D0256537

CANADIAN Almanac & DIRECTORY 1982

135th year of publication

Editor Susan Bracken

Copp Clark Pitman
A division of Copp Clark Limited
Toronto

© Copp Clark Pitman 1982

All rights reserved. No part of the material covered by this copyright may be reproduced in any form or by any means (whether electronic, mechanical or photographic) for storage in retrieval systems, tapes, discs, or for making multiple copies without the written permission of the publisher.

Code 140850
ISBN 0-7730-4046-3

Printed and bound in Canada.

0773040463 858 772 5101
HAMPSHIRE COUNTY LIBRARY
R917.10025 7045872

TABLE OF CONTENTS

Section A ▪ Canadian Directory

Section B ▪ Almanac Information

Section C ▪ Canadian Information and Statistics

Section D ▪ Canadian Law Firms and Lawyers

FREQUENTLY USED INFORMATION

TOPICAL TABLE OF CONTENTS

For detailed references, see Index.

For late changes, see Addenda.

TOPICAL TABLE OF CONTENTS

TOPICAL TABLE OF CONTENTS

Section A

CANADIAN DIRECTORY

Be Up to Date!

Check your Addenda at back of this book.

Additions and late corrections to material in Part A that appear in the addenda include:

Associations

Banks

Book Publishers

Churches

Government

Libraries

Manitoba Election Results

Schools

Translators

TV Stations

CHARTERED BANKS

(See Index for Bank of Canada; Federal Business Development Bank; and Canada Mortgage & Housing Corp., which are Crown Corporations, listed in the Government Section)

Chartered banks in Canada are incorporated either by Special Act of the Canadian Parliament or by Letters Patent and are governed by the Bank Act (Chapter 40 of the Statutes of 1980-81). The Bank Act provides the banks with their charters and establishes the legislation framework for Canada's banking system. The present Bank Act came into effect on December 1, 1980.

The Bank Act provides for the incorporation of two classes of banks. Schedule A banks are those banks in which no one shareholder or group of associated shareholders own more than 10 per cent of the bank's voting shares. Schedule B banks are those banks that are permitted to be closely held upon incorporation. Schedule A and Schedule B banks have the same general powers, restrictions and obligations under the Bank Act.

Foreign banks are permitted to incorporate 'foreign bank subsidiaries' under the Bank Act and to commence business in Canada on the basis of reciprocal treatment for Canadian banks. Foreign banks that incorporate in Canada are required to obtain a licence from the Minister of Finance. Foreign bank subsidiaries are Schedule B banks under the Bank Act.

The Bank Act provides chartered banks a number of specific powers including the authority to: open branches; lend money and make advances, with or without security; issue subordinated debentures, subject to terms and conditions; acquire and hold real property for the bank's actual use and occupation; take, and set conditions for realization on security; pay interest on a debt payable to a bank and charge interest on a loan, advance or any debt or liability of the bank; and subject to terms and conditions, engage in financial leasing, factoring, venture capital and data processing.

The Bank Act embodies many provisions designed for the protection of creditors and shareholders including requirements related to minimum cash reserves, shareholders' audits by public accountants and government inspection. No chartered bank in Canada has failed since 1923.

INSPECTOR-GENERAL OF BANKS, Dept. of Finance, Ottawa, Ont. K1A 0G5 — William A. Kennett

BANK OF BRITISH COLUMBIA

Capital Paid up........$17,418,000
Rest Account........$41,503,000
(Mar. 31, 1981)

Head Office—1725 Two Bentall Centre, 555 Burrard St., Vancouver, B.C. V7X 1K1; (604/668-4499)
Chairman & Chief Executive Officer—Trevor W. Pilley
President & Chief Operating Officer—D.E. McGeachan
Executive Vice President—V. Dobb
Executive Vice President, International—F. P. Darling
Senior Vice President, Corporate Credit—R.J. Fruin
Senior Vice President, Pacific Division—G.R. Wallace
Senior Vice President, Alberta Division—D.C. Wollstein
Senior Vice President, International Banking—Henry J. Bow
Vice President, Human Resources—O.G. West
Vice President & Chief Inspector—Hugh Dalgleish
Vice President & Controller—John Thomas
Vice President, Systems & Administration—P.N. McEachern
Senior Vice President, Investments—A. E. Miles-Pickup
Senior Vice President, Corporate Banking—Duncan Campbell
Vice President, Credit Alberta Division—E.N. Myrholm
Vice President, Marketing & Consumer Services—M.S. Rogers
Vice President—L.J. Fowler
Secretary—D. M. Clark, Q.C.
Branches: B.C. 35; Alta. 12

CANADIAN COMMERCIAL BANK

Head Office: 1801 Toronto Dominion Tower, Edmonton Centre, Edmonton, Alta. T5J 2Z1; (403/425-1220)
Toronto Office: 4900 First Canadian Place, Toronto, Ont. M5K 1E5; (416/869-3454)

Capital Paid up........$37,267,000
Rest Account........$13,398,000
(Mar. 31, 1981)

Chairman—Wm. H. McDonald (Toronto)
Chief Executive Officer—G. Howard Eaton (Edmonton)
President, Chief Operating Officer—R.A. Splane (Edmonton)
Executive Vice President—R.E.P. Allan (Los Angeles)
Executive Vice President—R.S. McCreath (Edmonton)
Executive Vice President—G.W.C. McLaughlan (Edmonton)
Executive Vice President—S.M. Stewart (Edmonton)

CANADIAN IMPERIAL BANK OF COMMERCE

Capital Paid up........$303,390,000
Rest Account........$1,023,160,000
(Mar. 31, 1981)

Head Office—Commerce Court, Toronto, Ont. M5L 1A2; (416/862-2211)
Chairman & Chief Executive Officer—R.E. Harrison
Vice Chairman & President—R.D. Fullerton
Vice Chairmen—J.A. Hilliker; C.M. Laidley
Vice Presidents—M.E. Jones; H. J. Lang; J. D. Leitch; André Monast; W. F. McLean; G. T. Richardson
Executive Vice Presidents—J. G. Bickford; C.W. Cole; L.G. Greenwood; A.W. Moysey
Senior Vice Presidents—E.S. Duffield; F.S. Duncanson; G.T. Ormston
Vice President & Controller—E. L. Pursey
Vice President & General Manager, International, Toronto—C.E. Langston
Vice President, U.S.A.—A.L. Flood
Vice President, Europe, Africa and the Middle East, London, Eng.—P.H. Nickels
Vice President, International Credits—I.R. Harrison
Vice President & Regional General Manager, Halifax—J. D. Simpson
Vice President & Regional General Manager (Quebec Region), Montreal—P.F. Leger
Vice President & Regional General Manager, Montreal—M.J.M. Casavant
Vice President, Main Branch, Commerce Court, Toronto—R.N. Brady
Vice President & Regional General Manager (Ontario Central West Region), Toronto—H.G. Mills
Vice President & Regional General Manager (Ontario Central East Region), Toronto—T.P.G. Morris
Senior Vice President & Regional General Manager (Toronto City Region), Toronto—G.T. Ormston
Vice President & Regional General Manager, Ottawa—M.L. Dufresne
Vice President & Regional General Manager, Hamilton—R.J. Bisset
Vice President & Regional General Manager, London—W.F. Spence
Vice President & Regional General Manager, Winnipeg—J.D. Haig
Vice President & Regional General Manager, Regina—J.B. Rogan
Vice President & Regional General Manager, Alberta North & Northwest Territories, Edmonton—J.G. Anderson
Vice President & Regional General Manager, Alberta South, Calgary—V.R.B. Nordheimer
Vice President & Regional General Manager, Vancouver & Lower Mainland, Vancouver—C.J. Shirley
Vice President & Regional General Manager, Vancouver Island, Interior & Yukon Region, Vancouver—G.W. Lewis
Branches: Alta. 199; B.C. 228; Man. 83; Yukon 6; N.B. 26; Nfld. 18; N.W.T. 8; Sask. 109; N.S. 38; Que. 206; Ont. 746; P.E.I. 8; International 95

CONTINENTAL BANK OF CANADA

Capital Paid up........$50,000,000
Rest Account........$50,000,000

(Mar. 31, 1981)
Head Office: Continental Place, 130 Adelaide St. W., Toronto, Ont. M5H 3R2
(416) 868-8000
Chairman of the Board—D.W. Maloney
President & Chief Executive Officer—S.F. Melloy
Executive Vice Presidents—A.P. Bolin, S.S. Ilaqua, D.A. Lewis, D.A. Rattee

THE MERCANTILE BANK OF CANADA

Capital Paid up....$40,000,000
Reserve Fund....$55,000,000
(Mar. 31, 1981)
Head Office—625 Dorchester Blvd. W., Montreal, P.Q. H3B 1R2; (514/871-2500)
President & Chief Executive Officer—R.L. Davidson
Executive Vice Presidents
Marketing—B.J. Guyette
Finance—N. Bossen
Corporate Services—R.M. Ray
Senior Vice President, Corporate Development—J.S. Ahern

BANK OF MONTREAL

Capital Paid up....$111,582,000
Rest Account....$1,152,579,000
(Mar. 31, 1981)
Head Office—129 St. James St. W., Montreal, P.Q. H2Y 1L6
(514) 877-7110
Chairman & Chief Executive Officer—W.D. Mulholland
Deputy Chairman—G.L. Reuber
President—W.E. Bradford
Vice Chairman—S.M. Davison
Vice Chairman—J.H. Warren
Vice Chairman & General Manager, Corporate Banking—H.M. MacDougall
Executive Vice President & Chairman, Credit Policy Committee—J.A. Whitney
Executive Vice President & General Manager, Domestic Banking—C.G. Stratton
Executive Vice President, Corporate Banking—J.D.C. de Jocas
Executive Vice President & General Manager, International Banking—W.B. Bateman
Vice President & Secretary—Robert Muir
Divisional Senior Vice Presidents:
Alberta—A.N. Tait, Calgary
British Columbia—D.G. Parker, Vancouver
Manitoba & Saskatchewan—A.E. Bates, Winnipeg
Central Ontario—G.L. Purcell
Metropolitan Ontario—R.M. Forster
Eastern & Northern Ontario—M.W. Barrett
Western Ontario—P.A. Franklin
Quebec—P. Macdonald, Montreal
Atlantic—J.R. Ellis, Halifax
Branches: Alta. 136; B.C. 168; Man. 73; N.B. 28; Nfld. 40; N.S. 34; Ont. 496; P.E.I. 5; Que. 225; Sask. 65; Yukon 2; N.W.T. 3

NATIONAL BANK OF CANADA

Capital Paid up....$89,819,292
Rest Account....$294,830,000
(Mar. 31, 1981)
Head Office: 500 Place d'Armes, Montreal, P.Q. H2Y 2W3
(514) 281-6611
Chairman of the Board & Chairman of the Executive Committee—Germain Perreault
President & Chief Executive Officer—Michel Bélanger
Executive Vice President & Chief Operating Officer—Gilles Mercure
Vice President & Secretary—Yvon Marcoux
Chief Accountant—Claude Garneau
Vice President, International—J.A. Seigneuret
Manager, Securities Dept.—Gaétan Parent
Branches: Quebec Division 687; Maritime Division 31; Ontario & Western Provinces Division 92

NORTHLAND BANK

Capital Paid up....$17,074,000
Rest Account....$4,373,000
(Mar. 31, 1981)
Executive Office—1200 Home Oil Tower, 324 8th Ave. S.W., Calgary, Alta. T2P 2Z2; (403/266-8901)
Chairman of the Board & Chief Executive Officer—R.A. Willson
Vice Chairman—N.A. Bromberger
President—W.A. Prisco
Senior Vice President—E.T. Young
Vice President, Finance—H.G. Green
Vice President, Credit—P.G. Saunderson
Vice President, Regions—G.A. Simpson
Vice President, Corporate Development—D.R. Watson
Secretary & General Counsel—A.W. Scarth, Q.C.
General Manager, Leasing—B.E. Reilly
Manager, Investments—D.M. Palmer
Branches: B.C. 2; Alta. 2; Sask. 2; Man. 1

THE BANK OF NOVA SCOTIA (Scotiabank)

Capital Paid up....$46,406,250
Rest Account....$1,050,992,188
(Mar. 31, 1981)
Executive Office—44 King St. W., Toronto, Ont. M5H 1H1; (416/866-6161)
Chairman & Chief Executive Officer—C. E. Ritchie
Deputy Chairman of the Board—A. H. Crockett
President & Chief Operating Officer—J. A. G. Bell
Senior Executive Vice President—W.S. McDonald
Executive Vice President—P.C. Godsoe
Senior Vice Presidents
Ontario Division—W.P. Meinig
Eastern Canada Division—C.F. Gill
Western Canada Division—R.J. Kavanagh
Corporate Banking—B.R. Birmingham
Canadian Commercial Banking—L.A. Shaw
Vice Presidents & General Managers
Canadian Commercial Banking—N.P. Penney
Nfld. & Labrador Regional Office—C. Bartlett
Nova Scotia Regional Office—R.C. McLeod
New Brunswick & P.E.I. Regional Office—G.M. Morrell
Quebec Regional Office—A. Bisson
Toronto Central Regional Office—E.D. MacNevin
Toronto Suburban Regional Office—H.L. Fawcett
Western & Northern Ontario Regional Office—L.A. Thurston
Eastern Ontario Regional Office—W.H. McMillan
Manitoba & N.W. Ontario Regional Office—E. Ranft
Saskatchewan Regional Office—D.A. Reed
Alberta & N.W.T. Regional Office—T.A. Cumming
B.C. & Yukon Regional Office—R.L. Mason
Latin America Regional Office—R. Cooke
North American International Regional Office—B.R. Birmingham
Caribbean Regional Office—R.G. Taylor
U.K., Europe, Mid-East, Africa Regional Office—L.L. Fox
Pacific Regional Office—K.S. Rowe
Canadian Branches: Alta. 118; B.C. 109; Man. 35; N.B. 55; Nfld. 60; N.S. 68; Ont. 413; P.E.I. 10; Que. 95; Sask. 49; Yukon 1; N.W.T. 1

THE ROYAL BANK OF CANADA

Capital Paid up....$233,861,000
Rest Account inc. Undivided Profits....$1,632,109,000
(Mar. 31, 1981)
Head Office—The Royal Bank of Canada Bldg., 1 Place Ville Marie, Box 6001, Montreal, P.Q. H3C 3A9
Chairman & Chief Executive Officer—Rowland C. Frazee
President—J.K. Finlayson (Toronto)
Vice Chairman—R.A. Utting (Montreal)
Vice Chairman—H.E. Wyatt (Calgary)
Executive Vice Presidents:
Finance & Investments—B.D. Gregson
National Accounts, Toronto—J.C. McMillan

Canada—A.H. Michell

World Trade & Merchant Banking, Toronto—R.G.P. Styles

International—A.R. Taylor

Affiliated Banks & Financial Organizations:

Chairman of the Board of Supervising Directors, RBC Holdings B.V. and RBC Houdstermaatschappij B.V. (London, Eng.)—R.C. Paterson

Senior Vice Presidents & General Managers:

R.B. Ashforth, Alberta (Calgary); J.E. Gleghorn, B.C. (Vancouver); W.D. Henry, Ontario (Toronto); F.P. Paradis, Quebec (Montreal); W.S. Snook, U.S. (New York)

Senior Vice Presidents:

L.E. Gillmoure, Operations & Systems

A.G. Halliwell, Commercial Bank–Canada

H.S. Hardy, Public Affairs

G.J. Johnson, Global Energy & Minerals Group (Calgary)

B.V. Kelly, International

W.A.R. MacDonald, Retail Bank–Canada

A.H. MacKenzie, Personnel

H.E. McClenaghan, Global Energy & Minerals Group (Calgary)

W.N. McFadyen, Commercial & Retail Banking, International

V.G. McKay, World Trade & Merchant Banking (Toronto)

M.O.P. Morrison, Retail Banking–Ontario (Toronto)

E.P. Neufeld, Chief Economist

M.J. Regan, National Accounts (Toronto)

J.C. Sinclair, Commercial Banking–Ontario (Toronto)

J.M. Walker, World Trade & Merchant Banking (Toronto)

Vice Presidents & General Managers:

J.G. Macpherson, Atlantic Provinces (Halifax)

W.C.C. Mackay, Middle East/Africa (London, Eng.)

J.B. McDonald, Manitoba (Winnipeg)

J.N.T. Rednall, Asia/Pacific (Hong Kong)

R.B. Robertson, Saskatchewan (Regina)

P.J. Rossiter, U.K., Ireland & Scandinavia (London, Eng.)

C.P. de Souza, Latin America & Caribbean (Coral Gables, Florida)

A. de Takacsy, Continental Europe (Paris)

Vice President & Treasurer—G.C. Aitken

Vice President & General Counsel—J.T. Burnett

Vice President & Comptroller—K.A. Smee

Chief Inspector—D.F.W. Bruce

Secretary—R.J. Moores

Branches: Alta. 153; B.C. 204; Man. 104; N.B. 31; Nfld. 20; N.S. 84; Ont. 586; P.E.I. 6; Que. 217; Sask. 102; Yukon & N.W.T. 6; International 84

In addition, the Royal Bank has financial interest in 113 Subsidiaries and Affiliates throughout the world.

THE TORONTO-DOMINION BANK

Capital Paid up..$175,183,000

Rest Account..$850,000,000

(Mar. 31, 1981)

Head Office—Box 1, Toronto Dominion Centre, Toronto, Ont. M5K 1A2; (416/866-8087)

Chairman & Chief Executive Officer—R.M. Thomson

President—R.W. Korthals

Banking correspondents in principal cities of the world.

Branches: Alta. 124; B.C. 116; Man. 58; N.B. 10; Nfld. 6; N.S. 14; Ont. 540; P.E.I. 2; Que. 96; Sask. 52; Yukon 2; N.W.T. 1

SAVINGS BANKS WITH FEDERAL CHARTERS

THE MONTREAL CITY & DISTRICT SAVINGS BANK

Capital Paid up..$3,000,000

Rest Account..$56,760,000

Head Office—262 St. James St. W., Montreal, P.Q. H2Y 1N1 (514) 284-3931

Chairman of the Board, President & Chief Executive Officer—Raymond Garneau

Executive Vice President & General Manager—Pierre Goyette

117 Branches in Quebec.

PROVINCE OF ONTARIO SAVINGS OFFICE

Head Office—19th floor, 77 Bloor St. W., Toronto, Ont. M7A 1A2; (416/965-1791)

Director, C.S. Costanza

Approved by the Legislature 1921.

21 Branches in Ontario.

PROVINCE OF ALBERTA TREASURY BRANCHES

Head Office—9925 109th St., Edmonton, Alta.

Mailing address—Box 1440, Edmonton, Alta. T5J 2N6

Phone—(403) 427-2721

Treasury Branches, established in 1938 by the Government of the Province of Alberta, render financial services similar to those offered by chartered banks, including current and savings accounts, loans, etc. They also act as agents for several Government Departments.

There are 113 Branches, 4 Sub-Branches, and 99 Agencies in Alberta.

TRUST COMPANIES AND LOAN COMPANIES IN CANADA

Trust companies act as executors, trustees and administrators under wills and trust agreements; as agents for the administration of estates and trusts; as transfer agents, registrars and bond trustees for corporations and as financial agents for individuals and corporations. They receive money on deposit and for guaranteed fixed term investment. They also offer participation in their own unit investment funds. Trust companies manage investments including those of the pension and profit sharing plans of corporations and personal retirement plans. They manage property and provide real estate sales services. Trust companies make various types of mortgage loans and some personal loans. Funds in their care are invested in investments authorized by their enabling legislation, for trustees or as directed, including mortgages, Federal, provincial, municipal bonds and corporate securities. A few trust companies accept appointments as authorized trustees in bankruptcy.

The principal function of loan companies is the lending of funds on the security of first mortgages, a high proportion of which are on residential property. Funds are obtained mainly by the sale of debentures to the public and by the acceptance of deposits through savings departments.

Trust Companies with name of person responsible for public relations and information.

The Acadia Trust Company
798 Prince St., Truro, N.S. B2N 1H1
(902) 895-5484
Secretary, Edsel M. Hamilton

Alcan Fiduciaries Ltd./Fiduciaires de l'Alcan Ltée
Box 6090, Montreal, P.Q. H3C 3H2

(514) 877-2340
Atlantic Trust Company of Canada
1741 Barrington St., Halifax, N.S. B3J 3C4
(902) 422-1701
The Bankers' Trust Company
630 Dorchester Blvd. W., Montreal, P.Q. H3B 1S6
(514) 876-7716
Bayshore Trust Company
1 St. Clair Ave. E., #700, Toronto, Ont. M4T 2V7
(416) 968-3372
The British Swiss Trust Company
83 Queen St., Box 1450, Charlottetown, P.E.I. C1A 7N3
(902) 892-1930
Cabot Trust Company
1055 Wilson Ave., #605, Downsview, Ont. M3K 1Y9
(416) 633-4400
Vice President, Peter V. Simone
Canada Permanent Mortgage Corporation
and Subsidiaries, including Canada Permanent Trust Co.
320 Bay St., Toronto, Ont. M5H 2P6
(416) 361-8205
Asst. Vice President, Public Relations, M.D. Sinclair
Canada Trust Company
A wholly owned subsidiary of Canada Trustco Mortgage Co.
Canada Trustco Mortgage Company
Canada Trust Tower, 275 Dundas St., London, Ont. N6A 4S4
(519) 673-6000
Canadian First Mortgage Corporation
Royal Trust Tower, Box 108, Toronto, Ont. M5X 1A4
(416) 869-1277
The Canadian Trust Company
c/o Montreal Trust Co., 1 Place Ville Marie, Montreal, P.Q. H3B 4A8
(514) 861-1681
Vice President & Managing Director, R.D. Quart
Central Trust Company
Head Office: (5151 Terminal Bldg.) Box 2343, Halifax, N.S. B3J 3C8
(902) 425-7390
Public Relations Contact, W.J. Kokesh, Asst. Vice President, Marketing
Citicorp Trust Company
First Canadian Place, Box 34, Toronto, Ont. M5X 1C3
(416) 360-5500
Citizens Trust Company
#1110, 595 Howe St., Vancouver, B.C. V6C 2T5
Columbia Trust Company
625 Howe St., Vancouver, B.C. V6C 2T6
Commercial Trust Company Ltd.
409 8th Ave. S.W., Calgary, Alta. T2P 1E3
(403) 262-3017
Community Trust Company Ltd.
2299 Bloor St. W., Toronto, Ont. M6S 1P1
(416) 763-2291
La Compagnie Fonciere du Manitoba (1967), Limitée
c/o Montreal Trust Co., 221 Portage Ave., Winnipeg, Man. R3B 2A6
(204) 943-0451
Treasurer, J.P. Allard
La Compagnie Sherbrooke Trust
(75 Wellington St. N.) Box 250, Sherbrooke, P.Q. J1H 5J2
(819) 563-4011
Continental Trust Company
145 King St. W., Toronto, Ont. M5H 2E2
(416) 366-9161
Co-operative Trust Company of Canada
Co-op Bldg., 333 3rd Ave. N., Saskatoon, Sask. S7K 2M2
(306) 244-1900
Corporate Secretary, W.J. Lipsett
Counsel Trust Company
390 Bay St., #501, Toronto, Ont. M5H 2Y2
(416) 364-6044
Vice President, Administration, Jack Phinn
Credit Foncier
612 St. James St., Montreal, P.Q. H3C 1E1
(514) 282-1880
Manager, Advertising Dept., Yvon Grant
Crown Trust Company
Box 38, One First Canadian Place, Toronto, Ont. M5X 1G4
(416) 364-4400
Vice President, Corporate Development, J.W. Beckerleg
District Trust Company
150 Fullarton St., London, Ont. N6A 4V6
(519) 434-6013
Asst. Secretary, Mrs. Jean N. Maybrey
The Dominion Trust Company
(81 Durham St. S.) Box 1117, Sudbury, Ont. P3E 4S6
Eaton Bay Mortgage Corporation
#2200, 181 University Ave., Toronto, Ont. M5H 3M7
(416) 868-0369
Public Relations Contact, Clifford Prupas
Eaton Bay Trust Company (Alberta)
#2200, 181 University Ave., Toronto, Ont. M5H 3M7
(416) 868-0369
Public Relations Contact, Clifford Prupas
Head Office: 209 8th Ave. S.W., Calgary, Alta. T2P 1B8
Eaton Bay Trust Company
1235 Bay St., Toronto, Ont. M5R 3L4
(416) 928-0611
Public Relations Contact, Clifford Prupas
The Effort Trust Company
240 Main St. E., Hamilton, Ont. L8N 1T5
Evangeline Savings & Mortgage Company
535 Albert St., Windsor, N.S. B0N 2T0
(902) 798-8326
Vice President, Admin., A. David Howell, R.I.A.
Family Trust Corporation
8 Wellington St. W., Markham, Ont. L3P 1A2
(416) 294-1372
The Fidelity Trust Company
10506 Jasper Ave., Edmonton, Alta. T5J 2W9
Head Office: 201 Portage Ave., Winnipeg, Man. R3B 2A1
Fiduciaires de la Cité et du District de Montréal Limitée
Montreal City & District Trustees Ltd.
1253 McGill College, Montréal, P.Q. H3B 2Z6
(514) 878-3351
Marketing Director, Normand Paquin
Fiducie Canadienne Italienne
Canadian Italian Trust Co.
6995 boul. St-Laurent, Montreal, P.Q. H2S 3E1
(514) 270-4121
Fiducie du Quebec
Quebec Trust
One Complexe Desjardins, Tour Sud, C.P. 34, Montréal, P.Q. H5B 1E4
(514) 281-8833
Fiducie Nord-Amérique
North America Trust
85 St. Catherine St. W., Montréal, P.Q. H2X 3P4
(514) 281-1818
Public Relations Contact, Hugo Valente, C.A.
Fiducie Pret et Revenu
Savings & Investment Trust
850 D'Youville, Québec, P.Q. G1K 7P3
(418) 692-1221
Financial Trust Company
21 St. Clair Ave. E., Penthouse Floor, Toronto, Ont. M4T 2T7
First City Trust Company
#600, 777 Hornby St., Vancouver, B.C. V6Z 1S4
(604) 668-5777
Manager, Public Relations, Jil A. Pratt
Fort Garry Trust Company
283 Portage Ave., Winnipeg, Man. R3B 2B6
(204) 944-7211
President, Brendan Calder
Greymac Mortgage Corporation
390 Bay St., 22nd Floor, Toronto, Ont. M5H 2Y2
(416) 862-0111
Guaranty Trust Company of Canada
366 Bay St., Toronto, Ont. M5H 2W5

(416) 863-5000
Guardian Trustco Inc.
(also Guardian Trust Company; Compagnie de Fiducie Guardian; Guardian Trustco International)
Head Office: 618 rue St-Jacques, Montreal, P.Q. H3C 1E3
(514) 842-8251; Telex: 05-25721
Toronto Office: 123 Yonge St., Toronto, Ont. M5C 1W4 (416/ 863-1100; Telex: 06-23837)
Hellenic Canadian Trust
Trust Hellenique Canadien
852 Jean Talon W., Montreal, P.Q. H3N 1S4
(514) 273-4233
Treasurer, D.J. Yantsulis
Heritage Savings & Trust Company
10126 101 St., Edmonton, Alta. T5J 0S4
(403) 429-6656
HFC Trust Limited
85 Bloor St. E., Toronto, Ont. M4W 1B4
Huronia Trust Company
2 Mississaga St. E., Orillia, Ont. L3V 6H9
(705) 325-2328
Managing Director, James L. Graham
Income Trust Company
181 Main St. W., Hamilton, Ont. L8P 4S1
(416) 528-9811
Industrial Mortgage & Trust Company
201 N. Front St., Sarnia, Ont. N7T 7T9
(519) 336-0490
Subsidiary of Royal Trust Co.
Inland Trust & Savings Corporation Ltd.
1080 Portage Ave., Winnipeg, Man. R3G 0S5
(204) 786-6016
The Interior Trust Company
#914, 504 Main St., Winnipeg, Man. R3B 1B8
(204) 942-6920
International Trust Company
Royal Bank Plaza, North Tower, Box 75, Toronto, Ont. M5J 2J2
Investors Group Trust Co. Ltd.
280 Broadway, Winnipeg, Man. R3C 3B6
(204) 943-0361
Kinross Mortgage Corporation
Commerce Court West, Toronto, Ont. M5L 1E5
(416) 862-3806
Macdonald Cartier Trust Company
165 Dundas St. W., Mississauga, Ont. L5B 2N6
(416) 276-2112
Mennonite Trust Ltd.
Waldheim, Sask. S0K 4R0
(306) 945-2080
Monarch Trust Company
21 St. Clair Ave. E., #1005, Toronto, Ont. M4T 1L9
(416) 922-4545
Montreal Trust Company
1 Place Ville Marie, Box 1900, Stn. B, Montreal, P.Q. H3B 3L6
(514) 861-1681
The Morgan Trust Company
#1440, 1 Place Ville Marie, Montreal, P.Q. H3B 2B4
(514) 878-3861
Secretary, Mme Justine Lacoste
Morgan Trust Company of Canada
#2710, Toronto Dominion Bank Tower, Toronto Dominion Centre, Toronto, Ont. M5K 1E7
Morguard Trust Company
6 Crescent Rd., Toronto, Ont. M4W 3K9
(416) 967-0880
The Municipal Trust Company
70 Collier St., Box 147, Barrie, Ont. L4M 4S9
National Trust Company, Limited
21 King St. E., Toronto, Ont. M5C 1B3
(416) 364-9141
Vice President, Marketing, Bruce F. Patterson
Norfolk Trust
250 3rd Ave. S., Saskatoon, Sask. S7K 1L9
(306) 244-4240
The North Canadian Trust Company
#104, 386 Broadway, Winnipeg, Man. R3C 3R6
(204) 944-8758
North West Trust Company
3rd Floor, 11456 Jasper Ave., Edmonton, Alta. T5K 0M1
(403) 482-6081
Vice President, Marketing, D.V. Roberts
Nova Scotia Savings & Loan Company
1645 Granville St., Halifax, N.S. B3J 2T3
(902) 423-1181
Pan-American Trust Company
119 Richmond St., Charlottetown, P.E.I. C1A 1H7
Administered by Montreal Trust Co.
Inquiries to, A.R. Reist
Peace Hills Trust Company
10232 112 St., Edmonton, Alta. T5K 1M4
Pioneer Trust Company
Box 576, Regina, Sask. S4P 3A3
(306) 569-2288
President, Will Klein
The Premier Trust Company
19 Richmond St. W., Toronto, Ont. M5H 1Z1
(416) 363-7043
Secretary, M.H. Wilson
Principal Savings & Trust Company
(10303 Jasper Ave., 2900 Principal Plaza), Box 2425, Edmonton, Alta. T5J 3N6
The Regional Trust Company
190 Division St., Welland, Ont. L3B 4A2
(416) 735-6671
Inquiries to, David R. Taylor
Royal Trust Corporation of Canada
Executive Office: Toronto Dominion Centre, Box 7500, Stn. A, Toronto, Ont. M5W 1P9
(416) 867-2000
Vice President, Public Relations, Lauchlin A. Chisholm
Registered Office: 700 the Dome Tower, Toronto Dominion Sq., Calgary, Alta. T2P 2Z3
Royal Trustco Limited
Executive Office: Toronto Dominion Bank Tower, Box 7500, Stn. A, Toronto, Ont. M5W 1P9
(416) 867-2000
Vice President, Public Relations, Lauchlin A. Chisholm
Registered Office: 76 Metcalfe St., Ottawa, Ont. K1P 5L8
Saskatchewan Trust Company
339 Main St. N., Moose Jaw, Sask. S6H 7A8
(306) 693-4881
Trust Officer, E.J. Sakundiak
Security Trust Company
5296 Yonge St., Willowdale, Ont. M2N 5R2
(416) 226-5313
Settlers Savings & Mortgage Corporation
877 Portage Ave., Winnipeg, Man. R3G 0N8
(204) 786-8508
Sherbrooke Trust
75 Wellington nord, Sherbrooke, P.Q. J1H 5B5
Subsidiary of Trust Général du Canada
Société Nationale de Fiducie
385 Sherbrooke St. E., Montréal, P.Q.H2X 1E5
(514) 844-2050
Standard Trust Company
69 Yonge St., #200, Toronto, Ont. M5E 1K3
(416) 868-6900
Sterling Trust Corporation
Sterling House, 220 Bay St., Toronto, Ont. M5J 2K8
(416) 364-7495
Inquiries to, Nancy Rodrigues
Teachers' Trust Company
5909 West Blvd., Vancouver, B.C. V6M 3X1
(604) 263-2371
Trust General du Canada
909 Boul. Dorchester W., Montreal, P.Q. H3B 2G7
(514) 866-9641

Vanguard Trust of Canada Limited
#5240, One First Canadian Place, Box 128, Toronto, Ont. M5X 1A4
(416) 868-0234
Secretary Treasurer, Phyllis Baldwin

Victoria and Grey Trust Company
165 University Ave., Toronto, Ont. M5H 3B8
(416) 860-8600
Director of Advertising, J.P. Mackenzie

Western Capital Trust Company
980 One Bentall Centre, 505 Burrard St., Vancouver, B.C. V7X 1M4

Yorkshire Trust Company
1100 Melville St., Vancouver, B.C. V6E 2W9
(604) 685-3711
Asst. General Manager, Marketing, Duart A. Campbell

STOCK EXCHANGES

THE TORONTO STOCK EXCHANGE

234 Bay St., Toronto, Ont. M5J 1R1
(416) 868-5100
Telex: 065 24038

The Board of Governors

Chairman, H.K. McMahon
Vice Chairman, M.J. Howe
Governors, Anne R. Dubin, Q.C.; St. Clair Balfour; E.B. Thomson; J.P. Bunting; C.B. Loewen; R.H. Canning; D.T.C. Moore; Bev Collombin; S. Davis; M.J. Howe; J.A. MacKnight; C.R. Younger

Executive Officers

President, J.P. Bunting
Vice President, Policy Development & Regulation, L.D. Pringle
Vice President, Markets & Market Development, H.W.F. McKay
Vice President, Administration, & Treasurer, A.C. Puley
Vice President, Operations, D. Unruh
Secretary, Ailsa M. Currie

Member Firms and Corporations

John C. L. Allen, Ltd., Box 155, Royal Bank Plaza, Toronto, Ont. M5J 2J4 (865-1090)

A. E. Ames & Co., 320 Bay St., Toronto, Ont. M5H 2P7 (867-4000)

Andras, Hatch & Hetherington Ltd., 4 King St. W., Toronto, Ont. M5H 1B8 (363-9151)

Arachnae Securities Ltd., Buttonville Airport, Markham, Ont. L3P 3J9 (297-3150)

Atlantic Securities Ltd., Box 3411, Halifax, N.S. B3J 3J1 (902/423-8391)

Bache Halsey Stuart Canada Ltd., 18 King St. E., Toronto, Ont. M5C 1E3 (860-3000)

Bawlf Securities Ltd., #400, 550 Burrard St., Vancouver, B.C. V6C 2J6 (604/687-9971)

Begg Securities Ltd., Main floor, 120 Adelaide St. W., Toronto, Ont. M5H 1T7 (869-1721)

Bell, Gouinlock & Co. Ltd., Ste. 1010, Box 110, First Canadian Place, Toronto, Ont. M5X 1B6 (364-2231)

Brault, Guy, O'Brien Inc., Box 279, Commerce Court Postal Stn., Toronto, Ont. M5L 1E9 (869-1373)

Brawley, Cathers Ltd., 11 King St. W., Toronto, Ont. M5H 1A7 (363-5821)

L. A. Brenzel Securities Ltd., 10 Temperance St., Toronto, Ont. M5H 1Y4 (863-1655)

Brink, Hudson & Lefever Ltd., #717, 837 W. Hastings St., Vancouver, B.C. V6C 1C1

Brown, Baldwin, Nisker Ltd., 100 Adelaide St. W., Toronto, Ont. M5H 1S3 (366-7663)

Alfred Bunting & Co. Ltd., 155 University Ave., Toronto, Ont. M5H 3B7 (364-3293)

Burgess Graham Securities Ltd., Box 175, Royal Bank Plaza, Toronto, Ont. M5J 2J4 (865-1060)

Burns Fry Ltd., Box 150, First Canadian Place, Toronto, Ont. M5X 1H3 (365-4000)

Caldwell Securities Ltd., Box 162, Toronto Dominion Centre, Toronto, Ont. M5K 1H6

Canavest House Ltd., Box 13, Commerce Court Postal Stn., Toronto, Ont. M5L 1A3 (862-1930)

Cassels, Blaikie & Co. Ltd., 110 Yonge St., Toronto, Ont. M5C 1V9 (362-6531)

Hector M. Chisholm & Co. Ltd., 11 Adelaide St. W., Toronto, Ont. M5H 1M9 (362-4731)

Connor, Clark & Co. Ltd., 390 Bay St., Ste. 2318, Toronto, Ont. M5H 2Y2 (862-7558)

W.J. Corcoran Co. Ltd., 4 King St. W., #1920, Toronto, Ont. M5H 1B6 (362-6515)

R. A. Daly & Co. Ltd., #800, 130 Adelaide St. W., Toronto, Ont. M5H 3R9 (362-6192)

Davidson Partners Ltd., Box 122, First Canadian Place, Toronto, Ont. M5X 1E9 (867-3300)

F. H. Deacon, Hodgson Inc., 105 Adelaide St. W., Toronto, Ont. M5H 1R4 (867-3000)

Dean Witter Reynolds (Canada) Inc., #1102, 181 University Ave., Toronto, Ont. M5H 3M7 (868-0303)

Dominick Corp. of Canada Ltd., Box 272, Royal Trust Tower, Toronto, Ont. M5K 1J5 (363-0204)

Dominion Securities Ltd., Box 21, Commerce Court S., Toronto, Ont. M5L 1A7 (362-5711)

Equitable Securities Ltd., Box 85, Royal Bank Plaza, Toronto, Ont. M5J 2J2 (865-7400)

First Marathon Securities Ltd., 11 Adelaide St. W., #700, Toronto, Ont. M5H 1M2 (869-3707)

Fraser, Dingman & Co. Ltd., 199 Bay St., Toronto, Ont. M5J 1L4 (364-3125)

Gardiner, Watson Ltd., 11 Adelaide St. W., 12th floor, Toronto, Ont. M5H 2R4 (862-8142)

Geoffrion, Leclerc Inc., 800 Dorchester Blvd. W., Montreal, P.Q. H3B 1Y8 (514/861-8811)

Gordon Securities Ltd., Box 67, Toronto Dominion Centre, Toronto, Ont. M5K 1E7 (364-9393)

Goulding, Rose & Turner Ltd., 11 King St. W., Toronto, Ont. M5H 1A3 (366-7701)

Greenshields Ltd., Ste. 3000, One First Canadian Place, Toronto, Ont. M5X 1E6 (366-8311)

Heritage Securities Corporation, #1404, 7 King St. E., Toronto, Ont. M5X 1R6 (863-1773)

Housser & Co. Ltd., 60 Yonge St., #1200, Toronto, Ont. M5E 1S1 (362-2701)

Houston, Willoughby & Co. Ltd., 1825 Cornwall St., Regina, Sask. S4P 2K4 (306/525-6731)

Jones, Gable & Co. Ltd., 110 Yonge St., Toronto, Ont. M5S 1T6 (362-5454)

Jones Heward & Co. Ltd., 141 Adelaide St. W., Ste. 909, Toronto, Ont. M5H 3L5 (367-1611)

Lafferty, Harwood & Partners Ltd., 500 St. Jacques St., #600, Montreal, P.Q. H2Y 3R3 (514/845-3166)

W. D. Latimer Co. Ltd., Box 96, Toronto Dominion Centre, Toronto, Ont. M5K 1G8 (363-5631)

Leeburn Securities Ltd., 11 Adelaide St. W., Ste. 707, Toronto, Ont. M5H 1M2 (367-9901)

Levesque, Beaubien Inc., Box 92, Royal Bank Plaza, Toronto, Ont. M5J 2J2 (865-0750)

Loewen, Ondaatje, McCutcheon & Co. Ltd., 7 King St. E., Toronto, Ont. M5C 1A2 (869-7211)

MacDougall, MacDougall & MacTier Inc., First Canadian Place, Box 11, Toronto, Ont. M5X 1A9 (362-1631)

J.D. Mack Ltd., Box 2052, 1813 Granville St., Halifax, N.S. B3J 2Z1 (902/422-7341)

Maison Placements Canada Inc., 11 King St. W., Toronto, Ont. M5H 1A3 (364-0165)

McCarthy Securities Ltd., #509, 55 Yonge St., Toronto, Ont. M5E 1J4 (862-9160)

McConnell & Co. Ltd., 8 King St. E., Toronto, Ont. M5C 1B5 (364-4461)
McDermid, Miller & McDermid Inc., #1000, 675 W. Hastings St., Vancouver, B.C. V6B 1N6 (604/682-7121)
McEwen, Easson Ltd., #1330, North Tower, Royal Bank Plaza, Box 72, Toronto, Ont. M5J 2J2 (865-0303)
McLean, McCarthy & Co. Ltd., Ste. 1504, 11 King St. W., Toronto, Ont. M5H 1A8 (368-2751)
McLeod Young Weir Ltd., Box 433, Toronto Dominion Centre, Toronto, Ont. M5K 1M2 (362-7311)
Merit Investment Corp., 155 University Ave., Ste. 400, Toronto, Ont. M5H 3B7 (867-6000)
Merrill Lynch, Royal Securities Ltd., Box 31, Toronto Dominion Centre, Toronto, Ont. M5K 1C2 (361-3100)
Midland Doherty Ltd., Box 25, Commercial Union Tower, Toronto Dominion Centre, Toronto, Ont. M5K 1B5 (361-6000)
Molson, Rousseau & Co., Ltd., 800 Place Victoria, Montreal, P.Q. H4Z 1G2 (514/866-1551)
Moss, Lawson & Co., Ltd., 48 Yonge St., Toronto, Ont. M5E 1G7 (867-2700)
Nesbitt Thomson Bongard Inc., Box 35, Royal Trust Tower, Toronto, Ont. M5K 1C4 (866-3000)
Odlum Brown & T. B. Read Ltd., 8 King St. E., Toronto, Ont. M5C 1B5 (363-8443)
A. E. Osler, Wills, Bickle, Ltd., Ste. 2350, South Tower, Box 60, Royal Bank Plaza, Toronto, Ont. M5J 2K6 (865-2000)
Pemberton Securities Ltd., Ste. 3450, Box 121, First Canadian Place, Toronto, Ont. M5X 1A4 (869-3690)
Peters & Co. Ltd., 312-4th Ave. S.W., Calgary, Alta. T2P 0H7 (403/261-4850)
Pitfield MacKay Ross Ltd., Box 54, Royal Bank Plaza, Toronto, Ont. M5J 2K5 (865-3500)
Rademaker, MacDougall & Co., 400, 409 Granville St., Vancouver, B.C. V6C 1T7 (604/687-0456)
Rasmussen, Sharp & Co. Ltd., 1200 McGill College Ave., Montreal, P.Q. H3B 4G7 (514/878-1841)
Research Securities of Canada Ltd., Ste. 1803, 4 King St. W., Toronto, Ont. M5H 1B6 (864-1200)
Richardson Securities of Canada, 130 Adelaide St. W., Toronto, Ont. M5H 3P5 (860-3400)
St. Lawrence Securities Ltd., 401 Bay St., Toronto, Ont. M5H 2Y4 (368-3811)
Scotia Bond Co. Ltd., Box 666, Halifax, N.S. B3J 2T3 (902/425-6900)
Security Trading Ltd., Ste. 4706, Manulife Centre, 44 Charles St. W., Toronto, Ont. M4Y 1R8 (961-2048)
Standard Securities Ltd., 185 Bay St., Toronto, Ont. M5J 1K6 (363-5911)
Tasse & Associes Ltee, 630 Dorchester Blvd. W., #1600, Montreal, P.Q. H3B 1T4 (514/879-2100)
Thomson, Kernaghan & Co. Ltd., 365 Bay St., Toronto, Ont. M5H 2V2 (368-3871)
Walwyn Stodgell Cochran Murray Ltd., Ste. 1900, York Centre, 145 King St. W., Toronto, Ont. M5H 3M1 (364-1131)
Watt, Carmichael Securities Ltd., Box 88, First Canadian Place, Toronto, Ont. M5X 1B1 (864-1500)
Westfield Securities Ltd., #2300, 300 5th Ave. S.W., Calgary, Alta. T2P 0L3 (403/232-1635)
Wood, Gundy Ltd., Box 274, Royal Trust Tower, Toronto, Ont. M5K 1M7 (362-4433)
Yorkton Securities Ltd., Ste. 1200, 11 King St. W., Toronto, Ont. M5H 1A3 (864-3500)

THE MONTREAL STOCK EXCHANGE

Box 61, Tour de la Bourse, 800 Victoria Sq., Montreal, P.Q. H4Z 1A9
(514) 871-2424
Telex: 012841

Executive Officers

Chairman, André Charron
President, R. Demers
Executive Vice President, Giovanni Giarrusso, C.A.

Member Firms

A.E. Ames & Co., #2900, 630 Dorchester Blvd. W., Montreal, P.Q. H3B 1W8 (879-1401)
Bache, Halsey, Stuart Canada Ltd., 4 Westmount Sq., Montreal, P.Q. H3Z 2R2 (934-5000)
Bell, Gouinlock Ltd., Suite 820, Sun Life Bldg., Montreal, P.Q. H3B 2W1 (875-2180)
Bontrad Inc., 800 Place Victoria, #3615, Tour de la Bourse, Montreal, P.Q. H4Z 1G8 (871-8511)
Brault, Guy, O'Brien Inc., Suite 1000, 635 Dorchester Blvd. W., Montreal, P.Q. H3B 1R8 (871-1175)
L. A. Brenzel Securities Ltd., 10 Temperance St., Toronto, Ont. M5H 1Y4 (416/863-1655)
Brown, Baldwin, Nisker Ltd., 100 Adelaide St. W., Toronto, Ont. M5H 1S3 (416/366-7663)
Alfred Bunting & Co. Ltd., Suite 2606, 1110 Sherbrooke St. W., Montreal, P.Q. H3A 1G8 (842-8726)
Burns Fry Ltd., Suite 1712, 1 Place Ville Marie, Montreal, P.Q. H3B 2C1 (875-2130)
Canavest House Ltd., Box 13 Commerce Court East, Toronto, Ont. M5L 1A3 (416/862-1930)
Casgrain & Cie Ltee, 625 Dorchester Blvd. W., #1705, Montreal, P.Q. H3B 1R2 (871-8080)
Hector M. Chisholm & Co. Ltd., 11 Adelaide St. W., Toronto, Ont. M5H 1M9 (416/362-4731)
R. A. Daly & Co. Ltd., Suite 1220, 1200 McGill College Ave., Montreal, P.Q. H3B 4G7 (861-9751)
Davidson Partners Ltd., 715 Victoria Sq., Montreal, P.Q. H2Y 2J2 (844-3722)
Deacon (F.H.), Hodgson Inc., #1010, 800 boul. Dorchester ouest, Montreal, P.Q. (871-7000)
Dean, Witter, Reynolds (Canada) Inc., 635 Dorchester Blvd. W., #1300, Montreal, P.Q. H3B 1S1 (871-0004)
Dominick Corp. of Canada Ltd., Suite 3434, 1 Place Ville Marie, Montreal, P.Q. H3B 3N6 (871-8111)
Dominion Securities Ltd., Suite 3000, 1155 Dorchester Blvd. W., Montreal, P.Q. H3B 2L6 (861-2581)
Equitable Securities Ltd., Suite 2406, Place Ville Marie, Montreal, P.Q. H3B 3M9 (Mtl.: 875-5198; Tor.: 416/875-5199)
First Canada Bond Share Corporation, 1155 Dorchester Blvd. W., #816, Montreal, P.Q. H3B 2H7 (875-0590)
Geoffrion, Leclerc Inc., Suite 1700, 800 Dorchester Blvd. W., Montreal, P.Q. H3B 1Y8 (861-8811)
Gordon Securities Ltd., Box 67, Toronto Dominion Centre, Toronto, Ont. M5K 1E7 (416/364-9393)
Goulding, Rose & Turner Ltd., 11 King St. W., #1300, Toronto, Ont. M5H 1A5 (416/366-7701)
John Graham & Co. Ltd., 100 Sparks St., Ottawa, Ont. (875-2585, Mtl.)
Greenshields Ltd., 4 Place Ville Marie, Montreal, P.Q. H3B 2E7 (861-3831)
Grenier, Ruel & Cie Inc., Suite 4004, Stock Exchange Tower, Montreal, P.Q. H4Z 1C7 (871-9000)
Jones Heward & Co. Ltd., 249 St. James St. W., Montreal, P.Q. H2Y 1M8 (845-6131)
Lafferty, Harwood & Partners Ltd., 500, rue St-Jacques, Montreal, P.Q. (845-3166)
W. D. Latimer Co. Ltd., 455 St-Antoine St. W., Montreal, P.Q. H2Z 1J1 (866-8763)
Levesque, Beaubien Inc., 360 o., rue St-Jacques, Montreal, P.Q. H2Y 1P5 (879-2222)
Loewen, Ondaatje, McCutcheon & Co. Ltd., Suite 313, 3 Place Ville Marie, Montreal, P.Q. H3B 2E3 (879-1644)
MacDougall, MacDougall & MacTier Ltd., #2000, Place du Canada, Montreal, P.Q. (871-9611)
J.D. Mack Ltd., 1813 Granville St., Halifax, N.S. (902/422-7341)
Maison Placements Canada Inc., Suite 1130, Place du Canada, Montreal, P.Q. H3B 2P7 (861-9761)
McLean, McCarthy Co. Ltd., Ste. 1504, 11 King St. W., Toronto, Ont. M5H 1A8 (416/368-2751)
McLeod, Young, Weir & Co. Ltd., Suite 4005, 1155 Dorchester Blvd. W., Montreal, P.Q. H3B 1V4 (861-5811)
McNeil, Mantha Inc., 614 St. James St. W., Montreal, P.Q. H2Y 1L9 (845-8201)

Mercier, Ouimet, Masse, Inc., Suite 1114, 2015 Peel St., Montreal, P.Q. H3A 1T8 (284-1838)
Merit Investment Corp., 155 University Ave., Ste. 400, Toronto, Ont. (416/867-6000)
Merrill, Lynch, Royal Securities Ltd., Suite 300, 800 Dorchester Blvd. W., Montreal, P.Q. H3B 1Y1 (392-7111)
Midland-Doherty Ltd., Suite 208, 3 Place Ville Marie, Montreal, P.Q. H3B 4C5 (879-1050)
Molson, Rousseau & Co. Ltd., #4528, Stock Exchange Tower, Montreal, P.Q. H4Z 1G2 (866-1551)
Nesbitt, Thomson, Bongard Inc., 355 St. James St. W., Montreal, P.Q. H2Y 1P1 (844-0131)
C. M. Oliver & Co. Ltd., 821 W. Hastings St., Vancouver, B.C. V6C 1B5 (604/684-9211)
A. E. Osler, Wills, Bickle Ltd., Suite 1060, 800 Dorchester Blvd. W., Montreal, P.Q. H3B 1X9 (879-1770)
Pitfield, Mackay, Ross Ltd., #2101, 1 Place Ville Marie, Montreal, P.Q. (876-5220)
Pope & Co., 15 Duncan St., Toronto, Ont. (416/593-5535)
Rasmussen, Sharp & Co. Ltd., Suite 1210, 1200 McGill College Ave., Montreal, P.Q. H3B 4G7 (878-1841)
Research Securities of Canada, Ltd., #300, 1155 Sherbrooke St. W., Montreal, P.Q. (281-1800)
Richardson Securities of Canada, Ste. 1540, 1155 Metcalfe St., Montreal, P.Q. H3B 2V6 (871-1115)
Saunders Hatt Ltd., 49 Wellington St. E., 1st Floor, Toronto, Ont. M5E 1C9 (416/862-7610)
Scotia Bond Co. Ltd., Suite 500, Barrington Tower, Scotia Sq., Halifax, N.S. (902/425-6900)
Shearson, Loeb, Rhoades (Canada) Inc., #1620, 1200 McGill College Ave., Montreal, P.Q. H3B 4G7 (878-1861)
Tasse & Associes, Ltée, 630 Dorchester Blvd. W., Montreal, P.Q. H2B 1T4 (879-2100)
D. W. Taylor & Co. Ltd., Suite 1215, 800 Dorchester Blvd. W., Montreal, P.Q. H3B 1X9 (871-1250)
Walwyn, Stodgell, Cochran & Murray, Ste. 510, 1200 McGill College, Montreal, P.Q. (871-9951)
Wood Gundy Ltd., 36th floor, 1 Place Ville Marie, Montreal, P.Q. H3B 3P2 (879-1222)
Yorkton Securities Ltd., Suite 4006, 1155 Dorchester Blvd. W., Montreal, P.Q. H3B 3V5 (861-4221)

Members with Restricted Trading Privileges (Senior Industrials Section only)

Wm. M. Molson, #100, 1303 Greene Ave., Montreal, P.Q. (932-4481)

Individual Members

Address: Tour de la Bourse, Montreal, P.Q. H4Z 1A9 (514/871-2424)

Crispino Adragna; Ahmad Athar; Ara Basmadjian; André Beaulieu; Prosper Benaim; Ronald Biron; Gilles Boivin; André Campeau; J.-R. Cardinal; G. Casey; F. Cavanagh; Roger Charland; Remo Costa; Jacques Dery; Pierre Dubeau; J.-P. Ferland; Donald Fortin; J.A. Gill; R.G. Lachapelle; Guy Lapierre; S.H. Lebel; R.J. Maude; Paul Morand; Eric Morissette; Huu Pituoc Nguyen; Gilles Ostiguy; Yvon Perron; H.-P. Roy; J.R. Schlybeurt

VANCOUVER STOCK EXCHANGE

Stock Exchange Tower, Box 10333, (609 Granville St.), Vancouver, B.C. V7Y 1H1
(604) 689-3334
Telex: 04-55480

The Board of Governors

Chairman, Ian A. Falconer
President, R.A. Scott

Member Firms

A. E. Ames & Co., 1625-555 Burrard St., Vancouver, B.C. V7X 1G5 (689-4422)
Bache, Halsey, Stuart Canada Ltd., 12th floor, 789 W. Pender St., Vancouver, B.C. V6C 1H2 (683-9242)
Blyth, Eastman Dillon & Co. Ltd., Ste. 1115, 595 Howe St., Vancouver, B.C. V6C 2T5 (689-4445)
Bond Street International Securities Ltd., Ste. 301, 580 Granville St., Vancouver, B.C. V6C 1X2 (687-7521)
Brink, Hudson & Lefever Ltd., 717-837 W. Hastings St., Vancouver, B.C. V6C 1C1 (688-0133)
Alfred Bunting & Co. Ltd., 155 University Ave., Toronto, Ont. M5H 3H7 (416/364-3293)
Burns Fry Ltd., #1700, 1055 W. Georgia St., Vancouver, B.C. V6E 3P3 (685-5181)
Canarim Investment Corp. Ltd., 1350, 409 Granville St., Vancouver, B.C. V6C 2J5 (688-8151)
Canarim Investment Corp. Ltd., Ste. 1130, 444 St. Mary Ave., Winnipeg, Man. R3C 3T1 (204/943-6587)
W.F. Christensen, #1710, 1177 W. Hastings St., Vancouver, B.C. V6E 2L3 (683-9611)
Continental, Carlisle, Douglas Ltd., 600-789 W. Pender St., Vancouver, B.C. V6C 1H7 (688-8331)
R.A. Daly & Co. Ltd., Box 42, Toronto Dominion Centre, Toronto, Ont. M5K 1E1 (416/362-6192)
Davidson, Partners Ltd., Box 122, First Canadian Place, Toronto, Ont. M5X 1E9 (416/867-3300)
F.H. Deacon, Hodgson Inc., 105 Adelaide St. W., Toronto, Ont. M5H 1R4 (416/867-3000)
Dominion Securities Ltd., Box 10024, Pacific Centre, Vancouver, B.C. V7Y 1B2 (687-9411)
Fisher Securities Corp., #1202, 750 W. Pender St., Vancouver, B.C. (681-1832)
Gardiner, Watson Ltd., 11 Adelaide St. W., 12th Floor, Toronto, Ont. M5H 2R4
Geoffrion Leclerc Inc., 800 Dorchester Blvd. W., #1700, Montreal, P.Q. H3B 1Y8 (514/861-8811)
Greenshields Ltd., Box 11126, 1055 W. Georgia St., Vancouver, B.C. V6E 3R1 (682-5811)
Houston, Willoughby Ltd., 1825 Cornwall St., Regina, Sask. S4P 3C9 (306/525-6731)
Jones, Gable & Co. Ltd., Ste. 101, 535 Thurlow St., Vancouver, B.C. V6E 3L3 (685-1481)
W. D. Latimer Co. Ltd., Box 96, Toronto Dominion Bank Tower, Toronto, Ont. M5K 1G8 (416/363-5631)
William E. Lewis, 630 Columbia St., New Westminster, B.C. V3M 1A5 (526-4466)
Loewen, Ondaatje, McCutcheon & Co. Ltd., Ste. 2716, 200 Granville St., Vancouver, B.C. V6C 1S6 (688-6701)
McDermid, Miller & McDermid Ltd., Ste. 1000, 675 W. Hastings St., Vancouver, B.C. V6B 1N6 (682-7121)
McLeod, Young, Weir Ltd., 1256-200 Granville St., Vancouver, B.C. V6C 2R4 (681-0111)
Mead & Co. Ltd., Ste. 802, 409 Granville St., Vancouver, B.C. V6G 2J5 (687-3833)
Merrill Lynch, Royal Securities Ltd., 158, 200 Granville St., Vancouver, B.C. V6C 1S4 (682-3311)
Merrill Lynch, Royal Securities Ltd., Box 31, Toronto Dominion Centre, Toronto, Ont. M5K 1C2(416/361-3303)
Midland Doherty Ltd., 11th Floor, Three Bentall Centre, 595 Burrard St., Vancouver, B.C. V7X 1C3 (688-2111)
Nesbitt Thomson Bongard Inc., Box 11512, #1500, 650 W. Georgia St., Vancouver, B.C. V6B 4N7 (683-1181)
Odlum Brown & T. B. Read Ltd., 1270-700 W. Georgia St., Vancouver, B.C. V7Y 1A3 (684-9332)
C. M. Oliver & Co. Ltd., 750 W. Pender St., Vancouver, B.C. V6C 1B5 (684-9211)
A.E. Osler, Wills, Bickle Ltd., Box 60, Royal Bank Plaza, Toronto, Ont. M5J 2K6 (416/865-2000)
Pemberton Securities Ltd., 2403-595 Burrard St., Vancouver, B.C. V7X 1K6 (688-8411)
Peters & Co. Ltd., 312 4th Ave. S.W., Calgary, Alta. T2P 0H7 (403/261-4850)
Pitfield Mackay Ross Ltd., Box 11536, #1995, 650 W. Georgia St., Vancouver, B.C. V6B 4S2 (683-8611)
Rademaker, MacDougall & Co., Ste. 400, 409 Granville St., Vancouver, B.C. V6C 1T7 (687-0456)
Richardson Securities of Canada, 500, 1066 W. Hastings St., Vancouver, B.C. V6C 2M4 (682-1751)

Union Securities Ltd., Ste. 211, 543 Granville St., Vancouver, B.C. V6C 1X8 (685-7000)
Walwyn Stodgell Cochran Murray Ltd., #1465, Two Bentall Centre, 555 Burrard St., Vancouver, B.C. V7X 1G7 (682-5955)
West Coast Securities Ltd., #511, 837 W. Hastings St., Vancouver, B.C. V6C 1B6 (681-1286)
Westfield Securities Ltd., #1616, 500 4th Ave. S.W., Calgary, Alta. T2P 2V6 (403/262-1901)
Wolverton & Co. Ltd., 534 Burrard St., Vancouver, B.C. V6C 2J9 (688-3477)
Wood, Gundy Ltd., 1700-700 W. Georgia St., Vancouver, B.C. V7Y 1A5 (683-8311)
Yorkshire Securities Ltd., #206, 595 Howe St., Vancouver, B.C. V6C 2T5 (669-7752)
Yorkton Securities Ltd., Suite 1200, 11 King St. W., Toronto, Ont. M5H 1A3 (416/864-3500)

THE ALBERTA STOCK EXCHANGE

3rd Floor, 300 5th Ave. S.W., Calgary, Alta. T2P 3C4
(403) 262-7791
Telex: 038-21793

Executive Officers

Chairman, R.G. Rogers
President, R.J. Milliken
Secretary Treasurer, W. D. Kaine
Governors, J.B. Kennedy, R.B. Brookes, W.W. Charlton, R.E. Ewing, A.J. Coote, J.M. Brandreth, R.B. Christie, R.G. Peters
Public Governor, G.H. Rose, Q.C.
Operations Manager, T.P. Callaghan
Clearing Manager, H.J. Hall

Member Firms

A.E. Ames & Co., #440, 407 8th Ave. S.W., Calgary, Alta. T2P 1E5
Bache Halsey Stuart Canada Ltd., #1812, 715 5th Ave. S.W., Calgary, Alta. T2P 2X6
Bell Gouinlock Ltd., Box 110, First Canadian Place, Toronto, Ont. M5X 1B6
Brault, Guy, O'Brien Inc., Box 279, Commerce Court Postal Stn., Toronto, Ont. M5L 1E9
Alfred Bunting & Co. Ltd., 155 University Ave., Toronto, Ont. M5H 3B7
Burns Fry Ltd., #299, 401 9th Ave. S.W., Calgary, Alta. T2P 3C5
Canarim Investment Corp. Ltd., Ste. 1350, 409 Granville St., Vancouver, B.C. V6C 2J5
Canavest House Ltd., Box 13, Commerce Court Postal Stn., Toronto, Ont. M5L 1A3
Charlton Investment Group Ltd., 220 Bow Valley Sq. Two, Box 9443, Calgary, Alta. T2P 2V7
Columbia Securities Ltd., #800, 602 12th Ave. S.W., Calgary, Alta. T2R 0H5
Continental Carlisle Douglas Ltd., 600-789 W. Pender St., Vancouver, B.C. V6C 1H7
R.A. Daly & Co. Ltd., 1406 Home Oil Tower, 324 8th Ave. S.W., Calgary, Alta. T2P 2Z2
Davidson Partners Ltd., First Canadian Place, Box 122, Toronto, Ont. M5X 1E9
F.H. Deacon, Hodgson Inc., 105 Adelaide St. W., Toronto, Ont. M5H 1R4
Dominion Securities (Alta.) Ltd., 1107, 333 7th Ave. S.W., Calgary, Alta. T2P 2Z1
First Marathon Securities Ltd., #700, 11 Adelaide St. W., Toronto, Ont. M5H 1M2
Gardiner Watson Ltd., #640, 401 9th Ave. S.W., Calgary, Alta. T2P 1G2
Gordon Securities Ltd., #960, 540 5th Ave. S.W., Calgary, Alta. T2P 0M4
Greenshields Ltd., 200, 407 2nd St. S.W., Calgary, Alta. T2P 2Y3
Heritage Securities Corp., #1404, 7 King St. E., Toronto, Ont. M5C 1A6
Houston Willoughby of Alta. Ltd., Ste. 1837, Toronto Dominion Tower, Edmonton Centre, Edmonton, Alta. T4J 2Z1
Jones, Gable & Co. Ltd., 110 Yonge St., Toronto, Ont. M5L 1T6
Lafferty, Harwood & Partners Ltd., 500 St. James St. W., Montreal, P.Q. H2Y 3R3
W. D. Latimer & Co. Ltd., Box 96, Toronto Dominion Centre, Toronto, Ont. M5K 1G8
L.O.M. Western Securities Ltd., 2716 Granville Sq., 200 Granville St., Vancouver, B.C. V6C 1S6
McDermid, Miller & McDermid Ltd., #305, 605 5th Ave. S.W., Calgary, Alta. T2P 3H5
McLeod, Young, Weir Ltd., 401 9th Ave. S.W., #885, Calgary, Alta. T2P 3C5
Merit Investment Corp., #400, 155 University Ave., Toronto, Ont. M5H 2Z5
Merrill Lynch, Royal Securities Ltd., 480 7th Ave. S.W., Calgary, Alta. T2P 0X7
Midland Doherty Ltd., #400, 605 5th Ave. S.W., Calgary, Alta. T2P 3H5
Moss, Lawson & Co. Ltd., 2nd floor, 330 5th Ave. S.W., Calgary, Alta. T2P OL4
Nesbitt, Thomson, Bongard Inc., M200, 345 4th Ave. S.W., Calgary, Alta. T2P 0H9
Odlum Brown & T.B. Read Ltd., Ste. 2470, 700 2nd Ave. S.W., Calgary, Alta. T2P 2W2
C. M. Oliver & Co. Ltd., 2nd Floor, 750 W. Pender St., Vancouver, B.C. V6C 1B5
Osler, Wills, Bickle Ltd., Main floor, 407 2nd St. S.W., Calgary, Alta. T2P 2Y3
Pemberton Securities Ltd., #1008, 324 8th Ave. S.W., Calgary, Alta. T2P 2Z2
Peters & Co. Ltd., 312 4th Ave. S.W., Calgary, Alta. T2P OH7
Pitfield, MacKay, Ross Ltd., #900, 700 4th Ave. S.W., Calgary, Alta. T2P 3J4
Richardson Securities of Canada, 6th floor, Toronto Dominion Sq., Box 730, Calgary, Alta. T2P 2M7
St. Lawrence Securities Ltd., #2315, 401 Bay St., Toronto, Ont. M5H 2Y4
Shearson Loeb Rhoades (Canada) Inc., 622 5th Ave. S.W., Calgary, Alta. T2P OM6
Walwyn Stodgell Cochran Murray Ltd., #680, 401 9th Ave. S.W., Calgary, Alta. T2P 3C5
Westfield Securities Ltd., #2300, 300 5th Ave. S.W., Calgary, Alta. T2P 3C4
Wood, Gundy Ltd., #1900, 300 5th Ave. S.W., Calgary, Alta. T2P 3C4

THE WINNIPEG STOCK EXCHANGE

#303, 167 Lombard Ave., Winnipeg, Man. R3B OT6
(204) 942-8431
Telex:

Governing Committee

President, J.T. Ethans
Vice President & Secretary Treasurer, F.W. Buchanan
Governors, H.R.G. Scrivener; W.J. Fischer; S.D. Cohen; R.A. Stafford; J.T. Ethans; J.G. Oborne

Member Firms

A. E. Ames & Co. Ltd., 280 Broadway Ave., Winnipeg, Man. R3C 0R8 (943-6411)
Bache Halsey Stuart Canada Ltd., #310, 360 Main St., Winnipeg, Man. R3C 3Z3 (944-8207)
Bell, Gouinlock & Co. Ltd., 201-209 Notre Dame Ave., Winnipeg, Man. R3B 1M9 (943-0611)
Burns Fry Ltd., 400-305 Broadway Ave., Winnipeg, Man. R3C 0R9 (947-1501)
Canarim Investment Corp. Ltd., 3rd fl., 52 Donald St., Winnipeg, Man. R3C 3Z6 (944-8616)
Dominion Securities Ltd., #770, 360 Main St., Winnipeg, Man. R3C 3Z3 (942-3431)
Dreman & Co. Ltd., 6th fl., 238 Portage Ave., Winnipeg, Man. R3C 0B1 (943-0691)
Greenshields Ltd., 1112, 363 Broadway Ave., Winnipeg, Man. R3C 3N9 (956-1020)
McLeod Young Weir Ltd., #990, 360 Main St., Winnipeg, Man. R3C 3Z3 (943-5461)

Merrill Lynch, Royal Securities Ltd., #100, 360 Main St., Winnipeg, Man. R3C 3Z3 (944-9267)

Midland Doherty Ltd., Richardson Bldg., 1200-1 Lombard Pl., Winnipeg, Man. R3B 0X3 (942-0311)

Nesbitt, Thomson, Bongard Inc., 330 Portage Ave., Winnipeg, Man. R3C 0C4 (942-2521)

Pitfield MacKay Ross Ltd., #600, 360 Main St., Winnipeg, Man. R3C 3Z3 (943-8461)

Richardson Securities of Canada, Richardson Bldg., 1 Lombard Pl., Winnipeg, Man. R3B 0X4 (943-9311)

Sellers, Dickson Securities Ltd., 2210-1 Lombard Pl., Winnipeg, Man. R3B 0X3 (943-2584)

Walwyn Stodgell Cochran Murray Ltd., 4th fl., 200 Portage Ave., Winnipeg, Man. R3C 0X2 (942-4251)

Wood, Gundy Ltd., 280 Broadway Ave., Winnipeg, Man R3C 0R8 (942-6141)

INSURANCE COMPANIES

Registered to conduct business in Canada under the Canadian and British Insurance Companies Act and the Foreign Insurance Companies Act. For companies registered in the various provinces and not listed below (marked *), contact the Superintendent of Insurance, each Province.

A.G.F. Réassurances
Life Branch, #2100, Place du Canada, Montreal, P.Q. H3B 2R8
Chief Agent, Colin Jack

A.G.F. Réassurances
Property & Casualty Branch, 360 St. James St., #2000, Montreal, P.Q. H2Y 1P5
Chief Agent, Ralph Davis

Abbey Life Insurance Company of Canada
3027 Harvester Rd., Burlington, Ont. L7N 3G9
(416) 639-6200
President, W.D. Millar

Abeille-Paix Réassurances
188 University Ave., Toronto, Ont. M5H 3C3
(416) 593-5222
Chief Agent, Sidney Gordon

*Abstainers Insurance Company
3228 South Service Rd., Burlington, Ont. L7N 3H8
(416) 639-9031
President, M.E. Schultz
Fire and auto insurance for abstainers

The Acadia Life Insurance Company
439 University Ave., Toronto, Ont. M5G 1Y8
(416) 596-6100
President, J.B. Murch

Adriatic Insurance Company
(Riunione Adriatica de Sicurta)
1075 Beaver Hall Hill, Montreal, P.Q. H2Z 1S6
(514) 866-6531
Chief Agent, J. Legault

Advocate General Insurance Company of Canada
#300, 363 Broadway, Winnipeg, Man. R3C 3N9
(204) 944-0629
President, J.P. Pereira

The Aetna Casualty & Surety Company
20 Toronto St., Toronto, Ont. M5C 2C4
(416) 863-8000
Chief Agent, Donald F. Duncan

Aetna Casualty Company of Canada
20 Toronto St., Toronto, Ont. M5C 2C4
(416) 863-8000
President, G.N. Farquhar

Aetna Insurance Company
2300 Yonge St., #2900, Toronto, Ont. M4P 2X3
(416) 366-8231
Chief Agent, Richard Calvert

Aetna Life Insurance Company
20 Toronto St., Toronto, Ont. M5C 2C4
(416) 863-8247
Chief Agent, D.F. Duncan

Affiliated FM Insurance Company
100 Alexis Nihon Blvd., #500, St-Laurent, P.Q. H4M 2P8
(514) 747-9961
Manager & Chief Agent, B.J. Hurley

*Alberta General Insurance Company
10221 104 St., Edmonton, Alta. T5J 1B7
(403) 422-2197
Chief Agent, Harold J. Simmons

*Alberta Motor Association Insurance Co.
(11230 110 St.), Box 370, Edmonton, Alta. T5L 4J7
(403) 474-0481
Chief Agent, D. Haughey

The Albion Insurance Company of Canada
#1100, 1 St. Clair Ave. W., Toronto, Ont. M4V 2Z1
(416) 968-2122
Chief Agent, J.R. Lowrie

Alexander Hamilton Life Insurance Company of America
85 Bloor St. E., Toronto, Ont. M4W 1B4
(416) 960-0982
Chief Agent, M.A. Castonguay

Allendale Mutual Insurance Company
100 Alexis Nihon Blvd., #500, St-Laurent, P.Q. H4M 2P8
(514) 747-9961
Manager & Chief Agent, B.J. Hurley

Alliance Mutual Life Insurance Company
680 Sherbrooke St. W., Montreal, P.Q. H3A 1E9
President, Hervé Belzile

Allianz Insurance Company
7 King St. E., #1212, Toronto, Ont. M5C 1A2
(416) 364-4373
Chief Agent, Ronald A. Griffin

Allstate Insurance Company
255 Consumers Rd., Willowdale, Ont. M2J 1R3
(416) 493-0550
Chief Agent, Gerald J. Fournier

Allstate Insurance Company of Canada
255 Consumers Rd., Willowdale, Ont. M2J 1R3
(416) 493-0550
President, Gerald J. Fournier

Allstate Life Insurance Company
255 Consumers Rd., Willowdale, Ont. M2J 1R3
(416) 493-0550
Chief Agent, Gerald J. Fournier

Allstate Life Insurance Company of Canada
255 Consumers Rd., Willowdale, Ont. M2J 1R3
(416) 493-0550
President, Gerald J. Fournier

Alpina Insurance Company Ltd.
188 University Ave., Toronto, Ont. M5H 3C3
(416) 593-6121
Chief Agent, R.N. Mackintosh

American Bankers Insurance Company of Florida
111 Merton St., Toronto, Ont. M4S 3A7
(416) 486-5305
Chief Agent, B.R. Thompson

American Bankers Life Assurance Company of Florida
111 Merton St., Toronto, Ont. M4S 3A7
(416) 486-5305
Chief Agent, B.R. Thompson

American Credit Indemnity Company of New York
623 Dominion Square Bldg., Montreal, P.Q. H3B 1G7
(514) 866-1788
Chief Agent, B.C. Westgate

American Health & Life Insurance Company
500 University Ave., 5th Floor, Toronto, Ont. M5G 1W1
(416) 598-4500

American Home Assurance Company
55 University Ave., Toronto, Ont. M5J 2H7
(416) 869-5000

Chief Agent, Gary A. McMillan
The American Insurance Company
Box 4060, Stn. A, Toronto, Ont. M5W 1L9
Chief Agent, J.L. Kirschbaum
American Life Insurance Company
55 University Ave., Toronto, Ont. M5J 2H7
(416) 869-5000
Chief Agent, Gary A. McMillan
American Mutual Liability Insurance Company
2655 Liruma Rd., Mississauga, Ont. L5K 2Y9
(416) 823-6202
Chief Agent, W.S. Utter
American National Fire Insurance Company
(305 4th Ave. N.), Box 1237, Saskatoon, Sask. S7K 3N7
(306) 244-7520
Chief Agent, K.R. Stephenson
American National Insurance Company
Box 262, Toronto Dominion Centre, Toronto, Ont. M5K 1J9
Chief Agent, A.F. Sellers
American Re-Insurance Company
20 Toronto St., Toronto, Ont. M5C 2B8
(416) 863-9850
Chief Agent, D.L. Breckles
The American Road Insurance Company
The Canadian Rd., Oakville, Ont. L6J 5C7
(416) 845-1123
Chief Agent, John B. Gregorovich
American United Life Insurance Company
c/o McLean & Kerr, 372 Bay St., #1000, Toronto, Ont. M5H 2X5
(416) 364-5371
Chief Agent, R.B. Cumine, Q.C.
Ancienne Mutuelle Accidents
(Société d'Assurances à forme mutuelle à cotisations fixes contre les accidents et autres risques)
2021 Union Ave., Montreal, P.Q. H3A 2V1
(514) 282-1914
Chief Agent, W.A. Major
*Anglo-Canada General Insurance Company
171 Queens Ave., London, Ont. N6A 5J7
(519) 679-9440
President, E.O. Shieck
Antigonish Farmers' Mutual Fire Insurance Company
Box 1535, Antigonish, N.S. B2E 2B9
(902) 863-3544
Treasurer & Manager, D.J. Chisholm
Argonaut Insurance Company
c/o Coopers & Lybrand, 28th Floor, Royal Centre, 1055 W. Georgia St., Vancouver, B.C.
Chief Agent, D.R. Sinclair
Arkwright-Boston Manufacturers Mutual Insurance Company
45 Charles St. E., Toronto, Ont. M4Y 1S2
(416) 920-5041
Chief Agent, L.C. Boughner
The Artisans, Life Insurance Cooperative Society
333 St-Antoine St. E., Montreal, P.Q. H2X 1R9
(514) 861-5781
Le Assicurazioni d'Italia
850 W. Hastings St., #502, Vancouver, B.C. V6C 1E1
Chief Agent, N.G. Williams
*L'Assomption Mutuelle d'Assurance-Vie
(770 Main St.), Box 160, Moncton, N.B. E1C 8L1
(506) 855-6040
*Atlantic Insurance Co. Ltd.
Box 970, Stn. C, St. John's, Nfld. A1C 5M3
General Manager, David Woolley
Atlantic Mutual Life Assurance Company
(140 Garfield St.), Box 489, Moncton, N.B. E1C 8L9
(506) 854-1811
Secretary, D.R. Lennox
Aviation & General Insurance Company Ltd.
Royal Bank Plaza, Box 2, Toronto, Ont. M5J 2J1
(416) 865-0252
Chief Agent, D.S. Barbeau
Balboa Insurance Company
Box 5071, Term. A, London, Ont. N6A 4M5
(519) 672-1070
Chief Agent, R.J. O'Brien
The Baloise Insurance Company Ltd.
40 University Ave., #214, Toronto, Ont. M5J 1J1
(416) 977-7438
Chief Agent, J.G. Dovey
Baltica-Skandinavia Insurance Company of Canada
111 Richmond St. W., #1012, Toronto, Ont. M5H 2G4
President, P.E. Lindblad
Bankers Life Company
c/o McLean & Kerr, 372 Bay St., #1000, Toronto, Ont. M5H 2X5
(416) 364-5371
Chief Agent, R.B. Cumine, Q.C.
*The Bay City General Insurance Company
505 York Blvd., Box 2018, Hamilton, Ont. L8N 3S3
(416) 525-5300
Managing Director, J.C. Stradwick
The Bee Fire, Hail etc Insurance Company
See Abeille
*Belair Insurance Company
5455 St-André, Montréal, P.Q. H2J 4A9
(514) 270-9111
General Manager, A. Faulkner
Beneficial Standard Life Insurance Company
#1201, 750 W. Pender St., Vancouver, B.C. V6C 1G8
Chief Agent, Maurice J. Calf
The Boiler Inspection and Insurance Company of Canada
8 King St. E., Toronto, Ont. M5C 1B5
(416) 363-5491
President, T.F. Cartwright
The British Aviation Insurance Company Ltd.
240 Eglinton Ave. E., Toronto, Ont. M4P 1K8
(416) 485-4461
Chief Agent, J.A. Redwood
*British Columbia Automobile Association Insurance Company (BCAA)
(999 W. Broadway), Box 9900, Vancouver, B.C. V6B 4H1
(604) 732-3911
Administration & Claims Manager, J.D. Harris
British Economic Insurance Company Limited
150 Consumers Rd., #403, Willowdale, Ont. M2J 1P8
Chief Agent, H.G.C. Innes
Buffalo Insurance Company
c/o Fasken & Calvin, Box 30, Toronto Dominion Centre, Toronto, Ont. M5K 1C1
(416) 366-8381
Chief Agent, F.D. Gibson
Business Men's Assurance Company of America
330 University Ave., Toronto, Ont. M5G 1R8
(416) 597-1456
Chief Agent, Gordon A. Gibbins
*Cabot Insurance Company Limited
Portugal Cove Rd. & Elizabeth Ave., St. John's, Nfld.
President, J.F. Munn
California-Western States Life Insurance Company
Box 49130, Three Bentall Centre, 595 Burrard St., Vancouver, B.C. V7X 1J5
Chief Agent, W.S. Owen
Calvert Fire Insurance Company
18 King St. E., #201, Toronto, Ont. M5C 2R6
(416) 869-0542
Chief Agent, C.F. Dumaresq
The Canada Accident & Fire Assurance Company
Box 441, Toronto Dominion Centre, Toronto, Ont. M5K 1L9
(416) 361-2500
Chairman, President & Chief Executive Officer, F.A. Saville
The Canada Life Assurance Company
330 University Ave., Toronto, Ont. M5G 1R8
(416) 597-1456
President, E.H. Crawford
Canada Security Assurance Company
60 Yonge St., Toronto, Ont. M5E 1H5

(416) 362-2961
President, R.H. Stevens
*Canada West Insurance Company
10603 107 Ave., Edmonton, Alta. T5H 3Z1
(403) 426-2200
President & General Manager, J.M. Connauton
The Canadian Commerce Insurance Company
111 Avenue Rd., #300, Toronto, Ont. M5R 3J8
(416) 961-5013
President, Ray F. Rush
Canadian General Insurance Company
Box 4030, Term. A, Toronto, Ont. M5W 1K4
(416) 593-1355
President, R.E. Bethell
Canadian General Life Insurance Company
105 Main St. E., Hamilton, Ont. L8N 1G6
(416) 528-6766
President, Charles P. Flood
Canadian Home Assurance Company
1075 Beaver Hall Hill, Montreal, P.Q. H2Z 1S6
(514) 866-6531
President, J.-P. Lussier
The Canadian Indemnity Company
Royal Bank Plaza, Box 26, Toronto, Ont. M5J 2J1
(416) 865-0182
President, H.B. Vannan
The Canadian Provincial Insurance Company
111 Avenue Rd., #300, Toronto, Ont. M5R 3J8
(416) 961-5013
President, Ray F. Rush
Canadian Reassurance Company
95 St. Clair Ave. W., Toronto, Ont. M4V 1N9
(416) 925-2261
President, Michel Sales
Canadian Reinsurance Company
95 St. Clair Ave. W., Toronto, Ont. M4V 1N9
(416) 925-2261
President, Michel Sales
The Canadian Surety Company
Canada Sq., 2180 Yonge St., Toronto, Ont. M4S 2C2
(416) 486-2800
President, John Robertson
*Canadian Universal Insurance Company Ltd.
1155 Dorchester Blvd. W., Montreal, P.Q. H3B 2K7
(514) 866-8444
President, M.H. Saval
Canners Exchange Subscribers at Warner Inter-Insurance Bureau
120 Bloor St. E., Toronto, Ont. M4W 1B7
(416) 924-7487
Chief Agent, Ian C. White, Q.C.
*La Capitale (Cie d'Assurance Générale)
C.P. 17100, Québec, P.Q. G1K 7X2
(418) 643-2700
The Capitol Life Insurance Company
c/o McLean & Kerr, 372 Bay St., #1000, Toronto, Ont. M5H 2X5
(416) 364-5371
Chief Agent, R.B. Cumine, Q.C.
Cardinal Insurance Company
171 Wilson Ave., Toronto, Ont. M5M 3A2
President, Antony Mendez
Carolina Life & Accident Insurance Company
6075 Yonge St., 3rd Floor, Willowdale, Ont. M4M 3W2
(416) 224-2235
Chief Agent, Iain S. Paterson
The Casualty Company of Canada
165 University Ave., Toronto, Ont. M5H 3B8
(416) 362-7231
President, F.G. Elliott
Centennial Insurance Company
4150 Ste-Catherine W., #620, Montreal, P.Q. H3Z 2R3
(514) 931-6234
Chief Agent, G. Gordon Symons
Central Mutual Insurance Company
20 Wood Glen Rd., Scarborough, Ont. M1N 2V7
Chief Agent, Sydney Barlow
The Century Insurance Company of Canada
1112 W. Pender St., Vancouver, B.C. V6E 2S1
(604) 683-6777
President, G.R. Elliott
Charter National Life Insurance Company
Box 38, Toronto Dominion Centre, Toronto, Ont. M5K 1C7
Chief Agent, James G. Torrance
Chateau Insurance Company
#2900, 2300 Yonge St., Toronto, Ont. M4P 2X3
(416) 488-3601
President, P.A. Bradbury
Chicago Title Insurance Company
c/o McLean & Kerr, 372 Bay St., #1000, Toronto, Ont. M5H 2X5
(416) 364-5371
Chief Agent, R.B. Cumine, Q.C.
Chrysler Insurance Company
#201, Plaza One Meadowvale Corporate Centre, 2000 Argentia Rd., Mississauga, Ont. L5N 1P7
(416) 826-5315
Chief Agent, G.G. Sampson
Chrysler Life Insurance Company of Canada
#201, Plaza One Meadowvale Corporate Centre, 2000 Argentia Rd., Mississauga, Ont. L5N 1P7
(416) 826-5240
Vice President, G.G. Sampson
Chubb Insurance Company of Canada
145 King St. W., #1200, Toronto, Ont. M5H 3L2
(416) 863-0550
President, Edward Dunlop
The Citadel General Assurance Company
1075 Bay St., Toronto, Ont. M5S 2W5
(416) 928-8500
President & Chief Executive Officer, J.E. Stephens
The Citadel Life Assurance Company
1075 Bay St., Toronto, Ont. M5S 2W5
(416) 928-8500
President & Managing Director, F.W. Tallman
Clare Mutual Fire Insurance Company
Belliveau's Cove, N.S. B0W 1J0
(902) 837-4418
Manager, J. Vincent Blin
*Coachman Insurance Company
Box 157, Stn. U, Toronto, Ont. M8Z 5P1
(416) 255-3417
College Retirement Equities Fund
#2300, 130 Adelaide St. W., Toronto, Ont. M5H 3C2
Chief Agent, J.T. DesBrisay, Q.C.
Cologne Life Reinsurance Company
2 St. Clair Ave. E., Toronto, Ont. M4T 2V6
(416) 960-3601
Chief Agent, William H. Gleed
Colonia Life Insurance Company
2 St. Clair Ave. E., Toronto, Ont. M4T 2V6
(416) 960-3601
President, William H. Gleed
Combined Insurance Company of America
Box 4081, Stn. A, Toronto, Ont. M5W 1M7
(416) 922-1922
Chief Agent, Peter Cherian
*Commerce & Industry Insurance Company of Canada
55 University Ave., Toronto, Ont. M5J 2H7
(416) 869-5000
Chief Agent, Gary A. McMillan
The Commerce Group Insurance Company
2450 boul. Girouard, St-Hyacinthe, P.Q. J2S 3B3
(514) 773-9701
President & Chief Executive Officer, Guy St. Germain
The Commercial Life Assurance Company of Canada
1303 Yonge St., Toronto, Ont. M4T 1X1
(416) 924-7311

Commercial Travelers Mutual Insurance Company
27 Queen St. E., Toronto, Ont. M5C 2M6
(416) 362-1366
Chief Agent, W.R. Adams
Commercial Union Assurance Company Limited
Box 441, Toronto Dominion Centre, Toronto, Ont. M5K 1L9
(416) 361-2500
President for Canada, F.A. Saville
Commercial Union Assurance Company of Canada
Box 441, Toronto Dominion Centre, Toronto, Ont. M5K 1L9
(416) 361-2500
President, Chief Executive Officer & Director, F.A. Saville
Commonwealth Insurance Company
715 Two Bentall Centre, 555 Burrard St., Vancouver, B.C. V7X 1J3
(604) 688-3631
President, John Watson
*La Concorde Compagnie d'Assurances Générales
255 St-Jacques ouest, Montréal, P.Q. H2Y 1M6
(514) 845-5251
President, Gérard Brunet
Compagnie Transcontinental de Réassurance
c/o Professional Reinsurance Consultants, 703 Evans Ave., Etobicoke, Ont. M9C 5A7
Chief Agent, Raymond Viger
Confederation Life Insurance Company
321 Bloor St. E., Toronto, Ont. M4W 1H1
(416) 967-8111
President, John A. Rhind
Connecticut General Life Insurance Company
c/o McLean & Kerr, 372 Bay St., #1000, Toronto, Ont. M5H 2X5
(416) 364-5371
Chief Agent, R.B. Cumine, Q.C.
Constellation Assurance Company
55 Yonge St., Toronto, Ont. M5E 1J6
(416) 360-1560
President & Chief Executive Officer, T.L. Bourk
Constitution Insurance Company of Canada
500 University Ave., Toronto, Ont. M5G 1V9
(416) 595-1300
Secretary Treasurer, Wm. H.N. Hitch
Continental Assurance Company
1075 Bay St., Toronto, Ont. M5S 2W5
(416) 928-8500
Chief Agent, F.W. Tallman
Continental Casualty Company
1075 Bay St., Toronto, Ont. M5S 2W5
(416) 928-8500
Chief Agent, J.E. Stephens
The Continental Insurance Company
Box 4024, Term. A, Toronto, Ont. M5W 1K1
(416) 860-4250
Chief Agent, W.W. Ward
The Contingency Insurance Company Ltd.
620 Dorchester Blvd. W., #402, Montreal, P.Q. H3B 1N8
Chief Agent, E.L. Clark
*Les Coopérants Compagnie d'Assurances Générale
1259 rue Berri, Montreal, P.Q. H2L 4C7
(514) 288-1502
Manager, Administration, Pierre Fecteau
Co-operative Fire & Casualty Company
1920 College Ave., Regina, Sask. S4P 1C4
(306) 347-6200
Chief Executive Officer, Teunis Haalboom
*Co-operative Hail Insurance Company Ltd.
(2709 13th Ave.), Box 777, Regina, Sask. S4P 3A8
(306) 522-8691
Manager, G.C. Ashdown
Co-operative Life Insurance Company
1920 College Ave., Regina, Sask. S4P 1C4
(306) 347-6200
Chief Executive Officer, Teunis Haalboom
*Co-operators Insurance Association
Priory Sq., Guelph, Ont. N1H 6P8
(519) 824-4400
Chief Executive Officer, Teunis Haalboom
*Co-operators Life Insurance Association
Priory Sq., Guelph, Ont. N1H 6P8
(519) 824-4400
Chief Executive Oficer, Teunis Haalboom
Cornhill Insurance Company Limited
111 Avenue Rd., #300, Toronto, Ont. M5R 3J8
(416) 961-5013
Chief Agent, Ray F. Rush
*Coronation Insurance Company
181 Bay St., Toronto, Ont.
(416) 869-0235
The Credit Life Insurance Company
Box 262, Toronto Dominion Centre, Toronto, Ont. M5K 1J9
Chief Agent, A.F. Sellers
Crown Life Insurance Company
120 Bloor St. E., Toronto, Ont. M4W 1B8
(416) 928-4500
President, R.C. Dowsett
CUMIS Insurance Society, Inc.
Box 5065, Burlington, Ont. L7R 4C2
(416) 632-1221
Executive Vice President & Chief Agent, J.L. Hervé Lanctôt
CUMIS General Insurance Company
Box 5065, Burlington, Ont. L7R 4C2
(416) 632-1221
President, J.L. Hervé Lanctôt
CUMIS Life Insurance Company
Box 5065, Burlington, Ont. L7R 4C2
(416) 632-1221
President, J.L. Hervé Lanctôt
CUNA Mutual Insurance Society
Box 5065, Burlington, Ont. L7R 4C2
(416) 632-1221
Executive Vice President & Chief Agent, J.L. Hervé Lanctôt
Desjardins Mutual Life Assurance Company
200 Ave. des Commandeurs, Lévis, P.Q. G6V 6R2
(418) 835-2000
Secrétaire, M. St-Cyr
The Dominion Insurance Corporation
Box 4024, Term. A, Toronto, Ont. M5W 1K1
(416) 860-4250
Vice President & Manager, W.W. Ward
The Dominion Life Assurance Company
111 Westmount Rd. S., Waterloo, Ont. N2J 4C6
(519) 888-5111
President, J.S. Acheson
The Dominion of Canada General Insurance Company
General Insurance: 165 University Ave., Toronto, Ont. M5H 3B8
(416) 362-7231
President, F.G. Elliott
The Dominion of Canada General Insurance Company
Life Insurance: (33 William St.), Box 9500, Kingston, Ont. K7L 5E8
*The Drake Insurance Company Limited
#605, 20 Victoria St., Toronto, Ont. M5C 2N8
(416) 368-5666
Eagle Star Insurance Company Limited
180 Bloor St. W., #201, Toronto, Ont. M5S 2V6
(416) 922-8065
Chief Agent, M.P. Greening
Eaton Bay Insurance Company
1235 Bay St., Toronto, Ont. M5R 3L4
(416) 928-0611
President, W.R. Livingston
Eaton/Bay Life Assurance Company
1235 Bay St., Toronto, Ont. M5R 3L4
(416) 928-0611
President, W.R. Livingston
Ecclesiastical Insurance Office Ltd.
(#1707, 2300 Yonge St.), Box 2401, Toronto, Ont. M4P 1E4
(416) 484-4555
Chief Agent, Peter Mangin

Economical Mutual Insurance Company
Box 700, Kitchener, Ont. N2G 4C1
(519) 888-8200
President & General Manager, J.T. Hill
*The Edmonton Canadian Insurance Company
See Canadian Surety Co.
Elite Insurance Company
#400, 1500 W. Georgia St., Vancouver, B.C. V6G 2Z6
(604) 682-4794
President, R.F. Lively
Emmco Insurance Company
45 Sheppard Ave. E., Willowdale, Ont. M2N 5W9
(416) 225-2315
Chief Agent, D.E. Wilson
*Empire Life Insurance Company
243-251 King St. E., Kingston, Ont. K7L 3A8
Employers Insurance of Wausau, A Mutual Company
#400, 55 University Ave., Box 25, Toronto, Ont. M5J 2H7
Chief Agent, J.B. Harrison
Employers Reinsurance Corporation
199 Bay St., 6th Floor, Toronto, Ont. M5J 1L4
(416) 362-6527
Chief Agent, J.L. Beamish
English & American Insurance Company Limited
48 Yonge St., #1060, Toronto, Ont. M5E 1G6
(416) 364-5485
Chief Agent, I.B. Manley
Equitable General Insurance Company
200 St. James St. W., Montreal, P.Q. H2Y 1M2
(514) 842-7801
President, Robert Bégin
The Equitable Life Assurance Society of the United States
1200 McGill College, #530, Montreal, P.Q. H3B 4G7
Chief Agent, Raymond Belhumeur
The Equitable Life Insurance Company of Canada
1 Westmount Rd. N., Waterloo, Ont. N2J 4C7
(519) 886-5110
President, D.L. MacLeod
The Excelsior Life Insurance Company
20 Toronto St., Toronto, Ont. M5C 2C4
(416) 863-8000
President, G.N. Farquhar
Family Life Assurance Company
300 5th Ave. S.W., Calgary, Alta. T2P 0L3
(403) 266-9000
President, J.H. Walsh
*Farm Mutual Reinsurance Plan Inc.
2445 Eagle St., Box 3428, Cambridge, Ont.
Federal Home Life Insurance Company
161 Eglinton Ave. E., #702, Toronto, Ont. M4P 1J7
Chief Agent, J.N. Drouin
Federal Insurance Company
145 King St. W., Toronto, Ont. M5H 3L2
(416) 863-0550
Chief Agent, P.B. Smith
Federated Life Insurance Company
Box 5800, Winnipeg, Man. R3C 3C9
(204) 786-6431
Chief Agent, R.E. Novog
Federated Mutual Insurance Company
Box 5800, Winnipeg, Man. R3C 3C9
(204) 786-6431
Chief Agent, R.E. Novog
Federation Insurance Company of Canada
275 St. James St. W., Montreal, P.Q. H2Y 1M9
(514) 842-1701
Managing Director, E.E. Ahl
Fidelity Insurance Company of Canada
4 King St. W., Toronto, Ont. M5H 3P4
(416) 366-1931
Vice President & Manager, G.A. Lightbound
Fidelity Life Assurance Company
1130 W. Pender St., #1600, Vancouver, B.C. V6E 2S2
(604) 669-2022
President & Chief Executive Officer, J.S.M. Cunningham
Financial Life Assurance Company of Canada
#1900, 10123 99th St., Edmonton, Alta. T5J 3H1
President, D.R. Urquhart
The Fire Insurance Company of Canada
c/o Desjardins, Ducharme, etc., #1200, 635 Dorchester Blvd. W., Montreal, P.Q. H3B 1R9
(514) 878-9411
Chief Agent, J.A. Desjardins
Fireman's Fund American Life Insurance Company
Box 4060, Stn. A, Toronto, Ont. M5W 1L9
(416) 963-7000
Chief Agent, J.L. Kirschbaum
Fireman's Fund Insurance Company
Box 4060, Stn. A, Toronto, Ont. M5W 1L9
(416) 963-7000
Chief Agent, J.L. Kirschbaum
Fireman's Fund Insurance Company of Canada
Box 4060, Stn. A, Toronto, Ont. M5W 1L9
(416) 963-7000
President, J.L. Kirschbaum
First National Insurance Company of America
Box 3000, Stn. A, Mississauga, Ont. L5A 3P6
(416) 828-2900
Chief Agent, J.C. McArthur
Ford Life Insurance Company
The Canadian Rd., Oakville, Ont. L6J 5C7
Chief Agent, John B. Gregorovich
Foremost Insurance Company Grand Rapids, Michigan
c/o McLean & Kerr, 372 Bay St., 10th Floor, Toronto, Ont. M5H 2X5
Chief Agent, R.B. Cumine, Q.C.
Foresters Indemnity Company
789 Don Mills Rd., Don Mills, Ont. M3C 1T9
(416) 429-3000
President, Peter Daly
The Franklin Life Insurance Company
c/o Cassels, Brock, 130 Adelaide St. W., Toronto, Ont. M5H 3C2
(416) 869-5300
Chief Agent, J.W. Graham
Frankona Ruckversicherungs - Aktien - Gesellschaft
Box 383, Commerce Court N., Toronto, Ont. M5L 1G3
Chief Agent, H.K. Ballantyne
GAN Incendie Accidents
(Compagnie Française D'Assurances Incendie, Accidents et Risques Divers)
c/o Robert Bradford Ltée, 360 St. James St., #920, Montreal, P.Q. H2Y 1P5
Chief Agent, Eric L. Clark
GAN VIE
(Compagnie Française D'Assurances sur la Vie)
c/o Robert Bradford Ltée, 360 St. James St., #920, Montreal, P.Q. H2Y 1P5
Chief Agent, Eric L. Clark
The General Accident Assurance Company of Canada
357 Bay St., 2nd Floor, Toronto, Ont. M5H 2T9
(416) 368-4733
President, L.G. Latham
General American Life Insurance Company
c/o Peat, Marwick, Mitchell & Co., 31st Floor, Commerce Court West, Toronto, Ont. M5L 1B2
Chief Agent, W.D. Cox
General Insurance Company of America
Box 3000, Stn. A, Mississauga, Ont. L5A 3P6
(416) 828-2900
Chief Agent, J.C. McArthur
General Reassurance Corporation
c/o Touche, Ross et Cie, 1 Place Ville Marie, #820, Montreal, P.Q. H3B 2A2
(514) 861-8531
Chief Agent, Wm. Highfield
General Reinsurance Corporation
First Canadian Place, Toronto, Ont. M5X 1B1
(416) 869-0490
Chief Agent, D.W. Bradford

General Security Assurance Corporation of New York
#1400, 635 Dorchester Blvd. W., Montreal, P.Q. H3B 1S3
Chief Agent, E.W. Tinmouth
General Security Insurance Company
See Le Groupe Desjardins, Assurances Générales
*Gerling Global General Insurance Company
480 University Ave., Toronto, Ont. M5G 1V6
(416) 598-4651
President, Dr. R.R. Kern
*Gerling Global Reinsurance Company
480 University Ave., Toronto, Ont. M5G 1V6
(416) 598-4651
President, Dr. R.R. Kern
*Gibraltar General Insurance Company
171 Queens Ave., London, Ont. N6A 5J7
(519) 679-9440
President, E.O. Shieck
Glacier National Life Assurance Company
750 W. Pender St., #1201, Vancouver, B.C. V6C 1G8
President, Maurice J. Calf
Globe Life Insurance Company
Two Robert Speck Pkwy., #1140, Mississauga, Ont. L4Z 1H8
Chief Agent, J.E. Harris
Gold Circle Insurance Company
#301, 74 Victoria St., Toronto, Ont. M5C 2A5
(416) 869-7500
President, Peter Kendrick
Gore Mutual Insurance Company
252 Dundas St., Cambridge (G), Ont. N1R 5T3
(519) 623-1910
Secretary, J.M. Gray
Grain Insurance & Guarantee Company
167 Lombard Ave., #906, Winnipeg, Man. R3B 0V9
(204) 943-0721
President & General Manager, A.C. Affleck
Great American Insurance Company
305 4th Ave. N., Box 1237, Saskatoon, Sask. S7K 3N7
(306) 244-7520
Chief Agent, K.R. Stephenson
The Great Eastern Insurance Company
#1880, Sun Life Bldg., Montreal, P.Q. H3B 2X5
(514) 861-4292
President, W.N. Johnston
The Great Lakes Reinsurance Company
55 Yonge St., #606, Toronto, Ont. M5E 1J4
(416) 364-2851
President, M.H. McLachlan
The Great-West Life Assurance Company
60 Osborne St. N., Winnipeg, Man. R3C 3A5
(204) 946-1190
President, K.P. Kavanagh
Le Groupe Desjardins – assurances générales
100 rte Trans Canada est, Lévis, P.Q. G6V 6P9
(418) 835-2698; Telex: 051-3480
Western Division: 1 Complexe Desjardins, #1722, Montreal, P.Q. H5B 1B1
President, C. LeBlanc
The Guarantee Company of North America
Place du Canada, 15th Floor, Montreal, P.Q. H3B 2R4
(514) 866-6351
President, G.A. Savage
Guardian Insurance Company of Canada
Box 4096, Stn. A, Toronto, Ont. M5W 1N1
(416) 863-4111
President, Norman Curtis
Guildhall Insurance Company Limited
188 University Ave., Toronto, Ont. M5H 3C3
(416) 593-5222
Chief Agent, Sidney Gordon
The Halifax Insurance Company
1303 Yonge St., Toronto, Ont. M4T 1W9
(416) 924-7311
President, W.L. Williams
Hannover Ruckversicherungs - Aktiengesellschaft
Box 447, Stn. A, Toronto, Ont. M5W 1E3
Chief Agent, Neil Cockcroft
The Hanover Insurance Company
1 St. Clair Ave. W., #1100, Toronto, Ont. M4V 2Z1
(416) 968-2122
Chief Agent, J.R. Lowrie
The Hartford Fire Insurance Company
401 Bay St., 9th Floor, Toronto, Ont. M5H 2Y7
(416) 364-7131
Chief Agent, J.M. McFadyen
Hartford Life Insurance Company
401 Bay St., 9th Floor, Toronto, Ont. M5H 2Y7
(416) 364-7131
Chief Agent, J.M. McFadyen
The Hartford Steam Boiler Inspection and Insurance Company
8 King St. E., Toronto, Ont. M5C 1B5
(416) 363-5491
Chief Agent, T.F. Cartwright
Helvetia Swiss Fire Insurance Company Limited
275 St. James St. W., Montreal, P.Q. H2Y 1M9
(514) 842-1701
Chief Agent, E.E. Ahl
Herald Insurance Company
155 University Ave., 10th & 11th Floors, Toronto, Ont. M5H 3L8
(416) 362-4481
President, G.A. Chellew
Highlands Insurance Company
c/o Fasken & Calvin, Toronto Dominion Centre, Box 30, Toronto, Ont. M5K 1C1
(416) 366-8381
Chief Agent, F. Douglas Gibson
The Home Insurance Company
790 Bay St., #1100, Toronto, Ont. M5G 2A4
(416) 595-0175
Vice President, D.R. Alexander
Ideal Mutual Insurance Company
44 Victoria St., #1413, Toronto, Ont. M5C 1Y2
(416) 864-1476
Chief Agent, A.J. Barnes
The Imperial Life Assurance Company of Canada
95 St. Clair Ave. W., Toronto, Ont. M4V 1N7
(416) 923-6661
President, W.G. Munro
INA Insurance Company of Canada
Box 447, Term. A, Toronto, Ont. M5W 1E3
(416) 484-0711
President, J.R. Soper
INA Life Insurance Company of Canada
141 Adelaide St. W., #709, Toronto, Ont. M5H 3L5
(416) 367-9163
Vice President, Stephen L. Wyss
Independence Life & Accident Insurance Company
c/o McLean & Kerr, 372 Bay St., #1000, Toronto, Ont. M5H 2X5
(416) 364-5371
Chief Agent, R.B. Cumine, Q.C.
*Industrial Life Insurance Company
1080 Chemin St-Louis, Québec, P.Q. G1K 7M3
(418) 688-8210
President, Robert Bégin
*Industrial General Insurance Company
1080 Chemin St-Louis, Québec, P.Q. G1K 7M3
(418) 688-8210
President, Robert Bégin
Insmor Mortgage Insurance Company
Box 56, Royal Trust Tower, Toronto Dominion Centre, Toronto, Ont. M5K 1E7
(416) 868-0880
President, Desmond R. Smith
Insurance Company of North America
Box 447, Term. A, Toronto, Ont. M5W 1E3
(416) 484-0711
Chief Agent, Victor Reid

*Insurance Corporation of British Columbia
Box 11131, Royal Centre, 1055 W. Georgia St., Vancouver, B.C. V6E 3R4
(604) 665-2800
President & General Manager, T.E. Holmes
The Insurance Corporation of Ireland, Limited
Box 63, Royal Bank Plaza, Toronto, Ont. M5J 2J2
(416) 865-0444
Chief Agent, K.W. Evans
Jevco Insurance Company
2021 Union Ave., #1150, Montreal, P.Q. H3A 2S9
President, J. Verdon
John Alden Life Insurance Company
1530 Gamble Place, Winnipeg, Man. R3T 1N6
(204) 453-9642
Chief Agent, W.R. Templin
John Deere Insurance Company of Canada
Box 1000, Grimsby, Ont. L3M 4H5
President, Michael Frank
John Hancock Mutual Life Insurance Company
c/o McLean & Kerr, 372 Bay St., #1000, Toronto, Ont. M5H 2X5
(416) 364-5371
Chief Agent, R.B. Cumine, Q.C.
Kanata Reinsurance Company
620 University Ave., #1201, Toronto, Ont. M5G 2C1
(416) 977-4800
Vice President, R.W. Easton
Kansa General Insurance Company
2021 Union Ave., #1150, Montreal, P.Q. H3A 2S9
(514) 284-9340
Chief Agent, Jean Verdon
*Kent General Insurance Corporation
40 Charlotte St., Saint John, N.B. E2L 2H6
(506) 693-5801
Manager, Gordon L. Ellerker
The Kings Mutual Insurance Company
Berwick, N.S. B0P 1E0
(902) 538-3187
Manager, D.C. Cook
The Laurentian Shield Insurance Company
(507 Place d'Armes, 4th Floor) Box 1780, Place d'Armes, Montreal, P.Q. H2Y 3L8
General Manager, Jean Baillargeon
*La Laurentienne (Cie d'Assurances Générales)
425 St-Amable, Québec, P.Q. G1K 7X5
(418) 647-5151
Director General, Jean Baillargeon
Laurier Life Insurance Company
295 The West Mall, Etobicoke, Ont. M9C 4Z9
(416) 626-6830
Chairman & President, H.D. Haney
Lawyers Title Insurance Corporation
#202, 738 Sheppard Ave. E., Willowdale, Ont. M2K 1C4
(416) 226-1254
Chief Agent, D.L. Gibson
Liberty Mutual Fire Insurance Company
1200 Eglinton Ave. E., Don Mills, Ont. M3C 1J2
(416) 445-8410
Chief Agent, J.R. Heinisch
Liberty Mutual Insurance Company
1200 Eglinton Ave. E., Don Mills, Ont. M3C 1J2
(416) 445-8410
Chief Agent, J.R. Heinisch
Life Insurance Company of North America
Box 447, Stn. A, Toronto, Ont. M5W 1E3
Chief Agent, Victor Reid
Life Investors Insurance Company of America
2nd Floor, 1040 South Service Rd., Box 574, Oakville, Ont. L6J 5B7
(416) 845-3622
Chief Agent, Gwendolyn L. Elliott
The Lincoln National Life Insurance Company
c/o McLean & Kerr, 372 Bay St., #1000, Toronto, Ont. M5H 2X5
(416) 364-5371
Chief Agent, R.B. Cumine, Q.C.
Lloyd's
See The Non-Marine Underwriters of London
*Lombard Insurance Company Ltd.
(439 University Ave.), Box 219, Term. A, Toronto, Ont. M5W 1B6
(416) 596-6244
Chief Agent, E.B. Dale
London & Midland General Insurance Company
Box 5071, Term. A, London, Ont. N6A 4M5
(519) 672-1070
Vice President & General Manager, R.J. O'Brien
The London Assurance
48 Yonge St., 9th Floor, Toronto, Ont. M5E 1G8
(416) 362-6392
Chief Agent, J.W. Evans
London-Canada Insurance Company
401 Bay St., 9th Floor, Toronto, Ont. M5H 2Y4
(416) 364-7131
President, J.M. McFadyen
London Life Insurance Company
London, Ont. N6A 4K1
(519) 432-5281
President, E.H. Orser
Lumbermens Mutual Casualty Company
88 University Ave., Toronto, Ont. M5J 1T6
(416) 593-6626
Chief Agent, D.E. Aitchison
Lumbermen's Underwriting Alliance
9350 Yonge St., #207, Richmond Hill, Ont. L4C 5J2
(416) 883-1611
Chief Agent, R.G. Wilbur
Maccabees Mutual Life Insurance Company
1120 Ouellette Ave., Windsor, Ont. N9A 1C8
(519) 253-7416
Chief Agent, Mrs. Cecile Richer
*The Manitoba Public Insurance Corporation
9th Floor, 330 Graham Ave., Winnipeg, Man. R3C 4A4
(204) 942-0331
President & General Manager, J.O. Dutton
The Manufacturers Life Insurance Company
200 Bloor St. E., Toronto, Ont. M4W 1E5
(416) 928-4100
President, E.S. Jackson
*Maplex General Insurance Company
3228 South Service Rd., Burlington, Ont. L7N 3H8
(416) 639-9031
President, M.E. Schultz
Fire & auto insurance for non-smokers.
Marine Indemnity Insurance Company of America
48 Yonge St., #1060, Toronto, Ont. M5E 1G6
(416) 364-5485
Chief Agent, I.B. Manley
Maritime Insurance Company Limited
60 Yonge St., Toronto, Ont. M5E 1H5
(416) 362-2961
Chief Agent, R.H. Stevens
The Maritime Life Assurance Company
(2701 Dutch Village Rd.), Box 1030, Halifax, N.S. B3J 2X5
President & Chief Executive Officer, M.L. Hepher
Markel Insurance Company of Canada
500 University Ave., #516, Toronto, Ont. M5G 1W1
(416) 598-4500
President, D. Reid
Maryland Casualty Company
1425 Mountain St., 3rd Floor, Montreal, P.Q. H3G 1Z3
Chief Agent, Raymond Miron
Massachusetts General Life Insurance Company
#700, 372 Bay St., Toronto, Ont. M5H 2X3
(416) 363-5056
Vice President Canada, R. Harrison
Massachusetts Indemnity & Life Insurance Company
c/o McLean & Kerr, 372 Bay St., #1000, Toronto, Ont. M5H 2X5

(416) 364-5371
Chief Agent, R.B. Cumine, Q.C.
Massachusetts Mutual Life Insurance Company
c/o McLean & Kerr, 372 Bay St., #1000, Toronto, Ont. M5H 2X5
(416) 364-5371
Chief Agent, R.B. Cumine, Q.C.
*Mennonite Mutual Hail Insurance Company
Box 100, Hepburn, Sask. S0K 1Z0
(306) 947-2141
Manager, H. Arneson
The Mercantile & General Reinsurance Company Limited
141 Adelaide St. W., Toronto, Ont. M5H 3N2
(416) 360-8350
Chief Agent, Life, I.G. Michie
Chief Agent, Fire & Casualty, D.M. Batten
The Mercantile & General Reinsurance Company of Canada
141 Adelaide St. W., #1104, Toronto, Ont. M5H 3N2
(416) 360-8350
President, D.M. Batten
Metropolitan Life Insurance Company
99 Bank St., Ottawa, Ont. K1P 5A3
(613) 231-4141
President, C.N. Armstrong
Midland Insurance Company
Box 262, Toronto Dominion Centre, Toronto, Ont. M5K 1J9
Chief Agent, A.F. Sellers
Ministers Life - A Mutual Life Insurance Company
c/o McLean & Kerr, 372 Bay St., #1000, Toronto, Ont. M5H 2X5
(416) 364-5371
Chief Agent, R.B. Cumine, Q.C.
The Minnesota Mutual Life Insurance Company
c/o McLean & Kerr, 372 Bay St., #1000, Toronto, Ont. M5H 2X5
(416) 364-5371
Chief Agent, R.B. Cumine, Q.C.
The Missisquoi & Rouville Insurance Company
Box 70, Frelighsburg, P.Q. J0J 1C0
(514) 298-5251
President & General Manager, L.R. Boast
The Monarch Life Assurance Company
333 Broadway Ave., Winnipeg, Man. R3C 0S9
(204) 949-1660
President, H. Thompson
Montreal Life Insurance Company
Box 850, Stn. B, Montreal, P.Q. H3B 3K7
(514) 842-9151
President, Nicholas Bauer
MONY Life Insurance Company of Canada
1500 Mony Life Tower, 797 Don Mills Rd., Don Mills Rd., Don Mills, Ont. M3C 1V2
(416) 429-2200
President & Chief Executive Officer, J.T. Birkenshaw
The Mortgage Insurance Company of Canada
401 Bay St., Box 14, Toronto, Ont. M5H 2Y4
(416) 366-6231
President, R.T. Ryan
Motors Insurance Corporation
1125B Leslie St., Don Mills, Ont. M3C 2K4
(416) 446-5100
Chief Agent, S.G. Stoker
Munich Reinsurance Company
55 Yonge St., Toronto, Ont. M5E 1J4
Chief Agent, Non-Life, John M. Coker (416/366-9206)
Chief Agent, Life, G.R. Minns (416/366-9587)
Munich Reinsurance Company of Canada
55 Yonge St., #1103, Toronto, Ont. M5J 1J4
(416) 366-9206
President, J.M. Coker
The Mutual Life & Citizens' Assurance Company Limited
c/o Hébert, LeHouillier & Associes, 1080 Beaver Hall Hill, #1915, Montreal, P.Q. H2Z 1S8
(514) 866-5314
Chief Agent, M. Le Houillier
The Mutual Life Assurance Company of Canada
227 King St. S., Waterloo, Ont. N2J 4C5
(519) 888-2262
President, J.H. Panabaker
The Mutual Life Insurance Company of New York
797 Don Mills Rd., Don Mills, Ont. M3C 1V2
(416) 429-2200
Chief Agent, H.D. Russel
Mutual of Omaha Insurance Company
500 University Ave., Toronto, Ont. M5G 1V8
(416) 598-4321
Chief Agent, Thomas Child
Mutuelle Générale Française Accidents
#2100, Place du Canada, Montréal, P.Q. H3B 2R8
Chief Agent, Robert Parizeau
Mutuelle Générale Française Vie
#2100, Place du Canada, Montréal, P.Q. H3B 2R8
Chief Agent, Robert Parizeau
National Employers' Mutual General Insurance Association Limited
300 St. Sacrement St., Montreal, P.Q. H2Y 1X6
(514) 844-2541
Chief Agent, A.T. McLean
National Fidelity Life Insurance Company
2025 Sheppard Ave. E., #2320, Willowdale, Ont. M2J 1V6
(416) 499-4004
Branch Manager, Imants Saksons
The National Life Assurance Company of Canada
522 University Ave., Toronto, Ont. M5G 1Y7
(416) 598-2122
President, C.T.P. Galloway
The National Reinsurance Company of Canada
#2100, Place du Canada, Montreal, P.Q. H3B 2R8
President & General Manager, Robert Parizeau
Nationwide Mutual Insurance Company
Box 262, Toronto Dominion Centre, Toronto, Ont. M5K 1J9
Chief Agent, A.F. Sellers
Netherlands Reinsurance Group N.V.
188 University Ave., Toronto, Ont. M5H 3C3
(416) 593-5222
Chief Agent, S. Gordon
New England Mutual Life Insurance Company
c/o Tory, Tory, Deslauriers & Binnington, Royal Bank Plaza, Box 20, Toronto, Ont. M5J 2K1
(416) 865-0040
Chief Agent, B.W. Shields
New England Reinsurance Corporation
401 Bay St., Toronto, Ont. M5H 2Y7
Chief Agent, J.M. McFadyen
New Hampshire Insurance Company
55 University Ave., Toronto, Ont. M5J 2H7
(416) 869-5000
Chief Agent, Gary A. McMillan
The New India Assurance Company Limited
#1100, 1 St. Clair Ave. W., Toronto, Ont. M4V 2Z1
(416) 968-2122
Chief Agent, J. Ross Lowrie
New Rotterdam Insurance Company
505 York Blvd., Box 2018, Hamilton, Ont. L8N 3S3
(416) 525-5300
Chief Agent, J.C. Stradwick
New York Life Insurance Company
443 University Ave., Toronto, Ont. M5G 1T8
(416) 598-2145
Chief Agent, H.G. Folliott
The New Zealand Insurance Company Limited
40 University Ave., #214, Toronto, Ont. M5J 1T1
(416) 977-7438
Chief Agent, J.G. Dovey
Niagara Fire Insurance Company
Box 4024, Term. A, Toronto, Ont. M5W 1K1
(416) 860-4250
Chief Agent, W.W. Ward

The Non-Marine Underwriters, Members of Lloyd's, London, England
635 Dorchester Blvd. W., #1400, Montreal, P.Q. H3B 1S3
(514) 861-8361
Chief Agent, J.A. Madill

The Nordisk Reinsurance Company Limited
188 University Ave., Toronto, Ont. M5H 3C3
(416) 593-5222
Chief Agent, Sidney Gordon

Norman Insurance Company Ltd.
c/o L'Union Canadienne, Cie d'Assurances, 2475 Laurier Blvd., Sillery, P.Q. G1V 4E4
(418) 651-3551
Chief Agent, Paul H. Brochu

North American Company for Property & Casualty Insurance
2 St. Clair Ave. W., Toronto, Ont. M4V 1L5
(416) 923-9865
Chief Agent, T.P. Flynn

North American Life & Casualty Company
#1500, 797 Don Mills Rd., Don Mills, Ont. M3C 1V2
(416) 429-2200
Chief Agent, H.D. Russel

North American Life Assurance Company
105 Adelaide St. W., Toronto, Ont. M5H 1R1
(416) 362-6011
President, A.G. McCaughey

North American Reassurance Company
c/o Canadian Reassurance Company, 95 St. Clair Ave. W., Toronto, Ont. M4V 1N6
(416) 925-2261
Chief Agent, Ralph G. Swail

North American Reinsurance Corporation
95 St. Clair Ave. W., Toronto, Ont. M4V 1N6
(416) 925-2261
Chief Agent, G.E.P. Eastwood

The North Waterloo Farmers Mutual Insurance Company
100 Erb St. E., Waterloo, Ont. N2J 4B1
Manager, Gordon MacIntyre

The North West Life Assurance Company of Canada
595 Howe St., 12th Floor, Vancouver, B.C. V6C 2T5
(604) 689-1211
Secretary, John W. Long

The Northern Life Assurance Company of Canada
London, Ont. N6A 4G3
(519) 439-0171
President & General Manager, G.L. Bowie

Northumberland General Insurance Company
Box 247, Toronto Dominion Centre, Toronto, Ont. M5K 1J5
(416) 364-9521
Chairman, P.E. Reeve

Norwich Union Fire Insurance Society Limited
60 Yonge St., Toronto, Ont. M5E 1H5
(416) 362-2961
Chief Agent, R.H. Stevens

The Norwich Union Life Insurance Society
60 Yonge St., Toronto, Ont. M5E 1H5
(416) 362-2961
Chief Agent, Hugh Taylor

Norwich Winterthur Reinsurance Corporation Ltd.
#2100, Place du Canada, Montreal, P.Q. H3B 2R8
Chief Agent, M.W. Donald

Nova Scotia General Insurance Company
35 Church St., Amherst, N.S. B4H 3A7
(902) 667-7281
President, R.M. Van Snick

NRG London Reinsurance Company Ltd.
#2100, Place du Canada, Montreal, P.Q. H3B 2R8
Chief Agent, Robert Parizeau

Occidental Life Insurance Company of California
Box 69, Stn. K, Toronto, Ont. M4P 2G4
(416) 486-2700
Chief Agent, D. Onstad

Occidental Life Insurance Company of Canada
Box 69, Stn. K, Toronto, Ont. M4P 2G4
(416) 486-2700
President, D. Onstad

Old Republic Insurance Company
505 York Blvd., Box 557, Hamilton, Ont. L8N 3K9
(416) 523-5587
Chief Agent, A.T. Chmiel

Old Republic Life Insurance Company
505 York Blvd., Box 557, Hamilton, Ont. L8N 3K9
(416) 523-5587
Chief Agent, A.T. Chmiel

Olympic Insurance Company
Canada Sq., 2180 Yonge St., 7th Floor, Toronto, Ont. M4S 2C2
Chief Agent, T.J. Gonsalves

The Omaha Indemnity Company
500 University Ave., 4th Floor, Toronto, Ont. M5G 1V9
(416) 595-1300
Chief Agent, Thomas Child

*Ontario Motorist Insurance Company
2 Carlton St., Toronto, Ont. M5B 1K4
(416) 964-3015
President, N.D. Gaskin

*Ontario Mutual General Insurance
Grand Valley, Ont. L0N 1G0
Manager, D.T. Tombs

*Ontario Mutual Insurance Association
2445 Eagle St. N., Cambridge, Ont. N3H 4S1
(519) 653-0366
Secretary Treasurer, Mel McIntyre, F.I.I.C.

The Orion Insurance Company Limited
#1100, 1 St. Clair Ave. W., Toronto, Ont. M4V 2Z1
(416) 968-2122
Chief Agent, J. Ross Lowrie

Pacific Employers Insurance Company
Box 447, Term. A, Toronto, Ont. M5W 1E3
(416) 484-0711
Chief Agent, Victor Reid

Pacific Mutual Life Insurance Company
105 Adelaide St. W., #900, Toronto, Ont. M5H 1R3
(416) 862-1309
Chief Agent, J.F. Perrett

*Pafco Insurance Company Limited
2489 Bloor St. W., Toronto, Ont. M6S 4X1
(416) 766-8271
President, W.G. Starr

Paragon Insurance Company of Canada
650 W. Georgia St., #1000, Box 11602, Vancouver, B.C. V6B 4N9
(604) 669-4247
Executive Vice President & General Manager, Simon R. Farrow

The Patriot Life Insurance Company
Box 5071, Term. A, London, Ont. N6A 4M5
(519) 672-6463
Chief Agent, R.J. O'Brien

The Paul Revere Life Insurance Company
(440 Elizabeth St.), Box 5044, Burlington, Ont. L7R 4C1
(416) 681-1180
Chief Agent, J.C. Davey

Pearl Assurance Company Limited
#201, 180 Bloor St. W., Toronto, Ont. M5S 2V6
Chief Agent, M.P. Greening

The Penn Mutual Life Insurance Company
c/o McLean & Kerr, #1000, 372 Bay St., Toronto, Ont. M5H 2X5
(416) 364-5371
Chief Agent, R.B. Cumine, Q.C.

Pennsylvania Life Insurance Company
2345 Stanfield Rd., Mississauga, Ont. L4Y 3Y3
(416) 272-0210
Chief Agent, R.B. Cumine, Q.C.

The Personal Insurance Company of Canada
703 Evans Ave., Toronto, Ont. M9C 5A7
(416) 621-6000
Executive Vice President & General Manager, H.P. Johne

Perth Insurance Company
210 Water St., Stratford, Ont. N5A 6V3
(519) 271-4250
President & General Manager, K.V. Salt
PHF Insurance Company
161 Eglinton Ave. E., #702, Toronto, Ont. M4P 1J7
Chief Agent, J.N. Drouin
Philadelphia Manufacturers Mutual Insurance Company
2 Dunbloor Rd., Islington, Ont. M9A 2E4
(416) 239-3936
Chief Agent, B.J. Kelly
Philadelphia Reinsurance Corporation
c/o Campbell, Sharp, etc., 55 University Ave., #800, Toronto, Ont. M5J 2K4
(416) 863-1234
Chief Agent, N.S. Reid
Phoenix Assurance Company Limited
Box 219A, Phoenix House, Toronto, Ont. M5W 1B6
(416) 596-6100
Chief Agent, J.B. Murch
Phoenix Assurance Company of Canada
Box 219A, Phoenix House, Toronto, Ont. M5W 1B6
(416) 596-6100
President, J.B. Murch
The Phoenix Insurance Company
c/o Cassels, Brock, 130 Adelaide St. W., Toronto, Ont. M5H 3C2
(416) 869-5300
Chief Agent, J.W. Graham
Phoenix Mutual Life Insurance Company
c/o Cassels, Brock, 130 Adelaide St. W., Toronto, Ont. M5H 3C2
(416) 869-5300
Chief Agent, J.W. Graham
Pictou County Farmers' Mutual Fire Insurance Company
Box 130, Pictou, N.S. B0K 1H0
Secretary Treasurer, R.C. MacKean
Pierce National Life Insurance Company
#101, 1766 W. Broadway, Vancouver, B.C. V6J 1Y1
(604) 736-4816
Chief Agent, John Douglas
*Pilot Insurance Company
90 Eglinton Ave. W., Box 703, Stn. K, Toronto, Ont. M4P 1E9
(416) 487-5141
President & Chief Executive Officer, Brian Greenslade
Pioneer Life Assurance Company
Box 3145, 1920 Broad St., Regina, Sask. S4P 3G7
(306) 565-0888
President, Will Klein
Pitts Insurance Company
201 King St., London, Ont. N6A 1C9
President, R.W. Trollope
Pitts Life Insurance Company
201 King St., London, Ont. N6A 1C9
President, R.W. Trollope
Pohjola Insurance Company Ltd.
(Vakuutusosakeyhtio Pohjola)
#2100, Place du Canada, Montreal, P.Q. H3B 2R8
Chief Agent, Robert Parizeau
Pool Insurance Company
220 Portage Ave., #810, Winnipeg, Man. R3C 0A5
(204) 942-0658
Manager, L.M. Heber
The Portage la Prairie Mutual Insurance Company
Portage la Prairie, Man.
(204) 857-3415
General Manager, H.G. Owens
Presbyterian Ministers' Fund
40 Wynford Dr., #310, Don Mills, Ont. M3C 1J5
Chief Agent, K.G. Clarke
La Préservatrice, A.I.R.D.
703 Evans Ave., Etobicoke, Ont. M9C 5A7
(416) 622-9020
Chief Agent, Raymond Viger
*La Prévoyance Compagnie d'Assurances
507 Place d'Armes, Montreal, P.Q. H2Y 2W8
(514) 842-6212
Director General, Jean Baillargeon
*Les Prévoyants du Canada – Assurance Générale
801 Sherbrooke St. E., Montreal, P.Q. H2L 1K8
(514) 527-3141
General Manager, R. Viger
*Prince Edward Island Mutual Fire Insurance Company
201 Water St., Summerside, P.E.I. C1N 1B4
(902) 436-2185
Principal Life Insurance Company of Canada
1600 Cambridge Bldg., 10024 Jasper Ave., Edmonton, Alta. T5J 1S3
Director, L.A. Patrick
Protection Mutual Insurance Company
#406, 141 Adelaide St. W., Toronto, Ont. M5H 3L5
(416) 869-3110
Chief Agent, B. Kealty
Providence Washington Insurance Company
401 Bay St., #2310, Toronto, Ont. M5H 2Y4
(416) 869-0264
Chief Agent, N.C. March
Provident Alliance Life Insurance Company
See The Patriot Life
Provident Life & Accident Insurance Company
c/o McLean & Kerr, 372 Bay St., #1000, Toronto, Ont. M5H 2X5
(416) 364-5371
Chief Agent, R.B. Cumine, Q.C.
*Provinces-Unies Assurances
2021 Union Ave., 12th Floor, Montreal, P.Q. H3A 2V1
(514) 282-1914
President, John Sylvain
Prudasco Assurance Company
635 Dorchester Blvd. W., Montreal, P.Q. H3B 1R7
President, I.D. Mair
The Prudential Assurance Company Limited (of England)
635 Dorchester Blvd. W., Montreal, P.Q. H3B 1R7
(514) 878-2361
Chief Agent, I.D. Mair
The Prudential Insurance Company of America
4 King St. W., Toronto, Ont. M5H 1B7
(416) 366-6971
Chief Agent, W.J.D. Lewis
Prudential Reinsurance Company of America
Box 116, Toronto Dominion Centre, Toronto, Ont. M5K 1G8
(416) 862-1228
Chief Agent, T.D. MacKenzie
QBE Insurance Limited
c/o Edward Lumley (Canada) Ltd., 300 St. Sacrement St., Montreal, P.Q. H2Y 1X6
(514) 844-2541
Chief Agent, A.T. McLean
Quebec Assurance Company
10 Wellington St. E., Toronto, Ont. M5E 1L5
(416) 366-7511
President, J. Robitaille
*Red River Valley Mutual Insurance Company
245 Centre Ave. E., Altona, Man. R0G 0B0
(204) 324-6434
General Manager, H.G. Heinrichs
Reinsurance Corporation of New York
c/o Coopers & Lybrand, 145 King St. W., Toronto, Ont. M5H 1V8
(416) 869-1130
Chief Agent, J.F. Knight
Reliable Life Insurance Company
505 York Blvd., Box 557, Hamilton, Ont. L8N 3K9
(416) 523-5587
President, A.T. Chmiel
Reliance Insurance Company
100 University Ave., 4th Floor, Toronto, Ont. M5J 1W1
(416) 593-6371
Chief Agent, R.J. McCormick

Retail Lumbermen's Inter-Insurance Exchange
#400, 191 Lombard Ave., Winnipeg, Man. R3B 0X1
(204) 942-5256
Chief Agent, F.L. Cvitkovitch, Q.C.
Royal Exchange Assurance of America Inc.
48 Yonge St., #1060, Toronto, Ont. M5E 1G6
(416) 364-5485
Chief Agent, I.B. Manley
Royal Insurance Company Limited (Life)
10 Wellington St. E., Toronto, Ont. M5E 1L5
(416) 366-7511
President, J. Robitaille
Royal Insurance Company of Canada
10 Wellington St. E., Toronto, Ont. M5E 1L5
(416) 366-7511
President, J. Robitaille
SAFECO Insurance Company of America
Box 3000, Stn. A, Mississauga, Ont. L5A 3P6
(416) 828-2900
Chief Agent, J.C. McArthur
SAFECO Life Insurance Company
Box 3000, Stn. A, Mississauga, Ont. L5A 3P6
(416) 828-2900
Chief Agent, J.C. McArthur
The Safeguard Life Assurance Company
1, Complexe Desjardins, Montreal, P.Q. H5B 1E2
(514) 281-8444
President, C. Gauthier
*La St-Maurice Compagnie d'Assurances
C.P. 428, Trois-Rivières, P.Q. G9A 5H4
(819) 379-8840
Président, F. Spenard
St. Paul Fire & Marine Insurance Company
55 University Ave., #200, Toronto, Ont. M5J 2L3
(416) 366-8301
Chief Agent, Barry Wilson
*The St. Paul Property & Liability Insurance
55 University Ave., Toronto, Ont. M5J 2L3
(416) 366-8301
General Manager, B.L. Wilson
*Saskatchewan Government Insurance
2260 11th Ave., Regina, Sask. S4P 0J9
(306) 565-1200
President, D. Murray Wallace
Saskatchewan Mutual Insurance Company
279 3rd Ave. N., Saskatoon, Sask. S7K 2H8
(306) 653-4232
Managing Director, Edward Statham
SCOR Reinsurance Company of Canada
55 University Ave., #300, Toronto, Ont. M5J 2H7
(416) 869-3670
President, P. Croizat
The Scottish Dominion Insurance Company Limited
620 Dorchester Blvd. W., #402, Montreal, P.Q. H3B 1N8
(514) 849-3641
Chief Agent, E.L. Clark
*Scottish & York Insurance Company
155 University Ave., Toronto, Ont. M5H 3M2
(416) 366-8181
Chief Agent, R.W. Broughton
Seaboard Surety Company
c/o Fasken & Calvin, Box 30, Toronto Dominion Centre, Toronto, Ont. M5K 1C1
(416) 366-8381
Chief Agent, F.D. Gibson
La Sécurité (Cie d'Assurances Générales du Canada)
See Le Groupe Desjardins
Security Casualty Company
700 Bay St., Toronto, Ont. M5G 1N4
(416) 598-0606
Chief Agent, George Ayton
Security Insurance Company of Hartford
Box 4030, Term. A, Toronto, Ont. M5W 1K4
Chief Agent, G. Symons
Security National Insurance Company
401 Bay St., #2310, Toronto, Ont. M5H 2Y4
(416) 869-0264
Manager, N.C. March
Sentry Insurance A Mutual Company
700 Bay St., Toronto, Ont. M5G 1N4
(416) 598-0606
Chief Agent, George Ayton
*Simcoe & Erie General Insurance Company
505 York Blvd., Box 557, Hamilton, Ont. L8N 3K9
(416) 525-5300
Managing Director, J.C. Stradwick
Skandia Insurance Company
55 University Ave., Toronto, Ont. M5J 2H7
(416) 862-0162
Chief Agent, P.W.G. Hall
*La Société d'Assurance des Caisses Populaires
See Le Groupe Desjardins
Société Anonyme Française de Réassurances
360 St. James St., #2000, Montreal, P.Q. H2Y 1P5
(514) 845-3261
Chief Agent, R. Davis, C.A.
Société Commerciale de Réassurance
Life Branch: #2100, Place du Canada, Montreal, P.Q. H3B 2R8
Chief Agent, Robert Parizeau
Société Commerciale de Réassurance
Property & Casualty Branch: 55 University Ave., #300, Toronto, Ont. M5J 2H7
(416) 869-3670
Chief Agent, P. Croizat
*Société Nationale d'Assurances
612 rue St-Jacques, bur. 601, Montreal, P.Q. H3C 3Y8
(514) 288-8711
Treasurer, P. Genest
The Sovereign General Insurance Company
Box 210, 300 5th Ave. S.W., Calgary, Alta. T2P 0L3
(403) 266-9000
Executive Vice President, D.J. Wilson
The Sovereign Life Assurance Company
Box 210, 300 5th Ave. S.W., Calgary, Alta. T2P 0L3
(403) 266-9000
President, J.H. Walsh
Sphere Reinsurance Company of Canada
20 Victoria St., #605, Toronto, Ont. M5C 2N8
(416) 364-7371
The Standard Life Assurance Company
1245 Sherbrooke St. W., Montreal, P.Q. H3G 1G3
(514) 284-6734
Chief Agent, A.S. Fernie
The Stanstead & Sherbrooke Insurance Company
Box 441, Toronto Dominion Centre, Toronto, Ont. M5K 1L9
(416) 361-2500
President, Chief Executive Officer & Director, F.A. Saville
State Farm Fire & Casualty Company
1801 Brimley Rd., Scarborough, Ont. M1P 3H3
(416) 291-1961
Chief Agent, J.R. MacKenzie
State Farm Life Insurance Company
1801 Brimley Rd., Scarborough, Ont. M1P 3H3
(416) 291-1961
Chief Agent, George Archambault
State Farm Mutual Automobile Insurance Company
1801 Brimley Rd., Scarborough, Ont. M1P 3H3
(416) 291-1961
Chief Agent, J.R. MacKenzie
State Mutual Life Assurance Company of America
c/o Cassels, Brock, 130 Adelaide St. W., Toronto, Ont. M5H 3C2
(416) 869-5300
Chief Agent, J.W. Graham
Stonewall Insurance Company
Box 262, Toronto Dominion Centre, Toronto, Ont. M5K 1J9
Chief Agent, A.F. Sellers

Storebrand International Reinsurance Company Ltd.
Life Branch: 110 Bloor St. W., #200, Toronto, Ont. M5S 2W7
(416) 961-2200
Chief Agent, Sidney Gordon
Storebrand International Reinsurance Company Ltd.
Property & Casualty Branch: 188 University Ave., Toronto, Ont. M5H 3C3
(416) 593-5222
Chief Agent, Sidney Gordon
The Strathcona General Insurance Company
331 Cooper St., #202, Ottawa, Ont. K2P 0G5
Secretary, J.P. O'Connor
Sun Alliance & London Assurance Company Limited
48 Yonge St., 9th Floor, Toronto, Ont. M5E 1G8
(416) 362-6392
Chief Agent, J.W. Evans
Sun Alliance Insurance Company
48 Yonge St., 9th Floor, Toronto, Ont. M5E 1G8
(416) 362-6392
President, J.W. Evans
Sun Life Assurance Company of Canada
Box 4150, Stn. A, Toronto, Ont. M5W 2C9
(416) 869-6000
Chairman & Chief Executive Officer, Thomas M. Galt
Swiss Reinsurance Company
95 St. Clair Ave. W., Toronto, Ont. M4V 1N6
(416) 925-2261
Chief Agent, R.F. Clark
Switzerland General Insurance Company Limited
Box 910, Place d'Armes, Montreal, P.Q. H2Y 3J5
(514) 842-1701
Chief Agent, E.E. Ahl
Symons General Insurance Company
45 Charles St. E., Toronto, Ont. M4Y 1S8
(416) 920-2801
President, G. Gordon Symons
Teachers Insurance & Annuity Association of America
165 University Ave.#2300, 130 Adelaide St. W., Toronto, Ont. M5H 3C2
(416) 869-5300
Chief Agent, J.T. DesBrisay, Q.C.
The Tokio Marine & Fire Insurance Company Limited
Box 4024, Stn. A, Toronto, Ont. M5W 1K1
(416) 860-4250
Chief Agent, W.W. Ward
Toro Assicurazioni S.P.A.
401 Bay St., #2310, Toronto, Ont. M5H 2Y4
(416) 869-0264
Chief Agent, Norman March
Toronto General Insurance Company
Box 4030, Term. A, Toronto, Ont. M5W 1K4
(416) 593-1355
President, R.E. Bethell
Toronto Mutual Life Insurance Company
112 St. Clair Ave. W., Toronto, Ont. M4V 2Y3
(416) 960-3463
President, J.T. English
Traders General Insurance Company
Box 4030, Term. A, Toronto, Ont. M5W 1K4
(416) 593-1355
President, R.E. Bethell
Trafalgar Insurance Company Ltd.
111 Avenue Rd., #300, Toronto, Ont. M5R 3K3
Chief Agent, R.F. Rush
Transamerica Insurance Company
See Canadian Surety Co.
Transatlantic Reinsurance Company
55 University Ave., #1000, Toronto, Ont. M5J 2H7
(416) 869-5000
Chief Agent, G.A. McMillan
Transit Insurance Company
250 Bloor St. E., #1201, Toronto, Ont. M4W 3K8
Secretary, P.C. Bookalam
Transport Indemnity Company
c/o Cassels, Brock, 130 Adelaide St. W., Toronto, Ont. M5H 3C2
(416) 869-5300
Transport Insurance Company
1130 ouest rue Sherbrooke, #800, Montreal, P.Q. H3A 2M8
(514) 381-9386
Chief Agent, A.F. Melling
*Transport Insurance of Dallas, Texas
1130 ouest rue Sherbrooke, #800, Montreal, P.Q. H3A 2M8
(514) 381-9386
Chief Agent, A.F. Melling
The Travelers Indemnity Company
c/o Cassels, Brock, 130 Adelaide St. W., Toronto, Ont. M5H 3C2
(416) 869-5300
Chief Agent, J.W. Graham
Travelers Indemnity Company of Canada
Travelers Tower, 400 University Ave., Toronto, Ont. M5G 1S7
(416) 595-7114
President, Daniel Damov
Travelers Insurance Company
c/o Cassels, Brock, 130 Adelaide St. W., Toronto, Ont. M5H 3C2
(416) 869-5300
Chief Agent, J.W. Graham
Travelers Life Insurance Company of Canada
Travelers Tower, 400 University Ave., Toronto, Ont. M5G 1S7
(416) 595-7114
President, Daniel Damov
Truck Insurance Exchange
Box 11128, Royal Centre, 1055 W. Georgia St., Vancouver, B.C. V6E 3R2
Chief Agent, M.A. Linsley
Unifund Assurance Company
95 Elizabeth Ave., St. John's, Nfld. A1B 1R7
(709) 737-1500
President, Paul Johnson
Unigard Mutual Insurance Company
c/o Price Waterhouse & Co., 1075 W. Georgia St., Vancouver, B.C. V6E 3G1
(604) 682-4711
Contact, Robert R. Gourley
*L'Union Canadienne Compagnie d'Assurances
2475 boul. Sir Wilfrid Laurier, Sillery, P.Q. G1V 4E4
(418) 651-3551
President & General Manager, P.H. Brochu
The Union Marine & General Insurance Company Limited
Box 219, Term. A, Toronto, Ont. M5W 1B6
(416) 596-6100
Chief Agent, J.B. Murch
Union Mutual Life Insurance Company
c/o McLean & Kerr, #1000, 372 Bay St., Toronto, Ont. M5H 2X5
(416) 364-5371
Chief Agent, R.B. Cumine
Union Reinsurance Company
188 University Ave., Toronto, Ont. M5H 3C3
(416) 593-5222
Chief Agent, Sidney Gordon
Unione Italiana Di Riassicurazione S.P.A.
#2100, Place du Canada, Montreal, P.Q. H3B 2R8
Chief Agent, Colin Jack
United American Insurance Company
1262 Don Mills Rd., #12, Don Mills, Ont. M3B 2W7
Chief Agent, Mrs. Helen E.V. Lewis
United Benefit Life Insurance Company
500 University Ave., Toronto, Ont. M5G 1V8
Chief Agent, Thomas Child
United Canada Insurance Company
155 University Ave., 8th Floor, Toronto, Ont. M5H 3B7
(416) 864-1287
Vice President, D.J. Reid
United States Fidelity & Guaranty Company
4 King St. W., 15th Floor, Toronto, Ont. M5H 3P4

(416) 366-1931
Chief Agent, G.A. Lightbound
United States Fire Insurance Company
155 University Ave., 10th & 11th Floors, Toronto, Ont. M5H 3L8
(416) 362-4481
Chief Agent, G.A. Chellew
The Unity Fire & General Insurance Company
111 Avenue Rd., #400, Toronto, Ont. M5R 3J8
(416) 961-5013
Chief Agent, R.F. Rush
*Upper Canada Insurance Company
67 Yonge St., #710, Toronto, Ont. M5E 1J8
(416) 363-8015
General Manager, Tom Hanson
Utica Mutual Insurance Company
c/o Fasken & Calvin, Box 30, Toronto Dominion Centre, Toronto, Ont. M5K 1C1
(416) 366-8381
Chief Agent, F.D. Gibson
Victoria Insurance Company of Canada
155 University Ave., Toronto, Ont. M5H 3B7
(416) 363-9404
Executive Vice President, R.W. Broughton
The Victory Insurance Company, Limited
Life Branch: 55 Yonge St., Toronto, Ont. M5E 1J4
(416) 366-9587
Chief Agent, G.R. Minns
The Victory Insurance Company, Limited
Fire & Casualty Branch: 188 University Ave., Toronto, Ont. M5H 3C3
(416) 593-5222
Chief Agent, Sidney Gordon
Warner Reciprocal Insurers
120 Bloor St. E., Toronto, Ont. M4W 1B7
Chief Agent, I.C. White
Washington National Insurance Company
105 Adelaide St. W., #900, Toronto, Ont. M5H 1R3
(416) 862-1309
Chief Agent, J.F. Perrett
The Waterloo Mutual Insurance Company
14 Erb St. W., Waterloo, Ont. N2J 4C8
(519) 886-4940
General Manager, K.I. Tyers
*Wausau Insurance Companies
#400, 55 University Ave., Toronto, Ont. M5J 2H7
(416) 862-8923
Chief Agent, J.B. Harrison
The Wawanesa Mutual Insurance Company
191 Broadway, Winnipeg, Man. R3C 3P1
(204) 985-3811
President, G.C. Trites
The Wawanesa Mutual Life Insurance Company
191 Broadway, Winnipeg, Man. R3C 3P1
(204) 985-3811
President, G.C. Trites
The Western Assurance Company
10 Wellington St. E., Toronto, Ont. M5E 1L5
(416) 366-7511
President, J. Robitaille
Western General Mutual Insurance Company
989 Dundas St., Box 37, Woodstock, Ont. N4S 7W6
(519) 539-9883
General Manager, C.D. Fleming
The Western Life Assurance Company
Box 67, Hamilton, Ont. L8N 3B3
(416) 527-3877
Vice President/Asst. Secretary, S.M. Szenasi
Marketing Vice President, G.R. Pearsall, CLU
Western Surety Company
Box 527, Regina, Sask. S4P 2G8
(306) 569-8800
President, L.C. Ell
*Western Union Insurance Company
640 8th Ave. S.W., Calgary, Alta. T2P 1G8
(403) 269-7961
President, D.J. Freeze
Winterthur Life Insurance Company
(360 Broadway, Winnipeg, Man. R3C 0T7)
Mailing: 1075 Bay St., Toronto, Ont. M5S 2B1
(416) 928-8500
Chief Agent, F.W. Tallman
The Yasuda Fire & Marine Insurance Company, Limited
Royal Bank Plaza, Box 26, Toronto, Ont. M5J 2J1
(416) 865-0182
Chief Agent, D.B. Bridge
*York Fire & Casualty Insurance Company
7699 Yonge St., Thornhill, Ont. L3T 1Z5
(416) 889-6204
President, W. Bryce
Zurich Insurance Company
188 University Ave., Toronto, Ont. M5H 3C3
(416) 593-6121
Chief Agent, R.N. Mackintosh
Zurich Life Insurance Company of Canada
188 University Ave., Toronto, Ont. M5H 3C4
(416) 593-4444
President, R.N. Mackintosh

LIBRARIES IN CANADA

Government Departments in Charge

ALBERTA:– Alberta Culture, Library Services, 16214 114 Ave., Edmonton, Alta. T5M 2Z5 (403/427-2556; Telex: 037-2055). Director, J. Forsyth

BRITISH COLUMBIA:– The Library Services Branch, (1250 Quadra St.) Parliament Bldgs., Victoria, B.C. V8V 1X4 (604/387-5277). Director, Peter Martin; (Regional Offices: 3907 15th Ave., Prince George, V2N 1A5 (562-7226); 1017 105th Ave., Dawson Creek, V1G 2L3 (782-8040); 18 9th Ave. S., Cranbrook, V1C 2L8 (489-3521); L50, 4946 Canada Way, Burnaby, V5G 1M3 (298-0422)).

MANITOBA: Public Library Services, Cultural Affairs & Historical Resources Dept., 139 Hamelin St., Winnipeg, Man. R3T 4H4 (204/453-7549)

NEW BRUNSWICK: New Brunswick Library Service, Director, A. Hall, 513 Union St., Box 6000, Fredericton, N.B. E3B 5H1 (506/453-2224)

NEWFOUNDLAND: Newfoundland Public Libraries Board, Chairman, Ms. Anne Hart; Chief Provincial Librarian, Pearce J. Penney; Deputy Chief Provincial Librarian, Joe Lavery; Administration Office: Arts & Culture Centre, Allandale Rd., St. John's, Nfld. A1B 3A3 (709/737-3964)

NOVA SCOTIA: Nova Scotia Provincial Library, 5250 Spring Garden Rd., Halifax, N.S. B3J 1E8 (902/424-5439)
Director, Mrs. Carin Somers; Public Libraries, Miss Elizabeth MacDonald; Information Services, Mrs. Lorraine McQueen; School Libraries, Miss Shirley Coulter; Technical Services, Miss Bertha Higgins

ONTARIO: Director of Libraries & Community Information, W. Grace Buller (acting), Ministry of Culture & Recreation, 77 Bloor St. W., Toronto, Ont. M5S 2R9 (416/965-2696)

PRINCE EDWARD ISLAND: Prince Edward Island Provincial Library, University Ave., Charlottetown, P.E.I. C1A 7N9 (902/892-3504); Director & Provincial Librarian, D.J. Scott.

QUEBEC: Public Library Service, Dept. of Cultural Affairs, 225 est Grande Allée, Quebec City, P.Q. G1R 5G5. Director, Pierre Matte (418/643-2140)

SASKATCHEWAN: Saskatchewan Provincial Library, 1352 Winnipeg St., Regina, Sask. S4P 3V7
Saskatchewan Library Development Board Chairman, Morris Anderson; Secretary, the Provincial Librarian, 1352 Winnipeg St., Regina, Sask. S4R 1J9 (306/565-2972)

Library Associations

CANADIAN LIBRARY ASSOCIATION, 151 Sparks St., Ottawa, Ont. K1P 5E3
(613) 232-9625
Executive Director, Paul Kitchen
Divisions at same address:
Canadian Association of Public Libraries
Canadian Association of College & University Libraries
Canadian Library Trustees' Association
Canadian School Library Association
Canadian Association of Special Libraries & Information Services

LIBRARY ASSOCIATION OF ALBERTA, Box 1357, Main PO, Edmonton, Alta. T5J 2N2. President, B.J. Busch, Head, Education Library, Univ. of Alberta, Edmonton, Alta. T6G 2G5

ATLANTIC PROVINCES LIBRARY ASSOCIATION, Secretary, c/o Dalhousie School of Library Service, Dalhousie Univ., Halifax, N.S. B3H 4H8 (902/424-3656)

BRITISH COLUMBIA LIBRARY ASSOCIATION, Box 46378, Stn. G, Vancouver, B.C. V6R 4G6

MANITOBA LIBRARY ASSOCIATION, c/o St. Vital Pub. Library, 6 Fermor Ave. W., Winnipeg, Man. R2M OY2 (204/257-1733)

ONTARIO LIBRARY ASSOCIATION, Executive Director, Diane Wheatley, 73 Richmond St. W., #402, Toronto, Ont. M5H 1Z4 (416/363-3388, 89)

QUEBEC LIBRARY ASSOCIATION/ASSOCIATION DES BIBLIOTHECAIRES DU QUEBEC, c/o Dawson College Library, 350 Selby St., Montreal, P.Q. H3Z 1W7 (514/931-2808)
French Secretary, Agnès Lassonde; English Secretary, Mrs. Sharon Huffman

SASKATCHEWAN LIBRARY ASSOCIATION, Box 3388, Regina, Sask. S4P 3H1

ASTED (Association pour l'avancement des sciences et des techniques de la documentation), 360, rue Le Moyne, Montreal, P.Q. H2Y 1Y3 (514/844-8023)—Director General, Lise Brousseau

BIBLIOGRAPHICAL SOCIETY OF CANADA/LA SOCIETE BIBLIOGRAPHIQUE DU CANADA, Box 1878, Guelph, Ont. N1H 7A1

BRITISH COLUMBIA ASSOCIATION OF LIBRARY TECHNICIANS (B.C.A.L.T.), Box 67515, Stn. O, Vancouver, B.C. V5W 3T9

CANADIAN ASSOCIATION OF LAW LIBRARIES, c/o Executive Secretary, Box 220, Adelaide St. PO, Toronto, Ont. M5C 2J1

CANADIAN ASSOCIATION OF LIBRARY SCHOOLS, c/o Adele Fasick, Faculty of Library Science, University of Toronto, Toronto, Ont.

CANADIAN COUNCIL OF LIBRARY SCHOOLS, c/o Dean K. Packer, Faculty of Library Science, University of Toronto, 140 St. George St., Toronto, Ont. M5S 1A1

CANADIAN HEALTH LIBRARIES ASSOCIATION (Association des bibliothèques de la santé du Canada): Treasurer, Sandra R. Duchow, c/o Royal Victoria Hospital, Medical Library, Room H4.01, 687 ave des Pins ouest, Montreal, P.Q. H3A 1A1 (514/842-1231, ext. 250)

CANADIAN LIBRARY EXHIBITORS' ASSOCIATION c/o Mrs. E. Hicks, 120 Beverly Glen Blvd., No. 59, Scarborough, Ont. M1W 1W6 (416/497-2416)

CORPORATION DES BIBLIOTHECAIRES PROFESSIONNELS DU QUEBEC, c/o the Executive Director, Colette Rivet, bibl. prof., 360 rue Le Moyne, Montreal, P.Q. H2Y 1Y3 (514/845-3327)

ONTARIO ASSOCIATION OF LIBRARY TECHNICIANS/ASSOCIATION DES BIBLIOTECHNICIENS DE L'ONTARIO (OALT/ABO), Box 682, Oakville, Ont. L6J 5C1, President, Paulette Thibault

SPECIAL LIBRARIES ASSOCIATION, 235 Park Ave. S., New York, N.Y. 10003, U.S.A.
Eastern Canada Chapter, President, Joyce Charlebois, Pratt & Whitney, Box 10, Longueuil, P.Q. J4K 4X9 (514/677-9411, ext. 7209)
Toronto Chapter, President, Betty A. Bassett, c/o Xerox Research Centre of Canada, Technical Information Centre, 2480 Dunwin Dr., Mississauga, Ont. L5L 1J9 (416/828-6200)

National Library Advisory Board

Nine persons are appointed to limited terms by the Governor in Council, and two persons are nominated by the Canada Council and the Association of Universities & Colleges of Canada. The following are *ex officio* members:

Elmer Smith, Director, Canada Institute for Scientific & Technical Information, National Research Council, Montreal Rd. (M-55), Ottawa, Ont. K1A OS2
W. I. Smith, Dominion Archivist, Ottawa
Erik J. Spicer, Parliamentary Librarian, Ottawa, Ont. K1A 0A9
J. Guy Sylvestre, National Librarian, Ottawa

ALBERTA

Public Libraries in Alberta

With Librarian

Area Code is 204

Parkland Regional Library

W.R. Bale, Librarian, Box 1000, Lacombe, Alta. T0C 1S0, 782-3850

Branches within Parkland Regional Library

Alix Public Library, Box 322, Alix, Alta. T0C 0B0 – 747-2595 – Mrs. Doris L. Ambury
Bentley Public Library, Box 179, Bentley, Alta. T0C 0J0 – 748-4044 – Mrs. Mary Wilson
Blackfalds Public Library, Box 220, Blackfalds, Alta. T0M 0J0 – 885-2343 – Mrs. Carol Griner
Bowden Public Library, Box 218, Bowden, Alta. T0M 0K0 – 224-3688 – D. Charlton
Caroline Public Library, Caroline, Alta. T0M 0M0 – 722-9905 – Mrs. Georgina O'Coin
Carstairs Public Library, Box 941, Carstairs, Alta. T0M 0N0 – 337-3237 (res.) – Mrs. Audrey Spensley
Clive Public Library, Box 82, Clive, Alta. T0C 0Y0 – 784-3366 – Hazel Orange
Cremona Municipal Library, Cremona, Alta. T0M 0R0 – 637-2177 (res.) – Flora Newsome
Delburne Public Library, Box 405, Delburne, Alta. T0M 0V0 – 749-2552 (res.) – Diana Powell
Didsbury Public Library, Box 305, Didsbury, Alta. T0M 0W0 – 335-3377 – Mrs. Elsie Phillips
Eckville Public Library, Box 492, Eckville, Alta. T0M 0X0 – 746-3240 –Mrs. Mary Williams (Apr./Sept.) Mrs. Fannie Kasper (Oct./Mar.)
Elnora Public Library, Box 674, Elnora, Alta. T0M 0Y0 – 773-3602 – Lulu Bergquist
Innisfail Public Library, Box 220, Innisfail, Alta. T0M 1A0 – 227-3376 – Miss Margaret Pendergast
Lacombe Public Library, Lacombe, Alta. T0C 1S0 –782-3433 – Mrs. Alice Gleeson
Lone Pine Public Library, R.R. 2, Didsbury, Alta. T0M 0W0 – 335-4536 (res.) – Christine Milne
Mirror Public Library, Box 63, Mirror, Alta. T0B 3C0 –788-3038 (res.) – Mrs. Eva Davenport
Mynarski Public Library, Box 7, Mynarski, Alta. T0M 1N0 – 886-4361 – Mrs. Jo-Anne Marshall
Nordegg Town Public Library, Nordegg, Alta. T0M 2H0 – 721-3946 (res.) – Mrs. Joan Leavitt
Olds Public Library, Box 968, Olds, Alta. T0M 1P0 –226-6460 – Mrs. P. Dalgetty
Ponoka Public Library, Box 1057, Ponoka, Alta. T0C 2H0 – 783-4431, ext. 34 – Betty Schell
Rimbey Public Library, Box 315, Rimbey, Alta. T0C 2J0 – 843-2841 – Mrs. Blanche Boorman
Rocky Mountain House Public Library, Box 1497, Rocky Mountain House, Alta. T0M 1T0 –845-2042 – Myrna G. Speers
Sundre Public Library, Box 539, Sundre, Alta. T0M 1X0 – 638-4000 – Eileen Miller

Sylvan Lake Public Library, Box 46, Sylvan Lake, Alta. T0M 1Z0 –887-2141 – Esther Dube

Water Valley Public Library, Water Valley, Alta. T0M 2E0 – 637-2441 (res.) – Mrs. Lorraine Yates

Yellowhead Regional Library

Paul Galibois, Librarian, Box 400, Spruce Grove, Alta. T0E 2C0 – 962-2003

Branches within Yellowhead Regional Library

Alberta Beach Public Library, Box 135, Alberta Beach, Alta. T0E 0A0 – 924-3430 –Mrs. Joyce Walters

Alder Flats Public Library, Alder Flats, Alta. T0C 0A0 –388-3881 –Lois Robinson

Barrhead Elem. Sch.-Public Library, Box 820, Barrhead, Alta. T0G 0E0 – 674-2160 – Susan McLaren

J.E. LaPointe Sch./Community Library, Box 510, Beaumont, Alta. T0C 0H0 – 988-5833 – Mrs. V. McGillivray

Breton Public Library, Box 447, Breton, Alta. T0C 0P0 –696-3552 (res.) – Mrs. Alma Gillies

Calmar Public Library, Box 63, Calmar, Alta. T0C 0V0 –985-3472 –Carol Nystrom

Darwell Public Library, Darwell, Alta. T0E 0L0 – 892-2436 – Edith Richardson

Drayton Valley Municipal Library, Box 398, Drayton Valley, Alta. T0E 0M0 – 542-2228 – Mrs. Lois Peterson

Duffield Public Library, Duffield, Alta. T0E 0N0 – 892-2500 (res.) – Mrs. C. Brown

Entwistle Public Library, Box 154, Entwistle, Alta. T0E 0S0 – 727-4332 – Mrs. Penny Deib

Fort Assiniboine Public Library, Fort Assiniboine, Alta. T0G 1A0 –584-3751 – Susan Monasmith

Keephills Public Library, R.R. 1, Duffield, Alta. T0E 0N0 – Mrs. Vanderwell

Lakedell Public Library, R.R. 1, Westerose, Alta. T0C 2V0 – 586-2415 – Ms. Y.M. Adair

Leduc Public Library, Box 216, Leduc, Alta. T9E 2Y1 –986-2637 – Mrs. Bev. Maksymec

Mayerthorpe Public Library, Box 810, Mayerthorpe, Alta. T0E 1N0 – 786-2404 –Mrs. Shirley Kvill

Millet Public Library, Box 30, Millet, Alta. T0C 1Z0 – 387-5222 – Daphne Marr

Neerlandia Public Library, Box 2, Neerlandia, Alta. T0G 1R0 – 674-5581 – Mrs. Wilma Wieranga

New Sarepta Public Library, Box 10, New Sarepta, Alta. T0B 3M0 – 941-3924 – Sonia Barker

Onoway Branch Library, Box 484, Onoway, Alta. T0E 1V0 – Mrs. Elizabeth Turnbull

Rich Valley Public Library, R.R. 1, Gunn, Alta. T0E 1A0 – 967-5692 – Sylvia Fitzgerald

Sangudo Public & High Sch. Library, Box 419, Sangudo, Alta. T0E 2A0 – 785-2212 – Mrs. Gisela Brown

Seba Beach Public Library, Box 159, Seba Beach, Alta. T0E 2B0 – Raymonde Milner

Spruce Grove Public Library, Box 2759, Spruce Grove, Alta. T0E 2C0 – 962-0522 – Paul Donaldson

Stony Plain Public Library, Box 1680, Stony Plain, Alta. T0E 2G0 – 963-5440 – Mrs. Nancy Jones

Thorsby Public Library, Box 30, Thorsby, Alta. T0C 2P0 – 789-3914 (res.) – Mrs. Leona Hankin

Tomahawk Public Library, Tomahawk, Alta. T0E 2H0 – 339-3950 (res.) – Frances Gilbert

Wabamun Public Library, Box 1, Wabamun, Alta. T0E 2K0 – 892-2204 (res.) – Mrs. Nesa Watt

Warburg Public Library, Box 291, Warburg, Alta. T0C 2T0 – 848-2391 – Gloria Farmer

Whitecourt Public Library, Box 150, Whitecourt, Alta. T0E 2L0 – 778-2900 – Mrs. Irene Karlzen

Winfield Branch Library, R.R. 1, Winfield, Alta. T0C 2X0 – 586-2415 – Mrs. Daphne Betlamini

Municipal Libraries in Alberta

Acme Municipal Library, Box 326, Acme, Alta. T0M 0A0 – 546-3845 – Mrs. Claire Jackson

Airdrie Municipal Library, Box 659, Airdrie, Alta. T0M 0B0 – 948-5907, loc. 241

Andrew Municipal Library, Box 449, Andrew, Alta. T0B 0C0 – 365-3501 – Nick Bugiak

Athabasca Municipal Library, Box 2099, Athabasca, Alta. T0G 0B0 –675-2735 – Mrs. Irene Robbins

The Banff Library, Box 996, Banff, Alta. T0L 0C0 – 762-2661 – George Stacey

Bashaw Municipal Library, Box 669, Bashaw, Alta. T0B 0H0 – 372-3953 (res.) – Mrs. Edna Percival

Beaverlodge Municipal Library, Box 119, Beaverlodge, Alta. T0H 0C0 – 354-2569 – Mrs. H. Hennig

Beiseker Municipal Library, Box 357, Beiseker, Alta. T0M 0G0 – 547-3883

Black Diamond Municipal Library, Box 213, Black Diamond, Alta. T0L 0H0 – 933-4075 (res.) – Mrs. Erma Brown

Bonnyville Municipal Library, Box 1438, Bonnyville, Alta. T0A 0L0 – 826-3071 – Patricia Perkins

Bow Island Municipal Library, Box 608, Bow Island, Alta. T0K 0G0 – Ms. Susan Anderson

Boyle Public Library, Box 9, Boyle, Alta. T0A 0M0 – 689-4161 – Ms. E. Baillie

Brooks Municipal Library, Box 1149, Brooks, Alta. T0J 0J0 – 362-2947 – Mrs. Karen Armbruster

Calgary Public Library, 616 Macleod Trail S.E., Calgary, Alta. T2V 0H5 – 266-4606 – John Dutton

Camrose Municipal Library, 4710 50 Ave., Camrose, Alta. T4V 0R8 – 672-4214 – Miss Donna Holowaychuk

Canmore Municipal Library, Box 757, Canmore, Alta. T0L 0M0 – 678-2468 (res.) – Jean Luthy

Cardston Municipal Library, Box 479, Cardston, Alta. T0K 0K0 – Mrs. Gertrude Worth

Cardston M.D. No. 6 Library, Cardston, Alta. T0K 0K0

Cereal Municipal Library, Box 21, Cereal, Alta. T0J 0N0 – 326-3853 – Mrs. Sandra Rude

Champion Municipal Library, Box 177, Champion, Alta. T0L 0R0 – 897-3833 – Mrs. R. Middleton

Claresholm Municipal Library, Box 548, Claresholm, Alta. T0L 0T0 – 625-4168 – Mrs. Evelyn Volstad

Coaldale Municipal Library, Box 840, Coaldale, Alta. T0K 0L0 – 345-4842 (res.) – Mrs. Pat McRae

(Cochrane) Nan Boothby Memorial Library, Box 996, Cochrane, Alta. T0L 0W0 – 932-4353 – Mrs. M. Beattie

Cold Lake Municipal Library, Box 430, Cold Lake, Alta. T0A 0V0

Consort Municipal Library, Consort, Alta. T0C 1B0 – 577-3654

Coronation Memorial Library, Box 453, Coronation, Alta. T0C 1C0 – 578-3445 – Miss M. Elliott

Crossfield Municipal Library, Box 355, Crossfield, Alta. T0M 0S0 – 946-4232 – Wendy Jacobson

Crowsnest Municipal Library, Box 365, Coleman, Alta. T0K 0M0

Czar Municipal Library, Box 33, Czar, Alta. T0B 0Z0 – 857-3958 – Shirley Usselman

Daysland Municipal Library, Box 446, Daysland, Alta. T0B 1A0 – 374-3730

Delia Municipal Library, Box 302, Delia, Alta. T0J 0W0 – 364-3777 – Mrs. Frances Anderson

Derwent Municipal Library, Derwent, Alta. T0B 1C0 – 741-3743 – Mrs. L. Bielech

Devon Municipal Library, Box 398, Devon, Alta. T0C 1E0 – 987-3720 – Helen Bulner

Drumheller Municipal Library, Box 1599, Drumheller, Alta. T0J 0Y0 – 823-5382 – Ms. Diane Hart

Duchess Municipal Library, Box 335, Duchess, Alta. T0J 0Z0 – 378-4369 – Mrs. M. Wilson

Eaglesham Municipal Library, Box 269, Eaglesham, Alta. T0H 1H0 – 359-3792 – Mrs. Freda King

Edgerton Public Library, Box 125, Edgerton, Alta. T0B 1K0

Edmonton Public Library, #7 Sir Winston Churchill Sq., Edmonton, Alta. T5J 2V4 – 423-2331 – Vince Richards

Edson Municipal Library, Box 249, Edson, Alta. T0E 0P0 – 723-6691 – Mrs. M. Ahlf

Elk Point Municipal Library, Box 750, Elk Point, Alta. T0A 1A0 – 724-3737 – Mrs. Diane Wolanuk

Evansburg Municipal Library, Box 339, Evansburg, Alta. T0E 0T0 – 727-3925 – Mrs. E. Lauer

BUSINESS REPLY CARD

No postage necessary if mailed in Canada

POSTAGE WILL BE PAID BY:

Canada Post Postes Canada

30866

Canadian Almanac & Directory

Copp Clark Pitman
517 Wellington St. West
Toronto, Ontario

M5V 9Z9

Help us keep improving the *Canadian Almanac & Directory*

Please take a few minutes to answer the following questions and return this postage-paid card. For your trouble we'll send you a handsome *Canadian Almanac & Directory* pen. Thank you.

1. Section I use most...
Please place a check mark beside the section which you use most frequently.

- ☐ Church & Religious Organization
- ☐ Commerce & Finance
- ☐ Cultural Directory
- ☐ Education Directory
- ☐ Electoral Districts
- ☐ Foreign & International
- ☐ Geographic Information
- ☐ Hospitals
- ☐ Historical & General Information
- ☐ Legal Section
- ☐ Postal Information
- ☐ Tourism
- ☐ Transportation
- ☐ Government Directory

2. Please add a section on...
Briefly itemize information you would like to see added to the *Canadian Almanac & Directory*.

____

____

____

____

____

3. How/Where I acquired my *Canadian Almanac & Directory*

I acquired my Canadian Almanac & Directory from: ______________________________

____

I acquired my Canadian Almanac & Directory in the month of ______________

4. How long have you used the *Canadian Almanac & Directory*?

______________ year(s)

Name ______________ Title ______________

Organization ______________________________

Address ______________________________

City ______________________________

Code ______________ Date ______________ Phone ______________

Fairview Municipal Library, Box 248, Fairview, Alta. T0H 1L0 – 835-2613 – Mrs. Helen Stephenson
Falher Municipal Library, Box 60, Falher, Alta. T0H 1M0 – 837-2776 – Blanche Gervais
(Fort Macleod)R.C.M.P. Centennial Library, Box 1479, Fort Macleod, Alta. T0L 0Z0 – 234-3880 – Mrs. Mary Ann Hardy
Fort McMurray Municipal Library, 10012 Franklin Ave., Fort McMurray, Alta. T9H 2K6 – 743-2121
Fort Saskatchewan Municipal Library, Box 3060, Fort Saskatchewan, Alta. T8C 2T1 – 998-4271 – Mrs. M.E. Redford
Fox Creek Municipal Library, Box 88, Fox Creek, Alta. T0H 1P0 – 622-2343 – Ms. Brenda English
Galahad Municipal Library, Box 63, Galahad, Alta. T0B 1R0 – Lorraine Shaver
Gibbons Municipal Library, Box 510, Gibbons, Alta. T0A 1N0 – 923-2626 – Mrs. Pat Wandler
Gleichen Municipal Library, Box 159, Gleichen, Alta. T0J 1N0
Grande Cache Municipal Library, Box 809, Grande Cache, Alta. T0E 0Y0 – 827-2081 – Mrs. Anne Tuke
Grand Centre Municipal Library, Box 1049, Grand Centre, Alta. T0A 1T0 – 594-5101
Grande Prairie Municipal Library, 10032 100 Ave., Grande Prairie, Alta. T8V 0V3 – 532-3580 – Mrs. Amy Soltys
Granum Municipal Library, Granum, Alta. T0L 1A0 – 687-3884 – Mrs. Lois Webster
Hairy Hill Municipal Library, Hairy Hill, Alta. T0B 1S0 – 768-3800 – Mrs. V. Kotelko
Hanna Municipal Library, Box 878, Hanna, Alta. T0J 1P0 – 854-4433
Hardisty Municipal Library, Box 371, Hardisty, Alta. T0B 1V0 – 888-3531 – Mrs. Bea Hahn
Hay Lakes Municipal Library, Box 10, Hay Lakes, Alta. T0B 1W0 – Mrs. Lue Lindseth
High Level Library, Box 1380, High Level, Alta. T0H 1Z0 – 926-3706
High Prairie Municipal Library, Box 397, High Prairie, Alta. T0G 1E0 – 523-3838
High River Centennial Library, Box 309, High River, Alta. T0L 1B0 – 625-2917 – Mrs. Lucille Dougherty
Hinton Municipal Library, c/o Harry Collinge School, Hinton, Alta. T0E 1B0 – 865-2363 – Mrs. H. Hart
Hughenden Municipal Library, Hughenden, Alta. T0B 2E0 – 856-3830
Irvine Municipal Library, Box 90, Irvine, Alta. T0J 1V0
Jasper Municipal Library, Box 1170, Jasper, Alta. T0E 1E0 – 852-3652 – Jane Fitzpatrick
Killam Municipal Library, Box 67, Killam, Alta. T0B 2L0 – Ms. Bonnie Freadrich
Kinuso Municipal Library, Box 60, Kinuso, Alta. T0G 1K0 – 775-3661 (res.) – Helen Chasse
Kitscoty Municipal Library, Box 23, Kitscoty, Alta. T0B 2P0 – 846-2287 – Mrs. F. Elliott
Lamont Municipal Library, Box 180, Lamont, Alta. T0B 2R0 – 895-2229 – Mrs. Alice Richards
Lethbridge Municipal Library, 810 5th Ave. S., Lethbridge, Alta. T1J 4C4 – 329-3233 – Duncan Rand
Lloydminster Municipal Library, 4602 49 Ave., Lloydminster, Alta. S9V 0T2 – 825-2618 – Mrs. M. Collinge
Longview Municipal Library, Box 189, Longview, Alta. T0L 1H0 – 558-3741 – Mrs. Gayle Harmon
Lougheed Municipal Library, Lougheed, Alta. T0B 2V0
Magrath Public Library, Box 295, Magrath, Alta. T0K 1J0 – 758-6498 – Hazel Dudley
Manning Municipal Library, Box 927, Manning, Alta. T0H 2M0 – 836-3054 – Mrs. V. Daigle
Mannville Municipal Library, Box 273, Mannville, Alta. T0B 2W0 – 763-3660 (res.) – Mrs. Jean Schock
Marwayne Municipal Library, Box 82, Marwayne, Alta. T0B 2X0 – 847-3930 – M. Wheat (Sec.)
McLennan Municipal Library, Box 298, McLennan, Alta. T0E 2L0 – 324-3767 – Mrs. M. Lucas
Medicine Hat Municipal Library, 414 First St. S.E., Medicine Hat, Alta. T1A 0A8 – 527-5551 – Robert Block
Medley Public Library, Box 1400, Medley, Alta. T0A 2M0 – 594-4254
Milk River Municipal Library, Box 579, Milk River, Alta. T0K 1M0 – 647-3793 – Mrs. Margaret Thielen
Morinville Municipal Library, Box 474, Morinville, Alta. T0G 1P0 – 939-3292 – Mrs. Pauline Wood
Morrin Municipal Library, Box 16, Morrin, Alta. T0J 2B0 – 772-3801 – Mrs. Marion Tiessen
Nampa Municipal Library, Box 156, Nampa, Alta. T0H 2P0 – 322-3805 – Hilda Mears
Nanton Municipal Library, Box 310, Nanton, Alta. T0L 1R0 – 486-2258 – Ms. Thelma Fanning
Newell County Library Board, Box 88, Gem, Alta. T0J 1M0 – The Board operates libraries at Gem, Rolling Hills and Scandia.
Okotoks Municipal Library, Box 310, Okotoks, Alta. T0L 1T0 – 938-2220 – Ms. Marge Proctor
Oyen Municipal Library, Box 299, Oyen, Alta. T0J 2J0 – 664-3580 – Mary McGregor
Paradise Valley Municipal Library, Paradise Valley, Alta. T0B 3R0 – 745-2277 – Mrs. E. McLaughlin
Peace River Municipal Library, Box 2100, Peace River, Alta. T0H 2X0 – 624-4076 – Mrs. Freda Bobak
Picture Butte Municipal Library, Picture Butte, Alta. T0K 1V0 – 732-9710 – Mrs. Doreen Warnock
Pincher Creek Municipal Library, Box 1173, Pincher Creek, Alta. T0K 1W0 – 627-3813 – Mrs. Betty Schmidt
Provost Municipal Library, Box 449, Provost, Alta. T0K 3S0 – 753-2801 – Mrs. Cecelia Phillips
Radway Municipal Library, Box 220, Radway, Alta. T0A 2V0 – 736-9907 – Mrs. Natalka Palichuk
Rainbow Lake Municipal Library, Box 266, Rainbow Lake, Alta. T0H 2Y0 – 956-3734 (res.) – M.R. Hayden
Raymond Municipal Library, Box 161, Raymond, Alta. T0K 2S0 – 752-3236 – Mrs. Dorothea Roberts
Red Deer Municipal Library, 4818 49 St., Red Deer, Alta. T4N 1T8 – 346-4515 – M.D. Coleman
Redcliff Municipal Library, Box 280, Redcliff, Alta. T0J 2P0 – 548-3335 – Mrs. Daisy Congdon
Redwater Municipal Library, Box 384, Redwater, Alta. T0A 2W0 – 735-3464 – Mrs. Anne Schmidt
Rockyford Municipal Library, Rockyford, Alta. T0J 2R0 – 533-3861 (res.) – Mrs. Carolyn Madge
Rumsey Municipal Library, Rumsey, Alta. T0J 2Y0
Rycroft Municipal Library, Box 248, Rycroft, Alta. T0H 3A0 – 765-3652 – Mrs. Marj Zahara
Ryley Municipal Library, Box 243, Ryley, Alta. T0B 4A0 – 663-3682 – Mrs. Harriett Ruddy
St. Albert Public Library, 4 Glenview Cres., St. Albert, Alta. T8N 0G2 – 459-7731 – P. Forsyth
St. Paul Municipal Library, Box 1328, St. Paul, Alta. T0A 3A0 – 645-4904 – Mrs. Lillian Massé
Sedgewick Municipal Library, Box 36, Sedgewick, Alta. T0B 4C0 – 384-3642 (res.) – Mrs. Mary Bruce
Sexsmith Municipal Library, Box 266, Sexsmith, Alta. T0H 3C0
Slave Lake Municipal Library, Box 1195, Slave Lake, Alta. T0G 2A0 – 849-5250 – Diane Garret
Smoky Lake Municipal Library, Smoky Lake, Alta. T0A 3C0 – 656-3674 – Mrs. Sophie Leskiw
Spirit River Municipal Library, Box 686, Spirit River, Alta. T0H 3G0 – 864-3543 – Ms. Cathy Howrish
Stavely Municipal Library, Box 83, Stavely, Alta. T0L 1Z0 – 549-2405 (res.) – Mrs. Alice Graham
Stettler Municipal Library, Box 1512, Stettler, Alta. T0C 2L0 – 742-2292 – Mrs. Dorothy Brownlee
Stirling Municipal Library, Box 232, Stirling, Alta. T0K 2E0 – 756-3859 (res.) – Mrs. Dianne Eby
County of Strathcona Municipal Library, 2001 Sherwood Dr., Sherwood Park, Alta. T3A 3J4 – 467-3513 – Mrs. H. Dowling
Strathmore Municipal Library, Box 939, Strathmore, Alta. T0J 3H0 – 934-5440 – Mrs. Doris Bessie
Swan Hills Municipal Library, Box 386, Swan Hills, Alta. T0G 2C0 – 333-4505 – Mrs. R. Spellman
Taber Municipal Library, Box 209, Taber, Alta. T0K 2G0 – 223-4343 – Mrs. Alice Avery
Three Hills Municipal Library, Box 207, Three Hills, Alta. T0M 2A0 – 443-5140 – Mrs. Edith Helton

Tilley Municipal Library, Box 70, Tilley, Alta. T0J 3K0 – 377-2233 – Mrs. M. Buday
Tofield Municipal Library, Box 479, Tofield, Alta. T0B 4J0 – 662-3474 (res.) – Mrs. D. Freebury
Trochu Municipal Library, Box 433, Trochu, Alta. T0M 2C0 – 442-3974 (res.) – Mrs. Lorene Adolf
(Two Hills) Alice Melnyk Public Library, Box 460, Two Hills, Alta. T0B 4K0 – 657-3553 – Marlene Hlewka
Valleyview Municipal Library, Box 844, Valleyview, Alta. T0H 3N0 – 524-5520 – Mrs. Kay Meldrum
Vegreville Municipal Library, Box 129, Vegreville, Alta. T0B 4L0 – 632-3491 – Mrs. Jean Kelly
Vermilion Municipal Library, Box 476, Vermilion, Alta. T0B 4M0 – 853-4288 – Mrs. Gwen Lewis
Veteran Municipal Library, Box 527, Veteran, Alta. T0C 2S0 – 575-2191 (res.) – Mrs. Shirley Kary
Viking Municipal Library, Box 27, Viking, Alta. T0B 4N0 – 336-3130 (res.) – Mrs. D. Caldwell
Vulcan Public Library, Box 92, Vulcan, Alta. T0L 2B0 – 485-2571 – Mrs. Pat Crosby
Warner Municipal Library, Box 271, Warner, Alta. T0K 2L0 – 642-3648 (res.) – Mrs. Evelyn Schoen
Waskatenau Public Library, Box 130, Waskatenau, Alta. T0A 3P0 – 358-2297 – Mrs. Cathy Zon
Westlock Municipal Library, Box 1198, Westlock, Alta. T0G 2L0 – 349-3060 – Kathleen Hathaway
Wetaskiwin Municipal Library, 4906 51 St., Wetaskiwin, Alta. T9A 2E9 – 352-4055 – Ms. L. Hamilton
Wildwood Municipal Library, Wildwood, Alta. T0E 2M0
Willingdon & Dist. Public Library, Box 270, Willingdon, Alta. T0B 4R0 – 367-2222 – Miss J. Chrunik
Willow Creek M.D. #26 Public Library, Box 518, Nanton, Alta. T0L 1R0 – c/o Mrs. Betty Lowe, Bd. Sec.
Youngstown Municipal Library, Box 296, Youngstown, Alta. T0J 3P0 – 779-2143 (res.) – Mrs. Jean Jackson

Community Libraries in Alberta

With Librarian

Alliance Community Library, Box 202, Alliance, Alta. T0B 0A0 – 879-3849 (res.) – Mrs. Clara Johnson
Amisk Community Library, Box 71, Amisk, Alta. T0B 0B0 – Mrs. Joyce Venema
Bassano Community Library, Box 145, Bassano, Alta. T0J 0B0 – Mrs. Molly Schelske
Berwyn Municipal Library, Box 178, Berwyn, Alta. T0H 0E0 – Mrs. Marie Olsen
Brocket Community Library, Box 70, Brocket, Alta. T0K 0H0 – 965-3939 – Jo-Ann Yellowhorn
Brownfield Community Library, Brownfield, Alta. T0C 0R0 – 578-2247 – Mrs. B. Lindmark
Brownvale Community Library, Brownvale, Alta. T0H 0L0 – 597-2250 – Mrs. Lynn Shelton
Caslan Community Library, Caslan, Alta. T0A 0R0 – 689-2505 (res.) – Mrs. Grace Bury
Castor Community Library, Box 699, Castor, Alta. T0C 0X0 – 882-3451 (res.) – Mr. Pat Bain
Cessford Community Library, Cessford, Alta. T0J 0P0 – 566-3743 – Mrs. B. Stringer
Debolt Community Library, Box 480, Debolt, Alta. T0H 1B0 – 957-3752 (res.) – Mrs. Norma Perkins
East Coulee Community Library, Box 576, East Coulee, Alta. T0J 1B0 – 822-3872 (res.) – Mrs. Cecilia Evans
Enchant Community Library, Box 3000, Enchant, Alta. T0K 0V0 – 792-2108 – Mrs. S. Severtson
Exshaw Community Library, Box 113, Exshaw, Alta. T0L 2C0 – 673-3656 – Mrs. Jean Cooper
Faust Community Library, Box 64, Faust, Alta. T0G 0X0 – 355-3666 – Mrs. E. Witt
Fawcett Community Library, Box 150, Fawcett, Alta. T0G 0Y0 – 954-3827 – Alice Frose
Flatbush Community Library, Box 82, Flatbush, Alta. T0G 0Z0 – 681-2107 (res.) – Mrs. Thelma Schwarz
Forestburg Community Library, Forestburg, Alta. T0B 1N0 – 582-3513 (res.) – Mrs. C. Shillinglaw
Fort Vermilion Community Library, Bag #4, Fort Vermilion, Alta. T0H 1N0 – 927-4279 – Pat Koenig (927-3750, res.)
Grimshaw Community Library, Box 588, Grimshaw, Alta. T0H 1W0 – 332-1110 (res.) – Mr. Bernice Glen
Hines Creek Community Library, Box 64, Hines Creek, Alta. T0H 2A0 – 494-3654 – Mrs. Ann Zavisha
Hussar Community Library, Box 54, Hussar, Alta. T0J 1S0 – 787-2134 (res.) – Mrs. Kay Isaak
Jarvie Community Library, Box 119, Jarvie, Alta. T0G 1H0 – 954-3935 – Mrs. Evelyn Mechalchuk (Sec.)
Keg River Community Library, Keg River, Alta. T0H 2G0 – 981-2128 – Mrs. A. Vos
La Crete Community Library, Box 609, La Crete, Alta. T0H 2H0 – 928-3913 – Brian Walker
Lac La Biche Community Library, Box 1588, Lac La Biche, Alta. T0A 2C0 – 623-7467 – Dr. J. McNinch
Linaria Community Library, R.R. 1, Westlock, Alta. T0G 2L0
Linden Community Library, Box 120, Linden, Alta. T0M 1J0 – 546-3757
Millarville Community Library, c/o Millarville School, Millarville, Alta. T0L 1K0 – Mrs. Loraine Debnam
Myrnam Community Library, Myrnam, Alta. T0B 3K0 – 336-3801 – Mrs. Ellen Yaremchuk
Newbrook Community Library, Box 208, Newbrook, Alta. T0A 2P0 – 576-3771 – Mrs. Olga Dozorec
Niton (Green Grove Community Library), Niton Junction, Alta. T0E 1S0 – 795-3782 – Mrs. June Priestley-Wright
Plamondon Community Library, Box 90, Plamondon, Alta. T0A 2T0 – 798-3840 – Emily Chevigny
Ralston Community Library, Ralston, Alta. T0J 2N0 – 544-3670 – Mrs. M. Myers
Rochester Community Library, Rochester, Alta. T0G 1Z0 – 698-3746 – Mrs. Theresa Betts
Stavely Community Library, Box 83, Stavely, Alta. T0L 1Z0 – 549-2405 (res.) – Mrs. Alice Graham
Vauxhall Community Library, Box 265, Vauxhall, Alta. T0K 2K0
Vimy Community Library, Box 29, Vimy, Alta. T0G 2J0 – 961-3014 – Mrs. Lindell G. Church
Wainwright Community Library, Box 1358, Wainwright, Alta. T0B 4P0 – 842-3605 – Mrs. K. Taylor
Wandering River Community Library, Box 37, Wandering River, Alta. T0A 3M0
Wanham Community Library, Wanham, Alta. T0H 3P0 – 694-3828 – Mrs. Olga Podruzny
Warner Community Library, Box 271, Warner, Alta. T0K 2L0 – 642-3648 (res.) – Mrs. Evelyn Schoen
Youngstown Community Library, Youngstown, Alta. T0J 3P0 – 779-2143 (res.) – Mrs. Jean Jackson

Special & College Libraries & Resource Centres in Alberta

With Contact Person (Librarian, unless otherwise indicated)

Area Code is 403

BANFF

Archives of the Canadian Rockies Library, Box 160, Banff, Alta. T0L 0C0 – 762-2291 – Edward J. Hart, Admr.
Banff Centre School of Fine Arts Library, Box 1020, Banff, Alta. T0L 0C0 – 762-6265 – Bob Foley
Mineral Springs Hospital Library, Banff, Alta. T0L 0C0 – 762-2222 – Mrs. E. Heikkila

BEAVERLODGE

Agriculture Canada, Research Station Library, Box 29, Beaverlodge, Alta. T0H 0C0 – 354-2212

CALGARY

Alberta Alcoholism & Drug Abuse Commission Library, 3rd floor, 1177 11th Ave. S.W., Calgary, Alta. T2R 0G5 – 244-2727 – M. Molly Taylor
Alberta Bible College Library, 599 Northmount Dr. N.W., Calgary, Alta. T2K 3J6 – 282-2994 – Aileen B. Case
Alberta Dept. of the Attorney General:
Judges' Library, Courthouse, 611 4 St. S.W., Calgary, Alta. T2P 1T5 – 261-7475 – Melody M. Hainsworth

Law Society of Alberta Library, same Librarian & address as Judges' Library

Provincial Court Library, Southern Alberta Region, 5th floor, 323 6th Ave. S.E., Calgary, Alta. T2G 4V1 – 261-3126 – Laura Scott

Alberta Dept. of Housing & Public Works Library, 10050 112th St., 10th floor, Calgary, Alta. T5K 1L9

Alberta Energy Co. Library, #2400, 639 5th Ave. S.W., Calgary, Alta. T2P 0M9

Alberta Gas Ethylene Co. Ltd. Library, #500, BP House, 333 5th Ave. S.W., Calgary, Alta. T2P 3B6 – 263-8130 – Carrie-Faye Smith

Alberta Heart Foundation Library, 2011 10 Ave. S.W., Calgary, Alta. T3C 0K4 – 244-0786 – J.L. Paquet

Alberta Petroleum Marketing Commission Library, #1000, 205 5th Ave. S.W., Calgary, Alta. T2P 2V7 – 262-8808

Alberta & Southern Gas Co. Ltd. Library, 240 4th Ave. S.W., Calgary, Alta. T2P 0H5 – 263-8320 – Marian S. Eagen

Alberta Vocational Centre Library, 332 6 Ave. S.E., Calgary, Alta. T2G 4S6 – 261-3930 – Nora Robinson

Amoco Canada Petroleum Co. Ltd. Library, 444 7 Ave. S.W., Calgary, Alta. T2P 0Y2 – 233-1451 – Frances M. Drummond

Anglican Diocese of Calgary Library, c/o Anglican Cathedral Church of the Redeemer, 602 1st St. S.E., Calgary, Alta. T2G 4W4 – 269-1905 – The Very Rev. D. Carter, Archivist

Arctic Institute of North America Library, 2500 University Dr., Calgary, Alta. T2N 1N4 – 284-5966 – W.R. Maes

Atkinson, McMahon Law Library, 750 IBM Bldg., 606 4th St. S.W., Calgary, Alta. T2P 1T1 – 269-4351

Baptist Leadership Training School Library, 4330 16th St. S.W., Calgary, Alta. T2T 4L5 – 243-3770 – Rev. Gerald Fisher, Principal

Beak Consultants Ltd. Library, #6, 3530 11A St. N.E., Calgary, Alta. T2E 6M7 – 276-4565 – Doreen Conn

Bennett Jones Law Library, #3200, 400 4th Ave. S.W., Calgary, Alta. T2P 0J4 – 267-3226 – Jennifer Martison

Berean Bible College Library, 460 31 Ave. N.W., Calgary, Alta. T2M 2P4 – 277-5616 – Miss Mary M. Macomber

BP Canada Technical Library, 333 5 Ave. S.W., Calgary, Alta. T2P 3B6 – 237-1236 – Ms. Sylvia Hoyling

Burnet, Duckworth & Palmer Law Library, 425 1 St. S.W., Calgary, Alta. T2P 3L8 – Kathy Kurceba

Calgary Board of Education, Media Services, 3610 9 St. S.E., Calgary, Alta. T2G 3C5 – 268-8538 – L.G. MacRae, Co-ordinator

Calgary General Hospital, Dept. of Educational Services Hospital Library, 841 Centre Ave. E., Calgary, Alta. T2E 0A1 – 268-9234 – Mrs. Elizabeth Kirchner

The Calgary Herald Library, 215 16 St. S.E., Calgary, Alta. T2P 0W8 – 269-6361 – Karen Liddiard

Calgary Power Ltd. Library, Box 1900, Calgary, Alta. T2P 2M1 – 267-7388 – Miss Shamim Kassam

Canada Cities Service Ltd. Library, 407 2nd St. S.W., Calgary, Alta. T2P 2M7 – 263-4330 – Anne Higgin

Canadian Music Centre Library, 9th floor, University Library Tower, Univ. of Calgary, Calgary, Alta. T2N 1N4 – 284-7403

Canadian Petroleum Association Library, #1500, 633 6th Ave. S.W., Calgary, Alta. T2P 2Y5 – 269-6721

Canadian Western Natural Gas Co. Ltd. Library, 140 6th Ave. S.W., Calgary, Alta. T2P 0P6 – 245-7403 – Ms. Shelley J. Weatherhead

Champlin Petroleum Co., Engr./Explr. Library, #2300, 715 5th Ave. S.W., Calgary, Alta. T2P 2X6 – 263-7070 – P. Joan Marks

Chevron Standard Ltd. Library, 400 5 Ave. S.W., Calgary, Alta. T2P 0L1 – 267-5910 – Terri Pieschel

Church of Jesus Christ of Latter Day Saints, Institute of Religion Library, 3120 32 Ave. N.W., Calgary, Alta. T2N 1N7 – 282-5426 – Merlin V. Olsen

City of Calgary Electric System Library, Box 2100, Calgary, Alta. T2P 2M5 – 268-1100 – Ann Savage

City of Calgary Engineering Dept. Library, Box 2100, Calgary, Alta. T2P 2M5 – 268-5807 – Miss S. Jadavji

City of Calgary Information Services, Box 2100, Calgary, Alta. T2P 2M5 – 268-5449 – Patricia J. Drake

City of Calgary Social Service Dept. Library, Box 2100, Calgary, Alta. T2P 2M5 – 268-5111

Code, Hunter Law Library, 640 7th Ave. S.W., Calgary, Alta. T2P 3A6 – 261-2800

Commonwealth Microfilm Library, 901 10 Ave. S.W., Calgary, Alta. T2R 0B5 – 245-2555 – Don Wurzer

Cook, Snowdon & Laird Law Library, #1700, 444 5 Ave. S.W., Calgary, Alta. T2P 2T8 – 278-4593 – W. Staehr

Energy Resources Conservation Board Library, 640 5 Ave. S.W., Calgary, Alta. T2P 3G4 – 261-8242 – Ms. E.A. Johnson

Esso Resources Canada Ltd., Library Information Centre, 25th floor, 237 4th Ave. S.W., Calgary, Alta. T2P 0H6 – L. Brodner

Esso Resources Canada Ltd., Research Dept. Library, 339 50 Ave. S.E., Calgary, Alta. T2G 2B3 – 259-0303 – V. Kohse

Fenerty, Robertson etc. Law Library, 39th floor, Bow Valley Sq. Two, 205 5th Ave. S.W., Calgary, Alta. T2P 2V7 –268-7055 – Mrs. S. London

Foothills Hospital Sch. of Nursing Library, 1403 29 St. N.W., Calgary, Alta. T2N 2T9 – 270-1460 – Ruth MacRae

Foothills Pipeline (Yukon) Ltd. Library, #1600, 205 5 Ave. S.W., Box 9083, Calgary, Alta. T2P 2V7 – 237-1480 – L. Marchese

Glenbow-Alberta Institute Library, Glenbow Centre, 130 9th Ave. S.E., Calgary, Alta. T2G 0P3 – 264-8300 – Leonard J. Gottselig

Gordon Atkins & Assoc. Architects Ltd. Library, 1909 17th Ave. S.W., Calgary, Alta. T2T 0E9 – 245-4545

Grace Hospital Library, 1402 8 Ave. N.W., Calgary, Alta. T2N 1B9 – 284-1141 – Dr. A. Rothwell, Chairman

Grand Lodge Library, 330 12th Ave. S.W., Calgary, Alta. T2R 0H2 – 262-1149 – M.P. Dunford

Gulf Canada Ltd. Library, Box 130, Calgary, Alta. T2P 2H7 – 233-3804 – D. Budrevics

Holy Cross Hospital, Medical Library, 2210 2 St. S.W., Calgary, Alta. T2S 1S6 – 266-7231 – Mumtaz Jivraj

Home Oil Co. Ltd. Library, #2300, 324 8th Ave. S.W., Calgary, Alta. T2P 2Z5 – 232-7207 – R.A. Muir

Hudson's Bay Oil & Gas Co. Ltd., Corporate Library, 700 2nd St. S.W., Calgary, Alta. T2P 2W1 – 231-6051 – C.G. Harvey

Husky Oil Operations Ltd. Information Centre, Box 6525, Calgary, Alta. T2P 3G7 – 267-8404 – F.W. Graham

Institute of Sedimentary & Petroleum Geology Library, 3303 33 St. N.W., Calgary, Alta. T2L 2A7 – 284-0301 – Marian Jones

Insurance Institute of Southern Alberta Library, #601, 630 8th Ave. S.W., Calgary, Alta. T2P 1G6 – 266-3427 – Mrs. N. Read

Kaiser Oil Ltd. Library, Box 6800, Stn. D, Calgary, Alta. T2P 0N1 – 266-7602 – Sheila Howard

Lavalin Centre Library, (Petroleum/Engr.), 909 5 Ave. S.W., Calgary, Alta. T2P 3G5 – 237-6500, loc. 314 – Sheila Ward

Law Society of Alberta, see Alta. Dept. of Attorney General, Calgary and Edmonton

Mason and Company Library, 1110 Bow Valley Sq. Two, 205 5 Ave. S.W., Calgary, Alta. T2P 2V7 – 263-2190 – Ms. Lou Selgensen

McDougall United Church Library, 8516 Athabasca St. S.E., Calgary, Alta. T2H 1S1 – 252-1620

McKinnon, Allen & Associates (Western) Ltd., Library, 631 42nd Ave. S.E., Calgary, Alta. T2G 1Y7 – 243-4345

McLaws & Co. Law Library, 407 8th Ave. S.W., Calgary, Alta. T2P 1E6 – 264-0580 – Susan L. Ross

Mobil Oil Canada Ltd. Library, Box 800, Calgary, Alta. T2P 2J7 – 268-7785 – Miss K. McNeely

Montreal Engineering Co. Ltd. Library, 125 9 Ave. S.E., Calgary, Alta. T2G 0P6 – 263-1680 – B. Bendell

Mount Royal College, Learning Resources Centre, 4825 Richard Rd. S.W., Calgary, Alta. T3E 6K6 – 246-6520 – Alan Dyment

National Film Board of Canada, Calgary Dist. Office, Film Library, (222 1st St. S.E.) Box 2959, Stn. M, Calgary, Alta. T2P 3C3 – 231-5414 – Ms. Doris Ostergaard

Norcen Energy Resources Ltd. Library, 715 5th Ave. S.W., Calgary, Alta. T2P 2X7 – 231-0887 – Gwendolyn Cameron

Northland Bank Library, #1200, 324 8th Ave. S.W., Calgary, Alta. T2P 2Z2 – 266-8901

NOVA: An Alberta Corporation, Library, Box 2535, Calgary, Alta. T2P 2N6 – 231-9100 – Murray Genoe

Panarctic Oils Ltd. Library, 703 6th Ave. S.W., Box 190, Calgary, Alta. T2P 2H6 – 269-0329 – Susan Tyrrell
PanCanadian Petroleum Ltd. Library, 125 9th Ave. S.E., Calgary, Alta. T2G 0P6 – 231-3439 – Marilyn Harvey
Parks Canada, Western Region Library, (220 4th Ave. S.E.) Box 2989, Stn. M, Calgary, Alta. T2P 3H8 – 231-4455
Petro-Canada Library, Box 2844, Calgary, Alta. T2P 3E3 – 232-8000 – M. Meadows
Pleasant Heights United Church Library, 1112 19 Ave. N.W., Calgary, Alta. T2M 0Z9 – 289-9281
St. David's United Church Library, 3303 Capitol Hill Cres. N.W., Calgary, Alta. T2M 2R2 – 284-2276
Shell Canada Resources Ltd., Technical Library, Box 100, Calgary, Alta. T2P 2H5 – 232-3512 – Sheila J. Jepps
Southern Alberta Institute of Technology, Learning Resources Centre, 1301 16 Ave. N.W., Calgary, Alta. T2M 0L4 – 284-8647 – Grace A. Armstrong
Sproule Associates Ltd. Library, 505 2nd St. S.W., Calgary, Alta. T2P 1N8 – 269-7951
Suncor Inc. Library, Box 38, Calgary, Alta. T2P 2V5 – 269-8126 – Mrs. P.J. Strong
Swedish Consulate Library, 420 47 Ave. S.W., Calgary, Alta. T2S 1C4 – 243-1093 – R. Zoumer, Consul
Texaco Canada Resources Ltd. Library, Box 3333, Calgary, Alta. T2P 2P8 – 267-0681 – Jeanne Shaw
Toronto Dominion Bank, Oil & Gas Dept. Library, 1700 Home Oil Tower, Toronto Dominion Sq., Calgary, Alta. T2P 2Z2 – 265-9020 – Mrs. V. Swanson
Total Petroleum (North America) Ltd. Library, 639 5 Ave. S.W., Calgary, Alta. T2P 0M9 – 265-9080 – K. Kabir
Transcanada Pipelines Ltd. Library, 407 8th Ave. S.W., Box 500, Calgary, Alta. T2P 2M7 – 269-5792 – Liz Winter
Union Oil Co. of Canada Ltd. Library, (335 8 Ave. S.W.) Box 999, Calgary, Alta. T2P 2K6 – 268-0303 – Julie Graham
University of Calgary Libraries, 2500 University Dr., Calgary, Alta. T2N 1N4 – 284-5954 – Alan H. MacDonald, Dir. of Libraries
Medical – A.K. Kirchner
Law – G. Starr
Social Sciences – G. Ghent
Arts & Humanities – W. Converth
Environment-Science-Technology – M. Sinkey
Development – E. Bouey
Walsh Young Law Library, 1500 Guinness House, Calgary, Alta. T2P 0Z8 – Susan L. Ross
Westmin Resources Ltd. Library, 1800 Bow Valley Square Three, 255 5th Ave. S.W., Calgary, Alta. T2P 3G8

CAMROSE

Camrose Lutheran College Library, Camrose, Alta. T4V 2R3 – 672-3381 – Asgeir Ingibergsson

COLLEGE HEIGHTS

Canadian Union College Library, College Heights, Alta. T0C 0Z0 – 782-6461 – K.H. Clouten

DIDSBURY

Mountain View Bible College Library, Box 190, Didsbury, Alta. T0M 0W0 – 335-3337 – Mrs. Sharon E. Quantz

EDMONTON

Alberta Alcoholism & Drug Abuse Commission, Film Library, 7th floor, 10909 Jasper Ave., Edmonton, Alta. T5J 3M9 – 427-7303
Alberta Association of Registered Nurses Library, 10256 112 St., Edmonton, Alta. T5K 1M6 – 426-0160 – Mrs. Lloanne Walker
Alberta Bureau of Statistics Library, 7th floor, 10820 98 Ave., Edmonton, Alta. T5K 0C8 – 427-3058
Alberta Council on Aging Resource Library, #324, 10010 105 St., Edmonton, Alta. T5J 1C8 – 423-7781
Alberta Dept. of Advanced Education & Manpower Library, 11160 Jasper Ave., Edmonton, Alta. T5K 0L1 – 427-5590 – Mrs. Pauline Howatt
Alberta Dept. of Agriculture, Departmental Library, 9718 107 St., Edmonton, Alta. T5K 2C8 – 427-2104 – Margaret Bhatnagar
Alberta Dept. of Agriculture, Film Library, 9718 107 St., Edmonton, Alta. T5K 2C8 – 427-2127 – R.H. Glanvill
Alberta Dept. of Agriculture, Branch Library, 6909 116 St., Edmonton, Alta. T6H 4P2 – 436-1165 – Frances L.M. Hewitt
Alberta Dept. of the Attorney General
Judges' Library, Law Courts Bldg., 1A Churchill Sq., Edmonton, Alta. T5J 0R2 – 423-7601 – Dr. George Solt
Law Society of Alberta Library, same Librarian and address as Judges' Library
Attorney General's Law Library, 4th Floor North, 9833 109 St., Edmonton, Alta. T5K 2E8 – 427-5021, 2 – Andrew Balazs
Provincial Court Libraries, Central Office, 7th floor, 9803 102A Ave., Edmonton, Alta. T5J 3A3 – O.M. Kizlyk
Alberta Dept. of Consumer & Corporate Affairs Resource Centre, 10065 Jasper Ave., 7th floor, Edmonton, Alta. T5J 3B1 – 427-5215 – Rean Modien
Alberta Dept. of Culture Library, 11th floor, CN Tower, 10004 104 Ave., Edmonton, Alta. T5J 0K5 – 427-2571 – Lucy M. Pana
Alberta Dept. of Culture, Historical Resources Library, 12845 102 Ave., Edmonton, Alta. T5N 0M6 – 427-1750 – J. Toon
Alberta Dept. of Economic Development Library, 11th floor, Pacific Plaza, Edmonton, Alta. T5J 3M8 – 427-4957
Alberta Dept. of Education Library, 4th floor, West Wing, Devonian Bldg., 11160 Jasper Ave., Edmonton, Alta. T5K 0L2 – 427-2985 – Mrs. Helen Skirrow
Alberta Dept. of Energy & Natural Resources Library, 9915 108 St., Edmonton, Alta. T5K 2C9 – 427-7425 – Carole Dawson
Alberta Dept. of the Environment Library, 14th floor, 9820 106 St., Edmonton, Alta. T5K 2J6 – 427-5870 – Ione Hooper
Alberta Dept. of Federal & Intergovernmental Affairs Library, 14th floor, South Tower, 10030 107 St., Edmonton, Alta. T5J 3E4 – 427-2611 – Anita Duncan
Alberta Dept. of Government Services, Information Services, #259, 9515 107 St., Edmonton, Alta. T5K 2C4 – 427-8224 – D. Bugeaud
Alberta Dept. of Hospitals & Medical Care, Hospital Services Library, Box 2222, Edmonton, Alta. T5J 2P4 – 427-8720 – Margaret Bradfield
Alberta Dept. of Housing & Public Works Library, 10th floor, 10050 112 St., Edmonton, Alta. T5K 1L9 – 427-8150 – Dolores Ogilvie
Alberta Dept. of Labour Library, IBM Bldg., 10808 99 Ave., Edmonton, Alta. T5K 0G2 – 427-8531 – Wendy Kinsella
Alberta Dept. of Municipal Affairs Library, 9th floor, Jarvis Bldg., 9925 107 St., Edmonton, Alta. T5K 2H9 – 427-4829 – Bettie Bayrak
Alberta Dept. of Recreation & Parks Library, 10363 108 St., Edmonton, Alta. T5J 1L7 – 427-7638 – M.N. Aston
Alberta Dept. of Social Services & Community Health Library, 6th floor, 10030 107 St., Edmonton, Alta. T5J 3E4 – 427-6412 – Judy E. Sponholz
Alberta Dept. of Solicitor General Library, 5th floor, 10310 Jasper Ave., Edmonton, Alta. T5J 1Y8 – 427-3421 – Mrs. Aileen Wright
Alberta Dept. of Tourism & Small Business Library, #1900, 10065 Jasper Ave., Edmonton, Alta. T5J 0H4 – 427-3685 – G. Winter
Alberta Dept. of Transportation Library, Room 159, 9630 106 St., Edmonton, Alta. T5K 2B8 – 427-8802 – Eleanor Chernenkoff
Alberta Government Telephones Library, 13th floor, 10020 100 St., Edmonton, Alta. T5J 0N5 – 425-3653 – Mrs. Y.M. Kyllo
Alberta Historical Resources Library, See Alta. Dept. of Culture
Alberta Hospital Library, Box 307, Edmonton, Alta. T5J 2J7 – 973-2268 – M. Pierre
Alberta Hospital Association Library, 6th floor, 10025 108 St., Edmonton, Alta. T5J 1K9 – 423-1776 – Pat Baxter
Alberta Human Rights Commission Library, #501, 10053 111 St., Edmonton, Alta. T5K 2H8 – 427-7661
Alberta Personnel Admin. Office Library, 12th floor, 9925 107 St., Edmonton, Alta. T5K 2H9 – 427-7895 – Lynda Peacock, Lib. Tech.
Alberta Power Ltd., See Canadian Utilities Ltd.

Alberta Research Council, Library Services, 4445 Calgary Trail S., Edmonton, Alta. T6H 5R7 – 438-1810 – Sharon M. Gee
Alberta Research Council, Interlibrary Loans, 11315 87 Ave., Edmonton, Alta. T6G 2C2 – 432-8123 – H.R. Csanyi
Alberta School for the Deaf Library, 6240 113 St., Edmonton, Alta. T6H 3L2 – 434-1481 – Charmaine Muise
Alberta Teachers' Association Library, 11010 142 St., Edmonton, Alta. T5N 2R1 – 453-2411 – Donna Dryden
Alberta Treasury Library, #404, 9515 107 St., Edmonton, Alta. T5K 2C3 – 427-7595 – Robin Brown
Alberta Treasury Payroll & Pensions Library, 12th Floor, Centre West, 10035 108 St., Edmonton, Alta. T5J 3G5 – 427-2782
Alberta Union of Provincial Employees Library, 10975 124 St., Edmonton, Alta. T5M 0J2 – 452-0333 – Frank Moorgen (Research Officer)
Alberta Vocational Centre Library, 10215 108 St., Edmonton, Alta. T5J 1L6 – 427-5488
AME Engineering Ltd. Library, #700, 10160 113 St., Edmonton, Alta. T5K 1M3 – 425-1710 – Darlene Elias
Associated Engineering Services Ltd. Library, 13140 St. Albert Trail, Edmonton, Alta. T5L 4R8 – 453-8111 – M. Davidson
Atmospheric Environment Service, See Canada Dept. of Environment
Banister Continental Ltd. Library, 9910 39 Ave., Edmonton, Alta. T5J 2R4 – 462-9430 – Louise Frank
Bishop & McKenzie Law Library, #2200, 10205 101 St., Edmonton, Alta. T5J 1V3 – 426-5550 – Joan Ennion
Boreal Institute for Northern Studies Library, CW401, Biological Sciences Bldg., Univ. of Alberta, Edmonton, Alta. T6G 2E9 – 432-4409 – Mrs. G.A. Cooke
L.A. Broughton Library, 6240 113 St., Edmonton, Alta. T6H 3L2 – 434-1481, ext. 224 – Charmaine Muise
Brownlee, Fryett Law Library, 803 Chancery Hall, #3 Sir Winston Churchill Sq., Edmonton, Alta. T5J 2C9 – 429-4821
Canada Dept. of Environment, Atmospheric Environment Service, Western Regional Library, 6325 103 St., Edmonton, Alta. T6H 5H6 – 437-1250 – A.S. Mann, Lib. Committee
Canada Dept. of Justice, Edmonton Region Library, 928 Royal Trust Tower, Edmonton, Alta. T5J 2Z2 – 420-2983 – Karen Buchanan
Canadian Forestry Service, Northern Forest Research Centre Library, 5320 122 St., Edmonton, Alta. T6H 3S5 – 435-7210 – D.J.S. Robinson
Canadian Mental Health Association, Alberta Division Library, Room 207, 10711 107 Ave., Edmonton, Alta. T5H 0W6 – 426-6665
Canadian Utilities Ltd. Library, 10040 104 St., Edmonton, Alta. T5J 2V6 – 420-7039 – Ms. Donna I. Humphries
Canadian Wildlife Service, Western & Northern Region Library, 10th floor, 9942 108 St., Edmonton, Alta. T5K 2J5 – 420-2537 – Peter A. Jordan
Cancer Research Unit, McEachern Laboratory, Resource Centre, Univ. of Alberta, Edmonton, Alta. T6G 2H7 – 432-3607
Centre for the Study of Mental Retardation, Resource Centre, Univ. of Alberta, 6-123d Education 2, Edmonton, Alta. T6G 2G5 – 432-4439 – Barbara McGowan
Charles Camsell General Hospital, The Peter Wilcock Library, 12815 115 Ave., Edmonton, Alta. T5M 3A4 – 453-5494 – Jan Jacobson
City of Edmonton Commissioner's Library, 3rd floor, City Hall, Edmonton, Alta. T5J 2R7 – 428-5446 – Mrs. H.P. Thursby
City of Edmonton, Edmonton Power Library, 7th Floor, 10250 101 St., Edmonton, Alta. T5J 3P4 – Mrs. Janet Marren
City of Edmonton, Business Development Dept. Library, #2410, 10235 101 St., Edmonton, Alta. T5J 3G1 – 428-5464 – A.G. Bleiken
City of Edmonton Law Dept. Library, 8th floor, City Hall, Edmonton, Alta. T5J 2R7 – 428-3506 – A. Massing, Barr. & Sol.
City of Edmonton, Parks & Recreation Dept., Edmonton Archives, 10105 112 Ave., Edmonton, Alta. T5G 0H1 – 479-2060 – Mrs. Helen LaRose, Manager
City of Edmonton Planning Dept. Library, 11th floor, 10020 101A Ave., Edmonton, Alta. T5J 3G2 – 428-2661
City of Edmonton Social Services Library, 6th floor, CN Tower, 10004 104 Ave., Edmonton, Alta. T5J 0K1 – 428-5914 – Miss V. Von Semmler
Concordia College Library, 7128 Ada Blvd., Edmonton, Alta. T5B 4E4 – 479-8481 – Mircea Panciuk
Consulate General of the Federal Republic of Germany Library, Box 363, Edmonton, Alta. T5J 2J6 – 429-6421
J.C. Cooke Library, Northwest Bible College, 11617 106 Ave., Edmonton, Alta. T5H 0S1 – 452-0808 – B.S. Fawcett
Cross Cancer Institute Library, 11560 University Ave., Edmonton, Alta. T6G 1Z2 – 432-8593 – Mrs. K. Sharma
Departments of Government, See Alberta Dept. etc.
Edmonton Art Gallery Library, #2 Sir Winston Churchill Sq., Edmonton, Alta. T5J 2C1 – 429-6781 – Brenda Banks
Edmonton Catholic School Dist., See Edmonton Separate School Board
Edmonton City, See City of
Edmonton General Hospital, Health Sciences Library, 11111 Jasper Ave., Edmonton, Alta. T5K 0L4 – 482-4421 – J. Vande Brink, Head Librn.
Edmonton Journal Library, 101 St. & 100 Ave., Edmonton, Alta. T5J 2S6 – 420-1919 – Mrs. Pat Garneau
Edmonton Power Library, See City of Edmonton
Edmonton Public School Board, Learning Resources Professional Centre, 10010 107A Ave., Edmonton, Alta. T5H 0Z8 – 429-5621, ext. 237 – Marilyn Elliott
Edmonton Separate School Board, Professional Library, 9807 106 St., Edmonton, Alta. T5K 1C2 – 429-7631 – Mrs. Carol Hornby
Edmonton Sun Newspaper Library, 10310 124 St., Edmonton, Alta. T5N 3Y3 – 482-7611, ext. 224 – John M. Sinclair
Environment Council of Alberta Library, 2100 College Plaza Tower 3, 8215 112 St., Edmonton, Alta. T6G 2M4 – 427-5792 – Colleen MacLachlan
Faculté Saint-Jean Bibliotheque, Univ. of Alberta, 8406 91 rue, Edmonton, Alta. T6C 4G9 – 466-2196 – Fr. Georges E. Durocher
Field & Field Law Library, #2000, 10235 101 St., Edmonton, Alta. T5J 3G1 – 423-3003 – S.D. Hillier
The GCG Engineering Partnership Library, 17420 Stony Plain Rd., Edmonton, Alta. T5S 1K6 – 483-8094 – Mrs. Heather Grimble
Genstar Cement Ltd. Library, Box 3961, Stn. D, (12640 156 St.), Edmonton, Alta. T5L 4P8 – 452-8290
Glenrose Provincial General Hospital, Medical Library, 10230 111 Ave., Edmonton, Alta. T5G 0B7 – 474-4541, ext. 265 – Mrs. E.M. Jamieson, Dir., Med. Records
Good Samaritan Society Library, 9649 71 Ave., Edmonton, Alta. T6E 5J2 – 439-6381 – Mrs. G. Ridge
Grace United Church Library, 6215 104 Ave., Edmonton, Alta. T6A 0X9 – 466-0916
Grant MacEwen Community College, Learning Resources Centre, 7319 29 Ave., Edmonton, Alta. T6K 2P1 – 462-5523 – Allen Watson, Co-ordinator
Hanson Materials Engineering Ltd. Library, 18 St. & 75 Ave., R.R. 2, Edmonton, Alta. T6C 4E6 –464-7916 – Norma Armstrong
Hardy Associates (1978) Ltd. Engineering Library, 4810 93 St., Box 746, Edmonton, Alta. T5J 2L4 – 436-2152 – A.R. Lechelt
Insurance Brokers' Association of Alberta Library, #200, 10240 124 St., Edmonton, Alta. T5N 1S9 – 482-6340
Japan External Trade Organization (JETRO), Information Centre, 10117 Jasper Ave., Edmonton, Alta. T5J 1W8 – 428-0866
Knox-Metropolitan United Church Library, 8307 109 St., Edmonton, Alta. T6G 1E1 – 439-1718 – Miss R.E. Hyndman, Chairman
Law Society of Alberta, see Alberta Dept. of Attorney General, Calgary and Edmonton
Legislature Library, 216 Legislature Bldg., Edmonton, Alta. T5K 2B6 – 427-2473 – D.B. McDougall
Milner & Steer Law Library, 9th floor, 10040 104 St., Edmonton, Alta. T5J 0Z7 – 425-8830 – Janet Darby
Misericordia Hospital, Weinlos Library, 16940 87th Ave., Edmonton, Alta. T5R 4H5 – 484-8811, ext. 291 – L. Herman

National Film Board of Canada, Film Library, 1003 103 Ave., Edmonton, Alta. T5J 0G9 – 420-3010
Newman Theological College Library, R.R. 8, Edmonton, Alta. T5L 4H8 – 459-6656 – Shirleyan Threndyle
North American Baptist College Library, 23 Ave. & 115 St., R.R. 3, Edmonton, Alta. T6H 4N7 – 437-1960 – A. Rapske
Northern Alberta Institute of Technology, Learning Resources Centre, 11762 106 St., Edmonton, Alta. T5G 2R1 – 427-9189 – Miss Jean Paul
Northern Forest Research Centre, See Canadian Forestry Service
Northwest Industries Technical Data Control Centre Library, Box 517, Municipal Airport, Edmonton, Alta. T5J 2K5 – 455-3161, ext. 223 – C.E. Buckley, Supvr.
Northwestern Utilities Ltd., See Canadian Utilities Ltd.
Nuclear Research Centre Physics Library, Univ. of Alberta, Edmonton, Alta. T6G 2N5 – 432-3637
Ombudsman's Office Library, 1630 Phipps-McKinnon Bldg., Edmonton, Alta. T5J 3G2 – 427-2756 – Ms. Diann Harry
Pollution & Environment Information Services, Corbett Hall, Univ. of Alberta, Edmonton, Alta. T6G 2N5 – 432-5068 – Gerald Wright
Public Utilities Board Library, 11th floor, 10055 106 St., Edmonton, Alta. T5J 2Y2 – 427-4901 – J. McKee
Robertson-Wesley United Church Library, 10209 123 St., Edmonton, Alta. T5N 1N3 – 482-1587
Rockliff Partnership Architects/Planners Library, 11207 103 Ave., Edmonton, Alta. T5K 2V9 – 426-7412 – Cheryl Sanford
Royal Alexandra Hospital Medical Library, 10240 Kingsway Ave., Edmonton, Alta. T5H 3V9 – 474-3431 – Deana Dryden – Nursing Library, Elizabeth Pass, Librarian
St. Joseph's College Library, Univ. of Alberta, Edmonton, Alta. T6G 2J5 – 433-1569 – Rev. John Janisse, C.S.B.
St. Joseph's Seminary, See Newman Theological College
St. Stephen's College, Centre for Continuing Education for Church Workers Library, 112 St. & 88 Ave., Edmonton, Alta. T6G 2J6 – 439-7311 – Mrs. Ruth Schrag
Schick Information Systems Library, 10011 80 Ave., Edmonton, Alta. T6E 1T4 – 432-7621
Stanley Associates Engineering Ltd. Library, 11748 Kingsway Ave., Edmonton, Alta. T5G 0X5 – 453-3441 – Mrs. Cathy Wang
Statistics Canada, User Services Library, #1000, 10025 106 St., Edmonton, Alta. T5J 1G9 – 420-3027 Alberta callers outside Edmonton dial 1-800-222-6400
Suncor Inc. Information Centre Library, 1100 Sun Life Place, Edmonton, Alta. T5J 3H9 – 426-7440, ext. 2251 – I.J. Caine
Syncrude Canada Ltd., Technical Information Service, Petroleum Plaza South, 9915 108 St., Edmonton, Alta. T5K 2G8 – J. Garvey
Syncrude Canada Ltd., Research Library, Box 5790, Edmonton, Alta. T6C 4G3 – 464-8400 – P.J. Bates, Info. Specialist
Transport Canada Western Regional Library, #10-76, 9820 107 St., Edmonton, Alta. T5K 1G3 – 420-3801 – Patricia Nelson
Transport Canada Western Region, Construction Branch Library, 7th Floor, 9820 107 St., Edmonton, Alta. T5K 1G3 – 420-3908 – Catherine Wolfe
Trigg, Woollett Consulting Ltd. Library, 10504 103 St., Edmonton, Alta. T5H 2V4 – 425-8905
Unifarm Library, 9934 106 St., Edmonton, Alta. T5K 1E1 – 423-1684 – W.J. Plosz, Exec. Dir.
University of Alberta Libraries, c/o Chief Librarian, University of Alberta, Edmonton, Alta. T6G 2J8 – 432-3790 – Bruce Peel
Computing Science Reading Room – Ms. Jennifer Penny
H.T. Coutts (Education) Library – Mrs. Betty Jean Busch
Health Sciences – Miss Phyllis J. Russell
Humanities & Social Sciences – Mohan Sharma
John Alexander Weir Memorial Law Library – Ms. L. MacPherson
John W. Scott Reading Room, University Hospital – Mrs. Sylvia Chetner
Mathematics Library – Masood Ahmad
Physical Sciences Library – Mrs. Marion Brady
Science Library – (vacant)
Special Collections– John Charles
Undergraduate Library – Mrs. Elizabeth Schwob
Dept. of Biochemistry – (vacant)
Dept. of Extension – Mrs. Sylvia Dubrule
Dept. of Geography – Mrs. H. Luoma
Dept. of Geology – Ms. J. Powell
Dept. of Music – James Whittle
Dept. of Political Science – Mrs. A. Lau
Dept. of Rural Economy – Miss Evelyn Shapka
Dept. of Sociology, Population Research Lab – Mrs. S. Williams-Major
University Map Collection – R. Whistance-Smith, Curator
Winspear Higgins Stevenson & Co. Library, 1900 Royal Trust Tower, Edmonton Centre, Edmonton, Alta. T5J 0W7 – 426-6880

FAIRVIEW

Fairview College Library, Box 3000, Fairview, Alta. T0H 1L0 – 835-2213 – Mrs. Olive Lancaster

FORT McMURRAY

Alberta Dept. of Attorney General, Provincial Court Library, Provincial Bldg., Franklin Ave., Fort McMurray, Alta. – 743-7195 – E. Kellsey
Keyano College Learning Resource Centre, 8115 Franklin Ave., Fort McMurray, Alta. T9H 2H7 – 791-2213, loc. 248 – R. Morris, Dir.
Syncrude Canada Ltd., Operations Library, Box 4009, Fort McMurray, Alta. T9H 3L1 – 791-8431 – A. Thomas

FORT SASKATCHEWAN

Fort Saskatchewan Correctional Institution Library, Box 10, Fort Saskatchewan, Alta. T8L 2P3 – 998-3701 – Kay Foran
Sherritt Gordon Mines Ltd., Sherritt Research Centre Library, Fort Saskatchewan, Alta. T8L 2P2 – 998-6419 – Derek Sim

GRANDE PRAIRIE

Grande Prairie General Hospital Library, 10409 98 St., Grande Prairie, Alta. T8V 2E8 – 532-7711 – Susan Black
Grande Prairie Regional College Library, Grande Prairie, Alta. T8V 4C4 – 532-8830, ext. 302 – Olga Anderson

HARDISTY

Hardisty General Hospital Library, Box 269, Hardisty, Alta. T0B 1V0 – 888-3742

GROUARD

Alberta Vocational Centre Library, Grouard, Alta. T0G 1C0 – 751-3915 – Bob Bruce

LACOMBE

Agriculture Canada, Research Station Library, Lacombe, Alta. T0C 1S0 – 782-3316 – Joy Otto
Canadian Union College Library, See College Heights, Alta.

LETHBRIDGE

Agriculture Canada, Research Station Library, Lethbridge, Alta. T1J 4B1 – 327-4561 – John P. Miska
Alberta Dept. of Attorney General & Law Society of Alberta Library, Court House, Lethbridge, Alta. T1J 3Z6 – 329-3266 – Joan Kiprick
Church of Jesus Christ of Latter Day Saints, Genealogical Library, 636 10 St. S., Lethbridge, Alta. T1J 2M8 – 327-5889 – Prudence R. Poulsen
Lethbridge Community College, Buchanan Resource Centre, Lethbridge, Alta. T1K 1L6 – 320-3352 – K. Lea, Lib. Supvr.
Lethbridge Correctional Institution Staff Library, Bag 3001, Lethbridge, Alta. T1J 3Z3 – 329-9414
The Lethbridge Herald Library, Box 670, Lethbridge, Alta. T1J 3Z7 – 328-4411 – Bernice Duguay
St. Michael's General Hospital Library, 13 St. & 9th Ave. S., Lethbridge, Alta. T1J 1X7 – 327-1531 – Mrs. Iris Mossey
University of Lethbridge Library, 4401 University Dr., Lethbridge, Alta. T1K 3M4 – 329-2261 – Paul Wiens

MAGRATH

Magrath Municipal Hospital Library, Box 550, Magrath, Alta. T0K 1J0 – 758-3464 – Dorothy Bennett

MEDICINE HAT

Alberta Law Society Library, Court House, Box 729, Medicine Hat, Alta. T1A 7G6 – 529-3666 – Beverly McKee

Church of Jesus Christ of Latter Day Saints, Medicine Hat Ward Library, Box 639, Medicine Hat, Alta. T1A 7G6 – Dr. Melvin Tagg
Hillcrest Christian College Library, 2801 13 Ave. S.E., Medicine Hat, Alta. T1A 3R1 – 526-6951 – Miss Ruth Leischner
Medicine Hat College Library, Medicine Hat, Alta. T1A 3Y6 – 527-7141 – Agatha Heinrichs

OLDS

Olds College Library, Olds, Alta. T0M 1P0 – 556-8323 – Garry Grisak, Lib. Co-ord.

RALSTON

Defence Research Establishment Suffield Library, Ralston, Alta. T0J 2N0 – 544-3701, ext. 208 – Miss L.A. Berg

RED DEER

The Advocate Newspaper Library, Box 520, Red Deer, Alta. T4N 5G3 – 343-2400 – Patricia Goulet
Alberta Law Society Library, Court House, 4836 Ross St., Red Deer, Alta. T4N 1X6 – 343-5220 – Susan Mamchur
The Michener Centre Staff Library, Box 5002, Red Deer, Alta. T4N 5Y5 – 343-5936 – Mrs. Judith Benson, Lib. Tech.
Red Deer College Library, Red Deer, Alta. T4N 5H5 – 342-3344 – Michael Brydges

TABER

Church of Jesus Christ of Latter Day Saints Library, Box 288, Taber, Alta. T0K 2G0 – 223-2785 – Florence P. Tufts

THREE HILLS

Prairie Bible Institute Library, Three Hills, Alta. T0M 2A0 – 443-5511 – Ron Jordahl

VERMILION

Lakeland College, Vermilion Campus Library, Vermilion, Alta. T0B 4M0 – 853-2971 – L. Herman

WAINWRIGHT

Wainwright Hospital Complex Library, Box 820, Wainwright, Alta. T0B 4P0 – 842-3324, loc. 45 – Mrs. Lorraine Murray

WETASKIWIN

Alberta Law Society Library, Court House, 4705 50 Ave., Wetaskiwin, Alta. T9A 0R8 – 352-9211, Loc. 303 – Susan O'-Connor

BRITISH COLUMBIA

Municipal Libraries in British Columbia

With Librarian

Area Code is 604

Burnaby Public Library, 4455 Alaska St., Burnaby, B.C. V5C 5T3 – 294-7234 – B.L. Bacon
Coquitlam Public Library, 901 Lougheed Hwy., Coquitlam, B.C. V3K 3T3 – 931-2416 – Miss Heather Harbord
Nelson Public Library, 719 Vernon St., Nelson, B.C. V1L 4G3 – 352-6333 – Mrs. Eva Walters
New Westminster Public Library, 716 6th Ave., New Westminster, B.C. V3M 2B3 – 521-8874 – Alan Woodland
North Vancouver City Public Library, 121 W. 14th St., North Vancouver, B.C. V7M 1P2 – 980-0581 – Miss Helen Moore
North Vancouver District Public Library, 1280 E. 27th St., North Vancouver, B.C. V7J 1S1 – 984-0286 – Miss Enid Dearing
Penticton Public Library, 785 Main St., Penticton, B.C. V2A 5E3 – 492-0024 – R.M. McIvor, Adm.
Port Moody Public Library, 2732 St. Johns St., Port Moody, B.C. V3H 2B7 – 939-1588 – I.C. Holter
Prince George Public Library, 425 Brunswick St., Prince George, B.C. V2L 2B7 – 563-9251 – Stan Smith
Prince Rupert Public Library, 101 6th Ave. W., Prince Rupert, B.C. V8J 1Y9 – 627-1345 – Miss Denise St. Arnaud
Richmond Public Library, 7691 Minoru Gate, Richmond, B.C. V6Y 1R8 – 273-6606 – J.A. Siqueira
Trail Public Library, 1051 Victoria St., Trail, B.C. V1R 3T3 – 364-1731 – Miss Deanne Williamson
Vancouver Public Library, 750 Burrard St., Vancouver, B.C. V6Z 1X5 – 682-5911 – Dr. G.C. Wootton, Dir.
Greater Victoria Public Library, 735 Broughton St., Victoria, B.C. V8W 3H2 – 382-7241 – D.W. Miller, Dir.
West Vancouver Memorial Library, 1950 Marine Dr., West Vancouver, B.C. V7V 1J8 – 926-3291 – Don Mills

Regional Libraries in British Columbia

With Director

Area Code is 604

Fraser Valley Regional Library, 34589 S. Fraser Way, Abbotsford, B.C. V2S 5Y1 – 859-7141 – W.H. Overend
Okanagan Regional Library, 1430 KLO Rd., Kelowna, B.C. V1Y 7X8 – 860-4033 – W.P. Lofts
Vancouver Island Regional Library, Strickland St., Nanaimo, B.C. V9R 5J7 – 754-6327 – F.T. White

Library Systems in British Columbia

With Director

Area Code is 604

Cariboo-Thompson Nicola Library System, 905 Laval Cres., Kamloops, B.C. V2C 5P5 – 374-8866 – H.E. Newsom
Greater Vancouver Library Federation, 1105 Commercial Dr., Vancouver, B.C. V5L 3X3 – 251-1147 – Miss Joy Scudamore

Regional Offices, British Columbia Library Services Branch

Cranbrook—18 9th Ave. S., Cranbrook, B.C. V1C 2L8
Dawson Creek—1017 105th Ave., Dawson Creek, B.C. V1G 2L3
Prince George—3907 15th Ave., Prince George, B.C. V2N 1A5
Vancouver—L50, 4946 Canada Way, Burnaby, B.C. V5G 4H7

Unaffiliated Public Library Associations in British Columbia

With Librarian

Area Code is 604

Alert Bay Community Library, Box 208, Alert Bay, B.C. V0N 1A0 – 974-5721 – Mrs. Joyce Wilby
Beaver Valley Community Library, Box 429, Fruitvale, B.C. V0G 1L0 – Mrs. Marcella Tjader
Castlegar & Dist. Community Library, 1005 3rd St., Castlegar, B.C. V1N 2A2 – Mrs. Judy Wearmouth
Gibsons Community Library, Box 109, Gibsons, B.C. V0N 1V0 – 886-2130 – Mrs. G. Rorke
Grand Forks Community Library, Box 1539, Grand Forks, B.C. V0H 1H0 – 442-3944 – Mrs. Monica Simcox
Greenwood Community Library, Box 279, Greenwood, B.C. V0H 1J0 – Mrs. Mary Kelly
Kaslo Community Library, Box 728, Kaslo, B.C. V0G 1M0 – Mrs. Joan Matthews
Kemano Community Library, Box 90, Kemano, B.C. V0T 1K0 – Mrs. Joan Verney
Kitimat Community Library, 169 Nechako Centre, Kitimat, B.C. V8C 1M8 – 632-6464 – Miss Julianne Ouron
Masset Community Library, Box 710, Masset, B.C. V0T 1M0 – Mrs. Claire Sim
Nakusp Community Library, Box 297, Nakusp, B.C. V0G 1R0 – 265-3363 – Ms. Evelyn Goodeil
Ocean Falls Community Library, Box 430, Ocean Falls, B.C. V0T 1P0 – 289-3211 – Mrs. Gisele Hoskinson
Pemberton Community Library, Box 430, Pemberton, B.C. V0N 2L0 – Mrs. Janet Naylor
Powell River Dist. Community Library, 4411 Michigan Ave., Powell River, B.C. V8A 2S3 – 485-4796 – Mrs. Byrl Ward
Rossland Community Library, Box 190, Rossland, B.C. V0G 1Y0 – 362-7611 – Mrs. Lois Haynes
Salmo Community Library, Box 458, Salmo, B.C. V0G 1Z0 – Mrs. Elsia Stewart

Saltspring Island Community Library, Box 366, Ganges, B.C. V0S 1E0 – George Wells, Sec.

Squamish Community Library, Box 1039, Squamish, B.C. V0N 3G0 – 892-3110 –

Terrace Community Library, 4610 Park Ave., Terrace, B.C. V8G 1V6 – 638-8177 – Ed Curell

North Central Associated Libraries

With Librarian

Area Code is 604

Burns Lake Community Library, Box 449, Burns Lake, B.C. V0J 1E0 – 692-3192 – Mrs. Margaret Foster

Fort St. James Community Library, Box 729, Fort St. James, B.C. V0J 1P0 – 996-7431 – Mrs. Arvilla Silver

Fraser Lake Community Library, Box 520, Fraser Lake, B.C. V0J 1S0 – 699-8888 – Mrs. Pat Fallat

Granisle Community Library, Box 550, Granisle, B.C. V0J 1W0 – 697-2713 – Mrs. Barbara Brokx

Hazelton Community Library, Box 323, Hazelton, B.C. V0J 1Y0 – 842-5961 – Mrs. Judy Kerr

Houston Community Library, Box 525, Houston, B.C. V0J 1Z0 – 845-2256 – Mrs. Darlene Thompson

McBride Community Library, Box 385, McBride, B.C. V0J 2E0 – 569-2411 – Mrs. M. Openshaw

Mackenzie Community Library, Box 790, Mackenzie, B.C. V0J 2C0 – 997-6343 – Mrs. Helen Stuparyk

Smithers Community Library, Box 55, Smithers, B.C. V0J 2N0 – 847-3043 – Ms. Patricia Moss

Valemount Community Library, Box 368, Valemount, B.C. V0E 2Z0 – 566-4367 – Mrs. Linda Hedberg

Vanderhoof Community Library, Box 825, Vanderhoof, B.C. V0J 3A0 – 567-4060 – Mrs. Marquerite Andros

Peace River Associated Libraries

With Librarian

Area Code is 604

Cassiar Community Library, Box 299, Cassiar, B.C. V0C 1E0 – Ms. Hilde Guderjahn

Chetwynd Community Library, Box 371, Chetwynd, B.C. V0C 1J0 – 788-2559 – Mrs. Mae McGraw

Dawson Creek Community Library, 1001 107A Ave., Dawson Creek, B.C. V1G 2S2 – 782-4661 – Les Szollosy

Fort Nelson Community Library, Box 627, Fort Nelson, B.C. V0C 1R0 – 774-6777 – Mrs. Margaret Keith

Fort St. John Community Library, 9711 100 Ave., Fort St. John, B.C. V1J 1Y2 – 785-3731 – Ms. Romi Haseo

Hudson's Hope Community Library, Box 18, Hudson's Hope, B.C. V0C 1V0 – 783-9414 – Mrs. Vicky Allen

Pouce Coup Community Library, Box 75, Pouce Coupe, B.C. V0C 2C0 – 786-5765 – Rev. G. Bullen

East Kootenay Associated Libraries

With Librarian

Area Code is 604

Cranbrook Community Library, 20 17th Ave. N., Cranbrook, B.C. V1C 3W8 – 426-4063 – Mrs. Patricia Armstrong

Creston Community Library, Box 1609, Creston, B.C. V0B 1G0 – 428-4141 – Mrs. Barbara Thomas

Elkford Community Library, Box 280, Elkford, B.C. V0B 1H0 – 865-2912 – Mrs. Yvonne Torgerson

Fernie Community Library, Box 448, Fernie, B.C. V0B 1M0 – 423-7017 – Mrs. Phyllis Buchan

Invermere Community Library, Box 989, Invermere, B.C. V0A 1K0 – 342-6416 – Mrs. Leslie Wynder

Kimberley Community Library, 115 Spokane St., Kimberley, B.C. V1A 2E5 – 427-3221 – Mrs. Beverly Varty

Sparwood Community Library, Box 1060, Sparwood, B.C. V0B 2G0 – 425-2299 – Mrs. Wendy Venne

Special & College Libraries & Resource Centres in British Columbia

With Contact Person (Librarian, unless otherwise indicated)

Area Code is 604

ABBOTSFORD

Fraser Valley College, Learning Resources Centre, 34194 Marshall Rd., Abbotsford, B.C. V2S 5E4 – 853-7441 – Winifred E. Harris

BURNABY

B.C. Institute of Technology Library, 3700 Willingdon Ave., Burnaby, B.C. V5G 3H2 – 434-5734 – Jos. E. Carver, Dean

B.C. Telephone Co. Library, 3777 Kingsway, Burnaby, B.C. V5H 3Z7 – 432-2671 – Elizabeth Murray

Church of Jesus Christ of Latter Day Saints Genealogical Library, 5280 Kincaid St., Burnaby, B.C. V5G 1V9 – 299-8656 – Duncan G.C. Tidmarsh

Microtel Pacific Research Ltd. Library, #105, 4664 Lougheed Hwy., Burnaby, B.C. V5C 5T5 – 294-0414, loc. 299 – V. Renzetti

Pacific Vocational Institute Library, 3650 Willingdon Ave., Burnaby, B.C. V5G 3H1 – 434-5722 – Jack Mounce

Simon Fraser University Libraries, c/o T.C. Dobb, Univ. Librarian, Burnaby, B.C. V5A 1S6 – 291-3265

- Archaeology, Anthropology, Law & Sociology – Mrs. Eve Szabo, 291-4654
- Biological Sciences – Maurice Deutsch, 291-3269
- Criminology – Brian Phillips, 291-4359
- Economics & Commerce – Mrs. Mary Roberts, 291-4655
- Education, Psychology & Recreation – Ms. Gail Tesch, 291-4652
- English Studies & Special Collections – Gene Bridwell, 291-4652
- External Loans – Miss Sylvia Bell, 291-3625
- Geography & Maps – Jack Corse, 291-4656
- Government Documents – Mrs. Pat Leger, 291-4651
- History & Political Science – Mrs. Helen Gray, 291-4654
- Languages, Literature – Miss Aleksandra Wawrzyszko, 291-3268
- Loans (Circulation) – Richard Malinski, 291-3274
- Monographs (Technical Services) – Ms. Cheryl Spencer, 291-3273
- Physical Sciences – Edward Weinstein, 291-4173
- Serials – Ms. Ann Liston, 291-3677

CAMPBELL RIVER

B.C. Law Library Foundation, Court House, 908C Alder St., Campbell River, B.C. V9W 2P6

CASTLEGAR

Selkirk College Library, Box 1200, Castlegar, B.C. V1N 3J1 – 365-5518

CHILLIWACK

B.C. Law Library Foundation, Court House, 77 College St., Chilliwack, B.C. V2P 4L7

Fraser Valley College, Learning Resources Centre, 45600 Airport Rd., Chilliwack, B.C. V2P 6P4 – 792-0025 – Winifred E. Harris

CLAYBURN

Western Pentecostal Bible College Library, Box 1000, Clayburn, B.C. V0X 1E0 – 853-7491 – Rev. Laurie M. Van Kleek

COMOX

North Island College, Instructional Materials Centre, 156 Manor Dr., Comox, B.C. V9N 6P7 – 339-5551 – Dr. L. Mithen

COURTENAY

B.C. Law Library Foundation, Court House, 420 Cumberland, Courtenay, B.C. V9N 5M6

CRANBROOK

B.C. Law Library Foundation, Court House, 102 11th Ave. S., Cranbrook, B.C. V1C 2P2

The Daily Townsman Newsp. Library, 31 7th Ave. S., Cranbrook, B.C. V1C 2J2 – 426-5201 – Craig McArthur

East Kootenay Community College Library, 32 9th Ave. S., Cranbrook, B.C. V1C 2L8 – 489-2751 – Ms. Catherine Campbell

DAWSON CREEK

B.C. Law Library Foundation, Court House, 1201 103rd Ave., Dawson Creek, B.C. V1G 3T9

Northern Lights College Library, 11401 8th St., Dawson Creek, B.C. V1G 4G2 – 782-5251

DUNCAN

B.C. Law Library Foundation, Court House, 238 Government St., Duncan, B.C. V9L 1A5

FORT ST. JOHN

B.C. Law Library Foundation, Court House, 10600 100 St., Fort St. John, B.C. V1J 4L6

GRANVILLE ISLAND

Emily Carr College of Art, See Vancouver

KAMLOOPS

Agriculture Canada, Research Station Library, 3015 Ord Rd., Kamloops, B.C. V2B 8A9 – 604/376-5565

B.C. Consumer Resource Centre, 521 Seymour St., Kamloops, B.C. V2C 2G8 – 374-5676

B.C. Law Library Foundation, Court Annex, 1165 Battle St., Kamloops, B.C. V2C 2N4 – 374-7415

Cariboo College Library, Box 3010, Kamloops, B.C. V2C 5N3 – 374-0123, loc. 300 – David Fox

KELOWNA

B.C. Law Library Foundation, Court House, 1420 Water St., Kelowna, B.C. V1Y 1J2 – 763-1787

Church of Jesus Christ of Latter Day Saints Genealogical Library, Glenmore & Ivans Sts., Kelowna, B.C.

Okanagan College, Muriel Ffoulkes Learning Resource Centre, 1000 KLO Rd., Kelowna, B.C. V1Y 4X8 – 762-5445 – G.J.F. Homer

KIMBERLEY

Sullivan Mine, Cominco Ltd. Library, Box 2000, Kimberley, B.C. V1A 2G3 – 427-3485 – E.E. Gold

LANGLEY

Trinity Western College Library, 7600 Glover Rd., Langley, B.C. V3A 4R9 – 888-7511 – David A. Twiest

MISSION

Westminster Abbey Library, Seminary of Christ the King, Mission, B.C. V2V 4J2 – 826-8975 – B. Aicher, osb

NANAIMO

B.C. Law Library Foundation, Court House, 35 Front St., Nanaimo, B.C. V9R 5J1 – 754-2111, loc. 278

Fisheries & Oceans Canada, Pacific Biological Station Library, Nanaimo, B.C. V9R 5K6 – 758-5202, loc. 240 – G. Miller

Malaspina College Library, 900 5th St., Nanaimo, B.C. V9R 5S5 – 753-3245

NELSON

B.C. Law Library Foundation, Court House, 320 Ward St., Nelson, B.C. V1L 1S6

The Daily News Library, 266 Baker St., Nelson, B.C. V1L 4H3 – 352-3552

David Thompson University Centre Library, 820 10th St., Nelson, B.C. V1L 3C7 – 352-2241 – R.J. Welwood, Dir.

NEW WESTMINSTER

B.C. Law Library Foundation, Court House, Begbie Sq., New Westminster, B.C. V3M 1C9 – 525-0931, loc. 258

CanOcean Resources Ltd. Library, 610 Derwent Way, New Westminster, B.C. V3M 5P8 – 524-4451 – Ron Simmer

Columbian Newspaper Library, Box 730, New Westminster, B.C. V3L 4Z7 – 521-2622 – Una Broughton

Douglas College Library, Box 2503, New Westminster, B.C. V3L 5B2 – 521-4851 – David R. Williams

International Pacific Salmon Fisheries Commission Library, Box 30, New Westminster, B.C. V3L 4X9 – 521-3771 – Mrs. F. Sato

McQuarrie Hunter Law Library, #400, 713 Columbia St., New Westminster, B.C. V3L 4Y6 – 526-1821 – B. Crawford

NORTH VANCOUVER

Capilano College Library, 2055 Purcell Way, North Vancouver, B.C. V7J 3H5 – 986-1911, ext. 241

Lions Gate Hospital Library, 230 E. 13th St., North Vancouver, B.C. V7L 2L7 – 988-3131, loc. 490 – Mrs. M.N. Marshall

PENTICTON

B.C. Law Library Foundation, Court House, 100 Main St., Penticton, B.C. V2A 5A5

PORT ALBERNI

B.C. Law Library Foundation, Court House, 4515 Elizabeth St., Port Alberni, B.C. V9Y 6L5

PORT COQUITLAM

Riverview Hospital Library, 500 Lougheed Hwy., Port Coquitlam, B.C. – 521-1911, loc. 521 – Min-Ja Laubental

POWELL RIVER

B.C. Law Library Foundation, Court House, 6953 Alberni St., Powell River, B.C. V8A 2B8

PRINCE GEORGE

B.C. Consumer Resource Centre, 395 Victoria St., Prince George, B.C. V2L 2J6 – 562-9331

B.C. Law Library Foundation, Court House, 1600 3rd Ave., Prince George, B.C. V2L 3G6 – 562-8131, loc. 414

The Citizen Newsp. Library, Box 578, Prince George, B.C. V2L 4T1 – 562-2441, loc. 287 – Lynda Jane Williams

City of Prince George Planning Library, 1100 Patricia Blvd., Prince George, B.C. V2L 3V9 – 564-5151 – c/o City Planner

College of New Caledonia Library, 3330 22nd Ave., Prince George, B.C. V2N 1P8 – 562-2131 – P. Seens

PRINCE RUPERT

B.C. Law Library Foundation, Court House, 100 Market Place, Prince Rupert, B.C. V8J 1B7

QUESNEL

B.C. Law Library Foundation, Court House, 350 Barlowe Ave., Quesnel, B.C. V2J 2C1

REVELSTOKE

B.C. Law Library Foundation, Court House, Box 2820, Revelstoke, B.C. V0E 2S0

RICHMOND

B.C. Geneaological Society Library, Box 94371, Richmond, B.C. V6Y 2A8 – 274-3659

MacDonald, Dettwiler & Assoc. Ltd. Library, 10280 Shellbridge Way, Richmond, B.C. V6X 2Z9 – 278-3411 – Judy Growe

ROSSLAND

B.C. Law Library Foundation, Columbia St., Rossland, B.C. V0G 1Y0

SALMON ARM

B.C. Law Library Foundation, Court House, Box 1990, Salmon Arm, B.C. V0E 2T0

SIDNEY

Agriculture Canada, Saanichton Research & Plant Quarantine Station Library, 8801 E. Saanich Rd., Sidney, B.C. V8L 1H3 – 656-1173

SMITHERS

B.C. Law Library Foundation, Court House, Smithers, B.C. V0J 2N0

SUMMERLAND

Agriculture Canada, Research Station Library, Summerland, B.C. V0H 1Z0 – 494-7711 – Mrs. V.B. Smith

SURREY

B.C. Hydro, Surrey Research Library, 12388 88th Ave., Surrey, B.C. V3W 7R7 – 591-0256 – Susan Robinson

TERRACE

Northwest Community College, Learning Resources Centre, Box 726, Terrace, B.C. V8G 4C2 – 635-6511 – Leo Wang

TRAIL

Cominco Ltd., Central Technical Library, Trail, B.C. V1R 4L8 – 364-4409 – Bob Lewis

The Times Newsp. Library, 1163 Cedar Ave., Trail, B.C. V1R 4B8 – 368-8551 – Nancy Rode

VANCOUVER

Agriculture Canada Library, 6660 N.W. Marine Dr., Vancouver, B.C. V6T 1X2 – 224-4355 – Miss C.M. Cutler

Alcohol & Drug Programs Library, Ministry of Health, 1755 W. Broadway, Vancouver, B.C. V6J 4S5 – 873-0263 – Wendy Holmes

Alliance Française (Centre for French Studies) Resource Centre, 6161 Cambie St., Vancouver, B.C. V5Z 3B2 – 327-0201 – Mrs. H. Wegmann

Associated Engineering Library, 1661 W. 8th Ave., Vancouver, B.C. V6J 1V1 – 736-7361, loc. 217 – John Lloyd

Bank of British Columbia Library, 11th floor, 555 Burrard St., Vancouver, B.C. V7X 1K1 – 668-4417 – Robert Rippon

Barbeau, McKercher & Co. Law Library, #2400, Oceanic Plaza, Box 12534, 1066 W. Hastings St., Vancouver, B.C. V6E 3X1 – 688-9411 – Mary Matthews

Boughton & Co. Law Library, #600, 890 W. Pender St., Vancouver, B.C. V6C 1K4 – 683-6631

Bourne, Lyall etc. Law Library, #1180, 505 Burrard St., Vancouver, B.C. V7X 1B8 – 685-2311 – Yvonne Turkenburg

Braidwood, Nuttall etc. Law Library, #1500, 510 W. Hastings St., Vancouver, B.C. V6B 1M6 – 689-3281

B.C. Hydro & Power Authority Library, 970 Burrard St., Vancouver, B.C. V6Z 1Y3 – 663-2660 – Eleanor Haydock

B.C. Hydro & Power Authority, Engineering Branch Library, Box 12121, 555 W. Hastings St., Vancouver, B.C. V6B 4T6 – 663-4101 – Elizabeth Preston

B.C. Labour Relations Board Library, 1620 W. 8th Ave., Vancouver, B.C. V6J 1V4 – 736-2421 – Heather Macdonald

B.C. Law Library Foundation, Court House, 800 Smithe St., Vancouver, B.C. V6Z 2E1 – 668-2841 – Joan Honeywell

B.C. Lions Society for Crippled Children Library, 177 W. 7th Ave., Vancouver, B.C. V5Y 1L8 – 873-1865 – Wm. J. Townsend

B.C. Lung Association Film Library, 906 W. Broadway, Vancouver, B.C. V5Z 1K7 – 731-4961

B.C. Medical Library Service, 1807 W. 10th Ave., Vancouver, B.C. V6J 2A9 – 736-5551 – William Fraser

B.C. Ministry of Human Resources Library, 800 Cassiar St., Vancouver, B.C. V5K 4N6 – 299-9131

B.C. Ministry of Tourism Film Library, 800 Hornby St., Vancouver, B.C. V6Z 2C5 – 668-2732

B.C. Research Library, 3650 Wesbrook Mall, Vancouver, B.C. V6S 2L2 – 224-4331 – Viona Coates

B.C. Resources Investment Corp., Corporate Information Centre, 1176 W. Georgia St., Vancouver, B.C. V6E 4B9 – 687-2600 – Jill Rowland

B.C. Teachers' Federation Resources Centre, #105, 2235 Burrard St., Vancouver, B.C. V6J 3H9 – 731-8121, loc. 260

B.C. Telephone Co., See Burnaby

B.C. Utilities Commission Library, #2100, 1177 W. Hastings St., Vancouver, B.C. V6E 2L7 – 689-1831 – C. Brian Tu

B.C. & Yukon Chamber of Mines Library, 840 W. Hastings St., Vancouver, B.C. V6C 1C8 – 681-5328 – Jack M. Patterson

Bull, Housser & Tupper Law Library, #3000, 1055 W. Georgia St., Vancouver, B.C. V6E 3R3 – 687-6575 – Susan Daly

Campney & Murphy Law Library, Box 49190, 595 Burrard St., Vancouver, B.C. V7X 1K9 – 684-2511 – Astrid V. Kenning

Canada Dept. of Justice Library, #1900, 1055 W. Georgia St., Vancouver, B.C. V6E 3P9 – 666-6887 – Judy Deavy

Canadian Music Centre B.C. Regional Branch, #3, 2007 W. 4th Ave., Vancouver, B.C. V6J 1N3 – 734-4622

Canadian Superior Exploration Library, Box 10104, 18th floor, 701 W. Georgia St., Vancouver, B.C. V7X 1C6 – 681-9426 – Judith Bradshaw

Cancer Control Agency of B.C. Library, 2656 Heather St., Vancouver, B.C. V5Z 3J3 – 873-6212, loc. 279 – David Noble

CBA Engineering Ltd. Library, 1425 W. Pender St., Vancouver, B.C. V6G 2S3 – 683-4131 – Bradley Lockner

Centre for Human Settlements, Audio Visual Viewing Library, Univ. of B.C., Vancouver, B.C. V6T 1W5 – 228-6265

CP Air Engineering Library, Operations Centre, Vancouver International Airport, Vancouver, B.C. V7B 1V1 – 270-5211

Chinese Nationalist League Library, 529 Gore Ave., Vancouver, B.C. V6A 2Z6 – 681-6022

City of Vancouver Health Dept. Library, 1060 W. 8th Ave., Vancouver, B.C. V6H 1C4 – 736-2033 – Patricia Young

City of Vancouver Planning Dept. Library, 453 W. 12th Ave., Vancouver, B.C. V5Y 1V4 – 873-7782 – Coralys Cuthbert

Clark, Wilson & Co. Law Library, 750 W. Pender St., Vancouver, B.C. V6C 2B8 – 684-6521 & 687-5700 – Mrs. Maureen Fauman

Columbia College Library, 1619 W. 10th Ave., Vancouver, B.C. V6J 2A2 – 731-2413 – Ms. Randi V. Smith

Cominco Ltd. Library, 200 Granville Sq., Vancouver, B.C. V6C 2R2 – 682-0611 – David A. Pepper

Consumer Resource Centre, 411 Dunsmuir St., Vancouver, B.C. V6B 1X4 – 668-2345

Coopers & Lybrand Library, 28th floor, 1055 W. Georgia St., Vancouver, B.C. V6E 3R2 – 682-7821, loc. 319 – Raquel Kupfer

Council of Forest Industries Library, #1800, 1055 W. Hastings St., Vancouver, B.C. V6E 2H1 – 684-0211 – Sheila Foley

The Court Yard Law Library, 131 Water St., Vancouver, B.C. V6B 4M3 – 689-1353 – Mrs. Maureen Fauman

Davis & Company Law Library, #1400, 1030 W. Georgia St., Vancouver, B.C. V6E 3C2 – 687-9444 – Joan Mulholland

Denison Mines Library, Box 11575, 650 W. Georgia St., Vancouver, B.C. V6B 4N7 – 669-2226, ext. 35 – Ann Johansen

Emily Carr College of Art Library, 1399 Johnston St., Granville Island, Vancouver, B.C. V6H 3R9 – 687-2345 – Ken Chamberlain

Farris, Vaughan & Co. Law Library, Box 10026, 700 W. Georgia St., Vancouver, B.C. V7Y 1B3 – 684-9151 – Fiona Anderson

Fisheries & Oceans Canada
- Vancouver Laboratory Library, 6640 N.W. Marine Dr., Vancouver, B.C. V6T 1X2 – 224-1366, loc. 44
- Fisheries Management Regional Library, 1090 W. Pender St., Vancouver, B.C. V6E 2N9 – Paulette Westlake
- Forintek Canada Corp., Western Laboratory Library, 6620 N.W. Marine Dr., Vancouver, B.C. V6T 1X2 – 224-3221, loc. 224 – Marion E. Johnson

Fraser Hyndman Law Library, 777 Hornby St., Vancouver, B.C. V6Z 1T3 – 687-3216 – Mrs. Maureen Fauman

Freeman & Co. Law Library, 16th floor, 1030 W. Georgia St., Vancouver, B.C. V6E 3C4 – 683-4201 – Harriet Spiro

Geological Survey of Canada Research Library, 5th floor, 100 W. Pender St., Vancouver, B.C. V6B 1R8 – 666-3812 – Miss M. Akehurst

Geological Survey of Canada, Publications & Map Sales, 100 W. Pender St., 6th Floor, Vancouver, B.C. V6B 1E8 – 666-1271 – Mrs. Olga Langenhaun

Greater Vancouver Regional District Library, (located at 2034 W. 12th Ave., 731-1155); mail: 2294 W. 10th Ave., Vancouver, B.C. V6K 2H9 – Mrs. F. Christopherson

Harper, Gray etc. Law Library, #3100, 650 W. Georgia St., Vancouver, B.C. V6B 4N7 – 687-0411 – Jennifer Finlay

Health & Welfare Canada, Health Protection Branch Library, 1001 W. Pender St., Vancouver, B.C. V6E 2M7 – 666-3147 – Elizabeth Hardacre

Insurance Corporation of B.C. Library, Box 11131, 1055 W. Georgia St., Vancouver, B.C. V6E 3R4 – 665-5976 – Norman Churchland

Insurance Institute of B.C. Library, #410, 800 W. Pender St., Vancouver, B.C. V6C 2V6 – 681-5491 – Ms. E. Gilchrist, Sec. Mgr.

Judges' Library, Superior & County Courts, Law Courts, 800 Smithe St., Vancouver, B.C. V6Z 2E1 – 668-2799

Justice Institute of B.C. Instructional Services, 4198 W. 4th Ave., Vancouver, B.C. V6R 4K1 – 228-9771

Ladner Downs Law Library, Box 10021, 700 W. Georgia St., Vancouver, B.C. V7Y 1A8 – 687-5744, loc. 152 – Anne Beresford

Lawson, Lundell etc. Law Library, 28th floor, 650 W. Georgia St., Vancouver, B.C. V6B 4R7 – 685-3456 – Gwendoline Hoar

Legal Services Society, Legal Resource Centre, Box 12120, 555 W. Hastings St., Vancouver, B.C. V6B 4N6 – 689-0741 – Ms. Sidney Sawyer

MacMillan Bloedel Research Ltd. Library, 3350 E. Broadway, Vancouver, B.C. V5M 4E6 – 254-5151, loc. 213 – Diana Wilimovsky
Macrae, Montgomery & Co. Law Library, #585, 555 Burrard St., Vancouver, B.C. V7X 1H8 – 689-555 – Jane Wostradowski
Northwest Baptist Theological College, (and Northwest Baptist Theological Seminary), Library, 3358 S.E. Marine Dr., Vancouver, B.C. V5S 3W3 – 433-2475 – H. Sturhahn
Owen, Bird Law Library, Box 49130, 595 Burrard St., Vancouver, B.C. V7X 1J5 – 688-0401 – Bonnie Shandro
Pacific Marine Training Institute, Library & Resource Centre, 2019 Dundas St., Vancouver, B.C. V5L 1J5 – 254-0741 – Ms. Kay Look
Pacific Press Ltd. Library, 2250 Granville St., Vancouver, B.C. V6H 3G2 – 732-2605 – Miss Shirley Mooney
Placer Development Ltd. Library, #800, 1030 W. Georgia St., Vancouver, B.C. V6E 3A8 – 682-7082 – Linda Martin
Price Waterhouse Library, 1075 W. Georgia St., Vancouver, B.C. V6E 3G1 – 682-4711, loc. 232 – Janet Parkinson
Ray, Wolfe etc. Law Library, 18th floor, 1030 W. Georgia St., Vancouver, B.C. V6E 3C1 – 684-1181 – Jay Maclean
Registered Nurses Association of B.C. Library, 2130 W. 12th Ave., Vancouver, B.C. V6K 2N3 – 736-7331 – Mrs. Pat Kolesar
Royal Bank of Canada Library, 1055 W. Georgia St., Box 11141, Vancouver, B.C. V6E 3S5 – 665-4069 – Judy Kornfeld
Royal Commission on Uranium Mining Library, 3724 W. Broadway, Vancouver, B.C. V6R 2C1 – 224-1716 – Keltie McCall
Russell & Dumoulin Law Library, #1700, 1075 W. Georgia St., Vancouver, B.C. V6E 3G2 – 688-3411 – Diana Hunt
St. Paul's Hospital Health Sciences Library, 1081 Burrard St., Vancouver, B.C. V6Z 1Y6 – 682-2344, loc. 2373 – Roberta Wong
Sandwell & Co. Library, 1550 Alberni St., Vancouver, B.C. V6G 1A4 – 684-8151, loc. 131 – Ruth Trifos
Satellite Video Exchange Society, Media/Video Library, 261 Powell St., Vancouver, B.C. V6A 1C3 – 688-4336
Shaughnessy Hospital Library, 4500 Oak St., Vancouver, B.C. V6H 3N1 – 876-6767 – Deborah Newstead
H.A. Simons Library, 425 Carrall St., Vancouver, B.C. V6B 2J6 – 664-4499 – Geoffrey White
SPARC of B.C. Library, #109, 2182 W. 12th Ave., Vancouver, B.C. V6K 2N4 – 736-6621 – Jenny Welsh
The Sun-Province Library, See Pacific Press
Swan Wooster Library, 1525 Robson St., Vancouver, B.C. V6G 1C5 – 684-2351 – Linda Hall
Teachers' Professional Library, Teachers' Centre, 123 E. 6th Ave., Vancouver, B.C. V5T 1J6 – 874-2617 – Miss M.L. Dunbar
Teck Mining Group Library, 1199 W. Hastings St., Vancouver, B.C. V6E 3T5 – 687-1117, loc. 268 – Elizabeth Watson
Touche Ross & Co. Library, #700, 1177 W. Hastings St., Vancouver, B.C. V6E 2L2 – 669-3343 – Linda King
UNICEF B.C. Committee Library, 739 W. Hastings St., Vancouver, B.C. V6C 1A1 – 687-9096
United Way of the Lower Mainland Library, 1625 W. 8th Ave., Vancouver, B.C. V6J 1T9 – 731-7781
University of B.C. Libraries, c/o Acting University Librarian, 1956 Main Mall, Vancouver, B.C. V6T 1Y3 – 228-3871 – Douglas McInnes
  Assoc. Librarian – I.F. Bell
  Asst. Librarian, Admin. Services – Erik de Bruijn
  Asst. Librarian, Collections – Anthony Jeffreys
  Asst. Librarian, Physical Planning – William Watson
  Asst. Librarian, Processing & Systems – R.W. MacDonald
  A/Asst. Librarian, Public Services – Wm. Watson
  Animal Resource Ecology Library – Mrs. A. Nelson
  Asian Studies – Miss T.K. Ng
  Crane Library for the Blind – Paul Thiele
  Curriculum Laboratory – Howard Hurt
  Data Library – Ms. Laine Ruus
  Fine Arts – Miss M. Dwyer
  Forestry/Agriculture – Mrs. M. Macaree
  Gifts & Exchanges – Graham Elliston
  Government Publications – Mrs. S. Dodson
  Humanities – Chuck Forbes
  Information & Orientation – Miss Joan Sandilands
  Interlibrary Loans – Ms. Margaret Friesen
  Law – Thomas Shorthouse
  Maps – Miss M. Wilson
  Mathematics – Reinder Brongers
  Music – Hans Burndorfer
  Reading Rooms – Nicholas Omelusik
  Record Collection – Douglas Kaye
  Science & Maths – Reinder Brongers
  Sedgewick Undergraduate – Ture Erickson
  Social Sciences – Miss L. Carrier
  Social Work – Mrs. E. de Bruijn
  Special Collections – Mrs. A. Yandle
  Woodward Biomedical – Miss A. Leith
  Biomedical Branch – George Freeman
Universities Council of B.C. Library, 500, 805 W. Broadway, Vancouver, B.C. V5Z 1K1 – 872-0245 – Theresa Boyce Iverson
Uranium Information Centre, c/o B.C. Research 3650 Wesbrook Mall, Vancouver, B.C. V6S 2L2 – 224-4331
Urbanics Consultants Library, #1410, 1090 W. Georgia St., Vancouver, B.C. V6E 3V7 – 669-2724 – Aurora Winter
Vancouver Art Gallery Association Library, 1145 W. Georgia St., Vancouver, B.C. V6E 3H2 – 682-5621, loc. 41 – Jean Martin
Vancouver Board of Trade Library, 5th floor, 1177 W. Hastings St., Vancouver, B.C. V6E 2K3 – 681-2111 – Maureen Devine
Vancouver City, See City of
Vancouver Community College Libraries, 675 W. Hastings St., Vancouver, B.C. V6B 1N2 – 688-1111 – C. Ross Carter, Dir. of College Resources
  Langara Library – Mary Anne Epp (324-5386)
    Audio Visual – Linda Prince (324-5459)
    Cataloging – Laurie Fredericksen (324-5457)
  King Edward Campus – Paul Cook (731-4614, loc. 55)
  Vancouver Vocational Institute – Ross Henderson (681-8111)
Vancouver General Hospital, School of Nursing Library, 2851 Heather St., Vancouver, B.C. V5Z 3J7 – 876-3211, loc. 3210 – Barbara Trip
Vancouver School of Theology Library, 6050 Chancellor Blvd., Vancouver, B.C. V6T 1X3 – 228-9031 – Paul Nathanson
Warnock Hersey Professional Services Ltd. Library, 125 E. 4th Ave., Vancouver, B.C. V5T 1G4 – 876-4111 – Inge McGarry
Westcoast Transmission Co. Ltd. Library, 1333 W. Georgia St., Vancouver, B.C. V6E 3K9 – 664-5517 – Mrs. Beatrice Yakimchuk
Woodward Stores (Vancouver) Ltd., Training & Development Library, 101 W. Hastings St., Box 8600, Vancouver, B.C. V6B 1H4 – 684-5231
Workers' Compensation Board Library, 5255 Heather St., Vancouver, B.C. V5Z 3L8 – 266-0211 – Barbara L. Sanderson

VERNON

B.C. Law Library Foundation, Court House, 3001 27th St., Vernon, B.C. V1T 4W5

VICTORIA

B.C. Law Library Foundation, Court House, 850 Burdett Ave., Victoria, B.C. V8W 1B4 – 387-3239
B.C. Ministry of Attorney General, See Justices Library
B.C. Ministry of Consumer & Corporate Affairs Library, 940 Blanshard St., Victoria, B.C. V8W 3E6 – 387-6831 – Frances Baskerville
B.C. Ministry of Education Library, Parliament Bldgs., Victoria, B.C. V8V 1X4 – 387-6279 – Mrs. N. Lofthouse
B.C. Ministry of Energy, Mines & Petroleum Resources Library, Parliment Bldgs., Victoria, B.C. V8V 1X4 – 387-6407, loc. 604 – Miss S.E. Ferris
B.C. Ministry of Environment, Departmental Library, Parliament Bldgs., Victoria, B.C. V8V 1X4 – 387-5195 – Ms. M. Palmer
B.C. Ministry of Finance, Finance Research Branch Library, #104, 617 Government St., Victoria, B.C. V8V 1X4 – 387-1471
B.C. Ministry of Forests Library, 1450 Government St., Victoria, B.C. V8W 3E7 – 387-3628 – S.E. Barker
B.C. Ministry of Health Library, Parliament Bldgs., Victoria, B.C. V8V 1X4 – 387-6627 – E.M. Woodworth
B.C. Ministry of Human Resources Library, See Vancouver

B.C. Ministry of Industry & Small Business Development Library, Parliament Bldgs., Victoria, B.C. V8V 1X4 – 387-3765 – Mrs. H.G. Bruce

B.C. Ministry of Labour Library, Parliament Bldgs., Victoria, B.C. V8V 1X4 – 387-5071

B.C. Ministry of Lands, Parks & Housing, Parks Library, Parliament Bldgs., Victoria, B.C. V8V 1X4 – 387-1978 – Mrs. S. Desrosiers

B.C. Ministry of Provincial Secretary & Government Services Library, Parliament Bldgs., Victoria, B.C. V8V 1X4 – 387-3751

B.C. Ministry of Tourism Library, 1117 Wharf St., Victoria, B.C V8W 2Z2 – 387-6415

B.C. Ministry of Transportation & Highways, Highways Library, 3-C, 940 Blanshard St., Victoria, B.C. V8W 3E6

B.C. Ministry of Universities, Science & Communication Library, Parliament Bldgs., Victoria, B.C. V8V 1X4 – 387-6008

B.C. Provincial Archives Library, Parliament Bldgs., Victoria, B.C. V8V 1X4 – 387-5886 – J.A. Bovey, Archivist

B.C. Provincial Museum Library, 601 Belleville St., Victoria, B.C. V8V 1X4 – 387-5533 – Mrs. Rose Rodgers

Camosun College Library, 1950 Lansdowne Rd., Victoria, B.C. V8P 5J2 – 592-1281 – Catherine Winter

Canada Institute for Scientific & Technical Information, See National Research Council etc.

The Daily Colonist, See Times-Colonist

Defence Research Establishment Pacific Library, c/o Forces Mail Office, Victoria, B.C. V0S 1B0 – 388-1665 – J.A. Wilson

Departments of Government, See B.C. Ministry of ...

Dominion Astrophysical Observatory, See National Research Council

Environment Canada, Canadian Forestry Service, Pacific Forest Research Centre Library, 506 W. Burnside Rd., Victoria, B.C. V8Z 1M5 – 388-3811 – Alice Solyma

Greater Victoria School Board Library, Media Centre, 2101 Cadboro Bay Rd., Victoria, B.C. V8R 5G4 – 592-1211 – Mrs. Win Cartwright, Elem. Lib. Co-ordinator

John Howard Society of Vancouver Island Library, #310, 620 View St., Victoria, B.C. V8W 1J6 – 386-3428 – Jeanette Maher

Justices' Library, The Law Courts, 850 Burdett Ave., Victoria, B.C. V8W 1B4 – 387-6056

Legislative Library, Parliament Bldgs., Victoria, B.C. V8V 1X4 – 387-6500 – J.G. Mitchell

Lester B. Pearson College of the Pacific Library, R.R. 1, Victoria, B.C. V8X 3W9 – 478-5591 – Mrs. M. McAvity

Maritime Museum Research Library, 28-30 Bastion Sq., Victoria, B.C. V8W 1H9 – 386-7622 – W.P. Yager, Admin. Officer

Ministries of Government, See B.C. Ministry of ...

National Research Council, Herzberg Institute of Astrophysics, Dominion Astrophysical Observatory Library, 5071 W. Saanich Rd., R.R. 5, Victoria, B.C. V8X 4M6 – 388-0298 – E.S. Leblanc

Royal Roads Military College Library, Victoria, B.C. V0S 1B0 – 388-1483 – C.C. Whitlock

Times-Colonist Library, 2621 Douglas St., Box 300, Victoria, B.C. V8W 2N4 – 382-7211 – Corinne Wong

University of Victoria Libraries, c/o Chief Librarian, University of Victoria, Victoria, B.C. V8W 2Y3 – D.W. Halliwell – 477-6911
- Curriculum Laboratory – D. Hamilton
- Government Documents – Mrs. F. Rose
- Interlibrary Loans – Mrs. B. Gibb
- Law – Miss D.M. Priestly
- Music & Audio Recordings – Mrs. S. Benet
- Special Collections – H.B. Gerwing
- University Map Collection – B. Turnbull

Victoria General Hospital, Health Sciences Library, 841 Fairfield Rd., Victoria, B.C. V8V 3B6 – 388-9121, loc. 330 – George E.A. Zizka

Victoria Medical Society/Royal Jubilee Hospital Library, 1900 Fort St., Victoria, B.C. V8R 1J8 – 595-9723 – Johann A. van Reenen

Victoria Times, See Times-Colonist

WEST VANCOUVER

Canada Dept. of Fisheries & Oceans, West Vancouver Laboratory Library, 4160 Marine Dr., West Vancouver, B.C. V7V 1N6 – 926-2447 – Kathleen Day

WILLIAMS LAKE

B.C. Law Library Foundation, Court House, 540 Borland St., Williams Lake, B.C. V2G 1R8

MANITOBA

Public Libraries in Manitoba

With Librarian

Area Code for Manitoba is 204

Boissevain & Morton Regional Library, Box 340, Boissevain, Man. R0K 0E0 – 534-6478 – Mrs. Anna Grace Diehl

Boyne Regional Library, Box 788, Carman, Man. R0G 0J0 – 745 3504 – Mrs. Rosella Semple

Bren Del Win Centennial Library, Box 584, Deloraine, Man. R0M 0M0 – 747-2415 – Ms. Lori Bell

Churchill Public Library, Box 459, Churchill, Man. R0B 0E0 – 675-2731 – Ms. Wendy Rolfe

Evergreen Regional Library, Box 1140, Gimli, Man. R0C 1B0 – 642-7912 – Mrs. Adriana Bouillet – Branches at Arborg and Riverton

Flin Flon Public Library, 58 Main St., Flin Flon, Man. R8A 1J8 – 687-3397 – Mrs. Dorothy Bridges

Gillam Public Library, Box 400, Gillam, Man. R0B 0L0 – 652-2617 – Mrs. Glynis Magnusson

Glenwood & Souris Regional Library, Box 760, Souris, Man. R0K 2C0 – 483-2757 – Mrs. Margaret Greaves

Jolys Regional Library, Box 118, St-Pierre-Jolys, Man. R0A 1V0 – 433-7729 – Mrs. Alice Bedard – Branch at St. Malo

Lac du Bonnet Regional Library, Box 216, Lac du Bonnet, Man. R0E 1A0 – 345-2653 – Mrs. Barbara Steed

Lakeland Regional Library, Box 970, Killarney, Man. R0K 1G0 – 523-4949 – Ms. L.G. Jewel Snowdon – Branches at Pilot Mound and Cartwright

Leaf Rapids Public Library, Leaf Rapids, Man. R0B 1W0 – 473-2741 – Mrs. Ann Ball

Minnedosa Regional Library, Box 1226, Minnedosa, Man. R0J 1E0 – 867-2585 – Ms. Shirley Metcalfe

North-West Regional Library, Box 999, Swan River, Man. R0L 1Z0 – 734-3880 – Ms. Jo-anne VanderWeyde – Branch at Benito

Parkland Regional Library, 31 First Ave. S.W., Dauphin, Man. R7N 1R9 – 638-6410 – Glenn Butchart – Branches at Dauphin and Birtle

Pinawa Public Library, Pinawa, Man. R0E 1L0 – 753-2496 – Mrs. Edna Graham

Portage la Prairie City Library, 170 Saskatchewan Ave. W., Portage la Prairie, Man. R1N 0M1 – 857-4271 – Mrs. Pat Mutala

Prairie Crocus Regional Library, Box 609, Rivers, Man. R0K 1X0 – 328-7613 – Mrs. Anne Harris

Rapid City Regional Library, Box 8, Rapid City, Man. R0K 1W0 – 826-2732 – Mrs. Margaret Northam

Reston District Library, Box 340, Reston, Man. R0M 1X0 – 877-3673 – Mrs. Emma St. Pierre

Rossburn Regional Library, Box 87, Rossburn, Man. R0J 1V0 – 859-2687 – Mrs. Rose Stefanuk

Russell & District Regional Library, Box 340, Russell, Man. R0J 1W0 – 773-3127 – Mrs. Agnes Burgess – Branch at Binscarth

Ste. Rose Regional Library, Ste. Rose du Lac, Man. R0L 1S0 – 447-2527 – Mrs. Rosanne Henson

Selkirk Community Library, 221 Mercy St., Selkirk, Man. R1A 2C8 – 482-6926 – Mrs. Dorothy Newton

South Central Regional Library, Box 1056, Morden, Man. R0G 1J0 – 822-4092 – Mrs. Iris Loewen – Branch at Winkler

South Interlake Regional Library, Box 908, Stonewall, Man. R0C 2Z0 – 467-8415 – Mrs. Dorothy Fleury

Southwestern Manitoba Regional Library, Box 670, Melita, Man. R0M 1L0 – 522-3923 – Barbara A. Walker – Branch at Pierson

Steinbach Public Library, Box 2050, Steinbach, Man. R0A 2A0 – 326-6841 – Mrs. Gladys Barkman

The Pas Public Library, Box 4100, The Pas, Man. R9A 1R2 – 623-2023 – Mrs. Roberta Day

Thompson Public Library, 81 Thompson Dr. N., Thompson, Man. R8N 0C3 – 677-3717 – Mrs. Peggy Henderson

Virden-Elkhorn Regional Library, Box 970, Virden, Man. R0M 2C0 – 748-3862 – Mrs. Hilda Kent – Branch at Elkhorn

Western Manitoba Regional Library, 1043 Rosser Ave., Brandon, Man. R7A 0L5 – 727-6648 – Mrs. Gliceria Dimaculangan – Branches at Carberry, Glenboro and Neepawa

Winnipeg Public Library, Main Branch, 251 Donald St., Winnipeg, Man. R3C 3P5 – 985-6472 – John S. Russell

- Brooklands Branch Library, 9 Dee St., Winnipeg, Man. R2R 0K8 – 633-5668
- Charleswood Branch Library, 5014 Roblin Blvd., Winnipeg, Man. R3R 0G7 – 837-3267
- Cornish Branch Library, 20 West Gate, Winnipeg, Man. R3C 2E1 – 783-5223
- Coronation Park Branch Library, 120 Eugenie St., Winnipeg, Man. R2H 0X7 – 233-7766
- Fort Garry Branch Library, 1360 Pembina Hwy., Winnipeg, Man. R3T 2B4 – 452-3201
- Henderson Branch Library, 1044 Henderson Hwy., Winnipeg, Man. R2K 2M5 – 339-4286
- McPhillips Branch Library, 1120 McPhillips St., Winnipeg, Man. R2X 2L3 – 586-4642
- Munroe Branch Library, 513 London St., Winnipeg, Man. R2K 2Z4 – 667-0956
- Osborne Branch Library, 700 Osborne St. S., Winnipeg, Man. R3L 2B9 – 475-5832
- River Heights Branch Library, 1520 Corydon Ave., Winnipeg, Man. R3N 0J6 – 489-5303
- St. Boniface Branch Library, 255 Cathedrale Ave., Winnipeg, Man. R2H 0J1 – 233-7755
- St. James Assiniboia Branch Library, 1910 Portage Ave., Winnipeg, Man. R3J 0J2 – 888-0880
- St. John's Branch Library, 500 Salter St., Winnipeg, Man. R2W 4M5 – 582-6431
- St. Vital Branch Library, 6 Fermor Ave., Winnipeg, Man. R2M 0Y2 – 257-0011
- Transcona Branch Library, 111 Victoria Ave., Winnipeg, Man. R2C 1S6 – 222-5293
- West End Branch Library, 823 Ellice Ave., Winnipeg, Man. R3G 0C3 – 775-7941
- West Kildonan Branch Library, 365 Jefferson Ave., Winnipeg, Man. R2V 0N3 – 589-5359
- Westwood Branch Library, 66 Allard Ave., Winnipeg, Man. R3K 0T3 – 837-3136
- William Ave. Branch Library, 380 William Ave., Winnipeg, Man. R3A 0J1 – 985-6487
- Windsor Park Branch Library, 955 Cottonwood Rd., Winnipeg, Man. R2J 1G3 – 253-1168

Special & College Libraries & Resource Centres in Manitoba

With Contact Person (Librarian, unless otherwise indicated)

Area Code for Manitoba is 204

BRANDON

Assiniboine Community College Library, 1430 Victoria Ave. E., Brandon, Man. R7A 5Z9 – 725-4530

Brandon General Hospital Library, 150 McTavish E., Brandon, Man. R7A 2B3 – 728-3321, loc. 399 – Ms. Kathy Eagleton

Brandon University Library, 270 18th St., Brandon, Man. R7A 6A9 – 728-9520 – Maria Szivos

Brandon Mental Health Centre, Reference & Lending Library, Box 420, Brandon, Man. R7A 5Z5 – 728-7110, ext. 287 – Marjorie McKinnon

CHURCHILL

Churchill Northern Studies Centre Library, Box 610, Churchill, Man. R0B 0E0 – 856-2842 – Wm. R. Erickson (act.)

PINAWA

Atomic Energy of Canada Ltd., Whiteshell Nuclear Research Establishment Library, Pinawa, Man. R0E 1L0 – 753-2311, loc. 244 – Gladys N. Gibson

PORTAGE LA PRAIRIE

David Winton Bell Memorial Library, Delta Waterfowl Research Station, R.R. 1, Portage la Prairie, Man. R1N 3A1 – 857-9125, 9872 – Shirley Rutledge

The Daily Graphic Library, Box 130, Portage la Prairie, Man. R1N 3B4 – 857-3427 – Y. Tashiro

ST. BONIFACE

See Winnipeg

THE PAS

Keewatin Community College, Learning Resources Centre, Box 3000, The Pas, Man. R9A 1M7 – 623-3416 – Jo Ann Brewster

WINNIPEG

Agriculture Canada, Research Station Library, 195 Dafoe Rd., Winnipeg, Man. R3T 2M9 – 269-2100 – M. Malyk

Aikins, MacAulay & Thorvaldson Law Library, #3, 333 Broadway, Winnipeg, Man. R3C 0T1 – 957-0050 – Mrs. Virginia Scott – A private legal library

Alcohol & Drug Education Service, William Potoroka Memorial Library, #107, 249½ Notre Dame Ave., Winnipeg, Man. R3B 1N8 – 942-2907 – Mrs. M. Belliveau

The Anna E. Wells Memorial Library, #202, 880 Portage Ave., Winnipeg, Man. R3G 0P1 – 786-5867 – Marilyn J. Hernandez

Atmospheric Environment Service, Central Region Library, 266 Graham Ave., Winnipeg, Man. R3C 0J8 – 949-4389 – R. Tortorelli

Balmoral Hall School Library, 630 Westminster Ave., Winnipeg, Man. R3C 3S1 – 786-8643 – Mrs. E. Law

Canada Dept. of Justice, Winnipeg Region Library, #301, 310 Broadway, Winnipeg, Man. R3C 0S6 – 949-2391 – P.M. Kremer

Canadian Association on Gerontology Resource Centre, Box 1859, Winnipeg, Man. R3C 3R1 – 944-2454

Canadian Association for the Mentally Retarded, Winnipeg Branch Library, #46, 825 Sherbrook St., Winnipeg, Man. R3A 1M5 – 783-7147 – Dave Wetherow, Exec. Dir.

Canadian Broadcasting Corp., Music & Record Library, Box 160, Winnipeg, Man. R3C 2H1 – 775-8351 – Don R. McLaren

Canadian Grain Commission Library, #1001, 303 Main St., Winnipeg, Man. R3C 3G7 – 949-3360 – Mrs. Lee Teal

Canadian National Institute for the Blind, Manitoba Division Library, 1031 Portage Ave., Winnipeg, Man. R3G 0R9 – 774-5421 – Mrs. E. Mourre

Canadian Wheat Board Library, 423 Main St., Winnipeg, Man. R3C 2P5 – 949-3437 – Nancy Brydges

The Citadel Life Library, 360 Broadway, Winnipeg, Man. R3C 0T7 – 956-1030 – Lynne Armer

Bibliothèque Universitaire du Collège St-Boniface, 200 ave de la Cathédrale, St-Boniface, Man. R2H 0H7 – 233-0210, ext. 130 – Marcel Boulet

- Collège Secondaire – Mme Gisèle Dupasquier (233-0210, ext. 152)
- Centre de Ressources – vacant (233-6474)

City of Winnipeg Environmental Planning Library, 100 Main St., Winnipeg, Man. R3C 1A5 – 985-5174 – Mrs. A. Thiesson

Crafts Guild of Manitoba Library, 183 Kennedy St., Winnipeg, Man. R3C 1S6 – 943-6281 – Miss A.M. Allen

D'Arcy & Deacon Law Library, #300, 286 Smith St., Winnipeg, Man. R3C 1K6 – 942-2271 – R. Anderson

Deer Lodge Hospital Library, 2109 Portage Ave., Winnipeg, Man. R3J 0L3 – 837-1301, ext. 374 – Mrs. J.L. Saunders

Departments of Government, See Manitoba Dept. of ...

Ducks Unlimited (Canada) Library, 1190 Waverley St., Winnipeg, Man. R3T 2E2 – 477-1760 – Marlene Hilland

Fillmore & Riley Law Library, #1400, One Lombard Place, Winnipeg, Man. R3B 0X5 – 956-2970 – Mrs. L. Nosworthy

Fisheries & Oceans, Freshwater Institute Library, 501 University Cres., Winnipeg, Man. R3T 2N6 – 269-7379 – K.E. Marshall

Great West Assurance Co. Library, 60 Osborne St. N., Winnipeg, Man. R3C 3A5 – 946-9225 – Mary F. Keelan

Health Sciences Centre Children's Library, Community Services Bldg., 685 William Ave., Winnipeg, Man. – 787-2511 – Gursharan Bawa

Health Sciences Centre, School of Nursing Library, 700 McDermot Winnipeg, Man. R3E 0T2 – 787-3416 – Ms. Rae Hovorka

Hudson's Bay Co. Library, 77 Main St., Winnipeg, Man. R3C 2R1 – 943-0881, ext. 133 or 269 – Carol Preston

Insurance Institute of Manitoba, #300, 213 Notre Dame Ave., Winnipeg, Man. R3B 1N3 – 956-1702 – Miss B.H. Rollo

Law Society of Manitoba Library, Law Courts, Broadway & Kennedy, Winnipeg, Man. R3C 0V7 – 943-5277 – Garth Niven

Legislative Library, 200 Vaughan St., Winnipeg, Man. R3C 0P8 – 946-7214 – Miss C. Clementine Combaz

Manitoba Association of Registered Nurses Library, 647 Broadway, Winnipeg, Man. R3C 0X2 – 774-3477, ext. 26 – Mrs. Eleanor Gowerluk

Manitoba Blue Cross Library, Box 1046, Winnipeg, Man. R3C 2X7 – 775-0161 – Dr. N.I. Corne

Manitoba Cancer Treatment & Research Foundation Library, 700 Bannatyne Ave., Winnipeg, Man. R3E 0V9 – 787-2136 – Isobel Steedman

Manitoba Dept. of Attorney General, Law Library, 5th floor, 405 Broadway, Winnipeg, Man. R3C 3L6 – 944-2895 – Walter Karlicki

Manitoba Dept. of Consumer & Corporate Affairs Library, 10th floor, Woodsworth Bldg., 405 Broadway, Winnipeg, Man. R3C 3L6 – 944-2658 – S. Norma Godavari
  Environment Library, 139 Tuxedo Blvd., Winnipeg, Man. R3N 0H6 – 895-5307 – S. Norma Godavari

Manitoba Dept. of Economic Development & Tourism Library, #648, 155 Carlton St., Winnipeg, Man. R3C 3H8 – 944-2036 – Miss F. Helen Paine

Manitoba Dept. of Education Library, Box 3, Main floor, 1181 Portage Ave., Winnipeg, Man. R3G 0T3 – 786-0218 – John Tooth

Manitoba Dept. of Finance, Federal-Provincial Relations & Research Library, #123, Legislative Bldg., Winnipeg, Man. R3C 0V8 – 944-3757 – Mrs. Beatrice Miller, i/c

Manitoba Dept. of Fitness, Recreation & Sport Resource Centre, #304, 379 Broadway, Winnipeg, Man. R3C 3N4 – 944-4398 – Daryl Steen

Manitoba Dept. of Health, See Anna E. Wells Memorial Library

Manitoba Dept. of Highways & Transportation Library, 215 Garry St., 16th floor, Winnipeg, Man. R3C 3Z1 – 944-3772 – Mrs. Gladys Bronevitch

Manitoba Dept. of Labour & Manpower, Research Branch Library, 409 Norquay Bldg., Winnipeg, Man. R3C 0P8 – 944-3412 – Mrs. L.M. Cooper

Manitoba Dept. of Municipal Affairs Library, #1436, 405 Broadway, Winnipeg, Man. R3C 3L6 – 944-4129 – Judy Stephenson

Manitoba Dept. of Natural Resources Library, Box 26, 1495 St. James St., Winnipeg, Man. R3H 0W9 – 786-9299 – Irene Hamerton

Manitoba Health Services Commission Library, 599 Empress St., Winnipeg, Man. R3C 2T6 – 786-7398 – D.A.T. Kowal

Manitoba Hydro Electric Board Library, 820 Taylor Ave., Winnipeg, Man. R3C 2P4 – 474-3614 – Margaret M. Gardiner

Manitoba Museum of Man & Nature Library, 190 Rupert Ave., Winnipeg, Man. R3B 0N2 – 956-2830 – V. Hatten

Mennonite Brethren Bible College Library, 77 Henderson Hwy., Winnipeg, Man. R2L 1L1 – 667-9560 – Herbert Giesbrecht

Ombudsman Library, #509, 491 Portage Ave., Winnipeg, Man. R3B 2E4 – 774-4491

Red River Community College, Learning Resources Centre, 2055 Notre Dame Ave., Winnipeg, Man. R3H 0J9 – 632-2232 – P. Bozyk

Rehabilitation Engineering Library, Health Sciences Centre Rehab., 800 Sherbrook St., Winnipeg, Man. R3A 1M4 – Dr. F.R. Tucker, i/c

Richardson Securities of Canada Library, Richardson Bldg., One Lombard Place, Winnipeg, Man. R3B 0Y2 – 988-5940 – Mrs. Agnes Unger

St. Amant Medical Library, 440 River Rd., Winnipeg, Man. R2M 3Z9 – 256-4301 – Marjorie Ramsay, A.R.T.

St. Andrew's College Library, Univ. of Manitoba, 475 Dysart Rd., Winnipeg, Man. R3T 2M7 – 269-3566 – Very Rev. Andrew Teterenko

St. Boniface General Hospital Library, 409 Taché Ave., Winnipeg, Man. R2H 2A6 – 237-2807, 8 – Dallas Bagby

St. Boniface School of Nursing Library, 431 Taché Ave., Winnipeg, Man. R2H 2A7 – 237-2953 – S. Leone Banks

Schwartz, McJannet etc. Law Library, 5th floor, 175 Carlton St., Winnipeg, Man. R3C 3H9 – 942-8101

Skwark, Myers etc. Law Library, #204, 215 Portage Ave., Winnipeg, Man. R3B 2A5 – 942-0501 – David R. James

Social Planning Council of Winnipeg Library, 412 McDermot Ave., Winnipeg, Man. R3A 0A9 – 943-2561 – E.T. Sale

Society for Crippled Children & Adults of Manitoba, Stephen Sparling Library, 825 Sherbrook St., Winnipeg, Man. R3A 1M4 – 786-5601 – Mrs. Barbara Wolfe

Statistics Canada Reference Centre, #602, 266 Graham St., Winnipeg, Man. R3C 0K4 – 949-3257 – W. Pawluk

Ukrainian Cultural & Educational Centre Library, 184 Alexander Ave. E., Winnipeg, Man. R3B 0L6 – 942-0218

Ukrainian Public Library, 603 Pritchard Ave., Winnipeg, Man. R2W 2K4 – 589-4397 – Anthony Bilecki

United Grain Growers Ltd. Library, 433 Main St., Box 6600, Winnipeg, Man. R3C 3A7 – 944-5572 – Mrs. Carole Rogers

United Health Services Corp. Library, Box 1046, Winnipeg, Man. R3C 2X7 – 775-0161 – Dr. N.I. Corne

University of Manitoba Libraries, c/o Director of Libraries, Univ. of Manitoba, Winnipeg, Man. R3T 2N2 – 474-9881, telex: 07-587721 – M.J. Sharrow, Dir.
  A/Asst. Director, Technical Services – R. Lincoln
  Asst. Director, Public Services – tba
  Asst. Director, Admin. Services – K.R. Bonin
  Systems Co-ordinator – P.J. Fawcett
  Administrative Studies – Judith Head
  Agriculture – Judith Harper
  Architecture & Fine Arts – Peter Anthony
  Dental Library – Doris Pritchard
  Education – Doreen Shanks
  Engineering – Yong-Ja Cho
  Law – Denis Marshall
  Medical – Audrey Kerr
  Music – Peter Anthony
  St. John's College – Arthur E. Millward
  St. Paul's College – Father Harold Drake
  Science – Vladimir N. Simosko

University of Winnipeg Library, 515 Portage Ave., Winnipeg, Man. R3B 2E9 – 786-7811, ext. 520 – R.C. Wright

Winnipeg Art Gallery, The Clara Lander Library, 300 Memorial Blvd., Winnipeg, Man. R3C 1V1 – 786-6641 – David Rozniatowski

Winnipeg Clinic Library, 425 St. Mary Ave., Winnipeg, Man. R3C 0N2 – 957-1900, ext. 357

Winnipeg Free Press Library, 300 Carlton St., Winnipeg, Man. R3C 3C1 – 943-9331 – Mrs. E. Langer

Winnipeg Sun Library, 290 Garry St., Winnipeg, Man. R3C 1H3 – 957-0710

NEW BRUNSWICK

Public Libraries in New Brunswick

With Librarian or Official

ALBERT-WESTMORLAND-KENT LIBRARY REGION, Box 708, Moncton, N.B. E1C 8M9 (506/389-2631)—Librarian, Claude Potvin

Units:
Dieppe Library Unit, 333 Acadia Ave., Dieppe, N.B. E1A 1G9 – 382-2710 – Mrs. Sylvie St. Onge
Dorchester Library Unit, Dorchester, N.B. E0A 1M0 – 379-2582 – Mrs. Harriet Robinson
Hillsborough Library Unit, Hillsborough, N.B. E0A 1X0 – Mrs. Dora Braam
Hopewell Cape Library Unit, Hopewell Cape, N.B. E0A 1Y0 – Shirley Teahan
Lewisville Library Unit, 100 Willowbend Dr., Lewisville, N.B. E1A 5P9 – 388-1571 – Mrs. Irene Ferguson
Moncton Library Unit, 51 Highfield St., Moncton, N.B. E1C 5N2 – 389-2631 – Miss Gwynneth Hughes
Port Elgin Library Unit, Port Elgin, N.B. E0A 2X0 – Mrs. Rose Johnson
Riverview Library Unit, 559 Coverdale Rd., Riverview, N.B. E1B 3K7 – 386-2438 – Miss Margaret MacMillan
Sackville Library Unit, Sackville, N.B. E0A 3C0 – 536-3184 – Mrs. Patricia Sims
St. Antoine Library Unit, Box 328, St. Antoine, N.B. E0A 2X0 – Miss Anise Melanson
St. Joseph Library Unit, St. Joseph, N.B. E0A 2Y0 – Mrs. Beatrice Légendre
Salisbury Library Unit, Box 56, Salisbury, N.B. E0A 3E0 – 372-9106 – Miss Margaret Crosthwaite
Shediac Library Unit, Box 1448, Shediac, N.B. E0A 3G0 – 532-9337 – Miss Gabrielle LeBlanc

YORK LIBRARY REGION, 4 Carleton St., Fredericton, N.B. E3B 5P4 (506/454-4481)—Librarian, Mrs. Paul Le Butt
(operating three bookmobiles and the following branches):
Chatham Public Library, Box 446, Chatham, N.B. E1N 3A8 – 773-6274 – Mrs. Patricia Clancy
Chipman Public Library, Chipman, N.B. E0E 1C0 – 339-5852 – Mrs. Marilyn Austin
Florenceville Public Library, Box 110, Florenceville, N.B. E0J 1K0 – 392-5294 – Mrs. Valerie Brooker
(Fredericton) Bibliothèque Dr. Marguerite Michaud, 715 Priestman St., Fredericton, N.B. E3B 5W7 – 455-1740 – Mrs. Mona Guerrette
Fredericton Public Library, 12 Carleton St., Fredericton, N.B. E3B 5P4 – 454-2431 – Alison Fitzgerald
Marysville Public Library, Canada St., Marysville, N.B. – 472-4196 – Mrs. Anne Marie Ottens
McAdam Public Library, McAdam, N.B. E0H 1K0 – 784-3103 – Mrs. Joan Phillips
Nackawic Public Library, Nackawic, N.B. E0H 1P0 – 575-2136 – Miss Linda Watson
Nashwaaksis Public Library, 364 Fulton Ave., Fredericton, N.B. E3A 1R6 – 472-4123 – Elizabeth Winsche
Oromocto Public Library, 54 Miramichi Rd., Oromocto, N.B. E0G 2P0 – 357-3329 – William Molesworth
Perth-Andover Public Library, Perth-Andover, N.B. E0J 1V0 – 273-2843 – Mrs. Joan Nicholson
Plaster Rock Public/School Library, Plaster Rock, N.B. E0J 1W0 – 356-8642 – Miss M. Edel Toner
Stanley Public Library, Stanley, N.B. E0H 1T0 – Mrs. Leota Henderson
Woodstock-York Sub-Headquarters, Box 1540, Woodstock, N.B. E0J 2B0 – 328-8663 – William Hegan
(Woodstock) L.P. Fisher Public Library, Box 1540, Woodstock, N.B. E0J 2B0 – 328-6880 – Mrs. Marion Lindsay

CHALEUR LIBRARY REGION, Box 607, Campbellton, N.B. E3N 3H1 (506/753-4500)—Librarian, Robert Richards
Units:
Atholville Library Unit, Atholville, N.B. E0K 1A0 – Mrs. Ginette Soucy
Bathurst Library Sub-Headquarters, 360 Douglas Ave., Bathurst, N.B. E2A 3Z1 – Mlle Claudette LeBlanc
Campbellton Library Unit, Box 607, Campbellton, N.B. E3N 3H1 – 753-5253 – James Katan
Caraquet Library Unit, C.P. 940, Caraquet, N.B. E0B 1K0 – 727-2070 – Mme Anita Theriault
Dalhousie Centennial Library, Dalhousie, N.B. E0K 1B0 – 684-2068 – Mrs. Mary Guitard
Shippegan Public Library, 244 J.D. Gauthier Blvd., Shippegan, N.B. E0B 2P0 – Mme Carole LeBouthillier
Tracadie Library Unit, C.P. 966, Tracadie, N.B. E0C 2B0 – 395-5387 – Mlle Irene Arsenault

SAINT JOHN LIBRARY REGION, 20 Hazen Ave., Saint John, N.B. E2L 3G8 (506/693-1191)—Librarian, Mrs. Eileen Travis
Units:
St. Croix Library Unit, 1 Budd Ave., St. Croix, N.B. E3L 1E8 – 466-4781 – Mrs. Elva Hatt
Saint John Free Public Library, 20 Hazen Ave., Saint John, N.B. E2L 3G8 – 693-1191 – Ian Wilson
Saint John Boys' & Girls' Room, Fairview Plaza, Lansdowne Ave., Saint John, N.B. E2K 3A1 – 657-3250– Mrs. Gertrude Haslett
Saint John East Branch Library, 545 Westmorland Rd., Saint John, N.B. E2J 2G5 – 696-7715 – Miss Pearl Hazen
Saint John West Branch Library, 621 Fairville Blvd., Saint John, N.B. E2M 4X5 – Mrs. Janet Currie
Sussex Library Unit, Box 1496, Sussex, N.B. E0E 1P0 – 433-4586 – Mrs. Patricia McCleave
Welshpool Library Unit, Welshpool, Campobello Island, N.B. E0G 3H0 – 782-2268 – Mrs. Glenna Cline

BIBLIOTHEQUE REGIONALE DU HAUT SAINT-JEAN, 50 rue Queen, Edmundston, N.B. E3V 3N4 (506/739-7331)—Librarian, Gilles Chiasson
Units:
Edmundston Library Unit, Edmundston, N.B. E3V 1V5 – 735-4713 – Jeanne Maddix
Grand Falls Library Unit, Grand Falls, N.B. E0J 1M0 – 473-1248 – Mrs. Joyce Shannon
Saint Leonard Library Unit, Saint Leonard, N.B. E0L 1M0 – 423-7787 – Mme Nicole Malenfant
St-Quentin Library Unit, St-Quentin, N.B. E0K 1J0 – 235-2513 – Yvette Quimper

Special & College Libraries & Resource Centres in New Brunswick

With Contact Person (Librarian, unless otherwise indicated)

Area Code for New Brunswick is 506

BATHURST

Collège Communautaire du Nouveau Brunswick, Campus de Bathurst, Division Technologie Bibliothèque, C.P. 1, Bathurst, N.B. E2A 3Z2 – 548-4591 – Lucien Chassé

EDMUNDSTON

Centre universitaire St-Louis-Maillet Students Library, 165 Hébert Boul., Edmundston, N.B. E3V 2S8 – 735-8804 – Gérard Lavoie

FREDERICTON

Agriculture Canada Library, Box 20280, Fredericton, N.B. E3B 4Z7 – 452-3260 – D.B. Gammon
Barristers' Society of New Brunswick Library, Justice Bldg., Room 305, Fredericton, N.B. E3B 5C2 – 453-2500 – Mrs. D. Hanson
Departments of Government, See New Brunswick Dept. of ...
Legislative Library, Legislative Bldg., Box 6000, Fredericton, N.B. E3B 5H1 – 453-2338 – Mlle Jocelyne LeBel, Dir.
Maritimes Forest Research Centre Library, Canadian Forestry Service, Box 4000, Fredericton, N.B. E3B 5P7 – 452-3541 – Barry Barner
New Brunswick Association of Registered Nurses Library, 231 Saunders St., Fredericton, N.B. E3B 1N6 – 454-5591 – Mrs. Barbara Thompson
New Brunswick Dept. of Agriculture & Rural Development Library, Box 6000, Fredericton, N.B. E3B 5H1 – 453-2258
New Brunswick Dept. of Commerce & Development Library, Box 6000, Fredericton, N.B. E3B 5H1 – 453-3608 – Pamela M. Spinney
New Brunswick Dept. of Education Library, Box 6000, Fredericton, N.B. E3B 5H1 – 453-3739 – Mrs. Germaine Burns
New Brunswick Dept. of the Environment Library, Box 6000, Fredericton, N.B. E3B 5H1 – 453-3700
New Brunswick Dept. of Fisheries Library, Box 6000, Fredericton, N.B. E3B 5H1 – 453-2251

New Brunswick Dept. of Health Library, #349, Centennial Bldg., Fredericton, N.B. E3B 5H1 – 453-2536 – Margaret Cooper

New Brunswick Dept. of Labour & Manpower Library, Box 6000, Fredericton, N.B. E3B 5H1 – 453-2722 – Geri E. Gadd

New Brunswick Dept. of Municipal Affairs Library, #450, Centennial Bldg., Fredericton, N.B. E3B 5H1 – 453-2171

New Brunswick Dept. of Natural Resources, Forests Branch Library, Box 6000, Fredericton, N.B. E3B 5H1 – 453-2485 – Mrs. I. Long

New Brunswick Dept. of Social Services Library, Box 6000, Fredericton, N.B. E3B 5H1 – 453-2039

New Brunswick Dept. of Youth, Recreation & Cultural Services Library, (York Tower, King's Place) Box 6000, Fredericton, N.B. E3B 5H1 – 453-2928 – Rino Levesque

New Brunswick Electric Power Commission Library, 527 King St., Fredericton, N.B. E3B 4X1 – 453-4353 – Mrs. Aileen W. Humes

New Brunswick Provincial Archives Library, Box 6000, Fredericton, N.B. E3B 5H1 – 453-2637 – Marion Beyea, Archivist

New Brunswick Research & Productivity Council Library, Box 6000, Fredericton, N.B. E3B 5H1 – 455-8994 – April L. James

Office of the Ombudsman Library, Box 6000, Fredericton, N.B. E3B 5H1 – 453-2789

University of New Brunswick Libraries, c/o University Librarian, Fredericton, N.B. E3B 5H5
University Librarian – Dr. G.E. Gunn (453-4740)
Education Resource Centre – Andrew Pope (453-3516)
Engineering Library – Everett R. Dunfield (453-4747)
Law Library – Ms. Anne Crocker (453-4669)
Science Library – Mrs. Eszter Schwenke (453-3566)

MONCTON

Atlantic Baptist College Library, Box 1004, Moncton, N.B. E1C 8P4 – 382-7550

Bibliothèque Champlain, Université de Moncton, Moncton, N.B. E1A 3E9 – 858-4073 – Albert Lévésque

Centre d'études acadiennes (bibliothèque), Université de Moncton, Moncton, N.B. E1A 3E9 – 858-4083 – Ronald LeBlanc

Centre de ressources pédagogiques, Faculté des sciences de l'éducation, Université de Moncton, Moncton, N.B. E1A 3E9 – 858-4356 – Berthe Boudreau

Ecole de droit (bibliothèque), Université de Moncton, Moncton, N.B. E1A 3E9 – 858-4569 – Mme Simonne Clermont

L'Evangeline Library, 80 Church St., C.P. 1050, Moncton, N.B. E1C 4Z2 – 855-5560 – Donald Langis

Moncton Barristers' Society Library, 770 Main St., Box 6011, Moncton, N.B. E1C 1E7 – 389-1649 – Jean M. Sawyer, Lib. Asst.

Moncton Hospital, Health Sciences Library, McBeath Ave., Moncton, N.B. E1C 6Z8 – 855-1600, ext. 340 – Mrs. I.W. Wallace

ROTHESAY

Colin Mackay Memorial Library, Rothesay College School, Rothesay, N.B. E0G 2W0 – 847-8224 – A.C.B. Savege

SACKVILLE

Canadian Wildlife Service, Atlantic Region Library, Box 1590, Sackville, N.B. E0A 3C0 – 536-3025 – Mrs. F.H. Anderson

Mount Allison University, Ralph Pickard Bell Library, Sackville, N.B. E0A 3C0 – 536-2040, ext. 375 – Theodore D. Phillips

ST. ANDREWS

Dept. of Fisheries & Oceans, Biological Station Library, St. Andrews, N.B. E0G 2X0 – 529-8854 – Ms. C.R. Garnett

SAINT JOHN

Church of England Institute Library, 116 Princess St., Saint John, N.B. E2L 1K4 – 693-2295 – Mrs. F.H. Burton

Insurance Institute of New Brunswick Library, Box 843, Saint John, N.B. E2L 4C3 – 652-2120 – D.E. MacDonald, A.I.I.C., i/c

New Brunswick Community College Library, Box 2270, Saint John, N.B. E2L 3V1 – 696-1860 – Dewan Sachdeva

New Brunswick Museum Library, 277 Douglas Ave., Saint John, N.B. E2K 1E5 – 693-1196 – Carol Rosevear

New Brunswick Telephone Co. Ltd. Library, One Brunswick Sq., Box 1430, Saint John, N.B. E2L 4K2 – 693-6845 – Mrs. Patricia Blenkhorn

Occupational Health & Safety Council of New Brunswick Library, Box 2239, Saint John, N.B. E2L 3V1 – 652-8261 – Mrs. C.F. McGowan

Palmer, O'Connell, Leger etc. Law Library, Box 1324, Saint John, N.B. E2L 4H8 – 642-2700 – Peter R. Forestell

Saint John Law Society Library, 110 Charlotte St., Saint John, N.B. E2L 2J4 – 658-2542 – Mrs. Marilyn Brown

The Telegraph-Times Library, 210 Crown St., Box 2350, Saint John, N.B. E2L 3V8 – 657-1230 – Peggy Goss

University of New Brunswick, Ward Chipman Library, Saint John, N.B. E2L 4L5 – 657-7310, ext. 217 – Kenneth M. Duff

NEWFOUNDLAND

Library Regions in Newfoundland

With Regional Librarian

Area Code is 709

Avalon Library Region: Arts & Culture Centre, St. John's, Nfld. A1B 3A3 – 737-3957 – Howard Saunders

Central Library Region: Box 499, Grand Falls, Nfld. A2A 2J9 – 489-9001 – Ralph Dale

Gander Library Region: Arts & Culture Centre, Gander, Nfld. A1V 1K6 – 651-2781 – Miss Patricia Wilson

Western Library Region: Bag 2007, Union St., Corner Brook, Nfld. A2H 6V7 – 634-7333 – Ms. Elinor Benjamin

Public Libraries in Newfoundland

With Librarian

Area Code is 709

Arnold's Cove Public Library, Arnold's Cove, Nfld. A0B 1A0 – 463-8707 – Mrs. Nina Marshall

Badger's Quay Memorial Library, Badger's Quay, Nfld. A0G 1B0 – 536-2010 – Mrs. Marian Hennebury

Baie Verte Public Library, Box 178, Baie Verte, Nfld. A0K 1B0 – 532-8361 – Mrs. Phyllis Hoven

Bay Roberts Public Library, Box 385, Bay Roberts, Nfld. A0A 1G0 – Linda Spencer

Bay St. George South Public Library, Highlands, Nfld. A0N 1N0 – 645-2660 – Mrs. Anita MacInnes

Bell Island Public Library, Wabana, Bell Island, Nfld. A0A 1H0 – 488-2413 – Mrs. Margaret Murphy

Bishop's Falls Public Library, Box 329, Bishop's Falls, Nfld. A0H 1C0 – 258-6244 – Mrs. Jean Sheppard

Bonavista Public Library, Box 400, Bonavista, Nfld. A0C 1B0 – 468-2185 – Mrs. Frances Sweetland

Botwood Public Library, Box 747, Botwood, Nfld. A0H 1E0 – 257-2091 – Mrs. Gwen Humphries

Brigus Public Library, Brigus, Nfld. A0A 1K0 – Mrs. June Walker

Buchans Public Library, Buchans, Nfld. A0H 1G0 – 672-3859 – Mrs. Alma White

Burgeo Public Library, Box 370, Burgeo, Nfld. A0M 1A0 – 886-2730 – Mrs. Harriet Strickland

Burin Public Library, Box 118, Burin, Nfld. A0E 1E0 – 891-1924 – Mrs. Joan Rowe

Cape St. George Public Library, Cape St. George, Nfld. A0N 1E0 – Mrs. Gladys Cornect

Carbonear Public Library, Box 928, Carbonear, Nfld. A0A 1T0 – 596-3382 – vacant

Carmanville Public Library, Carmanville, Nfld. A0G 1N0 – 534-2370 – Mrs. Gloria Gillingham

Cartwright Public Library, Cartwright, Nfld. A0K 1V0 – 938-7393 – Mrs. Hilda Clarke

Joseph E. Clouter Memorial Library, Catalina, Nfld. A0C 1J0 – 489-3045 – Mrs. June Lodge

Centreville Public Library, Box 100, Centreville, Nfld. A0G 4P0 – 678-2700 – Mrs. Gertrude Collins

Change Islands Public Library, Change Islands, Nfld. A0G 1R0 – 621-4181 – Mrs. Christine Hoffe
Channel-Port aux Basques Public Library, Box 790, Port aux Basques, Nfld. A0M 1C0 – 695-3471 – Mrs. Brenda Ingram
Churchill Falls Public Library, Box 160, Churchill Falls, Nfld. A0R 1A0 – 925-3281 – Mrs. Lynn Betts
Clarenville Public Library, Box 250, Clarenville, Nfld. A0E 1J0 – 466-7634 – Mrs. Elizabeth Perry
Codroy Valley School & Public Library, Upper Ferry, Codroy Valley, Nfld. A0N 1H0 – 955-2940 – Mrs. Wilfrieda Bungey
Conception Bay South Public Library, Box 580, Manuels, Nfld. A0A 2Y0 – 834-4241 – Mrs. Glenda Quinn
Cormack Public Library, Cormack, Nfld. A0K 2E0 – Marie Morris
Corner Brook City Library, Sir Richard Squires Bldg., Corner Brook, Nfld. A2H 6J8 – 639-9111 – Charles Cameron
Cow Head Public Library, Cow Head, Nfld. A0K 2A0 – 243-2467 – Mrs. Joan Hewlin
Daniel's Harbour Public Library, Daniel's Harbour, Nfld. A0K 2C0 – Mrs. Edith Guinchard
Dark Cove Public Library, Dark Cove, Nfld. A0G 1T0 – 674-5052 – Mrs. Marjorie Lane
Deer Lake Public Library, Box 629, Deer Lake, Nfld. A0K 2E0 – 635-3671 – Mrs. Worneta Cramm
Dover Public Library, Dover, Nfld. A0G 1X0 – 537-5763 – Mrs. Melita Noble
Fogo Public Library, Fogo, Nfld. A0G 2B0 – 226-2210 – Mrs. Cynthia Coish
Fortune Public Library, Fortune, Nfld. A0E 1P0 – 832-0232 – Mrs. Fay Dominie
Fox Harbour Public Library, Fox Harbour, Nfld. A0B 1V0 – 227-2271 – Mrs. Florence Spurvey
Freshwater Public Library, Freshwater, Nfld. A0B 1W0 – 227-3801 – Mrs. Rita Coffey
Gander Public Library, 100 Elizabeth Dr., Gander, Nfld. A1V 1G7 – 256-3282 – Mrs. Jean Greening
Garnish Public Library, Garnish, Nfld. A0E 1T0 – Mrs. Anne Riley
Gaultois Public Library, Gaultois, Nfld. A0H 1N0 – Mrs. Gerty Howse
Glenwood Public Library, Glenwood, Nfld. A0G 2K0 – Mrs. Virginia Fry
Glovertown Public Library, Glovertown, Nfld. A0G 2L0 – 533-6688 – Mrs. Dorothy Roach
Grand Bank Public Library, Grand Bank, Nfld. A0E 1W0 – 832-0310 – Mrs. Mildred Watts
(Grand Falls) Harmsworth Public Library, Arts & Culture Centre, Grand Falls, Nfld. A2A 1W9 – 489-2303 – Ms. Betty Wyatt
Greenspond Public Library, Greenspond, Nfld. A0G 2N0 – Mrs. Ruth Woodland
(Happy Valley) Melville Public Library, Box 944, Happy Valley, (Lab.) Nfld. A0P 1E0 – 896-8045 – Mrs. Hyra Skoglund
Harbour Breton Public Library, Harbour Breton, Nfld. A0H 1P0 – 885-2165 – Mrs. Vivian Bennett
Harbour Grace Public Library, Harbour Grace, Nfld. A0A 2M0 – 596-3895 – Mrs. Marjorie Davis
Hare Bay Public Library, Hare Bay, Nfld. A0G 2P0 – 537-2391 – Mrs. Ada Smith
Harry's Harbour Public Library, Harry's Harbour, Nfld. A0J 1E0 – Mrs. Rachel Moore
Hermitage Public Library, Hermitage, Nfld. A0H 1S0 – 883-2421 – Mrs. Nina Engram
King's Point Public Library, King's Point, Nfld. A0J 1H0 – Mrs. Greta Noble
Labrador City Public Library, 306 Hudson Dr., Labrador City, Lab. (Nfld.) A2V 1L5 – 944-2190 –
L'Anse au Loup Public Library, L'Anse au Loup, Nfld. A0K 3L0 – 927-5542 – Mrs. Ruth O'Brien
(Lark Harbour) Blow Me Down School & Public Library, Lark Harbour, Nfld. A0L 1H0 – 681-2620 – Mrs. Norma Pickett
LaScie Public Library, LaScie, Nfld. A0K 3M0 – Mrs. Rowena Morey
Lewisporte Public Library, Lewisporte, Nfld. A0G 3A0 – 535-2519 – Mrs. Liza Sutherland
Lourdes School & Public Library, Lourdes, Nfld. A0N 1R0 – 642-5322 – Mrs. Elizabeth Snook
Lumsden Public Library, Lumsden, Nfld. A0G 3E0 – Mrs. Cindy Norman
Marystown Public Library, Box 92, Marystown, Nfld. A0E 2M0 – 279-1507 – Mrs. Josephine Kelly
Mount Pearl Public Library, Box 37, Mount Pearl, Nfld. A1N 2C1 – 368-3603 – Mrs. Margaret Noseworthy
(Musgrave Harbour) John B. Wheeler Memorial Library, Musgrave Harbour, Nfld. A0G 3J0 – 655-2730 – Mrs. Ena Flynn
Norris Arm Public Library, Box 100, Norris Arm, Nfld. A0G 3M0 – 653-2531 – Mrs. Judith Rowsell
Norris Point Public Library, Norris Point, Nfld. A0K 3V0 – Mrs. Lucy Hillier
Old Perlican Public Library, Old Perlican, Nfld. A0A 3G0 – Mrs. Judith Barter
Pasadena Public Library, Pasadena, Nfld. A0L 1K0 – 686-2792 – Mrs. Judith Skinner
Placentia Public Library, Placentia, Nfld. A0B 2Y0 – 227-3621 – Mrs. Gertrude Sullivan
Point Leamington Public Library, Box 76, Point Leamington, Nfld. A0H 1Z0 – Mrs. Emma Rolfe
(Port au Port East) Curran Memorial Library, Point au Mal Rd., Port au Port East, Nfld. A0N 1T0 – 648-9401 – Mrs. Eileen Hann
Port au Port West School & Public Library, Port au Port West, Nfld. A0N 1T0 – 648-9921 – Mrs. Dorothy Alexander
Port Saunders Public Library, Box 118, Port Saunders, Nfld. A0K 4H0 – 861-3690 – Mrs. Kay Hamlyn
Pouch Cove Public Library, Pouch Cove, Nfld. A0A 3L0 – 335-2650 – Mrs. Diane Mulley
(Ramea) Marie S. Penney Memorial Library, Box 59, Ramea, Nfld. A0M 1N0 – 625-2344 – Mrs. Marlene Augustus
Robert's Arm Public Library, Box 119, Robert's Arm, Nfld. A0J 1R0 – 652-3100 – Mrs. Rowena Ryan
Rocky Harbour Public Library, Rocky Harbour, Nfld. A0K 4N0 – 458-2900 – Mrs. Johan Sparkes
St. Alban's Public Library, Box 10, St. Alban's, Nfld. A0H 2E0 – Mrs. Gabriella Drew
St. Anthony Public Library, Box 38, St. Anthony, Nfld. A0K 4S0 – 454-2585 – Mrs. Bernice Smith
(St. Bride's) Cape Shore Public Library, St. Bride's, Nfld. A0B 2Z0 – 337-2360 – Mrs. Mary Coffey
St. George's Public Library, St. George's, Nfld. A0N 1Z0 – 647-3808 – Mrs. Zita MacDonnell
St. John's City Library System, Arts & Culture Centre, St. John's, Nfld. A1B 3A3 – 737-3951 – Mrs. Mary C. Jones
St. Lawrence Public Library, St. Lawrence, Nfld. A0E 2V0 – 873-2650 – Mrs. Ena Edwards
St. Lunaire-Griquet Public Library, St. Lunaire, Nfld. A0K 2X0 – Mrs. Mae Bussey
Seal Cove Public Library, Box 70, Seal Cove, Nfld. A0K 5E0 – 531-4101 – Mrs. Madeline Parsons
(Sops Arm) Naskapi School & Public Library, Sops Arm, Nfld. A0K 5K0 – 482-7301 – Mrs. Judith Decker
Southern Harbour Public Library, Southern Harbour, Nfld. A0B 3H0 – 463-8740 – Miss Bride Whiffen
Spaniard's Bay Public Library, Spaniard's Bay, Nfld. A0A 3X0 – Mrs. Ellie Vokey
Springdale Public Library, Box 100, Springdale, Nfld. A0J 1T0 – Mrs. Golda Burton
(Stephenville) Kindale Public Library, 16 Glendale, Stephenville, Nfld. A2N 2K3 – 643-4262 – Gilbert Higgins
Stephenville Crossing Public Library, Stephenville Crossing, Nfld. A0N 2C0 – Mrs. Kay Lucus
Summerford Public Library, Summerford, Nfld. A0G 4E0 – Miss Karen Wheeler
Torbay Public Library, Site 6, Box 39, Torbay, Nfld. A0A 3Z0 – 437-6571 – Mrs. Marie Evans
Trepassey Public Library, Trepassey, Nfld. A0A 4B0 – 438-2044 – Ted Winter
Twillingate Public Library, Twillingate, Nfld. A0G 4M0 – 884-5928 – Mrs. Harriet Scott
Upper Island Cove Public Library, Upper Island Cove, Nfld. A0A 4E0 – 589-2090 – Mrs. Clara Peckford

Victoria Public Library, Victoria, Nfld. A0A 4G0 – 596-3682 – Mrs. Hilda Stevens
Wabush Public Library, Box 179, Wabush, Nfld. A0R 1B0 – 282-3479 – Alfreda Harkins
Wesleyville Public Library, Wesleyville, Nfld. A0G 4R0 – Mrs. Mary Howse
Whitbourne Public Library, Whitbourne, Nfld. A0B 3K0 – 759-2461 – Mrs. Olive Noseworthy
Windsor Memorial Public Library, Box 1000, Windsor, Nfld. A0H 2H0 – 489-9352 – Mrs. Joyce Gregory
Winterton Public Library, Winterton, Nfld. A0B 3M0 – Miss Betty Pitcher
(Woody Point) Edgar L. Roberts Memorial Library, Woody Point, Nfld. A0K 1P0 – Mrs. Sylvia Deans

Special & College Libraries & Resource Centres in Newfoundland

With Contact Person (Librarian, unless otherwise indicated)

Area Code for Newfoundland is 709

CORNER BROOK
Bowaters Newfoundland Ltd. Library, Corner Brook, Nfld. A2H 6J4 – 634-5151 – J.L. Barron
Sir Wilfred Grenfell College Library, Corner Brook, Nfld. A2H 6P9 – 639-8981 – Elizabeth Behrens
Western Memorial Regional Hospital, Health Sciences Library, Box 2005, West Valley Rd., Corner Brook, Nfld. A2H 6J7 – 634-5101 – Walter S. MacPherson

GANDER
James Paton Memorial Hospital, Medical Library, Gander, Nfld. A1V 1P7 – 651-2500 – Mrs. C. Candow

ST. ANTHONY
Charles Curtis Memorial Hospital, Library, St. Anthony, Nfld. A0K 4S0 – 454-8881, ext. 246

ST. JOHN'S
Atlantic Development Council Library, Bldg. 102, Churchill Ave., St. John's, Nfld. A1A 1N1 – 737-4090 – K. Walsh
Board of Trade Community Data Centre, (169-173 Water St.) Box 5127, St. John's, Nfld. A1C 5V5 – 726-2961 – B.J. Tilley, Gen. Manager
Canadian National Institute for the Blind, Tape Library, 70 The Boulevarde, St. John's, Nfld. A1A 1K2 – 754-1180
City of St. John's Planning Library, City Hall, Box 908, St. John's, Nfld. A1C 5M2 – 726-8820, ext. 311/312 – B. Newell, Planning Techn.
College of Fisheries, Navigation, Marine Engineering & Electronics, Library, Parade St., Box 4920, St. John's, Nfld. A1C 5R3 – 726-5272, ext. 218 – M. Farmer
College of Trades & Technology Library, Prince Philip Dr., Box 1693, St. John's, Nfld. A1C 5P7 – 753-9360 – P. Rahal
Curtis, Dawe & Co. Law Library, 139 Water St., Box 337, St. John's, Nfld. A1C 5J9 – 722-5181
Departments of Government, See Newfoundland Dept. of ...
Dr. Charles A. Janeway Child Health Centre Library, Pleasantville, St. John's, Nfld. A1A 1R8 – 778-4344 – Miss J. Wheeler
Environment Canada, Newfoundland Forest Research Centre Library, Box 6028, E.E.P.O., St. John's, Nfld. A1C 5X8 – 737-4672 – Mrs. C.E. Philpott
General Hospital, Nursing Library, Forest Rd., St. John's, Nfld. A1A 1E5 – 737-6789 – Mrs. E. McGrath
Grace General Hospital, Medical Library, Le Marchant Rd., St. John's, Nfld. A1E 1P9 – 778-6796 – Mrs. Elizabeth Duggan – K. Walsh, Nursing
Insurance Institute of Newfoundland Library, Box 9412, Stn. B, St. John's, Nfld. A1A 2Y3 – 722-1649 – Doris Cook
Law Society of Newfoundland Library, Court House, Box 1028, St. John's, Nfld. A1C 5M3 – 753-7770 – Miss Suzanna Duke
Legislative Library, House of Assembly, Confederation Bldg., St. John's, Nfld. A1C 5T7 – 737-3604 – Miss N.J. Richards
Memorial University Libraries, c/o University Librarian, St. John's, Nfld. A1B 3Y1 – 737-7428
University Librarian – Margaret Williams
Assoc. Librarian – Richard H. Ellis
Curriculum Materials Centre – Alison Mews
Education – Barbara Eddy
Health Sciences – Isabel Hunter
Ocean Engineering Info. Centre – Judith Whittick

Newfoundland Dept. of Development Library, Confederation Bldg., St. John's, Nfld. A1C 5T7 – 737-2785

Newfoundland Dept. of Education Library, 951 Charter Ave., St. John's, Nfld. A1A 1R2 – 737-2612 – Norman Harris

Newfoundland Dept. of Environment Library, Box 4750, St. John's, Nfld. A1C 5T7 – 737-2562

Newfoundland Dept. of Forest Resources & Lands Library, Bldg. 810, Pleasantville, St. John's, Nfld. A1C 5T7

Newfoundland Dept. of Justice, Law Library, Confederation Bldg., St. John's, Nfld. A1C 5T7 – 737-2861 – Mrs. Mona B. Pearce

Newfoundland Dept. of Labour & Manpower Library, Beothuck Bldg., Crosbie Place, St. John's, Nfld. A1C 5T7 – 737-2729 – Mrs. N.M. Fosnaes

Newfoundland Dept. of Mines & Energy, Mineral Development Division Library, 95 Bonaventure Ave., St. John's, Nfld. A1C 5T7 – 737-3159

Newfoundland Dept. of Municipal Affairs & Housing, Planning Library, Confederation Bldg., St. John's, Nfld. A1C 5T7 – 737-3087 – Ruth Wilson

Newfoundland Dept. of Rural, Agricultural & Northern Development Library, 6th floor, Atlantic Place, St. John's, Nfld. A1C 5T7 – 737-3172 – Irvine Mullett

Newfoundland Dept. of Social Services Library, Confederation Bldg., St. John's, Nfld. A1C 5T7 – 737-3590 – Mrs. V. Hoyles

Newfoundland Dept. of Tourism, Recreation & Culture, Library, (146-148 Forest Rd.), Confederation Bldg., St. John's, Nfld. A1C 5T7

Newfoundland Labrador Development Corp. Library, 44 Torbay Rd., Box 9548, St. John's, Nfld. A1A 2Y4 – 753-3560 – Mrs. Heddy M. Peddle

Newfoundland & Labrador Hydro Library, Box 9100, Philip Place, St. John's, Nfld. A1A 2X8 – 737-1325 – Mrs. Margaret Miller

Newfoundland Teachers' Association Information Centre, 3 Kenmount Rd., St. John's, Nfld. A1B 1W1 – 726-3223 – Jean Brown

Northwest Atlantic Fisheries Centre Library, Dept. of Fisheries & Oceans, Box 5667, St. John's, Nfld. A1C 5X1 – 737-2022 – Audrey Conroy

Ombudsman Library, 49-55 Elizabeth Ave., St. John's, Nfld. A1C 5T7 – 753-7730, or 737-3704

Provincial Archives of Newfoundland & Labrador, Library, Military Rd., St. John's, Nfld. A1C 2C9 – 753-9380, 90, 98 – David J. Davis, Prov. Archivist

St. Clare's Mercy Hospital, Medical Library, 3rd Floor E., St. Clare Ave., St. John's, Nfld. A1C 5B8 – 778-3414 – Eileen E. Woll

St. Clare's Mercy Hospital, School of Nursing Library, Le Marchant Rd., St. John's, Nfld. A1C 5B8 – 778-3577 – Dora M. Braffet

Seventh-Day Adventist Academy Library, 106 Freshwater Rd., St. John's, Nfld. A1C 2N8 – 579-0968 – Alex Garland

The Telegram Newsp. Library, 275-277 Duckworth St., St. John's, Nfld. A1C 5X7 – 726-2060 – Evelyn Power

Waterford Hospital, Health Services Library, Waterford Bridge Rd., St. John's, Nfld. A1E 4J8 – 368-6061, ext. 269 – Daniel Peyton

NOVA SCOTIA

Regional Public Libraries in Nova Scotia

With Librarian

Area Code for Nova Scotia is 902

Annapolis Valley Regional Library, Box 339, Annapolis Royal, N.S. B0S 1A0 – 532-2260 – Mrs. Vivian Walker

Sub-Headquarters: Bookmobile #2, Box 625, Kentville, N.S. B4N 3X7 – 678-6319 – Morley Wills

Branches within Annapolis Valley

Berwick Library, Main St., Berwick, N.S. B0P 1E0 – 538-9517

Bridgetown Library, Town Hall, Bridgetown, N.S. B0S 1C0 – 665-2758 – Mrs. Robert Ruggles

Hantsport Library, Hantsport High School, Hantsport, N.S. B0P 1P0 – 684-3488 – Mrs. Diane Thompson

Kentville Library, Church St., Kentville, N.S. B4N 2M6 – 678-3650 – Mrs. Kathleen Corbin

Kingston Library, Victoria St., Kingston, N.S. B0P 1R0 – 765-2800 – Mrs. Barbara McLaughlin

Lawrencetown Library, Main St., Lawrencetown, N.S. B0S 1M0 – Mrs. Elsie Whitman

Middleton Library, Town Hall, Middleton, N.S. B0S 1P0 – 825-4835 – Mrs. Sandra Hickey

Port Williams Library, Community Centre, Port Williams, N.S. B0P 1T0 – 542-3005 – Mrs. Edith Woodworth

Windsor Library, Community Centre, Windsor, N.S. B0N 2T0 – 798-2536 – Mrs. Margaret Hamilton

Wolfville Library, Main St., Wolfville, N.S. B0P 1X0 – 542-3037 – Miss Wanda Atwell

Cape Breton Regional Library, 110 Townsend St., Sydney, N.S. B1P 5C9 – Miss M.L. Fraser

Branches within Cape Breton Regional Library

Baddeck Library, Chebucto St., Baddeck, N.S. B0E 1B0 – 295-2055 – Miss Cynthia MacIntyre

Dominion Library, Dominion, N.S. B0A 1E0 – Mrs. Anne Godwin

Donkin Library, Donkin, N.S. B0A 1G0 – Mrs. Diane Reid

Florence Library, Florence, N.S. B0C 1J0 – Mrs. Anne Burton

Glace Bay Library, 36 Union St., Glace Bay, N.S. B1A 2P5 – 849-8657 – Miss Isabel Abernethy

Louisbourg Library, Louisbourg, N.S. B0A 1M0 – Mrs. Marjorie MacDonald

Main-a-Dieu Library, Credit Union Bldg., Main-a-Dieu, N.S. B0A 1N0 – Mrs. Lillian Murray

New Waterford Library, New Waterford, N.S. – 862-2892 – Mrs. Joan Connors

North Sydney Library, North Sydney, N.S. – 794-3897 – Mrs. Daphne Webber

(Reserve Mines) Tompkins Memorial Library, Reserve Mines, N.S. B0A 1V0 – Mrs. John MacIntyre

(Sydney) James McConnell Memorial Library, 190 Bentinck St., Sydney, N.S. B1P 1G8 – 562-3161 – Miss M.L. Fraser

(Sydney Mines) Martha Hollett Memorial Library, Sydney Mines, N.S. – 736-3219 – Mrs. Dorothy Hawboldt

Colchester-East Hants Regional Library, 754 Prince St., Truro, N.S. B2N 1G9 – 895-4183 – Ms. Reay Freve

(Service includes two bookmobiles and three branch libraries at Truro, Stewiacke and Tatamagouche)

Cumberland Regional Library, Confederation Memorial Bldg., Box 220, Amherst, N.S. B3H 3Z2 – Miss Beverly True

Dartmouth Regional Library, 100 Wyse Rd., Dartmouth, N.S. B3A 1M1 – 466-7623 – Aileen Lewis

Branch in Dartmouth

Woodlawn Branch Library, 114 Woodlawn Rd., Dartmouth, N.S. B2W 3X8 – 434-6196

Eastern Counties Regional Library, Murray St., Box 250, Mulgrave, N.S. B0E 2G0 – 747-2598 – Mrs. Kerstin Mueller

Branches in Eastern Counties

Canso Branch Library, Canso, N.S. B0H 1H0 – 366-2955 – Mrs. Sandra Dixon

Drs. Coody & Tompkins Memorial Library, Margaree Forks, N.S. B0E 2A0 – 248-2821 – Mrs. Aurea Gillis

Mulgrave Branch, c/o Regional Headquarters

Port Hawkesbury Branch Library, Strait Area Education Centre, Port Hawkesbury, N.S. B0E 2V0 – 625-2729

Sherbrooke Branch Library, Sherbrooke, N.S. B0J 3C0 – 522-2180 – Mrs. Betty Theriault

Halifax City Library, 5381 Spring Garden Rd., Halifax, N.S. B3J 1E9 – Miss Diane MacQuarrie

(also operating one branch in north Halifax)

Halifax County Regional Library, Box 300, Armdale PO, Halifax, N.S. B3L 4K3 – 477-6265 – Ms. Mary McCullough

Pictou-Antigonish Regional Library, Civic Bldg., Box 276, New Glasgow, N.S. B2H 5E3 – 752-6217 – Ann Green

Branches within Pictou-Antigonish Region

Antigonish Library, Box 1741, Antigonish, N.S. B2G 2M5 – 863-4276 – Grace MacKinnon

New Glasgow Library, Box 276, New Glasgow, N.S. B2H 5E3 – 752-0022 – Mrs. Carol MacMillan

Pictou Library, Box 622, Pictou, N.S. B0K 1H0 – 485-5021 – Mrs. June Grosvold

Stellarton Library, Box 1372, Stellarton, N.S. B0K 1S0 – 755-1638 – Mrs. Gail Meikle

Trenton Library, Box 612, Trenton, N.S. B0K 1X0 – 752-5181 – Mrs. Shelley MacLean

Westville Library, Box 627, Westville, N.S. B0K 2A0 – 396-5022 – Mrs. Sylvia Hale

South Shore Regional Library, Box 34, Bridgewater, N.S. B4W 2W6 – 543-2548 – Gloria Hardy

(Two bookmobiles and three branches at Bridgewater, Lunenburg and Liverpool)

Western Counties Regional Library, 405 Main St., Yarmouth, N.S. B5A 1G3 – 742-2486 – Miss Barbara Kincaid

Special & College Libraries & Resource Centres in Nova Scotia

With Contact Person (Librarian, unless otherwise indicated)

Area Code for Nova Scotia is 902

AMHERST

Maritime Resource Management Service, Information Division Library, Box 310, 16 Station St., Amherst, N.S. B4H 3E3 – 667-7231, ext. 67 – Margaret E. Campbell

ANTIGONISH

Angus L. Macdonald Library, St. Francis Xavier University, Antigonish, N.S. B2G 1C0 – 867-2267 – Rev. Charles Brewer

BEDFORD

Atmospheric Environment Service Library, 1496 Bedford Hwy., Bedford, N.S. B4A 1E5 – 835-9529 – A.D. Gates

CHURCH POINT

Université Sainte-Anne (Bibliothèque), Church Point, N.S. B0W 1M0 – 769-2114 – Gustave Doucet

DARTMOUTH

Bedford Institute of Oceanography Library, Box 1006, Dartmouth, N.S. B2Y 4A2 – 426-3675 – J.E. Sutherland

Canadian Coast Guard, Marine Library, Box 1013, Dartmouth, N.S. B2Y 3Z7 – 426-5182 – G.M. Ritchie

Dartmouth Regional Vocational School Library, 21 Woodlawn Rd., Dartmouth, N.S. B2W 2R7 – 434-2020, ext. 33 – John Vincent

Defence Research Establishment Atlantic Library, (9 Grove St.), Box 1012, Dartmouth, N.S. B2Y 3Z7 – 426-3100, loc. 135 – Mrs. D.I. Collins

Hermes Electronics Ltd. Library, (40 Atlantic St.), Box 1005, Dartmouth, N.S. B2Y 4A1 – 466-7491, loc. 141 – Pamela Harris

Imperial Oil Ltd. Library, Box 1001, Dartmouth, N.S. B2Y 3Z7 – 424-7207 – R.W. Shay
MacLaren-Marex Inc. Library, 1000 Windmill Rd., Dartmouth, N.S. B3B 1L7 – 469-0932, ext. 41 – Ms. Hedy Armour
Nova Scotia Hospital, Health Sciences Library, Drawer 1004, Dartmouth, N.S. B2Y 3Z9 – 469-7500, loc. 710 – Mrs. Marjorie A. Cox
Nova Scotia Research Foundation Corp. Library, Box 790, Dartmouth, N.S. B2Y 3Z7 – 424-8670 – Miss Helen I. Hendry
Transport Canada Marine Safety Library, Box 1013, Dartmouth, N.S. B2Y 3Z7 – 426-5182 – Gaylen Ritchie

HALIFAX

Armbrae Academy Library, 1400 Oxford St., Halifax, N.S. B3H 3Y8 – 423-7920 – Carol F. Salton
Art Gallery of N.S. Library, Box 2262, (6152 Coburg Rd.), Halifax, N.S. B3J 3C8 – Bernard Riordan
Atlantic Institute of Education Library, 5244 South St., Halifax, N.S. B3J 1A4 – 425-5430, ext. 32 – Mrs. Diane Brooks
Atlantic Provinces Economic Council Library, One Sackville Place, Halifax, N.S. B3J 1K1 – 422-6516
Atlantic School of Theology Library, 640 Francklyn St., Halifax, N.S. B3H 3B5 – 423-7986 – Alice W. Harrison
Attorney General's Library, (3rd Floor, Provincial Admin. Bldg., Hollis St.), Box 7, Halifax, N.S. B3J 2L6 – 424-7699 – Ms. Margaret Murphy
Cambridge Military Library, 1565 Queen St., R.A. Park, Halifax, N.S. B3J 2H9 – 426-5142 – M/Cpl. Pyle
Camp Hill Hospital Library, 1763 Robie St., Halifax, N.S. B3H 3G2 – 423-1371, ext. 287 – Verona Hall
Canada Dept. of Justice Library, 12th floor, 1791 Barrington St., Halifax, N.S. B3J 3L1 – 426-3260 – Ms. Payne
Canadian Broadcasting Corp., Music & Record Library, Box 3000, (5600 Sackville St.), Halifax, N.S. B3J 3E9 – 422-8311 – D.S. Leadbeater
Chronicle Herald & Mail Star Newsp. Library, (1650 Argyle St.), Box 610, Halifax, N.S. B3J 2T2 – 426-3080
City of Halifax, Engineering & Works Dept. Library, 3rd Floor, Duke St. Tower, Scotia Sq., Halifax, N.S. B3J 3A5
City of Halifax, Planning Information Office, City Hall Basement, Halifax, N.S. B3J 3A5 – 426-7652 – Donita Boyd, Planning & Info. Officer
City of Halifax, Social Development Division Library, City Hall, 3rd Floor, Halifax, N.S. B3J 3A5 – 426-8716 – Karen Traversy, Admr.
Civil Service Commission Library, Box 943, Halifax, N.S. B3J 2V9 – 424-4132
Cox, Downie & Co. Law Library, Box 2380, Halifax, N.S. B3J 3E4 – 423-6262 – Daniel M. Campbell
Dalhousie University Libraries, c/o University Librarian, Halifax, N.S. B3H 4H8
- University Librarian – Mrs. Dorothy L. Cooke (424-3601)
- Institute of Public Affairs (B3H 3J5) – Mrs. Faustina Chen (424-2526)
- Health Sciences – Ann Nevill (424-2458)
- Law – Christian Wiktor (424-2124)
- Maritime Sch. of Social Work (B3H 3J5) – Mrs. J.O. Hattie (424-3760)

Departments of Government, See Nova Scotia Dept. of ...
Fisheries & Oceans Canada, Maritimes Regional Library, Box 550, Halifax, N.S. B3J 2S7 – 426-3972 – Anna Oxley
Halifax City, See City of Halifax
Halifax Infirmary Library, 1335 Queen St., Halifax, N.S. B3J 2H6 – 428-3058 – Dr. Anitra Laycock
Institute of Public Affairs, See Dalhousie Univ.
Halifax Regional Vocational School Library, 1825 Bell Rd., Halifax, N.S. B3H 2Z4 – 422-8301, ext. 33 – Ms. Joanne Morris
Kitz, Matheson etc. Law Library, Box 247, Halifax, N.S. B3J 2N9 – 429-5050 – Linda Keddy
Legislative Library, See Nova Scotia Legislative
King's College Library, 3rd floor, King's College, Coburg Rd., Halifax, N.S. B3H 2A1 – 422-1271, ext. 29 – Ms. Lane
Maritime Conservatory of Music Library, 5920 Gorsebrook Ave., Halifax, N.S. B3H 1G2 – 423-6995 – Mrs. Sharon Harland
Maritime School of Social Work, See Dalhousie Univ.
Maritime Telegraph & Telephone Co. Ltd., Information Resource Centre, Box 880, Halifax, N.S. B3J 2W3 – 421-4570 – Mrs. Joan Fage, M.L.S.
Mount Saint Vincent University Library, Halifax, N.S. B3M 2J6 – 443-4450, ext. 120 – Lucien Bianchini
National Research Council of Canada Library, 1411 Oxford St., Halifax, N.S. B3H 3Z1 – 426-8250 – A.R. Taylor
Nova Scotia Barristers' Society Library, Law Courts, 1815 Upper Water St., Halifax, N.S. B3J 1S7 – 422-1491 – Linda Keddy
Nova Scotia College of Art & Design Library, 5163 Duke St., Halifax, N.S. B3J 3J6 – 422-7381 – John Murchie
Nova Scotia Commission on Drug Dependency Library, 5668 South St., Halifax, N.S. B3J 1A6 – 424-4270 – Ms. E. Cardoza
Nova Scotia Dept. of Agriculture, See Truro
Nova Scotia Dept. of Attorney General, See Attorney General
Nova Scotia Dept. of Consumer Affairs Library, Box 998, Halifax, N.S. B3J 2X3 – 424-4690
Nova Scotia Dept. of Culture, Recreation & Fitness, Library, (1531 Grafton St.), Box 864, Halifax, N.S. B3J 2V2 – 424-7734 – Ms. Genni Archibald
Nova Scotia Dept. of Development Library, (5151 George St.), Box 519, Halifax, N.S. B3J 2R7 – 424-5807 – Donald Purcell
Nova Scotia Dept. of Education, Education Media Services, 5250 Spring Garden Rd., Halifax, N.S. B3J 1E8 – 424-5445 – Mrs. Audrey McSweeney
Nova Scotia Dept. of Environment Library, (1690 Hollis St.), Box 2107, Halifax, N.S. B3J 3B7 – 424-8600 – Janice Laufer
Nova Scotia Dept. of Finance, Federal-Provincial Taxation & Fiscal Relations Library, Box 187, Halifax, N.S. B3J 2N3 – 424-4160 – Ms. Theresa MacLean
Nova Scotia Dept. of Fisheries Library, 1690 Hollis St., Box 2223, Halifax, N.S. B3J 3C4 – 424-7653 – Ms. Mary Evans
Nova Scotia Dept. of Health Library, Box 488, Halifax, N.S. B3J 2R8 – 424-5411 – Joyce Kublin
Nova Scotia Dept. of Highways Library, Box 188, Halifax, N.S. B3J 2N2 – 424-4036
Nova Scotia Dept. of Labour & Manpower Library, Box 697, Halifax, N.S. B3J 2T8 – 424-4313 – Marie DeYoung
Nova Scotia Dept. of Mines & Energy Library, (2nd Floor, 1690 Hollis St.), Box 1087, Halifax, N.S. B3J 2X1 – 424-8633 – Valerie Brisco
Nova Scotia Dept. of Municipal Affairs Library, Box 216, Halifax, N.S. B3J 2M4 – 424-4094 – Mrs. Audrey Manzer
Nova Scotia Dept. of Social Services Library, (4th Floor, Johnston Bldg.), Box 696, Halifax, N.S. B3J 2T7 – 424-4383 – Jane Phillips
Nova Scotia Dept. of Tourism Library, Box 456, Halifax, N.S. B3J 2R5 – 424-5908 – Ms. Sandra Martinello
Nova Scotia Human Rights Commission Library, Box 2221, Halifax, N.S. B3J 3C4 – 424-4111 – Leslie Sansom
Nova Scotia Institute of Technology Library, (Leeds St.), Box 2210, Halifax, N.S. B3J 3C4 – 424-4224 – Nola D. Brennan
Nova Scotia Legislative Library, Province House, Granville St., Halifax, N.S. B3J 2P8 – 424-5932 – Miss S.B. Elliott
Nova Scotia Museum Library, 1747 Summer St., Halifax, N.S. B3H 3A6 – 429-4610 – Miss Susan Whiteside
Nova Scotia Nautical Institute Library, Box 578, Pier 21, Halifax, N.S. B3J 2S9 – 424-3290 – Ms. F. Campbell
Nova Scotia Power Corp. Library, Box 910, Halifax, N.S. B3J 2W5 – 424-2928 – B.N. MacKenzie
Ombudsman Library, Box 2152, Halifax, N.S. B3J 3B7 – 424-6780 – Miss Muriel Hogan
Parks Canada Atlantic Regional Library, Historic Properties, Upper Water St., Halifax, N.S. B3J 1S9 – 426-7529 – Ms. Pat O'Neill
Public Archives of Nova Scotia Library, 6016 University Ave., Halifax, N.S. B3H 1W4 – 423-9115 – Hugh A. Taylor, Archivist
Public Works Canada Atlantic Regional Library, 1190 Barrington St., Box 2247, Halifax, N.S. B3J 3C9 – 426-7891 – Ms. F.A. Bradley
St. Mary's University Library, Halifax, N.S. B3H 3C3 – 422-7361, ext. 182 – Ronald A. Lewis
Technical University of Nova Scotia Library, Halifax, N.S. B3J 2X4 – 429-8300 – M.R. Hussain

Tourism Industry Association of Nova Scotia Library, 5871 Spring Garden Rd., Halifax, N.S. B3H 1Y2 – 423-4480 – Exec. Dir.
University of King's College Library, Coburg Rd., Halifax, N.S. B3H 2A1 – 422-1271 – Mrs. Mary H. Lane
Victoria General Hospital Library, 1270 Tower Rd., Halifax, N.S. B3H 2Y9 – 428-2429 – Frank Oram

KENTVILLE

Agriculture Canada, Research Station Library, 32 Main St., Kentville, N.S. B4N 1J5 – 678-2171, ext. 213 – Jerry R. Miner

LOUISBOURG

Fortress of Louisbourg National Historic Park, Resource Centre, Louisbourg, N.S. B0A 1M0 – 733-2280 – Mrs. M.E. MacMullin

SYDNEY

Canadian Coast Guard College Library, Box 4500, Sydney, N.S. B1P 6L1 – 539-1631 – D.N. MacSween
Cape Breton Development Corp. Library, Box 1330, Sydney, N.S. B1P 6K3 – 539-6300 – Arlene Canning
College of Cape Breton Library, Box 5300, Sydney, N.S. B1P 6L2 – 539-5300, loc. 358 – Sister Rita Marie MacInnis, C.N.D.
St. Rita Hospital, School of Nursing Library, Churchill Dr., Sydney, N.S. B1S 1B4 – 539-3740, ext. 261 – Mrs. Patricia Keough

TRURO

Nova Scotia Agricultural College Library, Box 550, Truro, N.S. B2N 5E3 – 895-1571 – B. Sodhi
Nova Scotia Dept. of Agriculture & Marketing – is located in the Nova Scotia Agricultural College
Nova Scotia Teachers' College Library, Truro, N.S. B2N 5G5 – 895-5347, ext. 230 – Dr. D.L. Burt
Patterson, Smith & Co. Law Library, (10 Church St.), Box 1068, Truro, N.S. B2N 5B9 – 895-1631 – Mrs. Brenda Anderson

WINDSOR JUNCTION

Nova Scotia Dept. of Highways, Materials Laboratory Library, Site #37, R.R. 1, Windsor Junction, N.S. B0N 2V0 – 861-1911, ext. 56

WOLFVILLE

Harold Campbell Vaughan Memorial Library, Acadia University, Wolfville, N.S. B0P 1X0 – 542-2201, loc. 215 – Isobel Horton

ONTARIO

Regional Library Systems in Ontario

With Director

Algonquin Regional Library System, 29 Mary St., Parry Sound, Ont. P2A 1E3 – 705/746-9161 – R.A. Smith
Central Ontario Regional Library System, 129 Church St. S., Richmond Hill, Ont. L4C 1W4 – 416/884-4395 – Dorothy Templin
Eastern Ontario Regional Library System, 200 Cooper St., #6, Ottawa, Ont. K2P 0G1 – 613/238-8457 – Larry Eshelman
Georgian Bay Regional Library System, 30 Morrow Rd., Barrie, Ont. L4N 3V8 – 705/726-8251 – R.J. Mackenzie
Lake Erie Regional Library System, 380 Saskatoon St., London, Ont. N5W 4R3 – 519/453-9100 – D.D. Sudar
Lake Ontario Regional Library System, 88 Wright Cres., Kingston, Ont. K7L 4T9 – 613/546-9400 – B.J. Robinson
Metropolitan Toronto Regional Library System, 789 Yonge St., Toronto, Ont. M4W 2G8 – 416/928-5050 – M. Allen (act.)
Midwestern Regional Library System, 637 Victoria St. N., Kitchener, Ont. N2H 5G4 – 519/576-5061 – Clint Lawson
Niagara Regional Library System, Box 490, St. Catharines, Ont. L2R 6W3 – 416/684-7411 – J.F. Bird, Chairman
North Central Regional Library System, 334 Regent St. S., Sudbury, Ont. P3C 4E2 – 705/675-6467 – R.C. Jones
Northeastern Regional Library System, 6 Al Wende Ave., Kirkland Lake, Ont. P2N 3G9 – 705/567-7043 – Brian Cahill
Northwestern Regional Library System, 910 Victoria Ave., Thunder Bay, Ont. P7C 1B4 – 807/623-2794 – A.G. Pepper
South Central Regional Library System, 220 Dundurn St. S., Hamilton, Ont. L8P 4K7 – 416/525-2610 – Mrs. M. Allwood
Southwestern Regional Library System, 660 Ouellette Ave., Windsor, Ont. N9A 1B9 – 519/258-2533 – Howard Ford

Municipal Public Libraries in Ontario

Listed alphabetically by name of library. Cross references have been inserted in major cities. Toronto cross-references include the suburbs.

Acton Library, 17 River St., Acton, Ont. L7J 1C2 – 519/853-0301 (a branch of the Halton Hills Library)
Addison Library, Addison, Ont. K0E 1A0
Agincourt Library, 3850 Sheppard Ave. E., Agincourt, Ont. M1T 3L4 – 416/293-7811
Ailsa Craig Branch, c/o Middlesex County Library
Airy Twp. Library, Box 208, Whitney, Ont. K0J 2M0 – 705/637-5471 – Mrs. T. Kuiack
Ajax Public Library, 65 Harwood Ave. S., Ajax, Ont. L1S 2H8 – 416/683-6911 – Mrs. J. Tate
Ajax, see also Village Library
Albany Band Library, Kashechewan, Ont. P0L 1S0 – Silas Wesley, Chief
Albert Campbell Dist. Library, 496 Birchmount Rd., Scarborough, Ont. M1K 1N8 – 416/698-1194
Albion-Bolton Library, 43 Ellwood Dr. W., Bolton, Ont. L0P 1A0 – 416/857-1400
Albion Library, 1515 Albion Rd., Rexdale, Ont. M9V 1B2 – 416/741-7734
Aldershot Branch, c/o Burlington Library
Alderwood Library, 525 Horner Ave., Toronto, Ont. M8W 2B9 – 416/251-5921
Alexandria, see Stormont, Dundas & Glengarry
Alfred Library, Box 329, Alfred, Ont. K0B 1A0 – 613/679-4404 – S. Bourque
Alfred Twp. Library, c/o Box 59, Lefaivre, Ont. K0B 1J0 – 613/679-4470 – Sister M. Chartrand
Allenford Branch, c/o Bruce County Library
Alliston Library, Box 1199, Victoria St. E., Alliston, Ont. L0M 1A0 – 705/435-5651 – Mrs. J. Owens
Almonte Library, Box 820, Almonte, Ont. K0A 1A0 – 613/256-1037 – Ms. K. Lohse
Alta Vista Library, 2516 Alta Vista Dr., Ottawa, Ont. K1V 7T1 – 613/236-0301
Alton Branch, c/o Caledon Library
Alvinston Branch, c/o Lambton County Library
Ambassador Library, 1564 Huron Church Rd., Windsor, Ont. N9C 2L1 – 519/253-7340
Ameliasburgh Twp. Library, Ameliasburgh, Ont. K0K 1A0 – J. Plamondon
Amesbury Park Library, 1565 Lawrence Ave. W., Toronto, Ont. M6L 1C3 – 416/244-6614
Amherstburg Branch, c/o Essex County Library
Amherstview Branch, c/o Lennox & Addington County Library
Ancaster Library, 300 Wilson St. E., Ancaster, Ont. L9G 2B9 – 416/648-6911 (a branch of the Wentworth County Library)
Annette Library, 145 Annette St., Toronto, Ont. M6P 1P3 – 416/769-5846
Arden Branch, c/o Kingston Twp. Centre 70 Library
Argyle Branch Library, 1925 Dundas St. E., London, Ont. N5V 1P7 – 519/451-7600
Arkona Branch, c/o Lambton County Library
Armstrong Twp. Library, C.P. 449, Earlton, Ont. P0J 1E0 – 705/563-2717
Arnprior Library, 35 Madawaska St., Arnprior, Ont. K7S 1R6 – 613/623-2279 – J. Barker
Arthur Branch, c/o Wellington County Library
Arthur Street Library, 285 Arthur St., Thunder Bay, Ont. P7B 1A9 – 807/344-3585
Arva Branch, c/o Middlesex County Library
Assiginack Public Library, Manitouwaning, Ont. P0P 1N0 – 705/859-3196
Athens Library, Box 309, Athens, Ont. K0E 1B0 – 613/924-2048 – Ms. M. Earl

Atikokan Library, Civic Centre, Atikokan, Ont. P0T 1C0 – 807/597-4406 – Eileen A. Nayda
Attawapiskat Band Library, c/o Emile Nokogee, Chief, via Moosonee
Atwood Branch, c/o Elma Twp. Library
Auburn Branch, c/o Huron County Library
Augusta Twp. Library, R.R. 2, Brockville, Ont. K6V 5T2 – 613/926-2449 – Mrs. D. Maloney
Aurora Library, 56 Victoria St., Aurora, Ont. L4G 1R2 – 416/727-9493 – P. McKee
Avon Branch, c/o Middlesex County Library
Avonmore, see Stormont, Dundas & Glengarry
Ayamichigay-Wegumick Band Library, Sandy Lake, via Favourable Lake, Ont. P0V 1V0
Aylmer Library, 62 Centre St., Aylmer, Ont. N5H 2G7 – 519/773-2439 (a branch of the Elgin County Library)
Ayr Branch, c/o Waterloo Regional Library
Azilda Library, Box 818, Azilda, Ont. P0M 1B0 – 705/983-2650
Baden Branch, c/o Waterloo Regional Library
Bailieboro Branch, c/o Cavan, Millbrook etc. Library
Balmertown Library, Box 58, Balmertown, Ont. P0V 1C0 – 807/735-2110 – Ms. A. Johnson
Bancroft Library, 14 Flint St., Box 127, Bancroft, Ont. K0L 1C0 – 613/332-3380 – Mrs. Sheila Hillen
Bangor, Wicklow & McClure Twp. Library, Municipal Bldg., Maynooth, Ont. K0L 2S0 – 613/338-2262 – Mrs. D. Millsum
Barrie Library, 37 Mulcaster St., Barrie, Ont. L4M 3M2 – 705/728-1010 – Mrs. S. Maley
Barriefield Branch, c/o Kingston Twp. Centre 70 Library
Barry's Bay Library, Box 970, Opeongo Line, Barry's Bay, Ont. K0J 1B0 – 613/756-2000 – Mrs. A. Lorbetskie
Barton Library, 571 Barton St. E., Hamilton, Ont. L8L 2Z4 – 416/527-8122
Base Borden Library, Box 430, CFB Borden, Ont. L0M 1C0 – 705/424-1200, loc. 2273
Batchewana Indian Band Library, Rankin Reserve 15D, #4, Sault Ste. Marie, Ont. P6A 5K9
Bath Branch, c/o Lennox & Addington County Library
Bathurst Heights Library, 3170 Bathurst St., Toronto, Ont. M6A 2A9 – 416/783-4283
Bayfield Branch, c/o Huron County Library
Bayham Twp. Branch, c/o Elgin County Library
Baysville Branch, c/o Lake of Bays Twp. Library
Bayview Village Library, 2901 Bayview Ave., Willowdale, Ont. M2K 1E6 – 416/223-6289
Beachburg Library, Main St., Beachburg, Ont. K0J 1C0 – 613/582-3556 – Mrs. H. Johnson
Beaches Library, 2161 Queen St. E., Toronto, Ont. M4M 1E4 – 416/691-9298
Beachville Branch, c/o Oxford County Library
Beamsville Branch, c/o Lincoln Library
Bear Island Library, Bear Island PO, Temagami, Ont. P0H 1C0 – 705/569-3743 – Mrs. J. Mattias
Beardmore Library, Box 9, Beardmore, Ont. P0T 1G0 – 807/875-2075
Beausoleil Band Library, Christian Island Elem. School, Christian Island, Cedar Point PO, Ont. L0K 1C0
Beaver Lake Service Point, c/o Walden Library
Beaverton Library, Box 89, Simcoe St., Beaverton, Ont. L0K 1A0 – 705/426-9283
Beechwood Branch, c/o Middlesex County Library
Beeton Library, Box 305, Beeton, Ont. L0G 1A0 – 416/729-3726 – Mrs. F. St. Peters
Belfountain Branch, c/o Caledon Library
Belgrave Branch, c/o Huron County Library
Belle River High School and Public Library, 333 South St., Belle River, Ont. N0R 1A0 – 519/728-1212
Belle River Library, Box 459, Belle River, Ont. N0R 1A0 – 519/728-2324 – Mrs. R. Ouellette
Belleville Library, 223 Pinnacle St., Belleville, Ont. K8N 3A7 – 613/968-6731 – D. Weismiller
Belleville, see also Wallbridge Rd.
Belmont & Methuen Twp. Library, Nephton, Ont. K0L 2T0 – Mrs. S. Mycroft
Belmont Branch, c/o Elgin County Library
Belmore Branch, c/o Huron County Library
Bendale Library, 1515 Danforth Rd., Scarborough, Ont. M1J 1H5 – 416/431-9141
Bériault Branch, c/o Gloucester Public Library
Bertie Library, 3717 Elm St., Ridgeway, Ont. L0S 1N0 – 416/894-1281
Big Grassy Band Library, Morson, Ont. P0W 1J0
Billings & East Allan Twp. Library, Kagawong, Ont. P0P 1J0 – 705/282-2611
Binbrook Branch, c/o Wentworth Library
Black Creek Library, 2141 Jane St., Downsview, Ont. M3M 1A2 – 416/244-9998
Black River-Matheson Public Library, 2nd St., Box 450, Matheson, Ont. P0K 1N0 – 705/273-2760
Blackburn Hamlet Branch, c/o Gloucester Public Library
Blenheim Branch, c/o Kent County Library
Blind River Library, Box 880, Blind River, Ont. P0R 1B0 – 705/356-7616 – Mrs. M. Sarazin
Bloomfield-Hallowell Union Library, Box 9, 36 Main St., Bloomfield, Ont. K0K 1G0 – 613/393-3900 – Ms. M. Sly
Bloomingdale Branch, c/o Waterloo Regional Library
Bloor & Gladstone Library, 1101 Bloor St. W., Toronto, Ont. M6H 1M7 – 416/536-3402
Bluevale Branch, c/o Huron County Library
Blyth Branch, c/o Huron County Library
Bobcaygeon Branch, c/o Victoria County Library
Bolton, see Albion-Bolton
Bond Head Library, Bond Head, Ont. L0G 1B0
Bonfield Library, 514 Yonge St., Bonfield, Ont. P0H 1E0 – 705/776-2641 – Mrs. Armelle Kingsbury
Bothwell Branch, c/o Kent County Library
Bourget Library, C.P. 311, Bourget, Ont. K0A 1E0 – 613/487-2377
Bowmanville Library, 62 Temperance St., Bowmanville, Ont. L1C 3A8 – 416/623-7322
Boys & Girls Library, 10 King St. W., Dundas, Ont. L9H 1T7 – 416/627-4721
Boys & Girls House Library, 40 St. George St., Toronto, Ont. M5S 2E4 – 416/593-5162 – Margaret C. Maloney
Bracebridge Library, 94 Manitoba St., Box 1537, Bracebridge, Ont. P0B 1C0 – 705/645-4171 – Ms. E. Smith
Bradford Library, Box 130, 35 John St. W., Bradford, Ont. L0G 1C0 – 416/775-6482 – Ms. A. Price
Brampton Public Library, (4 Corners Branch), 65 Queen St. E., Brampton, Ont. L6W 3L6 – 416/453-2444 – Ms. Marilyn Read
Brampton, see also Chinguacousy
Brantford Library, 73 George St., Brantford, Ont. N3T 2Y3 – 519/756-2220
Brantford, see also St. Paul Ave.
Brentwood Library, 36 Brentwood Rd. N., Toronto, Ont. M8X 2B5 – 416/233-2105
Bridlewood Library, 2900 Warden Ave., Scarborough, Ont. M1W 2S8 – 416/499-4284
Brigden Branch, c/o Lambton County Library
Brighton Library, Box 129, Brighton, Ont. K0K 1H0 – 613/475-2511 – Mrs. I. Carter
Brights Grove Branch, c/o Lambton County Library
Brinston, see Stormont, Dundas & Glengarry
Brock Twp. Library, Box 208, Church St., Sunderland, Ont. L0C 1H0 – 705/357-3109
Brockville Library, Box 100, Brockville, Ont. K6V 5T7 – 613/342-3936
Brodie Street Library, 216 S. Brodie St., Thunder Bay, Ont. P7E 1C2 – 807/622-6446
Bromley-St. Michael's Library, Box 130, Douglas, Ont. K0J 1S0
Brookbanks Library, 210 Brookbanks Dr., Don Mills, Ont. M3A 2T8 – 416/445-0822
Brooklin Library, Vipond Rd., Brooklin, Ont. L0B 1C0 – 416/655-3191
Broughdale Branch Library, 247 Epworth Ave., London, Ont. N6A 2M2
Brownsville Branch, c/o Oxford County Library
Bruce County Library, Box 16000, 662 Gustavus St., Port Elgin, Ont. N0H 2C0 – 519/832-2181 – Mrs. J. Johnston

Bruce Mines & Plummer Union Library, Box 162, Bruce Mines, Ont. P0R 1C0 – 705/785-3370 – Mrs. M. Walker
Brucefield Branch, c/o Huron County Library
Brussels Branch, c/o Huron County Library
Burford Twp. Library, 1 King St. W., Burford, Ont. N0E 1A0 – 519/449-5371 – Mrs. R. Massicotte
Burgessville Branch, c/o Oxford County Library
Burks Falls, Armour & Ryerson Union Library, 106 Yonge St., Box 190, Burk's Falls, Ont. P0A 1C0 – 705/382-3327 – Mrs. K. Purdie
Burleigh-Anstruther Union Library, Apsley, Ont. K0K 1A0 – Mrs. E.M. Reddick
Burlington Library, 2331 New St., Burlington, Ont. L7R 1J4 – 416/639-3611
Burlington, see also New Appleby
see also Tyandaga
Burnhamthorpe Library, 1350 Burnhamthorpe Rd. E., Mississauga, Ont. L4Y 3V9 – 416/625-4314
Burnt River Branch, c/o Victoria County Library
Burritt's Rapids Branch, c/o Oxford-on-Rideau Twp. Library
Byron Branch Library, 1295 Commissioners Rd. W., London, Ont. N6K 1C9 – 519/471-4000
Cache Bay Library, Box 54, Cache Bay, Ont. P0H 1G0 – 705/753-3305 – Mrs. Y. Bonenfant
Caistorville Branch, c/o West Lincoln Twp. Library
Caldwell Twp. Library, Box 59, Verner, Ont. P0H 2M0 – 705/594-2800 – Mme A. Charlebois
Caledon Library, Box 788, 43 Ellwood Dr. W., Bolton, Ont. L0P 1A0 – 416/857-1400
Caledon East Library, Municipal Complex, Caledon East, Ont. L0N 1E0 – 416/584-2273 (a branch of the Caledon Library)
Caledon Village Branch, c/o Caledon Library
Caledonia Library, see Haldimand Library
Calvin Park Library, 88 Wright Cres., Kingston, Ont. K7L 4T9 – 613/546-2582
Cambray Branch, c/o Victoria County Library
Cambridge Library, 20 Grand Ave. N., Cambridge, Ont. N1S 2K6 – 519/621-0460
Cambridge, see also Hespeler and Preston
Cambridge-St. Albert Library, Box 99, St. Albert, Ont. K0A 3C0 – 613/987-2143
Cambridge Twp. Library, Limoges, Ont. K0A 2M0
Camden East Branch, c/o Lennox & Addington County Library
Cameron Branch, c/o Victoria County Library
Camlachie Branch, c/o Lambton County Library
Campbellford Branch, c/o Northumberland Union Library
Cannington Branch, c/o Brock Twp. Library
Capreol Library, Box 520, Morin St., Capreol, Ont. P0M 1H0 – 705/858-1622 – V. Wood
Carden Branch, c/o Victoria County Library
Cardiff Branch, c/o Haliburton County Library
Cardinal Library, Box 182, Victoria St., Cardinal, Ont. K0E 1E0 – Mrs. M. Kennedy
Cargill Branch, c/o Bruce County Library
Carleton Place Library, 101 Beckwith St., Carleton Place, Ont. K7C 2T3 – 613/257-2702 – Mrs. B. Walsh
Carlingwood Library, 281 Woodroffe Ave., Ottawa, Ont. K2A 3W4 – 613/236-0301
Carlisle Branch, c/o Wentworth Library
Carnarvon Twp. Library, Mindemoya, Ont. P0P 1S0
Carson Branch Library, 465 Quebec St., London, Ont. N5W 3Y3 – 519/438-4287
Casimir, Jennings & Appleby Twp. Library, Box 66, St. Charles, Ont. P0M 2W0 – 705/867-2888 – Mrs. L. Lafontaine
Casselman Library, C.P. 340, Casselman, Ont. K0A 1M0 – 613/764-5505 – Mrs. T. Chenier
Cavan, Millbrook Union Library, Box 40, Millbrook, Ont. L0H 1G0 – 705/932-2872 – Mrs. K. Packman
Cayuga Branch, c/o Haldimand Library
Cedarbrae Dist. Library, 545 Markham Rd., Scarborough, Ont. M1H 2A1 – 416/431-2222
Centennial Library, 578 Finch Ave. W., Willowdale, Ont. M2R 1N7 – 416/665-2931
Centennial Library, 3870 Richmond Rd., Nepean, Ont. K2H 5C4 – 613/828-5142
Central Library, 5126 Yonge St., Willowdale, Ont. M2N 5N9 – 416/225-8891
Centralia Branch, c/o Huron County Library
Centre Wellington Branch, c/o Wellington County Library
Centreton Branch, c/o Northumberland Union Library
Chalk River Library, Box 160, Chalk River, Ont. K0J 1J0 – 613/589-2966
Chapleau Twp. Library, Box 910, Chapleau, Ont. P0M 1K0 – 705/864-0852 – Mrs. E. Morin
Charles Connor Memorial Library, King Side Rd. at Yonge, Oak Ridges, Ont. L0G 1P0 – 416/773-5533
Charles M. Shields Library, Box 400, 99 Bloor Ave., South Porcupine, Ont. P0N 1H0 – 705/235-4974
Charles R. Sanderson Library, 327 Bathurst St., Toronto, Ont. M5T 1J1 – 416/366-4664
Chatham Library, 120 Queen St., Chatham, Ont. N7M 2G6 – 519/354-2940 – Miss L. Brown
Chesley Branch, c/o Bruce County Library
Chesterville, see Stormont, Dundas & Glengarry
Children's Branch, c/o London Library
Chinguacousy Branch Library, 150 Central Park Dr., Bramalea, Ont. L6T 1B4 – 416/793-4636
Chippawa Library, 3763 Main St., Niagara Falls, Ont. L2G 6B3 – 416/295-3541
Christian Island Library, Cedar Point PO, Christian Island, Ont. L0K 1C0
City Hall Public Library, Nathan Phillips Sq., Toronto, Ont. M5H 2N3 – 416/366-6330
Claremont Library, Claremont, Ont. L0H 1E0 – 416/649-3341
Clarence Creek Library, Clarence Creek, Ont. K0A 1N0
Clarke Library, Centre & Church Sts., Orono, Ont. L0B 1M0 – 416/983-5507
Clarkson-Lorne Park Library, 1474 Truscott Dr., Mississauga, Ont. L5J 1Z2 – 416/822-1241
Cliffcrest Library, 2977 Kingston Rd., Scarborough, Ont. M1M 1P1 – 416/266-5697
Clifford Branch, c/o Wellington County Library
Clinton Branch, c/o Huron County Branch
Cloyne Branch, c/o Kingston Twp. Centre 70 Library
Cobalt Library, 32 Lang St., Box 135, Cobalt, Ont. P0J 1C0 – 705/679-8120 – Mrs. B. Eno
Cobden Library, Box 40, Cobden, Ont. K0J 1K0 – 613/646-2385 – Ms. B. Wallace
Coboconk Branch, c/o Victoria County Library
Cobourg Library, 18 Chapel St., Cobourg, Ont. K9A 1H9 – 416/372-9271 – Ms. V. Scott
Cochrane Library, 143 3rd St., Box 700, Cochrane, Ont. P0L 1C0 – 705/272-4178
Codrington Branch, c/o Northumberland Union Library
Colborne Library, Box 190, Colborne, Ont. K0K 1S0 – 416/355-3430 – Mrs. Ann Hill
Coldstream Branch, c/o Middlesex County Library
Coldwater Library, Box 278, Main St., Coldwater, Ont. L0K 1E0 – 705/686-3601 – Mrs. M. Beach
Collingwood Library, 100 2nd St., Collingwood, Ont. L9Y 1E5 – 705/445-1571 – Mrs. M.E. Sandell
Collingwood Twp. Library, Marsh St., Clarksburg, Ont. N0H 1J0 – 519/590-3574 – Mrs. P. Brown
Comber Branch, c/o Essex County Library
Concession Library, 565 Concession St., Hamilton, Ont. L8V 1A8 – 416/383-2322
Concord Branch, c/o Vaughan Public Libraries (Concord: 416/669-2528)
Coniston Library, Box 230, 30 2nd Ave., Coniston, Ont. P0M 1M0 – 705/694-5511
Conmee Twp. Library, R.R. 1, Kakabeka Falls, Ont. P0T 1W0 – 807/577-9392 – Mrs. F.M. Pajamaki, Clerk
Constance Lake Band Library, Constance Lake Reserve, Calstock, Ont. P0L 1B0
Cookstown Library, Municipal Bldg., Queen St., Cookstown, Ont. L0L 1L0 – Mrs. D. Crawford
Copper Cliff Centennial Library, 11 Balsam St., Copper Cliff, Ont. P0M 1N0 – 705/673-1155, ext. 45
Cornwall Library, Box 939, Cornwall, Ont. K6H 5V1 – 613/932-4796

Corunna Branch, c/o Lambton County Library
Cosby, Mason & Martland Twp. Library, Box 30, Noelville, Ont. P0M 2N0 – 705/898-2965 – Ms. C. Prevost
Cottam Branch, c/o Essex County Library
Couchiching Band Library, Box 723, Fort Frances, Ont. P9A 3N1 – 807/274-9607
Courtright Branch, c/o Lambton County Library
Cramahe Twp. Library, Town Hall, Percy St., Castleton, Ont. K0K 1M0 – 416/344-7612 – Mrs. S. Palmer
Cranbrook Branch, c/o Huron County Library
Creemore Library, 179 Mill St., Creemore, Ont. L0M 1G0 – 705/466-3011 – Mrs. E. Wines
Crediton Branch, c/o Huron County Library
Crysler, see Stormont, Dundas & Glengarry
Crystal Beach Library, Box 370, 56 Belfast St., Crystal Beach, Ont. L0S 1B0 – 416/894-1783
Cumberland Twp. Library, Box 15, R.R. 3, Navan, Ont. K0A 2S0 – 613/835-2526 – Ms. P. Cocker
Curran Library, Curran, Ont. K0B 1C0
Curve Lake Indian Band Library, Curve Lake, Ont. K0L 1R0 – 705/657-3217
Dalkeith, see Stormont, Dundas & Glengarry
Dalton Twp. Branch, c/o Victoria County Library
Dashwood Branch, c/o Huron County Library
Dawes Rd. Library, 416 Dawes Rd., Toronto, Ont. M4B 2E8 – 416/757-8649
De La Fosse Library, 729 Park St. S., Peterborough, Ont. K9J 3T3 – 705/745-8653
Deep River Library, Box 278, Deep River, Ont. K0J 1P0 – 613/584-4244 – Mrs. I.M. Cox
Deer Lake Band Library, via Favourable Lake PO, Sandy Lake, Ont. P0V 1V0
Deer Park Library, 40 St. Clair Ave. E., Toronto, Ont. M4T 1M9 – 416/921-3177
Delaware Branch, c/o Middlesex County Library
Delhi Twp. Library, 192 Main St., Delhi, Ont. N4B 2M2 – 519/582-1791 – Mrs. K. Harrison
Deloro Branch, c/o Marmora & Deloro Union Library
Delta Branch, c/o South Crosby Union Library
Deseronto Library, Box 302, Main St., Deseronto, Ont. K0K 1X0 – 613/396-2744
Dokis Reserve Library, Monetville PO, Monetville, Ont. P0M 2K0
Don Mills Library, 888 Lawrence Ave. E., Don Mills, Ont. M3C 1P6 – 416/449-3711
Dorchester Branch, c/o Middlesex County Library
Dorion Public Library, R.R. 1, Community Centre, Dorion, Ont. P0T 1K0 – 807/857-2318
Dorset Branch, c/o Haliburton County Library
Dowling Branch, c/o Onaping Falls Library
Downeyville Branch, c/o Victoria County Library
Downsview Library, 2793 Keele St., Downsview, Ont. M3M 2G3 – 416/636-4510
Drayton Library, Box 130, Drayton, Ont. N0G 1P0 – Mrs. J. Robertson
Dresden Branch, c/o Kent County Library
Drumbo Branch, c/o Oxford County Library
Drummond Library, 5929 Main St., Niagara Falls, Ont. L2G 5Z7 – 416/354-2633
Dryden Library, 36 Van Horne Ave., Dryden, Ont. P8N 2A7 – 807/223-4314
Dubreuilville Library, Dubreuilville, Ont. P0S 1B0 – 705/884-2284
Dufferin-St. Clair Library, 1625 Dufferin St., Toronto, Ont. M6H 3L9 – 416/652-1460
Dundalk Library, Box 190, Main St., Dundalk, Ont. N0C 1B0 – 519/923-3248 – Mrs. D. Black
Dundas Library, 18 Ogilvie St., Dundas, Ont. L9H 2S2 – 416/627-3507 – Mrs. D. Bryden
Dundas, see also Boys & Girls
Dungannon Branch, c/o Huron County Library
Dungannon, Mayo Union Library, Hermon Public School, R.R. 4, Bancroft, Ont. K0L 1C0 – 613/332-2897 – Mrs. N. Vandusen
Dunnville Library, 106 Main St. W., Dunnville, Ont. N1A 1W1 – 416/774-4240
Dunsford Branch, c/o Victoria County Library
Durham Library, Box 706, Durham, Ont. N0G 1R0 – 519/369-2107 – Mrs. D.M. Smith
Dutton Branch, c/o Elgin County Library
Dwight, see Irwin Memorial Library
Eagle Lake Band Library, Eagle Lake, Ont. P0V 1S0 – 807/223-5526
Ear Falls Twp. Library, Box 369, Ear Falls, Ont. P0V 1T0 – 807/222-3209
East Branch, see Belleville
East Branch, see Cornwall
East Branch Library, Churchill Plaza, Sault Ste. Marie, Ont. P6A 5L1 – 705/949-2553
East Gwillimbury Library, Box 370, 8 Bradford St., Holland Landing, Ont. L0G 1H0 – 416/895-1782 – Mrs. Karen Bruce
East Oxford Branch, c/o Oxford County Library
East York Library, 2 Thorncliffe Park Dr., Unit 34, Toronto, Ont. M4H 1H2 – 416/423-6218
Eastman Resource Centre, Box 99, Kars, Ont. K0A 2E0
Eatonville Library, 430 Burnhamthorpe Rd., Islington, Ont. M9B 2B1 – 416/622-2840
Edward D. Jones Branch, c/o Gloucester Public Library
Edwardsburg Twp. Library, Box 28, Spencerville, Ont. K0E 1X0 – 613/658-5575 – Mrs. E.E. Smith
Eganville Library, Box 39, Eganville, Ont. K0J 1T0 – 613/628-2400
Eglinton Square Library, 50 Eglinton Sq., Scarborough, Ont. M1L 2K1 – 416/755-3986
Eilber & Devitt Twps. Union Library, Box 129, Mattice, Ont. P0L 1T0 André Sauchon, Clerk
Eldon Twp. Branch, c/o Victoria County Library
Elgin Branch, c/o South Crosby Union Library
Elgin County Library, 153 Curtis St., St. Thomas, Ont. N5P 3Z7 – 519/633-0815
Elk Lake Library, Pine St., Elk Lake, Ont. P0J 1G0 – 705/678-2340
Elliot Lake Library, 1 Mary Walk, Elliot Lake, Ont. P5A 1Z9 – 705/848-7454 – B. Fazekas
Elma Twp. Library, Atwood, Ont. N0G 1B0 – 519/356-2865 – Mrs. Alma Leslie
Elmira Branch, c/o Waterloo Regional Library
Elmvale Acres Library, 1910 St. Laurent Blvd., Ottawa, Ont. K1G 1A4 – 613/236-0301
Elmwood Branch, c/o Bruce County Library
Elora Library, Elora, Ont. N0B 1S0 – Mrs. C. Broome
Embro Branch, c/o Oxford County Library
Embrun Branch, c/o Russell Twp. Library
Emeryville Branch, c/o Essex County Library
Emo Twp. Library, Mill St., Box 334, Emo, Ont. P0W 1E0 – 807/482-2575
Englehart Library, Third St., Box 809, Englehart, Ont. P0J 1H0 – 705/544-2100 – Ms. J. King
Ennismore Twp. Library, Ennismore, Ont. K0L 1T0 – 705/292-9892
Enterprise Branch, c/o Lennox & Addington County Library
Erin Branch, c/o Wellington County Library
Erin Twp. Library, Box 129, 115 Main St., Hillsburgh, Ont. N0B 1Z0 – 519/855-4010 – Ms. A. Higginbottom
Espanola Public Library, Box 1187, Espanola, Ont. P0P 1C0 – 705/869-2940 – Mrs. A. Wagner
Essa Twp. Library, Box 580, Angus, Ont. L0M 1B0 – 705/424-6531
Essex Branch, c/o Essex County Library
Essex County Library, 360 Fairview Ave. W., Essex, Ont. N8M 1Y3 – 519/776-5241 – E.R. George
Ethel Branch, c/o Huron County Library
Etobicoke Library, Box 501, Etobicoke, Ont. M9C 5G1 – 416/248-5681
Euphrasia Twp. Library, Kimberley, Ont. N0C 1G0 – Mrs. E. Brooks
Evelyn Gregory Library, 120 Trowell St., Toronto, Ont. M6M 1L7 – 416/653-6185
Exeter Branch, c/o Huron County Library
Fairview Library,
see North York

Falconbridge Library, Box 480, 63 Edison St., Falconbridge, Ont. P0M 1S0 – 705/693-2423
Fauquier Library, Centre Communautaire, Fauquier, Ont. P0L 1G0 – 705/339-4511
Fenelon Falls Branch, c/o Victoria County Library
Fergus Library, 190 St. Andrew St. W., Fergus, Ont. N1M 1N5 – 519/843-1180 – Mrs. D. Mackenzie
Field Twp. Library, 110 Morin St., Field, Ont. P0H 1M0 – Mme T. Lafond
Finch, see Stormont, Dundas & Glengarry
Flemingdon Park Library, 747 Don Mills Rd., Don Mills, Ont. M3C 1T2 – 416/424-4108
Flesherton Library, 10 Eliza St., Flesherton, Ont. N0C 1E0 – 519/924-2241
Florence Branch, c/o Lambton County Library
Flos-Elmvale Library, Box 256, Queen St., Elmvale, Ont. L0L 1P0 – 705/322-1482 – Mrs. L.J. Lyons
Foldens Branch, c/o Oxford County Library
Fordwich Branch, c/o Huron County Library
Forest Branch, c/o Lambton County Library
Forest Heights Library, 251 Fischer Dr., Kitchener, Ont. N2M 4X8 – 519/743-0271
Forest Hill Library, 700 Eglinton Ave. W., Toronto, Ont. M5N 1C3 – 416/787-0179
Fort Erie Library, 136 Gilmore Rd., Fort Erie, Ont. L2A 2M1 – 416/871-2546 – Ms. N. Harsanyi
Fort Frances Library, 363 Church St., Fort Frances, Ont. P9A 1C9 – 807/274-9879 – Mrs. M. Sedgwick
Fort William Indian Band Library, Box 786, Stn. STB, Thunder Bay, Ont. P7C 3Y0 – 807/623-9543
Frankford Library, Box 550, 12 Trent St. N., Frankford, Ont. K0K 2C0 – 613/398-7572 – Mrs. J. Turner
Freelton Branch, c/o Wentworth Library
Front of Escott Twp. Library, R.R. 2, Mallorytown, Ont. K0E 1R0 – 613/659-3800 – Ms. R. Phillips
Front of Leeds & Lansdowne Twp. Library, Box 5, Lansdowne, Ont. K0E 1L0 – 613/659-2216 – Mrs. K. Lackie
Front of Yonge Twp. Library, Mallorytown, Ont. K0E 1R0 – 613/923-5032 – Mrs. J. Koerber
Frontenac County Library, see Kingston Twp. Centre 70 Library
Gallanough Memorial Library, 1 Brooke St., Thornhill, Ont. L4J 2K7 – 416/881-2828 (a branch of the Vaughan Public Libraries)
Gananoque Library, 100 Park St., Gananoque, Ont. K7G 2Y5 – 613/382-2436 – J. Love
Garden Hill Branch, c/o Northumberland Union Library
Garden River Band Library, Site 5, Box 7, R.R. 4, Sault Ste. Marie, Ont. P6A 5K9 – 705/248-2333
Garson Library, 214 Orell St., Garson, Ont. P0M 1V0 – 705/693-2729
George H. Locke Library, 3083 Yonge St., Toronto, Ont. M4N 2K7 – 416/483-8578
Georgetown, see Halton Hills
Georgian Bay Twp. Library, Box 119, Mactier, Ont. P0C 1H0 – 705/375-5430 – Mrs. M. Keall
Georgina Public Library, 200 Church St., Keswick, Ont. L4P 1J7 – 416/476-5762 – A.A. Cameron
Geraldton Library, 405 2nd St. W., Box 40, Geraldton, Ont. P0T 1M0 – 807/854-1490 – Mrs. D. Mikkonen
Gerrard-Ashdale Library, 1432 Gerrard St. E., Toronto, Ont. M4L 1Z6 – 416/466-2913
Gibson Reserve Library, Box 327, Bala, Ont. P0C 1A0
Glanworth Branch, c/o Middlesex County Library
Glen Morris Library, Glen Morris, Ont. N0B 1W0 – 519/621-9760
Glencoe Branch, c/o Middlesex County Library
Gloucester Public Library, 2536 Innes Rd., #202, Ottawa, Ont. K1B 4C5 – 613/824-8366 – R.W. Price
Goderich Branch, c/o Huron County Library
Golden Lake Indian Band Library, Golden Lake, Ont. K0J 1X0 – 613/625-2180
Gooderham Branch, c/o Haliburton County Library
Gore Bay Union Library, Box 225, Gore Bay, Ont. P0P 1H0 – 705/282-2382 – Mrs. D.E. Porter
Gorrie Branch, c/o Huron County Library
Goulbourn Twp. Public Library, Box 760, (444 Main St. S.), Stittsville, Ont. K0A 3G0 – Marek J. Czuma
Grafton Branch, c/o Northumberland Union Library
Grand Bend Branch, c/o Lambton County Library
Grand Valley Library, Box 129, Main St., Grand Valley, Ont. L0N 1G0 – 519/928-5622 – Ms. S. Leighton
Grantham Library, Scott & Vine Sts., St. Catharines, Ont. L2M 3W4 – 416/934-7511
Granton Branch, c/o Middlesex County Library
Gravenhurst Library, 275 Muskoka Rd. S., Box 1120, Gravenhurst, Ont. P0C 1G0 705/687-3382 – Miss R. Kirton
Greensville Branch, c/o Wentworth Library
Grimsby Library, 25 Adelaide St., Grimsby, Ont. L3M 1X2 – 416/945-5142 – Barry Church
Guelph Library, 100 Norfolk St., Guelph, Ont. N1H 4J6 – 519/824-6220 – N. McLeod
Guildwood Library, 123 Guildwood Pkwy., Unit 6, Scarborough, Ont. M1E 4V2 – 416/266-4787
Hagerman Twp. Library, Dunchurch, Ont. P0A 1G0 – 705/389-3311 – Mrs. L. Bell
Hagersville Branch, c/o Haldimand Library
Haileybury Library, 545 Lakeshore, Box 1090, Haileybury, Ont. P0J 1K0 – 705/672-3707 – Mrs. K. Sroka
Haldimand Library, Caithness St. W., Caledonia, Ont. N0A 1A0 – 416/765-2634 – Ms. J. Booth
Haliburton Branch, c/o Haliburton County Library
Haliburton County Library, Box 119, Maple St., Haliburton, Ont. K0M 1S0 – 705/457-2241 – S. McDougall
Halton Hills Public Library, 9 Church St., Georgetown, Ont. L7G 2A3 – 416/877-2681 – Mrs. B. Cornwell
Hamilton Library, 55 York Blvd., Hamilton, Ont. L8R 3K1 – 416/529-8111 – Mrs. J. McAnanama
Hamilton, see also
- Barton
- Concession
- Locke
- Kenilworth
- Mount Albion
- Picton Branch
- Red Hill
- Sherwood
- South Central Regional
- Terryberry
- Westdale
- Wentworth

Hammond Library, Hammond, Ont. K0A 2A0
Hanover Library, 341 10th St., Hanover, Ont. N4N 1P5 – 519/364-1420 – S.J. Hanns
Harrietsville Branch, c/o Middlesex County Library
Harrington Branch, c/o Oxford County Library
Harriston Library, Elora St., Harriston, Ont. N0G 1Z0 – Mrs. D. Pike
Harrow Branch, c/o Essex County Library
Hartington Branch, c/o Kingston Twp. Centre 70 Library
Hastings Library, Box 130, Hastings, Ont. K0L 1Y0 – 705/696-2111 – Mrs. L. Preston
Havelock Library, Box 464, 14 George St., Havelock, Ont. K0L 1Z0 – 705/778-2621
Hawkesbury Library, 550 Higginson St., Hawkesbury, Ont. K6A 1H1 – 613/632-6656 – Miss T. Legault
Head, Clara & Maria Twp. Public Library, Stonecliffe, Ont. K0J 2K0 – 613/586-2698
Hearst Library, Box 7000, 10th St., Hearst, Ont. P0L 1N0 – 705/362-4770 – J. Aubin
Hensall Branch, c/o Huron County Library
Hepworth Branch, c/o Bruce County Library
Hespeler Library, 5 Tannery St., Cambridge, Ont. N3C 2C1 – 519/658-4412
Hickson Branch, c/o Oxford County Library
High Park Library, 228 Roncesvalles Ave., Toronto, Ont. M6R 2L7 – 416/536-9583
Highgate Branch, c/o Kent County Library
Highland Creek Library, 277 Old Kingston Rd., West Hill, Ont. M1C 1B4 – 416/282-7211
Highland Grove Branch, c/o Haliburton County Library

Hillcrest Library, 5801 Leslie St., Willowdale, Ont. M2H 1J8 – 416/493-6247
Hilton Union Library, Hilton Beach, Ont. P0R 1G0 – Mrs. E. Allison
Holland Landing Library, c/o East Gwillimbury Library
Honey Harbour Branch, c/o Georgian Bay Twp. Library
Humber Bay Library, 200 Parklawn Rd., Toronto, Ont. M8Y 3J1 – 416/251-7721
Humber Summit Library, 2990 Islington Ave., Weston, Ont. M9L 2K6 – 416/749-5528
Humphrey Twp. Library, R.R. 2, Parry Sound, Ont. P2A 2W8 – 705/732-4526 – Mrs. M. Hammel
Huntsville Library, 7 Minerva St., Box 1029, Huntsville, Ont. P0A 1K0 – 705/789-5232 – Miss D. Burton
Huron County Library, 66 Waterloo St. S., Goderich, Ont. N7A 4A4 – 519/524-7751 – W. Partridge
Ingleside, see Stormont, Dundas & Glengarry
Ignace Library, Box 480, Ignace, Ont. P0T 1T0 – 807/934-2548 – Ms. C. Ferguson
Ilderton Branch, c/o Middlesex County Library
Ingersoll Branch, c/o Oxford County Library
Inglewood Branch, c/o Caledon Library
Innerkip Branch, c/o Oxford County Library
Innisfil Twp. Library, Stroud, Ont. L0L 2M0 – 705/436-1681 – Mrs. N. Watson
Inverary Branch, c/o Kingston Twp. Centre 70 Library
Inwood Branch, c/o Lambton County Library
Iron Bridge Library, Box 339, Iron Bridge, Ont. P0R 1H0 – 705/843-2192
Iroquois Falls Library, Box 860, 725 Synagogue St., Iroquois Falls, Ont. P0K 1G0 – 705/232-5722 – Mrs. Trudy Groome
Iroquois Library, Box 39, Iroquois, Ont. K0E 1K0 – Mrs. C. Graham
Iroquois of St. Regis Indian Band Library, Box 579, Cornwall, Ont. K6H 5T3 – 514/575-2222
Irwin Memorial Public Library, Irwin Memorial Pub. School, Dwight, Ont. P0A 1H0 – 705/635-2232
James F. Cox Library, 85 Marmora St., Trenton, Ont. K8V 2J2 – 613/392-4656
James Twp. Library, Elk Lake, Ont. P0J 1G0
Jane-Dundas Library, 620 Jane St., Toronto, Ont. M6S 4A6 – 416/769-4123
Janet St. Library, Janet St., Port Colborne, Ont. L3K 2E7 – 416/835-2926
Jarvis Library, 17 Main St. N., Jarvis, Ont. N0A 1J0 – 519/587-4746
Jess Hann Library, Lake Vista Sq., 199 Wentworth St. W., Oshawa, Ont. L1J 6P4 – 416/728-2441
Jones Ave. Library, 118 Jones Ave., Toronto, Ont. M4M 2Z9 – 416/466-9057
Jordan Branch, c/o Lincoln Library
Kaladar, Anglesea & Effingham Twp. Library, R.R. 1, Flinton, Ont. K0H 1P0 – Mrs. B.Y. Brushey
Kanata Library, 241 Penfield Dr., Kanata, Ont. K2K 1M8 – 613/592-2712 – Mrs. J. Dodsworth
Kapuskasing Library, 24 Mundy Ave., Kapuskasing, Ont. P5N 1P9 – 705/335-3363 – Mrs. A. McElwee
Kars Library, Box 99, Kars, Ont. K0A 2E0
Kearney & Area Library, Box 32, Kearney, Ont. P0A 1M0 – Mrs. E. Dault
Keewatin Library, Box 602, 1008 Ottawa St., Keewatin, Ont. P0X 1C0 – 807/547-2145 – Mrs. S. Clancy
Kemptville Library, Box 538, 207 Prescott St., Kemptville, Ont. K0G 1J0 – 613/258-5577 – Mrs. H. Groskopf
Kenilworth Library, 103 Kenilworth Ave. N., Hamilton, Ont. L8H 4R6 – 416/544-8705
Kenora Library, 24 Main St. E., Kenora, Ont. P9N 1S7 – 807/468-7091 – Mrs. E. Roussin
Kent County Library, 455 Grand Ave. W., Chatham, Ont. N7L 1C5 – 519/352-2520 – R. Burford
Keswick Branch, c/o Georgina Public Library
Kilbride Library, Kilbride Public School, Kilbride, Ont. L0P 1G0 – 416/335-6394
Killaloe Station Library, Killaloe Station, Ont. K0J 2A0 – 613/757-2211 – M. MacKay
Kincardine Library, Box 88, Queen St., Kincardine, Ont. N0G 2G0 – 519/396-3289 (a branch of the Bruce County Library)
King Twp. Library, Box 399, King Side Rd., King City, Ont. L0G 1K0 – 416/833-5101 – L. Bruce
Kingfisher Lake Band Library, Kingfisher Lake, Ont. P0V 1Z0
Kingscourt Library, 115 Kirkpatrick St., Kingston, Ont. K7K 2P4 – 613/546-0698
Kingston Library, 130 Johnson St. E., Kingston, Ont. K7L 1X8 – 613/549-8888 – Mrs. M.C. Cartwright
Kingston, see also
  Calvin Park
  Kingscourt
Kingston Twp. Centre '70 Library, 130 Days Rd., Kingston, Ont. K7M 3P8 – 613/389-2616 – C. Peppler
Kingsville Branch, c/o Essex County Library
Kinmount Branch, c/o Victoria County Library
Kintore Branch, c/o Oxford County Library
Kirkland Lake Library, 10 Kirkland St. E., Kirkland Lake, Ont. P2N 3K2 – 705/567-7966 – Mrs. J. Bennetts
Kirkton Branch, c/o Huron County Library
Kitchener Library, 85 Queen St. N., Kitchener, Ont. N2H 2H1 – 519/743-0271 – I.L. Matthews
Kitchener, see also
  Forest Heights
  Stanley Park
Kleinburg Library, c/o Vaughan Public Libraries (Kleinburg: 416/893-1248)
Komoka Branch, c/o Middlesex County Library
Korah Library, 496 Second Line W., Sault Ste. Marie, Ont. P6C 2K4 – 705/949-2871
Lake Helen Library, Old School Bldg., Box 326, Nipigon, Ont.
Lake of Bays Twp., see Irwin Memorial
Lakefield Library, Box 220, Lakefield, Ont. K0L 2H0 – 705/652-8623 – Mrs. J. Binnington
Lakelet Branch, c/o Huron County Library
Lakeview Library, 1110 Atwater Ave., Mississauga, Ont. L5E 1M9 – 416/274-5027
Lambeth Branch, c/o Middlesex County Library
Lambton County Library, 546 Niagara St., Box 100, Wyoming, Ont. N0N 1T0 – 519/845-3324 – R. Baker
Lambton Mall Branch Library, 1362 Lambton Mall Rd., Sarnia, Ont. N7S 5A1 – 519/542-2580 (a branch of the Lambton County Library)
Lanark Library, Box 249, George St., Lanark, Ont. K0G 1K0 – 613/259-2000 – Mrs. G. Affleck
Lancaster, see Stormont, Dundas & Glengarry
Landon Branch Library, 167 Wortley Rd., London, Ont. N6C 3P6 – 519/439-6240
Larder Lake Library, Box 66, 107 Government Rd., Larder Lake, Ont. P0K 1L0 – 705/643-2222
LaSalle Branch, c/o Essex County Library
Leamington Library, 1 John St., Leamington, Ont. N8H 1H1 – 519/326-3441 – Mrs. R.C. Sackett
Leaside Library, 165 McRae Dr., Toronto, Ont. M4G 1S8 – 416/425-1044
Lennox & Addington County Library, 37 Dundas St. W., Napanee, Ont. K7R 1Z5 – 613/354-2585 – A.B. Geddes
Levack Branch, c/o Onaping Falls Library
Limehouse Branch, c/o Halton Hills Library
Lincoln Library, Box 460, Beamsville, Ont. L0R 1B0 – 416/563-7014 – B. Church
Lindsay Library, 190 Kent St. W., Lindsay, Ont. K9V 2Y6 – 705/324-5632 – M. Tahiliani
Linwood Branch, c/o Waterloo Regional Library
Lion's Head Branch, c/o Bruce County Library
Listowel Library, 260 Main St. W., Listowel, Ont. N4W 1A3 – 519/291-4621 – Ms. J.L. Ballantyne
Little Britain Branch, c/o Victoria County Library
Little Current Library, Little Current, Ont. P0P 1K0 – 705/368-2444 – Ms. C. Paisley
Lively, see Walden Public Library
Locke Library, 285 Locke St. S., Hamilton, Ont. L8P 4C2 – 416/522-7154
London Library, 305 Queens Ave., London, Ont. N6B 3L7 – 519/432-7166 – E.S. Beacock

London, see also
Argyle
Broughdale
Byron
Carson
Landon
Northland
Northridge
Westminster
Westmount
Westown
White Oaks
Long Branch Library, 3500 Lakeshore Blvd. W., Toronto, Ont. M8W 1N6 – 416/251-5481
Long Lake Reserve Library, c/o Chief Gabriel Echum, Longlac, Ont.
Long Sault, see Stormont, Dundas & Glengarry
Longlac Library, Box 760, Longlac, Ont. P0T 2A0 – 807/876-4515 – Mrs. F. Emmons
Lucan Branch, c/o Middlesex County Library
Lucknow Branch, c/o Bruce County Library
Lutterworth Branch, c/o Haliburton County Library
Lyn Library, Lyn, Ont. K0E 1M0
Lynden Branch, c/o Wentworth Library
Lyndhurst Branch, c/o South Crosby etc. Union Library
Mactier Branch, c/o Georgian Bay Twp. Library
Madoc Library, 20 Davidson St., Madoc, Ont. K0K 2K0 – 613/473-4456 – Mrs. R. Sporring
Main Street Library, 137 Main St., Toronto, Ont. M4E 2V9 – 416/694-6054
Malden Road Branch, c/o Essex County Library
Malton Library, 3540 Morningstar Dr., Malton, Ont. L4T 1Y2 – 416/677-5878
Mandaumin Branch, c/o Lambton County Library
Manilla Branch, c/o Victoria County Library
Manitou Library, Box 450, Emo, Ont. P0W 1E0 – 807/482-2479
Manitouwadge Twp. Library, Community Centre, Manitouwadge, Ont. P0T 2C0 – 807/826-3913
Manotick Library, Box 430, Ann St., Manotick, Ont. K0A 2N0 – 613/692-3854
Maple Acres Library, Box 59, Fenwick, Ont. L0S 1C0 – 416/892-5226
Maple Branch, c/o Vaughan Public Libraries
Mara Twp. Library, Brechin, Ont. L0K 1B0 – Mrs. A. Lambert
Marathon Public Library, Box 400, Marathon, Ont. P0T 2E0 – 807/229-0740
March Twp., see Kanata
Markdale Library, 21 Main St. E., Box 499, Markdale, Ont. N0C 1H0 – 519/986-3436
Markham Library Central Administration, 7755 Bayview Ave., Thornhill, Ont. L3T 4T1 – 416/881-4804 – R. Osborne
Markham Centennial Library, 199 Main St. N., Markham, Ont. L3P 1Y4 – 416/294-2782
Marmora, Deloro, Marmora & Lake Twps. Union Library, 37 Forsythe St., Marmora, Ont. K0K 2M0 – 613/472-3122 – Mrs. R. McCoy
Marten Falls Library, c/o Sandy Moonias, Ogoki Post, Ont. P0T 2L0
Mary J.L. Black Library, 151 W. Brock St., Thunder Bay, Ont. P7E 4H9 – 807/623-1529
Massey Twp. Public Library, Box 40, Massey, Ont. P0P 1P0 – 705/865-2641 – Mrs. Lilliane Richer
Matchedash Twp. Library, R.R. 1, Coldwater, Ont. K0K 1E0 – 705/686-7994 – Mrs. J. Flemming
Mattagami Indian Band Library, Box 148, Gogama, Ont. P0M 1W0 – 705/894-2072
Mattawa Library, 362 Main St., Mattawa, Ont. P0H 1V0 – 705/744-5550 – Mrs. M. Nesseth
Mattice-Van Cote Library, Box 129, Mattice, Ont. P0L 1T0 – 705/364-5301
Maxville, see Stormont, Dundas & Glengarry
McGarry Twp. Library, 59 Connell Ave., Box 250, Viginiatown, Ont. P0K 1X0 – 705/634-2312
McGregor Branch, c/o Essex County Library
McGregor Park Library, 2219 Lawrence Ave. E., Scarborough, Ont. M1P 2P5 – 416/759-6757
McLaughlin Bldg. Library, 65 Bagot St., Oshawa, Ont. L1H 1N2 – 416/579-6111
Meaford Library, Box 970, 15 Trowbridge St., Meaford, Ont. N0H 1Y0 – 519/538-3500 – Mrs. D. Binsted
Melbourne Branch, c/o Middlesex County Library
Merivale Branch Library, 1541 Merivale Rd., Nepean, Ont. K2G 3J4 – 613/224-7874
Merlin Branch, c/o Kent County Library
Merrickville Library, Main St., Merrickville, Ont. K0G 1N0 – 613/269-3326 – Mrs. J.R. Ogilvie
Metcalfe Branch, c/o Osgoode Twp. Library
Michipicoten Twp. Library, Box 950, Wawa, Ont. P0S 1K0 – 705/856-2062 – Mrs. A. Fleming
Middlesex County Library, Centennial Bldg., Arva, Ont. N0M 1C0 – 519/438-8368 – Miss E. McPherson
Midland Library, 320 King St., Midland, Ont. L4R 3M6 – 705/526-5811 – Mrs. E. Goodburne
Mildmay-Carrick Branch, c/o Bruce County Library
Millgrove Branch, c/o Wentworth Library
Milton Library, 45 Bruce St., Milton, Ont. L9T 2L5 – 416/878-2879 – Mrs. S. Conway
Milverton Library, 27 Main St. S., Milverton, Ont. N0K 1M0 – 519/595-8395 – Mrs. B. Engeland
Mimico Centennial Library, 47 Station Rd., Toronto, Ont. M8V 2R1 – 416/259-8489
Minden Branch, c/o Haliburton County Library
Mississauga Central Library, 110 Dundas St. W., Mississauga, Ont. L5B 1H3 – 416/279-7002
Mississauga, see also
Burnhamthorpe
Clarkson-Lorne Park
Lakeview
Malton
Park Royal
Port Credit
Sheridan Mall
Streetsville
Woodlands
Mitchell Library, 105A St. Andrew St., Mitchell, Ont. N0K 1N0 – 519/348-9234 – J. Thorup
Molesworth Branch, c/o Huron County Library
Monkton Branch, c/o Elma Twp. Library
Moonbeam Library, rue Albert, C.P. 249, Moonbeam, Ont. P0L 1V0 – 705/367-2462
Mooretown Branch, c/o Lambton County Library
Moose Creek, see Stormont, Dundas & Glengarry
Moose Factory Island Library, Box 219, Moose Factory Island, Ont. P0L 1W0 – 705/658-4897
Morningside Library, 4521 Kingston Rd., Scarborough, Ont. M1E 2P1 – 416/282-3485
Morrisburg, see Stormont, Dundas & Glengarry
Mount Albert Branch, c/o East Gwillimbury Library
Mount Albion Library, 110 Gordon Drummond Dr., Hamilton, Ont. L8G 1P5 – 416/560-1315 (a branch of the Wentworth Library)
Mount Brydges Branch, c/o Middlesex County Library
Mount Dennis Library, 1123 Weston Rd., Toronto, Ont. M6N 3S3 – 416/762-1101
Mount Elgin Branch, c/o Oxford County Library
Mount Forest Library, Box 309, Mount Forest, Ont. N0G 2L0 – Mrs. J. Butt
Mount Hope Branch, c/o Wentworth Library
Mount Pleasant Branch, c/o Cavan etc. Union Library
Mountain Grove Branch, c/o Kingston Twp. Centre 70 Library
Murillo Library, Murillo Town Hall, Murillo, Ont. P0T 2G0 807/935-2903
Murray Twp., see Northumberland Union
Muskoka Lakes Twp. Library, Box 189, Port Carling, Ont. P0B 1J0 – 705/765-5650
Muskrat Dam Library, c/o Mrs. Clara Beard, Muskrat Dam, via Pickle Lake, Ont. P0V 3A0
Naicatchewenin Band Library, R.R. 1, Devlin, Ont. P0W 1C0 – 807/486-3407

Nairn Branch, c/o Middlesex County Library
Nakina Improvement District Library, c/o Mrs. K.M. Manuel, Nakina, Ont. P0T 2H0 – 807/329-5982
Nanticoke Library, Box 130, Selkirk, Ont. N0A 1P0 – 416/776-2127 – Mrs. G. Bell
Napanee Public Library, 37 Dundas St. W., Napanee, Ont. K7R 1Z5 – 613/354-2525 (a branch of the Lennox & Addington County Library)
Napier Branch, c/o Middlesex County Library
Naughton Branch, c/o Walden Library
Nepean Library, 16 Rowley Ave., Nepean, Ont. K2G 1L9 – 613/224-4338 – M. Sinclair
Nepean, see also
Centennial
Merivale
New Appleby Library, 5111 New St., Burlington, Ont. L7L 1V2 – 416/639-3611
New Dundee Branch, c/o Waterloo Regional Library
New Hamburg Branch, c/o Waterloo Regional Library
New Liskeard Library, Whitewood Ave., Box 668, New Liskeard, Ont. P0J 1P0 – 705/647-4215 – Mrs. F.G. Landry
New Toronto Library, 110 11th St., Toronto, Ont. M8V 3G5 – 416/252-7254
Newboro Branch, c/o South Crosby etc. Union Library
Newburgh Branch, c/o Lennox & Addington County Library
Newbury Branch, c/o Middlesex County Library
Newcastle Public Library, 62 Temperance St., Bowmanville, Ont. L1C 3A8 – 416/623-7322 – Mrs. B. Schon
Newcastle Memorial Library, 20 King St. W., Newcastle, Ont. L0A 1H0 – 416/987-4844
Newington, see Stormont, Dundas & Glengarry
Newmarket Library, 438 Park Ave., Newmarket, Ont. L3Y 1W1 – 416/895-5196
Newton Robinson Library, R.R. 2, Bradford, Ont. L0G 1C0 – 705/458-4515
Niagara Falls Library, 4848 Victoria Ave., Niagara Falls, Ont. L2E 4C5 – 416/356-8080 – Miss D. Vanslyke
Niagara Falls, see also
Chippawa
Drummond
Stamford Centre
Niagara-on-the-Lake Library, Box 430, Niagara-on-the-Lake, Ont. L0S 1J0 – 416/468-2023 – Mrs. G. Molson
Nickel Centre Library, 214 Orell St., Garson, Ont. P0M 1V0 – 705/693-2729 – Mrs. L. Bergeron
Nikola Budimir Library, 1310 Grand Marais Rd. W., Windsor, Ont. N9E 1E4 – 519/969-5880
Nipigon Twp. Library, Box 728, 25 Third St., Nipigon, Ont. P0T 2J0 – 807/887-3142
Nobleton Branch, c/o King Twp. Library
Norfolk Twp. Library, Box 159, Langton, Ont. N0E 1G0 – 514/586-3522 – G. Bailey
Norland Branch, c/o Victoria County Library
Normanby Twp. Library, Ayton, Ont. N0G 1C0 – 519/665-7784
North Bay Library, 271 Worthington St. E., North Bay, Ont. P1B 1H1 – 705/474-4830 – A. Maizen
North Branch, see Cornwall
North Gower Library, Box 280, North Gower, Ont. K0A 2T0 – 613/489-3909
North Himsworth Twp. Library, Lansdowne St., Box 249, Callander, Ont. P0H 1H0 – Ms. N. Alkins
North Shore Public Library, Box 329, Spanish, Ont. P0P 2A0 – 705/844-2300
North Simcoe Library, Chalet Plaza, 1050 Simcoe St. N., Oshawa, Ont. L1G 4W5 – 416/576-6040
North York Library, 35 Fairview Mall Dr., Willowdale, Ont. M2J 4S4 – 416/494-6838 – G.C. Barhydt
North York, other libraries cross-references are listed with Toronto
Northern District Library, 40 Orchard View Blvd., Toronto, Ont. M4R 1B9 – 416/484-6087
Northland Branch Library, 1280 Huron St., London, Ont. N5Y 4M2 – 519/451-8140 – Ms. J. Hedges
Northridge Branch Library, 1444 Glenora Dr., London, Ont. N5X 1V2 – 519/439-4331
Northumberland Union Library, R.R. 1, Trenton, Ont. K8V 5P4 – 613/392-4435 – Mrs. W. Brown
Northwest Library, 650 South Pelham St., Welland, Ont. L3C 3C8 – 416/735-4231
Norwich Branch, c/o Oxford County Library
Norwood Library, Box 100, Norwood, Ont. K0L 2V0 – Mrs. M. Ferguson
Oakland Twp. Library, Oakland St., Scotland, Ont. N0E 1R0 – 519/446-0181
Oak Ridges, see Charles Conner
Oakville Library, 120 Navy St., Oakville, Ont. L6J 2Z4 – 416/845-3405
Oakville, see also
White Oaks
Woodside
Oakwood Branch, c/o Victoria County Library
Odessa Branch, c/o Lennox & Addington County Library
Ogilvie Rd. Branch, c/o Gloucester Public Library
Oil Springs Branch, c/o Lambton County Library
Ojibways of Manitou Library, Box 450, Emo, Ont. P0W 1E0 – 807/482-2479
Omemee Branch, c/o Victoria County Library
Ompah Branch, c/o Kingston Twp. Centre 70 Library
Onaping Branch, c/o Onaping Falls Library
Onaping Falls Library, Box 520, Dowling, Ont. P0M 1R0 – 705/855-9028 – Pat Terrick
Oneida Indian Band Branch, c/o Middlesex County Library
Orangeville Library, 144 Broadway Ave., Orangeville, Ont. L9W 2Z7 – 519/941-0610
Orillia Library, 36 Mississaga St. W., Orillia, Ont. L3V 3A6 – 705/325-2338 – Miss K. McKinnon
Osborne Collection, see Boys & Girls House, Toronto
Osgoode Twp. Library, Box 103, Main St., Osgoode, Ont. K0A 2W0 – Miss J. Geymonat
Oshawa Public Library, 65 Bagot St., Oshawa, Ont. L1H 1N2 – 416/579-6111 – Miss R.P. Brooking
Oshawa, see also
Jess Hann
McLaughlin Bldg.
North Simcoe
Otonabee Twp. Library, Box 16, Keene, Ont. K0L 2G9 – 705/295-6814
Ottawa Library, 120 Metcalfe St., Ottawa, Ont. K1P 5M2 – 613/236-0301 – G. Frappier
Ottawa, see also
Alta Vista
Carlingwood
Elmvale Acres
Rideau
Rockcliffe Park
St. Laurent
South
West Branch
Otterville Branch, c/o Oxford County Library
Owen Sound Library, 824 First Ave. W., Owen Sound, Ont. N4K 4K4 – 519/376-6623 – A.D. Armitage
Owens-Williamson-Idington Twps. Library, ave de l'Eglise, C.P. 69, Val Rita, Ont. P0L 2G0 – Ms. C.M. Bélanger
Oxford County Library, 93 Graham St., Woodstock, Ont. N4S 6J8 – 519/537-3322 – Mrs. M.J. Webb
Oxford Mills Library, Oxford Mills, Ont. K0G 1S0 – 613/258-5040
Oxford-on-Rideau Twp. Library, Burritts Rapids, Ont. K0G 1B0 – 613/269-3636 – Mrs. D. Steacy
Paisley Branch, c/o Bruce County Library
Pakenham Twp. Library, Box 99, Pakenham, Ont. K0A 2X0 – 613/624-5430 – Mrs. T. Barratt
Palmerston Library, 560 Palmerston Ave., Toronto, Ont. M6G 2P7 – 416/531-2486
Palmerston Branch, c/o Wellington County Library
Pape/Danforth Library, 701 Pape Ave., Toronto, Ont. M4K 3S6 – 416/465-1221
Paris Library, 12 William St., Paris, Ont. N3L 1K7 – 519/442-2433 – Mrs. A. Cesnulis
Park Royal Library, 2425 Park Royal Shopping Plaza, Truscott Dr., Mississauga, Ont. L5J 2B4 – 416/822-3476

Parkdale Library, 1303 Queen St. W., Toronto, Ont. M6K 1L6 – 416/532-6548
Parkhill Branch, c/o Middlesex County Library
Parkside Library, 500 Parkside Dr., Waterloo, Ont. N2L 5J4 – 519/885-1920
Parliament Street Library, 269 Gerrard St. E., Toronto, Ont. M5A 2G3 – 416/924-7122
Parry Sound Library, 29 Mary St., Parry Sound, Ont. P2A 1E3 – 705/746-9601 – R. Hall
Pefferlaw Library, c/o Georgina Public Library (Pefferlaw: 705/437-1514)
Pelee Island Library, Pelee Island, Ont. N0R 1M0 – 519/724-2022
Pelham Public Library, Box 830, Fonthill, Ont. L0S 1E0 – 416/892-6443 – Mrs. F. Morabito
Pembroke Library, 237 Victoria St., Pembroke, Ont. K8A 4K5 – 613/732-8844 – S. Mehta
Pen Centre Library, Pen Centre Shopping Centre, Glendale Ave., St. Catharines, Ont. L2T 2K9 – 416/682-3568
Penetanguishene Library, Box 159, 3 Simcoe St., Penetanguishene, Ont. L0K 1P0 – 705/549-7164
Percy Twp. Library, Main & Church Sts., Warkworth, Ont. K0K 3K0
Perry Twp. Library, Emsdale, Ont. P0A 1J0 – Mrs. B. Marshall
Perth Public Library, 127 Gore St. E., Perth, Ont. K7H 1Z7 – 613/267-1224 – Miss F. Cunningham
Perth-Dupont Library, 1531 Dupont St., Toronto, Ont. M6P 3S3 – 416/535-7188
Petawawa Village & Twp. Union Library, 16 Civic Centre Rd., Petawawa, Ont. K8H 3H5 – 613/687-2227 – Mrs. P. Pollard
Peterborough District Library Office, 474 George St. N., Peterborough, Ont. K9H 3R7 – 705/748-5881
Peterborough Library, 345 Aylmer St. N., Peterborough, Ont. K9H 3V7 – 705/745-5382 – Ms. Anne C. Smith
Peterborough, see also
De La Fosse
Petrolia Branch, c/o Lambton County Library
Pic Heron Library, Heron Bay, Ont.
Pickering Library, Box 368, 1340 Rougemount Dr., Pickering, Ont. L1V 2R6 – 416/284-0623 – Mrs. T. Driesschen
Picton Branch Library, 502 James St. N., Hamilton, Ont. L8L 1J3 – 416/528-7453
Picton Library, Box 260, Main St., Picton, Ont. K0K 2T0 – 613/476-5962 – Mrs. V. Creasy
Pine Ridge Union Library, Box 160, Milbrook, Ont. L0A 1G0 – 705/932-2168
Plantagenet Village Library, Plantagenet, Ont. K0B 1L0
Plattsville Branch, c/o Oxford County Library
Pleasant View Library, 575 Van Horne Ave., Willowdale, Ont. M2J 4S8 – 416/492-9141
Point Edward Library, 220 Michigan Ave., Point Edward, Ont. N7V 1E8 – 519/336-3291 – Mrs. M. Campbell
Porcupine, see Whitney
Port Burwell Branch, c/o Elgin County Library
Port Carling Library, Community Centre, Box 189, Port Carling, Ont. P0B 1J0 – 705/765-5650
Port Colborne Library, 310 King St., Port Colborne, Ont. L3K 4H1 – 416/834-6512 – Miss A.K. Jones
Port Colborne, see also Janet St.
Port Credit Library, 20 Lakeshore Rd. E., Mississauga, Ont. L5G 1C8 – 416/278-3437
Port Dalhousie Library, Brock St., St. Catharines, Ont. L2N 5E1 – 416/934-2621
Port Dover Centennial Library, 413 Main St., Port Dover, Ont. N0A 1N0 – 519/583-0622
Port Elgin Library, Box 609, Goderich St., Port Elgin, Ont. N0H 2C0 – 519/832-2201 (a branch of the Bruce County Library)
Port Franks Branch, c/o Lambton County Library
Port Hope Library, 31 Queen St., Port Hope, Ont. L1A 2Y8 – 416/885-4712 – Ms. Victoria Owen
Port Lambton Branch, c/o Lambton County Library
Port McNicoll Library, Box 160, First Ave., Port McNicoll, Ont. L0K 1R0 – 705/534-3761 – Mrs. A. Hancox
Port Robinson Branch, c/o Thorold Library
Port Rowan Branch, c/o Norfolk Twp. Library
Port Stanley Branch, c/o Elgin County Library
Port Union Library, 5530 Lawrence Ave. E., Scarborough, Ont. M1C 3B2 – 416/282-7428
Portland Branch, c/o South Crosby etc. Union Library
Powassan & Dist. Union Library, 196 Main St. W., Powassan, Ont. P0H 1Z0 705/724-3618 – Mrs. M. Hall
Prescott Library, Box 430, Dibble St. W., Prescott, Ont. K0E 1T0 – 613/925-4340 – Mrs. A. Steiner
Preston Library, 435 King St. E., Cambridge, Ont. N3H 3N1 – 519/653-3632
Princeton Branch, c/o Oxford County Library
Putnam Branch, c/o Middlesex County Library
Queensville Branch, c/o East Gwillimbury Library
Radcliffe Twp. Library, Box 93, Combermere, Ont. K0J 1L0 – Ms. H. Kern
Rainy River Library, 202 4th St., Rainy River, Ont. P0W 1L0 – 807/852-3375 – Ms. R. Bynkoski
Ramore Branch, c/o Black River Matheson Library
Rayside-Balfour Library, Box 1720, Chelmsford, Ont. P0M 1L0 – 705/855-9333 – Mrs. J. Vaillancourt
Red Hill Library, 75 Centennial Pkwy. N., Stoney Creek, Ont. L8E 2P2 – 416/561-2835
Red Lake Twp. Library, Box 348, 147 Howey St., Red Lake, Ont. P0V 2M0 – 807/727-2230
Red Rock Improvement District Library, Box 285, Salls St., Red Rock, Ont. P0T 2P0 – 807/886-2558 – Mrs. B. Anderson
Reference Library, 52 James St. S., Hamilton, Ont. L8P 2Y8 – 416/529-8111
Regency Mall Library, 469 Bouchard St., Sudbury, Ont. P3E 2K8 – 705/673-1155, ext. 44
Renfrew Library, 13 Railway Ave. E., Renfrew, Ont. K7V 3A9 – 613/432-8151 – C. Pugh
Rexdale Branch Library, 2243 Kipling Ave., Rexdale, Ont. M9W 4L5 – 416/741-1170
Richmond Branch, c/o Goulbourn Twp. Library
Richmond Hill Library, 24 Wright St., Richmond Hill, Ont. L4C 4A1 – 416/884-9288 – Mrs. E. Rowland
Richvale Library, 54 Pearson Ave., Richvale, Ont. L4J 2C8 – 416/889-2847
Richview Branch Library, Islington at Summercrest, Box 501, Etobicoke, Ont. M9C 5G1 – 416/248-5681
Rideau Library, 377 Rideau St., Ottawa, Ont. K1N 5Y6 – 613/236-0301
Ridgetown Branch, c/o Kent County Library
Ripley Branch, c/o Bruce County Library
Riverdale Library, 370 Broadview Ave., Toronto, Ont. M4K 2M8 – 416/466-2197
Riverside Library, 6275 Wyandotte St. E., Windsor, Ont. N8S 1N5 – 519/945-7568
Rockcliffe Park Library, 350 Springfield Rd., Rockcliffe Park, Ottawa, Ont. K1M 0K7 – 613/745-2562 – Mrs. W. Loftus
Rockland Library, Box 819, Rockland, Ont. K0A 3A0 – 613/446-5680 – Mme O. Dalrymple
Rockton Branch, c/o Wentworth Library
Rocky Bay Library, Rocky Bay Indian Reserve #1, MacDiarmid, Ont. P0J 2B0 – 807/885-3191 – T. Hardy
Rodney Branch, c/o Elgin County Library
Rolph, Buchanan Twp. Library, Deep River, Ont. K0J 1P0 – 613/584-2714 – Mrs. J. Ward
Roseneath Branch, c/o Northumberland Union Library
Ross Twp. Library, Forester's Falls, Ont. K0J 1V0 – 613/646-2543 – Mrs. D. McLaughlin
Rosseau Library, Box 8, Rosseau, Ont. P0C 1J0 – 705/732-4231 – Mrs. S. Grenkie
Runnymede Library, 2178 Bloor St. W., Toronto, Ont. M6S 1M8 – 416/767-1051
Russell Twp. Library, Box 280, 472 Concession St., Russell, Ont. K0A 3B0 – 613/445-5331 – Ms. I.E. Kinkaid
Ruthven Branch, c/o Essex County Library
S. Walter Stewart Library, 170 Memorial Park Ave., Toronto, Ont. M4J 2K5 – 416/425-8222
Sabaskong Band Library, Box 160, Nester Falls, Ont. P0X 1K0 – 807/484-2510
St. Andrews West, see Stormont, Dundas & Glengarry
St. Catharines Library, 54 Church St., St. Catharines, Ont. L2R 7K2 – 416/688-6103 – Miss J.E. Munro

St. Catharines, see also
Grantham
Pen Centre
Port Dalhousie
St. Clair Beach Branch, c/o Essex County Library
St. Clements Branch, c/o Waterloo Regional Library
St. George Library, Main St., Saint George, Ont. N0E 1N0 – 519/448-1300
St. Helen's Branch, c/o Huron County Library
St. Isidore-de-Prescott Library, Centre Paroissial Joseph Roy, St. Isidore-de-Prescott, Ont. K0C 2B0 – 613/524-2252
St. Jacobs Branch, c/o Waterloo Regional Library
St. Joseph Twp. Library, Richards Landing, Ont. P0R 1J0 – 705/246-2353
St. Laurent Library, 847 St. Laurent Blvd., Ottawa, Ont. K1K 3A7 – 613/236-0301
St. Mary's Library, Box 700, Church St. N., St. Mary's, Ont. N0M 2V0 – 519/284-3346 – Mrs. D.J. Coles
St. Pascal-Baylon Library, St. Pascal Baylon, Ont. K0A 3N0
St. Paul Ave. Library, 441 St. Paul Ave., Brantford, Ont. N3R 4N8 – 519/753-2179
St. Thomas Library, 153 Curtis St., St. Thomas, Ont. N5P 3Z7 – 519/631-6050 – Mrs. C. Kneeshaw
Saltfleet Branch, c/o Wentworth County Library
Sandhurst Branch, c/o Lennox & Addington County Library
Sarnia Library, 124 S. Christina St., Sarnia, Ont. N7T 2M6 – 519/337-3291
Sarnia, see also East Branch
Sauble Beach Branch, c/o Bruce County Library
Saugeen Band Library, Chippawa Hill, Ont. N0H 1H0 – 705/797-2218
Sault Ste. Marie Library, 50 East St., Sault Ste. Marie, Ont. P6A 3C3 – 705/949-2152 – B.R. Ingram
Sault Ste. Marie, see also
Korah
Steelton
Savant Lake Library, General Delivery, Savant Lake, Ont. P0V 2S0 – 807/584-2277
Scarborough Library Admin. & Support Services, 1076 Ellesmere Rd., Scarborough, Ont. M1P 4P4 – 416/291-1991 – P. Bassnett
Schomberg Branch, c/o King Twp. Library
Schreiber Library, Box 39, Schreiber, Ont. P0T 2S0 – 807/824-2477
Schumacher Library, 56 First Ave., Box 800, Schumacher, Ont. P0N 1G0 – 705/264-3545
Scott Branch, c/o Uxbridge Twp. Library
Scugog Memorial Library, 269 Queen St., Box 459, Port Perry, Ont. L0B 1N0 – 416/985-7686 – Mrs. G. Milne
Seaforth Branch, c/o Huron County Library
Seeley's Bay Branch, c/o South Crosby etc. Union Library
Seine River Reserve Library, Mine Centre, Ont. P0W 1H0
Selkirk Branch, see Nanticoke
Seminole Library, 4285 Seminole St., Windsor, Ont. N8Y 1Z5 – 519/945-6467
Shackleton & Machin Twp. Library, Box 40, Fauquier, Ont. P0L 1G0
Sharbot Lake Branch, c/o Kingston Twp. Centre 70 Library
Shedden Branch, c/o Elgin County Library
Sheffield Branch, c/o Wentworth Library
Sheguiandah Band Library, c/o Miss Rita Osawabine, Sheguiandah, Ont. P0P 1W0 – 705/368-2781
Shelburne Library, Box 127, Owen Sound St., Shelburne, Ont. L0N 1S0 – 519/925-2168 – Mrs. I.E. Porter
Sheppard Centre Library, 4841 Yonge St., Willowdale, Ont. M2N 5X3 – 416/222-5188
Sheridan Mall Library, 2225 Erin Mills Pkwy., Mississauga, Ont. L5K 1T9 – 416/823-4106
Sherwood Library, 1104 Fennell Ave. E., Hamilton, Ont. L8T 1R9 – 416/389-8977
Sherwood, Jones & Burns Twp. Library, Wilno, Ont. K0J 2N0 – 613/756-3217
Sheshegwaning Band Library, Sheshegwaning, Ont. P0P 1X0 – 705/283-3292
Shetland Branch, c/o Lambton County Library
Sidney Twp. Library, 1 Haig St., Batawa, Ont. K0K 1E0 – 613/398-7344
Simcoe County Library, County Admin. Centre, Midhurst, Ont. L0L 1X0 – 705/726-9300 – Maurice G. Allen
Simcoe Library, 23 Argyle St., Simcoe, Ont. N3Y 1V6 – 519/426-3506 – A.K. Ganju
Sioux Lookout Library, Box 1028, Sioux Lookout, Ont. P0V 2T0 – 807/737-3660 – Mrs. S.D. Sanders
Sioux Narrows Improvement Dist. Library, Box 417, Sioux Narrows, Ont. P0X 1N0 – 807/226-5204 – Miss G. North
Six Nations Band Library, Ohsweken, Ont. N0A 1M0 – 519/445-2954
Skead Branch, c/o Nickel Centre Library
Smith Twp. Library, Ward St., Bridgenorth, Ont. K0L 1H0 – 705/292-5065
Smiths Falls Library, 81 Beckwith St. N., Smiths Falls, Ont. K7A 2B9 – 613/283-2911 – Mrs. H. McCabe
Smithville Branch, c/o West Lincoln Twp. Library
Smooth Rock Falls Library, Box 670, 6th Ave., Smooth Rock Falls, Ont. P0L 2B0 – 705/338-2318 – Ms. J. Landry
Snowdon Library, R.R. 1, Minden, Ont. K0M 2K0 – 705/286-2049 – Mrs. Marjorie Brown
Sombra Branch, c/o Lambton County Library
South Library, 1049 Bank St., Ottawa, Ont. K1S 3W9 – 613/236-0301
South Central Library, Churchill, Ont. L0L 1K0 – 705/456-2671
South Crosby etc. Union Library, Box 89, Elgin, Ont. K0G 1E0 – 613/359-5358 – Mrs. P. Little
South Elmsley Twp. Library, Lombardy Public School, R.R. 1, Lombardy, Ont. K0G 1L0 – 613/283-0860 – Mrs. L. Covell
South Marysburgh Twp. Library, King St., Milford, Ont. K0K 2P0 – Mrs. A. James
South Mobile Library Services, (Ottawa), 1049 Bank St., Ottawa, Ont. K1S 3W9 – 613/236-0301
South Mountain, see Stormont, Dundas & Glengarry
South Porcupine, see Charles M. Shields
South River-Machar Union Library, Box 190, Hwy. 11 N. at Marie St. E., South River, Ont. P0A 1X0 – 705/386-0222
South Walkerville Library, 1425 Tecumseh Rd. E., Windsor, Ont. N8W 1C2 – 519/253-3600
Southampton Branch, c/o Bruce County Library
Spaced-Out Library, 40 St. George St., Toronto, Ont. M5S 2E4 – 416/484-8015
Spadina Rd. Library, 10 Spadina Rd., Toronto, Ont. M5R 2S7 – 416/967-7167
Spanish River Indian Reserve Library, Box 420, Massey, Ont. P0P 1P0 – 705/865-5421
Springfield Branch, c/o Elgin County Library
Stamford Centre Library, 3643 Portage Rd. N., Niagara Falls, Ont. L2J 2K8 – 416/357-0410
Stanhope Branch, c/o Haliburton County Library
Stanley Park Library, 251 Kenneth St., Kitchener, Ont. N2A 1W5 – 519/743-0271
Stayner Library, Box 160, 201 Huron St., Stayner, Ont. L0M 1S0 – 705/428-3595 – Mrs. J. Trotter
Steelton Library, 283 Wellington St. W., Sault Ste. Marie, Ont. P6A 1H6
Stella Branch, c/o Lennox & Addington County Library
Stevensville Branch, c/o Fort Erie Library
Stirling Library, 43 Front St., Stirling, Ont. K0K 3E0 – 613/395-2837 – Mrs. B. Faulkner
Stittsville, see Goulbourn Twp.
Stoney Creek Library, 10 2nd St. N., Stoney Creek, Ont. L8G 1Y6 – 416/662-2211 (a branch of the Wellington County Library)
Stoney Point Branch, c/o Essex County Library
Stormont, Dundas & Glengarry County Library, 150 Edward St., Box 939, Cornwall, Ont. K6H 5V1 – 613/933-6195 – Mrs. A. Nyland
Stratford Library, 19 St. Andrew St., Stratford, Ont. N5A 1A2 – 519/271-0220 – Ms. S. Bonsteel
Strathroy Library, 34 Frank St., Strathroy, Ont. N7G 2R4 – 519/245-1290 – Miss J. Cummer
Streetsville Library, 112 Queen St. S., Mississauga, Ont. L5M 1K8 – 416/826-3001

Stroud Library, Stroud, Ont. L0L 2M0 – 705/436-1681
Sturgeon Falls Library, Main & William Sts., Box 180, Sturgeon Falls, Ont. P0H 2G0 – 705/753-2620 – Ms. C. Marion
Sucker Creek Indian Band Library, Box 21, R.R. 1, Little Current, Ont. P0P 1K0 – 705/368-2228
Sudbury Library, 74 MacKenzie St., Sudbury, Ont. P3C 4X8 – 705/673-1155
Sudbury Library Information & Reference Services, Civic Sq., West Tower, 200 Brady St., Sudbury, Ont. P3E 5K3 – 705/673-1155
Sudbury, see also Regency Mall
Sunderland, see Brock Twp.
Sundridge Library, Box 111, Main St., Sundridge, Ont. P0A 1Z0 – Mrs. F. Therien
Sunnidale Twp. Library, New Lowell, Ont. L0M 1N0 – 705/424-6288 – Mrs. J. Smith
Sutton Centennial Branch Library, Box 338, High St., Sutton, Ont. L0E 1R0 – 416/722-5702
Swansea Memorial Library, 95 Lavinia Ave., Toronto, Ont. M6S 3H9 – 416/769-1513
Swastika Branch, c/o Kirkland Lake Library
Sydenham Branch, c/o Kingston Twp. Centre 70 Library
Tamworth Branch, c/o Lennox & Addington County Library
Tara Branch, c/o Bruce County Library
Tavistock Branch, c/o Oxford County Library
Taylor Memorial Library, 1440 Kingston Rd., Scarborough, Ont. M1N 1R3 – 416/698-3481
Tecumseh Branch, c/o Essex County Library
Tecumseh Mall, 7716 Tecumseh Rd. E., Windsor, Ont. N8T 1E9 – 519/945-7323
Teeswater Branch, c/o Bruce County Library
Temagami Band Council Library, c/o G. Potts, Bear Island, Lake Temagami, Ont. P0H 1C0
Terrace Bay Library, Box 369, Terrace Bay, Ont. P0T 2W0 – 807/825-3819
Terryberry Library, 100 Mohawk Rd. W., Hamilton, Ont. L9C 1W1 – 416/388-7515
Thamesford Branch, c/o Oxford County Library
Thamesville Branch, c/o Kent County Library
Thedford Branch, c/o Lambton County Library
Thessalon Library, Box 549, Thessalon, Ont. P0R 1L0 – 705/842-2306 – Ms. H. Hoover
Thornbury Library, Box 357, 33 Bruce St., Thornbury, Ont. N0H 2P0 – 519/599-3681 – Mrs. L. Reid
Thorncliffe Library, 48 Thorncliffe Park Dr., Toronto, Ont. M4H 1J7 – 416/421-4791
Thornhill Community Centre Library, 7755 Bayview Ave., Thornhill, Ont. L3T 4T1 – 416/881-5668
Thornhill Gallanough Library, c/o Vaughan Public Libraries (Thornhill: 881-2828)
Thornhill Village Library, 10 Colborne St., Thornhill, Ont. L3T 1Z6 – 416/881-8299
Thorold Library, 1 Ormond St. S., Thorold, Ont. L2V 1X9 – 416/227-2581
Thunder Bay Library, 285 Arthur St., Thunder Bay, Ont. P7B 1A9 – 807/344-3585 – G. Burgess
Thunder Bay, see also
  Arthur St.
  Brodie St.
  Mary J.L. Black
Tilbury Branch, c/o Kent County Library
Tillsonburg Library, 2 Library Lane, Tillsonburg, Ont. N4G 3P9 – 519/842-5571 – M. Scholtz
Timmins Library, 236 Algonquin Blvd. E., Timmins, Ont. P4N 1B2 – 705/264-0665
Tiverton Branch, c/o Bruce County Library
Tobermory-St. Edmunds Branch, c/o Bruce County Library
Todmorden Library, Pape & Torrens Aves., Toronto, Ont. M4K 3W6 – 416/425-9977
Toronto Library, 40 Orchard View Blvd., Toronto, Ont. M4R 1B9 – 416/484-8015 – L. Fowlie
Toronto, see also
  Agincourt
  Albert Campbell
  Alderwood
  Albion
  Amesbury Park
  Annette
  Bathurst Heights
  Bayview Village
  Beaches
  Bendale
  Black Creek
  Bloor & Gladstone
  Boys & Girls House
  Brentwood
  Bridlewood
  Brookbanks
  Cedarbrae Dist.
  Centennial (Willowdale)
  Central (Willowdale)
  Charles R. Sanderson
  City Hall
  Cliffcrest
  Dawes Rd.
  Deer Park
  Don Mills
  Downsview
  Dufferin-St. Clair
  East York
  Eatonville
  Eglinton Square
  Etobicoke
  Evelyn Gregory
  Fairview
  Flemingdon Park
  Forest Hill
  George H. Locke
  Gerrard-Ashdale
  Guildwood
  Highland Creek
  High Park
  Hillcrest
  Humber Bay
  Humber Summit
  James F. Cox
  Jane-Dundas
  Jones Ave.
  Leaside
  Long Branch
  Main St.
  McGregor Park
  Mimico Centennial
  Morningside
  Mount Dennis
  New Toronto
  Northern Dist.
  North York
  Palmerston
  Pape/Danforth
  Parkdale
  Parliament St.
  Perth-Dupont
  Pleasant View
  Port Union
  Rexdale Branch
  Richview Branch
  Riverdale
  Runnymede
  Scarborough Admin.
  Sheppard Centre (Willowdale)
  Spaced-Out
  Spadina Rd.
  S. Walter Stewart
  Swansea Memorial
  Taylor
  Thorncliffe
  Victoria Village
  Weston
  Woodside Square

Woodview Park
Wychwood
York (Borough)
Yorkdale
Yorkville
York Woods
Tottenham Library, Box 339, 18 Queen St., Tottenham, Ont. L0G 1W0 – 416/936-2291 – Mrs. D. Smith
Trenton Library, 18 Albert St., Trenton, Ont. K8V 4S3 – 613/394-3381
Trenton, see also James F. Cox
Tweed Library, 21 Spring St., Tweed, Ont. K0K 3J0 – Mrs. Mabel McCulloch
Tyandaga Library, 1500 Upper Middle Rd., Burlington, Ont. L7P 3P5 – 416/639-3611
Tyendinaga Twp. Library, Box 10, Shannonville, Ont. K0K 3A0 – 613/962-3303
Unionville Library, 221 Main St., Unionville, Ont. L3R 2H3 – 416/297-2641
Uxbridge Twp. Library, 9 Toronto St. S., Uxbridge, Ont. L0C 1K0 – 416/852-5231 – Mrs. M. O'Regan
Valley East Library, Box 700, Val Caron, Ont. P0M 3A0 – 705/897-6250 – Mrs. G. Mullen
Valley Heights Branch, c/o Norfolk Twp. Library
Vanier Library, 300 White Fathers Ave., Ottawa, Ont. K1L 7L5 – 613/745-0861 – A. Hebert
Vankleek Hill Library, Box 520, Vankleek Hill, Ont. K0B 1R0 – 613/678-2216 – Mrs. M. Boucher
Vaughan Public Libraries, Merino Rd., Maple, Ont. L0J 1E0 – 416/832-2959 – Mrs. S.J. Hall
Verner, see Caldwell Twp.
Vernon Branch, c/o Osgoode Twp. Library
Vespra Twp. Library, Minesing, Ont. L0L 1Y0
Victoria County Library, 32 William St. N., Lindsay, Ont. K9V 4A1 – 705/324-3104 – Miss M.B. Gibson
Victoria Harbour Library, Victoria Harbour, Ont. L0K 2A0 – 705/534-3582
Victoria Village Library, 184 Sloane Ave., Toronto, Ont. M4A 2C4 – 416/755-6691
Vienna Branch, c/o Elgin County Library
Village Library, 58 Church St. N., Pickering, Ont. L1V 2H8 – 416/683-1140
W. Clarence Sinclair Library, New Sudbury Shopping Centre, 1349 LaSalle Blvd., Sudbury, Ont. P3A 1Z2 – 705/673-1155, ext. 43
Wainfleet Twp. Library, Wainfleet, Ont. L0S 1V0 – 416/899-1277 – Mrs. M.I. Dilts
Walden Public Library, Box 189, Lively, Ont. P0M 2E0 – 705/692-4848 – Mrs. B. Mukherjee, Adm.
Walkerton Library, Drawer 250, 253 Durham St. E., Walkerton, Ont. N0G 2V0 – 519/881-3240 (a branch of the Bruce County Library)
Wallaceburg Library, 209 James St., Wallaceburg, Ont. N8A 2N4 – 519/627-5292 – Joan Stearns (a branch of the Kent County Library)
Wallbridge Rd. Branch, c/o Sidney Twp. Library
Walpole Island Branch, c/o Lambton County Library
Walton Branch, c/o Huron County Library
Wardsville Branch, c/o Middlesex County Library
Warkworth Library, Church at Main Sts., Warkworth, Ont. K0K 3K0
Warwick Branch, c/o Lambton County Library
Wasaga Beach Public Library, 60 19th St., c/o Box 12, Site 1, R.R. 1, Wasaga Beach, Ont. L0L 2P0 – Mrs. C. Downer
Waterdown Branch, c/o Wentworth County Library
Waterford Branch, c/o Nanticoke Library
Waterloo Library, 35 Albert St., Waterloo, Ont. N2L 5E2 – 519/886-1310 – J.J. Brown
Waterloo, see also Parkside
Waterloo Regional Library, 7th floor, Marsland Centre, 20 Erb St. W., Waterloo, Ont. N2J 4G7 – 519/885-9590 – Miss K. Manley
Waters Branch, c/o Walden Library
Watford Branch, c/o Lambton County Library
Waubaushene Library, Waubaushene, Ont. L0K 2C0 – 705/538-1122
Webbwood Library, Webbwood, Ont. P0P 2G0 – 705/869-2389 – Mrs. C. Frost
Welland Library, 140 King St., Welland, Ont. L3B 3J3 – 416/734-6210 – Miss S.L. Jones
Welland, see also Northwest
Wellandport Branch, c/o West Lincoln Twp. Library
Wellesley Branch, c/o Waterloo Regional Library
Wellington County Library, Wellington Place, R.R. 1, Fergus, Ont. N1M 2W3 – 519/846-5761 – P. Harvie
Wellington Library, 261 Main St., Box 370, Wellington, Ont. K0K 3L0 – 613/399-2023 – Miss B. Webster
Wendover Library, Wendover, Ont. K0A 3K0
Wentworth Library, 67 Sanders Blvd., Hamilton, Ont. L8S 3J8 – 416/526-4126 – I. Calbick
West Branch Library, 18 Rosemount Ave., Ottawa, Ont. K1Y 1P4 – 613/236-0301
West Carleton Twp. Library, Box 220, Carp, Ont. K0A 1L0 – 613/839-5412 – Miss M.A. Nicholson
West Hill, see Highland Creek
West Lincoln Twp. Library, Box 164, Smithville, Ont. L0R 2A0 – 416/957-3756
West Lorne Branch, c/o Elgin County Library
West Nissouri Branch, c/o Middlesex County Library
Westdale Library, 955 King St. W., Hamilton, Ont. L8S 1K9 – 416/528-1668
Westminster Branch Library, 690 Osgoode Dr., London, Ont. N6E 2G2 – 519/685-1333
Westmount Branch Library, 507 Village Green Ave., London, Ont. N6J 4G4 – 519/473-4708 – Ms. E. Floody
Weston Library, 2 King St., Weston, Ont. M9N 1K9 – 416/241-3116
Westown Branch Library, 301 Oxford St. W., London, Ont. N6H 1S6 – 519/439-6456
Westport Library, Box 28, Westport, Ont. K0G 1X0 – 613/273-3223 – Miss R. McCan
Wheatley Branch, c/o Kent County Library
Whitby Library, 405 Dundas St. W., Whitby, Ont. L1N 6A1 – 668-6531 – Mrs. Margaret McFadyen
Whitchurch-Stouffville Library, 65 Main St. W., Stouffville, Ont. L0H 1L0 – 416/640-2395 – G. Schlukbier
White Oaks Branch Library, 1380 Ernest Ave., London, Ont. N6E 2H8 – 519/685-6465 – H. McIntyre
White Oaks Library, 70 McCraney St., Oakville, Ont. L6H 1H9 – 416/844-8464
Whitefish Branch, c/o Walden Library
Whitefish Lake Band Library, Box 39, Naughton, Ont. P0M 2M0 – 705/692-9618
Whitefish River Band Library, c/o Miss Pauline Andrews, Whitefish River Indian Reserve, Birch Island, Ont. P0P 1A0 – 705/285-4310
Whitevale Branch, c/o Pickering Library
Whitney Library, Box 160, 118 Martin St., Porcupine, Ont. P0N 1C0 – 705/235-5185
Wiarton Branch, c/o Bruce County Library
Wicksteed Twp. Library, Box 539, Hornepayne, Ont. P0M 1Z0 – 705/868-2285
Wikwemikong Indian Band Library, Box 112, Wikwemikong, Ont. P0P 2J0 – 705/859-3122
Wilberforce Branch, c/o Haliburton County Library
Williamsburgh, see Stormont, Dundas & Glengarry
Williamstown, see Stormont, Dundas & Glengarry
Winchester, see Stormont, Dundas & Glengarry
Windsor Library, 850 Ouellette Ave., Windsor, Ont. N9A 4M9 – 519/258-8111 – F.C. Israel
Windsor, see also
Ambassador
Nikola Budimir
Riverside
Seminole
South Walkerville
Tecumseh Mall
Wingham Branch, c/o Huron County Library
Winona Branch, c/o Wentworth Library

Wollaston-Limerick Twp. Library, Box 129, Coe Hill Public School, Coe Hill, Ont. K0L 1P0 – 613/337-5711 – Mrs. A. Russell

Woodbridge Library, Woodbridge Ave., Woodbridge, Ont. L4L 1A8 – 416/851-1296 (a branch of the Vaughan Public Libraries)

Woodlands Library, 1030 McBride Ave., Mississauga, Ont. L5C 1L6 – 416/275-7087

Woodside Library, 1274 Rebecca St., Oakville, Ont. L6L 1Z2 – 416/827-3321

Woodside Sq. Library, 1571 Sandhurst Circle, Unit 30, Scarborough, Ont. M1V 1V2 – 416/291-9437

Woodstock Library, 445 Hunter St., Woodstock, Ont. N4S 4G7 – 519/539-4801 – Ms. C. Croke

Woodview Branch, c/o Burleigh, Anstruther Library

Woodview Park Library, 16 Bradstock Rd., Weston, Ont. M9M 1M8 – 416/742-7242

Woodville Branch, c/o Victoria County Library

Wychwood Library, 1431 Bathurst St., Toronto, Ont. M5R 3J2 – 416/532-0462

Wyoming Branch, c/o Lambton County Library

Yarker Branch, c/o Lennox & Addington County Library

York Borough Library, 1745 Eglinton Ave. W., Toronto, Ont. M6E 2H4 – 416/781-5208 – B. Derer

York Woods Library, 1785 Finch Ave. W., Downsview, Ont. M3N 1M6 – 416/630-9585

Yorkdale Library, Yorkdale Shopping Centre, Toronto, Ont. M6A 2T9 – 416/781-8150

Yorkville Library, 22 Yorkville Ave., Toronto, Ont. M4W 1L4 – 416/922-4913

Zurich Branch, c/o Huron County Library

Special & College Libraries & Resource Centres in Ontario

With Contact Person (Librarian, unless otherwise indicated)

AGINCOURT

See Toronto

ARNPRIOR

Federal Study Centre Library, Box 40, Arnprior, Ont. K7S 3H2 – 613/623-4227 – A.B. Moorhead

BARRIE

Georgian College (AA & T) Library, One Georgian College Dr., Barrie, Ont. L4M 3X9 – Jean M. Neice, i/c

Simcoe County Law Association Library, Court House, 30 Poyntz St., Barrie, Ont. L4M 1M1 – 705/728-1221, ext. 54 – Mrs. E. Garner

BELLEVILLE

The Intelligencer Newsp. Library, 45 Bridge St., Belleville, Ont. K8N 1L5 – 613/962-9171 – H.M. Morton

Loyalist College Library, Box 4200, Belleville, Ont. K8N 5B9 – 613/962-9501 – R. Boyce

BRAMPTON

The Daily Times Library, 33 Queen St. W., Brampton, Ont. L6Y 1M1 – 416/457-2020

Northern Telecom Canada Ltd., Dept. 3070 – Library, 8200 Dixie Rd., Box 3000, Brampton, Ont. L6V 2M6 – Mrs. Beverly J. Law

Sheridan College (AA & T), Brampton Campus Library, McLaughlin Rd., Box 7500, Brampton, Ont. L6V 1G6 – 416/459-7533 – Margaret Bram

Vanier Centre for Women, Library, (205 McLaughlin Rd.) Box 1150, Brampton, Ont. L6V 2M5 – 416/459-9100, ext. 158 – Mrs. Angelika Zanotti

BRANTFORD

Brant County Law Association Library, Court House, Brantford, Ont. N3T 2J3 – 519/752-1744 – T.A. Whitbread

Burtch Correctional Centre, Library, Box 940, Brantford, Ont. N3T 5S6 – 519/484-2421 – Miss Carol Holden

Mohawk College (AA & T), Braneida Campus Library, Elgin St., Brantford, Ont. N3T 5V2 – 519/759-7200 – Mrs. Marilyn McDermott

Mohawk College (AA & T), Brantford General Nursing Library, 235 St. Paul Ave., Brantford, Ont. N3R 5Z3 – 519/759-2770 – Mrs. Joan Redmond

BROCKVILLE

AEL Microtel Limited Library, 100 Strowger Blvd., Brockville, Ont. K6V 5W8 – 613/342-6621 – Linda Eyre

St. Lawrence College (AA & T), Learning Resource Centre, 20 Parkedale Ave., Brockville, Ont. – 613/345-0660 – Gloria Reinbergs

BURLINGTON

Canada Centre for Inland Waters Library, 867 Lakeshore Rd., Box 5050, Burlington, Ont. L7R 4A6 – 416/637-4282 – Eve Dowie

Canadian Canners Ltd. Research Centre Library, 1101 Walker's Line, Burlington, Ont. L7N 2G4 – 416/335-9700 – Mrs. G. Smithson

City of Burlington, Clerk's Department Library, 426 Brant St., Burlington, Ont. L7R 2G2 – 416/335-7701 – Mrs. Thelma Kerr

CUMIS Life Insurance Co. Library, Box 5065, Burlington, Ont. L7R 4C2 – 416/632-1221 – Mrs. Marlene McIntosh

Westinghouse Canada Ltd., Electronic Systems Division Library, Box 5009, Burlington, Ont. L7R 4B3 – 416/528-8811, ext. 4226 – Mrs. Elizabeth J. Jackson

CARLETON PLACE

Leigh Instruments Ltd., Technical Library, Box 82, Carleton Place, Ont. K7C 3P3 – 613/238-4400 (direct Ottawa line); 257-3883, ext. 304 – Mrs. Betty G. Robertson

CHALK RIVER

Atomic Energy of Canada Ltd. Library, Chalk River, Ont. KOJ 1JO – 613/584-3311 via Deep River, 613/687-5581 via Pembroke – H. Greenshields

Petawawa National Forestry Institute Library, Environment Canada, Chalk River, Ont. K0J 1J0 – 613/589-2880, ext. 337 – Mrs. R.B. Reiche, Library Clerk

CHATHAM

The Daily News Library, 45 Fourth St., Chatham, Ont. N7M 5M6 – 519/354-2000

St. Clair College (AA & T), Thames Campus Resource Centre, 1001 Grand Ave. W., Box 2017, Chatham, Ont. N7M 5W4 – 519/354-9100, ext. 232 – Ada Berti

Union Gas Ltd., Library Services, 50 Keil Dr. N., Chatham, Ont. N7M 5M1 – 519/352-3100, ext. 2594 – Mrs. A. Steen

CORNWALL

Parks Canada, Ontario Region Library, (132 2nd St. E.), Box 1359, Cornwall, Ont. K6H 5V4 – 613/933-7951, ext. 211 – Michel R. Jesmer, Lib. Tech.

Transport Canada Training Institute Library, 1950 Montreal Rd., Cornwall, Ont. K6H 6L2 – 613/938-4411 – D. Harding

DON MILLS

See Toronto

DOWNSVIEW

See Toronto

ETOBICOKE

See Toronto

GUELPH

Conestoga College (AA & T), Guelph Campus Library, 460 Speedvale Ave. W., Guelph, Ont. N1H 6N6 – 519/824-9390 – Barbara J. Cowan

Guelph Correctional Centre Library, Box 3600, Guelph, Ont. N1H 6P3 – 519/822-0020 – H.F. Steele

Guelph University Library, c/o Chief Librarian, Guelph, Ont. N1G 2W1 – 519/824-4120, ext. 2159
- Chief Librarian – Mrs. Margaret Beckman
- Associate Librarian – Dr. J.B. Black
- Asst. Librarian, Information Services – Mrs. E.M. Pearson
- Asst. Librarian, Systems & Development – L.T. Porter
- Divisions:
- Library Business Office – F. Stewart
- Circulation – Mrs. P. Hock
- Collections Librarian – J. Moldenhauer
- Documentation & Media Resource Centre – Mrs. V. Gillham

Humanities & Social Science – B. Katz
Library Personnel Office – Mrs. J. Hill
Technical Processing – Mrs. E. Tom
Science & Veterinary Science – D. Hull
Systems & Data Processing – D. Paterson

Reorganized Church of Jesus Christ of Latter Day Saints (Canada) Ltd., Research Library, 390 Speedvale Ave. E., Guelph, Ont. N1E 1N5 – 519/822-4150 – Donald H. Comer

Uniroyal Ltd., Research Labs Library, 120 Huron St., Guelph, Ont. N1H 6N3 – 519/822-3790, ext. 58 – Lorna Cole

HAILEYBURY

Northern College (AA & T), School of Mines Library, Box 849, Haileybury, Ont. P0J 1K0 – 705/672-3376 – Mrs. Maureen Taeger

HAMILTON

Agro, Zaffiro & Associates Law Library, (15 King St. W., 9th Floor), Box 1069, Hamilton, Ont. L8N 3G6 – 416/528-6703 – Anne Grady

Board of Education, See Education Centre

Canadian Baptist Archives, McMaster Divinity College, Hamilton, Ont. L8S 4K1 – 416/525-9140, ext. 4401 – Miss Judith Colwell

Chedoke-McMaster Hospitals, Chedoke Division Library, (Sanatorium Rd.), Box 2000, Stn. A, Hamilton, Ont. L8N 3Z5 – 416/388-0240, ext. 242 – Mrs. Elsie Mathews

City of Hamilton, City Hall Library, 71 Main St. W., Hamilton, Ont. L8P 1H4 – 416/527-0241, ext. 320 – S.G. Hollowell

Dofasco Inc., Main Office Library, Box 460, Hamilton, Ont. L8N 3J5 – 416/544-3761, ext. 2794 – Mrs. M. Gucma

Education Centre Library, 100 Main St. W., Hamilton, Ont. L8P 1H6 – 416/527-5092, ext. 308 – Mrs. E.B. Langhammer

Hamilton Academy of Medicine Library, 286 Victoria Ave. N., Hamilton, Ont. L8L 5G4 – 416/528-1611 – Miss B. McKinlay

Hamilton City, See City of Hamilton

Hamilton Law Association Library, Court House, 50 Main St. E., Hamilton, Ont. L8N 1E9 – 416/522-1563 – Ms. W. Hearder-Moan

Hamilton Spectator Reference Library, 44 Frid St., Hamilton, Ont. L8N 3G3 – 416/526-3315 – Jean M. Tebbutt

McMaster University Libraries, c/o University Librarian, Hamilton, Ont. L8S 4L6 – 416/525-9140, ext. 2070
University Librarian – Graham R. Hill
Associate Librarians:
Readers Services – Margaret Maggs
Science & Engineering – Harold Siroonian
Technical Services – Marju Kraav
Health Sciences – Beatrix Robinow
Associate Director, Library Admin. – Arthur Lawrence
Director of Research Collections – Charlotte Stewart
Business Library – Sheila Pepper
Map Library – Kate Donkin

Mohawk College (AA & T), Library, 135 Fennell Ave. W., Box 2034, Hamilton, Ont. L8N 3T2 – 416/389-4461 – Thomas R. Drynan
Chedoke Health Sciences Library, Box 2034, Hamilton, Ont. L8N 3T2 – 416/389-4461, ext. 561 – Mrs. June Shore
And See Brantford, Ont.

Royal Botanical Gardens Library, Box 399, Hamilton, Ont. L8N 3H8 – 416/527-1158, ext. 46 – Mrs. Ina Vrugtman

St. Joseph's Hospital Library, 50 Charlton Ave. E., Hamilton, Ont. L8N 1Y4 – 416/522-4941, ext. 410 – Mrs. S.L. Rogers

Society of Management Accountants of Canada Library, 154 Main St. E., Box 176, Hamilton, Ont. L8N 3C3 – 416/525-4100 – Mrs. H. Hill

Stelco Inc., Central Library, Stelco Tower, 100 King St. W., Hamilton, Ont. L8N 3T1 – 416/528-2511
Central Library – Mrs. L.P. Murphy
Research Library – D.W. Rosenplot
Engineering Services Library – J.A. DeYoung
Head Office Library – Ms. G. Davidson

Westinghouse Canada Ltd., See Burlington

HARROW

Agriculture Canada, Research Station Library, Harrow, Ont. N0R 1G0 – 519/738-2251 – Eric A. Champagne

HAWKESBURY

Algonquin College (AA & T), Hawkesbury Campus Resource Centre, 517 McGill St., Hawkesbury, Ont. K6A 1R1 – 613/632-0003

C.I.P. Research Ltd. Library, Hawkesbury, Ont. K6A 2H4 – 613/632-4121 – Mrs. M.E. Cranford

HEARST

College Universitaire de Hearst (Bibliothèque), Box 580, Hearst, Ont. P0L 1N0 – 705/362-4841 – Johanne Morin

HURON PARK

Centralia College of Agricultural Technology, Library, Huron Park, Ont. N0M 1Y0 – 519/228-6691 – Mrs. Marie Kenney

ISLINGTON

See Toronto

KEMPTVILLE

Kemptville College of Agricultural Technology, Library, Kemptville, Ont. K0G 1J0 – 613/258-3411, ext. 256 – V.M. Healy

KINGSTON

Alcan International Ltd., Kingston Laboratories Technical Library, Box 8400, Kingston, Ont. K7L 4Z4 – 613/549-4500 – Miss E.M. Vanags

Du Pont Canada Inc., Customer Technical Centre, Box 3500, Kingston, Ont. K7L 5A1 – 613/544-6000, ext. 7194 – L.A. Collins

Du Pont Canada Inc., Research Centre & Kingston Works, Box 5000, Kingston, Ont. K7L 5A5 – 613/544-6400, ext. 504 – Betty F. Swerbrick

Hotel-Dieu Hospital (Religious Hospitallers of St. Joseph), Library, Brock & Sydenham Sts., Kingston, Ont. K7L 3H6 – 613/544-3310, ext. 361 – Miss Lynda Silver

Kingston General Hospital, Medical Library, Stuart St., Kingston, Ont. K7L 2V7 – 613/547-5023 – Mrs. E. Scott

Kingston Psychiatric Hospital, Staff Library, Bag 603, Kingston, Ont. K7L 4X3 – 613/546-1101, ext. 216 – Mae Morley

National Defence College of Canada, and the Canadian Land Forces Command & Staff College, Library, Fort Frontenac, Kingston, Ont. K7K 2X8 – 613/545-5829 – Santosh K. Kamra

Queen's University Libraries, c/o Chief Librarian, Kingston, Ont. K7L 5C4 – 613/547-6637
Chief Librarian – Mrs. Margot B. McBurney
Associate Librarian – Mrs. Lin Good
Asst. Librarian (Personnel) – Miss M.E. Skeith
Asst. Librarian (Systems) – G.W. Clevenger
Business Officer – P. Schell
Units in Douglas Library:
Acquisitions – Miss D. Cook
Cataloguing – Miss S. Denyer
Central Collection Services – D. Wang
Documents – Mrs. S. Casey
Information & Reference – Peter Girard
Special Collections – W.F.E. Morley
Branch and Faculty Libraries:
Co-ordinator, Branches – V. Mahalingam
Art – Miss E. Albrich
Biology – Mrs. J. Stevenson
Chemical Engineering – see Dupuis Hall
Chemistry – Mrs. Wendy Innis
Civil Engineering – Mrs. P. Egan
Dupuis Hall – Mrs. B. Walls
Education – Mrs. G. Wright
Electrical Engineering – vacant
Geological Sciences – D.A. Redmond
Health Sciences (Bracken) – Miss V. Parker
Law Library – Mrs. I. Bessette
Mathematics – Mrs. D. Nuttall
Mechanical Engineering – Mrs. K. Paget
Mining Engineering – see Dupuis Hall
Music – Miss E. Albrich

Physics – Miss Catherine Johnson
Psychology – Miss Helen Cobb
Supervisor, Science/Engineering Br. – Miss A. Laing

Royal Military College of Canada, Library, Kingston, Ont. K7L 2W3 – 613/545-7305
Chief Librarian – R.K.C. Crouch (545-7229)
Special Collections – C.R. Watt (545-7260)
Technical Services – vacant
Humanities & Social Sciences – Maj. (ret.) A.S.J. Bake (545-7330)
Science/Engineering – Mrs. N. Turkington (545-7312)

St. Lawrence College (AA & T), Library, Kingston, Ont. K7L 5A6 – 613/544-5400, ext. 196 – S. Raichman

The Whig-Standard Library, 306 King St. E., Kingston, Ont. K7L 3B4 – 613/544-5000 – Heather Stewart

KIRKLAND LAKE

Northern College (AA & T), Resource Centre, 140 Government Rd. E., Kirkland Lake, Ont. P2N 3L8 – 705/567-9291, ext. 148 – T.O. Wright, Supvr.

KITCHENER

Conestoga College (AA & T), Resource Centre, 299 Doon Valley Dr., Kitchener, Ont. N2G 4M4 – 519/653-2511, ext. 214

Kitchener-Waterloo Hospital, Library, 835 King St. W., Kitchener, Ont. N2G 1G3 – 519/742-3611, ext. 2235 – Mrs. T. Bisch

Kitchener-Waterloo Record Library, 225 Fairway Rd. S., Kitchener, Ont. N2G 4E5 – 519/894-2231 – Penny Coates – (in-house newspaper library)

St. Mary's Hospital Library, Kitchener, Ont. N2M 1B2 – 519/744-3311 – Mrs. M. Mathews

Waterloo Law Association Library, Court House, 20 Weber St. E., Kitchener, Ont. N2H 1C3 – 519/742-9090 – Mrs. M. Goyder

LAKEFIELD

Lakefied College School Library, Lakefield, Ont. K0L 2H0 – 705/652-3324 – Mrs. Gwen Morawetz

LEAMINGTON

Point Pelee National Park, Library, R.R. 1, Leamington, Ont. N8H 3V4 – 519/326-1161

LINDSAY

Sir Sandford Fleming College (AA & T), Frost Campus Educational Resource Centre, Box 8000, Lindsay, Ont. K9V 5E6 – 705/324-9144 – Mrs. Joan Webster

LONDON

Agriculture Canada, London Research Centre Library, University Sub Post Office, London, Ont. N6A 5B7 – 519/679-4452 – Josephine Giesbrecht

Brescia College Library, 1285 Western Rd., London, Ont. N6G 1H2 – 519/432-8353 – Sister Pierina Caverzan

Canadian Library of Family Medicine, Medical Bldg., University of Western Ontario, London, Ont. N6A 5C1 – 519/679-2537 – Miss Dorothy Fitzgerald

Children's Psychiatric Research Institute Library, Box 2460, Term. A, London, Ont. N6A 4G6 – 519/471-2540, ext. 255 – Mrs. Asta Hansen

City of London, Main Library, City Hall, 300 Dufferin Ave., Box 5035, London, Ont. N6A 4L9 – 519/679-5414 – G.A. McInnis (Contact)
Also Planning Dept. Library
Also Social Services Dept. Library

Fanshawe College (AA & T), Library, Box 4005, London, Ont. N5W 5H1 – 519/452-4100 – Miss A.K. Frost

Huron College, Silcox Memorial Library, 1349 Western Rd., London, Ont. N6G 1H3 – 519/438-7224, ext. 13, 35 – Victoria E. Ripley

King's College Library, London, Ont. N6A 2M3 – 519/433-3491, ext. 44 – Peter D. Mitchell

Labatt Brewing Co. Ltd., Central Research Library, Box 5050, London, Ont. N6A 4M3 – 519/673-5324 – Mrs. Marliese Lehwaldt

Lerner & Associates Law Library, (80 Maple St.), Box 2335, Stn. A, London, Ont. N6A 4G4 – 519/672-4131 – Kathryn Ferris

London City, See City of London

London Free Press Editorial Library, Box 2280, London, Ont. N6A 4G1 – 519/679-1111, ext. 257 – Edythe Cusack

Middlesex Law Association Library, (Court House), Box 5600, Term. A, London, Ont. N6A 2P3 – 519/679-7046 – Ms. J.V. Gulliver

St. Joseph's Hospital, Medical Library, 268 Grosvenor St., London, Ont. N6A 4V2 – 519/439-3271 – Mrs. Louise Lin

St. Peter's Seminary Library, 1040 Waterloo St. N., London, Ont. N6A 3Y1 – 519/432-9739, ext. 70 – Lois Côté

3M Canada Inc., Technical Information Centre, Box 5757, London, Ont. N6A 4T1 – 519/451-2500, ext. 2486 – Lorraine Polk

University Hospital, Library Services, Box 5339, Stn. A, London, Ont. N6A 5A5 – 519/673-3464 – Miss S.A. Gillespie

University of Western Ontario Libraries, c/o Director of Libraries, London, Ont. N6A 3K7 – 519/679-3165
Director of Libraries – Dr. Robert Lee
Business – Alan Burk
Education – Mrs. Anna Holman
Engineering – Miss Bogdana Brajsa
Health Sciences – Larry Lewis
Law – Dr. Margaret Banks
Music – Merwin Lewis
Natural Sciences – John Macpherson

University of Western Ontario, School of Library & Information Science, London, Ont. N6A 5B9 – 519/679-3542 – Mrs. Pat Nicholls

MAPLE

Ontario Ministry of Natural Resources, Research Branch Library, Maple, Ont. L0J 1E0 – 416/832-2761 – Mrs. Sandra Louet

MAITLAND

Du Pont Canada Inc. Library, Box 611, Maitland, Ont. K0E 1P0 – 613/348-3611, ext. 301 – Hilary Perrott

MIDLAND

Huronia Historical Parks, Resource Centre, Box 160, Midland, Ont. L4R 4K8 – 705/526-7838 – Mrs. Michelle Quealey

MISSISSAUGA

Abitibi-Price Inc., Research Centre Library, Sheridan Park, Mississauga, Ont. L5K 1A9 – 416/822-4770 – Mrs. J.A. Armstrong

Allied Chemical Canada Ltd. Library, 201 City Centre Dr., Mississauga, Ont. L5B 2T4 – 416/276-9211

Atomic Energy of Canada Ltd., Engineering Company Library, Sheridan Park, Mississauga, Ont. L5K 1B2 – 416/823-9040 – Mrs. C.C. Byrne

Canada Systems Group Library, 2599 Speakman Dr., Mississauga, Ont. L5K 1B1 – 416/822-5200, ext. 289 – Janet Bycio

C-I-L Inc., Chemicals Research Laboratory Library, Sheridan Park, Mississauga, Ont. L5K 2L3 – 416/823-7160 – Mrs. Joan Leishman

Cominco Ltd., Product Research Centre Library, Sheridan Park, Mississauga, Ont. L5K 1B4 – 416/822-2022 – Miss K. Szachlewicz

Domglas Inc., Corporate Library, Sheridan Park, Mississauga, Ont. L5K 2C9 – 416/823-3860 – Mary MacKinnon

Dunlop Research Centre Library, Sheridan Park, Mississauga, Ont. L5K 1Z8 – 416/822-4711 – Mrs. S.A. Morrison

Du Pont Canada Inc., Central Library, Box 2300, Streetsville PO, Mississauga, Ont. L5M 2J4 – 416/821-5781 – Mrs. Martha G. Pettit

Du Pont Canada Inc., Legal Library, 6700 Century Ave., Mississauga, Ont. L5M 2H3 – 416/821-5504 – Joan E. Leedale

Duracell Inc., Research Library, 2333 North Sheridan Way, Mississauga, Ont. L5K 1A7 – 416/823-4410 – Mrs. Marni Lyttle

Erindale College Library, 3359 Mississauga Rd. N., Mississauga, Ont. L5L 1C6 – 416/828-5235 – H.L. Smith

Golder Associates Ltd. Library, 3151 Wharton Way, Mississauga, Ont. L4X 2B6 – 416/625-0094 – Marry Anne Smyth, Lib. Techn.

Gulf Canada Ltd., Research & Development Dept. Library, 2489 North Sheridan Way, Sheridan Park, Mississauga, Ont. L5K 1A8 – 416/822-6770 – Miss A. Neilson

Inco Metals Co., Library, Sheridan Park, Mississauga, Ont. L5K 1Z9 – 416/822-3322 – L. Green

Ontario Concrete Pipe Association Library, #202, 2345 Stanfield Rd., Mississauga, Ont. L4Y 3Y3 – 416/270-8575 – Mrs. M. Peck

Ontario Research Foundation, Library, Sheridan Park, Mississauga, Ont. L5K 1B3 – 416/822-4111 – Carl K. Wei

Peel Board of Education, J.A. Turner Professional Library, 73 King St. W., Mississauga, Ont. L5B 1H5 –

Sheridan College (AA & T), Credit Valley Campus School of Nursing Library, 2186 Hurontario St., Mississauga, Ont. L5B 1M9 – 416/279-3731 – Elda Dunham, Lib. Techn.

Sheridan College (AA & T), Lorne Park Campus School of Crafts & Design Library, 1460 South Sheridan Way, Mississauga, Ont. L5H 1Z7 – 416/274-3685 – Madeleine La Pointe, Lib. Techn.

Smith, Kline & French Canada Ltd., Medical Library, 1940 Argentia Rd., Mississauga, Ont. L5N 2V7 – 416/821-2200, ext. 291 – Mary Smith

United Co-operatives of Ontario, Library, (151 City Centre Dr.), Box 527, Stn. A, Mississauga, Ont. L5A 3A4 – 416/270-3560 – Mrs. H.J. Carnell

Warner-Lambert Research Institute Library, Sheridan Park, Mississauga, Ont. L5K 1B4 – 416/822-3520

Xerox Research Centre of Canada, Technical Information Centre, 2480 Dunwin Dr., Mississauga, Ont. L5L 1J9 – 416/828-6200, ext. 306 – Betty A. Bassett

NEPEAN

Carleton Board of Education Library, 133 Greenbank Rd., Nepean, Ont. K2H 6L3 – 613/820-1820, ext. 312

NEW LISKEARD

Ecole St-Michel (Bibliothèque), New Liskeard, Ont. P0J 1P0 – 705/647-6614 – Juliette Aubé

NIAGARA FALLS

Acres Consulting Services Ltd. Library, (5259 Dorchester Rd.), Box 1001, Niagara Falls, Ont. L2E 6W1 – 416/354-3831, ext. 247 – Mrs. A. McKay

The Review Library, Corner Valley Way & Morrison, Niagara Falls, Ont. L2E 6T6 – 416/358-5711 – G. Herbison

NORTH BAY

Education Centre Library, Box 5001, North Bay, Ont. P1B 8K9 – 705/474-7600 – Garth Poff – Serving Canadore College and Nipissing University

Forest Products Accident Prevention Association Library, Box 270, North Bay, Ont. P1B 8H2 – 705/472-4120 – Ms. R. Molloy

The Nugget Newsp. Library, Box 570, North Bay, Ont. P1B 8J6 – 705/472-3200 – Mrs. N. Floyd

NORTH YORK

See Toronto

OAKVILLE

Appleby College Library, Oakville, Ont. L6K 3P1 – 416/845-4681 – Ms. Elizabeth Gibb

Shell Research Centre Library, Box 2100, Oakville, Ont. L6J 5C7 – 416/827-1141, ext. 339 – Lan C. Sun

Sheridan College (AA & T), Oakville Campus Library, 1430 Trafalgar Rd., Oakville, Ont. L6H 2L1 – 416/823-9730 – Ms. C. Zuraw

Welding Institute of Canada Library, 391 Burnhamthorpe Rd. E., Oakville, Ont. L6J 6C9 – 416/845-9881 – B. Bryan

ORILLIA

Georgian College (AA & T), Library, (825 Memorial Ave.), Box 2316, Orillia, Ont. L3V 6S2 – Joanne R. Shea, i/c

OSHAWA

Durham College (AA & T), Main Library & Simcoe Resource Centre, Box 385, Oshawa, Ont. L1H 7L7 – 416/576-0210, ext. 214 – Susan L. Barclay

Kingsway College Library, Box 605, Oshawa, Ont. L1H 7M6 – 416/725-6557 – Ms. Glenda-mae Greene

Oshawa General Hospital Library, 24 Alma St., Oshawa, Ont. L1G 2B9 – 416/576-8711, ext. 334 – Mrs. S.E. Hendricks

OTTAWA

Affairs of the Moment, Information Centre, 18 Third Ave., Ottawa, Ont. K1S 2J6 – 613/236-2976 – Charlotte McEwen

Agriculture Canada, Departmental Library, Sir John Carling Bldg., Ottawa, Ont. K1A 0C5 – 613/995-5219 – Mrs. M.L. Morton

Agriculture Canada, Neatby Library, K.W. Neatby Bldg., Ottawa, Ont. K1A 0C5 – M.C. Charette

Agriculture Canada, Animal Diseases Research Institute Library, Box 11300, Stn. H, Ottawa, Ont. K2H 8P9 – 613/998-9320

Agriculture Canada, Entomology Research Library, Ottawa, Ont. K1A 0C6 – 613/996-1665 – R. Sharrett

Agriculture Canada, Ottawa Research Station Library, Ottawa, Ont. K1A 0C6 – 613/995-9428

Agriculture Canada, Plant Research Library, Ottawa, Ont. K1A 0C6 – 613/996-1665 – Mrs. E. Gavora

Agudath Israel Congregation, Malca Pass Memorial Library, 1400 Coldrey Ave., Ottawa, Ont. K1Z 7P9 – 613/728-1750 – Frieda Lauterman

Algonquin College (AA & T), Byron Campus Resource Centre, 2135 Knightsbridge Rd., Ottawa, Ont. K2A 0R3 – 613/728-4945 – Mme M. Jennings

Algonquin College (AA & T), Colonel By Campus Resource Centre, 281 Echo Dr., Ottawa, Ont. K1S 1N3 – 613/237-5257 – Mrs. I. Stark

Algonquin College (AA & T), Heron Park Campus Resource Centre, 1644 Bank St., Ottawa, Ont. K1V 7Y6 – 613/731-9441 – Miss B. Dowd

Algonquin College (AA & T), Parkdale Campus Resource Centre, 725 Parkdale Ave., Ottawa, Ont. K1Y 4K9 – 613/725-2195 – Mrs. I. Bond

Algonquin College (AA & T), Rideau Campus Resource Centre, 200 Lees Ave., Ottawa, Ont. K1S 0C5 – 613/237-8103 – Mrs. I. Stark

Algonquin College (AA & T), Woodroffe Campus Resource Centre, Ottawa, Ont. K2G 1V8 – 613/725-7302 – James Feeley

Association of Universities & Colleges of Canada, Library, 151 Slater St., Ottawa, Ont. K1P 5N1 – 613/563-3670 – Mrs. Hazel Roberts

Atomic Energy of Canada Ltd., Commercial Product Division Library, Box 6300, Stn. J, Ottawa, Ont. K2A 3W3 – 613/592-2790, loc. 254 – Herb Fletcher

Atomic Energy Control Board Library, Box 1046, Ottawa, Ont. K1P 5S9 – 613/995-1359, 593-7903 – Helen T. Booth

Auditor General's Office Library, 11th Floor, West Tower, 240 Sparks St., Ottawa, Ont. K1A 0G6 – 613/995-3763 –

Bank of Canada Library, Wellington St., Ottawa, Ont. K1A 0G9 – 613/563-8246 – Mrs. S. Balatti

Bell-Northern Research Library, Box 3511, Stn. C, Ottawa, Ont. K1Y 4H7 – 613/596-2469 – Mrs. M. Towaij

Boy Scouts of Canada Library, Box 5151, Stn. F, Ottawa, Ont. K2C 3G7 – 613/224-5131 – Mrs. M. Crampton

Brewers Association of Canada Library, 151 Sparks St., #805, Ottawa, Ont. K1P 5E3 – 613/232-9601

Canada Centre for Remote Sensing, see Dept. of Energy, Mines etc.

Canada Council Library, 255 Albert St., Ottawa, Ont. K1P 5V8 – 613/237-3400 – Mrs. Elizabeth Adamitz

Canada Employment & Immigration Commission Library, Ottawa, Ont. K1A 0J9 – 819/994-2603 – P.E. Sunder-Raj

Canada Institute for Scientific & Technical Information, National Research Council, Bldg. M-55, Montreal Rd., Ottawa, Ont. K1A 0S2 – 613/993-1600 – E.V. Smith, Dir.

Branch Libraries (NRC):

- Administration – Mrs. D. McColm (993-1517)
- Aeronautical & Mechanical Engineering – Mrs. L. Fletcher (993-9361)
- Building Research – Mrs. J. Waudby-Smith (993-2180)
- Chemistry – Mrs. N. Ross (993-2266)
- Dominion Astrophysical Observatory (Victoria) – E. Leblanc (604/388-0298)

Electrical Engineering – Miss M. Hubbard (993-2006)
Energy – Dr. D. Holmes (993-3861)
Materials Research Institute (Mtl.) – Miss L. Venne (514/935-8513)
Physics – Miss M. VanBuskirk (993-2483)
Sussex Bldg. – Mrs. M. Schade (992-9151)
Uplands – Mrs. A. Gorman (998-3327)

Canada Labour Relations Board Library, Tower D, 4th Floor, Sussex Dr., Ottawa, Ont. K1A 0X8 – 613/995-0895 – Judith Rubin

Canada Mortgage & Housing Corp., Canadian Housing Information Centre, Montreal Rd., Ottawa, Ont. K1A 0P7 – 613/746-4611

Canadian Broadcasting Corp., Head Office Library, 1500 Bronson Ave., Box 8478, Ottawa, Ont. K1G 3J5 – 613/731-3111, ext. 561 – Normand Deschamps
CBC Branch libraries include:
Documentation Centre
Historical Section-Archives
Northern Service Reference Centre
Program Archives

Canadian Centre for Films on Art, 75 Albert St., #B-20, Ottawa, Ont. K1P 5E7 – Peter Dyson-Bonter (Act. Dir.)

Canadian Conservation Institute Library, c/o National Museums of Canada, Ottawa, Ont. K1A 0M8 – 613/998-3721

Canadian Co-ordinating Council on Deafness, Information Resource Centre, 55 Parkdale Ave., Ottawa, Ont. K1Y 1E5 – 613/728-0936 – Alrick Huebener

Canadian Council on Social Development Library, (55 Parkdale Ave.), Box 3505, Stn. C, Ottawa, Ont. K1Y 4G1 – 613/728-1865 – Pat Redhead

Canadian Dental Association, Sydney Wood Bradley Memorial Library, 1815 Alta Vista Dr., Ottawa, Ont. K1G 3Y6 – 613/523-1770 – J.G. D'Aoust, D.D.S.

Canadian Export Association Library, #250, 99 Bank St., Ottawa, Ont. K1P 6B9 – 613/238-8888 – Mrs. M. Kane

Canadian Film Institute, National Film Library, 75 Albert St., Ottawa, Ont. K1P 5E7 – 613/232-2495 – Peter Dyson-Bonter, Dir.

Canadian Government Expositions Centre, Technical Library, Supply & Services Canada, 440 Coventry Rd., Ottawa, Ont. K1A 0T1 – 613/993-9732

Canadian Hospital Association Library, 410 Laurier Ave. W., #800, Ottawa, Ont. K1R 7T6 – 613/238-8005, ext. 38 & 58 – Diane Thomson & Louise Gibson

Canadian Human Rights Commission Library, 257 Slater St., 4th Floor, Ottawa, Ont. K1A 1E1 – 613/996-4597 – Ann E. Hall

Canadian Hunger Foundation Library, 323 Chapel St., Ottawa, Ont. K1N 7Z2 – 613/237-0180

Canadian Intergovernmental Conference Secretariat, Intergovernmental Documents Centre, (66 Slater St.), Box 488, Stn. A, Ottawa, Ont. K1N 8V5 – 613/995-2341 – André Gareau, Head

Canadian International Development Agency, See Hull, Quebec

Canadian Labour Congress Library, 2841 Riverside Dr., Ottawa, Ont. K1V 8X7 – 613/521-3400, ext. 52 – Mrs. Dawn Dobson

Canadian Lung Association Library, #908, 75 Albert St., Ottawa, Ont. K1P 5E7 – 613/237-1208

Canadian Medical Association Library, Box 8650, Ottawa, Ont. K1G 0G8 – 613/731-9331, ext. 144 – Mrs. K. Beaudoin

Canadian Museums Association, Documentation Centre, 331 Cooper St., #400, Ottawa, Ont. K2P 0G5 – 613/233-5653 – Micheline M. Boucher, Lib. Techn.

Canadian Nurses Association Library, 50 The Driveway, Ottawa, Ont. K2P 1E2 – 613/237-2133 – Mrs. Linda Solomon Shiff

Canadian Police College Library, (St. Laurent Blvd. N. & Sandridge Rd.), Box 8900, Ottawa, Ont. K1G 3J2 – 613/993-9500 – Joan Beavis

Canadian Radio-Television & Telecommunications Commission Library, Ottawa, Ont. K1A 0N2 – 613/997-4484 – M. Anschutz – library located at 1, Promenade du Portage, Hull

Canadian Rights & Liberties Federation, National Resource Centre, 323 Chapel St., Ottawa, Ont. K1N 7Z2 – 613/235-8978

Canadian Teachers' Federation, George G. Croskery Memorial Library, 110 Argyle St., Ottawa, Ont. K2P 1B4 – 613/232-1505 – Mrs. M. Moll

Canadian Transport Commission Library, Ottawa, Ont. K1A 0N9 – 819/997-7642 – M.H. Lovelock

Canadian War Museum Library, 330 Sussex Dr., Ottawa, Ont. K1A 0M8 – 613/996-4708 – L. Kosche

Canadian Wildlife Service, Ontario Regional Library, Environment Canada, 1725 Woodward Dr., 5th Floor, Ottawa, Ont. K1A 0E7 – 613/998-4693, ext. 31 – Katherine L. Mahoney

Canadian Wood Council Library, 85 Albert St., Ottawa, Ont. K1P 6A4 – 613/235-7221 – R.F. DeGrace

CANMET, see Dept. of Energy, Mines etc.

Carleton County Law Library, Court House, 2 Daly Ave., Ottawa, Ont. K1N 6E2 – 613/233-7386 – Mrs. W.T. Walsh

Carleton University, MacOdrum Library, Colonel By Drive, Ottawa, Ont. K1S 5J7 – 613/231-2683 – G.H. Briggs

Chief Electoral Officer Library, 440 Coventry Rd., Ottawa, Ont. K1A 0M6 – 613/993-2975

Children's Aid Society Library, 1370 Bank St., Ottawa, Ont. K1H 7Y3 – 613/737-1832 – Mrs. Jane Sorbie, Co-ord.

Coaching Association of Canada, See Sport Information Resource Centre, Vanier

Collège Dominicain de Philosophie et de Théologie (Bibliothèque), 96 ave Empress, Ottawa, Ont. K1R 7G2 – 613/233-5696 – J.-J. Robillard, o.p.

Commissioner of Official Languages Library, 66 Slater St., Ottawa, Ont. K1A 0T8 – 613/995-7717 – Beryl Hunter

The Conference Board of Canada Library, 25 McArthur Rd., #100, Ottawa, Ont. K1L 6R3 – 613/746-1261 – Mrs. T. Bruneau

Consumers' Association of Canada Library, 2660 Southvale Cres., Level 3, Ottawa, Ont. K1B 5C4 – 613/238-4840 – Marion G. Fuller

Defence Research Establishment Ottawa Library, Ottawa, Ont. K1A 0Z4 – 613/596-9386 – T. Matiisen

Dept. of Communications, Research Centre, Box 11490, Stn. H, Ottawa, Ont. K2H 8S2 – 613/596-9250

Dept. of Consumer & Corporate Affairs Library, Ottawa, Ont. K1A 0C9 – 819/997-1632 – Miss C. MacLaurin

Dept. of Energy, Mines & Resources:
Earth Physics Branch Library, 1 Observatory Cres., Ottawa, Ont. K1A 0Y3 – 613/995-5558 – W.M. Tsang
Surveys & Mapping Branch Library, 615 Booth St., Ottawa, Ont. K1A 0E9 – 613/995-4071 – Mrs. V.E. Hoare
CANMET Library, 555 Booth St., Ottawa, Ont. K1A 0G1 – 613/995-4132 – Miss G.M. Peckham
Canada Centre for Remote Sensing Library, 717 Belfast Rd., Ottawa, Ont. K1A 0Y7 – 613/995-1210 – B. McGurrin
Geological Survey of Canada Library, 601 Booth St., Ottawa, Ont. K1A 0E3 – 613/995-4151 – Miss A.E. Bourgeois
Resource Economics Library, 580 Booth St., Ottawa, Ont. K1A 0E4 – 613/995-9351 – B. Scollie

Dept. of the Environment, Library, Ottawa, Ont. K1A 1C7 – 819/997-2485 – Mrs. A.M. Bystram

Dept. of External Affairs, Library, Lester B. Pearson Bldg., Sussex Dr., Ottawa, Ont. K1A 0G2 – 613/996-8691 – Mrs. Ruth M. Thompson

Dept. of Finance & Treasury Board, Library, 17th Floor, Place Bell Canada, Ottawa, Ont. K1A 0G5 – 613/593-6146 – M.I. Aitken

Dept. of Indian Affairs & Northern Development, Library, Ottawa, Ont. K1A 0H4 – 819/997-0799 – Mrs. Ramma Kamra – library located at Les Terrasses de la Chaudière, Hull

Dept. of Industry, Trade & Commerce, Main Library, 235 Queen St., Ottawa, Ont. K1A 0H5 – 613/992-4947 – S. Rush

Dept. of Insurance, Library, 16th Floor, 140 O'Connor St., Ottawa, Ont. K1A 0H2 – 613/996-5162 – Miss Luanne Larose

Dept. of Justice, Library, Justice Bldg., Wellington St., Ottawa, Ont. K1A 0H8 – 613/995-0144 – Miss Susan Geggie

Dept. of Labour, Library, Ottawa, Ont. K1A 0J2 – 819/997-3540 – V.S. MacKelvie

Dept. of National Defence, Departmental Library, 101 Colonel By Drive, 2 N.T., Ottawa, Ont. K1A 0K2 – 613/996-0831 – R. Van den Berg

National Defence Branch Libraries include:
Computer Services Library
Construction & Property Technical Library
Defence Headquarters Technical Library
Defence Scientific Information Service
Directorate of History Library
Judge Advocate Library
Land Technical Library
Mapping & Charting Library
Maritime Technical Library
Medical Centre Library
Mobile Command Library (St-Hubert, P.Q.)

Dept. of National Health & Welfare, Departmental Library, Brooke Claxton Bldg., Ottawa, Ont. K1A 0K9 – 613/992-5743 – D. Dolan
Health Protection Branch Libraries:
Laboratory Centre for Disease Control (K1A 0L2)
Environmental Health (K1A 0L2)
Sir. Frederick G. Banting Research Centre (K1A 0L2)
Health Services & Promotion Branch Library (K1A 1B4)
Medical Services Branch Library (K1A 0L3)

Dept. of National Revenue, See Revenue Canada

Dept. of Public Works, Library, Sir Charles Tupper Bldg., Riverside Dr., Ottawa, Ont. K1A 0M2 – 613/998-8350

Dept. of Regional Economic Expansion, Library, Ottawa, Ont. K1A 0M4 – 819/997-6075 – D. Bays

Dept. of the Secretary of State, See Hull

Dept. of the Solicitor General, 340 Laurier Ave. W., Ottawa, Ont. K1A 0P8 – 613/995-6898

Dept. of Supply & Services, Departmental Library, 123 Slater St., Ottawa, Ont. K1A 0S5 – 613/997-7850 – Louis P. Landreville

Dept. of Supply & Services, Expositions Centre Technical Library, See Canadian Government Expositions Centre

Dept. of Transport, Library & Information Centre, 330 Sparks St., Ottawa, Ont. K1A 0N5 – 613/996-7121 – Serge G. Campion

Dept. of Veterans Affairs, Library, 284 Wellington St., Ottawa, Ont. K1A 0P4 – 613/593-4155 – Miss Joceline Cousineau

Dominion Bridge Co. Ltd. Library, Box 3246, Stn. C, Ottawa, Ont. K1Y 4J5 – 613/238-3472 – J.E. Capogreco

Le Droit (Bibliothèque), 375 rue Rideau, Ottawa, Ont. K1N 5Y7 – 613/560-2711 – Alice Mimeault

Economic Council of Canada Library, Box 527, Stn. B, Ottawa, Ont. K1P 5V6 – 613/993-1914 – Ms. Irene Lackner

Eldorado Nuclear Ltd., Research & Development Library, #400, 255 Albert St., Ottawa, Ont. K1P 6A9 – 613/238-5222 – Mrs. Mary Cochrane

Embassy of Chile, Library, 56 Sparks St., #801, Ottawa, Ont. K1P 5A9 – 613/235-4402

Embassy of Guatemala, Library, 294 Albert St., #500, Ottawa, Ont. K1P 6E6 – 613/237-3941

Embassy of Ireland, Library, 170 Metcalfe St., Ottawa, Ont. K2P 1P3 – 613/233-6281 – Mrs. L. McKee

Embassy of Pakistan, Library, 170 Metcalfe St., Ottawa, Ont. K2P 1P3 – 613/238-7881

Embassy of Poland, Library, 443 Daly Ave., Ottawa, Ont. K1N 6H3 – 613/236-0468 – Tomasz Przygoda

Embassy of U.S.S.R., Press & Information Centre, 400 Stewart St., #1108, Ottawa, Ont. K1N 6L2 – 613/236-7228 – Erlyne Allinotte

Export Development Corp. Library, Box 655, Ottawa, Ont. K1P 5T9 – 613/237-2570, ext. 266 – Miss A. James

Expositions Centre Technical Library, See Canadian Government Expositions Centre

Farm Credit Corp. Library, Box 2314, Stn. D, Ottawa, Ont. K1P 6J9 – 613/996-6606 – Louise Neveu

Federal Court of Canada, Library, Wellington St., Ottawa, Ont. K1A 0H9 – 613/992-8037 – Ms. Diana Gazda, Law Librarian

Federation des droits et liberties, see Canadian Rights & Liberties

Foreign Investment Review Agency Library, Box 2800, Stn. D, Ottawa, Ont. K1P 6A5 – 613/995-9603 – Mrs. Heather Hannaford

Forintek Canada Corp., Eastern Laboratory Library, 800 Montreal Rd., Ottawa, Ont. K1G 3Z5 – 613/744-0963 – Marjorie Wickens

Geological Survey of Canada, see Dept. of Energy, Mines etc.

Goldberg, Shinder & Co. Law Library, 307 Gilmour St., Ottawa, Ont. K2P 0P7 – 613/237-4922 – Gary Steinberg

Gowling & Henderson Law Library, 160 Elgin St., Ottawa, Ont. K1N 8S3 – 613/232-1781 – Mrs. Christina Wright

Heritage Canada Foundation Library, (275 Maclaren St.), Box 1358, Stn. B, Ottawa, Ont. K1P 5R4 – 613/237-1867 or 237-1066 – Helen Smith

Hewitt, Hewitt, Nesbitt, Reid Law Library, 75 Albert St., #604, Ottawa, Ont. K1P 5E7 – 613/563-0202 – Pam Buckingham

High Commission for Jamaica, Library, 85 Range Rd., Ottawa, Ont. K1N 8J6 – 613/233-9311

High Commission for Malaysia, Information Centre, 60 Boteler St., Ottawa, Ont. K1N 8Y7 – 613/237-5182

High Commission for New Zealand, Library, 99 Bank St., #801, Ottawa, Ont. K1P 6G3 – 613/238-5991

High Commission for Sri Lanka, Library, 85 Range Rd., Ottawa, Ont. K1N 8J6 – 613/233-8449 – R.S. Withane

Hôpital Général d'Ottawa, Library, 43 rue Bruyère, Ottawa, Ont. K1N 5C8 – 613/231-3128 – Diane R. Couture

International Communication Agency, See United States International etc.

International Development Research Centre Library, Box 8500, Ottawa, Ont. K1G 3H9 – 613/996-2321, ext. 211 – Sharon E. Henry (Deputy)

Inuit Tapirisat of Canada Library, 176 Gloucester St., 3rd Floor, Ottawa, Ont. K2P 0A6 – 613/238-8181 – Debbie Brisebois

Jewish Community Centre Library, 151 Chapel St., Ottawa, Ont. K1N 7Y2 – 613/232-7306 – Mrs. Miriam Paghis

Law Reform Commission Library, 130 Albert St., #809, Ottawa, Ont. K1A 0L6 – 613/996-7851 – Miss E. Irene Roy

Library of Parliament, Ottawa, Ont. K1A 0A9
Parliamentary Librarian – Erik J. Spicer (613/992-3122)
Assoc. Parliamentary Librarian – Richard Paré (992-2427)
Asst. Parliamentary Librarian – vacant (992-6478)

Macdonald, Afleck Law Library, 100 Sparks St., Ottawa, Ont. K1P 5B7 – 613/236-9521

Macdonald Cartier Library, 178 Queen St., Ottawa, Ont. K1P 5E1 – 613/238-6111

Management Information Centre, Privy Council Office, Blackburn Bldg., Ottawa, Ont. K1A 0A3 – 613/992-7608 – M. Ryan

Metric Commission Canada, SIM Research Unit, 240 Sparks St., 1st Floor East, Ottawa, Ont. K1A 0H5 – 613/996-8584

Metropolitan Life Insurance Co. Library, 99 Bank St., Ottawa, Ont. K1P 5A3 – 613/231-3531 – Miss Marjorie A. Purvis

Ministry of State for Science & Technology, Library, 270 Albert St., Ottawa, Ont. K1A 1A1 – 613/992-7851 – Miss Carol Barton

National Air Photo Library, Dept. of Energy, Mines & Resources, 615 Booth St., #180, Ottawa, Ont. K1A 0E9 – 613/995-4560 – Miss Dianne Rombough

National Capital Commission Library, 161 Laurier Ave. W., Ottawa, Ont. K1P 6J6 – 613/992-4130 – Miss C. Amyotte

National Energy Board Library, 473 Albert St., #962, Ottawa, Ont. K1A 0E5 – 613/996-3509 – Mrs. M.J. Hurley

National Film Board, Phototheque, Tunney's Pasture, Ottawa, Ont. K1A 0M9 – 613/593-5826

National Film Library, See Canadian Film Institute

National Gallery of Canada Library, Ottawa, Ont. K1A 0M8 – 613/992-6861 – Miss J. Hunter

National Harbours Board, Secretariat, Tower A, 14th Floor, 320 Queen St., Ottawa, Ont. K1A 0N6 – 613/992-0180

National Indian Brotherhood, Library & Info Services, 222 Queen St., #500, Ottawa, Ont. K1P 5V9

National Library, Ottawa, Ont. K1A 0N4 – 613/996-1623 – J.G. Sylvestre

National Map Collection, Public Archives of Canada, Ottawa, Ont. K1A 0N3 – 613/998-3923 – Mrs. B. Kidd

National Museums of Canada Library, Ottawa, Ont. K1A 0M8 – 613/998-4425 – Mrs. Valerie Monkhouse

National Postal Museum Library, 180 Wellington St., Ottawa, Ont. K1A 1C6 – 613/995-8085 – Cimon Morin

National Research Council, See Canada Institute for Scientific & Technical etc.

The Navy League of Canada Library, 4 Queen Elizabeth Dr., Ottawa, Ont. K2P 2H9 – 613/232-2784 – W.J. Hodge

Ottawa Board of Education, Professional Development Library, 330 Gilmour St., Ottawa, Ont. K2P 0P9 – 613/563-2400 – G. Genier

Ottawa Citizen Library, 1101 Baxter Rd., Ottawa, Ont. K2C 3M4 – 613/596-3746 – S.D. Proulx

Ottawa Civic Hospital Library, 1053 Carling Ave., Ottawa, Ont. K1Y 4E9 – 613/725-4459 – Miss M. Brown

Ottawa Journal Library, 365 Laurier Ave. W., Ottawa, Ont. K1G 3K6 – 613/563-3757 – Marion Barron

Patent Office Library, Place du Portage, Ottawa, Ont. K1A 0E1 – 613/997-2525 – Mary I. Morris, Ref. Services

Parliament, Library of, See Library of Parliament

Planned Parenthood Federation of Canada Library, 1226A Wellington St., Ottawa, Ont. K1Y 3A1 – 613/722-3484 – Eleanor Roine

Post Office Dept., Library, Confederation Heights, Ottawa, Ont. K1A 0B1 – 613/998-4463

Privy Council Library, Blackburn Bldg., Ottawa, Ont. K1A 0A3 – 613/992-7608 – M. Ryan

Professional Institute of the Public Service, Library, 786 Bronson Ave., Ottawa, Ont. K1S 4G4 – 613/237-6310

Public Archives of Canada, 395 Wellington St., Ottawa, Ont. K1A 0N3 – 613/992-6534 – Normand St-Pierre

Public Service Commission Library, #936, West Tower, 300 Laurier Ave. W., Ottawa, Ont. K1A 0M7 – 613/992-4808 – A. Campbell

Public Service Staff Relations Board Library, Box 1525, Stn. B, Ottawa, Ont. K1P 5V2 – 613/996-1206 – Charlene Elgee

Revenue Canada - Customs & Excise Library, 2nd Floor, Connaught Bldg., Sussex Dr., Ottawa, Ont. K1A 0L5 – 613/995-0007 – Dianne L. Parsonage

Revenue Canada - Taxation Library, Ottawa, Ont. K1A 0L8 – 613/996-9896 – L. Wilkinson

Roads & Transportation Association of Canada Library, 1765 St. Laurent Blvd., Ottawa, Ont. K1G 3V4 – 613/521-4052 – Françoise M. Brunet & Iona M. DeBow

Royal Architectural Institute of Canada Library, 151 Slater St., #1104, Ottawa, Ont. K1P 5H3 – 613/232-7165

Royal Canadian Mint Library, 355 River Rd., 6th Floor, Ottawa, Ont. K1A 0G8 – 613/993-3614 – June Ouellette

Royal Canadian Mounted Police Library, 1200 Alta Vista Dr., #B203A, Ottawa, Ont. K1A 0R2 – 613/993-3225 – Mrs. Nadene Grattan Garrett
- Scientific Information Centre (Rm. 160 CPS Bldg., Lab Tower) – Paulette St-Amour (993-3800)

Royal Ottawa Hospital Library, 1145 Carling Ave., Ottawa, Ont. K1Z 7K4 – 613/722-6521, ext. 372 – Mrs. Evelyn Chow

Saint Paul University Library, 223 Main St., Ottawa, Ont. K1S 1C4 – 613/236-1393 – Gaston Rioux

Science Council of Canada, Library, 100 Metcalfe St., Ottawa, Ont. K1P 5M1 – Ms. F. Bonney

Smart & Biggar Law Library, 70 Gloucester St., Ottawa, Ont. K1P 5Y6 – 613/232-2486 – Mrs. Cathryn Laver

Soloway, Wright & Co. Law Library, 170 Metcalfe St., Ottawa, Ont. K2P 1P3 – 613/236-0111 – Mrs. Norma Vincent

Southam Library, 362 Mariposa Ave., Ottawa, Ont. K1M 0T3 – 613/749-5954 – R.D. Rice

Sport Information Resource Centre, See Vanier, Ont.

Statistics Canada, Library, R.H. Coats Bldg., 2nd Floor, Ottawa, Ont. K1A 0T6 – 613/992-0673 – Mrs. G. Ellis

Supreme Court Library, Wellington St., Ottawa, Ont. K1A 0J1 – R. Boult, Q.C., Chief Lib., 613/992-9720; G. Howell, Asst. Lib., 995-6355

Tariff Board Library, 365 Laurier Ave., Ottawa, Ont. K1A 0G7 – 613/996-8541 – Mrs. L. Cyr

Tax Review Board Library, 381 Kent St., Ottawa, Ont. K1A 0M1 – 613/996-4762 – Mrs. N.C. Mecher

Telesat Canada Library, See Vanier, Ont.

Tourism Reference & Data Centre, Canadian Government Office of Tourism, 235 Queen St., Ottawa, Ont. K1A 0H6 – 613/995-2754

United States International Communication Agency, 150 Wellington St., 3rd Floor, Ottawa, Ont. K1P 5A4 – 613/238-5045

University of Ottawa Library System, 65 Hastey Ave., Ottawa, Ont. K1N 9A5 – 613/231-6892
- University Chief Librarian – Yvon Richer
- Morisset Library (Humanities & Social Sciences), 65 Hastey Ave. – Yvon Richer
- Vanier Library (Medicine, Science & Engineering), 11 Somerset St. E. – Dr. David Holmes (231-2324)
- Law Library, 57 Copernicus St. – tba (231-5739)
- Teacher Education Library, 651 Cumberland St. – tba (231-5986)
- Music Library, 1 Stewart St. – Debra Begg (231-5717)
- Nursing Library, 770 King Edward Ave. – Myra Owen (231-3218)
- Institute for International Co-operation Documentation Centre, 14 Henderson St. – William D. Ward (231-4240)

Vanier Institute of the Family, Resource & Information Centre, #207, 151 Slater St., Ottawa, Ont. K1P 5H3 – 613/232-7115 – Ms. S.L. Campbell

OWEN SOUND

Georgian College (AA & T), Learning Resources Centre, Box 700, (1150 8th St. E.), Owen Sound, Ont. N4K 5R4 – 519/376-0682, ext. 48 – G.A. Kerr

PEMBROKE

Algonquin College (AA & T), Upper Ottawa Valley Campus Resource Centre, 315 Pembroke St. E., Pembroke, Ont. K8A 3K2 – 613/735-1041 – Ms. L. Stilborn

PERTH

Algonquin College (AA & T), Lanark Campus Resource Centre, 7 Craig St., Perth, Ont. K7H 1X7 – 613/267-2859 – Mrs. C. Ebbs

PETERBOROUGH

Thomas J. Bata Library of Trent University, Peterborough, Ont. K9J 7B8 – 705/748-1550 – Prof. B. Heeney

Canadian General Electric Co. Ltd., Engineering Library, 107 Park St. N., Peterborough, Ont. K9J 7B5 – 705/742-7711, ext. 439 – Mrs. L. Madisso

Peterborough Examiner Library, Box 389, Peterborough, Ont. K9J 6Z4 – 705/745-4641 – Vivian Hall

Sir Sandford Fleming College (AA & T), Brealey Campus Library, Brealey Dr., Peterborough, Ont. K9J 7B1 – 705/743-5610 – Janice Coughlin

Sir Sandford Fleming College (AA & T), McDonnel Campus Library, Box 653, Peterborough, Ont. K9J 6Z8 – 705/743-5620 – R. Veenman

PORT HOPE

Eldorado Nuclear Ltd. Refinery Library, 215 John St., Port Hope, Ont. L1A 3A1 – 416/885-4511 – Mrs. Dorothy Kingman

REXDALE

See Toronto

RICHMOND HILL

David Dunlap Observatory Library, Dept. of Astronomy, University of Toronto, Box 360, Richmond Hill, Ont. L4C 4Y6 – 416/884-2112 or 884-9562 – Lynda Colbeck

ST. CATHARINES

Brock University, DeCew Campus Library, St. Catharines, Ont. L2S 3A1 – 416/684-7201 – James W. Hogan

City of St. Catharines, Planning Dept. Library, Box 3012, Church St., St. Catharines, Ont. L2R 7C2 – 416/688-5600, ext. 270 – Robert Steele

City of St. Catharines, Engineering Dept. Library, Box 1385, Canada Trust House, James St., St. Catharines, Ont. L2R 7J8 – 416/688-5600, ext. 296 – Miss Dianne James

Genaire Ltd. Library, Box 84, St. Catharines, Ont. L2R 6R4 – 416/684-1165 – Valerie Patterson

Niagara College (AA & T), Mack Centre Nursing Library, 178 Queenston St., St. Catharines, Ont. L2R 2Z7 – 416/688-5310, ext. 276 – Miss N. Rolls

Niagara College (AA & T), Welland Vale Campus Library, 59 Welland Vale Rd., Box 340, St. Catharines, Ont. L2R 6V6 – 416/684-4315 – M. Edelman

Rodman Hall Arts Centre Library, 109 St. Paul Cres., St. Catharines, Ont. L2S 1M3 – 416/684-2925 – Mrs. Susan Dickinson

SARNIA

Big Sisters of Ontario Resource Centre, c/o Big Sisters of Sarnia, 681 Oxford St., Sarnia, Ont. N2T 6Z7

Dow Chemical of Canada Ltd. Library, Box 1012, Sarnia, Ont. N7T 7K7 – 519/339-3663 – Miss B.R. Buchanan

Imperial Oil Limited Library, Box 3022, Sarnia, Ont. N7T 7M1 – 519/339-2471 – N.J. Gaspar

Lambton College (AA & T), Resource Centre, Box 969, Sarnia, Ont. N7T 7K4 – 519/542-7751, ext. 287 – Margaret Turner

Polysar Ltd. Library, Sarnia, Ont. N7T 7M2 – 519/337-8251, ext. 7711 – D.J. Clarkson

SAULT STE. MARIE

Algoma College Library, Sault Ste. Marie, Ont. P6A 2G4 – 705/949-2101 – Dr. R.J. Bazillion, Lib. Adm.

Algoma Steel Corp. Ltd., Quality Control & Metals Research Library, Queen St. W., Sault Ste. Marie, Ont. P6A 5P2 – 705/945-2344, 2341 – A. Haft and B. Morin-Strom

General Hospital, Health Sciences Library, 941 Queen St. E., Sault Ste. Marie, Ont. P6A 2B8 – 705/254-5181, ext. 315 – Mrs. Kathy You

Great Lakes Forest Research Centre Library, Canadian Forestry Service, Box 490, Sault Ste. Marie, Ont. P6A 5M7 – 705/949-9461, ext. 205 – S. Burt

Plummer Memorial Public Hospital, Medical Library, 969 Queen St. E., Sault Ste. Marie, Ont. P6A 2C4 – 705/254-5161, ext. 297 – Mrs. Kathy You

Sault College (AA & T), Resource Centre, 443 Northern Ave., Box 60, Sault Ste. Marie, Ont. P6A 5L3 – 705/949-2050 – W. Cole, Mgr.

The Sault Star Library, 145 Old Garden River Rd., Sault Ste. Marie, Ont. P6B 5A5 – 705/253-1111, ext. 285 – Joan Dorse

SCARBOROUGH

See Toronto

SUDBURY

Cambrian College (AA & T), Library, 1400 Barrydowne Rd., Sudbury, Ont. P3A 3V8 – 705/566-8101, ext. 320 – Bernard Brégaint

Huntington University Library, Laurentian Campus, Sudbury, Ont. P3E 2C6 – 705/673-4126 – J. Ceccarelli

Laurentian Hospital, Medical Library, 41 Ramsey Lake Rd., Sudbury, Ont. P3E 5J1 – 705/522-2200, ext. 215 – Mrs. Simone Hamilton

Laurentian University Library, Ramsey Lake Rd., Sudbury, Ont. P3E 2C6 – 705/675-1151 – A.H. Mrozewski

Ontario Ministry of Education Library, 199 Larch St., Sudbury, Ont. P3E 5P9 – George Whalen

Sudbury General Hospital Library, 700 Paris St., Stn. B, Sudbury, Ont. P3E 3B5 – 705/674-3181, ext. 238 – Donald M. Hawryliuk, B.A., M.L.S.

THOROLD

Ontario Paper Co. Ltd., Library, Thorold, Ont. L2V 3Z5 – 416/227-1121 – Mrs. I. Ridgway

THUNDER BAY

Confederation College (AA & T), Resource Centre, Box 398, Stn. F, Thunder Bay, Ont. P7C 4W1 – 807/475-6241

Lakehead Psychiatric Hospital, Staff Library, Box 2930, N. Algoma, Thunder Bay, Ont. P7B 5G4 – 807/344-3571, ext. 287 – Mrs. Kathy Cameron

Lakehead University, Library, Thunder Bay, Ont. P7B 5E1 – 807/345-2121, ext. 205

Old Fort William Resource Centre, Vickers Heights Post Office, Thunder Bay, Ont. P0T 2Z0 – 807/577-8461, ext. 43 – Mrs. Jacqueline Baker

Ontario Ministry of Education, Teachers' Resource Library, 435 James St. S., Box 5000, Thunder Bay, Ont. P7C 5G6 – 807/475-1550 – Mrs. Fay Nagy

TORONTO (and Metropolitan Area, including Agincourt, Don Mills, Downsview, Etobicoke, Islington, North York, Rexdale, Scarborough, Weston, Willowdale)

Acres Consulting Services Ltd. Library, 480 University Ave., Toronto, Ont. M5G 1V2 – 416/595-2086 – Elske M. Bosma

Addiction Research Foundation Library, 33 Russell St., Toronto, Ont. M5S 2S1 – 416/595-6144 – R.J. Hall

Aird & Berlis Law Library, #1500, 145 King St. W., Toronto, Ont. M5H 2J3 – 416/364-1241

Alcohol & Drug Concerns, Audio Visuals, 15 Gervais Dr., #603, Don Mills, Ont. M3C 1Y8 – 416/449-4933 – Miss O. Hussey

A.E. Ames & Co. Ltd. Library, 320 Bay St., Toronto, Ont. M5H 2P7 – 416/867-4058 – W.M. Malcom

Arthur Anderson & Co. Library, Box 29, Toronto Dominion Centre, Toronto, Ont. M5K 1B9 – 416/366-6243, ext. 210 – Mary O'Neill

Anglican Church of Canada, Chancellor R.V. Harris Memorial Library, 600 Jarvis St., Toronto, Ont. M4Y 2J6 – 416/924-9192, ext. 291 – Miss A.M. Hedderick

Anthroposophical Society of Canada Library, 81 Lawton Blvd., Toronto, Ont. M4V 1Z6 – 416/488-2886 – Miss B. Gunther

Archives of Ontario, Library, 77 Grenville St., Queen's Park, Toronto, Ont. M7A 2R9 – 416/965-4039 – Miss E. Harlow

Art Gallery of Ontario, The Edward P. Taylor Reference Library, 317 Dundas St. W., Toronto, Ont. M5T 1G4 – 416/977-0414, ext. 339, 340, 341 – Karen McKenzie

Arthritis Society, National Office Library, #420, 920 Yonge St., Toronto, Ont. M4W 3J7 – 416/967-1414 – Miss J.M. Attwood

Atlin, Goldenberg & Co. Law Library, 439 University Ave., 22nd Floor, Toronto, Ont. M5G 1Y8 – 416/598-1400 – Janet Grice

Atmospheric Environment Service Library, Environment Canada, 4905 Dufferin St., Downsview, Ont. M3H 5T4 – 416/667-4880 – Miss M.M. Skinner

Audit Bureau of Circulations, Library of Print Media Circulation Statistics, #503, 335 Bay St., Toronto, Ont. M5H 2R3 – 416/366-8949 – Mrs. Lorraine King, Mgr.

Howard E. Bacon Library, See Metro Toronto Assn. for Mentally Retarded

Bank of Montreal, Technical Information Centre, 245 Consumers Rd., Willowdale, Ont. M2J 1S2 – 416/493-2440 – Janice Reynolds

Bank of Montreal, Technical Information Centre, Box 7000, Scarborough, Ont. M1S 4M5 – 416/498-8800, ext. 4522 – Carol Diakun

Bank of Nova Scotia, General Office Library, 44 King St. W., Toronto, Ont. M5H 1H1 – 416/866-6257 – Mrs. Beverley Kent

Bank of Nova Scotia, Systems Library, 10 Gateway Blvd., Don Mills, Ont. M3C 3A1 – 416/424-3551 – Penni Lee

Bechtel Canada Ltd. Library, 15th Floor, 250 Bloor St. E., Toronto, Ont. M4W 3K5 – 416/928-1671 – Elke M. Warwas

BEC Information Service, (Built Environment Co-ordinators), 1947 Avenue Rd., Toronto, Ont. M5M 4A2 – 416/783-4277 – Jill Roughley

Bell Canada, Information Resource Centre, 393 University Ave., 6th Floor, Toronto, Ont. M5G 1W9 – 416/599-7096 – Vivian Lung

Beth Tzedec Congregational Library, 1700 Bathurst St., Toronto, Ont. M5P 3K3 – 416/781-5658, ext. 30 – Samuel Simchovitch

Black Resources & Information Centre Library, 427 Bloor St. W., 2nd Floor, Toronto, Ont. M5S 1X7 – 416/960-3697

Blake, Cassels & Graydon Law Library, Box 25, Commerce Court West, Toronto, Ont. M5L 1A9 – 416/863-2650 – Judith Smith

Blaney, Pasternak & Co. Law Library, 365 Bay St., #1100, Toronto, Ont. M5H 2V3 – 416/364-9421, ext. 267 – Arlene Levy

Board of Education Library, 155 College St., Toronto, Ont. M5T 1P6 – 416/598-4931, ext. 430 – F. Eugene Gattinger

Board of Trade of Metropolitan Toronto, Resource Centre, Box 60, Three First Canadian Place, Toronto, Ont. M5X 1C1 – 416/366-6811 – Valerie Dolegowski

Borden & Elliot Law Library, 250 University Ave., Toronto, Ont. M5H 3E5 – 416/593-5511 – Mary M. Zorko

Brinco Ltd. Library, 20 King St. W., 10th Floor, Toronto, Ont. M5H 1C4 – 416/868-6970 – Mrs. Deborah M. Kelly

British Information Services, 200 University Ave., Toronto, Ont. M5H 3E3 – 416/593-1290 – K. Heald
Bureau of Municipal Research Library, #404, 73 Richmond St. W., Toronto, Ont. M5H 1Z4 – 416/363-9265 – Mrs. J. Milne
Burns Fry Limited Library, Box 150, One First Canadian Place, Toronto, Ont. M5X 1H3 – 416/365-4444 – Ann Rait
Campbell, Godfrey & Lewtas Library, Box 36, Toronto Dominion Centre, Toronto, Ont. M5K 1C5 – 416/362-2401 – Miss Clare Lyons
Canada Dept. of Employment & Immigration, Branch Library, 4900 Yonge St., #700, Willowdale, Ont. M2N 6A8 – 416/224-4524 – Stan Feldman
Canada Dept. of Justice, Toronto Region Library, Box 57, Toronto Dominion Centre, Toronto, Ont. M5K 1E7 – 416/369-4241 – c/o Library Clerk
Canada Dept. of Public Works, Ontario Regional Library, 4900 Yonge St., Willowdale, Ont. M2N 6A6 – 416/224-4233 – Rocco Cornacchia
Canada Life Assurance Co. Library, 330 University Ave., Toronto, Ont. M5G 1R8 – 416/597-1456, ext. 266 – Miss Gloria F.L. Johns
Canada Packers Inc. Library, 2211 St. Clair Ave. W., Toronto, Ont. M6N 1K4 – 416/766-4311, ext. 680 – Miss F.M. Misiak
Canada Permanent Trust Co. Library, 320 Bay St., Toronto, Ont. M5H 2P6 – 416/361-8383 – Mrs. Florence Haynes
Canada Wire & Cable, Technical Library, 147 Laird Dr., Toronto, Ont. M4G 3W1 – 416/421-8800 – Mrs. Dianne Crompton
Canadian Association–Latin America & Caribbean, Library, 42 Charles St. E., Toronto, Ont. M4Y 1T4 – 416/964-6068 – Maria A. Escriu
Canadian Association for Mentally Retarded, John Orr Foster Memorial Reference Library, Kinsmen NIMR Bldg., York Univ., 4700 Keele St., Downsview, Ont. M3J 1P3 – 416/661-9611 – M.A. Hutton
Canadian Bible Society Library, 10 Carnforth Rd., Toronto, Ont. M4A 2S4 – 416/757-4171 – Rev. Howard G. Zurbrigg
Canadian Book Publishers Council Library, 45 Charles St. E., #701, Toronto, Ont. M4Y 1S2 – 416/964-7231
Canadian Broadcasting Corp., Reference Library, (415 Yonge St.), Box 500, Term. A, Toronto, Ont. M5W 1E6 – 416/925-3311, ext. 2097 – Elizabeth Jenner
Program Archives – Pat Kellogg (925-3311, ext. 4614)
TV Current Affairs Library – Cynthia Fisher (925-3311, ext. 3201)
Canadian Centre for Philanthropy Resource Centre, 12 Shepherd St., 3rd Floor, Toronto, Ont. M5H 3A1
Canadian Co-operative Credit Society, Resource Centre, (300 The East Mall), Box 800, Stn. U, Toronto, Ont. M8Z 5R2 – 416/232-1262 –
Canadian Council of Christians & Jews, John D. Hayes Library of Human Relations, 49 Front St. E., Toronto, Ont. M5E 1B3 – 416/364-3101 – Jeane Kotick
Canadian Credit Institute Library, 931 Yonge St., Toronto, Ont. M4W 2H6 – 416/962-9911 – W.J. Hambly
Canadian Deaf Information Centre, 2395 Bayview Ave., Willowdale, Ont. M2L 1A2 – 416/449-9651
Canadian Education Association Library, 252 Bloor St. W., Toronto, Ont. M5S 1V5 – 416/924-7721 – Ms. Diane Sibbett
Canadian Environmental Law Research Foundation Library, 5th Floor South, 8 York St., Toronto, Ont. M5J 1R2 – 416/366-9717
Canadian Forces College Library, 215 Yonge Blvd., Toronto, Ont. M5M 3H9 – 416/484-5742 – Miss M. Ash
Canadian Foundation for Economic Education, Resource Centre, 252 Bloor St. W., #S.560, Toronto, Ont. M5S 1V5 – 416/968-2236 – Judy Jackson
Canadian Hearing Society Library, 60 Bedford Rd., Toronto, Ont. M5R 2K2 – 416/964-9595 – Mrs. J.A. Scott
Canadian Gas Research Institute Library, 55 Scarsdale Rd., Don Mills, Ont. M3B 2R3 – 416/447-6465, ext. 75 – Margot Clarice
Canadian Imperial Bank of Commerce, Information Centre, Commerce Court, Toronto, Ont. M5L 1A2 – 416/862-3352 – Jane Cooney
C-I-L Inc. Library, 1330 Castlefield Ave., Toronto, Ont. M6B 4B3 – 416/787-2411 – Miss M.E. Fitzpatrick
C-I-L Inc. Patent Library, Box 200, Stn. A, Toronto, Ont. – Mrs. Y. D'Souza – Law Library also c/o this address
Canadian Institute of International Affairs Library, 15 King's College Circle, Toronto, Ont. M5S 2V9 – 416/979-1851 – Mrs. Jane Barrett
Canadian Institute of Religion & Gerontology Library, 296 Lawrence Ave. E., Toronto, Ont. M4N 1T7 – 416/483-1879 – Mrs. Catherine Pritchard
Canadian Institute of Steel Construction Library, 201 Consumers Rd., #300, Willowdale, Ont. M2J 4G8 – 416/491-4552
Canadian Jesuit Missions Library, 833 Broadview Ave., Toronto, Ont. M4K 2P9 – 416/466-1195 – Peter Nash, s.j.
Canadian Jewish Congress Library, 150 Beverley St., Toronto, Ont. M5T 1Y6 – 416/977-3811 – Dr. Edmond Y. Lipsitz
Canadian Life Insurance Association Library, 55 University Ave., Toronto, Ont. M5J 2K7 – 416/364-6295 – Mrs. B.R. Mander
Canadian Memorial Chiropractic Library, 1900 Bayview Ave., Toronto, Ont. M4G 3E6 – 416/482-2340, ext. 60 – J. Claire Callaghan
Canadian Mental Health Association Library, 2160 Yonge St., 3rd Floor, Toronto, Ont. M4S 2Z3 – 416/484-7750
Canadian Music Centre Library, 1263 Bay St., Toronto, Ont. M5R 2C1 – 416/961-6601 – H.A. Mutsaers
Canadian National Institute for the Blind Library, 1929 Bayview Ave., Toronto, Ont. M4G 3E8 – 416/486-2579 – F. Hébert
Canadian Nuclear Association Library, 111 Elizabeth St., 11th Floor, Toronto, Ont. M5G 1P7 – 416/977-6152 – D. McArthur
Canadian Paraplegic Association Library, 520 Sutherland Drive, Toronto, Ont. M4G 3V9 – 416/422-5640 – Mrs. Helen Peterson
CN Telecommunications, Great Lakes Region Library, 151 Front St. W., Toronto, Ont. M5J 1G1 – 416/860-2418 – Shirley K. Smith
Canadian Press Library, 36 King St. E., Toronto, Ont. M5C 2L9 – 416/364-0321 – Elizabeth Shewan
Canadian Real Estate Association Library, 99 Duncan Mill Rd., Don Mills, Ont. M3B 1Z2 – 416/445-9910 – Ms. M.L. Weatherwax
Canadian Red Cross Library, 95 Wellesley St. E., Toronto, Ont. M4Y 1H6 – 416/923-6692, ext. 232 – Mrs. C. Pepper
Canadian Rehabilitation Council for the Disabled, Resource Centre, One Yonge St., #2110, Toronto, Ont. M5E 1E5 – Maureen Vasey, Dir., Info.
Canadian Restaurant & Foodservices Association, Resource Centre, 80 Bloor St. W., #904, Toronto, Ont. M5S 2V1 – 416/923-8416 – Joyce Reynolds, Info. Specialist
Canadian Standards Association Information Centre, 178 Rexdale Blvd., Toronto, Ont. M9W 1R3 – 416/744-4058 – Ms. B. Esson, Mgr., Info. Resources Group
Canadian Tax Foundation Library, 130 Adelaide St. W., Box 6, Toronto, Ont. M5H 3P5 – 416/863-9784 – Mrs. M. Robinson
Canadian Thoroughbred Horse Society Library, Box 172, Rexdale, Ont. M9W 5L1 – 416/675-3602 – Don M. Amos
Carr-McLean Co. Library, 461 Horner Ave., Toronto, Ont. M8W 4X2 – 416/252-3371 – W.G. Carr
Catholic Information Centre, 830 Bathurst St., Toronto, Ont. M5R 3G1 – 416/534-2326 – Mrs. Joan DesLauriers
Centennial College (AA & T), Resource Centre, Box 631, Stn. A, Scarborough, Ont. M1K 5E9 – 416/439-7180, ext. 228 – Frances Davidson-Arnott
Central Baptist Seminary Library, 95 Jonesville Cres., Toronto, Ont. M4A 1H3 – 416/752-1976 – Mrs. Ruth L. Kraulis
Centre for Christian Studies Library, 77 Charles St. W., Toronto, Ont. M5S 1K5 – 416/923-1168 – Mrs. R.H.N. Davidson
Le Centre Communautaire Francophone de Toronto (Centre d'information), 435 ouest, Queen's Quay, Toronto, Ont. M5V 1A2 – 416/367-1950 – Ann-Marie Couffin, Dir.
Church of Jesus Christ of Latter Day Saints, Microfilm Library, 95 Melbert Rd., Box 247, Etobicoke, Ont. M9C 4V3 – 416/621-4607 – Brian J. Margetson
Citadel General Assurance Co., Information Centre, 1075 Bay St., Toronto, Ont. M5S 2W5 – 416/928-8540 – Christine Macdonald

City of Toronto, Planning & Development Dept. Library, 20th Floor, East Tower, City Hall, Toronto, Ont. M5H 2N2 – 416/367-7182 – Georgina Moravec

Civic Garden Centre Library, 777 Lawrence Ave. E., Don Mills, Ont. M3C 1P2 – 416/445-1552 – Mrs. P. MacKenzie

C-I-L, listed under Canadian

Civil Service Commission Library, Frost Bldg. South, Queen's Park, Toronto, Ont. M7A 1Z5 (located at 9th floor, 151 Bloor St. W.) – 416/965-7096 – Miss M. Williams

Clarkson, Gordon & Co. Library, Box 251, Royal Trust Tower, Toronto Dominion Centre, Toronto, Ont. M5K 1J7 – 416/864-1234 – Jean Parriss

CN, listed under Canadian

Collins Canada Rockwell International Library, 150 Bartley Dr., Toronto, Ont. M4A 1C7 – 416/757-1101, ext. 320 – Joan Hall

Confederation Life Insurance Co. Library, 321 Bloor St. E., Toronto, Ont. M4W 1G9 – 416/967-8326 – Ms. Lynne M. Cousins

Commonwealth Microfilm Library, 760 Gordon Baker Dr., Willowdale, Ont. M2H 3B4 – 416/497-8140

Connaught Laboratories Ltd. Library, 1755 Steeles Ave. W., Willowdale, Ont. M2R 3T4 – 416/667-2921, 2 – Mrs. Elaine Selke

Consumers' Gas Co. Library Services, (500 Consumers Rd.), Box 650, Scarborough, Ont. M1K 5E3 – 416/492-5490 – Donna M. Ivey

Continental Bank Library, 130 Adelaide St. W., Toronto, Ont. M5H 3R2 – 416/868-8401 – Betty Magee

Convention & Tourist Bureau of Metropolitan Toronto Information Centre, Box 510, #110, Toronto Eaton Centre, 220 Yonge St., Toronto, Ont. M5B 2H1 – 416/979-3133

Council of Ontario Universities, Library, 130 St. George St., #8039, Toronto, Ont. MS 2T4 – 416/979-2165 – William Sayers, Dir. of Communications

County of York Law Association Library, Court House, 361 University Ave., Toronto, Ont. M5G 1T3 – A.M. MacIver

Cowan Memorial Library, The Church Army in Canada, 397 Brunswick Ave., Toronto, Ont. M5R 2Z2 – 416/924-9279 – Sister Dianne Nelson

J.W. Crane Memorial Library, (Sponsored by the Canadian Geriatrics Research Society), 351 Christie St., Toronto, Ont. M6G 3C3 – 416/537-6000 – Mrs. Elaine Duwors

Crown Life Insurance Co. Library, 120 Bloor St. E., Toronto, Ont. M4W 1B8 – 416/928-4650 – Miss H. Elizabeth Angus

Currie, Coopers & Lybrand Ltd. Library, 145 King St. W., Toronto, Ont. M5H 1J8 – 416/366-1921, ext. 545 – S. Abram

Datacrown Inc. Library, 650 McNicholl Ave., Willowdale, Ont. M2H 2E1 – 416/499-1012, ext. 502 – Lucille Slack, Mgr. Lib. Services

Defence & Civil Institute of Environmental Medicine Library, Box 2000, Downsview, Ont. M3M 3B9 – 416/633-4240, ext. 209 – R. Cheung

DeHavilland Aircraft of Canada Ltd. Library, Garratt Blvd., Downsview, Ont. M3K 1Y5 – 416/633-7310 – Mrs. C. Parsons

Departments of Government, See Ontario Ministry of ...

Doctors Hospital, Alexander Raxlen Memorial Library, 45 Brunswick Ave., Toronto, Ont. M5S 2M1 – 416/963-5464 – Mrs. Tsai-o Wong

Dominion Securities Ltd. Library, Box 21, Commerce Court South, Toronto, Ont. M5L 1A7 – 416/362-5711 – Mrs. S. Dummett

Ecumenical Forum of Canada Library, 11 Madison Ave., Toronto, Ont. M5R 2S2 – 416/924-9351 – Ms. M. MacKinnon

Environment Canada, Environmental Protection Service Library, 25 St. Clair Ave. E., 7th Floor, Toronto, Ont. M6P 4B9 – 416/966-5840 – Nancy L. Urbankiewicz

Erco Industries Corporate Library, 2 Gibbs Rd., Islington, Ont. M9B 1R1 – 416/239-7111, ext. 213 – Douglas G. Suarez

Esso Chemical Canada Library, 2300 Yonge St., Toronto, Ont. M5W 1K3 – 416/488-6600, ext. 377 – Carole Gray

Etobicoke Education Centre Resource Library, 1 Civic Centre Court, Etobicoke, Ont. M9C 2B3 – 416/626-4360 – Alice Guignard

Ewart College Library, 156 St. George St., Toronto, Ont. M5S 2G1 – 416/979-2501 – Dr. Margaret Webster, Prin.

Falconbridge Nickel Mines Ltd., Information Centre, Box 40, Commerce Court West, Toronto, Ont. M5L 1B4 – 416/863-7230 – Stewart Collett, Mgr.

Fasken & Calvin Law Library, Box 30, Toronto Dominion Centre, Toronto, Ont. M5K 1C1 – 416/366-8381 – Ms. Bettina Hakala

Financial Times of Canada Library, #500, 920 Yonge St., Toronto, Ont. M4W 3L5 – 416/922-1133 – Ms. J. Wachna

Foster Advertising Co. Ltd. Library, 40 St. Clair Ave. W., Toronto, Ont. M4V 1M6 – 416/928-8090 – Lou Salvucci

Fraser & Beatty Law Library, Box 100, First Canadian Place, Toronto, Ont. M5X 1B2 – 416/863-4527 – Mrs. Joan Hudson

Friends House Library, 60 Lowther Ave., Toronto, Ont. M5R 1C7 – 416/921-0368

Gage Publishing Ltd. Editorial Library, 164 Commander Blvd., Agincourt, Ont. M1S 3C7 – 416/293-8141 – Gordon Cluett

General Foods Ltd. Library, 2200 Yonge St., Toronto, Ont. M5W 1J6 – 416/484-5492 – C. Symon

George Brown College (AA & T), Resource Centre, Box 1015, Stn. B, Toronto, Ont. M5T 2T9 – 416/967-1212, ext. 224 – Mrs. R.L. Edwards, Dir.

Glaxo Canada Ltd. Library, 1025 The Queensway, Toronto, Ont. – 416/252-2281 – Dr. V. Chivers Wilson

The Globe and Mail Ltd. Library, 444 Front St. W., Toronto, Ont. M5V 2S9 – 416/361-5000 – Ms. Amanda Valpy

Goodman and Carr Law Library, 2800 York Centre, 145 King St. W., Toronto, Ont. M5H 3K1 – 416/868-1234 – C. Malcolm

Gulf Canada Central Library, Box 460, Stn. A, Toronto, Ont. M5W 1E5 – 416/924-4141 – Wendy A. Davis (Asst.)

John D. Hayes Library of Human Relations, See Canadian Council of Christians & Jews

F.H. Hayhurst Co. Ltd. Library, 55 Eglinton Ave. E., Toronto, Ont. M4P 1G9 – 416/487-4371, ext. 315 – Ann Sargent

C.M. Hincks Treatment Centre, Saul A. Silverman Library, 440 Jarvis St., Toronto, Ont. M4Y 2H4 – 416/924-1164, ext. 63 – Mrs. Betty Mair

Holden, Murdoch & Finlay Law Library, Box 80, First Canadian Place, Toronto, Ont. M5X 1B1 – 416/863-5686

Hospital for Sick Children Library, 555 University Ave., Toronto, Ont. M5G 1X8 – 416/597-1500, loc. 1446 – Mrs. I. Jeryn

Humber College (AA & T), Learning Resource Centre, Lakeshore One Campus, 3199 Lakeshore Blvd. W., Toronto, Ont. M8V 1K8 – Margaret Trott, Co-ord.
Lakeshore Two Campus, 56 Queen Elizabeth Blvd. (252-5571)
Keelesdale Campus, 88 Industry Rd. (763-4571)

Huntec (70) Ltd. Library, 25 Howden Rd., Scarborough, Ont. M1R 5A6 – 416/751-8055 – Mrs. J. Kurantsin-Mills

Imperial Life Assurance Co. of Canada Library, 95 St. Clair Ave. W., Toronto, Ont. M4V 1N7 – 416/923-6661 – Miss P. Stewart

Imperial Oil Ltd. Library, 111 St. Clair Ave. W., Toronto, Ont. M5W 1K3 – 416/968-4866 – Miss M. Greenwood

Inco Metals Co. of Canada Ltd., Business Library, Box 44, One First Canadian Place, Toronto, Ont. M8X 1S2 – 416/361-7641 – Cynthia Smith, M.A., M.L.S.

Indusmin Limited Technical Centre, 1933 Leslie St., Don Mills, Ont. – 416/445-6720 – Yvonne Postill

Industrial Accident Prevention Association, Occupational Safety & Health Reference Library, 2 Bloor St. E., Toronto, Ont. M4W 3C2 – 416/965-8888 – Marion Frank

Institute of Chartered Accountants of Ontario, The Merrilees Library, 69 Bloor St. E., Toronto, Ont. M4W 1B3 – 416/962-1841 – Theresa Wolak

Institute of Municipal Assessors of Ontario, #2, 180 Yorkland Blvd., Willowdale, Ont. M2J 1R5 – 416/492-1331 – Ms. K.F. McGillivray

IBM Canada Ltd., Laboratory Library, Dept. 835, 1150 Eglinton Ave. E., Don Mills, Ont. M3C 1H7 – 416/443-3136 – Mrs. Rose Yan

Inco Ltd. Library, Box 44, One First Canadian Place, Toronto, Ont. M5X 1C4 – 416/361-7641 – Mrs. C.M. Smith

Italian Chamber of Commerce of Toronto Library, 159 Bay St., #313, Toronto, Ont. M5J 1J7 – 416/364-6551 – Mrs. Marina Del Grande

Jewish Public Library of Toronto, 22 Glen Park Ave., Toronto, Ont. M6B 2B9 – 416/781-6282 – Mrs. Rose Miskin, and Ms. Kaila Cramer
John Howard Society of Ontario, 980 Yonge St., #407, Toronto, Ont. M4W 2J5 – 416/925-2205
Kilborn Limited Library, 2200 Lakeshore Blvd. W., Toronto, Ont. M8V 1A4 – 416/252-5311 – Maureen M. Roe
Kingsmill Jennings Law Library, #4700, Box 124, One First Canadian Place, Toronto, Ont. M5X 1G1 – 416/362-2672 – Miss Doreen Balston
Knox College Library, 59 St. George St., Toronto, Ont. M5S 2E6 – 416/978-4504
Land Compensation Board Library, 10 King St. E., Toronto, Ont. M5C 1C3 – 416/965-6027 – Y. Fernandes
Lash, Johnston Law Library, 24th Floor, North Tower, Royal Bank Plaza, Toronto, Ont. M5J 2J1 – 416/865-1100 – Joan C. Murphy
Law Society of Upper Canada Library, Osgoode Hall, 130 Queen St. W., Toronto, Ont. M5H 2N6 – 416/362-5811 – Glen W. Howell
Legislative Library, Research & Information Services, Legislative Bldg., Queen's Park, Toronto, Ont. M7A 1A2 – 416/965-4545 – R. Brian Land, Dir.
The Lummus Company Canada Limited, Engineering Library, 251 Consumers Rd., Willowdale, Ont. M2J 4H4 – 416/493-4123 – Mrs. Sybil Salt
MacLaren Engineers, Planners & Scientists Inc., Library, 1220 Sheppard Ave. E., #100, Willowdale, Ont. M2K 2T8 – 416/499-0880 – A.M. Croxford
Maclean-Hunter Library, 481 University Ave., Toronto, Ont. M5W 1A7 – 416/596-5244 – Ms. M. Duncan
The Manufacturers Life Insurance Company, Business Library, 200 Bloor St. E., Toronto, Ont. M4W 1E4 – 416/928-4104 – Mrs. Oriole P. Anderson
Marsh & Mclennan Ltd. Information Centre, One First Canadian Place, Box 58, Toronto, Ont. M5X 1G2 – 416/868-2623 – Angela Agostino
Massey College Library, 4 Devonshire Place, Toronto, Ont. M5S 2E1 – 416/978-2893 – D.G. Neill
McCarthy & McCarthy Law Library, Box 48, Toronto Dominion Centre, Toronto, Ont. M5K 1E6 – 416/362-1812 – Mary Percival
McKim Advertising Ltd. Library, Box 99, Commerce Court East, Toronto, Ont. M5L 1E1 – 416/863-5471
McKinsey & Company Research Library, 80 Bloor St. W., Toronto, Ont. M5S 2V1 – 416/922-2200 – Lorraine Mazzocato
McMillan Binch Law Library, Box 38, Royal Bank Plaza, Toronto, Ont. M5J 2J7 – 416/865-7161 – Judith A. Ryll
The Merrilees Library, See Institute of Chartered Accountants
Metropolitan Separate School Board, Professional Library, 146 Laird Drive, Toronto, Ont. M4G 3V8 – 416/421-8950, ext. 289, 330 – Mrs. Patricia A. Berry
Metropolitan Toronto Association for the Mentally Retarded, Howard E. Bacon Memorial Library, 8 Spadina Rd., Toronto, Ont. M5R 2S7 – 416/968-0650 – Adrienne Wykes, Asst. Librn.
Midland Doherty Ltd. Library, Box 25, Commercial Union Tower, Toronto Dominion Centre, Toronto, Ont. M5K 1B5 – 416/361-6063 – Mrs. Ilme Regina
The Migraine Foundation Library, 390 Brunswick Ave., Toronto, Ont. M5R 2Z4 – 416/920-4916 – Miss Rosemary Dudley
Miller, Thomson Law Library, #1100, 21 King St. E., Toronto, Ont. M5C 1A9 – 416/361-0055 – D. Melnykas
Minden, Gross & Co. Law Library, 111 Richmond St. W., #600, Toronto, Ont. M5H 2H5 – 416/362-3711
Mining Association of Canada, Reference Library, 36 Toronto St., Toronto, Ont. M5C 2C2 – 416/363-8019
Ministries of Government, See Ontario Ministry of ...
Mount Sinai Hospital, Sidney Liswood Library, 600 University Ave., Toronto, Ont. M5G 1X5 – 416/596-4614 – Dr. J. Jimenez
Munich-London Mgmt. Corporation Ltd. Library, 55 Yonge St., Toronto, Ont. M5E 1J4 – 416/366-9587 – Mrs. S. Beer
National Cancer Institute of Canada Library, #1001, 130 Bloor St. W., Toronto, Ont. M5S 2V7 – 416/961-7223 – Dr. R.A. Macbeth
National Institute on Mental Retardation, See Canadian Association for Mentally Retarded
Needham, Harper & Steers, Information Service Centre Library, 130 Adelaide St. W., 20th Floor, Toronto, Ont. M5H 3P5 – 416/364-1492 – Linda Dominitz
Noranda Sales Corp., Sales Library, Box 45, Commerce Court West, Toronto, Ont. M5L 1B6 – 416/867-7036 – Ms. Karen Hammond
North American Life Assurance Co. Library, 105 Adelaide St. W., Toronto, Ont. M5H 1R1 – 416/362-6011 – Mrs. Dulcie Klyne
Northern Miner Library, 7 Labatt Ave., Toronto, Ont. M5A 3P2 – 416/368-3481
Northern Pigment Limited Library, Box 1, Stn. N, Toronto, Ont. M8V 3S5 – 416/251-1161
Northern Telecom Canada Ltd. Library, 304 The East Mall, Islington, Ont. M9B 6E4 – 416/232-2000 – E. Daniel
North York Board of Education, F.W. Minkler Library, 5050 Yonge St., Willowdale, Ont. M2N 5N8 – 416/225-4661, ext. 395 – H.P. Greaves
North York General Hospital, W. Keith Welsh Library, 4001 Leslie St., Willowdale, Ont. M2K 1E1 – 416/492-4748 – Mrs. Fred W. Brett
Occupational Safety, See Industrial Acc. Prev. Assn.
Office of the Ombudsman Library, 125 Queen's Park, Toronto, Ont. M5S 2C7 – 416/596-3300
Ontario Archaeological Society Library, Box 241, Stn. P, Toronto, Ont. M5S 2S8
Ontario Bible College, J. Wm. Horsey Library, 25 Ballyconnor Ct., Willowdale, Ont. M2M 4B3 – 416/226-6380 – James Johnson
Ontario Cancer Institute Library, 500 Sherbourne St., Toronto, Ont. M4X 1K9 – 416/924-0671, ext. 265 – Carol Morrison
Ontario Crafts Council, Craft Resource Centre, 346 Dundas St. W., Toronto, Ont. M5T 1G5 – 416/979-3551 – Sandra Dunn
Ontario Chamber of Commerce Library, 5th Floor, 2323 Yonge St., Toronto, Ont. M4P 2C9 – 416/482-5222 – E.L. Roscow
Ontario College of Art Library, 100 McCaul St., Toronto, Ont. M5T 1W1 – 416/977-5311 – Ian Carr-Harris
Ontario Economic Council Library, 81 Wellesley St. E., Toronto, Ont. M6C 3Y5 – 416/965-4315 – Ann M. Chin
Ontario Educational Communications Authority, see TV Ontario
Ontario Energy Board Library, 14 Carlton St., 9th Floor, Toronto, Ont. M5B 1K5 – 416/963-0821 – Miss L. Holder
Ontario Film Institute Library, 770 Don Mills Rd., Toronto, Ont. M3C 1T3 – 416/429-4100 – Sherrie Brethour
Ontario Genealogical Society Library, Box 66, Stn. Q, Toronto, Ont. M4T 2L7 – 416/921-4606 – D. Grant Brown
Ontario Hydro Library, 700 University Ave., Toronto, Ont. M5G 1X6 – 416/592-2716 – M.D. Taylor
Ontario Institute for Studies in Education, Library, 252 Bloor St. W., Toronto, Ont. M5S 1V6 – 416/923-6641 – Miss S.K. Wigmore
Ontario Labour Relations Board Library, 400 University Ave., 4th Floor, Toronto, Ont. M7A 1V4 – 416/965-0206 – Ms. B.A. Mathias
Ontario Law Reform Commission Library, 16th Floor, 18 King St. E., Toronto, Ont. M5C 1C5 – 416/965-4761 – Elizabeth Page
Ontario Legislature, see Legislative Library
Ontario Medical Association Library, 240 St. George St., Toronto, Ont. M5R 2P4 – 416/925-3264 – Ms. Jan Greenwood
Ontario Ministry of Agriculture & Food, Library, 801 Bay St., 3rd Floor, Toronto, Ont. M7A 2B2 – 416/965-1816 – Ken Sundquist
Ontario Ministry of Attorney General, Crown Law Office Library, 18 King St. E., 3rd Floor, Toronto, Ont. M5C 1C5 – 416/965-4714 – Ms. Elaine Norman
Ontario Ministry of Community & Social Services, Library, 6th Floor, 880 Bay St., Toronto, Ont. M7A 1E9 – 416/965-2300 – Mrs. I. Shlapak
Ontario Ministry of Correctional Services, Library, 2001 Eglinton Ave. E., Scarborough, Ont. M1L 4P1 – 416/750-3481 – T.J.B. Anderson

Ontario Ministry of Culture & Recreation, Library/Resource Centre, 77 Bloor St. W., 9th Floor, Toronto, Ont. M7A 2R9 – 416/965-6763 – Mrs. Renata Grodski (Mrs. Marjorie B. Howard, Co-ord.)

Ontario Ministry of Education, Information Centre, Mowat Block, Queen's Park, Toronto, Ont. M7A 1L2 – 416/965-1451 – Miss Carol Fordyce, Mgr.

Ontario Ministry of Energy, Library, 12th Floor, 56 Wellesley St. W., Toronto, Ont. M7A 2B7 – 416/965-9174 – N. Pierobon

Ontario Ministry of the Environment, Departmental Library, 135 St. Clair Ave. W., 1st Floor, Toronto, Ont. M4V 1P5 – 416/965-7978

Ontario Ministry of the Environment, Air Resources Branch Library, 880 Bay St., 4th Floor, Toronto, Ont. M5S 1Z8 – 416/965-6343

Ontario Ministry of the Environment, Laboratory Library, Resources Rd., Islington, Ont. M9W 5L1 – 416/248-3048 – N. McIlroy

Ontario Ministry of Health, Public Health Labs Library, Box 9000, Stn. A, Toronto, Ont. M5W 1R5 – 416/248-3165 – Doris Standing

Ontario Ministry of Health, Library, 7th Floor, 15 Overlea Blvd., Toronto, Ont. M4H 1A9 – 416/965-7881 – Miss V. Brunka

Ontario Ministry of Industry & Tourism, Library, 900 Bay St., Toronto, Ont. M7A 2E2 – 416/965-3365 – Mrs. M. Enge

Ontario Ministry of Intergovernmental Affairs, Library, Frost Bldg. North, 1st Floor, Queen's Park, Toronto, Ont. M7A 1Y8 – 416/965-2314 – Miss B.A.B. Weatherhead

Ontario Ministry of Labour, Library, 400 University Ave., Toronto, Ont. M7A 1T7 – 416/965-1641 – Douglas A. Armstrong

Ontario Ministry of Municipal Affairs & Housing, Library, 56 Wellesley St. W., 2nd Floor, Toronto, Ont. M5S 2S3 – 416/965-9720 – F. Szucs

Ontario Ministry of Natural Resources, Mines Library, 77 Grenville St., #812, Toronto, Ont. M5S 1B3 – 416/965-1352 – Ms. N. Thurston

Ontario Ministry of Northern Affairs, Library, 9th Floor, 10 Wellesley St. E., Toronto, Ont. M4Y 1G2 – 416/965-7577 – Mrs. Glenda J. Schultz

Ontario Ministry of Revenue, Library, 77 Bloor St. W., 3rd Floor, Toronto, Ont. M7A 1X8 – 416/965-3892 – Miss Lorna Brown

Ontario Ministry of Transporation & Communications, Library & Information Centre, 1st Floor Central Bldg., 1201 Wilson Ave., Downsview, Ont. M3M 1J8 – 416/248-3591 – Mrs. S.A. Pavlin

Ontario Ministry of Treasury & Economics, Library, 1st Floor, Frost Bldg. North, Queen's Park, Toronto, Ont. M7A 1Y8 – 416/965-2314 – Miss B.A. Weatherhead

Ontario Office of Fire Marshal Library, Ministry of the Solicitor General, 590 Keele St., #341, Toronto, Ont. M6N 4X2 – 416/965-4855 – Mrs. Nancy Carlucci

Ortho Pharmaceutical (Canada) Ltd. Library, 19 Green Belt Dr., Don Mills, Ont. M3C 1L9 – 416/449-9444 – Marta Bodnar

Ontario Provincial Police, Training & Development Centre Library, 291 Sherbourne St., Toronto, Ont. M5A 2R9 – 416/965-5421 – F.C. Harvey

Ontario Puppetry Association Library, 10 Skyview Cres., Toronto, Ont. M2J 1B8 – 416/494-7011 – K.B. McKay

Ontario Science Centre Library, 770 Don Mills Rd., Don Mills, Ont. M3C 1T3 – 416/429-4100 – Dale Munro

Ontario Trucking Association Library, 555 Dixon Rd., Rexdale, Ont. M9W 1H8 – 416/247-7131 – Mrs. Dorothy Myles

Ontario Welfare Council Library, 1240 Bay St., Toronto, Ont. M5R 2A7 – 416/961-4771 – The Librarian

Orthopedic Arthritic Hospital Library, 43 Wellesley St. E., Toronto, Ont. M4Y 1H1 – 416/967-8545 – Mrs. Sallee Baigent

Peat Marwick & Partners Library, Box 31, Commerce Court Postal Stn., Toronto, Ont. M5L 1B2 – 416/863-3441 – Mrs. S.A. Layton

Polar Gas Project Library, Box 90, Commerce Court West, Toronto, Ont. M5L 1H3 – 416/869-2675 – Mrs. Jennifer Wentworth

Pontifical Institute of Mediaeval Studies Library, 113 St. Joseph St., Toronto, Ont. M5S 1J4 – 416/921-3151 – D.F. Finlay

Price Waterhouse & Co. Library, Box 51, Toronto Dominion Centre, Toronto, Ont. M5K 1G1 – 416/863-1133 – Mrs. Dorothy Sedgwick

Proctor & Redfern Ltd., Consulting Engineers & Planners, Library, 75 Eglinton Ave. E., Toronto, Ont. M4P 1H3 – 416/486-5225 – Mrs. T. Dam

Prudential Insurance Co. of America Library, King & Yonge Sts., Toronto, Ont. M5H 1B7 – 416/366-6971 – Mrs. J. Ireland

Queen Street Mental Health Centre, Health Sciences Library, 1001 Queen St. W., Toronto, Ont. M6J 1H3 – 416/535-8501, ext. 171 – Mary-Ann Georges

Reed Ltd. Technical Information Centre, 145 King St. W., Toronto, Ont. M5H 1J8 – 416/862-5485 – Jim Drake

Reed Stenhouse Ltd. Library, Royal Trust Tower, Box 250, Toronto Dominion Centre, Toronto, Ont. M5K 1J6 – 416/868-5520 – G.R.E. Bromwich

Registered Nurses' Association of Ontario Library, 33 Price St., Toronto, Ont. M4W 1Z2 – 416/923-3523 – Mary Boite

Rio Algom Ltd. Library, 120 Adelaide St. W., Toronto, Ont. M5H 1W5 – 416/367-4299 – Penny Lipman

Royal Astronomical Society of Canada Library, 124 Merton St., Toronto, Ont. M4S 2Z2 – 416/484-4960 – F.L. Troyer

Royal Bank of Canada, Information Resources Centre, Royal Bank Plaza, Toronto, Ont. M5J 2J5 – 416/865-2780 – Mrs. Jane Dysart

Royal Canadian Military Institute Library, 426 University Ave., Toronto, Ont. M5G 1S9 – 416/597-0286 – Lt. Col. W.G. Heard

Royal Ontario Museum Library, 100 Queen's Park, Toronto, Ont. M5S 2C6 – 416/978-3671 – Gene Wilburn

Royal Trust Corporation of Canada, Investment Research Library, (Royal Trust Tower), Box 7500, Stn. A, Toronto, Ont. M5W 1P9 – 416/867-2928 – Ms. Anita Frank

Ryerson Polytechnical Institute Library, 50 Gould St., Toronto, Ont. M5B 1E8 – 416/595-5331 – John North

St. Augustine's Seminary Library, 2661 Kingston Rd., Scarborough, Ont. M1M 1M3 – 416/261-7207, ext. 36 – Sr. Madeline Connolly

St. Joseph's Health Centre, George Pennal Library, 30 The Queensway, Toronto, Ont. M6R 1B5 – 416/534-9531, ext. 629 – Julia Chan

St. John's Convalescent Hospital, Beeston Staff Library, 285 Cummer Ave., Willowdale, Ont. M2M 2G1 – 416/226-6780, ext. 458 – Mrs. B. Friedman

St. Michael's Hospital, Health Science Library, 30 Bond St., Toronto, Ont. M5B 1W8 – 416/360-4941 – Mrs. Anita Wong

Scarborough Board of Education, A.B. Patterson Professional Library, Level 2, 140 Borough Drive, Scarborough, Ont. M1P 4N6 – 416/296-7515 – MaryLu Brennan

Scarborough General Hospital, Health Sciences Library, 3050 Lawrence Ave. E., Scarborough, Ont. M1P 2V5 – 416/438-2911 – Ms. A. Kubjas

Seneca College (AA & T), Library, 43 Sheppard Ave. E., Willowdale, Ont. M2N 2Z8 – 416/491-5050, ext. 244 – D. Massey

Shell Canada Ltd. Library, 505 University Ave., Toronto, Ont. M5G 1X4 – 416/597-7111

Shibley, Righton & McCutcheon Law Library, 401 Bay St., Box 32, Toronto, Ont. M5H 2Z1 – 416/363-9381 – Mrs. Florence Hall

Saul A. Silverman Library, See C.M. Hincks Treatment Centre

Simpsons, Training Dept. Library, 7th Floor, 176 Yonge St., Toronto, Ont. M5C 2L7 – 416/861-6406

Statistics Canada Library, 25 St. Clair Ave. E., Toronto, Ont. M4T 1M4 – 416/966-6586 – Sandra McIntyre

Stikeman, Elliott, & Co. Law Library, Box 85, Commerce Court West, Toronto, Ont. M5L 1B9 – 416/869-5500 – Carol Frymer

Strathy, Archibald and Seagram Law Library, Box 438, Commerce Court West, Toronto, Ont. M5L 1J3 – 416/862-7525 – Catherine J. McLoughlin

Sun Life Assurance Co. of Canada Library, Box 4150, Stn. A, Toronto, Ont. M5W 2C9 – 416/869-6908 – Miss M. Walsh

Sus-Wal Editorial Library, 130 Harlandale Ave., Willowdale, Ont. M2N 1P3

Sunnybrook Medical Centre Library, 2075 Bayview Ave., Toronto, Ont. M4N 3M5 – 416/486-3880 – Linda McFarlane

Thomson, Rogers Law Library, 390 Bay St., #3100, Toronto, Ont. M5H 1W2 – 416/868-3309 – Mrs. Dianne D. Sydij

Toronto Board of Education, See Board of Education

Toronto Dominion Bank, Dept. of Economic Research Library, 55 King St. W., Toronto, Ont. M5K 1A2 – 416/866-8068 – Ruth P. Smith

Toronto East General & Orthopaedic Hospital, Medical Library, 825 Coxwell Ave., Toronto, Ont. M4C 3E7 – 416/461-8272, ext. 275 – Mrs. K. Hauw

Toronto General Hospital, Fudger Library, 101 College St., Toronto, Ont. M5G 1L7 – 416/595-3549, 3429 – Mrs. D. Cowper

Toronto Star Newspapers Ltd., Library, One Yonge St., Toronto, Ont. M5E 1E6 – 416/367-2420 – Carol Lindsay

Toronto Stock Exchange Library, 55 Yonge St., 8th Floor, Toronto, Ont. M5E 1J8 – 416/868-5326 – Miss S. Foster

Toronto Sun Library, 333 King St. E., Toronto, Ont. M5A 3X5 – 416/868-2257 – Julie Kirsh

Toronto Transit Commission Library, 1900 Yonge St., Toronto, Ont. M4S 1Z2 – 416/481-4252 – Mrs. Adrian Gehring

Toronto Western Hospital, Health Sciences Library, 399 Bathurst St., Toronto, Ont. M5T 2S8 – 416/369-5750 – Miss Elizabeth A. Reid

Tory, Tory, DesLauriers & Binnington Law Library, Royal Bank Plaza, Box 20, Toronto, Ont. M5J 2K1 – 416/865-0040 – Laurel C. Murdoch

TV Ontario Library, 2180 Yonge St., Toronto, Ont. M4S 2C1 – 416/484-2651 – Cheryl Zimmerman

Ukrainica Canadiana Library, 4 Island View Blvd., Toronto, Ont. M8V 2P4 – 416/255-9090 – S. Pavvluk

UNICEF Canada Library, 443 Mt. Pleasant Rd., Toronto, Ont. M4S 2L8 – 416/482-4444

Union Carbide Canada Ltd. Library, 123 Eglinton Ave. E., Toronto, Ont. M4P 1J3 – 416/487-1311, ext. 1160 – K. Martha Nagata

United Church of Canada Archives, Victoria University, 73 Queen's Park Cres. E., Toronto, Ont. M5S 2C4 – 416/978-3832 – Rev. Glenn Lucas

United Empire Loyalists Association of Canada, Loyalist Reference Library, 23 Prince Arthur Ave., Toronto, Ont. M5R 1B2 – 416/923-7921 – E.J. Chard

United States Info Service Library, 360 University Ave., Toronto, Ont. M5G 1S4 – 416/595-1700, ext. 217 – Sharon Shulda

University of Toronto, Central University Library, Toronto, Ont. M5S 1A5 – 416/978-2292 – R.H. Blackburn, Chief Librarian

- John P. Robarts Research Library – (978-2294)
- Science & Medicine Library – Mrs. G. Bishop (978-2284)
- Sigmund Samuel Library – Miss S. Laidlaw (978-2280)
- Thomas Fisher Rare Book Library – R. Landon (978-5285)
- University Archives – D. Rudkin (978-2277)

Aerospace Studies – Mrs. A. Luik (667-7712)
Anthropology – Mrs. T. Ireland (978-3296)
Architecture – Mrs. P. Manson-Smith (978-2649)
Astronomy (David Dunlap Observatory) – Miss Z. Sterns (884-2112)
Audio Visual – Ms. L. Avison (978-6522)
Best Institute Library – Kathy Baier (978-2588)
Botany – Mrs. E. Chamberlain (978-3538)
Chemistry – Ms. D. Allen (978-3587)
Computer Science – Mrs. S. Johnston (978-2987)
Criminology – Mrs. C. Matthews (978-7068)
Dentistry – Mrs. S. Goddard (978-2796)
*East Asian – Mrs. Anna U (978-3300)
Education – Miss M. Shortt (978-3224)
Emmanuel College – Rev. R.G. Bracewell (978-3864)
*Engineering – Miss E. Brown (978-6494)
Environmental Studies – Mrs. J. Eichmanis (978-7429)
Erindale College – H. Smith (828-5236)
Fine Art – Miss A. Retfalvi (978-3290)
Forestry – Mrs. J. Bohne (978-6016)
Geology – Miss L.A. Eschenauer (978-3024)
Industrial Relations – W. Roulston (978-2928)
Institute for Child Study – Mrs. M. Herman (978-5086)
Joint Program on Transportation (York U & U of T) – Ms. A. Poole (978-6424)
Knox College Caven Library – Mrs. A.H. Burgess (978-4508)
Law – C. Attalai (978-3719)
Library Science – Mrs. D. Henderson (978-7060)
Management Studies – Miss B. Dance (978-3421)
*Map Library – Miss J. Winearls (978-3372)
Massey College – D. Neill (978-2893)
Mathematics – Mrs. C. Graham (978-8624)
Music – Miss K. McMorrow (978-3734)
New College – Mrs. J. Guillaume (978-2493)
Pathology – Mrs. S. Duda (978-2558)
*Pharmacy – Miss B.A. Gallivan (978-2872)
Physics (including Geophysics) – Mrs. B. Chu (978-5188)
Policy Analysis, Inst. for – Mrs. U. Greenberg (978-8623)
St. Michael's College – Rev. J.B. Black, c.s.b. (921-3151)
Scarborough College – J. Ball (284-3246)
Trinity College – Mrs. F. Finch (978-2653)
Victoria College – Dr. R. Brandeis (978-3825)
Wycliffe College – Mrs. L. Hassell (979-2870)
Zoology (including Great Lakes Institute) – Ms. R. O'Grady (978-3515)
(*Administered by Central Library)

Warner-Lambert Reference Library, 2200 Eglinton Ave. E., Scarborough, Ont. M1K 5C9 – 416/750-2360 – Mrs. Edna Allen

Wellesley Hospital Library, 160 Wellesley St. E., Toronto, Ont. M4Y 1J3 – 416/966-6617 – Mrs. V. Empey

Women's College Hospital Library, 76 Grenville St., Toronto, Ont. M5S 1B2 – 416/966-7468 – Miss Margaret Robins

Wood Gundy Ltd. Library, Box 274, Royal Trust Tower, Toronto Dominion Centre, Toronto, Ont. M5K 1M7 – 416/362-4433, ext. 426 – Ms. A. Robinson

Workmen's Compensation Board Library, 2 Bloor St. E., Toronto, Ont. M4W 3C3 – 416/965-8722 – Ms. M. Griffith

York Board of Education, Professional Library, 2 Trethewey Dr., Toronto, Ont. M6M 4A8 – 416/653-2270 – Sheila Moll, Pat Steenbergen

York-Finch General Hospital, Thomas J. Malcho Memorial Library, 2111 Finch Ave. W., Downsview, Ont. M3N 1N1 – 416/744-2500 – Mrs Joyce Jones

York University, Scott Library, 4700 Keele St., Downsview, Ont. M3J 2R2 – 416/667-2235 – Anne Woodsworth, Director of Libraries

Asst. Director (Public Services) – Ellen Hoffmann
Asst. Director (Technical Services) – Rasma Rugelis
Government Documents (Admin. Studies Bldg., M3J 2R6) – F. Anne Cannon (667-2545)
Law Library (Osgoode Hall, M3J 2R5) – B.J. Halévy (667-3939)
Leslie Frost Library, 2275 Bayview Ave., Toronto, Ont. M4N 3M6 – Phyllis Platnick, Head
Steacie Science Library (M3J 2R3) – B.B. Wilks (667-3927)

YWCA Women's Resource Centre, 15 Birch Ave., Toronto, Ont. M4V 1E1 – 416/925-3137 – Elaine Berns (Co-ord.)

Youthdale Treatment Centre Library, 20 Spadina Rd., 5th Floor, Toronto, Ont. M5R 2S7 – 416/967-7466 – Marg Matheson

VANIER

Sport Information Resource Centre, 333 River Rd., Vanier, Ont. K1L 8B9 – 613/746-5357 – Gilles Chiasson

Royal Canadian Mint, See Ottawa

Telesat Canada Library, 333 River Rd., Vanier, Ont. K1L 8B9 – 613/746-5920 – Ms. Eileen Foster

VINELAND STATION

Agriculture Canada, Research Station Library, Vineland Station, Ont. L0R 2E0 – 416/562-4113, ext. 41 – N. Gibson-MacDonald

Ontario Ministry of Agriculture & Food, Horticultural Research Institute Library, Vineland Station, Ont. L0R 2E0 – 416/562-4141, ext. 61 – Mrs. J. Wanner

WATERLOO

Conestoga College (AA & T), Waterloo Campus Library, 435 King St. N., Waterloo, Ont. N2J 2Z5 – 519/885-0300 – Dora Paterson, Lib. Techn.

Conrad Grebel College Library, Waterloo, Ont. N2L 3G6 – 519/885-0220 – Sam Steiner

Dominion Life Assurance Company Library, 111 Westmount Rd. S., Waterloo, Ont. N2J 4C6 – 519/888-5320 – Venilia Sperling – An in-Company library, not open to the public

Mutual Life Assurance Co. of Canada Library, 227 King St. S., Waterloo, Ont. N2J 4C5 – 519/888-2262 – Leslie Day

Renison College Library, Waterloo, Ont. N2L 3G4 – 519/884-4400 – Barbara Smucker

St. Jerome's College Library, Waterloo, Ont. N2L 3G3 – 519/884-8110 – Mrs. B. Lanktree

St. Paul's United College Library, Westmount Rd. N., Waterloo, Ont. N2L 3G5 – 519/885-1460 – Irma Kadela

University of Waterloo, Library, Waterloo, Ont. N2L 3G1 – 519/885-1211 – Murray C. Shepherd, University Librarian
- Assoc. Librarian, Reader Services – Bruce MacNeil
- Assoc. Librarian, Support Services – C. David Emery
- Asst. Librarian, E.M.S. Divisional Library – Carolynne Presser
- Asst. to Librarian, Admin. – Lorraine Beattie
- Administrative Asst. – vacant
- Head, University Map Library – Richard Pinnell
- Cataloguing Dept. Head – Bill Oldfield
- Government Publications – Lois Claxton
- Serials Dept. Head – Boris Bruder
- Arts Circulation Dept. Head – Elaine Reaman
- Arts Reference Dept. Head – Tom Eadie
- Asst. Librarian for Systems – Gene Damon
- E.M.S. Circulation Dept. Head – Claudine McDonald
- E.M.S. Reference Dept. Head – Faye Abrams
- Co-ordinator of Machine-Assisted Reference Service – Irwin Rodin

Waterloo Public Interest Research Group Resource Centre, University of Waterloo, Waterloo, Ont. N2L 3G1 – 519/884-9020

Wilfrid Laurier University, Central Library, Waterloo, Ont. N2L 3C5 – 519/884-1970 – Erich R.W. Schultz, University Librarian
- Acquisitions – Mrs. Norma McClenaghan
- Bibliographic Searching – Mrs. Joan Mitchell
- Cataloguing Dept. Head – Dr. Wasyl Sirskyj
- Circulation Dept. Head – Howard Parkinson
- Documents Dept. Head – Mrs. Inez Cawley
- Reference & Collections Development Head – John Arndt
- Serials Dept. Head – Richard Woeller
- Systems – Herbert Schwartz

WELLAND

Atlas Steels Library, Welland, Ont. L3B 5R7 – 416/735-5661

Niagara College (AA & T), Learning Resource Centre, Welland, Ont. L3B 5S2 – 416/735-2211 – S.J. Kees

WEST HILL

Scarborough College Library, 1265 Military Trail, West Hill, Ont. M1C 1A4 – 416/284-3245 – J.L. Ball

WESTON

See Toronto

WHITBY

Ontario Ministry of Health, Whitby Psychiatric Hospital, Library, Box 613, Whitby, Ont. L1N 5S9 – 416/668-5881, ext. 263 – E. Evans

WILLOWDALE

See Toronto

WINDSOR

Essex Law Association Library, County Court House, 245 Windsor Ave., Windsor, Ont. N9A 1J2 – 519/252-8418 – Anne Matthewman

International Joint Commission Library, 100 Ouellette Ave., 8th Floor, Windsor, Ont. N9A 6T3 – 519/256-7821 – Patricia Murray

St. Clair College (AA & T), Library, 2000 Talbot Rd., Windsor, Ont. N9A 6S4 – 519/966-1656 – Anita Blair

University of Windsor, Central Library, 401 Sunset, Windsor, Ont. N9B 3P4 – 519/253-4232 – Albert Mate, Acting University Librarian
- Assoc. Librarian, Info. Services – Albert Mate
- Assoc. Librarian, Tech. Services – Conrad Reitz
- Cataloguing Dept. Head – Mrs. Aline Soules
- Circulation Dept. Head – Mrs. Patricia Suttor
- Collections Development Dept. Head – Mrs. Johanna Foster
- Education Librarian – Thomas Robinson
- Government Documents Librarian – Miss Jeanette McGrath
- Interlibrary Loans Head – Mrs. Martha Wolfe (act.)
- Monographs Dept. Head – Miss Wendy Fraser
- Reference Dept. Head – Mrs. Martha Wolfe
- Serials Dept. Head – Mrs. Idalia Rappé
- Law Librarian – Paul Murphy

The Windsor Star Library, Ferry & Pitt Sts., Windsor, Ont. N9A 4M5 – 519/255-5672 – Mrs. Frances Curry

WOODSTOCK

Western Ontario Breeders Library, Box 457, Woodstock, Ont. N4S 7Y7 – 519/539-9831 – Vicki Davey – Livestock & Veterinary Journals

---

PRINCE EDWARD ISLAND

Public Libraries in Prince Edward Island

With Librarian

Area Code for P.E.I. is 902

Charlottetown, Confederation Centre Library, Box 7000, Charlottetown, P.E.I. C1A 8G8 – 892-7932 – Miss Brenda Brady

Branch Public Libraries:

Abram Village (Bibliothèque Publique), Abram Village, P.E.I. C0B 2E0 – Mme Lucia Arsenault

Alberton Public Library, Alberton, P.E.I. C0B 1B0 – Mrs. Blanche England

Bradalbane Public Library, Bradalbane, P.E.I. C0A 1E0 – Mrs. Grace Murray

Cornwall Public Library, Cornwall, P.E.I. C0A 1H0 – Elmer Power

Crapaud Public Library, Crapaud, P.E.I. C0A 1J0 – 658-2145 – Mrs. Olga Stordy

Georgetown Public Library, Georgetown, P.E.I. C0A 1L0 – Miss Genevieve Solomon

Hunter River Public Library, Hunter River, P.E.I. C0A 1N0 – Mrs. Dorothy Bolger

Kensington Public Library, Kensington, P.E.I. C0B 1M0 – Mrs. Katherine Carrier

Kinkora Public Library, Kinkora, P.E.I. C0B 1N0 – Doug Kirby

Montague Public Library, Montague, P.E.I. C0A 1R0 – 838-2863 – Mrs. Melissa Yorston

Morell Public Library, Morell, P.E.I. C0A 1S0 – Mrs. Frances Cobb

Mount Stewart Public Library, Mount Stewart, P.E.I. C0A 1T0 – Mrs. Betty Affleck

Murray Harbour Public Library, Murray Harbour, P.E.I. C0A 1V0 – Mrs. Valda Hume

Murray River Public Library, Murray River, P.E.I. C0A 1W0 – Mrs. Leona Giddings

O'Leary Public Library, O'Leary, P.E.I. C0B 1V0 – Mrs. Lila MacNeill

Port Borden Public Library, Port Borden, P.E.I. C0B 1X0 – Alfred Chappell

St. Peter's Bay Public Library, St. Peter's Bay, P.E.I. C0A 2A0 – Mrs. Mary Larkin

Souris Public Library, Souris, P.E.I. C0A 2B0 – Mrs. Kathleen Poole

Summerside Public Library, 247 Central St., Summerside, P.E.I. C1N 3M5 – Mrs. Goldie MacDonald

Tignish Public Library, Tignish, P.E.I. C0B 2B0 – Mrs. Theresa Wasnidge

Tyne Valley Public Library, Tyne Valley, P.E.I. C0B 2C0 – Mrs. Edna Walker

Wellington Public Library, Wellington, P.E.I. C0B 2E0 – 854-2736 – Mrs. Mae Arsenault

Special & College Libraries in Prince Edward Island

With Librarian or Official

Area Code for P.E.I. is 902

CHARLOTTETOWN

Agriculture Canada, Research Station Library, Box 1210, Charlottetown, P.E.I. C1A 7M8 – 892-5461 – Barrie Stanfield

Holland College, Charlottetown Centre Library, Weymouth St., Charlottetown, P.E.I. C1A 4Z1 – 892-4191, ext. 158 – Ian MacIntosh

Institute of Man & Resources Reference Library, Box 2008, Charlottetown, P.E.I. C1A 1A4 – 892-0361 – Katherine Arnold

Legislative Library, Box 7000, Charlottetown, P.E.I. C1A 7M8 – 892-7932

Planning Library, Box 2000, Charlottetown, P.E.I. C1A 7N8 – 892-3504, ext. 29 – Marion Kielly

University of Prince Edward Island, Library, Charlottetown, P.E.I. C1A 4P3 – 892-1243 – C. Merritt Crockett

QUEBEC

Public Libraries in Quebec

With Librarian

Abitibi-Témiscamingue (Bibliothèque régionale), C.P. 266, (19 11e rue), Noranda, P.Q. J9X 5A6 – 819/762-4305 – Norman Fink

Alma (Bibliothèque municipale), 50 St. Joseph sud, Alma, P.Q. G8B 3E4 – 418/668-3339 – Mlle Joanne Déry

Amos (Bibliothèque municipale), 42 rue Principale nord, Amos, P.Q. J9T 2K6 – 819/732-6070 – Mlle Claire Sénéclauze

Amqui (Bibliothèque municipale), 123A, rue Desbiens, #215, Amqui, P.Q. G0J 1B0 – 418/629-4216 – Mme Ludgère Fournier

Anjou (Bibliothèque municipale), 7500 Goncourt, Anjou, P.Q H1K 3Y3 – 514/352-4440, poste 256 – Mme Louise Guillemette-Labory

Arthabaska (Bibliothèque municipale), a/s Hôtel de Ville, 841 boul Bois-Francs sud, Arthabaska, P.Q. G6P 5W3 – 819/357-2346 – Mme Thérèse Nadeau

Asbestos (Bibliothèque), 189 rue du Roi, Asbestos, P.Q. J1T 1S4 – 819/879-4363 – Mme Luce Godbout

Aylmer (Bibliothèque municipale), 74 rue Principale, Aylmer, P.Q. J9H 3L7 – 819/684-5360 – Mlle Laurette Mackey

Baie Comeau (Bibliothèque municipale), 41 ave Mance, Baie Comeau, P.Q. G4Z 1N1 – 418/296-4750 – Mme L. Thériault

Baie-d'Urfé (Bibliothèque publique), 20,551 Chemin du Bord du Lac, Baie-d'Urfé, P.Q. H9X 1R3 – 514/457-3274 – Mme Ann Cumyn

Bas-St-Laurent-Gaspésie (Bibliothèque régionale), (31 rue des Ecoliers), C.P. 430, Cap-Chat, P.Q. G0J 1E0 – 418/786-5597 – Gilles Rochette

Beaconsfield (Bibliothèque municipale), 303 boul. Beaconsfield, Beaconsfield, P.Q. H9W 4A7 – 514/697-9040 – Mlle Thérèse Shaw

Beauharnois (Bibliothèque municipale), 33 Richardson, Beauharnois, P.Q. J6N 2T4 – 514/429-3083 – Mlle Lise Ranger

Beauport Library System, 577 ave Royale, Beauport, P.Q. G1E 6P4 – 418/667-8554 – Denis Couture

Beloeil (Bibliothèque municipale), (542 boul. Laurier), C.P. 33, Beloeil, P.Q. J3G 4S8 – 514/467-7872 – Jean Lasnier

Blainville (Bibliothèque municipale), 1050 boul. Labelle, Blainville, P.Q. J7C 2N6 – 514/430-8680 – Mme Maud Lefebvre

Boisbriand (Service du Livre), 940 Grande-Allée, Boisbriand, P.Q. J7G 2J7 – 514/435-1954, poste 62 – Mme Andrée Chartrand

Boucherville (Bibliothèque municipale), 500 Rvière-aux-Pins, Boucherville, P.Q. J4B 2Z7 – 514/655-3131, poste 219 – Florian Dubois

Brossard (Bibliothèque municipale), 3200 boul. Lapinière, Brossard, P.Q. J4Z 2L4 – 514/676-0201 – Y.-A. Lacroix

Candiac (Bibliothèque municipale), 9 boul. Montcalm, #450, Candiac, P.Q. J5R 3L5 – 514/659-2855 – Mme Maryse Hansen

Cap-de-la-Madeleine (Bibliothèque municipale), 45 rue Dorval, C.P. 368, Cap-de-la-Madeleine, P.Q. G8T 7W6 – 819/375-1666 – Mme France S. Bisson

Chambly (Bibliothèque municipale), 56 rue Martel, Chambly, P.Q. J3L 1V3 – 514/658-1778 – Pierre-Yves Blanchard

Charlesbourg (Bibliothèque municipale), 5420 Villa St-Vincent, Charlesbourg, P.Q. G1H 4B6 – 418/628-8672 – Mlle Louise Allard

Châteauguay (Bibliothèque municipale), 15 boul. Maple, Châteauguay, P.Q. J6J 3P7 – 514/691-1934 – René Richer

Chibougamau (Bibliothèque municipale), 505 rue Wilson, Chibougamau, P.Q. G8P 1K2 – 819/748-2688, poste 22 – Mlle Lise Matte

Chicoutimi (Bibliothèque municipale), 455 rue Racine est, Chicoutimi, P.Q. G7H 1T5 – 418/543-6881 – Mlle Odette Madore

Coaticook (Bibliothèque municipale), 34 rue Principale est, Coaticook, P.Q. J1A 1N2 – 819/849-4013 – Rock Létourneau

Côte-Nord (Bibliothèque régionale), 405 Brochu, Sept-Iles, P.Q. G4R 2W9 – 418/962-1020 – Johan Nadeau

Côte-Saint-Luc (Bibliothèque municipale), 7101 Côte-Saint Luc, Côte-Saint-Luc, P.Q. H4V 1J2 – 514/481-5676 – Mlle Eleanor London

Cowansville (Bibliothèque municipale), 220 place Municipale, Cowansville, P.Q. J2K 1T4 – 514/263-4071 – Mlle Anne-Marie Duchaine

Des Portages (Bibliothèque régionale), 184 Fraser, Rivière-du-Loup, P.Q. G5R 1C8 – 418/867-1682 – Yves Savard

Deux-Montagnes (Bibliothèque municipale), 200 rue Henri-Dunant, Deux-Montagnes, P.Q. J7R 2W6 – 514/473-2702 – Mlle Michelle Dupuis

Dorval (Bibliothèque municipale), 1401 Chemin du Bord du Lac, Dorval, P.Q. H9S 2E5 – 514/631-3575 – Mlle Eleanore Schonfeld

Drummondville (Bibliothèque municipale), 405 rue Saint-Jean, Drummondville, P.Q. J2B 5L7 – 819/472-7679 – Pierre Meunier

Estrie (Bibliothèque régionale), 4155 rue Brodeur, Sherbrooke, P.Q. J1L 1K4 – 819/565-9744 – Normand Bernier

Fermont (Bibliothèque municipale), C.P. 10, Fermont, P.Q. G0G 1J0 – 418/287-3227 – Mme Lise Landry

Gagnon (Bibliothèque publique), C.P. 520, Gagnon, P.Q. G0G 1K0 – 418/532-4471 – Mme Pauline Bellavance

Gatineau (Bibliothèque municipale), 381 boul. Maloney, Gatineau, P.Q. J8P 1E3 – 819/663-9254 – Bernard Lehoux

Granby (Bibliothèque municipale), 125 rue Principale, Granby, P.Q. J2G 2T9 – 514/372-6678 – Jose-Luis Fuenzalida

Grand-Mère (Bibliothèque municipale), 650 8e rue, Grand-Mère, P.Q. G9T 6K1 – 819/538-5555 – Mme Janine Vaugeois-Patry

Greenfield Park (Bibliothèque municipale), 147 boul. Churchill, Greenfield Park, P.Q. J4V 2M2 – 514/672-7500 – Simon Tremblay

Hull (Bibliothèque municipale), (25 rue Laurier), C.P. 1970, Succ. B, Hull, P.Q. J8X 3Y9 – 819/777-4341 – Denis Boyer

Institut national canadien pour les aveugles, (Bibliothèque publique), 1181 rue Guy, Montreal, P.Q. H3H 2K6 – 514/931-7221, poste 71 – Jeannine Tardif

Institut Nazareth et Louis Braille, (Bibliothèque publique), 1255 rue Beauregard, Longueuil, P.Q. J4K 2M3 – 514/463-1710 – Mlle Suzanne Olivier

Jonquière (Bibliothèque municipale), Hôtel de Ville, Carré Davis, Jonquière, P.Q. G7S 4L1 – 418/548-7456 – Mme Mireille Boudreault

Kirkland (Bibliothèque municipale), 17000 boul. Hymus, Kirkland, P.Q. H9J 2W2 – 514/695-2317 – Mme J.C. Weyergangs

La Baie (Bibliothèque municipale), 491, 2e rue, Ville de La Baie, (Port Alfred), P.Q. G7B 2C9 – 418/544-1151 – Mlle Anne Lebel

Lac Brome, (Pettes Memorial Library), C.P. 177, (rue Principale), Lac Brome, P.Q. J0E 1V0 – 514/243-6128 – Mlle Catherine Fraser

Lac Etchemin (Bibliothèque municipale), C.P. 370, Lac Etchemin, P.Q. G0R 1S0 – 418/625-4521 – Mme Roberte Maheux

Lachine (Bibliothèque municipale), 3100 rue Saint-Antoine, Lachine, P.Q. H8S 4B8 – 514/637-2568 – J.H. Beauchamp

Lachute (Bibliothèque municipale), 55 Harriet, Lachute, P.Q. J8H 4H6 – 514/562-4092 – Mme Madeleine Thérien

La Malbaie (Bibliothèque publique), (395 St-Etienne), C.P. 715, La Malbaie, P.Q. G0T 1J0 – 418/665-6027 – Mme R.B. Gagné

Lasalle (Bibliothèque municipale), 414 rue Lafleur, Lasalle, P.Q. H8R 3H6 – 514/366-2582 – Mme Anna Rovira

La Tuque (Bibliothèque municipale), C.P. 787, (575 rue St-Eugène), La Tuque, P.Q. G9X 3P6 – 819/523-3100 – Mlle Georgette Brassard

Laval (Bibliothèque municipale), 6200 boul. des Laurentides, Laval, P.Q. H7H 1N5 – 514/625-1924 – Mlle Angèle Pintal

Lévis (Bibliothèque municipale), 17 rue Notre-Dame, Lévis, P.Q. G6V 4A3 – 418/833-4444 – Mlle Michele Lamoureux

Longueuil (Bibliothèque municipale), 100 rue St-Laurent ouest, C.P. 5000, Longueuil, P.Q. J4K 4Y7 – 514/670-1410 – Yves Ouimet

Loretteville (Bibliothèque municipale), 307 rue Racine, Loretteville, P.Q. G2B 1E7 – 418/842-1921, poste 27 – Marc Doré

Lorraine (Bibliothèque municipale), 10 ch. de la Meuse, Lorraine, P.Q. J6Z 2T2 – 514/621-2421 – Mme Jeannine Gauthier

Magog (Bibliothèque municipale), C.P. 42, Magog, P.Q. J1X 3W7 – 819/843-1330 – Mme H. Milne

Malartic (Bibliothèque municipale), C.P. 4170, (870 rue Royale), Malartic, P.Q. J0Y 1Z0 – 819/757-4449 – Mme Lucille Mikolajczak

Marieville (Bibliothèque municipale), C.P. 908, (1801 rue du Pont), Marieville, P.Q. J0L 1J0 – 514/460-4988 – François Huet

Matane (Bibliothèque municipale), 230 ave Saint-Jérôme, Matane, P.Q. G4W 3A2 – 418/562-2333 – Nicol Gauthier

Mauricie (Bibliothèque régionale), 3125 rue Girard, Trois-Rivières, P.Q. G9A 5K8 – 819/375-9623 – Pierre L'Hérault

Mirabel (Bibliothèque municipale), 13908 rte 117, C.P. 239, St-Janvier, Mirabel, P.Q. J0N 1L0 – 514/430-4563 – Lucie Laperrière

Mont-Laurier (Bibliothèque municipale), C.P. 1227, (469 rue Madone), Mont-Laurier, P.Q. J9L 1S4 – 819/623-1833 – Marcel Bouchard

Montreal (Bibliothèque municipale), 5500 rue Fullum, Montreal, P.Q. H2G 2H3 – 514/872-2900 – Jacques Panneton

Montreal Region Sud (Bibliothèque), 275 Conrad Pelletier, Montreal, P.Q. J5R 4V1 – 514/659-9119 – Gaston Blais

Montreal-Est (Bibliothèque municipale), 11,111 rue Notre Dame est, Montreal-Est, P.Q. H1B 2V7 – 514/645-7431, loc. 272 – Jean Ko

Montreal-Nord (Bibliothèque municipale), 4740 rue Charleroi, Montreal-Nord, P.Q. H1G 2S9 – 514/325-4655 – Mme Raymonde Turbide

Mont-Royal (Bibliothèque J.P. Dawson), 1967 boul. Graham, Mont-Royal, P.Q. H3R 1G9 – 514/342-1892 – Mme Sharon Huffman

Outaouais (Bibliothèque régionale), C.P. 3000, 221 Chemin Freeman, Hull, P.Q. J8Z 1V7 – 819/771-7345 – J.-P. Germain

Outremont (Bibliothèque municipale), 544 rue Davaar, Outremont, P.Q. H2V 3A8 – 514/274-9451 – Guy Laverdière

Pierrefonds (Bibliothèque de la Montée St-Jean), 4913 boul. St-Jean, Pierrefonds, P.Q. H9H 2A9 – 514/626-7633

Pincourt (Bibliothèque municipale), 62 Mgr. Langlois, Pincourt, P.Q. J7V 5C1 – Mlle Micheline Perreault

Plessisville (Bibliothèque), 1699 rue St-Calixte, Plessisville, P.Q. G6L 1R2 – 819/362-6628 – Mlle Francine Therrien

Pointe-aux-Trembles (Bibliothèque municipale), 11953 rue Notre-Dame est, Pointe-aux-Trembles, P.Q. H1B 2Y6 – 514/645-5381 – Roland Gagné

Pointe-Claire (Bibliothèque municipale), 100 Douglas Shand, Pointe-Claire, P.Q. H9R 4V1 – 514/695-0222 – Mlle Claire Côté

Port-Cartier-Est (Bibliothèque municipale), 40, ave Parent, Port-Cartier-Est, P.Q. G5B 2G5 – 418/766-2346, loc. 39 – Jean-Didier Larrue

Quebec (Bibliothèque régionale), 3022 Chemin Ste-Foy, Ste-Foy, P.Q. G1X 1P6 – 418/658-4423 – Réal Messier

Quebec (Bibliothèque municipale), 37 rue Ste-Angèle, Quebec, P.Q. G1R 4G5 – 418/694-6357 – Philippe Sauvageau

Répentigny (Bibliothèque municipale), 437 rue Notre-Dame, Répentigny, P.Q. J6A 2T3 – 514/581-3320

Rimouski (Bibliothèque municipale), C.P. 710, Rimouski, P.Q. G5L 7C7 – 418/724-3164 – Mme Madeleine Villeneuve

Rivière-du-Loup (Bibliothèque publique), 435 rue Lafontaine, Rivière-du-Loup, P.Q. G5R 3B9 – 418/862-4252 – Denis Boisvert

Roberval (Bibliothèque municipale), 243 Menard, Roberval, P.Q. G8H 1P4 – 418/275-2333 – Mme Francine Lachance

Rosemère (Bibliothèque municipale), 239 Grande-Côte, Rosemère, P.Q. J7A 1K2 – 514/621-6132 – Mlle Thérèse Bélisle

Rouyn-Noranda (Bibliothèque municipale), 201 Dallaire, Rouyn, P.Q. J9X 4T5 – 819/762-0944 – Jean-Paul Lessard

Roxboro (Bibliothèque municipale), 110 rue Cartier, Roxboro, P.Q. H8Y 1G8 – 514/684-8247 – Mlle Zipporah Shnay

Saguenay-Lac St-Jean (Bibliothèque régionale), 100 rue Price ouest, Alma, P.Q. G8B 4S1 – 418/662-6425 – J.-M. Bourgeois

St-Basile-le-Grand (Bibliothèque municipale), 22 rue Savaria, St-Basile-le-Grand, P.Q. J0L 1S0 – 514/653-0287 – Mme Denise Gingras

St-Bruno-de-Montarville (Bibliothèque municipale), 1605 rue Montarville, C.P. 567, St-Bruno-de-Montarville, P.Q. J3V 3T8 – 514/653-2474 – Mlle Luce Bernardin

St-Eustache (Bibliothèque municipale), 80 boul. Arthur-Sauvé, St-Eustache, P.Q. J7R 2H7 – 514/472-0601 – Mme Monique Khouzam

St-Félicien (Bibliothèque municipale), 1058 boul. Sacré-Coeur, St-Félicien, P.Q. G0W 2N0 – 418/679-0251 – Mlle Francine Ménard

St-Hubert (Bibliothèque municipale), 5900 boul. Cousineau, St-Hubert, P.Q. J3Y 7K8 – 514/676-7744 – Mme Kim Mychau Neuyen

St-Hyacinthe (Bibliothèque publique), 1775 rue Duvernay, St-Hyacinthe, P.Q. J2S 1Z2 – 514/773-1830 – Mme Pauline Archambault

St-Jacques-de-Montcalm (Bibliothèque municipale), C.P. 370, (16 rue Maréchal), St-Jacques-de-Montcalm, P.Q. J0K 2R0 – 514/839-3926 – Mme M.F. Lafortune

St-Jean (Bibliothèque municipale), C.P. 1025, (203 rue Jacques-Cartier), St-Jean, P.Q. J3B 6T3 – 514/347-1305 – Serge Bessette

St-Jérôme (Bibliothèque municipale), 374 rue Laviolette, St-Jérôme, P.Q. J7Y 2S9 – 514/436-1772 – Mlle Jacqueline Desjardins

St-Lambert (Bibliothèque municipale), 490 ave Mercille, St-Lambert, P.Q. J4P 2L5 – 514/465-4508 – Mme Madeleine Fink

St-Laurent (Bibliothèque municipale), 1380 rue de l'Eglise, St-Laurent, P.Q. H4L 2H2 – 514/744-6411 – Mme Marie-Louise Simon

St-Léonard (Bibliothèque municipale), 8420 boul. Lacordaire, St-Léonard, P.Q. H1R 3G5 – 514/321-7635 – Mme Huguette Deschênes

St-Pierre (Bibliothèque publique), 69 5ième Ave., St-Pierre, P.Q. H8R 1P1 – 514/364-5153

St-Raphael-de-l'Ile-Bizard (Bibliothèque municipale), 510 rue de l'Eglise, St-Raphael-de-l'Ile-Bizard, P.Q. H9C 1G9 – 514/626-2047 – Mlle Helene Rouette

St-Romuald (Bibliothèque municipale), 1263 rue Commerciale, St-Romuald, P.Q. G6W 5M5 – 418/839-6422 – Mme Jacqueline Chartier-Lapointe
Ste-Foy (Biliothèque municipale), 999 Place de Ville, Ste-Foy, P.Q. G1V 4E1 – 418/657-4252 – Gilbert Blondeau
Ste-Geneviève-de-Pierrefonds (Bibliothèque municipale), 13 rue Chauret, Ste-Geneviève-de-Pierrefonds, P.Q. H9H 2X2 – 514/626-8922 – Pierre Forgues
Ste-Julie (Bibliothèque municipale), 477 Jules-Choquet, Ste-Julie, P.Q. J0L 2C0 – 514/649-4730 – Mlle Nicole Perras
Ste-Thérèse (Bibliothèque municipale), C.P. 100, (150 boul. Ducharme), Ste-Thérèse, P.Q. J7E 4H7 – 514/430-6860 – Léonard Nadeau
Salaberry-de-Valleyfield (Bibliothèque municipale), 75 rue St-Jean-Baptiste, Salaberry-de-Valleyfield, P.Q. J6T 1Z6 – 514/371-4353 – Mme Monique Chagnon
Sept-Iles (Bibliothèque municipale), 500 ave Joliette, Sept-Iles, P.Q. G4R 2B4 – 418/964-3355 – Mme Jocelyne Boudreau
Shawinigan (Bibliothèque municipale), C.P. 550, Shawinigan, P.Q. G9N 6V6 – 819/537-0021 – Fabien Larochelle
Sherbrooke (Bibliothèque municipale), 165 rue Bank, Sherbrooke, P.Q. J1H 1G8 – 819/565-5860 – Allen Dufour
Sorel (Bibliothèque municipale), 145 rue Georges, Sorel, P.Q. J3P 1C7 – 514/743-4013 – Mlle Danielle Blanchard-Girouard
Terrebonne (Bibliothèque municipale), C.P. 540, (754 rue St-Pierre), Terrebonne, P.Q. J6W 1E4 – 514/471-4042 – Mlle Ginette Lapointe
Trois-Pistoles (Bibliothèque municipale), Hôtel de Ville, Trois-Pistoles, P.Q. G0L 4K0 – 418/851-2374 – Mme Nicole Sirois
Trois-Rivières (Bibliothèque municipale), C.P. 1713, Place de l'Hôtel de Ville, Trois-Rivières, P.Q. G9A 5L9 – 819/374-3521 – Armand Allard
Val-d'Or (Bibliothèque municipale), C.P. 400, (600 7e rue), Val-d'Or, P.Q. J9P 3P3 – 819/824-2666 – Mlle Yvette Morissette
Verdun (Bibliothèque municipale), 5955 ave Bannantyne, Verdun, P.Q. H4H 1H6 – 514/768-1149 – André Fortier
Victoriaville (Bibliothèque municipale), 19 rue des Forges, Victoriaville, P.Q. G6P 6T2 – 819/758-8441 – Mme Johanne Perreault
Warwick (Bibliothèque municipale), C.P. 577, (104 rue St-Louis), Warwick, P.Q. J0A 1M0 – 819/358-6187 – Mlle Gaby Bernard
Westmount (Bibliothèque municipale), 4574 rue Sherbrooke ouest, Westmount, P.Q. H3Z 1G1 – 514/935-8531 – Mme Norah Bryant

Special & College Libraries & Resource Centres in Quebec

With Contact Person (Librarian, unless otherwise indicated)

ALMA

Collège d'Alma (Bibliothèque), 675 ouest. boul. Auger, Alma, P.Q. G8B 2B7 – 418/668-2381

ARTHABASKA

Hotel-Dieu d'Arthabaska (Bibliothèque), 5 rue Quesnel, Arthabaska, P.Q. G6P 6N2 – 819/357-2031, loc 216 – Mlle Micheline Leclair

ARVIDA

Alcan International Ltd., Technical Information Centre, Box 250, Arvida, P.Q. G7S 4K8 – 418/548-1121, ext. 2844 – Miss Paquerette Leclerc

BEACONSFIELD

L'Atelier a votre santé, (bibliothèque), 101 Amherst Rd., Beaconsfield, P.Q. H9W 5Y7 – 514/694-2777 – Jane Edwards

CAP-ROUGE

Campus Notre-Dame-de-Foy (Bibliothèque), 5000, St-Félix, Cap-Rouge, P.Q. G0A 1K0 – 418/872-8041 – Albert Pruneau

CHARLESBOURG

Jardin zoologique de Québec (Bibliothèque), 8191 ave du Zoo, Charlesbourg, P.Q. G1C 4G4 – 418/643-2310 – Jeannine Gagné

CHICOUTIMI

Hôpital de Chicoutimi Inc., (Bibliothèque), 305, rue St-Vallier, C.P. 5006, Chicoutimi, P.Q. G7H 5H6 – 418/509-2195, ext. 302 – Angèle Tremblay
Seminaire de Chicoutimi (Bibliothèque), 679 Chabanel, Chicoutimi, P.Q. G7H 1Z7 – 418/549-1786 – Clément-J. Simard
Société historique du Saguenay (bibliothèque), C.P. 456, Chicoutimi, P.Q. G7H 5C8 – 418/549-2805 – Roland Bélanger, archiviste
Université du Québec (Bibliothèque), 930 est rue Jacques Cartier, Chicoutimi, P.Q. G7H 2B1 – 418/545-5642

DOLLARD DES ORMEAUX

Provincial Association of Protestant Teachers of Quebec, Resource Centre, 84 J Brunswick Blvd., Dollard des Ormeaux, P.Q. H9B 2C5 – 514/683-9330 – Evelyn Athanasiou, Clerk

DORVAL

See Montreal

DRUMMONDVILLE

CEGEP Bourgchemin, Campus Drummondville (Bibliothèque), 415 rue des Ecoles, Drummondville, P.Q. J2B 1J3 – 819/478-4671

GASPE

CEGEP de la Gaspésie (Bibliothèque), C.P. 590, Gaspé, P.Q. G0C 1R0 – 418/368-2201
L'Hôtel-Dieu de Gaspé, bibliothèque médicale, C.P. 120, Havre de Gaspé, Gaspé, P.Q. G0C 1R0 – 418/368-3301, loc. 626 – Mathilda Adams, responsable

GRANBY

College de Granby, (Bibliothèque), 50 St-Joseph, Granby, P.Q. J2G 6T6 – 514/372-6614

HAUTERIVE

CEGEP de Hauterive (Bibliothèque), 537 boul. Blanche, Hauterive, P.Q. G5C 2B2 – 418/589-5707

HULL

Bibliothèque centrale de prêt de l'Outaouais et des Laurentides, inc., C.P. 3000, (221 Chemin Freeman), Hull, P.Q. J8Z 1V7 – 819/771-7345 – J.-P. Germain
Canada Employment & Immigration Commmn., See Ottawa
Canadian International Development Agency, Development Information Centre, Place du Centre, 200 Promenade du Portage, Hull, P.Q. – 819/997-6212
Canadian Radio-Television Commn., See Ottawa
Canadian Transport Commn., (15 Eddy St.), See Ottawa
CEGEP de l'Outaouais (Bibliothèque), 333 boul. Cité des Jeunes, Hull, P.Q. J8Y 6M5 – 819/770-4012 – J. Walther
Centre Hospitalier Pierre Janet (Bibliothèque), 20 Pharand, Hull, P.Q. J9A 1K7 – 819/771-7761 – Nguyen Lam
Centre Hospitalier Régional de l'Outaouais, Bibliothèque, 116 blvd. Lionel-Emond, Hull, P.Q. J8Y 1W7 – 819/776-1581, poste 349 – André-P. Racine
Dept. of Consumer & Corporate Affairs, See Ottawa
Dept. of Environment, See Ottawa
Dept. of Indian Affairs, See Ottawa
Dept. of Labour, See Ottawa
Dept. of Regional Economic Expansion, See Ottawa
Dept. of Secretary of State Library, (15 Eddy St., Hull) Ottawa, Ont. K1A 0M5 – 819/997-5391 – Claire Renaud-Frigon
E.B. Eddy Forest Products Ltd. Library, Hull, P.Q. J8X 3Y7 – 819/595-6025 – Olive Stalker
Hôpital du Sacré Coeur (Bibliothèque), 230 boul. Gamelin, Hull, P.Q. J8Y 1W7 – André-Paul Racine
Université du Québec à Hull, (bibliothèque), C.P. 1250, Succ. B, Hull, P.Q. J8X 3X7 – 819/776-8381 – André Chénier

JOLIETTE

CEGEP de Joliette (Bibliothèque), 20 sud rue St-Charles, Joliette, P.Q. J6E 4T1 – 514/759-1661
Centre Hospitalier Regional de Lanaudière, (Bibliothèque), 1000 boul. Ste-Anne, Joliette, P.Q. J6E 6J2 – 514/759-8222 – Francine Garneau

JONQUIERE

College de Jonquière (Bibliothèque), 65 rue St-Hubert, Jonquière, P.Q. G7X 7W2 – 418/547-2191 – J.-P. Dufour

KIRKLAND

Merck Frosst Laboratories, Research Library, Box 1005, Kirkland, P.Q. H9R 4P8 – 514/695-7920, ext. 463 – Mrs. Claire B. Kelly

LACHINE

Dominion Engineering Works Ltd. Library, 795 1st Ave., Lachine, P.Q. H8S 2S8 – 514/634-3411 – Celine Bourdages

Rolls-Royce Canada Ltd. Library, Box 1000, Montreal AMF, 9500 Côte de Liesse Rd., Montreal, P.Q. H4Y 1B7 – 514/631-3541 – J.W. Beverage

LA POCATIERE

Agriculture Canada, Library, C.P. 400, La Pocatière, P.Q. G0R 1Z0 – 418/856-3141 – J. Deschênes

CEGEP de La Pocatière (Bibliothèque), 140 40 Ave., La Pocatière, P.Q. G0R 1Z0 – 418/856-1525

Institut de technologie agricole, centre de documentation, (Quebec Dept. of Agriculture), La Pocatière, P.Q. G0R 1Z0 – 418/856-1110, poste 233 – R.-D. Langlois

LaSALLE (see also Montreal)

CEGEP André Laurendeau (Bibliothèque), 1111 Lapierre, LaSalle, P.Q. H8N 2J4 – 514/364-3320

Monsanto Canada Ltd. Library, 425 St. Patrick St., LaSalle, P.Q. H8N 2H3 – 514/366-4850, ext. 247 – Mrs. E. Hayward

LAUZON

CEGEP de Lévis-Lauzon, (Bibliothèque), 205 Mgr Ignace Bourget, Lauzon, P.Q. G6V 6Z9 – 418/833-5110 – Germain Bouffard

LAVAL

Collège Montmorency, (Bibliothèque), 475 boul. de l'Avenir, Laval, P.Q. H7N 5H9 – 514/667-5100 – Rolland Danis (résp.)

Commission Scolaire des Mille-Iles, (Bibliothèque), 213 boul. Ste-Rose, (Ste-Rose), Laval, P.Q. H7L 1L7 – 514/625-6951 – F. Lynette

LENNOXVILLE

Bishop's University, John Basset Memorial Library, Lennoxville, P.Q. J1M 1Z7 – 819/569-9551 – Germain Belisle

LEVIS

College de Levis (Bibliothèque), 9 rue Mgr. Gosselin, Lévis, P.Q. G6V 5K1 – 418/837-7544 – Roger Audet

Confédération des Caisses Populaires et d'Economie Desjardins du Québec, Centre de Documentation, 100 ave des Commandeurs, Lévis, P.Q. G6V 7N5 – 418/835-2468

Desjardins Mutual Life Assurance Co. Library, 200 Ave. des Commandeurs, Lévis, P.Q. G6V 6R2 – 418/835-2000 – Jean Carrier

Hotel-Dieu de Levis (Bibliothèque), 143 rue Wolfe, Lévis, P.Q. G6V 3Y9 – 418/833-7121, ext. 1.274 – Colette Audant

LONGUEUIL

College Edouard-Montpetit (Bibliothèque), 945 Chemin Chambly, Longueuil, P.Q. J4H 3M6 – 514/679-2630, loc. 155 – Gisèle Laramée-Pépin

Health & Welfare Canada, Bibliothèque régionale, Direction générale de la protection de la santé, 1001 ouest, blvd. Saint-Laurent, Salle 321, Longueuil, P.Q. J4K 1C7 – 514/283-5472 – E.A. Ferenczy

Institut Nazareth et Louis Braille, See Public Libraries in Quebec

Materials Research Institute Library, National Research Council, 1000 De Serigny, #620, Longueuil, P.Q. J4K 5B1 – 514/677-3606 – Miss L. Venne

Pratt & Whitney Aircraft of Canada Ltd. Library, Box 10, 1000 Marie-Victorin, Longueuil, P.Q. J4K 4X9 – 514/677-9411 – Joyce Charlebois

MATANE

CEGEP de Matane (Bibliothèque), 616 St-Rédempteur, Matane, P.Q. G4W 3P7 – 418/562-1240 – Colette Côté

MONTREAL

Abbott Laboratories Ltd. Library, Box 6150, Montreal, P.Q. H3C 3K6 – 514/341-6880 – Mrs. Micheline Allard

Advocates Library, See Barreau du Quebec

Air Canada Library, 1 Place Ville Marie, 38th Floor, Montreal, P.Q. H3B 3P7 – 514/874-4841 – Iris L. Land

Alcan Aluminium Ltd. Library, Box 6090, 1 Place Ville Marie, Montreal, P.Q. H3C 3H2 – 514/877-2610 – Mrs. Ellen A. Johnston

Allan Memorial Institute of Psychiatry Library, 1025 Pine Ave. W., Montreal, P.Q. H3A 1A1 – 514/842-1251, ext. 269 – Felicitas Kirchenberger

Association des Courtiers d'Assurances, see Insurance Brokers Association

Association de l'immeuble du Québec (Bibliothèque), 1080 Beaver Hall Hill, #1100, Montreal, P.Q. H2Z 1T8 – 514/866-7641

Association Paritaire de Prévention pour la Santé et la Sécurité du Travail du Québec, Centre de documentation, 50 Place Cremazie, #812, Montreal, P.Q. H2P 2T5 – 514/389-8295 – Lise Locas, documentaliste/recherchiste

Atomic Energy of Canada Ltd. Library, 2001 University St., 9th Floor, Montreal, P.Q. H3A 2N2 – 514/282-9680, loc. 202 – Susan Nish

Atwater Library of Mechanics' Institute of Montreal, 1200 Atwater Ave., Montreal, P.Q. H3Z 1X4 – 514/935-7344 – Mrs. Heather Connolly

Aviation Electric Ltd., Engineering Library, Box 2140, St-Laurent, Montreal, P.Q. H4L 4X8 – 514/744-2811, ext. 424 – Carole Hernandez

Bank of Montreal, Head Office Library, Box 6002, Stn. A, Montreal, P.Q. H3C 3B1 – 514/877-6890 – Nancy C. Leclerc

Banque Nationale du Canada, (Bibliothèque), 221, rue St-Jacques, Montreal, P.Q. H2Y 1M7 – 514/281-3220 – Nicole Lavigne

Barreau de Montréal, (Bibliothèque), Palais de Justice, Montreal, P.Q. H2Y 1B6 – 514/873-3083 – Arthur Perrault

Bell Canada Information Resource Centre, 1050 Beaver Hall Hill, Main Floor, Montreal, P.Q. H3C 3G4 – 514/870-3364 – B. Eskelson

Bibliothèque de la Ville de Montreal, See City of Montreal

Bibliothèque nationale du Québec, 1700, rue St-Denis, Montreal, P.Q. H2X 3K6 – 514/873-4553 – Jean-Remi Brault

Board of Trade, See Montreal Board etc.

Building Products of Canada Ltd. Library, 10500 Côte de Liesse Rd., #200, Montreal, P.Q. H8T 3E3 – 514/636-6810 – Mrs. C. Rose

Bureau de Surveillance du Cinema, Centre de Documentation, 360 rue McGill, Montreal, P.Q. H2Y 2E9 – 514/873-2371 – Pierre Saucier

Cae Electronics Ltd. Reference Library, Box 1800, St-Laurent Stn., Montreal, P.Q. H4L 4X4 – 514/341-6780, ext. 644 – Mrs. S. Holloway

Caisse de Depot et Placement du Québec (Bibliothèque), C.P. 74, La Tour de la Bourse, Montreal, P.Q. H4Z 1B4 – 514/873-2460 – Pauline Lefebvre

Canada Cement Lafarge Ltd. Library, 606 Cathcart, Montreal, P.Q. H3B 1L7 – 514/861-1411

Canada Dept. of Employment & Immigration, Regional Library, 550 Sherbrooke St. W., 4th Floor, Montreal, P.Q. H3A 1B9 – 514/283-4695 – Claudine Lussier

Canada Dept. of Justice, Montreal Region Library, 500 Place d'-Armes, Montreal, P.Q. H2Y 2W2 – 514/283-4975

Canada Dept. of Regional Economic Expansion, Documentation Centre, 800 Square Victoria, C.P. 247, Montreal, P.Q. H4Z 1E8 – 514/283-7266 – Rita Désilets, Clerk

Canadair Ltd. Library, Box 6087, Montreal, P.Q. H3C 3G9 – 514/744-1511, ext. 263 – Mrs. M. Levesque

CBC, Engineering Library, 7925 Côte St-Luc Rd., Montreal, P.Q. H4W 1R5 – 514/488-2551 – Mrs. E. Mercer

CBC, Reference Library, Box 6000, Montreal, P.Q. H3C 3A8 – 514/285-3854 – Michelle Bachand

Canadian Chamber of Commerce, Library, 1080 Beaver Hall Hill, Montreal, P.Q. H2Z 1T2 – 514/866-4334

Canadian Heritage of Quebec, Library, 563 Côte St-Antoine, Montreal, P.Q. H3Y 2K5 – 514/481-5796 – Miss Alice M.S. Lighthall

Canadian Institute of Hypnotism Library, 3465 Côte des Neiges, #91, Montreal, P.Q. H3H 1T7 – 514/937-4488 – Mrs. Jeanne Rigaud
Canadian Jewish Congress Library, 1590 Ave. Dr. Penfield, Montreal, P.Q. H3G 1C5 – 514/931-7531
Canadian Liquid Air Ltd. Library, 1155 Sherbrooke St. W., Montreal, P.Q. H3A 1H8 – 514/842-5431 – Mrs. D. Hammond
Canadian Marconi Co. Library, 2442 Trenton, Montreal, P.Q. H3P 1Y9 – 514/341-7630, ext. 577 – Mrs. M. Benjamin
Canadian Music Centre Library, 1259 rue Berri, bur. 300, Montreal, P.Q. H2L 4C7 – 514/849-9175
Canadian National Railway, Dechief Library, 935 Lagauchetière St. W., Montreal, P.Q. H3C 3N4 – 514/877-4407 – Mrs. K.M. Elliott
Photographic – Miss Susan R. Gallagher
Public Affairs – Mrs. D. Webb
Canadian Olympic Association, Information Centre, Olympic House, Cité du Havre, Montreal, P.Q. H3C 3R4 – 514/861-3371 – Pierre Labelle
Canadian Pacific Ltd. Library, Box 6042, Stn. A, Windsor Stn., Montreal, P.Q. H3C 3E4 – 514/395-6762 – Ms. D. Wolfenden
Canadian Psychoanalytic Society Library, 7000 Côte des Neiges Rd., Montreal, P.Q. H3S 2C1 – 514/738-6105 – Mrs. N. Gargour, Exec. Sec.
Canadian Pulp & Paper Association Library, 2300 Sun Life Bldg., Montreal, P.Q. H3B 2X9 – 514/866-6621
Canadian Telephone Employees Association Library, #1270, Place du Canada, Montreal, P.Q. H3B 2N2 – 514/861-9963 – Miss E.A. Fenton
Canadian Tobacco Manufacturers Council Library, 1808 Sherbrooke St. W., Montreal, P.Q. H3H 1E5 – 514/937-7428 – Myrna Cain
Canatom Inc. Library, C.P. 420, Tour de la Bourse, Montreal, P.Q. H4Z 1K3 – 514/879-4722 – Marie-Anna Myers
CEGEP, See College de ...
Celanese Canada Inc. Library, Box 6170, Stn. A, Montreal, P.Q. H3C 3K8 – 514/871-5789 – Miss L. Trevaskis
Centre d'Animation de Developpement et de Recherche en Education (CADRE), 1940 boul. Henri-Bourassa est, Montreal, P.Q. H2B 1S2 – 514/381-8891 – Jean-Luc Roy
Centre Canadien d'Oecumenisme, (Canadian Centre for Ecumenism), Bibliothèque, 2065 ouest, rue Sherbrooke, Montreal, P.Q. H3H 1G6 – 514/937-9176, poste 6 – Réginald Goulet, s.j.
Centre de diffusion de la Documentation Scientifique et technique française, See Informatech Franco-Québec
Centre Hospitalier Côte-des-Neiges, (Bibliothèque), 4565 Queen Mary Rd., Montreal, P.Q. H3W 1W5 – 514/344-3905 – Jocelyne Blain-Juneau
Centre Hospitalier Jacques-Viger, Bibliothèque Médicale, 1051, rue St-Hubert, Montreal, P.Q. H2L 3Y5 – Jocelyne Blain-Juneau
Centre interculturel Monchanin (Bibliothèque), 4917 St. Urbain St., Montreal, P.Q. H2T 2W1 – 514/288-7229 – Réal Bathalon
Centre de Recherches en Relations Humaines (Bibliothèque), 2715 chemin côte Ste-Catherine, Montreal, P.Q. H3T 1B6 – 514/738-8076 – Jacqueline Leduc
Chait, Salomon, Gelber & Partners Library, 1 Place Ville Marie, #1901, Montreal, P.Q. H3B 2C3 – 514/879-1353 – Mrs. Shaké Hagopian
Charette, Fortier, Hawey et Cie, Touche, Ross et Cie, (Bibliothèque), 1 Place Ville Marie, Montreal, P.Q. H3B 2A2 – 514/861-8531, loc. 367 – Mrs. N. Bouchard
Chateau Ramezay Museum Library, 280 est, rue Notre Dame, Montreal, P.Q. H2Y 1C5 – 514/861-7182 – Jacques Poulin
Ciba-Geigy Canada Ltd. Library, 205 Bouchard Blvd., Dorval, P.Q. H9S 1B1 – 514/631-4841 – Dr. E. Pungartnik
La Cinémathèque québecoise (bibliothèque), 335 de Maisonneuve est, Montreal, P.Q. H2X 1K1 – 514/845-8118
City of Montreal Archives, #16, 275 Notre Dame St. E., Montreal, P.Q. H2Y 1C6 – 514/872-2678 – Henri Gerin-Lajoie
City of Montreal Planning Library, 85 Notre Dame St. E., Montreal, P.Q. H2Y 1B5
Clarkson, Gordon Co. Library, 630 Dorchester Blvd. W., #2000, Montreal, P.Q. H3B 1T9 – 514/875-6060 – Linda Cunnington
College Ahuntsic (Bibliothèque), 9155 rue St-Hubert, Montreal, P.Q. H2M 1Y8 – 514/389-5921 – Philippe Arlen
College André-Grasset (Bibliothèque), 1001 Crémazie Blvd. E., Montreal, P.Q. H2M 1M3 – 514/381-0539 – Jean-Pierre Lussier
College Bois-de-Boulogne (Bibliothèque), 10,555 rue Bois-de-Boulogne, Montreal, P.Q. H4N 1L3 – 514/332-3000
College Jean-de-Brebeuf (Bibliothèque), 5625 rue Decelles, Montreal, P.Q. H3T 1W4 – 514/342-1320, loc. 261 – Mrs. Lise Lemire
College LaSalle (Documentation Centre), 2015 rue Drummond, Montreal, P.Q. H3G 1W7 – 514/842-3823 – Lise Harnois-Godard
College de Maisonneuve (Bibliothèque), 3800 est Sherbrooke, Montreal, P.Q. H1X 2A2 – 514/254-7131 – C. Gabriel Allard, c.s.c.
College Marguerite-Bourgeoys (Bibliothèque), 4873, ave Westmount, Montreal, P.Q. H3Y 1X9 – 514/487-2420, poste 27 – Mlle Francine Caisse
College Marie-Victorin (Bibliothèque), 7000, rue Marie-Victorin, Montreal, P.Q. H1G 2J6 – 514/321-0150 – Marcel Houle
College O'Sullivan (Bibliothèque), 1191 de la Montagne, Montreal, P.Q. H3G 1Z2 – 514/866-4622 – Krishna Pal
College de Rosemont (Bibliothèque), 6400 16ieme ave., Montreal, P.Q. H1X 2S9 – 514/376-1620, poste 259 – Gilles Cusson & Serge Ostiguy
College Stanislas (Bibliothèque), 780 boul. Dollard, Outremont, P.Q. H2V 3G5
College de Vieux-Montreal (Bibliothèque), 255 est rue Ontario, Montreal, P.Q. H2X 3M8 – 514/284-7315
Commission des Ecoles Catholiques de Montreal (Bibliothèque), 3737 est, rue Sherbrooke, Montreal, P.Q. H1X 3B3 – 514/525-6001
Commission des Services Juridiques, Bibliothèque et Centre de documentation, 2 Complexe Desjardins, #1404, Montreal, P.Q. H5B 1B3 – 514/873-3562 – Bernard Desrosiers – not open to public
Commission de Transport de la Communaute Urbaine de Montreal (Bibliothèque), 159 ouest St-Antoine, Montreal, P.Q. H2Z 1H3 – 514/877-6046 – Victor Itesco
Communauté urbaine de Montreal, Service de planification (bibliothèque), 2 Complexe Desjardins, Montreal, P.Q. H2B 1E6 – 514/872-6856 – Guy Gravel, Dir.
Concordia University, Main Library, 1455 de Maisonneuve Blvd. W., Montreal, P.Q. H3G 1M8 – 514/879-2820 – Telex: 05-25517 – Dr. P.E. Filion, Dir. of Libraries
Conservatoire d'art Dramatique (Bibliothèque), 100 rue Notre Dame est, Montreal, P.Q. H2Y 1C1 – 514/873-4283 – Mrs. Odette Le Sourd
Convention & Visitors' Bureau of Greater Montreal Ltd., Documentation Centre, Mart F, 49 Frontenac, Box 889, Place Bonaventure, Montreal, P.Q. H5A 1E6 – 514/871-1129
Corporation professionnelle des Médecins du Québec, Informathèque, 1440 St. Catherine St. W., #914, Montreal, P.Q. H3G 1S5 – 514/878-4441 – Mrs. Marthe Salvail
Currie, Coopers & Lybrand Information Centre, 630 Dorchester Blvd. W., Montreal, P.Q. H3B 1W5 – 514/866-3721, loc. 228 – Johan Mady
Dawson College Library, 1001 Sherbrooke St. E., Montreal, P.Q. H2L 1L3 – 514/525-2501, ext. 293
Desjardins, Ducharme & Co. Law Library, 635 W. Dorchester Blvd., #1200, Montreal, P.Q. H3B 1R9 – 514/878-9411 – Jacques Cartier
Le Devoir (Bibliothèque), 211 rue du St-Sacrement, Montreal, P.Q. H2Y 1X1 – 514/844-3361 – Gilles Pare
Domtar Inc. Library, Box 7210, 395 de Maisonneuve Blvd. W., Montreal, P.Q. H3C 3M1 – 514/282-5039 – Elyse Therrien
Douglas Hospital Centre, Staff Library, 6875 LaSalle Blvd., Montreal, P.Q. H4H 1R3 – 514/761-6131, loc. 394 – Mrs. Elaine Mancina
Ecole de Musique Vincent-d'Indy (Bibliothèque), 628 ch. de la Côte Ste-Catherine, Outremont, P.Q. H2V 2C5 – 514/731-8751 – Mme Jeannette Pinard

Ecole Polytechnique, Campus de l'Université de Montréal (Bibliothèque), C.P. 6079, Succ. A, Montreal, P.Q. H3C 3A7 – 514/344-4847 – Roger Bonin

Environmental Protection Service Library, 1550 de Maisonneuve ouest, #410, Montreal, P.Q. H3G 1N2 – 514/283-4670 – Jocelyne Sénécal

Evelyn Wood International Reading Dynamics Institute Library, #EW2, 450 Sherbrooke St. E., Montreal, P.Q. H2L 1J8 – 514/844-1941 – Deb McDougall

Facultes de la Compagnie de Jesus, Bibliothèque de Théologie, 5605, rue Decelles, Montreal, P.Q. H3T 1W4 – 514/737-1465 – Claude-Roger Nadeau, s.j., Dir.

Federal Business Development Bank Library, 360 St. James St. W., #320, Montreal, P.Q. H2Y 1P5 – 514/283-7632 – Julia E. McIntosh

Federation des Administrateurs des Services de Santé et des Services Sociaux du Québec (Bibliothèque), 4237 rue de Bordeaux, Montreal, P.Q. H2H 1Z4 – 514/526-0875

Fédération des médecins omnipraticiens du Québec, Centre de documentation, 1440 ouest rue Ste-Catherine, #1100, Montreal, P.Q. H3G 1R8 – 514/878-1911 – Ghislaine Lincourt, dir., lib. techns.

Fondation Lionel-Groulx Centre de recherche, #257, 261 ave Bloomfield, Montreal, P.Q. H2V 3R6 – 514/271-4759

The Fraser-Hickson Institute Free Library, 4855 Kensington, Montreal, P.Q. H3X 3S6 – 514/489-5301 – Miss Margery W. Trenholme, Chief Librn.

Gazette, See Montreal Gazette

Gestas Inc. Library, 410 St. Nicholas, Montreal, P.Q. H2Y 2P5 – 514/288-5611, loc. 48 – Monique Dumont

Grand Seminaire de Montreal (Bibliothèque), 2065 rue Sherbrooke ouest, Montreal, P.Q. H3H 1G6 – 514/932-9918 – Jacques Viger

Hôpital General Juif, Sir Mortimer B. Davis (Bibliothèque médicale), 3755 Côte St. Catherine Rd., Montreal, P.Q. H3T 1E2 – 514/342-3111, loc. 325 – Ms. A. Greenberg

Hôpital Hôtel-Dieu de Montreal, Bibliothèque médicale, 3840 rue St-Urbain, Montreal, P.Q. H2W 1T8 – 514/844-0161, ext. 592 – Mme G. Boyer-Caya

Hôpital Jean-Talon, Bibliothèque médicale, 1385 Jean-Talon est, Montreal, P.Q. H2E 1S6 – 514/273-5151, poste 420 – Pierrette Galarneau

Hôpital L.H. Lafontaine, Bibliothèque médicale, 7401 Hochelaga, Montreal, P.Q. H1N 3M5 – 514/253-8200, ext. 740 – Camil Lemire

Hôpital Maisonneuve, Bibliothèque médicale, 5415 de l'Assomption, Montreal, P.Q. H1T 2M4 – 514/254-8341, loc. 334 – Hélène Lauzon

Hôpital Notre Dame, Bibliothèque médicale, C.P. 1560, Succ. C, Montreal, P.Q. H2L 4K8 – 514/876-6862 – Mme M. L'Espérance

Hôpital Ste-Justine pour les Enfants, Centre d'information sur la Santé de l'Enfant, 3175 chemin Ste-Catherine, Montreal, P.Q. H3T 1C5 – 514/731-4931, ext. 339 – Pierrette Dubuc

Frank W. Horner Ltd. Research Library, (5485 Ferrier St.), Box 959, Stn. A, Montreal, P.Q. H3C 2W6 – 514/731-3931, ext. 216 – Miss R. Robinson

C.D. Howe Institute Library, #2064, 1155 Metcalfe St., Montreal, P.Q. H3B 2X7 – 514/879-1254 – Barry Norris

Hydro-Québec (Bibliothèque), 75 ouest boul. Dorchester, Montreal, P.Q. H2Z 1A4 – 514/289-2149 – C.A. Bonin

Imasco Foods Ltd. Library, 4945 Ontario est, Montreal, P.Q. H1V 1M2 – 514/255-2811 – Mme Louise Pichet

Imperial Tobacco Ltd. Corporate Library, Box 6500, Montreal, P.Q. H3C 3L6 – 514/932-6161 – Mrs. Y. Mukherjee
Research Librarian – Miss R. Ayoung

Industrial Grain Products Ltd., Research & Development Library, Box 6089, Montreal, P.Q. H3C 3H1 – 514/866-7961 – Ms. Muriel Henri

Informatech France-Québec, Place Bonaventure, 20 Edison, etage E, B.P. 160, Montreal, P.Q. H5A 1A7 – 514/875-8931

Institut Albert Prévost (Centre de Documentation), 6555 ouest boul. Gouin, Montreal, P.Q. H4K 1B3 – 514/333-4284 – Lise Daneau

Institut Canadien d'Education des Adultes, Centre de documentation, 506 est Ste-Catherine, #800, Montreal, P.Q. H2L 2C7 – 514/842-2766 – Micheline Séguin

Institut de Diagnostic et de Recherches Cliniques, Centre de documentation, 110 ave des Pins ouest, Montreal, P.Q. H2W 1R7 – 514/842-1481, ext. 275 – Mme L.D. Bielmann, Head Librn.

Institut d'histoire de l'Amerique française, Centre de recherche Lionel-Groulx, 257-261 ave Bloomfield, Montreal, P.Q. H2V 3R6 – 514/271-4759 – Juliette Rémillard, relationniste

Institut International de Lecture Dynamique, See Evelyn Wood

Institut National des Viandes (Bibliothèque), 10216 Lajeunesse, Montreal, P.Q. H3L 2E2 – 514/389-8241

Institut National Canadien pour les Aveugles, See Public Libraries in Quebec

Institute of Occupational & Environmental Health Library, #410, 1130 Sherbrooke St. W., Montreal, P.Q. H3A 2M8 – 514/844-4955 – P.V. Pelnar, M.D.

Institut Philippe Pinel de Montreal (Bibliothèque), 10905 est, boul. Henri-Bourassa, Montreal, P.Q. H1C 1H1 – 514/648-8461 – Normand Beaudet

Insurance Brokers Association of Quebec Library, 300 Leo Pariseau, #801, Montreal, P.Q. H2W 2N1 – 514/842-2591 – Charles Thibault, Dir. Gén.

Insurance Institute of Quebec Library, 261 St. James St. W., Montreal, P.Q. H2Y 1M6 – 514/845-2238 – Susan McKay

International Civil Aviation Organization Library, 1000 Sherbrooke St. W., Montreal, P.Q. H3A 2R2 – 514/285-8208 – Mrs. F. Ismail

Jewish General Hospital, See Hôpital General Juif

Jewish Public Library, 5151 Cote St. Catherine Rd., Montreal, P.Q. H3W 1M6 – 514/735-6535 – Niaomi Caruso

Johnson & Higgins Willis Faber Ltée, Employee Benefit Plan Library, C.P. 191, Tour de la Bourse, Montreal, P.Q. H4Z 1E2 – 514/878-1781 – Mary J. Norton

Johnson & Johnson Ltd. Research Library, 7101 Notre Dame St. E., Montreal, P.Q. H1N 2G4 – 514/252-5029 – Lilian Smyth

KHD Canada Library, 4660 Hickmore Ave., Montreal, P.Q. H3T 1K2 – 514/735-4411, ext. 207 – Sharon E. McKay

Kidney Foundation of Canada, Information Centre, 1650 de Maisonneuve Blvd. W., #400, Montreal, P.Q. H3H 2P3 – 514/934-4806

Lapointe, Rosenstein Law Library, 1117 St. Catherine St. W., #903, Montreal, P.Q. H3B 1H9 – 514/849-5311 – Denis Boudreault

Lavery, O'Brien Law Library, 3100, 2 Complexe Desjardins, C.P. 156, Montreal, P.Q. H5B 1G4 – 514/288-7811, poste 306 – Ginette Choquette

Lethbridge Rehabilitation Centre, Medical Library, 7005 de Maisonneuve Blvd. W., Montreal, P.Q. H4B 1T3 – 514/487-1770, ext. 220 – Jane Petrov

Loto Québec (Société des Loteries et Courses du Québec), Centre de documentation, 2000 Berri, Montreal, P.Q. H2L 4N5 – 514/873-5213

Lower Canada College Library, 4090 Royal Ave., Montreal, P.Q. H4A 2M5 – 514/482-9916 – Mrs. M.E. Drummond

Maimonides Hospital, Pollack Library, 5795 Caldwell Ave., Montreal, P.Q. H4W 1W3 – 514/483-2121 – Mrs. S.H. Bresinger

Maison Bellarmin (Bibliothèque), 25 ouest rue Jarry, Montreal, P.Q. H2P 1S6 – 514/387-2541 – E. Desrochers

Marianopolis College Library, 3880 Côte des Neiges Rd., Montreal, P.Q. H3H 1W1 – 514/931-8792 – Dr. R.R. Grodzicky

Marius Barbeau (Centre de documentation), 6560 Chambord, Montreal, P.Q. H2G 3B9 – 514/274-5655 – Isabelle Robidas

Materials Research Institute, See Longueuil

Marsh & McLennan Limited (Insurance Brokers), Research & Information Centre, 1801 McGill College Ave., #800, Montreal, P.Q. H3A 2N4 – 514/285-1104 – Mrs. E. Rennie, Contact

McGill University, Central Library, 3459 McTavish St., Montreal, P.Q. H3A 1Y1 – 514/392-4953 – Miss Marianne Scott, Director of Libraries (392-4949)

Area Librarians
Humanities-Social Sciences – Miss Alison Cole (392-4937)
Law – M. Renshawe (392-5060)
Life Sciences – Mrs. F. Groen (392-3059)
Physical Sciences-Engineering – R. Freese (392-5712)
Undergraduate – Dr. H. Moller (392-6779)

Blackader-Lauterman – Mrs. Eva Doelle (392-4960)
Blacker-Wood – Miss E. MacLean (392-4955)
Botany-Genetics – Miss W. Patrick (392-5829)
Dentistry – Miss Jean Fensom (392-4926)
Education – Mrs. J. Gagné (392-8812)
Engineering – Mrs. J. Wygnanski (392-5913)
Howard Ross (Management) – Mrs. M. Judah (392-5795)
Islamic Studies – Mrs. R. Dirlik (392-5197)
Law – M. Renshawe (392-5060)
Library Science – Mrs. S. Both (392-5931)
Macdonald Campus – Miss J. Finlayson (457-2000, loc. 297)
Map & Air Photo – Miss L. Dubreuil (392-5492)
Marine Sciences – R. Freese (392-5723)
Mathematics – R. Freese (392-8273)
McLennan – Miss A. Cole (392-4937)
Medical – Mrs. F. Groen (392-3059)
Meteorology – R. Freese (392-8237)
Marvin Duchow Music – Miss K. Toomey (392-4281)
Northern Studies – Ms. Carol Bekar (392-8233)
Nursing – M.A. Flower (392-5027)
Osler Library – P. Teigen (392-4329)
Physical Sciences – R. Freese (392-5712)
Religious Studies – Miss N. Johnston (392-4832)
Rutherford Physics – R. Freese (392-4785)
Social Work – Mrs. E. Raby (392-5054)
Undergraduate – Dr. H. Moller (392-6779)

Mechanics' Institute, See Atwater

William M. Mercer Ltd., Information Centre, 1801 McGill College Ave., Montreal, P.Q. H3A 2N4 – 514/285-1802, ext. 418 – Lonnie Brodkin-Schneider

Mental Hygiene Institute, See Peel Centre

Mercantile Bank of Canada Library, (625 Dorchester West, #1001), C.P. 520, Succ. A, Montreal, P.Q. H3C 2T6 – 514/871-2524

Ministère des Affairs Sociales (Bibliothèque), 6161 rue St-Denis, #416, Montreal, P.Q. H2S 2R5 – G. Darlington

Ministère de L'Education, Centrale des Bibliothèque, 1685 est rue Fleury, Montreal, P.Q. H2C 1T1 – 514/381-8891 – Gertrude S. de Carufel

Ministère de l'Immigration (Bibliothèque), 355 rue McGill, Montreal, P.Q. H2Y 2E8 – 514/873-3255 – Denis Robichaud

Ministère du Loisir, de la Chasse et de la Pêche, Bibliothèque de la Faune, 5075 rue Fullum, Montreal, P.Q. H2H 2K3 – 514/873-4693 – Richard Mathieu, Chief Librarian

Ministère du Travail (Bibliothèque), 255 est boul. Cremazie, Montreal, P.Q. H2M 1L5 – 514/873-3624 – Roch Mercier

Monsanto Canada Ltd. Library, 425 St. Patrick St., LaSalle, P.Q. H8N 2H3 – 514/366-4850 – Ethel Hayward

Montreal Association for Mentally Retarded, Documentation Centre, 8605 Berri St., 3rd Floor, Montreal, P.Q. H2P 2G5 – 514/381-2307 – Michelle Jacques

Montreal Board of Trade Library, 1080 Beaver Hall Hill, 6th Floor, Montreal, P.Q. H2Z 1S9 – 514/878-4651 – Mrs. Jeannette Lemay

Montreal Chest Hospital Centre, Medical Library, 3650 St. Urbain, Montreal, P.Q. H2X 2P4 – 514/849-5201, ext. 310 – Marianne Constantine

Montreal Children's Hospital, Medical Library, 2300 Tupper St., Montreal, P.Q. H3H 1P3 – 514/937-8511, ext. 374 – Mrs. D. Sirois

Montreal City, See City of Montreal

Montreal Engineering Co. Ltd. Library, Box 6088, Stn. A, Montreal, P.Q. H3C 3Z8 – 514/286-3519 – Ms. P. Kamichaitis

Montreal Gazette Library, Box 4300, Place d'Armes, Montreal, P.Q. H2Y 3S1 – 514/282-2771 – Agnes McFarlane

Montreal General Hospital, Medical Library, 1650 Cedar Ave., Montreal, P.Q. H3G 1A4 – 514/937-6011, loc. 775 – Ms. Kathryn Vaughn

Montreal Military & Maritime Museum, MacDonald Stewart Library, Box 1024, Stn. A, Montreal, P.Q. H3C 2W9 – 514/861-6738 – Mrs. Elizabeth F. Hale

Montreal Museum of Fine Arts, See Musée des beaux-arts

Montreal Neurological Institute Library, 3801 University St., Montreal, P.Q. H3A 2B4 – 514/284-4651 – Mrs. Marina Boski

Musée d'Art Contemporain (Bibliothèque), Cité du Havre, Montreal, P.Q. H3C 3R4 – 514/873-2878 – Isabelle Montplaisir

Musée des beaux-arts de Montreal (Bibliothèque), 3400 av. du Musée, Montreal, P.Q. H3G 1K3 – 514/285-1600 – Juanita M. Toupin

National Library of Quebec, See Bibliothèque Nationale

National Film Board of Canada (Library), (3155 Côte de Liesse Rd.), Box 6100, Stn. A, Montreal, P.Q. H3C 3H5 – 514/333-3141 – Rose-Aimee Todd

National Research Council, See Materials Research, Longueuil

National Theatre School Library, 5030 St-Denis, Montreal, P.Q. H2J 2L8 – 514/842-7954 – Beatrice DeVreeze

Nesbitt Thomson Securities Ltd. Library, 355 St. James St. W., Montreal, P.Q. H2Y 1P1 – 514/844-0131 – Miss L. Cahill

Office de la Langue Française (Bibliothèque), 800 Victoria Sq., Montreal, P.Q. H4Z 1G8 – 514/873-5291 – Denis Rousseau

Oratoire St-Joseph, Bibliothèque Sainte-Croix, 3800 Ch. Reine-Marie, Montreal, P.Q. H3V 1H6 – 514/733-8211, loc. 234 – Miss Mariette Reeves

Ordre des infirmieres et infirmiers du Québec, Centre de documentation, 4200 Dorchester W., Montreal, P.Q. H3Z 1V4 – 514/935-2501 – Denise Mailhot

Peel Centre, C.L.S.C. Metro, (Bibliothèque), 3647 Peel St., Montreal, P.Q. H3A 1X1 – 514/844-8435

Phillips, Halperin Law Library, #1400, Place du Canada, Montreal, P.Q. H3B 2P8 – 514/878-3371 – L. Pass

Phillips & Vineberg Law Library, 1 Place Ville Marie, #930, Montreal, P.Q. H3B 2A5 – 514/866-8541 – Stephanie Alyanakian

Polish Institute of Arts & Sciences Library, 3479 Peel St., Montreal, P.Q. H3A 1W7 – 514/392-5958 – Anna Poray-Wybranowska

Presbyterian College Library, 3495 University St., Montreal, P.Q. H3A 2A8 – 514/288-5256 – Rev. Daniel Shute

La Presse (Bibliothèque), 7 ouest rue St-Jacques, Montreal, P.Q. H2Y 1K9 – 514/285-7007 – Fernand Drouin

Price, Waterhouse & Co. Library, 1200 McGill College Ave., Montreal, P.Q. H3B 2G4 – 514/879-9050, ext. 388 – Mrs. Martha Nugent

Protestant School Board of Greater Montreal, Professional Library, 6000 Fielding Ave., Montreal, P.Q. H3X 1T4 – 514/482-6000, loc. 223

Quebec Real Estate Association, See L'association de l'immeubles

Queen Elizabeth Hospital, Medical Library, 2100 Marlowe Ave., Montreal, P.Q. H4A 3L6 – 514/488-2311, ext. 333 – Ms. S.L. Mullan

Radio-Québec, Centre des ressources documentaires, 655 rue Parthenais, Montreal, P.Q. H2K 3R7 – 514/873-5243 – Nicole Charest

Reader's Digest Magazines Ltd., Editorial Library, 215 Redfern, Montreal, P.Q. H3Z 2V9 – 514/934-0751 – Colette Nishizaki

Reddy Memorial Hospital, Medical Library, 4039 Tupper St., Montreal, P.Q. H3Z 1T5 – 514/933-7511, loc. 256 – Judith P. Gibbons

Rehabilitation Institute of Montreal Library, 6300 Darlington Ave., Montreal, P.Q. H3S 2J4 – 514/735-3741, ext. 212

Robinson, Cutler & Assoc. Law Library, 800 Place Victoria, #612, Montreal, P.Q. H4Z 1H6 – 514/878-2631, ext. 55 – Ms. Lesley-Ann Lawrence

Royal Bank of Canada Information Resources, 1 Place Ville Marie, Box 6001, Montreal, P.Q. H3C 3A9 – 514/874-6647 – Anthea Downing

Royal Victoria Hospital, Medical Library, 687 Pine Ave. W., Montreal, P.Q. H3A 1A1 – 514/842-1231, ext. 250 – Miss Sandra Duchow

St. Mary's Hospital, Medical Library, 3830 Lacombe Ave., Montreal, P.Q. H3T 1M5 – 514/344-3317 – Lucile Lavigueur

Shawinigan Consultants Inc. Library, 620 Dorchester Blvd. W., Montreal, P.Q. H3B 1N8 – 514/878-9311, loc. 229 – Dorothy Leonard

Shell Canada Ltd. Engineering Library, 10501 Sherbrooke St. E., Montreal-Est, P.Q. – 514/645-1661, ext. 404 – Mrs. Idelle Blakey

Sherwin-Williams Co. of Canada Ltd. Library, 2875 Centre St., Box 489, Montreal, P.Q. H3C 2T4 – 514/933-8611, ext. 206 – Shirley Brown

SIDBEC-DOSCO (Bibliothèque), C.P. 249, Succ. A, Montreal, P.Q. H3C 2S6 – 514/583-3361, loc. 605 et 614 – Mrs. Asta Sokov

Société d'Archéologie et de Numismatique (Bibliothèque), 280 Notre Dame est, Montreal, P.Q. H2Y 1C5 – 514/861-7182

La Société Dentaire de Montreal (Bibliothèque), 9428 De-Bretonvilliers, Montreal, P.Q. H2M 2B1 – 514/387-1125

Société d'Energie de la Baie James (Bibliothèque), 800 de Maisonneuve blvd. est, 14th Floor, Montreal, P.Q. H2L 2A7 – 514/844-3741, loc. 733 – Lisa Galante

Société National de Diffusion Educative & Culturelle Inc. (Bibliothèque), 4935 rue Jarry est, Montreal, P.Q. H1R 1Y2

Spiegel & Kravetz Law Library, 1155 Dorchester Blvd. W., #3406, Montreal, P.Q. H3B 3T3 – 514/875-2100 – Mtre. Cecile K. Solomon

Squibb Canada Inc. Library, 2365 Côte de Liesse Rd., Montreal, P.Q. H4N 2M7 – 514/331-7423

Sun Life Assurance Co. of Canada Library, Box 6075, Montreal, P.Q. H3C 3G5 – 514/866-6411, ext. 364 – Celia Donnelly

Surete du Québec, Centre de documentation, 1701 Parthenais, Montreal, P.Q. H2L 4K7 – 514/395-5687 – Jeannine Morin

Surveyor, Nenninger & Chenevert Inc. (Bibliothèque), Complexe Desjardins, Box 10, Montreal, P.Q. H5B 1C8 – 514/282-9551 – Madeleine C. Lambert

The Tourism-Leisure Documentation Library, Centre for Research in Tourism Development, Box 599, Stn. A, Montreal, P.Q. H3C 2T6

Trafalgar School for Girls Library, 3495 Simpson St., Montreal, P.Q. H3G 2J7 – 514/935-2644 – Mrs. Jeanne Burck

Transportation Development Centre, Library, 1000 Sherbrooke St. W., Box 549, Montreal, P.Q. H3A 2R3 – 514/283-4008 – Judith V. Nogrady

L'Union des Municipalités du Québec, 922 est, rue de Liège, Montreal, P.Q. H2P 1L1 – 514/387-2576

Université de Montréal, Service des bibliothèques, C.P. 6128, Montreal, P.Q. H3C 3J7 – 514/343-7643
- Directeur – Arlette Joffe-Nicodème
- Directeur adjoint – Claire Audet
- Adjoint administratif – Maurice Brisson
- Co-ordonnateur des collections – Hedwidge Barbeau-Côté
- Co-ordonnateur-Services aux usagers – Clément Tremblay
- Co-ordonnateur-Services informatises – Gilles Chaput
- Co-ordonnateur à la gestion – Michel Goulet
- Services techniques – Ginette Darbon
- Acquisitions – Suzanne Simoneau
- Catalogue – Marc Joanis et Christiane Robert-Guertin
- Periodiques – Monique Lecavalier
- Pret entre bibliothèques – Ginette Gagnier
- Droit – Paquerette Ranger
- Theologie philosophie – Françoise Beaudet
- E.P.C. – Marielle Durand
- Education Physique – Lise Mayrand
- Musique – Claude Soulard
- Psycho-Education – Yolande Beaudoin
- Santé – Thérèse Peternell
- Para-Médicale – Johanne Hopper
- Optometrie – Denise Lacroix
- Sciences humaines et sociales – Richard Greene
- Bibliothèconomie – Pierre Sultana
- Géographie – Francine Caplette
- Bibliothèques scientifiques – Gilles Picard
- Aménagement – Jacqueline Pelletier
- Biologie et diététique – Vesna Blazina
- Botanique – tba
- Chimie – Corinne Haumont
- Géologie – Clément Arwas
- M.I.P. (mathématiques, informatique, physique) – Jules Giroux
- Médecine vétérinaire – Jean-Paul Jetté
- Collections Baby et Melzack – Lucie Robitaille

Université du Québec à Montréal (Bibliothèques), C.P. 8888, Montreal, P.Q. H3C 3P8
- Administrateur délégué – Roch Meynard
- Directeur administratif – Julien Laperrière
- Service des Acquisitions – Mme Danièle Lamarche
- Service de la Codification – André Champagne
- Bibliothèque Centrale – Conrad Corriveau
- Service au Public – Mlle Lisette Dupont
- Collections Spéciales – Jean-Yves Gendreau
- Bibliothèque des Arts – Mlle Daphné Dufresne
- Bibliothèque de Musique – Rénald Beaumier
- Bibliothèque des Sciences – Conrad Corriveau
- Bibliohèque des Sciences de l'Education – Marcel Dupuis
- Bibliothèque des Sciences Juridiques – Mlle Micheline Drapeau

Vanier College, Snowdon Media Resource Centre, 5160 Decarie, Montreal, P.Q. H3X 2H9 – 514/333-4030 – Judith Stonehewer

Viau, Bélanger & Associés Law Library, 2810 Tour de la Bourse, Place Victoria, Montreal, P.Q. H4Z 1E6 – 514/878-3081 – Manh Tien Thai

Warnock Hersey Professional Services Ltd. Library, 128 Elmslie St., LaSalle, P.Q. H8R 1V8 – 514/366-3100

Young Women's Christian Association Library, 1355 Dorchester Blvd. W., Montreal, P.Q. H3G 1T3 – 514/866-9941

MOUNT ROYAL

See Montreal

NICOLET

Seminaire de Nicolet (Bibliothèque), 700 boul. Louis Frechette, Nicolet, P.Q. J0G 1E0 – 819/293-4838 – Gilles Proulx

ORSAINVILLE

Ministère Loisir, Chasse et Peche, Bibliothèque de la Faune, 9530 rue de la Faune, Orsainville, P.Q. G1G 5E5 – 418/643-8554 – Francine Morneau

OUTREMONT

See Montreal

POINTE AUX TREMBLES

Union Carbide Canada Ltd. Library, Box 700, Pointe aux Trembles, P.Q. H1B 5K8 – 514/645-5311, ext. 312 – Mrs. A.M. de Jesus

POINTE CLAIRE

Lakeshore General Hospital, Medical Library, 160 Stillview Rd., Pointe Claire, P.Q. H9R 2Y2 – 514/695-1310, ext. 233 – Mrs. Aimée Muther

Merck Frosst Research Library, C.P. 1005, Pointe Claire, P.Q. H9R 4P8 – 514/695-7920, ext. 463 – Mrs. Claire B. Kelly

Noranda Research Centre Library, 240 Hymus Blvd., Pointe Claire, P.Q. H9R 1G5 – 514/697-6640 – Miss S. Courtis

Pulp & Paper Research Institute of Canada Library, 570 boul. Saint-Jean, Pointe Claire, P.Q. H9R 3J9 – 514/697-4110 – Miss A. Finnemore

QUEBEC (See also Ste-Foy)

Archives nationales du Québec, Bibliothèque, C.P. 10450, Ste-Foy, P.Q. G1V 4N1 – 418/643-8904 – Miss Colette Barry

L'Association de Paralysie Cerebrale du Quebec, Centre de Documentation, 525 boul. Hamel, Sous-sol Aile A, local A-50, Québec, P.Q. G1M 2S8 – 418/529-5371 – Rock Gadreau

Barreau de Quebec (Bibliothèque), Palais de Justice, #202, Québec, P.Q. G1R 4P6 – 418/643-4267

Bibliothèque de la Législature, Hôtel du Gouvernement, Québec, P.Q. G1A 1A5 – 418/643-2896 – Jacques Prémont

Centre Hospitalier Jeffery Hale, Bibliothèque médicale, 1250 chemin Ste-Foy, Québec, P.Q. G1S 2M6 – 418/683-4471, poste 238 – Henriette Grenier

Centre Hospitalier Robert Giffard, Bibliothèque médicale, 2601 de la Canardière, Québec, P.Q. G1J 2G3 – 418/663-5300 – Yolande Plamondon

Centre Hospitalier St-François D'Assise, Bibliothèque Medico-Administrative, 10 de l'Espinay, Québec, P.Q. G1L 3L5 – 418/529-7311, loc. 305 – Marie-Paule Genest, S.F.A., Chief

Cerebral Palsy, See L'Association de Paralysie Cerebrale

College François-Xavier Garneau (Bibliothèque), 1660 boul. de l'Entente, C.P. 6300, Sillery, Québec, P.Q. G1T 2S5 – 418/688-8310 – Andrée Lachance

Collège des Jésuites (Bibliothèque), 1150 St-Cyrille W., Québec, P.Q. G1S 1V7 – 418/681-0107 – Georges-H. Gamache, s.j.

Collège Jésus-Marie de Sillery, (Bibliothèque), 2047 Chemin Saint-Louis, Québec, P.Q. G1T 1P3 – 418/683-1148 – Jeanne Paré

College Limoilou (Bibliothèque), C.P. 1400, Québec, P.Q. G1K 7H3 – 418/694-7400

Compagnie d'Assurance Générale, La Capitale, Centre de documentation, C.P. 16040, Québec, P.Q. G1K 7X8 – 418/643-2324 – N. Roy

Commission des Accidents du Travail (Bibliothèque), 524 Bourdages, Ch. 261, C.P. 1200, Québec, P.Q. G1K 7E2 – 418/643-2362 – Louis Taché

Court House Library, See Barreau de Québec

Fondation Universitas, See Ste-Foy

Hôpital de l'Enfant Jésus, Bibliothèque médicale, 1401 18ème rue, Québec, P.Q. G1J 1Z4 – 418/694-5686 – Madeleine Dumais

Hôpital du Saint-Sacrement, Bibliothèque médicale, 1050 chemin Ste-Foy, Québec, P.Q. G1S 4L8 – 418/688-7560 – Bernadette Drolet

Legislature Library, See Bibliothèque de la Legislature

Literary & Historical Society of Quebec Library, 44 St. Stanislas St., Quebec, P.Q. G1R 4H3 – 418/694-9147 – Mrs. C. Dooley

Ministère de l'Agriculture, Pêcheries et Alimentation, Bureau de documentation scientifique et technique (bibliothèque), 200A Chemin Ste-Foy, 1er étage, Québec, P.Q. G1R 4X6 – 418/643-1830 – Pierre Noreau

Ministère de l'Agriculture, Pêcheries et Alimentation, Direction générale des pêches maritimes (Bibliothèque), 2700 Einstein, Quebec, P.Q. G1P 3W8

Ministère des Communications, Bibliothèque administrative, Edifice H, 875 est Grande-Allée, Québec, P.Q. G1R 4Y8 – 418/643-2377 – Louise Lindsay
also 1037 De La Chevrotière, Quebec, P.Q. G1R 4Y7 – 643-1515

Ministère des Consommateurs, co-op. et institutions financières (bibliothèque), 800 Place d'Youville, 7e étage, Québec, P.Q. G1R 4Y5 – 418/643-5236 – Francine Breton

Ministère de l'Energie et des Ressources, (Bibliothèque), 1530 boul. de l'Entente, Québec, P.Q. G1S 4N6 – 418/643-4624 – Normand Guérette – libraries also at 200B chemin Ste-Foy and 8 rue Cook

Ministère des finances, centre de documentation, 1025 St-Augustin, Edifice C, Québec, P.Q. G1R 4Z6 – 418/643-4426 – J.G. Gosselin

Ministère de l'Industrie, du Commerce et du Tourisme, Bibliothèque centrale, 710 Place d'Youville, Québec, P.Q. G1R 4Y4 – 418/643-5081

Ministère de la Justice (Bibliothèque), 1200 route de l'Eglise, 4e étage, Ste-Foy, P.Q. G1V 4M1 – 418/643-8409 – Michel Ricard

Ministère du Revenu (Bibliothèque), 3800 rue Marly, Ste-Foy, P.Q. G1X 4A5 – 418/643-6255 – Mme V. Roy

Ministère des Transports, Centre de documentation, 700 est boul. St-Cyrille, 31e ét., Québec, P.Q. G1R 5H1

Musée du Québec, (Bibliothèque), Parc des Champs de Bataille, Québec, P.Q. G1A 1A3 – 418/643-7134 – F. Lafortune

Office de la Langue Français (Bibliothèque), 62 St-Cyrille est, Québec, P.Q. G1R 5A9 – Mme Monique Charbonneau

Office de Planification et de Developpement du Québec (Bibliothèque), Complexe G, bloc 2, 1er étage, Québec, P.Q. G1R 5E6 – 418/643-1607 – Mme Suzanne P. Garneau

Office des professions du Québec, Direction de la documentation, 930 chemin Ste-Foy, Québec, P.Q. G1S 2L4 – 418/643-6409 – André Contant

Le Protecteur du Citoyen (Centre de documentation), 14 rue Haldimand, Québec, P.Q. G1R 4N4 – 418/643-2688 – Michele Pourchelle

Quebec Departments of Government, See Ministère ...

Régie de l'Assurance-Maladie du Québec (Bibliothèque), C.P. 6600, Québec, P.Q. G1K 7T3 – 418/643-9415 – Clément Sirois

Régie des Rentes du Québec (Bibliothèque), C.P. 5200, Québec, P.Q. G1K 7S9 – 418/643-8250 – Nicole Paquin

Le Soleil Ltée (Bibliothèque), 390 est rue St-Vallier, Québec, P.Q. G1K 7J6 – 418/647-3369 – Pierre Mathieu, Directeur

Université Laval Bibliothèque, Ste-Foy, Québec, P.Q. G1K 7P4
Directeur – Mme Céline Cartier
Directeur adjoint – Claude Bonnelly
Directeur du secteur de l'exploitation et du developpement – Bernard Vinet
Directeur du secteur des services techniques – Lucien Papillon

Université du Québec (Médiathèque), 2875 boul. Laurier, Ste-Foy, Québec, P.Q. G1V 2M3 – 418/657-2578

RIMOUSKI

Université du Québec à Rimouski (Bibliothèque), 300 ave des Ursulines, Rimouski, P.Q. G5L 3A1 – 418/724-1470 – Gérard Mercure

RIVIERE-DU-LOUP

Collège de Rivière-du-Loup (Bibliothèque), 80 Frontenac, Rivière-du-Loup, P.Q. G5R 1R1 – 418/862-6903, ext. 325 – Alain Roberge

ROUYN-NORANDA

Collège du Nord-Ouest (Bibliothèque), CP. 8000, Rouyn-Noranda, P.Q. J9X 5M5 – 819/762-0931, poste 134 – P.S. Allard, o.m.i.

Université du Québec, Centre d'études universitaires dans l'-ouest québécois (bibliothèque), C.P. 8000, Rouyn-Noranda, P.Q. J9X 5M5 – 819/762-0971 – S. Allard, resp.

STE-ANNE-DE-BELLEVUE

Arctic Biological Station Library, Dept. of Fisheries & Oceans, 555 St-Pierre, Ste-Anne-de-Bellevue, P.Q. H9X 3R4 – 514/457-3660, ext. 40 – Mrs. June Currie

CEGEP John Abbott (Bibliothèque), C.P. 2000, Ste-Anne-de-Bellevue, P.Q. H9X 3L9 – 514/457-6610

ST-BENOIT-DU-LAC

Abbaye Saint-Benoît-du-Lac (Bibliothèque), Saint-Benoît-du-Lac, P.Q. J0B 2M0 – 819/843-2567 – Rev. M. Chamberlain

ST-FELICIEN

College de St-Félicien (Bibliothèque), 1298 rue Leclerc, St-Félicien, P.Q. – 418/677-1880

STE-FOY (see also Québec)

Agriculture Canada, Bibliothèque, Station de Recherches, 2560 boul. Hochelaga, Ste-Foy, P.Q. G1V 2J3 – 418/694-4017 – Paul-R. Venne

College Ste-Foy (Bibliothèque), 2410 ch. Ste-Foy, Québec, P.Q. G1V 1T3 – 418/657-3511

Environnement Canada, Bibliothèque de la Faune et des Eaux interieures, C.P. 10,325, Ste-Foy, P.Q. G1V 4H5 – 418/694-7062 – M. Kroon

Environnement Canada, Centre de Recherches Forestieres des Laurentides (Bibliothèque), C.P. 3800, Ste-Foy, P.Q. G1V 4C7 – 418/694-4428 – Monique Kroon

Fondation Universitas (Bibliothèque), 2600 boul. Laurier, #220, Ste-Foy, P.Q. G1V 2L1 – 418/651-8975

Parcs Canada, Centre de Documentation, 1141 route de l'Eglise, C.P. 10,275, Ste-Foy, P.Q. G1V 4H5 – 418/694-7380 – Hélène D'Amours-Rezenthel, Lib. Tech.

ST-GEORGES

Seminaire de Saint-Georges, Bibliothèque du Collegial, Saint-Georges, P.Q. G5Y 3G1 – 418/228-8896 – Dominique Giguère

ST-HYACINTHE

Collège de Saint-Hyacinthe (Bibliothèque), 3000 rue Boullé, St-Hyacinthe, P.Q. J2S 7C7 – 514/773-6800 – Jacques Lefebvre

Faculté de Médecine vétérinaire (bibliothèque), Université de Montreal, C.P. 5000, St-Hyacinthe, P.Q. J2S 7C6 – 514/773-8521 – Jean-Paul Jeté

ST-HUBERT

Dept. of National Defence, Mobile Command HQ Library, St-Hubert, P.Q. J3Y 5T5 – 514/671-3711, loc. 242 – Mrs. M. Finlay

ST-JEAN

CEGEP St-Jean-sur-Richelieu (Bibliothèque), C.P. 1018, St-Jean-sur-Richelieu, P.Q. J3B 7B1 – 514/347-5301

Collège Militaire Royal de Saint-Jean (Bibliothèque), St-Jean, P.Q. J0J 1R0 – 514/346-2131, loc. 606 – A. Lamirande

ST-JEROME

CEGEP St-Jérôme (Bibliothèque), 455 rue Fournier, St-Jérôme, P.Q. J7Z 4V2 – 514/436-1580

ST-LAMBERT

Champlain Regional College Resource Centre, 900 Riverside Dr., St-Lambert, P.Q. J4P 3P2 – 514/672-7360, ext. 221 – Beverley Brucha

ST-LAURENT (see also Montreal)

Atomospheric Environment Service Library, 100 boul. Alexis-Nihon, 3rd Floor, St-Laurent, P.Q. H4M 2N6 – 514/333-3020 – Jacques Miron

Ayerst Laboratories Library, 1025 Laurentian Blvd., St-Laurent, P.Q. H4R 1J6 – 514/744-6771 – Nicole Barrette-Pilon

CEGEP de St-Laurent (Bibliothèque), 625 boul. Ste-Croix, St-Laurent, P.Q. H4L 3X7 – 514/747-6521

Centre Hospitalier de St-Laurent (Bibliothèque médicale), 1275 Côte Vertu, Ville St-Laurent, P.Q. H4L 4V2 – 514/747-4771

Produits Chimiques Allied Canada Ltée (Bibliothèque), 750 Laurentian Blvd., #400, St-Laurent, P.Q. H4M 2M5 – 514/748-8771

Smith, Kline & French Medical Research Library, 300 Laurientien Blvd., St-Laurent, P.Q. H4M 2L6 – 514/747-6565, ext. 312

STE-THERESE-DE-BLAINVILLE

CEGEP Lionel-Groulx (Bibliothèque), 100 rue Duquet, Ste-Thérèse-de-Blainville, P.Q. J7E 3G6 – 514/430-3120

SALABERRY-DE-VALLEYFIELD

See Valleyfield

SENNEVILLE

Domtar Inc. Research Centre Library, Senneville, P.Q. H9X 3L7 – 514/457-6810 – Barbara G. Bolton

SEPT-ILES

CEGEP de Sept-Iles (Bibliothèque), 175 de la Vérendrye, Sept-Iles, P.Q. G4R 5B7 – 418/962-9848 – Denis Couture

SHAWINIGAN

Collège de Shawinigan (Bibliothèque), 2263 blvd. du Collège, Shawinigan, P.Q. G9N 6V8 – 819/539-6401 – Colette Caron

SHERBROOKE

Centre Hospitalier St-Vincent de Paul, Bibliothèque médicale, 300 rue King est, Sherbrooke, P.Q. J1G 1B1 – 819/563-2366 – Gilberte Poirier

College du Sacre-Coeur (Bibliothèque), 155 Belvédère nord, Sherbrooke, P.Q. J1H 4A7 – 819/569-9457

Collège de Sherbrooke (Bibliothèque), 475 rue Parc, Sherbrooke, P.Q. J1H 5M7 – 819/563-3150, poste 233 – Gaétan Roy

Grand Séminaire (Bibliothèque), 130 Cathédrale, C.P. 430, Sherbrooke, P.Q. J1H 5K1 – 819/563-9934, ext. 38 – Irène Desruisseaux

Hôtel-Dieu de Sherbrooke (Bibliothèque), 580 sud, rue Bowen, Sherbrooke, P.Q. J1G 2E8 – 819/569-2551, ext. 226 – Louise Saucier

Séminaire de Sherbrooke (Biliothèque), 195 rue Marquette, Sherbrooke, P.Q. J1H 1L6 – 819/563-2050, ext. 31 – Rev. C. Pelletier

Société d'Histoire des Cantons de l'Est (Bibliothèque), C.P. 1141, (1304 Portland), Sherbrooke, P.Q. J1H 5L5 – 819/562-0616 – Miss Marie-Jeanne Daigneau

Université de Sherbrooke, Bibliothèque generale, Sherbrooke, P.Q. J1K 2R1
Dir. des bibliothèques – Guy Cloutier (819/565-5611)
Bibliothèque de droit – Guy Tanguay (565-2905)
Bibliothèque générale – Pierre Lafrance (565-5507)
Bibliothèque de Médecine – Germain Chouinard (565-2096)
Bibliothèque des sciences – Michel Beaudoin (565-5476)

SILLERY

See Quebec City

SOREL

QIT - Fer et Titane Inc., att. La Bibliothèque, C.P. 560, Sorel, P.Q. J3P 5P6 – 514/742-6671 – C. Stroemgren

STANSTEAD

Stanstead College (Bibliothèque), Stanstead, P.Q. J0B 3E0 – 819/876-5577 – Mrs. J. Philip

THETFORD MINES

College de la Région de L'Amiante, Centre de ressources educatives, 671 boul. Smith sud, Thetford Mines, P.Q. G6G 1N1 – 418/338-8591, ext. 247 – Ronald Levesque

TROIS-RIVIERES

CEGEP de Trois-Rivières (Bibliothèque), 3500 de Courval, Trois-Rivières, P.Q. G9A 5E6 – 819/376-1721 – Denis Simard

Conservatoire de Musique (Bibliothèque), (587 rue Radisson), C.P. 1146, Trois-Rivières, P.Q. G9A 2A8 – 819/375-7748 – Guy Lefebvre, bibliotechnicien

Hôpital St-Joseph, Bibliothèque médicale, 731 rue Ste-Julie, Trois-Rivières, P.Q. G9A 1Y1 – 819/379-8112, ext. 276 – Solange De-Rouyn

Hôpital Ste-Marie, Bibliothèque médicale, 1991 boul. du Carmel, Trois-Rivières, P.Q. G8Z 3R9 – 819/379-4130, ext. 215 – Lucie Grondin

Séminaire St-Joseph (Bibliothèque), C.P. 548, Trois-Rivières, P.Q. G9A 5J1 – 819/378-5167 – Jérôme Laperrière

VALCARTIER

Defence Research Establishment Valcartier (Bibliothèque), Box 8800, Courcelette, P.Q. G0A 1R0 – 418/844-4271 – R. Menard

VALLEYFIELD

College de Valleyfield (Bibliothèque), 169 Champlain, Valleyfield, P.Q. J6T 1X6 – 514/373-9441 – Yves Castonguay

VARENNES

Institut de Recherche d'Hydro-Québec (Bibliothèque), C.P. 1000, Varennes, P.Q. J0L 2P0 – 514/652-8325 – Michel Leclerc

VAUDREUIL

Hoffmann-La Roche Ltd. Library, 1000 boul. Roche, Vaudreuil, P.Q. J7V 6B3 – 514/487-8428 – Mrs. Cecile Johnson

VERDUN

Centre Culturel (Bibliothèque), 5955 ave. Bannantyne, Verdun, P.Q. H4H 1H6 – 514/768-1140 – A. Fortier

Douglas Hospital, See Montreal

VICTORIAVILLE

CEGEP de Victoriaville (Bibliothèque), C.P. 68, Victoriaville, P.Q. G6P 6S4 – 819/758-1571

VILLE-VANIER

Hôpital Christ-Roi (Bibliothèque), 300 W. Hamel, Ville-Vanier, P.Q. G1M 2R9 – 418/687-1717 – Gratien Gélinas

SASKATCHEWAN

Public Libraries in Saskatchewan

With Librarian

Area Code is 306

Chinook Regional Library

Michael Keaschuk, Librarian, 1240 Chaplin St. W., Swift Current, Sask. S9H 0G8 – 773-3186 – Telex 071-21129

Branches within Chinook Regional Library

Abbey Branch Library, Box 185, Abbey, Sask. S0N 0A0 – 689-2202 – Mrs. Marilyn Turgeon

Admiral Branch Library, Box 152, Admiral, Sask. S0N 0B0 – Mrs. Mary Green

Burstall Branch Library, Box 84, Burstall, Sask. S0N 0H0 – 679-2177 – Mrs. Judy Winter

Cabri Branch Library, Cabri, Sask. S0N 0J0 – 587-2500 – Mrs. Bertha Davidson

Central Butte Branch Library, Box 276, Central Butte, Sask. S0H 0T0 – 796-2222 – Mrs. Virginia Hemsworth

Chaplin Branch Library, Box 225, Chaplin, Sask. S0H 0V0 – 395-2227 – Mrs. Margaret Wakeford

Climax Branch Library, Climax, Sask. S0N 0N0 – 293-2006 – Mrs. Sue Smith

Consul Branch Library, Consul, Sask. S0N 0P0 – Mrs. Linda Brown

Eastend Branch Library, Box 91, Eastend, Sask. S0N 0T0 – Mrs. Joyce Turvey

Fox Valley Branch Library, Fox Valley, Sask. S0N 0V0 – 666-2045 – Mrs. Anne Metz

Frontier Branch Library, Frontier, Sask. S0N 0W0 – 296-2244 – Mrs. Sharon Stolz

Glentworth Branch Library, Glentworth, Sask. S0H 1V0 – Mrs. Meryle Iwanicki

Gouldtown Branch Library, Gouldtown, Sask. S0H 1W0 – Mrs. Mary Shygera

Gravelbourg Branch Library, Box 745, Gravelbourg, Sask. S0H 1X0 – 648-3177 – Mrs. Rose Bolen

Gull Lake Branch Library, Box 653, Gull Lake, Sask. S0N 1A0 – 672-3277 – Mrs. Pearl Weston

Hazlet Branch Library, Box 73, Hazlet, Sask. S0N 1E0 – 678-2155 – Mrs. Pat Horn

Herbert Branch Library, Box 176, Herbert, Sask. S0H 2A0 – 784-2484 – Mrs. Zelda Wiebe

Hodgeville Branch Library, Hodgeville, Sask. S0H 2B0 – 677-2223 – Mrs. Betty Haubrich

Kincaid Branch Library, Kincaid, Sask. S0H 2J0 – 264-3226 – Mrs. Olive Wilson

Lafleche Branch Library, Lafleche, Sask. S0H 2K0 – 472-5466 – Mrs. Debbie Williamson

Leader Branch Library, Leader, Sask. S0N 1H0 – 628-3830 – Mrs. Lou Hegg

Mankota Branch Library, Mankota, Sask. S0H 2W0 – 478-2331 – Mrs. Doreen McCallum

Maple Creek Branch Library, Box 760, Maple Creek, Sask. S0N 1N0 – 667-3522 – Mrs. V. Bethel

Morse Branch Library, Morse, Sask. S0H 3C0 – 629-3335 – Mrs. Bea Murdock

Pennant Branch Library, Pennant, Sask. S0N 1X0 – 626-3316 – Mrs. Merle Croteau

Piapot Branch Library, Box 73, Piapot, Sask. S0N 1Y0 – Mrs. Frances Saunderson

Ponteix Branch Library, Box 700, Ponteix, Sask. S0N 1Z0 – 625-3353 – Mrs. Marie Kouri

Prelate Branch Library, Box 40, Prelate, Sask. S0N 2B0 – 673-2340 – Wendel Kosolofski

Robsart Branch Library, Robsart, Sask. S0N 2G0 – Mrs. Lavone Smiley

Sceptre Branch Library, Box 128, Sceptre, Sask. S0N 2H0 – 623-4244 – Mrs. Mina Anderson

Shaunavon Branch Library, Box 1116, Shaunavon, Sask. S0N 2M0 – 297-3844 – Mrs. Dorothy Rose

Simmie Branch Library, Box 111, Simmie, Sask. S0N 2N0 – Mrs. Helen Carleton

Stewart Valley Branch Library, Stewart Valley, Sask. S0N 2P0 – Mrs. Freida Gray

Swift Current Branch Library, 411 Herbert St. E., Swift Current, Sask. S9H 1M5 – 773-4301 – Mrs. Joan Olesen

Tompkins Branch Library, Tompkins, Sask. S0N 2S0 – 622-2255 – Mrs. Emily Mitchell

Val Marie Branch Library, Val Marie, Sask. S0N 2T0 – 298-2122 – Mrs. Florette Kane

Vanguard Branch Library, Vanguard, Sask. S0N 2V0 – 582-2244 – Mrs. Doris Burns

Webb Branch Library, Webb, Sask. S0N 2X0 – 674-2200 – Mrs. Florence Bollman

Lakeland Library Region

Ms. Joylene Campbell, Librarian, Box 813, North Battleford, Sask. S9A 2Z3 – 445-6108 – Telex 074-25157

Branches within Lakeland Library Region

Area Code is 306

Battleford Branch Library, Box 220, Battleford, Sask. S0M 0E0 – 937-2346 – Vi Loscombe

Borden Branch Library, Borden, Sask. S0K 0N0 – 997-4517 – Helen Sutherland

Cut Knife Library, Cut Knife, Sask. S0M 0N0 – 398-2294 – Dale Wettlaufer

Denzil Branch Library, Denzil, Sask. S0L 0S0 – 358-2085 – Rose Reiniger

Edam Branch Library, Edam, Sask. S0M 0V0 – 397-2223 – Trudy McMurphy

Glaslyn Branch Library, Glaslyn, Sask. S0M 0Y0 – Helen Cherwoniak

Goodsoil Branch Library, Goodsoil, Sask. S0M 1A0 – 238-4622 – Emillie Stremick

Hafford Branch Library, Hafford, Sask. S0J 1A0 – 549-2213 – Jean Krsacok

Lashburn Branch Library, Lashburn, Sask. S0M 1H0 – 285-3546 – Colleen Carruthers

Loon Lake Branch Library, Loon Lake, Sask. S0M 1L0 – 837-2147 – Edith Farn

Macklin Branch Library, Macklin, Sask. S0L 2C0 – 753-2075 – Josie Zoller

Maidstone Branch Library, Maidstone, Sask. S0M 1M0 – 893-2576 – Joyce Weston

Makwa Branch Library, Makwa, Sask. S0M 1N0 236-4708 – Lynda Bertrand

Marsden Branch Library, Marsden, Sask. S0M 1P0 – 826-5666 – Evelyn Powers

Maymont Branch Library, Maymont, Sask. S0M 1T0 – 389-2006 – Gladys Brehon

Meadow Lake Branch Library, Meadow Lake, Sask. S0M 1V0 – 236-5396 – Jean Gorst

Medstead Branch Library, Medstead, Sask. S0M 1W0 – 342-4744 – Pauline Bovair

Meota Branch Library, Meota, Sask. S0M 1X0 – 892-2034 – Bernice Tait

Mervin Branch Library, Mervin, Sask. S0M 1Y0 – 845-2207 – Irene Palen

Mosquito Branch Library, Box 941, North Battleford, Sask. S9A 2Z3 – 937-3634 – Valerie Stone

Neilburg Branch Library, Neilburg, Sask. S0M 2C0 – 823-4234 – Hazel Mackie

North Battleford Branch Library, 1081 100th St., North Battleford, Sask. S9A 0V2 – 445-3206 – Ron Berntson

Onion Lake Branch Library, Onion Lake, Sask. S0M 2E0 – 344-4530 – Dora Cardinal

Paradise Hill Branch Library, Paradise Hill, Sask. S0M 2G0 – 344-2206 – Mary Scotton

Paynton Branch Library, Paynton, Sask. S0M 2J0 – 895-2175 – Bev Webb

Pehtokahanopewin Branch Library, Box 187, Cut Knife, Sask. S0M 0N0 – 398-2925 – Valerie Bonaise

Pierceland Branch Library, Pierceland, Sask. S0M 2K0 – 839-2166 – Shirley Dimion

Rabbit Lake Branch Library, Rabbit Lake, Sask. S0M 2L0 – 824-2106 – Laura Ricketts

Radisson Branch Library, Radisson, Sask. S0K 3L0 – 827-2118 – Gerry Scott

Red Pheasant Branch Library, Box 176, Cando, Sask. S0K 0V0 – Merinda Bugler

St. Walburg Branch Library, St. Walburg, Sask. S0M 2T0 – 248-3250 – G. Etcheverry

Saskatchewan Hospital Public Library, North Battleford, Sask. S9A 2X8 – 445-9411, ext. 223 – Doris Allan

Speers Branch Library, Speers, Sask. S0M 2V0 – 246-2114 – Joyce Koliniak
Sweet Grass Branch Library, Box 80, Gallivan, Sask. S0M 0X0 – 937-2974 – Barbara Albert
Thunderchild Branch Library, Box 381, Turtleford, Sask. S0M 2Y0 – 845-2662 – Dorothy Jack
Turtleford Branch Library, Box 146, Turtleford, Sask. S0M 2Y0 – 845-2074 – Pat Pizzey
Waterhen Lake Branch Library, Waterhen Lake, Sask. S0M 3B0 – Delphine Fiddler

Palliser Regional Library

Ms. Cora Greer, Librarian, Box 2500, Moose Jaw, Sask. S6H 6Y2 – 693-3669 – Telex 071-29221

Branches within Palliser Regional Library

Area Code is 306

Assiniboia Branch Library, Box 1075, Assiniboia, Sask. S0H 0B0 – 642-3631 – Mrs. Gladys Reid
Avonlea Branch Library, Avonlea, Sask. S0H 0C0 – 868-2076 – Mrs. Gwen Hickey
Bethune Branch Library, Bethune, Sask. S0G 0H0 – 638-3046 – Mrs. Mildred Kistner
Briercrest Branch Library, Briercrest, Sask. S0H 0K0 – 799-2137 – Mrs. Eleanor Anderson
Bushell Park Branch Library, CFB Moose Jaw, Bushell Park, Sask. S0H 0N0 – 693-5375 – Mrs. Barbara Tease
Caronport Branch Library, Caronport, Sask. S0H 0S0 – 756-2244 – Mrs. Evelyn Budd
Coronach Branch Library, Coronach, Sask. S0H 0Z0 – 267-3260 – Mrs. Maxine Thurlow
Craik Branch Library, Craik, Sask. S0H 0V0 – 734-2388 – Mrs. Mildred Bakken
Davidson Branch Library, Davidson, Sask. S0G 1A0 – 567-2022 – Mrs. Jenny Scott
Elbow Branch Library, Elbow, Sask. S0H 1J0 – 854-2244 – Mrs. Charlotte Cafferata
Holdfast Branch Library, Holdfast, Sask. S0G 2H0 – 488-2140 – Mrs. Josephine Burkhart
Imperial Branch Library, Imperial, Sask. S0G 2J0 – 963-2272 – Mrs. Dorothy Lucas
Loreburn Branch Library, Loreburn, Sask. S0H 2S0 – 644-2172 – Mrs. Velma Vaughan
Moose Jaw Public Library, 461 Langdon Cres., Moose Jaw, Sask. S6H 0H6 – 692-2787 – Miss Anne Warriner
Mortlach Branch Library, Mortlach, Sask. S0H 3E0 – 355-2202 – Mrs. Phyllis Wolf
Mossbank Branch Library, Mossbank, Sask. S0H 3G0 – 354-2474 – Vera Wilet
Riverhurst Branch Library, Riverhurst, Sask. S0H 3P0 – 353-2112 – Mrs. Florence Miller
Rockglen Branch Library, Rockglen, Sask. S0H 3R0 – 476-2350 – Mrs. Dini Miller
Rouleau Branch Library, Rouleau, Sask. S0G 4H0 – 776-2322 – Mrs. Jean Mountain
Tugaske Branch Library, Tugaske, Sask. S0H 4B0 – 759-2215 – Mrs. Nola Rudd
Willow Bunch Branch Library, Willow Bunch, Sask. S0H 4K0 – 473-2227 – Mrs. Irene Porter
Wood Mountain Branch Library, Wood Mountain, Sask. S0H 4L0 – 266-2110 – Mrs. Shirley Punga

Parkland Regional Library

Stan Skrzeszewski, Librarian, 95A Broadway W., Yorkton, Sask. S3N 0L9 – 783-7022 – Telex 074-21536

Branches within Parkland Regional Library

Area Code is 306

Annaheim Branch Library, Annaheim, Sask. S0K 0G0 – 598-2155 – Mrs. Beverly Pappenfus
Balcarres Branch Library, Box 640, Balcarres, Sask. S0G 0C0 – 334-2966 – Mrs. Elaine Chatterson
Bredenbury Branch Library, Bredenbury, Sask. S0A 0H0 – 898-2299 –Mrs. Lois Smandych
Buchanan Branch Library, Buchanan, Sask. S0A 0J0 – 592-2144 – Mrs. Marie Kupchinski
Calder Branch Library, Box 70, Calder, Sask. S0A 0K0 – 742-2060 – Mrs. Marlene Balabuk
Canora Branch Library, Box 694, Canora, Sask. S0A 0L0 – 563-6877 – Mrs. Hughina Samuels
Churchbridge Branch Library, Box 530, Churchbridge, Sask. S0A 0M0 – 896-2322 – Mrs. Clara Bender
Cupar Branch Library, Cupar, Sask. S0G 0Y0 – 723-4376 – Mrs. Marie Reed
Earl Grey Branch Library, Earl Grey, Sask. S0G 1J0 – 939-2212 – Mrs. Doreen Bundus
Elfros Branch Library, Box 70, Elfros, Sask. S0A 0V0 – 328-2175 – Mrs. Stella Stephanson
Esterhazy Branch Library, Esterhazy, Sask. S0A 0X0 – 745-6406 – Mrs. Helen Staples
Foam Lake Branch Library, Box 181, Foam Lake, Sask. S0A 1A0 – 272-3660 – Mrs. Elin Reynolds
Govan Branch Library, Box 40, Govan, Sask. S0G 1Z0 – 484-2122 – Mrs. Margaret Roland
Invermay Branch Library, Invermay, Sask. S0A 1M0 – 593-2242 – Mrs. Betty Brezinski
Ituna Branch Library, Ituna, Sask. S0A 1N0 – 795-2672 – Mrs. Daisy Ivey
Jedburgh Branch Library, Jedburgh, Sask. S0A 1R0 – 647-2452 – Mrs. Adele Polegi
Kamsack Branch Library, Box 1870, Kamsack, Sask. S0A 1S0 – 542-3787 – Carl Eggenschwiler
Kelliher Branch Library, Box 161, Kelliher, Sask. S0A 1V0 – 675-2110 – Miss Ethel North
Kelvington Branch Library, Box 429, Kelvington, Sask. S0A 1W0 – 327-4322 – Mrs. Shirley Lalonde
Lake Lenore Branch Library, Lake Lenore, Sask. S0K 2J0 – 368-2391 – Mrs. Lucille Eberle
Langenburg Branch Library, Langenburg, Sask. S0A 2A0 – 743-2432 – Mrs. Joyce Angus
Lemberg Branch Library, Box 339, Lemberg, Sask. S0A 2B0 – 335-2369 – Mrs. Anna Mann
Leroy Branch Library, Box 310, Leroy, Sask. S0K 2P0 – 286-3334 – Mrs. Aletha Stein
Lestock Branch Library, Box 186, Lestock, Sask. S0A 2G0 – 274-2048 – Mrs. Luelle Frisko
Lintlaw Branch Library, Lintlaw, Sask. S0A 2H0 – 325-2033 – Mrs. Sharon Kowaski
Lipton Branch Library, Lipton, Sask. S0G 3B0 – 336-2288 – Mrs. Marlene Huber
Macnutt Branch Library, Box 150, Macnutt, Sask. S0A 2K0 – 742-4221 – Mrs. May Frederiksen
Melville Branch Library, Box 489, Melville, Sask. S0A 2P0 – 728-2171 – Mrs. Ferne Mattison
Muenster Branch Library, Muenster, Sask. S0K 2Y0 – 682-5252 – Mrs. Sally Muench
Neudorf Branch Library, Neudorf, Sask. S0A 2T0 – 748-2553 – Mrs. Isabel Lintott
Norquay Branch Library, Box 460, Norquay, Sask. S0A 2V0 – 594-2522 – Mrs. Marlene Jacquemart
Pelly Branch Library, Pelly, Sask. S0A 2Z0 – 595-2124 – Mrs. Jeannette Robson
Punnichy Branch Library, Punnichy, Sask. S0A 3C0 – 835-2176 – Mrs. Bertha Schlosser
Quill Lake Branch Library, Box 271, Quill Lake, Sask. S0A 3E0 – 383-2592 – Mrs. Marina Humenny
Rose Valley Branch Library, Rose Valley, Sask. S0E 1M0 – 322-2001 – Mrs. Sandra Hanson
Saltcoats Branch Library, Saltcoats, Sask. S0A 3R0 – 744-2911 – Mrs. Irene Wilson
Semans Branch Library, Semans, Sask. S0A 3S0 – 524-2224 – Mrs. Edith Murney
Southey Branch Library, Southey, Sask. S0G 4P0 – 726-2907 – Mrs. Marilyn Hornoi
Spalding Branch Library, Spalding, Sask. S0K 4C0 – 872-2184 – Mrs. Dora Knutson
Springside Branch Library, Springside, Sask. S0A 3V0 – 792-2022 – Mrs. Viola Rodgerson
Spy Hill Branch Library, Box 160, Spy Hill, Sask. S0A 3W0 – 534-4526 – Mrs. Jeanette Blakley

Stockholm Branch Library, Stockholm, Sask. S0A 3Y0 – 793-2102 – Mrs. Joyce Banga
Strasbourg Branch Library, Box 331, Strasbourg, Sask. S0G 4V0 – 725-4301 – Mrs. Patricia Kelln
Sturgis Branch Library, Sturgis, Sask. S0A 4A0 – 548-2824 – Mrs. Margaret Moritz
Wadena Branch Library, Box 297, Wadena, Sask. S0A 4J0 – 338-2293 – Mrs. Norah Stroshein
Watson Branch Library, Box 489, Watson, Sask. S0K 4V0 – 287-3642 – Mrs. Lynn Knafelc
Wishart Branch Library, Box 58, Wishart, Sask. S0A 4S0 – 576-2150 – Mrs. Angeline Hall
Wynyard Branch Library, Box 477, Wynyard, Sask. S0A 4T0 – 554-2133 – Mrs. Alda Cooper
Yorkton Branch Library, 93 Broadway W., Yorkton, Sask. S3N 0L9 – 783-3523 – Larry Joseph

Southeast Regional Library

Miss Barbara Blyth, Librarian, Box 550, Weyburn, Sask. S4H 2K7 – 842-3432 – Telex 071-2820

Branches within Southeast Regional Library

Area Code is 306

Alameda Public Library, Box 144, Alameda, Sask. S0C 0A0 – 489-2066 – Laura Griffin
Arcola Public Library, Arcola, Sask. S0C 0G0 – 455-2212 – Isabelle George
Balgonie Public Library, Balgonie, Sask. S0G 0E0 – 637-2332 – Irene Gerhardt
Bengough Public Library, Box 391, Bengough, Sask. S0C 0K0 – 268-2022 – Myrel Cairns
Big Beaver Public Library, Big Beaver, Sask. S0H 0G0 – 267-4540 – Wanda Duperreault
Bienfait Public Library, Box 214, Bienfait, Sask. S0C 0M0 – 388-2223 – Hilda Carlson
Broadview Public Library, Broadview, Sask. S0G 0K0 – 696-2414 – Donna Petrie
Carievale Public Library, Carievale, Sask. S0C 0P0 – Sarah Dalziel
Carlyle Public Library, Box 417, Carlyle, Sask. S0C 0R0 – 453-6120 – Joan Zander
Carnduff Public Library, Carnduff, Sask. S0C 0S0 – 482-3255 – Jennie Small
Ceylon Public Library, Ceylon, Sask. S0C 0T0 – Marguerite Arnott
Estevan Public Library, 1037 2nd St., Estevan, Sask. S4A 0L6 – 634-3933 – Freda Evans
Fillmore Public Library, Fillmore, Sask. S0G 1N0 – 722-3369 – Dolores MacKay
Fort Qu'Appelle Public Library, Fort Qu'Appelle, Sask. S0G 1S0 – A.J. White
Frobisher Public Library, Box 235, Frobisher, Sask. S0C 0Y0 – 486-2140 – Beatrice Johnstone
Gainsborough Public Library, Gainsborough, Sask. S0C 0Z0 – 685-2229 – Irene Smith
Grenfell Public Library, Grenfell, Sask. S0G 2B0 – 697-2455 – Mary Keedwell
Indian Head Public Library, Box 986, Indian Head, Sask. S0G 2K0 – 695-3922 – Leone Tuttle
Kennedy Public Library, Box 217, Kennedy, Sask. S0G 2R0 – Marie Bourhis
Kipling Public Library, Box 608, Kipling, Sask. S0G 2S0 – Amy McFarlane
Lake Alma Public Library, Lake Alma, Sask. S0C 1M0 – Emily Stadler
Lampman Public Library, Box 9, Lampman, Sask. S0C 1N0 – Blandina Walter
Lumsden Public Library, Lumsden, Sask. S0G 3C0 – 485-2433 – Bessie Hill
Manor Public Library, Manor, Sask. S0C 1R0 – 448-2020 – Caroline Thomas
Maryfield Public Library, Maryfield, Sask. S0G 3K0 – 646-2143 – Ruby Graham
Midale Public Library, Box 206, Midale, Sask. S0C 1S0 – 458-2263 – Corrine Sjodin
Milestone Public Library, Milestone, Sask. S0G 3L0 – 436-2112 – Blanche Solberg
Montmartre Public Library, Montmartre, Sask. S0G 3M0 – 424-2029 – Pat Chittenden
Moosomin Public Library, Box 462, Moosomin, Sask. S0G 3N0 – 435-2107 – Joan Bird
Odessa Public Library, Odessa, Sask. S0G 3S0 – Lynn Herauf
Ogema Public Library, Ogema, Sask. S0C 1Y0 – Viola Kazell
Oungre Public Library, Oungre, Sask. S0C 1Z0 – 456-2870 – Carol Kuntz
Oxbow Public Library, Oxbow, Sask. S0C 2B0 – 483-5175 – Helen Kingsbury
Pangman Public Library, Pangman, Sask. S0C 2C0 – Audrey Kessler
Qu'Appelle Public Library, Qu'Appelle, Sask. S0G 4A0 – 699-2279 – Elizabeth Desrochers
Radville Public Library, Radville, Sask. S0C 2G0 – Juliette LaBelle
Redvers Public Library, Redvers, Sask. S0C 2H0 – 452-3255 – Connie Wells
Regina Beach Public Library, Regina Beach, Sask. S0G 4C0 – Avis Black
Rocanville Public Library, Rocanville, Sask. S0A 3L0 – 645-2088 – Amanda Parks
Stoughton Public Library, Stoughton, Sask. S0G 4T0 – Melita Jess
Torquay Public Library, Box 61, Torquay, Sask. S0C 2L0 – 923-2172 – G. Kvammen
Tribune Public Library, Tribune, Sask. S0C 2M0 – Elizabeth Porth
Trossachs Public Library, Trossachs, Sask. S0C 2N0 – 842-5920 – Joan Klippenstein
Wapella Public Library, Wapella, Sask. S0G 4Z0 – Rachel Carlson
Wawota Public Library, Wawota, Sask. S0G 5A0 – 739-2375 – Jean Taylor
Weyburn Public Library, 45 Bison Ave. N.E., Weyburn, Sask. S4H 0H9 – 842-4352 – Marlene Yurkowski
White Bear Public Library, Box 520, White Bear Development Co., Carlyle, Sask. S0C 0R0 – Irean Smith
Whitewood Public Library, Whitewood, Sask. S0G 5C0 – 735-4233 – Ellen Miskiman
Windthorst Public Library, Windthorst, Sask. S0G 5G0 – Marguerite Tholl
Yellow Grass Public Library, Yellow Grass, Sask. S0G 5J0 – Dorothy Erb

Wapiti Regional Library

Joel Levis, Librarian, 145 12th St. E., Prince Albert, Sask. S6V 1B7 – 764-0712 – Telex 074-29188

Branches within Wapiti Regional Library

Alvena Branch Library, Alvena, Sask. S0K 0E0 – Mrs. D. Oleskiw
Arborfield Branch Library, Arborfield, Sask. S0E 0A0 – Mrs. Ivy Dyck
Archerwill Branch Library, Archerwill, Sask. S0E 0B0 – Mrs. Lena Numedahl
Big River Branch Library, Big River, Sask. S0J 0E0 – Mrs. Mabel Hodgson
Birch Hills Branch Library, Birch Hills, Sask. S0J 0G0 – Mrs. Florence Saxton
Bjorkdale Branch Library, Bjorkdale, Sask. S0E 0E0 – Mrs. Wesalean Abra
Blaine Lake Branch Library, Blaine Lake, Sask. Blaine Lake, Sask. S0J 0J0 – Mrs. Christine Cheveldayoff
Canwood Branch Library, Canwood, Sask. S0J 0K0 – Miss H. Butz
Carrot River Branch Library, Carrot River, Sask. S0E 0L0 – Mrs. Ina Wolowidnyk
Choiceland Branch Library, Choiceland, Sask. S0J 0M0 – Mrs. Patricia Black
Christopher Lake Branch Library, Christopher Lake, Sask. S0J 0N0 – Mrs. Judi Selkirk
Crooked River Branch Library, Crooked River, Sask. S0E 0R0 – Mrs. Judy Mahoney

Crystal Springs Branch Library, Crystal Springs, Sask. S0K 1A0 – Mrs. Ethel LaRoche

Cudworth Branch Library, Cudworth, Sask. S0K 1B0 – Mrs. Rose Wunderlich

Debden Branch Library, Debden, Sask. S0J 0S0 – Mrs. Aline Grimard

Gronlid Branch Library, Gronlid, Sask. S0E 0W0 – Mrs. Janis Keller

Hudson Bay Branch Library, Hudson Bay, Sask. S0E 0Y0 – Mrs. Sharon Grant

Humboldt Branch Library, Humboldt, Sask. S0K 2A0 – Mrs. Madeleine Thompson

James Smith Branch Library, Kinistino, Sask. S0J 1H0 – Mrs. Betsy McLeod

Kinistino Branch Library, Kinistino, Sask. S0J 1H0 – Mrs. Evelyn Sjolin

Leask Branch Library, Leask, Sask. S0J 1M0 – Mrs. Marjorie Duncan

Leoville Branch Library, Leoville, Sask. S0J 1N0 – Mrs. A. Laventure

Marcelin Branch Library, Marcelin, Sask. S0J 1R0 – Mrs. D. Sutherland

Meath Park Branch Library, Meath Park, Sask. S0J 1T0 – Mrs. Darlene Child

Melfort Branch Library, Melfort, Sask. S0E 1A0 – Mrs. Helen Kaminski

Meskanaw Branch Library, Meskanaw, Sask. S0K 2W0 – Mrs. Betty Selnes

Mistatim Branch Library, Mistatim, Sask. S0E 1B0 – Mrs. Agnes Hrbachek

Naicam Branch Library, Naicam, Sask. S0K 2Z0 – Mrs. Dorothy Anderson

Nipawin Branch Library, Nipawin, Sask. S0E 1E0 – Miss Marjorie Ross

Paddockwood Branch Library, Paddockwood, Sask. S0J 1Z0 – Mrs. Therese Gobeil

Pilger Branch Library, Pilger, Sask. S0K 3G0 – Mrs. Sharon Doepker

Porcupine Plain Branch Library, Porcupine Plain, Sask. S0E 1H0 – Mrs. Janis Franklin

Prairie River Branch Library, Prairie River, Sask. S0E 1J0 – Mrs. Petress Foga

Prince Albert Branch Library, Prince Albert, Sask. S6V 1B7 – Mrs. Eleanor Acorn

Provincial Correctional Centre Library, 29th St. W. & Central, Prince Albert, Sask. – Al Demerais

Red Earth Branch Library, Red Earth, Sask. S0E 1K0 – Ms. Mary Whitehead

Ridgedale Branch Library, Ridgedale, Sask. S0E 1L0 – Mrs. Shirley Surman

St. Benedict Branch Library, St. Benedict, Sask. S0K 3T0 – Mrs. Louise Meidl

St. Brieux Branch Library, St. Brieux, Sask. S0K 3V0 – Mrs. Betty Mahussier

Saskatchewan Penitentiary Public Library, Prince Albert, Sask. S6V 5R6 – Harry Walls

Shell Lake Branch Library, Shell Lake, Sask. S0J 2G0 – Mrs. L. Christiansen

Shellbrook Branch Library, Shellbrook, Sask. S0J 2E0 – Mrs. Hazel Barkway

Smeaton Branch Library, Smeaton, Sask. S0J 2J0 – Mrs. Joan Falloon

Spiritwood Branch Library, Spiritwood, Sask. S0J 2M0 – Mrs. Mary Schira

Star City Branch Library, Star City, Sask. S0E 1P0 – Mrs. Florence Pace

Sturgeon Lake Branch Library, Sturgeon Lake, Sask. S0E 1P0 – Ms. Melinda Daniels

Tisdale Branch Library, Tisdale, Sask. S0E 1T0 – Mrs. Edwina Schulz

Wakaw Branch Library, Wakaw, Sask. S0K 4P0 – Mrs. Melinda Johnson

Waskesiu Branch Library, Waskesiu, Sask. S0J 2Y0 – Mrs. Grace Dickinson

Weekes Branch Library, Weekes, Sask. S0E 1V0 – Mrs. Elda Grisdale

Weldon Branch Library, Weldon, Sask. S0J 3A0 – Mrs. Lorna Olsen

White Fox Branch Library, White Fox, Sask. S0J 3B0 – Mrs. Violet Johnson

Zenon Park Branch Library, Zenon Park, Sask. S0E 1W0 – Mrs. Alice Valois

Wheatland Regional Library

Bruce Cameron, Librarian, 806 Duchess St., Saskatoon, Sask. S7K 0R3 – 652-5077 – Telex 074-2662

Branches within Wheatland Regional Library

Area Code is 306

Allan Branch Library, Box 40, Allan, Sask. S0K 0C0 – 257-4222 – Mrs. Theresa Usselman

Beechy Branch Library, Box 257, Beechy, Sask. S0L 0C0 – 859-2032 – Mrs. Ella Holden

Biggar Branch Library, Box 357, Biggar, Sask. S0K 0M0 – 948-3911 – Mrs. Connie Eamon

Bruno Branch Library, Box 2, Bruno, Sask. S0K 0S0 – 369-2353 – Mrs. A. Krentz

Coleville Branch Library, Box 45, Coleville, Sask. S0L 0K0 – 965-2551 – Mrs. Chris Scott

Colonsay Branch Library, Box 172, Colonsay, Sask. S0K 0Z0 – 255-2662 – Mrs. Rose Hanson

Delisle Branch Library, Box 340, Delisle, Sask. S0L 0P0 – 493-2302 – Miss Rosalind Sandy

Dinsmore Branch Library, Box 369, Dinsmore, Sask. S0L 0T0 – 846-2011 – Mrs. Bertha Pflug

Dodsland Branch Library, Box 291, Dodsland, Sask. S0L 0V0 – 356-2180 – Mrs. Flora Campbell

Eatonia Branch Library, Box 100, Eatonia, Sask. S0L 0Y0 – 967-2224 – Mrs. Loretta Wiseman

Elrose Branch Library, Elrose, Sask. S0L 0Z0 – 378-2808 – Mrs. Catherine McDonald

Eston Branch Library, Box 487, Eston, Sask. S0L 1A0 – 962-3513 – Miss Joanne Portz

Hanley Branch Library, Box 263, Hanley, Sask. S0G 2E0 – 544-2546 – Mrs. Sonja English

Kenaston Branch Library, Box 41, Kenaston, Sask. S0G 2N0 – 252-2130 – Mrs. Doreen Kerpan

Kerrobert Branch Library, Box 104, Kerrobert, Sask. S0L 1R0 – 834-5211 – Mrs. B. Farquhar

Kindersley Branch Library, Box 1627, Kindersley, Sask. S0L 1S0 – 463-4141 – Mrs. Alice Lewis

Kyle Branch Library, Box 370, Kyle, Sask. S0L 1T0 – 375-2566 – Mrs. Margaret Larson

Landis Branch Library, Box 247, Landis, Sask. S0K 2K0 – 658-2177 – Mrs. Vera Halter

Lanigan Branch Library, Box 70, Lanigan, Sask. S0K 2M0 – 365-2472 – Mrs. Eva Klaassen

Lucky Lake Branch Library, Box 164, Lucky Lake, Sask. S0L 1Z0 – 858-2246 – Miss Joy McGregor

Luseland Branch Library, Box 40, Luseland, Sask. S0L 2A0 – 372-4808 – Mrs. Loverne Mercier

Nokomis Branch Library, Box 38, Nokomis, Sask. S0G 3R0 – 528-2251 – Mrs. Irene Proseilo

Osler Branch Library, Box 190, Osler, Sask. S0K 3A0 – 239-2155 – Mrs. Linda Ens

Outlook Branch Library, Box 547, Outlook, Sask. S0L 2N0 – 867-8823 – Mrs. Frances Davison

Perdue Branch Library, Box 253, Perdue, Sask. S0K 2C0 – 237-4227 – Mrs. Mabel Ellis

Plenty Branch Library, Box 70, Plenty, Sask. S0L 2R0 – 932-2045 – Mrs. Joyce Saxton

Rosetown Branch Library, Box 1208, Rosetown, Sask. S0L 2V0 – 882-3566 – Mrs. Jean Backlund

Rosthern Branch Library, Box 127, Rosthern, Sask. S0K 3R0 – 232-5377 – Mrs. Phyllis Henschel

Sonningdale Branch Library, Box 40, Sonningdale, Sask. S0K 4B0 – 237-9533 – Mrs. Dorothy Elliott

Stranraer Branch Library, Box 34, Stranraer, Sask. S0L 3B0 – 377-4670 – Mrs. Linda Ek

Unity Branch Library, Unity Sask. S0K 4L0 – 228-2802 – Mrs. Joyce Thurlow
Viscount Branch Library, Box 117, Viscount, Sask. S0K 4M0 – 944-2155 – Mrs. Henriette Morelli
Watrous Branch Library, Box 460, Watrous, Sask. S0K 4T0 – 946-3369 – Mrs. Magdolene Chamney
Wilkie Branch Library, Box 189, Wilkie, Sask. S0K 4W0 – 843-2616 – Mrs. Francis Weber
Young Branch Library, Box 288, Young, Sask. S0K 4Y0 – 259-2227 – Mrs. Lenore Mintkawetz

Regina Public Library

Ron Yeo, Librarian, 2311 12th Ave., Regina, Sask. S4P 0N3 – 569-7570 – Telex 071-2398

Saskatoon Public Library

Ms. Alice Turner, Librarian, 311 23rd St. E., Saskatoon, Sask. S7K 0J6 – 664-9556 – Telex 074-2661

Branches in Saskatoon

Carlyle King Library, 3130 Laurier Dr., Saskatoon, Sask. S7K 0J6 – 664-9592 – Linda Smith
Mayfair Library, 602 33rd St. W., Saskatoon, Sask. S7H 2C4 – 664-9591 – Gloria Kostyniuk
Sutherland Library, Central Ave. & 105th St., Saskatoon, Sask. S7H 2C4 – 664-9593 – Shirley Mogenson, Lib. Asst.
J.S. Wood Library, 1801 Lansdowne Ave., Saskatoon, Sask. S7H 2C4 – 664-9590 – Molly Stayner

Special & College Libraries & Resource Centres in Saskatchewan

With Contact Person (Librarian, unless otherwise indicated)

Area Code for Saskatchewan is 306

BATTLEFORD

Battleford National Historic Park, Campbell Innes Memorial Library, Box 70, Battleford, Sask. S0M 0E0 – 937-2621 – Mrs. M.A. Simpson, Supt.
Law Society of Saskatchewan Library, Court House, Battleford, Sask. S0M 0E0 – Mrs. Eileen G. Curry

CARONPORT

Briercrest Bible Institute, Archibald Library, Caronport, Sask. S0H 0S0 – 756-2321 – Allan Johnson

HUMBOLDT

Prairie Agricultural Machinery Institute Library, Box 1900, Humboldt, Sask. S0K 2A0 – 682-2555 – Miss Bernie Jansen

LA RONGE

Dept. of Northern Saskatchewan Library, Box 5000, La Ronge, Sask. S0J 1L0 – 425-4496 – Linda Maurer

MOOSE JAW

Aldersgate College, Wilson Memorial Library, Box 460, Moose Jaw, Sask. S6H 4P1 – 692-1816 – Mrs. Ruth Huston
Law Society Library, Court House, Moose Jaw, Sask. S6H 4P1 – 693-6105 – Paul Bozak
Saskatchewan Technical Institute Library, Box 1420, Moose Jaw, Sask. S6H 4R4 – 693-8236 – Ken Sagal
The Times Herald Library, 44 Fairford St. W., Moose Jaw, Sask. S6H 6E4 – 692-6441 – Joyce Walter

MUENSTER

St. Peter's Abbey & College Library, Box 10, Muenster, Sask. S0K 2Y0 – 682-3373 – Br. Bede M. Hubbard

PRINCE ALBERT

IDIG (Institute for the Development of Indian Government) Library, Dept. of Indian & Northern Affairs, 154 8th St. E., Prince Albert, Sask. S6V 5T2 – 764-5241 – Mrs. K. Toews
Law Society of Saskatchewan Library, Court House, Prince Albert, Sask. S6V 4W7 – 763-7273 – J.V. Hicks
Saskatchewan Dept. of Tourism & Renewable Resources, Forestry Branch Library, #300, Provincial Court Bldg., Prince Albert, Sask. S6V 1B5 – 922-3133
Saskatchewan Penitentiary Library, Box 160, Prince Albert, Sask. S6V 5R6 – 764-1586 – H. Walls
Victoria Union Hospital, Medical Library, 1200 24 St. W., Prince Albert, Sask. S6V 5T4 – 764-1551 – Mrs. J.I. Ryan, R.R.L.

REGINA

Agriculture Canada, Regional Development & International Affairs Branch Library, #101, 2050 Cornwall St., Regina, Sask. S4P 2K6 – 569-5545 – Miss H.C. Vanstone, Lib. Techn.
Agriculture Canada, Research Station Library, Box 440, Regina, Sask. S4P 3A2 – 585-0255 – Miss H.C. Vanstone, Lib. Techn.
Alcoholism Commission of Saskatchewan Library, 3475 Albert St., Regina, Sask. S4S 6X6 – 565-4656 – Ms. Susan Whittick
Allan Blair Memorial Clinic, Oncology Library, 1555 Pasqua St., Regina, Sask. S4T 4L8 – 527-9651, ext. 203
Atmospheric Environment Service, Weather Office Library, Terminal Bldg., Regina Airport, Regina, Sask. S4P 3W5 – 359-5740
Campion College Library, University of Regina, Regina, Sask. S4S 0A2 – 586-4242 – Ms. Myfanwy Truscott
Canada Dept. of Indian Affairs & Northern Development Library, 2332 11th Ave., Regina, Sask. S4P 2G7 – 359-6470 – Ernie Elkington
Canada Dept. of Regional Economic Expansion, PFRA Library, Canadian Motherwell Bldg., Regina, Sask. S4P 0R5 – 359-5100 – C. Kosack
Canadian Bible College Library, 4400 4th Ave., Regina, Sask. S4T 0H8 – 545-1515 – Ms. Marguerite Porter
Canadian Schizophrenia Foundation Library, 2229 Broad St., Regina, Sask. S4P 1Y7 – 527-7969 – Doris Rands
Consumer Affairs Resource Centre, see Sask. Dept. of Consumer Affairs
Court of Appeal Library, Court House, 2425 Victoria Ave., Regina, Sask. S4P 3V7 – 565-5411 – Mrs. R.M. Lidster
Departments of Government, See Saskatchewan Dept. of ...
Environment Canada, Inland Waters Directorate Library, 1901 Victoria Ave., Regina, Sask. S4P 3R4 – 359-5306 – Joan Prentice-Naqvi, B.A., M.L.
Gabriel Dumont Institute Library, 2505 11th Ave., #300, Regina, Sask. S4P 0A6 – 522-5691 – Sarah Lochhead
Law Society of Saskatchewan Library, Court House, Regina, Sask. S4P 3E4 – 569-8020 – D.T. MacEllven
Leader-Post Ltd. Library, 1964 Park St., Regina, Sask. S4S 3G4 – 527-8511, ext. 234 – Gloria Moor
Legislative Library, Room 234, Legislative Bldg., Regina, Sask. S4S 0B3 – 565-2277 – Ms. Christine MacDonald
Luther College, George W. Thorn Library, University of Regina, Regina, Sask. S4S 0A2 – 584-0255 – Mrs. Thelma Nabe
Museum of Natural History Library, Wascana Park, Regina, Sask. S4P 3V7 – 565-2808 – Mrs. R. Apperley
National Film Board Library, 2nd Floor, 1917 Broad St., Regina, Sask. S4P 1Y1 – 359-5012 – Tanya Owen
Ombudsman Library, 2310 Scarth St., Regina, Sask. S4P 3V7 – 565-6211
Pasqua Hospital Library, 4101 Dewdney Ave., Regina, Sask. S4T 1A5 – 527-9641, loc. 370 – Mrs. Leona Lang
Plains Health Centre Library, 4500 Wascana Pkwy., Regina, Sask. S4S 5W9 – 584-6426 – Beth Silzer
Prairie Farm Rehabilitation Administration, See Canada Dept. of Regional Economic Expansion
Provincial Library, 1352 Winnipeg St., Regina, Sask. S4P 3V7 – 565-2972
Regina Board of Education Library, 1870 Lorne St., Regina, Sask. S4P 2L9 – 569-3610 – Connie Acton
Regina General Hospital, Medical Library, 14th St. & St. Johns St., Regina, Sask. S4P 0W5 – 359-4444, ext. 4314 – Mrs. A. Belva Park, Reg. N., R.R.L.
Royal Canadian Mounted Police Training Academy Library, Box 6500, Regina, Sask. S4P 3J7 – 359-5824 – Ruth Hoffert
Saskatchewan Archives Library, 5th Floor, Library Bldg., University of Regina, Regina, Sask. S4S 0A2 – 565-4066 – Ian Wilson
Saskatchewan Bureau of Statistics Library, 2nd Floor, West Wing, T.C. Douglas Bldg., Regina, Sask. S4S 6X6 – 565-6333 – Shirley Sebastian
Saskatchewan Dept. of Agriculture Library, Walter Scott Bldg., Regina, Sask. S4S 0B1 – 565-5151 – Rhona A. Wright
Saskatchewan Dept. of Attorney General Library, 2476 Victoria Ave., Regina, Sask. S4P 3V7 – 565-5487 – A. Matz

Saskatchewan Dept. of Consumer & Commercial Affairs, Resource Centre, 1871 Smith St., Regina, Sask. S4P 3V7 – 565-5549 – Edith Berg

Saskatchewan Dept. of Continuing Education, Policy Planning & Information Systems Branch Resource Centre, 1855 Victoria Ave., Regina, Sask. S4P 3V5 – 565-5923

Saskatchewan Dept. of Co-operation Library, 2055 Albert St., Regina, Sask. S4P 3V7 – 565-5807 – Mrs. Rae French

Saskatchewan Dept. of Culture & Youth Library, 11th Floor, Avord Tower, 2002 Victoria Ave., Regina, Sask. S4P 3V7 – Gillian McCreary

Saskatchewan Dept. of Education Library, 7th Floor, Parkview Place, 2220 College Ave., Regina, Sask. S4P 3V7 – 565-5977 – Jane Naisbitt

Saskatchewan Dept. of Environment Library, 5th Floor, 1855 Victoria Ave., Regina, Sask. S4P 3V5 – 565-6125 – Mrs. S.G. Bellamy

Saskatchewan Dept. of Health Library, 3475 Albert St., Regina, Sask. S4S 6X6 – 565-3090 – M. Smigarowski

Saskatchewan Dept. of Highways & Transportation, Planning Branch Library, 1855 Victoria Ave., Regina, Sask. S4P 3V5 – 565-4777 – Roger P. Couturier, Dir.

Saskatchewan Dept. of Industry & Commerce Library, 7th Floor, Sask. Power Bldg., Regina, Sask. S4P 3V7 – 565-2254 – Ms. C. McNabb

Saskatchewan Dept. of Labour, Departmental Library, 1914 Hamilton St., 6th Floor, Regina, Sask. S4P 4V4 – 565-2429 – Fraser Russell

Saskatchewan Dept. of Labour, Occupational Health & Safety Division Library, 1150 Rose St., Regina, Sask. S4P 3V7 – 565-4494 – Susan Johnson

Saskatchewan Dept. of Labour, Women's Division Library, 1914 Hamilton St., Regina, Sask. S4P 4V4 – 565-2465 – Jane Coombe

Saskatchewan Dept. of Mineral Resources, Publications Office, 1914 Hamilton St., Regina, Sask. S4P 4V4 – 565-2528 – Mrs. Terry Theiss, i/c

Saskatchewan Dept. of Revenue, Supply & Services, Systems Centre Library, 3475 Albert St., Regina, Sask. S4S 6X6 – 565-2090 – H. Haig

Saskatchewan Dept. of Social Services Library, 1920 Broad St., Regina, Sask. S4P 3V6 – 565-3605 – Ms. Janice Watson

Saskatchewan Dept. of Tourism & Renewable Resources, Program Planning Branch Library, 3211 Albert St., Regina, Sask. S4S 5W6 – 565-3015

Saskatchewan Dept. of Urban Affairs Library, 1791 Rose St., Regina, Sask. S4S 0B1 – 565-2781 – D.W. Bennett

Saskatchewan Economic Development Corporation Library, 1106 Winnipeg St., Regina, Sask. S4R 6N9 – 565-7233 – Geraldine Vance

Saskatchewan Genealogical Society Library, Box 1894, Regina, Sask. S4P 3E1 – Beth White

Saskatchewan Government Executive Council, Photographic Art Library, Legislative Bldg., Regina, Sask. S4S 0B3 – 565-6298 – Dorothy Redlin

Saskatchewan Government Insurance, Ellen Basler Library, 4th Floor, 2260 11th Ave., Regina, Sask. S4P 0J9 – 565-1681

Saskatchewan Highway Traffic Board Library, 2260 11th Ave., 12th Floor, Regina, Sask. S4P 3V7 – 565-4039 – Karen Yuzik

Saskatchewan Housing Corporation Library, 9th Floor, 2500 Victoria Ave., Regina, Sask. S4P 3X2 – 565-4177 – Robert Hawkins

Saskatchewan Indian Federated College Library, University of Regina, Regina, Sask. S4S 0A2 – 584-8333 – Heather West

Saskatchewan Piping Industry, Joint Training Board Library, 1366 Cornwall St., Regina, Sask. S4R 2H5 – 522-4237 – Mrs. Jill Collins

Saskatchewan Power Corp. Library, Victoria & Scarth, Regina, Sask. S4P 0S1 – 525-7650

Saskatchewan Public Service Commission Resource Centre, 3211 Albert St., Regina, Sask. S4S 5W6 – 565-7517 – Beth Miller

Saskatchewan Registered Nurses Association Library, 2066 Retallack St., Regina, Sask. S4T 2K2 – 527-4643 – Jean Passmore

Saskatchewan Supt. of Insurance, Insurance & Real Estate Branch Library, #308, 1919 Rose St., Regina, Sask. S4P 3V7 – 565-2957 – D.M. King

Sask Tel Library, 2nd Floor, 2121 S. Railway St., Regina, Sask. S4P 2Y4 – 347-2237 – Basil Pogue

Saskatchewan Wheat Pool, Research Division Library, 2625 Victoria Ave., Regina, Sask. S4P 2Y6 – 569-4480 – A.D. McLeod, Dir., i/c

SASKMEDIA Resource Distribution Centre, 1112 Winnipeg St., Regina, Sask. S4P 3S7 – 565-5104 – Ms. N. Exner

University of Regina Library, Regina, Sask. S4S 0A2 – 584-4295
University Librarian – S. Harland
Assoc. Librarian, Public Services – Miss M.A. Hammond
Assoc. Librarian, Technical Services – S. Fielden
Education – D. Affleck
Fine Arts – Miss L. Eley

Wascana Hospital Library, 23rd Ave. & Ave. G, Regina, Sask. S4S 0A5 – 359-9230 – Lily Walter

Wascana Institute Resource & Information Centre, 4635 Wascana Pkwy., Regina, Sask. S4P 3A3 – 565-4321 – Pran Vohra

SASKATOON

Agriculture Canada, Research Station Library, 107 Science Cres., Saskatoon, Sask. S7N 0X2 – 343-8214 – E. Watson

Canada Dept. of Regional Economic Expansion Library, #814, 601 Spadina Cres. E., Saskatoon, Sask. S7K 3G8 – 665-4386 – David W. Giffen

Canadian Wildlife Service, Prairie Migratory Bird Research Centre Library, 115 Perimeter Rd., University of Saskatchewan Campus, Saskatoon, Sask. S7N 0X4 – 665-4096 – Mrs. D. Lapp

College of Emmanuel & St. Chad Library, 1337 College Dr., Saskatoon, Sask. S7N 0W6 – 343-3206 – Rosa Ho

Co-operative College of Canada Library, #141, 105 St. W., Saskatoon, Sask. S7N 1N3 – 373-0474 – Mrs. Leona Olson

Federation of Saskatchewan Indians, Saskatchewan Indian Cultural College Library, Box 3085, Saskatoon, Sask. S7K 3S9 – located at 1030 Idylwyld Dr. N. – 244-1146, ext. 46 – Maria Ahenakew

Kelsey Institute of Applied Arts & Sciences Library, Box 1520, Saskatoon, Sask. S7K 3R5 – 664-6417 – D.F. Robertson

Law Society of Saskatchewan Library, Court House, Saskatoon, Sask. S7K 3G7 – 664-5141 – Peta J. Bates

Lutheran Theological Seminary, Otto Olson Memorial Library, 114 Seminary Cres., Saskatoon, Sask. S7N 0X3 – 343-8204, ext. 01 – Mary Mitchell

MacNeill Clinic Library, 912 Idylwyld Dr. N., Saskatoon, Sask. S7K 0M5 – 664-5800 – Sophia Thompson

McKercher, McKercher, Stack etc. Law Library, 3rd Floor, 374 3rd Ave. S., Saskatoon, Sask. S7K 1M5 – 653-2000

Mohyla Institute Library, 1240 Temperance St., Saskatoon, Sask. S7N 0P1 – 653-1944 – F.J. Kindrachuk

National Research Council of Canada, Prairie Regional Laboratory Library, 110 Gymnasium Rd., Saskatoon, Sask. S7N 0W9 – 665-5256 – Mrs. Flora Chen

Nutana Collegiate Institute, Memorial Library & Art Gallery, 411 11th St. E., Saskatoon, Sask. S7N 0E9 – 653-1677 – Philip Listoe

POS Pilot Plant Corp. Library, University of Saskatchewan Campus, Saskatoon, Sask. S7N 2R4 – 665-7791 – Mark H. Reineke

St. Andrew's College Library, Saskatoon, Sask. S7N 0W3 – 343-6631 – Ms. Rosa Ho

St. Paul's Hospital Library, 1702 20th St. W., Saskatoon, Sask. S7M 0Z9 – 664-1438 – Patricia Munroe

St. Thomas More College, Shannon Library, 1437 College Dr., Saskatoon, Sask. S7N 0W6 – 343-4561 – Dr. Margot King

The Saskatoon Gallery & Conservatory Corp. (Mendel Art Gallery), Library, (950 Spadina Cres. E.), Box 569, Saskatoon, Sask. S7K 3L6 – 664-9610 – Joan Steel

Saskatchewan Association for the Mentally Retarded Library, 103 Central Chambers, 219 22nd St. E., Saskatoon, Sask. S7K 0G4 – 653-0141

Saskatchewan Real Estate Association Library, 2602 8th St. E., Saskatoon, Sask. S7H 0V7 – 373-3350 – Peggy Simenson

Saskatchewan Research Council Library, 30 Campus Dr., Saskatoon, Sask. S7N 0X1 – 664-5454 – S. Neary
Saskatchewan Teachers' Federation, Stewart Resources Centre, 2317 Arlington Ave., Box 1108, Saskatoon, Sask. S7K 3N3 – 373-7808 – Susan Dyer
Saskatoon Gallery & Conservatory Corporation Library, 950 Spadina Cres. E., Box 569, Saskatoon, Sask. S7K 3L6 – 664-9610 – Joan Steel
Saskatoon Mental Health Centre Library, 165 3rd Ave. S., Saskatoon, Sask. S7K 1L8 – 664-6500 – Donna Welykochy
Star-Phoenix Newspaper Library, 204 5 Ave. N., Saskatoon, Sask. S7K 2P1 – 664-8223 – Don Perkins
University of Saskatchewan, c/o Director of Libraries, Saskatoon, Sask. S7N 0W0 – 343-4216
University Librarian – N.A. Brown
Assoc. Librarian – M.M. Brady
Asst. Director of Libraries (Public Services) – P.A. Greig
Asst. Director of Libraries (Systems & Planning) – C. Lunau
Health Sciences – W. Sweaney
Instructional Resources – M. Baldock
Law – E. Stanek
Veterinary Medicine – J. James
Western Development Museum, George Shepherd Library, 2610 Lorne Ave. S., Box 1910, Saskatoon, Sask. S7K 3R5 – 652-1910

SWIFT CURRENT

Agriculture Canada, Research Station Library, Box 1030, Swift Current, Sask. S9H 3X2 – 773-4621 – Miss K.E. Wilton

WEYBURN

Souris Valley Extended Care Hospital, Medical Library, Box 2001, Weyburn, Sask. S4H 2L7 – 842-7481, loc. 344
Weyburn Psychiatric Centre Staff Library, Box 1056, Weyburn, Sask. S4H 2L4 – 842-5461 – Helen Sayyeau

WILCOX

Athol Murray College of Notre Dame, Lane Hall Memorial Library, Box 280, Wilcox, Sask. S0G 5E0 – 732-2080, ext. 29 – Ellen Basler

YORKTON

Parkland Community College, University Division Library, 185 Gladstone Ave. N., S3N 2A9 – 782-6166 – Sister Cornelia Mantyka

YUKON LIBRARIES

The Library Services Branch, Department of Library/Information Resources, Government of the Yukon Territory is responsible for a variety of services including the direct provision of public library service to Yukon communities, centralized acquisition and processing of school library materials, and the centralization and distribution of a 16mm film collection. Other branches of the department include the Yukon Archives which includes records management services to all Territorial Government Departments. Public Library Service is provided through a system of small community book stations and branch libraries. Branch libraries are maintained in Dawson City, Elsa, Faro, Haines Junction, Mayo, Watson Lake, Whitehorse.

Library Services Branch: Jean Dirksen, Territorial Librarian, Box 2703, Whitehorse, Yukon Y1A 2C6.

Dept. of Library/Information Resources: Garth Graham, Director, Box 2703, Whitehorse, Yukon Y1A 2C6.

NORTHWEST TERRITORIES LIBRARIES

Library service for the Northwest Territories is based on a Territorial Library System, with the Headquarters of the service at Hay River, N.W.T. The name is Northwest Territories Public Library Services and there are member libraries at Aklavik; Cambridge Bay; Cape Dorset; Coppermine; Eskimo Point; Fort McPherson; Fort Norman; Fort Simpson; Fort Smith; Frobisher Bay; Hay River (in conjunction with the headquarters); Igloolik; Inuvik; Nanisivik; Norman Wells; Pangnirtung; Pine Point; Rankin Inlet; Spence Bay; Tuktoyaktuk and Yellowknife.

Special & College Libraries in the Territories

With Contact Person (Librarian, unless otherwise indicated)

Area Code for the Territories is 403

INUVIK

Inuvik Scientific Resource Centre, Box 1430, Inuvik, N.W.T. – 979-3838

WHITEHORSE

Environmental Protection Service Library, Room 225, Federal Bldg., Whitehorse, Y.T. Y1A 2B5 – 667-6487 – Wendy Chambers
Law Library, Yukon Supreme Court, Whitehorse, Y.T. Y1A 2B5 – 667-4431 – Dorothy DeHart

YELLOWKNIFE

Canadian Forces Northern Region Headquarters Reference Library, Box 6666, Yellowknife, N.W.T. X1A 2R3 – 873-4011, ext. 43
Government In-Service Library, Government of the N.W.T., Yellowknife, N.W.T. X1A 2L9
Indian & Northern Affairs Library, Box 1500, Yellowknife, N.W.T. X1A 2R3 – 920-8252 – Mrs. M.V. Huber, act.

ART GALLERIES AND MUSEUMS

THE NATIONAL MUSEUMS OF CANADA

West Tower, L'Esplanade Laurier, 300 Laurier Ave. W., Ottawa, Ont. K1A 0M8
(613) 995-9832

The National Museums of Canada is a Crown Corporation established in 1968 to federate under one administration four existing museum activities: the National Museum of Natural Sciences; the National Museum of Man (including the Canadian War Museum); the National Gallery of Canada; and the National Museum of Science & Technology (including the National Aeronautical Collection). The corporation reports to Parliament through the Secretary of State.

Secretary General, Ian Christie Clark
Asst. Secretary General, National Programs, R.W. Nichols
Asst. Secretary General, Corporate Management, Jacques Coulombe
Director, Information Services, J.-A. Sorel

National Museum of Natural Sciences

Metcalfe & McLeod Sts., Ottawa
(613) 996-3102

The Museum consists of six divisions: Botany, Mineral Sciences, Palaeobiology, Vertebrate Zoology, Invertebrate Zoology, and Interpretation and Extension. Six exhibit halls on Birds, Mammals, Prehistoric Life, Geology, Animal Life, and Plant Life and a special exhibit area are in the Victoria Memorial Museum Building. Large research collections are maintained by the Museum and these collections are open to study by qualified students and others.

Director, Dr. Louis Lemieux
Asst. Director, Operations & Research, F.H. Schultz
Asst. Director, Administration, C. Eades
Senior Scientist, E.L. Bousfield
Scientific Advisor, Dr. D.J. Faber
Botany Division, Chief, Dr. J.H. Soper
Verterbrate Zoology Division, Chief, Dr. H. Ouellet
Invertebrate Zoology Division, Chief, C. Gruchy
Palaeobiology Division, Chief, Dr. D.A. Russell
Mineral Sciences Division, Chief, R. Williams
Interpretation & Extension Division, Chief, J.S. Whiting

Zooarchaeological Identification Centre, Head, Mrs. A. Rick
Public Relations Officer, Louise Leclair

The National Museum of Man

Metcalfe & McLeod Sts., Ottawa
(613) 992-3497

The National Museum of Man is concerned with the archaeology, ethnology, physical anthropology, ethnolinguistics, ethnohistory, folklore and history of Canada. Its study collections, which are open to research by properly qualified students, include archaeological, ethnological and physical anthropology specimens, also historic and folk culture materials. Folksong collections include Indian, French-Canadian, British-Canadian and new Canadian recordings. Scientific and educational publications are available for distribution. The Canadian War Museum (330 Sussex Dr.), a component of the National Museum of Man, is concerned with research collections, exhibits and publications in Canadian military history.

Director, Dr. William E. Taylor, Jr.
Asst. Director, Operations, Mike Carrol
Asst. Director, Public Programs, Frank Corcoran
Archaeological Survey of Canada, Chief, Dr. Roger Marois
Canadian Ethnology Service, Chief, Annette McFayden Clark
Canadian Centre for Folk Culture Studies, Chief, Dr. Pierre Crépeau
History Division, Chief, Dr. Fred J. Thorpe
Canadian War Museum, Chief Curator, Lee F. Murray
Education & Cultural Affairs Division, Chief, Lorna Kee, act.
National Programs Division, Chief, Sylvie Morel-Hall, act.

The National Gallery of Canada

Lorne Bldg., Elgin & Slater Sts., Ottawa
(613) 992-4636

The permanent collection of the National Gallery consists mainly of painting, sculpture, prints and drawings from the European and Canadian schools. In 1957 the development of a Conservation and Scientific Research Division, as applied to works of art, was begun and is now the Canadian Conservation Institute, a component of the National Museums of Canada.

Exhibitions of art collections from its own holdings, from private and public sources and from abroad are organized and circulated nationally and internationally. Services offered to the general public across Canada include films, publications and reproduction of works of art. Lecture tours are organized.

Director, vacant
Special Advisor, J. Martin
Building Project Leader, Gyde V. Shepherd
Asst. Director, Public Programs, vacant
Asst. Director, Admin., K. Krug
Asst. Director, Collections & Research, Brydon Smith
Asst. Curator of Contemporary Art, Jessica Bradley
Research Curator of Canadian Art, J.R. Ostiguy
Curator, Canadian Art, Charles Hill
Asst. Curator, Early Canadian Art, R. Fox
Curator of Drawings, Mimi Cazort
Curator of Prints, D. Druick
Curator of Photography, J. Borcoman
Curator of European Art, Myron Laskin, Jr.
Asst. Curator of European Art, Catherine Johnston
Head, Restoration & Conservation Laboratory, Ursus Dix
Chief Librarian, Jacqueline Hunter
Chief, Exhibitions, Darcy Edgar
Head of Publications, P. Smith
Head, Education Services, Lorna Johnson
Registrar, A. Fronton
Chief of Information & Public Relations, Janine Smiter

National Museum of Science & Technology

1867 St. Laurent Blvd., Ottawa
(613) 998-4566

Visitors to this museum are invited to work the exhibits themselves, to learn in a concrete way the abstract principles that underlie such technologies as ground transportation, aviation, agriculture, shipping, industrial technologies, physics, computer science and astronomy, from early times to the present. Clocks, automobiles and buggies, trains and fire engines, music boxes and telephones make up some of the Museum's many collections.

The National Aeronautical Collection, part of the National Museum of Science and Technology, is in three hangars at Rockcliffe Airport, Ottawa. Forty four of the ninety-eight aircraft in the collection are on display, showing the history of flight, with emphasis on Canadian achievements.

Director, Dr. D.M. Baird
Executive Asst., J.P. Malone
Asst. Director, Administration, R. Mayost
Curators:
- Aviation & Space, R.W. Bradford
- Agricultural Technology, T.A. Brown
- Industrial Technology, R.J. Corby
- Communications Technology, E.A. DeCoste
- General Technology, J.J. Dost
- Registrar, R. Tropea

ALBERTA

Provincial Museum of Alberta

12845 102 Ave., Edmonton, Alta. T5N 0M6
(403) 427-1730

Major collections and exhibits of Alberta's natural and human history, including habitat groups, dinosaurs, native cultures, social history. Frequent changing exhibits from other collections, loan exhibits throughout Canada. Bookshop, publications information service, films, lectures, live demonstrations and performances. Special programs for schools and other groups.

Director, Dr. John Lunn
Head Curator of Natural History, David A. E. Spalding
Head Curator of Human History, Eric C. Waterton
Public Programs Supervisor, Charles Williams
Exhibition Supervisor, Gordon E. Johnston
Conservator, Elizabeth Mibach

The Edmonton Art Gallery

2 Sir Winston Churchill Sq., Edmonton, Alta. T5J 2C1
(403) 429-6781

Collections: Canadian art; international contemporary art; Canadian painting from Krieghoff to present, sculpture, graphics; photographs.

Research Fields: Western Canadian art, historical and contemporary art; sculpture, graphics; photography; ceramics; art criticism.

Activities: Guided tours; lectures; films; gallery talks; concerts; dance recitals; rental gallery, formally organized education programs for children and adults, docent program workshops and seminars, temporary travelling and extension exhibitions; Junior Gallery and experimental art education.

Facilities: 2,000 + vol. library of art reference books, slides, periodicals and catalogues available for inter-library loans and research by permission; 8 exhibition rooms; 210 seat auditorium; classrooms. Art books; handicrafts; ceramics, prints and reproductions for sale.

Glenbow-Alberta Institute

130 9th Ave. S.E., Calgary, Alta. T2G 0P3 (403) 264-8300

The Institute and its subsidiaries, Glenbow Foundation and Luxton Museum Ltd., operate two museums in Alberta: the Luxton Museum in Banff and the Glenbow Museum in Calgary.

Director, Duncan F. Cameron

Glenbow Museum

130 9th Ave. S.E., Calgary, Alta. T2G 0P3
264-8300

The Glenbow Museum has an exhibition program that is intended to interpret the history of man through his art and lifestyles, with emphasis on the history of western Canada, and features Glenbow's own permanent collection and world-class, travelling exhibits. The Museum also has an Archives; Library; an Education & Extension Department; Art Department; Ethnology Department; Cultural History Department; Mineralogy Section; and a Museum Shop.

The Luxton Museum

Box 850, Banff, Alta. T0L 0C0
(403) 762-2388

The Luxton Museum features displays and dioramas of early native life in western Canada.

Other Museums and Art Galleries in Alberta

Alberta Beach: Garden Park Farm Museum, Alberta Beach, Alta. T0E 0A0 (15 buildings and 222,000 displays on 3 acres). Guided tours and teaching of cement sculpture, stone work & taxidermy. Director, John H. Oselies.

Alix: Alix Wagon Wheel Regional Museum, c/o Mrs. Alice Whitfield, Alix, Alta. T0C 0B0 (403/747-2462)

Andrew: Andrew & Dist. Local History Museum, Andrew, Alta. T0B 0C0, Suprv., Mrs. G. Topolnisky (403/365-3606)

Ardrossan: Alberta Game Farm, 15 miles east of Edmonton on Hwy. 14. 3,000 animals of 100 species. Open year round. Guided tours. Director, Dr. Al Oeming, R.R. 4, Sherwood Park, Alta. T8A 3K4 (403/922-3013)

Banff: Peter & Catharine Whyte Foundation: Archives of the Canadian Rockies: collections of photographs, maps, books, tape recordings and manuscripts pertaining to the mountain areas of Western Canada; Peter Whyte Gallery program of continually changing exhibits from other collections as well as its own collection of mountain paintings. Administrator, E.J. Hart, 111 Bear St., Box 160, T0L 0C0 (403/762-2291)

Banff: Banff Natural History Museum. Director, Park Supt., Box 900, T0L 0C0 (403/762-3324, loc. 231)

Banff: Luxton Museum, see Glenbow-Alberta Institute

Banff: Walter Phillips Gallery, The Banff Centre, Box 1020, T0L 0C0 (403/762-6281)

Barrhead: Centennial Museum, Barrhead, Alta. T0G 0E0, President, E. Nicol

Beaverlodge: South Peace Centennial Museum, Director, Gordon McLean, Box 493, T0H 0C0 (403/354-8869)

Calgary: Alta. College of Art Gallery, (contemporary temporary exhibitions) Curator, Val Greenfield, 1301-16th Ave. N.W., T2M 0L4 (403/284-8661)

Calgary: Centennial Planetarium (Planetarium & Aero-Space Science Centre & Fort Calgary Interpretive Centre), Director, S. Wieser, Mewata Park, T2P 2M5 (403/264-2030)

Calgary: Heritage Park. Manager, W. J. Campbell, 1900 Heritage Dr. S.W., T2V 2X3 (Pioneer Village) (403/255-1182)

Calgary: Lord Strathcona's Horse (Royal Canadians) Regimental Museum, Bldg. BG, Currie Barracks, Canadian Forces Base Calgary, T3E 1T8 (403/242-6610)

Calgary: Nickle Arts Museum, University of Calgary, 2500 University Dr. N.W., T2N 1N4. Administrator, Richard Graburn (403/284-7234)

Calgary: P.P.C.L.I. Regimental Museum, Currie Barracks, T3E 1T8, Curator, Regimental Adjutant (403/246-7525)

Calgary: Sam Livingston Fish Hatchery, 1440 17A St. S.E., T2G 4T9, Supt., W. Schenk (403/261-6561)

Calgary: Univ. of Calgary Museum of Zoology, Univ. of Calgary, T2N 1N4, Curator, A.P. Russell (403/284-5269)

Camrose: Camrose & Dist. Museum Society, T4V 0M3. President, A.J. Vikse, 4702 50th St. (403/672-5350)

Cardston: C.O. Card Home & Museum and Old Court House Museum, Box 280, T0K 0K0

Castor: Castor & Dist. Museum, Box 92, T0C 0X0

Claresholm: Willow Creek Historical Museum. Custodian, Mrs. Mae Weber, Box 397, T0L 0T0 (403/625-3427)

Claresholm: Claresholm Museum, c/o Recreation Dept., Box 1000, T0L 0T0 (403/625-3381)

Cochrane: Cochrane Ranche Historic Site, c/o Alta. Culture, Historic Sites Service, Old St. Stephen's College, 8820 112 St., Edmonton, Alta. T6G 2P8 (403/932-3242; 427-5708)

Colinton: Kinnoull Park, Box 61, T0G 0R0 (403/695-4535)

Coutts: Belmore's Altamont Museum, Box 176, T0K 0N0. King size 'One in a Million' Educational displays, with something for everyone from a postage stamp to a 1903 oil rigg including Art and Natural History. Curator, B.H. Schultz (403/344-3888)

Czar: Prairie Panorama Museum, Custodian, Mrs. Harold Almberg, Czar, Alta. T0B 0Z0

Drumheller: Dinosaur Fossil Museum, 335 1st St. E., Box 2135, T0J 0Y0 (403/823-2593)

Drumheller: Homestead Antique Museum, Box 700, T0J 0Y0 (403/823-2600)

Duchess: Frontier Memorial Arena & Museum, c/o Mrs. June Endersby, Duchess, Alta. T0J 0Z0 (403/378-4671)

Dunvegan: Historic Dunvegan (c/o Alberta Culture, Historic Sites Service, Old St. Stephen's College, 8820 112 St., Edmonton, Alta. T6G 2P8) (403/427-5708)

Edmonton: Man & Telecommunication, Alta. Government Telephones' historic and current display, Vista 33, 33rd floor, Telephone Tower, 10020-100 St., Box 2411, T5J 0N5 (403/425-3978)

Edmonton: George McDougall Museum, Fort Edmonton Park, Whitemud Rd., T5J 0K1

Edmonton: Oblate Archives. Archivist, Dr. E. O. Drouin, o.m.i., 9916-110 St., T5K 1J3 (403/488-6277)

Edmonton: Parks & Recreation, 10th floor, CN Tower, T5J 0K1 (403/428-3534):
- General Manager, H. Monroe
- Artifacts & Restoration Centre, Saskatchewan Drive & Old Fort Rd. (434-0644)
- City of Edmonton Archives, 10105 112 Ave., T5G 0H1 (479-2060)
- Fort Edmonton, Whitemud Rd. (436-5566)
- John Janzen Nature Centre, Whitemud Rd. (434-7446)
- John Walter Site, 10627 93 Ave. (436-5565)
- Muttart Conservatory, 9626 96A St. (428-3664)
- Queen Elizabeth Planetarium, Coronation Park (452-9100)
- Valley Zoo, 132 St. & Buena Vista Rd. (483-5511)

Edmonton: Rutherford House, 11153 Saskatchewan Dr. (c/o Alberta Culture, Historic Sites Service, Old St. Stephen's College, 8820 112 St., T6G 2P8) (403/427-3995; 427-5708)

Edmonton: Ukrainian Museum of Canada, President, Mrs. N. Seniw, 10611 110 Ave., T5H 1H7

Edmonton: Univ. of Alta., Ring House Gallery, T6G 2E2, Director, H. Collinson

Elk Island: Elk Island National Park, R.R. #1, Fort Saskatchewan, Alta. T8L 2N7 (403/998-3781)

Elk Point: Fort George Museum, Box 66, T0A 1A0

Evansberg: Pembina Lobstick Historical Museum, c/o A. L. Fausak, Evansberg, Alta. T0E 0T0

Fort Macleod: Historical Museum, Box 776, T0L 0Z0, Director/Curator, Grant Tolley

Fort Saskatchewan: Museum & Historic Site, 10104 101 St., T8L 1V9 (403/998-2407)

Girouxville: Girouxville Museum & Sanctuaire N-D de Lourdes, Box 129, T0H 1S0

Grande Prairie: Pioneer Museum, Box 687, T8V 3A8, President, Bert Tieman (403/532-2897; museum phone 532-5482)

Hanna: Pioneer Museum. Secretary, Mrs. R. Walker, Box 1137, T0J 1P0 (403/854-4244)

High Prairie: High Prairie & Dist. Museum & Historical Society, Secretary, Wm. E. Marx, Box 1464, T0G 1E0 (403/523-3838)

High River: Museum of the Highwood, Curator, Don King, Box 456, T0L 1B0 (403/652-3080; museum phone 652-7156)

Hinton: Alta. Forest Service Museum, 1176 Switzer Dr., T0E 1B0 (403/865-3361)

Iddesleigh: Rainy Hills Pioneer Exhibits, Iddesleigh, Alta. T0J 1T0, President, Mrs. Lucille Olson (403/898-2511)

Innisfail: Historical Village Museum, Box 642, T0M 1A0 (403/227-9025) May-Sept. 1

Irvine: Irvine Museum, Box 90, T0J 1V0 (403/834-3923)
Islay: Morrison Museum of the Country School, c/o Allen Ronaghan, Box 120, T0B 2J0
Lethbridge: Fort Whoop-up, Box 1074, T1J 4A2. General Manager, Earl A. Simmonds (403/329-0444)
Lethbridge: Sir Alexander Galt Museum. Supervisor, W. J. (Jack) Elliott, Community Services Dept., T1J 0P6 (403/328-6455)
Lethbridge: Southern Alta. Art Gallery, 601 3rd Ave. S., T1J 0H4 (403/327-8770)
Lethbridge: Univ. of Lethbridge Art Gallery, Lethbridge, Alta. T1K 3M4, Director, B.J. McCarroll (403/379-2691)
Lloydminster: Barr Colony Museum, 5011 49 Ave., S9V 0T8 (403/825-6184)
Lougheed: Iron Creek Museum, Box 6, T0B 2V0
Medicine Hat: Medicine Hat Museum & Art Gallery, 1302 Bomford Cres. S.W., T1A 5E6. Director, T.A. Willock (403/527-6266)
Mundare: Museum of the Basilian Fathers, Box 379, T0B 3H0 (403/764-3860)
Oyen: Crossroads Museum, Box 9, T0J 2J0
Patricia: Dinosaur Provincial Park, Dept. of Recreation & Parks, Parks Division, Box 60, Patricia, Alta. T0J 2K0 (403/378-4587)
Peace River: Centennial Museum, Box 747, T0H 2X0, Director, Murray Cook (403/624-4261)
Pincher Creek: Pincher Creek Museum & Kootenai Brown Historical Park, Box 1226, T0K 1W0 (403/627-3684)
Ponoka: Alta. Hospital Museum, Box 1000, T0C 2H0 – temporarily closed for re-org.
Ponoka: Fort Ostell Museum, Box 2192, T0C 2H0
Red Deer: Red Deer & Dist. Museum & Archives, Box 762, T4N 5H2. Director, F. Morris Flewwelling (403/343-6844)
Rimbey: Pas-ka-Poo Historical Park, c/o Mrs. R. White, Rimbey, Alta. T0C 2J0
Rosebud: Centennial Museum. Rosebud Lion's Club, c/o Jim Finley, Pres., Rosebud, Alta. TOJ 2TO
St. Albert: Father Lacombe Museum. Curator, Mrs. Arlene Borgstede, Box 98, T8N 1N2 (403/459-8601)
Sangudo: Lac Sainte Anne & Dist. Historical Society Pioneer Museum, c/o Mrs. F. Weiss, Box 55, T0E 2A0 (403/785-2481)
Smoky Lake: Fort Victoria Museum, Box 178, T0A 3C0
Stony Plain: Multicultural Heritage Centre, 5411 51st St., T0E 2G0 (403/963-2777)
Viking: Viking Historical Museum, President, John Heslop, Box 232, T0B 4N0 (403/336-3406)
Wainwright: Wainwright Museum, c/o Battle River Historical Society, Box 99, T0B 4P0. Secretary, Mrs. W.C. Taylor (403/842-3183)
Wetaskiwin: Reynolds Museum, Hwy. 2A, 1,000 Antique & Classic Cars, Trucks, 600 Gas Tractors, 200 Steam Engines, Gas Engines, Motorcycles, Airplanes, Carriages, Sleighs. Also Bicycles, Machinery, Weapons, Guns, Fossils, Indian & Eskimo Artifacts, etc., Open Daily May 1 to Oct. 1, Box 6780, T9A 2G4 (403/352-5201)
Willingdon: Historic Village & Pioneer Museum, Box 147, T0B 4R0

BRITISH COLUMBIA

British Columbia Provincial Museum

Heritage Court, 601 Belleville St., Victoria, B.C. V8V 1X4
(604) 387-3701

Founded in 1886, the B.C. Provincial Museum has specialized in zoology, botany, archaeology and ethnology with the addition over the years of divisions in history, marine biology and linguistics. Service divisions cover the fields of Conservation, Education and Extension, Display and Administration.

Director, R. Y. Edwards
Asst. Director, W.D. Barkley
Administrative Officer, D. Lockhart
Division Curators
- Archaeology, D. N. Abbott
- Aquatic Zoology, Dr. A.E. Peden
- Botany, Dr. R.T. Ogilvie
- Entomology, R. Cannings
- Ethnology, P. L. Macnair
- Modern History, D. T. Gallacher
- Linguistics, Dr. B. Efrat
- Vertebrate Zoology, Dr. E.H. Miller

Service Divisions
- Chief Conservator, R.B. Renshaw-Beauchamp
- Chief of Exhibits, A.M. James
- Chief of Education & Extension, Shirley Cuthbertson
- Museums Advisor, J. Adams

Other Museums and Art Galleries in British Columbia

Abbotsford: Matsqui-Sumas-Abbotsford Museum Society, 2313 Ware St., V2S 3C6. Curator, Mrs. Diane Kelly (604/853-0313)
Alert Bay: Public Library & Museum, Box 208, V0N 1A0 (604/974-5721)
Ashcroft: Ashcroft Museum, Box 129, VOK 1AO (604/453-9161)
Atlin: Atlin Museum, Box 111, VOW 1AO. President, Shirley Connoly
Barkerville: Barkerville Historic Park, Barkerville, B.C. VOK 1BO (Curator, 604/994-3209)
Black Creek: Miracle Beach Provincial Park Nature House, R.R. 1, VOR 1CO, Attn.: District Supt.
Britannia Beach: B.C. Museum of Mining, Box 155, VON 1JO (604/688-8735)
Burnaby: Burnaby Art Gallery. Fine Arts Exhibits, 6344 Gilpin St., V5G 2J3 (604/291-9441)
Campbell River: Campbell River & Dist. Museum & Archives, 1235 Island Hwy., V9W 2C7. Curator, Ms. Jay S. Stewart (604/287-3103)
Chilliwack: Canadian Military Engineers Museum, C.F.S.M.E., M.P.O. 612, CFB Chilliwack, B.C. VOX 2EO
Cranbrook: The Railway Museum, 1 Van Horne St. N. (Box 400, V1C 4H9) (604/489-3918). Open year round, daily June-Sept., 5 days/week Oct-May. Features the last restored A-Class CPR dining car in Canada, and other 1929 CPR cars.
Duncan: B.C. Forest Museum, R.R. 4, V9L 3W8 (administered by the B.C. Forest Museum Society) (604/748-9389)
Fort Steele: Fort Steele Provincial Historic Park, Park Manager, Struan Robertson, Fort Steele, B.C. V0B 1N0 (604/489-3351) Open year round. (Restored 1890's Boom Town of the East Kootenays)
Gilford Island: Na Wa La Gwa Tsi, Box 177, Alert Bay, B.C. V0N 1A0
Grand Forks: Boundary Museum Society, Box 422, V0H 1H0 (604/442-3737)
Greenwood: Greenwood Museum, (Old Jail, Old Supreme Court), Box 399, VOH 1JO. Curator Secretary, Art Gough
Harrison Mills: Kilby Historic Park, 215 Kilby Rd., VOM 1LO. Park Suprv., C.T. Wood (604/796-9576)
Hazelton: Ksan Indian Village Museum, Box 326, V0J 1Y0 (604/842-5544)
Kamloops: Kamloops Museum & Archives, 207 Seymour St., V2C 2E7. Curator/Archivist, Ken Favrholdt (604/372-9931)
Kaslo: Langham Cultural Society Galleries, Box 1000, V0G 1M0
Kelowna: Father Pandosy Mission Restoration Committee of the Okanagan Historical Society. Chairman, G.D. Cameron, 1073 Guisachan Rd., V1Y 7X3 (604/762-6078)
Kelowna: Kelowna Centennial Museum, and National Exhibit Centre, 470 Queensway, V1Y 6S7. Curator, Ursula Surtees (604/763-2417)
Nanaimo: Centennial Museum, 100 Cameron Rd., V9R 2X1. Curator, Barrie Hardcastle (604/753-1821)
Nelson: Kootenay Museum, 402 Anderson St., V1L 3Y3. Curator, W. A. Fetterley
New Westminster: Irving House Historic Centre and Royal City Museum, 302 Royal Ave., V3L 1H7. Curator, Archie W. Miller (604/521-7656)

North Vancouver: Ecology Centre, Lynn Canyon Park (c/o Dist. Municipal Hall, 355 W. Queens Rd., North Vancouver, B.C. V7L 4K1) (604/987-5922)

North Vancouver: North Shore Museum & Archives, Director, W.H.J. Baker, 209 W. 4th St., V7M 1H8 (604/987-5618)

Osoyoos: Osoyoos Museum & Archives, Box 791, VOH 1VO (604/495-6723) Open daily May to Sept.

Penticton: Penticton Art Gallery, 785 Main St., V2A 5E3. Director, John R. Taylor (604/493-2928)

Penticton: R.N. (Reg) Atkinson Museum, 785 Main St., V2A 5E3, Curator, Jos. G. Harris (604/492-6025)

Prince George: Fort George Regional Museum, Box 1779, V2L 4V7. President, T. Williams, Coordr., D. McCallum (604/562-1612)

Prince Rupert: Museum of Northern B.C., Box 669, V8J 3S1 (604/624-3207)

Princeton: Princeton & Dist. Pioneer Museum, Box 687, V0X 1W0

Shuswap Lake: Nature House, R.R. 1, Chase, B.C. V0E 1M0, Park Supervisor, P. V. Rathbone (604/955-2217)

Vancouver: Kenneth G. Heffel Fine Art Inc., 2247 Granville St., V6H 3G1 (604/732-6505)

Vancouver: Vancouver Museums & Planetarium, 1100 Chestnut St., V6J 3J9 (604/736-4431). Includes Centennial Museum, Maritime Museum, (including the R.C.M.P. schooner St. Roch), and H. R. MacMillan Planetarium.

Vancouver: The Vancouver Art Gallery, 1145 W. Georgia St., V6E 3H2, Director, Luke Rombout (604/682-5621)

Vancouver: Univ. of B.C. Museum of Anthropology, Vancouver, B.C. V6T 1W5, Director, Dr. Michael Ames (604/228-3825)

Vancouver: Univ. of B.C., The M.Y. Williams Geological Museum, Vancouver, B.C. V6T 2B4, Head of Dept. of Geological Sciences, H.J. Greenwood, Ph.D.; Curator, J. Nagel (604/228-5586)

Vernon: Vernon Museum, Art Gallery & Archives, 3009-32nd Ave., V1T 2L8 (604/542-3142)

Victoria: Helmcken House Museum, 638 Elliott St., V8V 1W1. Maintained by Provincial Archives, c/o Min. of Provincial Secretary, Parliament Bldgs., V8W 1X4. Resident Curator, Mrs. M. Pettigrew (604/387-3440)

Victoria: Art Gallery of Greater Victoria, 1040 Moss St., V8V 4P1. Director, Patricia E. Bovey (604/384-4101)

Victoria: Craigflower Manor Historic House, 110A Island Hwy., V9B 1E9. Maintained by Heritage Conservation Branch, c/o Min. of Provincial Secretary, Parliament Bldgs. Resident Curator, Mrs. J. Thompson (604/387-3067)

Victoria: Maritime Museum of B.C., 28 Bastion Sq., V8W 1H9. Director, Capt. A.K. Cameron (604/385-4222; 386-7622)

Victoria: Point Ellice House, 2616 Pleasant St., V8T 4V3 (604/385-3837) (maintained by Min. of Provincial Secretary & Government Services, Parliament Bldgs., Victoria, B.C.)

Victoria: Provincial Archives of B.C., Parliament Bldgs., V8V 1X4. Archivist, John A. Bovey (604/387-5885)

Wells: Wells Museum, Wells Historical Society, Box 244, V0K 2R0

MANITOBA

Manitoba Museum of Man and Nature

190 Rupert Ave., Winnipeg, Man. R3B 0N2
(204) 956-2830

Seven permanent galleries and Alloway Hall which houses temporary and travelling exhibitions. *Permanent galleries are: Orientation* (in which the main theme of the Museum is expounded); *Earth History* (provides the broad geological background of the province which set the stage for the evolution of man and nature in the province); *Grasslands* (in the south of Manitoba); *Urban* (a section of Winnipeg, reconstructed as it might have been in 1920); *Nonsuch* (a replica of the 17th century Hudson Bay ship); *Arctic-Subarctic* (how native people and white man have interrelated with their environment); and *Boreal Forest* (coniferous trees, towering cliffs and icy streams).

The *Planetarium* provides educational and entertaining programs for the general public and school groups in the 287-seat Star Theatre. It also maintains a 7,500 square foot exhibit hall, the *Hall of Astronomy,* which deals with various topics in astronomy and space travel.

Also: The Education and Extension Departments provides special programs for schools and other groups; live demonstrations and performances; films; lectures; gift shop; book shop.

Executive Director, Dr. H. D. Hemphill
Museum Director, Dr. R.E. Wrigley
Planetarium Director, R.J. Ballantyne
Administrative Director, T.W. Nickle

The Winnipeg Art Gallery

300 Memorial Blvd., Winnipeg, Man. R3C 1V1
(204) 786-6641

History: Founded in 1912, the gallery opened in its present location in 1971.

Collections: A permanent collection of over 11,000 works of art that includes: Canadian, Inuit (largest collection in the Western World), Lord and Lady Gort Collection (Gothic and Renaissance panel painting), Masters prints and drawings (15th to 20th C.), Modern European, Decorative Arts and Photography.

Facilities: 120,000 sq. ft. building with 9 major galleries; 25,000 sq. ft. outdoor sculpture court; Clara Lander Library – 11,100 volume collection; Muriel Richardson Auditorium – 325 seats; studio facilities, lecture and seminar rooms, Gallery Shop, Gallery Restaurant, Art Rental and Sales Gallery.

Activities: guided tours, lectures, films, concerts, dance-recitals, drama, studio art classes, extension exhibitions, and courses in conjunction with the University of Winnipeg.

Other Museums and Art Galleries in Manitoba

Austin: Man. Agricultural Museum, 2 miles S. of No. 1 Hwy. on No. 34 Hwy. Admr., T. Farley, Box 10, R0H 0C0 (204/637-2354) (pioneer artifacts; homesteaders' village; annual Thresherman's Reunion & Stampede)

Boissevain: Beckoning Hills Museum, Hwy 10, President, Cecil Deacon, Boissevain, Man. R0K 0E0 (204/534-6468)

Bowsman: McKay's Museum, 12 miles N.E. of Bowsman on Lenswood Rd., R0L 0H0 (204/238-4412)

Brandon: Brandon Allied Arts Council, 1036 Louise Ave., R7A 0Y1. Executive Director, Mrs. Mary Louise Perkios (204/727-1036)

Brandon: B. J. Hales Museum of Natural History, Arts & Library Bldg., Brandon Univ., R7A 6A9 (204/728-9520, ext. 407). Curator, Barbara Robinson (Contact person: Dr. Robin Giles, Dean of Science)

Carman: Dufferin Historical Museum, Kings Park, Carman, Man. R0G 0J0. Contact, L. Shilson (204/745-2742)

Carman: Heaman's Antique Autorama, Hwy. 3, R0G 0J0 (204/745-6865)

Churchill: Eskimo Museum. Curator, Brother Jacques Volant, o.m.i., Churchill, Man. R0B 0E0 (204/675-2252)

Cook's Creek: Cook's Creek Heritage Museum, Hwy. 212, North of "UC Grotto Church". Slavics & Religious Artifacts, outdoor pioneer machinery. (via R.R. 2, Dugald, Man. R0E 0K0) (204/444-2248)

Dauphin: The Fort Dauphin Museum, 140 Jackson Ave., Box 181, R7N 2V1 (204/638-6630)

Dauphin: Pioneer Cottage Museum, #20 Hwy. East, Mrs. George Dowler, Owner (204/638-7454)

Dauphin: McCallum's Museum, Hwy. 5 West, Russ McCallum, Owner (204/638-7247)

Elkhorn: Man. Automobile Museum. Antique Autos and Agric. Machines. Curator, Cliff Clarke, Box 266, Elkhorn, Man. R0M 0N0 (204/845-2296)

Emerson: Gateway Stopping Place, Secretary, Miss Jessie Johnston, Box 220, Emerson, Man. R0A 0L0 (204/373-2721)

Eriksdale: Eriksdale Museum, Railway Ave. S., R0C 0W0 (204/739-5408)
Gardenton: Ukrainian Museum & Village and Park, Gardenton, Man. R0A 0M0
Gladstone: Gladstone Museum, Gladstone, Man. R0J 0T0 (204/385-2138)
Glenora: Claude Grayston Museum, Glenora, Man. R0K 0Y0
Grandview: Crossley Pioneer Museum, 5 miles n. and 1 mile w. of Grandview (ROL OYO) (204/546-2335). Polished rock collection.
Grandview: The Watson Crossley Community Museum, ROL OYO. Open daily, June 15 to Labour Day. Historical and agricultural.
Hadashville: Conservation Training Area Museum, Hadashville, Man. R0E 0X0 (mail address: 900 Corydon Ave., Winnipeg, Man. R3M OY4)
Killarney: J. A. Victor David Museum, 414 Williams Ave., Box 805, R0K 1G0 (204/523-8466)
La Broquerie: Musée St. Joachim, La Broquerie, Man. R0A 0W0 (204/424-5509)
La Riviere: Archibald Historical Museum, Box 97, R0G 1A0. Curator, Wm. R. Wallcraft (204/242-2825)
Melita: Antler River Historical Museum, Melita, Man. R0M 1L0 (204/522-3936)
Miami: Miami Pioneer Museum, 3rd St., R0G 1H0
Minnedosa: Minnedosa & Dist. Co-operative Museum, 42 2nd Ave. N.E., Minnedosa, Man. R0J 1E0. President, Mrs. M.S. Shorrock (204/867-3444)
Morden: Morden & Dist. Museum of Paleontology & Pioneer Artifacts, Morden Recreation Centre, Gilmour & 2nd Sts., R0G 1J0
Neepawa: Don Murray's Museum of History, 4 miles west of Neepawa to Hwy. 464, 5 miles south, ½ mi. east, (R0J 1H0) (204/476-2460)
Pilot Mound: Pilot Mound Centennial Museum, Centennial Bldg., Broadway St., R0G 1P0
Portage la Prairie: The Fort-La-Reine Museum & Pioneer Village, Hwys. 1A & 26, Secretary Manager, Box 744, R2Y OA9 (204/857-3259, or call Chamber of Commerce, 857-7778)
Rapid City: Rapid City Museum & Cultural Centre, Box 211, R0K 1W0
Reston: The Historical Museum, Reston, Man. R0M 1X0
Roblin: Keystone Pioneer Museum, 4½ miles east of Robin on Hwy. 5, Roblin, Man. R0L 1P0 (204/937-2935)
St. Georges: Musée de St-Georges Museum, Curator, Jean Dupont, St. Georges, Man. ROE 1VO (204/367-2927)
St. Malo: Musée 'Le Pionnier', Hwy. 59 & Beach Rd., R0A 1T0
Shilo: Royal Canadian Artillery Museum. Canadian Forces Base, Bldg. C2, R0K 2A0 (204/765-2282)
Shoal Lake: Spruce Haven Museum, Shoal Lake, Man. R0J 1Z0. Museum opened on request only.
Snowflake: Star Mound School Museum Park, Snowflake, Man. R0G 2K0 (phone Bert Moir, 204/876-4695)
Souris: Hillcrest Pioneer Museum, Souris, Man. R0K 2C0. c/o Eva Barclay (204/483-2569)
Steinbach: Mennonite Village Museum, Box 1136, R0A 2A0 (Hwy. 12, 1 mile north of Steinbach). Manager, Peter Goertzen
Swan River: Swan Valley Museum, Box 628, Swan River, Man. R0L 1Z0. Secretary Treasurer, Mrs. Alice Filuk (204/734-2504)
The Pas: The Sam Waller Little Northern Museum, 1359 Gordon Ave. (Box 185, R9A 1K4)
Virden: Pioneer Home Museum of Virden & Dist., 390 King St. W., R0M 2C0 (204/748-1659)
Waskada: Waskada Pioneer Museum, Waskada, Man. R0M 2E0 (204/673-2450)
West Kildonan: Seven Oaks House Museum, Pioneer Farm Home, Rupertsland & Mac St. Maintained by Community of West Kildonan, 1760 Main St., R2V 1Z7 (204/338-4671). Open May 15 to Labour Day.
Winkler: Pembina Thresherman's Museum Inc. (Steam Threshing Equipment; Antiques; Buildings; Thresherman's Reunion), Box 1103, Winkler, Man. R0G 2X0 (204/325-8208). Located 3½ miles east of Morden on No. 3 Hwy. Open weekends May to Sept.
Winnipeg: Aquatic Hall of Fame & Museum of Canada Inc., Pan-Am Pool, 25 Poseidon Bay, R3M 3E4 (204/284-4030)
Winnipeg: Dalnavert (Macdonald House), 61 Carlton St., R3C 1N7, (204/943-2835). Director, Tim Worth
Winnipeg: Historical Museum of St. James-Assiniboia, 3180 Portage Ave., R3K 0Y5 (204/888-8706)
Winnipeg: Ivan Franko Museum, 603 Pritchard Ave., R2W 2K4. Director, Anthony Bilecki (204/589-4397)
Winnipeg: Provincial Archives of Man., 200 Vaughan St., R3C 1T5, Provincial Archivist, Peter Bower (204/944-3971)
Winnipeg: Ross House, Western Canada's First Post Office, (June 1st - Labour Day) Higgins Ave. Maintained by Manitoba Historical Society, 190 Rupert Ave., R3B ON2 (204/943-7037)
Winnipeg: Royal Winnipeg Rifles Regimental Museum, Room 208, Minto Armoury, 969 St. Matthews Ave., R3G OJ7, Curator, M.M. Abrams, C.D. (204/783-0880)
Winnipeg: Le Musée de St. Boniface, 494 ave Taché, C.P. 6, St-Boniface, Man. R2H 3B4) (204/247-4500)
Winnipeg: St. Volodymyr Ukrainian Catholic Centre Museum, 418 Aberdeen Ave., R2W 1V7
Winnipeg: Seven Oaks House Museum, (c/o Community of West Kildonan, 1760 Main St., Winnipeg, Man. R2V 1Z7) (204/338-4671)
Winnipeg: Ukrainian Museum of Canada, Manitoba Branch, 1175 Main St., R2W 3S4 (204/334-6531)
Winnipeg: Ukrainian Cultural & Educational Centre, 184 Alexander Ave., R3B OL6 (204/942-0218)
Winnipeg: Univ. of Man. Museums, Gallery III; Mineralogy Museum; Natural History Museum; Planetarium.
Winnipeg: Upstairs Gallery, 266 Edmonton St., R3C 1R9 (204/943-2734)
Whiteshell Provincial Park: Nutimik Lake Museum, on Prov. Rd. 307 near Nutimik Lake, address: Seven Sisters Falls, Man. R0E 1Y0 (204/348-2203)
Woodlands: Woodlands Pioneer Museum, Woodlands, Man. R0C 3H0

NEW BRUNSWICK

New Brunswick Museum

277 Douglas Ave., Saint John, N.B. E2K 1E5
(506) 693-1196
President, William H. Patterson
Director, David Ross
History Curator, Gregg Finley
Art Curator, R. M. Percival
Exhibits Chief, E. Milota
Natural Science Curator, S.W. Gorham
Librarian, Carol Rosevear

Other Museums and Art Galleries in New Brunswick

Aulac: Fort Beausejour National Historic Park, Supt., David Taylor, Aulac, N.B. EOA 3CO (506/536-0720)
Campobello Island: Franklin Roosevelt Summer Cottage & Park, Box 9, Welshpool, N.B. E0G 3H0 (506/752-2922)
Caraquet: Le Musée Acadien, C.P. 420, E0B 1K0 (506/727-3269)
Chatham: Miramichi Natural History Museum, 149 Wellington St., E1N 1L7 – President, J.R. Martin, 13 Henderson St.
Dalhousie: Chaleur History Museum/Musée Historique Chaleur, Co-ordinator, Mrs. Kathleen Archibald, Box 1717, E0K 1B0 (506/684-4685)
Dorchester: The Keillor House, (Westmorland Centennial Museum), Building & History: Sylvia Yeoman, Rocklyn, Dorchester, N.B. E0A 1M0 (506/379-2205); other information: Manager, Keillor House, 379-6633
Edmundston: Musée du Madawaska/Madawaska Museum, Box 462, E3V 3L1 (506/739-7254), Curator, Jean Pelletier
Fredericton: Beaverbrook Art Gallery. Curator, Ian G. Lumsden, Box 605, E3B 5A6 (506/455-6551)

Fredericton: Military Compound Board, Box 6000, E3B 5H1, Secretary, R.A. MacDiarmid (506/453-2636)
Fredericton: Provincial Archives, Box 6000, E3B 5H1. Provincial Archivist, Marion Beyea (506/453-2637)
Fredericton: Univ. of N.B. Burden Academy, c/o Public Relations Office, UNB, Box 4400, Fredericton, N.B. E3B 5A3 (506/453-4793)
Fredericton: Univ. of N.B. Art Centre. Curator, Marjory Donaldson; Director, Bruno Bobak, E3B 5A2 (506/453-4623)
Fredericton: York-Sunbury Historical Society Museum, Box 1312, E3B 5C8 (506/455-6041), Curator, Brent Wilson
Gagetown: Queens County Museum (Sir Leonard Tilley Birthplace), Gagetown, N.B. E0G 1V0. Director, Miss P. Jenkins.
Grand Harbour: Grand Manan Museum. Eric Allaby, Grand Manan Island, E0G 1X0 (506/662-3524)
Hampton: Kings County Museum (Kings County Historical Society), Hampton, N.B. E0G 1Z0, Curator, W.H. Dalling
Hopewell Cape: Albert County Museum, located in former ancient Gaol at Hopewell Cape, also 1904 County Courthouse and 1846 Arts & Crafts Bldg., and Agriculture Bldg. with old farm machines. Open June 15 to Sept., c/o Mrs. Iris MacGillivray, Box 505, Moncton, N.B. E1C 8L9
Moncton: Art Gallery, Univ. of Moncton, E1A 3E9. Director, Marc Pitre (506/858-4082)
Moncton: Free Meeting House, c/o Moncton Museum. Open, summer season.
Moncton: Moncton Museum Inc., 20 Mountain Rd., E1C 2J8, Director, Keith A. Wickens (506/854-1001). Open all year.
Moncton: Musée Acadien, Université de Moncton, E1A 3E9. Director, Jean Daigle (506/858-4082)
Oromocto: CFB Gagetown Military Museum, CFB Gagetown, N.B. E0G 2P0, Curator, Sgt. W.A. Green (506/357-8401, ext. 630)
Sackville: Owens Art Gallery, Sackville, N.B. E0A 3C0. Director, T. Keilor Bentley (506/536-2040, ext. 270)
St. Andrews: The Blockhouse, Nat. Historic Site, Box 160, St. Andrews, N.B. E0G 2X0 (open June to Sept.)
St. Andrews: Huntsman Marine Laboratory, Museum & Aquarium, St. Andrews, N.B. E0G 2X0 (506/529-3979)
St. Andrews: The Ross Memorial Museum, 188 Montague St., E0G 2X0, Curator, Mrs. Ruth Spicer
St. Andrews: Sunbury Shores Arts & Nature Centre, Box 100, St. Andrews, N.B. E0G 2X0 (506/529-3386)
St-Jacques: Musée Automobile Museum, c/o Box 180, E0L 1K0 (506/735-8769)
Saint John: G. E. Barbour Store, (restoration), R. Brenan, Box 1130, Sussex, N.B. EOE 1PO (506/433-2260)
Saint John: Loyalist House, 120 Union St., E2L 1A3. Supervisor, W. F. Merritt (506/652-3590)
Saint John: Martello Tower, Saint John West, E2K 1E5 Supervisor, W. A. Schofield (506/672-5792)
Woodstock (Old): County Court House Restoration, Carleton County Historical Society, Inc., Woodstock, N.B. E0J 2B0. President, Mrs. Lena Perley (506/328-2468)

NEWFOUNDLAND

Newfoundland Museum

Duckworth St., St. John's, Nfld. A1C 1G9
(709) 737-2460
Director, Martin L. Bowe

Other Museums and Art Galleries in Newfoundland

Corner Brook: Arts & Culture Centre, Box 100, A2H 6C3, Manager, G. W. Neal (709/639-9251)
Gander: Aviation Exhibit, Gander Airport, c/o J. D. James, Airport General Manager, Gander, Nfld. A1V 1W8 (709/256-3857)
Gander: Arts & Culture Centre, 50 Airport Blvd., A1V 1K6. Manager, Una Joseph (709/256-7575)
Grand Falls: Arts & Culture Centre, Cromer Ave., A2A 1W9, Manager, R. S. Pye (709/489-5741)
St. John's: Provincial Archives of Nfld. & Labrador, St. John's, Nfld. A1C 2C9, Provincial Archivist, David J. Davis (709/753-9390)
St. John's: Arts & Culture Centre, Box 1854, A1C 5P9, Director of Cultural Affairs, John C. Perlin (709/737-3650)
Stephenville: Arts & Culture Centre, 141 Massachusetts Dr., A2N 3A5, Manager, Laura Lush (709/643-4571)

NOVA SCOTIA

Nova Scotia Museum

1747 Summer St., Halifax, N.S. B3H 3A6
(902) 429-4610

Established in 1868, the museum exhibits illustrate the social and natural history of Nova Scotia. There are also frequently changing exhibits on various subjects. Building contains administrative and curatorial offices, laboratories and reference library. Administers a province wide complex of historic sites and buildings. School classes and loans and public programming.

Director, J. Lynton Martin

Other Museums and Art Galleries in Nova Scotia

Annapolis Royal: Fort Anne National Historic Park. Area Supt., J. A. Hall, Annapolis Royal, N.S. B0S 1A0 (902/532-2397)
Annapolis Royal: McNamara House (circa 1780), St. George St., c/o Box 503, B0S 1A0 (902/532-2041)
Annapolis Royal: North Hills Museum, Granville Ferry. c/o Box 503, Annapolis Royal, N.S. B0S 1A0 (902/532-2168) Open May 15 to Oct. 15
Annapolis Royal: Pickels & Mills Exhibit Centre, St. George St., c/o Box 503, BOS 1AO (902/532-2041)
Annapolis Royal: O'Dell Inn Museum (Victorian Stagecoach Inn), St. George St., c/o Box 503, B0S 1A0 (902/532-2041)
Baddeck: The Alexander Graham Bell National Historic Park, Box 159, Baddeck, N.S. B0E 1B0. Supt., John W. Stephens (902/295-2069)
Balmoral Mills: Balmoral Grist Mill, c/o Curator, Branch Museums, N.S. Museum, Halifax, B3H 3A6 (902/429-4610) (open May 15 to Oct. 15)
Barrington: Woolen Mill, Cape Sable Historical Society, Barrington, N.S. B0W 1E0. Open daily with attendants June 15-Sept. 30. (902/637-2185)
Barrington: Old Meeting House, c/o Cape Sable Historical Society, Box 152, B0W 1S0. Open daily with attendants June 15-Sept. 30.
Bridgewater: DesBrisay Museum/National Exhibit Centre, Bridgewater, N.S. B4V 2W9, Curator, Gary Selig (902/543-4033)
Bridgewater: Dean Wile Carding Mill, c/o Curator Des Brisay Museum, Bridgewater (902/543-4033)
Clementsport: Old St. Edwards Church, c/o the Rector, Clementsport, Annapolis Co., N.S. B0S 1E0 (restored Loyalist Church of 1783) Open to public during summer season.
Dartmouth: Dartmouth Heritage Museum, Wyse Rd., B3A 1M1 (902/463-3183)
Denmark: Sutherland Steam Mill, c/o Curator, Branch Museums, N.S. Museum, Halifax, N.S. B3H 3A6 (Open May 15 to Oct. 15)
Glace Bay: Miners' Museum, c/o Director, Roger Hill, Quarry Point, Glace Bay, N.S. B1A 5T8 (902/849-4522)
Guysborough: Old Court House Museum, Guysborough, N.S. B0H 1N0 (902/533-4008)
Halifax: Anna Leonowens Art Gallery, N.S. College of Art & Design, 5163 Duke St., B3J 3J6
Halifax: Army Museum, The Citadel, Box 3666, South Postal Stn., B3J 3K6, Curator, D.E. Graves (902/422-5979)

Halifax: Art Gallery of N.S., 6152 Coburg Rd., Box 2262, B3J 3C8. Curator, Bernard Riordon (902/424-7542)

Halifax: Dalhousie Art Gallery, Dalhousie Univ. Arts Centre, University Ave., B3H 3J5 (902/424-2195)

Halifax: Dalhousie Univ., R. L. de C. H. Saunders Museum of Anatomy. Curator, Head of Anatomy Dept., B3H 4H7 (902/424-3591)

Halifax: Maritime Command Museum, CFB Halifax, Gottingen St. (mailing: Admiralty House, CFB Halifax, FMO Halifax, B3K 2X0) (902/426-5210)

Halifax: Mount Saint Vincent Art Gallery, Seton Academic Centre, Mount Saint Vincent Univ., B3M 2J6. Director, Mrs. Mary Sparling (902/443-4450, loc. 160) Open daily.

Halifax: Art Gallery & Historical Museum, Public Archives of N.S., B3H 1W4, Provincial Archivist, Hugh A. Taylor (902/423-9115)

Halifax: Saint Mary's Univ. Art Gallery, Saint Mary's Univ., Robie St., B3H 3C3 (902/423-7727)

Liverpool: Perkins House, c/o Curator, Simeon Perkins Museum, Box 1078, B0T 1K0 (902/354-4058) (open May 15 to Oct. 15)

Louisbourg: S & L (Sydney & Louisburg) Railway Museum. Curator, James Hickman, R.R. 1, Bras D'Or, C.B., N.S. Open June 1 to Oct. 15

Louisbourg: The Fortress of Louisbourg National Historic Park, Park Supt., J. B. Fortier, Louisbourg, N.S. B0A 1M0 (902/733-2280)

Maitland: Lawrence House, c/o Curator, Branch Museums, N.S. Museum, Halifax, B3H 3A6 (902/429-4610). Open daily May 15 to Oct. 15.

Minudie: King Seaman School Museum, c/o Minudie Tourist Council, R.R. 2, River Hebert, N.S. BOL 1GO (902/251-2041). Open daily July 1 to Labour Day.

Mount Uniacke: Uniacke House, c/o Curator, Branch Museums, N.S. Museum, Halifax, B3H 3A6 (902/429-4610). (open May 15 to Oct. 15)

Musquodoboit Harbour: Musquodoboit Railway Museum, Musquodoboit Harbour, N.S. B0J 2L0. Curator, D. E. Stephens (902/889-2084, res.). Open daily July and August.

New Ross: Ross Farm Museum, New Ross, N.S. B0J 2M0. Curator, A Hiltz (902/389-2210). Open daily May 15 to Oct. 15

Oyster Ponds - Jeddore: Fisherman's Life Museum, c/o Curator, Branch Museums, N.S. Museum, Halifax, N.S. B3H 3A6 (902/429-4610). Open May 15 to Oct. 15.

Parrsboro: Parrsboro Geological Museum, c/o Chamber of Commerce, Box 297, B0M 1S0 (902/254-3266)

Pictou: McCulloch House, and Hector Nat. Exhibition Centre, Old Haliburton Rd., Pictou, B0K 1H0 (902/485-4563)

Pictou: Mic Mac Museum, R.R. 1, B0K 1H0, Owners, Mr. & Mrs. Kenneth Hopps (902/485-4723)

Port Royal: The Habitation, Parks Canada, Port Royal, N.S. BOS 1KO (902/532-2898)

Shelburne: Ross-Thomson House, c/o President, Shelburne Historical Society, B0T 1W0 (902/875-3821)

Shelburne: Shelburne County Museum, Shelburne, N.S. B0T 1W0. Open daily May 15 to Oct. 15. Winter by appointment only.

Sherbrooke Village: c/o Project Director, Box 285, Sherbrooke, Guysborough Co., N.S. B0J 3C0 (902/522-2400)

Springhill: Miners Museum, c/o Brian Fuller, Springhill, N.S. B0M 1X0 (902/597-3449)

Starr's Point: Prescott House, c/o Curator, Branch Museums, N.S. Museum, Halifax, B3H 3A6 (902/429-4610). (open May 15 to Oct. 15)

Sydney: Cossit House, c/o Old Sydney Society, Box 912, B1P 6J4 (902/539-7973). Open May 15 to Thanksgiving.

Sydney: Old Sydney Museum, c/o Old Sydney Society, Box 912, B1P 6J4 (902/564-6619)

Tatamagouche: Sunrise Trail Museum, Tatamagouche, N.S. B0K 1V0. Contact Ray Carruthers (902/657-2679). Open during summer season. Features puppets of giantess Anna Swan and her husband Capt. Martin Van Burin Bates.

Tupperville: Tupperville School Museum, c/o Mrs. Ralph E. Bent, Bridgetown, R.R. 3, N.S. B0S 1C0 (902/665-2004). Open daily mid May to mid Sept.

Windsor: "Clifton" Haliburton House, c/o Curator, Branch Museums, N.S. Museum, Halifax, B3H 3A6 (902/429-4610). Open daily from May 15 to Oct. 15.

Wolfville: Wolfville Historical Museum, Randall House, 175 Main St., B0P 1X0 (902/542-9775). (open daily June 15 to Sept. 15)

Yarmouth: Yarmouth County Historical Society Museum, Curator, E. J. Ruff, 22 Collins St., B5A 3C8 (902/742-5539)

Yarmouth: Firefighters Museum of N.S., 451 Main St., B5A 1G9. Curator, Mrs. Helen Goodwin (902/742-5525). Open all year.

ONTARIO

Royal Ontario Museum

100 Queen's Park, Toronto, Ont. M5S 2C6
(416) 978-3690

The Royal Ontario Museum is Canada's largest public Museum and is a major research institution consisting of 25 curatorial departments in the fields of art and archaeology and the natural sciences and a number of departments dealing with education, communication and administration.

The Museum offers a variety of programs and activities including special exhibitions, concerts, lectures, literary readings, film programs, and planetarium shows in the Theatre of the Stars of the McLaughlin Planetarium.

Director, Dr. James E. Cruise
Assoc. Director, Curatorial, Mrs. Barbara Stephen
Asst. Director, Education & Communication, R. McCartney Samples
Asst. Director, Administration & Facilities, C. Gordon G. Bristowe
Head, Programs & Public Relations, David A. Young
Canadiana, Curator-in-Charge, D. Webster
Egyptian, Curator, N.B. Millett
Ethnology, Curator-in-Charge, H. Fuchs
European, Curator-in-Charge, H. Hickl-Szabo
Greek & Roman, Curator, Neda Leipen
Far Eastern, Assoc. Curator-in-Charge, Dr. James Hsu
New World Archaeology, Assoc. Curator-in-Charge, Dr. Peter Storck
Textiles, Assoc. Curator, J. Vollmer
West Asian, Curator-in-Charge, Dr. Louis Levine

Botany, Curator, Dr. John McAndrews
Entomology, Curator-in-Charge, Dr. David Barr
Ichthyology & Herpetology, Curator-in-Charge, Dr. E.J. Crossman
Invertebrate Palaeontology, Assoc. Curator-in-Charge, Dr. Peter von Bitter
Invertebrate Zoology, Curator-in-Charge, Dr. David Barr
Mammalogy, Curator-in-Charge, Dr. R.L. Peterson
Mineralogy & Geology, Curator-in-Charge, Dr. Sydney Lumbers
Ornithology, Assoc. Curator-in-Charge, Dr. Allan Baker
Vertebrate Palaeontology, Curator-in-Charge, Dr. Christopher McGowan

McLaughlin Planetarium

The Star Theatre of the ROM's McLaughlin Planetarium seats 355 people in a temperature-controlled environment. The complex Zeiss planetarium instrument in the centre reproduces the motions of the moon, sun and planets, and shows constellation figures and thousands of stars on the dome, which is 75 feet in diameter.

Assoc. Curator, Dr. T.R. Clarke

Education Services

The Department organizes school tours, produces learning resource materials, sends its certified teachers with artifacts to schools, and provides professional development courses for Ontario teachers.

Head, R. Miles

Extension Services

The Extension Services Department offers circulating and modular exhibitions to local museums, libraries, shopping centres, schools and service organizations throughout the province.

Head, A. Foss

Public Services

ROMbus tours, ROM World Civilization and Life Science Tours, walking tours during summer, identification service by curatorial departments.

ROM Renovation and Expansion

The ROM is currently undergoing a major program of renovation and expansion. For complete information on the renovation program please call 978-3703.

Art Gallery of Ontario

317 Dundas St. W., Toronto, Ont. M5T 1G4
(416) 977-0414
Cable: Galeon
Director, W.J. Withrow
Manager, Public Affairs, Alex MacDonald

Other Museums and Art Galleries in Ontario

Adolphustown: Old Hay Bay Church, Secretary, Board of Trustees, Mrs. Donald Hough, R.R. 2, Napanee, Ont. K7R 3K7

Adolphustown: United Empire Loyalist Museum. Chairman, Board of Directors, W. J. VanKoughnett, 41 Mill St., Napanee, Ont.

Algonquin Park: Algonquin Park Museum, Min. of Natural Resources, Box 219, Whitney, Ont. K0J 2M0. Park Naturalist, Dan Strickland (705/633-5592)

Algonquin Park: Pioneer Logging Exhibit, Min. of Natural Resources, Box 219, Whitney, Ont. K0J 2M0. Park Naturalist, Dan Strickland (705/633-5592)

Alliston: South Simcoe Pioneer Museum, Secretary, M. Campbell, Municipal Office, L0M 1A0

Amherstburg: Fort Malden National Historic Park. Supt., Harry J. Bosveld, 100 Laird Ave., Box 38, N9V 2Z2 (519/736-5416)

Arnprior: Arnprior & Dist. Museum, 35 Madawaska St., K7M 1R6 Curator, Mrs. Janet Carmichael (613/623-4902)

Atikokan: Atikokan Centennial Museum, Civic Centre, Atikokan, Ont. P0T 1C0. Director/Curator, Jo-Anne Lachapelle (807/597-6585)

Atikokan: Dawson Trail Camp Grounds, French Lake Quetico Park, Atikokan, Ont. POT 1CO. Curator, Shan Walshe (807/929-3552)

Atikokan: Atikokan Historical Park, Legion Point, Atikokan, Ont. P0T 1C0 (summer months). Director/Curator, Jo-Anne Lachapelle (807/597-6585)

Bancroft: Bancroft Historical Museum Society, Box 239, K0L 1C0 (613/332-1884)

Belleville: Hastings County Museum, 257 Bridge St. E., K8N 1P4, Director, Mrs. Mary Simonds (613/962-2329)

Blind River: Blind River Timber Village Museum, Box 1125, P0R 1B0, Chairman, Henry Provencher

Borden: Canadian Forces Base Borden Military Museum, CFB Borden, L0M 1C0 (705/424-1200, ext. 2331)

Bothwell: Fairfield Museum. Curator, Rev. S.H. Brenton, Bothwell, Ont. NOP 1CO (519/692-4397)

Bowmanville: Bowmanville Museum, 37 Silver St., L1C 3K9 (416/623-2734) Curator, Mrs. Marion Veinot

Bowmanville: Darlington Prov. Park Pioneer Home, R.R. #2, L1C 3K3, Park Supt., B. D. Swaile (416/723-4341)

Brampton: Peel Museum & Art Gallery. Director, Wm. D.W. Barber, 3 Wellington St. E., L6W 1Y1 (416/451-9051)

Brantford: Art Gallery of Brant, Box 1747, 76 Dalhousie St., N3T 5V7, Director, Richard Pottruff (519/753-7581)

Brantford: Bell Homestead, 94 Tutelo Heights Rd., N3T 1A1, Curator, J. Brian Studier (519/756-6220)

Brantford: Brant County Museum, 57 Charlotte St., N3T 2W6 (519/752-2483), Director, Wm. R. Robbins

Brantford: Glenhyrst Arts Council, 20 Ava Rd., N3T 5G9, Admr., Elsie Kerrigan (519/756-5932)

Brighton: Presqu'ile Provincial Park Museum, R.R. #4, Brighton, KOK 1HO. Park Supt., G. E. Cox (613/475-2204)

Bruce Mines: Bruce Mines Museum, Taylor Hwy. 17. Curator, A. M. Henderson, Taylor St., P0R 1C0 (705/785-3426)

Burlington: Joseph Brant Museum, 1240 North Shore Blvd. E., L7S 1C5, Curator, Ms. Shirley E. Hartt (416/634-3556)

Cayuga: Haldimand County Museum & Pioneer Log Cabin, Box 38, N0A 1E0 (416/772-5880). Curator, Ms. Rene Tunney

Chatham: Chatham-Kent Museum, Curator, Mrs. Mary G. Creasey, 59 William St. N., N7M 4L3 (519/352-8540)

Cobalt: Cobalt's Northern Ontario Mining Museum, Silver St. (Box 215, POJ 1CO) (705/679-8301)

Cobourg: Art Gallery of Cobourg. Director, Anne Kolisnyk, Victoria Hall, 55 King St. W., K9A 2M2 (416/372-0333)

Collingwood: Collingwood Museum, Memorial Park, 35 St. Paul St., L9Y 3Z5

Comber: Tilbury West Agricultural Museum, 3 miles south of Comber on Hwy. 77. Secretary, D.H. McMillan, Box 158, N0P 1J0

Cornwall: Inverarden Regency Cottage & Museum. Curator, Ian Bowering; East Front, Box 773, K6H 5T5 (613/938-9585)

Cornwall: United Counties Museum. Curator, Mrs. C. S. MacKinnon, 731 Second St. W., Box 773, K6H 5T5 (613/932-2381)

Dryden: Dryden Dist. Museum, 284 Government St., P8N 2P3 (phone Chamber of Commerce, 807/223-4671)

Dundas: Dundas Historical Society Museum. Curator, Miss Olive Newcombe, 139 Park St. W., L9H 5G1 (416/627-7412)

Dunvegan: The Glengarry Scottish Museum, c/o Committee Chairman, Mrs. M.L. Loewen, Box 42, KOC 1JO (613/527-2284)

Elliot Lake: Elliot Lake Nuclear & Mining Museum, Municipal Offices, 45 Hillside Dr. N., P5A 1X5, off Hwy. 108. Curator, R.E. Manuel (705/848-2287) (logging and wildlife display). Open year round.

Elora: Wellington County Museum, R.R. 1, Fergus, Ont. N1M 2W3, Director, Ken Seiling (519/846-5169). Open year round.

Fanshawe Dam: Fanshawe Pioneer Village, see London.

Fenelon Falls: Fenelon Falls Museum, c/o Mrs. Bessie Christian, 18 Francis St. E., KOM 1NO

Fergus: see Elora

Forest: Forest-Lambton Museum. Curator, Miss E. M. Powell, R.R. #1, N0N 1J0 (519/786-5884)

Fort Erie: Old Fort Erie, Niagara Parks Commission, Box 150, Niagara Falls, Ont. L2E 6T2. Manager, T. Shaughnessy (416/871-0540)

Fort Frances: Fort Frances Museum & Recreational Cultural Centre, Curator, Darryl Allan, 259 Scott St., P9A 1G8 (807/274-7891)

Fort Frances: Tower Lookout Historical Museum, Pither's Point Park (Summer months). Curator, Darryl Allan, c/o Fort Frances Museum, 259 Scott St., P9A 1G8 (807/274-7891)

Frankville: Montgomery House, c/o Kitley Historical Association, Frankville, Ont. K0E 1H0, President, David Allen

Gananoque: Gananoque Historical Museum, 10 King St. E. Curator, Mrs. Ralph Scott, Box 214, K7G 2T7 (613/382-3829)

Goderich: Huron County Pioneer Museum. Curator, Raymond Scotchmer, 110 North St., N7A 2T8

Golden Lake: Golden Lake Algonquin Museum. Curator, Philip Comnonda, Box 28, KOJ 1XO (613/625-2027)

Gore Bay: Gore Bay Museum, c/o Town Clerk, Box 298, Gore Bay, Ont. POP 1HO (705/282-2420)

Grafton: Barnum House Museum. Curator, G. G. Young, Grafton, Ont. K0K 2G0 (416/349-2724). Open daily 12-5 p.m. during July & Aug. and Sundays, 1-5 p.m. May 7 to Thanksgiving, other days by request.

Gravenhurst: Muskoka Steamships & Historical Society, Box 1283, P0C 1G0 (705/687-2612)

Grimsby: Grimsby Public Art Gallery, 25 Adelaide St., L3M 1X2 Director, Michael Dobson. (416/945-3246)

Grimsby: The Stone Shop Museum (a local History Museum) 271 Main St. W. c/o Curator, Miss Florence E. Martin, Box 244, L3M 4G5 (416/945-4453)

Guelph: Colonel John McCrae Birthplace, Water St., Box 601, N1H 6L3 (519/821-1094)

Guelph: Guelph Civic Museum, 6 Dublin St. S., N1H 4L5. Director, Ian Vincent (519/836-1221)

Guelph: Macdonald Stewart Art Centre, 358 Gordon St., N1G 1Y1. Director, Judith Nasby (519/837-0010)

Hamilton: Art Gallery of Hamilton, 123 King St. W., L8P 4S8, Director, Glen E. Cumming (416/527-6610)

Hamilton: Jordan Museum of the Twenty, see Jordan, Ont.

Hamilton: McMaster University Planetarium, Gilmour Hall, Rm. 120, (L8S 4L8) (416/525-9140, ext. 4721)

Hamilton: Dundurn Castle, Dundurn Park, York Blvd., L8R 3H1. Curator, Miss Marilyn Soules (416/522-5313)

Hamilton: Hamilton Military Museum, York Blvd., Dundurn Park, L8R 3H1. (416/523-5681)

Hamilton: Children's Museum, 1072 Main St. E., L8M 1N6. Curator, Miss Marjorie Johnston (416/649-9285)

Hamilton: "Whitehern", Restored McQuesten Residence, 41 Jackson St. W., L8P 1L3, adjoining the City Hall (Curator, George L. Harrod) (416/522-5664)

Hamilton-Wentworth: Wentworth Heritage Village, Rockton, Ont. L0R 1X0 (519/621-2595), Curator, Barry Lord

Huntsville: Muskoka Pioneer Village, c/o U.E. Buchner, Director, Box 2802, P0A 1K0 (705/789-7576)

Iroquois: Carman House Museum, Carman Rd. S., c/o Municipal Clerk, Box 249, K0E 1K0 (613/652-4422)

Jordan: Ball's Falls Historical Park, Curator, Miss Christine Ranger, 6th Ave., R.R. #1, L0R 1S0 (416/562-5235)

Jordan: Jordan Museum of the Twenty, 6 miles west of St. Catharines on Hwy. 8. Director, H. Crowfoot, Box 85, Campden, Ont. LOR 1GO (416/562-5242)

Kenora: Lake of the Woods Museum, Memorial Park on Main St., Director, Reg Reeve (mailing address, Box 497, P9N 3X5) (807/468-8865)

Kingston: Agnes Etherington Art Centre, Director, R.F. Swain, Queen's Univ., K7L 3N6 (613/547-6551)

Kingston: Bellevue National Historic Park, 35 Centre St., K7L 4E5, Supt., E. R. Friel (613/542-3858)

Kingston: The Canadian Forces Communications & Electronics Museum, CFB Kingston, K7L 2Z2 (613/545-5395) Curator, Sgt. Carter, T.F.

Kingston: Frontenac County Schools Museum, 5 Clergy St. E., K7L 3H7. Curator, Miss Beth Hogan (613/544-9113)

Kingston: Marine Museum of the Great Lakes, 55 Ontario St., K7L 2Y2, Executive Director, Maurice D. Smith (613/542-2261)

Kingston: Murney Tower Museum. Curator, Fred A. McConnell, Poplar Grove, R.R. 1, K7L 4V1 (613/542-4687, res.)

Kingston: Old Fort Henry. Manager, D.H. Clark, Box 213, K7L 4V8 (613/542-7388)

Kingston: Queen's University Geological Museum, Miller Hall, Union St., K7L 3N6. Chairman, Dr. Leigh Smith (613/547-2854)

Kingston: The Royal Military College of Canada Museum, Fort Frederick, K7L 2W3, (613/549-1333). Committee Chairman, J.G. Pike; Secretary, Raymond Dignum

Kirkland Lake: Museum of Northern History. Chairman F. T. O'-Connor; Curator, Bruce Turner, 20 Duncan Ave. N., Box 730, P2N 1H4 (705/567-3600)

Kitchener: Kitchener-Waterloo Art Gallery. Director, Brad Blain, 101 Queen St. N., N2H 6P7 (519/579-5860). Open all year.

Kitchener: Doon Pioneer Village & Waterloo County Hall of Fame, R.R. #2, Kitchener, N2G 3W5 (401 Inter. 34) (519/893-4020)

Kitchener: Woodside National Historic Park. A/Supt., Ms. Jane Humphries, 528 Wellington St. N., N2H 5L5 (519/742-5273). Open all year.

Kleinburg: The McMichael Canadian Collection, Kleinburg, Ont. L0J 1C0, Director, Dr. R. McMichael (416/893-1121)

Lang: Lang water powered grist mill, Otonabee Region Conservation Authority (Mrs. E.A. Wright, 727 Lansdowne St. W., Peterborough, Ont. K9J 1Z2, 705/745-5791)

Lang/Hope: Water powered saw mill, Otonabee Region Conservation Authority (Mrs. E.A. Wright, 727 Lansdowne St. W., Peterborough, Ont. K9J 1Z2, 705/745-5791)

Lang: Century Village; living museum village, 16 km south east of Peterborough. Curator, Dr. Margaret MacKelvie, R.R. #3, Keene, Ont. K0L 2G0 (705/743-0380)

Leamington: Point Pelee National Park, R.R. #1, N8H 3V4, Supt., D. A. MacEachern (519/326-3204)

Lindsay: Victoria County Historical Society Museum, 435 Kent St. W., Secretary, Miss Berle Coulter, 66 Colborne St. W., K9V 3S9 (705/324-4782)

London: Centennial Museum, London Historical Museums, an agency of London Public Library Board, Director, E. S. Beacock; Curator, Christopher Severance, 325 Queens Ave., N6B 3L7 (519/432-7166, ext. 64)

London: Fanshawe Pioneer Village. Upper Thames River Conservation Authority, R.R. #6 (mail: Box 6278, Stn. D, N5W 5S1) (519/451-2800)

London: London Regional Art Gallery, 421 Ridout St. N., N6A 4H5 (519/672-4580). Director, Nancy H. Poole (int.); Asst. Director & Curator, P. O'Brien

London: Eldon House, London Historical Museums, an agency of London Public Library Board, Director, E. Stanley Beacock; Curator, Christopher Severance, 481 Ridout St. N. (mailing address, 325 Queens Ave., N6B 3L7) (519/432-7166, ext. 64 or 67)

London: Lawson Museum, Grosvenor Lodge, London Historical Museums, an agency of the London Public Library Board. Director, E. Stanley Beacock; Curator, Christopher Severance. 1017 Western Rd. (mailing address, 325 Queens Ave., N6B 3L7) (519/432-7166, ext. 64, or 433-6171)

London: Museum of Indian Archaeology (London), Lawson-Jury Bldg., 1600 Attawandaron Rd., N6G 3M6 (519/473-1360) Director, Dr. W.D. Finlayson; Curator, Robert Pihl

London: Storybook Gardens. Director of Parks, M. C. Chapman, c/o Public Utilities Commission, Box 2700, N6A 4H6 (519/473-2500)

London: The Royal Canadian Regiment Museum, Wolseley Hall, CFB London, N5Y 4T7 (519/679-5173)

London: McIntosh Art Gallery, Univ. of Western Ont., N6A 3K7, Curator, M. Stubbs (519/679-3181)

Madoc Township: O'Hara Mill, c/o Moira River Conservation Authority, 217 N. Front St., Belleville, Ont. K8P 3C3 (613/968-3434)

Manotick: Watson's Mill. Curator & Owner, Rideau Valley Conservation Authority, Box 599, Mill St., K0A 2N0 (613/692-3571)

Meaford: Meaford Museum. Curator, Wade Wilson, R.R. 4, NOH 1YO (519/538-3891)

Meldrum Bay: Manitoulin Historical Marine Museum & Library. Curator, T. Tomlinson, Water St., POP 1RO (705/283-3243). Open daily except Sundays, June 15 to Labour Day.

Merrickville: The Blockhouse Museum. (Corres. to Secretary, Merrickville & Dist. Historical Society, Box 294, K0G 1N0, 613/269-3614) Open daily July & Aug.

Midland: Huronia Museum & Gallery of Historic Huronia, Little Lake Park. Curator, Vern Farrow, Box 638, L4R 4P4 (705/526-2844)

Midland: Sainte-Marie among the Hurons (1639-1649) c/o Huronia Historical Parks, Box 160, Midland, Ont. L4R 4K8 (705/526-7838)

Midland: Martyrs' Shrine, Midland, Ont. L4R 4K3. Director, Rev. J. Winston Rye, S.J. (705/526-6121)

Milton: Halton Museum, Curator, Mrs. E. Brittain, R.R. #3, L9T 2X7 (416/878-3232)

Minesing: Simcoe County Museum. Director, Robert E. Fisher, R.R. #2, L0L 1Y0 (705/728-3721)

Morpeth: Rondeau Provincial Park Interpretive Centre, Min. of Natural Resources, R.R. #1, N0P 1X0 (519/674-3169)

Morrisburg: Upper Canada Village. c/o W. J. Patterson, Supt. of Historic Sites, St. Lawrence Parks Commission, Box 740, K0C 1X0 (613/543-2911)

Napanee: Allan Macpherson House, Curator, Mrs. Doris Connolly, Box 183, K7R 3M3 (613/354-5982)

Napanee: Lennox & Addington County Museum, Director, W.J. Foster, (97 Thomas St. E.) Box 160, K7R 3M3 (613/354-3027)

Niagara Falls: Circus World, 4848 Clifton Hill, L2G 3N4

Niagara Falls: Potvin Museum Skylon Tower. Owner, R. Delrae, 5510 Woodland Blvd., L2G 5K5 (416/356-2319)

Niagara Falls: Ripley's Believe it or not Museum, Clifton Hill, L2G 3N4. Manager, Doug Beaupit (416/356-2238)

Niagara Falls: Louis Tussaud's Wax Museum. Manager, Kenneth Wallington, 4915 Clifton Hill, L2G 3N5 (416/358-5103)

Niagara Falls: Lundy's Lane Historical Museum, 5810 Ferry St., L2G 1S9, Curator, Mrs. M.A. Tabaka (416/358-5082)

Niagara Falls: Niagara Falls Museum, Ltd. Curator, L. Wolffe, 5651 River Rd., Box 960, L2E 6V8 (416/356-2151)

Niagara Falls: Oak Hall, Portage Rd. S., Curator, L. Burns, Niagara Parks Commission, Box 150, L2E 6T2 (416/356-2241)

Niagara Falls: School of Horticulture, Niagara Parks Commission, Supt. Roland Barnsley, Box 150, L2E 6T2 (416/356-8554)

Niagara-on-the-Lake: Fort George National Historic Park. Supt., W. Haldorson, Box 787, L0S 1J0 (416/468-2741)

Niagara-on-the-Lake: McFarland House, The Niagara Parks Commission, Niagara Parkway, c/o M. S. Cushing, Niagara Parks Commission, Box 150, L2E 6T2 (416/356-2241)

Niagara-on-the-Lake: Niagara Historical Museum. Curator, Liza Whealy, 43 Castlereagh St., Box 208, L0S 1J0 (416/468-3912)

Norwich: Norwich & Dist. Museum & Archives Complex. Administrator, Mrs. Johan Hopkins, Box 413, N0J 1P0 (519/863-3638)

Oakville: Old Post Office & Thomas House Museum, Lakeside Park, 168 Lakeshore Rd. (Dir./Curator, M. Fergusson, Box 395, L6J 5A8) (416/845-3952)

Oakville: Taras H. Shevchenko Museum. Curator, P. Prokop, 1363 Dundas St. W., L6J 4Z2 (Toronto office: 42 Roncesvalles Ave., M6R 2K3, 416/535-1063)

Oil Springs: Oil Museum of Canada. Mgr., C. Bridges, Oil Springs, Ont. N0N 1P0 (519/834-2840). Open summer months, daily 10-5 inc. weekends & holidays.

Orillia: Stephen Leacock Memorial Home. Director/Curator, Jay Cody, Atherley Rd. (Box 625, Orillia) (705/326-9357)

Oshawa: Canadian Automotive Museum, General Manager, G.J. Brackett, 99 Simcoe St. S., L1H 4G7 (416/576-1222)

Oshawa: Henry House Museum, Lakeview Park (Curator, Mrs. F.C. Anderson, 6 Henry St., L1H 7Y5, 416/728-6331)

Oshawa: The Robert McLaughlin Gallery, Civic Centre, L1H 3Z3. Director, Ms. Joan Murray (416/576-3000)

Ottawa: Bytown Museum. President & Curator, Dr. B. R. MacKay, 193 Carling Ave., Ottawa.

Ottawa: Governor General's Foot Guards Museum, Drill Hall, Cartier Sq., K1A 0K2 (phone Curator, 613/235-2712)

Ottawa: Laurier House, Curator, Valerie Proctor, 335 Laurier Ave. E., K1N 6R4 (613/992-8142)

Ottawa: Public Archives of Canada, Exhibition Services Division, 395 Wellington St., K1A 0N3 (613/996-3580)

Ottawa: National Film Board Photo Gallery, 150 Kent St., 613/992-0841 (mailing: NFB Still Photography Division, Tunney's Pasture, Ottawa, Ont. K1A 0N1)

Ottawa: Museum of Canadian Scouting. Curator, P. M. O. Evans, 1345 Baseline Rd., Box 5151, Stn. F., K2C 3G7 (613/224-5131)

Owen Sound: County of Grey Owen Sound Museum, 975-6th St. E., N4K 1G9. Director, A. W. Landen

Owen Sound: Tom Thomson Memorial Art Gallery, 840 1st Ave. W., Box 312, N4K 5P5, Director, James Logan (519/376-1932)

Pembroke: Champlain Trail Museum, 1032 Pembroke St. E., (Curator, Mrs. Carl Price, R.R. 2, K8A 6W3) (613/582-3521)

Penetanguishene: Penetanguishene Centennial Museum, 8 Burke St., L0K 1P0. Curator, Douglas Dubeau

Penetanguishene: Historic Naval & Military Establishments (1817-1856) c/o Min. of Culture & Recreation, Huronia Historical Parks, Box 160, Midland, Ont. L4R 4K8 (705/526-7838)

Perth: Archibald W. Campbell Memorial Museum. Curator, Mrs. D. McDonald, Matheson House, Gore St., Box 222, K7H 1H4. (613/267-1947)

Peterborough: Art Gallery of Peterborough, 2 Crescent St., K9J 2G1 (705/743-9179)

Peterborough: Century Village. Curator, Mrs. M. McKelvie, Lang Village in Township of Otonabee. (c/o W. D. Armstrong, Administrator, County of Peterborough, Court House, Peterborough, Ont. K9H 3M3) (705/743-0380)

Peterborough: Peterborough Centennial Museum & Archives; Museum of the Trent-Severn Waterway. Director, D. A. Smithies, Armour Hill, Hunter St. E., Box 143, K9J 6Y5 (705/743-5180)

Port Carling: Port Carling Pioneer Museum, Box 432, P0B 1J0, Curator, Mrs. Marion Brittain (705/765-5367)

Port Rowan: Backhouse Mill, (519/586-2201) c/o Long Point Region Conservation Authority, Box 525, Simcoe, Ont. N3Y 4N5 (426-4623)

Port Rowan: Backus Agricultural Museum Complex, (519/586-2201) c/o Long Point Region Conservation Authority, Box 525, Simcoe, Ont. N3Y 4N5 (426-4623)

Prescott: Fort Wellington Nat. Historic Park, Dibble St. E., Box 479, K0E 1T0, (613/925-2896), Interpretation Officer, Ron Dale

Queenston: MacKenzie House, The Niagara Parks Commission, c/o M. S. Cushing, Niagara Parks Commission, Box 150, Niagara Falls, Ont. L2E 6T2 (416/356-2241) Not open to public.

Richard's Landing: see St. Joseph's Island.

Rockton: Wentworth Pioneer Village, see Hamilton-Wentworth

St. Catharines: Mountain Mills Museum. Curator, D.W. Robson, R.R. #1, Fonthill, Ont. L0S 1E0 (416/682-4634)

St. Catharines: Rodman Hall Arts Centre. Director, A. Peter Harris, 109 St. Paul Cres., L2S 1M3 (416/684-2925)

St. Catharines: St. Catharines Historical Museum. Administrator Curator, Arden Phair, 343 Merritt St., L2T 1K7 (416/227-2962)

St. George: Adelaide Hunter Hoodless Homestead, c/o Mrs. John Charlton, Secretary, Homestead Committee, Federated Women's Institutes of Canada, 5 Bayly Dr., Paris, Ont. N3L 2R1 (519/442-3450)

St. Joseph's Island: Fort St. Joseph National Historic Park, Box 220, Richard's Landing, Ont. P0R 1J0 (705/246-2664, summer only) (Nov. to Apr.: Irv Mazurkiewicz, 132 Second St. E., Cornwall, Ont. K6H 5V4)

St. Joseph's Island: St. Joseph Island Museum. Curator, Mrs. Ada Tranter, Richard's Landing, Ont. P0R 1J0 (705/246-2601)

St. Marys: St. Marys Dist. Museum, 177 Church St. S., N0M 2V0 (Contact, Mary Smith, 519/284-2293)

St. Thomas: Elgin County Pioneer Museum. Curators, Mr. & Mrs. J.J. Kirby, 32 Talbot St., N5P 1A3 (519/631-6537)

Sarnia: Sarnia Public Library & Art Gallery, 124 Christina St. S., N7T 2M6, Director, R. T. Bradley (519/337-3291)

Scarborough: Scarborough Historical Museum (Cornell House & McCowan Log Cabin), Thomson Memorial Park, c/o Box 593, Stn. A, M1K 5C4 (phone Ann Braithwaite, 416/438-5436)

Sharon: Sharon Temple Museum, Sharon, Ont. LOG 1VO (416/478-2389) Manager, Ruth Mahoney

Sheguiandah: Sheguiandah, Little Current, Howland Centennial Museum, Sheguiandah, Ont. P0P 1W0, Director, John Dunlop (705/368-2367)

Shelburne: Dufferin County Pioneer Museum, Box 957, L0N 1S0

Simcoe: Eva Brook Donly Museum, 109 Norfolk St. S., N3Y 2W3, Curator, William Yeager (519/426-1583)

Sioux Lookout: Sioux Lookout Museum. Curator, Mrs. Elva E. Walsh, Box 113, POV 2TO (807/737-2040)

Sombra: Sombra Township Museum, Curator, R. Grant, Box 99, N0P 2H0 (519/892-3672)

Stoney Creek: Battlefield House, 77 King St. W., Box 161, L8G 1H9 (416/662-8458) Curator, Mrs. Ann Boyer

Stratford: The Gallery/Stratford, 54 Romeo St., N5A 4S9. Director, Paul D. Bennett (519/271-5271)

Sturgeon Falls, Township of Springer: Sturgeon River House Museum, Box 1390, P0H 2G0 (705/753-0570)

Sudbury: Musée du Centre Franco-Ontarien de Folklore. Conservateur, Rév. P. Germain Lemieux, S.J., Place St-Joseph, P3C 5N4 (705/675-6493)

Sudbury: Laurentian Univ. Art Gallery, 11th floor, Library Tower, Laurentian Univ., P3E 2C6. (c/o Dept. of Cultural Affairs, 705/675-1151, ext. 400)

Sudbury: Laurentian Univ. Museum & Arts Centre, John St. off Drinkwater Overpass (c/o Dept. of Cultural Affairs, Laurentian Univ., P3E 2C6, 705/675-1151, ext. 400)

Sutton West: Eildon Hall (Sibbald Memorial Museum). c/o Supt., Sibbald Point Provincial Park, R.R. #2, L0E 1R0 (416/722-3268)

Teeterville: Windham Township Pioneer Museum. Curator, Mrs. Yates Eaker, 117 Henry St., Delhi, Ont. N4B 2G1

Thunder Bay: Chippewa Park Zoo, c/o Parks & Recreation Dept., 950 Memorial Ave., P7B 4A2 (807/623-2711, ext. 351)

Thunder Bay: 1910 Logging Museum, Centennial Park, c/o Parks & Recreation Dept., 950 Memorial Ave., P7B 4A2 (807/683-6511)

Thunder Bay: Thunder Bay Museum. Curator, G. Noble, 219 May St. S., P7E 1B5 (807/623-0801)

Timmins: Timmins Museum, Nat. Exhibition Centre, Legion Dr., South Porcupine, Ont., Director, Mrs. Lydia Ross Alexander (705/264-1331, ext. 158)—Mailing: c/o City of Timmins, 220 Algonquin Blvd. E., Timmins, Ont. P4N 1B3

Tobermory: The Peninsula & St. Edmunds Township Museum. Curator, Miss C. E. Wyonch, R.R. #1, N0H 2R0

Toronto: Black Creek Pioneer Village, Jane St. at Steeles Ave., Administrator, Russell K. Cooper, 5 Shoreham Dr., Downsview, Ont. M3N 1S4 (416/661-6600)

Toronto: Campbell House, 160 Queen St. W., Toronto, Ont. M5H 3H3 (416/597-0227). Administrator, Miss H. Halchuk

Toronto: Casa Loma. Manager, Major R.R. Hilliard, C.D., 1 Austin Terrace, M5R 1X8 (416/923-1171)

Toronto: Colborne Lodge, High Park. Curator, Mrs. N. Wronski (Toronto Historical Board, Stanley Barracks, Exhibition Place, M6K 3C3) (416/595-1567)

Toronto: Craven Foundation Vintage Automobile Museum & Restoration Centre, 760 Lawrence Ave. W., M6A 1B9 (416/789-3432)

Toronto: Historic Fort York. Curator, C. Bourque, Strachan & Fleet St. (416/366-6127) (Toronto Historical Board, Stanley Barracks, Exhibition Place, M6K 3C3)

Toronto: H.M.C.S. Haida, Ontario Place, Commanding Officer, Lt.-Cdr. N. J. Russell, C.D., R.C.N. (Rtd.), Box 703 (Streetsville), Mississauga, Ont. L5M 2C2

Toronto: Marine Museum of Upper Canada. c/o Managing Director, (Toronto Historical Board, Stanley Barracks, Exhibition Place, M6K 3C3) (416/-595-1567)

Toronto: Mackenzie House. Curator, Mrs. N. Wronski, 82 Bond St. (Toronto Historical Board, Stanley Barracks, Exhibition Place, M6K 3C3) (416/595-1567)

Toronto: Ont. Science Centre. Director-General, Dr. J. Tuzo Wilson, Eglinton Ave. & Don Mills Rd., Don Mills, Ont. M3C 1T3 (416/429-4100)

Toronto: The Queen's Own Rifles of Canada Regimental Museum. Curator, Lt.-Col. W. T. Barnard, Casa Loma, 1 Austin Terrace, M5R 1X8 (416/425-3604)

Toronto: Scadding Cabin, foot of Dufferin St., CNE grounds. (c/o Toronto Historical Board, Stanley Barracks, Exhibition Place, Toronto, Ont. M6K 3C3–416/595-1567)

Toronto: Ukrainian Museum of Canada, Eastern Branch, Ukrainian Women's Association of Canada, 620 Spadina Ave., Toronto, Ont. M5S 2H4 (416/923-3318)

Toronto: East York, Todmorden Mills Historic Site, 67 Pottery Rd. (Mailing address, 550 Mortimer Ave., Toronto, Ont. M4J 2H2) Curator, Eleanor Darke (416/425-2250)

Toronto: University College Historic Site, Archivist, Prof. Humphrey Milnes, Univ. of Toronto, M5S 1A1 (416/978-3183)

Wasaga Beach: Nancy Island Historic Site, c/o Supt., Wasaga Beach Provincial Park, Min. of Natural Resources, Box 183, Wasaga Beach, Ont. L0L 2P0 (705/429-2516)

Waterloo: UW Arts Centre Gallery, Univ. of Waterloo, Waterloo, Ont. N2L 3G1, (519/885-4281) Administrator, Marlene Bryan

Waupoos: North Marysburgh Museum, Prince Edward County. Curator, Mrs. Ruth Mordaunt, R.R. #4, Picton, Ont. K0K 2T0 (613/476-5185) (Early settlers home furnished with nineteenth century artifacts).

Wellington: Wellington Community Historical Museum, Main St. Curator, Mrs. R. V. Armstrong, Box 55, K0K 3L0 (613/399-3041)

Westport: Rideau District Museum, Westport, Ont. K0G 1X0 Curator, Mrs. Margaret Kane

Whitby: Whitby Arts Inc. "The Station" Gallery, Henry & Victoria Sts., Box 124, L1N 5R7 (416/668-4185) Director, Linda Paulocik

Whitby: Whitby Historical Society Museum, summer location, Lynde House, 960 Dundas St. W. (Mailing address, Box 281, L1N 5S1) (phone Margaret Kennedy, 416/668-2683)

White Lake: Waba Cottage Museum, located at White Lake, Ont. (c/o Mrs. Arnold Somerville, 65 Stadacona St., Arnprior, Ont. K7S 1C4; 613/623-2263)

Williamstown: The Nor'Westers & Loyalist Museum, Box 69, K0C 2J0 (613/347-3547)

Willowdale: Gibson House Museum, c/o North York Historical Board, 5172 Yonge St., M2N 5P6 (416/225-0146)

Windsor: Hiram Walker Historical Museum. Curator, R. A. Douglas, 254 Pitt St. W., N9A 5L5 (519/253-1812)

Windsor: The Art Gallery of Windsor, 445 Riverside Dr. W., N9A 6T8 Director, Kenneth Saltmarche; Curator, Ted Fraser (519/258-7111)

Woodstock: Oxford Museum, City Square, N4S 1C4, Curator, Don Milton (519/537-8411)

PRINCE EDWARD ISLAND MUSEUMS & ART GALLERIES

Alberton: Alberton Museum (reconstruction of early Prince Edward Island home). c/o The Curator, Alberton, P.E.I. C0B 1B0

Charlottetown: Confederation Centre Art Gallery & Museum, Charlottetown, P.E.I. C1A 7L9, works by Robert Harris; contemporary fine crafts, permanent collection. Director, Moncrieff Williamson (902/892-2464)

Charlottetown: Public Archives of P.E.I. Archivist, N. J. de Jong, Box 1000, C1A 7M4 (902/892-7949)

Miscouche: Musée Acadien/Acadian Museum (folk museum). Custodian, Sr. Marguerite Richard, c.n.d., Miscouche, P.E.I. C0B 1T0 (902/436-5614)

Montague: Garden of the Gulf Museum (pioneer history museum). President, Harold MacLeod, Montague, P.E.I. C0A 1R0 (902/838-2467)

New London: Lucy Maud Montgomery Birthplace, Chairman, Rev. F.W.P. Bolger, 14 Confederation St., Charlottetown, P.E.I. C1A 5V4 (902/892-3651)

QUEBEC

Musée du Quebec

Parc des Champs de Bataille, Quebec, P.Q. G1S 1C8
(418) 643-4173
Director, Pierre Lachapelle
Chief Librarian, F. Lafortune

One of the most important museums in Canada. Prestigious collections of 17th, 18th and 19th century art. Collection of contemporary art, folk art, etc. Library, Ciné-Musée, Educational Service. Varied temporary exhibitions. Ethnology, antique Québecois furniture.

Other Museums and Art Galleries in Quebec

Amos: Centre Culturel d'Amos, 42 principale nord, J9T 2K6 (819/732-6541)

Aylmer East: The Canadian Golf Museum. Curator, W. Lyn Stewart, (Correspondence: 1962 Lauder Dr., Ottawa, Ont. K2A 1B1) 613/722-9544

Baie Comeau: Le Musée de Baie-Comeau et le Centre d'exposition Paul Provencher, 43 rue Mance, C.P. 273, G4Z 2H1 (418/296-9690). Directeur, Mme Thérèse Paris Gagnon

Baie Saint-Paul: Centre d'Art Baie St-Paul, 4, boul. Faford, C.P. 789, G0A 1B0 (418/435-3681)

Beloeil: Centre Culturel, 600 rue Richelieu, C.P. 210, J3G 4S9

Carillon: Musée Carillon Museum, Carillon, P.Q. J8H 3X2 (514/737-3861)

Caughnawaga: Musée Kateri Tekakwitha, C.P. 70, J0L 1B0 (514/632-6030)

Chicoutimi: Le Musée du Saguenay-Lac-St-Jean, Ste. 30, 534 Jacques Cartier est, G7H 1Z6 (418/545-9400). Directeur, Mme Renée Wells Gagnon

Eaton: Compton County Historical & Museum Society. Secretary, Mrs. E. S. Heatherington, Box 413, Cookshire, P.Q. J0B 1M0 (819/875-3109)

Fort Chambly: Fort Chambly Parc historique national, Agent d'-accueil et d'interpretation, 2 Richelieu St., Chambly (mailing: Parcs Canada, 1369 de Bourgogne, Chambly, P.Q. J3L 1Y4)

Joliette: Musée d'Art de Joliette, Directeur, Bernard Schaller, 145 rue Wilfrid Corbeil, C.P. 132, J6E 3Z3 (514/756-0311)

Knowlton: Town of Brome Lake; Brome County Historical Museum & Archives, Box 690, J0E 1V0, (514/243-6782), Curator, Miss Marion L. Phelps. Open daily in June, July and August, 10 a.m. to 5 p.m., by appointment in winter.

La Pocatière: Musée François-Pilote, La Pocatière, P.Q. G0R 1Z0, Directeur, Paul-André Leclerc, CEGEP de La Pocatière (418/856-3145)

Longueuil: Musée Historique Charles Le Moyne, 4 est. rue Saint-Charles, J4H 1A9

Montreal: Archives nationales du Québec, 100 est rue Notre-Dame, H2Y 1C1 (514/873-3064). Directeur, Jacques Grimard

Montreal: Bank of Montreal Museum, 129 St. James St. W., H2Y 1L6, Freeman Clowery (514/877-6892)

Montreal: Chateau Ramezay Museum, 280 Notre Dame St. E., H2Y 1C5, Directeur, Jacques Poulin

Montreal: Dow Planetarium, 1000 St. Jacques St. W., H3C 1G7 (514/872-4530)

Montreal: McCord Museum, 690 Sherbrooke St. W., H3A 1E9 (514/392-4778)

Montreal: Musée des beaux-arts de Montréal, 3400, av. du Musée, H3G 1K3 (514/285-1600), Jean Trudel, directeur

Montreal: "The Telephone Historical Collection". Historian, Bell Canada, 8th floor, 1050 Beaver Hall Hill, H3C 3G4 (514/870-5214)

Montreal: Musée de l'Eglise Notre-Dame, 426, rue Saint Sulpice, H2Y 2V5

Montreal: Musée Marguerite Bourgeoys, 400, est rue Saint-Paul, H2Y 1H4 (514/845-9991)

Montreal: Musée de l'Oratoire Saint-Joseph, 3800, Chemin Reine-Marie, H3V 1H6. Directeur, Paul LeDuc, c.s.c. (514/733-8211)

Montreal: Museum of Contemporary Art/Musée d'art contemporain, Cité du Havre, H3C 3R4, Directeur, Louise Letocha (514/873-2878)

Montreal: Royal Canadian Ordnance Corps Museum, 6560 Hochelaga St., Box 6109, H3C 3H7, Curator, Leo Lavigne (514/255-8811, ext. 241)

Montreal: Saidye Bronfman Centre, 5170, Côte St. Catherine Rd., H3W 1M7 (514/739-2301)

Montreal: Sir George Williams Art Galleries, Concordia Univ., 1455 de Maisonneuve Blvd., H3G 1M8 (514/879-5917)

Montreal: The Society of the Montreal Military & Maritime Museum, The Old Fort-St. Helen's Island, Box 1024, Stn. A, H3C 2W9 (514/861-6738)

Mont St. Hilaire: Mont St. Hilaire Nature Conservation Centre, 422 rue des Moulins, J3G 4S6, Director, Michel Drew (514/467-1755)

Nicolet: Musée du Séminaire de Nicolet. Conservateur, Gilles Proulx, 700, boul. Louis-Fréchette, JOG 1EO (819/293-4838)

Odanak: Musée des Abénaquis d'Odanak, Co. Yamaska. Administrateur, Esther Nolett-Sioui, Odanak, P.Q. J0G 1H0 (514/568-2600). Open daily June 1st to Oct. 1st. Weekends all year.

Pointe Claire: Pointe Claire Cultural Centre, Stewart Hall, 176 Lakeshore Rd., H9S 4J7 (514/695-3312)

Quebec: Aquarium de Québec, Ministère Loisir Chasse et Pêche, 1675 ave du Parc, Ste-Foy, P.Q. G1W 4S3. Directeur, P.-J. Paulhus (418/643-5023)

Quebec: Archives nationales du Quebec, Centre de la Capitale, C.P. 10450, Ste-Foy, P.Q. G1V 4N1 (418/643-2167). Conservateur, Robert Garon

Quebec: Maison Maillou, 17, rue Saint-Louis, G1R 4R5 (418/692-3853)

Quebec: Musée des Augustines de l'Hôtel-Dieu de Québec, 32 rue Charlevoix, G1R 3R9. Conservateur, S. Claire Gagnon (418/692-2492, poste 47)

Quebec: Musée de Géologie et de Minéralogie, Université Laval, G1K 7P4. Conservateur, André Lévesque (418/656-2195)

Quebec: Musée du Séminaire, 6 rue de l'Université, G1R 4R7. Conservateur, Abbé Jean-Marie Thivierge

Quebec: La Vieille Maison des Jésuites (début 18ième siècle); Association des créateurs et artisans de Sillery, 2320 chemin du Foulon, Sillery, P.Q. G1T 1X4 (418/653-4776)

St. Constant: Canadian Railway Museum, 122A St. Pierre St. (Box 148, J0L 1X0) (514/632-2410)

Saint-Laurent: Musée d'Art de Saint-Laurent, 615 boul. Sainte-Croix, H4L 3X7 Director, Gérard Lavallee (514/747-7367)

Stanbridge East: Missisquoi Historical Society Inc., Box 186, J0J 2HO (514/248-3153) (Missisquoi Museum: Cornell Mill, Hodge's Store, Bill's Barn)

Trois-Rivières: Archives nationales du Québec, Centre Régional de la Mauricie/Bois-Francs, 225 des Forges, #208, G9A 2G7. Responsable, Yvon Martin (819/379-8253)

Vaudreuil: Musée régional de Vaudreuil-Soulanges, 431, boul. Roche, J7V 2N3, Directeur, Jean Lavoie. Open all year Wed. to Sun., 2-9 p.m. (514/455-2092)

SASKATCHEWAN

Saskatchewan Museum of Natural History

Wascana Park, College & Albert, Regina, Sask. S4P 3V7
(306) 565-2815
Director, Dr. John Storer
Supervisor, Archaeological Research, Ian Dyck
Supervisor, Natural History Research, David Baron
Supervisor, Museum Services, Mrs. Ruby Apperley
Design Consultant, Fred W. Lahrman

Major collections and exhibits of Saskatchewan's natural and human history, including archaeology, entomology, botany, natural history and paleontology. In addition the museum is responsible for nature centres in provincial parks and Trans Canada campgrounds.

Publication of informational booklets and nature notes, bookshop, research library, guided tours, information services, lectures, films, teachers' workshops, and summer film programs for all ages.

Other Museums and Art Galleries in Saskatchewan

Batoche: Batoche National Historic Site, S0K 0K0 Supt., Mrs. M. A. Simpson (306/423-6100)

Battleford: The Fred Light Museum, Curator, F.G. Light, Box 310, S0M 0E0 (306/937-7111)

Denare Beach: Northern Gateway Museum, c/o Mrs. Anne Wiebe, Flin Flon, Man. R8A 1M6 (204/687-5000)

Eastend: Eastend Museum. Collector & Custodian, Henri Lebastard, Box 250, S0N 0T0 (306/295-3508, 3512)

Foam Lake: Foam Lake Museum, Box 395, S0A 1A0. Director, B.E. White

Kindersley: Kindersley Plains Museum, Box 599, S0L 1S0, Secretary, Mrs. J. Helfrich (306/463-4141)

Maple Creek: Oldtimer's Museum, Jasper St. (306/667-2474). (Operated by The Southwestern Sakatchewan Old Timers Association, Secretary, Marj Boyer, Box 1540, S0N 1N0)

Moose Jaw: Western Development Museum, Manager, J. Kaiser, Box 185, S6H 4N8 (306/693-6556)

North Battleford: Western Development Museum & Pioneer Village, Jct. of Nos. 16 & 40 Hwys. E., Manager, Alex Balych, Box 183, North Battleford, Sask. S9A 2Y1 (306/445-8033)

Prince Albert: Lund Wildlife Exhibit, Nesbet Park, River St. W., S6V 0K6

Regina: Diefenbaker Homestead, c/o Wascana Centre Authority, 3475 Albert St., Box 7111, S4P 3S7 (306/584-8660) Public Relations Officer, Marilyn Fox

Regina: Plains Historical Museum, Box 1363, S4P 3B8

Regina: Royal Canadian Mounted Police Museum, Depot Division, Box 6500, S4P 3J7, Director, Malcolm J. H. Wake; Curator, E. McCann (306/359-5837)

Regina: Telorama, SASK TEL, 2350 Albert St., S4P 2Y4, Supervisor, Ted Cholod (306/347-2004)

Riverhurst: F. T. Hill Museum, Riverhurst, Sask. S0H 3P0 (306/353-2112). Curator, Gilmore Krislock (gun collection; Indian artifacts, pioneer items)

Rocanville: Rocanville & Dist. Museum Society, Box 239, Rocanville, Sask. S0A 3L0 (306/645-2605)

St. Walburg: Imhoff Art Gallery, St. Walburg, Sask. S0M 2T0 (306/248-3818)

Saskatoon: Museum of Ukrainian Arts & Crafts, 202 Ave. M.S., S7M 2K4 (306/244-8438)

Saskatoon: Western Development Museum, Manager, David F. Klatt, 2610 Lorne Ave. S., Box 1910, S7K 3S5 (306/652-8900)

Shaunavon: Grand Coteau Heritage and Cultural Centre - Natural history museum, heritage museum, art gallery and public library. Centre St., Shaunavon, S0N 2M0. Curator, Mrs. Déserée J. Rowley, Box 966, 306/297-3882

Spy Hill: Wolverine Hobby & Historical Society Museum, Main St., S0A 3W0, contact Mrs. George Barker (306/534-2032)

Swift Current: Swift Current Museum, Box 1477, Swift Current, Sask. S9H 3X5 (306/773-9888). Curator, Mrs. Clarence Wilson, 105 Chaplin St. E.

Waskesiu Lake: Prince Albert National Park Interpretive Centre, Waskesiu Lake, Sask. S0J 2Y0 (306/663-5322). Town of Waskesiu in the National Park, under the direction of the Chief Park Naturalist.

Weyburn: Soo Line Historical Museum, Hwy. 39 East (Old Power House). Box 1016, S4H 2L2, Curator-Manager, Lavine Stepp (306/842-2922)

Yorkton: Western Development Museum, Manager, Tom Waiser, No. 16 Hwy. W., Box 98, S3N 2V6 (306/783-8361)

YUKON MUSEUMS

Burwash Landing: Kluane Museum of Natural History (Tourist Info. & native handicraft), Alaska Hwy. Mile 1093, Yukon Y1A 3V4

Dawson City: Dawson City Museum & Historical Society, Box 303, Y0B 1G0

Dawson City: Klondike National Historic Sites, Project Manager, Parks Canada, Box 390, Y0B 1G0

Teslin: George Johnston Memorial Museum, Teslin, Yukon Y0A 1B0

Whitehorse: MacBride Museum, 1st Ave. & Wood St., Box 4037, Y1A 3S9

ZOOLOGICAL GARDENS

British Columbia

Vancouver: Stanley Park Zoological Gardens, 2099 Beach Ave., Vancouver, B.C. V6G 1Z4 (604/681-1146)

Alberta

Calgary: Calgary Zoo & Prehistoric Park, St. George's Island, Calgary, Alta. T2G 3H4 (403/265-9310)

Edmonton: Valley Zoo, c/o 10th floor, CN Tower, Edmonton, Alta. T5J 0K1 (403/483-5511)

Saskatchewan

Saskatoon: Forestry Farm Park, Sutherland Sub. P.O., Saskatoon, Sask. S7N 2H0 (306/373-0494)

Manitoba

Winnipeg: Assiniboine Park Zoo, 2355 Corydon Ave., Winnipeg, Man. R3P 0R5 (204/888-3634)

Ontario

Peterborough: Riverview Park & Zoo, Peterborough Utilities Commission, Box 449, Peterborough, Ont. (705/745-4615)

Rockton: African Lion Safari, Rockton, Ont. (519/623-2620)

Thunder Bay: Chippewa Park Zoo, c/o Parks & Recreation Dept., 950 Memorial Ave., Thunder Bay, Ont. P7B 4A2 (807/623-2711, ext. 355)

Toronto: Metro Toronto Zoo, Box 280, West Hill, Ont. M1E 4R5 (416/284-8181)

Wasaga Beach: Wasaga Zoo, Wasaga Beach, Ont. (416/429-5522)

Quebec

Bonaventure: Jardin zoologique de la Gaspésie, C.P. 64, Bonaventure, P.Q. G0C 1S0

Charlesbourg: Jardin Zoologique de Quebec/Quebec Zoological Garden, 8191 ave du Zoo, Charlesbourg, P.Q. G1G 4G4 (418/643-2310)

Granby: Zoological Garden, (Société Zoologique de Granby), 347 Bourget, Granby, P.Q. J2G 1E8 (514/372-9113,4)

Montreal: Zoological Park & Aquarium, c/o Raymond Roth, Director, La Ronde, St. Helen Island, Montreal, P.Q. H3C 1A0 (514/872-5674)

St. Felicien: Zoological Garden, C.P. 520, St. Felicien, P.Q. G0W 2N0 (418/679-0543)

BOTANICAL GARDENS

Montreal Botanical Garden, 4101 E. Sherbrooke St., Montreal, P.Q. H1X 2B2 (514/872-4543)

Arboretum, c/o Ottawa Research Station, Research Branch, Agriculture Canada, Ottawa, Ont. K1A 0C6 (613/995-9827)

Devonian Botanic Garden of the Univ. of Alta., Univ. of Alta., Edmonton, Alta. T6G 2E9 (403/987-3054)

Univ. of B.C. Botanical Garden, Univ. of B.C., 6501 N.W. Marine Dr., Vancouver, B.C. V6T 1W5 (604/228-3928)

Royal Botanical Gardens, Box 399, Hamilton, Ont. L8N 3H8 (416/527-1158)

BOOK PUBLISHERS

The following is a list of major Canadian Book Publishers, Distributors and Publishers' Representatives.

Academic Press Canada
55 Barber Green Rd., Don Mills, Ont. M3C 2A1
(418) 444-7331 – ISBN 0-7747

Addison-Wesley (Canada) Ltd.
36 Prince Andrew Place, Box 580, Don Mills, Ont. M3C 2T8
(416) 447-5101 – ISBN 0-201
Distributors: U.K.—Addison-Wesley Limited, London; Europe—Addison-Wesley Publishers B.V., Amsterdam, and InterEditions, Paris; South America—Fondo Educativo Interamericano, S.A., Panama.

Agence de Distribution Populaire
955 rue Amherst, Montreal, P.Q. H2L 3K4
(514) 523-1182; Telex 05-24667

Alcuin Society
Box 94108, Richmond, B.C. V6Y 2A2
(604) 274-1877 – ISBN 0-919026

All About Us/Nous Autres Canada Inc.
Box 1985, Ottawa, Ont. K1P 5R5
(613) 828-6968 – ISBN 0-919970

Thomas Allen & Son Ltd.
250 Steelcase Rd. E., Markham, Ont. L3R 2S3
(416) 495-9126; Telex 06-966-716 – ISBN 0-919028

Allyn & Bacon, Canada, Ltd.
791 St. Clair Ave. W., Toronto, Ont. M6C 1B8
(416) 654-3221 – ISBN 0-205

Annick Press Ltd.
23 Homewood Ave., Willowdale, Ont. M2M 1K1
(416) 221-4802 – ISBN 0-920236
Distributor: Firefly Books Ltd., 3520 Pharmacy Ave., Unit 1C, Scarborough, Ont. M1W 2T8

Anson-Cartwright Editions
229 College St., Toronto, Ont. M5T 1R4
(416) 979-2441 – ISBN 0-919974

Aquila Communications Ltd.
476 Richmond St. W., Toronto, Ont. M5V 1Y2
(416) 363-0928

A.R.C. Publications
Box 3044, Vancouver, B.C. V6B 3X5
(604) 929-7558 – ISBN 0-88985

The Avondale Press
Box 451, Willowdale, Ont. M2N 5T1
(416) 773-5115 – ISBN 0-9690452

Aya Press
Box 303, Stn. A, Toronto, Ont. M5W 1C2
(416) 782-9984 – ISBN 0-920544

Ballantine Books of Canada
5390 Ambler Dr., Mississauga, Ont. L4W 1Y7
(416) 624-0672 – ISBN 0-345

Bantam Books Canada Inc.
60 St. Clair Ave. E., Ste. 601, Toronto, Ont. M4T 1N5
(416) 922-4970 – ISBN 0-553

Barrdawn Sales Ltd.
2220 Midland Ave., Unit 75, Scarborough, Ont. M1R 3E6
(416) 292-9808

Beaverbooks Ltd.
150 Lesmill Rd., Don Mills, Ont. M3B 2T5
(416) 449-0030

Bell & Howell Canada Ltd.
(Bell & Howell is a publishers' representative)
Audio Visual Products Division, 230 Barmac Dr., Weston, Ont. M9L 2X5
(416) 746-2200; Telex 065-27166

Bellhaven House
Wholly-owned subsidiary of the Book Society, at Book Society's address.
ISBN 0-88774

Bestsellers, Inc.
17 Queen St. E., #439, Toronto, Ont. M5C 1P9
(416) 364-2428 – ISBN 0-86507

Between the Lines
97 Victoria St. N., Kitchener, Ont. N2H 5C1
(519) 576-2640

Book Center Inc.
1140 Beaulac St., Montreal, P.Q. H4R 1R8
(514) 332-4154 – ISBN 0-920094

Book Society of Canada Ltd.
(4386 Sheppard Ave. E.) Box 200, Agincourt, Ont. M1S 3B6
(416) 293-4175 – ISBN 0-7725

Books By Kids
23 Homewood Ave., Willowdale, Ont. M2M 1K1
(416) 221-4802 – ISBN 0-919984
Distributor: Firefly Books Ltd., 3520 Pharmacy Ave., Unit 1C, Scarborough, Ont. M1W 2T8

Borealis Press Ltd.
9 Ashburn Dr., Ottawa, Ont. K2E 6N4
(613) 224-6837 – ISBN 0-919594, 0-88887

Boston Mills Press
98 Main St., Erin, Ont. N0B 1T0
(519) 833-2407 – ISBN 0-919822

Bow-Dell Publishing Ltd.
#101, 2020 King St. E., Hamilton, Ont. L8K 6B9
(416) 547-7994

Brault & Bouthillier Ltée
700 rue Beaumont, Montreal, P.Q. H3N 1V5
(514) 273-9186 – ISBN 0-88537

Breakwater Books Ltd.
277 Duckworth St., Box 2188, St. John's, Nfld. A1C 6E6
(709) 722-6680 – ISBN 0-919948

Brick Books
Box 219, Ilderton, Ont. NOM 2AO
(519) 666-0283 – ISBN 0-919626

B. Broughton Co. Ltd.
123 Queen St. E., Toronto, Ont. M5C 1S1
(416) 863-1656

Brunswick Press
Box 3370, Fredericton, N.B. E3B 5A2
(506) 455-0461 – ISBN 0-88790

Burke Publishing (Canada) Ltd.
91 Station St., Ajax, Ont. L1S 3H2
(416) 683-3800

Burroughs & Company
A Division of The Carswell Company Ltd.
#280, 1520 4th St. S.W., Calgary, Alta. T2R 1H5
(403) 269-5356

Butterworth & Co. (Canada) Ltd.
2265 Midland Ave., Scarborough, Ont. M1P 4S1
(416) 292-1421 – ISBN 0-409

Butterworth & Co. (Western Canada)
409 Granville St., Ste. 856, Vancouver, B.C. V6C 1T2
(604) 684-4116 – ISBN 0-409

Caitlin Press
Box 35550, Stn. E, Vancouver, B.C. V6M 4G8
(604) 539-2769 – ISBN 0-920576

Campbell's Publishing Ltd.
#201, 1150 Rockland Ave., Victoria, B.C. V8V 3H7
(604) 383-0225

Canada Law Book Ltd.
240 Edward St., Aurora, Ont. L4G 3S9
(416) 727-4245; Toronto line: 859-3880
ISBN 0-88804

CBC Merchandising
Canadian Broadcasting Corporation
Box 500, Stn. A, Toronto, Ont. M5W 1E6
(416) 925-3311 – ISBN 0-88794

Canadian Government Publishing Centre
Supply & Services Canada, (located at Hull, P.Q.), mailing: Ottawa, Ont. K1A OS9
(613) 994-3475 – ISBN 0-662, 0-660

Carlton House
91 Station St., Ajax, Ont. L1S 3H2
(416) 683-3800 – ISBN 0-920572

Carswell Legal Publications
A Division of The Carswell Company Ltd.
2330 Midland Ave., Agincourt, Ont. M1S 1P7
(416) 291-8421; Telex 065-25289 – ISBN 0-459

Carswell Legal Publications
A Division of The Carswell Company Ltd.
815 W. Hastings St., Vancouver, B.C. V6C 1B4
(604) 685-8171
CCH Canadian Limited
6 Garamond Court, Don Mills, Ont. M3C 1Z5
(416) 441-2992 – ISBN 0-88796
Centre de Diffusion Editions Paulines
3965 est. boul. Henri-Bourassa, Montreal, P.Q. H1H 1L1
(514) 322-7341 – ISBN 0-88840
Centre Educatif et Culturel Inc.
8101, boul. Métropolitain, Anjou, P.Q. H1J 1J9
(514) 351-6010 – ISBN 2-7617
Centre Pédagogique Inc.
2299, Versant Nord, Ste-Foy, P.Q. G1N 4G2
(418) 688-1943 – ISBN 0-88816
Cercle Littéraire Esotérique
2692 rue Beaubien est, Montreal, P.Q. H1Y 1G7
(514) 721-1880 – ISBN 2-89042
Le Cercle du Livre de France Ltée
8955, boul. St-Laurent, Montréal, P.Q. H2N 1M6
(514) 384-4131 – ISBN 2-89051
Cerebrus Publishing Co. Ltd.
300 Esna Park Dr., Markham, Ont. L3R 1H3
(416) 495-0371 – ISBN 0-920016
Choice Publications Ltd.
491 Brimley Rd., Unit 25, Scarborough, Ont. M1J 1A4
(416) 264-3324 – ISBN 0-920138
Clarke, Irwin & Company Ltd.
791 St. Clair Ave. W., Toronto, Ont. M6C 1B8
(416) 654-3211 – ISBN 0-7720
Clock House Publications
Box 103, Peterborough, Ont. K9J 6Y5
(705) 742-6809 – ISBN 0-919134
Cloudburst Press Ltd.
Mayne Island, B.C. VON 2JO
(604) 539-2923 – ISBN 0-88930
The Coach House Press
401 (rear) Huron St., Toronto, Ont. M5S 2G5
(416) 979-2217 – ISBN 0-88910
Coles Publishing Co. Ltd.
90 Ronson Dr., Rexdale, Ont. M9W 1C1
(416) 249-9121 – ISBN 0-7740
The College of Cape Breton Press
Box 5300, Sydney, N.S. B1P 6L2
(902) 539-5300
Collier Macmillan Canada, Ltd.
Service, 539 Collier-MacMillan Dr., Cambridge, Ont. N1R 5W9 (519) 621-2440, Toronto line (416) 823-7250, 7251; Sales & Editorial Offices, 1125B Leslie St., Don Mills, Ont. M3C 2K2 (416) 449-6030
ISBN 0-02
Collins Publishers
100 Lesmill Rd., Don Mills, Ont. M3B 2T5
(416) 445-8221; Telex 06-966 673 – ISBN 0-00
Computofacts
209 Sheppard Ave. E., Willowdale, Ont. M2N 5W2
(416) 222-4361 – ISBN 0-919640
Copp Clark Pitman
(A Division of Copp Clark Ltd.)
517 Wellington St. W., Toronto, Ont. M5V 1G1
(416) 366-4911; Telex: 06-217849
ISBN 0-7730
Corpus Information Services Ltd.
1450 Don Mills Rd., Don Mills, Ont. M3B 2X7
(416) 445-7101 – ISBN 0-919217
Crabtree Publishing Co. Ltd.
102 Torbrick Ave., Toronto, Ont. M4J 4Z5
(416) 466-1906 – ISBN 0-86505
Cross Country Press
5572 Clark St., Montreal, P.Q. H2T 2V4
(514) 279-4816 – ISBN 0-916696
Cumming Publishers
Box 23, Stratford, Ont. N5A 6S8
ISBN 0-88988
Daniel Books of Toronto
Box 488, Adelaide PO, Toronto, Ont. M5C 2J6
(416) 922-2912
Richard De Boo Ltd.
81 Curlew Dr., Don Mills, Ont. M3A 3P7
(416) 445-4940 – ISBN 0-88820
Deluge Editions
1538 Sherbrooke St. W., Montreal, P.Q. H3G 1L5
(514) 931-5905 – ISBN 0-920068
Deneau Publishers & Co. Ltd.
281 Lisgar St., Ottawa, Ont. K2P 0E1
(613) 233-4075 – ISBN 0-88879
J.M. Dent & Sons (Canada) Ltd.
100 Scarsdale Rd., Don Mills, Ont. M3B 2R8
(416) 447-7221 – ISBN 0-460
Distributors: U.S.—Educational Activities, Inc.; U.K.—J.M. Dent & Sons Ltd.; Canada – Van Nostrand Reinhold Ltd.
Marcel Didier (Canada) Ltee
2050 Bleury St., Ste. 500, Montreal, P.Q. H3A 2J4
(514) 288-7191; Telex 055-61003
ISBN 2-89144
Diliton Publications Inc.
Box 1351, St. Catharines, Ont. L2R 7J8
(416) 662-2808 – ISBN 0-920642
Discovery Press
Box 46295, Vancouver, B.C. V6R 4G6
(604) 228-8606 – ISBN 0-919624
DMR Inc.
317 Benjamin-Hudon, Montreal, P.Q. H4N 1J1
(514) 331-4540; Telex 05-825646
Dodd, Mead & Co. (Canada) Ltd.
See Hollinger House Ltd.
ISBN 0-396
Dominie Press Ltd.
345 Nugget Ave., Unit 15, Agincourt, Ont. M1S 4J4
(416) 291-5857 – ISBN 0-88751
Doubleday Canada Ltd.
105 Bond St., Toronto, Ont. M5B 1Y3
(416) 977-7891 – ISBN 0-385
Douglas & McIntyre Ltd.
1615 Venables St., Vancouver, B.C. V5L 2H1
(604) 254-7191; Telex 04-508616
ISBN 0-88894
Dundurn Press Ltd.
Box 245, Stn. F, Toronto, Ont. M4Y 2L5
(416) 368-9390 – ISBN 0-919670
Ecrits des Forges
2095 rue Sylvain, Trois-Rivières, P.Q. G8Y 2H6
(819) 375-9561 – ISBN 2-89046-002
Eden Press Inc.
245 Victoria Ave., #12, Westmount, P.Q. H3Z 2M6
(514) 931-3910 – ISBN 0-88831
Edi Compo Inc.
1027 Ste-Hélène, Longueuil, P.Q. J4K 3S1
(514) 463-3930 – ISBN 2-89066
Editeur Officiel du Québec
1283 boul. Charest Ouest, Quebec, P.Q. G1N 2C9
(418) 643-5150 – ISBN 2-551-
Editions Agence d'Arc
6872 rue Jarry est, St-Léonard, P.Q. H1P 3C1
(514) 321-0241 – ISBN 0-88586
Editions Aquila Ltée
3785 Côte de Liesse, Montréal, P.Q. H4N 2N5
(514) 747-2408 – ISBN 0-88510; 2-89054
Editions Archambault Inc.
500 est rue Ste-Catherine, Montreal, P.Q. H2L 2C6
(514) 849-6201
Editions Bellarmin
8100 boul. St-Laurent, Montréal, P.Q. H2P 2L9
(514) 387-2541 – ISBN 2-89007
Editions Champlain Ltee
107 Church St., Toronto, Ont. M5C 2G5
(416) 364-4345 – ISBN 0-920936
Editions Cheminements Ltee
C.P. 54, (St-Martin) Laval, P.Q.H7V 3P4

(514) 687-4571
Editions Coopératives Albert St-Martin
5089 rue Garnier, Montreal, P.Q. H2J 3T1
(514) 525-4346 – ISBN 2-89035
Editions Cosmos Enr.
C.P. 697, Sherbrooke, P.Q. J1H 5K5
(819) 563-1117 – ISBN 0-7765
Editions d'Acadie Ltée
120 rue Victoria, C.P. 885, Moncton, N.B. E1C 8N8
(506) 854-3490 – ISBN 2-7600
Editions du Boréal Express
C.P. 418, Stn. Youville, Montréal, P.Q. H2P 2V6
(514) 336-9551 – ISBN 2-89052
Editions de l'Ecureuil Noir
19650 boul. Bécancour, St-Grégoire (Nicolet), P.Q. G0X 2T0
(819) 233-2927
Editions de l'Espoir Ltée
55 Adrien Robert, Hull, P.Q. J8Y 3S3
(819) 777-2113
Editions de l'Hexagone Enr.
C.P. 337, Bur. Postal N, Montreal, P.Q. H2X 3M4
(514) 843-8653 – ISBN 2-89006
Editions du Levrier
5375, ave Notre-Dame de Grâce, Montréal, P.Q. H4A 1L2
(514) 481-5603 – ISBN 0-919274
Les Editions du Noroit
C.P. 244, St-Lambert, P.Q. J4P 3N8
(514) 671-7718 – ISBN 2-89018
Editions du Pélican
Box 1182, Québec, P.Q. G1K 7C3
(418) 692-0330 – ISBN 2-89011
Editions du Renouveau Pédagogique Inc.
8925, boul. Saint-Laurent, Montréal, P.Q. H2N 1M5
(514) 384-2690 – ISBN 2-7613
Editions du Richelieu Ltée
C.P. 216, 142 rue St-Pierre, Saint-Jean, P.Q. J3B 5W3
(514) 347-5326 – ISBN 0-88520
Editions du Seuil Ltee
539 boul Lebeau, St-Laurent, P.Q. H4N 1S2
(514) 336-3941 – ISBN 2-0200
Editions de l'Université d'Ottawa
65 Hastey Ave., Ottawa, Ont. K1N 6N5
(613) 231-2270 – ISBN 2-7603
Editions Ecole Active
2244 rue Rouen, Montréal, P.Q. H2K 1L5
(514) 527-3425 – ISBN 2-89069
Editions l'Etincelle (SCE)
3449 rue St-Denis, Montreal, P.Q. H2X 3L1
(514) 843-4344 – ISBN 2-89019
Editions Etudes Vivantes Ltée
6700 ch. Côte de Liesse, St-Laurent, P.Q. H4T 1E3
(514) 341-6690
Editions Fides
235 est, boul. Dorchester, Montréal, P.Q. H2X 1N9
(514) 861-9621 – ISBN 0-7755
Editions FM Les
1113, rue Desnoyers, St-Vincent-de-Paul, Laval, P.Q. H7C 1Y6
(514) 324-0712 – ISBN 2-89047
Les Editions Françaises Inc.
1411 rue Ampère, C.P. 395, Boucherville, P.Q. J4B 5B0
(514) 641-0514 – ISBN 0-7756
Editions Guy Maheux Inc.
7705 boul. de l'Acadie, #101, Montreal, P.Q. H3N 2W1
(514) 272-3256 – ISBN 2-89042
Les Editions Heritage
300 ave Arran, St-Lambert, P.Q. J4R 1K5
(514) 672-6710 – ISBN 0-7773
Editions HRW Ltée (Les)
8035, rue Jarry est, Anjou, Montréal, P.Q. H1J 1H6
(514) 351-7810 – ISBN 0-03
Editions Hurtubise HMH Ltée
7360 Boul. Newman, LaSalle, P.Q. H8N 1X2
(514) 364-0323 – ISBN 0-7758
Editions internationales Alain Stanké
2127, rue Guy, Montréal, P.Q. H3H 2M1
(514) 935-7452 – ISBN 2-7604-0
Editions Leméac Inc.
5111, rue Durocher, Montréal, P.Q. H2V 3X7
(514) 274-0354 – ISBN 2-7609
Editions Marcel Broquet Inc.
C.P. 310, Laprairie, P.Q. J5R 3Y3
(514) 659-4819 – ISBN 2-89000
Editions Marie-France Ltee
3688 rue Fleury est, Montreal-Nord, P.Q. H1H 2S6
(514) 322-6834 – ISBN 2-89168
Editions Mirabel
8925 boul. Saint-Laurent, Montréal, P.Q. H2N 1M5
(514) 384-2690 – ISBN 2-89041
Editions Naaman
C.P. 697, Sherbrooke, P.Q. J1H 5K5
(819) 563-1117; 566-2341 – ISBN 2-89040
Editions Parti Pris
947 Duluth est, Montreal, P.Q. H2L 1B7
(514) 523-0810 – ISBN 0-88512/2-7602
Editions Pedagogia (Inc.)
see Les Editions Françaises
Les Editions La Liberté Inc.
3020 ch. Ste-Foy, Ste-Foy, P.Q. G1X 3V6
(418) 658-3763 – ISBN 2-89084
Editions La Presse
7 rue Saint-Jacques, Montréal, P.Q. H2Y 1K9
(514) 285-6981 – ISBN 2-89043
Les Editions Projets Inc.
342 terrasse Saint-Denis, Montréal, P.Q. H2X 1E8
(514) 845-4126 – ISBN 2-89038
Editions Québec-Amérique
450 est, rue Sherbrooke, bur. 801, Montreal, P.Q. H2L 1J8
(514) 288-2371
Les Editions St-Yves Inc.
C.P. 9638, Ste-Foy, P.Q. G1V 4C2
(418) 651-1073 – ISBN 2-89034
Edu-Media Holdings Ltd.
One Adam St., Box 1240, Kitchener, Ont. N2G 4H1
(519) 578-5410 – ISBN 0-88979
Encyclopaedia Britannica Publications Ltd.
2 Bloor St. W., Ste. 1100, Toronto, Ont. M4W 3J1
(416) 925-9531 – ISBN 0-7738
Engendra Press Ltd.
Box 235, Westmount Stn., Montreal, P.Q. H3Z 2T2
(514) 933-1282 – ISBN 0-919830
Enterprises culturelles Enr.
399 rue des Conseillers, Laprairie, P.Q. J5R 4H6
(514) 659-1282 – ISBN 2-7614
EPC Educational Progress Co. Ltd.
See Hayes Publishing Ltd.
M.F. Feheley Publishers
5 Drumsnab Rd., Toronto, Ont. M4W 3A4
(416) 964-3722 – ISBN 0-919880
Fforbez Publications Ltd.
2133 Quebec St., Vancouver, B.C. V5T 2Z9
(604) 872-7325 – ISBN 0-88976
Fiddlehead Poetry Books
c/o English Dept., U.N.B., Bag Service 45555, Fredericton, N.B. E3B 6A5
(506) 453-4675
ISBN 0-920110, 0-919196, 0-919197, 0-86492
Fideler Representatives & Consultants
Box 35460, Vancouver, B.C. V6M 4G8
(604) 266-2217
Fitzhenry & Whiteside Limited
150 Lesmill Rd., Don Mills, Ont. M3B 2T5
(416) 449-0030 – ISBN 0-88902
Formac Publishing Ltd.
Box 1688, 86 College St., Antigonish, N.S.
(902) 863-1166 – ISBN 0-88780
Samuel French (Canada) Ltd.
80 Richmond St. E., Toronto, Ont. M5C 1P1
(416) 363-3536 – ISBN 0-573
Frontier Books
Box 1228, Stn. A, Surrey, B.C. V3S 2B3

(604) 596-5245 – ISBN 0-919214
Gage Publishing Limited
164 Commander Blvd., Agincourt, Ont. M1S 3C7
(416) 293-8141 – Telex 065-25374 – ISBN 0-7715
Gateway Sales
A Division of G.R. Welch Co.
960 Gateway, Burlington, Ont. L7L 5K7
(416) 681-2760
General Merchandising
30 Lesmill Rd., Don Mills, Ont. M3B 2T6
(416) 445-3333 – Telex 06-986664
General Paperbacks
25 Torbay Rd., Markham, Ont. L3R 1H1
(416) 495-9111
General Publishing Co. Limited
30 Lesmill Rd., Don Mills, Ont. M3B 2T6
(416) 445-3333; Telex: 06-986664
ISBN 0-7736
Ginn and Company
3771 Victoria Park Ave., Scarborough, Ont. M1W 2P9
(416) 497-4600 – ISBN 0-7702
GLC Publishers Ltd.
115 Nugget Ave., Agincourt, Ont. M1S 3B1
(416) 291-2926 – ISBN 0-88874
Globe/Modern Curriculum Press
200 Steelcase Rd. E., Markham, Ont. L3R 1G2
(416) 495-0564 – ISBN 0-88996
Gray's Publishing Ltd.
Box 2160, Sidney, B.C. V8L 3S6
(604) 656-4454 – ISBN 0-88826
Greey de Pencier Books
59 Front St. E., Toronto, Ont. M5E 1B3
(416) 364-3333 – ISBN 0-919872
Griffin House Publishers
461 King St. W., Toronto, Ont. M5V 1K7
(416) 864-1400 – ISBN 0-88760
Grolier Ltd.–Grolier Ltée
16 Overlea Blvd., Toronto, Ont. M4H 1A6
(416) 425-1924 – ISBN 0-7172
Guardian Books
99 Niagara St., St. Catharines, Ont. L2R 4L3
(416) 682-5614 – ISBN 0-920376
Guerin Editeur Ltée
4574, rue Saint-Denis, Montreal, P.Q. H2J 2L3
(514) 842-3481 – ISBN 2-7601
Guidance Centre
1000 Yonge St., Toronto, Ont. M4W 2K8
(416) 978-3206 – ISBN 0-7713
Guinness Publishing Ltd.
Box 35460, Vancouver, B.C. V6M 4G8
(604) 266-2217 – ISBN 0-919228
Hancock House Publishers Ltd.
10 Orwell St., North Vancouver, B.C. V7J 3K1
(604) 980-4113
Harlequin Enterprises Ltd.
Executive Offices, 225 Duncan Mills Rd., Don Mills, Ont. M3B 3K9
(416) 445-5860 – ISBN 0-373
Harvest House Ltd.
4795 St. Catherine St. W., Montreal, P.Q. H3Z 1S8
(514) 932-0666 – ISBN 0-88772
Hayes Publishing Ltd.
3312 Mainway, Burlington, Ont. L7M 1A7
(416) 335-0393
D.C. Heath Canada Ltd.
100 Adelaide St. W., Ste. 1600, Toronto, Ont. M5H 1S9
(416) 362-6483, 7597 – ISBN 0-669
Herald Press
117 King St. W., Kitchener, Ont. N2G 4M5
(519) 743-9731 – ISBN 0-8361
Heritage House Publishing Co. Ltd.
5543 129th St., Surrey, B.C. V3W 4H4
(604) 596-5245 – ISBN 0-919214
Hollinger House Ltd.
25 Hollinger Rd., Toronto, Ont. M4B 3G2
(416) 751-4520 – ISBN 0-7710
Holt, Rinehart & Winston of Canada Ltd.
55 Horner Ave., Toronto, Ont. M8Z 4X6
(416) 255-4491 – ISBN 0-03
U.S. Distributor: Holt, Rinehart & Winston Inc., 383 Madison Ave., New York, N.Y. 10017, U.S.A.
Houghton Mifflin Canada Ltd.
150 Steelcase Rd. W., Markham, Ont. L3R 1B2
(416) 495-1755 – ISBN 0-395
Hounslow Press
(A Division of Anthony R. Hawke, Ltd.)
124 Parkview Ave., Willowdale, Ont. M2N 3Y5
(416) 225-9176 – ISBN 0-88882
House of Anansi Press Ltd.
35 Britain St., Toronto, Ont. M5A 1R7
(416) 363-5444 – ISBN 0-88784
(distributed in Canada and the U.S. by U. of T. Press)
House of Grant (Canada) Ltd.
98 Scarsdale Rd., Don Mills, Ont. M3B 2R8
(416) 447-7221
Canadian distributor: Van Nostrand Reinhold Ltd.
House of Learning Ltd.
Box 152, Stratford, Ont. N5A 6T1
(519) 393-6144
Hurtig Publishers Ltd.
10560 105 St., Edmonton, Alta. T5H 2W7
(403) 426-2359 – ISBN 0-88830
Hyperion Press Ltd.
300 Wales Ave., Winnipeg, Man. R2M 2S9
(204) 256-9204 – ISBN 0-920534
Inner City Books
Box 1271, Stn. Q, Toronto, Ont. M4T 2P4
(416) 484-4562 – ISBN 0-919123
Institute of Psychological Research, Inc./Institut de Recherches psychologiques, inc.
34 ouest, rue Fleury, Montréal, P.Q. H3L 1S9
(514) 382-3000 – ISBN 0-88509
International Self-Counsel Press Ltd.
306 W. 25th St., North Vancouver, B.C. V7N 2G1
(604) 986-3366 – ISBN 0-88908
Inter-Varsity Press
(IVP is a Publishers' Representative)
1875 Leslie St., Unit 10, Don Mills, Ont. M3B 2M5
(416) 447-4001 – ISBN 0-88918
ISER Publications (Institute of Social & Economic Research)
Memorial University of Nfld., St. John's, Nfld. A1C 5S7
(709) 737-8156 – ISBN 0-919666
Le Jour
955 rue Amherst, Montreal, P.Q. H2L 3K4
(514) 523-1182 – ISBN 0-7760
Canadian distributor: Agence de distribution Populaire, 955 Amherst
Kids Can Press
585½ Bloor St. W., Toronto, Ont. M6G 1K5
(416) 534-3141 – ISBN 0-919964
Canadian Distributor: Fitzhenry & Whiteside
Kosoy Travel Guides
40 Shallmar Blvd., Toronto, Ont. M6C 2J9
(416) 783-8578 – ISBN 0-919632
Lancelot Press Ltd.
Box 425, Hantsport, N.S. BOP 1PO
(902) 684-9129 – ISBN 0-88999
J.M. LeBel Enterprises Ltd.
10372 60 Ave. (Box 4224, Edmonton, Alta. T6E 4T2)
(403) 439-4717 – ISBN 0-920008
Lenbrook Industries Ltd.
1145 Bellamy Rd., Scarborough, Ont. M1H 1H5
(416) 438-4610 – ISBN 0-672
Lester and Orpen Dennys Ltd.
78 Sullivan St., Toronto, Ont. M5T 1C1
(416) 863-6402 – ISBN 0-919630
Librairie Beauchemin Ltée
381 ouest rue St-Jacques, bur. 400, Montreal, P.Q. H2Y 3S2
(514) 842-1427 – ISBN 2-7616

Librairie Déom
1773 rue St-Denis, Montréal, P.Q. H2X 3K4
(514) 845-2320 – ISBN 2-89020
Librairie Garneau Ltée
8955, Boul. St-Laurent, Montreal, P.Q. H2N 1M6
(514) 384-8760 – ISBN 0-7757
Librairie L.S.C.
2244 rue Rouen, Montréal, P.Q. H2K 1L5
(514) 527-3425 – ISBN 2-89069
Lidec Inc.
1083 rue Van Horne, Montreal, P.Q. H2V 1J6
(514) 274-6521 – ISBN 2-7608
J.B. Lippincott Co. of Canada Ltd.
75 Horner Ave., Toronto, Ont. M8Z 4X7
(416) 252-5277
Little, Brown & Co. (Canada) Ltd.
See Hollinger House Ltd.
ISBN 0-400
James Lorimer & Co., Publishers
35 Britain St., Toronto, Ont. M5A 1R7
(416) 362-4762 – ISBN 0-88862
LR Associates Publishing Ltd.
Box 302, Agincourt, Ont. M1S 3TO
(416) 264-2834 – ISBN 0-88845
Canadian distributor: Sports & Fitness Book Service, 3549 St. Clair Ave. E., Scarborough, Ont. M1K 1L6 (416/264-2834)
Macdonald-Raintree Canada
2020 King St. E., #101, Hamilton, Ont. L8K 6B9
Macmillan of Canada
A Division of Gage Publishing
146 Front St. W., #685, Toronto, Ont. M5J 1G2
(416) 597-1060 – ISBN 0-7715
La Maison de l'Education Inc.
10,485 boul. Saint Laurent, Montréal, P.Q. H3L 2P1
(514) 384-4844
McAinsh & Co. Ltd.
10 Carnforth Rd., Toronto, Ont. M4A 2S5
(416) 755-7708
also: 730 W. Broadway, Vancouver, B.C. V5Z 1G8 (604/872-5310)
McClelland & Stewart Ltd.
See Hollinger House Ltd.
ISBN 0-7710
McGill-Queen's University Press
1020 Pine Ave. W., Montreal, P.Q. H3A 1A2
(514) 392-4421 – ISBN 0-7735
McGraw-Hill Ryerson Ltd.
330 Progress Ave., Scarborough, Ont. M1P 2Z5
(416) 293-1911 – ISBN 0-07
McLeod Publishing
30 Lesmill Rd., Don Mills, Ont. M3B 2T6
(416) 445-3333; Telex: 06-986664
ISBN 0-919292
Charles E. Merrill Publishing
Bell & Howell Canada Ltd., Audio Visual Products Division, 230 Barmac Dr., Weston, Ont. M9L 2X5
(416) 746-2200; Telex: 065-27166
Methuen Publications
2330 Midland Ave., Agincourt, Ont. M1S 1P7
(416) 291-8421 – ISBN 0-458
Mika Publishing Co.
Box 536, Belleville, Ont. K8N 5B2
(613) 962-4022
ISBN 0-919302, 0-919303
Mitchell Press Ltd.
Box 6000, Vancouver, B.C. V6B 4B9
(604) 731-5211 – ISBN 0-88836
R.G. Mitchell Family Books Ltd.
(Mitchell is a Publishers' Representative)
565 Gordon Baker Rd., Willowdale, Ont. M2H 2W2
(416) 499-4615
Monarch Press
3547 Bathurst St., Toronto, Ont. M6A 2C7
(416) 783-5725
Mosaic Press/Valley Editions
Box 1032, Oakville, Ont. L6J 5E9
(416) 844-0963 – ISBN 0-88962
Moyer Vico Corp.
25 Milvan Dr., Weston, Ont. M9L 1Z1
(416) 749-2222
Musson Book Co.
30 Lesmill Rd., Don Mills, Ont. M3B 2T6
(416) 445-3333; Telex: 06-986664
ISBN 0-7737
Nelson Canada Ltd.
1120 Birchmount Rd., Scarborough, Ont. M1K 5G4
(416) 752-9100 – ISBN 0-17
Nelson, Foster & Scott
30 Lesmill Rd., Don Mills, Ont. M3B 2T6
(416) 445-3333; Telex: 06-986664
ISBN 0-919324
New American Library of Canada Ltd.
81 Mack Ave., Scarborough, Ont. M1L 1M8
(416) 699-7193
ISBN 0-451, 0-452, 0-453
New Press
30 Lesmill Rd., Don Mills, Ont. M3B 2T6
(416) 445-3333; Telex 06-986664
ISBN 0-88770
NeWest Publishers Ltd.
#204, 10711 107 Ave., Edmonton, Alta. T5H 0W6
(403) 426-6382 – ISBN 0-920316
Oberon Press
401a Inn of the Provinces, Ottawa, Ont. K1R 7S8
(613) 238-3275 – ISBN 0-88750
Overseas Distributor: Dobson Books Ltd., 80 Kensington Church St., London, W8 4BZ, Eng.
October Publications
Box 3104, Stn. D, Willowdale, Ont. M2R 3G5
ISBN 0-919660
Ontario Publishing Co. Ltd.
33 Kern Rd., Don Mills, Ont. M3B 1S9
(416) 447-7295 – ISBN 0-919354
Optimum Publishing International Inc.
511 Place d'Armes, Montréal, P.Q. H2Y 2W7
(514) 844-8468 – ISBN 0-88890
Outcrop – The Northern Publishers
Box 1114, Yellowknife, N.W.T.
(403) 873-6152
Oxford University Press
70 Wynford Drive, Don Mills, Ont. M3C 1J9
(416) 441-2941 – Telex 06-966518 – ISBN 0-19
Pagurian Press Ltd.
13 Hazelton Ave., Toronto, Ont. M5R 2E1
(416) 968-0255
ISBN 0-919364, 0-88932
Canadian Distributor: Clarke Irwin Ltd.
PaperJacks Ltd.
330 Steelcase Rd., Markham, Ont. L3R 2M1
(416) 495-1261 – ISBN 0-7701
Pathfinder Press Ltd.
1317 rue Ste-Catherine est, Montreal, P.Q. H2L 2H4
(514) 856-9848 – ISBN 0-87348
Peguis Publishers Ltd.
462 Hargrave St., Winnipeg, Man. R3A OX5
(204) 956-1486 – ISBN 0-919566
Pendragon House Ltd.
2525 Dunwin, Mississauga, Ont. L5L 1T2
(416) 828-0400 – ISBN 0-88761
Distributors: U.S.A.—Pendragon House Inc., 2898 Joseph Ave., Campbell, Calif. 95008; Pendragon House of Connecticut Inc., Mystic, Conn.; U.K.—Pendragon House, U.K. Ltd., Lizard Town, S. of Helston, Cornwall TR12 7PG, Eng.
Pendulum Press Inc.
Canadian Distributor: School Book Fairs Ltd., 2201 Dunwin Dr., Mississauga, Ont. L5L 1A3
(416) 828-6620 – ISBN 0-88301
Penguin Books Canada Ltd.
2801 John St., Markham, Ont. L3R 1B4

(416) 495-1571 – ISBN 0-14
Pergamon Press Canada Ltd.
150 Consumers Rd., Ste. 104, Willowdale, Ont. M2J 1P9
(416) 497-8337; Telex: 065-25460 – ISBN 0-08
Petheric Press Ltd.
Box 8171, Halifax, N.S. B3K 5L9
(902) 422-4194 – ISBN 0-919380
PMA Books
(Published by Peter Martin Associates Ltd.)
150 Browning Ave., Toronto, Ont. M4K 1W5
(416) 463-5329 – ISBN 0-88778
The Prairie Publishing Co.
Box 264, Stn. C, Winnipeg, Man. R3M 3S7
(204) 885-6496 – ISBN 0-919576
Prentice-Hall Canada Inc.
1870 Birchmount Rd., Scarborough, Ont. M1P 2J7
(416) 293-3621 – ISBN 0-13
Distributors:
Prentice-Hall International Inc., 66 Wood Lane End, Hemel Hempstead, Herts, HP2 4GR, Eng. (U.K. & Europe)
Prentice-Hall International, Englewood Cliffs, N.J. 07632 (U.S.A.)
Prentice-Hall of Australia Pty. Ltd., Box 151, Brookvale, N.S.W. 2100 Aust. (Australia)
Les Presses de l'Université de Montréal
C.P. 6128, Succ. A, Montréal, P.Q. H3C 3J7
(514) 343-6929 – ISBN 2-7606
Distributors: Europe—Librairie L'Ecole, 11, rue de Sèvres, Paris 75006, France; U.S.A.—Global Library Marketing Service, Rt. 127, Contoocook, New Hampshire 03229
Les Presses de l'Université du Québec
2875, boul. Laurier, Ste-Foy, Québec, P.Q. G1V 2M3
(418) 657-2426 – ISBN 2-7605
Les Presses de l'Université Laval
C.P. 2447, Québec, P.Q. G1K 7R4
(418) 656-3001 – ISBN 2-7637
Les Presses Laurentiennes
1645 ave Notre Dame, C.P. 130, Notre-Dame-des-Laurentides, P.Q. GOA 2SO
(418) 849-8403 – ISBN 2-89015
Presses Select Ltée
1555 ouest rue Louvain, Montreal, P.Q. H4N 1G6
(514) 387-6268 – ISBN 2-89132
Progress Books
71 Bathurst St., 3rd floor, Toronto, Ont. M5V 2P6
(416) 368-5336 – ISBN 0-919396
Pulp Press
Box 3868, Vancouver, B.C. V6B 3Z3
(604) 687-4233 – ISBN 0-88978
Queenston House Publishing Co. Ltd.
102 Queenston St., Winnipeg, Man. R3N OW5
(204) 489-6862 – ISBN 0-919866
Ragweed Press Inc.
Box 2023, Charlottetown, P.E.I. C1A 7N7
(902) 892-4121 – ISBN 0-920304
Random House of Canada Ltd.
5390 Ambler Dr., Mississauga, Ont. L4W 1Y7
(416) 624-0672 – ISBN 0-394
Renouf Publishing Co. Ltd.
2182 St. Catherine St. W., Montreal, P.Q. H3H 1M7
(514) 937-3519 – ISBN 0-88852
Le Sablier Inc.
C.P. 120, Boucherville, P.Q. J4B 5E6
(514) 861-2764/5 – ISBN 0-919428
Saunders of Toronto Ltd.
250 Steelcase Rd. E., Markham, Ont. L3R 2S3
(416) 495-9126 – ISBN 0-88762
W.B. Saunders Company Canada Ltd.
1 Goldthorne Ave., Toronto, Ont. M8Z 5T9
(416) 251-3787; Telex: 06-984657
ISBN 0-7216
SBF Media Ltd.
See Pendulum Press
Scholar's Choice Ltd.
225 Duncan Mill Rd., 6th Floor, Don Mills, Ont. M3B 3K9
ISBN 0-88809
Scholastic-TAB Publications Ltd.
123 Newkirk Rd., Richmond Hill, Ont. L4C 3G5
(416) 883-5300; Telex 610-492-2620
Science Research Associates (Canada) Limited
707 Gordon Baker Rd., Willowdale, Ont. M2H 2S6
(416) 497-7707 – Telex 065-25182 SCIRECAN
ISBN 0-574
Seal Books
See Bantam Books
Simon & Pierre Publishing Co. Ltd.
69 Sherbourne St. (Box 280, Adelaide St. P.O., Toronto, Ont. M5C 2J4)
(416) 363-6767 – ISBN 0-88924
Socadis Inc.
350, boul. Lebeau, St-Laurent, P.Q. H4N 1W6
(514) 331-3300; Telex 05-826568
Sono Nis Press
1745 Blanshard St., Victoria, B.C. V8W 2J8
(604) 382-1024; 382-0516
ISBN 0-919462
Steel Rail Publishing
Box 4357, Stn. E, Ottawa, Ont. K1S 5B3
(613) 232-6382 – ISBN 0-88791
Steiner Book Centre
151 Carisbrooke Cres., North Vancouver, B.C. V7N 2S2
(604) 986-2444 – ISBN 0-919924
Samuel-Stevens, Publishers Ltd.
250 Merton St., Toronto, Ont. M4S 1B1
(416) 489-6811 – ISBN 0-88866
Summerthought Ltd.
Box 1420, Banff, Alta. TOL OCO
(403) 762-3919 – ISBN 0-919934
Synaxis Press
Box 404, Chilliwack, B.C. V2P 6J7
(604) 858-7750 – ISBN 0-919672
Talon Books
#201, 1019 E. Cordova, Vancouver, B.C. V6A 1M8
(604) 255-5915 – ISBN 0-88922
Totem Books
Paperback division of Collins Publishers
Tree Frog Press Ltd.
10717 106 Ave., Edmonton, Alta. T5H 3Y9
(403) 425-1505 – ISBN 0-88967
Trinity Press
A Division of G.R. Welch Co.
960 Gateway, Burlington, Ont. L7L 5K7
(416) 681-2760
Tundra Books/Les Livres Toundra
1434 Ste Catherine St. W., #308, Montreal, P.Q. H3G 1R4
(514) 932-5434 – ISBN 0-88776
Canadian Distributor: Collins Publishers
U.S. Distributor: Tundra Books of Northern N.Y., Box 1030, Plattsburgh, N.Y. 12901
University of Alberta Press
450, Athabasca Hall, Univ. of Alta., Edmonton, Alta. T6G 2E8
(403) 432-3662 – ISBN 0-88864
University of British Columbia Press
#303, 6344 Memorial Rd., UBC, Vancouver, B.C. V6T 1W5
(604) 228-3259, 228-5959 – ISBN 0-7748
University of Ottawa Press
65 Hastey Ave., Ottawa, Ont. K1N 6N5
(613) 231-2270 – ISBN 2-7603
University of Toronto Press
63a St. George St., Toronto, Ont. M5S 1A6
(416) 667-7791 – Telex 06-219583 – ISBN 0-8020
Vanguard Publications
See Pathfinder Press
Van Nostrand Reinhold Ltd.
1410 Birchmount Rd., Scarborough, Ont. M1P 2E7
(416) 751-2800; Telex 06-963546
ISBN 0-442
Véhicule Press
Box 125, Succ La Cité, Montreal, P.Q. H2X 3M0
(514) 524-2355 – ISBN 0-919890

Vesta Publications Ltd.
Box 1641, Cornwall, Ont. K6H 5V6
(613) 932-2135 – ISBN 0-919806

Wadsworth Publishers of Canada Ltd.
400 Esna Park Dr., Markham, Ont. L3R 1H5
(416) 495-2090

G.R. Welch Co. Ltd.
960 Gateway, Burlington, Ont. L7L 5K7
(416) 681-2760 – ISBN 0-919532

Western Producer Prairie Books
Box 2500, Saskatoon, Sask. S7K 2C4
(306) 665-3548 – ISBN 0-88833

Wiley, John, & Sons Canada Ltd.
22 Worcester Rd., Rexdale, Ont. M9W 1L1
(416) 675-3580 – ISBN 0-471

Wilfrid Laurier University Press
Alumni Hall, Wilfrid Laurier Univ., Waterloo, Ont. N2L 3C5
(519) 884-7300 – ISBN 0-88920

Women's Educational Press
Room 313, 280 Bloor St. W., Toronto, Ont. M5S 1W1
(416) 922-9447 – ISBN 0-88961

Xerox Canada Inc.
See Ginn and Company

CANADIAN NEWSPAPER AND MAGAZINE DIRECTORY

(Source: "Canadian Advertising Rates & Data", a publication of Maclean-Hunter, with kind permission; and Canadian Periodical Publishers Association)

NEWSPAPERS

(listed alphabetically within provinces)

Alberta Daily Newspapers

CALGARY: The Calgary Sun (morning), 830-10th Ave. S.W. (T2R 0B1)—403/263-7730
The Herald (evening) Southam Press, 215 16 St. S.E.

EDMONTON: The Edmonton Sun (morning) 10310 124th St. (T5N 1R2)—403/482-7611
Edmonton Journal (evening) Southam Press, 10006-101 St. (T5J 2S6)—403/425-9120

FORT McMURRAY: Fort McMurray Today (afternoon), 9701 Franklin Ave. (Bag 4008, T9H 3G1)—403/743-8186

GRANDE PRAIRIE: Daily Herald-Tribune (afternoon), 10604-100 St. (T8V 2M5)—403/532-1110

LETHBRIDGE: The Lethbridge Herald (evening) 504-7th St. S. (T1J 3Z7)—403/328-4411

LLOYDMINSTER: Daily Times, 4828 44 St. (S9V OG8) — 403/825-5522

MEDICINE HAT: News (evening) Southam Press, 3257 Dunmore Rd. S.E. —403/527-1101

RED DEER: Advocate (evening), 2950 Bremner Ave. (Box 520, T4N 5G3)—403/343-2400

Alberta Weekly Newspapers

Airdrie & Dist. Echo (Wed.) Box 580, Airdrie, Alta. TOM OBO—403/948-7280

Airdrie, Rocky View Times (Wed.) Box 580, TOM OBO — 403/948-7280

Alliance Enterprise (Wed.) Box 99, Sedgewick, Alta. T0B 4C0—403/384-3641

Athabasca Echo (Wed.) Box 1800, T0G 0B0—403/675-2414

Banff Crag & Canyon (Wed.) Box 129, T0L 0C0—403/762-2453

Barrhead Leader (Tue.) Box 10, T0G 0E0—403/674-3823

Bashaw Star (Wed.) Box 188, T0B 0H0—403/372-3608

Bassano Times (Wed.) Box 780, T0J 0B0—403/472-3636

Beaverlodge & Dist. Advertiser (Wed.) Box 300, T0H 0C0—403/354-2460

Beverly Page (15 & 30), 11407-50 St., Edmonton, Alta.—403/479-3959

Blairmore, The Pass Herald (Wed.) Box 960, T0K 0E0—403/562-2248

Blairmore, The Pass Promoter (Wed.) Box 1019, T0K 0E0—403/562-8884

Bonnyville Nouvelle (Tue.) Box 1200, T0A 0L0—403/826-3876

Bow Island, The 40-Mile County Commentator (Wed.) Box 580, T0K 0G0—403/545-2358

Bowden Eyeopener (Wed.) Box 70, TOM OKO — 403/224-3624

Bragg Creek Pioneer (eo Wed.) Box 776, Cochrane, Alta. TOL 0W0 – 403/932-2055

Brooks Bulletin (Wed.) Box 1450, T0J 0J0—403/362-5571

Calgary, The Jewish Star (Wed.) 2315 98th Ave. S.W., T2V 4S7 – 403/238-0010

Calgary, North Hill News (Wed.) Box 3160, Stn. B, T2M 0H7 – 403/276-9311

Calgary, North Side Mirror (Tue.) 830 10th Ave. S.W., T2R 0B1 – 403/263-7730

Calgary, Rocky View News (Tue.) Box 3160, Stn. B, T2M OH7—403/276-9311

Calgary, The Roundup (Thur.) CFB Calgary, T3E 1T8—403/242-5055

Calgary, Rural Ad-Viser, Bag 3820, Stn. B, T2M 4R3 – 403/277-9319

Calgary, South Side Mirror (Wed.) 830 10th Ave. S.W., T2R 0B1 – 403/263-7730

Camrose, The Booster (Tue.) 4925-48 St., T4V 1L7—403/672-3142

Camrose Canadian (Wed.) Box 1600, T4V 1X6—403/672-4421

Canmore, The Hoodoos Highlander (Wed.) Box 657, TOL OMO — 403/274-8134

Carbon Village Press (Tue.) Box 69, TOM OBO—403/935-4688

Cardston Chronicle (Tue.) Box 8, TOK OKO — 403/653-3607

Carstairs Community Press (Wed.) Box 519, T0M 0N0—403/337-3588

Castor Advance (Thur.) Box 120, T0C 0X0—403/882-4044

Claresholm Local Press (Thur.) Box 520, T0L 0T0—403/625-4474

Coaldale Sunny South News (Wed.) Box 30, T0K 0L0—403/345-3081

Cochrane Times (Wed.) Box 776, TOL OWO—403/932-2055

Cold Lake Courier (eo Wed.) CFB, Box 2350, Medley, Alta. T0A 2M0—403/594-5206

Coleman Review (Wed.) Box 130, Creston, B.C. VOB 1GO—604/428-2711

Consort Enterprise (Wed.) Box 129, T0C 1B0—403/577-3611

Coronation Review (Wed.) Box 70, T0C 1C0—403/578-4111

Cremona Town Crier (eo Wed.) Box 776, Cochrane, Alta. TOL 0W0 – 403/932-2055

Delburne & District Journal (eo Thur.) Box 70, T0M 0V0—403/749-2319

Didsbury Booster & Mountain View County News (Wed.) Box 760, Didsbury, Alta. T0M 0W0—403/335-3301

Drayton Valley Western Review (Wed.) Box 120, T0E 0M0—403/542-5380

Drumheller Mail (Wed.) Box 1629, T0J 0Y0—403/823-2580

Eckville Examiner (Wed.) Box 380, Rimbey, Alta. T0C 2J0—403/843-2231

Edmonton, Le Franco-Albertain (Fri.) 10014 109 St., T5J 1M4—403/423-5672

Edmonton, The Jewish Star (Wed.) 2315 98th Ave. S.E., Calgary, Alta. T2V 4S7 – 403/238-0010

Edmonton, The Native People (Fri.) 9311 60 Ave., T6E OC2 — 403/437-1212

Edmonton, North Edmonton Examiner (Wed.) 15113 Stony Plain Rd., T5P 3Y2 — 403/483-7070

Edmonton, Southeast Edmonton Examiner (Wed.) 15113 Stony Plain Rd., T5P 3Y2 – 403/483-7070

Edmonton, Southwest Edmonton Examiner (Wed.) 15113 Stony Plain Rd., T5P 3Y2 – 403/483-7070

Edmonton, West Edmonton Examiner (Wed.) 15113 Stony Plain Rd., T5P 3Y2 — 403/483-7070

Edmonton, Western Catholic Reporter (Mon.) 10562 109 St., T5H 3B2—403/420-1330
Edson Leader (Wed. & Sat.) Box 1510, T0E 0P0—403/723-3301
Elk Point Sentinel (Wed.) Box 608, TOA 1AO — 403/724-3534
Fairview Post (Wed.) Box 200, T0H 1L0—403/835-4925
Falher, Smoky River Express (Wed.) Box 644, T0H 1M0—403/837-2585
Fort Macleod, Macleod Gazette (Wed.) Box 720, T0L 0Z0—403/553-3891
Fort McMurray Express (Wed.) 8323 Fraser Ave., T9H 1W9 – 403/743-1605
Fort Saskatchewan, The Record (Wed.) 9921 101 St., T8L 1V6—403/998-7070
Fort Vermilion, The Northern Pioneer (Wed.) Box 1018, TOH 1NO—403/927-3731
Grand Centre, Cold Lake Sun (Tue.) Box 268, TOA 1TO—403/594-5881
Grande Cache Mountaineer (Wed.) Box 660, T0E 0Y0—403/827-3539
Grande Prairie Booster (Wed.) 10022-99 Ave., T8V 0R9—403/532-0606
Grande Prairie, The Rural Route (Wed.) 10604 100 St., T8V 2M5—403/532-1110
Grimshaw, The Mile Zero News (Thur.) Box 1010, TOH 1WO—403/332-2215
Grimshaw North Peace Pictorial (Tue.) Bag 600, Grimshaw, Alta. T0H 1W0—403/332-4573
Hanna Herald (Tue.) Box 790, T0J 1P0—403/854-3075
High Level Echo (Wed.) Box 240, T0H 1Z0—403/926-2000
High Prairie, South Peace News (Wed.) Box 1000, T0G 1E0—403/423-4484
High River Times (Thur.) Box 489, T0L 1B0—403/652-2034
Hinton Parklander (Wed.) Box 100, T0E 1B0—403/865-3115
Innisfail Booster (Wed.) Box 262, TOM 1AO—403/227-3477
Innisfail Province (Tue.) Box 9, T0M 1A0—403/227-3612
Irricana Five Village Weekly (Tue.) Box 40, TOM 1BO—403/935-4688
Jasper Booster (Wed.) Box 940, T0E 1E0—403/852-3620
Lac La Biche Post (Tue.) Box 508, T0A 2C0—403/623-4221
Lacombe Globe (Wed.) Box 519, T0C 1S0—403/782-3498
Lamont, Elk Island Triangle (Wed.) 4704 51st St., T0B 2R0 – 403/365-3939
Leduc Representative (Tue. & Thur.) Box 220, T9E 2Y1—403/986-2271
Lethbridge, The Ad-Viser (1 & 15) 1233-2nd Ave. S.—403/328-5114
Lloydminster Meridian Booster (Tue. & Thur.) Box 830, S9V 1C2—403/875-3362
Manning Banner Post (Wed.) Box 686, T0H 2M0—403/836-3588
Mannville Reflections (Tue.) Box 444, T0B 2W0 – 403/763-3066
Mayerthorpe, The Freelancer (Mon.) Box 785, TOE 1NO—403/786-2602
Morinville Mirror (Wed.) Box 1649, T0G 1P0 – 403/939-2133
Nanton News (Thur.) Box 429, T0L 1R0—403/486-2023
Okotoks, The Western Wheel, Box 238, TOL 1TO—403/938-4855
Olds Gazette (Wed.) Box 820, T0M 1P0—403/556-3351
Onoway, The Tribune (Wed.) Box 570, TOE 1VO — 403/967-2236
Oyen Echo (Fri.) Box 420, T0J 2J0—403/664-3622
Peace River Record-Gazette (Wed.) Box 399, T0H 2X0—403/624-2591
Pincher Creek Echo (Wed.) Box 1000, T0K 1W0—403/627-3252
Ponoka Herald (Tue.) Box 669, T0C 2H0—403/783-3074
Ponoka News & Advertiser (Mon.) Box 1270, T0C 2H0—403/783-4320
Provost News (Wed.) Box 180, T0B 3S0—403/753-2564
Raymond Review (Wed.) Box 315, T0K 2S0—403/752-3635
Red Deer Shopper (Wed. & Fri.) Box 709, T4N 5H3—403/346-3356
Red Deer, Central Alberta Ad-Viser (Wed.) Box 709, T4N 5H3—403/346-3356
Red Deer, Central Alberta Parkland News (Wed.) Box 520, T4N 5G3 – 403/343-2400
Red Deer County News (1st Fri.) Box 190, Sylvan Lake, Alta. T0M 1Z0—403/887-2331
Redwater-Thorhild News (Wed.) Box 40, Westlock, Alta. T0G 2L0—403/342-3033
Rimbey Record (Tue.) Box 380, T0C 2J0—403/843-2231
Rocky Mt. House, The Mountaineer (Wed.) Box 1750, T0M 1T0—403/845-3334
Rycroft, The Central Peace Signal (Wed.) Box 250, T0H 3A0 – 403/765-3604
St. Albert & Sturgeon Gazette (Wed.) Box 263, St. Albert, Alta. T8N 1N3—403/458-2240
St. Paul Journal (Wed.) Box 159, T0A 3A0—403/645-3342
Sedgewick, The Community Press (Wed.) Box 99, T0B 4C0—403/384-3641
Sherwood Park, The News (Wed./Fri.) 235 Chippewa Rd., T8A 4E6—403/464-3044
Slave Lake, Lakeside Leader (Wed.) Box 849, TOG 2AO—403/849-4380
Slave Lake Scope (Tue.) Box 541, T0G 2A0—403/849-4350
Smoky Lake Signal (Wed.) Box 328, TOA 3CO—403/656-4114
Spruce Grove, The Grove Examiner (Wed.) Box 2190, TOE 2CO—403/962-4257
Standoff, Kainai News (1 & 15) Box 58, TOL 1YO—403/737-3784
Stettler Actioneer (Wed.) Box 2140, T0C 2L0—403/742-3532
Stettler Independent (Wed.) Box 310, T0C 2L0—403/742-2395
Stony Plain Reporter (Tue.) Box 780, T0E 2G0—403/963-2291
Strathmore Standard (Wed.) Box 119, T0J 3H0—403/934-3021
Sundre Round-Up (Wed.) Box 599, T0M 1X0—403/638-3577
Swan Hills Grizzley Gazette (Tue.) Box 10, Barrhead, Alta. TOG OEO — 403/674-3823
Sylvan Lake News (Tue.) Box 190, T0M 1Z0—403/887-2331
Taber Times (Wed.) Box 2020, T0K 2G0—403/223-2266
Three Hills Capital (Wed.) Box 158, T0M 2A0—403/443-5133
Tofield Mercury (Thur.) Box 1600, Camrose, Alta. T4V 1X6—403/672-4421
Trochu Community Voice (Tue.) Box 246, TOM 2CO—403/935-4688
Valleyview Valley Views (Wed.) Box 787, T0H 3N0—403/524-3490
Vauxhall Advance (Thur.) Box 302, T0K 2K0 – 403/654-2122
Vegreville Observer (Thur.) Box 160, T0B 4L0—403/632-2353
Vermilion Standard (Wed.) Box 750, T0B 1M0—403/853-5344
Viking, The Weekly Review (Wed.) Box 240, TOB 4NO—403/336-3422
Vulcan Advocate (Wed.) Box 389, T0L 2B0—403/485-2036
Wainwright Star-Chronicle (Wed.) Box 1090, T0B 4P0—403/842-4465
Westlock Hub (Tue.) Box 1290, T0G 2L0—403/342-3600
Westlock News (Wed.) Box 40, T0G 2L0—403/342-3033
Wetaskiwin News Advertiser (Wed.) Box 6540, T9A 2G2—403/352-2231
Wetaskiwin Times (Wed.) Box 6900, T9A 2G5—403/352-2221
Whitecourt Star (Wed.) Box 630, T0E 2L0—403/778-3977
Wildwood, The Grand Trunk Poplar Press (Wed.) Box 359, T0E 2M0 – 403/786-2602

British Columbia Daily Newspapers

BURNABY: The Burnaby Columbian: see listing under New Westminster Columbian
COQUITLAM: The Coquitlam Columbian: see listing under New Westminster Columbian
CRANBROOK: Daily Townsman, 31 7th Ave. S. (V1C 2J2)—604/426-5201
DAWSON CREEK: Peace River Block News, Box 180 (V1G 4G6) — 604/782-4888
FORT ST. JOHN: Alaska Hwy. News, 9916 98th St. (V1J 3T8)—604/785-5631

KAMLOOPS: Daily Sentinel (evening; Sun. morning) Thomson Newspapers Ltd., 206 Seymour St. (V2C 2E6)—604/372-7731

KELOWNA: Daily Courier (evening), Thomson (B.C.) Newspapers Ltd., 550 Doyle Ave. (V1Y 7V1)—604/762-4445

KIMBERLEY: The Daily Bulletin, 335 Spokane St. (V1H 2E7)—604/427-2233

KITIMAT: Daily Herald, see Terrace

NANAIMO: Daily Free Press (evening), Thomson Co. Ltd., 225 Commercial St. (Box 69, V9R 5K5)—604/753-3451

NELSON: Daily News (morning) 266 Baker St. (V1L 4H3)—604/352-3552

NEW WESTMINSTER: The Columbian (evening) The Columbian Co. Ltd., Box 730 (V3L 4Z7)—604/521-2622

PENTICTON: Herald (evening), Thomson Co. Ltd., 186 Nanaimo Ave. W. (V2A 1N4)—604/492-4002

PORT ALBERNI: Alberni Valley Times (evening), 4918 Napier St. (Box 400) (V9Y 7N1)—604/723-8171

PRINCE GEORGE: The Citizen (evening), Southam Press, Box 578 (V2L 4T1)—604/562-2441

PRINCE RUPERT: Daily News (evening) Box 580 (V2L 4S8)—604/624-6781

SURREY: The Surrey Columbian: see listing under New Westminster Columbian

TERRACE: The Daily Herald, 3212 Kalum St. (V8G 2M9) — 604/635-6357

TRAIL: Times (afternoon) 1163 Cedar Ave. (V1R 4B8)—604/368-8551

VANCOUVER: The Columbian, see New Westminster

Sun Province (Sun: evening; Province: morning), 2250 Granville St. (V6H 3G2)—604/732-2513

VERNON: Daily News (evening) 3309-31st Ave. (V1T 2G7)—604/545-0671

VICTORIA: Times Colonist (morning & evening), Box 300 (V8W 2N4)—604/382-7211

British Columbia Weekly Newspapers

Abbotsford, Sumas & Matsqui News (Wed.) 34375 Cyril St., Abbotsford, B.C. V2S 2H5—604/853-1144

Agassiz-Harrison Advance (Thur.) Box 436, Agassiz, B.C. V0M 1A0—604/796-2288

Aldergrove Star (Wed.) Box 220, V0X 1A0—604/856-8303

Armstrong Advertiser (Wed.) Box 610, V0E 1B0—604/546-3121

Ashcroft, The Journal (Wed.) Box 190, Ashcroft, B.C. V0K 1A0—604/453-2261

Barriere Bulletin (Thur.) Box 281, VOE 1EO—604/672-5898

Bowen Island Undercurrent (eo Fri.) Hummingbird Lane, VON 1GO —604/947-9573

Burnaby Today (Wed.) 7774 Royal Oak Ave., V5J 2L7 — 604/521-2622

Burns Lake District News (Wed.) Box 309, Burns Lake, B.C. V0J 1E0—604/692-7526

Cache Creek, The Pioneer (Tue.) Box 610, VOK 1HO—604/457-6626

Campbell River Courier (Fri.) Box 310, V9W 5B5—604/287-7464

Campbell River Mirror (Wed.) Box 459, V9W 5C1—604/287-9227

Campbell River, The Upper Islander (Wed.) Box 159, V9W 5A7 —604/287-7464

Castlegar News (Sun. & Wed.) Box 3007, V1N 3H4—604/365-7266

Castlegar News Times Advisor (Tue.) 266 Baker St., Nelson, B.C. V1L 4H3 - 604/352-3552

Chase Shuswap Weekly (Thur.) Box 667, Merritt, B.C. V0K 2B0 —604/378-9915

Chetwynd Echo (Wed.) Box 750, V0C 1J0—604/788-2246

Chetwynd Pioneer (Thur.) Box 600, V0C 1J0 - 604/788-3255

Chilliwack Progress (Wed.) 36 Spadina Ave., V2P 6H9—604/792-1931

Clearwater Times (Wed.) Box 1102, V0E 1N0—604/674-3343

Colwood, Juan de Fuca News (Tue.) 2788 Millstream Rd., Victoria, B.C. V9B 3S6—604/478-5528

Comox Totem Times (eo Thur.) CFB Comox, Lazo, B.C. V0R 2K0 —604/339-2211, ext. 249

Coquitlam, The Enterprise (Tue.) Ste. 4, 1111 Austin Ave., V3K 3P4—604/931-4461

Coquitlam Herald (Tue.) 3028 Flint St., V3B 4H4 - 604/941-6641

Coquitlam Today (Tue.) 1530 Prairie Rd., Port Coquitlam, B.C. V3B 1T4 - 604/521-2622

Courtenay Comox District Free Press (Wed. & Fri.) Box 3039, Courtenay, B.C. V9N 5N3 —604/334-4446

Courtenay, The North Island Advertiser (eo Thur.) Box 3013, V9N 5N3—604/338-8872

Cranbrook, Courier Merchandiser (Mon.) 31 7th Ave. S., V1C 2J2—604/426-5201

Cranbrook, The Kootenay Advertiser (Mon.) 1502 2nd St. N., V1C 3L2—604/489-3455

Creston Review (Wed.) Box 130, V0B 1G0—604/428-2711

Creston Valley Advance (Mon. Thur.) Box 1279, V0B 1G0—604/428-2266

Dawson Creek Mirror (Wed.) 1701 Alaska Ave., V1G 1P5 - 604/782-9424

Delta, North Delta Sentinel (twice mthly.) Ste. 2, 9325-120th St., V4C 6R8—604/588-0271

Delta Optimist (Wed.) 5020 48 Ave., V4K 3N5—604/946-4451

Delta Sunshiner (Tue.) 1171 56th St., V4L 2A2 - 604/943-0255

Duncan Cowichan Leader (Thur.) Box 910, Duncan, B.C. V9L 3Y2—604/746-4471

Duncan Cowichan Pictorial (Mon.) Box 765, Duncan, B.C. V9L 3Y1—604/746-4451

Duncan Cowichan News (Wed.) Box 774, Duncan, B.C. V9L 3Y1 —604/748-3032

Enderby Commoner (Fri.) Box 610, Armstrong, B.C. V0E 1B0—604/546-2316

Esquimalt Lookout (2nd & 4th Thur.) CFB Esquimalt, FMO Victoria, B.C. VOS 1BO—604/385-0313

Fernie Free Press (Wed.) Box 1320, V0B 1M0—604/423-4414

Fort Nelson News (Wed.) Box 600, V0C 1R0—604/774-2357

Fort St. James Caledonia Courier (Tue.) Box 1007, Vanderhoof, B.C. V0J 3A0 - 604/567-9258

Fort St. John Town & Country (Thur.) 9916 98th St., V1J 3T8—604/785-5631

The Fraser Lake Bugle (Tue.) Box 1007, Vanderhoof, B.C. VOJ 3AO — 604/567-9062

Ganges, Gulf Islands Driftwood (Wed.) Box 250, Ganges, B.C. V0S 1E0—604/537-2211

Gibsons Sunshine Coast News (Tue.) Box 460, V0N 1V0—604/886-2622

Gold River, The Record (2 & 4 Mon.) Box 398, VOP 1GO — 604/283-2347

Golden Gazette (Fri.) Box 273, V0A 1H0—604/344-5909

Golden Star (Wed.) Box 149, V0A 1H0—604/344-5251

Grand Forks Gazette (Wed.) Box 700, V0H 1H0—604/442-2191

Hope Standard (Wed.) Box 1090, V0X 1L0—604/869-2421

Houston Today (Wed.) Box 899, V0J 1Z0 - 604/845-2890

Invermere Valley Echo (Thur.) Box 70, V0A 1K0—604/342-9216

Kamloops News (Mon. Wed. Fri.) 309 Tranquille Rd., V2B 3G5 —604/554-2551

Kaslo Pennywise (Wed.) Box 430, VOG 1MO—604/353-2602

Kelowna Capital News (Wed.) 287 Bernard Ave., V1Y 6N2—604/763-7114

Kelowna, Central Okanagan Capital News (Sat.) 287 Bernard Ave., V1Y 6N2—604/763-7114

Kelowna-Rutland Progress (Wed.) 172 Asher Rd., Kelowna, B.C. V1X 3H6—604/765-2991

Kitimat News Advertiser (Tue.) 626 Enterprise Ave.—604/632-6144

Kitimat, Northern Sentinel (Thur.) 626 Enterprise Ave.—604/632-6144

Ladysmith-Chemainus Chronicle (Wed.) 23 High St., Ladysmith, B.C. V0R 2E0—604/245-2277

Lake Cowichan, The Lake News (Wed.) Box 962, V0R 2G0—604/749-3143

Langford Goldstream Gazette (Wed.) 9-721 Station Rd., V9B 2S1—604/478-9552

Langley Advance (Wed.) Box 3310, V3A 4R6—604/534-8641

Langley, Suburban Shopping News (Mon.) 5737 203 A St., Box 3398, V3A 1W7—604/534-8658
Langley Times (Wed.) #102, 20560 56th Ave., V3A 4S1 – 604/533-4157
Lantzville Log (mthly) Box 114, V0R 2H0 – 604/390-4471
Lillooet, Bridge River-Lillooet News (Wed.) Box 709, V0K 1V0 —604/256-4322
Logan Lake Leader (Wed.) Box 190, Ashcroft, B.C. V0K 1A0 – 604/453-2261
Lumby Review (Wed.) Box 160, V0E 2G0—604/547-9075
Mackenzie, The Times (Wed.) Box 609, V0J 2C0—604/997-6675
Maple Ridge, The Gazette (Wed.) Box 100, V2X 7E9—604/463-4191
Maple Ridge, The News (Wed.) 22325 Lougheed Hwy., V2X 2T3 —604/467-6941
Maple Ridge Sunday Gazette/Herald (Sun.) Box 100, V2X 7E9 – 604/463-4191
McBride Robson Valley Courier (Wed.) Box 130, McBride, V0J 2E0—604/569-2697
Merritt Herald (Wed.) Box 9, V0N 2B0—604/378-4242
Merritt Merrittonian (Tue.) Box 667, V0K 2B0—604/378-9915
Merritt, News-Advertiser Focus (Mon.) Box 9, VOK 2BO — 604/378-4241
Mission, Fraser Valley Record (Wed.) 33047 First Ave., V2V 1G2 —604/826-6221
Nakusp, Arrow Lake News (Wed.) Box 10, V0G 1R0—604/265-4215
Nanaimo Times (Tue. & Thur.) Box 486, V9R 5L5—604/753-3277
Nelson, The Kootenay Grapevine (Wed.) 501D Vernon St., V1L 4E9 – 604/354-4481
Nelson Pennywise (Wed.) Box 560—604/353-2602
Nelson West Kootenay Today (Fri.) 266 Baker St., Nelson, B.C. V1L 4H3—604/352-3552
New Denver, Nakusp, Slocan Valley Pennywise (mid. & last Wed.) Box 430, Kaslo, B.C. VOG 1MO — 604/353-2602
North & West Vancouver, North Shore News (Wed. & Sun.) 1139 Lonsdale Ave., N. Vancouver, B.C. V7M 2H4 — 604/980-0511
Okanagan Falls Viewpoint (Wed.) Box 448, VOH 1RO—604/497-5191
Oliver Chronicle (Thur.) Box 880, V0H 1T0—604/498-3711
100 Mile House Free Press (Wed.) Box 459, V0K 2E0—604/395-2219
Osoyoos Times (Thur.) Box 359, V0H 1V0—604/495-7225
Parksville, The Arrowsmith Star (Wed.) Box 1300, V0R 2S0—604/248-3202
Parksville-Qualicum Beach Progress (Tue.) Box 368, Parksville, B.C. V0R 2S0—604/248-6161
Penticton, Tri-Lake Recorder (Tue.) 409 Okanagan Ave., V2A 3K1 — 604/493-3717
Penticton Western News Advertiser (Wed.) 121 Westminster Ave., V2A 1J7 —604/492-0444
Port Hardy, North Island Gazette (Wed.) Box 458, V0N 2P0—604/949-6225
Powell River News (Wed.) 4548 Marine Dr., V8A 2K4—604/485-4255
Powell River Town Crier (Mon.) 4548 Marine Dr., V8A 2K4—604/485-4255
Princeton Similkameen Spotlight (Wed.) Box 340, Princeton, B.C. V0X 1W0—604/295-3535
Quesnel Cariboo Observer (Tue./Thur.) Box 4460, Quesnel, B.C. V2J 3J4—604/992-2121
Revelstoke Review (Wed.) Box 20, V0E 2S0—604/837-2193
Revelstoke, This Week in Revelstoke (Fri.) Box 2209, V0E 2S0 – 604/837-2500
Richmond News (Wed.) #118, 3633 No. 3 Rd., V6X 2B9—604/270-8031
Richmond Review (Wed. & Fri.) 8271 Westminster Hwy., V6X 1A7—604/273-7744
Salmo-Fruitvale Pennywise, Box 430, Kaslo, B.C. V0G 1M0 – 604/353-2602
Salmon Arm Guide (Mon. & Thur.) Box 1270, V0E 2T0 – 604/832-9461
Salmon Arm Observer (Wed.) Box 550, V0E 2T0—604/832-2131
Sechelt, The Press (Tue.) Box 676, V0N 3A0—604/885-5121
Sidney Peninsula Free Press (Wed.) 9803 3rd St., Sidney, B.C. V8L 3A6 — 604/656-0141
Sidney Review (Wed.) Box 2070, V8L 3S5—604/656-1151
Smithers Interior News (Wed.) Box 2560, V0J 2N0—604/847-3266
Sooke Mirror (Wed.) Box 339, V0S 1N0—604/642-5752
Sparwood, The Crowsnest Clarion (Thur.) Box 66, V0B 2G0—604/425-7787
Squamish Citizen Shopper (Thur.) Box 1128, V0N 3G0—604/892-3018
Squamish, The Howe Sound & Dist. Advertiser (eo Tue.) Box 501, V0N 3G0 — 604/898-5014
Squamish Times (Tue.) Box 107, V0N 3G0—604/892-5131
Summerland Review (Thur.) Box 309, V0H 1Z0—604/494-5406
Surrey Leader (Wed.) Box 1180, Stn. A, V3S 4R2—604/574-4191
Surrey-Delta Messenger (Wed.) 10692 135A St., Box 275, Surrey, B.C. V3T 4W8 —604/588-4458
Surrey-North Delta Today (Mon.) #2, 13634 104th St., Surrey, B.C. V3T 1W2 – 604/521-2622
Terrace Northern Times (Mon.) Box 880, V8G 4R1—604/638-1188
Ucluelet-Tofino, The Westcoaster (Wed.) Box 66, Ucluelet, B.C. V0R 3A0—604/726-4201
Valemount, Canoe Mountain Echo (Wed.) Box 423, V0E 2Z0 — 604/566-4668
Vancouver Free Press (Thur.) 2110 W. 4th Ave., V6K 1N6 — 604/734-5520
Vancouver, Highland Echo (Grandview) (Thur.) 1720 Graveley St., V5L 3B1—604/253-7030
Vancouver, Highland Echo (Hastings East) (Thur.) 1720 Graveley St., V5L 3B1—604/253-7030
Vancouver, Jewish Western Bulletin (Thur.) 3268 Heather St., V5Z 3K5—604/879-6575
Vancouver, The Link (1/15) Box 76873, Stn. S, V5R 5T3 — 604/879-4815
Vancouver, North Shore News (Wed.) #202, 1139 Lonsdale Ave., North Vancouver, B.C. V7M 2H4—604/980-0511
Vancouver, North Shore Sunday News (Sun.) #202, 1139 Lonsdale Ave., North Vancouver, B.C. V7M 2H4—604/980-0511
Vancouver, The Overseas Times (1/15) 4270 Fraser St. — 604/873-9315
Vancouver, Le Soleil de Colombie (Fri.) 3213 Cambie St., V5Z 2W3—604/879-6924
Vancouver, South Vancouver Review (Wed. closest to 1/15) 5608 Victoria Dr., V5P 3W4 —604/327-0221
Vancouver, The Vancouver Courier (Thur.) 6244 East Blvd., V6M 3V7 – 604/266-1171
Vancouver, The Vancouver Herald (Wed. 1/15) 2619 Alma St., V6R 3S1 – 604/228-1717
Vancouver, The Vancouver News (15/30) 4270 Fraser St., V5V 4G1 – 604/873-9315
Vancouver, West Ender (Thur.) 1035 Davis St., V6E 1M5 – 604/682-0686
Vancouver Western News (Wed.) 4380 W. 10th Ave., V6R 2H7 – 604/224-4413
Vanderhoof, Nechako Chronicle (Thur.) Box 440, V0J 3A0—604/567-4465
Vanderhoof, Omineca Advertiser (Tue.) Box 1007, VOJ 3AO—604/567-9258
Vedder Crossing, The Mountaineer (eo Wed.) CFB Chilliwack, VOX 1ZO—604/858-3311
Vernon This Week (Wed.) 2700 32nd St., V1T 5L6—604/545-4461
Victoria, Oak Bay Star (Wed.) 1534 Monterey Ave., V8S 4V9 — 604/595-3741
Victoria, The Sportscaster (Wed.) 836 View St., V8W 1K2—604/382-2131
Victoria, Victoria's Monday Magazine (Thur.) 823 Broughton St., V8W 1E5—604/382-6188

Westbank-Peachland News Advertiser (Thur.) 172 Asher Rd., Kelowna, B.C. V1X 3H6—604/765-2991
Whistler, The Whistler Question (Thur.) Box 126, VON 1BO—604/932-5131
White Rock, The Peace Arch News (Wed.) Box 131, V4B 4Z7—604/531-1711
White Rock & Surrey Sun (Tue.) Box 127, White Rock, B.C. V4B 4Z7—604/531-5588
Williams Lake, Laketown News (Wed.) 1158 S. Mackenzie Ave., V2G 3X9 — 604/392-6501
Williams Lake, The Tribune (Tue. & Thur.) 188 N. 1st Ave., V2G 1Y8 —604/392-2331

Manitoba Daily Newspapers

BRANDON: The Brandon Sun (evening) Con., 501 Rosser Ave. (R7A 5Z6)—204/727-2451
DAUPHIN: Daily Bulletin, 120 1st Ave. N.E. (R7N 1A5)—204/638-4420
FLIN FLON: Reminder (evening) Box 727 (R8A 1N5) —204/687-3454
PORTAGE LA PRAIRIE: Daily Graphic (evening) Box 130 (R1N 3B4)—204/857-3427
ROBLIN: The News, Box 299, 182 Main St. (ROL 1PO)—204/937-2517
SWAN RIVER: Report, Box 1629 (R0L 1Z0)—204/734-2729
THOMPSON: Citizen (evening) Box 887 (R8N 1N8)—204/677-2920
WINNIPEG: Free Press (evening) 300 Carlton St. (R3C 3C1)—204/943-9331
The Winnipeg Sun (morning) #100, 290 Garry St. (R3C 1H3) – 204/957-0710

Manitoba Weekly Newspapers

Altona Red River Valley Echo (Wed.) Box 720, Altona, Man. R0G 0B0—204/324-6431
Baldur Gazette (Wed.) Box 188, R0K 0B0—204/535-2127
Beausejour Manitoba Beaver (Wed.) Box 1148, R0E 0C0—204/268-1155
Belmont News (Tue.) Box 70, R0K 0C0—204/537-2441
Benito Standard (Fri.) Box 424, R0L 0C0—204/539-2772
Birtle Eye-Witness (Thur.) Box 430, R0M 0C0—204/842-3349
Boissevain Recorder (Wed.) Box 220, R0K 0E0—204/534-6479
Brandon, Westman Rural (Tue.) 501 Rosser Ave., R7A 5Z6 —204/727-2451
Carberry News-Express (Thur.) Box 220, R0K 0H0—204/834-2153
Carman, The Valley Leader (Wed.) Box 70, R0G 0J0—204/745-2051
Cartwright, S. Manitoba Review (Wed.) Box 249, R0K 0L0—204/529-2342
Dauphin Herald (Wed.) Box 548, R7N 2V4—204/638-4420
Dauphin, Parkland Enterprise (Wed.) Box 548, R7N 2V4—204/638-4420
Deloraine Times & Star (Wed.) Box 407, R0M 0M0—204/747-2249
Gilbert Plains Maple Leaf (Wed.) Box 250, R0L 0X0—204/548-2691
Gladstone Age-Press (Wed.) Box 135, R0J 0T0—204/385-2592
Glenboro Gazette (Wed.) Box 10, R0K 0X0—204/827-2343
Grand Beach Spotlight (2nd Thur.) Box 1, R0E 0S0—204/754-2282
Grandview Exponent (Wed.) Box 39, R0L 0Y0—204/546-2555
Hamiota Echo (Thur.) Box 70, R0M 0T0—204/764-2733
Killarney Guide (Tue.) Box 670, R0K 1G0—204/523-4611
Lac du Bonnet Springfield Leader (Tue.) Box 910, Lac du Bonnet, Man. R0E 1A0—204/345-8611
Lynn Lake, The Northern Breeze (Wed.) Box 148, R0B 0W0—204/356-2547
Manitou Western Canadian (Wed.) Box 190, R0G 1G0—204/242-2555
Melita New Era (Wed.) Box 426, R0M 1L0—204/522-3491
Miniota Herald (Thur.) Box 70, Hamiota, Man. R0M 0T0—204/764-2733
Minnedosa Tribune (Thur.) Box 930, R0J 1E0—204/867-3816
Morden Pembina Times (Wed.) Box 130, Morden, Man. R0G 1J0—204/822-4421
Morris, The Scratching River Post (Mon.) Box 160, ROG 1KO—204/746-2823
Neepawa Press (Thur.) Box 939, R0J 1H0—204/476-2309
Pilot Mound Sentinel Courier (Wed.) Box 179, R0G 1P0—204/825-2772
Portage la Prairie, Portage Leader-MacGregor Herald (Wed.) Box 130, R1N 3B4—204/857-3427
Reston Recorder (Thur.) Box 10, R0M 1X0—204/877-3321
Rivers Gazette-Reporter (Wed.) Box 70, R0K 1X0—204/328-7580
Roblin Review (Wed.) Box 938, R0L 1P0—204/937-4404
Rossburn Review (Thur.) Box 130, R0J 1V0—204/759-2644
Russell Banner (Wed.) Box 100, R0J 1W0—204/773-2069
St. Boniface, La Liberté (Thur.) Box 96, R2H 3B4—204/247-4823
Selkirk Enterprise & Lake Centre News (Wed.) Box 187, Selkirk, Man. R1A 2B2—204/482-3721
Shilo, The Shilo Stag (eo Thur.) 857-18th St., Brandon, Man. R7A 5B8—204/728-3037
Shoal Lake Star (Thur.) Box 160, R0J 1Z0—204/759-2644
Souris Plaindealer (Wed.) Box 488, R0K 2C0—204/483-2108
Steinbach, The Carillon (Wed.) 377 Main St., R0A 2A0—204/326-3421
Stonewall, Argus & Teulon Times (Wed.) Box 190, R0C 2Z0—204/467-2421
Stonewall, The Interlake Spectator (Wed.) Box 190, R0C 2Z0—204/467-2421
Swan River Report (Wed.) Box 1629, R0L 1Z0—204/734-2729
Swan River Star & Times (Thur.) Box 670, R0L 1Z0—204/734-3858
The Pas, Opasquia Times (Wed. Fri.) Box 750, R9A 1K8—204/623-3435
Thompson Nickel Belt News (Wed.) Box 887, R8N 1N8—204/677-4534
Treherne, The Times (Thur.) Box 50, R0G 2V0—204/723-2542
Virden Empire Advance (Wed.) Box 250, R0M 2C0—204/748-3931
Winnipeg Central City News (eo Wed.) 396 Selkirk Ave., R2W 2M2 – 204/589-4343
Winnipeg, The Jewish Post (Thur.) Box 3777, Stn. B, R2W 3R6 —204/633-5575
Winnipeg, Metro One (Tue.) 1397 Erin St., R3E 2S9 – 204/786-6446
includes:
Herald (Elmwood, E. & N. Kildonan, Transcona)
Metro One (St. James, Assiniboia, Charleswood)
Lance (Fort Garry, St. Vital)
Marketplace (Wpg.)
Winnipeg Times (Wed.) 1397 Erin St., R3E 2S9 – 204/786-6446
Winnipeg Voxair (eo Wed.) CFB Winnipeg, Westwin, Man. R2R OTO — 204/832-1311, ext. 502
Winnipeg, The Western Jewish News (Thur.) 400, 259 Portage Ave., R3C 2G6—204/942-6361
Woodworth Times (Thur.) Box 70, Hamiota, Man. R0M 0T0—204/764-2733

New Brunswick Daily Newspapers

FREDERICTON: Gleaner (evening) Box 3370 (E3B 5A2)—506/455-6671
MONCTON: L'Evangeline (morning), 80 Church St.—506/855-5560
Times and Transcript (Times: morning; Transcript: evening), Box 1001 (E1C 8P3)—506/382-9321
SAINT JOHN AND LANCASTER: The Telegraph-Journal/The Evening Times-Globe (Telegraph-Journal: morning; Times-Globe evening), Crown St. at Union, Saint John (E2L 3V8)—506/657-1230

New Brunswick Weekly Newspapers

Bathurst Northern Light (Wed.) Box N, E2A 3Z3—506/546-4491
Bathurst, Le Point (Wed.) fr., Box W, E2A 3Z6—506/548-8924
Campbellton, L'Aviron (Wed.) fr., Box 637, E3N 3H1—506/753-7637
Campbellton Graphic (Wed.) 15 Ritchie St.—506/753-5752
Campbellton Tribune (Wed.) Box 486, E3N 3G9—506/753-4413
Cap Pelé, La Boueille (Wed.) C.P. 329, EOA 1JO — 506/532-4401
Caraquet, Le Voilier (Wed.) fr., Box 878, E0B 1K0—506/727-2928
Chatham, Miramichi Weekend (Fri.) Box 250 - 506/622-1600
Chatham, Northumberland News (Wed.) Box 517, E1N 3A8 — 506/773-9431
Dalhousie News (Wed.) Box 160, E0K 1B0—506/684-5544
Edmundston, Le Madawaska (Wed.) biling., 20 St.-François, E3V 1E3—506/735-5575
Edmundston, La Republique (Wed.) fr., Box 410, Rimouski, P.Q. G5L 7C4 — 418/723-4800
Grand Falls, Cataract Weekly (Wed.) biling., 208 Main St., E0J 1M0—506/473-3117
Grand Falls, see Perth Andover
Hartland Observer (Wed.) Box 330, E0J 1N0—506/375-4458
Newcastle, Miramichi Leader (Wed.) Box 500, E1V 3M6—506/622-1600
Oromocto Post (Wed.) 101 Hersey St., E2V 2G5—506/357-9813
Perth-Andover, Victoria County Record (Wed.) Box 990, EOJ 1VO—506/328-8863
Riverview, The Recorder (Wed.) 1 Trites Rd., E1B 2V5—506/386-3524
Sackville, The Tribune-Post (Wed.) Box 1530, E0A 3C0—506/536-2500
St. Stephen St. Croix Courier (Wed.) 47 Milltown Blvd., St. Stephen, N.B. E3L 1G4—506/466-3220
Sussex Kings County Record (Wed.) Box 40, E0E 1P0—506/433-1070
Woodstock, The Bugle (Wed.) Box 130, E0J 2B0—506/328-8863

Newfoundland Daily Newspapers

CORNER BROOK: The Western Star (evening) Box 460 (A2H 6E7)—709/634-4348
ST. JOHN'S: The Daily News (morning) Box 8835, Stn. A (A1B 3V2)—709/726-1810
Telegram (evening) 273 Duckworth St. (A1C 5X7)—709/726-2060

Newfoundland Weekly Newspapers

Burin, Southern Gazette (Wed.) Box 8660, St. John's, Nfld. - 709/279-3188
Carbonear, The Compass (Wed.) Box 8660, St. John's, Nfld.—709/596-6458
*Channel-Port aux Basques, The Gulf News (Wed.)—709/955-2715
*Clarenville Packet (Thur.)—709/466-2243
*Corner Brook Humber Log (Wed.)—709/639-9203
*Gander Beacon (Wed./Fri.)—709/256-4371
*Grand Falls Advertiser (Mon. Thur.)—709/489-2162
*Harbour Breton, The Coaster (eo Fri.) — 709/489-9856
Labrador City, The Aurora (Wed.) Box 423, A2V 2K7—709/944-2957
*Lewisporte, The Pilot (Wed.)—709/535-6910
Marystown, The Burin Post (Wed.) Box 8835, Stn. A, St. John's, Nfld.—709/726-1810
Port Union Fishermen's Advocate (Fri.) Box 68, A0C 2J0—709/469-2221
St. Anthony, The Northern Pen (Wed.) Box 207, A0K 4S0 - 709/454-2191
Stephenville, The Georgian (Wed.) Box 283, A2N 2Z4—709/643-4531

**Box 129, Grand Falls, Nfld. A2A 2J4*

Nova Scotia Daily Newspapers

AMHERST: Daily News (morning) Box 280 (B4H 3Z2)—902/667-5102
HALIFAX: The Chronicle-Herald (morning) and The Mail-Star (evening) 1650 Argyle St. (B3J 2T2)—902/426-2811
NEW GLASGOW: The Evening News (evening) 352 E. River Rd. (B2H 5E2)—902/752-3000
SACKVILLE: Bedford-Sackville Daily News, 446 Main Hwy., Lower Sackville (B4C 2S9) — 902/865-0942
SYDNEY: Cape Breton Post (evening) 75 Dorchester St. (B1P 6K6)—902/564-5451
TRURO: The Daily News (evening) Ind., 6 Louise St. (B2N 5C3) —902/893-9405

Nova Scotia Weekly Newspapers

Amherst, The Citizen (Sat.) Box 280, B4H 3Z5—902/667-5116
Annapolis Royal, The Spectator (Wed.) Box 250, Bridgetown, N.S. B0S 1C0—902/665-4441
Antigonish, The Casket (Thur.) Box 1300—902/863-4370
Berwick Register (Wed.) Box 640, B0P 1E0—902/538-8810
Bridgetown Monitor (Wed.) Box 250, B0S 1C0—902/665-4441
Bridgewater Bulletin (Wed.) Box 89, B4W 2W6—902/543-2457
Bridgewater, South Shore News (Wed.) Box 366, B4V 2W9 - 902/543-9161
Cornwallis Ensign (CFB) (Wed.) Box 280, B0S 1H0—902/638-8536
Dartmouth Free Press (Wed.) Box 698, B2Y 3Y9—902/469-2494
Digby Courier (Thur.) Box 670, B0V 1A0—902/245-4715
Digby, The Mirror (Wed.) Box 880, Middleton, N.S. B0S 1P0—902/825-3457
Greenwood, The Aurora (CFB) (Wed.) Box 99, CFB Greenwood, N.S. B0P 1N0—902/765-3391, ext. 440
Halifax, Maritime Command Trident (CFB) (eo Wed.) Box 3308, Halifax—902/423-2135
Inverness, The Oran (Thur.) Box 100, B0E 1N0 - 902/258-2253
Kentville, The Advertiser (Wed.) Box 430, B4N 3X4—902/678-2121
Liverpool Advance (Wed.) Box 10, B0T 1K0—902/354-3441
Lunenburg Progress Enterprise (Wed.) Box 89, B4V 2W6—902/543-2457
Middleton Examiner (Tue.) Box 1090, B0S 1P0 - 902/765-4775
North Sydney, Northside/Victoria Times (Wed.) Box 220, B2A 3N3 - 902/794-4713
Oxford Journal (Wed.) Box 10, B0M 1P0—902/447-2051
Pictou Advocate (Wed.) Box 1000, B0K 1H0—902/485-4327
Port Hawkesbury, The Scotia Sun (Wed.) Box 599, B0E 2V0—902/625-1900
Port Joli, The Rural Delivery, Box 8, B0T 1S0 - 902/683-2763
Shearwater, The Warrior (eo Wed.) Box 190, B0J 3A0 - 902/463-5111
Shelburne, The Coast Guard (Wed.) Box 100, B0T 1W0—902/875-3244
Springhill & Parrsboro Record (Wed.) Box 670, B0M 1X0—902/597-3731
Sydney, Micmac News (15th) Box 344, B1P 6H2—902/539-0045
Truro, The Weekly Record (Wed.) Box 946, B2N 5G7 - 902/895-7947
Windsor Hants Journal (Wed.) Box 550, B0N 2T0—902/798-8371
Yarmouth, Le Courrier de la Nouvelle-Ecosse (Thur.) fr., 4 Alma St., B5A 3E6—902/742-9119
Yarmouth, The Vanguard (Wed.) Box 128, B5A 4B1—902/742-7111

Ontario Daily Newspapers

BARRIE: Examiner (evening), 16 Bayfield St. (L4M 4T6)—705/726-6537
BELLEVILLE: The Intelligencer (evening), 45 Bridge St. E. (K8N 1L5)—613/962-9171

BRAMPTON: Daily Times (evening), 33 Queen St. W. (L6Y 1M1)—416/451-2020; Toronto line 864-1710

BRANTFORD: Expositor (evening) 53 Dalhousie St. (N3T 5S8) —519/756-2020

BROCKVILLE: Recorder and Times (evening) 23 King St. W., Box 10 (K6V 5T8)—613/342-4441

CAMBRIDGE-GALT: Daily Reporter (evening) 26 Ainslie St. S. (N1R 3K1)—519/621-3810

CHATHAM: Daily News (evening) 45 Fourth St., Box 2007 (N7M 2G4)—519/354-2000

COBOURG: Daily Star (afternoon), 415 King St. W., K9A 3P9—416/372-0131

CORNWALL: Standard-Freeholder (afternoon), 44 Pitt St. (K6J 3P3)—613/933-3160

FORT FRANCES: Daily Bulletin, Box 339 (P9A 3M7)—807/274-5373

GUELPH: Mercury (evening) 8-14 Macdonnell St. (N1H 6P7)—519/822-4310

HAMILTON: Spectator (evening) Southam Press, 44 Frid St. (L8N 3G3)—416/526-3333

KENORA: Daily Miner & News (evening) 33 Main St. S. (Box 1620, P9N 3X7)—807/468-5555

KINGSTON: Whig-Standard (evening) 306 King St. (K7L 4Z7)—613/544-5000

KIRKLAND LAKE: Northern Daily News (evening) 8 Duncan Ave. (P2N 3L4)—705/567-5321

KITCHENER: Kitchener-Waterloo Record (afternoon) 225 Fairway Rd. S. (N2G 4E5)—519/894-2231

LINDSAY: Post (evening) 15 William St. N. (K9V 3Z9)—705/324-2114

LONDON: London Free Press (morning), 369 York St., Box 2280 (N6A 4G1) – 519/679-1111

NIAGARA FALLS: Review (evening) 4801 Valley Way (L2E 6T6) —416/358-5711

NORTH BAY: Nugget (evening) 259 Worthington St., Box 570 (P1B 8J6)—705/472-3200

ORILLIA: Packet and Times (evening) 31 Colborne St. E. (L3V 1T4)—705/325-1355

OSHAWA: The Oshawa Times (evening) 44 Richmond St. W. (L1G 1C8)—416/723-3474

OTTAWA: The Citizen (evening) 1101 Baxter Rd., Box 5020 (K2C 3M4)—613/829-9100
Le Droit (evening) 375 Rideau St. (K1N 5Y7)—613/560-2747

OWEN SOUND: Sun-Times (evening) Box 56 (N4K 5P2)—519/376-2250

PEMBROKE: Observer (evening) 186 Alexander St. (K8A 4L9)—613/732-3691

PETERBOROUGH: Examiner (evening) 400 Water St. (K9J 6Z4) —705/745-4541

PORT COLBORNE: see Welland-Port Colborne Tribune

PORT HOPE: Guide (evening) Box 296 (L1A 3W4)—416/885-2471

ST. CATHARINES: Standard (evening) 17 Queen St. (L2R 5G5) —416/684-7251

ST. THOMAS: Times-Journal (evening) 16 Hincks St. (N5P 3W6)—519/631-2790

SARNIA: Observer (evening) 140 S. Front St. (N7T 7M8)—519/344-3641

SAULT STE. MARIE: Star (noon & evening) Box 460 (P6A 5M5) —705/253-1111

SIMCOE: Reformer (evening) 105 Donly Dr., N3Y 4L2—519/426-5710

SIOUX LOOKOUT: Daily Bulletin, Box 668 (P0V 2T0)—807/737-2161

STRATFORD: The Beacon-Herald (evening) 108 Ontario St. (N5A 3H2)—519/271-2220

SUDBURY: Star (evening), 33 McKenzie St. (P3C 4Y1)—705/674-5271

THUNDER BAY: Times-News/Chronicle-Journal (Times- News: morning; Chronicle-Journal: evening) 75 S. Cumberland St. (P7B 1A3)—807/344-3535

TIMMINS: Press (evening), 125 Cedar St. S. (P4N 2G9)—705/264-2215

TORONTO: Corriere Canadese (afternoon) 1000 Lawrence Ave. W. (M6A 1P2)—416/789-1171
Daily Racing Form (morning), 245 Carlaw Ave. (M4M 2S7)—416/465-5487
The Globe and Mail (morning) 444 Front St. W. (M5V 2S9)—416/361-5411
The Toronto Star (morning & evening), One Yonge St. (M5E 1E6) – 416/367-2233
The Toronto Sun (morning) 333 King St. E. (M5A 3X5)—416/868-2333

WATERLOO: see Kitchener-Waterloo Record

WELLAND: Welland-Port Colborne Tribune (evening), Thomson Newspapers Ltd., 228 E. Main St. (L3B 3W8)—416/732-2411

WINDSOR: The Windsor Star (morning & evening) 167 Ferry St. (N9A 4M5) – 519/255-5640

WOODSTOCK: Woodstock-Ingersoll Sentinel Review (evening) Thomson Newspapers, 16 Brock St. (N4S 8A5)—519/537-2341

Ontario Weekly Newspapers

Acton Free Press (Wed.) 59 Willow St. N., L7J 1Z8—519/853-2010

Agincourt, see Toronto

Ajax, see Toronto

Alexandria, Glengarry News (Wed.) Box 10, K0C 1A0—613/525-2020

Alexandria, Le Point (fr.) (Tue.) 126 rue Principale, K0C 1A0 – 613/525-1815

Alliston Herald (Wed.) Box 280, L0M 1A0—705/435-6228

Alliston, The Reporter (Wed.) Box 998, LOM 1AO— 705/435-5616

Almonte Gazette (Wed.) Box 130, K0A 1A0—613/256-1311

Amherstburg Echo (Wed.) Box 10, N9V 2Z2—519/736-2147

Amherstview-Kingston, The Heritage (Wed.) 3 Manitou W., Amherstview, Ont. K7N 1B5—613/389-8884

Ancaster News Journal (Wed.) 393 Wilson St. E., L9G 3L4—416/561-1090

Arnprior Chronicle (Wed.) 116 John St. N., K7S 2N6—613/623-4406

Arnprior Guide (Wed.) Box 339, K7S 3H6—613/623-4237

Arthur Enterprise-News (Wed.) 222 George St., Box 310, N0G 1A0—519/484-2410

Atikokan Progress (Wed.) Box 220, P0T 1C0—807/597-2731

Aurora/Newmarket Banner (Wed.) 10 Tempo Ave., Willowdale, Ont. M2H 2N8—416/493-1300

Aylmer Express (Wed.) 17-23 King St., N5H 1Z2—519/773-3126

Ayr News (Wed.) 40 Piper St., N0B 1E0—519/632-7432

Bancroft Times (Wed.) 93 Hastings St. N., KOL 1CO—613/332-2300

Barrie Banner (Wed. & Fri.) 124 Brock St., L4N 2M2—705/726-0573

Barry's Bay, This Week in the Madawaska Valley (Wed.) Box 220, K0J 1B0—613/756-2944

Beaverton Express (Wed.) Box 10, L0K 1AO—705/426-7443

Beeton-Schomberg Record Sentinel (Wed.) Box 310, Beeton, Ont. LOG 1AO—416/729-2287

Belle River, North Essex News (Wed.) Box 429, N0R 1A0—519/728-1082

Blenheim News-Tribune (Wed.) Box 160, N0P 1A0—519/676-3321

Blyth Standard (Wed.) Box 10, N0M 1H0—519/523-9646

Bobcaygeon Independent (Thur.) 100 Prince St. W., K0M 1A0—705/738-2212

Bolton Enterprise (Wed.) 10 Tempo Ave., Willowdale, Ont. M2H 2N8—416/493-1300

Borden, The Borden Citizen (CFB) (Wed.) L0M 1C0—705/424-1200

Bothwell Times (Wed.) Box 40, N0P 1CO—519/695-2803

Bowmanville Canadian Statesman (Wed.) Box 190, L1C 3K9—416/623-3303

Bracebridge Examiner (Thur.) Box 1049, POB 1CO—705/645-8771

Bracebridge Herald-Gazette (Wed.) Box 1600, P0B 1C0—705/645-2255

Bradford/West Gwillimbury Witness (Wed.) Box 1090, Bradford, Ont. L0G 1C0—416/883-4830
Brampton Guardian (Wed.) 30 Victoria Cres., L6T 1E4—416/791-1739
Brantford, Brant News (Wed.) Box 532, N3T 5N9—519/759-5550
Brighton Independent (Wed.) Box 1030, K0K 1H0—613/475-0255
Brussels Post (Wed.) Box 50, N0G 1H0—519/527-0240
Burford Advance (Wed.) Box 100, N0E 1A0—519/449-2441
Burks Falls-Powassan Almaguin News (Wed.) Box 518, Burks Falls, Ont. P0A 1C0—705/382-3843
Burlington Gazette (Tue.) 496 Brant St., L7R 2G4—416/639-5500
Burlington Post (Wed. & Sat.) 2321 Fairview St., L7R 2E3—416/632-4444

Caledon Citizen (Wed.) 22 Mill St., #11, Orangeville, Ont. L9W 2M3—519/941-2230
Caledonia, Grand River Sachem (Wed.) Box 160, N0A 1A0—416/765-2770
Cambridge Times (Wed.) 1315 Bishop St., N1R 6J9 —519/653-7168
Campbellford Herald (Wed.) Box 970, K0L 1L0—705/653-3684
Cannington Gleaner (Wed.) Box 10, Beaverton, Ont. L0K 1A0—705/426-7443
Carleton Place, The Canadian (Wed.) Box 430, K7C 3P5—613/257-1303
Cayuga, Regional News (Wed.) Box 418, NOA 1EO—416/772-3365
Chapleau Sentinel (Thur.) Box 158, P0M 1K0—705/864-0640
Chesley Enterprise (Wed.) Box 250, N0G 1L0—519/363-2414
Chesterville Record (Wed.) Box 368, K0C 1H0—613/448-2321
Clinton News-Record (Thur.) Box 39, N0M 1L0—519/482-3443
Cobden Sun (Wed.) Box 100, K0J 1K0—613/646-2380
Cochrane Northland Post (Wed.) Box 10, P0L 1C0—705/272-4363
Colborne, The Citizen (Wed.) Box 399, K0K 1S0—613/475-0255
Colborne Chronicle (Wed.) Box 400, K9A 4L1—416/372-0131
Coldwater Journal (Wed.) Box 280, L0K 1E0 — 705/686-7283
Collingwood Enterprise-Bulletin (Wed.) Box 98, L9Y 1HE—705/445-4611
Collingwood Times (Wed.) Box 187, L9X 3Z5—705/445-2171
Cornwall, Le Journal (Fri.) French. 113 Montreal Rd., K6H 1B2—613/938-1433
Cornwall Weekly News (Wed.) biling. Box 1467, K6H 5V5—613/932-2991
Courtright St. Clair Gazette (Wed.) Box 99, Sarnia, Ont. N7T 7H8—519/336-1100
Creemore Star (Wed.) Box 70, L0M 1G0—705/466-2002

Deep River North Renfrew Times (Wed.) Box 310, Deep River, Ont. K0J 1P0—613/584-4161
Delhi News-Record (Wed.) 222 Argyle St., N4B 2Y1 —519/582-2510
Deseronto, The Quinte Scanner (Wed.) Box 410, K0K 1X0—613/396-3431
Dorchester, The Signpost (Thur.) 95 Hamilton Rd. E., N0L 1G0—519/268-7337
Downsview, see Toronto
Drayton, The Community News (Thur.) Box 189, N0G 1P0—519/638-3066
Dresden, North Kent Leader (Wed.) Box 490, N0P 1M0—519/683-4485
Dryden Observer (Wed.) Box 3009, P8N 2Y9—807/223-2381
Dundalk Herald (Thur.) Box 280, N0C 1B0—519/923-2203
Dundas-Ancaster Recorder (Tue.) Box 513, Hamilton, Ont. L8N 3H8—416/385-7192
Dundas Star Journal (Wed.) Box 4, L9H 5E7—416/664-4455
Dunnville Chronicle (Wed.) 131 Lock St. E., N1A 1J6—416/774-5855
Durham Chronicle (Thur.) Box 230, N0G 1R0—519/369-2504
Dutton Advance (Wed.) Box 220, N0L 1J0—519/762-2310

Eganville Leader (Wed.) Box 310, K0J 1T0—613/628-2332
Elliot Lake Standard (Wed. & Fri.) Box 86, P5A 2J6—705/848-7195
Elmira Independent (Wed.) 15 King St., N3B 2R1—519/669-5155
Elmira Signet (Wed.) 4 Arthur St. S., N0B 1R0—519/669-5123
Elmvale Huronia Holiday (Wed. Summer) Box 339, L0L 1P0—705/322-1871
Elmvale Lance (Wed.) Box 609, Midland, Ont. L4R 4L3—705/526-2283
Erin Advocate (Wed.) Box 160, N0B 1T0—519/833-9603
Espanola, Mid-North Monitor (Wed.) Box 1126, P0P 1C0—705/869-2860
Essex Free Press (Fri.) 16 Centre St., N8M 1N9—519/776-8511
Etobicoke, see Toronto
Exeter Times-Advocate (Thur.) Box 880, N0M 1S0—519/235-1331

Fenelon Falls Gazette (Thur.) Box 340, K0M 1N0—705/887-2940
Fergus-Elora News Express (Wed.) Box 130, Fergus, Ont. N1M 2W7—519/843-1310
Fergus, The Wellington Advertiser (Mon.) Box 252, N1M 1P1—519/843-5410
Flesherton Advance (Thur.) Box 280, Dundalk, Ont. N0C 1B0—519/923-2203
Fonthill Herald (Tue.) Box 550, Pelham, Ont. L0S 1E0—416/892-6022
Forest Standard (Wed.) Box 220, N0N 1J0—519/873-5242
Fort Erie Times Review (Wed.) Box 70, L2A 5M6—416/871-3100
Fort Frances Times (Wed.) Box 339, P9A 3M7—807/274-5373
Frankford Advertiser (Thur.) Box 270, K0K 2C0—613/398-6771

Gananoque Reporter (Wed.) 79 King St. E., K7G 1E8—613/382-2156
Georgetown, Halton Hills Herald (Wed.) 45 Guelph St., L7G 3Z6—416/877-2201
Georgetown Independent (Wed.) 30 Main St. S., L7G 3G4—416/877-5266
Geraldton Times-Star (Wed.) Box 490, P0T 1M0 - 807/854-1919
Glencoe-Alvinston Transcript & Free Press (Thur.) Box 400, Glencoe, Ont. N0L 1M0—519/287-2615
Goderich Signal-Star (Wed.) Box 220, Industrial Park, N7A 4B6—519/524-8331
Gore Bay, Manitoulin Recorder (Wed.) Box 235, P0P 1H0—705/282-2003
Grand Valley Star & Vidette (Wed.) Box 40, L0N 1G0—519/928-2822
Gravenhurst Banner (Thur.) 141 Bay St., P0C 1G0 - 705/687-6674
Gravenhurst News (Thur.) Box 609, P0G 1G0—705/687-2259
Grimsby Independent (Wed.) Box 310, L3M 4G5—416/945-9264
Guelph This Week (Wed.) 219 Silvercreek Pkwy. N., Unit 17 —519/821-2643

Hagersville, The Haldimand Press (Thur.) Box 369, N0A 1H0—416/768-3111
Haliburton County Echo (Wed.) Box 360, K0M 1S0—705/457-1037
Halton, see Toronto
Hamilton City Journal (Wed.) 178 King St. W., Box 4, Dundas, Ont. L9H 5E7—416/664-4455
Hamilton Mountain News (Wed.) Box 208, Stoney Creek, Ont. L8G 3X9—416/561-1090
Hamilton Recorder (Wed.) Box 513, Main PO, L8N 3H8—416/385-7192
Hanover & Dist. Advertisers News (Wed.) Box 67, N4N 3C3 – 519/364-2001
Hanover Post (Wed.) Box 67, N4N 3C3—519/364-2001
Harriston Review (Wed.) Box 370, N0G 1Z0—519/338-2341
Harrow News (Wed.) Box 310, N0R 1G0—519/738-2542
Hastings Star (Wed.) Box 250, Marmora, Ont. K0K 2M0—613/472-2431
Havelock Citizen (Wed.) Box 250, Marmora, Ont. KOK 2MO—613/472-2431
Hawkesbury, Le Carillon (Wed.) fr., 176 Canada Atlantique, Box 69, K6A 2R6—613/632-4155
Hawkesbury, Express (Fri.) biling. 228 James St., K6A 1S8 – 613/632-0191
Hawkesbury, Le Moniteur & The Echo (Sat.) biling., Box 69, K6A 2R6—613/632-4155
Hearst, Le Nord (Wed.) fr., Box 1748, POL 1NO—705/362-8464
Hillsburgh, The Local Paper (1st mo.) Box 310, N0B 1Z0 – 519/855-6125

Huntsville Forester (Wed.) Box 940, P0A 1K0—705/789-5541
Huntsville, Muskoka Free Press (Wed.) Box 1210, POA 1KO—705/789-9651
Ignace Driftwood (Wed.) Box 989, POT 1TO — 807/934-6482
Ingersoll Times (Wed.) Box 38, N5C 3K1—519/842-4255
Innisfil Scope, see Stroud
Iroquois Post (Wed.) Box 400, K0E 1M0—613/652-4806
Iroquois Falls, The Enterprise (Wed.) Box 834, 'A', P0K 1G0—705/232-4081
Kanata Standard (eo Fri.) Box 13061, K2K 1X3 — 613/592-1084
Kapuskasing Northern Times (Wed.) Box 8, P5N 2Y1—705/335-2283
Kemptville Weekly Advance (Wed.) Box 669, K0G 1J0—613/258-3451
Kincardine, The Independent (Wed.) Box 1240, N0G 2G0—519/396-3111
Kincardine News (Wed.) Box 340, N0G 2G0—519/396-2963
King City, see Toronto
Kingston This Week (Wed.) 677 Gardiners Rd., K7M 3Y4—613/389-7400
Kingsville Reporter (Wed.) 17 Chestnut St., N9Y 1J9—519/733-2211
Kitchener (East) The Citizen (Wed.) 1005 Ottawa St. N., N2A 1H2 — 519/893-8500
Lakefield Leader (Thur.) 96 Queen St., Box 610, K0L 2H0—705/652-8518
Lambeth News-Star (Thur.) 1 Rutledge St., N0L 1S0—519/652-3421
Leamington Post & News (Wed.) Box 520, N8H 3W5—519/326-4434
Lincoln, The Post Express (Wed.) Box 400, Beamsville, Ont. L0R 1B0—416/563-8231
Lindsay, The Post Mercury (Tue.) 15 William St. N., K9V 3Z8—705/324-2114
Lindsay This Week (Wed.) 64 Lindsay St. S., K9V 2M2—705/324-8600
Lindsay, The Thursday Post (Wed.) 15 William St. N., K9V 3Z8—705/324-2114
Listowel Banner (Wed.) Box 97, N4W 3H2—519/291-1660
Little Current Manitoulin Expositor (Wed.) Box 369, P0P 1K0—705/368-2744
London, The Byron Advocate (mthly 1st Mon.) 469 Boler Rd., N6K 2K8—519/471-7245
London Tribune (Thur.) 364 Richmond St., N6A 3C3 – 519/432-2695
Lucknow Sentinel (Wed.) Box 400, N0G 2H0—519/528-2822
Mac Tier, Muskoka Lakes-Georgian Bay Beacon (Thur.) Box 250, P0C 1H0—705/375-5551
Madoc Review (Wed.) Box 250, Marmora, Ont. K0K 2M0—613/472-2431
Malton, see Mississauga
Manitouwadge Echo (Wed.) Box 550, POT 2CO—807/826-3788
Marathon Mercury (Wed.) Box 369, P0T 2E0—807/229-1520
Markdale Standard (Thur.) Box 465, N0C 1H0—519/986-3151
Markham/Thornhill Economist & Sun (Thur.) 72B Main St. N., Markham, Ont. L3P 1X5—416/481-4481
Marmora Herald (Wed.) Box 250, K0K 2M0—613/472-2431
Mattawa Recorder (Wed.) 341 McConnell St., Box 67, POH 1VO—705/744-5361
Meaford Express (Wed.) Box 700, N0H 1Y0—519/538-1421
Midland, The Free Press (Wed. & Fri.) 248 First St., L4R 3N8—705/526-5431
Midland Friday Times (Fri.) Box 609, L4R 4L3—705/526-2283
Midland Times (Wed.) Box 609, L4R 4L3—705/526-2283
Mildmay Town & Country Crier (eo Thur.) Box 190, N0G 2J0—519/367-2681
Milton Canadian Champion (Wed.) 191 Main St. E., L9T 1N7—416/878-2341
Milton Weekly Tribune (Wed.) 181 Main St. E., L9T 1N7—416/878-8185
Milverton Sun (Wed.) Box 456, N0K 1M0—519/595-8921
Minden, The Highlands Express (Wed.) R.R. 2, KOM 2KO—705/489-2036
Minden, The Times (Wed.) Box 97, K0M 2K0—705/286-1288
Mississauga, L'Express de Mississauga (eo Tue.) Box 127, Stn. F, Toronto, Ont. M4Y 2L4 – 416/922-3750
Mississauga, Malton Mercury (Thur.) 7205 Goreway Dr., L4T 2T9—416/677-4940
Mississauga, Malton Review (Wed.) 7205 Goreway Dr., L4T 2T9—416/676-9384
Mississauga, Meadowvale Review (Wed.) 93 Queen St. S., L5M 1K7—416/826-3425
Mississauga News (Wed.) 3145 Wolfedale Rd., L5C 3A9—416/279-2211
Mississauga Review (Wed.) Box 159, Stn. A, L5A 2Z7—416/826-3425

Mitchell Advocate (Wed.) Box 669, N0K 1N0—519/348-8431
Morrisburg Leader (Wed.) Box 891, K0C 1X0—613/543-2987
Mount Albert, The Communicator (Wed.) Box 123, L0G 1M0—416/473-2425
Mount Forest Confederate (Wed.) Box 130, N0G 2L0—519/323-1550
Nanticoke Times (Wed.) Box 1000, Waterford, Ont. N0E 1Y0—519/443-8664
Napanee Beaver (Wed.) Box 278, K7R 3M4—613/354-5326
New Hamburg Independent (Wed.) 100 Huron St., N0B 2G0—519/662-1240
New Liskeard, Temiskaming Speaker (Wed.) Box 580, P0J 1P0—705/647-6791
Newcastle Independent (Wed.) Box 190, Bowmanville, Ont. L1C 3K9 — 416/623-3303
Newcastle & Millbrook Reporter (Wed.) Box 130, Newcastle, Ont. L0A 1H0—416/987-4704
Newmarket/Aurora Era (Wed.) 30 Charles St., Newmarket, Ont. L3Y 3V8—416/362-5981
Newmarket, York Regional Topic (Tue.) Box 141, Newmarket, Ont. L3Y 4Z4—416/883-4830
Niagara-on-the-Lake, Niagara Advance (Wed.) Box 760, L0S 1J0—416/468-3283
Nipigon Gazette (Wed.) Box 1057, P0T 2J0—807/887-3712
North Bay Sun (Wed.) Box 1301, P1B 8K5—705/474-6733
North York, see Toronto
Norwich Gazette (Wed.) Box 459, N0J 1P0—519/842-4255
Norwood Register (Wed.) Box 250, Marmora, Ont. K0K 2M0—613/472-2431
Oakville Beaver (Wed.) 467 Speers Rd., L6K 3S4—416/845-3824

Orangeville Banner (Wed. & Fri.) 37 Mill St., L9W 2M4—519/941-1350
Orangeville Citizen (Wed.) 22 Mill St., #11, L9W 2M3—519/941-2230
Orillia, The Wednesday Nighter (Wed.) Box 2237, L3V 6S1—705/325-2306
Orono Weekly Times (Wed.) Box 209, L0B 1M0—416/983-5301
Oshawa This Week (Wed.) 865 Farewell Ave., Box 481, L1H 2PO—416/579-4400
Oshawa This Weekend (Sat.) 865 Farewell Ave., L1H 6N8—416/579-4400
Ottawa, Centretown News (eo Sun.) Carleton Univ., K1S 5B6—613/231-6388
Ottawa, The Nepean Clarion (Tue.) Box 5166, Stn. F, K2C 3H4—613/225-8513
Paisley Advocate (Wed.) Box 250, Chesley, Ont. NOG 1LO — 519/363-2414
Palmerston Observer (Wed.) Box 757, N0G 2P0—519/343-2440
Paris Star (Thur.) 36 Grand River St. N., N3L 2M2—519/442-2621
Parkhill Gazette (Thur.) Box 400, N0M 2K0—519/294-6264
Parry Sound Beacon (Thur.) 51 James St., P2A 1T6 – 705/375-5551
Parry Sound, North Star (Tue. & Thur.) Box 370, P2A 2X4—705/746-5331
Penetanguishene Citizen (Wed.) Box 609, Midland, Ont. L4R 4L3—705/526-2283

Penetanguishene Friday Citizen (Fri.), as above
Perth Courier (Wed.) Box 156, K7H 3E3—613/267-1100
Petrolia Advertiser Topic (Wed.) Box 40, N0N 1R0—519/882-1770
Petrolia Enniskillen Gazette (Wed.) Box 99, Sarnia, Ont. N7T 7H8—519/336-1100
Petrolia, The Grand Bend Sun (Thur.) Box 40, NON 1RO — 519/882-1770
Pickering, see Toronto
Picton Gazette (Wed. & Fri.) Box 80, K0K 2T0—613/476-3201
Point Edward Gazette (Wed.) 287 N. Front St., Sarnia, Ont. N7T 5S6—519/336-1100
Port Colborne News (Wed.) Box 130, L3K 4E3—416/835-2411
Port Dover Maple Leaf (Fri.) 351 Main St., N0A 1N0—519/583-0112
Port Elgin, The Beacon Times (Wed.) Box 580, N0H 2C0—519/832-9001
Port Perry Star (Wed.) Box 90, L0B 1N0—416/985-7383
Prescott Journal (Wed.) Box 549, K0E 1T0—613/925-4265
Rainy River Record (Thur.) Box 280, P0W 1L0—807/852-3366
Red Lake District News (Thur.) Box 328, P0V 2M0—807/727-2618
Renfrew Mercury (Wed.) Box 400, K7V 4A8—613/432-3655
Richmond Hill, See Toronto
Ridgetown Dominion (Wed.) 11 Ebenezer St. W., N0P 2C0—519/674-3232
Riverside News (Wed.) Box 396, Walkerville, Windsor, Ont. N8Y 4S2—519/945-1013
Rockland, Bonjour Chez-Nous (Wed.) fr., Box 1149, KOA 3AO—613/446-5871
Rodney Mercury (Wed.) Box 188, N0L 2C0—519/785-0310
St. Marys Journal-Argus (Wed.) Box 1030, N0M 2V0—519/284-2440
Sarnia Gazette (Wed.) 287 Front St. N., Box 99, N7T 7H8—519/336-1100
Sarnia, Lambton County Gazette (Wed.) 287 Front St. N., Box 99, N7T 7H8—519/336-1100
Scarborough, See Toronto
Schomberg-Nobleton, see Tottenham
Seaforth, Huron Expositor (Thur.) Box 69, N0K 1W0—519/527-0240
Shelburne Free Press & Economist (Wed.) Box 100, L0N 1S0—519/925-2832
Sioux Lookout, Northwest Explorer (Wed.) Box 989, P0V 2P0 – 807/737-2959
Sioux Lookout, Wawatay News (mthly) Box 1180, POV 2TO — 807/737-2957
Smiths Falls Record-News (Wed.) Box 158, K7A 4T1—613/283-3182
Stayner Sun (Wed.) Box 80, L0M 1S0—705/428-2638
Stirling News-Argus (Wed.) Box 100, K0K 3E0—613/395-3321
Stittsville News (Wed.) Box 610, K0A 3G0—613/836-1357
Stoney Creek News (Wed.) Box 208, L8G 3X9—416/664-4455
Stouffville, see Toronto
Stratford, The County Neighbours (Wed.) 108 Ontario St., N5A 6T6 – 519/271-2220
Strathroy Age-Dispatch (Wed.) 8 Front St., N7G 1Y4—519/245-2370
Streetsville, see Toronto
Stroud, The Innisfil Scope (Wed.) Gen Delivery, LOL 2MO—705/737-1383
Sturgeon Falls Tribune (Wed.) biling. Box 900, P0H 2G0—705/753-2930
Sudbury, Le Voyageur (Wed.) fr., Box 1180, P3E 4S7—705/673-3687
Sudbury, Northern Life (Wed.) 31 Cedar St., P3E 1A3—705/673-5667
Sutton, Lake Simcoe Advocate (Wed.) 179 Simcoe Ave., Keswick, Ont. L4P 1V7—416/722-3289
Tara Leader (Wed.) Box 250, Chesley, Ont. N0G 1L0 — 519/363-2414
Tavistock Gazette (Wed.) Box 70, N0B 2R0—519/655-2341
Teeswater News (Wed.) Box 250, N0G 2S0—519/396-3111
Terrace Bay News (Wed.) Box 579, P0T 2W0—807/825-3747
Thamesford Town Crier (Wed.) Box 399, NOM 2MO—519/485-3631
Thamesville Herald (Thur.) 133 London Rd., N0P 2K0—519/692-3825
Thessalon, The Sentinel (Tue.) 199 Main St., P0R 1L0 – 705/842-2504
Thornbury Review-Herald (Wed.) Box 190, N0H 2P0—519/599-3030
Thornbury Valley Courier (Thur.) Box 700, Meaford, Ont. NOH 1YO — 519/538-1421
Thornhill, See Toronto
Thorold News (Thur.) Box 86, L2V 3Y7—416/227-1141
Thunder Bay, Lakehead Living (Wed.) Box 100, P7C 4V5—807/623-5423
Tilbury Times (Wed.) Box 490, N0P 2L0—519/682-0411
Tillsonburg News (Mon. Wed. Fri.) Box 190, N4G 4H5—519/842-4255

Toronto Metro Area

Agincourt News (Wed.) 4246 Sheppard Ave. E., Agincourt, Ont.—416/291-2583
Ajax News Advertiser (Wed.) 130 Commercial Ave., Ajax, Ont. L1S 2H5—416/683-5110
Brampton Guardian (Wed.) 30 Victoria Cres., Brampton, Ont. L6T 1E4—416/791-1739
Downsview, The Jane Corridor (Mthly.) Box 2331, Stn. C, Downsview, Ont. M3N 2V8—416/635-5776
Etobicoke Advertiser-Guardian (Wed.) 10 Tempo Ave., Willowdale, Ont. M2H 2N8 — 416/493-1300
Etobicoke Consumer (Wed.) 10 Tempo Ave., Willowdale, Ont. M2H 2N8 — 416/493-1300
Etobicoke Reporter (Wed.) Box 400, Stn. T, Toronto, Ont. M6B 4A3—416/630-2180
King City, King Twp. Weekly (Wed.) Box 1036, King City, Ont. LOG 1KO—416/833-4533
Malton Messenger (Wed.) Box 215, Malton PO, Mississauga, Ont. L4T 3B6—416/678-0152
Malton Review (Wed.) 7205 Goreway Dr., Mississauga, Ont. L4T 2T9—416/676-9384
Markham/Thornhill Consumer (Wed.) 10 Tempo Ave., Willowdale, Ont. M2H 2N8 — 416/493-1300
Markham/Thornhill Economist & Sun (Thur.) 728 Main St. N., Markham, Ont. L3P 1X5—416/481-4481
Meadowvale Review (Wed.) 93 Queen St. S., Mississauga, Ont. L5M 1K7—416/826-3425
Mississauga, L'Express de Mississauga (eo Tue.) Box 127, Stn. F, Toronto, Ont. M4Y 2L4 – 416/922-3750
Mississauga News (Wed.) 3145 Wolfedale Rd., Mississauga, Ont. L5C 3A9—416/279-2211
Mississauga Review (Wed.) Box 159, Stn. A, Mississauga, Ont. L5A 2Z7—416/826-3425
North York Consumer (Wed.) 10 Tempo Ave., Willowdale, Ont. M2H 2N8 — 416/493-1300
North York, Downsview Reporter (Wed.) Box 400, Stn. T, Toronto, Ont. M6B 4A3—416/630-2180
North York Mirror (Wed.) 10 Tempo Ave., Willowdale, Ont. M2H 2N8—416/493-1300
North York News (Wed.) 4246 Sheppard Ave. E., Agincourt, Ont.—416/291-2583
North York, Yorkview Reporter (Wed.) Box 400, Stn. T, Toronto, Ont. M6B 4A3—416/630-2180
Oakville Beaver (Wed.) 467 Speers Rd., Oakville, Ont. L6K 3S4—416/845-3824
Pickering Consumer, see Ajax
Pickering Post (Wed.) 4246 Sheppard Ave. E., Agincourt, Ont. —416/291-2583
Pickering's Bay News (Wed.) 1730 McPherson Crt., Unit 18, Pickering, Ont. L1W 3E6—416/683-1561

Richmond Hill, York Regional Topic (Tue.) Box 1090, Bradford, Ont. L0G 1C0 — 416/883-4830
Richmond Hill/Thornhill Liberal (Wed.) 10 Tempo Ave., Willowdale, Ont. M2H 2N8—416/493-1300
Scarborough Consumer (Wed.) 10 Tempo Ave., Willowdale, Ont. M2H 2N8—416/493-1300
Scarborough Mirror (Wed.) 10 Tempo Ave., Willowdale, Ont. M2H 2N8—416/493-1300
Scarborough News (Wed.) 4246 Sheppard Ave. E., Agincourt, Ont.—416/291-2583
Scarborough Reporter (Wed.) Box 400, Stn. T, Toronto, Ont. M6B 4A3—416/630-2180
Scarborough, West Hill Reporter (Wed.) Box 400, Stn. T, Toronto, Ont. M6B 4A3—416/630-2180
Stouffville Tribune (Thur.) 54 Main St. W., Stouffville, Ont. LOH 1LO—416/640-2100
Streetsville Booster (1st Tue.) 24 Falconer Dr., Mississauga, Ont. L5N 1B1—416/826-3672
Streetsville Review (Wed.) Box 640, Mississauga, Ont. L5M 2C2—416/826-3425
Toronto, Bloor West Village (mthly.) 2259 Bloor St. W., Toronto, Ont. M6S 1N8 - 416/767-3644
Toronto, Canadian Jewish News (Thur.) 562 Eglinton Ave. E., Ste. 401, Toronto, Ont. M4P 1P1—416/481-2087
Toronto, The Catholic Register (Sat.) 67 Bond St., Toronto, Ont. M5B 1X6—416/362-6822
Toronto City Dweller (1st week) 95 Trinity Sq., Toronto, Ont. M5A 3C7—416/367-0297 (editions: Ward 6; Eglinton-Yonge; St. Clair-Yonge; Cabbagetown/Ward 7; Thorncliffe)
Toronto Clarion (eo Wed.) 73 Bathurst St., Toronto, Ont. M5V 2P6—416/363-4404
Toronto Contrast (Fri.) 28 Lennox St., Toronto, Ont. M6G 1J4 —416/537-3461
Toronto, The Downtowner (eo Wed.) 33 Britain St., Toronto, Ont. M5A 3Z3 — 416/362-6739
Toronto, East End Express (Wed.) 9398 Danforth Ave., Toronto, Ont. M4J 1L8—416/293-5893
Toronto, East End News (Wed.) 4246 Sheppard Ave. E., Agincourt, Ont.—416/291-2583
Toronto Express, Le, (Tue.) fr., Box 127, Stn. F, Toronto, Ont. M4Y 2L4—416/922-3750
Toronto Jewish Press (eo Fri.) Box 142, Downsview, Ont. M3M 3A3—416/633-0202
Toronto, Share (Sat.) Ste. B, 1573 Eglinton Ave. W., Toronto, Ont. M6E 2G9 - 416/782-5298
Toronto, Silverthorn & Dist. News (2nd wk) 72 Cloverdale Rd., Toronto, Ont. M6N 3L5—416/656-7171
Toronto Tribune Weekly Newspapers (Thur.) 2533 Gerrard St. E., Scarborough (Includes Beaches; Danforth; Gerrard; Leaside; Scarboro)—416/699-9695
Toronto, Upper Yonge Villager (1st mthly) 181 Sheldrake Blvd., Toronto, Ont. M4P 2B1 - 416/486-1471
Toronto Ward 7 News (eo Fri.) 315 Dundas St. E., Toronto, Ont. M5A 2A2—416/363-9650
Toronto Ward 8 News (eo Fri.) 947 Queen St. E., Toronto, Ont. M4M 1J9—416/463-4277
Toronto Ward 9 Community News (eo Tue.) 907 Kingston Rd., Toronto, Ont. M4E 1S4—416/698-1164
Toronto, West Toronto News Express (mthly) 202 Ossington Ave., Toronto, Ont. M6J 2Z7—416/534-4201
Toronto Wright Media Ltd. (Thur.) 95 Research Rd., Toronto, Ont. M4G 2G8—416/425-6037 (Includes East Toronto Weekly; East York Times; Forest Hill Journal; Leaside Advertiser; North Toronto Free Press; North Toronto Herald; The St. Clair Examiner)
West Hill News (Wed.) 4246 Sheppard Ave. E., Agincourt, Ont. M1S 1T5—416/291-2583
Willowdale Reporter (Wed.) Box 400, Stn. T, Toronto, Ont. M6B 4A3—416/630-2180
Woodbridge Advertiser (Tue.) Palgrave, Ont. L0N 1P0—416/361857-2638
Woodbridge & Vaughan News (Wed.) 10 Tempo Ave., Willowdale, Ont. M2H 2N8—416/493-1300
end of Toronto Metro Area

Tottenham-Schomberg-Nobleton News (Wed.) Box 70, Tottenham, Ont. L0G 1W0—416/936-4205
Tottenham Times (Wed.) Box 310, Beeton, Ont. LOG 1AO—416/729-2287
Trenton Contact (Wed.) CFB Trenton, Box 40, Astra, Ont. KOK 1BO—613/392-2811
Trenton Trentonian (Mon. Wed. Fri.) Quinte & Stewart Sts., Box 130, K8V 5R3—613/392-6501
Tweed News (Wed.) Box 550, K0K 3J0—613/478-2017
Uxbridge Times Journal (Wed.) 191 Main St., L0C 1K0—416/852-3361
Vankleek Hill Review (Wed.) Box 160, K0B 1R0—613/678-3327
Vaughan, The Courier (Wed.) Box 462, Kleinburg, Ont. LOJ 1CO — 416/893-1139
Walkerton Herald-Times (Thur.) 110 Durham St. E., N0G 2V0—519/881-1600
Wallaceburg Courier-Press (Wed.) Box 86, N8A 4L5—519/627-1488
Wallaceburg News (Wed.) Box 2, N8A 4L5—519/627-2243
Warkworth Journal (Thur.) Box 159, K0K 3K0—705/924-2423
Wasaga Beach Times (Wed.) Box 254, LOP 2PO — 705/429-5577
Waterdown Flamborough Review (Wed.) Box 20, Waterdown, Ont. L0R 2H0—416/689-4841
Waterloo Chronicle (Wed.) 92 King St. S. —519/886-2830
Watford Guide-Advocate (Wed.) Box 99, N0M 2S0—519/876-2809
Wawa Algoma News Review (Wed.) Box 528, POS 1KO—705/856-2267
Welland Consumer News (Tue.) Box 458, L3B 5R2 — 416/735-6422
Welland, Journal L'Ecluse (fr.) (Wed.) 810 rue Main est, L3B 3Y4 - 416/735-8925
West Carleton Banner (Wed.) Box 279, Carp, Ont. KOA 1LO — 613/839-2888
West Hill, See Toronto
West Lincoln Review (Wed.) Box 40, Smithville, Ont. L0R 2A0—416/957-3315
West Lorne Sun (Wed.) Rodney, Ont. N0L 2C0—519/785-0310
Westport & Rideau Valley Mirror (Wed.) Box 130, Westport, Ont. K0G 1X0—613/273-2021
Wheatley Journal (Thur.) Box 10, N0P 2P0—519/825-4541
Whitby Free Press (Wed.) Box 206, L1N 5S1—416/668-6111
Wiarton Echo (Wed.) Box 220, N0H 2T0—519/534-0645
Willowdale, See Toronto
Winchester Press (Thur.) Box 398, K0C 2K0—613/774-2524
Windsor, Le Rempart (Wed.) fr., 2418 Ave. Central, N8W 4J3 – 519/948-4139
Windsor, The Times (Wed.) 5130 Halford Dr., N9A 6J3—519/737-6143
Wingham Advance-Times (Wed.) Box 390, N0G 2W0—519/357-2320
Woodbridge, See Toronto
Wyoming-Plympton Gazette (Wed.) 287 Front St. N., Sarnia, Ont.—519/336-1100
Zurich Citizen News (Thur.) Box 190, N0M 2T0—519/235-1331

Prince Edward Island Daily Newspapers

CHARLOTTETOWN: Guardian and Patriot (Guardian: morning; Patriot: evening), 165 Prince St. (C1A 4R7)—902/894-8506
SUMMERSIDE: Journal-Pioneer (evening), 4 Queen St. (C1N 3N8)—902/436-2121

Prince Edward Island Weekly Newspapers

Montague, The Eastern Graphic (Wed.) Box 790—902/838-2515
Summerside, Gulf Wings (2 & 4 Tue.) CFB Summerside, Slemon Park, P.E.I. C0B 2A0—902/436-6177
Summerside, La Voix Acadienne (Wed.) fr., 340 rue Court, C1N 4K2—902/436-6005

Quebec Daily Newspapers

CHICOUTIMI: Le Quotidien (morning), 1051 Talbot Blvd. (G7H 4B5)—418/545-4480

GRANBY: La Voix de L'Est (evening), 136 Main St. (J2G 2V4)—514/372-5433

MONTREAL: Le Devoir (morning) 211 St. Sacrement St. (H2Y 1X1)—514/844-3361

The Gazette (morning) 1000 St. Antoine St. (H3C 3R7)—514/282-2750

Le Journal de Montreal (morning), 155 Port-Royal W. (H3L 2B3)—514/382-1312

La Presse (evening) Ind., 7 St. James St. W. (H2Y 1K9)—514/285-7306

QUEBEC: Le Journal de Québec (morning), 450 Bechard St., Ville de Vanier, P.Q. (G1K 7P2)—418/683-1573

Le Soleil (evening), 390 St. Vallier E. (G1K 7J6)—418/647-3270

SHERBROOKE: Record (evening) Box 1200 (J1H 5L6)—819/569-9525

La Tribune (morning), 1950 Roy St. (J1K 2X8)—819/569-9201

TROIS-RIVIERES: Le Nouvelliste (morning) 500 St. Georges St. (G9A 5J6)—819/376-2501

Quebec Weekend Newspapers

CHICOUTIMI: Progres-Dimanche (Sun.) 1051 Talbot Blvd. (G7H 4B5)—418/545-4474

MONTREAL: Allo Police (Sun.) 1800 Parthenais St. (H2K 3S4)—514/527-5730

Dimanche Derniere Heure (Sun.) 5701 Christophe Colombe (H2S 2E9)—514/274-2501

Dimanche-Matin (Sun.) 5701 Christophe-Colomb (H2S 2E9)—514/274-2501

Echos Vedettes (Sat.) 225 Roy St. E. (H2W 1M5)—514/282-9600

Le Grand Journal Illustré (Sat.) 225 Roy St. E. (H2W 1M5)—514/282-9600

Le Journal de Montreal, 155 Port Royal W. (H3L 2B3) — 514/382-8800

Le Nouveau Samedi (Sat.) 225 Roy St. E. (H2W 1M5) —514/527-3161

Nouvelles Illustrees (Sat.) 225 Roy St. E. (H2W 1M5)—514/282-9600

La Patrie (Sat.) 5960 Rosemont Blvd. (H1M 1G6)—514/254-9475

Petit Journal (Sat.) 5960 Rosemont Blvd. (H1M 1G6)—514/254-9475

Photo-Journal (Sat.) 5960 Rosemont Blvd. (H1M 1G6)—514/254-9475

Photo-Vedettes (Sat.) 225 Roy St. E. (H2W 1M5)—514/282-9600

Sunday Express (Sun.) 225 Roy St. E. (H2W 1M5)—514/282-9600

Tele-Radiomonde (Sat.) 225 Roy St. E. (H2W 1M5)—514/282-9600

Quebec Weekly Newspapers in French

Acton Vale, Journal Acton Régional (Wed.) C.P. 1138, J0H 1A0 – 514/546-3772

Alma, Le Lac Saint-Jean (Wed.) Box 520, G8B 5W1—418/668-4545

Amos, Le Reflet d'Amos (Wed.) 25 1ère Ave. est, J9T 1H2—819/732-5449

Amqui, L'Avant-Poste Gaspesien (Wed.) Box 1600, G0J 1B0—418/620-3443

Asbestos, Le Citoyen (Wed.) Box 208, J1T 3N1—819/879-5409

Baie Comeau/Hauterive, Le Nordic (Sat.) 3 Place La Salle, Baie Comeau, P.Q. G4Z 1J8—418/296-3350

Baie Comeau/Hauterive Plein Jour sur Manicouagan (Wed.) 3 Place La Salle, Baie Comeau, P.Q. G4Z 1J8 — 418/296-3350

Beauport, Reflet de Mon Milieu (10th) 809 Blvd. Des Chutes, G1A 2C5—418/661-5103

Bedford, Le Journal des Rivières (Tue.) biling. 16 Rivière St., J0J 1A0—514/248-3353

Beloeil, Guide D'Achat de la Rive Sud (mthly) biling., 513 boul. Laurier, J3G 4H8 – 514/464-5120

Beloeil, L'Oeil Regional (Wed.) biling. 513 Laurier Blvd., J3G 4H8—514/467-1821

Boucherville, see Montreal

Bromont, Le Regional (Tue.) Box 69, JOE 1LO—514/534-2001

Cabano, Le Touladi (Wed.) 177B Commerciale, G0L 1E0 – 418/854-2322

Cap-aux-Meules, Le Radar (Wed.) C.P. 580, G0B 1B0—418/986-2345

Cap-de-la-Madeleine, L'Hebdo (Wed.) 943 Thibeau, G8T 7B1—819/379-1490

Chambly, Le Journal (Tue.) 2336 Bourgogne, J3L 2A2—514/658-6516

Chandler, Le Havre (Wed.) biling., Box 410, Rimouski, P.Q. G5L 7G4—418/723-4800

Charlesbourg-Est, Reflet de Mon Milieu (15th) 809 boul des Chutes, Beauport, P.Q. G1E 2C5 – 418/661-5103

Chibougamau, La Sentinelle (Wed.) Box 250, G8P 2K7—819/276-6406

Chicoutimi, Le Réveil (Wed.) 73 rue Du Pont, G7X 7W4—418/547/2601

Coaticook, Le Progres (Wed.) Box 150—819/849-3616

Cowansville, Le Guide (Tue.) biling., 245 rue Principale, J2K 1J4—514/263-5288

Dolbeau, Le Point (Wed.) 1891 Sacre-Coeur, G8L 2A4—418/276-5110

Donnacona, Le Courrier de Portneuf (Tue.) 274, rue Notre-Dame, GOA 1TO—418/285-0211

Dorion, see Montreal

Drummondville, L'Express (Tue.) 393 Heriot, J2B 1B1—819/477-3773

Drummondville, La Parole (Wed.) 1159 St. Joseph Blvd., J2C 2C8—819/478-8171

Drummondville, Le Regional (Tue.) 1159 St-Joseph Blvd., J2C 2C8 – 819/478-8171

Drummondville, Le Voltigeur (Tue.) 447, rue Lindsay, J2B 1G9—819/472-1195

Farnham, L'Avenir de Brome-Missisquoi (Mon.) Box 88, J2N 2R4—514/293-4732

Forestville Plein Jour Saguenay (Wed.) 15 ieme Ave., G0T 1E0 – 418/296-3350

Gaspé, Le Pharillon (Wed.) Box 410, Rimouski, P.Q. G5L 7C4—418/723-4800

Granby, La Nouvelle Revue (Wed.) 154, rue Principale, J2G 2V6—514/372-3605

Grand'Mere, Le Pont (Wed.) Box 55, G9T 5K7 — 819/538-1923

Hull, Le Regional (Wed.) 65 Adrien-Robert, J8Y 3S3—819/776-1063

Huntingdon, Le Gleaner (Wed.) biling., Box 130, J0S 1H0—514/264-5364

Joliette, L'Etoile du Nord (Wed.) 540 rue St-Thomas, J6E 3R4 – 514/759-3575

Jonquiere, Le Réveil (Wed.) Box 520, G7X 7W4—418/547-2601

L'Annonciation, L'Hebdo de la Rouge (Wed.) 947 rue Ouimet, C.P. 428, St-Jovite, P.Q. J0T 2H0 – 819/275-3795

L'Annonciation, Journal Le Nord (Tue.) Box 820, JOT 1TO—819/425-3337

La Baie, Le Réveil, see Jonquiere

Lac Etchemin, La Voix du Sud (Wed.) Box 400, G0R 1S0—418/625-7471

Lac Megantic, L'Echo de Frontenac (Tue.) 5040 boul. des Vétérans, G6B 2G5—819/583-1630

Lachine, see Montreal

Lachute, L'Argenteuil (Wed.) Box 220, J8H 3X3—514/562-2494

La Malbaie, Le Confident (Tue.) Box 848, GOT 1JO—418/665-3925

La Malbaie, Le Plein Jour Charlevoix (Wed.) 15 ieme Ave., Forestville, P.Q. G0T 1E0 – 418/296-3350

La Pocatière, Le Kamouraska (Wed.) Box 410, Rimouski, P.Q. G5L 7C4—418/723-7877

La Prairie, see Montreal

LaSalle, see Montreal
La Tuque, L'Echo (Wed.) Box 310, G9X 3P3—819/523-4575
Laval, see Montreal
Levis, Le Peuple-Tribune (Wed.) Box 1216, G6V 6W8—418/833-1225
Longueuil, see Montreal
Lotbinière, Le Peuple de Lotbinière (Tue.) 1033 rue Bergeron, St-Agapit, P.Q. GOS 1ZO—418/888-3926
Louiseville, L'Echo de Louiseville/Berthier (Wed.) 80 St-Martin St., J5V 1B4—819/228-2766
Magog, Le Progres de Magog (Wed.) 287 rue Principale, J1X 2A8—819/843-2961
Malartic, Le Courier de Malartic (Wed.) C.P. 4020, JOY 1ZO — 819/757-4712
Maniwaki, La Gatineau (Wed.) 455 Ste-Cecile, J9E 1K9—819/449-1725
Maniwaki, La Gazette (Wed.) 212 Notre Dame, J9E 2J5—819/449-2233
Mascouche, Le Trait d'Union (Wed.) 2906 Ste-Marie, JON 1CO —514/474-2488
Matane, La Voix Gaspésienne (Wed.) 305 de la Gare—418/562-4040
Mirabel, see Montreal
Mont Joli, L'Information (Wed.) Box 70, G5H 3K8—418/775-4381
Mont Laurier, L'Echo de la Lievre (Wed.) Box 57, J9L 3G9—819/623-1262
Montmagny, Peuple/Courrier (Wed.) Ste. 100, 1 Place de l'Eglise, C.P. 430, G5V 3S7—418/248-0415

Montreal Metropolitan Area

Ahuntsic Contact (Wed.) 2633 boul. Le Corbusier, #100, Chomedey, Laval, P.Q. H7S 2E8 — 514/687-4900
Ahuntsic, Courrier Ahuntsic (Wed.) biling., 317 Montmorency, Laval-des-Rapides, P.Q. H7N 1X1—514/667-4360
Beauharnois-Chateauguay, L'information Regional (Wed.) 110A St-Jean Baptiste, Chateauguay, P.Q. J6K 3A8 — 514/691-3863
Boucherville, La Seigneurie (Wed.) biling., 414 boul. Marie-Victorin, J3B 1W4 - 514/655-1967
Dorion, Le Courrier Express (Wed.) C.P. 37, J7V 5V8 - 514/455-6191
Dorion, L'Etoile de L'Outaouais St-Laurent (Thur.) Box 160, Dorion, P.Q. J7V 5W1—514/455-6111
Lachine Messenger (Wed.) biling., 1015 Notre Dame, Lachine, P.Q. H8S 2C3—514/637-2381
La Prairie, Le Reflet (Wed.) biling., 9 boul. Montcalm N., Candiac, P.Q. J5R 3L5 — 514/659-9146
LaSalle Messenger (Tue.) biling., 9216 Bolvin Rd., LaSalle, P.Q. H8R 2E7—514/363-5656
Laval, Courrier-Laval (Wed.) 317 Montmorency, Laval-des-Rapides, P.Q. H7N 1X1—514/667-4360
Laval, Journal Contact Laval (Wed.) 2633 Le Corbusier, #100, Chomedey, Laval, P.Q. H7S 2E8—514/687-4900
Longueuil Courrier Mag (Wed.) 267 ouest rue St-Charles, Longueuil, P.Q. J4H 1E3—514/463-2730
Longueuil, Le Courrier du Sud/South Shore Courier (Wed.) biling., 267 St-Charles St. W., Longueuil, P.Q. J4H 1E3—514/463-2730
Mirabel, La Concorde (Tue.) 53 St-Eustache, St-Eustache, P.Q. J7R 1Y2—514/473-1700
Montreal, Le Centre-Ville (Tue.) 1317 E. Marie-Ann, Montreal, P.Q. H2J 2C3 - 514/521-2129
Montreal, Le Courrier Metropolitain (Tue.) 1470 est, rue Fleury, Montreal, P.Q. H2C 1S1—514/389-5324
Montreal, Le Guide de Montreal-Nord (Wed.) biling. 11881 Edger, Montreal North, P.Q.—514/322-4642
Montreal, Le Guide Mont-Royal (Wed.) Ste. 2, 4566 de La-Roche, Montreal, P.Q. H2J 3J6—514/527-8329
Montreal Hebdos Metropolitains, 5699 Christophe Colomb, Montreal, P.Q. H2S 2G4—514/527-8329
L'Avenir de l'Est (Tue.)
Flambeau de l'Est (Tue.)
Guide du Nord (Tue.)
Journal de Rosemont (Wed.)
Nouvelles de l'Est (Tue.)
St. Leonard & New Rosemont (Wed.)
Montreal, Journal Liason St-Louis (mthly 4th) 3950 ave Hôtel de Ville, Montreal, P.Q. H2W 2G7 - 514/844-7454
Montreal, Nun's Island Journal (Thur.) biling., 1880 Centre St., Montreal, P.Q. H3K 1N9 — 514/932-1455
Montreal, The Oracle (Wed.) biling., Ste. 14, 2425 Grand Blvd., Montreal, P.Q. H4B 2X2—514/489-6323
Montreal, Le Progrès de Villeray (Tue.) biling., 7577 St-Hubert, Montreal, P.Q. H2R 2N7—514/279-8419
Montreal, Le Progrès du Nord (Wed.) biling., 7577 St-Hubert, Montreal, P.Q. H2R 2N7—514/279-8419
Montreal, La Voix Populaire (Tue.) biling. 1735 de l'Eglise, Montreal, P.Q. H4E 1G6—514/768-4777
Pointe Claire, Cites Nouvelles (Thur.) 15718 ouest boul. Gouin, #5, St-Genevieve, P.Q. H9H 1C4 - 514/620-0781
St-Bruno, Le Journal de St-Bruno (Wed.) biling., 1507 rue Roberval, Ste. 1, St-Bruno de Montarville, P.Q. J3V 3P8—514/653-3685
St-Eustache, L'Eveil des Deux Rives (Wed.) 53 rue St-Eustache, St-Eustache, P.Q. J7R 2L2—514/472-3440
St-Eustache, Le Mirabel de St-Eustache (Tue.) 15 St-Eustache, St-Eustache, P.Q. J7R 2L1 - 514/472-9966
St-Hubert, Le Parapet (15/30) CFB Montreal, St-Hubert, P.Q. J3Y 5T4—514/671-3711
St-Lambert, Courrier Mag Expansion (Wed.) biling., Ste. 202, 1136 Victoria, Ville Lemoyne, St-Lambert, P.Q. J4R 1R1—514/465-1211
St-Laurent News (Wed.) biling., 6525 Somerled Ave., Montreal, P.Q. H4V 1S7—514/482-2545
St-Léonard, Le Journal de St-Léonard (Tue.) 6615 rue Jarry, Montreal, P.Q. H1P 1W5 — 514/327-2834
St-Michel, Le Nouveau Journal (Wed.) Fr. & It., #1, 8052 boul. St-Michel, Montreal, P.Q. H1Z 3E1 - 514/721-4911
Ste-Thérèse, Le Nor-Info (Wed.) 40 rue Turgeon, Ste-Thérèse, P.Q.—514/435-6537
Ste-Thérèse, La Voix des Milles Iles (Wed.) Box 190, Ste-Thérèse, P.Q. J7E 4J2—514/435-8791
Terrebonne, La Révue de Terrebonne (Wed.) Box 55, Terrebonne, P.Q. J6W 3L5—514/471-3948
Vaudreuil, L'Echo de Vaudreuil-Soulanges (Tue.) biling., Box 160, Dorion, P.Q. J7V 5W1—514/455-6111
Verdun, Messager de Verdun Messenger (Wed.) biling., 3132 LaSalle Blvd., Verdun, P.Q. H4G 1Y9—514/768-2544

End of Montreal Metropolitan Area

Neuville Hebdo de Portneuf Frin.) Box 220, G0A 2R0—418/876-2456
New Richmond, Le Journal Chaleur (Wed.) Box 410, Rimouski, P.Q. G5L 7C4—418/723-4800
Nicolet Courrier-Sud (Tue.) 3255 Marie Victorin, JOG 1EO—819/293-4551
Plessisville, La Feuille d'Erable (Wed.) Box 160, G6L 2Y7—819/362-7049
Quebec, Reflet de Mon Milieu Orleans (10th) 809 boul. des Chutes, Beauport, P.Q. G1E 2C5 - 418/661-5103
Repentigny, L'Artisan (Wed.) 142A Notre-Dame St., J6A 2P4—514/581-5120
Rimouski, Le Nouvel-Est (Wed.) 148 de la Cathedrale, G5L 5H8 - 418/724-5915
Rimouski, Le Progrès Echo (Wed.) #203, 192 est, St-Germain, Box 410, G5L 7C4—418/723-4800
Rimouski, Le Rimouskois (Wed.) Box 460, G5L 7C5—418/723-2571
Rivière-du-Loup, Le Portage (Tue.) 122 rue Lafontaine, C.P. 1178, G5R 4C3 — 418/867-1465
Rivière-du-Loup, St-Laurent Echo (Wed.) Box 1026, G5R 4C3 - 418/862-1774
Roberval, L'Etoile du Lac (Wed.) 840 Arthur St., G8H 2M7—418/275-2911
Rouyn-Noranda, La Frontière (Wed.) 82 Perreault St. W.—819/762-4361
St-André Avellin, Le Bulletin La Petite Nation (Tue.) Box 240, JOV 1WO —819/983-2616

St-Bruno, see Montreal
St-Eustache, see Montreal
St-Georges (Beauce), Beauce Nouvelle (Tue.) 12625 1st Ave. E., St-Georges est, P.Q. G5Y 2E8—418/228-8634
St-Georges (Beauce), L'Eclaireur-Progres (Wed.) 12625 1st Ave. E., St-Georges est, P.Q. G5Y 2E8—418/228-8858
St-Hyacinthe, Le Courrier (Wed.) 655 Ste-Anne, Box 340—514/773-6028
St-Hyacinthe, Le Journal Maskoutain (Wed.) 2605 Dessaulles – 514/773-1034
St-Hyacinthe Nouveau Clairon (Wed.) Box 276, J2S 7B6—514/774-5375
St-Jean, L'Aladin (eo Thur.) CFB St-Jean Richelain JOJ 1RO—514/346-2131
St-Jean, Le Canada Français (Wed.) 84 Richelieu, J3B 6X3—514/347-0323
St-Jean, Journal Le Régional (mthly) 169 boul. du Seminaire, J3B 5K4 — 514/347-8328
St-Jerome, Courrier-Laurentides (Wed.) 317 Montmorency, Laval-des-Rapides, P.Q. H7N 1X1—514/667-4360
St-Jerome, L'Echo du Nord (Wed.) Box 500, J7Z 5V2—514/436-5381
St-Jerome, Le Mirabel (Tue.) Box 276, J7Z 5T9—514/436-5381
St-Joseph (Beauce), La Vallée de la Chaudière (Wed.) Box 130, G0S 2V0—418/397-5796
St-Jovite, Le Messager Régional (Tue.) Box 428, J0T 2H0—819/425-2407
St-Lambert, see Montreal
St-Laurent, see Montreal
St-Pascal de Kamouraska, Le Placoteux (Mon.) C.P. 181, G0L 3Y0 – 418/492-2706
St-Tite, Le Dynamique de la Mauricie (Wed.) Box 520, G0X 3H0 —418/365-6262
Ste-Adele, Le Journal des Pays D'en Haut (Wed.) Box 1890, Ste-Adele, P.Q. JOR 1LO—514/229-6664
Ste-Agathe des Monts, Le Sommet Echo des Laurentides (Wed.) biling. 145 St-Venant St., J8C 2P5—819/326-3534
Ste-Foy, L'Appel (Wed.) 2715 Restigouche St., G1V 1E3—418/651-7944
Ste-Foy, Reflet de Mon Milieu (15th) 809 boul. des Chutes, Beauport, P.Q. G1E 2C5 – 418/661-7733
Ste-Julie, L'Information (Tue.) Box 359, JOL 2CO—514/649-0719
Ste-Marie, Beauce Media (Tue.) C.P. 400, Ste-Marie-de-Beauce, P.Q. G0S 2Y0 – 418/387-8000
Ste-Marie (Beauce), Le Guide (Wed.) Box 100, GOS 2YO—418/387-5408
Ste-Thérèse, see Montreal
Sept-Iles, L'Elan Sept-Ilien (Thur.) Ste. 226, 456 Arnaud, G4R 3B1—418/968-1230
Sept-Iles, Le Nord Est (Wed.) 365 boul. Laure, G4R 1X2 – 418/962-9941
Sept-Iles/Port Cartier, Le Nordic Regional (Sat.) 365 boul. Laure, Sept-Iles, P.Q. G4R 1X2—418/962-4100
Shawinigan, Hebdo du St-Maurice (Wed.) Box 67, G9N 2L4—819/537-5111
Shawville, The Equity (Wed.) biling. Box 430, JOX 2YO—819/647-2204
Sherbrooke, La Nouvelle du Haut St-François (Wed.) Box 490, East Angus, P.Q. JOB 1RO—819/832-2461
Sorel, Le Courrier Riviera (Wed.) 38a Augusta, J3P 1A3—514/742-1002
Sorel, Les 2 Rives (Tue.) 77 Georges St., J3P 1B9 — 514/742-9409
Sorel, La Voix Metropolitaine (Tue.) 82 rue Roi, J3P 4M8—514/743-8466
Sorel, La Voix du Samedi (Sat.) 82 rue Roi, J3P 4M8—514/743-8466
Temiscamingue, Le Journal Temiscamien (Wed.) Box 219, Ville Marie, P.Q. JOZ 3WO — 819/629-2618
Terrebonne, see Montreal
Thetford Mines, Courrier Frontenac (Tue.) Box 789, G6G 5V3—418/338-3157
Thetford Mines, Le Progres-Carrousel (Tue.) Box 699, G6G 5X1 —418/335-5995
Trois Pistoles, Le Courrier (Wed.) Box 400, G0L 4K0—418/851-3644
Val Bélair, Le Mercredi Soir (Wed.) C.P. 70, G0A 4T0 – 418/843-4173
Val d'Or, L'Echos Abitibien (Wed.) 1085 3rd Ave., J9P 1T5—819/825-3755 (inc. Amos; LaSarre; Malartic; Matagami)
Valcartier, Adsum (Wed.) Room 234, 513 CFB Bldg., 500 Valcartier, G0A 1RO—418/844-5598
Valleyfield, Le Soleil du St-Laurent (Wed.) Box 98, Beauharnois, P.Q. J6N 3C1—514/692-8555
Valleyfield, Le St-François Journal (Tue.) 211 Victoria St., J6T 1A8—514/371-6222
Verdun, see Montreal
Victoriaville, La Nouvelle (Tue.) Box 504, G6P 5T3—819/752-6718
Victoriaville, L'Union des Cantons de l'Est (Tue.) 370 Girouard, G5P 6S8—819/357-2065
Windsor, L'Etincelle (Wed.) 13 rue St-Georges—819/845-2705

Quebec Weekly Newspapers in English

See also Weekly Newspapers in French (for bilingual papers)

Aylmer, The Reporter (Thur.) 195 Main St., J9H 6J8—819/684-3418
Buckingham Post (Wed.) 585 James St., J8L 2R7—819/986-8557
Chelsea, The Low Down to Hull and Back News (Thur.) JOX 1NO — 819/827-0321
Gaspé Peninsula Spec (Tue.) Box 99, New Carlisle, P.Q. GOC 1ZO—418/752-5400
Hudson, Lake of Two Mountains Gazette (Thur.) Box 70, J0P 1H0—514/458-5482
Huntingdon Gleaner (Wed.) biling. Box 130, J0S 1H0—514/264-5364
Lachute Watchman (Wed.) Box 220, J8H 3X3—514/562-2494
Lennoxville, The Township Sun (mthly 1st) C.P. 28, J1M 1Z3 – 819/566-7424
Montreal, The Monitor (Wed.) 6525 Somerled Ave., H4V 1S7—514/482-2545
Montreal, Nun's Island Journal (Wed.) biling., 1880 Centre St., H3K 1H9—514/932-1455
Montreal, Outremont News (Wed.) 2425 Grand Blvd., #20, H4B 2X2 – 514/481-2769
Montreal, The Suburban, 8170 Wavell Rd., Cote St-Luc, H4W 1M3—514/484-1107:
- Cote des Neiges East Edition (Wed.) biling.
- Cote St-Luc Edition (Wed.) biling.
- Dollard des Ormeaux Edition (eo Wed.) biling.
- Laval (Chomedey) Edition (Wed.) biling.
- New Bordeaux Edition (eo Wed.) biling.
- Notre Dame de Grace Edition (Wed.) (Engl.-Ital.)
- St-Laurent Edition (Wed.) biling.
- Town of Mount Royal Edition (eo Wed.) biling.
- Westmount Edition (eo Wed.) biling.

Montreal, West Central Courrier (mthly 18th) Box 806, Stn. H, H3G 2M8 – 514/845-3024
Pointe Claire News & Chronicle (Thur.) 15 Cartier Ave., H9S 4R7 — 514/695-9150
Quebec Chronicle-Telegraph (Wed.) 980 Holland Ave., G1S 3T1 —418/527-2591
Rock Island, Stanstead Journal (Thur.) Box 130, J0B 2K0—819/876-5153
Rouyn-Noranda Press (Thur.) 82 Perreault St. W., Rouyn, P.Q.—819/762-4000
St-Eustache (Deux Monts) The Victory (Wed.) 53 St-Eustache, J7R 2L2—514/472-3440
Tenaga, see Chelsea
Town of Mount Royal Weekly Post (Thur.) biling. 233 Dunbar Ave., H3P 2H4—514/739-3302
Val d'Or, The Star (Wed.) 1095 3rd Ave., J9P 4A9—819/825-3755

Westmount Examiner (Thur.) 155 Hillside Ave., H3Z 2Y8 — 514/932-3157

Saskatchewan Daily Newspapers

LLOYDMINSTER: See Alberta
MOOSE JAW: Times-Herald (evening) 44 Fairford St. W. (S6H 1V1)—306/692-6441
PRINCE ALBERT: Herald (evening) 30-10th St. E. (S6V 5R9)—306/764-4276
REGINA: The Leader-Post (evening) 1964 Park St. (S4P 3G4)—306/565-8211
SASKATOON: Star-Phoenix (evening), 204-5th Ave. N. (S7K 2P1)—306/664-8340

Saskatchewan Weekly Newspapers

Assiniboia Times (Wed.) S0H 0B0—306/642-4432
Balcarres, The Local Exchange (Tue.) Box 940, Fort Qu'Appelle, Sask. S0G 1S0 – 306/332-5526
Battleford Telegraph (Fri.) Box 338, SOM OEO — 306/937-2647
Bengough-Coronach Big Muddy Roundup (Thur.) Box 370, Radville, Sask. SOC 2GO—306/869-2202
Biggar Independent (Wed.) Box 40, S0K 0M0—306/948-3344
Birch Hills Gazette (Thur.) Box 340, Kinistino, Sask. S0J 1H0—306/864-2266
Broadview Express (Thur.) Box 69, Grenfell, Sask. S0G 2B0—306/697-2722
Canora Courier (Wed.) Box 746, S0A 0L0—306/563-5131
Carlyle Observer (Wed.) Box 160, S0C 0R0 – 306/453-2525
Carlyle, The Prairie Progress (Wed.) Box 160, SOC ORO — 306/453-2525
Carnduff Gazette-Post News (Wed.) Box 220, S0C 0S0—306/482-3252
Carrot River Observer (Wed.) Box 2014, Nipawin, Sask. S0E 1E0—306/862-4618
Craik Weekly News (Thur.) Box 360, S0G 0V0—306/734-2313
Cut Knife, Highway 40 Courier (Wed.) Box 400, S0M 0N0—306/398-2221
Davidson Leader (Wed.) Box 723, S0G 1A0—306/567-2047
Elrose Review (Wed.) Box 70, S0L 0Z0—306/378-2255
Esterhazy Potashville Miner-Journal (Wed.) Box 1000, Esterhazy, Sask. S0A 0X0—306/745-2331
Estevan Mercury (Wed.) Box 730, S4A 2A6—306/634-2654
Eston Press (Wed.) Box 787, S0L 1A0—306/962-3221
Foam Lake Review (Wed.) Box 550, S0A 1A0—306/272-3262
Fort Qu'Appelle Times (Wed.) Box 940, S0G 1S0—306/332-5526
Grenfell Sun (Wed.) Box 69, S0G 2B0—306/697-2722
Gull Lake Advance (Tue.) Box 628, S0N 1A0—306/672-3373
Hafford, The Big Country Voice (Thur.) Box 70, SOJ 1A0—306/549-2149
Herbert Herald (Wed.) Box 399, S0H 2A0—306/784-2422
Hudson Bay Post-Review (Wed.) Box 10, S0E 0Y0—306/865-2771
Humboldt Journal (Thur.) Box 970, S0K 2A0—306/682-2561
Indian Head-Wolseley News (Wed.) Box 70, Indian Head, Sask. S0G 2K0—306/695-3565
Ituna News (Thur.) Box 550, Foam Lake, Sask. S0A 1A0—306/272-3262
Kamsack Times (Thur.) Box 746, Canora, Sask. S0A 0L0—306/563-5131
Kelvington Radio (Thur.) Box 100, Wadena, Sask. S0A 4J0—306/338-2231
Kerrobert Citizen (Wed.) Box 1150, Kindersley, Sask. SOL 1SO — 306/463-4611
Kindersley Clarion (Wed.) Box 1150, S0L 1S0—306/463-4611
Kinistino Post (Wed.) Box 340, S0J 1H0—306/864-2266
Kipling Citizen (Thur.) S0J 2S0—306/736-2535
La Ronge, Northland News (Wed.) Box 1350, S0J 1L0—306/425-3344
Lanigan, Last Mountain Ad-Visor (Wed.) Box 249, S0K 2M0 – 306/365-3071
Leader News (Wed.) Box 1150, Kindersley, Sask. SOL 1SO—306/463-4611
Macklin Mirror (Wed.) Box 100, SOL 2CO—306/753-2424
Maidstone Mirror (Thur.) Box 308, S0M 1M0—306/893-2251
Maple Creek News (Wed.) Box 1360, S0N 1N0—306/667-2133
Meadow Lake Progress (Wed.) Box 879, S0M 1V0—306/236-5265
Melfort Journal (Wed.) Box 1300, S0E 1A0—306/752-5737
Melville Advance (Wed.) Box 1420, S0A 2P0—306/728-5448
Moosomin World-Spectator (Wed.) Box 250, S0G 3N0—306/435-2445
Nipawin Journal (Wed.) Box 2014, S0E 1E0—306/862-4618
Nipawin, N.E. Region Community Booster (2/4 Fri.) Box 2014, SOE 1EO—306/862-4618
Nokomis Times (Wed.) Box 340, S0G 3R0—306/528-2020
Norquay North Star (Thur.) Box 746, Canora, Sask. S0A 0L0—306/563-5131
North Battleford Advertiser-Post (Wed.) Box 160, S9A 2Y1—306/445-7261
North Battleford, CCA Rodeo News (1 & 15) Box 276, S9A 2Y3—306/445-3233
North Battleford News-Optimist (Tue. Fri.) Box 430, S9A 2Y5—306/445-4401
Outlook, The Outlook (Thur.) Box 279, S0L 2N0—306/867-8262
Oxbow Herald (Wed.) Box 420, S0C 2B0—306/483-2323
Preeceville Progress (Thur.) Box 746, Canora, Sask. S0A 0L0—306/563-5131
Radville Star (Thur.) Box 370, S0C 2G0—306/869-2202
Redvers, The Optimist (Wed.) Box 490, S0C 2H0—306/452-3363
Regina, Journal L'eau Vive (Wed.) 2604 rue Centrale, S4N 2N9—306/525-8934
Rosetown Eagle (Wed.) Box 130, S0L 2V0—306/882-2232
Rosthern, Saskatchewan Valley News (Thur.) Box 10, S0K 3R0—306/232-4255
Saskatoon, The Saskatoon Commentator (Wed.) 717-2nd Ave. N., S7K 2C9—306/652-7556
Semans, Hi-Way 15 Gazette (Wed.) Box 10, Wynyard, Sask. S0A 4T0—306/554-2224
Shaunavon Standard (Wed.) Box 729, S0N 2M0—306/297-2711
Shellbrook Chronicle (Wed.) Box 10, S0J 2E0—306/747-2442
Spiritwood Herald (Thur.) Box 10, Shellbrook, Sask. S0J 2E0—306/747-2442
Star City & Naicam Echo-Sentinel (Wed.) Box 2014, Nipawin, Sask. S0E 1E0—306/862-4618
Stoughton Times (Wed.) Box 69, Grenfell, Sask. SOG 2BO—306/697-2722
Swift Current, The Southwest Booster (Tue.) Box 1330, S9H 3X4—306/773-9321
Swift Current Sun (Tue. & Thur.) Box 670, S9H 3W7—306/773-3116
Tisdale Recorder (Wed.) Box 1660, S0E 1T0—306/873-4515
Unity Northwest Herald (Wed.) Box 309, S0K 4L0—306/228-2267
Wadena News (Wed.) Box 100, S0A 4J0—306/338-2231
Wakaw Recorder (Thur.) Box 9, S0K 4P0—306/233-4325
Watrous Manitou (Thur.) Box 100, S0K 4T0—306/946-3343
Watson Witness (Wed.) Box 129, S0K 4V0—306/287-3245
Weyburn Review (Wed.) Box 400, S4H 2K4—306/842-7487
Whitewood Herald (Tue.) Box 160, S0G 5C0—306/735-2230
Wilkie Press (Wed.) Box 309, Unity, Sask. S0K 4L0—306/228-2267
Windthorst Independent (Wed.) Box 69, Grenfell, Sask. S0G 2B0—306/697-2722
Wynyard Advance (Wed.) Box 10, S0A 4T0—306/554-2224
Yorkton Enterprise (Wed.) Box 520, S3N 2W4—306/782-2481
Yorkton This Week (Wed.) Box 1300, S3N 2X3—306/783-2465

Territories Newspapers

FORT SMITH (N.W.T.): Slave River Journal (Thur.) Box 990, XOE OPO—403/872-2784

FROBISHER BAY (N.W.T.): Nunatsiaq News (Fri.) Box 8, X0A 0H0—819/979-5357
HAY RIVER (N.W.T.): Tapwe (Wed.) Box 130
The Hub (Wed.) Box 1250, X0E 0R0—403/874-6577
INUVIK: The Drum (Wed.) Box 2600, XOE OTO — 403/979-2623
WHITEHORSE (YUKON): Star (daily) 2149 2nd Ave., Y1A 1C5—403/667-4481
Yukon Indian News (eo Thur.) 22 Nisutlin Dr., Y1A 3S5 — 403/667-7631
Yukon News (Wed.) 211 Wood St., Y1A 2E4—403/667-6285
YELLOWKNIFE (N.W.T.): News of the North (Fri.) Box 2820, XOE 1HO—403/873-8109
Native Press (twice mthly.) Box 1919, XOE 1HO—403/873-2661
Yellowknifer (Wed.) Box 2820, X0E 1H0—403/873-8109

FOREIGN LANGUAGE PUBLICATIONS

(excluding French and English)

ARABIC: Arab Directory (annually) Box 508, Stn. F, Toronto, Ont. M4Y 2L8—416/922-0283
Arab News of Toronto (semi-monthly) Box 508, Stn. F, Toronto, Ont. M4Y 2L8—416/922-0283
ARC Arabic Journal (semi-monthly) #203, 834 Yonge St., Toronto, Ont. M4W 2H1 - 416/922-1685
Canada & Arab World, Ottawa (semi-monthly) Box 508, Stn. F, Toronto, Ont. M4Y 2L8—416/922-0283
Canadian Arab World Review (monthly) 10935 Jeanne Mance St., Montreal, P.Q. H3L 3C7—514/331-5550
Canadian Middle East Journal (monthly) 285 Jean Talon St. E., Montreal, P.Q. H2R 1S9—514/272-8267
Islam Canada (monthly) Box 771, Stn. B, Willowdale, Ont. M2K 2R1
Liban au Canada (monthly) 7497 St-Denis St., Montreal, P.Q. H2R 2E5—514/270-5633
The Source (monthly) Box 9420, Ottawa, Ont. K1G 3V1—613/737-4425
ARMENIAN: Abaka (weekly) 663 Jarry ouest, Montreal, P.Q. H3N 1G3 - 514/273-0855
BYELORUSSIAN: Bielaruski Holas (monthly) 24 Tarlton Rd., Toronto, Ont. M5P 2M4—416/488-0048
CHINESE: Chinatown News: see Consumer Magazines
Chinese Canadian Bulletin (monthly) 3289 Main St., Vancouver, B.C. V5V 3M6—604/872-2810
Chinese Express (daily) #203, 530 Dundas St. W., Toronto, Ont. M5T 1H3 - 416/977-7551
The Chinese Times (daily) 1 E. Pender St., Vancouver, B.C. V6A 1S9—604/685-8812
The Chinese Voice (daily) 233 Main St., Vancouver, B.C. V6A 2S7—604/684-6828
The Chinese Way (twice a month) #209, 145 Keefer St., Vancouver, B.C. V6A 1X3 - 604/684-2281
National Capital Chinese Community Newsletter (monthly) 565 Somerset St., Ottawa, Ont. K1R 5K1 — 613/820-3370
The New Republic (daily) 531 Main St., Vancouver, B.C. V6A 2V1—604/683-8033
Shing Wah Daily News (evening) 12 Hagerman St., Toronto, Ont. M5G 1A7—416/977-3745
CROAT, SERB & SLOVENIAN: Bratstvo (monthly) 345 Dovercourt Rd., Toronto, Ont. M6J 3E4—416/533-5473
Glas Kanadskih Srba (weekly) 1297 Drouillard Rd., Windsor, Ont. N8Y 2R6—519/945-8311
Hrvatski Glas (weekly) Ste. 8, 9 Mill St. (Box 310, Acton, Ont. L7J 1G4)
Kanadski Srbobran (weekly) 335 Britannia Ave., Hamilton, Ont. L3H 1Y4—416/549-4079
Nase Novine (weekly) 10 St. Mary St., Ste. 505, Toronto, Ont. M4Y 2L8—416/961/8018
Slovenska Drzava (monthly) 1115 Bay St., Toronto, Ont. M5S 2B3—416/532-4746
Vrijeme (semi-annually) Box 35697, Vancouver, B.C. V6M 4G9 - 604/731-5450
DANISH: Modersmaalet (eo week) Box 306, Oakville, Ont. L6J 5A2—416/845-9484
DUTCH: Calvinist-Contact (weekly) 99 Niagara St., St. Catharines, Ont. L2R 4L3
Duca-Post (bi-monthly) Box 1100, Willowdale, Ont. M2N 5W5—416/223-8502
Hollandia News (eo Mon.) Box 966, Chatham, Ont. N7M 5L3—519/354-4071
De Hollandse Krant (monthly) 5423 Brydon Cres., Langley, B.C. V3A 4A3—604/534-1739
De Nederlandse Courant (bi-weekly) Box 2236, Stn. B, Scarborough, Ont. M1N 2E9—416/264-2672
Pioneer (monthly) c/o Council of the Reformed Church in Canada, R.R. 4, Cambridge, Ont. N1R 5S5 - 519/623-4860
The Windmill Herald (eo Mon.) Box 533, New Westminster, B.C. V3L 4Y8—604/524-0184
ESTONIAN: Meie Elu (weekly) 958 Broadview Ave., Toronto, Ont. M4K 2R6—416/466-0951
Vaba Eestlane (Tue. & Fri.) Box 70, Stn. C, Toronto, Ont. M6J 3M7
FINNISH: Aikamme (quarterly) Box 76979, Vancouver, B.C. V5R 5T3—604/437-0132
Canadan Uutiset (weekly) 218 Wilson St., Thunder Bay, Ont. P7B 1M8—807/344-1611
Vapaa Sana (Tue. & Thur.) 400 Queen St. W., Toronto, Ont. M5V 2A6—416/368-7221
GERMAN: Kanada Kurier (weekly) 955 Alexander Ave., Winnipeg, Man. R3C 2X8 - 204/774-1883
Die Mennonitische Post (semi-monthly) Box 1926, Steinbach, Man. ROA 2AO—204/326-6790
Mennonitische Rundschau (bi-weekly) 159 Henderson Hwy., Winnipeg, Man. R2L 1L4—204/667-3560
Der Osterreicher (semi-monthly) Box 355, Stn. Z, Toronto, Ont. M5N 2Z5 — 416/483-2149
Pazifische Rundschau (semi-monthly) Box 2033, Vancouver, B.C. V6B 3R6—604/277-5246
Die Zeit (weekly) Room 303-4, 455 Spadina Ave., Toronto, Ont. M5S 2G9—416/979-2434
GREEK: Acropolis (monthly) Ste. 5, 2160 W. 39th Ave., Vancouver, B.C. V6M 1T5—604/266-6137
Evdomada (weekly) 59 Cambridge Ave., Toronto, Ont. M4K 2L1—416/461-3519
Greek Canadian Action (monthly) 8085 Birnam, Montreal, P.Q. H3N 2T6—514/271-9325
Greek Canadian Reportage (weekly) 7438 Durocher St., Montreal, P.Q. H3N 2A3—514/279-2610
Greek Canadian Tribune (weekly) 5619 Park Ave., Montreal, P.Q.—514/272-6873
Hellenic Free Press (bi-weekly) 819A Bloor St. W., Toronto, Ont. M6G 1M1 - 416/532-4431
Hellenic Hamilton News (monthly) 23 Myrtle Ave., Hamilton, Ont. L8M 2E8 - 416/529-2380
Hellenic View (semi-monthly) Box 2045, Vancouver, B.C. V6B 3R6
GUJARATI: Gujarat Vartman (monthly) 86 Pilkey Cres., Scarborough, Ont. M1B 2A9 — 416/281-2736
Subras (monthly) 51 Hillside Ave., Toronto, Ont. M8V 1S7 — 416/251-7182
HINDI: Bharati (monthly) 1433 Bloor St. W., Toronto, Ont. M6P 3L6—416/536-4737
HUNGARIAN: Kanadai Magyarsag (weekly) 412 Bloor St. W., Toronto, Ont. M5S 1X5—416/924-2502
Magyar Elet (weekly) 6 Alcina Ave., Toronto, Ont. M6G 2E8—416/654-2551
Menorah-Egyenloseg (weekly) 26 Oxford St., Toronto, Ont. M5T 1N9
Sporthirado (weekly) 3 Meadowbrook Rd., Toronto, Ont. M6B 2S3—416/783-4936
ICELANDIC: Logberg-Heimskringla (weekly) 1400, 191 Lombard Ave., Winnipeg, Man. R3B OX1 — 204/943-9945
INDIAN: Canadian India Star: See Consumer Magazines
The Canadian India Times: See Consumer Magazines
India Calling: See Consumer Magazines
The Link: See Weekly Newspapers (Vancouver)

ITALIAN: Ciao! Magazine (monthly) 1081 Bas de L'Assomption Nord, L'Assomption, P.Q. J0K 1G0 - 514/376-1540
Il Cittadino Canadese (weekly) 6896 St. Lawrence Blvd., Montreal, P.Q. H2S 3C7—514/277-3181
Comunita Viva (monthly) Box 429, Stn. D, Toronto, Ont. M6P 3K1—416/656-2192
Corriere Canadese, see Toronto Daily Newspapers
Corriere Illustrato (weekly) 1000 Lawrence Ave. W., Toronto, Ont. M6A 1P2—416/789-1171
Corriere Italiano (weekly) 6900 St. Denis St., Montreal, P.Q.—514/279-4536
Donna (semi-monthly) 2924 Dufferin St., Toronto, Ont. M6B 3T7 — 416/787-2806
L'Eco D'Italia (weekly) 1441 Commercial Dr., Vancouver, B.C. V5L 3X8—604/255-6201
La Gazzetta (weekly) 501 Erie St. W., Windsor, Ont. N9A 3X8 —519/253-8883
Giornale Di Sicilia (weekly) 7581 Jane St., Concord, Ont. L4K 1B1 - 416/669-5442
Insieme (weekly) 9652 St. Michel Blvd., Montreal, P.Q. H1H 3G5—514/388-2691
Il Mormoratore (monthly) Box 394, Calgary, Alta. T2S 0A7—403/278-4580
The Newsletter (monthly) Box 233, Stn. N, Toronto, Ont. M8V 3T2—416/255-8631
Il Nuovo Mondo Edmonton (monthly) 4545 118 Ave., Edmonton, Alta. T5W 1A8 - 403/471-4136
Nuovo Mondo Toronto (monthly) 1185A St. Clair Ave. W., Toronto, Ont. M6B 1B5—416/656-6775
L'Ora Di Ottawa (weekly) Box 9028, Stn. A, Ottawa, Ont. K1G 3T8—613/232-5689
Il Rincontro (monthly) 7092 St. Laurent Blvd., Montreal, P.Q. H2S 3E2—514/272-0344
Il Settimanale (semi-monthly) 1725 Eglinton Ave. W., Toronto, Ont. M6E 2H1—416/782-5140
Il Settimanale di Montreal (weekly) 6615 Jarry St. E., Montreal, P.Q. H1P 1W5—514/327-2614
La Sicilia (semi-monthly) 1725 Eglinton Ave. W., Toronto, Ont. M6E 2H1 - 416/789-5513
Il Tevere (weekly) 369 Old Weston Rd., Toronto, Ont. M6N 3A9—416/656-7800
La Tribuna Italiana (monthly) #4, 1989 Jean Talon St. E., Montreal, P.Q. H2E 1T9—514/374-1542
Vita Italiana (weekly) Box 163, Stn. L, Toronto, Ont. M6E 4Y5
La Voce d'Italia (semi-monthly) 6736 Monk Blvd., Montreal, P.Q. H4E 3J1—514/769-5711

JAPANESE: The Continental Times (Tue. & Fri.) 417 Dundas St. W., Toronto, Ont. M5T 1G6—416/366-1888
The New Canadian (Tue. & Fri.) 479 Queen St. W., Toronto, Ont. M5V 2A9—416/366-5005

JEWISH: The Hebrew Journal (weekly) 304 Adelaide St. W., Toronto, Ont. M5V 1P6—416/363-7424
The Jewish Eagle (weekly) 4180 De Courtrai, Suite 218, Montreal, P.Q. H3S 1C3—514/735-6577
The Jewish Post: see Weekly Newspapers (Winnipeg)
Jewish Standard: see Magazine Section
Jewish Western Bulletin: see Weekly Newspapers (Vancouver)
North York Downsview Reporter: see Weekly Newspapers (Tor.)
The Toronto Jewish Press: see Weekly Newspapers (Tor.)
Western Jewish News: see Weekly Newspapers (Winnipeg)

KOREAN: The Canada News (semi-weekly) 928 Queen St. W., Toronto, Ont. M6J 1G6—416/533-2361
The Korean Journal (weekly) 257 Olive Ave., Willowdale, Ont. M2N 4P5—416/267-0745
The Koreanna (weekly) 1212 Brisbane Ave., Port Coquitlam, B.C. V3J 5L1 - 604/931-2136
The Minjoong Shinmoon (weekly) #306, 741 Broadview Ave., Toronto, Ont. M4K 2P6 - 416/469-1103
New Korea Times (weekly) 344 Bloor St. W., Ste. 606, Toronto, Ont.—416/925-3250

LATVIAN: Latvija-Amerika (weekly) 125 Broadview Ave., Toronto, Ont. M4M 2E9—416/465-7902

LITHUANIAN: Nepriklausoma Lietuva (weekly) 7722 George St., Ville LaSalle, P.Q. H8P 1C4—514/366-6220
Teviskes Ziburiai (weekly) 2185 Stavebank Rd., Mississauga, Ont. L5C 1T3—416/275-4672

MALAYALAM: Malayalee (semi-monthly) 275 Lansdowne Ave., Toronto, Ont. M6K 2W2 — 416/766-6361
Voice of Kerala (semi-monthly) 155 Walton St., Port Hope, Ont. L1A 1N7

NORWEGIAN: Norrona (1 & 15) 8594 Sunbury Place, Delta, B.C. V4C 3Y7—604/581-8930

PAKISTANI: Eastern News (semi-monthly) 3100 Dixie Rd., Mississauga, Ont. L4Y 3W4 — 416/272-0259
Fortnightly Al-Hilal (1 & 15) 338 Hollyberry Trail, Willowdale, Ont. M2H 2P6
Shama (monthly) Box 1061, Stn. B, Mississauga, Ont. L4Y 3W4 - 416/272-0259

PHILIPINO: Balita (semi-monthly) Box 392, Stn. A, Toronto, Ont. M5W 1C2 — 416/276-3267
Silangan (monthly) Ste. 311, 310 Donald St., Winnipeg, Man. R3B 2H4—204/943-3214

POLISH: Czas (weekly) 1150 Main St., Winnipeg, Man. R2W 3S6 —204/582-4392
Glos Polski-Gazeta Polska (weekly) 1089 Queen St. W., Toronto, Ont. M6J 1H5—416/533-9469
The Polish Canadian Courier (semi-monthly) Box 161, Stn. P, Toronto, Ont. M5S 2JO—416/921-1069
Zwiazkowiec (Mon. & Wed.) 1638 Bloor St. W., Toronto, Ont. M6P 4A8—416/531-2491

PORTUGUESE: A Voz de Portugal (weekly) 4136 boul. St-Laurent, Montreal, P.Q. H2W 1Y8 - 514/844-0388
Correio Portugues (15 & 30) 793 Ossington Ave., Toronto, Ont. M6G 3T8—416/532-9894
Desporto (weekly) 629 Dufferin St., Toronto, Ont. M6K 2B2—416/532-6067
Jornal Acoreano (weekly) 1123 Dundas St. W., Toronto, Ont. M6J 1W9 — 416/532-3195
Jornal Do Emigrante (semi-monthly) Box 628, Stn. N, Montreal, P.Q. H2X 3M6
Mundo (weekly) 946 College St., Toronto, Ont. M6H 1A5 - 416/535-8199
O Lusitano (eo week) Box 3485, Cambridge, Ont. N3H 5C6—519/653-6988
O Mensageiro (bi-weekly) 6926 Tyne St., Vancouver, B.C. V5S 3M6—604/435-9018
Portugal Ilustrado (semi-monthly) Unit 133, 60 Hanson Rd., Mississauga, Ont. L5B 2P6 - 416/279-8368
Sentinela (semi-monthly) Box 65532, Stn. F, Vancouver, B.C. V5N 5K5—604/874-7416

PUNJABI: Asia Times (semi-monthly) 1433 Bloor St. W., Toronto, Ont. M6P 3L6—416/536-4717
Indo Canadian Times (semi-monthly) Box 118, Surrey, B.C. V3T 4W4—604/584-9220
Perdesi Panjab (semi-monthly) 853 Gladstone Ave., Toronto, Ont. M6H 3J7—416/531-3640
Punjabi Patarka (semi-monthly) Box 287, Stn. W, Toronto, Ont. M6M 4Z2

ROMANIAN: Cuvantul Romanesc (monthly) Box 4217, Stn. D, Hamilton, Ont. L8V 4L6—416/387-1832
Ecouri Romanesti (monthly) 1862 Eglinton Ave. W., Toronto, Ont. M6E 2J4—416/787-8633

SCANDINAVIAN: The Scandinavian Canadian Businessman (monthly) Box 306, Oakville, Ont.—416/845-9484

SLOVAK: Kanadske Listy (monthly) Box 520, Stn. D, Toronto, Ont. M6P 3K1
Kanadsky Slovak (weekly) 1736 Dundas St. W., Toronto, Ont. M6K 1V5—416/364-4075
Novy Domov (bi-weekly) 450 Scarborough Golf Club Rd., Scarborough, Ont. M1G 1H1 - 416/439-4354
Slovensky Hlas (monthly) c/o Canadian Slovak Benefit Society, Box 1705, Stn. A, Windsor, Ont. N9A 6Y1

SPANISH: El Popular (Mon. Wed. & Fri.) Box 1108, Adelaide St. Stn., Toronto, Ont. M5C 2K5 - 416/967-5326
Latino (weekly) #501, 344 Bloor St. W., Toronto, Ont. M5S 1W9 - 416/967-0042

Quincenario Hispano (15 & 30) 1836 W. 11th Ave., Box 76884, Stn. S, Vancouver, B.C. V6J 2C5

SWEDISH: Canada-Svensken (1 & 15) Box 653, Stn. F, Toronto, Ont. M4Y 2N6

Nya Svenska Pressen (eo week) Ste. 1009, 207 W. Hastings St., Vancouver, B.C. V6B 1H7—604/688-4023

UKRAINIAN: Batkivshchyna (monthly) 362 Bathurst St., Toronto, Ont. M5T 2S6

The Canadian Farmer (weekly) 842 Main St., Box 3717, Stn. B, Winnipeg, Man. R2W 3R6—204/589-5101

Homin Ukrainy (weekly) 140 Bathurst St., Toronto, Ont. M5V 2R3—416/368-3443

Lemko News (monthly) Box 68, Stn. E, Toronto, Ont. M6H 4E1

Moloda Ukraina (monthly) Box 40, Stn. M, Toronto, Ont. M6S 4T2

My I Svit (monthly) c/o Art Museum, E. Service Rd., Q.E.W., Niagara Falls, Ont. L2E 6S5

Nasha Meta (weekly) 278 Bathurst St., Toronto, Ont. M5T 2S3—416/368-3519

Novy Shliakh (weekly) 297 College St., Toronto, Ont. M5T 1S2—416/960-3424

New Pathway Annual (annually) 297 College St., Toronto, Ont. M5T 1S2—416/960-3424

Nowi Dni (monthly) Box 126, Stn. N, Toronto, Ont. M8V 3S4

Oko (monthly) 3370 St. Zotique St. E., Montreal, P.Q. H1X 1C8 - 514/728-8931

Postup (weekly) 418 Aberdeen Ave., Winnipeg, Man. R2W 1V7—204/582-1940

Promin (monthly) Box 3551, Stn. B, Winnipeg, Man. R2W 3R4

Svitlo (monthly) 286 Lisgar St., Toronto, Ont. M6J 3G9—416/535-6483

Ukrainski Visti (weekly) 10967-97th St., Edmonton, Alta. T5H 2M8—403/422-5708

Ukrainsky Holos (weekly) 842 Main St., Box 3629, Stn. B, Winnipeg, Man. R2W 3R4—204/589-5101

Vilne Slovo (weekly) 196 Bathurst St., Toronto, Ont. M5T 2R8—416/368-7282

Vilne Slovo Annual (annually) 196 Bathurst St., Toronto, Ont. M5T 2R8—416/368-7282

Yunak (monthly) 2150 Bloor St. W., Toronto, Ont. M6S 1M8—416/769-7855

Zhinochy Svit (monthly) Box 234, Stn. M, Toronto, Ont. M6S 4T3

URDU: Akhbar-I-Gulrang (semi-monthly) Box 355, Stn. O, Toronto, Ont. M4A 2N9—416/498-6377

Imrose (semi-monthly) 89 John Dabor Trail, Scarborough, Ont. M1B 2P5 - 416/281-5338

The Messenger (semi-monthly) Box 2114, Stn. B, Scarborough, Ont. M1N 2E5 — 416/267-8006

The Pakeeza International (monthly) Unit 21, 21 Lexington Ave., Rexdale, Ont. M9V 2G4 — 416/745-1866

Punjab (monthly) 1433 Bloor St. W., Toronto, Ont. M6P 3L6—416/536-4737

CONSUMER MAGAZINES

(listed alphabetically by name of publication)

L'Actualité (monthly) 481 University Ave., Toronto, Ont. M5W 1A7—416/596-5311

Age D'or Vie Nouvelle (semi-monthly) 1415 rue Jarry est, Montreal, P.Q. H2E 2Z7 - 514/374-4700

Alberta Fishing Guide (annually) 3728 44 Ave., Red Deer, Alta. T4N 3H5 - 403/347-5079

Alberta Magazine (bi-monthly) #202, 10734 107 Ave., Edmonton, Alta. T5H 0W8 - 403/428-9578

Alberta Report (weekly) 11648 142 St., Edmonton, Alta. T5M 1V4 — 403/452-8442

Alberta Wild Rose Quarter Horse Journal (monthly) Box 550, Nanton, Alta. T0L 1R0 - 403/486-2144

Alive (6 times a year) 8592 Fraser St., Box 67333, Vancouver, B.C. V5W 3T1—604/321-4811

Alive Magazine (irregular) Box 1331, Guelph, Ont. N1H 6N8

Alive & Well Magazine (10 times a year) 7 Geneva St., St. Catharines, Ont. L2R 4M2—416/688-9460

Almanach Chasse et Peche (annually) 385 St. Jacques St. W., Montreal, P.Q. H2Y 1N9 - 514/842-1427

Almanach du Peuple (annually) 385 St. Jacques St. W., Montreal, P.Q. H2Y 1N9 - 514/842-1427

Almanach Jardin (annually) 385 St. Jacques St. W., Montreal, P.Q. H2Y 1N9 - 514/842-1427

Almanach Moderne (annually) 9393 Ave. Edison, Montreal, P.Q. H1J 1T5—514/353-7660

Almanach Sports et Loisirs (annually) 385 St. Jacques St. W., Montreal, P.Q. H2Y 1N9 - 514/842-1427

Alternatives, see Scholarly Publications

Angel – Canada's Entertainment Newsmag (bi-monthly) 65 Helena Ave., Toronto, Ont. M6G 2H3 - 416/652-1302

Angler & Hunter in Ontario (monthly) Box 1541, Peterborough, Ont. K9J 7H7—705/748-3891

The Antigonish Review (4 times a year) St. Francis Xavier Univ., Antigonish, N.S. B2G 1C0

Antiques & Art (bi-monthly) 2227 Granville St., Vancouver, B.C. V6H 3G1 - 604/734-4944

Arms Collecting (quarterly) Box 390, Bloomfield, Ont. K0K 1G0—613/393-2980

Artmagazine (5 times a year) Ste. 408, 234 Eglinton Ave. E., Toronto, Ont. M4P 1K5—416/488-1100

ArtsAtlantic (quarterly) Box 848, Charlottetown, P.E.I. C1A 7L9 - 902/892-2464

Arts/Canada (bi-monthly) 3 Church St., Toronto, Ont. M5E 1M2—416/863-0212

Arts West (bi-monthly) Box 8243, Stn. F, Calgary, Alta. T2J 2V4—403/243-1916

Athletica (monthly) Box 4981, Vancouver, B.C. V6B 4A6—604/683-5038

Athletics (9 times a year) Ont. Track & Field Association, 160 Vanderhoof Ave., Toronto, Ont. M4G 4B8 - 416/429-7701

The Atlantic Advocate (monthly) Box 3370, Fredericton, N.B. E3B 5A2—506/455-6671

Atlantic Insight (monthly) 6088 Coburg Rd., Halifax, N.S. B3H 1Z4—902/423-7365

The Atlantic Salmon Journal (quarterly) #109, 1434 Ste-Catherine St. W., Montreal, P.Q. H3G 1R4 - 866-6668

L'Auberge via Québecair (monthly) 252 rte 171, St-Etienne de Lauzon, P.Q. G0S 2L0 — 418/831-5317

Audio Scene Canada (monthly) 481 University Ave., Toronto, Ont. M5W 1A7—416/596-5895

Autoclub (quarterly) 2600 Laurier Blvd. (Box 9600, Ste-Foy, P.Q. G1V 4K8)—418/653-2600

Autosport Canada (monthly) 3045 Universal Dr., Mississauga, Ont. L4X 2E2—416/625-5300

Babillard (monthly) #310, 407 St. Laurent, Montreal, P.Q. H2Y 2Y5 — 514/866-4707

Ballet-Hoo (4 times a year) 289 Portage Ave., Winnipeg, Man. R3B 2B4—204/956-0183

Best Wishes (quarterly) 37 Hanna Ave., Toronto, Ont. M6K 1X4—416/362-6412

Better Business Bureau Trufax Directory & Consumer Guide (annually) 321 Bloor St. E., #901, Toronto, Ont. M4K 3K6 — 416/961-0084

Boating News (monthly) 26 Coal Harbour Wharf, 566 Cardero St., Vancouver, B.C. V6G 2W7—604/684-1643

The Body Politic, A Magazine for Gay Liberation (monthly) Box 7289, Stn. A, Toronto, Ont. M5W 1X9—416/977-6320

Bonjour (monthly) Ste. 715, 620 Cathcart St., Montreal, P.Q. H3B 1M1—514/866-0126

Books in Canada (monthly) 366 Adelaide St. E., 4th floor, Toronto, Ont. M5A 1N4—416/363-5426

Bottin Local (annually) 4060 Monselet St., Montreal, P.Q. H1H 2C5—514/326-9650

Bottin Vert-Green Selector (annually) 3035 Boul L'Assomption, Montreal, P.Q. H1N 2H2—514/254-5302

Branching Out (quarterly) Box 4098, Edmonton, Alta. T6E 4S8—403/433-4021

Breakaway, see BUSINESS, Business Publications

Breakthrough for Women (monthly) Box 506, Stn. A, Toronto, Ont. M5W 1E4 - 416/968-3664

Briar Patch (monthly) 2138 McIntyre St., Regina, Sask. S4P 2R7 — 306/525-2949
The Bride & Groom Magazine (6 times a year) Box 175, Downsview, Ont. M3M 3A3—416/636-7781
B.C. Fishing Guide (annually) #202, 1132 Hamilton St., Vancouver, B.C. V6B 2S2 - 604/687-1581
B.C. Freshwater Fishing Guide (annually) 1375 W. 57th Ave., Vancouver, B.C. V6P 1S7—604/261-5951
B.C. Hunting Guide (annually) #202, 1132 Hamilton St., Vancouver, B.C. V6B 2S2 - 604/687-1581
B.C. Outdoors (monthly) Ste. 202, 1132 Hamilton St., Vancouver, B.C. V6B 2S2—604/687-1581
B.C. Sea Angling Guide (annually) 1375 W. 57th Ave., Vancouver, B.C. V6P 1S7—604/261-5951
B.C. Soccer Magazine (monthly) 17231 57A Ave., Surrey, B.C. V3S 5A8 - 604/576-1611
B.C. Sport Salmon Fishing News (bi-monthly) Box 730, New Westminster, B.C. V3L 4Z7 - 604/521-2622
Broadcast Week (weekly) The Globe and Mail Ltd., 444 Front St. W., Toronto, Ont. M5V 2S9—416/361-5411
Le Bulletin des Agriculteurs, See Farm Publications
The Business & Professional Woman, see Business Magazines, category "Business"
CA Magazine, see Business Magazines, category "Business"
Calgary Magazine (monthly) #200, 139 17th Ave. S.W., Calgary, Alta. T2S OA1—403/265-1054
Calgary New Homes Guide (quarterly) #158, 1224 53 Ave. N.E., Calgary, Alta. T2E 7E2 - 403/275-9457
Calgary Women's Newspaper (11 times a year) 320 5th Ave. S.E., Calgary, Alta. T2G OE5 — 403/262-1873
Camping Canada (6 times a year) Ste. 221, 3414 Park Ave., Montreal, P.Q. H2X 2H5—514/282-0191
Canada & The World (monthly) 481 University Ave., Toronto, Ont. M5W 1A7—416/596-5819
Canada Crafts Magazine (bi-monthly) #102, 2453 Yonge St., Toronto, Ont. M4P 2E8 - 416/485-8284
Canada Rides (monthly) Box 6818, Stn. D, Calgary, Alta. T2P 2E7 - 403/277-4751
Canadian Amateur (11 times a year) c/o Canadian Amateur Radio Federation Inc., 3 Kirkstall Ave., Nepean, Ont. K2G 3M2 - 613/226-8686
The Canadian Art Investors Guide (quarterly) Box 519, Stn. Z, Toronto, Ont. M5N 2Z6
Canadian Automobile Repair & Maintenance (quarterly) Box 67, West Hill, Ont. M1E 4R4 - 416/266-6241
Canadian Aviation (monthly) 481 University Ave., Toronto, Ont. M5W 1A7—416/596-5791
Canadian Boating (monthly) Suite 204, 5200 Dixie Rd., Mississauga, Ont. L4W 1E4—416/625-5277
Canadian Business (monthly) 59 Front St. E., Toronto, Ont. M5E 1R5—416/364-4266
Canadian Churchman (monthly) Anglican Church of Canada, 600 Jarvis St., Toronto, Ont. M4Y 2J6—416/924-9192
Canadian Coin News (eo Tue.) 1567 Sedlescomb Dr., Mississauga, Ont. L4X 1M5—416/625-4700
Canadian Collector (bi-monthly) #406, 27 Carlton St., Toronto, Ont. M5B 1L2 - 416/977-0770
Canadian Consumer/Le Consommateur canadien (bi-monthly) 2660 Southvale Cres., Level 3, Ottawa, Ont. K1B 5C4
Canadian Curling News (7 times a year) #303, 234 Eglinton Ave. E., Toronto, Ont. M4P 1K5 — 416/481-3371
Canadian Dimension (8 times a year) #801, 44 Princess St., Winnipeg, Man. R3B 1K2 — 204/957-1519
Canadian Do-It-Yourself Magazine (quarterly) Unit 3, 2000 Ellesmere Rd., Scarborough, Ont. M1H 2W4 - 416/438-1153
Canadian Equestrian (bi-monthly) #5, 1470 Rupert St., North Vancouver, B.C. V7J 1E9 - 604/985-6126
The Canadian Forum (monthly) 70 The Esplanade, 3rd floor, Toronto, Ont. M5E 1R2 — 416/364-2431
Canadian Geographic (bi-monthly) 488 Wilbrod St., Ottawa, Ont. K1N 6M8 — 613/236-7493
The Canadian Guider (9 times a year) 50 Merton St., Toronto, Ont. M4S 1A3—416/487-5281
Canadian Homeowner (monthly) #100, 1751 Richardson St., Montreal, P.Q. H3K 1G6 - 514/931-4487
The Canadian Horse (monthly) 148 King Rd. E., King City, Ont. L0G 1K0 - 416/833-6200
Canadian India Star (1 & 15) 1433 Bloor St. W., Toronto, Ont. M6P 3L6—416/536-4737
The Canadian India Times (1 & 3 Thur.) 403 Catherine St., Ottawa, Ont. K1R 5T6—613/235-2554
Canadian Heritage (5 times a year) Box 1358, Stn. B, Ottawa, Ont. K1P 5R4 - 613/237-1066
Canadian Jewish Outlook (monthly) #4, 2414 Main St., Vancouver, B.C. V5T 3E3—604/874-1323
Canadian Lawyer, see Business Magazines, category "Legal"
The Canadian Leader (monthly) Box 5112, Stn. F, Ottawa, Ont. K2C 3H4—613/224-5131
Canadian Living (monthly) 112 Merton St., Toronto, Ont. M4S 2Z7—416/482-8600
The Canadian Log House (annually) Box 1205, Prince George, B.C. V2L 4V3

The Canadian Military Journal (4 times a year) Suite 8, 3450 Durocher St., Montreal, P.Q. H2X 2E1—514/845-2049
Canadian Motorcycle Rider (quarterly) 3rd Floor, 2066 Queen St. W., Toronto, Ont. M4E 1C9 - 416/690-0566
Canadian Motorist (7 times a year) 2 Carlton St., Toronto, Ont. M5B 1K4—416/964-3075
Canadian Motorsport Annual (annually) 3045 Universal Dr., Mississauga, Ont. L4X 2E2 - 416/625-5300
Canadian Musician (bi-monthly) 2453 Yonge St., #3, Toronto, Ont. M4P 2E8 — 416/485-8284
Canadian Pool & Patio (annually) 1450 Don Mills Rd., Don Mills, Ont. M3B 2X7—416/445-6641
Canadian Public Policy/Analyse de Politiques (quarterly) Univ. of Guelph, Room 039, Arts Bldg., Guelph, Ont. N1G 2W1—519/824-4120, ext. 3330
The Canadian Rider (monthly) 491 Book Rd. W., Ancaster, Ont. L9G 3L3—416/648-2035
Canadian Rodeo News (monthly) #223, 2116 27th Ave. N.E., Calgary, Alta. T2E 7A6
Canadian Secretary, see Business Magazines, category "Office Equipment"
Canadian Skater (6 times a year) 333 River Rd., Vanier, Ont. K1L 8B9—613/746-5953
Canadian Sportsman (weekly May to Oct., bi-weekly Oct. to May) Box 190, 25 Townline Rd., Tillsonburg, Ont. N4G 4H6—519/842-4824
Canadian Stamp News (eo Tue.) 1567 Sedlescomb Dr., Mississauga, Ont. L4X 1M5—416/625-4700
Canadian Theatre Review (quarterly) 200B Admin. Studies, York Univ., Downsview, Ont. M3J 1P3—416/667-3768
Canadian UFO Report (quarterly) Box 455 (Streetsville), Mississauga, Ont. L5M 2B9 — 416/826-6073
Canadian Workshop (monthly) Unit 6, 3781 Victoria Park Ave., Scarborough, Ont. M1W 3K5 - 416/492-7330
Canadian Yachting (monthly) 6th Floor, 425 University Ave., Toronto, Ont. M5G 1T6 - 416/596-5022
Canadian Zionist (bi-monthly) Suite 822, 1310 Greene Ave., Montreal, P.Q. H3Z 2B2—514/934-0804
Cape Breton's Magazine (3 times a year) Wreck Cove, Cape Breton, N.S. BOC 1HO—902/929-2372
Carguide (annually) Ste. 105, 1255 Yonge St., Toronto, Ont. M4T 1W6—416/922-7197
The Ceramic Hobbyist (6 times a year) Ste. 110, 2175 Sheppard Ave. E., Willowdale, Ont. M2J 1W8—416/491-3556
C'est Pour Quand (twice a year) 1476 St-Zotique St. E., Montreal, P.Q. H2G 1H1—514/273-8449
Chatelaine (monthly) English edition: 481 University Ave., Toronto, Ont. M5W 1A7—416/596-5422; French edition: 625 President Kennedy Ave., Montreal, P.Q. H3A 1K5—514/845-5141
Chef Novati (monthly) 259 Beaumont St., (Box 22, Stn. A, Montreal, P.Q. H3N 1T3) - 514/271-5398
Chickadee (10 times a year) 59 Front St. E., Toronto, Ont. M5E 1B3—416/364-3333

Chimo (8 times a year) 1455 Peel St., Montreal, P.Q. H3A 1T5—514/284-9111
Chinatown News (semi-monthly) 459 E. Hastings St., Vancouver, B.C. V6A 1P5—604/254-2533
Chinook (quarterly) Box 427, Brampton, Ont. L6V 2L4—416/459-2446
City Magazine (twice a year) 35 Britain St., Toronto, Ont. M5A 1R7—416/362-4762
City Scene (weekly) Box 3160, Stn. B, Calgary, Alta. T2M 4L7 – 403/276-9311
City Woman (5 times a year) 2300 Yonge St., Toronto, Ont. M4P 1E4—416/482-8260
Clin D'Oeil (monthly) 100 ave. Dresden, Mont-Royal, P.Q. H3P 2B6 – 514/735-6361
Coda (bi-monthly) Box 87, Stn. J, Toronto, Ont. M4J 4X8—416/368-3149
Comics Heritage (monthly) 300 Arran Ave. (Box 8, St. Lambert, P.Q. J4P 3N4)—514/672-6710
Common Cents (quarterly) Box 3282, Stn. D, Willowdale, Ont. M2R 3G6 – 416/361-1234
The Commonwealth (bi-weekly) 1630 Quebec St., Regina, Sask. S4P 1J2—306/522-3293
The Condominium (monthly) Box 286, Stn. R, Toronto, Ont. M4G 3Z9 — 416/429-4600
Contemporary Verse II (quarterly) Box 32, Univ. Centre, Univ. of Manitoba, Winnipeg, Man. R3T 1E0 – 204/474-9860
Content (6 times a year) 91 Raglan Ave., Toronto, Ont. M6C 2K7—416/651-7799
Co-operative Consumer (bi-weekly) Box 1050, Saskatoon, Sask. S7K 3M9—306/244-3118
The Corinthian (monthly) 10077-C Yonge St., Richmond Hill, Ont. L4X 1T7 – 416/883-5863
The Cottager (bi-monthly) #202, 309 Cooper St., Ottawa, Ont. K2P 0G5 – 613/235-7156
Country Estate (6 times a year) Country Estate Magazine Ltd., R.R. 1, Terra Cotta, Ont. LOP 1NO — 416/838-2800
Country Guide (monthly) 1760 Ellice Ave., Winnipeg, Man. R3H OB6—204/774-1861
Country Ways (quarterly) 1345 Johnston Rd., White Rock, B.C. V4B 3Z3 – 604/536-7622
Coup d'oeil sur le Saguenay-Lac-St-Jean (quarterly) 623 Louis-Hemon, Chicoutimi, P.Q. G7H 5W2 – 418/543-6392
Cradle Club Magazine (quarterly) #301, 12 Sheppard St., Toronto, Ont. M5H 3A1 — 416/367-1133
Craftnews (8 times a year) 346 Dundas St. W., Toronto, Ont. M5T 1G5 – 416/977-3551
CROC (monthly) 464 rue St-Jean, Vieux-Montreal, P.Q. H2Y 2S1 – 514/844-3911
Cross-Canada Writers' Quarterly (quarterly) Box 277, Stn. F, Toronto, Ont. M4Y 2L7 – 416/690-0917
The Curler (4 times a year) Ste. 504, 56 Esplanade St. E., Toronto, Ont. M5E 1A7—416/363-6002
Cycle Canada (monthly) 290 Jarvis St., Toronto, Ont. M5B 2C5—416/868-6318

Dance in Canada (quarterly) Ste. 325, 100 Richmond St. E., Toronto, Ont. M5C 2P9—416/368-4793
The Deaf Canadian Magazine (monthly) Box 1291, Edmonton, Alta. T5J 2M8
Decoration Chez-soi (monthly) 100 Dresden Ave., Mount Royal, P.Q. H3P 2B6—514/735-6361
Decormag (monthly) 181 Saint-Paul E., Vieux-Montreal, P.Q. H2Y 1G8—514/866-9894
The Democrat (monthly) 517 E. Broadway, Vancouver, B.C. V5T 1X4—604/879-4601
Descant (3 times a year) Box 314, Stn. P, Toronto, Ont. M5S 2S8 — 604/766-9241
Destinations, see Westworld
Discovery for Seniors & 50 Plus (monthly) 2 College St., #107, Toronto, Ont. M5G 1K3 – 416/968-0913
Diver Magazine (8 times a year) 1601 Granville St., Vancouver, B.C. V6Z 2B3—604/689-8688
Dogs in Canada (monthly) Ste. 500, 3 Church St., Toronto, Ont. M5E 1M2—416/363-2018

Ears (biennially) #603, 3 Church St., Toronto, Ont. M5E 1M2 – 416/362-7611
Eastern Provincial Inflight (8 times a year) 6088 Coburg Rd., Halifax, N.S. B3H 1Z4 — 902/423-7365
Easy Living (monthly) #203, 13309 72nd Ave., Surrey, B.C. V3W 2N5 – 604/591-5101
Echoes (quarterly) #254, 40 Orchard View Blvd., Toronto, Ont. M4R 1B9—416/487-4416
Edmonton Magazine (monthly) 10610 105 Ave., Edmonton, Alta. T5H OL2—403/423-3807
Electronics Today International (monthly) Unit 6, 25 Overlea Blvd., Toronto, Ont. M4H 1B1—416/423-3262
Elite (monthly) Ste. 204, 234 Eglinton Ave. E., Toronto, Ont. M4P 1K5—416/487-7183
enRoute Magazine (monthly) 2973 Weston Rd. (Box 510, Weston, Ont. M9N 3R3)—416/741-1112
en Voyage (6 times a year) Ste. 200B, 674 Place Publique, Ste-Dorothee, Laval, P.Q. H7X 1G1—514/689-0288
Enterpriser (monthly) Box 3891, Stn. C, Ottawa, Ont. K1Y 4M5 – 613/722-3461
Epicure (7 times a year) 49 Avenue Rd., Toronto, Ont. M5R 2G3 – 416/968-3359
L'Estrie (monthly) Box 1296, Sherbrooke, P.Q. J1H 5L7—819/563-3339
Evasion (7 times a year) 1429 Crescent St., Montreal, P.Q. H3G 2B2 – 514/842-6478

The FM Guide (monthly) #203, 1659 Bayview Ave., Toronto, Ont. M4G 3C1—416/481-2209
Fat City (monthly) Box 12, Fredericton, N.B. E3B 4Y2 – 506/454-3022
Femme (monthly) 465 Deslauriers St., Ville St-Laurent, P.Q. H4N 1W2—514/332-3149
File Magazine (quarterly) 217 Richmond St. W., 2nd floor, Toronto, Ont. M5G 1W2 – 416/977-1685
Financial Post Magazine (monthly) 481 University Ave., Toronto, Ont. M5W 1A7—416/596-5649
Flare (10 times a year) 481 University Ave., Toronto, Ont. M5W 1A7 — 416/596-5462
Focus on Entertainment (weekly) The Citizen, 150 Brunswick St., Prince George, B.C. V2L 4T1 — 604/562-2441
The Freemason (4 times a year) Box 250, Pefferlaw, Ont. LOE 1NO—705/437-2083
Friday (bi-weekly) #306, 130 Merton St., Toronto, Ont. M4A 1A4 – 416/485-7634
Fuse (bi-monthly) 31 Dupont Ave., Toronto, Ont. M5R 1V3 – 416/967-9309
Future Focus (quarterly) 632 Queen St. W., Toronto, Ont. M6J 1E4 – 416/362-4561

Gam on Yachting (monthly) 39A Colborne St., Toronto, Ont. M5E 1E3—416/363-4707
Gastown & Vancouver Today (semi-annually) Box 91045, W. Vancouver, B.C. V7V 3N3—604/922-5891
La Gazette Sportive (monthly) 166 Ch. Dufferin, Hampstead, P.Q. H3X 2Y1 – 514/484-3960
Geos (quarterly) Energy, Mines & Resources Canada, Ottawa, Ont. K1A OE4—613/995-3065
Good Health (6 times a year) #201, 801 York Mills Rd., Don Mills, Ont. M3B 1X7 – 416/444-4952
Grain (quarterly) Box 1885, Saskatoon, Sask. S7K 3S2
Great Expectations/Les Grands Espoirs (quarterly) 45 Charles St. E., Toronto, Ont. M4Y 1S2—416/964-8903
Gryphon Theatre News (quarterly) 124 Brock St., Barrie, Ont. L4N 2M2 – 705/726-0573
Guelph Magazine (monthly) 19 Prospect Ave., Guelph, Ont. N1E 4W7 – 519/821-1830

Halifax (monthly) Box 2172, Halifax, N.S. B3J 3C4 — 902/423-7675
Hamilton Magazine (monthly) 110 George St., Hamilton, Ont. L8P 1E2—416/528-0436
Hands Magazine (6 times a year) Box 867, Stn. F, Toronto, Ont. M4Y 2N7 – 416/964-8705
Harness World (semi-monthly) biling., Box 100, Cote-des-Neiges, Montreal, P.Q. H3S 2S4—514/739-8723

Harrowsmith (8 times a year) Camden House Publishing, Camden East, Ont. KOK 1JO—613/378-6661
Health (quarterly) 76 Avenue Rd., Toronto, Ont. M5R 2H1—416/923-8405
Hi-Rise (6 times a year) Unit 121, 95 Leeward Glenway, Don Mills, Ont. M3C 2Z6 - 416/424-1393
The Hockey News (weekly) #314, 214 King St. W., Toronto, Ont. M5H 1K4 — 416/598-1753
Home Decor Canada (quarterly) 481 University Ave., Toronto, Ont. M5W 1A7—416/596-5884
Home Improvement (twice a year) 382 W. Broadway, Vancouver, B.C. V5Y 1R2 - 604/879-4144
Homemaker's Magazine (10 times a year) 2300 Yonge St., Toronto, Ont. M4P 1E4—416/482-8260
Horse Journal B.C. (quarterly) 124 8th St. W., North Vancouver, B.C. V7M 3H2 - 604/985-8711
Horses All (monthly) Box 550, Nanton, Alta. TOL 1RO—403/486-5445
Humanist in Canada (quarterly) Box 157, Victoria, B.C. V8W 2M6
Huronia Week (weekly) Box 339, Elmvale, Ont. LOL 1PO
Igalaaq (monthly) #201, 2910 Carling Ave., Ottawa, Ont. K2B 7J7 — 613/820-8777
Image de la Mauricie (monthly) 564 Blvd. Des Prairies, Cap-de-la-Madeleine, P.Q. G8T 1K9—819/378-2176
Image des Laurentides (4 times a year) Ste. 200, 1000 Labelle Blvd., St-Jerome, P.Q. J7Z 5N6—514/436-8532
Impulse (4 times a year) Box 901, Stn. Q, Toronto, Ont. M4T 2P1 - 416/925-2933
India Calling (bi-weekly) #1908, 41 Mabelle Ave., Islington, Ont. M9A 5A9 — 416/233-9577
Interculture (quarterly) 4917 St. Urbain, Montreal, P.Q. H2T 2W1 - 514/288-7229
Interface (monthly) 6427 112 Ave., Edmonton, Alta. T5W 0N9 - 403/479-5931
International Journal (quarterly) 15 King's College Circle, Toronto, Ont. M5S 2V9—416/979-1851
Jam - Just About Me (4 times a year) 1 Fairleigh Cres., Toronto, Ont. M6C 3R7 - 416/781-6188
Jet-Set International (quarterly) 6285 Ave. Cairns, Anjou, P.Q. H1K 4B1 — 514/351-0716
The Jewish Post, see Weekly Newspapers (Winnipeg)
Jewish Standard (semi-monthly) #139, 67 Mowat Ave., Toronto, Ont. M6K 3E3—416/537-2696
Journal UFO (quarterly) Box 455 (Streetsville), Mississauga, Ont. L5M 2B9 — 416/826-6073
Kan'at'a (3 times a year) Aircom Publishing, 92 Isabella St., Toronto, Ont. M4Y 1N8—416/960-5139
Key to Toronto (monthly) 59 Front St. E., Toronto, Ont. M5E 1B3—416/364-3333
Kin (bi-monthly) Association of Kinsmen Clubs, Box KIN, 1920 Hal Rogers Dr., Cambridge, Ont. N3H 5C6 - 519/653-1920
The Last Post (8 times a year) Suite 302, 454 King St. W., Toronto, Ont. M5V 1L6—416/366-1134
Legion Magazine (monthly) Ste. 504, 359 Kent St., Ottawa, Ont. K2P 0R6—613/235-8741
Leisure Life (twice a year) Box 220, Goderich, Ont. N7A 4B6 - 519/524-8331
Leisure Wheels (8 times a year) Box 7302, Stn. E, Calgary, Alta. T3C 3M2 - 403/249-1755
Lionage (5 times a year) #B16, 5740 Yonge St., Willowdale, Ont. M2M 3T4 — 416/451-7888
Log Home Guide (4 times a year) Muir Publishing, Gardenvale, P.Q. H9X 1BO — 514/457-2045
London & Company (monthly) 393 William St., London, Ont. N6B 3C9 - 519/672-2331
London Magazine (bi-monthly) 287 Queens Ave., London, Ont. N6B 1X2 - 519/434-1177
Le Lundi (weekly) 9922 boul. St-Laurent, Montreal, P.Q. H3L 3R2 - 514/382-8443
Maclean's (weekly) English edition: 481 University Ave., Toronto, Ont. M5W 1A7—416/596-5311; French edition: 625 President Kennedy Ave., Montreal, P.Q. H3A 1K5—514/845-5141; West edition: Ste. 600, 1111 Melville St., Vancouver, B.C. V6E 3V6—604/683-8254
Le Magazine Affaires, see BUSINESS, Business Publications
Le Magazine Illustre (weekly) 9922 boul. St-Laurent, Montreal, P.Q. H3L 3R2 - 514/382-8443
Magazine Vivre (monthly) 225 Roy St. E., Montreal, P.Q. H2W 1M5—514/282-9600
Maigrir et Rester Belle (monthly) 3820 boul. Ste-Rose, Fabreville, Laval, P.Q. H7P 5B9 - 514/622-5530
Les Maisons du Quebec (6 times a year) 2950 Lemire Blvd., Drummondville, P.Q. J2B 7J6—819/477-6646
Malahat Review (quarterly) Univ. of Victoria, Box 1700, Victoria, B.C. V8W 2Y2 — 604/477-6911
Manitoba Motorist (bi-monthly) #76, 1313 Border St., Winnipeg, Man. R3H 0X4 - 204/633-1720
Marquee (bi-monthly) 300 Richmond St. W., Toronto, Ont. M5V 1X2—416/368-7004
Mennonite Mirror (10 times a year) Ste. 201, 818 Portage Ave., Winnipeg, Man. R3G 0N4—204/786-2289
Metro Telecaster (weekly) Box 128, Yarmouth, N.S. B5A 4B1—902/742-7111
Millions Magazine (monthly) 44 Wellington St. E., #401, Toronto, Ont. M5E 1C8 — 416/361-0844
Mon Amie (monthly) #2420, 505 Sherbrooke St. E., Montreal, P.Q. H2L 4N3 - 514/849-2429
Monarchy Canada (4 or 5 times a year) #203, 3050 Yonge St., Toronto, Ont. M4N 2K4 - 416/482-4157
Mon Bébé (twice a year) 1476 St-Zotique St. E., Montreal, P.Q. H2G 1H1—514/273-8449
Mon Marche (4 times a year) 7160 Pie IX Blvd., Montreal, P.Q. H2A 2G4 — 514/729-2874
Moncton Telecaster (weekly) 1 Trites Rd., Riverview, N.B. E1B 2V5 — 506/855-6855
Montreal Calendar Magazine (monthly) 65 Front St. E., Toronto, Ont. M5E 1B6—416/869-1260
Montreal Ce Mois-Ci (monthly) 65 Front St. E., Toronto, Ont. M5E 1B6—416/869-1260
Montreal Review (8 times a year) #1003, 1538 Sherbrooke St. W., Montreal, P.Q. H3G 1L5 - 514/931-5905
Montreal Scop (monthly) Room 232, 1253 McGill College, Montreal, P.Q. H3B 2Y4—514/933-3333
Moto Journal (monthly) 290 Jarvis St., Toronto, Ont. M5B 2C5 — 416/868-6318
Motoneigiste Canadien (annually) Ste. 221, 3414 Park Ave., Montreal, P.Q. H2X 2H5—514/282-0191
Motor Miniatures (quarterly) 3045 Universal Dr., Mississauga, Ont. L4X 2E2 - 416/625-5300
Moving House & Home (4 times a year) 26 Berkeley St., Toronto, Ont. M5A 3V7 — 416/363-6246
Moving to .... (publications)#201, 801 York Mills Rd., Don Mills, Ont. M3B 1X7 — 416/447-7783
Music Magazine (bi-monthly) Ste. 202, 56 The Esplanade, Toronto, Ont. M5E 1A7—416/364-5938
Nature Canada (quarterly) Ste. 203, 75 Albert St., Ottawa, Ont. K1P 6G1—613/238-6154
The New Democrat (8 times a year) 184 Main St., Toronto, Ont. M5E 2W1 - 416/699-6637
The Newfoundland Herald (weekly) Box 2015, St. John's, Nfld. A1C 5R7 - 709/726-7060
The Newfoundland Magazine (monthly) Box 304, Corner Brook, Nfld. A2H 6C9 - 709/634-3109
Newfoundland TV Topics (weekly) Box 8660, St. John's, Nfld. A1B 3T7 - 709/722-8500
Nordic Canada (annually) 531 Deslauriers, Montreal, P.Q. H4N 1W2 — 514/337-2941
Northward Journal (quarterly) Box 340, Moonbeam, Ont. POL 1VO—705/367-2556
Nous (monthly) 465 Deslauriers St., Ville St-Laurent, P.Q. H4N 1W2 - 514/332-3164
1001 Decorating Ideas (quarterly) 5445 De Gaspé St., Montreal, P.Q. H2T 3B2—514/273-7274

Odyssey (bi-monthly) 298 Avenue Rd., Toronto, Ont. M4V 2H1 —416/922-5938
The Ontario Amateur (bi-monthly) c/o Radio Society of Ontario, Box 246, Port Credit Stn., Mississauga, Ont. L5G 4L8
Ontario Craft (quarterly) 346 Dundas St. W., Toronto, Ont. M5T 1G5 - 416/977-3551
Ontario Out of Doors (monthly) #202, 3 Church St., Toronto, Ont. M5E 1M2 - 416/368-3011
The Ontario Showcase (monthly) 1567 Sedlescomb Dr., Mississauga, Ont. L4X 1M5 - 416/625-4700
Opera/Canada (4 times a year) Ste. 433, 366 Adelaide St. E., Toronto, Ont. M5A 1N4—416/363-0395
Orah Magazine (monthly) Room 900, 1310 Greene Ave., Westmount, P.Q. H3Z 2B2—514/482-2285
Ottawa Magazine (monthly) 345 O'Connor St., Ottawa, Ont. K2P 1V9 — 613/238-4736
Our Generation (quarterly) 3981 St-Laurent Blvd., Montreal, P.Q. H2W 1Y5 — 514/844-4076
Outdoor Canada (8 times a year) 935A Eglinton Ave. E., Toronto, Ont. M4G 4B5—416/429-5550
Owl (10 times a year) 59 Front St. E., Toronto, Ont. M5E 1B3—416/364-3333
The Pacific Hosteller (quarterly) 3425 W. Broadway, Vancouver, B.C. V6R 2B4 - 604/736-2674
Pacific Tribune (weekly) #101, 1416 Commercial Dr., Vancouver, B.C. V5L 3X9—604/251-1186
Pacific Yachting (monthly) 202, 1132 Hamilton St., Vancouver, B.C. V6B 2S2—604/687-1581
Parachute (quarterly) C.P. 730, Stn. N, Montreal, P.Q. H2X 3N4 — 514/522-9167
Parents D'aujourd'hui (monthly) 1429 Crescent St., Montreal, P.Q. H3G 2B2 - 514/842-6478
Perception (bi-monthly) 55 Parkdale, Box 3505, Stn. C, Ottawa, Ont. K1Y 4G1—613/728-1865
Performance (6 times a year) #200, 129 Yorkville Ave., Toronto, Ont. M5R 1C4 — 416/923-3700
Performing Arts in Canada (quarterly) 52 Avenue Rd., Toronto, Ont. M5R 2G3—416/921-2601
Perspectives (weekly) 231 rue St-Jacques, Montreal, P.Q. H2Y 1M6 — 514/282-2224
Perspectives (monthly) 623 Queen St. W., Toronto, Ont. M6J 1E4 - 416/362-4561
Pharma-Prix Beauté Magazine (4 times a year) 38 Wellington St. E., Toronto, Ont. M5E 1C7 - 416/363-9466
Photo Canada (bi-monthly) 481 University Ave., Toronto, Ont. M5W 1A7—416/596-5869
Photo Communique (4 times a year) Box 129, Stn. M, Toronto, Ont. M6S 4T2 — 519/535-0407
Photo Life (monthly) 9th Floor, 225 Duncan Mill Rd., Don Mills, Ont. M3B 3K9
Playboard (monthly) 7560 Lawrence Dr., Burnaby, B.C. V5A 1T6 —604/420-6115
Presbyterian Record (monthly) 50 Wynford Dr., Don Mills, Ont. M3C 1J7—416/441-1111
Prestige Beauté (bi-monthly) #302, 204 ouest Notre-Dame, Montreal, P.Q. H2Y 1T4 - 514/845-0132
Pro Pocket Guide Magazine (4 times a year) 10th Floor, 2 St. Clair Ave. E., Toronto, Ont. M4T 2R1 - 416/961-8647
Probe Post (bi-monthly) Pollution Probe Fdn., 12 Madison Ave., Toronto, Ont. M5R 2S1 - 416/978-7016
Pulse (weekly) 225 Fairway Rd., Kitchener, Ont. N2G 4E5—519/579-2231
Quarry (quarterly) Box 1061, Kingston, Ont. K7L 4X5 - 613/544-5400, ext. 165
Quebec Chasse et Peche (monthly) 5786 Christophe-Colomb, Montreal, P.Q. H2S 2G1—514/270-9241
Quebec Rock (monthly) C.P. 115, Stn. H, Montreal, P.Q. H3G 2K5 - 514/842-5853
Quebec Science (monthly) 2875 Laurier Blvd., Ste-Foy, P.Q. G1V 2M3—418/657-2426
Quebec Soccer (monthly) 9652 St-Michel Blvd., Montreal, P.Q. H1H 5G6 — 514/387-0664
Quebec Yachting (bi-monthly) 995 Lakeshore Dr., Dorval, P.Q. H9S 2C8 — 514/636-6342
Queen's Quarterly, see Scholarly Publications
Quest (8 times a year) 2300 Yonge St., Toronto, Ont. M4P 1E4—416/482-8260
Racquets-Canada (6 times a year) 6th Floor, 425 University Ave., Toronto, Ont. M5G 1T6 - 416/596-5022
Raincoast Chronicles, Box 119, Madeira Park, B.C. VON 2HO—604/883-2730
Reader's Digest/Selection du Reader's Digest (monthly) 215 Redfern Ave., Montreal, P.Q. H3Z 2V9—514/934-0751
Les Recettes du Chef (monthly) 465 Deslauriers, Ville St-Laurent, P.Q. H4N 1W2—514/332-3149
Regina (annually) 1150 8th Ave., Regina, Sask. S4R 1C9 - 306/525-2304
Regina Nite-Life (monthly) 1150 8th Ave., Regina, Sask. S4R 1C9 - 306/525-2304
Relations (monthly) 8100 St. Laurent Blvd., Montreal, P.Q. H2P 2L9—514/387-2541
Renovation Bricolage (monthly) 100 Dresden St., Mount Royal, P.Q. H3P 2B6—514/735-6361
Renovation West (monthly) #605, 402 W. Pender St., Vancouver, B.C. V6B 1T6 - 604/687-8117
Resourcebook, see EDUCATION, Business Publications
Revue Trafic Routier (monthly) #210A, 3019 Sherbrooke St. E., Montreal, P.Q. H1W 1B2 - 514/527-2149
Rikka (quarterly) Box 6031, Stn. A, Toronto, Ont. M5W 1P4 - 416/968-3656
Room of Ones Own (quarterly) Box 46160, Stn. G, Vancouver, B.C. V6R 4G5—604/733-3529
Sailing (6 times a year) 40 Wellington St. E., Toronto, Ont. M5E 1C7 - 416/366-3538
Saint John Telecaster (weekly) 2 Second St., Yarmouth, N.S. B5A 4B1 - 902/742-7111
The Saskatchewan Motorist (bi-monthly) 200 Albert St. N., Regina, Sask. S4R 5E2—306/543-5677
Saskatchewan Ski Journal (6 times a year) 413 Hilliard St. E., Saskatoon, Sask. S7J OE7
Saturday Night (10 times a year) 69 Front St. E., Toronto, Ont. M5E 1R3—416/362-5907
Scene Changes (9 times a year) 8 York St., Toronto, Ont. M5J 1R2 — 416/366-2938
Scope Camping News (6 times a year) Merton Publications Ltd., Hyde Park, Ont. NOM 1ZO — 519/471-9109
Scope/Wheelers Canadian Campground Guide (annually) Merton Publications, Hyde Park, Ont. NON 1ZO—519/471-9109
The Scottish Banner (monthly) Box 200, Stn. H, Toronto, Ont. M4C 5J2 - 416/690-3810
Scrumdown (monthly) Box 65631, Stn. F, Vancouver, B.C. V5N 5K5 — 604/254-2233
Seasons (4 times a year) 355 Lesmill Rd., Don Mills, Ont. M3B 2W8 — 416/444-8419
Sel & Poivre (4 times a year) 100 Dresden Ave., Mount Royal, P.Q. H3P 2B6 - 514/735-6361
Select Home Designs (twice a year) 382 W. Broadway, Vancouver, B.C. V5Y 1R2—604/879-4144
Sentier (monthly) 2170 Charland, Montreal, P.Q. H1Z 1B1 — 514/381-9243
The Sentinel (6 times a year) 94 Sheppard Ave. W., Willowdale, Ont. M2N 1M5—416/223-1690
Shoppers Drug Mart Beauty Magazine (4 times a year) 38 Wellington St. E., Toronto, Ont. M5E 1C7—416/363-9466
Ski Canada (6 times a year) 6th Floor, 425 University Ave., Toronto, Ont. M5G 1T6 - 416/596-5022
Ski Quebec (5 times a year) 531 Deslauriers, Ville St-Laurent, P.Q. H4N 1W2—514/337-2941
Ski-Runner (4 times a year) 95 King St. E., Toronto, Ont. M5C 1G4—416/368-1331
Ski Trails (8 times a year) Ste. 8, 2375 York St., Vancouver, B.C. V6K 1C8—604/681-5922
Ski World (6 times a year) Box 1274, Kelowna, B.C. V1Y 7V8 — 604/763-4649
Skyword (12 times a year) 1334 Seymour St., Vancouver, B.C. V6B 3P3 - 604/682-6311
Snow, see Westworld

Snowmobile Buyer's Guide (annually) Suite 221, 3414 Park Ave., Montreal, P.Q. H2X 2H5—514/282-0191
Snowmobile Canada (4 times a year) Ste. 221, 3414 Park Ave., Montreal, P.Q. H2X 2H5—514/282-0191
Snowmobile Sports (4 times a year) Ste. 105, 1255 Yonge St., Toronto, Ont. M4T 1W6—416/922-9412
Snowmobile Sports Annual (annually) Ste. 105, 1255 Yonge St., Toronto, Ont. M4T 1W6—416/922-7197
Soccer Canada (6 times a year) 49 St. Nicolas St., Toronto, Ont. M4Y 1W6 — 416/922-0007
Soccer Illustrated (monthly) 3 Church St., Toronto, Ont. M5E 1M2 - 416/363-9161
Son Hi-Fi Magazine (6 times a year) 1843 Tupper St., Montreal, P.Q. H3H 1N3 - 514/937-9609
Sound Canada (monthly) 7240 Woodbine Ave., Markham, Ont. L3R 1A4—416/495-6523
Sound Heritage Series (quarterly) Sound & Moving Image Division, Provincial Archives of B.C., Victoria, B.C. V8V 1X4
South Shore Magazine (weekly) Box 89, Bridgewater, N.S. B4V 2W6 - 902/543-2457
Spare Time (5 times a year) 69 Wyndham St. N., Guelph, Ont. N1H 4E7 - 519/836-0261
Sportmania (monthly) 8724 Foucher, Montreal, P.Q. H2M 1V3 — 514/384-6811
The Sports Journal (monthly) #B4, 416 Meridian Rd. S.E., Calgary, Alta. T2A 1X2—403/273-5141
Sports Club Magazine (10 times a year) 531 Deslauriers, Ville St-Laurent, P.Q. H4N 1W2—514/337-2941
Sportsmen's Show Magazine (annually) #221, 3414 Park Ave., Montreal, P.Q. H2X 2H5 - 514/282-0191
Sportwest (6 times a year) 1200 Hornby St., Vancouver, B.C. V6Z 2E2 - 604/687-3333
Squash (5 times a year) 54 Springhouse Sq., Agincourt, Ont. M1W 2X1 - 416/497-0930
The Standardbred Magazine (bi-weekly) Box 150, Acton, Ont. L7J 2M3—519/853-1090
Star Week (weekly) One Yonge St., Toronto, Ont. M5E 1E6—416/367-2219
Status of Women News (4 times a year) Ste. 306, 40 St. Clair Ave. E., Toronto, Ont. M4T 1M9—416/922-3246
Stereo Guide (5 times a year) 6 Byng Ave., Brampton, Ont. L6Y 1L1 - 416/298-6121
Summer, see Westworld
Sunday Sun Television (Calgary) (weekly) 830 10th Ave. S.W., Calgary, Alta. T2R 0B1 - 403/263-7730
Sunday Sun Television (Edmonton) (weekly) 10310 124 St., Edmonton, Alta. T5N 1R2—403/482-7631
Sunday Sun Television (Toronto) (weekly) 333 King St. E., Toronto, Ont. M5A 3X5—416/868-2333
SuperFare (10 times a year) 24 Ryerson Ave., Toronto, Ont. M5T 2P3 — 416/364-9833
Take 5 Rag Mag (quarterly) 1438 9th Ave. S.E., Calgary, Alta. T2G 0T5 - 403/266-4186
Teen Generation (8 times a year) 481 University Ave., Toronto, Ont. M5W 1A7 - 416/596-5467
Tee-off (14 times a year) Box 8700, Don Mills, Ont. M3C 2T9—416/444-1171
Tele Horaire (weekly) 155 Port Royal St. W., Montreal, P.Q. H3L 2B3—514/382-1312
Le Téléphone Rouge (annually) 545 Grande Allée est, Québec, P.Q. G1R 2J5 - 418/529-8466
Téléprobec 5 (weekly) 7 St-James St. W., Montreal, P.Q. H2Y 1K9—514/285-7306
Tele-Soleil (weekly) 390 St-Vallier St. E., Quebec, P.Q. G1K 7J6 - 418/647-3270
Le Temps (monthly) #500, 325 Dalhousie St., Ottawa, Ont. K1N 7G2 - 613/237-6050
Le Temps de Vivre (monthly) 9393 Edison Ave., Montreal, P.Q. H1J 1T4 — 514/351-7460
This Magazine, see Business Publications, Education
Thornhill Month (monthly) Box 250, Thornhill, Ont. L3T 3N3 — 416/495-1743
Thunder Bay Guest (17 times a year) 837 Fort William Rd., Thunder Bay, Ont.—807/345-2587
Thunder Bay TV Guide (weekly) 87 N. Hill St., Thunder Bay, Ont. P7A 5V6—807/345-0412
Time (weekly) #1100, 620 University Ave., Toronto, Ont. M5G 2C5 - 416/595-1229
Today Magazine (weekly) 2180 Yonge St., #1702, Toronto, Ont. M4S 3A2 — 416/485-1552
Today's Bride (twice a year) 335 Lesmill Rd., Don Mills, Ont. M3B 2V1 — 416/441-3030
Today's Woman (4 times a year) 38 Wellington St. E., Toronto, Ont. M5E 1C7 - 416/363-6124
Toronto Calendar Magazine (monthly) 65 Front St. E., Toronto, Ont. M5E 1B6—416/869-1260
Toronto Life Magazine (monthly) 59 Front St. E., Toronto, Ont. M5E 1B3—416/364-3333 (inc. Design & Decor Guide; Fashion Magazine; Restaurant & Gourmet Guide)
Touring & Travel (6 times a year) 4th floor, 199 Bay St., Toronto, Ont. M5J 1L4—416/364-8442
Tout pour la Mariée (quarterly) 6285 Cairns Ave., Montreal, P.Q. H1K 9Z9—514/353-9155
Trace (quarterly) #330, 144 Front St. W., Toronto, Ont. M5J 2L7 - 416/593-4545
Trader's Post (monthly) Box 60, 3 First Canadian Place, Toronto, Ont. M5X 1C1 — 416/366-1681
Travel Times (7 times a year) #806, 1010 St. Catherine St. W., Montreal, P.Q. H3B 3R5—514/878-1973
Travelife (5 times a year) 12th Floor, 797 Don Mills Rd., Don Mills, Ont. M3C 1V2 - 416/424-1300
Trellis (6 times a year) 777 Lawrence Ave. E., Don Mills, Ont. M3C 1P2—416/445-1552
Trot (monthly) 148 King Rd. E., King City, Ont. L0G 1K0 - 416/833-6200
Trufax Directory, see Better Business Bureau
TV Book, The Brandon Sun (weekly) 501 Rosser Ave., Brandon, Man. R7A 5Z6 — 204/727-2451
TV Close-up (weekly) Ad Ventures Ltd., 308 4th Ave. N., Saskatoon, Sask. S7K 2L7 — 306/244-1377
TV Facts - Central Ontario (weekly) #2009, 110 Erskine Ave., Toronto, Ont. M4P 1Y4 - 416/483-7333
TV Facts Magazine (weekly) 29½ Simcoe St. S., Oshawa, Ont. L1H 4G1 — 416/579-9217
TV Guide (weekly) 2nd Floor, 124 Merton St., Toronto, Ont. M4S 2Z7—416/482-8600
TV Hebdo (weekly) Ste. 1100, 1001 de Maisonneuve Blvd. E., Montreal, P.Q. H2L 4P9—514/527-9601
TV Journal, see Ottawa Journal Mag.
TV News (weekly) 1252 Kingsway, Box 2362, Stn. A, Sudbury, Ont. P3E 4S8—705/560-4465
TV Nite (weekly) 815 Pine St., Box 2100, Timmins, Ont. P4N 7J8 - 705/264-4282
TV Plus (weekly) #1100, 1001 de Maisonneuve Blvd. E., Montreal, P.Q. H2L 4P9 - 514/527-9601
TV Scene (weekly) Winnipeg Free Press, 300 Carlton St., Winnipeg, Man. R3C 3C1—204/943-9331
TV/Times (weekly) 321 Bloor St. E., Toronto, Ont. M4W 1G9—416/925-2881
TV Times (weekly) 101 Marsh Dr., Quesnel, B.C. V2J 3K3—604/992-2713
TV Week (weekly) #320, 9940 Lougheed Hwy., Burnaby, B.C. V3J 1N3 - 604/936-2191
United Church Observer (monthly) 85 St. Clair Ave. E., Toronto, Ont. M4T 1M8—416/925-5931
Vancouver Calendar Magazine (monthly) 65 Front St. E., Toronto, Ont. M5E 1B6—416/869-1260
Vancouver Guideline (weekly) 285 E. 1st Ave., Vancouver, B.C. V5T 1A8 - 604/873-1646
Vancouver Magazine (monthly) 1205 Richards St., Vancouver, B.C. V6B 3G3 — 604/685-5374
Vancouver Symphony VSO (4 times a year) 873 Beatty St., Vancouver, B.C. V6B 2M6—604/689-1411
Victoria Guideline (weekly) 285 E. 1st Ave., Vancouver, B.C. V5T 1A8 - 604/873-1646
Victoria's Monday Magazine (weekly) 823 Broughton St., Victoria, B.C. V8W 1G5—604/382-6188

Video Scene (4 times a year) #306, 542 Mount Pleasant Rd., Toronto, Ont. M4S 2M7 - 416/482-1696
Vie des Arts (quarterly) 373 ouest, rue St-Paul, Montreal, P.Q. H2Y 2A7—514/282-0205
Vie et Camping (5 times a year) Ste. 221, 3414 Park Ave., Montreal, P.Q. H2X 2H5—514/282-0191
Village Squire (monthly) Box 10, Blyth, Ont. NOM 1HO—519/523-9646
Vintage Vehicles of Canada (bi-monthly) 3045 Universal Dr., Mississauga, Ont. L4X 2E2—416/625-5300
Virus Montreal (monthly) C.P. 187, Succ. E, Montreal, P.Q. H2T 3A7 - 514/842-9749
Vivre au Quebec (quarterly) 5707 Waverly St., Montreal, P.Q. H2T 2Y2—514/272-4513
Voice of the Vaad (twice a year) #117, 5491 Victoria Ave., Montreal, P.Q. H3W 2P9—514/739-6363
Votre Automobile (quarterly) Box 67, West Hill, Ont. M1E 4R4 - 416/266-6241
Wardair World (5 times a year) 6299 Airport Rd., Mississauga, Ont. L4V 1N3—416/671-3100
Waterloo Region (quarterly) 225 Fairway Rd., Kitchener, Ont. N2G 4E5 - 519/894-1630
Waves (3 times a year) 79 Denham Dr., Thornhill, Ont. L4J 1P2 - 416/889-6703
Western Canada Outdoors (bi-monthly) 1219 100th St. (Box 430, North Battleford, Sask. S9A 2Y5)—306/445-7477
Western Labour (4 times a year) 10070 151 St., Edmonton, Alta. T5P 1Y3 - 403/483-3401
Western Living (monthly) #303, 2930 Arbutus St., Vancouver, B.C. V6J 3Y9—604/736-8121
Western People (bi-weekly) Box 2500, Saskatoon, Sask. S7K 2C4 - 306/665-3500
Western Producer, see Farm Publications
Western Sportsman (quarterly) Box 737, Regina, Sask. S4P 3A8 — 306/352-8384
Western Thoroughbred (annually) Box 30048, Stn. B, Calgary, Alta. T2M 4N7 - 403/245-1070
Westworld (8 times a year) 999 W. Broadway (Box 6680, Vancouver, B.C. V6B 4L4)—604/732-1371
What's on Voici Ottawa-Hull (monthly) 345 O'Connor St., Ottawa, Ont. K2P 1V9—613/238-4736
Wheelspin News (26 times a year) 3045 Universal Dr., Mississauga, Ont. L4X 2E2—416/625-5300
Whiskey Jack (bi-monthly) 1601 Granville St., Vancouver, B.C. V6Z 2B3 - 604/689-8688
Wildlife Crusader (6 times a year) 1870 Notre Dame Ave., Winnipeg, Man. R3E 3E6—204/633-5967
Windsor this Month (12 times a year) Box 1029, Stn. A, Windsor, Ont. N9A 6P4—519/256-7162
Wine & Dine (quarterly) Ste. M, 580 Place de la Fontaine, Nun's Island, Montreal, P.Q. H3E 1G7 - 514/766-7004
The Wine Press (7 times a year) 636 Church St., Toronto, Ont. M4Y 2G3 — 416/922-4066
Wine Tidings (8 times a year) #5, 2140 Grey Ave., Montreal, P.Q. H4A 3N4 — 514/481-5892
Winnipeg Magazine (monthly) #201, 177 Lombard Ave. E., Winnipeg, Man. R3B 0W5 —204/944-1441

RELIGIOUS PUBLICATIONS

The Anglican (monthly) 135 Adelaide St. E., Toronto, Ont. M5C 1L8—416/363-6021
The Atlantic Baptist (monthly) Box 756, Kentville, N.S. B4N 3X9 —902/678-6868
The B.C. Catholic (weekly) 150 Robson St., Vancouver, B.C. V6B 2A7—604/683-0281
Calvinist Contact (weekly) 99 Niagara St., St. Catharines, Ont. L2R 4L3—416/682-8311
The Canadian Baptist (monthly) 217 St. George St., Toronto, Ont. M5R 2M2—416/922-5163
The Canadian Churchman, see Consumer Magazines
Canadian Ecumenical News (7 times a year) #209, 1811 W. 16th Ave., Vancouver, B.C. V6J 2M3 — 604/736-1613
The Canadian Messenger (monthly) Jesuit Fathers, 833 Broadview Ave., Toronto, Ont. M4K 2P9—416/466-1195
Catholic New Times (bi-weekly) 80 Sackville St., Toronto, Ont. M5A 3E5—416/361-0761
The Catholic Register (weekly) 67 Bond St., Toronto, Ont. M5B 1X6—416/362-6822
The Christian Inquirer (monthly) 228 Jarvis St., Fort Erie, Ont. L2A 2S5 - 416/871-3188
Communicate (monthly exc. Aug.) Box 600, Beaverlodge, Alta. T0H 0C0
The Diocesan Times (monthly) 5732 College St., Halifax, N.S. B3H 1X3
Faith Today (6 times a year) Box 103, Stn. D, Scarborough, Ont. M1R 4Y7 — 416/495-9644
The Gospel Herald (monthly) Box 94, Beamsville, Ont. L0R 1B0 —416/563-7503
Huron Church News (monthly) 220 Dundas St., London, Ont. N6A 4W3 — 519/434-6893
Living Message (monthly) Anglican Church Women, Box 820, Petrolia, Ont. N0N 1R0
Mennonite Brethren Herald (bi-weekly) 159 Henderson Hwy., Winnipeg, Man. R2L 1L4—204/667-3560
Messenger (monthly) Box 345, Wasaga Beach, Ont. L0L 2P0 — 705/429-2275
The New Brunswick Anglican (monthly) Tracy, N.B. E0G 3C0—506/368-2617
The New Freeman (weekly) Box 6609, Stn. A, Saint John, N.B. E2L 4S1—506/652-3667
L'Oratoire (bi-monthly) 3800 Queen Mary Rd., Montreal, P.Q. H3V 1H6—514/733-8211
Orthodoxy Canada (bi-monthly) Box 404, Chilliwack, B.C. V2P 6J7 - 604/858-7750
The Pentecostal Testimony (monthly) 10 Overlea Blvd., Toronto, Ont. M4H 1A5—416/425-1010
Prairie Messenger (weekly) Box 190, Muenster, Sask. S0K 2Y0 —306/682-5245
The Shepherd (11 times a year) 247 1st Ave. N., Saskatoon, Sask. S7K 4H5
Studies in Religion/Sciences Religieuses (quarterly) c/o Charles Davis, Dept. of Religion, Concordia University, Montreal, P.Q. H3G 1M8 - 514/879-2843
The United Church Observer (monthly) 85 St. Clair Ave. E., Toronto, Ont. M4T 1M8—416/925-5931
Western Catholic Reporter (weekly) 10562 109 St., Edmonton, Alta. T5H 3B2—403/420-1330

UNIVERSITY & SCHOOL PUBLICATIONS

Alumni Gazette (4 times a year) Room 11, Univ. of Western Ont., Alumni Hall, London, Ont. N6A 5B9
Alumni Journal (quarterly) Univ. of Manitoba, Room 139, University Centre, Winnipeg, Man. R3T 2N2
Alumni-News, Ottawa (quarterly) Univ. of Ottawa Alumni Secretariat, Ottawa, Ont. K1N 6N5
The Argus, Lakehead Univ., see Campus Plus
Arthur, Trent Univ., see Campus Network
The Athenaeum, Acadia Univ., see Campus Plus
Balcony Square, Scarborough College, see Campus Plus
Bandersnatch, John Abbot College, see Campus Plus
BCIT Link (weekly) B.C. Inst. of Technology, 3700 Willingdon Ave., Burnaby, B.C. V5G 3H2
Bricklayer, Red Deer College, see Campus Plus
Brock Press, Brock Univ., see Campus Plus
The Brunwickian (weekly) Box 4400, Univ. of N.B., Fredericton, N.B. E3B 5A3
Bugle, Champlain College, see Campus Plus
Bulletin (bi-weekly) Univ. of Toronto, 45 Willcocks St., Toronto, Ont. M5S 1A1
The Campus, Bishop's Univ., see Campus Plus
Canada & The World, see Consumer Magazines
Canadian Campus Mag. Career Directory (annually) #1201, 55 Bloor St. W., Toronto, Ont. M4W 3K2
Caper Chronicle, Cape Breton College, see Campus Plus
Capilano Courier, Capilano College, see Campus Plus
The Carillon, Univ. of Regina, see Campus Plus
The Charlaton, Carleton Univ., see Campus Plus
The Chevron, Box 363, Waterloo, Ont. N2J 4A4

The Chronicle (bi-weekly) Durham College, Box 385, Oshawa, Ont. L1H 7L7
Clan Macdonald Annual (annually) Macdonald College, Box 98, Macdonald College, P.Q. H0A 1C0
Concordia Magazine (monthly) Concordia Univ., 7141 Sherbrooke St. W., Montreal, P.Q. H4B 1R6
The Cord, Sir Wilfrid Laurier Univ., see Campus Plus
Coven, Humber College, see Campus Network
Dalhousie Gazette, Dalhousie Univ., see Campus Plus
Les Diplomés, Univ. de Montreal, #3, 2910 boul. Edouard Montpetit, Montreal, P.Q. H3T 1J7
The Emery Weal, Southern Alta. Institute of Technology, see Campus Network
The End, Vanier College, see Campus Plus
Excalibur, York Univ., see Campus Network
The Eyeopener, Ryerson Polytech. Inst., see Campus Network
Free Press, College of New Caledonia, see Campus Plus
The Fulcrum/La Rotonde (weekly) 85 Hastey Ave., Rm. 07, Ottawa, Ont. K1N 8Z4
Gateway, Univ. of Alberta, see Campus Plus
The Gauntlet, Univ. of Calgary, see Campus Network
The Gazette (semi-weekly) Room 244, Univ. Community Centre, Univ. of Western Ontario, London, Ont. N6A 3K7
The Georgian (weekly) Georgian College, 1 Georgian College Dr., Barrie, Ont. L4M 3X9
Golden Words (weekly) Engineering Soc., Clark House, Queen's Univ., Kingston, Ont.
Goliard, Okanagan College, see Campus Plus
The Green & White (quarterly) Univ. of Sask., Memorial Union Bldg., Saskatoon, Sask. S7N 0W0
Impact, Algonquin College, see Campus Plus
Imprint, Univ. of Waterloo, see Campus Plus
The Journal, St. Mary's Univ., see Campus Plus
Kootenay Reporter, Selkirk College, see Campus Plus
Lambda, Laurentian Univ., see Campus Plus
The Lance, Univ. of Windsor, see Campus Plus
The Link, Concordia Univ., see Campus Plus
The MacEwan Journal (weekly) 8020 118 Ave., Edmonton, Alta. T5B 0R8
The Manitoban, Univ. of Manitoba, see Campus Plus
The Martlet (weekly) Univ. of Victoria, Box 1700, Victoria, B.C. V8W 2Y2
McGill Daily, McGill Univ., see Campus Plus
The McGill News (quarterly) 3605 Mountain St., Montreal, P.Q. H3G 2M1
Medium II, Erindale College, see Campus Plus
The Meliorist, Univ. of Lethbridge, see Campus Plus
Mount Allison Record (3 times a year) Mount Allison Univ., Hillcrest House, Sackville, N.B. E0A 3C0
The Muse, Memorial Univ., see Campus Plus
New Edition, New College, see Campus Network
The Newspaper, U. of T., see Campus Network
Obiter Dicta, Osgoode Hall, see Campus Network
Oblique Times, Seneca College, see Campus Plus
The Ontarion, Univ. of Guelph, see Campus Network
Oracle, Centennial College, see Campus Network
Other Press, Douglas College, see Campus Plus
Other Side, Lambton College, see Campus Network
Pacific Progress (bi-weekly) Pacific Voc. Inst., 3650 Willingdon Ave., Burnaby, B.C. V5G 3H1
The Peak, Simon Fraser Univ., see Campus Plus
Phoenix, Mohawk College, see Campus Plus
Picaro, Mount St. Vincent Univ., see Campus Plus
Plant, Dawson College, see Campus Plus
Plumbers Pot (9 times yearly) McConnell Engineering Bldg., McGill Univ., Box 6070, Montreal, P.Q. H3C 3G1
Le Polyscope (24 times a year) 2500 Marie-Guyard Ave., Box 501, Snowdon, Montreal, P.Q.
The Projector, Red River College, see Campus Plus
The Pro Tem, Glendon College, see Campus Plus
The Quad (annually) Bishop's Univ., Box 2133, Lennoxville, P.Q. JOB 1ZO
Queen's Journal (Tues. & Fri.) Queen's Univ., Kingston, Ont.
Queen's Quarterly, see Scholarly Publications
Quill, Brandon Univ., see Campus Plus
Reflector, Mount Royal College, see Campus Plus
La Rotonde (weekly) Univ. of Ottawa, 85 Hastey Ave., Rm. 07, Ottawa, Ont. K1N 5N6
Ryersonian (daily) Ryerson Polytech. Institute, 50 Gould St., Toronto, Ont. M5B 1E8
The Saint, St. Clair College, see Campus Network
Savant (weekly) Vancouver College, 100 W. 49th Ave., Vancouver, B.C. V5Y 2Z6
The Sheaf, Univ. of Sask., see Campus Plus
Sheridan Sun (weekly) Sheridan College, 1430 Trafalgar Rd., Oakville, Ont. L6H 2L1
The Silhouette, McMaster Univ., see Campus Plus
Snowdon Press, Vanier College, see Campus Plus
Spoke, Conestoga College, see Campus Network
Student, Ukrainian Students' Union, see Campus Plus
Sunshine News (monthly) #14A, 465 King St. E., Toronto, Ont. M5A 1L6
Toike Oike (9 times a year) Univ. of Toronto, 2nd floor, Engineering Annex, Toronto, Ont. M5S 2E4
U.B.C. Alumni Chronicle (quarterly) 6251 Cecil Green Park Rd., Vancouver, B.C. V6T 1X8
The Ubyssey, Univ. of B.C., see Campus Plus
Uniter, Univ. of Winnipeg, see Campus Plus
University Affairs (monthly) Assn. of Universities & Colleges of Canada, 151 Slater St., Ottawa, Ont. K1P 5N1
The Varsity, Univ. of Toronto, see Campus Plus
Le Vieil Escollier (4 times a year) Laval Univ., Cité Universitaire, Quebec, P.Q. G1K 7P4
Western News (weekly) Univ. of Western Ontario, Room 130, Stevenson-Lawson Bldg., London, Ont. N6A 5B8
The Winters Seer (8 times a year) 029 Winters College, 4700 Keele St., Downsview, Ont. M3J 1P5
Xaverian, St. Francis Xavier Univ., see Campus Plus

THE CAMPUS NETWORK, 310 Davenport Rd., Toronto, Ont. M5R 3K2 – 416/925-6358

CAMPUS PLUS, 3rd floor, 124 Merton St., Toronto, Ont. M4S 2Z2 – 416/481-7283

SCHOLARLY PUBLICATIONS

Acadiensis (biennial) Univ. of N.B., Campus House, Fredericton, N.B. E3B 5A3
Alternatives: Journal of Friends of the Earth, Canada (quarterly) Trent Univ., Peterborough, Ont. K9J 7B8
Atlantis (twice a year) Box 294, Acadia Univ., Wolfville, N.S. BOP 1XO
B.C. Journal of Special Education (quarterly) Special Education Association, c/o Dept. of Special Education, UBC, Vancouver, B.C. V6T 1W5
B.C. Studies, Univ. of B.C., 2021 West Mall, Vancouver, B.C. V6T 1W5
Canadian Historical Review (quarterly) Univ. of Toronto Press, Front Campus, Toronto, Ont. M5S 1A6
Canadian Journal of Economics (quarterly) Univ. of Toronto Press, Front Campus, Toronto, Ont. M5S 1A6
Canadian Journal of Education/Revue Canadienne de l'Education (quarterly) c/o Faculty of Education, Univ. of Victoria, Victoria, B.C. V8W 2Y2
Canadian Journal of Higher Education/La Revue Canadienne d'enseignement supérieur, c/o Canadian Society for the Study of Higher Education, A.D. Gregor, Dept. of Educational Administration & Foundations, Univ. of Manitoba, Winnipeg, Man. R3T 2N2
Canadian Journal of Mathematics (bi-monthly) Univ. of Toronto Press, Front Campus, Toronto, Ont. M5S 1A6
Canadian Public Policy (quarterly) Rm. 039, Arts Bldg., Univ. of Guelph, Guelph, Ont. N1G 2W1

Canadian Review of Sociology & Anthropology (quarterly) Concordia Univ., 1455 Boul. de Maisonneuve ouest, Montreal, P.Q. H3G 1M8

Emergency Librarian (bi-monthly) Box 46258, Stn. G, Vancouver, B.C. V6R 4G6

Free! The Newsletter of Free Materials & Services, Box 46258, Stn. G, Vancouver, B.C. V6R 4G6

Journal of Canadian Art History (twice a year) Concordia Univ., 1395 Dorchester Blvd. W., VA 258, Montreal, P.Q. H3G 2M5

Journal of Canadian Studies/Revue d'études Canadiennes (quarterly) Trent Univ., Peterborough, Ont. K9J 7B8

Monographs in Education (twice a year) Univ. of Manitoba, Faculty of Education, Winnipeg, Man. R3T 2N2

Northward Journal (quarterly) Box 340, Moonbeam, Ont. P0L 9Z9

Nova Scotia Historical Review (quarterly) Public Archives of N.S., 6016 University Ave., Halifax, N.S. B3H 1W4

Queen's Quarterly (quarterly) 130 L. Albert St., Queen's Univ., Kingston, Ont.

Scholarly Publishing (quarterly) Univ. of Toronto Press, Front Campus, Toronto, Ont. M5S 1A6

Tourism Management Review (quarterly) Box 599, Stn. A, Montreal, P.Q. H3C 2T6

University Affairs (AUCC)(10 times a year) Association of Universities & Colleges, 151 Slater St., Ottawa, Ont. K1P 5N1

University of Toronto Quarterly (quarterly) Univ. of Toronto Press, Front Campus, Toronto, Ont. M5S 1A6

FARM PUBLICATIONS

Agri-book Magazine (annually) Box 1060, Exeter, Ont. NOM 1SO—519/235-2400

Agrologist (quarterly) 907 Burnside Bldg., 151 Slater St., Ottawa, Ont. K1P 5H4—613/232-9459

Alberta Farm Life (weekly) 10330 104 St., Edmonton, Alta. T5J 1C2—403/425-1610

Beans in Canada, see Agri-book

Breeder & Feeder (monthly) 590 Keele St., Toronto, Ont. M6N 3E3—416/766-9217

Le Bulletin Des Agriculteurs (monthly) Ste. 1100, 110 Cremazie Blvd. W., Montreal, P.Q. H2P 1B9—514/382-4350

Butter-Fat (bi-monthly) Box 9100, Vancouver, B. C. V6B 4G4—604/420-6611

Calgary Livestock Market Journal (monthly) #203, 2635 Portland St., Calgary, Alta. T2B 4M8 — 403/265-5169

Canada Poultryman (monthly) 605 Royal Ave., New Westminster, B.C. V3M 1J4—604/526-8525

Canada's Who's Who Of The Poultry Industry (annually) 605 Royal Ave., New Westminster, B.C. V3M 1J4—604/526-8525

Canadian Aberdeen-Angus News (9 times a year) Box 277, Lethbridge, Alta. T1J 3Y7—403/328-1448

Canadian Ayrshire Review (monthly) 1160 Carling Ave., Ottawa, Ont. K1Z 7K6—613/728-8192

Canadian Charolais Banner (monthly) 2424A 2nd Ave. S.E., Calgary, Alta. T2E 6J9—403/273-7404

Canadian Fruitgrower (9 times a year) 222 Argyle Ave., Delhi, Ont. N4B 2Y2—519/582-2510

Canadian Guernsey Breeders' Journal (9 times a year) 368 Woolwich St., Guelph, Ont.—519/836-2141

Canadian Hereford Digest (monthly) 5160 Skyline Way N.E., Calgary, Alta. T2E 6V1 — 403/274-1734

Canadian Jersey Breeder (monthly) 343 Waterloo Ave., Guelph, Ont. N1H 3K1—519/821-9150

Canadian Swine (quarterly) R.R. 5, Cambridge, Ont. N1R 5S6

The Canadian Tobacco Grower (10 times a year) 222 Argyle Ave., Delhi, Ont. N4B 2Y2—519/582-2510

Canadian Wool Grower (twice a year) Box 9, Carleton Place, Ont. K7C 3P3—613/257-2714

Cash Crop Farming (11 times a year) 222 Argyle Ave., Delhi, Ont. N4B 2Y2—519/582-2510

Cattlemen (monthly) 1760 Ellice Ave., Winnipeg, Man. R3H 0B6 —204/774-1861

Le Cooperateur Agricole (monthly) Box 500, Youville Stn., Montreal, P.Q. H2P 2W2—514/384-6450

Co-Operative Consumer (25 times a year) Box 1050, Saskatoon, Sask. S7K 3M9—306/244-3118

Corn in Canada, see Agri-book

Corn-Soy Guide (semi-annually) 1760 Ellice Ave., Winnipeg, Man. R3H 0B6—204/774-1861

Country Guide (monthly) 1760 Ellice Ave., Winnipeg, Man. R3H 0B6—204/774-1861

Country Life in British Columbia (monthly) 1345 Johnston Rd., White Rock, B.C. V4B 3Z3 - 604/536-7622

County Farm (monthly) (491 Book Rd.) Box 65, Ancaster, Ont. L9G 3L3 - 416/648-2035

Crops Guide (annually) 1760 Ellice Ave., Winnipeg, Man. R3H 0B6—204/774-1861

Crossroads (weekly) Box 390, Wingham, Ont.—519/357-2320

Dairy Contact (monthly) 334 9th Ave. N.E., Calgary, Alta. T2E OV6—403/233-0767

Dairy Guide (bi-monthly) 1760 Ellice Ave., Winnipeg, Man. R3H 0B6—204/774-1861

Drainage Contractor, see Agri-book

Eastern Ontario Farmer (weekly) Box 7400, Stn. E, London, Ont. N5Y 4X3—519/473-0010

Economic Planning (6 times a year) Box 42, Snowdon Stn., Montreal, P.Q. H3X 3T3 - 514/737-7615

Elevator Manager & Farm Supply Store Operator, see Agri-book

Farm and Country (semi-monthly) 7th floor, 950 Yonge St., Toronto, Ont. M4W 2J4—416/924-6209

Farm Focus (semi-monthly) Box 128, 2 Second St., Yarmouth, N.S.—902/742-7111

The Farm Gate (monthly) 15 King St. (Box 280, Elmira, Ont. N3B 2Z7)—519/669-5155

Farm Light & Power (10 times a year) 2352 Smith St., Regina, Sask. S4P 2P6—306/525-3305

Farm News (bi-weekly) Box 70, Tottenham, Ont. LOG 1WO

Farm Trends (monthly) 9934 106 St., Edmonton, Alta. T5K 1E1 - 403/423-1684

Farm Update (twice a month) Box 850, Exeter, Ont. N0M 1S0 - 519/235-1331

The Farmer (monthly) Box 400, Iroquois, Ont. KOE 1KO—613/652-4806

Farmer's Finder - Equipment News (bi-weekly) 1393 Aimco Blvd., Mississauga, Ont. L4W 1Y3 — 416/625-3460

The Farmer's Insight (monthly) 799 Erskine Ave., Peterborough, Ont. K9J 5V1 - 705/743-4771

Farming Today (semi-monthly) Box 130, Mount Forest, Ont. N0G 2L0 - 519/323-1550

Farm'n Family (eo Tues) Box 456, Milverton, Ont. N0K 1M0 - 519/595-8921

Feather Fancier (monthly) R.R. 5, Forest, Ont. N0N 1J0 - 519/899-2364

The Forage Book, see Agri-book

Free Press Report on Farming (monthly) 300 Carlton St., Winnipeg, Man. R3C 3C1—204/943-9331

Grainews (monthly) Box 6600, Winnipeg, Man. R3C 3A7 - 204/944-5571

The Grower (monthly) 303 Ontario Food Bldg., 165 The Queensway, Toronto, Ont. M8Y 1H8—416/255-4473

Herd Health & Hygiene, see Agri-book

Hog Guide (bi-monthly) 1760 Ellice Ave., Winnipeg, Man. R3H 0B6—204/774-1861

Hog Market Place Quarterly (quarterly) 7th floor, 950 Yonge St., Toronto, Ont. M4W 2J4—416/924-6209

Holstein-Friesian Journal (monthly) 335 Lesmill Rd., Don Mills, Ont. M3B 2V1—416/441-3030

Huron Soil & Crop News (annually) Exeter Times-Advocate, Exeter, Ont.—519/235-1331

Hygiene du Troupeau, see Agri-book

The Limousin Leader (monthly) #105, 2116 27th Ave. N.E., Calgary, Alta. T2E 7A6—403/230-2155

Macdonald Journal (monthly) Macdonald College, Box 284, Ste. Anne de Bellevue, P.Q. HOA 1CO—514/457-2000

Maine-Anjou Canada (6 times a year) 334 9th Ave. N.E., Calgary, Alta. T2E 0V6 - 403/265-8073

Le Mais au Canada, see Agri-book

The Manitoba Co-Operator (weekly) Room 908, 220 Portage Ave., Winnipeg, Man. R3C 0A5 - 204/942-0224

Le Meunier Quebecois (monthly) 915 St-Cyrille Blvd., Quebec, P.Q. G1S 1T7 - 418/688-9227

N.B. Farm & Forest (semi-monthly) Box 130, Woodstock, N.B. EOJ 2BO — 506/328-8863

Niagara Farmers' Monthly (monthly) Box 52, Smithville, Ont. L0R 2A0

Northern Alberta Farmer (weekly) 9921 101 St., Fort Saskatchewan, Alta. T8L 1V6 - 403/998-7070

Ontario Milk Producer (monthly) 50 Maitland St., Toronto, Ont. M4Y 1C7—416/920-2700

Potatoes in Canada, see Agri-book

Le Producteur Agricole (monthly) Box 1367, Place d'Estrie, Bedford, P.Q. JOJ 1AO—514/248-3356

Le Producteur de Lait Quebecois (monthly) 515 ave Viger, Montreal, P.Q. H2L 2P2 - 514/288-6141

Le Producteur de Porc (quarterly) Box 1367, Bedford, P.Q. JOJ 1AO — 514/248-3356

Rabbits in Canada (monthly) Clay Publishing Co. Ltd., Bewdley, Ont. K0L 1E0—416/797-2281

Le Richelieu Agricole (weekly) 84B Richelieu St., St-Jean, P.Q. J3B 6X3 - 514/861-4624

The Rural Voice (5 times a year) Box 10, Blyth, Ont. N0M 1H0 - 519/527-0240

Saskatchewan Stockgrower (monthly) Box 849, Maple Creek, Sask. S0N 1N0

Shorthorn News (8 times a year) Gummer Bldg., Guelph, Ont. N1H 2S8—519/822-6841

Simmental Country (monthly) #13, 4101 19th St. N.E., Calgary, Alta. T2E 7C4—403/230-2471

La Terre de Chez Nous (weekly) 515 Viger Ave., Montreal, P.Q. H2L 2P2—514/288-6141

Union Farmer (monthly) 250C 2nd Ave S., Saskatoon, Sask. S7K 2M1—306/652-9465

The Valley Farmer (monthly) Box 158, Smiths Falls, Ont. K7A 4T1 - 613/283-3182

Voice of the Elgin Farmer (semi-monthly) Box 490, Main St., Dresden, Ont. NOP 1MO—519/683-4485 (also: Voice of the Essex Farmer, Voice of the Kent Farmer, Voice of the Lambton Farmer, Voice of the Middlesex Farmer)

Western Hog Journal (quarterly) 10319 Princess Elizabeth Ave., Edmonton, Alta. T5G 0Y5 — 403/474-8288

Western Livestock and Agricultural News (monthly) 215 Inglewood Bldg., 11802-124 St., Edmonton, Alta. T5L 0M3—403/453-2553

Western Ontario Farmer (weekly) Box 7400, Stn. E, London, Ont. N5Y 4X3—519/473-0010

Western Producer (weekly) Box 2500, Saskatoon, Sask. S7K 2C4—306/665-3500

World of Beef & Stockman's Recorder (monthly) #105, 2116 27th Ave. N.E., Calgary, Alta. T2E 7A6 — 403/230-2155

BUSINESS PUBLICATIONS

ADVERTISING & MARKETING: A-V Canada (quarterly) 481 University Ave., Toronto, Ont. M5W 1A7—416/596-5877

Canadian Advertising Rates & Data (monthly) 481 University Ave., Toronto, Ont. M5W 1A7—416/596-5890

Canadian Industry Shows & Exhibitions (annually) 481 University Ave., Toronto, Ont. M5W 1A7—416/596-5890

Canadian Premiums & Incentives (bi-monthly) 481 University Ave., Toronto, Ont. M5W 1A7—416/596-5738

Conventions & Meetings Canada (annually) 505 Consumers Rd., #303, Willowdale, Ont. M2J 4V8—416/494-7766

Marketing (weekly) 481 University Ave., Toronto, Ont. M5W 1A7—416/596-5858

Media Forum (6 times a year) #307, 85 Scarsdale Rd., Don Mills, Ont. M3B 2R2 - 416/447-7263

Media West (semi-monthly) #601, 510 W. Hastings St., Vancouver, B.C. V6B 1L8 - 604/689-2021

Meetings, Conferences & Conventions (Financial Post) (annually) 481 University Ave., Toronto, Ont. M5W 1A7—416/596-5649

Meetings & Incentive Travel (bi-monthly) 1450 Don Mills Rd., Don Mills, Ont. M3B 2X7 — 416/445-6641

Meetings Canada (monthly) Box 490, Stn. T, Toronto, Ont. M6B 4C2 — 416/364-1310

The National List of Advertisers (annually) 481 University Ave., Toronto, Ont. M5W 1A7—416/596-5890

Le Publicitaire (18 times a year) Ste. 639, 1010 Ste Catherine St. W., Montreal, P.Q. H3B 1G7—514/875-2565

Sales & Marketing Management in Canada (10 times a year) #303, 416 Moore Ave., Toronto, Ont. M4G 1C9 — 416/424-4441

Stimulus (alternate months) Suite 721, 67 Yonge St., Toronto, Ont. M5E 1J8—416/368-1764

Stimulus Adnews & Information (weekly) #906, 67 Yonge St., Toronto, Ont. M5E 1J8 - 416/368-1764

AIR CONDITIONING: see HEATING, etc.

ARCHITECTURE: ARQ Architecture Quebec (4 times a year) 1463 Prefontaine, Montreal, P.Q. H1W 2N6 - 514/523-6832

Architects Forum (10 times a year) 970 Richards St., Vancouver, B.C. V6B 3C1 — 604/683-8588

Architecture-Concept (6 times a year) #200, 6725 Darlington Ave., Montreal, P.Q. H3S 2J7 - 514/731-3524

Batiment, see BUILDING

The Canadian Architect (monthly) 1450 Don Mills Rd., Don Mills, Ont. M3B 2X7—416/445-6641

Canadian Architect's Yardsticks for Costing (annually) 1450 Don Mills Rd., Don Mills, Ont. M3B 2X7—416/445-6641

Canadian Building, see BUILDING

Canadian Interiors, see INTERIOR DESIGN

Canadian Workshop, see Consumer Magazines

Construction Canada (6 times a year) #1206, 1 St. Clair Ave. W., Toronto, Ont. M4V 1K6 - 416/922-3159

Renovation Bricolage, see Consumer Magazines

Sweet's Canadian Construction Catalogue File (annually) 330 Progress Ave., Scarborough, Ont. M1P 2Z5—416/293-1931

AUTOMOTIVE, ACCESSORIES: L'Automobile (monthly) Suite 3, 5020 de Salaberry, Montreal, P.Q.—514/331-9764; Suite 101, 109 Vanderhoof Ave., Toronto, Ont. M4G 2J2—416/425-9021

Automotive Marketer (quarterly) Suite 101, 109 Vanderhoof Ave., Toronto, Ont. M4G 2J2—416/425-9021

Automotive Retailer (monthly) 1687 W. Broadway, Vancouver, B.C. V6J 1X5—604/731-2108

Automotive Service Data Book (annually) 481 University Ave., Toronto, Ont. M5W 1A7—416/596-5787

Bodyshop (bi-monthly) Suite 101, 109 Vanderhoof Ave., Toronto, Ont. M4G 2J2—416/425-9021

Canadian Automotive Aftermarket Directory/Marketing Guide (annually) Ste. 101, 109 Vanderhoof Ave., Toronto, Ont. M4G 2J2—416/425-9021

Canadian Automotive Trade (monthly) 481 University Ave., Toronto, Ont. M5W 1A7—416/596-5787

Helicopters in Canada (quarterly) #158, 1224 53 Ave. N.E., Calgary, Alta. T2E 7E2 - 403/275-9457

Jobber News (monthly) Suite 101, 109 Vanderhoof Ave., Toronto, Ont. M4G 2J2—416/425-9021

Motor in Canada (monthly) 1077 St. James St., Box 6900, Winnipeg, Man. R3C 3B1—204/775-0201

Revue-Moteur (monthly) 625 President Kennedy Ave., Montreal, P.Q. H3A 1K5—514/845-5141

Service Station & Garage Management (monthly) Suite 101, 109 Vanderhoof Ave., Toronto, Ont. M4G 2J2—416/425-9021

Taxirama (6 times a year) C.P. 278, Succ. Ahuntsic, Montreal, P.Q. H3L 3N8 - 514/337-3990

AVIATION: Aerospace Canada (4 times a year) 481 University Ave., Toronto, Ont. M5W 1A7—416/596-5791

Airborne (monthly) #511, 250 Consumers Rd., Willowdale, Ont. M2J 4V6

Airforce (4 times a year) 424 Metcalfe St., Ottawa, Ont. K2P 2C3—613/236-4673

Aviation Quebec (monthly) 5786 Christophe-Colomb, Montreal, P.Q. H2S 2G1—514/270-9241

Calgary Airport Business Directory (annually) #158, 1224 53 Ave. N.E., Calgary, Alta. T2E 7E2 - 403/275-9457

The Canadian Aircraft Operator (semi-monthly) Box 669, Streetsville Postal Stn., Mississauga, Ont. L5M 2C2—416/826-2287

Canadian Aviation (monthly) 481 University Ave., Toronto, Ont. M5W 1A7—416/596-5791

Canadian Flight (bi-monthly) Box 563, Stn. B, Ottawa, Ont.—613/236-4901

Edmonton Airport Business Directory (annually) #158, 1224 53 Ave. N.E., Calgary, Alta. T2E 7E2 - 403/275-9457

ICAO Bulletin (monthly) 1000 Sherbrooke St. W., Montreal, P.Q. H3A 2R2—514/285-8220

Skyads (6 times a year) 3317 Bloor St. W., Toronto, Ont. M8X 1E7 - 416/236-1048

Toronto Airport Business Directory (annually) #158, 1224 53 Ave. N.E., Calgary, Alta. T2E 7E2 - 403/275-9457

Vancouver Airport Business Directory (annually) #158, 1224 53 Ave. N.E., Calgary, Alta. T2E 7E2 - 403/275-9457

Wings (monthly) #158, 1224 53 Ave. N.E., Calgary, Alta. T2E 7E2 - 403/275-9457

BAKING, BAKERS' SUPPLIES: (See also FOOD) Bakers Journal (bi-monthly) 106 Lakeshore Rd. E., Ste. 209, Mississauga, Ont. L5G 1E3—416/271-1366

Focus on the Baking Industry (monthly) 2425 Truscott Dr., Mississauga, Ont. L5J 2B4 - 416/823-7350

Food in Canada, see FOOD

La Fournee (bi-monthly) Suite 203, 6841 St. Hubert, Montreal, P.Q. H2S 2M8—514/273-7217

BARBERS, BEAUTICIANS: Canadian Hairdresser (12 times a year) Suite 204, 5200 Dixie Rd., Mississauga, Ont. L4W 1E4—416/625-5277

CBC Coiffure Beaute Charme (monthly) C.P. 7730, Charlesbourg, P.Q. G1G 5W6 - 418/651-3347

BEEKEEPING: Canadian Beekeeping (monthly) Arnott & Son, Orono, Ont. L0B 1M0

BEVERAGES: Canadian Beverage Review (bi-monthly) 106 Lakeshore Rd. E., Ste. 209, Mississauga, Ont. L5G 1E3—416/271-1366

Food in Canada, see FOOD

BOOKS, STATIONERY, GIFTS, GAMES: Books in Canada, see Consumer Magazines

Canadian Publishers' Directory (twice a year) 59 Front St. E., Toronto, Ont. M5E 1B3—416/364-3333

Quill & Quire (monthly) 59 Front St. E., Toronto, Ont. M5E 1B3—416/364-3333

BREWING: Beverage Alcohol Reporter, see HOTELS

BROADCASTING: Broadcast Technology (bi-monthly) Box 423, Stn. J, Toronto, Ont. M4J 4Y8 — 416/463-5304

Broadcaster (monthly) 7 Labatt Ave., Toronto, Ont. M5A 3P2—416/363-6111

BUILDING: Action Entretien et Salubrité (6 times a year) 245 Lindsay St., Drummondville, P.Q. J2C 1P2 — 819/477-6811

Alumni News (6 times a year) Box 115, Westmount, P.Q. H3Z 2T1 — 514/932-9922

Bâtiment (monthly) 481 University Ave., Toronto, Ont. M5W 1A7—416/596-5762

B.S.D.A. Survey (bi-monthly) 3875 Canada Way, Burnaby, B.C. V5G 1G6—604/435-4447

B.C. Building Tradesman (4 times a year) 124 W. 8th St., North Vancouver, B.C. V7M 3H2 - 604/985-8711

Buildcore Index (annually) 1 Sparks Ave., Willowdale, Ont. M2H 2W1 - 416/493-2280

Building Guide (6 times a year) 1450 Don Mills Rd., Don Mills, Ont. M3B 2X7 - 416/445-6641

Building Management & Maintenance News (6 times a year) 56 Esplanade, Toronto, Ont. M5E 1A7—416/363-6002

Building Operating Manager (bi-monthly) #503, 56 The Esplanade, Toronto, Ont. M5E 1A7 - 416/363-6002

Building Supply Dealer (monthly) 481 University Ave., Toronto, Ont. M5W 1A7—416/596-5799

Canadian Building (monthly) 481 University Ave., Toronto, Ont. M5W 1A7—416/596-5762

Genie-Construction, see ENGINEERING CONSTRUCTION

Heavy Construction News, see ENGINEERING CONSTRUCTION

L.B.M.A.O. Reporter (bi-monthly) Lumber & Building Materials Association, Unit F, 4500 Sheppard Ave. E., Scarborough, Ont. M1S 3R6 - 416/298-1731

Quart de Rond (bi-monthly) Ste. 102, 4270 Jean Talon St. E., Montreal, P.Q. H1S 1G7—514/376-8541

Real Estate Development Annual (annually) 481 University Ave., Toronto, Ont. M5W 1A7—416/596-5762

Sanitation Canada (6 times a year) 838 Mount Pleasant Rd., Toronto, Ont. M4P 2L3 - 416/485-2014

Select Home Designs, see Consumer Magazines

Southam Building Guide (bi-monthly) 1450 Don Mills Rd., Don Mills, Ont. M3B 2X7—416/445-6641

Sweet's Canadian Construction Catalogue File, see ARCHITECTURE

Western Construction & Industry (monthly) 200, 633 Portage Ave., Winnipeg, Man. R3B 2Z9—204/775-0387

BUSINESS: Action Canada France (10 times a year) Ste. 826, 1080 Beaver Hall Hill, Montreal, P.Q. H2Z 1S8—514/866-0178

Administrative Digest, see OFFICE EQUIPMENT

Les Affaires (weekly) #903, 465 St-Jean St., Montreal, P.Q. H2Y 3S4 - 514/842-6491

Alberta Business (weekly) Ste. 130, 14315 118th Ave., Edmonton, Alta. T5L 4S6 - 403/451-1802

Alberta Commercial Directory (annually) #205, 7710 5th St. S.E., Calgary, Alta. T2H 2L9 - 403/253-9023

Alberta Inc. (monthly) #601, 510 W. Hastings St., Vancouver, B.C. V6B 1L8 - 604/689-2021

Benefits Canada (bi-monthly) 481 University Ave., Toronto, Ont. M5W 1A7—416/596-5919

B.C. Business (monthly) #601, 510 W. Hastings St., Vancouver, B.C. V6B 1L8—604/689-2021

B.C. Commercial Directory (annually) 4400 Dominion St., Burnaby, B.C. V5G 4G4 — 604/438-5535

Business (monthly) #29, 43 Victoria St., Toronto, Ont. M5C 2A2 — 416/364-3325

Businessbeat (monthly) 50 LePage Court, Downsview, Ont. M3J 1Z9 - 416/638-0039

Business Journal (Metro Toronto) (10 times a year) Box 60, 3 First Canadian Place, Toronto, Ont. M5X 1C1—416/366-6811

Business Life (monthly) #100, 3016 19th St. N.E., Calgary, Alta. T2E 6Y9 - 403/230-3131

The Business & Professional Woman (5 times a year) 796 Carlaw Ave., #18, Toronto, Ont. M4K 3L2

The Business Quarterly (quarterly) School of Business Admin., University of Western Ontario, London, Ont. N6A 3K7 - 519/679-6287

Business Review (4 times a year) 1494 Regent Ave. W., Winnipeg, Man. R2C 3A8 - 204/224-2267

CA Magazine (monthly) 250 Bloor St. E., Toronto, Ont. M4W 1G5—416/962-1242

CGA Magazine (9 times a year) #740, 1176 W. Georgia St., Vancouver, B.C. V6E 4A2 - 604/669-3555

CTM: The Human Element (6 times a year) #301, 542 Mt. Pleasant Rd., Toronto, Ont. M4S 2M7 — 416/483-9666

Canadian Association Executive (bi-monthly) Box 194, Stn. P, Toronto, Ont. M5S 2S7 — 416/961-1028

The Canadian Banker & ICB Review (bi-monthly) Box 282, Royal Trust Tower, Toronto-Dominion Centre, Toronto, Ont. M5K 1K2—416/362-6092

Canadian Business (monthly) #214, 56 The Esplanade, Toronto, Ont. M5E 1R5—416/364-4266

The Canadian Jaycee (bi-monthly) 39 Leacock Way, Kanata, Ont. K2K 1T1—613/592-2450

The Canadian Manager (5 times a year) 2175 Sheppard Ave. E., Ste. 110, Willowdale, Ont. M2J 1W8 — 416/491-0777

Caribbean Business News (monthly) #332, 111 Queen St. E., Toronto, Ont. M5C 1S2 - 416/368-6404

Commerce (monthly) 1080 Beaver Hall Hill, Montreal, P.Q. H2Z 1T1—514/866-1728

Commerce Alberta (6 times a year) 124 W. 8th St., North Vancouver, B.C. V7M 3H2 - 604/985-8711

Commerce B.C. (6 times a year) 124 W. 8th St., North Vancouver, B.C. V7M 3H2 - 604/985-8711

Commerce News (monthly) #600, 10123 99 St., Edmonton, Alta. T5J 3G9 — 403/426-4620
Commercial News (monthly) Ste. 400, 5251 Duke St., Halifax, N.S. B3J 1P3—902/422-6447
Consumer Power Package, 1450 Don Mills Rd., Don Mills, Ont. M3B 2X7—416/445-6641
Cost and Management (6 times a year) 154 Main St. E., Hamilton, Ont. L8N 1G9—416/525-4100
Digest Business & Law Journal (daily) 38 Dundas St. E., Toronto, Ont. M5B 1C4—416/363-0401
Directory of Directors (annually) 481 University Ave., Toronto, Ont. M5W 1A7—416/596-5573
Edmonton Commerce & Industry Report on Business (monthly) Ste. 215, 11802 124 St., Edmonton, Alta. T5L OM3—403/454-5540
Ensemble (bi-weekly) 2030 Blvd. Père Lelièvre, Quebec, P.Q. G1P 2X1—418/527-3467
Executive (monthly) 1450 Don Mills Rd., Don Mills, Ont. M3B 2X7—416/445-6641
Finance (weekly) #200, 381 Notre Dame W., Montreal, P.Q. H2Y 1V2 — 514/849-7709
The Financial Post (weekly) 481 University Ave., Toronto, Ont. M5W 1A7—416/596-5672
Financial Times of Canada (weekly) Ste. 500, 920 Yonge St., Toronto, Ont. M4W 3L5—416/922-1133
Gestion (4 times a year) #200B, 674 Place Publique, Ste-Dorothée, Laval, P.Q. H7X 1G1 — 514/689-2982
Globe and Mail Report on Business (daily) 444 Front St. W., Toronto, Ont. M5V 2S9 — 416/361-5411
Independent Business Forum (monthly) #1500, 1176 W. Georgia St., Vancouver, B.C. V6E 4A2 - 604/669-7208
Influential Business (6 times a year) #524, 470 Granville St., Vancouver, B.C. V6C 1V5 — 604/687-7070
Initiatives (4 times a year) Suite 206, 1380 Gilford, Montreal, P.Q. H2J 1R8—514/526-3309
International (quarterly) 2973 Weston Rd. (Box 1011, Stn. A, Weston, Ont. M9N 3R4)—416/741-1112
Investor's Digest of Canada (twice a month) 481 University Ave., Toronto, Ont. M5W 1A7—416/596-5664
Italian Chamber of Commerce Bulletin (quarterly) Suite 412, 1255 Phillips Sq., Montreal, P.Q. H3B 3G1—514/866-0070
Italy Canada Trade (quarterly) Suite 313, 159 Bay St., Toronto, Ont. M5J 1J7—416/364-6551
Le Magazine Affaires (10 times a year) #903, 465 St-Jean St., Montreal, P.Q. H2Y 3S4 - 514/842-6491
Magazine MBA (bi-monthly) #100-D, 1800 rue Bercy, Montreal, P.Q. H2K 4K5 - 514/526-3753
Manitoba Business (6 times a year) #201, 177 Lombard St. E., Winnipeg, Man. R3B OW5—204/944-1441
Manitoba Trade Directory (annually) 1077 St. James St. (Box 6900), Winnipeg, Man. R3C 3B1—204/775-0201
Middle East Directory & Information (annually) #204, 834 Yonge St., Toronto, Ont. M4W 2H1 - 416/922-0283
Northern Ontario Business (10 times a year) 31 Cedar St., Sudbury, Ont. P3E 1N3 - 705/673-5667
Ontario Business (monthly) 2323 Yonge St., Toronto, Ont. M4P 2C9 — 416/482-5222
Ontario Business News (10 times a year) 9th floor, Hearst Block, Queen's Park, Toronto, Ont. M7A 2E1 — 416/965-1576
Le Point (annually) 1080 Beaver Hall Hill, Montreal, P.Q. H2Z 1T1—514/866-1728
Regina Business Directory (annually) 1150 8th Ave., Regina, Sask. S4R 1C9 - 306/525-2304
Resource Development (6 times a year) Box 91760, West Vancouver, B.C. V7V 4S1 - 604/986-7361
Saskatchewan Business (8 times a year) #201, 177 Lombard St. E., Winnipeg, Man. R3B 3B1 — 204/944-1441
Saskatoon Business Directory (annually) 1150 8th Ave., Regina, Sask. S4R 1C9 - 306/525-2304
The Financial Post Survey of Industrials (annually) 481 University Ave., Toronto, Ont. M5W 1A7—416/596-5585
The Financial Post Survey of Markets (annually) 481 University Ave., Toronto, Ont. M5W 1A7—416/596-5585
Toronto Business Magazine (monthly) 105 Main St., Unionville, Ont. L3R 2G1—416/297-2922
Trade and Commerce (monthly) 1077 St. James St., Box 6900, Winnipeg, Man. R3C 3B1—204/775-0201
Trufax (10 times a year) 321 Bloor St. E., Toronto, Ont. M4W 3K6—416/961-0237
Financial Post Western Business (weekly) 481 University Ave., Toronto, Ont. M5W 1A7 - 416/596-5672
Western Ontario Business (eo Mon.) Box 7400, Stn. E, London, Ont. N5Y 4X3—519/472-7601

CERAMICS: Canadian Clay & Ceramics (bi-monthly) 2175 Sheppard Ave. E., Suite 110, Willowdale, Ont. M2J 1W8—416/491-0777

CHEMICALS, CHEMICAL PROCESSING: Canadian Chemical, Pharmaceutical & Product Directory (annually) #200, 6725 Darlington Ave., Montreal, P.Q. H3S 2J7 - 514/731-3524
Canadian Chemical Processing (every 6 weeks) 1450 Don Mills Rd., Don Mills, Ont. M3B 2X7—416/445-6641
Canadian Process Equipment & Control News (bi-monthly) 745 Mount Pleasant Rd., Toronto, Ont. M4S 2N5—416/481-6483
Chemical Buyers Guide (annually) 1450 Don Mills Rd., Don Mills, Ont. M3B 2X7—416/445-6641
Chemistry in Canada (monthly) Ste. 906, 151 Slater St., Ottawa, Ont. K1P 5H3—613/233-0075

CIVIL SERVICE: Civil Service Review (quarterly) 233 Gilmour St., Ottawa, Ont. K2P 0P1—613/236-9931
RA News (8 times a year) 2451 Riverside Dr., Ottawa, Ont. K1H 7X7—613/733-5100

CLOTHING, FURNISHINGS: Buyers Market (twice a year) 400, 259 Portage Ave. (Box 87, Winnipeg, Man. R3C 2G6)—204/942-6361
Canadian Apparel Manufacturer (quarterly) Ste. 307, 4920 de Maisonneuve Blvd. W., Montreal, P.Q. H3Z 1N1—514/487-2272
Canadian Clothing Journal (bi-monthly) #139, 67 Mowat Ave., Toronto, Ont. M6K 3E3—416/534-7158
Children's Apparel Merchandising Aids (quarterly) Suite 304, 8235 Mountain Sights Ave., Montreal, P.Q. H4P 2B4—514/731-7774
Ego (quarterly) Ste. 101, 5445 De Gaspé Ave., Montreal, P.Q. H2T 3B2—514/273-7274
Elan-Image (quarterly) 3484 Mountain St., Montreal, P.Q. H3G 2A6—514/288-9426
Men's Wear of Canada (monthly) 380 Wellington St. W., Toronto, Ont. M5V 1W3 - 416/366-4608
Style (monthly) 481 University Ave., Toronto, Ont. M5W 1A7—416/596-5754

COMMUNICATIONS: Communications Systems (4 times a year) 3535 Lakeshore Blvd. W., Toronto, Ont. M4W 1P4 - 416/255-4416

CONSTRUCTION: Alberta Construction (6 times a year) 1494 Regent Ave. W., Winnipeg, Man. R2C 3A8—204/224-2267
Construction Sightlines (6 times a year) 124 W. 8th St., North Vancouver, B.C. V7M 3H2 - 604/985-8711
Fraser's Construction & Building Directory (annually) 481 University Ave., Toronto, Ont. M5W 1A7—416/596-5086
Information-Construction (monthly) 5800 boul. L.H. Lafontaine, Anjou, P.Q. H1M 1S7 - 514/353-9960
Toronto Construction News (bi-monthly) #419, 720 Spadina Ave., Toronto, Ont. M5S 2T9 - 416/961-1028

CONTROLS & INSTRUMENTATION SYSTEMS: Canadian Controls & Instruments (monthly) 481 University Ave., Toronto, Ont. M5W 1A7—416/596-5960

CONVENTIONS: see also ADVERTISING
Canadian Industry Shows & Exhibitions (annually) 481 University Ave., Toronto, Ont. M5W 1A7 - 416/596-5890

COSMETICS: Beauty (6 times a year) 38 Wellington St. E., Toronto, Ont. M5E 1C7 — 416/363-9466
Cosmetics (bi-monthly) Ste. 201, 801 York Mills Rd., Don Mills, Ont. M3B 1X7—416/449-2304

CREDIT: The Atlantic Co-Operator (monthly) Box 1386, Antigonish, N.S. B2G 2L7—902/863-2776
Ontario Credit Union News (quarterly) 180 Duncan Mill Rd., Don Mills, Ont. M3B 3K3—416/441-2900

La Semaine Commerciale (weekly) Box 310, Stn. B, Quebec, P.Q. G1K 7B1—418/839-4388

DAIRY PRODUCTS: Modern Dairy (bi-monthly) #101, 702 Weston Rd., Toronto, Ont. M6N 3R2—416/766-8390

DATA PROCESSING: CIPS Review (6 times a year) 243 College St., 5th floor, Toronto, Ont. M5T 2Y1 — 416/593-4040

Canadian Computer Census (annually) 5th floor, 243 College St., Toronto, Ont. M5T 2Y1 — 416/593-4040

Canadian Datasystems (monthly) 481 University Ave., Toronto, Ont. M5W 1A7—416/596-5919

Computer Data (monthly) #1201, 55 Bloor St. W., Toronto, Ont. M4W 3K2 - 416/967-6200

Computing Canada (26 times a year) Ste. 106, 211 Consumers Rd., Willowdale, Ont. M2J 4G8—416/497-9562

Data Product News (4 times a year) 481 University Ave., Toronto, Ont. M5W 1A7 — 416/596-5919

Info Carrières (semi-monthly) 254 ave. Bloomfield, Outremont, P.Q. H2V 3R4 - 514/270-5481

Info Digest (annually) see Info Carrières

Info Mag (4 times a year) see Info Carrières

Informatique et Bureautique (monthly) 7045 Park Ave., #100, Montreal, P.Q. H3N 1X7 - 514/276-4211

Informatique Québec (monthly) 254 Ave. Bloomfield, Montreal, P.Q. H2V 3R4 — 514/270-4795

DENTISTRY: Canadian Dental Management (monthly) #200, 6725 Darlington Ave., Montreal, P.Q. H3S 2J7 - 514/731-3524

Canadian Dental Nurses & Assistants Association Journal (quarterly) 1009 2nd Ave. S., Box 516, Lethbridge, Alta. T1J 3Z4

Dental Guide (annually) 1450 Don Mills Rd., Don Mills, Ont. M3B 2X7—416/445-6641

Journal Dentaire du Quebec (monthly) 601 Côte Vertu, St-Laurent, P.Q. H4L 1X8 - 514/748-6561

The Journal of the Canadian Dental Association (monthly) 1815 Alta Vista Dr., Ottawa, Ont. K1G 3Y6—613/523-1770

Ontario Dentist (monthly) 1450 Don Mills Rd., Don Mills, Ont. M3B 2X7 - 416/445-7101

Oral Health (monthly) 1450 Don Mills Rd., Don Mills, Ont. M3B 2X7—416/445-6641

DEPARTMENT, CHAIN STORES: Volume Retail Merchandising (monthly) Ste. 501, 32 Front St. W., Toronto, Ont. M5J 2H9—416/869-1735

DRUGS: The Canadian Journal of Hospital Pharmacy (bi-monthly) University Hospital, Saskatoon, Sask. S7N 0W8—306/343-2898

Canadian Journal of Pharmaceutical Sciences (quarterly) #104, 1815 Alta Vista Dr., Ottawa, Ont. K1G 3Y6 - 613/523-7877

Canadian Pharmaceutical Journal (monthly) #104, 1815 Alta Vista Dr., Ottawa, Ont. K1G 3Y6 - 613/523-7877

Drug Merchandising (monthly) 481 University Ave., Toronto, Ont. M5W 1A7—416/596-5736

Le Pharmacien (monthly) 481 University Ave., Toronto, Ont. M5W 1A7—416/596-5736

Québec Pharmacie (monthly) 5115 rue St-Denis, Montreal, P.Q. H2J 2M1 - 514/273-0644

EDUCATION: The ATA Magazine (4 times a year) 11010 142nd St., Edmonton, Alta. T5N 2R1—403/453-2411

The Alberta School Trustee (6 times a year) 12310 105 Ave., Edmonton, Alta. T5N OY4—403/482-7311

The B.C. Teacher (5 times a year) Suite 105, 2235 Burrard St., Vancouver, B.C. V6J 3H9—604/731-8121

The CAUT/ACPU Bulletin (7 times a year) 75 Albert St., Ottawa, Ont. K1P 5E7—613/237-6885

Canadian Journal of Education (4 times a year) c/o Faculty of Education, University of B.C., Vancouver, B.C. V6T 1Z5 - 604/228-3595

Canadian Teacher (5 times a year) Box 102, Stn. R, Toronto, Ont.—416/499-1061

Canadian Vocational Journal (quarterly) Suite 608, 251 Bank St., Ottawa, Ont. K2P 1X3—613/232-1028

College Canada (8 times a year) Ste. 203, 211 Consumers Rd., Willowdale, Ont. M2J 4G8—416/497-7361

Educational Digest (bi-monthly) 481 University Ave., Toronto, Ont. M5W 1A7—416/596-5884

Les Enseignants (monthly) 767 Demers St., Saint Jean, P.Q. J3B 4W1—514/348-8718

Ligne Directe (6 times a year) 2336 Chemin Ste-Foy, Sainte-Foy, P.Q. G1V 1S5—418/658-5711

The Manitoba Teacher (monthly) 191 Harcourt St., Winnipeg, Man. R3J 3H2—204/888-7961

Ontario Education (5 times a year) Suite 303, 4195 Dundas St. W., Toronto, Ont. M8X 1Y4—416/239-1101

Orbit (5 times a year) 252 Bloor St. W., Toronto, Ont. M5S 1V6—416/923-6641

OSSTF Forum (5 times a year) 60 Mobile Dr., Toronto, Ont. M4A 2P3—416/751-8300

OTF Interaction (4 times a year) Ste. 700, 1260 Bay St., Toronto, Ont. M5R 2B5—416/966-3424

P.A.C.T. (monthly) 1880 Centre St., Montreal, P.Q. H3K 1H9 - 514/932-1454

Quebec Home & School News (5 times a year) 4795 St. Catherine St. W., Montreal, P.Q. H3Z 1S8—514/933-3664

The Reporter (monthly) 1260 Bay St., 6th floor, Toronto, Ont. M5R 2B4—416/925-2493

Resourcebook (annually) 425 University Ave., 6th Floor, Toronto, Ont. M5G 1T6 - 416/596-5014

La Revue Information (monthly) #100, 7855 boul. L.H. Lafontaine, Anjou, P.Q. H1K 4E4 - 514/353-7511

The School Trustee (5 times a year) #400, 2222 13th Ave., Regina, Sask. S4P 3M7—306/569-0750

The Sentinel (monthly) 84J Brunswick Blvd., Dollard des Ormeaux, P.Q. H9B 2C5—514/683-9330

Short Courses & Seminars (twice a year) Box 84, Stn. A, Willowdale, Ont. M2N 5S7—416/636-2230

This Magazine (bi-monthly) 70 The Esplanade, Toronto, Ont. —416/364-2431

ELECTRICAL EQUIPMENT: CEDA-Current (bi-monthly) Ste. 201, 20 Holly St., Toronto, Ont. M4S 2E8—416/487-3461

Electrical Blue Book (annually) Ste. 405, 20 Holly St., Toronto, Ont. M4S 2E8—416/487-3461

Electrical Business (monthly) Ste. 405, 20 Holly St., Toronto, Ont, M4S 2E8—416/487-3461

Electrical Contractor & Maintenance Supervisor (monthly) 481 University Ave., Toronto, Ont. M5W 1A7—416/596-5727

Electrical Equipment News (monthly) 1450 Don Mills Rd., Don Mills, Ont. M3B 2X7—416/445-6641

Le Maitre Electricien (monthly) Ste. 209, 7333 Desroserais St., Anjou, P.Q. H1M 2X6—514/353-9830

Le Monde de L'Electricité (monthly) 20 Holly St., Ste. 405, Toronto, Ont. M4S 2E8—416/487-3461

Le Repertoire des produits electriques (annually) #405, 20 Holly St., Toronto, Ont. M4S 2E6 — 416/487-3461

TCEM Showguide (annually) #405, 20 Holly St., Toronto, Ont. M4S 2E6 — 416/487-3461

ELECTRONICS: Canadian CES Journal (monthly) Box 569, Don Mills, Ont. M3C 2T6—416/444-7054

Canadian Electronics Engineering (monthly) 481 University Ave., Toronto, Ont. M5W 1A7—416/596-5727

CEE Electronics Directory & Buyers' Guide (annually) 481 University Ave., Toronto, Ont. M5W 1A7—416/596-5727

EIC (Electronique, Industrielle et Commerciale) (quarterly) 50 Aubin St., Repentigny, P.Q. J6A 1M7 — 514/581-1494

Electronic Procurement Index for Canada (annually) 1450 Don Mills Rd., Don Mills, Ont. M3B 2X7—416/445-6641

Electronic Products & Technology (6 times a year) 3535 Lakeshore Blvd. W., Toronto, Ont. M8W 1P4 — 416/255-4416

Electronics & Communications (bi-monthly) 1450 Don Mills Rd., Don Mills, Ont. M3B 2X7—416/445-6641

Electronics Today, see Consumer Magazines

Micros (monthly) 583 Ellice Ave., Winnipeg, Man. R3B 1Z7 - 204/783-7064

ENERGY: See also SCIENCE etc

Energy Management Canada (6 times a year) 3535 Lakeshore Blvd. W., Toronto, Ont. M8W 1P4 — 416/255-4416

ENGINEERING: The B.C. Professional Engineer (monthly) 1201 Melville St., Vancouver, B.C. V6E 2X9 —604/685-3241

B.C. Technologist (4 times a year) #203, 4400 Dominion St., Burnaby, B.C. V5G 4G3 — 604/433-0548

Canadian Consulting Engineer (monthly) 1450 Don Mills Rd., Don Mills, Ont. M3B 2X7—416/445-6641
Dimensions (6 times a year) 1027 Yonge St., Toronto, Ont. M4W 3E5 - 416/961-1100
Engineering (every 4 weeks) 1300 Bay St., Toronto, Ont. M5R 3K8 - 416/928-0500
Engineering Digest (10 times a year) Ste. 501, 32 Front St. W., Toronto, Ont. M5J 2H9—416/869-1735
Engineering Journal (6 times a year) 1450 Don Mills Rd., Don Mills, Ont. M3B 2X7 — 416/445-7101
L'Ingenieur (bi-monthly) Box 6079, Stn. A, Montreal, P.Q. H3C 3A7—514/344-4764
Ontario Technologist (6 times a year) #253, 40 Orchard View Blvd., Toronto, Ont. M4R 2G1 - 416/488-1175
Plan (monthly) Ste. 1100, 2075 University St., Montreal, P.Q. H3A 1K8—514/845-6141

ENGINEERING CONSTRUCTION: Alberta Construction Industry Directory/Purchasing Guide (annually) Ste. 406, 315 10th Ave. S.E., Calgary, Alta. T2G OW2—403/265-4750
British Columbia Construction Industry Directory (annually) 4411 208th St., Langley, B.C. V3H 2H7 - 604/534-3643
Canadian Contractors Equipment Magazine (monthly) Ste. 108, 215 Morrish Rd., West Hill, Ont. M1C 1E9—416/284-0231
The Canadian Surveyor (4 times a year) Box 5378, Stn. F, Ottawa, Ont. K2C 3J1 — 613/224-9851
Central Ontario Construction Industry Directory, see Construction Industry Directory, below
Construction Alberta News (Mon. & Wed.) Ste. 220, 11 Fairway Dr., Edmonton, Alta. T6J 2W4—403/436-6970
Construction Industry Directory/Purchasing Guide (annually) Box 6900, 1077 St. James St., Winnipeg, Man. R3C 3B1—204/775-0201 (separate guides for: Eastern Ontario; Central Ontario; Manitoba; Northern Ontario; Northwestern Ontario; Ontario Golden Horseshoe; Saskatchewan; South Central Ontario; Southwestern Ontario; Toronto & Area)
Construction West (monthly) 2000 W. 12th Ave., Vancouver, B.C. V6J 2G2—604/731-1171
Daily Commercial News and Construction Record (daily) 34 St. Patrick St., Toronto, Ont. M5T 1V1—416/598-2222
Engineering and Contract Record (monthly) 1450 Don Mills Rd., Don Mills, Ont. M3B 2X7—416/445-6641
Equipment Journal (every 3 weeks) Ste. 36, 150 Lakeshore W., Mississauga, Ont. L5H 3R2—416/274-4883
Equipment Trader (every 2 weeks) Blairmore, Alta. (Box 1320, Fernie, B.C. VOB 1MO)—604/423-4561
Génie-Construction (monthly) Suite 201, 310 Victoria Ave., Montreal, P.Q. H3Z 2M9—514/487-2302
Heavy Construction News (bi-weekly) 481 University Ave., Toronto, Ont. M5W 1A7—416/596-5840
In-Site (monthly) Ste. 220, 11 Fairway Dr., Edmonton, Alta. T6J 2W4—403/436-6970
Journal of Commerce (twice weekly) 2000 W. 12th Ave., Vancouver, B.C. V6J 2G2—604/731-1171
Journal Constructo (twice a week) Ste. 70A, 100 Montarville, Box 280, Boucherville, P.Q. J4B 5J6—514/655-3880
Machinerie Lourde (monthly) 245 Lindsay St., Drummondville, P.Q. J2C 1P2—819/477-6811
Mart (monthly) #202, 6841 St. Hubert, Montreal, P.Q. H2S 2M8 — 514/273-7261
Northpoint (quarterly) 6070 Yonge St., Willowdale, Ont. M2M 3Z6—416/222-5481
The Ontario Construction Guide (annually) #405, 20 Holly St., Toronto, Ont. M4S 2E6 — 416/487-3461
The Ontario Land Surveyor (quarterly) 6070 Yonge St., Willowdale, Ont. M2M 3Z3 — 416/222-5482
Quebec Construction (weekly) #903, 465 St-Jean St., Montreal, P.Q. H2Y 3S4 - 514/842-6491
Supply Post (monthly) Box 46619, Stn. G, Vancouver, B.C. V6R 4G8 - 604/263-0312

EXPORTS: Canadian Exporter (quarterly) Unit 3, 2000 Ellesmere Rd., Scarborough, Ont. M1H 2W4 — 416/438-1153
Export Canada (annually) Box 1048, Stn. A, Surrey, B.C. V3S 4P5—604/596-9426

FARM IMPLEMENTS: Farm Equipment Quarterly (quarterly) Box 1060, Exeter, Ont. NOM 1SO—519/235-2400

FARM SUPPLIES, FEEDS & MILLING: Feed & Farm Supply Dealer (bi-monthly) 1077 St. James St., Box 6900, Winnipeg, Man. R3C 3B1—204/775-0201
Le Meunier Quebecois (monthly) 915 St-Cyrille Blvd., Quebec, P.Q. G1S 1T7—418/688-9227

FINANCIAL (see also BUSINESS): Benefits Canada (bi-monthly) 481 University Ave., Toronto, Ont. M5W 1A7—416/596-5919
The Financial Post (weekly) 481 University Ave., Toronto, Ont. M5W 1A7—416/596-5649

FIRE PROTECTION: The Canadian Firefighter (bi-monthly) Box 37, Stn. M, Toronto, Ont. M6S 4T2—416/233-2516
Firefighting in Canada (bi-monthly) 222 Argyle Ave., Delhi, Ont. N4B 2Y2—519/582-2510

FISHERIES: Canadian Fisherman & Ocean Science (monthly) #200, 6725 Darlington Ave., Montreal, P.Q. H3S 2J7 - 514/731-3524
Canadian Fishing Report (monthly) Box 818, Stn. B, Ottawa, Ont. K1P 5P9 — 613/232-5204
The Fisherman (twice a month) 138 E. Cordova St., Vancouver, B.C. V6A 1K9 — 604/683-9655
The Sou'Wester (bi-weekly) Box 128, 2 Second St., Yarmouth, N.S.—902/742-7111
Western Fisheries (monthly) Ste. 202, 1132 Hamilton St., Vancouver, B.C. V6B 2S2—604/687-1581

FLOOR COVERINGS: Floor Covering News (monthly) 481 University Ave., Toronto, Ont. M5W 1A7—416/596-5942

FLORISTS: Canadian Florist, Greenhouse & Nursery (monthly) 1090 Aerowood Dr., Unit #1, Mississauga, Ont. L4W 1B7 — 416/828-6896
United Florists of Canada Membership Journal & Directory (4 times a year) 350 Bay St., Toronto, Ont. M5H 3N9 — 416/368-6121

FOOD & FOOD PROCESSING: Canadian Food & Packaging Directory (annually) #200, 6725 Darlington Ave., Montreal, P.Q. H3S 2J7 - 514/731-3524
Canadian Institute of Food Science & Technology Journal (quarterly) #104, 150 Consumers Rd., Willowdale, Ont. M2J 1P9
Focus on Food Service (monthly) 2425 Truscott Dr., Mississauga, Ont. L5J 2B4 - 416/823-7350
Food in Canada (monthly) 481 University Ave., Toronto, Ont. M5W 1A7—416/596-5876

FOOTWEAR: Canadian Footwear Journal (9 times a year) 1450 Don Mills Rd., Don Mills, Ont. M3B 2X7—416/445-6641
Footwear Forum (monthly) #307, 85 Scarsdale Rd., Don Mills, Ont. M3B 2R2 - 416/447-7263

FOREST & LUMBER INDUSTRIES: "ABC" British Columbia Lumber Trade Directory & Year Book (biennially) 355 Burrard St., Marine Bldg., Vancouver, B.C. V6C 2G6—604/685-4385
British Columbia Lumberman (monthly) 2000 W. 12th Ave., Vancouver, B.C. V6J 4M8—604/731-1171
Canadian Forest Industries (monthly) 1450 Don Mills Rd., Don Mills, Ont. M3B 2X7—416/445-6641
Canadian Pulp & Paper Industry (6 times a year) 481 University Ave., Toronto, Ont. M5W 1A7—416/596-5829
The Forestry Chronicle (bi-monthly) Box 5000, Macdonald College, P.Q. HOA 1CO—514/457-9131
Forêt-Conservation (monthly) 915 St. Cyrille St. W., Ste. 210, Quebec, P.Q. G1S 1T8—418/681-3588
Hiballer Forest Magazine (monthly) #202, 4455 Juneau St., Burnaby, B.C. V5C 4C4 - 604/294-6341
Journal of Logging (monthly) #260, 10691 Shellbridge Way, Richmond, B.C. V6X 2W8—604/270-8981
N.B. Farm & Forest, see Farm Publications
Operations Forestières et de Scierie (monthly) Room 201, 310 Victoria Ave., Montreal, P.Q. H3Z 2M9—514/487-2302
The Truck Logger (monthly) 124 W. 8th St., North Vancouver, B.C. V7M 3H2 - 604/985-8711

FUNERAL SERVICE: Canadian Funeral Director (monthly) Suite 5, 1658 Victoria Park Ave., Scarborough, Ont. M1R 1P7—416/755-7050

Canadian Funeral News (monthly) #105, 2116 27th Ave. N.E., Calgary, Alta. T2E 7A6—403/230-2155

FUR TRADE: Fur Trade Journal (incorporating Maritime Fur Breeder; Canadian Fur; Fur of Canada; American Fur Breeder) (monthly) The Clay Publishing Co., Bewdley, Ont. K0L 1E0 —416/797-2281

FURNITURE, HOME FURNISHINGS: Canadian Furniture & Furnishings Directory (annually) #200, 6725 Darlington Ave., Montreal, P.Q. H3S 2J7 – 514/731-3524

Decormag, see Consumer Magazines

Furniture & Furnishings Magazine (monthly) 380 Wellington St. W., Toronto, Ont. M5V 1E3—416/366-4608

Furniture Production & Design/Meubles (bi-monthly) #200, 6725 Darlington Ave., Montreal, P.Q. H3S 2J7 – 514/731-3524

Furniture Retailer (6 times a year) #200, 6725 Darlington Ave., Montreal, P.Q. H3S 2J7 – 514/731-3524

GARDEN SUPPLIES: See also LANDSCAPING

Jardins et Pelouses (3 times a year) #221, 3414 Park Ave., Montreal, P.Q. H2X 2H5 — 514/282-0191

Lawn & Garden Trade (6 times a year) Ste. 221, 3414 Park Ave., Montreal, P.Q. H2X 2H5—514/282-0191

GAS (see also PETROLEUM): Propane/Canada (6 times a year) Ste. 406, 315 10th Ave. S.E., Calgary, Alta. T2G 0W2—403/265-4750

GENERAL RETAIL TRADE: Canadian Distributor & Retailer, see GROCERY TRADE

Shopping Centre Canada (5 times a year) 481 University Ave., Toronto, Ont. M5W 1A7 — 416/596-5251

GIFTS: see also JEWELLERY

Gift Magazine (6 times a year) 380 Wellington St. W., Toronto, Ont. M5V 1E3 – 416/366-4608

Gifts & Tablewares (6 times a year) 1450 Don Mills Rd., Don Mills, Ont. M3B 2X7—416/445-6641

GOVERNMENT: B.C. Municipal Year Book (annually) Box 46475, Stn. G, Vancouver, B.C. V6R 4G7 – 604/228-9213

Civic Public Works (monthly) 481 University Ave., Toronto, Ont. M5W 1A7—416/596-5955

Government Purchasing Guide (bi-monthly) Suite 706, 43 Eglinton Ave. E., Toronto, Ont. M4P 1A2—416/483-8767

Municipal World (monthly) Box 399, 360 Talbot St., St. Thomas, Ont. N5P 3V3—519/633-0031

Nato Review (bi-monthly) Public Relations Division, Dept. of External Affairs, Pearson Bldg., 125 Sussex Dr., Ottawa, Ont. K1A 0G2

La Revue Municipale (monthly) Ste. 203, 6841 St-Hubert, Montreal, P.Q. H2S 2M8—514/273-7217

Towns & Cities Magazine (quarterly) #200, 6725 Darlington Ave., Montreal, P.Q. H3S 2J7 – 514/731-3524

Western Municipal Product News (3 times a year) Box 3512, Stn. B, Calgary, Alta. T2M 4M2 – 403/288-9375

GROCERY TRADE: L'Alimentation au Quebec (monthly) 7160 Boul Pie IX, Montreal, P.Q. H2A 2G4—514/729-2874

Canadian Distributor & Retailer (monthly) #7, 880 Decarie Blvd., St. Laurent, P.Q. H4L 3L9 — 514/744-4518

Canadian Grocer (monthly) 481 University Ave., Toronto, Ont. M5W 1A7—416/596-5762

L'epicier (monthly) 625 President Kennedy Ave., Montreal, P.Q. H3A 1K5—514/845-5141

Western Grocer (bi-monthly) 200, 633 Portage Ave., Winnipeg, Man. R3B 2Z9—204/775-0387

HARDWARE TRADE: Canadian Hardware, Electrical & Building Supply Directory (annually) #200, 6725 Darlington Ave., Montreal, P.Q. H3S 2J7 – 514/731-3524

Canadian Hardware-Housewares Retailing (monthly) #200, 6725 Darlington Ave., Montreal, P.Q. H3S 2J7 – 514/731-3524

Centre (8 times a year) Unit 3, 2000 Ellesmere Rd., Scarborough, Ont. M1H 2W4—416/438-1153

Hardware Merchandising (monthly) 481 University Ave., Toronto, Ont. M5W 1A7—416/596-5799

Quincaillerie-Matériaux (monthly) 481 University Ave., Toronto, Ont. M5W 1A7—416/596-5799

HEATING, PLUMBING, AIR CONDITIONING: Canadian Woodstove & Fireplace Retailer (annually) #221, 8414 Park Ave., Montreal, P.Q. H2X 2H5 – 514/282-0191

Environment Systems Industries (monthly) 109 Vanderhoof Ave., Toronto, Ont. M4G 2J2—416/425-9021

Heating, Plumbing, Air Conditioning (monthly) 1450 Don Mills Rd., Don Mills, Ont. M3B 2X7—416/445-6641

Heating, Plumbing, Air Conditioning Buyers' Guide (annually) 1450 Don Mills Rd., Don Mills, Ont. M3B 2X7—416/445-6641

Plomberie-Chauffage et Climatisation (monthly) Ste. 201, 310 Victoria Ave., Montreal, P.Q. H3Z 2M9—514/487-2302

HOSPITALS, HEALTH CARE: Administration Hospitalière et Sociale (6 times a year) 8 St-Joseph Blvd. E., Montreal, P.Q. H2T 1G8—514/849-6961

The Alternate Review (bi-monthly) Box 2430, Stn. A, Oshawa, Ont. L1H 7V6 – 416/571-0332

Canadian Health Record Association Recorder (5 times a year) 187 King St. E., Oshawa, Ont. L1H 1C3—416/728-9743

Canadian Hospital Directory (annually) 25 Imperial St., Toronto, Ont. M5P 1C1—416/481-2244

Canadian Journal of Medical Technology (4 times a year) Box 830, Hamilton, Ont. L8N 3N8—416/528-8642

Catholic Health Association of Canada Review (bi-monthly) 312 Daly Ave., Ottawa, Ont. K1N 6G7—613/238-8471

Dimensions in Health Service (monthly) 25 Imperial St., Toronto, Ont. M5P 1C1—416/481-2244

Health Care (monthly) 1450 Don Mills Rd., Don Mills, Ont. M3B 2X7—416/445-6641

Health Care Digest (bi-monthly) 1450 Don Mills Rd., Don Mills, Ont. M3B 2X7—416/445-6641

Hospital Trustee (bi-monthly) 25 Imperial St., Toronto, Ont. M5P 1C1—416/481-2244

Respiratory Technology (6 times a year) 146 Corbett Dr., Winnipeg, Man. R2Y 1V2 – 204/889-4901

Techno-Information (bi-monthly) 1150 St-Joseph Blvd. E., Montreal, P.Q. H2J 1L5

HOTELS, RESTAURANTS: Barrique et Marmite (monthly) 2949 Soissons, Montreal, P.Q. H3S 1W1—514/733-5288

Beverage Alcohol Reporter (monthly) Ste. 2, 130 Willowdale Ave., Willowdale, Ont. M2N 4Y2—416/222-2557

Beverage Canada (7 times a year) Ste. 204, 5200 Dixie Rd., Mississauga, Ont. L4W 1E4—416/625-5277

B.C. Hotelman (monthly) 124 W. 8th St., North Vancouver, B.C. V7M 3H2 – 604/985-8711

Canadian Hospitality (monthly) 124 W. 8th St., North Vancouver, B.C. V7M 3H2 – 604/985-8711

Canadian Hotel & Restaurant (monthly) 481 University Ave., Toronto, Ont. M5W 1A7—416/596-5782

Canadian Hotel & Restaurant's "Hotel/Motel Lodging" (monthly) 481 University Ave., Toronto, Ont. M5W 1A7—416/596-5782

The Canadian Inn Business (6 times a year) 108 Harvard Rd., Guelph, Ont. N1G 2Z2 – 416/494-4644

Foodservice & Hospitality (9 times a year) 85 Bloor St. E., #405, Toronto, Ont. M4W 1A9—416/923-8888

Frozen Foods/Canada (annually) 481 University Ave., Toronto, Ont. M5W 1A7—416/596-5782

L'Hospitalité (quarterly) 481 University Ave., Toronto, Ont. M5W 1A7—416/596-5782

Hôtellerie Restauration (10 times a year) Suite 410, 1500 Stanley St., Montreal, P.Q. H3A 1R3—514/843-4953

Ontario Innkeeper (bi-monthly) 1494 Regent Ave. W., Winnipeg, Man. R2C 3A8—204/224-2267

Prairie Hotelman (monthly) 1494 Regent Ave. W., Winnipeg, Man. R2C 3A8—204/224-2267

TIANS – The Traveller & Travel Industry Reporter (monthly) Box 128, Yarmouth, N.S. B5A 4B1 – 902/742-7111

Wrigley's Hotel-Motel Directory (annually) 7385 Laburnum St., Vancouver, B.C. V6P 5N2—604/261-2300

INDUSTRIAL (See also BUSINESS, and PURCHASING): Byers National Industrial Directory (annually) 1885 Wilson Ave., Weston, Ont. M9M 1A2—416/741-2827

Canadian Engineering & Industrial Year Book (annually) #200, 6725 Darlington Ave., Montreal, P.Q. H3S 2J7 - 514/731-3524

Canadian Industrial Equipment News (monthly) 1450 Don Mills Rd., Don Mills, Ont. M3B 2X7—416/445-6641

Industrial Management (10 times a year) 1289 Marlborough Crt., Oakville, Ont. L6H 2R9—416/842-2884

Industrial Product Ideas (6 times a year) 481 University Ave., Toronto, Ont. M5W 1A7—416/596-5819

Maintenance Engineering Management (7 times a year) 1289 Marlborough Crt., Oakville, Ont. L6H 2R9—416/842-2884

Market (monthly) Box 5355, Stn. A, Toronto, Ont. M5W 1N6 — 416/979-2082

Modern Power & Engineering (monthly) 481 University Ave., Toronto, Ont. M5W 1A7—416/596-5712

National Factory & Equipment News (bi-monthly) 150 Milner Ave., Unit 11, Scarborough, Ont. M1S 3R3 - 416/298-3488

New Equipment News (monthly) Ste. 501, 32 Front St. W., Toronto, Ont. M5J 2H9—416/869-1735

Ontario Industrial Magazine (monthly) Unit 11, 150 Milner Ave., Scarboro, Ont. M1S 3R3—416/298-3488

Plant Digest (bi-monthly) 335 Lesmill Rd., Don Mills, Ont. M3B 2V1 — 416/444-1179

Plant Management & Engineering (monthly) 481 University Ave., Toronto, Ont. M5W 1A7—416/596-5787

Produits Pour L'Industrie Quebecoise (bi-monthly) 3860 Côte Vertu #220, St-Laurent, P.Q. H4R 1V4—514/337-2177

Le Quebec Industriel (monthly) 625 President Kennedy Ave., Montreal, P.Q. H3A 1K5—514/845-5141

Shop (monthly) 1450 Don Mills Rd., Don Mills, Ont. M3B 2X7 —416/445-6641

INDUSTRIAL SAFETY: Canadian Occupational Safety (bi-monthly) 222 Argyle Ave., Delhi, Ont. N4B 2Y2—519/582-2510

Prevention (monthly) #812, 50 Place Cremazie, Montreal, P.Q. H2P 2T5 - 514/389-8295

INSTITUTIONS: Canadian Home Economics Journal (quarterly) #203, 151 Slater St., Ottawa, Ont. K1P 5H3—613/232-9791

Guide Des Institutions Joncas, Joncas Institutional Guide (annually) 250 Faillon W., Montreal, P.Q. H2R 2V7—514/274-3541

Journal of the Canadian Dietetic Association (quarterly) Ste. 214, 7 Pleasant Blvd., Toronto, Ont. M4T 1K2—416/925-2225

INSURANCE: Alberta Insurance Directory (annually) Box 35070, Stn. E, Vancouver, B.C. V6M 4G1 - 604/681-4531

The B.C. Agent (6 times a year) Box 35070, Stn. E, Vancouver, B.C. V6M 4G1—604/681-4531

British Columbia Insurance Directory (annually) Box 35466, Stn. E, Vancouver, B.C. V6M 4G8—604/681-4531

Canadian Insurance (monthly) 100 Simcoe St., Toronto, Ont. M5H 3G2—416/593-1310

Canadian Insurance Claims Directory (annually) Univ. of Toronto Press, Front Campus, Toronto, Ont. M5S 1A6

Canadian Journal of Life Insurance (6 times a year) Box 365, Elmira, Ont. N3B 2Z7 — 519/669-2693

Canadian Risk Management & Business Insurance (bi-monthly) Suite 101, 109 Vanderhoof Ave., Toronto, Ont. M4G 2J2—416/425-9021

Canadian Underwriter (monthly) Suite 101, 109 Vanderhoof Ave., Toronto, Ont. M4G 2J2—416/425-9021

Corporate Insurance in Canada (annually) 100 Simcoe St., Toronto, Ont. M5H 3G2—416/593-1310

General Insurance Register (annually) 100 Simcoe St., Toronto, Ont. M5H 3G2—416/593-1310

The Insurance Marketer (annually) Suite 101, 109 Vanderhoof Ave., Toronto, Ont. M4G 2J2—416/425-9021

LUAC Forum (monthly) Life Underwriters Association, 41 Lesmill Rd., Don Mills, Ont. M3B 2T3—416/444-5251

Regards (bi-monthly) C.P. 985, Tour Cité Branch, Montreal, P.Q. H2W 2N1 - 514/842-2591

Risk, see Canadian Risk Management, above

Toronto Insurance Directory (annually) #101, 109 Vanderhoof Ave., Toronto, Ont. M4G 2J2 — 416/425-9021

INTERIOR DESIGN & DECOR (See also ARCHITECTURE): Canadian Interiors (monthly) 481 University Ave., Toronto, Ont. M5W 1A7—416/596-5869

The Designer (annually) 1450 Don Mills Rd., Don Mills, Ont. M3B 2X7—416/445-6641

JEWELLERY & GIFTWARE: Bijou (monthly) Suite 205, 2950 Masson St. E., Montreal, P.Q. H1Y 1X4—514/728-3685

Canadian Jeweller (monthly) 481 University Ave., Toronto, Ont. M5W 1A7—416/596-5863

Canadian Jewellery & Giftware Directory (annually) #200, 6725 Darlington Ave., Montreal, P.Q. H3S 2J7 - 514/731-3524

Gift Magazine, see GIFTS

Jewellery World (bi-monthly) 33 Marmot St., Toronto, Ont. M4S 2T4—416/488-5803

JOURNALISM: Content (bi-monthly) 91 Raglan Ave., Toronto, Ont. M6C 2K7—416/651-7733

Press Review (quarterly) Box 368, Stn. A, Toronto, Ont. M5W 3X1—416/368-0512

LANDSCAPING: Gardenland (monthly) Stupple & Buttenham, R.R. 2, Hamilton, Ont. L8N 2Z7—416/689-4640

Landscape Ontario (5 times a year) #103, 3034 Palstan Rd., Mississauga, Ont. L4Y 2Z6—416/276-6177

Landscape Trades (6 times a year) #103, 3034 Palstan Rd., Mississauga, Ont. L4Y 2Z6 — 416/276-6177

LAUNDRY, DRY CLEANING: Canadian Cleaner & Launderer (bi-monthly) Room 307, 4920 de Maisonneuve Blvd. W., Montreal, P.Q. H3Z 1N1—514/487-2272

Cleantario (6 times a year) #1, 16A Wyndham St., Guelph, Ont. N1H 4E5 - 514/836-6183

LEATHER: Canadian Footwear & Leather Directory (annually) #200, 6725 Darlington Ave., Montreal, P.Q. H3S 2J7 - 514/731-3524

Luggage & Leather Goods News (9 times a year) 380 Wellington St. W., Toronto, Ont. M5V 1E3—416/366-4608

LEGAL: The Advocate (bi-monthly) 4765 Pilot House Rd., West Vancouver, B.C. V7W 1J2

Annuaire Téléphonique Judiciaire du Quebec (annually) Ste. 2302, 1115 Sherbrooke St. W., Montreal, P.Q. H3A 1H3—514/288-4124

Canadian Bar Review (quarterly) Canadian Bar Association, 130 Albert St., Ottawa, Ont. K1P 5G4 — 613/237-2925

Canadian Lawyer (6 times a year) #401, 56 The Esplanade, Toronto, Ont. M5E 1A7 - 416/368-7746

Chitty's Law Journal (monthly) 620 Sheppard Ave. W., Downsview, Ont. M3H 2S1—416/630-6952

Family Law Review (4 times a year) 620 Sheppard Ave. W., Downsview, Ont. M3H 2S1—416/630-6952

Legal Medical Quarterly (4 times a year) 620 Sheppard Ave. W., Downsview, Ont. M3H 2S1—416/630-6952

National (monthly) Canadian Bar Association, Ste. 1700, 130 Albert St., Ottawa, Ont. K1P 5G4—613/237-2925

The Ontario Reports (weekly except Aug.) 240 Edward St., Aurora, Ont. L4G 3S9 - 416/859-3880

La Revue du Notariat (5 times a year) Box 130, Outremont, P.Q. H2V 4M8

Toronto Legal Directory (annually) Univ. of Toronto Press, Front Campus, Toronto, Ont. M5S 1A6

LITERARY (See also Consumer Magazines): Canadian Author & Bookman (quarterly) 24 Ryerson Ave., Toronto, Ont. M5T 2P3 — 416/868-6916

Canadian Library Journal (bi-monthly) 151 Sparks St., Ottawa, Ont. K1P 5E3

Dalhousie Review (quarterly) Dalhousie University, Halifax, N.S. B3H 4H8

MANUFACTURING: see TRADE

MARKETING: See ADVERTISING

MATERIALS HANDLING & DISTRIBUTION: Materials Handling Handbook & Directory of Buying Sources (annually) 481 University Ave., Toronto, Ont. M5W 1A7—416/596-5708

Materials Management & Distribution (monthly) 481 University Ave., Toronto, Ont. M5W 1A7—416/596-5708

MEDICAL: (see also HOSPITALS)

L'Actualité Médicale (eo week) #324, 50 Place Cremazie, Montreal, P.Q. H2P 2S9 - 514/381-9308

Annals of the Royal College of Physicians & Surgeons of Canada (quarterly) 74 Stanley Ave., Ottawa, Ont. K1M 1P4 —613/746-8177
British Columbia Medical Journal (monthly) 1807 W. 10th Ave., Vancouver, B.C. V6J 2A9—604/736-5551
The Bulletin of the Academy of Medicine, Toronto (twice a year) 288 Bloor St. W., Toronto, Ont. M5S 1V8—416/922-1134
Canadian Anaesthetists' Society Journal (bi-monthly) 178 St. George St., Toronto, Ont. M5R 2M7—416/923-1449
Canadian Doctor (monthly) #201, 310 Victoria Ave., Westmount, P.Q. H3Z 2M9—514/487-2302
Canadian Emergency Services News (6 times a year) #105, 2116 27th Ave. N.E., Calgary, Alta. T2E 7A6 — 403/230-2155
Canadian Family Physician (monthly) 4000 Leslie St., Willowdale, Ont. M2K 2R9—416/493-7513
Canadian Journal of Neurological Sciences (quarterly) #GF543, 700 William Ave., Winnipeg, Man. R3E OZ3
Canadian Journal of Ophthalmology (quarterly) 1867 Alta Vista Dr., Ottawa, Ont. K1G 3G2 - 613/731-6493
The Canadian Journal of Optometry (quarterly) Ste. 2001, 210 Gladstone Ave., Ottawa, Ont. K2P OY6—613/238-2006
Canadian Journal of Psychiatry (8 times a year) 190 Main St., Unionville, P.Q. L3R 2G9—416/297-2030
Canadian Journal of Public Health (bi-monthly) 1335 Carling Ave., Ste. 210, Ottawa, Ont. K1Z 8N8—613/725-3769
The Canadian Journal of Radiography Radiotherapy Nuclear Medicine (bi-monthly) c/o A. Mattila, Suite 410, 280 Metcalfe St., Ottawa, Ont. K2P 1R7—613/234-0012
The Canadian Journal of Surgery (bi-monthly) 1867 Alta Vista Dr., Ottawa, Ont. K1G 0G8—613/731-9331
The Canadian Medical Association Journal (eo week) 1867 Alta Vista Dr., Ottawa, Ont. K1G 0G8—613/731-9331
Clinical Biochemistry (bi-monthly) Suite 906, 151 Slater St., Ottawa, Ont. K1P 5H3 - 613/233-5623
Le Courrier médical (eo Tues.) 481 University Ave., Toronto, Ont. M5W 1A7 - 416/596-5748
The Journal (monthly) Addiction Research Foundation, 33 Russell St., Toronto, Ont. M5S 2S1—416/595-6053
Journal of the Canadian Association of Radiologists (quarterly) Suite 806, 1440 St. Catherine St. W., Montreal, P.Q. H3G 1R8—514/866-2035
Journal of the Canadian Chiropractic Association (quarterly) 1900 Bayview Ave., Toronto, Ont. M4G 3E6 - 416/482-2850
Journal of Otolaryngology (bi-monthly) 190 Main St., Unionville, Ont. L3R 2G9—416/297-2030
Journal of Rheumatology (6 times a year) 190 Main St., Unionville, Ont. L3R 2G9—416/297-2030 (Toronto phone: 967-1414)
Le Médecin du Quebec (monthly) Suite 1100, 1440 St. Catherine St. W., Montreal, P.Q. H3G 1R8—514/878-1911
The Medical Post (eo week) 481 University Ave., Toronto, Ont. M5W 1A7—416/596-5748
Medicine North America (monthly) 1 rue Pacifique, Ste-Anne-de-Bellevue, P.Q. H9X 1B0 - 514/457-2427
Modern Medicine of Canada (monthly) 1450 Don Mills Rd., Don Mills, Ont. M3B 2X7—416/445-6641
Newfoundland Medical Association Journal (quarterly) O'-Mara Martin Bldg., Rawlins Cres., St. John's, Nfld. A1C 2E4 —709/726-7424
Nova Scotia Medical Bulletin (bi-monthly) Sir Charles Tupper Medical Bldg., Halifax, N.S.—902/423-8166
Ontario Medical Review (monthly) 240 St. George St., Toronto, Ont. M5R 2P4—416/925-3264
Ontario Medical Technologist (quarterly) #206, 234 Eglinton Ave. E., Toronto, Ont. M4P 1K5
Ontario Nursing Homes (6 times a year) 6075 Yonge St., Willowdale, Ont. M2M 3W2 - 416/224-2282
Ontario Optician (9 times a year) 601 Euclid St., Whitby, Ont. L1N 5B9 - 416/668-9776
The Ontario Psychologist (quarterly) 1407 Yonge St., Ste. 402, Toronto, Ont. M4T 1Y7—416/961-5552
Physician's Management Manuals (monthly) 1 rue Pacifique, Ste-Anne-de-Bellevue, P.Q. H9X 1BO — 514/457-2423
Physiotherapy Canada (6 times a year) 25 Imperial St., Toronto, Ont. M5P 1B9
Psychiatric Journal of the University of Ottawa (4 times a year) 501 Smyth Rd., Ottawa, Ont. K1H 8L6 - 613/526-1690
L'Union Medicale du Canada (monthly) Ste. 510, 1440 rue St. Catherine, Montreal, P.Q. H3G 2P9—514/866-2053
The University of Toronto Medical Journal (4 times a year) Medical Bldg., University of Toronto, Toronto, Ont. M5S 1A8—416/978-8730
La Vie Medicale au Canada Français (monthly) Ste. 310, 785 Plymouth Ave., Mount Royal, P.Q. H4P 1B4—514/735-5191
Western Medical News (monthly) 10216 128th St., Surrey, B.C. V3T 2Z3 - 604/581-0244

METALWORKING: Canadian Machinery and Metalworking (monthly) 481 University Ave., Toronto, Ont. M5W 1A7—416/596-5720
Metalworking Production & Purchasing (bi-monthly) Box 460, Milliken, Ont. LOH 1KO—416/297-3222
Production Machinery & Equipment (10 times a year) 1295 Matheson Blvd., Mississauga, Ont. L4W 1R1 - 416/624-2000

MILITARY: Canadian Defence Quarterly (quarterly) Ste. 1300, 100 Adelaide St. W., Toronto, Ont. M5H 1S3—416/364-9344

MINING: CIM Bulletin (monthly) Ste. 400, 1130 Sherbrooke St. W., Montreal, P.Q. H3A 2M8—514/842-3461
CIM Directory (annually) see above
CIM Reporter (8 times a year) see above
Canadian Mines Handbook (annually) 7 Labatt Ave., Toronto, Ont. M5A 3P2—416/368-3481
Canadian Mining Journal (monthly) #201, 310 Victoria Ave., Westmount, P.Q. H3Z 2M9—514/487-2302
Canadian Mining Journal's Reference Manual & Buyers Guide (annually) #201, 310 Victoria Ave., Westmount, P.Q. H3Z 2M9—514/487-2302
The Financial Post Survey of Mines (annually) 481 University Ave., Toronto, Ont. M5W 1A7—416/596-5585
Mining Review (bi-monthly) 124 W. 8th St., North Vancouver, B.C. V7M 3H2 - 604/985-8711
The Northern Miner (weekly) 7 Labatt Ave., Toronto, Ont. M5A 3P2—416/368-3481
Western Miner (monthly) 1201 Melville St., Vancouver, B.C. V6E 2X9 - 604/685-3241

MOTION PICTURES: Cinema/Canada (10 times a year) 834 Ave. Bloomfield, Montreal, P.Q. H2V 3S6 — 514/272-5354
Cinema/Quebec (10 times a year) Box 309, Outremont Stn., Montreal, P.Q. H2V 4N1—514/272-1058
CinéMag (eo week) 834 Ave. Bloomfield, Montreal, P.Q. H2V 3S6 — 514/272-5354
Film World (monthly) 1000 Lawrence Ave. W., Toronto, Ont. M6A 1P2 — 416/789-1171
Motion (bi-monthly) Box 5490, Stn. A, Toronto, Ont. M5W 1N7—416/488-5314

MOTOR TRUCKS & BUSES: Atlantic Truck Transport Review (4 times a year) #7A, 567 Coverdale Rd., Riverview, N.B. E1B 3K7 — 506/386-4413
B.C. Motor Transport Directory (annually) 4090 Graveley St., Burnaby, B.C. V5C 3T6 - 604/299-7407
Bus and Truck Transport (monthly) 481 University Ave., Toronto, Ont. M5W 1A7—416/596-5930
Canadian Driver/Owner (bi-monthly) 481 University Ave., Toronto, Ont. M5W 1A7—416/596-5930
Canadian Highway Carriers Guide (annually) 1450 Don Mills Rd., Don Mills, Ont. M3B 2X7—416/445-6641
Canadian Special Truck Equipment Manual (annually) 481 University Ave., Toronto, Ont. M5W 1A7—416/596-5930
Eastern Canadian Trucker (monthly) #101, 109 Vanderhoof Ave., Toronto, Ont. M4G 2J2 - 416/425-9021
L'Echo du Transport (10 times a year) 435 rue Norman, Ville St-Pierre, P.Q. H8R 1A4 - 514/486-7386
Guide du Transport par Camion Inc. (annually) B.P. 1188, Pointe Claire, P.Q. H9S 5K7 - 514/694-3695
Heavy Truck Equipment News (18 times a year) 1730 Aimco Blvd., Mississauga, Ont. L4W 1Y3 — 416/625-3460
M.T.A. Ship-By-Truck Directory (annually) 25 Bunting St., Winnipeg, Man. R2X 2P5 — 204/632-6600

Manitoba Highway News (bi-monthly) 25 Bunting St., Winnipeg, Man. R2X 2P5 — 204/632-6600
Motor Truck (monthly) Suite 101, 109 Vanderhoof Ave., Toronto, Ont. M4G 2J2—416/425-9021
Ontario Ship-By-Truck Directory (annually) 555 Dixon Rd., Rexdale, Ont. M9W 1H8 - 416/247-7131
Saskatchewan Shippers Directory (annually) 1494 Regent Ave. W., Winnipeg, Man. R2C 3A8 — 204/224-2267
Saskatchewan Trucking (quarterly) 124 W. 8th St., North Vancouver, B.C. V7M 3H2 - 604/985-8711
Transport Commercial (8 times a year) 625 President Kennedy Ave., Montreal, P.Q. H3A 1K5—514/845-5141
Transport Routier du Quebec (monthly) 1259 Berri St., 4th floor, Montreal, P.Q. H2L 4C7—514/849-1217
Truck Canada (monthly) #200, 6725 Darlington Ave., Montreal, P.Q. H3S 2J7 - 514/731-3524
La Voix de l'Ancai (monthly) 245 Lindsay St., Drummondville, P.Q. J2C 1P2—819/477-6811
Western Motor Fleet (bi-monthly) 200, 633 Portage Ave., Winnipeg, Man. R3B 2Z9—204/775-0387

MUNICIPAL, PUBLIC WORKS: See GOVERNMENT

MUSIC & MUSIC TRADES: Canadian Music Directory (annually) #200, 6725 Darlington Ave., Montreal, P.Q. H3S 2J7 - 514/731-3524
Canadian Music Industry Directory (annually) 6 Brentcliffe Rd., Toronto, Ont. M4G 3Y2—416/425-0257
Canadian Music Trade (6 times a year) #3, 2453 Yonge St., Toronto, Ont. M4P 2E8 — 416/485-8284
Canadian Musician, see Consumer Magazines
RPM Weekly (weekly) 6 Brentcliffe Rd., Toronto, Ont. M4G 3Y2—416/425-0257

NURSING: A A R N News Letter (11 times a year) 10256-112 St., Edmonton, Alta. T5K 1M6—403/426-0160
Canadian Journal of Psychiatric Nursing (bi-monthly) 1854 Portage Ave., Winnipeg, Man. R3J 0G9 - 204/775-4111
The Canadian Nurse, L'Infirmière Canadienne (monthly) 50 The Driveway, Ottawa, Ont. K2P 1E2—613/237-2133
Nursing Quebec (6 times a year) 4200 Dorchester Blvd. W., Montreal, P.Q. H3Z 1V4 - 514/935-2501

OFFICE EQUIPMENT: Administrative Digest (monthly) 1450 Don Mills Rd., Don Mills, Ont. M5B 2X7—416/445-6641
Le Bureau (bi-monthly) 481 University Ave., Toronto, Ont. M5W 1A7—416/596-5923
Canadian Office (monthly) #1201, 55 Bloor St. W., Toronto, Ont. M4W 3K2—416/967-6200
Canadian Secretary (4 times a year) 481 University Ave., Toronto, Ont. M5W 1A7—416/596-5923
Comda Key (6 times a year) 15 Dyas Rd., Don Mills, Ont. M3B 1V7—416/441-1717
Office Equipment & Methods (monthly) 481 University Ave., Toronto, Ont. M5W 1A7—416/596-5923

PACKAGING: Canadian Packaging (monthly) 481 University Ave., Toronto, Ont. M5W 1A7—416/596-5744

PAINT & FINISHES: Coatings (bi-monthly) Ste. A, 86 Wilson St., Oakville, Ont. L6K 3G5 - 416/844-9773
Decorating Dealer (quarterly) Ste. 70, 1262 Don Mills Rd., Don Mills, Ont. M3B 2W7—416/444-5289

PARK, PLAYGROUND, ARENA EQUIPMENT: Pool Industry Canada (5 times a year) 1450 Don Mills Rd., Don Mills, Ont. M3B 2X7—416/445-6641
Recreation Canada (5 times a year) 333 River Rd., Ottawa, Ont. K1L 8B9 - 613/746-7740
Recreation Saskatchewan (monthly) Box 160, North Battleford, Sask. S9A 2Y1—306/445-7264

PERSONNEL: See PUBLIC & INDUSTRIAL RELATIONS

PETROLEUM OIL & GAS: Alberta Oil & Gas Directory (annually) #908, 10235 101 St., Edmonton, Alta. T5J 3G1 - 403/426-4993
Canadian Oil & Gas Handbook (annually) 7 Labatt Ave., Toronto, Ont. M5A 3P2 - 416/368-3481
Canadian Oil Register (annually) 330-9th Ave. S.W., Calgary, Alta. T2P 1K8—403/269-3161
Canadian Petroleum (monthly) #110, 330 9th Ave. S.W., Calgary, Alta. T2P 1K8—403/269-1334
Drilling Canada (bi-monthly) #110, 330 9th Ave. S.W., Calgary, Alta. T2P 1K8 - 403/269-1334
Drillsite (monthly) #200, 918 6th Ave. S.W., Calgary, Alta. T2P 0V5 — 403/266-5621
Energy (monthly) Ste. B8, 118 11th Ave. S.E., Calgary, Alta. T2G 0X5 - 403/266-5301
Energy Forum (4 times a year) 481 University Ave., Toronto, Ont. M5W 1A7 - 416/596-5928
Energy Processing/Canada (6 times a year) Ste. 406, 315 10th Ave. S.E., Calgary, Alta. T2G 0W2—403/265-4750
The Journal of Canadian Petroleum Technology (quarterly) Ste. 400, 1130 Sherbrooke St. W., Montreal, P.Q. H3A 2M8 —514/842-3461
Oilweek (weekly) Ste. 200, 918 6th Ave. S.W., Calgary, Alta. T2P 0V5—403/266-5621
The Roughneck (monthly) #2A 1440A 17 St. S.W., Calgary, Alta. T2T 2C9—403/245-2445

PHOTOGRAPHY: Camera Canada (quarterly) 90 Betty Ann Dr., Willowdale, Ont. M2N 1X2 - 416/223-8175
Canadian Directory of Professional Photography (annually) 318 Royal Bank Bldg., Edmonton, Alta. - 403/428-0850
Canadian Photography (monthly) 481 University Ave., Toronto, Ont. M5W 1A7—416/596-5877
OVO Magazine (quarterly) 307 Ste-Catherine ouest, Montreal, P.Q. H2X 2A3 - 514/849-6253
Professonal Photgraphers of Canada (6 times a year) 318 Royal Bank Bldg., Edmonton, Alta. - 403/428-0850

PLASTICS: Canadian Plastics (monthly) 1450 Don Mills Rd., Don Mills, Ont. M3B 2X7—416/445-6641
Canadian Plastics Directory and Buyers' Guide (annually) 1450 Don Mills Rd., Don Mills, Ont. M3B 2X7—416/445-6641
Plastics Business (6 times a year) #405, 20 Holly St., Toronto, Ont. M4S 2E6 - 416/487-3461

POLICE: Scarlet & Gold (annually) #813, 675 W. Hastings St., Vancouver, B.C. V6B 1N2

POWER & POWER PLANTS: Modern Power & Engineering (monthly) 481 University Ave., Toronto, Ont. M5W 1A7—416/596-5712

PRINTING: Canadian Community Publisher (monthly) #201, 12 Shuter St., Toronto, Ont. M5B 1A7—416/366-4277
Canadian Printer and Publisher (monthly) 481 University Ave., Toronto, Ont. M5W 1A7—416/596-5884
The Graphic Monthly (bi-monthly) 30 Titan Rd., Toronto, Ont. M8Z 5Y2 - 416/231-4393
Le Maitre Imprimeur (monthly) 480 Mont Royal Ave. E., Montreal, P.Q. H2J 1W4—514/842-2751
Printaction (monthly) Ste. 506, 355 St. Clair Ave. W., Toronto, Ont. M5P 1N4—416/923-5538

PRODUCT ENGINEERING & DESIGN: Design Engineering (monthly) 481 University Ave., Toronto, Ont. M5W 1A7—416/596-5819
Design Product News (bi-monthly) Box 460, Milliken, Ont. L0H 1K0—416/297-3222

PUBLIC & INDUSTRIAL RELATIONS: The Canadian Personnel & Industrial Relations Journal (6 times a year) #803, 11 Adelaide St. W., Toronto, Ont. M5H 1L9—416/363-9453

PUBLISHING: See BOOKS

PULP & PAPER: Canadian Pulp and Paper Industry (monthly) 481 University Ave., Toronto, Ont. M5W 1A7—416/596-5829
Forêt et Papier (6 times a year) 625 President Kennedy Ave., Montreal, P.Q. H3A 1K5—514/845-5141
Pulp & Paper Canada (monthly) #201, 310 Victoria Ave., Westmount, P.Q. H3Z 2M9—514/487-2302 (also publishers of the annual Business Directory and the Reference Manual & Buyers' Guide)

PURCHASING: Canadian Trade Index (annually) One Yonge St., Toronto, Ont. M5E 1J9—416/363-7261
Fraser's Canadian Trade Directory (annually) 481 University Ave., Toronto, Ont. M5W 1A7—416/596-5086
Government Purchasing Guide (bi-monthly) Ste. 706, 43 Eglinton Ave. E., Toronto, Ont. M4P 1A2—416/483-8767
Modern Purchasing (monthly) 481 University Ave., Toronto, Ont. M5W 1A7—416/596-5949

Purchasing in Western Canada (monthly) #601, 510 W. Hastings St., Vancouver, B.C. V6B 1L8—604/689-2021
Purchasing Management Digest (6 times a year) 1289 Marlborough Crt., Oakville, Ont. L6H 2R9—416/842-2884
Telex Gold Pages (annually) 740 Notre Dame St. W., Montreal, P.Q. H3C 3X6—514/877-5681
RADIO, TV: Audio Marketnews (monthly) Ste. 603, 3 Church St., Toronto, Ont. M5E 1M2—416/362-7611
Canadian CES Journal (monthly) 93 Railside Rd., Don Mills, Ont. M3A 1B2 - 416/444-7054
Home Goods Retailing (monthly) 481 University Ave., Toronto, Ont. M5W 1A7—416/596-5942
REAL ESTATE: Canadian Real Estate (monthly) 99 Duncan Mill Rd., Don Mills, Ont. M5B 1Z2—416/445-9910
Habitabec (weekly) 8620 Berri St., Montreal, P.Q. H2P 2G4—514/389-5944
RENTAL EQUIPMENT: Canadian Rental Service (bi-monthly) Box 247, Stn. A, Weston, Ont. M9N 3M7 — 416/241-4724
SCIENCE & RESEARCH: Canadian Journal of Applied Sport Sciences (4 times a year) Box 2274, Windsor, Ont. N8Y 4R8 — 519/969-8188
Canadian Journal of Spectroscopy (bi-monthly) 1253 McGill College, Ste. 175, Montreal, P.Q. H3B 2Y5 — 514/866-8236
Canadian Renewable Energy News (monthly) Box 4869, Stn. E, Ottawa, Ont. K1S 5B4 — 613/238-5591
Canadian Research (8 times a year) 481 University Ave., Toronto, Ont. M5W 1A7—416/596-5721
Laboratory Product News (7 times a year) 1450 Don Mills Rd., Don Mills, Ont. M3B 2X7—416/445-6641
The Microscopical Society of Canada Bulletin (quarterly) Rm. 79, 150 College St., Toronto, Ont. M5S 1A1 - 416/978-8896
Physics in Canada (6 times a year) Suite 903, 151 Slater St., Ottawa, Ont. K1P 5H3—613/237-3392
Quebec Science, see Consumer Magazines
SECURITY: Canadian Security (bi-monthly) 93 Railside Rd., Don Mills, Ont. M3A 1B2 - 416/444-7054
National Loss Prevention (4 times a year) Box 982, Stn. B, Willowdale, Ont. M2K 2T6 - 416/222-9629
SHIPPING, MARINE: Boating Business (quarterly) Box 673, Parry Sound, Ont. P2A 2Z1—705/732-2095
The Canadian Forwarder (bi-weekly) 3440 Trenholme Ave., Montreal, P.Q. H4B 1X9—514/481-5802
Canadian Ports and Seaway Directory (annually) 1450 Don Mills Rd., Don Mills, Ont. M3B 2X7—416/445-6641
Canadian Shipping and Marine Engineering (monthly) 5200 Dixie Rd., Mississauga, Ont. L4W 1E4—416/625-5277
Captain Lillie's Coast Guide & Radiotelephone Directory (biennially) 355 Burrard St., Marine Bldg., Vancouver, B.C. V6C 2G6—604/685-4385
Great Lakes Navigation (annually) Ste. 504, 1434 St. Catherine St. W., Montreal, P.Q. H3G 1R4—514/861-6715
Harbour & Shipping (monthly) 355 Burrard St., Marine Bldg., Vancouver, B.C. V6C 2G6—604/685-4385
Marine Equipment Directory (annually) Ste. 504, 1434 St. Catherine St. W., Montreal, P.Q. H3G 1R4—514/861-4371
Marine Trades (4 times a year) Suite 204, 5200 Dixie Rd., Mississauga, Ont. L4W 1E4—416/625-5277
Montreal Port Guide (annually) Ste. 504, 1434 St. Catherine St. W., Montreal, P.Q. H3G 1R4—514/861-4371
Ports Annual, see above
Quebec Port Guide, see above
Seaports and the Shipping World (monthly) 4634 St. Catherine St. W., Montreal, P.Q. H3Z 2W6—514/934-0373
SPORTING GOODS: Canadian Camping & RV Dealer (bi-monthly) Ste. 221, 3414 Park Ave., Montreal, P.Q. H2X 2H5—514/282-0191
Canadian Motorcycle Dealer News (monthly) 2066 Queen St. E., Toronto, Ont. M4E 1C9 - 416/690-0566
Canadian Pool & Spa Marketing (5 times a year) Box 282, Stn. Q, Toronto, Ont. M4T 2M1 — 416/486-8549
Canadian Sporting Goods & Playthings Directory (annually) #200, 6725 Darlington Ave., Montreal, P.Q. H3S 2J7 - 514/731-3524
The Greenmaster (8 times a year) Ste. 32, 698 Weston Rd., Toronto, Ont. M6N 3R3—416/767-2550
Motorcycle Dealer & Trade (monthly) 290 Jarvis St., Toronto, Ont. M5B 2C5—416/868-6318
Ski Industry Bulletin (4 times a year) 306 Youville Sq., Ste. B-10, Montreal, P.Q. H2Y 2B6
Sporting Goods Canada (6 times a year) 481 University Ave., Toronto, Ont. M5W 1A7—416/596-5955
Sporting Goods Trade (8 times a year) 380 Wellington St. W., Toronto, Ont. M5V 1E3—416/366-4608
Sports Marketing Canada (6 times a year) 9851 Parkway Blvd., Montreal, P.Q. H1J 1P3 - 514/353-4747
Vehicules de Recreation Trade (twice a year) Ste. 221, 3414 Park Ave., Montreal, P.Q. H2X 2H5—514/282-0191
STATIONERY: Canadian Office Products & Stationery (bi-monthly) 1450 Don Mills Rd., Don Mills, Ont. M3B 2X7—416/445-6641
TELECOMMUNICATIONS: Telex Directory (annually) 740 Notre Dame St. W., Montreal, P.Q. H3C 3X6—514/877-5681
TELEVISION: Cable Communications Magazine (monthly) 4 Smetana Dr., Kitchener, Ont. N2B 3B8 - 519/744-4111
TEXTILES: Canadian Textile Directory (annually) #200, 6725 Darlington Ave., Montreal, P.Q. H3S 2J7 - 514/731-3524
Canadian Textile Journal (monthly) Ste. 307, 4920 de Maisonneuve Blvd. W., Montreal, P.Q. H3Z 1N1—514/487-2272
TOYS: Canadian Variety Merchandise Directory (annually) #200, 6725 Darlington Ave., Montreal, P.Q. H3S 2J7 - 514/731-3524
Toys & Games (bi-monthly) 380 Wellington St. W., Toronto, Ont. M5V 1E3—416/366-4608
TRADE: Canada Commerce (monthly) Dept. of Industry, Trade & Commerce, 235 Queen St., Ottawa, Ont. K1A 0H5 - 613/995-7489
TRANSPORTATION, TRAFFIC, SHIPPING: Air Cargo Canada (monthly) Box 370, Stn. Q, Toronto, Ont. M4T 2M5—416/486-0516
Air Transportation Annual (annually) Ste. 504, 1434 St. Catherine St. W., Montreal, P.Q. H3G 1R4—514/861-4371
Canadian Guide (bi-monthly) Box 1040, Stn. B, Burlington, Ont. L7P 3S9—416/335-0373
Canadian Highway Carriers Guide (annually) 1450 Don Mills Rd., Don Mills, Ont. M3B 2X7—416/445-6641
Canadian Transportation & Distribution Management (monthly) 1450 Don Mills Rd., Don Mills, Ont. M3B 2X7—416/445-6641
Quarterly Report on Transportation (quarterly) 1289 Marlborough Ct., Oakville, Ont. L6H 2R9 - 416/842-2884
Toronto Trade & Transport (annually) Ste. 504, 1434 St. Catherine St. W., Montreal, P.Q. H3G 1R4—514/861-4371
TRAVEL (See also HOTELS, RESTAURANTS): Agent West Traveletter (weekly) 1256 W. Pender St., Vancouver, B.C. V6E 2S8 - 604/688-0481
Bulletin Voyages (weekly) Ste. 502, 1121 St. Catherine St. W., Montreal, P.Q. H3B 1J5—514/845-3237
Canadian Travel Courier (eo week) 481 University Ave., Toronto, Ont. M5W 1A7—416/596-5806
Canadian Travel News (eo week) 1450 Don Mills Rd., Don Mills, Ont. M3B 2X7—416/445-6641
Canadian Travel Press (eo Thur.) Ste. 1300, 100 Adelaide St. W., Toronto, Ont. M5H 1S3—416/364-9344
Executive Travel Canada (annually) #303, 505 Consumers Rd., Willowdale, Ont. M2J 4V8—416/494-7766
Journal des Voyages (weekly) C.P. 547, Succ. Snowdon, Montreal, P.Q. H3X 3T7 — 514/483-1682
Marketing Voyages (monthly) 1121 St. Catherine St. W., Montreal, P.Q. H3B 1J5—514/845-3237
Personnel Guide to Canada's Travel Industry (twice a year) Ste. 1300, 100 Adelaide St. W., Toronto, Ont. M5H 1S3—416/364-9344
Quebec Voyages (twice a year) #502, 1121 St. Catherine St. W., Montreal, P.Q. H3B 1J5 — 514/845-3237
Tote Airline Timetables & Travel Digest (monthly) #443, 69 Sherbourne St., Toronto, Ont. M9A 4X1 — 416/364-6830
Tourisme + (10 times a year) #408, 1410 Stanley St., Montreal, P.Q. H3A 1P8 - 514/845-2171
Travel North America (quarterly) #306, 130 Merton St., Toronto, Ont. M4A 1A4 - 416/485-7634

Travelweek Bulletin (twice a week) Box 575, Stn. F, Toronto, Ont. M4Y 2L8 — 416/363-9026

VENDING & VENDING EQUIPMENT: Automatic Merchandising in Canada (6 times a year) 106 Lakeshore Rd. E., #209, Mississauga, Ont. L5G 1E3 – 416/271-1366

Canadian Coin Box Magazine (monthly) Box 187, Owen Sound, Ont. N4K 5P4—519/376-9680

Canadian Vending Magazine (bi-monthly) Box 187, Owen Sound, Ont. N4K 5P4—519/376-9680

VETERINARY: Canadian Journal of Comparative Medicine (quarterly) 360 Bronson Ave., Ottawa, Ont. K1R 6J3—613/236-1162

The Canadian Veterinary Journal, La Revue Veterinaire Canadienne (monthly) 360 Bronson Ave., Ottawa, Ont. K1R 6J3—613/236-1162

Le Medecin Veterinaire du Québec (quarterly) 190 Main St., Unionville, P.Q. L3R 2G9 — 416/297-2030

WATER TREATMENT: Canadian Water Well (quarterly) Box 1060, Exeter, Ont. NOM 1SO—519/235-2400

Eau du Quebec (quarterly) 6290 Perinault, Bur. 2, Montreal, P.Q. H4K 1K5—514/337-4446

Water & Pollution Control (monthly) 1450 Don Mills Rd., Don Mills, Ont. M3B 2X7—416/445-6641

WELDING: Canadian Welder & Fabricator (monthly) 1077 St. James St., Box 6900, Winnipeg, Man. R3C 3B1—204/775-0201

WOODWORKING: Le Bois Ouvre (bi-monthly) 214 rue Perreault, Victoriaville, P.Q. G6P 5E9 — 819/752-7315

TRANSLATORS AND INTERPRETERS

All persons listed are available for work on a freelance basis. There are other members of the professional associations but their employment precludes their working independently.

Abbreviations used in this list:

Arabic	Arab.
Chinese	Chi.
Czech	Cz.
Danish	Dan.
Dutch	Du.
English	Eng.
French	Fr.
German	Ger.
Greek	G.
Iranian	Iran.
Italian	It.
Japanese	Jap.
Norwegian	Nor.
Polish	Pol.
Portuguese	Port.
Roumanian	Roum.
Russian	Russ.
Serb-Croatian	S.Cr.
Spanish	Span.
Swedish	Swed.
Turkish	Turk.

Sources:

Association of Translators & Interpreters of Ontario, #1406, One Nicholas St., Ottawa, Ont. K1N 7B7 (613/233-6395)

Canadian Translators & Interpreters Council, Box 452, Stn. A, Ottawa, Ont. K1N 8V5 – Administrator, J.C. Carisse

Corporation of Translators and Interpreters of New Brunswick, Box 427, Fredericton, N.B. E3B 4Z9 (506/452-3407)

Société des traducteurs du Québec/Translators Society of Quebec, 1010, rue Ste-Catherine ouest, bur. 340, Montréal, P.Q. H3B 1G1 (514/861-1783)

Alberta

CALGARY

Lord-Cotter, Danielle, 1101 42nd St. S.W., Calgary, Alta. T3C 1Z2 (403/242-3187) *Eng.-Fr.*

EDMONTON

Bullock-Quail, Brenda A., #1201, 10045 118 St., Edmonton, Alta. T5K 2K2 *Eng.-Fr. / Fr.-Eng.*

New Brunswick

EDMUNDSTON

Savoie, Françoise, 14 Guérette St., Edmundston, N.B. E3V 1N9 (Home: 506/739-8133) *Eng.-Fr.*

Thériault, Florine, 34 d'Amours St., Edmundston, N.B. E3V 1X8 (Home: 506/735-4375; Work: 735-8804) *Eng.Fr./Fr.-Eng.*

FREDERICTON

Beggs, Wendy, 266 rue Northumberland, Fredericton, N.B. E3B 3J7 (506/454-6875, res.) *Fr.-Eng.*

Bézier, Dominique, 29 Mountain Dr., Fredericton, N.B. E3B 5M7 (Home: 506/454-3790; Work: 453-2920) *Eng.-Fr.*

Daigle, Bernice, 179 Beaconsfield St., Fredericton, N.B. E3B 5H3 (Home: 506/455-8638; Work: 453-2520) *Eng.-Fr.*

Duval, Paul, 538 promenade Hillcrest, Fredericton, N.B. E3A 2X7 (506/472-8668, res.) *Eng.-Fr.*

Epstein, Margaret, 69 Dickson St., Fredericton, N.B. E3A 4Y8 (Home: 506/472-6186; Work: 453-2920) *Fr.-Eng.*

Juhel, Dominique E., 508 rue Lisgar, Bat 7, app 2, Fredericton, N.B. E3B 3B2 (506/455-4229, res.) *Eng.-Fr.*

LeBlanc, Valmond, 95 Linden Cres., Fredericton, N.B. E3A 5A1 (Home: 506/472-0214; Work: 453-2648) *Eng.Fr./Fr.-Eng.*

Pardons, Claude, 550 Dufferin St., Bldg. 5, Apt. 1, Fredericton, N.B. E3B 3A9 (Home: 506/454-0917) *Eng.-Fr.*

Patenaude, Lise M., 25 Cambridge Cres., Fredericton, N.B. E3B 4N8 (506/455-2123, res.) *Eng.-Fr.*

Pelletier, Annette, Box 52, Site 4, S.S. #3, Fredericton, N.B. E3B 5W9 (Home: 506/454-1488) *Eng.-Fr.*

Saint-Laurent, Léopold, 18 Kent St., Manor Place, Fredericton, N.B. E3A 4Y1 (Home: 506/472-3963; Work: 453-2470) *Eng.-Fr. / Fr.-Eng.*

MONCTON

Lapointe, Marc, 54 Henry St., Moncton, N.B. E1C 5B7 (Home: 506/854-9891; Work: 854-9891) *Eng.-Fr.*

Snow, Odette, 104 Miller Dr., Moncton, N.B. E1C 7T2 (Home: 506/384-6021) *Eng.-Fr.*

RICHIBUCTO

Arsenault, J.-Léonard, Box 625, Richibucto, N.B. EOA 2MO (Home: 506/523-9871) *Eng.-Fr.*

ST-LOUIS-DE-KENT

Arseneault, Alphonse-A., Box 68, St-Louis-de-Kent, N.B. EOA 2Z0 (Home: 506/876-2562) *Eng.-Fr.*

Nova Scotia

WOLFVILLE

Ledwidge, Dr. F., Box 947, Wolfville, N.S. BOP 1XO (902/542-5276) *Eng.-Fr. / Fr.-Eng.*

Ontario

BRAMPTON

Kummel, Dr. E.G., 5 Crescent Hill Dr. S., Brampton, Ont. L6S 2P2 (416/793-2799) *Eng.-Ger./Ger.-Eng.*

KANATA, see Ottawa-Hull

KINGSTON

Davies, Elizabeth M., #46, 258 Queen Mary Rd., Kingston, Ont. K7M 2B2 *Port.-Eng. / Fr.-Eng.*

KITCHENER/WATERLOO

Fischer, Helmuth A., 665 Belmont Ave. W., Kitchener, Ont. N2M 1N9 (519/742-3325) *Ger.-Eng.*

Souan, Anne-Marie, 665 Belmont Ave. W., Kitchener, Ont. N2M 1N9 (519/742-3325) *Eng.-Fr.*

LONDON

Toth, Jacqueline C., 701 Adelaide St. N., London, Ont. N5Y 2L4 (519/686-5008) *Eng.-Fr.*

MISSISSAUGA

Côté, Michel, 625 Atwater, Mississauga, Ont. L5G 2A8 (416/ 278-2518) *Eng.-Fr./Fr.-Eng.*

NEPEAN

See Ottawa

NIAGARA FALLS

Bogdanovic, Nikola, 7063 Dirdene St., Niagara Falls, Ont. L2E 5N6 (416/354-4760) *Russ.-Eng. / S.Cr.-Eng.*

OAKVILLE

Armstrong, Helene B., 1081 Jutland Place, Oakville, Ont. L6H 2V3 (416/845-7705) *Eng.-Fr.*

Lanouette-Bubbs, Gisele, 1200 Lambeth Rd., Oakville, Ont. L6H 2C8 (416/844-0995) *Eng.-Fr.*

ORLEANS, see Ottawa-Hull

OTTAWA-HULL

Bauer, Charles, 378, rue Cunningham, Ottawa, Ont. K1H 6B4 (613/731-8019; 521-3400) *Eng.-Fr./Fr.-Eng.*

Bessens, Marie-Claire, 2161 Blossom Dr., Ottawa, Ont. K1H 6G6 (613/737-3551) *Eng.-Fr. / Span.-Fr.*

Boch, Ana Ruth, 20 Parker Ave., Ottawa, Ont. K2G 3A7 (613/ 224-1269) *Du.-Eng.*

Bouvier, Yvan, 11, rue Villeneuve, Hull, P.Q. J8Y 1L1 (819/ 777-7427) *Eng.-Fr.*

Bruyere, Eugene, 529, rue Blair, Ottawa, Ont. K1G OJ3 (613/ 231-3537) *Eng.-Fr./Fr.-Eng.*

Bullock-Quail, Brenda A., 54, rue Cholette, Hull, P.Q. J8Y 1J8 (819/778-2106) *Eng.-Fr./Fr.-Eng.*

Campagna, Manuel-M., Box 80, Stn. B, Ottawa, Ont. K1P 6C3 (613/236-2798) *Eng.-Fr./It.-Fr.*

Charbonneau, Henri, #21, 525 boul. St-Laurent, Ottawa, Ont. K1K 2Z9 (613/746-9107) *Eng.-Fr.*

Chicoyne-Lefebvre, Mme Louise, 26, rue Fréchette, Hull, P.Q. J8Y 5P9 (819/776-5174) *Eng.-Fr.*

Desparois, Richard, 28, rue Fontainebleau, Touraine (Gatineau), P.Q. J8T 1G7 (819/568-3698) *Eng.-Fr./Fr.-Eng.*

Dreyfus, Hélène M., 200 Rideau Terrace, #603, Ottawa, Ont. K1M 0Z3 (819/643-3470; 613/741-1320) *Fr.-Eng.*

Edridge, Sylvia, 52 Barrow Cres., Kanata, Ont. K2L 2K1 (613/ 997-3899) *Eng.-Fr. / Fr.-Eng.*

Eveleigh, Raymond, 333 rue Chapel, app 1004, Ottawa, Ont. K1N 8Y8 *Eng.-Fr.*

Gagner-Scott, Mme Renée, 25, rue Chouinard, app. 215, Hull, P.Q. J8Y 1E8 (819/776-2622) *Eng.-Fr.*

Gagnon, Mlle Marthe, 110, rue Stewart, app. 20, Ottawa, Ont. K1N 6J6 (613/238-6616) *Eng.-Fr./Fr.-Eng.*

Giroux, Michel, 48, rue Nice, Touraine, P.Q. J8T 4W3 (819/ 568-7428) *Eng.-Fr.*

Gravelle, Paul-André, 286, rue Wilbrod, app. 31, Ottawa, Ont. K1N 6M2 (613/234-8849; 819/997-1375) *Eng.-Fr./Fr.-Eng.*

Harrison, Joan, 883 Hamlet Rd., Ottawa, Ont. K1G 1R3 (613/ 731-0339) *Fr.-Eng.*

Henley, Laure, 530 rue Laurier ouest, app. 1906, Ottawa, Ont. K1R 7T1 (613/238-2752) *Eng.-Fr.*

Hyde, Peter John, Box 3574, Stn. C, Ottawa, Ont. K1Y 4J7 (613/237-6188) *Russ.-Eng. / Fr.-Eng.*

Irwin-Carrière, Kathleen, 1814 Applegrove Court, Ottawa, Ont. K1J 6S5 (613/745-1109) *Eng.-Fr./Fr.-Eng.*

Jury, Janet, #2, 75 Stewart St., Ottawa, Ont. K1N 6H9 (613/ 236-7400) *Fr.-Eng. / Span.-Eng.*

Keen, Elena, 1935 Sharel Dr., Ottawa, Ont. K1H 6W3 (613/ 523-2633) *Span.-Eng./Fr.-Eng.*

Lambert, Jean, 2111 ch. de Montreal, #153, Ottawa, Ont. K1J 8M8 (613/741-4423) *S.Cr.-Eng.*

Lane, Dr. Alexander, 40 Boteler St., Apt. 701, Ottawa, Ont. K1N 9C8 (613/238-4443) *Eng.-Du. / Fr.-Du.*

Leck, Glenys H., R.R. 3, Russell, Ont. KOA 3BO (613/445-5454) *Fr.-Eng.*

Libert, P.-E., 1433, boul. Morley, Ottawa, Ont. K2C 1R4 (613/ 225-8330) *Eng.-Fr.*

Macewicz, Lisa, 658 Sherbourne Rd., Ottawa, Ont. K2A 3H3 (613/728-4732) *Ger.-Eng.*

Malherbe, Jean-Luc, 630 Gaines Dr., Ottawa, Ont. K1J 7W6 (613/744-0007) *Eng.-Fr./Ger.-Fr.*

McNicoll, Bernard, #2, 5 rue Heney, Ottawa, Ont. K1N 5V5 (613/234-2810) *Eng.-Fr.*

Méchin, Bernard, 6 Glen Park Dr., Ottawa, Ont. K1B 3Z2 (613/ 824-5619) *Eng.-Fr./Ger.-Fr. / Span.-Fr.*

Naim, Joseph, 101 Sherway Dr., Ottawa, Ont. K2J 1P8 (613/ 825-3518) *Eng.-Fr./Eng.-Fr.-Arab.*

Nekrassoff, Dr. Vladimir N. (President, Canadian Translators & Interpreters Council, and Association of Translators & Interpreters of Ontario), 1218 Meadowlands Dr. E., Apt. 608, Ottawa, Ont. K2E 6K1 (613/225-5307) *Ger.-Eng.*

Patry, Réjean, 530 ouest av. Laurier, app 2309, Ottawa, Ont. K1R 7T1 (613/236-3697; 995-2610) *Eng.-Fr.*

Phillips, Geoffrey, 65 Inverness Ave., Ottawa, Ont. K2E 6N6 (613/224-6833) *Russ.-Eng.*

Quesnel-Bédard, Andrée, 1350, rue Potvin, Templeton-Est, P.Q. J8P 1P8 (819/663-9575; 613/233-2200) *Eng.-Fr.*

Rebetez, Suzanne, 261, rue Cooper, app. 809, Ottawa, Ont. K2P OG3 (613/235-9610) *Eng.-Fr./Span.-Fr.*

Riedel, Dr. Dieter, 2125 Killarney Dr., Ottawa, Ont. K2A 1R4 (613/995-2658) *Ger.-Eng.*

Rouisse, Emérienne, 100, rue Empress, app. 811, Ottawa, Ont. K1R 7S6 (613/236-3286) *Eng.-Fr.*

Sinclair, Don A., 940 Beaudry St., Ottawa, Ont. K1K 3S1 (613/ 746-1224) *Russ.-Eng. / Du.-Eng.*

Smith, Markland, 111, rue Wurtemburg, app. 1214, Ottawa, Ont. K1N 8M1 (613/238-2675) *Fr.-Eng./Eng.-Fr.*

Walsh, Mignonne, 43 ave. Reid, Ottawa, Ont. K1Y 1S5 (613/ 722-5343) *Eng.-Fr. / Fr.-Eng.*

Wilbee, Paul Earl, #804, 163 MacLaren St., Ottawa, Ont. K2P 2G4 (613/234-6749) *Fr.-Eng.*

PERKINS

See Ottawa-Hull

RUSSELL, see Ottawa-Hull

SOUTHAMPTON

Breede, Dagmar, Box 489, Southampton, Ont. N0H 2L0 (519/ 797-5218) *Du.-Eng.*

SUDBURY

Arbuckle, Anne-Francoise M., 37 Lancaster Dr., Sudbury, Ont. P3E 3R5 (705/674-0476; 675-1151, poste 466) *Eng.-Fr.*

Arbuckle, John, 37 Lancaster Dr., Sudbury, Ont. P3E 3R5 (705/674-0476) *Eng.-Fr./Fr.-Eng.*

Parent, Isabelle, 1170 Ramsey View Crt., Apt. 503, Sudbury, Ont. P3E 2E4 (705/522-5179) *Eng.-Fr.*

TORONTO (including boroughs)

Arnaudon, Daniel-Henry, 214 St. George St., Apt. 408, Toronto, Ont. M5R 2N8 (416/968-1538) *Eng.-Fr.*

Bebbington, Françoise, 51 Rands Rd., Ajax, Ont. L1S 3H6 (416/683-3609) *Eng.-Fr.*

Benais, Raoul, 20 rue Carlton, Box 632, Toronto, Ont. M5B 2H5 *Eng.-Fr.*

Bhabha, Anne, 2234 Lawrence Ave. W., Weston, Ont. M9P 2A1 (416/248-1613) *Eng.-Fr.*

Bloom, Hyman, Box 743, Stn. Q, Toronto, Ont. M4T 2N5 (416/ 656-5793) *Fr.-Eng.*

Charlez, Georges, 358 Davenport Rd., Toronto, Ont. M5R 1K6 (416/923-7371) *Eng.-Fr./Fr.-Eng.*

Czarnecki, Mark, 758 Euclid Ave., Toronto, Ont. M6G 2V2 (416/532-6508) *Fr.-Eng.*

d'Oliveira, J.A., 25 Sunny Glenway, #315, Don Mills, Ont. M3C 2Z5 *Fr.-Eng.*

Dupont, Ernest, 111B Jefferson Ave., Toronto, Ont. M6K 3E4 (416/537-8172; 366-5405) *Eng.-Fr. / Fr.-Eng.*

Filius, Noele, 500 Duplex Ave., Apt. 1002, Toronto, Ont. M4R 1V6 (416/485-0954) *Eng.-Fr./Fr.-Eng.*

Fuhrman, Robert P., 511, The West Mall, Apt. 1811, Etobicoke, Ont. M9C 1G5 (416/622-1970; 863-0263) *Fr.-Eng./ Ger.-Eng./Cz.-Eng./Eng.-Fr./Eng.-Ger./Eng.-Cz.*

Gabrini, Michel, 1992 Yonge St., Ste. 302, Toronto, Ont. M4S 1Z7 (416/488-5905) *Eng.-Fr.*

Gatien, Emile, 210 Markland Dr., app. 911, Etobicoke, Ont. M9C 1R2 (416/621-2994) *Fr.-Eng.*

Gauthier, Gérard, #15G, 20 Prince Arthur Ave., Toronto, Ont. M5R 1B1 (416/967-1362) *Eng.-Fr./Fr.-Eng.*

Haynes, Donald H., 7 Walmer Rd., Apt. 1705, Toronto, Ont. M5R 2W8 (416/967-6943) *Ger.-Eng.*

Hoff, Jean Connell, 45 Southport St., Apt. 1409, Toronto, Ont. M6S 3N5 (416/769-7124) *Jap.-Eng.*

Hsia, Chester Chih-Chuan, 83 Deep Dene Dr., West Hill, Ont. M1C 1L9 (416/282-8316) *Eng.-Chi./Chi.-Eng.*

Jope, Dr. James, 50 Stephanie St., Apt. 2401, Toronto, Ont. M5T 1B3 (416/977-2807) *Du.-Eng.*

Lista, Luciano, 651 College St., Toronto, Ont. M6G 1B7 *Eng.-It.*

Metz, Charles, 37 Don Valley Dr., Toronto, Ont. M4K 2J1 (416/924-9379) *Eng.-Fr. / Fr.-Eng.*

O'Brien-Hitching, Patrick, 11 Breezewood Dr., Toronto, Ont. M8Y 2B9 (416/233-8693) *Eng.-Swed. / Swed.-Eng.*

Okuda, Francine, 100 Marlow Ave., Toronto, Ont. M4J 3V1 (416/466-5934) *Eng.-Fr.*

Roland, Jacques, 90 Eglinton Ave. W., Ste. 125, Toronto, Ont. M4R 2E4 (416/487-1576) *Eng.-Fr.*

Staples, Micheline, 96 Belsize Dr., Toronto, Ont. M4S 1L7 (416/487-3136) *Eng.-Fr.*

Stillich, Stefan W., 185 Bay St., #704, Toronto, Ont. M5J 1K6 (416/364-5666) *Eng.-Du. / Du.-Eng. / Fr.-Eng. / Swed.-Eng. / Nor.-Eng. / Dan.-Eng.*

Velvart, Germaine, 245 Hollywood Ave., Willowdale, Ont. M2N 3K7 (416/222-4351) *Eng.-Fr.*

VANIER, see Ottawa-Hull

WALKERTON

Voisin, Lucille, 16 rue George, C.P. 1118, Walkerton, Ont. N0G 2V0 (519/881-2951) *Eng.-Fr.*

WINDSOR

Gallerno, Mariette, 3971 Lennon Court, Windsor, Ont. N9G 2E4 (519/966-2565) *Eng.-Fr.*

Quebec

ANJOU, see Montreal

AYLMER (see also Ottawa-Hull)

Gamas, Gilles, 69 Atholl Doune, Aylmer, P.Q. J9J 1B9 (819/770-8777) *Eng.-Fr.*

Simard, Mme Gisèle, 552, cr. John Egan, Aylmer, P.Q. J9H 3V7 (819/684-0143) *Eng.-Fr./Fr.-Eng.*

Veilleux, Gaston, 37 ch. Foley, Aylmer, P.Q. J9H 2E6 (819/684-1377) *Eng.-Fr.*

BAIE-D'URFE, see Montreal

BEACONSFIELD, see Montreal

BEAUREPAIRE, see Montreal

BOUCHERVILLE, see Montreal

BROSSARD (see also Montreal)

Pelletier-Landry, Micheline, 6450 boul. Milan, app. 102, Brossard, P.Q. J4Z 2B2 (514/678-0999) *Eng.-Fr.*

CHAMBLY, see Montreal

CHARLESBOURG

Brousseau, Jean-Luc, 6382, rue des Citelles, Charlesbourg, P.Q. G1G 1E6 (418/623-5247) *Eng.-Fr. / Fr.-Eng.*

CHOMEDEY, see Montreal

DEUX MONTAGNES, see Montreal

DOLLARD DES ORMEAUX, see Montreal

DORVAL, see Montreal

DUVERNAY, see Montreal

FOSTER

Dubuc, Serge, Chemin Doucet, C.P. 57, Foster, P.Q. JOE 1RO (514/539-0980) *Eng.-Fr.*

GATINEAU

Delorme, Robert, 168 est boul. du Progrès, Gatineau, P.Q. J8T 2E4 (819/568-0097) *Eng.-Fr.*

GREENFIELD PARK, see Montreal

HAMPSTEAD, see Montreal

HULL, see Ottawa

IBERVILLE

Bernard-Frégeault, Mme Hélène, 158, rue Bernadette, Iberville, P.Q. J2X 4E6 (514/347-4512) *Eng.-Fr.*

ILE-DES-SOEURS, see Montreal

ILE-PERROT, see Montreal

JOLIETTE, see Montreal

L'ACADIE

Fournel-Paquin, Mme Gertrude, 204, Ruisseau des Noyers, L'Acadie, P.Q. JOJ 1HO (514/347-7061) *Eng.-Fr.*

LACHINE, see Montreal

LACOLLE

Legault, Mlle M.-G., C.P. 146, Lacolle, P.Q. JOJ 1JO (514/246-2225) *Eng.-Fr.*

LaSALLE, see Montreal

LAVAL, see Montreal

LAVAL-SUR-LE-LAC, see Montreal

LONGUEUIL, see Montreal

MARTINVILLE

Dorin, Henri, Domaine du Puyjalon, Martinville, P.Q. JOB 2AO (819/835-5570) *Eng.-Fr.*

MONTREAL (including surrounding areas)

Adlerblum, Armand, 4145 Blueridge Cres., app. 17, Montreal, P.Q. H3H 1S7 (514/842-4437) *Eng.-Fr. / Fr.-Eng.*

Aganian, Dikran, 1440, av. Bernard ouest, app. 4, Outremont, P.Q. H2V 1W3 (514/272-6372) *Eng.-Fr.*

Ali, Mme Michèle, 306 av. Hickson, St-Lambert, P.Q. J4P 2R1 (514/672-5014) *Eng.-Fr.*

Anderson, Mlle Linda, 11 chemin Salisbury, Pointe Claire, P.Q. H9S 3Z2 (514/697-4447) *Fr.-Eng.*

April, Mlle Nicole, 1050, rue Mackay, 3e étage, Montreal, P.Q. H3G 2H1 (514/861-6487) *Eng.-Fr.*

Arcache, Henri, 4000 ouest, de Maisonneuve, app. 1903, Westmount, P.Q. H3Z 1J9 (514/283-2172) *Eng.-Fr.*

Arcand, Mlle Claire, 10480, rue Meunier, Montreal, P.Q. H3L 2Z4 (514/387-6642) *Eng.-Fr./Fr.-Eng.*

Archambault, Mme J. Michelle, 5793, av. Trans Island, Montreal, P.Q. H3B 3W3 (514/731-8959) *Eng.-Fr./Fr.-Eng.*

Arsenault, Mme Murielle, c.a., 560, boul. Henri-Bourassa ouest, bur. 114, Montreal, P.Q. H3L 3P5 (514/332-9070) *Eng.-Fr.*

Aspler, Moses, 6523, chemin Baily, Montreal, P.Q. H4V 1A1 (514/486-2162) *Fr.-Eng.*

Ayotte-Champagne, Mme Lucille, 6545, rue Chambord, Montreal, P.Q. H2G 3C1 (514/274-4751, 285-2316) *Eng.-Fr.*

Ayotte-Yakhloufi, Mme Louise, 2670, boul. Saint-Joseph est, app. 2, Montreal, P.Q. H1Y 2A6 (514/525-2260) *Eng.-Fr.*

Azuelos Chétrit, Mme Dina, 5999, av. Monkland, app. 1406, Montreal, P.Q. H4A 1H1 (514/483-2140) *Eng.-Fr.*

Azuelos, Claude, 3540 rue Limoges, St-Laurent, P.Q. H4K 1Y3 (514/874-2469) *Eng.-Fr.*

Baptiste, Mme Marie-Laure, 5362, av. Louis-Colin, Montreal, P.Q. H3T 1T4 (514/738-1464) *Eng.-Fr.*

Barsamian, Edouard, Place Concorde, 3355 ch. Queen Mary, app. 204, Montreal, P.Q. H3V 1A5 (514/739-9174) *Eng.-Fr.*

Barta, Mme Micheline, 6630, rue Sherbrooke ouest, app. 1009, Montreal, P.Q. H4B 1N7 (514/488-4811) *Eng.-Fr./Fr.-Eng.*

Baudelle, Mme Gemma, 1595 St-Germain, Ville de St-Laurent, P.Q. H4L 3S7 (514/747-3472) *Eng.-Fr./Span.-Fr./It.-Fr./Port.-Fr.*

Beaugrand-Champagne, Jules, 2711, boul. Edouard-Montpetit, app. 10, Montreal, P.Q. H3T 1J6 (514/733-3980) *Eng.-Fr./Fr.-Eng.*

Beccat, J.-P., 33, ch. Côte Ste-Catherine, app. 1401, Montreal, P.Q. H2V 2A1 (514/849-3665) *Eng.-Fr./Fr.-Eng.*

Bélanger, Gilles, 11125, av. Audoin, Montreal Nord, P.Q. H1H 5G1 (514/323-0006) *Eng.-Fr.*

Bélanger-Moyson, Christine, 517, place Ambroise, Saint-Lambert, P.Q. J4S 1S7 (514/672-6775) *Eng.-Fr./Fr.-Eng.*

Béliveau, Roger, 9330, av. de Galinée, Montreal, P.Q. H2M 2A6 (514/384-8099) *Eng.-Fr./Fr.-Eng.*

Bellerose, Mme Marguerite P., 70, 6e ave., app. 5, Ile-Perrot, P.Q. J7V 4V2 (514/453-5779) *Eng.-Fr./Fr.-Eng.*

Belleville, Marcel, 5885, rue Madore, Montreal, P.Q. H1M 1H3 (514/256-4824) *Eng.-Fr.*

Belva, Mme C.C., 2710, rue de Beaurivage, Montreal, P.Q. H1L 5W4 (514/353-7394) *Eng.-Fr.*

Bertrand, Mlle Francine, 2300, rue St-Mathieu, app. 504, Montreal, P.Q. H3H 2J8 (514/937-7665) *Eng.-Fr.*

Blais-Ialenti, Mme Diane, 40, rue de l'Anse-de-Miquelon, Laval-sur-le-Lac, P.Q. H7Y 1V7 (514/689-2569) *Eng.-Fr.*

Boffin, L. John, 6, rue Woodcroft, Dollard-des-Ormeaux, P.Q. H9A 1G6 (514/684-7480) *Span.-Eng.*

Boivineau, Roger, 5003, av. Grosvenor, Montreal, P.Q. H3W 2M2 (514/737-4078) *Eng.-Fr.*

Bouchard, Roger, C.P. 158, Succ. Bourassa, Montreal, P.Q. H2C 3E9 (514/388-4344) *Eng.-Fr./Fr.-Eng.*

Boudreau, Yvon, 9177, rue St-Denis, Montreal, P.Q. H2M 1N9 (514/389-4717) *Eng.-Fr.*

Bourgeois, Denise, 6280 Northcrest Place, app 620, Montréal, P.Q. H3S 2N1 (514/731-2896) *Eng.-Fr./Fr.-Eng.* (Interpreter)

Boutin-Quesnel, Mme Rachel, 191, boul. Curé-Labelle, Sainte-Rose (Laval), P.Q. H7L 2Z9 (514/622-4378) *Eng.-Fr.*

Boyer, Mlle Thérèse, 2045, rue Closse, app. 4-A, Montreal, P.Q. H3H 1Z7 (514/937-4032) *Eng.-Fr./Fr.-Eng./Span.-Fr./Span.-Eng./Port.-Fr./Port.-Eng.*

Brody, K.D., 4242 West Hill Ave., Montreal, P.Q. H4B 2S7 (514/487-0644) *Fr.-Eng.*

Brunet, J.-P., 3, place Belle-Rive, app. 1009, Laval, P.Q. H7V 1B2 (514/681-9568) *Eng.-Fr./Fr.-Eng.*

Burke, Mlle Sheila, 250, av. Lansdowne, app. 9, Westmount, P.Q. H3Z 2L3 (514/937-4349) *Fr.-Eng.*

Buteau, Mlle M.F., 8449, rue Lajeunesse, Montreal, P.Q. H2P 2E7 (514/387-4391) *Eng.-Fr./Fr.-Eng.*

Caillé, Sylvain, 1530 av. Docteur-Penfield, app. 300, Montreal, P.Q. H3G 1C1 (514/933-7689) *Eng.-Fr.*

Caouette, Mlle Diane, 2308, rue Beaubien est, Montreal, P.Q. H2G 1M9 (514/721-0988) *Span.-Fr./Ger.-Fr./It.-Fr.*

Cardinal-Laurin, Mme Jacqueline, 28, av. Kelvin, Outremont, P.Q. H2V 1T2 (514/733-1804) *Eng.-Fr.*

Castro, Mme Micheline, 1078, boul. Bellevue, Greenfield Park, P.Q. J4V 1J9 (514/676-6013) *Fr.-Span.*

Chamaillard, Gaston-Gilles, 7555 est, boul. Gouin, Montréal, P.Q. H1E 1A7 (514/648-2296) *Eng.-Fr.*

de Chancenotte, Mme Jacq., 18 Anworth, Westmount, P.Q. H3Y 2E7 (514/935-4564) *Eng.-Fr.*

Charette, Mme Yolande, 2970 rue Martigny, Longueuil, P.Q. J4L 1V6 (514/468-0981) *Eng.-Fr.*

Charland, Gérard, 446 rue des Moulins, Mont St-Hilaire, P.Q. J3G 4S6 (514/467-1253) *Eng.-Fr.*

Chevalier, Mme Colette, 5291, rue McKenna, Montreal, P.Q. H3T 1T9 (514/737-7278) *Eng.-Fr.*

Chliapnikoff, Véra, 8222, av. de l'Epée, app. 2, Montreal, P.Q. H3N 2G1 (514/277-9255) *Eng.-Fr./Fr.-Eng./Russ.-Ger./Ger.-Russ.*

Christophory, Mme Christine, 346 Linnet Cres., Dorval, P.Q. H9S 2K9 (514/631-1490) *Eng.-Fr.*

Clarke, Mme B. Denise, 4961, av. Dornal, Montreal, P.Q. H3W 1W1 (514/737-2012) *Eng.-Fr.*

Clas, André, 7405, rue Maynard, Montreal, P.Q. H3R 2B3 (514/733-1295) *Eng.-Fr.*

Claxton, Mme Patricia, 5138, Côte St-Antoine, Montreal, P.Q. H4A 1N7 (514/489-5597) *Fr.-Eng.*

Cloutier, Denis, 208 rue Pierre-Conefroy, Boucherville, P.Q. J4B 1K6 (514/655-2114) *Eng.-Fr. / Fr.-Eng.*

Connolly, J.-G., 10355, rue Verville, Montreal, P.Q. H3L 3E6 (514/387-8727) *Eng.-Fr.*

Constant, Mme Blandine, 3630, rue Berne, Brossard, P.Q. J4Z 2P2 (514/676-0482) *Eng.-Fr.*

Coppin, Mrs. Mary, 2156, Sherbrooke St. W., Apt. 16, Montreal, P.Q. H3H 1G7 (514/933-8572) *Fr.-Eng.*

Corbin, Lise, 4960 rue Barclay, app 6, Montreal, P.Q. H3W 1E2 (514/735-2838) *Eng.-Fr.*

Côté, Nancy, 748, av. Rockland, Outremont, P.Q. H2V 2Z6 (514/274-4610) *Fr.-Eng.*

Courtois, Colette, 5539, av. Woodbury, app. 9, Montreal, P.Q. H3T 1S5 (514/731-1378) *Eng.-Fr.*

Couture, Yvon, 2590, rue Tadoussac, Laval, P.Q. H7E 3V6 (514/661-9523) *Eng.-Fr./Fr.-Eng.*

Cunio, Renée, 3330, av. Ridgewood, app. 40, Montreal, P.Q. H3V 1C1 (514/285-8125) *Fr.-Eng./Eng.-Fr./Span.-Eng./It.-Eng.*

Daigneault, Mlle Simonne, 7425, chemin Canora, app. 312, Montreal, P.Q. H3P 2H9 (514/738-9236) *Eng.-Fr.*

Daoust, André, 5466, av. Isabella, Montreal, P.Q. H3X 1R6 (514/489-9583) *Eng.-Fr.*

De Grace, J.-Gérard, 3460, av. Simpson, app. 603, Montreal, P.Q. H3G 2J4 (514/937-8829) *Eng.-Fr.*

De Grandpré, J.-P., 6840, 10e ave., Montreal, P.Q. H1Y 2J2 (514/722-9293) *Eng.-Fr.*

Deschamps, René, 1985, rue Bellevue, St-Bruno, P.Q. J3V 3X3 (514/653-3268) *Eng.-Fr.*

Descoteaux, Diane, 3250 av. Forest Hill, app. 206, Montreal, P.Q. H3V 1C8 (514/738-2078) *Eng.-Fr.* also Trois-Rivières

Desjardins, Suzanne, 4326, av. Earnscliffe, Montreal, P.Q. H4A 3E8 (514/486-8940) *Eng.-Fr.*

Desrochers, André, 226, av. Willowdale, Outremont, P.Q. H3T 1G7 (514/738-7901) *Eng.-Fr./Fr.-Eng.*

Desrochers, Mme Mireille, 10, rue de Montmagny, Boucherville, P.Q. J4B 4H4 (514/655-1959) *Eng.-Fr./Fr.-Eng.*

Divirgilio, Mme Lise, 3000, boul. Gouin ouest, Montreal, P.Q. H3M 1B6 (514/334-8178) *Eng.-Fr./Fr.-Eng./It.-Fr./It.-Eng./Span.-Fr./Span.-Eng.*

Dorais, Rupert, 6070, rue de Terrebonne, Montreal, P.Q. H4A 1B9 (514/486-7715) *Eng.-Fr./Fr.-Eng.*

Dubuc, Mme H. Chrétien, 605, rue Berwick, Mont-Royal, P.Q. H3R 2A1 (514/737-8813) *Eng.-Fr.*

Dufresne, Mme Claudine, 745, place Fortier, app. 907, St-Laurent, P.Q. (514/336-6249) *Eng.-Fr.*

Dugal, Pierre, 10347, av. de l'Esplanade, Montreal, P.Q. H3L 2Y1 (514/384-4347) *Eng.-Fr.*

Duhamel-Vanderveken, Mme Lucie, 343 rue Pine, St-Lambert, P.Q. J4P 2N7 (514/671-8962) *Eng.-Fr.*

Dupont, André, 3450, place Decelles, app. 41, Montreal, P.Q. (514/737-4530) *Eng.-Fr.*

Dyke, Patricia, 12184, rue Louis-Jadon, Montréal, P.Q. H4K 1T7 (514/331-4286) *Eng.-Fr./Fr.-Eng.*

Epitaux, Mlle Jacq., 5538, av. Decelles, app. 2, Montreal, P.Q. H3T 1W5 (514/735-5065) *Eng.-Fr.*

Favreau, André, 357, av. de Bretagne, Longueuil, P.Q. J4H 1R2 (514/677-3583) *Eng.-Fr.*

Favreau-Beauvais, Mme Françoise, 232, av. Curzon, St-Lambert, P.Q. J4P 2V2 (514/672-8717) *Eng.-Fr.*

Filiatrault, Jean, 12122, rue Daigle, Montreal, P.Q. H4J 1S7 (514/334-8897) *Eng.-Fr.*

Fontana, Mme M.-T., 4381, Circle Rd., Pierrefonds, P.Q. H9H 2G8 *Eng.-Fr./Fr.-Eng./It.-Fr.*

Fournier, Mme Rita Labonté, 2150, boul. de Maisonneuve ouest, app. 1003, Montreal, P.Q. H3H 1L2 (514/933-4739) *Eng.-Fr./Fr.-Eng.*

Fourtet, Mlle Monique, 851, chemin du Lac Renaud, Ste-Adèle, P.Q. JOR 1LO (514/229-2662) *Fr.-Eng.*

Franquet-Kraushaar, Mme Nelly, 4801, boul. de Maisonneuve ouest, Westmount, P.Q. H3Z 1M4 (514/935-5000) *Eng.-Fr./Ger.-Fr.*

Frenette, Raymond, 559, rue Church, Beaurepaire, P.Q. H9W 3T5 (514/695-6634) *Eng.-Fr.*

Ftaya, Mme Madeleine, 1745, ave Cedar, app. 809, Montreal, P.Q. H3G 1A7 (514/935-3982) *Eng.-Fr./Fr.-Eng./Arab.-Eng.*

Gaber, Fakhry, 2460, rue Paton, St-Laurent, P.Q. H4M 1C8 (514/744-2087) *Eng.-Fr./Fr.-Arab./Eng.-Arab./Arab.Fr.*

Gagné-Robert, Mme Marie, 870, rue Rouillard, Mont-St-Hilaire, P.Q. (514/464-3466) *Eng.-Fr./Fr.-Eng.*

Gagnon, P.-O., 2860, cr. de la Marquise, Brossard, P.Q. J4Y 1P4 (514/656-6171) *Eng.-Fr.*

Gagnon, Roland, 50A, 22e Ave., St-Marthe-sur-le-Lac, P.Q. JOW 1PO (514/472-5888) *Eng.-Fr.*

Gallant, Mme Nicole, 5228, rue Versailles, Pierrefonds, P.Q. H8Z 2P9 (514/626-3512) *Eng.-Fr.*

Gareau, Richard, 1464, rue de Val-Brillant, Laval, P.Q. H7Y 1T6 (514/689-1249) *Eng.-Fr. / Fr.-Eng.*

Garneau, Edouard, 1509, rue Sherbrooke ouest, app. 62, Montreal, P.Q. H3G 1L7 (514/935-4727) *Eng.-Fr./Fr.-Eng.*

Gascon, Mme Rolande, 6375, av. de Vimy, Montreal, P.Q. H3S 2R5 (514/733-1773) *Eng.-Fr.*

Gauthier, Pierre, 632, Place du May, Ste-Thérèse en Haut, P.Q. J7E 2L5 (514/435-0898) *Eng.-Fr.*

Gauthier, Mme Viviane, 579, av. Champagneur, Outremont, P.Q. H2V 3P4 (514/273-1197) *Eng.-Fr./Ger.-Fr.*

Gauvin, Claude, 797, av. Lavallée, Laval, P.Q. H7E 2W6 (514/661-2121) *Eng.-Fr.*

Gémar, J.-C., 3809, av. Kent, Montreal, P.Q. H3S 1N4 (514/341-6716) *Eng.-Fr.*

Germain, Mlle Marthe, 256 9e ave, Deux-Montagnes, P.Q. J7R 3M3 *Eng.-Fr.*

Giguère-Boyer, Mme Jacq., 136, rue Sénécal, Montreal, P.Q. H8P 2B1 (514/366-3848) *Eng.-Fr./Fr.-Eng.*

Gilcher, Mme Rachel, 465, av. Berwick, Mont-Royal, P.Q. H3R 1Z8 (514/733-0904) *Eng.-Fr.*

Gingras, Mme Madeleine, 3975, rue Berri, Montreal, P.Q. H2L 4H2 (514/849-0249) *Eng.-Fr.*

Giocondese, Mlle Denise, 2210 rue Prud'homme, Montreal, P.Q. H4A 3H2 (514/487-5551) *Eng.-Fr./Span.-Fr./It.-Fr.*

Girard, Mme Louise, R.R. 1, Mont-Tremblant, P.Q. JOT 1ZO (514/425-2673) *Eng.-Fr.*

Girard-Larocque, Mme Henriette, 12105, av. Henri-Beau, Saraguay, Montreal, P.Q. H4K 2E6 (514/332-5285) *Eng.-Fr.*

Globensky, Mme Claire, 19 des Bouleaux, C.P. 1221, St-Sauveur, P.Q. J0R 1R0 (514/227-5952) *Eng.-Fr.*

Gomez, Luis J., 840, 47e Ave., Lachine, P.Q. H8T 2R3 (514/283-3013) *Eng.-Span.*

Gosselin, Yves, 113, rue Morley, Greenfield Park, P.Q. J4V 2Z1(514/672-9574) *Eng.-Fr.*

Goulet-Bonin, Mme Jeanne, 3022, boul. Langelier, Montreal, P.Q. H1N 3A6 (514/254-5700) *Eng.-Fr.*

Granier, Mme Monique, "Li Pimparrin", 200, rue Casgrain, Longueuil, P.Q. J4L 1K9 (514/674-6352) *Eng.-Fr./Span.-Fr.*

Graziano, Mme Simonetta, 26, ch. McLynn, Dollard-des-Ormeaux, P.Q. (514/684-8897) *Fr.-It./Eng.-It.*

Grossman, Liliane, 39 Holton Ave., Westmount, P.Q. H3Y 2E9 (514/989-1687; 937-2152) *Fr.-Eng. / Span.-Eng. / It.-Eng.*

Guay, Gaston, 12240, rue Dépatie, Montreal, P.Q. H4J 1X2 (514/334-1017) *Eng.-Fr.*

Hais, Mlle Tatiana, 4877, rue de la Peltrie, Montreal, P.Q. H3W 1K6 (514/739-5354) *Fr.-Russ./Russ.-Fr./Roum.-Fr./Fr.-Roum./Span.-Fr./Fr.-Span.*

Habra, Mme Jocelyne, 4, ave. Crestwood, Montreal Ouest, P.Q. H4X 1N2 (514/488-4589) *Eng.-Fr.*

Harder, Mlle Carolyn, 4488, rue Ste-Catherine ouest, app. 702, Westmount, P.Q. H3Z 1R7 (514/937-6560) *Fr.-Eng./Span.-Eng./It.-Eng./Port.-Eng./Eng.-Span.*

Hérard, Roland, 670, av. Gentilly, Duvernay, P.Q. H7E 2Y5 (514/661-4968) *Eng.-Fr.*

Heuet-Fauteux, Mme G., 65, av. Brittany, app. 412, Mont-Royal, P.Q. H3P 1A4 (514/341-4266) *Eng.-Fr./Fr.-Eng.*

Heurtel, J.-P., 442, rue Rockland, Mont-Royal, P.Q. H3P 2W8 (514/739-7261) *Eng.-Fr.*

Horguelin, Mme Hélène, 3256, av. Lacombe, Montreal, P.Q. H3T 1L7 (514/737-4620) *Eng.-Fr.*

Houde, Raymond, 3440, boul. Henri-Bourassa est, Montreal Nord, P.Q. H1H 5M2 (514/663-5579) *Eng.-Fr.*

Houde, Mme Raymonde, 7090 rue Cannes, Montreal, P.Q. H1S 2P8 (514/327-1077) *Eng.-Fr.*

Houle, Edouard, C.P. 150, Dollard-des-Ormeaux, P.Q. H9G 2H5 (514/861-4474) *Eng.-Fr. / Fr.-Eng.*

Hozer, Mme Liliane, 32, 90e ave., Chomedey, P.Q. H7W 3K6 (514/681-9722) *Eng.-Fr.*

Hudon, J.L., 4807, av. Victoria, Montreal, P.Q. H3W 2M9 (514/487-7312) *Eng.-Fr./Fr.-Eng.*

Ieraci, Mme Michelle, 4598, av. Marcil, Montreal, P.Q. H4A 3A1 (514/486-4705) *Eng.-Fr.*

Jammal, Mme Amal, 4996, av. Roslyn, Montreal, P.Q. H3W 2L2 (514/341-3876) *Eng.-Fr.*

Janelle-Gascon, Mme Christiane, 4095, ch. Côte-des-Neiges, app. 25, Montreal, P.Q. H3H 1W9 (514/733-5387) *Eng.-Fr.*

Joannides, Mme Io, 55, av. de Vimy, Outremont, P.Q. H3S 2P9 (514/731-6779) *Eng.-Fr./Fr.-Eng./G.-Fr./G.-Eng.*

Jones, Mme Nicole, 415, rue Gohier, St-Laurent, P.Q. H4L 3H6 (514/748-8672) *Eng.-Fr.*

Jurisic, Mlle Vida, 3555, ch. Côte-des-Neiges, app. 310, Montreal, P.Q. H3H 1V2 (514/931-2157) *Fr.-Eng.*

Kearns Pierre-Antoine, Mme Suzanne, 1635, rue Dudemaine, app. 3, Montreal, P.Q. H3M 1R2 (514/336-2180) *Eng.-Fr./Fr.-Eng.*

Khayat, Clément, 4992, ch. du Souvenir, Chomedey-ouest, Laval, P.Q. H7W 4L7 (514/688-7078) *Eng.-Fr.*

Khlok, Diman, 672, av. Grosvenor, Westmount, P.Q. H3V 2S8 (514/487-3177) *Eng.-Fr./Ger.-Fr.*

Kory, Manfred, 1117 Ste-Catherine ouest, bur. 423, Montreal, P.Q. H3B 1H9 (514/844-4860) *Eng.-Ger./Ger.-Eng.*

Lacoursière, Hervé, 1161, rue Grenade, Chambly, P.Q. J3L 3B9 (514/658- 6221) *Eng.-Fr./Fr.-Eng.*

Lafontaine, Mme Françoise, 72 Roselawn Cres., Mont-Royal, P.Q. H3P 1H9 (514/739-1892) *Eng.-Fr.*

Laforce, Luc, 3040, rue Somerset, St-Laurent, P.Q. H4K 1R6 (514/334-8464) *Eng.-Fr./Fr.-Eng./Ger.-Fr./Ger.Eng./Span.-Fr./Span.-Eng./It.-Fr./It.-Eng./Port.-Fr./Port.-Eng.*

Lagacé, Henri, 5576, av. Wilderton, Montreal, P.Q. H3T 1R9 (514/737-8014) *Eng.-Fr.*

Laliberté, Roger, C.P. 156, Beaconsfield, P.Q. H9W 5T7 (514/697-4033) *Eng.-Fr./Fr.-Eng.*

Lara, J.-P., 185 rue Séraphin Marion, Boucherville, P.Q. J4B 6T8 (514/655-5046) *Eng.-Fr.*

Laroche-Kahanov, Mme Claire, 29, ch. Finchley, Hampstead, P.Q. H3X 2Z6 (514/486-2430) *Eng.-Fr.*

La Rue, Mlle Chantal, 695, rue St-Charles ouest, app. 608, Longueuil, P.Q. J4H 1H2 (514/679-2019) *Eng.-Fr.*

Latouche, Pierre, 4384, av. Coolbrook, Montreal, P.Q. H4A 3G2 (514/482-5199) *Eng.-Fr.*

Laurin, Mlle Germaine, 1692, boul. St-Joseph est, app. 4, Montreal, P.Q. H2J 1M9 (514/527-1734) *Eng.-Fr./Fr.-Eng.*

Laurin, J.-G., 13, Plateau Belmont, Repentigny, P.Q. J6A 3N8 (514/581-3297) *Eng.-Fr.*

Lavigueur, Mlle Huguette, 1509, rue Sherbrooke ouest, app. 5, Montreal, P.Q. H3G 1M1 (514/935-1605) *Eng.-Fr.*

Legault-Bégin, Mme Madeleine, 2670, rue Rosemère, Duvernay, Laval, P.Q. H7E 2K1 (514/669-0576) *Eng.-Fr.*

Léger-Farkas, Mme Louise, 286, rue Green, St-Lambert, P.Q. J4P 1T2 (514/672-1980) *Eng.-Fr.*

Lemaire, Christian, 4911 Côte des Neiges, app. 409, Montreal, P.Q. H3V 1H7 (514/738-3538) *Eng.-Fr.*

Lemieux, Bernard, 11000, rue de St-Réal, Montreal, P.Q. H3M 2Y4 (514/332-1894) *Eng.-Fr.*

LeThullier, Jacques, 4040, av. Wilson, Montreal, P.Q. H4A 2T9 (514/483-2094) *Eng.-Fr.*

Lette, Mme Maryrose, 27, av. McNider, Outremont, P.Q. H2V 3X4 (514/871-3838) *Eng.-Fr./Fr.-Eng./Ger.-Fr./Fr.-Ger.*

Levac, Patrice, 65, rue de Tilly, Boucherville, P.Q. J4B 4N9 (514/655-9151) *Eng.-Fr.*

Lévesque, Paul, 3010 boul. St-Joseph est, app 2, Montreal, P.Q. H1Y 2B5 (514/273-6757) *Eng.-Fr.*

Lévy, Moise, 176, pr. Schubert, Dollard-des-Ormeaux, P.Q. H9B 2E4 (514/684-9692) *Eng.-Fr./Fr.-Eng./Fr.-Span./Eng.-Span.*

Liboiron, Mlle Micheline, 7560, rue Marquette, app. 2, Montreal, P.Q. H2E 2E4 (514/729-5935) *Eng.-Fr.*

Longtin, Mme Odile, 1730, Croissant Séguin, Brossard, P.Q. J4X 1K8 (514/671-6474) *Eng.-Fr.*

Lucassian, Vartan, 65, rue Sherbrooke est, app. 1806, Montreal, P.Q. H2X 1C4 (514/282-0122) *Eng.-Span./Span.-Eng.*

Mailhot, Gérard, 6963, place de Nevers, Montreal, P.Q. H4K 1E4 (514/334-7047) *Eng.-Fr.*

Manson-Daoust, Mme Aline, 5466, av. Isabella, Montreal, P.Q. H3X 1R6 (514/489-9583) *Eng.-Fr.*

Marchand, Mlle Lise, 486, rue Maple, St-Lambert, P.Q. J4P 2S4 (514/672-5287) *Eng.-Fr./Fr.-Eng.*

Marécat, F.J., 187, Rang du petit Côteau, Verchères, P.Q. JOL 2RO (work: 514/282-5657) *Eng.-Fr.*

Margulies, Mme Dorothée, 4530, ch. de la Côte-des-Neiges, app. 1408, Montreal, P.Q. H3V 1G1 (514/737-7505) *Eng.-Fr./Fr.-Eng./Roum.-Fr./Roum.-Eng./Ger.-Fr./Ger.-Eng.*

Marquette, P.R., 1055, rue Vanier, St-Laurent, P.Q. H4L 1S8 (514/744-6254) *Eng.-Fr./Fr.-Eng.*

Marquis, Roland, 6649A St-Denis, Montréal, P.Q. H2S 2S1 (514/277-1820) *Eng.-Fr.*

Massy, G., 5500, rue Snowdon, app. 501, Montreal, P.Q. H3X 1Y6 (514/488-5448) *Eng.-Fr.*

Mathan, Mlle Claudine, 3181, boul. Edouard-Montpetit, app. 12, Montreal, P.Q. H3T 1K3 (514/735-0537) *Eng.-Fr.*

Mathan, Mme Eva, 152, rue Pierre-Boucher, Boucherville, P.Q. J4B 5B4 (514/655-7806) *Eng.-Fr.*

Mayer, Mlle Rochelle, 252, rue Cabano, LaSalle, P.Q. H8R 2M1 (514/364-1350) *Eng.-Fr.*

Melby, E.K., 226, rue Ste-Anne, Varennes, P.Q. JOL 2PO (514/652-2107) *Fr.-Eng.*

Meurice, Pierre, 5290, rue Louis-Collin, Montreal, P.Q. H3T 1T3 (514/731-6269) *Eng.-Fr./Fr.-Eng.*

Meyer, Serge, 4820, av. Wilson, Montreal, P.Q. H3X 3P2 (514/489-4206) *Eng.-Fr.*

Michaud, Mme Adèle, 6632, av. Monkland, Montreal, P.Q. H4B 1H4 (514/482-9543) *Eng.-Fr./Span.-Fr./Fr.-Eng.*

Michaud, P.G., c.r., 620, rue Cathcart, bur. 752, Montreal, P.Q. H3B 1M1 (514/866-9575) *Eng.-Fr.*

Miles, Mme Céline, 25, Magnolia Rd., Baie-d-Urfé, P.Q. H9X 3K7 (514/457-9311) *Eng.-Fr.*

Monty, Mme Marie-José, 10, av. Ingleside, Westmount, P.Q. H3Q 1N3 (514/933-0800) *Eng.-Fr.*

Morand, Alain, 1920, rue de Lorimier, Longueuil, P.Q. J4K 3N7 (514/651-5153) *Eng.-Fr.*

Moreau, Mme Andrée, 3460 rue Peel, app. 811, Montreal, P.Q. H3A 2M1 (514/286-9128) *Eng.-Fr.*

Morin, Mlle Carmelle, 6616, rue de Normanville, Montreal, P.Q. H2S 2B9 (514/271-4037) *Eng.-Fr.*

Morin, Mlle Michelle, 10560, av. Hogue, Montreal, P.Q. H3L 3J2 (514/337-8772) *Eng.-Fr.*

Murray, Mme Jacq., 148, rue du Béarn, St-Lambert, P.Q. J4S 1K7 (514/671-3469) *Eng.-Fr.*

Myers, Hugh, 768, rue Maréchal, Longueuil, P.Q. J4L 2C5 (514/670-0946) *Fr.-Eng.*

Olivier, Daniel, 21, rue d'Ailleboust, Joliette, P.Q. J6E 6K1 (514/759-1187) *Eng.-Fr.*

Orvoine, Mme F.A., 672, av. Grosvenor, Westmount, P.Q. H3V 2S8 (514/487-3177) *Eng.-Fr.*

Ouanès, Mlle Danièle, 3480, rue Simpson, app. 408, Montreal, P.Q. H3G 2N7 (514/933-2439) *S.Cr.-Fr.*

Ouimet, Mme Germaine, 10970, rue de Florence, Montreal, P.Q. H3L 2K9 (514/389-0895) *Eng.-Fr./Span.-Fr.*

Pageau-Goyette, Mme Nycol, 432, Place Jacques Cartier, Montreal, P.Q. H2Y 3B3 (514/866-2648) *Eng.-Fr./Fr.-Eng.*

Papavasil, Mme Jeannette, 6001, ch. Côte-St-Luc, app. 209, Montreal, P.Q. H3X 2G4 (514/482-8715) *Fr.-Eng./Turk.-Fr./Turk.-Eng./G.-Fr./G.-Eng.*

Parenteau, Mme Nicole, 106, rue de Touraine, St-Lambert, P.Q. (514/277-8703) *Eng.-Fr.*

Partensky, J.-P., 520, rue de Gaspé, bur. 510, Ile-des-Soeurs, P.Q. H3E 1G1 (514/761-3775) *Eng.-Fr./Span.-Fr.*

Pellerin, Jacques, 2072, rue Notre-Dame-de-Grâce, Longueuil, P.Q. J4J 3G8 (work: 514/283-6829) *Eng.-Fr.*

Péloquin-Jourdain, Mme Pauline, 11230, av. du Bois-de-Boulogne, Montreal, P.Q. H3M 2X3 (514/334-1663) *Eng.-Fr.*

Phaneuf, Frédéric, 11915, rue Guertin, Montreal, P.Q. H4J 1V7 (514/334-3186) *Eng.-Fr./Fr.-Eng.*

Pilozzi-Korfage, Mme Liane, 3570, av. Ridgewood, app. 303, Montreal, P.Q. H3V 1C2 (514/738-2046) *Eng.-Fr./It.-Fr.*

Pinault, Mme Louise, 221, chemin Forest, Beaconsfield, P.Q. H9W 2N1 (514/697-1658) *Fr.-Eng.*

Plaice, Mme H.M., 5380, boul. St-Joseph, Lachine, P.Q. H8T 1S4 (514/634-2485) *Fr.-Eng.*

Plouffe, Mme Christine, 2, Parklane Place, Dollard-des-Ormeaux, P.Q. H9G 1B9 *Eng.-Fr.*

Poirier-Asch, Mme Huguette, 509, rue Laplante, app. 2, LaSalle, P.Q. H8R 3B7 (514/366-5727) *Eng.-Fr.*

Pollet, R.J., 1920, rue des Cèdres, St-Bruno de Montarville, P.Q. J3V 3M3 (514/653-2237) *Fr.-Eng./Eng.-Fr.*

Pottier, Michel, 5171, av. MacMahon, Montreal, P.Q. H4V 2B8 (514/487-3184) *Eng.-Fr.*

Pranno-Bisson, Raymonde, 895 rue Cardinal, Ville St-Laurent, P.Q. H4L 3E3 (514/747-4413) *Eng.-Fr. / Fr.-Eng.*

Pratt, Mme Audrey, 4339, av. Hingston, Montreal, P.Q. H4A 2J8 (work: 514/873-4954) *Fr.-Eng.*

Progneaux, Francis, 5179, av. Clanranald, Montreal, P.Q. H3X 2S5 (514/486-9853) *Eng.-Fr.*

Quijano, J.-P., 304, av. Querbes, Outremont, P.Q. H2V 3W3 (514/845-0219) *Eng.-Fr.*

Raymond-Dandonneau, Mme Louise, 4388, rue Marcil, Montreal, P.Q. H4A 2Z8 (514/486-2925) *Eng.-Fr.*

Rémillard, Louis, 10390, av. London, Montreal Nord, P.Q. H1H 4H5 (514/322-9986) *Eng.-Fr.*

Ricard, Mme Kelly, 3652, rue Northcliffe, Montreal, P.Q. H4A 3K7 (514/486-2435) *Fr.-Eng.*

Richter-Wilde, Eva, 1805 du Bocage, St-Bruno, P.Q. J3V 4M7 (514/653-3469) *Fr.-Eng. / Ger.-Eng.*

Riopel, Mlle Michelle, 25, av. Brittany, app. 308, Mont-Royal, P.Q. H3P 1A2 (514/739-9064) *Eng.-Fr./Fr.-Eng.*

Rivard, Mlle Cécile, 5970, 21e ave., app. 407, Montreal, P.Q. H1X 2G4 (514/727-2414) *Eng.-Fr.*

Rochette, Gilles, 5673 Monkland, Montreal, P.Q. H4A 1E5 (514/487-0732) *Eng.-Fr.*

Rogers, B.J., 24 Cedars Dr., Baie-d'Urfé, P.Q. H9X 2T4 (514/524-1115) *Fr.-Eng.*

Rosenthal, Mme Heather, 603, rue Powell, Montreal, P.Q. H3R 1L7 (514/733-6258) *Fr.-Eng./Ger.-Eng.*

Rouleau, J.-P., 2525, Havre-de-Iles, #606A, Laval, P.Q. H7W 4C4 (514/688-4874) *Eng.-Fr.*

Sabella, Marcel, 4165, rue Mackenzie, Montreal, P.Q. H3S 1E7 (514/737-2569) *Eng.-Fr.*

Saint-Georges, Mlle Isabelle, 4063 av. Marcil, Notre-Dame-de-Grâce, P.Q. H4A 2Z7 (514/482-0755) *Eng.-Fr.*

Saint-Martin, Mlle Hélène, 1225, rue St-Marc, app. 303, Montreal, P.Q. H3H 2E7 (514/932-8786) *Eng.-Fr.*

Samman, Mlle Aurore, 625, rue Milton, app. 1403, Montreal, P.Q. H2X 1W7 (514/843-3585) *Eng.-Fr.*

Schneider, Mme Colette, 4922, av. Bessborough, Montreal, P.Q. H4V 2S3 (514/488-4994) *Eng.-Fr.*

Séguin, Marcel, 4496, rue Maplewood, Pierrefonds, P.Q. H9A 1B3 (514/626-4873) *Eng.-Fr.*

Sénécal, Mlle Laurette, 283, rue de Salaberry, St-Jean, P.Q. J3B 6R8 (514/348-4951) *Eng.-Fr.*

Sévigny, Mme Doris, 10055, rue de la Roche, Montreal, P.Q. H2C 2N9 (514/387-0303) *Fr.-Eng./Eng.-Fr.*

Sokolowsky, Mlle Hertha, 4145, boul. Décarie, app. 5, Montreal, P.Q. H4A 3J8 (514/481-5735) *Fr.-Eng./Ger.-Eng./Span.-Eng.*

Spilka, Mme Irène Vachon, 4928, rue Piedmont, Montreal, P.Q. H3V 1E2 (514/731-7010) *Eng.-Fr./Span.-Fr.*

Stoian, Mme Lyliane, 662 de Gaspé, Ile-des-Soeurs, P.Q. H3E 1H1 (514/7615495) *Eng.-Fr./Ger.-Fr./Roum.-Fr.*

Storch, Mme R.-A., 555, av. Curzon, St-Lambert, P.Q. J4P 2V9 (514/465-3695) *Eng.-Fr.*

Tanguay, Raymond, 990, av. Pratt, Outremont, P.Q. H2V 2V1 (514/739-1257) *Eng.-Fr.*

Tessier, Armand, 9788, av. du Sacré-Coeur, Montreal, P.Q. H2C 2S2 (514/389-5594) *Eng.-Fr./Fr.-Eng.*

Thériault, Mme Denise, 11744, av. Alfred, Montreal, P.Q. H1G 5C1 (514/322-4290) *Eng.-Fr./Span.-Fr.*

Tousignant, Mlle J.R., 3550, rue Jeanne-Mance, Montreal, P.Q. H2X 3P7 (514/843-8612) *Fr.-Eng./Eng.-Fr.*

Touzin-Bauer, Mme Lucie, app 2, 3068, boul. Edouard-Montpetit, Montreal, P.Q. H3T 1J7 (514/342-3862) *Ger.-Fr.*

Tremblay, Mlle Monique, 365 rue de Châteauguay, app. 248, Longueuil, P.Q. J4H 3X5 *Eng.-Fr.*

Trenner, Mlle Simone, 625, rue Milton, app. 1801, Montreal, P.Q. H2X 1W7 (514/843-6142) *Eng.-Fr./Ger.-Fr.*

Trindall, Mme Anne, 4449, rue Johnson, Pierrefonds, P.Q. H9H 1V4 (work: 514/747-6565) *Fr.-Eng.*

Trottier-Drouault, Mme Marie, 371, rue Willowdale, Outremont, P.Q. H3T 1H1 (514/733-9753) *Eng.-Fr.*

Turgeon, Mme Thérèse, 12441, rue Gratton, Pointe-aux-Trembles, P.Q. H1B 1J6 *Eng.-Fr./Fr.-Eng.*

Valentine, Mlle Monique, 2425, av. Madison, app. 2, Montreal, P.Q. H4B 2T5 (514/486-4978) *Eng.-Fr./Fr.-Eng.*

Van Becelaere, Mme Pascale, 364, ave. Querbes, Outremont, P.Q. H2V 3W3 (514/277-3404) *Eng.-Fr.*

Van den Eynden, Paul, 130, rue Dieppe, Pointe Claire, P.Q. H9R 1X6 (work: 514/697-4383) *Eng.-Du./Russ.-Du./Fr.-Du./Ger.-Du.*

Vanderveken, Alain, 343 rue Pine, St-Lambert, P.Q. J4P 2N7 (514/671-8962) *Eng.-Fr./Russ.-Fr.*

Vanier, Mlle Claire, 170, av. Lockhart, Mont-Royal, P.Q. H3P 1Y1 (514/737-0808) *Eng.-Fr.*

de Vienne, Bernard, 1260, av. McGregor, Montreal, P.Q. H3G 1B6 (514/284-9118) *Eng.-Fr.*

Vinals-Hernandez, Mercedes, 3244, av. Lacombe, Montreal, P.Q. H3T 1L7 (514/735-0984) *Eng.-Fr. / Span.-Fr. / Eng.-Span. / Fr.-Span.*

Vineberg, Mme Allyna, 5757, av. Westluke, Montreal, P.Q. H4W 2N6 (514/489-4704) *Eng.-Fr./Fr.-Eng.*

Vinet, Mlle Louise, 5472, av. Notre-Dame-de-Grâce, Montreal, P.Q. H4A 1L4 (514/486-0237) *Eng.-Fr.*

Vinet, Mlle Madeleine, 5116A, av. Casgrain, Montreal, P.Q. H2T 1W7 (514/271-9206) *Fr.-Eng./Eng.-Fr.*

Walter, Mlle Christine, 200 Elgar, app 109, Ile-des-Soeurs, P.Q. H3E 1C8 (work: 514/526-0465) *Eng.-Fr.*

Watel, Mme Claudie, c/o Traductions Watel Inc., 437, av. Grosvenor, app. 9, Westmount, P.Q. H3Y 2S5 (514/937-0746) *Eng.-Fr.*

Weil-Brenner, Richard, 6725 Monkland Ave., Montreal, P.Q. H4B 1H9 (514/488-4707) *Eng.-Fr./Fr.-Eng.*

Wuidart, Mme Yolande, 237, av. Dresden, Mont-Royal, P.Q. H3P 2B9 (514/731-1879) *Eng.-Fr.*

MONT-ROYAL, see Montreal

MONT-ST-HILAIRE, see Montreal

MONT-TREMBLANT, see Montreal

NOTRE-DAME-DE-GRACE, see Montreal

ORSAINVILLE, see Montreal

OUTREMONT, see Montreal

PIERREFONDS, see Montreal

POINTE-AUX-TREMBLES, see Montreal

POINTE-CLAIRE, see Montreal

QUEBEC

Chaput, Mme Sylvie, 1120 Ch. Ste-Foy, Quebec, P.Q. G1S 2M3 (418/527-1137) *Eng.-Fr.*

Dufresne, Mme Suzanne, R.R. 3, B.P. 3705, St-Pamphile, Co. de l'Islet, P.Q. G0R 3X0 (418/359-2760) *Eng.-Fr.*

Foster, Mme Vivianne, 600, av. Laurier, app. 205, Quebec, P.Q. G1R 2L5 (418/524-8970) *Fr.-Eng.*

Juhel, D.-N.-P., Langues et Linguistique, Université Laval, Québec, P.Q. G1K 7P4 *Eng.-Fr.*

Pouliot, Mlle Loraine, 1018 de Montigny, Sillery, P.Q. G1S 3T7 *Eng.-Fr.*

Simard, Claude, 714 ave. Joffre, Quebec, P.Q. G1S 3L6 (418/527-0613) *Eng.-Fr./Span.-Fr.*

Simard, Mme Hélène, 1185, rue Belvédère, app. 3, Quebec, P.Q. G1S 3G4 (418/681-6808) *Fr.-Eng.*

Wells, Mme Claire, 1490, rue Beaulieu, app. 603, Quebec, P.Q. G1S 4M8 (418/527-5131) *Eng.-Fr.*

REPENTIGNY, see Montreal

RIMOUSKI

Lebel, Mme Monique, 579, boul. St-Germain ouest, Rimouski, P.Q. G5L 3R7 (418/723-3834) *Eng.-Fr.*

RIVIERE-BEAUDETTE

Smith, Mlle Patricia, 1015 ch. Ste-Claire, Rivière-Beaudette, P.Q. J0P 1R0 (514/269-2716) *Fr.-Eng. / Ger.-Eng.*

STE-ADELE, see Montreal

ST-BRUNO, see Montreal

STE-FOY

Bartlett, Mme Micheline, 2833, rue Poitiers, Ste-Foy, P.Q. G1W 2B7 (418/651-3971) *Fr.-Eng.*

Boulay, Dr Jacques, 857, rue du Chanoine-Martin, Ste-Foy, P.Q. G1V 3P6 (418/651-1967) *Eng.-Fr.*

Fournier, P.-A., 1259, av. Nelles, Ste-Foy, P.Q. G1W 3B3 (418/651-1674) *Eng.-Fr./Fr.-Eng./It.-Fr./It.-Eng.*

Lafontaine, Mme E., 748, av. Maskinongé, Ste-Foy, P.Q. G1X 2N4 (418/653-3019) *Fr.-Du./Eng.-Du./Eng.-Fr./Du.-Fr.*

Lemaire, Mme M.-C., 1596, av. Tournai, Ste-Foy, P.Q. G1W 3X9 (418/651-1525) *Eng.-Fr.*

de Léry, Mme Ethel, 786, av. Moreau, Ste-Foy, P.Q. G1V 3A7 (418/653-3630) *Eng.-Fr.*

Matuszewski, Mme Janine, 2580, rue Gregg, Ste-Foy, P.Q. G1W 1J8 (418/658-2993) *Eng.-Fr.*

Nakos-Aupetit, Mme Dorothy, 2276, ch. Ste-Foy, app. 804, Ste-Foy, P.Q. G1V 1S7 (418/658-0877) *Eng.-Fr.*

Pfalzgraf, Mme Marie, 3332, rue Périgny, Ste-Foy, P.Q. G1X 1Z8 (418/656-1919) *Eng.-Fr.*

Resendes, Alberto, 845, boul. Pie XII, Ste-Foy, P.Q. G1X 3T2 (418/656-1634) *Fr.-Port./Port.-Fr.*

Roberts, Mme Roda, 2969, rue Summerside, Ste-Foy, P.Q. G1X 2E9 (418/653-9312) *Fr.-Eng.*

Schwab, Wallace, 1190, av. Colbert, app. 303, Ste-Foy, P.Q. G1V 3Y7 (418/658-7565) *Fr.-Eng./Span.-Eng.*

ST-GEDEON-DE-BEAUCE

Rancourt, Suzy, C.P. 87, St-Gedeon-de-Beauce, P.Q. G0M 1T0 (418/582-3823) *Eng.-Fr.*

ST-JEAN, see Montreal

ST-JEAN CHRYSOSTOME

Bédard, Pierre, 943 de Vinci nord, St-Jean Chrysostome, P.Q. G0S 2T0 *Eng.-Fr.*

ST-LAMBERT, see Montreal

ST-LAURENT, see Montreal

STE-MARTHE-SUR-LE-LAC, see Montreal

ST-REDEMPTEUR

Chartré-Viel, Mme Marie, 1305, rue des Cèdres, C.P. 618, St-Rédempteur-de-Lévis, P.Q. G0S 3B0 (418/831-3198) *Eng.-Fr.*

ST-ROMUALD

Mercier, Raymond, 51, place du Paysan, St-Romuald, P.Q. G6W 2W2 (418/839-4326) *Eng.-Fr.*

STE-ROSE, see Montreal

ST-SAUVEUR, see Montreal

STE-THERESE EN HAUT, see Montreal

SARAGUAY, see Montreal

SHERBROOKE

Collinge, Pierre, R.R. 1, Sherbrooke, P.Q. J1H 5G9 (819/864-9409) *Eng.-Fr.*

Mugnier, André, 243 nord, boul. Queen, Sherbrooke, P.Q. J1H 3R1 (819/563-9731) *Eng.-Fr.*

TOURAINE (see also Ottawa-Hull)

McKee, John J.M., 25 Des Rapides, Touraine, P.Q. J8T 5K2 (568-1872) *Span.-Eng./Fr.-Eng./Port.-Eng./Russ.-Eng./Arab.-Eng.*

TROIS-RIVIERES

Descoteaux, Mme Diane, 5275, rue d'Orléans, Trois-Rivières-Ouest, P.Q. G8Y 3X9 (819/379-3851) *Eng.-Fr.*

Dumoulin, Mlle Luce, 569, rue St-Paul, Trois-Rivières, P.Q. G9A 1H7 (819/379-3851) *Eng.-Fr.*

Larose, Robert, 1898, rue Jean-Nicolet, Trois-Rivières, P.Q. G9A 1B8 (819/375-4337) *Fr.-Eng.*

Verrette, Mme Claudette, 3755, rue Jean-Talon, Trois-Rivières, P.Q. G8Y 2G8 (819/374-5952) *Eng.-Fr.*

Vitale, Geoffrey, C.P. 500, Trois-Rivières, P.Q. G9A 5H7 (819/376-5295) *Eng.-Fr./Fr.-Eng.*

VARENNES, see Montreal

VERCHERES, see Montreal

WESTMOUNT, see Montreal

BROADCASTING STATIONS IN CANADA

LIST OF AM BROADCASTING STATIONS

Post Office address same as in first column, except where otherwise noted
CBC Stations are indicated by asterisk*
French Language stations are indicated by dagger†

LOCATION	CALL		FREQ.
Abbotsford, B.C.	CFVR	Fraser Valley Broadcasters Ltd., 2722 Allwood St., V2T 3R8 (604/859-5277)	850
Ajax, Ont.	CHOO	Community Communications Inc., 97 McMaster Ave., L1S 2E6 (416/683-4131)	1390
Alert Bay, B.C.	*CBRY	Studio at Vancouver (CBU)	1340
Alice Arm, B.C.	*CBKL	Studio at Prince Rupert (CFPR)	1150
Alma, P.Q.	†CFGT	Radio Lac St-Jean Ltée, 790 Sud, ave. Du Pont, G8B 2V4 (418/662-3461)	1270
Altona, Man.	CFAM	Golden West Broadcasting Ltd., Box 950, R0G 0B0 (204/324-6464)	950
Amherst, N.S.	CKDH	Tantramar Broadcasting Ltd., 32 Church St., Box 8, B4H 3A8 (902/667-3875)	900
Amos, P.Q.	†CHAD	See Radio Nord Inc., Rouyn	1340
Amqui, P.Q.	†CFVM	La Radio de la Matapedia Ltee, C.P. 1840, G0J 1B0 (418/629-2025)	1220
Andover, N.B.	*CBAN	Studio at Fredericton (CBZ)	1140
Antigonish, N.S.	CJFX	Atlantic Broadcasters, 85 St. Ninian St., B2G 9Z9 (902/863-4580)	580
Arichat, N.B.	*†CBHH	Studio at Moncton (CBAF)	610
Armstrong, Ont.	*CBOL	Studio at Thunder Bay (CBQ)	1450
Asbestos, P.Q.	†CJAN	Radio Victoriaville Ltée, C.P. 57, J1T 1S4 (819/879-5430)	1340
Ashcroft, B.C.	*CBWA	Studio at Vancouver (CBU)	860
Atikokan, Ont.	*CBLA	Re-broadcasting CBQ, Thunder Bay	1490
Atikokan, Ont.	CFAK	See Border Broadcasting, Fort Frances	1240
Baie Comeau, P.Q.	*CBMI	Studio at Montreal (CBM)	1140
Baie-Comeau, P.Q.	†CKBH	Communications Manicouagan Inc., Box 260, G4Z 2H1 (418/296-8414)	790
Baie Verte, Nfld.	*CBNL	Studio at Grand Falls (CBC)	1400
Baie Verte, Nfld.	CKIM	See Colonial Broadcasting, St. John's	1240
Bancroft, Ont.	*CBLV	Studio at Toronto (CBL)	600
Bancroft, Ont.	CJNH	See Quinte Broadcasting, Belleville	1240
Banff, Alta.	*CBRB	Studio at Calgary (CBR)	860
Barrie, Ont.	CKBB	Four Seasons Radio Ltd., 129 Ferris Lane, Box 950, L4M 4V1 (705/726-9500)	950
Barrington, N.S.	*CBAC	Studio at Halifax (CBH)	540
Barry's Bay, Ont.	*CBEQ	Studio at Ottawa (CBO)	1340
Bathurst, N.B.	CKBC	Bathurst Broadcasting Co. Ltd., 176 Main St., Box G, E2A 3Z2 (506/546-4461)	1360
Beardmore, Ont.	*CBLE	Studio at Thunder Bay (CBQ)	1240
Beaver Creek, Y.T.	CBDM	See CFWH, Whitehorse	690
Bella Bella, B.C.	*CBTB	Studio at Vancouver (CBU)	630
Belle Cote, N.B.	*†CBHF	Studio at Moncton (CBAF)	1230
Belleville, Ont.	CBLC	Loyalist College, Box 4200 (613/962-9501) closed circuit	
Belleville, Ont.	CJBQ	Quinte Broadcasting Co. Ltd., 45 Bridge St. E., Box 488, K8N 1L5 (613/968-5555)	800
Blairmore, Alta.	*CBXL	Studio at Calgary (CBR)	860
Blairmore, Alta.	CJPR	Lethbridge Broadcasting Ltd., Box 840, T0K 0E0 (403/562-2806)	1490

LOCATION	CALL		FREQ.
Blind River, Ont.	CJNR	Huron Broadcasting Ltd., 10 Lawton St., P0R 1B0 (705/356-2209)	730
Blind River, Ont.	*†CJBC-6	Studio at Toronto (CJBC)	1010
Blue River, B.C.	*CBKM	Studio at Vancouver (CBU)	1150
Boissevain, Man.	CJRB	Golden West Broadcasting Ltd., Box 950, Altona, Man. R0G 0B0 (204/324-6464)	1220
Bonavista Bay, Nfld.	*CBGY	Studio at Gander (CBG)	750
Bonfield, Ont.	*†CJBC-8	Studio at Toronto (CJBC)	990
Bonnyville, Alta.	CIOK	See OK Radio, Westlock	1310
Boss Mountain, B.C.	*CBKH	Studio at Vancouver (CBU)	1150
Bralorne, B.C.	*CBRZ	Studio at Vancouver (CBU)	630
Brampton, Ont.	CKMW	See Toronto	
Brandon, Man.	CKLQ	Riding Mountain Broadcasting Ltd., Box 1570, R7A 6N6 (204/725-1570)	1570
Brandon, Man.	CKX	Western Manitoba Broadcasters Ltd., 2940 Victoria Ave., R7A 6A5 (204/728-1150)	1150
Brantford, Ont.	CKPC	Telephone City Broadcast Ltd., 571 West St., N3T 5P8 (519/759-1000)	1380
Bridgewater, N.S.	CKBW	Acadia Broadcasting Co. Ltd., 215 Dominion St., B4V 2G8 (902/543-2401)	1000
Britt, Ont.	*CBEZ	Studio at Toronto (CBL)	1240
Brockville, Ont.	CFJR	Eastern Ont. Broadcasting Co. Ltd., Box 666, K6V 5V9 (613/345-1666)	1450
Brooks, Alta.	CKBR	Dinosaur Broadcasting (1957) Ltd., Box 180, T0J 0J0 (403/362-3418)	1340
Burnaby, B.C.	CSFU	Simon Fraser University, V5A 1S6 (604/291-3727) closed circuit	
Burns Lake, B.C.	CFLD	See CFBV Ltd., Smithers	1400
Cabano, P.Q.	†CJAF	See Radio CJFP Ltée, Rivière-du-Loup	1240
Cache Creek, B.C.	*CBKS	Studio at Vancouver (CBU)	1450
Calgary, Alta.	*CBR	CBC, Box 2640, T2P 2M7 (403/283-8361)	1010
Calgary, Alta.	CHQR	Radio QR Ltd., 830 9th Ave. S.W., T2P 1L7 (403/263-5522)	810
Calgary, Alta.	CFCN	CFCN Communications Ltd., Broadcast House, Box 7060, Stn. E, T3C 3L9 (403/246-7111)	1060
Calgary, Alta.	CKXL	Moffat Communications Ltd., 804-16th Ave. S.W., Box 1140, T2P 2M7 (403/264-8000)	1140
Calgary, Alta.	CFAC	Calgary Broadcasting Co. Ltd., 1301 17th Ave. S.W., T2T 0C5 (403/244-9311)	960
Calgary, Alta.	CJSW	University of Calgary, #118, MacEwan Hall, T2N 1N4 (403/282-4222) closed circuit	
Calgary, Alta.	CMRC	Mount Royal College, 4825 Richard Rd. S.W., T3E 6K6 (403/246-6366) closed circuit	
Calais, N.B.	WQDY	WQDY Inc., Box 305, St. Stephen, N.B. E3L 1G5 (506/466-4848)	1230
Cambridge, Ont.	CFTJ	Galt Broadcasting Ltd., 46 Main St., N1R 1V4 (519/621-7510)	960
Campbell River, B.C.	CFWB	CFCP Radio Ltd., #117, 1180 Ironwood Rd., V9W 5P7 (604/287-7106)	1490
Campbellton, N.B.	CKNB	Restigouche Broadcasting Co. Ltd., 100 Water St., Box 340, E3N 3G7 (506/753-4415)	950
Camrose, Alta.	CFCW	CFCW Radio Ltd., 4872-50th St., T4V 1P8 (403/672-3151)	790
Canso, N.S.	*CBAR	Studio at Halifax (CBH)	1230
Caraquet, N.B.	†CJVA	Radio Acadie Ltée, CP 970, E0B 1K0 (506/727-4426)	810
Carbonear, Nfld.	CHVO	See Colonial Broadcasting, St. John's	
Carmacks, Y.T.	*CBQF	See CFWH, Whitehorse	990
Cartwright, Nfld.	*CBNK	Studio at Happy Valley (CFGB)	570
Cassiar, B.C.	*CBDG	See CFWH, Whitehorse	1340
Castlegar, B.C.	*CBUD	Studio at Vancouver (CBU)	1080
Castlegar, B.C.	CKQR	Valley Broadcasters Ltd., 601 Columbia Ave., V1N 1G9 (604/365-7225)	1230
Causapscal, P.Q.	*†CJBM	Studio at Matane (CBGA)	1450
Chapais, P.Q.	*CBMD	Studio at Montreal (CBM)	1400
Chapais, P.Q.	*†CBJ-2	Studio at Chicoutimi (CBJ)	1140
Chapais, P.Q.	†CFED	See CJMD Inc., Chibougamau	1340
Chapleau, Ont.	*CBLC	Studio at Toronto (CBL)	1090
Chapleau, Ont.	*†CJBC-9	Studio at Toronto (CJBC)	1340
Charlottetown, P.E.I.	CFCY	CFCY Radio Ltd., 51 University Ave., Box 1060, C1A 7M7 (902/892-1066)	630
Charlottetown, P.E.I.	CHTN	Northumberland Broadcasting Co. Ltd., Box 1190, C1A 7M8 (902/892-8591)	1190
Charlottetown, P.E.I.	CIMN	University of P.E.I., C1A 4P3 (902/892-4121) closed circuit	
Chase, B.C.	*CBUH	Studio at Vancouver (CBU)	860
Chatham, Ont.	CFCO	Greatlakes Broadcasting, Box 630, N7M 5K9 (519/352-3000)	630
Cheticamp, N.B.	*†CBHE	Studio at Moncton (CBAF)	1380
Chetwynd, B.C.	*CBUZ	Studio at Vancouver (CBU)	1170
Chibougamau, P.Q.	*†CBJ-1	Studio at Chicoutimi (CBJ)	540
Chibougamau, P.Q.	*CBMF	Studio at Montreal (CBM)	710
Chibougamau, P.Q.	†CJMD	Radio CJMD Chibougamau Inc., 618 6e rue, G8P 2T9 (819/276-4171)	1240
Chicoutimi, P.Q.	*†CBJ	CBC, CP 790, G7H 5E7 (418/545-4321)	1580
Chicoutimi, P.Q.	†CJMT	CJMT Ltée, C.P. 5200, G7H 5B4 (418/543-1517)	1420
Chilliwack, B.C.	CHWK	Fraser Valley Broadcasters Ltd., Meadowbrook 5, Box 386, V2P 6J7 (604/795-5711)	1270
Christina Lake, B.C.	*CBRI	Studio at Vancouver (CBU)	1080
Churchill, Man.	*CHFC	Studio at Winnipeg (CBW)	1230
Churchill Falls, Nfld.	*CBQA	Studio at Happy Valley (CFGB)	610
Clarenville, Nfld.	CKVO	See Colonial Broadcasting, St. John's	710

LOCATION	CALL		FREQ.
Clearwater, B.C.	*CBKZ	Studio at Vancouver (CBU)	860
Clearwater, B.C.	CHNL-1	See NL Broadcasting Ltd., Kamloops	1400
Clinton, B.C.	*CBUU	Studio at Vancouver (CBU)	1070
Clova, P.Q.	*†CBV-3	Studio at Quebec (CBV)	990
Coal Harbour, B.C.	*CBKO	Studio at Vancouver (CBU)	540
Cobourg, Ont.	CHUC	Radio CHUC Ltd., Box 520, K9A 4L3 (416/372-5401)	1450
Coleman, Alta.	*CBXC	Studio at Calgary (CBR)	1450
Collingwood, Ont.	CKCB	Four Seasons Radio Ltd., Box 339, L9Y 3Z7 (705/445-2011)	1400
Copper Creek, B.C.	*CBXH	Studio at Vancouver (CBU)	1450
Corner Brook, Nfld.	*CBY	CBC, Box 610, A2H 6G1 (709/634-3141)	990
Corner Brook, Nfld.	CFCB	Humber Valley Broadcasting Co. Ltd., Box 2020, A2H 6H5 (709/634-3111)	570
Cornwall, Ont.	†CFIX	Les Communications Franco Communications Ltd., 1308 Pitt St., K6J 3T6 (613/932-3356)	1170
Cornwall, Ont.	CJSS	Tri-Co Broadcasting Ltd., 237 Water St. E., Box 969, K6H 5V1 (613/932-5180)	1220
Courtenay, B.C.	CFCP	CFCP Radio Ltd., 1595 Cliffe Ave., V9N 2K6 (604/334-2421)	1440
Cow Head Harbour, Nfld.	*CBNI	Studio at Corner Brook (CBY)	600
Cranbrook, B.C.	*CBRR	Studio at Vancouver (CBU)	860
Cranbrook, B.C.	CKEK	EK Radio Ltd., 28 8th Ave. S., V1C 2K3 (604/426-2224)	570
Creston, B.C.	*CBRM	Studio at Vancouver (CBU)	740
Creston, B.C.	CFKC	Kokanee Broadcasting, 341 Canyon St., Box 310, V0B 1G0 (604/428-5385)	1340
Crowsnest Pass, Alta.	CJPR	See Lethbridge Broadcasting Ltd., Lethbridge	1490
Dartmouth, N.S.	CFDR	Dartmouth Broadcasting Ltd., Box 1007, B2Y 3Z7 (902/469-9231)	790
Dauphin, Man.	CKDM	Dauphin Broadcasting Co. Ltd., 3rd Ave., N.E., R7N 2V5 (204/638-3230)	730
Dawson, Y.T.	*CBDE	See CFWH, Whitehorse	560
Dawson Creek, B.C.	CJDC	CJDC Ltd., 901 102nd Ave., V1G 2B6 (604/782-3341)	1350
Deep River, Ont.	*†CBOF-3	Studio at Ottawa (CBOF)	730
Deep River, Ont.	*CBLI	Studio at Ottawa (CBO)	1110
Degelis, P.Q.	CFVD	Radio Degelis Inc., Box 1370, G0L 1H0 (418/853-3370)	1370
Destruction Bay, Y.T.	*CBDL	See CFWH, Whitehorse	940
Digby, N.S.	*†CBAE	Studio at Moncton (CBAF)	990
Digby, N.S.	CKDY	See Annapolis Valley Radio, Kentville (Digby ph.: 902/245-2111)	1420
Dolbeau, P.Q.	†CHVD	Placements Claude St-Arnault Inc., 1975 Walberg Blvd., G8L 1J5 (418/276-3333)	1230
Donald Station, B.C.	*CBWD	Studio at Vancouver (CBU)	900
Drumheller, Alta.	CJDV	Dinosaur Broadcasting (1957) Ltd., Box 1480, T0J 0Y0 (403/823-3384)	910
Drummondville, P.Q.	†CHRD	Radio Drummond (1980) Inc., 2070 St-Georges, J2C 5G6 (819/472-5458)	1480
Dryden, Ont.	*CBLD	Re-broadcasting CBQ, Thunder Bay	1010
Dryden, Ont.	CKDR	Lake of the Woods Broadcasting, 122 King St., Box 580, P8N 2Z3 (807/223-2355)	900
Dubreuilville, Ont.	*†CJBC-11	Studio at Toronto (CJBC)	540
Duncan, B.C.	CKAY	CKAY Radio (1979) Ltd., 160 Jubilee St., V9L 1W7 (604/748-5259)	1500
Ear Falls, Ont.	*CBOI	Re-broadcasting CBQ, Thunder Bay	690
Ear Falls, Ont.	CKEF	c/o Fawcett Broadcasting, see CKDR, Dryden	1490
Edgewood, B.C.	*CBXW	Studio at Vancouver (CBU)	860
Edmonton, Alta.	*CBX	CBC, Box 555, T5J 2P4 (403/469-2321)	740
Edmonton, Alta.	CFCW	CFCW Radio Ltd., 4752 99 St., T6E 5H5 (403/437-7879)	790
Edmonton, Alta.	CFRN	Sunwapta Broadcasting Ltd., Broadcast House, 18520 Stony Plain Rd., Box 5030, Stn. E, T5P 4C2 (403/484-3311)	1260
Edmonton, Alta.	CHED	Radio Station CHED Ltd., 10006 107th St., T5J 1J3 (403/424-2111)	630
Edmonton, Alta.	*†CHFA	CBC, 8830 85th St., #1507, CP 555, T5J 2P4 (403/465-0911)	680
Edmonton, Alta.	CHQT	CHQT Broadcasting Ltd., 10154-103 St., T5J 0X8 (403/424-1131)	1110
Edmonton, Alta.	CJCA	Edmonton Broadcasting Co. Ltd., 10230 108 St., T5J 2X3 (403/423-4930)	930
Edmonton, Alta.	CKUA	Alta. Educational Communications Corp., 10526 Jasper Ave., T5J 1Z7 (403/428-7595)	580
Edmundston, N.B.	*CBAM	Studio at Fredericton (CBZ)	1320
Edmundston, N.B.	†CJEM	Edmundston Radio Ltd., 174 Church St., C.P. 188, E3V 1K2 (506/735-3351)	570
Edson, Alta.	*CBXD	Studio at Edmonton (CBX)	1340
Edson, Alta.	CJYR	Yellowhead Broadcasting Ltd., 4813 4th Ave., Box 1450, T0E 0P0 (403/723-4461)	970
Elliot Lake, Ont.	*CBEC	Studio at Toronto (CBL)	1090
Elliot Lake, Ont.	CKNR	Huron Broadcasting Ltd., 15 Charles Walk, P5A 2A2 (705/848-3608)	1340
Elliot Lake, Ont.	*†CJBC-5	Studio at Toronto (CJBC)	1440
Elsa, Y.T.	*CBOD	See CFWH, Whitehorse	560
Espanola, Ont.	*†CJBC-7	Studio at Toronto (CJBC)	990
Espanola, Ont.	CKNS	Huron Communication Co. Ltd., 377 Station Rd., Box 1910, P0P 1C0 (705/869-4930)	930
Espanola, Ont.	*CBLP	Studio at Toronto (CBL)	1240
Estevan, Sask.	CJSL	Soo Line Broadcasting, 1132 5th St., S4A 2A4 (306/634-7224)	1280
Falher, Alta.	*†CBXY	Studio at Edmonton (CHFA)	1490
Faro, Y.T.	*CBQK	See CFWH, Whitehorse	1230
Fernie, B.C.	*CBRF	Studio at Vancouver (CBU)	730
Fernie, B.C.	CFEK	EK Radio Ltd., Box 1170, V0B 1M0 (604/423-4449)	1240

LOCATION	CALL		FREQ.
Field, B.C.	*CBRD	Studio at Vancouver (CBU)	860
Field, Ont.	*†CJBC-14	Studio at Toronto (CJBC)	1440
Flin Flon, Man.	CFAR	Arctic Radio Corp. Ltd., 316 Green St., Box 430, R8A 1N3 (204/687-3469)	590
Flowers Cove, Nfld.	*CBND	Studio at Corner Brook (CBY)	1450
Foleyet, Ont.	*CBLF	Studio at Toronto (CBL)	1450
Forestville, P.Q.	†CFRP	See Radio Cote-Nord Inc., Hauterive	620
Fort Chipewyan, Alta.	*CBKE	See CFYK, Yellowknife	1450
Fort Frances, Ont.	CFOB	Border Broadcasting Ltd., 242 Scott St., Box 800, P9A 3M9 (807/274-5341)	800
Fort Franklin, N.W.T.	*CBQO	See CHAK, Inuvik	1230
Fort Good Hope, N.W.T.	*CBQE	See CHAK, Inuvik	920
Fort McMurray, Alta.	*CBKF	Studio at Edmonton (CBX)	1450
Fort McMurray, Alta.	CJOK	See OK Radio, Westlock	1230
Fort McPherson, N.W.T.	*CBQM	See CHAK, Inuvik	680
Fort Nelson, B.C.	*CBDA	Studio at Vancouver (CBU)	1240
Fort Nelson, B.C.	CFNL	See Northern Lights Broadcasting Ltd., Fort St. John	590
Fort Norman, N.W.T.	*CBQI	See CHAK, Inuvik	920
Fort Providence, N.W.T.	*CBQC	See CFYK, Yellowknife	
Fort Rae, N.W.T.	*CBQB	See CFYK, Yellowknife	1200
Fort Resolution	*CBQD	See CFYK, Yellowknife	1150
Fort Simpson, N.W.T.	*CBDO	See CFYK, Yellowknife	690
Fort Smith, N.W.T.	*CBDI	See CFYK, Yellowknife	860
Fort St. James, B.C.	CIFJ	See Prince George Broadcasting Ltd., Prince George	1480
Fort St. James, B.C.	*CBUV	Studio at Prince Rupert (CFPR)	1070
Fort St. John, B.C.	*CBUW	Studio at Vancouver (CBU)	1170
Fort St. John, B.C.	CKNL	Northern Lights Broadcasting Ltd., Box 6310, V1J 4H8 (604/785-6634)	560
Fort Vermilion, Alta.	*CBKC	Studio at Edmonton (CBX)	1460
Fraserdale, Ont.	*CBEW	Studio at Toronto (CBL)	1400
Fraser Lake, B.C.	CIFL	See Prince George Broadcasting Ltd., Prince George	1450
Fredericton, N.B.	CFNB	Radio Atlantic (1970) Ltd., 125 Hanwell Rd., Box 217, E3B 4Z4 (506/455-5501)	550
Fredericton, N.B.	*CBZ	CBC, 1160 Regent St., Box 1538, E3B 5G2 (506/455-8974)	970
Fredericton, N.B.	CHSR	University of New Brunswick, Box 4400, E3B 5A3 (506/453-4999)	700
Fredericton, N.B.	CIHI	Radio One Ltd., 364 Argyle St., E3B 1T9 (506/455-2444)	1260
Frobisher Bay, N.W.T.	*CFFB	CBC, Box 490, X0A 0H0 (403/979-5353)	1210
Gagnon, P.Q.	*CBMG	Studio at Montreal (CBM)	1400
Gander, Nfld.	*CBG	CBC, 98 Sullivan Ave., Box 369, A1V 1W7 (709/256-4311)	1450
Gander, Nfld.	CFYQ	See Q Radio 930 Ltd., St. John's	1350
Gander, Nfld.	CKGA	See Colonial Broadcasting, St. John's	730
Gaspé, P.Q.	*CBMH	Studio at Montreal (CBM)	1230
Geraldton, Ont.	*CBLG	Studio at Thunder Bay (CBQ)	730
Geraldton, Ont.	*†CJBC-15	Studio at Toronto (CJBC)	900
Gillam, Man.	*CBWG	Studio at Winnipeg (CBW)	1400
Gloverton, Nfld.	*CBNG	Studio at Gander (CBG)	1090
Gold Bridge, B.C.	*CBTG	Studio at Vancouver (CBU)	860
Golden, B.C.	CKGR	See Hall-Gray Broadcasting Co. Ltd., Salmon Arm	1400
Gold River, B.C.	*CBKJ	Studio at Vancouver (CBU)	740
Goose Bay, Lab., Nfld.	CFLN	See Humber Valley Broadcasting, Corner Brook	1230
Granby, P.Q.	†CHEF	La Voix de l'Est Ltée, 136 Principale, J2G 2V4 (514/372-2433)	1450
Grand Bank, Nfld.	CKYQ	Q Radio 930, Fortune Hwy., Box 189, A0E 1W0 (709/832-2650)	610
Grand Falls, N.B.	CKMV	See Edmundston Radio Ltd., Edmundston	1490
Grand Falls, Nfld.	*CBT	CBC, Lind Ave., Box 218, A2A 2J7 (709/489-2102)	540
Grand Falls, Nfld.	*CBAB	Studio at Fredericton (CBZ)	1350
Grand Falls, Nfld.	CKCM	See Colonial Broadcasting, St. John's	620
Grand Forks, B.C.	*CBRJ	Studio at Vancouver (CBU)	860
Grand Forks, B.C.	CKGF	Boundary Broadcasting Ltd., 128-11th St. N.E., Box 1570, V0H 1H0 (604/442-8221)	1340
Grand Sault, N.B.	†CKMV	Studio at Edmundston (CJEM)	1490
Grande Cache, Alta.	*CBWI	Studio at Edmonton (CBX)	1450
Grande Cache, Alta.	CKYR-1	See Yellowhead Broadcasting Ltd., Edson	1230
Grande Prairie, Alta.	CFGP	Northern Broadcasting Corp. Ltd., 10008-103rd Ave. T8V 1B8 (403/532-1050)	1050
Grande Prairie, Alta.	CJXX	Pioneer Broadcasting Ltd., 9913 100th Ave., T8V 0V1 (403/539-5599)	
Granisle, B.C.	*CBKG	Studio at Prince Rupert (CFPR)	920
Granisle, B.C.	CHLD	See CFBV Ltd., Smithers	1480
Gravelbourg, Sask.	*CBKF-1	Studio at Regina (CBKF)	690
Gravelbourg, Sask.	*†CFRG	c/o 1840 McIntyre St., Regina, Sask. (306/523-6641)	690
Greenwood, B.C.	*CBRO	Studio at Vancouver (CBU)	740
Guelph, Ont.	CJOY	CJOY Ltd., 75 Speedvale Ave. E., N1E 6M3 (519/824-7000)	1460
Haines Junction, Y.T.	*CBDF	See CFWH, Whitehorse	860
Haliburton, Ont.	*CBLY	Studio at Toronto (CBL)	1400
Halifax, N.S.	*CBH	CBC, 5600 Sackville St., Box 3000, B3J 3E9 (902/422-8311)	860
Halifax, N.S.	CHNS	Maritime Broadcasting Co. Ltd., 5230 Tobin St., Box 400, B3J 2R2 (902/422-1651)	960

LOCATION	CALL		FREQ.
Halifax, N.S.	CJCH	Radio CJCH 920 Ltd., 2885 Robie St., B3J 2Z4 (902/453-2524)	920
Halifax, N.S.	CKDU	Dalhousie University, Student Union Bldg., B3H 4J2 (902/424-2487)	610
Hamilton, Ont.	CHML	Radio M L Ltd., 848 Main St. E., L8M 1M1 (416/549-2411) (Toronto line: 924-2844)	900
Hamilton, Ont.	CHMR	Mohawk College, 135 Fennell Ave. W., L8N 3T2 (416/389-1335) closed circuit	
Hamilton, Ont.	CJJD	CJJD Radio Ltd., 2 King St. W., L8P 1A1 (416/526-1280)	1280
Hamilton, Ont.	CKOC	Armadale Communications Ltd., 73 Garfield St. S., Box 1150, L8N 3P5 (416/545-5885)	1150
Happy Valley, Nfld.	*CFGB	White Bldg., Box 736, A0P 1E0 (709/896-2911)	1340
Hauterive, P.Q.	†CHLC	CFRP Radio Cote-Nord Inc., 399 de Puyjalon, G5C 2Z7 (418/589-3771)	580
Hawkesbury, Ont.	†CHPR	See Les Communications Franco Communications Ltd., Cornwall	1170
Hay River, N.W.T.	*CBDJ	See CFYK, Yellowknife	1490
Hazelton, B.C.	CKBY	See CFBV Ltd., Smithers	1490
Hearst, Ont.	†CFLH	See Mid Canada Corp., Timmins	1340
Hearst, Ont.	*CBLZ	Studio at Toronto (CBL)	1400
Hearst, Ont.	*†CJBC-3	Studio at Toronto (CJBC)	1110
High Level, Alta.	*CBKD	Studio at Edmonton (CBX)	1230
High River, Alta.	CHRB	Palliser Broadcasting Ltd., Box 1280, T0L 1B0 (403/652-2472)	1280
Hinton, Alta.	*CBXI	Studio at Edmonton (CBX)	1450
Hinton, Alta.	CIYR	See Yellowhead Broadcasting Ltd., Edson	1230
Hope, B.C.	CKGO	Fraser Valley Broadcasters Ltd., Box 1600, V0X 1L0 (604/869-9313)	1240
Hopedale, Nfld.	*CBNN	Studio at Happy Valley (CFGB)	1490
Hornepayne, Ont.	*CBLH	Studio at Thunder Bay (CBQ)	1010
Houston, B.C.	CHBV	See CFBV Ltd., Smithers	1450
Hudson, Ont.	*CBQW	Re-broadcasting CBQ, Thunder Bay	1340
Hudson, Ont.	CKHD	c/o Fawcett Broadcasting, see CKDR, Dryden	1450
Hudson Hope, B.C.	*CBXU	Studio at Vancouver (CBU)	940
Hull, P.Q.	†CKCH	CKCH Radio Ltée, 72 Laval St., J8X 3H3 (819/777-2771)	970
Huntsville, Ont.	CFBK	Muskoka-Parry Sound Broadcasting Ltd., 15 Main St. E., Box 820, P0A 1K0 (705/789-4461)	630
Ignace, Ont.	*CBES	Re-broadcasting CBQ, Thunder Bay	690
Ignace, Ont.	CKIG	c/o Fawcett Broadcasting, see CKDR, Dryden	1340
Inuvik, N.W.T.	*CHAK	CBC, Bag Service No. 8, X0E 0T0 (403/979-2871)	860
Jaffray, B.C.	*CBKW	Studio at Vancouver (CBU)	740
Jasper, Alta.	*CBXJ	Studio at Edmonton (CBX)	860
Jasper, Alta.	CKYR	See Yellowhead Broadcasting Ltd., Edson	1450
Joliette, P.Q.	†CJLM	Radio Joliette Ltd., 854 Papineau St., J6E 2L6 (514/759-0772)	1350
Jonquiere, P.Q.	†CKRS	CKRS-Radio, 38 rue Cantin, C.P. 59, G7X 7V8 (418/547-3681)	590
Joutel, P.Q.	*†CBFW	Studio at Montreal (CBF)	990
Kamloops, B.C.	CHNL	NL Broadcasting Ltd., Lansdowne St. & 6th, Box 610, V2C 1Y6 (604/372-2292)	610
Kamloops, B.C.	CFJC	Twin Cities Radio Ltd., 460 Pemberton Ter., V2C 1T5 (604/372-3322)	550
Kamloops, B.C.	CMMD	Cariboo College, Box 3010 (604/374-0123, loc. 227) closed circuit	
Kapuskasing, Ont.	*CBOK	Studio at Toronto (CBL)	1090
Kapuskasing, Ont.	CKAP	Kapuskasing Broadcasting Co. Ltd., 24 Byng Ave., P5N 1X5 (705/335-2379).	580
Kapuskasing, Ont.	†CFLK	See Mid Canada Corp., Timmins	1230
Kaslo, B.C.	*CBUG	Studio at Vancouver (CBU)	860
Kedgewick, N.B.	*†CBAK	Studio at Moncton (CBAF)	990
Kelowna, B.C.	CKOV	Okanagan Broadcasters Ltd., 1491 Pandosy St., Box 100, V1Y 7N3 (604/762-3331)	630
Kelowna, B.C.	CKIQ	Four Seasons Radio Ltd., 2419 Hwy. 97 N., V1X 4J2 (604/860-8600)	1150
Kenora, Ont.	CJRL	Lake of the Woods Broadcasting Ltd., 128 Main St. S., Box 2490, P9N 3X8 (807/468-3181)	1220
Kentville, N.S.	CKEN	Annapolis Valley Radio Ltd., Radio Centre, Box 310, B4N 1H5 (902/678-2111)	1490
Keremeos, B.C.	*CBKY	Studio at Vancouver (CBU)	1350
Kimberley, B.C.	*CBRK	Studio at Vancouver (CBU)	900
Kingston, Ont.	CFRC	Queen's University, Carruthers Hall, K7L 3N6	1490
Kingston, Ont.	CKLC	St. Lawrence Broadcasting Co. Ltd., 99 Brock St., Box 1380, K7L 4Y5 (613/544-1380)	1380
Kingston, Ont.	CKWS	Frontenac Broadcasting Co. Ltd., 170 Queen St. E., K7K 1B2 (613/544-2340)	960
Kirkland Lake, Ont.	CJKL	Kirkland Lake Broadcasting Ltd., 6 Hudson Bay Ave., Box 430, P2N 3J4 (705/567-3366)	560
Kirkland Lake, Ont.	*†CJBC-1	Studio at Toronto (CJBC)	1090
Kispiox, B.C.	*CBTB	Studio at Prince Rupert (CFPR)	990
Kitchener, Ont.	CHYM	Greatlakes Broadcasting System, 305 King St. W., N2G 4E4 (519/743-2611).	570
Kitchener, Ont.	CXLR	Conestoga College, 299 Doon Valley Dr., N2G 4M4 (519/653-2511, loc. 302) closed circuit	
Kitchener, Ont.	CKKW	C A P Communications Ltd., Box 1090, N2G 4E9 (519/579-1090)	1090
Kitimat, B.C.	CKTK	Skeena Broadcasters Ltd., 350 City Centre, V8C 1T6 (604/632-2102)	1230
Kitsault, B.C.	*CBKL	Studio at Prince Rupert (CFPR)	1150
Kitwanga, B.C.	*CBKK	Studio at Prince Rupert (CFPR)	630

LOCATION	CALL		FREQ.
Labrador City, Nfld.	*CBDQ	Studio at Happy Valley (CFGB)	1490
Lac-Edouard, P.Q.	*†CBV-2	Studio at Quebec (CBV)	710
Lac Etchemin, P.Q.	†CIRB	See Radio Beauce Inc., Ville St-Georges Est	1240
Lac La Hache, B.C.	*CBUY	Studio at Vancouver (CBU)	1340
Lac Megantic, P.Q.	*CBMO	Studio at Montreal (CBM)	1240
Lac Megantic, P.Q.	†CKFL	Radio CKFL Ltée, 3852 Quebec Central, G6B 2C6 (819/583-0663)	1400
Lachute, P.Q.	†CJLA	Radio Lachute Inc., 385 rue Principale, J8H 1Y1 (514/462-8862)	630
Lake Windermere, B.C.	*CBUQ	Studio at Vancouver (CBU)	860
Langley, B.C.	CJJC	CJJC Radio Ltd., 20590 Fraser Hwy., V3A 4G2 (604/534-5341)	800
L'Annonciation, P.Q.	†CKLR	See Radio CKML Inc., Mont Laurier	1490
La Pocatière, P.Q.	†CHGB	Radio La Pocatière Ltée, 508 4th Ave., C.P. 550, G0R 1Z0 (418/856-1310)	1310
Larry's River, N.S.	*CBAU	Studio at Halifax (CBH)	1370
La Sarre, P.Q.	†CKLS	See Radio Nord Inc., Rouyn	1240
Latchford, Ont.	*CBLQ	Studio at Toronto (CBL)	1450
La Tuque, P.Q.	*CBME	Studio at Montreal (CBM)	990
La Tuque, P.Q.	†CFLM	Radio La Tuque Ltd., 529 rue St-Louis, Box 310, G9X 2X3 (819/523-4575)	1240
Laval, P.Q.	†CKLM	Entreprises Tele-Capital, 1600 est boul. St Martin, H7G 4R8 (514/668-0100)	1570
Leamington, Ont.	CHYR	CHYR Radio (Div. of Rogers Radio Broadcasting Ltd.), 23 Erie St. N., N8H 3W1 (519/326-6171) (Windsor line: 776-7303)	730
Lebel-sur-Quevillon, P.Q.	*†CBFM	Studio at Montreal (CBF)	1400
Lebel-sur-Quevillon, P.Q.	*CBMK	Studio at Montreal (CBM)	1230
Lethbridge, Alta.	CJOC	Lethbridge Broadcasting Ltd., 1015-3rd Ave. S., Box 820, T1J 3Z9 (403/320-1220)	1220
Lethbridge, Alta.	CHEC	Southern Alta. Broadcasting Ltd., 401 Mayor Magrath Dr., T1J 3L8 (403/329-4144)	1090
Lethbridge, Alta.	CLCC	Lethbridge Community College, T1K 1L6 (403/327-2141) closed circuit	
Levis, P.Q.	†CFLS	Radio Etchemin Inc., 5 est. trans-Canada, C.P. 2000, G6V 6P5 (418/833-2151)	1240
Lillooet, B.C.	*CBUL	Studio at Vancouver (CBU)	860
Lindsay, Ont.	CKLY	Greg-May Broadcasting Ltd., 249 Kent St. W., K9V 2Z3 (705/324-9103)	910
Lloydminster, Alta.	CKSA	Sask.-Alta. Broadcasters Ltd., 5026-50th St., T9V 1P3 (403/875-3321)	1080
Lockeport, N.S.	*CBHD	Studio at Halifax (CBH)	740
London, Ont.	CFPL	CFPL Broadcasting Ltd., 369 York St., Box 2580, N6A 4H3 (519/438-8391)	980
London, Ont.	CJBK	Middlesex Broadcasters Ltd., 743 Wellington Rd. S., Box 1290, Stn. A, N6A 5A2 (519/686-2525)	1290
London, Ont.	CKSL	London Broadcasters Ltd., 343 Richmond St., Box 1410, N6A 5J2 (519/432-4181)	1410
Longlac, Ont.	*CBLL	Studio at Thunder Bay (CBQ)	1400
Longueuil, P.Q.	†CHRS	See St-Jean	1090
Lynn Lake, Man.	*CBDU	Studio at Winnipeg (CBW)	1170
Lytton, B.C.	*CBRE	Studio at Vancouver (CBU)	1080
Mackenzie, B.C.	*CBWF	Studio at Vancouver (CBU)	900
Mackenzie, B.C.	CKMK	See Radio Station CKPG Ltd., Prince George	1240
Malartic, P.Q.	*CBMN	Studio at Montreal (CBM)	1230
Manitouwadge, Ont.	*CBEB	Studio at Thunder Bay (CBQ)	1010
Maniwaki, P.Q.	*†CBOF-1	Studio at Ottawa (CBOF)	990
Maniwaki, P.Q.	*CBON	Studio at Ottawa (CBO)	1230
Maniwaki, P.Q.	†CKMG	See CKML Inc., Mont Laurier	1340
Marathon, Ont.	*CBLM	Studio at Thunder Bay (CBQ)	1090
Marystown, Nfld.	CHCM	See Colonial Broadcasting, St. John's	560
Marystown, Nfld.	*CBNM	Studio at St. John's (CBN)	740
Matachewan, Ont.	*†CJBC-10	Studio at Toronto (CJBC)	1110
Matagami, P.Q.	*†CBFR	Studio at Montreal (CBF)	1140
Matane, P.Q.	*†CBGA	CBC, 155 St. Sacrement, C.P. 2000, G4W 3P7 (418/562-0290)	1250
Matane, P.Q.	†CHRM	Les Communications Matane Inc., 800 ave du Phare ouest, G4W 1V7 (418/562-4141)	1290
Mattawa, Ont.	*†CBOF-5	Studio at Ottawa (CBOF)	1090
Mattawa, Ont.	*CBLO	Studio at Toronto (CBL)	1240
Maynooth, Ont.	*CBOD	Studio at Toronto (CBL)	1400
Mayo, Y.T.	*CBDC	See CFWH, Whitehorse	1230
McAdam, N.B.	*CBAX	Studio at Fredericton (CBZ)	600
McBride, B.C.	*CBXM	Studio at Vancouver (CBU)	860
Meadow Lake, Sask.	CJNS	Northwestern Broadcasting Co. Ltd., Centre St., Box 1660, S0M 1V0 (306/236-6494)	1240
Medicine Hat, Alta.	CHAT	Monarch Broadcasting Co. Ltd., 1111 Kingsway, Box 1270, T1A 7H5 (403/529-1270)	1270
Medley, Alta.	CHCL	CFB, Box 1220, T0A 2M0	1450
Mégantic, P.Q.	*†CBFB	Studio at Montreal (CBF)	990
Melfort, Sask.	CJVR	Radio CJVR Ltd., 611 Main St. N., Box 1420, S0E 1A0 (306/752-2867)	1420
Merritt, B.C.	*CBUP	Studio at Vancouver (CBU)	860
Merritt, B.C.	CJNL	See NL Broadcasting Ltd., Kamloops	1230
Meteghan, N.B.	*†CBAH	Studio at Moncton (CBAF)	580
Mica Dam, B.C.	*CBXA	Studio at Vancouver (CBU)	1150

LOCATION	CALL		FREQ.
Middleton, N.S.	CKAD	See Annapolis Valley Radio, Kentville (Middleton ph.: 902/825-3322)	1350
Midland, Ont.	CKMP	Telemedia Ontario Inc., 490 Dominion Ave., L4R 1P6 (705/526-2268)	1230
Midway, B.C.	*CBXS	Studio at Vancouver (CBU)	1150
Mindemoya, Ont.	*CBEN	Studio at Toronto (CBL)	540
Minto, N.B.	*†CBAI	Studio at Moncton (CBAF)	1320
Mississauga, Ont.	CFRE	Erindale College, 3359 Mississauga Rd., L6B 2S7 (416/828-5310) closed circuit	
Mississauga, Ont.	CJMR	CJMR 1190 Radio Ltd., Box 1190, Port Credit PO, L3G 4M3 (416/279-1190)	1190
Moncton, N.B.	*†CBAF	CBC, 250 Archibald St., CP 950, E1C 8N8 (506/855-3370)	1300
Moncton, N.B.	CKCW	CKCW Radio Ltd., 1000 St. George Blvd. (506/855-1220)	1220
Moncton, N.B.	*CBA	CBC, 250 Archibald St., Box 950, E1C 8N8 (506/388-3061)	1070
Mont-Apica, P.Q.	CKMA	Stn. CKMA, CFB Mont Apica, P.Q. G0A 2P0	1340
Mont Brun, P.Q.	*†CBFI	Studio at Montreal (CBF)	990
Mont Laurier, P.Q.	†CKML	CKML Inc., 515 Paquette Blvd., J9L 1K9 (819/623-1011)	610
Montmagny, P.Q.	†CKBM	Radio CKBM Inc., 120 St-Jean Baptiste est, G5V 1K5 (418/248-0801)	1490
Montreal, P.Q.	*†CBF	CBC, Box 6000, H3C 3A8 (514/285-3211)	690
Montreal, P.Q.	*CBM	CBC, Box 6000, H3C 3A8 (514/285-3211)	940
Montreal, P.Q.	CFCF	CFCF Inc., 405 Ogilvy Ave., H3N 1M4 (514/273-6311)	600
Montreal, P.Q.	(Multiling.) CFMB	CFMB Ltd., 35 York St., Westmount, H3Z 2Z5 (514/483-2362)	1410
Montreal, P.Q.	CJAD	CJAD Ltd., 1411 rue du Fort, #300, H3H 2R1 (514/989-2523)	800
Montreal, P.Q.	†CJMS	CJMS Radio-Montréal Ltée, 1700 Berri St., H2L 4E8 (514/849-6221)	1280
Montreal, P.Q.	†CKAC	CKAC Ltée, 1400 Metcalfe St., H3A 1X4 (514/845-5155)	730
Montreal, P.Q.	CKGM	Maisonneuve Broadcasting Corp. Ltd., 1310 Greene Ave., Westmount, H3Z 2B5 (514/931-6251)	980
Montreal, P.Q.	†CKLM	See Laval	1570
Montreal, P.Q.	CKO	CKO All News Radio Ltd., 203 Hymus Blvd., Pointe Claire, P.Q. (514/697-1470)	1470
Montreal, P.Q.	CRSG	Concordia University, 1455 de Maisonneuve Blvd. W., #647, H3G 1M8 (514/879-4598)	
Moose Jaw, Sask.	CHAB	Moffat Communications Ltd., 116 Main St. N., S6H 3J7 (306/692-6464)	800
Moosonee, Ont.	*CBEY	Studio at Toronto (CBL)	1340
Moosonee, Ont.	CHMO	James Bay Broadcasting Corp. Inc., Box 400, P0L 1Y0 (705/336-2953)	1450
Murdochville, P.Q.	*CBMJ	Studio at Montreal (CBM)	1400
Nain, Nfld.	*CBNZ	Studio at Happy Valley (CFGB)	740
Nakina, Ont.	*CBLN	Studio at Thunder Bay (CBQ)	1240
Nakusp, B.C.	*CBUM	Studio at Vancouver (CBU)	900
Nanaimo, B.C.	CHUB	Nanaimo Broadcasting Corp. Ltd., 22 Esplanade Cres., Box 1570, V9R 4Y7 (604/753-4341)	1570
Natal, B.C.	*CBXN	Studio at Vancouver (CBU)	1400
Nelson, B.C.	CKKC	KC Broadcasting, (702 Stanley St.) Box 250, V1L 5P9 (604/352-7277)	1390
New Carlisle, P.Q.	†CHNC	La Cie Gaspésienne de Radiodiffusion Ltée, Principale St. & Perron Blvd., C.P. 610, G0C 1Z0 (418/752-2215)	610
Newcastle, N.B.	CFAN	CFAN Broadcasting Co. Ltd., 245 Pleasant St., Box 338, E1V 3M5 (506/622-3311)	790
New Denver, B.C.	*CBUI	Studio at Vancouver (CBU)	740
New Glasgow, N.S.	CKEC	Hector Broadcasting Co. Ltd., 84 Provost St., Box 519, B2H 5E7 (902/752-4200)	1320
New Hazelton, B.C.	*CBRH	Studio at Prince Rupert (CFPR)	1170
New Liskeard, Ont.	CJTT	Kirkland Lake Broadcasting Co. Ltd., Box 1058, P0J 1P0 (705/647-7334)	1230
Newmarket, Ont.	CKAN	CKAN Radio Ltd., Box 1480, L3Y 4X1 (416/898-1100)	1480
New Westminster, B.C.	CKNW	Radio NW Ltd., 8th Ave. & McBride Blvd., V3L 2C1 (604/522-2711)	980
Niagara Falls, Ont.	CJRN	CJRN/710 Inc., Box 710, 4668 St. Clair Ave., L2E 6X7 (416/356-6710)	710
Noranda, P.Q.	*CBMA	Studio at Montreal (CBM)	1450
Noranda, P.Q.	†CKRN	Radio Nord Inc., 380 Murdoch St., J9X 1G5 (819/762-0741)	1400
Norman Wells, N.W.T.	*CBDW	See CHAK, Inuvik	990
North Battleford, Sask.	CJNB	Northwestern Broadcasting Co. Ltd., 1711-100th St., Box 1460, S9A 2Z5 (306/445-2478)	1050
North Bay, Ont.	CFCH	Northern Broadcasting Ltd., Box 3000, P1B 8K8 (705/474-2000)	600
North Bay, Ont.	CRTV	Canadore College, Box 5001, P1B 8K9 (705/474-7600) closed circuit	
North Bend, B.C.	*CBRN	Studio at Vancouver (CBU)	740
Norway House, Man.	CJNC	Native Communications Inc., R0B 1B0 (204/359-6764)	
Oakville, Ont.	CHWO	CHWO Radio Ltd., 490 Wyecroft Rd., L6K 2H1 (416/845-2821)	1250
Oakville, Ont.	CORS	Sheridan College, 1430 Trafalgar Rd., L6H 2L1 (416/845-3311) closed circuit	
Oliver, B.C.	*CBUA	Studio at Vancouver (CBU)	730
Oliver, B.C.	CKOO-1	See CKOK, Penticton	1490
100 Mile House, B.C.	*CBUS	Studio at Vancouver (CBU)	860
100 Mile House, B.C.	CKBX	Cariboo Broadcasters Ltd., Box 939,, V0K 2E0 (604/395-3848)	1240
Orillia, Ont.	CFOR	Orillia Broadcasting Ltd., 241 West St. N., Box 550, L3V 6K2 (705/326-3511).	1570
Oshawa, Ont.	CKAR	Grant Broadcasting Ltd., 360 King St. W., L1J 2K2 (416/571-1350) (Toronto line: 686-1350)	1350
Osoyoos, B.C.	*CBUR	Studio at Vancouver (CBU)	900

LOCATION	CALL		FREQ.
Osoyoos, B.C.	CKOO	Okanagan Radio Ltd., Box 539, V0N 1V0 (604/495-7226)	1240
Ottawa, Ont.	*CBO	Chateau Laurier Hotel, Box 3220, Stn. C, K1Y 1E4 (613/725-3511)	920
Ottawa, Ont.	*†CBOF	Chateau Laurier Hotel, CP 3220, Succ. C, K1Y 1E4 (613/725-3511)	1250
Ottawa, Ont.	CFRA	Radio Station CFRA Ltd., 150 Isabella St., K1S 5A3 (613/233-6241)	580
Ottawa, Ont.	CHOR	University of Ottawa, 85 Hastey St., K1N 6N5 (613/231-5826) closed circuit	
Ottawa, Ont.	†CJRC	CJRC Radio Capitale Ltée, 681 Belfast Rd., K1G 0Z4 (613/237-7100) (Montreal line: 514/861-3109)	1150
Ottawa, Ont.	CFGO	CFGO Radio Ltd., 88 Argyle Ave., K2P 1B4 (613/238-6500)	1440
Ottawa, Ont.	CKOY	Key Radio Ltd., #1900, Place de Ville, Tower B, 112 Kent St., K1P 6J1	1310
Owen Sound, Ont.	CFOS	Grey & Bruce Broadcasting Co. Ltd., 270-9th St. E., N4K 1N7 (519/376-2030)	560
Parent, P.Q.	*†CBV-1	Studio at Quebec (CBV)	1240
Parksville, B.C.	CHPQ	Anchor Developments, Box 1570, Nanaimo, B.C. V9R 5N3	1370
Parry Sound, Ont.	CFBQ	Muskoka-Parry Sound Broadcasting Ltd., 24A William St., P2A 1V1 (705/746-2163)	1340
Parson, B.C.	*CBKR	Studio at Vancouver (CBU)	740
Peace River, Alta.	CKYL	Peace River Broadcasting Corp. Ltd., 9811-100th Ave., Box 1150, T0H 2X0 (403/624-2535)	610
Pemberton, B.C.	*CBXX	Studio at Vancouver (CBU)	1240
Pembroke, Ont.	CHOV	Ottawa Valley Broadcasting Co. Ltd., 179 Pembroke St. E., Box 100, K8A 6X2 (613/735-6807)	1350
Penticton, B.C.	CKOK	Okanagan Radio Ltd., 33 Carmi Ave., V2A 3G4 (604/492-2800)	800
Petawawa, Ont.	*†CBOF-2	Studio at Ottawa (CBOF)	1240
Peterborough, Ont.	CHEX	Kawartha Broadcasting Co. Ltd., Box 659, K9J 6Z9 (705/742-7708)	980
Peterborough, Ont.	CKPT	Radio CKPT 1420 Ltd., 340 George St. N., Ste. 403, K9J 6Y8 (705/742-8844)	1420
Pine Point, N.W.T.	*CBDV	See CFYK, Yellowknife	880
Plaster Rock, N.B.	*CBAD	Studio at Fredericton (CBZ)	990
Plessisville, P.Q.	†CKTL	Radio Plessisville Ltée, 1646 Ave. St-Laurent, CP 160, G6L 2Y7 (819/362-3737)	1420
Pohenegamook, P.Q.	†CHRT	See Radio CJFP Ltée, Rivière-du-Loup	1450
Pomquet, N.B.	*†CBHG	Studio at Moncton (CBAF)	1340
Portage la Prairie, Man.	CFRY	Portage-Delta Broadcasting Co. Ltd., 1500 Saskatchewan Ave. W., R1N 0N6 (204/857-5111)	920
Port Alberni, B.C.	CJAV	CJAV Radio Ltd., 2970 3rd Ave., V9Y 7N4 (604/723-2455)	1240
Port Alice, B.C.	*CBUX	Studio at Vancouver (CBU)	1170
Port au Choix, Nfld.	CFNW	See Humber Valley Broadcasting, Corner Brook	790
Port-aux-Basques, Nfld.	*CBNE	Studio at Corner Brook (CBY)	1370
Port-aux-Basques, Nfld.	CFGN	See Humber Valley Broadcasting, Corner Brook	1230
Port Cartier, P.Q.	*CBMB	Studio at Montreal (CBM)	990
Port Cartier, P.Q.	†CIPC	Radio Sept-Iles Inc., 8 boul. des Iles, Ste. 220 (418/766-6868)	710
Port Elgin, Ont.	CFPS	See CFOS, Owen Sound	1490
Port Hardy, B.C.	*CBRW	Studio at Vancouver (CBU)	630
Port Hardy, B.C.	CFNI	CFCP Radio Ltd., Box 1240, V0N 2P0 (604/949-6500)	1240
Port Hawkesbury, N.S.	CIGO	Eastern Broadcasters Ltd., Light Industrial Park, Box 1410, B0E 2V0 (902/625-1220)	1410
Port Saunders, Nfld.	*CBNJ	Studio at Corner Brook (CBY)	740
Powell River, B.C.	CHQB	Sunshine Coast Broadcasting Co., 6816 Courtenay St., V8A 1X1 (604/485-4207)	1280
Prince Albert, Sask.	CKBI	Central Broadcasting Co. Ltd., 22 10th St., S6V 3A5 (306/763-7421)	900
Prince George, B.C.	CHPG	Privately owned re-broadcaster of CBU, Vancouver	1490
Prince George, B.C.	*†CBRG	Studio at Vancouver (see CBUF-FM)	1150
Prince George, B.C.	CKPG	Radio Station CKPG Ltd., 1220-6th Ave., V2L 3M8 (604/564-8861)	550
Prince George, B.C.	CJCI	CJCI Radio, 1940 3rd Ave., V2M 5X5 (604/564-2524)	620
Prince Rupert, B.C.	*CFPR	CBC, 346 Stiles Pl., Box 99, V8J 3P4 (604/624-2161)	860
Prince Rupert, B.C.	CHTK	Skeena Broadcasters Ltd., 300 2nd Ave. W.	560
Princeton, B.C.	*CBRP	Studio at Vancouver (CBU)	860
Princeton, B.C.	CINL	See NL Broadcasting Ltd., Kamloops	1400
Procter, B.C.	*CBUO	Studio at Vancouver (CBU)	900
Pukatawagan, Man.	*CBDS	Studio at Winnipeg (CBW)	690
Quebec, P.Q.	*†CBV	Radio Canada, 2505 Laurier Blvd., Ste-Foy, G1V 2X2 (418/656-9440)	980
Quebec, P.Q.	†CHRC	Télé-Capitale Ltée, 2136, Ste-Foy Rd., Box 8080, G1K 7W1 (418/688-8080)	800
Quebec, P.Q.	†CJRP	CJRP Radio Provinciale Ltée, 1300 boul. Laurier, G1S 1L8 (418/688-1060)	1060
Quebec, P.Q.	†CKCV	C.K.C.V. (Que.) Ltée, 800 d'Youville Sq., Ste. 2100, G1R 4W7 (418/694-1280)	1280
Quesnel, B.C.	*CBRQ	Studio at Vancouver (CBU)	740
Quesnel, B.C.	CKCQ	Cariboo Broadcasters Ltd., 160 Front St., V2J 2K1 (604/992-7046)	920
Quinan, N.B.	*†CBAS	Studio at Moncton (CBAF)	600
Radium Hot Springs, B.C.	*CBKV	Studio at Vancouver (CBU)	900
Rainbow Lake, Alta.	*CBXX	Studio at Edmonton (CBX)	1240
Rankin Inlet, N.W.T.	*CBQR	See CFFB, Frobisher Bay	1160
Red Deer, Alta.	CKRD	Central Alta. Broadcasting Co. (1961) Ltd., 2840 Bremner Ave., T4N 5H6 (403/343-0850)	850
Red Deer, Alta.	CKGY	Park Country Broadcasting Ltd., Box 339, T4N 5E9 (403/343-1170)	1170
Red Lake, Ont.	*CBEA	Re-broadcasting CBQ, Thunder Bay	1010
Red Rock, Ont.	*CBLR	Studio at Thunder Bay (CBQ)	1010

LOCATION	CALL		FREQ.
Regina, Sask.	*CBK	CBC, 1840 McIntyre St., S4P 2R1 (306/523-6641)	540
Regina, Sask.	CJME	Midwest Broadcasters Ltd., 2526 11th Ave., Box 1300, S4P 3B9 (306/569-1300)	1300
Regina, Sask.	CKCK	Armadale Communications Ltd., Victoria Ave. & Park St., Box 6200, S4P 3H7 (306/522-8591)	620
Regina, Sask.	CKRM	Harvard Communications, 2060 Halifax St., Box 9800, S4P 3J4 (306/352-5661)	980
Renfrew, Ont.	CKOB	Opeongo Broadcasting Co. Ltd., 282 Raglan St. S., Box 96, K7V 4A2 (613/432-6428)	1400
Revelstoke, B.C.	*CBRA	Studio at Vancouver (CBU)	860
Revelstoke, B.C.	CKCR	Hall-Gray Broadcasting Co. Ltd., Box 1420, V0E 2S0 (604/837-2149)	1340
Richmond, B.C.	C-ISL	South Fraser Broadcasting Ltd., #20, 11151 Horseshoe Way, V7A 4S5 (604/274-9940)	940
Richmond Hill, Ont.	CFGM	CFGM Broadcasting Ltd., 10254 Yonge St., L4C 3B7 (416/961-1320)	1320
Rimouski, P.Q.	*†CJBR	CBC, 273 St-Jean Baptiste St. O., G5L 4J8 (418/723-2217)	900
Rivière-du-Loup, P.Q.	†CJFP	CJFP Ltée, 1 rue Frontenac, G5R 1R7 (418/862-8241)	1400
Roberval, P.Q.	†CHRL	Radio Roberval Inc., 568 boul. St-Joseph, G8H 2K6 (418/275-1831)	910
Rogers Pass, B.C.	*CBWR	Studio at Vancouver (CBU)	1150
Rogersville, N.B.	*†CBAQ	Studio at Moncton (CBAF)	1530
Rolphton, Ont.	*CBEO	Studio at Ottawa (CBO)	1230
Rolphton, Ont.	*†CBOF-4	Studio at Ottawa (CBOF)	1400
Rosetown, Sask.	CKKR	Goose Lake Broadcasting Co. Ltd., Box 490, S0L 2V0 (306/882-2686)	1330
Ross River, Y.T.	*CBQJ	See CFWH, Whitehorse	990
Sable River, N.S.	*CBAV	Studio at Halifax (CBH)	1240
Sackville, N.B.	CHMA	Mount Allison University, E0A 3C0 (506/536-2040) closed circuit	
Ste-Agathe-des-Monts, P.Q.	†CJSA	Radio Sainte-Agathe Inc., 3 est rue Principale, J8C 1J2 (819/326-1230)	1230
St. Albert, Alta.	CKST	St. Albert Broadcasting Ltd., 8610 McKenney Ave., T8N 2T7 (403/458-9722)	1070
Ste-Anne-des-Monts, P.Q.	†CJMC	Radio du Golfe Inc., Box 820, G0E 2G0 (418/763-5522)	1490
St. Anthony, Nfld.	*CBNA	Studio at Corner Brook (CBY)	600
St. Boniface, Man.	*†CKSB	CBC, 607 Langevin St. C.P. 160, R3C 2H1 (204/247-4843)	1050
St. Catharines, Ont.	CKTB	Niagara Dist. Broadcasting Co. Ltd., Yates & St. Paul Sts., Box 610, L2R 6X7 (416/684-1174)	610
St. Catharines, Ont.	CHSC	Radio Station CHSC Ltd., 36 Queenston St., L2R 7C7 (416/682-6691)	1220
St. Catharines, Ont.	CJRN	See Niagara Falls	
St. Catharines, Ont.	CRBC	Brock University, L2S 3A1 (416/688-2013) closed circuit	
St. Fintans, Nfld.	*CBNB	Studio at Corner Brook (CBY)	740
Ste-Foy, P.Q.	See Quebec		
St. George, N.B.	*CBAW	Studio at Fredericton (CBZ)	740
St. Georges-de-Beauce, P.Q.		See Ville St-Georges Est	
St-Hyacinthe, P.Q.	†CKBS	Radio St-Hyacinthe Ltée, 855 ave Ste-Marie, J2S 4R9 (514/774-6486)	1240
St-Jean, P.Q.	†CHRS	Radio Rive-Sud (CHRS) Ltée, 2019, Taschereau Blvd., Longueuil, P.Q. J4K 2Y1 (514/674-6238)	1090
Saint John, N.B.	CFBC	Fundy Broadcasting Co. Ltd., Box 930, E2L 4E2 (506/652-1680)	930
Saint John, N.B.	CHSJ	N.B. Broadcasting Co., Crown & Union St., E2L 3T4 (506/657-3410)	1150
Saint John, N.B.	*CBD	CBC, Hilyard Place, Main St., Box 2358, E2L 3V6 (506/642-7710)	1110
St. John's, Nfld.	*CBN	CBC, Duckworth St., Box 12010, Stn. A, A1B 3T8 (709/753-1300)	640
St. John's, Nfld.	CHMR	Memorial University, Box A-119, A1C 5S7 (709/753-9702) closed circuit	
St. John's, Nfld.	CJYQ	Radio CJYQ 930 Ltd., 221 Duckworth St., Box 6180, A1C 5X8 (709/753-4040)	930
St. John's, Nfld.	VOAR	Seventh Day Adventist Church, 106 Freshwater Rd., A1C 2N8 (709/579-2104)	1230
St. John's, Nfld.	VOCM	The Colonial Broadcasting System Ltd., Kenmount Rd., Box 8-590, Stn. A, A1B 3P5 (709/726-5590)	590
St. John's, Nfld.	VOWR	Wesley United Church Radio Bd., Box 7430, A1E 3Y5 (709/579-9233)	800
St-Jovite, P.Q.	†CKSJ	See CKML Inc., Mont Laurier	1400
St-Lazare, Man.	*†CKSB-2	Studio at St-Boniface (CKSB)	860
Ste-Marie de Beauce, P.Q.	†CJVL	Clival, Inc., President Kennedy Blvd., C.P. 1360, G0S 2Y0 (418/387-1360)	1360
St-Pamphile, P.Q.	†CHAL	See Radio la Pocatiere Ltée, La Pocatiere	1350
St. Paul, Alta.	CIOK	See OK Radio, Westlock	1310
St-Quentin, N.B.	*†CBAL	Studio at Moncton (CBAF)	1230
St-Rose-du-Lac, Man.	*†CKSB-1	Studio at St-Boniface (CKSB)	860
St. Stephen, N.B.	*CBAD	Studio at Fredericton (CBZ)	990
St. Thomas, Ont.	CHLO	Souwesto Broadcasters Ltd., 133 Curtis St., N5P 3T8 (519/631-3910)	1570
Salmo, B.C.	*CBUN	Studio at Vancouver (CBU)	740
Salmon Arm, B.C.	*CBUC	Studio at Vancouver (CBU)	860
Salmon Arm, B.C.	CKXR	Hall-Gray Broadcasting Co., Box 69, V0E 2T0 (604/832-2161)	580
Sanmaur, P.Q.	*†CBV-4	Studio at Quebec (CBV)	1340
Sarnia, Ont.	CHOK	Sarnia Broadcasters Ltd., 148 Front St. N., N7T 7K5 (519/336-1070)	1070
Sarnia, Ont.	CKJD	Rogers Radio Broadcasting Ltd., 546 N. Christina St., N7T 5W6 (519/336-1110)	1110
Saskatoon, Sask.	*†CFNS	c/o 1840 McIntyre St., Regina, Sask. S4P 2R1 (306/523-6641)	860
Saskatoon, Sask.	CFQC	CFQC Broadcasting Ltd., 216-1st Ave. N., S7K 3W3 (306/665-8600)	600
Saskatoon, Sask.	CJWW	Western World Communications, 345 4th Ave. S., S7K 5S5 (306/244-1975)	1370

LOCATION	CALL		FREQ.
Saskatoon, Sask.	CKOM	Saskatoon Community Broadcasting Co., 3333 8th St. E., S7H 0W3 (306/374-3690)	1250
Sault Ste Marie, Ont.	CFYN	Gilder Broadcasting Ltd., Box 1050, P6A 5N5 (705/942-1050)	1050
Sault Ste Marie, Ont.	CKCY	Huron Broadcasting Co., Box 370, P6A 5M2 (705/254-7111)	920
Sayward, B.C.	*CBKU	Studio at Vancouver (CBU)	630
Schefferville, P.Q.	*CBDN	Studio at Montreal (CBM)	570
Schreiber, Ont.	*CBLB	Studio at Thunder Bay (CBQ)	1340
Searston, Nfld.	*CBNH	Studio at Corner Brook (CBY)	1340
Senneterre, P.Q.	*CBMM	Studio at Montreal (CBM)	540
Senneterre, P.Q.	*†CBFC	Studio at Montreal (CBF)	710
Sept-Iles, P.Q.	*CBMC	Studio at Montreal (CBM)	1190
Sept-Iles, P.Q.	†CKCN	Radio Sept-Iles Inc., 106 Napoleon St., G4R 3L7 (418/962-3838)	560
Shalalth, B.C.	*CBKN	Studio at Vancouver (CBU)	1340
Shaunavon, Sask.	CJSN	Frontier City Broadcasting Co., c/o Box 370, Swift Current, Sask. S9H 3V8	1490
Shawinigan, P.Q.	†CKSM	The Shawinigan Falls Broadcasting Co. Ltd., Edifice Hotel de Ville., C.P. 695, G9N 6V9 (819/537-8824)	1220
Sheet Harbour, N.S.	*CBAZ	Studio at Halifax (CBH)	1230
Shelburne, N.S.	*CBAP	Studio at Halifax (CBH)	1140
Sherbrooke, P.Q.	†CHLT	Telemedia Communications Ltd., 25 Bryant St., J1J 3Z5 (819/563-6363)	630
Sherbrooke, P.Q.	†CJRS	CJRS Radio Sherbrooke Ltée, 2655 King St. W., J1L 1C1 (819/567-8951)	1510
Sherbrooke, P.Q.	CKTS	Télémedia Communications, 25 King St. W., J1H 1N4 (819/563-9090)	900
Simcoe, Ont.	CHNR	Simcoe Broadcasting Co. Ltd., 39 Kent St. N., N3Y 3S1 (519/426-7700)	1600
Sioux Lookout, Ont.	*CBLS	Re-broadcasting CBQ, Thunder Bay	1240
Sioux Lookout, Ont.	CKSI	c/o Fawcett Broadcasting, see CKDR, Dryden	1400
Slocan City, B.C.	*CBUJ	Studio at Vancouver (CBU)	860
Smithers, B.C.	CFBV	CFBV Ltd., 1139 Queen St., Box 335, V0J 2N0 (604/847-2521)	1230
Smiths Falls, Ont.	CJET	Rideau Broadcasting Ltd., Jasper Rd. Box 630, K7A 4T6 (613/283-4630)	630
Smooth Rock Falls, Ont.	*†CJBC-2	Studio at Toronto (CJBC)	540
Sorel, P.Q.	†CJSO	Radio Richelieu (1979) Ltée, 59A du Prince, J3P 4J5 (514/743-3318)	1320
Sorrento, B.C.	*CBKX	Studio at Vancouver (CBU)	1080
Spanish, Ont.	*CBED	Studio at Toronto (CBL)	1400
Squamish, B.C.	*CBRU	Studio at Vancouver (CBU)	1350
Steinbach, Man.	CHSM	See Golden West Broadcasting Ltd., Altona	1250
Stephenville, Nfld.	*CBNC	Studio at Corner Brook (CBY)	1190
Stephenville, Nfld.	CFSX	See Humber Valley Broadcasting, Corner Brook	910
Stettler, Alta.	CHOA	Dinosaur Broadcasting, Box 1840, T0C 2L0 (403/742-2462)	1400
Stewart, B.C.	*CBKA	Studio at Prince Rupert (CFPR)	1450
Stratford, Ont.	CJCS	Telemedia Ontario Inc., 178 Ontario St., Box 904, N5A 6W3 (519/271-2450)	1240
Sturgeon Falls, Ont.	*†CJBC-4	Studio at Toronto (CJBC)	1400
Sudbury, Ont.	†CFBR	The Sudbury Broadcasting Co. Ltd., C.P. 700, P3E 4R9 (705/674-6401)	900
Sudbury, Ont.	CHNO	The Sudbury Broadcasting Co. Ltd., Box 700, P3E 4R9 (705/674-6401)	550
Sudbury, Ont.	CKSO	United Broadcasting Ltd., 336 Ash St., P3C 2A1 (705/674-0711)	790
Summerland, B.C.	CKSP	Okanagan Radio Ltd., Main St., Box 1170, V0H 1Z0 (604/494-1524)	1450
Summerside, P.E.I	CJRW	Gulf Broadcasting Co. Ltd., 218 Water St., C1N 1B3 (902/436-2201)	1240
Sussex, N.B.	CJCW	CJCW Broadcasting Ltd., Box 5900, E0E 1P0 (506/433-4522)	590
Swift Current, Sask.	CKSW	Frontier City Broadcasting Co. Ltd., Box S9H 3V8 (306/773-4605)	570
Swift River, Y.T.	*CBDX	See CFWH, Whitehorse	970
Sydney, N.S.	*CBI	CBC, 285 Alexander St., Box 700, B1P 6H7 (902/539-5050)	1140
Sydney, N.S.	CHER	Radio Cape Breton Ltd., 751 Alexandra St., B1S 2H3 (902/539-8500)	950
Sydney, N.S.	CJCB	Celtic Investments Ltd., Radio Bldg., 318 Charlotte St., Box 1270, B1P 6K2 (902/564-5596)	1270
Taber, Alta	CKTA	See Southern Alta. Broadcasting Ltd., Lethbridge	1570
Tahsis, B.C.	*CBXP	Studio at Vancouver (CBU)	1350
Temagami, Ont	*CBEU	Studio at Toronto (CBL)	1340
Temiscaming, P.Q.	†CKVT	See CKVM, Ville Marie	1340
Terrace, B.C.	CFTK	Skeena Broadcasters Ltd., 4625 Lazelle Ave., V8G 1S4 (604/635-6316)	590
Terrace, B.C.	*†CBWK	Studio at Vancouver (see CBUF-FM)	990
Terrace Bay, Ont.	*CBEH	Studio at Thunder Bay (CBQ)	1010
Teslin, Y.T.	*CBDK	See CFWH, Whitehorse	940
The Pas, Man.	CJAR	Arctic Radio Corp. Ltd., Box 2980, R9A 1R7 (204/623-5307)	1240
Thetford Mines, P.Q.	†CKLD	Radio Megantic Ltée, C.P. 69, G6G 5S3 (418/335-7533)	1330
Thompson, Man.	CHTM	Arctic Radio Corp. Ltd., 201 Hayes Rd., R8N 1M5 (204/778-7361)	610
Thunder Bay, Ont.	*CBQ	CBC, 213 Myles St. E., P7C 1J5 (807/622-5811)	800
Thunder Bay, Ont.	CJLB	Leader Broadcasting Corp., Box 3448, P7B 5J9 (807/344-2404)	1230
Thunder Bay, Ont.	CKPR	H.F. Dougall Co. Ltd., 87 North Hill St., P7A 5V6 (807/344-3526)	580
Tillsonburg, Ont.	CKOT	Tillsonburg Broadcasting Co. Ltd., 77 Broadway, Box 10, N4G 4H3 (519/842-4281)	1510
Timmins, Ont.	†CFCL	Mid Canada Communications Corp., C.P. 620, P4N 7H8 (705/264-4211)	620
Timmins, Ont.	CKGB	Telemedia Ontario Inc., 155 Pine St. S., Box 1046, P4N 7H8 (705/264-2351)	680
Tofino, B.C.	*CBXZ	Studio at Vancouver (CBU)	630
Toronto, Ont.	CBFM	George Brown College, Box 1015, Stn. B, M5T 2T9 (416/967-1212) closed circuit	
Toronto, Ont.	*CBL	CBC, Box 500, Term. A, M5W 1E6 (416/925-3311)	740

LOCATION	CALL		FREQ.
Toronto, Ont.	CFGM	See Richmond Hill	
Toronto, Ont.	CFRB	CFRB Ltd., 2 St. Clair Ave. W., M4W 1L6 (416/924-5711)	1010
Toronto, Ont.	CFTR	Radio Rogers Ltd., 25 Adelaide St. E., M5C 1H3 (416/864-2016)	680
Toronto, Ont.	CHBR	Humber College, Box 1900, Rexdale (416/675-3111) closed circuit	
Toronto, Ont.	(Biling.) CHIN	Radio 1540 Ltd., 637 College St. M6G 1B6 (416/531-9991)	1540
Toronto, Ont.	CHUM	CHUM Ltd., 1331 Yonge St. M4T 1Y1 (416/925-6666)	1050
Toronto, Ont.	*†CJBC	CBC, Box 500, Term. A, M5W 1E6 (416/925-3311)	860
Toronto, Ont.	CJCL	Telemedia Ontario Inc., 464 Yonge St., M4Y 1W9 (416/923-0921)	1430
Toronto, Ont.	CJS	Scarborough College, 1265 Military Trail, West Hill, M1C 1A4 (416/284-3143) closed circuit	
Toronto, Ont.	CKCC	Centennial College, 651 Warden Ave., Scarborough, M1L 3Z6 (416/694-3033) closed circuit	
Toronto, Ont.	CKEY	KEY Radio Ltd., One Yonge St., M5E 1G1 (416/361-1281)	590
Toronto, Ont.	CKLN	Ryerson Institute, 50 Gould St., M5B 1E8 (416/595-1477) closed circuit	
Toronto, Ont.	CKMW	CKMR Radio, 83 Kennedy Rd. S., Brampton, Ont. L6W 3P3 (416/453-7111)	790
Toronto, Ont.	CRSC	Seneca College, 1750 Finch Ave. E., Willowdale, M2N 5T7 (416/491-5050) closed circuit	
Toronto, Ont.	UTR	University of Toronto, 91 St. George St., M5S 2E8 (416/978-4563) closed circuit	
Trail, B.C.	CJAT	Kootenay Broadcasting Co. Ltd., 1560 2nd Ave., V1R 1M4 (604/368-5511)	610
Trenton, Ont.	CJBR	See Belleville	800
Trenton, Ont.	CJTN	Quinte Broadcasting Ltd., 31 Quinte St., Box 9, K8V 5R1 (613/392-1237)	1270
Trois-Rivières, P.Q.	†CHLN	Radio Trois-Rivières Inc., 3550 Royal Blvd., G9A 5G8 (819/374-3556)	550
Trois-Rivières, P.Q.	†CJTR	CJTR Radio Trois-Rivières Ltée, City Hall Sq., 12th floor, Place Royale, 1350 rue Royale, G9A 4J4 (819/375-4855)	1140
Truro, N.S.	CKCL	Colchester Broadcasting Co. Ltd., 840 Prince St., Box 788, B2N 5E8 (902/895-4491)	600
Tuktoyaktuk, N.W.T.	(Biling.) CFCT	Tuktoyaktuk Broadcasting Soc., Bag 7000, X0E 1C0 (403/977-2277)	600
Ucluelet, B.C.	*CBXQ	Studio at Vancouver (CBU)	540
Uranium City, Sask.	*CBDH	Studio at Regina (CBK)	880
Val d'Or, P.Q.	*CBML	Studio at Montreal (CBM)	570
Val d'Or, P.Q.	†CKVD	See Radio Nord Inc., Rouyn	900
Valemount, B.C.	*CBKI	Studio at Vancouver (CBU)	1450
Valleyfield, P.Q.	†CFLV	Radio Valleyfield Ltée, 249 Victoria St., Salaberry-de-Valleyfield, P.Q. J6T 1A9 (514/373-1370)	1370
Vancouver, B.C.	*CBU	CBC, 700 Hamilton St., Box 4600, V6B 4A2 (604/665-8000)	690
Vancouver, B.C.	CFUN	CHUM Western Ltd., 1900 W. 4th Ave., V6J 1M6 (604/731-9222)	1410
Vancouver, B.C.	CHQM	Q Broadcasting Ltd., 1134 Burrard St., V6Z 1Y8 (604/682-3141)	1320
Vancouver, B.C.	CJOR	Jim Pattison Industries Ltd., 840 Howe St., V6Z 1N6 (604/669-6060)	600
Vancouver, B.C.	CJVB	Great Pacific Broadcasting Ltd., 814 Richards St., V6B 3A7 (604/688-9931)	1470
Vancouver, B.C.	CKLG-LG73	Moffat Communications Ltd., 1006 Richards St., V6B 1S8 (604/681-7511)	730
Vancouver, B.C.	CKWX	CKWX Radio Ltd., 1275 Burrard St., V6Z 1Z8 (604/684-5131)	1130
Vancouver, B.C.	CNBC	Vancouver Community College, 100 W. 49th Ave., V5Y 2Z6 (604/324-5335) closed circuit	
Vanderhoof, B.C.	CIVH	See Prince George Broadcasting Ltd., Prince George	1340
Verdun, P.Q.	†CKVL	Radio Futura Ltd., 211 Gordon Ave., H4G 2R2 (514/766-2311)	850
Vermilion Bay, Ont.	*CBEL	Re-broadcasting CBQ, Thunder Bay	1510
Verner, Ont.	*†CJBC-13	Studio at Toronto (CJBC)	1360
Vernon, B.C.	CJIB	Interior Broadcasters Ltd., 3313 32nd. Ave., V1T 2E1 (604/545-2141)	940
Vernon, B.C.	CKAL	Seabrook Broadcasting Ltd., 8808 Hwy. 97 South, V1B 1W2 (604/545-9222)	1050
Victoria, B.C.	CAMO	Camosun College, 1950 Lansdowne Ave., V8P 5J2 (604/592-1113) closed circuit	
Victoria, B.C.	CJVI	Island Broadcasting Co. Ltd., 817 Fort St., V8W 1H6 (604/382-0900)	900
Victoria, B.C.	CKDA	Capital Broadcasting System Ltd., 1450 Douglas St., Box 1220, V8W 2S5 (604/384-9311)	1220
Victoria, B.C.	CFAX	CFAX Radio 1070 Ltd., 825 Broughton St., V8W 1E5 (604/386-1070)	1070
Victoriaville, P.Q.	†CFDA	Radio Victoriaville Ltée, 55 St. Jean Baptiste St., C.P. 490, G6P 6T3 (819/752-5545)	1380
Ville Marie, P.Q.	†CKVM	Radio Témiscamingue Inc., 62 Sainte-Anne St., J0Z 3W0 (819/629-2710)	710
Ville St-Georges Est, P.Q.	†CKRB	Radio Beauce Inc., 32 20th St., C.P. 100 (418/228-1460)	1460
Wabowden, Man.	*CBWB	Studio at Winnipeg (CBW)	690
Wabush, Labrador, Nfld.	CFLW	See Humber Valley Broadcasting, Corner Brook	1340
Waterloo, Ont.	CILR	Wilfrid Laurier University, N2L 3C5 (519/884-2741)	820
Watson Lake, Y.T.	*CBDB	See CFWH, Whitehorse	990
Wawa, Ont.	*CBLJ	Studio at Toronto (CBL)	1440
Wawa, Ont.	CJWA	Huron Broadcasting Co., 73 Broadway, Box 1220, P0S 1K0 (705/856-2328)	1240
Wawa, Ont.	*†CJBC-12	Studio at Toronto (CJBC)	1090
Wedgeport, N.B.	*†CBAA	Studio at Moncton (CBAF)	990
Welland, Ont.	CHOW	Wellport Broadcasting Ltd., Regional Rd. 23, L3B 3N5 (416/732-4433)	1470
Welland, Ont.	CRNC	Niagara College, Box 1005 (416/735-2211) closed circuit	
Westlock, Alta.	CFOK	OK Radio Group Ltd., Box 1800, T0G 2L0 (403/420-6283)	1370
Wetaskiwin, Alta.	CJOI	Parkland Radio Ltd., 5008 50th Ave., T9A 0S4 (403/352-6006)	1440

LOCATION	CALL		FREQ.
Weyburn, Sask.	CFSL	Soo Line Broadcasting Co. Ltd., Souris Ave. & 3rd St., S4H 2K2 (306/842-4666)	1190
Weymouth, N.B.	*†CBAG	Studio at Moncton (CBAF)	1550
Whitecourt, Alta.	CFYR	See Yellowhead Broadcasting Ltd., Edson	1400
Whitehorse, Y.T.	*CFWH	CBC, Box 4430, 3103 3rd Ave., Y1A 1E5 (403/667-6261)	570
Whitehorse, Y.T.	CKRW	Klondike Broadcasting Co. Ltd., #203, 4103 4th Ave., Y1A 1H6 (403/667-4247)	610
White River, Ont.	*CBLW	Studio at Thunder Bay (CBQ)	1010
Williams Lake, B.C.	*CBRL	Studio at Vancouver (CBU)	860
Williams Lake, B.C.	CKWL	Cariboo Broadcasters Ltd., 83 S. 1st Ave., V2G 1H4 (604/392-6551)	570
Windsor, N.S.	CFAB	See Annapolis Valley Radio, Kentville (Windsor ph.: 902/798-2111)	1450
Windsor, Ont.	*CBE	CBC, 267 Pelissier St., N9A 4K5 (519/254-5116)	1550
Windsor, Ont.	*†CBEF	CBC, 267 rue Pelissier, N9A 4K5 (519/254-5116)	540
Windsor, Ont.	CING	St. Clair College, 2000 Talbot Rd. W., N9A 6S4 (519/966-1656) closed circuit	
Windsor, Ont.	CJAM	University of Windsor, Univ. Centre Bldg., N9B 3P4 (519/254-1494)	
Windsor, Ont.	CKLW	CKLW Radio Broadcasting Ltd., 1640 Ouellette Ave., N8X 1L1 (519/258-8888)	800
Windsor, Ont.	CKWW	Radio Windsor Canadian Ltd., 1150 Ouellette Ave., N9A 1E2 (519/252-5751)	580
Wingham, Ont.	CKNX	CKNX Broadcasting Ltd., Carling Terrace & John St., N0G 2W0 (519/357-1310)	920
Winkler, Man.	CISV	Sun Valley Radio Inc., Box 1530, R0G 2X0 (204/325-9506)	1530
Winnipeg, Man.	*CBW	CBC, 541 Portage Ave., Box 160, R3C 2H1 (204/774-2541)	990
Winnipeg, Man.	CFRW	CHUM (Man.) Ltd., 432 Main St., R3B 2Z7 (204/957-0000)	1300
Winnipeg, Man.	CJOB	Radio OB Ltd., 930 Portage Ave., R3G 0P8 (204/786-2471)	680
Winnipeg, Man.	CKJS	CKJS Ltd., 191 Lombard Ave., R3B 0X1 (204/947-6641)	810
Winnipeg, Man.	CKRC	Armadale Communications Ltd., Free Press Bldg., 300 Carlton St., Box 9700, R3C 3E5 (204/942-2231)	630
Winnipeg, Man.	CKY	Moffat Communications Ltd., Polo Park, R3G 0L7 (204/775-0371)	580
Woodstock, N.B.	CJCJ	Carleton-Victoria Broadcasting Co. Ltd., 131 Queen St., E0J 2B0 (506/328-6661)	920
Woodstock, Ont.	CKDK	Oxford Broadcasting Co. Ltd., 290 Dundas St., Box 100, N4S 7W7 (519/539-7451)	1340
Woody Point, Nfld.	*CBNF	Studio at Corner Brook (CBY)	740
Wrigley, N.W.T.	*CBQG	See CFYK, Yellowknife	1280
Yarmouth, N.S.	*†CBAJ	Studio at Moncton (CBAF)	1230
Yarmouth, N.S.	CJLS	Radio CJLS Ltd., 22 Main St., B5A 1C8 (902/742-7175)	1340
Yellowknife, N.W.T.	*CFYK	CBC, Box 160, X0E 1H0 (403/873-3464)	1340
Yellowknife, N.W.T.	CJCD	CJCD Radio Ltd., Box 218, X1A 2N2 (403/920-2523)	1240
Yorkton, Sask.	CJGX	Yorkton Broadcasting Co. Ltd., 2nd Ave., Tower Theatre Bldg., Box 9400, S3N 1G2 (306/782-2256)	940

LIST OF FM BROADCASTING STATIONS

Post Office address same as in first column except where otherwise noted.
CBC Stations are indicated by asterisk*.
French language stations are indicated by dagger†

LOCATION	CALL		FREQ.
Aiyansh, B.C.	*CBYA-FM	Studio at Vancouver (CBU-FM)	102.3
Alert, N.W.T.	CHAR-FM	c/o Box 310, Belleville, Ont. K0K 3S0	105.9
Alert Bay, B.C.	*CBRY-FM	Studio at Vancouver (See CBU-AM)	105.1
Ashcroft, B.C.	CFFM-FM	See Twin Cities Radio, Kamloops	95.3
Baldy Mountain, Man.	*CBWW-FM	Studio at Winnipeg (see CBW-AM)	105.3
Barrie, Ont.	CHAY-FM	CHAY Ltd., Box 937, L4M 4Y6 (705/737-3511)	93.1
Beauval, Sask.	*CBKB-FM	Studio at Regina (see CBK-AM)	101.5
Bellegarde, Sask.	*†CBKF-FM-4	Studio at Regina (CBKF-FM)	91-9
Belleville, Ont.	*†CJBC-17-FM	Studio at Toronto (see CJBC-AM)	95.5
Belleville, Ont.	CIGL-FM	Quinte Broadcasting Co. Ltd., 45 Bridge St. E., Box 488, K8N 1L5 (613/968-5555)	97.1
Bonnington, B.C.	*CBUD-FM	Studio at Vancouver (See CBU-AM)	92.3
Boston Bar, B.C.	CKGO-1-FM	c/o Fraser Valley Broadcasters Ltd. (see CKGO-AM, Hope)	
Brampton, Ont.	CFNY-FM	See Toronto	102.1
Brandon, Man.	*CBWV-FM	Studio at Winnipeg (see CBW-AM)	97.9
Brandon, Man.	CJCM-FM	Western Man. Broadcasters Ltd., 2940 Victoria Ave., R7A 6A5 (204/728-1150)	96.1
Brandon Man.	*†CKSB-8-FM	Studio at St-Boniface (see CKSB-AM)	99.5
Brantford, Ont.	CKPC-FM	The Telephone City Broadcast Ltd., 571 West St., N3T 5P8 (519/753-2664)	92.1
Buffalo Narrows, Sask.	*CBKD-FM	Studio at Regina (see CBK-AM)	103.5
Burlington, Ont.	CING-FM	Burlington Broadcasting Inc., 4144 S. Service Rd., L7L 4X5 (416/681-1079)	107.9
Burns Lake, B.C.	*CBXB-FM	Studio at Prince Rupert (see CFPR-AM)	99.1
Calais, N.B.	WQDY-FM	WQDY-FM Inc., Box 305, St. Stephen, N.B. E3L 1G5 (506/466-4848)	92.7

LOCATION	CALL		FREQ.
Calgary, Alta.	CHFM-FM	Moffat Communications Ltd., 804 16th Ave. S.W., Box 1140, T2P 2M7 (403/264-3696)	95.9
Calgary, Alta.	*†CBRF-FM	Studio at Edmonton (see CHFA-AM)	103.9
Calgary, Alta.	CKO-FM	CKO All News Radio Ltd., 332 17th Ave. S.W., T2S 0A8 (403/266-4007)	103.1
Calgary, Alta.	CJAY-FM	CFCN Communications Ltd., Broadcast House, Box 7060, Stn. E, T3C 3L9 (403/246-7252)	92.1
Calgary, Alta.	*CBR-FM	CBC, 1724 Westmount Blvd., Box 2640, T2P 2M7 (403/283-8361)	102.1
Calgary, Alta.	CKUA-FM	See Alta. Educational Communications Corp., Edmonton	93.7
Cambridge Bay, N.W.T.	*CBIN-FM	See CFFB, Frobisher Bay (AM list)	105.1
Canal Flats, B.C.	*CBYC-FM	Studio at Vancouver (CBU-FM)	91.5
Canmore, Alta.	*CBRC-FM	Studio at Calgary (see CBR-AM)	97.9
Cape Dorset, N.W.T.	*CBIH-FM	See CFFB-AM, Frobisher Bay	105.1
Charlottetown, P.E.I.	*CBCT-FM	CBC, 430 University Ave., Box 2230, C1A 8B9 (902/892-3591)	96.9
Chase, B.C.	CFFM-FM	See Twin Cities Radio, Kamloops	93.1
Chateh, Alta.	*CBXA-FM	Studio at Edmonton (see CBX-AM)	103.5
Chatham, Ont.	*CBEE-FM	Studio at Windsor (see CBE-AM)	95.1
Cheticamp, N.B.	*†CBHI-FM	Studio at Moncton (see CBAF-AM)	103.9
Chicoutimi, P.Q.	*†CBJ-FM	CBC, C.P. 790, G7H 1R6 (418/543-7747)	100.9
Chicoutimi, P.Q.	*CBJE-FM	Studio at Montreal (see CBM-AM)	107.9
Chilliwack, B.C.	*†CBUF-FM-1	Studio at Vancouver (CBUF-FM)	102.1
Churchill Falls, Lab., Nfld.	CFLC-FM	See Humber Valley Broadcasting, Corner Brook (AM list)	97.9
Church Point, N.B.	*†CBAC-FM	Studio at Moncton (see CBAF-AM)	95.9
Clearwater, B.C.	CFFM-FM-2	See Twin Cities Radio, Kamloops	92.7
Clinton, B.C.	CFFM-FM-4	See Twin Cities Radio, Kamloops	106.5
Cobourg, Ont.	CFMX-FM	Radio CHUC Ltd., Box 520, K9A 4L3 (416/372-5401)	103.1
Cooper Creek, B.C.	*CBXH	Studio at Vancouver (CBU-AM)	101.7
Coppermine, N.W.T.	*CBIO-FM	See CHAK-AM, Inuvik	105.1
Cornwall, Ont.	*†CBOF-6-FM	Studio at Ottawa (see CBOF-AM)	98.1
Cornwall, Ont.	*CBOC-FM	Studio at Ottawa (see CBO-AM)	95.5
Cornwall, Ont.	CFLG-FM	Tri-County Broadcasting Ltd., 237 Water St. E., Box 969, K6H 5V1 (613/932-5180)	104.5
Crawford Bay, B.C.	*CBTE-FM	Studio at Vancouver (CBU-FM)	99.7
Dawson Creek, B.C.	*CBKQ-FM	Studio at Vancouver (see CBU-AM)	93.7
Deer Lake, Nfld.	CFDL-FM	See Humber Valley Broadcasting, Corner Brook (AM list)	97.9
Downsview, Ont.	CKRY-FM	York University, 4700 Keele St., M3J 1P3 (416/667-3919) closed circuit	
Drummondville, P.Q.	*†CBF-FM-1	Studio at Montreal (CBF-FM)	104.3
Dryden, Ont.	*CBQH-FM	See CBQ-AM, Thunder Bay	100.9
Dryden, Ont.	*†CKSB-6-FM	Studio at St-Boniface, Man. (see CKSB-AM)	102.7
Easterville, Man.	*CBWE-FM	Studio at Winnipeg (see CBW-AM)	95.5
Edmonton, Alta.	*CBX-FM	CBC, Box 555, T5J 2P4 (403/469-2321)	93.3
Edmonton, Alta.	CIRK-FM	CIRK-FM Radio, 10230 108 St., T5J 2X3 (403/428-8597)	99.5
Edmonton, Alta.	CKXM-FM	Sunwapta Broadcasting Ltd., Broadcast House, Jasper Hwy., Box 5030, Stn. E, T5P 4C2 (403/483-2596)	100.3
Edmonton, Alta.	CKO-FM	CKO All News Radio Ltd., 12316 Jasper Ave., #230, T5N 3K5 (403/482-5606)	101.9
Edmonton, Alta.	CKRA-FM	CKRA-FM Radio, 4752 99 St., T6E 5H5 (403/437-4996)	96.0
Edmonton, Alta.	CKUA-FM	Alta. Educational Communications Corp., 10526 Jasper Ave., T5J 1Z7 (403/428-7595)	98.1
Eskimo Point, N.W.T.	*CBIG-FM	See CFFB-AM, Frobisher Bay	105.1
Exshaw, Alta.	*CBRE-FM	Studio at Calgary (see CBR-AM)	100.7
Fairford, Man.	*CBWZ-FM	Studio at Winnipeg (see CBW-AM)	104.3
Fisher Branch, Man.	*CBWX-FM	Studio at Winnipeg (see CBW-AM)	95.7
Flin Flon, Man.	*†CKSB-4-FM	Studio at St-Boniface (see CKSB-AM)	99.9
Fond du Lac, Sask.	*CBKG-FM	Studio at Regina (see CBK-AM)	100.1
Fort Fraser, B.C.	*CBXR-FM	Studio at Prince Rupert (see CFPR-AM)	102.9
Fort George, P.Q.	*CBMP-FM	Studio at Montreal (see CBM-AM)	105.1
Fort George, P.Q.	*†CBFG-FM	Studio at Montreal (see CBF-AM)	103.5
Fort McMurray, Alta.	*†CHFA-6-FM	Studio at Edmonton (see CHFA-AM)	101.5
Fox Lake, Alta.	*CBXX-FM	Studio at Edmonton (see CBX-AM)	96.9
Fraser Lake, B.C.	*CBBR-FM	Studio at Prince Rupert (see CFPR-AM)	102.9
Fredericton, N.B.	*CBZ-FM	See CBZ-AM, Fredericton	101.5
Fredericton, N.B.	*†CBZF-FM	Studio at Moncton (see CBAF-AM)	102.3
Gods Lake Narrows, Man.	*CBWN-FM	Studio at Winnipeg (see CBW-AM)	99.9
Golden, B.C.	*CBXE-FM	Studio at Vancouver (CBU-FM)	101.7
Grand Manan, N.B.	*CBZA-FM	Studio at Fredericton (see CBZ-AM)	95.0
Grande Prairie, Alta.	*†CHFA-5-FM	Studio at Edmonton (see CHFA-AM)	90.5
Grande Prairie, Alta.	CKUA-FM	See Alta. Educational Communications Corp., Edmonton	100.9
Grand Rapids, Man.	*CBWH-FM	Studio at Winnipeg (see CBW-AM)	101.5
Guelph, Ont.	CFRU-FM	University of Guelph, 2nd Floor, University Centre, N1G 2W1 (519/824-4120)	93.3
Guelph, Ont.	CKLA-FM	CJOY Ltd., 75 Speedvale Ave. E., N1E 6M3 (519/824-7000)	106.1
Halifax, N.S.	*CBH-FM	CBC, Box 3000, B3J 3E9 (902/422-8311)	102.7
Halifax, N.S.	CHFX-FM	Maritime Broadcasting Co. Ltd., 5230 Tobin St., B3H 1S2 (902/425-5210)	101.9

LOCATION	CALL		FREQ.
Halifax, N.S.	C100-FM	Radio CJCH 920 Ltd., 2885 Robie St., B3J 2Z4 (902/453-2524)	100.1
Hamilton, Ont.	CFMU-FM	CFMU, Room 301, Hamilton Hall, McMaster University, L8S 4K1 (519/528-9888)	93.3
Hamilton, Ont.	CKDS-FM	Radio M L Ltd., 11 Springer Ave., L8M 2W7 (416/549-2453) (Toronto line: 924-2844)	95.3
Hinton, Alta.	*†CHFA-4-FM	Studio at Edmonton (see CHFA-AM)	100.7
Hope, B.C.	*CBUF-FM	Studio at Vancouver (see CBU-AM)	92.3
Houston, B.C.	*CBUR-FM	Studio at Prince Rupert (see CFPR-AM)	102.1
Hull/Ottawa	†CIMF-FM	Telemedia Communications Ltd., 150 Edmonton St., Hull, P.Q. J8Y 3S6 (819/770-2463)	94.9
Igloolik, N.W.T.	*CBII-FM	See CFFB, Frobisher Bay (AM list)	105.1
Ile-a-la-Crosse, Sask.	*CBKC-FM	Studio at Regina (see CBK-AM)	105.1
Ilford, Man.	*CBWS-FM	Studio at Winnipeg (see CBW-AM)	94.7
Jackhead, Man.	*CBWY-FM	Studio at Winnipeg (see CBW-AM)	92.7
Jean D'Or, Alta.	*CBXH-FM	Studio at Edmonton (see CBX-AM)	102.5
Kamloops, B.C.	*†CBUF-FM-6	Studio at Vancouver (CBUF-FM)	96.5
Kamloops, B.C.	*CBYK-FM	Studio at Vancouver (CBU-FM)	94.1
Kamloops, B.C.	CFFM-FM	Twin Cities Radio Ltd., 460 Pemberton Terrace, V2C 1T5 (604/372-3322)	98.3
Kamloops, B.C.	CMMD-FM	Cariboo College, Box 3010 (604/374-0123)	
Kelowna, B.C.	*CBTK-FM	Studio at Vancouver (CBU-FM)	95.7
Kelowna, B.C.	*†CBUF-FM-2	Studio at Vancouver (CBUF-FM)	99.1
Kelowna, B.C.	CHIM-FM	Okanagan Broadcasters Ltd., Box 100, V1Y 7N3 (604/762-3331)	104.7
Kenora, Ont.	*CBQX-FM	See CBQ-AM, Thunder Bay	98.7
Kenora, Ont.	*†CKSB-7-FM	Studio at St-Boniface, Man. (see CKSB-AM)	93.5
Kentville, N.S.	CKWM-FM	Annapolis Valley Radio Ltd., Box 310, B4N 1H5 (902/678-2111)	97.7
Kingston, Ont.	*†CJBC-18-FM	Studio at Toronto (see CJBC-AM)	99.5
Kingston, Ont.	*CBBK-FM	Studio at Toronto (see CBL-AM)	107.5
Kingston, Ont.	CFLY-FM	St. Lawrence Broadcasting Co. Ltd., 99 Brock St., K7L 4Y5 (613/544-1380)	98.3
Kingston, Ont.	CFMK-FM	Frontenac Broadcasting Co. Ltd., 170 Queen St., K7K 1B2 (613/544-2340)	96.3
Kingston, Ont.	CFRC-FM	Queen's University, see CFRC-AM	91.9
Kitchener, Ont.	CFCA-FM	Central Ontario Television Ltd., 864 King St. W., N2G 4E9 (519/576-1053)	105.3
Kitchener, Ont.	CKGL-FM	Greatlakes Broadcasting System, 305 King St. W., N2G 4E4 (519/743-2611).	96.7
Kitchener, Ont.	CKWR-FM	Wired World Inc., Box 2035, Stn. B, N2H 6K8 (519/579-1150)	98.7
Kitimat, B.C.	*†CBUF-FM-5	Studio at Vancouver (CBUF-FM)	105.1
Kitimat, B.C.	*CBUK-FM	Studio at Prince Rupert (see CFPR-AM)	101.1
La Loche, Sask.	*CBKE-FM	Studio at Regina (see CBK-AM)	95.5
La Pocatière, P.Q.	†CHGB-FM	Radio La Pocatière Ltée, 508 4th Ave., C.P. 550, G0R 1Z0 (418/856-1310)	102.9
La Ronge, Sask.	*CBXA-FM	CBC, Box 959, S0J 1L0 (306/425-3324)	105.9
Laval, P.Q.	†CFGL-FM	Stereo Laval Inc., 3 Place Laval, H7N 1A2 (514/663-7550)	105.7
Leaf Rapids, Man.	*CBWP-FM	Studio at Winnipeg (see CBW-AM)	94.5
Lethbridge, Alta.	*†CHFA-1-FM	Studio at Edmonton (see CHFA-AM)	104.3
Lethbridge, Alta.	*CBRX-FM	Studio at Calgary (see CBR-AM)	100.1
Lethbridge, Alta.	CILA-FM	Lethbridge Broadcasting Ltd., Box 820, T1J 3Z9 (403/328-1077)	107.7
Lethbridge, Alta.	CKUA-FM	See Alta. Educational Communications Corp., Edmonton	99.3
Liverpool, N.S.	CKBW-FM-1	See CKBW-AM, Bridgewater	94.5
London, Ont.	*CBBL-FM	Studio at Toronto (see CBL-FM)	100.5
London, Ont.	CFPL-FM	CFPL Broadcasting Ltd., 369 York St., Box 2580, N6A 4H3 (519/434-4551)	95.9
London, Ont.	CHRW-FM	University of Western Ontario, Rm. 42, U.C.C. Bldg., N6A 3K7 (519/679-2479)	
London, Ont.	CIXX-FM	Radio Fanshawe Inc., 1460 Oxford St. E., N5W 5H1 (519/453-2810)	106.9
London, Ont.	CJBX-FM	BX-93 Country Radio, c/o Middlesex Broadcasters Ltd., Box 5593, N6A 5H8 (519/685-3693)	92.7
London, Ont.	HBB-FM	H.B. Beal Technical School, 525 Dundas St., N6B 1W5 (519/432-7581) closed circuit	
Longueuil, P.Q.	†CIEL-FM	Stereo Laval Inc., 87 St. Charles o., J4H 1C5 (514/527-8321)	98.5
Lytton, B.C.	CFFM-FM	See Twin Cities Radio, Kamloops	106.1
Manigotagan, Man.	*CBWA-FM	Studio at Winnipeg (see CBW-AM)	101.3
Margaree, N.B.	*†CBHJ-FM	Studio at Moncton (see CBAF-AM)	101.9
Masset, B.C.	*CBTM-FM	Studio at Prince Rupert (see CFPR-AM)	103.9
Medicine Hat, Alta.	CKUA-FM	See Alta. Educational Communications Corp., Edmonton	97.3
Merritt, B.C.	CFFM-FM-3	See Twin Cities Radio, Kamloops	103.9
Moncton, N.B.	CFQM-FM	CFQM-FM Broadcasting Ltd., 1000 St. George Blvd. (506/855-1039)	103.9
Montreal, P.Q.	*†CBF-FM	CBC, 1400 Dorchester Blvd. E., C.P. 6000, H3C 3A8 (514/285-3211)	100.7
Montreal, P.Q.	*CBM-FM	CBC, 1400 Dorchester Blvd. E., C.P. 6000, H3C 3A8 (514/285-3211)	93.5
Montreal, P.Q.	CFQR-FM	CFCF Inc., 405 Ogilvy Ave., H3N 1M4 (514/273-6311)	92.5
Montreal, P.Q.	CHOM-FM	Maisonneuve Broadcasting Corp. Ltd., 1355 Greene Ave., H3Z 2A5 (514/935-2425)	97.7
Montreal, P.Q.	(Multiling.) CINQ-FM	Radio Centre-Ville, 3981, boul. St-Laurent, H2W 1Y5 (514/288-1731)	102.3
Montreal, P.Q.	CITE-FM	Telemedia Communications Ltd., 1184 St. Catherine St. W., H3B 1K1 (514/866-3741)	107.3
Montreal, P.Q.	CJFM-FM	Standard Broadcasting Corp., 1411 rue du Fort, H3H 2R1 (514/989-CJFM)	95.9
Montreal, P.Q.	†CKMF-FM	Supravox Corp. Ltd., 225 est, rue Roy, Ste. 26, H2W 1M5 (514/282-3943)	94.3

LOCATION	CALL		FREQ.
Moose Lake, Man.	*CBWC-FM	Studio at Winnipeg (see CBW-AM)	99.9
Nelson House, Man.	*CBWO-FM	Studio at Winnipeg (see CBW-AM)	93.7
New Aiyansh, B.C.	*CBYA-FM	Studio at Prince Rupert (see CFPR-AM)	102.3
New Westminster, B.C.	CFMI-FM	Radio NW Ltd., 815 McBride Plaza, V3L 2C1 (604/521-4808)	101.1
North Bay, Ont.	*CBCN-FM	Studio at Toronto (see CBL-AM)	96.1
North Bay, Ont.	*†CBJN-FM	Studio at Toronto (see CJBC-AM)	95.1
North Bay, Ont.	CKAT-FM	Telemedia Ontario Inc., Box 3000, P1B 8K8 (705/474-3693)	93.7
Nouveau Comptoir, P.Q.	*†CBFW-FM	Studio at Montreal (see CBF-AM)	103.5
Nouveau Comptoir, P.Q.	*CBMW-FM	Studio at Montreal (see CBM-AM)	105.1
Ocean Falls, B.C.	*CBXO-FM	Studio at Vancouver (CBU-FM)	92.1
100 Mile House, B.C.	CFFM-FM	See Twin Cities Radio, Kamloops	99.7
Orillia, Ont.	*CBCO-FM	Studio at Toronto (see CBL-AM)	105.9
Oshawa, Ont.	CKQT-FM	Grant Broadcasting Ltd., 360 King St. W., L1J 2K2 (416/571-1350) (Toronto line: 686-1350)	94.9
Osnaburgh, Ont.	*CBQN-FM	See CBQ-AM, Thunder Bay	104.5
Ottawa, Ont.	*CBO-FM	Chateau Laurier Hotel, Box 3220, Stn. C., K1Y 1E4 (613/725-3511)	103.3
Ottawa, Ont.	*†CBOF-FM	Chateau Laurier Hotel, C.P. 3220, Succ. C, K1Y 1E4 (613/725-3511)	102.5
Ottawa, Ont.	CFMO-FM	Radio Station CFRA Ltd., 150 Isabella St., K1S 5A3 (613/233-6731)	93.9
Ottawa, Ont.	CHEZ-FM	CHEZ-FM Inc., 126 York St., Ste. 509, K1N 5T5 (613/563-1919)	106.1
Ottawa, Ont.	CKCU-FM	CKCU-FM Radio, Room 517, Unicentre, Carleton University, K1S 5B6	93.1
Ottawa, Ont.	CKBY-FM	KEY Radio Ltd., Ottawa Division, Ste. 1900, Tower B, Place de Ville, 112 Kent St., K1P 6J1 (613/238-6862)	105.3
Ottawa, Ont.	CKO-FM-1	CKO All News Radio Ltd., 69 Sparks St., K1P 5A5 (613/238-2555)	106.9
Oxford House, Man.	*CBWM-FM	Studio at Winnipeg (see CBW-AM)	95.5
Pangnirtung, N.W.T.	*CBIJ-FM	See CFFB, Frobisher Bay (AM list)	105.1
Peace River, Alta.	*CBXG-FM	Studio at Edmonton (see CBX-AM)	93.9
Peace River, Alta.	*†CHFA-3-FM	Studio at Edmonton (see CHFA-AM)	92.5
Peace River, Alta.	CKUA-FM	See Alta. Educational Communications Corp., Edmonton	96.9
Penetanguishene, Ont.	*†CJBC-19-FM	Studio at Toronto (see CJBC-AM)	96.5
Penetanguishene, Ont.	*CBCM-FM	Studio at Toronto (see CBL-AM)	107.5
Penticton, B.C.	*CBTP-FM	Studio at Vancouver (see CBU-AM)	93.3
Penticton, B.C.	CKOR-FM	Okanagan Radio Ltd., 33 Carmi Ave., V2A 3G4 (604/492-2800)	97.1
Peterborough, Ont.	*CBCP-FM	See CBL-AM, Toronto	93.5
Peterborough, Ont.	CKQM-FM	Radio CKPT 1420 Ltd., 340 George St. N., Ste. 403, K9J 6Y8 (705/742-8844)	105.1
Peterborough, Ont.	CFMP-FM	Kawartha Broadcasting Co. Ltd., Box 659, K9J 6Z9 (705/748-6101)	101.5
Pickle Lake, Ont.	*CBQP-FM	See CBQ-AM, Thunder Bay	105.1
Pikangikum, Ont.	*CBQU-FM	See CBQ-AM, Thunder Bay	103.1
Pincher Creek, Alta.	*CBRP-FM	Studio at Calgary (see CBR-AM)	97.5
Pinehouse Lake, Sask.	*CBKJ-FM	Studio at Regina (see CBK-AM)	94.1
Pond Inlet, N.W.T.	*CBIK-FM	See CFFB, Frobisher Bay (AM list)	105.1
Port-au-Port, N.B.	*†CBFN-FM	Studio at Moncton (see CBAF-AM)	94.3
Port Clements, B.C.	*CBYB-FM	Studio at Prince Rupert (see CFPR-AM)	102.9
Port Hope Simpson, Nfld.	*CBNP-FM	Studio at Happy Valley (see CFGB-AM)	105.1
Port Radium, N.W.T.	*CBIP-FM	See CHAK-AM, Inuvik	105.1
Prince George, B.C.	*†CBUF-FM-4	Studio at Vancouver (CBUF-FM)	95.5
Pritchard, B.C.	CFFM-FM	See Twin Cities Radio, Kamloops	106.3
Quebec, P.Q.	*†CBV-FM	CBC, C.P. 10400, Ste-Foy, P.Q. G1V 2X2 (418/656-9440)	95.3
Quebec, P.Q.	*CBVE-FM	Studio at Montreal (see CBM-AM)	104.7
Quebec, P.Q.	†CHOI-FM	Entreprises Télé-Capitale Ltée, 2136 Chemin Ste-Foy, Ste-Foy, P.Q. G1K 7W1 (418/687-9810)	98.1
Quebec, P.Q.	†CKRL-FM	Laval University, G1K 7P4 (418/656-5675)	89.1
Queen Charlotte City, B.C.	*CBYQ-FM	Studio at Prince Rupert (see CFPR-AM)	104.9
Radisson, P.Q.	*†CBFR-FM	Studio at Montreal (see CBF-AM)	100.1
Red Deer, Alta.	*†CHFA-2-FM	Studio at Edmonton (see CHFA-AM)	103.5
Red Deer, Alta.	CFCR-FM	Central Alberta Broadcasting, 2840 Bremner Ave., Box 5555, T4N 5H6	98.9
Red Deer, Alta.	CKUA-FM	See Alberta Educational Communications Corp., Edmonton	101.3
Red Lake, Ont.	*CBEA-FM	See CBQ-AM, Thunder Bay	90.5
Regina, Sask.	CBK-FM	CBC, 1840 McIntyre St., S4P 2R1 (306/352-6641)	96.9
Regina, Sask.	*†CBKF-FM	CBC, 1840 McIntyre St., S4P 2R1 (306/352-6641)	97.7
Regina, Sask.	CFMQ-FM	Harvard Communications, 2060 Halifax St., Box 9800, S4P 3J4 (306/525-9195)	92.1
Resolute, N.W.T.	*CBIL-FM	See CFFB, Frobisher Bay (AM list)	105.1
Richibucto, N.B.	*†CBHM-FM	Studio at Moncton (see CBAF-AM)	98.5
Rimouski, P.Q.	*†CJBR-FM	CBC, 273 St-Jean Baptiste St. o., G5L 4J8 (418/723-2217)	101.5
St. Andrews, Nfld.	CFCV-FM	See Humber Valley Broadcasting, Corner Brook (AM list)	97.7
St. Anthony, Nfld.	CFNN-FM	See Humber Valley Broadcasting, Corner Brook (AM list)	97.9
St. Catharines, Ont.	CHSC-FM	Radio Station C.H.S.C. Ltd., 36 Queenston St., L2R 7C7 (416/682-6691)	105.7
St. Catharines, Ont.	CJQR-FM	Niagara Dist. Broadcasting Co. Ltd., Yates & St. Paul Sts., Box 610, L2R 6X7 (416/684-1174)	97.7
Ste-Adele, P.Q.	†CIME-FM	Diffusion Laurentide Inc., 400 Ste-Adele Blvd., C.P. 1260, J0R 1L0 (514/430-3300)	99.5
St-Fabien-de-Panet, P.Q.	*†CBV-5-FM	Studio at Quebec (see CBV-AM)	96.5
Ste-Foy, P.Q.	See Quebec		

LOCATION	CALL		FREQ.
Saint John, N.B.	CFBC-FM	Fundy Broadcasting Co. Ltd., 68 Carleton St., E2L 2Z4 (506/652-1680)	98.9
Saint John, N.B.	*CBZ-FM	CBC (see CBZ-AM, Fredericton)	101.5
St. John's, Nfld.	*CBN-FM	CBC, Box 12010, Stn. A, A1B 3T8 (709/737-4140)	106.9
St. John's, Nfld.	CHOZ-FM	Nfld. Broadcasting Ltd., Box 2020, A1C 5S2 (709/579-5015)	93.9
Sandy Lake, Ont.	*CBQV-FM	See CBQ-AM, Thunder Bay	101.1
Sarnia, Ont.	*CBEG-FM	Studio at Windsor (see CBE-AM)	106.3
Saskatoon, Sask.	*CBKS-FM	CBC, 5 CN Towers	105.5
Saskatoon, Sask.	CFMC-FM	General Broadcasting Ltd., 1221 8th St. E., S7H 0S5 (306/343-1608)	103.9
Saskatoon, Sask.	CJUS-FM	CJUS-FM, Audio-Visual Centre, University of Saskatchewan, S7N 0W0	89.7
Sault Ste. Marie, Ont.	*CBSM-FM	Studio at Sudbury (see CBCS-FM)	89.5
Sault Ste. Marie, Ont.	CHAS-FM	Gilder Broadcasting Ltd., Box 1050, 254 Queen St. E., P6A 5N5 (705/942-1050)	100.5
Sault Ste. Marie, Ont.	Q104-FM	Huron Broadcasting Ltd., 119 East St., Box 370, P6A 5M2 (705/254-7111)	104.3
Savant Lake, Ont.	*CBQL-FM	See CBQ-AM, Thunder Bay	104.9
Savona, B.C.	CFFM-FM	See Twin Cities Radio, Kamloops	101.9
Shelburne, N.S.	CKBW-FM-2	See CKBW-AM, Bridgewater	93.1
Sherbrooke, P.Q.	†CITE-FM-1	Telemedia Communications Ltd., 25 Bryant St., J1J 3Z5 (819/566-6655)	102.7
Sioux Narrows, Sask.	*CBQS-FM	See CBQ-AM, Thunder Bay	95.7
Smithers, B.C.	*CBRS-FM	Studio at Prince Rupert (see CFPR-AM)	97.5
Smiths Falls, Ont.	CKUE-FM	Rideau Broadcasting Ltd., Jasper Rd., Box 1200, K7A 4T4 (613/283-4630)	101.1
Snow Lake, Man.	*CBWL-FM	Studio at Winnipeg (see CBW-AM)	95.5
Southend, Sask.	*CBKD-FM	Studio at Regina (see CBK-FM)	91.7
South Indian Lake, Man.	*CBWQ-FM	Studio at Winnipeg (see CBW-AM)	95.5
Stanley Mission, Sask.	*CBKI-FM	Studio at Regina (see CBK-AM)	95.5
Stony Rapids, Sask.	*CBKH-FM	Studio at Regina (see CBK-AM)	93.3
Sudbury, Ont.	*CBCS-FM	CBC, 15 Fir St., P3C 2A9 (705/675-2451)	99.9
Sudbury, Ont.	*†CBON-FM	CBC, 15 Fir St., P3C 2A9 (705/675-2451)	98.1
Sudbury, Ont.	CIGM-FM	United Broadcasting Ltd., 336 Ash St., P3C 5N2 (705/674-0711)	92.7
Sudbury, Ont.	CJMX-FM	Sudbury Broadcasting (1977) Ltd., Box 700, P3E 4R9 (705/674-6401)	105.3
Swift Current, Sask.	CJGL-FM	Grasslands Broadcasting Co., Box 370, S9H 3W2 (306/773-1505)	94.1
Sydney, N.S.	*CBI-FM	CBC, Box 700, B1P 6H7 (902/539-5050)	105.9
Sydney, N.S.	CJCB-FM	Celtic Investments Ltd., 313 Charlotte St., B1P 6K2 (902/564-5596)	94.9
Terrace, B.C.	*CBRC-FM	Studio at Prince Rupert (see CFPR-AM)	95.3
Terrace, B.C.	*†CBUF-FM-3	Studio at Vancouver (CBUF-FM)	96.9
The Pas, Man.	*†CKSB-3-FM	Studio at St-Boniface (see CKSB-AM)	93.7
The Pas, Man.	*CBWJ-FM	Studio at Winnipeg (see CBW-AM)	94.5
Thompson, Man.	*CBWK-FM	CBC, 7 Selkirk St., R8N 0M4 (204/677-2454)	100.9
Thompson, Man.	*†CKSB-5-FM	Studio at St-Boniface (see CKSB-AM)	99.9
Thunder Bay, Ont.	CJSD-FM	H.F. Dougall Co. Ltd., 87 North Hill St., P7A 5V6 (807/344-3526)	94.3
Tillsonburg, Ont.	CKOT-FM	Tillsonburg Broadcasting Co. Ltd., 77 Broadway, Box 10, N4G 4H3 (519/842-4281)	101.3
Timmins, Ont.	CFTI-FM	Telemedia Ontario Inc., Box 1046, P4N 7H8 (705/267-1134)	92.1
Toronto, Ont.	*CBL-FM	CBC, Box 500, Term. A, M5W 1E6 (416/925-3311)	94.1
Toronto, Ont.	CFNY-FM	Mutual Broadcasting 1980 Ltd. Canada, 83 Kennedy Rd. S., Brampton, Ont. (416/453-7452)	102.1
Toronto, Ont.	CHCR-FM	Humber College, Box 1900, Rexdale, M9W 5L7 (416/675-3111) closed circuit	
Toronto, Ont.	CHFI-FM	Rogers Radio Broadcasting Ltd., 25 Adelaide St. E., M5C 1H3 (416/864-2070)	98.1
Toronto, Ont.	(multi-ling.) CHIN-FM	Radio 1540 Ltd., 637 College St., M6G 1B6 (416/531-9991)	100.7
Toronto, Ont.	CHUM-FM	CHUM Ltd., 1331 Yonge St., M4T 1Y1 (416/925-6666)	104.5
Toronto, Ont.	CJRT-FM	CJRT-FM Inc., 297 Victoria St., M5B 1W1 (416/595-5281)	91.1
Toronto, Ont.	Q107-FM	Radio IWC Ltd., Ste. 3000, 2 Bloor St. E., M4W 1A8 (416/967-3445)	107.
Toronto, Ont.	CKFM-FM	CFRB Ltd., 2 St. Clair Ave. W., M4V 1L6 (416/922-9999)	99.9
Toronto, Ont.	CKO-FM	CKO All-News Network, 65 Adelaide St. E., M5C 1K6 (416/862-7200)	99.1
Trail, B.C.	*CBTA-FM	Studio at Vancouver (see CBU-AM)	106.7
Trois-Rivières, P.Q.	*†CBF-FM-1	Studio at Montreal (see CBF-AM)	100.1
Truro, N.S.	CKTO-FM	Colchester Broadcasting Co. Ltd., 840 Prince St., Box 788, B2N 5E8 (902/895-4491)	100.9
Vancouver, B.C.	*CBU-FM	CBC, 700 Hamilton St., Box 4600, V6B 4A2 (604/684-0246)	105.7
Vancouver, B.C.	*†CBUF-FM	CBC, 700 Hamilton St., Box 4600, V6B 4A2 (604/665-8000)	97.7
Vancouver, B.C.	CFRO-FM	Vancouver Co-operative Radio, 337 Carrall St., V6B 2J4 (604/684-8494)	102.7
Vancouver, B.C.	CHQM-FM	Q Broadcasting Ltd., 1134 Burrard St., V6Z 1Y8 (604/682-3141)	103.5
Vancouver, B.C.	CITR-FM	University of B.C., V6T 2A5 (604/228-3017) closed circuit	88.9
Vancouver, B.C.	CFOX-FM	Moffat Communications Ltd., 1006 Richards St., V6B 1S8 (604/681-7511)	99.3
Vancouver, B.C.	CJAZ-FM	Selkirk Communications Ltd., 1275 Burrard St., V6Z 1Z8 (604/684-5131)	92.1
Vancouver, B.C.	CKO-FM	CKO All News Radio Ltd., 2780 E. Broadway, V5M 1Y8 (604/665-8000)	96.1
Vanderhoof, B.C.	*CBRV-FM	Studio at Prince Rupert (see CFPR-AM)	96.7
Verdun, P.Q.	†CKOI-FM	Radio Futura Ltd., 211 Gordon Ave., H4G 2R2 (514/769-8585)	96.9
Vernon, B.C.	*CBYV-FM	Studio at Vancouver (see CBU-AM)	105.5
Victoria, B.C.	CFMS-FM	Capital Broadcasting Systems Ltd., 1450 Douglas St., Box 1220, V8W 2S5 (604/384-9311)	98.5

LOCATION	CALL		FREQ.
Waasagomach, Man.	*CBWD-FM	Studio at Winnipeg (see CBW-FM)	101.5
Waterloo, Ont.	CKMS-FM	Radio Waterloo Inc., Univ. of Waterloo, N2L 3G1 (519/886-2567)	94.5
Williams Lake, B.C.	CFFM-FM	See Twin Cities Radio, Kamloops	97.5
Windsor, Ont.	*CBE-FM	See CBE-AM list	89.9
Windsor, Ont.	CJOM-FM	Radio Windsor Canadian Ltd., 1120 Ouellette Ave., N9A 1C9 (519/252-7313)	88.7
Windsor, Ont.	CKLW-FM	CKLW Radio Broadcasting Ltd., 1640 Ouellette Ave., Box 480, N9A 6M6 (519/258-8888)	93.9
Wingham, Ont.	CKNX-FM	FM 102, 215 Carling Terrace, N0G 2W0 (519/357-1310)	101.7
Winnipeg, Man.	*CBW-FM	CBC, 541 Portage Ave., Box 160, R3C 2H1 (204/775-8351)	98.3
Winnipeg, Man.	CHIQ-FM	CHUM (Man.) Ltd., 432 Main St., R3B 2Z7 (204/957-0000)	94.3
Winnipeg, Man.	CHMM-FM	Radio OB Ltd., 930 Portage Ave., R3G 0P8 (204/772-0426)	97.5
Winnipeg, Man.	CITI-FM	Moffat Communications Ltd., Polo Park, R3G 0L7 (204/773-0371)	92.1
Winnipeg, Man.	CJUM-FM	CJUM-FM Inc., 310 University Centre, University of Manitoba (204/269-9690)	101.5
Winnipeg, Man.	CKWG-FM	Armadale Communications (see CKRC-AM)	103.1
Woss Camp, B.C.	*CBTW-FM	Studio at Vancouver (see CBU-AM)	92.9
Zenon Park, Sask.	*†CBKF-FM-3	Studio at Regina (see CBKF-FM)	93.5

TELEVISION STATIONS

CBC Stations are indicated by an asterisk*
French Language stations are indicated by dagger†
Stations in **bold** letters are original broadcasters. The balance are re-broadcast, relay, and satellite stations.

CALL LETTERS	LOCATION	CHANNEL
CFJC-TV-8	Adams Hill, B.C. (see Chase, B.C.)	11
*†CBST-7	Aguanish, P.Q. (see CBGAT, Matane)	8
*CBUT-16	Alert Bay, B.C. (see CBUT, Vancouver)	11
CHIL-TV-1	Alexis Creek, B.C. (see CFJC, Kamloops)	8
CIAC-TV	Alexis Creek, B.C. (see CHAN, Vancouver)	11
CKCC-TV-1	Alice Arm, B.C. (see CFTK, Terrace)	7
*†CBAFT-3	Allardville, N.B. (see CBAFT, Moncton)	3
†CKRS-TV-4	Alma, P.Q. (see CKRS, Jonquière)	4
CHWM-TV-1	Alta Lake, B.C. (see CHEK, Victoria)	7
CKBI-TV-1	Alticane, Sask. (see CKBI, Prince Albert)	10
CIAL-TV-1	Anahim Lake, B.C. (see CHAN, Vancouver)	5
CJCH-TV-1	Annapolis Valley, N.S. (see CJCH, Halifax)	10
†CHAU-TV-9	Anse a Valleau, P.Q. (see CHAU, Carleton)	7
CJCB-TV-2	Antigonish, N.S. (see CJCB, Sydney)	9
CJAP-TV	Argentia, Nfld. (see CJON, St. John's)	3
CKTK-TV-8	Aristazabol Is., B.C. (see CFTK, Terrace)	5
CHAC-TV-2	Ashcroft, B.C. (see CHAN, Vancouver)	2
CJAC-TV-2	Ashcroft, B.C. (see CFJC, Kamloops)	5
CFRN-TV-4	Ashmount, Alta. (see CFRN, Edmonton)	12
*CBIT-9	Aspen, N.S. (see CBIT, Sydney)	2
*CBXT-1	Athabasca, Alta. (see CBXT, Edmonton)	8
*CBWCT-1	Atikokan, Ont. (see CBWT, Winnipeg)	7
*CFAT-TV-2	Atlin, B.C. (satellite fed affiliate)	4
	Avola, B.C. (see CHAN, Vancouver)	13
*†CBGAT-7	Baie Comeau, P.Q. (see CBGAT, Matane)	7
†CFER-TV	Baie Comeau, P.Q. (see CFER, Rimouski)	11
*†CBST-8	Baie Johan Beetz, P.Q. (see CBGAT, Matane)	7
†CKRT-TV-1	Baie-St-Paul, P.Q. (see CKRT, Rivière-du-Loup)	2
*CBNAT-1	Baie Verte, Nfld. (see CBNT, St. John's)	3
*CBNAT-24	Baie Verte, Nfld. (see CBNT, St. John's)	12
*CBEIT	Baker Lake, N.W.T. (satellite fed relay station)	9
*CBWST	Baldy Mountain, Man. (see CBWT, Winnipeg)	8
CHEX-TV-1	Bancroft, Ont. (see CHEX, Peterborough)	4
CKGN-TV-2	Bancroft, Ont. (see CFGN, Toronto)	2
*CBRT-1	Banff, Alta. (see CBRT, Calgary)	5
CFCN-TV-2	Banff, Alta. (see CFCN, Calgary)	7
CFAC-TV-2	Banff, Alta. (see CFAC, Calgary)	13
CKRD-TV-2	Banff, Alta. (see CKRD, Red Deer)	10
	Barkerville, B.C. (see Wells, B.C.)	
CKVR-TV	**Barrie, Ont.** (CKVR Channel 3 Ltd., Box 519, L4M 4T9) 705/726-9711	3
CKTV-TV-1	Barriere, B.C. (see CFJC, Kamloops)	12
CKTV-TV-2	Barriere, B.C. (see CHAN, Vancouver)	7
	Barriere #2, B.C. (see CHAN, Vancouver)	8
CFAC-TV-3	Bassano, Alta. (see CFAC, Calgary)	8
CFCN-TV-7	Bassano, Alta. (see CFCN, Calgary)	6
CBRT-5	Bassano, Alta. (see CBRT, Calgary)	11
*CBXAT-6	Battle River, Alta. (see CBXT, Edmonton)	9
*CBNT-27	Bay L'Argent, Nfld. (see CBNT, St. John's)	8

CALL LETTERS	LOCATION	CHANNEL
*CBIT-17	Bay St. Lawrence, N.S. (see CBIT, Sydney)	13
CJCB-TV-5	Bay St. Lawrence, N.S. (see CJCB, Sydney)	7
*CBLAT-5	Beardmore, Ont. (see CBLT, Toronto)	9
†CKRN-TV-3	Bearn, P.Q. (see CKRN, Rouyn-Noranda)	3
CHBC-TV-9	Beaton, B.C. (see CHBC, Kelowna)	8
*CBKBT	Beauval, Sask. (see CBKST, Saskatoon)	7
*CFBF-TV	Beaver Creek, Yukon (satellite fed affiliate)	7
*CBUBT-11	Beaverfoot Range, B.C. (see CBUT, Vancouver)	40
*CBXAT-14	Beaverlodge, Alta. (see CBXT, Edmonton)	4
CJDC-TV-3	Beaverlodge, Alta. (see CJDC, Dawson Creek, B.C.)	4
CKDI-TV-1	Bella Bella, B.C. (see CFTK, Terrace)	9
*CBUIT-3	Bella Coola, B.C. (see CBUT, Vancouver)	13
*†CBKFT-9	Bellegarde, Sask. (see CBWFT, Winnipeg)	26
*CBNT-23	Belleoram, Nfld. (see CBNT, St. John's)	7
*†CBLFT-13	Belleville, Ont. (see CBLFT, Toronto)	15
CJOH-TV-2	Belleville, Ont. (see CJOH, Ottawa)	6
*CBRT-10	Bellevue, Alta. (see CBRT, Calgary)	57
CKBI-TV-5	Big River, Sask. (see CKBI, Prince Albert)	9
*CBWT-1	Big Trout Lake, Ont. (see CBWT, Winnipeg)	13
CKAM-TV-3	Blackville, N.B. (see CKCW, Moncton)	9
*†CBGAT-8	Blanc-Sablon, P.Q. (see CBGAT, Matane)	3
*CBIT-13	Blue Mountain, N.S. (see CBIT, Sydney)	7
CFJC-TV-13	Blue River, B.C. (see CFJC, Kamloops)	3
	Blue River, B.C. (see CHAN, Vancouver)	13
CKLT-TV-2	Boiestown, N.B. (see CKCW, Moncton)	7
CHSJ-TV-3	Boiestown, N.B. (see CHSJ, Saint John)	13
CHSJ-TV-1	Bon Accord, N.B. (see CHSJ, Saint John)	6
CJWB-TV	Bonavista, Nfld. (see CJON, St. John's)	10
*CBYT-3	Bonne Bay, Nfld. (see CBYT, Corner Brook)	2
*CBUDT	Bonnington, B.C. (see CBUT, Vancouver)	13
*†CBXFT-1	Bonnyville, Alta. (see CBXFT, Edmonton)	6
CITL-TV-4	Bonnyville, Alta. (see CITL, Lloydminster)	7
CKSA-TV-2	Bonnyville, Alta. (see CKSA, Lloydminster)	9
CFJC-TV-16	Boss Mtn., B.C. (see CFJC, Kamloops)	7
CJFC-TV-1	Boston Bar, B.C. (see CFJC, Kamloops)	5
CJFC-TV-2	Boston Bar, B.C. (see CHAN, Vancouver)	3
CHAT-TV-3	Bow Island, Alta. (see CHAT, Medicine Hat)	2
*CBUT-4	Bowen Island, B.C. (see CBUT, Vancouver)	13
CHAN-TV-2	Bowen Island, B.C. (see CHAN, Vancouver)	3
CHAN-TV-5	Brackendale, B.C. (see CHAN, Vancouver)	9
CKX-TV	**Brandon, Man.** (Western Man. Broadcasters Ltd., 2940 Victoria Ave., R7A 6A5) 204/728-1150	5
CKYB-TV	Brandon, Man. (see CKY, Winnipeg)	4
*CBNAT-18	Brent's Cove, Nfld. (see CBNT, St. John's)	10
*CIBR-TV	Brisco, B.C. (satellite fed affiliate)	11
CFCN-TV-3	Brooks, Alta. (see CFCN, Calgary)	9
CFAC-TV-5	Brooks, Alta. (see CFAC, Lethbridge)	3
*CBNAT-2	Buchans, Nfld. (see CBNT, St. John's)	13
*CBKDT	Buffalo Narrows, Sask. (see CBKST, Saskatoon)	11
CJDC-TV-2	Bullhead Mountain, B.C. (see CJDC, Dawson Creek)	8
*CBRT-8	Burmis, Alta. (see CBRT, Calgary)	47
CFAC-TV-4	Burmis, Alta. (see CFAC, Lethbridge)	3
CFCN-TV-4	Burmis, Alta. (see CFCN, Calgary)	5
CKHS-TV	Burns Lake, B.C. (see CHAN, Vancouver)	13
CBCH-TV-2	Burns Lake, B.C. (see CFTK, Terrace)	4
†CKRT-TV-4	Cabano, P.Q. (see CKRT, Rivière-du-Loup)	5
CHAC-TV-1	Cache Creek, B.C. (see CHAN, Vancouver)	12
CJAC-TV-1	Cache Creek, B.C. (see CFJC, Kamloops)	10
CJCH-TV-6	Caledonia, N.S. (see CJCH, Halifax)	6
*†CBRFT	Calgary, Alta. (see CBXFT, Edmonton)	16
***CBRT**	**Calgary, Alta.** (CBC, 1724 Westmount Blvd., Box 2640, T2P 2M7) 403/283-8361	9
CFAC-TV	**Calgary, Alta.** (Calgary Television Ltd., 955 Rideau Rd. S.W., T2S 0S4) 403/243-3491	2
CFCN-TV	**Calgary Alta.** (CFCN Television Ltd., Box 7060, Stn. E, T3C 3L9) 403/246-7111	4
*CBENT	Cambridge Bay, N.W.T. (satellite fed relay station)	9
*CBUT-8	Campbell River, B.C. (see CBUT, Vancouver)	3
*CBUT-9	Campbell River, B.C. (see CBUT, Vancouver)	82
	Campbell River, B.C. (see CHEK, Victoria)	13
CHCR-TV	Campbellton, N.B. (see CHSJ, Saint John)	4
CKCD-TV	Campbellton, N.B. (see CKCW, Moncton)	7
CFNV-TV-1	Camp Woss, B.C. (see CHEK, Victoria)	3
*CFTE-TV-1	Camsell River, N.W.T. (satellite fed affiliate)	12
*CBUBT-1	Canal Flats, B.C. (see CBUT, Vancouver)	12
CJCH-TV-1	Canning, N.B. (see CJCH, Halifax)	10
CHBC-TV-8	Canoe, B.C. (see CHBC, Kelowna)	6

CALL LETTERS	LOCATION	CHANNEL
CFJC-TV-14	Canoe Mtn., B.C. (see Valemount)	8
*CHCB-TV-1	Cape Broyle, Nfld. (see CBNT, St. John's)	3
CJBL-TV-13	Cape Broyle, Nfld. (see CJON, St. John's)	13
*CBEJT	Cape Dorset, N.W.T. (satellite fed relay station)	9
*CFCZ-TV	Carcross/Tagish, Yukon (satellite fed affiliate)	13
*CBRT-12	Cardston, Alta. (see CBRT, Calgary)	2
†CHAU-TV	**Carleton, P.Q.** (Télévision de la Baie-des-Chaleurs, Inc., C.P. 100, G0C 1J0) 418/364-3344	5
CIEW-TV	Carlyle, Sask. (see CICC, Yorkton)	7
*CFYC-TV	Carmacks, Yukon (satellite fed affiliate)	13
*CBNT-21	Cartwright, Nfld. (see CBNT, St. John's)	9
*CBUET	Cassiar, B.C. (satellite fed relay station)	7
*CBUAT-2	Castlegar, B.C. (see CBUT, Vancouver)	3
CKTN-TV-1	Castlegar, B.C. (see CHAN, Vancouver)	5
CFSB-TV-3	Cathedral Point, B.C. (see CFTK, Terrace)	13
*†CBGAT-5	Causapscal, P.Q. (see CBGAT, Matane)	6
CHKC-TV-3	Cawston, B.C. (see CHBC, Kelowna)	3
CFCC-TV-2	Cedarvale, B.C. (see CFTK, Terrace)	11
CHBC-TV-6	Celista, B.C. (see CHBC, Kelowna)	3
†CJPM-TV-1	Chambord, P.Q. (see CJPM, Chicoutimi)	10
†CHAU-TV-4	Chandler, P.Q. (see CHAU, Carleton)	7
*†CBFAT-1	Chapais, P.Q. (see CBFT, Montreal)	12
†CIVP-TV	Chapeau, P.Q. (see Radio Quebec, Hull)	23
*†CBOFT-1	Chapeau, P.Q. (see CBOFT, Ottawa)	11
CFCL-TV-6	Chapleau, Ont. (see CFCL, Timmins)	7
*†CBAFT-5	Charlottetown, P.E.I. (see CBAFT, Moncton)	31
***CBCT**	**Charlottetown, P.E.I.** (CBC, Box 2230, 430 University Ave., C1A 8B9) 902/892-3591	13
CKCW-TV-1	Charlottetown, P.E.I. (see CKCW, Moncton, N.B.)	5
CFJC-TV-8	Chase, B.C. (see CFJC, Kamloops)	11
CHSH-TV-2	Chase (Adams Hill), B.C. (see CHAN, Vancouver)	13
CHSH-TV-1	Chase (White Lake), B.C. (see CHAN, Vancouver)	7
*CBXAT-7	Chateh, Alta. (see CBXT, Edmonton)	5
CKAM-TV-2	Chatham, N.B. (see CKCW, Moncton)	10
*†CBLFT-10	Chatham, Ont. (see CBLFT, Toronto)	48
CICO-TV	Chatham, Ont. (see CICA, Toronto)	59
CKCO-TV-3	Chatham, Ont. (see CKCO, Kitchener)	42
CJCC-TV	Cherryville, B.C. (see CHAN, Vancouver)	13
CJWR-TV-1	Cherryville, B.C. (see CHBC, Kelowna)	10
*†CBHFT-4	Cheticamp, N.S. (see CBAFT, Moncton)	10
*CBIT-2	Cheticamp, N.S. (see CBIT, Sydney)	2
CBCD-TV-2	Chetwynd, B.C. (see CJDC, Dawson Creek)	7
*†CBFAT	Chibougamau, P.Q. (see CBFT, Montreal)	5
*CBJET	Chicoutimi, P.Q. (see CBMT, Montreal)	58
†CJPM-TV	**Chicoutimi, P.Q.** (C.J.P.M.-T.V. Inc., Box 600, G7H 5C8) 418/549-2576	6
†CKRS-TV-2	Chicoutimi, P.Q. (see CKRS, Jonquière)	2
*CBUT-2	Chilliwack, B.C. (see CBUT, Vancouver)	3
CHAN-TV-1	Chilliwack, B.C. (see CHAN, Vancouver)	11
*CBUAT-7	Christina Lake, B.C. (see CBUT, Vancouver)	13
*CHFC-TV	Churchill, Man. (see CBWT, Winnipeg)	8
*CBNLT-1	Churchill Falls, Nfld. (see CBNLT, Labrador City)	9
*†CBST-4	Churchill Falls, Nfld. (see CBGAT, Matane)	13
*CBNT-10	Clarenville, Nfld. (see CBNT, St. John's)	7
CJCV-TV-10	Clarenville, Nfld. (see CJON, St. John's)	10
CHCW-TV-1	Clearwater, B.C. (see CFJC, Kamloops)	2
CHCW-TV-2	Clearwater, B.C. (see CHAN, Vancouver)	10
*†CBSAT	Clermont, P.Q. (see CKRT, Rivière-du-Loup)	31
CFJC-TV-4	Clinton, B.C. (see CFJC, Kamloops)	9
CHTS-TV-1	Clinton, B.C. (see CHAN, Vancouver)	13
†CHAU-TV-8	Cloridorme, P.Q. (see CHAU, Carleton)	5
*CBNAT-16	Coachman's Cove, Nfld. (see CBNT, St. John's)	8
CHEK-TV-4	Coal Harbour, B.C. (see CHEK, Victoria)	10
*CBUT-20	Coal Harbour, B.C. (see CBUT, Vancouver)	8
*CBRT-11	Coleman, Alta. (see CBRT, Calgary)	17
CFAC-TV-6	Coleman, Alta. (see CFAC, Lethbridge)	12
CKCP-TV-1	Coleman, Alta. (see CFCN, Calgary)	8
CKCK-TV-1	Colgate, Sask. (see CKCK, Regina)	12
*CJOC-TV	Come By Chance, Nfld. (see CJON, St. John's)	5
*CICH-TV-2	Come By Chance, Nfld. (see CBNT, St. John's)	11
*CBNAT-8	Conche, Nfld. (see CBNT, St. John's)	13
*CBEOT	Coppermine, N.W.T. (satellite fed relay station)	9
CICM-TV-1	Cormorant, Man. (see CBWT, Winnipeg)	4
***CBYT**	**Corner Brook, Nfld.** (CBC, Hospital Hill, Box 610, A2H 6G1) 709/634-3141	5
CJWN-TV	Corner Brook, Nfld. (see CJON, St. John's)	10
CJOH-TV-1	Cornwall, Ont. (see CJOH, Ottawa)	8

CALL LETTERS	LOCATION	CHANNEL
CKRD-TV-1	Coronation, Alta. (see CKRD, Red Deer)	10
	Cottam, Ont. (see CKGN, Toronto)	
*CBIT-10	Country Harbour Mines, N.S. (see CBIT, Sydney)	6
*CBUT-1	Courtenay, B.C. (see CBUT, Vancouver)	9
CHAN-TV-4	Courtenay, B.C. (see CHAN, Vancouver)	13
*CBYT-6	Cow Head, Nfld. (see CBYT, Corner Brook)	8
*CBUBT	Cranbrook, B.C. (see CBUT, Vancouver)	59
CFCN-TV-10	Cranbrook, B.C. (see CFCN, Calgary, Alta.)	8
*CBUCT-1	Crawford Bay, B.C. (see CBUT, Vancouver)	5
*CBUCT-2	Creston, B.C. (see CBUT, Vancouver)	3
	Crawford Bay, B.C. (see CHAN, Vancouver)	7
*CBUCT-4	Crescent Valley (see CBUT, Vancouver)	33
CKTN-4	Creston, B.C. (see CHAN, Vancouver)	12
CFMH-TV-1	Crimson Lake, Alta. (see CFRN, Edmonton)	9
*CBWNT	Cross Lake, Man. (see CBWT, Winnipeg)	12
*CBWIT-2	Cumberland House, Sask. (see CBWT, Winnipeg)	9
*CBCP-TV-2	Cypress Hills, Sask. (see CJFB, Swift Current)	2
CKYD-TV	Dauphin, Man. (see CKY, Winnipeg)	12
*CBDDT	Dawson, Y.T. (satellite fed relay station)	7
CJDC-TV	**Dawson Creek, B.C.** (Radio Station CJDC Ltd., 901 102nd Ave., V1G 2B6) 604/782-3341	5
*†CBKFT-3	Debden, Sask. (re-b. CBKFT-1, Saskatoon)	22
*CBYAT	Deer Lake, Nfld. (see CBYT, Corner Brook)	12
CJLW-TV-7	Deer Lake, Nfld. (see CJON, St. John's)	7
*CFDB-TV	Destruction Bay, Yukon (satellite fed affiliate)	9
*†CBHFT-6	Digby, N.S. (see CBAFT, Moncton)	58
*CBHT-7	Digby, N.S. (see CBHT, Halifax)	52
*CBIT-16	Dingwall, N.S. (see CBIT, Sydney)	12
CJCB-TV-3	Dingwall, N.S. (see CJCB, Sydney)	9
CKLT-TV-2	Doaktown, N.B. (see CKCW, Moncton)	10
CKAM-TV-4	Doaktown, N.B. (see CHSJ, Saint John)	8
*CBUBT-4	Donald Station, B.C. (see CBUT, Vancouver)	3
CHBC-TV-12	Downie, B.C. (see CHBC, Kelowna)	9
*†CBLFT-16	Driftwood, Ont. (see CBLFT, Toronto)	74
*CBRT-2	Drumheller, Alta. (see CBRT, Calgary)	5
*CBRT-14	Drumheller, Alta. (see CBRT, Calgary)	3
CFCN-TV-1	Drumheller, Alta. (see CFCN, Calgary)	10
CFAC-TV-1	Drumheller, Alta. (see CFAC, Calgary)	8
*CBWDT	Dryden, Ont. (see CBWT, Winnipeg)	9
*†CBWFT-9	Dryden, Ont. (see CBWFT, Winnipeg)	6
*CBWJT	Ear Falls, Ont. (see CBWT, Winnipeg)	13
CJFB-TV-1	Eastend, Sask. (see CJFB, Swift Current)	2
†CHLG-TV-4	Eastmain, P.Q. (satellite fed relay station)	5
*CBWHT-2	Easterville, Man. (see CBWT, Winnipeg)	11
CKHF-TV-1	East Georgia, B.C. (see CFTK, Terrace)	9
*CBIT-14	Eden Lake, N.S. (see CBIT, Sydney)	17
***CBXT**	**Edmonton, Alta.** (CBC, Box 555, T5J 2P4) 403/469-2321	5
***†CBXFT**	**Edmonton, Alta.** (CBC, Box 555, T5J 2P4) 403/469-2321	11
CFRN-TV	**Edmonton, Alta.** (Sunwapta Broadcasting Ltd., Box 5030, Stn. E, T5P 4C2) 403/484-3311	3
CITV-TV	**Edmonton, Alta.** (Allarco Broadcasting Ltd., 5325 104 St., T6H 5B8) 403/436-1250	13
†CBAFT	Edmundston, N.B. (see CBAFT, Moncton)	13
CHCN	Edmundston, N.B. (see CHSJ, Saint John)	6
CJGR-TV-1	Elk Falls Lookout, B.C. (see CHAN, Vancouver)	49
*†CBLFT-6	Elliot Lake, Ont. (see CBLFT, Toronto)	12
CICI-TV-1	Elliot Lake, Ont. (see CICI, Sudbury)	3
CKNC-TV-1	Elliot Lake, Ont. (see CKNC, Sudbury)	7
*CBNT-7	Elliston, Nfld. (see CBNT, St. John's)	4
CKEL-TV-3	Elrose, Sask. (see CFQC, Saskatoon)	11
CKEL-TV-1	Elrose, Sask. (see CJFB, Swift Current)	7
CKEL-TV-2	Elrose, Sask. (see CBKST, Saskatoon)	13
*CBKHT-1	Elsa, Y.T. (see CBKHT, Keno Hill)	9
	Endako, B.C. (see CKPG, Prince George)	6
CFEN-TV-1	Enderby, B.C. (see CHBC, Kelowna)	4
CFEN-TV-2	Enderby, B.C. (see CHAN, Vancouver)	11
CHBC-TV-5	Enderby, B.C. (see CHBC, Kelowna)	72
*CBEHT	Eskimo Point, N.W.T. (satellite fed relay station)	9
*†CBLFT-7	Espanola, Ont. (see CBLFT, Toronto)	11
CIEW-TV	Estevan, Sask. (see CICC, Yorkton)	7
CFSS-TV	Estevan, Sask. (see CKOS, Yorkton)	3
CBCA-TV	Etzikom, Alta. (see CHAT, Medicine Hat)	12
*CBRT-3	Exshaw, Alta. (see CBRT, Calgary)	6
CHGR-TV-1	Exshaw, Alta. (see CFCN, Calgary)	7
*CBWGT-2	Fairford, Man. (see CBWT, Winnipeg)	7
*†CBXFT-2	Falher, Alta. (see CBXFT, Edmonton)	6

CALL LETTERS	LOCATION	CHANNEL
CFAW-TV	Falkland, B.C. (see CHAN, Vancouver)	12
CFWS-TV-1	Falkland, B.C. (see CHBC, Kelowna)	10
*CBDBT	Faro, Y.T.(satellite fed relay station)	8
*CBNT-5	Fermeuse, Nfld. (see CBNT, St. John's)	11
CJFR-TV	Fermeuse, Nfld. (see CJON, St. John's)	13
*†CBST-5	Fermont, P.Q. (see CBGAT, Matane)	7
*CBUBT-9	Fernie, B.C. (see CBUT, Vancouver)	8
*CBNT-38	Ferryland, Nfld. (see CBNT, St. John's)	4
*CBUBT-13	Field, B.C. (see CBUT, Vancouver)	11
CFFY-TV-1	Field, B.C. (see CFCN, Calgary)	4
*CBWGT	Fisher Branch, Man. (see CBWT, Winnipeg)	10
CKYA-TV	Fisher Branch, Man. (see CKY, Winnipeg)	8
*CBNAT-20	Fleur de Lys, Nfld. (see CBNT, St. John's)	5
*CBWBT	Flin Flon, Man. (see CBWT, Winnipeg)	10
*†CBWFT-2	Flin Flon, Man. (see CBWFT, Winnipeg)	3
CKYF-TV	Flin Flon, Man. (see CKY, Winnipeg)	13
*CBNAT-6	Fogo Island, Nfld. (see CBNT, St. John's)	2
*CBKAT-2	Fond du Lac, Sask. (see CBKAT, Uranium City)	10
*CBKAT-1	Ford Bay, Sask. (see CBKAT, Uranium City)	13
*CBXBT	Fort Chipewyan, Alta. (see CBXT, Edmonton)	10
*CBWCT	Fort Frances, Ont. (see CBWT, Winnipeg)	5
CKPG-TV-3	Fort Fraser, B.C. (see CKPG, Prince George)	6
†CBFGT	Fort George, P.Q. (see CBFT, Montreal)	9
*CBXT-6	Fort McMurray, Alta. (see CBXT, Edmonton)	9
CHAK-TV-1	Fort McPherson, N.W.T. (see CHAK, Inuvik)	13
*CBUGT	Fort Nelson, B.C. (satellite fed relay station)	8
*CBEBT-3	Fort Providence, N.W.T. (re-b. CBEBT-2, Lake Desmarais)	9
*CBKT-3	Fort Qu'Appelle, Sask. (see CBKT, Regina)	5
CKTV	Fort Qu'Appelle, Sask. (see CKCK, Regina)	11
CFSJ-TV-1	Fort St. James (Murray Ridge), B.C. (see CHAN, Vancouver)	10
CFFS-TV	Fort St. James #2, B.C. (see CHAN, Vancouver)	3
CKPG-TV-5	Fort St. James. B.C. (see CKPG, Prince George)	5
*CBEGT	Fort Simpson, N.W.T. (satellite fed relay station)	9
*CBEAT	Fort Smith, N.W.T. (satellite fed relay station)	8
*CBNT-33	Fortune, Nfld. (see CBNT, St. John's)	9
*CBXAT-5	Fort Vermilion, Alta. (see CBXT, Edmonton)	11
CFDF-TV-1	Fountain, B.C. (see CHAN, Vancouver)	5
*CBXT-7	Fox Creek, Alta. (see CBXT, Edmonton)	5
*CBNAT-10	Fox Harbour, Nfld. (see CBNT, St. John's)	7
*CBXAT-10	Fox Lake, Alta. (see CBXT, Edmonton)	9
CKX-TV-1	Foxwarren, Man. (see CKX, Brandon)	11
*CBLCT	Fraserdale Ont. (see CFCL, Timmins)	7
CFFL-TV-1	Fraser Lake, B.C. (see CHAN, Vancouver)	9
CFFL-TV-2	Fraser Lake, B.C. (see CKPG, Prince George)	6
*†CBAFT-1	Fredericton, N.B. (see CBAFT, Moncton)	5
CHSJ-TV	Fredericton, N.B. (see CHSJ, Saint John)	4
*CFFB-TV	Frobisher Bay, N.W.T. (satellite fed relay station)	8
*CBUAT-3	Fruitvale/Montrose, B.C. (see CBUT, Vancouver)	9
*†CBST-10	Gagnon, P.Q. (see CBGAT, Matane)	9
*CBNT-14	Gambo, Nfld. (see CBNT, St. John's)	8
CJGN-TV	Gander, Nfld. (see CJON, St. John's)	2
†CHAU-TV-6	Gaspé, P.Q. (see CHAU, Carleton)	13
CFGW-TV-1	Gaspé West, P.Q. (see CHSJ, Saint John)	6
*CBLAT	Geraldton, Ont. (relay of CBLT, Toronto)	13
*†CBST-9	Gethsemani, P.Q. (see CBGAT, Matane)	9
*CBWLT	Gillam, Man. (see CBWT, Winnipeg)	8
*CBYT-12	Gillams, Nfld. (see CBYT, Corner Brook)	13
CHRP-TV-3	Glacier, B.C. (see CHAN, Vancouver)	11
CHRP-TV-4	Glacier, B.C. (see CHBC, Kelowna)	13
	Glenanan, B.C. (see CHAN, Vancouver)	3
*CBNT-13	Glovertown, Nfld. (see CBNT, St. John's)	3
*CBWXT	Gods Lake Narrows, Man. (see CBWT, Winnipeg)	13
CJGB-TV-1	Gold Bridge, B.C. (see CHAN, Vancouver)	6
CJGB-TV-2	Gold Bridge, B.C. (see CFJC, Kamloops)	3
*CBUBT-2	Golden, B.C. (see CBUT, Vancouver)	13
CJGR-TV-3	Gold River, B.C. (see CHAN, Vancouver)	2
*CBUT-12	Gold River, B.C. (see CBUT, Vancouver)	7
***CFLA-TV**	**Goose Bay, Lab., Nfld.** (CBC, Box 925, Stn. A, A0P 1S0) 709/896-2466	8
*CBIT-8	Goshen, N.S. (see CBIT, Sydney)	5
CJOX-TV	Grand Bank, Nfld. (see CJON, St. John's)	2
CKSA-TV-2	Grande Centre, Alta. (see CKSA, Lloydminster)	9
CJCN-TV	Grand Falls, Nfld. (see CJON, St. John's)	4
*CBNAT	Grand Falls, Nfld. (see CBNT, St. John's)	11

CALL LETTERS	LOCATION	CHANNEL
CKSR-TV-1	Grand Forks, B.C. (see CHAN, Vancouver)	7
*CBUAT-1	Grand Forks, B.C. (see CBUT, Vancouver)	5
*CBXAT	Grande Prairie, Alta. (see CBXT, Edmonton)	10
CFRN-TV-1	Grande Prairie, Alta. (see CFRN, Edmonton)	13
CJDC-TV	Grande Prairie, Alta. (see CJDC, Dawson Creek)	5
*CBWHT	Grand Rapids, Man. (see CBWT, Winnipeg)	8
*CBWHT-1	Grand Rapids, Man. (see CBWT, Winnipeg)	15
*†CBGAT-3	Grande Vallée, P.Q. (see CBGAT, Matane)	11
CIGR-TV-1	Granisle, B.C. (see CHAN, Vancouver)	7
CHTL-TV-2	Granisle (Snow Shoe Island), B.C. (see CFTK, Terrace)	6
*CBKGT	Gravelbourg, Sask. (see CJFB-TV, Swift Current)	45
*†CBKFT	Gravelbourg, Sask. (see CBWFT, Winnipeg)	39
CKBI-TV-3	Greenwater Lake, Sask. (see CKBI, Prince Albert)	4
CFGI-TV-1	Gribbell Island, B.C. (see CFTK, Terrace)	12
CHBC-TV-5	Grindrod, B.C. (see CHBC, Kelowna)	72
*†CBGAT-9	Gros Morne, P.Q. (see CBGAT, Matane)	4
CBUIT-4	Hagensborg, B.C. (see CFTK, Terrace)	9
*CFHJ-TV	Haines Junction, Yukon (satellite fed relay affiliate)	13
***CBHT**	**Halifax, N.S.** (CBC, Box 3000, B3J 3E9) 902/422-8311	3
*†CBHFT	Halifax, N.S. (see CBAFT, Moncton)	13
CJCH-TV	**Halifax, N.S.** (Atlantic Television System Ltd., 2885 Robie St., B3J 2Z4) 902/453-4000	5
CFGN-TV	Hamilton, Ont. (see CFGN, Toronto)	6/22
CHCH-TV	**Hamilton, Ont.** (Niagara Television Ltd., 163 Jackson St. W., L8N 3A6) 416/522-1101; Toronto direct: 366-9688	11
*CBNAT-23	Hampden, Nfld. (see CBNT, St. John's)	13
CFCN-TV-1	Hand Hills, Alta. (see CFCN, Calgary)	12
*CBNT-22	Harbour Breton, Nfld. (see CBNT, St. John's)	13
*CBYT-10	Harbour Le Cou, Nfld. (see CBYT, Corner Brook)	5
*CNTT-29	Harbour Mille, Nfld. (see CBNT, St. John's)	13
*CBNAT-19	Harbour Round, Nfld. (see CBNT, St. John's)	12
*†CBST-11	Harrington Harbour, P.Q. (see CBGAT, Matane)	8
†CFER-TV	Hauterive, P.Q. (see CFER, Rimouski)	11
*†CBST-18	Havre-Aubert, P.Q. (see CBGAT, Matane)	18
*†CBST-1	Havre St. Pierre, P.Q. (see CBGAT, Matane)	12
*CBEBT-1	Hay River, N.W.T. (see CBEBT, Pine Point)	7
*CBYT-9	Hawkes Bay, Nfld. (see CBYT, Corner Brook)	5
CFST-TV-1	Hazelton, B.C. (see CFTK, Terrace)	9
*†CBLFT-5	Hearst, Ont. (see CBLFT, Toronto)	7
CFCL-TV-4	Hearst, Ont. (see CFCL, Timmins)	4
CIHL-TV	Hendrix Lake, B.C. (see CHAN, Vancouver)	12
*CBNT-24	Hermitage, Nfld. (see CBNT, St. John's)	4
*CBNT-18	Hickman's Harbour, Nfld. (see CBNT, St. John's)	4
*CBXAT-4	High Level, Alta. (see CBXT, Edmonton)	8
*CBXAT-2	High Prairie, Alta. (see CBXT, Edmonton)	2
*CBXT-3	Hinton, Alta. (see CBXT, Edmonton)	8
CKPG-TV-1	Hixon, B.C. (see CKPG, Prince George)	10
*CBUT-21	Holberg, B.C. (see CBUT, Vancouver)	2
CFKY-TV-1	Holberg #1, B.C. (see CHEK, Victoria)	4
CFSH-TV-1	Holberg #2, B.C. (see CHEK, Victoria)	8
*CBUT-6	Hope, B.C. (see CBUT, Vancouver)	9
*CBLAT-6	Hornepayne, Ont. (see CBLT, Toronto)	13
CFHO-TV	Houston, B.C. (see CHAN, Vancouver)	8
CFTK-TV-10	Houston, B.C. (see CFTK, Terrace)	2
CICC-TV-3	Hudson Bay, Sask. (see CICC, Yorkton)	11
CKOS-TV-2	Hudson Bay, Sask. (see CKOS, Yorkton)	9
CJDC-TV-1	Hudson Hope, B.C. (see CJDC, Dawson Creek)	11
CFTK-TV-11	Hudsons Bay Mtn., B.C. (near Telkwa) (see CFTK, Terrace)	7
†CHOT-TV	**Hull, P.Q.** (Radio Nord, 171 Jean Proulx, J8Z 1W5) 819/770-1040	40
†CIVO-TV	**Hull, P.Q.** (Radio Québec, 749B boul. St-Joseph, J8Y 4B7) 819/771-3257	30
CKCO-TV-4	Huntsville, Ont. (see CKCO, Kitchener)	11
CKVR-TV-2	Huntsville, Ont. (see CKVR, Barrie)	8
*CBWDT-2	Ignace, Ont. (see CBWT, Winnipeg)	13
*CBKCT	Ile-a-la-Crosse, Sask. (see CBKST, Saskatoon)	9
*†CBIMT	Iles-de-la-Madeleine, P.Q. (see CBAFT, Moncton)	12
*CBIT-15	Ingonish, N.S. (see CBIT, Sydney)	2
CHAK-TV	Inuvik, N.W.T. (satellite fed relay station)	6
CFWL-TV-1	Invermere, B.C. (see CFCN, Calgary)	6
*CBUBT-3	Invermere, B.C. (see CBUT, Vancouver)	2
CJCB-TV-1	Inverness, N.S. (see CJCB, Sydney)	6
*CBYT-2	Irishtown, Nfld. (see CBYT, Corner Brook)	7
CJWN-TV-6	Irishtown, Nfld. (see CJON, St. John's)	3
*CBWBT-2	Island Falls, Sask. (see CBWT, Winnipeg)	7
*CBWGT-1	Jackhead, Man. (see CBWT, Winnipeg)	5

CALL LETTERS	LOCATION	CHANNEL
*CBXT-4	Jasper, Alta. (see CBXT, Edmonton)	5
*CBXAT-13	Jean Cote, Alta. (see CBXT, Edmonton)	31
*CBXAT-9	Jean D'Or, Alta. (see CBXT, Edmonton)	13
CHTV-TV-1	Jenpeg, Man. (see CBWT, Winnipeg)	8
†CKRS-TV	**Jonquière, P.Q.** (Radio Saguenay Ltée, 175 Sir-Wilfrid-Laurier, G7X 7X3) 418/542-4551	12
†CJDG-TV-3	Joutel, P.Q. (see CKRN, Rouyn-Noranda)	12
CFWL-TV-2	Jubilee Mountain, B.C. (see CFCN, Calgary, Alta.)	8
CFTK-TV-7	Juskatla, B.C. (see CFTK, Terrace)	2
CFJC-TV	**Kamloops, B.C.** (Inland Broadcasters (1969) Ltd., 460 Pemberton Terrace, V2C 1T5) 604/372-3322	4
CHKM-TV	Kamloops, B.C. (see CHAN, Vancouver)	6
CFCL-TV-3	Kapuskasing, Ont. (see CFCL, Timmins)	2
*†CBLFT-4	Kapuskasing, Ont. (see CBLFT, Toronto)	12
CITO-TV-2	Kapuskasing, Ont. (see CICI, Sudbury)	10
CFCL-TV-2	Kearns, Ont. (see CFCL, Timmins)	2
CITO-TV-1	Kearns, Ont. (see CICI, Sudbury)	11
†CHAU-TV-11	Kedgwick, N.B. (see CHAU, Carleton, P.Q.)	2
*CBUAT-4	Kelly Mountain, B.C. (see CBUT, Vancouver)	13
CHBC-TV	**Kelowna, B.C.** (Okanagan Valley Television Co. Ltd., 342 Leon Ave., V1Y 6J2) 604/762-4535	2
CHKL-TV	Kelowna, B.C. (see CHAN, Vancouver)	5
CFTK-TV-5	Kemano, B.C. (see CFTK, Terrace)	2
*CBKHT	Keno Hill, Y.T. (satellite fed relay station)	13
*CBWAT	Kenora, Ont. (see CBWT, Winnipeg)	8
*†CBWFT-7	Kenora, Ont. (see CBWFT, Winnipeg)	2
CHKC-TV-1	Keremeos, B.C. (see CHBC, Kelowna)	4
CHKC-TV-2	Keremeos, B.C. (see CHAN, Vancouver)	9
CFTK-TV-4	Kildala, B.C. (see CFTK, Terrace)	5
CHVT-TV-1	King Island, B.C. (see CFTK, Terrace)	9
*†CBLFT-14	Kingston, Ont. (see CBLFT, Toronto)	32
CFGN-TV	Kingston, Ont. (see CFGN, Toronto)	2
CJOH-TV-3	Kingston, Ont. (see CJOH, Ottawa)	6
CKWS-TV	**Kingston, Ont.** (Frontenac Broadcasting, Co. Ltd., 170 Queen St., K7K 1B2) 613/544-2340	11
CITO-TV-1	Kirkland Lake, Ont. (see CICI, Sudbury)	11
*†CBLFT-8	Kitchener, Ont. (see CBLFT, Toronto)	76
CFGN-TV	Kitchener, Ont. (see CFGN, Toronto)	6
CICO-TV	Kitchener, Ont. (see CICA, Toronto)	28
CKCO-TV	**Kitchener, Ont.** (Central Ontario Television Ltd., 864 King St. W., N2G 4E9) 519/578-1313; Toronto direct: 416/456-2930	13
CFWC-TV-2	Kitwancool, B.C. (see CFTK, Terrace)	13
CFWK-TV-1	Kitwanga, B.C. (see CFTK, Terrace)	13
CFKK-TV-1	Klemtu, B.C. (see CFTK, Terrace)	2
CFKB-TV-2	Kokish, B.C. (see CHEK, Victoria)	9
	Kootenay Lake, B.C. (see CHAN, Vancouver)	10
CKCC-TV-1	Kwinatahl, B.C. (see CFTK, Terrace)	7
***CBNLT**	**Labrador City, Nfld.** (CBC, Box 576, A2V 2L3) 709/944-3616	13
*†CBST-3	Labrador City, Nfld. (see CBGAT, Matane)	11
*CBWT-2	Lac du Bonnet, Man. (see CBWT, Winnipeg)	4
*†CBVT-4	Lac-Etchemin, P.Q. (see CBVT, Quebec)	55
*CBXT-5	Lac La Biche, Alta. (see CBXT, Edmonton)	10
CFRN-TV-5	Lac La Biche, Alta. (see CFRN, Edmonton)	2
*†CBVT-3	Lac Megantic, P.Q. (see CBVT, Quebec)	2
*†CHLG-TV-7	Laforge, P.Q. (satellite fed affiliate)	12
*CBEBT-2	Lake Desmarais, N.W.T. (re-b. CBEBT-1, Hay River)	13
*CBRT-4	Lake Louise, Alta. (see CBRT, Calgary)	12
CFLL-TV-1	Lake Louise, Alta. (see CFCN, Calgary)	6
CFLL-TV-2	Lake Louise, Alta. (see CFAC, Calgary)	7
CFSB-TV-1	Lalakata Point, B.C. (see CFTK, Terrace)	11
*CBKDT-2	La Loche, Sask. (see CBKST, Saskatoon)	13
*CBNT-35	Lamaline, Nfld. (see CBNT, St. John's)	18
*CBYT-13	Lark Harbour, Nfld. (see CBYT, Corner Brook)	13
*CBKST-2	La Ronge, Sask. (see CBKST, Saskatoon)	12
*CBNAT-21	La Scie, Nfld. (see CBNT, St. John's)	9
CJLS-TV	La Scie, Nfld. (see CJON, St. John's)	9
*†CBST-13	La Tabatière, P.Q. (see CBGAT, Matane)	4
*†CBVT-2	La Tuque, P.Q. (see CBVT, Quebec)	3
*CBNT-36	Lawn, Nfld. (see CBNT, St. John's)	6
CJLN-TV	Lawn, Nfld. (see CJON, St. John's)	10
CKJC-TV-2	Leader, Sask. (see CFQC, Saskatoon)	13
CKJC-TV-1	Leader, Sask. (see CBKST, Saskatoon)	7
*CBWQT	Leaf Rapids, Man. (see CBWT, Winnipeg)	13
†CJDG-TV-2	Lebel-sur-Quevillon, P.Q. (see CKRN, Rouyn-Noranda)	12
CFCC-TV-1	Legate Creek, B.C. (see CFTK, Terrace)	7
*CBKST-3	Leoville, Sask. (see CBKST, Saskatoon)	12
*†CBXFT-3	Lethbridge, Alta. (see CBXFT, Edmonton)	23

CALL LETTERS	LOCATION	CHANNEL
*CBRT-6	Lethbridge, Alta. (see CBRT, Calgary)	10
CFAC-TV	**Lethbridge, Alta.** (Lethbridge Television Ltd., Box 1120, T1J 4A4) 403/327-1521	7
CFCN-TV-5	Lethbridge, Alta. (see CFCN, Calgary)	13
CFMZ-TV-1	Lillooet, B.C. (see CFJC, Kamloops)	2
CFDF-TV-2	Lillooet, B.C. (see CHAN, Vancouver)	13
CILY-TV-1	Lillooet #2, B.C. (see CHAN, Vancouver)	8
CHTV-TV-3	Limestone, Man. (see CBWT, Winnipeg)	10
†CJDG-TV	Lithiums Mines, P.Q. (see CKRN, Rouyn-Noranda)	8
CKTV-TV-1	Little Fort, B.C. (see CFJC, Kamloops)	12
*CBNT-8	Little Heart's Ease, Nfld. (see CBNT, St. John's)	11
*CBHT-1	Liverpool, N.S. (see CBHT, Halifax)	12
CITL-TV	**Lloydminster, Alta.** (Mid-West Television Ltd., 5026 50th St., T9V 1P3) 403/875-3321	4
CKSA-TV	**Lloydminster, Alta.** (Mid-West Television Ltd., 5026 50th St., T9V 1P3) 403/875-3321	2
*CBIT-7	Lochaber, N.S. (see CBIT, Sydney)	33
CHLK-TV-1	Logan Lake, B.C. (see CFJC, Kamloops)	11
CHLK-TV-2	Logan Lake, B.C. (see CHAN, Vancouver)	13
*†CBLFT-9	London, Ont. (see CBLFT, Toronto)	40
CFGN-TV	London, Ont. (see CFGN, Toronto)	6
CFPL-TV	**London, Ont.** (CFPL Broadcasting Ltd., Box 2880, N6A 4H9) 519/686-8810	10
CICO-TV	London, Ont. (see CICA, Toronto)	18
CHTV-TV-2	Long Spruce, Man. (see CBWT, Winnipeg)	12
*CBUHT-2	Loos, B.C. (see CBUT, Vancouver)	6
*CBNT-34	Lord's Cove, Nfld. (see CBNT, St. John's)	9
CFRN-TV-7	Lougheed, Alta. (see CFRN, Edmonton)	7
CFBA-TV-1	Louise Island, B.C. (see CFTK, Terrace)	3
CHID-TV-1	Lumby, B.C. (see CHBC, Kelowna)	4
CHID-TV-2	Lumby, B.C. (see CHAN, Vancouver)	9
*CBNT-20	Lumsden, Nfld. (see CBNT, St. John's)	12
*CBWRT	Lynn Lake, Man. (see CBWT, Winnipeg)	8
CHWS-TV-1	Lytton, B.C. (see CFJC, Kamloops)	11
CILY-TV-2	Lytton, B.C. (see CHAN, Vancouver)	8
CHPL-TV-1	Mabel Lake, B.C. (see CHAN, Vancouver)	13
CHPP-TV-1	Mabel Lake, B.C. (see CHBC, Kelowna)	8
*CBIT-4	Mabou, N.S. (see CBIT, Sydney)	10
CIMK-TV-1	Mackenzie, B.C. (see CHAN, Vancouver)	9
CKPG-TV-4	Mackenzie, B.C. (see CKPG, Prince George)	6
*CBWYT	Mafeking, Man. (see CBWT, Winnipeg)	2
*CBMT-2	Magog, P.Q. (see CBMT, Montreal)	30
....	Makkovik, Nfld. (satellite fed affiliate)	9
CFFI-TV-1	Malakwa, B.C. (see CHBC, Kelowna)	4
CFFI-TV-2	Malakwa, B.C. (see CHAN, Vancouver)	11
CFCL-TV-5	Malartic, P.Q. (see CFCL, Timmins)	5
†CKHQ-TV-1	Manicouagan, P.Q. (see CBGAT, Matane)	10
†CKHQ-TV-6	Manicouagan, P.Q. (see CBGAT, Matane)	13
*CBWGT-3	Manigotagan, Man. (see CBWT, Winnipeg)	22
*CBLAT-1	Manitouwadge, Ont. (see CBLT, Toronto)	8
*CBXAT-3	Manning, Alta. (see CBXT, Edmonton)	12
CHAT-TV-2	Maple Creek, Sask. (see CHAT, Medicine Hat, Alta.)	10
*CBLAT-4	Marathon, Ont. (see CBLT, Toronto)	11
*CBIT-5	Margaree, N.S. (see CBIT, Sydney)	8
CKMJ	Marquis, Sask. (see CKCK, Regina)	7
*†CBGAT-8	Marsoui, P.Q. (see CBGAT, Matane)	12
CBXAT	Marten Mtn., Alta. (see CBXT, Edmonton)	11
*CHMB-TV	Martin Bay, B.C. (satellite fed affiliate)	13
*CBNT-3	Marystown, Nfld. (see CBNT, St. John's)	5
CJMA-TV-11	Marystown, Nfld. (see CJON, St. John's)	11
CHMH-TV-1	Masset, B.C. (see CFTK, Terrace)	8
†CJDG-TV-4	Matagami, P.Q. (see CKRN, Rouyn-Noranda)	7
***†CBGAT**	**Matane, P.Q.** (CBC, 155 St-Sacrement St., C.P. 2000, G4W 3P7) 418/562-0290	9
†CFER-TV	Matane, P.Q. (see CFER, Rimouski)	11
*CBKHT-2	Mayo, Y.T. (see CBKHT, Keno Hill)	7
*CBUHT-3	McBride, B.C. (see CBUT, Vancouver)	2
....	McBride, B.C. (see CHAN, Vancouver)	12
*CBWUT	McCusker Lake, Man. (see CBWT, Winnipeg)	10
CITL-TV-3	Meadow Lake, Sask. (see CITL, Lloydminster)	3
CKSA-TV-1	Meadow Lake, Sask. (see CKSA, Lloydminster)	8
CFCN-TV-8	Medicine Hat, Alta. (see CFCN, Calgary)	8
CHAT-TV	**Medicine Hat, Alta.** (Monarch Broadcasting Co. Ltd., Box 1270, T1A 7H5) 403/548-3911	6
CKBQ-TV	Melfort, Sask. (see CFQC, Saskatoon)	2
CKX-TV-2	Melita, Man. (see CKX, Brandon)	9
CFJC-TV-3	Merritt, B.C. (see CFJC, Kamloops)	8
CFZQ-TV-1	Mica Creek (site 1), B.C. (see CHBC, Kelowna)	9
CHMC-TV-1	Mica Creek (site 1), B.C. (see CHAN, Vancouver)	7

CALL LETTERS	LOCATION	CHANNEL
CHMC-TV-2	Mica Creek (site 2), B.C. (see CHAN, Vancouver)	4
CFZQ-TV-2	Mica Creek Village, B.C. (see CHBC, Kelowna)	5
†CKHQ-TV-3	Micoua, P.Q. (see CBGAT, Matane)	12
*†CBHFT-5	Middleton, N.S. (see CBAFT, Moncton)	46
*CBHT-6	Middleton, N.S. (see CBHT, Halifax)	8
	Midway, B.C. (see CHAN, Vancouver)	3
CKMY-TV-1	Midway, B.C. (see CHBC, Kelowna)	7
*CBUT-32	Midway, B.C. (see CBUT, Vancouver)	7
*CIMC-TV-1	Mildred Lake, Alta. (satellite fed affiliate)	6
*CBNAT-5	Millertown, Nfld. (see CBNT, St. John's)	7
CHEX-TV-2	Minden, Ont. (see CHEX, Peterborough)	10
*CBNAT-14	Ming's Bight, Nfld. (see CBNT, St. John's)	10
CFMT-TV-3	Minto, B.C. (see CFJC, Kamloops)	3
***†CBAFT**	**Moncton, N.B.** (CBC, 250 Archibald St., Box 950, E1C 8N8) 506/855-3370	11
CHMT-TV	Moncton, N.B. (see CHSJ, Saint John)	7
CKCW-TV	**Moncton, N.B.** (ATV New Brunswick Ltd., Box 5004, E1C 8R6) 506/855-1224	2
CFGW-TV-2	Mont Blanc, Percé, P.Q. (see CHSJ, Saint John)	8
*†CBGAT-1	Mont-Climont, P.Q. (see CBGAT, Matane)	11
CJML-TV-1	Monte Lake, B.C. (see CFJC, Kamloops)	8
*†CBFT-2	Mont-Laurier, P.Q. (see CBFT, Montreal)	3
*†CBGAT-4	Mont-Louis, P.Q. (see CBGAT, Matane)	2
*†CBGAT-10	Mont-Louis-en-Haut, P.Q. (see CBGAT, Matane)	19
*†CBFT-1	Mont-Tremblant, P.Q. (see CBFT, Montreal)	11
***†CBFT**	**Montreal, P.Q.** (CBC, Box 6000, 1400 Dorchester Blvd. E., H3C 3A8) 514/285-3211	2
***CBMT**	**Montreal, P.Q.** (CBC, Box 6000, 1400 Dorchester Blvd. E., H3C 3A8) 514/285-3211	6
CFCF-TV	**Montreal, P.Q.** (CFCF Inc., 405 Ogilvy Ave., H3N 1M4) 514/273-6311	12
†CFTM-TV	**Montreal, P.Q.** (Télé-Métropole Inc., 1600 Maisonneuve Blvd. E., Box 170, Stn. C, H2L 4P6) 514/526-9251	10
†CIVM-TV	**Montreal, P.Q.** (Radio-Québec, 1000, rue Fullum, H2K 3L7) 514/873-4611	17
*CBKST-5	Montreal Lake, Sask. (see CBKST, Saskatoon)	11
***CBKT-1**	**Moose Jaw, Sask.** (CBC, 127 Main St. N., S6H 0V9) 306/693-4683	4
*†CBKFT-10	Moose Jaw, Sask. (see CBWFT, Winnipeg)	16
CKMJ-TV	Moose Jaw, Sask. (see CKCK, Regina)	7
*CBWIT-1	Moose Lake, Man. (see CBWT, Winnipeg)	9
*CBCO-TV-1	Moosonee, Ont. (see CFCL, Timmins)	9
*CBUBT-8	Morrissey Ridge, B.C. (see CBUT, Vancouver)	21
*CBUBT-7	Mount Baker, B.C. (see CBUT, Vancouver)	10
CHRP-TV-2	Mount Begbie, B.C. (see CHBC, Kelowna)	9
CKHF-TV-2	Mount Dolly, near Stewart, B.C. (see CFTK, Terrace)	11
CFHM-TV-1	Mount Hamilton, B.C. (see CFJC, Kamloops)	7
CFHM-TV-2	Mount Hamilton, B.C. (see CHAN, Vancouver)	9
*CBUBT-12	Mount Hunter, B.C. (see CBUT, Vancouver)	53
CFTK-TV-8	Mount Parizeau, B.C. (see CFTK, Terrace)	5
CHQC-TV-1	Mount Poole, B.C. (see CFTK, Terrace)	4
*CBNAT-9	Mount St. Margaret, Nfld. (see CBNT, St. John's)	9
CHMW-TV-1	Mount Wells, B.C. (see CFTK, Terrace)	12
*CBUBT-14	Moyie, B.C. (see CBUT, Vancouver)	6
CKVS-TV-1	Moyie, B.C. (see CFAC, Lethbridge)	5
*†CBHFT-2	Mulgrave, N.S. (see CBAFT, Moncton)	7
*CBIT-1	Mulgrave, N.S. (see CBIT, Sydney)	12
*†CBGAT-2	Murdochville, P.Q. (see CBGAT, Matane)	6
†CHAU-TV-11	Murdochville, P.Q. (see CHAU, Carleton)	5
*CBNT-11	Musgrave, Nfld. (see CBNT, St. John's)	9
*CBNAT-7	Musgrave Harbour, Nfld. (see CBNT, St. John's)	7
*CBNT-17	Musgravetown, Nfld. (see CBNT, St. John's)	9
*CBNBT	Nain, Nfld. (satellite fed relay station)	9
CJNP-TV-1	Nakusp, B.C. (see CHBC, Kelowna)	2
CJNP-TV-3	Nakusp, B.C. (see CHAN, Vancouver)	7
CHNI-TV	Narrows Inlet, B.C. (see CHEK, Victoria)	10
CFTK-TV-6	Nass Camp, B.C. (near Lava Lake) (see CFTK, Terrace)	5
*CBUBT-10	Natal, B.C. (see CBUT, Vancouver)	11
CKTN-TV-3	Nelson, B.C. (see CHAN, Vancouver)	3
*CBUCT	Nelson, B.C. (see CBUT, Vancouver)	9
*CBWPT	Nelson House, Man. (see CBWT, Winnipeg)	11
CHCN-TV	Newcastle, N.B. (see CHSJ, Saint John)	6
CKAM-TV-1	Newcastle, N.B. (see CKCW, Moncton)	10
CFKB-TV-1	Newcastle Ridge, B.C. (see CHEK, Victoria)	7
*CBUCT-6	New Denver, B.C. (see CBUT, Vancouver)	17
	New Denver/Silverton, B.C. (see CHAN, Vancouver)	13
*CBHT-5	New Glasgow, N.S. (see CBHT, Halifax)	7
CJCB-TV-4	New Glasgow, N.S. (see CJCB, Sydney)	2
CFJC-TV-12	Nicola, B.C. (see CFJC, Kamloops)	10
*CBUT-15	Nimpkish, B.C. (see CBUT, Vancouver)	9

CALL LETTERS	LOCATION	CHANNEL
CFNV-TV-2	Nimpkish, B.C. (see CHEK, Victoria)	6
CFST-TV-1	Nine Mile Mtn., B.C. (see CFTK, Terrace)	9
CKBI-TV-4	Nipawin, Sask. (see CKBI, Prince Albert)	10
†CKRN-TV	**Noranda, P.Q.** (Radio Nord Inc., 380 Mudoch St., J9K 1G5) 819/762-0741	4
CFJC-TV-16	Noranda Mines, B.C. (see CFJC, Kamloops)	7
*CBEDT	Norman Wells, N.W.T. (satellite fed relay station)	9
CICC-TV-2	Norquay, Sask. (see CICC, Yorkton)	7
CKOS-TV-1	Norquay, Sask. (see CKOS, Yorkton)	13
CKBI-TV-2	North Battleford, Sask. (see CKBI, Prince Albert)	7
CFQC-TV-2	North Battleford, Sask. (see CFQC, Saskatoon)	6
CHNB-TV	**North Bay, Ont.** (Mid Canada Communications (Canada) Corp., Box 3220, P1B 8K3) 705/476-3111	4
CKNY-TV	**North Bay, Ont.** (Mid Canada Communications (Canada) Corp., Box 3220, P1B 8K3) 705/476-3111	10
*CBNT-11	Northeast Brook, Nfld. (see CBNT, St. John's)	4
*CBIT-6	Northeast Margaree, N.S. (see CBIT, Sydney)	13
	North Forks, B.C. (see CHAN, Vancouver)	7
CKAM-TV	North Shore, N.S. (see CKLT, Saint John)	12
*CBWOT	Norway House, Man. (see CBWT, Winnipeg)	9
*†CBSNT	Notre-Dame-des-Monts, P.Q. (see CKRT, Rivière-du-Loup)	40
*†CBFWT	Nouveau-Comptoir, P.Q. (see CBFT, Montreal)	9
CKLT-TV-1	Oakland, N.B. (see CKCW, Moncton)	3
CFTK	Ocean Falls, B.C. (see CFTK, Terrace)	2
*CFOF-TV	Ocean Falls, B.C. (satellite fed relay station)	2
	Oil Springs, Ont. (see CKGN, Toronto)	
CHKC-TV-5	Olalla, B.C. (see CHAN, Vancouver)	11
CHKC-TV-2	Olalla, B.C. (see CHBC, Kelowna)	6
*†CBST-15	Old Fort Bay, P.Q. (see CBGAT, Matane)	7
CKKM-TV	Oliver, B.C. (see CHAN, Vancouver)	3
CHBC-TV-3	Oliver, B.C. (see CHBC, Kelowna)	8
CFJC-TV-6	100 Mile House, B.C. (see CFJC, Kamloops)	5
CITM-TV	100 Mile House, B.C. (see CHAN, Vancouver)	3
*CBWDT-4	Osnaburgh, Ont. (see CBWT, Winnipeg)	13
***†CBOFT**	**Ottawa, Ont.** (Radio Canada, C.P. 3220, Succ. C, K1Y 1E4) 613/725-3511	9
***CBOT**	**Ottawa, Ont.** (CBC, Box 3220, Stn. C, K1Y 1E4) 613/725-3511	4
CHRO-TV	**Ottawa, Ont.** (CHRO Television, 200 Isabella St., K1S 1V7)	5
CICO-TV	Ottawa, Ont. (see CICA, Toronto)	24
CJOH-TV	**Ottawa, Ont.** (C.J.O.H. Broadcasting Ltd., Box 5813, Stn. F, K2C 3G6) 613/224-1313	13
CHOT-TV	Ottawa, see Hull	
CKGN-TV-6	Ottawa, Ont. (see CFGN, Toronto)	6
*CBWVT	Oxford House, Man. (see CBWT, Winnipeg)	8
CFON-TV-1	Oyen, Alta. (see CFCN, Calgary)	2
CFON-TV-2	Oyen, Alta. (see CHAT, Medicine Hat)	7
*CBNAT-12	Pacquet, Nfld. (see CBNT, St. John's)	6
*CBKDT-1	Palmbere Lake, Sask. (see CBKST, Saskatoon)	8
*CBEKT	Pangnirtung, N.W.T. (satellite fed relay station)	9
*†CBTB-TV-1	Parent, P.Q. (FCP station)	12
CKGN-TV	Paris, Ont. (see CFGN, Toronto)	6
CKVR-TV-1	Parry Sound, Ont. (see CKVR, Barrie)	12
CFWL-TV-2	Parsons, Alta. (see CFCN, Calgary)	8
CJWN-TV-5	Pasadena, Nfld. (see CJON, St. John's)	8
	Pavilion Lake, B.C. (see CHAN, Vancouver)	7
*†CFAH-TV-1	Patuniq, P.Q. (satellite fed affiliate)	11
*CBXAT-1	Peace River, Alta. (see CBXT, Edmonton)	7
CFRN-TV-2	Peace River, Alta. (see CFRN, Edmonton)	3
CHPT-TV-1	Peachland, B.C. (see CHBC, Kelowna)	4
CIPL-TV	Peachland, B.C. (see CHAN, Vancouver)	9
CKPI-TV-1	Pearse Island, B.C. (see CFTK, Terrace)	4
*CBWBT-3	Pelican Narrows, Sask. (see CBWT, Winnipeg)	6
*CFPC-TV	Pelly Crossing, Y.T. (satellite fed affiliate)	12
*CBUFT	Pemberton, B.C. (see CBUT, Vancouver)	4
CHPV-TV-1	Pemberton, B.C. (see CHEK, Victoria)	9
CHRO-TV	**Pembroke, Ont.** (Mid Canada Communications (Canada) Corp., Box 100, 3 Forest Lea Rd., K8A 6X2) 613/735-1036	5
*†CBLFT-15	Penetanguishene, Ont. (see CBLFT, Toronto)	34
CHBC-TV-1	Penticton, B.C. (see CHBC, Kelowna)	13
CHKL-TV-1	Penticton, B.C. (see CHAN, Vancouver)	10
†CHAU-TV-5	Percé, P.Q. (see CHAU, Carleton)	2
*†CBLFT-12	Peterborough, Ont. (see CBLFT, Toronto)	44
CFGN-TV	Peterborough, Ont. (see CFGN, Toronto)	2
CHEX-TV	**Peterborough, Ont.** (Kawartha Broadcasting Co. Ltd., Box 659, K9J 6Z9) 705/742-0451	12
CHLG-TV-2	Petite Opinaca, P.Q. (satellite fed relay station)	3
*CBNT-37	Petty Harbour, Nfld. (see CBNT, St. John's)	13
CJPH-TV	Petty Harbour, Nfld. (see CJON, St. John's)	11
*CBUT-30	Phoenix, B.C. (see CBUT, Vancouver)	15

CALL LETTERS	LOCATION	CHANNEL
*CBWDT-5	Pickle Lake, Ont. (see CBWT, Winnipeg)	9
*CBWDT-6	Pikangikum, Ont. (see CBWT, Winnipeg)	7
CFPM-TV-1	Pikwitonei, Man. (see CBWT, Winnipeg)	12
*CBRT-9	Pincher Creek, Alta. (see CBRT, Calgary)	15
CHPC-TV-1	Pincher Creek, Alta. (see CFAC, Calgary)	9
CHPC-TV-2	Pincher Creek, Alta. (see CFCN, Calgary)	11
*†CBWFT-6	Pine Falls, Man. (see CBWFT, Winnipeg)	11
*CBEBT	Pine Point, N.W.T. (satellite fed relay station)	4
*CBKST-6	Pinehouse Lake, Sask. (see CBKST, Saskatoon)	10
CFJC-TV-18	Pine Valley, B.C. (see CFJC, Kamloops)	2
CIPT-TV	Pitt River, B.C. (see CHEK, Victoria)	10
CHAT-TV-1	Pivot, Alta. (see CHAT, Medicine Hat)	4
*CBNT-2	Placentia, Nfld. (see CBNT, St. John's)	12
*CBXT-8	Plamondon, Alta. (see CBXT, Edmonton)	4
*CBIT-3	Pleasant Bay, N.S. (see CBIT, Sydney)	8
*CBELT	Pond Inlet, N.W.T. (satellite fed relay station)	9
CBCP-TV-3	Ponteix, Sask. (see CJFB, Swift Current)	3
*†CBKFT-7	Ponteix, Sask. (see CBWFT, Winnipeg)	22
*CBUT-3	Port Alberni, B.C. (see CBUT, Vancouver)	4
CHEK-TV-3	Port Alberni, B.C. (see CHEK, Victoria)	11
†CKRS-TV-1	Port Alfred, P.Q. (see CKRS, Jonquiere)	9
*CBUT-17	Port Alice, B.C. (see CBUT, Vancouver)	10
CKPA-TV-1	Port Alice #1, B.C. (see CHEK, Victoria)	2
CKPA-TV-2	Port Alice #2, B.C. (see CHEK, Victoria)	7
*†CBFNT	Port au Port, Nfld. (see CBFT, Montreal)	13
*CBYT-4	Port-aux-Basques, Nfld. (see CBYT, Corner Brook)	3
CJPQ-TV	Port-aux-Basques, Nfld. (see CJON, St. John's)	7
*CBNT-32	Port Blandford, Nfld. (see CBNT, St. John's)	2
†CHAU-TV-3	Port Daniel, P.Q. (see CHAU, Carleton)	10
*CBUT-19	Port Hardy, B.C. (see CBUT, Vancouver)	6
CFKB-TV-3	Port Hardy, B.C. (see CHEK, Victoria)	3
CJCB-TV-6	Port Hawkesbury, N.S. (see CJCB, Sydney)	3
*CBNAT-12	Port Hope Simpson, Nfld. (see CBNT, St. John's)	12
*CBYT-8	Portland Creek, Nfld. (see CBYT, Corner Brook)	13
*CBUT-18	Port McNeill, B.C. (see CBUT, Vancouver)	2
*CFEB-TV	Port Radium, N.W.T. (satellite fed affiliate)	9
CJTV-TV-1	Port Renfrew, B.C. (see CHAN, Vancouver)	11
*CBNT-1	Port Rexton, Nfld. (see CBNT, St. John's)	13
CBCD-TV-1	Pouce Coupe, B.C. (see CJDC, Dawson Creek)	7
*†CBKFT-2	Prince Albert, Sask. (re-b. CBKFT-1, Saskatoon)	3
CKBI-TV	**Prince Albert, Sask.** (Central Broadcasting Co. Ltd., 22 10th St. W., S6V 3A5) 306/763-7421	5
CKPG-TV	**Prince George, B.C.** (Q Broadcasting Ltd., 1220 6th Ave., V2L 3M8) 604/564-8861	2
CIFG-TV	Prince George, B.C. (see CHAN, Vancouver)	12
CFTK-TV-1	Prince Rupert, B.C. (see CFTK, Terrace)	6
CHNJ-TV-1	Princeton, B.C. (see CHAN, Vancouver)	11
CHGP-TV-1	Princeton, B.C. (see CHBC, Kelowna)	5
CFJC-TV-19	Pritchard, B.C. (see CFJC, Kamloops)	2
CHKM-TV-1	Pritchard, B.C. (see CHAN, Vancouver)	9
CFJC-TV-12	Promontory Mtn., B.C. (see CFJC, Kamloops)	10
CITL-TV-2	Provost/Macklin, Alta. (see CITL, Lloydminster)	6
CKSA-TV-4	Provost/Macklin, Alta. (see CKSA, Lloydminster)	12
*CBWBT-1	Pukatawagan, Man. (see CBWT, Winnipeg)	11
CKPM-TV-1	Puntzi, B.C. (see CHAN, Vancouver)	2
*CBUHT-1	Purden Lake, B.C. (see CBUT, Vancouver)	10
†CFCM-TV	**Quebec, P.Q.** (Entreprises Télé-Capital Ltée, C.P. 2026, G1K 7N2) 418/688-9330	4
†CIVQ-TV	Quebec, P.Q. (see CIVM, Montreal)	15
CKMI-TV	**Quebec, P.Q.** (Entreprises Télé-Capital Ltée, C.P. 2026, G1K 7N2) 418/688-9330	5
***†CBVT**	**Quebec, P.Q.** (CBC, Box 10400, Ste-Foy, P.Q. G1V 2X2) 418/656-9400	11
CHQC-TV-1	Queen Charlotte City, B.C. (see CFTK, Terrace)	4
CFJC-TV-11	Quesnel, B.C. (see CFJC, Kamloops)	7
CKCQ-TV-1	Quesnel, B.C. (see CKPG, Prince George)	13
CITM-TV-2	Quesnel, B.C. (see CHAN, Vancouver)	8
*CFRL-TV	Rabbit Lake, Sask. (satellite fed affiliate)	12
*†CBFRT	Radisson, P.Q. (see CBFT, Montreal)	8
*CBUBT-5	Radium Hot Springs, B.C. (see CBUT, Vancouver)	77
*CBYK-TV-1	Rae/Edzo, N.W.T. (see CFYK, Yellowknife)	10
*CBXAT-8	Rainbow Lake, Alta. (see CBXT, Edmonton)	11
*CBNT-25	Ramea, Nfld. (see CBNT, St. John's)	13
CJRA-TV-10	Ramea, Nfld. (see CJON, St. John's)	10
*CBNT-19	Random Island, Nfld. (see CBNT, St. John's)	43
*CBECT	Rankin Inlet, N.W.T. (satellite fed relay station)	9
*†CBOFT-2	Rapides-des-Joachims, P.Q. (see CBOFT, Ottawa)	8
CKRD-TV	**Red Deer, Alta.** (C.H.C.A. Television Ltd., 2840 Bremner Ave., T4N 5H6) 403/343-0850	6

CALL LETTERS	LOCATION	CHANNEL
CFRN-TV-6	Red Deer, Alta. (see CFRN, Edmonton)	8
*CBWET	Red Lake, Ont. (see CBWT, Winnipeg)	10
CJRR-TV-11	Red Rocks, Nfld. (see CJON, St. John's)	11
***CBKT**	**Regina, Sask.** (CBC, 1840 McIntyre St., S4P 2R1) 306/352-6641	9
*CBKFT	Regina, Sask. (see CBWFT, Winnipeg)	13
CKCK-TV	**Regina, Sask.** (Harvard Communications Ltd., Box 2000, S4P 3E5) 306/569-2000	2
*CBKRT	Regina, Sask. (see CBKMT, Moose Jaw)	9
*CBEMT	Resolute, N.W.T. (satellite fed relay station)	9
CHRP-TV-1	Revelstoke, B.C. (see CHAN, Vancouver)	7
CHRP-TV-2	Revelstoke, B.C. (see CHBC, Kelowna)	7
CFQC-TV-3	Richmond Lake, Sask. (see CFQC, Saskatoon)	83
†CFER-TV	**Rimouski, P.Q.** (Entreprises Télé-Capital Ltée, 465 boul. Ste-Anne, Pointe-au-Père, P.Q. G0K 1G0) 418/722-6011	11
†*CJBR-TV	**Rimouski, P.Q.** (CBC, 273 St-Jean Baptiste ouest, G5L 4J8) 418/723-2217	3
CKRR-TV-1	Rimrock, B.C. (see CFJC, Kamloops)	9
CKRR-TV-2	Rimrock, B.C. (see CHAN, Vancouver)	11
	Riverhead, Nfld. (see CBNT, St. John's)	5
CJFB-TV-3	Riverhurst, Sask. (see CJFB, Swift Current)	10
CHEK-TV-2	River Jordan, B.C. (see CHEK, Victoria)	11
†CHAU-TV-7	Rivière-au-Renard, P.Q. (see CHAU, Carleton)	7
*†CBST-6	Rivière-au-Tonnère, P.Q. (see CBGAT, Matane)	2
†CKRT-TV	**Rivière-du-Loup, P.Q.** (C.K.R.T.-T.V. Ltée, 1 rue Frontenac, G5R 1R7) 418/862-8241	7
*†CBST-16	Rivière St-Paul, P.Q. (see CBGAT, Matane)	21
†CKRS-TV-3	Roberval, P.Q. (see CKRS, Jonquière)	8
	Rock Creek/Kettle Valley, B.C. (see CHAN, Vancouver)	13
*CBUT-33	Rock Creek, B.C. (see CBUT, Vancouver)	33
CFMH-TV-2	Rocky Mountain House, Alta. (see CFRN, Edmonton)	9
*CBNAT-22	Roddickton, Nfld. (see CBNT, St. John's)	11
*CFRR-TV-1	Ross River, Y.T. (see CBDBT, Faro)	12
*CBYT-11	Rose Blanche, Nfld. (see CBYT, Corner Brook)	9
†CKRN-TV	**Rouyn-Noranda, P.Q.** (Radio Nord, Inc., 380 Murdoch, Box 70, Noranda, P.Q. J9X 5C2) 819/762-0741	4
CITO-TV-1	Rouyn-Noranda, P.Q. (see CICI, Sudbury)	11
*CBNT-4	St. Alban's, Nfld. (see CBNT, St. John's)	9
CJST-TV-13	St. Alban's, Nfld. (see CJON, St. John's)	13
*CBYT-5	St. Andrews, Nfld. (see CBYT, Corner Brook)	6
*†CBGAT-11	Ste-Anne-des-Monts (see CBGAT, Matane)	8
*CBNAT-4	St. Anthony, Nfld. (see CBNT, St. John's)	6
*†CBST-14	St-Augustin, P.Q. (see CBGAT, Matane)	2
*CBNT-30	St. Bernard's, Nfld. (see CBNT, St. John's)	6
*†CBKFT-4	St. Brieux, Sask. (re-b. CBKFT-1, Saskatoon)	7
*†CBVT-5	St. Fabien-de-Panet, P.Q. (see CBVT, Quebec)	13
*†CBVT-1	St-Georges-de-Beauce, P.Q. (see CBVT, Quebec)	6
*†CBAFT-1	Saint John, N.B. (see CBAFT, Moncton)	5
CHSJ-TV	**Saint John, N.B.** (N.B. Broadcasting Co. Ltd., 335 Union St., Box 2000, E2L 3T4) 506/657-3410	4
CKLT-TV	Saint John, N.B. (see CKCW, Moncton)	9
CJON-TV	**St. John's, Nfld.** (Nfld. Broadcasting Co. Ltd., Box 2020, A1C 5S2) 709/579-5015	6
***CBNT**	**St. John's, Nfld.** (CBC, 239 Kenmount Rd., Box 12010, Stn. A, A1B 3T8) 709/737-4140	8
*CBNT-12	St. Jones Within, Nfld. (see CBNT, St. John's)	9
*CBNT-28	St. Lawrence, Nfld. (see CBNT, St. John's)	12
CJXL-TV-10	St. Lawrence, Nfld. (see CJON, St. John's)	10
*†CBWFT-3	St. Lazare, Man. (see CBWFT, Winnipeg)	13
†CHAU-TV-1	Ste Marguerite-Marie, P.Q. (see CHAU, Carleton)	2
†CHAU-TV-10	St. Martin, N.B. (see CHAU, Carleton, P.Q.)	9
*CBNT-6	St. Mary's, Nfld. (see CBNT, St. John's)	10
*†CBSPT	St-Pamphile, P.Q. (see CKRT, Rivière-du-Loup)	3
†CKRT-TV-3	St-Patrice-de-Rivière-du-Loup, P.Q. (see CKRT, Rivière-du-Loup)	13
†CHAU-TV-2	St. Quentin, N.B. (see CHAU, Carleton)	10
*†CBGAT-7	St-Rene, P.Q. (see CBGAT, Matane)	30
†CKRT-TV-2	Ste. Rose du Dégelis, P.Q. (see CKRT, Rivière-du-Loup)	2
*†CBWFT-4	Ste. Rose du Lac, Man. (see CBWFT, Winnipeg)	3
CJSH-TV	St. Shotts, Nfld. (see CJON, St. John's)	10
†CKRT-TV-5	St. Urbain, P.Q. (see CKRT, Rivière-du-Loup)	10
*CBNT-26	St. Vincent's, Nfld. (see CBNT, St. John's)	7
CBUAT-5	Salmo, B.C. (see CBUT, Vancouver)	8
CHBC-TV-4	Salmon Arm, B.C. (see CHBC, Kelowna)	9
CFSA-TV-1	Salmon Arm, B.C. (see CHAN, Vancouver)	13
*CBWDT-7	Sandy Lake, Ont. (see CBWT, Winnipeg)	10
CKSR-TV	Santa Rosa, B.C. (see CHAN, Vancouver)	83
*†CBLFT-17	Sarnia, Ont. (see CBLFT, Toronto)	68
CKCO-TV-3	Sarnia, Ont. (see CKCO, Kitchener)	42
CKGN-TV-29	Sarnia, Ont. (see CFGN, Toronto)	29
CFQC-TV	**Saskatoon, Sask.** (CFQC Broadcasting Ltd., 216 1st Ave. N., S7K 3W3) 306/665-8600	8

CALL LETTERS	LOCATION	CHANNEL
*†CBKFT-1	Saskatoon, Sask. (see CBWFT, Winnipeg)	13
***CBKST**	**Saskatoon, Sask.** (CBC, CN Tower, Midtown Plaza, S7K 1J5) 306/244-1911	11
CICO-TV	Sault Ste. Marie, Ont. (see CICA, Toronto)	20
CJIC-TV	**Sault Ste. Marie, Ont.** (Huron Broadcasting Ltd., 119 East St., P6A 3C7) 705/254-7111	5
CKCY-TV	**Sault Ste. Marie, Ont.** (Huron Broadcasting Ltd., 119 East St., P6A 3C7) 705/254-7111	2
*CBWDT-3	Savant Lake, Ont. (see CBWT, Winnipeg)	8
CFSC-TV-1	Savona, B.C. (see CHAN, Vancouver)	13
CFSC-TV-2	Savona, B.C. (see CFJC, Kamloops)	8
*CBUT-10	Sayward, B.C. (see CBUT, Vancouver)	4
*†CBST-2	Schefferville, P.Q. (see CBGAT, Matane)	9
*CBSET-1	Schefferville, P.Q. (see CBMT, Montreal)	7
*CBNAT-15	Seal Cove, Nfld. (see CBNT, St. John's)	7
*†CBST	Sept-Iles, P.Q. (see CBGAT, Matane)	13
†CFER-TV	Sept-Iles, P.Q. (see CFER, Rimouski)	11
CJBT-TV-1	Shalalth, B.C. (see CHAN, Vancouver)	11
CJBT-TV-2	Shalalth, B.C. (see CFJC, Kamloops)	5
*CBCP-TV-1	Shaunavon, Sask. (see CJFB, Swift Current)	7
*CBHT-4	Sheet Harbour, N.S. (see CBHT, Halifax)	11
*CBHT-2	Shelburne, N.S. (see CBHT, Halifax)	8
*CBIT-11	Sherbrooke, N.S. (see CBIT, Sydney)	4
CHLT-TV	**Sherbrooke, P.Q.** (CHLT-TV Inc., 3330 King St. W., J1L 1C9) 529/565-7777	7
†CKSH-TV	**Sherbrooke, P.Q.** (Television St-François Inc., 2295 King St. W., J1J 3W7) 819/563-9890	9
CJSM-TV-1	Sherridon, Man. (see CBWT, Winnipeg)	5
CJON-TV-4	Signal Hill, Nfld. (see CJON, St. John's)	10
*CBWDT-1	Sioux Lookout, Ont. (see CBWT, Winnipeg)	12
*CBWAT-1	Sioux Narrows, Ont. (see CBWT, Winnipeg)	4
CHCS-TV-1	16 Mile House, B.C. (see CHAN, Vancouver)	7
CHBC-TV-7	Skaha Lake, B.C. (near Penticton) (see CHBC, Kelowna)	7
*CBXAT-11	Slave Lake, Alta. (see CBXT, Edmonton)	11
*CBUCT-5	Slocan, B.C. (see CBUT, Vancouver)	39
CFHO-TV-1	Smithers, B.C. (see CHAN, Vancouver)	13
CFTK-TV-2	Smithers, B.C. (see CFTK, Terrace)	5
*CBWKT	Snow Lake, Man. (see CBWT, Winnipeg)	8
CKYS-TV	Snow Lake, Man. (see CKY, Winnipeg)	11
CKSC-TV-1	Soda Creek, B.C. (see CFJC, Kamloops)	4
CKSC-TV-2	Soda Creek, B.C. (see CHAN, Vancouver)	2
CFKB-TV-4	Sointula, B.C. (see CHEK, Victoria)	5
CHEK-TV-1	Sooke, B.C. (see CHEK, Victoria)	13
CFSB-TV-2	South Bentinck Arm, Narrows, B.C. (see CFTK, Terrace)	13
	South End, Sask. (c/o CBKST, Saskatoon)	13
*CBWQT-1	South Indian Lake, Man. (see CBWT, Winnipeg)	10
CJON-TV-5	South Side Hill, Nfld. (see CJON, St. John's)	2
CJNA-TV-1	Spence's Bridge, B.C. (see CFJC, Kamloops)	3
CJNA-TV-2	Spence's Bridge, B.C. (see CHAN, Vancouver)	7
*CBUBT-6	Spillimacheen, B.C. (see CBUT, Vancouver)	69
CKBI-TV-6	Spiritwood, Sask. (see CKBI, Prince Albert)	9
*CBNAT-13	Springdale, Nfld. (see CBNT, St. John's)	13
CHAN-TV-3	Squamish, B.C. (see CHAN, Vancouver)	7
*CBUT-5	Squamish, B.C. (see CBUT, Vancouver)	11
*CBKST-4	Stanley Mission, Sask. (see CBKST, Saskatoon)	8
CKBQ-TV	Star City, Sask. (see CFQC, Saskatoon)	2
*CBYT-1	Stephenville, Nfld. (see CBYT, Corner Brook)	8
CJSV-TV	Stephenville, Nfld. (see CJON, St. John's)	4
*CFCS-TV	Stewart Crossing, Y.T. (satellite fed affiliate)	9
*CBKAT-3	Stony Rapids, Sask. (see CBKAT, Uranium City)	7
CFQC-TV-1	Stranraer, Sask. (see CFQC, Saskatoon)	3
*CBKST-1	Stranraer, Sask. (see CBKST, Saskatoon)	9
*†CHST-TV	Strathcona Sound, N.W.T. (satellite fed affiliate)	9
*†CBLFT-1	Sturgeon Falls, Ont. (see CBLFT, Toronto)	7
*†CBLFT-2	Sudbury, Ont. (see CBLFT, Toronto)	13
CICI-TV	**Sudbury, Ont.** (Mid Canada Communications (Canada) Corp., 699 Frood Rd., Box 400, P3E 5A3) 705/674-0711	5
CICO-TV	Sudbury, Ont. (see CICA, Toronto)	19
CKNC-TV	**Sudbury, Ont.** (Mid Canada Communications (Canada) Corp., 699 Frood Rd., Box 400, P3C 5A3) 705/674-8301	9
CFJL-TV-1	Sundre, Alta. (see CFCN, Calgary)	13
*CBIT-12	Sunnybrae, N.S. (see CBIT, Sydney)	6
*CBNT-31	Swift Current, Nfld. (see CBNT, St. John's)	5
CJSC-TV	Swift Current, Nfld. (see CJON, St. John's)	10
CJFB-TV	**Swift Current, Sask.** (Swift Current Telecasting Co. Ltd., Box 160, S9H 3V7) 306/733-7266	5
CKMC-TV	Swift Current, Sask. (see CKCK, Regina)	12
CJCB-TV	**Sydney, N.S.** (ATV Cape Breton Ltd., Box 469, B1P 6H5) 902/562-5511	4
***CBIT**	**Sydney, N.S.** (CBC, 285 Alexandra St., Box 700, B1P 6H7) 902/539-5050	5

CALL LETTERS	LOCATION	CHANNEL
*†CBHFT-3	Sydney, N.S. (see CBAFT, Moncton)	13
*CBUHT	Tabor Mountain, B.C. (see CBUT, Vancouver)	78
CKTN-TV-2	Taghum, B.C. (see CHAN, Vancouver)	23
*CBUT-14	Tahsis, B.C. (see CBUT, Vancouver)	9
CFAL-TV-1	Tasu, B.C. (see CFTK, Terrace)	11
CIAL-TV-2	Tatla Lake, B.C. (see CHAN, Vancouver)	9
CFTK-TV-2	Telkwa, B.C. (see CFTK, Terrace)	7
	Telkwa, B.C. (see CHAN, Vancouver)	4
CKNY-TV	Temiscaming, P.Q. (see CICI, Sudbury, Ont.)	
*†CBFST-2	Temiscaming, P.Q. (see CKRN, Rouyn)	12
CFTK-TV	**Terrace, B.C.** (Skeena Broadcasters Ltd., 4625 Lazelle Ave., V8G 1S4) 604/635-6316	3
CFTV-TV-1	Terrenceville, Nfld. (see CBNT, St. John's)	12
CJNF-TV	Terrenceville, Nfld. (see CJON, St. John's)	10
*CFTN-TV-1	Teslin, YT (satellite fed affiliate)	13
*†CBST-12	Tête-a-la-Baleine (see CBGAT, Matane)	6
*CBUHT-4	Tête Jaune, B.C. (see CBUT, Vancouver)	10
CFQC-TV	The Battlefords, Sask. (see CFQC, Saskatoon)	6
*†CBWFT-1	The Pas, Man. (see CBWFT, Winnipeg)	6
*CBWIT	The Pas, Man. (see CBWT, Winnipeg)	7
CKYP-TV	The Pas, Man. (see CKY, Winnipeg)	12
*†CBWFT-5	Thompson, Man. (see CBWFT, Winnipeg)	5
*CBWTT	Thompson, Man. (see CBWT, Winnipeg)	7
CESM-TV	**Thompson, Man.** (CESM-TV Ltd. (closed circuit), 49 Severn Cres., R8N 1M7) 204/677-4576	3/4
CKYT-TV	Thompson, Man. (see CKY, Winnipeg)	9
CKPR-TV	**Thunder Bay, Ont.** (Thunder Bay Electronics Ltd., 87 North Hill St., P7A 5V6) 807/344-9685	2
CHFD-TV	**Thunder Bay, Ont.** (Thunder Bay Electronics Ltd., 87 North Hill St., P7A 5V6) 807/344-9685	4
CICO-TV	Thunder Bay, Ont. (see CICA, Toronto)	9
CJTM-TV-1	Ticket Portage, Man. (see CBWT, Winnipeg)	4
*†CBLFT-3	Timmins, Ont. (see CBLFT, Toronto)	9
CFCL-TV	**Timmins, Ont.** (Mid Canada Communications (Canada) Corp., 681 Pine St. N., Box 620, P4N 7G3) 705/264-4211	6
CITO-TV	Timmins, Ont. (see CICI, Sudbury)	3
CKBI-TV-6	Tisdale, Sask. (see CKBI, Prince Albert)	13
*CBUT-22	Tofino, B.C. (see CBUT, Vancouver)	10
GIGR-TV	Topley Landing, B.C. (see CHAN, Vancouver)	11
CHTL-TV-1	Topley Landing (Shoulder Mtn.), B.C. (see CFTK, Terrace)	9
***CBLT**	**Toronto, Ont.** (CBC, 354 Jarvis St., Box 500, Term. A, M5W 1E6) 416/925-3311	5
***†CBLFT**	**Toronto, Ont.** (CBC, C.P. 500, Succ. A, M5W 1E6) 416/925-3311	25
CFTO-TV	**Toronto, Ont.** (CFTO-TV Ltd., Box 9, Agincourt, Ont. M4A 2M9) 416/291-9111	9
CKGN-TV	**Toronto, Ont.** (Global Communications Ltd., 81 Barber Greene Rd., Don Mills, Ont. M3C 2A2) 416/446-5311 (Transmitting from Paris, Ont.)	6/22
CFMT-TV	Multi-ling. **Toronto, Ont.** (Channel 47, 545 Lakeshore Blvd. W., M5V 2N8) 416/593-4747	47
CICA-TV	**Toronto, Ont.** (TV Ontario, 2180 Yonge St., M4S 2C1) 416/484-2600	19
CITY-TV	**Toronto, Ont.** (Channel Seventynine Ltd., 99 Queen St. E., M5C 2M1) 416/867-7979	79
*CBUAT	Trail, B.C. (see CBUT, Vancouver)	11
*CBUAT-6	Trail, B.C. (see CBUT, Vancouver)	52
CKTN-TV	Trail, B.C. (see CHAN, Vancouver)	8
CJTA-TV-1	Trepassey, Nfld. (see CBNT, St. John's)	4
CJTP-TV	Trepassey, Nfld. (see CJON, St. John's)	10
*CBNT-16	Trinity, Nfld. (see CBNT, St. John's)	2
†CKRT-TV-6	Trois-Pistoles, P.Q. (see CKRT, Rivière-du-Loup)	5
†CHEM-TV	**Trois-Rivières, P.Q.** (CHEM-TV Inc., 1400 rue des Cyprès, G8Y 4S3) 819/376-8880	8
†CKTM-TV	**Trois-Rivières, P.Q.** (Télévision St-Maurice (1976) Inc., 4141 boul. St-Jean, C.P. 277, G9A 5G3) 819/377-1441	13
*CBYT-7	Trout River, Nfld. (see CBYT, Corner Brook)	13
*CBEPT	Tuktoyaktuk, N.W.T. (satellite fed relay station)	8
*CBUT-7	Ucluelet, B.C. (see CBUT, Vancouver)	7
CKUP-TV-1	Ucluelet, B.C. (see CHAN, Vancouver)	6
	Upper Salmon River, Nfld. (see CBNT, St. John's)	10
CKAM-TV	Upsalquitch Lake, N.B. (see CKCW, Moncton)	12
*CBKAT	Uranium City, Sask. (satellite fed relay station of CBKMT, Moose Jaw)	8
	Uxbridge, Ont. (see CKGN, Toronto)	
†CIVA-TV	Val d'Or, P.Q. (see Radio Québec, Montréal)	12
*CBUHT-5	Valemount, B.C. (see CBUT, Vancouver)	6
CFJC-TV-14	Valemount, B.C. (see CFJC, Kamloops)	8
	Valemount, B.C. (see CHAN, Vancouver)	4
CJFB-TV-2	Val Marie, Sask. (see CJFB, Swift Current)	2
***†CBUFT**	**Vancouver, B.C.** (CBC, C.P. 4600, V6B 4A2) 604/665-8000	26
***CBUT**	**Vancouver, B.C.** (CBC, 700 Hamilton St., Box 4600, V6B 2R5) 604/665-8000	2
CHAN-TV	**Vancouver, B.C.** (B.C. Television Broadcasting System Ltd., Box 4700, V6B 4A3) 604/420-2288; Telex: 043-54784	8
CKVU-TV	**Vancouver, B.C.** (Western Approaches Ltd., 180 W. 2nd Ave., V5Y 1C2) 604/876-1344	21
KVOS-TV	**Vancouver, B.C.** (KVOS-TV (B.C.) Ltd., 1000 Mainland St., V6B 4W5) 604/681-1212	12

CALL LETTERS	LOCATION	CHANNEL
CKIN-TV-1	Vanderhoof, B.C. (see CHAN, Vancouver)	8
CKVA-TV-1	Vavenby, B.C. (see CHAN, Vancouver)	8
*†CBWFT-8	Vermillion Bay, Ont. (see CBWFT, Winnipeg)	74
CHBC-TV-2	Vernon, B.C. (see CHBC, Kelowna)	7
CHKL-TV-2	Vernon, B.C. (see CHAN, Vancouver)	12
CHEK-TV	**Victoria, B.C.** (B.C. Television Broadcasting Ltd., Box 4700, Vancouver, B.C. V6B 4A3) 604/477-1821.	6
†CKRS-TV-1	Ville de la Baie, P.Q. (see CKRS, Jonquière)	9
†CKRN-TV-2	Ville Marie, P.Q. (see CKRN, Rouyn-Noranda)	6
*CBWWT	Waasagomach, Man. (see CBWT, Winnipeg)	9
*CBXAT-12	Wabasca, Alta. (see CBXT, Edmonton)	7
*CBWMT	Wabowden, Man. (see CBWT, Winnipeg)	10
CITL-TV-1	Wainwright, Alta. (see CITL, Lloydminster)	5
CKSA-TV-3	Wainwright, Alta. (see CKSA, Lloydminster)	8
CJWS-TV	Wakeman Sound, B.C. (see CHEK, Victoria)	7
CFSS-TV	Warmley, Sask. (see CICC, Yorkton)	3
*CBRT-7	Waterton Park, Alta. (see CBRT, Calgary)	4
CJWP-TV-1	Waterton Park, Alta. (see CFAC, Lethbridge)	12
CJWP-TV-2	Waterton Park, Alta. (see CFCN, Calgary)	6
*CBDAT	Watson Lake, Y.T. (satellite fed relay station)	8
*CBLAT-3	Wawa, Ont. (see CBLT, Toronto)	9
*CBNT-15	Wellington/Hare Bay, Nfld. (see CBNT, St. John's)	24
CKWB-TV	Wells/Barkerville, B.C. (see CHAN, Vancouver)	11
	Wells, B.C. (see CKPG, Prince George)	9
*CBNT-9	Wesleyville, Nfld. (see CBNT, St. John's)	5
CFWS-TV-2	Westwold, B.C. (see CHBC, Kelowna)	12
CIEW-TV	Weyburn, Sask. (see CICC, Yorkton)	7
CFSS-TV	Weyburn, Sask. (see CKOS, Yorkton)	3
CFRN-TV-3	Whitecourt, Alta. (see CFRN, Edmonton)	12
*CBXT-2	Whitecourt, Alta. (see CBXT, Edmonton)	9
*CFWH-TV	Whitehorse, Y.T. (satellite fed relay station)	6
WHTV-TV	**Whitehorse, Y.T.** (Northern Television Systems Ltd., 203, 4103 4th Ave., Y1A 1H6) 403/667-4247	9
*CFAT-TV-1	White Mountain, YT (satellite fed affiliate)	10
*CBLAT-2	White River, Ont. (see CBLT, Toronto)	12
CKCO-TV-2	Wiarton, Ont. (see CKCO, Kitchener)	2
CFJC-TV-5	Williams Lake, B.C. (see CFJC, Kamloops)	8
CITM-TV-1	Williams Lake, B.C. (see CHAN, Vancouver)	13
CKCK-TV-2	Willow Bunch, Sask. (see CKCK, Regina)	6
*CBKT-2	Willow Bunch, Sask. (see CBKT, Regina)	10
*†CBKFT-8	Willow Bunch, Sask. (see CBWFT, Winnipeg)	21
	Willow Point, B.C. (see CHAN, Vancouver)	12
***CBET-TV**	**Windsor, Ont.** (CBC, 825 Riverside Drive W., Box 1609, N9A 1K7) 519/255-3411	9
*†CBEFT	Windsor, Ont. (see CBLFT, Toronto)	78
CICO-TV	Windsor, Ont. (see CICA, Toronto)	32
CFGN-TV	Windsor, Ont. (see CFGN, Toronto)	22
CKNX-TV	**Wingham, Ont.** (CKNX Broadcasting Ltd., 215 Carling Terrace, N0G 2W0) 519/357-1310	8
*CBUCT-3	Winlaw, B.C. (see CBUT, Vancouver)	12
***CBWT**	**Winnipeg, Man.** (CBC, Portage Ave. & Young St., Box 160, R3B 2G1) 204/775-8351	6
***†CBWFT**	**Winnipeg, Man.** (CBC, Portage Ave. & Young St., C.P. 160, R3B 2G1) 204/775-8351	3
CKND-TV	**Winnipeg, Man.** (CanWest Broadcasting Ltd., Box 60, 603 St. Mary's Rd., R2M 4A5) 204/233-3304	9
CKY-TV	**Winnipeg, Man.** (Moffat Communications Ltd., Polo Park, R3G 0L7) 204/775-0371	7
CJGR-TV-2	Wokas Lake, B.C. (see CHAN, Vancouver)	11
*CBUT-11	Wokas Lake, B.C. (see CBUT, Vancouver)	60
CKLT-TV-1	Woodstock, N.B. (see CKCW, Moncton)	3
*CBUT-13	Woss Camp, B.C. (see CBUT, Vancouver)	12
CHSS-TV	Wynyard, Sask. (see CKOS, Yorkton)	6
CICC-TV-1	Wynyard, Sask. (see CICC, Yorkton)	12
CHYT-TV-1	Yale, B.C. (see CBUT, Vancouver)	4
*CBHT-3	Yarmouth, N.S. (see CBHT, Halifax)	11
*†CBHFT-1	Yarmouth, N.S. (see CBAFT, Moncton)	3
CJCH-TV-7	Yarmouth, N.S. (see CJCH, Halifax)	13/40
CABL	**Yellowknife, N.W.T.** (Mackenzie Media Ltd., Box 1469, X0E 1H0) 403/873-2226	3/12
*CFYK-TV	Yellowknife, N.W.T. (satellite fed relay station)	8
*CBYT-14	York Harbour, Nfld. (see CBYT, Corner Brook)	9
CKOS-TV	**Yorkton, Sask.** (Yorkton Television Co. Ltd., 95 E. Broadway, S3N 2V9) 306/783-3685	5
CICC-TV	**Yorkton, Sask.** (Yorkton Television Co. Ltd., 95 E. Broadway, S3N 2V9) 306/783-3685	10
*†CBKFT-5	Zenon Park, Sask. (re-b. CBKFT-1, Saskatoon)	21

ALPHABETICAL LIST OF COMMUNITY ANTENNA TELEVISION SYSTEMS BY TRANSMITTING LOCATION

Abbotsford-Clearbrook, B.C.	M.S.A. Cablevision Ltd., 31450 Marshall Rd., Box 2125, Clearbrook PO, Abbotsford, B.C. V2T 3X8 (604/859-4848)
Acton, Ont	Halton Cable Systems Ltd., 11 Main St. N., Acton, Ont. L7J 1V9 (519/853-1270)

Airdrie, Alta.	See Calgary Cable TV, Calgary
Ajax-Pickering, Ont.	Maclean-Hunter Cable TV Ltd., 91 Station St., Unit #3, Ajax, Ont. L1S 3H2 (416/683-1751)
Alliston, Ont.	Borden Cable TV/FM, 129 Victoria St. W., Alliston, Ont. L0M 1A0 (705/435-4601)
Alma, P.Q.	Cablovision Alma Inc., 590 Collard St., Alma, P.Q. G8B 1N2 (418/668-3318)
Almonte, Ont.	See Ottawa Cablevision, Ottawa
Altona, Man.	See Valley Cable, Carman
Amherst, N.S.	Central Cable Television Ltd., Box 99, Amherst, N.S. B4H 3Y6 (902/667-7201)
Ancaster, Ont.	See Western Co-Axial, Hamilton
Angus, Ont.	See Borden Cable, Alliston
Anjou, P.Q.	See Cablevision Nationale, Montréal
Annieville, B.C.	See Delta Cable Television, Delta
Antigonish, N.S.	Antigonish Cablevision Ltd., Box 1441, 30 College St., Antigonish, N.S. B2G 2L7 (902/863-5888)
Arnprior, Ont.	Arnprior Cablevision Ltd., 12 Elgin St. W., Arnprior, Ont. K7S 1N3 (613/623-6541) See also Ottawa Cablevision, Ottawa
Arthabaska, P.Q.	See Cablevision Nationale, Victoriaville
Arthur, Ont.	See Country Cable, Listowel
Asbestos, P.Q.	Cablovision Inc., 334 Rue Saint-Edmond, Asbestos, P.Q. J1T 2A5 (819/879-5222)
Ascot Canton, P.Q.	See Cablevision Nationale, Sherbrooke
Athabasca, Alta.	See Northern Cablevision, Edmonton
Atikokan, Ont.	Nor-Video Services Ltd., 24 Hematite, Box 1840, Atikokan, Ont. P0T 1C0 (807/597-6050)
Aurora, Ont.	Aurora Cable TV Ltd., Box 151, Aurora, Ont. L4G 3H3 (416/272-6951)
Ayer's Cliff, P.Q.	Transvision Magog, Division Ayer's Cliff, c/o Magog address
Aylmer, Ont.	East Elgin Cable TV Ltd., 18 Sydenham St. E., Aylmer, Ont. N5H 1L2 (519/773-3162)
Aylmer, P.Q.	See Télécâble Laurentien, Hull
Baden, Ont.	See Grand River Cable TV, Kitchener
Bagotville, P.Q.	Video Dery Ltée, 338 Rue Albert, C.P. 1154, Bagotville, P.Q. G7B 3P3 (418/544-3358)
Baie Comeau, P.Q.	Cablovision Baie Comeau Inc., 26 La Salle, Baie Comeau, P.Q. G4Z 1K3 (418/296-2440)
Baie St-Paul, P.Q.	Cablovision Baie St-Paul, Inc., 21 boul. Fafard, C.P. 778, Baie St-Paul, Charlevoix, P.Q. G0A 1B0
Balm Beach, Ont.	See Maclean-Hunter Cable TV, Midland
Banff, Alta.	Banff Community Antenna Ltd., Box 241, Banff, Alta. T0L 0C0 (403/762-2023)
Barkers Point, N.B.	See City Cablevision, Fredericton
Barrhead, Alta.	See QCTV, Edmonton
Barrie, Ont.	Barrie Cable TV/FM, 61 Patterson Rd., Barrie, Ont. L4N 3V9 (705/728-3644)
Bathurst, N.B.	North East Cablevision Ltd., Box 880, Bathurst, N.B. E2A 4H7 (506/548-8991)
Beach Grove, B.C.	See Delta Cable Television, Delta
Beachville, Ont.	See Western Cable TV, Woodstock
Beardmore, Ont.	See Modern Radio, Geraldton
Beaumont, Alta.	See Capital Cable, Edmonton
Beausejour, Man.	See Interlake Cable TV, Selkirk
Beauport, P.Q.	See Cablevision Nationale, Montréal
Bedford, N.S.	See Metrovision Ltd., Sackville
Beechville, N.S.	See Halifax Cablevision, Halifax
Belleville, Ont.	Cablevue (Quinte) Ltd., 160 Front St., Box 149, Belleville, Ont. K8N 4Z9 (613/968-5523)
Bellevue, Alta.	See Crowsnest Pass
Beloeil, P.Q.	Télécable Videotron, 3700 Boul. Losch, St-Hubert, P.Q. J3Y 5T6 (514/656-2111)
Beresford, N.B.	See North East Cablevision, Bathurst
Bernieres, P.Q.	See Télécable de la Rive-Sud, Levis
Bible Hill, N.S.	See Eastern Cablevision, Truro
Bishop's Falls, Nfld.	See Central Cable, Grand Falls
Blainville, P.Q.	See Video Cable Service, Laval
Block House, N.S.	Tri Town Cable T.V. Ltd., Box 84, Block House, N.S. B0J 1E0 (902/624-8305)
Blueberry Creek, B.C.	See Cable West TV, Montrose
Boisbriand, P.Q.	See Video Cable Service, Laval
Boissevain, Man.	See Westman Media, Brandon
Bolton, Ont.	Albion Cable T.V. Ltd., 4856 Yonge St., Willowdale, Ont. M2N 5N2 (416/857-1802)
Bonnyville, Alta	See Northern Cablevision, Edmonton
Borden (C.F.B.), Ont.	See Borden Cable, Alliston
Boundary Bay, B.C.	See Delta Cable Television, Delta
Bowden, Alta.	See QCTV, Edmonton
Bow Island, Alta.	See Taber Cable Television, Taber
Bowmanville, Ont.	See Pine Ridge Cable TV, Oshawa
Bracebridge, Ont.	See Gravenhurst Cable, Gravenhurst
Bradford, Ont.	See Jarmain Cable T.V., Newmarket
Brampton, Ont.	Rogers Cable TV, Brampton, 13 Hansen Rd. S., Brampton, Ont. L6W 3H6 (416/456-2280)
Brandon, Man.	Westman Media Cooperative Ltd., Box 1086, Brandon, Man. R7A 6A3 (204/727-6413)
Brantford, Ont.	Jarmain Cable TV, Box 1074, Brantford, Ont. N3T 5S7 (519/759-3020)
Breslau, Ont.	See Grand River Cable TV, Kitchener

Bridgeport, Ont.	See Grand River Cable TV, Kitchener
Bridgewater, N.S.	See Tri Town Cable TV, Block House
Brights Cove, Ont.	See Maclean Hunter Cable TV, Sarnia
Brooklin, Ont.	See Pine Ridge Cable TV, Oshawa
Brooklyn, N.S.	See Able Cablevision, Liverpool
Brooklyn, N.S.	See Viking Cable T.V., Yarmouth
Brooks, Alta.	Brooks Community Television, Box 1828, Brooks, Alta. T0J 0J0 (403/362-6511)
Burlington, Ont.	Burlington Cablenet, 1245 #5 Hwy., Box 216, Burlington, Ont. L7R 3Y2 (416/335-4655)
Burnaby, B.C.	See Vancouver Cablevision, Vancouver
Burnaby, B.C.	West Coast Cablevision Ltd., 6665 E. Hastings St., Burnaby, B.C. V5B 1S1 (604/291-6691)
Bushell Park CFB, Sask.	See Prairie Co-Ax TV, Moose Jaw
Caledon, Ont.	See Rogers Cable TV, Brampton
Calgary, Alta.	Calgary Cable T.V. Ltd., 2001 27th Ave. N.E., Calgary, Alta. T2E 7E5 (403/230-1841)
Calgary, Alta.	Community Antenna Television Ltd., 3003 Macleod Trail S.E., Calgary, Alta. T2G 2P8 (403/261-0970)
Cambridge (Galt), Ont.	See Grand River Cable TV, Kitchener
Campbell River, B.C.	Campbell River T.V. Association, 594-11th Ave., Campbell River, B.C. V9W 4G4 (604/287-8801)
Camp Borden, Ont.	See Borden Cable, Alliston
Camrose, Alta.	Cable TV Camrose/Wetaskiwin, 4910 46th St., Camrose, Alta. T4V 1H1 (403/672-8839)
Cap-de-la-Madeleine, P.Q.	Cablevision Nationale, Ltee, C.P. 484, Cap-de-la-Madeleine, P.Q. G8T 7W6 (819/375-0161)
Carberry, Man.	See Westman Media, Brandon
Cardston, Alta.	See QCTV, Edmonton
Carillon Gardens, Ont.	See Cie Cable Vision de Hawkesbury, Hawkesbury
Carleton Place, Ont.	See Ottawa Cablevision, Ottawa
Carman, Man.	Valley Cable Vision Limited, Box 1266, Morden, Man. R0G 0J0 (204/822-5635)
Castlegar, B.C.	See Cable West TV, Montrose
Caughnawaga (Reserve), P.Q.	See Cablevision Nationale, Montreal
Central Saanich, B.C.	See Saanich Cablevision, Sidney
Chapais, P.Q.	See Gagnon TV, St-Felicien
Charlesbourg, P.Q.	See Cablevision Nationale, Montreal
Charlottetown, P.E.I.	Island Cablevision Ltd., Box 1750, Charlottetown, P.E.I. C1A 7N4 (902/569-4101)
Charny, P.Q.	See Telecable de la Rive-Sud, Lévis
Chateauguay, P.Q.	See Cablevision Nationale, Montréal
Chatham, N.B.	See Miramichi Cable Ltd., Newcastle
Chatham, Ont.	Chatham Cable TV Ltd., 491 Richmond St., Chatham, Ont. N7M 1R2 (519/352-8270)
Chesley, Ont.	See Saugeen Telecable, Hanover
Chibougamau, P.Q.	See Gagnon TV, St-Felicien
Chilliwack, B.C.	CableNet Chilliwack, 25 Nowell St. S., Chilliwack, B.C. V2P 7G7 (604/792-4626)
Clair, N.B.	See Edmundston Cablevision, Edmundston
Claresholm, Alta.	See QCTV, Edmonton
Clearbrook, B.C.	See M.S.A. Cablevision, Abbotsford
Clementsport, N.S.	See Digby Cable TV, Digby
Clinton, Ont.	Airland Communication Services Ltd., R.R. 2, Clinton, Ont. N0M 1L0 (519/245-2200)
Clinton, Ont.	Bluewater Cable TV Ltd., R.R. 2, Clinton, Ont. N0M 1L0 (519/482-9233)
Clinton, Ont.	Ex-Con Cablevision Ltd., R.R. 2, Clinton, Ont. N0M 1L0 (519/482-9233)
Coaldale, Alta.	See Cablevision Lethbridge, Lethbridge
Coaticook, P.Q.	Transvision Coaticook Inc., 85 rue Child, Coaticook, P.Q. J1A 2B2 (819/849-4028)
Cobalt, Ont.	See Clear Crest Cable TV, New Liskeard
Cobourg, Ont.	Northumberland Cable TV Ltd., 10 King St. E., Cobourg, Ont. K9A 1K7 (416/372-2274)
Cochrane, Alta	See Calgary Cable TV, Calgary
Cochrane, Ont.	See Timmins Cable Services, Timmins
Collingwood, Ont.	Maclean-Hunter Cable TV Ltd., 100 Mountain Rd., #1, Collingwood, Ont. L9Y 3Z8 (705/445-3400)
Comox, B.C.	See Comox Valley CableNet, Courtenay
Comox Valley, B.C.	See Comox
Conestoga, Ont.	See Grand River Cable TV, Kitchener
Coquitlam, B.C.	See Fraser Cablevision, Port Coquitlam
Corner Brook, Nfld.	Shellbird Cable Ltd., Box 604, Corner Brook, Nfld. A2H 6G7 (709/639-9161)
Cornwall, Ont.	Cornwall Cablevision, 517 Pitt St., Cornwall, Ont. K6J 3R4 (613/932-6451)
Cornwallis, N.S.	See Digby Cable TV, Digby
Corunna, Ont.	See Maclean Hunter Cable TV, Sarnia
Cote Saint-Luc, P.Q.	See Cable TV Ltée, Montréal
Côte Saint-Luc, P.Q.	See Cablevision Nationale, Montréal
Courtenay, B.C.	Comox Valley CableNet Ltd., 1591 McPhee Ave., Courtenay, B.C. V9N 3A6 (604/334-4741)
Cowansville, P.Q.	Transvision Cowansville Inc., 354 Rue Principale, Granby, P.Q. J2G 2W6 (514/378-7905)
Cowichan Bay, B.C.	See Cowichan Cablevision, Duncan
Cowley, Alta.	See Crowsnest Cablevision, Crowsnest Pass

Crescent Beach, B.C.	See White Rock Cablevision, White Rock
Creston, B.C.	Creston Cabled-Video Ltd., Box 2880, Creston, B.C. V0B 1G0 (604/428-5317)
Crowsnest Pass, Alta.	Crowsnest Cablevision Ltd., Box 400, Bellevue, Alta. T0K 0C0 (403/562-2889)
Cultus Lake, B.C.	See CableNet, Chilliwack
Cumberland, B.C.	See Comox Valley CableNet, Courtenay
Cumberland, Ont	See Skyline Cablevision, Ottawa
Danville, P.Q.	Trans-Vision de Danville Inc., 12 Du Carmel, C.P. 570, Danville, P.Q. J0A 1A0 (819/839-2711)
Dartmouth, N.S.	Dartmouth Cable TV Ltd., 190 Victoria Rd., Box 1011, Dartmouth, N.S. B2Y 4A4 (902/469-9540)
Dauphin, Man.	See Westman Media, Brandon
D'Auteuil, P.Q.	See Video Cable Service, Laval
Dayton, N.S.	See Viking Cable T.V., Yarmouth
Deauville, P.Q.	See Cablevision Nationale, Sherbrooke
Deep River, Ont.	Deep River Video Ltd., Box 23, (Wylie Rd.), Deep River, Ont. K0J 1P0 (613/584-4488)
Deer Lake, Nfld.	See Shellbird Cable, Corner Brook
Deloraine, Man.	See Westman Media, Brandon
Delta, B.C.	Delta Cable Television Ltd., 5381-48th Ave., Delta, B.C. V4K 1W7 (604/946-7676)
Des Chenes, P.Q.	See Télécâble Laurentien, Hull
Deux Montagnes, P.Q.	See Video Cable Service, Laval
Devon, Alta.	See QCTV, Edmonton
Didsbury, Alta.	See QCTV, Edmonton
Dieppe, N.B.	See Cable Service Ltd., Moncton
Digby, N.S.	Digby Cable TV, Box 1090, Digby, N.S. B0V 1A0 (902/245-2519)
Disraeli, P.Q.	Transvision (Disraeli) Inc., 142 Rue St-Thomas, Disraeli, P.Q. G0N 1E0 (418/449-2700)
Dolbeau, P.Q.	Dolbeau TV Service Inc., 245 7ième Ave., Dolbeau, P.Q. G8L 1Y3 (418/276-2291)
Don Mills, Ont.	See Rogers Cable TV, Toronto
Dorval, P.Q.	See Cable TV Inc., Montreal
Douglastown, N.B.	See Miramichi Cable Ltd., Newcastle
Drayton Valley, Alta.	See QCTV, Edmonton
Drumheller, Alta.	See QCTV, Edmonton
Drummond, N.B.	See M.V. Cablevision, Grand Falls
Drummondville, P.Q.	Cablestrie Inc., 1960 boul. Lemire, Drummondville, P.Q. J2B 6X5 (819/477-3939)
Dryden, Ont.	Dryden Community T.V., 61A King St., Dryden, Ont. P8N 1B7 (807/223-5525)
Duncan, B.C.	Cowichan Cablevision Ltd., 35 Queens Rd., Duncan, B.C. V9L 2W1 (604/748-9113)
Dundas, Ont.	See Western Co-Axial, Hamilton
Durham, Ont.	See Saugeen Telecable, Hanover
Earlstown, P.Q.	See Lennoxville Transvision, Lennoxville
East Angus, P.Q.	Transvision East Angus-Weedon Inc., 257 St. Jean W., East Angus, P.Q. J0B 1R0 (819/832-3023)
East York, Ont.	See Rogers Cable T.V., Toronto
Edmonton, Alta.	Capital Cable TV Ltd., 7024-101st Ave., Edmonton, Alta. T6A 0H7 (403/468-7111)
Edmonton, Alta.	Northern Cablevision Ltd., 5358 89th St., Edmonton, Alta. T6E 5P9 (403/465-3489)
Edmonton, Alta.	QCTV Ltd., 10538-114th St., Edmonton, Alta. T5H 3J7 (403/425-8410)
Edmundston, N.B.	Edmundston Cablevision Ltd., 9 Hill St., Edmundston, N.B. E3V 1H7 (506/735-3371)
Edson, Alta.	See QCTV, Edmonton
Elkford, B.C.	See Fernie Television, Fernie (604/865-2463)
Elk Valley, B.C.	See Fernie Television, Fernie
Ellershouse, N.S.	See Windsor Cable TV, Windsor
Elmira, Ont.	See Grand River Cable TV, Kitchener
English Bluff, B.C.	See Delta Cable Television, Delta
Enoch, Alta.	See QCTV, Edmonton
Estevan, Sask	Estevan CableNet, (Div. of CableNet Ltd.), 1229 4th St., Estevan, Sask. S7A 0W8 (306/634-3822)
Etobicoke, Ont.	See Maclean-Hunter Cable TV, Toronto
Etobicoke, Ont.	See Rogers Cable T.V., Toronto
Exeter, Ont.	See Ex-Con Cablevision, Clinton
Fabreville, P.Q.	See Video Cable Service, Laval
Fairfield Island, B.C.	See CableNet, Chilliwack
Fall River, N.S.	See Metrovision Ltd., Sackville
Fernie, B.C.	Fernie Television Ltd., Box 1769, Fernie, B.C. V0B 1M0 (604/425-6442)
Fletcher's Lake, N.S.	See Metrovision Ltd., Sackville
Fonthill, Ont.	See Armstrong Communications, Welland
Fort Frances, Ont.	Norwont Ltd., Box 1840, Atikokan, Ont. P0T 1C0 (807/274-5522)
Fort Macleod, Alta.	See QCTV, Edmonton
Fort McMurray, Alta.	ABC Cable TV, Alta. Broadcasting Corp. Ltd., #200, 208 Beacon Hill Dr., Fort McMurray, Alta. T9H 2R1 (403/743-3717)
Fort Saskatchewan, Alta.	See Capital Cable, Edmonton
Fredericton, N.B.	City Cablevision Ltd., 594 Queen St., Box 1569, Fredericton, N.B. E3B 5G3 (506/454-3319)
Frost Village, P.Q.	See Waterloo T.V., Waterloo, P.Q.
Fruitvale, B.C.	See Cable West TV Ltd., Montrose
Gander, Nfld.	Omni Cable, Box 74, Gander, Nfld. A1V 1W5 (709/651-2345)
Gentilly, P.Q.	Video-Centre, 4050 des Verdiers, Gentilly, P.Q. G0X 1G0 (819/298-2792)

Georgetown, Ont.	See Halton Cable, Acton
Geraldton, Ont.	Modern Radio & TV Systems, 112 3rd Ave. N.E., Box 910, Geraldton, Ont. P0T 1M0 (807/854-1569)
Gibson's Landing, B.C.	See Coast Cable Vision, Sechelt
Girardville, P.Q.	See Téléval Inc., Roberval
Gladstone, Man.	See Westman Media, Brandon
Gloucester, Ont.	See Skyline Cablevision, Ottawa
Goderich, Ont.	See Bluewater Cable TV, Clinton
Golden, B.C.	Golden Television Ltd., Box 574, 818 E. 10th Ave., Golden, B.C. V0A 1H0 (604/344-6627)
Gore Bay, Ont.	Gore Bay Community TV System, Box 295, Gore Bay, Ont. P0P 1H0 (705/282-2091)
Goulbourn, Ont.	See Ottawa Cablevision, Ottawa
Granby, P.Q.	Transvision (Granby) Inc., 354 Rue Principale, Granby, P.Q. J2G 2W6 (514/378-7905)
Grande Cache, Alta.	See Nothern Cablevision, Edmonton
Grande Centre, Alta.	See Northern Cablevision, Edmonton
Grand Falls, N.B.	M.V. Cablevision Ltd., Box 1658, Grand Falls, N.B. E0J 1M0 (506/473-4771)
Grand Falls, Nfld.	Central Cable Systems, Box 636, Grand Falls, Nfld. A2A 2K2 (709/489-9071)
Grand-Mère, P.Q.	Cablodistribution Le Rocher Inc., 1360, 6e Ave., Grande-Mère, P.Q. G9T 2J6 (819/538-3889)
Grande Prairie, Alta.	See Nothern Cablevision, Edmonton
Granum, Alta.	See QCTV, Edmonton
Gravenhurst, Ont.	Gravenhurst Cable System Ltd., Box 327, Gravenhurst, Ont. P0C 1G0 (705/687-3765)
Greendale, B.C.	See CableNet, Chilliwack
Greenfield Park, P.Q.	See Cablevision Nationale, Montréal
Greensville, Ont.	See Western Co-Axial, Hamilton
Grimsby, Ont.	Grimsby Cable T.V. Ltd., 27 Kingsway Blvd., Grimsby, Ont. L3M 3E4 (416/945-4932)
Guelph, Ont.	Maclean Hunter Cable TV, 18 MacDonnell St., Guelph, Ont. N1H 6M1 (519/824-2030)
Haileybury, Ont.	See Clear Crest Cable TV, New Liskeard
Halfmoon Bay, B.C.	See Coast Cable Vision, Sechelt
Halifax, N.S.	Halifax Cablevision Ltd., Box 8660, Halifax, N.S. B3K 5M3 (902/453-2800)
Hamilton, Ont.	Hamilton Co-Axial, 1120 Main St. E., Hamilton, Ont. L8M 1P1 (416/547-2376)
Hamilton, Ont.	Maclean-Hunter Cable TV, 212 James St. S., Hamilton, Ont. L8P 3B1 (416/522-0123)
Hamilton, Ont.	See Niagara Co-Axial, Stoney Creek
Hamilton, Ont.	Northgate Cable T.V. Ltd., 110 King St. W., #640, Hamilton, Ont. L8P 4T8 (416/522-1400)
Hamilton, Ont.	Western Co-Axial Ltd., 110 King St. W., Hamilton, Ont. L8P 4T8 (416/522-3012)
Hanover, Ont.	Saugeen Telecable Ltd., Box 56, 275-10th St., Hanover, Ont. N4N 1P1 (519/364-2131)
Hantsport, N.S.	See Windsor Cable TV, Windsor
Harrietsfield, N.S.	See Halifax Cablevision, Halifax
Harriston, Ont.	See Country Cable, Listowel
Hauterive, P.Q.	See Cablovision Baie Comeau Inc., Baie Comeau
Hawkesbury, Ont.	Cie Cable Vision de Hawkesbury, Ltée., 305 Laurier St., Hawkesbury, Ont. K6A 2A3 (613/632-2514)
Hearst, Ont.	See Timmins Cable Services, Timmins
Hermitage, P.Q.	See Transvision Magog, Magog
Herring Cove, N.S.	See Halifax Cablevision, Halifax
Hespeler, Ont.	See Grand River Cable TV, Kitchener
Highland Park, N.S.	See Metrovision Ltd., Sackville
High River, Alta.	See QCTV, Edmonton
Hilden, N.S.	See Eastern Cablevision Ltd., Truro
Hinton, Alta.	Rocky Mountain CATV Ltd., Box 3140, Hinton, Alta. T0E 1C0 (403/865-2745)
Holland Landing, Ont.	See Jarmain Cable T.V., Newmarket
Hope, B.C.	Hope Cable Television Ltd., Box 489, Hope, B.C. V0X 1L9 (604/869-2618)
Hull, P.Q.	Télécâble Laurentien Inc., 5 rue Morin, Hull, P.Q. J8X 2M5 (819/771-7715)
Huntingdon, P.Q.	See Lennoxville Transvision, Lennoxville
Huntsville, Ont.	Maclean-Hunter Cable TV, 20 West St. S., Huntsville, Ont. P0A 1K0 (705/789-2731)
Ingersoll, Ont.	See Western Cable TV, Woodstock
Innisfail, Alta.	See QCTV, Edmonton
Iroquois Falls, Ont.	See Timmins Cable Services, Timmins
Jasper, Alta.	Jasper Community Television Ltd., Box 489, Jasper, Alta. T0E 1E0 (403/852-4851)
Kaleden, B.C.	See Penticton Cable T.V., Penticton
Kamloops, B.C.	Kamloops Cablenet Ltd., 180 Briar Ave., Kamloops, B.C. V2B 1C1 (604/376-7204)
Kanata, Ont.	See Ottawa Cablevision, Ottawa
Kapuskasing, Ont.	See Timmins Cable Services, Timmins
Kaslo, B.C.	Kaslo Television Ltd., Box 1056, Kaslo, B.C. V0G 1M0 (604/353-2547)
Kelowna, B.C.	Kelowna Cable T.V. Ltd., Box 550, Kelowna, B.C. V1Y 7P2 (604/762-4433)
Killarney, Man.	See Westman Media, Brandon
Kimberley, B.C.	Kootenay Enterprises Ltd., c/o Box 1769, Fernie, B.C. V0B 1M0 (604/427-2463)
Kincardine, Ont.	Kincardine Cable TV Ltd., Box 1028, 223 Bruce Ave., Kincardine, Ont. N0G 2G0 (519/396-7802)
Kingsgate, B.C.	See Creston Cabled-Video, Creston

Kingston, Ont.	Kingston Cablenet Ltd., 335 King St. E., Kingston, Ont. K7L 3B5 (613/544-6311)
Kingsville, Ont.	See Essex Cable T.V., Leamington
Kinnaird, B.C.	See Cable West TV, Montrose
Kirkland, P.Q.	See Cable TV Inc., Montréal
Kirkland Lake, Ont.	Fred Lang TV Ltd., 29 Prospect Ave., Kirkland Lake, Ont. P2N 2V3 (705/567-9383)
Kitchener, Ont.	Grand River Cable TV Ltd., 85 Grand Crest Pl., Box 488, Kitchener, Ont. N2G 4A8 (519/893-2101)
Kitimat, B.C.	See Skeena Broadcasters, Terrace
La Baie, P.Q.	See Video Déry, Bagotville
Lac aux Sables, P.Q.	Gilles Buisson, 800, Rue Principale, Lac aux Sables, P.Q. G0X 1M0 (418/336-2988)
Lachine, P.Q.	See Cablevision Nationale, Montréal
Lachute, P.Q.	Transvision Magog Inc., Division Lachute, c/o 15 St-Patrice O., Magog, P.Q. J1X 1V8 (819/843-3358)
Lac Megantic, P.Q.	Megantic Transvision Inc., 5084 rue Frontenac, Lac Megantic, P.Q. G6B 1H3 (819/583-0432)
Lacombe, Alta.	See QCTV, Edmonton
Lac St-Jean, P.Q.	See Cablovision Alma Inc., Alma
Ladner, B.C.	See Delta Cable Television, Delta
La Dore, P.Q.	See Gagnon TV, St-Felicien
Lakeside, N.S.	See Halifax Cablevision, Halifax
Lakeview Heights, B.C.	See Kelowna Cable TV, Kelowna
Lambeth, Ont.	See Maclean-Hunter Cable TV, London
Lancaster Park, Alta.	See Capital Cable, Edmonton
Langley, B.C.	See Western Cablevision, Surrey
La Pocatière, P.Q.	Cablodistribution de la Côte du Sud Inc., C.P. 500, La Pocatière, P.Q. G0R 1Z0 (418/856-2253)
La Salle, P.Q.	See Cable TV Ltée, Montréal
La Tuque, P.Q.	Electro-Vision (La Tuque) Inc., 333 St-Joseph, La Tuque, P.Q. G9X 1L3 (819/523-3737)
Lauzon, P.Q.	See Telecable de la Rive-Sud, Lévis
Laval, P.Q.	Video Cable Service (Div. of Treeford Ltd.), 3665 boul. Ste-Rose, Fabreville, Laval, P.Q. H7P 1C5 (514/622-1880)
Laval, P.Q.	See Cablevision Nationale, Montréal
Laval-sur-le-Lac, P.Q.	See Video Cable Service, Laval
Leamington, Ont.	Essex Cable T.V. Ltd., 94 Talbot St. E., Leamington, Ont. N8H 1L3 (519/326-4423)
Leduc, Alta.	See Capital Cable, Edmonton
Lemoyne, P.Q.	See Cablevision Nationale, Montréal
Lennoxville, P.Q.	Lennoxville Transvision Inc., 114 Queen St., Lennoxville, P.Q. J1M 1J6 (819/567-7969)
Lethbridge, Alta.	Cablevision Lethbridge, (Div. of CableNet Ltd.), 728 13th St. N., Lethbridge, Alta. T1H 2T1 (403/328-1222)
Lévis, P.Q.	Telecable de la Rive-Sud Inc., 150 Trans Canada Est, C.P. 1246, Lévis, P.Q. G6V 6R8 (418/833-1920)
Lindsay, Ont.	Lindsay CATV System Ltd., 55 George St. W., Lindsay, Ont. K9V 4V6 (705/324-4217)
Listowel, Ont.	Country Cable Ltd., 360 Wallace Ave. N., Listowel, Ont. N4W 1L4 (519/291-3551); 1-800-265-3227
Little River, B.C.	See Comox Valley CableNet, Courtenay
Liverpool, N.S.	Able Cablevision Ltd., 212 Main St., Box 449, Liverpool, N.S. B0T 1K0 (902/354-3424)
Lloydminster, Alta.	See QCTV, Edmonton
Loggieville, N.B.	See Miramichi Cable Ltd., Newcastle
London, Ont.	London Cable TV, 800 York St., London, Ont. N6A 5B1 (519/672-7704)
London, Ont.	Maclean-Hunter TV Ltd., 499 MacGregor Ave., London, Ont. N6J 2K9 (519/433-0141)
Longueuil, P.Q.	See Cablevision Nationale, Montréal
Loretteville, P.Q.	See Cablevision Nationale, Montréal
L'Orignal, Ont.	See Cie Cable Vision de Hawkesbury, Hawkesbury
Lower Nicola, B.C.	See Merritt Cablevision Ltd., Merritt
Lower Sackville, N.S.	See Metrovision Ltd., Sackville
Lucerne, P.Q.	See Télécâble Laurentien, Hull
Lundbreck, Alta.	See Crowsnest Cablevision, Crowsnest Pass
Lunenburg, N.S.	See Tri Town Cable TV, Block House
Magog, P.Q.	Transvision Magog Inc., 15 O. Rue St. Patrice, Magog, P.Q. J1X 1V8 (819/843-3358)
Mahone Bay, N.S.	See Tri Town Cable TV, Block House
Malartic, P.Q.	See Cablevision du Nord de Québec, Val d'Or
Manheim, Ont.	See Grand River Cable TV, Kitchener
Manitouwadge, Ont.	See Lakeshore Community Television, Terrace Bay
Maple Ridge, B.C.	See Fraser Cablevision, Port Coquitlam
Marathon, Ont.	See Lakeshore Community Television, Terrace Bay
Markham, Ont.	See Classic Communications, Richmond Hill
Marysville, N.B.	See City Cablevision, Fredericton
Matsqui, B.C.	See M.S.A. Cablevision, Abbotsford
McMasterville, P.Q.	See Télécâble Videotron, Beloeil
Meaford, Ont.	See Maclean-Hunter Cable TV, Owen Sound

Medicine Hat, Alta. .... Cablevision Medicine Hat Ltd., 1111 Kingsway Ave. S.E., Medicine Hat, Alta. T1A 2Y1 (403/527-5586)
Melita, Man. .... See Westman Media, Brandon
Merritt, B.C. .... Merritt Cablevision Ltd., Box 908, 2040 Granite Ave., Merritt, B.C. V0K 2B0 (604/378-2568)
Mersey Point, N.S. .... See Able Cablevision, Liverpool
Michel, B.C. .... See Fernie Television Ltd., Fernie
Midland, Ont. .... Maclean-Hunter Cable TV Ltd., Box 489, Balm Beach Rd., Midland, Ont. L4R 4L3 (705/526-5031)
Milton, N.S. .... See Able Cablevision, Liverpool
Milton, Ont. .... See Halton Cable, Acton
Minnedosa, Man. .... See Westman Media, Brandon
Mission, B.C. .... See Fraser Cablevision, Port Coquitlam
Mississauga-Streetsville, Ont. .... See Maclean-Hunter Cable TV, Toronto
Mississauga, Ont. .... Rogers Cable TV, 90 Dundas St. W., Mississauga, Ont. L5B 2T5 (416/270-2424)
Mistassini, P.Q. .... See Dolbeau TV Service, Dolbeau
Moncton, N.B. .... Cable Service Ltd./Ltée, 90 Driscoll Cres., Box 1310, Moncton, N.B. E1C 8T6 (506/854-8700)
Montmagny, P.Q. .... La Belle Vision Inc., 70 rue du Palais de Justice, C.P. 445, Montmagny, P.Q. G5V 3S7 (418/248-5697)
Mont-Rolland, P.Q. .... See Télédiffusion Ste-Adele Inc., Ste-Adele
Montreal, P.Q. .... Cable TV Inc., 8360 Mayrand St., Montreal, P.Q. H4P 2E1 (514/731-7951)
Montreal, P.Q. .... Cablevision Nationale Ltée, 90 Beaubien St. W., Montréal, P.Q. H2S 1V7 (514/270-6031) Telex: 055-60633
Montreal Est, P.Q. .... See Cablevision Nationale, Montréal
Montreal Nord, P.Q. .... See Cablevision Nationale, Montréal
Montreal Ouest, P.Q. .... See Cablevision Nationale, Montréal
Montrose, B.C. .... Cable West TV Ltd., 1471 Pemberton Ave., North Vancouver, B.C. V7P 2R9 (604/985-2151)
Moose Jaw, Sask. .... Prairie Co-Ax TV Ltd., 201 Manitoba St. E., Box 760, Moose Jaw, Sask. S6H 4P5 (306/693-8585)
Moose Jaw, Sask. .... Teletheatre (Moose Jaw) Ltd., 201 Manitoba St. E., Box 760, Moose Jaw, Sask. S6H 4P5 (306/693-8607)
Morden, Man. .... See Valley Cable Vision, Carman
Morinville, Alta. .... See QCTV Ltd., Edmonon
Mount Denson, N.S. .... See Windsor Cable TV, Windsor
Mount Forest, Ont. .... See Country Cable, Listowel
Mount Pleasant, Ont. .... See Jarmain Cable TV, Brantford
Mount Royal, P.Q. .... See Cable TV Inc., Montréal
Nackawic, N.B. .... See Woodstock Community TV, Woodstock
Nanaimo, B.C. .... Cable West TV Ltd., 711 Poplar St., Nanaimo, B.C. V9S 5L8 (604/754-5571)
Naramata, B.C. .... See Penticton Cable T.V., Penticton
Nashwaaksis, N.B. .... See City Cablevision, Fredericton
Natal,B.C. .... See Fernie Television, Fernie
Neepawa, Man. .... See Westman Media, Brandon
Nelson, B.C. .... See Cable West TV, North Vancouver (604/352-3322)
Nelson, N.B. .... See Miramichi Cable Ltd., Newcastle
Nepean, Ont. .... See Ottawa Cablevision, Ottawa
Newcastle, Ont. .... See Pine Ridge Cable TV, Oshawa
Newcastle, N.B. .... Miramichi Cable Ltd., 366 Water St., Newcastle, N.B. E1V 1X3 (506/622-0016)
New Dundee, Ont. .... See Grand River Cable TV, Kitchener
New Glasgow, N.S. .... K-Vision Services Ltd., Box 157, New Glasgow, N.S. B2H 5E2 (902/752-0310)
New Hamburg, Ont. .... See Grand River Cable TV, Kitchener
New Liskeard, Ont. .... Clear Crest Cable T.V. Ltd., Box 271, New Liskeard, Ont. P0J 1P0 (705/647-5394)
Newmarket, Ont. .... Jarmain Cable T.V. Ltd., 20 Gladman Ave., Newmarket, Ont. L3Y 1W5 (416/895-5169)
New Westminster, B.C. .... See Western Cablevision, Surrey
Niagara Falls, Ont. .... See Armstrong Communications, Welland
Nicholson, B.C. .... See Golden Television, Golden
Nigadoo, N.B. .... See North East Cablevision, Bathurst
Nipigon, Ont. .... See Lakeshore Community Television, Terrace Bay
Normandin, P.Q. .... See Téléval Inc., Roberval
North Bay, Ont. .... Maclean Hunter Cable TV, 240 Fee St., Box 3170, North Bay, Ont. P1B 8S4 (705/472-6580)
North Bench, B.C. .... See Golden Television, Golden
North Cowichan, B.C. .... See Cowichan Cablevision, Duncan
North Delta, B.C. .... See Delta Cable Television, Delta
North Hatley, P.Q. .... Transvision Magog, Division North Hatley, c/o Magog address
North Saanich, B.C. .... See Saanich Cablevision, Sidney
North Vancouver, B.C. .... Cable West TV Ltd., 1471 Pemberton Ave., North Vancouver, B.C. V7P 2R9 (604/985-2151)
North York, Ont. .... See Rogers Cable TV, Toronto
North York, Ont. .... See Maclean-Hunter Cable TV, Toronto
North York, Ont. .... See York Cablevision, Toronto
Nottawa, Ont. .... See Maclean-Hunter Cable TV, Collingwood

Oakville, Ont.	Oakville Cablenet, 447 Speers Rd., Oakville, Ont. L6K 3S7 (416/844-2230)
Ocean Park, B.C.	See White Rock Cablevision, White Rock
Okanagan Falls, B.C.	See Penticton Cable T.V., Penticton
Okotoks, Alta.	See QCTV, Edmonton
Olds, Alta.	See QCTV, Edmonton
Oliver, B.C.	Oliver Tele-Vue Ltd., 307 Main St., Box 790, Oliver B.C. V0H 1T0 (604/498-3630)
Omerville, P.Q.	See Transvision Magog, Magog
One Hundred Mile House, B.C.	See Central Interior Cablevision, Prince George
Orangeville, Ont.	Orangeville Cable-Vu Ltd., 10 Mill St., Orangeville, Ont. L9W 2M3 (519/941-4030)
Orillia, Ont.	Orillia Cable TV/FM, 505 Memorial Ave., Box 937, Orillia, Ont. L3V 6K8 (705/325-1376)
Oromocto, N.B.	See City Cablevision, Fredericton
Oshawa, Ont.	Pine Ridge Cable TV, 301 Marwood Dr., Oshawa, Ont. L1H 1J4 (416/579-2232)
Osoyoos, B.C.	See Oliver Telé-Vue, Oliver
Ottawa, Ont.	Skyline Cablevision Ltd., 1810 St. Laurent Blvd., Ottawa, Ont. K1G 0N2 (613/731-8250)
Ottawa, Ont.	Ottawa Cablevision Ltd., 475 Richmond Rd., Box 6315, Stn. J, Ottawa, Ont. K2A 3Y8 (613/725-3581)
Otterburn, P.Q.	See Télécable Videotron, Beloeil
Outremont, P.Q.	See Cablevision Nationale, Montréal
Owen Sound, Ont.	Maclean-Hunter Cable TV Ltd., 320 8th St. E., Owen Sound, Ont. N4K 1L4 (519/376-5195)
Paisley, Ont.	See Southport Cable TV, Port Elgin
Palmerston, Ont.	See Country Cable, Listowel
Paris, Ont.	See Jarmain Cable T.V., Brantford
Parksville, B.C.	District 69 Cablevision Inc., Box 880, Parksville, B.C. V0R 2S0 (604/248-3444)
Parry Sound, Ont.	Radio & T.V. Distribution Ltd., Box 338, 100 Parry Sound Rd., Parry Sound, Ont. P2A 2X4 (705/746-2659)
Pembroke, Ont.	Pembroke Cablevision Ltd., 223 Mackay St., Pembroke, Ont. K8A 1C3 (613/735-6819)
Penetanguishene, Ont.	See Maclean-Hunter Cable TV, Midland
Penticton, B.C.	Penticton Cable T.V. Ltd., 379 Martin St., Penticton, B.C. V2A 6K9 (604/492-5832)
Perkinsfield, Ont.	See Maclean-Hunter Cable TV, Midland
Petawawa, Ont.	See Pembroke Cablevision, Pembroke
Peterborough, Ont.	Peterborough Cable T.V. Ltd., 685 The Queensway, Box 876, Peterborough, Ont. K9J 7J6 (705/742-9264)
Petersburg, Ont.	See Grand River Cable TV, Kitchener
Petit-Rocher, N.B.	See North East Cablevision, Bathurst
Pickering, Ont.	Pickering Cable TV Ltd., 751 McKay Rd., Ste. 1, Pickering, Ont. L1W 3E2 (416/683-9800)
Picton, Ont.	Quinte Cablevision Ltd., 185 Main St., Box 590, Picton, Ont. K0K 2T0 (613/476-2722)
Pictou, N.S.	See K-Vision Services, New Glasgow
Piedmont, P.Q.	See Télédiffusion Ste-Adele Inc., Ste-Adele
Pierrefonds, P.Q.	See Cable TV Inc., Montréal
Pinawa, Man.	See Winnipeg Videon, Winnipeg
Pincher Creek, Alta.	See Crowsnest Cablevision, Crowsnest Pass
Pitt Meadows, B.C.	See Fraser Cablevision, Port Coquitlam
Plessisville, P.Q.	Claire-Vue Inc., 37 Rue St-Joseph O., CP 274, Thetford Mines, P.Q. G6G 3N7 (819/335-6620)
Plymouth, N.S.	See K-Vision Services, New Glasgow
Point Edward, Ont.	See Maclean Hunter Cable TV, Sarnia
Pointe aux Trembles, P.Q.	See Cablevision Nationale, Montréal
Pointe Claire, P.Q.	See Cable TV Ltée, Montréal
Pointe-Verte, N.B.	See North East Cablevision, Bathurst
Ponoka, Alta.	See QCTV, Edmonton
Port Alberni, B.C.	Alberni Cable Television Ltd., 3744 Third Ave., Port Alberni, B.C. V9Y 4G1 (604/723-6295)
Port Alfred, P.Q.	See Video Dery, Bagotville
Port-aux-Basques, Nfld.	Gateway Cable Ltd., Box 219, Port-aux-Basques, Nfld. A0M 1C0 (709/695-7278)
Port Colborne, Ont.	See Armstrong Communications, Welland
Port Coquitlam, B.C.	Fraser Cablevision Limited, 1820 Kingsway Ave., Port Coquitlam, B.C. V3C 1S5 (604/941-9431)
Port Elgin, Ont.	Southport Cable TV Ltd., Box 1330, Port Elgin, Ont. N0H 2C0 (519/832-6851)
Port Guichon, B.C.	See Delta Cable Television, Delta
Port Hope, Ont.	See Northumberland Cable TV, Cobourg
Port McNicoll, Ont.	See Maclean-Hunter Cable TV, Midland
Port Moody, B.C.	See Fraser Cablevision, Port Coquitlam
Port Perry, Ont.	See Compton Cable TV, Uxbridge
Port Stanley, Ont.	See Allview Cable, St. Thomas
Preston, Ont.	See Grand River Cable TV, Kitchener
Prince Albert, Sask.	Community T.V. Ltd., 22-10th St. W., Prince Albert, Sask. S6V 3A5 (306/763-7633)
Prince George, B.C.	Central Interior Cablevision Ltd., 470 Third Ave., Prince George, B.C. V2L 3B9 (604/562-1345)
Prince Rupert, B.C.	See Skeena Broadcasters, Terrace
Qualicum Beach, B.C.	See District 69 Cablevision, Parksville

Québec, P.Q.	Cablevision Nationale Inc., 336 rue du Roi, #101, Quebec, P.Q. G1K 2W5 (418/529-9361)
Quesnel, B.C.	See Central Interior Cablevision, Prince George
Raymond, Alta.	See QCTV, Edmonton
Redcliff, Alta.	See Cablevision Medicine Hat, Medicine Hat
Red Deer, Alta.	Cable West TV Ltd., 6123 48 Ave., Red Deer, Alta. T4N 5Z9 (403/346-6633)
Red Rock, Ont.	See Lakeshore Community Television, Terrace Bay
Regina, Sask.	Cable Regina, #102, 1911 Park St., Regina, Sask. S4N 5Y4 (306/569-3510)
Renfrew, Ont.	Renfrew Cablevision, 363 Raglan St. S., Renfrew, Ont. K7V 1R6 (613/432-4811)
Revelstoke, B.C.	Revelstoke Cable T.V. Ltd., Box 651, 309 MacKenzie Ave., Revelstoke, B.C. V0E 2S0 (604/837-2800)
Richmond, B.C.	See Vancouver Cablevision, Vancouver
Richmond, Ont.	See Ottawa Cablevision, Ottawa
Richmond Hill, Ont.	Classic Communications Ltd., 244 Newkirk Rd., Richmond Hill, Ont. L4C 3S5 (416/884-8111)
Rivers, Man.	See Westman Media, Brandon
Riverview, N.B.	See Cable Service Ltd., Moncton
Rivière-du-Loup, P.Q.	Le Cable de Rivière-du-Loup Ltée, 1 Rue Frontenac, Rivière-du-Loup, P.Q. G5R 1R7 (418/867-1478)
Rivière-Ouelle, P.Q.	See Cablodistribution de la Côte du Sud, La Pocatière
Rivière-Verte, P.Q.	See Le Cable de Rivière-du-Loup, Rivière-du-Loup
Roberval, P.Q.	Televal Inc., 698 rue Otis, Roberval, P.Q. G8H 2J4 (418/275-3773)
Robson, B.C.	See Cable West TV, Montrose
Rockcliffe, Ont.	See Skyline Cablevision, Ottawa
Rock Forest, P.Q.	See Cablevision Nationale, Sherbrooke
Rock Island, P.Q.	Border Community TV Inc., Box 238, Stanstead, P.Q. J0B 3E0 (819/786-2408)
Rosedale, B.C.	See CableNet Chilliwack, Chilliwack
Rosemere, P.Q.	See Video Cable Service, Laval
Rossland, B.C.	See Cable West TV, North Vancouver
Saanich, B.C.	Davin Enterprises Ltd., 4526 Viewmont Ave., Victoria, B.C. V8Z 6A9 (604/479-8611)
Saanich, B.C.	See Saanich Cablevision, Sidney
Sackville, N.S.	Metrovision Ltd., 367 Hwy. #1, Lower Sackville, N.S. B4C 2R7 (902/865-3020)
Ste-Adele, P.Q.	Télédiffusion Sainte-Adèle Inc., 422 Ch. Ste-Marguerite, Ste-Adèle, P.Q. J0R 1L0 (514/229-4555)
St. Albert, Alta.	See Capital Cable, Edmonton
St. Andre, N.B.	See M.V. Cablevision, Grand Falls
Ste-Angele-de-Laval, P.Q.	Venant Deshaies, 2, rue Bourgeois, Ste-Angele-de-Laval, P.Q. (819/222-5544)
St-Antonin, P.Q.	See Le Cable de Rivière-du-Loup, Rivière-du-Loup
St-Aubert, P.Q.	See Cablodistribution de la Côte du Sud, La Pocatière
St-Basile, N.B.	See Edmundston Cablevision, Edmundston
St-Basile, P.Q.	See Télécable Videotron, Beloeil
St-Bruno, P.Q.	See Télécable Videotron, Beloeil
St. Catharines, Ont.	Maclean-Hunter Cable TV, 45 Wright St., St. Catharines, Ont. L2P 3K6 (416/688-2555)
St-Croix, N.S.	See Windsor Cable TV, Windsor
St-David, P.Q.	See Telecable de la Rive-Sud, Lévis
St-Elie d'Orford, P.Q.	See Cablevision Nationale, Sherbrooke
St-Emile, P.Q.	See Cablevision Nationale, Montreal
Ste-Eustache, P.Q.	See Video Cable Service, Laval
St-Evariste, P.Q.	La Guadeloupe Télévision Inc., St-Evariste, P.Q. G0M 1S0 (418/459-6844)
St-Felicien, P.Q.	Gagnon TV Ltée, 1117 rue Monseigneur Bluteau, St-Felicien, P.Q. G0W 2N0 (418/679-0953)
St-Felix du Cap Rouge, P.Q.	See Cablevision Nationale, Montreal
Ste-Flore, P.Q.	See Cablodistribution Le Rocher, Grand'Mère
Ste-Foy, P.Q.	See Cablevision Nationale, Montréal
St. George, Ont.	See Jarmain Cable TV, Brantford
St-Georges-de-Champlain, P.Q.	See Cablodistribution La Rocher, Grand'Mère
St-Hilaire, P.Q.	See Télécable Videotron, Beloeil
St-Hubert, P.Q.	See Télécable Videotron, Beloeil
St. Jacobs, Ont.	See Grand River Cable TV, Kitchener
St. Jacques, N.B.	See Edmundston Cablevision, Edmundston
St-Jean, P.Q.	See Cablodistribution de la Côte du Sud, La Pocatière
St-Jean Chrysostome, P.Q.	See Télécable de la Rive-Sud, Lévis
Saint John, N.B.	Fundy Cablevision Ltd., 55 Waterloo St., Saint John, N.B. E2L 4V9 (506/657-5000)
St. John's, Nfld.	Avalon Cablevision, Box 8596, St. John's, Nfld. A1B 3P2 (709/753-7760)
St-Lambert, P.Q.	See Cablevision Nationale, Montréal
St. Lazare, Man.	St. Lazare Cable TV, c/o Box 160, St. Lazare, Man. R0M 1Y0 (204/683-2335)
St-Leonard, N.B.	See M.V. Cablevision, Grand Falls
St-Léonard, P.Q.	See Cablevision Nationale, Montréal
St-Louis-de-Pintendre, P.Q.	See Télécable de la Rive-Sud, Lévis
Ste-Louise, P.Q.	See Cablodistribution de la Côte du Sud, La Pocatière
St-Marc, P.Q.	Télécable de l'Annonciation Enrg., 26 de L'Islet, St-Marc, P.Q. J0L 2E0 (514/584-3976)
Ste-Marthe, P.Q.	See Cablevision Nationale, Cap-de-la-Madeleine
St-Marthe, P.Q.	Société TV Ste-Marthe Enrg., Ste-Marthe de Gaspé, P.Q. G0E 2H0 (418/288-5575)

St-Nazaire, P.Q.	See Cablovision Alma Inc., Alma
St-Nicolas, P.Q.	See Télécable de la Rive-Sud, Lévis
St-Pacôme, P.Q.	See Cablodistribution de la Côte du Sud, La Pocatière
St. Paul, Alta.	See Northern Cablevision, Edmonton
St-Pierre, P.Q.	See Cablevision Nationale, Montreal
St-Raymond, P.Q.	Video Dery Ltée, C.P. 697, 131 rue St-Joseph, St-Raymond de Portneuf, P.Q. G0A 4G0 (418/337-2413)
St-Redempteur, P.Q.	See Télécable de la Rive-Sud, Lévis
St-Rock, P.Q.	See Cablodistribution de la Côte du Sud, La Pocatière
St-Romauld, P.Q.	See Télécable de la Rive-Sud, Lévis
Ste-Rose, P.Q.	See Video Cable Service, Laval
St-Sauveur, P.Q.	See Télédiffusion Ste-Adele Inc., Ste-Adele
Ste-Thérèse, P.Q.	See Video Cable Service, Laval
St. Thomas, Ont.	Allview Cable Service, 658 Talbot St., St. Thomas, Ont. N5P 1C8 (519/631-5060)
St-Thomas Didyme, P.Q.	See Téléval Inc., Roberval
St-Tite, P.Q.	J. Bergeron & Frère Ltée, 363 Rue St-Paul, St-Tite, Cte. Laviolette, P.Q. G0X 3H0 (418/365-6175)
Salmon River, N.S.	See Eastern Cablevision, Truro
Saltair, B.C.	See Cowichan Cablevision, Duncan
Sardis, B.C.	See CableNet Chilliwack, Chilliwack
Sarnia, Ont.	Maclean Hunter Cable TV, 1550 Confederation St., Box 218, Sarnia, Ont. N7T 7J1 (519/337-3703)
Saskatoon, Sask.	Saskatoon Telecable, 345 4th Ave. S., Box 1950, Saskatoon, Sask. S7K 3S5 (306/664-2121)
Sault Ste. Marie, Ont.	Lake Superior Cablevision, Division of Huron Broadcasting Ltd., 672 Queen St. E., Sault Ste. Marie, Ont. P6A 2A4 (705/949-3901)
Sawyerville, P.Q.	Transvision Sawyerville Inc., 224 Cate, Sherbrooke, P.Q. J1J 2P3 (819/569-2219)
Scarborough, Ont.	Scarboro Cable TV/FM, Unit 33, 705 Progress Ave., Scarborough, Ont. M1H 2X2 (416/438-6370)
Schreiber, Ont.	Ray Sisson Cable TV, Box 84, Schreiber, Ont. P0T 2S0
Sechelt, B.C.	Coast Cable Vision Ltd., Box 218, Sechelt, B.C. V0N 3A0 (604/885-3224)
Selkirk, Man.	Interlake Cable TV Ltd., Box 243, Selkirk, Man. R1A 2B2 (204/785-8701)
Shakespeare, Ont.	See Grand River Cable TV, Kitchener
Sharon, Ont.	See Jarmain Cable TV, Newmarket
Shawinigan, P.Q.	See La Belle Vision, Trois-Rivières
Sherbrooke, P.Q.	Cablevision Nationale Inc., 725 Terrasse, Sherbrooke, P.Q. J1H 1T7 (819/569-5997)
Sherwood Park, Alta.	See Capital Cable, Edmonton
Shilo (C.F.B.), Man.	Shilo Cablevision, Box 40, C.F.B. Shilo, Man. R0K 2A0 (204/765-2586)
Shipton, P.Q.	See Trans-Vision de Danville, Danville
Sidney, B.C.	Saanich Cablevision Ltd., 9769 2nd St., Sidney, B.C. V8L 3C5 (604/656-3111)
Sillery, P.Q.	See Cablevision Nationale, Montréal
Silverwood, N.B.	See City Cablevision, Fredericton
Simcoe, Ont.	Clearview Cable TV Ltd., Box 327, Simcoe, Ont. N3Y 2T3 (519/426-7360)
Smooth Rock Falls, Ont.	See Timmins Cable Services, Timmins
Sooke, B.C.	Urban Cablevision Ltd., 2614 Sooke Rd., Victoria, B.C. V9B 1Y2 (604/474-2111)
Souris, Man.	See Westman Media, Brandon
Southampton, N.B.	See Woodstock Community TV, Woodstock
Southampton, Ont.	See Southport Cable TV, Port Elgin
South Slocan, B.C.	South Slocan Television Co-Operative Assn., South Slocan, B.C. V0G 2G0 (604/359-7313)
Sparwood, B.C.	See Fernie Television, Fernie
Spruce Grove, Alta.	See Capital Cable, Edmonton
Stellarton, N.S.	See K-Vision Services, New Glasgow
Stephenville, Nfld.	Bay St. George Cablevision, Box 566, Stephenville, Nfld. A2N 3B4 (709/643-5114)
Stettler, Alta.	See QCTV, Edmonton
Stittsville, Ont.	See Ottawa Cablevision, Ottawa
Stonewall, Man.	See Interlake Cable TV, Selkirk
Stoney Creek, Ont.	See Northgate Cable TV, Hamilton
Stoney Creek, Ont.	Niagara Co-Axial Ltd., 12 Mountain Ave. S., Stoney Creek, Ont. L8G 2V4 (416/662-8972)
Stony Plain, Alta.	See Capital Cable, Edmonton
Stouffville, Ont.	See Classic Communications, Richmond Hill
Stratford, Ont.	See Grand River Cable TV, Kitchener
Strathroy, Ont.	See Airland Communication, Clinton
Sudbury, Ont.	Sudbury Cable Services Ltd., 500 Barrydowne Rd., Unit 15, Sudbury, Ont. P3A 3T3 (705/560-1560)
Summerland, B.C.	See Penticton Cable T.V., Penticton
Surrey, B.C.	See White Rock Cablevision, White Rock
Surrey, B.C.	Western Cablevision Ltd., 10445-138th St., Surrey, B.C. V3T 4K4 (604/588-9331)
Sussex, N.B.	Kings County Cable Ltd., Box 1428, Sussex, N.B. E0E 1P0 (506/433-4520)
Sydney, N.S.	Cape Breton Cablevision Ltd., Box 138, Sydney, N.S. B1P 6G9 (902/539-0625)
Swan River, Man.	See Westman Media, Brandon
Taber, Alta.	Taber Cable Television Ltd., Box 1448, Taber, Alta. T0K 2G0 (403/223-3331)
Tavistock, Ont.	See Grand River Cable TV, Kitchener
Terrace, B.C.	Skeena Broadcasters Ltd., 4625 Lazelle Ave., Terrace, B.C. V8G 1S4 (604/635-6316)

Terrace Bay, Ont.	Lakeshore Community Television Ltd., Box 700, Terrace Bay, Ont. P0T 2W0 (807/825-3305)
Teulon, Sask.	See Interlake Cable TV, Selkirk
Thetford Mines, P.Q.	Thetford Video Inc., C.P. 274, 37 O. Rue St-Joseph, Thetford Mines, P.Q. G6G 3N7 (418/335-6620)
Thompson, Man.	CESM-TV Ltd., 49 Severn Cres., Thompson, Man. R8W 1M7 (204/677-4576)
Thornburn, N.S.	See K-Vision Services, New Glasgow
Thorold, Ont.	See Maclean-Hunter Cable TV, St. Catharines
Thunder Bay, Ont.	Maclean-Hunter Cable TV Ltd., 215 Van Norman St., Thunder Bay, Ont. P7A 4B7 (807/345-1211)
Tillsonburg, Ont.	Till-Cable T.V. Ltd., 86 Brock St. E., Tillsonburg, Ont. N4G 1Z9 (519/842-5242)
Timberlea, N.S.	See Halifax Cablevision, Halifax
Timmins, Ont.	Timmins Cable Services Ltd., Box 1429, Timmins, Ont. P4N 7N2 (705/267-6434)
Toronto, Ont.	Graham Cable TV/FM, 35 Scarlett Rd., Toronto, Ont. M6N 4J8 (416/762-3622)
Toronto, Ont.	Maclean-Hunter Cable TV Ltd., 27 Fasken Dr., Rexdale, Ont. M9W 1K7 (416/675-5930)
Toronto, Ont.	Rogers Cable T.V., 855 York Mills Rd., Don Mills, Ont. M3B 1Z1 (416/446-6500)
Toronto, Ont.	See Scarboro Cable, Scarboro
Toronto, Ont.	Willowdowns Cable Vision Ltd., 979 Alness St., Downsview, Ont. M3J 2J1 (416/661-9252)
Touraine, P.Q.	See Télécâble Laurentien, Hull
Trail, B.C.	See Cable West TV, North Vancouver
Trenton, N.S.	See K-Vision Services, New Glasgow
Trenton, Ont.	See Cablevue (Quinte), Belleville
Trois-Rivières, P.Q.	La Belle Vision Inc., 1579 St. Phillippe, Trois-Rivières, P.Q. G9A 5L6 (819/379-9121)
Truro, N.S.	Eastern Cablevision Ltd., 69 Walker St., Truro, N.S. B2N 4A8 (902/895-1515)
Union, Ont.	See Allview Cable, St. Thomas
Union Bay, B.C.	See Comox Valley CableNet, Courtenay
Uxbridge, Ont.	Compton Cable T.V. Ltd., Box 73, Uxbridge, Ont. L0B 1N0 (416/985-8171)
Val d'Or, P.Q.	Cablevision du Nord de Québec Inc., 45 boul. Hotel de Ville, Val d'Or, P.Q. J9P 2M5 (819/825-5133)
Valleyfield, P.Q.	Valleyfield Transvision Inc., 135 Alexandre St., Valleyfield, P.Q. J6S 3K5 (514/373-6616)
Vancouver, B.C.	Vancouver Cablevision Limited, 5594 Cambie St., Vancouver, B.C. V5Z 3A2 (604/324-3355)
Vanier, Ont.	See Skyline Cablevision, Ottawa
Vanier, Ont.	See Cablevision Nationale, Montreal
Vankleek Hill, Ont.	See Cie Cablevision, Hawkesbury
Vaughan, Ont.	See Classic Communications, Richmond Hill
Vauxhall, Alta.	See Taber Cable Television, Taber
Vedder Crossing, B.C.	See CableNet Chilliwack, Chilliwack
Vegreville, Alta.	See QCTV, Edmonton
Vermilion, Alta.	See QCTV, Edmonton
Victoria, B.C.	See Davin Enterprises, Saanich
Victoria, B.C.	See Urban Cablevision, Sooke
Victoria, B.C.	Victoria Cablevision Ltd., 3690 Shelbourne St., Victoria, B.C. V8P 4H3 (604/477-1884)
Victoria Harbour, Ont.	See Maclean-Hunter Cable TV, Midland
Victoriaville, P.Q.	Cablevision Nationale Inc., C.P. 248, Victoriaville, P.Q. G6P 6S9 (819/758-0501)
Viking, Alta.	See QCTV, Edmonton
Ville de Laval, P.Q.	See Cable TV Ltée, Montréal
Vimont, P.Q.	See Cablevision Nationale, Montréal
Vimont, P.Q.	See Video Cable Service, Laval
Virden, Man.	See Westman Media, Brandon
Wainwright, Alta.	See Northern Cablevision Ltd., Edmonton
Walkerton, Ont.	See Saugeen Telecable, Hanover
Wallaceburg, Ont.	See Maclean Hunter Cable TV, Sarnia
Warden, P.Q.	See Waterloo T.V., Waterloo, P.Q.
Waterloo, Ont.	See Grand River Cable TV, Kitchener
Waterloo, P.Q.	Waterloo T.V. Cable, 6003 Foster St., Waterloo, P.Q. J0E 2N0 (514/539-1808)
Waterville, P.Q.	See Lennoxville Transvision, Lennoxville
Waverley, N.B.	See Dartmouth Cable TV, Dartmouth
Weedon, P.Q.	See Transvision East Angus, East Angus
Welland, Ont.	Armstrong Communications Ltd., Box 159, Welland, Ont. L3B 5P2 (416/735-3331)
Wellington, N.S.	See Metrovision Ltd., Sackville
Westbank, B.C.	See Kelowna Cable TV, Kelowna
West Bench, B.C.	See Penticton Cable T.V., Penticton
West Flamboro Cty., Ont.	See Western Co-Axial, Hamilton
West Hill, Ont.	See Wired City Communications, Scarboro
Westlock, Alta.	See QCTV, Edmonton
West Vancouver, B.C.	See Cable West TV, North Vancouver
Westville, N.S.	See K-Vision Services, New Glasgow
Wetaskiwin, Alta.	See Cable TV, Camrose
Weyburn, Sask.	Weyburn CableNet, (Div. of CableNet Ltd.), 35-5th St. N.E., Weyburn, Sask. S4H 0Y9 (306/842-4236)

Whitby, Ont.	See Pine Ridge Cable TV, Oshawa
Whitecourt, Alta.	See Northern Cablevision, Edmonton
Whitehorse, Y.T.	Northern Television Systems Ltd., Suite 203, 4103 4th Ave., Whitehorse, Y.T. Y1A 1H6 (403/667-4247)
White River, Ont.	See Lakeshore Community TV, Terrace Bay
White Rock, B.C.	White Rock Cablevision Ltd., 15239 16th Ave., Surrey, B.C. V4A 1R6 (604/531-2322)
Williams Lake, B.C.	See Central Interior Cablevision, Prince George
Windsor, N.S.	Windsor Cable TV Ltd., Box 640, Windsor, N.S. B0N 2T0 (902/798-8313)
Wingham, Ont.	See Country Cable, Listowel
Winkler, Man.	See Valley Cable Vision, Carman
Winnipeg, Man.	Greater Winnipeg Cablevision Ltd., 930 Nairn Ave., Winnipeg, Man. R2L 0X8 (204/667-4610)
Winnipeg, Man.	Winnipeg Videon Inc., 651 Stafford St., Box 806, Winnipeg, Man. R3C 2N9 (204/475-9170)
Winterburn, Alta.	See QCTV, Edmonton
Woodstock, N.B.	Woodstock Community T.V. Ltd., 629 Main St., Box 1165, Woodstock, N.B. E0J 2B0 (506/575-8460)
Woodstock, Ont.	Western Cable TV Ltd., Box 363, Woodstock, Ont. N4S 7Y1 (519/539-9521)
Yahk, B.C.	See Creston Cabled-Video, Creston
Yarmouth, N.S.	Viking Cable T.V. Ltd., 25 Shaw Ave., Yarmouth, N.S. B5A 4C4 (902/742-9117)
Yarrow, B.C.	See CableNet Chilliwack, Chilliwack
Yellowknife, N.W.T.	Mackenzie Media Ltd., Box 1469, Yellowknife, N.W.T. X1A 2P1 (403/873-2226)

RELIGIOUS ORGANIZATIONS AND MISSIONARY SOCIETIES

THE ANGLICAN CHURCH OF CANADA

-not confirmed for 1982-

ARCHBISHOPS

Primate of the Anglican Church of Canada—Most Rev. E. W. Scott B.A., D.D., 600 Jarvis St., Toronto, Ont. M4Y 2J6

Most Rev. Lewis S. Garnsworthy, Archbishop of Toronto and Metropolitan of Ecclesiastical Province of Ontario, 135 Adelaide St. E., Toronto, Ont. M5C 1L8

Most Rev. T. D. Somerville, B.A., B.D., D.D., Archbishop of New Westminster and Metropolitan of Ecclesiastical Province of British Columbia, 692 Burrard St., Vancouver, B.C. V6C 2L1

Most Rev. F.H.W. Crabb, B.D., D.D., Archbishop of Athabasca, Metropolitan of the Ecclesiastical Province of Rupert's Land, Box 279, Peace River, Alta. TOH OXO

Most Rev. R. L. Seaborn, M.A., B.D., D.D., Archbishop of Eastern Newfoundland & Labrador and Metropolitan of Ecclesiastical Province of Canada, 67 Portugal Cove Rd., St. John's, Nfld. A1B 2M2

DIOCESE & BISHOP (WITH DATE OF CONSECRATION)

Algoma—Rt. Rev. F. F. Nock, 1975, Box 1168, Sault Ste. Marie, Ont.

The Arctic—Rt. Rev. J. R. Sperry, 1974; Rt. Rev. J.C.M. Clarke, Suffragan Bishop, 1979, 1055 Avenue Rd., Toronto

Athabasca—Most Rev. F. H. W. Crabb, 1975, Box 279, Peace River, Alta. T0H 2X0

Brandon—Rt. Rev. J. F. S. Conlin, B.A., L.Th., D.D., 1975, 341 13th St., Brandon, Man. R7A 4P8

British Columbia—Rt. Rev. Hywel Jones, 1980, 912 Vancouver St., Victoria, B.C. V8V 3V7

Caledonia—Rt. Rev. D. W. Hambidge, A.L.C.D., B.D., D.D., 1969, 208 Fourth Ave. W., Prince Rupert, B.C. V8J 1P5

Calgary—Rt. Rev. M. L. Goodman, B.A., D.D., 1968, 3015 Glencoe Rd. S.W., Calgary, Alta. T2S 2L9

Cariboo—Rt. Rev. J. S. P. Snowden, 1974, 360 Nicola St., Kamloops, B.C.

Edmonton—Rt. Rev. E. Kent Clarke, 1976, 10033-84th Ave., Edmonton, Alta. T6E 2S6

Fredericton—Rt. Rev. H. L. Nutter, B.A., M.A., B.S. Litt., D.D., 1971, 791 Brunswick St., Fredericton, N.B. E3B 1H8

Huron—Rt. Rev. T. D. B. Ragg, B.A., B.D., D.D., 1974, Rt. Rev. M.C. Robinson, B.A., Suffragan Bishop, 1974, and Rt. Rev. G.H. Parke-Taylor, M.A., B.D., D.D., 1976, 4-220 Dundas St., London, Ont. N6A 1H3

Keewatin—Rt. Rev. H. J. P. Allan, B.A., B.D., 1974, Box 118, Kenora, Ont. P9N 3X1

Kootenay—Rt. Rev. R. E. F. Berry, B.A., B.D., D.D., 1971, Box 549, Kelowna, B.C. V1Y 7P2

Montreal—Rt. Rev. R. A. Hollis, 1975, 1444 Union Ave., Montreal, P.Q. H3A 2B8

Moosonee—Rt. Rev. Caleb J. Lawrence, 1980, Box 841, Schumacher, Ont. P0N 1G0

Newfoundland (East)—Rt. Rev. Martin Mate, 1980, 67 Portugal Cove Rd., St. John's, Nfld. A1B 2M2

Newfoundland (Central)—Rt. Rev. M. Genge, M.A., L.Th., D.D., 1976, 34 Fraser Rd., Gander, Nfld. A1V 1K7

Newfoundland (West)—Rt. Rev. S.S. Payne, 1978, Ste. 311, Millbrook Mall, Corner Brook, Nfld. A2H 4R5

New Westminster—Most Rev. T. D. Somerville, B.D., D.D., 1968, #101, 325 Howe St., Vancouver, B.C. V6V 1Z7

Niagara—Rt. Rev. J. C. Bothwell, B.A., B.D., D.D., 1971, 67 Victoria Ave. S., Hamilton, Ont. L8N 2S8

Nova Scotia—Rt. Rev. L.F. Hatfield, M.A., D.D., 1976, 5732 College St., Halifax, N.S. B3H 1X3

Ontario—Rt. Rev. H. G. Hill, 1975, 90 Johnson St., Kingston, Ont. K7L 1X7

Ottawa—Rt. Rev. W. J. Robinson, B.A., D.D., 1970, and Most Rev. W.W. Davis, B.D., D.D., D.C.L., LL.D., 1958, Assistant Bishop, 71 Bronson Ave., Ottawa, Ont. K1R 6G6

Qu'Appelle—Rt. Rev. M.G. Peers, B.A., D.D., 1977, 1501 College Ave., Regina, Sask. S4P 1B8

Quebec—Rt. Rev. A. Goodings, B.A., B.D., D.D., 1977, 36 rue Desjardins, Quebec, P.Q. G1R 4L5

Rupert's Land—Rt. Rev. B. Valentine, M.A., B.D., D.D., 1969, 935 Nesbitt Bay, Winnipeg, Man. R3T 1W6

Saskatchewan—Rt. Rev. H. V. R. Short, B.A., B.D., D.D., 1970, Box 1088, Prince Albert, Sask. S6V 5S6

Saskatoon—Rt. Rev. D. A. Ford, B.A., D.D., 1970, Box 1965, Saskatoon, Sask. S7K 3S5

Toronto—Most Rev. L. S. Garnsworthy, B.A., D.D., 1968, Rt. Rev. A.A. Read, B.A., D.D., Suffragan Bishop, 1972, and Rt. Rev. H.V. Stiff, 1969, Assistant Bishop, 135 Adelaide St. E., Toronto, Ont. M5C 1L8

Yukon—Rt. Rev. J. T. Frame, B.A., L.Th., S.T.B., D.D., 1968, Box 4247, Whitehorse, Yukon

ECCLESIASTICAL PROVINCES OF CANADA

Ecclesiastical Divisions—(a) Province of Canada, comprising the Dioceses of Nova Scotia, Quebec, Montreal, Fredericton, Eastern Newfoundland & Labrador, Central Newfoundland, Western Newfoundland. (b) Province of Ontario, comprising Toronto, Huron, Ontario, Algoma, Niagara, Ottawa, Moosonee. (c) Province of Rupert's Land, comprising Rupert's Land, Saskatchewan, Athabasca, Qu'Appelle, Calgary, Keewatin, Edmonton, Brandon, Saskatoon, and The Arctic. (d) Province of British Columbia, comprising British Columbia, Caledonia, New Westminster, Kootenay, Cariboo, Yukon.

GENERAL SYNOD OF CANADA

Comprising Clerical and Lay Representatives of all the Dioceses in Canada.

Official Year Book of The Anglican Church of Canada, giving ecclesiastical information and list of clergy is published by the Anglican Book Centre, from 600 Jarvis St., Toronto, Ont. M4Y 2J6 (416/924-9192)

General Secretary of General Synod, The Ven. H. St. C. Hilchey, M.A., B.D., D.D., 600 Jarvis St.

Prolocutor, Chancellor J.H.C. Harradence, 685 20th St., Prince Albert, Sask. S6V 4H4

General Treasurer, J. R. Ligertwood, C.A., 600 Jarvis St.

Hon. Clerical Secretary, The Ven. C. Wilkins, 692 Burrard St., Vancouver, B.C. V6C 2L1

Hon. Lay Secretary, E.H. Fisher, 5732 College St., Halifax, N.S. B3H 3S5

MISSIONARY SOCIETY OF THE CHURCH

Executive Secretary, Rev. T. M. Anthony, B.A., S.T.B.

Treasurer, J. R. Ligertwood, C.A.

ADMINISTRATION AND FINANCE

Director, John R. Ligertwood

PENSIONS

Director, Ven. Ernest Hobson

PROGRAM OF GENERAL SYNOD

Executive Director of Program, Rev. L. Clarke Raymond

Director of Personnel Resources, Rev. Richard G. Johns

Director of Planning, Rev. William E. Lowe

Director of National & World Program, Rev. Thomas M. Anthony

Secretary, Primate's World Relief & Development Fund, George H. Cram

Ecumenical Officer, Rev. James Boyles

Archivist, Mrs. Teresa Thompson

Librarian, Miss Alice Marie Hedderick

ANGLICAN BOOK CENTRE

Director, Rev. Michael J. Lloyd

CANADIAN CHURCHMAN

Editor, Jerrold F. Hames

LIVING MESSAGE

Editor, Mrs. Rita Baker

CHURCH STATISTICS (1977 REPORT)

Total Parish enrolment	1,001,927
Total number of clergy	2,693
Total number of Licensed Lay Readers	1,642
Total number of Congregations	3,072
Total number of Dioceses	30

Total number of Sunday Schools 1,815
Teachers 13,481
Total Scholars 93,381

THE APOSTOLIC CHURCH IN CANADA

General Headquarters, Penygroes, Carms, S. Wales, U.K.
Canadian Headquarters, 27 Castlefield Ave., Toronto, Ont. M4R 1G3 (416/292-1811)
President, Rev. D. S. Morris, 685 Park St. S., Peterborough, Ont. K9J 3S9
National Secretary, Rev. S. M. Hammond, 43 Marlbank Rd., Agincourt, Ont. M1T 1Y6
Missionary Secretary, Rev. S. M. Hammond

The Apostolic Church in Canada is a branch of the Apostolic Church which originated in Great Britain as a result of the religious awakening there in 1904.

NEW APOSTOLIC CHURCH-CANADA

Headquarters, 65 Northfield Dr., Box 1615, Waterloo, Ont. N2J 4J2
(519) 884-2862
President, M. Kraus
Secretary, H. Rempel

APOSTOLIC CHURCH OF PENTECOST OF CANADA, INC.

General Office, #4, 3026 Taylor St. E., Saskatoon, Sask. S7J 4J2
(306) 374-1944; cable "Apostolic"
Moderator, Rev. Daniel W. Breen
Missionary Council Chairman, Rev. Edward G. Bradley
Clerk Treasurer, Bryan W. Conrad
"End Times Messenger" is the official voice of the Church – Editor, Irvin W. Ellis, 1338 Tyrol Rd., West Vancouver, B.C. V7S 2L6

BAHA'I FAITH

The Baha'i Faith, which was founded in 1844, has its headquarters in Haifa, Israel, and claims adherents in 136 independent states and 204 significant territories and islands. Canadian Baha'is are located in some 1500 centres throughout the country, 300 of which elect local Spiritual Assemblies. The National Spiritual Assembly of the Baha'is of Canada was incorporated by Act of Parliament in 1949.

Secretary, J. D. Martin, 7200 Leslie St., Thornhill, Ont. L3T 2A1 (416/889-8168)

BAPTIST FEDERATION OF CANADA

This Federation is composed of the Baptist Convention of Ontario and Quebec, the United Baptist Convention of the Atlantic Provinces, the Baptist Union of Western Canada, and the Union D'Eglises Baptistes Françaises au Canada. It is organized for fellowship and co-operation, but it does not exercise formal jurisdiction over its constituent members.

National Office, 219 St. George St., Toronto, Ont. M5R 2M2
(416) 922-4775
General Secretary Treasurer, Rev. R. Michael Steeves, B.A., B.D.

BAPTIST CONVENTION OF ONTARIO AND QUEBEC

217 St. George St., Toronto, Ont. M5R 2M2
(416) 922-5163
General Secretary, Rev. Dr. Ronald F. Watts
Treasurer, Peter Kaups
Dept. of Christian Education, Rev. Wm. Steeper
Dept. of the Ministry, Rev. George Scott
Dept. of Communications, Rev. Phil Karpetz
Dept. of Canadian Missions, Rev. Albert E. Coe

"THE CANADIAN BAPTIST" official publication of the Baptist Convention of Ontario and Quebec and the Baptist Union of Western Canada, 217 St. George St., Toronto, Ont. M5R 2M2—Editor, Rev. Dr. W.H. Jones

BAPTIST UNION OF WESTERN CANADA

Executive Minister, Rev. Douglas N. Moffat, 4404-16 St. S.W., Calgary, Alta. T2T 4H9 (403/243-6880, 81)
Asst. to the Executive Minister, Dr. C. Howard Bentall
Treasurer, Michael Packer
Principal, Baptist Leadership Training School, Rev. Donald Fraser, 4330 16 St. S.W., Calgary, Alta. T2T 4H9
Principal, Carey Hall, Univ. of B.C., Dr. Roy D. Bell, 5920 Iona Dr., Vancouver, B.C. V6T 1J6
Director of Field Education, Carey Hall, Rev. Philip Collins

AREA MINISTERS

Alberta: Rev. G.R. Fisher, c/o 4404 16 St. S.W., Calgary, Alta. T2T 4H9 (403/243-6880)
B.C.: Rev. Tom Oshiro, 201 7 St., New Westminster, B.C. V3M 3K2 (604/522-0232)
Manitoba: Rev. Jack Farr, 61 Columbus Cres., Winnipeg, Man. R3K 0C5 (204/885-3025)
Saskatchewan: Rev. B.A. Medgett, 4306 79 Cambridge Ave., Regina, Sask. S4N 5N4 (306/352-6165)

UNION D'EGLISES BAPTISTES FRANCAISES AU CANADA

(Union of French Baptist Churches in Canada)
3674 rue Ontario est, Montreal, P.Q. H1W 1R9
(514) 526-6643
General Secretary, J.S. Gilmour

UNITED BAPTIST CONVENTION OF ATLANTIC PROVINCES

1655 Manawagonish Rd., Saint John, N.B. E2M 3Y2
(506) 674-2006
President, L.G. Brace, 16 Alice Ave., Moncton, N.B. E1E 2H8
Executive Minister and Editor of the Year Book, Dr. Keith R. Hobson
Administrator Treasurer, Rev. W. E. O'Grady
Director of Training, Mrs. Mary Raymond
Director of Evangelism, Rev. Roy D. Campbell
President, Women's Missionary Union, Mrs. Evelyn Smith, 13A Marilyn Dr., Dartmouth, N.S. B2Y 3X8
Secretary, Women's Missionary Union, Mrs. Dorothy Brooks, Apt. 215, 6969 Bayers Rd., Halifax, N.S. B3L 2B8
President, Atlantic Baptist Young People's Convention, Greg Pike, Box 1004, Moncton, N.B. E1C 8P4
Editor of The Atlantic Baptist, Rev. George E. Simpson, Box 756, Kentville, N.S. B4N 3X9
Chairman, Board of Baptist Men, Kenneth Phillips, 401 Robie St., Truro, N.S. B2N 1L9

CANADIAN BAPTIST OVERSEAS MISSION BOARD

217 St. George St., Toronto, Ont. M5R 2M2
(416) 922-5163
Chairman, Mrs. Catherine Stratton, Sarnia, Ont.
General Secretary, Rev. R.C. Berry, B.A., B.D.
Associate Secretaries: Dr. P. V. Allaby, Dr. J.F. Keith, M.E.C. Lang

THE FELLOWSHIP OF EVANGELICAL BAPTIST CHURCHES IN CANADA

74 Sheppard Ave. W., Willowdale, Ont. M2N 1M3
(416) 223-8696
General Secretary, Dr. R.W. Lawson

THE BIBLE HOLINESS MOVEMENT

Established 1949, Incorporated 1957
A missionary movement in Canada, Philippines, Nigeria, India, U.S.A., Ghana, Liberia, Haiti and Kenya.
International Leader, Evangelist Wesley H. Wakefield, Vancouver, B.C.
International Headquarters, Box 223, Stn. A, Vancouver, B.C. V6C 2M3 (604/683-1833; cable: "Hallelujah")
Official Gazette, "Truth on Fire!" Field Council meets annually.

THE OLD HOLY CATHOLIC CHURCH IN CANADA

The church has a membership of approx. 4,500 people and operates 15 parishes Canada wide.

Canadian Bishop in Charge, The Most Rev. Rainer Laufers, D.D., 1117 St. Catherine St. W., Ste. 313, Montreal, P.Q. H3B 1H9 (514/845-4471)

Chancellor & Vicar General, Rev. Jean Laplante, 385 Place de la Louisanne, Apt. 712, Longueuil, P.Q. J4H 1A8

Vicariate of Denver, Rev. William Bushnell, Administrator, 6011 East Mineral Place, Englewood, Colorado, U.S.A. 80112

Diocesan Secretary, Rev. Thomas Nesbitt

Liturgical Counsellor, Rev. Gaetan Giroux

Diocesan Procurer Prison Ministry, Rev. Guy Potvin

OLD HOLY CATHOLIC CHURCH IN NORTH AMERICA

Canadian Address: Box 94, Stn. Z, Toronto, Ont. M5N 2Z3

Prime Bishop, Most Rev. Francis P. Facione, D.D.

Canadian Representative & Auxiliary Bishop of Michigan, Most Rev. A.G. Johnston-Cantrell, D.D.

Headquarters: 3827 Old Creek Rd., Troy, Mich. 48084 U.S.A.

CHRISTIAN CHURCH (DISCIPLES OF CHRIST)

39 Arkell Rd., R.R. 2, Guelph, Ont. N1H 6H8

(519) 823-5190

There are in Canada 39 Churches with a membership of 4,700 and 52 ministers.

Executive Minister, tba

Executive Administrator, Mrs. Emily Leland (int.)

THE CHRISTIAN & MISSIONARY ALLIANCE IN CANADA

Box 7900, Stn. B, Willowdale, Ont. M2K 2R6

President, Rev. M.P. Sylvester

Eastern & Central Canadian District Supt., Rev. R.J. Gould

Western Canadian District Supt., Rev. H.A. Town

Midwest Canadian District Supt., Rev. Arnold Downey

Canadian Pacific District Supt., Rev. G.R. Fowler

Churches, 241; Members, 37,800; Foreign Missionaries, 114

CHRISTIAN SCIENCE IN CANADA

The Church of Christ, Scientist, or Christian Science denomination, in Canada includes more than 80 congregations from British Columbia to Newfoundland, as well as organizations of Christian Scientists at some 12 colleges and universities. Each church is a branch of The Mother Church, The First Church of Christ, Scientist, in Boston, Massachusetts, but the congregations are governed democratically by the local membership. Christian Scientists in Canada have held regular services since the 1880s, shortly after the denomination was founded in 1879 by New England religious leader Mary Baker Eddy. The Church has no ordained clergy, and Sunday and Wednesday services are conducted by lay Readers elected from the congregation. Sunday Schools are open to young people up to the age of 20. Each branch church maintains a public Reading Room where visitors find a quiet place to read the Bible and Christian Science literature, including the Church's well-known daily newspaper *The Christian Science Monitor*. Communications may be addressed to A.W. Phinney, Manager, Committee on Publication, Christian Science Center, Boston, MA 02115. Phone: 617/262-2300

THE CHURCH ARMY IN CANADA

Headquarters and Training Centre, 397 Brunswick Ave., Toronto, Ont. M5R 2Z2 (416/924-9279)

Director, Capt. R. A. Taylor

Warden, Rev. Canon Leslie Hunt, B.A., B.D., M.Th., D.D.

All information regarding training and program or literature may be obtained from the Director.

THE EVANGELICAL ALLIANCE MISSION OF CANADA, INC.

70 Froom Cres., Regina, Sask.

(306) 525-5444

Mailing Address: Box 980, Regina, Sask. S4P 3B2

General Director, Richard M. Winchell

Administrative Secretary, Sam Archer

FREE METHODIST CHURCH IN CANADA

Number of members, 19,000

CANADIAN JURISDICTIONAL CONFERENCE

President, Bishop Donald N. Bastian, 96 Elmbrook Cres., Etobicoke, Ont. M9C 5E2 (416/622-4094)

Executive Secretary Treasurer, Rev. Claude A. Horton, 833-D Upper James St., Hamilton, Ont. L9C 3A3 (416/385-1145)

Vice President, Rev. W.D. Kinney

CANADA WEST CONFERENCE

Secretary, Rev. Clarence F. Lyons, c/o Box 460, Moose Jaw, Sask. S6H 4P1 (306/692-5539)

CANADA GREAT LAKES CONFERENCE

Secretary, Rev. J. W. Hyndman, 53 Kirkpatrick Ave., Dryden, Ont. P8N 2G2

CANADA EAST CONFERENCE

Secretary, Rev. Carl V. Bull, 210 Bayfield St., Barrie, Ont. L4M 3B6 (705/728-6644)

Organ of the Church, *The Canadian Free Methodist Herald*

Editor, Rev. Gary R. Walsh, 833-D Upper James St., Hamilton, Ont. L9C 3A3 (416/387-6370)

Official Schools, Lorne Park College Foundation, Director, Rev. C.A. Horton, 833D Upper James, Hamilton (385-1145); Aldersgate College, Moose Jaw, Sask., President, Dr. J. Leon Winslow, Box 460, Moose Jaw, Sask. S6H 4P1 (306/692-1816)

GOSPEL MISSIONARY UNION OF CANADA

Operating mission stations in South America, Central America, Europe, Africa, Alaska.

Offical Organ, "The Gospel Message"

Canadian Headquarters, 2121 Henderson Hwy., Winnipeg, Man. R2G 1P8 (204/338-7831)

Director of Public Ministries, Rev. John Harder

Director of Administration, Rev. Jake Goertzen

THE LUTHERAN CHURCH

Lutherans in Canada: 716,000. Ordained ministers 955; congregations 1,029; membership of congregations 301,088; Theological Seminaries 3; Colleges 3.

Common Agency

LUTHERAN COUNCIL IN CANADA

500-365 Hargrave St., Winnipeg, Man. R3B 2K3

(204) 942-0096

Executive Director, W.A. Schultz, C.A.

Executive Secretary, Theology, Rev. N.J. Threinen, Th.D.

Executive Secretary, Mission & Ministry, Rev. L.C. Gilbertson

Participating Churches in Council

LUTHERAN CHURCH IN AMERICA-CANADA SECTION

President, Rev. G.W. Luetkehoelter, #211, 2281 Portage Ave., Winnipeg, Man.

Executive Secretary, Rev. J.M. Zimmerman, D.D., 600 Jarvis St., Toronto, Ont. M4Y 2J6 (416/961-8917)

Eastern Canada Synod—LCA—50 Queen St. N., 3rd floor, Kitchener, Ont. N2H 6P4; Rev. William D. Huras, President

Central Canada Synod—LCA—211-2281 Portage Ave., Winnipeg, Man.; Rev. G.W. Luetkehoelter, President

Western Canada Synod—LCA—9901-107th St., Edmonton, Alta.; Rev. Donald W. Sjoberg, President

THE EVANGELICAL LUTHERAN CHURCH OF CANADA

247 1st Ave. N., Saskatoon, Sask. (306/653-0133); Rev. S. Theodore Jacobson, Th.D., President

THE LUTHERAN CHURCH-CANADA

3022 E. 49 Ave., Vancouver, B.C. V5S 1K9 (604/433-4744); Rev. E.M. Treit, President

Ont. Dist.—149 Queen St. S., Kitchener, Ont.; Rev. Albin J. Stanfel, President

Man.-Sask. Dist.—1927 Grant Dr., Regina, Sask.; Rev. Roy K. Holm, President

Alta.-B.C. Dist.—7119-112 Ave., Edmonton, Alta.; Rev. Edwin Lehman, D.D., President

THE MENNONITES IN CANADA

Mennonite Central Committee (Canada): 1483 Pembina Hwy., Winnipeg, Man. R3T 2C8 (204/475-3550)

There are approx. 70,000 members of Mennonite Churches in Canada.

CONFERENCES

Canadian Conference of the Mennonite Brethren Church of North America
Moderator, Dave Redekop, 101 Lamont Blvd., Winnipeg, Man. R3P 0E7

Evangelical Mennonite Mission Conference
Moderator, Ed Stoesz, 232 Nassau St., Winnipeg, Man. R3L 2H8

Evangelical Mennonite Conference
Moderator, Edwin Plett, Box 80, R.R. 1, Ste. Anne, Man. R0A 1R0

Sommerfelder Mennonite Conference
Representative, Bishop J.A. Friesen, Sommerfelder Mennonite Church, Lowe Farm, Man. R0G 1E0

Rheinlaender Mennonite Conference
Representative, Allen Kehler, Box 1002, Altona, Man. R0G 0B0

Chortitzer Mennonite Conference
Representative, Bishop H.K. Schellenberg, Box 226, Steinbach, Man. R0A 2A0

Mennonite Conference of Ontario
Moderator, Glenn Brubacher, 800 King St. E., Kitchener, Ont. N2G 2M6

Conference of Mennonites in Canada
Moderator, Jake Franson, Smithville, Ont. L0R 2A0

Western Ontario Mennonite Conference
Moderator, Nelson Scheifele, 24 Dunbar Rd. N., Waterloo, Ont. N2L 2C7

Northwest Mennonite Conference
Moderator, Merlin Stauffer, 9431 75th St., Edmonton, Alta. T6C 2H6

Brethren in Christ
Moderator, Bishop Harvey Sider, 1301 Niagara Pkwy., R.R. 1, Fort Erie, Ont. L2A 5M4

Old Colony Mennonite
Representative, Abram Driedger, Box 601, Winkler, Man. R0G 2X0

Markham-Waterloo Conference
Moderator, Leonard Freeman, R.R. 1, Fergus, Ont. N1M 2W3

HIGH SCHOOLS

Mennonite Collegiate Institute, Box 39, Gretna, Man. R0G 0V0

Westgate Mennonite Collegiate, 86 Westgate St., Winnipeg, Man. R3C 2E1

Rosthern Junior College, Rosthern, Sask. S0K 3R0

United Mennonite Educational Institute, R.R. 5, Leamington, Ont. N8H 3V8

Mennonite Brethren Collegiate Institute, 173 Talbot Ave., Winnipeg, Man. R2L 0P6

Eden Christian College, R.R. 3, Niagara-on-the-Lake, Ont. L0S 1J0

Rockway Mennonite School, 111 Doon Rd., Kitchener, Ont.

BIBLE SCHOOLS

Columbia Bible Institute, 2940 Clearbrook Rd., Clearbrook, B.C. V2T 2Z8

Elim Bible Institute, Box 120, Altona, Man. R0G 0B0

Swift Current Bible Institute, Box 1268, Swift Current, Sask. S9H 3X4

Winkler Bible Institute, Box 1540, Winkler, Man. R0G 2X0

COLLEGES

Conrad Grebel College, Waterloo, Ont. N2L 3G6

Canadian Mennonite Bible College, 600 Shaftesbury Blvd., Winnipeg, Man. R3P 0M4

Mennonite Brethren Bible College, 77 Henderson Hwy., Winnipeg, Man. R2L 1L1

Steinbach Bible College, Box 1420, Steinbach, Man. R0A 2A0

CHURCH OF JESUS CHRIST OF LATTER-DAY SAINTS (MORMONS)

(Established 1830)

Canadian Public Communications Office, 1235 Bay St., #505, Toronto, Ont. M5R 1A5

Office of the Presiding Bishopric, 50 East North Temple, Salt Lake City, Utah 84150 U.S.A.

There is no paid ministry in the Church of Jesus Christ of Latter-day Saints, all officers and missionaries being sustained at their own expense.

The total number of Mormons in Canada is 74,900.

STAKES OF ZION IN CANADA WITH PRESIDENTS

Calgary Alberta Stake—R.H. Walker, 930 Prospect Ave. S.W., Calgary, Alta. T2T 0W5

Calgary Alberta North Stake—M.B. Manley, 6111 Touchwood Dr. N.W., Calgary, Alta. T2K 5R7

Calgary Alberta South Stake—C.L. Robertson, 13031 Canso Place S.W., Calgary, Alta. T2J 2T8

Calgary Alberta West Stake—L.A. Rosenvall, 6309 Dalbeattie Hill N.W., Calgary, Alta. T3A 1M3

Cardston Alberta Stake—F.N. Spackman, Box 218, Cardston, Alta. T0K 0K0

Cranbrook British Columbia Stake—B.J. Erickson, 2509 Third St. S., Cranbrook, B.C. V1C 4W4

Edmonton Alberta Stake—W.D. Wilde, 5108 112 St., Edmonton, Alta. T6H 3J2

Edmonton Alberta East Stake—B.L. Stringham, 6608 92A Ave., Edmonton, Alta. T6B 0T6

Hamilton Ontario Stake—C.M. Warner, 91 Owen Ave., Kitchener, Ont. N2B 2L7

Lethbridge Alberta Stake—H.L. Matkin, 1715 12th Ave. S., Lethbridge, Alta.

Lethbridge Alberta East Stake—B.C. Stringham, 433D Mayor Magrath Dr., Lethbridge, Alta. T1J 3L3

London Ontario Stake—H. Crookell, 62 Queen Anne Circle, London, Ont. N6H 4B7

Montreal Quebec Stake—G.C. Pelchat, 541 Blackwood St., Greenfield Park, P.Q. J4V 1H4

Ottawa Ontario Stake—B.E. Lee, 6098 Vineyard Dr., Orleans, Ont. K1C 2K2

Raymond Alberta Stake—J.D. Bridge, Box 358, Raymond, Alta. T0K 2S0

Saskatoon Saskatchewan Stake—N.W. Burt, Box 88, Clavet, Sask. S0K 0Y0

Taber Alberta Stake—K.E. Francis, Box 89, Taber, Alta. T0K 2G0

Toronto Ontario Stake—C.L. Merkley, 2 The Outlook, Islington, Ont. M9B 2X6

Toronto Ontario East Stake—J.B. Smith, 79 Alpaca Dr., Scarborough, Ont. M1J 2Z9

Vancouver B.C. South Stake—R.C. Bulpitt, 13254 15A Ave., Surrey, B.C. M1J 2Z9

Vancouver B.C. Stake—R.W. Komm, 1384 Chartwell Dr., West Vancouver, B.C. V7S 2R5

Vernon B.C. Stake—J.R. Burnham, 3201 19th St., Vernon, B.C. V1T 4B6

Victoria B.C. Stake—H.L. Biddulph, 4020 Haro Rd., Victoria, B.C. V8N 4B2

Winnipeg Manitoba Stake—L.L. Clapson, 300 Victoria Cres., Winnipeg, Man. R2M 1X9

In addition there are Missions in Calgary, Toronto, Montreal, Halifax, Vancouver and Winnipeg, and Institutes of Religion in Calgary, Edmonton, Lethbridge, Regina, Saskatoon and Vancouver

THE REORGANIZED CHURCH OF JESUS CHRIST OF LATTER-DAY SAINTS

World Headquarters, Saints Auditorium, Independence Mo. U.S.A.

Canadian Headquarters: 390 Speedvale Ave. E., Guelph, Ont. N1E 1N5 (519/822-4150)

Founded April 6, 1830 by Joseph Smith, Jr. and reorganized under the leadership of the founder's son, Joseph Smith III in 1860. Church is established in 30 countries in addition to the United States and Canada. Biennial world conference is held in Independence, Missouri. Current president is Wallace B. Smith, great-grandson of the original founder.

Church officers in Canada:

Regional President, D.H. Comer

Bishop of Canada & Regional Bishop, D.F. Silverthorn

District Presidents:

Alta.: Al Mogg, #1040, 3730 50 St. N.W., Calgary, Alta. T3A 2V9

B.C.: Vic Suddaby, 2406 Oranda, Coquitlam, B.C. V2K 3A4

Chatham, Ont.: George Morden, R.R. 5, Forest, Ont. N0N 1J0

Grand River, Ont.: Wm. McCarty, 43 Cedar Waxwing, Elmira, Ont. N3B 1E5

London, Ont.: Jack Wright, 859 Valetta St., London, Ont. N6H 2Z4

Niagara, Ont.: Don Saul, 4229 Longmoor Dr., Burlington, Ont. L7L 5A1

Northern Ont.: Clair Shepherdson, Box 525, New Liskeard, Ont. P0J 1P0

Ottawa, Ont.: Wilburt Canniff, 1 Cedarcrest Ave., Ottawa, Ont. K2E 5P7

Owen Sound, Ont.: Alma Leeder, Box 192, Wiarton, Ont. N0H 2T0

Sask.: Frank Ward, 411 Preston Ave., Saskatoon, Sask. S7H 2V1

Toronto, Ont.: B.A. Taylor, 1443 Bathurst St., Toronto, Ont. M5R 3J2

Office of Public Information:

Saints Auditorium, Box 1059, Independence, Missouri 64051, U.S.A.

THE ORTHODOX CHURCH

There are approximately 316,610 (1971 Census) Greek Orthodox adherents in Canada. This number includes various nationalities, such as the Ukrainians, Greeks, Russians, Syrians, Roumanians, Bulgarians and Armenians.

Ukrainian Greek-Orthodox Church of Canada

Headquarters, 9 St. Johns Ave., Winnipeg, Man. R2W 1G8

Primate, Metropolitan of Winnipeg & of all Canada, His Beatitude Metropolitan ANDREW (Metiuk), Winnipeg

Most Rev. Archbishop BORIS (Yakowkewich), Edmonton

Most Rev. Archbishop NICHOLAS (Debryn), Toronto

Rt. Rev. Bishop WASYLY (Fedak), Saskatoon

Governing Body, Consistory of the Ukrainian Greek-Orthodox Church of Canada composed of nine clergy, nine laymen and all Bishops, presided over by the Metropolitan.

Executive Body, Praesidium of the Consistory

Chairman of the Praesidium, Very Rev. Dr. H. Udod (204/586-3093)

Secretary, Very Rev. S. Jarmus

Parishes number 300.

Official Publication, "The Herald," Winnipeg.

Greek Orthodox Church

Greek Orthodox Churches in Canada

Representing the Greek Orthodox Diocese of Toronto (Canada), His Grace Bishop Sotirios of Toronto, 27 Teddington Park Ave., Toronto, Ont. M4N 2C4 (416/481-2223)

Belleville: Holy Trinity, Box 483.

Calgary: St. Demetrios, One Tamarac Cres. S.W.

Edmonton: St. George, 10056-114th St., T5K 1R2
All Saints: 5824 118 Ave., T5W 1E4

Halifax: St. George, 1279 Queen St., B3J 3J1

Hamilton: St. Demetrios, 22 Head St., L8R 1P9
Koimisis Tis Theotokou, 233 E. 15th St., L9A 4G1

Montreal: Holy Trinity, 8 Sherbrooke St. W. H2X 1X1
St. George, 2455 Cote St. Catherine Rd., H3T 1A8
Archangels, 11801 Ave. Elie Blanchard Blvd., St-Laurent, H4J 1R7
Koimisis Tis Theotokou, 7700 de l'Epee, St. Pk. Ext., H3N 2E6
Sts. Constantine & Helen, 11400 Gouin Blvd. W., Roxboro, H8Y 1X8
Evangelismos Tis Theotokou, 777 St. Roch St., H3N 2K3
St. Nicholas, 3780 du Souvenir, Chomeday, Laval, P.Q. H7V 1X8
St. Markella Chiopolitis, 100 Bernard Ave. W., H2T 2K1

Ottawa: Koimisis Tis Theotokou, 1315 Prince of Wales Dr., K2C 1N2

Quebec: Evangelismos Tis Theotokou, 17 St. Cyrille St. E., G1R 2A3

Regina: St. Paul, 3000 Argyle St., S4S 2B2

St. Catharines: St. Katherine, 124 Queenston St., L2R 2Z3

Saint John: St. Nicholas, 33 Dorchester St.

Sarnia: St. Demetrios, 204 N. East St., N7T 6X7

Saskatoon: Koimisis Tis Theotokou, 1020 Dufferin Ave., S7H 2G1

Thunder Bay: Holy Trinity, 830 St. Paul St., P7C 3L6

Toronto: Sts. Constantine and Helen, 1 Brookhaven Dr., M6M 4N6
Holy Trinity, 54 Clinton St., M6G 2Y3
St. George, 115 Bond St., M5B 1Y2
Evangelismos Tis Theotokou, 136 Sorauren Ave., M6R 2E4
St. Demetrios, 30 Thorncliffe Park Dr., M4H 1L3
St. Irene, 66 Gough Ave., M4K 3N8
St. Nicholas, 3840 Finch Ave. E., Scarborough, Ont. M1W 4R6
St. Ephrasinia, 1008 Dovercourt Rd., M6H 2X8
All Saints, 222 Burbank Dr., Willowdale, Ont. M2K 1P8

Vancouver: St. George, 4500 Arbutus St., V6J 4A2
St. Nicholas, 5817 Victoria Dr., V5P 3W5

Windsor: Holy Cross, 65 Ellis St. E., N8X 2G8

Winnipeg: St. Demetrios, 2255 Grant Ave., R3P 0S2

The Antiochian Orthodox Church

The Antiochian Orthodox Community in Canada with a membership of about 100,000 is under the jurisdiction of the Patriarch of Antioch and all the East, with headquarters in Damascus, Syria. The Primate of the Church in North America is His Eminence Metropolitan Philip Saliba.

Inquiries regarding the Antiochian Orthodox Community in Canada may be addressed to V. Rev. Antony Gabriel, Pastor of St. George Orthodox Church in Montreal with headquarters at 555-575 Jean Talon St. E., Montreal, P.Q. H2R 1T8 (514/276-8533)

There are five churches in Canada, two in Montreal and one each in Ottawa, Toronto an Edmonton. Also attached to these churches are missions in Trois-Rivières, Shawinigan, Grand'Mère, and Joliette in Quebec and Cornwall, London and Windsor in Ontario.

The Byelorussian Autocephalic Orthodox Church

In Canada: The Parish of St. Kizyla of Turau, 524 St. Clarens Ave., Toronto, Ont. M6H 3W7 (416/537-1705); Rt. Rev. Bishop Mikalay

Parish Executive Chairman, W. Nowicki

Secretary, M. Ganko

Treasurer, Maria Ganko

The Sisterhood President, Mrs. V. Radek

Secretary, Mrs. M. Ganko

Treasurer, Mrs. N. Filanovic

OVERSEAS MISSIONARY FELLOWSHIP (China Inland Mission)

General Director, J.H. Taylor III

Home Director, D.J. Michell

Secretary Treasurer, M.W. Bartlett

Pacific Representative, Doug Shortt, #516, 9867 Manchester Dr. Burnaby, B.C. V3N 4P6

Western Canada Representative, Nick Gawryletz, Box 777, Three Hills, Alta. T0M 2A0

Eastern Canada Representative, B.J. Gibson, 1058 Avenue Rd., Toronto, Ont. M5N 2C6
Atlantic Provinces Representative, A. Gordon Watts, (act.), 25 Greenwood Dr., Dartmouth, N.S. B2W 3S4
Offices of the Mission—Canadian Headquarters, 1058 Avenue Rd., Toronto, Ont. M5N 2C6 (416/485-0427)

THE PENTECOSTAL ASSEMBLIES OF CANADA

The number of adherents estimated at 136,000, 1,054 Ordained Ministers and 950 churches.
General Superintendent, Rev. Robt. W. Taitinger
Head Office, 10 Overlea Blvd., Toronto, Ont. M4H 1A5 (416/425-1010)
General Secretary, Rev. C. Yates
General Treasurer, Rev. A. G. Richards
Official Publication, "The Pentecostal Testimony"
Editor, Miss Joy E. Hansell
Executive Directors:
Overseas Missions, Rev. W.C. Cornelius
Christian Education & Youth, Rev. W.A. Griffin
Home Missions and Bible Colleges, Rev. R. M. Argue
Women's Ministries, Mrs. Elma Scratch
Full Gospel Publishing House, Manager, Victor T. Smalridge

DISTRICT SUPERINTENDENTS

Alta.: Rev. I. Roset, 11617 106 Ave., Edmonton, Alta. T5H OS1
B.C.: Rev. J. M. House, 5641 176A St., Surrey, B.C. V3S 4G8
Man.: Rev. W. G. Reinheimer, 3081 Ness Ave., Winnipeg, Man. R2Y 2G3
Maritime Provinces: Rev. A. Donald Moore, Box 1184, Truro, N.S. B2N 5H1
E. Ont. & Que.: Rev. Gordon R. Upton, Box 1600, Belleville, Ont. K8N 5J3
W. Ont.: Rev. H.J. Cantelon, 3419 Mainway, Burlington, Ont. L7M 1A9
Sask: Rev. J. C. Tyler, 1219 Idylwyld Dr., Saskatoon, Sask. S7L 1A1

BRANCH CONFERENCES

East Slavic: Rev. Walter Senko, R.R. 1, Wilsonville, Ont. N0E 1Z0
Finnish: Rev. Veikko Kyllonen, Secretary, 1615 William St., Apt. 302, Vancouver, B.C. V5L 2R3
French: Rev. Oscar Masseau, 29 Papineau St., Valleyfield, P.Q. J6G 4J6
German: Rev. Gustav Kurtz, 5 Manitou Dr., Kitchener, Ont. N2C 2J6
West Slavic: Rev. Peter Kerychuk, 7104 39 Ave., Edmonton, Alta. T6K OR5

EDUCATIONAL INSTITUTIONS

The Eastern Pentecostal Bible College, 780 Argyle St., Peterborough, Ont. K9H 5T2 (705/745-7450)
President, Rev. G.O. Atkinson
Central Pentecostal College, 1303 Jackson Ave., Saskatoon, Sask. S7H 2M9 (306/374-6655)
President, Rev. Dr. Kenneth B. Birch, B.A., D.Min.
Northwest Bible College, 11617 106th Ave., Edmonton, Alta. T5H 0S1 (403/452-0808)
President, Rev. E. A. Francis
Western Pentecostal Bible College, Box 1000, Clayburn, B.C. V0X 1E0 (604/853-7491)
President, Rev. L. T. Holdcroft
Berea Bible Institute, 1711 Henri-Bourassa E., Montreal, P.Q. H2C 1J5 (514/388-1498)
Principal, Rev. André Gagnon

MISSIONARIES

235 missionaries working in West Indies, Argentina, Brazil, Liberia, South Africa, Mozambique, Kenya, Tanzania, Zambia, Zimbabwe, Hong Kong, Taiwan, Thailand, Macao, Malawi and Eastern Europe.

THE PRESBYTERIAN CHURCH IN CANADA

Church Offices, 50 Wynford Dr., Don Mills, Ont. M3C 1J7 (416) 441-1111

The total number of Presbyterians in Canada, 872,335 (1971 census)

OFFICERS OF THE GENERAL ASSEMBLY

Moderator, Dr. A.F. MacSween, B.A., D.D.
Principal Clerk, Rev. D. C. MacDonald, B.A., D.D.
Treasurer, R. R. Merifield, Q.C., Toronto
(Latest Statistics to December 31st 1979)
Synods 8; Presbyteries 44; Congregations 1055; Communicants on roll 166,190; Ministers 993; Church School pupils 47,395; Amount raised for all purposes $36,466,240

BOARDS & COMMITTEES OF THE GENERAL ASSEMBLY

Administrative Council—Chairman, E.F. Bell, Winnipeg, Man.; Secretary, Rev. D. C. MacDonald, B.A., D.D., Don Mills, Ont.
Comptroller, N.H. Green, M.B.A., Don Mills, Ont.
Congregational Life—Chairman, Dr. M.A. McCuaig, B.A., B.D., D.Min., Ottawa, Ont.; General Secretary, Rev. W. L. Young, Don Mills, Ont.
Board of World Mission—Chairman, Mrs. W.H. Henry, Willowdale, Ont.; Secretary, Rev. George A. Malcolm, B.A., B.D., M.Th., Don Mills, Ont.
Board of Ministry—Chairman, Rev. W. Little, B.A., B.D., Th. M., Cambridge, Ont.; Secretary, Dr. J.W. Evans, B.A., B.Ed., D.D., Don Mills, Ont.
Ewart College, Toronto—Chairman, Rev. J.K. English, B.A., B.D., Calgary, Alta.; Principal, Miss Margaret Webster, B.A., M.Ed., D.D.
Knox College, Toronto—Board Chairman, F. Arnold Beale, Hamilton, Ont.; Principal, Rev. J.C. Hay, M.A., B.D., Ph.D., Toronto, Ont.
Presbyterian College, Montreal—Senate Chairman & Principal, Rev. W.J. Klempa, M.A., B.D., Ph.D.
Board of Education—Chairman, Rev. J. Ferguson, B.A., D.D., Stratford, Ont.
Pension Board—Chairman, Rev. E. Herron, Wallaceburg, Ont.
Lending Fund Committee—Chairman, Rev. H. McWilliams, B.A., M.Div., Islington, Ont.
Committee on History—Convener, Rev. Fred Rennie, B.A., B.D., M.Th., Cornwall, Ont.
Committee on Ecumenical Relations—Convener, Mrs. J. A. Johnston, Hamilton, Ont.
The Record Committee—Chairman, John Ball, Ottawa, Ont.; Editor, Rev. J.R. Dickey, B.A., B.D., Don Mills, Ont.

THE EIGHT SYNODS WITH CLERKS

Synod of the Atlantic Provinces—Rev. E.H. Bean, B.Th., B.D., D.D., Sydney, N.S.
Synod of Que. & Eastern Ont.—D. Fulford, Ottawa, Ont.
Synod of Toronto & Kingston—Rev. P.G. MacInnes, B.A., Toronto, Ont.
Synod of Hamilton & London—Dr. R.D. MacDonald, C.D., B.A., D.D., Kincardine, Ont.
Synod of Man. & N.W. Ont.—Rev. J.D. Marnoch, B.A., Winnipeg, Man.
Synod of Sask.—Rev. W.A. Donovan, B.A., Kipling, Sask.
Synod of Alta.—Mrs. Joyce Evans, Calgary, Alta.
Synod of B.C.—Rev. Ian Morrison, Vancouver, B.C.

WOMEN'S MISSIONARY SOCIETIES

President, Western Division, Miss Isabella Hunter, 50 Wynford Dr., Don Mills, Ont.
President, Eastern Division, Mrs. Murchison, Charlottetown, P.E.I.

THE RELIGIOUS SOCIETY OF FRIENDS QUAKERS

The Religious Society of Friends originated in England in the 17th Century. Its distinctive Christian witness has been based on what has been called "The Inner Light". Quakers believe that "there is something of God in every man", and that human personality is of great importance. From this conviction arises the Quaker way of worship and the well-known interest in peace, penal reform, and other questions involving the use of goodwill in overcoming evil.

CANADIAN YEARLY MEETING

Canadian Yearly Meeting of The Religious Society of Friends was formed in 1955, amalgamating Canada Yearly Meeting, Genesee Yearly Meeting and Canada Yearly Meeting (Conservative).

Presiding Clerk, Edward Bell, 2339 Briar Hill Dr., Ottawa, Ont. K1H 7A7

Secretary of Yearly Meeting, Mrs. Dorothy Muma (922-2632)

Clerk of Representative Meeting, Betty Polster, Argenta, B.C. VOG 1BO

President of the Canadian Friends' Foreign Missionary Board, Beatrice M. Petrie, R.R. 2, Pickering, Ont. L1V 2P9

Official Organ, "The Canadian Friend", 60 Lowther Ave., Toronto, Ont. M5R 1C7

THE CANADIAN FRIENDS' SERVICE COMMITTEE

This Committee performs the home and overseas service work of Canadian Friends.

Clerk, Nancy Pocock, 60 Lowther Ave., Toronto, Ont. M5R 1C7

ROMAN CATHOLIC CHURCH IN CANADA

The Hierarchy

Apostolic Nunciature, 724 Manor Ave., Ottawa, Ont. K1M 0E3 (613) 746-4914

Apostolic Pro-Nuncio, His Excellency the Most Rev. Angelo Palmas

Counsellor, Msgr. Dante Pasquinelli

Secretaries to the Apostolic Nunciature, Msgr George Paniculam, Fr. Gerard Yelle

Provinces Ecclesiastiques
Ecclesiastical Provinces

QUEBEC (1844)

(A.) Quebec (1674); (D.) Trois-Rivières (1852); (D.) Chicoutimi (1878); (D.) Amos (1938); (D.) Ste-Anne-de-la-Pocatière (1951); (D.) Rouyn-Noranda (1974)

HALIFAX (1852)

(A.) Halifax (1842); (D.) Charlottetown (1829); (D.) Antigonish (1844); (D.) Yarmouth (1953)

TORONTO (1870)

(A.) Toronto (1841); (D.) Hamilton (1856); (D.) London (1855); (D.) Thunder Bay (1952); (D.) St. Catharines (1958)

ST-BONIFACE (1871)

(A.) St-Boniface (1847)

OTTAWA (1886)

(A.) Ottawa (1847); (D.) Pembroke (1898); (D.) Mont-Laurier (1913); (D.) Timmins (1915-1938); (D.) Hearst (1938); (D.) Hull (1963)

MONTREAL (1887)

(A.) Montréal (1836); (D.) Valleyfield (1892); (D.) Joliette (1904); (D.) St-Jean-de-Québec (1933); (D.) St-Jérôme (1951)

KINGSTON (1889)

(A.) Kingston (1826); (D.) Peterborough (1882); (D.) Alexandria (1890); (D.) Sault Ste. Marie (1904)

ST. JOHN'S (1904)

(A.) St. John's, Nfld. (1847); (D.) Grand Falls (1856); (D.) St. George's (1904)

VANCOUVER (1908)

(A.) Vancouver (1890); (D.) Victoria (1846); (D.) Nelson (1936); (D.) Kamloops (1945)

EDMONTON (1912)

(A.) Edmonton (1871-1912); (D.) Calgary (1912); (D.) St. Paul (1948)

WINNIPEG (1915)

(A.) Winnipeg (1915)

REGINA (1915)

(A.) Regina (1910); (D.) Prince Albert (1907-1933); (D.) Gravelbourg (1930); (D.) Saskatoon (1933); (A.N.) St. Peter's of Muenster (1911-1921)

MONCTON (1936)

(A.) Moncton (1936); (D.) Saint John, N.B. (1842); (D.) Bathurst (1860-1938); (D.) Edmundston (1944)

RIMOUSKI (1946)

(A.) Rimouski (1867); (D.) Gaspe (1922); (D.) Hauterive (1945)

SHERBROOKE (1951)

(A.) Sherbrooke (1874); (D.) St-Hyacinthe (1852); (D.) Nicolet (1885)

GROUARD-MCLENNAN (1967)

(A.) Grouard-McLennan (1927); (D.) Prince George (1916); (D.) Mackenzie-Fort Smith (1862); (D.) Whitehorse (1944)

KEEWATIN-LE PAS (1967)

(A.) Keewatin-Le Pas (1910); (D.) Churchill-Baie D'Hudson (1931); (D.) Moosonee (1938); (D.) Labrador-Schefferville (1945)

UKRAINIAN (1956)

(A.) Winnipeg (1956); (D.) Toronto (1956); (D.) Saskatoon (1956); (D.) Edmonton (1956); (D.) New Westminster (1974)

Division des Archidioceses

QUEBEC

Quebec: L.A. Vachon, Archevêque; L. Audet, J.-P. Labrie, Auxiliaires

Trois-Rivières: L. Noel, Evêque

Chicoutimi: Jean-Guy Couture, Evêque; R. Pedneault, Auxiliaire

Amos: G. Drainville, Evêque

Ste-Anne-de-la-Pocatière: G. H. Lévesque, Evêque

Rouyn-Noranda: Jean-Guy Hamelin, Evêque

HALIFAX

Halifax: J. M. Hayes, Archbishop

Charlottetown: F. J. Spence, Bishop

Antigonish: W. E. Power, Bishop

Yarmouth: A. E. Burke, Evêque

TORONTO

Toronto: G.E. Carter, Archbishop; A.M. Ambrozic, R.B. Clune, M.P. Lacey, L.J. Wall, Auxiliaries

Hamilton: P. E. Reding, Bishop; J.H. MacDonald, Auxiliary

London: J.M. Sherlock, Bishop

Thunder Bay: J.A. O'Mara, Bishop

St. Catharines: T. Fulton, Bishop

ST-BONIFACE

St-Boniface: A. Hacault, Archevêque

OTTAWA

Ottawa: J. A. Plourde, Archevêque; G. Bélisle, Auxiliaire; J.M. Beahen, Auxiliary

Pembroke: J. R. Windle, Bishop

Mont-Laurier: Jean Graton, Evêque

Timmins: J. Landriault, Evêque

Hearst: R. A. Despatie, Evêque

Hull: A. Proulx, Evêque

MONTREAL

Montréal: P. Grégoire, Archevêque; V. Bélanger, A. M. Cimichella, J.-M. Lafontaine, Gérard Tremblay, Jude St-Antoine, Auxiliaires; L. P. Whelan, L. Crowley, Auxiliaries

Valleyfield: R. Lebel, Evêque

Joliette: R. Audet, Evêque

St-Jean-de-Québec: B. Hubert, Evêque

St-Jérôme: C. Valois, Evêque

KINGSTON

Kingston: J. L. Wilhelm, Archbishop

Peterborough: J.L. Doyle, Bishop

Alexandria: Eugène P. LaRocque, Evêque

Sault Ste. Marie: A. Carter, Bishop; G. Dionne, Auxiliary; B. F. Pappin, Auxiliary

ST. JOHN'S, NFLD.

St. John's, Nfld.: A.L. Penney, Archbishop

Grand Falls: J.F. MacDonald, Bishop

St. George's: R. McGrath, Bishop

VANCOUVER
Vancouver: J. Carney, Archbishop; L. Sabatini, Auxiliary
Victoria: R. De Roo, Bishop
Nelson: W. E. Doyle, Bishop
Kamloops: A. Exner, Bishop

EDMONTON
Edmonton: J. N. MacNeil, Archbishop
Calgary: P. J. O'Byrne, Bishop
Saint-Paul: R. Roy, Evêque

WINNIPEG
Winnipeg: G. B. Cardinal Flahiff, Archbishop

REGINA
Regina: C. Halpin, Archbishop
Prince Albert: L. Morin, Evêque
Gravelbourg: N. Delaquis, Evêque
Saskatoon: J. P. Mahoney, Bishop
St. Peter's of Muenster: J. Weber, Ordinary

MONCTON
Moncton: D. Chiasson, Archevêque
Saint John, N.B.: A. Gilbert, Bishop
Bathurst: E. Godin, Evêque
Edmundston: F. Lacroix, Evêque

RIMOUSKI
Rimouski: G. Ouellet, Archevêque
Gaspé: B. Blanchet, Evêque
Hauterive: Roger Ebacher, Evêque

SHERBROOKE
Sherbrooke: J. M. Fortier, Archevêque
Saint-Hyacinthe: Louis-de-Gonzague Langevin, Evêque
Nicolet: A. Martin, Evêque

GROUARD-MCLENNAN
Grouard-McLennan: H. Legaré, Archevêque
Prince George: F. J. O'Grady, Bishop
Mackenzie-Fort Smith: P. Piché, Evêque
Whitehorse: H. O'Connor, Bishop

KEEWATIN-LE PAS
Keewatin-Le Pas: P. Dumouchel, Archevêque
Churchill-Baie D'Hudson: O. Robidoux, Evêque
Moosonee: J. LeGuerrier, Evêque
Labrador-Schefferville: P. Sutton, Evêque

UKRAINIAN
Winnipeg: M. Hermaniuk, Eparch
Toronto: I. Borecky, Eparch
Saskatoon: A. Roborecki, Eparch
Edmonton: N. Savaryn, Eparch; Martin Greschuk, Auxiliary
New Westminster: Jerome I. Chimy, Eparch

SLOVAKIAN
Toronto: M. Rusnak, Eparch

GREEK MELKITE CATHOLIC
Montreal: M. Hakim, Apostolic exarch

THE SALVATION ARMY IN CANADA

Headquarters for Canada and Bermuda: 20 Albert St., (Box 4021, Stn. A, Toronto, Ont. M5W 2B1)
Territorial Commander, Commr. John D. Waldron
Chief Secretary, Col. Harry Read
Field Secretary, Col. Edward Read
Financial Secretary, Lt.-Col. N. Sampson
Personnel Secretary, Lt.-Col. Calvin Ivany
Property Secretary, Major Wm. Kerr
Editor-in-Chief, Major Dudley Coles
Education Secretary, Brig. Gordon Holmes
Information Services Secretary, Major Ken Evenden
Music Secretary, Capt. Robert Redhead
Printing & Publishing Secretary, Brig. Cyril Gillingham
Red Shield Services Secretary, Major Donald McMillan
Trade Secretary, Brig. W. Vernon Marsland
Women's Organizations President, Mrs. Commr. John D. Waldron
Territorial Home League Secretary, Lt.-Col. Evelyn Hammond
Territorial League of Mercy Secretary, Mrs. Col. Harry Read
Territorial Youth Secretary, Major Roy Calvert
Correctional Services Secretary, Major James Tackaberry
Men's Social Services Secretary, Lt.-Col. Melvin Hamilton
Territorial Public Relations Secretary, Major Frederick Halliwell
Senior Citizens' Services Secretary, Brig. Robert Weddell
Women's Social Services Secretary, Lt.-Col. Doris Routly

TRAINING COLLEGE
The William Booth Memorial Training College, 2130 Bayview Ave., Toronto, Ont.; Principal, Major Edwin Brown
The William Booth Memorial College for Officers' Training, 21 Adams Ave., St. John's, Nfld.; Principal, Major David Hammond

DIVISIONAL HEADQUARTERS
Address, "The Divisional Commander"
Alta.: Bank of Commerce Bldg., Room 404, 10102-101st St., Edmonton, Alta. T5J 0S5 (403/423-2111)
Bermuda: Box 412, Hamilton, Bermuda (809/292-0601)
B.C. North: 1500-10 Ave. E., Box 490, Prince Rupert, B.C. V8J 3R2 (604/624-2773)
B.C. South: 555 W. Hastings St., Ste. 1540, Vancouver, B.C. V6B 4N6 (Box 12135) (604/682-2841)
Man. & N.W. Ont.: 400 Colony St., Room 301, Winnipeg, Man. R3B 2P4 (204/774-1993)
Maritime: 1329 Barrington St., Halifax, N.S. B3J 1Y9 (902/423-7603)
Metropolitan Toronto: 171 Millwood Rd., Toronto, Ont. M4S 1J6 (416/485-0731)
Mid-Ont.: 218 Front St., Box 577, Belleville, Ont. K8N 5B2 (613/962-0336)
Nfld. (Central): 1 Junction Rd., Grand Falls, Nfld. A2A 2K2 (709/489-5839)
Nfld. (Eastern): 146 Campbell Ave., St. John's, Nfld. A1E 2Z8 (709/579-2022)
Nfld. (Western): #202, 10 Manin St., Corner Brook, Nfld. (Box 1018, A2H 6J3) (709/639-8632)
Northern Ont.: 27 Coldwater St. E., Box 427, Orillia, Ont. L3V 6J8 (705/325-4416)
Que. & E. Ont.: 2000 Notre Dame St. W., Montreal, P.Q. H3J 1M8 (514/937-2832)
Sask.: 2040 McIntyre St., Regina, Sask. S4P 2R6 (306/527-1631)
S. Ont.: 28 Rebecca St., Hamilton, Ont. L8R 1B4 (416/528-9863)
W. Ont.: 330 Queen's Ave., Box 875, Stn. B, London, Ont. N6A 4Z3 (519/433-6106)

SEVENTH-DAY ADVENTIST CHURCH IN CANADA

CANADIAN UNION CONFERENCE
President, L. L. Reile
Secretary, P.F. Lemon
Secretary of the Dept. of Public Affairs, D.D. Devnich, 1148 King St. E., Oshawa, Ont. L1H 1H8 (416/723-3401)
Health Institutions, North York Branson Hospital, 555 Finch Ave. W., Willowdale, Ont. M2R 1N5
Publishing House, Pacific Publishing Association, Box 306, Oshawa, Ont. L1H 7L5

PROVINCIAL CONFERENCES WITH SECRETARIES
Alta.: C.G. Patterson, Box 5007, Red Deer, Alta. T4N 6A1
B.C.: G. Deboer, Box 1000, Abbotsford, B.C. V2S 4P5
Man.-Sask.: G. Gray, 1004 Victoria Ave., Saskatoon, Sask. S7N 0Z8
Maritime: Reid Coolen, 120 Salisbury Rd., Moncton, N.B. E1E 1A6
Ont.: T. McLeary, 1110 King St. E., Oshawa, Ont. L1H 7M1
Que. S.D.A. Church Association: T. W. Staples, 940 Ch. Chambly, Longueuil, P.Q. J4H 3M3
S.D.A. Church in Nfld.: 106 Freshwater Rd., St. John's, Nfld. A1C 2N8
Educational Institutions, Kingsway College, Oshawa, Ont. L1H 7L3; Canadian Union College, College Heights, Alta. T0C 0Z0

THE SYNAGOGUE IN CANADA

Synagogues in Canada are autonomous, responsible to no superiors and not organized in an hierarchical manner. Any group of Jews may form a synagogue which does not necessarily require the services of a Rabbi, and any individual is allowed to lead in the recital of prayers.

There are four movements in Judaism — Orthodox, Conservative, Reform and Reconstructionist. The Orthodox movement is the most traditional and the Reconstructionist the most liberal, vis-a-vis the movement's adherence to Mosaic and Rabbinic law.

There is an organization of synagogues which joins together Jewish leaders of all persuasion to discuss and deal with issues that affect the entire Jewish community.

Areas of direct concern include: strengthening membership and participation in synagogue life, the state of the Jewish family and marriage, aging and the aged, legislative enactments affecting religious observances, chaplaincy services, Jewish education, religious broadcasting, and religious functions for small Jewish communities. This organization is the National Religious Department of Canadian Jewish Congress. One hundred fifty synagogues of all denominations are registered with this Department. For further information, contact Rabbi Robert Sternberg, Executive Director, National Religious Department, Canadian Jewish Congress, 1590 Ave. Docteur Penfield, Montreal, P.Q. H3G 1C5 (514/931-7531)

Some synagogues are affiliated with the parent organizations of their own movements:

Orthodox — Union of Orthodox Jewish Congregations of America

Conservative — United Synagogue of America

Reform — Union of American Hebrew Congregations

Other Canadian congregations are not affiliated with any of these parent organizations. In all cases, none of the parent organizations have any authority over its constituent members.

CANADIAN UNITARIAN & UNIVERSALIST CHURCHES & FELLOWSHIPS

There is a membership of about 5,000, comprised of 18 Churches, and 31 Fellowships (lay groups). The Churches and Fellowships are members of the Unitarian Universalist Association, 25 Beacon St., Boston, Mass. 02108 and of the Canadian Unitarian Council, 175 St. Clair Ave. W., Toronto, Ont. M4V 1P7 (416/921-4506)

OFFICERS OF CANADIAN UNITARIAN COUNCIL

President, Brian Reid
Secretary, Rev. Vernon Nichols
Treasurer, Miss Anna M. MacIver
Administrative Secretary, Mrs. Thelma Peters

THE UNITED CHURCH OF CANADA

Headquarters: 85 St. Clair Ave. E., Toronto, Ont. M4T 1M8
(416) 925-5931

STATISTICS FOR 1979

Pastoral Charges: 2,382
Missionaries: 110 in 16 countries
Ministers: 3,599
Members: 907,222
Preaching Places: 4,271

The United Church of Canada was formed in 1925 through the union of the Methodist Church, the Congregational Union of Canada and the Councils of Local Union Churches, and 70 per cent. of the Presbyterian Church in Canada. On January 1, 1968, the Canada Conference of the Evangelical United Brethren became part of The United Church of Canada. The United Church is a full member of the World Methodist Council, the World Alliance of Reformed Churches (Presbyterian and Congregational) and the Canadian and World Council of Churches.

THE GENERAL COUNCIL

The General Council is the highest legislative body of The United Church of Canada. The Moderator is elected at each meeting of the General Council to hold office until the following Council.

Moderator, The Rt. Rev. Lois M. Wilson
Secretary, Rev. Donald G. Ray
Deputy Secretary (Regionalism & Personnel), Rev. Albion R. Wright
Deputy Secretary (Theology & Faith), Rev. Peter G. White
Personnel Officer, Margaret Fortin
Research Officer, Rev. David Stone
Archivist-Historian, Rev. C. Glenn Lucas, 73 Queen's Park Cr. E., Toronto, Ont. M5S 2C4 (416/978-3832)

PERIODICAL "The United Church Observer"

Editor, Hugh B. McCullum
Advertising, Jack Wells
Circulation, Gordon Mason

The Administrative Divisions

DIVISION OF COMMUNICATION

Secretary, Rev. Frank Brisbin
Regional Relations, Rev. Keith Woollard
Education for Mission & Stewardship, Rev. Robert Plant
News Services, Ms. Alayne Scanlon
Audio-Visuals Consultant, Mrs. Margaret Nix

Media Services: 315 Queen St. E., Toronto, Ont. M5A 1S7
(416) 366-9221
Director, Rev. Earl Leard
Services include TV & Films; Radio; Still Pictures; Cassettes; Photos

CANEC Publishing & Supply House: 47 Coldwater Rd., Don Mills, Ont. M3B 1Y9
(416) 449-7440
General Manager, Alun Hughes

DIVISION OF FINANCE

Secretary, Douglas Borgal
Dept. of the Treasury: Treasurer, Wm. Davis
Dept. of Pensions: Secretary, Rev. Douglas Weatherburn
Dept. of Stewardship Services: Secretary, Rev. M. Jewitt Parr

DIVISION OF MINISTRY PERSONNEL & EDUCATION

Secretary, Rev. Howard M. Mills
Division includes Career Development; Personnel Services; Student Services & Field Education; Grants & Admissions

DIVISION OF MISSION IN CANADA

Secretary, Rev. Howard L. Brox
Division includes Christian Development; Church in Society; Curriculum Resources; Evangelism; Ministry with Adults, Laity; Marriage & Family Life; Persons of Special Need; Social Issues; Youth; Senior Adults; Resource; French-English Relations; Human Rights & International Affairs; and Hospitals & Medical Work–Supt., Dr. W.D. Watt, 6762 Cypress St., Vancouver, B.C. V6P 5L8, 604/266-5426

DIVISION OF WORLD OUTREACH

Secretary, Rev. Garth Legge
Caribbean & Latin America, Rev. Garth Legge
Africa, Rev. James Kirkwood
Asia, Rev. Frank Carey
Inter-Faith Dialogue, Dr. John Berthrong
Personnel, Ms. Janet MacPherson
World Development, Service & Relief, Ms. Glenna Graham
Administration, Rev. Fred Bayliss

EXECUTIVE SECRETARIES OF CONFERENCES

Alta.: Rev. P.A. Cline, 6724 99 St., Edmonton, Alta. T6E 5B8 (403/432-0287)
Bay of Quinte: Rev. Peter McKellar, 218 Barrie St., Kingston, Ont. K7L 3K3 (613/549-2503)
B.C.: 1955 W. 4th Ave., Vancouver, B.C. V6J 1M7 (604/682-7556)
Hamilton: Mrs. Irene Parker, Box 100, Carlisle, Ont. L0R 1H0 (416/659-3343)

London: Rev. L.T.C. Harbour, 359 Windermere Rd., London, Ont. N6G 2K3 (519/672-1930)
Manitoba: Rev. W.J. Hickerson, 120 Maryland St., Winnipeg, Man. R3G 1L1 (204/786-8911)
Manitou: Rev. F.A. Sorensen, 366 McIntyre St., North Bay, Ont. P1B 2Z1 (705/474-3350)
Maritime: Rev. J.H. Tye, Box 1560, Sackville, N.S. E0A 3C0 (506/536-1334)
Montreal & Ottawa: Rev. Richard Allen, #204, 352 Dorval Ave., Dorval, P.Q. H9S 3H8 (514/613-8594)
Nfld: Rev. Boyd Hiscock, Box 248, St. John's, Nfld. A1C 5J2 (709/576-4011)
Saskatchewan: Rev. R.S. Harper, 1805 Rae St., Regina, Sask. S4T 2E3 (306/525-9155)
Toronto: Rev. W.H. Walsh, #321, 85 St. Clair Ave. E., Toronto, Ont. M4T 1L8 (416/967-1880)

BOARDS OF TRADE & CHAMBERS OF COMMERCE IN CANADA

The Canadian Chamber of Commerce Headquarters, Commerce House, 1080 Beaver Hall Hill, Montreal, P.Q. H2Z 1T2 (514/866-4334)
President, S.F. Hughes

CC—Chamber of Commerce; BT—Board of Trade; Ag—Agriculture

CANADIAN COUNCIL INTERNATIONAL CHAMBER OF COMMERCE

President, B.G. Côté, Director, Kruger Inc., Montreal
General Manager, R. Lorne Seitz, Room 710, 1080 Beaver Hall Hill, Montreal, P.Q. H2Z 1T2 (514/866-4334)

CANADA–UNITED KINGDOM CHAMBER OF COMMERCE

Secretary, Brian Burrows, 3 Lower Regent St., London, SW1Y 4NZ, England – (01) 839-1838

LA FEDERATION DES JEUNES CHAMBRES DU CANADA FRANCAIS

Secrétaire executif, Pierre Gauthier, 2745, rue Masson, Montréal, P.Q. H1Y 1W6 (514/721-4919)

NORTHWESTERN ONTARIO ASSOCIATED CHAMBERS OF COMMERCE

Box 263, Fort Frances, Ont. P9A 3M6
(807) 274-3057
Secretary Treasurer, H.A.L. Tibbetts, Fort Frances

ATLANTIC PROVINCES TRANSPORTATION COMMISSION

236 St. George St., Ste. 210, Box 577, Moncton, N.B. E1C 8L9
(506) 855-0031
Telex: 014-2842
Chairman, Elwood L. Dillman, Hantsport, N.S.
General Manager, Craig S. Dickson, Moncton, N.B.

CANADA JAYCEES

President, Cyril Mills
Executive Director, Ken R. McAra, 39 Leacock Way, Kanata, Ont. K2K 1T1 (613/592-2450)

WHITEHORSE CHAMBER OF COMMERCE

302 Steele St., Whitehorse, Yukon Y1A 2C5
(403) 667-7545

YELLOWKNIFE CHAMBER OF COMMERCE

Box 906, Yellowknife, N.W.T. XOE 1HO
(403) 873-3131
Secretary Manager, Mrs. T. Bossert

CHAMBER OF COMMERCE FOR BELGIUM & LUXEMBOURG IN CANADA

B.P. 548, Station NDG, Montreal, P.Q. H4A 3P8
(514) 488-8229
Executive Secretary, P. van Emmerik

BRAZIL-CANADA CHAMBER OF COMMERCE

Head Office, 11 Adelaide St. W., Ste. 307, Toronto, Ont. M5H 1L9 (416/364-4634)
General Manager, L.A. Bourgeois
West Coast Representative, Ingrid Megnis Derviller, Box 5132, Main PO, Vancouver, B.C. V6B 4B2 (604/669-5625)

CANADA-JAPAN TRADE COUNCIL

75 Albert St., Ste. 903, Ottawa, Ont. K1P 5E7
(613) 233-4047
President, N. Gregor Guthrie

CANADIAN GERMAN CHAMBER OF INDUSTRY & COMMERCE INC.

2015 Peel St., Ste. 1110, Montreal, P.Q. H3A 1T8
(514) 844-3051
General Manager, U. Harnack
480 University Ave., Ste. 1410, Toronto, Ont. M5G 1V6
(416) 598-3355
Manager, R. Steinbrink
Main Floor Lobby, Hotel Macdonald, Edmonton, Alta. T5J ON6
(403) 420-6611
Manager, E. Goetting

ITALIAN CHAMBER OF COMMERCE OF MONTREAL

1255 Phillips Sq., #1109, Montreal, P.Q. H3B 3G1
(514) 866-0070
President, Giovanni Giarrusso

ITALIAN CHAMBER OF COMMERCE OF TORONTO

159 Bay St., Ste. 313, Toronto, Ont. M5J 1J7
(416) 364-6551, 364-9055
Managing Director, A. Valeri

SWISS-CANADIAN CHAMBER OF COMMERCE INC.

1572 Docteur Penfield Ave., Montreal, P.Q. H3G 1C4
(514) 937-5822

CHAMBERS OF MINES

ALBERTA CHAMBER OF RESOURCES

14th Floor, 10025 106 St., Edmonton, Alta. T5J 1G4
(403) 420-1030
Managing Director, Harold V. Page, P. Eng.
Employment and membership services to the Mineral Resource Industries.

BRITISH COLUMBIA & YUKON CHAMBER OF MINES

Manager, J.M. Patterson, 840 W. Hastings St., Vancouver, B.C. V6C 1C8 (604/681-5328)

CHAMBER OF MINES OF EASTERN BRITISH COLUMBIA

Secretary Treasurer, G.A. Murray, 215 Hall St., Nelson, B.C. V1L 5X4 (604/352-5242)

ALBERTA

Alberta Chamber of Commerce, #212, 10201-104 St., Edmonton, Alta. T5J 1B2
General Manager, B.G. Day, (403) 424-0531

Acme & Dist. CC & Ag, T0M 0A0
Acadia Valley CC, T0J 0A0
Airdrie CC, T0M 0B0
Alix CC, T0C 0B0
Ashmont BT, T0A 0C0
Athabasca CC, T0G 0B0
Banff-Lake Louise CC, T0L 0C0
Barrhead CC, T0G 0E0
Bashaw & Dist. CC, T0B 0H0
Bassano CC, T0J 0B0
Beaverlodge & Dist. CC, T0H 0C0
Beiseker & Dist. CC, T0M 0G0
Bentley CC, T0C 0J0
Berwyn CC, T0H 0E0
Big Valley Comm. Action Centre, T0J 0C0
Blackfalds CC, T0M 0J0
Bonnyville CC, T0A 0L0
Bowden CC, T0M 0K0
Bow Island CC, T0K 0G0
Boyle & Dist. CC, T0A 0M0
Breton & Dist. CC, T0C 0P0
Brooks CC, T0J 0J0
Calgary CC, Manager, C. M. Black, 273 One Palliser Sq., 125-9 Ave. S.E., T2G 0P6
Calmar & Dist. CC, T0C 0V0
Camrose CC, T4V 0K6
Carbon & Dist. CC, T0M 0L0
Cardston & Dist. CC, T0K 0K0
Carstairs & Comm. CC, T0M 0N0
Castor & Dist. BT, T0C 0X0
Cereal & Dist. BT, T0J 0N0
Chauvin & Dist. BT, T0B 0V0
Chipman CC, T0B 0W0
Claresholm CC, T0L 0T0
Coaldale CC, T0K 0L0
Cochrane CC, T0L 0W0
Cold Lake CC, T0A 0V0
Condor CC, T0M 0P0
Consort CC, T0K 1B0
Coronation Comm. CC, T0C 1C0
Coutts CC, T0K 0N0
Crossfield & Dist. CC, T0M 0S0
Crowsnest Pass CC
Devon CC, T0C 1E0
Didsbury & Dist. CC, T0M 0W0
Drayton Valley CC, T0E 0M0
Drumheller & Dist. CC, T0J 0Y0
Eckville CC, T0M 0X0
Edgerton & Dist. BT, T0B 1K0
Edmonton CC, General Manager, J. Chesney, 600, 10123 99 St., T5J 3G9
Edson CC, T0E 0P0
Egremont BT, T0A 0Z0
Elk Point CC, T0A 1A0
Empress CC, T0J 1E0
Fairview & Dist. CC, T0H 1L0
Falher CC, T0H 1M0
Foothills CC, Black Diamond, Alta. T0L 0H0
Foremost & Dist. CC, T0K 0X0
Fort Assiniboine CC, T0G 1A0
Fort Macleod & Dist. CC, T0L 0Z0
Fort McMurray CC, T0A 1K0
Fort Sask. CC & Ag, T0B 1P0
Fort Vermilion Area BT, T0H 1N0
Glendon CC, T0A 1P0
Grand Centre & Dist. CC, T0A 1T0
Grande Cache CC, T0E 0Y0
Grande Prairie CC, T8V 1B9
Grimshaw CC, T0H 1W0
Hanna CC, T0J 1P0
Hardisty CC, T0B 1V0
High Level & Dist. CC, T0H 1Z0
High Prairie CC, T0G 1E0
High River CC, T0L 1B0
Hines Creek & Dist. CC, T0H 2A0
Hinton & Dist. CC, T0E 1B0
Holden CC, T0B 2C0
Hythe & Dist. CC, T0H 2C0
Innisfail CC, T0M 1A0
Irma & Dist. CC, T0B 2H0
Irricana & Dist. CC, T0M 1B0
Jasper Park CC, T0E 1E0
Killam & Dist. CC, T0B 2L0
Kinuso & Dist. CC, T0G 1K0
Lac La Biche CC, T0A 2C0
Lacombe & Dist. BT, T0C 1S0
La Crete CC, T0H 2H0
Lamont & Dist. CC, T0B 2R0
Leduc & Dist. CC, T0C 1V0
Lethbridge CC, T1J 0P7
Lloydminster CC, S9V 0P7
Magrath & Dist. CC, T0K 1J0
Manning CC & Ag., T0H 2M0
Mannville CC, T0B 2W0
Marwayne & Dist. CC, T0B 2X0
Mayerthorpe & Dist. CC, T0E 1N0
McLennan CC, T0H 2L0
Medicine Hat CC, Manager, D.G. Oliphant, Box 670, T1A 7G6
Milk River & Dist. CC, T0K 1M0
Morinville BT, T0G 1P0
Myrnam CC, T0B 3K0
Nanton & Dist. CC, T0L 1R0
Onoway & Dist. CC, T0E 1V0
Oyen & Dist. CC, T0J 2J0
Peace River CC, T0H 2X0
Picture Butte & Dist. CC, T0K 1V0
Pincher Creek & Dist. CC, T0K 1W0
Pine Lake CC, T0M 1S0
Ponoka CC, T0C 2H0
Provost & Dist. CC, T0B 3S0
Radway CC, T0A 2V0
Rainbow Lake CC, T0H 2Y0
Raymond & Dist. CC, T0K 1Y0
Redcliff CC, T0J 2P0
Red Deer CC, P. Henry, Box 708, T4N 5H2
Rimbey CC, T0C 2J0
Rocky Mountain House CC, T0M 1T0
St. Albert & Dist. CC, T8N 1N2
St. Paul CC, T0A 3A0
Sangudo & Dist. CC, T0E 2A0
Sedgewick BT, T0B 4C0
Sherwood Park & Dist. CC, T8A 2A6
Slave Lk. & Dist. CC, T0G 2A0
Smith & Dist. CC, T0G 2B0
Smoky Lake & Dist. CC, T0A 3C0
Spirit River CC, T0H 3G0
Spruce Grove & Dist. CC, T0E 2C0
Stettler CC, T0C 2L0
Stony Plain & Dist. CC, T0E 2G0
Strathmore & Dist. CC, T0J 3H0
Sundre & Dist. CC, T0M 1X0
Swan Hills CC, T0G 2C0
Taber CC, T0K 2G0
Thorhild & Dist. CC, T0A 3J0
Thorsby & Dist. CC, T0C 2P0
Two Hills CC, T0B 4K0
Valleyview & Dist. CC, T0H 3N0
Vegreville CC, T0B 4L0
Vermilion CC, T0B 4M0
Veteran BT, T0C 2S0
Viking & Dist. CC, T0B 4N0
Vilna & Dist. CC, T0A 3L0
Wainwright & Dist. CC, T0B 4P0
Warner & Dist. CC, T0K 2L0
Waterton Lakes CC, T0K 2M0

Westlock & Dist. CC, T0G 2L0
Wetaskiwin & Dist. CC & Ag, T9A 1W7
Whitecourt CC, T0E 2L0

BRITISH COLUMBIA

Canadian Chamber of Commerce, Regional Office, 626 W. Pender St., #901, Vancouver, B.C. V6B 1V9 (604/681-5541)
Vancouver Office Manager, Miss M.J. Henderson

Area Code is 604

Abbotsford-Clearbrook CC, V2S 3P9 (859-9651)
Alberni Valley CC, Jo-Ann Nicklin, Box 190, Port Alberni, B.C. V9Y 7M7 (724-2048)
Aldergrove & Dist. CC, V0X 1A0 (856-2517)
Bowen Island CC, R.R. 1, VON 1GO (947-2222)
Burnaby CC, A. J. Macdonald, #10, 6035 Sussex Ave., V5H 3C1 (437-8464)
Cache Creek & Dist. CC, Box 460, VOK 1HO (457-9229)
Campbell River & Dist. CC, Box 400, V9W 5B6 (287-3912)
Castlegar & Dist. CC, Box 3001, V1N 3H4 (365-5337)
Central Coast CC, Box 40, Bella Bella, B.C. VOT 1BO (957-2378)
Chase & Dist. CC, V0E 1M0 (679-8432)
Chemainus-Crofton & Dist. CC, V0R 1K0 (246-9820)
Chetwynd CC, V0C 1J0 (788-9956)
Chilliwack CC, 5 First Ave., V2P 7E5 (792-4231)
Clinton & Dist. CC, V0K 1K0 (459-2645)
Coquitlam CC, Box 1124, V3J 6Z4 (461-0444)
Courtenay-Comox CC, V9N 5N4 (336-2486)
Cranbrook CC, Box 84, V1C 4H6 (426-5914)
Creston CC, V0B 1G0 (428-4342)
Cumberland CC, V0R 1S0 (334-3181)
Dawson Creek CC, D. D. McCartney, 10100-13th St., V1G 3W2 (782-4868)
Delta CC, 6005 No. 17 Hwy., V4K 3N3 (946-4232)
Duncan-Cowichan CC, Box 669, Duncan, B.C. (746-4421)
Enderby & Dist. CC, Box 1000, VOE 1VO
Fernie BT, V0B 1M0 (423-6913)
Fort Langley CC, c/o Box 394, V0X 1J0 (888-1555)
Fort Nelson CC, V0C 1R0 (774-2956)
Fort St. James CC, Box 1164, V0J 1P0
Fort St. John & Dist. CC (785-6037)
Gibsons & Dist. CC, Box 1190, VON 1VO (885-2691)
Golden & Dist. CC, Box 677, VOA 1HO (344-5204)
Grand Forks & Dist. BT, V0H 1H0 (442-2833)
Greenwood BT, Box 430, VOM 1JO (445-6398)
Hope & Dist. CC, Box 370, VOX 1LO (869-9941)
Houston & Dist. CC, V0J 1Z0
Kamloops (Greater) CC, C. J. Forget, Box 488, V2C 5L2 (372-7722)
Kelowna CC, Manager, Wm. Stevenson, Box 398, V1Y 7N8 (769-4140)
Kimberley & Dist. CC, V1A 2Y5 (427-3666)
Langley CC, Box 3422, V3A 4R8 (888-4892)
Likely CC, Box 79, VOL 1NO (790-2310)
Maple Ridge CC, V2X 2T2 (463-3366)
Merritt & Dist. CC, V0K 2B0 (378-6676)
Mission & Dist. CC, V2V 4J3 (826-6914)
Nakusp CC, V0G 1R0 (265-4143)
Nanaimo (Greater) CC, Manager, Mrs. Alice Hutchins, 100 Cameron Rd., V9R 2X1 (753-1191)
Nelson CC, V1L 4B4 (352-3433)
New Westminster CC, Manager, R. S. Macdonell, 333 Brunette, V3L 3E7 (521-7781)
North Vancouver CC, Manager, Mrs. M.J. Pitt-Brooke, 131 E. 2nd St., V7L 1C2 (987-4488)
Oliver CC, V0H 1T0 (498-4296)
Osoyoos CC, V0H 1V0 (495-7142)
Parksville & Dist. CC, V0R 2S0 (248-3613)
Pemberton & Dist. CC, V0N 2L0 (894-6530)
Penticton CC, Executive Manager, Ross Axworthy, Jubilee Pavilion, 185 Lakeshore Dr., V2A 1B7 (492-4103)
Port Hardy & Dist. CC, V0N 2P0 (949-6412)
Port McNeill & Dist. CC, V0N 2R0 (956-3333)
Powell River CC, Box 70, V8A 4Z5 (485-4051)
Prince George CC, 1198 Victoria St., V2L 2L2 (562-2454)
Prince Rupert CC, Mrs. B.A. Grodecki, Box 158, V8J 3P6 (624-2296)
Princeton & Dist. CC, V0X 1W0 (295-6862)
Queen Charlotte Is. CC, Box 69, V0T 1M0 (626-5048)
Quesnel & Dist. CC, 703 Carson Ave., V2J 2B6 (992-8716)
Revelstoke CC, Box 490, V0E 2S0 (837-5345)
Richmond CC, Manager, Irene Vennard, 8060 Granville St., (278-2822)
Rossland CC, V0G 1Y0
Salmon Arm & Dist. CC, V0E 2T0 (832-6247)
Salt Spring Island CC, V0S 1E0 (537-5571)
Sayward CC, Box 70, V0P 1R0 (282-3749)
Sechelt Dist. CC, V0N 3A0 (885-3216)
Sidney & North Saanich CC, V8L 3S3 (656-3616)
Slocan Dist. CC, Box 488, New Denver, B.C. V0G 1S0
Smithers & Dist. CC, V0J 2N0 (847-9854)
Squamish & Dist. CC, V0N 3G0 (892-5919)
Surrey Regional CC, 15105A 105 Ave., Surrey, B.C. V3R 7G9 (581-7130)
Terrace Dist. CC, V8G 4A2
Tofino-Long Beach CC, V0R 2Z0 (725-3356)
Trail CC, Ms. J.I. Turner, 1300 Cedar Ave., V1R 4C2 (368-3144)
Ucluelet/Port Albion CC, Box 161, Ucluelet, B.C. VOR 3AO (726-7741)
Valemount CC (non-member)
Vancouver BT, Managing Director, B. Pepper, #500, 1177 W. Hastings, V6E 2K3 (681-2111)
Vanderhoof & Dist. CC, Box 126, VOJ 3AO (567-2500)
Vernon CC, General Manager, Lew V. Rossner, 3700-33rd St., V1T 5T6 (545-0771)
Victoria (Greater) CC, Manager, Brian J. Small, 1020 Government St., V8W 1X7 (383-7191)
West Vancouver CC, Madge Germain, Box 91026, V7V 3N3 (926-6614)
Whistler Mountain Dist. CC, V0N 1B0 (932-5491)
White Rock CC, V4B 1C4 (536-6844)
Williams Lake & Dist. CC, Box 4330, V2G 2V4 (392-4360)
Windermere Dist. CC, Box 249, VOA 1KO (342-6514)

MANITOBA

Manitoba Chamber of Commerce, #401, 177 Lombard Ave., Winnipeg, Man. R3B 0W8
(204) 942-2561
Executive Director, Alex Milton

Area Code is 204

Altona CC, R0G 0B0 (324-6731)
Binscarth CC, R0J 0G0 (532-2279)
Birch River CC, R0L 0E0 (236-4280)
Birtle CC, R0M 0C0
Boissevain CC, R0K 0E0 (534-2433)
Brandon CC, General Manager, Rick Chrest, Box 548, R7A 5Z7 (727-5431)
Carberry CC, R0K 0H0 (834-3349)
Carman CC, R0G 0J0 (745-2467)
Crystal City CC, R0K 0N0 (873-2331)
Dauphin CC, 21-2 Ave. N.W., R7N 1H1 (638-4838)
Deloraine CC, R0M 0M0
Emerson CC, R0A 0L0 (373-2029)
Erickson CC, R0J 0P0 (636-2431)
Flin Flon CC (687-3444)
Gimli CC, R0C 1B0 (642-5284)
Gladstone CC, R0J 0T0
Glenboro CC, R0K 0X0 (827-2729)
Grandview CC, R0L 0Y0 (546-2834)
Hamiota CC, R0M 0T0
Inglis CC, R0J 0X0 (564-2401)
Kenton CC, R0M 0Z0 (828-2371)
Killarney CC, R0K 1G0 (523-7011)
La Broquerie CC, R0A 0W0 (424-5423)
Lac du Bonnet CC, R0E 1A0
Lynn Lake CC, Box 229, R0B 0W0 (356-8019)
MacGregor CC, R0H 0R0 (685-2130)
Manitou CC, R0G 1G0 (242-2801)
McCreary CC, R0J 1B0 (835-2456)

Melita CC, R0M 1L0 (522-3463)
Minnedosa CC, R0J 1E0 (867-2279)
Morden CC, R0G 1J0 (822-5630)
Neepawa CC, Box 726, R0J 1H0 (476-5292)
Pilot Mound CC, R0G 1P0 (825-2022)
Piney CC, R0A 1K0 (423-2207)
Plum Coulee CC, R0G 1R0
Portage la Prairie CC, Secretary Manager, Mrs. Joyce Brooker, 160 Saskatchewan Ave., R1N 0M1 (857-7778)
Rapid City CC, R0K 1W0 (826-2090)
Reston CC, R0M 1X0 (877-3877)
Roblin CC, R0L 1P0 (937-2792)
Russell CC, Box 205, R0J 1W0 (773-2099)
Ste Anne CC, R0A 1R0 (422-8870)
St. Boniface CC, 41 St. Mary's Rd., St. Boniface, Winnipeg, Man. R2H 1H6 (247-6991)
St. Claude CC, R0G 1Z0
St. Jean Baptiste CC, R0G 2B0 (758-3393)
St. James-Assiniboia CC, 200 Berry St., St. James, Man. R3J 1N2 (888-1574)
St. Malo CC, R0A 1T0 (347-5610)
St. Pierre CC, R0A 1V0 (433-7645)
St. Vital CC, 644 Oakenwald, Winnipeg, Man. R3T 1M7 (452-8426)
Selkirk CC, Box 189, R1A 2B2 (482-6926)
Shoal Lake CC, R0J 1Z0
Sprague CC, R0A 1Z0 (437-2173)
Steinbach CC, R0A 2A0 (326-9566)
Stonewall CC, R0C 2Z0 (467-8343)
Swan River CC, R0L 1Z0 (734-3737)
Teulon CC, R0C 3B0 (886-2826)
The Pas CC (623-3862)
Thompson CC (677-5171)
Virden CC, R0M 2C0 (748-3955)
Wasagaming CC, R0J 2H0
Winkler CC, Box 808, R0G 2X0 (325-4301)
Winnipeg CC, General Manager, W. W. Draper, 177 Lombard Ave., R3B 0W7 (944-8484)
Winnipegosis CC, R0L 2G0

ATLANTIC PROVINCES

Atlantic Provinces Chamber of Commerce, 1111 Main St., #305, Moncton, N.B. E1C 1H3
(506) 854-0480
Executive Vice President, Mike Cahill

New Brunswick

Allardville CC, EOB 1AO
Baie-Ste-Anne CC, E0C 1A0
Bath CC, E0J 1E0
Bathurst CC, Manager, Mrs. Geraldine Mason, Box 620, E2A 3Z4
Blackville CC, E0C 1C0
Buctouche CC, E0A 1G0
Campbellton CC, E3N 3G7
Campobello Island CC, EOG 3LO
Canterbury BT, E0H 1C0
Caraquet CC, E0B 1K0
Charlotte Co. CC, EOG 2XO
Chatham CC, E1N 3A6
Clair CC, E0L 1B0
Collette CC, EOA 2TO
Deer Island CC, E0G 2G0
Edmundston CC, Manager, Renaud Bard, Box 338, E3V 3K9
Fredericton CC, Manager, Michael Ross, Box 275, E3B 4Y9
Grand Falls & Dist. CC, E0J 1M0
Grand Manan BT, EOG 2MO
Hampton & Area CC, E0G 1Z0
Hartland CC, E0J 1N0
Inkerman CC, E0B 1S0
Lameque CC, E0B 1V0
Maisonnette CC, E0B 1X0
McAdam CC, E0H 1K0
Memramcook CC, E0A 2C0
Miramichi BT, E0H 1A0
Greater Moncton CC, General Manager, Darryl Goyetche, Box 1009, E1C 8P2
Neguac CC, E0C 1S0
Newcastle CC, E1V 3M2
Oromocto CC, E2V 2G5
Petit Rocher CC, E0B 2E0
Petite Riviere de L'Ile CC, E0B 2C0
Plaster Rock CC, EOJ 1WO
Rivière-du-Portage CC, EOC 1YO
Richibucto CC, EOA 2MO
St. Andrews CC, EOG 2XO
Saint Francois CC, EOL 1JO
Saint John BT, General Manager, Lynda Heffernan, 2nd floor, Admiral Beatty Hotel, King Sq., E2L 1E5
St. Leonard CC, EOL 1MO
Saint Quentin CC, E0K 1J0
St. Raphael-Pigeon Hill CC, E0B 2N0
St. Stephen CC, E3L 2X3
St. Simon CC, EOB 1LO
Shediac & Area CC, E0A 3G0
Shippegan CC, E0B 2P0
Sussex CC, EOE 1PO

Nova Scotia

Amherst CC, B4H 3Y6
Annapolist Dist. BT, B0S 1A0
Annapolis Valley Affiliated BT, Manager, Dianne LeGard, Box 1149, Middleton, N.S. B0S 1P0
Antigonish CC, B2G 2L8
Bear River BT, B0S 1B0
Bedford BT, B4A 2X3
Berwick BT, B0P 1E0
Bridgetown BT, B0S 1C0
Bridgewater CC, B4V 1N1
Canso BT, B0H 1H0
Chester CC, B0J 1J0
Dartmouth CC, Manager, Mrs. M. Gilbert, 12 Portland St., B2Y 1G9
Digby BT, B0V 1A0
Grand Narrows & Dist. BT, B0A 1C0
Guysborough BT, B0H 1N0
Halifax BT, General Manager, G. Lummis, 5251 Duke St., #400, B3J 1P3
Industrial Cape Breton, Manager, W. MacDonald, Box 131, Sydney, N.S. B1P 6G9
Isaac's Harbour Dist. BT, B0H 1S0
Kentville & Area BT, B4N 3X1
Lunenburg BT, B0J 2C0
Middleton & Dist. BT, B0S 1P0
Musquodoboit Harbour BT, B0J 2L0
New Glasgow CC, B2H 1J5
North Queens BT, BOT 1BO
Parrsboro CC, B0M 1S0
Pictou CC, B0K 1H0
Port Hawkesbury CC, B0E 2V0
River Bourgeois CC, BOE 2XO
Riverdale CC, BOE 1JO
Riverport & Dist. BT, B0J 2W0
Sackville & Dist. CC, B4C 2S8
St. Peters & Dist. CC, B0E 3B0
Sheet Harbour BT, B0J 3B0
South Queens CC, B0T 1K0
South Shore Associated BTs, B0T 1B0
Springhill CC, B0M 1X0
Tiverton & Dist. BT, B0V 1G0
Truro CC, Secretary Manager, A. Thomson, Box 54, B2N 5B6
United BT, BOJ 2KO
Windsor BT, B0N 2T0
Whycocomach & Dist. BT, B0E 2K0
Wolfville BT, B0P 1X0
Yarmouth CC, Manager, Rupert White, Box 425, B5A 4B3

Prince Edward Island

Charlottetown CC, General Manager, Keith Mullins, Box 67, C1A 7K2
Crapaud-Victoria CC, C0A 1J0
Eastern Kings CC, COA 2BO
Greater Summerside CC, General Manager, Earl Cannon, 267 Water St., C1B 1B5
Kensington Area CC, C0B 1M0
Montague Regional CC, C0A 1R0
West Prince CC, C0B 1V0

Newfoundland & Labrador

Baie Verte CC, AOK 1BO
Botwood CC, A0H 1E0
Burgeo CC, A0M 1A0
Channel Port Aux Basques CC, A0M 1C0
Clarenville CC, A0E 1J0
Corner Brook CC, A2H 6E6
Deer Lake CC, A0K 2E0
Gander CC, Manager, Box 159, A1V 1W6
Glovertown CC, A0G 2L0
Grand Falls CC, Manager, Walter Tucker, Box 272, A2A 2J7
Harbour Grace BT, AOA 2MO
Ingornachoix CC, A0K 3B0
Labrador North CC, A0P 1C0
Labrador West CC, Box 444, AOR 1BO
Lewisporte CC, A0G 3A0
Pasadena CC, AOL 1KO
St. Anthony CC, AOK 4SO
St. John's BT, General Manager, Bruce Tilley, Box 5127, A1C 5V5
Springdale CC, A0J 1T0
Stephenville CC, Box 28, A2N 2Y7
Twillingate CC, A0G 4M0
Windsor CC, A0H 2H0

ONTARIO

Ontario Chamber of Commerce, 2323 Yonge St., 5th floor, Toronto, Ont. M4P 2C9
(416) 482-5222
General Manager, J.G. Carnegie

Acton CC, Box 415, L7J 2M7 (519/853-0925)
Ajax CC, Box 97, L1S 3C2 (416/683-0291)
Amherstburg-Anderdon & Malden Dist. CC, Box 162, Amherstburg, Ont. N9V 2Z3 (519/736-7272)
Atikokan CC, 119 Pine Cres., POT 1CO
Atwood Dist. CC, Main St., NOG 1BO (519/356-2431)
Ayr & Dist. CC, N0B 1E0 (519/632-7302)
Bancroft & Dist. CC, Box 539, K0L 1C0 (613/332-2143)
Barrie CC, R. J. Hollywood, 2 Fred Grant St., L4M 3G6 (705/726-6573)
Beaver Valley CC, Box 477, Thornbury, Ont. N0H 2P0 (519/599-3322)
Belleville CC, D. L. Sutton, Box 726, K8N 5B3 (613/962-4597)
Belmore CC, R.R. 1, Wroxeter, Ont. NOG 1MO (519/335-3696)
Blenheim & Dist. CC, 20 Catherine St., NOP 1AO (519/676-3841)
Blind River CC, P0R 1B0
Bobcaygeon CC, 34 Bolton St., K0M 1A0 (705/738-2202)
Bothwell & Dist. CC, 184 Main St. N., NOP 1CO (519/695-2732)
Bowmanville CC, 54 Loscombe Dr., L1C 3S9 (416/623-5573)
Bracebridge CC, Box 578, P0B 1C0
Bradford CC, Box 476, L0G 1C0 (416/775-3381)
Brampton BT, 55 Queen St. E., L6W 2A8 (416/451-1122)
Brantford CC, Box 1294, N3T 5T6 (519/753-2617)
Brockville CC, Victoria Bldg., K6V 3P5 (613/342-6553)
Brodhagen & Dist. CC, R.R. 5, Mitchell, Ont. N0K 1N0 (519/345-2438)
Burlington CC, Box 103, L7R 3X8 (416/639-0174)
Caledonia Regional CC, Box 5, NOA 1AO (416/765-4454)
Cambridge CC, 785 Coronation Blvd., N1R 6H7 (519/621-8030)
Campbellford CC, Box 376, K0L 1L0 (705/653-1551)
Cannington CC, Box 9, LOE 1EO
Capreol & Dist. CC, Box 858, POM 1HO
Chapleau Area CC, Box 365, P0M 1K0 (705/864-1442)
Chatham CC, Hugh McMillan, 275 King St. W., N7M 1E9 (519/352-7540)
Cobourg CC, 55 King St. W., K9A 2M2 (416/372-5831)
Cochrane BT, Box 1468, P0L 1C0 (705/272-4926)
Collingwood CC, 101 Hurontario St., L9Y 2L9 (705/445-0221)
Comber CC, NOP 1JO
Cornwall CC, Box 338, K6H 5Y1 (613/933-4004)
Delhi CC, Box 11, N4B 2W8 (519/582-0280)
Dryden Dist. CC, Miss R. Scharenberg, 284 Government St., P8N 2P3 (807/223-2622)
Dunnville CC, Box 124, N1A 2W9 (416/774-6791)
Durham & Dist CC, Box 800, NOG 1RO (519/369-5750)
Dutton & Dunwich CC, 197 Nancy St., Dutton, Ont. N0L 1J0 (519/762-5212)
Elk Lake & Dist. CC, P0J 1G0 (705/678-2100)
Elliot Lake CC, Box 1, P5A 2J6 (705/848-3974)
Elmira & Woolwich CC, 5 First St. E., Elmira, Ont. N3B 2E3 (519/669-2605)
Elmwood & Dist. CC, R.R. 2, N0G 1S0 (519/363-6042)
La CC d'Embrun, Box 734, R.R. 2, K0A 1W0 (613/443-5751)
Emo CC, Box 420, POW 1EO (807/482-2477)
Englehart & Dist. CC, Box 171, P0J 1H0 (705/544-2542)
Erin Dist. CC, Box 451, NOB 1TO (519/833-9991)
Espanola & Dist. CC, Box 1248, P0P 1C0 (705/869-1944)
Essex & Dist. CC, 82 Victoria Ave., N8M 1M7 (519/776-7193)
Fenelon Falls CC, K0M 1N0 (705/887-2989)
Fergus CC, Box 3, N1M 2W7 (519/846-9254)
Flesherton & Dist. CC, N0C 1E0 (519/924-2742)
Fort Erie CC, Box 1098, Stn. B, L2A 5N9 (416/871-3803)
Fort Frances CC, Box 237, P9A 3M6 (807/274-5773)
Frontenac (Central) BT, Box 202, Sydenham, Ont. KOH 2TO (613/376-3204)
Gananoque CC, 240 Pine St., K7G 1C8 (613/382-3250)
Georgetown CC, Box 111, L7G 4T1 (416/877-7119)
Georgina CC, Box 850, Sutton West, Ont. LOE 1RO (416/722-8650)
Geraldton Dist. CC, Box 128, P0T 1M0 (807/854-1100)
Gorrie CC, N0G 1X0 (519/335-3959)
Grand Bend Area CC, Box 248, N0M 1T0 (519/238-2501)
Gravenhurst BT, Box 129, P0C 1G0 (705/687-4432)
Grimsby & Dist. CC, Box 264, L3M 4G5 (416/945-8319)
Guelph CC, Box 1268, N1H 6N6 (519/822-8081)
Hagersville Dist. CC, Box 70, NOA 1HO (416/768-3368)
Haliburton Highlands CC, Box 147, Minden, Ont. K0M 2K0 (705/286-1760)
Hamilton CC, 155 James St. S., L8P 3A5 (416/522-1151)
Harrow (Harrow & Colchester S. CC), Box 888, N0R 1G0 (519/738-2402)
Hastings Dist. CC, K0L 1Y0 (705/696-2416)
Hawkesbury CC, Box 322, K6A 2R9 (613/632-3374)
Honey Harbour, Port Severn & Dist. CC, R.R. 1, Port Severn, Ont. L0K 1S0 (705/756-2644)
Huntsville Senior CC, Box 1470, P0A 1K0 (705/789-4771)
Ignace CC, Box 217, P0T 1T0
Ingersoll Dist. CC, Box 121, N5C 2H2 (519/485-3530)
Innisfil CC, Box 122, R.R. 2, Stroud, Ont. LOL 2MO (705/436-3430)
Iroquois Falls & Dist. CC, Box 840, P0K 1C0 (705/232-4645)
Kapuskasing & Dist. CC, 21 Government Rd., P5N 2X5 (705/335-2332)
Kenora CC, Box 1500, P9N 3X7 (807/468-5762)
Killaloe CC, R.R. 2, K0J 2A0 (613/757-2075)
Kingston & Dist. CC, Box 486, K7L 2Z1 (613/548-4453)
Kirkland Lake CC, Box 966, P2N 3L1 (705/567-5444)
Kitchener CC, Box 2367, Stn. B, N2H 6M2 (519/576-5000)
Lakefield CC, Water St., K0L 2H0 (705/652-3141)
Larder Lake CC, 136 Godfrey St., POK 1LO (705/643-2119)
Leamington Dist. CC, 7 Cameo Dr., N8H 1J1 (519/326-3159)
Lindsay CC, 200 Kent St. W., K9V 2Y8 (705/324-2393)
Listowel CC, Box 232, N4W 3H4 (519/291-1551)
London CC, Box 3295, N6A 4K3 (519/432-7551)
Mattawa CC, 559 McConnell, POH 1VO (705/744-2540)
Meaford & Dist. CC, Box 1298, N0H 1Y0 (519/538-1945)
Midland CC, 578 King St., L4R 3M9 (705/526-7884)
Millbrook CC, L0A 1G0

Milton CC, Box 52, L9T 2Y3 (416/878-3179)
Mississauga BT, 100 City Centre Dr., L5B 2C9 (416/276-4357)
Morrisburg CC, Box 288, K0C 1X0 (613/543-3170)
Newcastle CC, Box 243, L0A 1H0 (416/987-4379)
New Dundee BT, Bridge St., NOB 2EO
New Hamburg BT, N0B 2G0 (519/662-1533)
Niagara Falls CC, 5433 Victoria Ave., L2G 3L1 (416/354-1601)
Niagara-on-the-Lake CC, Box 1043, L0S 1J0 (416/468-2326)
North Bay & Dist. CC, 509 Main St. E., P1B 1B7 (705/472-8480)
North Lambton CC, Box 752, Forest, Ont. NON 1JO (519/873-2319)
Norwich CC, Box 307, N0J 1P0 (519/863-6160)
Oakville & Dist. CC, 345 Lakeshore Rd. E., L6J 1J5 (416/845-6613)
Omemee & Dist. CC, King St., K0L 2W0 (705/799-5083)
Orangeville CC, Box 101, L9W 2Z5 (519/941-0490)
Orillia & Dist. CC, C. E. Shaver, Sundial Rd., R.R. 3, Orillia, Ont. L3V 6H3 (705/326-4424)
Orleans CC, Box 512, K1C 1S9 (613/824-1428)
Oshawa CC, Box 2067, L1H 7V4 (416/728-1683)
Ottawa BT, 100 Kent St., 27th floor, K1P 5R7 (613/236-3631)
D'Ottawa, La CC (Française), 418B, rue Rideau, K1N 5Z1 (613/238-4816)
Owen Sound CC, W. J. Graham, City Hall, Owen Sound, Ont. N4K 2H4 (519/376-6261)
Parry Sound CC, 2 Louisa St., P2A 2V4 (705/746-9012)
Pembroke CC, Box 365, K8A 6X6 (613/735-5381)
Penetanguishene CC, Box 90, L0K 1P0 (705/549-7225)
Perth CC, 80 Gore St. E., K7H 1H9 (613/267-3200)
Peterborough CC, 135 George St. W., K9J 3G6 (705/742-8881)
Plantagenet CC, Box 294, KOB 1CO
Plattsville & Dist. BT, Box 203, N0J 1S0 (519/684-7421)
Pointe au Baril CC, Box 67, P0G 1K0 (705/366-2211)
Pontypool CC, Box 34, L0A 1K0 (705/277-2329)
Port Colborne (Greater) CC, 76 Main St. W., L3K 3V2 (416/834-9765)
Port Dover BT, Box 239, N0A 1N0 (519/583-1350)
Port Elgin & Dist. CC, Box 69, NOH 2CO (519/832-9306)
Port Hope CC, 27 Queen St., L1A 2Y8 (416/885-5519)
Port Rowan – Long Point CC, Secretary, Ms. P. Stark, R.R. 3, Port Rowan, Ont. N0E 1M0 (519/586-2801)
Prescott CC, Box 2000, K0E 1T0 (613/925-2354)
Prince Edward CC, R.R. 4, Picton, Ont. K0K 2T0 (613/476-4203)
Rainy River CC, POW 1LO
Red Lake Dist. CC, Box 430, POV 2MO
Renfrew CC, Box 220, K7V 4A4 (613/432-4848)
Richmond Hill CC, Box 155, L4C 4Y2
Ridgetown CC, Box 522, NOP 2CO (519/674-3272)
St. Catharines CC, Box 940, L2R 6Z4 (416/684-2361)
St. Isidore CC, 5 Lamoureux, KOC 2BO (613/524-2801)
St. Thomas BT, 538 Talbot St., N5P 1C4 (519/631-1981)
Sarnia & Dist. CC, 224 N. Vidal St., N7T 5Y3 (519/336-2400)
Sauble Beach CC, R.R. 2, Hepworth, Ont. N0H 1PO (519/422-1685)
Sault Ste. Marie & Dist. CC, 360 Great Northern Rd., P6B 4Z7 (705/949-7152)
Scugog CC, Box 29, Port Perry, Ont. L0B 1N0 (416/985-8571)
Seaforth CC, Box 579, N0K 1W0 (519/527-0195)
Seeleys Bay & Dist. CC, Box 111, K0H 2N0 (613/387-3420)
Simcoe CC, 76 Kent St. S., N3Y 2Y1 (519/426-5867)
Sioux Lookout CC, Box 577, POV 2TO (807/737-1614)
Smiths Falls CC, 77 Beckwith St. N., K7A 2B8 (613/283-1334)
Smithville Dist. CC, Box 40, LOR 2AO (416/957-3315)
Southampton CC, Box 261, NOH 2LO (519/797-5066)
Stoney Creek CC, Box 69, L8G 3X7 (416/664-4000)
Stratford CC, 38 Albert St., N5A 3K3 (519/271-5140)
Sudbury & Dist. CC, 144 Durham St., P3E 3M8 (705/673-7133)
Tavistock BT, Box 586, N0B 2R0 (519/655-2201)
Temagami CC, Box 57, P0H 2H0 (705/569-3637)
Thessalon CC, Box 119, P0R 1L0 (705/842-5015)
Thorold CC, Box 66, L2R 6R4 (416/227-2382)
Thousand Islands CC, Box 36, Lansdowne, Ont. K0E 1L0 (613/382-2291)
Thunder Bay CC, Box 2000, P7C 4Y4 (807/622-9643)
Tilbury CC, Box 1355, NOP 2LO (519/682-2019)
Tillsonburg CC, Box 113, N4G 4H3 (519/842-5571)
Timmins-Porcupine CC, Box 985, Timmins, Ont. P4N 7H6 (705/264-4321)
Tobermory CC, Box 250, NOH 2RO
Toronto, BT of Metropolitan Toronto, General Manager, J. A. Collins, Box 60, Three, First Canadian Place, Toronto, Ont. M5X 1C1 (416/366-6811)
Tottenham Dist. CC, 20 Alexander St., LOG 1WO (416/936-4251)
Trenton CC, Box 536, K8V 4N6 (613/392-7635)
Tri Town CC, Box 1724, New Liskeard, Ont. POJ 1PO
Tweed & Dist. CC, Secretary, Mrs. S. Frost, Box 448, K0K 3J0 (613/478-2616)
Valley East CC, Box 519, Hanmer, Ont. P0M 1Y0
Vaughan CC, Box 441, Concord, Ont. L4K 1B2 (416/669-2215)
Victoria Harbour CC, Box 53, LOK 2AO (705/534-3938)
Walkerton CC, Box 1344, N0G 2V0 (519/881-3193)
Wallaceburg CC, Box 11, N8A 4L5 (519/627-1141)
Wasaga Beach CC, Box 10, L0L 2P0 (705/429-2247)
Waterloo CC, 5 Bridgeport Rd. W., N2L 2X9 (519/886-2440)
Wawa Dist. CC, POS 1KO
Welland (Greater) CC, 55 Main St. E., L3B 2P8 (416/732-7515)
Wellesley & Dist. BT, 178 Queen St. E., N0B 2T0 (519/656-2054)
West Nipissing CC, Box 840, Sturgeon Falls, Ont. POH 2GO (705/753-1079)
Westport CC, Secretary, Mrs. J. McNally, Box 157, K0B 1X0 (613/273-2803)
Whitby CC, Box 268, L1N 5S1 (416/668-4506)
Whitchurch-Stouffville CC, Box 1500, Stouffville, Ont. LOM 1LO (416/640-5993)
Whitney CC, KOJ 2MO
Windsor CC, R. F. Richardson, 500 Riverside Dr., N9A 5K6 (519/256-2641)
Woodstock CC, Box 24, N4S 7W5 (519/539-3083)
Zurich & Dist. CC, N0M 2T0 (519/236-4371)

QUEBEC

Province of Quebec Chamber of Commerce, 500 St-François Xavier, Montreal, P.Q. H2Y 2T6
(514) 844-9571
Executive Vice President, J. P. Létourneau

Amos CC, J9T 1N6 (819/732-8100)
Ancienne Lorette CC, G2E 2T9 (418/872-1762)
Anse-Au-Griffon CC, G0E 1A0 (418/892-5382)
Baie Comeau CC, G4Z 2R4 (418/296-2010)
Batiscan CC, G0X 1A0 (418/362-2358)
Beauport CC, G1C 4J6 (418/524-5121)
Bécancour CC, G0X 1B0 (819/294-6633)
Bedford CC, JOJ 1AO (514/248-7267)
Bic CC, G0L 1B0 (418/736-4452)
Boisbriand CC, J7G 1X4 (514/430-3867)
Bois Des Filion CC, J6Z 1H9 (514/621-4210)
Bonaventure CC, G0C 1E0 (418/534-3788)
Cabano CC, G0L 1E0 (418/854-2325)
Cacouna CC, G0L 1G0 (418/862-4615)
Cap-de-la-Madeleine CC, G8T 7N6 (819/379-3373)
Cap-des-Rosiers CC, G0E 1E0 (418/892-5272)
Caplan CC, G0C 1H0 (418/388-2144)
Carleton CC, G0C 1J0 (418/364-3251)
Causapscal CC, G0J 1J0 (418/756-3213)
Chambly CC, J3L 1E4 (514/658-7597)
Chambord CC, G0W 1G0 (418/342-6343)
Chandler CC, G0C 1K0 (418/689-3520)
Chapais CC, G0W 1H0 (418/745-2779)
Charlesbourg CC, G1G 2L5 (418/626-5514)
Chateauguay CC, J6J 2R1 (514/691-3311
Chicoutimi CC, G7H 5G4 (418/543-5941)
Cowansville CC, J2K 3H6 (514/263-5555)
Daveluyville CC, G0Z 1C0 (819/367-2664)
Disraeli CC, G0N 1E0 (418/449-2029)
Dolbeau CC, Box 460, G8L 1B8 (418/276-3530)
Donnacona CC, G0A 1T0 (418/285-2600)
Drummondville CC, C.P. 188, J2B 5L2 (819/472-5245)
Duparquet CC, J0Z 1W0 (819/948-2266)

East Angus CC, J0B 1R0 (819/832-3474)
East Broughton CC, G0N 1G0 (418/427-2432)
Fabre CC, J0Z 1Z0 (819/724-3131)
Farnham CC, J2N 1L5 (514/293-7313)
Forestville CC, G0T 1E0 (418/587-4484)
Frampton CC, G0R 1M0 (418/479-5253)
Franklin Centre CC, JOS 1NO (514/827-2745)
Fugèreville CC, J0Z 2A0 (819/748-3241)
Gaspé CC, G0C 1R0 (418/368-2201)
Gatineau CC, J8T 3C5 (819/561-2345)
Granby CC, C.P. 363, J2G 2T8 (514/372-6100)
Grande-Rivière CC, G0C 1V0 (418/385-2279)
Grand-Mère CC, G9T 5K7 (819/538-8676)
Ham-Nord CC, GOP 1AO (819/344-2484)
Hauterive CC, G5V 1V1 (418/589-4240)
Hâvre St-Pierre CC, G0G 1P0 (418/538-2400)
Hemmingford CC, JOL 1HO (514/247-2926)
Hull CC, J8Y 4B4 (819/770-0800)
Huntingdon CC, J0S 1H0 (514/264-6204)
Iles de la Madeleine CC, GOB 1BO (418/986-2460)
Isle d'Orleans CC, G0A 3W0 (418/228-8896)
Isle Verte CC, G0L 1K0 (418/898-2513)
Joliette CC, J6E 3Z6 (514/759-6363)
Jonquière CC, G7X 7J9 (418/548-3586)
La Baie CC, G7B 2B6 (418/544-6936)
Labelle CC, J0T 1H0 (819/686-2031)
Lac-aux-Sables CC, GOX 1MO (418/336-2988)
Lac-Drolet CC, G0Y 1C0 (819/549-2922)
Lac-du-Cerf CC, JOW 1SO (819/597-2525)
Lac Mégantic CC, G6B 1H2 (819/583-4662)
Lacolle CC, J0J 1J0 (514/246-2853)
Lac Simon CC, J0V 1W0 (819/983-2616)
Lake Massawippi CC, J0B 2C0 (819/838-5830)
La Minerve CC, JOT 1SO (819/686-2606)
L'Annonciation CC, JOT 1TO (819/275-5561)
La Pêche (Gatineau) CC, JOX 2WO (819/456-2592)
Lasalle CC, H8P 2A2 (514/366-4556)
La Sarre CC, J9Z 1X5 (819/333-5535)
L'Ascension CC, J0T 1W0 (819/275-3027)
Laval CC, 1435 W. St-Martin (514/388-0512)
La Vallée de St-Sauveur CC, J0R 1R0 (514/227-2564)
Lavaltrie CC, J0K 1H0 (514/586-2962)
Lebel sur Quévillon CC, J0Y 1X0 (819/755-3206)
L'Epiphanie CC, J0K 1J0 (514/588-5229)
Lévis CC, G6V 6N6 (418/833-3333)
Loretteville-Neufchâtel CC, G2A 2M3 (418/842-8989)
Lorrainville CC, J0Z 2R0 (819/629-3274)
L'Ouest de l'Ile CC, H9R 1C4 (514/697-4228)
Louiseville CC, J5V 2N8 (819/228-5575)
Magog-Orford CC J1X 3W8 (819/843-3494)
Malartic CC, J0Y 1Z0 (819/757-4289)
Mansonville CC, J0E 1X0 (514/292-5757)
Marieville CC, JOL 1JO (514/658-8081)
Mascouche CC, JON 1CO (514/474-2774)
Matagami CC, JOY 2AO (819/739-2277)
Matane CC, G4W 3N2 (418/566-2637)
Matapedia CC, G0J 1V0 (418/865-2221)
Mirabel CC, JON 1JO (514/258-3291)
Montebello CC, J0V 1L0 (819/423-5506)
Mont-Joli CC, G5H 3K9 (418/775-4366)
Mont-Laurier CC, J9L 3N7 (819/585-2555)
Montmagny CC, G5V 3S5 (418/248-5646)
Montréal CC, André Vallerand, d.g., 1080 Beaver Hall Hill, H2Z 1T2 (514/866-2861)
Montreal BT, E. Lorne Tracey, 1080 Beaver Hall Hill, H2Z 1T2 (514/878-4651)
Murdochville CC, GOE 1WO (418/784-2360)
Napierville CC, J0J 1L0 (514/245-3391)
Neuville CC, G0A 2R0 (418/529-3353)
Nicolet CC, J0G 1E0 (819/293-6125)
Nominingue CC, J0W 1R0 (819/278-3678)
Notre-Dame-du-Lac CC, G0L 1X0 (418/899-6837)
Notre-Dame-du-Nord CC, J0Z 3B0 (819/723-2068)
Notre-Dame du Portage CC, G0L 1Y0 (418/862-0640)
Nouvelle CC, G0C 2G0 (418/794-2554)
Percé CC, G0C 2L0 (418/782-2258)
Pierreville CC, JOG 1JO (514/568-3321)
Plessisville CC, G6L 2E1 (819/362-7395)
Pont Rouge CC, GOA 2XO (418/875-2725)
Port-Cartier CC, G5B 1B7 (418/766-2242)
Port Daniel CC, G0C 2N0 (418/396-5421)
Princeville CC, G0P 1E0 (819/364-5355)
Québec CC, Pierre Talbot, 17 St-Louis, G1R 3Y8 (418/692-3853)
Rawdon CC, J0K 1S0 (514/834-2282)
Repentigny CC, J6A 2T8 (514/581-1000)
Richmond (région de) CC, JOB 2HO (819/826-5814)
Rimouski CC, G5L 7C1 (418/723-2322)
Rive Sud CC, C.P. 27, Longueuil, P.Q. J4H 3W2 (514/463-2121)
Rivière-au-Renard CC, G0E 2A0 (418/269-5231)
Rivière-Bleue CC, G0L 2B0 (418/854-3640)
Rivière-du-Loup CC, G5R 1G8 (418/862-5243)
Roberval CC, G8H 2L8 (418/275-3504)
Rougemont CC, J0L 1M0 (514/469-3218)
Rouyn-Noranda CC, J9X 5B2 (819/762-9937)
Ste-Agathe CC, J8C 2P5 (819/326-3534)
St-Alban CC, G0A 3B0 (418/268-3831)
St-Alphonse Rodriguez CC, JOK 1WO (514/376-9740)
Ste-Anne-de-Bellevue CC, H9X 1A2 (514/457-5831)
Ste-Anne-des-Monts CC, GOE 2GO (418/763-5505)
Ste-Anne-de la Pérade CC, G0X 2J0 (418/328-3315)
St-Anselme CC, G0R 2N0 (418/885-9252)
St-Bruno CC, J3V 1W3 (514/653-0248)
St-Bruno de Guiges CC, JOZ 2GO (819/629-2921)
St-Camile de Bellechasse CC, GOR 2SO (418/595-2277)
Ste-Catherine d'Alexandrie CC, JOL 1EO (514/632-3205)
Ste-Claire CC, G0R 2V0 (418/883-3391)
St-Come CC, JOK 2BO (514/883-6507)
Ste-Croix de Lotbinière CC, GOS 2HO (418/926-3115)
St-Damien de Brandon CC, JOK 2EO (514/835-7634)
St-Donat CC, JOT 2CO (819/424-2833)
St-Esprit CC, J0K 2L0 (514/622-6960)
St-Eugene de Guigues CC, J0Z 3L0 (819/785-3461)
St-Eustache CC, J7R 1N1 (514/473-0933)
St-Fabien CC, G0L 2Z0 (418/869-2859)
St-Félicien CC, GOW 2NO (418/679-2344)
Ste-Foy CC, G1V 4B8 (418/651-7181)
St-Fréderic (Beauce) CC, G0N 1P0 (418/426-2309)
St-Gabriel de Brandon CC, J0K 2N0 (514/835-7667)
St-Hubert-de-Témiscouata CC, G0L 3L0 (418/497-3593)
St-Hyacinthe CC, J2S 7T2 (514/773-7463)
St-Jean CC, J3B 6Z8 (514/346-2544)
St-Jean de Matha CC, J0K 2S0 (514/886-2777)
St-Jérôme CC, J7Z 5L3 (514/436-6434)
St-Joseph-du-Lac CC, J0N 1M0 (514/472-2980)
Ste-Julie CC, JOL 2CO (514/656-5420)
Ste-Julienne CC, J0K 2T0 (514/831-3211)
St-Justine CC, G0R 1X0 (418/383-3801)
St-Lambert-de-Lévis CC, G0S 2W0 (418/889-9701)
St-Léonard, Co. Portneuf CC, G0A 4A0 (418/337-2632)
St-Léonard d'Aston CC, JOC 1MO (819/399-2122)
St-Lin-des-Laurentides CC, J0R 1C0 (514/439-3704)
St-Louis de France CC, GOX 2XO (819/374-4823)
St-Louis-du-Ha-Ha CC, G0L 3S0 (418/854-5224)
Ste-Marie-de-Beauce CC, G0S 2Y0 (418/387-5060)
St-Mélanie CC, JOK 3AO (514/671-4536)
St-Pacôme CC, G0L 3X0 (418/852-2785)
St-Pascal de Kamouraska CC, G0L 3Y0 (418/492-3127)
St-Paul L'Ermite CC, J5Z 1K4 (514/284-0426)
St-Paul (Montmagny) CC, GOR 3YO (418/469-2195)
Ste-Perpétue-de-L'Islet CC, G0R 3Z0 (418/359-2232)
St-Prosper CC, G0M 1Y0 (418/228-9759)
St-Raymond CC, G0A 4G0 (418/337-2900)
St-Sebastien CC, G0Y 1M0 (819/652-2000)
Ste-Sophie-New Glasgow CC, J0R 1S0 (514/436-9559)
Ste-Thérèse de Gaspé CC, J0C 1V0 (418/385-3111)
St-Ubalde CC, G0A 4L0 (418/277-2065)
Senneterre CC, J0Y 2M0 (819/737-2278)
Sept-Iles CC, G4R 4J9 (418/968-3488)
Shawinigan CC, C.P. 397, G9N 6V1 (819/536-5197)
Sherbrooke CC, C.P. 591, J1J 2G2 (819/569-3133)

Sorel-Tracy Metropolitain CC, J3P 5N9 (514/742-0018)
Squatec CC, GOL 4HO (418/855-2208)
Temiscaming CC, J0Z 3R0 (819/627-3256)
Terrebonne CC, J6W 3L5 (514/471-3731)
Thetford Mines CC, G8G 6X3 (418/335-3441)
Trois-Pistoles CC, G0L 4K0 (418/851-3644)
Trois-Rivières CC, Mario Côté, C.P. 1045, G9A 5K4 (819/375-9628)
Val-David CC, J0T 2N0 (819/322-6042)
Val d'Or CC, J9P 4P4 (819/825-3703)
Valleyfield CC, J6T 1C2 (514/371-3911)
Val Morin CC, JOT 2RO (819/322-2415)
Varennes CC, J0L 2P0 (514/652-2584)
Vaudreuil CC, J7V 2W4 (514/455-6735)
Villebois CC, J0Z 3V0 (819/868-4351)
Ville-Marie CC, JOZ 3WO (819/629-2218)
Windsor CC, J1S 1W5 (819/845-2636)
Woburn CC, GOY 1RO (418/544-2671)

SASKATCHEWAN

Saskatchewan Chamber of Commerce, 2314 11th Ave., Ste. 203, Regina, Sask. S4P 0K1

(306) 352-2671
Executive Director, R. C. Finlay

Aberdeen & Dist. CC, Box 100, S0K 1K8
Arborfield & Dist. CC, Box 769, SOE OAO
Aylsham BT, Box 61, SOE OCO
The Battlefords CC, Box 1000, North Battleford, Sask. S9A 3E6
Biggar CC, Box 178, S0K 0M0
Big River BT, c/o Sandra's Beauty Salon, SOJ OEO
Bjorkdale CC, Box 100, S0E 0E0
Blaine Lake BT, Box 218, S0J 0J0
Broadview Dist. CC, Box 610, S0G 0K0
Bruno CC, Box 340, S0K 0S0
Cabri CC, S0N 0J0
Canora & Dist. CC, Box 746, S0A 0L0
Carlyle CC, Box 276, S0C 0R0
Consul & Comm. BT, Box 103, S0N 0P0
Coronach CC, Box 60, S0H 0Z0
Cut Knife CC, SOM ONO
Davidson CC, Box 2, S0G 1A0
Delisle & Dist. CC, Box 28, S0L 0P0
Dinsmore BT, S0L 0T0
Eastend CC, Box 534, S0N 0T0
Edam & Dist. BT, Box 56, S0M 0V0
Esterhazy & Dist. CC, Box 788, S0A 0X0
Estevan CC, 1102 4th St., S4A OW6
Eston BT, SOL 1AO
Foam Lake & Dist. CC, Box 867, S0A 1A0
Fort Qu'Appelle CC, Box 777, S0G 1S0
Fox Valley CC, Box 72, S0N 0V0
Gravelbourg BT, Box 82, S0H 1X0
Grenfell Dist. CC, S0G 2B0
Gull Lake & Dist. CC, Box 262, S0N 1A0
Herbert & Dist. CC, SOH 2AO
Hudson Bay & Dist. CC, Box 1298, S0E 0Y0
Humboldt & Dist. CC, Box 1440, S0K 2A0
Kamsack CC, Box 1957, SOA 1SO
Kelvington & Dist. CC, Box 819, S0A 1W0
Kenaston & Dist. CC, Box 207, S0G 2N0
Kerrobert CC, Box 201, S0L 1R0
Kindersley CC, Box 125, S0L 1S0
Kipling CC, SOG 2SO
Langenburg & Dist. CC, Box 298, S0A 2A0
La Ronge Dist. CC, Box 286, S0J 1L0
Lashburn & Dist. CC, Box 488, S0M 1H0
Leader BT, Box 358, S0N 1H0
Lintlaw Dist. CC, Box 220, SOA 2HO
Lloydminster CC, Manager, Mrs. R. McCullough, 4919-50th Ave., S9V 0P7 (875-4390)
Lucky Lake CC, Box 38, S0L 1Z0
Maidstone CC, Box 461, S0M 1M0
Maple Creek CC, Box 729, S0N 1N0
Martensville BT, Box 14, S0K 2T0
Meadow Lake CC, Box 1168, S0M 1V0
Melfort & Dist. CC, Box 2002, S0E 1A0
Melville & Dist. CC, Box 429, S0A 2P0
Mistatim & Dist. CC, Box 42, S0E 1B0
Moose Jaw CC, Manager, Mrs. M. Ellard, Box 1359, 1201 Main St. N., S6H 4R3 (692-6414)
Moosomin CC, S0G 3N0
Naicam Dist. CC, Box 433, S0K 2Z0
Nipawin & Dist. CC, Box 177, S0E 1E0
Norquay CC, Box 507, S0A 2V0
Ogema CC, Box 234, S0C 1Y0
Outlook CC, Box 279, S0L 2N0
Pelly Dist. CC, Box 25, S0A 2Z0
Perdue & Dist. CC, S0K 3C0
Pontiex CC, Box 416, S0N 1Z0
Preeceville & Dist. CC, Box 722, S0A 3B0
Prince Albert CC, Manager, G. A. Rimmer, 3700 Marquis Rd., Box 2200, S6V 6Z1 (764-6222)
Radisson BT, Box 68, S0K 3L0
Radville CC, c/o Radville Co-op, S0C 2G0
Redvers CC, c/o Redvers Agencies Ltd., S0C 2H0
Regina CC, Executive Director, W.L. Whelan, 2145 Albert St., S4P 2V1 (527-4658)
Rosetown & Dist. CC, Box 592, S0L 2V0
Rosthern CC, Box 234, S0K 3R0
St. Victor CC, Box 40, S0H 3T0
St. Walburg CC, S0M 2T0
Saskatoon BT, Commissioner, Bert Salloum, Bessborough Hotel, S7K 3G8 (244-2151)
Shaunavon CC, c/o Great West Life, S0N 2M0
Shell Lake CC, Box 15, S0J 2G0
Spiritwood & Dist. CC, c/o Spiritwood High School, S0J 2M0
Swift Current CC, Manager, Mrs. D. Veitenheimer, #8, 244 1st St. N.E., (773-7268)
Tisdale & Dist. CC, Box 219, S0E 1T0
Unity & Dist. CC, Box 745, S0K 4L0
Uranium City CC, Box 876, S0J 2W0
Wadena CC, Box 1043, S0A 4Z0
Waskesiu CC, c/o T. Brown, 50 Pearson Ct., Prince Albert, Sask.
Watson & Dist. CC, Box 35, S0K 4V0
Wawota CC, S0G 5A0
Weyburn CC, Manager, W.A. Shields, 4 4th St. N.E., S4H 0X7 (842-4738)
Whitewood CC, Box 160, S0G 5C0
Wilkie CC, Box 776, S0K 4W0
Wolseley & Dist. CC, S0G 5H0
Wynyard & Dist. CC, Box 126, S0A 4T0
Yorkton CC, Box 1051, 131 Broadway St. E., S3N 2X3 (783-4368)

ASSOCIATIONS, SOCIETIES, ETC.

Note:—*The Editor wishes to list as many important associations and societies as possible, and would be grateful if the Secretary of any organization, unlisted here, would send information concerning such to the Editor, Canadian Almanac & Directory, 130 Harlandale Ave., Willowdale, Ont. M2N 1P3.*

ABILITY FUND

See Canadian Rehabilitation Council

ACCIDENT PREVENTION ASSOCIATIONS

ALBERTA SAFETY COUNCIL
#201, 10526 Jasper Ave., Edmonton, Alta. T5J 1Z7
(403) 428-7555
General Manager, R.D. Novikoff

Branches: Calgary, Edmonton

ASSOCIATION PARITAIRE DE PREVENTION POUR LA SANTE ET LA SECURITE DU TRAVAIL
50 Place Crémazie, #812, Montreal, P.Q. H2P 2T5
(514) 389-8295
General Manager, Mrs. Suzanne Blais-Grenier

BRITISH COLUMBIA SAFETY COUNCIL
#200, 3316 Kingsway, Vancouver, B.C. V5R 5K7
(604) 438-8281
General Manager, C.R. Rustemeyer

CANADA SAFETY COUNCIL
1765 Blvd. St. Laurent, Ottawa, Ont. K1G 3V4
(613) 521-6881
President, W.L. Higgitt
Traffic Safety Manager, G.M. Currie
Public Safety Manager, R.M. Plunkett
Occupational Safety Manager, A.R. Bray
Manager, Communication, P.G. Green, A.B.C.

CONSTRUCTION SAFETY ASSOCIATION OF ONTARIO
74 Victoria St., Toronto, Ont. M5C 2A5
(416) 366-1501
General Manager, L. Sylvester

ELECTRICAL UTILITIES SAFETY ASSOCIATION OF ONTARIO, INC.
81 Kelfield St., Unit 1, Rexdale, Ont. M9W 5A3
(416) 249-7837
Manager & Secretary Treasurer, Jack Craig

FOREST PRODUCTS ACCIDENT PREVENTION ASSOCIATION
Box 270, North Bay, Ont. P1B 8H2
(705) 472-4120
General Manager, James D. Nugent

INDUSTRIAL ACCIDENT PREVENTION ASSOCIATION, ONTARIO
2 Bloor St. E., Toronto, Ont. M4W 3C2
(416) 965-8888
Executive Vice President & General Manager, J.V. Findlay

Included in the Industrial Accident Prevention Association are ten Class Associations as per the following list. The address of all is 2 Bloor St. E., Toronto, Ont. M4W 3C2 and the Secretary Treasurer is J.V. Findlay.

Ceramics & Stone Accident Prevention Association
Chemical Industries Accident Prevention Association
Food Products Accident Prevention Association
Grain, Feed & Fertilizer Accident Prevention Association
Leather, Rubber & Tanners Accident Prevention Association
Metal Trades Accident Prevention Association
Ontario Retail Accident Prevention Association
Printing Trades Accident Prevention Association
Textile & Allied Industries Accident Prevention Association
Woodworkers Accident Prevention Association

MANITOBA SAFETY COUNCIL
#202, 213 Notre Dame Ave., Winnipeg, Man. R3B 1N3
(204) 949-1085
Executive Director, D.A.J. Herbert

MINES ACCIDENT PREVENTION ASSOCIATION
199 Bay St., 10th floor, Toronto, Ont. M5J 1L4
(416) 364-9301
Executive Director, J.M. Hughes
Secretary Treasurer, R.G. Horncastle
Field Office Director, L.C. MacDonald, 290 Second Ave. W., North Bay, Ont. P1B 3K9 (705/472-4140)

MOTOR VEHICLE SAFETY ASSOCIATION
Secretary, Ed. Cox, c/o Teledyne Transport, 610 Dixon Rd., Rexdale, Ont. M9W 1J1 (416/245-2022)

NOVA SCOTIA SAFETY COUNCIL
3627 Joseph Howe Dr., Halifax, N.S. B3L 4H8
(902) 454-9621
Manager, L.M. Delbridge

ONTARIO PULP & PAPER MAKERS SAFETY ASSOCIATION
91 Kelfield St., Rexdale, Ont. M9W 5A4
(416) 249-8591
Manager & Secretary Treasurer, W.C. Lockhart

ONTARIO SAFETY LEAGUE
82 Peter St., Toronto, Ont. M5V 2G5
(416) 362-1516
President & General Manager, S.F. Andrunyk

QUEBEC FOREST INDUSTRIALS SAFETY ASSOCIATION
3350 Wilfrid Hamel Blvd., #300, Quebec, P.Q. G1P 2J9
(418) 872-6126/27
General Manager, J. Turgeon, F. Eng.

QUEBEC LOGGING SAFETY ASSOCIATION INC.
(Association de Securité des Exploitations Forestieres du Quebec Inc.)
directeur général, Edmour Garon, 580 Grande Allée est, Quebec, P.Q. G1R 2K2 (418/522-5135)

QUEBEC PULP & PAPER SAFETY ASSOCIATION INC.
(Association de Securité des Pates et Papiers du Quebec Inc.)
directeur général, Edmour Garon, 580 Grande Allée est, Quebec, P.Q. G1R 2K2 (418/522-1638)

QUEBEC SAFETY LEAGUE
6785 St-Jacques St. W., Montreal, P.Q. H4B 1V3
(514) 482-9110
President & General Manager, Yves R. Mondoux

SASKATCHEWAN ROAD BUILDERS SAFETY ASSOCIATION
11 Robinson Cres., Regina, Sask. S4R 3R1
(306) 545-0660

SASKATCHEWAN SAFETY COUNCIL
348 Victoria Ave., Regina, Sask. S4N OP6
(306) 527-3197, or 527-5870
Executive Director, L.R. Donnelly

TRANSPORTATION SAFETY ASSOCIATION OF ONTARIO, INC.
2 Bloor St. E., 9th floor, Toronto, Ont. M4W 3C2
(416) 965-8911
General Manager, Harry I. Melnyk

WORKERS' COMPENSATION BOARD, ACCIDENT PREVENTION DEPARTMENT
Box 1150, Halifax, N.S. B3J 2Y2
(902) 424-3986

ACCOUNTANTS' ASSOCIATIONS

(See also "Chartered")

Society of Management Accountants of Canada

Executive Vice President, J. W. Ross, M.B.A., R.I.A., F.S.M.A.C., 154 Main St. E., Box 176, Hamilton, Ont. L8N 3C3 (416/525-4100)

SOCIETY OF MANAGEMENT ACCOUNTANTS OF ALBERTA
Executive Director, K. Crowder, R.I.A., #810, 505 5th St. S.W., Calgary, Alta. T2P 3J2 (403/269-5341)

SOCIETY OF MANAGEMENT ACCOUNTANTS OF BRITISH COLUMBIA
Executive Director, W.C. Easton, R.I.A., Box 11548, #1575, 650 W. Georgia St., Vancouver, B.C. V6B 4W7 (604/687-5891)

SOCIETY OF MANAGEMENT ACCOUNTANTS OF MANITOBA
Executive Director, E. Orpin, R.I.A., F.S.M.A.C., #808, 386 Broadway, Winnipeg, Man. R3C 3R6 (204/943-1538)

SOCIETY OF MANAGEMENT ACCOUNTANTS OF NEW BRUNSWICK
Regional Executive Director, G.D. Pollock, Ph.D., Box 543, Halifax, N.S. B3J 1V8 (902/422-5836)

SOCIETY OF MANAGEMENT ACCOUNTANTS OF NEWFOUNDLAND
Regional Executive Director, G.D. Pollock, Ph.D., Box 543, Halifax, N.S. B3J 1V8 (902/422-5836)

SOCIETY OF MANAGEMENT ACCOUNTANTS OF NOVA SCOTIA
Regional Executive Director, G.D. Pollock, Ph.D., Box 543, Halifax, N.S. B3J 1V8 (902/422-5836)

SOCIETY OF MANAGEMENT ACCOUNTANTS OF ONTARIO
Executive Director, E. W. Scott, R.I.A., F.S.M.A.C., 154 Main St. E., Box 176, Hamilton, Ont. L8N 3C3 (416/525-4100)

SOCIETY OF MANAGEMENT ACCOUNTANTS OF PRINCE EDWARD ISLAND
Regional Executive Director, G.D. Pollock, Ph.D., Box 543, Halifax, N.S. B3J 1V8 (902/422-5836)

LA CORPORATION PROFESSIONNELLE DES COMPTABLES EN ADMINISTRATION INDUSTRIELLE DU QUEBEC
Director General, J.K. Archibald, 1425 Mountain St., Montreal, P.Q.

SOCIETY OF MANAGEMENT ACCOUNTANTS OF SASKATCHEWAN
Executive Director, Mrs. R.S. Lowery, 2221 14th Ave., Regina, Sask. S4P OX9 (306/565-0949)

Canadian Certified General Accountants' Association

National Office, #740, 1176 W. Georgia St., Vancouver, B.C. V6E 4A2 (604/669-3555)
Executive Vice President, D.J. MacDonald, P.Eng.

Provincial Offices

CERTIFIED GENERAL ACCOUNTANTS ASSOCIATION OF THE YUKON
Box 5358, Whitehorse, Yukon Y1A 4Z2
(403) 667-6401

CERTIFIED GENERAL ACCOUNTANTS ASSOCIATION OF BRITISH COLUMBIA
Executive Director, G.F. McKinnon, 1555 W. 8th Ave., Vancouver, B.C. V6J 1T5 (604/732-1211)

CERTIFIED GENERAL ACCOUNTANTS ASSOCIATION OF ALBERTA
Calgary: Executive Director, C.L. Fuerst, F.C.G.A., 223 14th St. N.W., Calgary, Alta. T2N 1Z6 (403/283-6620) Toll free: 1-800-322-1078
Edmonton: #101, 9924 106th St., Edmonton, Alta. T5K 1E2 (403/428-0689)

CERTIFIED GENERAL ACCOUNTANTS' ASSOCIATION OF THE N.W.T.
Box 2915, Yellowknife, N.W.T. X0E 1H0
(403) 873-5620

CERTIFIED GENERAL ACCOUNTANTS' ASSOCIATION OF SASKATCHEWAN
#408, 333 25th St. E., Saskatoon, Sask. S7K 0L4
(306) 244-9660

CERTIFIED GENERAL ACCOUNTANTS ASSOCIATION OF MANITOBA
Executive Director, L. Hampson, C.G.A., #300, 260 St. Mary Ave., Winnipeg, Man. R3C 0M6 (204/944-9766)

CERTIFIED GENERAL ACCOUNTANTS ASSOCIATION OF ONTARIO
Executive Director, G.W. Fuller, C.G.A., 4th floor, 480 University Ave., Toronto, Ont. M5G 1V2 (416/593-1103)

LA CORPORATION PROFESSIONNELLE DES C.G.A. DU QUEBEC
Executive Director, F.R. Plante, C.G.A., 3ieme etage, 152 rue Notre Dame est, Montreal, P.Q. H2Y 3P6 (514/861-1823)

CERTIFIED GENERAL ACCOUNTANTS ASSOCIATION – ATLANTIC REGION
Executive Director, J.C. Richard, Box 5100, 236 St. George St., Moncton, N.B. E1C 8R2
(represents the provinces of New Brunswick, Nova Scotia, Prince Edward Island and Newfoundland, and the affiliated islands of Bermuda, Bahamas and Belize)
N.S.: Asst. Executive Director, H. MacDonald, Box 953, Dartmouth, N.S. B2Y 3Z6 (902/463-2700)

Guild of Industrial, Commercial & Institutional Accountants

President, W. Harold Ross, I.C.I.A.
Registrar, Garfield Brown, I.C.I.A.
Chairman, Publicity, M. Melnyk, I.C.I.A., Box 7, Stn. C, Toronto, Ont. M6J 3M7 (416/241-3440)

Canadian Institute of Accredited Public Accountants

Secretary Treasurer, C.S. Massey, 39 Wilson St. W., Ancaster, Ont. L9G 1N1 (416/648-1774)

Provincial Institutes

Alta.: M. Bell, Treasurer, 1710C Centre St. N., Calgary, Alta. T2E 2S4
B.C.: D.F. McBride, 800 W. Pender St., 3rd floor, Vancouver, B.C. V6C 2V8 (604/684-1838)
Man.: Mrs. Joyce Jurkow, 5640 Betsworth Ave., Winnipeg, Man. R3R 0J6 (204/889-1958)
Ont.: W.P. Fazackerley, A.P.A., 1420 Tecumseh Rd. E., Windsor, Ont. N8W 1C1
Que.: Ralph M. Bell, A.P.A., 670 Hyde Park Ave., Dorval, P.Q. H9P 1Z6 (514/636-0211)
Sask.: Mrs. Isabelle Strelioff, A.P.A., 322 Auld Place, Saskatoon, Sask. S7H 4X1

Institute of Internal Auditors, Inc.

Head Office, 249 Maitland Ave., Altamonte Springs, Florida, 32701 (305/830-7600)
International President, S.C. Gross (act.)

Chapters in Canada with Presidents

Calgary: N. Karbonik, Gulf Canada, Box 130, Calgary, Alta. (403/233-3002)
Edmonton: R.W. Grainger, Workers' Comp. Bd., Box 2514, Edmonton, Alta. T2P 2H7 (403/427-1276)
Montreal: J.-P. Larrivee, Metro-Richelieu, C.P. 152, Montreal, P.Q. H5B 1B3
N.S.: D.C. Wright, Maritime T & T, Box 880, Halifax, N.S. B3J 2W3 (902/421-5909)
Ottawa: Al Ericksen, Treasury Bd., 11 Birchview Rd., Ottawa, Ont. K2G 3G3 (613/996-1292)
Quebec: Florian Coutu, C.S.S.T., 524 Bourdages, #350, Quebec, P.Q. G1K 7E2 (418/643-5870)
Sask.: Dennis Down, 248 Logan Circle, Regina, Sask. S4S 5P9
Toronto: J.H. Pether, Canada Packers, 95 St. Clair Ave. W., Toronto, Ont. M4V 1P2 (416/766-4311)
Vancouver: P.D. Jeffrey, Okanagan Helicopters, Internat. Airport South, Vancouver, B.C. V7B 1A5 (604/278-5502)
Winnipeg: Dave Hildebrand, Civic Centre, 510 Main St., Winnipeg, Man. R3B 1B9 (204/946-0387)

ACTORS FUND OF CANADA

64 Shuter St., Toronto, Ont. M5B 2G7
(416) 869-1295
President, Jane Mallett

ADDICS (Alcohol & Drug Dependency Information & Counselling Services)

#205, 818 Portage Ave., Winnipeg, Man. R3G 0N4
(204) 775-1233
Executive Director, S.A. Steinmann

ADMINISTRATIVE MANAGEMENT SOCIETY

Headquarters: Willow Grove, Pa. 19090
Attn: John E. Harmon, Executive Secretary

Canadian Chapters with Secretaries

Brantford: Glenn Cherry, Hostein-Friesian Association of Canada, Box 610, Brantford, Ont. N3T 5R4
Calgary: J.D. Scott, C.G.A., Gulf Canada Ltd., Box 130, Calgary, Alta. T2P 2H7
Edmonton: Don Macdonald, Canada Packers Inc., Box 39, Edmonton, Alta. T5J 2H3
Grand Valley: Ray D'Aguilar, A.E.S. Data Ltd., 114 Radcliffe Dr., Kitchener, Ont. N2E 1Y5
Hamilton: Carol Angel, Cumis General Ins. Co., Box 5065, Burlington, Ont. L7R 4C2
International: Allen Gable, Port Huron School District, 1799 Krafft Rd., Port Huron, Mi. 48060
London: (TBA)
Montreal: W. Grandy, Imperial Tobacco Ltd., 3810 St. Antoine St. W., Montreal, P.Q. H4C 1B5
Ottawa: Lucille Wood, Civil Service Co-operative Credit Society, 400 Albert St., Ottawa, Ont. K1R 5B2

Regina: W. Anderson, The Cooperators, 1920 College Ave., Regina, Sask. S4P 1C4
Toronto: W.A. Wharton, Work Wear Corp., 17 Benton Rd., Toronto, Ont. M6M 3G3
Vancouver: Dawn Noble, Canadian Trust, 901 W. Pender St., Vancouver, B.C. V6C 1L7
Victoria: (TBA)
Winnipeg: R.G. Kellow, Manitoba Hydro, Box 815, Winnipeg, Man. R3C 2P4

ADMINISTRATIVE OFFICERS ASSOCIATION, CITIES OF NEW BRUNSWICK

President, Charles Shannon, City Solicitor, Box 130, Fredericton, N.B. E3B 4Y7 (506/455-9426)
Secretary, Bob Bouchard, City Treasurer, PO Drawer D, Bathurst, N.B. E2A 3Z1 (506/546-6651)

ADVERTISING AGENCY ASSOCIATION OF ALBERTA

Treasurer, Roy Elander, c/o Francis, Williams & Johnson Ltd., #644, 700 6th Ave. S.W., Calgary, Alta. T2P 0T8

ADVERTISING AGENCY ASSOCIATION OF BRITISH COLUMBIA

Secretary Treasurer, Godfrey J. Mead, c/o Godfrey J. Mead Advertising Ltd., #901, 100 Park Royal S., West Vancouver, B.C. V7T 1A2 (604/926-8661)

ADVERTISING AGENCY PRINT PRODUCTION ASSOCIATION (ONTARIO)

President, Ken Mullen, c/o Ogilvy & Mather (Canada) Ltd., 100 University Ave., Toronto, Ont. M5J 1V5 (416/593-7711)

THE ADVERTISING & SALES CLUB OF TORONTO

73 Richmond St. W., Toronto, Ont. M5H 1Z4
(416) 366-4643
Managing Director, R.A. (Bob) Morten

ADVERTISING AND SALES EXECUTIVES CLUB OF MONTREAL

900 Dorchester Blvd. W., Montreal, P.Q. H3B 1X8
(514) 866-1668
Managing Director, Ms. J. Kulhanek

ADVERTISING STANDARDS COUNCIL

1240 Bay St., Room 302, Toronto, Ont. M5R 2A7
(416) 961-6311
Director, E. Crandell

Regional Offices

LE CONSEIL DES NORMES DE LA PUBLICITE
#200, 1499 Bleury St., Montreal, P.Q. H3A 2H5

ADVERTISING STANDARDS COUNCIL—PRAIRIE REGION, MANITOBA
Box 1001, Winnipeg, Man. R3C 2W3

ALBERTA ADVERTISING STANDARDS COUNCIL, CALGARY
Box 6630, Stn. D, Calgary, Alta. T2P 2E4

ALBERTA ADVERTISING STANDARDS COUNCIL, EDMONTON
Box 9009, Stn. E, Edmonton, Alta. T5P 4K1

ADVERTISING STANDARDS COUNCIL, BRITISH COLUMBIA REGION
Box 3005, Vancouver, B.C. V6B 3X5

ADVERTISING STANDARDS COUNCIL, SASKATCHEWAN
Box 1322, Regina, Sask. S4P 3B8

ADVERTISING STANDARDS COUNCIL—MARITIME REGION
Box 394, Stn. M, Halifax, N.S. B3J 2P8

AEROBATICS CANADA

Box 1052, Stn. B, Ottawa, Ont. K1P 5R1
President, J.P. Hunt, Ottawa
Secretary Treasurer, D.D. Picklyk, 4 Lansfield Way, Nepean, Ont. K2G 3V8 (613/225-0262)

AFRICAN VIOLET SOCIETY OF CANADA

President, Mrs. Laura McLellan, 119 Wesley St., Moncton, N.B. E1C 4V9
Secretary, Mrs. Hilda Lewis, 202 Spring Park Rd., Charlottetown, P.E.I. C1A 3Y9 (902/894-9455)

HOUSE PLANT SOCIETY OF MONTREAL
President, Mrs. Louise Johnson, 119 Maple Ave., Hudson Heights, P.Q. J0P 1J0

AGGREGATE PRODUCERS ASSOCIATION OF ONTARIO

3701 Chesswood Dr., Ste. 209, Downsview, Ont. M3J 2P6
(416) 630-4747
General Manager, R.P. Cook

AGRICULTURE ASSOCIATIONS

(See separate listings for poultry, egg and livestock associations)

Agricultural Institute of Canada

151 Slater St., Ste. 907, Ottawa, Ont. K1P 5H4
(613) 232-9459
General Manager, W.E. Henderson

Provincial Divisions

ALBERTA INSTITUTE OF AGROLOGISTS
Registrar, K.C. Davies, P.Ag., #1, 12415 Stony Plain Rd., Edmonton, Alta. T5N 3N3 (403/482-5104)

BRITISH COLUMBIA INSTITUTE OF AGROLOGISTS
Registrar, Margaret E. McDonald, P.Ag., 4631 E. Hastings St., Burnaby, B.C. V5C 2K6 (604/294-5939)

MANITOBA INSTITUTE OF AGROLOGISTS
Registrar, Donald I. Cook, Managra Consultants, 511 Madison St., Winnipeg, Man. R3H 0L6 (204/775-3392)

NEW BRUNSWICK INSTITUTE OF AGROLOGISTS
Registrar, Roy Bush, P.Ag., Agriculture Canada Research Station, Box 20280, Fredericton, N.B. E3B 4Z7 (506/455-9931)

NOVA SCOTIA INSTITUTE OF AGROLOGISTS
Registrar, M.E. Neary, Box 550, Truro, N.S. B2N 5E3 (902/895-1571)

ONTARIO INSTITUTE OF PROFESSIONAL AGROLOGISTS
Registrar, S.W. Kennady, Box 5002, 8185 Yonge St., Bay Hill Mews, Thornhill, Ont. L3T 4S5 (416/881-5516)

PRINCE EDWARD ISLAND INSTITUTE OF AGROLOGISTS
Secretary Treasurer, Wayne Dickieson, Box 1600, Charlottetown, P.E.I. C1A 7N3 (902/892-5465)

SASKATCHEWAN INSTITUTE OF AGROLOGISTS
Registrar, N.R. Bray, #206, 4401 Albert St., Regina, Sask. S4S 6B6 (306/584-7247)

Affiliated Societies

Canadian Agricultural Economics Society
Canadian Consulting Agrologists' Association
Canadian Pest Management Society
Canadian Society of Agricultural Engineering
Canadian Society of Agronomy
Canadian Society of Animal Science
Canadian Society of Extension
Canadian Society for Horticultural Science
Canadian Society of Soil Science

Alberta Association of Agricultural Societies

9718 107 St., Edmonton, Alta. T5K 2C8
(403) 427-2171

Alberta Beekeepers Association

Box 8454, Stn. F, Edmonton, Alta. T6H 5H3 (403/438-0976)
Secretary Treasurer, Louise Kinley

Alberta Horticultural Association
Secretary, Mrs. Muriel Conner, Box 223, Lacombe, Alta. T0C 1S0
Treasurer, Mrs. D. Adamson, Box 1083, Lacombe, Alta. T0C 1S0 (403/782-3053)

Alberta Irrigation Projects Association
-not confirmed for 1982-
Secretary Treasurer, D. Berry, Box 140, Vauxhall, Alta. T0K 2K0 (403/654-2111)

Alberta Milk Producers' Association
Secretary, R.T. Bocock, Box 244, R.R. 6, Edmonton, Alta. T5B 4K3 (403/973-6091)

Alberta Potato Growers' Association
Secretary Manager, R.E. Marfleet, 220F 12A St. N., Lethbridge, Alta. T1H 2J1 (403/328-7018)

Alberta Wheat Pool
Box 2700, 505 2nd St. S.W., Calgary, Alta. T2P 2P5
(403) 267-4910
President, A.J. Macpherson

Allied Farm Services of Canada
210 Oxford St. E., London, Ont. N6A 1T6
(519) 673-1940

Association des Apiculteurs de l'Ouest du Quebec
(beekeepers)
-not confirmed for 1982-
Secretary, Gérard Binette, 148, rue Principale, Aylmer, P.Q. J9H 3M4 (819/684-6219)

Association des Apiculteurs de la Région de Quebec
(beekeepers)
Secretary, Robert Villeneuve, 58, rue de la Colombière est, Quebec, P.Q. G1L 1R1 (418/626-2067)

Association des Jardiniers-Maraichers de la Région de Montreal
(market gardeners)
805, rue du Marché Central, Ste. 102, Montreal, P.Q. H4N 1K2 (514/387-8319)
Director, Gaetan Amyot
Secretary, Mlle Chantal Yelle

Association Professionnelle des Meuniers du Quebec Inc.
(feed manufacturers and dealers)
915, boul. St-Cyrille ouest, bur. 105, Sillery, P.Q. G1S 1T8
(418) 688-9227

Association des Technologistes Agricoles Inc.
(agricultural technologists)
President, M.-A. Lessard, C.P. 308, St-Hyacinthe, P.Q. J2S 7B6

British Columbia Blueberry Co-op Association
5400 No. 6 Rd., Richmond, B.C. V6V 1T1
(604) 278-2731 & 278-6316
Manager, Norm Constantine

British Columbia Coast Vegetable Co-op Association
13631 Vulcan Way, Richmond, B.C. V6V 1K4
(604) 278-6234
General Manager, David Gibson

British Columbia Federation of Agriculture
846 Broughton St., Victoria, B.C. V8W 1E4
(604) 383-7171
Manager, Jack Wessel

British Columbia Fruit Growers' Association
Secretary Manager, D.M. Cheyne, #203, 1636 Pandosy St., Kelowna, B.C. V1Y 1P7 (604/762-5226)

British Columbia Grape Growers' Association
Box 1060, Kelowna, B.C. V1Y 7P7
(604) 762-4652
Secretary, Connie Bielert

British Columbia Lower Mainland Farmers' Co-op Association
272 E. Pender St., Vancouver, B.C. V6A 1T7
(604) 683-7024
Secretary, Jerry Hong

British Columbia Milk Board
Chairman, E.C. Daum, 800 S. Cassiar St., Vancouver, B.C. V5K 4N6 (604/299-9131)

British Columbia Raspberry Growers' Association
#204, 2589 Cedar Park Place, Clearbrook, B.C. V2T 3S4
(604) 853-1312
Manager, C. Penner

British Columbia Seed Potato Growers' Association
Box 202, Ladner, B.C. V4K 3N6
(604) 946-8338
Secretary, Noel Roddick

Canadian Agricultural Economics Society
#907, 151 Slater St., Ottawa, Ont. K1P 5H4 (613/232-9459)

Canadian Co-operative Wool Growers Limited
Box 9, Carleton Place, Ont. K7C 3P3
(613) 257-2714
General Manager, R.J. Cleland

Canadian Consulting Agrologists' Association
#22, 44 Wellington St. E., Toronto, Ont. M5E 1C8
(416) 364-4055
Manager, Clive R. Tisdale, P. Ag.

Canadian Dairy & Food Industries Supply Association
R.R. 1, Bradford, Ont. L0G 1C0
(416) 939-2545
Secretary, D.F. Thompson

Canadian Federation of Agriculture
111 Sparks St., Ottawa, Ont. K1P 5B5
(613) 236-3633
Executive Secretary & Treasurer, David Kirk

Member Organizations
British Columbia Federation of Agriculture
Canadian Horticultural Council
Co-operative Federée de Québec
Dairy Farmers of Canada
Manitoba Farm Bureau
New Brunswick Federation of Agriculture
Nova Scotia Federation of Agriculture
Ontario Federation of Agriculture
Prince Edward Island Federation of Agriculture
Quebec Farmers Association
Saskatchewan Federation of Agriculture
Unifarm
L'Union des Producteurs Agricoles
United Grain Growers Limited

Canadian Feed Industry Association
Box 2080, Stn. D, Ottawa, Ont. K1P 5W3
(613) 238-6421
President, C.L. Friend, CAE
Divisions
Alta.: Secretary, Hugh Campbell, 11643 79th Ave., Edmonton, Alta. T6G 0P8
B.C.: Secretary, B.H. Creelman, 5678 182nd St., Surrey, B.C. V3S 4M6
Que.: Secretary, Rene Aubrey, Box 64, St. Jerome, P.Q. J7Z 5T7 (514/438-1214)
Man.: Secretary, Ms. C. Hall, Winnipeg Chamber of Commerce, 177 Lombard Ave., Winnipeg, Man. R3B 0W5 (204/944-8484)
Ont.: Secretary, Dr. D. Mitchell, 77 City Centre Dr., #101G, Mississauga, Ont. L5B 1M5 (416/276-1720)
Sask.: Secretary, Gordon Janzen, Box 1050, Saskatoon, Sask. (306/244-3347)
Atl.: Secretary, A.G. Lelacheur, Box 404, Sackville, N.B. E0A 3C0

Canadian Fruit Wholesalers Association
1568 Carling Ave., Ottawa, Ont. K1Z 7M5
(613) 725-1118
Executive Vice President, W. Daman

Canadian Honey Council
Secretary Treasurer, F. Rathje, Box 480, Bassano, Alta. TOJ OBO (403/472-3934)

Canadian Horticultural Council
1568 Carling Ave., Ottawa, Ont. K1Z 7M5
(613) 725-1118
Affiliated Societies
Canadian Fruit Wholesalers Association
Canadian Mushroom Growers' Association
Canadian Potato Chip Association

Canadian Mushroom Growers' Association
1568 Carling Ave., Ottawa, Ont. K1Z 7M5
(613) 725-1118
Executive Secretary, H.R. Taylor

Canadian Pest Management Society
Secretary, John A. Scott, Pesticides Division, Plant Products & Quarantine Directorate, Agriculture Canada, K.W. Neatby Bldg., Ottawa, Ont. K1A OC6 (613/995-5880)

Canadian Plowing Council
Secretary, Robert Timbers, (60 Reach St.) Box 1180, Uxbridge, Ont. L0C 1K0 (416/869-3751)
Provincial Secretaries
B.C.: C. Thomson, 10045 Fairbanks Cres., Chilliwack, B.C. V2P 5L9
Alta.: Mrs. Tara Foote, Box 122, Wanham, Alta. T0H 3P0
Ont.: R.T. McMahon, c/o Agricultural & Horticultural Societies Branch, Ministry of Agriculture & Food, Legislative Bldg., Toronto, Ont. M7A 2B2
Que.: Martin Van Lierop, Quebec Provincial Plowmen's Association, Box 284, Macdonald-Stewart Bldg., Macdonald College, P.Q. H9X 1C0 (514/457-2000, loc. 261)
N.B.: David M. Gilchrist, 169 Burpee St., Fredericton, N.B. E3A 1M6
P.E.I.: Raynall MacNeill, Box 1600, Charlottetown, P.E.I. C1A 7N3

Canadian Seed Growers' Association
Box 8455, Ottawa, Ont. K1G 3T1
(613) 236-0497
Executive Director, W.K. Robertson

Canadian Seed Trade Association
408 Gertrude Ave., Winnipeg, Man. R3L OM6
(204) 284-1842

Canadian Society of Agricultural Engineering
151 Slater St., #907, Ottawa, Ont. K1P 5H4
(613) 232-9459

Canadian Society of Agronomy
Secretary, Dr. R.J. McLaughlin, Dept. of Crop Science, University of Guelph, Guelph, Ont. N1G 2W1

Canadian Society of Animal Science
Secretary, Dennis McKnight, P.Ag., Centralia College, Huron Park, Ont. N0M 1Y0 (519/228-6691)

Canadian Society of Extension
#907, 151 Slater St., Ottawa, Ont. K1P 5H4
Secretary Treasurer, Lyall MacLachlan
President, Douglas Pletsch

Canadian Society for Horticultural Science
Secretary, E.W. Toop, Dept. of Plant Science, University of Alberta, Edmonton, Alta. T6G 2E1 (403/432-2653)

Canadian Society of Soil Science
Secretary, Dr. R.B. McKercher, Dept. of Soil Science, University of Saskatchewan, Saskatoon, Sask. S7N 0W0 (306/343-2501)

Canola Council of Canada
#301, 433 Main St., Winnipeg, Man. R3B 1B3
also Box 438, Saskatoon, Sask. S7K 3L6

Central Alberta Dairy Pool
Box 550, Red Deer, Alta. T4N 5G4
(403) 346-2074; Telex 03-83121
Manager, K.A. Johnstone

Christian Farmers Federation of Western Canada
10020 108 St., Edmonton, Alta. T5J 1K6
(403) 428-6981
President, Lambert Tuininga

Conseil de l'Alimentation du Quebec
(food)
Vice Président exécutif, Léonard Roy, 50 ouest, boul. Crémazie, bur. 304, Montreal, P.Q. H2P 2S9 (514/381-5331)

Conseil de l'Industrie Laitière du Québec Inc.
(dairy industry)
Vice président exécutif, Léonard Roy, 50 ouest, boul. Crémazie, bur. 304, Montreal, P.Q. H2P 2S9 (514/381-5331)

Conseil des Viandes du Canada
(meat packing plants)
Secretary, Roland Soucy, 689, rue Couves, Greenfield Park, P.Q. J4V 1T7 (514/672-3760)

Co-op Atlantic
Secretary, Gilles Menard, Box 750, Moncton, N.B. E1C 8N5 (506/858-6065)

Co-operative Federée de Quebec
Secretary, Marcel Gingras, Box 500, Youville Station, Montreal, P.Q. H2P 2W2 (514/384-6450)

Dairy Bureau of Canada
20 Holly St., Ste. 400, Toronto, Ont. M4S 2E6
(416) 485-4453

Dairy Farmers of Canada
111 Sparks St., Ottawa, Ont. K1P 5B5
(613) 236-9997

Dairy Producers Co-operative Limited
Box 560, Regina, Sask. S4P 3A5

(306) 525-0321
Manager, G.H. Pedersen

Dairymen's Association of Western Ontario
Secretary Treasurer, W.M. Broad, 21 Ridge Blvd., Tillsonburg, Ont. N4G 2S6 (519/424-9139)

Fédération des Associations Apicoles du Quebec
(beekeepers)
C.P. 656, St-Hyacinthe, P.Q. J2S 7P5
(514) 774-0158

Fédération des Producteurs de Lait du Quebec
(milk producers)
-not confirmed for 1982-
Président, Réjean Grégoire, 515, ave. Viger, Montreal, P.Q. H2L 2P2 (514/288-6141, poste 224)

Fédération des Producteurs de Pommes du Quebec
(apple growers)
Secretary, Mario Limoges, 515, ave. Viger, Montreal, P.Q. H2L 2P2 (514/288-6141)

Flax Growers Western Canada
Box 832, Regina, Sask. S4P 3B1
(306) 586-7006

Holland Cheese Exporters Association
Box 163, Toronto Dominion Centre, Toronto, Ont. M5K 1H6
(416) 368-2669

International Flying Farmers
Headquarters: Mid Continent Airport, Box 9124, Wichita, Kansas 67277
Canadian Executive Secretary, Charles F. Burbank, R.R. 1, Shelburne, Ont. L0N 1S0 (519/925-2065)
Asst. Canadian Executive Secretary, G.M. Sinclair, 26 Eddy Place, Saskatoon, Sask. S7K 1A1 (306/653-2462)
There are five chapters in Canada (with about 2,000 members) which elect presidents each year. Contact the Executive Secretary for up to date names and addresses.

Junior Farmers' Association of Ontario
President, Bill Emmott, R.R. 3, Brantford, Ont. N3T 5L6
Secretary, (tba) c/o Parliament Bldgs., Toronto, Ont. (416/965-1241)

Manitoba Co-op Honey Producers
-not confirmed for 1982-
General Manager, D. Robertson, 625 Roseberry St., Winnipeg, Man. R3H OT2 (204/774-5566)

Manitoba Dairy Association
Secretary, C. Vincent, Agriculture Services Complex, University of Manitoba, Winnipeg, Man. R3T 2N2 (204/269-1220)

Manitoba Farm Bureau
Secretary, R.O. Douglas, 437 Assiniboine Ave., Winnipeg, Man. R3C OY5 (204/943-2509)

Maritime Farmers Council
Secretary, Keith Russell, Box 750, Moncton, N.B. E1C 8N5 (506/858-6037)

National Dairy Council of Canada
#704, 141 Laurier Ave. W., Ottawa, Ont. K1P 5J3
(613) 238-4116
President, K.L. Matte

National Farmers Union
National Office: 250C 2nd Ave. S., Saskatoon, Sask. S7K 2M1
(306) 652-9465
Executive Secretary, Stuart Thiesson
Regional Offices:
Region 1: Box 8, Perth, N.B. EOJ 1VO (506/273-2914)
Region 3: 5 Douglas St., Guelph, Ont. N1H 2S8 (519/836-2515)
Region 5: 902 St. James St., Winnipeg, Man. R3G 3J7 (204/774-3596)
Region 6: 1717 13th Ave., Regina, Sask. S4P OV4 (306/525-8729)
Region 7: 10047 80th Ave., Edmonton, Alta. T6E 1T4 (403/433-2528)
Region 8: Ste. 2, 1001 102nd Ave., Dawson Creek, B.C. V1G 2B9 (604/782-8171)

New Brunswick Federation of Agriculture
Secretary, T. Demma, R.R. 6, Fredericton, N.B. E3B 4X7 (506/454-9642)

New Brunswick Fruit Growers' Association
Secretary, Elizabeth Burke, R.R. 6, Island View, Fredericton, N.B. E3B 4X7 (506/454-9636)

New Brunswick Potato Agency
Secretary Manager, J.P. Drozdowski, Box 238, Florenceville, N.B. EOJ 1K0 (506/392-6909)

New Brunswick Strawberry Growers Association
Secretary, Dennis G. Foreman, Foreman's Strawberry Farm, Stanley, N.B. E0H 1T0

New Brunswick Vegetable Growers Association
Secretary, Tom Demma, R.R. 6, Fredericton, N.B. E3B 4X7 (506/454-9642)

Newfoundland Federation of Agriculture
Box 759, Bishops Falls, Nfld. A0H 1C0
Secretary, A.O. Gill

Newfoundland Vegetable Marketing Associates Ltd.
Box 190, Deer Lake, Nfld. A0K 2E0
(709) 635-5171, 5172

Northern Alberta Dairy Pool
-not confirmed for 1982-
Box 367, Edmonton, Alta. T5J 2J8
(403) 451-3890
Manager, W. McBride

Northern Ontario Dairymen's Association
Secretary, D.S. Harrison, Box 532, North Bay, Ont. P1B 8J1 (705/472-8880)

Nova Scotia Beekeepers Association
Secretary, Earl Blades, Box 1421, Truro, N.S. B2N 5V2 (902/895-7591)

Nova Scotia Blueberry Producers Association
Secretary, Sybil Brown, R.R. 1, Bass River, N.S. B0M 1L0 (902/668-2908)

Nova Scotia Federation of Agriculture
Secretary, Lester Settle, Box 784, Truro, N.S. B2N 5E8 (902/893-2293)

Nova Scotia Fruit Growers' Association
Secretary Manager, Alex G. Buchanan, Research Station, 24 Main St., Kentville, N.S. B4N 1J5 (902/678-7366)

Nova Scotia Greenhouse Growers Association
Secretary, Cathy Kehoe, c/o Avon Valley Greenhouses, Falmouth, N.S. B0P 1L0

Nova Scotia Maple Syrup Producers Association
Secretary, Karen Dickinson, R.R. 3, Southampton, N.S. B0M 1W0

Nova Scotia Milk Producers Association
Secretary, Box 784, Truro, N.S. B2N 5E8 (902/893-2293)

Nova Scotia Raspberry Growers Association
Secretary, Mrs. Boyd Corkum, Chester Basin, N.S. B0J 1K0

Nova Scotia Vegetable & Potato Growers Association
Secretary, Richard Melvin, R.R. 2, Canning, N.S. B0P 1H0

Office des Producteurs de Lait du Quebec
(industrial milk producers)
Secretary, Roch Morin, 515 ave. Viger, Montreal, P.Q. H2L 2P2 (514/288-6141)

Ontario Beekeepers' Association
President, Erle Byer, R.R. 2, Markham, Ont. L3P 3J3
Secretary, Prof. P.W. Burke, Graham Hall, University of Guelph, Guelph, Ont.

Ontario Creamerymen's Association
Executive Manager, H.W. Dunsdon, 75 Erie Ave., Brantford, Ont. N3S 2G1 (519/752-8631)

Ontario Dairy Council
#300, 40 Wynford Dr., Don Mills, Ont. M3C 1J6
(416) 445-7734
President, T.D. Kane

Ontario Farm Drainage Association
Secretary Treasurer, Wm. J. Amos, Box 189, Parkhill, Ont. N0M 2K0 (519/294-0061)

Ontario Federation of Agriculture
General Manager, Jack Hale, 491 Eglinton Ave. W., #500, Toronto, Ont. M5N 1A8 (416/485-3333)

Ontario Food Processors Association
Executive Vice President, E.L. Chudleigh, 2395 Cawthra Rd., Ste. 1, Mississauga, Ont. L5A 2W8 (416/276-6727)

Ontario Fruit & Vegetable Growers' Association
President, Don Bonter, R.R. 1, Carrying Place, Ont. K0K 1L0
Secretary, J. Van der Zalm, 301 Ontario Food Terminal, 165 The Queensway, Toronto, Ont. M8Y 1H8 (416/255-4473)

Ontario Grain & Feed Dealers Association
Executive Vice President, Dr. J.D. Mitchell, 77 City Centre Dr., Mississauga, Ont. L5B 1M5 (416/276-6980)

Ontario Maple Syrup Producers' Association
Box 340, Elmvale, Ont. L0L 1P0
(705) 322-2231

Ontario Milk Transport Association
555 Dixon Rd., Rexdale, Ont. M9W 1H8
(416) 247-7131
Executive Secretary, John D. Wishart

Ontario Tender Fruit Institute
Secretary, E.L. Chudleigh, 2395 Cawthra Rd., Ste. 1, Mississauga, Ont. L5A 2W8 (416/276-6727)

Ordre des Agromes du Quebec
(Professional Corporation of Agrologists)
262 ouest, boul. Henri-Bourassa, Montreal, P.Q. H3L 1N6
(514) 337-9510

Palliser Wheat Growers Association
#219, 3806 Albert St., Regina, Sask. S4S 3R2
(306) 586-5866
Executive Director, Don Baron

Prince Edward Island Beekeepers' Co-operative Association Ltd.
Box 1114, Charlottetown, P.E.I. C1A 7M8
Secretary, Ruby Bakker

Prince Edward Island Dairy Producers Association
Secretary, Art MacRae, Farm Centre, 420 University Ave., Charlottetown, P.E.I. C1A 7Z5 (902/892-6422)

Prince Edward Island Federation of Agriculture
Secretary, Eric Hammill, Farm Centre, 420 University Ave., Charlottetown, P.E.I. C1A 7Z5 (902/892-6913)

Prince Edward Island Soil & Crop Improvement Association
Attn.: Raynall MacNeill, Box 1600, Charlottetown, P.E.I. C1A 7N3 (902/892-5465)

Prince Edward Island Vegetable Growers Co-op Association
-not confirmed for 1982-
Manager, Don Read, 81 Sherwood Rd., Box 1494, Charlottetown, P.E.I. C1A 7N1 (902/892-5361)

Quebec Dairy Council
Executive Vice President, Leonard Roy, #304, 50 Cremazie Blvd. W., Montreal, P.Q. H2P 2S9 (514/381-5331)

Quebec Farmers Association
Executive Secretary, Steve Gruber, Box 284, Extension Dept., Macdonald College, P.Q. H9X 1C0 (514/457-2000, loc. 251)

Quebec Young Farmers' Provincial Federation
Secretary Manager, Ann Louise Carson, Box 284, Extension Dept., Macdonald College, P.Q. H9X 1C0 (514/457-2000, loc. 277)

Rapeseed Growers Association of Saskatchewan
Box 2066, Saskatoon, Sask. S7K 3S7
(306) 343-6878

Rural Education & Development Association
Director, John Melicher, 14815 119 Ave., Edmonton, Alta. T5L 2N9 (403/451-5959)

Saskatchewan Beekeepers Association
Secretary Treasurer, John Gruszka, 4th Floor, McIntosh Mall, 800 Central Ave., Prince Albert, Sask. S6V 6Z2 (306/922-9770)

Saskatchewan Federation of Agriculture
Secretary, G. Carlson, Box 1637, Regina, Sask. S4P 3C4 (306/525-3366)

Saskatchewan Horticultural Association
Secretary, B.J. Porter, Plant Industry Branch, Saskatchewan Agriculture, Walter Scott Bldg., Regina, Sask. S4S 0B1 (306/565-4670)

Saskatchewan Wheat Pool
Secretary, J.O. Wright, 2625 Victoria Ave., Regina, Sask. S4P 2Y6 (306/569-4228)

Society of Ontario Nut Growers
Secretary, Mrs. Joyce McEwan, R.R. 1, Beamsville, Ont. L0R 1B0
Editor, "Song News", R.D. Campbell, R.R. 1, Niagara Pkwy., Niagara-on-the-Lake, Ont. L0S 1J0 (416/262-4927)

Strawberry Growers Association of Nova Scotia
Secretary, Ms. Donna Langille, Box 784, Truro, N.S. B2N 5E8 (902/893-2293)

Unifarm
Executive Director, W. Plosz, 14815 119 Ave., Edmonton, Alta. T5L 4W2 (403/451-5912)

L'Union des Cultivateurs Franco-Ontariens
Secretary, C.A. Hurtubise, 2 rue Lapointe, C.P. 32, Bourget, Ont. K0A 1E0

L'Union des Producteurs Agricoles
Secretary, J.-C. Blanchette, 515 Viger Ave., Montreal, P.Q. H2L 2P2 (514/288-6141)

United Grain Growers Limited
Secretary, J.A. White, 433 Main St., Winnipeg, Man. R3C 3A7 (204/944-5411)

Vegetable Growers' Association of Manitoba
Secretary, Garth Stone, 717 Norquay Bldg., Winnipeg, Man. R3C 0P8

Western Agricultural Conference
Box 1637, Regina, Sask. S4P 3C4
(306) 525-3366
Affiliates:
Manitoba Farm Bureau
Saskatchewan Federation of Agriculture
Unifarm
United Grain Growers Ltd.

Western Greenhouse Growers Co-op Association
Manager, Phil Beale, 6462 Beresford St., Burnaby, B.C. V5E 1B6 (604/438-6161)

THE AIR CADET LEAGUE OF CANADA
424 Metcalfe St., Ottawa, Ont. K2P 2C3
(613) 235-1409

Authorized by Minister of National Defence to raise and administer Royal Canadian Air Cadet Squadrons.
Patron, The Governor-General of Canada
Executive Director, Arthur Macdonald
Assistant Executive Director, Richard Logan
Provincial Committees with Chairmen
B.C.: W.P. Cumberland, 1812 Hamilton St., New Westminster, B.C. V3M 2P4
Alta.: D. Rognvaldson, 8813 98 St., Grande Prairie, Alta. T8V 2C9
Sask.: G.A. Coffey, Box 416, Carlyle, Sask. S0C 0R0
Man.: L. Grieve, 39 McMasters Rd., Winnipeg, Man. R3T 2Y2
Northwestern Ont.: R. Angove, 280 Hinton Ave., Thunder Bay, Ont. P7A 7E4
Ont.: J.M. Donnelly, 101 Wedgewood Dr., Kitchener, Ont. N2B 1E6
Que.: B. Clement, 138 130th St., Shawinigan Sud, P.Q. G9P 4K9
N.B.: I. Von Richter, Box 3325, Stn. B, Saint John, N.B. E2M 4X9
N.S.: R. Horne, Box 100, Milford Station, N.S. B0N 1Y0
P.E.I.: R.D. McKinnon, Box 48, Alberton, P.E.I. C0B 1B0
Nfld.: J. Russell, Bldg. 805, Apt. 58, Pleasantville, St. John's, Nfld. A1A 1R4
Yukon/NWT: R. Paulin, Box 1347, Yellowknife, N.W.T.

AIR INDUSTRIES ASSOCIATION OF CANADA
Suite 601, 116 Albert St., Ottawa, Ont. K1P 5G3
(613) 232-4297
President, J.M. DesRoches

AIR MANAGEMENT ASSOCIATION OF ONTARIO
-not confirmed for 1982-
Secretary Treasurer, J.U. Thornton, Armadale Co. Ltd., Buttonville Airport, Markham, Ont. L3P 3J9 (416/297-2600)

AIR TRANSPORT ASSOCIATION OF CANADA
747, 99 Bank St., Ottawa, Ont. K1P 6B9
(613) 233-7727
President & Chief Executive Officer, A. C. Morrison

ALBERTA ASSESSORS ASSOCIATION
Executive Secretary Treasurer, J. E. Fritch, 13104 136 Ave., Edmonton, Alta. T5L 4B3 (403/454-4053)

ALBERTA ASSOCIATION FOR CAPITALIST EDUCATION
-not confirmed for 1982-
14604 13th St. N.E., Box 7456, Stn. E, Calgary, Alta. T3E 3M3
(403) 276-8107
Secretary Treasurer, Bill Donaldson

ALBERTA ASSOCIATION OF MUNICIPAL DISTRICTS & COUNTIES
Executive Director, J. D. Edworthy, 4504 101 St., Edmonton, Alta. T6E 5G9 (403/436-9375)

ALBERTA ASSOCIATION OF SUMMER VILLAGES
Executive Director, Wm. Gowan-Smith, 7604 86 Ave., Edmonton, Alta. T6E 1H7 (403/465-3928)

ALBERTA AVIATION COUNCIL
220 Terminal Bldg., Municipal Airport, Edmonton, Alta. T5G 0W6
(403) 454-7569
General Manager & Treasurer, F.B. Davis

ALBERTA CONSTRUCTION LABOUR RELATIONS ASSOCIATION
14040 128 Ave., Edmonton, Alta. T5L 4M8
President, George Durocher

ALBERTA COUNCIL ON AGING
#324, 10010 105 St., Edmonton, Alta. T5J 1C4
(403) 423-7781
Executive Director, Rein Selles

ALBERTA FEDERATION OF ROCK CLUBS
Secretary, Mrs. Anne Newson, Lot 31, 9200 Blackfoot Trail S.E., Calgary, Alta. T2J 0T2 (403/253-3421)
Editor, 'Fossil Trails', Dave Engberg, 47 Garland Cres., Sherwood Park, Alta. T8A 2P7 (467-0520)

ALBERTA FISH & GAME ASSOCIATION
Secretary Manager, Paul L. J. Morck, 6024 103 St., Edmonton, Alta. T6H 2H6 (403/434-0655)

ALBERTA FOREST PRODUCTS ASSOCIATION
#204, 11710 Kingsway Ave., Edmonton, Alta. T5G 0X5
(403) 452-2841
General Manager, Arden A. Rytz

ALBERTA FUNERAL INFORMATION SERVICE
#105, 2116 27 Ave. N.E., Calgary, Alta. T2E 7A6
(403) 230-2115
Chairman, Luke Lafrance
Branch at Edmonton, Alta.

THE ALBERTA GENEALOGICAL SOCIETY
Box 12015, Edmonton, Alta. T5J 3L2
Branches at Brooks, Edmonton, Grande Prairie, Lethbridge, Medicine Hat, Red Deer and Wetaskiwin

ALBERTA MOTION PICTURE INDUSTRIES ASSOCIATION
345 Birks Bldg., Edmonton, Alta. T5J 1A1
(403) 423-4692
Executive Secretary, Len Stahl

ALBERTA MUSEUMS ASSOCIATION
Box 4036, Stn. C, Calgary, Alta. T2T 5M9
(403) 264-8300
President, J. Gibson

ALBERTA RURAL MUNICIPAL ADMINISTRATORS ASSOCIATION
Secretary Treasurer, O.W. Likness, County of Flagstaff, Sedgewick, Alta. T0B 4C0 (403/384-3537)

ALBERTA URBAN MUNICIPALITIES ASSOCIATION
Executive Director, T.P. Buchanan, 8712 105 St., Edmonton, Alta. T6E 5V9 (403/433-4431)

ALBERTA URBAN MUNICIPAL ADMINISTRATORS ASSOCIATION
Secretary, Bev Lehman, Box 371, Onoway, Alta. T0E 1V0 (403/967-3020)

ALCOHOL & DRUG CONCERNS, INC.
Room 603, 15 Gervais Dr., Don Mills, Ont. M3C 1Y8
(416) 449-4933

ALCOHOLICS ANONYMOUS, TORONTO
Intergroup Office, 272 Eglinton Ave. W., Toronto, Ont. M4R 1B2 (416/487-5591)
There are approx. 3,000 AA groups in Canada.

ALLERGY INFORMATION ASSOCIATION
President, Susan Dagish, Room 7, 25 Poynter Dr., Weston, Ont. M9R 1K8 (416/244-9312)

ALLIANCE FRANCAISE
1633 Riverside Dr., Ottawa, Ont. K1G OE5
(613) 733-0588
Directeur des Cours, Claude Suire

ALLIANCE FRANCAISE DE TORONTO
895 Yonge St., Toronto, Ont. M4W 2H2
(416) 922-2014
Director, André Petit

ALLIANCE FOR LIFE
#203, 379 Broadway Ave., Winnipeg, Man. R3C 0T9

There are member organizations in every province. For local addresses, contact the Staff Secretary, at the above address.

ALLIED BEAUTY ASSOCIATION
#1001, 2 Sheppard Ave. E., Willowdale, Ont. M2N 5Y7
(416) 225-2359

ALLIED BOATING ASSOCIATION OF CANADA
4800 Dundas St. W., Suite 210, Islington, Ont. M9A 1B1
(416) 236-2497

ALLIED INDIAN & METIS SOCIETY
2716 Clark Dr., Vancouver, B.C. V5N 3H6
(604) 874-9610

ALTRUSA INTERNATIONAL, INC.
International Headquarters, 8 S. Michigan Ave., Chicago 60603, Ill. (312/236-5894)
Executive Director, Mrs. Dorothy E. Kuehlhorn, address as above.

Altrusa Clubs in Canada
Alta.: Calgary, Edmonton
B.C.: Nanaimo, Vancouver
Man.: Winnipeg
Ont.: Hamilton, Ottawa, Thunder Bay
Que.: Montreal, Quebec

AMALGAMATED CONSTRUCTION ASSOCIATION OF BRITISH COLUMBIA
2675 Oak St., Vancouver, B.C. V6H 2K3
(604) 736-6311
Attn.: H.M. Alexander

AMERICAN BUREAU OF SHIPPING (Canadian Branch)
Ste. 520, Roy Bldg., 1657 Barrington St., Halifax, N.S. B3J 2A1
(902) 423-6236
Contact, K. Nicol, Sr. Surveyor

AMERICAN CONTRACT BRIDGE LEAGUE
2200 Democrat Rd., Memphis, Tenn. 38116
(901) 332-5586

There are Canadian Units, with elected officials, in all provinces and duplicate bridge clubs in many cities. The ACBL will supply free copies of the Directory of Affiliated Duplicate Bridge Clubs.

AMERICAN MARKETING ASSOCIATION (British Columbia Chapter)
c/o Moira Silcox, 1155 Homer St., Vancouver, B.C. V6B 4J3

AMERICAN MARKETING ASSOCIATION (Montreal Chapter)
C.P. 1299, Succ. Desjardins, Montreal, P.Q. H5B 1C4
(514) 387-2384

AMERICAN MARKETING ASSOCIATION (Quebec Chapter)
c/o Michel Daviault, 1283 La Lorraine, Ste-Foy, P.Q. G1W 3Y5

AMERICAN MARKETING ASSOCIATION (Toronto Chapter)
c/o Domar Duplicating Service, 145 Yonge St., Toronto, Ont. M5C 1W9 (416/364-7237)

AMERICAN SOCIETY OF HEATING, REFRIGERATION & AIR CONDITIONING ENGINEERS (Ontario Chapter)
15 Toronto St., #702, Toronto, Ont. M5C 2E3
(416) 364-1223
Executive Secretary, Mrs. Susan Cooke

AMERICAN SOCIETY FOR INFORMATION SCIENCE (Student Chapter, University of Alberta)
c/o W.J. Kurmey, Faculty of Library Science, Univ. of Alta., Edmonton, Alta. T6G 2J4 (403/432-4578)

AMERICAN SOCIETY FOR INFORMATION SCIENCE (Western Canada Chapter)
c/o Ms. Rodney Muir, 2300 Home Oil Tower, 324 8th Ave. S.W., Calgary, Alta. T2P 2Z5

AMERICAN SOCIETY FOR QUALITY CONTROL
National Headquarters, 161 W. Wisconsin Ave., Milwaukee, Wis. 53203
(414) 272-8575
Executive Director, Wayne L. Kost
Regional Director, Irving E. Willard, NCR Canada, Ltd., 580 Weber St. N., Waterloo, Ont. N2J 4G5(519/884-1710)

AMERICAN WATER WORKS ASSOCIATION (Ontario Section)
45 23rd St., Toronto, Ont. M8V 3M6
(416) 252-7060

AMERICAN WOMAN'S CLUB
1010 14 Ave. S.W., Calgary, Alta. T2R OP1 (403/244-4443)
Secretary, Mrs. Eric Waldman (282-5169)

AMNESTY INTERNATIONAL (Canadian Section - English Speaking)
2101 Algonquin Ave., Ottawa, Ont. K2A 1T1
(613) 722-1988 / Cable: AMSTY CANAD

THE ANGLICAN YOUTH MOVEMENT
All correspondence should be addressed to The Anglican Youth Movement, 600 Jarvis St., Toronto, Ont. M4Y 2J6 (416/924-9192)

THE ANIMAL DEFENCE & A-V SOCIETY OF B.C.
Box 391, Stn. A, Vancouver, B.C. V6C 2N2
(604) 929-4574
Treasurer, Elsie Kozak

ANTHROPOSOPHICAL SOCIETY IN CANADA
81 Lawton Blvd., Toronto, Ont. M4V 1Z6
Secretary, G. Wilson (416/488-2886)

APPAREL MANUFACTURERS ASSOCIATIONS

APPAREL MANUFACTURERS ASSOCIATION OF ONTARIO
430 King St. W., Ste. 100, Toronto, Ont. M5V 1L5
(416) 364-5746
Executive Director, F.J. Bryan

ASSOCIATED CLOTHING MANUFACTURERS, P.Q. INC.
Ste. 205, 1030 Cherrier St., Montreal, P.Q. H2L 3M2
(514) 526-0434
Executive Director, Lionel Rubin

BRITISH COLUMBIA FASHION & NEEDLE TRADES ASSOCIATION
608 Marine Bldg., 355 Burrard St., Vancouver, B.C. V6C 2G8
(604) 685-8131
Secretary, W.E. Gordon

CANADIAN APPAREL MANUFACTURERS INSTITUTE
#804, 141 Laurier Ave. W., Ottawa, Ont. K1P 5J3
(613) 238-7743
Executive Director, Peter Clark

CHILDREN'S APPAREL MANUFACTURERS ASSOCIATION
8235 Mountain Sights, Ste. 304, Montreal, P.Q. H4P 2B4
(514) 731-7774
Executive Director, B. Rogers

LINGERIE & LOUNGEWEAR MANUFACTURERS ASSOCIATION OF CANADA
2015 Peel St., 3rd floor, Montreal, P.Q. H3A 1T8
(514) 845-0141
Executive Director, Avrum Orenstein

MEN'S CLOTHING MANUFACTURERS ASSOCIATION OF ONTARIO
430 King St. W., Ste. 100, Toronto, Ont. M5V 1L5
(416) 364-5746
Executive Director, F.J. Bryan

MEN'S CLOTHING MANUFACTURERS ASSOCIATION OF QUEBEC
1030 Cherrier St., Ste. 205, Montreal, P.Q. H2L 1H9
(514) 526-0434
Executive Director, Lionel Rubin

MONTREAL DRESS & SPORTSWEAR MANUFACTURERS GUILD
9250 Park Ave., Ste. 300, Montreal, P.Q. H2N 1Z2
(514) 384-3800
Executive Director, L. Peters

TORONTO DRESS & SPORTSWEAR MANUFACTURERS GUILD
410 Adelaide St. W., Toronto, Ont. M5V 1S8
(416) 363-1066/7
Executive Director, I. Cordes

APPRAISAL INSTITUTE OF CANADA
Ste. 309, 93 Lombard Ave., Winnipeg, Man. R3B 3B1
(204) 942-0751
Executive Vice President, W. T. O'Brien

Provincial Associations

Alta.: Secretary, R.C. Delamater, 10806 123 St., Edmonton, Alta. T5M 0C6
B.C.: Secretary, Mrs. E. Getz, #601, 626 W. Pender St., Vancouver, B.C. V6B 1V9
Man.: Secretary, L.M. Morton, 863 Dale Blvd., Winnipeg, Man. R3R 1R4
Ont.: Executive Director, P. Burton, 5468 Dundas St. W., Ste. 330, Islington, Ont. M9B 6E3
Sask.: Secretary, D.D. Genereaux, #503, 508 Main St., Saskatoon, Sask. S7N 0C1

There are Local Chapters with elected secretaries in all major population areas across Canada. Contact the head office, above, for current addresses.

ARCHITECTS' ASSOCIATIONS

ROYAL ARCHITECTURAL INSTITUTE OF CANADA
151 Slater St., Suite 1104, Ottawa, Ont. K1P 5H3
(613) 232-7165
Executive Director, tba

ALBERTA ASSOCIATION OF ARCHITECTS
Executive Secretary, Gerard Tersmette, Duggan House, 10515 Saskatchewan Dr., Edmonton, Alta. T6E 4S1 (403/432-0224)

THE ARCHITECTURAL INSTITUTE OF BRITISH COLUMBIA
Executive Director, Ian G. King, 970 Richards St., Vancouver, B.C. V6B 3C1 (604/683-8588)

MANITOBA ASSOCIATION OF ARCHITECTS
Executive Secretary, Mrs. Helene C. Peters, 2nd Floor, 100 Osborne St. S., Winnipeg, Man. R3L 1Y5 (204/452-6613)

ARCHITECTS' ASSOCIATION OF NEW BRUNSWICK
Executive Secretary, Mrs. Freda M. Large, Box 910, Rothesay, N.B. E0G 2W0 (506/847-3940)

NEWFOUNDLAND ASSOCIATION OF ARCHITECTS
Honorary Secretary Treasurer, J.K. Dobbs, Box E5204, St. John's, Nfld. A1C 5V9 (709/778-2416)

NOVA SCOTIA ASSOCIATION OF ARCHITECTS
Executive Secretary, Mrs. Diane Scott, 5991 Spring Garden Rd., Ste. 630, Halifax, N.S. B3H 1Y6 (902/423-7607)

ONTARIO ASSOCIATION OF ARCHITECTS
Executive Director, Brian Parks, 50 Park Rd., Toronto, Ont. M4W 2N5 (416/929-0623)

ARCHITECTS' ASSOCIATION OF PRINCE EDWARD ISLAND
Secretary, Peter W. Hyndman, Box 1766, Charlottetown, P.E.I. C1A 7N4 (902/892-8908)

ORDRE DES ARCHITECTES DU QUEBEC
Secretary, Antoine Ghattas, 1825 Dorchester Blvd. W., Montreal, P.Q. H3H 1R4 (514/937-6168)

THE SASKATCHEWAN ASSOCIATION OF ARCHITECTS
Executive Secretary, Mrs. E. C. Hippe, #101, 701 Broadway Ave., Saskatoon, Sask. S7N 1B3 (306/242-0733)

ARCHITECTURAL ALUMINUM ASSOCIATION OF CANADA
15 Toronto St., #702, Toronto, Ont. M5C 2E3
(416) 364-1223

Executive Secretary, Mrs. Susan Cooke

ARCHITECTURAL CONSERVANCY OF ONTARIO
191 College St., Toronto, Ont. M5T 1P7
(416) 598-3051

ARCHITECTURAL METAL ASSOCIATION
55 York St., Suite 512, Toronto, Ont. M5J 1S2
(416) 363-8374
Secretary, F. Young

ARCHITECTURAL WOODWORK MANUFACTURERS ASSOCIATION OF CANADA
#242, 4299 Canada Way, Burnaby, B.C. V5G 1H3
(604) 438-6616
Secretary, E. Russell

THE ARCTIC INSTITUTE OF NORTH AMERICA
University of Calgary, 2500 University Dr. N.W., Calgary, Alta. T2N 1N4
(403) 284-3387

Established in 1945 to encourage and support scientific research pertaining to the polar regions.
Executive Director, Dr. P. Schledermann, Calgary

ARCTIC PETROLEUM OPERATORS' ASSOCIATION
Executive Director, Dr. G.H. Jones, #1902, 727 6th Ave. S.W., Calgary, Alta. T2P 0V1 (403/265-1161)

ARMY, NAVY & AIR FORCE VETERANS IN CANADA
Dominion Secretary Treasurer, J. C. McArthur, 275 Slater St., #1502, Ottawa, Ont. K1P 5H9 (613/232-0222)

Provincial Commands with Secretaries
Alta.: Al Cox, 57 Thornlee Cres. N.W., Calgary, Alta. T2K 2W2
B.C.: T. E. Fontaine, #200, 951 E. 8th Ave., Vancouver, B.C. V5T 4L2
Man.: C.A. Myall, 275 Garry St., Winnipeg, Man. R3C 1H9
N.S.: H. Carruthers, Ste. 31, 5320 Torbin St., Halifax, N.S. B3H 1S2
Ont.: M. Rogers, 408 Royal York Rd., Toronto, Ont. M8Y 2R5
Que.: J. Betournay, Box 113, Pointe-Aux-Trembles, P.Q. H1B 5K1
Sask.: O.M. Grasley, Box 1947, Moose Jaw, Sask. S6H 7N6

ART SOCIETIES IN CANADA
(See Government listings for Provincial Arts Councils)

CANADIAN CONFERENCE OF THE ARTS
141 Laurier Ave. W., #707, Ottawa, Ont. K1P 5J3
(613) 238-3561
Patron, The Governor General of Canada
National Director, John Hobday
(Contact Conference of the Arts for up-to-date addresses and phone numbers of member organizations)

CANADIAN CRAFTS COUNCIL
Ste. 16, 46 Elgin St., Ottawa, Ont. K1P 5K6
(613) 235-8200
Executive Director, Peter Weinrich

For list of affiliated and associated associations contact Executive Director.

CANADIAN GUILD OF CRAFTS QUEBEC
Managing Director, Miss Virginia J. Watt, 2025 Peel St., Montreal, P.Q. H3A 1T6 (514/849-6091)

Affiliated members:
Dyehouse Maison du Batik, Box 306, Montreal, P.Q. H4A 3P6
Le Fil d'Ariane, 130 rue du Port, Montréal, P.Q. H2Y 2N8
Phoenix Natural Science Association, c/o Mrs. J.G. Telfer, 148Kenaston Ave., Montreal, P.Q. H3R 1H2
Pointe Claire Cultural Centre, Stewart Hall, 176 Lakeshore Rd., Pointe Claire, P.Q. H9S 4J7
Volunteer Committee, The Montreal Museum of Fine Arts, 3400 Ave. du Musée, Montreal, P.Q. H3G 1K1
Women's Art Society of Montreal, c/o Mrs. A. Hreno, 774 Upper Belmont, Montreal, P.Q. H3Y 1K4

CONSEIL DES ARTS DE LA COMMUNAUTE URBAINE DE MONTREAL
2 Complexe Desjardins, C.P. 129, Montreal, P.Q. H5B 1E6
(514) 872-2074
Secretary General, F.F. Biondi

EMBROIDERERS' ASSOCIATION OF CANADA INC.
7 Garden Dr., Grimsby, Ont. L3M 3X8
(416) 945-4945

ONTARIO ASSOCIATION OF ART GALLERIES
38 Charles St. E., 2nd floor, Toronto, Ont. M4Y 1T3
(416) 920-8378
Director, R. O'Donal

ONTARIO CRAFTS COUNCIL
346 Dundas St. W., Toronto, Ont. M5T 1G5
(416) 977-3551

The Ontario Crafts Council is an umbrella organization whose aim is to encourage the development, marketing, and preservation of crafts. The Council represents craftsmen to the public, government and commerce.

CRAFT RESOURCE CENTRE
The Craft Resource Centre is an information service and reference library for the Ontario Crafts Council.

THE GUILD SHOP
140 Cumberland St., Toronto, Ont. M5R 1A8
(416) 921-1721

The Guild Shop, operated by the Ontario Crafts Council, offers for sale the finest in Canadian crafts.

VISUAL ARTS ONTARIO
417 Queen's Quay W., Toronto, Ont. M5V 1A2
(416) 366-1607
Executive Director, W. J. S. Boyle

Member groups at same address:
Canadian Society of Painters in Water Colour
Ont. Crafts Council
Ont. Society for Education through Art
Ont. Society of Artists
The Print & Drawing Council of Canada
Sculptor's Society of Canada
Society of Canadian Artists

THE ARTHRITIS SOCIETY
Ste. 420, 920 Yonge St., Toronto, Ont. M4W 3J7
(416) 967-1414
Associate Managing Director, Mrs. S.L. McConnell
Director of Finance & Administration, Mrs. B.D. Thorn
Director of Development, John Travis

Division Offices:
Alta.: #339, 805 5th St. S.W., Calgary, Alta. T2P 1W3
B.C.: 895 W. 10th Ave., Vancouver, B.C. V5Z 1L7
Man.: 825 Sherbrook St., Winnipeg, Man. R3A 1M5
N.B.: 43 Brunswick St., Fredericton, N.B. E3B 1G5
Nfld.: Box 4211, St. John's, Nfld. A1C 5Z7
N.S.: 5516 Spring Garden Rd., Halifax, N.S. B3J 1G6
Ont.: Ste. 420, 920 Yonge St., Toronto, Ont. M4W 3J7
P.E.I.: Box 1537, Charlottetown, P.E.I. C1A 7N3
Que.: Ste. 802, 2075 University, Montreal, P.Q. H3A 2L1
Sask.: 864 Victoria Ave. E., Regina, Sask. S4N 0P2

ASPHALT ROOFING TECHNICAL COMMITTEE
55 York St., Suite 512, Toronto, Ont. M5J 1S2
(416) 363-8374
Secretary, F. Young

ASSEMBLEE DES EVEQUES DU QUEBEC
1225 est, boul. St-Joseph, Montreal, P.Q. H2J 1L7

(514) 274-4323
Secrétaire général, S. Gisèle Turcot, s.b.c.

ASSISTANCE MEDICALE INTERNATIONALE (AMI)

(International Medical Assistance (IMA))
3450 rue de Lorimier, Montreal, P.Q. H2K 3X6
(514) 526-2311
Directrice Générale, Ghislaine Bélanger

ASSOCIATED CREDIT BUREAUS OF CANADA

250 Merton St., Toronto, Ont. M4S 1E4
(416) 484-0822

Branches & Managers

ALBERTA

CB Calgary: #260, 1016 68 Ave. S.W. (Box 5218, Stn. A, Calgary, Alta. T2H 1X3), Priscille Gauthier (403/259-3355)
Collectrite Services Ltd.: #502, 1300 8 St. S.W., Calgary, Alta. T2R 1B2, B. Matthews (403/265-6191)
CB Drumheller: Western Garage Bldg., 3rd Ave. W. (Box 1857, Drumheller, Alta. TOJ OYO), Suzanne Goldie (403/823-3235)
CB Edmonton: Box 9117, Stn. E, Edmonton, Alta. T5P 4K2, D.E. Emberly (403/483-0216)
Edmonton Collectrite Services: Box 9117, Stn. E, Edmonton, Alta. T5P 4K2, G. McTavish (403/483-0216)
CB Athabasca: 8127 Fraser Ave., Fort McMurray, Alta. T9H 1W5, G. Tucknott (403/743-1144)
CB Grande Prairie: 10009 101 Ave., Grande Prairie, Alta. T8V OX9, Garry Martin (403/532-8542)
CB Lethbridge: 1277 3rd Ave. S. (Box 172, Lethbridge, Alta. T1J OK3), B.R. Matthews (403/328-1781)
CB Medicine Hat: Box 1268, Medicine Hat, Alta. T1A 7M9, G.A. Tellman (403/526-2846)
CB Red Deer: #35, 4917 48 St., Red Deer, Alta. T4N 1S8, Ed Kisling (403/343-3176)

BRITISH COLUMBIA CREDIT BUREAUS

CB Abbotsford: #202, 33119 S. Fraser Way, Abbotsford, B.C., A.A. Wright (604/853-2787)
Burns Lake (Reporting): located at CB Smithers, Box 1074, Smithers, B.C., I. Oevermann (604/847-2628)
CB Burns Lake (Collection): 322 Yellowhead (Box 538, Burns Lake, B.C. VOJ 1EO), I. Oevermann (604/847-9721)
CB Campbell River: #202, 437 10th Ave. (Box 99, Campbell River, B.C. V9W 4Z9), D.C. Drummond (604/287-7134)
CB Cloverdale: Box 1163, Stn. A, Cloverdale, B.C., H.M. Read
CB Courtenay: Box 3277, 493A Puntledge Rd., Courtenay, B.C., D.C. Drummond (604/334-4481)
CB Cranbrook, Kimberley Dist.: Ste. 201, 16 11th Ave. S., Cranbrook, B.C. V1C 2P1, D.E. Nilson (604/489-2345)
CB Dawson Creek: 1200 103 Ave., Dawson Creek, B.C. V1G 2G9, N.D. Robertson (604/782-3317)
CB Duncan: 145 Kenneth St. (Box 91, Duncan, B.C.), D. Skaife (604/748-8181)
CB Fort St. John: #203, 10343 100 Ave., Fort St. John, B.C. V1J 1Y8, R.T. Phelps (604/785-6731)
CB Kamloops: 539 Tranquille Rd., Kamloops, B.C. V2B 3H5, J.W. Barber (604/554-2331)
CB Kelowna: #202, 1583 Ellis St. (Box 666, Kelowna, B.C. V1Y 7P2), L.J. Olynick (604/762-3344)
CB Kitimat: 370 Century House, Box 222, Kitimat, B.C., E. Lewis (604/632-3141)
CB Nanaimo: Box 583, Nanaimo, B.C. V9R 5L5, Ed Kisling (604/753-4356)
CB Nelson: 373 Baker St., Nelson, B.C. V1L 4H6, E. Legge (604/352-5526)
CB Penticton: #202, 69 Nanaimo St. E., Penticton, B.C., Donna Carsience (604/492-2835)
CB Port Alberni: Box 326, Port Alberni, B.C. V9Y 7M8, M.R. Conway (604/723-7361)
CB Powell River: 4695A Marine Ave., Powell River, B.C. V8A 2L2, R.C. Gulash (604/485-6246)
CB Prince George: Box 40, 101, 1157 5th Ave., Prince George, B.C. V2L 4R9, B.L. Stearns (604/563-1551)
CB Prince Rupert: #2, 220 6th St. (Box 533, Prince Rupert, B.C.), J.D. McNish (604/624-6701)
CB Quesnel: Box 4731, 345 Reid St., Quesnel, B.C. V2J 3J9, B. Black (604/992-5527)
CB Revelstoke: 100 Fourth St. E. (Box 219, Revelstoke, B.C. VOE 2SO), M.J. Patrick (604/837-2242)
CB Smithers: 3839 Second Ave. (Box 1074, Smithers, B.C.), I. Oevermann (604/847-2628)
CB Trail: #1, 1310 Cedar Ave., Trail, B.C. V1R 4C2, Sharon Stewart (604/368-3383)
CB Vancouver: 400 Robson St., Vancouver, B.C., K. Downie (604/685-5111)
CB Vernon: #1, 3316A 30th Ave., Vernon, B.C. V1T 2C3, S.M. Mitchell (604/545-5354)
CB Victoria: Box 8, 106, 826 N. Park St., Victoria, B.C. V8W 2M2, R.J. Cribbs (604/388-4366)
CB Whitehorse: 312 Wood St., Whitehorse, Y.T. Y1A 2E6, Marilyn Gibb (403/667-4294)
CB Williams Lake: #101, 197 N. 2nd Ave., Williams Lake, B.C. V2G 1Z5, G.A. Smith (604/392-7126)

MANITOBA CREDIT BUREAUS

CB Brandon: 801 13th St., Box 125, Brandon, Man. R7A 5Y6, A.B. Dalgleish (204/727-6444)
CB Dauphin: 30 1st Ave. N.W., Dauphin, Man. R7H 1H1, Sylvia Leskiw (204/638-3333)
CB Flin Flon: 78 Main St., Flin Flon, Man. R8A 1K1, Alma Hill (204/687-7504)
CB Portage La Prairie: 102 Ideal Bldg., 20 3rd St. N.E., Portage La Prairie, Man. R1N 1N4, A.B. Dalgleish (204/857-3491)
CB Northern Man.: 3, 91 Churchill Dr., Thompson, Man. R8N OL5, Melva Graham (204/677-4529)
CB Winnipeg: #400, 215 Garry St., Winnipeg, Man. R3C 3Y7 A.B. Dalgleish (204/944-9966)

NEW BRUNSWICK CREDIT BUREAUS

CB Bathurst (Affiliated Credit Bureau): 2nd floor, 176 Main St. (Box 630, Bathurst, N.B.), F. Power (506/546-9921)
CB Fredericton: 404 Queen St., Box 1075, Fredericton, N.B., E. MacEwen (506/454-3311)
CB Moncton: 236 St. George St. (Box 1009, Moncton, N.B. E1C 8P2), D. Arnold (506/382-3049)
Moncton Collection Bureau: 15A Granville St. (Box 1454, Summerside, P.E.I. C1N 4K4), A.A. Johnston (902/436-9140)
CB Saint John: Box 249, 219 Wentworth St., Saint John, N.B. E2L 3Y2 A.J. Donovan (506/657-4270)

NEWFOUNDLAND CREDIT BUREAUS

CB Corner Brook: 53 West St. (Box 336, Corner Brook, Nfld.), B. Waterman (709/634-4016)
CB Central Nfld.: High St. (Box 395, Grand Falls, Nfld.), A. Frampton (709/489-2285)
CB St. John's: 157 Water St. (Box 278, St. John's, Nfld. A1C 5J7), F.M. Barnes (709/753-7030)

NOVA SCOTIA CREDIT BUREAUS

CB Antigonish: 273 Main St., Antigonish, N.S., J.R. Stewart (902/863-2707)
CB South Shore, Bridgewater Branch, Credit Clearing Centre: 180 Dufferin St. (Box 278, Bridgewater, N.S. B4V 2X1), H.L. Boone (902/543-4611)
CB Twin Cities: 6080 Young St., Ste. 301, Halifax, N.S. B3K 5L2, W.P. Doull (902/453-2822)
CB Kentville: 403 Main St. (Box 67, Kentville, N.S. B4N 3W1), J.A. Andersen (902/678-3261)
CB New Glasgow: Box 395, New Glasgow, N.S. B2H 5E5, J.R. Stewart (902/752-8355)
CB Sydney: 363 Charlotte St. (Box 427, Sydney, N.S. B1P 1C8), S. Colbourne (902/539-3670)
CB Truro: 63 Duke St. (Box 97, Truro, N.S. B2N 5B6), C. MacVicar (902/893-9444)
Truro Merchants CB: 24 Louise St. (Box 704, Truro, N.S. B2N 5E5), A. Torraville (902/895-5461)
CB South Shore Yarmouth Branch: Box 506, 14 Kirk St., Yarmouth, N.S. B5A 4B4, E.R. Glencross (902/742-7137)

ONTARIO CREDIT BUREAUS

CB Barrie: 46 Mary St., Box 337, Barrie, Ont. L4M 4T5, Ross Waterhouse (705/726-6552)

CB Belleville: 377 Front St. (Box 236, Belleville, Ont. K8N 5A2), (613/962-0781)

CB Brampton: 27 John St., Brampton, Ont. L6W 3L1, H. Lockwood (416/451-4030)

CB Brantford: 154 Dalhousie St., Brantford, Ont. N3T 5P2, M. Matyas (519/756-2300)

CB Brockville: Box 602, Brockville, Ont. K6V 3P7, J. Hill (613/342-0171)

CB Cambridge: 61 Ainslie St. N., Box 607, Cambridge, Ont. N1R 5W1, A. Ferguson (519/621-4260)

CB Chatham: 231 William St. S., Chatham, Ont. N7M 5K4, C.C. Mifflin (519/352-0400)

CB Cobourg: Box 554, Cobourg, Ont. K9A 4L3, Wm. Grandy (416/372-2211)

CB Cornwall: 31 Second St. (Box 1059, Cornwall, Ont. K6H 5V2), C. Poirier (613/932-9301)

CB Guelph: 485 Silvercreek Pkwy. N., Unit 16, Guelph, Ont. N1H 6K9, O. Wilson (519/822-0681)

CB Hamilton: 170 Jackson St. E., Hamilton, Ont. L8N 3K8, A.F. Adams (416/525-4420)

Collectrite Hamilton: 636 Main St. E. (M.P.O. Box 977, Hamilton, Ont. L8N 1L5), Betty Millar (416/525-7300)

CB Kenora-Dryden: 14 Earl Ave., Dryden, Ont. P8N 1X3, E. Hampe (807/223-2338)

CB Kingston: 258 Bagot St. (Box 523, Kingston, Ont. K7L 4W5), M. Massey (613/962-0781)

CB Kirkland Lake: Box 1104, Kirkland Lake, Ont. P2N 3L6, M. Baird (705/567-5271)

CB Kitchener Waterloo: 31 College St., Kitchener, Ont. N2G 3Z6, J.G. Bowman (519/744-6192)

CB Lindsay: Box 32, Lindsay, Ont. K9V 4R8, I.F. McClure (705/324-3588)

CB London: 240 Wharncliff Rd. N., Ste. 204-206, London, Ont. N6H 4P2, E. Laing (519/423-8301)

CB Midland: 522 Elizabeth St., #33, Midland, Ont. L4R 4K8, P. Mattar (705/526-5468)

CB Newmarket: Box 29, Newmarket, Ont. L3Y 4W4, J. Arnold (519/895-5141)

CB Niagara Falls (Reporting): Box 186, St. Catharines, Ont. L2R 6S7, E.W. Bower (416/227-6140)

CB Niagara Falls (Collection): Box 58, Niagara Falls, Ont. L2E 6S8, J.T. Wilson (416/356-1381)

CB North Bay: Box 198, North Bay, Ont. P1B 1A8, R. Kouris (705/472-9120)

CB Oakville: Box 99, Oakville, Ont. L6J 4Z9, R.K. Henderson (416/845-7193)

CB Orillia: Box 66, Orillia, Ont. L3V 5J9, G. Showers (705/326-7347)

CB Oshawa: 286 King St. W. (Box 236, Oshawa, Ont. L1H 7L2), J.M. Hatt (416/725-6591)

CB Ottawa: 368 Slater St., Box 2050, Stn. D, Ottawa, Ont. K1P 5X6, A.D. Sinclair (613/236-0251)

Ottawa Collection: McGrath Canada Ltd., 111 Rideau St., Ottawa, Ont. K1N 5X1, M. McGrath (613/237-8420)

CB Owen Sound: R.R. 3, Chatsworth, Ont., and Box 696, Owen Sound, Ont., W.M. Pearson (519/794-3500)

CB Pembroke: Box 308, Pembroke, Ont. K8A 6X6, P.J. Moore (613/735-6891)

CB Peterborough: Box 111, Peterborough, Ont. K9H 2L2, I.F. McClure (705/742-4293)

CB St. Catharines: Box 186, St. Catharines, Ont. L2R 6S7, E.W. Bower (416/227-6140)

CB St. Thomas: 55 Curtis St., St. Thomas, Ont. N5P 3T5, B. Herbert (519/631-1050)

CB Sarnia: Box 400, Sarnia, Ont. N7T 5X2, G.M. McSweeney (519/336-6111)

CB Sault Ste. Marie: Box 1107, Sault Ste. Marie, Ont. P6A 5N7, J. Luxton (705/254-7545)

CB Stratford: 21 Market Place, Stratford, Ont. N5A 1A4, D.C. Forster (519/271-6211)

CB Sudbury: Box 2514, Stn. A, Sudbury, Ont. P3E 4S9, E.A. Beaudoin (705/560-6080)

CB Thunder Bay: Box 783, Thunder Bay, Ont. P7C 4X5, W.G. Waite (807/622-3981)

CB Timmins: Box 908, Timmins, Ont. P4N 6H8, T.J. Laporte (705/264-5281)

CB Greater Toronto: 60 Bloor St. W., 12th floor, Toronto, Ont. M4W 3C1, R.M. Cox (416/964-5200)

Toronto Collection Collectrite (Central): 1240 Bay St., Ste. 600, Toronto, Ont. M4R 2A7, M. Grant (416/961-9622)

CB Welland: 91 East Main St., Welland, Ont. L3B 3W4, B.C. Smith (416/732-7521)

CB Windsor: 305 Victoria Ave., Windsor, Ont. N9A 6R2, D.C. Larkin (519/253-4481)

Windsor Collection Service: Box 1209, Windsor, Ont. N9A 6R2, E.B. Hassberger (519/256-3421)

CB Woodstock: 601 Dundas St., Woodstock, Ont. M4S 7W8, H. Wark (519/539-8196)

PRINCE EDWARD ISLAND CREDIT BUREAUS

CB Charlottetown: Box 751, Charlottetown, P.E.I., J.W. Johnston (902/894-8525)

CB Summerside: Box 1454, Summerside, P.E.I., A.A. Johnston (902/436-9115)

QUEBEC CREDIT BUREAUS

CB Alma: see Chicoutimi

CB Baie Comeau: 3 Place La Salle, Ste. 103, Baie Comeau, P.Q., A. Giguere (418/296-3318)

CB Chicoutimi: 901 boul. Talbot, #401, Chicoutimi, P.Q. G7H 4B5, D. Boivin (418/543-0211)

CB Drummondville: Box 70, Drummondville, P.Q. J2C 1J8, L. Fontaine (819/478-2522)

CB Granby: Box 124, Granby, P.Q. J2G 8E4, C. Gaudreau (514/372-5838)

CB Joliette: c/o 4875 Metropolitain Blvd., St-Leonard, P.Q. H1R 2J3, M. Globensky (514/327-4222)

CB Matane: Box 307, Matane, P.Q. G4W 3N2, G. Levesque (418/562-3835)

CB Montreal: 4875 Metropolitain Blvd., St-Leonard, P.Q. H1R 2J3 M. Globensky (514/327-4222)

Montreal Collection: Collectrite Inc., 1420 rue Montarville, C.P. 210, St-Bruno, P.Q. H3V 4P9, R. Amyot (514/653-4296)

CB Quebec: 580 Grande Allée est, Quebec, P.Q. G1R 2K2, R. Gingras (418/529-8971)

CB Rimouski: Box 878, Rimouski, P.Q. G5L 3J6, R. Poirier (418/723-3335)

CB Lower St. Lawrence: 600 rue Lafontaine, Ste. 201 (Box 577, Riviere du Loup, P.Q. G5R 3C6), P. Levesque (418/862-8235)

CB Rouyn: Box 727, Rouyn, P.Q., H. Boucher (819/762-4351)

CB St-Hyacinthe: 1625 St. Antoine, St-Hyacinthe, P.Q. J2S 3L3, Y. Drainville (514/774-6475)

CB St-Jean: Box 514, St-Jean, P.Q. J3B 4K1, L. Tougas (514/346-4404)

CB St-Jérôme: Box 333, St-Jérôme, P.Q. J7Z 5L2, M. Globensky (514/438-4148)

CB Sept Iles: Edifice 'Le Concorde', 350 Smith, Ste. 48 (Box 880, Sept Iles, P.Q. G4R 4L4), J. Boutin (418/962-9414)

CB Shawinigan: Bureau Credit de la Mauricie, 550 Bonaventure (Box 1084, Trois-Rivières, P.Q. G9A 2B5), R. Gingras (819/536-2509)

CB Sherbrooke: 740 Galt St. W., 3rd floor, Sherbrooke, P.Q. J1H 1Z3, Y. Drainville (819/556-2882)

CB Sorel/Tracy: 51 rue George, #1, Sorel, P.Q. J3P 5N7, Y. Drainville (514/743-5506)

CB Thetford Mines: 97 S. Notre Dame St., Thetford Mines, P.Q. G6G 5T6, J.M. Lachance (418/335-2907)

CB Trois Rivières: Box 1084, Trois Rivieres, P.Q. G9A 2B5, R. Gingras (819/375-9644)

CB Val D'Or: C.P. 939, 812 3e Ave., Val D'Or, P.Q., D. Morneau (819/824-9661)

CB Valleyfield: Box 253, Valleyfield, P.Q. J6T 1P1, J.C. Bedard (514/373-5055)

SASKATCHEWAN CREDIT BUREAUS

CB Estevan: 1213 5th St., Estevan, Sask. S4A 0Z5, R.K. McCuaig (306/634-4784)

CB Lloydminster: Drawer 826, Lloydminster, Sask. S9V 1C2, D. Hutchinson (403/825-3315)

CB Medicine Hat: Box 1268, Medicine Hat, Alta., G.A. Tellman (403/526-2846)

CB Moose Jaw: No. 8, 46 High St. E., Moose Jaw, Sask. S6H OB8, H.J. Tobias (306/693-3677)

CB North Battleford: #2, 1092 101 St. (Box 85, North Battleford, Sask. S9A 2X6), L.M. Sutton (306/445-9439)

CB Prince Albert: #103, 70 17th St. W., Prince Albert, Sask. S6V 3X3, H. Wheaton (306/764-1481)

CB Regina: 315 McCallum Hill Bldg., Regina, Sask. S4P 2G6, K. Wood (306/527-4176)

CB Saskatoon Reporting Ltd.: 321B 4th Ave. N., Saskatoon, Sask. S7K 1K7, J. McKinnon (306/652-5262)

Saskatoon Collection: 321C 4th Ave. N., Saskatoon, Sask. S7K 1K7, P. Vogan (306/652-4012)

CB Swift Current: Box 278, Swift Current, Sask. S9H OA9, L.G. Mang (306/773-7235)

CB Yorkton: 41 Broadway W., #035, Yorkton, Sask. S3N 2W8, W.M. Rieben (306/783-6588)

ASSOCIATION OF ADMINISTRATIVE ASSISTANTS

(Association des adjoints administratifs)
Box 5107, Stn. A, Toronto, Ont. M5W 1N4
Corresponding Secretary, Miss I. Hanna, 239 Belvidere St., Winnipeg, Man. R3J 2H1 (204/837-5381, 988-5296)

The Association sponsors an Administrative Correspondence Course through School of Continuing Studies, University of Toronto. All graduates receive certificates. In addition, member-graduates receive designating letters Q.A.A. (Qualified Administrative Assistant).

THE ASSOCIATION FOR THE ADVANCEMENT OF CHRISTIAN SCHOLARSHIP

229 College St., Toronto, Ont. M5T 1R4
(416) 979-2331
Executive Officer, R. E. Vander Vennen

ASSOCIATION OF ARCHITECTURAL TECHNOLOGISTS OF ONTARIO

40 Orchard View Blvd., #253, Toronto, Ont. M4R 1B9
(416) 481-2426
Administrative Secretary, Pamela Brown

ASSOCIATION BELGIQUE-CANADA

President, J. Dupre, Q.C., 1600 est, boul. St-Martin, Place Val des Arbres, Tour B, 6e étage, Duvernay-Laval, P.Q. H7G 4S7 (514/668-5200)

Manager, Downes Ryan, 5580, Gatineau ave, apt. 9, Montreal, P.Q. H3T 1X7 (514/733-9061)

ASSOCIATION DE BIENFAISANCE ET DE RETRAITE DES POLICIERS DE LA COMMUNAUTE URBAINE DE MONTREAL

480 rue Gilford, Montreal, P.Q. H2J 1N3
(514) 288-9113
Président, Jacques Perron

ASSOCIATION OF BOOK PUBLISHERS OF BRITISH COLUMBIA

1622 W. 7th Ave., Vancouver, B.C. V6J 1S5
(604) 734-1611

ASSOCIATION OF BRITISH COLUMBIA PROFESSIONAL FORESTERS

#406, 837 W. Hastings St., Vancouver, B.C. V6C 1B6
(604) 687-8027

ASSOCIATION OF CANADIAN ADVERTISERS

180 Bloor St. W., #1010, Toronto, Ont. M5S 2V6
(416) 964-3805
President, John Foss

ASSOCIATION OF CANADIAN BIBLE COLLEGES

Secretary, Rev. Isaac Bergen, c/o Bethany Bible College, Box 160, Hepburn, Sask. S0K 1Z0 (306/947-2175)

ASSOCIATION OF CANADIAN BISCUIT MANUFACTURERS

1185 Eglinton Ave. E., Ste. 101, Don Mills, Ont. M3C 3C6
(416) 429-1074

ASSOCIATION OF CANADIAN CAREER COLLEGES

Executive Director, A.E. Pocius, Box 340, 1 Wellington St., Brantford, Ont. N3T 5N3 (519/753-8689)

ASSOCIATION OF CANADIAN CLUBS

#309, 222 Queen St., Ottawa, Ont. K1P 5V9
(613) 236-8288
National Director, N.A. Mence

ASSOCIATION OF CANADIAN DISTILLERS

350 Sparks St., Ste. 506, Ottawa, Ont. K1R 7S8
(613) 238-8444
Executive Secretary, Conrad Pilon

ASSOCIATION OF CANADIAN FINANCIAL CORPORATIONS

#1001, 21 St. Clair Ave. E., Toronto, Ont. M4T 1L9
(416) 967-4277
President, Carne Bray

ASSOCIATION OF CANADIAN FIRE MARSHALS & FIRE COMMISSIONERS

Secretary Treasurer, Len Adrian, Box 488, Edmonton, Alta. (403/420-3291)

Roster of Fire Marshals & Commissioners

Dominion Fire Commissioner, G.A. Hope, Dept. of Public Works, Ottawa, Ont. K1A 0M2 (613/998-4617)

Alta.: W. D. MacKay, 7th floor, IBM Bldg., 10808 99 Ave., Edmonton, Alta. T5K 0G2 (403/427-8392)

B.C.: G.R. Anderson, 2780 E. Broadway, Vancouver, B.C. V5M 1Y8 (604/251-3131)

Man.: A. Thorimbert, Ste. 510, 401 York Ave., Winnipeg, Man. R3C 0P8 (204/944-3322)

N.B.: G.R. Elliott (act.), Box 6000, Fredericton, N.B. E3B 5H1 (506/453-2134)

Nfld.: John N. Cardoulis, Dept. of Justice, Pleasantville Fire Stn., St. John's, Nfld. A1C 5T7 (709/726-1050)

N.W.T.: L.D. McPhee, Government of the N.W.T., Yellowknife, N.W.T. X0E 1H0

N.S.: Charles Findlay, Box 697, Halifax, N.S. B3J 2T8 (902/424-5721)

Ont.: John Bateman, 590 Keele St., Toronto, Ont. M6N 4X2 (416/965-4844)

P.E.I.: C.R. Kennedy, Box 2000, Charlottetown, P.E.I. C1A 7N8 (902/892-0221)

Que.: G. Lamothe, Director General of Fire Prevention, 1279 boul. Charest ouest, Quebec, P.Q. G1N 4K7 (418/643-2014)

Sask.: M.G.G. Fisher, 1150 Rose St., Regina, Sask. S4P 3V7 (306/565-4516)

Yukon: Larry Hipperson, Box 2703, Whitehorse, Yukon Y1A 2C6 (403/667-5217)

Canadian Forces Fire Marshal, Lt. Col. L. MacLean, National Defence Hdqs., 101 Colonel By Dr., Ottawa, Ont. K1A OK2 (613/992-7651)

ASSOCIATION CANADIENNE-FRANCAISE DE L'ALBERTA

#203, 10008-109e rue, Edmonton, Alta. T5J 1M4
President, Roger Lalonde (403/423-1680)

ASSOCIATION CANADIENNE-FRANCAISE DE L'ONTARIO

Président général, Yves Saint-Denis, 325, rue Dalhousie, Pièce 500, Ottawa, Ont. K1N 7G2 (613/237-6050)

ASSOCIATION OF CANADIAN FRANCHISORS

#1005, 88 University Ave., Toronto, Ont. M5J 1T9
(416) 595-0022
Executive Director, Howard Rose

ASSOCIATION OF CANADIAN INDUSTRIAL DESIGNERS

President, Jacques Giard, c/o School of Industrial Design, Carleton University, Colonel By Dr., Ottawa, Ont. K1S 5B6 (613/231-5526)

ASSOCIATION DES DESIGNERS INDUSTRIELS DU CANADA (QUEBEC)

432 Place Jacques Cartier, Montréal, P.Q. H2Y 3B3
(514) 861-1909

ASSOCIATION OF CANADIAN INDUSTRIAL DESIGNERS (MANITOBA)

Box 1722, Winnipeg, Man. R3C 0K0

ASSOCIATION OF CANADIAN INDUSTRIAL DESIGNERS (ONTARIO)

55 University Ave., #600, Toronto, Ont. M5J 2H7
(416) 862-1799
Administrative Secretary, Audrey Duff

ASSOCIATION OF CANADIAN KNIGHTS OF THE SOVEREIGN & MILITARY ORDER OF MALTA

Lock Box 252, Tour de la Bourse, Montreal, P.Q. H4Z 1E8
(514) 861-3073
President, Lieut.-Col. Simon Parent
Vice President, Dr. Philippe Garigue, B.Sc., Ch.D., F.R.S.C.

ASSOCIATION OF CANADIAN MAP LIBRARIES

c/o National Map Collection, Public Archives of Canada, 395 Wellington St., Ottawa, Ont. K1A 0N3 (613/995-1077)

ASSOCIATION OF CANADIAN PENSION MANAGEMENT

2 Bloor St. W., #503, Toronto, Ont. M4W 3E2
(416) 964-1260
Executive Director, A.L. Vincent

ASSOCIATION OF CANADIAN PUBLISHERS

70 The Esplanade, 3rd floor, Toronto, Ont. M5E 1R2
(416) 361-1408
Executive Director, Phyllis Yaffe

ASSOCIATION CANADIENNE DE LA RADIO ET DE LA TELEVISION DE LANGUE FRANCAISE INC.

857, Madeleine-de-Verchères, Québec, P.Q. G1S 4K6

ASSOCIATION CANADIENNE DES REDACTEURS AGRICOLES DE LANGUE FRANCAISE

(agricultural editors)
Secretary, André Laprise, 3940 Nicolet, St-Hyacinthe, P.Q. J2S 7H1 (514/285-3013)

ASSOCIATION OF CANADIAN UNIVERSITY PRESSES

(Association des Presses Universitaires Canadiennes)
Secretary, Ian Montagnes, University of Toronto Press, Toronto, Ont. M5S 1A6 (416/978-2231)

ASSOCIATION OF CANADIAN VENTURE CAPITAL COMPANIES

c/o President, A.G. Fells, SB Capital Corp. Ltd., 85 Bloor St. E., #506, Toronto, Ont. M4W 1A9 (416/967-5439)

ASSOCIATION CANADO-AMERICAINE

1343, 1ère Rue, Trois-Rivières, P.Q. G8Y 2T3
(819) 376-7981
Gérant, Henri Lemay

ASSOCIATION DES CENTRES D'ACCUEIL DU QUEBEC

65 est, Sherbrooke, Ste. 110, Montreal, P.Q. H2X 1C4
(514) 845-0171
Directeur général, Pierre Cloutier

ASSOCIATION DES CHEFS DE POLICE ET POMPIERS DU QUEBEC

1701 Parthenais St., Room 131 (C.P. 1400, Succ C, Montreal, P.Q. H2L 4K7)
(514) 523-6183
Secretary Treasurer, P.-A. Duchesneau

ASSOCIATION OF COMMUNITY INFORMATION CENTRES IN ONTARIO

Contact: Rexdale Community Information Directory

Member Centres (Listed Alphabetically by Location)

Information Agincourt, 3333 Finch Ave. E., Agincourt, Ont. M1W 2R9 (416/494-6912)
Contact Alliston, 66 Victoria St. W., Alliston, Ont. L0M 1A0 (705/435-4900)
Amherstburg, Anderdon & Malden Community Service Centre, 272 Sandwich St. S., Amherstburg, Ont. N9V 2A6 (519/736-5471)
Ancaster Information Centre Inc., 314 Wilson St. E., Ancaster, Ont. L9G 2B9 (416/648-6675)
Community Information & Help Centre of Aylmer, 49 Talbot St. E., Aylmer, Ont. N5H 1H3 (519/773-5301)
Information Barrie, 37 Mulcaster St., Barrie, Ont. L4M 3M2 (705/728-2662)
Caledon Information Centre, 23 Mill St., Box 701, Bolton, Ont. L0P 1A0 (416/857-1050)
Information Brampton, 150 Central Park Dr., Bramalea, Ont. L6T 1B4 (416/457-9612)
Brantford Information Centre, 16 Market St., Box 113, Brantford, Ont. N3T 5M3 (519/753-3171)
Information Burlington, 2331 New St., Burlington, Ont. L7R 1J4 (416/639-4212)
Brock Information Centre, 30 Allan St., Box 131, Cannington, Ont. L0E 1E0 (705/432-2636)
Share Info, Box 632, Cobourg, Ont. K9A 4L3 (416/372-8913)
Collingwood & District Information Centre, 125 Napier St., Collingwood, Ont. L9Y 1R9 (705/445-0641)
Information Dundas, 10 Market St. S., Dundas, Ont. L9H 4G5 (416/627-5461)
Woolwich Community Information Centre, 69 Arthur St. S., Elmira, Ont. N3B 2M8 (519/669-5139)
Community Information - Essex, 115 Talbot St. N., Essex, Ont. N8M 2C5 (519/776-6262)
Guelph Information, 161 Waterloo Ave., Guelph, Ont. N1H 3G9 (519/821-0632)
Community Information Service Hamilton-Wentworth, 42 James St. N., Hamilton, Ont. L8R 2K2 (416/528-0104)
Community Information Centre, 18 Queen St. N., Kitchener, Ont. N2H 2G8 (519/579-3800)
South Essex Community Council, 18 Selkirk Ave., Leamington, Ont. N8H 1G3 (519/326-8629)
Information London, 294 Dundas St., Ste. 109, London, Ont. N6B 1T6 (519/432-2211)
Malton Community Council, Westwood Mall, 7205 Goreway Dr., Malton, Ont. L4T 2T9 (416/677-6585)
Information Markham, 199 Main St. N., Markham, Ont. L3P 1Y4

(416/294-3733 or 297-3459)
Contact Telephone Information & Referral Centre, Box 423, Midland, Ont. L4R 4L1 (705/526-9333)
Information Niagara, 5017 Victoria Ave., Niagara Falls, Ont. L2E 4C9 (416/356-4636)
Information Oakville, 120 Navy St., Oakville, Ont. L6J 2Z4 (416/845-3255)
Information Dufferin, 70 1st St., #102, Orangeville, Ont. L9W 2E5 (519/941-0363)
Information Orillia, 18 Peter St. N., Orillia, Ont. L3V 4Y7 (705/326-7743)
Information Oshawa Inc., 50 Centre St. S., Oshawa, Ont. L1H 3Z7 (416/728-6233)
Community Information Centre of Ottawa-Carleton, 377 Rideau St., Ottawa, Ont. K1N 5Y6 (613/238-2101)
Information Gloucester, 2339 Ogilvie Rd. (Beacon Hill Shopping Centre), Ottawa, Ont. K1T 8M6 (613/741-0770)
The Olde Forge Community Resource Centre, 2730 Carling Ave., Ottawa, Ont. K2B 7J1 (613/829-9777)
Information Paris, 63 Grand River St. N., Paris, Ont. N3L 2M3 (519/442-4343)
Peterborough Information Centre, 281 King St., Peterborough, Ont. K9J 2S4 (705/743-2523)
Information Scugog, Box 1066, Port Perry, Ont. L0B 1N0 (416/985-8461)
Rexdale Community Information Directory, 1530 Albion Rd., Rexdale, Ont. M9V 1B4 (416/741-1553)
Helpmate Information & Referral Services, 10 Trench St., Richmond Hill, Ont. L4C 4Z3 (416/883-2234)
Information Niagara (Branch Office), 348 St. Paul St., St. Catharines, Ont. (416/682-6611)
St. Thomas Elgin Information Centre, 538 Talbot St., St. Thomas, Ont. N5P 1C4 (519/631-1100)
Information Sarnia-Lambton, 224 N. Vidal St., Sarnia, Ont. N7T 5Y3 (519/336-2422)
Community Information Centre, 8 Albert St. E., Sault Ste. Marie, Ont. P6A 2H6 (705/949-6565)
Community Information Centre Haldimand-Norfolk, 85 Pond St., Simcoe, Ont. N3Y 2T5 (519/426-6655)
Stratford Information Centre, 19 St. Andrews St., Stratford, Ont. N5A 1A2 (519/271-7080)
Strathroy-Middlesex Multi-Service Centre, 90 Albert St., Strathroy, Ont. N7G 1V5 (519/245-4330)
Information Tillsonburg, 185 Ralph St., Tillsonburg, Ont. N4G 3Y9 (519/842-9007)
Bloor Bathurst Information Centre, 1006 Bathurst St., Toronto, Ont. M5R 3G8 (416/531-4613)
Community Information Centre of Metropolitan Toronto, 34 King St. E., Toronto, Ont. M5C 1E5 (416/863-0505)
Neighbourhood Information Centre, 81 Barrington Ave., Toronto, Ont. M4C 2G3 (416/698-1626)
Neighbourhood Information Post, 265 Gerrard St. E., Toronto, Ont. M5A 2G3 (416/924-2543)
Parkdale Community Information Centre, 1303 Queen St. W., Toronto, Ont. M6K 1L6 (416/532-7939)
YMCA Action Service Contact Centre, 185 5th St., Toronto, Ont. M8V 2Z5 (416/255-5322)
Information Flamborough, 15 Mill St., Box 240, Waterdown, Ont. L0R 2H0 (416/689-7880)
Community Information Fairview, Box 2273, Fairview Mall, 1800 Sheppard Ave. E., Willowdale, Ont. M2J 4G6 (416/493-0752)
Link Information & Referral, 5126 Yonge St., Willowdale, Ont. M2N 5N9 (416/223-9727)
Windsor-Essex Community Information Service, 65 Wyandotte St. W., Windsor, Ont. N9A 5W6 (519/253-6351)
Vaughan Community Information, 132 Woodbridge Ave., Woodbridge, Ont. L4L 2S7 (416/851-2333)
Information Oxford, Box 955, Woodstock, Ont. N4S 8A3 (519/539-4889)

ASSOCIATION FOR COMPUTING MACHINERY INC.

1133 Ave. of the Americas, New York, N.Y. 10036
(212) 265-6300
Executive Director, Sidney Weinstein
Executive Secretary, Mrs. Irene Hollister

ASSOCIATION OF CONCERN FOR ULTIMATE REALITY & MEANING

15 St. Mary St., Toronto, Ont. M4Y 2R5
General Secretary, Tibor Horvath (416/922-2476, 922-8419)

ASSOCIATION OF CONSTRUCTION SUPERINTENDENTS

President, H. Sytsma, C.C.S., 602 Willard Ave., Toronto, Ont. M6S 3S3 (416/766-1794)

THE ASSOCIATION OF CONSULTING ENGINEERS OF CANADA

Managing Director, H. R. Pinault, 130 Albert St., Suite 616, Ottawa, Ont. K1P 5G4 (613/236-0569)

ASSOCIATION DES INGENIEURS-CONSEILS DU QUEBEC

1010 ouest, rue Ste-Catherine, bur. 303, Montreal, P.Q. H3B 1G1
(514) 879-1717
Directeur général, Marcel Desrochers

CONSULTING ENGINEERS OF ONTARIO

1027 Yonge St., Toronto, Ont. M4W 3E5
(416) 961-2457
Executive Director, Ross F. Reid

NOVA SCOTIA CONSULTING ENGINEERS ASSOCIATION

Secretary Treasurer, Tom Swanson, c/o Alderney Consultants Ltd., 157 Main St., Dartmouth, N.S. B2X 1S1 (902/434-0044)

CONSULTING ENGINEERS OF BRITISH COLUMBIA

2675 Oak St., Vancouver, B.C. V6H 2K3
(604) 736-6311
Attn.: J.H. Bennett

ASSOCIATION OF CONSULTING ENGINEERS OF SASKATCHEWAN

2220 12th Ave., Ste. 220, Regina, Sask. S4P OM8
(306) 527-8266
General Manager, Reg Bing-Wo

CONSULTING ENGINEERS OF ALBERTA

A/Executive Director, Harold Page, #1403, 10025 106 St., Edmonton, Alta. T5J 1G4 (403/420-1030)

ASSOCIATION OF CONSULTING ENGINEERS OF MANITOBA

Secretary, R. McKnight, c/o #640, 175 Hargrave St., Winnipeg, Man. R3C 3R8 (204/942-6481)

ASSOCIATION OF COUNTIES & REGIONS OF ONTARIO

100 University Ave., #1100, Toronto, Ont. M5J 1V6
(416) 593-1477
Executive Director, Sheila Richardson

ASSOCIATION OF CULTURAL EXECUTIVES

1916 Tupper St., Montreal, P.Q. H3H 1N5
(514) 937-9488
President, Peter Swann
Directors, David Silcox, William Boyle, Shirley Gibson, Richard d'Anjou

ASSOCIATION CULTURELLE FRANCO-CANADIENNE DE LA SASKATCHEWAN

514 ave Victoria est, #210, Regina, Sask. S4N 0N7
(306) 569-2188
Directeur général, Florent Bilodeau

ASSOCIATION DES DISTRIBUTEURS D'ARTICLES DE BUREAU DU QUEBEC

(Quebec Office Products Distributors' Association)
30 de l'Epée, Montreal, P.Q. H2V 3S9
(514) 273-3696
Secretary Treasurer, Dave Gagnon

ASSOCIATION FRANCE-CANADA INC.
429, ave Viger, Montreal, P.Q. H2L 2N9
(514) 849-3695 (p.m.)

ASSOCIATION FOR THE HEARING HANDICAPPED
c/o St. Andrew's School, 11342 127 St., Edmonton, Alta. T5M OR4 (403/455-1904)
Coordinator, Mary Holdgrafer

ASSOCIATION OF IROQUOIS & ALLIED INDIANS
R.R. 3, Wallaceburg, Ont. N8A 4K9
(519) 627-1475
President, Charles Cornelius

THE ASSOCIATION OF JUNIOR LEAGUES, INC.
825 Third Ave., New York, N.Y. 10022 (212/355-4380)
An international voluntary service organization with 244 Junior Leagues in the U.S., Canada and Mexico. Membership over 135,000. Incorporated 1921.
President, Margaret M. Graham
Executive Director, Deborah L. Seidel

FEDERATION OF JUNIOR LEAGUES OF CANADA
366 Victoria Ave., Montreal, P.Q. H3Z 2N4 (514/489-9896)
1981-82 Co-Chairman, Mrs. Molly Murray, 3198 Travers Ave., West Vancouver, B.C. V7V 1G3 (604/922-6304)
In Canada, there are eight Junior Leagues.
Alta.: Calgary, Edmonton
B.C.: Vancouver
Man.: Winnipeg
N.S.: Halifax
Ont.: Hamilton-Burlington, Toronto
Que.: Montreal

THE ASSOCIATION OF KINSMEN CLUBS
1920 Hal Rogers Dr., Box KIN, Cambridge, Ont. N3H 5C6
(519) 653-1920
Executive Director, W. Daniel Lamey

ASSOCIATION OF LEGAL COURT INTERPRETERS & TRANSLATORS
2114 St. Lawrence Blvd., Montreal, P.Q. H2X 2T2
(514) 845-3111
President, Henri Keleny, C.C.S.
Translations Manager, Nicholas Czako, M.A., D.Ed.

ASSOCIATION OF MAJOR POWER CONSUMERS IN ONTARIO
#201, 15 Toronto St., Toronto, Ont. M5C 2E3
(416) 363-9634
Executive Director, T.B. Lounsbury

ASSOCIATION OF MANITOBA MUSEUMS
190 Rupert Ave., Winnipeg, Man. R3B ON2
(204) 956-2830

ASSOCIATION OF MARINE UNDERWRITERS OF BRITISH COLUMBIA
325 Howe St., Vancouver, B.C. V6C 2A3
(604) 683-8471
Secretary Treasurer, J.L. Lewis

ASSOCIATION OF MEMBERS & STAFF, ALBERTA LANDLORD & TENANT ADVISORY BOARDS
10237 98th St., Edmonton, Alta. T5J 0M7
(403) 424-6633

ASSOCIATION OF METIS & NON-STATUS INDIANS
1170 8th Ave., Regina, Sask. S4R 1C9
(306) 525-6721
Executive Director, Tim Low

ASSOCIATION OF MUNICIPAL ADMINISTRATORS, NOVA SCOTIA
-not confirmed for 1982-
Box 817, Dartmouth, N.S. B2Y 3Z3
Secretary, Tom Rath (902/466-7401, loc. 175)

ASSOCIATION OF MUNICIPAL CLERKS & TREASURERS OF ONTARIO
100 University Ave., Ste. 1108, Toronto, Ont. M5J 1V6
(416) 593-1400
Secretary Treasurer, Gordon E. Gunning

ASSOCIATION OF MUNICIPAL ELECTRICAL UTILITIES (OF ONTARIO)
700 University Ave., Toronto, Ont. M5G 1X6
(416) 592-3807
General Manager, W.R. Mathieson

ASSOCIATION OF MUNICIPAL TAX COLLECTORS OF ONTARIO
Secretary, Ms. Dorothy Robertson, Town of Wasaga Beach, Box 110, Wasaga Beach, Ont. L0L 2P0 (705/429-3844)

ASSOCIATION OF MUNICIPALITIES OF ONTARIO
100 University Ave., Ste. 902, Toronto, Ont. M5J 1V6
(416) 593-1441
Executive Director, MacDonald Dunbar

ASSOCIATION NATIONALE DES ETUDIANTS ET ETUDIANTES DU QUEBEC
232 ouest, Jean-Talon, Montréal, P.Q. H2R 2X5
(514) 277-5826
Publishes: Le Québec Etudiant

ASSOCIATION OF NOVA SCOTIA HAIRDRESSERS
159 Portland St., 3rd Floor, Dartmouth, N.S. B2Y 1H9
(902) 463-3599
Business Manager, Elaine Josey

ASSOCIATION OF ONTARIO HOUSING AUTHORITIES
#405, 111 Avenue Rd., Toronto, Ont. M5R 3J8
(416) 923-6830
Executive Director, A. Le Masurier

ASSOCIATION OF ONTARIO LOCKSMITHS
6004A Yonge St., Willowdale, Ont. M2M 3V9
(416) 221-5294
President, Ron Smuk

ASSOCIATION OF ONTARIO ROAD SUPERINTENDENTS
Secretary Treasurer, William Taylor, Varna, Ont. NOM 2RO (519/482-3276)

ASSOCIATION DES PARENTS CATHOLIQUES DU QUEBEC
3675, rue St-Hubert, Montreal, P.Q. H2L 3Z9
(514) 526-0844, 5
Présidente, Adeline Mathieu
Secrétaire, Fernande Bruyère

ASSOCIATION OF PENSIONERS & INJURED WORKMEN OF ONTARIO
1878 Danforth Ave., Toronto, Ont. M4C 1J4
(416) 421-9344
President, Antonino Brancati

ASSOCIATION OF POSTAL OFFICIALS OF CANADA
141 Laurier Ave., Ste. 904, Ottawa, Ont. K1P 5J3
(613) 235-4361
National Secretary Treasurer, G.R. Santamaria

L'ASSOCIATION PROFESSIONNELLE DES EVALUATEURS-CONSEILS DU QUEBEC INC.
C.P. 1742, Place d'Armes, Montreal, P.Q. H2Y 3L5
(514) 844-1026
Secretary Treasurer, Jean-Guy Paquette, ing. c.a., c.a.c.

ASSOCIATION DES PROPRIETAIRES DE CINEMA DU QUEBEC INC.
(Association of Cinema Owners of Quebec Inc.)
3720 Van Horne, Suite 4-5, Montreal, P.Q. H3S 1R8
(514) 738-2715
Executive Secretary, T. Cleary, Dollard Des Ormeaux

ASSOCIATION FOR THE PROTECTION OF FUR-BEARING ANIMALS
1316 E. 12th Ave., Vancouver, B.C. V5N 1Z9
Secretary, Mrs. Elsie Kozak (604/874-5816, 874-3717)

ASSOCIATION OF QUEBEC INDUSTRIAL COMMISSIONERS
800 Place Victoria, pièce 4130, C.P. 617, Montreal, P.Q. H4Z 1J8
(514) 878-9025
Président, Jean Lafrenière

ASSOCIATION OF QUEBEC MUNICIPAL ENGINEERS
2075, rue University, Ste. 1100, Montreal, P.Q. H3A 1K8
(514) 845-5303

ASSOCIATION QUEBECOISE DU JEUNE THEATRE
952 rue Cherrier, Montréal, P.Q. H2L 1H7
(514) 526-5967
Permanents, Hélène Castonguay, Suzanne Lemire

ASSOCIATION QUEBECOISE DES TECHNIQUES DE L'EAU
(water technicians)
6290 rue Périnault, bur. 2, Montréal, P.Q. H4K 1K5
(514) 337-4446
Directeur général, Raymond Larivée

ASSOCIATION QUEBECOISES DES PARCS ZOOLOGIQUES
1449 rue Leclaire, Montreal, P.Q. H1V 2Z4
Secretary Treasurer, Raymond Roth (res.: 514/259-5544; bus.: 872-5674)

ASSOCIATION DES REALISATEURS DE FILMS DU QUEBEC
(film editors)
-not confirmed for 1982-
C.P. 460, Stn. C, Montreal, P.Q. H2L 4K4
(514) 526-0473
Président, Michel Bouchard

THE ASSOCIATION OF REGISTERED PROFESSIONAL FORESTERS OF NEW BRUNSWICK
500 Beaverbrook Ct., Fredericton, N.B. E3B 5X4
(506) 454-8435
Executive Director, E.L. Hughes

ASSOCIATION FOR SOCIAL PSYCHOLOGY
Box 152, Stn. O, Toronto, Ont. M4A 2N3

A non-profit educational foundation for study and support of research in psychology, philosophy, parapsychology, and the social and natural sciences.
Secretary, Ann Skirko

ASSOCIATION FOR SYSTEMS MANAGEMENT
Ste. 600, 55 University Ave., Toronto, Ont. M5J 2H7
(416) 364-4018
President, R. Jackson
Senior Vice President, R. Meredith

ASSOCIATION OF TRANSLATORS & INTERPRETERS OF ONTARIO
#1406, One Nicholas St., Ottawa, Ont. K1N 7B7
(613) 233-6395

ASSOCIATION OF UNITED UKRAINIAN CANADIANS
42 Roncesvalles Ave., Toronto, Ont. M6R 2K3
(416) 535-1063
National Executive Committee, Secretary, W. Harasym

Provincial Secretaries
Man.: M. Mokry, 595 Pritchard Ave., Winnipeg, Man. R2W 2K4 (204/582-9269)
Sask.: Mrs. Anne Lapchuk, 1809 Toronto St., Regina, Sask. S4P 1M7
Alta.: G. Solomon, 10553 A 97 St., Edmonton, Alta. T5H 2L4 (403/424-2553)
B.C.: 805 E. Pender St., Vancouver, B.C. V6A 1V9

ASSOCIATION OF WOMEN ELECTORS OF METRO TORONTO
#601, 100 Adelaide St. W., Toronto, Ont. M5H 1S3
(416) 366-0195

THE ASSOCIATION OF WORKERS' COMPENSATION BOARDS OF CANADA
16 Limcombe Dr., Thornhill, Ont. L3T 2V5
Executive Director, K.B. Harding

ATHLETIC ORGANIZATIONS

Alberta Games Council
#302, 1520 4 St. S.W., Calgary, Alta. T2R 1H5
(403) 261-6700
Managing Director, Max Gibb

Alberta Snowmobile Association
-not confirmed for 1982-
Box 4647, South Stn., Edmonton, Alta. T6E 55

Alpine Club of Canada
Box 1026, Banff, Alta. TOL OCO
(403) 762-4481
Manager, Ron Matthews

American League of Professional Baseball Clubs
280 Park Ave., New York, N.Y. 10017
(212) 682-7000

TORONTO BLUE JAYS BASEBALL CLUB
Box 7777, Adelaide St. PO, Toronto, Ont. M5C 2K7
(416) 595-0077

Aquatic Federation of Canada
President, E.C. Godfrey, C.A., 2 Varbow Place, Calgary, Alta. T3A 0B6

Arctic Winter Games Corporation
President, Ted Richard, Box 939, Yellowknife, N.W.T.
(403) 873-4456

Association of Canadian Underwater Councils
333 River Rd., Vanier, Ont. K1L 8B9
(613) 746-5797
Executive Director, E. Jane Arkell

Association Québécoise de Canoe-Kayak de Vitesse
1415 rue Jarry est, Montréal, P.Q. H2E 2Z7
(514) 374-4700

Basketball Canada (C.A.B.A.)
333 River Rd., Vanier, Ont. K1L 8B9
(613) 746-5723
Executive Director, G. Gruson

Biathlon Canada
25 cr. Notre-Dame, Duvernay, Laval, P.Q. H7E 3Z7
(514) 737-7860
Secrétaire général, Sandy Kerekes

Bowling Federation of Canada
333 River Rd., Tower A, Vanier, Ont. K1L 8B9
(613) 744-0685
Executive Director, David F. Baird

British Columbia Snow Vehicle Association
-not confirmed for 1982-
3311 30th Ave., Vernon, B.C. V1T 2C9
(604) 542-6124
Secretary Manager, W.C. Shields

Canada Games Council
#502, 169 Pioneer Ave., Winnipeg, Man. R3C OH2
(204) 949-3675

Canadian Academy of Sport Medicine
Attn.: Dr. Peter Fowler, c/o Sport Medicine Council of Canada, 333 River Rd., Vanier, Ont. K1L 8B9

Canadian Amateur Bobsleigh & Luge Association
#2200, 1000 Sherbrooke St. W., Montreal, P.Q. H3A 2P2
Executive Director, J.D. Coulson

Canadian Amateur Boxing Association
-not confirmed for 1982-
Box 1980, Timmins, Ont. P4N 7X2
President, Stuart Charbula (Timmins) 705/235-5613
Vice President, Technical, Fred G. Mitchell, 806 University Dr., Saskatoon, Sask. S7N OJ6 (306/652-5749)
Vice President, Finance, Bill Starr, Box 70, Punnichy, Sask. S0A 3C0 (306/835-2050)

Canadian Amateur Diving Association Inc.
Tower B, 10th floor, 333 River Rd., Vanier, Ont. K1L 8B9
(613) 745-3898
Executive Director, Mark Lowry

Canadian Amateur Federation of Body Building
President, S.L. Pukalo, 713 Munroe Ave., Winnipeg, Man. R2K 1J1 (204/667-2003)
General Secretary, Winston Roberts, 201 Grenier St., St. Rose, Laval, P.Q. H7L 3E4 (514/622-8931)

Canadian Amateur Football Association
333 River Rd., Vanier, Ont. K1L 8B9
(613) 746-5750
Executive Director, Bill Robinson

Canadian Amateur Hockey Association
333 River Rd., Vanier, Ont. K1L 8B9
(613) 746-0238
Executive Director, Hal Lewis

Canadian Amateur Hockey Association Services
129 Yorkville Ave., Ste. 200, Toronto, Ont. M5R 1C4
(416) 923-3700

Canadian Amateur Modern Pentathlon Association
(Associan Canadienne de Pentathlon Moderne)
President, Sandy Kerekes, 25 cr. Notre-Dame, (Duvernay), Laval, P.Q. H7E 3Z7

Canadian Amateur Netball Association
Box 6044, Stn. A, Toronto, Ont. M5W 1P4
President, Mrs. Rachael Flood (519/622-2300)

Canadian Amateur Rowing Association
333 River Rd., Vanier, Ont. K1L 8B9
(613) 746-5758
Executive Director, Rodger Sellars

Canadian Amateur Speed Skating Association
333 River Rd., Vanier, Ont. K1L 8B9
(613) 741-0620
Executive Director, R.H. Belanger

Canadian Amateur Swimming Association
333 River Rd., Vanier, Ont. K1L 8B9
(613) 741-5111
Executive Vice President, Douglas Fraser

Canadian Amateur Synchronized Swimming Association
333 River Rd., Vanier, Ont. K1L 8B9
(613) 745-8923
Executive Director, Rick Johnson

Canadian Amateur Water Polo Association, Inc.
333 River Rd., Vanier, Ont. K1L 8B9
(613) 745-4053

Canadian Amateur Wrestling Association
333 River Rd., Vanier, Ont. K1L 8B9
(613) 746-3894
Executive Director, Cam MacIntyre

Canadian Amputee Sports Association
President, Gerry Sorensen, 28 St. Laurent St., St. John's, Nfld. A1A 2V2
Sports Technical Director, Graham Knox, 730 Upper Wellington St., Hamilton, Ont. L9A 3R3

Canadian Association for Disabled Skiing
Box 2077, Banff, Alta. T0L 0C0
(403) 762-3519
Executive Co-ordinator, Jerry Johnston

Canadian Automobile Sport Clubs
Box 97, Willowdale, Ont. M2N 5S7
(416) 222-5411 or 5458
Executive Director, R.J. Hanna
Regional Offices:
Atlantic: c/o Kenneth Vaughan, 706 Blythwood Ave., Riverview, N.B. E1B 2H6
B.C.: 1200 Hornby St., BC Sport Admin. Bldg., Vancouver, B.C. V6Z 1W2
Ontario: Box 965, Stn. A, Scarborough, Ont. M1K 5E4
Prairie: c/o 760 Cathcart St., Winnipeg, Man. R3R 2T6
Que.: 1415 Jarry St., Montreal, P.Q. H2E 2Z7

Canadian Badminton Association
333 River Rd., Vanier, Ont. K1L 8B9
(613) 746-5831
Executive Director, D.W. Kilfoyle

Canadian Ball Hockey Association
2201 Riverside Dr., Ste. 314, Ottawa, Ont. K1H 8K9
(613) 737-4546
Executive Vice President, Alan Tomalty (819/997-6922)

ONTARIO BALL HOCKEY ASSOCIATION
Box 381, Stn. P, Toronto, Ont. M5S 2S9
President, Ken White (416/463-7024)

NOVA SCOTIA BALL HOCKEY ASSOCIATION
Box 3010 South, Halifax, N.S. B3J 3G6
President, Wayne Doran (902/479-3174)

BRITISH COLUMBIA BALL HOCKEY ASSOCIATION
1200 Hornby St., Vancouver, B.C. V6Z 2E2
Ross Cameron (604/524-8732)

NEWFOUNDLAND BALL HOCKEY ASSOCIATION
17 Field St., St. John's, Nfld. A1C 4J3
Secretary Treasurer, Paul Barron (709/726-4576)

MANITOBA BALL HOCKEY ASSOCIATION
#2, Grassington Bay, Winnipeg, Man. R2N 1E4
President, Bob Sims (204/256-0990)

ALBERTA BALL HOCKEY ASSOCIATION
9935 86th Ave., Edmonton, Alta. T6E 2L8
President, John Geiger (403/433-2744)

NEW BRUNSWICK BALL HOCKEY ASSOCIATION
1146 Rothesay Rd., Saint John, N.B. E2H 2H8
(506) 696-8408

Canadian Billiards & Snooker Referees' Association
Secretary, G. Duncan, 24 Northey Dr., Willowdale, Ont. M2L 2S9 (416/444-4144)

Canadian Blind Sport Association
-not confirmed for 1982-
3701 Danforth Ave., Scarborough, Ont. M1N 2G2
(416) 694-9563
Executive Director, Murry G. Minshall

Canadian Boating Federation
4597 Kingston Rd., #203-5, Scarborough, Ont. M1E 2P3
(416) 281-1534
Executive Director, Victor R. Waring

Canadian Canoe Association
333 River Rd., Vanier, Ont. K1L 8B9
(613) 746-5455
Executive Director, Jean Matheson, A.C.I.S.

Canadian Casting Federation
c/o P. Edwards, Toronto Sportsmen's Association, 61 Edgehill Rd., Islington, Ont. M9A 4N1 (416/233-3297)

Canadian Colleges Athletic Association
President, Al Hoffman, St. Clair College, 2000 Talbot Rd. W., Windsor, Ont. N9A 6S4 (519/966-1656, ext. 220)

Canadian Council of Snowmobile Organizations
-not confirmed for 1982-
3311 30th Ave., Vernon, B.C. V1T 2C9
(604) 542-6124
Secretary, William C. Shields

Canadian Cricket Association
Box 809, Adelaide St. PO, Toronto, Ont. M5C 2K1

Canadian Cycling Association
333 River Rd., Vanier, Ont. K1L 8B9
(613) 746-5753
Executive Director, Roger Ouellette

Canadian Equestrian Federation
333 River Rd., Vanier, Ont. K1L 8B9
(613) 745-0296
Executive Director, Col. W.D. Little

Canadian Federation of Amateur Baseball (Baseball Canada)
333 River Rd., Vanier, Ont. K1L 8B9
(613) 745-9315
Executive Director, Paul E. Lavigne

Canadian Federation of Amateur Rollerskaters
President, M.L. Pope, 4716 Elbow Dr. S.W., Calgary, Alta. T2S 2K8 (403/243-5543)

Canadian Fencing Association
333 River Rd., Vanier, Ont. K1L 8B9
(613) 745-8497
Executive Director, Cheryl Hassen

Canadian Field Hockey Council
333 River Rd., Vanier, Ont. K1L 8B9
(613) 746-7693
Executive Director, A.M. Egan

Canadian Figure Skating Association
333 River Rd., Vanier, Ont. K1L 8B9
(613) 746-5953
Executive Director, Douglas Gunter

Canadian 5 Pin Bowlers' Association
7138 Fisher St. S.E., Calgary, Alta. T2H 0W5
(403) 253-7496
National Program Co-ordinator, A.G. Hong

ALBERTA 5 PIN BOWLERS' ASSOCIATION
c/o Don Sim, President, 831 Maplewood Cres. S.E., Calgary, Alta. T2J 1T3

BOWLERS' ASSOCIATION OF BRITISH COLUMBIA
c/o Bob Grant, President, 1855 Humber Cres., Port Coquitlam, B.C. V3C 2V8

MANITOBA 5 PIN BOWLERS' ASSOCIATION
c/o Gerald Sidkoski, President, 451 Oakview Ave., Winnipeg, Man. R2K 0S6

NEW BRUNSWICK 5 PIN BOWLERS' ASSOCIATION
c/o Roy Goving, President, 500 St. Johns, Chatham, N.B. E1N 2S6

NEWFOUNDLAND 5 PIN BOWLERS' ASSOCIATION
c/o Fred Hawco, President, Flat Rock, Box 2, Site 10, R.R. 1, Torbay, St. John's, Nfld.

NORTHERN ONTARIO 5 PIN BOWLERS' ASSOCIATION
c/o Frank Massaro, President, 96 Burriss St., Thunder Bay, Ont. P7A 3E4

NORTHWEST TERRITORIES 5 PIN BOWLERS' ASSOCIATION
c/o Jim White, President, Box 8888, Yellowknife, N.W.T. X1A 2R3

NOVA SCOTIA 5 PIN BOWLERS' ASSOCIATION
c/o Jim Miles, President, Box 359, Greenwood, N.S. B0P 1N0

ONTARIO 5 PIN BOWLERS' ASSOCIATION
c/o Jack Hales, President, 21 Progress Ct., Unit 14, Scarborough, Ont. M1G 3V4

PRINCE EDWARD ISLAND 5 PIN BOWLERS' ASSOCIATION
c/o Ernest Doucette, President, 385 N. Market St., Summerside, P.E.I. C1N 1L7

QUEBEC 5 PIN BOWLERS' ASSOCIATION
c/o Marc Potvin, President, 602 rue Matte, Buckingham, P.Q. J8L 2Y4

SASKATCHEWAN 5 PIN BOWLERS' ASSOCIATION
c/o John Hoffman, President, 3337 Queen St., Regina, Sask. S4S 2E8

Canadian Football League
Ste. 1800, 11 King St. W., Toronto, Ont. M5H 1A3
(416) 366-8591
Commr., J.G. (Jake) Gaudaur
Secretary Treasurer, G.B. Fulton
Director of Information, Gordon Walker
Director of Officiating, W.H. (Bill) Fry
Montreal Alouettes, Olympic Stadium, Box 100, Stn. M, Montreal, P.Q. H1V 3L6
Ottawa Rough Riders, Lansdowne Park, Ottawa, Ont. K1S 3W7
Toronto Argonauts, Exhibition Stadium, Exhibition Place, Toronto, Ont. M6K 3C3
Hamilton Tiger Cats, 78 Balsam Ave. N. (Box 172, Hamilton, Ont. L8N 3A2)
Winnipeg Blue Bombers, 1465 Maroons Rd., Winnipeg, Man. R3G OL6
Saskatchewan Roughriders, 2940 10th Ave. (Box 1277, Regina, Sask. S4P 3B8)
Calgary Stampeders, McMahon Stadium (1817 Crowchild Trail N.W., Calgary, Alta. T2M 4R6)
Edmonton Eskimos, 9023 111 Ave., Edmonton, Alta. T5B 0X3
B.C. Lions, Empire Stadium (Box 69010, Stn. K, Vancouver, B.C. V5K 4W3)

Canadian Greyhound Racing & Breeders Association
Secretary, Mrs. C. McIlveen, Alexander Blvd., Baldwin, Ont. LOE 1AO (416/722-5394)

ONTARIO GREYHOUND BREEDERS ASSOCIATION INC.
Secretary Treasurer, Clara McIlveen, Alexander Blvd., Baldwin, Ont. LOE 1AO (416/722-5394)

Canadian Gymnastics Federation
333 River Rd., Vanier, Ont. K1L 8B9
(613) 746-3714
Executive Director, Terence Phillips

Canadian Handball Association
President, Les Robinson, 311 Habkirk Dr., Regina, Sask. S4S 6A9 (306/586-9270)

Canadian Highland Games Council
President, Andy McDonald, 63 Brant Ave., Brantford, Ont. N3T 3H2 (519/753-5027)

Canadian Interuniversity Athletic Union
333 River Rd., Vanier, Ont. K1L 8B9
(613) 744-2875
Executive Vice President, Bob Pugh

Canadian Jiu-jitsu Association
President, Ronald Forrester, 1309 Falgarwood Dr., Oakville, Ont. L6H 2L7 (416/844-8750)

Canadian Lacrosse Association
333 River Rd., Vanier, Ont. K1L 8B9
(613) 746-5727
Executive Director, Bob Oliver
Technical Director, John Tobias

Canadian Ladies Curling Association
333 River Rd., Vanier, Ont. K1L 8B9
(613) 741-7126
Technical Director, Garry DeBlonde

Canadian Ladies Lawn Bowling Council
President, Miss Marilyn Sutherland, 30 Lincolnwood Dr., Sherwood, P.E.I. C1A 6H5
First Vice President, Mrs. M. MacLellan, 2691 Oxford St., Halifax, N.S. B3L 2T9

Canadian Lawn Bowling Council
Secretary Treasurer, J.A. (Ab) McBride, 5926 Larch St., Vancouver, B.C. V6M 4E4

Canadian Maccabiah Games Association Inc.
1225 Hodge St., Montreal, P.Q. H4N 2B5
(514) 748-7711
National Secretary, Nicki H. Lang

Canadian Men's Field Hockey Assocation
333 River Rd., Vanier, Ont. K1L 8B9
(613) 746-0060; Telex: 053 3660

Canadian Olympic Association
Head Office & Secretariat, Olympic House, Cité du Havre, Montreal, P.Q. H3C 3R4
(514) 861-3371
Secretary, Maurice Allan, 160 Ave. Claude, Dorval, P.Q.

Canadian Orienteering Association
333 River Rd., Vanier, Ont. K1L 8B9
(613) 741-9427
Executive Director, Colin Kirk

Canadian Platform Tennis Association
47 Whitehall Rd., Toronto, Ont. M4W 2C5
(416) 964-7370

Canadian Professional Boxing Federation
President, Murray Sleep, 6053 Pepperell St., Halifax, N.S. B3H 2N8(902/423-1709)
Secretary Treasurer, Ken Weston, 26 Gourok Ave., Dartmouth, N.S. B2X 2B3 (902/435-1938)

Member Commissions

MONTREAL ATHLETIC COMMISSION
275 est, rue Notre Dame, Montreal, P.Q. H2Y 1B6
(514) 282-7363
Secretary, Jean-Guy Prescott

NOVA SCOTIA BOXING AUTHORITY
Box 2175, Dartmouth East PO, Dartmouth, N.S. B2W 3Y2
(902) 435-1938

MANITOBA BOXING & WRESTLING COMMISSION
Chairman, Jim Trifunov, #912, 200 Ronald St., Winnipeg, Man. R3J 3J3 (204/944-3535)

QUEBEC ATHLETIC COMMISSION
President, Rosaire Clermont, 1160 Salaberry Ave., Quebec, P.Q. G1R 2V9 (418/523-8818)

CALGARY BOXING & WRESTLING COMMISSION
Vice Chairman, Glen Dempsey, 910A 14 Ave. S.W., Calgary, Alta. (403/245-3288)

VANCOUVER ATHLETIC COMMISSION
Chairman, Dave Brown, 4280 Venables St., Burnaby, B.C. V5C 2Z9 (604/298-2230)

EDMONTON BOXING & WRESTLING COMMISSION
Secretary Treasurer, Ron Hayter, 2nd floor, City Hall, Edmonton, Alta. T5J 2R7 (403/428-5457)

MONCTON BOXING & WRESTLING COMMISSION
Chairman, Richard Murphy, 28 Lorentz Dr., Moncton, N.B. E1E 2TA

HALIFAX ATHLETIC COMMISSION
Chairman, David Johnson, 2508 Poplar St., Halifax, N.S. B3L 2Y8 (902/425-5862)

ONTARIO ATHLETIC COMMISSION
Jim Vipond, Athletic Commissioner, 555 Yonge St., 3rd floor, Toronto, Ont. (416/963-0844)

NANAIMO BOXING & WRESTLING COMMISSION
Chairman, J.B. Martin, Martin-McAfee & Co., Box 248, Nanaimo, B.C. V9R 5K9

Canadian Professional Golfers Association
See Golf Associations

Canadian Professional Rodeo Association
#223, 2116 27 Ave. N.E., Calgary, Alta. T2E 7A6
(403) 230-3407
General Manager, Keith Hyland

Canadian Racing Drivers Association
Ste. 404, 11 Yorkville Ave. (Box 5310, Stn. A, Toronto, Ont. M5W 1N6)
(416) 924-0533

Canadian Racquetball Association
333 River Rd., Vanier, Ont. K1L 8B9
(613) 745-1247
Executive Director, John Hamilton

Canadian Recreational Canoeing Association
Box 54, Hyde Park, Ont. NOM 1ZO
(519) 473-2109
Executive Director, Mrs. June Mahood

THE NEWFOUNDLAND CANOEING ASSOCIATION
Box 4351, St. John's, Nfld. A1C 5Z7

P.E.I. RECREATIONAL CANOEING ASSOCIATION
4 Vista St., Charlottetown, P.E.I. C1A 3S9

CANOE NOVA SCOTIA
Box 3010, South, (5516 Spring Garden Rd.), Halifax, N.S. B3S 3S6

CANOE NEW BRUNSWICK
R.R. 1, Hopewell Cape, Albert Co., N.B. E0A 1Y0

FEDERATION QUEBECOISE DU CANOT-CAMPING INC.
1415 est rue Jarry, Montreal, P.Q. H2E 2Z7

ONTARIO RECREATIONAL CANOEING AFFILIATION
c/o Canoe Ontario, 160 Vanderhoof Ave., Toronto, Ont. M4G 4B8

MANITOBA RECREATIONAL CANOEING ASSOCIATION
c/o T. Easton, 133 Woodhaven Blvd., Winnipeg, Man. R3J 3K2

SASKATCHEWAN CANOE ASSOCIATION
Box 6064, Saskatoon, Sask. S7K 4E5

ALBERTA RECREATIONAL CANOEING ASSOCIATION
11241 34A Ave., Edmonton, Alta. T6J 3M4

RECREATIONAL CANOEING ASSOCIATION OF BRITISH COLUMBIA
c/o K. Spain, Box 1160, Stn. A, Surrey, B.C. V3S 4P6

THE YUKON VOYAGEURS CANOE AND KAYAK CLUB
c/o K. Sylvestre, 12 Tagish Rd., Whitehorse, Yukon

NORTHWEST TERRITORIES
c/o C. Grant, Box 1382, Yellowknife, N.W.T. X1A 2P1

Canadian Rugby Union
333 River Rd., Vanier, Ont. K1L 8B9
(613) 745-0434
Executive Director, Stephen Baines

Canadian School Sports Federation
333 River Rd., Vanier, Ont. K1L 8B9
(613) 746-3258
A/Executive Director, Gail Gibson

Canadian Ski Association
333 River Rd., Vanier, Ont. K1L 8B9
(613) 746-3324
Executive Director, John Newton

Canadian Snowshoers Union
44 Toulon, Touraine, P.Q. J8T 4V6
1st Vice President, Ronald Goudie

Canadian Soccer Association
333 River Rd., Vanier, Ont. K1L 8B9
(613) 746-5847
Executive Director, Eric King

ALBERTA SOCCER ASSOCIATION
Executive Director, Kevan Pipe, 13 Mission Ave., St. Albert, Alta. T8N 1H6 (403/458-7111)

BRITISH COLUMBIA SOCCER ASSOCIATION
c/o Keith Liddiard, 1200 Hornby St., Vancouver, B.C. V6C 1W2

CANADIAN YOUTH SOCCER ASSOCIATION
c/o Chris Bellamy, Youth Development Co-ordinator, Canadian Soccer Association, 333 River Rd., Vanier, Ont. K1L 8B9 (613/746-0060)

MANITOBA SOCCER ASSOCIATION
Executive Director, David Kerr, 1700 Ellice Ave., Winnipeg, Man. R3H 0B1 (204/786-5641)

SOCCER NEW BRUNSWICK
c/o Mrs. Doreen Thompson, President, 106 Westview St., Fredericton, N.B. E3A 1W9

NEWFOUNDLAND SOCCER ASSOCIATION
c/o Mrs. Angela King, Executive Director, Box 9064, St. John's, Nfld. A1A 2X3

SOCCER NOVA SCOTIA
c/o Bruce Henderson, 5516 Spring Garden Rd., Ste. 401, (Box 3010 South, Halifax, N.S. B3J 3G6)

THE ONTARIO SOCCER ASSOCIATION
c/o Brian Avey, Executive Director, 160 Vanderhoof Ave., Toronto, Ont. M4G 4B8

PRINCE EDWARD ISLAND SOCCER ASSOCIATION
c/o Tom Wallis, President, 69 Trafalgar St., Charlottetown, P.E.I. C1A 3Z4

QUEBEC SOCCER FOOTBALL FEDERATION
c/o Michel Cardinal, Executive Administrator, 1415 Jarry St. E., Montreal, P.Q. H2E 2Z7

SASKATCHEWAN SOCCER ASSOCIATION
c/o Peter Senko, Executive Director, 2205 Victoria Ave., Regina, Sask. S4S 0S4

Canadian Sport Parachuting Association
333 River Rd., Ottawa, Ont. K1L 8B9
(613) 749-0152
Executive Director, D.E. Holmes

Canadian Squash Racquets Association
333 River Rd., Vanier, Ont. K1L 8B9
(613) 741-6786
Executive Director, James R. Ball
Program Co-ordinator, Alan Baird

Canadian Table Tennis Association
333 River Rd., Vanier, Ont. K1L 8B9
(613) 746-7645
Executive Director, Maurice Hayes

Canadian Team Handball Federation
333 River Rd., Vanier, Ont. K1L 8B9
(613) 745-4607
Executive Director, Bob Gadoua

Canadian Tenpin Federation
President, Mrs. Joan W. Esary, 2687 Hoskins Rd., North Vancouver, B.C. V7J 3A6 (604/985-9625)

Canadian Track & Field Association
355 River Rd., Vanier, Ont. K1L 8C1
(613) 744-1160
Director General, Geoff Elliott

Canadian Trotting Association
233 Evans Ave., Toronto, Ont. M8Z 1J6
(416) 252-3565
Executive Vice President & General Manager, W.G. Bryant
Director of Publicity & Public Relations, Michel Corbeil

Canadian Volleyball Association
333 River Rd., Vanier, Ont. K1L 8B9
(613) 746-5811
Executive Director, Ian Stoddart

Canadian Water Ski Association
333 River Rd., Vanier, Ont. K1L 8B9
(613) 746-5446
Executive Director, Mrs. Elaine Barnes

Canadian Weightlifting Federation
(Halterophile Canadienne)
333 River Rd., Vanier, Ont. K1L 8B9
(613) 749-7237
Executive Director, K. Nesbitt

Canadian Wheelchair Sports Association
333 River Rd., Vanier, Ont. K1L 8B9
(613) 741-2463
Executive Director, John R. Smyth

Canadian White Water Affiliation
c/o Roger Parsons, 15 Langside Ave., Weston, Ont. M9N 3E2 (416/244-1022)

Provincial Affiliates

CANOE NOVA SCOTIA
Box 3010 South, Halifax, N.S.

ONTARIO WILD WATER AFFILIATION
1579 Applewood Rd., Mississauga, Ont. L5E 2M2 (416/274-4630)

MANITOBA KAYAK ASSOCIATION
c/o Wray Pearce, President, 710 Rosedale Ave., Winnipeg, Man. R3L 1M8 (204/452-7689)

ALBERTA WHITE WATER ASSOCIATION
c/o Dale O'Brien, President, 11215 53 Ave., Edmonton, Alta. T6H OS6

WHITE WATER CANOEING ASSOCIATION OF BRITISH COLUMBIA
c/o Sport B.C., 1200 Hornby St., Vancouver, B.C. V6Z 1W2

Canadian Women's Field Hockey Association
c/o 333 River Rd., Vanier, Ont. K1L 8B9

Canadian Yachting Association
333 River Rd., Vanier, Ont. K1L 8B9
(613) 746-5861
Executive Director, Geoff Wheatly

Coaching Association of Canada
333 River Rd., Vanier, Ont. K1L 8B9
(613) 746-5693
President, Dr. Geoff R. Gowan
Vice President, Administration, Gerry McCready

Commonwealth Games Association of Canada
President, Kenneth P. Farmer, 90 Easton Ave., Montreal West, P.Q. H4X 1L2 (514/488-4983)
Hon. Secretary, Neil J. Farrell, Box 3763, Stn. C, Hamilton, Ont. L8H 7N1 (416/560-2408)

Curl Canada
333 River Rd., Vanier, Ont. K1L 8B9
(613) 741-7126
Executive Director, J.W. McLeod

Federation of Canadian Archers
333 River Rd., Vanier, Ont. K1L 8B9
(613) 741-3610
Executive Director, Nick Timtsenko
Technical Director, Ms. Kathy Millar

Federation Canadienne de Pentanque Inc.
1415 rue Jarry est, Montreal, P.Q. H2E 2Z7
(514) 374-4700, loc. 291
Executive Director, Gerard Galliano

Federation of Silent Sports of Canada
2125 W. 7th Ave., Vancouver, B.C. V6K 1X9
(604) 736-7391 (voice & TTY)

Golf Associations

ALBERTA GOLF ASSOCIATION
Secretary, G.R. Beavers, 200H Haddon Rd. S.W., Calgary, Alta. T2P 2Y6 (403/259-6261)

BRITISH COLUMBIA GOLF ASSOCIATION
Secretary, Robert E. Maze, #322, 1675 W. 8th Ave., Vancouver, B.C. V6J 1V2

CANADIAN PROFESSIONAL GOLFERS ASSOCIATION
General Manager, Robert H. Hoble, 59 Berkeley St., Toronto, Ont. M5A 2W5 (416/368-6104)

CANADIAN LADIES GOLF ASSOCIATION
Executive Director, L. John Whamond, 333 River Rd., Ottawa, Ont. K1L 8B9 (613/746-5564)

CANADIAN WOMEN'S SENIOR GOLF ASSOCIATION
-not confirmed for 1982-
National Secretary, Mrs. C.W. Bourke, 7811 Yonge St., Apt. 811, Thornhill, Ont. L3T 4S3

MANITOBA GOLF ASSOCIATION
Administrative Centre for Recreation & Sport, 1700 Ellice Ave., Winnipeg, Man. R3H 0B1
(204) 786-5641
Executive Director, D.I. MacDonald
Tournament Secretary, R.V. Brown

ONTARIO GOLF ASSOCIATION
Executive Director, W.J. Williams, 400 Esna Park Dr., Unit 11, Markham, Ont. L3R 1H5 (416/495-5238)

QUEBEC GOLF ASSOCIATION
Executive Director, C.H. Gribbin, 3300 Cavendish Blvd., Room 250, Montreal, P.Q. H4B 2M8 (514/481-0471)

ROYAL CANADIAN GOLF ASSOCIATION
Golf House, R.R. 2, Oakville, Ont. L6J 4Z3 (416/844-0516)

SASKATCHEWAN GOLF ASSOCIATION
Secretary Treasurer, Harold W. Dunlop, 30 Deborah Cres., Saskatoon, Sask. S7J 2W8

NON-SMOKERS' JUNIOR GOLF ASSOCIATION
28 Tuna Ct., Don Mills, Ont. M3A 3L1
(416) 444-9501
Executive Director, Dr. A.J. Longo

Hockey Canada
333 River Rd., Vanier, Ont. K1L 8B9
(613) 746-3153

Horseshoe Canada Association
35 O'Neil Cres., Saskatoon, Sask. S7N 1W7
(306) 373-5184
President, Jack Adams

HORSESHOES BRITISH COLUMBIA
Executive Member, Bernie Lepper, 34 N. Howard Ave., Burnaby, B.C. V5B 1J5
(604) 298-0638

ALBERTA HORSESHOE PITCHERS ASSOCIATION
Executive Member, Bob Moodie, 1314 3rd Ave. N., Lethbridge, Alta. T1H 0J3
President, Laurence Johns, 9828 91 Ave., Grande Prairie, Alta. T8V 0G2 (403/532-3921)

SASKATCHEWAN HORSESHOE PLAYERS ASSOCIATION
Executive Member, Sharon Ellison, Box 441, Raymore, Sask. S0A 3J0

MANITOBA HORSESHOE PITCHERS ASSOCIATION
Executive Member, Ivens Reddon, Box 235, Carberry, Man. R0K 0H0

ONTARIO HORSESHOE PITCHERS ASSOCIATION
Executive Member, Merv Lichty, Box 73, R.R. 1, Waterloo, Ont. N2J 4G8
(519) 884-0697

LA FEDERATION DES CLUBS DE FERS DU QUEBEC
Executive Member, Fernand Dutremble, 290 Boul. Fiset, Sorel, P.Q. J3P 3R1

MARITIME PROVINCES HORSESHOE PLAYERS ASSOCIATION
Public Relations, Clark Brown, 6 Honeydale Cres., Spryfield, Halifax, N.S. B3R 2G9

NOVA SCOTIA HORSESHOE PITCHERS ASSOCIATION
Executive Director, W.E. Dean, Sr., Box 748, 152 N. Foord St., Stellarton, N.S. B0K 1S0 (902/752-2580)

NEW BRUNSWICK HORSESHOE PITCHERS ASSOCIATION
Executive Director, Raymond Hebert, 205 Highland View, Lewisville, N.B. (506/854-0770)

PRINCE EDWARD ISLAND HORSESHOE PITCHERS ASSOCIATION
Executive Director, Clinton Glydon, 105 Fitzroy St., Charlottetown, P.E.I. (902/892-6987)

International Pentadic Committee
3549 St. Clair Ave. E., Scarborough, Ont. M1K 1L6
(416) 264-2834

Inuit-Dene Games
-not confirmed for 1982-
Box 2656, Inuvik, N.W.T. X0E 0T0
(403) 979-3220
Co-ordinator, Ernie Bernhardt

Judo Canada
333 River Rd., Vanier, Ont. K1L 8B9
(613) 749-2127
Executive Director, Miss C. Potvin

National Hockey League
960 Sun Life Bldg., Montreal, P.Q. H3B 2W2
(514) 871-9220
Director of Information, Ron Andrews

CANADIAN TEAMS
Calgary Flames, Box 1540, Stn. M, Calgary, Alta. T2P 3B9
Edmonton Oilers, Edmonton Coliseum, Edmonton, Alta. T5B 4M9 (403/474-8561)
Montreal Canadiens, 2313 St. Catherine St. W., Montreal, P.Q. H3H 1N2 (514/932-6131), Publicity & Information Director, Claude Mouton
Quebec Nordiques, Colisée de Quebec, Quebec, P.Q. G1L 4W7 (418/529-4161)
Toronto Maple Leafs, Maple Leaf Gardens, 60 Carlton St., Toronto, Ont. M5B 1L1, Director of Public Relations, Stan Obodiac
Vancouver Canucks, Pacific Coliseum, 100 N. Renfrew St., Vancouver, B.C. V5K 3N7, Public Relations Director, Norm Jewison
Winnipeg Jets, #15, 1430 Maroons Rd., Winnipeg, Man. R3G 0L5 (204/772-9491)

AMERICAN TEAMS
Boston Bruins, 150 Causeway St., Boston, Mass. 02114
Buffalo Sabres, 140 Main St., Buffalo, N.Y. 14202
Chicago Black Hawks, 1800 W. Madison St., Chicago, Ill. 60612
Colorado Rockies, One McNichols Plaza, Denver, Col. 80204
Detroit Red Wings, 600 Civic Center Dr., Detroit, Mich. 48226
Hartford Whalers, One Civic Center Plaza, Hartford, Conn. 06103
Los Angeles Kings, Box 10, Inglewood, Calif. 90306
Minnesota North Stars, 7901 Cedar Ave. S., Bloomington, Minn. 55420
New York Islanders, Nassau Veterans Memorial Coliseum, Hempstead Turnpike, Uniondale, N.Y. 11553
New York Rangers, 4 Pennsylvania Plaza, New York, N.Y. 10001
Philadelphia Flyers, The Spectrum, Pattison Place, Philadelphia, Pa. 19148
Pittsburgh Penguins, Gate #7, Civic Arena, Pittsburgh, Pa. 15219
St. Louis Blues, 5700 Oakland Ave., St. Louis, Mo. 63110
Washington Capitals, Capital Centre, One Harry S. Truman Dr., Landover, Maryland 20786

National Karate Association
-not confirmed for 1982-
President, M. Tsurouka, 605 Indian Rd., Toronto, Ont. M6P 2C4 (416/532-8221)

National League Baseball
One Rockefeller Plaza, Ste. 1602, New York, N.Y. 10020
(212) 582-4213
President, Charles S. Feeney
Secretary, Phyllis Collins
Administrator/Director of Public Relations, Blake Cullen

MONTREAL BASEBALL CLUB LTD.
Box 500, Stn. M, Montreal, P.Q. H1V 3P2
(514) 253-3434
President & General Manager, John J. McHale

National Retriever Club of Canada
Secretary Treasurer, Judge G.H. McConnell, 232 Pandora Cres., Kitchener, Ont. N2H 3E6

National Sport & Recreation Centre
333 River Rd., Vanier, Ont. K1L 8B9
(613) 746-0060

The Centre offers administrative, consultative and referral services to national sport and recreation organizations in Canada.
President, Hugh Glynn

National Youth Bowling Council
335 Nugget Ave., Unit 11, Scarborough, Ont. M1S 4J3
(416) 292-3433
National Administrator, Carl Malcolmson

New Brunswick Federation of Snowmobile Clubs
President, John LaBonville, Box 810, R.R. 3, Bathurst, N.B. E2A 4G8
Secretary, Mrs. Gregory Green, R.R. 5, Grand Falls, N.B. E0J 1M0

North American Soccer League
Ste. 3500, 1133 Ave. of the Americas, New York, N.Y. 10036
(212) 575-0066

TORONTO BLIZZARD
Exhibition Stadium, Exhibition Place, Toronto, Ont. M6K 3C3
(416) 977-4625

VANCOUVER WHITECAPS SOCCER CLUB
3683 E. Hastings St., Vancouver, B.C. V5K 2B1

(604) 291-8811
General Manager, Tony Waiters

Ontario Federation of Snowmobile Clubs
Box 318, Port Sydney, Ont. P0B 1L0
(705) 385-2773
Executive Secretary, Mrs. Vera Van Alstine

The Ontario Jockey Club
Box 156, Rexdale, Ont. M9W 5L2
(416) 675-6110

Ontario Minor Hockey Association
56 Applefield Dr., Scarboro, Ont. M1P 3X9
(416) 757-9538

Ringette Canada
President, B.F. Mattern, 66 Madera Cr., Winnipeg, Man. R2P 0C5 (204/633-1372)

Royal Canadian Golf Association
See Golf Associations

Saskatchewan Snowmobile Association
Box 1881, Moose Jaw, Sask. S6H 7N6
(306) 692-5947

Shooting Federation of Canada
333 River Rd., Vanier, Ont. K1L 8B9
(613) 746-1588

Snoman Inc.
(Snowmobilers of Manitoba)
Box 1577, Winnipeg, Man. R3C 2Z4
President, Harry Knysh, 1245 College Ave., Winnipeg, Man. R2X 1B8 (204/582-2507, res.; 946-0471, bus.)

Snowmobile Association of Nova Scotia
Box 1377, North Stn., Halifax, N.S. B3K 5H7
Secretary, Alma Russell, 10 Little Fox Lane, Halifax, N.S. B3M 3J1 (902/443-0409)

Soaring Association of Canada
Box 1173, Stn. B, Ottawa, Ont. K1P 5A0
(613) 489-2038, 822-1797
Executive Director, J.W. Leach

Softball Canada (CASA)
355 River Rd., 12th Floor, Vanier, Ont. K1L 8C1
(613) 746-5735
Executive Director, Claude Deschamps
Technical Director, John Stevens

Sports Federation of Canada
The Sports Federation's membership includes the majority of sport and recreation governing bodies in Canada.
Address: 333 River Rd., Tower A, Vanier, Ont. K1L 8B9
(613) 741-2374
Executive Director, Jo-Ann Sincennes

Provincial Sports Federations

SPORT ALBERTA
Percy Page Recreation Centre, 13 Mission Ave., St. Albert, Alta. T8N 1H6
(403) 458-0440
Office Manager, Lea Samuel
Calgary Office: 7138 Fisher St. S.E., Calgary, Alta. T2H 0W5, General Manager, Lyle Leslie

SPORT B.C.
1200 Hornby St., Vancouver, B.C. V6Z 2E2
(604) 687-3333
Executive Director, Tom Walker

MANITOBA SPORTS FEDERATION
1700 Ellice Ave., Winnipeg, Man. R3H 0B1
(204) 786-5641
Executive Director, George Fraser

SPORT NEW BRUNSWICK
43 Brunswick St., Fredericton, N.B. E3B 1G5
(506) 455-3685

NEWFOUNDLAND & LABRADOR SPORTS FEDERATION
Box 1597, St. John's, Nfld. A1C 5P3
(709) 753-7039
Executive Director, Denis Murphy

SPORT NOVA SCOTIA
5516 Spring Garden Rd. (Box 3010, South, Halifax, N.S. B3J 3G6)
(902) 425-5450
Executive Director, Al Smith

SPORT ONTARIO
Secretary, Wm. Hoyle, 6 Bridgetown Dr., Etobicoke, Ont. M9C 2P4 (416/964-8745)

SPORT PRINCE EDWARD ISLAND
Box 302, Charlottetown, P.E.I. C1A 7K7
(902) 894-8879
Executive Director, Don LeClair

SOCIETE DES SPORTS DU QUEBEC
1415 Jarry St. E., Montreal, P.Q. H2E 2Z7
(514) 374-4700, ext. 337, 339
Coordonnateur de l'information, Claude Dufour

SASK SPORT
2205 Victoria Ave., Regina, Sask. S4P OS4
(306) 522-3651
General Manager, C.E. Springstein

YUKON SPORTS FEDERATION
302 Steele St., Whitehorse, Yukon
President, Judy Saunders

SPORT NORTH FEDERATION
Box 336, Yellowknife, N.W.T. X0E 1H0
(403) 873-7770
Executive Director, Dave Hurley

Tennis Canada
Tower B, 10th Floor, 355 River Rd., Vanier, Ont. K1L 8B9
(613) 746-5593
Executive Director, D.H. Steele

ATLANTIC ASSOCIATION OF BROADCASTERS
Box 930, Saint John, N.B. E2L 4E2
(506) 652-1680

ATLANTIC CANADA INSTITUTE
Tucker Park, Saint John, N.B. E2L 4L5
(506) 657-7310
Chairman, Board of Directors, William Prouty
President, Laurent Lavoie

A non-profit organization in the field of alternate education whose emphasis is on Atlantic studies in art, history, literature, economics, and ethnic culture.

ATLANTIC COUNCIL OF CANADA
15 King's College Circle, Toronto, Ont. M5S 2V9
(416) 979-1875
Chairman, Marvin Gelber
President, Gerald Wright

ATLANTIC PETROLEUM ASSOCIATION
-not confirmed for 1982-
Box 1145, Halifax, N.S. B3J 2X1
(902) 429-2980

ATLANTIC PROVINCES ART GALLERY ASSOCIATION
President, Mrs. Patricia Grattan, Curator, Memorial University Art Gallery, Arts & Culture Centre, St. John's, Nfld. A1C 5S7 (709/753-1200)

ATLANTIC PUBLISHERS ASSOCIATION
Killam Library, Dalhousie University, Halifax, N.S. B3H 4H8
(902) 424-3525
Executive Director, Angela Rebeiro

ATLANTIC QUEEN CRAB ASSOCIATION
R.C. Stirling, Box 991, Dartmouth, N.S. B2Y 3Z6 (902/463-7790)

ATLANTIC SALMON ASSOCIATION
1434 St. Catherine St. W., Ste. 109, Montreal, P.Q. H3G 1A4
(514) 866-6668
Executive Director, Michael Price
Editor, "The Atlantic Salmon Journal", B.J. McGuire
Admin. Asst., Patricia Villeneuve

AUDIT BUREAU OF CIRCULATIONS
Canadian Member Service Office, Ste. 503, 335 Bay St., Toronto, Ont. M5H 2R3 (416/366-8949)
Manager, Mrs. Lorraine King
Canadian Directors, Robert J. Galloway, Campbell Soup Co. Ltd., Toronto; L. M. Hodgkinson, Maclean-Hunter Ltd., Toronto; Peter W. Hunter, McConnell Advertising Co. Ltd., Toronto; E.H. Wheatley, Pacific Press, Vancouver

AUTOMOBILE ASSOCIATIONS
See also Safety Leagues

Antique & Classic Car Club of Canada
-not confirmed for 1982-
Box 1304, Stn. A, Toronto, Ont. M5W 1G7
Secretary, Peter Weatherhead

L'Association des Proprietaires d'Autobus du Quebec
225 est, boul. Charest, Ste. 107, Quebec, P.Q. G1K 3G9
(418) 522-7131
Secretary, Paul Noreau

Automobile Protection Association
Montreal: 292 St. Joseph Blvd. W., Montreal, P.Q. H2V 2N7 (514/273-1733)
Ottawa: 255 Argyle Ave., Ottawa, Ont. K2P 1B8 (613/235-9941)

Automotive Industries Association of Canada
1306 Wellington St., Room 305, Ottawa, Ont. K1Y 3B2
(613) 728-5821
President, T.H. Whellams
Official Publication, "The Aftermarket"

Automotive Parts Manufacturers' Association of Canada
55 York St., Toronto, Ont. M5J 1R7
(416) 366-9673
President, P.J. Lavelle

Automotive Retailers' Association (Alberta)
10171 107 St., Edmonton, Alta. T5J 1J5
(403) 423-5010
Executive Director, D.A. Achilles

Automotive Trades Association (Manitoba) Inc.
#202, 419 Graham Ave., Winnipeg, Man. R3C 0M3
(204) 943-8501, 943-8502
Manager, Marc Boisselle

Automotive Trades Association of Ontario
Unit 17, 705 Progress Ave., Scarborough, Ont. M1H 2X1
(416) 438-6855
Executive Director, D.S. Prowse

Canadian Automobile Association
1775 Courtwood Cres., Ottawa, Ont. K2C 3J2
(613) 237-2105
Executive Vice President, R. B. Erb

Affiliated with the Canadian Automobile Association are the following provincial associations.

ALBERTA MOTOR ASSOCIATION
Provincial Headquarters, 11230 110th St., Edmonton, Alta. (403/474-0461)
Banff: AMA Branch, Box 343, T0L 0C0 (403/762-2266)
Calgary: AMA, 905-11th Ave. S.W., T2R 0E9 (403/244-9731)
Camrose: AMA Branch, 4807 Fiftieth St., T4V 1P4 (403/672-3391)
Edmonton: AMA, 109 St. & Kingsway Ave. (403/474-8601)
Fort McMurray: AMA Branch, #105, 9911 MacDonald Ave., T9H 1S7 (403/743-2433)
Grande Prairie: AMA Branch, 10828-100th St., T8V 2M8 (403/532-4421)
Lethbridge: AMA, 608-5th Ave. S., T1J 4B9 (403/328-1181)
Medicine Hat: AMA, 2710 13th Ave. S.E., T1A 7G5 (403/527-1166)
Peace River: AMA Branch, 9611 100 St., T0H 2X0
Red Deer: AMA Branch, 5913 Gaetz Ave., T4N 4C4 (403/346-3306)
Stettler: AMA Branch, 5003-51st Ave., T0C 2L0 (403/742-2871)

BRITISH COLUMBIA AUTOMOBILE ASSOCIATION
Provincial Headquarters, 999 W. Broadway, Vancouver, B.C. V5Z 1K5 (604/732-3911)
Chilliwack: BCAA Branch, Southgate Shopping Centre, 419 Yale Rd. W., V2P 2M6 (604/792-4664)
Kamloops: BCAA Branch, 243 Seymour St., V2C 2E7 (604/372-9577)
Nanaimo: BCAA Branch, Northbrook Shopping Mall, 2115 Departure Bay Rd., V9S 3V5 (604/758-7377)
Nelson: BCAA Branch, 556 Baker St., V1L 4H9 (604/352-3535)
New Westminster: BCAA Branch, 755-6th St., V3L 3C6 (604/521-3791)
Penticton: BCAA Branch, 339 Martin St., V2A 5K9 (604/492-7016)
Prince George: BCAA Branch, 690 Victoria St., V2L 2K4 (604/563-0417)
Richmond: BCAA Branch, #115 Lansdowne Plaza, 4940 No. 3 Rd., V6X 3A5 (604/278-4646)
Vancouver: BCAA Branch, 999 W. Broadway, V5Z 1K5 (604/732-3911)
Vancouver: BCAA Branch, 740 Marine Dr., North Vancouver, B.C. V7M 1H4
Victoria: BCAA Branch, 1075 Pandora Ave., V8V 3P7 (604/382-8171)

MANITOBA MOTOR LEAGUE
Winnipeg: 870 Empress St., Winnipeg, Man. R3G 3H3 (204/786-5411)
Brandon: MML Branch, 940 Princess St., R7A OP6 (204/727-1394)
Portage La Prairie: MML Branch, 238 Saskatchewan Ave. E., R1N 0K9

MARITIME AUTOMOBILE ASSOCIATION
Saint John (N.B.): Haymarket Square (Head Office), Saint John, N.B. E2L 3N6 (506/657-3470)
Moncton (N.B.): MAA Branch, 80 Mapleton Rd., E1C 7W8 (506/384-4586)
Halifax (N.S.): MAA Branch, 7169 Chebucto Rd., B3L 1N5 (902/425-5220)

NEWFOUNDLAND & LABRADOR AUTOMOBILE ASSOCIATION
Box 8454, Stn. A, St. John's, Nfld. A1B 3N9

ONTARIO MOTOR LEAGUE

Provincial Headquarters, 2 Carlton St., Ste. 619, Toronto, Ont. M5B 1K4 (416/924-8793)
Barrie: OML TC Branch, 320 Bayfield St., L4M 3C1
Belleville: OML Eastern Ont. Club, 183 Pinnacle St., K8N 3A5 (613/968-4733)
Brampton: OML Brampton, 239 Queen St. E., L6W 2B6
Brantford: HAC Branch, 431 St. Paul Ave., N3R 4N8 (519/756-6321)
Burlington: HAC Branch, 491 Brant St., L7R 2G5
Cambridge: OML-Tri County Branch, 175 Hespeler Rd., N1R 3H6
Chatham: OML Branch, 810 Richmond St., N7M 5K8 (519/351-2222)
Clinton: OML Branch, 7 Rattenbury St. E., N0M 1L0 (519/482-9300)
Cobourg: OML Branch, 31 King St. W., Box 356, K9A 4K8
Guelph: OML Tri County Club, Wellington St. Plaza, 94 Gordon St., N1H 4H6 (519/821-9940)
Hamilton: Hamilton Automobile Club, 393 Main St. E., L8N 1J7 (416/525-1210)
Islington: OML Toronto, 5233 Dundas St. W., M9B 1A6 (416/231-4181)
Kingston: OML Eastern Ont. Club, 2300 Princess St., K7M 3G4 (613/546-2679)
Kitchener: OML Tri-County Club, 836 Courtland Ave. E., N2C 1K3 (519/576-1020)
London: OML London Motor Club, 1069 Wellington Rd. S., N6E 2H6 (519/453-3140)
London: OML Branch, 285 King St., N6B 3M6 (519/679-0740)
Mississauga: OML Toronto Club, Square One, 33 City Centre Dr., L5B 2N5 (416/275-2501)
Niagara Falls: OML Branch, 4444 Drummond Rd., L2E 6C6
North Bay: OML NBC Branch, 190 McIntyre St. W., P3B 1Y6 (705/474-8230)
Oakville: HAC Branch, 125 Navy St., L6J 2Z5 (416/845-9680)
Orangeville: OML Branch, 150 First St., L9W 3T7
Oshawa: OML TC Branch, 340 King St. W., L1J 2J9 (416/723-5203)
Ottawa: OML Ottawa Club, Lincoln Fields Centre, 1354 Richmond Rd., K2B 7Z3 (613/820-1890)
Owen Sound: OML Branch, 187 Tenth St. W., N4K 3R1 (519/376-1940)
Parry Sound: OML Nickel Belt Club, 70 Joseph St., P2A 2G5 (705/746-9000)
Peterborough: OML Peterborough Club, 238 Lansdowne St., Box 1957, K9j 7X7 (705/745-5747)
St. Catharines: OML Niagara Peninsula Club, Box 144, 76 Lake St., L2R 6S3 (416/688-0321)
St. Thomas: OML Elgin Norfolk Club, 1091 Talbot St., N5P 1G4 (519/631-6490)
Sarnia: OML Branch, Box 100, 889 London Rd., N7T 7H8 (519/336-6101)
Sault Ste. Marie: OML TC Branch, 344 Queen St. E., P6A 1Z1 (705/942-4600)
Simcoe: OML ENC, 44 Peel St., N3Y 1S2 (519/426-7230)
Strathroy: OML London Club, 87 Colborne St., N7G 2M1 (519/245-0530)
Sudbury: OML Nickel Belt Club, Regent Place, 1769 Regent St. S., P3E 3Z7 (705/522-0000)
Thunder Bay: OML Northwestern Division, 585 Memorial Ave., P7B 3Z1 (807/345-1261)
Timmins: OML-Nickel Belt Branch, The 101 Mall, 38 Pine St. N., P4N 6K6
Toronto: OML Toronto Club, 2 Carlton St., M5B 1K4 (416/964-3111)
Windsor: OML Essex County Automobile Club, 1215 Ouellette Ave., N8X 1J3 (519/255-1212)
Woodstock: OML London Motor Club, 976 Dundas St., N4S 1H3 (519/539-5676)

QUEBEC AUTOMOBILE CLUBS

Brossard: ATCM Brossard, 1670 Blvd. Provencher, G4W 2Z6
Chicoutimi: QAC Chicoutimi, 1401 Blvd. Talbot, G7H 6E1
Laval: Touring Club, Montreal, 1200 W. St. Martin Blvd., H7S 2E4 (514/669-0823)
Montreal: Automobile et Touring Club de Montréal, 1425 rue de la Montagne, H3G 2R7 (514/288-7111)
Ste-Foy: Quebec Auto Club, 2600 Laurier Blvd., G1V 2L1 (418/653-2600)
Trois-Rivières: Quebec Automobile Club, 3748 Des Forges Blvd., G8Y 4R2 (819/376-9393)

SASKATCHEWAN MOTOR CLUB

Provincial Headquarters, 200 Albert St. N., Regina, Sask. S4R 5E2 (306/543-5679)
Estevan: SMC Branch, 1330 4th St., S4A OZ2 (306/634-6441)
Moose Jaw: SMC Branch, 80 Caribou St. W., S6H 2J6 (306/693-5195)
North Battleford: SMC Branch, 2002-100th St., S9A 0X5 (306/445-9451)
Prince Albert: SMC Branch, 68-13th St. W., S6V 3E8 (306/764-6818)
Regina: SMC Branch, 200 Albert St. N., S4R 5E2 (306/543-5679)
Saskatoon: SMC Branch, 321-4th Ave. N., S7K 2L9 (306/653-1833)
Swift Current: SMC Branch, 300 Begg St. W., S9H 0H6 (306/773-3194)
Yorkton: SMC Branch, 159 Broadway St. E., S3N 3K6 (306/783-6536)

Canadian Automotive Electric Association

3335 Yonge St., Suite 403, Toronto, Ont. M4N 2L9
(416) 489-0221
Executive Secretary, A. J. Bishop

Canadian Carwash Association

Box 130, Stn. W, Toronto, Ont. M6M 4Z2
(416) 247-8361
Executive Secretary, T. Snyders
Affiliated with International Carwash Association

Canadian Truck Dealers

2 Sheppard Ave. E., #1902, Willowdale, Ont. M2N 5Y7
(416) 224-5166

La Corporation des Concessionnaires d'Automobiles du Quebec Inc.

880 Chemin Ste-Foy, #910, Québec, P.Q. G1S 2L2
(418) 683-2991
Executive Director, Denys Demers
Affiliated Branches
Eastern Townships Automobile Dealers Association
North Shore Automobile Dealers Association
Eastern Quebec Automobile Dealers Association
Laurentian Automobile Dealers Association
Mauricie Automobile Dealers Association
Montreal Automobile Dealers Association
North-Western Quebec Automobile Dealers Association
Outaouais Automobile Dealers Association
Quebec Automobile Dealers Association
Richelieu Automobile Dealers Association
Saguenay, Lac St-Jean Automobie Dealers Association

Dominion Automobile Association

201 King St., London, Ont. N6A 4T3
(519) 434-2185

Alta.: 513 8th Ave. S.W., Calgary, Alta. T2P 1G3 (403/266-6777)
9912 109th St., Edmonton, Alta. T5K 1H5 (403/422-1330)
740 4th Ave. S., Lethbridge, Alta. T1J ON9 (403/328-4241)
B.C.: 207 W. Hastings St., Vancouver, B.C. V6B 1H7 (604/683-3914)
Man.: 310 Donald St., Winnipeg, Man. R3B 2H4 (204/943-9630)
N.B.: #390, 110 Crown St., Saint John, N.B. E2L 2X7 (506/652-7719)
N.S.: 1030 S. Park St., Halifax, N.S. B3H 2W3 (902/423-2280)
Ont.: #804, 10 St. Mary St., Toronto, Ont. M4Y 1P9 (416/924-8429)

331 Cooper St., Ottawa, Ont. K2P OG5 (613/233-6297)
P.E.I.: 64 University Ave., Charlottetown, P.E.I. C1A 4K9
Que.: 5980 Côte des Neiges, Montreal, P.Q. H3S 1Z5 (514/731-7671)
20 rue St-Jean, Quebec, P.Q. G1R 1N6 (418/529-5173)
#201, 234 rue Dufferin, Sherbrooke, P.Q. J1H 5K7 (Zenith 30450)
Sask.: 2325 11th Ave., Regina, Sask. S4P OK2 (306/352-6333)

Federation of Automobile Dealer Associations of Canada
2 Sheppard Ave. E., Ste. 1902, Willowdale, Ont. M2N 5Y7
(416) 224-5161

Motor Vehicle Manufacturers' Association
25 Adelaide St. E., Ste. 1602, Toronto, Ont. M5C 1Y7
(416) 364-9333
President, J.G. Dykes

National Automotive Trades Association of Canada
1687 W. Broadway, Vancouver, B.C. V6J 1X5
(604) 731-2108
Executive Vice President, Ron Baldwin

Nova Scotia Automobile Dealers' Association
-not confirmed for 1982-
Box 5125, Halifax, N.S. B3L 4M7
(902) 455-0434

Ontario Retail Gasoline & Automotive Service Association
#102, 101 Queensway W., Mississauga, Ont. L5B 2P7
(416) 276-7512
Co-ordinator, Wm. J. Burkimsher

Organization of Registered Automobile Dealers in Ontario
#129B, 17 Queen St. E., Toronto, Ont. M5C 1P9
(416) 368-2765
Managing Director, E.H. van Slyke

Saskatchewan Motor Dealers' Association
#6, 1235 Albert St., Regina, Sask. S4R 2R4
(306) 522-8868

Vintage Automobile Racing Association of Canada
c/o 302 Merton St., Toronto, Ont. M4S 1A9
(416) 484-1533

Western Motor Association (Canada) Ltd.
-not confirmed for 1982-
14004 121 Ave., Edmonton, Alta. T5L 2S9
(403) 455-6895

BAKERY COUNCIL OF CANADA
#1101, 130 Bloor St. W., Toronto, Ont. M5S 2X7
(416) 364-2696
Managing Director, Charles W. Tisdall

BAR ASSOCIATIONS
See Law Societies

BENEVOLENT & PROTECTIVE ORDER OF ELKS CANADA
Grand Secretary Treasurer, R. K. Coulling, 4908 Dewdney Ave., Regina, Sask. S4T 1B8 (306/543-9010)

BETTER BUSINESS BUREAU OF CANADA INC.
2 Bloor St. E., Ste. 3034, Toronto, Ont. M4W 3J5 (416) 925-3141
President, R.D. Etches (acting)

Local Bureaus

BETTER BUSINESS BUREAU OF NEWFOUNDLAND & LABRADOR LTD.
Manager, L.F. Miller, (2 Adelaide St.) Box 516, St. John's, Nfld. A1C 5K4 (709/722-2222)

BETTER BUSINESS BUREAU OF NEW BRUNSWICK
General Manager, H.J. McLellan, 331 Elmwood Dr., #2, Moncton, N.B. E1C 8P2

BETTER BUSINESS BUREAU OF NOVA SCOTIA
General Manager, Ann E. Janega, 1722 Granville St., Box 2124, Halifax, N.S. B3J 3B7 (902/422-6581)

BETTER BUSINESS BUREAU OF QUEBEC INC./BUREAU D'ETHIQUE COMMERCIALE DE QUEBEC INC.
General Manager, Raymond Perreault, 475 rue Richelieu, Quebec, P.Q. G1R 1K2 (418/523-2555)

BETTER BUSINESS BUREAU OF MONTREAL, INC.
President & General Manager, tba, 2055 Peel St., Ste. 460, Montreal, P.Q. H3A 1V4 (514/286-9281)

BETTER BUSINESS BUREAU OF OTTAWA & HULL, INC.
General Manager, L.L. Smith, Sovereign Bldg., 71 Bank St., Ste. 503, Ottawa, Ont. K1P 5N2 (613/233-3562)

BETTER BUSINESS BUREAU OF METROPOLITAN TORONTO, INC.
President, Paul J. Tuz, 321 Bloor St. E., 9th floor, Toronto, Ont. M4W 3K6 (416/961-0088)

BETTER BUSINESS BUREAU OF HAMILTON & DISTRICT
General Manager, Robert Irvine, 170 Jackson St. E., Hamilton, Ont. L8N 1L4 (416/526-1111)

BETTER BUSINESS BUREAU OF WATERLOO REGION
Manager, Pat Tallman, 58 Scott St., Kitchener, Ont. N2H 2R1 (519/579-3080)

BETTER BUSINESS BUREAU OF WINDSOR & DISTRICT
General Manager, Joseph Amort, 500 Riverside Dr. W., Windsor, Ont. N9A 5K6 (519/258-7222)

BETTER BUSINESS BUREAU OF WINNIPEG
Manager, T.S. Durham, 365 Hargrave St., Room 204, Winnipeg, Man. R3B 2K3 (204/943-1486)

BETTER BUSINESS BUREAU OF REGINA
Executive Director, Richard Eastman, #3, 1942 Hamilton St., Regina, Sask. S4P 2C4

BETTER BUSINESS BUREAU OF CALGARY, INC.
Manager, David S. Oakes, 630-8th Ave. S.W., Ste. 404, Calgary, Alta. T2P 1G6 (403/269-3905)

BETTER BUSINESS BUREAU OF EDMONTON & NORTHERN ALBERTA
President, H. J. Stutt, 600 Guardian Bldg., 10240-124th St., Edmonton, Alta. T5N 3W6 (403/482-2341)

BETTER BUSINESS BUREAU OF THE MAINLAND OF BRITISH COLUMBIA
Executive Vice President, Bryan F. Denham, 12th floor, Sun Tower, 100 W. Pender St., Vancouver, B.C. V6B 1S3 (604/682-2711)

BETTER BUSINESS BUREAU OF VANCOUVER ISLAND
Manager, D.M. Ryan, M37 - 635 Humboldt St., Victoria, B.C. V8W 1A7 (604/386-6348)

BIG BROTHERS OF CANADA
Cumis Bldg., 151 North Service Rd. (Box 758, Burlington, Ont. L7R 3Y7)
(416) 639-0461
Executive Vice President, Frank D. Fogwell
Director of Agency Programs & Services, Clifford Hall
Director of Public Relations & Special Projects, James Weber
Administrative Assistant, Helen Turpin
There are 155 Big Brother Associations in Canada.

BIG SISTERS ASSOCIATION OF ONTARIO
34 Huntley St., Toronto, Ont. M4Y 2L1
President, Izetta Hobbs

BIOLOGICAL PHOTOGRAPHIC ASSOCIATION INC.
Lake Ontario Chapter
Chairman, J. Atkinson
Treasurer, J. Atkinson, Medical Photography Dept., Sunnybrook Medical Center, 2075 Bayview Ave., Toronto, Ont. M4N 3M5 (416/486-3258)

THE BIOMASS ENERGY INSTITUTE INC.
1329 Niakwa Rd., Winnipeg, Man. R2J 3T4
(204) 257-3891
Executive Director, E.E. Robertson, P.Eng.

BLACK RESOURCES & INFORMATION CENTRE
427 Bloor St. W., Toronto, Ont. M5S 1X7
(416) 960-3697
Executive Director, Clyde McNeil

BMI CANADA LTD.
See Performing Rights of Canada

THE BOLSHEVIK UNION
-not confirmed for 1982-
C.P. 892, Succ. Tour de la Bourse, Montreal, P.Q. H4Z 1K2
Box 5707, Stn. A, Toronto, Ont. M5W 1N8

BOOK & PERIODICAL DEVELOPMENT COUNCIL
86 Bloor St. W., #260, Toronto, Ont. M5S 1M5
(416) 964-2655
Executive Director, Nancy Fleming

BOOK PUBLISHERS' PROFESSIONAL ASSOCIATION
c/o Jerry Trainer, President, Dell Publishing Inc., 20 Brimwood Blvd., Unit 29, Agincourt, Ont. M1V 1B7 (416/291-1347)

BOY SCOUTS OF CANADA
National Council
Offices, Box 5151, Stn. F, Ottawa, Ont. K2C 3G7
(613) 224-5131
Chief Scout of Canada, H. E. the Governor-General of Canada
President, W.B. Tilden
National Commr., Lt.-Gen. A.C. Hull, C.M.M., D.F.C., C.D. (Ret'd.)
Chief Executive, J. P. Ross
International Commr., R.K. Groome, Montreal
Provincial Scout Executives
Alta. & Sask.: D. A. Dick, 14205-109 Ave., Edmonton, Alta. T5N 1H5 (403/454-8561)
B.C. & Yukon: F. B. Hathaway, 719 W. 16th Ave., Vancouver, B.C. V5Z 1S8 (604/879-6818)
Man.: L. Wilcox, 883 Notre Dame Ave., Winnipeg, Man. R3E OM4 (204/786-6661)
N.B.: H. C. Northcott, 55 Rothesay Ave., Saint John, N.B. E2J 2B2 (506/657-2290)
N.S.: D. M. Duncan, Box 2003, Halifax, N.S. B3J 1Z1 (902/423-9227)
Nfld.: F. J. Kavanagh, 15 Terra Nova Rd., St. John's, Nfld. A1B 1E7 (709/722-0931)
Ont.: J. E. Turner, 9 Jackes Ave., Toronto, Ont. M4T 1E2 (416/923-2461)
P.E.I.: E. G. Kerr, Box 533, Charlottetown, P.E.I. C1A 7L1 (902/894-4777)
Que.: J. Blain, 2001 Trans-Canada Hwy., Dorval, P.Q. H9P 1J1 (514/683-3004)

THE BOY'S BRIGADE IN CANADA
Executive Secretary, C.D. (Danny) Reesor, 115 St. Andrew's Rd., Scarborough, Ont. M1P 4N2 (416/431-6052)

BOYS & GIRLS CLUBS OF CANADA
National Director, Ronald S. Wylie, 620 Wilson Ave., 3rd floor, Downsview, Ont. M3K 1Z3 (416/635-6402)

BREEDERS' ASSOCIATIONS
See Livestock Associations

BREWERS ASSOCIATION OF CANADA
151 Sparks St., Suite 805, Ottawa, Ont. K1P 5E3
(613) 232-9601
President & Chief Executive Officer, Kenneth R. Lavery

BRITISH COLUMBIA ASSOCIATION OF BROADCASTERS
President, John Skelly, CHNL Radio, Box 610, Kamloops, B.C. (604/372-2292)

BRITISH COLUMBIA ASSOCIATION OF LEARNING MATERIALS & EDUCATIONAL REPRESENTATIVES
1622 W. 7th Ave., Vancouver, B.C. V6V 1S5
(604) 773-2011

BRITISH COLUMBIA AVIATION COUNCIL
International Airport South, Box 23529, Vancouver, A.M.F., B.C. V7B 1W2
(604) 278-9330
Executive Officer, Ron Heath

BRITISH COLUMBIA BOATBUILDERS' ASSOCIATION
#608, 355 Burrard St., Vancouver, B.C. V6C 2G8
(604) 685-8131
Secretary, Ernie Gordon

BRITISH COLUMBIA DRAMA ASSOCIATION/ THEATRE B.C.
572 Beatty St., Vancouver, B.C. V6B 2L3
(604) 688-3836

BRITISH COLUMBIA FILM INDUSTRY ASSOCIATION
1237 Richards St., Vancouver, B.C. V6B 3G4
(604) 684-4712
President, Peter Bryant

BRITISH COLUMBIA FLOOR COVERING ASSOCIATION
2675 Oak St., Vancouver, B.C. V6H 2K3
(604) 736-6311
Secretary, Gay Woodward

BRITISH COLUMBIA GENEALOGICAL SOCIETY
Box 94371, Richmond, B.C. V6Y 2A8
(604) 274-3659

BRITISH COLUMBIA GRAIN SHIPPERS CLEARANCE ASSOCIATION
355 Burrard St., Vancouver, B.C. V6C 2G8
(604) 682-6832

BRITISH COLUMBIA HOUSING FOUNDATION
#106, 198 W. Hastings St., Vancouver, B.C. V6B 1H2
(604) 684-3515

BRITISH COLUMBIA INSULATION CONTRACTORS ASSOCIATION
#242, 4299 Canada Way, Burnaby, B.C. V5G 1H3
(604) 438-6616
Secretary Manager, E. Russell

BRITISH COLUMBIA LOG SPILL RECOVERY CO-OP ASSOCATION
Box 52, #1102, 1166 Alberni St., Vancouver, B.C. V6E 3Z3
(604) 685-2251

BRITISH COLUMBIA MARITIME EMPLOYERS ASSOCIATION
45 Dunlevy Ave., Vancouver, B.C. V6A 3A3
(604) 688-1155
President, N.G. Cunningham
Executive Vice President, P.N. Monk
Secretary, Mrs. Yu Oi Yip

BRITISH COLUMBIA MUSEUMS ASSOCIATION
The Secretary Treasurer, c/o British Columbia Provincial Museum, 675 Belleville St., Victoria, B.C. V8V 1X4 (604/387-3315)

BRITISH COLUMBIA NATIVE WOMEN'S SOCIETY
293 1st Ave., Kamloops, B.C. V2C 3J3
(604) 374-9412
President, Mildred Gotfriedson, C.M.

BRITISH COLUMBIA OYSTER GROWERS' ASSOCIATION
Box 970, Ladysmith, B.C. VOR 2EO
(604) 245-2939
Secretary, Mrs. P. Irvine

BRITISH COLUMBIA PAINT MANUFACTURERS' ASSOCIATION
-not confirmed for 1982-
2918 W. 44th St., Vancouver, B.C. V6N 3K4
(604) 266-2013

BRITISH COLUMBIA PARKINSON'S DISEASE ASSOCIATION
1195 W. 8th Ave., Vancouver, B.C. V6H 1C5
(604) 734-2221
Executive Director, J.R. Hopkins

BRITISH COLUMBIA SOFT DRINK ASSOCIATION
#608, 355 Burrard St., Vancouver, B.C. V6C 2G8
(604) 685-8131
Secretary, Ernie Gordon

BRITISH COLUMBIA STUDENTS' FEDERATION
c/o Student Society, Simon Fraser University, Burnaby, B.C. V5A 1S6 (604/291-4677)
Publishes: The B.C. Student

BRITISH-ISRAEL-WORLD FEDERATION (CANADA), INC.
313 Sherbourne St., Toronto, Ont. M5A 2S3 (416/921-5996)
Secretary, D.V. Cunningham, Apt. 207, 321 Sherbourne St., Toronto, Ont. M5A 2C3

BROADCAST EDUCATION ASSOCIATION OF CANADA
President, Gary Parkhill, c/o Radio & TV Program, Conestoga College, 299 Doon Valley Dr., Kitchener, Ont. N2G 4M4 (519/653-2511)

BROADCAST EXECUTIVES SOCIETY
#2115, 65 Queen St. W., Toronto, Ont. M5H 2M5
(416) 366-9567

BROADCAST RESEARCH COUNCIL OF CANADA
2 Bloor St. W., Box 409, Toronto, Ont. M4W 3E2
Information from Leona Ross, 416/961-1255

BROADCASTERS PROMOTION ASSOCIATION
248 W. Orange St., Lancaster, Pa. 17603
(717) 397-5727
Administrative Secretary, P. Evans

THE BROKER-DEALERS' ASSOCIATION OF ONTARIO
Executive Secretary & General Counsel, Donald McNeill, 11 Adelaide St. W., Suite 609, Toronto, Ont. M5H 1L9 (416/363-0345)

BUILDING OWNERS & MANAGERS ASSOCIATION OF CANADA
325 Howe St., Ste. 601, Vancouver, B.C. V6C 1Z7
(604) 684-3916
Executive Vice President, D. T. Bain

BUILDING OWNERS & MANAGERS ASSOCIATION INTERNATIONAL
1221 Massachusetts Ave. N.W., Washington, D.C. 20005
Executive Vice President, Gardner S. McBride

Other Affiliates
Pacific Apartment Management Association
Ste. 601, 325 Howe St., Vancouver, B.C. V6C 1Z7
Executive Director, Donald T. Bain

BBM BUREAU OF MEASUREMENT
120 Eglinton Ave. E., Toronto, Ont. M4P 1E3
(416) 486-5055

BUREAU OF MUNICIPAL RESEARCH
#404, 73 Richmond St. W., Toronto, Ont. M5H 1Z4
(416) 363-9265
Executive Director, Ms. Mary Lynch

BUSINESS COUNCIL ON NATIONAL ISSUES
#806, 90 Sparks St., Ottawa, Ont. K1P 5B4
(613) 238-3727

BYELORUSSIAN CANADIAN ALLIANCE
National Headquarters, 524 St. Clarens Ave., Toronto, Ont. M6H 3W7
Secretary General, Dr. R. Zuk-Hryskievic (705/728-7581)
Branch Offices in London, Montreal, Ottawa, Sudbury, Toronto.

CALGARY DOWNTOWN BUSINESS ASSOCIATION
#302, 513 8 Ave. S.W., Calgary, Alta. T2P 1G3
(403) 269-1193
General Manager, A. Jonassen

CAMPING ASSOCIATIONS
See Travel and Tourism Associations

CANADA CHINA FRIENDSHIP ASSOCIATION
33 E. Hastings St., Vancouver, B.C. V6A 1M9
(604) 681-4916
Hon. Chairman, Rev. Earl Willmott

CANADA EMPLOYMENT & IMMIGRATION UNION
Ste. 1004, 233 Gilmour St., Ottawa, Ont. K2P OP2
(613) 236-9634
President, Robert E. Sonier

CANADA-ISRAEL COMMITTEE
60 Bloor St. W., Ste. 1003, Toronto, Ont. M4W 3B8
(416) 924-0755
Director of Research, Shira Herzog Bessin

CANADA PEACE PARK ASSOCIATION
c/o Lester B. Pearson Peace Park, R.R. 3, Tweed, Ont. K0K 3J0
Chairman, Roy Cadwell

CANADA STUDENT EXCHANGE PROGRAM
(Inter-provincial student exchange)
1117 St. Catherine St. W., #521, Montreal, P.Q. H3B 1H9
(514) 845-9163
Executive Director, R.G. Beale

CANADA-USSR ASSOCIATION INC.
#202, 165 Bloor St. E., Toronto, Ont. M4W 1A9
(416) 922-4217
President, Michael Lucas

CANADA'S NATIONAL BIBLE HOUR
11440 Kingsway Ave., Edmonton, Alta. T5G 0X4
Director, Hon. Ernest C. Manning
Chairman, O. A. Kennedy
Executive Secretary, Mrs. J.F. Wagstaff

CANADIAN ABORTION RIGHTS ACTION LEAGUE
Box 935, Stn. Q, Toronto, Ont. M4T 2P1
(416) 961-1507
Attn.: K. Hammond

CANADIAN ACADEMY OF FILM AND TELEVISION ARTS AND SCIENCES
345 Allard Ave., Dorval, P.Q. H9S 3C1
(514) 484-0714
Secretary Treasurer, Peter Benison

CANADIAN ACADEMY OF RECORDING ARTS & SCIENCES (CARAS)
89 Bloor St. E., Toronto, Ont. M4W 1A9
(416) 922-5029

CANADIAN ADVERTISING ADVISORY BOARD
1240 Bay St., Room 305, Toronto, Ont. M5R 2A7
(416) 961-6311
Secretary, S. Keeler

CANADIAN ADVERTISING RESEARCH FOUNDATION
Chairman, Bob Scott
Treasurer, John Foss
Secretary, Heather McLeod, #1010, 180 Bloor St. W., Toronto, Ont. M5S 2V6 (416/964-3832)

CANADIAN ADVERTISING AND SALES ASSOCIATION
73 Richmond St. W., #205, Toronto, Ont. M5H 1Z4
(416) 366-1809

CANADIAN AERONAUTICS & SPACE INSTITUTE
#60, 75 Sparks St., Ottawa, Ont. K1P 5A5
(613) 234-0191
Executive Secretary, P. A. Cobbett
Branches, Montreal, Ottawa, Toronto, Winnipeg, Vancouver, Edmonton, Halifax-Dartmouth, Calgary, Quebec, Sault Ste. Marie, Trenton-Kingston, Oshawa.

CANADIAN AGRICULTURAL CHEMICALS ASSOCIATION
Ste. 710, 116 Albert St., Ottawa, Ont. K1P 5G3
(613) 232-6802
Executive Director, Jacques Chevalier

CANADIAN AIR LINE EMPLOYEES' ASSOCIATION
6455 Northam Dr., Mississauga, Ont. L4V 1J2
(416) 678-1551
President, J.T. Saunders
Executive Vice Presidents, P. Lindsay; G. C. Pryce

CANADIAN AIR LINE FLIGHT ATTENDANTS ASSOCIATION
#860, 1200 W. 73rd Ave., Vancouver, B.C. V6P 6G5
(604) 266-1421
Affiliated Branches
Toronto Regional Office—CALFAA, #303, 6303 Airport Rd., Mississauga, Ont. L4V 1R8 (416/678-7080)
Montreal Regional Office—CALFAA, #812, 2075 University St., Montreal, P.Q. H3A 2R7 (514/849-3747)

CANADIAN AIR LINE PILOTS ASSOCIATION
1300 Steeles Ave. E., Brampton, Ont. L6T 1A2
(416) 453-8210
Executive Administrator, Philip Brady

CANADIAN AIR TRAFFIC CONTROL ASSOCIATION
#604, 1 Nicholas St., Ottawa, Ont. K1N 7B7
(613) 232-9413
Managing Director, H.J. Brennen

CANADIAN ALLIED TEXTILE TRADES ASSOCIATION
135 Liberty St., Toronto, Ont. M6K 1A7
(416) 535-2137

CANADIAN AMATEUR RADIO FEDERATION
c/o Don Slater, Box 356, Kingston, Ont. K7L 4W2

CANADIAN AMPHIBIAN & REPTILE CONSERVATION SOCIETY
President, Wayne F. Weller, 9 Mississauga Rd., Mississauga, Ont. L5H 2H5

CANADIAN APPLIANCE MANUFACTURERS ASSOCIATION
#1608, One Yonge St., Toronto, Ont. M5E 1R1
(416) 862-7152

CANADIAN ARBITRATION, CONCILIATION & AMICABLE COMPOSITION CENTRE INC.
c/o Institute for International Cooperation, University of Ottawa, Ottawa, Ont. K1N 6N5
(613) 231-5862; Telex: 0533338
President, Prof. L. Kos-Rabcewicz-Zubkowski
Note:- This is not an association, but is a non-profit corporation that conducts research, and provides training and information in the field of conciliation and arbitration.

CANADIAN ARCTIC RESOURCES COMMITTEE
#11, 46 Elgin St., Ottawa, Ont. K1P 5K6
(613) 236-7379
Executive Director, Murray Coolican

CANADIAN ART MUSEUMS DIRECTORS' ORGANIZATION
President, Jean Trudel, Director, The Montreal Museum of Fine Arts, 3400 ave du Musée, Montréal, P.Q. H3G 1K3 (514/285-1600)

CANADIAN ASSOCIATION OF ADMINISTRATORS OF LABOUR LEGISLATION
(Association Canadienne des Administrateurs de la Legislation Ouvriere)
-not confirmed for 1982-

Secretary Treasurer, Gloria M. Kunka, Director, Federal Provincial Relations, Policy Co-ordination & Liaison, Labour Canada, Ottawa, Ont. K1A 0J2 (819/997-1333)

CANADIAN ASSOCIATION OF AERIAL SURVEYORS
46 Elgin St., Ottawa, Ont. K1P 5K6
(613) 232-8770
President, Donald W. McLarty

CANADIAN ASSOCIATION OF BROADCAST CONSULTANTS
Secretary Treasurer, E.A. Bogdanowicz, c/o Imagineering Ltd., 95 Barber Greene Rd., #112, Don Mills, Ont. M3C 3E9

CANADIAN ASSOCIATION OF BROADCAST REPRESENTATIVES INC.
(L'Association Canadienne des representatives en radiodiffusion inc.)
Box 251, Stn. F, Toronto, Ont. M4Y 2L5
President, Bob Alexander
Vice President, Radio, Bob Munro
Vice President, Television, Ross McCreath
Secretary Treasurer, Dick Sienko

THE CANADIAN ASSOCIATION OF BROADCASTERS
165 Sparks St., Box 627, Stn. B, Ottawa, Ont. K1P 5S2
(613) 233-4035
Chairman of the Board, J.E. Ansell
President, G.G.E. Steele

CANADIAN ASSOCIATION OF BUSINESS VALUATORS
15 Toronto St., #702, Toronto, Ont. M5C 2E3
(416) 366-7720
Executive Secretary, Mrs. Susan Cooke

CANADIAN ASSOCIATION OF CHIEFS OF POLICE
Ste. 1002, 116 Albert St., Ottawa, Ont. K1P 5G3
(613) 233-1106

CANADIAN ASSOCIATION OF CONVENTION BUREAUX
63 Dalewood Cres., Hamilton, Ont. L8S 4B5
(416) 522-7676
Executive Director, William Cockman

ONTARIO ASSOCIATION OF CONVENTION BUREAUX
Address, etc. same as above

CANADIAN ASSOCIATION OF THE DEAF
2395 Bayview Ave., Willowdale, Ont. M2L 1A2
President, Eleanor McPeake

Regional Affiliates
Eastern Canada Association of the Deaf
Gallaudet Canadian Club of Washington, D.C.
Ontario Association of the Deaf

CANADIAN ASSOCIATION OF EQUIPMENT DISTRIBUTORS
#1411, 130 Albert St., Ottawa, Ont. K1P 5G4
(613) 233-3474
General Manager, J.W. Hopper

CANADIAN ASSOCIATION OF EXHIBITIONS
Box 409, Stn. C, Toronto, Ont. M6J 3P5
(416) 595-1375
Director, G.H. Awde
Secretary, Pat Roberts

CANADIAN ASSOCIATION OF EXPOSITION MANAGERS
29 Sabrina Dr., Weston, Ont. M9R 2J4
(416) 244-8871
Executive Secretary, Robert McBeth
President, Georgia Prassas, Ontario Marketing Productions, Toronto

THE CANADIAN ASSOCIATION OF FIRE CHIEFS INC.
#1590, 7 Liverpool Ct., Ottawa, Ont. K1B 4L2
(613) 749-3825
Executive Director, Emile Therien

CANADIAN ASSOCIATION OF FLEET SUPERVISORS
Box 1188, Coquitlam, B.C. V3J 6Z9
President, John Tessier

CANADIAN ASSOCIATION OF GEOGRAPHERS
President, Dr. J. Keith Fraser, Dept. of Environment, Ottawa, Ont. K1A 0H3
Secretary Treasurer, J.D. Booth, Burnside Hall, McGill Univ., 805 Sherbrooke St. W., Montreal, P.Q. H3A 2K6 (514/392-5496)

CANADIAN ASSOCIATION ON GERONTOLOGY
Box 1859, Winnipeg, Man. R3C 3R1
(204) 944-2454

CANADIAN ASSOCIATION FOR HEALTH, PHYSICAL EDUCATION & RECREATION
National Office, 333 River Rd., Vanier, Ont. K1L 8B9
(613) 746-0060, ext. 260, or 746-5909
Executive Director, Dr. Thomas Bedecki

CANADIAN ASSOCIATION FOR HUMANE TRAPPING
5 Sultan St. (Box 934, Stn. F, Toronto, Ont. M4Y 2N9)
(416) 922-7030
President, Prof. D.C. Baillie

CANADIAN ASSOCIATION OF ICE INDUSTRIES INC.
10 Shorncliffe Rd., Islington, Ont. M9B 3S3
(416) 231-7247

CANADIAN ASSOCIATION FOR INFORMATION SCIENCE
Box 776, Stn. G, Calgary, Alta. T3A 2G6
President, Margaret Telfer, Infomart, Toronto (416/598-4000)

CANADIAN ASSOCIATION OF INVESTMENT CLUBS (1961)
President, A.D.H. Smith, Box 122, Ste. 3700, First Canadian Place, Toronto, Ont. M5X 1E9 (416/867-3457)

CANADIAN ASSOCIATION FOR LABORATORY ANIMAL SCIENCE
2627 Morley Trail N.W., Calgary, Alta. T2M 4G6
(403) 284-2928
Executive Secretary Treasurer, Mrs. Evalyn M. Neilson
Regional Chapters in Vancouver, Calgary, Edmonton, Saskatoon, Winnipeg, Ottawa, Toronto, London, Kingston, Montreal, St. John's, Halifax.

CANADIAN ASSOCIATION—LATIN AMERICA & CARIBBEAN
42 Charles St. E., Toronto, Ont. M4Y 1T4
(416) 964-6068
Executive Director, Keith O. Hillyer

CANADIAN ASSOCIATION OF MANAGEMENT CONSULTANTS
#915, 1243 Islington Ave., Toronto, Ont. M8X 1Y9
(416) 231-4122
Executive Director, Herb Breithaupt

CANADIAN ASSOCIATION OF MANUFACTURERS OF MEDICAL DEVICES
480 Garyray Dr., Weston, Ont. M9L 1P8
(416) 745-9210
Executive Director, E.R. Hillrich

CANADIAN ASSOCIATION OF MARKETING RESEARCH ORGANIZATIONS
15 Toronto St., #702, Toronto, Ont. M5C 2E3
(416) 364-1223
Executive Secretary, Mrs. Susan Cooke

CANADIAN ASSOCIATION FOR THE MENTALLY RETARDED
Kinsmen NIMR Bldg., York Univ. Campus, 4700 Keele St., Downsview, Ont. M3J 1P3
(416) 661-9611
Executive Vice President, Dr. Hugh Lafave

Executive Directors, Provincial Associations

ALBERTA ASSOCIATION FOR THE MENTALLY RETARDED
Reg Peters, 11728 Kingsway Ave., Edmonton, Alta. T5G 0X5 (403/451-3055)

BRITISH COLUMBIA ASSOCIATION FOR THE MENTALLY RETARDED
Alan Etmanski, Airport Sq., #155, 1200 W. 73rd Ave., Vancouver, B.C. V6P 6G5 (604/266-1146)

CANADIAN ASSOCIATION FOR THE MENTALLY RETARDED, MANITOBA DIVISION
Dale Kendel, 46, 825 Sherbrook St. W., Winnipeg, Man. R3A 1M5 (204/786-4819)

CANADIAN ASSOCIATION FOR THE MENTALLY RETARDED, NEW BRUNSWICK DIVISION
Rev. R. Stewart Clarke, 107 Queen St., Moncton, N.B. E1C 1K5 (506/855-6262)

CANADIAN ASSOCIATION FOR THE MENTALLY RETARDED, NEWFOUNDLAND AND LABRADOR DIVISION
President, Bob Johnston, Box 4489, St. John's, Nfld. A1C 6C8

CANADIAN ASSOCIATION FOR THE MENTALLY RETARDED, NOVA SCOTIA DIVISION
President, William Powroz, #915, 45 Alderney Dr., Dartmouth, N.S. B2Y 2N6 (902/469-1174)

ONTARIO ASSOCIATION FOR THE MENTALLY RETARDED
John N. Haddad, 1376 Bayview Ave., Toronto, Ont. M4G 3A3 (416/483-4348)

CANADIAN ASSOCIATION FOR THE MENTALLY RETARDED, PRINCE EDWARD ISLAND DIVISION
Box 280, Charlottetown, P.E.I. C1A 7K4 (902/894-3714)

QUEBEC ASSOCIATION FOR THE MENTALLY RETARDED
Mlle Lorraine Boyer, 1193 Place Phillips, #3950, Montreal, P.Q. H3B 3E1 (514/282-3483)

SASKATCHEWAN ASSOCIATION FOR THE MENTALLY RETARDED
W. J. Dolan, 103 Central Chambers, 219 22nd St. E., Saskatoon, Sask. S7K 0G4 (306/653-0141)

CANADIAN ASSOCIATION OF MOTION PICTURE PRODUCERS
950 Yonge St., #1000, Toronto, Ont. M4W 2J4
(416) 964-6661

CANADIAN ASSOCIATION OF OILWELL DRILLING CONTRACTORS
#414, 603 7 Ave. S.W., Calgary, Alta. T2P 2T5
(403) 264-4311

CANADIAN ASSOCIATION OF OPTOMETRISTS
210 Gladstone Ave., Suite 2001, Ottawa, Ont. K2P 0Y6
(613) 238-2006
Executive Director, D. N. Schaefer

Provincial Associations

ALBERTA OPTOMETRIC ASSOCIATION
#2, 9333 50 St., Edmonton, Alta. T6B 2L5

BRITISH COLUMBIA OPTOMETRIC ASSOCIATION
Executive Secretary, Mrs. Nina Cline, #414, 1033 Davie St., Vancouver, B.C. V6E 1M7 (604/685-1810)

MANITOBA OPTOMETRIC SOCIETY
#886, 167 Lombard Ave., Winnipeg, Man. R3B 0V3

THE NEWFOUNDLAND OPTOMETRIC ASSOCIATION
Box 307, Clarenville, Nfld. A0E 1J0

NEW BRUNSWICK OPTOMETRICAL SOCIETY
Secretary Treasurer, Dr. Keith Fullarton, Box 1889, Woodstock, N.B. E0J 2B0 (506/328-9335)

NOVA SCOTIA OPTOMETRICAL ASSOCIATION
Executive Director, Jim Lotz, Box 3393, South Stn., Halifax, N.S. B3J 3J1 (902/423-3263)

ONTARIO ASSOCIATION OF OPTOMETRISTS
President, Dr. Barry Winters, #914, 40 St. Clair Ave. W., Toronto, Ont. M4V 1M2 (416/923-1173)

PRINCE EDWARD ISLAND OPTOMETRICAL ASSOCIATION
Secretary, Dr. J.M. Rusk, Box 1508, Summerside, P.E.I. C1N 4K4 (902/436-3287)

L'ASSOCIATION PROFESSIONNELLE DES OPTOMETRISTES DU QUEBEC
Directeur executif, Guy Lamoureux, 614 ouest, St-Jacques, Ste. 302, Montreal, P.Q. H3C 1E2 (514/849-8051)

SASKATCHEWAN OPTOMETRIC ASSOCIATION
Registrar, Dr. J. Holmes, Box 880, North Battleford, Sask. S9A 0V6 (306/446-3373)

CANADIAN ASSOCIATION OF PETROLEUM PRODUCTION ACCOUNTING
Box 36, Calgary, Alta. T2P 2G9
President, Diane Knight (403/264-9380)
Secretary, Gail Fraser (403/263-1500)

CANADIAN ASSOCIATION OF PHYSICISTS
151 Slater St., Suite 903, Ottawa, Ont. K1P 5H3
(613) 237-3392
Honorary Secretary Treasurer, Dr. Dr. B.G. Gregory, I.N.R.S. Energie, Université du Québec
Executive Secretary, Mona L. Jento

CANADIAN ASSOCIATION FOR THE PREVENTION OF CRIME
55 Parkdale Ave., Ottawa, Ont. K1Y 1E5
(613) 728-1865
Executive Director, W.T. McGrath

A national organization active in crime prevention and promoting good criminal justice services for all Canadians. Publishes the Canadian Journal of Criminology and other literature; sponsors the bi-ennial Canadian Congress on the Prevention of Crime.

CANADIAN ASSOCIATION OF PRIMARY AIR CARRIERS, INC.
c/o Secretary, W.M. Swystun, Q.C., Box 23439, Vancouver AMF, B.C. V7B 1W1 (604/273-9531)

CANADIAN ASSOCIATION FOR PRODUCTION & INVENTORY CONTROL
President, J. Paterson
Secretary, B. Smith, 197 Pellett Ave., Weston, Ont. M9N 2P5 (416/244-8810)

CANADIAN ASSOCIATION OF RECYCLING INDUSTRIES
67 Yonge St., #1003, Toronto, Ont. M5E 1J8
(416) 362-4521
Executive Director, Stanley T. Parker

CANADIAN ASSOCIATION OF SEXUAL ASSAULT CENTRES
c/o Yvette Perreault, B.C. Regional Representative, #4, 45 Kingsway, Vancouver, B.C. V5T 3H7
(604) 872-8212

CANADIAN ASSOCIATION OF SOCIAL WORKERS
55 Parkdale Ave., 4th floor, Ottawa, Ont. K1Y 1E5
(613) 728-1865
Executive Director, Gweneth J. Gowanlock, M.S.W.

CANADIAN ASSOCIATION IN SUPPORT OF THE NATIVE PEOPLES
16 Spadina Rd., #302, Toronto, Ont. M5R 2S7
(416) 964-0169

CANADIAN ASSOCIATION OF TEMPORARY SERVICES
#614, 390 Bay St., Toronto, Ont. M5H 2Y2
(416) 361-1445
Executive Director, Thomas E. Reid

CANADIAN ASSOCIATION OF TOKEN COLLECTORS
Secretary, Ken Palmer, 10 Wesanford Place, Hamilton, Ont. L8P 1N6 (416/528-3649)

CANADIAN ASSOCIATION FOR THE WELFARE OF PSYCHIATRIC PATIENTS
Box 39, Stn. J, Toronto, Ont. M4J 4X8
(416) 691-3499
Executive Director, Miss G. Tori Salter

CANADIAN ASSOCIATION OF WOMEN BUSINESS OWNERS
15 Toronto St., #702, Toronto, Ont. M5C 2E3
(416) 364-1223
Executive Secretary, Mrs. Susan Cooke

CANADIAN ASSOCIATION OF WOMEN EXECUTIVES
One First Canadian Place, #4800, Box 192, Toronto, Ont. M5X 1A6
(416) 366-2520
Administration Manager, Amanda M. Curtis

THE CANADIAN AUTHORS ASSOCIATION
24 Ryerson Ave., Toronto, Ont. M5T 2P3
(416) 868-6916
Secretary, (vacant)

Branches in Calgary, Edmonton, Hamilton, Kamloops, Kitchener-Waterloo, London, Montreal, New Brunswick, Nova Scotia, Okanagan, Ottawa, Sarnia, Toronto, Vancouver, Victoria, and Winnipeg elect secretaries annually. Write to the Toronto Address for up to date information.

CANADIAN AUTOMATIC MERCHANDISING ASSOCIATION
85 Ellesmere Rd., #203, Scarborough, Ont. M1R 4B8
(416) 447-0652
Executive Director, D. A. Blowe

CANADIAN AUTOMATIC SPRINKLER ASSOCIATION
3638 Victoria Park Ave., Willowdale, Ont. M2H 3B2
(416) 497-2100
President, William Clark

CANADIAN AVIATION HISTORICAL SOCIETY
Box 224, Stn. A, Willowdale, Ont. M2N 5S8
President, F.W. Hotson (416/278-7757)
Secretary, J.A. Biehler
Membership Secretary, S. D. Benner
Editor, W. J. Wheeler

THE CANADIAN BANKERS' ASSOCIATION
Box 282, Toronto Dominion Centre, Toronto, Ont. M5K 1K2
(416) 362-6092
President, Robert M. MacIntosh

CANADIAN BATTERY MANUFACTURERS ASSOCIATION
One Yonge St., Ste. 1400, Toronto, Ont. M5E 1J9
(416) 363-7261
Manager, James A. Rankin

CANADIAN BIBLE SOCIETY
#100, 10 Carnforth Rd., Toronto, Ont. M4A 2S4
(416) 757-4171
General Secretary, Rev. Kenneth G. McMillan, B.A., M.Div., D.D.
Resource Director, Rev. Dr. Russell T. Hall
Director, Scriptures for Canada, Rev. Howard G. Zurbrigg, B.A., M.Div.
Stewardship Director, Rev. Gunter Flemke, B.Th.
Director of French Work, Rev. Daniel Racine, L.L., M.Ed.

District Offices & Secretaries

B.C.: 593 Richards St., Vancouver, B.C. V6B 3A1 (604/681-9345)
Hamilton: Rev. D. B. Thierry, 196 Main St. E., Hamilton, Ont. L8N 1H3 (416/522-9104)
Man.: Rev. D. S. Collins, 308 Kennedy St., Winnipeg, Man. R3B 2M6
Montreal: Rev. Dr. R. S. Johnston; Rev. D. Racine, 1450 Union Ave., Montreal, P.Q. H3A 2B8 (514/844-3367)
N.B.: Rev. G. Boyd Butt, 117 Germain St., Saint John, N.B. E2L 2E9 (506/652-1390)
Nfld.: Rev. G.E. Benson, St. John's, Nfld.
North Alta.: Rev. Robert H. Grey, 10345 Jasper Ave., Edmonton, Alta. T5J 1Y5 (403/428-1802)
North Sask.: Rev. G. E. Ward, 250 Second Ave. S., Saskatoon, Sask. S7K 1K9
North West: Rev. S.B. Nafziger, Suite 200, 1835 Yonge St., Toronto, Ont. M4S 1Y1
Northern Ont.: Rev. R. S. Magee, 847 Main St. W., North Bay, Ont. P1B 2V8
N.S.: Rev. Byron Howlett, Box 183, Halifax, N.S. B3J 2M4 (902/423-3545)
Ottawa: Rev. M. C. Thomas, 315 Lisgar St., Ottawa, Ont. K2P 0E1 (613/236-3401)
P.E.I.: Rev. G. Boyd Butt, 170 Kent St., Charlottetown, P.E.I. C1A 1N9 (902/892-6931)
Que.: Rev. Dr. R. S. Johnston; Rev. D. Racine, 1025 rue St. Jean, Quebec, P.Q. G1R 1R9
South Alta.: Rev. R. R. Mohr, 117-7th Ave. S.W., Calgary, Alta. T2P 0W5 (403/262-4277)
South Sask.: Rev. G.E. Ward, 2127 Albert St., Regina, Sask. S4P 2V1
Upper Canada: Rev. A. Brndjar, 10 Carnforth Rd., Toronto, Ont. M4A 2S4
Western Ont.: Rev. D.L. Howlett, 424 Waterloo St., London, Ont. N6B 2P2 (519/432-6663)

CANADIAN BOARD OF MARINE UNDERWRITERS
15 Toronto St., #702, Toronto, Ont. M5C 2E3
(416) 264-1223/4

CANADIAN BOILER SOCIETY
One Yonge St., Ste. 1400, Toronto, Ont. M5E 1J9
(416) 363-7261

CANADIAN BOOK INFORMATION CENTRE
70 The Esplanade, 3rd floor, Toronto, Ont. M5E 1A6
(416) 362-6555
National Manager, Serge Lavoie
Branches:
Killam Library, Dalhousie University, Halifax, N.S. B3H 4H8 (902/424-3410), Regional Manager, Angela Rebeiro
1622 W. 7th Ave., Vancouver, B.C. V6J 1S5 (604/734-2011), Regional Manager, Paulette Kerr

CANADIAN BOOK PUBLISHERS' COUNCIL
45 Charles St. E., Toronto, Ont. M4Y 1S2
(416) 964-7231
Executive Director, Mrs. Jacqueline Nestmann-Hushion
Affiliated Societies
SCHOOL GROUP
45 Charles St. E., Suite 701, Toronto, Ont. M4Y 1S2
President, Hugh Furneaux, Copp Clark Pitman
COLLEGE GROUP
45 Charles St. E., Suite 701, Toronto, Ont. M4Y 1S2
President, James Rogerson, John Wiley & Sons Canada Ltd.
TRADE PUBLISHERS' GROUP
45 Charles St. E., Ste. 701, Toronto, Ont. M4Y 1S2
President, John Neale, McClelland & Stewart Ltd.
PAPERBACK GROUP
45 Charles St. E., Ste. 701, Toronto, Ont. M4Y 1S2
President, Peter J. Waldock, Penguin Books Canada Ltd.

CANADIAN BOOKSELLERS ASSOCIATION
56 The Esplanade, Ste. 400, Toronto, Ont. M5E 1A7
(416) 361-1529
Executive Director, Bernard E. Rath
Convention Manager, Irene Read

CANADIAN BROADCASTING LEAGUE
Box 1504, Ottawa, Ont. K1P 5R5
(613) 232-1591

CANADIAN BRUSH, BROOM & MOP MANUFACTURERS ASSOCIATION
#512, 55 York St., Toronto, Ont. M5J 1S2
(416) 363-8374
Secretary, Frank Young

CANADIAN BUILDING OFFICIALS ASSOCIATION
Secretary, R.V. Hebart, 1940 Orchard Way, West Vancouver, B.C. V7V 4G3
Secretaries of the Provincial Associations
BUILDING INSPECTORS ASSOCIATION OF BRITISH COLUMBIA
T.N. Blackall, 3904 W. 4th Ave., Vancouver, B.C. V6R 1P5 (604/732-4828)
ALBERTA BUILDING OFFICIALS ASSOCIATION
Denis O'Brien, 3204 10th St. N.W., Calgary, Alta.
SASKATCHEWAN BUILDING OFFICIALS ASSOCIATION
W.G. Sully, City Hall, Yorkton, Sask.
MANITOBA BUILDING OFFICIALS ASSOCIATION
S. Wolf, Room 508, 401 York Ave., Winnipeg, Man. R3C OP8 (204/944-3403)
ONTARIO BUILDING OFFICIALS ASSOCIATION
Ray Weido, Corp. of Town of Milton, 251 Main St. E., Milton, Ont. L9T 1P1 (416/878-7211)
L'ASSOCIATION QUEBECOISE DES AGENTS DU BATIMENT ING.
Léo Paul Trépanier, 37 boul. Brien, Repentigny, P.Q. J6A 4R9 (514/872-3124, bur.; 581-0795, res.)
NEW BRUNSWICK BUILDING OFFICIALS ASSOCIATION
c/o Richard Greene, CHMC, Box 2235, Stn. C, Saint John, N.B. E2L 3V1 (506/658-4988)
BUILDING INSPECTORS ASSOCIATION OF NOVA SCOTIA
Mansel Eisan, Box 300, Armdale, Halifax Co., N.S. B3L 4K3
PRINCE EDWARD ISLAND BUILDING OFFICIALS ASSOCIATION
H.W. Foster MacKinnon, Box 98, Charlottetown, P.E.I. C1A 7K2 (902/894-5552, bus.; 675-2324, res.)
NEWFOUNDLAND AND LABRADOR BUILDING OFFICIALS ASSOCIATION
Harvey Gabriel, 55 Philip Dr., Corner Brook, Nfld. A2H 6B2

CANADIAN BUSINESS AIRCRAFT ASSOCIATION, INC.
#1212, 275 Slater St., Ottawa, Ont. K1P 5H9
(613) 236-5611
Executive Director, H.F. Protheroe

CANADIAN BUSINESS EQUIPMENT MANUFACTURERS ASSOCIATION INC.
#212, Yorkdale Place, 1 Yorkdale Rd., Toronto, Ont. M6A 3A1
(416) 789-0508
General Manager, D.J. Flood

CANADIAN CABLE TELEVISION ASSOCIATION
Ste. 405, 85 Albert St., Ottawa, Ont. K1P 6A4
(613) 232-2631
Director of Public Affairs, S.E. Cornell

CANADIAN CANCER SOCIETY
130 Bloor St. W., #1001, Toronto, Ont. M5S 2V7
(416) 961-7223
Executive Vice President, Dr. R.A. Macbeth, Toronto
Secretary Treasurer, Alan Martin
Provincial Divisions
Alta.: Main Floor, 1134-8th Ave. S.W., Calgary, Alta. T2P 1J5 (403/263-3120)
B.C. & Yukon: 955 W. Broadway, Vancouver, B.C. V5Z 3X8 (604/736-1211)
Man.: 960 Portage Ave., Winnipeg, Man. R3G 0R4 (204/786-8438)
N.B.: (61 Union St.) Box 2089, Saint John, N.B. E2L 3T5 (506/652-7600)
Nfld.: Pippy Place (Box 8921, St. John's, Nfld. A1B 3R9) (709/753-6520)
N.S.: 1485 South Park St., Halifax, N.S. B3J 2L1 (902/423-6550)
Ont.: 185 Bloor St. E., 6th floor, Toronto, Ont. M4W 3G5 (416/923-7474)
P.E.I.: 51 University Ave., 3rd floor, Charlottetown, P.E.I. C1A 7K2 (902/894-9675)
Que.: 1118 St. Catherine St. W., Montreal, P.Q. H3B 1H5 (514/866-2613)
Sask.: 4219 Dewdney Ave., Regina, Sask. S4T 1A9 (306/525-5817)

CANADIAN CARPET INSTITUTE
1080 Beaver Hall Hill, Suite 1002, Montreal, P.Q. H2Z 1T6
(514) 866-2081
President, P. T. Nance

CANADIAN CATHOLIC BIBLICAL ASSOCIATION
3377 Bayview Ave., Willowdale, Ont. M2M 3S4
(416) 225-9019
Secretary, Sister Mary Louise Brooks, C.S.J.

CANADIAN CATHOLIC HISTORICAL ASSOCIATION
-not confirmed for 1982-
95 St. Joseph St., Toronto, Ont. M5S 2R9
(416) 651-5619

A National society for the promotion of interest in the history of the Catholic Church.

Secretary, English Section, Mrs. Joan Lenardon, St. Peter's Seminary, 1040 Waterloo St., London, Ont. N6A 3Y1 (519/438-6752)

Secretary, French Section, Rev. Louis-Philippe Normand, 8844 est, rue Notre-Dame, Montreal, P.Q. H1L 3M4

CANADIAN CATHOLIC ORGANIZATION FOR DEVELOPMENT & PEACE

2111 Centre St., Montreal, P.Q. H3K 1J5
(514) 932-5136
Executive Director, Jacques Champagne

CANADIAN CENTRAL REGISTRY OF SUBSCRIPTION REPRESENTATIVES, INC.

15 Toronto St., #702, Toronto, Ont. M5C 2E3
(416) 364-1223
Executive Secretary, Mrs. Susan Cooke

CANADIAN CENTRE FOR PHILANTHROPY

12 Shepherd St., 3rd Floor, Toronto, Ont. M5H 3A1
Executive Director, Allan Arlett

CANADIAN CERAMIC SOCIETY

Ste. 110, 2175 Sheppard Ave. E., Willowdale, Ont. M2J 1W8
(514) 491-2886
Executive Director, Harold Taylor

THE CANADIAN CEREBRAL PALSY ASSOCIATION

National Office, 15 Toronto St., #301, Toronto, Ont. M5C 2E3
(416) 364-0445
Co-ordinator, Jo-Anne Y. Bolger

Provincial Affiliates

CEREBRAL PALSY ASSOCIATION OF BRITISH COLUMBIA
#204, 579 Granville St., Vancouver, B.C. V6C 1Y7
(604) 669-0756
Executive Director, J.P. Grocott

CEREBRAL PALSY ASSOCIATION IN ALBERTA
#5 St. Margaret School, 3320 Carol Dr. N.W., Calgary, Alta. T2L 0K7 (403/282-9111)
Executive Director, William Donahoo

MANITOBA CEREBRAL PALSY ASSOCIATION
c/o Brian Stewart, 364 Whytewold Rd., Winnipeg, Man. R3J 2W5 (204/944-8101)

ONTARIO FEDERATION FOR THE CEREBRAL PALSIED
#300, 2010 Yonge St., Toronto, Ont. M4S 1Z9
(416) 485-6913, 485-7065

L'ASSOCIATION DE PARALYSIE CEREBRALE DU QUEBEC INC./ QUEBEC CEREBRAL PALSY ASSOCIATION
525 boul. Hamel est, Sous-Sol/Aile A, #50, Québec, P.Q. G1M 2S8
(418) 529-5371
Directeur General, Mme Pauline Demers

ATLANTIC CEREBRAL PALSY ASSOCIATION
President, Harold Pollock, 24 Bristol St., Fredericton, N.B. E3B 4W2

PRINCE EDWARD ISLAND CEREBRAL PALSY ASSOCIATION INC.
President, Richard Montigny, Box 2702, Charlottetown, P.E.I. C1A 8C3 (902/675-2354)

THE CANADIAN CHEMICAL PRODUCERS' ASSOCIATION

#805, 350 Sparks St., Ottawa, Ont. K1R 7S8
(613) 237-6215
President, J.M. Bélanger
Secretary Treasurer, D. L. Mackenzie

CANADIAN CIRCULATION MANAGERS' ASSOCIATION

Secretary, M. E. Fearnall, The Sun-Times, Box 200, Owen Sound, Ont. N4K 5P2 (519/376-2250)

CANADIAN CIRCULATIONS AUDIT BOARD, INC.

44 Eglinton Ave. W., Ste. 705, Toronto, Ont. M4R 1A1
(416) 487-2418
President, General Manager & Secretary, Patrick Sweeney

CANADIAN CIVIL LIBERTIES ASSOCIATION

229 Yonge St., Suite 403, Toronto, Ont. M5B 1N9
(416) 363-0321
General Counsel, A. Alan Borovoy
Administrative Co-ordinator, Helen Cainer

THE CANADIAN CLUB OF MONTREAL

(LE CERCLE CANADIEN DE MONTREAL)
Windsor Hotel, 1170 Peel St., Ste. 1121, Montreal, P.Q. H3B 2T4
(514) 861-0022

THE CANADIAN CLUB OF NEW YORK

One East Sixtieth St., New York, N.Y. 10022, U.S.A.
Plaza 3-6161
President, Reid Lighton
Club Secretary, Ms. Barbara Kalista

THE CANADIAN CLUB OF TORONTO

159 Bay St., #724, Toronto, Ont. M5J 1J7
(416) 364-5590
Secretary Treasurer, S.L. Rodway

CANADIAN COALITION FOR NUCLEAR RESPONSIBILITY

Box 236, Snowdon Stn., Montreal, P.Q. H3X 3T4
(514) 842-1471

CANADIAN COLLECTORS' ASSOCIATION

Representative: B.A. Yolleck, Ste. 305, 491 Eglinton Ave. W., Toronto, Ont. M5N 1A8 (416/487-7644)

INTERNATIONAL COLLECTORS' ASSOCIATION
Canadian Representative, B.A. Yolleck, Ste. 305, 491 Eglinton Ave. W., Toronto, Ont. M5N 1A8 (416/487-7644)

CANADIAN COMMITTEE ON THE STATUS OF WOMEN

Chairman, Ms. D. Flaherty, 200 Clearview Ave., Apt. 2326, Ottawa, Ont. K1Z 8M2 (613/722-5364)

CANADIAN COMMUNITY NEWSPAPERS ASSOCIATION

12 Shuter St., Ste. 201, Toronto, Ont. M5B 1A2
(416) 366-4277
Executive Director, Jim Dills

Provincial Associations

ALBERTA WEEKLY NEWSPAPERS ASSOCIATION
Bill Draayer, 11 Fairway Dr., #213, Edmonton, Alta. T6J 2W4 (403/436-1405)

ATLANTIC COMMUNITY NEWSPAPERS ASSOCIATION
Jim MacNeill, Box 790, Montague, P.E.I. C0A 1R0 (902/838-2515)

BRITISH COLUMBIA & YUKON COMMUNITY NEWSPAPERS ASSOCIATION
Mrs. Marge Dunning, #1004, 207 W. Hastings St., Vancouver, B.C. V6B 1H7 (604/684-4713)

MANITOBA COMMUNITY NEWSPAPERS ASSOCIATION
B. McCallum, #401, 280 Smith St., Winnipeg, Man. R3C 1K2 (204/942-8818)

ONTARIO WEEKLY NEWSPAPERS ASSOCIATION
E.C. Lydan, Box 451, Oakville, Ont. L6J 5A8 (416/844-0184)

QUEBEC
c/o OWNA, Box 451, Oakville, Ont. L6J 5A8

SASKATCHEWAN WEEKLY NEWSPAPERS ASSOCIATION
Don Telfer, Box 970, Humboldt, Sask. S0K 2A0

CANADIAN CONFERENCE OF CATHOLIC BISHOPS

(Conference des Eveques Catholiques du Canada)
90 Parent Ave., Ottawa, Ont. K1N 7B1
(613) 236-9461

The national association of the Roman Catholic Cardinals, Archbishops and Bishops of Canada.

General Secretaries, Rev. D. Murphy (English Sector); André Vallée, P.M.E. (French Sector)

CANADIAN CONFERENCE OF MOTOR TRANSPORT ADMINISTRATORS

1765 St. Laurent Blvd., Ottawa, Ont. K1G 3V4
(613) 526-0550
Executive Director, Jo-Anne Knight

CANADIAN CONGRESS FOR LEARNING OPPORTUNITIES FOR WOMEN (CCLOW)

29 Prince Arthur Ave., Toronto, Ont. M5R 1B2
(416) 964-0563

CANADIAN CONSTRUCTION ASSOCIATION

2nd floor, 85 Albert St., Ottawa, Ont. K1P 6A4
(613) 236-9455
President & Chief Executive Officer, Robert E. Nuth

Provincial & Major Cities Associations

ALBERTA CONSTRUCTION ASSOCIATION
10569 109 St., Box 3830, Stn. D, Edmonton, Alta. T5G 4J8, President, Gordon Alexander (403/420-0055)

ALBERTA ROADBUILDERS ASSOCIATION
10147-119 St., Edmonton, Alta. T5K 1Z1, Executive Director, R. M. McFarland (403/488-3363)

ASSOCIATION DES CONSTRUCTEURS DE ROUTES ET GRANDS TRAVAUX DU QUEBEC
435 Grande-Allée est, Quebec, P.Q. G1R 2J5, Directeur administratif, Jacques Guay (418/529-2949)

BRITISH COLUMBIA CONSTRUCTION ASSOCIATION
#208, 1999 Marine Dr., North Vancouver, B.C. V7P 3J3, President, P. Sorensen (604/984-9724)

BRITISH COLUMBIA ROADBUILDERS' ASSOCIATION
400-698 Seymour St., Vancouver, B.C. V6B 3K7, General Manager, D. W. Spooner (604/681-9251)

CALGARY CONSTRUCTION ASSOCIATION & CALGARY GENERAL CONTRACTORS ASSOCIATION
2540 5 Ave. N.W., Calgary, Alta. T2N OT5, Executive Director, R.M. Scrimgeour (403/283-5555)

THE CONSTRUCTION ASSOCIATION OF MONTREAL & THE PROVINCE OF QUEBEC
4970 Place de la Savane, Montreal, P.Q. H4P 1Z6, General Manager, Jacques Théoret (514/739-2381)

CONSTRUCTION ASSOCIATION OF NEW BRUNSWICK INC.
98 Prospect St., Box 1282, Fredericton, N.B. E3B 5C8, Executive Director, R. E. Porter (506/455-5770)

CONSTRUCTION ASSOCIATION OF NOVA SCOTIA
Box 1476, North Stn., Halifax, N.S. B3K 5H7, President, J.F. Rowe (902/429-6760)

CONSTRUCTION ASSOCIATION OF PRINCE EDWARD ISLAND
Box 728, Charlottetown, P.E.I. C1A 7L3, General Manager, Francis Reid (902/892-2072)

EDMONTON CONSTRUCTION ASSOCIATION
Box 3807, Stn. D, Edmonton, Alta. T5L 4J8, Executive Vice President, J.A. Norton (403/483-1130)

LA FEDERATION DE LA CONSTRUCTION DU QUEBEC
1045 Chemin Ste-Foy, Quebec, P.Q. G1S 2L8, General Manager & Executive Secretary, Michel Cliche (418/687-1992)

FREDERICTON CONSTRUCTION ASSOCIATION
Box 275, 20 Woodstock Rd., Fredericton, N.B. E3B 4Y9, Executive Director, Michael H. Ross (506/455-8871)

MANITOBA HEAVY CONSTRUCTION ASSOCIATION INC.
Box 86, St. James Postal Stn., Winnipeg, Man. R3J OH4, Manager, Harry Budgell (204/772-3375)

NEWFOUNDLAND & LABRADOR CONSTRUCTION ASSOCIATION
Box 8008, Stn. A, St. John's, Nfld. A1B 3M7, Manager, L. Rossiter (709/753-8920)

NEWFOUNDLAND & LABRADOR ROAD BUILDERS ASSOCIATION
Box 9381, Stn. B, St. John's, Nfld. A1A 2Y3, Manager, J. Seymour (709/722-3429)

NIAGARA CONSTRUCTION ASSOCIATION
Box 983, 34 Scott St., St. Catharines, Ont. L2R 6Z4, Manager, Mrs. Catharine Tribble (416/682-6661)

NOVA SCOTIA ROAD BUILDERS ASSOCIATION
Box 5125, Armdale, N.S. B3L 4M7, Secretary Treasurer, M. Thompson (902/455-8228)

ONTARIO GENERAL CONTRACTORS ASSOCIATION
Ste. 402, 15 Toronto St., Toronto, Ont. M5C 2E3 (416/360-1590), Executive Director, Bryn Lloyd

ONTARIO ROAD BUILDERS' ASSOCIATION
325 Eddystone Ave., Downsview, Ont. M3N 1H8, General Manager, M. F. Macdonald (416/743-1242)

OTTAWA CONSTRUCTION ASSOCIATION
196 Bronson Ave., Ottawa, Ont. K1R 6H4, General Manager, Wm. P. Becker (613/236-0488)

PRINCE EDWARD ISLAND ROADBUILDERS ASSOCIATION
Box 1901, Charlottetown, P.E.I. C1A 7N5, General Manager, F. W. Curtis (902/894-9514)

REGINA CONSTRUCTION ASSOCIATION
1935 Elphinstone, Regina, Sask. S4P 3B8, Secretary Manager, E.G. Smillie (306/352-2618)

ROAD BUILDERS' ASSOCIATION OF NEW BRUNSWICK
Box 1061, Fredericton, N.B. E3B 5C2, Secretary Manager, D. L. Forbes (506/454-5079)

ROAD BUILDERS & HEAVY CONSTRUCTION ASSOCIATION OF SASKATCHEWAN
Box 1757, Regina, Sask. S4P 3C6, Executive Director, D. A. Wagg (306/525-0171)

SASKATCHEWAN CONSTRUCTION ASSOCIATION
Box 1757, Regina, Sask. S4P 3C6, President, J. E. Chase (306/525-0171)

TORONTO CONSTRUCTION ASSOCIATION
1 Sparks Ave., Willowdale, Ont. M2H 2W1, Executive Director, J. Clifford Bulmer (416/499-4000)

WESTERN CANADA ROADBUILDERS ASSOCIATION
Box 1757, Regina, Sask. S4P 3C2, Executive Secretary, D.A. Wagg (306/525-0171)

THE WINNIPEG CONSTRUCTION ASSOCIATION
290 Burnell St., Winnipeg, Man. R3G 2A7, Executive Vice President, G. L. Greasley (204/774-2431)

YUKON CONTRACTORS ASSOCIATION
106 Lambert St., No. 2, Whitehorse, Y.T. Y1A 1Z2, Secretary, Mrs. Corinne Cyr (403/667-2451)

NORTHWEST TERRITORIES CONSTRUCTION ASSOCIATION
Box 1425, Hay River, N.W.T. XOE ORO, President, Harold Rattai (403/874-2491)

CANADIAN CO-OPERATIVE CREDIT SOCIETY

Box 800, Stn. U, Toronto, Ont. M8Z 5R2
(300 The East Mall, Toronto)
(416) 232-1262
Telex: 06 967677 – Cable: COOPCAN
Chief Executive Officer, George S. May
Affiliated with World Council of Credit Unions, Madison, Wisc. 53701

CANADIAN CO-ORDINATING COUNCIL ON DEAFNESS

55 Parkdale Ave., Ottawa, Ont. K1Y 1E5

(613) 728-0936
TTY: (613) 728-0954

The Council is an umbrella organization to enable the various local and provincial associations concerned with deafness and hard of hearing persons to better achieve their aims.

Provincial Councils:

NEWFOUNDLAND CO-ORDINATING COUNCIL ON DEAFNESS
Box 9125, St. John's, Nfld. A1A 2X3

CO-ORDINATING COUNCIL ON DEAFNESS OF NOVA SCOTIA
c/o School of Human Communication Disorders, Fenwick Tower, Dalhousie University, Halifax, N.S. B3H 1R2

PRINCE EDWARD ISLAND ASSOCIATION FOR THE HEARING IMPAIRED
Box 2063, Charlottetown, P.E.I. C1A 7N7

NEW BRUNSWICK CO-ORDINATING COUNCIL ON DEAFNESS
Box 182, Petit Rocher, N.B. E0B 2E0

QUEBEC CENTRE FOR THE HEARING IMPAIRED
c/o Institution des Sourds de Montreal, 7400 St-Laurent Blvd., Montreal, P.Q. H2R 2Y1

ONTARIO CO-ORDINATING COUNCIL FOR THE HEARING IMPAIRED
60 Bedford Rd., Toronto, Ont. M5R 2K2

MANITOBA CO-ORDINATING COUNCIL FOR THE HEARING IMPAIRED
Box 244, Stn. C, Winnipeg, Man. R3M 3S7

SASKATCHEWAN CO-ORDINATING COUNCIL ON DEAFNESS
2811 Assiniboine Ave., Regina, Sask. S4S 1E2

ALBERTA CO-ORDINATING COUNCIL ON DEAFNESS
Box 605, Edmonton, Alta. T5J 2K8

COUNCIL OF ORGANIZATIONS SERVING THE HEARING IMPAIRED OF BRITISH COLUMBIA
2125 W. 7th Ave., Vancouver, B.C. V6K 1X9

CANADIAN COPPER & BRASS DEVELOPMENT ASSOCIATION

55 York St., Toronto, Ont. M5J 1R7
(416) 363-8826
Executive Director, R. Wardell

CANADIAN COPYRIGHT INSTITUTE

#260, 86 Bloor St. W., Toronto, Ont. M5S 1M5
(416) 921-8478
Chairman, Dr. M.O. Edwardh

CANADIAN CORPS ASSOCIATION

201 Niagara St., Toronto, Ont. M5V 1C9
(416) 363-0694

Dominion Command Officers

President, E. V. Heesaker
Dominion Secretary, Mrs. S. Wood Heesaker

Provincial Command Officers

Ont.: President, D.G. Foster, 2323 Lakeshore Blvd. W., Apt. 803, Toronto, Ont. M8V 1B8
Que.: President, F. Blanchette, 4643 Colonial, Montreal, P.Q.
Western: President, N. Seabrook, 11157 102 St., Edmonton, Alta. T5G 2C9
Northern Command: President, R. Pickering, 446 Ryadon, Temiscaming, P.Q. JOZ 3RO
U.S. Command: President, Ray Fluker, 25010 Roan St., Warren, Mich. 48089

THE CANADIAN CORPS OF COMMISSIONAIRES

100 Gloucester St., Suite 503, Ottawa, Ont. K2P 0A4
(613) 236-4936
Patron-in-Chief, H. E. The Rt. Hon. Edward Schreyer
Chairman, Major A.E. Bruce
Secretary Treasurer, Lt. Col. J.E. de Hart

Affiliated Society

CANADIAN CORPS OF COMMISSIONAIRES (TORONTO & REGION)
80 Church St., Toronto, Ont. M5C 2G1
Commandant, Col. M.E. Rich (416/364-4496)

CANADIAN CORRUGATED CASE ASSOCIATION

Ste. 1400, One Yonge St., Toronto, Ont. M5E 1J9
(416) 363-7261

THE CANADIAN COUNCIL OF THE BLIND

National Office, 96 Ridout St. S., London, Ont. N6C 3X4 (519/434-4339)
Executive Director, Paul J. Chovancek

Number of clubs in Canada 91; as follows: Maritimes, 17; Nfld., 3; Que., 18; Ont., 32; Man., 2; Sask., 4; Alta., 3; B.C., 12

CANADIAN COUNCIL ON CHILDREN & YOUTH

323 Chapel St., Ottawa, Ont. K1N 7Z2
(613) 238-6520
Executive Director, Andrew Cohen

CANADIAN COUNCIL OF CHRISTIANS & JEWS

49 Front St. E., Toronto, Ont. M5E 1B3
(416) 364-3101
President, Victor C. Goldbloom, M.D.

Divisions

Pacific: 736 Granville St., Vancouver, B.C. V6Z 1G3 (604/684-6024), Director, Dr. Charles Paris
Western: 2nd floor, 110 11th Ave. S.E., Calgary, Alta. T2G OX6 (403/262-3354), Director, Robert Lucas
Central: 224 Phoenix Bldg., Winnipeg, Man. R3B 2J4 (204/943-9155), Director, Mrs. Olga Fuga
Ontario: 49 Front St. E., Toronto, Ont. M5E 1B3 (416/364-3101)
Quebec: 1010 St. Catherine St. W., Montreal, P.Q. (514/866-1929), Director, Michel Bravay
Atlantic: 1657 Barrington St., Halifax, N.S., Director, Brenda Taylor
Human Relations Library, 49 Front St. E., Toronto, Ont.

THE CANADIAN COUNCIL OF CHURCHES

40 St. Clair Ave. E., Toronto, Ont. M4T 1M9
(416) 921-4152
General Secretary, The Rev. Donald W. Anderson, S.T.B., M.A., Th.D.

CANADIAN COUNCIL OF ENGINEERING TECHNICIANS & TECHNOLOGISTS

Ste. 602, 350 rue Sparks St., Ottawa, Ont. K1R 7S8
(613) 238-8123
Executive Secretary, Dr. J.T. McCarthy

Provincial Affiliates:

ALBERTA SOCIETY OF ENGINEERING TECHNOLOGISTS
240 One Thornton Court, Edmonton, Alta. T5J 2E7
(403) 425-0626
Executive Director, Brian McCormack

THE SOCIETY OF ENGINEERING TECHNOLOGISTS OF BRITISH COLUMBIA
Ste. 203, 440 Dominion St., Burnaby, B.C. V5G 4G3
(604) 433-0548
Executive Director, J.E. Leech

THE MANITOBA SOCIETY OF CERTIFIED ENGINEERING TECHNICIANS & TECHNOLOGISTS
#5, 1767 Portage Ave., Winnipeg, Man. R3J OE7
(204) 885-2788
Registrar, Mrs. T. Whiteman

THE NEW BRUNSWICK SOCIETY OF CERTIFIED ENGINEERING TECHNICIANS & TECHNOLOGISTS
123 York St., Fredericton, N.B. E3B 3N6
(506) 454-6124
Registrar, H. Orville Scott

THE ASSOCIATION OF ENGINEERING TECHNICIANS & TECHNOLOGISTS OF NEWFOUNDLAND
Box 4202, St. John's, Nfld. A1C 5Z7
(709) 368-0685
Registrar, Lloyd Murchy

THE SOCIETY OF CERTIFIED ENGINEERING TECHNICIANS & TECHNOLOGISTS OF NOVA SCOTIA
Box 601, Halifax, N.S. B3J 2R7
(902) 443-0148
Registrar, G.E. MacDonald

THE ONTARIO ASSOCIATION OF CERTIFIED ENGINEERING TECHNICIANS & TECHNOLOGISTS
40 Orchard View Blvd., Ste. 253, Toronto, Ont. M4R 2G1
(416) 488-1175
Executive Director, P.W. Newman

THE PRINCE EDWARD ISLAND SOCIETY OF CERTIFIED ENGINEERING TECHNOLOGISTS
Box 1436, Charlottetown, P.E.I. C1A 7N1
(902) 892-6531
Registrar, Ross Barnes

LA CORPORATION PROFESSIONNELLE DES TECHNOLOGUES DES SCIENCES APPLIQUEES DU QUEBEC
4152 rue St-Denis, Montreal, P.Q. H2W 2M5
(514) 845-3247
Directeur général, Roméo Malenfant, t.s.

THE SOCIETY OF ENGINEERING TECHNICIANS & TECHNOLOGISTS OF SASKATCHEWAN
Ste. 220, 2220 12th Ave., Regina, Sask. S4P OM8
(306) 527-8266
Registrar, Reg. Bing-Wo

CANADIAN COUNCIL OF FURNITURE MANUFACTURERS

(Le Conseil Canadien des Fabricants de Meubles)
39 Elysée, Place Bonaventure, C.P. 1002, Montreal, P.Q. H5A 1E9
(514) 866-3631
General Manager, Claude Jutras

Provincial Associations

ONTARIO FURNITURE MANUFACTURERS ASSOCIATION
International Centre, 6900 Airport Rd., Mississauga, Ont. L4V 1E8
(416) 677-6561
General Manager, Ken Campbell

FURNITURE WEST
#96, 1313 Border St., Winnipeg, Man. R3H OX4
(204) 632-5529
Manager, J. Malko

QUEBEC FURNITURE MANUFACTURERS ASSOCIATION INC.
Box 1002, Place Bonaventure, Montreal, P.Q. H5A 1E9
(514) 866-3631
General Manager, Claude Jutras

CANADIAN COUNCIL FOR INTERNATIONAL CO-OPERATION

321 Chapel St., Ottawa, Ont. K1N 7Z2
(613) 236-4547
Executive Director, Richard Harmston

CANADIAN COUNCIL OF LAND SURVEYORS

#210, 14964 121A Ave., Edmonton, Alta. T5V 1A3
(403) 452-1856

ALBERTA LAND SURVEYORS' ASSOCIATION
Secretary Treasurer, G.K. Allred, A.L.S., #210, 14964 121A Ave., Edmonton, Alta. T5V 1A3 (403/452-7662)

CORPORATION OF LAND SURVEYORS OF THE PROVINCE OF BRITISH COLUMBIA
Secretary Treasurer, A.W. Burhoe, #101, 655 Douglas St., Victoria, B.C. V8V 2P9 (604/382-4323)

THE ASSOCIATION OF MANITOBA LAND SURVEYORS
Secretary Treasurer, E. Barrie Flower, Lower Level, 171 Donald St., Winnipeg, Man. R3C 1M4 (204/943-6972)

THE ASSOCIATION OF NEW BRUNSWICK LAND SURVEYORS
Secretary Treasurer, Ralph G. Brown, Box 22, Fredericton, N.B. E3B 4Y2 (506/454-2834)

ASSOCIATION OF NEWFOUNDLAND LAND SURVEYORS
Secretary Treasurer, Bob Power, Box 4155, St. John's, Nfld. A1C 5S5 (709/229-4358)

ASSOCIATION OF NOVA SCOTIA LAND SURVEYORS
Secretary Treasurer, G.E. Streb, 5450 Cornwallis St., Halifax, N.S. B3K 1A9 (902/423-2058)

ASSOCIATION OF ONTARIO LAND SURVEYORS
Executive Director, Lorraine Setterington, 6070 Yonge St., Willowdale, Ont. M2M 3Z3 (416/222-5482)

ASSOCIATION OF PRINCE EDWARD ISLAND LAND SURVEYORS
Secretary Treasurer, Brian Potter, Box 818, Charlottetown, P.E.I. C1A 7L9 (902/894-5531)

ORDRE DES ARPENTEURS-GEOMETRES DU QUEBEC
Secretary, J. Roland Pelletier, 917 Mgr. Grandin, Ste-Foy, Québec, P.Q. G1V 3X8 (418/656-0730)

SASKATCHEWAN LAND SURVEYORS' ASSOCIATION
Secretary Treasurer, M.R. Skelton, #5, 2700 Montague St., Regina, Sask. S4S 0J9 (306/584-9131)

THE CANADIAN COUNCIL OF PROFESSIONAL ENGINEERS

General Manager, Claude Lajeunesse, Ph.D., P. Eng., 116 Albert St., Suite 401, Ottawa, Ont. K1P 5G3 (613/232-2474)

Provincial Associations

THE ASSOCIATION OF PROFESSIONAL ENGINEERS, GEOLOGISTS & GEOPHYSICISTS OF ALBERTA
1010 One Thornton Court, Edmonton, Alta. T5J 2E7
(403) 426-3990
Executive Director & Registrar, A.C. Milroy, P. Eng.

ASSOCIATION OF PROFESSIONAL ENGINEERS OF BRITISH COLUMBIA
2210 W. 12th Ave., Vancouver, B.C. V6K 2N6
(604) 736-9808
Managing Director & Registrar, D. C. Lambert, P. Eng.

ASSOCIATION OF PROFESSIONAL ENGINEERS OF THE PROVINCE OF MANITOBA
#640, 175 Hargrave St., Winnipeg, Man. R3C 3R8
(204) 942-6481
Managing Director & Registrar, tba

THE ASSOCIATION OF PROFESSIONAL ENGINEERS OF NEW BRUNSWICK
123 York St., Fredericton, N.B. E3B 3N6
(506) 454-3296
Executive Director, Sheila W. McLeod

ASSOCIATION OF PROFESSIONAL ENGINEERS OF NEWFOUNDLAND
Box 8414, Postal Stn. A, St. John's, Nfld. A1B 3N7
(709) 753-7714
General Manager, Capt. John F. Power, C.D.

THE ASSOCIATION OF PROFESSIONAL ENGINEERS OF NOVA SCOTIA
Box 129, 1888 Brunswick St., #902, Halifax, N.S. B3J 2M4
(902) 429-2250
Executive Secretary Treasurer & Registrar, F.J. MacDonald, P.Eng.

THE ASSOCIATION OF PROFESSIONAL ENGINEERS OF ONTARIO
1027 Yonge St., Toronto, Ont. M4W 3E5
(416) 961-1100
Executive Director, A.C. Cagney, P.Eng.

ASSOCIATION OF PROFESSIONAL ENGINEERS OF PRINCE EDWARD ISLAND
Box 278, Charlottetown, P.E.I. C1A 4B1
(902) 892-9174
Secretary Registrar, D. C. Champion, P. Eng.

ORDRE DES INGENIEURS DU QUEBEC
1100/2075, rue University, Montréal, P.Q. H3A 1K8
(514) 845-6141
Directeur général, Jacques Soucy, ing.

THE ASSOCIATION OF PROFESSIONAL ENGINEERS OF SASKATCHEWAN
2220-12th Ave., Ste. 220, Regina, Sask. S4P 0M8
(306) 527-8266
Registrar, R. Bing-Wo, P. Eng.

ASSOCIATION OF PROFESSIONAL ENGINEERS OF YUKON TERRITORY
President, J.A. Cormie, P.Eng., Box 4125, Whitehorse, Y.T. Y1A 3S9 (403/667-6727)

CANADIAN COUNCIL FOR RACIAL HARMONY
-not confirmed for 1982-
Box 202, Stn. J, Toronto, Ont. M4J 4Y1
(416) 463-4246
Executive Director, J. Bhadauria

CANADIAN COUNCIL OF REHABILITATION WORKSHOPS
234 Adelaide St. E., Toronto, Ont. M5A 1M9
(416) 862-0970
Executive Director, Tom Stuckey

ONTARIO REHABILITATION WORKSHOP COUNCIL
same address and phone
Executive Director, Jack Amos

CANADIAN COUNCIL OF RESOURCE & ENVIRONMENT MINISTERS
60 Bloor St. W., Ste. 701, Toronto, Ont. M4W 3B8
Executive Director, R.G. Barrens

CANADIAN COUNCIL ON SMOKING & HEALTH
725 Churchill Ave., Ottawa, Ont. K1Z 5G7
(613) 722-3419
Executive Director, Kurt Baumgartner

THE CANADIAN COUNCIL ON SOCIAL DEVELOPMENT
Executive Director, T.M. Hunsley, Ottawa
Business Address, 55 Parkdale Ave., Box 3505, Stn. C, Ottawa, Ont. K1Y 4G1 (613/728-1865)

The Council, established in 1920, is a national association of organizations and individual citizens devoted to the development of sound and comprehensive social policies for Canada. It provides authoritative information and technical advice on income security, law and social development, housing, social planning and citizen participation, personal social services and health; conducts research; sponsors national and regional conferences, seminars and institutes on social issues, and provides a means of cooperative planning and action between public and private agencies. The policies and programs of the Council are determined by its members with the help of a nationally representative board of governors. Council publications include the bi-monthly, bilingual periodical *Perception,* a directory of Canadian welfare services, pamphlets and reports.

CANADIAN COUNCIL OF WAR VETERANS' ASSOCIATIONS
16 Kingslake Rd., Willowdale, Ont. M2J 3C9
(416) 491-2211
President, John E. Denniston
Executive Secretary, J. W. Trotter

Operating Camp Maple Leaf, Inc. (a free summer camp for underprivileged children), R.R. #1, Peterborough, Ont. Also operating Camp Maple Leaf Marina on Pigeon Lake, R.R. #1, Peterborough, Ont.

CANADIAN CROSSROADS INTERNATIONAL
National Office: 361 Windermere Rd., London, Ont. N6G 2K3
(519) 434-1148
Francophone Office: 3500 ave. Laval, Montréal, P.Q. H2X 3C8
(514) 844-7938

A service organization providing sponsorship to Canadians to learn through participation in development projects in Third World Countries, and sponsorship to Third World people to participate in development projects in Canada.

CANADIAN CULTURAL SOCIETY OF THE DEAF, INC.
1503, 360 Cumberland Ave., Winnipeg, Man. R3B 1T4
Executive Director, Forrest C. Nickerson

CANADIAN CYSTIC FIBROSIS FOUNDATION
161 Eglinton Ave. E., Ste. 503, Toronto, Ont. M4P 1J5
(416) 485-9149
President, M.R. Houghton
Secretary, Harry Brown
Executive Director, Cathleen Morrison

There are regional directors throughout Canada. Contact the above office for names and addresses.

CANADIAN DAILY NEWSPAPER PUBLISHERS ASSOCIATION
General Manager, J. E. Foy, 321 Bloor St. E., Ste. 214, Toronto, Ont. M4W 1E7 (416/923-3567)

CANADIAN DANCE TEACHERS ASSOCIATION
Room 25, 501 Yonge St., Toronto, Ont. M4Y 1Y4
(416) 924-7204
Secretary, L. Pastor

CANADIAN DIABETES ASSOCIATION
123 Edward St., Ste. 601, Toronto, Ont. M5G 1E2
(416) 593-4311
Executive Director, Mrs. Marie Virgin

CANADIAN DIAMOND DRILLING ASSOCIATION
#719, 74 Victoria St., Toronto, Ont. M5C 2A5
(416) 364-4680
Secretary Manager, David Holland

THE CANADIAN DIETETIC ASSOCIATION
Central Office, 7 Pleasant Blvd., Ste. 214, Toronto, Ont. M4T 1K2
(416) 925-2225
Executive Director, Eleanor Sortome

Provincial Associations

ALBERTA REGISTERED DIETITIANS ASSOCIATION
Box 3874, Stn. D, Edmonton, Alta. T5L 4K1
and
Box 2208, Stn. M, Calgary, Alta. T2P 2M4

BRITISH COLUMBIA DIETETIC ASSOCIATION
#B100, 1089 W. Broadway, Vancouver, B.C. V6H 2V3
(604) 732-3121

DIETETIC ASSOCIATION OF MANITOBA
#208, 93 Lombard Ave., Winnipeg, Man. R3B 3B1
(204) 943-3215

NEW BRUNSWICK DIETETIC ASSOCIATION
Box 321, Fredericton, N.B. E3B 4Y9

NEWFOUNDLAND DIETETIC ASSOCIATION
c/o President, Miss Carmel Bailey, Dietitian, St. Clare's Mercy Hospital, LeMarchant Rd., St. John's, Nfld. A1C 5B8

NOVA SCOTIA DIETETIC ASSOCIATION
Box 8841, Stn. A, Halifax, N.S. B3K 5M5

ONTARIO DIETETIC ASSOCIATION
234 Eglinton Ave. E., Ste. 402, Toronto, Ont. M4P 1K5

(416) 484-6818

PRINCE EDWARD ISLAND DIETETIC ASSOCIATION
Box 2575, Charlottetown, P.E.I. C1A 8C2
(902) 436-4760

CORPORATION PROFESSIONNELLE DES DIETETISTES DU QUEBEC
934 est, rue Ste-Catherine, bur. 240, Montreal, P.Q. H2L 2E9
(514) 842-7923

SASKATCHEWAN DIETETIC ASSOCIATION
c/o President, E.D. Misskey, 27 La Verendrye Way, Regina, Sask. S4S 5Z6

CANADIAN DIRECT MAIL/MARKETING ASSOCIATION
#405, 150 Consumers Rd., Willowdale, Ont. M2J 1P9
(416) 494-8585
President, Frank C. Ferguson

THE CANADIAN ECONOMICS ASSOCIATION
President, Prof. R.J. Wonnacott
Secretary Treasurer, Prof. Richard Arnott, Dept. of Economics, Queen's University, Kingston, Ont. K7L 3N6 (613/547-3122)
Organs "The Canadian Journal of Economics", "La Revue Canadienne d'économique", c/o Dept. of Economics, Univ. of B.C., Vancouver, B.C. V6T 1Y2; and, "Canadian Public Policy/Analyse de Politique," c/o Dept. of Economics, Univ. of Guelph, Guelph, Ont. N1G 2W1

CANADIAN ELECTRICAL ASSOCIATION
General Manager, D. C. Campbell, Ste. 580, One Westmount Sq., Montreal, P.Q. H3Z 2P9 (514/937-6181)

CANADIAN ELECTRICAL DISTRIBUTORS ASSOCIATION (CEDA INC.)
Executive Director & Secretary, S.G. Wild, 620 Wilson Ave., Ste. 250, Downsview, Ont. M3K 1Z3 (416/636-2792)

CANADIAN ENVIRONMENTAL LAW ASSOCIATION
8 York St., Fifth Floor South, Toronto, Ont. M5J 1R2
(416) 366-9717
Director of Litigation, Grace Patterson
Counsel, Robert Timberg, Toby Vigod

CANADIAN EXECUTIVE SERVICE OVERSEAS
1130 Sherbrooke St. W., Montreal, P.Q. H3A 2M8
(514) 282-0556

CANADIAN EXPORT ASSOCIATION
President, T.M. Burns
Secretary, J. D. Moore, Ste. 250, 99 Bank St., Ottawa, Ont. K1P 6B9 (613/238-8888)

CANADIAN FARM & INDUSTRIAL EQUIPMENT INSTITUTE
720 Guelph Line, #307, Burlington, Ont. L7R 4E2
(416) 632-8483
General Manager, Brent M. Hamre

CANADIAN FASTENERS INSTITUTE
14th floor, One Yonge St., Toronto, Ont. M5E IJ9
(416) 363-7261
Attn.: J.A. Rankin

THE CANADIAN FEDERATION OF BUSINESS & PROFESSIONAL WOMEN'S CLUBS
Head Office, 56 Sparks St., Room 308, Ottawa, Ont. K1P 5A9
(613) 234-7619

CANADIAN FEDERATION OF CHEFS DE CUISINE
c/o National Treasurer, M. Beaulieu, 220 Lucerne, Rosemere, P.Q. J7B 1A4 (514/430-0613)

CANADIAN FEDERATION OF FARM EQUIPMENT DEALERS
Box 288, North Battleford, Sask. S9A 2M4

Affiliated Societies

FARM EQUIPMENT DEALERS' ASSOCIATION OF ALBERTA & BRITISH COLUMBIA
Ste. G, 3801 21st St. N.E., Calgary, Alta. T2E 6T5
(403) 277-7581

ASSOCIATION DES MARCHANDS DE MACHINES ARATOIRES DE LA PROVINCE DE QUEBEC
11 Dutch Ave., Bedford, P.Q. JOJ 1AO
(514) 248-7946

ONTARIO RETAIL FARM EQUIPMENT DEALERS' ASSOCIATION
3601 Lawrence Ave. E., Scarborough, Ont. M1G 1P5
(416) 439-3726

SASKATCHEWAN-MANITOBA IMPLEMENT DEALERS' ASSOCIATION
#10, 2602 8th St. E., Saskatoon, Sask. S7H OV7
(306) 373-8755

CANADIAN FEDERATION OF FILM SOCIETIES
Box 484, Stn. A, Toronto, Ont. M5W 1E4
Chairman, Arne Ljungstrom (416/449-3143)

THE CANADIAN FEDERATION OF HUMANE SOCIETIES
101 Champagne St., Ottawa, Ont. K1S 4P3
(613) 728-2516
Patron, The Governor General of Canada
Executive Director, Neal Jotham

ALBERTA S.P.C.A.
Ste. A, 12231 Fort Rd., Edmonton, Alta. T5B 4H2
(403) 471-2020

BRITISH COLUMBIA S.P.C.A.
#218, 470 Granville St., Vancouver, B.C. V6C 1V5
(604) 681-7271

CANADIAN S.P.C.A.
5215 Jean Talon W., Montreal, P.Q. H4P 1X4
(514) 735-2711

ONTARIO HUMANE SOCIETY
8064 Yonge St., Thornhill, Ont. L4J 1W3
(416) 226-9555

TORONTO HUMANE SOCIETY
111 River St., Toronto, Ont. M5A 4C2
(416) 362-2273
Executive Director & Secretary Treasurer, John E. Ridout

NOVA SCOTIA S.P.C.
5737 McCully St., Halifax, N.S. B3K 1R2
(902) 454-5824

SASKATCHEWAN S.P.C.A.
518 Ave. K. South, Saskatoon, Sask. S7M 2E2
(306) 652-7212

CANADIAN FEDERATION FOR THE HUMANITIES
151 Slater St., Ste. 415, Ottawa, Ont. K1P 5H3
(613) 238-6112
Executive Director, Viviane Launay-Elbaz

CANADIAN FEDERATION OF INDEPENDENT BUSINESS
4141 Yonge St., #100, Willowdale, Ont. M2P 2A6
(416) 222-8022
President, John Bulloch

CANADIAN FEDERATION OF INSURANCE AGENTS & BROKERS ASSOCIATIONS

General Manager, F. G. Funston, Ste. 1306, 69 Yonge St., Toronto, Ont. M5E 1K3 (416/367-1831)

Affiliated Society

INDEPENDENT INSURANCE AGENTS & BROKERS OF ONTARIO
67 Yonge St., Ste. 633, Toronto, Ont. M5E 1J8 (416/364-4475)
General Manager, K.W. Martin

Other Provincial Associations

INSURANCE BROKERS' ASSOCIATION OF ALBERTA
#200, 10240 124 St., Edmonton, Alta. T5N 3W6
(403) 482-6340
Secretary Manager, Frank Easton

INSURANCE AGENTS ASSOCIATION OF BRITISH COLUMBIA
325 Howe St., Vancouver, B.C. V6C 2A3
(604) 683-8471
Secretary Manager, J.L. Lewis

INSURANCE AGENTS' ASSOCIATION OF MANITOBA, INC.
#301A, 310 Donald St., Winnipeg, Man. R3B 2H4
(204) 943-4709

INSURANCE BROKERS' ASSOCIATION OF QUEBEC/ASSOCIATION DES COURTIERS D'ASSURANCES DE LA PROVINCE DE QUEBEC
300 Leo Pariseau, Ste. 801, Montreal, P.Q. H2W 2N1
(514) 842-2591
Directeur Général, Charles Thibault

INSURANCE AGENTS ASSOCIATION OF SASKATCHEWAN
#8, 2700 Montague St., Regina, Sask. S4S 0J9
(306) 586-7177
Secretary Manager, K.E. Anderson

CANADIAN FEDERATION OF RETAIL GROCERS

Box 336, Peterborough, Ont. K9J 6G1
(705) 742-6684
President, K.V. Gadd

CANADIAN FERTILIZER INSTITUTE

350 Sparks St., Ste. 602, Ottawa, Ont. K1R 7S8
(613) 238-8121
President, R. W. Neal

Regional Affiliates

MARITIME PLANT FOOD PRODUCERS
Box 2920, Charlottetown, P.E.I. C1A 8C5 (902/894-7303)

THE FERTILIZER INSTITUTE OF ONTARIO
#203, Dixie Plaza, 1250 South Service Rd., Mississauga, Ont. L5E 1V4 (416/274-2870)

QUEBEC FERTILIZER INC.
c/o Agrex Advertising Inc., 4080 Wellington St., #11, Montreal, P.Q. H4G 1V4 (514/761-4548)

WESTERN CANADA FERTILIZER ASSOCIATION
724 Oakhill Place S.W., Calgary, Alta. T2V 3X9 (403/281-6345)

CANADIAN FIBREBOARD TECHNICAL COMMITTEE

55 York St., Suite 512, Toronto, Ont. M5J 1S2
(416) 363-8374
Chairman, Jacques Grignon
Secretary, F. Young

CANADIAN FILM EDITORS GUILD

Box 46, Stn. A, Toronto, Ont. M5W 1A2
(416) 485-3222
President, Brian Ravok, cfe

CANADIAN FILM INSTITUTE

(Institut Canadien du Film)
#911, 75 Albert St., Ottawa, Ont. K1P 5E7
(613) 238-6748
President, Judith Crawley
Executive Director, Frederik Manter

CANADIAN FILM & TELEVISION ASSOCIATION

8 King St. E., #1505, Toronto, Ont. M5C 1B5
(416) 363-0296
General Manager, John Teeter

CANADIAN FIRE SAFETY ASSOCIATION

1750 Finch Ave. E., Willowdale, Ont. M2N 5T7
(416) 424-1295
President, Gerry Landmesser

CANADIAN FLUID POWER ASSOCIATION

One Yonge St., Ste. 1400, Toronto, Ont. M5E 1J9
(416) 363-7261
Attn.: Ms. Sue Jones

CANADIAN FOLK ARTS COUNCIL

263 Adelaide St. W., 5th Floor, Toronto, Ont. M5H 1Y2
(416) 977-8311
Director General, Leon Kossar

Le Conseil canadien des arts populaires

1499 de Bleury, Ste. 200, Montreal, P.Q. H3A 2H5
(514) 844-2551
Co-Director General, Guy Landry

Members of CFAC/CCAP

Canadian Folk Society, Vancouver, B.C.
Alberta Folk Arts Council
Multicultural Council of Saskatchewan
Manitoba Heritage & Folk Arts Council
Ontario Folk Arts Council
Regroupement des organismes nationaux loisirs du Québec
New Brunswick Folk Arts Council
Nova Scotia Folk Arts Council
Multicultural Association of Nova Scotia (MANS)
Prince Edward Island Multicultural Council
Newfoundland & Labrador Multicultural & Folk Arts Council

CANADIAN FOOD BROKERS ASSOCIATION

50 River St., Toronto, Ont. M5A 3N9
(416) 364-2134
President, Ian C. Kennedy

CANADIAN FOOD PROCESSORS ASSOCIATION

1409, 130 Albert St., Ottawa, Ont. K1P 5G4
(613) 233-4049
Executive Vice President, E.T. Banting

CANADIAN FORESTERS LIFE INSURANCE SOCIETY

84 Market St., Brantford, Ont. N3T 2Z7
(519) 753-3461
President, G.E. Short
Executive Vice President & General Manager, A.R. Davis
Vice President, Administration, J.N. Jepson
Vice President, Investments, R.L. Williamson
Vice President, Marketing, W.R. Shepherd
Controller, J.W. Shaddick
Actuary, Marlene L. Anderson

CANADIAN FORESTRY ASSOCIATION

A Federation of Provincial Forestry Assns.
Executive Director, A. D. Hall, 185 Somerset St. W., Ottawa, Ont. K2P 0J2 (613/232-1815)

Provincial Associations

ALBERTA FORESTRY ASSOCIATION
Manager, Greg P. Stevens, 311 Alberta Block, 10526 Jasper Ave., Edmonton, Alta. T5J 1Z7 (403/428-7582)

CANADIAN FORESTRY ASSOCIATION OF BRITISH COLUMBIA
General Manager, R. H. Lyster, 1200 W. Pender St., Room 410, Vancouver, B.C. V6E 2S9 (604/683-7591)

CANADIAN FORESTRY ASSOCIATION OF NEW BRUNSWICK
Executive Director, J. B. Kelly, 43 Brunswick St., Fredericton, N.B. E3B 1G5 (506/455-8372)

MANITOBA FORESTRY ASSOCIATION
Secretary Manager, Dianne Beaven, 900 Corydon Ave., Winnipeg, Man. R3M 0Y4 (204/453-3182)

NEWFOUNDLAND FOREST PROTECTION ASSOCIATION
Chairman, Education Committee, Richard Sparkes, Dept. of Forest Resources & Lands, 6th Floor, Atlantic Place, St. John's, Nfld. A1C 5T7 (709/737-3245)

NOVA SCOTIA FORESTRY ASSOCIATION
Secretary Manager, Gordon Maybee, R.R. 1, Debert, N.S. B0M 1G0 (902/662-3193)

ONTARIO FORESTRY ASSOCIATION
Executive Vice President, J. D. Coats, Rm. 209, 150 Consumers Rd., Willowdale, Ont. M2J 1P9 (416/493-4565)

QUEBEC FORESTRY ASSOCIATION
Director General, Albert Roy, 915 St. Cyrille St. W., Quebec, P.Q. G1S 1T8 (418/681-3588)

SASKATCHEWAN FORESTRY ASSOCIATION
Manager, Don MacKinnon, 692 Cuelenaere St., Prince Albert, Sask. S6V 2S9 (306/763-2189)

CANADIAN FORGINGS ASSOCIATION
One Yonge St., Ste. 1400, Toronto, Ont. M5E 1J9
(416) 363-7261
Manager, J.A. Rankin

CANADIAN FOUNDRY ASSOCIATION
Box 2270, Orillia, Ont. L3V 6S1
(705) 326-3895
Executive Vice President, J.L. Reade

CANADIAN 4-H COUNCIL
323 Chapel St., Ottawa, Ont. K1N 7Z2
(613) 232-7108
General Manager, B.M. Shane

Federal & Provincial Directors
Alta.: Irene M. Leavitt, Dept. of Agriculture, Edmonton, Alta.
B.C.: Dave Freed, B.C. Ministry of Agriculture, Summerland, B.C.
Man.: Bill Martin, Man. Dept. of Agriculture, Winnipeg, Man.
N.B.: Michel Gauthier, Dept. of Agriculture & Rural Development, Fredericton, N.B.
Nfld.: Mervie Ford, Dept. of Tourism, St. John's, Nfld.
N.S.: Jack Redden, N.S. Dept. of Agriculture & Marketing, Truro, N.S.
Ont.: Janet Horner, Ont. Ministry of Agriculture & Food, Toronto, Ont.
P.E.I.: Gwyneth Jones, P.E.I. Dept. of Agriculture & Forestry, Charlottetown, P.E.I.
Que.: Ann Louise Carson, Extension Division, Macdonald College, P.Q.
Sask.: Patricia Katz, University of Saskatchewan, Saskatoon, Sask.
Federal: W.G. Robinson, Agriculture Canada, Ottawa, Ont.

THE CANADIAN FRATERNAL ASSOCIATION
Secretary Treasurer, A. Stewart, 789 Don Mills Rd., Don Mills, Ont. M3C 1T9 (416/429-3000, ext. 211)

CANADIAN FREIGHT ASSOCIATION
Western Headquarters: #1100, 215 Garry St., Winnipeg, Man. R3C 3P3 (204/942-3488), Chairman, K.W. Juvonen
Eastern Headquarters: 1162 Ste. Antoine St. W., Montreal, P.Q. H3C 1B5 (514/861-8331), Chairman, P.J. Lavallée

CANADIAN FROZEN FOOD ASSOCIATION
130 Albert St., Ste. 1409, Ottawa, Ont. K1P 5G4
(613) 233 9400
Executive Director, C.J. Kyte

CANADIAN FOUNDATION FOR ILEITIS & COLITIS
National Office: 294 Spadina Ave., Toronto, Ont. M5T 2E7
(416) 366-2776
Executive Director, D.E. Scott
Chapters in most major cities in Canada.

CANADIAN FOUNDATION FOR THE STUDY OF INFANT DEATHS
181 Belsize Dr., Toronto, Ont. M4S 1L9
(416) 488-3260
National Co-ordinator, Mrs. Peggy Lyons

CANADIAN GAS ASSOCIATION
55 Scarsdale Rd., Don Mills, Ont. M3B 2R3
(416) 447-6465; Telex: 06 966824
President, D.E. Alderson

CANADIAN GAS PROCESSORS ASSOCIATION
-not confirmed for 1982-
#102, 118 4th Ave. S.W., Calgary, Alta. T2P 0H3
(403) 232-5836

CANADIAN GAS RESEARCH INSTITUTE
55 Scarsdale Rd., Don Mills, Ont. M3B 2R3
(416) 447-6465; Telex: 06 966824
President, W.H. Dalton

CANADIAN GEMMOLOGICAL ASSOCIATION
Box 1106, Stn. Q, Toronto, Ont. M4T 2P2
(416) 362-2436

CANADIAN GIFT & TABLEWARE ASSOCIATION
68 Carnforth Rd., Toronto, Ont. M4A 2K7
(416) 497-5771

CANADIAN GEOTECHNICAL SOCIETY
700 EIC Bldg., 2050 Mansfield St., Montreal, P.Q. H3A 1Z2
(514) 842-8121
Staff Representative, Moira F. Meddings

CANADIAN GIRLS IN TRAINING (CGIT)
40 St. Clair Ave. E., #200, Toronto, Ont. M4T 1M9
(416) 961-2036
Chairperson, (National Association), Miss Mary-Lou Funston

CANADIAN GOLF SUPERINTENDENTS ASSOCIATION
698 Weston Rd., Ste. 32, Toronto, Ont. M6N 3R3
(416) 767-2550
President, Randy Scott

CANADIAN GROCERY BAG MANUFACTURERS ASSOCIATION
116 Albert St., Ste. 710, Ottawa, Ont. K1P 5G3
(613) 232-2406
Executive Secretary, Jacques Chevalier

CANADIAN GROCERY DISTRIBUTORS' INSTITUTE
#410, 750 boul. Laurentien, Montreal, P.Q. H4M 2M4
(514) 747-6566
President, R.C. Bertrand

CANADIAN HARDWARE & HOUSEWARES MANUFACTURERS' ASSOCIATION
411 Guildwood Pkwy., Scarborough, Ont. M1E 1R3
(416) 284-7911
Executive Director, P.J. Risdon

CANADIAN HARDWOOD PLYWOOD ASSOCIATION

27 Goulburn Ave., Ottawa, Ont. K1N 8G7
(613) 233-6205
Secretary, J.F. McCracken

THE CANADIAN HEARING SOCIETY

(Non Profit) Services for the Deaf and Hard of Hearing.
Head Office: 60 Bedford Rd., Toronto, Ont. M5R 2K2 (416/964-9595) TTY 964-2066
Executive Director, Denis Morrice

Regional Offices

127 Bayfield St., Barrie, Ont. L4M 3B3 (705/737-3190, voice or TTY)
Box 882, #105, 143 Wellington St. W., Chatham, Ont. N7M 5L3 (519/354-9347, voice or TTY)
402A Concession St., Hamilton, Ont. L9A 1B7 (416/389-1353, TTY 389-2724)
15 Ocean Ave. W., Kenora, Ont. P9N 3P1 (807/468-7230)
(Recreation Centre, Bagot St.) Box 1101, Kingston, Ont. K7L 4Y5 (613/544-1927, TTY 544-2765)
396 Queen's Ave., Ste. 102, London, Ont. N6B 1X7 (519/433-0169, TTY 433-1920)
71 Bank St., 4th Floor, Ottawa, Ont. K1P 5N2 (613/236-0509, TTY 236-0902)
St. Joseph's Hospital, 384 Rogers St., Peterborough, Ont. K9H 7B6 (705/743-1573, TTY 743-1621)
137 Wellington St., 2nd Floor, Sarnia, Ont. N7T 1G4 (519/337-8307, voice or TTY)
473 Queen St. E., 2nd Floor, Sault Ste. Marie, Ont. P6A 1A7 (705/256-6505, voice or TTY)
174 Larch St., Ste. 301, Sudbury, Ont. P3E 1C6 (705/675-7151, TTY 675-1722)
135 N. Syndicate Ave., Ste. 203, Thunder Bay, Ont. P7C 3V3 (807/622-5141, TTY 622-1295)
Waterloo: 1342 King St. E., Kitchener, Ont. N2G 2N7 (519/744-6811, TTY 744-6901)
1082 Wyandotte St. E., Windsor, Ont. N9A 3K2 (519/253-7241, TTY 254-1704)
1453 Prince Rd., Windsor Western Hospital, Windsor, Ont. N9A 3Z4 (519/253-6102)

CANADIAN HEART FOUNDATION

1 Nicholas St., Ste. 1200, Ottawa, Ont. K1N 7B7
(613) 237-4361
Executive Director, E. McDonald

Provincial Heart Foundations

BRITISH COLUMBIA HEART FOUNDATION
1212 W. Broadway, Vancouver, B.C. V6H 3V2
(604) 736-4404

ALBERTA HEART FOUNDATION
2011 10th Ave. S.W., Calgary, Alta. T3C 0K4
(403) 244-0786

SASKATCHEWAN HEART FOUNDATION
279 3rd Ave. N., Saskatoon, Sask. S7K 2H8
(306) 244-2124

MANITOBA HEART FOUNDATION
301 Canada Bldg., 352 Donald St., Winnipeg, Man. R3B 2H8
(204) 942-0195

ONTARIO HEART FOUNDATION
576 Church St., Toronto, Ont. M4Y 2S1
(416) 962-3600

QUEBEC HEART FOUNDATION
1455 Peel St., Ste. M-31, Montreal, P.Q. H3A 1T5
(514) 288-8141

NOVA SCOTIA HEART FOUNDATION
408 Roy Bldg., Box 1585, Halifax, N.S. B3J 2Y3
(902) 423-7530

NEW BRUNSWICK HEART FOUNDATION
28 Germain St., Saint John, N.B. E2L 2E5
(506) 657-2062

CANADIAN HEART FOUNDATION, NEWFOUNDLAND DIVISION
152 Water St., Box 5819, St. John's, Nfld. A1C 5X3
(709) 753-8521

CANADIAN HEART FOUNDATION, PRINCE EDWARD ISLAND DIVISION
Box 279, Charlottetown, P.E.I. C1A 7K4
(902) 894-8297

CANADIAN HEMOPHILIA SOCIETY

National Office, Chedoke Centre, Patterson Bldg. (Box 2085, Hamilton, Ont. L8N 3R5) (416/387-2677)
President, Ken Poyser (Edmonton)
Executive Director, (vacant)
Chapters in all provinces with elected presidents. Contact national office for up to date names and addresses.

WORLD FEDERATION OF HEMOPHILIA
President, Frank L. Schnabel, 1170 Peel St., Room 1126, Montreal, P.Q. H3B 2T4 (514/866-0442)

THE CANADIAN HERITAGE OF QUEBEC

2025 Peel St., Montreal, P.Q. H3A 1T6
President, C.J.G. Molson (514/481-5796)

THE CANADIAN HISTORICAL ASSOCIATION

c/o Public Archives of Canada, Ottawa, Ont. K1A 0N3 (613/233-7885)
English Secretary, Norman Hillmer
French Secretary, Andrée Lévesque

Affiliated Societies

Alta. Historical Society, H. A. Dempsey, Editor, Alta. History, 95 Holmwood Ave., Calgary, Alta. T2K 2G7 (403/289-8149)
American Antiquarian Society, 185 Salisbury St., Worcester, Mass. 01609 (617/755-5221)
American Geographical Society, Broadway at 156th St., New York, N.Y. 10032 (212/234-8100)
Archives of Anglican Provincial Synod of B.C., 6050 Chancellor Blvd., Vancouver, B.C. V6T 1X3 (604/228-9031, loc. 59)
Finnish Canadian Historical Society, President, Leo Raaska, Box 911, Sudbury, Ont. P3E 4S4
Glenbow-Alta. Institute, 9th Ave. & 1st St. S.E., Calgary, Alta. T2G 0P3 (403/264-8300)
Heritage Canada, Box 1358, Stn. B, Ottawa, Ont. K1P 5R4
Hudson Historical Society, Box 802, Hudson, P.Q. J0P 1H0
Kent Historical Society, Bert Wees, Secretary, R.R. #1, Chatham, Ont. N7M 5J1 (519/352-6672)
Lake St. Louis Historical Society, Box 1024, Stn. A, Montreal, P.Q. H3C 2W9
Lennox & Addington Historical Society, James Eadie, 165 Union St., Napanee, Ont.
Literary & Historical Society of Quebec, Box 399, Quebec, P.Q. G1R 4R2 (418/694-9147)
Minnesota Historical Society, 690 Cedar St., St. Paul, Minn. 55101 (612/296-6126)
N.S. Historical Society, Box 895, Armdale, N.S. B3G 4K5
The Ont. Historical Society, 1466 Bathurst St., Toronto, Ont. M5R 3J3 (416/536-1353)
Sask. History & Folklore Society, c/o J.L. Constantine, 448 29th St. E., Prince Albert, Sask. S6V 1Y7
La Société d'archéologie et de numismatique de Montréal, 280 est, rue Notre-Dame, Montréal, P.Q. H2Y 1C5
La Société historique de la Côte-Nord, 43 Mance, Baie-Comeau, P.Q. G4Z 2H1 (418/296-5561, loc. 53)
La Société historique de la Côte du Sud, Col. de Ste-Anne, La Pocatière, Kamouraska, P.Q. G0R 1Z0
La Société historique de la Gaspésie, C.P. 680, Gaspé, P.Q. G0C 1R0 (418/368-5710)
La Société historique du Nouvel-Ontario, Roger Lavoie, Université de Sudbury, Sudbury, Ont. P3E 2C6 (705/673-5661)
La Société historique du Saguenay, Archiviste, Roland Bélanger, C.P. 456, Chicoutimi, P.Q. G7H 5C8
La Société historique de Saint-Boniface, C.P. 125, Saint Boniface, Man. R2H 3B4

Toronto Historical Board, c/o BGen. J.A. McGinnis, Managing Director, Stanley Barracks, Exhibition Place, Toronto, Ont. M6K 3C3 (416/595-1567)

Univ. of Iowa Libraries, Serials Dept., Iowa City, Iowa 52242 U.S.A.

Women's Wentworth Historical Society, c/o Mrs. W.A. Freeman, President, 39 Binkley Cres., Hamilton, Ont.

York Pioneer & Historical Society, c/o Janet H. Watt, President, Box 481, Stn. K, Toronto, Ont. M4P 2G9

Yukon Historical & Museums Association, Box 4357, Whitehorse, Yukon

THE CANADIAN HOME ECONOMICS ASSOCIATION

151 Slater St., Ottawa, Ont. K1P 5H3
(613) 232-9791

CANADIAN HOSTELLING ASSOCIATION

(Association Canadienne de L'Ajisme)
National Office: 333 River Rd., Vanier, Ont. K1L 8B9
(613) 746-0060

Regional Offices

Nfld.—Box 1815, St. John's, Nfld. A1C 5P9 (709/753-8603)

P.E.I.—Box 1718, Charlottetown, P.E.I. C1A 7N4 (902/894-7700)

N.S.—5516 Spring Garden Rd. (Box 3010 South, Halifax, N.S. B3J 1G6) (902/425-5450)

The Trail Shop Co-operative Ltd.—6260 Quinpool Rd., Halifax, N.S. B3L 1A3 (902/423-8736)

Que.—1320 Sherbrooke St. W., Montreal, P.Q. H3G 1H9 (514/842-9048)

Ont.—8 York St., 2nd floor, Toronto, Ont. M5J 1R2 (416/368-1848)

National Capital—#109, 150 Metcalfe St., Ottawa, Ont. K2P 1P1 (613/233-7738)

Ont. Great Lakes—8 York St., Toronto, Ont. M5J 1R2 (416/368-1848)

Man.—1700 Ellice Ave., Winnipeg, Man. R3H 0B1 (204/786-5641)

Sask.—2205 Victoria Ave., Regina, Sask. S4P 0S4 (306/522-3651)

Alta. & North West—10926 88th Ave., Edmonton, Alta. T6G 0Z1 (403/432-7798)

Mountain—#203, 1414 Kensington N.W., Calgary, Alta. T2N 3P9 (403/283-5551)

B.C.—3425 W. Broadway, Vancouver, B.C. V6R 2B4 (604/736-2674)

B.C. Pack & Boots Shop—3425 W. Broadway, Vancouver, B.C. V6R 2B4 (604/738-3128)

B.C. Pack & Boots Shop—#10, 720 Yates Mall, Victoria, B.C. V8W 1L5 (604/383-2144)

Yukon—Box 4762, Whitehorse, Y.T. Y1A 4N6 (403/667-4471)

CANADIAN HOUSEHOLD GOODS CARRIERS' TARIFF BUREAU ASSOCIATION

222 Dixon Rd., Weston, Ont. M9P 3S5
(416) 243-3443
Executive Vice President & General Manager, W. D. McConnell

CANADIAN HOUSEWIVES REGISTER

Betty Dalgliesh, 399 Sunset Dr., Oakville, Ont. L6L 3N3 (416/827-6196)

CANADIAN HOUSING DESIGN COUNCIL

Executive Director, Peter S. van Es, C.M.H.C. National Office, Montreal Rd., Ottawa, Ont. K1A 0P7 (613/748-2515/6)

CANADIAN HUNGER FOUNDATION

323 Chapel St., Ottawa, Ont. K1N 7Z2
(613) 237-0180
Executive Director, John Laidlaw

A non-profit development organization. It is the official non-government representative in Canada of the Freedom from Hunger Campaign of the United Nations Food & Agriculture Organization.

CANADIAN IMPORTERS ASSOCIATION INC.

World Trade Centre, 60 Harbour St., Toronto, Ont. M5J 1B7
Phone: (416) 862-0002
Cable Address: "IMPORTANT", Toronto
Telex: 065-24115
Telecopier: (416) 862-0665
President, Keith G. Dixon

CANADIAN INDEPENDENT RECORD PRODUCTION ASSOCIATION

144 Front St. W., Ste. 330, Toronto, Ont. M5J 2L7
(416) 593-4545

CANADIAN INDUSTRIAL ADVERTISERS

Secretary Treasurer, Lincoln Whiffen, c/o Urban Associates, 940 Main St. W., Hamilton, Ont. L8S 1B1 (416/525-7168)

CANADIAN INDUSTRIAL COMMUNICATIONS ASSEMBLY

15 Toronto St., #702, Toronto, Ont. M5C 2E3
(416) 362-4500

CANADIAN INDUSTRIAL SUGAR USERS

1185 Eglinton Ave. E., Ste. 101, Don Mills, Ont. M3C 3C6
(416) 429-1004
Co-Ordinating Secretary, S.K. Watanabe

THE CANADIAN INDUSTRIAL TRAFFIC LEAGUE

General Manager, Thos. J. McTague, 67 Yonge St., Suite 708, Toronto, Ont. M5E 1J8 (416/863-1944)

CANADIAN INFANTRY ASSOCIATION

Honorary Secretary Treasurer, Col. L.E. Barclay, C.D., Box 2303, Ottawa, Ont. K1P 5W5 (613/232-2242)

CANADIAN INFORMATION PROCESSING SOCIETY

243 College St. W., 5th floor, Toronto, Ont. M5T 2Y1
(416) 593-4040
Executive Secretary, Mrs. M. J. Hart
Branches in Calgary, Edmonton, Fredericton, Halifax, Hamilton, Kingston, Kitchener-Waterloo, London, Montreal, Nanaimo, Ottawa, Regina, Saint John, N.B., St. John's, Nfld., Saskatoon, Toronto, Vancouver, Victoria and Winnipeg.

CANADIAN INSTITUTE OF ACTUARIES

(Institut Canadien des Actuaires)
275 Slater St., #1505, Ottawa, Ont. K1P 5H9
Secretary, Claude Genest

CANADIAN INSTITUTE OF CERTIFIED ADMINISTRATIVE MANAGERS

One St. Clair Ave. E., #605, Toronto, Ont. M4T 2V7
(416) 960-8234
President, A.E. Ballantyne, C.A.M., C.I.A., M.C.I.

INSTITUTE OF CERTIFIED ADMINISTRATIVE MANAGERS OF ONTARIO

One St. Clair Ave. E., #605, Toronto, Ont. M4T 2V7
(416) 675-7500
President, A.S. Best, C.A.M. (675-7500)

TORONTO CHAPTER, INSTITUTE OF CERTIFIED ADMINISTRATIVE MANAGERS

Box 5145, Term. A, Toronto, Ont. M5W 1N4
President, Eric Brueggemann, C.A.M. (296-8571)

CANADIAN INSTITUTE OF COST REDUCTION

2468 Wyndale Cres., Ottawa, Ont. K1H 7A6

(613) 731-0900
Director, James V. Thoppil

CANADIAN INSTITUTE OF FOOD SCIENCE & TECHNOLOGY

Ste. 38, 46 Elgin St., Ottawa, Ont. K1P 5K6
(613) 233-8992
Executive Director, A.H.M. Greene

CANADIAN INSTITUTE OF FORESTRY

Manager, A. G. Racey, Box 5000, Macdonald College, P.Q. H9X 1C0 (514/457-9131)

CANADIAN INSTITUTE OF HYPNOTISM

Medical Towers Bldg., 3465 Cote des Neiges, #51, Montreal, P.Q. H3H 1T7
(514) 937-4488
Executive Director, M. Kershaw
Executive Secretary, Mrs. J. Rigaud

CANADIAN INSTITUTE OF INTERNATIONAL AFFAIRS

15 King's College Circle, Toronto, Ont. M5S 2V9
(416) 979-1851

A non-profit organization in the field of public education, with specific relation to international affairs and Canada's role in the world.

President, Clarence Shepard, Q.C.
Executive Director, Jacques Rastoul

CANADIAN INSTITUTE OF MANAGEMENT

Administrator, H. L. Taylor, C.I.M., P. Mgr., 2175 Sheppard Ave. E., Ste. 110, Willowdale, Ont. M2J 1W8 (416/493-0155)

THE CANADIAN INSTITUTE OF MINING & METALLURGY

Executive Director, G.F. Skilling
Secretary Treasurer, John Robertson, #400, 1130 Sherbrooke St. W., Montreal, P.Q. H3A 2M8 (514/842-3461)

CANADIAN INSTITUTE FOR ORGANIZATION MANAGEMENT

Conducted by the Canadian Chamber of Commerce in co-operation with the Institute of Association Executives.
Director, Roger Stanion
Administrator, Bill Eggertson, #710, 1080 Beaver Hall Hill, Montreal, P.Q. H2Z 1T2 (514/866-4334)

CANADIAN INSTITUTE OF PARAPSYCHOLOGY

85A Seyton Dr., Ottawa, Ont. K2H 8Y7
(613) 820-8419
President, Dr. J.P. Rae
Secretary, Dr. B.W. Fearon

CANADIAN INSTITUTE OF PLANNERS

46 Elgin St., Ste. 30, Ottawa, Ont. K1P 5K6
(613) 233-2105

CANADIAN INSTITUTE OF PLUMBING & HEATING

#414 Parkview Sq., 5468 Dundas St. W., Islington, Ont. M9B 6E3
(416) 232-2600
President, L. G. Ecroyd

THE CANADIAN INSTITUTE OF PUBLIC HEALTH INSPECTORS

#206, 1330 15 Ave. S.W., Calgary, Alta. T3C 3N6
(403) 245-0680
Executive Secretary Treasurer, Lilli Anne Zahara, C.P.H.I.(C), R.S.

CANADIAN INSTITUTE OF PUBLIC REAL ESTATE COMPANIES

#2806, 390 Bay St., Toronto, Ont. M5H 2Y2
(416) 863-0471
Executive Director, M.A. Galway

CANADIAN INSTITUTE OF QUANTITY SURVEYORS

Ste. 704A, 43 Eglinton Ave. E., Toronto, Ont. M4P 1A2
(416) 485-4850
President, Harland C. Lindsay

NOVA SCOTIA ASSOCIATION OF QUANTITY SURVEYORS

Box 8774, Stn. A, Halifax, N.S. B3K 5M4
Chairman, L. White

ONTARIO INSTITUTE OF QUANTITY SURVEYORS

Ste. 704A, 43 Eglinton Ave. E., Toronto, Ont. M4P 1A2
(416) 485-4850
President, Eric R. Foster

QUANTITY SURVEYORS OF QUEBEC INC.

8285 Mountain Sights, Ste. 204, Montreal, P.Q. H4P 2B3
(514) 737-8877
Chairman, M. Caputo

ASSOCIATION OF QUANTITY SURVEYORS OF ALBERTA

c/o Derek A. Sanft, Maxam Contracting Ltd., #100, 3016 10th Ave. N.E., Calgary, Alta. T2A 6A3
Chairman, J. Pettie

QUANTITY SURVEYORS SOCIETY OF BRITISH COLUMBIA

1250 Homer St., Vancouver, B.C. V6B 2Y5
(604) 681-0296
President, R. Wells

CANADIAN INSTITUTE OF RELIGION & GERONTOLOGY

296 Lawrence Ave. E., Toronto, Ont. M4N 1T7
(416) 483-1879
Executive Director, Sister St. Michael Guinan

CANADIAN INSTITUTE OF STEEL CONSTRUCTION

201 Consumers Rd., Suite 300, Willowdale, Ont. M2J 4G8
(416) 491-4552
Chairman of the Board, J.G. Marshall
President, H.A. Krentz

THE CANADIAN INSTITUTE OF SURVEYING

Executive Manager, J.B. O'Neill, "The Canadian Surveyor", Box 5378, Stn. F, Ottawa, Ont. K2C 3J1 (613/224-9851)
Chairman, Editorial Committee, L. Sebert

CANADIAN INSTITUTE OF TIMBER CONSTRUCTION

100 Bronson Ave., Ottawa, Ont. K1R 6G8
(613) 234-9456
Executive Director, D. R. Douglas

CANADIAN INSTITUTE OF TRAFFIC & TRANSPORTATION

44 Victoria St., #515, Toronto, Ont. M5C 1Y2
(416) 363-5696
General Manager, B.A. Parkin, Toronto

CANADIAN INTERNATIONAL FREIGHT FORWARDERS ASSOCIATION INC.

Box 156, Place d'Armes, Montreal, P.Q. H2Y 3E9
(514) 697-2111
Secretary Manager, George A. Sloan

CANADIAN ITALIAN BUSINESS & PROFESSIONAL ASSOCIATION OF TORONTO

750 Oakdale Rd., #54, Downsview, Ont. M3N 2Z4
(416) 743-7730
President, Vito Giovannetti

General Manager, Robert Dante Martella

CANADIAN JEWELLERS ASSOCIATION

General Manager, Wm. Basztyk, Royal York Hotel, 100 Front St. W., Toronto, Ont. M5J 1E3 (416/368-8372)

THE CANADIAN KENNEL CLUB

2150 Bloor St. W., Toronto, Ont. M6S 4V7
(416) 763-4391

CANADIAN KITCHEN CABINET ASSOCIATION

(Association Canadienne des Cabinets de Cuisine)
80 Flaming Roseway, Willowdale, Ont. M2N 5W8
(416) 226-0642
Executive Vice President, P.E. Woodger

CANADIAN LABOUR CONGRESS

2841 Riverside Dr., Ottawa, Ont. K1V 8X7
(613) 521-3400

The Canadian Labour Congress (CLC) is Canada's major national trade union centre, representing more than 100 affiliated national and international unions with a total membership of 2.3 million. Its principal role is to represent the interests of its affiliates—and workers in general—on the national level.

The CLC charters 12 federations of labour (one in each province and one each in the Yukon and the Northwest Territories) and 120 community labour councils. These bodies concern themselves particularly with matters respectively within the jurisdiction of their province or their community.

Internationally, the CLC plays a prominent role in both the International Labor Organization (a tripartite UN agency) and the International Confederation of Free Trade Unions.

President, Dennis McDermott
Secretary Treasurer, Donald Montgomery
Executive Vice Presidents, Shirley G.E. Carr; Julien Major

Departmental Directors

Organization, Ed. Johnston
Education, Larry Wagg
Research & Legislation, Ronald W. Lang
International Affairs, John Harker

Departmental Co-ordinators

Political Education Department, Patrick Kerwin
Public Relations Department, Charles Bauer
Social & Community Programs, Jim MacDonald
Union Label Trades & Services Department, Secretary Treasurer, Rhéal Bastien
Production Manager, Myles Hayes

Regional Directors

Pacific: Director of Organization, W.V. Smalley; Director of Education, Art Kube, Office: 228, 4925 Canada Way, Burnaby, B.C. V5G 1M1
Prairie: Director of Organization, E. W. Norheim; Director of Education, A. Walker. Office: 2709 12th Ave., Ste. 107, Regina, Sask. S4T 1J3
Ont.: Director of Organization, Ralph Ortlieb; Director of Education, Jim Brechin, 206, 15 Gervais Drive, Don Mills, Ont. M3C 1Y8
Que.: Regional Director of Organization, Jean-Jacques Jauniaux, 2112 Frontenac St., 2nd floor, Montreal, P.Q. H2K 2Z3
Atl.: Director of Organization, Allister MacLeod, 96 Norwood Ave., Ste. 208, Moncton, N.B. E1C 6L9 (506/389-9805); Director of Education, J. H. Stafford, Box 6951, Stn. A, 133 Prince William St., Saint John, N.B. E2L 4S4

Provincial Federations of Labour with Secretaries

Alta.: E. A. Mitchell, #306, 11010-142 St., Edmonton, Alta. T5N 2R1 (403/451-0810)
B.C.: Dave MacIntyre, 3110 Boundary Rd., Burnaby, B.C. V5M 4A2
Man.: J. A. Coulter, #104, 570 Portage Ave., Winnipeg, Man. R3C 0G4
N.B.: John Thebeau, Box 524, 96 Norwood Ave., Moncton, N.B. E1C 6L9 (506/382-0804)
Nfld. & Labrador: Austin Thorne, Box 6114, St. John's, Nfld. A1C 5X8 (709/754-1660)
N.S.: Leo McKay, #313, 6074 Lady Hammond Rd., Halifax, N.S. B3K 2R7 (902/454-6735)
N.W.T.: Ms. Jo Showalter, Box 969, Yellowknife, N.W.T. X0E 1H0
Ont.: Terry Meagher, #202, 15 Gervais Drive, Don Mills, Ont. M3C 1Y8 (416/441-2731)
P.E.I.: S. Hennessey, Box 185, One Jordon Cres., Charlottetown, P.E.I. C1A 7K6 (902/892-7331)
Que.: Fernand Daoust, 1290 St-Denis St., 5th Floor, Montreal, P.Q. H2X 3J7 (514/288-7431)
Sask.: Dave Maki, 2709-12th Ave., Room 103, Regina, Sask. S4T 1J3
Yukon: Angela Dornian, 106 Strickland St., Whitehorse, Yukon Y1A 2J5

OFFICIAL PUBLICATION

"Canadian Labour", 2841 Riverside Dr., Ottawa, Ont. K1V 8X7

Member Unions in the Canadian Labour Congress

Amalgamated Clothing & Textile Workers Union, #601, 15 Gervais Dr., Don Mills, Ont. M3C 1Y8
Amalgamated Transit Union, 3400 Riverspray Cres., Apt. 1106, Mississauga, Ont. L4Y 3M5
American Federation of Grain Millers, 46 Guildford Ct., London, Ont. N6J 3Y1
American Federation of Musicians of the U.S. & Canada, #404, 86 Overlea Blvd., Toronto, Ont. M4H 1C6
Association of Canadian Television & Radio Artists, 105 Carlton St., Toronto, Ont. M5B 1M2
Bakery, Confectionery & Tobacco Workers' International Union, 58 Danby Ave., Downsview, Ont. M3H 2J5
Brotherhood of Maintenance of Way Employees, 1708 Bank St., Ottawa, Ont. K1V 7Y6
Brotherhood of Railroad Signalmen, #505, 130 Slater St., Ottawa, Ont. K1P 5H6
Brotherhood of Railway, Airline & Steamship Clerks, Freight Handlers, Express & Station Employees, #690, 2085 Union Ave., Montreal, P.Q. H3A 2C3
Brotherhood of Railway Carmen of the U.S. & Canada, 286 Randill St., Chateauguay, P.Q. J6J 2P3
Canadian Actors' Equity Association, 64 Shuter St., Toronto, Ont. M5B 2G7
Canadian Air Line Dispatchers' Association, 19 Sparklett Cres., Brampton, Ont. L6Z 1M7
Canadian Air Line Employees' Association, 6455 Northam Dr., Mississauga, Ont. L4V 1J2
Canadian Air Line Flight Attendants' Association, Ste. 860, 1200 W. Broadway, Vancouver, B.C. V6P 6G5
Canadian Brotherhood of Railway, Transport & General Workers, 2300 Carling Ave., Ottawa, Ont. K2B 7G1
Canadian Marine Officers' Union, 9670 Notre Dame St. E., Montreal, P.Q. H1L 3P8
Canadian Merchant Service Guild, 1150 Morrison Dr., Ottawa, Ont. K2H 8S9
Canadian Paperworkers Union, 1155 Sherbrooke St. W., 15th floor, Montreal, P.Q. H3A 2N3
Canadian Seafood Workers' Union, R.R. 1, Lunenburg, N.S. B0J 2C0
Canadian Union of Postal Workers, 280 Metcalfe St., Ottawa, Ont. K2P 1R7
Canadian Union of Public Employees, 21 Florence St., Ottawa, Ont. K2P 0W6
Canadian Union of United Brewery, Flour, Cereal, Soft Drink & Distillery Workers, #311, 255 Morningside Ave., West Hill, Ont. M1E 3E6
Communications Workers of Canada, 301, 25 Cecil St., Toronto, Ont. M5T 1N1
Distillery, Rectifying, Wine & Allied Workers' International Union of America, 11 Monette St., Delson, P.Q. J0L 1G0
Energy & Chemical Workers' Union, #44, 9912 100 St., Edmonton, Alta. T5K 1C5

Fédération des Auteurs et des Artistes du Canada, 1290 St. Denis St., 6th floor, Montreal, P.Q. H2X 3J7
Grain Services Union, Rm. 202, 1810 Albert St., Regina, Sask. S4P 2S8
Graphic Arts International Union, #600, 1110 Finch Ave. W., Toronto, Ont. M3J 2T2
Hotel & Restaurant Employees' & Bartenders' International Union, 1410 Stanley St., Ste. 500, Montreal, P.Q. H3A 1P8
International Alliance of Theatrical Stage Employees & Moving Picture Machine Operators of U.S. & Canada, 69 Weir St. S., Hamilton, Ont. L8K 3A5
International Association of Bridge, Structural & Ornamental Iron Workers, 212 King St. W., Suite 216, Toronto, Ont. M5H 1K5
International Association of Fire Fighters, #906, 233 Gilmour St., Ottawa, Ont. K2P OP2
International Association of Heat & Frost Insulators & Asbestos Workers, 71 Rossander Crt., Scarborough, Ont. M1J 2B6
International Association of Machinists & Aerospace Workers, #400, 287 MacLaren St., Ottawa, Ont. K2P OL9
International Association of Siderographers, 47 Larkspur Dr., Ottawa, Ont. K2H 6K8
International Brotherhood of Boilermakers, Iron Ship Builders, Blacksmiths, Forgers & Helpers, 2 Dunbloor Rd., #107, Islington, Ont. M9A 2E4
International Brotherhood of Electrical Workers, Ste. 401, 45 Sheppard Ave. E., Willowdale, Ont. M2N 5Y1
International Brotherhood of Firemen & Oilers, 1434 St. Catherine St. W., Suite 305, Montreal, P.Q. H3G 1R3
International Brotherhood of Painters & Allied Workers, 9 Aspen Ave., Toronto, Ont. M4B 2Z1
International Brotherhood of Pottery & Allied Workers, 737 Millwood Rd., Toronto, Ont. M4G 1V7
International Federation of Professional & Technical Engineers, #1203, 5 Tangreen Crt., Willowdale, Ont. M2M 3Z1
International Jewelry Workers' Union, R.R. #3, Belleville, Ont. K8N 4Z3
International Ladies' Garment Workers' Union, 307, 333 Chabanel St. W., Montreal, P.Q. H2N 2H2
International Leather Goods, Plastics & Novelty Workers' Union, #301, 7200 Hutchison St., Montreal, P.Q. H3N 1Z2
International Longshoremen's & Warehousemen's Union, 2681 E. Hastings St., Vancouver, B.C. V5K 1Z5
International Longshoremen's Association, 20 Flamingo Dr., Halifax, N.S. B3M 1S7
International Molders' & Allied Workers' Union, 951 Dufferin St., Toronto, Ont. M6H 4B3
International Plate Printers', Die Stampers, & Engravers' Union of North America, Box 347, Old Colony Rd., Manotick, Ont. KOA 2NO
International Printing & Graphic Communications Union, 15 Gervais Dr., Room 605, Don Mills, Ont. M3C 1Y8
International Typographical Union, 40 Athabaska Ave., Willowdale, Ont. M2M 2T7
International Union of Allied Novelty & Production Workers, 147-149 E. 26th St., New York, N.Y. 10010
International Union of Bricklayers & Allied Craftsmen, 226 Queen St. W., Toronto, Ont. M5V 1Z6
International Union of Electrical, Radio & Machine Workers, 15 Gervais Dr., 5th floor, Don Mills, Ont. M3C 1Y8
International Union of Elevator Constructors, 22 Montcalm Blvd. S., Candiac, P.Q. J5R 3M5
International Union of Operating Engineers, 706-200 Consumers Rd., Willowdale, Ont. M2J 4R4
International Woodworkers of America, 1285 W. Pender St., 5th Floor, Vancouver, B.C. V6E 4B2
Labourers' International Union of North America, Ste. 105, 1210 Sheppard Ave. E., Willowdale, Ont. M2K 2S5
Letter Carriers' Union of Canada, 887 Richmond Rd., Ottawa, Ont. K2A OG8
Marine Workers' Federation, Box 175, Dartmouth, N.S. B2Y 3Y3
Maritime Fishermen's Union, Box 506, Richibucto, N.B. E0A 2M0
Metal Polishers, Buffers, Platers & Helpers International Union, #822 105 Rowena Dr., Don Mills, Ont. M3A 1R3
National Association of Broadcast Employees & Technicians, c/o Ste. 735, 1010 St. Catherine St. W., Montreal, P.Q. H3B 3R3
National Union of Provincial Government Employees, #200, 265 Carling Ave., Ottawa, Ont. K1S 2E1
Components:
Alta. Union of Provincial Employees, 10975 124 St., Edmonton, Alta. T5M OJ2
B.C. Government Employees Union, 4911 Canada Way, Burnaby, B.C. V5G 3W3
Man. Government Employees Association, 360 McMillan Ave., Winnipeg, Man. R3L 0N2
Nfld. Association of Public Employees, Box 1085, St. John's, Nfld. A1C 5M5
N.S. Government Employees' Association, Box 5300, Sydney, N.S.
Ontario Liquor Control Board Union, 3063 Southcreek Rd., Mississauga, Ont. L4X 2E9
Ontario Public Service Employees Union, 1901 Yonge St., Toronto, Ont. M4S 2Z5
P.E.I. Public Service Association Inc., Box 1116, Enman Cres., R.R. 7, Charlottetown, P.E.I. C1A 7M8
Sask. Government Employees Association, 1440 Broadway, Regina, Sask. S4P 1E2
Office & Professional Employees' International Union, 1290 St-Denis St., Suite 26, Montreal, P.Q. H2X 3J7
Pattern Makers' League of North America, 1589 Kelly, St. Sauveur des Monts, P.Q. J0R 1R0
Public Service Alliance of Canada, 1100-233 Gilmour St., Ottawa, Ont. K2P 0P2
Retail, Wholesale & Department Store Union, 15 Gervais Dr., Room 310, Don Mills, Ont. M3C 1Y8
Seafarers' International Union of Canada, 634 St. Jacques St. W., Montreal, P.Q. H3C 1E7
Service Employees' International Union, #1400, 67 Yonge St., Toronto, Ont. M5E 1P5
Sheet Metal Workers' International Association, #260, 7851 Jarry St. E., Ville d'Anjou, P.Q. H1J 2C3
Shipyard General Workers' Federation of B.C., 1219 Nanaimo St., Vancouver, B.C. V5L 4T5
Telecommunications Workers Union, 5261 Lane St., Burnaby, B.C. V5H 4A6
The Newspaper Guild, #2028, 1755 Courtwood Cres., Ottawa, Ont. K2C 3J2
United Association of Journeymen & Apprentices of the Plumbing & Pipe Fitting Industry of the U.S. & Canada, 310 Broadway, Suite 702, Winnipeg, Man. R3C 0S6
United Automobile, Aerospace & Agricultural Implement Workers of America International Union, 205 Placer Court, Willowdale, Ont. M2H 3H9
United Brotherhood of Carpenters & Joiners of America, 1235 40th Ave. N.W., Calgary, Alta. T2K 0G3
United Cement, Lime & Gypsum Workers' International Union, 34 Burton St., Belleville, Ont. K8P 1E6
United Electrical, Radio & Machine Workers of America, 10 Codeco Court, Don Mills, Ont. M3A 1A2
United Fishermen & Allied Workers' Union, 138 E. Cordova St., Vancouver, B.C. V6A 1K9
United Food & Commercial Workers International Union, #305, 15 Gervais Dr., Don Mills, Ont. M3C 1Y8
United Garment Workers of America, 59 Kushner Cres., Winnipeg, Man. R2P OP2
United Glass & Ceramic Workers of North America, 408 Royal York Rd., Toronto, Ont. M8Y 2R5
United Hatters', Cap & Millinery Workers' International Union, #301, 7200 Hutchinson St., Montreal, P.Q. H3N 1Z2
United Mine Workers of America, District 26, Box 129, Commercial Bldg., Glace Bay, N.S. B1A 5V2; District 18, 224-9th Ave. S.W., Room 401, Calgary, Alta. T2P 1K2
United Paperworkers' International Union, 57 Cleaveholm Dr., Georgetown, Ont. L7G 3E3
United Rubber, Cork, Linoleum & Plastic Workers of America, 2249 Yonge St., Suite 301, Toronto, Ont. M4S 2B1

United Steelworkers of America, 55 Eglinton Ave. E., 8th floor, Toronto, Ont. M4P 1P5
United Telegraph Workers, 501 Yonge St., Ste. 20, Toronto, Ont. M4Y 1Y4
United Textile Workers of America, 4377 Notre Dame St. W., Montreal, P.Q. H4C 1R9
United Transportation Union, #709, 99 Bank St., Ottawa, Ont. K1P 6B9
Upholsterers' International Union of North America, 7330 Chateaubriand, Montreal, P.Q. H2R 2L6

CANADIAN LEAGUE FOR THE LIBERATION OF UKRAINE

140 Bathurst St., Toronto, Ont. M5V 2R3
(416) 366-9350

CANADIAN LIFE & HEALTH INSURANCE ASSOCIATION INC.

(Association canadienne des compagnies d'assurances de personnes inc.)

20 Queen St. W., #2500, Toronto, Ont. M5H 3S2 (416/977-2221)
666 ouest, rue Sherbrooke, Montréal, P.Q. H3A 1E7 (514/845-6173)
Executive Vice President, Gerald M. Devlin, Q.C.
Senior Vice President, Frank C. Dimock
Secretary, Kent G. Cook

THE CANADIAN LINGUISTIC ASSOCIATION

(Association canadienne de Linguistique)

Founded in 1954 with the aim of advancing the scientific study of linguistics and language in Canada.
Publication, "The Canadian Journal of Linguistics/La Revue canadienne de Linguistique", (semi-annual).
Secretary, D. Wilson, Queen's Univ., Kingston, Ont. K7L 3N6 (613/547-3180)

CANADIAN LUMBER STANDARDS ADMINISTRATIVE BOARD

#1475, 1055 W. Hastings St., Vancouver, B.C. V6E 2E9
(604) 684-0211, loc. 285
Manager, Norm Midtdal

CANADIAN LUMBERMEN'S ASSOCIATION

Executive Director, J. F. McCracken, 27 Goulburn Ave., Ottawa, Ont. K1N 8C7 (613/233-6205)

CANADIAN LUNG ASSOCIATION

75 Albert St., Ste. 908, Ottawa, Ont. K1P 5E7
(613) 237-1208
Executive Director, E.S. Hershfield, M.D.

Provincial Associations

BRITISH COLUMBIA LUNG ASSOCIATION
906 W. Broadway, Vancouver, B.C. V5Z 1K7
(604) 731-4961

ALBERTA LUNG ASSOCIATION
10618 124 St., Edmonton, Alta. T5N 3X4
(403) 482-6527

SASKATCHEWAN LUNG ASSOCIATION
Fort San, Sask. SOG 1TO
(306) 332-5985

MANITOBA LUNG ASSOCIATION
2nd floor, 629 McDermot Ave., Winnipeg, Man. R3A 1P6
(204) 774-5501

ONTARIO LUNG ASSOCIATION
157 Willowdale Ave., Willowdale, Ont. M2N 4Y7
(416) 221-3483

ASSOCIATION PULMONAIRE DU QUEBEC
264 rue Chénier, Québec, P.Q. G1K 1R2
(418) 524-4254

NEW BRUNSWICK LUNG ASSOCIATION
123 York St., #3, Fredericton, N.B. E3B 5E3
(506) 455-8961

NOVA SCOTIA LUNG ASSOCIATION
17 Alma Cres., Fairview, Halifax, N.S. B3N 2C4
(902) 443-8141

PRINCE EDWARD ISLAND LUNG ASSOCIATION
Provincial Sanatorium, Charlottetown, P.E.I. C1A 2K1
(902) 894-7331

NEWFOUNDLAND TB & RD ASSOCIATION
Box 5250, St. John's, Nfld. A1C 5W1
(709) 726-4664

YUKON TB & HEALTH ASSOCIATION
Box 4754, Whitehorse, Y.T. Y1A 4N6
(403) 667-7462

CANADIAN MACHINE BUILDERS' ASSOCIATION

President, J. Havlik, 695 Bishop St., Box 3430, Cambridge (Preston), Ont. N3H 4V2
Toronto phone: (416) 364-6208

CANADIAN MANAGEMENT CENTRE OF AMA/ INTERNATIONAL

100 University Ave., #303, Toronto, Ont. M5J 1V6
(416) 593-4600

THE CANADIAN MANUFACTURERS' ASSOCIATION

One Yonge St., Toronto, Ont. M5E 1J9
(416) 363-7261
President & Executive Director, Roy A. Phillips
Vice President & Secretary, W.D.H. Frechette
Ottawa Representative, L. Albert Deschamps, #812, La Promenade Bldg., 151 Sparks St., Ottawa, Ont. (613/233-8423)

Divisions

Alta.: Ed Benson, Manager, #227 One Thornton Ct., Jasper Ave. at 99 St., Edmonton, Alta. T5J 2E7 (403/426-6622)
B.C.: Frank S. Kenny, Manager, 608 Marine Bldg., 355 Burrard St., Vancouver, B.C. V6C 2G8 (604/685-8131)
Man.-Sask.: John L.R.S. Ross, Manager, 408 Power Bldg., 428 Portage Ave., Winnipeg, Man. R3C OE2 (204/942-5467)
N.B.-P.E.I.: Gerald R. Cluney, Manager, Ste. 312, 236 St. George St., Moncton, N.B. E1C 1W1 (506/389-1591)
N.S.-Nfld.: Peter O'Brien, Manager, Ste. 510, 1888 Brunswick St., Halifax, N.S. B3J 3J8 (902/422-4477)
Ont.: V.R. Denholm, Manager, One Yonge St., Toronto, Ont. M5E 1J9 (416/363-7261)
Que.: Claude Dessureault, Executive Officer, Ste. 904, 1080 Beaver Hall Hill, Montreal, P.Q. H2Z 1S8 (514/866-7774)

CANADIAN MANUFACTURERS OF CHEMICAL SPECIALTIES ASSOCIATION

Ste. 710, 116 Albert St., Ottawa, Ont. K1P 5G3
(613) 232-6616
Executive Director, Jacques Chevalier

CANADIAN MASONRY CONTRACTORS' ASSOCIATION

#201, 1013 Wilson Ave., Downsview, Ont. M3K 1G1
(416) 636-6778
Executive Director, W. N. Fraser

Affiliated Societies

ONTARIO MASONRY CONTRACTORS' ASSOCIATION
METRO MASON CONTRACTORS ASSOCIATION
CANADA MASONRY CENTRE
Address and Executive Director as above

CANADIAN MEAT COUNCIL

(Conseil des Viandes du Canada)
General Manager, D.M. Adams

A/Secretary, L.M. Campbell, 5233 Dundas St. W., Islington, Ont. M9B 1A6 (416/239-8411)

CANADIAN MEDIA DIRECTORS' COUNCIL

Secretary Treasurer, S. Bonfield, c/o Needham, Harper & Steers of Canada Ltd., 130 Adelaide St. W., Toronto, Ont. M4P 3P5 (416/364-1492)

CANADIAN MEDIC-ALERT FOUNDATION INC.

176 St. George St., Toronto, Ont. M5R 2N1 (416/923-2451)
A Medical identification service. International 24 hour emergency toll-free switch board, 209-634-4917.
Managing Director, G.G. Jarvis

CANADIAN MENTAL HEALTH ASSOCIATION

(L'Association canadienne pour la santé mentale)
2160 Yonge St., Toronto, Ont. M4S 2Z3
(416) 484-7750
General Director, George Rohn

Provincial Executive Directors

Alta.: #201B, 10711-107th Ave., Edmonton, Alta. T5H OW6 (403/426-6665)
B.C.: Ronald Brown, 692 E. 26th Ave., Vancouver, B.C. V5V 2H7 (604/873-1633)
Man.: William Martin, 330 Edmonton St., Winnipeg, Man. R3B 2L2 (204/942-3461)
N.B.: Ken Ross, 43 Brunswick St., Fredericton, N.B. E3B 1G5 (506/455-5231)
Nfld.-Labrador: R.J. Vardy, Box 5788, 93 Water St., St. John's, Nfld. A1C 5X3 (709/753-8550)
N.W.T.: Box 2580, Yellowknife, N.W.T. X0E 1H0 (403/873-3190)
N.S.: Andrew J. Crook, 5739 Inglis St., Halifax, N.S. B3H 1K5 (902/422-5800)
Ont.: Howard Richardson, 8 Pailton Cres., 2nd floor, Toronto, Ont. M4S 2H8 (416/487-5361)
P.E.I.: Allan James, Box 785, 57 Queen St., Charlottetown, P.E.I. C1A 4A5 (902/894-9952)
Que.: P.-M. Gélinas, 550 Sherbrooke St. W., Suite 1080, Montreal, P.Q. H3A 1B9 (514/849-3291)
Sask.: Huntley Schaller, 1810 Albert St., Regina, Sask. S4P 2S8 (306/525-5601)

CANADIAN METEOROLOGICAL & OCEANOGRAPHIC SOCIETY

-not confirmed for 1982-
6325 103 St., Edmonton, Alta. T6H 5H6
President, Dr. J. Maybank
Corresponding Secretary, P.J. Kociuba (403/437-1250)
Publication: "Atmosphere–Ocean" (quarterly)
Local centres at Halifax, Quebec, Montreal, Rimouski, Ottawa, Toronto, Winnipeg, Regina-Saskatoon, Edmonton-Calgary, Vancouver, and Victoria.

CANADIAN METRIC ASSOCIATION

Box 35, Fonthill, Ont. L0S 1E0
(416) 358-0171 (office); 892-3800 (res.)
Secretary, A. J. Mettler
President & Editor, J.B. Reid, Toronto phone 960-3288

CANADIAN MICROGRAPHIC SOCIETY

Box 6084, Stn. J, Ottawa, Ont. K2A 1T1
(613) 233-1701
Administrative Secretary, A. Currie

CANADIAN MOTHERCRAFT SOCIETY

32 Heath St. W., Toronto, Ont. M4V 1T3
(416) 920-3515
President, Martin Rabinovitch

CANADIAN MOTION PICTURE DISTRIBUTORS ASSOCIATION

#1703, 22 St. Clair Ave. E., Toronto, Ont. M4T 2S4
(416) 961-1888
Executive Director, Millard S. Roth

CMPDA Division Film Boards

MARITIME FILM BOARD
President, Don McKelvie, c/o Universal Films, 77 Germain St., Saint John, N.B. E2A 4T4 (506/652-1600)

L'ASSOCIATION CANADIENNE DES DISTRIBUTEURS DE FILMS DE MONTREAL
President, Jean-Paul Hurtubise, c/o Universal Films, 8444 St. Laurent Blvd., Montreal, P.Q. H2P 2M3 (514/382-8475)

TORONTO FILM BOARD
Executive Director, Millard S. Roth, #1703, 22 St. Clair Ave. E., Toronto, Ont. M4T 2S4 (416/961-1888)

WINNIPEG FILM BOARD
President, Roy Walkey, c/o Universal Films, 583 Ellice Ave., Winnipeg, Man. R3B 1Z7 (204/786-3397)

CALGARY FILM BOARD
President, Don Popow, c/o Paramount Films Distribution (Can) Ltd., 1410 11th Ave. S.W., Calgary, Alta. T3C OM8 (403/245-4306)

VANCOUVER FILM BOARD
President, R. Rickard, c/o Warner Bros. Pictures, 2182 W. 12th Ave., #202, Vancouver, B.C. V6K 2N4 (604/731-5351)

CANADIAN MOTORCYCLE ASSOCIATION

500 James St. N., Hamilton, Ont. L8L 1J3
(416) 522-5705
Executive Officer, Mrs. M. Bastedo

CANADIAN MUSEUMS ASSOCIATION

331 Cooper St., Ste. 400, Ottawa, Ont. K2P OG5
(613) 233-5653
Executive Director, tba

CANADIAN MUSIC PUBLISHERS ASSOCIATION

111 Avenue Rd., Toronto, Ont. M5R 3J8
(416) 922-4170

CANADIAN MUSICAL REPRODUCTION RIGHTS AGENCY LTD.

111 Avenue Rd., Toronto, Ont. M5R 3J8
(416) 922-4170
President, Alexander Mair
General Manager, C.C. Devereux

THE CANADIAN NATIONAL INSTITUTE FOR THE BLIND

National Office, 1929 Bayview Ave., Toronto, Ont. M4G 3E8
(416) 486-2550
Managing Director, R. Mercer

Provincial Divisions

Alta.: 12010 Jasper Ave., Edmonton, Alta. T5K 0P3 (403/488-4871)
B.C-Yukon: 350 E. 36th Ave., Vancouver, B.C. V5W 1C6 (604/321-2311)
Man.: 1031 Portage Ave., Winnipeg, Man. R3G 0R9 (204/774-5421)
Maritime: 6136 Almon St., Halifax, N.S. B3K 1T8 (902/453-1480)
Nfld. & Labrador: 70 The Blvd., St. John's, Nfld. A1A 1K2 (709/754-1180)
Ont.: 1929 Bayview Ave., Toronto, Ont. M4G 3E8 (416/486-2521)
Que.: 1181 rue Guy, Montreal, P.Q. H3H 2K6 (514/931-7221)
Sask.: 2550 Broad St., Regina, Sask. S4P 3E1 (306/525-2571)

CANADIAN NATIONAL MILLERS ASSOCIATION

151 Slater St., Ste. 205, Ottawa, Ont. K1P 5H3
(613) 238-2293

CANADIAN NATURE FEDERATION
#203, 75 Albert St., Ottawa, Ont. K1P 6G1
(613) 238-6154
Conservation Director, Rick Pratt
Managing Director, Peggy Heppes
Editor of *Nature Canada*, Arnet Sheppard

A national non-profit conservation organization dedicated to the protection of wildlife and wild lands. Publishes Canada's only national nature magazine, *Nature Canada*.

CANADIAN NUCLEAR ASSOCIATION
111 Elizabeth St., Toronto, Ont. M5G 1P7
(416) 977-6152/Telex: 06-23741
President, Dr. Norman Aspin
General Manager, James A. Weller
Also at same address etc. is the **Canadian Nuclear Society,** (the Technical Society of the CNA): President, George R. Howey

CANADIAN NUMISMATIC RESEARCH SOCIETY
Secretary, Ken Palmer, 10 Wesanford Place, Hamilton, Ont. L8P 1N6 (416/528-3649)

CANADIAN NURSERY TRADES ASSOCIATION
#103, 3034 Palstan Rd., Mississauga, Ont. L4Y 2Z6
(416) 276-6640
Executive Director, R.W. Cheesman

Provincial Associations

BRITISH COLUMBIA NURSERY TRADES ASSOCIATION
#230, 10330 152nd St., Surrey, B.C. V3R 4G8
(604) 585-2225

LANDSCAPE ALBERTA NURSERY TRADES ASSOCIATION
10215 176 St., Edmonton, Alta. T5S 1M1
(403) 489-1991

LANDSCAPE SASKATCHEWAN
Box 460, Carnduff, Sask. SOC OSO
(306) 482-3410

MANITOBA NURSERY & LANDSCAPE ASSOCIATION
104 Parkside Dr., Winnipeg, Man. R3J 3P8
(204) 888-9880

LANDSCAPE ONTARIO
#103, 3034 Palstan Rd., Mississauga, Ont. L4Y 2Z6
(416) 276-6177

SOCIETE QUEBECOISE DE L'HORTICULTURE ORNEMENTALE
Jardin Van Den Hende, Université Laval, Ste-Foy, P.Q. G1K 7P4
(418) 659-3561

ATLANTIC PROVINCES NURSERY TRADES ASSOCIATION
1232 Bedford Hwy., Bedford, N.S. B4A 1C6
(902) 835-8591

CANADIAN OCEAN INDUSTRIES ASSOCIATION
One Yonge St., #1400, Toronto, Ont. M5E 1J9
(416) 363-7261
Manager, A.C. Dick

CANADIAN OFFICE MACHINE DEALERS' ASSOCIATION
15 Dyas Rd., Don Mills, Ont. M3B 1V7
(416) 441-1717
Executive Director, Ms. D.J. Brisebois

CANADIAN OFFICE PRODUCTS ASSOCIATION
1243 Islington Ave., Suite 604, Toronto, Ont. M8X 1Y9
(416) 239-2737
Executive Vice President, E. G. Freeman

CANADIAN OILFIELD MANUFACTURERS ASSOCIATION
5003 109A Ave., Edmonton, Alta. T6A 1S6
(403) 468-2078
Business Development Director, Peter Stephenson, c/o 1021 Toronto Dominion Tower, Edmonton, Alta. T5J 2Z1

CANADIAN ORAL HISTORY ASSOCIATION
(Société canadienne d'histoire orale)
Box 301, Stn. A, Ottawa, Ont. K1N 8V3
Editor, Canadian Oral History Association *Journal*, Richard Lochead

CANADIAN ORGANIZATION FOR THE SIMPLIFICATION OF TRADE PROCEDURES
President, J.G. Patry, 151 Sparks St., Room 302, Ottawa, Ont. K1P 5E3 (613/995-2814)

THE CANADIAN OSTEOPATHIC AID SOCIETY
Executive Secretary, Mrs. Marguerite Torney, 575 Waterloo St., London, Ont. N6B 2R2 (519/439-5521)

CANADIAN OUTDOOR MEASUREMENT BUREAU
Ste. 1610, 439 University Ave., Toronto, Ont. M5G 1Y8
(416) 598-4672
President, J.H.C. Penaligon

CANADIAN OUTDOOR POWER EQUIPMENT ASSOCIATION
One Yonge St., Ste. 1400, Toronto, Ont. M5E 1J9
(416) 363-7261
Manager, A.C. Dick

CANADIAN OWNERS & PILOTS ASSOCIATION (COPA)
Box 734, Ottawa, Ont. K1P 5S4
(613) 236-4901
General Manager, W.N. Peppler

CANADIAN PAINT & COATINGS ASSOCIATION
515 St. Catherine St. W., #825, Montreal, P.Q. H3B 1B4
(514) 285-6381
Executive Vice President, R.W. Murry

CANADIAN PAINTING CONTRACTORS ASSOCIATION
85 Ellesmere Rd., #218, Scarborough, Ont. M1R 4B9
(416) 444-7958
President, K. N. Edgar

THE CANADIAN PAPER BOX MANUFACTURERS' ASSOCIATION INC.
Executive Director, W. T. Bainbridge, 185 Bay St., Toronto, Ont. M5J 1K6 (416/364-7362)

CANADIAN PAPER TRADE ASSOCIATION
55 York St., Room 512, Toronto, Ont. M5J 1S2
(416) 363-8374
Secretary, F. Young

CANADIAN PARAPLEGIC ASSOCIATION
520 Sutherland Dr., Toronto, Ont. M4G 3V9
(416) 422-5640
Managing Director, M.E. Ryan
Lyndhurst Hospital: 520 Sutherland Dr., Toronto, Ont. M4G 3V9 —Administrator, R.F. Swan (416/422-5551)

Provincial Divisions

Alta.: Executive Director, Rick Hiatt, 18131 107 Ave., Edmonton, Alta. T5S 1K4 (403/489-7731)
B.C.: Executive Director, D. L. Mowat, 780B S.W. Marine Dr., Vancouver, B.C. V6P 5Y7 (604/324-3611)

Man.: Executive Director, John Lane, 825 Sherbrook St., Winnipeg, Man. R3A 1M5 (204/786-4753)
N.B.: Executive Director, Bev. Hallam, 43 Brunswick St., Room 203, Fredericton, N.B. E3B 1G5 (506/455-9607)
Nfld.: Executive Director, A. Rose, 21 Factory Lane, St. John's, Nfld. (709/579-6742)
N.S.: Executive Director, D.E. Curren, Fenwick Place, 5599 Fenwick St., Halifax, N.S. B3H 1R2 (902/423-1277)
Ont.: Executive Director, W.K. Rowe, 520 Sutherland Dr., Toronto, Ont. M4G 3V9 (416/422-5640)
Que.: (Association des Paraplégiques du Québec), Executive Director, Gaetan Bourgoin, 4545 Queen Mary Rd., Montreal, P.Q. H3W 1W4 (514/344-3890)
Sask.: Executive Director, D. E. McFadyen, 325 5th Ave. N., Saskatoon, Sask. S7K 2P7 (306/652-9644)

CANADIAN PARENTS FOR FRENCH
Box 8470, Main Terminal, Ottawa, Ont. K1G 3H6
(613) 749-3430
National Chairman, Janet Poyen, 568 Lansdowne Ave., Calgary, Alta. T2S 0Z7

CANADIAN PARKS/RECREATION ASSOCIATION
Executive Director, Denny Neider, 333 River Rd., Tower B, Vanier, Ont. K1L 8B9 (613/746-7740)

CANADIAN PEACE CONGRESS
671 Danforth Ave., Room 301-302, Toronto, Ont. M4J 1L3
(416) 469-3422
President, Rev. John Morgan
Executive Secretary, Mrs. J. Vautour

Affiliated Councils

ALBERTA PEACE COUNCIL
11622 74th Ave., Edmonton, Alta. T6G OG2

BRITISH COLUMBIA PEACE COUNCIL
#712, 207 W. Hastings St., Vancouver, B.C. V6B 1H7

MANITOBA PEACE COUNCIL
476 St. Anthony Ave., Winnipeg, Man. R2V OS5
(204) 582-4248

NOVA SCOTIA PEACE COUNCIL
246 Herbert St., Sydney, N.S. B1P 3T2

ONTARIO PEACE COUNCIL
Box 4518, Stn. D, Hamilton, Ont. L8V 4S7

OTTAWA PEACE COUNCIL
45 Kilbarry Cres., Ottawa, Ont. K1K OH2

REGINA PEACE COUNCIL
1147 Argyle St., Regina, Sask. S4T 3R6

SASKATCHEWAN PEACE COUNCIL
118 Cumberland Ave. N., Saskatoon, Sask. S7N 1M2

CANADIAN PEACE RESEARCH INSTITUTE
Gryffin Lodge, Huntsville, Ont. P0A 1K0
Directors, Norman & Pat Alcock

CANADIAN PENSION CONFERENCE
#407, 3 Church St., Toronto, Ont. M5E 1M2
(416) 368-8253
Executive Director, Al Warson
President, Wm. L. Kennedy, Union Carbide Canada, Toronto
Regional Chairmen in every area of Canada. Contact Executive Director for up to date names and addresses.

CANADIAN PENSIONERS CONCERNED INC.

ONTARIO DIVISION
51 Bond St., Toronto, Ont. M5B 1X1
(416) 368-5222

NOVA SCOTIA DIVISION
#200, Tower One, 7001 Mumford Rd., Halifax, N.S. B3L 2H9

CANADIAN PERIODICAL PUBLISHERS ASSOCIATION
54 Wolseley St., Toronto, Ont. M5T 1A5
(416) 362-2546
Executive Director, Sherrill Cheda

CANADIAN PETROLEUM ASSOCIATION
1500, 633 6 Ave. S.W., Calgary, Alta. T2P 2Y5
(403) 269-6721
Executive Director, Ian R. Smyth
Secretary & General Counsel, D.B. Macnamara

Provincial Divisions

B.C.: 880 Douglas St., Victoria, B.C. V8W 2B7, Manager, G.S. Bryson (604/388-4121)
Sask.: 915 McCallum-Hill Bldg., Regina, Sask. S4P 2G6, Manager, W. W. Spicer (306/523-4461)
Ottawa: 400-130 Albert St., Ottawa, Ont. K1P 5G4, Manager, J. Deacey (613/237-5515)
Pipeline: #1500, 633 6 Ave. S.W., Calgary, Alta. T2P 2Y5, Administrator, R.J. Frocklage (403/269-6721)

CANADIAN PHILOSOPHICAL ASSOCIATION
Simard Hall, University of Ottawa, Ottawa, Ont. K1N 6N5
(613) 238-2607
Executive Secretary, Mrs. Jeanne Laviolette

CANADIAN PHOTOGRAPHIC TRADE ASSOCIATION
Ste. 200, 3500 Dufferin St., Downsview, Ont. M3K 1N2
(416) 635-5040

CANADIAN PHYTOPATHOLOGICAL SOCIETY
Secretary, Dr. H. Harding, Agriculture Canada Research Stn., 107 Science Cres., Saskatoon, Sask. S7N 0X2 (306/343-8214)
Treasurer, Dr. R.J. Copeman, Plant Science Dept., U.B.C., Vancouver, B.C. V6T 2A2 (604/228-4586)

CANADIAN PICTURE PIONEERS
175 Bloor St. E., Toronto, Ont. M4W 1C8
(416) 929-0865
President, Jack Bernstein

CANADIAN POLICE ASSOCIATION
268 Lakeshore Rd. E., Mississauga, Ont. L5G 1H1
(416) 278-3884

Affiliated Society

OTTAWA POLICE ASSOCIATION LTD.
353 Dalhousie St., Suite 201, Ottawa, Ont. K1N 7G1

CANADIAN POLISH CONGRESS
Head Executive Board, 288 Roncesvalles Ave., Toronto, Ont. M6R 2M4 (416/532-2876)
Secretary General, K.F. Klimaszewski
Ottawa Office: c/o Mrs. M. Gawalewicz, 1852 Cloverlawn Cr., Ottawa, Ont. K1J 6V2

THE CANADIAN POLITICAL SCIENCE ASSOCIATION
Secretary Treasurer, N.H. Chi, Carleton University, Ottawa, Ont. K1S 5B6 (613/231-7160)
Organ, "The Canadian Journal of Political Science/La Revue Canadienne de Science Politique," c/o The Press, Wilfrid Laurier Univ., Waterloo, Ont. N2L 3C5

CANADIAN POOL CAR OPERATORS ASSOCIATION INC.
Room 111, 1117 Ste. Catherine St. W., Montreal, P.Q. H3B 1H9
(514) 849-9721
General Manager, N.A. Emblem

CANADIAN PORT & HARBOUR ASSOCIATION
60 Harbour St., Toronto, Ont. M5J 1B7
(416) 863-2026

CANADIAN PORTLAND CEMENT ASSOCIATION
116 Albert St., Ottawa, Ont. K1P 5G3
(613) 236-9471
President, Lance C. DeCory

Provincial Branches
Alta.: #1210, 10055 106 St., Edmonton, Alta. T5J 2Y2 (403/423-5101)
B.C.: #201, 1155 W. Pender St., Vancouver, B.C. V6E 2P4 (604/685-0582)
Maritimes: 1660 Hollis St., Halifax, N.S. B3J 1V7 (902/423-7317)
Ont.: 365 Bloor St. E., #1402, Toronto, Ont. M4W 3L4 (416/924-1159)
Que.: 1010 Ste. Catherine St. W., Montreal, P.Q. H3B 1G1 (514/866-1882)

CANADIAN POSTMASTERS & ASSISTANTS ASSOCIATION
National Secretary Treasurer, J. G. Gélinas, Suite 1204, 130 Albert St., Ottawa, Ont. K1P 5G4 (613/232-2404)

CANADIAN POTATO CHIP ASSOCIATION
1568 Carling Ave., Ottawa, Ont. K1Z 7M5
(613) 725-1118
Executive Secretary, H.R. Taylor

CANADIAN POWER SQUADRONS
(Canadian Headquarters)
26 Golden Gate Court, Scarborough, Ont. M1P 3A5
(416) 293-2438

THE CANADIAN PRESS
36 King St. E., Toronto, Ont. M5C 2L9
(416) 364-0321
General Manager & Secretary, Keith Kincaid

Regional Bureaus
Edmonton, Alta.: Graham Trotter, Chief of Bureau, 10025 102 St., Edmonton, Alta. T5J 2X8 (403/428-6107)
Vancouver, B.C.: Fred Chafe, Chief of Bureau, 1455 Seventh Ave. W., Vancouver, B.C. V6H 1S1 (604/731-3191)
Winnipeg, Man.: Joe Dupuis, Chief of Bureau, 300 Carlton St., Winnipeg, Man. R3B 2K6 (204/942-8188)
Halifax, N.S.: Gordon Grant, Chief of Bureau, 2021 Brunswick St., Halifax, N.S. B3K 2Y5 (902/422-8496)
Ottawa, Ont.: Arch MacKenzie, Chief of Bureau, 140 Wellington St., Ottawa, Ont. K1P 5P7 (613/238-4142)
Toronto, Ont.: Mel Sufrin, Managing Editor; Peter Buckley, General News Editor; Chris Nichols, Chief of Ontario Service; Jack Picketts, Chief of Picture Service, 36 King St. E, Toronto, Ont. M5C 2L9 (416/364-0321)
Montreal, P.Q.: Guy Rondeau, Chief of Bureau, 245 St. James St. W., Montreal, P.Q. (514/849-6154)
Quebec, P.Q.: Pierre Tourangeau, Chief of Bureau, Le Soleil Bldg., 390 St. Vallier E., Quebec, P.Q. G1K 3P6 (418/529-9416)
London, England: Frank Mackey, Staff Correspondent, 83-86 Farringdon St., London Eng. C4A 4BS (01-353-6355)
New York, N.Y.: Al Colletti, Chief Correspondent, 50 Rockefeller Plaza, New York, N.Y. 10020 (212/247-1333)
Washington, D.C.: Carl Mollins, Chief Correspondent, 2021 K St. N.W., #606, Washington, D.C. 20006 (202/833-5324)

CANADIAN PRESTRESSED CONCRETE INSTITUTE
85 Albert St., Ottawa, Ont. K1P 6A4
(613) 232-2619
Executive Director, J. W. Cumming

CANADIAN PRINTING INK MANUFACTURERS ASSOCIATION
Box 294, Kleinburg, Ont. LOJ 1CO
(416) 851-1118
Secretary Treasurer, Boyd W. Browne

CANADIAN PROFESSIONAL DRIVER EDUCATION ASSOCIATION
3745 Bloor St. W., Islington, Ont. M9B 1A2
(416) 231-4125

CANADIAN PROFESSORS FOR PEACE IN THE MIDDLE EAST
60 Bloor St W., Ste. 912, Toronto, Ont. M4W 3B8
(416) 922-3596
National Chairman, Professor Harry Crowe
National Director, Dr. Eva Dessen

CANADIAN PROGRESS CLUB NATIONAL
Executive Secretary Treasurer, Mrs. Lee Irwin, 67 Yonge St., Ste. 532, Toronto, Ont. M5E 1J8 (416/364-8095)

CANADIAN PROPERTY MANAGERS ASSOCIATION
4141 Yonge St., Willowdale, Ont. M2P 2A7
(416) 493-5380
President, R. Hume

CANADIAN PROPERTY TAX AGENTS ASSOCIATION, INC.
2249 Yonge St., Ste. 304, Toronto, Ont. M4S 2B1
(416) 481-6666
Executive Secretary, Mrs. Maureen Marquardt

CANADIAN PUBLIC HEALTH ASSOCIATION
1335 Carling Ave., Ste. 210, Ottawa, Ont. K1Z 8N8
(613) 725-3769
Executive Director, Gerald H. Dafoe

THE CANADIAN PUBLIC RELATIONS SOCIETY, INC.
(La Société canadienne des Relations publiques, inc.)
220 Laurier Ave. W., #720, Ottawa, Ont K1P 5Z9
(613) 232-1222
Vice President, Administration, P. H. Macleod, APR

There are affiliated societies with elected Officers in every province. Contact the Ottawa office for latest list.

CANADIAN PULP & PAPER ASSOCIATION
2300 Sun Life Bldg., Montreal, P.Q. H3B 2X9
(514) 866-6621
Secretary, Gordon P. Minnes

CANADIAN RACING PIGEON UNION
Secretary Treasurer, Mrs. Dorothy Joseph, R.R. 4, London, Ont. N6A 4B8 (519/681-1092)

CANADIAN RAILROAD HISTORICAL ASSOCIATION
See 'Railroad Associations'

CANADIAN RAILWAY LABOUR ASSOCIATION
Ste. 513, 130 Albert St., Ottawa, Ont. K1P 5G4
(613) 236-6945
Executive Secretary, E.G. Abbot

CANADIAN RAILWAY & TRANSIT MANUFACTURERS ASSOCIATION
One Yonge St., #1400, Toronto, Ont. M5E 1J9
(416) 363-7261
Manager, A.C. Dick

THE CANADIAN REAL ESTATE ASSOCIATION
99 Duncan Mill Rd., Don Mills, Ont. M3B 1Z2
(416) 445-9910
President, Eric Charman
Vice President, Sylvio Huneault
Vice President, Raymond Buxton

BRITISH COLUMBIA REAL ESTATE ASSOCIATION
#105, 1847 W. Broadway, Vancouver, B.C. V6J 1Y6
(604) 731-2196

ALBERTA REAL ESTATE ASSOCIATION
1410 1st St. S.W., Calgary, Alta. T2R OV8
(403) 264-5581

SASKATCHEWAN REAL ESTATE ASSOCIATION
2602 8th St. E., Saskatoon, Sask. S7H OV7
(306) 373-3350

MANITOBA REAL ESTATE ASSOCIATION
1240 Portage Ave., Winnipeg, Man. R3G OT6
(204) 786-5679

ONTARIO REAL ESTATE ASSOCIATION
99 Duncan Mill Rd., Don Mills, Ont. M3B 1Z2
(416) 445-9910

QUEBEC REAL ESTATE ASSOCIATION/ASSOCIATION DE L'IMMEUBLE DU QUEBEC
1080 Beaver Hall Hill, #1100, Montreal, P.Q. H2Z 1T8
(514) 866-7641

NEW BRUNSWICK REAL ESTATE ASSOCIATION
Box 6681, Stn. A, Saint John, N.B. E2L 4S1
(506) 657-4333

NOVA SCOTIA REAL ESTATE ASSOCIATION
6132 Quinpool Rd., Halifax, N.S. B3L 1A3
(902) 423-9145

PRINCE EDWARD ISLAND REAL ESTATE ASSOCIATION
202 Queen St., Charlottetown, P.E.I. C1N 4B6
(902) 892-8734

NEWFOUNDLAND REAL ESTATE ASSOCIATION
Box 1126, Corner Brook, Nfld. A2H 6T2
(709) 634-3564

YUKON REAL ESTATE ASSOCIATION
Box 5292, Whitehorse, Y.T. Y1A 1A1
(403) 667-2229

CANADIAN RECORDING INDUSTRY ASSOCIATION
89 Bloor St. E., Toronto, Ont. M4W 1A9
(416) 967-7272
President, W. B. Robertson

CANADIAN RED CROSS SOCIETY
95 Wellesley St. E., Toronto, Ont. M4Y 1H6
(416) 923-6692
Honorary President, His Excellency, The Governor General of Canada
Chairman National Executive Committee, Wm. R. Livingston
National Commissioner, H. Tellier (416/923-6692)

Provincial Divisions

Alta.-N.W.T.: 737 13th Ave. S.W., Calgary, Alta. T2R 1J1; Commissioner, G.S. Hogg (403/233-2901)
B.C.-Yukon: 4750 Oak St., Vancouver, B.C. V6H 2N9; Commissioner, B. R. Howard, E.D. (604/879-7551)
Man.: 226 Osborne St. N., Winnipeg, Man. R3C 1V4; Commissioner, C. King (204/772-2551)
N.B.: 1 Bayard Drive (Hospital Hill), Saint John, N.B. E2L 3L5; Commissioner, J. C. McVicar (506/657-6500)
Nfld.: 7 Wicklow St., St. John's, Nfld. A1B 4A4; Commissioner, Norman A. Winter (709/754-0461)
N.S.: 1940 Gottingen St., Halifax, N.S. B3J 2H2; Commissioner, K. P. Bendelier (902/423-9181)
Ont.: 460 Jarvis St., Toronto, Ont. M4Y 2H5; Commissioner, James T. West (416/923-6692)
P.E.I.: 62 Prince St., Charlottetown, P.E.I. C1A 4R2; Commissioner, James Bentham (902/894-8551)
Que.: 2170 Dorchester Blvd. W., Montreal, P.Q. H3H 1R6; Commissioner, Fernand Delhaes (514/937-7761)
Sask.: 2571 Broad St., Regina, Sask. S4P 3B4; Commissioner, J.H. McMurtry (306/352-4601)

CANADIAN REGISTRY OF INTERPRETERS OF THE DEAF
Box 219, Brooklin, Ont. LOB 1CO
(416) 655-4434

CANADIAN REHABILITATION COUNCIL FOR THE DISABLED
One Yonge St., Suite 2110, Toronto, Ont. M5E 1E5
(416) 862-0340
National Executive Director, J. R. Sarney

Members

ALBERTA REHABILITATION COUNCIL FOR THE DISABLED
#303 Kingsway Garden Mall, 109 St. & Kingsway, Edmonton, Alta. T5G 3A6 (403/474-8391); Executive Director, J.H. Killick
Calgary Branch: #410, 5920 1A St. S.W., Calgary, Alta. T2H 0G3 (403/259-2602); Regional Adm., R.K. Thompson

THE BRITISH COLUMBIA LIONS SOCIETY FOR CRIPPLED CHILDREN
Head Office: 177 W. 7th Ave., Vancouver, B.C. V5Y 1L8 (604/873-1865); Executive Director, Wm. J. Townsend (Branches: 3937 Quadra St., Victoria, B.C. V8X 1J5; and R.R. 1, Sorrento, B.C. V0E 2W0)

CANADIAN FOUNDATION FOR POLIOMYELITIS & REHABILITATION, ALBERTA CHAPTER
Box 3067, Stn. B, Calgary, Alta. T2M 4L6; Secretary, D.J. Ooms (403/284-1161)

CANADIAN HEMOPHILIA SOCIETY
Chedoke Hospital Patterson Bldg., Box 2085, Hamilton, Ont. L8N 3R5 (416/387-2677); Executive Director, E.T. Gurney

CANADIAN REHABILITATION COUNCIL FOR THE DISABLED, NEW BRUNSWICK BRANCH INC.
43 Brunswick St., Fredericton, N.B. E3B 1G5 (506/454-5990); Executive Director, Randy Dickinson

CANADIAN REHABILITATION COUNCIL FOR THE DISABLED, NOVA SCOTIA CHAPTER
2004 Gottingen St., Halifax, N.S. B3K 3A9 (902/429-3420); Executive Director, Miss Caroline Macdougall

CANADIAN WHEELCHAIR SPORTS ASSOCIATION
333 River Rd., Vanier, Ont. K1L 8B9 (613/741-2463); Executive Director, John Smyth

THE EASTER SEAL SOCIETY (Ontario)
(formerly Ontario Soc. for Crippled Children)
350 Rumsey Rd., Toronto, Ont. M4G 1R8 (416/425-6220); Executive Director, Ian Bain

FEDERATION DES LOISIRS ET SPORTS POUR HANDICAPES DU QUEBEC
1415 est, rue Jarry, Bureau R-32, Montreal, P.Q. H2E 2Z7; Directeur Général, Roger Mondor (514/374-4700, poste 378 ou 379)

THE KINSMEN REHABILITATION FOUNDATION OF BRITISH COLUMBIA
2256 W. 12th Ave., Vancouver, B.C. V6K 2N5; Executive Director, Ed Sherwood (604/736-8841)

LOISIRS POUR LES HANDICAPES INC.
#116, 1800 ouest, boul. Dorchester, Montreal, P.Q. H3H 2H2 (514/935-1100)

NEWFOUNDLAND SOCIETY FOR THE CARE OF CRIPPLED CHILDREN & ADULTS
Bldg. 567, St. John's Place, Box 1403, Pleasantville, St. John's, Nfld. A1C 5N5; Executive Director, Hubert W. Hall (709/754-1970)

ONTARIO MARCH OF DIMES
90 Thorncliffe Park Dr., Toronto, Ont. M4H 1M5; Executive Director, Ms. Andria Spindel (416/425-0501)

Ability Centres:

Barrie: 70 Collier St., #704, Barrie, Ont. L4M 4Z2
Hamilton: 508 Wellington St. N., Hamilton, Ont. L8L 5B3
Kingston: 2 Cataraqui St., Kingston, Ont. K7K 1Z7
Kitchener: 141 Weber St. S., Waterloo, Ont. N2J 2A9
London: 627 Maitland St., London, Ont. N5Y 2V7
Oshawa: 141 Thornton Rd. S., Oshawa, Ont. L1G 5Y1

Ottawa: 80 Colonnade St. N., Nepean, Ont. K2E 7G2
Peel: 2 Robert Speck Pkwy., #750, Mississauga, Ont. L4Z 1H8
St. Catharines: 3 Lowell Ave., St. Catharines, Ont. L2R 2C7
Sault Ste. Marie: 180 Gore St., Sault Ste. Marie, Ont. P6A 1M2
Sudbury: 35 Elm St. E., #309, Sudbury, Ont. P3C 1S3
Thunder Bay: 237 Camelot St., Thunder Bay, Ont. P7A 4B2
Timmins: 429 Spruce St. S., Timmins, Ont. P4N 2N6
Toronto: 585 Trethewey Dr., Toronto, Ont. M6M 4B8 (416/248-6206)
Welland: 160 E. Main St., Welland, Ont. L3B 3W8

PRINCE EDWARD ISLAND COUNCIL OF THE DISABLED INC.
Box 2128, Charlottetown, P.E.I. C1A 7N7; Executive Director, Kevin Edgecombe (902/892-9149)

QUEBEC EASTER SEAL SOCIETY/LA SOCIETE DES TIMBRES DE PAQUES DE LA PROVINCE DU QUEBEC
Box 1030, Stn. B, Montreal, P.Q. H3B 3K5 (514/866-1969); Executive Director, L.A. McClintock

QUEBEC MARCH OF DIMES FOR THE DISABLED
Ste. 475, 1253 McGill College Ave., Montreal, P.Q. H3B 2Y5; Executive Director, W.V. Messervey (514/866-3689)

QUEBEC SOCIETY FOR CRIPPLED CHILDREN
1455 Rochon St., St-Laurent, Montreal, P.Q. H4L 1W1; Executive Director, Tony Shorgan (514/748-8816)

ROTARY CLUB OF CHARLOTTETOWN, EASTER SEAL COMMITTEE
Box 608, Charlottetown, P.E.I. C1A 7L3; Executive Director, R. Anderson

SASKATCHEWAN COUNCIL FOR CRIPPLED CHILDREN & ADULTS
1410 Kilburn Ave., Saskatoon, Sask. S7M 0J8; Executive Director, J. Wasilenko (306/653-1694)

SOCIAL PLANNING & REVIEW COUNCIL OF BRITISH COLUMBIA
#109, 2182 W. 12th Ave., Vancouver, B.C. V6K 2N4; Executive Director, Virginia Langdon (604/736-4367)

THE SOCIETY FOR CRIPPLED CHILDREN & ADULTS OF MANITOBA
825 Sherbrook St., Winnipeg, Man. R3A 1M5; Executive Director, J. A. Carmichael (204/786-5601)

CANADIAN RESEARCH INSTITUTE FOR THE ADVANCEMENT OF WOMEN

151 Slater St., #415, Ottawa, Ont. K1P 5H3
(613) 563-3576
President, Dr. Ann Hall

CANADIAN RESEARCH MANAGEMENT ASSOCIATION

Secretary, W.R. Stadelman, Ontario Research Foundation, Sheridan Park, Mississauga, Ont. L5K 1B3 (416/822-4111)

CANADIAN RESTAURANT & FOODSERVICES ASSOCIATION

Head Office: Nu-West Centre, 80 Bloor St. W., Ste. 904, Toronto, Ont. M5S 2V1
Executive Vice President, R.C. Huddart
(416) 923-8416
Ottawa Office: 85 Albert St., 16th floor, Ottawa, Ont. K1P 6A4
(613) 236-6255

ALBERTA RESTAURANT & FOODSERVICES ASSOCIATION
Executive Director, Mrs. Elizabeth Baker, 1330 15th Ave. S.W., #121, Calgary, Alta. T3C 3N6 (403/245-0677)

BRITISH COLUMBIA RESTAURANT & FOODSERVICES ASSOCIATION
Executive Director, Don Bellamy, 1267 Kingsway, Vancouver, B.C. V5V 3E2 (604/879-8801)

MANITOBA RESTAURANT ASSOCIATION
Executive Director, Mrs. Lena Corley, 68B Donald St., Winnipeg, Man. R3C 1L6 (204/942-8724)

HOSPITALITY NEW BRUNSWICK
Executive Director, Mrs. Audrey Williston, 349 King St., Fredericton, N.B. E3B 1E4 (506/454-2615)

NEWFOUNDLAND RESTAURANT ASSOCIATION
Executive Director, Haydn A. Johns, 137 Le Marchant Rd., St. John's, Nfld. A1C 2H3 (709/753-8657)

NOVA SCOTIA RESTAURANT & FOODSERVICES ASSOCIATION
Secretary, Box 3128, South, Halifax, N.S. B3J 3G6 (902/423-7111)

ONTARIO RESTAURANT & FOODSERVICES ASSOCIATION
Executive Director, D.C. Needham, c/o Park Plaza Hotel, Ste. 302, 170 Bloor St. W., Toronto, Ont. M5S 1T9 (416/920-4354)

PRINCE EDWARD ISLAND RESTAURANT & FOODSERVICES ASSOCIATION
President, J.W. Lawrence, 12 Pope Ave., Charlottetown, P.E.I. C1A 6N3

ASSOCIATION DES RESTAURANTEURS DU QUEBEC
Executive Director, Claude Blondeau, 2161 Ste-Catherine est, Montreal, P.Q. H2K 2H9 (514/527-3686)

CANADIAN RETAIL BUILDING SUPPLY COUNCIL

4500 Sheppard Ave. E., Scarboro, Ont. M1S 3R6
President, Herb Hardy (416/298-1731)
Secretary Treasurer, Gordon Wade

Affiliated Associations

ATLANTIC BUILDING SUPPLY DEALERS ASSOCIATION
Box 441, Amherst, N.S. B4H 3Z5
(902) 667-7914
Executive Director, Paul Landry
Official Publication, "Lumberin' Round"

THE BUILDING SUPPLY DEALERS ASSOCIATION OF BRITISH COLUMBIA
3875 Canada Way, Burnaby, B.C. V5G 1G6
(604) 435-4447
Executive Director, Gordon F. Wade
Official Publication, "B.S.D.A. Monthly Survey"

THE LUMBER & BUILDING MATERIALS ASSOCIATION OF ONTARIO
4500 Sheppard Ave. E., Scarboro, Ont. M1S 3R6
(416) 298-1731
Executive Vice President, Herbert C. Hardy
Official Publication "LBMAO Reporter"

ASSOCIATION DES DETAILLANTS DE MATERIAUX DE CONSTRUCTION DU QUEBEC
4270 est rue Jean Talon, bur. 102, Montreal, P.Q. H1S 1G7
(514) 376-8541
Directeur exécutif, Maurice Rhéaume
Official Publication, "Quart de Rond"

WESTERN RETAIL LUMBERMEN'S ASSOCIATION
601-228 Notre Dame Ave., Winnipeg, Man. R3B 1N7
(204) 957-1077
Executive Director, Mike Kearney

CANADIAN RETAIL HARDWARE ASSOCIATION

6800 Campobello Rd., Mississauga, Ont. L5N 2L8
(416) 821-3470
Executive Director, Thomas M. Ross

CANADIAN RIGHTS & LIBERTIES FEDERATION

(Fédération Canadienne des droits et libertés)
323 Chapel St., Ottawa, Ont. K1N 7Z2
(613) 235-8978

Member Associations

NEWFOUNDLAND LABRADOR HUMAN RIGHTS ASSOCIATION
Box 4247, St. John's, Nfld. A1C 5Z7
(709) 754-0690

PRINCE EDWARD ISLAND CIVIL LIBERTIES ASSOCIATION
Box 1834, Charlottetown, P.E.I. C1A 7N5
(902) 894-9260

COMITE DES DROITS DE L'HOMME DU NORD-EST DU N.B.
Edifice Municipal, Lameque, N.B. E0B 1V0
(506) 344-2216

LA LIGUE DES DROITS ET LIBERTES
1825 rue Champlain, Montreal, P.Q.
(514) 527-8551

CANADIAN CIVIL LIBERTIES ASSOCIATION, WINDSOR REGION
c/o C. Wydrzynski, Faculty of Law, University of Windsor, Windsor, Ont. N9B 3P4

CIVIL LIBERTIES ASSOCIATION, NATIONAL CAPITAL REGION
78 Daly Ave., Ottawa, Ont. K1N 6E4
(613) 238-7368

SASKATCHEWAN ASSOCIATION ON HUMAN RIGHTS
#305, 116 Third Ave. S., Saskatoon, Sask.
(306) 244-1933
Branches at Esterhazy, Moose Jaw and Regina

ALBERTA HUMAN RIGHTS & CIVIL LIBERTIES ASSOCIATION
#105, 11147 82 Ave., Edmonton, Alta.

LETHBRIDGE CITIZENS HUMAN RIGHTS COUNCIL
1011 4th Ave. S., Lethbridge, Alta. T1J 0P7

BRITISH COLUMBIA CIVIL LIBERTIES ASSOCIATION
Box 24833 Vancouver, B.C. V5T 4E9
(604) 685-4284
There are also independent Civil Liberties Associations in British Columbia at Kamloops, Kelowna, Powell River, Prince George, Quesnel, South Okanagan, Victoria, and Williams Lake

Other Associations

NOVA SCOTIA CIVIL LIBERTIES ASSOCIATION
1519 Dresden Row, Halifax, N.S.
(902) 425-3070

KINGSTON CIVIL LIBERTIES ASSOCIATION
c/o Ned Frank, 55 Earl St., Kingston, Ont.

CANADIAN CIVIL LIBERTIES ASSOCIATION
#403, 229 Yonge St., Toronto, Ont. M5B 1N9
(416) 363-0321

CIVIL LIBERTIES ASSOCIATION, HAMILTON REGION
Box 104, McMaster University, Hamilton, Ont. L8S 1L0

HUMAN RIGHTS COMMITTEE, SUDBURY & REGION
251 Lorne St. S., Sudbury, Ont. P3C 4P8
(705) 674-4338

CALGARY CIVIL LIBERTIES ASSOCIATION
c/o Maureen Lashuk, Sch. of Social Welfare, University of Calgary, Calgary, Alta.

MANITOBA ASSOCIATION FOR RIGHTS & LIBERTIES
425 Elgin Ave., Winnipeg, Man. R3A 1P2

CANADIAN ROOFING CONTRACTORS' ASSOCIATION
Ste. 710, 116 Albert St., Ottawa, Ont. K1P 5G3
(613) 232-6724
Executive Director, Jacques Chevalier

CANADIAN ROSE SOCIETY
20 Portico Dr., Scarborough, Ont. M1G 3R3
(416) 439-0693
Executive Secretary, Mrs. A. Hunter

Affiliate

PRINCE EDWARD ISLAND ROSE SOCIETY
Secretary, J.C. Sutherland, 129 Fitzroy St., Charlottetown, P.E.I. C1A 7N3 (902/894-3553)

CANADIAN SANITATION STANDARDS ASSOCIATION
Secretary Treasurer, David Armstrong, Box 6090, Stn. A, Toronto, Ont. M5W 1P5 (416/278-7886)

CANADIAN SAVE THE CHILDREN FUND (CANSAVE)
720 Spadina Ave., 4th floor, Toronto, Ont. M5S 2W3
(416) 960-3190
National Director, Gordon Ramsay

THE CANADIAN SCHIZOPHRENIA FOUNDATION
2229 Broad St., Regina, Sask. S4P 1Y7
(306) 527-7969
General Director, I. J. Kahan
Branches in Calgary, Edmonton, Halifax, Kamloops, Lethbridge, Lloydminster, Montreal, Ottawa, Regina, Saskatoon, Thunder Bay, Toronto, Vancouver, Victoria, Windsor, Winnipeg

CANADIAN SCIENCE WRITERS' ASSOCIATION
Secretary Treasurer, Bob Morrow, c/o Ontario Hydro, 700 University Ave., Toronto, Ont. M5G 1X6 (416/592-3327)

CANADIAN SEAPLANE PILOTS ASSOCIATION
Secretary Treasurer, Bruce Winnacott, 950 Aviation Rd., Mississauga, Ont. L5G 4H9 (416/251-4464)

CANADIAN SECURITIES INSTITUTE
Box 225, Commerce Court S., Toronto, Ont. M5L 1E8
(416) 364-9130
Director, E.A. Harvie

THE CANADIAN SEMIOTICS ASSOCIATION
(Association Canadienne de Sémiotique)
Secretary Treasurer, Professor Marie Grenier-Francoeur, Département des Littératures, Université Laval, Québec, P.Q. G1K 7P4
President, Louis Francoeur, Université Laval

CANADIAN SHEET STEEL BUILDING INSTITUTE
201 Consumers Rd., Ste. 305, Willowdale, Ont. M2J 4G8
(416) 493-8780

CANADIAN SHIPOWNERS ASSOCIATION
(National Organization of Canadian Deep Sea Owners/Operators)
#703, 350 Sparks St., Ottawa, Ont. K1R 7S8
(613) 232-3539

THE CANADIAN SHIPPERS' COUNCIL
Ste. 250, 99 Bank St., Ottawa, Ont. K1P 6B9
(613) 238-8888
Secretary, J.D. Moore

CANADIAN SHOE RETAILERS' ASSOCIATION
2510 Yonge St., Toronto, Ont. M4P 2H7
(416) 487-7011
General Manager, Jack Shand

CANADIAN SILK & SYNTHETIC TEXTILES ASSOCIATION, INC.
(Association Canadienne de la Soie et des Textiles Synthétiques, Inc.)
#1005, 1155 Dorchester Blvd. W., Montreal, P.Q. H3B 2J2
(514) 866-8205

CANADIAN SKI INSTRUCTORS' ALLIANCE
3300 Cavendish Blvd., #645, Montreal, P.Q. H4B 2M8
(514) 489-5334
Executive Director, Nicole O'Gallagher
Toronto Office: 160 Vanderhoof Ave., Toronto, Ont. M4G 4B8 (416/421-6700)

CANADIAN SKI PATROL SYSTEM
4531 South Clark Place, Box 921, R.R. 5, Ottawa, Ont. K1G 3N3
(613) 822-2245, 6

Charitable, non-profit organization dedicated to safety and service to the skiing public.
National President, Nick Cartwright (1981-82)

CANADIAN SOCIETY OF AIR SAFETY INVESTIGATORS

Box 2098, Bramalea, Ont. L6T 3S3
(416) 838-3910
President, Roger W. Smith (Canadair)
Vice President, R.W. Slaughter (Transport Canada)
Secretary Treasurer, Capt. J.D. Gallagher (Air Canada)

CANADIAN SOCIETY OF APPRAISERS

Box 100-431, 2 Bloor St. W., Toronto, Ont. M4W 3E2
President, John Elliott, Oakville (827-4800)

CANADIAN SOCIETY OF BIBLICAL STUDIES

Executive Secretary, Peter Richardson, Principal, University College, Univ. of Toronto, Toronto, Ont. M5S 1A1 (416/978-3160)

CANADIAN SOCIETY OF CHILDREN'S AUTHORS, ILLUSTRATORS & PERFORMERS

90 Falcon St., Toronto, Ont. M4S 2P5
(416) 922-7736

CANADIAN SOCIETY FOR CIVIL ENGINEERING

#700, 2050 Mansfield St., Montreal, P.Q. H3A 1Z2
(514) 842-8121
President, P.M. Wright
General Manager, R.J. Thibault

CANADIAN SOCIETY FOR ELECTRICAL ENGINEERING

Ste. 700, 2050 Mansfield St., Montreal, P.Q. H3A 1Z2
(514) 842-8121
President, D. Mukhedkar
General Manager & Chief Executive Officer, (vacant)

CANADIAN SOCIETY OF EXPLORATION GEOPHYSICISTS

#229, 640 5th Ave. S.W., Calgary, Alta. T2P 3G4
(403) 262-0015
Secretary, B.W. Curts

CANADIAN SOCIETY OF FORENSIC SCIENCE

#303, 171 Nepean St., Ottawa, Ont. K2P 0B4
(613) 235-7112
Secretary, Rita C. Charlebois, Centre of Forensic Sciences, 25 Grosvenor St., Toronto, Ont. M7A 2G8
Editor, A.M. Headrick, 171 Nepean St.

CANADIAN SOCIETY FOR INDUSTRIAL SECURITY INC.

National Secretary Treasurer, Ms. B.P. Cannell, Box 8157, Ottawa, Ont. K1G 3H7 (613/828-9613)

CANADIAN SOCIETY OF LANDSCAPE ARCHITECTS

Box 3304, Stn. C, Ottawa, Ont. K1Y 4J5
Component provincial organizations in B.C., Alberta, Saskatchewan, Manitoba, Ontario, Quebec, and the Atlantic Provinces. Contact Ottawa address for information.

CANADIAN SOCIETY FOR MECHANICAL ENGINEERING

#700, 2050 Mansfield St., Montreal, P.Q. H3A 1Z2
(514) 842-8121
President, R.E. Chant
General Manager, R.J. Thibault

CANADIAN SOCIETY OF MILITARY MEDALS & INSIGNIA

Box 1263, Guelph, Ont. N1H 6H6
(519) 822-3993
Editor, Ross W. Irwin

CANADIAN SOCIETY FOR NON-DESTRUCTIVE TESTING

President, George Shewchuk, c/o Mohawk College, 135 Fennell Ave. W., Hamilton, Ont. L8N 3T2 (416/387-1655)

CANADIAN SOCIETY OF PETROLEUM GEOLOGISTS

#229, 640 5th Ave. S.W., Calgary, Alta. T2P 3G4
Secretary, K.R. Arthur, Chevron Standard Ltd., 400 5 Ave. S.W., Calgary, Alta. T2P 0L7 (403/267-5910)

CANADIAN SOCIETY OF PLANT PHYSIOLOGISTS

Secretary, W.C. Kimmins, Biology Dept., Dalhousie University, Halifax, N.S. B3H 4J1 (902/424-3545)
Treasurer, Ragai Ibrahim, Biology Dept., Concordia University, Montreal, P.Q. H3G 1M8 (514/879-2877)
East Director, Andre D'Aoust, Centre de Recherches Forestieres des Laurentide, Ste-Foy, P.Q. G1V 4C7 (418/653-1728)

CANADIAN SOCIETY FOR THE PREVENTION OF CRUELTY TO ANIMALS

See Canadian Federation of Humane Societies

CANADIAN SOCIETY FOR THE PREVENTION OF CRUELTY TO CHILDREN

National office: 298 First St., Box 700, Midland, Ont. L4R 4P4
(705) 526-5647
President, E.T. Barker, M.D., D.Psych., F.R.C.P.(C)
Official Publication: Journal of the CSPCC (Quarterly)

CANADIAN SOCIETY OF SAFETY ENGINEERING, INC.

Box 3035, Stn. B, Rexdale, Ont. M9V 2G2
(416) 675-3955
Executive Manager, Peter Fletcher
Chapters in Newfoundland, Labrador, Nova Scotia, New Brunswick, Quebec, Ontario, Manitoba, Saskatchewan, Alberta, British Columbia, and members at large throughout North America and the World.

CANADIAN SOFT DRINK ASSOCIATION

67 Yonge St., Suite 1528, Toronto, Ont. M5E 1J8
(416) 869-1642
Executive Director, T. P. Gregor, C.A.E.

CANADIAN SPEECH & HEARING ASSOCIATION

-not confirmed for 1982-
Administrative Secretary, Anita Yates, c/o Room 308, Corbett Hall, University of Alberta, Edmonton, Alta. T6G 2G4
(For names and addresses of provincial representatives and associations, contact the administrative secretary).

CANADIAN SPORTING ARMS & AMMUNITION ASSOCIATION

Ste. 710, 116 Albert St., Ottawa, Ont. K1P 5G3
(613) 232-2406
Executive Secretary, Jacques Chevalier

CANADIAN SPORTING GOODS ASSOCIATION

(Association Canadienne d'Articles de Sport)
1315 de Maisonneuve Blvd. W., #702, Montreal, P.Q. H3G 1M4
(514) 845-6113
Executive Director, Miss G. Deschamps

CANADIAN STANDARDS ASSOCIATION
178 Rexdale Blvd., Rexdale, Ont. M9W 1R3
(416) 744-4000
President, J. E. Kean

CANADIAN STEEL CONSTRUCTION COUNCIL
201 Consumers Rd., Ste. 300, Willowdale, Ont. M2J 4G8
(416) 491-9898
Chairman, H.A. Krentz
Public Relations Consultant, R. E. Richardson

CSCC is a trade association made up of the four basic Canadian steel mills and four steel institutes representing the fabricators of steel used in construction.

CANADIAN STEEL ENVIRONMENTAL ASSOCIATION
One Yonge St., #1400, Toronto, Ont. M5E 1J9
(416) 363-7261
Manager, Sue Jones

CANADIAN STEEL INDUSTRY RESEARCH ASSOCIATION
One Yonge St., #1400, Toronto, Ont. M5E 1J9
(416) 363-7261
Secretary, Sue Jones

CANADIAN STEEL SERVICE CENTRE INSTITUTE
345 Lakeshore Rd. E., #501, Oakville, Ont. L6J 1J5
(416) 842-1861
General Manager, W.A. Firstbrook

Provincial Chapters

Alta.: President, R.G. Siegel, 9525 60th Ave., Edmonton, Alta. T6E 0C3
B.C.: Executive Secretary, Felix Smalley, 2675 Oak St., Vancouver, B.C. V6H 2K3
Eastern Canada: Secretary, Margot Langendorf, c/o 2055 Bishop St., 3rd floor, Montreal, P.Q. H3G 2E8 (514/849-8673)
Man.: President, Ken Oakley, 1424 Willson Place, Winnipeg, Man. R3T 0Y3
Ont.: Executive Secretary, J. Teeter, 8 King St. E., #1505, Toronto, Ont. M5C 1B5 (416/363-0296)
Sask.: Burt Weisner, Box 3253, Regina, Sask. S4P 3H1

CANADIAN SUGAR INSTITUTE
#1904, 7 King St. E., Toronto, Ont. M5C 1A2
(416) 368-8091
President, M. W. Davidson

CANADIAN TECHNICAL ASPHALT ASSOCIATION
Box 1387, Victoria, B.C. V8W 2W3
(604) 385-8721
Secretary Treasurer, R. Noble, P. Eng.

CANADIAN TECHNION SOCIETY
2828 Bathurst St., #603, Toronto, Ont. M6B 3A7
(416) 789-2501

CANADIAN TELECOMMUNICATIONS CARRIERS ASSOCIATION
Ste. 700, One Nicholas St., Ottawa, Ont. K1N 7B7
(613) 560-2600

CANADIAN TESTING ASSOCIATION
National Office, Box 13033, PO Kanata, Ottawa, Ont. K2K 1X3
(613) 836-3010
Executive Secretary, Helene Fortin
Ont. Chapter: 159 Bay St., Suite 207, Toronto, Ont. M5J 1J7
Admin. Secretary, Mace Mair (416/366-1495)
Que. Chapter: 163 Mère d'Youville, Boucherville, P.Q. J4B 2V8
Admin. Secretary, M. Latraverse (514/655-3472)

CANADIAN TEXTILES INSTITUTE
President & Executive Vice President of Affiliated Associations, E. L. Barry
Head Office, 1002 Commerce House, 1080 Beaver Hall Hill, Montreal, P.Q. H2Z 1T6 (514/866-2081)

Affiliated Associations

Canadian Carpet Institute
Cordage Institute of Canada
Knitters Association of Canada
Institute of Carpet Undercushion Mfrs.
Institute of Commission Dyers, Finishers & Printers

CANADIAN TOBACCO MANUFACTURERS COUNCIL
1808 Sherbrooke St. W., Montreal, P.Q. H3H 1E5
(514) 937-7428
Executive Director, Norman J. McDonald
Executive Secretary, C.M. Seymour

CANADIAN TOY COLLECTORS' SOCIETY
President, R.J. Pride, 27 Greta Court, Hamilton, Ont. L9C 4V1

CANADIAN TOY MANUFACTURERS ASSOCIATION
Box 294, Kleinburg, Ont. L0J 1C0
(416) 851-1118
President, Boyd W. Browne

CANADIAN TRANSMISSION ASSOCIATION
25 Hughson St. S., #508, Hamilton, Ont. L8N 2A5
(416) 522-5161
President, Gordon King

CANADIAN TRANSPORT TARIFF BUREAU ASSOCIATION
#807, 155 Rexdale Blvd., Rexdale, Ont. M9W 5Z8
(416) 741-7805
General Manager, R.A. Blackborow

CANADIAN TRUCK TRAILER MANUFACTURERS ASSOCIATION
Box 294, Kleinburg, Ont. LOJ 1CO
(416) 851-1118
Secretary Treasurer, Boyd W. Browne

CANADIAN TRUCKING ASSOCIATION
National Office, 130 Albert St., Suite 300, Ottawa, Ont. K1P 5G4
(613) 236-9426
Executive Director, A. Kenneth Maclaren

Provincial Affiliates

ALBERTA TRUCKING ASSOCIATION
5112 3rd St. S.E. (Box 5520, Stn. A, Calgary, Alta. T2H 1X9)
(403) 253-8401
General Manager, R. J. Drinnan

ATLANTIC PROVINCES TRUCKING ASSOCIATION
567 Coverdale Rd., Ste. 7A, Moncton, N.B. E1B 3K7
(506) 386-4413
Executive Director, Dale Elliott

BRITISH COLUMBIA MOTOR TRANSPORT ASSOCIATION
4090 Graveley St., N. Burnaby, B.C. V5C 3T6
(604) 299-7407
General Manager, R. E. Hunt

ONTARIO TRUCKING ASSOCIATION
555 Dixon Rd., Rexdale, Ont. M9W 1H8
(416) 247-7131
Executive Vice President, Stephen Flott

MANITOBA TRUCKING ASSOCIATION
25 Bunting St., Winnipeg, Man. R2X 2P5
(204) 632-6600
General Manager, Al Harris

SASKATCHEWAN TRUCKING ASSOCIATION
1335 Wallace St., Regina, Sask. S4N 3Z5
(306) 569-9696
General Manager, Brett G. Filson

TRUCKING ASSOCIATION OF QUEBEC, INC.
4855 Boyer St., #100, Montreal, P.Q.
(514) 527-1356
Executive Vice President, Jacques Alary

NORTHWEST TERRITORIES MOTOR TRANSPORT ASSOCIATION
Box 506, Yellowknife, N.W.T. XOE 1HO
(403) 873-8751
Secretary Manager, Lupcia Klowak

YUKON TRANSPORT ASSOCIATION
Box 274, Whitehorse, YT
Secretary Manager, Lesley Lane

CANADIAN UNICEF COMMITTEE
See Diplomatic Section of the Almanac

CANADIAN URBAN TRANSIT ASSOCIATION
234 Eglinton Ave. E., Ste. 301, Toronto, Ont. M4P 1K5
(416) 481-3309
Executive Director, Al Cormier

CANADIAN VETERINARY MEDICAL ASSOCIATION
360 Bronson Ave., Ottawa, Ont. K1R 6J3
(613) 236-1162
Executive Director, J.-C. Carisse

Provincial Secretaries or Registrars

Alta.: Dr. J.P. Best, #208, 9509 156th St., Edmonton, Alta. T5P 4J5 (403/489-5007)
B.C.: Dr. J.A. Forsyth, Room 250, 1070 W. Broadway, Vancouver, B.C. V6H 1E7 (604/733-9312)
Man.: Dr. Mait Sundmark, Box 1646, Winnipeg, Man. R3C 2Z6 (204/269-1220)
N.B.: Dr. L.B. Donald, Box 20280, Fredericton, N.B. E3B 4Z7 (506/455-9931)
Nfld.: Dr. R.D. Dunphy, Box 7400, St. John's, Nfld. A1E 3Y5 (709/364-4234)
N.S.: Dr. T. Mouris, Box 432, Wolfville, N.S. B0P 1X0
Ont.: F.J. Murphy, 340 Woodlawn Rd. W., Ste. 24-25, Guelph, Ont. N1H 7K6 (519/824-5600)
P.E.I.: Dr. E.S. Howatt, Box 10, Kensington, P.E.I. C0B 1M0 (902/836-3410)
Que.: Dr. H.-P. Girouard, 2200 ave Pratte, #301, St-Hyacinthe, P.Q. J2S 4B6 (514/774-1427)
Sask.: Dr. W.H. Reeker, 139 Mayfair Cres., Regina, Sask. S4S 4J1 (306/586-9344)

CANADIAN WAFERBOARD ASSOCIATION
240 Duncan Mill Rd., #604, Don Mills, Ont. M3B 1Z4
(416) 445-3263
Technical Director, W.M. McCance

CANADIAN WAREHOUSING ASSOCIATION
President, D.I. Kentish, #213, 111 Peter St., Toronto, Ont. M5V 2H1 (416/363-1455)

CANADIAN WATER RESOURCES ASSOCIATION
Secretary, F.A. Ross, c/o Lethbridge Northern Irrigation District, 334 13th St. N., Lethbridge, Alta.

CANADIAN WATER SYSTEM MANUFACTURERS ASSOCIATION
One Yonge St., #1400, Toronto, Ont. M5E 1J9
(416) 363-7261
Manager, Sue Jones

CANADIAN WELDING BUREAU
254 Merton St., Toronto, Ont M4S 1A9
(416) 487-5415
General Manager, R.A. Dunn

Branch Offices

Atlantic Region: 5664 Stanley St., Halifax, N.S. B3K 2G1 (902/455-0891)
Alberta District: 5224 99th St., Edmonton, Alta. T6E 3N7 (403/436-2774)
B.C. District: 5760 Minoru Blvd., Richmond, B.C. V6X 2A9 (604/278-7826)
Midwest Region: 50 Paramount Rd., Winnipeg, Man. R2X 2W3 (204/632-6316)
Ontario Region: 254 Merton St., Toronto, Ont. M4S 1A9 (416/487-5415)
Quebec Region: 149 Oneida Dr., Pointe Claire, P.Q. H9R 1A9 (514/694-1539/2064)

CANADIAN WHOLESALE HARDWARE ASSOCIATION
6800 Campobello Rd., Mississauga, Ont. L5N 2L8
(416) 821-3470
Administrative Officer, H.E. Harvey

CANADIAN WILDLIFE FEDERATION
1673 Carling Ave., #106, Ottawa, Ont. K2A 1C4
(613) 725-2191
Executive Vice President, K.A. Brynaert

CANADIAN WIND ENGINEERING ASSOCIATION
Chairman, H.W. Teunissen, Atmospheric Environment Service, 4905 Dufferin St., Downsview, Ont. M3H 5T4 (416/667-4910)

CANADIAN WINDOW & DOOR MANUFACTURERS ASSOCIATION
27 Goulburn Ave., Ottawa, Ont. K1N 8C7
(613) 233-6205
Executive Vice President, J.F. McCracken

CANADIAN WINE INSTITUTE
One Yonge St., Ste. 2104, Toronto, Ont. M5E 1E5
(416) 363-5769
General Manager, N. Plumridge

CANADIAN WOLF DEFENDERS
Box 3480, Stn. D, Edmonton, Alta. T5L 4J3
(403) 479-7369
President, Arne Jonasson

CANADIAN WOMAN'S CHRISTIAN TEMPERANCE UNION
National Headquarters, #302, 30 Gloucester St., Toronto, Ont. M4Y 1L6 (416/922-0757)
Provincial Unions in all provinces, with elected representatives. Contact national headquarters for names.

CANADIAN WOOD COUNCIL
85 Albert St., Ottawa, Ont. K1P 6A4
(613) 235-7221
Executive Director, R. F. DeGrace

CANADIAN WOODWORK MANUFACTURERS ASSOCIATION
Secretary, Morley Halberstadt, 64 Signet Dr., Weston, Ont. M9L 1T1 (416/741-6000)

CANADIANS FOR CANADA
Box 159, First Canadian Place, Toronto, Ont. M5X 1H4
(416) 865-0807

CARE CANADA
1312 Bank St., Ottawa, Ont. K1S 5H7
(613) 521-7081
National Director, Thomas Kines

Administrative Services Director, Domenico Ricci
Program Director, Rheal Cousineau

Affiliated Branches

Vancouver: Glen Ringdal, Box 86668, North Vancouver, B.C. V7L 4L2
Calgary: Mrs. B. Hanson, 2628 Cochrane Rd. N.W., Calgary, Alta. T2M 4H7
Toronto: C. J. Harris, Box 99, Terminal M, Toronto, Ont. M6S 4T2

CARE-RING (ONTARIO)

1066 Avenue Rd., Toronto, Ont. M5N 2C6
(416) 486-0620
Chairman, Mrs. June Laking

CARIBBEAN CULTURAL COMMITTEE

632B Yonge St., Toronto, Ont. M4Y 1Z8
(416) 925-5435
Chairman, Peter Marcelline

CARIBOO LUMBER MANUFACTURERS' ASSOCIATION

#301, 197 Second Ave. N., Williams Lake, B.C. V2G 1Z5
(604) 392-7778
President, J.C. Kerr
Manager, J.M. Taylor

THE CATHOLIC WOMEN'S LEAGUE OF CANADA

3081 Ness Ave., Winnipeg, Man. R2Y 2G3
(204) 885-4856, 889-6964
Executive Secretary, Valerie J. Fall

CATHOLIC YOUTH ORGANIZATION OF TORONTO

570-A Jarvis St., Toronto, Ont. M4Y 2H9
(416) 920-2393
Executive Director, L. G. Urszenyi

C. D. HOWE INSTITUTE

#2064, 1155 Metcalfe St., Montreal, P.Q. H3B 2X7
(514) 879-1254
Editor, Romana Cap

CENTRAIDE CANADA

(See United Way)

CENTRAL CANADA BROADCASTERS' ASSOCIATION

8th floor, 165 Sparks St., Ottawa, Ont. K1P 5R4
(613) 233-4035
Executive Secretary, Gerry Acton

CENTRAL FOREST PRODUCTS ASSOCIATION

14G-1975 Corydon Ave., Winnipeg, Man. R3P 0R1
(204) 489-5749
Secretary Manager, A. Stuesser

CENTRAL ONTARIO INDUSTRIAL RELATIONS INSTITUTE

Ste. 200, 85 Richmond St. W., Toronto, Ont. M5H 2C9
(416) 368-2364
General Counsel, R.A. Williamson

CENTRE COMMUNAUTAIRE FRANCOPHONE DE TORONTO

435 Queen's Quay W., Toronto, Ont. M5V 1A2
(416) 367-1950
Directeur, Mme Anne-Marie Couffin

CERAMIC TILE CONTRACTORS ASSOCIATION OF BRITISH COLUMBIA

-not confirmed for 1982-

2675 Oak St., Vancouver, B.C. V6H 2K3
(604) 736-6311
Secretary, Nancy Trant

THE CHAMPLAIN SOCIETY

Address communications to Executive Secretary Treasurer, Royal York Hotel, 100 Front St. W., Toronto, Ont. M5J 1E3 (416/363-8310)

CHARTERED ACCOUNTANTS' ASSOCIATIONS

INSTITUTE OF CHARTERED ACCOUNTANTS OF ALBERTA
(Incorporated 1910)
Executive Director, V. W. Dzurko, F.C.A., #201, 10080 Jasper Ave., Edmonton, Alta. T5J 1V9 (403/424-7391)

ATLANTIC PROVINCES ASSOCIATION OF CHARTERED ACCOUNTANTS
(Incorporated 1977)
Director of Education, R. Bowes, C.A., Box 489, Halifax, N.S. B3J 2R7 (902/425-7974)

INSTITUTE OF CHARTERED ACCOUNTANTS OF BERMUDA
(Incorporated 1972)
Executive Director, S. Gascoigne, B.A., M.Ed., Box 1625, Hamilton 5, Bermuda

INSTITUTE OF CHARTERED ACCOUNTANTS OF BRITISH COLUMBIA
Executive Director, J. D. Manson, F.C.A., 562 Burrard St., Vancouver, B.C. V6C 2K8 (604/681-3264)

CANADIAN INSTITUTE OF CHARTERED ACCOUNTANTS
(Incorporated 1902)
Executive Director, K.C. Fincham, F.C.A., 250 Bloor St. E., Toronto, Ont. M4W 1G5 (416/962-1242)

INSTITUTE OF CHARTERED ACCOUNTANTS OF MANITOBA
(Incorporated 1886)
Executive Director, C. O. Gilmore, F.C.A., #1200, 363 Broadway, Winnipeg, Man. R3C 3N9 (204/942-8248)

NEW BRUNSWICK INSTITUTE OF CHARTERED ACCOUNTANTS
(Incorporated 1916)
Executive Director, V.D. Lindley, 107 Germain St., Saint John, N.B. E2L 2E9 (506/652-3980)

INSTITUTE OF CHARTERED ACCOUNTANTS OF NEWFOUNDLAND
(Incorporated 1949)
Secretary, W. Drover, C.A., 70 Portugal Cove Rd., St. John's, Nfld. A1B 2M3 (709/753-7566)

INSTITUTE OF CHARTERED ACCOUNTANTS OF NOVA SCOTIA
(Incorporated 1900)
Executive Director, Ross Towler, C.A., #914, 5161 George St., Halifax, N.S. B3J 1M7 (902/425-3291)

INSTITUTE OF CHARTERED ACCOUNTANTS OF ONTARIO
(Founded 1879)
Executive Director, D.A. Wilson, F.C.A.
Institute Office, 69 Bloor St. E., Toronto, Ont. M4W 1B3
(416) 962-1841

INSTITUTE OF CHARTERED ACCOUNTANTS OF PRINCE EDWARD ISLAND
(Incorporated 1921)
Executive Secretary, E. Shea, C.A., Box 301, Charlottetown, P.E.I. C1A 7K7

ORDRE DES COMPTABLES AGREES DU QUEBEC
(Incorporated 1880)
Executive Director, A. Desrochers, C.A., 680 Sherbrooke St. W., 7th floor, Montreal, P.Q. H3A 2S3 (514/288-3256)

THE INSTITUTE OF CHARTERED ACCOUNTANTS OF SASKATCHEWAN
(Incorporated 1908)
Executive Director, J.A. Florek, C.A., #530, 1867 Hamilton St., Regina, Sask. S4P 2C2 (306/523-0900)

THE INSTITUTE OF CHARTERED ACCOUNTANTS OF THE NORTHWEST TERRITORIES
(Incorporated 1977)

Box 2433, Yellowknife, N.W.T. X0E 1H0

INSTITUTE OF CHARTERED ACCOUNTANTS OF THE YUKON TERRITORY
(Incorporated 1977)
Executive Director, J.D. Manson, Institute Administrative Office, 562 Burrard St., Vancouver, B.C. V6C 2K8 (604/681-3264)

THE CHEMICAL INSTITUTE OF CANADA
151 Slater St., Ste. 906, Ottawa, Ont. K1P 5H3
(613) 233-5623
Executive Director & Secretary, T. H. Glynn Michael, F.C.I.C.

Major local sections include Atlantic, Edmonton, Hamilton, Montreal, Ottawa, Sarnia, Saskatoon, Toronto, Vancouver, Wellington-Waterloo. These elect representatives annually. Contact the head office for latest names.

The Institute also maintains Student Chapters at most universities and technological colleges in Canada.

Official Publications: "Chemistry in Canada", "Canadian Journal of Chemical Engineering"

Constituent Societies

CANADIAN SOCIETY FOR CHEMICAL TECHNOLOGY
151 Slater St., Ste. 906, Ottawa, Ont. K1P 5H3
(613) 233-5623
Executive Secretary, Barry Bockus, A.C.I.C.

CANADIAN SOCIETY FOR CHEMICAL ENGINEERING
151 Slater St., Ste. 906, Ottawa, Ont. K1P 5H3
(613) 233-5623
Executive Secretary, Barry Bockus, A.C.I.C.

The society maintains eight Local Sections: Calgary, Edmonton, Montreal, Sarnia, Toronto, Vancouver, Kingston, Ottawa and student chapters at the following universities: Alberta, British Columbia, Ecole Polytechnique, Calgary, Laval, McGill, McMaster, New Brunswick, Nova Scotia Technical College, Ottawa, Queen's, Saskatchewan, Toronto, Waterloo, Royal Military College (Kingston), Lakehead, and Windsor.

Affiliated Societies

CANADIAN SOCIETY OF CLINICAL CHEMISTS
151 Slater St., #906, Ottawa, Ont. K1P 5H3
(613) 233-562
Executive Secretary, N.L. Chellingworth

QUEBEC RUBBER & PLASTICS GROUP
Box 220, Sherbrooke, P.Q. J1H 5H8
Secretary, J. Totsch

ONTARIO RUBBER GROUP
Secretary, I.E. Rowan, Uniroyal Ltd.

ASSOCIATION OF THE CHEMICAL PROFESSION OF ONTARIO
151 Slater St., Ste. 906, Ottawa, Ont. K1P 5H3
(613) 233-5623
Secretary, W.A. James, Ph.D.

ORDRE DES CHIMISTES DU QUEBEC
934, est, rue Ste-Catherine, Bur. 250, Montreal, P.Q. H2L 2E9
(514) 844-3644
President, Jean Claude Richer
Secretary, Réal Laliberte

THE CHESS FEDERATION OF CANADA
Business Manager, J. Berry, Box 7339, Ottawa, Ont. K1L 8E4
(613) 741-4242

The Federation co-ordinates chess play across Canada. The magazine *Chess Canada Echecs*, which gives results of completed tournaments, news of upcoming events, games and analysis, and books and equipment for sale, is sent free to all members bi-monthly.

CHESS FOUNDATION OF CANADA
c/o L. Kirstein, Chairman, 1455 Charlebois Ave., Orleans, Ont. K1E 1J8

CANADIAN CORRESPONDENCE CHESS ASSOCIATION
General Secretary, G. Ruben, 1319 Poprad Ave., Pickering, Ont. L1W 1K9

CHILDBIRTH EDUCATION ASSOCIATION OF TORONTO
33 Price St., Toronto, Ont. M4W 1Z2
(416) 924-1628

CHILDREN'S REHABILITATION & CEREBRAL PALSY ASSOCIATION
1195 W. 8th Ave., Vancouver, B.C. V6H 1C5
(604) 734-2221
Executive Director, J.R. Hopkins

CHINESE NATIONALIST LEAGUE OF CANADA
529 Gore Ave., Vancouver, B.C. V6A 2Z6
(604) 681-6022
Secretary General, Y.L. Wong

CHIROPRACTIC ORGANIZATIONS

Canadian Chiropractic Association
1900 Bayview Ave., Toronto, Ont. M4G 3E6
(416) 487-5459
Executive Director, Dr. J.L. Watkins

Provincial Associations

ALBERTA CHIROPRACTIC ASSOCIATION
Secretary, S.A. Marcoux, 10106 111 Ave., #203, Edmonton, Alta. T5G 0B4 (403/477-5171)

BRITISH COLUMBIA CHIROPRACTIC ASSOCIATION
Secretary, B. Alderson, D.C., #213, 736 Granville St., Vancouver, B.C. V6Z 1G3 (604/681-8028)

MANITOBA CHIROPRACTORS' ASSOCIATION
Secretary, J.K. Bloomer, D.C., #121, 388 Donald St., Winnipeg, Man. R3B 2J4 (204/943-3955)

NEW BRUNSWICK CHIROPRACTORS' ASSOCIATION
Secretary, R.C. Randall, D.C., 126 Steadman St., Moncton, N.B. E1C 4P6 (506/855-1110)

NOVA SCOTIA CHIROPRACTORS' ASSOCIATION
Secretary, B. Stephenson, M.A., D.C., 50 Hawthorn St., Antigonish, N.S. B2G 1A4 (902/863-6924)

ONTARIO CHIROPRACTIC ASSOCIATION
Executive Director, R.C. Lafferty, 1900 Bayview Ave., Toronto, Ont. M4G 3E6 (416/482-2707)

PRINCE EDWARD ISLAND CHIROPRACTIC ASSOCIATION
Secretary, M. Gamble, D.C., 40 Upper Queen St., Summerside, P.E.I.

QUEBEC ASSOCIATION OF CHIROPRACTORS
Executive Secretary, Miss Suzanne Lamanque, 1344 Jean-Talon St. E., Montreal, P.Q. H2E 1S1 (514/273-5391)

QUEBEC ORDER OF CHIROPRACTORS
50 Cremazie Place, #921, Montreal, P.Q. H2P 2T6
(514) 382-5821

CHIROPRACTORS' ASSOCIATION OF SASKATCHEWAN
Secretary, Mrs. June Bredin, #1, 3420A Hill Ave., Regina, Sask. S4S 0W9 (306/585-1411)

Chiropractic Boards

CANADIAN CHIROPRACTIC EXAMINING BOARD
Chairman, J.A. Langford, D.C., 423 Colborne St., London, Ont. N6B 2T2

BOARD OF DIRECTORS OF CHIROPRACTIC OF ONTARIO
Secretary, S.W. Stolarski, D.C., 20 Prince Arthur Ave., Ste. 15D, Toronto, Ont. M5R 1B1 (416/922-6355)

ADVISORY BOARD
Chairman, R.A. Oswald, D.C., 102 King St. E., Stoney Creek, Ont. L8G 1K6

Chiropractic Council

CANADIAN COUNCIL OF CHIROPRACTIC ROENTGENOLOGY
President, V. Thomson, D.C., 3367 Bloor St. W., Toronto, Ont. M8X 1G2

CHRETIENS D'AUJOURD'HUI
242 1073 boul. St-Cyrille ouest, Québec, P.Q. G1S 4R5
(418) 688-1211
A Catholic Action movement for men.
Secretary, (TBA)

MOUVEMENT DES FEMMES CHRETIENNES
A Catholic action movement for women.
Same address and phone as Chretiens D'Aujourd'hui

CHRISTIAN CHILDREN'S FUND OF CANADA
1407 Yonge St., Toronto, Ont. M4T 1Y8
(416) 922-2767
National Director, P.G. Harris

CHRISTIAN REFORMED WORLD RELIEF COMMITTEE OF CANADA
Box 5070 (760 Brant St., #408), Burlington, Ont. L7R 3Y8
(416) 637-3434
Director, H. Veldstra

CHRISTMAS TREE GROWERS' ASSOCIATION OF ONTARIO INC.
Secretary, R. Drysdale, 234 Delhi, Downsview, Ont. M3H 1A8

LA CINEMATHEQUE QUEBECOISE
335 de Maisonneuve est, Montreal, P.Q. H2X 1K1
(514) 845-8118
Directeur général, Robert Daudelin

CITIES ASSOCIATION OF NEW BRUNSWICK
500 Beaverbrook Court, Fredericton, N.B. E3B 5X4
(506) 455-1501
Executive Secretary, R. Ogilvie

CITIZENSHIP COUNCIL OF MANITOBA
700 Elgin Ave., Winnipeg, Man. R3E 1B2
(204) 772-0346
Executive Director, Mrs. Elizabeth Willcock

CIVITAN INTERNATIONAL IN CANADA
Civitan's slate of officers is elected annually after the Almanac deadline. For up to date information contact:
Frank J. Bulgarella, Executive Administrator, Civitan International, Box 2102, Birmingham, Ala. 35201

CLAY BRICK ASSOCIATION OF CANADA
5218 Yonge St., Willowdale, Ont. M2N 5P6
(416) 225-7763
Managing Director, J. F. Cutler

CLUB MINI BARMAN
(a mini-bottle collectors' club)
C.P. 126, Rosemount, Montreal, P.Q. H1X 3B6

COAL ASSOCIATION OF CANADA
#210, 909 5th Ave. S.W., Calgary, Alta. T2P 0N8
(403) 262-1544 Telex: 03-827596
President, G.T. Page

COALITION FOR LIFE
280 Albert St., #410, Ottawa, Ont. K1P 5G8
(613) 232-0024
Executive Director, Don McPhee

COLOR PHOTOGRAPHIC ASSOCIATION OF CANADA, INC.
Secretary, Miss Loretta Dean, 104 John St., Thornhill, Ont. L3T 1Y5 (416/889-2153)

LE COMITE DIOCESAIN D'ACTION CATHOLIQUE
A group for the co-ordination of Catholic Action Associations in the Quebec diocese.
Action Catholique de Milieu, 435 du Roi, Quebec, P.Q. G1K 2X1 (418/525-6187)

COMMITTEE FOR AN INDEPENDENT CANADA
-not confirmed for 1982-
National Office: 46 Elgin St., Ste. 48, Ottawa, Ont. K1P 5K6 (613/238-2730)

COMMITTEE FOR ORIGINAL PEOPLE'S ENTITLEMENT
Box 2000, Inuvik, N.W.T. XOE OTO
(403) 979-3510
Executive Director, Peter Green

COMMITTEE ON SEALS & SEALING
8064 Yonge St., Thornhill, Ont. L4J 1W3
(416) 226-9110
Secretary, T.I. Hughes

COMMONWEALTH PARLIAMENTARY ASSOCIATION
(Canadian Branch)
Box 950, Parliament Bldgs., Ottawa, Ont. K1A 0X2
(613) 996-6111
Presidents, Senator the Hon. Jean Marchand, P.C. (Speaker of the Senate); Hon. Jeanne Sauvé, P.C., M.P. (Speaker of the House of Commons)
Vice Presidents, Rt. Hon. Pierre Trudeau, P.C., M.P. (Prime Minister); Rt. Hon. Joseph Clark, P.C., M.P. (Leader of the Opposition)
Executive Secretary Treasurer, Ian G. Imrie

COMMONWEALTH PRESS UNION
President, The Lord Astor of Hever, *The Times,* London, England.

Canadian Section
Chairman, Donald G. Campbell, Maclean Hunter Ltd., Toronto
Honorary Chairman, Michael Davies, The Whig-Standard, Kingston
Vice Chairman, Frank G. Swanson, The Calgary Herald, Calgary
Honorary Secretary Treasurer, T.J. McCarthy, The Spectator, Box 300, Hamilton, Ont. L8N 3G3 (416/526-3203)

COMMUNITY LEGAL EDUCATION ONTARIO
111 Queen St. E., Ste. 310, Toronto, Ont. M5C 1S2
(416) 363-0466
Managing Director, Wendy L. Geyer
Hamilton: 25 Hughson St. S., #504, Hamilton, Ont. L8N 2A5 (416/523-4461); Program Director, Madeline Yakimchuk

COMPASSION OF CANADA
Box 5591, London, Ont. N6A 5G8
(519) 686-6788
(An independent charitable organization that provides sponsors for children in third world countries)
Director of Communications, Rev. Robert Ripley

COMPOSERS, AUTHORS & PUBLISHERS ASSOCIATION OF CANADA, LTD.
1240 Bay St., Toronto, Ont. M5R 2C2 (416/924-4427)
1245 Sherbrooke St. W., Montreal, P.Q. H3G 1G2 (514/288-4755)
1 Alexander St., Vancouver, B.C. V6A 1B2 (604/689-8871)

General Manager, John V. Mills, OC, Q.C.

COMPRESSED GAS ASSOCIATION INC.
Canadian Division
2003 Foxcroft Ave., Mississauga, Ont. L5J 2J6
(416) 278-2456
Secretary, F.R. Adams

CONFECTIONERY MANUFACTURERS ASSOCIATION OF CANADA
1185 Eglinton Ave. E., Ste. 101, Don Mills, Ont. M3C 3C6
(416) 429-1046
General Manager, Philip Moyes

LA CONFEDERATION DES CAISSES POPULAIRES ET D'ECONOMIE DESJARDINS DU QUEBEC
100 ave des Commandeurs, Lévis, P.Q. G6V 7N5
(418) 835-7323
President, Raymond Blais

CONFEDERATION OF INDIANS OF QUEBEC
President, Joe Stacey, Box 810, Caughnawaga, P.Q. JOL 1BO (514/632-7321)

CONFEDERATION OF RESIDENT & RATEPAYERS ASSOCIATIONS
Attn.: Susan Kee, c/o Social Planning Council, 185 Bloor St. E., Toronto, Ont. M4W 3J3 (416/961-9831)

CONFEDERATION DES SYNDICATS NATIONAUX
(Trade Unions)
1601 deLorimier, Montréal, P.Q. H2K 4M5
(514) 286-2121

The Confédération is a Canadian organization affiliated with the World Confederation of Labour and confines its activity mostly to the Province of Quebec although it has some locals in Ontario, in New Brunswick, and one in Newfoundland.

It comprises 9 federations, 22 Central Councils and 1,600 syndicates. It has approximately 220,000 members.

President, Norbert Rodrigue
General Secretary, Sylvio Gagnon
Official Organ, "Le Travail"
Director, Michel Rioux

THE CONFERENCE BOARD OF CANADA
25 McArthur Rd., Ste. 100, Ottawa, Ont. K1L 6R3
(613) 746-1261
President, Dr. James R. Nininger

CONSEIL ACADIEN DE COOPERATION CULTURELLE (EN ATLANTIQUE)
Ste. 206, 120 rue Victoria, Moncton, N.B. E1C 1P9
(506) 388-3045
Directeur, Maurice A. Léger

Organismes membres:

- Le conseil de promotion et de diffusion de la culture (Nouveau-Brunswick), a/s Ginette Ste-Marie, Directeur général, 261 rue Lutz, Moncton, N.B. E1C 5G4 (506/382-0764)
- Le Secteur culturel de la fédération acadienne de la Nouvelle-Ecosse, a/s Jules Chiasson, animateur culturel, Les Trois Pignons, Chéticamp, N.S. B0E 1H0 (902/224-2642)
- Le comité culturel de la Société Saint-Thomas-d'Aquin de l'Ile-du-Prince-Edouard, a/s Liliane Gaudet, C.P. 1362, Summerside, P.E.I. C1N 3K5 (902/436-4881)
- La fédération des francophones de Terre-Neuve et du Labrador, a/s Françoise Enguehard, animateur culturel, C.P. 9274, Succ. B, St. John's, Nfld. A1A 2X9 (709/726-4900)

CONSEIL DES TRADUCTEURS ET INTERPRETES DU CANADA
(Canadian Translators & Interpreters Council)
C.P. 452, Succ. A, Ottawa, Ont. K1N 8V5
Administrator, J.-C. Carisse
Organ: META

CONSTRUCTION MANAGEMENT LABOUR BUREAU LTD.
Box 8628, Stn. A, Halifax, N.S. B3K 5M3
(902) 429-6763
Director, Labour Relations, Merrill C. Brinton

CONSTRUCTION SPECIFICATIONS CANADA
#1206, 1 St. Clair Ave. W., Toronto, Ont. M4V 1K6
(416) 922-3159
Executive Vice President, René Gaulin

CONSUMER ELECTRONICS INDUSTRIES
#1608, One Yonge St., Toronto, Ont. M5E 1R1
(416) 862-7152

CONSUMERS' ASSOCIATION OF CANADA
Southvale Plaza, 2660 Southvale Cres., Level III, Ottawa, Ont. K1B 5C4
(613) 238-4840
President, Mrs. Janice Kerr, 406 Prince St., Truro, N.S. B2N 1E5

There are provincial affiliates in all provinces, with annually elected officials. Contact the national office for names.

CO-OPERATIVE UNION OF CANADA
237 Metcalfe St., Ottawa, Ont. K2P 1R2
(613) 238-6711; Telex: 053-4406
Executive Director, Bruce Thordarson

CORPORATION OF MASTER PIPE MECHANICS OF QUEBEC
2475 Blvd. Sir Wilfrid Laurier, Quebec, P.Q. G1T 1C4 (418/653-8376)
Ste. 265, 1400 Sauve St. W., Montreal, P.Q. H4N 1C5 (514/332-6171)

CORPORATION PROFESSIONNELLE DES TRAVAILLEURS SOCIAUX DU QUEBEC
(Social Workers)
5757 Decelles Ave., Ch. 335, Montreal, P.Q. H3S 2C3
(514) 731-2749

CORPORATION OF QUEBEC CHARTERED MUNICIPAL OFFICERS
1100 De La Chevrotière, Québec, P.Q. G1K 7X2
(418) 643-1998
Attn.: Georges Delisle

CORPORATION OF QUEBEC MUNICIPAL SECRETARIES
(La Corporation des Secrétaires Municipaux du Québec Inc.)
580 Grande Allée est, #325, Québec, P.Q. G1R 2K2
(418) 647-4518
Attn.: Marie-Andrée Levasseur

CORPORATION DES SERVICES D'AMBULANCE DU QUEBEC
-not confirmed for 1982-
939 rue Paradis, Roberval, Lac St-Jean, P.Q. G8H 2J9
(418) 275-4424
Secretary, Ghislain Harvey

CORPORATION OF TRANSLATORS & INTERPRETERS OF NEW BRUNSWICK
Box 427, Fredericton, N.B. E3B 4Z9
(506) 452-3407

CORRUGATED STEEL PIPE INSTITUTE
Ste. 207, Crestview Plaza, 1640 Crestview Ave., Mississauga, Ont. L5G 3P9

(416) 274-2354
General Manager, William A. Porter

COSTI-IIAS Immigrant Services
1215A St. Clair Ave. W., Toronto, Ont. M6E 1B5
(416) 652-1033

COUCHICHING INSTITUTE ON PUBLIC AFFAIRS
20 Eglinton Ave. E., Ste. 203, Toronto, Ont. M4P 1A9
(416) 489-9212
Executive Director, Michael Wilson

COUNCIL FOR BUSINESS & THE ARTS IN CANADA
Box 7, 401 Bay St., Toronto, Ont. M5H 2Y4
(416) 869-3016
President & Chief Executive Officer, Arnold Edinborough

COUNCIL OF CANADIAN FILMMAKERS
Box 1003, Stn. A, Toronto, Ont. M5W 1G5
(416) 869-0716

COUNCIL OF CANADIAN PERSONNEL ASSOCIATIONS
11 Adelaide St. W., #803, Toronto, Ont. M5H 1L9
(416) 363-9453

THE COUNCIL FOR CANADIAN UNITY
2055 Peel St., Ste. 1000, Montreal, P.Q. H3A 1V4
(514) 849-5303; Telex: 055-61492
Executive Director, Mr. Jocelyn L. Beadoin

COUNCIL OF CATHOLIC CHARITIES OF TORONTO
67 Bond St., Toronto, Ont. M5B 1X5
(416) 363-1301
Executive Director, Rev. Paul Lennon, M.S.W.

COUNCIL ON DRUG ABUSE
56 Esplanade St. E., Toronto, Ont. M5E 1A7
(416) 367-0183
Secretary, Mrs. H. Colme

COUNCIL OF FOREST INDUSTRIES OF BRITISH COLUMBIA
1055 W. Hastings, Vancouver, B.C. V6E 2H1
(604) 684-0211
President & Chief Executive Officer, D. A. S. Lanskail

COUNCIL OF PRINTING INDUSTRIES OF CANADA
159 Bay St., Suite 808, Toronto, Ont. M5J 1J7
(416) 362-2528
General Manager, Franklyn R. Smith

CREDIT BUREAUS
See "Associated Credit Bureaus"

CREDITEL OF CANADA LTD.
National Office, 931 Yonge St., Toronto, Ont. M4W 2H6
(416) 924-8461
President & General Manager, M. A. Desautels, B.A., LL.M.
Secretary Treasurer, A.D. Stirling

Regional Offices with Managers

Central: Ian D. Macdonald, 931 Yonge St., Toronto, Ont. M4W 2H6 (416/924-8461)
Eastern: M. L'Heureux, 7170 St. Lawrence Blvd., Montreal, P.Q. H2S 3E2 (514/270-7111)
Pacific: D. Ainslie, Ste. 125, Sperling Plaza, 6400 Roberts St., Burnaby, B.C. V5G 4C9 (604/291-2281)
Prairie: A. J. Breen, 1038 Portage Ave. W., Winnipeg, Man. R3C 3B9 (204/774-4486)
Western: R. Drummond, 10441 123rd St., Edmonton, Alta. T5N 1N8

THE CRIMINAL LAWYERS ASSOCIATION
-not confirmed for 1982-
Treasurer, John M. Rosen, 390 Bay St., Ste. 1520, Toronto, Ont. M5H 2Y2 (416/364-8500)

CROSS-CANADA WRITERS' WORKSHOP
Box 277, Stn. F, Toronto, Ont. M4Y 2L7
(416) 690-0917
Founder, Ted Plantos

CU AND C HEALTH SERVICES SOCIETY
22 E. 8th Ave., Vancouver, B.C. V5T 1R4
(604) 879-5711
General Manager, D.D. Schreck, Ph.D.

CUMBA
Secretary & General Manager, D.M. Tripp, 562 Eglinton Ave. E., Toronto, Ont. M4P 1B9 (416/487-5451)

CZECHOSLOVAK NATIONAL ASSOCIATION OF CANADA
740 Spadina Ave., Toronto, Ont. M5S 2J2
(416) 925-0557
President, J.G. Corn, C.A.
Secretary General, Prof. Dr. Victor Fic

DAIRY ASSOCIATIONS
See Agriculture Associations

DANCE ASSOCIATIONS
See Music Associations

DATA PROCESSING MANAGEMENT ASSOCIATION OF TORONTO
Box 116, Stn. F, Toronto, Ont. M4Y 2L4
(416) 445-8287
President, R. Paolucci

DAUGHTERS OF ENGLAND BENEVOLENT SOCIETY
Grand Secretary, Miss I. G. Luckett, Box 29, Cookstown, Ont. L0L 1L0 (705/458-4440)

DEAF CANADIAN READERS' ASSOCIATION
Box 1291, Edmonton, Alta. T5J 2M8
(403) 462-3323
President & Executive Director, David Burnett

DEAFNESS COMMUNICATIONS
(Canadian Registry of Interpreters for the Deaf)
Box 219, Brooklin, Ont. L0B 1C0
(416) 655-4434
President, E. Marshall Wick

DECISION CANADA
800 Stock Exchange Tower, Place Victoria, Ste. 2810, Montreal, P.Q. H4Z 1E6
(514) 878-3081
President, Robert Dostie

DEFENCE MEDICAL ASSOCIATION OF CANADA
Secretary Treasurer, Col. J.E. Lawson, 565 Shelley Ave., Ottawa, Ont. K1G 0S1

DENE NATIONAL OFFICE
-not confirmed for 1982-
Box 2338, Yellowknife, N.W.T. X0E 1H0
(403) 873-4081

DENTAL ORGANIZATIONS

Canadian Dental Association

Executive Director, Hubert E. Drouin, 1815 Alta Vista Dr., Ottawa, Ont. K1G 3Y6 (613/523-1770)

National Dental Examining Board of Canada

Registrar, Dr. G. Kravis, 100 Bronson Ave., Suite 807, Ottawa, Ont. K1R 6G8 (613/236-5912)

Provincial Licensing Bodies

ALBERTA DENTAL ASSOCIATION

Registrar, Dr. B.P. Martinello, #101, 8230 105 St., Edmonton, Alta. T6E 5H9 (403/432-1012)

COLLEGE OF DENTAL SURGEONS OF BRITISH COLUMBIA

Registrar, Dr. G.R. Thordarson, 1125 W. 8th Ave., Vancouver, B.C. V6H 3N4 (604/736-3621)

MANITOBA DENTAL ASSOCIATION

Registrar, Dr. U.R. Claman, #300, 296 Kennedy St., Winnipeg, Man. R3B 2M6 (204/942-5211)

NEW BRUNSWICK DENTAL SOCIETY

Executive Director, Registrar, Dr. J.G. Thompson, 79 Neck Rd., Quispamsis, Rothesay, N.B. E0G 2W0 (506/847-4243)

NEWFOUNDLAND DENTAL BOARD

Registrar, Dr. Bruce L. Bowden, 205 LeMarchant Rd., St. John's, Nfld. A1C 2H5 (709/579-1213)

PROVINCIAL DENTAL BOARD OF NOVA SCOTIA

Registrar, Dr. S. G. Bagnall, #206, 2745 Dutch Village Rd., Halifax, N.S. B3L 4G7 (902/454-5449)

THE ROYAL COLLEGE OF DENTAL SURGEONS OF ONTARIO

Registrar Secretary Treasurer, Dr. K. F. Pownall, 230 St. George St., Toronto, Ont. M5R 2N5 (416/961-6555)

DENTAL ASSOCIATION OF PRINCE EDWARD ISLAND

Secretary Registrar, Dr. R.D. Wenn, Box 280, Cornwall, P.E.I. C0A 1H0 (902/892-9234)

ORDRE DES DENTISTES DU QUEBEC

Director General, Dr. Pierre-Yves Lamarche, 801 Sherbrooke St. E., Ste. 303, Montreal, P.Q. H2L 1K7 (514/526-6638)

COLLEGE OF DENTAL SURGEONS OF SASKATCHEWAN

Secretary, Dr. G. H. Peacock, 105 21st St. E., #811, Saskatoon, Sask. S7K 0B3 (306/244-5072)

Provincial Dental Associations

NEWFOUNDLAND DENTAL ASSOCIATION

Secretary, Dr. T.J. Gushue, Box 9505, St. John's, Nfld. A1A 2Y4 (709/579-2362)

NOVA SCOTIA DENTAL ASSOCIATION

Executive Director, D.V. Pamenter, #206, 2745 Dutch Village Rd., Halifax, N.S. B3L 4G7

ONTARIO DENTAL ASSOCIATION

Executive Director, John C. Gillies, C.A.E., 234 St. George St., Toronto, Ont. M5R 2P1 (416/922-3900)

Other Dental Associations

ALBERTA DENTAL ASSISTANTS ASSOCIATION

50 Chinook Dr. S.W., Calgary, Alta. T2V 2P6
(403) 255-5905

ASSOCIATION OF REGISTERED DENTAL TECHNICIANS

-not confirmed for 1982-
1962 Yonge St., Ste. 206, Toronto, Ont. M4S 1Z4
(416) 482-3008
Executive Director, Bernard Mullen, R.D.T.

CANADIAN DENTAL HYGIENISTS' ASSOCIATION

-not confirmed for 1982-
Executive Secretary, Mrs. Judy Dickey, 46 James St., Aylmer, P.Q. J9H 4S6 (819/684-9102)

CANADIAN DENTAL NURSES & ASSISTANTS ASSOCIATION

Executive Director, Ms. Elaine Wesley, SS1-1-21, Lethbridge, Alta. T1J 4B3 (403/328-1948)

CANADIAN SOCIETY OF DENTISTRY FOR CHILDREN

c/o Dr. D.L. Rife, 2953 Bathurst St., Toronto, Ont. M6B 3B2 (416/783-0419)

GOVERNING BOARD OF DENTAL TECHNICIANS OF ONTARIO

11A Glen Watford Dr., Ste. 10, Agincourt, Ont. M1S 2B8
(416) 293-7921
Secretary Registrar, tba

ONTARIO DENTAL NURSES & ASSISTANTS ASSOCIATION

#406, 345 Dixon Rd., Weston, Ont. M9R 1S6
(416) 245-6129

ROYAL COLLEGE OF DENTISTS OF CANADA

#614, 170 St. George St., Toronto, Ont. M5R 2M8
(416) 964-7263
Registrar, Dr. J.E. Speck

DESK & DERRICK CLUB OF CALGARY

President, Gladys P. Wells, c/o Home Oil Co. Ltd., #2300, 324 8th Ave. S.W., Calgary, Alta. T2P 2Z5 (403/232-7165)

DIRECTORS GUILD OF CANADA

#47, 3 Church St., Toronto, Ont. M5E 1M2
(416) 364-0122

The Directors Guild of Canada was formed in 1961 to represent the interests of Professional Film and Television Directors, Unit Production Managers and Assistant Directors, Trainee Assistant Directors (Production Assistants), and Art Directors.

National Executive Secretary, P.J. Currie
Western Representative, Michael Steele, 744 W. Hastings St., #119, Vancouver, B.C. V6C 1A5

DIRECT SELLERS ASSOCIATION

390 Bay St., Ste. 1506, Toronto, Ont. M5H 2Y2
(416) 368-1089
President, Leonard C. Webster
Secretary, Ruth C. Peet

DISABLED VETERANS' ASSOCIATION

438 W. Pender St., Vancouver, B.C. V6B 1T5
(604) 683-3633

DOMINION OF CANADA ENGLISH SPEAKING ASSOCIATION

Box 2, Moncton, N.B. E1C 8R9
(506) 384-8074
President, James London, 9 Purdy Ave., Moncton, N.B.

THE DOMINION OF CANADA RIFLE ASSOCIATION

Cottage Row, CFB Ottawa North, K1A 0K4
(613) 741-6356
Executive Vice President, Major C.M. Brown
Executive Director, Robert B. Muir

DOMINION CHARTERED CUSTOMS HOUSE BROKERS ASSOCIATION

46 Elgin St., Ste. 18, Ottawa, Ont. K1P 5K6
(613) 238-3394; Telex: 053-4474
Executive Vice President, J. Norman Leigh

There are Divisions in every province, plus one each in Toronto and Montreal. For names of elected officers contact the head office.

DOMINION CIVIL SERVICE VETERANS ASSOCIATION

1403 Gerrard St. E., Toronto, Ont. M4L 1Z5
(416) 465-0477

DOMINION MARINE ASSOCIATION
350 Sparks St., Ste. 703, Ottawa, Ont. K1R 7S8
(613) 232-3539
President, R/Adm. R. W. Timbrell

DOOR & HARDWARE INSTITUTE
(Ontario Chapter)
1622 Magenta Court, Mississauga, Ont. L5G 3A7
(416) 278-8491

DOWNTOWN HALIFAX BUSINESS ASSOCIATION
Box 761, 1541 Barrington St., Halifax, N.S. B3J 1Z5
(902) 423-6658
Executive Manager, W.H. McCurdy

DOWNTOWN VICTORIA ASSOCIATION
319 Sayward Bldg., 1207 Douglas St., Victoria, B.C. V8W 2E7
(604) 383-2111
Executive Manager, Mrs. Gerry Parker

DRUGGISTS' ASSOCIATIONS
See Pharmaceutical Associations

DRY CLEANERS & LAUNDERERS INSTITUTE (ONTARIO)
49 Eglinton Ave. E., Toronto, Ont. M4P 1G6
(416) 481-6881
Managing Director, J. J. Dillon

DUCKS UNLIMITED (CANADA)
Conservation of waterfowl habitat.
Head Office, 1190 Waverley St., Winnipeg, Man. R3T 2E2
(204) 477-1760
Executive Vice President, D. S. Morrison
Public Relations, C.A. Radimer

Provincial Branches with Managers

Alta.: A. C. Burns, 10422 169 St., Edmonton, Alta. T5P 3X6 (403/484-1187)
B.C.: T.K. Slater, 2-345 Victoria St., Kamloops, B.C. V2C 2A3 (604/374-8307)
Man.: R.B. Fowler, 1190 Waverley St., Winnipeg, Man. R3T 2E2 (204/477-1760)
Maritimes: A.S. Glover, Box 61, 32 Church St., Amherst, N.S. B4H 3Y6 (902/667-8726)
Ont.: R.L. Renwick, 240 Bayview Dr., Unit 10, Barrie, Ont. L4N 4Y8 (705/726-3825)
Que.: G. Arseneault, 929 Boul. du Séminaire, St-Jean, P.Q. J3A 1B6 (514/348-6811)
Sask.: D. Chekay, Box 4465, 1606 4th Ave., Regina, Sask. S4P 3W7 (306/569-0424)

DUTCH CANADIAN SOCIETY OF MANITOBA INC.
Box 525, Winnipeg, Man. R3C 2J3
(204) 339-5674
President, George de Jonge, 1154 Salter St., Winnipeg, Man. R2V 2J1

DX RADIO CLUBS

CANADIAN INTERNATIONAL DX RADIO CLUB
169 Grandview Ave., Winnipeg, Man. R2G 0L4
Executive Secretary, Lorne Jennings

CANADIAN S-W-L INTERNATIONAL
Box 142, Thunder Bay, Ont. P7C 4V5
(807) 577-9182

HANDICAPPED AID PROGRAM – CANADIAN BRANCH (CHAP)
6 Coolbreeze Ave., Pointe Claire, P.Q. H9S 5G4
(514) 697-4969 (evenings)

UNIVERSITY OF MANITOBA DX CLUB
Box 131, University Centre, Winnipeg, Man. R3T 2N2
(204) 474-8233

EAR BONE BANK OF BRITISH COLUMBIA
865 W. 10th Ave., Vancouver, B.C. V5Z 1L7
(604) 874-6312
Director, A. Blokmanis, M.B.B.S., F.R.C.S.(C), F.R.A.C.S.

EASTCOAST PETROLEUM OPERATORS ASSOCIATION
#1902, 727 6th Ave. S.W., Calgary, Alta. T2P 0V1
(403) 265-1161
Executive Director, Dr. G.H. Jones

EASTER SEALS ASSOCIATIONS
See 'Canadian Rehabilitation Council'

EDUCATIONAL & SCHOLARLY ORGANIZATIONS

Alberta Federation of Home & School Associations
#6, 416 83rd Ave. S.E., Calgary, Alta. T2H 1N3
(403) 252-4171

Association of Atlantic Universities
Ste. 702, 6080 Young St., Halifax, N.S. B3K 5L2
(902) 453-2775

Association for Bright Children - A.B.C.
General Secretary, Fred Speed, c/o University of Toronto Schools, 371 Bloor St. W., Toronto, Ont. M5S 2R8

L'Association des cadres scolaires du Québec
2014 boul. Charest ouest, bur. 205, Québec, P.Q. G1N 4N6
Directeur exécutif, Fernand Langlais

Association of Canadian Career Colleges
(L'Association Canadienne des Collèges Carrière)
One Wellington St., Box 340, Brantford, Ont. N3T 5N3
(519) 753-8689

Association of Canadian Community Colleges
(Association des Collèges Communautaires du Canada)
211 Consumers Rd., Ste. 203, Willowdale, Ont. M2J 4G8
(416) 497-6661
Executive Director, J.P.R. LaRose

Association canadienne française pour l'avancement des sciences
-not confirmed for 1982-
2730, chemin Côte Ste Catherine, C. P. 6060, Montreal, P.Q. H3C 3A7
(514) 342-1411, 12
Secretaire, Serge Hamel

Association des colleges du Quebec (ACQ)
1940 boul. Henri-Bourassa est, Montréal, P.Q. H2B 1S2
(514) 381-8891
Secrétaire général, Jean-Marie Saint-Germain

Association des Commissions Scolaires du Diocese de Quebec
100 Begon, Ste-Foy, P.Q. G1X 3M4
(418) 653-8738

Association for Early Childhood Education, Ontario
212 King St. W., #503, Toronto, Ont. M5H 1K5
(416) 598-1205
Toronto branch: 2498 Yonge St., Toronto, Ont. M4P 2H8

Association d'Education du Quebec
1990 ouest, boul. Charest, bur. 220, Québec, P.Q. G1N 4K8

(418) 681-0178
Directeur général, Michel Simard

Association des Institutions d'Enseignement Secondaire (AIES)

1940 est, boul. Henri-Bourassa, Montreal, P.Q. H2B 1S2
(514) 381-8891
Secrétaire général, Gilles-André Grégoire

Association des Institutions de Niveaux Prescolaire et Elementaire du Quebec

1940 est. boul. Henri-Bourassa, Montreal, P.Q. H2B 1S2
(514) 381-8891
President, H. Landry

Association nationale des étudiants et étudiantes du Québec

232 ouest rue Jean-Talon, Montréal, P.Q. H2R 2X5
(514) 277-5826
Publishes: Le Québec Etudiant

Association of Student Councils (Canada)

44 St. George St., Toronto, Ont. M5S 2E4
(416) 979-2604
Offices in Vancouver, Edmonton, Saskatoon, Ottawa, Halifax.

Association of Universities & Colleges of Canada

(Association des Universités et Collèges du Canada)
151 Slater St., Ottawa, Ont. K1P 5N1
(613) 563-3562
President, Dr. L.I. Barber, University of Regina
Executive Director/Directeur administratif, A.K. Gillmore

Associate Members

ASSOCIATION OF CANADIAN FACULTIES OF DENTISTRY
Executive Director, Dr. G.W. Myers, Faculty of Dentistry, Dentistry-Pharmacy Centre, The University of Alberta, Edmonton, Alta. T6G 2H7 (403/432-5762)

ASSOCIATION OF CANADIAN FACULTIES OF ENVIRONMENTAL STUDIES
Executive Secretary, P.C. Brother, Faculty of Environmental Studies, University of Waterloo, Waterloo, Ont. N2L 3G1 (519/885-1211, ext. 2796)

ASSOCIATION OF CANADIAN MEDICAL COLLEGES
Executive Director, Dr. Douglas Waugh, 151 Slater St., Ottawa, Ont. K1P 5N1 (613/237-0070)

ASSOCIATION OF CANADIAN UNIVERSITY INFORMATION BUREAUS
Secretary, Robert Raeburn, Director, University Relations & Information Office, The University of Manitoba, Winnipeg, Man. R3T 2N2 (204/474-8174)

ASSOCIATION OF DEANS OF PHARMACY OF CANADA
Secretary Treasurer, Dr. Mervyn Huston, Faculty of Pharmacy & Pharmaceutical Sciences, Room 318, Dentistry-Pharmacy Bldg., The University of Alberta, Edmonton, Alta. T6G 2N5 (403/432-3362)

ASSOCIATION OF FACULTIES OF AGRICULTURE IN CANADA
Secretary Treasurer, Dean A.D. Ells, Technical & Vocational Training, N.S. Agricultural College, Truro, N.S. B2N 5E3 (902/895-1571, ext. 235)

ASSOCIATION OF FACULTIES OF VETERINARY MEDICINE IN CANADA
Secretary Treasurer, Dr. J. Robert Saunders, Western College of Veterinary Medicine, Veterinary Microbiology, University of Saskatchewan, Saskatoon, Sask. S7N 0W0 (306/344-5533)

ASSOCIATION OF REGISTRARS OF UNIVERSITIES & COLLEGES OF CANADA
Secretary Treasurer, L.A. Towe, Asst. Registrar, Brock University, East Block, Rm. A-206, St. Catharines, Ont. L2S 3A1 (416/684-7201, ext. 262)

ASSOCIATION OF SCHOOLS OF OPTOMETRY OF CANADA
Secretary Treasurer, Dr. J.V. Lovasik, School of Optometry, Faculty of Science, University of Waterloo, Waterloo, Ont. N2L 3G1 (519/885-1211, ext. 3654)

ASSOCIATION OF UNIVERSITY FORESTRY SCHOOLS OF CANADA
Secretary Treasurer, Dr. A.J. Kayll, Director, School of Forestry, Lakehead University, Thunder Bay, Ont. P7B 5E1 (807/345-2121)

ASSOCIATION OF URBAN & REGIONAL PLANNING PROGRAMS IN CANADIAN UNIVERSITIES
Secretary Treasurer, Dr. Don Detomasi, Urbanism Program Division, Faculty of Environmental Design, 10th Floor, Earth Sciences Bldg., University of Calgary, Calgary, Alta. T2N 1N4 (403/284-6601)

CANADIAN ASSOCIATION OF COLLEGE & UNIVERSITY LIBRARIES
Secretary Treasurer, David Jones, Asst. Science Librarian, University of Alberta, 4-85, Cameron Library, Edmonton, Alta. T6G 2J8 (403/432-3785)

CANADIAN ASSOCIATION OF COLLEGE & UNIVERSITY STUDENT SERVICES
Secretary Treasurer, Michel Leduc, Directeur du Service de l'aide financière, Université d'Ottawa, 85 Hastey, Ottawa, Ont. K1N 6N5 (613/231-2482)

CANADIAN ASSOCIATION OF DEANS OF EDUCATION
Secretary Treasurer, Dr. P.B. Park, Dean, Faculty of Education, University of Western Ontario, London, Ont. N6G 1G7 (519/679-3292)

CANADIAN ASSOCIATION OF DEANS OF ARTS & SCIENCE
Secretary Treasurer, Dr. Peter Morand, Dean, Faculty of Science & Engineering, University of Ottawa, 32 Somerset St. W., Marion Hall, Ottawa, Ont. K1N 9B4 (613/231-2407)

CANADIAN ASSOCIATION OF GRADUATE SCHOOLS
Secretary Treasurer, Dr. S.G. French, Dean, Faculty of Graduate Studies, Concordia University, 1455 de Maisonneuve Blvd. W., Montreal, P.Q. H3G 1M8 (514/879-7320)

CANADIAN ASSOCIATION OF SCHOOLS OF SOCIAL WORK
Executive Director, Dennis Kimberley, 151 Slater St., Room 909, Ottawa, Ont. K1P 5N1 (613/563-3554)

CANADIAN ASSOCIATION OF UNIVERSITY BUSINESS OFFICERS
Executive Director, K. Clements, 151 Slater St., Ottawa, Ont. K1P 5N1 (613/563-3542)

CANADIAN ASSOCIATION FOR UNIVERSITY CONTINUING EDUCATION
Secretary, Dean Ken MacKeracher, Continuing Education Division, Ryerson Polytechnical Institute, 50 Gould St., Toronto, Ont. M5B 1E8 (416/595-5420)

CANADIAN ASSOCIATION OF UNIVERSITY DEVELOPMENT OFFICERS
Secretary, H.B. Rooney, Development Officer, University of Western Ontario, Rm. 108A, Stevenson-Lawson Bldg., London, Ont. N6A 5B8 (519/679-2551)

CANADIAN ASSOCIATION OF UNIVERSITY RESEARCH ADMINISTRATORS
Secretary Treasurer, Gilbert Laporte, Directeur de la recherche, Ecole des Hautes Etudes Commerciales, 5255, av. Decelles, Montréal, P.Q. H3T 1V6 (514/343-4374)

CANADIAN ASSOCIATION OF UNIVERSITY SCHOOLS OF NURSING
Executive Secretary, Mrs. Kathy Lauzon, Room 1200, 151 Slater St., Ottawa, Ont. K1P 5N1 (819/684-1797)

CANADIAN ASSOCIATION OF UNIVERSITY SCHOOLS OF REHABILITATION
Secretary Treasurer, Prof. Edith Aston, Co-ordinator, Physical Therapy Program, School of Physical & Occupational Therapy, McGill University, 3654 Drummond St., Montreal, P.Q. H3G 1Y5 (514/392-4307)

CANADIAN COMMITTEE OF UNIVERSITY BIOLOGY CHAIRMEN
Secretary, Dr. William Threlfall, Dept. of Biology, Memorial University, St. John's, Nfld. A1B 3X9 (709/753-1200, ext. 2142)

CANADIAN COUNCIL OF LIBRARY SCHOOLS
Chairman, Mrs. V.S. Sessions, Director, Graduate School of Library Science, McGill University, McLennan Library Bldg., Montreal, P.Q. H3A 1Y1 (514/392-5934)

CANADIAN COUNCIL OF UNIVERSITY PHYSICAL EDUCATION ADMINISTRATORS
Secretary Treasurer, Dr. D.R. Riley, Chairman, Dept. of Physical Education, McGill University, 475 Pine Ave. W., Montreal, P.Q. H2W 1S4 (514/392-4733)

CANADIAN INTERUNIVERSITY ATHLETIC UNION
Executive Vice President, R.W. Pugh, 11th floor, 333 River Rd., Vanier, Ont. K1L 8B9 (613/746-4015)

CANADIAN UNIVERSITY SERVICE OVERSEAS
Executive Director, Ian Smillie, 151 Slater St., Ottawa, Ont. K1P 5H5 (613/563-3598)

COMMITTEE OF CANADIAN LAW DEANS
Secretary, Dean John Brierley, Faculty of Law, McGill University, 3644 Peel St., Montreal, P.Q. H3A 1W9 (514/392-5120)

COUNCIL OF CANADIAN UNIVERSITY CHEMISTRY CHAIRMEN
Secretary Treasurer, Dr. A. Knight, Chairman, Dept. of Chemistry, University of Saskatchewan, Saskatoon, Sask. S7N 0W0 (306/343-2954)

CANADIAN FEDERATION OF DEANS OF MANAGEMENT & ADMINISTRATIVE STUDIES
Secretary, Dr. W.B. Crowston, Dean, Faculty of Administrative Studies, York University, 434 Admin. Studies Bldg., 4700 Keele St., Downsview, Ont. (416/667-2210)

INTER-UNIVERSITY COUNCIL ON ACADEMIC EXCHANGES WITH THE USSR & EASTERN EUROPE
Chairman, Treasurer, Dr. E. Heier, Dept. of Germanic & Slavic Languages, University of Waterloo, Waterloo, Ont. N2L 3G1 (519/885-1211, ext. 2259)

Canadian Association for Adult Education
29 Prince Arthur Ave., Toronto, Ont. M5R 1B2
(416) 964-0559
Executive Director, Ian Morrison

Canadian Association of Business Education Teachers
c/o Canadian Teachers' Federation, 100 Argyle Ave., Ottawa, Ont. K2P 1B4 (613/232-1505)

Canadian Association for Children and Adults with Learning Disabilities
Kildare House, 323 Chapel, Ottawa, Ont. K1N 7Z2
(613) 238-5721
Executive Director, June Bourgeau
See Ontario Association below alphabetically

Canadian Association of Independent Schools
1451 Avenue Rd., Toronto, Ont. M5N 2H9
(416) 483-3519
Executive Secretary, Mrs. Pamela McPherson

Canadian Association of School Administrators
252 Bloor St. W., Suite N1201, Toronto, Ont. M5S 1V5
(416) 922-6570
Executive Director, R.G. Taylor

Canadian Association of University Teachers
75 Albert St., Ste. 1001, Ottawa, Ont. K1P 5E7
(613) 237-6885
Executive Secretary, D. C. Savage

Affiliated Societies

CONFEDERATION OF ALBERTA FACULTY ASSOCIATIONS
315, 11010 142 St., Edmonton, Alta. T5N 2R1
President, Prof. Eugene Falkenberg, University of Lethbridge

CONFEDERATION OF UNIVERSITY FACULTY ASSOCIATIONS OF BRITISH COLUMBIA
President, Dr. Brian Sagar, University of B.C.

MANITOBA ORGANIZATION OF FACULTY ASSOCIATIONS
Chairman, Prof. Meir Serfaty, Brandon University

FEDERATION OF NEW BRUNSWICK FACULTY ASSOCIATIONS
President, Prof. Arsène Richard, Université de Moncton

NOVA SCOTIA CONFEDERATION OF UNIVERSITY FACULTY ASSOCIATIONS
President, Prof. Derek Wood, St. Francis Xavier University

ONTARIO CONFEDERATION OF UNIVERSITY FACULTY ASSOCIATIONS
40 Sussex Ave., Toronto, Ont. M5S 1J7
Chairman, Dr. Sarah J. Shorten, University of Western Ontario

FEDERATION DES ASSOCIATIONS DE PROFESSEURS DES UNIVERSITES DU QUEBEC
2715 Côte Ste Catherine, Montreal, P.Q. H3T 1B6
Secrétaire général, René-Serge Larouche
President, Prof. Jean-Louis Roy, Université McGill

Canadian Bureau for International Education
(Bureau Canadien de L'Education Internationale)
141 Laurier St., Ste. 809, Ottawa, Ont. K1P 5J3
(613) 237-4820
Executive Director, J.R. McBride

Canadian Catholic School Trustees' Association
67 Bond St., Toronto, Ont. M5B 1X5
(416) 368-3049
Executive Secretary, Rev. P.H. Fogarty, C.S.C.

The Canadian College of Teachers
Secretary Treasurer, Ronald E. Johnston, 7546 10 Ave., Edmonton, Alta. T6K 2T6 (403/462-5103)

Canadian Education Association
A/Executive Director, R.E. Blair, 252 Bloor St. W., Toronto, Ont. M5S 1V5 (416/924-7721)

Canadian Federation of University Women
Université de Montréal, C.P. 6128, Succ. A, Montréal, P.Q. H3C 3J7
(514) 733-3142
Secrétaire générale, Laurie Mainville

Canadian Guidance & Counselling Association
c/o Faculty of Education, Univ. of Ottawa, 651 Cumberland St., Room 212, Ottawa, Ont. K1N 6N5 (613/234-2572)

The Canadian Home & School & Parent-Teacher Federation, Inc.
240 Eglinton Ave. E., Suite 204, Toronto, Ont. M4P 1K8
(416) 487-9939
President, Ms. Kirsti Jarvis
Executive Secretaries, Mrs. Joan Saul, Mrs. Kay Wright

Canadian Mathematical Society
577 King Edward, Ottawa, Ont. K1N 6N5
(613) 231-2223
Executive Director & Secretary, Dr. G.P. Wright

The Canadian Research Centre for Anthropology
Saint Paul Univ., 223 Main St., Ottawa, Ont. K1S 1C4
(613) 236-1393, ext. 215
Director, M. Doucet, F.I.C.

Canadian School Trustees' Association
Ste. 507, 30 Metcalfe St., Ottawa, Ont. K1P 5L4
(613) 236-9153

Executive Director, C. H. Witney

Provincial Associations

ALBERTA SCHOOL TRUSTEES' ASSOCIATION

Executive Director, Dr. L.W. Ferguson, 12310 105 Ave., Edmonton, Alta. T5N OY4 (403/482-7311)

BRITISH COLUMBIA SCHOOL TRUSTEES ASSOCIATION

Executive Director, Dr. H. Armstrong, 1155 W. 8th Ave., Vancouver, B.C. V6H 1C5 (604/734-2721)

MANITOBA ASSOCIATION OF SCHOOL TRUSTEES

Executive Director, N. Harvey, 191 Provencher Blvd., Winnipeg, Man. R2H OG6 (204/233-1595)

NEW BRUNSWICK SCHOOL TRUSTEES' ASSOCIATION

Executive Director, David Coughey, 701 Churchill Row, Fredericton, N.B. E3B 1P7 (506/454-3291)

FEDERATION OF SCHOOL BOARDS OF NEWFOUNDLAND

Executive Secretary, Kevin Breen, Box 9085, Stn. B, St. John's, Nfld. A1A 2X3 (709/722-7171)

NOVA SCOTIA SCHOOL BOARDS ASSOCIATION

Executive Director, Janet C. Carney, #816, 1888 Brunswick St., Halifax, N.S. B3J 3J8 (902/423-6461)

ONTARIO SCHOOL TRUSTEES' COUNCIL

Executive Director, Dr. Donal Déiseach, #500, 2 Bloor St. W., Toronto, Ont. M4W 3E2 (416/961-8825)

PRINCE EDWARD ISLAND ASSOCIATION OF SCHOOL BOARDS

Executive Director, Dr. Helen MacDonald, 45 Fitzroy St., Charlottetown, P.E.I. C1A 1R4 (902/892-6355)

QUEBEC ASSOCIATION OF PROTESTANT SCHOOL BOARDS

Executive Director, David Wadsworth, #315, 1410 Stanley St., Montreal, P.Q. H3A 1P8 (514/849-8661)

SASKATCHEWAN SCHOOL TRUSTEES' ASSOCIATION

Executive Director, J.A. Volk, #400, 2222 13th Ave., Regina, Sask. S4P 3M7 (306/569-0750)

Canadian Society for Education Through Art

Secretary General, D.G. Storey, 3186 Newbould Court, Malton, Ont. L4T 1R9

ONTARIO SOCIETY FOR EDUCATION THROUGH ART

417 Queen's Quay W., Toronto, Ont. M5V 1A2
(416) 366-1607

Canadian Teachers' Federation

Secretary General, Norman M. Goble, 110 Argyle Ave., Ottawa, Ont. K2P 1B4 (613/232-1505)

Provincial Members

ALBERTA TEACHERS' ASSOCIATION

Executive Secretary, Dr. B. T. Keeler, 11010-142 St., Edmonton, Alta. T5N 2R1 (403/453-2411)

BRITISH COLUMBIA TEACHERS' FEDERATION

General Secretary, R. M. Buzza, 105-2235 Burrard St., Vancouver, B.C. V6J 3H9 (604/731-8121)

MANITOBA TEACHERS' SOCIETY

General Secretary, W.J. Pindera, 191 Harcourt St., Winnipeg, Man. R3J 3H2 (204/888-7961)

NEW BRUNSWICK TEACHERS' ASSOCIATION

Executive Director, J.S. MacKinnon, Box 752, Fredericton, N.B. E3B 5R6 (506/455-8921)

L'ASSOCIATION DES ENSEIGNANTS FRANCOPHONES DU NOUVEAU-BRUNSWICK

Directeur général, Ronald LeBreton, C.P. 712, Fredericton, N.B. E3B 5B4 (506/454-2654)

NEWFOUNDLAND TEACHERS' ASSOCIATION

Executive Secretary, William O'Driscoll, 3 Kenmount Rd., St. John's, Nfld. A1B 1W1 (709/726-3223)

NORTHWEST TERRITORIES TEACHERS' ASSOCIATION

Executive Director, B.W. Lyons, Box 2340, Yellowknife, N.W.T. X1A 2P7 (403/873-8501)

NOVA SCOTIA TEACHERS UNION

Executive Secretary, Norman H. Fergusson, Box 1060, Armdale, Halifax, N.S. B3L 4L7 (902/477-5621)

ONTARIO TEACHERS' FEDERATION

Secretary Treasurer, W. A. Jones, 1260 Bay St., Toronto, Ont. M5R 2B5 (416/966-3424)

Associations of Teachers Affiliated with OTF:

Federation of Women Teachers' Assns. of Ont., Executive Secretary, Dr. F. Henderson, 1260 Bay St., Toronto, Ont. M5R 2B8 (416/964-1232)

Ont. Secondary School Teachers' Federation, General Secretary, L. M. Richardson, 60 Mobile Dr., Toronto, Ont. M4A 2P3 (416/751-8300)

Ont. Public School Men Teachers' Federation, General Secretary, Dr. R. Ross Andrew, 1260 Bay St., Toronto, Ont. M5R 2B7 (416/928-1128)

Ont. English Catholic Teachers' Association, Executive Director, F. Griffin, 1260 Bay St., Toronto, Ont. M5R 2B4 (416/925-2493)

L'Association des enseignants franco-ontariens, Secrétaire général, Jacques Schryburt, 1427, chemin Ogilvie, pièce 202, Ottawa, Ont. K1J 8M7 (613/741-6604)

PRINCE EDWARD ISLAND TEACHERS' FEDERATION

General Secretary, James L. Blanchard, Box 6000, Charlottetown, P.E.I. C1A 8B4 (902/569-4157)

PROVINCIAL ASSOCIATION OF CATHOLIC TEACHERS (QUEBEC)

Secretary General, Robert R. Dobie, 2005 St. Marc St., Montreal, P.Q. H3H 2G8 (514/935-8612)

PROVINCIAL ASSOCIATION OF PROTESTANT TEACHERS OF QUEBEC

President, Harvey Weiner, 84J Brunswick Blvd., Dollard des Ormeaux, P.Q. H9B 2C5 (514/683-9330)

SASKATCHEWAN TEACHERS' FEDERATION

General Secretary, Dr. S. McDowell, Box 1108, Saskatoon, Sask. S7K 3N3 (306/373-1660)

YUKON TEACHERS' ASSOCIATION

200-107 Main St., Whitehorse, Y.T. Y1A 2A7 (403/667-7009)

Canadian University Press

#202, 126 York St., Ottawa, Ont. K1N 5T5
(613) 232-2881

Canadian Vocational Association

(Association Canadienne de la Formation Professionnelle)
Central Headquarters, 251 Bank St., Suite 608, Ottawa, Ont. K2P 1X3 (613/232-1028)

The Objectives of the Association are to promote and foster vocational-technical education in Canada.

Secretary Treasurer, D.A. White

Centre d'animation de developpement et de recherche en education (CADRE)

1940 est, boul. Henri-Bourassa, Montreal, P.Q. H2B 1S2
(514/381-8891)
Directeur général, Mathieu Girard

Commonwealth Scholarship & Fellowship Committee

c/o The Association of Universities & Colleges of Canada, 151 Slater St., Ottawa, Ont. K1P 5N1
(613) 563-3551
Secretary, Guy d'Auray

Council of Ministers of Education, Canada

252 Bloor St. W., Suite S500, Toronto, Ont. M5S 1V5
(416) 964-2551
Executive Director, Dr. Lucien Perras

Council of Ontario Universities

130 St. George St., Suite 8039, Toronto, Ont. M5S 2T4
(416) 979-2165
Executive Director, Dr. E.J. Monahan

Deputy to the Executive Director & Secretary, G.G. Clarke
Director of Research, E.K. DesRosiers
Director of Communications, W. Sayers

The Early Childhood Educators of Canada
Box 307, Brampton, Ont. L6V 2L3
Director & Co-ordinator, Editor of Newsletter, Lynn P. Barkley (416/252-2730, res.)

Educational Research Institute of British Columbia
#400, 515 W. 10th Ave., Vancouver, B.C. V5Z 4A8
(604) 873-3801
Executive Director, Mrs. A. Sojonky

Fédération des cégeps
1940, boul. Henri-Bourassa est, Montréal, P.Q. H2B 1S2
(514) 381-8891
Directeur général, Paul G. Lemire

Federation of Catholic Parent-Teacher Associations of Ontario
President, Vern Blanchard, 1096 Dublin St., Sudbury, Ont. P3A 1R6 (705/566-0298)

Federation of Independent School Associations
150 Robson St., Vancouver B.C. V6B 2A7
(604) 684-6023, 684-7846
A provincial organization, acting as spokesman for the Independent Schools of B.C.
Executive Director, G. Ensing

Institut Canadien d'Education des Adultes
-not confirmed for 1982-
National co-ordinating body for the Adult Education movement in French-speaking Canada.
Directeur général, Paul Bélanger, 506 est, St. Catherine St., Suite 800, Montréal, P.Q. H2L 2C7 (514/842-2766)

Manitoba Educational Research Council
693 Taylor Ave., Winnipeg, Man. R3M 3T8
(204) 452-7962
Executive Director, tba

National Union of Students
2nd floor, 126 York St., Ottawa, Ont. K1N 5T5
(613) 232-7394
Executive Officer, John Doherty

New Brunswick Federation of Home & School Associations
(La Fédération des Associations Foyer-Ecole du Nouveau Brunswick, Inc.)
87 Winter Ave., Moncton, N.B. E1C 5X3
(506) 854-6121
Executive Secretary, Shirley A. Dobson

Ontario Association for Children with Learning Disabilities
1901 Yonge St., #504, Toronto, Ont. M4S 2Z3
(416) 487-4107
Executive Director, Mrs. Rosemary Underwood

Ontario Association for Continuing Education
8 York St., Toronto, Ont. M5J 1R2
(416) 366-2374

Ontario Association for Curriculum Development
Secretary Treasurer, Kaspar Pold, c/o Edgewood Junior P.S., 230 Birkdale Rd., Rm. 29, Scarborough, Ont. M1P 3S4 (416/755-8212)

Ontario Association of Education Administrative Officials
1260 Bay St., #530, Toronto, Ont. M5R 2B1
(416) 920-1915
Secretary, Elizabeth Walty

Ontario Association of School Business Officials
252 Bloor St. W., Suite N-1201, Toronto, Ont. M5S 1V5
(416) 923-3107
Executive Secretary, J.W. Boich

Ontario Council for Leadership in Educational Administration
Ste. N665, 252 Bloor St. W., Toronto, Ont. M5S 1V5
(416) 923-6641, ext. 558
Executive Director, P.E. Angelini

Ontario Educational Association
252 Bloor St. W., Suite C24, Toronto, Ont. M5S 1V7
(416) 920-1915
Secretary, Irene Chalupka

Ontario Educational Research Council
1260 Bay St., Toronto, Ont. M5R 2B1
(416) 923-3061
Secretary, Dr. H. O. Barrett

Ontario Federation of Students
643 Yonge St., Toronto, Ont. M4Y 1Z9
(416) 925-3825

Ontario Municipal & Provincial Education Officers' Association
Executive Secretary, Leon MacLeod, 168 St. George St., Brantford, Ont. N3R 1V8 (519/753-8816)

Parent Co-operative Preschools International
20551 Lakeshore Rd., Baie d'Urfe, P.Q. H9X 1R3
(514) 457-3291

QUEBEC COUNCIL OF PARENT PARTICIPATION PRESCHOOLS
20551 Lakeshore Rd., Baie d'Urfé, P.Q. H9X 1R3 (514/457-3291)

Presse étudiante du Québec
C.P. 216, Succ. Beaubien, Montreal, P.Q. H2G 3C9
(514) 725-1331

Regroupement des associations étudiantes universitaires du Québec
3480 McTavish, Montreal, P.Q. H3A 1X9
(514) 392-8923

The Rhodes Scholarship Trust
Secretary, R.A. Fletcher, M.A., D.Phil., D.S.C., Rhodes House, Oxford, England
General Secretary for the Rhodes Scholarships in Canada, A. R. A. Scace, Box 48, Toronto-Dominion Centre, Toronto, Ont. M5K 1E6 (416/362-1812)

Provincial Secretaries
Alta.: D.G. McKenzie, Esq., 2200 Royal Trust Tower, Edmonton, Alta. T5J 1V3
B.C.: M.J. Brown, Esq., Ste. 2238, 200 Granville St., Vancouver, B.C. V6C 1S4
Man.: Prof. W.F. Neville, c/o Office of the Vice President, Rm. 202, Admin. Bldg., University of Manitoba, Winnipeg, Man. R3T 2N2
N.B. & N.S.: J. G. Godsoe, Box 997, Halifax, N.S.
Nfld.: Keith J. H. Mercer, 19 Craigmiller Ave., St. John's, Nfld.
Ont.: J. M. Farley, Box 451, Toronto Dominion Centre, Toronto, Ont. M5K 1M5
Que.: M. Vennat, 1155 Dorchester Blvd. W., Suite 3900, Montreal, P.Q. H3B 3V2

Sask.: K. E. Norman, College of Law, Univ. of Sask., Saskatoon, Sask.

Eleven Scholarships of the value of £2,010 per year, tenable at Oxford University for 2 or 3 years, are awarded annually to Canadian university students 19 to 24 years of age.

Apply to University Registrars or Provincial Secretaries of Selection Committees for particulars and application forms. Closing date Oct. 25th each year.

Société Nationale de Diffusion educative & Culturelle Inc. (SONDEC)
Ste. 230, 8770 Langelier, Montreal, P.Q. H1P 3E8
(514) 324-4010

Toronto Montessori Institute
8569 Bayview Ave., Thornhill, Ont. L3T 2A1
(416) 889-6882
Course Co-ordinator, Audrey Sillick

University & College Placement Association
43 Eglinton Ave. E., 10th Floor, Toronto, Ont. M4P 1A2
(416) 485-3330
Executive Director, C.W. Gartley

The Workers' Educational Association of Canada
134 Carlton St., Toronto, Ont. M5A 2K1
(416) 924-2275
Secretary, Mrs. Maurice Coulter

World University Service of Canada
(1404 Scott St.) Box 3000, Stn. C, Ottawa, Ont. K1Y 4M8
(613) 725-3121
Executive Director, William W. McNeill

ELECTRICAL BUREAU OF CANADA
#1608, 1 Yonge St., Toronto, Ont. M5E 1R1
(416) 862-7152

ELECTRICAL CONTRACTORS ASSOCIATION OF ALBERTA
11507 120 St., Edmonton, Alta. T5G 2Y4
(403) 451-2412

ELECTRICAL CONTRACTORS ASSOCIATION OF BRITISH COLUMBIA
Ste. 265, 4299 Canada Way, Burnaby, B.C. V5G 1H3
(604) 435-4186
General Manager, Ross Kinneard

ELECTRICAL CONTRACTORS ASSOCIATION OF MANITOBA
Box 737, Winnipeg, Man. R3C 2L4
(204) 774-2431

ELECTRICAL CONTRACTORS ASSOCIATION OF NEW BRUNSWICK
Box 322, Fredericton, N.B. E3B 4Y9
(506) 455-7627
Managing Consultant, Stuart F. Card

ELECTRICAL CONTRACTORS ASSOCIATION OF ONTARIO
161 Eglinton Ave. E., Ste. 605, Toronto, Ont. M4P 1J5
(416) 486-1290
Executive Vice President, Norman W. Purdy

ELECTRICAL CONTRACTORS ASSOCIATION OF SASKATCHEWAN
1939 Elphinstone St., Box 1757, Regina, Sask. S4P 3C6
(306) 525-0171
Secretary Manager, D.A. Wagg

ELECTRICAL & ELECTRONIC MANUFACTURERS ASSOCIATION OF CANADA
One Yonge St., Ste. 1608, Toronto, Ont. M5E 1R1
(416) 862-7152
and, 77 Metcalfe St., #809, Ottawa, Ont. K1P 5L6
(613) 237-6847

THE EMPIRE CLUB OF CANADA
Royal York Hotel, 100 Front St. W., Toronto, Ont. M5J 1E3
(416) 364-2878
Secretary, Leland H. Ausman

EMPLOYERS' COUNCIL OF BRITISH COLUMBIA
800 W. Pender St., #1130, Vancouver, B.C. V6C 2V6
(604) 684-3384
Director, Administration, Barbara G. Cranna

ENERGY PROBE
43 Queen's Park Cres. E., Toronto, Ont. M5S 2C3
(416) 978-7014
Co-ordinator, Jan Marmorek

THE ENGINEERING INSTITUTE OF CANADA
General Manager, Robert J. Thibault, Ing., M.E.I.C., 2050 Mansfield St., Suite 700, Montreal, P.Q. H3A 1Z2 (514/842-8121)

THE ENGLISH-SPEAKING UNION OF THE COMMONWEALTH
Headquarters, Dartmouth House, 37 Charles St., London, Eng. W1X 8AB
Patron, H.M. The Queen
President, H.R.H. Prince Philip
Chairman, Sir Patrick Dean, G.C.M.G.
Canadian Headquarters, 60 St. Clair Ave. W., #1, Toronto, Ont. M4V 1M7 (416/923-6731)
Patron, H.E. The Governor-General
Canadian National President, R.H. McNairn
Canadian Chairman, M.K. Kenny
Canadian Executive Secretary, Audrey S. Hunt

ENTOMOLOGICAL SOCIETY OF CANADA
1320 Carling Ave., Ottawa, Ont. K1Z 7K9
(613) 725-2619
Secretary, John E. Laing, Dept. of Environmental Biology, University of Guelph, Guelph, Ont. N1G 2W1

For names and addresses of provincial representatives, who are elected annually, contact the Ottawa address.

ENVELOPE MAKERS INSTITUTE OF CANADA
1500 Stanley St., Ste. 315, Montreal, P.Q. H3A 1R3
(514) 849-0347
General Manager, V.G. Baker

ENVIRONMENTAL ORGANIZATIONS

ALBERTA ENVIRONMENTAL GROUPS
(Listed Alphabetically by Location)

The Alpine Club of Canada, Box 1026, Banff, Alta. T0L 0C0 (403/762-4481)
Bow Valley Naturalists, Box 1693, Banff, Alta. T0L 0C0
Alta. Wilderness Association, Box 6398, Stn. D, Calgary, Alta. T2P 2E1 (403/283-2025)
The Alpine Club of Canada, Calgary Section, Box 1995, Calgary, Alta. T2P 2M2
Calgary Eco-Centre, #204, 223 12 Ave. S.W., Calgary, Alta. T2R 0G9
Calgary Field Naturalists Society, c/o Secretary, Box 981, Calgary, Alta. T2P 2K4
Chinook Trail Association, Box 6623, Stn. D, Calgary, Alta. T2P 2E4

National & Provincial Parks Association of Canada, (Calgary-Banff Chapter), Sub. P.O. 91, Univ. of Calgary, Calgary, Alta. T2N 1N4

National Trail Association of Canada, Box 6623, Stn. D, Calgary, Alta. T2P 2E4

Sierra Club of Alberta, Box 342, Stn. G, Calgary, Alta. T3A 2G3 (403/283-2025)

Society for the Promotion of Responsible Environmental Education, Room 538, Education Tower, University of Calgary, Calgary, Alta. T2N 1N4 (403/284-5645)

Alta. Forestry Association, President, Arden A. Rytz, 311 Alta. Block, 10526 Jasper Ave., Edmonton, Alta. T5J 1Z7

The Alpine Club of Canada, Edmonton Section, c/o Mrs. Jo Ann Creore, 10512 132nd St., Edmonton, Alta. T5N 1Z5

Canadian Society of Environmental Biologists, Alta. Chapter, Box 12, Substation 11, Univ. of Alta., Edmonton, Alta. T6G 2E0

Canadian Wolf Defenders, Box 3480, Stn. D, Edmonton, Alta. T5L 4J3

Edmonton Bird Club, Box 4441, Edmonton, Alta. T6E 4T5

Edmonton Natural History Club, Box 1582, Edmonton, Alta. T5J 2N9

Federation of Alberta Naturalists, Box 1472, Edmonton, Alta. T5J 2N5

Interdisciplinary Committee for Environmental Quality, D.C. Wighton, Co-ordinator, c/o Dept. of Genetics, Univ. of Alta., Edmonton, Alta. T6G 2E9 (403/432-3606)

National & Provincial Parks Association of Canada, (Edmonton Chapter), 3071 116 St., Edmonton, Alta. T6J 3T2

Outdoors Unlittered, #45, 9912 106 St., Edmonton, Alta. T5K 1C5 (403/429-0517)

Waskahegan Trail Association, Box 131, Edmonton, Alta. T5J 2G9

Lethbridge Naturalists' Society, c/o D.W.A. Roberts, President, 2129 18th Ave. S., Lethbridge, Alta. T1K 1C7 (403/327-4710)

Red Deer River Naturalists, Box 785, Red Deer, Alta. T4N 5H2

Buffalo Lake Naturalists, c/o Box 1414, Stettler, Alta. T0C 2L0 (403/742-3846)

BRITISH COLUMBIA ENVIRONMENTAL GROUPS
(Listed Alphabetically by Location)

Environmental Studies, c/o David Brown, 350 Dogwood St., Campbell River, B.C. V9W 2X9 (604/286-6282)

Sierra Club, Campbell River Group, c/o Mrs. Shirley Duncan, Chairman, 1410 Evergreen Rd., Campbell River, B.C. V9W 3S2 (604/287-3468)

Kootenay Mountaineering Club, Box 3195, Castlegar, B.C. V1N 3H5 (604/362-7723)

Chilliwack Field Naturalists Club, Box 23, Chilliwack, B.C. V2P 6H7

Comox-Strathcona Natural History Society, c/o Phil Capes, R.R. #1, Comox, B.C. V9N 5N1 (604/339-2708)

Cranbrook Dist. Rod & Gun Club, Box 333, Cranbrook, B.C. V1C 4H8

International Wildlife Protection Association, Box 728, Kamloops, B.C. V2C 5M4

Probe British Columbia, 681 Richmond Ave., Kamloops, B.C. V2B 1T4 (604/376-8220)

Canadian Coalition for Nuclear Responsibility (Kelowna Branch), c/o John Moelaert, Box 1093, Kelowna, B.C. V1Y 7P8 (604/764-4949)

Central Okanagan Naturalists Club, Box 396, Kelowna, B.C. V1Y 7N8

Kelowna S.P.E.C., c/o Peter Chataway, Box 673, Kelowna, B.C. V1Y 7P2

Recycling Council of B.C. Society, 759 Crowley Ave., Kelowna, B.C. V1Y 7G6

Maple Ridge S.P.E.C., c/o Julie Koehn, 25425 Johnson Ave., Maple Ridge, B.C. V2X 4A4 (604/467-6028)

The Conserver Society, Box 201, McBride, B.C. VOJ 2EO

Nanaimo S.P.E.C. Office, Box 132, Nanaimo, B.C. (604/758-3711)

Voice of Women, c/o Mrs. Alice Coppard, Box 235, Nanaimo, B.C. V9R 5K9

Nelson S.P.E.C., c/o Mike Jesson, 924 Observatory St., Nelson, B.C. (604/352-9412)

New Westminster S.P.E.C., c/o Dorothy Beach, 1907 River Rd., New Westminster, B.C.

Arctic International Wildlife Range Society, c/o Mrs. Nancy Russel LeBlond, 917 Leovista Ave., North Vancouver, B.C. V7R 1R1 (604/988-3513, 986-0586)

South Okanagan Environmental Coalition, Box 188, Penticton, B.C. V2A 6K3

Port Coquitlam & District Hunting & Fishing Club, Box 122, Port Coquitlam, B.C. V3C 3V5 (604/942-9736)

Sierra Club, West Kootenay Group, c/o Colleen King, Chairman, R.R. 1, South Slocan, B.C. V0G 2G0

Sierra Club, Okanagan Group, c/o Katy Madsen, Chairman, R.R. 2, Summerland, B.C. V0H 1Z0 (604/494-8424)

Okanagan Similkameen Parks Society, Box 787, Summerland, B.C. V0H 1Z0

B.C. Wildlife Federation, 5659 176 St., Surrey, B.C. V3S 4C5

The Alpine Club of Canada, (Vancouver Section) Box 2839, Vancouver, B.C. V6B 3W7

B.C. Research Council, 3650 Wesbrook Mall, Vancouver, B.C. V6S 2L2

B.C. Water & Waste Association, c/o W.G. Mills, CBA Engineering Ltd., 1425 W. Pender St., Vancouver, B.C. V6G 2S3

Federation of B.C. Naturalists, #100, 1200 Hornby St., Vancouver, B.C. V6Z 2E2

Federation of Mountain Clubs of B.C., Box 33768, Stn. D, Vancouver, B.C. V6J 4L6

Fisheries Association of B.C., Room 400, 100 W. Pender St., Vancouver, B.C. V6B 1R8

Northwest Wilderness Society of the Unitarian Church, 949 W. 49th Ave., Vancouver, B.C. V5Z 2T1 (604/261-7204)

Outdoors Unlittered, #502, 455 Granville St., Vancouver, B.C. V6C 1V2 (604/669-2488)

Recreation Society of B.C., 1200 Hornby St., Vancouver, B.C. V6Z 1W2

Sierra Club, Vancouver Group, c/o Outdoor Recreation Council, 1200 Hornby St., Vancouver, B.C. V6Z 1W2 (604/687-3333)

Vancouver S.P.E.C. Energy Information Centre, 2150 Maple St., Vancouver, B.C. V6J 3T3

West Coast Environmental Law Association, #1001, 207 W. Hastings St., Vancouver, B.C. V6B 1H7 (604/684-7378)

Nechako Valley Wildlife Conservation Association, Box 1077, Vanderhoof, B.C. V0J 3A0

Amalgamated Conservation Society, Box 741, Victoria, B.C. V8W 2P9 (President, Cam Vaesen, 604/382-6601)

Citizens Association to Save the Environment, 6002 W. Saanich Rd., R.R. 5, Victoria, B.C. V8X 4M6

Greater Victoria Environmental Centre, 536A Yates St., Victoria, B.C. V8W 1K8 (604/388-5317)

Sierra Club, Victoria Group, c/o Ms. Sharon Chow, Chairman, 2611 Roseberry Ave., Victoria, B.C. V8R 3T8 (604/595-0655)

Sierra Club of Western Canada, Regional Office, 536A Yates St., Victoria, B.C. V8W 1K8 (604/386-5255)

Thetis Park Nature Sanctuary Association, Secretary, Mrs. Eleanor Hendy, #203, 260 Curry St., Victoria, B.C. V8S 3C1 (604/595-5108)

Victoria Fish & Game Protective Association, President, Gord Davies, Box 93, Victoria, B.C. V8W 2M1 (604/477-2393)

Victoria Natural History Society, Box 1747, Victoria, B.C. V8W 2Y1

West Vancouver S.P.E.C., c/o Anne Ferris, 6009 Eagleridge Dr., West Vancouver, B.C. V7W 1W7 (604/921-7950)

Scout Island Nature Centre, Causeway Rd., Box 4575, Williams Lake, B.C. V2G 2V6

Williams Lake Field Naturalists, Box 4575, Williams Lake, B.C. V2G 2V6

MANITOBA ENVIRONMENTAL GROUPS
(Listed Alphabetically by Location)

Brandon Natural History Society, President, Roy Everitt, Newdale, Man. R0J 1J0

The Biomass Energy Institute Inc., 1329 Niakwa Rd., Winnipeg, Man. R2J 3T4

Ducks Unlimited (Canada), 1190 Waverley St., Winnipeg, Man. R3T 2E2

Man. Environmental Council, Box 139, 139 Tuxedo Ave., Winnipeg, Man. R3N OH6 (204/895-5317)

Man. Naturalists Society, 214-190 Rupert Ave., Winnipeg, Man. R3B 0N2 (204/943-9029)

Man. Wildlife Federation, Executive Secretary, P. Murphy, 1770 Notre Dame Ave., Winnipeg, Man. R3E 3K2 (204/633-5967)

National & Provincial Parks Association of Canada, (Man. Chapter), c/o Parks Committee, Man. Naturalists Society, 214-190 Rupert Ave., Winnipeg, Man. R3B 0N2 (204/943-9029)

Solar Energy Society of Canada, #303, 870 Cambridge St., Winnipeg, Man. R3M 3H5 (204/284-3076)

Wildlife Foundation of Manitoba (including Fort Whyte Nature Centre), Box 124, Fort Whyte PO, Man. R0G 0R0 – Located at 2505 McGllivray Blvd., Winnipeg, 204/895-7001)

Zoological Society of Manitoba, c/o W.S. Neal, #1006, 167 Lombard Ave., Winnipeg, Man. R3B 0V3

NEW BRUNSWICK ENVIRONMENTAL GROUPS
(Listed Alphabetically by Location)

Conservation Council of N.B., 180 Saint John St., Fredericton, N.B. E3B 4A9 (506/454-6062)

Fredericton Field Naturalists Club, c/o Harold Hatheway, 50 Beechwood Cres., Fredericton, N.B. E3B 2S8 (506/455-7540)

The Kindness Club, c/o Mrs. H. J. Flemming, 252 Waterloo Row, Fredericton, N.B. E3B 1Z3 (a children's organization) (506/455-6186)

Moncton Naturalists Club, c/o Dr. M. F. Majka, Regional Lab., Arden St., Moncton, N.B. E1C 4B7

Barbara Richardson Wildlife Foundation, Box 77, St. Andrews, N.B. E0G 2X0 (506/529-3074)

Sunbury Shores Arts & Nature Centre Inc., Box 100, St. Andrews, N.B. E0G 2X0 (506/529-3386)

Saint John Naturalists Club, 277 Douglas Ave., Saint John, N.B. E2K 1E5 (506/693-1196)

NORTHWEST TERRITORIES ENVIRONMENTAL GROUPS

C.O.P.E., Committee for Original People's Entitlement, President, Sam Raddi, Box 2000, Inuvik, N.W.T. X0E 0T0

The Metis Association of the N.W.T., Box 1375, Yellowknife, N.W.T.

NOVA SCOTIA ENVIRONMENTAL GROUPS
(Listed Alphabetically by Location)

Atlantic Canada Section American Water Works Association, c/o W.H. Gates, Public Service Commission of Halifax, Box 608, Halifax, N.S. B3J 2T1

Ecology Action Centre, c/o S. Holtz, Research Co-ord., Forrest Bldg., Dalhousie Univ., Halifax, N.S. B3H 3J5

N.S. Wildlife Federation, Box 654, Halifax, N.S. B3J 2T3

ONTARIO ENVIRONMENTAL GROUPS
(Listed Alphabetically by Location)

The Ganaraska Trail Association, Box 1136, Barrie, Ont. L4M 5E2

Pollution Probe Barrie, c/o W.D. Beckett, 381 Edgehill Dr., R.R. 2, Barrie, Ont. L4M 4S4

Quinte-Hastings Recreational Trail Association, Box 1333, Belleville, Ont. K8N 5J1

Federation of Ontario Hiking Trail Associations, Box 422, Cambridge, Ont. N1R 5V5 (416/298-7250)

Federation of Ontario Naturalists, 355 Lesmill Rd., Don Mills, Ont. M3B 2W8 (416/444-8419)

Halton Field Naturalists, 6 Shelley St., Georgetown, Ont. L7G 3W9

Maitland Trail Association, Box 443, Goderich, Ont. N7A 4C7

Guelph Field Naturalists, Box 1401, Guelph, Ont. N1H 6N8 (519/821-5965)

Guelph Trail Club, Box 1, Guelph, Ont. N1H 6J6

The Bruce Trail Association, Box 857, Hamilton, Ont. L8N 3N9 (416/529-6821)

Hamilton Naturalists Club, Box 5182, Stn. E, Hamilton, Ont. L8S 4L3

Iroquoia Bruce Trail Club, Box 183, Hamilton, Ont. L8N 3A2 (President, Frank Birch)

Kingston Field Naturalists, Box 831, Kingston, Ont. K7L 4X6

Rideau Trail Association, c/o Mrs. Cathy Cutts, Box 15, Kingston, Ont. K7L 4V6 (613/542-5414)

Jack Miner Migratory Bird Foundation, Inc., Box 39, Kingsville, Ont. N0R 1H0 (519/733-4034)

Grand Valley Trails Association, Box 1233, Kitchener, Ont. N2G 4G8

McIlwraith Field Naturalists, c/o Mrs. W. G. Wake, 1354 Langmuir Ave., London, Ont. N5W 2G6 (519/455-4903)

Thames Valley Trail Association, Box 821, Term. B, London, Ont. N6A 4Z3

Beaver Valley Bruce Trail Club, Box 1327, Meaford, Ont. N0H 1Y0

South Peel Naturalists Club, Box 91, Port Credit Stn., Mississauga, Ont. L5G 4L5

Committee of a Thousand, President, N. Mitchinson, 7945 Watson St., Niagara Falls, Ont. L2H 1E4

Pollution Control Association of Ontario, c/o T. Davey, Box 790, Oak Ridges, Ont. L0G 1P0

Durham Recycling Centre, 717 Wilson Rd. S., Unit 4, Oshawa, Ont. L1H 6E9, Treasurer, Ms. Glenda Gies

Canadian Arctic Resources Committee, 46 Elgin St., Room 11, Ottawa, Ont. K1P 5K6 (613/236-7379)

Canadian Forestry Association, 185 Somerset St. W., Ottawa, Ont. K2P 0J2 (613/232-1815)

Canadian Nature Federation, Managing Director, P. Heppes, #203, 75 Albert St., Ottawa, Ont. K1P 6G1 (613/238-6154)

Canadian Wildlife Federation/La Fédération Canadienne de la Faune, Executive Vice President, K. A. Brynaert, 1673 Carling Ave., Ste. 106, Ottawa, Ont. K2A 1C4 (613/725-2191)

National & Provincial Parks Association of Canada, (Ottawa-Hull Chapter), Box 3072, Stn. D, Ottawa, Ont. K1P 6H6 (613/238-6404)

Ottawa Field Naturalists Club, Box 3264, Stn. C, Ottawa, Ont. K1Y 4J5 (613/722-3050)

Pace (Petroleum Association for Conservation of the Canadian Environment), 400-130 Albert St., Ottawa, Ont. K1P 5G4 (613/236-9122)

Pollution Probe Ottawa, #54, 53 Queen St., Ottawa, Ont. K1P 5C5 (613/235-9266)

The RA Outdoor Club, Ottawa Civil Service, 2451 Riverside Dr., Ottawa, Ont. K1H 7X7

Youth Science Foundation, 151 Slater St., Ottawa, Ont. K1P 5H3 (613/238-1671)

Ont. Federation of Anglers & Hunters, Inc., Box 28, Peterborough, Ont. K9J 6Y5 (705/748-3115)

Willow Beach Field Naturalists, c/o Bob Trennum, 97 Dorset St. W., Port Hope, Ont. L1A 1G4

Long Point Bird Observatory, Box 160, Port Rowan, Ont. N0E 1M0 (519/586-2909)

Ont. Bird Banding Association, c/o Long Point Bird Observatory, Box 160, Port Rowan, Ont. N0E 1M0 (519/586-2909)

Richmond Hill Naturalists Club, c/o Mrs. Peter Addison, 55 Trench St., Richmond Hill, Ont. L4C 3W6 (416/884-2787)

Sault Naturalists, Box 1043, Sault Ste. Marie, Ont. P6A 5N7

Voyageur Trail Association, Box 66, Sault Ste. Marie, Ont. P6A 5L2

Dufferin Hi-Land Bruce Trail Club, Box 354, Shelburne, Ont. L0N 1S0 (519/925-3514)

Elgin Hiking Trail Club, Box 11, St. Thomas, Ont. N5P 3T5

St. Thomas Field Naturalists, Secretary, Mrs. Hugh Pryce-Jones, 73 Metcalfe St., St. Thomas, Ont. N5R 3K6

Avon Trail Association, Box 384, Stratford, Ont. N5A 6T3

Norfolk Field Naturalists, c/o President, D.M. Dean, Box 277, Tillsonburg, Ont. N4G 4H8

Air Pollution Control Association, Ont. Section, President, R. Butler, Box 259, Stn. U, Toronto, Ont. M8Z 5P1

Algonquin Wildlands League, #308, 47 Colborne St., Toronto, Ont. M5E 1E3 (416/366-3494)

The Brodie Club, c/o Dr. Howard Savage, Dept. of Anthropology, Univ. of Toronto, Toronto, Ont. M5S 1A1

Canadian Environmental Law Association, 5th Floor South, 8 York St., Toronto, Ont. M5J 1R2 (416/366-9717)

Canadian National Committee of the International Association on Water Pollution Research, c/o Institute for Environmental Studies, Univ. of Toronto, Toronto, Ont. M5S 1A4 (416/978-3486)
Canadian Society of Environmental Biologists, Box 962, Stn. F, Toronto, Ont. M4Y 2N9
Conservation Council of Ont., 45 Charles St. E., 6th floor, Toronto, Ont. M4Y 1S2 (416/961-6830)
Elsa Wild Animal Appeal of Canada, Box 864, Stn. K, Toronto, Ont. M4P 2H2, President, Ms. Betty Henderson (416/489-8862)
National & Provincial Parks Association of Canada, Ste. 308, 47 Colborne St., Toronto, Ont. M5E 1E3 (416/366-3494)
Nature Conservancy of Canada, 2180 Yonge St., Suite 1704, Toronto, Ont. M4S 2E7 (416/486-1011)
Ontario Section, American Water Works Association, c/o J.D. Pawley, 45 23rd St., Toronto, Ont. M8V 3M6
Pollution Probe, c/o Ecology House, 12 Madison Ave., Toronto, Ont. M5R 2S1 (416/978-6155)
Quetico Foundation, 170 University Ave., Toronto, Ont. M5H 3B5 (416/593-1391)
Sierra Club of Ont., 47 Colborne St., Suite 308, Toronto, Ont. M5E 1E3 (416/366-6692)
Toronto Bruce Trail Club, Box 44, Stn. M, Toronto, Ont. M6S 4T2 (416/487-4260)
Toronto Field Naturalists, c/o Mrs. Ida Hanson, 83 Joicey Blvd., Toronto, Ont. M5M 2T4 (416/488-7304)
Underwater Club of Canada, Box 26, Adelaide Post Office, Toronto, Ont. M5C 2H8
World Wildlife Fund, Ste. 201, 60 St. Clair Ave. E., Toronto, Ont. M4T 1N5 (416/923-8173)
Zero Population Growth of Canada Inc., c/o Dept. of Zoology, Univ. of Toronto, Toronto, Ont. M5S 1A1 (416/978-6404)
K-W Probe, Room 212, Environmental Studies Bldg. I, Univ. of Waterloo, Waterloo, Ont. N2L 3G1 (519/885-1211, ext. 3780)
Waterloo Public Interest Research Group, c/o Univ. of Waterloo, Waterloo, Ont. N2L 3G1 (519/884-9020)
West Elgin Nature Club, c/o Colin Kittmer, Box 394, West Lorne, Ont. N0L 2P0 (519/768-1671)

QUEBEC ENVIRONMENTAL GROUPS
(Listed Alphabetically by Location)

Centre Ecologique de Port-au-Saumon, St-Fidèle, Charlevoix, P.Q. G0T 1T0 (winter mailing: C.P. 1000, Rigaud, P.Q. J0P 1P0) (418/434-2209; 514/451-0526)
Makivik Corporation, Box 179, Fort Chimo, P.Q. J0M 1C0
Memphremagog-Conservation, Inc., Box 55, R.R. 1, Georgeville, P.Q. J0B 1T0 (819/843-1394)
The St-Francis Valley Naturalists' Club Inc., Box 222, Lennoxville, P.Q. J1M 1Z4
Association Quebecoise des Techniques de l'Eau, c/o Bertrand Samson, 6290 Perinault, Ste. 2, Montreal, P.Q. H4K 1K5
Canadian Coalition for Nuclear Responsibility, Box 236, Snowdon Stn., Montreal, P.Q. H3X 3T4 (514/842-1471)
La Société d'animation du Jardin et de l'Institut botaniques de Montréal, c/o Denis Barabé, 4101 est, rue Sherbrooke, Montreal, P.Q. H1X 2B2
Les Cercles des Jeunes Naturalistes, 4101 est, rue Sherbrooke, #124, Montreal, P.Q. H1X 2B2 (514/255-6111)
Que. Wildlife Conservation Association, 1245 Sherbrooke St. W., Room 1260, Montreal, P.Q. H3G 1G2
Que. Wildlife Federation/Fédération québécoise de la faune, 319 est, St-Zotique, Montréal, P.Q. H2S 1L5
Société pour Vaincre la Pollution, B.P. #65, Place d'Armes, Montréal, P.Q. H2Y 3E9 (514/844-5477)
STOP, (Society to Overcome Pollution), 1361 Greene Ave., Montreal, P.Q. H3Z 2A5 (514/932-7267)
La Société Linnéenne de Qué. Inc., Aquarium, Pont de Québec, Ste-Foy, P.Q. G1W 4S3 (418/653-8186)
La Société Zoologique de Qué. Inc., Jardin Zoologique de Qué., 8191 Ave. du Zoo, Orsainville, Québec, P.Q. G1G 4G4
The Morgan Arboretum Association, Box 500, Macdonald College, Ste-Anne de Bellevue, P.Q. H9X 1C0 (514/457-2000)
Société Zoologique de la Mauricie, Inc., c/o M.G.L. Bellavance, D.C., Box 401, Trois-Rivières, P.Q. G9A 5G4 (819/374-6717)

SASKATCHEWAN ENVIRONMENTAL GROUPS
(Listed Alphabetically by Location)

Whooping Crane Conservation Association, Box 995, Indian Head, Sask. S0G 2K0 (306/695-2047)
South Sask. Wildlife Association, Box 164, Moose Jaw, Sask. S6H 4N8
ECAC (Environmental Crisis Action Committee), Dept. of Biology, Univ. of Regina, Regina, Sask. S4S 0A2
Outdoors Unlittered, #202, 1819 Cornwall St., Regina, Sask. S4P 2K4 (306/584-2425)
Saskatchewan Natural History Society, Box 1784, Saskatoon, Sask. S7K 3S1
Saskatoon Natural History Society, c/o Mary Gilliland, 902 University Dr., Saskatoon, Sask. S7N 0K1 (306/652-5970)
Saskatoon Environmental Society, Box 1372, Saskatoon, Sask. S7K 3N9
Western Canada Water & Sewage Conference, Box 6070, Saskatoon, Sask. S7K 4E5
Swift Current Museum & Natural History Society, Curator, Mrs. Clarence Wilson, (105 Chaplin St. E.) Box 1477, Swift Current, Sask. S9H 3X5 (306/773-9888)

EPILEPSY CANADA
#1125, 123 Edward St., Toronto, Ont. M5G 1E2
Executive Director, Mrs. Joan Kent

EPILEPSY ONTARIO
2160 Yonge St., 1st floor, Toronto, Ont. M4S 2A9
(416) 489-2825
Executive Director, Mrs. Sally Sullivan

EQUIPMENT LESSORS ASSOCIATION OF CANADA
350 Sparks St., Ste. 602, Ottawa, Ont. K1R 7S8
(613) 238-8122
Executive Vice President, R.W. Neal

ESPERANTO ASSOCIATION OF CANADA
Box 2159, Sidney, B.C. V8L 3S3
(604) 656-5283
President, Wallace G. du Temple

ETHNIC PRESS ASSOCIATION OF BRITISH COLUMBIA
Box 2033, Vancouver, B.C. V6B 3R6
(604) 277-5246
Secretary, Baldwin Ackerman

ETHNIC PRESS ASSOCIATION OF ONTARIO
President, V. Mauko, 1115 Bay St., Toronto, Ont. M5S 2B3 (416/923-7021)

EVANGELICAL FELLOWSHIP OF CANADA
Box 8800, Stn. B, Willowdale, Ont. M2K 2R6
(416) 497-4796
President, Rev. Charles Yates

EXECUTIVE CLUB
491 Lawrence Ave. W., Toronto, Ont. M5M 1C7
(416) 789-5347

EXPERIMENTAL AIRCRAFT ASSOCIATION OF CANADA
Box 94248, Richmond, B.C. V6Y 2A6
President, C.R. Goguillot

EXPRESS TRANSPORT ASSOCIATION
Room 204, 1253 McGill College Ave., Montreal, P.Q. H3B 2Y5
(514) 866-3469

EYE BANK OF CANADA
(Ontario Division)
1929 Bayview Ave., Toronto, Ont. M4G 3E8

(416) 486-2520
Executive Secretary, Mrs. Anne Wolf

FAMILY PLANNING
See Planned Parenthood

FEDERAL SUPERANNUATES NATIONAL ASSOCIATION
National Secretary Treasurer, F.J. Lancaster, #402, 233 Gilmour St., Ottawa, Ont. K2P 0P2 (613/234-9663)

FEDERATED WOMEN'S INSTITUTES OF CANADA INC.
National Office, Room 28, 46 Elgin St., Ottawa, Ont. K1P 5K6
(613) 234-1090

Provincial Affiliates with Secretaries

Alta. Women's Institutes, Mrs. Sylvia McKinley, #201, 7203 101 Ave., Edmonton, Alta. T6A OH9 (403/469-1254)
B.C. Women's Institutes, Mrs. Ida M. Boyd, 545 Superior St., Victoria, B.C. V8V 1T7 (604/382-6442)
Man. Women's Institutes, Mrs. L. E. Parker, 880 Portage Ave., Winnipeg, Man. R3G OP1 (204/786-3436)
N.B. Women's Institutes, Mrs. Anna Manzer, 25 Waggoner's Lane, Fredericton, N.B. E3B 2L2 (506/454-0798)
Nfld. & Labrador Women's Institutes, Miss Jane Robinson, Box 4056, St. John's, Nfld. A1C 5Y2
N.S. Women's Institutes, Mrs. N. Mosher, Cumming Hall, N.S.A.C., Truro, N.S. B2N 5E3 (902/895-1571, ext. 278)
Federated Women's Institutes of Ont., Miss Mary Campbell, 8th floor, 801 Bay St., Toronto, Ont.
P.E.I. Women's Institutes, Ms. Lois Thomson, Box 2000, Charlottetown, P.E.I. C1A 7N8 (902/892-4101)
Que. Women's Institutes, Mrs. Sheila Washer, Box 258, Macdonald College, P.Q. H9X 1CO (514/457-2006, loc. 278)
Sask. Women's Institutes, Miss M. Pattillo, Extension Div., Univ. of Sask., Saskatoon, Sask.

FEDERATION ACADIENNE DE LA NOUVELLE-ECOSSE
1106 South Park, Halifax, N.S. B3H 2W7
(902) 422-1324
Executive Director, Jean Comeau

FEDERATION DES ADMINISTRATEURS DES SERVICES DE SANTE ET DES SERVICES SOCIAUX DU QUEBEC
4237 rue de Bordeaux, Montreal, P.Q. H2H 1Z4
(514) 526-0875

FEDERATION OF ALBERTA STUDENTS
Room 270, SUB, University of Alberta, Edmonton, Alta. T6G 2J7
(403) 432-5288
Publishes: Alberta Student Voice

FEDERATION OF ASSOCIATIONS ON THE CANADIAN ENVIRONMENT
1335 Carling Ave., Ste. 210, Ottawa, Ont. K1Z 8N8
(613) 725-1881
President, R.A. Goodings, P.Eng.

FEDERATION DES ASSOCIATIONS DE MUSICIENS EDUCATEURS DU QUEBEC
Président, Jean Genest, 361 rue Vendôme, Québec, P.Q. G1P 3M2 (418/683-1660)

FEDERATION OF CANADIAN MUNICIPALITIES
#1318, 112 Kent St., Ottawa, Ont. K1P 5P2
(613) 237-5221
Executive Director, Glenys Parry

THE FEDERATION OF ENGINEERING & SCIENTIFIC ASSOCIATIONS
234 St. George St., Toronto, Ont. M5R 2P1
(416) 922-7612
Executive Asst., Mrs. Mabell E. LeClair

Affiliated Societies

Society of Ontario Hydro Management & Professional Staff
Society of Professional Engineers & Associates, AECL Engineering Co.
Association of Engineers - Bell Canada
Professional Engineers Group, Toronto Hydro-Electric System
Professional Engineers Group, Canadian General Electric
Association of Scientific & Technical Employees of CIP Research
Northern Telecom Engineering Council
Northern Electric, London Professional Association
Seaway Engineers' Association
Professional Engineers Group, Canadian Standards Association
Westinghouse Association of Professional Employees
City of Calgary Professional Engineers Association
Salaried Employees Alliance, Computing Devices Co.
Government of Ontario Professional Employees Group
SPAR Professional & Allied Technical Employees Association
Commercial Products Professional Employees Association, AECL
Professional Staff Association, Research Council of Alberta

FEDERATION OF ETHNIC GROUPS OF QUEBEC, INC.
Box 543, Snowdon Stn., Montreal, P.Q. H3X 3T7
(514) 481-7909
President, Dr. Kévork Baghdjian (739-0314)

FEDERATION OF METRO TENANTS' ASSOCIATIONS
#233, 366 Adelaide St. E., Toronto, Ont. M5V 3X9
(416) 364-1564
Chairman, Kenn Hale

FEDERATION OF MUSEUMS, HERITAGE & HISTORICAL SOCIETIES OF NOVA SCOTIA
5516 Spring Garden Rd., Ste. 305, Halifax, N.S. B3J 1G6
(902) 423-4677
Executive Director, Elizabeth Ross

FEDERATION OF NORTHERN ONTARIO MUNICIPALITIES
Secretary Treasurer, W.G. Lindsay, Civic Centre, Sault Ste. Marie, Ont.

THE FEDERATION OF ONTARIO COTTAGERS' ASSOCIATIONS INC.
215 Morrish Rd., Ste. 105, Scarborough, Ont. M1C 1E9
(416) 284-2305
Executive Director, A.O. Shingler

Largest ratepayers group in the province of Ontario, representing about 300,000 lakefront owners across the province

FEDERATION OF ONTARIO HIKING TRAIL ASSOCIATIONS
Box 422, Cambridge, Ont. N1R 5V5

FEDERATION OF ONTARIO NATURALISTS
FON Conservation Centre, Moatfield Park, 355 Lesmill Rd., Don Mills, Ont. M3B 2W8
(416) 444-8419, 10
General Manager, Mike Singleton

FEDERATION OF PRINCE EDWARD ISLAND MUNICIPALITIES
Executive Director, Joseph E. Coady, Box 98, City Hall, Charlottetown, P.E.I. C1A 7K2 (902/894-5552)

FEDERATION DES POMPIERS PROFESSIONNELS DU QUEBEC
1551 Boul. St-Joseph est, Montreal, P.Q. H2J 1M8
(514) 522-4488
President, Alfred Morin

FEDERATION OF RUSSIAN CANADIANS
6 Denison Ave., Toronto, Ont. M5T 2M4
(416) 368-8101

FEDERATION OF SASKATCHEWAN INDIANS
1114 Central Ave., Box 1644, Prince Albert, Sask. S6V 4V6
(306) 764-3411
Office Manager, Priscilla Bear

FINANCIAL EXECUTIVES INSTITUTE CANADA
#207, 141 Adelaide St. W., Toronto, Ont. M5H 3L5
(416) 366-3007
Chairman, C.L. Bishop
Vice Chairman, I.C. Ferrier
President, Kenneth H. Smith, Toronto
Executive Vice President, Douglas G. Simpson
Chapters in Calgary, Edmonton, Hamilton, Maritime Provinces, Montreal, Ottawa, Southwestern Ontario, Toronto, Winnipeg and Vancouver

FINNISH ORGANIZATION OF CANADA
957 Broadview Ave., Toronto, Ont. M4K 2R5
(416) 421-9020
Executive Secretary, Helen Tarvainen

FIRE PREVENTION CANADA (FIPRECAN) ASSOCIATION
#1590, 7 Liverpool Ct., Ottawa, Ont. K1B 4L2
(613) 749-8200
Executive Director, Emile J. Therien

FISHERIES COUNCIL OF CANADA
77 Metcalfe St., Room 603, Ottawa, Ont. K1P 5L6
(613) 238-7751
President, K. M. Campbell

Provincial Affiliates

FISHERIES ASSOCIATION OF BRITISH COLUMBIA
J.N. Spitz, Room 400, 100 W. Pender St., Vancouver, B.C. V6B 1R8 (604/684-6454)

PRINCE RUPERT FISHERMEN'S COOPERATIVE ASSOCIATION
R.A. Shumka, Box 520, Prince Rupert, B.C. V8J 3R7 (604/624-2146)

PRINCE RUPERT FISH EXCHANGE
L. Nolin, c/o B.C. Packers Ltd., Box 220, Prince Rupert, B.C. (604/628-3245)

VANCOUVER WHOLESALE FISH DEALERS ASSOCIATION
J.W. Nicholls, c/o J.W. Nicholls Co. Ltd., 2115 Commissioner St., Vancouver, B.C. V5L 1A6 (604/253-7828)

FISH & SEAFOOD ASSOCIATION OF ONTARIO
A. Jefferson, c/o B.C. Packers Ltd., 4195 Dundas St. W., #326, Toronto, Ont. M8X 1Y4 (416/233-6231)

LAKE ERIE FISH PACKERS & PROCESSORS ASSOCIATION
Gordon Omstead, Omstead Foods Ltd., Box 520, Wheatley, Ont. N0P 2P0 (519/825-4611)

L'ASSOCIATION QUEBECOISE DE L'INDUSTRIE DE LA PECHE
L. Morisset, c/o Primonor Inc., C.P. 307, Succ. B, Québec, P.Q. G1K 7B1 (418/694-4375)

QUEBEC SEAFOODS DISTRIBUTORS ASSOCIATION
G. Couture, c/o National Sea Products Ltd., 7881 Boul. Decarie, 4th Fl., Montreal, P.Q. H4P 2H2 (514/735-2741)

NEW BRUNSWICK FISH PACKERS ASSOCIATION
G.R. Cluney, 236 St. George St., Moncton, N.B. E1C 1W1 (506/389-1591)

ATLANTIC FISHING VESSEL ASSOCIATION
R.C. Stirling, Box 991, Dartmouth, N.S. B2Y 3Z6 (902/463-7790)

SEAFOOD PRODUCERS ASSOCIATION OF NOVA SCOTIA
R.C. Stirling, Box 991, Dartmouth, N.S. B2Y 3Z6 (902/463-7790)

PRINCE EDWARD ISLAND SEAFOOD PROCESSORS ASSOCIATION
G. Gorman, Box 694, Charlottetown, P.E.I. C1A 7L3 (902/894-4368)

FISHERIES ASSOCIATION OF NEWFOUNDLAND & LABRADOR LTD.
E.A. Harvey, Box 8900, St. John's, Nfld. A1B 3R9 (709/726-7223)

FISHING VESSEL OWNERS ASSOCIATION OF BRITISH COLUMBIA
#203, 8041 Granville St., Vancouver, B.C. V6P 4Z5
(604) 261-5218
Secretary Treasurer, Luiz M. Souza, MBE AE

FLOORCOVERING INSTITUTE OF ONTARIO
19 27th St., Toronto, Ont. M8W 2X2
(416) 259-1607
General Manager & Treasurer, Clare C. Weeks

THE FORCES HELP SOCIETY & LORD ROBERTS' WORKSHOP
For Imperial and Commonwealth Ex-Service Men and Women.
c/o the Director of the Service Bureau, Royal Canadian Legion, Dominion Command, 359 Kent St., Ottawa, Ont. K2P 0R7 (613/235-4391)

FOOTWEAR & LEATHER INSTITUTE OF CANADA
7575 Trans Canada Hwy., #406, St-Laurent, P.Q. H4T 1V6
(514) 337-6812

THE FORTUNE SOCIETY OF CANADA, INC.
278 Havelock St., Toronto, Ont. M6H 3B9
(416) 532-6779
President, Wm. Sharp

FOSTER PARENTS PLAN OF CANADA
153 St. Clair Ave. W., Toronto, Ont. M4V 1P8
(416) 920-1654
National Director, E. Munro Ashkanase

FOUNDATIONS

La fondation d'action familiale et sociale inc
636, rue Quebec, Sherbrooke, P.Q. J1H 3M2
(819) 566-6365
President, Trefflé Michaud

This Foundation has a very limited capital, the interest from which is allocated to welfare services in the region 05, Province of Quebec.

Alberta Law Foundation
#315W, 131 9th Ave. S.W., Calgary, Alta. T2P 1K1
(403) 264-4701

Public funds from interest on solicitors' trusts are expended on law research, reform, libraries, law education and programs.

Executive Manager, S. B. Laing

Alberta Orange Foundation for Children
c/o Mrs. P. Horton, 2419 25A St. S.W., Calgary, Alta. T3E 1Z1
(403) 249-1431

To aid needy children in the Province of Alberta.

Associated Medical Services, Inc.
50 Prince Arthur Ave., Ste. 105, Toronto, Ont. M5R 1B5
(416) 924-3368
President, Dr. J.B. Neilson

This charitable organization has as its primary object the support of a "Hannah Institute" for the history of medicine.

The Atkinson Charitable Foundation
One Yonge St., Toronto, Ont. M5E 1E5
(416) 368-5152

Incorporated in 1942 under Letters Patent, Province of Ont., for religious, charitable, or educational purposes within Ontario.

Trustees: President, Mrs. H. C. Hindmarsh; William J. Campbell; Mrs. J. H. Crang, Jr.; Harry A. Hindmarsh; Beland H. Honderich; Burnett M. Thall

The Banting Research Foundation
c/o Faculty of Medicine, McMurrich Bldg., University of Toronto, Toronto, Ont. M5S 1A8
(416) 978-4952
Chairman, W.J. Farmery
Vice Chairman, E.H. Crawford
Honorary Secretary Treasurers, M.J. Sole, M.D., F.R.C.P. (C); C.H. Tator, M.D., Ph.D., F.A.C.S., F.R.C.S. (C); E.B. Marliss, M.D., F.R.C.P. (C)

Baxter-Temple Carmichael Foundation
For charitable work mainly in the Sudbury area.
c/o Valin, Innes & Carroll, 105 Durham St. S., Sudbury, Ont. P3E 3M9 (705/673-3655)

R.A. Beamish Foundation
306 Faircrest Rd., Ottawa, Ont. K1H 5E3
(613) 733-6285
President, R. L. Beamish

Max Bell Foundation
Box 122, Toronto Dominion Centre, Toronto, Ont. M5K 1H1
(416) 364-2814
Correspondence to, Donald S. Rickerd

The Foundation has a Western Canadian orientation and provides grants in the fields of Health Services, The Media, Oceans and Inland Waters, Physical Fitness and Sports, Veterinary Medicine, and Canada and the Asian Pacific.

H. G. Bertram Foundation
c/o Personal Trust Dept., Royal Trust Corp., Box 980, Hamilton, Ont. L8N 3R2

To aid charitable organizations in Ontario with preference to those operating in the town and surrounding district of Dundas.

J. P. Bickell Foundation
National Trust Co., 21 King St. E., Toronto, Ont. M5C 1B3
(416) 364-9141
Secretary, P. J. Sewell

Restricted to charitable and worthy objectives in Ontario.

E. W. Bickle Foundation
Box 90, 1 First Canadian Place, Toronto, Ont. M5X 1C5
(416) 492-5244
Secretary Treasurer, Miss E. Joan Williams

The Birks Family Foundation
1240 Phillips Square, Montreal, P.Q. H3B 3H4
(514) 392-2566
Correspondence to the Secretary

The Boissevain & Morton Foundation
Box 120, Boissevain, Man. ROK OEO
(204) 534-2961
Executive Director, E.J. Clark

Community Trust for charitable, educational and cultural purposes in the district.

Fondation J. Armand Bombardier
C.P. 370, 1000 rue J.A. Bombardier, Valcourt, P.Q. JOE 2LO
(514) 532-2258
Manager, Camille Rouillard, M.V.

Grants are divided into three parts: Education; Health & Welfare; and Missionaries to foreign countries.

No application forms needed.

British Columbia Medical Services Foundation
1199 W. Pender St., 9th floor, Vancouver, B.C. V6E 2R1
(604) 688-2204

For the support of research and services related to clinical medicine and the health sciences in British Columbia.

The Samuel and Saidye Bronfman Family Foundation
1916, rue Tupper, Montreal, P.Q. H3H 1N5
(514) 937-9480
Executive Director, Dr. Peter C. Swann

The current areas of interest are:

1) Children with learning disabilities.
2) The Canadian North and Native peoples.
3) Social problems concerned with the elderly.
4) "Heritage Projects" projects with particular but not exclusive reference to Montreal.
5) "Added Dimensions" - Support to organizations whose creative initiatives can be given wider dissemination by additional means and through other media.

The Burton Charitable Foundation
#1606, 141 Adelaide St. W., Toronto, Ont. M5H 1V7
President, Mrs. A.K. Stuart

Calgary & District Foundation
402 Palliser Sq. W., 131 9th Ave. S.W., Calgary, Alta. T2P 1K1
(403) 264-4701
Executive Director, H.C. Paillefer

The Canada Studies Foundation
(La Fondation d'Etudes du Canada)
252 Bloor St. W., Toronto, Ont. M5S 1V5
(416) 922-4149
Director, R.M. Anderson
Directeur associé, Benoît Robert

The Foundation's objective is to encourage national understanding of significant Canadian questions by students in schools throughout Canada. It facilitates bilingual, intercultural, and interprovincial curriculum development activities by classroom teachers and their students, supported by resource personnel from the universities, departments of education, school boards, and community groups.

Canada West Foundation
245 West Palliser Square, Calgary, Alta. T2P 1K1
(403) 264-9535
President, Dr. David K. Elton

The chief objective of the Foundation is to strengthen the position of the West within Confederation.

It is presently engaged in major studies on Canadian Confederation, Coal as a Western Resource, Western Agriculture–Policy and Potential, and Western Canada's Water Supply and Potential.

Canadian Environmental Law Research Foundation
8 York St., 5th Floor South, Toronto, Ont. M5J 1R2
(416) 366-9717
Executive Director, Adele Worland

The Canadian Foundation for the Advancement of Pharmacy
123 Edward St., #303, Toronto, Ont. M5G 1E2
(416) 979-2024

A voluntary alliance of all branches of the profession of pharmacy. The Foundation is an assistance organization, receiving contributions annually and disbursing the funds in the form of fellowships, research and special grants, individual merit awards, loans etc., in accordance with the needs of Pharmacy.
Executive Secretary Treasurer, L. J. Haskett

Canadian Foundation for Economic Education

252 Bloor St. W., #S560, Toronto, Ont. M5S 1V5
(416) 968-2236

Canadian Nurses Foundation

50 The Driveway, Ottawa, Ont. K2P 1E2
(613) 237-2133

The purposes of the Foundation are to provide bursaries and scholarships to nurses for graduate study, to support nursing research, and to solicit, acquire, accept or receive monies in support of the Foundation. Available to graduate nurses who are members of the Canadian Nurses Association who plan to study at the graduate level in a health-related discipline.
Secretary Treasurer, Ginette Rodger

Canadian Progress Charitable Foundation

Ste. 532, 67 Yonge St., Toronto, Ont. M5E 1J8
(416) 364-8095
Executive Secretary, Mrs. Lee Irwin

The main project is to assist the Deaf in Canada, and in particular, the multi-handicapped Deaf.

Canadian Restaurant Association Foundation

69 King George's Rd., Toronto, Ont. M8X 1L8
(416) 231-0568

The Foundation provides scholarships and bursaries to encourage young men and women who attend universities and colleges to gain education in the area of foodservice management. The Foundation also provides research funding for projects related to food service management and techniques.
Executive Secretary, Mrs. Patricia Kennedy

Canadian-Scandinavian Foundation

c/o Geography Dept., McGill Univ., 805 Sherbrooke St. W., Montreal, P.Q. H3C 3G1

Scholarships and grants for studies, research, fine arts, etc. in Scandinavian countries for Canadian Students.
Correspondence to, Dr. Jan Lundgren, 514/392-8084

Canadian Society for Non-Destructive Testing Foundation

Managing Director, Wm. R. Mercer, c/o Mohawk College, 135 Fennell Ave. W., Hamilton, Ont. L8N 3T2 (416/387-1655)

Canadian Tax Foundation

(L'Association canadienne d'etudes fiscales)
130 Adelaide St. W., Box 6, Toronto, Ont. M5H 3P5
(416) 863-9784
Director, Douglas J. Sherbaniuk
Secretary, Ms. Patricia Hillmer
Treasurer, John W. Buckell

The Canadian Tax Foundation was established in 1945 as an independent tax research organization, sponsored by the Canadian Bar Association and the Canadian Institute of Chartered Accountants. Its purpose is to provide both the tax-paying public and the governments of Canada with the benefit of expert, impartial research into current problems of taxation and government finance.
Publications, Canadian Tax Journal, Tax Papers, Tax Memos, The National Finances, Conference Proceedings, etc.

Canadian Veterinary Research Trust Fund

(Fondation canadienne pour la recherche veterinaire)
360 Bronson Ave., Ottawa, Ont. K1R 6J3
(613) 236-1162
Secretary, J.-C. Carisse

To provide financial support for veterinary clinical research in Canada with emphasis on areas unlikely to receive assistance from traditional sources.

The Canadian Writers' Foundation, Inc.

(La Fondation des Ecrivains Canadiens)
90 Kenilworth St., Box 3071, Stn. C, Ottawa, Ont. K1Y 4J3
(613) 728-0602
Secretary Treasurer, Mrs. M. Kim

The Canadian Writers' Foundation is a benevolent trust operated on a purely voluntary basis for the benefit of distinguished Canadian writers who have fallen upon difficult days by reason of physical disability or the waning of their earning capacity in their advanced years.

Cancer Research Society Inc.

Box 183, 19 Esterel, Place Bonaventure, Montreal, P.Q. H5A 1A9
(514) 861-9227

The Society collects and raises funds expressly for research on cancer.
President, Flora Caplan

The Floyd S. Chalmers Fund

c/o Ontario Arts Council, 151 Bloor St. W., Toronto, Ont. M5S 1T6 (416/961-1660)

To support creation of innovative work in performing arts and advance career training for performing artists. Ontario residents only. No operating or capital grants. Organizations can commission, but grants are to individuals only.

Sir Winston Churchill Scholarship Foundation

10328 130 St., Edmonton, Alta. T5N 1X6
(403) 452-6187
Chairman, Dr. Harvey D. Hebb

To provide an award of an $10,000 scholarship for a graduate student of the University of Alberta to attend Churchill College, Cambridge. Priority to the study of energy.

Community Foundation of Ottawa & District

c/o United Way, 85 Plymouth St., Ottawa, Ont. K1S 3E2
(613) 236-9585
Secretary, W.A. Gamble

This Foundation is dormant at present.

Construction Specifications Foundation

#1206, 1 St. Clair Ave. W., Toronto, Ont. M4V 1K6
(416) 922-3159

To further education and research in matters pertaining to construction documents and to promote publication and distribution thereof.
Executive Vice President, René Gaulin

C.L. Copland Family Foundation

610 ave. Victoria, Westmount, P.Q. H3Y 2R9
Correspondence to the Treasurer, Michael Carpenter

The Craven Foundation

760 Lawrence Ave. W., Toronto, Ont. M6A 1B8
(416) 789-3432
General Manager, Frank H. Francis

Operates The Craven Foundation Automobile Museum and Restoration Centre in Toronto, and also provides travelling exhibits of vintage cars throughout Canada.

Crestview Foundation

#770, 999 8th St. S.W., Calgary, Alta. T2R 1J5
(403) 245-3781
Secretary Treasurer, W.G.H. Robinson

Grants restricted to a small number of capital projects in Western Canada, primarily in Alberta.

Crown Zellerbach Canada Foundation
815 W. Hastings St. (Box 2079, Vancouver, B.C. V6B 3T1)
(604) 668-4218

Main Fields of Interest: Arts & culture, conservation, the handicapped, recreation, safety, social and youth agencies.

Eligibility: Corporate donations are designed to aid organizations in operating areas where the company has plants, offices and employs a substantial number of people. Organizations which serve a wide segment of the community, and are local or provincial in nature, are given priority.

Value: Varies from $100 to $10,000.

C.S.T. Foundation
#603, 797 Don Mills Rd., Don Mills, Ont. M3C 1V1
(416) 429-2608

A charitable, non-profit organization devoted to the promotion of savings on the part of parents and others to provide opportunities for the children in whom they are interested to achieve university or college education. The Foundation sponsors the Canadian Scholarship Trust Plan, and other projects related to the financing of higher education. There are C.S.T. offices in the major cities of every province.
Executive Vice Presidents, W.E. Brumwell, W.R. Lloyd

J. W. Dafoe Foundation
Chairman, A. E. Tarr, 615 South Dr., Winnipeg, Man. R3T 0C1
Honorary Secretary, W. D. Smith, History Dept., Univ. of Man., Winnipeg, Man. R3T 2M8

The purpose of the Foundation is the promotion of international understanding and co-operation.

The Devonian Group of Charitable Foundations
#770, 999 8th St. S.W., Calgary, Alta. T2R 1J5
(403) 245-3781
Secretary Treasurer, W.G.H. Robinson

Supports selected projects in the areas of public parks, applied scientific research and historic preservation, mainly in Western Canada.

The De Waan Foundation
c/o Rene Laham, 1340 Chattaway Ave., Ottawa, Ont. K1H 7S3

Dominion Textile Foundation
-not confirmed for 1982-
1950 ouest, rue Sherbrooke, Montreal, P.Q. H3H 1E7
(514) 937-5711
Secretary, C.M. Beck

Donner Canadian Foundation
President, D. S. Rickerd, Box 122, Toronto Dominion Centre, Toronto, Ont. M5K 1H1
Phone: (416) 869 1091

A private foundation which makes grants in the following four fields: law reform and penology in Canada, Canadian foreign policy, the native peoples of Canada, and Canada's north.

The Eaton Foundation
1 Dundas St. W., Toronto, Ont. M5B 1C8
(416) 591-3423

For charitable purposes in fields of education, environment, health, culture, social development, within Canada only. No grants to private individuals.
Chairman, F. F. McEachren

Fondation Edouard-Montpetit
1479 boul. Mont-Royal, Outremont, P.Q. H2V 2J6
(514) 739-9596
Correspondence to: François Desmarais

Sir Joseph Flavelle Foundation
National Trust Co. Ltd., 21 King St. E., Toronto, Ont. M5C 1B3
(416) 364-9141
Secretary, P. J. Sewell

General charities in the province of Ontario.

The Sandford Fleming Foundation
Box 816, Waterloo, Ont. N2J 4C2
(519) 885-0910

For the encouragement of industry-university co-operation in engineering education.

The Ford Foundation
Secretary, Howard Dressner, 320 East 43rd St., New York 10017, N.Y. (212/573-5000)

Harry E. Foster Charitable Foundation
-not confirmed for 1982-
40 St. Clair Ave. W., Toronto, Ont. M4V 1M6
(416) 928-8009
Executive Director, John C. McCrea

Supports religious, charitable and educational activities with a particular interest in the field of mental retardation.

The James Franceschini Foundation
372 Bay St., Suite 902, Toronto, Ont. M5H 2W9
(416) 368-2352
Secretary, M.L. Palmer

Funds primarily for medical research and the establishment of scholarships.

The Gairdner Foundation
255 Yorkland Blvd., Ste. 220, Willowdale, Ont. M2J 1S3
(416) 493-3101

Awards are bestowed to those, in the field of medical science, who have made significant contributions in the conquest of disease, and the relief of human suffering. Selections are made from international nominations received from specially appointed confidential correspondents, and are reviewed and assessed by a Panel of Review and Medical Advisory Board, set up by the Foundation.
Executive Director, T. V. Kenney

Glenbow-Alberta Institute
130 9th Ave. S.E., Calgary, Alta. T2G 0P3
(403) 264-8300
Director, Duncan F. Cameron

To collect, preserve and document, art, artifacts, printed and non-printed materials pertaining to the history of Western Canada. Major museum, art gallery, library and archives; international collections with emphasis on the development of the Canadian West.

The Elizabeth Greenshields Foundation
1814 Sherbrooke St. W., Montreal, P.Q. H3H 1E4

To assist young painters and sculptors with their education. Applicants must have already embarked upon their studies and have advanced to the point where they could submit examples if so requested.

Grenfell Labrador Medical Mission
Supporting Association of the International Grenfell Association
501 Dovercourt Ave., Ottawa, Ont. K2A 0T7

Toronto Branch, 227 Bloor St. E., Toronto, (416 924-7090), operating the Grenfell Workroom where Toronto produced Grenfell Cards and Made-in-Newfoundland Handicrafts are sold. Proceeds help provide medical and health services through hospitals, nursing stations and air ambulance along the northern coast of Newfoundland and Labrador.

Fondation Lionel-Groulx
#257, 261 ave Bloomfield, Outremont, P.Q. H2V 3R6
(514) 271-4759

For the study of the history of French Canada.

President, Dr. Jacques Genest, m.d.
Secretary, Mme Juliette Rémillard

Fondation Père Eusèbe Ménard
65, rue de Castelnau ouest, Montréal, P.Q. H2R 2W3
(514) 274-7645

For the support of the Missionaries of the Holy Apostles in their promotion of sacerdotal vocations in the third world.
Executive Director, Marcel Arès

The Hamber Foundation

The purpose of the Foundation is to assist and support such general charitable and educational purposes as the development of preventive medicine; scientific research for the increase of human knowledge, education (in particular the occasional needs of the universities), cultural and creative arts, and athletics. Preference is given to specific single projects. The causes and organizations to be benefitted by the Foundation should be those carrying on their work within the Province of British Columbia, and must qualify as a charitable organization under the Canadian Income Tax Act.
President, G.W. MacLaren
Secretary Treasurer, Mrs. M.D.S. Herbert, c/o The Permanent, Box 10152, Pacific Centre, Vancouver, B.C. V7Y 1E5 (604/689-0611)

The Hamilton Foundation
C. K. MacGillivray, F.C.A., 314 Wilson St., Ancaster, Ont. L9G 2B9 (416/648-2061, 648-6056)

Grants restricted to the Hamilton Metro area.

Audrey S. Hellyer Charitable Foundation
President, Suite 202, 1262 Don Mills Rd., Don Mills, Ont. M3B 2W7
(416) 445-1121

Financial support to religious, educational and welfare institutions.

The J. William Horsey Foundation
3080 Yonge St., Ste. 5044, Toronto, Ont. M4N 3N1
President & Treasurer, W.G. Horsey

For general charitable purposes in the fields of religion and education.

The Hospital for Sick Children Foundation
555 University Ave., Toronto, Ont. M5G 1X8
(416) 597-1500, ext. 2217,8
President, Claus A. Wirsig
Vice President, Mary MacDonald

To provide funds for The Hospital for Sick Children and to make grants to outside organizations for activities directed toward improving the health and well-being of children in Canada.

Charles H. Ivey Foundation
201 Consumers Rd., #105, Willowdale, Ont. M2J 4G8
Secretary, C. R. Ivey

The Richard Ivey Foundation
380 Wellington St., London, Ont. N6A 5C3
(519) 673-1280
Research Officer, Susan L. McLean

To support projects in health and education, social development and the environment, and the arts. Emphasis is placed on applications with reference to London and Southwestern Ontario, although projects of significance to the Province of Ontario or to Canada as a whole are considered.

The Richard and Jean Ivey Fund
Ste. 2200, 380 Wellington St., London, Ont. N6A 5B5
(519) 679-0870
Secretary-Treasurer, K.L. Sumner

The Jewish Foundation of Manitoba
Room 204, 370 Hargrave St., Winnipeg, Man. R3B 2K1
(204) 943-0406

Funds for general charitable purposes.
Executive Director, I. Peltz

The Thos. J. Johnston Foundation
1901 Avenue Rd., Toronto, Ont. M5M 3Z9
(416) 783-3117
Executive Secretary, A. K. Kingsmill

The Oakah L. Jones Foundation
145 King St. W., Ste. 1500, Toronto, Ont. M5H 2J3
(416) 364-1241
Director & Secretary, Graham D. Worley, Q.C.

For the support and advancement of the arts, the sciences, social institutions, law, education and religion.

The W. K. Kellogg Foundation
Secretary, 400 North Ave., Battle Creek, Michigan 49016 (616/965-1221)

For the application of knowledge to solve human problems in the areas of health, education and agriculture.

The Leon and Thea Koerner Foundation

To assist and support development projects by registered charitable organizations in the fields of higher education, culture, health and welfare in British Columbia. The foundation does not support existing normal operations, meet annual deficits or aid in building programs.
Secretary, J. E. Duff, The Permanent, Box 10152, Pacific Centre, Vancouver, B.C. V7Y 1E5 (604/689-0611)

The Kresge Foundation
2401 W. Big Beaver Rd., Box 3151, Troy, Michigan 48084
(313) 643-9630
President, A.H. Taylor, Jr.

Grant Eligibility: The Foundation principally makes challenge grants to tax exempt (U.S.) financially sound, well-established, fully accredited institutions operating in the following fields: Four-year college and university education; Health care and related services; Welfare; Conservation; The arts; Care of the young or old.

Areas of Interest: Foundation grants to eligible institutions are primarily made toward: construction and major renovation projects; Purchase of major, movable, capital equipment having a unit cost of not less than $50,000; Purchase of real estate.

Please write for application guidelines.

The Kroeker Foundation, Inc.
Box 1450, Winkler, Man. R0G 2X0
(204) 325-4333
Secretary, W.E. Kroeker

Laidlaw Foundation
Miss M. C. Thomas, 60 St. Clair Ave. E., Suite 203, Toronto, Ont. M4T 1N5 (416/964-3614)

Grants in support of experimental and demonstration projects in the fields of child development, environmental and conservation projects and the arts.

Law Foundation of British Columbia
#900, 1199 W. Pender St., Vancouver, B.C. V6E 2R1
(604) 688-2204

Funds for legal education, legal research, legal aid, law reform and the establishment, operation and maintenance of law libraries.
Research Director, M.E. Jacobsen

Law Foundation of Nova Scotia
Box 325, Halifax, N.S. B3J 2N7
(902) 422-8335
Executive Director, Mrs. Mary Helleiner

Constance Lethbridge Foundation
7005 ouest, boul. de Maisonneuve, Montreal, P.Q. H4B 1T3
(514) 487-1770
Assistant Secretary Treasurer, Miss Maryke Muller

To fund the Constance Lethbridge Centre in the City of Montreal.

The Life Underwriters Association of Canada Educational Foundation
41 Lesmill Rd., Don Mills, Ont. M3B 2T3
(416) 444-5251

Funds for the advancement of education (particularly with relation to the life insurance business) by the provision of lectures, scholarships, prizes, medals, bursaries, books, etc.
Secretary, A. W. Lingard

Masonic Foundation of Ontario
Box 217, 363 King St. W., Hamilton, Ont. L8N 3C9
Secretary Treasurer, T.J. Arthur

Provides bursaries for medical research in universities and colleges in Ontario.

The John and Margaret Ann Wilson McConnell Memorial Foundation
Box 786, Bracebridge, Ont.
Secretary, Mrs. D. C. Thomas

J. W. McConnell Foundation Inc.
Ste. 510, 1130 Sherbrooke St. W., Montreal, P.Q. H3A 2T1
(514) 288-2133

The R. Samuel McLaughlin Foundation
c/o National Trust Co. Ltd., 21 King St. E., Toronto, Ont. M5C 1B3 (416/364-9141)

Incorporated in 1951 under Letters Patent, Province of Ontario, for such charitable purposes for the benefit of people as may seem expedient from time to time to the trustees of the Corporation including (but without limiting the said discretion of the trustees) the expenditure of income in such manner as shall constitute a charitable object in the advancement of learning, teaching and education particularly in the medical and health and physical and mental therapy fields.
Secretary, P. J. Sewell

The McLean Foundation
Secretary Treasurer, 95 St. Clair Ave. W., 16th floor, Toronto, Ont. M4V 1P2 (416/964-6802)

Grants to registered charitable organizations.

The Fiona Mee Foundation
59 Front St. E., Toronto, Ont. M5E 1B3
(416) 364-3333

For the establishment and operation of the Fiona Mee Literary Journalism Award.

The Molson Foundation
Box 1600, Place d'Armes, Montreal, P.Q. H2Y 3L3
(514) 527-5151

Of primary interest to the Foundation are innovative projects in the fields of health and welfare, education, social development, national development and the humanities for which "seed" money is provided.

The Foundation generally makes one payment grants but, in certain circumstances, will also make commitments for grants payable over a period of up to five years. The majority of grants approved are in the $5,000 to $50,000 range; however, grants over $50,000 constitute the major part of funds distributed. Only Canadian charitable organizations which are registered with the Department of National Revenue are eligible.

The Foundation does not normally give consideration to appeals for a) Annual maintenance, budget deficits or endowment campaigns; b) Conferences, seminars, workshops; c) Scholarships, bursaries, student aid; d) Publication of books, magazines, films, tapes or other media of communication.
Secretary, S. T. Molson

F. K. Morrow Foundation
67 Yonge St., Room 808, Toronto, Ont. M5E 1J8
(416) 364-4124
President, Rev. Msgr. J. G. Fullerton, P.H.

The M.S.I. Foundation
#401, 10454 82 Ave., Edmonton, Alta. T6E 4Z7
(403) 433-2502
Director, Ian Walker

For the provision and promoting of medical and allied health services to the people of Alberta.

National Action Committee on the Status of Women Charitable & Educational Trust
40 St. Clair Ave. E., #306, Toronto, Ont. M4T 1M9
(416) 922-3246

Newman Foundation
89 St. George St., Toronto, Ont. M5S 2E8
(416) 979-2468

Maintenance and support of Roman Catholic chaplaincy on University of Toronto campus.
Correspondence to, Managing Director

Nickle Family Foundation
#402, 630 6th Ave. S.W., Calgary, Alta. T2P 0S8
(403) 269-3157
President, Carl O. Nickle

Grants to registered organizations involved in educational, cultural and community projects in Alberta.

Ontario Heritage Foundation
77 Bloor St. W., 7th floor, Toronto, Ont. M7A 2R9
(416) 965-9504

Established in 1967 by the Government of Ontario, to acquire and preserve property of historical, architectural, aesthetic, scenic, archaeological or recreational importance. As a Crown agency, it may accept donations of such property.
Chairman, John White

OTA Education Foundation, Inc.
555 Dixon Rd., Rexdale, Ont. M9W 1H8
(416) 247-7131
Executive Director, Stephen P. Flott

The Parkinson Foundation of Canada
Manulife Centre, Ste. 232, 55 Bloor St. W., Toronto, Ont. M4W 1A6
(416) 964-1155
Secretary Treasurer, Mrs. Mimi Feutl

The P.S.I. Foundation
Ste. 304, 4881 Yonge St., Willowdale, Ont. M2N 5X3
(416) 226-6323

Established in 1970 by the physicians of Ontario for charitable and educational purposes related to health, the science and practice of medicine and the healing arts. Projects undertaken in Ontario only. Annual report available on request.
Executive Director, C. A. Bond, F.C.G.A.

The Pillars Trust Fund
2005 St. Marc St., Montreal, P.Q. H3H 2G8
(514) 937-2301

Quebec-Labrador Foundation (Canada) Inc.
(Fondation Quebec Labrador du Canada Inc.)

c/o Guardian Trust Co., 1st Floor, 614 rue St-Jacques, Montreal, P.Q. H3C 1E2
(514) 842-8251
Secretary & Director, Ormonde H. Barrett

To help provide for higher education for qualified young men and women from the Quebec-Labrador region; to maintain a summer youth volunteer program for school and college age students from Canada and the United States.

The Queen Elizabeth II Canadian Fund to Aid in Research on the Diseases of Children

Jeanne Mance Bldg., Tunney's Pasture, Ottawa, Ont. K1A 0W9
(613) 996-8176
Secretary, Miss Mary-Anne Lipke

The Quetico Foundation

170 University Ave., Toronto, Ont. M5H 3B5
(416) 593-1391
Honorary Chairman, John B. Ridley
Joint Chairmen, Dr. O.M. Solandt, L.C. Bonnycastle

The Foundation has "as potential objects of its interest all lakeland, wilderness and other appropriate areas within the Province of Ontario deemed worthy of preservation by reason of their scenic and recreational values."

The Francis F. Reeve Foundation

300, 535 7th Ave. S.W., Calgary, Alta. T2T OY4
(403) 266-8931

Charitable and educational funds for YWCA, YMCA, Boys Clubs of Canada, Churches and certain students.
President, G.J. McKay

Regina Community Foundation

Ste. 202, 1102 Angus St., Regina, Sask. S4T 1Y5
(306) 527-8177

Grants in Regina area only, for health, welfare, recreation, education and the arts.
Manager, J. Ambler

The Julius Richardson Foundation Inc.

c/o 5425 Bessborough Ave., Montreal, P.Q. H4V 2S7
(514) 481-0461

A foundation to support the Montreal Julius Richardson Convalescent Hospital.

The Rockefeller Foundation

1133 Ave. of the Americas, New York, N.Y. 10036
(212) 869-8500
Secretary, Laurence D. Stifel

The Foundation's activities are concentrated in five areas of fundamental importance to mankind through programs directed toward the conquest of hunger and its attendant ills, toward the solution of problems of population, toward the resolution of conflicts in international relations, and, especially within the United States, toward equal opportunity for all, and toward cultural development. The Foundation's program is carried out through three closely related procedures. First is the making of grants to universities, research institutes, and other qualified agencies conducting work within the scope of the Foundation's program; second is the acceptance by the Foundation of active responsibility for certain co-operative projects; the third is advanced training, through two types of fellowship programs: 1) regular fellowship awards for advanced studies for individuals from those developing countries in which the Foundation has active programs; and 2) special fellowship awards primarily in support of domestic program objectives and open to qualified candidates on a competitive basis.

The Stephen B. Roman Foundation

Box 40, Royal Bank Plaza, Toronto, Ont. M5J 2K2
(416) 865-1991

Fondation Léo Roy

540, ave. Royale, Beauport, P.Q. G1E 1Y1
(418) 667-0149
President, Dr. Guy Marcoux, M.D.

To promote the works of Léo Roy (who was a musician and composer) and to help young talents from Quebec.

St. James Scholarship Foundation

241 Conway St., Winnipeg, Man. R3J 2M2
(204) 888-0643
Secretary Treasurer, Doug Kurtz

To receive donations to provide investment income for scholarships presented to selected students at the five high schools in St. James-Assiniboia.

The Colonel Harland Sanders Charitable Organization Inc.

2000 Jane St., Weston, Ont. M9N 2V2
(416) 249-7656

Saskatchewan Law Foundation

#620, 2220 12th Ave., Regina, Sask. S4P OM8
(306) 352-1121

The Sellers Foundation

2410, One Lombard Place, Winnipeg, Man. R3B 0X3
(204) 943-2584

For support of medical research projects, and the work of the Anglican Church, primarily in Western Canada.
Chairman, G. H. Sellers

Shaw Festival Theatre Foundation

Box 774, Niagara-on-the-Lake, Ont. LOS 1JO
(416) 468-2153

A.E. Silverwood Foundation

c/o Silverwood Dairies Limited, 6303 Airport Rd., Mississauga, Ont. L4V 1R8
(416) 678-9350

Conn Smythe Research Foundation for Crippled Children

350 Rumsey Rd., Toronto, Ont. M4G 1R8
(416) 425-6220, ext. 234
Director of Research, Dr. Walter H. Johnson

To support and help co-ordinate research throughout Ontario into the causes, prevention and special treatment of physically handicapping conditions in young people.

Chris Spencer Foundation

c/o Douglas, Symes & Brissenden, 16th floor, 409 Granville St., Vancouver, B.C. V6C 1V1

Funds for organizations providing scholarships for students entering B.C. universities for the first time and to promote good citizenship among young people. Limited to Greater Vancouver and Lower Fraser Valley area.

The Strathcona Trust

For the encouragement of physical training and military drill in the public schools. Canadian Forces Cadet Corps, organized in connection with public schools of all provinces, are eligible to participate in the benefits of the Trust.
Secretary to the Executive Council, c/o Director General Reserves & Cadets, Dept. of National Defence, Ottawa, Ont. K1A 0K2 (613/593-5313)

Fondation de la Famille Terrienne

10819, rue St-Denis, Montreal, P.Q. H3L 2J6
(514) 384-1442
President, Jacques de Broin, 4621 Coolbrook, Montreal, P.Q. H3X 2K7

To honour outstanding rural families for their accomplishments and interest in social affairs.

La Fondation Tex-Scope Inc.
3000, rue Boulle, St-Hyacinthe, P.Q. J2S 7C7
(514) 773-6800
Secretary Treasurer, Marcel R. Prescott

To promote textile knowledge by funding scholarships for students at the St-Hyacinthe Junior College Textile Department.

Ukrainian Canadian Research Foundation Inc.
4 Island View Blvd., Toronto, Ont. M8V 2P4
(416) 255-9090
Secretary Treasurer, Stephen Kalin

The principal aim of the Foundation is to study the Ukrainian ethnic group in Canada. This is achieved by supporting the research of scholars, publishing research and establishing a library and archives.

Fondation Universitas du Canada
(Universitas Foundation of Canada)
2590 boul. Laurier, 9e étage, Ste-Foy, P.Q. G1V 4M6
(418) 651-8975

A non profit organization whose aim is to give university scholarships to children registered by their parents.
Secretary, Gaetan Bélanger, M.Sc.C.

Vancouver Foundation
9th floor, 1199 W. Pender St., Vancouver, B.C. V6E 2R1
(604) 688-2204

The Vancouver Foundation is a philanthropic organization with funds for research, demonstration projects, experimental activities and, in some cases, sustaining support for agencies, societies and other institutions. Being limited to British Columbia and principally active in Greater Vancouver, it is concerned with the mental, physical, moral, educational and cultural well-being of residents.

The Victoria Foundation
877 Island Rd., Victoria, B.C. V8S 2V1
(604) 592-2132
Correspondence to, E. E. Chamberlin

The W. Garfield Weston Foundation
22 St. Clair Ave. E., Ste. 2001, Toronto, Ont. M4T 2S3
(416) 922-4673
Governor & Secretary, Roger A. Lindsay

The Winnipeg Foundation
Executive Director, Alan G. Howison, 800-305 Broadway, Winnipeg, Man. R3C 3J7 (204/944-7165)

Community Trust for charitable, educational and cultural purposes in Greater Winnipeg.

Mr. and Mrs. P.A. Woodward's Foundation
1177 W. Hastings St., Ste. 1912, Vancouver, B.C. V6E 2L5
(604) 682-8116
Secretary, J.N. Bell

For health projects which benefit the people of British Columbia.

The Writers Development Trust
24 Ryerson Ave., Toronto, Ont. M5T 2P3
(416) 868-6910

FOUR NATIONS CONFEDERACY INC.
#500, 275 Portage Ave., Winnipeg, Man. R3B 2B3
(204) 944-8245

FREELANCE EDITORS' ASSOCIATION OF CANADA
Box 113, Stn. Z, Toronto, Ont. M5N 2Z3
(416) 968-3154
President, Grace Deutsch

FUNERAL SERVICE ASSOCIATION OF CANADA
Ste. 602, 350 Sparks St., Ottawa, Ont. K1R 7S8
(613) 238-8124
Executive Director, J.T. McCarthy

FUR TRADE ASSOCIATION OF CANADA (ONTARIO) INC.
185 Spadina Ave., Toronto, Ont. M5T 2C6
(416) 368-7049
Executive Director, H. R. Bockner

GAYS FOR EQUALITY
Box 27, University Centre, University of Manitoba, Winnipeg, Man. R3T 2N2 (204/269-8678)

GENETICS SOCIETY OF CANADA
Ste. 907, 151 Slater St., Ottawa, Ont. K1P 5H4
(613) 232-9459

THE GEOLOGICAL ASSOCIATION OF CANADA
Secretary Treasurer, Dr. A.V. Morgan, Dept. of Earth Sciences, Univ. of Waterloo, Waterloo, Ont. N2L 3G1 (519/885-1211, ext. 3029)

GERMAN-CANADIAN BUSINESS & PROFESSIONAL ASSOCIATION
159 Bay St., Ste. 1023, Toronto, Ont. M5J 1J7
(416) 863-9453
Manager, Mrs. Ingeborg Bibersteiner

GIFT PACKAGING & GREETING CARD ASSOCIATION
c/o Richard B. Cairns, Chairman, 2 Hallcrown Place, Willowdale, Ont. M2J 1P6 (416/492-1300)

GIRL GUIDES OF CANADA, INC.
50 Merton St., Toronto, Ont. M4S 1A3
(416) 487-5281
Chief Commissioner, Mrs. J.E. Currah, Burlington, Ont.
Deputy Chief Commissioners, Mrs. G.R. McCague, Alliston, Ont.; Mrs. R.R. Coldwell, Bathurst, N.B.; Mrs. L.W. Howell, Scarborough, Ont.

Provincial Commissioners
Alta.: Mrs. T.F. Clement, 10359 Whyte Ave., #200, Edmonton, Alta. T6E 1Z9
B.C.: Mrs. J. Runcie, 1462 W. 8th Ave., Vancouver, B.C. V6H 1E1
Man.: Mrs. K.W. Clark, 200-267 Edmonton St., Winnipeg, Man. R3C 1S2
N.B.: Mrs. R. Coldwell, Ste. 215, 70 Crown St., Saint John, N.B. E2L 2X6
Nfld.: Mrs. N. Crane, Bldg. 566, St. John's Pl., Pleasantville, St. John's, Nfld. A1A 1S3
N.W.T.: Mrs. Judith Comerford, Box 2835, Yellowknife, N.W.T. X0E 1H0
N.S.: Mrs. C.J. Stone, 1871 Granville St., Halifax, N.S. B3J 1Y1
Ont.: Mrs. I.M. Gracey, 50 Merton St., Toronto, Ont. M4S 1A3
P.E.I.: Mrs. Elizabeth Jensen, 100 Upper Prince St., Charlottetown, P.E.I.
Que.: Mrs. W.H. Steers, 1939 Maisonneuve Blvd. W., Montreal, P.Q. H3H 1K3
Sask.: Mrs. V.J. Andreas, 1362A Lorne St., Regina, Sask. S4R 2K1
Yukon: Mrs. J. Pollock, Box 5133, Whitehorse, Yukon Y1A 4S3
Guides Catholiques du Canada (secteur français), Mlle Ghislaine Clavet, 3827 St. Hubert, Montreal, P.Q.

GLASS CONTAINER COUNCIL OF CANADA
Ste. 1310, 67 Yonge St., Toronto, Ont. M5E 1J8
(416) 364-4109
Executive Director, H.E. Dalton

GLAZING CONTRACTORS ASSOCIATION (B.C.)
2675 Oak St., Vancouver, B.C. V6H 2K3
(604) 736-6311

GOETHE INSTITUTE
German Cultural Centre, 1067 Yonge St., Toronto, Ont. M4W 2L2
(416) 924-3327
Director, Dr. Helmut Liede

GOLF ASSOCIATIONS
See Athletic Associations

GRAPHIC ARTS INDUSTRIES ASSOCIATION
75 Albert St., Suite 906, Ottawa, Ont. K1P 5E7
(613) 236-7208
President, J.B. Linklater

Affiliated Societies

L'Association des Maîtres-Imprimeurs de Montréal Inc.
Atlantic Provinces Graphic Arts Association
Calgary Graphic Arts Association
Canadian Bank Cheque Manufacturers
Canadian Business Forms Association
Canadian Book Manufacturing Association
Canadian Printing Ink Manufacturers' Association
Council of Printing Industries, Toronto
East Central Ont. Graphic Arts Association
Employing Printers' Association of Montreal, Inc.
Graphic Arts Association of B.C.
Graphic Arts Industries Association, Edmonton Branch
Graphic Arts Industries Association, Montreal Branch
Graphic Arts Industries Association, Toronto Branch
Man. Graphic Arts Industries Association
Ottawa Graphic Arts Association
Sask. Graphic Arts Association
South Western Ont. Branch, GAIA

GREAT LAKES WATERWAYS DEVELOPMENT ASSOCIATION
Ste. 606, 116 Albert St., Ottawa, Ont. K1P 5G3
(613) 233-8779
President & General Manager, D.S. Rothwell

GREENPEACE FOUNDATION
2623 W. 4th Ave., Vancouver, B.C. V6K 1P8
(604) 736-0321
President, Dr. Pat Moore

GROCERY PRODUCTS MANUFACTURERS OF CANADA
Head Office, 170 Laurier Ave. W., Suite 703, Ottawa, Ont. K1P 5V5 (613/236-0583)
Admin. Office, Ste. 101, 1185 Eglinton Ave. E., Don Mills, Ont. M3C 3C6 (416/429-4444)

GYRO INTERNATIONAL
Secretary Treasurer, J.H. Harding, 1096 Mentor Ave., Box 489, Painesville, Ohio, 44077 (216/352-2501)

HAIRDRESSERS' ASSOCIATION OF BRITISH COLUMBIA
1777 W. 3rd Ave., Vancouver, B.C. V6J 1K7
(604) 736-9891

HANG GLIDERS ASSOCIATION OF CANADA
#10, 441 5th Ave. S.W., Calgary, Alta. T2P 2V1
(403) 277-2606
President, Cliff Kakish

BRITISH COLUMBIA HANG GLIDING ASSOCIATION
c/o Sport B.C., 1200 Hornby St., Vancouver, B.C. V6Z 2E2

ALBERTA HANG GLIDING ASSOCIATION
Box 4063, Stn. C, Calgary, Alta. T2T 5M9
(403) 277-2606

MANITOBA HANG GLIDING ASSOCIATION
#303, 122 Weatherstone Place, Winnipeg, Man. R2J 2S8

ONTARIO HANG GLIDING ASSOCIATION
234 Argyle St., Ottawa, Ont. K2P 1B9

ASSOCIATION DE VOL LIBRE DU QUEBEC INC.
C.P. 332, Succ. St-Laurent, Montréal, P.Q. H4L 4V6

NEWFOUNDLAND HANG GLIDING ASSOCIATION
Box 203, Mount Pearl, Nfld. A1N 2C2

THE HEALTH LEAGUE OF CANADA
A National Citizen's Committee for World Health Organization.
76 Avenue Rd., Toronto, Ont. M5R 2H1
(416) 923-8405
President, Mrs. Reginae Tait
Director, Dr. D.F. Damude
Official publication, "HEALTH".

HEATING, REFRIGERATING & AIR CONDITIONING INSTITUTE OF CANADA
5468 Dundas St. W., Ste. 226, Islington, Ont. M9B 6E3
(416) 239-8191
General Manager, S. K. Cryer

LES HEBDOS REGIONAUX
(French Weeklies Association of Canada)
81, rue Saint-Pierre, Quebec, P.Q. G1K 4A3
(418) 694-0381
General Manager, Jean Longval

HELLENIC FEDERATION OF PARENTS & GUARDIANS OF GREATER MONTREAL
(Federation Hellenique des Parents et Guardians de Montreal)
451 Ogilvy Ave., Montreal, P.Q. H3N 1M7
(514) 279-3155, 279-3808
Director, Peter Ferentinos

THE HERALDRY SOCIETY OF CANADA
Honorary Secretary, F. D'Alton Gooderham, 125 Lakeway Dr., Ottawa, Ont. K1L 5A9 (613/745-5701)
Publication, "Heraldry in Canada" (quarterly)

HERITAGE CANADA
Box 1358, Stn. B, Ottawa, Ont. K1P 5R4
(613) 237-1066
Executive Director, Jacques Dalibard

Participating Associations

ALBERTA HERITAGE SOCIETIES
(Listed alphabetically by location)

Alta. Historical Resources Foundation, 102 8th Ave. S.E., Calgary, Alta. T2G OK6
Heritage Park Society, 900 Heritage Dr. S.W., Calgary, Alta. T2V 2X3
Historical Society of Alta., c/o Dr. H.A. Dempsey, 95 Holmwood Ave. N.W., Calgary, Alta. T2K 2G7
Society for the Preservation of Architectural Resources, c/o Faculty of Environ. Design, Univ. of Calgary, Calgary, Alta. T2N 1N4
Fort Edmonton Historical Foundation, Box 8645, Stn. L, Edmonton, Alta. T6C 4J4
Old Strathcona Foundation, 8520 104 St., Edmonton, Alta. T6E 4G4
Society for the Protection of Architectural Resources, 11047 81 Ave., Edmonton, Alta. T6G 0S3

Fort Macleod Historical Association, Box 776, Fort Macleod, Alta. TOL OZO
Fort Saskatchewan Historical Society, 10104 101 St., Fort Saskatchewan, Alta. T8L 1V9
Rainy Hills Historical Society, Iddesleigh, Alta. TOJ 1TO
Innisfail & Dist. Historical Society, Box 642, Innisfail, Alta. TOM 1AO
Leduc & Dist. Historical Society, Box 1385, Leduc, Alta. T9E 2Y8
Red Deer & Dist. Museum Society, Box 762, Red Deer, Alta. T4N 5H2
Albert Lacombe Historical Foundation, c/o 30 Sir Winston Churchill Ave., St. Albert, Alta. T8N 3A3

BRITISH COLUMBIA HERITAGE SOCIETIES
(Listed alphabetically by location)
Matsqui-Sumas-Abbotsford Museum Society, Heritage Committee, 2313 Ware St., Abbotsford, B.C. V2S 3C6
Atlin Historical Society, Box 111, Atlin, B.C. VOW 1AO
Bowen Island Historians, R.R. 1, Bowen Island, B.C. VON 1GO
Burnaby Historical Society, 5530 Ewart St., Burnaby, B.C. V5J 2W4
Cranbrook Archives, Museum & Landmark Foundation, Box 400, Cranbrook, B.C. V1C 4H9
Creston & Dist. Historical Society, Box 1123, Creston, B.C. VOB 1GO
South Peace Historical Society, Box 2033, Dawson Creek, B.C. V1G 4K8
Fernie & Dist. Historical Society, Box 1527, Fernie, B.C. VOB 1MO
Langham Cultural Society, Box 555, Kaslo, B.C. VOG 1MO
Mission Historical Society, 33201 2nd Ave., Mission, B.C. V2V 1J9
City of Nanaimo Heritage Advisory Committee, City Hall, 455 Wallace St., Nanaimo, B.C. V9R 5J6
Nanaimo Historical Society, Box 933, Nanaimo, B.C. V9R 5N2
Okanagan Historical Society, Box 847, Penticton, B.C. V2A 7G1
Powell River Historical Museum Association, Box 42, Powell River, B.C. V8A 4Z5
Cariboo Historical Society (Quesnel Branch), 1582 Beach Cres., Quesnel, B.C. V2J 4J6
Richmond Historical & Museum Society, 3111 Shell Rd., Richmond, B.C. V6X 2P3
Steveston Historical Society, 3811 Moncton St., Richmond, B.C. V7E 3A0
Riondel Historical Society, Riondel, B.C. VOB 2BO
Trail Historical Society, Box 405, Trail, B.C. V1R 4L7
Native Sons of B.C. (Post #2), c/o S.P. Greenwood, 2292 W. 37th Ave., Vancouver, B.C. V6M 1P1
Vancouver Historical Society, Box 3071, Vancouver, B.C. V6B 3X6
West Coast Railway Association Inc., Box 2790, Vancouver, B.C. V6B 3X2
Nechako Valley Historical Society, c/o Mrs. Jill Vickers, Box 1318, Vanderhoof, B.C. VOJ 3AO
Hallmark Society, Box 1204, Victoria, B.C. V8W 2T6
Wells Historical Society, Box 244, Wells, B.C. VOK 2RO
White Rock Historical Society, Box 264, White Rock, B.C. V4B 5C6

MANITOBA HERITAGE SOCIETIES
(Listed alphabetically by location)
Assiniboine Historical Society, c/o Glen Olmstead, 1502 Lorne Ave. E., Brandon, Man. R7A 1X2
Flin Flon Historical Society, Box 294, Flin Flon, Man. R8A 1J8
The Pas Historical Society, Box 547, The Pas, Man.
Festival du Voyageur, c/o 219 Provencher Blvd., St. Boniface, Man. R2H 3B5
Heritage St-Norbert Inc., c/o 1124 rue des Trappistes, St. Norbert, Man. R3V 1B8
Le Comité du Coq Gaulois, C.P. 61, St-Pierre-Jolys, Man. R0A 1V0
Swan Valley Historical Society, Box 397, Swan River, Man. ROL 1ZO
Charleswood Historical Society Inc., 1018 Charleswood Rd., Winnipeg, Man. R3S 1A2
Fort Garry Historical Society, 650 Riverwood Ave., Winnipeg, Man. R3T 1K4
Man. Historical Society, 190 Rupert Ave., Winnipeg, Man. R3B ON2

NEW BRUNSWICK HERITAGE SOCIETIES
(Listed alphabetically by location)
Société Historique Nicolas Denys, Case 6, Site 19, Bertrand, N.B. EOB 1JO
St. Michael's Museum Association, c/o John Connell, 12 Alexandra St., Chatham, N.B. E1N 1P8
Peninsula Heritage Inc., c/o W. Murray, R.R. 1, Clifton Royal, N.B. EOG 1NO
Fredericton Heritage Trust, Box 546, Fredericton, N.B. E3B 5A6
Kings County Historical Society, Hampton, N.B. E0G 1Z0
Heritage Moncton, 15 Fairview Dr., Moncton, N.B. E1C 3C5
Miramichi Historical Society, 225 Mary St., Newcastle, N.B. E1V 1Z3
Rothesay Area Heritage Trust, Box 692, Rothesay, N.B. EOG 2WO
St. Andrews Civic Trust, Box 484, St. Andrews, N.B. EOG 2XO
Quaco Historical & Library Society Inc., Quaco Museum, St. Martins, N.B. EOG 2ZO
Carleton County Historical Society, Inc., c/o Miss C.L. Chase, Box 898, Woodstock, N.B. EOJ 2EO

NEWFOUNDLAND HERITAGE SOCIETIES
(Listed alphabetically by location)
Carbonear Heritage Society, Carbonear, Nfld. A0A 1T0
Placentia Area Historical Society, Box 359, Placentia, Nfld. AOB 2YO
Nfld. Historic Trust, Box 5542, St. John's, Nfld. A1C 5W4
St. John's Heritage Foundation, Box 5246, St. John's, Nfld. A1C 5W1

NOVA SCOTIA HERITAGE SOCIETIES
(Listed alphabetically by location)
Annapolis Royal Development Commission, Box 278, Annapolis Royal, N.S. B0S 1A0
Historic Restoration Society of Annapolis County, Box 503, Annapolis Royal, N.S. B0S 1A0
Cole Harbour Rural Heritage Society, Bissett Rd., R.R. 1, Dartmouth, N.S. B2W 3X7
Dartmouth Museum Society, 1 Ellenvale Ave., Dartmouth, N.S. B2W 2W2
Heritage Trust of N.S., Box 217, Halifax, N.S. B3J 2M4
Kings Historical Society, Box 11, Kentville, N.S. B4N 1S4
Lunenburg Heritage Society, Box 674, Lunenberg, N.S. BOJ 2CO
Committee for the Preservation of Mining Heritage of Pictou County, 103 North Ave., New Glasgow, N.S. B2H 2E2
Yarmouth County Historical Society, c/o Helen Hall, 22 Collins St., Yarmouth, N.S. B5A 3C8

ONTARIO HERITAGE SOCIETIES
(Listed alphabetically by location)
Glengarry Historical Society, Box 416, Alexandria, Ont. KOC 1AO
North Lanark Historical Society, Box 218, Almonte, Ont. KOA 1AO
Amherstburg Historic Sites, 1117 Front Rd. S., Amherstburg, Ont. N9V 2M4
Local Architectural Conservation Advisory Committee, 271 Sandwich St. S., Amherstburg, Ont. N9V 2A5
Ancaster Township Historical Society, Box 163, Ancaster, Ont. L9G 3L4
Arnprior Historical Society, 277 Elgin St. W., Arnprior, Ont. K7S 1P6
Aurora & Dist. Historical Society, Box 356, Aurora, Ont. L4G 3H4
Heritage Aylmer, 219 Talbot St. E., Aylmer, Ont. N5H 1H6
Association of Barrie Citizens, Box 521, Barrie, Ont. L4M 4Y6
Simcoe County Historical Association, Box 144, Barrie, Ont. L4M 4S9

Hastings County Historical Society, Box 1418, Belleville, Ont. K8N 5J1
Tecumseth & West Gwillimbury Historical Society, Box 171, Bond Head, Ont. L0G 1B0
Architectural Conservancy of Ontario (Brant County), 117 Dufferin Ave., Brantford, Ont. N3T 4P9
Save Our Heritage Org., Box 578, Brighton, Ont. K0K 1H0
Brockville & Dist. Historical Society, Box 195, Brockville, Ont. K6V 5V2
Ont. Genealogical Society (Leeds & Grenville Branch), Box 536, Brockville, Ont. K6V 5V7
Burlington Historical Society, 3047 Woodland Park Dr., Burlington, Ont. L7N 1K8
Heritage Cambridge, Box 181, Cambridge (Galt), Ont. N1R 5T6
Riverside Park Neighbourhood Association, 89 Kensington Place, Chatham, Ont. N7M 2X7
East Durham Historical Society, c/o Foster Russell, Box 636, Cobourg, Ont. K9A 4L3
The Society for the Restoration of Victoria Hall, #203, 107 King St. W., Cobourg, Ont. K9A 2M4
Collingwood & Dist. Historical Society, c/o Anne Stockwood, 255 Maple St., Collingwood, Ont. L9Y 2R1
Seventh Town Historical Society, c/o J.E. Wannamaker, R.R. 1, Consecon, Ont. K0K 1T0
Stormont, Dundas & Glengarry Historical Society, Box 773, Cornwall, Ont. K6H 5T5
Delta Mill Society, Box 222, Delta, Ont. K0E 1S0
Dundas Heritage Association, 1 Victoria St., Dundas, Ont. L9H 2B7
Pelham Historical Society, c/o General Delivery, Fonthill, Ont. L0S 1E0
Architectural Conservancy of Ont. (Huron Co. Branch), 35 Wellington St. S., Goderich, Ont. N7A 3S5
Grimsby Historical Society, Box 294, Grimsby, Ont. L3M 1R8
Guelph Historical Society, Box 1502, Guelph, Ont. N1H 6N9
Heritage Hamilton Foundation, Box 166, Hamilton, Ont. L8N 3A2
Ont. Genealogical Society (Hamilton Branch), Box 904, Hamilton, Ont. L8N 3P6
Harrow Early Immigrant Research Society, Box 53, Harrow, Ont. NOR 1GO
Frontenac Historic Foundation, Box 27, Kingston, Ont. K7L 4V6
Ont. Genealogical Society (Kingston Branch), Box 1394, Kingston, Ont. K7L 5C6
Ont. Genealogical Society (Waterloo-Wellington Branch), Box 603, Kitchener, Ont. N2G 4A2
Waterloo Historical Society, Box 552, Stn. C, Kitchener, Ont. N2G 4A2
Kleinburg Binder Twine Festival, Box 6, Kleinburg, Ont. LOJ 1CO
Christ Church Restoration Committee, Box 427, Lakefield, Ont. KOL 2HO
Architectural Conservancy of Ont. (London), Box 22, Stn. B, London, Ont. N6A 4V3
Heritage London Foundation, Box 1761, Stn. A, London, Ont. N6A 5M9
London & Middlesex Historical Society, Box 303, Stn. B, London, Ont. N6A 4W1
Ont. Genealogical Society (London Branch), Box 871, Stn. B, London, Ont. N6A 4Z3
Merrickville & Dist. Historical Society, Box 294, Merrickville, Ont. KOG 1NO
Niagara Falls Heritage Foundation, 5616 Royal Manor Dr., Niagara Falls, Ont. L2G 1E6
Old St. John's Stamford Heritage Association, 3428 Portage Rd., Niagara Falls, Ont. L2J 2K4
Associated Concerned Townspeople of Old Niagara, Box 567, Niagara-on-the-Lake, Ont. LOS 1JO
Historical Committee of North Bay, 652 Copeland St., North Bay, Ont. P1B 3C8
Ont. Genealogical Society (Nipissing Dist. Branch) Box 93, North Bay, Ont. P1B 8G8
Rideau Township Historical Society, Box 232, North Gower, Ont. KOA 2TO
Oakville Historical Society, (168 Lakeshore Rd. E.) Box 395, Oakville, Ont. L6J 5A8
Dufferin County Historical Society, 209 Zina St., Orangeville, Ont. L9W 1E9
Orillia Historical Society, c/o 235 Laclie St., Orillia, Ont. L3V 4N5
Oshawa & Dist. Historical Society, c/o Donald Fox, 412 Simcoe St. N., Oshawa, Ont. L1G 4T6
Carleton-West-Russell Historical Society, #5, 65 Riverdale, Ottawa, Ont. K1S 1R1
Heritage Ottawa, (62 John St.) Box 510, Ottawa, Ont. K1P 5P6
Historical Society of Ottawa, Box 523, Stn. B, Ottawa, Ont. K1P 5P6
Ont. Genealogical Society (Ottawa Branch), Box 8346, Ottawa, Ont. K1G 3H8
Local Architectural Conservation Advisory Committee, c/o City Hall, Owen Sound, Ont.
Billy Bishop Heritage, Box 535, Owen Sound, Ont. N4K 5R1
Owen Sound Historical Society, c/o Murray Telford, 975 6th Ave. W., Owen Sound, Ont. N4K 5G6
Ottawa Valley Historical Society, Box 985, Pembroke, Ont. K8A 7M5
Ont. Genealogical Society (Kawartha Branch), Box 162, Peterborough, Ont. K9J 6Y8
Peterborough Historical Society, Hutchison House, 270 Brock St., Peterborough, Ont. K9H 2P9
Petrolia Heritage Committee, Box 1278, Petrolia, Ont. NON 1RO
Ont. Genealogical Society (Bruce Grey Branch), Box 1606, Port Elgin, Ont. N0H 2C0
Heritage Ganaraska Foundation, Box 1793, Port Hope, Ont. L1A 4B4
Lake Scugog Historical Society, Box 489, Port Perry, Ont. LOB 1NO
Grenville County Historical Society, Box 982, Prescott, Ont. KOE 1TO
Heritage Renfrew, Box 11, Renfrew, Ont. K7V 4A2
Goulbourn Twp. Historical Society, c/o Brian Bowrin, R.R. 3, Richmond, Ont. KOA 2ZO
Ridgetown & Dist. Historical Society, Box 248, Ridgetown, Ont. NOP 2CO
Welland Canals Preservation Association, Box 1224, St. Catharines, Ont. L2R 7A7
St. Marys on the Thames Historical Society, c/o Dr. Jim Smibert, St. Marys, Ont. N0M 2V0
Heritage St. Marys (L.A.C.A.C.), Box 998, St. Mary's, Ont. N0M 2V0
Norfolk Historical Society, 109 Norfolk St. S., Simcoe, Ont. N3V 2W3
Porcupine Camp Historical Society, Box 452, South Porcupine, Ont. P0N 1H0
Avon Valley Historical Society, Court House, Stratford, Ont. N5A 5S4
Perth Co. Historical Board, Court House, Stratford, Ont. N5A 5S4
Stratford Local Architectural Conservation Adv. Committee, Clerk's Office, City Hall, Stratford, Ont. N5A 2L1
Ont. Genealogical Society (Sudbury Dist. Branch), c/o Sudbury Public Library, 200 Brady St., Sudbury, Ont. P3E 5K3
Sudbury Local Architectural Conservancy Adv. Committee, c/o Gary Peck, 167 Shelley Dr., Sudbury, Ont. P3A 2S6
Sudbury Centennial Foundation, c/o Sudbury Regional Multicultural Centre, 150 Durham St. S., Box 1312, Stn. B, Sudbury, Ont. P3E 4S7
Society for Preservation of Historic Thornhill, Box 224, Thornhill, Ont. L3T 3N1
Ont. Genealogical Society (Thunder Bay Dist.), Box 373, Stn. F, Thunder Bay, Ont. P7E 4V9
Bruce County Historical Society, Box 182, Tiverton, Ont. N0G 2T0
Architectural Conservancy Ontario (Toronto), c/o Mrs. K. Spratley, 285 Heath St. E., Toronto, Ont. M4T 1T3
Don Vale Property Owners Association, 276 Carlton St., Toronto, Ont. M5A 2L5

Ont. Genealogical Society (Toronto Branch), Box 74, Stn. U, Toronto, Ont. M8Z 5M4
United Empire Loyalists (Governor Simcoe Branch), Box 44, Stn. K, Toronto, Ont. M4P 2G1
Waterdown-East Flamborough Heritage Society, Box 1044, Waterdown, Ont. L0R 2H0
Ont. Genealogical Society (Essex County Branch), Box 2, Stn. A, Windsor, Ont. N9A 6J5
Essex County Historical Society, 254 Pitt St. W., Windsor, Ont. N9A 5L5
Ont. Genealogical Society (Oxford Branch), Box 1092, Woodstock, Ont. N4S 8A5
Oxford Historical Society, c/o Don Milton, Oxford Museum, City Square, Woodstock, Ont. N4S 1C4

PRINCE EDWARD ISLAND HERITAGE SOCIETIES

P.E.I. Heritage Foundation, Box 922, Charlottetown, P.E.I. C1A 7L9

QUEBEC HERITAGE SOCIETIES
(Listed alphabetically by location)

Société d'histoire des Iles Percées, C.P. 234, Boucherville, P.Q.
Hudson Historical Society, Box 802, Hudson Heights, Como, P.Q. J0P 1H0
Compton County Historical & Museum Society, R.R. 5, Cookshire, P.Q. J0B 1M0
Société Historique de la Cote-du-Sud, 100, 4e Ave., C.P. 937, La Pocatière, P.Q. G0R 1Z0
Société Historique du Marigot Inc., C.P. 432, Succ. A, Longueuil, P.Q. J4H 3Z2
Richmond County Historical Society, Box 280, Melbourne, P.Q. J0B 2B0
Canadian Heritage of Quebec, 2025 Peel St., Montreal, P.Q. H3A 1T6
Heritage Montreal, 418 rue Bonsecours, Montreal, P.Q. H2Y 3C4
Save Montreal (Sauvons Montréal), Box 158, Succ. La Cité, Montreal, P.Q. H2W 2M9
Historical Society of the Gatineau, Old Chelsea, P.Q. J0X 2N0
La Corporation du Vieux Moulin Marcoux, C.P. 130, Pont-Rouge, P.Q. G0A 2X0
Ste-Anne de Bout de l'Ille Heritage Society, Box 22, Ste-Anne de Bellevue, P.Q. H9X 3L4
Seigneurie des Aulnaies, St-Roch des Aulnaies, P.Q. G0R 4E0
La Société d'histoire des Cantons de l'Est, C.P. 1141, Sherbrooke, P.Q. J1H 5L5
Centre Communautaire Guerin, Co. Témiscamingue, P.Q. J0Z 2E0
La Société d'Histoire de la Région d'Arthabaska, c/o Pierre Labbe, 116 Lafrance, #3, Victoriaville, P.Q. G6P 4Y6
Metis Beach Community Association, Box 585, Westmount, P.Q. H3Z 2T6

SASKATCHEWAN HERITAGE SOCIETIES
(Listed alphabetically by location)

Moose Jaw Historical Society, c/o Barry Elmer, 1138 13th Ave. N.W., Moose Jaw, Sask. S6H 6G1
Prince Albert Branch, Sask. Genealogical Society, c/o Jeannine Megaffin, MacDowall, Sask. S0K 2S0
Prince Albert Historical Society, Box 531, Prince Albert, Sask. S6V 5R8
Heritage Regina, c/o G.R. Bothwell, Box 581, Regina, Sask. S4P 3A3
Saskatoon Heritage Society, c/o 118 9th St. E., Saskatoon, Sask. S7N 0A1

YUKON HERITAGE SOCIETIES

Klondike Heritage Committee, Box 303, Dawson City, Y.T. Y0B 1G0

HOSPITAL ASSOCIATIONS

Canadian Administrative Housekeepers Association

Box 3340, Stn. C, Ottawa, Ont. K1Y 4J5
(416) 595-4116
Secretary, P. White

Canadian Association of Hospital Auxiliaries

410 Laurier Ave. W., Ottawa, Ont. K1R 7T6
(613) 238-8005, ext. 35

Canadian College of Health Service Executives

410 Laurier Ave. W., Ste. 805, Ottawa, Ont. K1R 7T3
(613) 235-7218
President, John M. Phin, M.D., M.H.A.
B.C. Education Services Office: 440 Cambie St., Vancouver, B.C. V6B 2N5, Director, Wayne Soucy
Atlantic Education Services Office: 2615 Northwood Terrace, Halifax, N.S. B3K 3S5, Director, Charles A. Shields, Jr.
Collège canadien des Directeurs de Services de Santé: 110 rue de la Barre, #216, Longueuil, P.Q. J4K 1A3, Director administratif, J.-C. Tremblay

Canadian Council on Hospital Accreditation

1815 Alta Vista Dr., Ottawa, Ont. K1G 3Y6
(613) 523-9154
Executive Director, Dr. A. L. Swanson

Canadian Hospital Association

410 Laurier Ave. W., Ste. 800, Ottawa, Ont. K1R 7T6
(613) 238-8005
President, Jean-Claude Martin

Provincial Associations

ALBERTA HOSPITAL ASSOCIATION

Executive Director, D.A. Macgregor, 10025 108th St., Edmonton, Alta. T5J 1K9 (403/423-1776)

BRITISH COLUMBIA HEALTH ASSOCIATION

Executive Director, Patricia M. Wadsworth, 440 Cambie St., Vancouver, B.C. V6B 2N6 (604/683-7421)

MANITOBA HEALTH ORGANIZATIONS, INC.

Executive Director, H.A. Crewson, 377 Colony St., Winnipeg, Man. R3B 2P5 (204/942-6591)

NEW BRUNSWICK HOSPITAL ASSOCIATION

Executive Director, V.R. Olive, Box 1418, 315 Regent St., Fredericton, N.B. E3B 5E3 (506/455-8626)

NEWFOUNDLAND HOSPITAL ASSOCIATION

Executive Director, R.J. Burnell, Box 8234, Stn. A, St. John's, Nfld. A1B 3N4

NORTHWEST TERRITORIES HOSPITAL ASSOCIATION

Executive Director, L.E. Todd, Box 10, Yellowknife, N.W.T. X0E 1H0 (403/873-3444)

NOVA SCOTIA ASSOCIATION OF HEALTH ORGANIZATIONS

Executive Director, J.F. Ingram, 5991 Spring Garden Rd., Halifax, N.S. B3H 1Y6 (902/429-4020)

ONTARIO HOSPITAL ASSOCIATION

Executive Director, R. Alan Hay, 150 Ferrand Dr., Don Mills, Ont. M3C 1H6 (416/429-2661)

HOSPITAL ASSOCIATION OF PRINCE EDWARD ISLAND

Secretary, E.Y. Porter, P.E.I. Hospital, Charlottetown, P.E.I. C1A 1T5 (902/894-8532)

ASSOCIATION DES HOPITAUX DU QUEBEC

Directeur général, Jacques A. Nadeau, 276 St. Jacques St., #310, Montreal, P.Q. H2Y 1N3 (514/842-4861)

SASKATCHEWAN HEALTH CARE ASSOCIATION

Executive Director, C.H. Helmsing, 1445 Park St., Regina, Sask. S4N 4C5 (306/525-2741)

Catholic Health Association of Canada

Executive Director, Everett MacNeil, 312 Daly Ave., Ottawa, Ont. K1N 6G7 (613/238-8471)
Regional Conferences in all provinces. Contact Ottawa address for names and addresses.

Hospital Auxiliaries Association of Ontario
150 Ferrand Dr., Don Mills, Ont. M3C 1H6
(416) 429-2661, ext. 265

Hospital Council of Metropolitan Toronto
123 Edward St., Ste. 1500, Toronto, Ont. M5G 1E2
(416) 595-0930
Executive Director, Neville C. Chenoy

Ontario Association of Directors of Hospital Volunteer Services
150 Ferrand Dr., Don Mills, Ont. M3C 1H6
(416) 429-2661, ext. 265

HOTEL ASSOCIATIONS
See 'Travel & Tourism'

HOTEL & RESTAURANT SUPPLIERS ASSOCIATION INC.
474 St-Alexis St., Montreal, P.Q. H2Y 2N6
(514) 844-8889
Executive Manager, G. A. Huot

HOUSING & URBAN DEVELOPMENT ASSOCIATION OF CANADA
15 Toronto St., 10th floor, Toronto, Ont. M5C 2E3
(416) 364-4135
Executive Vice President, B. J. Bernard
Branches in B.C., Alta., Man., Sask., Ont., Que., and Atlantic Regions

THE HUGUENOT SOCIETY OF CANADA
Membership Secretary, Mrs. Alma Secord Mills, 11 Athlone Rd., Toronto, Ont. M4J 4H1 (416/425-8570)

HUNGARIAN CANADIAN FEDERATION
840 St. Clair Ave. W., Toronto, Ont. M6C 1C1
(416) 654-4926

HUNTINGTON SOCIETY OF CANADA
13 Water St. N., #3, Box 333, Cambridge, Ont. N1R 3B2
(519) 622-1002
Executive Director, R.M. Walker

IMPERIAL OFFICERS' ASSOCIATION
c/o Capt. C.P.F. Baillie, M.C., Box 428, Adelaide St. PO, Toronto, Ont. M5C 2J5 (416/925-1461)

IODE, National Chapter of Canada
Head Office, 40 Orchard View Blvd., Ste. 254, Toronto, Ont. M4R 1B9
(416) 487-4416
President, Mrs. W.G. Alexander
There are Chapters in every Province and Territory.

INDEPENDENT CANADIAN BUSINESSMEN ASSOCIATION OF SASKATCHEWAN
1800 College Ave., Regina, Sask. S4P 1C1
(306) 522-7035
Executive Director, J. Prosper Fernando

THE INDEPENDENT ORDER OF FORESTERS
Forester House, 789 Don Mills Rd., Don Mills, Ont. M3C 1T9
(416) 429-3000
Executive Secretary, A.N. Karim

INDEPENDENT ORDER OF ODD FELLOWS

GRAND LODGES, I.O.O.F.

Alta.: Grand Secretary, Kermit L. Moe, #602, 604 1st St. S.W., Calgary, Alta. T2P 1M7 – not confirmed for 1982
B.C.: Grand Secretary, J. Main, 1443 W. 8th Ave., Vancouver, B.C. V6H 1C9 (604/733-6126)
Man.: Grand Secretary, George Dusenbury, Odd Fellows Temple, 293 Kennedy St., Winnipeg, Man. R3B 2M7 (204/942-8815)
Atlantic Provinces: Grand Secretary, Sam Gordon, Box 182, New Glasgow, N.S. B2H 5E2
Ont.: Grand Secretary, R. E. Yager, 310 O'Connor Dr., Toronto, Ont. M4J 2T9 (416/421-4810)
Que.: Grand Secretary, Ralph Bernard, PGM, 78 Bourgeois, Granby, P.Q. J2G 4A9 (514/378-5523)
Sask.: Grand Secretary, Joe Beresh, 207 Somerset Block, Regina, Sask. S4P 2N4

GRAND ENCAMPMENTS, I.O.O.F.

Alta.: Grand Scribe, G.W. Ireland, 13035 123A Ave., Edmonton, Alta. T5L 2Y8
B.C.: Grand Scribe, J. Main, 1443 W. 8th Ave., Vancouver, B.C. V6H 1C9 (604/733-6126)
Atlantic Provinces: Grand Scribe, Sam Gordon, Box 371, Westville, N.S. B0K 2A0
Ont.: Grand Scribe, Glynn A. Scarrow, 2184 Caroline St. E., Burlington, Ont. L7R 1M3

REBEKAH ASSEMBLIES

Alta.: Secretary, Mrs. Mary Lockhart, #604 Lougheed Bldg., 604 1st St. S.W., Calgary, Alta. T2P 1M7 (403/262-6049) – not confirmed for 1982
B.C.: Secretary, Mrs. Evelyn Livingstone, 2832 E. 42nd Ave., Vancouver, B.C. V5R 2Y4 (604/434-7051)
Man.: Secretary, Mrs. Nessie Stewart, 299 Kennedy St., Winnipeg, Man. R3B 2M8 (204/943-8155) – not confirmed for 1982
Maritimes: Secretary, Mrs. Muriel W. Stroud, Box 775, New Glasgow, N.S. B2H 5G2 (902/752-2697)
Ont.: Secretary, Miss Lillian Borden, 3416 Dundas St. W., #203A, Toronto, Ont. M6S 2S1 (416/767-0939)
Que.: Secretary, Miss Viola Noble, Box 128, Richmond, P.Q. J0B 2H0 (819/826-2496)
Sask.: Secretary, Miss Rose May, 1680 Angus St., Regina, Sask. S4T 1Z2 (306/527-8048)

INDEPENDENT PETROLEUM ASSOCIATION OF CANADA
#700, 707 7 Ave. S.W., Calgary, Alta. T2P 0Z2
(403) 232-1530
Managing Director, J. D. Porter

INDEXING & ABSTRACTING SOCIETY OF CANADA
c/o 114 Hillsdale Ave. W., Toronto, Ont. M5P 1G5

INDIAN ASSOCIATION OF ALBERTA
Room 202, Kingsway Court, 11710 Kingsway Ave., Edmonton, Alta. T5J 0X5
(403) 452-7221
President, E. Stienhauer

INDIAN HOMEMAKERS ASSOCIATION OF BRITISH COLUMBIA
#102, 423 W. Broadway, Vancouver, B.C. V5Y 1R4
(604) 876-4929
President, Rose Charlie

INDIAN RIGHTS FOR INDIAN WOMEN
(National Committee)
10831 130 St., Edmonton, Alta. T5M 0Z2

INDUSTRIAL CARTAGE ASSOCIATION OF METRO TORONTO
111 Peter St., Ste. 213, Toronto, Ont. M5V 2H1
(416) 368-0059
Executive Vice President, J.N. Nickell

INDUSTRIAL DEVELOPERS ASSOCIATION OF CANADA
#602, 350 Sparks St., Ottawa, Ont. K1R 7S8
(613) 238-1490

Executive Secretary, R.W. Neal

INDUSTRIAL FIRST AID ATTENDANTS ASSOCIATION OF BRITISH COLUMBIA

#110, 10691 Shellbridge Way, Richmond, B.C. V6X 2W8
(604) 270-7446

INDUSTRIAL INSTRUMENT MANUFACTURERS ASSOCIATION

One Yonge St., Ste. 1400, Toronto, Ont. M5E 1J9
(416) 363-7261
Manager, James A. Rankin

INDUSTRIAL MANAGEMENT CLUBS OF CANADA

One Yonge St., Toronto, Ont. M5E 1J9
(416) 363-7261
Executive Director, John Martin

INDUSTRIAL TRUCK ASSOCIATION OF CANADA

One Yonge St., Ste. 1400, Toronto, Ont. M5E 1J9
(416) 363-7261

LES INDUSTRIELS DES ARTS GRAPHIQUES DE QUEBEC

81, rue St-Pierre, Québec, P.Q. G1K 4A3
(418) 694-1970
Secretary Treasurer, Léopold Dubuc

INGLES HOUSE

344 Dundas St. W., Toronto, Ont. M5T 1G5
(416) 977-6250

A residence for girls 16-22 where group living and family atmosphere are maintained. Sponsored by the Anglican Church. Superintendent, Miss Dorothy Fraleigh, Reg.N.

INNOVATION MANAGEMENT INSTITUTE OF CANADA

Box 6291, Stn. J, Ottawa, Ont. K2A 1T4
(613) 224-2940
President, Alan Sargant

L'INSTITUT CANADIEN-FRANCAIS D'OTTAWA

316 Dalhousie St., Ottawa, Ont. K1N 7E7
(613) 745-6130
Secretary, L. Paul Boucher

INSTITUT D'HISTOIRE DE L'AMERIQUE FRANCAISE

261 ave. Bloomfield, Montreal, P.Q. H2V 3R6
(514) 271-4759
President, René Durocher
Treasurer, Jean-Claude Robert
Official Publication, "Revue d'histoire de l'Amerique Française" (quarterly)

INSTITUT NATIONAL DE LA RECHERCHE SCIENTIFIQUE

C.P. 7500, Sainte-Foy, P.Q. G1V 4C7
(418) 657-2560
Directeur général, André Lemay

INSTITUTE OF APPLIED METAPHYSICS

R.R. 3, Tweed, Ont. KOK 3JO
(613) 478-3510
President, Winifred G. Barton

INSTITUTE OF ASSOCIATION EXECUTIVES

Ste. 500, 121 Richmond St. W., Toronto, Ont. M5H 2K1
(416) 367-1134
President, H.H. Perry, C.G.A., C.A.E.

INSTITUTE OF CANADIAN ADVERTISING

8 King St. E., Suite 401, Toronto, Ont. M5C 1B5
(416) 368-2981
President, Keith B. McKerracher

THE INSTITUTE OF CHARTERED ENGINEERS OF CANADA (ICEC)

(L'Institut des ingénieurs agréés du Canada (IIAC))
Box 415, Downsview, Ont. M3M 3A8
(416) 481-5043

THE INSTITUTE OF CHARTERED SECRETARIES & ADMINISTRATORS

General Manager, R.W. Pogson, C.A., Aff., 372 Bay St., Toronto, Ont. M5H 1R7 (416/363-8925)
Branches and Chapters with elected representatives in: Victoria & Vancouver, B.C.; Calgary & Edmonton, Alta.; Winnipeg, Man.; Toronto & Ottawa, Ont.; Montreal, P.Q.; Halifax, N.S.; and St. John's, Nfld.

INSTITUTE OF EDIBLE OIL FOODS

#101, 1185 Eglinton Ave. E., Don Mills, Ont. M3C 3C6
(416) 429-1004
Executive Director, Philip Moyes

THE INSTITUTE OF ELECTRICAL & ELECTRONICS ENGINEERS, INC.

345 East 47th St., New York, N.Y. 10017

The IEEE, founded in 1884, is the world's largest professional engineering society. Its objectives are scientific and educational, directed toward the advancement of the theory and practice of electrical engineering, electronics, radio, and the allied branches of engineering and the related arts and sciences.

IEEE CANADIAN REGION OFFICE

Manager, George G. Armitage, 7061 Yonge St., Thornhill, Ont. L3T 2A6 (416/881-1930)

IEEE has 18 Local Sections with volunteer officers who are elected annually, in the following areas of Canada: Bay of Quinte; Canadian Atlantic & Newfoundland; Hamilton; Kitchener-Waterloo; London; Montreal; Newfoundland-Labrador; New Brunswick; Northern Canada; Ottawa; Quebec City; St. Maurice; Saskatchewan; Southern Alberta; Toronto; Vancouver; Victoria; Winnipeg. Contact the Canadian Regional Office for up to date information.

INSTITUTE OF ENGLISH & FRENCH CONVERSATION INC.

(Institut de Conversation Anglaise et Francaise Inc.)
575 Jarry St. E., Montreal, P.Q. H2P 1V6
(514) 279-0678
Executive Director, Roger Hénault

INSTITUTE OF MANAGEMENT CONSULTANTS OF ONTARIO

#915, 1243 Islington Ave., Toronto, Ont. M8X 1Y9
(416) 231-4120
Executive Director, Herb Breithaupt

INSTITUTE OF MANAGEMENT CONSULTANTS OF QUEBEC

315 Dorchester E., #1800, Montreal, P.Q. H2X 3P3
(514) 284-0382

INSTITUTE OF MUNICIPAL ASSESSORS OF ONTARIO

Executive Director, Ms. K. F. McGillivray, 180 Yorkland Blvd., Willowdale, Ont. M2J 1R5 (416/492-1331)

INSTITUTE OF POWER ENGINEERS

920 Yonge St., #216, Toronto, Ont. M4W 3C7
(416) 922-6615
National Secretary, Norman L. Parker

THE INSTITUTE OF PUBLIC ADMINISTRATION OF CANADA

897 Bay St., Toronto, Ont. M5S 1Z7
(416) 923-7319, 923-7310
President, W.B. Brittain
National Secretary, Jean-Louis Caron
National Treasurer, J.L. Pickard
Executive Director, J.M. Galimberti

INSTITUTE FOR RESEARCH ON PUBLIC POLICY

2149 Mackay St., Montreal, P.Q. H3G 2J2
(514) 879-8533
President, Gordon Robertson

THE INSTITUTION OF ELECTRONIC & RADIO ENGINEERS

151 Slater St., Room 300, Ottawa, Ont. K1P 5H3
(613) 234-5513
Administrative Secretary, Mrs. E. Voyer

INSULATION CONTRACTORS ASSOCIATION OF QUEBEC

Secretary Treasurer, J.-C. Corbeil, 31 de Vouziers, Lorraine, P.Q. J6Z 3H5 (514/621-6831)

INSURANCE BUREAU OF CANADA

13th floor, 181 University Ave., Toronto, Ont. M5H 3M7
(416) 362 2031
President, J.L. Lyndon
General Manager, C.L. Wilcken

MONTREAL OFFICE
Ste. 920, 1080 Beaver Hall Hill, Montreal, P.Q. H2Z 1S8
(514) 866 9801
Manager, R. Medza

HALIFAX OFFICE
1505 Barrington St., 12th floor, Halifax, N.S. B3J 3K5
(902) 429-2730
Manager, G.M. Walsh

EDMONTON OFFICE
Ste. 1105, 10080 Jasper Ave., Edmonton, Alta. T5J 1V9
(403) 423 2212
Manager, R.A.S. Cooper

VANCOUVER OFFICE
409 Granville St., Ste. 1050, Vancouver, B.C. V6C 1W9
(604) 684 3635
Manager, B.E.T. Stanhope

THE INSURANCE INSTITUTE OF CANADA

President, J. C. Rhind, F.I.I.C., C.A.E., 55 University Ave., Toronto, Ont. M5J 2H7 (416/366-1601)

INSURANCE INSTITUTE OF SOUTHERN ALBERTA
Secretary, Mrs. N. Read, 630 8th Ave. S.W., Apt. 601, Calgary, Alta. T2P 1G6 (403/266-3427)

INSURANCE INSTITUTE OF NORTHERN ALBERTA
Secretary, Ms. J. Fortier, #506, 10169 104 St., Edmonton, Alta. T5J 1A5 (403/424-1268)

INSURANCE INSTITUTE OF BRITISH COLUMBIA
Secretary, Ms. Ethel Gilchrist, #410, 800 W. Pender St., Vancouver, B.C. V6C 2V6

INSURANCE INSTITUTE OF MANITOBA
Secretary Treasurer, Betty Rollo, #300, 213 Notre Dame Ave., Winnipeg, Man. R3B 1N3 (204/956-1702)

INSURANCE INSTITUTE OF NEW BRUNSWICK
Secretary, Miss Mary E. Kellier, A.I.I.C., Box 843, Saint John, N.B. E2L 4C3 (506/652-2120)

INSURANCE INSTITUTE OF NEWFOUNDLAND
Secretary, Ms. Doris Cook, Box 9412, Stn. B, St. John's, Nfld. A1A 2Y3

INSURANCE INSTITUTE OF NOVA SCOTIA
Secretary, Miss G. Peters, Box 1561, Halifax, N.S. B3J 2Y3

INSURANCE INSTITUTE OF ONTARIO
General Manager, J. C. Rhind, F.I.I.C., C.A.E., 55 University Ave., Toronto, Ont. M5J 2H7 (416/366-1601)

INSURANCE INSTITUTE OF PRINCE EDWARD ISLAND
Secretary, Mrs. Elsie Brown, Box 811, Charlottetown, P.E.I. C1A 7L9 (902/892-3547)

INSURANCE INSTITUTE OF QUEBEC
President, Gerry Gallagher, 261 St. James St., Montreal, P.Q. H2Y 1M6

INSURANCE INSTITUTE OF EASTERN QUEBEC
Secretary, Mrs. L. Blanchet, 2022 Lavoisier, Bur. 184, Ste-Foy, P.Q. G1N 4L5

INSURANCE INSTITUTE OF SASKATCHEWAN
Secretary, Mrs. L. Hameluck, Box 1791, Regina, Sask. S4P 3C6

INSURERS' ADVISORY ORGANIZATION

180 Dundas St. W., Toronto, Ont. M5G 1Z9
(416) 597-1200
President, E.F. Belton
Executive Secretary, Mrs. M. Ronco
Atlantic Regional Office: #810, 1660 Hollis St. (Box 938, Halifax, N.S. B3J 2V9) 902/429-4333
Ontario Regional Office: 180 Dundas St. W., Toronto, Ont. M5G 1Z9 416/597-1200
Pacific Regional Office: #350, 409 Granville St., Vancouver, B.C. V6C 1W5 604/681-3111
Prairie Regional Office: #204, 3030 2nd Ave. S.E. (Box 747, Stn. J, Calgary, Alta. T2A 6A6) 403/248-8313
Quebec Regional Office: 300, rue Léo Pariseau, Montréal, P.Q. H2W 2N1 514/285-1201

Printing Division: B. Fuller, 180 Dundas St. W., Toronto, Ont. M5G 1Z9 (416/597-1200)
School of Loss Control Technology: 7 Crouse Rd., Scarborough, Ont. M1R 3A9 (416/752-0043)

INTER-AMERICAN COMMERCIAL ARBITRATION COMMISSION (Canadian Section)

c/o Institute for International Co-operation, University of Ottawa, Ottawa, Ont. K1N 6N5
(613) 231-5862, 231-4910

INTERGOVERNMENTAL COMMITTEE ON URBAN & REGIONAL RESEARCH

#625, 123 Edward St., Toronto, Ont. M5G 1E2
(416) 966-5629
Executive Director, S. Lavoie

INTERIOR DESIGNERS OF CANADA

Box 752, Stn. B, Ottawa, Ont. K1P 5P8
(613) 238-6675

Provincial Associations

REGISTERED INTERIOR DESIGNERS INSTITUTE OF ALBERTA
1331 Montreal Ave. S.W., Calgary, Alta.

INTERIOR DESIGNERS' INSTITUTE OF BRITISH COLUMBIA
#205, 1836 W. 5th Ave., Vancouver, B.C. V6J 1P3

INTERIOR DESIGNERS' INSTITUTE OF MANITOBA
468 Academy Rd., Winnipeg, Man. R3N 0C7
(204) 489-6234

ASSOCIATION OF INTERIOR DESIGNERS OF NOVA SCOTIA
c/o 6113 Shirley St., Halifax, N.S. B3H 2N1
(902) 469-9468)

INTERIOR DESIGNERS OF ONTARIO
185 Bloor St. E., Toronto, Ont. M4W 1C8
(416) 921-2127

LA SOCIETE DES DECORATEURS-ENSEMBLIERS DU QUEBEC
Studio G, 451 rue St-Sulpice, Montreal, P.Q. H2Y 2V9
(514) 288-9046

INTERIOR DESIGNERS OF SASKATCHEWAN
#60, 158 2nd Ave. N., Saskatoon, Sask. S7N 2B3
(306) 653-0282

INTERNATIONAL AIR TRANSPORT ASSOCIATION

Director General, Knut Hammarskjold
Corporate Secretary, A. M. Black
Public Information Director, D.R. Kyd
Director, Public Relations (Western Hemisphere), D.B. Pengelly
Manager, Information Services, J.F. Brindley
Head Office, 2000 Peel St., Montreal, P.Q. H3A 2R4 (514/844-6311)
Geneva Office, 26, chemin de Joinville, Box 160, 1216 Cointrin, Geneva, Switzerland (022) 98.33.66

INTERNATIONAL ASSOCIATION OF BUSINESS COMMUNICATORS (CANADA DISTRICT 1)

Box 8812, Ottawa, Ont. K1G 3J1
District Vice President, Canada, David Barr, Alberta Treasury, #423, 9515 107th St., Edmonton, Alta. T5J 2C3
Chapter locations in Canada: Vancouver Island, Vancouver, Yellowknife, Edmonton, Calgary, Regina/Saskatoon, Winnipeg, Northern Ontario, London, Toronto, Ottawa/Hull, Montreal, Atlantic Canada.
International Office: 870 Market St., #940, San Francisco, Ca. 94102

INTERNATIONAL ASSOCIATION FOR SUICIDE PREVENTION (CANADA) INC.

#700, 71 Bank St., Ottawa, Ont. K1P 5N2

INTERNATIONAL CIVIL AVIATION ORGANIZATION (ICAO)

1000 Sherbrooke St. W., Montreal, P.Q. H3A 2R2
(514) 285-8220
Attn.: Public Information Officer

INTERNATIONAL COUNCIL OF MUSEUMS
ICOM Museums–Musées Canada

331 Cooper St., Ste. 400, Ottawa, Ont. K2P OG5
(613) 233-5653

INTERNATIONAL DYNAMIC READING INSTITUTE

Rm. 464, 450 Sherbrooke E., Montreal, P.Q. H2L 1J8
(514) 844-1944
Director General, Joel M. Bonn
Registraire (francophone division), Rita Kaloust
Registrar (English Division), Debi McDougall

INTERNATIONAL GEOGRAPHICAL UNION
Canadian Committee for Geography

Chairman, Romain Paquette, Université de Sherbrooke
Secretary, J. Keith Fraser, Dept. of the Environment, Ottawa, Ont. K1A 0H3 (613/997-1171)

The purposes of the National Committee are: 1. To promote the study of geographical problems of international significance. 2. To facilitate professional contacts between Canadian geographers and those in other countries. 3. To organize Canadian participation in International Geographical Congresses.

INTERNATIONAL GRAPHOANALYSIS SOCIETY

BRITISH COLUMBIA CHAPTER
President, Mrs. Penny Bowell, 888 Riverside Rd., Nanaimo, B.C. V9S 5G7

ONTARIO CHAPTER
President, Patricia Girouard, 54 Wineva Ave., Toronto, Ont. M4E 2T2 (416/690-1397)

QUEBEC CHAPTER
President, Guy Montambeault, 1424 Madrid, Rock Forest, P.Q. J0B 2J0

INTERNATIONAL LABOUR ORGANIZATION
Canada Branch

75 Albert St., #202, Ottawa, Ont. K1P 5E7
(613) 233-1114
Director, J.R.W. Whitehouse

INTERNATIONAL MEDITATION SOCIETY

(Canadian Section)
1099 W. 8th Ave., Vancouver, B.C. V6H 1C3

INTERPROVINCIAL ASSOCIATION OF STEVEDORING CONTRACTORS

360 rue St-Jacques St., Ste. 1225, Montreal, P.Q. H2Y 1P5
(514) 842-7966

INTER-VARSITY CHRISTIAN FELLOWSHIP

745 Mount Pleasant Rd., Toronto, Ont. M4S 2N5
(416) 487 3431
General Director, James Berney

INUIT TAPIRISAT OF CANADA

176 Gloucester, 3rd floor, Ottawa, Ont. K2P OA6
(613) 238-8181
President, Michael Amarook

INVENTORS ASSOCIATION OF CANADA

Box 281, Swift Current, Sask. S9H 3V6
(306) 773-7762
Secretary & General Manager, Mrs. Phyllis Tengum

INVESTMENT DEALERS' ASSOCIATION OF CANADA

Box 217, Commerce Court S., Toronto, Ont. M5L 1E8
(416) 364-6133
Secretary, E.M. Andrews
Regional Director, M. Tardif, #1110, 1080 Beaver Hall Hill, Montreal, P.Q. H2Z 1S8 (514/878-2854)
Regional Director, R. E. Granger, Box 49151, The Bentall Centre, Vancouver, B.C. V7X 1J1 (604/683-1338)
Regional Director, D.W. Grant, #280, 700 Fourth Ave. S.W., Calgary, Alta. T2P 3J4 (403/262-6393)

THE INVESTMENT FUNDS INSTITUTE OF CANADA

Ste. 210, 8 King St. E., Toronto, Ont. M5C 1B5
(416) 363-2158
President, Keith A. Douglas
Secretary Treasurer, John Kaszel

Education Division

THE CANADIAN INVESTMENT FUNDS COURSE
Ste. 210, 8 King St. E., Toronto, Ont. M5C 1B5

Quebec Branch

C.I.L. House, 630 Dorchester Blvd. W., #2960, Montreal, P.Q.
(514) 866-5421
Director, J. Kaszel

IPMS CANADA

(An association for aeronautical scale modelling)
-not confirmed for 1982-
Box 626, Stn. B, Ottawa, Ont. K1P 5P7
National Director, R.D. Migliardi

IRISH PROTESTANT BENEVOLENT SOCIETY

#210, 1117 St. Catherine St. W., Montreal, P.Q. H3B 1H9
(514) 288-4478

JAMAICAN CANADIAN ASSOCIATION
Box 532, Term. A, Toronto, Ont. M5W 1E4
(416) 783-4004

JAPAN SOCIETY OF CANADA
Secretary, 8155 Rousselot St., Montreal, P.Q. H2E 1Z7 (514/524-0718)

JAPANESE CANADIAN CITIZENS ASSOCIATION
Box 383, Stn. K, Toronto, Ont. M4P 2G7
(416) 461-5765

JESUIT FATHERS OF UPPER CANADA
69 Marmaduke Ave., Toronto, Ont. M6R 1T3
(416) 763-4664
Major Superior, Rev. Wm. F. Ryan, s.j.

Affiliated Society

CANADIAN JESUIT MISSIONS
833 Broadview Ave., Toronto, Ont. M4K 2P9
(416) 466-1195
Executive Officers, Rev. Peter Nash, S.J. (International); Rev. James Farrell, S.J. (Canadian); Rev. F. West, S.J.

JE VEUX GRANDIR (I Want to Grow)
4560 Beaconsfield Ave., Montreal, P.Q. H4A 2H7

JEWISH ORGANIZATIONS

B'NAI B'RITH
15 Hove St., 2nd floor, Downsview, Ont. M3H 4Y8
(416) 633-6224
Executive Vice President, Frank Dimant

CANADIAN ASSOCIATION OF REFORM RABBIS
President, Rabbi Lawrence Englander, Temple Solel Congregation, 2399 Folkway Dr., Mississauga, Ont. L5L 2M6 (416/828-5915)

CANADIAN FOUNDATION FOR JEWISH CULTURE
150 Beverley St., Toronto, Ont. M5T 1Y6
(416) 977-3811
Executive Secretary, Dr. Edmond Y. Lipsitz

CANADIAN JEWISH CONGRESS
National Office, 1590 Dr. Wilder Penfield Ave., Montreal, P.Q. H3G 1C5
(514) 931-7531
National Executive Vice President, Alan Rose
Regional Offices:
150 Beverley St., Toronto, Ont. M5T 1Y6
370 Hargrave St., Room 203, Winnipeg, Man. R3B 2K1
950 W. 41st Ave., Vancouver, B.C. V5Z 2N7

CANADIAN ORT ORGANIZATION
5165 Sherbrooke St. W., Ste. 208, Montreal, P.Q. H4A 1T6
(514) 481-2787
National Executive Director, Mac Silver

THE CANADIAN ZIONIST FEDERATION
1310 Greene Ave., Montreal, P.Q. H3Z 2B2
(514) 934-0804
Executive Vice President, Dr. Leon Kronitz

HADASSAH-WIZO ORGANIZATION OF CANADA
1310 Greene Ave., 9th floor, Montreal, P.Q. H3Z 2B8
(514) 937-9431
National Executive Vice President, Miss Lily Frank

JEWISH CHILD & FAMILY SERVICE
165 Garry St., Winnipeg, Man. R3C 1G9
(204) 943-6425
Executive Director, Edward Moscovitch, M.S.W., R.S.W.

JEWISH COMMUNITY CENTRE OF TORONTO
President, Bernard S. Dales
Head Office: 4588 Bathurst St., Willowdale, Ont. M2R 1W6 (416/636-1880)
Includes the Koffler Centre of the Arts, Leah Posluns Theatre, and the Northern, Bloor and Northeast Branches.

JEWISH IMMIGRANT AID SERVICES OF CANADA (JIAS)
National Executive Vice President, Dr. Joseph Kage, 5151 Côte Ste. Catherine Rd., 2nd floor, Montreal, P.Q. H3W 1M6 (514/342-9351)
Ontario Office, 638A Sheppard Ave. W., Ste. 221, Downsview, Ont. M3H 2S1 (416/630-6481)
Western Office, 370 Hargrave St., Winnipeg, Man. R3B 2K1 (204/943-0406)

JEWISH NATIONAL FUND
Ste. 300, 1980 Sherbrooke St. W., Montreal, P.Q. H3H 2M7
(514) 934-0313
National Executive Vice President, Michael D. Yarosky

LABOR ZIONIST MOVEMENT OF CANADA
-not confirmed for 1982-
4770 Kent Ave., Suite 300, Montreal, P.Q. H3W 1H2
(514) 342-9710
Central Region, 272 Codsell Ave., Downsview, Ont.
Western Region, 1727 Main St., Winnipeg, Man.

LEAGUE FOR HUMAN RIGHTS OF CANADIAN B'NAI B'RITH
National Office: 15 Hove St., #250, Downsview, Ont. M3H 4Y8 (416/633-6224), Executive Vice President, Frank Dimant
Central Region: 15 Hove St., #250, Downsview, Ont. M3H 4Y8 (416/633-6224), Central Region Director, Alan Shefman
Eastern Region: Ligue Pour les Droits de L'Homme de B'nai B'rith, 4480 Cote de Liesse, #107, Montreal, P.Q. H4N 2R1 (514/731-7396), Eastern Region Director, Arthur Hiess
Mid West Region: 235 Garry St., #201, Winnipeg, Man. R3C 1H2 (204/942-2597), Mid West Region Director, H.L. Ross

NATIONAL COUNCIL OF JEWISH WOMEN OF CANADA
1111 Finch Ave. W., #401, Downsview, Ont. M3J 2E5
(416) 633-1251
National President, Mrs. Helen Marr
Executive Secretary, Mrs. Florence Greenberg

UNITED JEWISH RELIEF AGENCIES OF CANADA
Officers and Offices as for the Canadian Jewish Congress.

UNION OF ORTHODOX JEWISH CONGREGATIONS
Eastern Canada Region
-not confirmed for 1982-
2855 Victor Doré, Montreal, P.Q. H3M 1T1
(514) 334-4610
President, Max M. Richler

WOMEN'S CANADIAN ORT
3101 Bathurst St., Ste. 404, Toronto, Ont. M6A 2A6
(416) 787-0339
National Executive Director, Diane Uslaner
Regional offices in Montreal, Toronto and Winnipeg.

JOHN MILTON SOCIETY FOR THE BLIND IN CANADA
40 St. Clair Ave. E., #202, Toronto, Ont. M4T 1M9
(416) 960-3953
Executive Secretary, Mrs. Ruth Banko

JOINT PROVINCIAL MINING ASSOCIATIONS
Secretary, G. Langlois, Manager, Quebec Metal Mining Association, #704, Two Quebec Place, Quebec, P.Q. G1R 2B5 (418/525-4706)
New Brunswick Metal Mining Association
Quebec Metal Mining Association
Quebec Asbestos Mining Association
Mines Accident Prevention Association of Ontario
Mining Association of Manitoba
Saskatchewan Mining Association
Alberta Chamber of Resources
The Mining Association of British Columbia

JUNIOR ACHIEVEMENT OF CANADA
3240 Bloor St. W., Toronto, Ont. M8X 1E4
(416) 236-1763

President, H. Edward Miskiman

JUNIOR FOREST WARDENS OF CANADA

#410, 1200 W. Pender St., Vancouver, B.C. V6E 2S9
(604) 683-7591

KABALARIAN PHILOSOPHY

908 W. 7th Ave., Vancouver, B.C. V5Z 1C3
(604) 736-2875
Administrator, I. H. Shearing

THE KIDNEY FOUNDATION OF CANADA

1650 de Maisonneuve Blvd. W., #400, Montreal, P.Q. H3H 2P3
(514) 934-4806

Provincial Offices

Alta.: #103, 5920 1A St. S.W., Calgary, Alta. T2H 0G3 (403/255-1113)
B.C.: 353 W. 7th Ave., Vancouver, B.C. V5Y 1M2 (604/874-9391-2)
Man.: 1121 One Lombard Place, Winnipeg, Man. R3B 1X3 (204/949-1858)
Nfld.: Box 7342, Stn. C, St. John's, Nfld. A1E 3Y5 (709/753-8999)
N.B.: Box 3121, Stn. B, Saint John, N.B. E2M 4X7 (506/672-9024)
N.S.: Box 3301, Halifax, N.S. B3J 3J1 (902/425-5341)
Ont.: 1300 Yonge St., #508, Toronto, Ont. M4T 1X3 (416/925-2836)
P.E.I.: 78 Goodwill Ave., Charlottetown, P.E.I. C1A 3E5 (902/894-7233)
Que.: 1650 de Maisonneuve Blvd. W., #400, Montréal, P.Q. H3H 2P3 (514/934-4844)
Sask.: c/o #905, 201 21st St. E., Saskatoon, Sask. S7K OB8 (306/652-9422)

KIWANIS INTERNATIONAL

EASTERN CANADA & CARIBBEAN DISTRICT

Casa Loma, 1 Austin Ter., Toronto, Ont. M5R 1X8
(416) 921-1297
Administrative Secretary, Win Robinson

WESTERN CANADA DISTRICT

Secretary Treasurer, A.F. Lough, 1 Taggart Pl., Regina, Sask. S4S 4G3

KNIGHTS OF COLUMBUS

P.O. Drawer 1670, New Haven, Conn.
Supreme Knight, Virgil C. Dechant
Supreme Secretary, Richard B. Scheiber

State Deputies

Alta.: Stanley K. Turner, Box 954, Brooks, Alta. T0J 0J0
B.C.: W.L. Cahill, 7249 McKay Ave., Burnaby, B.C. V5J 3S8
Man.: S.J. Chrobak, 2654 Henderson Hwy., Winnipeg, Man. R2E OC3
N.B.: Yvon Poitras, 169 Canada Rd., Box 252, St. Quentin, N.B. E0K 1J0
Nfld.: Nicholas F. Hurley, North River, Conception Bay, Nfld. AOA 3CO
N.S.: John C. Thomas, 2850 Connaught Ave., Halifax, N.S. B3L 3A1
Ont.: John Rodina, 188 Margaret Ave., Apt. 611, Kitchener, Ont. N2H 4J3
P.E.I.: Rev. Eric J. Dunn, Box 907, Charlottetown, P.E.I. C1A 7L9
Que.: Charles A. Dery, 248 Vallieres, Chicoutimi-Nord, P.Q. G7G 1P8
Sask.: William Baryluk, 1709 1st St., Estevan, Sask. S4A 0H5

KNIGHTS OF PYTHIAS

Supreme Secretary, J. O. Pritchard, 47 N. Grant St., Room 201, Stockton, Calif., 95202.

Grand Domains in Canada

Alta.: Grand Secretary, Byron R. Rutt, Box 968, Coaldale, Alta. TOK OLO
B.C.: Grand Secretary, M. Wilson, 447 Penticton Ave., Penticton, B.C. V2A 2M5 (604/492-6520)
Man.: Deputy Supreme Chancellor, Walter Tod, 15 Tod Drive, St. Vital, Man.
Man. (Kenton): Deputy Supreme Chancellor Kenton, C. H. Finnie
Maritime Provinces: Grand Secretary, Glenn D. Heighton, 30 Lindsay St., Riverview, N.B. E1B 3A1 (506/386-8604)
Ont.: Grand Secretary, Arnold Phillips, 74 Brucewood, Toronto, Ont. M6A 2G8
Que.: Grand Secretary, Jack Derrick, 6600 Mountain Heights, Montreal, P.Q. H3W 2Z6
Sask.: Grand Secretary, S. Poulton, 377 Athabasca St. E., Moose Jaw, Sask. S6H 0L7 (306/692-5767)

KTAQAMKUK ILNUI SAQIMAWOUTIE

(Newfoundland Indian Government)
Conn River, Baie d'Espoir, Nfld. A0H 1J0
(709) 882-2303, 4; Telex: 016 4990

LABRADOR INUIT ASSOCIATION

-not confirmed for 1982-
Box 70, Nain, Labrador AOP 1LO
(709) 922-2942
Executive Director, Jim Lyall

LAKE OF THE WOODS CHILD DEVELOPMENT CENTRE

(221 Main St. S.) Box 2110, Kenora, Ont. P9N 3X8
Executive Director, Patrick Mulgrew

LAMBTON INDUSTRIAL SOCIETY

242A Indian Rd. S., #212-S, Sarnia, Ont. N7T 3W4
(519) 344-2412
Manager, Dr. J. A. McCoubrey

LAST POST FUND

A patriotic society organized with the purpose of seeing that no ex-service member of British Empire Forces shall suffer pauper burial and oblivion at death.

Dominion Headquarters, Suite 921, 685 Cathcart St., Montreal, P.Q. H3B 1M7 (514/866-2888)
Dominion Secretary Treasurer, Capt. A.J. Lawrence
Secretary Treasurer, Que. Branch, Capt. A.J. Lawrence
Secretary Treasurer, Ont. Branch, R. Noble, 26 St. Clair Ave. E., #811, Toronto, Ont. M4T 1M2 (416/923-1608)
Secretary Treasurer, Man. Branch, Clifford A. Spencer, 361 Mandeville St., Winnipeg, Man. R3V 2G8
Secretary Treasurer, Sask. Branch, J. W. Dodds, 2214 York Ave. S., Saskatoon, Sask. S7J 1J1
Secretary Treasurer, Southern Alta. Branch, R. Martin, 1609 Kensington Rd. N.W., #110, Calgary, Alta. T2N 3R2
Secretary Treasurer, Northern Alta. Branch, J.W. Ritchie, Box 335, Edmonton, Alta. T5J 2J6
Secretary Treasurer, B.C. Branch, Maj. F.C. Smith, 510 W. Hastings St., #318, Vancouver, B.C. V6B 1L8
Secretary Treasurer, Nfld. Branch, C. D. Moyst, D.V.A., Sir Humphrey Gilbert Bldg., Duckworth St., St. John's, Nfld.
Local Representatives, D. Large, 134 Richmond St., Charlottetown, P.E.I. C1A 7K7; P.R. Mawhinney, 19 Bayview Dr., Saint John, N.B. E2M 4C9; A. R. Tripp, 6 Little Fox Lane, Kearney Lake, Halifax, N.S.

LATVIAN NATIONAL FEDERATION IN CANADA

491 College St., Toronto, Ont. M6G 1A5
(416) 922-5418
Secretary Treasurer, K.J. Tannis

LAW SOCIETIES IN CANADA

THE ADVOCATES' SOCIETY

160 Queen St. W., Toronto, Ont. M5H 3H3
(416) 597-0243

Executive Director, Helen Halchuk

BARREAU DE MONTREAL/THE BAR OF MONTREAL
Palais de Justice, Montreal, P.Q. H2Y 1B6
(514) 866-9392
Director General, Mtre Maurice Boileau

THE BAR OF THE PROVINCE OF QUEBEC/BARREAU DU QUEBEC
Palais de Justice, bur. 9.80, 1 est, Notre Dame, Montreal, P.Q. H2Y 1B6
(514) 866-3901
Director General, Micheline Audette Filion

THE BAR OF QUEBEC CITY/BARREAU DE QUEBEC
Palais de Justice, Ste. 201, Quebec, P.Q. G1R 4P6
(418) 692-4192
Executive Secretary, Mrs. Justine Jobin

THE BARRISTERS' SOCIETY OF NEW BRUNSWICK
Box 1063, Fredericton, N.B. E3B 5C2
(506) 455-6458
Secretary Treasurer, Paul M. LeBreton

THE CANADIAN BAR ASSOCIATION
130 Albert St., Ste. 1700, Ottawa, Ont. K1P 5G4
(613) 237-2925; Telex: 053-3349
President, A. William Cox, Q.C., Box 2380, 800 Corporation Tower, Halifax, N.S. B3J 3E5 (902/423-6262)
Vice President, Paul D.K. Fraser, #1570, 777 Hornby St., Vancouver, B.C. V6Z 1T3 (604/687-3216)
Executive Director, John R. Griner, R.I.A., C.A.E.
Deputy Executive Director, N. Roger Gauthier

CANADIAN CANON LAW SOCIETY
233 Main St., Ottawa, Ont. K1S 1C4
(613) 236-1393
Executive Secretary, Rev. Francis G. Morrisey, o.m.i.

CHAMBER OF NOTARIES OF QUEBEC
630 Dorchester Blvd. W., Ste. 1700, Montreal, P.Q. H3B 1T6
(514) 879-1793
General Director, J.B. Coupal

THE COUNTY OF YORK LAW ASSOCIATION
Court House, 361 University Ave., Toronto, Ont. M5G 1T3

HAMILTON LAW ASSOCIATION
50 Main St. E., Hamilton, Ont. L8N 1E9
(416) 522-1563
Executive Secretary, Ms. W. Hearder-Moan

THE LAW SOCIETY OF ALBERTA
344 12th Ave. S.W., Calgary, Alta. T2R 0H2
(403) 266-6036
Secretary Treasurer, W.B. Kelly, Q.C.

THE LAW SOCIETY OF BRITISH COLUMBIA
#300, 1148 Hornby St., Vancouver, B.C. V6Z 2C4
(604) 688-9461
Secretary, T.V. McCallum

THE LAW SOCIETY OF MANITOBA
#1400, 155 Carlton St., Winnipeg, Man. R3C 3H8
(204) 942-5571
Chief Executive Officer, Graeme Garson

THE LAW SOCIETY OF NEWFOUNDLAND
Court House, Box 1028, St. John's, Nfld. A1C 5M3
(709) 753-7770
Secretary, Francis P. Fowler
Executive Director, Lawrence E. Collins

THE LAW SOCIETY OF PRINCE EDWARD ISLAND
17 West St., Charlottetown, P.E.I. C1A 5S5
Secretary Treasurer, Theodore Reagh

THE LAW SOCIETY OF SASKATCHEWAN
(2425 Victoria Ave.) Box 4320, Regina, Sask. S4P 3W6
(306) 569-8242
Secretary Treasurer, Iain A. Mentiplay

THE LAW SOCIETY OF UPPER CANADA
Osgoode Hall, Toronto, Ont. M5H 2N6
(416) 362-5811
Secretary, Kenneth Jarvis, Q.C.

NOVA SCOTIA BARRISTERS' SOCIETY
Law Courts, 1815 Upper Water St., Halifax, N.S. B3J 1S7
(902) 422-1491
Secretary Treasurer, Gail Salsbury

THE SAINT JOHN LAW SOCIETY
Box 7289, Stn. A, Saint John, N.B. E2L 4S6
(506) 652-1970
Secretary Treasurer, D.H. Aiton

THE SOCIETY OF NOTARIES PUBLIC OF BRITISH COLUMBIA
Ste. 1401, 736 Granville St., Vancouver, B.C. V6Z 1G3
(604) 681-4516
Secretary, Bernard W. Hoeter, Ph.D.

YUKON LAW SOCIETY
Box 4444, Whitehorse, Y.T. Y1A 3T5
(403) 668-4405
President, D.G. Kidd

LEAGUE OF CANADIAN POETS
175 Carlton St., Toronto, Ont. M5A 2K3
(416) 928-0714
Director, Arlene Lampert

LEBANESE SYRIAN CANADIAN ASSOCIATION OF QUEBEC
(Association Canadienne Libanaise Syrienne du Quebec)
40 est, rue Jean Talon, Montreal, P.Q. H2R 1S3
(514) 274-3583

LIBRARY ASSOCIATIONS
See Libraries Section of the Almanac

THE LIFE INSURANCE INSTITUTE OF CANADA
Ste. 1400, 55 University Ave., Toronto, Ont. M5J 2K7
(416) 364-6295
Secretary Treasurer, Debbie Cole-Gauer

THE LIFE UNDERWRITERS ASSOCIATION OF CANADA
Executive Vice President, R. L. Kayler, Q.C., LL.B., C.L.U.
Senior Vice President & Executive Director, A. W. Lingard, 41 Lesmill Rd., Don Mills, Ont. M3B 2T3 (416/444-5251)

THE INSTITUTE OF CHARTERED LIFE UNDERWRITERS
The educational organization of the L.U.A. of C.
Director of Institute Services, Graham Goulden, C.L.U., 41 Lesmill Rd., Don Mills, Ont. M3B 2T3 (416/444-5251)

LIONS CLUBS INTERNATIONAL
District A
1407 Yonge St., Ste. 403, Toronto, Ont. M4T 1Y7
(416) 923-0935

LITERARY TRANSLATORS ASSOCIATION
964 rue Cherrier, Montreal, P.Q. H2L 1H7

LIVESTOCK AND BREEDERS' ASSOCIATIONS

Alberta Salers Association
#201, 1200 26th Ave. S.E., Calgary, Alta. T2G 4M8
(403) 266-7360

Alberta Provincial Sheep Breeders' Co-operative Association
Secretary, Leroy Emerson, Box 1480, Edmonton, Alta. T5J 2N5

Appaloosa Horse Club of Canada
Box 3036, Stn. B, Calgary, Alta. T2M 4L6
(403) 276-6778

There are regional clubs in every area of Canada. Contact the Calgary address for up-to-date addresses.

Association des Eleveurs de Bovins de Boucherie Pur-Sang du Québec
(Pure-bred beef cattle breeders)
Secretary, Eileen Morgan, 400, rue Parc, Sherbrooke, P.Q. J1E 2J9 (819/563-5651)

Association des Eleveurs de Bovins Canadiens
President, Fernand Charpentier, St-Guillaume d'Upton, Cte Yamaska, P.Q. J0C 1L0 (819/396-5206)

Association des Eleveurs de Bovins Charolais
(Charolais cattle breeders)
Secretary, Pierre Tétreault, St-Armand, P.Q. J0J 1T0 (514/248-7690)

Association des Eleveurs de chevaux Clydesdale du Québec
(breeders of Clydesdale horses)
Secretary, M. Beaudoin, C.P. 51, Durham Sud, P.Q. J0H 2C0 (819/858-2657)

Association Professionnelle des Producteurs de Fourrure du Québec
(fur animal breeders)
Secretary, Mme Pierrette Lessard, 90 rue Venne, St-Jacques (Co. Montcalm), P.Q. J0K 2R0 (514/839-3494)

Association Quarter Horse du Quebec
(Quarter horse breeders)
Secretary, J.-J. Carrier, C.P. 104, St-Charles (Cté Bellechasse), P.Q. G0R 2Y0 (418/887-3178)

Ayrshire Breeders Association of Canada
1160 Carling Ave., Ottawa, Ont. K1Z 7K6
(613) 728-8192
Secretary Manager, John D. McCaig

Ayrshire Breeders Club of British Columbia
10922 143A St., Surrey, B.C. V3R 3M3
(604) 581-7666
Secretary, Alice McKay

Beef Producers of Nova Scotia
Secretary, Lester Settle, Box 784, Truro, N.S. B2N 5E8 (902/893-2293)

British Columbia Artificial Insemination Centre
General Manager, Gordon Souter, Box 40, Milner, B.C. V0X 1T0 (604/530-1141)

British Columbia Cattlemen's Association
Secretary Manager, Henry Blazowski, 10145 E. Trans Canada Hwy., R.R. 2, Kamloops, B.C. V2C 2J3 (604/573-3611)

British Columbia Charolais Association
President, Doug Baker, R.R. 2, Grand Forks, B.C. V0H 1H0

British Columbia Goat Breeders' Association
Secretary, Bev Helman, 5727 Ross Rd., R.R. 1, Mt. Lehman, B.C. V0X 1V0

British Columbia Guernsey Breeders' Association
Secretary Treasurer, George M. White, 2578 Bradner Rd., R.R. 6, Aldergrove, B.C. V0X 1A0 (604/856-5341)

British Columbia Livestock Producers' Co-op Association
General Manager, Bruce Whyte, R.R. 2, Kamloops, B.C. V2C 2J3 (604/573-3939)

British Columbia Mink Producers' Association
Secretary, Mrs. Louise Peterson, 326 Bradner Rd., R.R. 1, Abbotsford, B.C. V2S 1M3 (604/856-6387)

British Columbia Pork Producers Association
2564 Montrose Ave., Abbotsford, B.C. V2S 3T3
(604) 853-9461
Secretary Manager, Elsie Waite

British Columbia Sheep Breeders' Co-op Association
Secretary, Mrs. H. Finch, R.R. 1, Cawston, B.C. V0X 1C0 (604/499-5717)

Canada Mink Breeders Association
58 Oakwood Ave. N., Mississauga, Ont. L5G 3L8
(416) 274-5812
Managing Director, Mrs. Doris E. Boyd, R.R. 1, Guelph, Ont. N1H 6H7

Canadian Aberdeen Angus Association
Box 663, Guelph, Ont. N1H 6L3
(519) 824-8760
General Manager, Jack Peaker

ALBERTA ABERDEEN ANGUS ASSOCIATION
Secretary, Miss Gail Pentland, Rm. 108, 2003 McKnight Blvd. N.E., Calgary, Alta. T2E 6L2 (403/277-2127)

BRITISH COLUMBIA ABERDEEN ANGUS ASSOCIATION
Secretary, Mrs. Lucille Turner, R.R. 2, Qualicum Beach, B.C. V0R 2T0 (604/752-6007)

MANITOBA ABERDEEN-ANGUS ASSOCIATION
Secretary, Mrs. Mary Van Daele, Box 123, Medora, Man. R0M 1K0 (204/665-2455)

MARITIME ABERDEEN-ANGUS ASSOCIATION
Secretary, Mrs. Iva Mutch, R.R. 3, Vernon Bridge, P.E.I. C0A 2E0 (902/651-2414)

NEW BRUNSWICK ABERDEEN ANGUS ASSOCIATION
Secretary, Mrs. George MacLean, R.R. 2, Centreville, N.B. E0J 1H0 (506/276-4412)

NOVA SCOTIA ABERDEEN-ANGUS ASSOCIATION
Secretary, Mrs. Nellie Hirst, R.R. 1, Bridgetown, N.S. B0S 1C0

ONTARIO ABERDEEN-ANGUS ASSOCIATION
Secretary, Cameron McTaggart, 50 Royal Rd., Aurora, Ont. L4G 1A9 (416/727-4923)

PRINCE EDWARD ISLAND ABERDEEN ANGUS BREEDERS' ASSOCIATION
Secretary, Mrs. Boyd Dixon, Clyde River, P.E.I. C0A 1H0 (902/675-3452)

ASSOCIATION ABERDEEN ANGUS DU QUEBEC
Secretary, James Houston, C.P. 289, Macdonald College, P.Q. H9X 1C0 (514/457-5315)

SASKATCHEWAN ANGUS ASSOCIATION
Secretary, L. Bernice Willms, Box 400, Dundurn, Sask. S0K 1K0 (306/492-4734)

Canadian American Saddle Horse Breeders Association
Secretary, Mrs. Donna G. Underwood, Box 908, Ridgetown, Ont. N0P 2C0 (519/674-3079)

Canadian Arabian Horse Registry
Secretary, Charles Hubschmid, Box 101, Bowden, Alta. T0M 0K0 (403/224-2136)

Canadian Belgian Horse Association
Secretary, R. Trepanier, Oka, P.Q. J0N 1E0

Canadian Blonde d'Aquitaine Association
#207, 1606 Centre St. N., Calgary, Alta. T2E 2R9

(403) 276-5771

Canadian Brown Swiss Association
343 Waterloo Ave., Guelph, Ont. N1H 3K1
(519) 821-2811
Secretary Treasurer, D.A. Taylor

ALBERTA BROWN SWISS ASSOCIATION
Secretary, Mrs. Freda Copithorne, Box 30049, Stn. B, Calgary, Alta. T2M 4N7

MANITOBA BROWN SWISS ASSOCIATION
Secretary, Isabel Hyndman, R.R. 1, Rapid City, Man. R0K 1W0

ONTARIO BROWN SWISS ASSOCIATION
Secretary, Mrs. Norma McConnell, R.R. 5, Kincardine, Ont. NOG 2GO

CLUB BROWN SWISS DU QUEBEC
Secretary, Mrs. Ellen Rohlfs, R.R. 3, Roxton Falls, P.Q. J0H 1E0

SASKATCHEWAN BROWN SWISS ASSOCIATION
Secretary, Mrs. Harriet Werschner, R.R. 5, Saskatoon, Sask. S7K 3V8

Canadian Cattle Breeders' Association
Secretary, Jean-Guy Bernier, #2, 211 12th Ave., Sherbrooke, P.Q. J1G 2V5 (819/567-1258)

Canadian Cattlemen's Association
West: #238, 2116 27 Ave. N.E., Calgary, Alta. T2E 7A6(403/277-2371) – not confirmed for 1982
East: #325, 590 Keele St., Toronto, Ont. M6N 3E3 (416/766-6871)
Ottawa: 111 Sparks St., #102, Ottawa, Ont. K1P 5B5 (613/233-5331)

Canadian Charolais Association
2320 41st Ave. N.E., Calgary, Alta. T2E 6W8
(403) 276-9242

Canadian Chianna Association
Secretary, Jim Carpenter, 1745 Broder St., Regina, Sask. S4N 5P1 (306/565-8822)

Canadian Finnsheep Breeders' Association
Secretary, Colin W. Ransom, 2740 Assiniboine Ave., Winnipeg, Man. R3J OB1

Canadian Galloway Association
Secretary, Mrs. Dianne S. Somers, Box 311, Blyth, Ont. NOM 1HO (519/523-9399)

ALBERTA-BRITISH COLUMBIA GALLOWAY ASSOCIATION
Secretary, Mrs. Donna Befus, 4339 19 St. N.W., Calgary, Alta. T2L 2B8 (403/282-3123)

SASKATCHEWAN GALLOWAY ASSOCIATION
Secretary, Floyd Currie, Box 565, Swift Current, Sask.

EASTERN CANADIAN GALLOWAY ASSOCIATION
Secretary, Robert Burns, Box 202, Norwood, Ont. K0L 2V0 (705/639-5642)

Canadian Gelbvieh Association
Bldg. 13, McCall Field, Calgary, Alta. T2P 2G3
(403) 277-2072
Secretary Manager, Ron Sturgeon

GELBVIEH ASSOCIATION OF ALBERTA
Secretary, Kaye James, R.R. 1, Okotoks, Alta. TOL 1TO (403/938-7634)

MANITOBA SASKATCHEWAN GELBVIEH ASSOCIATION
Secretary, Dr. Ron Hill, 129 Columbia Dr., Saskatoon, Sask. S7K 1E8 (306/653-4658)

Canadian Goat Society
Box 518, Uxbridge, Ont. L0C 1K0
(416) 852-7594
Secretary Manager, John Hunter

Canadian Guernsey Breeders Association
Secretary, Donald MacKenzie, 368 Woolwich St., Guelph, Ont. N1H 3W6 (519/836-2141)

Canadian Hackney Society
Secretary, Mrs. E.L. Burke, Box 59, Port Stanley, Ont. NOL 2AO

Canadian Hays Converter Association
Secretary, S.B. Williams, Ste. 509, 6707 Elbow Dr. S.W., Calgary, Alta. T2V OE5 (403/253-2345)

Canadian Hereford Association
5160 Skyline Way N.E., Calgary, Alta. T2E 6V1
(403) 275-2662
General Manager, Duncan J. Porteous

Provincial Associations

BRITISH COLUMBIA HEREFORD ASSOCIATION
Secretary, Keith Miller, R.R. 1, Salmon Arm, B.C. V0E 2T0 (604/832-4329)

ALBERTA HEREFORD ASSOCIATION
Secretary, John Hay, Box 910, Innisfail, Alta. TOM 1A0 (403/227-5246)

SASKATCHEWAN HEREFORD ASSOCIATION
Secretary, Harold Lees, Box 1336, Regina, Sask. S4P 3B8 (306/545-2333)

MANITOBA HEREFORD ASSOCIATION
Secretary, Alva D. Jones, Box 592, Killarney, Man. R0K 1G0 (204/523-4594)

ONTARIO HEREFORD ASSOCIATION
Secretary, John Slaght, Box 68, Langton, Ont. N0E 1G0 (519/875-4803)

ASSOCIATION HEREFORD DU QUEBEC
Secretary, Real Fortin, C.P. 7041, Quebec, P.Q. G1G 5E1 (418/628-5559)

MARITIMES HEREFORD ASSOCIATION
Secretary, Glen K. Cotton, Box 1113, Charlottetown, P.E.I. C1A 7M8 (902/672-2031)

Canadian Highland Cattle Society
Secretary Treasurer, Emmerson Smith, R.R. 3, McGinnis Rd., Westbank, B.C.

Canadian Horse Breeders Association
Secretary, Réal Sorel, Roxton Pond, P.Q. JOE 1ZO (514/372-7744)

Canadian Jersey Cattle Club
343 Waterloo Ave., Guelph, Ont. N1H 3K1
(519) 821-1020
Secretary Manager, C. Honderich

PRINCE EDWARD ISLAND JERSEY BREEDERS' ASSOCIATION
Secretary, Wayne Boswell, Marshfield, P.E.I. (902/894-5713)

NOVA SCOTIA JERSEY BREEDERS' CLUB
Secretary, Jack Adamson, R.R. 2, Scotsburn, N.S. B0K 1R0

NEW BRUNSWICK JERSEY BREEDERS' ASSOCIATION
Secretary, R.J. Curtis, N.B. Dept. of Agriculture, Box 6000, Fredericton, N.B. E3B 5H1 (506/453-2483)

ASSOCIATION DES ELEVEURS DE JERSEY DU QUEBEC
Secretary, Hugh MacDonald, R.R. 2, Lennoxville, P.Q. J1M 2A3

ONTARIO JERSEY CLUB
Secretary Treasurer, J. Grisdale, 343 Waterloo Ave., Guelph, Ont. N1H 3K1 (519/821-1130)

MANITOBA JERSEY BREEDERS' ASSOCIATION
Secretary, Grace Copp, Box 231, Brandon, Man. R7A 5Y8

SASKATCHEWAN JERSEY BREEDERS' ASSOCIATION
Secretary, Fred Thompson, Fairlight, Sask.

ALBERTA JERSEY CATTLE CLUB
Secretary, J.A. McPherson, 203 Alberta Stock Yards Bldg., 2635 Portland St. S.E., Calgary, Alta. T2G 4M8

BRITISH COLUMBIA JERSEY BREEDERS' ASSOCIATION
Secretary, Ken Anderlini, 2041 248th St., R.R. 4, Aldergrove, B.C. V0X 1A0

Canadian Lacombe (Swine) Breeders' Association
Secretary, George Croome, Box 122, Breton, Alta. T0C 0P0 (403/696-2458)

Canadian Landrace Swine Breeders Association
Secretary, William T. New, 21 Thomson St., Barrie, Ont. L4N 1X4

Canadian Limousin Association
#10, 6115 4 St. S.E., Calgary, Alta. T2H 2A5
(403) 253-7309

ALBERTA LIMOUSIN ASSOCIATION
c/o Voris Molsberry, R.R. 1, Leduc, Alta. T9E 2X1 (403/986-3716)

BRITISH COLUMBIA LIMOUSIN ASSOCIATION
c/o Norene Chutter, Box 2509, Merritt, B.C. V0K 2B0 (604/378-4955)

MANITOBA LIMOUSIN ASSOCIATION
c/o Alfred Yeomans, Box 159, Alexander, Man. (204/752-2292)

ONTARIO LIMOUSIN ASSOCIATION
c/o R.G. Snyder, 167 Lexington Rd., Waterloo, Ont. N2J 4G8 (519/885-0751)

QUEBEC LIMOUSIN ASSOCIATION
c/o J.-M. Lavoie, 45 St-Germain est, Rimouski, P.Q. G5L 1A3 (418/723-8438)

SASKATCHEWAN LIMOUSIN ASSOCIATION
c/o Miss Terry Karwandy, Box 332, Cabri, Sask. S0N 0J0 (306/587-2712)

The Canadian Luing Cattle Association
Secretary Treasurer, Mrs. R.J. Luft, Kathyrn, Alta. TOM 1EO (403/935-4414)

Canadian Maine-Anjou Association
General Manager, B.G. Kitchen, 2424C 2nd Ave. S.E., Calgary, Alta. T2E 6J9 (403/273-8219)

Canadian Meuse-Rhine-Ijssel Association
Box 235, Claresholm, Alta. T0L 0T0
(403) 625-2256

The Canadian Morgan Club
Secretary, Mrs. Peggy MacDonald, Box 2147, Leduc, Alta. T9E 2Z3
Treasurer, George Wade, Box 295, Kentville, N.S. B4N 2M9

Canadian Murray Grey Association
Secretary, Mrs. D. Burrrington, Box 605, Red Deer, Alta. T4N 5G6 (403/343-1355)

Canadian National Live Stock Records
2417 Holly Lane, Ottawa, Ont. K1V 7P2
(613) 731-7110

Canadian National Silver Fox Breeders Association
Executive Secretary, Mrs. Myrna Gallant, 292 Water St., Summerside, P.E.I. C1N 1B8 (902/836-5139)

Canadian Palomino Horse Association
Secretary, Arthur McCornock, R.R. 4, Picton, Ont. KOK 2TO (613/476-5323)

Canadian Parthenay Association
Secretary, Miss P.A. Attridge, Box 817, Cambridge (Galt), Ont. N1R 5W6 (519/621-5191)

Canadian Percheron Association
Secretary, Bruce A. Roy, Box 9, Cremona, Alta. T0M 0R0 (403/337-2342)

Canadian Pinzgauer Association
#409, 604 1 St. S.W., Calgary, Alta. T2P 1M7
(403) 265-7236

ALBERTA PINZGAUER ASSOCIATION
Box 761, Cardston, Alta. T0K 0K0
(403) 642-3922

SASKATCHEWAN PINZGAUER ASSOCIATION
Box 311, Hodgeville, Sask. SOH 2BO
(306) 677-2634

Canadian Pony Society
Secretary, Mrs. Barbara Anness, Box 324, Woodbridge, Ont. L4L 1B2

Canadian Pork Council
111 Sparks St., Ottawa, Ont. K1P 5B5
(613) 236-3633

Canadian Quarter Horse Association
Secretary, Lucille Katzman, Box 170, R.R. 4, Saskatoon, Sask. S7K 3J7

Canadian Red Poll Cattle Association
Secretary Manager, A.G. Howard, Box 237, Crystal City, Man. R0K 0N0 (204/873-2243, bus.; 873-2283, res.)

Canadian Romagnola-Marchigiana (Romark) Association
Box 177, Jarvie, Alta. T0G 1H0
(403) 954-2119
Secretary Manager, Mrs. Charlotte Schrader
The Alberta Romark Association is at the same address.

Canadian Santa Gertrudis Association
Secretary, J.W. Aldred, Box 122, Port Perry, Ont. L0B 1N0

Canadian Sheep Breeders Association
Secretary, D.J. Stevenson, R.R. 1, Egbert, Ont. L0L 1N0 (705/458-9780)

Provincial Associations

ALBERTA SHEEP BREEDERS ASSOCIATION
Secretary, L.B. Hubbard, Box 1060, Calgary, Alta. T2P 2K8

BRITISH COLUMBIA PURE BRED SHEEP BREEDERS' ASSOCIATION
Secretary, Mrs. W.V. McCabe, 2500 272 St., R.R. 5, Aldergrove, B.C. VOX 1AO (604/856-6647)

MANITOBA SHEEP ASSOCIATION
Secretary, Marni Fisher, 545 University Cres., Winnipeg, Man. R3T 2N2

NEW BRUNSWICK SHEEP BREEDERS' ASSOCIATION
Secretary, Lloyd McEwen, R.R. 3, Hampton, N.B. E0G 1Z0

NOVA SCOTIA SHEEP BREEDERS ASSOCIATION
Secretary, Angus Rouse, R.R. 2, Debert, N.S. B0M 1G0

ONTARIO SHEEP ASSOCIATION
Secretary, F. E. Winger, R.R. 1, Stevensville, Ont. L0S 1S0 (416/382-2688)

PRINCE EDWARD ISLAND SHEEP BREEDERS' ASSOCIATION
Secretary, Ross Tarvis, R.R. 3, Hunter River, P.E.I. C0A 1N0

SOCIETE DES ELEVEURS DE MOUTONS DU QUEBEC
Secretary, Ghislain Jobin, 4452 Notre Dame, St-Augustin, P.Q. GOA 3EO

SASKATCHEWAN SHEEP BREEDERS' ASSOCIATION
Secretary, Ab Gorrill, Box 104, Bulyea, Sask. SOG OLO (306/725-4820)

Canadian Shorthorn Association
Gummer Bldg., 5 Douglas St., Guelph, Ont. N1H 2S8
(519) 822-6841

Constituent Associations

CANADIAN DUAL PURPOSE SHORTHORN SOCIETY
Secretary, Maurice Knott, R.R. 1, Clarksburg, Ont. N0H 1J0

THE CANADIAN LINCOLN RED ASSOCIATION
Secretary, Mrs. Judy McDonald, Makwa Ranches, Box 644, Rocky Mountain House, Alta. TOM 1TO

Provincial Associations

ALBERTA SHORTHORN ASSOCIATION
Secretary, Mrs. Nadine Hymas, Box 275, Standard, Alta. T0J 3G0

BRITISH COLUMBIA SHORTHORN BREEDERS' ASSOCIATION
Secretary Treasurer, Ron Carter, 9002 168 St., Surrey, B.C. V3S 4N7

MANITOBA SHORTHORN ASSOCIATION
Secretary, Murray Martin, 1312 10th St., Brandon, Man. R7A 4A6

NEW BRUNSWICK SHORTHORN BREEDERS ASSOCIATION
Secretary, Brian DuPlessis, Dept. of Agriculture, Fredericton, N.B. E3B 5H1 (506/453-2483)

NOVA SCOTIA SHORTHORN ASSOCIATION
Secretary Treasurer, Dean Cole, R.R. 3, Middle Musquodoboit, N.S. B0N 1X0 (902/384-2783)

ONTARIO SHORTHORN CLUB
Secretary, Glenn Frosch, R.R. 2, Puslinch, Ont. N0B 2J0

PRINCE EDWARD ISLAND SHORTHORN BREEDERS ASSOCIATION
Secretary, Miss S. Boswall, Charlottetown R.R. 3, P.E.I. C1A 7J7 (902/892-4201)

QUEBEC SHORTHORN ASSOCIATION/CLUB SHORTHORN DU QUEBEC
Secretary, Normand Champagne, C.P. 585, Berthierville, P.Q. J0K 1A0 (514/836-4494)

SASKATCHEWAN SHORTHORN ASSOCIATION
Secretary, Grant Alexander, Goodwater, Sask. S0C 1E0

Canadian Simmental Association
#13, 4101 19 St. N.E., Calgary, Alta. T2E 7C4
(403) 230-1831
General Manager, James B. MacKay

Canadian Standard Bred Horse Society
233 Evans Ave., Toronto, Ont. M8Z 1J6
(416) 252-3565

Canadian Swine Breeders' Association
Secretary, J. Leonard McQuay, R.R. 5, Cambridge, Ont. N1R 5S6 (519/621-0392)

Canadian Tarentaise Association
Secretary, E.L. Reesor, Box 73, Walsh, Alta. T0J 3L0 (403/937-2216)

Canadian Thoroughbred Horse Society
Box 172, Rexdale, Ont. M9W 5L1
(416) 675-3602; Telex: 06-989526
National Executive Secretary, Mrs. W.E. Kenny

Provincial Divisions

Alta.: Box 1060, Calgary, Alta. T2P 2K8 (403/269-3941)
B.C.: 4023 E. Hastings St., Burnaby, B.C. V5C 2J1 (604/291-1461)
Man.: #808, 10 Valhalla Dr., Winnipeg, Man. R2G OX9 (204/338-4552)
Que.: c/o Jacques Cartier Co., 1100 Norman St., Lachine, P.Q. H8S 1A6 (514/634-3481)
Ont.: Box 172, Rexdale, Ont. M9W 5L1 (416/675-3602)
Sask.: Box 51, Milden, Sask. SOL 2LO (306/935-4705)

Canadian Trakehner Horse Society
Secretary, Harry Zimmermann, Box 176, Dundas, Ont. L9H 5G1 (416/627-0947)

Canadian Welsh Black Cattle Society
Site 5, Box 6, Hanna, Alta. TOJ 1PO
(403) 854-2402

Clydesdale Horse Association of Canada
Secretary, J. Douglas Charles, 1501 Arlington Ave., Saskatoon, Sask. S7H 2Y3 (306/374-4904)

Fédération Chevaline du Québec
(Quebec Equine Federation)
515 Viger St. E., Montreal, P.Q. H2L 2P2
(514) 288-6141
Executive Secretary, Jacques Bonneau, agr.

Federation Ovine du Quebec
Secretary, M.-Y. Ribardière, 1821 Cédar, Mascouche Heights, Terrebonne, P.Q. J0N 1T0 (514/477-0600)

Holstein Friesian Association of Canada
Box 610, Brantford, Ont. N3T 5R4
(519) 752-5401
Secretary, D.H. Clemons

Provincial Branches

B.C.: Secretary, Dan T. Schmidt, 1615 Highview St., Abbotsford, B.C. V2P 3G6
Alta.: Secretary, Doug Bienert, Box 39, Millet, Alta. T0C 1Z0
Sask.: Secretary, A.J. Sawatsky, 2801 MacEachern Ave., Saskatoon, Sask. S7J 1B4 (306/343-6733)
Man.: Secretary, A.H. Steinke, 84 Regatta Rd., Winnipeg, Man. R2G 2Y6
Ont.: (Holstein-Friesian Association of Canada, Brantford) Secretary, J.G. Snyder, Box 193, Brantford, Ont. N3T 5M8
Que.: Secretary, Pierre Léonard, #200, 201 est, rue Crémazie, Montreal, P.Q. H2M 1L2 (514/388-1184)
N.B.: Secretary, Ernest Jarvis, Box 744, Fredericton, N.B. E3B 5B4
N.S.: Secretary, Mrs. F.F. Hamilton, R.R. 5, Truro, N.S.
P.E.I.: (Prince Edward Island Holstein Breeders' Association) Secretary, S. MacArthur, Union Rd., R.R. 3, Charlottetown, P.E.I. C1A 7J7 (902/892-1948)

Manitoba Beef Cattle Performance Association
Box 232, Douglas, Man. R0K 0R0
(204) 763-4696

Manitoba Cattle Producers Association
c/o Charlene Oswald, #330, 125 Garry St., Winnipeg, Man. R3C 3P2

National Chinchilla Breeders of Canada
Secretary, Mrs. D.M. Bigras, Box 64, Carleton Place, Ont. K7C 3P3 (613/257-3898)

New Brunswick Ayrshire Breeders Association
Secretary, Frank A. Waterston, R.R. 1, Penobsquis, N.B. E0E 1L0

New Brunswick Cattle Producers Association
Secretary, Tom Demma, R.R. 6, Fredericton, N.B. E3B 4X7 (506/454-9642)

New Brunswick Dairy Goat Association
Secretary, Pat Ritchie, R.R. 3, Nackawic, N.B. E0H 1P0

New Brunswick Draft Horse Association
Secretary, Norman Powell, Welsford, N.B. EOG 3GO (506/486-2924)

New Brunswick Fur Farmers Association
Secretary, Graden Young, 13 Toth St., Riverview, N.B. E1B 3Y4 (506/386-2806)

New Brunswick Guernsey Cattle Club
Secretary, Ernest Eagles, Box 279, Sussex, N.B. E0E 1P0

New Brunswick Pork Producers Association
Secretary, Watson E. Cudmore, Box 750, Moncton, N.B. E1C 8N5 (506/858-6324)

Newfoudland Swine Producers Association
Box 82, R.R. 1, Portugal Cove, Nfld. AOA 3KO

Nova Scotia Chinchilla Breeders Association
President, Charlie R. Jodrey, 75 Lake Major Rd., R.R. 1, Dartmouth, N.S. B2W 3X7 (902/434-3485)
Secretary Treasurer, Mary Anne Jodrey

Nova Scotia Fox Breeders Association
Box 550, Truro, N.S. B2N 5E3

Nova Scotia Guernsey Breeders Club
Secretary, Ronald G. Barrett, R.R. 1, Bridgetown, N.S. B0S 1C0

Nova Scotia Mink Breeders' Association
Secretary, Ruby Mullen, R.R. 2, Weymouth, N.S. B0W 3T0 (902/837-5926)

Office des Producteurs de Porcs du Québec
President, Donald Desprès, C.P. 930, Bedford, P.Q. JOJ 1AO (514/248-3386)

Ontario Cattlemen's Association
Manager, G.W. Hedley, 590 Keele St., Toronto, Ont. M6N 3E3 (416/766-9217)

Pork Producers Association of Nova Scotia
Secretary, Ms. Donna Langille, Box 784, Truro, N.S. B2N 5E8 (902/893-2293)

Prince Edward Island Artificial Breeders' Association
Secretary, A. Stedman, Box 1600, Charlottetown, P.E.I. C1A 7N3 (902/892-3770)

Prince Edward Island Guernsey Breeders' Association
Secretary, Constance Coles, Winsloe R.R. 2, P.E.I. COA 2HO (902/894-7744)

Prince Edward Island Swine Breeders' Association
Secretary, Barbara Crabbe, Box 1600, Charlottetown, P.E.I. C1A 7N3 (902/892-5465)

Salers Association of Canada
Secretary, Alex J. McTaggart, #201, 1200 26 Ave. S.E., Calgary, Alta. T2G 4M8 (403/266-7360)

Saskatchewan Stock Growers Association
Secretary, Don J. Perrin, Box 849, Maple Creek, Sask. SON 1NO (306/667-3661)

Sheep Producers Association of Nova Scotia
Secretary, R.N. Evans, R.R. 1, Kingston, N.S. B0P 1R0 (902/765-2917)

Société Ayrshire du Québec
Secretary, Bernard Prévost, R.R. 1, Compton, P.Q. J0B 1L0 (819/837-2559)

Société des Eleveurs de Chevaux Belges du Québec
(breeders of Belgian horses)
Secretary, G.-E. Mayrand, 226 Quintal, Ville de Laval, P.Q. H7N 4W2 (514/669-7724)

Société des Eleveurs de Chevaux Canadiens
(breeders of Canadian horses)
Secretary, Réal Sorel, Chemin Grande-Ligne, Roxton Pond, P.Q. JOE 1ZO (514/372-7744)

Société des Eleveurs de Porcs du Québec
(swine breeders)
Secretary, Hélène Michon, C.P. 8495, Ste-Foy, P.Q. G1V 4N5 (418/659-2936)

Société des Eleveurs de Porcs Landrace du Québec
(Landrace swine breeders)
Secretary, Ghislain Jobin, 4452 Notre-Dame, St-Augustin, P.Q.G0A 3E0

Western Ontario Breeders Inc.
General Manager, R.J. McDonald, Box 457, Woodstock, Ont. N4S 7Y7 (519/539-9831)

Western Stock Growers Association
Stockmen's Centre, Ste. 101, 2116 27th Ave. N.E., Calgary, Alta. T2E 7A6
(403) 276-3328

THE LORD'S DAY ALLIANCE OF CANADA
Box 457, Islington PO, Islington, Ont. M9A 4X4
(416) 625-8759
Executive Director, Les Kingdon
Treasurer, D. J. Hicks

LOYAL ORANGE ASSOCIATION

Grand Orange Lodge of Canada
Grand Secretary, Norman Ritchie, 94 Sheppard Ave. W., Willowdale, Ont. M2N 1M5 (416/223-1690)

Ladies' Orange Benevolent Association of Canada
Grand Secretary, Mrs. Edith Halliday, 101, 6831 Arcola St., Burnaby, B.C. V5E 1H4 (604/526-6847)

Provincial Lodges

GRAND ORANGE LODGE OF BRITISH COLUMBIA
Grand Secretary, G. A. Ferguson, 2449 Chilcott Ave., Port Coquitlam, B.C. V3B 1Y5

GRAND LODGE OF ALBERTA
Grand Secretary, W.L. Rideout, 11226 68 St., Edmonton, Alta. T5B 1N5

GRAND ORANGE LODGE OF SASKATCHEWAN
Grand Secretary, Marvin L. Potter, Box 1, Nokomis, Sask. SOG 3RO (306/528-2106)

GRAND ORANGE LODGE OF MANITOBA
Grand Secretary, T. W. Robinson, 2312 Rosser Ave., Brandon, Man. R7B 0E3 (204/727-4025)

GRAND ORANGE LODGE OF ONTARIO WEST
Grand Secretary, D. J. Worden, Box 149, Atwood, Ont. NOG 1BO

GRAND ORANGE LODGE OF ONTARIO EAST
Grand Secretary, J. H. Book, 500 Evered Ave., Ottawa, Ont. K1Z 5K8

GRAND LODGE OF QUEBEC
Grand Secretary, William Curren, Box 38, R.R. 2, Brownsburg, P.Q. JOV 1AO (514/533-4938)

GRAND LODGE OF PRINCE EDWARD ISLAND
Grand Secretary, John Panton, Belfast, P.E.I. COA 1BO (902/659-2927)

GRAND LODGE OF NOVA SCOTIA
Grand Secretary, H.W. Vardy, Box 23, North Sydney, N.S. B2A 3M1 (902/794-4066)

GRAND ORANGE LODGE OF NEW BRUNSWICK
Grand Secretary, D.J. Thomas, R.R. 1, Westfield, N.B. E0G 3J0 (506/468-2978)

GRAND ORANGE LODGE OF NEWFOUNDLAND & LABRADOR
Grand Secretary, Gerald Crane, Box 214, Spaniard's Bay, Nfld. AOA 3XO

LOYAL TRUE BLUE ASSOCIATION
Supreme Grand Secretary, Mrs. Edna Bullions, Box 902, Southampton, Ont. N0H 2L0

LUMBER & BUILDING MATERIALS ASSOCIATION OF ONTARIO INC.
4500 Sheppard Ave. E., Unit F, Scarborough, Ont. M1S 3R6
(416) 298-1731
Executive Vice President, Herbert C. Hardy

MACHINERY & EQUIPMENT MANUFACTURERS' ASSOCIATION OF CANADA
Ste. 701, 116 Albert St., Ottawa, Ont. K1P 5G3
(613) 232-7213
Chairman, W.L. Mallory
President, J.R. Romanow

MAGAZINES CANADA
1240 Bay St., Suite 300, Toronto, Ont. M5R 2A7
(416) 922-3181
President, John S. Crosbie

MAKIVIK CORPORATION
Box 179, Fort Chimo, P.Q. J0M 1C0
(819) 964-2925

MALTESE CANADIAN SOCIETY OF TORONTO
3278 Dundas St. W., Box 57, Stn. D, Toronto, Ont. M6P 3J5
(416) 767-3645

MANITOBA ARCHAEOLOGICAL SOCIETY INC.
Box 1171, Winnipeg, Man. R3C 2Y4

MANITOBA ASSOCIATION OF URBAN MUNICIPALITIES
Executive Director, Ms. R.I. Zimberg, #203, 377 Henderson Hwy., Winnipeg, Man. R2K 2H2 (204/667-6585)

MANITOBA AVIATION COUNCIL
#211, 207 Fort St., Winnipeg, Man. R3C 1E2
(204) 957-1819
President, Ralph Danbert

MANITOBA HISTORICAL SOCIETY
190 Rupert Ave., Winnipeg, Man. R3B 0N2
(204) 943-7037
President, Prof. Wm. P. Thompson

MANITOBA INSTITUTE OF MANAGEMENT
193 Sherbrook St., Winnipeg, Man. R3C 2B7
(204) 786-5401
Executive Director, Glen A. Husack

MIM Management Centre also at above address

MANITOBA MUNICIPAL SECRETARY TREASURERS' ASSOCIATION
Secretary, Mel Didyk, 3550 Main St., R.R. 1B, Winnipeg, Man. R3C 2E4
Treasurer, J.B. Goossen, Box 40, Ste. Anne, Man. ROA 1RO (204/422-5929)

MASONIC ORDER

Provincial Lodges

GRAND LODGE OF BRITISH COLUMBIA A.F. & A.M.
Grand Secretary, C. Lorimer, 1495 W. 8th Ave., Vancouver, B.C. V6H 1C9 (604/736-8941)

GRAND LODGE OF ALBERTA A.F. & A.M.
Grand Secretary, M. P. Dunford (30), 330-12th Ave. S.W., Calgary, Alta. T2R 0H2

GRAND LODGE OF MANITOBA A.F. & A.M.
Grand Secretary, J.E. Reesor Bingeman, Masonic Memorial Temple, 420 Corydon Ave., Winnipeg, Man. R3L 0N8 (204/453-7410)

GRAND LODGE A.F. & A.M. OF CANADA, IN THE PROVINCE OF ONTARIO
Grand Secretary, R.E. Davies, Box 217, Hamilton, Ont. L8N 3C9 (416/528-8644)

GRAND LODGE OF QUEBEC A.F. & A.M.
Grand Secretary, W. Gordon Parker, 2295 St. Mark St., Montreal, P.Q. H3H 2G9 (514/933-6739)

GRAND LODGE OF NEW BRUNSWICK A.F. & A.M.
Grand Secretary, M.W. Dalton, Masonic Temple, Box 6430, Stn. A, Saint John, N.B. E2L 4R8 (506/652-2390)

GRAND LODGE A.F. & A.M. OF NOVA SCOTIA
Grand Secretary, W.H. Francis, Box 214, Halifax, N.S. B3J 2M4 (902/423-6149)

GRAND LODGE OF PRINCE EDWARD ISLAND A.F. & A.M.
Grand Secretary, Keith MacKinnon, PGM, Box 337, Charlottetown, P.E.I. C1A 7K7

Royal Arch Masons of Canada
Grand Chapter, R.A.M. of Manitoba, Grand Scribe E, E. E. Smith, 981 Dorchester Ave., Winnipeg, Man. R3M 0P9 (204/453-3915)
Grand Chapter, R.A.M. of N.B., Grand Scribe E, E. H. Wadman, Box 535, Moncton, N.B. E1C 8L9
Grand Chapter, R.A.M. of N.S., Grand Secretary, L.C. Armstrong, Box 227, Armdale PO, Halifax, N.S. B3L 4K1 (902/876-7300)
Grand Chapter of Canada in the Province of Ontario, Grand Z, Frederick Scott, 41 Fairfield Ave. N., Hamilton, Ont. L8H 5G9
Grand Scribe E, Robert T. Rigby, Toronto, Ont.
Office, #505, 3500 Dufferin St., Toronto, Ont. M3K 1N1 (416/638-2813)
Grand Chapter, R.A.M. of Que., Grand Scribe E, E.H.J. Platt, 50 Prince Edward Ave., Otterburn Heights, P.Q. J3H 1V4
Grand Chapter, R.A.M. of Sask., Grand Scribe E, R.E. Glaze, Box 237, Tisdale, Sask. SOE 1TO

Royal & Select Masters of Ontario
Grand Recorder, Hugh E. Fackrell, 423 Forest Ave., St. Thomas, Ont. N5R 5G2 (519/631-5414) – not confirmed, 1982

Cryptic Rite Masons of Western Canada, R. & S.M.
(covering Man., Sask., Alta. and B.C.)
Grand Recorder, L. S. Churchill, Box 86124, N. Vancouver, B.C. V7L 4J5 (604/980-0267)

The Supreme Grand Council of the Eastern Jurisdiction of Canada
(Covering Que., Nfld., P.E.I., N.B., and N.S.)

Grand Recorder, M. I. Comp. F. C. Morrison, Box 279, New Glasgow, N.S. B2H 5E4 (902/752-8307)

The Masonic & Military Order of Knights of the Red Cross of Constantine, K.H.S. and St. John the Evangelist

Grand Recorder, G. O. Smith, 8 Marion Cres., Barrie, Ont. L4M 2L3 (705/728-2665)

Ancient Arabic Order of the Nobles of the Mystic Shrine for North America

A.A.O.N.M.S. Temples in Canada

Al Azhar Temple: Recorder, Tom S. Walker, Sub PO Box 58, 6403 Bowness Rd. N.W., Calgary, Alta. T3B 0E0 (403/239-0030)

Gizeh Temple: Recorder, Cecil E. Rees, 3550 Wayburne Dr., Burnaby, B.C. V5G 3K9 (604/291-7707)

Khartum Temple: Recorder, D. F. Law, 529 Wellington Cres., Winnipeg, Man. R3M 0A5 (204/453-8718)

Luxor Temple: Recorder, H. T. Dykeman, Box 2084, Saint John, N.B. E2L 3T5 (506/657-3561)

Philae Temple: Recorder, 276 Bedford Hwy. (Box 9050, Stn. A, Halifax, N.S. B3K 5M7) (902/443-4469)

Mocha Temple: Recorder, F. Duane Miller, 468 Colborne St., London, Ont. N6B 2T3 (519/672-1391)

Rameses Temple: Temple Administrator, Ed Morgan, Box 158, Stn. C, Toronto, Ont. M6J 3M9

Karnak Temple: Recorder, Douglas M. Hodge, Room 301, 2295 St. Mark St., Montreal, P.Q. H3H 2G9 (514/935-7728)

Tunis Temple: Recorder, Stanley G. Davis, Box 8572, Ottawa, Ont. (613/993-2796)

Wa Wa Temple: Recorder, B. E. Wilford, 2065 Hamilton St., Regina, Sask. S4P 2E1 (306/569-2294)

MASTER INSULATORS' ASSOCIATION OF ONTARIO INC.

5799 Yonge St., #301, Willowdale, Ont. M2M 3V3
(416) 226-6977
Manager, H.W. Near

MASTER PAINTERS & DECORATORS ASSOCIATION OF BRITISH COLUMBIA

7171 Buller Ave., Burnaby, B.C. V5J 4S1
(604) 438-7578
Manager, Norman R.V. Faiers

MATCH - International Centre

(Development Agency/Women's Organization)
#401, 171 Nepean St., Ottawa, Ont. K2P 0B4
(613) 238-1312
Information Officer, Murielle Vachon

MECHANICAL CONTRACTORS ASSOCIATION OF CANADA

President, J. A. Long, Ste. 408, 116 Albert St., Ottawa, Ont. K1P 5G3 (613/232-0492)

Provincial Executives

Alta.: J. H. Curtis, Northern District, #210, 11803 125 St., Edmonton, Alta. T5L OS1 (403/283-7567)

D. McCorquindale, C.A.E., Southern District, 608 25th St. N.W., Calgary, Alta. T2N 2S8

B.C.: V.J. Traynor, #230, 4259 Canada Way, Burnaby, B.C. V5G 1H1

Man.: L. A. Winder, #206, 666 St. James St., Winnipeg, Man. R3G 3J5

N.B.: W. Duffie, MCA New Brunswick, 105 Prospect St. W., Fredericton, N.B. E3B 2T7

Nfld.: M. O'Keefe, Box 913, St. John's, Nfld. A1C 5L7

N.S.: J. Rowe, Construction Association of N.S., Box 1476, Halifax, N.S. B3K 5H7 (902/429-6760)

Ont.: W. Nicholls, Ste. 309, 701 Evans Ave., Etobicoke, Ont. M9C 1A3 (416/621-5351)

P.E.I.: F. Reid, Construction Association of P.E.I., Box 728, Charlottetown, P.E.I. C1A 7L3

Que.: C. Larochelle, Corp. of Master Pipe Mechanics of Que., 2475 boul Sir Wilfrid Laurier, Ste. 61, Quebec, P.Q.

Sask.: E. Ritson, MCA Saskatchewan, #303, 2631 28th Ave., Regina, Sask. S4S 6X3 (306/586-6755)

MEDIA CLUB OF CANADA

Box 504, Stn. B, Ottawa, Ont. K1P 5P6
(613) 237-0628
Executive Director, Elizabeth Hammond
Regional Directors in every province. Contact Ottawa address for list.

MEDICAL ORGANIZATIONS

The associations listed here are professional medical voluntary associations. (See also 'Hospital Associations' and 'Nursing Associations' and 'Pharmaceutical Associations')

Academy of Medicine, Ottawa

Box 8223, 1867 Alta Vista Dr., Ottawa, Ont. K1G 3H7
(613) 733-2604
Executive Secretary, Mrs. Gladys M. St. Louis

Acupuncture Foundation of Canada

10 St. Mary St., #503, Toronto, Ont. M4Y 1P9
(416) 961-4131

Association des médecins de langue française du Canada

1440 Ste-Catherine ouest, Ste. 510, Montreal, P.Q. H3G 2P9
(514) 866-2053
Président, Dr Paul Duchastel
Vice présidente et présidente désigné, Dr Monique Boivin-Lesage

Association professionnelle des paramédicaux du Québec

C.P. 2165, St-Romuald, P.Q. G6W 5M5
(418) 839-5690

Canadian Association of Electroencephalograph Technologists Inc.

-not confirmed for 1982-

Secretary, R. Zaglul, EEG Lab, North York General Hospital, 4001 Leslie St., Willowdale, Ont. M2K 1E1 (416/492-4619)

Canadian Association of Gastroenterology

Secretary, Dr. Michael Lichter, Jewish General Hospital, 3755 Côte St. Catherine Rd., Montréal, P.Q. H3T 1E2

Canadian Association of Medical Microbiologists

Secretary Treasurer, Dr. J.H. Thornley, Dept. of Laboratory Medicine, Henderson General Hospital, Concession St., Hamilton, Ont. L8V 1C3 (416/389-4411, ext. 357)

Canadian Association of Medical Radiation Technologists

280 Metcalfe St., Ste. 410, Ottawa, Ont. K2P 1R7
(613) 234-0012
Executive Director, A.A. Mattila, R.T., APR, B.Mgt., F.R.S.H.
Branches in British Columbia, Alberta, Manitoba, Saskatchewan, Newfoundland, Ontario, Quebec, New Brunswick, Nova Scotia, Prince Edward Island.

Canadian Association of Occupational Therapists

25 Imperial St., Toronto, Ont. M5P 1B9
(416) 481-3317
Executive Director, Mrs. M. Seanne Wilkins, O.T.(C)
There are Provincial Societies in every province with elected officers. Contact Toronto address for list.

Canadian Association of Pathologists

Secretary Treasurer, Dr. T.F. McElligott, Dept. of Pathology, Hotel Dieu Hospital, Kingston, Ont. K7L 3H6

Canadian Association of Physical Medicine & Rehabilitation

University Hospital (Dept. of Rehabilitation Medicine), 339 Windermere Rd., London, Ont. N6A 5A5
Secretary, Dr. M.G.P. Cameron (519/673-3513)

The Canadian Association of Radiologists

1440 St. Catherine St. W., Suite 806, Montreal, P.Q. H3G 1R8
(514) 866 2035
Executive Secretary, Mrs. A. E. Pentecost
There are provincial councillors throughout Canada. Contact Montreal address for list.

Canadian Association of Rehabilitation Personnel

160 Eglinton Ave. E., #305, Toronto, Ont. M4P 1G3
(416) 481-9111

Canadian Cardiovascular Society

Secretary, Dr. James F. Symes, 1455 Peel St., Room M-31, Montreal, P.Q. H3A 1T5 (514/288-8141)

Canadian College of Forensic Medicine

Secretary, Richard Isaac, M.D., LL.B., F.C.L.M., #605, 190 St. George St., Toronto, Ont. M5R 2N4

Canadian Council of Blue Cross Plans

c/o 150 Ferrand Dr., Don Mills, Ont. M3C 1H6
Secretary, L.R. Furlong, Moncton
Contact, B.A. Mead (416/429-2661)

Canadian Dermatological Association

Secretary, Raymond Lessard, M.D., 11, Côte du Palais, Quebec, P.Q. G1R 2J6 (418/694-5200)

Canadian Federation of Biological Societies

Honorary Secretary Treasurer, Dr. G.R.F. Davis, Box 498, Sub 6, Saskatoon, Sask. S7N 0W0

Member Societies

CANADIAN PHYSIOLOGICAL SOCIETY
Secretary, Dr. R.S. Smith, Dept. of Surgery, University of Alberta, Edmonton, Alta.

PHARMACOLOGICAL SOCIETY OF CANADA
Secretary, Dr. R. Capek, Dept. of Pharmacology, Rm. 715, McIntyre Medical Bldg., McGill University, Montreal, P.Q. H3G 1Y6

CANADIAN ASSOCIATION OF ANATOMISTS
Secretary, B.H. Bressler, Dept. of Anatomy, University of B.C., Vancouver, B.C. V6T 1W5

CANADIAN BIOCHEMICAL SOCIETY
Secretary, Dr. B.D. McLennan, Dept. of Biochemistry, University of Saskatchewan, Saskatoon, Sask. S7N 0W0

NUTRITION SOCIETY OF CANADA
Secretary, F. Farmer, Box 276, Macdonald College, Ste-Anne-de-Bellevue, P.Q. H9X 1C0

CANADIAN SOCIETY FOR CELL BIOLOGY
Secretary, Dr. D. Pallota, Dept. of Biology, Laval University, Quebec, P.Q. G1V 4G2

CANADIAN SOCIETY FOR IMMUNOLOGY
Secretary, A. Froese, Dept. of Immunology, Univ. of Man., 730 William Ave., Winnipeg, Man. R3E 0W3

SOCIETY OF TOXICOLOGY OF CANADA/SOCIETE DE TOXICOLOGIE DU CANADA
Executive Director, Gordon Krip, Ph.D., Box 517, Beaconsfield, P.Q. H9W 5V1

Canadian Federation of Voluntary Health Plans

c/o 150 Ferrand Dr., Don Mills, Ont. M3C 1H6
Secretary, S.P. Brannan, Halifax
Contact, B.A. Mead (416/429-2661)

Canadian Health Record Association

187 King St. E., Oshawa, Ont. L1H 1C3
(416) 728-1678
Executive Director, Mrs. Janet Milner

Canadian Liver Foundation

42 Charles St. E., #510, Toronto, Ont. M4Y 1T4
(416) 964-1953
Executive Director, Valerie M. Price

ONTARIO FOUNDATION FOR DISEASES OF THE LIVER
42 Charles St. E., #510, Toronto, Ont. M4Y 1T4

The Canadian Medical Association

Secretary General, R.G. Wilson, M.D.,C.M., Box 8650, Ottawa, Ont. K1G 0G8 (613/731-9331)

Provincial Divisions

ALBERTA MEDICAL ASSOCIATION
9901 108th St., Edmonton, Alta. T5K 1G8
(403) 423-2295
Executive Director, Dr. R.F. Clark

BRITISH COLUMBIA MEDICAL ASSOCIATION
1807 W. 10th Ave., Vancouver, B.C. V6J 2A9
(604) 736-5551
Executive Director, Dr. F. Norman Rigby

MANITOBA MEDICAL ASSOCIATION
125 Sherbrook St., Winnipeg, Man. R3C 2B5
(204) 947-0421
Executive Vice President, R.P.H. Sprague

NEW BRUNSWICK MEDICAL SOCIETY
#209, 565 Priestman St., Fredericton, N.B. E3B 5X8
(506) 454-7745
Secretary, Dr. J.S. Bennett

NEWFOUNDLAND MEDICAL ASSOCIATION
O'Mara Martin Bldg., Rawlins Cross, St. John's, Nfld. A1C 2E4
(709) 726-7424
Executive Director, Gerald Lynch

MEDICAL SOCIETY OF NOVA SCOTIA
Sir Charles Tupper Bldg., 10th floor, Halifax, N.S. B3H 4H7
(902) 423-8166
Executive Secretary, Douglas Peacocke

ONTARIO MEDICAL ASSOCIATION
240 St. George St., Toronto, Ont. M5R 2P4
(416) 925-3264
General Secretary, Dr. E.J. Moran

PRINCE EDWARD ISLAND MEDICAL SOCIETY
279 Richmond St., Charlottetown, P.E.I. C1A 1J7
(902) 892-7527
Executive Secretary, Marilyn Lowther

QUEBEC MEDICAL ASSOCIATION
Ste. 1010, 1010 Sherbrooke St. W., Montreal, P.Q. H3A 2R7
(514) 282-1443
Executive Director, Dr. Gerald Caron

SASKATCHEWAN MEDICAL ASSOCIATION
211 Fourth Ave. S., Saskatoon, Sask. S7K 1N1
(306) 244-2196
Executive Director, Dr. E.H. Baergen

Affiliated Societies

CANADIAN ANAESTHETISTS' SOCIETY
178 St. George St., Toronto, Ont. M5R 2M7
(416) 923-1449
Honorary Secretary, Dr. D.V. Catton

CANADIAN ASSOCIATION OF MEDICAL CLINICS
500 Parliament St., Toronto, Ont. M4X 1P4

(416) 966-3641
Executive Director, D.O. Evelyn

Canadian Medical & Biological Engineering Society
Room 183, M-50, National Research Council of Canada, Ottawa, Ont. K1A OR8
(613) 993-2482
National Executive Secretary, N. Durie

Canadian Medical Protective Association
Carling Sq., 560 Rochester St. (Box 8225, Ottawa, Ont. K1G 3H7)
(613) 236-2100
Secretary Treasurer, Dr. F. Norman Brown

Canadian Neurological Society
Secretary Treasurer, Dr. Robert F. Nelson, Dept. of Medicine (Neurology), Health Sciences Centre, Ottawa General Hospital, 501 Smythe Rd., Ottawa, Ont. K1G 8L6

Canadian Ophthalmological Society
Box 8844, Ottawa, Ont. K1G 3J2
(613) 731-6493
Executive Director, J. Paul Le Bel

Canadian Orthopaedic Association
1117 St. Catherine St. W., Ste. 225, Montreal, P.Q. H3B 1H9
(514) 844-9818
Secretary, Dr. J.J. Wiley

Canadian Orthoptic Society
Secretary Treasurer, Pamela Fairchild, 4694 De La Peltrie, Montreal, P.Q. H3W 1K3

Canadian Osteopathic Association
575 Waterloo St., London, Ont. N6B 2R2
(519) 439-5521
Administrative Secretary, Mrs. Marguerite Torney
Provincial Affiliates
B.C.: Flora Barr, D.O., 461 Martin St., Penticton, B.C. V2A 5L1
Ont.: Wm. K. Church, D.O., 85 Neywash St., Orillia, Ont. L3V 1X4 (705/326-9551)
Prairie: Doris M. Tanner, D.O., 2228 Albert St., Regina, Sask. S4P 2V2

Canadian Otolaryngological Society
c/o McMaster Bldg., 170 Elizabeth St., #668, Toronto, Ont. M5G 1E8
(416) 597-1500, ext. 1559
Secretary, Dr. Wm. Crysdale, Hospital for Sick Children, Toronto
Editor, Dr. P. W. Alberti

Canadian Paediatric Society
Executive Vice President, Dr. V. Marchessault, Centre hospitalier universitaire de Sherbrooke, Sherbrooke, P.Q. J1H 5N4 (819/563-9844)

Canadian Physiotherapy Association
25 Imperial St., Toronto, Ont. M5P 1B9
(416) 485-1139
Executive Director, Mrs. Nancy Christie
Branches and/or Districts in all provinces.

Canadian Podiatry Association
President, Dr. N. Mathews, #217, 624 6th St., New Westminster, B.C. (604/521-7110)
Treasurer, Dr. I. Kaufman, 718 Second St. E., Cornwall, Ont. K6H 2A2
Secretary, Dr. S. Sackman, 37 Alvin Ave., Toronto, Ont. M4T 2A7 (416/967-6400)

Provincial Associations
Ont.: President, Dr. S. Freelan, 3415 Dixie Rd., Mississauga, Ont. L4Y 2B1 (416/625-6662)
B.C.: President, Dr. L. Virgil, #3, 811 Anderson Rd., Richmond, B.C. V6Y 1S1
Man.: President, Dr. J. Sinclair, 502 Boyd Bldg., Winnipeg, Man.
Alta.: Representative, Dr. R. Gorman, 528 Tegler Bldg., 10189 101 St., Edmonton, Alta. T5J OT8
Maritimes: Representative, Dr. Allen Sellars, 66 Waterloo St., Saint John, N.B.
Que.: Representative, Dr. Claude La Liberté, 1210 av. Franco-eur, Cap Rouge, P.Q.

Canadian Psychiatric Association
225 Lisgar St., Suite 103, Ottawa, Ont. K2P 0C6
(613) 234-2815
Chief Administrative Officer, Mrs. L. C. Metivier

Canadian Psychoanalytic Society (1967) Inc.
7000 Côte des Neiges Rd., Montreal, P.Q. H3S 2C1
(514) 738-6105
Executive Secretary, Mrs. N. Gargour

Canadian Psychological Association
Executive Director, Dr. T.V. Hogan, 558 King Edward Ave., Ottawa, Ont. K1N 7N6 (613/238-4409)

Canadian Society of Aviation Medicine
c/o Academy of Medicine, 288 Bloor St. W., Toronto, Ont. M5S 1V8
(416) 922-1134
Executive Secretary, Miss M.E. Wilson

Canadian Society of Chemotherapy
1329 Highgate Rd., Ottawa, Ont. K2C 2Y5

Canadian Society for Clinical Investigation
Secretary, Dr. Paul Kelly, Centre de Recherches en Endocrinologie Moléculaire, Le Centre Hospitalier de l'Université Laval, 2705 boul. Laurier, Québec, P.Q. G1V 4G2 (418/656-8253)

Canadian Society of Cytology
Secretary Treasurer, Dr. G.H. Anderson, Director of Laboratories, Cancer Control Agency of B.C., 2656 Heather St., Vancouver, B.C. V5Z 3J3

Canadian Society of Electroencephalographers Electromyographers & Clinical Neurophysiologists
c/o Dr. Andrew Eisen, President, C.S.E.E.C.N., Centre Hospitalier Universitaire, Université de Sherbrooke, Sherbrooke, P.Q. J1H 5N4 (819/563-5555)

Canadian Society of Laboratory Technologists
Box 830, Hamilton, Ont. L8N 3N8
(416) 528-8642
Executive Director, E. Valerie Booth

Canadian Society of Respiratory Technologists
395 Waterloo St., Winnipeg, Man. R3N 0S7
(204) 452-1207
Executive Secretary, H. Friesen
Official journal: 'Respiratory Technology'

Canadian Surgical Trade Association
131 John St. S., Ste. 106, Hamilton, Ont. L8N 2C3
(416) 522-2435
Executive Secretary, Fred Beldham

Canadian Urological Association
-not confirmed for 1982-
Dr. G.A. Farrow, Ste. 407, Medical Arts Bldg., 170 St. George St., Toronto, Ont. M5R 2M8 (416/962-0452)

College of Family Physicians of Canada
4000 Leslie St., Willowdale, Ont. M2K 2R9
(416) 493-7513
Executive Director, Dr. D. I. Rice
Editor of Official Journal, "Canadian Family Physician" Margaret McCaffery

Corporation professionnelle des orthophonistes et audiologistes du Quebec
(Speech & Hearing Society)
4770 rue de Salaberry, Montreal, P.Q. H4J 1H6
(514) 332-9090
Présidente, Fabienne Desroches, M.O.A.
Secrétaire trésorière, Monique Hébert-Talbot, M.A.

Federation of Medical Women of Canada
#201A, 1815 Alta Vista Dr., Ottawa, Ont. K1G 3Y6
(613) 731-1026

International Society of Endocrinology
1110 Pine Ave. W., Room 22, Montreal, P.Q. H3A 1A1
(514) 842-7548

The Medical Council of Canada
Address all communications to The Registrar, 1867 Alta Vista Dr., Box 8234, Ottawa, Ont. K1G 3H7 (613/521-6012)

Provincial Licensing Bodies

COLLEGE OF PHYSICIANS & SURGEONS OF ALBERTA
Registrar, L.H. le Riche, M.B., Ch.B., 9901 108 St., Edmonton, Alta. T5K 1G9 (403/422-6184)

COLLEGE OF PHYSICIANS & SURGEONS OF BRITISH COLUMBIA
Registrar, J.A. Hutchison, F.R.C.P. (C), 1807 W. 10th Ave., Vancouver, B.C. V6J 2A9 (604/736-5551)

COLLEGE OF PHYSICIANS & SURGEONS OF MANITOBA
Registrar, Dr. J.B. Morison, Ste. 1410, 155 Carlton St., Winnipeg, Man. R3C 3H8 (204/947-1694)

MEDICAL COUNCIL OF NEW BRUNSWICK
Registrar, Eric D. McCartney, M.D., F.R.C.S. (C), 10 Prince Edward St., Saint John, N.B. E2L 4M5 (506/652-5221)

NEWFOUNDLAND MEDICAL BOARD
Registrar, Dr. G.M. Brownrigg, 47 Queen's Rd., St. John's, Nfld. A1C 2A7 (709/726-8546)

PROVINCIAL MEDICAL BOARD OF NOVA SCOTIA
Registrar, Dr. M.R. Macdonald, #315, 5675 Spring Garden Rd., Halifax, N.S. B3J 1H1 (902/422-5823)

COLLEGE OF PHYSICIANS & SURGEONS OF ONTARIO
Registrar, Dr. M.E. Dixon, 64 Prince Arthur Ave., Toronto, Ont. M5R 1B4 (416/961-1711)

THE MEDICAL COUNCIL OF PRINCE EDWARD ISLAND
Registrar, Dr. S. MacDonald, 206 Spring Park Rd., Charlottetown, P.E.I. C1A 3Y9 (902/894-5316)

PROFESSIONAL CORPORATION OF PHYSICIANS OF QUEBEC/ CORPORATION PROFESSIONNELLE DES MEDECINS DU QUEBEC
President & Secretary General, Dr. A. Roy, 1440 St. Catherine St. W., Room 914, Montreal, P.Q. H3G 1S5 (514/878-4441)

COLLEGE OF PHYSICIANS & SURGEONS OF SASKATCHEWAN
Registrar, A.W. Thomson, M.D., C.M., 211 Fourth Ave. S., Saskatoon, Sask. S7K 1N1 (306/244-7355)

Medical Group Management Association of Canada
4101 E. Louisiana Ave., Denver, Colorado 80222
(303) 753-1111
Executive Director, Richard V. Grant, Ph.D.

Ontario Psychiatric Association
-not confirmed for 1982-
Executive Secretary, Mrs. Sharon Sanders, 9 Cherry St., London, Ont. N6H 1H5 (519/433-7628)

Ontario Psychological Association
1407 Yonge St., Ste. 402, Toronto, Ont. M4T 1Y7
(416) 961-5552
Executive Secretary, Grace Brooker

Royal College of Physicians & Surgeons of Canada
Executive Director, Dr. James H. Darragh, 74 Stanley Ave., Ottawa, Ont. K1M 1P4 (613/746-8177)

The Society of Obstetricians & Gynaecologists of Canada
288 Bloor St. W., Toronto, Ont. M5S 1V8
(416) 923-3513
Executive Director, Mrs. Ruth Stockdale

MEMORIAL SOCIETY ASSOCIATION OF CANADA
Box 96, Stn. A, Weston, Ont. M9N 3M6
(416) 241-6274

Affiliated Societies

ALBERTA
Calgary Co-op Memorial Society Ltd., Box 6443, Stn. D, Calgary, Alta. T2P 2E1
Memorial Society of Edmonton & District, 9326 157 St., Edmonton, Alta. T5R 2B1
Memorial Society of Grande Prairie, Box 471, Grande Prairie, Alta. T8V 3A7
Lloydminster, Vermilion & District Memorial Society, 4729 45 St., Lloydminster, Sask. S9V OH6
Memorial Society of Red Deer & District, Box 817, Red Deer, Alta. T4N 5H2
Memorial Society of Southern Alberta, 924 20th St. E., Lethbridge, Alta. T1J 3J7

FUNERAL PLANNING & MEMORIAL SOCIETY OF MANITOBA
790 Banning St., Winnipeg, Man. R3E 2H9

MEMORIAL SOCIETY OF NEW BRUNSWICK
Box 622, Fredericton, N.B. E3B 5A6

MEMORIAL & FUNERAL PLANNING ASSOCIATION OF NEWFOUNDLAND
Box 9183, St. John's, Nfld. A1A 2X9

NOVA SCOTIA
Memorial Society of Cape Breton, Box 934, Sydney, N.S. B1P 6J4
Greater Halifax Memorial Society, Box 291, Armdale, Halifax, N.S. B3L 4K1

ONTARIO
Memorial Society (Quinte), Box 477, Belleville, Ont. K8N 5B2
Memorial Society of Guelph, Box 1784, Guelph, Ont. N1H 7A1
Hamilton Memorial Society, Box 164, Hamilton, Ont. L8N 3A2
Memorial Society of Kingston, Box 1081, Kingston, Ont. K7L 4Y5
Kitchener-Waterloo Memorial Society, Box 113, Kitchener, Ont. N2G 3W9
Memorial Society of London, Box 1729, Stn. A, London, Ont. N6A 5H9
Niagara Peninsula Memorial Society, Box 2102, 4500 Queen St., Niagara Falls, Ont. L2E 6Z2
Ottawa Memorial Society, R.R. 7, 62 Steeple Hill Cres., Nepean, Ont. K2H 7V2
Memorial Society of Northern Ontario, Box 2563, Stn. A, Sudbury, Ont. P3A 4S9
Memorial Society of Peterborough & Dist., Box 1795, Peterborough, Ont. K9J 7X6
Memorial Society of Thunder Bay, Box 501, Stn. F, Thunder Bay, Ont. P7C 4W4

Toronto Memorial Society, Box 96, Stn. A, Weston, Ont. M9N 3M6
Memorial Society of Windsor, Box 481, Windsor, Ont. N9A 6M6

QUEBEC

L'Association Funeraire de Montreal, Box 400, Stn. C, Montreal, P.Q. H2L 4K3

MEMORIAL SOCIETY OF SASKATCHEWAN

Box 1846, Saskatoon, Sask. S7K 3S2

Non-Member Societies

MEMORIAL SOCIETY OF BRITISH COLUMBIA

#410, 207 W. Hastings St., Vancouver, B.C. V6B 1J3
Nanaimo Branch, Box 177, Nanaimo, B.C. V9R 5K9
Victoria Branch, Box 685, Victoria, B.C. V8W 2P9

MENSA CANADA SOCIETY

(The high I.Q. Society)
Box 505, Stn. S, Toronto, Ont. M5M 4L8
(416) 485-0406
Administrator, Julie Richards

MENTAL PATIENTS ASSOCIATION

2146 Yew St., Vancouver, B.C. V6K 3G7
(604) 738-5177

METIS ASSOCIATION OF THE NORTHWEST TERRITORIES

Box 1375, Yellowknife, N.W.T. XOE 1HO
(403) 873-3505

METRO CHINESE CENTRE FOR SOCIAL SERVICE & CULTURE

202 St. Patrick St., Toronto, Ont. M5T 1V4
(416) 598-3920
President, John B. Mak

METRO TORONTO LEGAL SECRETARIES ASSOCIATION

Box 5644, Stn. A, Toronto, Ont. M5W 1N8
(416) 922-4581
President, Miss Linda Brooks

THE MIGRAINE FOUNDATION

390 Brunswick Ave., Toronto, Ont. M5R 2Z4
(416) 920-4916
A non profit organization for migraine information, research, etc.

MILLWORK MANUFACTURERS ASSOCIATION

#242, 4299 Canada Way, Burnaby, B.C. V5G 1H3
(604) 438-6616
Secretary, E. Russell

MINERALOGICAL ASSOCIATION OF CANADA

c/o Royal Ontario Museum, 100 Queen's Park, Toronto, Ont. M5S 2C6
Subscription Manager, R. I. Gait
Official Publication, "The Canadian Mineralogist"

THE MINING ASSOCIATION OF CANADA

Ste. 705, 350 Sparks St., Ottawa, Ont. K1R 7S8 (613/233-9391)
Ste. 409, 36 Toronto St., Toronto, Ont. M5C 2C2 (416/363-8019)
Managing Director, John L. Bonus, Ottawa

MODEL AERONAUTICS ASSOCIATION OF CANADA, INC.

112 Cowan Ave., Box 9, Oakville, Ont. L6J 4Z5
(416) 844-8764
President, Gordon Van Tighem, Calgary

MONARCHIST LEAGUE OF CANADA

Dominion Secretary, Mrs. Felicity Burton, 2 Wedgewood Cres., Ottawa, Ont. K1B 4B4 (613/824-5225)
Library & Archives: #203, 3050 Yonge St., Toronto, Ont. M4N 2K4 (416/482-4157)

MOPED ASSOCIATION OF CANADA

6 Farmstead Rd., Willowdale, Ont. M2L 2G2
(416) 444-6387
Executive Director, Jack H. Hemmings

MOTION PICTURE THEATRE ASSOCIATIONS OF CANADA

175 Bloor St. E., Toronto, Ont. M4W 1C8
(416) 929-0865
President, Chris Salmon

MOTOR TRANSPORT INDUSTRIAL RELATIONS BUREAU OF ONTARIO INC.

48 Belfield Rd., Rexdale, Ont. M9W 1G1
(416) 247-6621
General Manager, John J. Cowan

MULTIPLE DWELLING STANDARDS ASSOCIATION

163 Beechwood Ave., Willowdale, Ont. M2L 1J9
(416) 449-7700
President & General Manager, Jan Schwartz

MULTIPLE SCLEROSIS SOCIETY OF CANADA

130 Bloor St. W., Ste. 700, Toronto, Ont. M5S 1N5
(416) 922-6065
Executive Director, Sheila Kieran
Division offices in Atlantic (Moncton), Que. (Montreal), Ont. (Toronto), Man. (Winnipeg), Sask. (Regina), Alta. (Edmonton), and B.C. (Vancouver).

MUNICIPAL ADMINISTRATIVE OFFICERS' ASSOCIATION OF NEW BRUNSWICK

(Association des Administrateurs Municipaux du Nouveaux-Brunswick)
President, Geoff Greenough, Deputy City Engineer, City of Moncton, 774 Main St., Moncton, N.B. E1C 1E8
Secretary, Sandra M. Allen, 390 King St., Ste. 3, Fredericton, N.B. E3B 1E3 (506/454-0240)

MUNICIPAL ENGINEERS ASSOCIATION

Secretary, R.A. Dempsey, P.Eng., County Engineer, County of Huron, Goderich, Ont. N7A 1M2

MUNICIPAL OFFICERS' ASSOCIATION OF BRITISH COLUMBIA

Secretary, W. Vollrath, Clerk, District of Surrey, 14245 56th Ave., Surrey, B.C. V3W 1J2 (604/591-4132) – to June, 1982

MUNICIPAL POLICE AUTHORITIES

Box 2161, Bramalea, Ont. L6T 3S4
(416) 793-4110
Secretary Treasurer, J.W. Montgomery

THE MUSCULAR DYSTROPHY ASSOCIATION OF CANADA

National Office, Ste. 1014, 74 Victoria St., Toronto, Ont. M5C 2A5
(416) 364-9079
Executive Director, J.J.G. Connors
Provincial chapters in Alberta, British Columbia, Saskatchewan, Manitoba, and Local chapters and committees in Ontario and Quebec.

MUSIC ORGANIZATIONS

(including Orchestras, Bands, Voice and Dance Groups)

ALBERTA BALLET COMPANY
9722 102 St., Edmonton, Alta. T5K 0X4
(403) 423-1332 (Toll free within Alberta 1-800-222-6406)
General Manager, Stanley Ware

ALBERTA MUSIC FESTIVAL ASSOCIATION
Secretary, Kathy Taft, #1, 7317 118 St., Edmonton, Alta. T6G 1S5 (403/436-6319, res.)

ALLIANCE CHORALE CANADIENNE
2118 est, Beaubien, Montreal, P.Q. H2G 1M6
(514) 729-7705
Alliance Chorale Alberta: 9942 82e ave., ste. 102, Edmonton, Alta. T6E 1Y9
Alliance Chorale Manitoba: 340 bld. Provencher, St-Boniface, Man. R2H 0G7
Alliance Chorale Ontario: 61 rue Wood, app 2, Kirkland Lake, Ont. P2N 3B7
Alliance Chorale du Quebec: 1415 Jarry est, Montréal, P.Q. H2E 2Z7
Alliance Chorale Nouveau-Brunswick: 236 St. Georges, #409, Moncton, N.B. E1C 1W1
Allicance Chorale Nouvelle-Ecosse: Meteghan, Cté Digby, N.S. B0W 2J0

ANNA WYMAN DANCE THEATRE
1705 Marine Dr., West Vancouver, B.C. V7V 1J5
(604) 926-8181

ASSOCIATED MANITOBA FESTIVALS, INC.
3rd floor, 200 Vaughan St., Winnipeg, Man. R3C 0V8
(204) 944-4578
Executive Director, Elizabeth Lupton Enns

THE ASSOCIATION OF CANADIAN ORCHESTRAS
56 the Esplanade, Ste. 311, Toronto, Ont. M5E 1A7
(416) 366-8834
Executive Director, Mrs. Betty Webster

ATLANTIC SYMPHONY ORCHESTRA
2011 Elm St., Halifax, N.S. B3L 2Y2
(902) 423-9294
Conductor, Victor Yampolsky
Executive Director, Mark J. Warren

LES BALLETS-JAZZ DE MONTREAL
1231, rue Ste Catherine ouest, Ste. 205, Montreal, P.Q. H3G 1P5
(514) 849-6071
Artistic Director, Genevieve Salbaing

BAROQUE STRINGS OF VANCOUVER
Manager, Ian Hampton, #301, 1209 Ridgeway Ave., Coquitlam, B.C. V3J 1S8 (604/939-9167)
Leader, Gwen Thompson

BARRIE CHAMBER MUSIC SOCIETY
Director, Lloyd Tufford, 22 Shirley Ave., Barrie, Ont. L4N 1M9 (705/728-5017)

BRANTFORD SYMPHONY ORCHESTRA ASSOCIATION
General Manager, Mrs. Diana Taylor, Box 101, Brantford, Ont. N3T 5M3 (519/759-8781)

BRITISH COLUMBIA MUSIC FESTIVAL ASSOCIATION
Secretary, Mrs. J.F.K. English, 329 Arnold Ave., Victoria, B.C. V8S 3L6 (604/598-7608)

CALGARY FESTIVAL CHORUS
President, Julie Jacques, 1201 Lismer Green, Varsity Courts, Calgary, Alta. T3B 2V7 (403/289-6228)

CALGARY MUSICIANS ASSOCIATION
#703, 630 8th Ave. S.W., Calgary, Alta. T2P 1G6
(403) 261-0783
Secretary Treasurer, Ray Petch

CALGARY PHILHARMONIC SOCIETY
#200, 505 5th St. S.W., Calgary, Alta. T2P 3J2
(403) 269-8201
General Manager, John F. Shaw

THE CALGARY YOUTH ORCHESTRA SOCIETY
4825 Richard Rd. S.W., Calgary, Alta. T3E 6K6
(403) 246-6451
Conductor & Music Director, F.C. Simpson

"CAMMAC" (Canadian Amateur Musicians/Musiciens Amateurs du Canada)
-not confirmed for 1982-
Music Library, Newsletter and Music Camp, Box 353, Westmount, P.Q. H3Z 2T5 (514/932-8755)

CANADIAN ASSOCIATION OF YOUTH ORCHESTRAS
(Association des Orchestres des Jeunes du Canada)
Box 1020, Banff, Alta. TOL OCO
(403) 762-6278
Executive Director, Roger Breault

THE CANADIAN BAND DIRECTORS ASSOCIATION
National Secretary, F. McKinnon, 21 Tecumseh St., Brantford, Ont. N3S 2B3 (519/753-1858)

CANADIAN BUREAU FOR THE ADVANCEMENT OF MUSIC
Music Bldg., Exhibition Place, Toronto, Ont. M6K 3C3
(416) 366-7551
Managing Director, Lt.-Col. C.O. Hunt, C.D.
National Co-ordinator, Nancy M. Owen

CANADIAN FEDERATION OF MUSIC TEACHERS' ASSOCIATIONS
President, Kathleen Fensom, 5 Weldon St., Sackville, N.B. E0A 3C0
Secretary Treasurer, Mrs. Doris W. Phillips, 812 Haig Rd., Ancaster, Ont. L9G 3G9 (416/648-4711)

CANADIAN LEAGUE OF COMPOSERS
c/o Josette Fitch, Canadian Music Centre, 1263 Bay St., Toronto, Ont. M5R 2C1 (416/964-1364)

CANADIAN MUSIC CENTRE
1263 Bay St., Toronto, Ont. M5R 2C1
(416) 961-6601
Calgary: 9th floor, University Library Tower, University of Calgary, Calgary, Alta. T2N 1N4 (403/284-7403)
Montreal: 1259, rue Berri, bur. 300, Montreal, P.Q. H2L 4C7 (514/849-9175)
Vancouver: No. 3, 2007 W. 4th Ave., Vancouver, B.C. V6J 1N3 (604/734-4622)

CANADIAN MUSIC COMPETITIONS INC./CONCOURS DE MUSIQUE DU CANADA INC.
1600 Berri, #267, Montréal, P.Q. H2L 4E4
(514) 844-8836
General Director, Claude Deschamps

CANADIAN MUSIC COUNCIL
36 Elgin St., Ottawa, Ont. K1P 5K5
(613) 238-5893
President, George Laverock
Secretary General, Guy Huot

CANADIAN MUSIC EDUCATORS ASSOCIATION
National Resource Centre, Box 1461, St. Catharines, Ont. L2R 7J8
(416) 684-4664
Music Resource Co-ordinator, Wallace Laughton

CANADIAN MUSIC FESTIVAL ADJUDICATORS ASSOCIATION
Secretary Treasurer, Christine Wilcosz-Thompson, 121 Robertson Ave., Chatham, Ont. N7M 3A9 (519/352-3679)

CANADIAN MUSIC PUBLISHERS ASSOCIATION
111 Avenue Rd., Ste. 702, Toronto, Ont. M5R 3J8
(416) 922-4170

CANADIAN OPERA COMPANY
417 Queen's Quay W., Toronto, Ont. M5V 1A2
(416) 363-6671
General Director, Lotfi Mansouri

CENTRE DE MUSIQUE CANADIENNE
1259 rue Berri, bur. 300, Montreal, P.Q. H2L 4C7
(514) 849-9175

CHAMBER PLAYERS OF TORONTO
Box 5428, Stn. A, Toronto, Ont. M5W 1N6

(416) 421-3425
Music Director / Admr., Winston Webber

LA COMPAGNIE DE DANSE EDDY TOUSSAINT
551 Mont Royal est, Montreal, P.Q. H2J 1W6
(514) 524-3749

CONCOURS INTERNATIONAL DE MONTREAL
106, ave. Dulwich, St. Lambert, P.Q. J4P 2Y7
(514) 671-3186

CONTEMPORARY DANCERS
2nd floor, 444 River Ave., Winnipeg, Man. R3L 0C7
(204) 452-1239
Executive Director, Tom Scurfield

DANCE IN CANADA ASSOCIATION
100 Richmond St. E., Ste. 325, Toronto, Ont. M5C 2P9
(416) 368-4793

DANCE NOVA SCOTIA (DANS)
Box 3595 South, Halifax, N.S. B3J 3J2
(902) 422-1749

EAST YORK SYMPHONY
550 Mortimer Ave., Toronto, Ont. M4J 2H2
(416) 461-9451
Conductor, Clifford Poole

EDMONTON OPERA ASSOCIATION
#503, 10102 101 St., Edmonton, Alta. T5J OS5
(403) 422-4919
Administrative Director, Lorin J. Moore
Artistic Director, Irving Guttman

EDMONTON SYMPHONY SOCIETY
11712 87th Ave., Edmonton, Alta. T6G OY3
(403) 439-2091
Executive Director & General Manager, W.R. Palmer
Music Director & Principal Conductor, Uri Mayer

ETOBICOKE PHILHARMONIC SOCIETY
511 The West Mall, #1206, Etobicoke, Ont. M9C 1G5
(416) 239-5665
Manager, Mrs. Peggy Pinkerton

FEDERATION OF CANADIAN MUSIC FESTIVALS
540 Cordova St., Winnipeg, Man. R3N 1A7
(204) 489-5850
Executive Director, G.M. Campbell

THE FEDERATION OF MUSIC FESTIVALS OF NOVA SCOTIA
Secretary, Mrs. R.E. Baker, 21 Oakburn Court, Clayton Park, Halifax, N.S. B3M 2W5 (902/443-2471)

LES GRANDS BALLETS CANADIENS
Maison de la Danse, 4869 rue St-Denis, Montréal, P.Q. H2J 2L7
(514) 849-8681
Directeur général, Colin McIntyre

GROUPE NOUVELLE AIRE
1270 rue Saint-André, ste 2, Montreal, P.Q. H2L 3S9
(514) 286-9697

HAMILTON PHILHARMONIC SOCIETY INC.
Hamilton Place, Box 2080, Stn. A, Hamilton, Ont. L8N 3Y7
(416) 526-8800
General Manager, Hamish Robertson
Music Director & Conductor, Boris Brott

THE HURONIA SYMPHONY ORCHESTRA
Conductor, Arthur G. Burgin, 222 Grove St. E., Barrie, Ont.
Treasurer, David B. Croft, Box 904, Barrie, Ont. L4M 4Y6

INTERNATIONAL SYMPHONY ORCHESTRA OF SARNIA & PORT HURON
1700 Winton Rd., Sarnia, Ont. N7V 4B9
(519) 542-5801
General Manager, Mrs. J.J. Kovac

INTERNATIONAL YOUTH SYMPHONY
Manager, Mrs. Matti Holli, 8717 Riverside Dr. E., Apt. 509, Windsor, Ont. N8S 1G6

JEUNESSES MUSICALES DU CANADA
5253 ave du Parc, Ste. 600, Montreal, P.Q. H2V 4P2
(514) 271-2566
Directeur, Jean-Claude Picard

KINGSTON SYMPHONY ASSOCIATION
Box 1616, Kingston, Ont. K7L 5C8
(613) 546-9729
Manager, C.S. Smith
Conductor, Dr. Alexander Brott

KITCHENER-WATERLOO SYMPHONY ORCHESTRA ASSOCIATION INC.
101 Queen St. N., Kitchener, Ont. N2H 6P7
(519) 745-4711
Music Director, Raffi Armenian
General Manager, A.R. Shaw

KIWANIS MUSIC FESTIVAL ASSOCIATION OF GREATER TORONTO
223 St. Clair Ave. W., Toronto, Ont. M4V 1R3
(416) 964-9094

LADIES' MORNING MUSICAL CLUB
1410 Guy St., Room 32, Montreal, P.Q. H3H 2L7
(514) 932-6796
Secretary Treasurer, Mme S.M. Gamache

LETHBRIDGE SYMPHONY ASSOCIATION
Box 1101, Lethbridge, Alta. T1J OW5
(403) 328-6808
Conductor, Stewart Grant
President, S.R. Wild

LONDON SYMPHONY ORCHESTRA
520 Wellington St., London, Ont. N6A 3P9
(519) 433-6912
General Manager, Wesanne McKellar
Music Director, Alexis Hauser

MANITOBA MUSIC COMPETITION FESTIVAL
3rd Floor, 200 Vaughan St., Winnipeg, Man. R3C 1T5
(204) 944-4575
Secretary, Miss Isobel Caldwell

MANITOBA OPERA ASSOCIATION
#121, 555 Main St., Winnipeg, Man. R3B 1C3
(204) 942-4567

MARIPOSA FOLK FOUNDATION
525 Adelaide St. E., Toronto, Ont. M5A 3W4
(416) 363-4009

McGILL CHAMBER ORCHESTRA
1745 Cedar Ave., Montreal, P.Q. H3G 1A7
(514) 935-4955
Conductor, Dr. Alexander Brott
Manager, Mrs. Lotte Brott, 5459 Earnscliffe Ave., Montreal, P.Q. H3X 2P8

THE MEN'S MUSIC CLUB
President, G.M. Campbell, 3rd Floor, 200 Vaughan St., Winnipeg, Man. R3C 1T5 (204/944-4575)

MISSISSAUGA SYMPHONIC ASSOCIATION
Administrative Director, Miss Lynn Osmond, 161 Lakeshore Rd. W., Mississauga, Ont. L5H 1G3 (416/274-1571)

MONTREAL CIVIC YOUTH ORCHESTRA
#809, 1155 Metcalfe St., Montreal, P.Q. H3B 2V6
(514) 878-9680
President, Sandra Wilson

MONTREAL INTERNATIONAL COMPETITION
Director general, Monique Marcil, 106 Dulwich Ave., St. Lambert, P.Q. J4P 2Y7 (514/671-3186)

MUSIC INDUSTRIES ASSOCIATION OF CANADA
#1101, 130 Bloor St. W., Toronto, Ont. M5S 2X7
(416) 964-2875
Executive Secretary, A. Kowalenko

NANAIMO SYMPHONY SOCIETY
Box 661, Nanaimo, B.C. V9R 5L9
Secretary, John Barker

NATIONAL ARTS CENTRE ORCHESTRA
(Orchestra du Centre National des Arts)

Box 1534, Stn. B, Ottawa, Ont. K1P 5W1
(613) 996-5051
Conductor & Music Director, Mario Bernardi
Manager, John D. Kieser

THE NATIONAL BALLET OF CANADA
St. Lawrence Hall, 157 King St. E., Toronto, Ont. M5C 1G9
(416) 362-1041
Artistic Director, Alexander Grant
Administrative Director, Robert Johnston

NATIONAL COMPETITIVE FESTIVAL OF MUSIC
546 Cordova St., Winnipeg, Man. R3N 1A7
(204) 489-5850

NATIONAL YOUTH ORCHESTRA ASSOCIATION OF CANADA
76 Charles St. W., Toronto, Ont. M5S 1K8
(416) 922-5031
General Director, John Brown

NEPEAN SYMPHONY ORCHESTRA
65 Bentley Ave., Nepean, Ont. K2E 6T7
(613) 224-5523
Conductor, James Wegg

NEW BRUNSWICK COMPETITIVE FESTIVAL OF MUSIC
Box 2022, Saint John, N.B. E2L 3T5

NEW BRUNSWICK FEDERATION OF MUSIC FESTIVALS INC.
-not confirmed for 1982-
Secretary, Mrs. Georges Lauzier, 190 Blvd. J.D. Gauthier, Shippegan, N.B. EOB 2PO (506/336-4323)

NEW BRUNSWICK YOUTH ORCHESTRA
Box 2204, Saint John, N.B. E2L 3V1
(506) 693-6533

NEW CHAMBER ORCHESTRA
1240 Bay St., Ste. 805, Toronto, Ont. M5R 2A7
(416) 691-4660
Musical Director, W. Phillips
Manager, Len Hanna

NEWFOUNDLAND SYMPHONY ORCHESTRA
-not confirmed for 1982-
Conductor, David Gray, c/o Arts & Culture Centre, Prince Philip Dr., St. John's, Nfld. A1C 5P9 (709/753-6492)

NIAGARA SYMPHONY ASSOCIATION
Box 401, St. Catharines, Ont. L2R 6V9
(416) 685-7358
General Manager, Ian Spraggon

NORTH YORK SYMPHONY ASSOCIATION
1210 Sheppard Ave. E., #109, Willowdale, Ont. M2K 1E3
(416) 499-2204
General Manager, Wm. E. Ward

OAKVILLE SYMPHONY ORCHESTRA INC.
Box 125, Oakville, Ont. L6J 4Z9
(416) 844-8197

ONTARIO CHORAL FEDERATION
208 Bloor St. W., Ste. 303, Toronto, Ont. M5S 1T8
(416) 925-5525

THE ONTARIO FEDERATION OF SYMPHONY ORCHESTRAS
56 the Esplanade, Ste. 311, Toronto, Ont. M5E 1A7
(416) 366-8834
Executive Director, Mrs. Betty Webster

ONTARIO MUSIC FESTIVAL ASSOCIATION INC.
223 St. Clair Ave. W., Toronto, Ont. M4V 1R3
(416) 964-6618
Secretary, Mrs. Dorcas Plant

OPERA CANADA
366 Adelaide St. E., Ste. 433, Toronto, Ont. M5A 3X9
(416) 363-0395

THE OPERA GUILD INC.
3001 Sherbrooke St. W., Apt. 202, Montreal, P.Q. H3Z 2X8
(514) 933-6951
President, Mrs. Maurice Berne
Honorary Secretary, Mrs. F. Beaudoin, Handfield

OPERA DE MONTREAL
Place des Arts, 1501 Jeanne-Mance St., Montreal, P.Q. H2X 1Z9
(514) 842-2141
Directeur artistique, Jean-Paul Jeannotte

ORCHESTRE SYMPHONIQUE DE MONTREAL
Place des Arts, 200, de Maisonneuve Blvd. W., Montreal, P.Q. H2X 1Y9
(514) 844-2867
Music Director, Charles Dutoit
Managing Director, Zarin Mehta

L'ORCHESTRE SYMPHONIQUE DE QUEBEC
350 est boul. St-Cyrille, bur 201, Québec, P.Q. G1R 2B4
(418) 643-5598
Directeur artistique, James DePreist
Directeur général, François Magnan

ORCHESTRE SYMPHONIQUE DE SHERBROOKE
C.P. 1022, Sherbrooke, P.Q. J1H 5L3
(819) 565-4692
President, Dr. Antoni Trias, 465 rue Montmagny, Sherbrooke

OSHAWA SYMPHONY ORCHESTRA
Box 444, Oshawa, Ont. L1H 7L5
(416) 579-6711
Conductor, Winston Webber, 322 Eglinton Ave. E., #1103, Toronto, Ont. M4P 1L6

OTTAWA CHORAL SOCIETY
Box 952, Stn. B, Ottawa, Ont. K1P 5R1
(613) 820-1700
Music Director, Brian Law

OTTAWA MUSIC FESTIVAL ASSOCIATION
Box 6091, Stn. J, Ottawa, Ont. K2A 1T2
(613) 746-7386

OTTAWA SYMPHONY ORCHESTRA
Box 3644, Stn. C, Ottawa, Ont. K1Y 4J7
Music Director, Brian Law
Manager, W.G. Robson, 1533 Caton St., Ottawa, Ont. K1H 6J3 (613/733-2548)

OTTAWA YOUTH ORCHESTRA
Secretary, Mrs. H.E. Morris, 1680 Mallard Dr., Ottawa, Ont. K2C 1A2 (613/225-4561)

THE PAULA ROSS DANCE SOCIETY
3488 W. Broadway, Vancouver, B.C. V6R 2B3
(604) 732-9513

PETERBOROUGH SYMPHONY ORCHESTRA
Box 1135, Peterborough, Ont. K9J 7H4
(705) 742-1992

PRINCE EDWARD ISLAND MUSIC FESTIVAL ASSOCIATION
Secretary, Mrs. Eunice Wonnacott, 45 Roper Dr., Charlottetown, P.E.I. C1A 6J1 (902/894-4363)

QUEBEC MUSIC COMPETITIONS INC./CONCOURS DE MUSIQUE DU QUEBEC INC.
1600 Berri St., Ste. 267, Montreal, P.Q. H2L 4E4
(514) 844-8836
Deputy General Director, Hélène M. Stevens

REGINA MODERN DANCE WORKSHOP
1915 Osler St., Regina, Sask. S4P 1W3
(306) 527-0656
Director, Jo-Ann R. Olyowsky

REGINA SYMPHONY ORCHESTRA
200 Lakeshore Dr., Regina, Sask. S4S OB3
(306) 586-9555
General Manager, Ann Hewat

RICHARD EATON SINGERS
Secretary, Brian Burrows, 600 West Chambers, 12220 Stony Plain Rd., Edmonton, Alta. T5N 3Y4 (403/482-5802)

THE ROYAL ACADEMY OF DANCING
Executive Secretary, Doreen Scouler, Ste. 209, 3050 Yonge St., Toronto, Ont. M4N 2K4 (416/489-2813)

THE ROYAL CANADIAN COLLEGE OF ORGANISTS
212 King St. W., Ste. 300A, Toronto, Ont. M5H 1K5
(416) 593-4025
Secretary, T.J. Hillier, Mus. Bac.

THE ROYAL WINNIPEG BALLET
289 Portage Ave., Winnipeg, Man. R3B 2B4
(204) 956-0183
General Manager, William Riske
Artistic Director, Arnold Spohr

THE SASKATCHEWAN MUSIC FESTIVAL ASSOCIATION
#210, 3806 Albert St., Regina, Sask. S4S 3R2
(306) 586-3388
Executive Director, Kathleen Keple

THE SASKATCHEWAN REGISTERED MUSIC TEACHERS' ASSOCIATION
c/o Hallie Inglis, #33, 2022 Lorne St., Regina, Sask. S4P 2M3 (306/522-8700)

THE SASKATOON SYMPHONY ORCHESTRA
Box 1361, Saskatoon, Sask. S7K 3N9
(306) 665-6414

ST. LAWRENCE CHOIR
Box 141, Lachine, P.Q. H8S 4A6
(514) 695-7148

SOCIETE PRO-MUSICA INC.
1270, Sherbrooke St. W., Montreal, P.Q. H3G 1H7 (514/845-0532)

SOUTHERN ALBERTA OPERA ASSOCIATION
#3, 6025 12 St. S.E., Calgary, Alta. T2H 2K1
(403) 252-9905
General Manager, Brian M. Hanson

SUDBURY SYMPHONY ORCHESTRA ASSOCIATION
St. Andrew's Place, Box 1015, 111 Larch St., Sudbury, Ont. P3E 4T5
(705) 673-1280
General Manager, C. Littlehales

THUNDER BAY SYMPHONY ORCHESTRA ASSOCIATION INC.
Box 2004, Thunder Bay, Ont. P7B 5E7
(807) 344-0631, or 344-0612
Conductor & Music Director, Dwight Bennett
General Manager, (vacant)

TORONTO DANCE THEATRE
80 Winchester St., Toronto, Ont. M4X 1B2
(416) 967-1365
Managing Director, Dr. Roger Jones

TORONTO MENDELSSOHN CHOIR
151 Bloor St. W., #455, Toronto, Ont. M5S 1S4
(416) 961-3840

TORONTO SYMPHONY
215 Victoria St., Toronto, Ont. M5B 1V1
(416) 363-0374
Managing Director, Walter Homburger
(also Toronto Symphony Youth Orchestra)

VANCOUVER BALLET SOCIETY
926 W. Broadway, Vancouver, B.C.
(604) 669-6714

VANCOUVER NEW MUSIC SOCIETY
Box 4941, Vancouver, B.C. V6B 4A6
(604) 669-0909

VANCOUVER OPERA ASSOCIATION
111 Dunsmuir St., Vancouver, B.C. V6B 1W8
(604) 682-2871

VANCOUVER PHILHARMONIC ORCHESTRA
-not confirmed for 1982-
Box 35406, Stn. E, Vancouver, B.C. V6M 4G5
Music Director, Jerry Domer

VANCOUVER SOCIETY FOR EARLY MUSIC
1254 W. 7th Ave., Vancouver, B.C. V6H 1B7
(604) 732-1610

VANCOUVER SYMPHONY SOCIETY
Conductor, Kazuyoshi Akiyama
Managing Director, Michael Allerton, 873 Beatty St., Vancouver, B.C. V6B 2M6 (604/689-1411)

VICTORIA SYMPHONY SOCIETY
Manager, J.A. Wilson, 631 Superior St., Victoria, B.C. V8V 1V1 (604/385-9771)

WESTERN BOARD OF MUSIC
Central Office: University of Alberta, Edmonton, Alta. T6G 2E6 (403/432-3264)
Chairman, Professor G.E. Lincoln

Representing the Music Departments of the Universities of Manitoba, Brandon, Saskatchewan, Regina, Alberta, Calgary and Lethbridge.

WESTERN CANADIAN OPERA SOCIETY
Box 5105, Vancouver, B.C. V6B 4A9
(604) 987-7465

WINDSOR SYMPHONY SOCIETY
586 Ouellette Ave., #307, Windsor, Ont. N9A 1B8
(519) 254-4337
Music Director & Conductor, Laszlo Gati
Manager, Margaret Krause

WINNIPEG SYMPHONY ORCHESTRA
Room 117, 555 Main St., Winnipeg, Man. R3B 1C3 (204/942-4576)
Artistic Advisor, Franz-Paul Decker
Executive Director, J.M. Mills

WOODSTOCK STRINGS
General Manager, Gordon Latford, R.R. 6 Woodstock, Ont. N4S 7W1 (519/537-5147)

YORK SYMPHONY ORCHESTRA INC.
Box 355, Richmond Hill, Ont. L4C 4Y6
Conductor, Clifford Poole, 33 Harbour Sq., Apt. 1835, Toronto, Ont. (416/869-0153)

THE NATIONAL ACTION COMMITTEE ON THE STATUS OF WOMEN
40 St. Clair Ave. E., Ste. 306, Toronto, Ont. M4T 1M9
(416) 922-3246
Official Publication: "Status of Women News"
Membership Publication: "Memo"

NATIONAL ANTI-POVERTY ORGANIZATION
3101B Hawthorne Rd., Ottawa, Ont. K1G 3V8
(613) 523-8001

NATIONAL ASSOCIATION OF CANADIAN RACE TRACKS INC.
Ste. 607, 555 Burnhamthorpe Rd., Etobicoke, Ont. M9C 2Y3
(416) 622-6561
Executive Vice President, David Gorman

NATIONAL ASSOCIATION OF FRIENDSHIP CENTRES
(an association of native peoples)
200 Cooper St., Ste. 3, Ottawa, Ont. K2P OG1
(613) 563-4844
Executive Director, Bill Lee

Provincial Offices
Alta.: 10172 117 St., Edmonton, Alta. T5K 1X3 (403/488-5112)
B.C.: c/o 319 N. Fraser Dr., Quesnel, B.C. V2J 1V8 (604/992-8347)
Man.: 503 Main St., #1004, Winnipeg, Man. R3B 1B8 (204/943-8082)
Ont.: 234 Eglinton Ave. E., Toronto, Ont. M4P 1K5 (416/484-1411)
Que.: 5333 Sherbrooke E., Apt. 1009B, Montreal, P.Q. H1T 3W2 (514/254-2257)
Sask.: 1950 Broad St., 2nd Floor, Regina, Sask. S4P 1X9 (306/523-4743)

NATIONAL ASSOCIATION OF TOBACCO & CONFECTIONERY DISTRIBUTORS
-not confirmed for 1982-
Longueuil Industrial Park, 2025 de la Métropole Ave., Longueuil, P.Q. J4G 1S9
(514) 679-2212
Executive Manager, John L. Cunningham

NATIONAL ASSOCIATION OF WOMEN & THE LAW
Box 197, Stn. B, Ottawa, Ont. K1P 6C4

NATIONAL CANCER INSTITUTE OF CANADA
130 Bloor St. W., #1001, Toronto, Ont. M5S 2V7
(416) 961-7223
Executive Vice President, Dr. R.A. Macbeth

NATIONAL CITIZENS' COALITION
Ste. 907, 100 Adelaide St. W., Toronto, Ont. M5H 1S3
(416) 869-3838
President, Colin Brown

NATIONAL CONCRETE PRODUCERS' ASSOCIATION
1013 Wilson Ave., #101, Downsview, Ont. M3K 1G1
(416) 635-7179
Executive Director, M.A. Patamia

NATIONAL COUNCIL OF CANADIAN LABOUR
53 Queen St., Suite 10, Ottawa, Ont. K1P 5C5
(613) 233-7852

The National Council of Canadian Labour is a federation of Canadian trade unions that stands for a policy of Canadian unionism.

Member unions are located in Que., Ont., Man., Sask., and Alta.

President, John Nelson, London
General Secretary, Clive Thomas, Ottawa

NATIONAL COUNCIL OF INDUSTRIAL MANAGEMENT CLUBS OF CANADA
One Yonge St., 14th floor, Toronto, Ont. M4E 1J1
(416) 363-7261
Executive Director, John Martin

THE NATIONAL COUNCIL OF WOMEN OF CANADA
270 MacLaren St., Ottawa, Ont. K2P 0M3
(613) 233-4953
President, Mrs. J.W. (Amy) Williams, 750 50th, Lachine, P.Q. H3J 2T8

THE NATIONAL COUNCIL OF YOUNG MEN'S CHRISTIAN ASSOCIATIONS OF CANADA (YMCA)
2160 Yonge St., Toronto, Ont. M4S 2A9
(416) 485-9447
General Secretary, R. G. Rogers
Business Administrator, J. O. Pollock
Geneva Park Conference Centre, Executive, Russell E. Davey

NATIONAL DESIGN COUNCIL
235 Queen St., Ottawa, Ont. K1A OH5
(613) 992-0341
Executive Director, P.C. Fredenburgh

NATIONAL FRATERNAL SOCIETY OF THE DEAF
Chief Canadian Agent, Roger McAuley, 49 Frey Cres., Scarborough, Ont. M1R 2C5 (416/757-5263)
Deputy Chief Agent, John Potts, 47 Jackman Ave., Toronto, Ont. M4K 2X5 (463-7111)

NATIONAL HOCKEY LEAGUE PLAYERS' ASSOCIATION
65 Queen St. W., #210, Toronto, Ont. M5H 2M5
(416) 868-6574
Executive Director, R. A. Eagleson

NATIONAL INDIAN BROTHERHOOD
222 Queen St., 5th Floor, Ottawa, Ont. K1P 5V9
(613) 236-0673
President, Delbert Riley

NATIONAL INSTITUTE OF GOVERNMENTAL PURCHASING, INC.
1735 Jefferson Davis Hwy., Arlington, VA 22202
Executive Vice President, Lewis E. Spangler
Canadian Education Committee of NIGP: Box 275, Etobicoke, Ont. M9C 4V3

NATIONAL INSTITUTE ON MENTAL RETARDATION
York Univ. Campus, 4700 Keele St., Downsview, Ont. M3J 1P3
(416) 661-9611
Director, Jacques Pelletier

NATIONAL MULTICULTURAL THEATRE ASSOCIATION
8 York St., 6th floor, Toronto, Ont. M5J 1R2
(416) 366-9694

THE NATIONAL PENSIONERS & SENIOR CITIZENS FEDERATION
3505 Lakeshore Blvd. W., Toronto, Ont. M8W 1N5
(416) 251-7042
President, Charles McDonald, #902, 8888 Riverside E., Windsor, Ont. N8S 1H2

NATIONAL & PROVINCIAL PARKS ASSOCIATION OF CANADA
47 Colborne St., Suite 308, Toronto, Ont. M5E 1E3
(416) 366-3494

Local Chapters
B.C.: Box 6007, Stn. C, Victoria, B.C. V8P 5L4
Calgary/Banff: Box 608, sub. P.O. 91, Univ. of Calgary, Calgary, Alta. T2N 1N4
Edmonton: c/o 3071 116 St., Edmonton, Alta. T6J 3T2
Ottawa/Hull: Box 400, Stn. A, Ottawa, Ont. K1N 8V4 (613/731-2243)
Algonquin: c/o #308, 47 Colborne St., Toronto, Ont. M5E 1E3
Sask.: Box 1624, Prince Albert, Sask. S6X 5T2

NATIONAL RETINITIS PIGMENTOSA FOUNDATION OF CANADA
1 Spadina Cres., #115, Toronto, Ont. M5S 2J5
(416) 368-3809
President, J.N. Marin
Executive Director, Mrs. Sandie Burke

NATIONAL SANITARIUM ASSOCIATION
Box 100, Commerce Court Postal Stn., Toronto, Ont. M5L 1B9
(416) 862-4537

THE NATIONAL SECRETARIES ASSOCIATION (INTERNATIONAL)
2440 Pershing Rd., Suite G-10, Kansas City, Missouri, 64108, U.S.A.
Executive Director, Audrey Forman, CPS (act.)

CANADA DISTRICT
Director, Sandra Godwin, 1816 Applegrove Court, Ottawa, Ont. K1J 6S5

ONTARIO DIVISION
President, Betty Akers, Churchill, Ont. L0L 1K9

EASTERN CANADA DIVISION
President, Linda Furlought, CPS, Capital Region Dev. Comn. Inc., 358 King St., Fredericton, N.B. E3B 1E3

WESTERN CANADA DIVISION
President, Vera N. Poulos, Murphy Oil Co., 540 5th Ave. S.W., Calgary, Alta. T2P 2M7

NATIONAL SOCIETY OF FUND RAISING EXECUTIVES (CANADIAN CHAPTER)
Chairman, John Martin, 28 Geneva Ave., Toronto, Ont. M5A 2J8

NATIONAL SURVIVAL INSTITUTE
229 College St., Toronto, Ont. M5T 1R4
(416) 593-1299
Executive Director, Beatrice Olivastri

NATIONAL UNION OF STUDENTS
2nd floor, 126 York St., Ottawa, Ont. K1N 5T5
(613) 232-7394
Executive Officer, John Doherty

NATIVE ALCOHOLISM COUNCIL OF MANITOBA
#203, 865½ Main St., Winnipeg, Man. R2W 2N9
(204) 947-1805
Executive Director, Stanley Fontaine, Jr.
Supervisor Counsellor, Ivy Domin

PRITCHARD HOUSE REHAB CENTRE
456 Pritchard Ave., Winnipeg, Man. R2W 2J7
(204) 582-6411
Supervisor, Elizabeth Fontaine

NATIVE BROTHERHOOD OF BRITISH COLUMBIA
#517, 193 E. Hastings St., Vancouver, B.C. V6A 1N7
(604) 685-2255

NATIVE CANADIAN CENTRE OF TORONTO
16 Spadina Rd., Toronto, Ont. M5R 2S8
(416) 964-9087
Executive Director, Edward Buller

NATIVE CLAN ORGANIZATION INC.
#620, 504 Main St., Winnipeg, Man. R3B 1B8
(204) 943-7357
Executive Director, Curtis Fontaine

NATIVE COUNCIL OF CANADA
5th Floor, 170 Laurier Ave. W., Ottawa, Ont. K1P 5V5
(613) 238-3511

NATIVE WOMEN'S ASSOCIATION OF CANADA
222 Queen St., 5th Floor, Ottawa, Ont. K1P 5V9
(613) 236-6057
Executive Director, Agnes Mills

THE NAVY LEAGUE OF CANADA
Affiliated with the Navy League of the World
National Headquarters, 4 Queen Elizabeth Dr., Ottawa, Ont. K2P 2H9
(613) 232-2784
National Secretary, W. J. Hodge

Divisions with Secretaries

Alta.: Northern Alta. Division, Mrs. E. Tomas, Box 19, Site 8, R.R. 2, Sherwood Park, Alta. T8A 3K2
Southern Alta. Division, Mrs. A. Thompson, #3 Brae Glen Court S.W., Calgary, Alta. T2W 1B6
B.C.: Mainland Division, Mrs. M. Lee, 1565 19th St., West Vancouver, B.C. V7V 3X5
Vancouver Island Division, Mrs. S.M. Walker, 8632 Llewellyn Place, Sidney, B.C. V8L 1G7
Man.: Man. Division, Miss M. Timoney, #905, 800 Corydon Ave., Winnipeg, Man. R3M OY3
N.B.: N.B. Division, Secretary, Box 6956, Stn. A, Saint John, N.B. E2L 4S4
Nfld.: Nfld. & Labrador Division, Mrs. J. Hallett, 8 Burns Place, St. John's, Nfld. A1A 2B6
N.S.: N.S. Mainland Division, I.A. MacPherson, Esq., Meander R.R. 3, New Port, N.S. B0N 2A0
Cape Breton Division, Mrs. C. Hillier, 26 East St., Sydney, N.S. B1N 1S4
Ont.: Ont. Division, J. Crist, 1107 Avenue Rd., Room 314, Toronto, Ont. M5N 2E4
P.E.I.: P.E.I. Division, W. Whittaker, Glenfinnan, R.R. 5, Charlottetown, P.E.I. C1A 7J8
Que.: Que. Division, Secretary, 4846 Sherbrooke St. W., Room 105, Westmount, P.Q. H3Z 1G8
Sask.: Sask. Division, P.T. Gellvear, 1825 Grant Dr., Regina, Sask. S4S 4V5

THE NEW BRUNSWICK COALITION OF STUDENTS
c/o The Students Union, University of N.B., Fredericton, N.B. E3B 5A3 (506/453-4955)

NEW BRUNSWICK FOREST PRODUCTS ASSOCIATION INC.
500 Beaverbrook Court, Fredericton, N.B. E3B 5X4
(506) 455-0998
Executive Director, D.D. Lockhart

NEWFOUNDLAND HISTORICAL SOCIETY
Colonial Bldg., Room 15, St. John's, Nfld. A1C 2C9
(709) 722-3191
Office Secretary, Mrs. Bobbie Robertson

NEWFOUNDLAND INSTITUTE FOR MANAGEMENT ADVANCEMENT & TRAINING
Box 9554, St. John's, Nfld. A1A 2Y4
(709) 753-3707
Executive Director, Raymond D. Martin

NEWFOUNDLAND & LABRADOR FEDERATION OF MUNICIPALITIES
Executive Director, William B. Titford, 197 Water St., Box 5756, St. John's, Nfld. A1C 5X3 (709/753-6820)

NEWFOUNDLAND OUTPORT NURSING & INDUSTRIAL ASSOCIATION (NONIA)
286 Water St., St. John's, Nfld. A1C 1B7
(709) 753-8062
Manageress, Miss Florence Chafe

NEWFOUNDLAND SHIPOWNERS, AGENTS & BROKERS ASSOCIATION
Box 8900, Stn. A, (90 O'Leary Ave.), St. John's, Nfld. A1B 3R9
(709) 726-7223; Telex 016-4785

NEWSPAPER ADVERTISING EXECUTIVES ASSOCIATION OF CANADA
President, George Willcocks, "The Calgary Herald", 206 7th Ave. S.W., Calgary, Alta. T2P 0W8 (403/269-6211)

THE NINETY-NINES INC.
(International Organization of Women Pilots)
c/o Toronto Airways, Buttonville Airport, Buttonville, Ont.
Eastern Canada Governor: Virginia Cunningham, R.R. 2, MacPherson Dr., Corbeil, Ont. P0H 1K0 (705/752-2002)
Western Canada Governor: Rosella Bjornson, Box 333, Stony Mountain, Man. R0C 3A0 (204/344-5993)

NON-SMOKERS' RIGHTS ASSOCIATION
455 Spadina Ave., #201, Toronto, Ont. M5S 2G8
(416) 595-1538
Executive Director, Garfield Mahood

THE NORTH AMERICAN TRACKLESS TROLLEY ASSOCIATION, INC.
Box 565, Oshawa, Ont. L1H 7L9
(416) 725-3943
Manager, Member Services, T.G.J. Gascoigne

NORTHERN AIR TRANSPORT ASSOCIATION
Box 2457, Yellowknife, N.W.T. X0E 1H0
(403) 873-4477
Secretary Treasurer, Joe Sparling

NORTHERN ASSOCIATION OF COMMUNITY COUNCILS, INC.
#411, 259 Portage Ave., Winnipeg, Man. R3B 2A9
(204) 949-1439

NORTHEASTERN ONTARIO MUNICIPAL ASSOCIATION
Secretary Treasurer, T.E. Monahan, Box 601, Matheson, Ont. P0K 1N0

NORTHWESTERN ONTARIO MUNICIPAL ASSOCIATION
Secretary Treasurer, J. MacDonald, City Hall, Brodie St., Thunder Bay, Ont. P7E 5V3 (807/623-2711, ext. 271)

NOVA SCOTIA DRAMA LEAGUE
5516 Spring Garden Rd., Ste. 305, Halifax, N.S. B3J 1G6
(902) 425-3876
Executive Director, Penelope Harwood

NOVA SCOTIA FOREST PRODUCTS ASSOCIATION
30 Mill St., Box 696, Truro, N.S. B2N 5E5
(902) 895-1179
Executive Director, Lorne E. Etter

NOVA SCOTIA INSTITUTE OF ASSESSORS
Secretary, Ms. Mora Smith, Box 706, Sydney, N.S. B1P 6H7 (902/539-4900)

NUCLEAR INSURANCE ASSOCIATION OF CANADA
180 Dundas St. W., Toronto, Ont. M5G 1Z9
(416) 597-1200
Manager, D.B. Wood

NURSING ASSOCIATIONS

The Alberta Association of Registered Nursing Orderlies
10112 124 St., Edmonton, Alta. T5N 1P6
Executive Secretary, John F. Nimeck

Canadian Association of Practical & Nursing Assistants
National Secretary, Mrs. Joan Hayman, R.R. 4, St. Stephen, N.B. E3L 2Y2 (506/466-1049)

Provincial Associations

ALBERTA ASSOCIATION OF REGISTERED NURSING ASSISTANTS
17410 107 Ave., Edmonton, Alta. T5S 1E9
(403) 483-8126
Executive Director, Kathleen L. Thompson

BRITISH COLUMBIA COUNCIL OF PRACTICAL NURSES
3405 Willingdon Ave., Burnaby, B.C. V5G 3H4
(604) 434-4247
Registrar, Ivy E. McGowan

LICENSED PRACTICAL NURSES ASSOCIATION OF BRITISH COLUMBIA
Secretary, Mrs. Gerrie Fehr, 695 Montague Rd., Nanaimo, B.C. V9R 3G4 (604/754-9170)

MANITOBA ASSOCIATION OF LICENSED PRACTICAL NURSES
Ste. 1, 130 Marion St., Winnipeg, Man. R2H OT4
(204) 233-0291

ASSOCIATION OF NEW BRUNSWICK REGISTERED NURSING ASSISTANTS
39 Coventry Cres., Fredericton, N.B. E3B 4P4
(506) 454-0747
Executive Director, Mrs. Inez Smith

NOVA SCOTIA ASSOCIATION OF CERTIFIED NURSING ASSISTANTS
5614 Fenwick St., Halifax, N.S. B3H 1P9

ONTARIO ASSOCIATION OF REGISTERED NURSING ASSISTANTS
112 Merton St., 3rd floor, Toronto, Ont. M4S 1A1
(416) 484-1369

PRINCE EDWARD ISLAND LICENSED NURSING ASSISTANTS ASSOCIATION
Box 1253, Charlottetown, P.E.I. C1A 7M8
(902) 566-1512

CORPORATION PROFESSIONNELLE DES INFIRMIERES ET INFIRMIERS AUXILIAIRES DU QUEBEC
1980 Sherbrooke ouest, bur. 920, Montreal, P.Q. H3H 1E8
(514) 932-1491

SASKATCHEWAN NURSING ASSISTANTS' ASSOCIATION
2066 Retallack St., Regina, Sask. S4T 2K2
(306) 527-4643

Canadian Nurses Association
50 The Driveway, Ottawa, Ont. K2P 1E2
(613) 237-2133
Executive Director, Ginette Rodger

Provincial Associations

ALBERTA ASSOCIATION OF REGISTERED NURSES
Executive Director, Miss Yvonne Chapman, 10256 112th St., Edmonton, Alta. T5K 1M6 (403/426-0160)

REGISTERED NURSES' ASSOCIATION OF BRITISH COLUMBIA
Executive Director, Miss Marilyn Carmack, 2855 Arbutus St., Vancouver, B.C. V6J 3Y8 (604/736-7331)

MANITOBA ASSOCIATION OF REGISTERED NURSES
Executive Director, Miss M. Louise Tod, 647 Broadway Ave., Winnipeg, Man. R3C 0X2 (204/774-3477)

NEW BRUNSWICK ASSOCIATION OF REGISTERED NURSES
Executive Director, Ms. Bonny Hoyt, 231 Saunders St., Fredericton, N.B. E3B 1N6 (506/454-5591)

ASSOCIATION OF REGISTERED NURSES OF NEWFOUNDLAND
Executive Secretary, Mrs. Violet Ruelokke, 55 Military Rd., St. John's, Nfld. A1C 2C5 (709/753-6040)

REGISTERED NURSES' ASSOCIATION OF NOVA SCOTIA
Executive Secretary, Mrs. Joan Mills, 6035 Coburg Rd., Halifax, N.S. B3H 1Y8 (902/423-6156)

REGISTERED NURSES' ASSOCIATION OF ONTARIO
Executive Director, Ms. Maureen Powers, 33 Price St., Toronto, Ont. M4W 1Z2 (416/923-3523)

ASSOCIATION OF NURSES OF PRINCE EDWARD ISLAND
Executive Director/Registrar, Marilyn Nicholson, 41 Palmers Lane, Charlottetown, P.E.I. C1A 5V7 (902/892-6322)

ORDRE DES INFIRMIERES ET INFIRMIERS DU QUEBEC
Executive Director & Secretary, Thérèse Guimond, 4200 Dorchester Blvd. W., Montreal, P.Q. H3Z 1V4 (514/935-2501)

SASKATCHEWAN REGISTERED NURSES' ASSOCIATION
Executive Director, Margaret Rosso, 2066 Retallack St., Regina, Sask. S4T 2K2 (306/527-4643)

NORTHWEST TERRITORIES REGISTERED NURSES' ASSOCIATION
Executive Director, Mrs. Dianne Mercredi, Box 2757, Yellowknife, N.W.T. XOE 1HO (403/873-4932)

Psychiatric Nurses Association of Canada
1854 Portage Ave., Winnipeg, Man. R3J 0G9
(204) 885-1298
Secretary, Marlene Fitzsimmons

Provincial Associations

PSYCHIATRIC NURSES' ASSOCIATION OF ALBERTA
Box 755, Ponoka, Alta. TOC 2HO
(403) 783-3102

REGISTERED PSYCHIATRIC NURSES ASSOCIATION OF BRITISH COLUMBIA
7790 Edmonds St., Burnaby, B.C. V3N 1B8
(604) 524-1396

REGISTERED PSYCHIATRIC NURSES' ASSOCIATION OF MANITOBA
1854 Portage Ave., Winnipeg, Man. R3J 0G9
(204) 888-4841

PSYCHIATRIC NURSES ASSOCIATION OF NOVA SCOTIA
Box 40, Waterville, N.S. B0P 1V0

PSYCHIATRIC NURSES' ASSOCIATION OF ONTARIO
52 Forest St., Guelph, Ont. N1G 1H9

SASKATCHEWAN PSYCHIATRIC NURSES' ASSOCIATION
Ste. D, 2835 13th Ave., Regina, Sask. S4T 1N6
(306) 522-6691

PSYCHIATRIC NURSES ASSOCIATION OF NORTHWEST TERRITORIES
Box 1102, Yellowknife, N.W.T. XOE 1HO

St. Elizabeth Visiting Nurses Association
90 Stinson St., Hamilton, Ont. L8N 1S2
(416) 522-6887
Executive Director, Mrs. Sharon Campbell

Victorian Order of Nurses for Canada
National Office, 5 Blackburn Ave., Ottawa, Ont. K1N 8A2
(613) 233-5694
National Director, Miss A. E. McEwen

NURSING HOMES ASSOCIATIONS

ASSOCIATED HOMES FOR SPECIAL CARE (NOVA SCOTIA)
President, H.R. Saulnier, Box 248, Meteghan, N.S. B0W 2J0 (902/645-2065)

NURSING HOME ASSOCIATION OF MANITOBA
#1201, 155 Carlton St., Winnipeg, Man. R3C 3H8
(204) 957-0905
Secretary Treasurer, K.A. Kurbis

ONTARIO NURSING HOME ASSOCIATION
6075 Yonge St., 5th floor, Willowdale, Ont. M2M 3W2
(416) 224-2282
Executive Director, J.K. Maynard

SASKATCHEWAN ASSOCIATION OF SPECIAL CARE HOMES
Ste. B, 1445 Park St., Regina, Sask. S4N 4C5
(306) 565-0744
Executive Director, B. Wasiuta

OMNICHILD FOUNDATION INC.
Yorkdale Shopping Centre, Unit 56, Toronto, Ont. M6A 2T9
(416) 783-2142

A non-profit medical service organization providing free medical aid to needy children of the developing countries.
Secretary, Mrs. H. F. Spitzen

ONE PARENT FAMILIES ASSOCIATION OF CANADA
2279 Yonge St., Ste. 17, Toronto, Ont. M4P 2C7
(416) 487-7976
Secretary, Sheila Neely

ONTARIO ARENAS ASSOCIATION INC.
Secretary Manager, C.C. Dahmer, Box 177, 6570 Frederica St., Niagara Falls, Ont. L2E 6T3 (416/358-5252)

ONTARIO ASSOCIATION OF ART GALLERIES
c/o Rory O'Donal, 38 Charles St. E., Toronto, Ont. M4Y 1T3 (416/920-8378)

ONTARIO ASSOCIATION OF CEMETERIES
c/o Robert D. Old, Elgin Mills Cemetery, 1723 Elgin Mills Rd. E., R.R. 2, Gormley, Ont. L0H 1G0 (416/887-9317)

ONTARIO ASSOCIATION OF CHIEFS OF POLICE
Secretary Treasurer, E.G. Snider, 25 Murray St., Barrie, Ont. L4N 2X1 (705/728-5588)

ONTARIO ASSOCIATION OF CHILDREN'S AID SOCIETIES
2323 Yonge St., #505, Toronto, Ont. M4P 2C9
(416) 481-5223
Executive Director, George Caldwell

THE ONTARIO ASSOCIATION OF CORRECTIONS & CRIMINOLOGY
-not confirmed for 1982-
Room 1601, 100 Adelaide St. W., Toronto, Ont. M5H 1S3
(416) 366-9511
President, A. B. Whitelaw, Q.C.
Secretary, Edith Bater, Unified Family Court, Hamilton

ONTARIO ASSOCIATION OF CREDIT COUNSELLING SERVICES
168 Lakeshore Rd. E., Box 248, Oakville, Ont.L6J 5A2
(416) 845-3851
Executive Director, Ronald M. Mason

ONTARIO ASSOCIATION OF FAMILY SERVICE AGENCIES
3rd floor, 17 Dundonald St., Toronto, Ont. M4Y 1K5
(416) 961-1632
Executive Director, Paddy Ann Pogsley

ONTARIO ASSOCIATION OF FIRE CHIEFS
55 King William St., Hamilton, Ont. L8R 1A2
(416) 522-1155
Secretary, Chief L.G. Saltmarsh

ONTARIO ASSOCIATION FOR MARRIAGE & FAMILY THERAPY
271 Russell Hill Rd., Toronto, Ont. M4V 2T5
(416) 485-1217
Secretary, Reesa Kassirer, M.S.W.

ONTARIO AVIATION COUNCIL
c/o Armadale Co., Toronto Buttonville Airport, Buttonville, Ont.
(416) 297-2600 –Toronto line 364-9483
Secretary, Mark Hinchcliffe

ONTARIO AVIATION ENTHUSIASTS SOCIETY
Box 72, Malton PO, Mississauga, Ont. L4T 3B5
Chairman, A.P. Cardadeiro (416/366-4153)

ONTARIO CHECKER ASSOCIATION
President, F.E. Kendall, 113 Maybourne Ave., Scarborough, Ont. M1L 2W5 (416/755-7854)

ONTARIO COALITION OF RAPE CRISIS CENTRES
5 Douglas St., 2nd Floor, Guelph, Ont. N1H 2S8
(519) 821-9191
Provincial Office Co-ordinator, Holly Cole

THE ONTARIO FEDERATION OF STUDENTS
643 Yonge St., Toronto, Ont. M4Y 1Z9
(416) 925-3825

ONTARIO ELECTRICAL LEAGUE
700 University Ave., Toronto, Ont. M5G 1X6
(416) 592-3861
Manager, D.A. Beattie

ONTARIO FAMILY COURT JUDGES' ASSOCIATION
Mailing address: Judge James Karswick, Secretary, Provincial Court (Family Division), 311 Jarvis St., Toronto, Ont. M5B 2C4
(416) 963-0660
Contact Person: Judge Karswick's Secretary

ONTARIO FILM ASSOCIATION, INC.
Box 366, Stn. Q, Toronto, Ont. M4T 2M5
Membership Secretary, Ms. J. Macdonald, 130 George Henry Blvd., #603, Willowdale, Ont. M2J 1G3 (416/494-2165)

ONTARIO FOREST INDUSTRIES ASSOCIATION
#1700, 130 Adelaide St. W., Toronto, Ont. M5H 3P5
(416) 368-6188
President, K.D. Greaves

ONTARIO FROZEN FOOD COUNCIL
Secretary, Joyce Bird, 2395 Cawthra Rd., #1, Mississauga, Ont. L5A 2W8 (416/276-6727)

THE ONTARIO GENEALOGICAL SOCIETY
Box 66, Stn. Q, Toronto, Ont. M4T 2L7
(416) 921-4606
Publication, "Families"

ONTARIO GOOD ROADS ASSOCIATION
Box 128, 354 Talbot St., St. Thomas, Ont. N5P 3T7
(519) 631-6820
Secretary Treasurer, B. J. McCaffery

ONTARIO HISTORICAL SOCIETY
78 Dunloe Rd., #207, Toronto, Ont. M5P 2T6
(416) 486-1232
Executive Asst., Sandra Morton

ONTARIO INDUSTRIAL DEVELOPMENT COUNCIL INC.
9835 Esplanade Dr., Windsor, Ont. N8R 1J7
(519) 735-3615

An organization of Industrial Development Officers of Ontario communities and of chartered banks, railroads, utilities and regional areas, and Government Officials of the Ontario Ministry of Industry & Tourism. The object of the Council is to provide a medium of conference and interchange of ideas on principles, practices and ethics in the field of industrial development at the municipal level.

Executive Secretary, Dianne Moore

ONTARIO INDUSTRIAL ROOFING CONTRACTORS' ASSOCIATION
Ste. 404, 5233 Dundas St. W., Islington, Ont. M9B 1A6
(416) 239-9655

ONTARIO INSURANCE ADJUSTERS ASSOCIATION
Group Box 16, Site 2, R.R. 1, Brechin, Ont. LOK 1BO
(705) 484-5561

ONTARIO LUMBER MANUFACTURERS' ASSOCIATION
159 Bay St., Suite 414, Toronto, Ont. M5J 1J7
(416) 367-9717
President, O.G. Korpela

ONTARIO MARINA OPERATORS ASSOCIATION
95 Manitoba St., #5, Bracebridge, Ont. P0B 1C0
(705) 645-6001

ONTARIO METIS & NON-STATUS INDIAN ASSOCIATION
5385 Yonge St., Ste. 30, Willowdale, Ont. M2N 5R7
(416) 226-2890
President, Duke Redbird

ONTARIO MORTGAGE BROKERS ASSOCIATION
3 Church St., #407, Toronto, Ont. M5E 1M2
(416) 364-4027
Secretary, Bernard Gershman

ONTARIO MOVERS ASSOCIATION
555 Dixon Rd., Rexdale, Ont. M9W 1H8
(416) 247-7131
Executive Director, Brian Crowe

ONTARIO MUNICIPAL ADMINISTRATORS' ASSOCIATION
100 University Ave., Ste. 1108, Toronto, Ont. M5J 1V6
(416) 593-1400
Secretary Treasurer, G.E. Gunning

ONTARIO MUNICIPAL ELECTRIC ASSOCIATION
2323 Yonge St., Toronto, Ont. M4P 2C9
(416) 483-7739
Executive Director, E.C. Nokes

ONTARIO MUNICIPAL PERSONNEL ASSOCIATION
100 University Ave., Ste. 902, Toronto, Ont. M5J 1V6
(416) 593-1441
Secretary Treasurer, Rita McCarthy

ONTARIO MUNICIPAL RECREATION ASSOCIATION
8 York St., Toronto, Ont. M5J 1R2
(416) 368-1709
Executive Director, Ms. P. Artkin

ONTARIO MUNICIPAL SOCIAL SERVICES ASSOCIATION
#509, 12 Sheppard St., Toronto, Ont. M5H 3A1
(416) 366-7145
Executive Director, Nathan Gilbert

ONTARIO MUNICIPAL WATER ASSOCIATION
President, C.J. Byrne, 1322 Lesperance Rd., Windsor, Ont. N8N 1X7
Secretary, A.L. Furanna, London Public Utilities Commission, 300 Dufferin Ave., Box 2700, London, Ont. N6A 4H6 (519/679-5470)
Treasurer, D.R. Larkworthy, Stratford Public Utilities Commission, 187 Erie St., Box 397, Stratford, Ont. N5A 6T5 (519/271-2020)

ONTARIO MUSEUM ASSOCIATION
38 Charles St. E., Toronto, Ont. M4Y 1T1
(416) 923-3868
Executive Director, John McAvity

ONTARIO MUZZLE LOADING ASSOCIATION
Director & Secretary, Linda Hounslow, 1465 Paddington Crt., Burlington, Ont. L7M 1W7 (416/639-1082)

ONTARIO PAINTING CONTRACTORS ASSOCIATION
#218, 85 Ellesmere Rd., Scarborough, Ont. M1R 4B9
(416) 444-7958
President & General Manager, Kelvin N. Edgar

ONTARIO PARKS ASSOCIATION
Secretary, W.H. Palmer, 15 Wintemute St., Fort Erie, Ont. L2A 2N7 (416/871-2518)

ONTARIO PLUMBING INSPECTORS ASSOCIATION
Secretary, F. Penfold, Gregory Rd., R.R. 3, St. Catharines, Ont. L2R 6P9 (416/685-9402)

ONTARIO PRESS COUNCIL
151 Slater St., Suite 708, Ottawa, Ont. K1P 5H3
(613) 235-3847
Executive Secretary, Fraser MacDougall

ONTARIO PROFESSIONAL FIRE FIGHTERS ASSOCIATION
555 Burnhamthorpe Rd., Ste. 210, Etobicoke, Ont. M9C 2Y3
(416) 622-1767
Executive Secretary Treasurer, Ed. Hothersall

ONTARIO PROFESSIONAL FORESTERS ASSOCIATION
10271 Yonge St., Ste. 303, Richmond Hill, Ont. L4C 3B5
(416) 884-7845
Executive Secretary, Mrs. M. J. Beresford

ONTARIO PROVINCIAL POLICE ASSOCIATION
119 Ferris Lane, Barrie, Ont. L4M 2Y1
(705) 728-6161
Executive Manager, J.M. Kingston

ONTARIO PUBLIC BUYERS ASSOCIATION
President, H.D. Patterson, Purchasing Agent, Town of Halton Hills, 36 Main St. S., Georgetown, Ont. L7G 4X1 (416/877-5185)
Secretary, Clifford Stewart, Purchasing Agent, Town of Richmond Hill, Box 300, Richmond Hill, Ont. (416/884-8101)

ONTARIO PUBLIC HEALTH ASSOCIATION
7 Carlis Place, Mississauga, Ont. L5G 1A8
(416) 274-4104
Secretary Treasurer, David Burton

ONTARIO SEWER & WATERMAIN CONTRACTORS ASSOCIATION
6299 Airport Rd., Ste. 702, Mississauga, Ont. L4V 1N3
(416) 677-0470
Executive Director, Clarence W. Delion

ONTARIO SHADE TREE COUNCIL
Executive Director, W. D. Truman, 7241 Jane St., Concord, Ont. L4K 1A7 (416/669-1827)

ONTARIO SHEET METAL & AIR HANDLING GROUP
1 Sparks Ave., Suite T6, (City of North York), Willowdale, Ont. M2H 2W1
(416) 497-2211
Executive Director, L. Cianfarani

TORONTO SHEET METAL & AIR HANDLING GROUP
As above

RESIDENTIAL SHEET METAL CONTRACTORS ORGANIZATION
As above

ONTARIO SNOWMOBILE INDUSTRY ASSOCIATION
Box 20, Stn. Q, Toronto, Ont. M4T 2P2
(416) 249-2677

ONTARIO SOCIETY FOR AUTISTIC CHILDREN
4800 Dundas St. W., #01, Islington, Ont. M9A 1B1
(416) 239-2462
Executive Director, B. Harrower

ONTARIO SWIMMING POOL ASSOCIATION
6 Lansing Sq., Ste. 217, Willowdale, Ont. M2J 1T5
(416) 496-1917
Administrator, Richard Hubbard

ONTARIO TEMPORAL BONE BANK
c/o Banting Institute, 100 College St., Toronto, Ont. M5G 1L5 (416/978-6103)
Co-ordinator, Mrs. Helen Bryce

ONTARIO TRAFFIC CONFERENCE
20 Carlton St., #121, Toronto, Ont. M5B 2H5
(416) 598-4138
Administrative Manager, A.M. Eason
A voluntary association founded for the improvement of traffic conditions and traffic safety in the municipalities of Ontario.

THE ONTARIO WATCHMAKERS ASSOCIATION
R.R. 1, Cookstown, Ont. LOL 1LO
(705) 458-9221
Executive Secretary, Robert Phillip

ONTARIO WATER WORKS EQUIPMENT ASSOCIATION
3526 Lakeshore Blvd. W., Toronto, Ont. M8W 1N7
(416) 259-4211
Secretary Treasurer, H.C. Greer

ONTARIO WELFARE COUNCIL, INC.
1240 Bay St., Suite 404, Toronto, Ont. M5R 2A7
(416) 961-4771
Executive Director, Elwood Springman

OPERATION EYESIGHT UNIVERSAL
Box 123, Calgary, Alta. T2P 2H6
(403) 283-6323
President, A.T. Jenkyns

ORDER OF THE EASTERN STAR
Grand Chapter of Ontario
Grand Secretary, Mrs. Mary Smith, Lutterworth Pines Dr., R.R. 1, Minden, Ont. K0L 2K0 (705/286-1715)

THE ORDER OF SONS OF ITALY IN CANADA
505 Jean Talon St. E., Montreal, P.Q. H2R 1T6
(514) 271-2281
Secretary, F. Pantaleo

L'ORDRE DES INGENIEURS FORESTIERS DU QUEBEC
2022, rue Lavoisier, bur. 165, Ste-Foy, P.Q. G1N 4L5
(418) 683-2379
Secrétaire général, Marc Côté, ing.f.

ORGAN DONORS CANADA
5326 Ada Blvd., Edmonton, Alta. T5W 4N7
(403) 474-9363
Executive Director, Mrs. Mae Cox

An organization to assist the process of anatomical gift giving in Canada.

ORGANISMES FAMILIAUX ASSOCIES DU QUEBEC
#310, 2335 Sherbrooke ouest, Montreal, P.Q. H3H 1G6
(514) 849-7347
Secrétaire général, Mme Denise Laporte-Dubuc

ORGANIZATON FOR THE AID & PROMOTION OF SEARCH & RESCUE
-not confirmed for 1982-
B208 Forrest Dr. Manor, Yellowknife, N.W.T. X0E 1H0
(403) 873-2582
Managing Director, Susan Milligan

ORGANIZATION OF SMALL URBAN MUNICIPALITIES (ONTARIO)
-not confirmed for 1982-
Secretary, B.W. Baxter, 55 King St. W., Cobourg, Ont. K9A 2M2 (416/372-2288)

ORTHODOX CHRISTIAN EDUCATIONAL SOCIETY
(Saints Kyril & Methody)
Box 404, Chilliwack, B.C. V2P 6J7
(604) 858-7750

THE OTTAWA FIELD-NATURALISTS' CLUB
Corresponding Secretary, E.F. Pope, Box 3264, Stn. C, Ottawa, Ont. K1Y 4J5
Editor of "The Canadian Field Naturalist", Dr. Francis R. Cook, c/o Herpetology Section, National Museum of Natural Sciences, Ottawa, Ont. K1A 0M8

OUTDOOR ADVERTISING ASSOCIATION OF CANADA
Ste. 1610, 439 University Ave., Toronto, Ont. M5G 1Y8
(416) 598-4672
President, J. H. C. Penaligon

OVERSEAS BOOK CENTRE
(Centre du livre pour outre-mer)

A non-profit, voluntary organization which provides books, educational supplies and paper to schools, training centres and libraries in over 80 developing countries. OBC also provides funds to local groups for the production of educational material in local languages and on relevant topics.
321 Chapel St., Ottawa, Ont. K1N 7Z2
(613) 232-3569
National Director, Robert Dyck

Affiliated Branches
B.C.: 7920 River Rd., Richmond, B.C. (604/261-0970)
Alta.: 10255 104th St., Edmonton, Alta. (403/466-0818, 427-8805)
2519 Richmond Rd. S.W., Calgary, Alta. (403/249-4141)
Sask.: 1306 Lorne Ave., Saskatoon, Sask. (306/374-4010)
Man.: 145 McDermot St., 4th floor, Winnipeg, Man. (204/889-7122)
Ont.: 896 Queen St. W., Toronto, Ont. (416/532-8310)
321 Chapel St., Ottawa, Ont. (613/232-3569)
Que.: 181 Bourget St., Montreal, P.Q. (514/934-0329)
N.S.: 5985 Inglis St., Halifax, N.S. (902/523-2850)

OXFAM-CANADA
251 Laurier St. W., Ste. 301, Ottawa, Ont. K1P 5J6
(613) 237-5236
National Secretary, Lawrence Cumming

Providing relief and development assistance to Third World peoples, and aiding certain Canadian projects, primarily northern native peoples.

PACKAGING ASSOCIATION OF CANADA
10 St. Mary St., Toronto, Ont. M4Y 1P9
(416) 929-3194
President, Lyn G. Jamison

PAHONIA–BYELORUSSIAN-CANADIAN PUBLISHERS & ART CLUB
524 St. Clarens Ave., Toronto, Ont. M6H 3W7
(416) 461-3992
Secretary, K. Akula

PAN MACEDONIAN ASSOCIATION
406 Danforth Ave., Toronto, Ont. M4J 1P4
(416) 463-4424

PARENT FINDERS INC.
120 Eglinton Ave. E., 7th Floor, Toronto, Ont. M4P 1E2
(416) 483-1358

PARENTS WITHOUT PARTNERS INC.
International Headquarters, 7910 Woodmont Ave., Washington, D.C. 20014
Canadian Office, 205 Yonge St., Toronto, Ont. M5B 1N2 (416/363-0960). Office hours 10 a.m. to 3 p.m. Closed Wed.

PARLIAMENTARY CENTRE FOR FOREIGN AFFAIRS & FOREIGN TRADE
60 Queen St., Ottawa, Ont. K1P 5Y7
(613) 237-0143
Director, Peter C. Dobell

PARTICIPaction
80 Richmond St. W., #805, Toronto, Ont. M5H 2A4
(416) 361-0514
President, Russ Kisby

An independent government funded organization to improve the fitness and sports participation of all Canadians.

PATENT & TRADEMARK INSTITUTE OF CANADA
Box 1298, Stn. B, Ottawa, Ont. K1P 5R3
(613) 234-0516
Recording Secretary, Mrs. Noreen Cassidy

PEOPLE OR PLANES
Box 159, Claremont, Ont. LOH 1EO
(416) 294-1396
Office Manager, Mrs. Pat McClennan

PERFORMING RIGHTS ORGANIZATION OF CANADA LTD.
41 Valleybrook Dr., Don Mills, Ont. M3B 2S6
(416) 445-8700

An organization to serve the creators and users of music in Canada.
625 President Kennedy Ave., #1601, Montreal, P.Q. H3A 1K2 (514/849-3294)
1462 W. Pender St., Vancouver, B.C. V6G 2S2 (604/6887851)

PERIODICAL PRESS ASSOCIATION
100 University Ave., #508, Toronto, Ont. M5J 1V6
(416) 593-5497
President, Allan Goldenberg

Constituent Associations

AGRICULTURAL PRESS ASSOCIATION OF CANADA
President, Allan Goldenberg

CANADIAN BUSINESS PRESS
President & Chief Executive Officer, Allan Goldenberg

MAGAZINE PUBLISHERS ASSOCIATION OF CANADA
Chairman, L.M. Hodgkinson

PERIODICAL WRITERS ASSOCIATION OF CANADA
24 Ryerson Ave., 1st floor, Toronto, Ont. M5T 2P3
(416) 868-6913
Executive Director, Anne Billings

PERSONNEL ASSOCIATION OF TORONTO INC.
Ste. 601, 2 Bloor St. W., Toronto, Ont. M4W 3E2
(416) 925-1169
Executive Director, R.W. Redford
Program Director, Wayne Lamon

PET FOOD MANUFACTURERS ASSOCIATION OF CANADA
Ste. 101, 1185 Eglinton Ave. E., Don Mills, Ont. M3C 3C6
(416) 429-1073
Manager, Ms. Susan Watanabe

PHARMACEUTICAL ASSOCIATIONS

Association of Canadian Community Pharmacists
321 Kerr St., Oakville, Ont. L6K 3B6
(416) 845-4276
Executive Secretary, D.A. Manore

Association of Deans of Pharmacy in Canada
Secretary Treasurer, Dr. M.J. Huston, Faculty of Pharmacy, University of Alberta, Edmonton, Alta. T6G 2N8

Association of Faculties of Pharmacy of Canada
Executive Director, Dr. J.A. Wood, c/o College of Pharmacy, University of Saskatchewan, Saskatoon, Sask. S7N OWO (306/343-4779)

Association Professionelle des Pharmaciens Salaries du Quebec
C.P. 609, Stn. N, Montreal, P.Q. H2X 3M6
President, Jean-Pierre Martel

Association Québécoise des Pharmaciens Propriétaires
5115 rue St-Denis, Montréal, P.Q. H2J 2M1
(514) 273-1721

Atlantic Provinces Pharmaceutical Advisory Council
Box 3363, Halifax South, N.S. B3J 3J1
(902) 422-8528

British Columbia Pharmacists' Society
1200 W. 73rd Ave., Ste. 604, Vancouver, B.C. V6P 6G5
(604) 263-2766

Canadian Academy of the History of Pharmacy
Executive Director, Ernst W. Stieb, c/o Faculty of Pharmacy, University of Toronto, Toronto, Ont. M5S 1A1 (416/978-2880)

Canadian Association of Pharmacy Students & Interns
Secretary Treasurer, Lynn Lemon, c/o Faculty of Pharmacy, University of Saskatchewan, Saskatoon, Sask.

Canadian Conference on Continuing Education in Pharmacy
President, Doreen E. Zinyk, Box 400, SUB 11, University of Alberta, Edmonton, Alta. T6G 2E0

Canadian Cosmetic, Toiletry & Fragrance Association
1819 Yonge St., Toronto, Ont. M4S 1X8
(416) 487-8111
President, N.R. Richardson
Director of Administration & Meetings, Miss S. Wissler

Canadian Drug Manufacturers Association
5100 Timberlea Blvd., Mississauga, Ont. L4W 2S5
(416) 624-7000, ext. 206
Chairman, Dr. V.J.V. Parks

Canadian Foundation for the Advancement of Pharmacy
See Foundations

The Canadian Pharmaceutical Association
1815 Alta Vista Dr., Ottawa, Ont. K1G 3Y6
(613) 523-7877
Executive Director, L.C. Fevang

Provincial Pharmaceutical Associations

ALBERTA PHARMACEUTICAL ASSOCIATION
Registrar, D.M. Cameron, 10615 124 St., Edmonton, Alta. T5N 1S5 (403/488-8152)

COLLEGE OF PHARMACISTS OF BRITISH COLUMBIA
Registrar, N.S. Thomas, #240, 1575 W. Georgia St., Vancouver, B.C. V6G 2V3 (604/683-6588)

MANITOBA PHARMACEUTICAL ASSOCIATION
Registrar, A.L. Jones, 187 St. Mary's Rd., Winnipeg, Man. R2H 1J2 (204/233-1411)

NEW BRUNSWICK PHARMACEUTICAL SOCIETY
Registrar, J.V. Robichaud, #305, 1077 St. George Blvd., Moncton, N.B. E1E 4C9 (506/855-5757)

NEWFOUNDLAND PHARMACEUTICAL ASSOCIATION
Secretary Registrar, 125 New Gower St., St. John's, Nfld. A1C 1J5

NOVA SCOTIA PHARMACEUTICAL SOCIETY
Registrar, G.B. Locke, Box 3363, Halifax South, N.S. B3J 3J1 (902/422-8528)

ONTARIO COLLEGE OF PHARMACISTS
Registrar, W.R. Wensley, 483 Huron St., Toronto, Ont. M5R 2R4

PRINCE EDWARD ISLAND PHARMACEUTICAL ASSOCIATION
Registrar, Ed Deschenes, Box 177, Summerside, P.E.I. C1N 1Y8

ORDRE DES PHARMACIENS DE QUEBEC
Directeur général et secrétaire, J.A. Nadeau, 1253 McGill College Ave., Ste. 160, Montreal, P.Q. H3B 2Y5 (514/861-2435)

SASKATCHEWAN PHARMACEUTICAL ASSOCIATION
Registrar, S.A. Lissack, #301, 2631 28th Ave., Regina, Sask. S4S 6X3 (306/584-2292)

Canadian Society of Governmental Pharmacists
President, E.V. Wilson, 695 Buxton Cr., Ottawa, Ont. K1V 7H7 (613/731-4511)

Canadian Society of Hospital Pharmacists
Executive Director, Mrs. D. Shaw, 123 Edward St., #303, Toronto, Ont. M5G 1E2 (416/979-2049)
Branches in British Columbia, Alberta, Saskatchewan, Manitoba, Ontario, Quebec, New Brunswick and Nova Scotia.

Canadian Society of Industrial Pharmacists
#104, 1815 Alta Vista Dr., Ottawa, Ont. K1G 3Y6
(613) 523-7877
President, F. Ruppel

Canadian Wholesale Drug Association
1200 Atwater Ave., Westmount, P.Q. H3Z 1X4
(514) 935-8713
Executive Vice President, W.B. Ward

Conference of Pharmacy Registrars of Canada
Chairman, N.S. Thomas, #240, 1575 W. Georgia St., Vancouver, B.C. V6G 2V3

Independent Retail Druggists Association of Quebec Inc.
4415 Notre Dame Blvd., Chomedey, Laval, P.Q. H7W 1T7
(514) 681-6093

Manitoba Society of Professional Pharmacists Inc.
187 St. Mary's Rd., St-Boniface, Man. R2H 1J2
(204) 233-6227

Ontario Pharmacists' Association
99 Avenue Rd., #707, Toronto, Ont. M5R 2G5
(416) 922-7740

Pharmaceutical Manufacturers Association of Canada
141 Laurier Ave. W., Room 1110, Ottawa, Ont. K1P 5J3
(613) 236-9993
President, G. Beauchemin

Pharmacy Association of Nova Scotia
(1526 Dresden Row) Box 3214, South Stn., Halifax, N.S. B3J 3H5
(902) 422-9583
Executive Director, J.J. Ryan

Pharmacy Examining Board of Canada
#303, 123 Edward St., Toronto, Ont. M5G 1E2
Registrar, John Creasy, B.Sc.Ph.

The Proprietary Association of Canada
350 Sparks St., Ste. 504, Ottawa, Ont. K1R 7S8
(613) 238-1814
President, J.D. Harper

PHOTO MARKETING ASSOCIATION INTERNATIONAL
Intl. Office: 3000 Picture Place, Jackson, Mich. 49201 U.S.A. (517/788-8100); Executive Manager, Roy S. Pung
Canadian Office: 6205 Airport Rd., #103, Mississauga, Ont. L4V 1E1 (416/677-2593)
Manager of Canadian Operations, Harold Bourne
Director of Canadian Activities, Donald Spring

PIONEER WOMEN'S ORGANIZATION OF CANADA
4770 Kent Ave., #304, Montreal, P.Q. H3W 1H2
(514) 735-6253
National Executive Director, Mrs. Irene Welik

Branch Offices
Toronto: 272 Codsell Ave., Downsview, Ont. M3H 3X2 (416/636-5425)
Montreal: 4770 Kent Ave., #303, Montreal, P.Q. H3W 1H2 (514/735-1679)
Winnipeg: 1727 Main St., Winnipeg, Man. R2V 1Z4 (204/334-3637)
Vancouver: 950 W. 41st St., Rm. G, Vancouver, B.C. V5Z 2N7 (604/266-8308)

PIPE LINE CONTRACTORS ASSOCIATION OF CANADA
203, 698 Seymour St., Vancouver, B.C. V6B 3K6
(604) 681-3458
Executive Director, G. R. Hodson

PLANNED PARENTHOOD FEDERATION OF CANADA
151 Slater St., #200, Ottawa, Ont. K1P 5H3
Executive Director, Marilyn Wilson

Member Associations

PLANNED PARENTHOOD ALBERTA
#206, 223 12th Ave. S.W., Calgary, Alta. T2R OG9
(403) 265-3360

PLANNED PARENTHOOD ASSOCIATION OF BRITISH COLUMBIA
#205, 5704 Balsam St., Vancouver, B.C. V6M 4B9
(604) 266-1381

PLANNED PARENTHOOD MANITOBA
#1000, 259 Portage Ave., Winnipeg, Man. R3B 2A9
(204) 943-6489

PLANNED PARENTHOOD NEW BRUNSWICK
(La Fédération du Nouveau Brunswick pour le planning des naissances)
Victoria Health Centre, 43 Brunswick St., Fredericton, N.B. E3B 1G5
(506) 454-1808

PLANNED PARENTHOOD NEWFOUNDLAND LABRADOR
Fort William Bldg., 21 Factory Lane, St. John's, Nfld. A1C 3J8
(709) 753-7333

PLANNED PARENTHOOD NORTHWEST TERRITORIES
Box 1680, Yellowknife, N.W.T. XOE 1HO
(403) 873-6112

PLANNED PARENTHOOD ASSOCIATION OF NOVA SCOTIA
1815 Hollis St., Halifax, N.S. B3J 1W3
(902) 423-2090

PLANNED PARENTHOOD ONTARIO
Box 505, Stn. A, Hamilton, Ont. L8N 3H8

PLANNED PARENTHOOD OF PRINCE EDWARD ISLAND
81 Prince St., Charlottetown, P.E.I. C1A 4R3

LA FEDERATION DU QUEBEC POUR LE PLANNING DES NAISSANCES
3826 St-Hubert, Montreal, P.Q. H2L 4A5
(514) 842-9501

PLANNED PARENTHOOD SASKATCHEWAN
#502, 245 Third Ave. S., Saskatoon, Sask. S7K 1M4
(306) 664-2050

YUKON PLANNED PARENTHOOD
207 Elliott St., Whitehorse, Yukon Y1A 2A1
(403) 667-2970

National Affiliates
Canadian Home Economics Association
Presbyterian Church in Canada
United Church in Canada

POLICE ASSOCIATION OF ONTARIO
268 Lakeshore Rd. E., Mississauga, Ont. L5G 1H1
(416) 278-3884

POLISH ALLIANCE OF CANADA
1638 Bloor St. W., Toronto, Ont. M6P 1A7
(416) 531-4826
President, H.M. Lopinski

POLITICAL ASSOCIATIONS

Communist Party of Canada
24 Cecil St., Toronto, Ont. M5T 1N2
(416) 979-2109
Party Leader, William Kashtan

Communist Party of Canada (Marxist-Leninist)
Box 264, Adelaide St. PO, Toronto, Ont. M5C 2J4
(514) 522-1373
Official Agent, Richard Daly

Progressive Conservative Party of Canada
161 Laurier Ave. W., 2nd Floor, Ottawa, Ont. K1P 5J2
(613) 238-6111
Leader, Rt. Hon. Joseph Clark, M.P.

Progressive Conservative Association of Canada

161 Laurier Ave. W., 2nd Floor, Ottawa, Ont. K1P 5J2
(613) 238-6111
National President, Peter Blaikie
National Director, tba

Provincial Associations

BRITISH COLUMBIA PROGRESSIVE CONSERVATIVE ASSOCIATION
Office: #401, 535 Thurlow St., Vancouver, B.C. V6E 3L2
(604) 687-6688
President, tba
Provincial Leader, Brian Westwood
Federal Organizer, Don Taylor

ALBERTA PROGRESSIVE CONSERVATIVE ASSOCIATION
Office: #32, 9912 106 St., Edmonton, Alta.
(403) 423-1624
Executive Director, Frank McMillan
Provincial Leader, Hon. Peter Lougheed, M.L.A.

SASKATCHEWAN PROGRESSIVE CONSERVATIVE ASSOCIATION
Office: #411, 1874 Scarth St., Regina, Sask. S4P 2G3
(306) 359-1055
President, J. Gary Lane, 2100 Smith St., Regina, Sask. S4P 2P2
Provincial Leader, Grant Devine, M.L.A.

MANITOBA PROGRESSIVE CONSERVATIVE ASSOCIATION
Office: 23 Kennedy St., Winnipeg, Man. R3C 1S5
(204) 942-8283
Executive Director, Annis Shaddy
President, Harold G. Piercy, #906, 386 Broadway, R3C 3R6
Provincial Leader, Hon. Sterling Lyon, Q.C., M.L.A.

ONTARIO PROGRESSIVE CONSERVATIVE PARTY
Office: 180 Dundas St. W., Ste. 301, Toronto, Ont. M5G 1Z8
(416) 979-3233
Executive Director, Patrick Kinsella
President, David McFadden, #1405, 480 University Ave., Toronto
Provincial Leader, Hon. William G. Davis, Q.C., M.P.P.

QUEBEC PROGRESSIVE CONSERVATIVE ASSOCIATION
Office: 625 President Kennedy, #803, Montreal, P.Q. H3A 1K2
(514) 284-0090
President, Marcel Danis

NEW BRUNSWICK PROGRESSIVE CONSERVATIVE ASSOCIATION
c/o Box 1026, Fredericton, N.B. E3B 5C2
(506) 455-5106
President, John Winslow, Woodstock, N.B. E0J 2B0
Provincial Leader, Hon. Richard B. Hatfield, M.L.A.

NOVA SCOTIA PROGRESSIVE CONSERVATIVE ASSOCIATION
Office: 1649 Hollis St., Halifax, N.S.
(902) 429-9470
President, John Grant, Box 2380, Halifax, N.S.
Provincial Leader, Hon. John M. Buchanan, Q.C., M.L.A.

PROGRESSIVE CONSERVATIVE ASSOCIATION OF PRINCE EDWARD ISLAND
Box 578, 53 Queen St., Charlottetown, P.E.I.
(902) 892-7556
President, John McQuaid, Box 2140, Charlottetown

PROGRESSIVE CONSERVATIVE ASSOCIATION OF NEWFOUNDLAND & LABRADOR
Box 8551, Stn. A, (320 Freshwater Rd.), St. John's, Nfld. A1B 3P2
(709) 753-6930
President, Mac Le Messurier, St. John's
Provincial Leader, Hon. Brian Peckford, M.H.A., Premier

WESTERN ARCTIC PROGRESSIVE CONSERVATIVE ASSOCIATION
Box 337, Hay River, N.W.T. X0E 0R0
(403) 874-2101, 874-6670
President, S.F. MacIntyre

YUKON PROGRESSIVE CONSERVATIVE ASSOCIATION
-not confirmed for 1982-
President, Hal Komish, Box 5005, Whitehorse, Y.T. Y1A 4S2
Territorial Leader, Chris Pearson, M.L.A.

PROGRESSIVE CONSERVATIVE WOMEN'S ASSOCIATION OF ONTARIO
c/o Party Headquarters, 180 Dundas St. W., Toronto, Ont. M5G 1Z8 (416/979-3250)
President, Mrs. Aase Hueglin, 5838 Mouland Ave., Niagara Falls, Ont. L2G 5N7

PROGRESSIVE CONSERVATIVE YOUTH FEDERATION
President, Greg Thomas, 178 Queen St., Ottawa, Ont. K1P 5E1

Feminist Party of Canada

Box 5717, Stn. A, Toronto, Ont. M5W 1A0
(416) 960-3427
Contact: Moira Armour

Liberal Party of Canada

102 Bank St., Ottawa, Ont. K1P 5N4
(613) 237-0740
National Leader, Rt. Hon. Pierre Elliott Trudeau, P.C., Q.C., M.P.
President, Norman MacLeod
Secretary, Gerry Clark
Treasurer, Gordon R. Dryden

Provincial Associations

LIBERAL PARTY OF CANADA (ALBERTA)
111 Greymac Bldg., 11745 Jasper Ave., Edmonton, Alta. T5K 0N5
(403) 482-4461
President, Darryl Raymaker

ALBERTA LIBERAL PARTY
111 Greymac Bldg., 11745 Jasper Ave., Edmonton, Alta. T5K 0N5
(403) 482-4461
President, John Borger

BRITISH COLUMBIA LIBERAL PARTY
Office: #201, 1894 W. Broadway, Vancouver, B.C. V6J 1Y9
(604) 736-2331
President, William McEwen

LIBERAL PARTY IN MANITOBA
Office: 140 Roslyn Rd., Winnipeg, Man. R3L 0G8
(204) 453-7343
President, John Petryshyn, #300, 203 Portage Ave., Winnipeg, Man. R3B 2A1 (204/942-5191)

NEW BRUNSWICK LIBERAL ASSOCIATION
715 Brunswick St., Fredericton, N.B. E3B 1H8
(506) 454-3321
President, Jack Stevens

LIBERAL ASSOCIATION OF NEWFOUNDLAND & LABRADOR
Office mailing address: Box 9006, St. John's, Nfld. A1A 2X3
(709) 754-1813
President, Philip Warren, 6 Preswick Place, St. John's, Nfld.

NOVA SCOTIA LIBERAL ASSOCIATION
Office: Ste. 1210, 1809 Barrington St., Box 723, Halifax, N.S. B3J 2T3
(902) 423-6129
President, Ralph F. Fiske, Halifax
Provincial Leader, A.M. (Sandy) Cameron

ONTARIO LIBERAL PARTY
Office: Ste. 310, 10 St. Mary St., Toronto, Ont. M4Y 1P9
(416) 961-3800
Executive Director, Charles Bates
President, Jim Evans

LIBERAL PARTY OF CANADA (ONTARIO)
Office: 34 King St. E., Ste. 200, Toronto, Ont. M5C 1E5
(416) 364-8200
Executive Director, Isobel Finnerty

LIBERAL PARTY OF PRINCE EDWARD ISLAND
Office mailing address: Box 2559, Charlottetown, P.E.I. C1A 8C2
(902) 892-3449

Executive Director, Percy Downe
President, Frank Callaghan

LIBERAL PARTY OF CANADA (QUEBEC)
Offices, 1440 St. Catherine St. W., Suite 725, Montreal, P.Q. H3G 1R8 (514/866-6391); 999 rue Bougainville, Québec, P.Q. G1S 3A7 (418/681-0049)
Président, Jean-Claude Dansereau
Director General, Léonce Mercier

SASKATCHEWAN LIBERAL ASSOCIATION
Office: 2149 Albert St., Regina, Sask. S4P 2V1
(306) 522-8507
Secretary, K. Pearl Brown
President, Jack Wiebe

NORTHWEST TERRITORIES LIBERAL ASSOCIATION
c/o Box 965, Yellowknife, N.W.T. X0E 1H0

YUKON LIBERAL ASSOCIATION
Box 4302, Whitehorse, Y.T. Y1A 3T3
President, John P. Hoyt

Libertarian Associations

LIBERTARIAN PARTY OF CANADA
Box 190, Adelaide St. PO, Toronto, Ont. M5C 2J1
(416) 363-0157
Leader, Linda Cain
President, Vince Miller

ONTARIO LIBERTARIAN PARTY
2086 Yonge St., Toronto, Ont. M4S 2A3
(416) 489-6057
Chairman, Robert Cumming

LIBERTARIAN FOUNDATION
909 Thurlow St., Vancouver, B.C. V6E 1W3
(604) 688-2308
Directors, Richard Bolstler, Michael A. Little

Mouvement National des Quebecois
82 ouest, rue Sherbrooke, Montreal, P.Q. H2X 1X3
(514) 849-4257

New Democratic Party
Federal Headquarters, 301 Metcalfe St., Ottawa, Ont. K1P 1R9
(613) 236-3613
Leader, Ed Broadbent, M.P.
Honorary President, David Lewis
President, Alvin Hewitt, Box 129, Perdue, Sask. SOK 3CO
Treasurer, Gordon Brigden, 3 Church St., Toronto, Ont. M5E 1M2
Secretary, Robin V. Sears, 301 Metcalfe St., Ottawa, Ont. K2P 1R9

Provincial Secretaries
Alta., Tom Brook, 5339 112 Ave., Edmonton, Alta. T5W 0N6 (403/477-1491)
B.C., Yvonne Cocke, 517 E. Broadway, Vancouver, B.C. V5T 1X4 (604/879-4601)
Man., John Walsh, 656 Broadway Ave., Winnipeg, Man. R3C OX3 (204/786-4857)
N.B., Judy Wilson, 335 Queen St., Fredericton, N.B. E3B 5C2 (506/454-8107)
Nfld., Gerry Panting, Box 5275, Water St. Stn., St. John's, Nfld. A1C 5W1 (709/753-3231)
N.S., Mary Morison, 1741 Barrington St., Halifax, N.S. B3J 2E4 (902/423-9217)
Ont., Jack Murray, 184 Main St., Toronto, Ont. M4E 2W1 (416/699-6637)
P.E.I., Nancy Anderson, Box 394, Charlottetown, P.E.I. C1A 7K7 (902/894-8298)
Que., J.P. Bourdouxhe, 180 est Dorchester, #220, Montreal, P.Q. H7R 2R8 (514/878-9301)
Sask., Larry Deters, 1630 Quebec St., Regina, Sask. S4P 1J2 (306/525-1322)
N.W.T., Box 2226, Yellowknife, N.W.T.
Yukon, Tony Penikett, Box 4584, Whitehorse, Y.T.

Parti Québécois
8790 Ave. du Parc, Montréal, P.Q. H2N 2Y6
(514) 384-7110
Président, René Lévesque
Trésorier, Philippe Bernard

Le Parti Credit Social du Canada
(The Social Credit Party of Canada)
-not confirmed for 1982-
Box 1162, Stn. B, Ottawa, Ont. K1P 5R2
Secretary, Robert Klinck

Parti des travailleurs du Québec
4518 rue St-Denis, Montréal, P.Q. H2J 2L3
(514) 844-4707
Secrétaire général, G. Lachance
Agent officiel, Johanne Perreault
Bureau politique, André Rousseau
Président région de Montréal, Maurice Gohier
Président région de l'Outaouais, Gilles Bourque

Union Nationale Party
-not confirmed for 1982-
130 Grande Allée ouest, Québec, P.Q. G1R 2G7
(418) 529 9651
Montreal office: 450 Sherbrooke Est, Ste. 1201, Montreal, P.Q. H2L 1J8

Union Populaire
6900 rue St-Hubert, Montreal, P.Q. H2S 2M9
(514) 272-5242
Président, Henri Laberge

POLLUTION PROBE
See 'Environmental Associations'

PORTABLE APPLIANCE MANUFACTURERS ASSOCIATION
#1608, One Yonge St., Toronto, Ont. M5E 1R1
(416) 862-7152

POULTRY AND EGG ASSOCIATIONS

Alberta Commercial Egg Producers' Association
Secretary, Jim Haggins, 3223 1 St. S.W., Calgary, Alta. T2S 1P9 (403/243-8758)

Association des Abattoirs Avicoles du Québec Inc.
(poultry processors)
Executive Vice President, J.M. Touchette, 540 ouest boul. Casavant, #5, St-Hyacinthe, P.Q. J2S 7S3 (514/773-8508)

Association des Classificateurs du Québec
(egg graders)
Secrétaire, Léo Bond, 1535 rue St-Charles, La Providence, P.Q. J2T 1X4 (514/773-8930)

Association des Producteurs d'Oeufs Québécois
Directeur, Jean-Pierre Barret, C.P. 930, Bedford, P.Q. JOJ 1AO (514/248-3386)

Atlantic Provinces Hatchery Federation
Secretary, Edwin Black, Box 1073, Sussex, N.B. E0E 1P0 (506/433-1206)

British Columbia Baby Chick Association
Secretary, D. Lanigan, 505 Hamm Rd., R.R. 1, Abbotsford, B.C. V2S 1M3 (604/859-7168)

British Columbia Broiler Growers Association
Secretary, Garth Bean, c/o Canada Farm Labour Pool, 33827 S. Fraser Way, Abbotsford, B.C. V2S 2C4

British Columbia Hatching Egg Producers' Association
Secretary, V. Kembel, 5274 248 St., R.R. 3, Aldergrove, B.C. VOX 1AO (604/856-8800)

British Columbia Turkey Association
Secretary, Colyn Welsh, #201, 5752 176 St., Surrey, B.C. V3S 4C8 (604/574-7447)

Canadian Broiler Council
Secretary Treasurer, J.E. Janzen, Box 5035, Burlington, Ont. L7R 3Y8 (416/335-4496)

Canadian Egg Producers Council
111 Sparks St., Ottawa, Ont. K1P 5B5
(613) 236-3633

Canadian Hatchery Federation
77 City Centre Dr., Mississauga, Ont. L5B 1M5
(416) 276-6982

Canadian Poultry & Egg Processors Council
5233 Dundas St. W., Islington, Ont. M9B 1A6
(416) 233-2001
Executive Vice President, D.G. McKenzie

Les Couvoiriers du Québec Inc.
(chicks producers)
C.P. 217, Beloeil, P.Q. J3G 4T1
(514) 467-2353

Fédération des Producteurs d'Oeufs de Consommation du Québec
Président, Ovila Lebel, 1355 Graham Bell, Parc Edison, Boucherville, P.Q. J4B 6A1 (514/655-6410)

Fraser Valley Egg Producers Association
Secretary, Garth Bean, 33827 S. Fraser Way, Abbotsford, B.C. V2S 2C4 (604/853-7471)

New Brunswick Egg Producers Association
Secretary, Richard Gorham, Chestnut Complex, 476 York St., Fredericton, N.B. E3B 3P7 (506/455-7605)

New Brunswick Poultry Council
-not confirmed for 1982-
Secretary, James Wilson, R.R. 1, River Glade, N.B. EOA 2PO (506/372-9145)

Nova Scotia Chicken Producers Association
Secretary Treasurer, Herbert Jansen, c/o N.S. Dept. of Agriculture & Marketing, Agricultural Centre, Kentville, N.S. (902/678-7365)
President, David Young, R.R. 2, Bridgewater, N.S.

Nova Scotia Egg & Pullett Producers Association
Secretary, Lester Settle, Box 784, Truro, N.S. B2N 5E8 (902/893-2293)

Ontario Hatcheries Association
Secretary Manager, J.D. Mitchell, Ph.D., 77 City Centre Dr., Mississauga, Ont. L5B 1M5 (416/276-6982)

Ontario Poultry Council
Secretary Manager, J.D. Mitchell, Ph.D., 77 City Centre Dr., Mississauga, Ont. L5B 1M5 (416/276-6982)

Prince Edward Island Egg Producers & Allied Industries Association
Secretary, G. Johnstone, Box 1600, Charlottetown, P.E.I. C1A 7N3 (902/892-5465)

Prince Edward Island Rural Beautification Society
Secretary, L.E. Arsenault, Box 1194, Charlottetown, P.E.I. C1A 7M8 (902/894-4008)

Saskatchewan Poultry Association
Secretary Treasurer, D.H. Conrad, c/o Provincial Veterinary Laboratory, 4840 Wascana Pkwy., Regina, Sask. S4S OB1 (306/565-6424)

Saskatchewan Poultry Council
Secretary Treasurer, D.H. Conrad, c/o Provincial Veterinary Laboratory, 4840 Wascana Pkwy., Regina, Sask. S4S OB1 (306/565-6424)

PRINT MEASUREMENT BUREAU

#502, 11 Yorkville Ave., Toronto, Ont. M4W 1L3
(416) 961-3205
General Manager, J.E. Chaplin

PRISONERS' AID SOCIETIES

BEVERLEY LODGE

A rehabilitation home for young ex-offenders operated by Anglican Houses. Ages 16 to 20.
Director, J.M. Falls, 69 Beaty Ave., Toronto, Ont. M6K 3B3 (416/532-9700)

CENTRE DE SERVICES SOCIAUX DU MONTREAL METROPOLITAIN (SERVICES SOCIAUX DANS LE DOMAINE DE LA JUSTICE)
4217 d'Iberville, Montreal, P.Q. H2H 2L5
(514) 526-0481
Executive Director, Pierre Couturier

JOHN HOWARD SOCIETIES
National Office: 55 Parkdale Ave., Ottawa, Ont. K1Y 1E5
(613) 728-1865
Executive Director, J.M. MacLatchie

Provincial Societies

Alta.: Executive Director, B.A. Pollick, #200, 1305 11th Ave. S.W., Calgary, Alta, T3C 3P6 (403/245-4333)
B.C.: Executive Director, Rev. Dr. L. McFerran, 435 W. Broadway, Vancouver, B.C. V5Y 1R4 (604/872-5651)
Vancouver Island: Executive Secretary, William A. Blondé, 620 View St., Victoria, B.C. V8W 1J6 (604/386-3428)
Man.: Executive Director, John Howard & Elizabeth Fry Society of Manitoba, Dave Kennedy, 1767 Portage Ave., Room 4, Winnipeg, Man. R3J 0E7 (204/889-6634)
N.B.: Executive Director, Ron Gionet, 120 Carlton St., Saint John, N.B. E2L 2Z7 (506/693-2507)
Nfld.: Executive Director, T. Carlson, 7 Garrison Hill, St. John's, Nfld. A1C 3Y7 (709/722-1848)
N.S.: Executive Director, C. R. MacDonald, 1657 Barrington St., #220, Halifax, N.S. B3J 2A1 (902/422-2640)
Ont.: Executive Director, G.C. MacFarlane, 980 Yonge St., Ste. 407, Toronto, Ont. M4W 2J5 (416/925-2205)
P.E.I.: Executive Director, Mrs. Donna Hartley, Box 1211, Charlottetown, P.E.I. C1A 7M8 (902/894-3525)
Que.: Executive Director, J. Zambrowsky, #515, 517 Pine Ave. W., Montreal, P.Q. H2W 1S4 (514/842-3451)
Sask.: Executive Director, J. Coflin, 2228 Osler St., Regina, Sask. S4P 1W8 (306/527-6657)

ONTARIO COUNCIL OF ELIZABETH FRY SOCIETIES (and The Elizabeth Fry Society of Toronto)
215 Wellesley St. E., Toronto, Ont. M4X 1G1
(416) 924-3708

PRISONER SOLIDARITY COLLECTIVE
Box 2, Stn. O, Toronto, Ont. M4A 2M8
(416) 925-6442

THE ST. LEONARD'S SOCIETY OF CANADA
1787 Walker Rd., Room 3, Windsor, Ont. N8W 3P2
(519) 254-9430

A national organization concerned with residences for released prisoners and their reintegration into society.
Executive Director, L.A. Drouillard

THE SALVATION ARMY
259 Victoria St., Toronto, Ont. M5B 1V7
(416) 598-2071, ext. 314

LE SERVICE DE READAPTATION SOCIALE INC.
1279, boul. Charest ouest, ste. 900, Québec, P.Q. G1N 4K7
(418) 687-1441

PRIVATE MOTOR TRUCK COUNCIL OF CANADA
#602, 350 Sparks St., Ottawa, Ont. K1R 7S8
(613) 238-6052; Telex 053-4238
President, Russell W. Neal

PROFESSIONAL ART DEALERS' ASSOCIATION OF CANADA
65 Queen St. W., Ste. 1800, Toronto, Ont. M5H 2M5
(416) 363-1768

PROFESSIONAL ASSOCIATION OF CANADIAN THEATRES
3 Church St., Ste. 301, Toronto, Ont. M5E 1M2
(416) 366-0159; 366-2449

PROFESSIONAL ASSOCIATION OF FOREIGN SERVICE OFFICERS
Ste. 1002, 130 Albert St., Ottawa, Ont. K1P 5G4
(613) 234-1391

THE PROFESSIONAL INSTITUTE OF THE PUBLIC SERVICE OF CANADA
(L'Institut Professionnel de la Fonction Publique du Canada)
786 Bronson Ave., Ottawa, Ont. K1S 4G4
(613) 237-6310
Executive Secretary, G.L. Mosley

Institute Regional Offices
Atlantic, W.N. Rogers, 6436 Quinpool Rd., Halifax, N.S. B3L 1A8
B.C. and Yukon, Joseph Clare, 1225 Granville Sq., 200 Granville St., Vancouver, B.C. V6C 1S4 (604/688-8238)
Ont., Gordon Randall, 383 Richmond St., Suite 913, London, Ont. N6A 3C4 (519/432-3483)
Prairies, Donald Murray, 845 Avord Tower Bldg., 2002 Victoria Ave., Regina, Sask. S4P 0R7
Que., Mrs. Pierrette Gosselin, Dominion Sq. Bldg., Suite 912, 1010 St. Catherine St. W., Montreal, P.Q. H3B 3R3

PROFESSIONAL MARKETING RESEARCH SOCIETY
Box 5155, Stn. A, Toronto, Ont. M5W 1N5
(416) 487-4893
President, Ian Lightstone

PROFESSIONAL PHOTOGRAPHERS OF CANADA
318 Royal Bank Bldg., Edmonton, Alta. T5J 1W8
(403) 428-0850
Executive Manager, Oma Marler, SPA, Cr Photog.

Provincial Associations

ALBERTA PROFESSIONAL PHOTOGRAPHERS ASSOCATION
16136 110B Ave., Edmonton, Alta. T5P 4E6
(403) 489-8157
Executive Secretary, Pat Eisenbarth

PROFESSIONAL PHOTOGRAPHERS ASSOCIATION OF BRITISH COLUMBIA
8060 Granville Ave., Richmond, B.C. V6Y 1P4
(604) 273-7787
Executive Secretary, Lois Richert

PROFESSIONAL PHOTOGRAPHERS OF MANITOBA
Box 1575, Winnipeg, Man. R3C 2Z4
(204) 586-1497
President, Andrew Ulicki

MARITIMES PROFESSIONAL PHOTOGRAPHERS ASSOCIATION
221 Reade St., Moncton, N.B. E1C 6S7
(506) 855-1376, 77
Secretary, Arnold Clow

PROFESSIONAL PHOTOGRAPHERS OF ONTARIO INC.
#202, 881 Eglinton Ave. W., Toronto, Ont. M6C 2C1
(416) 789-5930
Membership Services Manager, Diane Reagin

LES PHOTOGRAPHES PROFESSIONNELS DU QUEBEC
C.P. 457, Succ N, Montreal, P.Q. H2X 3N3
(514) 284-0048
Sécretaire administratif, Gerald Garant

SASKATCHEWAN PROFESSIONAL PHOTOGRAPHERS ASSOCIATION
401 2nd Ave. N., Saskatoon, Sask. S7K 2C1
c/o David Brown (306/653-5353)

PROGRAMME D'EXCHANGE DES ETUDIANTS DU QUEBEC
(Student exchange within the province of Quebec)
1117 St. Catherine St. W., #521, Montreal, P.Q. H3B 1H9
(514) 845-9163
Directeur executif, Robert G. Beale

PROPANE GAS ASSOCIATION OF CANADA INC.
#1202, 500 4th Ave. S.W., Calgary, Alta. T2P 2V6
(403) 263-0450
Executive Director & General Manager, Col. L.G. (Greg) Doiron
Association Secretary, Joan Low

PROSPECTORS & DEVELOPERS ASSOCIATION
#219-220, 159 Bay St., Toronto, Ont. M5J 1J7
(416) 362-1969

PROVINCE OF QUEBEC SOCIETY FOR THE PROTECTION OF BIRDS INC.
(La Société Quebecoise de Protection des Oiseaux, Inc.)
Secretary, Miss Elizabeth Barber, 4832 de Maisonneuve Blvd. W., Westmount, P.Q. H3Z 1M5 (514/937-0224)

PROVINCIAL JUDGES ASSOCIATION OF ONTARIO (CRIMINAL DIVISION)
Secretary, Judge D.V. Latimer, Provincial Court (Criminal Division), 491 Steeles Ave. E., Milton, Ont. L9T 1Y7 (416/878-4161)

PROVINCIAL-MUNICIPAL COUNCIL OF NEW BRUNSWICK
Ste. 3, 390 King St., Fredericton, N.B. E3B 1E3
(506) 454-0240
Executive Secretary, Sandra M. Allen

PROVINCIAL (ONTARIO) ASSOCIATION OF COMMITTEES OF ADJUSTMENT & LAND DIVISION COMMITTEES
Secretary Treasurer, Rona Bihun, Box 7000, 1151 Bronte Rd., Oakville, Ont. L6J 6E1 (416/827-2151)

PUBLIC SERVICE ALLIANCE OF CANADA
(Alliance de la Fonction Publique du Canada)
Headquarters Offices/Siege Social, 233 Gilmour, Ottawa, Ont. K2P 0P1
(613) 560-4200
National President, A.I. Stewart
Executive Secretary, W.E. Brassington

PULP & PAPER RESEARCH INSTITUTE OF CANADA
570 St. John's Blvd., Pointe Claire, P.Q. H9R 3J9
(514) 697-4110
President & Chief Executive Officer, Bernard W. Burgess

PUPPETRY GROUPS

ADAMS MARIONETTES
27 Ladore Ave., Brampton, Ont. L6Y 1V4
(416) 459-1740

CANADIAN PUPPET FESTIVALS
c/o Leo Velleman, Chester, N.S. BOJ 1JO (902/275-3171)

CREATIVE PUPPETEERS ASSOCIATION
2419 Chicoutimi Dr. N.W., Calgary, Alta. T2L OW2
(403) 282-4392

THE FRIENDLY PUPPET PEOPLE
5 Parmalea Cres., Weston, Ont. M9R 2X8
(416) 248-2865

ONTARIO PUPPETRY ASSOCIATION
171 Avondale Ave., Glen Avon Pub. Sch., Willowdale, Ont. M2N 2V4
(416) 222-9029
Secretary, R. Tilroe

UNIMA CANADA
c/o Mrs. Pat Overgaard, Treasurer, 886 Keith Rd., West Vancouver, B.C. V7T 1M3 (604/922-3721)

PURCHASING MANAGEMENT ASSOCIATION OF CANADA
80 Richmond St. W., Toronto, Ont. M5H 2A4
(416) 366-5859
Branches in major centres of all Provinces.

QUARTER CENTURY IN AVIATION CLUB
7719 Yukon St., Vancouver, B.C. V5X 2Y4
(604) 263-9685
Secretary, J.C. Cooke

QUEBEC ASSOCIATION OF MUNICIPAL ASSESSORS
C.P. 1234, Complexe Desjardins, Montreal, P.Q. H5B 1C3
(514) 645-0443
Attn.: Guy Campion

QUEBEC BUILDING MATERIALS DEALERS' ASSOCIATION
4270 est Jean-Talon, #102, Montréal, P.Q. H1S 1G7
(514) 376-8541
Executive Director, Maurice Rhéaume

QUEBEC FEDERATION OF POLICEMEN
480 Gilford, Montreal, P.Q. H2J 1N3
(514) 849-6012

THE QUEBEC FOREST INDUSTRIES ASSOCIATION LTD.
500 Grande Allée E., Suite 508, Quebec, P.Q. G1R 2J7
(418) 522-4027
Chairman of the Board, J.S. Hermon
President & General Manager, Anatole Côté
Assistant Manager & Secretary, J.-Wilfrid Turcotte

QUEBEC JEWELLERS' CORPORATION
Ste. 205, 2950 Masson, Montreal, P.Q. H1Y 1X2
(514) 728-3685
Executive Secretary, Réal Savard

QUEBEC LUMBER MANUFACTURERS ASSOCIATION
3555 boul. Hamel ouest, #200, Québec, P.Q. G2E 2G6
(418) 872-5610

QUEBEC MASTER ROOFERS ASSOCIATION
1400 Sauve St. W., Ste. 230, Montreal, P.Q. H4N 1C5
(514) 331-5628
Executive Director, H.D. Lamarre

QUEBEC PROVINCIAL HOME BUILDERS ASSOCIATION
5800 boul. Louis-H. Lafontaine, Anjou, P.Q. H1M 1S7
(514) 353-9960
Directeur général, Omer Beaudoin Rousseau

MONTREAL METROPOLITAN HOME BUILDERS ASSOCIATION
3300 Côte Vertu, Ste. 112, Ville St-Laurent, P.Q. H4R 2B7
(514) 334-8722
Executive Vice President, Pierre-Paul Aird

QUEBEC WHOLESALE GROCERS ASSOCIATION
8615 St. Laurent Blvd., #300, Montreal, P.Q. H2P 2M9
(514) 381-8888
President, Bernard P. Turcot

QUEBEC WHOLESALE LUMBER ASSOCIATION
Room 316, 620 Cathcart St., Montreal, P.Q. H3B 1M1
(514) 861-7149
Secretary Treasurer, Mrs. T. Lamarre

QUOTA INTERNATIONAL, INC.
Ste. 908, 1828 L St. N.W., Washington 20036, D.C.
(202) 331-9694
Executive Director, Mrs. Dora Lee Haynes, Washington, D.C.
There are Quota Clubs in the following places in Canada:
Alberta: Lethbridge, Medicine Hat, Wainwright
Manitoba: Brandon, Winnipeg
New Brunswick: Fredericton, Moncton, Saint John
Nova Scotia: Halifax
Ontario: Barrie, Collingwood, Gloucester, Hamilton, Huronia, London, Nepean, Orillia, Ottawa, Owen Sound, Peterborough, Sarnia, St. Thomas, Sudbury
Saskatchewan: Estevan, Lloydminster, Weyburn

RADIO BUREAU OF CANADA - RBC
43 Eglinton Ave. E., Toronto, Ont. M4P 1A2
(416) 482-2222
President, Lou Tameanko

RADIO TELEVISION NEWS DIRECTORS' ASSOCIATION (CANADA)
Secretary, Dave Rogers, c/o Canadian Bankers' Association, Box 282, Commercial Union Tower, Toronto Dominion Centre, Toronto, Ont. M5K 1K2 (416/362-6092)

RAILROAD ASSOCIATIONS

ALBERTA PIONEER RAILWAY ASSOCIATION
Box 6102, Stn. C, Edmonton, Alta. T5B 4K5

CANADIAN RAILROAD HISTORICAL ASSOCIATION
Secretary, Bernard Martin, Box 148, St-Constant, P.Q. J0L 1X0 (514/632-2410)
Provincial Divisions
Calgary & South Western: Secretary, L. M. Unwin, #60, 6100 4th Ave. N.E., Calgary, Alta. T2A 5Z8
Crowsnest & Kettle Valley: Secretary, Al Davies, Box 400, Cranbrook, B.C. V1C 4H9 (604/426-5584)
Niagara: Secretary, G.S. Rout, Box 593, St. Catharines, Ont. L2R 6W8 (416/935-0493)
Ottawa: Secretary, Bruce Keer, Bytown Railway Society Inc., Box 141, Stn. A, Ottawa, Ont. K1N 8V1 (613/226-5569)
Pacific Coast: Secretary, R. Keillor, Box 1006, Stn. A, Vancouver, B.C. V6C 2P1 (604/732-5123)
Rocky Mountain: Secretary, Cameron Ward, Box 6102, Stn. C, Edmonton, Alta. T5B 2N0 (403/435-2995)
Toronto & York: Secretary, H. Lowry, Box 5849, Terminal A, Toronto, Ont. M5W 1P3 (416/431-4454)

Windsor-Essex: Secretary, Ken Garber, 300 Cabana Rd. E., Windsor, Ont. N9G 1A2 (519/966-3478)
St. Lawrence Valley: Secretary, Jean-Pierre Chartrand, Box 99, Ste-Dorothée, P.Q. H7X 2T4 (514/689-0385)

MIDWESTERN RAIL ASSOCIATION (1975) INC.
-not confirmed for 1982-
Box 1855, Winnipeg, Man. R3C 3R1
(204) 942-4632

ONTARIO RAIL ASSOCIATION INC.
Box 64, Brampton, Ont. L6V 2K7
(416) 282-6343

THE RAILWAY ASSOCIATION OF CANADA
1117 Ste. Catherine St. W., Montreal, P.Q. H3B 1H9
(514) 849-4274
General Manager, J.M. Beaupré

SCOTIAN RAILROAD SOCIETY INC.
Box 798, Armdale PO, Halifax, N.S. B3L 4K5
(902) 477-7536

THE VINTAGE LOCOMOTIVE SOCIETY INC.
Box 217, St. James PO, Winnipeg, Man. R3J 3R4
(204) 284-2690

WEST COAST RAILWAY ASSOCIATION
Box 2790, Vancouver, B.C. V6B 3X2
(604) 987-5926

READY MIXED CONCRETE ASSOCIATION OF ONTARIO
1183 Finch Ave. W., Suite 306, Downsview, Ont. M3J 2G2
(416) 636-8763
General Manager, S. C. Cosby

REFRIGERATED TRUCKING ASSOCIATION OF ONTARIO
555 Dixon Rd., Rexdale,Ont. M9W 1H8
(416) 247-7131
Executive Secretary, John D. Wishart

REGINA DOWNTOWN BUSINESS ASSOCIATION
#106, 1855 Scarth St., Regina, Sask. S4P 2G9
(306) 352-2955
Secretary Manager J.H. Richards

RETAIL COUNCIL OF CANADA
214 King St. W., #212, Toronto, Ont. M5H 1K4
(416) 598-4684
President, Alasdair McKichan
Vice President & General Manager, Food, Tim Carter
Manager, Member Services, Pat Porth
Manager, Research, Mel Fruitman
Manager, Administration, Holly Andrews

RETAIL MERCHANTS ASSOCIATION OF CANADA, INC.
1780A Birchmount Rd. (Box 262, Agincourt, Ont. M1S 3B6)
(416) 291-7535
National Manager, George Crompton

Provincial Associations
Alta.: J. Robinson, General Manager, 230, 9930 106th St., Edmonton, Alta. T5K 1C7 (403/428-6781)
Atlantic: R. Legere, President, Box 90, Memramcook, N.B. E0A 2C0 (506/758-9061)
B.C.: Mrs. Joan Wallace, General Manager, 1975 Maple St., Vancouver, B.C. V6J 3S9 (604/736-0368)
Man.: W. Michaluk, President, #301, 232 Portage Ave., Winnipeg, Man. R3C 0B1 (204/943-4719)
Ont.: J. Gillespie, President, 1780A Birchmount Rd., Scarborough, Ont. M1P 2H8 (416/291-7903)
Sask.: R. Will, Secretary Manager, 129 2nd Ave. N., Saskatoon, Sask. S7K 2A9 (306/664-2557)

ROADS & TRANSPORTATION ASSOCIATION OF CANADA
1765 St. Laurent Blvd., Ottawa, Ont. K1G 3V4
(613) 521-4052; Telex: 053-3334
Executive Vice President, W.H. Yeates
Executive Director, N.G.S. Brown
Technical Information Manager, C.A. Davies

THE ROCKY MOUNTAIN RAMBLERS ASSOCIATION
1001 7 Ave. S.W., Calgary, Alta. T2P 1A8
(403) 282-1330

ROSICRUCIAN ORDER, AMORC
Supreme Grand Lodge and World headquarters, Rosicrucian Park, San José, California
Imperator & Chief Executive Officer, Ralph M. Lewis

Principal Lodges in Canada
Mount Royal Lodge, AMORC, 2295 St-Marc, Box 160, Victoria Stn., Montreal, P.Q. H3Z 2V5
Loge Atlas, AMORC, C.P. 162, Succ. R, Montreal, P.Q. H2S 3K6 (514/274-8911)
Loge Pyramide, AMORC, C.P. 112, Limoilou, P.Q. G1L 4T8
Toronto Lodge, AMORC, 831 Broadview Ave., Toronto, Ont. M4K 2P9 (416/465-0143)
Vancouver Lodge, AMORC, 805 W. 23rd Ave., Vancouver, B.C. V5Z 2B1 (604/876-9910)

ROTARY CLUBS IN CANADA
(Members of Rotary International)
Secretariat of Rotary International, 1600 Ridge Ave., Evanston, Ill. 60201

In Canada, there are approx. 490 Rotary clubs. There are approx. 19,100 Rotary clubs in 156 countries throughout the world.

THE ROYAL ASTRONOMICAL SOCIETY OF CANADA
124 Merton St., Toronto, Ont. M4S 2Z2
(416) 484-4960
Executive Secretary, Ms. Rosemary Freeman
President, Dr. Ian Halliday
National Secretary, R.P. Broughton
National Treasurer, Mrs. Marie Fidler
Librarian, F. Troyer

Centres at
Alta.: Edmonton, Calgary
B.C.: Vancouver, Victoria
Man.: Winnipeg
Nfld.: St. John's
N.S.: Halifax
Ont.: Ottawa, Kingston, Toronto, Hamilton, Niagara Falls, London, Kitchener-Waterloo, Windsor
Que.: Quebec, Montreal and Centre d'Astronomie de Montreal
Sask.: Saskatoon
Toronto Centre Secretary, John Perkins, c/o McLaughlin Planetarium, 100 Queen's Park, Toronto, Ont. Publications, A bimonthly Journal and annual Observer's Handbook.

ROYAL CANADIAN AIR FORCE ASSOCIATION
National Headquarters, 424 Metcalfe St., Ottawa, Ont. K2P 2C3
(613) 236-1074

An aerospace and community service organization of airminded citizens based on the traditions of the Royal Canadian Air Force. Seventy-five branches in Canada, the United States of America and Germany.

General Manager, Len Lapeer

ROYAL CANADIAN FLYING CLUBS ASSOCIATION

President, W. P. Paris, Ste. 103, 1815 Alta Vista Dr., Ottawa, Ont. K1G 3Y6 (613/733-0520)

THE ROYAL CANADIAN GEOGRAPHICAL SOCIETY

488 Wilbrod St., Ottawa, Ont. K1N 6M8
(613) 236-7493
General Manager & Editor, D. Maclellan, Ottawa, Ont.
Official publication, "Canadian Geographic"

ROYAL CANADIAN HUMANE ASSOCIATION

Secretary Treasurer, Mrs. Mary J. Heels, Box 5155, Stn. E, Hamilton, Ont. L8S 4L3 (416/522-5770)

ROYAL CANADIAN INSTITUTE

191 College St., Toronto, Ont. M5T 1P9
(416) 979-2004
Executive Secretary, Mrs. G.M. Mudge, B.A.

THE ROYAL CANADIAN LEGION

Dominion Headquarters, Legion House, 359 Kent St., Ottawa, Ont. K2P 0R7
(613) 235-4391
Dominion Secretary, J. E. A. J. Lamy
Tuberculosis Veterans' Section Representative, R.J. Crowe, 2128 York Ave., Saskatoon, Sask.
Imperial Veterans' Representative, W.C. Janes, 25 Connemara Pl., St. John's, Nfld. A1A 3E3

Provincial Commands with Secretaries

Alta.: D.W. Bennett, Box 3067, Stn. B, Calgary, Alta. T2M 4L6
B.C.: L. H. Harrison, 3026 Arbutus St., Vancouver, B.C. V6J 4P7
Man.: A.K. Baker, 563 St. Mary's Rd., Winnipeg, Man. R2M 3L6
N.B.: R. Horncastle, Box 3426, Stn. B, Saint John, N.B. E2M 4X9
Nfld. & Lab.: Frank Wall, Box 5745, St. John's, Nfld.
N.S.: Ms. Bonnie MacPhee, Box 7116, North Stn., Halifax, N.S. B3K 5J5
Ont.: R.A. Cleator, 218 Richmond St. W., Toronto, Ont. M5V 1V8
P.E.I.: V. E. King, Box 134, Charlottetown, P.E.I. C1A 7K2
Que.: G. Calver, 1253 McGill College Ave., Montreal, P.Q. H3B 2Y5
Sask.: J.D. Bridges, 1836 Cornwall St., Regina, Sask. S4P 2K2

ROYAL CANADIAN MOUNTED POLICE VETERANS' ASSOCIATION

Secretary, J.A. Turnbull, 1634 Dorion Ave., Ottawa, Ont. K1G OJ8 (613/733-1491)

THE ROYAL CANADIAN NAVAL BENEVOLENT FUND

Head Office, Box 505, Stn. B, Ottawa, Ont. K1P 5P6
(613) 236-7389
Secretary Treasurer, Lieut. L.M. Langstaff, C.D., R.C.N., (Ret'd.)
Secretary, Western Committee, CDR A.C. Tassie, C.D., R.C.N., (Ret'd.), Canadian Forces Base Esquimalt, F.M.O. Victoria, B.C. VOS 1BO (604/383-6264)
Secretary, Eastern Committee, M. H. Keeler, Room 109, Admin. Bldg., Canadian Forces Base Halifax, F.M.O. Halifax, N.S. B3K 2XO (902/429-0654)

THE ROYAL LIFE SAVING SOCIETY CANADA

64 Charles St. E., 2nd Floor, Toronto, Ont. M4Y 1T1
(416) 966-5126
Executive Director, Miss Jocelyn Palm

THE ROYAL PHILATELIC SOCIETY OF CANADA

Secretary, Ms. R. Gould, Box 1054, Stn. A, Toronto, Ont. M5W 1G5 (416/362-4798)

ROYAL SOCIETY OF ARTS

John Adam St., London WC2, Eng.

Honorary Corresponding Members in Canada

Alta.: Prof. P.D. Walton, M.Sc., Ph.D., 14204 57th Ave., Edmonton, Alta. T6H 1B3
B.C.: Squadron Leader Clarence S. Goode, R.A.F. (ret), M. Institute R.E., Senior Fellow in Canada, 4690 Cordova Bay, Victoria, B.C. V8X 3V7
N.B.: Prof. D. S. Fensom, B.A.Sc., F.R.I.C., Dept. of Biology, Mount Allison Univ., Sackville, N.B. E0A 3C0
Ont.: E. P. Weeks, M.A., M.Litt., D.Phil., 542 Broadview Ave., Ottawa, Ont. K2A 2L4
Toronto (Hon. Corresponding Member): Raymond A. Munro, C.M., O.St.J., G.C.L.J., Kt.B., C.L., G.C.T.L., K.C.L.J., #703, 141 Adelaide St. W., Toronto, Ont. M5H 3L5
Toronto (Hon. Chairman): John J. Arena, S.B.St.J., K.C.L.J., K.C.T.L., M.L., F.S.A. (Scot.), 104 Adelaide St. W., Toronto, Ont. M5H 1S2
Que.: Lawrence M. Lande, O.C., S.M., B.A., LL.B., D.Litt., 4870 Cedar Cres., 4th floor, Montreal, P.Q. H3A 1W5
Sask.: Prof. Louis B. Jaques, M.A., Ph.D., D.Sc., F.R.S.C., 682 University Dr., Saskatoon, Sask. S7N 0J2

ROYAL SOCIETY OF CANADA

Executive Secretary, E. H. P. Garneau, 344 Wellington St., Ottawa, Ont. K1A 0N4 (613/992-3468)

RUBBER ASSOCIATION OF CANADA

100 University Ave., #501, Toronto, Ont. M5J 1V6
(416) 593-5207
President, J. Doran Moore

RURAL MUNICIPAL SECRETARY TREASURERS' ASSOCIATION

Secretary Treasurer, Wm. L. Burbank, 312 Scott Block, Moose Jaw, Sask. S6H 0B9 (306/693-1329)

RURAL ONTARIO MUNICIPAL ASSOCIATION

Secretary Treasurer, D. W. Rodgers, 100 University Ave., Ste. 902, Toronto, Ont. M5J 1V6 (416/593-1441)

ST. ANDREW'S SOCIETY OF MONTREAL

1195B Sherbrooke St. W., Montreal, P.Q. H3A 1H9
(514) 842-2030
General Secretary, Mrs. O. Gauthier

ST. ANDREW'S SOCIETY, TORONTO

Honorary Secretary, John F. Mitchell, c/o Cassels, Mitchell, #1800, 390 Bay St., Toronto, Ont. M5H 2G3 (416/364-3221)

THE ST. DAVID'S SOCIETY OF TORONTO

-not confirmed for 1982-
Secretary, Harry Hinton, 273 Old Orchard Grove, Toronto, Ont. M5M 2E6 (416/789-7231, bus.; 487-8623, res.)

ST. JOHN AMBULANCE

THE PRIORY OF CANADA OF THE MOST VENERABLE ORDER OF THE HOSPITAL OF ST. JOHN OF JERUSALEM

National Headquarters, 312 Laurier Ave. E., Ottawa, Ont. K1N 6P6
(613) 236-7461
Prior, H. E. The Governor General of Canada
Chancellor, BGen. C.J. Laurin, O.B.E.
Priory Secretary, D. W. Cunnington

Provincial Councils

Alta.: 10055-110th St., Edmonton, Alta. T5K 1J5 (403/424-8291)
B.C.: 6111 Cambie St., Vancouver, B.C. V5Z 3B2 (604/321-2651)
Man.: 535 Doreen St., Winnipeg, Man. R3G 3H5
N.B.: 200 Miles St., Fredericton, N.B. (506/472-1012)
Nfld.: Suite 30, King George V Institute, 93 Water St., Box 5489, St. John's, Nfld. A1C 5W4 (709/726-4200)
N.W.T.: Box 2640, Yellowknife, N.W.T. X0E 1H0 (403/873-5658)

N.S.: 5516 Spring Garden Rd., #209, Halifax, N.S. B3J 1G7 (902/454-5826)
Ont.: 46 Wellesley St. E., Toronto, Ont. M4Y 1G5 (416/923-8411)
Federal District, 30 The Driveway, Ottawa, Ont. K2P 1C9 (613/236-3626)
P.E.I.: 145 Pownal St., Charlottetown, P.E.I. C1A 3W7 (902/894-8356)
Que.: 405 de Maisonneuve Blvd. E., Montreal, P.Q. H2L 4J5 (514/842-4801)
Sask.: 2625 3rd Ave., Regina, Sask. S4T 0C8 (306/522-7226)

St. John Ambulance has branches in almost every community to co-ordinate demands for voluntary service by the Brigade (14,221 members), and arrange instructional programs in Safety Oriented First Aid, patient care in the home and related subjects.

SASKATCHEWAN ASSOCIATION OF RURAL MUNICIPALITIES
2075 Hamilton St., Regina, Sask. S4P 2E1
(306) 527-3577
Executive Secretary, Lorne Wilkinson

SASKATCHEWAN HISTORY & FOLKLORE SOCIETY
President, Rhoda M. Hall, 107 1st Ave. N.W., Weyburn, Sask. S4H 1N7 (306/842-4247)
Administrator, R.J. Wood, Box 1238, Moose Jaw, Sask. S6H 4P9 (306/693-6900)

SASKATCHEWAN MUNICIPAL HAIL INSURANCE ASSOCIATION
2100 Cornwall St., Regina, Sask. S4P 2K7
(306) 569-1852
Manager, K.E. Hanson

SASKATCHEWAN MUSEUMS ASSOCIATION
2205 Victoria Ave., Regina, Sask. S4P 0S4
(306) 522-3651; telex: 071-2476
Executive Director, Virginia Hatch

SASKATCHEWAN URBAN MUNICIPALITIES ASSOCIATION
#200, 1819 Cornwall St., Regina, Sask. S4P 2K4
(306) 525-3727
Executive Director, R. Wankling

SATELLITE VIDEO EXCHANGE SOCIETY
-not confirmed for 1982-
261 Powell St., Vancouver, B.C. V6A 1G3
(604) 688-4336

SCITEC (ASSOCIATION OF THE SCIENTIFIC, ENGINEERING & TECHNOLOGICAL COMMUNITY OF CANADA)
(l'association des scientifiques, ingenieurs et technologistes du Canada)
#805, 151 Slater St., Ottawa, Ont. K1P 5H3
(613) 232-0240
General Secretary, Mrs. Heather N. Hogan

SENIOR CITIZENS' FORUM OF MONTREAL
1800 Dorchester Blvd. W., Montreal, P.Q. H3H 2H2
(514) 937-7401
Executive Director, Mrs. Suzel T.-Perron

SHIPPING FEDERATION OF CANADA
President, J. A. Crichton, # 326 Board of Trade Bldg., 300 St. Sacrement St., Montreal, P.Q. H2Y 1X4 (514/849-2325)

SHOE INDUSTRY SUPPLIERS' ASSOCIATION OF CANADA
Ste. 710, 1010 Ste. Catherine St. W., Montreal, P.Q. H3B 3R4
(514) 878-9337

SHOE MANUFACTURERS ASSOCIATION OF CANADA
Ste. 710, 1010 Ste. Catherine St. W., Montreal, P.Q. H3B 3R4
(514) 878-9337

SIERRA CLUB OF ALBERTA
Box 342, Stn. G, Calgary, Alta. T3A 2G3
(403) 283-2025

SIERRA CLUB OF ONTARIO
47 Colborne St., Toronto, Ont. M5E 1E3
(416) 366-6692

SIERRA CLUB OF WESTERN CANADA
Regional Office, 536A Yates St., Victoria, B.C. V8W 1K8
(604) 386-5255

SIGN ASSOCIATION OF CANADA
1262 Don Mills Rd., Ste. 104, Don Mills, Ont. M3B 2W7
(416) 447-1128
General Manager, F.E. Church

THE SOAP & DETERGENT ASSOCIATION OF CANADA
1185 Eglinton Ave. E., Ste. 101, Don Mills, Ont. M3C 3C6
(416) 429-1074
Manager, S.K. Watanabe

SOCIAL PLANNING COUNCILS
Alta.—Edmonton Social Planning Council, #418, 10010 105 St., Edmonton, Alta. T5J 1C4 (403/423-2031)
B.C.—Social Planning & Review Council of B.C., #109, 2182 W. 12th Ave., Vancouver, B.C. V6K 2N4 (604/736-4367)
Man.—Social Planning Council of Winnipeg, 412 McDermot Ave., Winnipeg, Man. R3A OA9 (204/943-2561)
N.B.—Saint John Human Development Council, Box 6125, Stn. A, Saint John, N.B. E2L 4R6 (506/642-7262)
Ont.—Social Planning & Research Council of Hamilton & Dist., 153½ King St. E., Hamilton, Ont. L8N 1B1 (416/522-1148)
Social Planning Council of Kitchener-Waterloo, 18 Queen St. N., Kitchener, Ont. N2H 2G8 (519/578-7430)
Social Planning Council of Niagara Falls, 5017 Victoria Ave., Niagara Falls, Ont. L2E 4C9 (416/356-2482)
Social Planning Council of Oakville & Dist., Box 163, Oakville, Ont. L6J 4Z5 (416/844-7705)
Social Planning Council of Oshawa-Whitby, 52 Simcoe St. S., Oshawa, Ont. L1H 4G3 (416/725-4774)
Social Planning Council of Ottawa-Carleton, 85 Plymouth St., Ottawa, Ont. K1S 3E2 (613/236-3658)
Social Planning & Research Council of Sarnia & Lambton, 785 Exmouth, Sarnia, Ont. N7T 5P7 (519/337-2271) – not confirmed for 1982
Lakehead Social Planning Council, 221 Bay St., Thunder Bay, Ont. P7B 1R1 (807/345-3631)
Social Planning Council of Metro Toronto, 185 Bloor St. E., 3rd floor, Toronto, Ont. M4W 3J3 (416/961-9831)

SOCIAL SCIENCE FEDERATION OF CANADA
Director, J.E. Trent, 151 Slater St., Ottawa, Ont. K1P 5H3 (613/238-6112)

LA SOCIETE DES CHEFS DE CUISINE ET PATISSIERS DE LA PROVINCE DE QUEBEC
1500, rue Stanley, Ste. 205, Montreal, P.Q. H3A 1R3
(514) 843-3641
President, Maurice Martin

SOCIETE DE DEVELOPPEMENT DU LIVRE ET PERIODIQUE
1151, Alexandre DeSève, Montreal, P.Q. H2L 2T7
(514) 524-7528

AFFILIATED SOCIETIES AT SAME ADDRESS
Association des Editeurs Canadiens
Société des Editeurs de Manuels Scolaires du Québec
Association des Libraires du Québec
Société Canadienne Français de Protection du Droit d'Auteur
Edi-Québec

ASSOCIATION DES DISTRIBUTEURS EXCLUSIFS DE LIVRES EN LANGUE FRANCAISE
1977 boul. Industriel, Chomedey, Laval, P.Q. H7S 1P6
(514) 667-9221

ASSOCIATION DES EDITEURS DE PERIODIQUES CULTURELS QUEBECOIS
C.P. 786, Succ. Place d'Armes, Montréal, P.Q. H2Y 3J2
(514) 523-7724
Secrétaire exécutif, Paul Cauchon

ASSOCIATION QUEBECOISE DES PRESSES UNIVERSITAIRES
C.P. 6128, Montréal, P.Q. H3C 3J7
(514) 343-6929

LA SOCIETE DES ECRIVAINS CANADIENS
Secretary General, Gérard Brady, 1161 boul. Vanier, Ville de Laval, P.Q. H7C 2N4 (514/661-3064)

UNION DES ECRIVAINS QUEBECOIS
964 rue Cherrier, Montréal, P.Q. H2L 1H7
(514) 526-6653
Secrétaire général, Jean Yves Collette

LA SOCIETE FRANCO-MANITOBAINE
194 blvd. Provencher, C.P. 145, St. Boniface, Man. R2H 3B4
(204) 233-4915
Executive Director, Lucille Roch

SOCIETE NATIONALE D'ASSURANCES
612 St-Jacques, Ste. 601, Montreal, P.Q. H3C 3Y8
(514) 288-8711
Directeur général, Henri Joli-Coeur

SOCIETE NATIONALE DES CHEMINS DE FER FRANCAIS
1500, rue Stanley, bur. 436, Montreal, P.Q. H3A 1R3
(514) 288-8255
Manager for Canada, Jacques J. Meinnier

LA SOCIETE SAINT-JEAN-BAPTISTE DE MONTREAL
82 rue Sherbrooke ouest, Montreal, P.Q. H2X 1X3
(514) 843-8851
Executive Secretary, G. Turcotte

LA SOCIETE ST-VINCENT DE PAUL
President, Marie-Claire G. Letarte, 777 des Glacis, Quebec, P.Q. G1R 3R1 (418/692-1948)

SOCIETE DES TRADUCTEURS DU QUEBEC
(The Translators' Society of Quebec)
1010, rue Ste-Catherine ouest, bur. 340, Montreal, P.Q. H3B 1G1
(514) 861-1783

SOCIETY OF ACCREDITED MORTGAGE BROKERS
3 Church St., #407, Toronto, Ont. M5E 1M2
(416) 364-4027
Secretary, Len J. Hanley

SOCIETY OF BRITISH COLUMBIA ASSESSMENT PERSONNEL
Secretary, Ms. J. Simonsen, #301, 4911 Canada Way, Burnaby, B.C. V5G 1M1

SOCIETY OF CHEMICAL INDUSTRY
Canadian Section
Honorary Secretary, David Scott, c/o Celanese Canada Inc., Chemicals Division, #2 Robert Speck Pkwy., #900, Mississauga, Ont. L4Z 1H8 (416/276-9333, ext. 68)

SOCIETY FOR GOODWILL SERVICES
234 Adelaide St. E., Toronto, Ont. M5A 1M9
(416) 362-4711
Executive Director, J. Philip Gandon

SOCIETY OF PLASTICS ENGINEERS INC., ONTARIO SECTION
President, Barry Wheeler, Toronto Plastics, 2045 Midland Ave., Scarborough, Ont. M1P 3E2 (416/293-1156)

SOCIETY OF THE PLASTICS INDUSTRY OF CANADA
1262 Don Mills Rd., Suite 104, Don Mills, Ont. M3B 2W7
(416) 449-3444
President, E. R. Evason
Branch Office: Mrs. Elise Gagnon, Regional Manager, 555 Dorchester Blvd. W., #1729, Montreal, P.Q. H2Z 1B1 (514/861-9851-52)

SOCIETY OF PUBLIC INSURANCE ADMINISTRATORS OF ONTARIO
President, G.R. Peterson, 150 Borough Dr., Scarborough, Ont. M1P 4N7 (416/296-7237)

SOCIETY FOR RECOGNITION OF CANADIAN TALENT, INC.
881 Eglinton Ave. W., Ste. 208, Toronto, Ont. M6C 2C1
(416) 787-4000
President, Alderman Ben Nobleman

SOCIETY FOR THE RETIRED & SEMI-RETIRED
10004 105 St., Edmonton, Alta. T5J 1C3
(403) 423-5510
Executive Director, Alice Henbest

SOLAR ENERGY SOCIETY OF CANADA INC.
#303, 870 Cambridge St., Winnipeg, Man. R3M 3H5
(204) 284-3076; 475-6339

SONS OF SCOTLAND BENEVOLENT ASSOCIATION
19 Richmond St. W., Toronto, Ont. M5H 1Y9
(416) 364-4213, 4
Secretary Treasurer, Robert J. Bell

SOROPTIMIST CLUBS IN CANADA
SOROPTIMIST INTERNATIONAL:
63 Bayswater Rd., London, W.2, England

An Association of Classified Service Clubs for professional and executive business women.

WESTERN CANADA REGION
Governor, Mrs. Marguerite Duguid, 1928 32nd St. S.W., Calgary, Alta. T3E 2R1 (403/249-3474)

EASTERN CANADA REGION
Governor, Mrs. Dorothy Bertrand, 5720 Cavendish Blvd., Apt. 1907, Montreal, P.Q. H4W 1S9 (514/482-7455) – not confirmed, 1982

SPECTROSCOPY SOCIETY OF CANADA
1253 McGill College, Ste. 175, Montreal, P.Q. H3B 2Y5
(514) 866-8236
Secretary, James Fydell

SPORT PARTICIPATION CANADA
See PARTICIPaction

STEEL CASTINGS INSTITUTE OF CANADA
72 Mississaga St. E., Box 2270, Orillia, Ont. L3V 6S1
(705) 326-3895
Executive Vice President, J.L. Reade

THE STEPHEN LEACOCK ASSOCIATES
Box 854, Orillia, Ont. L3V 6K8
(705) 325-6546, winter; 375-2146, summer
Corresponding Secretary, Mrs. J. Bradley

STUDENT CHRISTIAN MOVEMENT OF CANADA
736 Bathurst St., Toronto, Ont. M5S 2R4
(416) 534-1352

THE STUDENTS UNION OF NOVA SCOTIA (SUNS)
Rm. 324, 6136 University Ave., Halifax, N.S. B3H 4J2
(902) 422-3649

SUFI – SOCIETY FOR UNDERSTANDING THE FINITE & THE INFINITE
#216, 120 George Henry Blvd., Willowdale, Ont. M2J 1G2
(416) 496-2214
President, Dr. M.Q. Baig

TANNERS ASSOCIATION OF CANADA
Box 294, Kleinburg, Ont. LOJ 1CO
(416) 851-1118
Executive Vice President, Boyd W. Browne

TEA COUNCIL OF CANADA
42 Charles St. E., Toronto, Ont. M4Y 1T4
(416) 922-3119
Corporate Secretary, Georgina DeCarlo

TEA & COFFEE ASSOCIATION OF CANADA
1185 Eglinton Ave. E., Ste. 101, Don Mills, Ont. M3C 3C6
(416) 429-1073
Executive Director, Shirley Cryderman

TECHNICAL SERVICE COUNCIL
(Le Conseil de Placement Professionnel)
President, Neil A. Macdougall, B.A.Sc., M. Com., P. Eng., #901, One St. Clair Ave. E., Toronto, Ont. M4T 2V7 (416/966-5030)
Branch, 816 7th Ave. S.W., Calgary, Alta. T2P 1A1 (403/269-7931)
Branch Manager, Keith Lott, 175 Hargrave St., Winnipeg, Man. R3C 3R8 (204/943-3484)
Branch Manager, C.H. Humble, 10709 Jasper Ave., Edmonton, Alta. T5J 3N3 (403/421-4444)
Pacific Area Manager, A.G. Tinker, 475 W. Georgia St., #1050, Vancouver, B.C. V6B 4M9 (604/682-8861)
Branch Manager, A. Lévesque, 555 Dorchester Blvd. W., Ste. 1120, Montreal, P.Q. H2Z 1B1 (514/866-2807)
Branch Manager, J.S.K. Williams, One St. Clair Ave. E., 10th Floor, Toronto, Ont. M4T 2V7 (416/966-5030)
Branch Manager, J. Forgeron, 1888 Brunswick St., Halifax, N.S. B3J 3J8 (902/422-7485)
Bryce, Haultain, Personnel Consultants, a TSC Division with locations in Toronto and Calgary

A non-profit placement service and personnel consulting organization, sponsored by industry and devoted to retaining Canadians with specialized and technical training in Canada. As a practical means of doing so, it has operated a placement service for engineers, scientists, executives, accountants, personnel and EDP staff and technologists since 1927. Studies of the supply of and demand for university graduates are published.

THE TEEN ASSOCIATION OF MODEL RAILROADING (Canadian Region)
President, Timothy M. Canfield, 409 Richards St., Nelson, B.C. V1L 5J9
Affiliated with The Teen Association of Model Railroading, New Carlisle, Ohio.

TELECASTER COMMITTEE
42 Charles St. E., Toronto, Ont. M4Y 1T5
(416) 928-6045
Co-ordinator, P. Beatty
Montreal Office: C.P. 170, Succ. C, Montreal, P.Q. H2L 4P6 (514/526-9251)
French Co-ordinator, M. Berubé

TELEVISION BUREAU OF CANADA, INC. (TvB)
65 Queen St. W., Ste. 2115, Toronto, Ont. M5H 2M5
(416) 862-1150
Secretary Treasurer, Gary Buss, Vice President, Director of Marketing & Sales, CHCH-TV

TERRAZZO TILE & MARBLE ASSOCIATION OF CANADA
#106, 3311 Bayview Ave., Willowdale, Ont. M2K 1G4
(416) 223-4460
Executive Director, John Grossi

TEXTILE TECHNICAL FEDERATION OF CANADA
4920 de Maisonneuve Blvd. W., Ste. 307, Montreal, P.Q. H3Z 1N1
(514) 487-2272
Executive Secretary, W.A.B. Davidson

THE THEOSOPHICAL SOCIETY IN CANADA
General Secretary, Ted G. Davy
Joint Editors of official journal of the Society, "The Canadian Theosophist", Mr. and Mrs. T. G. Davy, 2307 Sovereign Cres. S.W., Calgary, Alta. T3C 2M3 (403/242-6905)

THERMAL INSULATION ASSOCIATION OF CANADA
#1101, 130 Bloor St. W., Toronto, Ont. M5S 2X7
(416) 964-3656
Executive Vice President, Terry Paupst

THUNDER BAY MULTICULTURAL ASSOCIATION
Box 2334, Thunder Bay, Ont. P7B 5E9
(807) 345-0551

Operates the Immigrant Information Centre, The Northwestern Ontario Folklore Festival and publishes the Northern Mosaic Newspaper.

THYROID FOUNDATION OF CANADA
63 Gibson Ave., Kingston, Ont. K7L 4R1
(613) 546-1576
President, Mrs. Diana Meltzer Abramsky

An organization devoted to furthering thyroid research and helping patients with thyroid dysfunction.

T.O.P.C.A.T. (The Organization Protecting Children Against Tobacco-Smoke)
Box 94592, Richmond, B.C. V6Y 2V6
President, C. Forward (604/681-3825)

TORONTO ASSOCIATION OF BUSINESS ECONOMISTS INC.
Box 6125, Stn. A, Toronto, Ont. M5W 1P5
President, J.J. Clinkard

TORONTO BLACK WATCH ASSOCIATION
44 York St., Toronto, Ont. M5J 1R4
(416) 868-9416

TORONTO & DISTRICT EXCAVATORS ASSOCIATION
4180 Dundas St. W., Toronto, Ont. M8X 1X8
(416) 233-3802
Manager, Wm. T. White

TORONTO & DISTRICT SQUARE & ROUND DANCE ASSOCIATION
30 Kingswell Cres., Scarborough, Ont. M1L 3E1
(416) 757-1620
Office Manager, Mrs. Vivian Priest

TORONTO EXECUTIVES ASSOCIATION INC.
Main Mezzanine, Royal York Hotel, Toronto, Ont. M5J 1E4
(416) 364-3001
General Manager & Co-ordinator, Mrs. Helen Faver

TORONTO FILM SOCIETY
President, Jaan Salk
Secretary, Helen Arthurs, 6 Lonsdale Rd., Toronto, Ont. M4V 1W3 (416/485-8474; 967-0259)

TORONTO HOME BUILDERS' ASSOCIATION
5218 Yonge St., Willowdale, Ont. M2N 5P6
(416) 226-0010
Executive Vice President, David A. Stupart

TORONTO HOME ECONOMICS ASSOCIATION
Box 285, Stn. S, Toronto, Ont. M5M 4L7
(416) 787-4777
Executive Director, Mrs. Mary Adams

TORONTO HUMANE SOCIETY
See Canadian Federation of Humane Societies

TORONTO ISLAND AIRPORT ASSOCIATION
1A Rosedale Rd., Toronto, Ont. M4W 2P1
(416) 923-2756
President, George S. Niblett

THE TORONTO SOCIETY OF FINANCIAL ANALYSTS
390 Bay St., 24th floor, Toronto, Ont. M5H 2R6
(416) 366-5755
Associated Organization
The Financial Analysts Federation

TORONTO VEGETARIAN ASSOCIATION
28 Walker Ave., Toronto, Ont. M4V 1G2
(416) 923-1933
Executive Director, Mrs. Barbara Jackson

TOURISM
See Travel

TOWNS OF NEW BRUNSWICK ASSOCIATION
Executive Secretary, Dr. Alex Savoie, 14 Guerrette St., Edmundston, N.B. E3V 1N9 (506/739-8133)

TRAFFIC INJURY RESEARCH FOUNDATION OF CANADA
171 Nepean St., 6th Floor, Ottawa, Ont. K2P 0B4
(613) 238-5235
Secretary, S. W. Ryan
Executive Director, Dr. H. M. Simpson

TRAIL RIDERS OF THE CANADIAN ROCKIES
Box 6742, Stn. D, Calgary, Alta. T2P 2E6
(403) 287-1746
Secretary Manager, Mrs. Barbara Henson

TRANS-CANADA ADVERTISING AGENCY NETWORK
696 Yonge St., #701, Toronto, Ont. M4Y 2A7
(416) 925-5544
Managing Director, W. S. Whitehead

TRANSPORT 2000 CANADA
Box 858, Stn. B, Ottawa, Ont. K1P 5P9
(613) 235-2865

TRAVEL & TOURISM ASSOCIATIONS
(If information is required on a specific locality, contact the Chamber of Commerce. See Index.)

ACTA (Alliance of Canadian Travel Associations)
130 Albert St., Ste. 1207, Ottawa, Ont. K1P 5G4
(613) 238-1361
Executive Director, Gareth J. Davies

Member Associations

ACTA ATLANTIC (ATIC)
c/o Box 1030, Charlottetown, P.E.I. C1A 7M4

ACTA QUEBEC (QATA)
410 Henri Bourassa Blvd. E., Montreal, P.Q. H3L 1C4
(514) 381-8541

ACTA ONTARIO (OTIC)
67 Yonge St., Ste. 1208, Toronto, Ont. M5E 1J8
(416) 366-1909

ACTA MANITOBA (MTIA)
Box 54, St. Boniface (208 Provencher Blvd.), Winnipeg, Man. R2H 3B4
(204) 888-1268

ACTA SASKATCHEWAN (SATA)
c/o Box 850, Yorkton, Sask. S3N 2X1
(306) 783-3653

ACTA ALBERTA (ATAA)
6320 Louise Rd. S.W., Calgary, Alta. T3E 5V5
(403) 246-8339

ACTA BRITISH COLUMBIA (ATA-BC)
#251, 409 Granville St., Vancouver, B.C. V6C 1T2
(604) 682-0516

Association of Convention Co-ordinators (Convention Planners)
15 Toronto St., #702, Toronto, Ont. M5C 2E3
(416) 364-1223
Executive Secretary, Mrs. Susan Cooke

Association des Terrains de Camping du Quebec
8775 Lacordaire, St-Léonard, P.Q. H1R 2A9
(514) 323-1604

Association of Children's Camps
#2, 1806 Avenue Rd., Toronto, Ont. M5M 3Z1
(416) 781-4717
Executive Director, Ms. Marjorie Booth

Canadian Camping Association
1806 Avenue Rd., #2, Toronto, Ont. M5M 3Z1
(416) 781-4717
Executive Director, Ms. Marjorie Booth

Affiliated Associations

BRITISH COLUMBIA CAMPING ASSOCIATION
1200 Hornby St., Vancouver, B.C. V6Z 1Z2
(604) 879-5108

ALBERTA CAMPING ASSOCIATION
c/o Y.M.C.A., 332 6th Ave. S.W., Calgary, Alta. T2P 0R5

-6156

...CHEWAN CAMPING ASSOCIATION
c/o Saskatoon Y.M.C.A., 25 22 St. E., Saskatoon, Sask. S7K 0C7
(306) 652-7151

MANITOBA CAMPING ASSOCIATION
Admin. Centre for Recreation & Sport, 1700 Ellice Ave., Winnipeg, Man. R3H 0B1
(204) 786-5641

ONTARIO CAMPING ASSOCIATION
1806 Avenue Rd., #2, Toronto, Ont. M5M 3Z1
(416) 781-0525

ASSOCIATION DES CAMPS DU QUEBEC
1415 est rue Jarry, Montreal, P.Q. H2E 2Z7
(514) 374-4700, ext. 447

NEW BRUNSWICK CAMPING ASSOCIATION
Dunlop Lane, Saint John, N.B. E2L 3C9

NOVA SCOTIA CAMPING ASSOCIATION
Box 3243 South, Halifax, N.S. B3J 3H5
(902) 424-4329

NEWFOUNDLAND & LABRADOR CAMPING ASSOCIATION
Box 4188, St. John's, Nfld. A1C 5Z7

Canadian Country Vacations Association
437 Assiniboine Ave., Winnipeg, Man. R3C OY5
(204) 943-8361
Co-ordinator, Mrs. Marguerite Manning

ALBERTA COUNTRY VACATIONS
R.R. 1, Chauvin, Alta. TOB OVO
(403) 858-2234
Secretary, Mrs. Georgina Taylor

MANITOBA FARM VACATIONS ASSOCIATION
437 Assiniboine Ave., Winnipeg, Man. R3C OY5
(204) 943-8361

NEW BRUNSWICK FARM VACATION ASSOCIATION
President, Mrs. Anita Connors, Smith Corner Farm, Harcourt R.R. 1, Kent Co., N.B. E0A 1T0 (506/785-4361)

ONTARIO VACATION FARM ASSOCIATION
Executive Director, Mrs. Lynda Clipsham, R.R. 2, Erin, Ont. N0B 1T0

SASKATCHEWAN FARM VACATIONS ASSOCIATION
c/o Mrs. Irene Lightbody, Box 24, Bateman, Sask. S0H 0E0

Canadian Holiday Home Exchange
Since 1972: associated with Air Canada & offices world wide. Offers vacationers no-cost international home-swap opportunities; specializes UK, Germany, France etc., USA & Canada. Listing & Directory $39.50.
Box 2416, Vancouver, B.C. V6B 3W7

Canadian Hostelling Association
333 River Rd., Vanier, Ont. K1L 8B9
(613) 746-0060
Executive Director, Robert Ernest Martin

CHA Newfoundland Hostel Association, Box 1815, St. John's, Nfld. A1C 5P9 (709/753-8603)
CHA P.E.I. Hostelling Association, Box 1718, Charlottetown, P.E.I. C1A 7N4 (902/894-9696)
CHA Nova Scotia Region, 5516 Spring Garden Rd., Box 3010 South, Halifax, N.S. B3J 1G6 (902/425-5450)
CHA Nova Scotia Region, 6260 Quinpool Rd., Halifax, N.S. B3L 1A3 (902/423-8736)
CHA Quebec Hostelling Association, 1324 Sherbrooke St. W., Montreal, P.Q. H3G 1H9 (514/842-9048)
CHA Ontario Region, 8 York St., 2nd Floor, Toronto, Ont. M5J 1R2 (416/368-1848)
CHA Ontario Region, National Capital Hostelling Association, 150 Metcalfe St., #109, Ottawa, Ont. K2P 1P1 (613/233-7738)
CHA Ontario Region, Great Lakes Division, 8 York St., 2nd Floor, Toronto, Ont. M5J 1R2 (416/368-1848)
CHA Manitoba Region, Manitoba Sports Recreation Centre, 1700 Ellice Ave., Winnipeg, Man. R3H 0B1 (204/786-5641)
CHA Saskatchewan Region, 2205 Victoria Ave., Regina, Sask. S4P 0S4 (306/522-3651)
CHA Alberta Hostelling Association, 10926 88th Ave., Edmonton, Alta. T6G 0Z1 (403/433-5513)
CHA Southern Alberta Hostelling Association, 1414 Kensington Rd. N.W., #203, Calgary, Alta. T2N 3P9 (403/283-5551)
CHA Northern Alberta Hostelling Association, 10926 88th Ave., Edmonton, Alta. T6G 0Z1 (403/432-7798)
CHA British Columbia Region, 3425 W. Broadway, Vancouver, B.C. V6R 2B4 (604/736-2674)
CHA British Columbia Region Packs & Boots Shop (Yates Mall), 720 Yates St., Unit 10, Victoria, B.C. V8W 1L5 (604/383-2144)
CHA Yukon Region, Box 4762, Whitehorse, YT Y1A 4N6 (403/667-2402)

Canadian Hotel Marketing & Sales Executives
15 Toronto St., #702, Toronto, Ont. M5C 2E3
(416) 364-1223
Executive Director, Mrs. Susan Cooke

CITC (Canadian Institute of Travel Counsellors)
67 Yonge St., #1208, Toronto, Ont. M5E 1J8
(416) 362-1325
Information & Office Manager, Jeff C. Bateman

CITC (QUEBEC & ATLANTIC)
c/o 1010 St. Catherine St. W., #16A, Montreal, P.Q.
(514) 871-9600

CITC (ONTARIO)
67 Yonge St., #1208, Toronto, Ont. M5E 1J8
(416) 362-1325

CITC (MANITOBA)
Box 2007, Winnipeg, Man.

CITC (SASKATCHEWAN)
Box 3686, Regina, Sask.

CITC (ALBERTA)
c/o 109th St. & Kingsway Ave., Edmonton, Alta. T5S 6G5
(403) 474-8700

CITC (BRITISH COLUMBIA)
c/o #411, 1200 W. 73rd Ave., Vancouver, B.C. V6P 6G5
(604) 263-3117

Canadian Manufactured Housing Institute
55 York St., Suite 512, Toronto, Ont. M5J 1S2
(416) 363-8374
Executive Vice President, Frank Young

Canadian Motor Coach Association
#1310, Tower B, Place de Ville, 112 Kent St., Ottawa, Ont. K1P 5P2
(613) 238-1800
Executive Director, H. Segal

Canadian Recreational Vehicle Association
55 York St., Ste. 512, Toronto, Ont. M5J 1S2
(416) 363-8374
Executive Vice President, Frank Young

Canadian Universities Travel Service Ltd.
44 St. George St., Toronto, Ont. M5S 2E4
(416) 979-2604
Offices in Vancouver, Edmonton, Saskatoon, Ottawa (2), Toronto and Halifax.
Publishers of "The Canadian Student Traveller"

Cape Breton Tourist Association
20 Keltic Dr., Sydney River, N.S. B1S 1P5
(902) 539-9876

Commercial Travellers' Associations

THE COMMERCIAL TRAVELLERS' ASSOCIATION OF CANADA
365 Bloor St. E., #1002, Toronto, Ont. M4W 3K2
(416) 924-7724
General Manager, T.J. Ruffell

MARITIME COMMERCIAL TRAVELLERS' ASSOCIATION
Secretary, R. F. Croft, Box 39, Halifax, N.S. B3J 2L4 (902/423-6738)

THE NORTH WEST COMMERCIAL TRAVELLERS' ASSOCIATION OF CANADA
General Manager & Secretary, John McWilliams
Head Office, North West Travellers' Bldg., 291 Garry St., Box 336, Winnipeg, Man. R3C 2H6 (204/957-1442)

THE GIDEONS INTERNATIONAL IN CANADA
501 Imperial Rd., Guelph, Ont. N1H 7A2
(519) 823-1140
Executive Director, David M. MacLeod

UNITED COMMERCIAL TRAVELERS OF AMERICA
Chief Agent for Canada, W. C. Shortt, 1001 Cloverdale Ave., Ste. 210, Victoria, B.C. V8X 4C9 (604/388-6440)
Grand Council, Ont.-Que.—Grand Secretary, Charles P. Newman, 5 Fleance Cres., Thornhill, Ont. L3T 3J8
Grand Council, Man.-Sask.-Alta.—Grand Secretary, J. B. Chrisp, 504-13th St. S., Brandon, Man. R7A 4R2
Grand Council, Oregon-Washington-B.C.—Grand Secretary, Donald Henning, 3135 Van Ave., Eugene, Ore. 97401
Grand Council, Atlantic Provinces—Grand Secretary, William C. Ball, 23 Colonel Gray Dr., Charlottetown, P.E.I. C1A 2S6

Hospitality New Brunswick

(Incorporating the New Brunswick Restaurant & Foodservices Association and the New Brunswick Hotel-Motel Association)
349 King St., Fredericton, N.B. E3B 1E4
(506) 454-2615

Hotel Association of Canada, Inc.

Executive Vice President, Dario J. Perfumo, #300, 428 Portage Ave., Winnipeg, Man. R3C 0E2

Provincial Associations

ALBERTA HOTEL ASSOCIATION
Executive Vice President, G. T. Barr, #804, 10080 Jasper Ave., Edmonton, Alta. T5J 1V9 (403/422-6530)

BRITISH COLUMBIA HOTELS ASSOCIATION
Executive Vice President, Lloyd W. Manuel, 1st floor, Hotel Vancouver, 900 W. Georgia St., Vancouver, B.C. V6C 1P9

THE MANITOBA HOTEL ASSOCIATION
Executive Vice President, D. J. Perfumo, #300, 428 Portage Ave., Winnipeg, Man. R3C 0E2 (204/942-0671)

PROVINCE OF QUEBEC HOTEL ASSOCIATION
Managing Director, Pierre Salvail, 1500 Stanley St., Montreal, P.Q. H3A 1R3 (514/849-1157)

HOTELS ASSOCIATION OF SASKATCHEWAN
Executive Vice President & Managing Director, J. R. Freestone, 404 Guaranty Trust Bldg., Regina, Sask. S4P 0J3 (306/522-7141)

Huronia Tourist Association

Simcoe County Bldg., Midhurst, Ont. L0L 1X0
(705) 726-9300, ext. 220

Institut de Tourisme et d'Hotellerie du Québec

401 de Rigaud, Montreal, P.Q. H2L 4P5
(514) 873-4163
Directeur général, Antoine Samuelli

International Association for Medical Assistance to Travellers

123 Edward St., #725, Toronto, Ont. M5G 1E2
(416) 977-6059

Kawartha Tourist Association

Box 802, Peterborough, Ont. K9J 7A2
(705) 743-5940
Secretary Manager, Ross Wiegand

Motel Associations

ACCOMMODATION MOTEL ONTARIO ASSOCIATION
Box 1563, Peterborough, Ont. K9J 7H7
(705) 745-4982
Executive Secretary, Mrs. Isabel Henderson

MOTEL ASSOCIATION OF ALBERTA
Box 5262, Stn. E, Edmonton, Alta. T5P 4C5
(403) 483-6987
Executive Director, G. G. Marshall

BRITISH COLUMBIA MOTELS, RESORTS & TRAILER PARKS ASSOCIATION
1251 Kingsway, Vancouver, B.C. V5V 3E2
(604) 879-7833; 879-4141
Managing Director, W.N. Cary

Muskoka Tourist Association

-not confirmed for 1982-
Box 58, Gravenhurst, Ont. P0C 1G0
(705) 687-3331

Northern Ontario Tourist Outfitters Association

Box 1140, North Bay, Ont. P1B 8K4
(705) 472-5552
Executive Director, Roger Liddle

Ontario Hotel & Motel Association

10 St. Mary St., #601, Toronto, Ont. M4Y 1P9
(416) 961-8440
Executive Vice President, Mrs. Nancy Towning

Ontario Ski Resorts Association

17 Mill St., Willowdale, Ont. M2P 1B3
(416) 485-8340
Executive Director, Donald K. McIlveen

Quebec Camping Association, Inc.

2233 Belgrave Ave., Montreal, P.Q. H4A 2L9
(514) 489-1541
Executive Secretary, Frances M. Kelly

Resorts Ontario

Sundial Dr. E., Box 2148, Orillia, Ont. L3V 6S1
(705) 325-9115 and (416) 363-1100
Telex: 06-875600
Managing Director, Mrs. Shirley Dobson

Tourism Industry Association of Canada

130 Albert St., Suite 1016, Ottawa, Ont. K1P 5G4
(613) 238-3883
President & Chief Executive Officer, F.G. Brander

Provincial & Major City Contacts

Alberta: Mrs. Gillian Nish, Executive Director, Travel Industry Association of Alta., #207, 1235 17th Ave. S.W., Calgary, Alta. T2T 0C2 (403/244-3384)
Calgary Tourist & Convention Association, 1300 6th Ave. S.W., Calgary, Alta. T3C 0H8 (403/263-8510)
City of Edmonton Travel Development Director, J.P. Learney, #2410, 10235 101 St., Edmonton, Alta. T5J 3G1 (403/428-5464)

British Columbia: Tourism Industry Association of B.C., Box 2323, New Westminster, B.C. V3L 5A4 (604/525-9019); Vice President, Dan Lacasse
Greater Vancouver Convention & Visitors Bureau, Pacific Centre Mall, Box 10171, Vancouver, B.C. V7Y 1H5 (604/682-2222)

uver Island Publicity Bureau, #M36, 635 Humboldt , Victoria, B.C. V8W 1A7 (604/382-3551)

Manitoba: Executive Vice President, Tourism Industry Association of Man., #232, 375 York Ave., Winnipeg, Man. R3C 3J3 (204/943-1551)

New Brunswick: Hospitality New Brunswick, 349 King St., Fredericton, N.B. E3B 1E4 (506/454-2615); President, C.K. DeGrace

Director of Promotion, Dept. of Tourism, Box 12345, Fredericton, N.B. E3B 5C3 (506/453-2377)

Saint John Visitor & Convention Bureau, Box 1971, Saint John, N.B. E2L 4L1 (506/658-2878)

Fredericton Visitors & Convention Bureau, Box 130, Fredericton, N.B. E3B 4Y7 (506/455-9426)

Newfoundland: Tourism Industry Association of Nfld., Box 2016, St. John's, Nfld. A1C 5R8 (709/737-3814) General Manager, A.J. Winsor

Dept. of Development, Tourism Branch, Box 2016, St. John's, Nfld. A1C 5R8 (709/737-2830)

St. John's Tourist Commission & Convention Bureau, City Hall, Box 1567, St. John's, Nfld. A1C 5P3 (709/722-7080); General Manager, J.C. Tessier

Nova Scotia: Tourism Industry Association of N.S., Gordon Harmer IV, Chief Executive Officer, 5871 Spring Garden Rd., Halifax, N.S. B3H 1Y2

Central Nova Tourist Association, Box 176, Stewiacke, N.S. B0N 2J0

Halifax Visitors & Convention Bureau, R.W. Chisholm, Director, Ste. 508, Market Mall, Scotia Sq., Box 1749, Halifax, N.S. B3J 3A5 (902/426-6448) Telex: 019-22641

Ontario: Visitors & Convention Services, Regional Municipality of Hamilton-Wentworth, 100 Main St. E., Hamilton, Ont. L8N 3V9 (416/526-4222)

Niagara Falls, Canada, Visitor & Convention Bureau, 5433 Victoria Ave., Niagara Falls, Ont. L2G 3L1 (416/356-6061)

Ottawa Visitors & Convention Bureau, 222 Queen St., 7th floor, Ottawa, Ont. K1P 5V9 (613/237-5150)

Convention & Tourist Bureau of Metropolitan Toronto, Box 510, Ste. 110, Toronto Eaton Centre, 220 Yonge St., Toronto, Ont. M5B 2H1 (416/979-3133)

Southwestern Ontario Travel Association, c/o Box 5035, London, Ont. N6A 4L9 (519/679-0211)

Metro. Toronto Travel Association, W.M. Duron, Executive Vice President, c/o Convention & Tourist Bureau of Metropolitan Toronto, Ste. 110, Box 510, 220 Yonge St., Toronto, Ont. M5B 2H1

Georgian Lakelands Travel Association, Simcoe County Bldg., Midhurst, Ont. LOL 1XO (705/726-9300)

Central Ont. Travel Association, A. Campagnola, Manager, Box 191, Peterborough, Ont. K9J 6Y8 (705/745-3780)

Eastern Ont. Travel Association, W.A. Elliott, Managing Director, Lansdowne Travel Centre, Reynolds Rd. & 1000 Islands Pkwy., Lansdowne, Ont. KOE 1LO (613/659-2188)

Northwest Ontario Travel Association, M.P. Duggan, Executive Director, Box 647, Kenora, Ont. P9N 3X6 (807/468-5853)

North of Superior Travel Association, Dan Fulcher, General Manager, 107 Johnson Ave., Thunder Bay, Ont. P7B 5X7

Cochrane Timiskaming Travel Association, (James Bay Frontier), Guy Lamarche, Manager, #119, The 101 Mall, Box 1162, Timmins, Ont. P4N 7H9 (705/264-9589)

Algoma Kinniwabi Travel Association, Udo Rauk, Manager, #203, 616 Queen St. E., Sault Ste. Marie, Ont. P6A 2A4

Rainbow Country Travel Association, 1543 Paris St., Sudbury, Ont. P3E 3B7 (705/522-0104)

Almaguin-Nipissing Travel Association, V. McKinnon, Manager, 269 Main St. W., North Bay, Ont. P1B 8H5 (705/474-6634)

Prince Edward Island: Tourism Industry Association of P.E.I., General Manager, John E. MacRae, Box 2050, Charlottetown, P.E.I. C1A 7N7 (902/892-8960)

P.E.I. Convention Bureau, Contact: Judith Hinton, Box 2077, Charlottetown, P.E.I. C1A 7N7 (902/892-5900)

Quebec: Alain Famy, Director of Marketing, Ministry of Industry, Commerce & Tourism, 1 Place Ville Marie, #2433, Montreal, P.Q. H3B 3M9 (514/873-7977)

City of Montreal, CIDEM-Tourism, Pierre Labrie, Commissioner, 155 Notre Dame St. E., Montreal, P.Q. H2Y 1B5 (514/872-4756)

Tourist & Convention Dept. of La Communaute Urbaine de Quebec, 399 est rue St-Joseph, Quebec, P.Q. G1K 3B5 (418/529-8771)

Montreal Convention & Visitors' Bureau, F Mart, 49 Frontenac, Box 889, Place Bonaventure, Montreal, P.Q. H5A 1E6 (514/871-1129)

Saskatchewan: Tourism Saskatchewan Inc., Box 3022, Regina, Sask. S4P 3G7 (306/584-3813)

Regina Tourist & Convention Bureau, 2145 Albert St., Regina, Sask. S4P 2V1 (306/527-6631) Executive Director, W.L. Whelan

Saskatoon Tourist & Convention Bureau, 610 Spadina Cres., Saskatoon, Sask. S7K 3G8 (306/242-1206) Manager, Pat Ettinger

Northwest Territories: Travel Industry Association, N.W.T., Isabelle Wilcox, Acting General Manager, Box 506, Yellowknife, N.W.T. X0E 1H0 (403/873-2122)

Yukon: Yukon Visitors Association, R.B. Redfern, Executive Director, 208D Steele St., Whitehorse, Y.T. Y1A 2C6

Klondike Visitors Association, Box 389, Dawson City, Y.T.

Travellers Aid Society of Metro Toronto

Room B23, Union Station, Toronto, Ont. M5J 1E6
(416) 366-7788

Western Guides & Outfitters Association

Box 3790, Smithers, B.C. V0J 2N0
(604) 847-9688

TRUCK LOGGERS ASSOCIATION

837 W. Hastings St., Vancouver, B.C. V6C 1B6
(604) 684-4291
General Manager, Don Mackenzie

THE TRUST COMPANIES ASSOCIATION OF CANADA

Ste. 400, 11 Adelaide St. W., Toronto, Ont. M5H 1L9
(416) 364-1207
Executive Vice President, William W. Potter
Director, Reseach & Administration, & Secretary, James Sayers

There are branches with elected Chairmen in every province. Contact the Toronto address, above, for up to date names.

UFO CENTRE

Box 54, Agincourt, Ont. M1S 3B4
Director, Henry H. McKay

UKRAINIAN CANADIAN COMMITTEE

(and Ukrainian Canadian Foundation of Taras Shevchenko)

National Office, 456 Main St., Winnipeg, Man. R3B 1B6
(204) 942-4627, 943-1927
Executive Director, Mrs. A. Wach, A.C.I.S.
Regional Offices, Montreal, P.Q.; Toronto, Ont.; Saskatoon, Sask.; Edmonton, Alta.; Vancouver, B.C.

There are many affiliated organizations across Canada.

UKRAINIAN CANADIAN STUDENTS' UNION (SUSK)

National Office, 191 Lippincott St., Toronto, Ont. M5S 2P3
(416) 968-1599
President, Mykhajlo Maryn

(Regional offices in Eastern and Western Canada, and constituent clubs on most campuses between Montreal and Victoria.)

UNION OF BRITISH COLUMBIA MUNICIPALITIES

313 6th St., New Westminster, B.C. V3L 3A7
(604) 526-4447
Executive Director, C.S.J. McKelvey

UNION DES FEMMES ARABES AU CANADA

3866 Kent St., Montreal, P.Q.
(514) 739-5186

UNION OF MANITOBA MUNICIPALITIES

Secretary Treasurer, W.H. Rusk, Box 536, Portage la Prairie, Man. R1N 3B9 (204/857-8666)

UNION DES MUNICIPALITES DU QUEBEC

-not confirmed for 1982-
922 est, rue de Liège, Montréal, P.Q. H2P 1L1
(514) 387-2576
Attn.: Luc Lacharité

UNION OF NOVA SCOTIA MUNICIPALITIES

Executive Director, Sherman Zwicker, #134, 1657 Barrington St., Halifax, N.S. B3J 2A1 (902/423-8331)

UNION OF ONTARIO INDIANS

27 Queen St. E., Toronto, Ont. M5C 1R5
(416) 366-3527
Executive Director, Bill Lee

UNITARIAN SERVICE COMMITTEE OF CANADA (USC CANADA)

Executive Director, Dr. Lotta Hitschmanova, 56 Sparks St., Ottawa, Ont. K1P 5B1 (613/234-6827)

UNITED CO-OPERATIVES OF ONTARIO

Chief Executive Officer, Julian L. Smith, Box 527, Stn. A, Mississauga, Ont. L5A 3A4 (416/270-3560)

THE UNITED EMPIRE LOYALISTS' ASSOCIATION OF CANADA

Dominion Headquarters: 23 Prince Arthur Ave., Toronto, Ont. M5R 1B2
(416) 923-7921
Editor of the Loyalist Gazette, E. J. Chard
Chairman, Dominion Headquarters, E. J. Chard

There are branches in every area of Canada. Contact the Toronto address above, for latest names and addresses.

UNITED NATIONS ASSOCIATIONS

See Diplomatic Section of the Almanac

THE UNITED SENIOR CITIZENS OF ONTARIO INC.

Office, 3505 Lakeshore Blvd. W., Toronto, Ont. M8W 1N5
(416) 252-2021
President, J. V. VanWaggoner, 99 17th St., Toronto, Ont. M8V 3K5

UNITED WAY/CENTRAIDE CANADA

Place de Ville, #915, 112 Kent St., Tower B, Ottawa, Ont. K1P 5P2
(613) 236-7041
Executive Director, Robert J. Myers

Member United Ways

ALBERTA UNITED WAYS

United Way of Calgary, 120 13th Ave. S.E., Calgary, Alta. T2G 1B3
United Way of Edmonton & Area, #420, 10010 105th St., Edmonton, Alta. T5J 1C4
United Way of Fort McMurray, Box 4011, Fort McMurray, Alta. T9H 3L3
Grande Prairie & Dist. United Way, 10011 103 Ave., Box 578, Grande Prairie, Alta. T8V 3A8
Lethbridge United Way, 1120 7th Ave. S., Lethbridge, Alta. T1J 1K5
United Way of Medicine Hat, Redcliff & Dist., 380 2nd St. S.E., Medicine Hat, Alta. T1A 7G7
United Way of Red Deer & Dist., 4315 55 Ave., Box 97, Red Deer, Alta. T4N 5E7

BRITISH COLUMBIA UNITED WAYS

Cowichan United Way, Box 11, Duncan, B.C. V9L 3X1
Elk Valley & Dist. United Way, Box 1589, Fernie, B.C. VOB 1MO
United Way of Kamloops, #2, 219 Victoria St., Kamloops, B.C. V2C 2A1
Central Okanagan United Way, Box 1117, Kelowna, B.C. V1Y 7P8
Kimberley & Dist. United Way, Box 185, Kimberley, B.C. V1A 2P5
Nanaimo & Dist. United Way, Box 304, Nanaimo, B.C. V9R 5L3
Powell River & Dist. United Way, Box 370, Powell River, B.C. V8Z 5C2
Prince George & Dist. United Appeal, Box 494, Prince George, B.C. V2L 4S6
United Way of Trail, 1199 Cedar Ave., Trail, B.C. V1R 2S2
United Way of British Columbia, 2210 W. 12th Ave., Vancouver, B.C. V6K 2N6
United Way of Lower Mainland, 1625 W. 8th Ave., Vancouver, B.C. V6J 1T9
Vernon & Dist. United Way, Box 533, Vernon, B.C. V1T 2M8
United Way of Greater Victoria, 1081 Fort St., Victoria, B.C. V8V 3K5

MANITOBA UNITED WAYS

Brandon & Dist. United Appeal, Box 21, Brandon, Man. R7A 5Y6
Minnedosa & Dist. United Way, Box 856, Minnedosa, Man. R0J 1E0
United Way of Morden & Dist. Inc., Box 1406, Morden, Man. R0G 1J0
Portage Plains United Way, Inc., Box 810, Portage la Prairie, Man. R1N 3C3
Winkler & Dist. United Way Inc., Box 1528, Winkler, Man. R0G 2X0
United Way of Winnipeg, 267 Edmonton St., #315, Winnipeg, Man. R3C 1S2

NEW BRUNSWICK UNITED WAYS

The United Way of Fredericton, Inc., 119 Smythe St., Fredericton, N.B.
United Way of Moncton, 25 Wilbur St., Moncton, N.B. E1C 8M9
Oromocto & Area United Way, Box 98, Oromocto, N.B. E2V 2G4
United Way of Greater Saint John Inc., 10 King St., Box 7152, Stn. A, Saint John, N.B. E2L 4S5

NOVA SCOTIA UNITED WAYS

United Way of Amherst, Box 535, Amherst, N.S. B4H 4A1
United Way of Halifax-Dartmouth Metro Area, Ste. 504, Market St. Mall, Scotia Sq., Halifax, N.S. B3J 1N9
United Way of Pictou County, Box 75, New Glasgow, N.S. B2H 3PO
United Way of Cape Breton County, 56 Inglis St., Sydney, N.S. B1P 6H1
Truro & Dist. United Way, 22 McLean St., (Box 32, Truro, N.S. B2N 5B6)

ONTARIO UNITED WAYS

The Ajax-Pickering United Way, 158 Harwood Ave. S., Ste. #1, Ajax, Ont. L1S 2H6
Barrie & Dist. United Way, Box 644, Barrie, Ont. L4M 4V1
United Community Services of Belleville & Dist. Inc., 240 William St., Box 815, Belleville, Ont. K8N 3K3
United Community Fund of Brantford & Brant County, 88½ Colborne St., Box 7, Brantford, Ont. N3T 5M3
United Way of Leeds & Grenville, Box 576, Brockville, Ont. K6V 5V7

Way of Cambridge, 24 Dale Ave., Box 13, Cambridge, N1R 5S9
United Community Fund of Chatham & Dist., 93 Centre St., Box 805, Chatham, Ont. N7M 5L1
Cobourg & Dist. United Way, Box 476, Cobourg, Ont. K9A 4L1
Collingwood & Dist. United Way, Box 442, Collingwood, Ont. L9Y 3Z7
United Way of Cornwall & Dist., (331 Water St. E.), Box 441, Cornwall, Ont. K6H 5T2
Deep River Dist. Community Chest, Box 188, Deep River, Ont. K0J 1P0
Peace Bridge Area United Way, 560 Central Ave., Fort Erie, Ont. L2A 5V6
United Way of Guelph, 161 Waterloo Ave., Guelph, Ont. N1H 3H9
United Way in Burlington & Hamilton Wentworth, 177 Rebecca St., Hamilton, Ont. L8R 1B9
United Way of Kingston & Dist., 162 Wellington St., Ste. 11, Kingston, Ont. K7L 3E2
Kirkland & Dist. United Way, Box 313, Kirkland Lake, Ont. P2N 3H7
United Way of Lindsay & Dist., 260 Kent St. W., Lindsay, Ont. K9V 2Z5
United Way of Greater London, 409 King St., London, Ont. N6B 1S5
United Way of Peel Region, 77 City Centre Dr., #207, Mississauga, Ont. L5B 1M5
United Way of Niagara Falls, 5017 Victoria Ave., Niagara Falls, Ont. L2E 4C9
United Way of Oakville, 95 Thomas St., Box 94, Oakville, Ont. L6J 4Z5
United Way, Oshawa-Whitby-Newcastle, 52 Simcoe St. S., Oshawa, Ont. L1H 4G3
United Way of Ottawa Carleton, 85 Plymouth St., Ottawa, Ont. K1S 3E2
United Fund of the Upper Ottawa Valley Inc., Box 727, Pembroke, Ont. K8A 6X9
United Way of Peterborough & Dist., 277 Stewart St., Peterborough, Ont. K9H 3M8
United Way of York Region, Box 195, Richmond Hill, Ont. L4C 4Y2
United Way of St. Catharines & Dist. Inc., 15 King St., St. Catharines, Ont. L2R 6Y3
Elgin-St. Thomas United Way Services, 6 Princess Ave., St. Thomas, Ont. N5R 3V2
United Way of Sarnia-Lambton, Box 548, Sarnia, Ont. N7T 7J4
United Way of Sault Ste. Marie, 8 Albert St. E., Sault Ste. Marie, Ont. P6A 2H6
United Way of Haldimand-Norfolk, 43 Kent St. S., Simcoe, Ont. N3Y 2X7
Stratford United Way, 15 Downie St., Box 186, Stratford, Ont. N5A 6T1
United Way of Sudbury, c/o Addiction Research Foundation, 144 Pine St., #203, Sudbury, Ont. P3C 1X3
United Way of Thunder Bay, 857 May St. N., Box 2000, Thunder Bay, Ont. P7C 4Y4
Porcupine United Appeal, 108 Balsam St. S., Box 984, Timmins, Ont. P4N 7H6
United Way of Greater Toronto, 156 Front St. W., 4th Floor, Toronto, Ont. M5J 1J3
United Way of Welland & Dist., 636 King St., Box 84, Welland, Ont. L3B 3L1
United Way of Windsor & Essex County, 2260 University Ave. W., Windsor, Ont. N9B 1E5
Woodstock United Way, 800 Dundas St., Box 354, Woodstock, Ont. N4S 7X6

PRINCE EDWARD ISLAND UNITED WAY

United Way of P.E.I., Box 247, Charlottetown, P.E.I. C1A 7K4

QUEBEC UNITED WAYS

Centraide Saguenay Lac-St-Jean, Mail 170, 55 rte 170, Secteur Arvida, Jonquière, P.Q. G7S 4L1
Centraide de l'ouest québécois, 72 rue Laval, #101, Hull, P.Q. J8X 3H3
Centraide Portage-Taché, C.P. 520, La Pocatière, P.Q. G0R 1Z0
Centraide Montreal, 493 ouest, rue Sherbrooke, Montreal, P.Q. H3A 1B6
Centraide Coeur du Québec, C.P. 340, Nicolet, P.Q. J0G 1E0
Centraide Quebec, C.P. 130, St-Sauveur, 180 Blouin, Ville Vanier, Quebec, P.Q. G1M 1E3
Centraide Richelieu-Yamaska, C.P. 426, St-Hyacinthe, P.Q. J2S 7B8
Centre des Services Sociaux de la Côte Filiale de Sept-Iles, 405 rue Brochu, #200, Sept-Iles, P.Q.

SASKATCHEWAN UNITED WAYS

Arborfield & Dist. United Appeal, Box 92, Arborfield, Sask. S0E 0A0
Canora United Appeal, Box 278, Canora, Sask. S0A 0L0
Elrose & Dist. United Appeal, Box 41, Elrose, Sask. S0L 0Z0
United Way of Estevan, Box 611, Estevan, Sask. S4A 2A5
Eston United Way, Box 245, Eston, Sask. S0L 1A0
Kindersley & Dist. United Appeal, Box 489, Kindersley, Sask. S0L 1S0
Lloydminster & Dist. United Way, Box 391, Lloydminster, Sask. S9V 0Y4
United Way of Moose Jaw, 55 High St. W., Box 1359, Moose Jaw, Sask. S6H 7A8
The Battlefords United Appeal, Box 94, North Battleford, Sask. S9A 0V6
United Way of Regina, 202, 1102 Angus St., Regina, Sask. S4T 1Y5
United Way of Saskatoon, #301, 115 2nd Ave. N., Saskatoon, Sask. S7K 2B1
Swift Current United Way, #205, Professional Bldg., Swift Current, Sask. S9H 0H9
Weyburn & Dist. United Appeal, 4 4th St., Weyburn, Sask. S4H 0X7
Yorkton & Dist. United Way, 131 E. Broadway, Box 44, Yorkton, Sask. S3N 2X3

UNORGANIZED COMMUNITIES ASSOCIATION OF NORTHERN ONTARIO

UCANO East: Executive Director, Louise Ladouceur, Box 200, Cartier, Ont. P0M 1J0 (705/965-2230)
UCANO West: Executive Director, Kathy Davis, R.R. 1, Hurkett, Ont. P0T 1K0 (807/857-2476)

URBAN DEVELOPMENT INSTITUTE (ONTARIO)

60 Bloor St. W., Box 12, Toronto, Ont. M4W 3B8
(416) 928-0491
General Manager, P. T. Erhardt

VANIER INSTITUTE OF THE FAMILY

(L'Institut Vanier de la Famille)
151 Slater St., #207, Ottawa, Ont. K1P 5H3
(613) 232-7115

A research institute to further the well-being of Canadian families.

Executive Director, William A. Dyson

VARIETY CLUB OF BRITISH COLUMBIA, TENT #47

#4, 1170 Bute St., Vancouver, B.C. V6E 1Z6
(604) 669-2313
Administrative Director, Ann Alderson

VARIETY CLUB OF ONTARIO, TENT #28

Ste. 1721, Loews Westbury Hotel, 475 Yonge St., Toronto, Ont. M4Y 1X7
(416) 961-7300
Chief Barker, R. Fraser Neal
Charitable No.: 0140921-05-13

VICTORIAN ORDER OF NURSES

(See Nursing Associations)

VISITES INTERPROVINCIALES
Box 669, Stn. K, Toronto, Ont. M4P 2H1 (416/488-5954)
220 est, Grande Allée, Ste. 760, Québec, P.Q. G1R 4R8 (418/529-5928)
Executive Officer, Mrs. M. Browne

VOICE OF WOMEN
(La Voix des Femmes)
National Office: 175 Carlton St., Toronto, Ont. M5A 2K3
(416) 922-2997

THE WAR AMPUTATIONS OF CANADA
Ste. 210, 2277 Riverside Dr., Ottawa, Ont. K1H 7X6 (613) 731-3821
Key Tag Service, 140 Merton St., Toronto, Ont. M4S 1A5 (416) 488-0600
Chief Executive Officer, H. C. Chadderton
Branches in Hamilton, Kingston, Ottawa, Montreal, Victoria, Vancouver, Calgary, Edmonton, Halifax, Saint John, Charlottetown, Toronto, Winnipeg, London, Windsor, Regina, Kitchener, St. John's, Quebec City.

WATERLOO PUBLIC INTEREST RESEARCH GROUP (WPIRG)
A student-funded independent research and educational organization.
c/o University of Waterloo, Waterloo, Ont. N2L 3G1
(519) 884-9020

THE WELDING INSTITUTE OF CANADA INC.
391 Burnhamthorpe Rd. E., Oakville, Ont. L6J 6C9
(416) 845-9881
Director General, Dr. N.F. Eaton

WESTCOAST ACTORS' SOCIETY
The Waterfront Theatre, 1512 Anderson St., Granville Island, Vancouver, B.C. V6H 3R6
(604) 689-3821

WESTERN ASSOCIATION OF BROADCAST ENGINEERS
Chairman, Dean Cross, c/o CKTV, #1 Hwy. E., Box 2000, Regina, Sask. S9H 3E5 (306/569-2000)

WESTERN ASSOCIATION OF BROADCASTERS
President, Norm Haines, CFCN, Calgary, Broadcast House, Box 7060, Stn. E, Calgary, Alta. (403/246-7111)

WESTERN CANADA CONCEPT
810 Courtney St., Victoria, B.C. V8W 1C4
(604) 385-1022

WESTERN FOOD PROCESSORS ASSOCIATION
#608, 355 Burrard St., Vancouver, B.C. V6C 2G8
(604) 685-8131
Manager, Ernie Gordon

WESTERN GRAIN ELEVATOR ASSOCIATION
#720, 360 Main St., Winnipeg, Man. R3C 3Z3
(204) 942-6835
Chairman, J.A. Tooth

WESTERN INSTITUTE FOR THE DEAF
2125 W. 7th Ave., Vancouver, B.C. V6K 1X9
(604) 736-7391
Executive Director, Gary W. Magarrell
Regional office at: #5, 671 Fort St., Victoria, B.C. V8W 1G7

WESTERN RE-INFORCING CONSTRUCTION ASSOCIATION
-not confirmed for 1982-
2675 Oak St., Vancouver, B.C. V6H 2K3
(604) 736-6311
Secretary, Nancy Trant

WESTERN RETAIL LUMBERMEN'S ASSOCIATION
#601, 228 Notre Dame, Winnipeg, Man. R3B 1N7
(204) 957-1077
Executive Director, Mike Kearney

WEST-FED
Head Office: 9949 77 Ave., Edmonton, Alta. T6E 1M6
(403) 433-5848
President, Elmer Knutson

Branches
2435 Burrard St., Vancouver, B.C. V6J 3J3 (604/738-4177)
Box 167A, R.R. 5, Winnipeg, Man. R3C 2Z2 (204/224-3449)
28 Coteau Ave., Weyburn, Sask. S4H 0G4 (306/842-4050)

THE WHOLESALE LUMBER DEALERS ASSOCIATION INC.
4195 Dundas S. W., Unit B-6, Toronto, Ont. M8X 1Y4
(416) 232-2042
Secretary Treasurer, Mrs. Theresa Murphy

WISE – Women in Science & Engineering
President, Claudette MacKay-Lassonde, Box 6067, Stn. A, Toronto, Ont. M5W 1P5 (416/592-4062)

WOMEN IN TRADES ASSOCIATION
#4, 730 Alexander St., Winnipeg, Man.
(204) 783-8501

THE WOMEN'S CANADIAN CLUB OF TORONTO
Room 212, 2 College St., Toronto, Ont. M5G 1K3
(416) 923-2900
President, Mrs. W.A. Dafoe

WORLD ENERGY CONFERENCE
Canadian National Committee
588 Booth St., Box 4511, Stn. E, Ottawa, Ont. K1S 5B5
(613) 593-4624
Secretary Treasurer, W.A. Harper

WORLD FEDERALISTS OF CANADA
46 Elgin St., Room 32, Ottawa, Ont. K1P 5K6
(613) 232-0647
Administrative Secretary, Mrs. Irene Watson

WORLD LITERACY OF CANADA
692 Coxwell Ave., Toronto, Ont. M4C 3B6
(416) 465-4667
Executive Director, Michael McMorrow

WRITERS' FEDERATION OF NOVA SCOTIA
5516 Spring Garden Rd., Halifax, N.S. B3J 3K6
(902) 423-8116
Director, Gregory M. Cook

THE WRITERS' UNION OF CANADA
24 Ryerson Ave., Toronto, Ont. M5T 2P3
(416) 868-6914, 6915
Executive Director, Mary Jacquest

Y.M.C.A.
See National Council of Young Men's Christian Associations of Canada

.W.H.A.
.sh Organizations, "Jewish Community Centre"

YOUNG WOMEN'S CHRISTIAN ASSOCIATION OF CANADA
National Office, 571 Jarvis St., Toronto, Ont. M4Y 2J1
(416) 921-2117
Executive Director, Mrs. Dana Stehr

YOUTH SCIENCE FOUNDATION
#805, 151 Slater St., Ottawa, Ont. K1P 5H3
(613) 238-1671

ZERO POPULATION GROWTH OF CANADA INC.
President, John Meyer, Dept. of Zoology, University of Toronto, 43 Queen's Park Circle, Toronto, Ont. M5S 1A1 (416/978-6404)

ZONTA CLUBS IN CANADA
International Headquarters, 35 E. Wacker Dr., Chicago, Ill. 60601
Executive Director, Valerie F. Levitan
Contact Chicago office for a list of Districts that include Zonta Clubs in Canada.

EXHIBITIONS IN CANADA

NOTE FROM THE EDITOR: The following list gives major exhibitions listed alphabetically by province and city. *Agricultural & Fall Fairs* include livestock judging, Chuckwagon and pony wagon races, street dances, crafts and baking displays and sales, Grandstand Shows, Baby contests, Dog shows, and horticultural and fruit and vegetable displays. Events special to a particular show are listed following the postal address.

Industrial & Trade Shows are of a constantly changing nature and users of this list are advised to do so with caution.

Alberta Agricultural & Fall Fairs
(Class 'B')

Camrose—Camrose Agric. Society, Box 1418, Camrose, Alta. T4V 1X3 (spring show, Apr.; summer fair, Aug.; fall show, Nov.)

Grande Prairie—Grande Prairie Agric. Society Fair, Box 370, Grande Prairie, Alta. T8V 3A5 (Aug.)

Edmonton—Northlands Farmfair & Canadian Finals Rodeo, Admin. Bldg., Box 1480, Edmonton, Alta. T5J 2N5 (Nov.)

Edmonton—Northlands Stock Show & Sale & Superodeo, Edmonton Northlands, Box 1480, Edmonton, Alta. (end Mar.)

Lloydminster—Lloydminster Agric. Exhibition Association, Box 690, Lloydminster, Sask.-Alta. S9V 0Y7 (403/825-5571) (stockade roundup, Nov.; Annual Bull Sale, Apr.; farm equipment showcase, Mar.)

Olds—Olds Agric. Society, Box 2035, Olds, Alta. TOM 1PO (Fair and Progressive Livestock Days, July)

Vegreville—Vegreville Exhibition Association Ltd., Box 280, Vegreville, Alta. T0B 4L0 (403/632-3950) (July)

Vermilion—Vermilion Agric. Society Fair, Box 1565, Vermilion, Alta. T0B 4M0 (403/853-4108) (livestock show, Apr.; summerfair, July; 4-H Show June & Aug.)

Alberta General Exhibitions

Calgary—Homexpo, 206, 540 12th Ave. S.W., Calgary, Alta. T2R 0H4 (403/264-7170) (Apr.)

Calgary—Calgary Exhibition & Stampede, Box 1060, Calgary, Alta. T2P 2K8 (403/261-0101)

Calgary—Home & Garden Show, Southex Exhibitions, #200, 1201 5th St. S.W., Calgary, Alta. T2R 1L1 (403/269-3161) (Jan.)

Calgary—Calgary Ski & Sport Show, c/o 444 Robson St., Vancouver, B.C. V6B 2P5 (604/684-3823)

Calgary—Sportsmen's Show, c/o Canadian National Sportsmen's Shows, #201, 4547 E. Hastings St., Burnaby, B.C. V5C 2K3 (604/291-6651)

Calgary—Roundup (Farm Equipment Show), Southex Exhibitions, #200, 1201 5th St. S.W., Calgary, Alta. T2R 1L1 (403/269-3161) (Fall)

Edmonton—Canadian Western Farm & Ranch Show, Southex Exhibitions, #200, 1201 5th St. S.W., Calgary, Alta. T2R 1L1 (403/269-3161) (Mar.)

Edmonton—Cantrade (International Canadian Trade Fair Ltd.), c/o Gregory O'Laughlin, Director, #310, 9939 Jasper Ave., Edmonton, Alta. T5J 2W8 (403/423-9920)

Edmonton—Home & Garden Show, Southex Exhibitions, #200, 1201 5th St. S.W., Calgary, Alta. T2R 1L1 (403/269-3161) (Spring)

Edmonton—Klondike Days Exposition, Northland Grounds, Edmonton, Alta. T5J 2N5 (end July) (entertainment, Midway, Thoroughbred Horse Racing and general exhibits)

Edmonton—Sportsmen's Show, c/o Canadian National Sportsmen's Shows, #201, 4547 E. Hastings St., Burnaby, B.C. V5C 2K3 (604/291-6651)

Lethbridge—Lethbridge & Dist. Exhibition, 3401 6th Ave. S.E., Lethbridge, Alta. T1J 1G6 (403/328-4491)

Medicine Hat—Medicine Hat Exhibition & Stampede, Box 1298, Medicine Hat, Alta. T1A 7N1

Red Deer—The Westerner Exposition Association, Box 176, Red Deer, Alta. T4N 5E8 (403/343-7800)

Alberta Industrial Exhibitions & Trade Shows

Calgary—Industrial/Business Equipment Exhibition, Southex Exhibitions*

Calgary—Gift Shows (Fall & Spring) Southex Exhibitions*

Calgary—National Petroleum Show, Southex Exhibitions*

Calgary—Petrochem Processing Conference & Exhibition, Southex Exhibitions*

Edmonton—Industrial/Business Equipment Exhibition, Southex Exhibitions*

**Southex Exhibitions, #200, 1201 5th St. S.W., Calgary, Alta. T2R 1L1 (403/269-3161)*

British Columbia Agricultural & Fall Fairs
(Class 'A' & 'B')

Agassiz—Agassiz Agric. & Horticultural Fair, c/o J. A. Freeman, Box 78, Agassiz, B.C. V0M 1A0 (604/796-2534) (Sept.)

Armstrong—Interior Provincial Exhibition Association, c/o G. Tatton, Secretary-Mgr., Box 490, Armstrong, B.C. V0E 1B0 (weekend after Labour Day)

Barriere—North Thompson Fall Fair, c/o Mrs. D. Clearwaters, Secretary, Little Fort, B.C. V0E 2C0 (Labour Day Weekend)

Bella Coola—Bella Coola Fall Fair Association, Box 637, Bella Coola, B.C. VOT 1CO (604/799-5947)

Chilliwack—Chilliwack Exhibition, c/o Patricia Carnegie, Evergreen Hall, 209 Corbould St. S., Chilliwack, B.C. V2P 4A6 (Aug.)

Cloverdale—Lower Fraser Valley Exhibition, c/o K.R. Berger, Secretary Manager, Box 1174, Stn. A, Surrey, B.C. V3S 4P6 (604/576-9461) (2nd weekend after Labour Day)

Dawson Creek—Dawson Creek Exhibition, c/o Mel Benson, #201, 1025 102nd Ave., Dawson Creek, B.C. V1G 2B9 (Aug.)

Duncan—Cowichan Exhibition, c/o the Secretary, 5855 Clement St., Duncan, B.C. V9L 3W2 (604/748-0822) (weekend after Labour Day)

Grand Forks—Grand Forks Fall Fair, Box 704, Grand Forks, B.C. VOH 1HO

Kamloops—Kamloops Exhibition Association, 479 Chilcotin St., Kamloops, B.C. V2H 1G4 (604/372-9611) General Manager, H.M. Ligtvoet (Provincial Bull Sale, Mar.; Provincial Winter Fair, late Sept.)

Nanaimo—Vancouver Island Exhibition Association, c/o the Secretary, Box 373, Nanaimo, B.C. V9R 5L3 (Aug.)

Prince George—Prince George Agric. & Industrial Association, c/o W. E. Woycik, Secretary, Box 955, Prince George, B.C. V2L 4V1

Saanichton—Saanich Fair, c/o the Secretary, Saanichton, B.C. V0S 1M0 (604/652-3314) (Labour Day weekend)

Salmon Arm—Salmon Arm & Shuswap Lake Agric. Association Fair, c/o the Secretary, Box 101, Salmon Arm, B.C. V0E 2T0 (Sept.)

Smithers—Bulkley Valley Agric. & Industrial Association Exhibition, c/o the Business Manager, Box 2281, Smithers, B.C. V0J 2N0 (604/847-3816) (Aug.)

British Columbia General Exhibitions

Abbotsford—Abbotsford International Air Show, Box 361, Abbotsford, B.C. V2S 4N9 (2nd week Aug.) (Flying Show, Displays, Conference)

New Westminster—Hyack Festival, 615 Clarkson St., New Westminster, B.C. V3M 1C7 (604/522-6894) (May) (Canoe Marathon Race, Grand Parade, Can/Am Quarter Midget Auto Racing, May Day, Car Rally, Lacrosse, Softball & Baseball Tournaments, Street Entertainment, Swim Meet, Square Dance Jubilee, Hyack Anvil Battery 21 Gun Salute)

Surrey—Pacific International Motorama, c/o Speed Sport Enterprises, 8748 N.E. 140th St., Bothwell, Washington, 98011

Vancouver—International Boat Show, Exhibition Park, c/o Canadian National Sportsmen's Shows, #201, 4547 E. Hastings St., Burnaby, B.C. V5C 2K3 (604/291-6651)

Vancouver—Hadassah Bazaar, c/o 950 W. 41st St., Vancouver, B.C. V5Z 2N7 (604/263-2778) (Nov.)

Vancouver—Home Show, c/o Southex Exhibitions, Ste. 202, 2695 Granville St., Vancouver, B.C. V6H 3H4 (Feb.)

Vancouver—Oktoberfest, 3rd floor, 73 Water St., Vancouver, B.C. V6B 1A1 (Sept./Oct.)

Vancouver—Pacific International Auto Show, c/o Western Show & Convention Management, 5400B Minoru Blvd., Richmond, B.C. V6X 2A9 (Jan.)

Vancouver—Pacific National Exhibition (PNE), Box 69020, Vancouver, B.C. V5K 4W3 (604/253-2311) (last 17 days Aug. through Labour Day)

Vancouver—Vancouver Ski & Sport Show, 444 Robson St., Vancouver, B.C. V6B 2B5 (604/684-3823) (Oct.)

Vancouver—Vancouver Sportsmen's Show, c/o Canadian National Sportsmen's Shows, #201, 4547 E. Hastings St., Burnaby, B.C. V5C 2K3 (604/291-6651)

Victoria—Victoria Exhibition, c/o Victoria Jr. Chamber of Commerce, 3880 Quadra St., Victoria, B.C. V8X 1H8 (604/383-4521) (complete week prior to May 24th holiday) (250 inside & outside exhibits, Midway)

British Columbia Industrial Exhibitions & Trade Shows (open to the public)

Vancouver—B.C. Business Show, Southex Exhibitions* (Nov.)

Vancouver—B.C. International Forest Industries Equipment Exhibition, Southex Exhibitions* (Sept., biennially '82, '84)

Vancouver—Vancouver Fall Gift Show, Southex Exhibitions*

Vancouver—Vancouver Spring Gift Show, Southex Exhibitions* (Apr.)

Vancouver—Pacific Industrial Equipment & Materials Handling Show, Southex Exhibitions* (Nov., biennially '82, '84)

Vancouver—Photo & Travel Show, Southex Exhibitions* (Mar.)

Vancouver—Vancouver Island Business Show, Southex Exhibitions* (Mar.)

Vancouver—Western Construction Materials & Equipment Show, Southex Exhibitions* (Nov., biennially '83, '85)

**Southex Exhibitions, #202, 2695 Granville St., Vancouver, B.C. V6H 3H4 (604/736-3331)*

Manitoba Agricultural & Fall Fairs

Brandon—Ag Ex 82, Box 977, Brandon, Man. R7A 5Z9 (204/728-1925) (Livestock show late Oct.)

Carman—Dufferin Agric. Society, c/o C.L. Withers, Box 937, Carman, Man. R0G 0J0 (July)

Dauphin—Dauphin Agric. Society Exhibition, c/o Norris G. Aitken, Box 459, Dauphin, Man. R7N 2V3 (June)

Morris—Man. Stampede & Exhibition, c/o J. J. Hamblin, General Manager, Box 307, Morris, Man. R0G 1K0 (204/746-2552) (mid July)

Portage la Prairie—Portage Industrial Exhibition Association, c/o W. Cochlan, Secretary Manager, Box 278, Portage la Prairie, Man. R1N 3B5 (July)

Swan River—Northwest Round-up & Exhibition, c/o Mrs. Sherry Clarke, Secretary Treasurer, Swan River, Man. R0L 1Z0 (July)

Virden—Virden Agric. Exhibition, c/o Miss Helen Reid, Box 1238, Virden, Man. R0M 2C0 (204/748-1719) (end July)

Manitoba General Exhibitions

Brandon—Provincial Exhibition of Man., Box 977, Brandon, Man. R7A 5Z9 (204/728-1925) (mid June) (Commercial & Agric. exhibits, casino, Midway, Feminine Fair, Photography & Fine Arts, Large Machinery Display)

Brandon—Royal Manitoba Winter Fair, Farm & Home Expo, Box 977, Brandon, Man. R7A 5Z9 (204/728-1925) (Apr.)

Winnipeg—Boat Show, c/o Canadian National Sportsmen's Shows, Box 168, Toronto Dominion Centre, Toronto, Ont. M5K 1H8

Winnipeg—Red River Exhibition, c/o Mo Renaud, 1430 Maroons Rd., Winnipeg, Man. R3G 0L5 (last full week June) (Miss Manitoba Pageant, International Band Competition, Art-Hort-Photo-Hand Competitions, Midway, Casino, Parades)

Winnipeg—Winnipeg Sportsmen's Show, c/o Canadian National Sportsmen's Shows, Box 168, Toronto Dominion Centre, Toronto, Ont. M5K 1H8 (416/862-7800) (Apr.)

Manitoba Industrial Exhibitions & Trade Shows (open to the public)

Winnipeg—Industrial/Business Equipment Exhibition, Southex Exhibitions, #200, 1201 5th St. S.W., Calgary, Alta. T2R 1L1 (403/269-3161)

New Brunswick Fall Fairs

Albert—Albert County Exhibition, c/o Donald Keiver, R.R. 1, Albert, N.B. EOA 1AO (mid-Sept.)

Gagetown—Queens Fair, c/o Mrs. Margaret Coghill, Gagetown, N.B. EOG 1VO (Sept.)

Petitcodiac—Westmorland County Fair, c/o Miss Brenda Wilson, Box 230, Petitcodiac, N.B. EOA 2HO (506/756-2620) (Aug.)

Saint-Basile—Madawaska Fair, c/o D.J. Lajoie, Saint-Basile, N.B. EOL 1HO (Aug.)

Saint Isidore—Exposition Regionale Agricole, c/o Elizabeth Robichaud, Saint Isidore, N.B. E0B 2L0

Ste-Marie—Kent County Fair, c/o Gerard Vienneau, Ste-Marie, N.B. EOA 3AO (end of Aug.)

Stanley—Stanley Fair, c/o Mrs. Sandra Dorcas, Box 85, Stanley, N.B. E0H 1T0 (end Aug.)

Woodstock—Woodstock Old Home Week, c/o the President, Box 666, Woodstock, N.B. EOJ 2BO (506/328-6483) (July)

New Brunswick General Exhibitions

Chatham—Miramichi Exhibition, c/o Florence Traer, Secretary Treasurer, Box 422, Chatham, N.B. E1N 3A5 (506/773-5133) (mid-Aug.) (Agric. & Livestock Show, Educational & Commercial Displays, Midway, Horticulture exhibits)

Fredericton—Fredericton Exhibition, Exhibition Court, Fredericton, N.B. E3B 1N2 (Sept.) (Commercial & Agric., Midway, Stage Shows, Harness Racing)

Fredericton—Provincial Livestock Show, c/o R.M. Colpitts, Dept. of Agriculture, Box 6000, Fredericton, N.B. E3B 5H1 (506/453-2483) (Sept.)

Saint John—Atlantic National Exhibition, Box 284, Saint John, N.B. E2L 3Y2 (506/696-2020) (Aug.) (Commercial & Agric., Horticulture, Talent Show, Harness Racing, Fireworks)

Shediac—Shediac Lobster Festival, Box 487, Shediac, N.B. E0A 3G0 (506/532-2421)

Shippegan—Provincial Fisheries Festival Inc. & Exhibition, Box 280, Shippegan, N.B. E0B 2P0 (July) (Midway, Shows, Competitions, Pageant, Dory Race, Fish Filleting Contest, Blessing of the Fleet)

New Brunswick Industrial Exhibitions & Trade Shows (open to the public)

Moncton—Atlantic Provinces Floorcovering Market, c/o Southex Exhibitions, 1450 Don Mills Rd., Don Mills, Ont. M3B 2X7 (416/445-6641) (Jan.)

Nova Scotia District & County Exhibitions

Antigonish—Eastern Nova Scotia Exhibition, c/o Don MacLellan, Manager, 48 Victoria St., Antigonish, N.S. B2G 1X3 (902/863-2781) (end Aug. or beg. Sept.)

Bear River—Digby Co. Exhibition, c/o Jack D. Harris, Secretary Treasurer, Bear River, N.S. B0S 1B0 (902/467-3608) (Aug/Sept weekend)

Bridgewater—South Shore Exhibition, 235 Dufferin St., Bridgewater, N.S. B4V 2G9 (end July)

Caledonia—Queens Co. Fair, c/o C. R. Cushing, Box 4, Caledonia, N.S. B0T 1B0 (902/242-2522) (Sept.)

Lawrencetown—Annapolis Co. Exhibition, c/o Donald Carven, Secretary Manager, Lawrencetown, N.S. B0S 1M0 (902/584-3339) (Aug.)

Middle Musquodoboit—Halifax Co. Exhibition, c/o Ross Ervin, Manager, Middle Musquodoboit, N.S. B0N 1X0 (902/378-2468) (Aug.)

North Sydney—Cape Breton County Exhibition, c/o Mullins Hood, Manager, R.R. 3, Bras d'Or, N.S. B0C 1B0 (902/794-3591) (Aug.)

Oxford—Cumberland Co. Exhibition, c/o Hollis Johnson, Manager, Oxford, N.S. BOM 1PO (end Aug. or beg. Sept.)

Pictou—Pictou North Colchester Exhibition, c/o Clarence MacCarthy, Manager, 175 St. Andrews St., Pictou, N.S. BOK 1HO (902/485-4057) (early Sept.)

Shelburne—Shelburne Co. Exhibition, c/o G. Bower, Manager, R.R. 1, Shelburne, N.S. BOT 1WO (902/875-3572) (Aug.)

Truro—N.S. Provincial Exhibition, David Coombes, Secretary Manager, Box 192, Truro, N.S. B2N 5C1 (902/893-9222) (Aug.)

Windsor—Atlantic Winter Fair, and Hants Co. Exhibition, c/o David Coombes, Secretary Manager, Windsor, N.S. B0N 2T0 (902/798-2609) (Oct.)

Yarmouth—Western N.S. Exhibition, c/o Rupert While, Manager, Box 425, Yarmouth, N.S. B5A 4B3 (Aug.)

Nova Scotia General Exhibitions

Amherst—Atlantic Building Supply Dealers Association, Box 441, Amherst, N.S. B4H 3Z5 (902/667-7914) (Sponsors of an annual building materials show—Jan.' 82 in Halifax)

Halifax—Atlantic Home Improvement Exhibit, see Amherst

Lunenburg—N.S. Fisheries Exhibition, and Fishermen's Reunion, c/o Beverly Cluett, President, Lunenburg, N.S. B0J 2C0 (Sept.) (Water Sports, Queen of the Sea Pageant, Live Fish Displays, Double Dory Races, Fish Filleting & Scallop Shucking, Ox-Pull, Midway, Entertainment)

Parrsboro—Lions' "Old Home Week" and Forestry Days, Box 305, Parrsboro, N.S. B0M 1S0. Exhibits & demonstrations of lapidary & crafts (2nd week Aug.)

Parrsboro—Rock Hound Round-up, Box 297, Parrsboro, N.S. BOM 1SO (Aug.)

Nova Scotia Industrial Exhibitions & Trade Shows (open to the public)

Halifax—Halifax International Boat Show, c/o Canadian National Sportsmen's Shows, Box 168, Toronto Dominion Centre, Toronto, Ont. M5K 1H8

Ontario Major Agricultural & Fall Fairs

Aylmer—Aylmer & East Elgin Agric. Show, Box 126, Aylmer, Ont. N5H 2R9 (519/773-3445) (Aug.)

Barrie—Barrie Fair, Box 217, Barrie, Ont. L4M 4T2 (705/737-3670) (2nd week before Labour Day)

Belleville—Quinte Exhibition & Raceway (Ben Bleeker Bldg., Yeoman & Bridge Sts.), Box 456, Belleville, Ont. K8N 5B2 (613/968-3266) (Sept.)

Caledonia—Haldimand's Caledonia Fair, c/o Emerson H. Peart, Box 1000, Caledonia, Ont. N0A 1A0 (416/765-6861) (end Sept.)

Dresden—Dresden Agric. Exhibition, c/o Mrs. Ann Moreland, Box 790, Dresden, Ont. N0P 1M0 (519/683-2429)

Kitchener—Central Ont. Exhibition, 400 East Ave., Kitchener, Ont. N2H 1Z6 (519/885-7123) (last week Aug. through Labour Day)

Lindsay—Lindsay Central Exhibition, c/o Secretary Manager, R.J. Hodgson, 37 Adelaide St. N., Lindsay, Ont. K9V 4K8 (705/324-5551) (3rd week aft. Labour Day)

London—Western Fair, Box 4550, Stn. C, London, Ont. N5W 5K3 (519/438-7203) (mid-Sept.)

Markham—Markham Agric. Fair, Box 373, Markham, Ont. L3P 3J8 (416/640-1576) (Oct. weekend before Thanksgiving)

Norwood—Norwood Fair, Box 41, Norwood, Ont. K0L 2V0 (705/639-5207) (Thanksgiving weekend)

Ottawa—Central Canada Exhibition, Lansdowne Park, Ottawa, Ont. K1S 3W7 (613/237-7220) (end Aug.)

Paris—Paris Fair, c/o J. H. Buck, Box 124, Paris, Ont. N3L 3E7 (519/632-7590) (Labour Day weekend)

Peterborough—Peterborough Exhibition, Morrow Park, Lansdowne St., Peterborough, Ont. K9J 1Y5 (705/742-5781) (week following Civic holiday)

Picton—Prince Edward County Fair, c/o Arthur McCornock, R.R. 4, Picton, Ont. K0K 2T0 (613/476-5323) (Sept.)

Renfrew—Renfrew Fair, c/o William Fadyk, Box 206, Renfrew, Ont. K7V 4A3 (613/432-5331) (early Sept.)

Rockton—Rockton World's Fair, c/o E.L. Betzner, R.R. 2, Dundas, Ont. L9H 5E2 (416/689-5652) (Thanksgiving weekend)

Simcoe—Norfolk County Fair, c/o K. S. McArthur, 172 South Dr., Simcoe, Ont. N3Y 1G6 (519/426-7280) (Oct.) (Warrior's Day Parade, Crowning of 'Ontario Flue Cured Tobacco King')

Stratford—Stratford Agric. Society (Ont. Spring Holstein Show; Ont. Pork Congress; Perth County Ag Week - all at Stratford Fairgrounds) c/o Don Odbert, Box 204, Stratford, Ont. N5A 6T1

Teeswater—Teeswater Fall Fair, c/o Mrs. Evan Smyth, R.R. 1, Formosa, Ont. N0G 1W0 (Oct.)

Thunder Bay—Canadian Lakehead Exhibition, Box 1203, Thunder Bay, Ont. P7C 4X9

Toronto—Royal Agricultural Winter Fair, The Coliseum, Exhibition Place, Toronto, Ont. M6K 3C3 (416/366-9051) (Nov.)

Tweed—Tweed Festival, Chamber of Commerce, Box 448, Tweed, Ont. KOK 3JO (July)

Welland—Niagara Regional Exhibition, 1100 Niagara St., Welland, Ont. L3C 1M6

Woodstock—Woodstock Fair, c/o W. B. Wallace, Box 234, Woodstock, Ont. N4S 7W8 (mid Aug.)

Ontario General Exhibitions

Guelph—Guelph Homeshow, 57 Garden St., Guelph, Ont. N1H 2Z9

Hamilton—Hamilton Home Show, c/o Ont. Marketing Productions Ltd., 69 Yorkville Ave., #301, Toronto, Ont. M5R 1B7 (416/961-2999)

Kitchener—Camperama, c/o 88 Ruskview Rd., Kitchener, Ont. N2M 4S3 (519/742-8219)

Kitchener—Oktoberfest, c/o Box 1053, Kitchener, Ont. N2G 4G1 (519/576-0571) (Oct.)

London—Autorama Rod & Custom Car Show, 16 Wakefield Cres., London, Ont. N5X 1Z7 (mid Mar.)

London—Poultry Industry Conference & Exhibition, c/o Box 4550, Term. C, London, Ont. N5W 5K3 (519/438-7203)

Milton—Steam Era, c/o G. Rayner, 5511 3rd Line, R.R. 1, Milton, Ont. L9T 2X5 – held at Milton Fair Grounds, Lab. Day weekend.

Mississauga—Motor Home Show & Trailer Show, Box 170, Stn. A, Weston, Ont. M9N 3M6 (416/244-5995) (Feb.)

Mississauga—Toronto International Auto Show, c/o R. T. Homewood, Show Manager, #W213, 2255 Sheppard Ave. E., Willowdale, Ont. M2J 4Y1 (Feb.)

North Bay—Northern Ont. Sportmen's Show, Memorial Gardens, North Bay, Ont. P1B 6G2 (end Apr.)

Ottawa—Autorama, Civic Centre, Ottawa (D & R Promotions, R.R. 2, Carp Rd., Carp, Ont. KOA 1LO) (613/836-2997)

Ottawa (office; show held in various centres)—Canada Wide Science Fair, c/o Youth Science Foundation, 151 Slater St., #805, Ottawa, Ont. K1P 5H3

Ottawa—Ottawa '82 (7th annual collector Car Auction, Flea-market & Show), Lansdowne Park, Ottawa (D & R Promotions, R.R. 2, Carp Rd., Carp, Ont. KOA 1LO) (613/836-2997)

Ottawa—Ottawa Home Show, c/o #308, 124 O'Connor St., Ottawa, Ont. K1P 5M9 (613/232-0766)

Ottawa—Ottawa Sportsmen's Show, c/o Canadian National Sportsmen's Shows, Box 168, Toronto Dominion Centre, Toronto, Ont. M5K 1H8 (Feb.)

Parry Sound—Festival of the Sound (Classical Music), c/o Chamber of Commerce, 2 Louisa St., Parry Sound, Ont. P2A 2V4 (Aug.)

Parry Sound—Maple Fest (annual Maple Syrup Festival) c/o Chamber of Commerce, 2 Louisa St., Parry Sound, Ont. P2A 2V4 (705/746-9012) (Apr.)

Toronto—Better Living Show, c/o Ont. Marketing Productions Ltd., 69 Yorkville Ave., #301, Toronto, Ont. M5R 1B7 (416/961-2999)

Toronto—Camping on Wheels, Box 168, Toronto Dominion Centre, Toronto, Ont. M5K 1H8 (Feb.)

Toronto—Canadian Craft Show, c/o 458 St. Clements Ave., Toronto, Ont. M5N 1M2 (Nov.)

Toronto—Canadian National Exhibition (CNE), Queen Elizabeth Bldg., Exhibition Place, Toronto, Ont. M6K 3C3 (416/366-7551) (Aug.)

Toronto—Caribana, see Metro International Caravan

Toronto—Do It Yourself Show, c/o Ont. Marketing Productions Ltd., 69 Yorkville Ave., #301, Toronto, Ont. M5R 1B7 (416/961-2999)

Toronto—Hadassah Bazaar, c/o Mrs. Martha Anshan, Executive Director, 788 Marlee Ave., Toronto, Ont. M6B 3K1 (416/789-4373) (Nov.)

Toronto—International Plowing Match & Farm Machinery Show, c/o Ont. Plowmen's Association, Agric. Societies Branch, Ministry of Agric. & Food, Legislative Bldgs., Toronto, Ont. M7A 2B2 (416/965-1091)(This show is held in a different area of the Province each year.)

Toronto—Metro International Caravan, 263 Adelaide St. W., Toronto, Ont. M5H 1Y2 (416/977-0466)

Toronto—Musicanada, c/o Music Industries Association of Canada, #1101, 130 Bloor St. W., Toronto, Ont. M5S 2X7 (416/964-2875)

Toronto—National Home Show, c/o Southex Exhibitions, 1450 Don Mills Rd., Don Mills, Ont. M3B 2X7 (Apr.)

Toronto—Ontario Place, 955 Lakeshore Blvd. W., Toronto, Ont. M6K 3B9 (daily Mid May to Mid Sept.) (416/965-7917)

Toronto—Speed Sport Toronto, Speed Sport Promotions Ltd., 4140 S. Lapeer Rd., Pontiac, Md. 48057 (Jan.)

Toronto—Sportsmen's Show, see Toronto Sportmen's Show

Toronto—TravelExp, c/o Canadian National Sportsmen's Shows, Box 168, Toronto Dominion Centre, Toronto, Ont. M5K 1H8 (416/862-7800) (Oct.)

Toronto—Toronto Sportsmen's Show, c/o Canadian National Sportmen's Shows, Box 168, Toronto Dominion Centre, Toronto, Ont. M5K 1H8 (Mar.)

Ontario Industrial Exhibitions & Trade Shows (open to the public)

London—Poultry Industry Exhibition, c/o J.D. Mitchell, Ont. Poultry Council, 77 City Centre Dr., Mississauga, Ont. L5B 1M5 (416/276-6983)

Mississauga—Toronto Furniture Show, c/o Box 1002, Place Bonaventure, Montreal, P.Q. H5A 1E9 (Jan.)

Toronto—Bakery Production Show of Ont., c/o P. Newell, Publicity Chairman, General Foods Ltd., 2200 Yonge St., Toronto, Ont. M5W 1J6 (416/491-2090) (biennially Oct. '82, '84)

Toronto—Canada Farm Show, c/o Industrial Trade Shows of Canada, 36 Butterick Rd., Toronto, Ont. M8W 3Z8 (416/252-3506) (Jan.)

Toronto (office; show held in various centres)—Canadian Computer Show, c/o Industrial Trade Shows of Canada, 36 Butterick Rd., Toronto, Ont. M8W 3Z8 (416/252-7791)

Toronto—Canadian Construction Show, c/o Industrial Trade Shows of Canada, 36 Butterick Rd., Toronto, Ont. M8W 3Z8 (416/252-7791) (Feb. '83)

Toronto—Canadian Environmental Exposition (CEX), 109 Vanderhoof Ave., Ste. 101, Toronto, Ont. M4G 2J2 (416/425-1427) (Apr. biennially '82, '84) (A Trade Show for the heating, plumbing, air conditioning and refrigerating industries, presented by the Canadian Institute of Heating & Plumbing, and the Heating, Refrigerating & Air Conditioning Institute of Canada)

Toronto—Canadian Mining & Aggregate Equipment Exhibition, c/o Southex Exhibitions, 1450 Don Mills Rd., Don Mills, Ont. M3B 2X7

Toronto—Canadian National Packaging Exposition, 10 St. Mary St., Toronto, Ont. M4Y 1P9 (416/929-3194) (biennial)

Toronto—Canadian Garden, Pool & Patio Show, c/o Southex Exhibitions, 1450 Don Mills Rd., Don Mills, Ont. M3B 2X7 (Feb.)

Toronto—Canadian Premium/Incentive Show & Conference, c/o Industrial Trade Shows of Canada, 36 Butterick Rd., Toronto, Ont. M8W 3Z8 (end Mar.)

Toronto—Chemical & Process Equipment Exhibition, c/o Southex Exhibitions, 1450 Don Mills Rd., Don Mills, Ont. M3B 2X7 (Oct.)

Toronto—Dockside '82, c/o Canadian National Sportsmen's Shows, Box 168, Toronto Dominion Centre, Toronto, Ont. M5K 1H8 (Sept.) (on-the-water boat show)

Toronto—Focus 82 The Toronto Photo Show, c/o Canadian National Sportsmen's Shows, Box 168, Toronto Dominion Centre, Toronto, Ont. M5K 1H8

Toronto—Gift Shows (Fall & Spring) c/o Southex Exhibitions, 1450 Don Mills Rd., Don Mills, Ont. M3B 2X7 (Feb.; Sept.)

Toronto—Graphic Trade '84 (International Centre of Commerce, Nov. '84 and every 3 yrs thereafter) c/o Southex Exhibitions, 1450 Don Mills Rd., Don Mills, Ont. M3B 2X7

Toronto—International Boat Show, c/o Canadian National Sportsmen's Shows, Box 168, Toronto Dominion Centre, Toronto, Ont. M5K 1H8 (Jan.)

Toronto—International Electrical, Electronics Conference & Exposition, c/o Southex Exhibitions, 1450 Don Mills Rd., Don Mills, Ont. M3B 2X7 (Sept. biennially '83, '85)

Toronto—International Gourmet Show, c/o Southex Exhibitions, 1450 Don Mills Rd., Don Mills, Ont. M3B 2X7 (Oct.)

Toronto—Jewellery Show, c/o Canadian Jewellers Association, Royal York Hotel, 100 Front St. W., Toronto, Ont. M5J 1E3 (416/368-8372) – not open to public; trade members only

Toronto—National Industrial Production & Machine Tool Show, c/o Industrial Trade Shows of Canada, 36 Butterick Rd., Toronto, Ont. M8W 3Z8 (416/252-7791) (May biennially '83, '85)

Toronto—Ont. Floorcovering Market, c/o Southex Exhibitions, 1450 Don Mills Rd., Don Mills, Ont. M3B 2X7

Toronto—Products Parade (Canadian Tire Corp.), c/o Southex Exhibitions, 1450 Don Mills Rd., Don Mills, Ont. M3B 2X7 (Sept.)

Toronto—Prospectors & Developers Association Show, Ste. 219, 159 Bay St., Toronto, Ont. M5J 1J7 (416/362-1969)

Winter Carnivals in Ontario

(Following are major Winter Carnivals in Ontario. For small, local Carnivals, contact Chamber of Commerce in area of interest).

Barrie Winter Carnival—Barrie Chamber of Commerce, Wilson Bldg., 2 Fred Grant St., Barrie, Ont. L4M 3G6 (3rd weekend Feb.)

'Bon Soo' Winter Carnival—Box 781, Sault Ste. Marie, Ont. (705/942-4001) (end Jan., early Feb.)
Mississauga Winter Carnival—(Huron Park Recreation Centre), c/o 1 City Centre Dr., Mississauga, Ont. L5B 1M2 (Feb.)
Owen Sound Winter Carnival—808 2nd Ave. E., Owen Sound, Ont. N4K 2H4 (mid. Jan.)
Penetanguishene Winterama—Penetanguishene Chamber of Commerce, Box 90, Penetanguishene, Ont. L0K 1P0
Tweed Winter Carnival—Tweed Chamber of Commerce, Box 448, Tweed, Ont. K0K 3J0 (Feb.)

Quebec Agricultural & Fall Fairs

(Class 'A')
Abitibi—Mme Gertrude Darveau, Ste-Gertrude, P.Q. J0Y 2L0 (819/732-2557) (Aug.)
Argenteuil—Mme Edna Hadley, C.P. 123, Lachûte, P.Q. J8H 3X3 (514/562-2903) (June)
Brome—F.A. Smith, C.P. 88, Brome, P.Q. JOE 1KO (514/538-3662) (Labour Day weekend)
Chicoutimi—Louis Boucher, C.P. 622, Chicoutimi, P.Q. G7H 5B1 (418/545-8597) (June)
Kamouraska—Jacques Bérubé, rte 230 ouest, St-Pascal, P.Q. GOL 3YO (418/492-2694) (Aug.)
Lotbinière—Expo St-Agapit Inc., c/o Raynald Champagne, St-Sylvestre, P.Q. G0S 3CO (418/596-2688) (Aug.)
Ormstown—H.L. McCaig, C.P. 239, Ormstown, P.Q. JOS 1KO (514/829-2776) (June)
Pontiac—Shawville Fair, c/o Everett McDowell, Box 449, Shawville, P.Q. J0X 2Y0 (819/647-3771) (Labour day wknd.)
Quebec—Expo-Quebec, Exhibition Park, 2205 ave du Colisée, Quebec, P.Q. G1L 4W7 (418/694-7141) (Aug.)
Richelieu—L.A. Forcier, 107 Principale, Yamaska, P.Q. JOG 1WO (514/742-0448) (June)
St-Félicien—Simon Bergeron, 1235 rang 3, St-Prime, P.Q. G0W 2W0 (418/251-3207) (Aug.)
St-Honoré-de-Beauce—Eugène Fortin, St-Honoré-de-Shenley, Beauce, P.Q. G0M 1V0 (418/485-6564) (Aug.)
Sherbrooke—Exposition de Sherbrooke, 360 rue Parc, Sherbrooke, P.Q. J1E 2J9 (819/563-5651) (Aug.)
Trois-Rivières—Exposition de Trois-Rivières, c/o Jean Alarie, C.P. 968, Trois-Rivières, P.Q. G9A 5K2 (819/374-2714) (Aug.)
District d'Arthabaska—Gérard Drouin, Parc de l'Exposition, Victoriaville, P.Q. G6P 4K1 (819/752-9727) (Aug.)
District de Drummond—Germain Lefebvre, 69 Pays Brûlé, Baieville, Yamaska, P.Q. J0G 1A0 (819/783-6620) (June)
District de Joliette—Exposition à Berthierville, c/o Mme Francine Sylvestre, C.P. 1228, Berthierville, P.Q. JOK 1AO (514/836-2687) (July)
District de la Mauricie—Mme Micheline Turcot, 430 Grande-Rivière, St-Barnabé-Nord, P.Q. G0Y 2K0 (819/264-5606) (July)
District de Mégantic—Emile Hardoin, 1200, rue Lamonde, Thetford Mines, P.Q. G6G 5S5 (418/335-6218) (July/Aug. weekend)
District de Montmagny—Roland Gaumond, 12 ave Fournier, Montmagny, P.Q. G5V 2X7 (418/248-3418) (Aug.)
District de Rimouski—R. St-Pierre, B.P. 486, R.R. 2, Rimouski, P.Q. G5L 7B5 (418/723-1666) (Aug.)
District de St-Hyacinthe—R. Robert, 740 rue Sacré-Coeur, St-Hyacinthe, P.Q. J2S 1V1 (514/773-9307) (July)

Quebec General Exhibitions

Montreal—Auto-Sport Show, c/o Speed Sport Promotions Ltd., 4140 S. Lapeer Rd., Pontiac, Md. 48057 (Nov.)
Montreal—Boat Show, Ste. 306, 5890 Monkland Ave., Montreal, P.Q. H4A 1G2 (514/489-8671) (Mar.)
Montreal—Camping Show, 1115 Forest St., Chomedey, Laval, P.Q. H7W 1V9 (514/687-7818)
Montreal—Salon International de l'Auto, 7575 Transcanada Hwy., Ste. 206, St-Laurent, P.Q. H4T 1V6 (514/331-6571) (Jan.)
Montreal—International Salon of Food & Agriculture, 10819 St-Denis, Montreal, P.Q. H3L 2J6 (514/384-1442) (Nov.)
Montreal—Man & His World, St. Helen's Island, Montreal, P.Q. H3C 1AO (514/872-6392) (mid June to Labour Day)
Montreal—Montreal Ski Show, Ste. 306, 5890 Monkland Ave., Montreal, P.Q. H4A 1G2 (514/489-8671) (Oct.)
Rouyn—Western Que. Regional Exhibition, Box 278, Rouyn, P.Q. J9X 2P4 (July) (Commercial, industrial, forestry, athletic, arts & crafts)

Quebec Industrial Exhibitions & Trade Shows (open to the public)

Montreal—Canadian International Footwear Exposition, Ste. 710, 1010 St. Catherine St. W., Montreal, P.Q. H3B 3R4 (514/878-9337) (Aug.) – Trade only
Montreal—Furniture Market, Box 1002, Place Bonaventure, Montreal, P.Q. H5A 1E9 (June)
Montreal—Gift Shows (Fall & Spring), c/o Southex Exhibitions, 1450 Don Mills Rd., Don Mills, Ont. M3B 2X7 (Mar.; Aug.)
Montreal—Hardware & Home Centre Show, c/o Don Blanchard & Associates, #1 Davidson Rd., Aurora, Ont. L4G 2A9 (Sept.) – Trade only
Montreal—International Salon of Farm Machinery, c/o 10819 St-Denis, Montreal, P.Q. H3L 2J6 (514/384-1442) (Apr.)
Montreal—International Salon of Poultry Industries, c/o 10819 St-Denis, Montreal, P.Q. H3L 2J6 (514/384-1442) (Apr.)
Montreal—Salon du Livre de Montreal, 1151 Alexandre Desève, Montreal, P.Q. H2L 2T7 (Nov.)
Quebec—Action-Expo ('Municipal & Public Works Show'), c/o Action-Expo Hexa Inc., 6841 St-Hubert, Ste. 203, Montreal, P.Q. H2S 2M8 (514/273-7217) (end Sept.)

Quebec Winter Carnivals

(There are two major Winter Carnivals in Quebec. Contact the Chamber of Commerce for information regarding smaller local Carnivals).
Carnaval-Souvenir de Chicoutimi (Winter Carnival)—67 ouest, rue Jacques Cartier, Chicoutimi, P.Q. G7J 1E9 (418/543-4438) (Feb.)
Quebec Winter Carnival—290 Joly St., Box 8, Quebec, P.Q. G1L 4T8 (418/626-3716) (Feb.)

Saskatchewan Agricultural & Fall Fairs

('Class B')
Battlefords Exhibition Northwest Territorial Days—c/o G. Brown, Box 668, North Battleford, Sask. S9A 2Y9 (306/445-2024) (July)
Estevan Agric. Society Exhibition—c/o D. Matchett, Box 100, Estevan, Sask. S4A 2A2 (306/634-2603) (July)
Lloydminster Agric. Exhibition Association Ltd., see Alberta
Melfort Agric. Society Exhibition—c/o J.M. Solsten, Box 816, Melfort, Sask. S0E 1A0 (July)
Moose Jaw The Home Town Fair, Moose Jaw Exhibition Co. Ltd.—c/o L.J. Cochrane, President, Box 1467, Moose Jaw, Sask. S6H 4R3 (July)
Prince Albert Exhibition Association—c/o W. J. Williams, Box 1538, Prince Albert, Sask. S6V 5T1 (July)
Swift Current Agric. & Exhibition Association Frontier Days—c/o F. L. Smith, Box 146, Swift Current, Sask. S9H 3V5 (306/773-2944) (July)
Weyburn Agric. Society Exhibition—c/o Ernest Obst, Manager, Box 699, Weyburn, Sask. S4H 2K8 (306/842-4052) (July)
Yorkton Agric. Society Stampede & Exhibition—c/o D. Litowitz, Box 908, Yorkton, Sask. S3N 2X1 (306/783-4800) (July)

Saskatchewan General Exhibitions

Regina—Canadian Western Agribition, Box 3535, Regina, Sask. S4P 3J8 (306/565-0565) (last week Nov.) (International livestock show; Mexabition; Agribition Rodeo & Horserama)
Regina—Buffalo Days Provincial Exhibition, Box 167, Regina, Sask. S4P 2Z6 (306/527-2674) (end July, early Aug.)
Regina—Regina Farm Fair, Box 167, Regina, Sask. S4P 2Z6 (306/527-2674) (Mar.)(Livestock & farm equipment, casino)
Regina—Spring Spectacular, Box 167, Regina, Sask. S4P 2Z6 (306/527-2674) (Apr.) (Horse show & Carnival, casino)
Saskatoon—Prairie Land Exhibition Corp., Box 407, Saskatoon, Sask. S7K 3L3 (July)

Saskatchewan Industrial Exhibitions & Trade Shows (open to the public)

Regina—Western Canada Farm Progress Show, Box 167, Regina, Sask. S4P 2Z6 (306/527-2674) (2nd last week in June) (Agricultural machinery, products, services, Ladies' program)

Regina—Home Expo, Box 167, Regina, Sask. S4P 2Z6 (306/527-2674) (Oct.) (Home building materials and services and allied products)

EDUCATION IN CANADA

ALBERTA BOARDS OF EDUCATION

The Department of Education, Devonian Bldg., 11160 Jasper Ave., Edmonton, administers 170 public and separate school boards in Alberta. Of this number there are 30 county and 30 divisional school boards; 21 school district boards in 11 cities; 41 district boards in towns, 41 rural school boards and school boards in 7 villages.

For Alberta Education officials see government listings.

The following are school boards in Cities:

Calgary Board of Education
Education Centre, 515 Macleod Trail S.E., Calgary, Alta. T2G 2L9
(403) 268-8211
Chief Supt. of Schools, A.J. Longmore
Supt., Planning & Information, A.B. Cuppy
Supt., Facility Services, J.B. Delaney
Supt., Instructional Services, Dr. W. Dickson
Supt., Finance, G.E. Jenkins
Supt., Personnel Services, K.A. Jesse
Public Relations Director, J. Willson

Calgary Catholic Board of Education
Catholic Sch. Centre, 300-Sixth Ave. S.E., Calgary, Alta. T2G 0G5
(403) 264-1610
Supt., John McCarthy, B.A., M.A.
Secretary Treasurer, B.A. Benning, M.Ed., M.B.A.
Information-Community Relations Officer, Irene Morrison, B.A.
Co-ordinator, Elementary, L. W. Bunyan, M.Ed., D.Ed.
Co-ordinator, Secondary, D.D. Taylor, B.Sc., B.Ed., M.Ed.
Co-ordinator, Pupil Personnel Services, J. W. Quinn, M.Ed., Ph.D.
Co-ordinator, Special Services, A. Kowalski, M.Ed., Ph.D.
Instructional Materials Centre, Supervisor, John Stoeber, B.Ed., M.S.C.E.D.

Camrose School District 1315
6211 48 Ave., Camrose, Alta. T4V OK4
(403) 672-5594
Supt., Dr. S. Grywalski
Secretary Treasurer, M.A. Ruhl

Camrose Catholic School District 60
4931 48 St., Camrose, Alta. T4V 1X7
(403) 672-2977

Edmonton Public School Board
10010-107 A. Ave., Edmonton, Alta. T5H 0Z8
(403) 429-5621
Supt., M. A. Strembitsky
Board Secretary, R.A. Jones
Treasurer, L.N. Jones
Purchasing Agent, D. Witwicky

Edmonton Catholic School District
9807-106 St., Edmonton, Alta. T5K 1C2
(403) 429-7631
Supt., Dr. John F. Brosseau
Secretary Treasurer, J. N. Walsh
Area Supts., L.J. Hanak, Dr. M.P. Klotz, F.P. O'Hara
Supt., Facilities & Planning, W.P. Pasternak

Grande Prairie School District 2357
10213 99 St., Grande Prairie, Alta. T8V 2H3
(403) 532-4491
Supt., D.R. Taylor
Secretary Treasurer, Mrs. M.M. Moffett

Grande Prairie Catholic School District 28
Catholic Education Centre, 10715 102 St., Grande Prairie, Alta. T8V 2X1
(403) 532-3015
Supt., D.E. Grant
Asst. Supt., P.S. Maguire
Secretary Treasurer, Mrs. A.M. Kinderwater

Lethbridge School District 51
433 15th St., Lethbridge, Alta. T1J 2Z5
(403) 327-4521
Secretary Treasurer, M. V. Crumley
Supt., Dr. R. P. Plaxton
Director, Curriculum & Instruction, E.J. Warnica
Director, Personnel & Material Resources, Dr. G. B. Probe
Director, Pupil Personnel Services, Dr. Roger Barnsley
Asst. Secretary Treasurer, D. A. Forbes
Facilities Co-ordinator, D. B. Attwell

Lethbridge Catholic School District 9
534 18 St. S., Lethbridge, Alta. T1J 3E7
(403) 329-0365
Supt., R. Himsl
Secretary Treasurer, N.L. Reilander

Lloydminster Public School Division
5017 46 St., Lloydminster, Alta. T9V 1R4
(403) 875-5541
Director of Education, E.C. Price
Supt., A.C. Dornstauder
Supt. of Administration, L. Hanson

Lloydminster Catholic School Division
5216 44 St., Lloydminster, Alta. T9V 1R6
(403) 875-8911
Secretary Treasurer, R.M. Zelinski

Medicine Hat School District 76
601-1st Ave. S.W., Medicine Hat, Alta. T1A 4Y7
(403) 526-1323
Supt., Dr. K. C. Sauer
Asst. Supt. & Secretary Treasurer, E. Murray
Asst. Supts., H. Storlien; F. Kramer

Medicine Hat Catholic Board of Education
1251 1st Ave. S.W., Medicine Hat, Alta. T1A 8B4
(403) 527-2292
Supt., F.B. Allore
Secretary Treasurer, A.J. Giesinger

Red Deer Public School District 104
4747-53 St., Red Deer, Alta. T4N 2E6
(403) 347-1101
Supt., Wm. T. Brownlee
Asst. Supt., A.B. Gibb
Administrative Asst., Mrs. D.F. Solty
Secretary Treasurer, R.E. Congdon
Co-ordinator of Pupil Personnel, Dr. Bruce Handley

Red Deer Catholic Board of Education
3827 39 St., Red Deer, Alta. T4N OY6
(403) 343-1055

Supt. of Schools, J. Docherty
Secretary Treasurer, T. Smiley

Wetaskiwin School District 264
5008A 51 Ave., Wetaskiwin, Alta. T9A OV1
(403) 352-6018
Supt., G. Johnson
Secretary Treasurer, C. Fraser

Wetaskiwin Roman Catholic Separate School District 15
5109 49 Ave., Wetaskiwin, Alta. T9A OP9
(403) 352-4648
Supt., T. Grinnel
Secretary Treasurer, A. Landstorfer

The following are Town School Districts, pop. over 10,000:

Fort McMurray School District 2833
9401 Franklin Ave., Fort McMurray, Alta. T9H 3Z7
(403) 743-3705
Supt., R. Prather
Secretary Treasurer, D. Hassen

Fort McMurray Catholic School District 32
#201, 9809 Main St., Fort McMurray, Alta. T9H 1T7
(403) 743-3325
Supt., G.A. Heck
Secretary Treasurer, Mrs. Josie Estoque

St. Albert School District 6
-not confirmed for 1982-
60 Sir Winston Churchill Ave., St. Albert, Alta. T8N OG4
(403) 458-2060
Supt., Dr. P.F. Bargen
Secretary Treasurer, G. Hargreaves

POST SECONDARY & PRIVATE INSTITUTIONS IN ALBERTA

Agricultural Colleges
Olds and Fairview are listed with Public Colleges at the end of the Alberta section.

Alberta College
10041 101 St., Edmonton, Alta. T5J 0S3
(403) 428-1851
President, S. G. McCurdy, M.A., Ph.D.

The University of Alberta
Edmonton, Alta. T6G 2E8
(403) 432-2325
Chairman, Board of Governors, J.L. Schlosser
President, M. Horowitz, Ed.D.
Vice President, Academic, R.G. Baldwin, Ph.D.
Vice President, Finance & Admin., L. C. Leitch, M.B.A.
Vice President, Planning & Development, R. E. Phillips, B.Sc.
Vice President, Research, J.G. Kaplan, Ph.D.
Comptroller, A.S. Knowler, B.Com.
Registrar, W.A. Blanchard, Ph.D.
Community Relations, Wm. A. Preshing, Ph.D.
Purchasing Agent, R. A. Bennett
Librarian, Bruce Peel
Bookstore Manager, J. Malone
Dean of Students, P. Sartoris, Ph.D.

FACULTIES WITH DEANS
Agriculture & Forestry, John P. Bowland, Ph.D.
Arts, T.H. White, Ph.D.
Business Admin. & Commerce, R.S. Smith, Ph.D.
Dentistry, G.W. Thompson, D.D.S.
Education, W.H. Worth, B.Ed., M.Ed., Ed.D.
Engineering, P.F.G. Adams, B.Eng., M.Eng., Ph.D.
Extension, C.M. Lockwood, M.B.A.
Graduate Studies & Research, John Forster, Ph.D.
Home Economics, Doris Badir, M.Sc.
Law, Frank D. Jones, LL.M.
Library Science, W.J. Kurmey, A.M. in L.S.
Medicine, D. F. Cameron, M.D.
Nursing, B. Harrington, B.N. (act.)
Pharmacy & Pharmaceutical Sciences, J.A. Bachynsky, Ph.D.
Physical Education & Recreation, R.G. Glassford, Ph.D.
Rehabilitation Medicine, F. B. Wilson, Ph.D.
Science, W.J. McDonald, Ph.D.
Faculté Saint-Jean, Gamila Morcos, Ph.D.

AFFILIATED COLLEGES
St. Joseph's College, Univ. of Alta., Edmonton, Alta., Principal, Rev. A. De Valk, M.A., S.T.B.
St. Stephen's College, Univ. of Alta., Edmonton, Alta., Principal, Dr. G.I. Mundle, D.Min.

Art Schools

THE ALBERTA COLLEGE OF ART
(Affiliated with the Southern Alta. Institute of Technology)
1301 16th Ave. N.W., Calgary, Alta. T2M 0L4
(403) 284-8655
Head, Kenneth Sturdy

THE BANFF CENTRE
Box 1020, Banff, Alta. TOL OCO
(403) 762-6100

The Banff Centre comprises a School of Fine Arts, School of Management and a Conference Division. The School of Fine Arts provides intermediate, advanced and professional training in the Visual and Performing Arts, both during the summer sessions and Winter Cycle programs. Management Programs offers courses in management studies, cultural resource management, resource management programs and Banff Wilderness Seminars for top executives.
Director, Dr. David S. R. Leighton

Athabasca University
12352 149 St., Edmonton, Alta. T5V 1G9
(403) 452-9990
Chairman of Governing Council, J.P.C. Elson, P.Eng.
President Emeritus, W.A.S. Smith, Ph.D.
President, S. Griew, Ph.D.
Vice President, Learning Services, R. Paul, Ph.D.
Vice President, University Services, N.O. Henry, M.A.
Vice President, Finance & Facilities, B.L. Snowden, M.B.A.
Registrar, J.R.Y. Scarlett, B.A.
Director of Applied Sciences, D.R. Thomas, D.B.A.
Director of Liberal Studies, vacant
Head, Institutional Studies, D.G. Shale, Ph.D.
Head, Instructional Development, D.O. Coldeway, Ph.D.
Director, Regional & Tutorial Services, A.G. Meech, M.A.
Head, Student Development Services, J. Brindley, B.A.
Director, Computing Services, D.W. Cowper, M.Ed.
Director, Media Services, P.A. Nedza, M.Ed.
Librarian, T.A. Edge, B.L.S.
Co-ordinator, Public Affairs, vacant

Calgary Christian School
2839 49 St. S.W., Calgary, Alta. T3E 3X9
(403) 242-2838, 242-2896

Calgary Seventh Day Adventist School
Box 23, Site 12, SS1, Calgary, Alta. T2M 4N3
(403) 286-5686

The University of Calgary
Calgary, Alta. T2N 1N4
(403) 284-5110

PRINCIPAL OFFICERS
Chancellor, J.L. Lebel, B.A., LL.B.

Chairman, Board of Governors, R. A. MacKimmie, Q.C., LL.B., LL.D.
President & Vice Chancellor, N.E. Wagner, B.A., M.Div., M.A., Ph.D.
Vice President, Academic, P. J. Krueger, B.Sc., M.Sc., D.Phil., F.C.I.C., F.R.I.C.
Vice President, Finance, H. W. Bliss, F.C.A.
Vice President, Services, H.A.R. de Paiva, B.Sc., M.S., Ph.D.
Registrar, Mrs. J. Turner
Librarian, A.H. MacDonald, B.A., B.L.S.

DEANS OF FACULTIES
Continuing Education, R.S. Chapman, B.Ed., M.Ed., Ph.D.
Education, R. F. Lawson, B.A., M.A., Ph.D.
Engineering, T. H. Barton, B.Eng., D.Eng., Ph.D., F.I.E.E.
Environmental Design, D.D. Detomasi, B.S., Ph.D.
Fine Arts, L.A. Robertson, B.Ed., M.F.A.
General Studies, R.G. Weyant, B.A., M.A., Ph.D.
Graduate Studies, J. B. Hyne, B.Sc., Ph.D., F.C.I.C.
Humanities, P.C. Craigie, M.A., Dip.Th., M.Th., Ph.D.
Law, J.P.S. McLaren, LL.B., LL.M.
Management, P.M. Maher, B.E., M.B.A., Ph.D.
Medicine, Dr. M. Watanabe (act.)
Nursing, Margaret Scott Wright, M.A., D.Phil.
Physical Education, Roger C. Jackson, B.A., M.P.E., Ph.D.
Science, T.A. Oliver, B.Sc., M.Sc., Ph.D.
Social Sciences, H. K. Betz, B.A., M.A., Ph.D.
Social Welfare, L. Richards, B.A., M.S.W., M.A., Phil. M., Ph.D.

DIRECTOR
Kananaskis Centre for Environmental Research, G. W. Hodgson, B.Sc., M.Sc., Ph.D.

Camrose Lutheran College
-not confirmed for 1982-
Camrose, Alta. T4V 2R3
(403) 672-3381
President, Rev. K. Glen Johnson, B.A., B.D., S.T.M.

Canadian Union College
College Heights, Alta. T0C 0Z0
(403) 782-3381
President, N. O. Matthews, Ph.D.
Academic Dean, tba
Business Manager, G. Wasylyshen, C.A.
Librarian, Keith H. Clouten, M.S.L.S.

College Heights Adventist Jr. Academy
Box 451, College Heights, Alta. T0C 0Z0
(403) 782-6212

Concordia College
7128 Ada Blvd., Edmonton, Alta. T5B 4E4
(403) 479-8481
Chairman, Board of Regents, Rev. Edwin Lehman
President, Dr. O.C. Walz
Registrar, Dr. Harry Lutzer
Academic Dean, Dr. Judith Meier
Director of Admissions, Dr. Harry Lutzer
Director of Development & Communications, Dr. Clyde Kaminska
Librarian, Mircea Panciuk

Coralwood Academy
-not confirmed for 1982-
13510 122 Ave., Edmonton, Alta. T5L 2V8
(403) 454-2173, 455-6946

East Edmonton Christian School
11515 36 St., Edmonton, Alta. T5W 2A9
(403) 479-4171

Edmonton Christian High School
14304 109 Ave., Edmonton, Alta. T5N 1H6
(403) 454-0791

Immanuel Christian School
802 6 Ave. N., Lethbridge, Alta. T1H 0S1
(403) 328-4783, school; 329-1750, bus. office

Lacombe Christian School
Box 1749, Lacombe, Alta. T0C 1S0
(403) 782-6531

University of Lethbridge
4401 University Dr., Lethbridge, Alta. T1K 3M4
(403) 329-2111
President, Dr. J.H. Woods
Vice President, Academic, Dr. O. G. Holmes
Vice President, Finance, J.A. Rae
Co-ordinator of Information Services, S. Heller
Vice President, Campus Development, R.F. Comstock
Purchasing Agent, Barry Kimery
Librarian, Paul Wiens
Bookstore Manager, L. Long

FACULTIES & DEANS
Arts & Science, Dr. A.F. Cassis
Education, Dr. J.M. Thorlacius

North Edmonton Christian School
13470 Fort Rd., Edmonton, Alta. T5A 1C5
(403) 475-2818

Northwest Bible College
11617 106 Ave., Edmonton, Alta. T5H 0S1
(403) 452-0808

Peace River Junior Academy
-not confirmed for 1982-
R.R. 1, Wanham, Alta. T0H 3P0
(403) 694-2205

Prairie Bible Institute
Three Hills, Alta. T0M 2A0
(403) 443-5511
President, Paul T. Maxwell
Vice President, Biblical Ministries, T.S. Rendall
Vice President, Business Admin., L. Birch
Vice President, General Education, K. Penner
Registrar, R. Malesky
Librarian, Ronald Jordahl
Bookstore Manager, J.A. Toliver

Red Deer Christian School
-not confirmed for 1982-
14 McVicar St., Red Deer, Alta. T4N 0M2
(403) 346-5795

Rocky Mountain House Christian School
Box 669, Rocky Mountain House, Alta. T0M 1T0

St. Matthews Lutheran School
Box 939, Stony Plain, Alta. T0E 2G0
(403) 963-2715

Strathcona-Tweedsmuir School
R.R. 2, Okotoks, Alta. T0L 1T0
(403) 938-4431

Tempo School
-not confirmed for 1982-
5603 148 St., Edmonton, Alta. T6H 4T7
(403) 434-1190

West Edmonton Christian School
14345 McQueen Rd., Edmonton, Alta. T5N 3L5

TECHNICAL & VOCATIONAL INSTITUTIONS IN ALBERTA

INSTITUTES OF TECHNOLOGY

The Southern Alberta Institute of Technology, F. C. Jorgenson, B.Ed., President, 1301-16th Ave. N.W., Calgary, Alta. T2M 0L4 (403/284-8300)

The Northern Alberta Institute of Technology, Dr. S.G. Souch, President, 11762-106 St., Edmonton, Alta. T5J 2R1 (403/427-9300)

The Banff Centre (Banff School of Fine Arts), Box 1020, Banff, Alta. T0L 0C0, Director, D. S. R. Leighton (403/762-6100)

VOCATIONAL CENTRES

Alberta Vocational Centre, D.E. Hubert, Supervisor, 10215-108 St., Edmonton, Alta. T5J 1L6 (403/427-2741)

Alberta Vocational Centre, J. E. Crowe, Supervisor, 332-6 Ave. S.E., Calgary, Alta. T2G 4S6 (403/261-3930)

Alberta Vocational Centre, F.J. Dumont, Supervisor, Grouard, Alta. T0G 1C0 (403/751-3915)

Alberta Vocational Centre, D.E. Langford, Supervisor, Box 417, Lac La Biche, Alta. T0A 2C0 (403/623-4441)

ALBERTA PETROLEUM INDUSTRY TRAINING CENTRE

10330 71 Ave., Edmonton, Alta. T6E 0W8, Supervisor, C. J. Frankovitch (403/427-2768)

PUBLIC COLLEGES

Fairview College, Box 3000, Fairview, Alta. T0H 1L0, President, Dr. F.J. Speckeen

Grande Prairie Regional College, 10726 106 Ave., Grande Prairie, Alta. T8V 4C4, President, Miss Dorothy Rowles (403/532-8830)

Grant MacEwan Community College, 400, 10150 100 St., Edmonton, Alta. T5J 0P5, President, J. L. Haar (403/425-8810)

Keyano College, 8115 Franklin Ave., Fort McMurray, Alta. T9H 2H7, President, D. Schmit (403/791-2213)

Lakeland College, 4420 50 Ave., Lloydminster, Alta. T9V 0W2, President, R.V. Murray (403/875-8828)

Lethbridge Community College, Lethbridge, Alta. T1K 1L6, President, G.L. Talbot (403/320-3209)

Medicine Hat College, 299 College Dr. S.E., Medicine Hat, Alta. T1A 3Y6, President, C. Meagher (403/527-7141)

Mount Royal College, 4825 Richard Rd. S.W., Calgary, Alta. T3E 6K6, President, Dr. D.N. Baker (403/246-6300)

Olds College, Olds, Alta. T0M 1P0, President, G.N. Crombie (403/556-8281)

Red Deer College, 56 Ave. & 32 St., Red Deer, Alta. T4N 5H5, President, Dr. W. G. Forbes, B.Sc., M.Sc., Ph.D. (403/346-3376)

BRITISH COLUMBIA BOARDS OF EDUCATION

The British Columbia Ministry of Education, has set up 75 School Districts, each headed by a Superintendent, in the province. Superintendents in districts with enrolments of 4,000 or more, are appointed by the district board of school trustees. The remainder are appointed by the Ministry. Elections for school trustees are held in November throughout the Province.

For officials of the Ministry of Education see government listings.

Following is information regarding School Boards in major population areas, listed alphabetically, then a complete list of Superintendents in the 75 School Districts.

School District 23 (Central Okanagan)

1940 Haynes Rd., Kelowna, B.C. V1X 5X7
(604) 860-8888
Secretary Treasurer, H. Peatman
Supt., M. Pendharkar
Director, Secondary Instruction, R. Garner
Director, Elementary Instruction, A. W. Webb
Asst. Secretary Treasurer, F. J. Lemieux
Director of Programs, D. Marson
Purchasing Agent, P. A. Leach

School District 33 (Chilliwack)

235 Yale Rd. E., Chilliwack, B.C. V2P 2P9
(604) 792-1321
Secretary Treasurer, R.D. Ingram
Supt., W.T. Fisher
Asst. Supt., D. A. MacAulay
Supervisor, Instruction, P.E. Halladay
Supervisor, Instruction, M. E. Folkman
Supervisor, Instruction, T. A. Bodman
Resource Centre, Librarian, Mrs. V. Rempel
Asst. Secretary Treasurer, D. J. Lockyer
Purchasing Agent, J. A. Edwards

School District 24 (Kamloops)

1383 9 Ave., Kamloops, B.C. V2C 3X7
(604) 374-0679
Secretary Treasurer, A. V. MacLeod
Supt., R. Lyon
Asst. Supts., R. G. Zacharias, T.D. Grieve, V. Mowbray
Co-ordinator of Resources Centre, R. Shaw
E.T.V. Co-ordinator, J. Farr
Director of Support Services, W. Pelly
Director of Finance & Data, J. Sheldon
Director of Admin. Services, H. F. Tedder

School District 68 (Nanaimo)

395 Wakesiah Ave., Nanaimo, B.C. V9R 3K6
(604) 754-5521
Secretary Treasurer, J.H. Thorpe, P.Eng.
Supt., N.B. Hoadley
Asst. Supt., School Operations, R.M.M. Kulai
Asst. Supt., Curriculum Services, J.R. White
Asst. Supt., Properties, A. F. Vanidour
Director of Finance, R. V. Mark
Supervisor of Purchasing, L.M. Tillapaugh

School District 7 (Nelson)

308 Anderson St., Nelson, B.C. V1L 3Y2
(604) 352-6681
Secretary Treasurer, H. S. Nunn
Supt., William Maslechko
Director of Instruction, J.T. Wayling
Resource Centre Director & Administrative Asst., Wm. Evin
Co-ordinator of Special Services, Dr. P.S. Johnston
French Co-ordinator, Gail Sumanik
Director of Adult Education, R. Maennling
Librarian, Mrs. A. Ward
Asst. Secretary Treasurer, David Brandon
Maintenance Supervisor, Fred Scott

School District 40 (New Westminster)

Box 790, 821 8th St., New Westminster, B.C. V3L 4Z8
(604) 522-1631
Secretary Treasurer, C.T. Condon
Supt., D. N. Weicker
Asst. Supt., G. Catherall

School District 44 (North Vancouver)

721 Chesterfield Ave., North Vancouver, B.C. V7M 2M5
(604) 987-8141
Secretary Treasurer, Leonard Berg
Supt., Dr. R. A. Wickstrom
Purchasing Manager, Tom Tennant
Asst. Secretary Treasurer, S. P. Dodd

School District 39 (Vancouver)

1595 W. 10th Ave., Vancouver, B.C. V6J 1Z8
(604) 731-1131
Supt., Dr. Dante Lupini
Deputy Supt., Dr. John Wormsbecker
Head of Business Admin., Alick Patterson
Head of Communication Services, C.G. Gosbee

School District 61 (Greater Victoria)

Box 700, Victoria, B.C. V8W 2R1
(604) 592-1211
Secretary Treasurer, Carl Warner
Supt., Allan Stables
Asst. Supt., Curriculum, Bernie Chandler
Asst. Supt., Teacher Personnel, Bill Garner, act.
Asst. Supt., School Support Services, Dennis Brammer
School Plant Manager, Keith Hawkins
Purchasing Supervisor, Mrs. Edith Cooke
Business Manager, Hugh Fraser

OTHER BRITISH COLUMBIA SCHOOL DISTRICTS

-not confirmed for 1982-

Fernie SD 1: Box 160, Fernie, B.C. V0B 1M0, 423-4117
Cranbrook SD 2: 703 Cranbrook St., Cranbrook, B.C. V1C 3S1, 426-3171
Kimberley SD 3: Box 70, Kimberley, B.C. V1A 2Y5, 427-2247
Windermere SD 4: Box 430, Invermere, B.C. V0A 1K0, 342-6313
Castlegar SD 9: Box 3339, Castlegar, B.C. V1N 3H6, 365-7731
Arrow Lakes SD 10: Box 340, Nakusp, B.C. V0G 1R0, 265-4418
Trail SD 11: 2079 Columbia Ave., Trail, B.C. V1R 1K7, 368-6434
Grand Forks SD 12: Box 640, Grand Forks, B.C. V0H 1H0, 442-8258
Kettle Valley SD 13: Box 640, Grand Forks, B.C. V0H 1H0, 442-8258
Southern Okanagan SD 14: Box 280, Oliver, B.C. V0H 1T0, 498-3481
Penticton SD 15: 274 Eckhardt Ave. E., Penticton, B.C. V2A 1Z4, 492-2721
Keremeos SD 16: Box 850, Princeton, B.C. V0X 1W0, 295-6914
Princeton SD 17: Box 850, Princeton, B.C. V0X 1W0, 295-6914
Golden SD 18: Box 1110, Golden, B.C. V0A 1H0, 344-5241
Revelstoke SD 19: Bag 5800, Revelstoke, B.C. V0E 2S0, 837-2102
Armstrong-Spallumcheen SD 21: Box 430, Armstrong, B.C. V0E 1B0, 546-3031
Vernon SD 22: Drawer 1028, Vernon, B.C. V1T 6M2, 542-3331
North Thompson SD 26: Box 1314, Clearwater, B.C. V0E 1N0, 674-3313
Cariboo-Chilcotin SD 27: 350 2nd Ave. N., Williams Lake, B.C. V2G 1Z9, 392-3345
Quesnel SD 28: 450 Bowron Ave., Quesnel, B.C. V2J 2H5, 992-6109
Lillooet SD 29: Box 820, Lillooet, B.C. V0K 1V0, 256-4282
South Cariboo SD 30: Box 250, Ashcroft, B.C. V0K 1A0, 453-9101
Merritt SD 31: Box 2280, Merritt, B.C. V0K 2B0, 378-5161
Hope SD 32: Box 700, Hope, B.C. V0X 1L0, 869-5141
Abbotsford SD 34: 2343 McCallum Rd., Abbotsford, B.C. V2S 3P5, 859-4891
Langley SD 35: 22259 48th Ave., Langley, B.C. V3A 3Z7, 534-7891
Surrey SD 36: 14225 56 Ave., Surrey, B.C. V3W 1H9, 594-0411
Delta SD 37: 4629 51st St., Delta, B.C. V4K 2V9, 946-4101
Richmond SD 38: 6891 No. 3 Rd., Richmond, B.C. V6Y 2B9, 278-9521
Burnaby SD 41: 5325 Kincaid St., Burnaby, B.C. V5G 1W2, 299-0611
Maple Ridge SD 42: 22462 119th Ave., Maple Ridge, B.C. V2X 2Z4, 463-6223
Coquitlam SD 43: 550 Poirier St., Coquitlam, B.C. V3J 6A7, 939-9201
West Vancouver SD 45: 1075 21st St., West Vancouver, B.C. V7V 4A9, 922-9151
Sunshine Coast SD 46: Box 220, Gibsons, B.C. V0N 1V0, 926-3717
Powell River SD 47: 4351 Ontario Ave., Powell River, B.C. V8A 1V3, 485-6271
Howe Sound SD 48: Box 250, Squamish, B.C. V0N 3G0, 892-5228
Central Coast SD 49: Box 130, Hagensborg, B.C. V0T 1H0, 982-2414
Queen Charlotte SD 50: Box 69, Queen Charlotte City, B.C. V0T 1S0, 559-8471
Prince Rupert SD 52: Box 517, Prince Rupert, B.C. V8J 3R6, 624-6717
Smithers SD 54: Box 2890, Smithers, B.C. V0J 2N0, 847-3261
Burns Lake SD 55: Box 2000, Burns Lake, B.C. V0J 1E0, 692-7141
Nechako SD 56: Box 680, Vanderhoof, B.C. V0J 3A0, 567-2284
Prince George SD 57: 1894 9th Ave., Prince George, B.C. V2M 6G6, 564-1511
Peace River South SD 59: 929 106th Ave., Dawson Creek, B.C. V1G 2N9, 782-8571
Peace River North SD 60: 9803 102nd St., Fort St. John, B.C. V1J 4B3, 785-6785
Sooke SD 62: 2227 Sooke Rd., Victoria, B.C. V9B 1W9, 478-1781
Saanich SD 63: Box 2010, Sidney, B.C. V8L 3S4, 656-1111
Gulf Islands SD 64: Box 10, Lake Cowichan, B.C. V0R 2G0, 749-6636
Cowichan SD 65: 2557 Beverly St., Duncan, B.C. V9L 2X3, 748-0321
Lake Cowichan SD 66: Box 10, Lake Cowichan, B.C. V0R 2G0, 749-6636
Qualicum SD 69: Box 790, Qualicum Beach, B.C. V0R 2T0, 752-9215
Alberni SD 70: 4690 Roger St., Port Alberni, B.C. V9Y 3Z4, 723-3565
Courtenay SD 71: 892 Harmston Ave., Courtenay, B.C. V9N 2X8, 338-5383
Campbell River SD 72: 425 Pinecrest Rd., Campbell River, B.C. V9W 3P2, 286-0651
Mission SD 75: 33046 4th Ave., Mission, B.C. V2V 1S6, 826-6286
Agassiz-Harrison SD 76: Box 700, Hope, B.C. V0X 1L0, 869-5141
Summerland SD 77: Box 339, Summerland, B.C. V0H 1Z0, 494-7511
Kitimat SD 80: 1515 Kingfisher Ave., Kitimat, B.C. V8C 1S5, 632-6124
Fort Nelson SD 81: Box 87, Fort Nelson, B.C. V0C 1R0, 774-2593
Vancouver Island West SD 84: 7451 Elmbridge Way, Richmond, B.C. V6X 1B8
Vancouver Island North SD 85: Box 90, Port Hardy, B.C. V0N 2P0, 949-6618
Creston-Kaslo SD 86: Box 1640, Creston, B.C. V0B 1G0, 428-2217
Stikine SD 87: Box 87, Fort Nelson, B.C. V0C 1R0, 774-2593
Terrace SD 88: Drawer 460, Terrace, B.C. V8G 4B5, 635-4931
Shuswap SD 89: Box 699, Salmon Arm, B.C. V0E 2T0, 832-2157
Nisgha SD 92: Gen. Delivery, New Aiyansh, B.C. V0J 1A0

BRITISH COLUMBIA CURRICULUM DEVELOPMENT BRANCH

St. Ann's Academy, 835 Humboldt St., Victoria, B.C.
Director of Curriculum, Dr. J.J. Mussio
Asst. Director, W. D. Oliver
Home Economics Consultants, Miss J. Campbell; Mrs. H. A. Krueger, 516 Michigan St., Victoria, B.C.
Asst. Director, Career Programs, J. Jupp, 835 Humboldt St.

POST SECONDARY & PRIVATE INSTITUTIONS IN BRITISH COLUMBIA

Art Schools

KOOTENAY SCHOOL OF ART

David Thompson University Centre, 820 10th St., Nelson, B.C. V1L 3C7
(604) 352-2241
Chairman, E.H. Underhill

EMILY CARR COLLEGE OF ART & DESIGN

1399 Johnston St., Granville Island, Vancouver, B.C. V6H 3R9
(604) 687-2345
Principal, R. C. Mayor

University of British Columbia

Vancouver, B.C. V6T 1W5
(604) 228-2211
Visitor, Lt. Gov. of British Columbia, the Hon. Henry P. Bell-Irving, D.S.O., O.B.E., E.D.
Chancellor, Hon. J.V. Clyne, B.A., C.C., K.G. St.J.
President, D. T. Kenny, M.A., Ph.D.
Vice President & Bursar, William White, F.C.G.A.
Vice President, University Services, James Kennedy, M.A., Ph.D.
Vice President, Academic & Provost, Michael Shaw, M.Sc., Ph.D., F.L.S., F.R.S.C., D.Sc., P.Ag., F.A.P.S.

DEANS
Agricultural Sciences, Warren Kitts, M.S.A., Ph.D., F.A.I.C.
Applied Science, L.M. Wedepol, B.Sc., Ph.D., F.I.E.E.
Arts, R. M. Will, B.A., M.A., Ph.D.
Commerce & Business Admin., Peter Lusztig, B.Com., M.B.A., Ph.D.
Dentistry, George Beagrie, F.D.S.R.C.S., D.D.S., F.R.C.D.
Education, Daniel Birch, Dip. Theol., B.R.E., B.A., M.A., Ph.D.
Forestry, J. A. F. Gardner, M.A., Ph.D., F.C.I.C., F.I.A.W.S.
Graduate Studies, Peter A. Larkin, M.A., D. Phil., F.R.S.C.
Law, K.M. Lysyk, Q.C., B.A., LL.B., B.C.L.
Medicine, William Webber, M.D.
Pharmaceutical Sciences, B. E. Riedel, C.D., M.Sc., Ph.D.
Science, C.V. Finnegan, B.A., M.S., Ph.D.

DIRECTORS & OTHER OFFICERS
Director, Institutional Analysis & Planning, Wm. L. Tetlow, B.G.E., M.A., Ph.D.
Co-ordinator of Animal Care, J. R. Gregg, M.R.C.V.S., M.A.
Director, Athletics & Sport Services, Robert Hindmarch, B.P.E., M.Sc., D.Ed.
Director, Botanical Garden, R. L. Taylor, B.Sc., Ph.D.
Director, Centre for Continuing Education, Jindra Kulich, B.A., M.A.
Director, Ceremonies, Benjamin Moyls, M.A., Ph.D.
Director, Computing Centre, A.G. Fowler, B.A., Sc., M.Sc.
Director, Information Services, Brant E. Ducey, B.A., M.A.
Director, International House, Rorri McBlane, B.A.
Director, Extra-sessional Studies (inc. Summer Session), N. S. Watt, B.P.E., M.S., Ed.D.
Executive Director, Univ. of B.C. Press, A. N. Blicq
Research Administrator, R. D. Spratley, B.Sc., Ph.D.
Librarian, (tba)
Registrar, Kenneth Young, B.A., B.Com.
Women Students' Office, L. Woolsey, M.A., Ph.D., Director
Director, Univ. Health Service & Health Service Hospital, Archibald M. Johnson, M.D., F.R.C.P.(C.).
Director, Counselling & Resources Centre, A. F. Shirran, M.A.
Director, Residences, Michael Davis, B.A., M.B.A.
Director, Student Awards, B. H. Hender, B. Com.
Director of Employee Relations, Robert Grant, B.A.
Director, Physical Plant, Neville Smith, B.A.Sc., P.Eng.
Associate Vice President & Treasurer, Allen Baxter, B.Com., C.A.
Bookstore Manager, J.K. Hedgecock
Director, Food Services, Christine Samson, B.Sc., Dip. Dietetics
Director, Purchasing, S. C. Potter
Executive Secretary, Univ. Resources Committee, (tba)

SCHOOLS WITH DIRECTORS
Architecture, Douglas Shadbolt, B.Arch., D.Eng. (Hon.), F.R.A.I.C.
Nursing, M.D. Willman, B.S.N., M.S.N., Ph.D.
Home Economics, R.H. Rodgers, B.A., M.A., Ph.D.
Librarianship, Basil Stuart-Stubbs, B.A., B.L.S.
Social Work, George M. Hougham, B.A., M.A., Ph.D.
Physical Education, W. Robert Morford, B.P.E., M.P.E., Ed.D.
Community Planning, B. Wiesman, B.Arch., M.Arch.
Rehabilitation Medicine, Mrs. T.A. Conine, B.Sc., M.A., D.H.S.

AFFILIATED COLLEGES
Vancouver School of Theology, Rev. J.P. Martin
St. Mark's College (Roman Catholic), Rev. Daniel Mulvihill, C.S.B., B.A., M.A., Ph.D.
Regent College, C.E. Armerding, A.B., B.D., M.A., Ph.D.

The Canadian Outward Bound Mountain School

Box 370, Keremeos, B.C. V0X 1N0
(604) 499-5582
Information from: #101, 1600 W. 6th Ave., Vancouver, B.C. V6J 1S5 (604/733-9104)

Short courses ranging from 10 to 24 days designed to reveal character and develop self-confidence through small group shared experiences in the Cascades of British Columbia. Mountaineering, including rock climbing, mountain rescue and back packing, is taught, not for its own sake but as a means of providing self discovery through adventure. The activities also include white water kayaking, except in the winter when the accent is on ski-touring. Courses are run for men or women over the age of 16 years as well as mixed courses for men and women over 18, and junior courses for young men and women between 14 and 16.

The Canadian School of Ballet Ltd.

1157 Sutherland Ave., Kelowna, B.C. V1Y 5Y2
(604) 764-7865
Director, Joyce Gearing

Columbia College

1619 W. 10th Ave., Vancouver, B.C. V6J 2A2
(604) 733-9151
Principal, Dr. Lorne J. Kavic
Vice Principal/Registrar, Robert Jeffery
Library Administrator, Randi Smith

B. Allan Mackie School of Log Building & Environmental Centre

Box 1205, Prince George, B.C. V2L 4V3

A wilderness workshop, operating year round, 42 km. from downtown Prince George where twentieth century log construction skills are taught.

Lester B. Pearson College of the Pacific

R.R. 1, Victoria, B.C. V8X 3W9
(604) 478-5591

A member of the United World Colleges with associated institutions in Wales and Singapore. A two year course leading to the International Baccalaureate. The College accepts young men and women on full scholarship after eleven years of education.

Chairman, Board of Trustees, Hon. John L. Nichol, O.C.
Director, Jack E. Matthews
Administrator, John D. Davis
Manager, Development & Public Affairs, John K. Glaab

Northwest Baptist Theological College & Seminary

3358 S.E. Marine Dr., Vancouver, B.C. V5S 3W3
(604) 433-2475
Principal Officer, D. Harris

Prince George College

College Rd., Box 7000, Prince George, B.C. V2N 3Z2
(604) 964-4455
Principal, Ken Dick

Royal Roads Military College

Victoria, B.C. V0S 1B0
(604) 388-2251

OFFICERS OF ADMINISTRATION
President, The Hon. J. Gilles Lamontagne, P.C, M.P. (Ottawa)
Commandant, Col. G.L. Logan
Vice Commandant, Cdr. R.S. Copley
Director of Studies, E. S. Graham, B.Sc., M.Sc., Ph.D., M.C.I.C., F.C.S., F.O.A.S.

Dean of Science, H.J. Duffus, n.d.c., B.A., B.A.Sc., D.Phil., P.Eng.
Dean of Arts, Dr. W. Rodney, D.F.C. and Bar, B.A., M.A., Ph.D.,, F.R.G.S., F.R.Hist.S.
Chief Administrative Officer, Major L. Wagar
Registrar, Col. (Ret'd.) A.D. Wallis, C.D., B.A., M.A.
Chaplains, Capt. J. Dabrowski; Capt. E.W. Taylor; Capt. R.L. Marchand
Comptroller, Capt. J.L. Chow
Staff Officer, Cadets & Military Training, Major K.W. Casson C.D.
Squadron Commanders, Capt. J.P. Molloy; Capt. P.J. Kendell; Lt. (N) D.B. Fodor; Capt. K.M. Psutka; Maj. K.R. Merkley
Personnel Administrative Officer, Capt. T. McCarthy, CD.
Librarian, C. C. Whitlock, B.A., B.Ed., B.L.S.
Director of Athletics, Capt. W. Keener, C.D., B.A., pjsc.

St. Michaels University School

Sr. Sch. Grades 8-12 (girls in gr. 10-12), 3400 Richmond Rd., Victoria, B.C. V8P 4P5 (604/592-2411)
Jr. Sch., Grades 1-7, 820 Victoria Ave., Victoria, B.C. V8S 4N3 (592-2411)
Headmaster, H. John P. Schaffter, M.A.

Seminary of Christ the King

Mission, B.C. V2V 4J2
(604) 826-8715
Rector, Rev. Augustine Kalberer, O.S.B.
Registrar, Rev. Lawrence Bilesky, O.S.B.

Simon Fraser University

Burnaby, B.C. V5A 1S6
(604) 291-3111
Chancellor, P.T. Coté, B.A., B.A.Sc., M.B.A., P.Eng.
President & Vice Chancellor, K. George Pedersen, B.A., M.A., Ph.D., F.C.C.T.
Registrar, H. M. Evans, C.D., B.A.
Purchasing Manager, A. Shane
Librarian, T.C. Dobb, B.A., B.L.S.
Bookstore Manager, B. F. Quan, B. Com.

FACULTIES AND DEANS

Arts, R.C. Brown, B.Sc., M.S., Ph.D.
  Depts.: Archaeology, Business Administration, Economics, English, Geography, History, Languages, Literatures & Linguistics, Philosophy, Political Science, Psychology, Sociology & Anthropology
  Programs: Mathematics, Joint Major in Psychology and Linguistics and Philosophy
Education, J.W.G. Ivany, B.Sc., Dip.Ed., M.A., Ph.D.
Interdisciplinary Studies, T.W. Calvert, B.Sc., M.S.E.E., Ph.D.
  Depts.: Centre for the Arts, Communication, Computing Science, Criminology, Kinesiology
  Programs: Africa/Middle East Studies, Canadian Studies, Latin American Studies, Women's Studies
Science, J.F. Cochran, B.A.Sc., M.A.Sc., Ph.D.
  Depts.: Biological Sciences, Chemistry, Mathematics, Physics
  Programs: Biochemistry, Biophysics, Chemical Physics, Geography, Mathematical Physics
Graduate Studies, B. Beirne, B.Sc., M.A., M.Sc., Ph.D., M.R.I.A.
Continuing Studies, J. Blaney, B.Ed., M.Ed., Ph.D.

Trinity Western College

Glover Rd. & College Lane, Langley, B.C. V3A 4R9
(604) 888-7511
President, Dr. Neil Snider
Dean of Academic Affairs, Dr. Ken Davis
Dean of Students, Arvid Olson
Director, Business Affairs, Doug Sneath
Director, Public Affairs, (tba)
Registrar, Mrs. Marijke Olson
Librarian, David Twiest
Comptroller, Harvey Ouellette
Bookstore Manager, Lauren Pedersen

Vancouver School of Theology

6000 Iona Dr., Vancouver, B.C. V6T 1L4
(604) 228-9031
Chairman, Board of Governors, Dr. George Morrison
Principal, Rev. J. P. Martin, B.A.Sc., B.D., Th.M., Ph.D.
Bursar, J. Ponech
Purchasing Agent, J. Ponech
Registrar, J. Bradley

University of Victoria

Victoria, B.C. V8W 2Y2
(604) 721-7211
Visitor, The Hon. Henry J. Bell-Irving, D.S.O., O.B.E., E.D., Lt.-Gov. of the Province of British Columbia
Chancellor, Ian McTaggart Cowan, O.C., Ph.D., LL.D., D.Env.St., D.Sc., F.R.S.C.
President & Vice Chancellor, Howard E. Petch, B.Sc., M.A., Ph.D.
Vice President, Academic, Alfred Fischer, B.Sc., M.Sc., Ph.D.
Vice President, Administration, J. Trevor Matthews, B.A., M.B.A.
Vice President, Finance, Robert W. McQueen, B.Com., C.A.

DEANS AND OTHER SENIOR ADMINISTRATIVE OFFICERS

Dean, Faculty of Arts & Science, Roger R. Davidson, B.Sc., M.A.,Ph.D.
Dean, Faculty of Education, Arthur Kratzmann, B.Ed., M.Ed., Ph.D.
Dean, Faculty of Fine Arts, Douglas G. Morton
Dean, Faculty of Graduate Studies, John M. Dewey, B.Sc., Ph.D.
Dean, Faculty of Human & Social Development, Robert W. Payne, B.A., Ph.D.
Dean, Faculty of Law, Lyman R. Robinson, B.A., LL.B., LL.M.
Executive Asst. to President, James E. Currie, B.Com., M.B.A.
Asst. to President, Staff Relations, Peter J. Vanderleeden
Registrar & Secretary, Board of Governors, Ron Ferry, B.A.
Admin. Registrar, Gordon J. Smiley, B.A.
Univ. Librarian, Dean W. Halliwell, M.A., B.L.S.

ACADEMIC CHAIRMEN AND DIRECTORS

Chairman, Dept. of Anthropology, Leland H. Donald, B.A., Ph.D.
Chairman, Dept. of Art & Music Education, Ian L. Bradley, B.Ed., M.Ed., Ed.D.
Chairman, Dept. of Biochemistry & Microbiology, Alastair T. Matheson, B.A., M.Sc., Ph.D.
Chairman, Dept. of Biology, John E. McInerney, B.Sc., M.Sc., Ph.D.
Chairman, Dept. of Chemistry, Alexander McAuley, B.Sc., Ph.D., D.Sc.
Director, School of Child Care, Roy Ferguson, B.A., Ph.D.
Chairman, Dept. of Classics, Samuel E. Scully, B.A., M.Litt., Ph.D.
Chairman, Dept. of Communication & Social Foundations, A.V. Olson, B.S., M.S., Ed.D.
Chairman, Dept. of Computer Science, B.L. Ehle, A.B., M.S., Ph.D.
Chairman, Dept. of Creative Writing, W. David Godfrey, B.A., M.A., Ph.D.
Chairman, Dept. of Economics, K.L. Avio, B.S., M.S., Ph.D. (act.)
Chairman, Dept. of English, Michael R. Best, B.A., Ph.D.
Chairman, Dept. of French Language & Literature, Jennifer R. Waelti-Walters, B.A., L. ès L., Ph.D.
Chairman, Dept. of Geography, W.R. Derrick Sewell, B.Sc. Econ., M.A., Ph.D.
Chairman, Dept. of Germanic Languages & Literature, R.T.K. Symington, B.A., Ph.D.
Chairman, Dept. of Hispanic & Italian Studies, Caroline Monahan, B.A., M.A., Ph.D. (act.)
Chairman, Dept. of History, Wesley T. Wooley, A.B., A.M., Ph.D.
Chairman, Dept. of History in Art, Charles R. Wicke, B.A., M.A., Ph.D.
Chairman, Dept. of Linguistics, Henry J. Warkentyne, B.A., M.A., Ph.D.
Chairman, Dept. of Mathematics, Roger R. Davidson, B.Sc., M.A., Ph.D.

Director, School of Music, Paul Kling, Artist Dip.
Director, School of Nursing, Dorothy J. Kergin, B.S.N., M.P.H., Ph.D.
Director, Centre for Pacific & Oriental Studies, R.C. Croizier, B.A., M.A., Ph.D.
Chairman, Dept. of Philosophy, Rodger G. Beehler, B.A., B.Phil., Ph.D.
Director, School of Physical Education, J.J. Jackson, Dip. P.E., M.Sc., Ph.D.
Chairman, Dept. of Physics, J.T. Weaver, Ph.D.
Chairman, Dept. of Political Science, A.H. Birch
Chairman, Dept. of Psychological Foundations in Education, Roger A. Ruth, B.S., M.S., Ph.D.
Chairman, Dept. of Psychology, L.D. Costa, M.A., Ph.D.
Director, School of Public Admin., A.R. Dobell, B.A., M.A., Ph.D.
Chairman, Dept. of Slavonic Studies, Gunter H. Schaarschmidt, M.A., Ph.D.
Chairman, Dept. of Social & Natural Sciences, Robert H. Fowler, B.A., M.A., Ph.D.
Director, School of Social Work, Brian Wharf, B.A., B.S.W., M.S.W., Ph.D.
Chairman, Dept. of Sociology, R. Alan Hedley, B.A., M.A., Ph.D.
Chairman, Dept. of Theatre, C.R. Hare, M.A., Dip.R.ADA.
Chairman, Dept. of Visual Arts, George W. Tiessen, B.F.A., M.F.A.

Western Pentecostal Bible College

Box 1000, Clayburn, B.C. V0X 1E0
(604) 853-7491, 2
Chairman, Board of Governors, J.M. House
President, L. Thomas Holdcroft
Purchasing Agent, Stanley A. Sharkey
Librarian, Laurie Van Kleek
Bookstore Manager, Caroline Coughlan

COMMUNITY COLLEGES, TECHNICAL & VOCATIONAL INSTITUTES IN BRITISH COLUMBIA

PROVINCIAL INSTITUTES

B.C. Institute of Technology, 3700 Willingdon Ave., Burnaby, B.C. V5G 3H2 (604/434-5734)
President, G.A. Thom
B.C. Mining School, Box 789, Rossland, B.C. V0G 1Y0
Emily Carr College of Art, 1399 Johnston St., Granville Island, Vancouver, B.C. V6H 2R9 (604/687-2345)
Principal, R. Mayor
David Thompson University Centre, 820 10th St., Nelson, B.C. V1L 3C7 (604/352-2241)
Co-ordinator, Campus Director, Dr. R.L. Williams
Justice Institute of B.C., 4180 W. 4th Ave., Vancouver, B.C. V6R 4J5 (604/228-9771)
Principal, Gerry B. Kilcup
Open Learning Institute, 7671 Alderbridge Way, Richmond, B.C. V6X 1Z9 (604/270-4131)
Principal, R.R. Jeffels
Pacific Marine Training Institute, 2019 Dundas St., Vancouver, B.C. V5L 1J5 (604/254-0741)
Principal, D. Hughes
Pacific Vocational Institute, 3650 Willingdon Ave., Burnaby, B.C. V5G 3H1
Principal, H.E. Justesen
Burnaby Campus, 3650 Willingdon Ave., Burnaby, B.C. V5C 3H1 (604/434-5722)
Maple Ridge Campus, Box 3000, Maple Ridge, B.C. V2X 8L3 (604/362-5377)
Sea Island Campus, Vancouver International Airport (South), 4440 Stark St., Richmond, B.C. V7B 1A1

COMMUNITY COLLEGES

Camosun College, 1950 Lansdowne Rd., Victoria, B.C. V8P 5J2 (604/592-1281)
Principal, Dr. Lloyd Morin
Capilano College, 2055 Purcell Way, North Vancouver, B.C. V7J 3H5 (604/986-1911)
Principal, Dr. Paul Gallagher
Cariboo College, Box 3010, Kamloops, B.C. V2C 5N3 (604/374-0123)
Principal, C.W. Brewster
College of New Caledonia, 3330 22 Ave., Prince George, B.C. V2N 1P8
Principal, Charles McCaffray
Douglas College, Box 2503, New Westminster, B.C. V3L 5B2 (604/521-4851)
Principal, R.H. Pridham
East Kootenay College, Box 8500, Cranbrook, B.C. V1C 5L7 (604/489-2751)
Principal, Dr. D. Lorne Ball
Fraser Valley College
East Campus: 45600 Airport Rd., Chilliwack, B.C. V2P 6T4 (604/792-0025)
Principal, Dr. B.D. Moore
West Campus: 34194 Marshall Rd., Abbotsford, B.C. V2S 5E4 (604/853-7441)
Malaspina College, 900 5th St., Nanaimo, B.C. V9R 5S5 (604/753-3245)
President, G.A. Sylvester
North Island College, 156 Manor Dr., Comox, B.C. V9N 6P7 (604/339-5551)
Principal, Dr. D. Wing
Northern Lights College, 11401 8th St., Dawson Creek, B.C. V1G 4G2 (604/782-5251)
Chief Executive Officer, J.B. Kassen
Northwest College, Box 726, Terrace, B.C. V8G 4C2 (604/635-6511)
Principal, Dr. D.V. George
Okanagan College, 1000 KLO Rd., Kelowna, B.C. V1Y 4X8 (604/762-5445)
Principal, P.L. Williams
Selkirk College, Box 1200, Castlegar, B.C. V1N 3J1 (604/365-7292)
Principal, Leo Perra
Vancouver Community College, Royal Bank Bldg., 675 W. Hastings St., Vancouver, B.C. V6B 1N2 (604/688-1111)
President, A.S. Manera

MANITOBA BOARDS OF EDUCATION

The Province of Manitoba is divided into 63 educational units: 47 School divisions; 10 Remote School Districts; 6 Special Revenue School Districts. Three of the six Special Revenue School Districts, two of the ten Remote School Districts, and one school division, are operated under the jurisdiction of Official Trustees. The remaining eight Remote School Districts, three Special Revenue Districts, and the 46 School Divisions are controlled by elected school boards. Elections are held in accordance with the Local Authorities Election Act.

All 63 educational units are responsible for the provision of elementary and secondary education.

For Department of Education officials, see government listings.

The following are School Divisions in major population areas, listed alphabetically.

Brandon School Division 40

1031 6th St., Brandon, Man. R7A 4K5
(204) 728-0184
Secretary Treasurer, D. J. Cornell
Supt., J. Leslie Milne
Asst. Supt., R. M. Swayze
Asst. Supt., H. L. Stewart
Asst. Secretary Treasurer & Purchasing Agent, E. H. Harrison

River East School Division 9
589 Roch St., E. Kildonan, Man. R2K 2P7
(204) 667-7130
Secretary Treasurer, E.F. Solomchuk
Supt., W.W. Melnyk
Asst. Supt., Dr. R.W. Cross
Asst. Supt., Personnel & Resources, G.R. Green
Deputy Asst. Supt., Pupil Personnel Services, W. Kormylo
Deputy Asst. Supt., Curriculum, E.C. Buller
Director, Material Resources, N.P. Guilbert
Consultant, Physical Education, Mrs. R.M. Vyse
Consultant, Music, Miss F. Duerksen
Asst. Secretary Treasurer, H. Wildeman
Purchasing Co-ordinator, E. Schoen
Director of Maintenance, R. Reimer
Director of Transportation, M. Kirkland

Flin Flon School Division 46
Box 578, Flin Flon, Man. R8A 1N4
(204) 687-3413
Secretary Treasurer, Ms. R.M. Ariko

St. James-Assiniboia School Division 2
2574 Portage Ave., Winnipeg, Man. R3J 0H8
(204) 888-7951
Director of Education & Secretary Treasurer, G.B. Buchholz
Supt. of Secondary Schools, D.N. Stefanson
Supt. of Elementary Schools, M.A. Yaremchuk
Asst. Supt. of Secondary Schools, T.M. Carlyle
Asst. Supt. of Elementary Schools, J.Z. Friesen
Manager of Business & Finance, H.K. Hardy
Information Officer, Donna Phillips

Winnipeg School Division 1
1577 Wall St. E., Winnipeg, Man. R3E 2S5
(204) 775-0231
Chief Supt., W.C. Lorimer
Executive Asst., D.A. Downie
Supt., Secondary Schools, J.C. Smyth
Supt., Elementary Schools, W.P. Solypa
Secretary Treasurer, J.R. Hayes
Director of Buildings, S. Baumel
Architect, W.I. Enns
Communications Officer, H.A. Marshall
Purchasing Agent, H.J. Roberts

MANITOBA SUPERVISORY & CONSULTATIVE STAFF

DEPARTMENTAL ADMINISTRATIVE SUPPORT SERVICES
Director, L.A. Floyde (204/786-0340)
Field Services Branch
Metro Region - #512A, 1181 Portage Ave., Winnipeg, Man. R3G OT3 (786-0120) M. Daeninck, J.R. McCurdy, E. Woods
North Eastern Region - #310, 1181 Portage Ave., Winnipeg, Man. R3G OT3 (786-0246) A. Delaquis, V.F. Sanderson, N.S. Toms
South Eastern Region - #512A, 1181 Portage Ave., Winnipeg, Man. R3G OT3 (786-0327) J.A. Duhamel, R.R. Partridge, R.L. McIntosh
Western Region - 107 Provincial Bldg., 340 9th St., Brandon, Man. R7A 6C2 (728-7000) J.M. Taylor, J. Shaw, C.D. Bollman
Dauphin Region - 27 2nd Ave. S.W., Dauphin, Man. R7N 3E5 (638-9111) L.W. Day, G. Takashima
Thompson Region - 59 Elizabeth Dr., Thompson, Man. R8N 1X4 (778-4411) J.H. Hjalmarson, J.L. McGinn
Manitoba Text Book Bureau, 277 Hutchings St., Winnipeg, Man. R2X 2R4, Manager, W.B. Woolston (633-6505)

TEACHER CERTIFICATION & RECORDS
Director, Dr. R.F. Constant (786-0323)
Supervisor of Records, Mrs. Gail Lancaster

BUREAU DE L'EDUCATION FRANCAISE
Sous ministre adjoint (Asst. Deputy Minister), Dr. R.J. Duhamel
Adjoint administratif (Executive Asst.), Normand Boisvert
Directeurs des programmes:
Curriculum, G. Roy
Support Services, G. Lécuyer
Second Language Consultants, C. Sortiriadis (Core French); E. Molgat (Immersion)
General Office & Inquiry, 786-0126

PROGRAM DEVELOPMENT DIRECTORATE
Director, S.A.I. Bullock (786-0295)
Curriculum Development Branch
Co-ordinator, S.A.I. Bullock (786-0295)
General Office & Information, 786-0321
Consultants:
English Language Arts, D.C. Bewell (786-0316)
Second Languages Other Than French, K. Fast (786-0310)
Social Studies, J. Lohrenz (786-0264)
Arts, G. Warren (786-0318)
Sciences, W. Soprovich (786-0314)
Vocational/Practical Arts, H.M. Draper (786-0171)
Mathematics, W. Watt (786-0191)
Special Education, P. Wilby (786-0172)
Publications Editor, J. Peterson (786-0336)
Curriculum Services Branch
Co-ordinator, A.J. Janzen (786-0319)
General Office and Information, 786-0317
Consultants:
English Language Arts, Elementary, D. Brummitt (786-0267)
English Language Arts, Secondary, W.C. Layne (786-0313)
Social Studies, G. McEwen (786-0335)
Business Education, I. Dryden (786-0247)
Mobile Reading Centre, R. Scott, L. Fraser (786-0143)
Industrial Arts, G. Happychuk (786-0283)
German Language, C. Hartwig (786-0298)
Ukrainian Language, S. Yurkiwsky (786-0265)
Middle Years, A. Johannson (786-0142)
Physical Education, R. LaPage (786-0268)
Mathematics, P.M. Luba (786-0122)
Career Guidance & Counselling, D. Lucas, T. Prins (786-0243)
Computer Services, D. McCaig (786-0118)
Learning Materials, G. Parasuik (786-0290)
Immigrant Education & English as a Second Language, A. Peters (786-0288)
Art, R. Harris (786-0272)
Learning Materials, M. Szakacs (786-0187)
Sciences, E. Uzwyshyn (786-0325)
Vocational Industrial Education, V. Mollot (786-0255)
Health, I. Wettlaufer (786-0263)
Early Childhood & Elementary, A. Berg (786-0240)
Measurement & Evaluation Branch, Co-ordinator, H. Schulz (786-0130)
Native Education Branch, Co-ordinator, F. Zaharia (786-0284)
Vocational Education Branch, Co-ordinator, F. Zaboroski (786-0230)
Co-operative Vocational Education Project, Co-ordinator, P. Vouk (786-0169)

SUPPORT SERVICES DIRECTORATE
Director, J. Dyck (786-0212)
Child Development & Support Services, Co-ordinator, N. Cenerini
General Office, 786-0210
Field Support Services
Consultants, Special Education, A. Stevens, J. Latter, D. Reynolds, G. Castillo, J. Fradette

REGIONS
Interlake, Regional Co-ordinator, M. Timgren (642-5242)
Parkland, Regional Co-ordinator, T. Borsa (638-9111)
North, Regional Co-ordinator, P. Martin (778-8335)
South Central, Regional Co-ordinator, D. Middleton (857-9711)
South East, M. McLearon (326-9829)

Correspondence Branch, Principal, D. Eirikson (775-8461)

POST SECONDARY & PRIVATE INSTITUTIONS IN MANITOBA

Art Schools

THE UNIVERSITY OF MANITOBA SCHOOL OF ART
Winnipeg, Man. R3T 2N2
(204) 474-9303
Director, R.C. Sakowski, act.

FORUM ART INSTITUTE
181 Higgins Ave., c/o CP Mail, Winnipeg, Man. R3B 0C2
(204) 946-3294
Administrator, Ms. Ruth Legris
Art Director, Nikola Bjelajac

Balmoral Hall
Residential and Day School for Girls
630 Westminster Ave., Winnipeg, Man. R3C 3S1
(204) 786-8643
Headmaster, N. Thomas Russell

Brandon University
Brandon, Man. R7A 6A9
(204) 728-9520
President, Dr. Harold J. Perkins
Executive Asst. to the President, Alison Long
Comptroller, Ross Eastley
Development Officer, D. R. MacKay
Purchasing Agent, M. Tapley
Information Officer, Barbara Biggar-Giesbrecht
Librarian, Maria Szivos

FACULTIES WITH DEANS
Arts, Dr. P.J.C. Hordern
Science, Dr. Robin Giles
Education, Dr. D. Hayes

SCHOOL WITH HEAD
School of Music, Dr. L. Watson

University of Manitoba
Winnipeg, Man. R3T 2N2
(204) 474-8880

PRINCIPAL OFFICERS
Chancellor, Isabel Auld
President & Vice Chancellor, Dr. Arnold Naimark
Vice President, Admin., Dr. D. O. Wells
Vice President, Academic, Dr. D.J. Lawless
Admissions, D. C. Bevis
Student Records, Brian Salt
Director of Finance, T. G. Falconer
Public Relations Officer, R. M. Raeburn
Printing & Publication Services, George Hnatiuk
Purchasing Agent, D. Coyle
Librarian, Ms. Marilyn Sharrow
Bookstore Manager, Helen Garlicki

FACULTIES WITH DEANS
Agriculture, R.C. McGinnis
Architecture, H.E. Thompson
Arts, F.G. Stambrook
Admin. Studies, R.G. Grandpre
Dentistry, Dr. A. Schwartz
Education, Eric D. MacPherson
Engineering, Edmund Kuffel
Graduate Studies, T.P. Hogan
Human Ecology, B.E. Macdonald
Law, J.R. London
Medicine, tba
Pharmacy, J.R. Murray
Science, C.C. Bigelow

SCHOOLS WITH DIRECTORS
Art, Alfred E. Hammer
Dental Hygiene, Shirley Gelskey
Medical Rehabilitation, (vacant)
Music, Paul Patterson
Nursing, June M. Bradley
Physical Education, Henry Janzen
Social Work, Mrs. Addie Penner

AFFILIATED AND CONSTITUENT INSTITUTIONS
St. Boniface College, 200 Cathedral Ave., Winnipeg, Man. R2H 0H7
Rector, Dr. R. J. A. Cloutier
St. John's College, Winnipeg, Man. R3T 2M5
Warden, J. R. Brown
St. Paul's College, Winnipeg, Man. R3T 2M6
Rector, Harold Kane
University College, Winnipeg, Man. R3T 2N2
Provost, A.M. Lansdown

AFFILIATED INSTITUTION
St. Andrew's College, Winnipeg, Man. R3T 2M7
Principal, P.A. Kondra

APPROVED TEACHING CENTRES
Canadian Mennonite Bible College, 600 Shaftesbury Blvd., Winnipeg, Man. R3P 0M4
President, Dr. George K. Epp
Canadian Nazarene College, 1301 Lee Blvd., Winnipeg, Man. R3T 2P7
President, Neil Hightower

St. John's-Ravenscourt School
400 South Dr., Winnipeg, Man. R3T 3K5
(204) 453-3016
Principal, John A. Messenger
Headmaster of Upper School, H.T. McCracken
Headmaster of Lower School, C.B. Kiddell
Business Manager, G. Braun
Librarian, Mrs. S. Ford

The University of Winnipeg
515 Portage Ave., Winnipeg, Man. R3B 2E9
(204) 786-7811
Chancellor, R.O.A. Hunter
Chairman, Board of Regents, R.K. Siddall
President, H. E. Duckworth
Vice President, J. Clake
Dean of Arts & Science, D. Kydon
Dean of Theology, Rev. A.M. Watts
Comptroller, J. K. A. Brown
Registrar, R. M. Bellhouse
Information Officer, J. S. McDiarmid
Purchasing Agent, B. Bater
Librarian, R. C. Wright
Bookstore Manager, W. Shand

ASSOCIATED INSTITUTION
Mennonite Brethren College of Arts, 77 Henderson Hwy., Winnipeg, Man.

COMMUNITY COLLEGES IN MANITOBA
Red River Community College, 2055 Notre Dame Ave., Winnipeg, Man. R3H 0J9 (204/632-2311)
Director, E.B. Angood
Assiniboine Community College, 1430 Victoria Ave. E., Brandon, Man. R7A 5Z9 (204/725-4530)
Director, A. A. Loveridge
Registrar, W.R. McCaughan
Community Relations Officer, C.A. Stevens
Keewatin Community College, Box 3000, The Pas, Man. R9A 1M7 (204/623-3416)
Director, Dr. T. Duff

NEW BRUNSWICK SCHOOL BOARDS

As a result of the implementation of the New Brunswick Schools Act, New Brunswick is divided into 37 school districts, replacing 422 school districts in operation previous to January 1, 1967.

The administration of public school education in each of the thirty-five school districts is the responsibility of a board of school trustees, two-thirds of whose members are elected, and one-third appointed by the Lieutenant Governor in Council.

For Department of Education officials see government listings.

The following are school districts containing large cities, listed alphabetically.

Board of School Trustees, District 27

Box 39, Harvey Stn., N.B. EOH 1HO
(506) 366-2058
Business Admin., E. H. McGee
Inspectors, John Hildebrand; R. McCormack

Board of School Trustees, District 15

27 John St., Box 1008, Moncton, N.B. E1C 8P2
(506) 855-1900
Director, A. H. McLeod
Supt., G. Mawhinney
Asst. Supt., A.B. Baglole
Accountant, P. Melanson
Transportation Officer, J.J. MacNeil
Purchasing Officer, R. Goodwin

Board of School Trustees, District 20

384 Lancaster Ave., Saint John, N.B. E2M 2L5
(506) 672-2500
Secretary, G. S. Brewer
District Supt., Earle W.H. Wood
Asst. Supt., Special Services, Mrs. Claire L. Correia
Asst. Supt., Personnel & Secondary Schools, F.S. McGillicuddy
Asst. Supt., Elementary & Intermediate Schools, Anne Marie McGrath
Asst. Supt., Admin. & Finance, G. S. Brewer
Director of Business, C. Finley
Director of Plant, A. F. Stewart
Director of Transportation, Ardith Thompson

POST SECONDARY & PRIVATE INSTITUTIONS IN NEW BRUNSWICK

Université de Moncton

Moncton, N.B. E1A 3E9
(506) 858-4000
Chancelier, Dr. Léon Richard
Recteur, Gilbert Finn
Vice recteur à l'enseignement et à la recherche, Léonard LeBlanc
Vice recteur, admin., Médard Collette
Secrétaire général, Gilles Long
Directeur du Service aux étudiants, Gilles Nadeau
Directeur des Services techniques, Eustache Haché
Adjoint au vice recteur à l'enseignement et à la recherche, Léopold Laplante
Directeur du Service administratifs, Arthur Girouard
Directeur de ressorce humaine et relations de travail, Clément Loubert
Registraire, Gérard Cormier
Directeur du Service de l'information et des relations publiques, Yves Chouinard
Directeur du développement, Rhéal Bérubé

DOYENS ET DIRECTEURS

Faculté des arts, Georges Amand Français
Faculté des sciences et de génie, Francis Weil
Faculté d'administration, Normand Roy
Ecole des sciences infirmières, Marcelle Dumont
Ecole des sciences domestiques, Marielle Préfontaine
Faculté des sciences d'éducation, Louis Malenfant
Education permanente, (tba)
Etudes supérieures et de la recherche, Clarence Jeffrey
Faculté des sciences sociales, Léandre Desjardins
Ecole de droit, Me Michel Bastarache

CENTRES UNIVERSITAIRES

Moncton: Brian T. Newbold, vice-recteur exécutif
St-Louis-Maillet: Normand Carrier, recteur adjoint
Shippegan: Jean-Guy Rioux, recteur adjoint

Mount Allison University

Sackville, N.B. E0A 3C0
(506) 536-2040
Chancellor, A.J. MacQueen, B.A., B.D., D.D., LL.D.
President & Vice Chancellor, G.R. MacLean, B.A., M.A., Ph.D.
Chairman, Board of Regents, Charles Llewellyn
Vice President, Academic, C.W.J. Eliot, B.A., M.A., Ph.D.
Vice President, Administrative, B. Ash, B.A., M.A., Ph.D.
Faculty of Arts, Dean, C.H.H. Scobie, M.A., B.D., Ph.D.
Faculty of Science, Dean, J.F. Read, B.Sc., Ph.D.
Registrar, D.A. Cameron, B.Sc., LL.D.

Netherwood School for Girls

Box 160, Rothesay, N.B. E0G 2W0
(506) 847-7496
Headmistress, Miss B.L. Crocker

New Brunswick Craft School & Centre

Box 6000, Fredericton, N.B. E3B 5H1
(506) 453-2305
Director of Crafts, George Fry
Director of Studies, Lyall Hallum

University of New Brunswick

Fredericton, N.B. E3B 5A3
(506) 453-4995
Other Campus at Tucker Park, Saint John, N.B.
(506) 657-7310
Vice President (Saint John), Dr. Thomas J. Condon, B.A., M.A., Ph.D.
Chancellor, Sir Max Aitken, Bart., D.S.O., D.F.C., LL.D.
President, James Downey, B.A., B.Ed., M.A., Ph.D.
Vice President, Academic, R.E. Burridge, B.Sc., M.S., Ph.D.
Vice President, Finance & Admin., J. F. O'Sullivan, B.B.A.
Comptroller, John O'Brien, R.I.A.
University Secretary, James Woodfield, B.A., Ph.D.
Registrar, Brian Ingram, B.A.
Personnel, J.D. Horn
Dean of Students, G. B. Thompson, B.P.E., M.Sc.
Purchasing Agent, Mrs. Betty Hamilton, B.A.
Bookstore Manager, D.G. McConnell
Librarian, Gertrude E. Gunn, B.A., M.A., M.L.S., Ph.D.

FACULTIES WITH DEANS

Administration, Eric N. West, B.Sc., M.Sc., Ph.D.
Arts, P.G. Kepros, B.Sc., M.Sc., Ph.D.
Science, D.G. Brewer, B.A., Ph.D.
Engineering, A.M. Stevens, B.Sc., M.Sc. (act.)
Forestry, J. W. Ker, B.A.Sc., M.F., D.For., D.Sc.
Law, Edward Veitch, M.A., LL.B.
Education, D. A. MacIver, B.Ed., M.Ed., Ph.D.
Nursing, Irene Leckie, B.Sc.N., M.S.N.
Physical Education & Recreation, W.W. MacGillivary, B.P.E., M.A., Ph.D.

SCHOOLS WITH DIRECTORS

Computer Science, W. Dana Wasson, B.Sc., S.M., Ph.D.

SCHOOL OF GRADUATE STUDIES & RESEARCH

Dean, R. J. Kavanagh, B.Sc., M.A.Sc., Ph.D., D.I.C.

AFFILIATED COLLEGES

Maritime Forest Ranger School
Director, H. W. Blenis
Kenya Technical Teachers College

ASSOCIATED INSTITUTION

St. Thomas University

St. Thomas University grants its own degrees, and has academic independence, but is situated on the campus of the Univ. of N.B., and receives administrative services from the Univ. of N.B.

Rothesay Collegiate School

Rothesay, N.B. E0G 2W0
(506) 847-8224
Headmaster, E.R. Larsen
Bursar, Miss Joan Goucher

St. Thomas University

Fredericton, N.B. E3B 5G3
(506) 455-3337
Chancellor, Most Rev. A. J. Gilbert
President, Rev. G. W. Martin
Vice President, Academic, Dr. J. W. Poole
Comptroller, Joseph Walsh
Registrar, Lawrence Batt
Information Officer, Evelyn Sweezey
Purchasing Agent, the Comptroller
Librarian of Harriet Irving Library, Dr. G. E. Gunn
Bookstore Manager, Doug McConnell

DEPARTMENT CHAIRMEN

Education, Robert Monterio
English, Russell Hunt
History, Herbert Goltz
Philosophy, Marc Smith
Psychology, Gary Hughes
Religious Studies, Jeffrey Kay
Romance Languages, Kay Robinson
Social Sciences, Sylvia Hale
Social Work, Michael Howorth

NEW BRUNSWICK COMMUNITY COLLEGE

Dept. of Continuing Education, Box 6000, Fredericton, N.B. E3B 5H1

Campus de Bathurst, Drawer I, Bathurst, N.B. E2A 3Z2 (548-4591), Principal, G.J. Raymond

Campus de Campbellton, Box 309, Campbellton, N.B. E3N 3G7 (753-7661), Principal, Edouard Maltais

Campus d'Edmundston, Box 70, Edmundston, N.B. E3V 3K7 (735-5589), Principal, L.F. LeBlanc

Campus de Grand-Sault, Box 1270, Grand Falls, N.B. EOJ 1MO (473-2980), Principal, Jerome Martin

Moncton Campus, Box 2100, Stn. A, Moncton, N.B. E1C 8H9 (384-9121), Principal, D.F. Bertelsen

St. Andrews Campus, Box 427, St. Andrews, N.B. EOG 2XO (529-8801), Principal, G.M. Tatton

Saint John Campus, Box 2270, Saint John, N.B. E2L 3V1 (696-1860), Principal, L.R. Fulton

Woodstock Campus, Box 1175, Woodstock, N.B. EOJ 2BO (328-6643), Principal, J.A. Budden

---

NEWFOUNDLAND BOARDS OF EDUCATION

There are presently 21 Integrated School Boards (Anglican, United Church & Salvation Army), 12 Roman Catholic School Boards, one Pentecostal Assemblies School Board, one Seventh Day Adventist School Board, a total of 35 School Boards.

In Newfoundland and Labrador School Board Members are partly appointed, partly elected. It is required that at least one third of the members of a school board be selected by popular vote.

For Department of Education officials see government listings.

Following are the school boards in St. John's and Corner Brook.

Avalon Consolidated School Board

Box 1980, St. John's, Nfld. A1C 5R5
(709) 754-0710
Supt., N. Kelland
Deputy Supt., J.J. Parsons
Asst. Supts., H.M. Peddle, W.C. Robbins, H.R. Tilley, W.F. Oakley
Business Administrator, F. P. Follett
Director of Plant Maintenance, P.J. Barnes

Seventh-Day-Adventist School Board

106 Freshwater Rd., St. John's, Nfld. A1C 2N8
(709) 576-4051
Supt., H.B. Alexander

Roman Catholic School Board for St. John's

Belvedere, Bonaventure Ave., St. John's, Nfld. A1C 3Z4
(709) 753-8530
District Supt., Br. A. F. Brennan, C.F.C.

Bay of Islands-St. George's Integrated School Board

Box 190, Corner Brook, Nfld. A2H 6C7
(709) 639-9823 (Asst. Supt.)
Secretary, Fredrica Hodder
Supt., H. Coates
Asst. Supts., Cluney Vincent, Jean Powers-Spence

Roman Catholic School Board, Humber-St. Barbe

Box 368, Corner Brook, Nfld. A2H 6G9
(709) 634-5052
Supt., G. Fallon
Asst. Supt., D. A. Rousseau
Business Manager, Margaret Goosney

NEWFOUNDLAND DIVISION OF INSTRUCTION, CURRICULUM SECTION

-not confirmed for 1982-

220 Lemarchant Rd., c/o Box 2017, St. John's, Nfld. A1C 5R9
(709) 737-2738

CONSULTANTS

English, E. Jones, Ph.D.
Social Studies, Melvin Regular
Mathematics, (TBA)
Music, Sr. Paschal Carroll, Ph.D.
Vocational, S. Marshall, B.Sc.
Art, Pamela Hall
French, Marie-Christine Halliday, Patrick Balsom
French Specialist (Cultural), Donald Dumont
Science, Wayne Oakley
Physical Education, James Saunders, B.P.E., B.Ed.
Reading, (TBA)

POST SECONDARY & PRIVATE INSTITUTIONS IN NEWFOUNDLAND & LABRADOR

Memorial University of Newfoundland

St. John's, Nfld. A1C 5S7
(709) 737-8000
Official Visitor, His Hon. The Lt.-Gov. The Hon. G. A. Winter, O.C., LL.D.
Chancellor, Paul Guy Desmarais, O.C., B.Comm., LL.D.
President & Vice Chancellor, L. Harris, B.A. (Ed.), M.A., Ph.D.
Vice President, Admin. & Finance, W. H. M. Selby, LL.B., F.C.C.A., F.C.I.S., F.B.I.M.
Vice President, Health Sciences, I. E. Rusted, B.A., M.Sc., M.D., C.M., F.R.C.P.(C.), F.A.C.P.

Vice President, Professional Schools & Community Services, A. A. Bruneau, B.A.Sc., D.I.C., Ph.D., P.Eng. (on leave)
Vice President, Student Affairs & Services, J. D. Eaton, B.P.H.E., M.A., Ph.D.
Asst. Vice President, Admin./Physical Operations, T. C. Noel, M.Sc.
Principal, Sir Wilfred Grenfell College, Corner Brook, C.F. Poole, B.A., M.A., Ph.D.
Registrar & Legal Counsel, W.W. Thistle, B.Sc. (Hons.), B.Ed., M.A., LL.B.
Librarian, Miss M. Williams, B.A., B.L.S.
Comptroller, B. J. Agriesti, B.Sc., C.P.A.

FACULTIES WITH DEANS

Arts, I. A. F. Bruce, M.A., Dip.Ed., Ph.D.
Business Admin., J.G. Barnes, B.A., B.Com., M.B.A., Ph.D.
Science, P.J. Heald, M.Sc., Ph.D., D.Sc., F.R.S., A.M.C.T.
Education, B.V. Paddock, B.A. (Ed.), M.Ed.
Engineering & Applied Science, R. T. Dempster, B.Sc., M.Sc., Ph.D., P.Eng.
Medicine, A. R. Cox, B.A., M.D., F.R.C.P. (C), F.A.C.P.
Graduate Studies, F. A. Aldrich, A.B., M.Sc., Ph.D., F.Z.S., F.A.A.S.
Division of Part-time Credit Studies, A.H. Roberts, B.A. (Hons.), Ed.M., Ed.D.

DIRECTORS

Administrative Services, Mrs. M. Frampton
Audio Visual Centre (Education), G. Fizzard, B.A. (Ed.), M.A., Ed.D.
Centre for Cold Ocean Resources Engineering, H.L. Snyder, B.Eng., P.Eng.
Community Resources Development, D.G. Rees, P.Eng.
Computing Services, I. Javad, M.Sc., D.Comp.Sc.
Counselling Centre, B.M. Schoenberg, B.A., M.A., Ed.D.
Educational Television Centre, D.B. Starcher, B.A., M.M.
Engineering Co-ordination, P.V. Young, B.Sc. (Eng.), A.R.S.M., F.R.S.A., C.Eng., P.Eng.
Extension Service, A.M. Sullivan, B.A. (Ed.), M.A., Ph.D.
Folklore & Language Archive, N.V. Rosenberg, B.A., M.A., Ph.D.
Institute for Educational Research & Development, R.K. Crocker, B.Sc., B.Ed., Ph.D.
Institute for Research in Human Abilities, P.A. Jones, B.A. (Ed.), M.Ed., Ph.D.
Institute of Social & Economic Research, L. Harris, B.A. (Ed.), M.A., Ph.D.
Junior Studies, G.K. Winter, B.Sc., M.Sc., Ph.D.
Marine Sciences Research Laboratory, D.R. Idler, D.F.C., B.A., M.A., Ph.D., F.R.S.C.
Medical Audio Visual Services, B.W. Payton, M.B., B.S., Ph.D.
School of Nursing, M.D. McLean, B.Sc.N., M.A.
Personnel, F. Rees, B.E.
P.J. Gardiner Institute for Small Business Studies, G.A. Pynn, B.Com., M.B.A.
School of Physical Education & Athletics, M.J. Foster, B.A., B.A. (Ed.), Dip.Phy.Ed., M.Sc.
Physical Planning & Operations, J.F. Heintze, El.Eng.
Research Office, N.J. Gogan, B.Sc., Ph.D.
Research Unit on Vector Pathology, M. Laird, M.Sc., Ph.D., D.Sc.
School of Social Work, J.V. Thompson, B.A., B.S.W., M.S.W., D.S.W.
Student Health Centre, R.O. Harpur, M.B., B.Ch., C.C.F.P.
Student Teaching (Education), H.A. Cuff, B.A. (Ed.), M.A., Ed.D.
Technical Services, L.E. Smith
Division of University Relations & Development, G.B. Woodland
Vocational Education, D.B. Camp, B.S.Ed., M.S.Ed.

AFFILIATED INSTITUTION

Christian Brothers College, Mono Mills, Ont. L9W 2Z2
Dean of Studies, Br. G.E. Fitzpatrick, B.A., M.A., M.Ed.

TECHNICAL & VOCATIONAL INSTITUTIONS IN NEWFOUNDLAND

College of Trades & Technology, St. John's, Principal, K. F. Duggan
College of Fisheries, Navigation, Marine Engineering & Electronics, St. John's, Principal, Dr. C.R. Barrett
District Vocational Schools are in the following places. Address: The Principal, District Vocational School, Nfld.
Baie Verte; Bell Island; Bonavista; Burin; Carbonear; Conception Bay South (Seal Cove); Clarenville; Corner Brook; Gander; Grand Falls; Happy Valley-Goose Bay, Lab.; Lewisporte; Placentia, Port aux Basques; St. Anthony; Springdale; Stephenville Crossing

NOVA SCOTIA BOARDS OF EDUCATION

For administrative purposes in education Nova Scotia is divided into 58 municipal units—20 rural or non-urban, 36 urban and 3 amalgamated areas. The local authority for each rural unit is the municipal school board; for each town or city unit, the board of school commissioners. Eleven regional vocational schools are administered by the Minister of Education and locally by regional vocational school boards. Two regional vocational schools and one composite high school are administered by amalgamated school boards. Any combination of municipal or urban boards may co-operate in the operation of a regional school attended by pupils from their several jurisdictions, in which case a regional school board, consisting of members appointed by the co-operating boards plus members appointed by the Governor-in-Council, is established to administer the regional school. There are 16 such regional boards.

Since 1978, school boards in Nova Scotia (other than regional vocational school boards) are partially elected and partially appointed. The membership of municipal and urban boards is one-third elected, one-third appointed by the Lieutenant Governor in Council and one-third appointed by the municipal council. Amalgamated boards have no provincial appointees but include elected members and members appointed by the participating municipal councils. Regional boards are appointed partly by the Lieutenant Governor in Council and partly by the participating school boards. Half of the latter appointees must be chosen from among elected school board members.

Enabling legislation of 1968 makes provision for the eventual replacement of all of the above-mentioned authorities by amalgamated school boards, each of which would assume jurisdiction over all public educational facilities—elementary, secondary, vocational and continuing—in its "Amalgamation Area." The legislation is permissive, and amalgamation is to take place after full agreement has been reached among the municipal councils of a designated area. In 1970, the first three amalgamated school boards were formed.

For Department of Education officials, see government listings.

Following are Amalgamated School Boards:

Kings County Amalgamated

Box 220, Kentville, N.S. B4N 3W8
(902) 678-2161
Secretary, B. Sewards
Supt., J.J. Keith
Director of Support Services, P.A.R. Jackson
Treasurer, R.E. MacMichael
Supervisors, Geo. Forsyth; D. Stockman

Northside-Victoria Amalgamated

245 Commercial St., North Sydney, N.S. B2A 3M3
(902) 794-4721
Secretary Treasurer, J.D. Peach
Supt., D. Lorne MacLellan
Accountant, Leonard Finney
Inspector, Mrs. Catherine Gardiner

Colchester-East Hants Amalgamated
Box 975, Truro, N.S. B2N 5G8
(902) 895-1511
Secretary Treasurer, A.R. Westlake
Supt., Michael J. MacNeil
Asst. Supt., C. Grant MacDonald
Business Admin., A.R. Westlake
Inspector, B. E. Hatherly

The following are School Boards in Cities:

Dartmouth Board of School Commissioners
Box 817, Dartmouth, N.S. B2Y 3Z3
(902) 463-7700
Secretary, Gerald Hubley
Supt., R.E. Harrison, M.Ed.
Asst. Supts., Gerald Hubley; Josephine V. Harris
City Administrator, C. A. Moir
Purchasing Agent, W. M. Whitman
Clerk Treasurer, B.S. Smith

Halifax Board of School Commissioners
1649 Brunswick St., Box 370, Halifax, N.S. B3J 2R1
(902) 426-7656
Director of Education, Karl W. Perry
Secretary Treasurer, D.F. Lugar
Asst. Director of Education (Education Services), S.A. Clancey
Asst. Director of Education (Instruction & Program), G.A. Mosher

Sydney Board of School Commissioners
266 Whitney Ave., Sydney, N.S. B1P 5A6
(902) 539-0940
Secretary Treasurer, George Boudreau
Supt., Angus MacKillop
Asst. Supt., T. J. Gallaway
Supervisor of Elementary Schools, Martin MacIntyre
Supervisor of Secondary Schools, Dr. Hayes MacNeil
Supervisor of Guidance, Charles MacDonald
Supervisor of Special Education, Nancy Nicol
Supervisor of Modern Languages, Robert Purcell
Supervisor of Property Service, Lawrence MacDonald

POST SECONDARY & PRIVATE INSTITUTIONS IN NOVA SCOTIA

Agricultural Colleges

N.S. AGRICULTURAL COLLEGE
Truro, N.S. B2N 5E3
(902) 895-1571
Principal, H. F. MacRae, B.Sc. (Agr.), M.Sc., Ph.D.
Vice Principal, I.M. Fraser, B.Sc., M.A.
Dean, Vocational & Technical Training, A. D. Ells, B.Sc. (Agr.), M.A.
Registrar, P. Y. Hamilton, B.Sc.(Agr.), M.Sc.
Dean of Students & Chaplain, Rev. D. I. MacEachern, B.A., B.D.
Librarian, B. S. Sodhi, B.A., M.A., Dip.L.Sc.

Art Schools

N.S. COLLEGE OF ART & DESIGN
5163 Duke St., Halifax, N.S. B3J 3J6
(902) 422-7381
President, Garry N. Kennedy
Dean, Alan Barkley
Registrar, Ms. Stephanie Smith
Director of Admissions, Scott MacDougall
Director of Information, Mary L. Barker

Acadia University
Wolfville, N.S. B0P 1X0
(902) 542-2201
President, Dr. J.R.C. Perkin, M.A., D.Phil. (Oxon) (act.)
Vice President, Academic, Dr. M.A. Gibson, B.Sc., M.Sc., Ph.D. (act.)
Vice President, Admin., & Treasurer, F. J. Elderkin, LL.B.
Dean of Students, J.A.H. Fraser, B.A., M.Ed., Ed.D.
Director of Admissions, Robert A. Stead, B.Sc.
Registrar, David J. Green, B.A., M.A.
Chaplain, Rev. Gordon A. Delaney, B.A., B.D., M.Th.
Comptroller, Harold D. Austin, B.A., R.I.A.
Director of Alumni Affairs & Development, William Parker, B.A.
Director of Personnel, Robert T. Flecknell, B.Sc.
Director of Physical Plant & Fire Marshal, Roy A. Fraser, B.Eng.
Asst. Director, Information Services, Bruce E. Cohoon, B.Comm., B.Ed.
Asst. Director, Alumni Affairs, Winnifred K. Horton, B.Sc., Dip.Sec.Sc.
Purchasing Agent, Douglas Timney
Librarian, R. Isobel Horton, B.A., B.L.S.
Bookstore Manager, Donald Mosher

FACULTIES AND SCHOOLS WITH DEANS
Faculty of Arts, E.A. Eagles, B.A., B.Ed., M.A.
Faculty of Science, E.E. Zinck, B.Sc., Ph.D.
School of Business Admin., D.L. Misener, B.Comm., B.Ed., M.S.
School of Computer Science, Thomasz Pietrzykowski, M.S., Ph.D.
School of Engineering, G.D. Theophilus, B.Eng., M.Sc., Ph.D.
School of Home Economics, Virginia Campbell, B.Sc., M.Sc., Ph.D.
School of Music, W.O. Stephens, L.Mus., B.Mus., B.A., M.Mus.
School of Recreation & Physical Education, J.D. Bayer, B.Phys.Ed., M.Sc.
School of Secretarial Science, Jean Elizabeth Marsh, B.A., M.A.
School of Education, W. R. MacDonald, B.A., B.Ed., M.A., A.I.E., Ed.D.

AFFILIATED COLLEGE
Acadia Divinity College, Wolfville, N.S.
Principal, Dr. Harold Mitton, B.A., B.D., D.D.

Armbrae Academy
1400 Oxford St., Halifax, N.S. B3H 3Y8
(902) 423-7920
Principal, Miss Jean Murray, M.A.

Atlantic School of Theology
640 Francklyn St., Halifax, N.S. B3H 3B5
(902) 423-6939
President & Registrar, Rev. Dr. G.R. Hatton
Librarian, Mrs. A. Harrison

The College of Cape Breton
Box 5300, Sydney, N.S. B1P 6L2
(902) 539-5300
President, Donald F. Campbell, Ph.D.
Director of Information & Public Relations, Stephen MacDonald, B.Ed.
Senior Vice President, John E. Terry, P.Eng.
Registrar, Donald V. Fewer, M.Ed.
Director, Continuing Education, Ora McManus, Ph.D.
College Librarian, Rita MacInnis, M.L.S.
Director, Beaton Institute, Robert Morgan, Ph.D.
Director, Athletics, Carl Buchanan, M.Sc.
Co-ordinator, Student Services, Bill MacQueen, B.A.
Chaplaincy, J.B. Doucette, M.A.
Director, Bras d'Or Institute, Donald Arseneau, D.Sc.
Co-directors, Family Life Institute, Kevin MacNeil, Ph.D., Vincent Kachafanas, M.D.
Director, Reading & Writing Development Centre, Patricia Campbell, M.A.Ed.
Director, Centre for International Studies, Brian Tennyson, Ph.D.
Academic Vice President, William M. Reid, Ph.D.
Dean of Technology & Trades, Robert Rudderham, P.Eng.
Dean of Arts & Science, William Gallivan, M.A.
Treasurer/Comptroller, T.M. MacNeil, M.R.A. (Dipl.)

Manager of Purchasing, Garnet C. Ward

Dalhousie University

Main Campus, Studley Campus, Coburg Rd., Halifax, N.S. B3H 3J5
(902) 424-2517
Also, Carleton Campus
Chancellor, Lady Beaverbrook
Chairman, Board of Governors, A.G. Archibald
Vice Chancellor & President, Dr. W.A. MacKay
Vice President, Academic & Research, Dr. G.A. Klassen
Dean, Student Services, Prof. E.T. Marriott
Awards Office, Director, G.G. Steedman
Vice President, Administration, Robbie Shaw
Alumni Director, B. G. Irwin
Registrar, Dr. A.J. Tingley
Information Officer, Derek Mann
Purchasing Agent, Robert J. Townshend
Librarian, Mrs. Dorothy J. Cooke
Bookstore Manager, Irving Kirk

FACULTIES WITH DEANS

Admin. Studies, Tom Kent
Medicine, Dr. J. D. Hatcher
Dentistry, Dr. I.C. Bennett
Health Professions, Dr. Robert Tonks
Law, Prof. William H. Charles
Graduate Studies, Dr. K. T. Leffek
Arts & Science, Dr. Donald Betts

SCHOOLS WITH DIRECTORS

Maritime School of Social Work, C. G. Gifford
School of Library Service, Dr. N. Horrocks
Institute of Public Affairs, K. Antoft
College of Pharmacy, Dr. D.K. Yung (act.)
School of Nursing, Prof. Margaret L. Bradley
School of Dental Hygiene, Prof. Kate MacDonald
School of Physiotherapy, Prof. D.A. Egan
School of Physical Education, Dr. L.J. Maloney

AFFILIATED COLLEGES

N.S. Technical University
President, Prof. Clair Callaghan
Mount Saint Vincent
President, Dr. Margaret Fulton
University of King's College
President, Dr. John Godfrey

The Gaelic College of Celtic Folk Arts & Highland Home Crafts

St. Ann's, Cape Breton, Box 9, Baddeck, N.S. B0E 1B0
(902) 295-2877
Executive Director, Leonard W. Jones

King's-Edgehill School

-not confirmed for 1982-
Co-Educational Boarding School, Grades 6 - 12
Windsor, N.S. B0N 2T0
(902) 798-2278
Headmaster, T.T. Menzies, M.A.

Maritime Conservatory of Music

"The Oakes", 5920 Gorsebrook Ave., Halifax, N.S. B3H 1G2
(902) 423-6995
Director, K.M. Mizerit
Office Manager, S.L. Harland

Mount Saint Vincent University

Halifax, N.S. B3M 2J6
(902) 443-4450

(Primarily concerned with the education of women, this university is co-ed with residence accommodation available for female students.)
Chancellor, Archbishop of Halifax, Most Rev. James M. Hayes, J.C.D., D.D.
President & Vice-Chancellor, E. Margaret Fulton, Ph.D.
Registrar, Diane Morris, A.B.
Vice President, Academic, Walter Shelton, Ph.D.
Dean of Humanities/Sciences, Sr. Patricia Mullins, Ph.D.
Dean of Human/Professional Development, Susan Clark, Ph.D.
Asst. to the President for Finance & Planning, Mary Moore, M.A.
Director of Continuing Education, Dr. Mairi Macdonald, Ed.D.
Executive Asst. to the President, Michael V. Merrigan, M.Ed.
Director of Public Relations & Development, Dulcie Conrad, M.F.A.
Director of Co-operative Education, Ivan Blake, M.A.
Director of Research & Special Projects, W.B. Ingalls, Ph.D.
Purchasing Agent, Marie Kelly
Librarian, Lucian Bianchini, M.L.S.
Bookstore Manager, Jean McKay

DEPARTMENTS

Biology; Business (Administration); Business (Public Relations); Chemistry; Economics; Education (Child Studies); Education; English; Fine Arts; History; Home Economics; Mathematics; Modern Languages; Philosophy; Political Studies; Psychology; Religious Studies; Secretarial Administration; Sociology/Anthropology; and Speech & Drama. Programs are also offered through the Centre for Continuing Education and Summer School.

Nova Scotia Teachers College

Arthur St., Truro, N.S. B2N 5G5
(902) 895-5347
Principal, A. G. MacIntosh, B.Sc., M.A., D.Litt.
Vice Principal, Margaret Swan, B.A., B.Ed., A.I.E.
Director, Classroom Experiences, L. C. Duval, B.A., B.Ed., M.A.
Director, Instructional Services, D. L. Burt, B.P.E., M.Ed., Ed.D.
Director, Student Services, W. B. Brooks, B.A., M.A.T., Ed.D.
Director, Continuing Education, K.W.R. Kerr, B.P.E., M.P.E.

St. Francis Xavier University

Antigonish, N.S. B2G 1C0
(902) 863-3300
President, Rev. Gregory MacKinnon, Ph.D.
Executive Vice President, Academic, J. J. MacDonald, Ph.D.
Vice President, Administration, J. T. Langley, M.S., C.G.A.
Comptroller, J. C. Hagar, B.Comm., C.G.A.
Registrar, B.V. Liengme, Ph.D.
Public Relations Director, K. Smith, D.P.R.
Manager Procurement Services, Lorris Keizer
Librarian, Rev. C. G. Brewer, M.A.
Bookstore Manager, Dave Renny

FACULTIES WITH DEANS

Arts, R.B. MacDonald, Ph.D.
Science, E.J. McAlduff, Ph.D.

SCHOOLS WITH DIRECTORS

Coady International Institute, A.A. MacDonald, Ph.D.
Extension Dept., Rev. G. E. Topshee, B.A.

AFFILIATED COLLEGE

Mount Saint Bernard College, Antigonish
Principal, Sr. Margaret MacDonell, Ph.D.

Saint Mary's University

Halifax, N.S. B3H 3C3
(902) 429-9780
Chancellor, Most Rev. James M. Hayes, J.C.D., D.D., Archbishop, Archdiocese of Halifax

OFFICERS OF ADMINISTRATION

President, Kenneth L. Ozmon, B.A., M.A., Ph.D.
Vice President, Academic, J.G. Jabbra, M.A., Ph.D.
Director of University Services, G.L. Noel, B.Eng.
Director of Development, C.A. Vaughan
Director of Continuing Education, A.J. Gordon, B.Sc., Ph.D.
Director of Alumni, L.W. Smith, B.A., B.Ed., M.A.
Director of Student Services, Robert Hayes, B.A.
Comptroller, (tba)

Registrar, Mrs. Elizabeth A. Chard, B.A., B.Ed., M.A.
Librarian, Ronald A. Lewis, B.A., M.Div., M.L.S.
Director of Information & Public Relations, Elizabeth Stevens, B.A.

FACULTIES WITH DEANS
Arts, T.J. Musial, M.S., B.A., Ph.D.
Commerce, S.H. Jopling, B. Mech. Eng., M.S., Ph.D.
Education, M.R. MacMillan, B.A., B.Ed., M.A., Ph.D.
Science, D.H. Williamson, B.Sc., Ph.D.

Technical University of Nova Scotia
(formerly N.S. Technical College)
Box 1000, Halifax, N.S. B3J 2X4
(902) 429-8300
President, J.C. Callaghan
Undergrad & postgrad degrees in Engineering, Architecture, Urban & Rural Planning, Applied Mathematics, Computer Science.

Université Sainte Anne
Church Point, N.S. BOW 1MO
(902) 769-2114
President, Charles Gaudet
Vice President, Academic, Dr. Sylvestre Muise
Vice President, Admin., Omer Blinn
Secretary General, & Registrar, G.C. Boudreau
Information Officer, G.C. Boudreau
Librarian, Gustave Doucet
Bookstore Manager, Gordon Comeau

NOVA SCOTIA TECHNICAL & VOCATIONAL INSTITUTIONS

REGIONAL VOCATIONAL SCHOOLS
Annapolis Reg. Vocational School, Box 940, Middleton, N.S. B0S 1P0, 902/825-3491, Principal, George E. Adams
Canso Reg. Vocational School, Box 2000, Reeves St., Port Hawkesbury, N.S. B0E 2V0, 902/625-2200, Principal, John MacEachern
Cape Breton Reg. Vocational School, Prince St., Sydney, N.S. B1P 5L2, 902/564-4574, Principal, Robert McVeigh
Colchester Reg. Vocational School, Box 850, Truro, N.S. B2N 5G6, 902/895-1511, Principal, M.C. MacNevin
Cumberland Reg. Vocational School, Box 550, Springhill, N.S. B0M 1X0, 902/597-3737, Principal, Donald Munroe
Dartmouth Reg. Vocational School, Woodlawn Rd., Dartmouth, N.S. B2W 2R7, 902/434-2020, Principal, G. J. O'Malley
Dr. George A. Burridge Reg. Vocational School, Pleasant St., Yarmouth, N.S. B5A 2L2, 902/742-3501, Principal, J. H. McLellan
Halifax Reg. Vocational School, 1825 Bell Rd., Halifax, N.S. B3H 2Z4, 902/422-8301, Principal, A. Van Gurp
Hants Reg. Vocational School, Box 2079, Windsor, N.S. B0N 2T0, 902/798-8349, Principal, Bernard Fetter
Kings Reg. Vocational School, Box 487, Kentville, N.S. B4N 3X3, 902/678-7341, Principal, Geoff. Wright
Lunenburg Reg. Vocational School, 75 High St., Bridgewater, N.S. B4V 1V8, 902/543-4608, Principal, N. L. Brown
Memorial High School, Box 300, Sydney Mines, N.S. B1V 2Y5, 902/736-6233, Principal, Norman Connors
Pictou Reg. Vocational School, Drawer 820, Stellarton, N.S. B0K 1S0, 902/752-2002, Principal, W. A. Moore
Shelburne Reg. Vocational School, Box 760, Shelburne, N.S. B0T 1W0, 902/875-3091, Principal, A. E. McCabe

OTHER INSTITUTIONS
N.S. Institute of Technology, Box 2210, Leeds St., Halifax, N.S. B3J 3C4, 902/424-4533, Principal, G.L. Williams
N.S. Land Survey Institute, Box 10, Lawrencetown, Annapolis County, N.S. B0S 1M0, 902/584-2226, Principal, J. F. Doig
N.S. Adult Vocational Training Centre, Box 1042, Point Edward, Sydney, N.S. B1P 6J7, 902/564-5484
N.S. Adult Vocational Training Centre, 450 Pleasant St., Dartmouth, N.S. B2Y 3S5, 902/463-7840, A/Principal, M.R. Kent
N.S. Nautical Institute, Pier 21, Box 578, Halifax, N.S. B3J 2S9, 902/424-3290, Principal, Capt. E.J. Samson
Correspondence Courses Section, Box 1650, Halifax, N.S. B3J 2Z2, 902/424-4054
N.S. Agricultural College, Box 550, Truro, N.S. B2N 5E3, 902/895-1571, Principal, Dr. H. F. MacRae

ONTARIO BOARDS OF EDUCATION

In Ontario there are a total of 76 elected Boards of Education with jurisdiction over a continuous and integrated program of elementary and secondary education. In Southern Ontario there are 38 administrative counties, four defined cities and six municipalities of Metropolitan Toronto. Designation of the remaining 28 school divisions in Northern Ontario under similar boards of education is contained in Ontario Regulation 283/68: School Divisions in the Territorial Districts.

There are 31 zones in Southern Ontario and 18 in Northern Ontario under the jurisdiction of county or district Roman Catholic combined separate school boards.

In addition to these large units of administration there are approximately 110 boards to administer school sections and zones in remote areas or on crown lands.

For Ministry of Education officials see government listings.

The following are School Boards in the six municipalities of Metropolitan Toronto:

Metropolitan Toronto School Board
155 College St., Toronto, Ont.
(416) 598-4620

The School Board serves as the co-ordinating agent in the administration of public school education in Metropolitan Toronto. The Board sets a common mill rate for public school purposes in Metro and distributes the financial resources on an equitable basis to each area board. The Board co-ordinates the capital program for construction and renovation of school facilities, and the negotiation of collective agreements between various Teacher Federations and other employee groups and the various boards. It operates the Schools for the Retarded (1,250 pupils) throughout Metro region.

Director & Secretary Treasurer, Charles G. Brown
Comptroller of Finance, D.G. Timmins
Director of Capital Program & Research, Dr. Gerald Ridge
Supt. of Academic Studies, M.P. Montgomery
Supt. of Employee Relations (Academic), Al Merritt
Supt. of Employee Relations (Academic), Harry Richards
Supt. of Special Services, F.J. Reynolds
Schools for Retarded Central Office, 203 College St. (598-4620)

East York Board of Education
840 Coxwell Ave., Toronto, Ont. M4C 2V3
(416) 465-4631
Director of Education & Secretary Treasurer, R.A. Dodds
Supt. of Business, R. J. McIntosh
Supt. of Operations, E.W. Taylor
Supt. of Program, W.W. Coulthard
Supt. of Student & Community Services, H.R. Ryckman
Asst. Supt. of Operations, F.J. Speer
Asst. Supt. of Schools, J.D. Hannah
Asst. Supt. of Schools, E.B. Lewis

North York Board of Education
5050 Yonge St., Willowdale, Ont. M2N 5N8
(416) 225-4661
Director of Education & Secretary Treasurer, K. Kinzinger
Asst. Director of Education, J.M. Prideaux
Executive Asst. to Director of Education & Supt. of Board Services, W.A. Dempsey
Controller of Finance & Plant, L.J.H. Campbell
Supt., Western Region, D.N. Hazell
Supt., Central Region, R.C. Brock

Supt., Eastern Region, M. Patt
Supt. of Personnel Services, E.C. Porter
Supt. of Educational Services, J.D. Connell
Educational Planning, Information & Evaluation Services Director, Dr. A.E. Virgin
Asst. Secretary, M.W. Milne
Co-ordinator of Communications, S. Gilchrist
Chief Librarian, F.W. Minkler Professional Library, H.P. Greaves
Manager of Purchasing, H.J. Baird

Etobicoke Board of Education

1 Civic Centre Court, Etobicoke, Ont. M9C 2B3
(416) 626-4360
Director of Education & Secretary Treasurer, G.H. Gillespie
Assoc. Director & Supt. of Admin., S.S. Sauro
Supt. of Program, Ralph Prentice
Supt. of Personnel & Supervision, M.F. Lafratta
Controller of Planning & Plant, H.W. Moore
Comptroller of Finance, S.M. MacKinlay
Asst. Supt. of Special Education, J.E. Everett
Asst. Supt. of Curriculum, A.L. Kozakavich
Asst. Supts. of Personnel & Supervision, W.A. Praskey, J.F. Tummon
Asst. Supt., Admin., M.M. Young
Regional Supts., L.G. Augustus, J.T. Hanes, J. Masewich, W.J. McIntosh, J. McMurray, G.L. Vipond, D.S. Watson, C.J. Yakimoff

Scarborough Board of Education

140 Borough Dr., Scarborough, Ont. M1P 4N6
(416) 296-7111
Director of Education, W.A. Parish
Asst. Director of Education, J.J. Watt
Supt. of Personnel, C.R. Mason
Supt. of Student & Community Services, J.P. McLoughlin
Supt. of Planning & Operations, J.W. Wade
Supt. of Program, C.A. Cowan
Comptroller of Finance, W. D. Mason
Supt. of Plant, T. A. Lennard
Communications Officer, C.A. Smith
Area Supts.: J.E. Barker; C. H. Carter; C.B. Cowan; R.E. Gray; A.G. McLeod; W. H. Milnes; R. J. Murrell; J. K. Phillips; D.B. Richards; M.F. Roberts, E.A. Vine

Toronto Board of Education

155 College St., Toronto, Ont. M5T 1P6
(416) 598-4931
Director of Education, E. N. McKeown, B.A., Ed.D.
Assoc. Director, R.W. Halford, B.A.
Supt. of Curriculum & Program, D.G. Rutledge, M.A.
Asst. Supt., Curriculum & Program (Business, Technical & Continuing Education), C.W. Taylor, B.A.
Asst. Supt., Curriculum & Program (Curriculum Development), Ouida M. Wright, M.A., Ph.D.
Supt. of Personnel, Helen Sissons, B.A., M.Ed.
Asst. Supt., Personnel, R. H. McGillivray, B.A., Ed.D.
Asst. Supt., Personnel, B. G. DeGraaf, C.D., B.A.Sc., P.Eng.
Supt. of Professional Services, Mitchell Lennox, B.A., M.E., Dip. C.S.
Asst. Supt., Special Education, M. Choma, B.A., M.Sc.
Comptroller of Finance, D. S. Paton, B.Com., C.A.
Comptroller of Buildings & Plant, M.J. Rose, B.A.Sc., M.Ed., P.Eng.
Area Supts.:
West Area, Mrs. Helen Banks, B.A., M.Ed.
Central Area, William A. McLauchlin, B.A., B.Ed.
East Area, W. George Hayes, B.A.
North Area, D. Bruce Snell, Mus. Bac., M.A.

Board of Education for the Borough of York

2 Trethewey Dr., Toronto, Ont. M6M 4A8
(416) 653-2270
Director of Education & Secretary Treasurer, D. J. Phillips
Supt. of Education, D.R. Hodgins
Supt. of Business, W. L. G. James
Supt. of Personnel, J.E. Fisher
Controller of Plant, L. Decaire
Librarian, Education Admin. Centre Library, Mrs. S. Moll
Chief Accountant, F. Huff
Purchasing Agent, T. Kular
Manager, Computer Services, R. L. Spencer
Personnel Officer, I. W. Baker
Communications Officer, Mrs. K. Cox

Metropolitan Separate School Board

146-150 Laird Dr., Toronto, Ont. M4G 3V8
(416) 421-8950
Director, B.E. Nelligan
Deputy Director, Academic, A.J. Barone
Deputy Director, Business & Finance, A.S. Meneguzzi
Scarborough/East York Region: Asst. Director, F.M. Weiss
Etobicoke/York Region: Asst. Director, L.S. Power
Toronto Region: Asst. Director, B. Farley
North York Region: Asst. Director, J. Lavin
Asst. Director, Secondary School Programs, Rev. F. Kavanagh, O.M.I.
Asst. Director, Curriculum & Special Services, P.R. Wharton
Supt., Teacher Personnel, J. Stewart
Supt., Buildings & Plant, F. O'Toole
Supt., Finance, J. Jasenec
Supt., Planning, H. Howard
Co-ordinator, Computer Services, L. LeMay
Co-ordinator, Purchasing, J. vanPinxteren
Co-ordinator, Public Relations, D. Burge
Asst. Supt., Library Services, Rev. W.J. Brown

The following are School Boards in the Four Defined Cities (as designated by the Ministry of Education):

Hamilton Board of Education

100 Main St. W., Hamilton, Ont. L8N 3L1
(416) 527-5092
Director of Education, A.J. Krever, B.A., M.Ed.
Supt. of Curriculum & Special Services, C.G.W. McKague, B.A., M.Ed.
Supt. of Operations, K.A. Rielly, B.A., B.Ed., M.Sc.Ed.
Secretary Treasurer & Business Administrator, Roy S. Cartmell, B.A.
Area Supts. of Education, P.W. Diebel, M.A., F.C.C.T.; J. Forrester, B.A., M.A., M.Ed.; L.H. LeRoy, B.A.; L.J. McLachlan, B.A., M.Ed.; W.D. Millar, B.A., M.Ed.; D. Rothwell, B.A., M.Ed.
Assoc. Supt. of Curriculum & Special Services, P.S. Beveridge, B.A., B.Ed., M.Ed.
Deputy Business Administrator, John Penner, B.A.
Deputy Administrator, Buildings, J. B. Singer, B.Sc. (Arch.)

Hamilton-Wentworth Roman Catholic Separate School Board

90 Mulberry St., Box 2012, Hamilton, Ont. L8N 3R9
(416) 525-2930
Director of Education, P. J. Brennan
Supt. of Supervision & Operations, J. A. Hansen
Supt. of Program, Development & Planning, P. Burns
Supt. of Business Admin., S. Simon
Asst. Supt. of Business, T. Mahony
Controller of Buildings & Plant, J. Cutler
Purchasing Agent, John Kopak
Area Supts.: Michael Prokopich; Sister Ruth Cornwell; Paul Blake; Edward Clinton; J. J. Grosso (Professional Development Officer)

London Board of Education

165 Elmwood Ave., Box 5873, London, Ont. N6A 4T5
(519) 439-2451
Director of Education, Dr. M. Hardy
Executive Secretary, T. R. Moore
Supt., Business, & Treasurer, J. H. Morris

Supt., Program, R. T. Macaulay
Supt., Operations, W. Ford
Controller of Finance, J. R. Smith
Asst. Supts., H. G. McTaggart; R. S. Campbell; H. Capes; D.A. Craig; J. Little
Area Supts., L. W. Hooper; J. Townshend; W. Traut; R.J. Gladwell; G.O. Thatcher

Ottawa Board of Education

330 Gilmour St., Ottawa, Ont. K2P 0P9
(613) 563-2211
Director of Education & Secretary of the Board, M.O. Beauchemin
Supt., Academic Affairs, J.E. Sutherland
Supt., Personnel, L.M. Tenace
Supt., Program, J.H. Burwell
Supt., Plant, R.H. Tully
Supt., Student Services, R.W.G. Darby
Librarian, Library Service Centre, G. Genier
Supt. of Business & Finance, H. B. McGregor
Executive Asst., Mrs. Joyce Roome
Purchasing Agent, William Cutler
Area Supts.: R. S. Campbell; R. M. Dunlop; A. E. Gray; Guy Lapensée; Charlotte Lemieux

Ottawa Roman Catholic Separate School Board

140 Cumberland St., Ottawa, Ont. K1N 7G9
(613) 237-5660
Director of Education & Secretary Treasurer, Pierre Xavier
Supt., French Schools, Gérard-A. Dubé
Supt., English Schools, George Moore
Supt., Business Management, Lucien Villeneuve
Purchasing Agent, Raymond Gougeon
Chief Accountant, (tba)
Information Officer, Eliane Gaudet

Windsor Board of Education

451 Park St. W., Windsor, Ont. N9A 6K1
(519) 253-4291
Secretary, R.H. Field
Director of Education, R. H. Field
Supt. of Operations, D. Cadwell
Supt. of Program, W. Glenn
Employee Relations Administrator, B. Piliotis
Personnel Manager, W.T. Mickle
Supt. of Business, R.A. Dureno
Manager, Purchasing & Supply, R. Brew
Area Supts.: G.S. Gall, E. Gordon, D.C. Hyland, F. Johnson, R.J. Martin, Z. Veres, T.C. Wear
Administrator of Continuing Education, J. Fleming

Windsor Roman Catholic Separate School Board

1485 Janette Ave., Windsor, Ont. N8X 1Z2
(519) 253-2481
Secretary Treasurer, Wm. McRae
Director of Education, Wm. McRae
Asst. Director of Education, R.J. O'Brien
Area Supt. of Business, W. E. Baker
Chief Purchasing Agent, L. Couture
Area Supts.: D. Dillbaldo; A. Knight; J. Molnar
Manager of Plant, R. Carter
Manager of Operations, W. Stephens

The following are Toronto Suburban Area School Boards:

Durham Board of Education

555 Rossland Rd. W., Oshawa, Ont. L1J 3H3
(416) 576-4600
Director of Education, K. D. Munroe
Supt., Operation, R. V. Sheffield
Supt. of Business & Treasurer, J. R. Backus
Supt. of Curriculum & Program, B. R. Walker
Asst. Supt. of Operations, R.D. Peel

Durham Roman Catholic Separate School Board

209 Simcoe St. N., Oshawa, Ont. L1G 4T1
(416) 576-6150
Director of Education & Treasurer, Dr. Earl Lagroix
Supts. of Education, Wm. J. Cooper, J.K. Henry, R. Ste. Marie
Supt. of Business, (tba)

Halton Board of Education

2050 Guelph Line, Box 5005, Burlington, Ont. L7R 3Z2
(416) 335-3663
Secretary, E. S. Lavender
Director of Education, E. S. Lavender
Supt., Instruction, R.G. Stoness
Supt., Program, R.T. Dixon
Supt., Special Services, R. Chapman
Supt. of Business & Finance, Mrs. Barbara Moore
Area Supts.: R. Warren (Finance); H.R. Lishman (Operations)

Peel Board of Education

73 King St. W., Mississauga, Ont. L5B 1H5
(416) 279-6010
Director of Education, J. A. Fraser
Supt. of Academic Affairs, C. L. Dobson
Supt. of Business Affairs, M.D. Roy
Comptroller of Finance, J. G. Whaley
Director of Administrative Services, Doug Paton
Supt. of Personnel, R.J. Lee
Supt. of Special Services, R.N. Chalmers
Supt. of Schools, Special Units, N.P. Volpe
Supt. of Program, W.J. Lambie
Supt. of Schools, Staff Development, C.J. Flack
Supt. of Operations, D.G. Lawson
Supt. of Operations, H.R. Jones
Supt. of Planning & Resources, F.J. Hughes
Supt. of Plant, D.P. Wilkinson
Chief Accountant, K. H. Dudman
Manager of Purchasing, W. H. Porter
Supts. of Schools: H.R. Harrower, W.E.M. King, R.D. Barber, J.L. Berges, W.F. Burns, C.S. Lethbridge, K.A. Foster, W.R. Quance, D.T. Hands

Wentworth County Board of Education

357 Wilson St. E., Ancaster, Ont. L9G 2C1
(416) 523-8621
Director of Education & Secretary, A.A. Greenleaf
Supt., Business & Finance, D. Webb
Supt., Curriculum, D. Story
Supt., Instruction, G. Carswell
Supt., Instruction, J. Long
Supt., Operations, J. Rumball
Supt., Plant, R. McElroy
Supt., Special Services, C.J. Ramsay
Purchasing Agent, J. Growcott

Dufferin-Peel Roman Catholic Separate School Board

100 Dundas St. W., Mississauga, Ont. L5B 1H6
(416) 270-4630
Director of Education & Secretary of Board, J. Hugel
Supt., Business Affairs, & Treasurer, R. E. LeMay
Controller of Finance, F. J. Dunn
Purchasing Agent, A. Mearns
Controller of Plant, A. Papineau
Supervisor, Revenue, B.F. Quigley
Asst. to the Director, L.J. Lucas
Supts. of Schools, B.J. Fleming; J.E. McGirr; D.D. Mullin; M.J. Obee; T. Reilly; J. Tokar; J. Vintar

Halton Roman Catholic Separate School Board

Box 308, Burlington, Ont. L7R 3Y2

(416) 632-6300
Secretary, Clifford G. Byrnes
Treasurer, Thomas P. Brady
Director of Education, Clifford G. Byrnes
Supts. of Education, T. A. Hennelly, D. Nolan
Supt. of Business & Finance, T. P. Brady
Asst. Supt. of Business & Finance, Jos. W. Birett
Supt., Building & Plant, John Birett
Maintenance Supervisor, G. E. Smith

The following are other amalgamated Boards of Education in Ontario:

Atikokan Board of Education
Atikokan, Ont. P0T 1C0
(807) 597-6941
Director of Education, L. L. Fontana
Brant County Board of Education
349 Erie Ave., Brantford, Ont. N3T 5V3
(519) 756-6301
Director of Education & Secretary, Dr. Glenn Watson
Bruce County Board of Education
Box 190, Chesley, Ont. N0G 1L0
(519) 363-2014
Director of Education, J. L. Bowers
Carleton Board of Education
133 Greenbank Rd., Nepean, Ont. K2H 6L3
(613) 820-1820
Director of Education, S.S. Katz
Central Algoma Board of Education
Box 10, Richards Landing, Ont. P0R 1J0
(705) 246-2441
Director of Education, W. R. F. Wilson
Chapleau Board of Education
Box 220, Chapleau, Ont. P0M 1K0
(705) 864-1750
Secretary, E. R. Freeborn
Cochrane-Iroquois Falls Board of Education
Box 820, Iroquois Falls A, Ont. P0K 1G0
(705) 232-4015
Director of Education, D. D. Powell
Dryden Board of Education
79 Casimir Ave., Dryden, Ont. P8N 2H4
(807) 223-5311
Director of Education, A.G. Lugli
The Dufferin County Board of Education
40 Amelia St., Orangeville, Ont. L9W 3T8
(519) 941-6191
Director of Education & Secretary Treasurer, W.S. Robinson
East Parry Sound Board of Education
Box 40, South River, Ont. P0A 1X0
(705) 386-2387
Director of Education, Joseph DiProfio
Elgin County Board of Education
400 Sunset Dr., St. Thomas, Ont. N5R 3C8
(519) 633-2700
Director of Education, C. R. Prosser
Espanola Board of Education
Box 429, Espanola, Ont. P0P 1C0
(705) 869-3103
Director of Education, D. R. Diebel
Essex County Board of Education
360 Fairview Ave. W., Essex, Ont. N8M 1Y4
(519) 776-6421
Director of Education, G. E. Seguin
Fort Frances-Rainy River Board of Education
338 Scott St., Fort Frances, Ont. P9A 1G9
(807) 274-9855
Director of Education, A. J. Gillies
Frontenac County Board of Education
220 Portsmouth Ave., Kingston, Ont. K7L 4X4
(613) 544-6920
Director of Education, R.E. Shadbolt
Geraldton Board of Education
Box 909, Geraldton, Ont. P0T 1M0
(807) 854-1470
Secretary, N.R. Labranche
Grey County Board of Education
Box 100, Markdale, Ont. N0C 1H0
(519) 986-3410
Director of Education, R. M. Hall
Haldimand Board of Education
Box 2000, Cayuga, Ont. N0A 1E0
(416) 772-3391
Director of Education, J. Fransen
Haliburton County Board of Education
Box 507, Haliburton, Ont. K0M 1S0
(705) 457-1980
Director of Education, J. D. Hodgson
Hastings County Board of Education
Education Centre, 156 Ann St., Belleville, Ont. K8N 1N9
(613) 966-1170
Director of Education, B.W. Mather
Hearst Board of Education
Box 7000, Hearst, Ont. P0L 1N0
(705) 362-4283
Business Administrator & Secretary Treasurer, J. Siska
Hornepayne Board of Education
Box 69, Hornepayne, Ont. P0M 1Z0
(807) 868-2253
Secretary, Mrs. J. Beatty
Huron County Board of Education
103 Albert St., Clinton, Ont. N0M 1L0
(519) 482-3496
Director of Education, D. J. Cochrane
Kapuskasing Board of Education
62 Devonshire Ave., Kapuskasing, Ont. P5N 1C3
(705) 335-6025
Director of Education, R.J.G. Pilon
Kenora Board of Education
Box 1270, Kenora, Ont. P9N 3X7
(807) 468-5571
Director of Education, Emil W. Uhrynuk
Kent County Board of Education
476 McNaughton Ave. E., Box 1000, Chatham, Ont. N7M 5L7
(519) 354-3770
Director of Education, J. David Mistele
Kirkland Lake Board of Education
Box 610, Kirkland Lake, Ont. P2N 3J9
(705) 567-3271
Director of Education, J. Yakubowski
Lakehead Board of Education
2135 Sills St., Thunder Bay, Ont. P7E 5T2
(807) 622-2122
Director of Education, Wally Beevor
Lake Superior Board of Education
Box 189, Schreiber, Ont. P0T 2S0
(807) 824-2201
Director of Education, M.A. Twomey
Lambton County Board of Education
200 Wellington St., Box 2019, Sarnia, Ont. N7T 7L3
(519) 336-1500
Director of Education, N. L. Cheeseman
Lanark County Board of Education
15 Victoria St., Perth, Ont. K7H 2H7
(613) 267-4210
Director of Education, D.J. Schoular
Leeds & Grenville County Board of Education
25 Central Ave. W., Brockville, Ont. K6V 5X1
(613) 342-0371
Director of Education, K. Wayne Tompkins
Lennox & Addington County Board of Education
(Box 70), 264 Camden Rd., Napanee, Ont. K7R 3M1
(613) 354-3391
Director of Education, J. C. McLeod
Lincoln County Board of Education
112 Oakdale Ave., St. Catharines, Ont. L2P 3J9
(416) 685-1551
Director of Education, R.S. Lawless

Manitoulin Board of Education
Box 489, Little Current, Ont. P0P 1K0
(705) 368-2860
Director of Education, F.J. Soplet
Michipicoten Board of Education
Box 560, Wawa, Ont. P0S 1K0
(705) 856-2309
Business Administrator, F. C. Springer
Middlesex County Board of Education
Hyde Park, Ont. N0M 1Z0
(519) 471-3510
Director of Education, F.S. Toll
Muskoka Board of Education
Box 750, Bracebridge, Ont. P0B 1C0
(705) 645-5282
Director of Education, C. R. Whitfield
Niagara South Board of Education
250 Thorold Rd. W., Welland, Ont. L3C 3W3
(416) 735-3840
Director of Education, M. L. Townsend
Nipigon-Red Rock Board of Education
Box 448, Red Rock, Ont. P0T 2P0
(807) 886-2243
Director of Education & Secretary, N.E. Sheffield
Nipissing Board of Education
Box 3110, North Bay, Ont. P1B 8H1
(705) 472-8170
Director of Education, R. J. Lynch
Norfolk Board of Education
Box 486, Simcoe, Ont. N3Y 4L7
(519) 426-7750
Director of Education, A.A. Burbidge
North Shore Board of Education
160 Spruce Ave., Elliot Lake, Ont. P5A 2C5
(705) 848-3661
Director of Education, W. Mair
Northumberland & Newcastle Board of Education
Box 470, 834 D'Arcy St., Cobourg, Ont. K9A 4L2
(416) 372-6871
Director of Education, D.C.D. Sifton, B.A., M.Ed.
Oxford County Board of Education
94 Graham St., Box 636, Woodstock, Ont. N4S 7Z8
(519) 539-4821
Director of Education, J. Young
Perth County Board of Education
426 Britannia St., Stratford, Ont. N5A 6A3
(519) 271-0930
Director of Education, R. K. Self
Peterborough County Board of Education
Box 719, 150 O'Carroll Ave., Peterborough, Ont. K9J 7A1
(705) 743-7431
Director of Education, R. J. Linton
Prescott & Russell County Board of Education
411 Stanley St., Hawkesbury, Ont. K6A 3E8
(613) 632-0144
Director of Education, F. Lortie
Prince Edward County Board of Education
Box 220, Bloomfield, Ont. K0K 1G0
(613) 393-3153
Director of Education, H.W. Jacobs
Red Lake Board of Education
Red Lake, Ont. P0V 2M0
(807) 727-2696
Director of Education & Secretary, S. Korchuk
Renfrew County Board of Education
1270 Pembroke St. W., Pembroke, Ont. K8A 4G4
(613) 735-0151
Director of Education, H. Hempstead
Sault Ste. Marie Board of Education
644 Albert St. E., Sault Ste. Marie, Ont. P6A 2K7
(705) 949-7690
Director of Education, George G. Gordon
Simcoe County Board of Education
99 Ferris Lane, Barrie, Ont. L4M 2Y2
(705) 728-7570
Director of Education, I. C. Harris
Stormont, Dundas & Glengarry County Board of Education
902 Second St. W., Cornwall, Ont. K6H 5S6
(613) 933-6990
Director of Education, T. R. Léger
Sudbury Board of Education
200 Brady St., Sudbury, Ont. P3E 5K3
(705) 674-3171
Director of Education, G. W. Thomson
Timiskaming Board of Education
Box 40, New Liskeard, Ont. P0J 1P0
(705) 647-7394
Director of Education, A. E. Tindall
Timmins Board of Education
Box 1020, Timmins, Ont. P4N 7H7
(705) 267-1151
Director of Education, W.C. Blake
Victoria County Board of Education
Box 420, Lindsay, Ont. K9V 4S3
(705) 324-6776
Director of Education, W. S. Perkins
Waterloo County Board of Education
Box 68, Kitchener, Ont. N2G 3X5
(519) 742-1751
Director of Education, W.T. Townshend
Wellington County Board of Education
500 Victoria Rd. N., Guelph, Ont. N1E 6K2
(519) 822-4420
Director of Education, W. G. Forsythe
West Parry Sound Board of Education
Box 245, Parry Sound, Ont. P2A 2X4
(705) 746-9372
Director of Education, G. A. Snider
York County Board of Education
60 Wellington St. W., Box 40, Aurora, Ont. L4G 3H2
(416) 889-0660
Director of Education, R.A. Cressman

The following are other County & District Combined Roman Catholic Separate School Boards in Ontario:

Brant County R.C.S.S. Board
Box 217, 322 Fairview Dr., Brantford, Ont. N3T 5M8
(519) 756-6369
Director of Education, J.J. Flynn
Bruce-Grey County R.C.S.S. Board
Box 187, Hanover, Ont. N4N 3C4
(519) 367-2636
Director of Education, W. A. Brown
Carleton R.C.S.S. Board
1695 Merivale Rd., Nepean, Ont. K2G 3R4
(613) 224-2222
Director of Education, William Crossan, Ph.D.
Cochrane-Iroquois Falls D.R.C.S.S. Board
Box 858, Iroquois Falls A, Ont. P0K 1G0
(705) 232-4061
Director of Education, R. Pilon
Dryden District R.C.S.S. Board
38 Park Cres., Dryden, Ont. P8N 1T6
(807) 223-4663
Secretary, L. W. Moehlen
Elgin County R.C.S.S. Board
21 Parish St., St. Thomas, Ont. N5R 4W7
(519) 631-8300
Director of Education, J. Tokar
Essex County R.C.S.S. Board
360 Fairview Ave. W., Essex, Ont. N8M 1Y5
(519) 776-6431
Director of Education, R.J. Reddam, B.A., M.Ed.
Fort Frances-Rainy River R.C.S.S. Board
555 Finders Ave., Fort Frances, Ont. P9A 3L2
(807) 274-6414
Director of Education & Secretary, E. E. Kirk

Frontenac, Lennox & Addington County R.C.S.S. Board
84 Stephen St. (Box 1058), Kingston, Ont. K7K 2C4
(613) 544-4927
Director of Education, F.J. Fowler
Geraldton R.C.S.S. Board
Box 370, Geraldton, Ont. P0T 1M0
(807) 854-1421
Secretary, J.P. Rochon
Haldimand-Norfolk R.C.S.S. Board
Box 278, Regional Rd. #40, Simcoe, Ont. N3Y 4L1
(519) 426-8370
Director of Education, L. L. Begley
Hastings-Prince Edward County R.C.S.S. Board
158 George St., Belleville, Ont. K8N 3H3
(613) 962-9571
Director of Education, D.S. O'Sullivan, B.A., M.A.
Hearst District R.C.S.S. Board
Box 1660, Hearst, Ont. P0L 1N0
(705) 362-4337
Business Administrator, A.R. Proulx, C.G.A., C.A.
Supervising Principal, R. Lebrun
Secretary, B. Gagnon
Huron-Perth County R.C.S.S. Board
Box 70, Dublin, Ont. N0K 1E0
(519) 345-2440
Director of Education, W. Eckert
Kapuskasing R.C.S.S. Board
75 Queen St., Kapuskasing, Ont. P5N 1H5
(705) 335-6091
Director of Education, J. Bidal
Kenora R.C.S.S. Board
200 First St. N., Kenora, Ont. P9N 2K4
(807) 468-9851
Business Administrator & Secretary Treasurer, W. O'Neill
Kent County R.C.S.S. Board
Baldoon Rd., Box 2003, Chatham, Ont. N7M 5L9
(519) 354-5170
Director of Education, E.H. Lozon
Kirkland Lake R.C.S.S. Board
Box 910, Kirkland Lake, Ont. P2N 3K9
(705) 567-3327
Director of Education, E. E. Forgues
Lakehead District R.C.S.S. Board
212 Miles St. E., Thunder Bay, Ont. P7C 4Y5
(807) 623-5581
Director of Education, G. S. O'Brien
Lambton County R.C.S.S. Board
774 London Rd., Sarnia, Ont. N7T 4Y1
(519) 336-6139
Director of Education, J. Pace
Lanark-Leeds & Grenville County R.C.S.S. Board
Box 427, Smiths Falls, Ont. K7A 4T4
(613) 283-5007
Director of Education, J. L. Jordan
Lincoln County R.C.S.S. Board
80 Grantham Ave., St. Catharines, Ont. L2P 3H1
(416) 682-8354
Director of Education, J. P. Skehin
London & Middlesex R.C.S.S. Board
Box 517, 401 Queens Ave., London, Ont. N6A 4X5
(519) 432-3493
Director of Education, K. J. Regan
Michipicoten R.C.S.S. Board
Box 560, Wawa, Ont. P0S 1K0
(705) 856-2309
Business Administrator, F.C. Springer
Nipissing District R.C.S.S. Board
1140 Front St., North Bay, Ont. P1B 6P2
(705) 472-1520
Director of Education, B.D. Giroux
North of Superior District R.C.S.S. Board
Selkirk Ave. (Box 610, Terrace Bay, Ont. P0T 2W0)
(807) 825-3246
Director of Education, P.M. Gillen
North Shore R.C.S.S. Board
Box 460, Blind River, Ont. P0R 1B0
(705) 356-2223
Director of Education, David R. Hubbert
Oxford County R.C.S.S. Board
Box 97, Woodstock, Ont. N4S 7W5
(519) 539-4877
Director of Education, F. J. Sloan, B.A., M.Ed.
Peterborough-Victoria-Northumberland & Newcastle R.C.S.S. Board
459 Reid St., Peterborough, Ont. K9H 4G7
(705) 748-4861
Director of Education, Peter L. Roach
Prescott & Russell County R.C.S.S. Board
Box 570, L'Orignal, Ont. K0B 1K0
(613) 675-4691
Director of Education, J.-P. Scott
Renfrew County R.C.S.S. Board
499 Pembroke St. W., Pembroke, Ont. K8A 5P1
(613) 735-1031
Director of Education, F. J. Turner
Sault Ste. Marie R.C.S.S. Board
169 Spring St., Sault Ste. Marie, Ont. P6A 3A4
(705) 949-4400
Director of Education, J.R. Cameletti
Simcoe County R.C.S.S. Board
99 Ferris Lane, Barrie, Ont. L4M 2Y2
(705) 728-7570
Director of Education, W.P. Bolger
Stormont-Dundas & Glengarry County R.C.S.S. Board
1104 1st St. E., Cornwall, Ont. K6H 1N6
(613) 933-1720
Director of Education, C. J. Lamarche
Sudbury District R.C.S.S. Board
201 Jogues St., Sudbury, Ont. P3C 5L7
(705) 673-5621
Director of Education, J. O. Tremblay
Timiskaming R.C.S.S. Board
Box 309, New Liskeard, Ont. P0J 1P0
(705) 647-7304
Director of Education, L. Charette
Timmins R.C.S.S. Board
36 Birch St. S., Timmins, Ont. P4N 2A5
(705) 267-1421
Director of Education, E. Baribeau
Waterloo County R.C.S.S. Board
91 Moore Ave., Box 1116, Kitchener, Ont. N2G 4G2
(416) 578-3660
Director of Education, J. F. Clifford
Welland County R.C.S.S. Board
300 Fitch St., Welland, Ont. L3C 4W6
(416) 735-0240
Director of Education, P.W. Ferron
Wellington County R.C.S.S. Board
75 Woolwich St., Guelph, Ont. N1H 6N6
(519) 821-4600
Director of Education, M. B. Kiely
York Region R.C.S.S. Board
21 Dunlop St., Richmond Hill, Ont. L4C 2M6
(416) 884-2711
Director of Education, J. Zupancic

MINISTRY OF EDUCATION REGIONAL OFFICES

NORTHWESTERN ONTARIO REGIONAL OFFICE
435 James St. S., Thunder Bay, Ont. P7C 5G6
(807) 475-1581
Regional Director, F. Poleschuk, B.A.
Supt., Supervisory Services, (tba)
Supt., Curriculum Services, W.Y. Morgan
Supt., Business & Finance, P. E. Workman

MIDNORTHERN REGIONAL OFFICE
199 Larch St., Sudbury, Ont. P3E 5P9
(705) 675-4436

Regional Director, C. E. Butcher, B.A., M.Ed.
Supt., Curriculum Services, R. Brulé, B.A., M.Ed.
Supt., Supervisory Services, D. R. Tovey, B.P.H.E., M.Ed.
Supt., Business & Finance, A. D. Venugopal, B. Comm.
Community Development Officer, M. L. Baird, M.Sc.

NORTHEASTERN ONTARIO REGIONAL OFFICE
Box 3020, Transportation & Communications Bldg., 477 McKeown Ave., North Bay, Ont. P1B 8K7
(705) 474-7210
Regional Director, J.J. Sullivan, B.A., M.Ed.
Supt., Curriculum Services, E. L. Houghton, B.A.
Supt., Supervisory Services, G.L. Spalding, B.A., M.A., M.Ed.
Supt., Business & Finance, J. W. Cable, C.G.A.
Community Schools, R. H. Shulman, B.A.

WESTERN ONTARIO REGIONAL OFFICE
759 Hyde Park Rd., London, Ont. N6H 3S6
(519) 472-1440
Regional Director, D. Kinchlea, B.A., P.Eng.
Supt., Curriculum, M.F. Cyze, B.A., M.Ed.
Supt., Supervision, D.G. MacLeod, B.A.
Supt., Business & Finance, K. A. Carter, B.Comm.
Community Schools, J. H. Wilson, B.A., B.L.S.

CENTRAL REGIONAL OFFICE
Heron's Hill Bldg., Suite 3201, 2025 Sheppard Ave. E., Willowdale, Ont. M2J 1W4
(416) 491-0330
Regional Director, J.W. Storey, B.A., M.Ed.
Supt., Curriculum Services, K. F. Telfer, B.S.A., M.Ed.
Supt., Business & Finance., A.C. Cunningham, C.G.A.
Supt., Education, E.R. McPherson, B.A., B.Ed. (act.)

EASTERN ONTARIO REGIONAL OFFICE
1580 Merivale Rd., 4th floor, Ottawa, Ont. K2G 4B5
(613) 225-2230
Regional Director, Ray Doyle, B.A., M.Ed.
Supt., Supervisory Services, J.A. Snetsinger, B.A., M.Ed. (act.)
Supt., Curriculum Services, A. Skillings, B.A.
Supt., Business & Finance, G.H. LaFramboise, B.Comm.

POST SECONDARY & PRIVATE INSTITUTIONS IN ONTARIO

Accountancy Programs
For information contact:
The Registrar, The Certified General Accountants Association of Ontario, 480 University Ave., Toronto, Ont. M5G 1V2 (416/593-1103)
Director of Education, The Institute of Chartered Accountants of Ontario, 69 Bloor St. E., Toronto, Ont. M4W 1B3 (416/962-1841)
The Registrar, The Society of Management Accountants of Ontario, Box 176, MPO, Hamilton, Ont. L8N 3C3 (Hamilton: 416/525-4100; Toronto: 416/363-8191; Ottawa: 613/238-8405)

Agricultural Colleges

KEMPTVILLE COLLEGE OF AGRICULTURAL TECHNOLOGY
Kemptville, Ont. K0G 1J0
(613) 258-3411
Principal, J. D. Curtis, B.S.A., M.Sc., P.Ag.
Assoc. Principal (Home Economics), R. I. Shaver, B.Sc.(H.Ec.)
Executive Officer, F. F. Lawson, B.Sc. (Admin.), M.C.I., P.Ag.

ONTARIO AGRICULTURAL COLLEGE
Univ. of Guelph, Guelph, Ont. N1G 2W1
(519) 824-4120
Dean, C. M. Switzer, B.S.A., M.S.A., Ph.D.

RIDGETOWN COLLEGE OF AGRICULTURAL TECHNOLOGY
Ridgetown, Ont. N0P 2C0
(519) 674-5456
Principal, J.A. MacDonald, B.S.A., M.S.A.
Executive Asst., G. D. Walker

CENTRALIA COLLEGE OF AGRICULTURAL TECHNOLOGY
Huron Park, Ont. N0M 1Y0
(519) 228-6691
Principal, J.D. Jamieson
Executive Officer, D. Milton

NEW LISKEARD COLLEGE OF AGRICULTURAL TECHNOLOGY
New Liskeard, Ont. P0J 1P0
(705) 647-6701
Principal, D.W. Taylor
Executive Officer, A. Labonte

Albert College
Belleville, Ont. K8P 1A6
(613) 968-5726
Headmaster, R.B. Napier

Alma College
St. Thomas, Ont. N5R 5B6
(519) 631-3880
Principal, Miss M.E. Bone, B.A.

Appleby College
Oakville, Ont. L6K 3P1
(416) 845-4681
Chairman of the Board, P.A.G. Cameron
Headmaster, A.S. Troubetzkoy, B.A.
Business Administrator, A.V. Robbins
Development Secretary, M.W. Des Roches
Bursar, Mrs. P.V. Carter
Librarian, Ms. E. Gibb

Art Schools

DUNDAS VALLEY SCHOOL OF ART
21 Ogilvie St., Dundas, Ont. L9H 2S1
(416) 628-6357

The School offers a wide range of courses in visual arts for Adults, Teens and Children, which include a full time program, and many weekend and summer classes. Part time courses include printmaking, drawing, painting, stained glass, sculpture, photography, advertising design and pottery.
Director, T. Hodgson

ONTARIO COLLEGE OF ART
100 McCaul St., Toronto, Ont. M5T 1W1
(416) 977-5311

Founded in 1876, the Ontario College of Art offers a four-year, post-secondary education in art and design. Graduating students are given an Associate of the Ontario College of Art Diploma (AOCA).
President, Paul D. Fleck
Business Administrator, Owen W. Wilson
Registrar, R.T. Begley
Librarian, Ian Carr-Harris
Financial Aid Officer, Suzanne Coxon
Placement Officer, Esther Levin
Senior Advisor & Director of Student Services, Mary Egan Haines
Director of Information Services & Alumni Affairs, Ruth Hammond
Personnel Officer, Nancy Hood

CHAIRMEN
Foundation Studies, David Hall-Humpherson
Industrial Design, William Poole
Dept. of Design, Joan Burt
Dept. of Communication & Design, Beresford Mitchell
Dept. of Photo/Electric Arts, Richard Hill
Liberal Arts Studies, Tom Gordon
Technological Studies, Michael Harmes
Fine Arts, John Newman
Experimental Arts, Gustav Weisman
General Studies, Mario Polidori

THREE SCHOOLS
296 Brunswick Ave., Toronto, Ont. M5S 2M7
(416) 920-8370
Executive Director, John Sime

ARTISTS WORKSHOP
Director, Barbara Wood

The Artists' Workshop operates morning, afternoon and evening classes in drawing, painting, sculpture, ceramics, photography, crafts, writing, printmaking and the performing arts, also a Junior Workshop for children aged from 5 to 14.

The Workshop is a non profit organization owned and operated by the *Three Schools.*

THE NEW SCHOOL OF ART

The New School of Art offers a three/four year full time day course. There are no pre-requisites, educational or otherwise, and no diplomas or certificates are issued. The number of students is strictly limited.

The School uses the premises of the Artists' Workshop in downtown Toronto.

OTTAWA SCHOOL OF ART
159 Forward Ave., Ottawa, Ont. K1Y 1K8
(613) 728-1897

Ashbury College
362 Mariposa Ave., Rockcliffe Park, Ottawa, Ont. K1M 0T3
(613) 749-5954
Headmaster, A.M. Macoun, M.A.
Director, Junior School, M.H.E. Sherwood
Director of Development, K. Cattell
Librarian, R. D. Rice

The Bishop Strachan School
298 Lonsdale Rd., Toronto, Ont. M4V 1X2
(416) 483-4325
Headmistress, Miss Ann Tottenham, B.A., B.Ed., S.T.B., S.T.M.
Principal, Junior School, Miss Alison Pearce, B.A., M.Ed., L.R.A.M.
Admin., Mrs. M.S. Stewart, B.A.

Branksome Hall
10 Elm Ave., Toronto, Ont. M4W 1N4
(416) 920-9741
Principal, Miss Allison Roach, B.A., M.Ed.

Brock University
St. Catharines, Ont. L2S 3A1
(416) 684-7201
Chancellor, Ralph Scott Misener
President & Vice Chancellor, Alan Earp
Vice President, Administration, T.B. Varcoe
Dean, Division of Humanities, Maurice Yacowar
Dean, Division of Social Services, L.A. Soroka
Dean, Division of Mathematics & Sciences, M. S. Gibson
Dean, College of Education, Peter Atherton
Director, Physical Education, A.G. Lowenberger
Registrar & Dean of Students, R.W. McGraw
Librarian, James Hogan
Secretary to the University, R. A. Nairn
Director, Liaison & Information, D.J. Geddie
Director, Part-time Programs, J.F. Bird

The Canadian Credit Institute
Box 500, Stn. F, Toronto, Ont. M4Y 2L8
(416) 962-9911
President & Dean, L.E. McGuire, M.C.I.
Registrar & Bursar, W. J. Hambly, F.C.I., 931 Yonge St., Toronto, Ont. M4W 2H6

Canadian Investment Funds Course
Education Division of The Investment Funds Institute of Canada, #210, 8 King St. E., Toronto, Ont. M5C 1B5 (416/363-2158)
Quebec Branch: 630 Dorchester Blvd. W., Montreal, P.Q. H3B 1X1 (514/866-5421)

Canadian Jewellers Institute
Royal York Hotel, 100 Front St. W., Toronto, Ont. M5J 1E3
(416) 368-8372
Correspondence courses only.
General Manager, Wm. Basztyk

Canadian Memorial Chiropractic College
1900 Bayview Ave., Toronto, Ont. M4G 3E6
(416) 482-2340
Chairman, Board of Governors, R. Luck, D.C.
President of College, D.C. Sutherland, D.C.
Dean, A.H. Adams, D.C.
Clinic Director, B. Schut, D.C.
Comptroller, M.A. Salak, C.A.
Librarian, J.C. Callaghan, B.A., M.L.S.

Carleton University
Colonel By Dr., Ottawa, Ont. K1S 5B6
(613) 231-4321
Chancellor, Gordon Robertson, C.C., M.A., LL.D., D. de l'Univ., F.R.S.C.

OFFICERS OF ADMINISTRATION
Chancellor, Gordon Robertson, C.C., M.A., LL.D., D. de l'Univ., F.R.S.C.
President & Vice Chancellor, William E. Beckel, B.A., M.Sc., Ph.D.
Vice President, Academic, T.J. Ryan, M.A., Ph.D.
Vice President, Administration, C.G. Watt, B.A.
Assoc. Vice President (Planning) & Director, Planning Analysis & Statistics, D.J. Brown, B.Sc., Ph.D.
Asst. Vice President (Admin.), F.G. McStravick, B.Com., C.A.
Dean of Arts, Naomi E.S. Griffiths, B.A., M.A., Ph.D.
Dean of Social Sciences, D.P. Forcese, M.A., Ph.D.
Dean of Engineering, J.S. Riordon, M.Eng., D.I.C., Ph.D., P.Eng.
Dean of Science, George B. Skippen, M.Sc., Ph.D.
Dean of Graduate Studies & Research, S.F. Wise, B.A., M.A., B.L.S.
Director, School of Architecture, M.R. Coote, M.Arch., M.R.A.I.C., R.I.B.A.
Director, Institute of Biochemistry, James Neelin, B.A., Ph.D.
Director, Institute of Canadian Studies, (tba)
Director, School of Commerce, A.J. Bailetti, B.S., M.B.A., Ph.D.
Director, School of Computer Science, J.E. Neilson, B.Sc., Ph.D.
Director, School of Continuing Education, Faith B. Gildenhuys, B.A., M.A., Ph.D.
Director, School of Industrial Design, Willem Gilles
Director, School of Journalism, G. Stuart Adam, B.J. M.A., Ph.D.
Director, The Norman Paterson School of International Affairs, John H. Sigler, A.B., M.A., Ph.D.
Director, The Paterson Centre for International Programs, D.M.L. Farr, B.A., M.A., D.Phil.
Director, School of Public Administration, A.M. Maslove, B.A., Ph.D.
Director, School of Social Work, Glenn Drover, B.A., B.Th., M.S.W., Ph.D.
Director, Institute of Soviet & East European Studies, Carl H. McMillan, Jr., M.A., Ph.D.
Librarian, Geoffrey Briggs, B.A., M.A., Dip. Lib., Dip. Arch.
Registrar, J.I. Jackson, D.F.C., B.A., M.F.A.
Clerk of Senate, H.H.J. Nesbitt, B.A., M.A., Ph.D., D.Sc., F.L.S., F.R.E.S., F.Z.S.
Secretary, Board of Governors, Donald C. McEown, B.A., Dip. Bus. Admin.
Director, Administrative Services, Douglas N. Brombal, B.A., Cert. Bus. Admin.
Director, Finance, Jack K. Kettles, B.Com., C.A.
Controller, Murray F. Sutherland, C.A.
Business Office Manager, Ronald Lahey, B.Com.
Director, Computing Services, J.G. Cushing
Statistician, William Pickett, B.Sc., M.Sc.
Director, Information, R. Gerald McKee, B.A.
Director, Development, Michael D. Roberts, B.A.
Director, Personnel, R.A. Brown, B.A.
Director, Awards Office, Coralie Bartley, B.A.
Chief, Security, Sam Grant
Bookstore Manager, Philip Gore, B.A.

Purchasing Manager, Russell Weir
Director, Physical Plant, Jack Cook, B.I.D.
Director, Admissions & Academic Records, James L. Sevigny, B.A., B.P.E.
Asst. Director of Admissions (Liaison), Student Liaison Office, Patrick O'Brien, B.A.
Director, Physical Recreation & Athletics, K.N. Harris, B.A., B.P.H.E., M.S.
Director, Health Services, Mary O'Brien, M.B., Ch.B., L.M.C.C.
Director, University Counselling Services, Vincent Giannandrea, B.A., M.A.

Central Baptist Seminary

95 Jonesville Cres., (North York) Toronto, Ont. M4A 1H3
(416) 752-1976
Chancellor, Dr. Jack Scott
President, Dr. James G. Wetherall (int.)
Dean, Rev. G. E. Barton
Librarian, Mrs. Ruth L. Kraulis
Bookstore Manager, J.A. Carnegie

Centre for Christian Studies

77 Charles St. W., Toronto, Ont. M5S 1K5
(416) 923-1168
President, Central Council, Mrs. Edith Shore
Principal, Miss Marion Niven, M.A.
Librarian, Mrs. Elfa Davidson, B.L.S.

Crescent School

2365 Bayview Ave., Willowdale, Ont. M2L 1A2
(416) 449-2556
Chairman of the Board, Ian Roberts
Headmaster, C. B. Gordon
Secretary to Headmaster, Admissions, Miss Eileen Coo
Bursar, Mrs. P. McDonnell

Ecumenical Forum of Canada

11 Madison Ave., Toronto, Ont. M5R 2S2
(416) 924-9351
Director, Arturo R. Chacon
Librarian, Ms. M. MacKinnon
Chairman of the Board, Dr. Cranford Pratt

The Fashion Institute of Canada

2436 Yonge St., Toronto, Ont. M4P 2H4
(416) 481-6477
Director, C. Norman
For "Board of Directors" see Shaw Colleges.

Federal Study Centre (Arnprior)

Box 40, Arnprior, Ont. K7S 3H2
(613) 623-4227
Principal, J. A. Gaumond
Head Admin., A. B. Moorhead
Head Operations, P. J. Kelly

Frontier College

Frontier College operates informal adult education and community education projects in approximately 100 locations throughout Canada.
Head Office, 31 Jackes Ave., Toronto, Ont. M4T 1E2
(416) 923-3591
Patron, His Excellency The Governor General of Canada
Chairman of the Board, A.L. Hepworth
President, Jack Pearpoint

University of Guelph

Guelph, Ont. N1G 2W1
(519) 824-4120
Chancellor, Hon. Dr. Pauline McGibbon
President & Vice Chancellor, D. F. Forster
Vice President, Academic, H.C. Clark
Vice President, Admin., C.C. Ferguson
Chairman of the Board, A.R. Marchment
Registrar, A. G. Holmes
Provost, R. P. Gilmor
Chief Librarian, M. Beckman
Director of Information, Douglas Waterston
Director, Alumni Affairs & Development, J. K. Babcock
Comptroller, N. M. Sullivan
Director, Admin. Services, J.H. Mason
Director, Physical Resources, W. A. Brown
Director, Personnel, R.G. Pella

COLLEGES WITH DEANS

College of Arts, D.R. Murray
College of Biological Science, K. Ronald
College of Family & Consumer Studies, Janet M. Wardlaw
College of Physical Science, E. B. MacNaughton
College of Social Science, J. Vanderkamp
Ont. Agricultural College, C. M. Switzer
Ont. Veterinary College, D.C. Maplesden
Faculty of Graduate Studies, C.L. Gyles
Office of Research, W. E. Tossell

SCHOOLS WITH DIRECTORS

Human Biology, L.A. Cooper (act.)
Hotel & Food Admin., T.F. Powers
Engineering, J.R. Ogilvie
Landscape Architecture, C. Man
Agricultural Economics & Extension Ed., E. L. Menzie
Part Time Studies & Continuing Education, M.W. Waldron
Rural Planning & Development, M.B. Lapping

Havergal College

1451 Avenue Rd., Toronto, Ont. M5N 2H9
(416) 483-3519
Chairman of the Board, H.F.C. Graham, B.Comm., M.B.A., F.C.A.
Principal, Miss Mary Dennys, B.A.
Business Manager, W. H. Swetman
Bursar, Mrs. D. Shreve
Librarian, Miss Sharon Doyle
Bookstore Manager, Miss Mary Taylor

Hillfield-Strathallan College

Fennell Ave. W., Hamilton, Ont. L9C 1G3
(416) 389-1367
Headmaster, M. B. Wansbrough
Asst. Headmaster, M. G. Loranger
Dean of Women, Mrs. J.C. Callaghan
Bursar, W. Fleming
Development Director, B.H. Kaye
Chairman of the Board, Mrs. J.J. Ryan
Librarian, Mrs. Carla Harstone
Bookstore Manager, Mrs. Lois McKay

Institute for Christian Studies

229 College St., Toronto, Ont. M5T 1R4
(416) 979-2331
Principal, Dr. B. Zylstra

Ontario Institute for Studies in Education

252 Bloor St. W., Toronto, Ont. M5S 1V6
(416) 923-6641

The Ontario Institute for Studies in Education is a college to study matters and problems relating to education; to disseminate the results of and assist in the implementation of the findings of educational studies; and to offer graduate instruction in education. The Institute is affiliated with the University of Toronto for degree-granting purposes.
Director, Bernard J. Shapiro, M.A.T., Ed.D.
Asst. Director (Academic), Michael Fullan, Ph.D.
Asst. Director (Field Services & Research), Doris W. Ryan, Ph.D.
Asst. Director (Planning & Resources), Mark Holmes, Ph.D.
Chairman of Board of Governors, Eugene E. Jacobs, B.Comm.

Kingsway College
Box 605, Oshawa, Ont. L1H 7M6
(416) 725-6557
President, Leroy Kuhn
Business Manager, John Guenin
Counselling & Records, Glenda-mae Greene

Lakefield College School
Lakefield, Ont. K0L 2H0
(705) 652-3324
Hon. Chairman, J. Page R. Wadsworth
Chairman of the Board, G.C. Mills
Headmaster, J. Terence M. Guest
Secretary Treasurer, Keith Scott
Librarian, Mrs. Gwen Morawetz
Bookstore Manager, Albert Branscombe

Lakehead University
Thunder Bay, Ont. P7B 5E1
(807) 345-2121
Chancellor, R.J. Prettie
President & Vice Chancellor, G.A. Harrower
Vice President, Admin., B. Mason
Vice President, Finance, G. H. Thompson
Dean of Students, K. Hearnden
Registrar, P.A. Paularinne
Director, Computer Centre, D. Watson
Director, Physical Plant, W. Armstrong
Director of Personnel, J. Knox
Chief Business Officer, L. A. Miller
Director, Information & Media Services, T.K. Diggle
Director of Residence, G.D. McLeod
Purchasing Manager, Ted Kurlick
Bookstore Manager, Mrs. Day Laban

DEANS
Arts, E.R. Zimmermann
Science, J.S. Mothersill
University Schools, R.G. Rosehart
Education, J.J. Stapleton

Laurentian University of Sudbury
Université Laurentienne de Sudbury
Ramsey Lake Rd., Sudbury, Ont. P3E 2C6
(705) 675-1151

Teaching is in French and English, certain faculties offering parallel programs in both languages.
President, H.B.M. Best, B.A., M.A., D.Ph.
Vice President, Admin., R.E. Chrysler, C.A.
Vice President, Academic, F.J. Turner, B.A., B.S.W., M.S.W., D.S.W.
Director of Services, R. Bertoli
Comptroller, R. Chrysler, C.A.
Director, Centre for Continuing Education, G. Lafrenière, B.A., L.Ph.
Director of Communications, D.C. Stone
Registrar, J. Porter, B.B.A., M.Ed.
Librarian, A. H. Mrozewski, M.A., B.L.S., M.L.S.
Directeur de l'enseignement en français, A. Girouard, B.A., L.Ph., L.Th., M.A.

FACULTIES AND DEANS
Humanities, P. Sabourin, B.A., M.A., D.U.
Professional Schools, W.J. Gerhard, B.Sc.N., M.Sc.N., Reg.N.
Science & Engineering, D.E. Goldsack, B.Sc., Ph.D.
Social Sciences, A.D. Gilbert, M.A., Ph.D.

SCHOOLS AND DIRECTORS
Commerce, (tba)
Education, R. Lallier, B.A., M.Ed.
Nursing, G. Viverais, Dip. P.H., M.H.Sc., Reg.N.
Physical Education, R.R. Wallingford, B.Sc., B.P.E., Ed.D.
Social Work, K.I. Bastin-Millar, B.A., M.S.W.
Translators, G.E. Pitcher, B.A., M.A., M.Litt., B.Ed.

FEDERATED COLLEGES

SUDBURY COLLEGE
President, Lucien Michaud, s.j., B.A., B.Ph., Ed.D.

HUNTINGTON COLLEGE
President & Principal, Ludo J. Winckel, B.A., Th.M., D.Th.
Registrar, Douglas Reynolds, B.A., M.Ed.

THORNELOE COLLEGE
Provost & Vice Chancellor, E.B. Heaven, M.A., L.Th., S.T.B.
Dean of Residence & Registrar, A.S. McGregor, M.A., B.Ed.

AFFILIATED COLLEGES
College de Hearst, Hearst, Ont. P0L 1N0
Directeur, R. Bernard, B.A., M.A.
Administrateur financier, R. Tremblay, B.A., B.Sc., M.A.
Secrétaire général, Danielle Coulombe, B.A.
Algoma College, Sault Ste. Marie, Ont. P6A 2G4
Chairman, Board of Trustees, D.G. Howell, B.Sc., Ph.D., Dip. Bact., M.R.C.V.S.
Dean, R.G. Ewing, M.A., Ph.D.
Registrar, Richard P. McCutcheon, B.A., M.A.
Nipissing College, North Bay, Ont. P1B 8L7
President, G. Zytaruk, B.A., B.Ed., M.A., Ph.D.
Registrar, D. L. Lawrence, B.Math., B.Ed.

Loretto Abbey
-not confirmed for 1982-
101 Mason Blvd., Toronto, Ont. M5M 3E2
(416) 484-4733

A day school under the direction of the Sisters of the Institute of the Blessed Virgin Mary.
Principal, High School, Sr. M. Evanne Hunter, I.B.V.M.
Principal, Junior School, Sr. Sheila Zettel, I.B.V.M.

McMaster University
Hamilton, Ont. L8S 4L8
(416) 525-9140

McMaster University is a non-denominational university consisting of Faculties of Business, Engineering, Humanities, Health Sciences, Science and Social Sciences under one Board of Governors and one Senate. McMaster Divinity College controlled by its own Board of Trustees and Senate and supported by the Baptist Convention of Ontario and Quebec is affiliated with the University.
Chairman, Board of Governors, F.M. Fell
President & Vice Chancellor & Chairman of Senate, Dr. Alvin A. Lee
Vice President, Admin., J.A. MacFarlane (act.)
Vice President, Academic, Dr. L.J. King
Asst. Vice President, Academic Services & Secretary of Senate, J. P. Evans
Registrar, A. L. Darling
Information Officer, G. S. Murray
Librarian, G.R. Hill
Bookstore Manager, R.C. Crawford

FACULTIES WITH DEANS
Humanities, (tba)
Social Sciences, Dr. P.J. George
Business, Dr. A.Z. Szendrovits
Science, Dr. D.W.L. Sprung
Engineering, (tba)
Health Sciences, Dr. J.F. Mustard

SCHOOLS WITH DIRECTORS AND/OR DEANS
Adult Education, Director, Dr. L. Oddie Munro
Graduate Studies, Dean, Dr. D.M. Shaw
Physical Education & Athletics, Director, Dr. M.E. Keyes
Social Work, Director, Prof. K. Kinanen

DIRECTORS
Information & Publications, P.F. Reesor (Asst.)
Physical Planning & Construction, L.V. Auger
Audio Visual Services, E.J.M. Crawley
Student Counselling Services, R. Heinzl
Data Processing & Computing Centre, Dr. G. L. Keech
Office of Research Services, Dr. A. C. Frosst

CONSTITUENT COLLEGE

McMaster Divinity College, McMaster Univ.
Principal, Dr. M.R. Hillmer

Medical Laboratory Technology

For information contact:

The Canadian Society of Laboratory Technologists, Box 830, Hamilton, Ont. L8N 3N8 (416/528-8642)

The National Ballet School

105 Maitland St., Toronto, Ont. M4Y 1E4
(416) 964-3780

A residential and day school, offering a combined classical ballet training and an enriched academic education for gifted children (Gr. 5-12). Graduate programs are also available.

Honorary Chairman, Dr. Vincent W. Bladen, O.C.
Chairman of the Board & President, P. David Payne
Treasurer, J.L. Cowperthwaite
Artistic Director & Ballet Principal, Betty Oliphant, LL.D., O.C.
Admin. Director & Academic Principal, G. Eldred

Nursing Education in Ontario

BASIC DEGREE PROGRAMS WITHIN UNIVERSITIES

Lakehead Univ., Thunder Bay, Ont. P7B 5E1
Laurentian Univ., Sudbury, Ont. P3E 2C6
McMaster Univ., Hamilton, Ont. L8S 4L8
Queen's Univ., Kingston, Ont. K7L 3N6
Ryerson Inst., 50 Gould St., Toronto, Ont. M5B 1E8
Univ. of Ottawa, Ottawa, Ont. K1N 6N5
Univ. of Toronto, Toronto, Ont. M5S 1A1
Univ. of Western Ontario, London, Ont. N6A 3K7
Univ. of Windsor, Windsor, Ont. N9B 3P4

DIPLOMA NURSING PROGRAMS

Within Colleges of Applied Arts & Technology

Algonquin College, 1385 Woodroffe Ave., Nepean, Ont. K2G 1V8
Cambrian College, 1400 Barrydowne Rd., Sudbury, Ont. P3A 3V8
Canadore College, Box 5001, North Bay, Ont. P1B 8K9
Centennial College, 651 Warden Ave., Scarborough, Ont. M1L 3Z6
Conestoga College, 299 Doon Valley Dr., Kitchener, Ont. N2G 4M4
Confederation College, Box 398, Stn. F, Thunder Bay, Ont. P7C 4W1
Durham College, Simcoe St. N., Oshawa, Ont. L1H 7L7
Fanshawe College, Box 4005, Terminal C, London, Ont. N5W 5H1
George Brown College, Box 1015, Stn. B, Toronto, Ont. M5T 2T9
Georgian College, 1 Georgian Dr., Barrie, Ont. L4M 3X9
Humber College, Box 1900, Rexdale, Ont. M9W 5L7
Lambton College, Box 969, Sarnia, Ont. N7T 7K4
Loyalist College, Box 4200, Belleville, Ont. K8N 5B9
Mohawk College, 135 Fennell Ave. W., Hamilton, Ont. L8N 3T2
Niagara College, Woodlawn Rd., Welland, Ont. L3B 5S2
Northern College, Box 2002, South Porcupine, Ont. PON 1HO
Northern College, 140 Government Rd. E., Kirkland Lake, Ont. P2N 3L8
St. Clair College, 2000 Talbot Rd. W., Windsor, Ont. N9A 6S4
St. Clair College, 1001 Grand Ave. W., Chatham, Ont. N7M 5L8
St. Lawrence College, Parkdale Ave., Brockville, Ont. K6V 5X3
St. Lawrence College, Windmill Point, Cornwall, Ont. K6H 4Z1
St. Lawrence College, New Court House, Box 6000, Kingston, Ont. K7L 5A6
Sault College, Box 60, Sault Ste. Marie, Ont. P6A 5L3
Seneca College, 1750 Finch Ave., Willowdale, Ont. M2J 2X5
Sheridan College, 1430 Trafalgar Rd., Oakville, Ont. L6H 2L1
Sir Sandford Fleming College, Box 653, Peterborough, Ont. K9J 7B1

Within Ryerson Polytechnical Institute

Ryerson Polytechnical Institute, 50 Gould St., Toronto, Ont. M5B 1E8

NURSING ASSISTANT PROGRAMS

Nursing Assistant Programs are offered at the following Colleges of Applied Arts & Technology: Canadore, Conestoga, Durham, Fanshawe, Georgian, Humber, Loyalist, Northern, St. Clair, St. Lawrence - Brockville, St. Lawrence - Kingston.

Also, at Regional Nursing Assistant Centres administered by the Ministry of Colleges & Universities at: Hamilton, London, Sudbury, Thunder Bay and Toronto.

Also, at hospital-based training centres at: McEachern Training Centre of Collingwood General & Marine Hospital, Collingwood; General Hospital, Cornwall; St. Joseph's Hospital, Elliot Lake; LaVerendrye Hospital, Fort Frances; Lake of the Woods Dist. Hospital, Kenora; Ross Memorial Hospital, Lindsay; Ottawa Civic Hospital, Ottawa; St. Vincent Hospital, Ottawa (in French and English); West Nipissing General Hospital, Sturgeon Falls (in French); Scarborough General Hospital, Toronto; Wingham & Dist. Hospital, Wingham.

Also, in years three and four of the High Sch. system at: H.B. Beal Secondary Sch., London; Huron Heights Secondary Sch., Newmarket; Kenner Collegiate Vocational Institute, Peterborough; Central Technical Sch., Toronto.

Ontario Bible College & Theological Seminary

25 Ballyconnor Court, Willowdale, Ont. M2M 4B3
(416) 226-6380
Chairman, L.C. Simmonds
President, Dr. V. Adrian
Chancellor, Dr. S. L. Boehmer

University of Ottawa

Ottawa, Ont. K1N 6N5
(613) 231-3311

PRINCIPAL OFFICERS

Chancellor, Mme Jules Léger, C.C., D.U.
Rector & Vice Chancellor, Roger Guindon, O.M.I., C.C., L.Ph., D.Th., LL.D.
Vice Rector, Academic, Antoine D'Iorio, B.Sc., Ph.D., F.R.S.C.
Asst. Vice Rector, Academic, Denis Carrier, M.Sc.Com., Dipl.E.S. (sc.pol.), D.U.P.
Director General, Student Services, Pierre Boulet, B.A., B.Com., M.Sc.Com.
Vice Rector, Admin., Pierre Bourgault, B.A., B.Sc., Ph.D.
Asst. Vice Rector, Admin., J. McCarthy, C.A., A.C.I.S.
Asst. Vice Rector, Supply & Services, Charles-H. Perron
Asst. Vice Rector, Staff Relations, Trefflé Lacombe, B.Comm., M.A.
Secretary, J.-M. Beillard, M.A. (Econ.), Ph.D.
Registrar, Raymond R. Labelle, B.A., L.Ph.
Head Librarian, F. Yvon Richer, B.A., B.L.S., M.L.S.
Director of Public Relations & Information Services, G. W. (Bill) Boss, B.A.
Chief of Protocol & Marshal at Convocation, Marcel Hamelin, B.A., L.esL., D.Litt., F.R.S.C.

FACULTIES WITH DEANS

Administration, (tba)
Programs: Business Admin., Health Admin., Institute for International Co-operation, Management Science, Public Admin.

Arts, Marcel Hamelin, B.A., L.èsL., D.Litt., F.R.S.C.
Depts: Classical Studies, Communication, English, Geography, History, Lettres françaises, Linguistics, Modern Languages & Literatures, Music, Philosophy, Religious Studies, Theatre, School of Translators & Interpreters, School of Urban & Regional Planning, Visual Arts

Education, M. Yves Poirier, B.A. (Ed.), M.Ed., Ph.D.
Sections: Educational Studies, Teacher Education

Health Sciences, G.D. Hurteau, B.A., M.D., F.R.C.S.Canadian
School: Human Kinetics, vacant (Director)
Depts.: Kinanthropology, Physical Education
School: Medicine, G.D. Hurteau (Director)

Depts.: Anaesthesia, Anatomy, Biochemistry, Epidemiology & Community Medicine, Family Medicine, Medicine, Microbiology & Immunology, Obstetrics & Gynaecology, Ophthalmology, Oto-Rhino-Laryngology, Paediatrics, Pathology, Pharmacology, Physiology, Psychiatry, Radiology, Surgery
School: Nursing, vacant (Director)
Law, Common Law Section, A.W.R. Carrothers, B.A., LL.B., LL.M., S.J.D., LL.D.; Civil Law Section, Raymond A. Landry, B.A., LL.L., Dipl. E.S.D.
Science & Engineering, (tba)
Depts: Biochemistry, Biochemistry (Nutrition & Dietetics), Biology, Chemical Engineering, Chemistry, Civil Engineering, Computer Science, Electrical Engineering, Geology, Mathematics, Mechanical Engineering, Physics
Social Sciences, (tba)
Depts: Criminology, Economics, Political Science, Recreology, Sociology
School: Psychology, Joseph-M. De Koninck, B.A., M.A.(Ps.), Ph.D. (Director)

SCHOOL WITH DEAN

Graduate Studies & Research, Paul B. Hagen, M.B., F.C.I.C.

SUPPORT SERVICES

Alumni Secretariat, Director, H. Olivier Pelletier, B.A.
Bookstore Services, Director, Michel Canivet
Chaplaincy, Director, Carl Kelly, O.M.I., M.A.
Computing Centre, Director, William J. Lamb
Financial Services, Director, Rhéo Brisson, C.A.
Health Services, Director, Luc Laroche, B.A., M.D.
Materials Management Services, Director, Pierre Gauvin, B.A., B.Sc.Com.
Physical Plant, Director, Normand Berthiaume, B.Sc.A.
Personnel Services, Director, Pierre Faucher, B.Sc.
Placement Office, Director, Diane Maisonneuve
Planning & Construction Services, Witold Kubasiewicz, Dipl. Eng. (Arch).
Continuing Education, Ralph G. Tross, B.S., M.S., Ph.D.
Univ. of Ottawa Press, Director, Léopold Lanctôt, O.M.I., B.A., L.Ph., L.Th., L.D.C.

FEDERATED UNIVERSITY

SAINT PAUL UNIV.

223 Main St., Ottawa, Ont. K1S 1C4
(613) 235-1421
Rector, Henri Goudreault, O.M.I., B.A., L.Ph., D.Th., L.S.S.
Vice Rector, Academic, Pierre Hurtubise, O.M.I., M.A., L.Ph., L.Hist. Eccl., L.Th., D. Hist.
Vice Rector, Admin., Jacques L'Heureux, O.M.I., L.Ph., L.Th.
General Secretary, Eugène Marcotte, O.M.I., M.A., L.Ph., D.Th.
Registrar, Eugène Marcotte, O.M.I., M.A., L.Ph., D.Th.
Chief Librarian, Gaston Rioux, O.M.I., B.A., L.Ph., L.Th., B.J.C., B.L.S.
Faculty of Canon Law
Dean, Francis G. Morrisey, O.M.I., L.Ph., L.Th., M.A., M.C.L., D.C.L.
Faculty of Theology
Dean, André Guindon, O.M.I., B.A., L.Ph., D.Th.
Institute of Pastoral Studies
Director, Arthur Lacerte, O.M.I., B.A., L.Th., L.Ph., L.Ped.
Institute of Mission Studies
Director, Marcel Doucet, F.I.C., L.Ph., L.Th., Ph.D.
Institute of Social Communications
Director, Marcel Patry, O.M.I., M.A., L.Ph., Ph.D., L.Th., D.Ph.

Pickering College

Residential school for boys, grades 7 to 13.
389 Second St., Newmarket, Ont. L3Y 4X2
(416) 895-1700
Chairman of the Board, Allan D. Rogers
Headmaster, Sheldon H. Clark, B.Ed., M.A.
Director, Academics, K. G. McLaren, B.A.
Business Manager, T. Douglas Clark

Pontifical Institute of Mediaeval Studies

59 Queen's Park Cres. E., Toronto, Ont. M5S 2C4
(416) 921-3151
President, Rev. J. Ambrose Raftis
Treasurer, Rev. W.M. Hayes
Secretary, Prof. James P. Reilly, Jr.
Director of Publications, Dr. Ron B. Thomson
Information Officer, the Secretary
Librarian, Rev. D. F. Finlay

Queen's University

Kingston, Ont. K7L 3N6
(613) 547-5511

PRINCIPAL OFFICERS

Chancellor, Agnes M. Benidickson, B.A., LL.D.
Rector, Jeremy Freedman
Vice Chancellor & Principal, R. L. Watts, B.A., M.A., D.Phil., O.C.
Vice Principal, Services, J.A. Bennett, B.Sc., M.Sc., Ph.D.
Vice Principal, Resources, R.J. Hand, B.Com., M.B.A.
Vice Principal, Health Sciences, H. G. Kelly, M.D., C.M., F.R.C.P.(C), F.A.C.P.
Registrar, K.L.S. Gunn, B.A., M.Sc., Ph.D., M.A.
Asst. Registrar, Admissions, D. N. Ellis, C.D., B.A.
Asst. Registrar, Awards, Mrs. Doris Laughton, M.A., Dip. Ed.
Asst. Registrar, Records, G. F. Hammond, B.Sc., M.Sc.
Secretary of the University & Board, J. W. Bannister, B.Com.
Executive Director, Communications & External Liaison, B. Trotter, B.A., M.A.
Secretary of the Senate, Miss Margaret Hooey, B.A., M.A.
Secretary of the Univ. Council, H.A.T. Fleming, B.A.
Dean of Women, Elspeth H. Baugh, B.A., M.A., Ph.D.
Univ. Chaplain, Rev. A. M. Laverty, B.A., B.D., D.D.
Director, Alumni Affairs, M. A. Gill, B.Sc.
News Dept., Manager, Brenda M. Large
Purchasing & Food Services, Manager, R. C. Webb, B.A., M.A.
Librarian, Margot B. McBurney, M.L.S.
Bookstore Manager, F. Gauchie
Physical Services Group, Co-ordinator, J.D. Finch
Liaison Office, Nancy Swain, B.A., B.Ed., M.Ed.
Agnes Etherington Art Centre, Director, Robert F. Swain, B.A.
Career Planning & Placement, M.J. Kelly, B.A.
Conference Services, Director, Alex Zikakis
Part-Time Studies & Faculty Services, Director, M.R. Wardle, B.Sc., M.Sc.
International Centre (Student), Kaspar Pold, B.A.
John Deutsch, Univ. Centre, Norman Hart, B.A., M.A.
Office of Research Services (School of Graduate Studies & Research), J.C. Beal, B.Sc. Eng., Ph.D.
Personnel Services, M.W. Wright, B.A.
Residences, Director, J.R. Davies, B.Sc., M.Sc.

DEANS

Faculty of Arts & Science, D. G. Sinclair, D.V.M., V.S., M.S.A., Ph.D.
Faculty of Applied Science, David Bacon, B.Sc., M.S., Ph.D.
Faculty of Education, T.R. Williams, B.Sc., M.A., Ph.D.
Faculty of Law, B.L. Adell, B.A., LL.B., D.Phil.
Faculty of Medicine, T. J. Boag, M.B., Ch.B., Dip. Psych., F.R.C.P., F.R.C.P. (C)
School of Graduate Studies & Research, Maurice Yeates, B.A., M.A., Ph.D.
School of Nursing, Alice J. Baumgart, Reg. N., B.Sc.N., M.Sc., Ph.D.
School of Business, J.R.M. Gordon, B.S.Sc., M.B.A., Ph.D.

DIRECTORS

School of Rehabilitation Therapy, Barrie Pickles, B.A., M.Sc.
School of Physical & Health Education, D. deF. Macintosh, M.B.E., B.A., M.Sc., Ph.D., D.Sc., F.R.C.S., F.C.I.C.
School of Urban & Regional Planning, G. J. F. Hodge, B.A., M.C.P., Ph.D.
Canadian Institute of Guided Ground Transport, C.E. Law, B.A.
School of Public Admin., T.J. Plunkett, B.A., M.A.
Industrial Relations Centre, W. Donald Wood, B.A., M.A., A.M., Ph.D.

Centre for Resource Studies, Int. Executive Director, Dr. B.W. Mackenzie
Carbohydrate Research Institute, W.A. Szarek, B.Sc., M.Sc., Ph.D.
Centre for International Relations, Nils Orvik, B.A., M.A., Ph.D.
Kingston Institute of Pastoral Care, Rev. R. Oakley Dyer, B.A., B.D., S.T.M.
Institute of Intergovernmental Relations, Richard Simeon, B.A., M.A., Ph.D.
Institute of Local Government, Katherine A. Graham, B.A., M.A.
Occupational Health & Safety Resource Centre, Ronald E.U. Lees, M.B., Ch.B., D.Ph., M.D., M.F.C.M.

PRINCIPAL
Theological College, B. R. Bater, B.A., M.A., B.D., S.T.M., Ph.D.

Radiological Technology
For information contact:
Executive Director, Ont. Society of Radiological Technologists, Box 1054, Brantford, Ont. N3T 5S7 (519/753-6037)

Ridley College
Box 3013, St. Catharines, Ont. L2R 7C3
(416) 684-8193
President, S.M. Irwin
Headmaster, H.J. Packard, M.A.
Headmaster, Lower School, Rev. D. P. Hunt, B.A., S.T.B.
Business Administrator, I. C. Wilson, C.D., C.I.M.
Resident Chaplain, Rev. G.S. Shantz, M.A.

Roman Catholic Theological Seminaries & Pre-Theological Schools in Ontario

DOMINICAN'S COLLEGE OF PHILOSOPHY & THEOLOGY
96 Empress Ave., Ottawa, Ont. K1R 7G2
(613) 233-5696
Chancellor, Very Rev. J.-M. Guay, o.p.
Regent of Studies, Very Rev. G.-D. Mailhiot, O.P.
Master of Studies, Rev. J. Marcoux, o.p.
Dean, Faculty of Philosophy, Rev. J. Lavoie, o.p.
Dean, Faculty of Theology, M. Gourgues, o.p.
Director, Institute of Pastoral Theology, Rev. J.-C. Breton, o.p.
Registrar, Rev. J. Marcoux, o.p.
Secretary Treasurer, Rev. T. R. Potvin, O.P.
Librarian, Rev. J.-J. Robillard, o.p.

HOLY REDEEMER COLLEGE (REDEMPTORISTS)
Windsor, Ont. N9G 1V8
(519) 969-2840
Rector, Rev. D. L. Egan, C.SS.R.
Vicar, Rev. J. D. Scanlan, C.SS.R.
Bursar & Principal, Rev. D. L. Egan, C.Ss.R.

IGNATIUS COLLEGE
Box 1238, Guelph, Ont. N1H 6N6
(519) 824-1250
Rector, Rev. Remi Limoges, S.J.
Director of Novices/Director of Studies, Rev. R. Yaworski, S.J.
Administrator/Registrar, Rev. Norbert MacKenzie, S.J.

PERES MONTFORTAINS (RESIDENCE DES ETUDIANTS)
463 Riverdale Ave., Ottawa, Ont. K1S 1S1
(613) 731-2271
Superior, Bruno Richard, s.m.m.

ST. AUGUSTINE'S SEMINARY
2661 Kingston Rd., Scarborough, Ont. M1M 1M3
(416) 261-7207
Rector, Very Rev. Brian Clough
Bursar, R. Kunihiro

ST. BASIL'S COLLEGE
95 St. Joseph St., Toronto, Ont. M5S 2R9
(416) 925-4368
Rector, Ken Decker, C.S.B.

ST. PETER'S SEMINARY
1040 Waterloo St. N., London, Ont. N6A 3Y1
(519) 432-1824
A Theological Seminary and Catholic College of Arts, affiliated with the University of Western Ontario through King's College.
Rector, Rev. F.B. Henry, B.A., M.A., S.T.L.
Dean of Philosophy & Registrar, Rev. M. T. Ryan, B.A., M.A., Ph.D.
Spiritual Director, Rev. P. E. Cavanagh, B.A., M.A., Ph.D.
Business Administrator, John Zadorsky, B.A.
Librarian, Miss L. Cote, B.A., B.L.S., M.L.S.

Royal Conservatory of Music of Toronto
Univ. of Toronto, 273 Bloor St. W., Toronto, Ont. M5S 1W2
(416) 978-3797
Principal, Ezra Schabas
Business Administrator, George Hoskins

Royal Military College of Canada
Kingston, Ont. K7L 2W3
(613) 545-7236
Commandant, Brig.-Gen. J.A. Stewart
Principal & Director of Studies, Dr. D.E. Tilley
Registrar, Dr. R. E. Jones
Director of Cadets, Lt.-Col. L.R. Larsen
Director of Admin., Cdr. D. Oke
Librarian, R.K.C. Crouch

FACULTIES WITH DEANS
Arts, Dr. H.H. Binhammer
Science, Dr. D.C. Baird
Engineering, Dr. A. C. Leonard
Graduate Studies & Research, Dr. J.B. Plant
Canadian Forces Military Division, Dr. W.F. Furter

Ryerson Polytechnical Institute
50 Gould St., Toronto, Ont. M5B 1E8
(416) 595-5300
Chairman of the Board, C. Graham
President, Dr. B. Segal
Asst. to President, R.E. Crow
Vice President, Academic, A.M. Gifford
Vice President, Admin., T.G. Sosa
Dean of Applied Arts, P. Nowack
Dean of Arts, T. Grier
Dean of Business, D. Sutton
Dean of Community Services, R. De Burger (act.)
Dean of Continuing Education, H. Innis (act.)
Dean of Technology, T.E. Wisz
Registrar, J. Brunzell
Director, Physical Resources, J. Ezyk
Director, Computing Centre, M. Kallaur
Director, Finance, P.G. Harry
Director, Information Services, T. O'Connor
Director, Institute Services, V. Jensen
Director, Personnel, R.D. Steadman
Director, Learning Resources Centre, J. North
Director, Private Funding, W. Macpherson
Manager, Purchasing Dept., O.H. Von Bogen
Manager, Bookstore, J. Ericson
Secretary of the Board of Governors, J. R. Gorman

St. Andrew's College
Aurora, Ont. L4G 3H7
(416) 727-3178
Chairman, Board of Governors, P.D.G. Harris
Headmaster, R. Bedard, B.A., B.Ed.
Asst. Headmaster, L. C. MacPherson, B.Sc., M.S. in Ed.
Bursar, H.S. Tetlock

St. Joseph's Morrow Park
3377 Bayview Ave., Willowdale, Ont. M2M 3S4
(416) 226-0330

A day school, grades 9-13, for girls directed by the Sisters of St. Joseph (Roman Catholic).
Principal, Sr. M. Bonaventure Sandford

St. Mildred's-Lightbourn School
1080 Linbrook Rd., Oakville, Ont. L6J 2L1
(416) 845-2386

Day School for Girls under The Sisters of the Church (Anglican).
Principal, Mrs. Doris Bull

Shaw Colleges
2436 Yonge St., Toronto, Ont. M4P 2H4
(416) 481-6477

BOARD OF DIRECTORS
President, D.R. Shaw, F.C.I.S.
Vice President, L.H. Porter, F.C.I.S.
Secretary Treasurer, W.S.G. Shaw
Director, P.M. Shaw
Shaw Central College, 2436 Yonge St., Ulric Francis, Senior Vice Principal

Teachers' Education (Faculties, Colleges & Schools of Education)
College of Education, Brock Univ., St. Catharines, Ont. L2S 3A1
Faculty of Education, Lakehead Univ., Thunder Bay, Ont. P7B 5E1
Ecole des sciences de l'éducation, Université Laurentienne, Chemin lac Ramsey, Sudbury, Ont. P3E 2C6
Faculty of Education, Nipissing Univ. College Education Centre, Box 5002, North Bay, Ont. P1B 8L7
Faculty of Education, Duncan McArthur Hall, Queen's Univ., Kingston, Ont. K7L 3N6
Teacher Education Section, Faculty of Education, Univ. of Ottawa, 651 Cumberland St., Ottawa, Ont. K1N 6N5
Faculté d'éducation, Université d'Ottawa, 651 rue Cumberland, Ottawa, Ont. K1N 6N5
Faculty of Education, Univ. of Toronto, 371 Bloor St. W., Toronto, Ont. M5S 2R7
Faculty of Education, Althouse College, The Univ. of Western Ontario, 1137 Western Rd., London, Ont. N6G 1G7
Faculty of Education, Univ. of Windsor, 600 Third Concession Rd., Windsor, Ont. N9B 3P4
Faculty of Education, York Univ., 4700 Keele St., Downsview, Ont. M3J 1P3

Toronto Baptist Seminary
337 Jarvis St., Toronto, Ont. M5B 2C7
(416) 925-3263
Principal, Rev. G. A. Adams, M.A., M.Div., D.D.

The Toronto French School
Office: 3229 Yonge St., Toronto, Ont. M4N 2L3
(416) 484-6533
Directeur, W. H. Giles, C.M., Q.C., B.A., M.Ed.

University of Toronto
Toronto, Ont.
(416) 978-2011

OFFICERS OF ADMINISTRATION
Chancellor, G. Ignatieff, C.C., B.A., M.A., LL.D., D.C.L., D.Litts.
Chairman of the Governing Council, T.A. Wardrop, Q.C., B.A.
President, J.M. Ham, B.A.Sc., S.M., Sc.D.
Vice President & Provost, D.W. Strangway, B.A., M.A., Ph.D., F.R.C.S., F.R.A.S.
Vice Provost, E. Kingstone, B.Sc., M.D.C.M., F.R.C.P. (C)
Vice Provost, W.G. Saywell, B.A., M.A., Ph.D.
Vice Provost, R.N. Wolff
Vice President, Research & Planning, & Registrar, David Nowlan
Vice President, Business Affairs, (tba)
Vice President, Personnel & Student Affairs, W. Alexander, B.S.P., M.Sc., Ph.D.
Vice President, Institutional Relations, D.G. Ivey
Comptroller, R.G. White, R.I.A.
University Ombudsman, E.A. McKee, M.A.
Chief Librarian, R. Blackburn, M.A., B.L.S., M.S., LL.D.
Director of Admissions, W. Kent, M.A.
Director of Student Awards, P.S. Phillips, B.A., C.A.
Director of Student Record Services, M.S. Lippard
Warden of Hart House, Richard M.H. Alway, B.A., M.A., M.Phil.
Co-ordinator of Campus Services, H.L. Reimer, B.A., B.P.A.E.D.
Director of the Advisory Bureau, D.M. Graham, B.A., M.A., Ph.D. (act.)
Director of Athletics, A.J. Fraser, B.Sc. (P.E.), M.A.
Director of Career Counselling & Placement Centre, R. Frankle, B.A.
Director of University Health Service, G.E. Wodehouse, M.C., M.D., F.R.C.P. (C), M.R.C.P.
Director of Housing Service, S. Mason, B.A.
Director of International Student Centre, E. Paterson, B.A.
Director of Information Services, Mrs. Elizabeth Wilson, B.A.
Director, Administrative Services, M.A. Malcolm
Director, Alumni Affairs, E.B.M. Pinnington
Director, Business Information Systems, R.J. McGimpsey
Executive Director, Innovations Foundation, G.P. Adamson
Director, Media Centre, L.D. Todgham
Director, Personnel Dept., R.F. Brown
Director, U. of T. Press, Harald Bohne
Director, Private Funding, Mrs. Lee MacLaren
Director, Computing Services, Dr. D.J. Cohen
Bookstore Manager, John D. Taylor

DEANS & ASSOCIATE DEANS
Applied Science & Engineering, Dean Gordon Slemon
Architecture & Landscape Architecture, Prof. Blanche L. Van Ginkel
Arts & Science, Dean Arthur M. Kruger
Vice Dean, Prof. Jacob Spelt
Assoc. Dean, Prof. R.E. Pugh
Assoc. Dean, Prof. J.R. Webster
Dentistry, Dean Richard Ten Cate
Education, Dean John C. Ricker
Forestry, Dean Vidar J. Nordin
Graduate Studies, Dean John Leyerle
Assoc. Dean, Div. 1, Prof. J.F. Burke
Assoc. Dean, Div. 2, Prof. L.R. Marsden
Assoc. Dean, Div. 3, Prof. James Keffer
Assoc. Dean, Div. 4, Prof. A.M. Zimmerman
Asst. Dean, Prof. E.A. McCulloch
Law, Dean Frank Iacobucci
Library Science, Dean Katherine H. Packer
Management Studies, Dean D.J. Tigert, B.A., M.B.A., Ph.D.
Assoc. Dean, Academic, Prof. Basil Kalymon
Asst. Dean, Donna Crossan
Medicine, Dean F.H. Lowy, B.A., M.D., C.H., F.R.C.P. (C)
Assoc. Dean, Academic, Dr. W.H. Francombe
Assoc. Dean, Basic Sciences, Dr. K.J. Dorrington
Assoc. Dean, Community Health, Prof. J.W. Browne
Assoc. Dean, Institutional Affairs, Dr. W.M. Paul
Assoc. Dean, Planning & Development, (tba)
Assoc. Dean, Undergraduate Affairs, Dr. Edward Llewellyn-Thomas
Asst. Dean, Continuing Medical Education, Dr. W.H. Francombe
Asst. Dean, Postgraduate Medical Education, Dr. R.H. Sheppard
Music, Dean R. Falck (act.)
Nursing, Dean Phyllis Jones
Pharmacy, Dean R.M. Baxter
Assoc. Dean, Dr. Ernst W. Stieb
Social Work, Dean Ralph Garber

DIRECTORS
Aerospace Studies, Prof. Jaap de Leeuw
Canadian Institute of Ukrainian Studies, Prof. G. Luckyj (Assoc.)
Institute of Child Study, Prof. M.F. Grapko
Centre of Criminology, Prof. A.N. Doob
Program in Transportation, Prof. Richard M. Soberman

David Dunlap Observatory, Prof. J.D. Fernie
Graduate Centre for Study of Drama, Prof. Michael Sidnell
Institute for Environmental Studies, Prof. Ian Burton
Institute for History & Philosophy of Science & Technology, Prof. B. Sinclair, B.A., M.A., Ph.D.
Centre for Industrial Relations, Prof. J.B. Kervin
Institute of Immunology, Dr. Bernhard Cinader
Centre for International Studies, Prof. Robert Spencer
Centre for Medieval Studies, Prof. N.P. Zacour
School of Physical & Health Education, Prof. R.J. Sheppard
Institute for Policy Analysis, Prof. R.M. Bird
Pontifical Institute for Medieval Studies, Prof. A. Rastis, C.S.B.
Centre for Reformation & Renaissance Studies, Prof. J.M. Estes
Centre for Religious Studies, Prof. Willard G. Oxtoby
Centre for Russian & East European Studies, Prof. G. Zukelin
Postgraduate Studies, Dentistry, Dr. Murray Hunt
Division of Studies in Medical Education, Dr. A. Rothman
Toronto School of Theology, Prof. I.G. Nicol
Transitional Year Program, Prof. A. Martin Wall
Centre for Urban & Community Studies, Prof. Larry S. Bourne
Continuing Studies, D. Green
Centre for South Asian Studies, Prof. J.F. Burke
Child in the City, Prof. H.F. Andrews

UNIVERSITY COLLEGES

Erindale College, 3359 Mississauga Rd., Mississauga, Principal, P. W. Fox, M.A., Ph.D.
Innis College, 2 Sussex Ave., Principal, Dennis Duffy, B.A., M.A., Ph.D.
Massey College, 4 Devonshire Pl., Master, Prof. J.N.P. Hume
New College, 40 Willcocks St., Principal, Robert Lockhart, B.A., M.A., Ph.D.
Scarborough College, 1265 Military Trail, Principal, Joan E. Foley, B.A., Ph.D.
University College, 15 King's College Circle, Principal, G.P. Richardson, B.Arch., B.Div., Ph.D.
Woodsworth College, 119 St. George St., Principal, Peter Silcox

FEDERATED COLLEGES

St. Michael's College, 50 St. Joseph St., President, Rev. Peter J.M. Swan
Trinity College, Hoskin Ave., Provost, Kenneth Hare
Victoria College, 73 Queen's Park Cres. E., Principal, Alexandra F. Johnston

AFFILIATED COLLEGES

Emmanuel College, 75 Queen's Park Cres. E., Principal, Dr. C.D. Jay
Knox College, 59 St. George St., Principal, Dr. Charles Hay
Royal Conservatory of Music, 273 Bloor St. W., Principal, Ezra Schabas
Wycliffe College, Hoskin Ave., Principal, R. Stackhouse, M.A., B.D., Ph.D.

University of Toronto Schools

371 Bloor St. W., Toronto, Ont. M5S 2R8
(416) 978-3212
Principal, H. D. Gutteridge, M.A.
Dean, Faculty of Education, J. C. Ricker

Trafalgar Castle School

Whitby, Ont. L1N 3W9
(416) 668-3358
Principal, C.T.C. Kamcke, M.A.
Dean, Mrs. Dorothy Perry, B.Sc., M.P.S.
Bursar & Business Administrator, Mrs. Harriet M. Lamb
Librarian, Miss D. Briar Collins, B.A., B.Ed.

Trent University

Peterborough, Ont. K9J 7B8
(705) 748-1011
Chairman of the Board, Erica Cherney, B.A.
Chancellor, Margaret Laurence, C.C., B.A., D.Litt., LL.D.
President & Vice Chancellor, D.F. Theall, M.A., Ph.D.
Vice President, Robert D. Chambers, B.A., B.Litt.
Dean of Arts & Science, David Gallop, M.A.
Executive Vice President, Secretary to the Board, J. E. Leishman, B.Com., C.A.
Dean of Graduate Studies, W.P. Adams, B.A., M.Sc., Ph.D.
Registrar & Secretary of the Senate, A. O. C. Cole, M.A.
Master of Peter Robinson College, Ian McLachlan, M.A.
Principal of Catharine Parr Traill College, Mrs. Nancy Sherouse, B.A.
Master of Champlain College, J.W. Burbidge, M.A., B.D., Ph.D.
Principal of Lady Eaton College, S. Dale Standen, B.A., M.A., Ph.D.
Master of Otonabee College, Elwood Jones, M.A., Ph.D.
Vice Dean & Principal of Julian Blackburn College, M.L. Rubinoff, M.A., Ph.D.

ADMINISTRATIVE PERSONNEL

Director of Admissions, A.P. Saxby, B.A.
Controller, A.A. van Hoeckel
Director of Personnel Services, Kenneth S. Hayes, B.A.
University Planning Officer, R.J. Bowman, B.A., M.Ed.
Director of Physical Plant & General Services, George Ross, P.Eng.
Operations Engineer, M.J. O'Brien, B.A.Sc., P.Eng.
Purchasing Officer, A.F. Wells
Director of Information, J.G. English, B.A.
Director of Athletics, P.S.B. Wilson, B.A.
Director of Health Service, Ruggles Pritchard, M.D.
Master Planning Architect, R.J. Thom, LL.D., F.R.A.I.C.
Bookstore Manager, William Jordan

Trinity College School

Port Hope, Ont. L1A 3W2
(416) 885-4072
Headmaster, A. C. Scott, M.A.
House Masters, M. A. Hargraft; P. E. Godfrey; A. M. Campbell; P.A. Hill; R. Reynolds; J.B. Geale

Upper Canada College, Toronto

Toronto, Ont. M4V 1W6
(416) 488-1125
Principal, R. H. Sadleir, M.A.
Vice Principal, T. M. Adamson, B.A.
Bursar, J. L. Coulton, M.A.

UPPER CANADA COLLEGE PREPARATORY SCHOOL

Headmaster, R. B. Howard, B.A. (488-1120)

University of Waterloo

Waterloo, Ont. N2L 3G1
(519) 885-1211
Chancellor, Josef Kates, B.A., M.A., Ph.D.
Chairman, Board of Governors, J.P.R. Wadsworth
President & Vice Chancellor, D.T. Wright, B.A.Sc., M.S., Ph.D.
President Emeritus, J.G. Hagey, B.A., LL.D.
Vice President, Academic, T. A. Brzustowski, B.A.Sc., A.M., Ph.D.
Vice President, Finance & Operations, A. B. Gellatly, B.A., C.G.A.
University Secretary, J. W. Brown, B.A.
Registrar, C. T. Boyes, B.A.
Librarian, M. C. Shepherd, B.Ed., M.L.S.
Dean of Women, Mrs. H. Marsden, B.A., M.A.
Comptroller, A. H. Headlam, C.A.
Director, Information Services, J. D. Adams, B.A.
Bookstore Manager, Mrs. E. Dodds

DEANS

Arts, R.K. Banks, B.A., M.A., Ph.D.
Engineering, W. A. E. McLaughlin, B.Sc., M.A.Sc., Ph.D.
Environmental Studies, J. G. Nelson, B.A., M.A., Ph.D.
Mathematics, J.A. George, B.Sc., M.Sc., Ph.D.
Science, R.N. Farvolden, B.Sc., M.Sc., Ph.D.
Human Kinetics & Leisure Studies, G. S. Kenyon, B.P.E., M.S., Ph.D.
Graduate Studies, L. A. K. Watt, B.Sc., M.S., Ph.D.

DIRECTORS
Academic Services, D. P. Robertson, B.Comm.
Counselling Services, J.L. Williams, B.A., M.A., Ph.D.
Athletics, C. A. W. Totzke, B.A.
Co-ordination, R. J. Wieser, B.E., P.Eng.
Part-time Studies & Continuing Education, J.C. Gray, B.A., M.A., Ph.D.
Warden of Residence, H. R. N. Eydt, M.Sc., Ph.D.
Physical Planning, Ernie Lappin, P.Eng.
Physical Plant, Sean Sloan, P.Eng.
Computing Services, Paul Dirksen, B.Sc., M.A.
Audio-Visual Centre, G. Downie
Admin. Services, W. G. Deeks
Personnel Services, E. S. Lucy, B.A.
Fund Raising, Jon Dellandrea, B.A., M.Ed.
Security, A.E. Romenco, B.A.

AFFILIATED COLLEGES
University of St. Jerome's College (N2L 3G3)
President, N.L. Choate, C.R., B.A., M.A.
Renison College (N2L 3G4)
Principal, Ian Campbell, B.A., M.Sc.
Conrad Grebel College (N2L 3G6)
President, R.A. Lebold, B.A., B.D., M.Th.
St. Paul's United College (N2L 3G5)
Principal, F.C. Gerard, M.A., B.D., S.T.M., Ph.D.

University of Western Ontario

London, Ont. N6A 5B8
(519) 679-2111

OFFICERS OF THE UNIVERSITY
President & Vice Chancellor, George E. Connell
Chairman, Board of Governors, G.F. Francolini
Chancellor, R.M. Ivey
Vice President, Academic, & Provost, J.C. Leith
Vice President, Health Sciences, Dr. D. Bocking
Vice President, Admin. & Finance, A. K. Adlington
Asst. Provost, A.J. Bjerring
Secretary of the Board of Governors, C.F. Way
Registrar, D.A. Chambers
Chief Librarian, R. E. Lee
Director of Finance, W. S. McBride
Executive Secretary of Senate, J. van Fleet

DEANS
Arts, Faculty of, J. G. Rowe
Business Admin., School of, C.B. Johnston
Dentistry, Faculty of, W. J. Dunn
Education, Faculty of, P. Park
Engineering Science, Faculty of, G.F. Chess
Graduate Studies, Faculty of, H.B. Stewart
Journalism, School of, (tba)
Law, Faculty of, P. Slayton
Library & Information Science, School of, W. J. Cameron
Medicine, Faculty of, M.J. Hollenberg
Music, Faculty of, J. Behrens
Nursing, Faculty of, Beverlee Cox
Part Time & Continuing Education, T.N. Guinsburg
Physical Education, W. L'Heureux
Science, Faculty of, J.B. Bancroft
Social Science, Faculty of, B. B. Kymlicka

ADMINISTRATIVE OFFICERS
Director, French/English Summer School at Trois-Pistoles, J. Metford
Chairman, Intercollegiate Athletics, G. Leyshon
Director, Computing Centre, H.S. Jones
Director, Student Health Services, Dr. F.L. Pattison
Director, Information Analysis & Systems, G. Harris
Director, Physical Plant, R. M. Yeo
Director, Purchasing, G.M. Hamilton
Comptroller, S. Finlayson
Director, Student Awards, J. McClure
Director, Student Services, T. F. Seiss
Director, Alumni Affairs, J. Ferguson
Director, University Relations & Information, L. T. Moore
Bookstore Manager, D. Mason

CENTRES, COUNCILS AND STUDY GROUPS
University Research Council, Research Officer, H. W. Baldwin
Centre for Radio Science, Director, P. A. Forsyth
Centre for Chemical Physics, Director, G.M. Bancroft
Systems Analysis, Control & Design Activity (SACDA), Director, J.R. Dickinson
Museum of Indian Archaeology, Director, W.D. Finlayson

AFFILIATED COLLEGES
Brescia College, 1285 Western Rd., London, Ont.
Principal, Sr. Dolores Kuntz
Huron College, 1349 Western Rd., London, Ont.
Principal, J. G. Morden
King's College, 266 Epworth Ave., London, Ont.
Principal, J.D. Morgan

Wilfrid Laurier University

75 University Ave. W., Waterloo, Ont. N2L 3C5
(519) 884-1970
Chairman of the Board, Robert McIntosh
President, Dr. Neale H. Tayler
Vice President, Academic, Dr. John Weir
Vice President, Admin. & Finance, J. Peter Venton
Information Officer, Richard K. Taylor
Registrar, J.T. Wilgar
Director of Personnel, Earl W. Rayner
Librarian, Erich R. Schultz
Bookstore Manager, Paul Fischer

DEANS
School of Business & Economics, Dr. Max Stewart
Faculty of Social Work, Dr. Sherman Merle
Waterloo Lutheran Seminary, Dr. Delton J. Glebe
Faculty of Arts & Science, Dr. Gerald Vallillee
Graduate Studies, Dr. Andrew Berczi
Faculty of Music, Dr. Gordon Greene

University of Windsor

Windsor, Ont. N9B 3P4
(519) 253-4232
Chairman of the Board, John McGivney, Q.C.

OFFICERS OF ADMINISTRATION
Chancellor, R.H. Rohmer, C.M.M., D.F.C., O.St.J., C.D., Q.C., B.A., LL.D.
Vice Chancellor & President, Mervyn Franklin, B.Sc., Ph.D.
Asst. Vice President, Operations, C. W. Morgan, B.Sc., M.B.A.
Asst. Vice President, Human Resources, John Dempster
Vice President, Academic, P.V. Cassano, B.A., M.A., Ph.D.
Asst. Vice President, Student Services, George McMahon, B.A., M.A.
Asst. Vice President, Community Relations & Development, J. Laframboise
Registrar, F.L. Smith, B.A.
Librarian, A.V. Mate, B.A., A.M., A.M.L.S.
Dean of Students, K.F. Long, M.A.
Secretary of Senate, & Executive Asst. to the President, Barbara H. Birch, B.A., M.A.
Director, Administrative Services, D. M. Drew, P.P.
Director, Computer Centre, L. F. Miernicke, B.B.A.
Director, Finance, J. E. Schiller, B.A.
Director, Physical Planning & Information Analysis, A. M. Marshall, B.Sc.
Director, Media Centre, E. Marzotto, B.A.Sc., M.A.Sc.
Director, Physical Plant, R.J. Nicodemo, B.A.
Director, Secondary School Liaison, J. Saso, B.A.
Manager, University Centre, Randy Johnston, Hon. B.A.
Director, Information Services, E. Havelock, M.A.

FACULTIES WITH DEANS
Arts, J.V. Brown, B.A., M.A., Ph.D.
Social Science, Walter Romanow, B.A., M.A., Ph.D.
Science & Mathematics, C. P. Gravenor, B.A., M.S., Ph.D.
Engineering, C. MacInnis, B.Sc., B.E., Ph.D., P.Eng.
Business Admin., George Neal, D.B.A. (int.)

Education, A. Stuart Nease, B.A., M.A.
Human Kinetics, R. Hermiston, B.A., B.P.H.E., M.S., Ph.D.
Law, Ronald W. Ianni, B.A., B.Comm., LL.B., Ph.D.
Law Librarian, P. T. Murphy, B.A., LL.B., M.S.L.S.
Graduate Studies, C.P.J. Crowley, C.S.B., B.A., M.A., Ph.D.

DIRECTORS
School of Computer Science, E.W. Channen, Ph.D. (int.)
School of Dramatic Art, G.L. Neilson, M.F.A.
School of Fine Arts, A.P. Doctor, B.F.A., M.F.A.
School of Music, Richard Householder, B.A., Master of Music
School of Nursing, Janet Rosenbaum, B.Sc.N., M.Sc.N.
School of Social Work, James Chacko, B.A., B.S.W., M.S.W.
Part-time Studies, G.V. Booth, Ph.D.

FEDERATED AND AFFILIATED INSTITUTIONS
Assumption University
President, Rev. D.G. Heath, C.S.B., B.A., S.T.B., M.Ed., D.Ed.
Holy Redeemer College
President, Rev. D.L. Egan, C.Ss.R., S.T.L.
Canterbury College
Principal, The Rev. F. T. Kingston, B.A., M.A., L.Th., B.D., D.Phil.
Iona College
Principal, Rev. J. C. Hoffman, B.A., B.D., Ph.D., S.T.M., Th.D.

York University
4700 Keele St., Downsview, Ont. M3J 1P3 (416/667-2100)
Glendon Campus, 2275 Bayview Ave., Toronto, Ont. M4N 3M6 (416/487-6132)

ADMINISTRATION
Chairman of the Board, John S. Proctor, LL.D.
Chancellor, John P. Robarts, P.C., C.C., Q.C., B.A., LL.B., LL.D., D.C.L.
President, H.I. Macdonald, O.C., B.Com., M.A., B.Phil., LL.D.
Vice President, Academic Affairs, Wm. C. Found, B.A., M.A., Ph.D.
Vice President, Employee & Student Relations, Wm. D. Farr, B.A., M.A.
Vice President, Finance & Development, G.G. Bell, M.B.E., C.D., B.S., M.A., Ph.D.
Vice President, University Services, Wm. W. Small, B.Com., M.A.
Secretary of the University, M.W. Ransom, B.A.
Dean of Research, B.H. Massam, B.Sc., M.A., Ph.D.
Director of Libraries, A. Woodsworth, B.F.A., B.L.S., M.L.S.
Director of Communications, S.M. Fisher, B.A.
Director of Bookstores, R. Barreto-Rivera, B.A.
Asst. Vice President, Computing Services, N.G. Foster
Asst. Vice President, Student Relations, J.A. Becker, B.A.Sc.
Asst. Vice President, Academic Planning, S.H. Levy, B.Sc., M.A.
Director of the Office of International Services, W.C. Found, B.A., M.A., Ph.D.
Registrar, M.A. Bider, B.A., M.A.
Comptroller, J.A. Heber, R.I.A.
Director of Academic Computing, Uriel Domb, B.Sc., M.Sc.
Director of Admissions, J.A.S. McNeil, B.A., B.P.E.
Director of Ancillary Services, A.R. Dawson, B.A.Sc.
Director of the Centre for Continuing Education, L.R. Duncan, B.A., B.P.E., M.Ed.
Director of Computer Systems Development, I.Y. Aharoni, B.A., M.B.A., C.D.P.
Director of the Counselling & Development Centre, H.P. Mandel, B.Sc., M.Sc., Ph.D.
Director of Development, P. Bryden, B.A.
Director of Facilities Planning & Management, A.R. Dawson, B.A.Sc.
Director of Financial Services, B.H. Wareham, B.A.
Director of Health Services, R.J. Wheler, M.D., C.C.F.P.
Director of Instructional Aid Resources, D.A. Homer, B.A.A.
Director of Personnel Services, D.J. Mitchell
Director of Physical Education & Athletics, F. Cosentino, B.A., B.P.E., M.A., Ph.D.
Director of Physical Plant, J.K. Armour, B.A.Sc.
Director of Purchasing, T.H. Jones
Director of Safety & Security Services, C.G. Dunn
Director of Student Awards, J.-A. Albright, B.A.

FACULTIES WITH DEANS
Administrative Studies, W.B. Crowston, B.A.Sc., S.M., Ph.D.
Arts, H. Kaplan, A.B., Ph.D.
Joseph E. Atkinson College, H.S. Crowe, M.C., B.A., M.A.
Education, A. Effrat, B.A., Ph.D.
Environmental Studies, R.D. Schwass, B.A., M.Ed., Ed.D.
Fine Arts, L.H. Lawrence, B.A., M.A.
Glendon College, Principal, P. Garigue, M.C., B.Sc., Ph.D., F.R.S.C.
Graduate Studies, D.V.J. Bell, B.A., A.M., Ph.D.
Osgoode Hall Law School, S.M. Beck, B.A., LL.B., LL.M.
Science, O.R. Lundell, B.A., Ph.D.

RESEARCH UNITS WITH DIRECTORS
Institute of Behavioural Research, A.H. Richmond, B.Sc., M.A., Ph.D.
Joint Program in Transportation, R.M. Soberman, B.Sc., S.M., Ph.D.
Centre for Research in Experimental Space Science, R.W. Nicholls, A.R.C.S., B.Sc., Ph.D., D.Sc., F. Inst. P., F.R.A.S., F.A.P.S., F.R.S.C.
Centre for Research on Environmental Quality, W.J. Megaw, B.Sc., D.Sc., F.I.P.
Centre for Research on Latin America and the Caribbean, L. Lefeber, B.A., Ph.D.
Joint Centre on Modern East Asia, D.C.M. Lary, B.A., Ph.D.
Transport Centre, R.M. Soberman, B.Sc., S.M., Ph.D.

ONTARIO TECHNICAL & VOCATIONAL INSTITUTIONS

COLLEGES OF APPLIED ARTS AND TECHNOLOGY
Algonquin College of Applied Arts & Technology, 1385 Woodroffe Ave., Nepean, Ont. K2G 1V8
(613) 725-7010
President, Dr. L. Isabelle
Cambrian College of Applied Arts & Technology, 1400 Barrydowne Rd., Stn. A, Sudbury, Ont. P3A 3V8
(705) 566-8101
President, Dr. J.T. Koski
Canadore College of Applied Arts & Technology, Box 5001, North Bay, Ont. P1B 8K9
(705) 474-7600
President, Dr. M.A. Hewgill
Centennial College of Applied Arts & Technology, Box 631, Stn. A, Scarborough, Ont. M1K 5E9
(416) 694-3241
President, I.B. McCauley
Conestoga College of Applied Arts & Technology, 299 Doon Valley Dr., Kitchener, Ont. N2G 4M4
(519) 653-2511
President, K.E. Hunter
Confederation College of Applied Arts & Technology, Box 398, Thunder Bay, Ont. P7C 4W1
(807) 475-6110
President, B.E. Curtis
Durham College of Applied Arts & Technology, Simcoe St. N., Box 385, Oshawa, Ont. L1H 7L7
(416) 576-0210
President, Melvin Garland
Fanshawe College of Applied Arts & Technology, Box 4005, London, Ont. N5W 5H1
(519) 452-4100
President, Harry Rawson
George Brown College of Applied Arts & Technology, Box 1015, Stn. B, Toronto, Ont. M5T 2T9
(416) 967-1212
President, D.E. Light
Georgian College of Applied Arts & Technology, One Georgian Dr., Barrie, Ont. L4M 3X9
(705) 728-1951
President, W.F.J. Busch

Humber College of Applied Arts & Technology, Box 1900, Rexdale, Ont. M9W 5L7

(416) 675-3111

President, Gordon Wragg

North Campus, 205 Humber College Blvd., Rexdale, Ont. M9W 5L7 (675-3111)

Keelesdale Campus, 88 Industry St., Weston, Ont. M6M 4L8 (763-4571)

Humber Lakeshore 1, 3199 Lakeshore Blvd. W., Toronto, Ont. M8V 1L1 (252-5571)

Humber Lakeshore 2, 56 Queen Elizabeth Blvd., Toronto, Ont. M8Z 1M1 (252-5571)

York Eglinton Centre, 1669 Eglinton Ave. W., Toronto, Ont. (781-5621)

Osler Campus, 5 Queenslea Ave., Weston, Ont. M9N 2K8 (244-5361)

Lambton College of Applied Arts & Technology, Box 969, Sarnia, Ont. N7T 7K4

(519) 542-7751

President, Brian U. Seville

Loyalist College of Applied Arts & Technology, Box 4200, Belleville, Ont. K8N 5B9

(613) 962-9501

President, H. Young

Mohawk College of Applied Arts & Technology, Box 2034, Hamilton, Ont. L8N 3T2

(416) 389-4461

President, K.L. McIntyre

Niagara College of Applied Arts & Technology, Woodlawn Rd., Box 1005, Welland, Ont. L3B 5S2

(416) 735-2211

President, Jacqueline P. Robarts

Northern College of Applied Arts & Technology, 140 Government Rd. E., Kirkland Lake, Ont. P2N 3L8

(705) 325-3211

President, J.H. Drysdale

St. Clair College of Applied Arts & Technology, 2000 Talbot Rd. W., Windsor, Ont. N9A 6S4

(519) 966-1656

President, R.B. McAusland

St. Lawrence College of Applied Arts & Technology, Newcourt House, King St. W., Kingston, Ont. K7L 5A6

(613) 544-5400

President, W.W. Cruden

College Administrative Services/Brockville Campus, 20 Parkedale Ave., Brockville, Ont. K6V 5X3, 345-0660, Principal, J.M. Butt

Cornwall Campus, Windmill Point, Cornwall, Ont. K6H 4Z1, 933-6080, Principal, A.L. Martin

Kingston Campus, King St. W., Kingston, Ont. K7L 5A6, 544-5400, Principal, G. Welch

The Sault College of Applied Arts & Technology, Box 60, Sault Ste. Marie, Ont. P6A 5L3

(705) 949-2050

President, P.R. Doyle

Seneca College of Applied Arts & Technology, 1750 Finch Ave. E., Willowdale, Ont. M2N 5T7

(416) 491-5050

President, Dr. W.T. Newnham

Sheridan College of Applied Arts & Technology, 1450 Trafalgar Rd., Oakville, Ont. L6H 2L1

(416) 845-9430

President, D.A. Shields

Sir Sandford Fleming College of Applied Arts & Technology, Peterborough, Ont. K9J 7B1

(705) 743-5610

President, David B. Sutherland

PRINCE EDWARD ISLAND REGIONAL ADMINISTRATIVE SCHOOL UNITS

As of July, 1972, previously existing school boards were consolidated to form five regional administrative school boards. Each board consists of fifteen elected members.

For Dept. of Education officials see government listings.

Unit 1

Box 57, Elmsdale, P.E.I. C0B 1K0 (902/853-2013)
Chairman, Harold Phillips
Supt., Thomas Hall
Business Manager, Harvey MacEwan

Unit 2

Box 2500, Summerside, P.E.I. C1N 4L9 (902/436-2133)
Chairman, J. E. Laughlin
Supt., L.B. Russell
Business Manager, A. Savidant

Unit 3

Box 1840, Charlottetown, P.E.I. C1A 7N6 (902/892-0281)
Chairman, Sibyl Cutcliffe
Supt., Parnell Garland
Business Manager, Eric Ellsworth

Unit 4

Box 700, Montague, P.E.I. C0A 1R0 (902/838-2944)
Chairman, Steve McQuaid
Supt., Ralph Stonefield
Business Manager, Wayne Hooper

Unit 5

Wellington Station, R.R. 3, P.E.I. C0B 2E0 (902/854-2975)
Chairman, Leo S. Arsenault
Supt., J. Albert Gallant

POST SECONDARY INSTITUTIONS IN PRINCE EDWARD ISLAND

University of Prince Edward Island

Charlottetown, P.E.I. C1A 4P3
(902) 892-4121
President & Vice Chancellor, Peter P.M. Meincke, B.Sc., M.A., Ph.D.
Chancellor, Dr. Gustave Gingras, C.C., M.D., F.R.S.A., LL.D., F.R.C.P.(C).
Chairman of the Board, Kenneth C. Grant, M.D.
Registrar, Michael F. Hennessey
Director of Administration & Finance, G. Dennis Clough
Business Manager, Murray S. Stevenson
Information Officer, Mrs. Marita McNulty
Purchasing Agent, G.J. Quinn
Librarian, Merritt Crockett
Bookstore Manager, Russell I. Stewart

FACULTIES WITH DEANS

Arts, Prof. Frank J. Ledwell, B.A., M.A.
Science, J.I. Dowling, B.Sc., M.Sc.
Education, D. Roy Campbell, B.A., M.A., Ph.D.

TECHNICAL & VOCATIONAL SCHOOLS IN PRINCE EDWARD ISLAND

Holland College Charlottetown Centre
Weymouth St., Charlottetown, P.E.I. C1A 4Z1, 892-4191
President, Dr. D. Glendenning

Holland College Summerside Centre
425 Granville St., Summerside, P.E.I. C1N 3C4, 436-9101
Principal, J. G. Gauthier

Holland College Royalty Centre
Enman Cres., West Royalty, P.E.I. C1A 7N9, 892-2401
Principal, Dr. I.A.B. Low

School of Visual Arts
Box 7500, Burns Ave., West Royalty, P.E.I. C1A 7N8, 892-2401

Marine & Fisheries Training School

Waterfront Mall, Summerside, P.E.I. C1N 1A9, 436-2215

EDUCATION IN QUEBEC

The Quebec educational system consists of two sectors: the public sector and the private sector. The provisions of the law for private education allow a control over the quality of teaching in the private institutions, as of December 18th, 1968.

THE PUBLIC SECTOR

The public sector comprises the nursery and primary schools administered by the local or integrated school boards, the high schools administered by the regional school boards, the colleges for general and professional education and the University of Quebec.

Since the law regarding the regrouping and administration of school boards came into effect on July 1st, 1972, there are 48 regional school boards and 203 local school boards. The elementary course usually lasts six years and the secondary course five years. According to the terms of regulation No. 7 secondary education is polyvalent in that the students may choose professional options at the same time as general options.

College education (given by the colleges of general and professional education or C.E.G.E.P.) is designed both for young people between the ages of 17 and 19 years who wish to continue their studies at university or who are orienting themselves toward the labour market, and for adults who wish to complete their general or professional training according to the demands of the labour market.

The University of Quebec consists of a network of educational and research establishments. The component elements are the university campuses of Montreal, Trois-Rivières, Chicoutimi, and Rimouski. Added to these are colleges and research institutes, such as the National School of Public Administration (E.N.A.P.) and the National Institute for Scientific Research (I.N.R.S.).

THE PRIVATE SECTOR

The private sector is composed of establishments of primary, secondary and even college education. These institutions are subsidized for 80% of the cost per pupil in the public school, if they are recognized as being of public interest. If they are not recognized as being of public interest, but are recognized for purposes of grants, they may receive a subsidy reaching 60% of the cost per pupil in the public school. Other institutions may receive a simple permit which does not make them eligible for any subsidy but which allows them to operate legally.

QUEBEC SCHOOL BOARDS

INTEGRATED SCHOOL BOARDS

Roman Catholic	29
Protestant	6
Common	4

LOCAL SCHOOL BOARDS

Roman Catholic	145
Protestant	19

REGIONAL SCHOOL BOARDS

Roman Catholic	40
Protestant	8
	Total 251

For Department of Education officials, see government listings.

The following are School Boards in large population centres:

La Commission Scolaire d'Arvida
218 rue Gilbert, C.P. 430, Jonquière (Secteur Arvida), P.Q. G7S 4L1
(418) 548-7181
Directeur général, Roch Laroche
Directeur des services de l'enseignement, Mlle Laurence Levesque
Secrétaire général, Edouard Brassard

La Commission Scolaire Baldwin Cartier
10, boul. des Sources, Pointe-Claire, P.Q. H9S 5K8
(514) 697-6320
Secretary General, Jean Raby
Director General, Raynald Laplante
Asst. Director General, L.J. Cassidy
Director of Education, French, Germain Hotte
Director of Education, English, Donald Myles
Director, Personnel Services, Gilles Perron
Director of Finance Services, Jean Ouellette
Purchasing, Ronald Longtin

La Commission Scolaire du Cap-de-la-Madeleine
41, rue Bellerive, C.P. 190, Cap-de-la-Madeleine, P.Q. G8T 7W2
(819) 378-6146
Directeur général, Réginald Vézina
Directeur général adjoint, directeur des services financiers, et directeur des services de l'equipement, Robert Rocheleau
Directeur des services aux élèves et directeur des services de l'enseignement, André Fortin
Sécretaire général, Lucien Lefebvre
Directeur du personnel, André Pelletier

La Commission Scolaire de Chicoutimi
36 est, rue Jacques-Cartier, Chicoutimi, P.Q. G7H 1W2
(418) 549-8210
Directeur général, J. J. Hudon
Directeur des services de l'enseignement, Benoit Dolbec
Adjoint au directeur des services de l'enseignement, Bernard Martel
Directeur général adjoint et directeur des services aux étudiants, Pierre Tchernof
Directeur des services du personnel, Ghislain Girard
Directeur des services de l'équipement, Rosaire Tremblay
Directeur des services financiers, Renald Bergeron
Directeur des services d'éducation aux adultes, Fernand Palin
Secrétaire général, Michel Cloutier

Protestant School Board of Greater Hull
170 Main St., Aylmer, P.Q. J9H 6K1
(819) 684-2477
Director General, H. A. Macdonald
Secretary General, Mrs. E. Biehler

Laurenval School Board
1105 Victor Morin, Duvernay, Laval, P.Q. H7G 4B8
(514) 668-4380
Director General, Gerald McConaghy
Director, Administrative Services, David Russell
Director, Instructional Services, Bruce Campbell
Director, Financial Services, Roger Drapeau
Director, Personnel, Jon Ed

La Commission des Ecoles Catholiques de Montreal
3737 est, rue Sherbrooke, Montreal, P.Q. H1X 3B3
(514) 525-6311
Directeur général, Me Maurice Brunet
Secrétaire général, Gaston Dugas
Trésorier, André Murphy
Directeur général adjoint, Laurent Portugais
Directeur général adjoint, Secteur anglais, John F. Geci
Sous-directeur général, délégué à l'administration, Hubert Comeau
Sous-directeur général, Secteur anglais, George Pajuk

Protestant School Board of Greater Montreal
6000 Fielding Ave., Montreal, P.Q. H3X 1T4
(514) 482-6000

Director General, M. R. Fox
Deputy Director General, K.I. Trasler
Secretary General, Mrs. O. Kowcz
Co-ordinator of Communications Services & Special Duties, R.C. Paterson
Director of Administrative & Financial Services, M. McDonald
Director of Accounting Services, F. Robinson
Director of Buildings & Equipment, H.C. Sylvia
Director of Systems & Data Processing, H. Daly
Purchasing Manager, W. Yarnell
Regional Director, Region 1, D.E. DeSilva
Regional Director, Region 2, W.H. Ford
Regional Director, Region 3, Mrs. A. Schlutz
Regional Director, Region 4, Miss A. MacLeish
Director of Instructional Services, G.G. Auchinleck
Director of Student Services, G.S. Conrod
Director of Personnel, R.T.B. Fairbairn
Librarian, Mrs. M. Montague

La Commission Scolaire Outaouais-Hull

122, rue St-Laurent, C.P. 1217, Hull, P.Q. J8X 3X7
(819) 771-8303
Directeur général, Monique Cyr

Catholic School Commission of Quebec

1460 St. Foy Rd., Quebec, P.Q. G1S 2N9
(418) 688-3211
Secretary General, Marc DesRoches
Director General, Fernand Paradis
Director, Secondary, Rémi Beaudoin
Director, Elementary, Thérèse Ouellet
Director, Adult Education, Jacques Vézina
Asst. Director General, Jean Guy Thiffault
Director of Equipment, Jacques Charland
Director of Personnel, J.-L. Chabot

Greater Quebec School Board

2046 Ch. St-Louis, Sillery, P.Q. G1T 1P4
(418) 688-8730
Primary Level (called the Greater Quebec School Board)
Director General, W. Pennefather
Asst. Director General, A.T. Bayne
Secretary General, J.B. Wetmore
Secondary Level (called the Eastern Quebec Regional School Board)
Director General, W. Pennefather
Asst. Director General & Director of Financial Services, V. Richard
Director of Educational Services, G. Jackson

St. Maurice Protestant School Board

1241 Nicholas Perrot St., Trois-Rivières, P.Q. G9A 1C2
(819) 374-3205
Secretary General, Mrs. F. D. Harnois
Principal, High School, W.A. Dousett

Verdun Catholic School Commission

1100, 5th Ave., Verdun, P.Q. H4G 2Z7
(514) 769-2771
Director General, Dr. John Oss
Asst., J. Plante
Purchasing, Pierre Lamanque
Asst., Pierre Primeau

DIRECTEURS DES BUREAUX REGIONAUX DIRECTORS OF REGIONAL OFFICES DEPARTMENT OF EDUCATION

Bas St-Laurent/Gaspésie, Fernand Dionne, 337 rue Moreault, Rimouski, P.Q. G5L 1P4
Saguenay/ Lac St-Jean, Roger Bellavance, 50, boul. Harvey, Jonquière, P.Q. G7X 8L6
Québec, Gérard Létourneau, 1020 Route de l'Eglise, Ste-Foy, P.Q. G1V 3V9
Trois-Rivières, (vacant), Edifice Capitanal, 2e étage, 100 rue Laviolette, Trois-Rivières, P.Q. G9A 5S9 (819/376-3711)
Cantons de l'Est, Bernard Desruisseaux, 740, ouest, rue Galt, Sherbrooke, P.Q. J1H 1Z3
Montréal-centre, Guy Dozois, 600 rue Fullum, 8e étage, Montréal, P.Q. H1K 4L1
Montréal-sud, Jacques Perreault, Edifice Montval, 6e étage, 201 Pl. Charles-Lemoyne, Longueuil, P.Q. J4K 2T5
Montréal-nord, Gilles Lapointe, 206 boul. Labelle, Ste-Thérèse, P.Q. J7E 2X7
Outaouais, Gilles Meilleur, 170 Hotel de Ville, Hull, P.Q. J8X 4S2
Nord-Ouest, Maurice Morand, 180 boul. Rideau, Noranda, P.Q. J9X 1N9
Côte-Nord, Claude Mathieu, 625, boul. Laflèche, (local 347), Hauterive, P.Q. G5C 1C5
Sept-Iles, Claude Mathieu, 106 rue Napoléon, Sept-Iles, Duplessis, P.Q. G4R 3L7

POST SECONDARY & PRIVATE INSTITUTIONS IN QUEBEC

Agricultural Colleges

MACDONALD CAMPUS OF McGILL UNIVERSITY
21,111 Lakeshore Rd., Ste-Anne-de-Bellevue, P.Q. H9X 1CO
(514) 457-2000
The Faculty of Agriculture (including the School of Food Science) of McGill University.

INSTITUT DE TECHNOLOGIE AGRICOLE ET ALIMENTAIRE
3230 rue Sicotte, C.P. 70, St-Hyacinthe, P.Q. J2S 2M2
(514) 773-7401
Directeur, Lionel D'Amours, B.S.A.; agr.

INSTITUTE OF AGRICULTURAL TECHNOLOGY
1, rue Poiré, La Pocatière, P.Q. GOR 1ZO
(418) 856-1110
Director, André Vézina

FACULTE DES SCIENCES DE L'AGRICULTURE ET DE L'ALIMENTATION UNIVERSITE LAVAL
Cité Universitaire, Quebec, P.Q. G1K 7P4
(418) 656-3496
Doyen, Dr. G.B. Martin

Art Schools

UNIVERSITE DU QUEBEC A MONTREAL, FAMILLE DES ARTS
Mailing: C.P. 8888, Succ. A, Montreal, P.Q. H3C 3P8
405 Ste Catherine St. E., Montreal
(514) 282-3661
Courses given lead to a "specialized baccalaureate" in one of the 10 disciplines offered.

ECOLE DES ARTS VISUELS DE L'UNIVERSITE LAVAL
Cité Universitaire, Quebec, P.Q. G1K 7P4
Directeur, Bernard Jasmin
Directeur adjoint, Lucien Hudon

Bishop's College School

Lennoxville, P.Q. J1M 1Z8
(819) 569-0657
Chairman of Board, H. G. Hallward
Headmaster, J. D. Cowans, M.A.
Comptroller, D. F. Watson, C.A.
Director of Admissions, D.A.G. Cruickshank, M.A.

Bishop's University

Lennoxville, P.Q. J1M 1Z7
(819) 569-9551
Chancellor, R.A. Bandeen, O.C., B.A., Ph.D., LL.D., D.C.L.
President, R.L. Denton, B.Sc., M.D., F.R.C.P. (C)
Vice President, B.Gen. J.P. Gautier, D.S.O., C.D., D.C.L.
Chairman of Executive Committee, D. Marler
Principal, C.I.H. Nicholl, B.Sc., M.A.Sc., Ph.D.
Dean, Karl J. Kuepper, Dr. Phil.
Registrar, G.J. Marcotte, B.A., M.A., P.Mgr.

Vice Principal Admin., J.-L. Grégoire, R.I.A.
Director of Athletics, B. Coulter
Director of Ancillary Services, W. Duncan
Director of University Health Services, P.G. Marosi, M.D.C.M.
Director of Buildings & Grounds, I.W. Saunders
Co-ordinator of Admissions, J. Wilson, B.A.
Co-ordinator of Continuing Education, H.B. Taylor

GRADUATE SCHOOL OF EDUCATION
Professor of Education, A. W. Jones, B.A., M.Ed.

LIBRARY
Librarian, G. Belisle, B. ès L., B.A., B.Ph., B. ès Sc. Biblio.
Bookstore Manager, Mrs. P. LePoidevin

Collège Militaire Royal de Saint-Jean
Saint-Jean, P.Q. J0J 1R0
(514) 346-2131
Commandant, Col. Y. Durocher, C.D., M.Eng.
Principal & Director of Studies, Prof. M. A. Benoit, C.D., N.D.C., B.Sc., M.Sc., Ph.D.
Director of Cadets, L.Col. G.R. Bourret, C.D., pcsc, B.Eng.
Director of Admin., Maj. (W) M.M. Langlais, C.D.
Secretary General, J. M. Jarry, B.A., L.Sc., L. Péd., M.Sc.
Librarian, A. Lamirande, B.A., B.L.S., B.Ed.

Concordia University
(514) 879-5995
Sir George Williams Campus: 1455 de Maisonneuve Blvd. W., Montreal, P.Q. H3G 1M8
Loyola Campus: 7141 Sherbrooke St. W., Montreal, P.Q. H4B 1R6
Chancellor, H. J. Hemens, Q.C.
Chairman of Board of Governors, C.A. Duff
Rector & Vice Chancellor, J. W. O'Brien
Vice Rector, Admin. & Finance, Graham Martin
Vice Rector, Academic, J.S. Daniel
Vice Rector, Academic, R.W. Breen
Asst. Vice Rector & Registrar, K.D. Adams
Asst. Vice Rector & Treasurer, W.M. Reay
Asst. Vice Rector & Director of Libraries, P.E. Filion

FACULTIES AND DEANS
Arts & Science, Division 1, Donat Taddeo
Division 2, J. Chaikelson
Division 3, M. Cohen
Division 4, Martin Singer
Commerce & Admin., P. Simon
Engineering, M.N.S. Swamy
Fine Arts, C.A. Emery
Graduate Studies, S.G. French

Conservatory of Music
Dept. of Cultural Affairs, 100 est, Notre-Dame, Montreal, P.Q. H2Y 1C1
(514) 873-4031
Director, Albert Grenier

Conservatory of Dramatic Art
Dept. of Cultural Affairs, 100 est Notre Dame, Montreal, P.Q. H2Y 1C1
(514) 873-4283
Director, Guy Beaulne

Institut International de Lecture Dynamique
450 est rue Sherbrooke, #464, Montreal, P.Q. H2L 1J8
(514) 844-1942
Directeur général, Joel Bonn
Attaché à l'information, Michel Galipeau
Registraire (francophone), Rita Kaloust
Bibliothécaire, Dale Ouimet

Université Laval
Cité Universitaire, Québec, P.Q. G1K 7P4
(418) 656-2131

ADMINISTRATION DE L'UNIVERSITE
Recteur, Jean-Guy Paquet
Vice recteur exécutif, André Dufour
Vice recteur à l'enseignement et à la recherche, Jacques Desautels
Vice recteur aux affaires professorales et étudiantes, Louis Trotier
Vice recteur aux affaires administratives, Fernand Gingras
Secrétaire général, Louis-Marie Babineau
Directeur de l'Ecole des gradués, Claude St-Pierre
Directeur général des programmes de cours de premier cycle, Benoît Dumais
Directeur de l'Extension de l'enseignement, André Bouchard
Directeur du service de promotion de l'éducation permanente, Napoléon LeBlanc
Registraire, Marc Boucher
Directeur du Service des relations publiques, André Barnard
Directeur de la Bibliothèque, Céline Cartier
Directeur du Service de l'audio-visuel, Emile Descoteaux
Directeur des Presses de l'Université, Claude Frémont
Directeur du Centre de traitement de l'information, Louis P.A. Robichaud
Directeur du Service de pédagogie universitaire, Jacques Parent
Directeur du Service des animaux de laboratoire, Richard Blondin (int.)
Directeur de Vie étudiante, Rémy Bergeron
Directeur du Service des finances, Mathieu Leclerc
Directeur du Service du personnel, René Madore
Directeur du Service d'organisation et méthodes, Yves Rouleau
Directeur du Service des terrains et bâtiments, Gérard Bisaillon
Directeur du Service des résidences, R.-R. Côté
Directeur du Service des approvisionnements, Gaston Lavoie
Directeur du Service alimentaire, J.-G. Pouliot
Directeur de l'Association des anciens, Ludger St-Pierre
Service de l'expansion, Marcel Vachon
Stations expérimentales, Jacques Pfalzgraf

LES DOYENS
Faculté des arts, J.-C. Blouin
Faculté de droit, Yvan Bernier
Faculté de foresterie et géodésie, Yvan Hardy
Faculté des lettres, Lorne Laforge
Faculté de médecine, Jean Rochon
Faculté de philosophie, Robert Plante
Faculté des sciences de l'administration, Claude LeBon
Faculté des sciences de l'agriculture et de l'alimentation, G.-B. Martin
Faculté des sciences de l'éducation, Henri Saint-Pierre
Faculté des sciences et de génie, Lucien Huot
Faculté des sciences sociales, André Beaudoin
Faculté de théologie, Pierre Gaudette

DIRECTEURS DES ECOLES
Ecole d'architecture, Takashi Nakajima
Ecole des arts visuels, Bernard Jasmin
Ecole de médecine dentaire, Roland Vallée
Ecole de musique, Pierre Thibault
Ecole de pharmacie, Jacques Dumas
Ecole de psychologie, F.-X. Desrosiers
Ecole de réadaptation, J. François
Ecole des sciences infirmières, Thérèse Fortier
Ecole de service social, Marcelle Laforest (int.)

Lower Canada College
4090 Royal Ave., Montreal, P.Q. H4A 2M5
(514) 482-9916
Headmaster, G. H. Merrill, M.A.
Business Manager, I.F. Le Lievre, C.A.
Librarian, Mrs. E. Drummond, B.L.S.
Bookstore Manager, P. S. Howard, M.A.

Marianopolis College
3880 Côte des Neiges, Montreal, P.Q. H3H 1W1
(514) 931-8792
President, Anna Mary Breen, C.N.D.

Academic Dean, Joyce Roberts, C.N.D.
Registrar, Françoise Boisvert, C.N.D.
Chief Librarian, Roman R. Grodzicky
Co-ordinator of Admissions, Carol Mizgala
Director of Student Services, G.E. McSheffrey
Information Officer, Sheilagh Litchfield-Johnson

McGill University

845 Sherbrooke St. W., Montréal, P.Q. H3A 2T5
(514) 392-4311
Chancellor, C.F. Harrington, C.D., B.A., B.C.L., C. St. J.
Chairman of Board, Alan B. Gold, Q.C., B.A., LL.M.
Principal & Vice Chancellor, David L. Johnston, A.B., LL.B., LL.D. (hon.)
Vice Principal, Academic, S.O. Freedman, B.Sc., M.D., C.M., F.R.S.C., F.R.C.P. (C), F.A.C.P.
Vice Principal, Admin. & Finance, J. Armour, A.A.C.C.A.
Vice Principal, Planning & Academic Services, E.J. Stansbury, M.A., Ph.D.
Vice Principal, Research, G. Maclachlan, B.Sc.,M.A., Ph.D.
Secretary General, C. M. McDougall, D.S.O., B.A.
Registrar, J. P. Schuller, B.A.
Director of Admissions Office, Peggy Sheppard, B.A., B.Ed.
Director of Libraries, Marianne Scott, B.A., B.L.S.
Director, Public Relations Office, Betsy Hirst, B.A., M.A.

DEANS OF FACULTIES

Agriculture, L.E. Lloyd, B.Sc. (Agr.), M.Sc., Ph.D.
Arts, M.P. Maxwell, M.A., Ph.D.
Dentistry, K.C. Bentley, D.D.S., M.D.C.M.
Education, George E. Flower, M.A., Ed.D.
Engineering, G. W. Farnell, B.A.Sc., S.M., Ph.D.
Graduate Studies & Research, G. Maclachlan, B.Sc., M.A.,Ph.D.
Law, J.E.C. Brierley, B.A., B.C.L., D.V.
Management, L. Picard, C.C., B.A., B.Phil., B.Sc.A., D.B.A.
Medicine, R.L. Cruess, M.D., F.R.C.S.C.
Music, Paul Pedersen, B.A., M.M., Ph.D.
Religious Studies, J. C. McLelland, M.A., B.D., Ph.D., D.D.
Science, S. Orvig, B.Sc., M.Sc., Ph.D., F.R.S.C.

DIRECTORS OF SCHOOLS

Architecture, D. Drummond, B.Arch.
Computer Science, M.M. Newborn, B.E.E., Ph.D.
Food Science, S.M. Weber, B.Sc. (H.Ec.), M.S., Ph.D.
Human Communication Disorders, K.K. Charan, M.A., Ph.D.
Library Science, V. Sessions, A.B., M.A., M.S.
Nursing, Joan Gilchrist, B.N., M.Sc.(Appl.), R.N.
Physical & Occupational Therapy, M.C. Piper, B.Sc., M.A., Ph.D.
Social Work, Myer Katz, B.A., M.S.W., Ph.D.
Urban Planning, D. Farley, B.Arch., M.Arch., M.C.P.
Centre for Continuing Education, J. A. Duff, M.A., C.A.

INCORPORATED COLLEGE

The Royal Victoria College

The Royal Victoria College is the Women's College of McGill University. All women undergraduates registered at McGill University are automatically members of the Royal Victoria College, which is not itself a teaching college. It provides residential accommodation for women students.

AFFILIATED THEOLOGICAL COLLEGES

The Montreal Diocesan Theological College, 3473 University St., Montreal, P.Q.
Principal, Canon A.C. Capon, M.A., B.D.
The United Theological College of Montreal, 3521 University St., Montreal, P.Q.
Principal, Pierre Goldberger, B.A.
The Presbyterian College of Montreal, 3495 University St., Montreal, P.Q.
Principal, W.J. Klempa, B.A., M.A., B.D., Ph.D.
Note: The above three colleges train students for the Ministry and grant certificates for ordination but they have remitted their degree-granting powers to the University.

Montreal Technical College Inc.

1863 Dorchester W., Montreal, P.Q. H3H 1R4
(514) 932-6444
Director, E. Kefalidis
Administrator, L. Cochrane

Université de Montréal

C.P. 6128, Succ. A, Montréal, P.Q. H3C 3J7
(514) 343-6111

MEMBRES DE L'ADMINISTRATION

Recteur, Paul Lacoste
Vice recteur aux études, Jacques Ménard
Vice recteur à la recherche, René J.A. Lévesque
Vice recteur à l'administration, Jacques Lucier
Vice recteur à la planification, Jacques St-Pierre
Vice recteur aux affaires professorales, Louis-Marie Tremblay
Secrétaire général, Jacques Boucher
Conseiller du recteur en relations universitaires internationales, Roger Gaudry
Directeur des finances, Raymond Chouinard
Registraire, Claude Saint-Arnaud

DOYENS

Faculté de l'aménagement, Colin H. Davidson
Faculté des arts et des sciences, Roland Rivest
Faculté de droit, Yves Ouellette
Faculté de l'éducation permanente, Guy Bourgeault
Faculté des études supérieures, Jacques Brazeau
Faculté de médecine dentaire, Alain Vaillancourt
Faculté de médecine véterinaire, Raymond S. Roy
Faculté de médecine, Yvon Gauthier
Faculté de musique, Henri Favre
Faculté des sciences infirmières, Marie-France Castonguay-Thibaudeau
Faculté de pharmacie, Julien Braun
Faculté des sciences de l'éducation, Jean-Louis Bernard
Faculté de théologie, Léonard Audet
Total: 13 facultés
plus: Département d'éducation physique, Yvan Girardin (dir. int.), et Ecole d'optométrie, Claude Beaulne (rattachés au Comité exécutif)

ECOLES AFFILIEES

Ecole Polytechnique, Roger P. Langlois
Ecole des Hautes Etudes Commerciales, Pierre Laurin

National Theatre School of Canada
Ecole Nationale de Théâtre du Canada

5030 St. Denis St., Montreal, P.Q. H2J 2L8, and 1182 St. Lawrence Blvd., Montreal, P.Q. H2X 2S5
(514) 842-7954
Director General, Richard C. Dennison
Administrative Director, Jean Pol Britte
Artistic Director, English Acting Course, Joel Miller
Artistic Director, French Acting Course, Michelle Rossignol
Director, Production Course, José Descombes

Université du Québec

2875 boul. Laurier, Ste-Foy, Québec, P.Q. G1V 2M3
(418) 657-3551

DIRECTION GENERALE

Président, Gilles Boulet
Vice président, Pierre Cazalis
Vice président aux affaires administratives et financières, Roger Lefrançois
Vice président à l'enseignement et à la recherche, Germain Gauthier
Vice président à la planification et aux communications, Pierre DeCelles
Secrétaire général, J.-P. Fortin
Directeur général des relations publiques, Serge de La Rochelle

UNIVERSITE DU QUEBEC A MONTREAL

C.P. 8888, Stn. B, Montreal, P.Q. H3C 3P8
Recteur, Claude Pichette
Secrétaire général, Pierre Brossard

UNIVERSITE DU QUEBEC A TROIS-RIVIERES

C.P. 500, Trois-Rivières, P.Q. G9A 5H7

Recteur, Louis-Edmond Hamelin
Secrétaire général, André Brousseau

UNIVERSITE DU QUEBEC A CHICOUTIMI
930 est rue Jacques Cartier, Chicoutimi, P.Q. G7H 2B1
Recteur, Gérard Arguin
Secrétaire général, Lucien Gendron

UNIVERSITE DU QUEBEC A RIMOUSKI
300, Ave des Ursulines, Rimouski, P.Q. G5L 3A1
Recteur, Pascal Parent
Secrétaire général, Bertrand Lepage

UNIVERSITE DU QUEBEC A HULL
118 rue Notre Dame, Hull, P.Q. J8X 3X7
Recteur, J.-R. Messier
Secrétaire général et vice recteur à l'administration et aux finances, Luc Chaput

INSTITUT NATIONAL DE LA RECHERCHE SCIENTIFIQUE
2700, rue Einstein, Ste-Foy, P.Q. G1V 4C7
Directeur, André Lemay
Secrétaire général, Guy Reeves

INSTITUT ARMAND-FRAPPIER
531, boul. des Prairies, Ville de Laval, P.Q. H7N 4Z3
Directeur, Aurèle Beaulnes
Secrétaire général, Marcel Préfontaine

ECOLE NATIONALE D'ADMINISTRATION PUBLIQUE
625, rue St-Amable, Québec, P.Q. G1R 2B5
Directeur général, Louis Brunel
Secrétaire général, Serge Raymond

ECOLE DE TECHNOLOGIE SUPERIEURE
180 est, rue Ste-Catherine, Montréal, P.Q. H2X 3M4
Directeur général, Roland-A. Dugré
Secrétaire général, Jocelyn Gagnon

CENTRE D'ETUDES D'ABITIBI-TEMISCAMINGUE
435 rue Gagné, Rouyn, P.Q. J9X 5C6
Directeur, Rémy Trudel

TELE-UNIVERSITE
214, ave St-Sacrement, Québec, P.Q. G1N 4M6
Directeur général, Pierre DeCelles (int.)
Secrétaire général, Robert Brulotte

Selwyn House School
95 Côte St. Antoine, Westmount, P.Q. H3Y 2H8
(514) 931-9481
Headmaster, R. Manion, M.A.

Université de Sherbrooke
2500 Boul. Université, Sherbrooke, P.Q. J1K 2R1
(819) 565-5970

ADMINISTRATION
Recteur, Claude Hamel, B.A., B.Sc.A., M.Sc.A., ing.
Vice recteur à l'enseignement et à la recherche, Gaston Denis, B.A., B.Sc.A., M.S., ing.
Vice recteur à l'administration, (tba)
Vice recteur aux relations avec les personnels et les étudiants, Richard Béland, B.Sc.écon., M.A., Ph.D.
Secrétaire général, Jean-Guy Fréchette, M.A., L.Ph., LL.L., D.E.S., LL.D.
Registraire, Guy Langevin
Directeur des finances, J.-C. Poulin
Public Relations Officer, Marc Bernier
Purchasing Agent, René Dorais
Librarian, Guy Cloutier

DOYENS
Faculté d'administration, Alain Cousineau
Faculté des arts, Jacques Plamondon, B.A., B.Ph., L.Ph., D. 3e cycle
Faculté de droit, Jacques Anctil, LL.L., D.E.S.
Faculté d'éducation, Valérien Harvey, B.Péd., L.Péd., Ph.D.
Faculté d'éducation physique et sportive, J.-G. Ouellet, B.A., M.Sc., Ph.D.
Faculté de médecine, Jean de Margerie, B.A., M.D., D.Phil. (Oxon), C.S.P.Q., F.R.C.S. (C), F.A.C.S.
Faculté des sciences, Aldée Cabana, B.Sc. (chimie), M.Sc. (chimie), Ph.D. (chimie)
Faculté des sciences appliquées, K.C. Johns, B.Eng., Ph.D.
Faculté de théologie, Jacques Fillion, B.A., L.Th.
Ecole de musique, B.J. Ellard, B.Mus., M.A., Ph.D.

DIRECTION GENERALE DE L'EDUCATION PERMANENTE
Directeur général, Robert Routhier, B.A., M.S.S.

AFFILIATED COLLEGE
Collège militaire Royal de Saint-Jean, Col. R.J. Evraire

Stanstead College
Stanstead, P.Q. J0B 3E0
(819) 876-2702
Headmaster, Barry Gallant, M.A.

The Study School
3233 The Boulevard, Montreal, P.Q. H3Y 1S4
(514) 935-9352
Principal, Mrs. Jean Scott, B.A., M.A.T.
Secretary Treasurer, Miss Ellen Goode, B.A.

Trafalgar School for Girls
3495 Simpson St., Montreal, P.Q. H3G 2J7
(514) 935-2644
Principal, Mrs. J. H. Doupe, M.Ed.
Bursar, Mrs. M. Panet-Raymond

Weston School Inc.
124 Ballantyne Ave. S., Montreal W., P.Q. H4X 2B3
(514) 488-9191
Principal, Elizabeth A. Goddard, B.Sc. (Hons.)

TECHNICAL & VOCATIONAL INSTITUTIONS IN QUEBEC

COLLEGES D'ENSEIGNEMENT GENERAL ET PROFESSIONNEL
GENERAL AND VOCATIONAL COLLEGES (C.E.G.E.P.)
Ahuntsic, 9155, rue St-Hubert, Montréal, P.Q. H2M 1Y8, 514/389-5921
Amiante, 671 sud boul. Smith, C.P. 669, Thetford Mines, P.Q. G6G 1N1, 418/338-8591
Andre Laurendeau, 1111, Lapierre, LaSalle, P.Q. H8N 2J4, 514/364-3320
Bois-de-Boulogne, 10555, av. Bois-de-Boulogne, Montréal, P.Q. H4N 1L3, 514/332-3000
Bourgchemin, 2200, ave Léon Pratte, C.P. 9000, St-Hyacinthe, P.Q. J2S 7C7, 514/773-6691
Campus Drummondville, 415, rue des Ecoles, Drummondville, P.Q. J2B 1J3, 819/478-4671
Campus de St-Hyacinthe, 3000, Boullé, St-Hyacinthe, P.Q. J2S 7C7, 514/773-6800
Campus Sorel-Tracy, 95, chemin Ste-Anne, Sorel, P.Q. J3P 1J6, 514/742-4557
Champlain Regional College, 1257 Queen Blvd. N., Box 5000, Sherbrooke, P.Q. J1H 5N1, 819/563-9661
Lennoxville Campus, McGreer Hall, Lennoxville, P.Q. J1M 2A1, 819/563-6881
St. Lambert/Longueuil Campus, 900 Riverside Dr., St. Lambert, P.Q. J4P 3P2, 514/672-7360
St. Lawrence Campus, 790 Nérée Tremblay, Ste-Foy, P.Q. G1V 4K2, 418/656-6921
Dawson, 485 McGill, Montreal, P.Q. H2Y 2H4, 514/931-8731
Edouard-Montpetit, 945, ch. de Chambly, Ville de Longueuil, P.Q. J4H 3M6, 514/679-2630
François-Xavier-Garneau, 1660 boul. Entente, C.P. 6300, Sillery, P.Q. G1T 2S5, 418/688-8310
Gaspésie, rue Jacques Cartier, C.P. 590, Gaspé, P.Q. G0C 1R0, 418/368-2201
Hauterive, 537 boul. Blanche, Hauterive, P.Q. G5C 2B2, 418/589-5707
Campus Mingan (Sept-Iles), 25 de la Verendrye, Sept-Iles, P.Q. G4R 1H2, 418/962-9848

Institut Maritime du Québec, 53 St-Germain est, Rimouski, P.Q. G5L 4B4, 418/724-2822

John Abbott, C.P. 2000, Ste-Anne-de-Bellevue, P.Q. H9X 3L9, 514/457-6610

Joliette, 20 sud, rue St. Charles, Joliette, P.Q. J6E 4T1, 514/759-1661

La Pocatière, 140 40 Ave., La Pocatière, Cté Kamouraska, P.Q. GOR 1ZO, 418/856-1525

Lévis-Lauzon, 205, Mgr Ignace Bourget, Lauzon, P.Q. G6V 6Z9, 418/833-5110

Limoilou, 1300, 8e Ave., C.P. 1400, Quebec, P.Q. G1K 7H3, 418/694-7400

Lionel-Groulx, 100, rue Duquet, Ste-Thérèse-de-Blainville, Cté Terrebonne, P.Q. J7E 3G6, 514/430-3120

Maisonneuve, 3800 est, rue Sherbrooke, Montréal, P.Q. H1X 2A2, 514/254-7131

Matane, 616 ave. St-Rédempteur, Matane, P.Q. G4W 1L1, 418/562-1240

Montmorency, 475 boul. de l'Avenir, Chomedey, Ville Laval, P.Q. H7N 5H9, 514/667-5100

Nord-Ouest (Rouyn-Noranda), 425 boul. du Collège, C.P. 1500, Rouyn, P.Q. J9X 5E5, 819/762-0931

Outaouais (Hull), 333, boul. Cité des Jeunes, C.P. 5220, Succ A, Hull, P.Q. J8Y 6M5, 819/770-4012

Heritage Campus, 124 rue Maisonneuve, C.P. 1757, Hull, P.Q. J8X 3Y8, 819/778-2270

Rimouski, 60 ouest, rue de l'Evêché, Rimouski, P.Q. G5L 4H6, 418/723-1880

Rivière-du-Loup, 8 rue Frontenac, Rivière-du-Loup, P.Q. G5R 1S8, 418/862-6903

Rosemont, 6400, 16e ave., Rosemont, Montreal, P.Q. H1X 2S9, 514/376-1620

Saguenay Lac St-Jean, 218, rue Gilbert, C.P. 850, Jonquière, P.Q. G7S 4R8, 418/548-7191

Collège d'Alma, 675 ouest, boul. Auger, Alma, P.Q. G8B 2B7, 418/668-2381

Collège de Chicoutimi, 534 est, Jacques-Cartier, Chicoutimi, P.Q., 418/549-9520

Collège de Jonquière, 65, rue St-Hubert, Jonquière, P.Q. G7X 7W2, 418/547-2191

Collège de St-Félicien, 1298, rue Leclerc, St-Félicien, P.Q., 418/677-1880

Sainte-Foy, 2410, ch. Ste-Foy, Quebec, P.Q. G1V 1T3, 418/657-3511

Saint-Jean-sur-Richelieu, 30 boul. du Séminaire, St-Jean-sur-Richelieu, C.P. 1018, Cté St-Jean, P.Q. J3B 7B1, 514/347-5301

Saint-Jérôme, 455, rue Fournier, Saint-Jérôme, P.Q. J7Z 4V2, 514/436-1580

Saint-Laurent, 625, boul. Ste-Croix, Ville St-Laurent, Montréal, P.Q. H4L 3X7, 514/747-6521

Shawinigan, 2263, boul. du Collège, C.P. 610, Shawinigan, P.Q. G9N 6V8, 819/539-6401

Sherbrooke, 475, rue du Parc, Sherbrooke, P.Q. J1H 5M7, 819/563-3150

Campus de Granby, 50 St-Joseph, Granby, P.Q. J2G 6T6, 514/372-6614

Trois-Rivières, 3500, rue de Courval, Trois-Rivières, P.Q. G9A 5E6, 819/376-1721

Valleyfield, 169, rue Champlain, C.P. 308, Valleyfield, P.Q. J6T 1K6, 514/373-9441

Vanier, 821 boul. Ste-Croix, St-Laurent, P.Q. H4L 3X9, 514/333-3811

Victoriaville, 475 est, rue Notre-Dame, C.P. 68, Victoriaville, P.Q. G6P 6S4, 819/758-1571

Vieux-Montreal, 255 est, rue Ontario, C.P. 1444, Stn. N, Montréal, P.Q. H2X 3M8, 514/284-7255

PRIVATE COLLEGES & SECONDARY SCHOOLS IN QUEBEC

Le Collège André-Grasset, 1001 est boul. Crémazie, Montréal, P.Q. H2M 1M3, 514/381-4293

Collège Bourget, 65 rue St-Pierre, C.P. 1000, Rigaud, P.Q. J0P 1P0, 514/451-5311

Collège Jean-de-Brébeuf (Pères Jesuites), 3200 ch. Ste-Catherine, Montréal, P.Q. H3T 1C1, 514/342-1320

Collège Jésus-Marie de Sillery, 2047, ch. St-Louis, Sillery, P.Q. G1T 1P3, 418/527-4566

Collège Marie-de-l'Incarnation, 725, rue Hart, Trois-Rivières, P.Q. G9A 4R9, 819/379-3223

Le Collège de Montréal, 1931 ouest rue Sherbrooke, Montréal, P.Q. H3H 1E3, 514/933-7397

Collège Mont-Saint-Louis, 1700 est, boul. Henri-Bourassa, Montréal, P.Q. H2C 1J3, 514/382-1560

Collège du Sacré-Coeur, 155, Belvédère nord, Sherbrooke, P.Q. J1H 4A7, 819/569-9457

Collège de Sainte-Anne de la Pocatière, 100, 4ième Ave., La Pocatière, P.Q. G0R 1Z0, 418/856-3012

Collège Stanislas, 780, boul. Dollard, Outremont, P.Q. H2V 3G5

Ecole Secondaire M.S.C., 50, ave. des Cascades, Beauport, Québec, P.Q. G1E 6B3, 418/661-6978

Grand Séminaire Saint-Thomas d'Aquin, Chicoutimi, P.Q. G7H 4J3, 418/549-2683

Séminaire de Chicoutimi, 679, Chabanel, Chicoutimi, P.Q. G7H 1Z7, 418/549-1138

Séminaire de Québec, C.P. 460, Québec, P.Q. G1R 4R7, 418/692-3981

Séminaire de Sherbrooke, 195 rue Marquette, Sherbrooke, P.Q. J1H 1L6, 819/563-2050

Séminaire Saint-Alphonse, (Pères Rédemptoristes), Ste-Anne-de-Beaupré, P.Q. G0A 3C0, 418/827-2751

Séminaire Saint-Joseph, Trois-Rivières, P.Q. G9A 5J1, 819/376-4459

Ecole Secondaire Saint-Sacrement, 901 rue St-Louis, Terrebonne, P.Q. J6W 1K1, 514/471-6615

SASKATCHEWAN BOARDS OF EDUCATION

Saskatchewan Schools are organized as below.

Public school divisions	88
Roman Catholic Separate school divisions	25
High school divisions	1
Municipal Corporation of Uranium City and District	1
	115

Under The Education Act, proclaimed 1979, school units and independent school districts became school divisions. All high school districts, with one exception, and all school districts in school units ceased to exist.

The members of school divisions are elected for a term of three years on the fourth Wednesday in October. For divisions situated wholly or in part within a town or city, elections are conducted by the town or city clerk. Elections in the other divisions are conducted by a returning officer appointed by the board of education.

For Department of Education officials, see government listings.

Following are School Boards in Cities:

Moose Jaw Separate School Board of Education

Box 1087, Moose Jaw, Sask. S6H 4P8
(306) 692-6419
Secretary Treasurer, J. Hataley
Director, B. A. Wittman
Chief Purchasing Agent, J. Hataley

Board of Education, Moose Jaw School Division No. 1

1075 Ninth Ave. N.W., Moose Jaw, Sask. S6H 4J6
(306) 693-4631
Secretary Treasurer, G. A. Parr
Director, R. E. Stephenson
Deputy Director, R. D. Thiessen
Program Development Officer, Divisions I & II, Barclay J.S. Cant

Program Development Officer, Divisions III & IV, John D. Livingston

Prince Albert Roman Catholic School Division No. 6
717 MacArthur Dr., Prince Albert, Sask. S6V 5X6
(306) 763-7461
Secretary Treasurer, W. E. Rodych
Director of Education, Leonard Donais
Business Manager, W. E. Rodych
Supervisor of Maintenance, B. Carlson

Prince Albert School Division No. 3
140 14th St. W., Prince Albert, Sask. S6V 3L2
(306) 764-1571
Director of Education, D.L. Hockley
Secretary Treasurer, V. UnRuh
Supt. of Education, G.A. Streeton
Director of Guidance & Special Education, T. L. Dice
Consultant, Special Education Section, Mrs. B. Butt
Consultant, Primary Section, Mrs. J. Bell
Consultant, Fine Arts Section, W.D. Stewart
Consultant, Outdoor & Physical Education Section, W.P. Mossman
Co-ordinator of Library Services, C.E. Lutkin
Supervisor of Facilities, D.G. Tornquist

Regina Public School Division No. 4
1600 4th Ave., Regina, Sask. S4R 8C8
(306) 569-3610
Director of Education, J. A. Burnett
Secretary Treasurer, W.B. Knoll
Supt., Program Development, A. Robb
Supt., Instruction, H. Braun
Supt., Educational Facilities, V.J. Gross
Asst. Supts., M.C.J. Boon, Mrs. K.M. Holm, E. Kucey, M. Popp, I.G. Wright
Asst. Supt., Business Affairs, S. Stirr
Asst. Supt., Personnel, R.A.H. Brown

Regina Roman Catholic Separate School Division No. 81
2160 Cameron St., Regina, Sask. S4T 2V6
(306) 525-0591
Secretary Treasurer, Inez A. Benesh
Director of Education, W. A. Herle
Supt. of Instruction, J.A. Holash
Supt. of Support & Special Services, R.J. Tourigny
Supt. of Educational Facilities, J.J. Hoffart

Saskatoon Board of Education Division No. 13
405 Third Ave. S., Saskatoon, Sask. S7K 1M7
(306) 244-2211
Director of Education, Dr. R.G. Fast
Executive Asst., W.G. Bender
Supt. of Schools (Secondary), Dr. R.B. Earl
Asst. Supts. (Secondary), M.R. Houghton, E.W. Robertson
Supt. of Schools (Elementary), Dr. M.J. Kindrachuk
Asst. Supts. (Elementary), Dr. D.R. Hill, R.F. Dilts, Mrs. P.J. Dickson
Supt. of Planning, Development & Research, Dr. D.L. Hicks
Asst. Supts. (Planning, Development & Research), Dr. D.H. Gleave, W. Krynowsky
Supt. of Business & Administration, Dr. H.O. Langlois
Secretary of the School Division & Internal Auditor, R.W. Walter
Asst. Supt. of Personnel, D.M. Keith
Asst. Supt. of Facilities, S.J. Warder

Swift Current Comprehensive High School Board
191-2nd Ave. N.E., Swift Current, Sask. S9H 3C6
(306) 773-9328
Director of Education, B. Ward
Supt. of Education, David McCabe
Business Administrator, C.D. Belter

Swift Current School Division No. 94
191-2nd Ave. N.E., Swift Current, Sask. S9H 2C6
(306) 773-9328
Director of Education, B. Ward
Supt. of Education, David McCabe
Business Administrator, C.D. Belter

REGIONAL SERVICES DIVISION, SASKATCHEWAN DEPARTMENT OF EDUCATION
Regional Directors of Education, S. Krochak, S.J. Malach, D.R. Henderson, W. Kalmakoff, Dr. D.G. Drozda, G.M. Baxter, O. Reiman
Supts. of Education (assigned to regional offices, and in charge of small school divisions and private schools): R.A. Allison, L.D. Keith, I.J. Church

POST SECONDARY & PRIVATE INSTITUTIONS IN SASKATCHEWAN

Art Schools

COLLEGE OF FINE ARTS, DEPT. OF VISUAL ARTS
Univ. of Regina, Regina, Sask. S4S 0A2
(306) 584-4872
President, L.I. Barber, O.C., B.A., B.Comm., M.B.A., D.B.A.
Assoc. Dean, Fine Arts, R.J.W. Swales, Ph.D.
Dept. Head, R.V.J. Gomez
Director, Norman Mackenzie Art Gallery, Ms. Carol Phillips, B.A. (act.)
Registrar, N. A. Stables, B.Comm., C.A.
Librarian, S. Harland, B.A., M.A., F.L.A.
Controller, S. G. Mann, B.A., B.Comm.

Aldersgate College
Box 460, Moose Jaw, Sask. S6H 4P1
(306) 693-7773
President, Dr. J. Leon Winslow
Dean of Academic, D.N. Ashton
Dean of Students, Rev. Ken Burton
Asst. to President in Development, E.R. Parkins

AFFILIATED COLLEGES
Seattle Pacific University, Seattle, Wash.
President, David L. McKenna
Spring Arbor College, Spring Arbor, Mich.
President, K.H. Coffman
Greenville College, Greenville, Ill.
President, W. Richard Stephens
Roberts Wesleyan College, Rochester, N.Y.
President, William Carothers

Athol Murray College of Notre Dame
Box 220, Wilcox, Sask. SOG 5EO
(306) 732-2080
(Residential, co-educational, inter-denominational; grades 9 through 12)
Chairman, Board of Regents, Murray R. Maynard
Chancellor, Frederick W. Hill
President, R. Martin Kenney
Registrar, Frank Germann

Campion College
Univ. of Regina, Regina, Sask. S4S OA2
(306) 586-4242
President, Jos. B. Gavin, S.J., B.A., M.A., Ph.L., S.T.L., Ph.D.
Dean, Thomas O'D. Hanley, S.J., B.A., B.Sc., Lic. Phil., Ph.D.
Business Manager, F. Marcia

Collège Mathieu
Gravelbourg, Sask. S0H 1X0
(306) 648-3105

Saskatchewan's only French High School with boarding facilities for boys and girls.
Chairman of the Board, Clotaire Denis
Vice Chairman, Gilles Piché
Executive Administrator, Réal Forest
Principal, A. Moquin
Bursar & Secretary Treasurer, Jeanne Beauregard
Dean of Students, Louis Morin

University of Emmanuel College The College of Emmanuel & St. Chad

Saskatoon, Sask. S7N 0W6
(306) 343-3030
Visitor, His Excellency, the Governor General of Canada
Chancellor, Rt. Rev. D.A. Ford, Bishop of Saskatoon
Principal & Vice Chancellor, (tba)
Vice Principal, Dr. D.R. Mawer, M.A., Ph.D.
Bursar, John Avant, B.Acc., F.I.A.
President of the Council, The Rt. Rev. M. Peers, Bishop of Qu'-Appelle
Information Officer, & Registrar, Mrs. Patricia Bays, B.A., M.A., S.T.B.
Librarian, Ms. R. Ho, M.L.S.

Luther College

Univ. of Regina, Regina, Sask. S4S 0A2
(306) 584-0255
Chairman of the Board, Harold Dietrich
President, Dr. Morris A. Anderson
Academic Dean, Dr. R.E. Miller
Co-ordinator of Student Services, Sr. Anne Keffer
Business Manager, Rein Sommerfeld
Director of Admissions, David Boesch

Lutheran Collegiate Bible Institute

Outlook, Sask. S0L 2N0
(306) 867-8971
President, Rev. G. Hoeflicker, B.A., M.Div.
Business Manager, Rev. A. N. Solheim, B.A., B.D.
High School Principal, R. Blacklock, B.A., M.A.

The University of Regina

Regina, Sask. S4S 0A2
(306) 584-4402 (Public Relations)
Visitor, The Honourable, The Lt.-Gov. of Saskatchewan C. Irwin McIntosh, K.St.J.
Chairman, Board of Governors, J.G. Wicijowski, B.Comm., F.C.A.
Chancellor, Hon. Judge A. Raynell Andreychuk, B.A., LL.B.
President & Vice Chancellor, Lloyd I. Barber, O.C., B.A., B.Comm., M.B.A., Ph.D.
A/Vice President, D.E. Shaw, B.Comm., M.A., Ph.D.
University Secretary, D. T. Lowery, B.Comm., C.A., R.I.A.
Controller, Stuart G. Mann, B.A., B.Comm.
Registrar, Nowell A. Stables, B.Comm., C.A.
Director of Physical Plant, Donald A. Larmour, B.E.
Director of University Services, R.R.F. Carter, R.I.A.
Librarian, Sidney Harland, B.A., M.A., F.L.A.
Dean of Arts, R. R. Robinson, B.A., D.Phil.
Assoc. Dean of Fine Arts, Robin Swales, B.A., Ph.D.
Dean of Education, G.E. Richert, B.Ed. M.Ed., Ph.D.
Dean of Graduate Studies, C.W. Blachford, B.E., M.S., Ph.D.
Dean of Engineering, W.B.H. Cooke, B.A.Sc., M.Sc., Ph.D.
A/Dean of Admin., M.R. Hutchings, B.A., M.B.A.
Dean of Science, W. B. McConnell, B.Sc., M.Sc., Ph.D.
Dean of Social Work, O.H. Driedger, B.Ch.Ed., B.A., M.S.W.
Director, School of Human Justice Services, P.L. Havemann, LL.B., LL.M.
Dean of Student Services, R.H. Archer, B.A., Ph.D.
Director, Bilingual Centre, Anita T. Dubé, B.Ed., M.A.T.
Director, Canadian Plains Research Centre, M. Evelyn Jonescu, B.A., B.Ed., M.A., Ph.D.
Director, Conservatory of Music, H. Leyton-Brown, D.F.C., Dip.Mus., F.G.S.M.
Director, Dept. of Physical Education, Neil B. Sherlock, B.Ed., M.Sc. in Phys. Ed.
Director, Norman Mackenzie Art Gallery, Carol Phillips (act.)
Dean of Extension, H. Kindred, B.E., B.Ed., M.Ed.
Director, Regina Energy Research Institute, L.W. Vigrass, B.E., M.Sc., Ph.D.
Director, Counselling Services, Charles Jillings, B.A., M.A. (act.)
Director, Regina Water Research Institute, Donald R. Cullimore, B.Sc., Ph.D.
Budget Officer, D.G. Bamford, B.Comm., M.A.
Director, Personnel Services, Miss J.M. Blake, B.A.
Manager, Dept. of Computing Services, C.C. Turnbull, B.A., M.A.
Director, Public Relations, Lyn Goldman, M.A., A.P.R.
Co-ordinator, Institutional Research, D. Neil Southam, B.E., M.Sc., B.Ed., B.A., R.I.A.

FEDERATED COLLEGES

Campion College
President, Joseph B. Gavin, S.J., B.A., Ph.L., M.A., M.A.Th., S.T.L., Ph.D.
Luther College
President, M. Anderson, B.A., B.Ed., M.A., LL.D.
Saskatchewan Indian Federated College
Director, Ida Wasacase

AFFILIATED COLLEGES

Canadian Theological College, Regina
President, David L. Rambo, B.S., M.A., M.Div., Ph.D.

Rosthern Junior College

-not confirmed for 1982-
Rosthern, Sask. S0K 3R0
(306) 232-4222
Principal, David Winter
Secretary, Bev Janzen

University of Saskatchewan

Saskatoon, Sask. S7N 0W0
(306) 343-2100
Visitor, The Hon. the Lt.-Gov. of Sask.
Chancellor, The Hon. Emmett M. Hall, C.C., Q.C., LL.D., D.C.L., D.Med.
Chairman, Board of Governors, Christine Pastershank, B.A.
President, L.F. Kristjanson, B.A., M.A., Ph.D.
Vice President (Academic), M.A. Preston, B.A., M.A., Ph.D., F.R.S.C.
Vice President (Admin.), E.B. Tinker, B.E., M.Sc., Ph.D.
Vice President (Special Projects), B.A. Holmlund, B.E., M.Sc.
University Secretary, N. K. Cram, C.D., B.A., B.Ed.
Registrar, J. A. Dorgan, B.S.A.
Controller, M.G. Sheppard, B. Comm., C.A., F.C.A.
Librarian, Nancy Brown, B.Sc., B.L.S., M.L.S., M.B.A.

FACULTIES WITH DEANS

Graduate Studies, K. J. McCallum
Agriculture, J. A. Brown
Arts & Science, (tba)
Commerce, P. Michael Maher
Dentistry, E.R. Ambrose
Education, (tba)
Engineering, P. N. Nikiforuk
Home Economics, T.J. Abernathy
Law, Donald H. Clark
Medicine, R. G. Murray
Nursing, Una Ridley
Pharmacy, Bruce Schnell
Physical Education, John Dewar
Veterinary Medicine, N. O. Nielsen

SCHOOLS WITH DIRECTORS

Physical Therapy, Victor Cottrell
Agriculture, J. R. Peters
Religious Studies, R. W. Nostbakken

AFFILIATED COLLEGES
College of Emmanuel and St. Chad
Principal, (tba)
Lutheran Theological Seminary, Saskatoon, Sask.
President, Dr. Wm. Hordern
St. Andrew's College, Saskatoon, Sask.
President, Rev. J.R. Donnelly
St. Peter's College, Muenster, Sask.
Principal, Rev. A.M. Britz

FEDERATED COLLEGE
St. Thomas More College, Saskatoon, Sask.
President, Rev. Leonard Kennedy

Western Christian College
North Weyburn, Sask. S0C 1X0
(306) 842-6551
President, Max D. Mowrer
Principal & Dean, E.D. Wieb
Librarian, M. Ensley
Bookstore Manager, Miss A. Tetreau

COMMUNITY COLLEGES, TECHNICAL & VOCATIONAL INSTITUTIONS—SASKATCHEWAN
Kesley Institute of Applied Arts & Sciences, Idylwyld Dr. & 33rd St., Saskatoon, Sask. S7K 3R5, 306/664-6350
Principal, K. P. Gunn
Saskatchewan Technical Institute, Saskatchewan St. & 6th Ave. N.W., Moose Jaw, Sask. S6H 4R4, 306/693-8221
Principal, A.J. Nicol
Wascana Institute of Applied Arts & Sciences, 4635 Wascana Pkwy., Regina, Sask. S4P 3A3, 306/565-4356
Principal, R. L. Meyer
Meadow Lake Regional Vocational Centre, Meadow Lake, Sask. S0M 1V0, 306/236-5683
Principal, B. Denluck

COMMUNITY COLLEGES
Carlton Trail Community College, 623 7th St., Box 720, Humboldt, Sask. S0K 2A0, 306/682-2623
Principal, Lorne Johnson
Coteau Range Community College, 637 Main St. N., Box 1329, Moose Jaw, Sask. S6H 4R3, 306/692-6431
Principal, Bill Nosen
Cumberland Community College, Box 2225, Nipawin, Sask. S0E 1E0, 306/862-9833
Principal, J.H. Battye
Cypress Hills Community College, 197 4th Ave. N.W., Swift Current, Sask. S9H 0T7, 306/773-1531
Principal, Dr. A. Gelowitz
Lakeland College, 4420 50th Ave., Lloydminster, Alta. T9V 0W2, 403/875-8828
President, R.V. Murray
La Ronge Region Community College, Box 509, La Ronge, Sask. S0J 1L0, 306/425-2480
Principal, Keith Goulet
Mistikwa Community College, 1381 101 St., Box 1360, North Battleford, Sask. S9A 3L8, 306/445-6288
Principal, Mrs. Jean Sternig (act.)
Natonum Community College, 1695 17th St. W., Prince Albert, Sask. S6V 6W2, 306/764-6671
Principal, Mel Curniski
Parkland Community College, 332 Main St., Box 790, Melville, Sask. S0A 2P0, 306/728-4471
Principal, Dr. Peter Hettinga
Prairie West Community College, Box 700, Biggar, Sask. S0K 0M0, 306/748-3363
Principal, Ron Parsons
Regina Plains Community College, 1801 Broad St., Regina, Sask. S4P 1X7, 306/569-3811
Principal, F. Harland
Sask. Indian Community College, 1030 Idylwyld Dr. N., Box 3085, Saskatoon, Sask. S7K 3S9, 306/244-4444
Principal, Oliver Cameron
Saskatoon Region Community College, 230 23rd St. E., Saskatoon, Sask. S7K 0J4, 306/244-1114
Principal, Betty Pepper
South East Region Community College, 22 Third St. N.E., Box 880, Weyburn, Sask. S4H 2L1, 306/842-7417
Principal, A. Yeaman
West Side Community College, Box 89, Beauval, Sask. S0M 0G0, 306/288-2113
Principal, Morris Onyskevitch

EDUCATION IN YUKON TERRITORY
HEAD OFFICE ADMINISTRATION
Supt. of Education, T.A. Weninger
Asst. Supt. of Education, D.A. Pritchard
Regional Supt. of Schools (Urban), D. Courtice
Asst. Regional Supt. of Schools (Urban), H. Weigel
Regional Supt. of Schools (Rural-North), D. Odin
Regional Supt. of Schools (Rural-South), J. Davis
Supt. of Curriculum & Instructional Services, W.O. Ferguson
Supervisor of Special Education, G. Rodney
Supervisor of Primary Instruction, J. McCrie
Director of Adult & Continuing Education, D. Roberts
Industrial Training Co-ordinator, K. Smith
Director of Recreation, B. Robb
Recreation Consultant, R. McCullough
Administrative Officer, S. Cawley
School Services Inspector, A. Fedoriak
Co-ordinator of French Language Program, M. Almstrom
Manpower Planning Co-ordinator, D. Sinclair
Co-ordinator, Women's Bureau, S. Rea
Manpower Development Officer, D. Dornian

EDUCATION IN NORTH WEST TERRITORIES
HEADQUARTERS
Deputy Minister of Education, B. Lewis
Asst. Deputy Minister (Planning), G. Mulders
Asst. Deputy Minister (Programs), F. Carnew
Registrar, J. Walker
Chief Financial Officer, C. MacKillop

HOSPITALS IN CANADA

Government Departments in Charge
ALBERTA:–Dept. of Hospitals & Medical Care, 420 Legislative Bldg., Edmonton, Alta. T5K 2B6 (403/427-3665)
Hospitals Section, 11010 101st St. (Hys Centre), Edmonton, Alta. T5J 2P4 (403/427-6093)
BRITISH COLUMBIA:–Ministry of Health, Hospital Programs, Parliament Bldgs., Victoria, B.C. V8V 1X4 (604/387-1066)
MANITOBA:–Dept. of Health, Education & Library Services Branch, 880 Portage Ave., Winnipeg, Man. R3G 0P1 (204/775-8682)
NEW BRUNSWICK:–Dept. of Health, Box 6000, Fredericton, N.B. E3B 5H1 (506/453-2542)
NEWFOUNDLAND:–Dept. of Health, Confederation Bldg., St. John's, Nfld. A1C 5T7 (709/737-3106)
NOVA SCOTIA:–Dept. of Health, Joseph Howe Bldg., Box 488, Halifax, N.S. B3J 2R8 (902/424-4310)
ONTARIO:–Ministry of Health, 10th floor, Hepburn Block, Queen's Park, Toronto, Ont. M7A 2C4 (416/965-5167)
PRINCE EDWARD ISLAND:–Dept. of Health & Social Services, Health Branch, Box 3000, Charlottetown, P.E.I. C1A 7P1 (902/892-5471)
QUEBEC:–Dept. of Social Affairs, 1075 Ste-Foy Rd., Quebec, P.Q. G1S 2M1 (418/643-4095)

SASKATCHEWAN:–Saskatchewan Health, 3475 Albert St., Regina, Sask. S4S 6X6 (306/565-3269)

ALBERTA

General Hospitals in Alberta

Athabasca - Athabasca Municipal Hospital, Box 240, TOG OBO, 403/675-2272

Banff - Mineral Springs Hospital, Box 1050, TOL OCO, 403/762-2222

Barrhead - Barrhead General Hospital, Box 880, TOG OEO, 403/674-2221

Bashaw - Bashaw General Hospital, Box 449, TOB OHO, 403/372-3731

Bassano - Bassano General Hospital, Box 120, TOJ OBO, 403/472-3520

Beaverlodge - Beaverlodge Municipal Hospital, Box 480, TOH OCO, 403/354-2136

Bentley - Bentley General Hospital, 4834 52 Ave., TOC OJO, 403/748-4115

Berwyn - Berwyn Municipal Hospital, Box 154, TOH OEO, 403/338-3926

Blairmore - Crowsnest Pass General Hospital, Box 510, TOK OEO, 403/562-2831

Bonnyville - St. Louis Hospital, Box 68, TOA OLO, 403/826-3311

Bow Island - Bow Island General Hospital, Box 399, TOK OGO, 403/545-2211

Boyle - Boyle General Hospital, Box 330, TOA OMO, 403/689-3731

Breton - Breton General Hospital, Box 340, TOC OPO, 403/696-3731

Brooks - Brooks Health Care Centre, Bag 300, TOJ OJO, 403/362-3456

Calgary - Southern Alberta Cancer Centre, 2104 2nd St. S.W., T2S 1S5, 403/263-0770

Calgary - Alberta Children's Provincial General Hospital, 1820 Richmond St. W., T2T 5C7, 403/245-7211

Calgary - Calgary General Hospital, 841 Centre Ave. E., T2E OA1, 403/268-9111

Calgary - Colonel Belcher Hospital, 1213 4th St. S.W.(address General Correspondence to: Metro Calgary & Rural General Hospital District #93, 940 8th Ave. S.W.), 403/264-1850

Calgary - Foothills Provincial General Hospital, 1403 29th St. N.W., T2N 2T9, 403/270-1110

Calgary - Holy Cross Hospital, 2210 2nd St. S.W. (address General Correspondence to: Metro Calgary & Rural General Hospital District #93, 940 8th Ave. S.W., 403/254-9880)

Calgary - Rockyview General Hospital, 7007 14th St. S.W. (address correspondence as above)

Calgary - Salvation Army Grace Hospital, 1402 8th Ave. N.W., T2N 1B9, 403/284-1141

Camrose - St. Mary's Hospital, 4607 53 St., T4V 1Y5, 403/672-4401

Canmore - Canmore Municipal Hospital, TOL OMO, 403/678-5536

Cardston - Cardston Municipal Hospital, 150 1st Ave. W., Box 310, TOK OKO, 403/653-4411

Carmangay - Little Bow Municipal Hospital, Box 160, TOL ONO, 403/643-3522

Castor - Our Lady of the Rosary Hospital, Box 329, TOC OXO, 403/882-3434

Cereal - Cereal Municipal Hospital, Box 39, TOJ ONO, 403/326-3838

Claresholm - Claresholm General Hospital, Box 610, TOL OTO, 403/625-3344

Coaldale - Coaldale Community Hospital, Box 1268, TOK OLO, 403/345-3777

Cold Lake - John Neil Hospital, Box 128, TOK OVO, 403/639-3322

Consort - Consort Municipal Hospital, Box 310, TOC 1BO, 403/577-3555

Coronation - Coronation Municipal Hospital, Box 250, TOC 1CO, 403/578-3803

Daysland - Daysland General Hospital, Box 27, TOB 1AO, 403/374-3746

Devon - Devon Civic Hospital, Box 438, TOC 1EO, 403/987-2191

Didsbury - Didsbury Municipal Hospital, Box 130, TOM OWO, 403/335-3414

Drayton Valley - Drayton Valley General Hospital, Box 838, TOE OMO, 403/542-5321

Drumheller - Drumheller General Hospital, Box 4500, TOJ OYO, 403/823-6500

Eckville - Eckville Municipal Hospital, Box 150, TOM OXO, 403/746-2201

Edmonton - Charles Camsell Hospital, 12815 115 Ave., T5M 3A4, 403/452-8770

Edmonton - Dr. W.W. Cross Cancer Institute, 11560 University Ave., T6G 1Z2, 403/432-8771

Edmonton - Edmonton General Hospital, 11111 Jasper Ave., T5K OL4, 403/482-4421

Edmonton - Glenrose Provincial Hospital, 10230 111 Ave., T5G OB7, 403/474-5451

Edmonton - Misericordia Hospital, 16940 87 Ave., T5R 4H5, 403/484-8811

Edmonton - Royal Alexandra Hospital, 10240 Kingsway Ave., T5H 3V9, 403/477-9601

Edmonton - University of Alberta Hospital, 8440 112 St., T6G 2B7, 403/432-8822

Edson - St. John's Hospital, Box 1810, TOE OPO, 403/723-3331

Elk Point - Elk Point Municipal Hospital, Box 9, TOA 1AO, 403/724-3847

Elnora - Elnora General Hospital, Box 659, TOM OYO, 403/773-3636

Empress - Empress Municipal Hospital, Box 159, TOJ 1EO, 403/565-3777

Fairview - Fairview General Hospital, Box 2201, TOH 1LO, 403/835-4941

Fort Macleod - Macleod Municipal Hospital, Box 520, TOL OZO, 403/553-4024

Fort McMurray - Fort McMurray Regional Hospital, #7 Hospital St., T9H 1P2, 403/791-6161

Fort Saskatchewan - Fort Saskatchewan General Hospital, 9430 95 St., T8L 1R8, 403/998-2256

Fort Vermilion - St. Theresa General Hospital, TOH 1NO, 403/927-3761 (mail to: Bag 400, High Level, Alta. TOH 1ZO)

Galahad - Galahad General Hospital, Box 88, TOB 1RO, 403/583-3788

Glendon - Glendon Municipal Hospital, Box 180, TOA 1PO, 403/635-3861

Grande Cache - Grande Cache General Hospital, Box 629, TOE OYO, 403/827-3701

Grande Prairie - Grande Prairie General Hospital, 10409 98 St., T8V 2E8, 403/532-7711

Hanna - Hanna General Hospital, Box 730, TOJ 1PO, 403/854-3331

Hardisty - Hardisty General Hospital, Box 269, TOB 1VO, 403/888-3742

High Level - High Level Community Health Centre, Bag 400, TOH 1ZO, 403/926-3791

High Prairie - High Prairie Regional Health Complex, TOG 1EO, 403/523-3341

High River - High River General Hospital, PO Bag 30, TOL 1BO, 403/652-2321

Hinton - Hinton General Hospital, 1280 Switzer Dr., TOE 1BO, 403/865-3333

Hythe - Hythe Municipal Hospital, Box 207, TOH 2CO, 403/356-3818

Innisfail - Innisfail General Hospital, Box 250, TOM 1AO, 403/227-3381

Islay - Islay Municipal Hospital, Box 55, TOB 2JO, 403/744-3795

Jasper - Seton General Hospital, Box 310, TOE 1EO, 403/852-3344

Killam - Killam General Hospital, TOB 2LO, 403/385-3741

Lac La Biche - Lac La Biche General Hospital, Box 507, TOA 2CO, 403/623-4404

Lacombe - Lacombe General Hospital, Box 1450, TOC 1SO, 403/782-3336
Lamont - Archer Memorial Hospital, TOB 2RO, 403/895-2211
Leduc - Leduc General Hospital, Box 550, T9E 1P2, 403/986-2231
Lethbridge - Lethbridge Municipal Hospital, 1802 9th Ave. S., T1J 1W5, 403/327-4531
Lethbridge - St. Michael's General Hospital, 1315 9th Ave. 'A' S., T1J 1X7, 403/327-1531
Lloydminster - Lloydminster Hospital, 4611 48 Ave., S9V OZ5, 306/825-2211
McLennan - Sacred Heart Hospital, Box 390, TOH 2LO, 403/324-3730
Magrath - Magrath Municipal Hospital, Box 550, TOK 1JO, 403/758-3214
Manning - Manning Municipal Hospital, Box 250, TOH 2MO, 403/836-3391
Mannville - Manville Municipal Hospital, Box 180, TOB 2WO, 403/763-3621
Mayerthorpe - Mayerthorpe General Hospital, Box 30, TOE 1NO, 403/786-2030
Medicine Hat - Medicine Hat & District Hospital, 666 5 St. S.W., T1A 4H6, 403/527-2211
Milk River - Border Counties General Hospital, Box 90, TOK 1MO, 403/647-3500
Mundare - Mary Immaculate Hospital, Box 349, TOB 3HO, 403/764-3730
Myrnam - Myrnam Municipal Hospital, TOB 3KO, 403/366-3870
Olds - Olds Municipal Hospital, Box 398, 403/556-3381
Oyen - Big Country Hospital, Box 150, TOJ 2JO, 403/664-3526
Peace River - Peace River Hospital Complex, Box 400, TOH 2XO, 403/624-2551
Picture Butte - Picture Butte Municipal Hospital, Box 430, TOK 1VO, 403/732-4611
Pincher Creek - Pincher Creek Municipal Hospital, Box 968, TOK 1WO, 403/627-3333
Ponoka - Ponoka General Hospital, Box 699, TOC 2HO, 403/783-3341
Provost - Provost Municipal Health Care Centre, Box 270, TOB 3SO, 403/753-2291
Raymond - Raymond Municipal Hospital, Box 599, TOK 2SO, 403/752-3357
Red Deer - Red Deer Regional Hospital Centre, 3942 50 A Ave., T4N 4E7, 403/343-4422
Redwater - Redwater General Hospital, Box 39, TOA 2WO, 403/429-4533
Rimbey - Rimbey General Hospital, Box 440, TOC 2JO, 403/843-2271
Rocky Mountain House - Rocky Mountain House General Hospital, Box 940, TOM 1TO, 403/845-3347
St. Albert - Sturgeon General Hospital, 78 McKenney Ave., T8N 1L9, 403/459-5501
St. Paul - St. Therese General Hospital, Box 880, TOA 3AO, 403/645-3331
Slave Lake - Slave Lake General Hospital, Box 330, TOG 2AO, 403/849-3732
Smoky Lake - George McDougall Memorial Hospital, Box 340, TOA 3CO, 403/656-3858
Spirit River - Central Peace General Hospital, Box 339, TOH 3GO, 403/864-3993
Stettler - Stettler General Hospital, Bag 500, TOC 2LO, 403/742-3321
Stony Plain - Stony Plain Municipal Hospital, Box 300, TOE 2GO, 403/963-2241
Sundre - Sundre General Hospital, Box 269, TOM 1XO, 403/638-3033
Taber - Taber General Hospital, Box 939, TOK 2GO, 403/223-4461
Three Hills - Three Hills Municipal Hospital, Box 340, TOM 2AO, 403/443-5232
Tofield - Tofield Municipal Hospital, Box 300, TOB 4JO, 403/662-3263
Trochu - St. Mary's Hospital, Box 100, TOM 2CO, 403/442-3955
Turner Valley - Turner Valley Municipal Hospital, Box 148, TOL 2AO, 403/933-4331
Two Hills - Two Hills Municipal Hospital, Box 160, TOB 4KO, 403/657-3344
Valleyview - Valleyview General Hospital, Box 358, TOH 3NO, 403/524-3356
Vegreville - St. Joseph's General Hospital, 5241 43 St., TOB 4LO, 403/632-2811
Vermilion - Vermilion Municipal Hospital, Box 1050, TOB 4MO, 403/853-5305
Viking - Viking General Hospital, Box 60, TOB 4NO, 403/336-4786
Vilna - Our Lady's Hospital, TOA 3LO, 403/636-3533
Vulcan - Vulcan Municipal Hospital, Box 299, TOL 2BO, 403/485-2206
Wainright - Wainright General Hospital, Box 820, TOB 4PO, 403/842-3324
Westlock - Immaculata Hospital, Box 1590, TOG 2LO, 403/349-3301
Wetaskiwin - Wetaskiwin General Hospital, 5505 50 Ave., T9A OT4, 403/352-3371
Whitecourt - Whitecourt General Hospital, Box 1080, TOE 2LO, 403/778-2285
Willingdon - Mary Immaculate Hospital, Box 179, TOB 4RO, 403/367-2288

Auxiliary Hospitals in Alberta

Calgary - Bethany Care Centre, 916 18A St. N.W., T2N 1C6, 403/289-3701
Calgary - *Cross Bow Auxiliary Hospital, 1011 Centre Ave. E., T2E OA3, 403/265-0220
Calgary - *Dr. Vernon Fanning Extended Care Centre, 722 16th Ave. N.E., T2E 6V7, 403/276-8551
Calgary - *Glenmore Park Auxiliary Hospital, 6909 14 St. S.W., T2V 1P6, 403/253-1131
Calgary - *Sarcee Auxiliary Hospital, 3504 29 St. S.W., T3E 2L3, 403/249-3146
Camrose - Bethany Auxiliary Hospital, 4501 47 St., T4V 1H9, 403/672-3176
Claresholm - Willow Creek Claresholm Auxiliary Hospital, 5202 5th St. E., TOL OTO, 403/235-3789
Didsbury - Mountain View Kneehill Auxiliary Hospital, Box 130, TOM OWO, 403/335-3533
Drumheller - J. Cramer Auxiliary Hospital, Box 1360, TOJ OYO, 403/823-5151
Edmonton - Allen Gray Auxiliary Hospital, 7510 89 St., T6C 3J8, 403/469-2371
Edmonton - Good Samaritan Hospital, 9649 71 Ave., T6E 5J2, 403/439-6381
Edmonton - *Dickinsfield Extended Care Centre, 14225 94 St., T5E 6C6, 403/478-9221
Edmonton - *Grandview Extended Care Centre, 6515 124 St., T6H 3V1, 403/436-4130
Edmonton - *Lynnwood Extended Care Centre, 8740 165 St., T5G 2R8, 403/489-7771
Edmonton - *Norwood Extended Care Centre, 11135 105 St., T5G 2M3, 403/474-5441
Edmonton - St. Joseph's Hospital, 107 St. & 82 Ave., T6E 2A8, 403/433-5831
Edmonton - Edmonton Veterans Home, 11440 University Ave., T6G 1Z1, 403/336-6401
Grande Prairie - Grande Prairie Auxiliary Hospital, 10409 98 St., T8V 2E8, 403/532-7711
Killam - Flagstaff Auxiliary Hospital, TOB 2LO, 403/385-3741
Lamont - Lamont Auxiliary Hospital, TOB 2RO, 403/895-2621
Lethbridge - Lethbridge Rehabilitation Hospital, 935 17th St. S., T1J 3E4, 403/328-5571
Lloydminster - Lloydminster Auxiliary Hospital, Box 1007, S9V OZ7, 306/875-2291
Medicine Hat - Medicine Hat & Dist. Hospital (Auxiliary Centre), Box 998, T1A 7H1, 403/527-2211
Peace River - Peace River Auxiliary Hospital, Box 400, TOH 2XO, 403/624-2551
Radway - Radway Health Care Centre, T0A 2V0, 403/736-3740

Red Deer - Dr. Richard Parsons Auxiliary Hospital, 3942 50A Ave., T4N 4E7, 403/343-4422
Rimbey - Rimbey Auxiliary Hospital, Box 440, TOC 2JO, 403/843-2626
Stettler - Dr. A.E. Kennedy Auxiliary Hospital, Bag 500, TOC 2LO, 403/742-4446
Vegreville - Minburn Auxiliary Hospital, Box 959, TOB 4LO, 403/632-2871
Wainright - Wainright & Dist. Health Care Centre, Box 820, TOB 4PO, 403/842-3324
Westlock - Thorhild Westlock Auxiliary Hospital, Box 1110, TOG 2LO, 403/349-3306
Wetaskiwin - Wetaskiwin Auxiliary Hospital, 5505 50th Ave., T9A OT4, 403/352-3371
Whitelaw - Hotel-Dieu of St. Joseph Auxiliary Unit, TOH 3TO, 403/596-3740

***Direct correspondence to: Calgary Auxiliary Hospital & Nursing Home District #7, 200 140 First Ave. S.W., Calgary Alta. T2P OA5**

***Direct Correspondence to: Edmonton Rural Auxiliary Hospital & Nursing Home District #24, 14225 94 St., Edmonton, Alta. T5E 6C6, 403/478-9221**

Federal Hospitals in Alberta

Cardston - Blood Indian Hospital, Box 490, TOK OKO, 403/653-3351
Gleichen - Blackfoot Health Care Centre, 403/734-3970
Medley - Canadian Forces Hospital, Cold Lake, Alta. TOA 2MO, 403/594-8104

Contract Hospitals in Alberta

Bonnyville - Duclos Hospital, TOA OLO, 403/826-3782
Desmarais - St. Martin's Health Centre, T0G 0T0, 403/891-3910

Federal Nursing Stations in Alberta

Federal Nursing Stations are located at Fort Chipewyan, Fox Lake and Hay Lake. All correspondence to: Medical Services Branch, Health & Welfare Canada, 401 Toronto Dominion Tower, Edmonton, Alta.

BRITISH COLUMBIA

Public Hospitals in British Columbia

*INDICATES TEACHING HOSPITAL

Abbotsford: Matsqui-Sumas-Abbotsford General Hospital (V2S 3P1)
Alert Bay: St. George's Hospital (VON 1AO)
Armstrong: Armstrong & Spallumcheen Hospital (VOE 1BO)
Ashcroft: Ashcroft & Dist. General Hospital (VOK 1AO)
Bella Coola: Bella Coola General Hospital (VOT 1CO)
Burnaby: Burnaby General Hospital (V5G 2X6)
Burns Lake: Burns Lake & Dist. Hospital (VOJ 1EO)
Campbell River: Campbell River & Dist. General Hospital (V9W 3V1)
Castlegar: Castlegar & Dist. Hospital (V1N 2H7)
Chemainus: Chemainus General Hospital (VOR 1KO)
Chetwynd: Chetwynd General Hospital (VOC 1GO)
Chilliwack: Chilliwack General Hospital (V2P 1P7)
Clearwater: Dr. Helmcken Memorial Hospital (VOE 1NO)
Comox: St. Joseph's General Hospital (V9N 4B1)
Cranbrook: Cranbrook & Dist. Hospital (V1C 3H9)
Creston: Creston Valley Hospital (VOB 1GO)
Dawson Creek: Dawson Creek Dist. Hospital (V1G 3W8)
Duncan: Cowichan Dist. Hospital (V9L 1E5)
Enderby: Enderby & Dist. Memorial Hospital (VOE 1VO)
Essondale: Eagle Ridge Hospital & Health Care Centre (VOM 1JO)
Fernie: Fernie Dist. Hospital (VOB 1MO)
Fort Nelson: Fort Nelson General Hospital (VOC 1RO)
Fort St. James: Stuart Lake Hospital (VOJ 1PO)
Fort St. John: Fort St. John General Hospital (VOC 2PO)
Ganges: Lady Minto Gulf Islands Hospital (VOS 1EO)
Golden: Golden & Dist. General Hospital (VOA 1HO)
Grand Forks: Boundary Hospital (VOH 1HO)
Hazelton: Wrinch Memorial Hospital (VOJ 1YO)
Hope: Fraser Canyon Hospital (VOX 1LO)
Invermere: Windermere Dist. Hospital (VOA 1KO)
Kamloops: Royal Inland Hospital (V2C 2T1)
Kaslo: Victorian Hospital (VOG 1MO)
Kelowna: Kelowna General Hospital (V1Y 1T2)
Kimberley: Kimberley & Dist. Hospital (V1A 2R6)
Kitimat: Kitimat General Hospital (V8C 1E7)
Ladysmith: Ladysmith & Dist. General Hospital (VOR 2EO)
Langley: Langley Memorial Hospital (V3A 4H4)
Lillooet: Lillooet Dist. Hospital (VOK 1VO)
Lytton: St. Bartholomew's Hospital (VOK 1ZO)
Mackenzie: Mackenzie & Dist. Hospital (VOJ 2CO)
Maple Ridge: Maple Ridge Hospital (V2X 7G5)
McBride: McBride & Dist. Hospital (VOJ 2EO)
Merritt: Nicola Valley General Hospital (VOK 2BO)
Mission: Mission Memorial Hospital (V2V 3H5)
Nakusp: Arrow Lakes Hospital (VOG 1RO)
Nanaimo: Nanaimo Regional General Hospital (V9S 2B7)
Nelson: Kootenay Lake General Hospital (V1L 2V1)
New Denver: Slocan Community Hospital (VOG 1SO)
New Westminster: Royal Columbia Hospital; Saint Mary's Hospital (V3L 1H6)
North Vancouver: Lions Gate Hospital (V7L 2L7)
Ocean Falls: Ocean Falls General Hospital (VOT 1PO)
Oliver: South Okanagan General Hospital (VOH 1TO)
100 Mile House: 100 Mile Dist. General Hospital (VOK 2EO)
Penticton: Penticton Regional Hospital (V2A 3G6)
Port Alberni: West Coast General Hospital (V9Y 4S1)
Port Alice: Port Alice Hospital (VON 2NO)
Port Hardy: Port Hardy Hospital (VON 2PO)
Powell River: Powell River General Hospital (V8A 4S3)
Prince George: Prince George Regional Hospital (V2M 1S2)
Prince Rupert: Prince Rupert Regional Hospital (V8J 2A6)
Princeton: Princeton General Hospital (VOX 1WO)
Queen Charlotte City: Queen Charlotte Islands General Hospital (VOT 1WO)
Quesnel: G.R. Baker Memorial Hospital (V2J 2K7)
Revelstoke: Queen Victoria Hospital (VOE 2SO)
Richmond: Richmond General Hospital (V6X 1A2)
Rossland: Mater Misericordiae Hospital (VOG 1YO)
Salmon Arm: Shuswap Lake General Hospital (VOE 2TO)
Sechelt: St. Mary's Hospital (VON 3AO)
Smithers: Bulkley Valley Dist. Hospital (VOJ 2NO)
Sparwood: Sparwood General Hospital (VOB 2GO)
Squamish: Squamish General Hospital (VON 3GO)
Stewart: Stewart General Hospital (VOT 1WO)
Summerland: Summerland General Hospital (VOH 1ZO)
Surrey: Surrey Memorial Hospital (V3V 1Z2)
Tahsis: Tahsis Hospital (VOP 1XO)
Terrace: Mills Memorial Hospital (V8G 2W7)
Tofino: Tofino General Hospital (VOR 2ZO)
Trail: Trail Regional Hospital (V1R 4M1)
Vancouver: A. Maxwell Evans Clinic
Vancouver: Cancer Control Agency of B.C. (V5Z 3J3)
Vancouver: Children's Hospital (V5X 1X2)
Vancouver: Grace Hospital (V5Z 3E6)
Vancouver: Mount Saint Joseph Hospital (V5T 3N4)
Vancouver: *St. Paul's Hospital, 1081 Burrard St. (V6Z 1Y6)
Vancouver: St. Vincent's Hospital (V5Z 2K4)
Vancouver: Shaughnessy Hospital
Vancouver: *Vancouver General Hospital, 855 12th Ave. W., V5Z 1M9
Vancouver: Univ. Health Service Hospital (V6T 1W5)
Vancouver: *Univ. of B.C. Health Sciences Centre Hospital (V6T 1W5)
Vanderhoof: St. John Hospital (VOJ 3AO)
Vernon: Vernon Jubilee Hospital (V1T 5L2)
Victoria: Royal Jubilee Hospital (V8R 1J8); Victoria General Hospital (V8V 3B6)
Waglisla: R.W. Large Memorial Hospital (VOT 1ZO)

White Rock: Peace Arch Dist. Hospital (V4B 2R4)
Williams Lake: Cariboo Memorial Hospital (V2G 2V3)

Private Hospitals in British Columbia
Cassiar: Cassiar Asbestos Corp. Private Hospital (VOC 1EO)
Mica Creek: Mica Creek Private Hospital (VOE 2LO)

Rehabilitation Hospitals in British Columbia
Vancouver: G.F. Strong Rehabilitation Centre; Holy Family Hospital; Pearson Hospital (poliomyelitis Pavilion); Shaughnessy Hospital; Sunny Hill Hospital for Children
Victoria: The Gorge Rd. Hospital; Queen Alexandra Hospital for Children

Red Cross Outpost Nursing Stations in British Columbia
There are Red Cross Outpost Nursing Stations at Alexis Creek, Atlin, Bamfield, Blue River, Edgewood, Kyuquot, Tatla Lake

Federal Government Hospitals in British Columbia
Masset: Canadian Forces Station Hospital Masset (VOT 1MO)
San Josef: Canadian Forces Station Hospital Holberg (VON 1ZO)

Extended Care Hospitals in British Columbia
Abbotsford: Menno
Bella Coola: Bella Coola General
Burnaby: Fellburn
Burns Lake: Burns Lake & Dist.
Campbell River: Campbell River & Dist. General
Chilliwack: Chilliwack General
Comox: St. Joseph's General
Cranbrook: Cranbrook & Dist.
Creston: Creston Valley
Delta: Delta Centennial
Duncan: Cowichan Dist.
Ganges: Lady Minto Gulf Islands
Golden: Golden & Dist. General
Kamloops: Overlander Extended Care
Kelowna: Kelowna General
Langley: Langley Memorial
Nanaimo: Nanaimo Regional General
Nelson: Mount St. Francis
New Westminster: Queen's Park
North Vancouver: Lions Gate
Penticton: Penticton Regional
Port Alberni: West Coast General
Pouce Coupe: Pouce Coupe Community
Powell River: Powell River General
Prince George: Prince George Regional
Prince Rupert: Prince Rupert Regional
Richmond: Richmond General
Saanichton: Saanich Peninsula
Salmon Arm: Shuswap Lake General
Sechelt: St. Mary's
Surrey: Surrey Memorial
Trail: Trail Regional
Vancouver: Holy Family; Louis Brier; Mount Saint Joseph; Pearson; St. Vincent's; Shaughnessy; Sunny Hill; Vancouver General (Banfield Pavilion)
Vernon: Vernon Jubilee
Victoria: Glendale Lodge; Gorge Rd.; Juan de Fuca Hospitals (Aberdeen, Glengarry, Mount Tolmie, Priory); Mount St. Mary; Queen Alexandra Hospital for Children; Royal Jubilee (Eric Martin Institute) (Psychiatric)–Memorial Pavilion
Waglisla: R.W. Large Memorial
White Rock: Peace Arch Dist.

Diagnostic & Treatment Centres in British Columbia
Cumberland: Cumberland General
Elkford: Elkford Diagnostic & Treatment Centre
Gold River: Gold River Health Clinic
Houston: Houston Hospital
Keremeos: Keremeos Diagnostic & Treatment Centre
Pemberton: Pemberton & Dist. Diagnostic & Treatment Centre
Vancouver: Vancouver Resources Board; The Arthritis Centre of B.C.; Children's Hospital Diagnostic & Treatment Centre; Narcotic Addiction Fdn. of B.C.

MANITOBA

Hospitals in Manitoba
Altona - Altona Community Memorial Health Centre, 24 5th Ave. N.E., Box 660, ROG OBO, 204/324-6411
Arborg - Arborg & Dist. Health Centre, Box 10, TOC OAO, 204/376-2272
Ashern - Lakeshore General Hospital, Hospital Ave. S., Box 110, ROC OEO, 204/768-2461
Baldur - Baldur Dist. Hospital, Elizabeth St., Box 128, ROK OBO, 204/535-2373
Beausejour - Beausejour Dist. Hospital, 150 1st St. S., Box 1178, ROE OCO, 204/268-1076
Benito - Benito Medical Nursing Unit, Box 220, ROL OCO, 204/539-2815
Birtle River - Birtle Dist. Health Services, Gertrude St., Box 10, ROM OCO, 204/842-3493
Boissevain - Boissevain Health Centre, Mill Rd. S., Box 899, ROK OEO, 204/534-2451
Brandon - Brandon General Hospital, 150 McTavish Ave. E., R7A 2B3, 204/728-3321
Carberry - Fox Memorial Hospital, 1st Ave., ROK OHO, 204/834-2144
Carman - Carman Memorial Hospital, 75 2nd St. S.E., Box 610, ROG OJO, 204/745-2021
Cartwright - Cartwright Dist. Hospital, Division St., Box 118, ROK OLO, 204/529-2483
Churchill - Churchill Health Centre, Churchill Town Centre, ROB OEO, 204/675-8881
Crystal City - Rock Lake Health Dist., Box 86, ROK ONO, 204/873-2132
Dauphin - Dauphin General Hospital, 625 3rd St. S.W., R7N 1R7, 204/638-3010
Deloraine - Deloraine Memorial Hospital, 109 Kellett St., Box 447, ROM OMO, 204/742-2745
Elkhorn - Elkhorn Medical Nursing Unit, Box 70, ROM ONO, 204/845-2575
Emerson - The Emerson Hospital, Main & Morris Sts., Box 68, ROA OLO, 204/373-2340
Erickson - Erickson Medical Nursing Unit, 3rd St., ROJ OPO, 204/636-2521
Eriksdale - Elizabeth M. Crowe Memorial Hospital, Railway Ave. N., Box 130, ROC OWO, 204/739-2611
Flin Flon - Flin Flon General Hospital, 4th Ave., Box 340, R8A 1N2, 204/687-7591
Gilbert Plains - Gilbert Plains District Hospital, 412 Main St. N., ROL OXO, 204/548-2161
Gillam - Gillam Hospital, Box 130, ROB OLO, 204/652-2600
Gimli - Johnson Memorial Hospital, 117 7 Ave., Box 250, ROC 1BO, 204/642-5116
Gladstone - Seven Regions Health Centre, Box 1000, ROJ OTO, 204/385-2968
Glenboro - Glenboro Dist. Hospital, Murray Ave., Box 310, ROK OXO, 204/827-2414
Grandview - Grandview Dist. Hospital, Mill St., Box 8, ROL OYO, 204/546-2261
Hamiota - Hamiota Dist. Health Centre, ROM OTO, 204/764-2412
Hartney - Hartney Medical Nursing Unit, River Ave., Box 280, ROM OXO, 204/858-2054
Hodgson - Percy E. Moore Hospital, Box 190, ROC 1NO, 204/645-2144
Killarney - Tri-Lake Health Centre, 86 Ellice Dr., Box 400, ROK 1GO, 204/523-4661

Leaf Rapids - Leaf Rapids Health Centre, Town Centre, Box 370, ROB 1WO, 204/473-2441
Lynn Lake - Lynn Lake Hospital, Camp St., Box 2030, ROB OWO, 204/356-2474
MacGregor - North Norfolk MacGregor Medical Nursing Unit, Grafton St. E., Box 250, ROH ORO, 204/685-2850
Manitou - Pembina Manitou Hospital, Mary St., Box 268, ROG 1GO, 204/242-2744
McCreary - McCreary/Alonso Health Centre, Box 250, ROJ 1BO, 204/835-2482
Melita - Melita Health Centre, Summit St., Box 459, ROM 1LO, 204/522-8197
Minnedosa - Minnedosa Dist. Hospital, 140 3rd Ave. S.W., Box 960, ROJ 1EO, 204/867-2701
Morden - Morden Dist. General Hospital, 30 Stephen St., Box 190, ROG 1JO, 204/822-4411
Morris - Morris General Hospital, 215 Railroad Ave., Box 519, ROG 1KO, 204/746-2301
Neepawa - Neepawa Dist. Memorial Hospital, 225 Walker Ave., Box 70, ROJ 1HO, 204/476-2394
Ninette - Norway House Hospital, Fort Island, R0B 1B0, 204/359-6731
Notre Dame de Lourdes - Notre Dame Medical Nursing Unit, Box 90, ROG 1MO, 204/248-2112
Pilot Mound - Pilot Mound Medical Nursing Unit, Box 61, ROG 1PO, 204/825-2733
Pinawa - Pinawa Hospital, Vanier St., Box 220, ROE 1LO, 204/753-2334
Pine Falls - Pine Falls General Hospital, 37 Maple St., Box 2000, ROE 1MO, 204/367-2400
Portage la Prairie - Portage Dist. General Hospital, 524 Broadway S., R1N 3A8, 204/857-8781
Reston - Reston Community Hospital, First St., Box 250, ROM 1XO, 204/877-3322
Rivers - Riverdale Hospital, 512 Quebec St., Box 428, ROK 1XO, 204/328-5321
Roblin - Roblin Dist. Health Centre, Hospital St., Box 940, ROL 1PO, 204/937-2142
Rossburn - Rossburn Dist. Hospital, 4th St., Box 40, ROJ 1VO, 204/859-2413
Russell - Russell Dist. Hospital, Alexandria Ave., Box 550, ROJ 1WO, 204/773-2125
Selkirk - Selkirk General Hospital, 161 Manchester Ave., R1A OB5, 204/482-5800
Shoal Lake - Shoal Lake Dist. Hospital, Jane St., Box 158, ROJ 1ZO, 204/759-2336
Snow Lake - Snow Lake Medical Nursing Unit, Box 10, ROB 1MO, 204/358-2300
Souris - Souris Dist. Hospital, 155 Struggle Ave., Box 10, ROK 2CO, 204/483-2121
Ste-Anne - Ste-Anne Hospital, 52 St. Gerard St., Box 10, ROA 1RO, 204/422-5645
St. Boniface - St. Boniface General Hospital, 409 Tache Ave., R2H 2A6, 204/233-8563
St. Claude - St. Claude Hospital, Roy St., Box 400, ROG 1ZO, 204/379-2211
St. Pierre - DeSalaberry Dist. Hospital, Joubert St., Box 320, ROA 1VO, 204/433-7808
Ste-Rose du Lac - Ste-Rose General Hospital, 3rd Ave. E., Box 60, ROL 1SO, 204/447-2131
Steinbach - Bethesda Health Service, Henry St., Box 939, ROA 2AO, 204/326-6411
Stonewall - Doctor Evelyn Memorial Hospital, 3rd St. W., Box 2000, ROC 2ZO, 204/467-5514
Swan Lake - Lorne Memorial Medical Nursing Unit, Box 40, ROG 2SO, 204/836-2132
Swan River - Swan River Valley Hospital, 111 9 Ave. S., Box 1450, ROL 1ZO, 204/734-3441
Teulon - Hunter Memorial Hospital, 3rd Ave. S.E., Box 89, ROC 3BO, 204/886-2422
The Pas - St. Anthony's General Hospital, 67 First St., Box 240, R9A 1K4, 204/623-6431
Thompson - Thompson General Hospital, Thompson Dr. S., R8N OC8, 204/677-2381
Treherne - Victoria-South Norfolk-Treherne Hospital, Kelly Ave. W., Box 130, ROG 2VO, 204/723-2133
Virden - Virden Dist. Hospital, 480 King St. E., Box 400, ROM 2CO, 204/748-1230
Vita - Vita Dist. Hospital, 1st Ave., Box 160, ROA 2KO, 204/425-3222
Wawanesa - Wawanesa & Dist. Memorial Hospital, George St., ROK 2GO, 204/824-2210
Whitemouth - Whitemouth Medical Nursing Unit, River Ave., ROE 2GO, 204/348-2316
Winkler - Bethel Hospital, 133 6th St., Box 1070, ROG 2XO, 204/325-4354
Winnipeg - Concordia Hospital, 1095 Concordia Ave., R2K 3S8, 204/667-1560
Winnipeg - Deer Lodge Hospital, 2109 Portage Ave., R3J OL3, 204/837-1301
Winnipeg - Grace General Hospital, 300 Booth Dr., R3J 3M7, 204/837-8311
Winnipeg - Health Sciences Centre, 800 Sherbrook St., R3A 1M4, 204/774-6511
Winnipeg - Misericordia General Hospital, 99 Cornish Ave., R3C 1A2, 204/774-6581
Winnipeg - Seven Oaks General Hospital, 2300 McPhillips St., R2V 3M3, 204/338-9353
Winnipeg - Victoria General Hospital, 2340 Pembina Hwy., R3T 2E8, 204/269-3570
Winnipeg - Winnipeg Municipal Hospital, 1 Morley Ave., R3L 2P4, 204/452-3411
Winnipegosis - Winnipegosis General Hospital, 34 Bridge St., Box 280, ROL 2GO, 204/656-4431

NEW BRUNSWICK

Public Hospitals in New Brunswick

*INDICATES TEACHING HOSPITAL.
Albert: The Albert County Hospital Inc.
Bath: Northern Carleton Hospital
Bathurst: Chaleur General Hospital
Black's Harbour: Fundy Hospital Association Ltd.
Campbellton: Hotel-Dieu de Saint Joseph; The Restigouche & Bay Chaleur
Soldiers' Memorial Hospital
Campobello: Campobello Health Centre
Caraquet: Hôpital de l'Enfant-Jesus
Chatham: Hotel Dieu Hospital
Dalhousie: East Restigouche Community Health Centre; Saint Joseph Hospital
Doaktown: Doaktown Health Services Centre
Edmundston: Edmundston Regional Hospital
Fredericton: Forest Hill Rehabilitation Centre; The Dr. Everett Chalmers Hospital
Fredericton Junction: Fredericton Junction Health Services Centre
Grand Falls: Grand Falls General Hospital Inc.
Harvey Station: Harvey Community Hospital Ltd.
Lameque: Hotel-Dieu de Saint-Joseph
McAdam: MacLean Memorial Hospital Ltd.
Minto: Dr. H.M. Gardiner Memorial Hospital
Moncton: Dr. Georges L. Dumont Hospital; The Moncton Hospital
Newcastle: Miramichi Hospital
North Head, Grand Manan: Grand Manan Hospital Ltd.
Oromocto: Oromocto Public Hospital
Perth: Hôtel-Dieu de Saint-Joseph
Petitcodiac: Petitcodiac Health Centre
Plaster Rock: Tobique Valley Hospital Inc.
Rexton: Rexton Health Services Centre
Sackville: The Sackville Memorial Hospital
Saint John: St. Joseph's Hospital; *Saint John Regional Hospital (Central), Waterloo St., E2L 4L2; Saint John Regional Hospital (Western), Box 3610

St. Quentin: Hotel Dieu de Saint Joseph
St. Stephen: The Charlotte County Hospital
Ste. Anne de Kent: L'Hôpital Stella Maris de Kent
Shediac: Shediac Regional Health Centre
Stanley: Stanley Health Services Centre
Sussex: Sussex Health Centre
Tracadie: Hôtel-Dieu de Saint-Joseph
Woodstock: The Carleton Memorial Hospital

Mental Hospitals in New Brunswick

Campbellton: Restigouche Hospital Centre
Saint John: Centracare

NEWFOUNDLAND

Hospitals in Newfoundland

*INDICATES TEACHING HOSPITAL.

Baie Verte: Baie Verte Peninsula Health Centre, AOK 1BO, 709/532-4281
Bell Island: Dr. Walter Templeman Hospital, A0A 1H0, 709/488-2821
Black Tickle: Black Tickle Nursing Stn., AOK 1NO
Bonavista: Bonavista Cottage Hospital, AOC 1BO, 709/468-7883
Bonne Bay: Bonne Bay Cottage Hospital, A0K 3V0, 709/458-2201, or 2211
Botwood: Botwood Cottage Hospital, AOH 1EO, 709/257-2833
Brookfield: Brookfield Hospital, AOG 1JO, 709/536-2406
Buchans: A.M. Guy Memorial Hospital, AOH 1GO, 709/672-3326
Burgeo: Burgeo Cottage Hospital, AOM 1AO, 709/886-3350
Burin: Burin Cottage Hospital, AOE 1EO, 709/891-1410
Carbonear: Carbonear General Hospital, AOA 1TO, 709/596-5081
Cartwright: Cartwright Nursing Stn., AOK 1VO
Channel: Channel Hospital, AOM 1CO, 709/695-2151
Charlottetown (Lab.): Charlottetown Nursing Stn., A0K 5Y0
Churchill Falls: Churchill Falls Hospital, AOR 1AO, 709/925-3381
Come by Chance: Come by Chance Cottage Hospital, AOB 1NO, 709/542-3500
Conche: Conche Nursing Stn., AOK 1YO
Corner Brook: Western Memorial Regional Hospital, A2H 6J7, 709/634-4393
Davis Inlet: Davis Inlet Nursing Stn., A0P 1A0
Flower's Cove: Flower's Cove Nursing Stn., AOK 2NO, 709/456-2209
Fogo: Fogo Hospital, AOG 2BO, 709/266-2222
Forteau: Forteau Nursing Stn., AOK 2PO
Gander: James Paton Memorial Hospital, A1V 1P7, 709/651-2500
Goose Bay: Melville Hospital, AOP 1SO, 709/896-2417
Grand Bank: Grand Bank Cottage Hospital, AOE 1WO, 709/832-2500
Grand Falls: Central Newfoundland Hospital, A2A 2E1, 709/489-6661
Harbour Breton: Harbour Breton Cottage Hospital, AOH 1PO, 709/885-2359
Harbour Deep: Harbour Deep Nursing Stn., A0K 2Z0
Hopedale: Hopedale Nursing Stn., AOP 1GO
Labrador City: Capt. Wm. Jackman Memorial Hospital, A2V 2K1, 709/944-2632
Makkovik: Makkovik Nursing Stn., AOP 1JO
Markland: Markland Cottage Hospital, AOB 3KO, 709/759-2300
Mary's Harbour: Mary's Harbour Nursing Stn., AOK 3PO
Nain: Nain Nursing Stn., AOP 1LO
North West River: North West River Hospital, AOP 1MO, 709/946-8351
Old Perlican: Old Perlican Cottage Hospital, AOA 3GO, 709/587-2200
Placentia: Placentia Cottage Hospital, AOB 2YO, 709/227-2013
Port Saunders: Port Saunders Hospital, AOK 4HO, 709/861-3533
Roddickton: Roddickton Community Health Centre, AOK 4PO
St. Anthony: Charles S. Curtis Memorial Hospital, AOK 4SO, 709/454-8881
St. John's: Children's Rehabilitation Centre, A1C 5N5, 709/754-1970
St. John's: *Dr. Charles A. Janeway Child Health Centre, A1A 1R8, 709/722-5100
St. John's: *Grace General Hospital, A1E 1P9, 709/778-6222
St. John's: Health Science Complex, Prince Philip Dr., A1B 3V6, 709/737-6300
St. John's: *St. Clare's Mercy Hospital, Le Marchant Rd., A1C 5B8, 709/778-3438
St. John's: St. Luke's Home, A1E 2B4, 709/579-8767
St. John's: *St. John's General Hospital, Forest Rd., A1A 1E5, 709/737-6300
St. John's: St. Patrick's Mercy Home, A1B 1S5, 709/726-2687
St. John's: Waterford Hospital, A1E 4J8, 709/368-6061
St. Lawrence: St. Lawrence Cottage Hospital, AOE 2VO, 709/873-2330
Springdale: Springdale Hospital, AOJ 1TO, 709/673-3913
Stephenville: Sir Thomas Roddick Hospital, A2N 2V6, 709/643-5131
Twillingate: Notre Dame Bay Memorial Hospital, AOG 4MO, 709/884-2131

NOVA SCOTIA

Health Units in Nova Scotia

The Province is divided into eight Health Units with a medical director in charge of each:

Atlantic Health Unit: Director, Dr. W. Butt, 1600 Bedford Hwy., Bedford, N.S. B4A 1E8, 902/835-7181
Cape Breton North Health Unit: Director, Dr. L.D. MacCormick, Prince St., Sydney, N.S. B1P 5L1, 902/564-4447
Cape Breton South Health Unit: Director, Dr. N.F. Macneill, Prince St., Sydney, N.S. B1P 5L1, 902/564-4448
Cobequid Health Unit: Director, (vacant), Box 40, Truro, N.S. B2N 5B6, 902/895-5321
Fundy Health Unit: Director, Dr. V.K. Rideout, 100 King St., Windsor, N.S. BON 2TO, 902/798-2264
Lunenberg-Queens Health Unit: Director, Dr. W. Butt, 583 King St., Bridgewater, N.S. B4V 1B3, 902/543-4685
Northumberland Health Unit: Director, Dr. S.D. Dunn, Box 310, Pictou, N.S. BOK 1HO, 902/485-4388
Western Health Unit: Director, Dr. V.K. Rideout, Box 338, Yarmouth, N.S. B5A 4B3, 902/742-7141

Hospitals in Nova Scotia

Advocate Harbour - Bayview Memorial Hospital, BOM 1AO, 902/392-2859
Amherst - Highland View Hospital, B3H 1N6, 902/667-3361
Annapolis Royal - Annapolis General Hospital, BOS 1AO, 902/532-2381
Antigonish - St. Martha's Hospital, B2G 2G5, 902/863-2830
Arichat - St. Anne Hospital, PO Drawer 30, BOE 1AO, 902/226-2826
Baddeck - Victoria County Hospital, Box 220, BOE 1BO, 902/295-2760
Berwick - Western Kings Memorial Hospital, BOP 1EO, 902/538-3111
Bridgewater - Dawson Memorial Hospital, B4V 2H1, 902/543-4603
Canso - Eastern Memorial Hospital, BOH 1HO, 902/366-2794
Cheticamp - Sacred Heart Hospital, Box 129, BOE 1HO, 902/224-2450
Dartmouth - Dartmouth General Hospital, Box 1016, B2Y 3Z7, 902/469-9523
Digby - Digby General Hospital, B0V 1A0, 902/245-2501

Glace Bay - Glace Bay Community Hospital, B1A 4Z8, 902/849-5531

Glace Bay - Glace Bay General Hospital, B1A 1K9, 902/849-5511

Guysborough - Guysborough Memorial Hospital, BOH 1NO, 902/533-3702

Halifax - Camp Hill Hospital, 1763 Robie St., B3H 3G2, 902/423-1371

Halifax - Halifax Civic Hospital, 5938 University Ave., B3H 1V9, 902/422-1731

Halifax - Grace Maternity Hospital, 5821 University Ave., B3H 1W3, 902/422-6501

Halifax - Halifax Infirmary Hospital, 1335 Queen St., B3J 2H6, 902/428-2700

Halifax - Izaak Walton Killam Hospital for Children, 5850 University Ave., B3J 3G9, 902/424-3100

Halifax - N.S. Rehabilitation Centre, 1341 Summer St., B3H 4K4, 902/422-1787

Halifax - Victoria General Hospital, 1278 Tower Rd., B3H 2Y9, 902/428-2110

Inverness - Inverness Consolidated Hospital, Box 610, BOE 1NO, 902/258-2100

Kentville - Valley Health Services Association, 186 Park St., B4N 1M7, 902/678-7381

Liverpool - Queens General Hospital, BOT 1KO, 902/354-3436

Lunenburg - Fishermen's Memorial Hospital, BOJ 2CO, 902/634-8801

Middle Musquodoboit - Musquodoboit Valley Hospital, BON 1XO, 902/384-2220

Middleton - Soldiers' Memorial Hospital, BOS 1PO, 902/825-3413

Musquodoboit Harbour - Twin Oaks Memorial Hospital, BOJ 2LO, 902/889-2200

Neil's Harbour - Buchanan Memorial Hospital, BOX 1NO, 902/336-2200

New Glasgow - Aberdeen Hospital, B2H 3S6, 902/752-8311

New Waterford - New Waterford Consolidated Hospital, B1H 3Z5, 902/862-6411

Pugwash - North Cumberland Hospital, Box 242, BOK 1LO, 902/243-2521

North Sydney - Northside General Hospital, B2A 1E3, 902/794-4725

Parrsboro - South Cumberland Hospital, Box 489, BOM 1SO, 902/254-2540

Pictou - Sutherland-Harris Hospital, Box 1059, BOK 1HO, 902/485-4381

Port Hawkesbury - Strait-Richmond Hospital, R.R. 1, Cleveland, N.S. B0E 1J0, 902/625-3100

Sheet Harbour - Eastern Shore Memorial Hospital, BOJ 3BO, 902/885-2554

Shelburne - Roseway Hospital, BOT 1WO, 902/875-3011

Sherbrooke - St. Mary's Memorial Hospital, Box 82, BOJ 3CO, 902/522-2882

Springhill - All Saint's Hospital, BOM 1XO, 902/597-3773

Sydney - St. Rita Hospital, B1S 1B4, 902/539-3740

Sydney - Sydney City Hospital, B1P 2H8, 902/539-6400

Sydney Mines - Harbour View Hospital, Box 128, B1V 2Y4, 902/736-6283

Tatamagouche - Lillian Fraser Memorial Hospital, BOK 1XO, 902/657-2382

Truro - Colchester Hospital, 207 Willow St., B2N 5A1, 902/895-5421

Windsor - Hants Community Hospital, BON 2TO, 902/798-8351

Wolfville - Eastern Kings Memorial Hospital, BOP 1XO, 902/542-2266

Yarmouth - Yarmouth Regional Hospital, B5A 2P5, 902/742-3541

Psychiatric Hospitals in Nova Scotia

Dartmouth - Nova Scotia Hospital, Box 1004, B2Y 3Z9, 902/469-7500

Halifax - Abbie J. Lane Hospital, 5909 Jubilee Rd., B3H 2E2, 902/425-5800

Sydney River - Cape Breton Hospital, Box 515, B1P 6H4, 902/539-3370

Waterville - Kings Regional Health & Rehab. Centre, B0P 1V0, 902/538-3103

ONTARIO

Psychiatric Hospitals in Ontario

See also list of Public Hospitals following.

Brockville - Brockville Psychiatric Hospital, Box 1050, K6V 5W7, 613/345-1461

Hamilton - Hamilton Psychiatric Hospital, Box 585, L9C 3N6, 416/388-2511

Kingston - Kingston Psychiatric Hospital, 752 King St. W., Box 603, K7L 4X3, 519/546-1101

London - London Psychiatric Hospital, Box 2532, Terminal A, N6A 4H1, 519/455-5110

North Bay - North Bay Psychiatric Hospital, Box 3010, P1B 8L1, 705/474-1200

Penetanguishene - Mental Health Centre, Box 698, LOK 1PO, 705/549-7431

St. Thomas - St. Thomas Psychiatric Hospital, Box 2004, N5P 3V9, 519/631-8510

Thunder Bay - Lakehead Psychiatric Hospital, 580 Algoma St. N., Box 2930, P7B 5G8, 807/344-3571

Toronto - Queen St. Mental Health Centre, 1001 Queen St. W., M6J 1H4, 416/533-8501

Whitby - Whitby Psychiatric Hospital, Box 613, L1N 5S9, 416/668-5881

Public Hospitals in Ontario

Ajax - Ajax & Pickering General Hospital, Harwood Ave. S., L1S 2J4, 416/683-2321

Alexandria - Glengarry Memorial Hospital, Box 760, KOC 1AO, 613/525-2222

Alliston - Stevenson Memorial Hospital, 200 Fletcher Cres., Box 4000, LOM 1AO, 705/435-6281

Almonte - Almonte General Hospital, Box 940, 75 Spring St., KOA 1AO, 613/256-2500

Arnprior - Arnprior & Dist. Memorial Hospital, 350 John St. N., K7S 3H4, 613/623-3166

Atikokan - Atikokan General Hospital, 120 Dorothy St., POT 1CO, 807/597-4216

Barrie - The Royal Victoria Hospital, 76 Ross St., L4N 1G4, 705/728-9802

Barrys Bay - St. Francis Memorial Hospital, Box 129, KOJ 1BO, 613/756-3044

Belleville - Belleville General Hospital, Box 428, 265 Dundas St. E., K8N 5A9, 613/968-5511

Blind River - St. Josephs General Hospital, Box 970, POR 1BO, 705/356-2265

Bowmanville - Memorial Hospital, 47 Liberty St. S., L1C 2N4, 416/623-3331

Bracebridge - South Muskoka Memorial Hospital, Box 1570, 75 Anne St., POB 1CO, 705/645-4404

Brampton - Peel Memorial Hospital, 20 Lynch St., L6W 2Z8, 416/451-1710

Brantford - St. Joseph's Hospital, 63 Park Rd. N., N3S 6T6, 519/753-8641

Brantford - The Brant Sanatorium, 25 Bell Lane, N3T 1E1, 519/753-2658

Brantford - The Brantford General Hospital, 200 Terrace Hill St., N3R 1G9, 519/752-7871

Brockville - Brockville General Hospital, 75 Emma St., K6V 1S8, 613/345-5645

Brockville - St. Vincent de Paul Hospital, 42 Garden St., K6V 2C3, 613/342-4461

Burlington - Joseph Brant Memorial Hospital, 1230 North Shore Blvd., L7R 4C4, 416/632-3730

Cambridge - Cambridge Memorial Hospital, Coronation Blvd., N1R 3G2, 519/621-2330
Campbellford - Campbellford Memorial Hospital, 146 Oliver Rd., Box 1027, KOL 1LO, 705/653-1140
Carleton Place - Carleton Place & Dist. Memorial Hospital, Box 476, 211 Lake Ave. E., K7C 3P5, 613/257-2200
Chapleau - Chapleau General Hospital, Broomhead Rd., Box 757, POM 1KO, 705/864-1520
Chatham - Public General Hospital, 106 Emma St., N7L 1A8, 519/352-6400
Chatham - St. Joseph's Hospital, 519 King St. W., N7M 1G8, 519/352-2500
Chesley - Chesley & Dist. Memorial Hospital, 39 Second St. S.E., NOG 1LO, 519/363-2340
Clinton - Clinton Public Hospital, 98 Shipley St., NOM 1LO, 519/482-3447
Cobourg - Cobourg Dist. General Hospital, 176 Chapel St., Box 340, K9A 4K9, 416/372-6811
Cochrane - Lady Minto Hospital at Cochrane, 156 8th St., Box 4000, POL 1CO, 705/272-4246
Collingwood - Collingwood General & Marine Hospital, 67 Moberly St., L9Y 1W9, 705/445-2550
Cornwall - Cornwall General Hospital, 510 Second St. E., K6H 1Z6, 613/932-3300
Cornwall - Hotel Dieu Hospital, 840 McConnell Ave., K6H 4M3, 613/932-4630
Cornwall - MacDonell Memorial Hospital, 211 Water St. W., Box 489, K6J 1A3, 613/933-4911
Deep River - Deep River & Dist. Hospital, McElligott St., Box 307, KOJ 1PO, 613/584-3333
Downsview - York Finch General Hospital, 2111 Finch Ave. W., M3N 1N1, 416/744-2500
Dryden - Dryden Dist. General Hospital, 58 Goodall St., P8N 1V8, 807/223-5261
Dunnville - Haldimand War Memorial Hospital, 206 John St., N1A 2P7, 416/774-7431
Durham - Durham Memorial Hospital, Chester & College Sts., Box 638, NOG 1RO, 519/369-2340
Elliot Lake - St. Joseph General Hospital, 70 Spine Rd., P5A 1X2, 705/848-7181
Englehart - Englehart & Dist. Hospital, Box 69, 61 5th St., POJ 1HO, 705/544-2301
Espanola - Espanola General Hospital, 79 Tudhope St., Box 1280, POP 1CO, 705/869-1420
Etobicoke - Queensway General Hospital, 150 Sherway Dr., M9C 1A5, 416/259-6671
Exeter - South Huron Hospital, 24 Huron St. W., Box 910, NOM 1SO, 519/235-2700
Fergus - Groves Memorial Community Hospital, 235 Union St. E., N1M 1W3, 519/843-2010
Fort Erie - Douglas Memorial Hospital, 230 Bertie St., L2A 1Z2, 416/871-6600
Fort Frances - La Verendrye General Hospital, 110 Victoria Ave., P9A 2B7, 807/274-3261
Georgetown - Georgetown & Dist. Memorial Hospital, Princess Ann Dr., L7G 2B8, 416/877-0111
Geraldton - Geraldton Dist. Hospital, Hogarth St., POT 1MO, 807/854-1862
Goderich - Alexandra Marine & General Hospital, 120 Napier St., N7A 1W5, 519/524-8323
Grimsby - West Lincoln Memorial Hospital, 167 Main St. E., L3M 1P3, 416/945-2253
Guelph - Community Psychiatric Hospital, 160 Delhi St., N1E 4J8, 519/821-2060
Guelph - Guelph General Hospital, 115 Delhi St., N1E 4J4, 519/822-5350
Guelph - St. Joseph's Hospital, 80 Westmount Rd., N1H 5H8, 519/824-2620
Hagersville - West Haldimand General Hospital, King & Parkview Rds., NOA 1HO, 519/768-3311
Hamilton - Chedoke-McMaster Hospital, Box 2000, Stn. A, Hamilton, Ont. L8N 3Z5 – Chedoke Division, Sanatorium Rd., 416/388-0240 –McMaster Division, Main St. W., 416/525-9140
Hamilton - Civic Hospitals, 237 Barton St. E., L8L 2X2, 416/527-0271
Hamilton - Hamilton General Hospital, 237 Barton St. E., L8L 2X2, 416/527-0271
Hamilton - Henderson General Hospital, 711 Concession St., L8V 1C3, 416/389-4411
Hamilton - St. Joseph's Hospital, 50 Charlton Ave. E., L8N 1Y4, 416/522-4941
Hamilton - St. Peter's Centre, 88 Maplewood Ave., L8M 1W9, 416/549-6525
Hanover - Hanover & Dist. Hospital, 90 7th Ave., N4N 1N1, 519/364-2340
Hawkesbury - Hawkesbury & Dist. General Hospital, 342 McGill St., K6A 1R7, 613/632-7031
Hearst - Notre-Dame Hospital, 1405 Edward St., Box 8000, POL 1NO, 705/362-4291
Hornepayne - Hornepayne Community Hospital, 274 Front St., Box 190, POM 1ZO, 807/868-2442
Huntsville - Huntsville Dist. Memorial Hospital, 14 Mill St., Box 5500, POA 1KO, 705/789-2311
Ingersoll - Alexandra Hospital, 29 Noxon St., N5C 1B8, 519/485-1700
Iroquois Falls - Anson General Hospital, 58 Anson Dr., Box 370, POK 1EO, 705/258-3911
Kapuskasing - Sensenbrenner Hospital, 10 Drury St., P5N 1K9, 705/335-6041
Kemptville - Kemptville Dist. Hospital, Concession Rd., Bag 2007, KOG 1JO, 613/258-3435
Kenora - Lake of the Woods Dist. Hospital, 21 Sylvan St. W., P9N 3W7, 807/468-9861
Kincardine - Kincardine & Dist. General Hospital, Queen St. N., R.R. 5, NOG 2GO, 519/396-3331
Kingston - Hotel Dieu Hospital, Sydenham St., K7L 3H6, 613/544-3310
Kingston - Kingston General Hospital, Stuart St., K7L 2V7, 613/547-2121
Kingston - Ongwanada Hospital, 117 Park St., K7L 1J9, 613/548-4417
Kingston - St. Mary's of the Lake Hospital, 340 Union St., Box 3600, K7L 5A2, 613/544-5220
Kirkland Lake - Kirkland & Dist. Hospital, 145 Government Rd. E., P2N 1R2, 705/567-5251
Kitchener - Kitchener-Waterloo Hospital, 835 King St. W., N2G 1G3, 519/742-3611
Kitchener - St. Mary's General Hospital, 911 Queens Blvd., N2M 1B2, 519/744-3311
Kitchener - The Freeport Hospital, 3570 King St. E., N2A 2W1, 519/893-2710
Leamington - Leamington Dist. Memorial Hospital, Talbot St. W., N8H 1N9, 519/326-6131
Lindsay - Ross Memorial Hospital, 10 Angeline St. N., K9V 4M8, 705/324-6111
Listowel - Listowel Memorial Hospital, 255 Elizabeth St. E., N4W 2P5, 519/291-3120
Little Current - Manitoulin Health Centre, 11 Meredith St., Box 640, POP 1KO, 705/368-2300
London - Parkwood Hospital, 81 Grand Ave., N6C 1M2, 519/433-8451
London - St. Joseph's Hospital, 268 Grosvenor St., N6A 4V2, 519/439-3271
London - St. Mary's Hospital, 35 Grosvenor St., N6A 1Y6, 519/438-6185
London - University Hospital, 339 Windermere Rd., Box 5339, Terminal A, N6A 5A5, 519/673-6500
London - Victoria Hospital, 375 South St., N6A 4G5, 519/432-5241
Manitouwadge - Manitouwadge General Hospital, Manitou Rd., POT 2CO, 807/826-3251
Marathon - Wilson Memorial General Hospital, Peninsula Rd., POT 2EO, 807/229-1740
Markdale - Centre Grey General Hospital, 55 Isla St., Box 406, NOC 1HO, 519/986-3040
Matheson - Bingham Memorial Hospital, 8th Ave., Box 70, POK 1NO, 705/273-2424

Mattawa - Mattawa General Hospital, 215 Third St., Box 70, POH 1VO, 705/744-5511
Meaford - Meaford General Hospital, 229 Nelson St. W., Box 340, NOH 1YO, 519/538-1311
Midland - Huronia Dist. Hospital, Box 760, L4R 4P4, 705/526-3751
Milton - Milton Dist. Hospital, Derry Rd. at Bronte St., L9T 2X5, 416/878-2383
Mississauga - The Mississauga Hospital, 100 Queensway W., L5B 1B8, 416/279-7330
Moosonee - James Bay General Hospital, Box 370, POL 1YO, 705/336-2266
Mount Forest - Louise Marshall Hospital, 630 Dublin St., Box 190, NOG 2LO, 519/323-2210
Napanee - Lennox & Addington County General Hospital, Postal Bag 3000, K7R 2Z4, 613/354-3301
Newbury - Four Counties General Hospital, NOL 1ZO, 519/693-4441
Newmarket - York County Hospital, 596 Davis Dr., L3Y 2P9, 416/895-4521
Niagara Falls - Greater Niagara General Hospital, 5546 Portage Rd., Box 1018, L2E 6X2, 416/358-0171
Niagara-on-the-Lake - Niagara Hospital, 176 Wellington St., Box 300, LOS 1JO, 416/468-3261
Nipigon - Nipigon Dist. Memorial Hospital, 148 Churchill St., Box 37, POT 2JO, 807/887-3026
North Bay - North Bay Civic Hospital, 750 Scollard St., P1B 5A4, 705/474-8600
North Bay - St. Joseph's General Hospital, 720 McLaren St., P1B 3L9, 705/472-6100
Oakville - Oakville-Trafalgar Memorial Hospital, 327 Reynolds St., L6J 3L7, 416/845-2571
Orangeville - Dufferin Area Hospital, 32 First St., L9W 2E1, 519/941-2410
Orillia - Orillia Soldiers' Memorial Hospital, 170 Colborne St. W., L3V 5S2, 705/325-2201
Oshawa - Oshawa General Hospital, 24 Alma St., L1G 2B9, 416/576-8711
Ottawa - Children's Hospital of Eastern Ontario, 401 Smyth Rd., K1H 8L1, 613/737-7600
Ottawa - Hopital Montfort, 713 Montreal Rd., K1K OT2, 613/746-4621
Ottawa - Ottawa Civic Hospital, 1053 Carling Ave., K1Y 4E9, 613/729-2511
Ottawa - Elizabeth Bruyere Health Centre, 43 Bruyere St., K1N 5C8, 613/231-2100
Ottawa - Ottawa Centre General Hospital, 501 Smyth Rd., K1G 8L6, 613/737-7777
Ottawa - Queensway-Carleton Hospital, 3045 Baseline Rd., K2H 8P4, 613/820-2000
Ottawa - Riverside Hospital of Ottawa, 1967 Riverside Dr., K1H 7W9, 613/731-6710
Ottawa - Royal Ottawa Hospital, 1145 Carling Ave., K1Z 7K4, 613/722-6521
Ottawa - Salvation Army Grace General Hospital, 1156 Wellington St., K1Y 2Z4, 613/728-4611
Ottawa - St. Vincent Hospital, 60 Cambridge St., K1R 7A5, 613/233-4041
Ottawa - The Perley Hospital, 43 Aylmer Ave., K1S 4R5, 613/236-7171
Owen Sound - Owen Sound General & Marine Hospital, 1201 6th Ave. W., N4K 5H3, 519/376-2121
Palmerston - Palmerston & Dist. Hospital, 500 Whites Rd., Box 130, NOG 2PO, 519/343-2030
Paris - The Willett Hospital, 238 Grand River St. N., N3L 2N7, 519/442-2251
Parry Sound - Parry Sound Dist. General Hospital, 10 James St., P2A 1T3, 705/746-9321
Parry Sound - St. Joseph's Hospital, 88 Church St., P2A 1Z3, 705/746-2111
Pembroke - Pembroke Civic Hospital, 425 Cecelia St., K8A 1S7, 613/735-6851
Pembroke - Pembroke General Hospital, 705 MacKay St., K8A 1G8, 613/732-2811
Penetanguishene - Penetanguishene General Hospital, 25 Jeffery St., LOK 1PO, 705/549-7442
Perth - The Great War Memorial Hospital, 33 Drummond St. W., K7H 2K1, 613/267-1500
Peterborough - Peterborough Civic Hospital, Weller St., K9J 7C6, 705/743-2121
Peterborough - St. Joseph's General Hospital, 384 Rogers St., K9H 7B6, 705/743-4251
Petrolia - Charlotte Eleanor Englehart Hospital, 447 Greenfield St., NON 1RO, 519/882-1170
Picton - Prince Edward County Memorial Hospital, Main St. E., Box 1900, KOK 2TO, 613/476-2181
Port Colborne - Port Colborne General Hospital, 260 Sugarloaf St., L3K 2N7, 416/834-4501
Port Hope - Port Hope & Dist. Hospital, 53 Wellington St., L1A 2M6, 416/885-6371
Port Perry - Community Memorial Hospital, 451 Paxton St., LOB 1NO, 416/985-7321
Red Lake - Red Lake Margaret Cochenour Memorial Hospital, Box 314, POV 2MO, 807/727-2231
Renfrew - Renfrew Victoria Hospital, 499 Raglan St. N., K7V 1P6, 613/432-4851
Rexdale - The Etobicoke General Hospital, 101 Humber College Blvd., M9V 1R8, 416/744-3400
Richmond Hill - York Central Hospital, 10 Trench St., L4C 4Z3, 416/883-1212
Sarnia - Sarnia General Hospital, 220 N. Mitton St., N7T 6H6, 519/344-3661
Sarnia - St. Joseph's Hospital, 290 Russell St. N., N7T 6S3, 519/336-6121
Sault Ste. Marie - General Hospital, 941 Queen St. E., P6A 2B8, 705/254-5181
Sault Ste. Marie - Plummer Memorial Public Hospital, 969 Queen St. E., P6A 2C4, 705/254-5161
Scarborough - Providence Hospital, 3276 St. Clair Ave. E., M1L 1W1, 416/759-9321
Scarborough - Scarborough General Hospital, 3050 Lawrence Ave. E., M1P 2V5, 416/438-2911
Seaforth - Seaforth Community Hospital, 24 Centennial Dr., NOK 1WO, 519/527-1650
Shelburne - Shelburne Dist. Hospital, Box 190, LON 1SO, 519/925-3340
Simcoe - Norfolk General Hospital, 365 West St., N3Y 1T7, 519/426-0750
Sioux Lookout - Sioux Lookout General Hospital, 5th Ave. S., Box 909, POV 2TO, 807/737-3700
Smiths Falls - Smiths Falls Community Hospital, 170 Elmsley St. N., K7A 2H9, 613/283-2330
Smooth Rock Falls - Smooth Rock Falls Hospital, 105 Second Ave., Box 219, POL 2BO, 705/338-2781
South Porcupine - Porcupine General Hospital, Bruce Ave., Box 850, PON 1HO, 705/235-3377
Southampton - Saugeen Memorial Hospital, 340 High St., Box 310, N0H 2L0, 519/797-3230
St. Catharines - Hotel Dieu Hospital, 155 Ontario St., L2R 5K3, 416/682-6411
St. Catharines - Niagara Peninsula Rehab Centre, 547 Glenridge Ave., Box 924, L2R 6Z4, 416/688-2980
St. Catharines - Shaver Hospital for Chest Diseases, 541 Glenridge Ave., Box 158, L2R 6S5, 416/685-1381
St. Catharines - St. Catharines General Hospital, 142 Queenston St., L2R 7C6, 416/684-7271
St. Marys - St. Marys Memorial Hospital, 267 Queen St. W., Box 940, NOM 2VO, 519/284-1330
St. Thomas - St. Thomas Elgin General Hospital, 189 Elm St., Box 2007, N5P 3W2, 519/631-2020
Stratford - Stratford General Hospital, 46 General Hospital Dr., N5A 2Y6, 519/271-2120
Strathroy - Strathroy Middlesex General Hospital, 395 Carrie St., Box 5001, N7G 3J4, 519/245-1550
Sturgeon Falls - West Nipissing General Hospital, 111 Springer Ave., POH 2GO, 705/753-3110
Sudbury - Laurentian Hospital, 41 Ramsey Lake Rd., P3E 5J1, 705/522-2200

Sudbury - Sudbury Algoma Hospital, 680 Kirkwood Dr., P3E 1X3, 705/675-9192
Sudbury - Sudbury General Hospital, 700 Paris St., P3E 3B5, 705/674-3181
Sudbury - Sudbury Memorial Hospital, 865 Regent St. S., P3E 3Y9, 705/673-8421
Temiskaming - Temiskaming Hospitals, Shepherdson Rd., New Liskeard, Ont. P0J 1P0, 705/647-8121
Terrace Bay - The McCausland Hospital, 314 Kenogami Rd., POT 2WO, 807/825-3695
Thunder Bay - General Hospital of Port Arthur, 460 N. Court St., P7A 4X6, 807/344-6621
Thunder Bay - Hogarth-Westmount Hospital, 300 N. Lillie St., P7C 4Y7, 807/623-7493
Thunder Bay - McKellar General Hospital, Ridgeway St., P7E 1G6, 807/623-5561
Thunder Bay - St. Joseph's General Hospital, 35 N. Algoma St., Box 3251, P7B 5G7, 807/344-2431
Tillsonburg - Tillsonburg Dist. Memorial Hospital, 167 Rolph St., Box 3100, N4G 4J2, 519/842-3611
Timmins - St. Mary's General Hospital, 41 Pine St. N., P4N 6K7, 705/267-2131
Toronto - Baycrest Hospital, 3560 Bathurst St., M6A 2E1, 416/789-5131
Toronto - Bloorview Hospital, see Willowdale
Toronto - Central Hospital, 333 Sherbourne St., M5A 2S5, 416/964-4150
Toronto - Clarke Institute of Psychiatry, 250 College St., M5T 1R8, 416/979-2221
Toronto - Etobicoke General Hospital, see Rexdale
Toronto - Hillcrest Hospital, 47 Austin Terrace, M5R 1Y8, 416/537-3421
Toronto - Humber Memorial Hospital, see Weston
Toronto - Lyndhurst Hospital, 520 Sutherland Dr., M4G 3V9, 416/422-5551
Toronto - Mount Sinai Hospital, 600 University Ave., M5G 1X5, 416/596-4200
Toronto - Northwestern General Hospital, 2175 Keele St., M6M 3Z4, 416/651-6111
Toronto - North York Branson Hospital, see Willowdale
Toronto - North York General Hospital, see Willowdale
Toronto - Ontario Crippled Children's Centre, 350 Rumsey Rd., M4G 1R8, 416/425-6220
Toronto - Orthopaedic & Arthritic Hospital, 43 Wellesley St. E., M4Y 1H1, 416/967-8500
Toronto - Providence Hospital, see Scarborough
Toronto - Queensway Hospital, see Etobicoke
Toronto - Red Cross Hospital, Ontario Division, 460 Jarvis St., M4Y 2H5, 416/923-6692
Toronto - St. Bernard's Convalescent Hospital, see Willowdale
Toronto - St. John's Convalescent Hospital, see Willowdale
Toronto - St. Joseph's Health Centre, 30 The Queensway, M6R 1B5, 416/534-9531
Toronto - St. Michael's Hospital, 30 Bond St., M5B 1W8, 416/360-4000
Toronto - Scarborough Centenary Hospital, see West Hill
Toronto - Scarborough General Hospital, see Scarborough
Toronto - Sunnybrook Medical Centre, 2075 Bayview Ave., M4N 3M5, 416/486-3000
Toronto - Support Services Hospital, Addiction Research Foundation, 33 Russell St., M5S 2S1, 416/595-6000
Toronto - The Doctors' Hospital, 45 Brunswick Ave., M5S 2M1, 416/923-5411
Toronto - The Donwood Institute, 175 Brentcliffe Rd., M4G 3Z1, 416/425-3930
Toronto - The Hospital for Sick Children, 555 University Ave., M5G 1X8, 416/597-1500
Toronto - The Princess Margaret Hospital, 500 Sherbourne St., M4X 1K9, 416/924-0671
Toronto - The Queen Elizabeth Hospital, 550 University Ave., M5G 2A2, 416/597-5111
Toronto - The Riverdale Hospital, St. Matthews Rd., M4M 2B5, 416/461-8251
Toronto - The Runnymede Hospital, 274 St. John's Rd., M6P 1V5, 416/762-7316
Toronto - The Salvation Army Grace Hospital, 650 Church St., M4Y 2G5, 416/925-2251
Toronto - Toronto Western Hospital, 399 Bathurst St., M5T 2S8, 416/369-5201
Toronto - The Wellesley Hospital, 160 Wellesley St. E., M4Y 1J3, 416/966-6604
Toronto - Toronto East General & Orthopaedic Hospital, 825 Coxwell Ave., M4C 3E7, 416/461-8272
Toronto - Toronto General Hospital, 101 College St., M5G 1L7, 416/595-3111
Toronto - Toronto Rehabilitation Centre, 345 Rumsey Rd., M4G 1R7, 416/425-6630
Toronto - West Park Hospital, 82 Buttonwood Ave., M6M 2J5, 416/243-3600
Toronto - Women's College Hospital, 76 Grenville St., M5S 1B2, 416/966-7111
Toronto - York Finch General Hospital, see Downsview
Trenton - Trenton Memorial Hospital, 242 King St. W., K8V 5S6, 613/392-2541
Uxbridge - The Cottage Hospital, Campbell Dr., LOC 1KO, 416/852-3341
Walkerton - County of Bruce General Hospital, 21 McGivern St., NOG 2VO, 519/881-1220
Wallaceburg - Sydenham Dist. Hospital, 325 Margaret Ave., Box 1320, N8A 2A7, 519/627-1461
Wawa - The Lady Dunn General Hospital, Government Rd., Box 179, POS 1KO, 705/856-2335
Welland - Welland County General Hospital, Third St., L3B 4W6, 416/732-6111
West Hill - Scarborough Centenary Hospital, 2867 Ellesmere Rd., M1E 4B9, 416/284-8131
Weston - Humber Memorial Hospital, 200 Church St., M9N 1M8, 416/249-8111
Whitby - Dr. Joseph O. Ruddy General Hospital, Gordon St., L1N 5T2, 416/668-6831
Wiarton - Bruce Peninsula & Dist. Memorial Hospital, 369 Mary St., Box 520, NOH 2TO, 519/534-1260
Willowdale - Bloorview Children's Hospital, 25 Buchan Court, M2J 4S9, 416/494-2222
Willowdale - North York Branson Hospital, 555 Finch Ave. W., M2R 1N5, 416/633-9420
Willowdale - North York General Hospital, 4001 Leslie St., M2K 1E1, 416/492-4520
Willowdale - St. Bernard's Convalescent Hospital, 685 Finch Ave. W., M2R 1P2, 416/635-8422
Willowdale - St. John's Convalescent Hospital, 285 Cummer Ave., M2M 2G1, 416/226-6780
Winchester - Winchester Dist. Memorial Hospital, 566 Louise St., KOC 2KO, 613/774-2420
Windsor - Hotel Dieu of St. Joseph Hospital, 1030 Ouellette Ave., N9A 1E1, 519/252-3631
Windsor - Metropolitan General Hospital, 1995 Lens Ave., N8W 1L9, 519/254-1661
Windsor - Salvation Army Grace Hospital, 339 Crawford Ave., N9A 5C6, 519/255-2100
Windsor - Windsor Western Hospital Centre, 1453 Prince Rd., N9C 3Z4, 519/253-4261
Wingham - Wingham & Dist. Hospital, 270 Carling Terrace, NOG 2WO, 519/357-3210
Woodstock - Woodstock General Hospital, 270 Riddell St., N4S 6N6, 519/537-5511

Red Cross Outposts in Ontario

Located at: - Bancroft, Burks Falls, Emo, Haliburton, Lions Head, Mindemoya, Minden, Rainy River, Richard's Landing, Thessalon.

General & Special Rehabilitation Hospitals and Units in Ontario

Chatham - Public General Hospital (Rehab. U.)
Hamilton - Hamilton Civic Hospital (Henderson General U.); Chedoke Continuing Care Centre (Brow Infirmary U.); Chedoke Hospital (Rehab. U.)
Kingston - Kingston General Hospital (Rehab. U.)

Kitchener - Freeport Hospital (U.); Kitchener-Waterloo Hospital (Rehab. U.)
London - Victoria Hospital (Rehab. U.); University Hospital (Rehab. U.)
North York - St. Bernard's Convalescent Hospital; St. John's Convalescent Hospital
Ottawa - Royal Ottawa Hospital; St. Vincent Hospital (U.)
Scarborough - The Providence Hospital (U.)
Sudbury - Laurentian Hospital
Thunder Bay - St. Joseph's General Hospital (U.); Hogarth-Westmount Hospital (Conv. U.)
Toronto - Hillcrest Hospital; Lyndhurst Hospital; Ontario Crippled Children's Centre; The Queen Elizabeth Hospital (U.); Riverdale Hospital (U.); Toronto Rehabilitation Centre
Windsor - I.O.D.E. (Rehab. U.)

Hospitals for Chronically Ill in Ontario

Many Public active treatment hospitals in addition to those listed below also have separate units for the chronically ill.
Brantford - Brantwood Residential Centre
Cornwall - MacDonell Memorial Hospital
Hamilton - Chedoke Continuing Care Centre (Brow Infirmary - Chronic Patients' Unit); St. Peter's Hospital
Kingston - Ongwanada Hospital; St. Mary's of the Lake Hospital
Kitchener - The Freeport Hospital
London - Parkwood Hospital; St. Mary's Hospital
Ottawa - The Perley Hospital; St. Vincent Hospital
St. Catharines - The Shaver Hospital
Scarborough - Providence Hospital
Thunder Bay - Memorial Hospital (Chronic Patients' Unit); Hogarth-Westmount Hospital (Chronic Patients' Unit)
Toronto - Baycrest Hospital; Bloorview Children's Hospital; Our Lady of Mercy Hospital; Queen Elizabeth Hospital; Riverdale Hospital (Chronic Patients' Unit); The Runnymede Hospital; The Salvation Army Grace Hospital
Windsor - Riverview Hospital

PRINCE EDWARD ISLAND

Government Hospitals in Prince Edward Island

The Hillsborough Hospital (for the mentally ill), Box 4000, Charlottetown, P.E.I. C1A 7P3, 902/892-3471
The Provincial Sanatorium & Rehabilitation Centre, McGill Ave., Charlottetown, P.E.I. C1A 2K1, 902/894-7331
Rehabilitation Centre, McGill Ave., Charlottetown, P.E.I. C1A 2K1, 902/892-1225

QUEBEC

Hospitals in Quebec

-not confirmed for 1982-
*INDICATES TEACHING HOSPITAL.
Alma: Hôtel-Dieu D'Alma (1964), 300, boul. Champlain Sud, G8B 3N8
Amos: Centre Hosp. Hôtel-Dieu D'Amos, 622, 4e rue ouest, J9T 2S2
Amqui: Hopital d'Amqui, 135, rue de l'Hopital, GOJ 1BO
Armagh: Corp. de l'Hopital d'Armagh, rue Principale, GOR 1AO
Arthabaska: *Hotel-Dieu d'Arthabaska, 5, rue Quesnel, G6P 6N2
Asbestos: Centre Hosp. d'Asbestos, 475, 3e ave., J1T 1X6
Baie Comeau: Centre Hosp. régional Baie Comeau/Hauterive (Pavillon Baie Comeau), 70, ave Mance, G4Z 1M9
Baie James: Centre Hosp. La Grande Rivière, Chantier L.G.2, JOY 2VO
Baie St-Paul: Centre Hosp. de Charlevoix, 47, boul. Fafard, GOA 1BO
Beauceville: Hopital St-Joseph de Beauceville ouest, 253, Cote de l'Hopital, GOM 1AO
Beauport: *Centre Hosp. Robert Giffard, 2601, de la Canardière, G1J 2G3
Beauport: *Clinique Roy Rousseau, 2579 Ch. de la Canardiere, G1J 2G2
Buckingham: Centre Hosp. de Buckingham, 155, rue MacLaren, J8L 1K5
Cap-aux-Meules: Centre de Santé de l'Archipel, C.P. 730, GOB 1BO
Cap-de-la-Madeleine: Hopital Cloutier, 155, rue Toupin, G8T 7W3
Caughnawaga: Kateri Memorial Hospital, C.P. 10, JOL 1BO
Chandler: Centre Hosp. de Chandler, 250, Mgr Ross, GOC 1KO
Charny: Hopital Notre-Dame d CCharny, 563, 10e rue, G6W 4Z8
Chibougamau: Hopital Chibougamau Ltee, 51, 3e rue, G8P 1N1
Chicoutimi: *Hopital de Chicoutimi Inc., Ave. Saint-Vallier, C.P. 1006, G7H 5H6
Chicoutimi Nord: Institut Roland-Saucier, 150, rue Pinel, G7G 3N8
Coaticook: Centre Hosp. de Coaticook, 138, rue Jeanne Mance, J1A 1W3
Cote Nord du Golfe St-Laurent: Centre de Santé de la Basse Côte Nord, G0G 1W0
Cowansville: Brôme-Missisquoi-Perkins Hospital, 950, rue Principale, J2K 1K3
Dolbeau: Centre Hosp. de Dolbeau, 2000, boul. Sacre-Coeur, G8L 2R5
Drummondville: *Hopital Ste-Croix, 570, rue Heriot, J2B 1C1
Escoumins: Centre Hosp. St-Alexandre, 4, rue de l'Hopital, C.P. 400, GOT 1KO
Fleurimont: *Centre Hosp. Universitaire de Sherbrooke, 3001, 12e ave nord, J1H 5N4
Fort George: Hopital Chashasipich (Baie James), JOM 1EO
Gagnon: Hopital de Gagnon, 233, 1e Ave., GOG 1KO
Gaspé: Hotel-Dieu de Gaspé, 215, Havre-de-Gaspé, GOC 1RO
Gaspé: Le Sanatorium Ross, C.P. 800, GOC 1RO
Granby: Centre Hosp. de Granby, 205, boul. Leclerc, J2G 1T7
Grand-Mère: Centre Hosp. Laflèche-Grand-Mère, 1650, 6e ave, G9T 2K4
Greenfield Park: *Hopital Charles Lemoyne, 121, boul. Taschereau, J4V 2H1
Hauterive: Centre Hosp. régional Baie Comeau/Hauterive (Pavillon Hauterive), 635, boul. Joliet, G5C 1P1
Havre-Saint-Pierre: Hopital St-Jean-Eudes, 1035, Promenade des Anciens, GOG 1PO
Hull: Centre Hosp. du Sacre-Coeur, 230, boul. Gamelin, J8Y 1W7
Hull: Centre Hosp. Pierre-Janet, 20, rue Pharand, J9A 1K7
Huntingdon: Huntingdon County Hosp., 198, rue Chateauguay, JOS 1HO
Joliette: Centre Hosp. régional Delanaudière (Pavillon St-Eusèbe), 585, boul. Manseau, J6E 3E5
Jonquière: Centre Hosp. Jonquière, 450, rue de l'Hopital, G7X 7X2
Kuujjuaq: Hopital de l'Ungava, C.P. 149, J0M 1C0
La Baie: Hopital de la Baie des Ha Ha, 100, Ave. du Parc, G7B 3P9
Lac Etchemin: Sanatorium Begin, rue du Sanatorium, GOR 4KO
Lachine: Centre Hosp. de Lachine, 650, 16e Ave., H8S 3N5
Lachine: Lachine General Hospital, 3320, rue Notre-Dame, H8T 1W8
Lachute: L'Hopital d'Argenteuil, 145, boul. de la Providence, J8H 3X5
Lac Megantic: Hopital Saint-Joseph, 3569, rue Laval, G6B 1A5
La Malbaie: Centre Hosp. Saint-Joseph de la Malbaie, 303, rue Saint-Etienne, GOT 1JO
L'Annonciation: Hopital des Laurentides, rue Principale nord, JOT 1TO
La Peche: Gatineau Memorial Hospital, Wakefield, C.P. 160, JOX 3GO

La Pocatière: Hopital de Notre-Dame-de-Fatima, 404, 12e rue, GOR 1ZO
LaSalle: Hopital General LaSalle, 8585, Terrasse Champlain, H8P 1C1
La Sarre: Centre Hosp. Saint-François-d'Assise, Chemin Macamic, J9Z 2X7
La Tuque: Hopital St-Joseph de La Tuque, 885, boul. Ducharme, G9X 3C1
Laval: Centre Métropolitain de Chirurgie Plastique Inc., 300, rue Desnoyers, H7G 4R1
Laval: *Cite de la Santé de Laval, 1755, boul. Rene Leannec, H7M 3L9
Lebel-sur-Quevillon: Hopital Lebel, 156, boul. Quevillon nord, JOY 1XO
Lévis: *Hotel-Dieu de Lévis, 143, rue Wolfe, G6V 3Z1
Loretteville: Corp. du Centre Hosp. Chauveau, 29, rue de l'Hopital, G2A 2T7
Louiseville: Hopital Comtois, 41, boul. Comtois, J5V 2H8
Magog: Hopital La Providence de Magog, 50, rue Saint-Patrice est, J1X 1T4
Malartic: Centre Hosp. de Malartic, 1141, rue Royale, JOY 1ZO
Maniwaki: La Corp. du Centre Hosp. de Maniwaki, 309, boul. Desjardins, J9E 2E7
Maria: Centre Hosp. Baie-des-Chaleurs, 419, rte 132, C.P. 600, GOC 1YO
Matagami: Centre Hosp. Isle-Dieu Inc., 130, Boul. Matagami, JOY 2AO
Matane: Centre Hosp. de Matane, 333, rue Thibault, G4W 2W5
Mont-Laurier: Hopital Ste-Croix, rue Mont-Laurier, J9L 3G3
Montmagny: Hôtel-Dieu de Montmagny, 350, boul. Tache ouest, R.R. 1, G5V 3R8
Montreal: *Centre Hosp. Thoracique de Montreal, 3650, rue St-Urbain, H2X 2P4
Montreal: Clinique Médicale de l'Est Inc., 30, boul. Saint-Joseph est, H2T 1G9
Montreal: Hopital Bellechasse, 3950, rue de Bellechasse, H1X 1J5
Montreal: *Hopital du Sacré-Coeur, Montréal, 5400, boul Gouin ouest, H4J 1C5
Montreal: Hopital General Fleury, 2180, rue Fleury est, H2B 1K3
Montreal: Hopital Jean-Talon, 1385, rue Jean-Talon est, H2E 1S6
Montreal: *Hopital Maisonneuve-Rosemont, 5415, boul de l'Assomption, H1T 2M4
Montreal: *Hopital Neurologique de Montreal, 3801, rue University, H3A 2B4
Montreal: *Hopital Notre-Dame, 1560, rue Sherbrooke est, H2L 4M1
Montreal: *Hopital Rivière-des-Prairies, 7070, boul. Perras, H1E 1A4
Montreal: Hopital Rosemont, 1970, boul Rosemont, H2G 1S8
Montreal: Hopital Ste-Jeanne d'Arc, 3570, rue Saint-Urbain, H2X 2N8
Montreal: *Hopital Ste-Justine, 3175, Côte Ste-Catherine, H3T 1C5
Montreal: *L'Hopital St-Luc, 1058 rue St-Denis, H2X 3J4
Montreal: Hopital St-Michel, 8040, 9e ave, H1Z 2Y9
Montreal: Hopital Santa-Cabrini, 5655, St-Zotique est, H1T 1P7
Montreal: *Hotel-Dieu de Montreal, 3840, rue St-Urbain, H2W 1T8
Montreal: *Institut de Cardiologie de Montreal, 5000, rue Belanger, est, H1T 1C8
Montreal: *Insitut de réadaptation de Montreal, 6300, ave Darlington, H3S 2J4
Montreal: *Institut Philippe-Pinel de Montreal, 10905, boul Henri-Bourassa est, H1C 1H1
Montreal: *Jewish General Hospital / Hopital Général Juif Sir Mortimer B. Davis, 3755, Cote Ste-Catherine, H3T 1E2
Montreal: *Montreal Children's Hospital / L'Hopital de Montréal pour enfants, 2300, rue Tupper, H3H 1P3
Montreal: *Montreal General Hospital / Hopital général de Montréal, 1650, ave Cedar, H3G 1A4
Montreal: *Queen Elizabeth Hospital / Hopital Reine Elizabeth de Montréal, 2100, ave Marlowe, H4A 3L6
Montreal: *Royal Victoria Hospital, 687, ave des Pins, H3A 1A1
Montreal: *St-Mary's Hospital / Centre Hosp. de St. Mary, 3830, ave Lacombe, H3T 1M5
Montreal: *Shriners Hospital for Crippled Children, 1529, Ave. Cedar, H3G 1A6
Murdochville: Hopital de Murdochville, 600, ave est, GOE 1WO
Nicolet: Hopital du Christ-Roi, 675, rue St-Jean-Baptiste, JOG 1EO
Noranda: Centre Hospitalier Rouyn-Noranda, 4, 9e rue, J9X 2B2
Notre-Dame-du-Lac: Hopital Notre-Dame-du-Lac, 58, rue de l'Eglise, GOL 1XO
Ormstown: The Barrie Memorial Hospital, rue Gale, JOS 1KO
Pointe-Claire: *Lakeshore General Hospital / Hopital général du Lakeshore, 160, Chemin Stillview, H9R 2Y2
Port Cartier: Centre de Santé de Port Cartier, 103, boul des Rochelois, G5B 1K5
Quebec: *Hopital du St-Sacrement, 1050, Chemin Ste-Foy, G1S 4L8
Quebec: *Hopital de l'Enfant-Jésus, 1401, 18e rue, G1J 1Z4
Quebec: *Hopital Jeffery Hale, 1250, Chemin Ste-Foy, G1S 2M6
Quebec: Hopital Notre-Dame-de-l'Esperance, 383, Chemin Ste-Foy, G1R 4V9
Quebec: *Hopital St-François-d'Assise, 10, rue de l'Espinay, G1L 3L5
Quebec: *L'Hotel Dieu de Quebec, 11, Côte du Palais, G1R 2J6
Quebec: *Hotel Dieu du Sacre-Coeur-de-Jésus, ave du Sacre-Coeur, G1N 2W1
Repentigny: L'Hopital Le Gardeur Inc., 141, rue Ethier, J6A 1N6
Rimouski: Hopital St-Joseph de Rimouski, 150, ave Rouleau, G5L 5T1
Rivière-du-Loup: L'Hotel Dieu de Rivière-du-Loup, 75, rue St-Henri, G5R 2A4
Roberval: Centre Psychiatrique de Roberval, 483, ave Bouchard, G8H 1K2
Roberval: Hotel-Dieu de Roberval, 140, ave Lizotte, G8H 1B9
St-Charles-Borromée: Centre Hosp. régional Delanaudière (Pavillon St-Charles), 1000, boul. Ste-Anne, J6E 6J2
St-Eustache: Centre Hosp. St-Eustache, 520, boul Sauve, J7R 4K6
St-Georges-Ouest: Hotel-Dieu Notre-Dame de Beauce, 1500, 18e rue, G5Y 4T8
St-Hyacinthe: Hopital Honore Mercier Inc., 2750, ave Laframboise, J2S 4Y8
St-Jean-Baptiste: Hopital de Mont Joli Inc., 800, ave du Sanatorium, G5H 3L6
St-Jean sur Richelieu: Hopital du Haut-Richelieu, 920, boul du Seminaire, J3A 1B7
St-Jean-de-Dieu: *Hopital Louis H. Lafontaine, Gamelin, H1N 3M5
St-Jérôme: Hotel-Dieu de St-Jérôme, 290, rue Montigny, J7Z 5T3
St-Laurent: Centre Hosp. Notre-Dame de L'Espérance de St-Laurent, 1275, Chemin Cote Vertu, H4L 4V2
St-Raymond: Hopital St-Raymond, 700, rue St-Cyrille, GOA 4GO
Ste-Agathe-des-Monts: Centre Hosp. Laurentien, 234, rue St-Vincent, J8C 2B8
Ste-Anne-de-Beaupre: Hopital Ste-Anne-de-Beaupre, 9974, rue Royale, GOA 3CO
Ste-Anne-des-Monts: Corp. de l'Hopital des Monts, 50, Belvedere, GOE 2GO
Ste-Foy: *Centre Hosp. de l'Université Laval, 2705, boul Laurier, G1V 4G2
Ste-Foy: *Hopital Laval, 2725, Chemin Ste-Foy, G1V 4G5
Salaberry de Valleyfield: Centre Hosp. de Valleyfield, 245, rue Salaberry, J6T 2J5
Schefferville: Centre Hosp. de Schefferville, 238, rue Hudson, GOG 1TO
Sept-Iles: Corp. de l'Hopital de Sept-Iles, 45, rue Pere Divet, G4R 3N7

Shawinigan Sud: Hopital Regional de la Mauricie, 50, 118eme rue, G9P 4E7
Shawville: Pontiac Community Hospital Inc., rue Clarendon, JOX 2YO
Sherbrooke: *Centre Hosp. St-Vincent de Paul, 300, rue King est, J1G 1B1
Sherbrooke: *Hotel-Dieu de Sherbrooke, 580, rue Bowen sud, J1G 2E8
Sherbrooke: *Centre Hosp. de Sherbrooke, 375, rue Argyle, J1J 3H5
Sorel: Hotel-Dieu de Sorel, 400, ave Hotel-Dieu, J3P 1N5
Temiscaming: CLSC de Témiscaming, 320, ave Thorne, JOZ 3RO
Thetford Mines, Hopital General de la Region de l'Amiante, 1717, rue Notre-Dame nord, G6G 2V4
Trois-Rivières: Centre Hosp. Cooke, 3950, Chemin Ste-Marguerite, G8Z 1X3
Trois-Rivières: *Centre Hosp. St-Joseph de Trois-Rivières, 731, rue Ste-Julie, G9A 1Y1
Trois-Rivières: *Centre Hosp. Ste-Marie, 1991, boul du Carmel, G8Z 3R9
Val d'Or: Centre Hosp. St-Sauveur, 725, 6e rue, J9P 3Y1
Vanier: *Hopital Christ-Roi, 300, boul Wilfrid Hamel, G1M 2R9
Verdun: *Centre Hosp. de Verdun, 4000, boul Lasalle, H4G 2A3
Verdun: *Hopital Douglas, 6875, boul. Lasalle, H4H 1R3
Ville-Marie: Centre de Santé Ste-Famille, 22, rue Notre-Dame, JOZ 3WO
Westmount: *Reddy Memorial Hospital, 4039, rue Tupper, H3Z 1T5

Extended Care Hospitals & Units in Quebec

Aylmer: Mont St-Jude Inc., 32, Chemin Fraser, J9H 2H8
Beauport: L'Hopital Saint-Augustin, 2135, Terrasse Cadieux, G1C 1Z2
Bedford: CLSC de Bedford, 14, rue de l'Hopital, JOJ 1AO
Bernierville: Hopital St-Julien, 220, rue Principale, GON 1NO
Berthierville: Hopital Le Chateau de Berthier Inc., 730, rue Frontenac, JOK 1AO
Coteau-Landing: Hopital Notre-Dame-de-Coteau-Landing Ltee, 37, rue Principale, JOP 1CO
Cote-Saint-Luc: Maimonides Hospital & Home for the Aged, 5795, ave Caldwell, H4W 1W3
Cowansville: Hopital St-Louis de Cowansville Inc., 133, rue Larouche, J2K 1T2
Deux-Montagnes: Centre Hospitalier Deux-Montagnes Inc., 2700, Chemin Oka, J7R 4K1
Drummondville: Centre Hospitalier Georges Frederic, 75, rue Saint-Georges, J2C 4G6
Gatineau: Hopital Notre Dame de Gatineau Ltee, 176, rue Brian, J8P 6J3
Granby: Hopital Notre-Dame de Granby (1967) Inc., 363, rue Notre Dame, J2G 3L4
Greenfield Park: Centre Hosp. Rive-sud Inc., 860, Chemin Victoria, J4V 1M8
Hull, ouest: Hopital de la Pieta, 273, rue Laurier, J8X 3W8
Jonquiere: Centre Hosp. Jonquière (Pavillon Arvida), Chemin Deschenes, G7X 6X2
Lachine: Bussey Chronic Hospital Reg'd., 2069, rue Saint-Joseph, H8S 4B7
Lac Megantic: Hopital Frere Andre, 4982, rue Champlain, G6B 1X8
LaSalle: Hopital Ste-Therese Inc., 9307, boul. Lasalle, H8R 2M7
Laval: *Hopital Juif de Convalescence, 3205, rue Alton Goldbloom, H7V 1R2
Laval: Hopital St-Jude de Laval Ltee, 4410, boul. Saint-Martin ouest, H7T 1C3
Longueuil: Hopital St-Felix de Longueuil Inc., 650, Chemin Chambly, J4H 3L8
Macamic: Centre Hospitalier St-Jean, JOZ 2SO
Metabetchouan: Centre Hospitalier de Metabetchouan, 40, rue de l'Hopital, GOW 2AO
Montreal: Catherine Booth Hospital Centre, 4375, ave Montclair, H4B 2J5
Montreal: Centre de Sante St-Henri Inc., 5205, rue Notre-Dame ouest, H4C 3L2
Montreal: Centre de Soins Prolonges de Monteal, 5155, rue Sainte-Catherine est, H1V 2A5
Montreal: *Centre Hospitalier Cote-des-Neiges, 4565, Chemin de la Reine Marie, H3W 1W5
Montreal: Centre Hospitalier Jacques Viger, 1051, rue Saint-Hubert, H2L 3Y5
Montreal: Centre Hospitalier J. Henri Charbonneau, 3095, rue Sherbrooke est, H1W 1B2
Montreal: Centre Hospitalier Notre-Dame de la Merci, 555, boul. Gouin ouest, H3L 1K5
Montreal: Centre Hospitalier Saint-Charles Borromee, 66, boul. Dorchester est, H2X 1N3
Montreal: Centre Hospitalier St-Georges Inc., 1205, rue Labelle, H2L 4C1
Montreal: Grace Dart Hospital, 6085, rue Sherbrooke est, H1N 1C2
Montreal: Hopital Bois-Menu Inc., 2710, boul. Gouin est, H2B 1Y6
Montreal: Hopital Chinois de Montreal, 7500, rue Saint-Denis, H2R 2E6
Montreal: L'Hopital des Convalescents de Montreal, 6363, Chemin Hudson, H3S 1M9
Montreal: Hopital du Tres-Saint-Redempteur, 3591, rue Sainte-Catherine est, H1W 2E6
Montreal: Hopital Jeanne-Mance Inc., 1640, rue Tillemont, H2E 1C2
Montreal: Hopital La Visitation, 161, boul. Henri-Bourassa ouest, H3L 1N2
Montreal: Hopital Marie Enfant, 5200, rue Belanger est, H1T 1C9
Montreal: Hopital Notre-Dame de Lourdes, 1870, boul. Pie IX, H1V 2C6
Montreal: Hopital Saint-Albert-Le-Grand, 4357, ave Charlemagne, H1X 2H2
Montreal: Hopital St-Denis Enr., 2870, boul. Rosemont, H1Y 1L7
Montreal: Hopital Saint-Joseph de la Providence, 11844, Bois-de-boulogne, H3M 2X7
Montreal: Hopital West End, 6935, rue Hamilton, H4E 3C8
Montreal: Jewish Hospital of Hope Centre / Centre Hosp. Juif de l'Espérance, 7745, rue Sherbrooke est, H1L 1A3
Montreal: *Julius Richardson Convalescent Hospital, 5425, ave Bessborough, H4V 2S7
Montreal: Villa Medica Inc., 225, rue Sherbrooke est, H2X 1C9
Montreal-Nord: Hopital Marie Clarac, 3530, boul. Gouin est, H1H 1B7
Montreal-Nord: Hopital Marie Claret, 3345, boul. Henri-Bourassa est, H1H 1H6
Montreal-Nord: Hopital Ste-Rita, 11720, ave Desy, H1G 4C3
Montreal-Nord: Hopital Sainte-Therese des Convalescents Enr., 11129, ave Ethier, H1H 3G8
Nicolet: Foyer de Nicolet, 175, ave d'Youville, JOG 1EO
Plessisville: CLSC de l'Erable, 1331, rue Saint-Calixte, G6L 1P4
Pohenegamook: CLSC des Frontières, C.P. 70, G0L 2T0
Pointe-aux-Trembles: Centre Le Cardinal Inc., 12940, rue Notre-Dame est, H1A 1R9
Pointe-aux-Trembles: Hopital Bourget Inc., 11570, rue Notre-Dame est, H1B 2X4
Pointe-aux-Trembles: Hopital Ste-Germaine Cousin Inc., 14241, ave Victoria est, H1A 1P2
Pointe-Claire: Centre Hospitalier Bayview Inc., 27 route Lakeshore, H9S 4H1
Quebec: Centre Hospitalier Notre-Dame du Chemin Inc., 510, Chemin Sainte-Foy, G1S 2J5
Quebec: Centre Hospitalier St-Francois Inc., 1604, 1ere Ave., G1L 3L6
Quebec: Centre Hospitalier St-Sacrement Ltee, 1165, Chemin Sainte-Foy, G1S 2M8
Quebec: Hopital Civique de Quebec, 2480, Chemin de la Canardiere, G1J 2G1
Quebec: Hopital Fleur de Lys (1968) Inc., 220, de la Sapiniere Dorion est, G1L 1P5

Quebec: *Hopital General de Quebec, 260, boul. Langelier, G1K 5N1
Quebec: Hopital Ste-Monique (1970) Inc., 3415, boul. Wilfrid Hamel, G1P 2J7
Rawdon: Heather Hospital Inc., 800, 3e Ave., JOK 1SO
Rivière-du-Loup: Hopital Saint-Joseph-Rivière-du-Loup, 28, rue Joly, G5R 3H2
Sainte-Agathe-des-Monts: Centre Hosp. Laurentien (Pavillon Préfontaine), 2, Prefontaine ouest, J8C 1C3
Sainte-Agathe sud: Hopital Mont-Sinai, Ch. Trudel, J8C 3A4
Sainte-Anne-de-Bellevue: Hopital Sainte-Anne-de-Bellevue, 305, rue Saint-Pierre, H9X 1Y9
Saint-Charles Borromée: Centre Hosp. régional Delanaudière (Pavillon Delanaudière), 1000, boul. Sainte-Anne, J6E 6J2
Saint-Georges: Centre Hospitalier de l'Assomption (St-Geo. de Beauce) Inc., 16750, route Kennedy, G5Y 2G4
Saint-Hubert: Centre Hospitalier St-Louis Enrg., 2065, rue Charles, J4T 1L7
Saint-Hubert: Centre Hospitalier Régina Ltée, 2042, boul. Marie, J4T 2B4
Saint-Hyacinthe: Hotel-Dieu de St-Hyacinthe, 1800, rue Dessaulles, J2S 2T2
Saint-Jean-Port-Joli: CLSC des Trois-Saumons, Ave de Gaspé, GOR 3GO
Saint-Jerome: Centre Hospitalier d'Youville, 531, rue Laviolette, J7Y 2T8
Saint-Lambert: Hopital St-Lambert, 831, ave Notre-Dame, J4R 1S1
Saint-Mathieu-de-Beloeil: Centre Hospitalier Beloeil Inc., 221, rue Brunelle, J3G 2M9
Saint-Michel: Hopital Notre-Dame de Lourdes Inc., 80, rue Principale, GOR 3SO
Saint-Michel-du-Squatec: Hopital Saint-Michel-du-Squateck, 10, rue Saint-Andre, GOL 4HO
Saint-Pacome: L'Hopital d'Anjou Inc., 127, rue Galarneau, GOL 3XO
Shawinigan: Centre Hospitalier Sainte-Therese de Shawinigan, 1705, ave Georges, G9N 2N1
Sherbrooke: *La Corp. de l'Hopital d'Youville de Sherbrooke, 1036, rue Belvedere Sud, J1H 4C4
Sorel: L'Hopital Général de Sorel, 151, rue Georges, J3P 1C8
Sorel: Hopital Richelieu Inc., 89, rue Prince, J3P 4J7
Trois-Pistoles: Centre de Sante Boisbouscache, 550, rue Notre-Dame est, GOL 4KO
Trois-Rivières: Centre Hospitalier Cooke, 3450, rue Ste-Marguerite, G8Z 1X3
Verdun: Hopital Champlain de Verdun, 1350, ave Leclair, H4H 2M7
Victoriaville: Centre Hospitalier des Bois-Francs, 61, ave de l'Ermitage, G6P 6X4
Waterloo: Centre Hospitalier de Waterloo, 5300, ave Courville, JOE 2NO
Windsor: Hopital St-Louis de Windsor, Inc., 23, rue Ambroise-Dearden, J1S 1G8

SASKATCHEWAN

Government-Aided Hospitals in Saskatchewan

Facilities approved under the Hospital Standards Act, for purposes of payment by the Sask. Hospital Services Plan.
*INDICATES TEACHING HOSPITAL

Area Code is 306

Arborfield: Union Hospital (SOE OAO) 769-8722
Arcola: Brock Union Hospital (SOC OGO) 455-2433
Assiniboia: Union Hospital (SOH OBO) 642-3351
Balcarres: Union Hospital (SOG OCO) 334-2636
Beechy: Union Hospital (SOL OCO) 859-2118
Bengough: Union Hospital (SOC OKO) 268-2944
Bienfait: Bienfait-Coalfields Union Hospital (SOC OMO) 388-2282
Biggar: Union Hospital (SOK OMO) 948-3323
Big River: Union Hospital (SOJ OEO) 469-2220
Birch Hills: Memorial Union Hospital (SOJ OGO) 749-3331
Borden: Union Hospital (SOK ONO) 997-2110
Broadview: Union Hospital (SOG OKO) 696-2441
Cabri: Union Hospital (SON OJO) 587-2623
Canora: Union Hospital (SOA OLO) 563-5621
Carrot River: Union Hospital (SOE OLO) 768-2722
Central Butte: Union Hospital (SOH OTO) 796-2190
Climax: Border Union Hospital (SON ONO) 293-2222
Coronach: Union Hospital (SOH OZO) 267-2022
Craik: Community Hospital (SOG OVO) 734-2288
Cudworth: St. Michael's Hospital (SOK 1BO) 256-3443
Cupar: Union Hospital (SOG OYO) 723-4411
Cut Knife: Union Hospital (SOM ONO) 398-4718
Davidson: Union Hospital (SOG 1AO) 567-2801
Delisle: Community Health & Social Centre (SOL OPO) 493-2323
Dinsmore: Union Hospital (SOL OTO) 846-2222
Dodsland: Union Hospital (SOL OVO) 356-2172
Eastend: Union Hospital (SON OTO) 295-3202
Eatonia: Union Hospital (SOL OYO) 967-2212
Edam: Lady Minto Union Hospital at Edam (SOM OVO) 397-2222
Elrose: Union Hospital (SOL OZO) 378-2882
Esterhazy: St. Anthony's Hospital (SOA OXO) 745-3973
Estevan: St. Joseph's General Hospital (S4A OH3) 634-3604
Eston: Union Hospital (SOL 1AO) 962-3667
Fillmore: Union Hospital (SOG 1NO) 722-3281
Foam Lake: Union Hospital (SOA 1AO) 272-3737
Gainsborough: Union Hospital (SOC OZO) 685-2277
Goodsoil: Union Hospital (SOM 1AO) 238-2100
Gravelbourg: St. Joseph's Hospital (SOH 1XO) 648-2565
Grenfell: Union Hospital (SOG 2BO) 697-2585
Gull Lake: Union Hospital (SON 1AO) 672-3337
Hafford: Union Hospital (SOJ 1AO) 549-2108
Herbert: Herbert-Morse Union Hospital (SOH 2AO) 784-2533
Hodgeville: Community Health & Social Centre (SOH 2BO) 677-2223
Hudson Bay: Union Hospital (SOE OYO) 865-2219
Humboldt: St. Elizabeth's Hospital (SOK 2AO) 682-2603
Ile a la Crosse: St. Joseph's Hospital (SOM 1CO) 833-2081
Imperial: Union Hospital (SOG 2JO) 963-2210
Indian Head: Union Hospital (SOG 2KO) 695-3878
Invermay: Invermay-Canora Union Hospital (SOA 1MO) 593-2133
Ituna: Union Hospital (SOA 1NO) 795-2622
Kamsack: Union Hospital (SOA 1SO) 542-2636
Kelvington: Union Hospital (SOA 1WO) 327-4711
Kerrobert: Union Hospital (SOL 1RO) 834-2733
Kincaid: Union Hospital (SOH 2JO) 264-3233
Kindersley: Union Hospital (SOL 1SO) 463-2613
Kinistino: Union Hospital (SOJ 1HO) 864-2525
Kipling: Memorial Union Hospital (SOG 2SO) 736-2553
Kyle: Kyle-Whitebear Union Hospital (SOL 1TO) 375-2251
Lafleche: Union Hospital (SOH 2KO) 472-5230
LaLoche: St. Martin's Hospital (SOM 1GO) 822-2011
Lampman: Union Hospital (SOC 1NO) 487-2561
Langenburg: Union Hospital (SOA 2AO) 743-2661
Lanigan: Union Hospital (SOK 2MO) 365-2022
LaRonge: LaRonge Hospital (SOJ 1LO) 425-2422
Leader: Union Hospital (SON 1HO) 628-3343
Leoville: Union Hospital (SOJ 1NO) 984-2136
Leroy: Community Health & Social Centre (SOK 2PO) 286-3288
Lestock: St. Joseph's Union Hospital (SOA 2GO) 274-2215
Lloydminster: Community Health Services Association Ltd. (S9V OY6) 825-8312
Lloydminster: Lloydminster Hospital (S9V OZ5) 825-2211
Loon Lake: Union Hospital (SOM 1LO) 837-2123
Lucky Lake: Union Hospital (SOL 1ZO) 858-2133
Macklin: St. Joseph's Hospital (SOL 2CO) 753-2115
Maidstone: Union Hospital (SOM 1MO) 893-2622
Mankota: Union Hospital (SOH 2WO) 478-2200

Maple Creek: Union Hospital (SON 1NO) 667-2611
Maryfield: Community Health & Social Centre (SOG 3KO) 646-2133
Meadow Lake: Union Hospital (SOM 1VO) 236-5656
Melfort: Union Hospital (SOE 1AO) 752-2811
Melfort: Parkland Hospital (SOE 1AO) 752-2767
Melville: St. Peter's Hospital (SOA 2PO) 728-5407
Midale: Union Hospital (SOC 1SO) 458-2300
Milden: Union Hospital (SOL 2LO) 935-2142
Montmartre: Union Hospital (SOG 3MO) 424-2155
Moose Jaw: Providence Hospital (S6H 4S7) 692-6471
Moose Jaw: Union Hospital (S6H 1H3) 692-1841
Moosomin: Union Hospital (SOG 3NO) 435-3303
Mossbank: Community Health & Social Centre (SOH 3GO) 354-2414
Neilburg: Neilburg & Dist. Union Hospital (SOM 2CO) 823-4262
Neudorf: Community Health & Social Centre (SOA 2TO) 748-2566
Nipawin: Union Hospital (SOE 1EO) 862-4643
Nokomis: Union Hospital (SOG 3RO) 528-2114
Norquay: The Norquay-Canora Union Hospital (SOA OLO) 594-2133
North Battleford: The Battlefords Union Hospital (S9A 1Z1) 445-2411
Outlook: Union Hospital (SOL 2NO) 867-8676
Oxbow: Union Hospital (SOC 2BO) 483-2366
Pangman: Union Hospital (SOC 2CO) 442-2044
Paradise Hill: Union Hospital (SOM 2GO) 344-2262
Ponteix: Union Hospital (SON 1ZO) 625-3379
Porcupine Plain: Porcupine-Carragana Union Hospital (SOE 1HO) 278-2233
Preeceville: Union Hospital (SOA 3BO) 547-2102
Prince Albert: Prince Albert Co-operative Health Centre (S6V OV7) 763-6466
Prince Albert: Victoria Union Hospital (S6V 5T4) 764-1551
Prince Albert: Holy Family Hospital (S6V 3R8) 922-2605
Quill Lake: Community Health & Social Centre (SOA 3EO) 383-2266
Rabbit Lake: Union Hospital (SOM 2LO) 824-2020
Radville: Community Hospital (SOC 2GO) 869-2711
Redvers: Union Hospital (SOC 2HO) 452-3553
Regina: Community Health Services Association (Regina) Ltd. (S4R 4A9) 543-7880
Regina: *Regina General Hospital (1400 14 Ave., S4P OW5) 359-4444
Regina: Pasqua Hospital (S4T 1A5) 527-9641
Regina: *South Sask. Hospital Centre (4500 Wascana Pkwy., S4S 5W9) 584-6211
Regina: Wascana Hospital (S4S OA5) 359-9339
Regina: Plains Health Centre (S4S 5W9) 584-6211
Rockglen: Union Hospital (SOH 3RO) 476-2105
Rosetown: Union Hospital (SOL 2VO) 882-2672
Rose Valley: Union Hospital (SOE 1MO) 322-2115
Rosthern: Union Hospital (SOK 3RO) 232-4811
St. Walburg: Union Hospital (SOM 2TO) 248-3355
Saskatoon: Community Health Services (Saskatoon) Association Ltd. (S7K 2C2) 652-0300
Saskatoon: *St. Paul's Hospital (1702 20th St. W., S7M OZ9) 382-3220
Saskatoon: *Saskatoon City Hospital (Queen St. & 7th Ave., S7K OM7) 242-6681
Saskatoon: Sanatorium, Chronic Care Unit (S7H 1L2) 644-6480
Saskatoon: *University Hospital (S7N OXO) 343-2112
Shaunavon: Union Hospital (SON 2MO) 297-2644
Shellbrook: Union Hospital (SOJ 2EO) 747-2603
Smeaton: Union Hospital (SOJ 2JO) 426-2051
Spalding: Union Hospital (SOK 4CO) 872-2022
Spiritwood: Union Hospital (SOJ 2MO) 883-2133
Strasbourg: Community Health & Social Centre (SOG 4VO) 725-3220
Swift Current: Union Hospital (S9H 2K1) 773-2851
Swift Current: Palliser Hospital (S9H 3G6) 773-8307
Theodore: Union Hospital (SOA 4CO) 647-2375
Tisdale: Tisdale Union Hospital (SOE 1TO) 873-2621
Turtleford: Riverside Memorial Union Hospital (SOM 2YO) 845-2195
Unity: Union Hospital (SOK 4LO) 228-2666
Uranium City: Municipal Hospital (SOJ 2WO) 498-2412
Vanguard: Union Hospital (SON 2VO) 582-2044
Wadena: Union Hospital (SOA 4JO) 338-2515
Wakaw: Union Hospital (SOK 4PO) 233-4611
Watrous: Union Hospital (SOK 4TO) 946-3341
Watson: Union Hospital (SOK 4VO) 287-3366
Wawota: Memorial Union Hospital (SOG 5AO) 739-2244
Weyburn: Souris Valley Hospital (S4H 2L7) 359-3911
Whitewood: Whitewood-Moosomin Union Hospital (SOG 3NO) 735-2688
Wilkie: Union Hospital (SOK 4WO) 843-2644
Willowbunch: Community Health & Social Centre (SOH 4KO) 473-2302
Wolseley: Memorial Union Hospital (SOG 5HO) 698-2377
Wynyard: Union Hospital (SOA 4TO) 554-2586
Yorkton: Union Hospital (S3N 2K6) 782-2401
Zenon Park: Community Health & Social Centre (SOE 1WO) 767-2221

Indian Health Services Units in Saskatchewan

Fort Qu'Appelle: Indian Hospital (SOG 1SO) 332-5611

MEMBERS - DOMINION CHARTERED CUSTOMS-HOUSE BROKERS ASSOCIATION

*Telephone — **Telex

British Columbia

ALDERGROVE

Border Brokers Inc., R.R.5 (VOX 1AO)
*604/534-0733 —**via Pacific Hwy.

BURNABY

Allcity Customs Brokers Ltd., #17, 7867 Express St.
*604/420-7030
Border Brokers Inc., 7867 Express St., Lake City (North Burnaby, V5A 1T2)
*604/420-3103 — **04-354692
G.M. Patry Ltd., 7867 Express St., Rm. 204 (V5A 1S7)
*604/420-4510

CRANBROOK

Federated Customs Brokers Ltd., Box 547 (V1C 4S1)
*604/426-5918 — **041-45191

DAWSON CREEK

Interior Brokers Ltd., 10504 10th St. (Box 728, V1G 4A7)
*604/782-5626 — **036-77166

HUNTINGDON

Border Brokers Inc., Box 79 (VOX 1MO)
*604/534-2522 — **via Pacific Hwy.
Highway Customs Brokers Ltd., Box 83 (V0X 1M0)
*604/853-7014
Pacific Customs Brokers Ltd. (affil. of International-Import), Box 76 (V0X 1M0)
*604/530-1811 — **04-363551

KAMLOOPS

Kamloops Customs Brokers (1974) Ltd., #6, 264 4th Ave. (V2C 1N5)
*604/372-9356/7 — **048-8163

KELOWNA

Kelowna Customs Broker Ltd., Box 909 (V1Y 7P5)
*604/762-0414 — **048-5229

KINGSGATE
Border Brokers Inc. (VOB 1VO)
*604/424-5540 — **041-45134
H.H. Smith Ltd., General Delivery (V0B 1V0)
*604/424-5458 — **038-49190

NANAIMO
Island Shipping Ltd., Box 32 (V9R 5K4)
*604/754-2305 — **044-6111

NEW WESTMINSTER
Courtney Agencies Ltd., Box 733 (V3L 4Z3)
*604/522-9741 — **04-54662
Milne & Craighead, 528 Carnarvon St., Box 696 (V3L 4Z3)
*604/522-4671 —**04-5856
New West Customs Brokers Ltd., #405, 549 Columbia St. (V3L 1B2)
*604/525-6671

NORTH BURNABY
See Burnaby

OSOYOOS
Canco Customs Brokers Ltd., Box 310 (V0H 1V0)
*604/495-7241 — **048-88220
Lorne Adams Customs House Broker, Box 658 (V0H 1V0)
*604/495-7110 — **048-88177
L. Topliss & Co. Ltd., Box 310 (V0H 1V0)
*604/495-7241 — **048-88220

PACIFIC HIGHWAY
A & A Contract Customs Brokers Ltd., 80 176th St., Surrey (V3S 5J9)
*604/531-2842
Border Brokers Inc., 45 176th St., Surrey (V3S 5J9)
*604/531-2944 — **04-351228
Highway Customs Brokers Ltd., 80 176th St., Surrey (V3S 4N8)
*604/536-2121
KN Customs Brokers, #2D, 120 176th St., Surrey (V3S 5J9)
*604/684-4531 — **04/51247
Pacific Customs Brokers Ltd., 73 176th St., Surrey (V3S 5J9)
*604/531-2966 — **04-365667
G.M. Patry Ltd., #26, 120 176th St., Surrey (V5S 5J9)
*604/536-4043
Peace Bridge Brokerage Ltd., R.R. 8, 80 176th St., Surrey (V3S 4N8)
*604/536-1221

PENTICTON
Adams, Lorne, Customs House Brokers, #192, 333 Martin St. (V2A 1L0)
*604/492-8105 — **048-88138
Canco Customs Brokers Ltd., 376 Main St. (V2A 5C3)
*604/493-2801 — **048-88154

PORT ALBERNI
Port Alberni Shipping Co. Ltd., 5026 Argyle St., Box 490 (V9Y 7M9)
*604/723-7373

POWELL RIVER
Powell River Shipping Service Ltd., Box 74 (V8A 4Z5)
*604/483-4232 — **044-6144

PRINCE GEORGE
Interior Brokers Ltd., 1360 5th Ave., Box 158 (V2L 4S1)
*604/562-4171 — **047-8676

PRINCE RUPERT
A.S. Bill, #221, 225 3rd St., Box 8 (V8J 3P4)
*604/624-5233 — **04-789148
E.T.S. Moore, 535 W. 3rd Ave., Ste. 4 (V8J 1M1)
*604/624-5133 — **c/o 047-89140

SURREY
See Pacific Highway

TRAIL
J.B. Hutton Corp., Box 488, Federal Bldg., Spokane St. (V1R 4L7)
*604/364-2219

VANCOUVER
A.B.C. Customs Brokers Ltd., 890 W. Pender St., #200 (V6C 1K6)
*604/685-8501 — **04-54306
Adanac Customs Brokers Ltd., 1690 W. Second Ave., Box 2147 (V6B 3T9)
*604/732-8611 — **04-54347
Allcity Customs Brokers Ltd., 355 Burrard St. (V6C 2G8)
*604/689-8228 — **04-55339
also: #220, 4840 Miller Rd., Box 23288, Vancouver AMF, B.C.
*604/270-1348 — **04-355664
Blaiklock Inc., Ste. 1815, 1050 W. Pender St. (V6E 3S7)
*604/689-8847 — **04-507739
Border Brokers Inc., 1100 W. Pender St., Box 2168 (V6B 4R5)
*604/684-0332 — **04-508713
also: Box 23160, Vancouver AMF (V7B 1V6)
*604/273-4521 — **04-355769
Brown & Fortunato, 505 Burrard St. (V7X 1M3)
*604/684-3030
Columbia Customs Brokers Ltd., 890 W. Pender St., #210 (V6C 2P8)
*604/687-7491 — **04-55239
Courtney Agencies Ltd., 355 Burrard St. (V6C 2G6)
*604/684-7505 — **04-54662
Davidson & Sons Customs Brokers Ltd., 1070 W. Pender St. (V6E 2N8)
*604/681-5132 — **04-53317
D.H.L. Customs Brokerage Ltd., Box 23424, Vancouver AMF (V7B 1W1)
*604/273-1955 — **04-355789
J.B. Ellis & Co., #690, 885 Dunsmuir St. (V6C 1N5)
*604/684-1254 — **04-55328
Elmac World Transport Ltd., 555 W. Hastings St. (V6B 4N6)
*604/688-8511
Emery Customs Brokerage Ltd., Box 23228, 484 Miller Rd., Vancouver AMF (V7B 1T8)
*604/278-7361
Federated Customs Brokers Ltd., 1199 W. Pender St., Ste. 530 (V6E 2R1)
*604/687-7641 — **04-508575
Hogg & Boxall Ltd., #1031, 355 Burrard St. (V6C 2G8)
*604/687-7468 — **04-355517
International-Import Customs Brokers Inc., #200, 1130 W. Pender St. (V6E 4A3)
*604/681-5277 — **04-54375
Johnston Forwarding Co. Ltd., Box 5300 (V6B 4B6)
*604/874-7371 — ** 045-1142
KN Customs Brokers, #400, 455 Granville St. (V6C 1V2)
*604/684-4531 — **04-51247
Lee & Drummond, #810, 1112 W. Pender St. (V6E 2N4)
*604/669-2201 — **04-51568
Leimar Transportation Services Ltd., #505, 1200 W. Pender St. (V6E 2S9)
*604/682-7421 — ** 04-51256
Leith & Dyke Ltd., #200, 1130 W. Pender St. (V6E 4A3)
*604/685-3555 — **04-53367
Lep International Inc., 837 W. Hastings St., Ste. 522 (V6C 1B6)
*604/685-8111 — **04-54583
Locher Evers International, #200, 1200 W. Pender St. (V6E 2T3)
*604/669-6622 — **04-508788
Thomas Meadows Co. Canada Limited, #515, 1199 W. Pender St. (V6E 2R6)
*604/687-7808 — **04-355549
Meir Cohen Customs Brokers Ltd., 2145 W. Broadway (V6K 2C7)

*604/734-8553 — **04-51271
Mendelssohn Commercial Ltd., 890 W. Pender St., #300 (V6C 1J9)
*604/687-5535 — ** 04-55232
Milne & Craighead, #500, 1111 W. Hastings St. (V6E 3V9)
*604/683-4121 — **04-51481
Pac-Ex Customs Brokers (B.C.) Ltd., #230, 890 W. Pender St. (V6C 1K5)
*604/687-1331
Pacific Customs Brokers (Airport) Ltd., (A.M.F.) Vancouver International Airport (V7B 1T9)
*604/273-3941 — **04-355687
Pacific Customs Brokers Ltd., 890 W. Pender St., #445 (V6C 1K8)
*604/681-5191
G.M. Patry Ltd., Box 23163, Vancouver AMF (V7B 1T9)
*604/278-4491
Peace Bridge Brokerage Ltd., Air Cargo Bldg. No. 1, Box 23066 (V7B 1T9)
*604/273-8634 — **04-355572
Professional Customs Brokers Canada Ltd., #270, One Bentall Centre, 505 Burrard St. (V7X 1M3)
*604/669-0645 — **04-51259
Ralph Long Ltd., #310, 890 W. Pender St. (V6C 1J9)
*604/669-1116 — **04-508506
Robinson Heath Western Ltd., #310, 890 W. Pender St. (V6C 1J9)
*604/684-6827 — **04-508788
Schenker of Canada Ltd., Box 12127, 555 W. Hastings St. (V6B 4N6)
*604/688-8511 — **04-53403
Trans Commerce Brokerage Co. Ltd., #413, 1200 W. Pender St. (V6E 2J6)
*604/684-1421
United Customs Brokers (Canada) Ltd., #812, 1112 W. Pender St. (V6E 2N4)
*604/688-5461 — **04-51568
A.C. Wright Customs Brokers (1967) Ltd., #202, 940 Station St. (V6A 2X5)
*604/681-4642 — ** 04-507742

VERNON

Thomas R. Jenner, #204, 3002 32nd Ave. (V1T 2L7)
*604/542-2700 — **048-85260

VICTORIA

Border Brokers Inc., #720, 1175 Douglas St., Box 1382 (V8W 2W3)
*604/382-3105 — **049-7357
King Bros. Ltd., 850 Gordon St., Box 577 (V8W 2P5)
*604/384-1174 — **049-7319
Victoria Customs Brokers Ltd., #117, 645 Fort St. (V8W 2W3)
*604/388-4435

Alberta

CALGARY

Allan & Johnston Ltd., #266, 220 4th Ave. S.E., Box 424, Stn. M (T2P 2J1)
*403/266-8686 — **038-22828
Alwoods Custom Brokers Ltd., Box 5305, Stn. A (T2H 1X6)
*403/243-8740 — **03-821807
Border Brokers Inc., #456, 220 4th Ave. S.E. (Box 1538, Stn. M)
*403/263-8171 — **03-822565
Border Brokers Inc. (Airport), #1, 1928 27th Ave. N.E. (Box 1538, Stn. M)
*403/263-8171 — ** 038-26530
Calgary Customs Brokers Ltd., #488, 220 4th Ave. S.E. (Box 160, Stn. M, T2P 2H6)
*403/269-4393
Cole McCubbin Ltd., Room 430, 640 12th Ave. S.W. (T2R 0H5)
*403/261-9612
Galvanic Customs Brokers Ltd., #130, 112 4th Ave. S.E. (T2G 4X6)
403/265-7595 — ** 03-827723
H.T. Higinbotham Ltd., 239 12th Ave. S.W., Box 6834, Stn. D (T2P 2E9)
*403/269-5591 — **038-24560
International-Import Customs Brokers Inc., #263, 220 4th Ave. S.E. (T2P 3C3)
*403/262-4656 — **03-824620
KN Customs Brokers, 1350 42 Ave. S.E. (T2G 4V6)
*403/243-3241 — **038-24615
Lawrence Customs Brokers (1970) Ltd., #268, 220 4th Ave. S.E. (Box 2718, Stn. M, T2P 3C2)
*403/262-2771 — **03-824640
Lep International Inc., 517 Centre St. S. (T2G 2C4)
*403/233-2940 — **03-824895
L.V. Mathews Customs Broker, 748 Acadia Dr. S.E. (T2J 0C5)
*403/278-4613
Milne & Craighead, 133 6th Ave. S.E. (T2G 0G3)
*403/263-7856 — *03-822567
Mendelssohn Commercial Ltd., #204, 112 3rd Ave. S.W. (T2P 0E7)
*403/266-5845 — **03-827840
Monico Customs Brokers Ltd., #484, 220 4th Ave. S.E. (T2G 4X3)
*403/269-4833 — **038-26675
Pac-Ex Customs Broker (Alta.) Ltd., 304 4th Ave. S.E. (T2G 0C7)
*403/265-5365 — **03-827504
Peace Bridge Brokerage Ltd., Box 404, Airport Bunk, 2100 78th Ave. N.E. (T2E 6W6)
*403/276-0732 — **03-821858
Professional Customs Brokers Canada Ltd., 110 3rd Ave. S.W. (T2G 4Y0)
*403/232-0097 — **038-26862
Schenker of Canada Ltd., 2020 32nd Ave. N.E. (T2E 6T4)
*403/265-7565 — **03-826633
H.H. Smith Ltd., #264, 220 4 Ave. S.E. (T2P 2J2)
*403/263-8050 — **03-849190
Southco Customs Brokers Ltd., 110 11th Ave. S.W. (T2R 0B8)
*403/265-5015 — **03-824667

COUTTS

Allan & Johnston Ltd., Box 159 (T0K 0N0)
*403/344-3732 — **03-849181
Border Brokers Inc., Box 9 (T0K 0N0)
*403/344-3810 — **03-849140
H.T. Higinbotham Ltd., Box 217 (T0K 0N0)
*403/344-3931 — **03-849141
International-Import Customs Brokers Inc., Box 216 (T0K 0N0)
*403/344-3882 — **038-49168
KN Customs Brokers, 112 Centre St. (T0K 0N0)
*403/344-3962 — **038-49324
Lawrence Customs Brokers Ltd., Box 87 (T0K 0N0)
*403/344-3855 — **03-849149
Milne & Craighead, Box 34 (T0K 0N0)
*403/344-3878 — **03-849127
Pac-Ex Customs Brokers (Alta.) Ltd., Box 158 (T0K 0N0)
*403/344-3977
Peace Bridge Brokerage Ltd., 115 1st Ave. S. (T0K 0N0)
*403/344-3842
H.H. Smith Ltd., Box 39 (T0K 0N0)
*403/344-3822 — **03-849190
Southco Customs Brokers Ltd., Box 146 (T0K 0N0)
*403/344-3813 — **03-849166

EDMONTON

Allan & Johnston Ltd., #1922, 10015 103rd Ave. (T5J OG9)
*403/426-3134 — **037-2998
Alwoods Customs Brokers Ltd., 10008 103 St., Box 808 (T5J 2L4)

*403/429-6206 — **037-2790
Anderson-Smyth Brokers Ltd., #1912, 10015 103rd Ave. (T5J 0H1)
*403/420-0773 — **037-2279
Border Brokers Inc., 10145 104th St. (T5J 1A4)
*403/429-4351 — *037-2425
Border Brokers Inc., Box 9807, Edmonton International Airport (T5J 2T2)
*403/955-7238 — **037-3018
Emery Customs Brokerage Ltd., Box 9819, Edmonton International Airport (T5J 2T2)
*403/955-7237 — **037-41752
H.T. Higinbotham Ltd., #1910, 10015 103 Ave. (T5J 0H1)
*403/423-5444 — **037-2329
International-Import Customs Brokers Inc., 430 Centennial Bldg., 103rd Ave. (T5J 0H1)
*403/429-6902 — **037-2983
KN Customs Brokers, 15305 128 Ave. (T5J 2M1)
*403/452-2651 — **037-2711
Lawrence Customs Brokers (1970) Ltd., 6005 103A St. (Box 838, T5J 2L4)
*403/437-1936 — **037-2612
Mid-West Customs Brokers, 10116 105th Ave. (T5H 0K2)
*403/426-2776 — **037-3460
Milne & Craighead, #1400, 10015 103rd Ave. (T5J 0H1)
*403/429-4241 — **037-2460
Peace Bridge Brokerage Ltd., Box 9836 (T5J 2T2)
*403/955-8555 — **037-42597
Professional Customs Brokers Canada Ltd., 10856 97th St.
*403/424-0056 — **037-3335
Schenker of Canada Ltd., 10015 103rd Ave. (T5J 0H1)
*403/420-6920 — **037-3986
H.H. Smith Ltd., #726, 10015 103rd Ave. (T5J 0H1)
*403/429-5582 — **03-8-49190
Southco Customs Brokers Ltd., 10116 105 Ave. (T5H 0K2)
*403/423-1292 — **03-72238

LETHBRIDGE
Border Brokers Inc., 740 4th Ave. S. (T1J 0N9)
*403/320-5712 — **038-49368
Rossiter Agencies (1976) Ltd., 324 7th St. S. (Box 818, T1J 3Z8)
*403/327-1541 — **03-849333
H.H. Smith Ltd., 740 4th Ave. S. (Box 635, T1J 3Z4)
*403/328-8141 — **038-49190

MEDICINE HAT
Southco Customs Brokers Ltd., Box 7 (T1A 7E5)
*403/526-3368

RED DEER
Alwoods Customs Brokers Ltd., 4805 48 St., #203A (T4N 1S7)
*403/346-2296

Saskatchewan

ESTEVAN
Marsh Agencies, Box 743 (S4A 2A6)
*306/634-3294
Percy H. Davis Ltd., Box 161, Minton (via Regway, SOC 1T0)
*306/895-2644

MOOSE JAW
Percy H. Davis Ltd., 227 Federal Bldg., Ross St. W., Box 646 (S6H 4P4)
*306/692-4323

NORTH BATTLEFORD
O. Maybuck, Customs Broker, #7, 1092 101st St. (Box 307, S9A 2Y3)
*306/445-5133

NORTH PORTAL
Border Brokers Inc., Box 88 (SOC 1WO)
*306/927-2055 — **071-20559
Percy H. Davis, P.O. Drawer 90 (SOC 1WO)
*306/927-2165 — **071-20558

PRINCE ALBERT
Prince Albert Customs Brokers, 160 17th St. W. (S6V 3X5)
*306/764-5536 — **074-29179

REGINA
Border Brokers Inc., Room 202, 2184 12th Ave. (S4P OM6)
*306/525-0395 — **071-2241
Lawrence Customs Brokers (1970) Ltd., 333 Dewdney Ave. (Box 697, S4S 2Z1)
*306/352-0955 — **071-2200
Percy H. Davis Ltd., 302 Towne Sq., 1919 Rose St. (S4P 3P1)
*306/523-2662 — *071-2673
Wessel Bros., Ltd., #302, 1919 Rose St. (S4P 3P1)
*306/352-2662 — **071-2673

SASKATOON
Border Brokers Inc., Room 209, 115 2nd Ave. N. (S7K 2B1)
*306/653-4393 — **074-2473
Pendlebury's Division, Percy H. Davis Ltd., 59 York Bldg., 158 Second Ave. N. (S7K 2B4)
*306/244-4847 — **074-2247

SWIFT CURRENT
Swift Current Customs Brokers, Box 1116 (S9H 3X3)
*306/773-4902

WEYBURN
A.W. Weir, 310 Souris Ave., Box 1088 (S4H OC7)
*306/842-2045 — **071-2821

Manitoba

BOISSEVAIN
J.J. Coleman, Box 759 (ROK OEO)
*204/727-0707

BRANDON
J.J. Coleman, 1112 Rosser Ave., Box 134 (R7A 5Y6)
*204/727-0707

EMERSON
Border Brokers Inc., Box 338 (ROA OLO)
*204/373-2182 — **07-57551
Emerson Custom Brokers (1973) Ltd., Box 299 (R0A 0L0)
*204/373-2549 — **07-57228
Peace Bridge Brokerage Ltd., Box 189 (R0A 0L0)
*204/373-2400 — **07-57204
Ramsay Agencies Ltd., Box 246 (R0A 0L0)
*204/373-2494
Samson-Shaen & Co. Ltd., an International-Import Co., Box 10 (R0A 0L0)
*204/373-2047 — ** 07-587605
Thomas L. Skinner, P.O. Drawer 400 (R0A 0L0)
*204/373-2085
Unicity Customs Brokers Ltd., Box 429 (R0A 0L0)
*204/373-2537 — ** 07-55134
Geo. H. Young & Co. Ltd., P.O. Drawer 100 (ROA OLO)
*204/373-2167 — **07-587551

GRETNA
Emerson Customs Brokers Ltd., Box 93 (R0G 0V0)
*204/327-5219

SPRAGUE
B.L. Fostey Customs Brokers Ltd., Box 76 (ROA 1ZO)
*204/437-2110

WINNIPEG
Border Brokers Inc., #1110, 215 Garry St. (R3C 3P3)
*204/943-8651 — **07-57866
Border Brokers Inc. (Airport), 215 Garry St., #1110 (R3C 3P3)
*204/775-0405 — **075-7504
E.M. Cave Customs Brokers Ltd., 270 Fort St. (R3C 1E5)
*204/943-2024
Cole McCubbin Ltd., #213, 207 Fort St. (R3C 1E3)
*204/944-7255 — **07-57340

International-Import Customs Brokers Inc., #400, 275 Portage Ave. (R3B 2B3)
*204/947-0681 — **07-57322
International-Import Customs Brokers Inc., Winnipeg International Airport, Air Canada Terminal, 2020 Sargent Ave. (R3H 0C9)
*204/947-0681 — **07-57322
KN Customs Brokers, 10 Hutchings St. (R3C 2S1)
*204/633-1030 — **07-57742
L & L Importing Services Ltd., #203, 2020 Sargent Ave. (R3H 0C9)
*204/744-5584 —**07-57369
Thomas Meadows & Co., Canada Ltd., Air Canada Cargo Terminal, 2020 Sargent Ave. (R3H OC9)
*204/774-5584 — **07-587557
Peace Bridge Brokerage Ltd., Box 1589 (R3C 2Z6)
204/786-6511 — **07-57627
Ramsay Agencies Ltd., #402, 138 Portage Ave. E. (R3C OA1)
*204/943-2588 — **07-55472
Samson-Shaen & Co. Ltd., an International-Import Co., #400, 275 Portage Ave. (R3B 2B3)
*204/947-0681 — **07-57322
Unicity Customs Brokers Ltd., #300, 296 Garry St. (R3C 1H8)
*204/943-6451 — **07-587630
Geo. H. Young & Co. Ltd., #503, 203 Portage Ave. (R3B 2X6)
*204/947-6851 — **07-57341

Ontario

ACTON
A.T.W. Customs Brokers, Box 60 (L7J 2M2)
*519/853-1110 — **06-97754

AGINCOURT
Affiliated Customs Brokers Ltd., #102, 2055 Kennedy Rd. (M1T 3G3)
*416/292-2145 — **06-23282

AJAX
Border Brokers Inc., Box 146 (L1S 3C2)
*416/683-0430 —**via Toronto
International-Import Customs Brokers Inc., 398 Bayley St. (Box 305, L1S 3C5)
*416/683-4911 — **06-967854
KN Customs Brokers, 43 Station Plaza (L1S 1S2)
*416/683-7341 — **06-22135

BARRIE
Barrie Customs Brokers Ltd., 79 Bayfield St. (L4M 3A7)
*705/728-4722
Binus & Garrett (Barrie) Ltd., Box 484
*705/728-2020 — **06-875528
KN Customs Brokers, Unit 3, 461 Dunlop St. (L4M 4S4)
*705/737-4600 — **06-22135

BELLEVILLE
International-Import Customs Brokers Inc., 229 University Ave., #1 (K8N 5B5)
*613/966-9344 — **06-63221
Peace Bridge Brokerage Ltd., 89 Station St., Box 907 (K8N 5B6)
*613/968-5800 —**06-62238
Tilley Customs Brokers Ltd., Box 545 (K8N 5B2)
*613/962-1618

BOWMANVILLE
Ivan W. Davie, Box 61, 51 Mearns Ave. (L1C 3L3)
*416/623-4138

BRACEBRIDGE
Bracebridge Customs Brokers, c/o C.E. Cryderman, Box 1137 (P0B 1C0)
*705/645-9293

BRAMPTON
Border Brokers Inc., 297 Rutherford Rd. S. (L6W 3J8)
*416/457-6430 — **via Toronto
Federated Customs Brokers Ltd., 297 Rutherford Rd. S. (L6W 3J8)
*416/459-7122 — **06-97717
International-Import Customs Brokers Inc., 297 Rutherford Rd. S. (L6W 3J8)
*416/451-2063 — **06-967854
KN Customs Brokers, 297 Rutherford Rd. S. (L6W 3J8)
*416/453-3191 — **06-22135
Lep International Inc., 239 Queen St. E. (L6W 2B6)
*416/456-2101
W.G. McKay Ltd., 297 Rutherford Rd. S. (L6W 3J8)
*416/453-2241 — **06-219785
Panalpina World Transport (Ontario) Ltd., 7347 Kimbel St. (L4T 3M6)
*416/677-4800
Robinson & Heath Ltd., 297 Rutherford Rd. S. (L6W 3J8)
*416/453-3655 — **06-219896
Henry Weiner Ltd., 46 Queen St. E. (L6V 1A2)
*416/453-7510 — **06-23125

BRANTFORD
F.S. Sellar (1976) Ltd., Box 156 (N3T 5M8)
*519/752-7891 — **061-81112

BROCKVILLE
Peace Bridge Brokerage Ltd., 61A King St. E., Box 665 (K6V 5V8)
*613/345-2573 — **066-36544
H.M. Wakely Ltd., 39 Parkdale Ave., Box 486 (K6V 5V7)
*613/342-0325 — **066-36575

CAMBRIDGE
Russell A. Farrow Ltd., 218 Samuelson St., South Waterloo Terminal Warehouse, Box 233 (N1R 5T8)
*519/621-6810 — **069-5232
M.J. Gross Ltd., 218 Samuelson St., Box 501 (N1R 5T8)
*519/621-7600

CARLETON PLACE
Mrs. Doris H. Frey, Box 152, Smiths Falls (K7A 4T1)
*613/282-2501

CHATHAM
B & B Custom-House Brokerage Co. Ltd., 1000 Richmond St., Box 400 (N7M 5K5)
*519/354-4010
Russell A. Farrow Ltd., Federal Bldg. (Box 74, N7M 5K1)
*519/354-1340 — **024-78536

COBALT
A.L. Herbert Ltd., Federal Bldg., Box 10 (POJ 1CO)
*705/679-8335

COBOURG
Bailey Custom Broker, Federal Bldg., 39 Queen St. (K9A 1M8)
*416/372-9880 — **06-981368

COLLINGWOOD
Foreman and Metheral, 367 Hurontario St., Box 164 (L9Y 2M5)
*705/445-1485

CORNWALL
Border Brokers Inc., 119 Sydney St. (Box 2019, K6H 6N8)
*613/938-7797 — **058-11595
Brown Customs Brokerage Ltd., 110 Sydney St., Box 847 (K6H 3H2)
*613/932-0914 — **05-811536

ETOBICOKE
See Toronto

FORT ERIE
Blaiklock Inc., Box 1208, Stn. B (L2A 5Y2)
*416/871-2228 — **061-5466
Border Brokers Inc., Box 1099, Stn. B (L2A 5N9)
*416/871-5700 — **061-5180
Currier & Smith Ltd., 51 Queen St. (L2A 1T7)

*416/871-7732
Russell A. Farrow Ltd., Box 118 (L2A 5Y2)
*416/871-2228
Federated Customs Brokers Ltd., 35 Walnut St. (L2A 1S9)
*416/871-1711 — **061-5168
Hawkyard Nolan Ltd., 39 Walnut St. (L2A 1S9)
*416/871-2488 — **061-5109
International-Import Customs Brokers Inc., 49 Walnut St. (Box 1070, Stn. B, L2A 5N8)
*416/871-2000 — **06-967854
KN Customs Brokers, 41 Queen St. (L2A 1T6)
*416/871-8055 — **061-15371
W.G. McKay Ltd., 39 Walnut St. (Box 1040, Stn. B, L2A 5N8)
*416/871-4200 — **061-5170
Thomas Meadows & Co. Canada Ltd., 35 Walnut St. (L2A 1S9)
*416/871-3232 — **061-5168
Mendelssohn Commercial Ltd., 25 Walnut St. (L2A 1S7)
*416/871-8822 — **061-5424
Peace Bridge Brokerage Ltd., 33 Walnut St., Box 40 (L2A 5M7)
*416/871-6500 — **061-5101
Robinson & Heath Ltd., 39 Walnut St. (L2A 1S9)
*416/871-5854 — **06-219896
J. MacD. Thomson Ltd., Box 1036, Stn. B (L2A 5N8)
*416/871-4841
Universal Customs Brokers Ltd., 35 Walnut St., Box 1250, Stn. B (L2A 5Y2)
*416/871-0220 — **061-5254
Henry Weiner Ltd., 27 Walnut St. (L2A 5N8)
*416/871-7401 — **061-5288
Wm. F. Willson Brokerage Ltd., 53 Walnut St., Box 1100, Stn. B (L2A 5N9)
*416/871-1310 — **061-5262

GALT

See Cambridge, Ont.

GEORGETOWN

Elliott Custom Brokers and Storage Ltd., Box 40 (L7G 4T1)
*416/877-5293

GUELPH

Karl K. Husson, 155 Suffolk St. W., Box 233 (N1H 6J9)
*519/822-2342
International-Import Customs Brokers Inc., 71 Dawson Rd. (N1H 1B1)
*519/821-5670 — **069-56553
Peace Bridge Brokerage Ltd., Box 982 (N1H 6N1)
*519/824-6700 — **06-956644

HAMILTON

Border Brokers Inc., #102, 400 Grays Rd. N., Stoney Creek, Ont. L8E 3J6
*416/560-1522 — **061-8630
Harte & Lyne Ltd., Box 124, Stn. A (L8N 3B7)
*416/561-1241 — **061-8947
International-Import Customs Brokers Inc., 400 Grays Rd., Stoney Creek (Box 61, Hamilton L8N 3A2)
*416/525-0651 — **06-967854
C.R. Kenney, 25 Hughson St. S. (L8N 2A5)
*416/522-1869 — **061-8462
Lyman Custom Brokers & Freight Forwarding, 20 Hughson St. S., #407 (Box 960, L8N 3P9)
*416/526-0550
KN Customs Brokers, Marine Terminal No. 8, Box 102, Stn. B (L8L 7T5)
*416/527-2981 — **061-8744
Peace Bridge Brokerage Ltd., Box 156 (L8N 3A2)
*416/560-5000 — **061-8318
Schenker of Canada Ltd., 605 James St. N. (L8L 1J9)
*416/525-8844
M.J. Urry & Co., Division of Thos. Meadows & Co. Canada Ltd., 32 James St. S., Box 860 (L8N 3N9)
*416/522-4628 — **061-8731
Wm. F. Willson Brokerage Ltd., 400 Grays Rd., #218, Stoney Creek, Ont. L8E 3J6
*416/560-1300

HANOVER

Hanover Travel Service & Customs Brokerage Ltd., 290 10th St., Box 126 (N4N 3C3)
*519/364-5221

KINGSTON

International-Import Customs Brokers Inc., 65 Clarence St. (K7L 1X2)
613/544-9196 — **06-63221
Peace Bridge Brokerage Ltd., 162 Wellington St., Box 516 (K7L 4W5)
*613/542-2373 — **066-3267

KITCHENER

Border Brokers Inc., Box 2096, Stn. B (N2H 6K8)
*519/743-8271 — **069-55254
Davidson Customs Brokers Ltd., 53 Overland Dr. (N2C 2B3)
*519/576-0870
Russell A. Farrow Ltd., 39 Overland Dr., Box 533 (N2C 2B3)
*519/744-8197 — **069-5232
International-Import Customs Brokers Inc., 49 Overland Blvd. (N2H 6M1)
*519/745-6896 — **069-56553
KN Customs Brokers, 190 Goodrich Dr. (N2C 2L3)
*519/893-6141 — **069-55403

LANSDOWNE

Border Brokers Inc., Box 246 (KOE 1LO)
*613/659-2244 — **066-36550
Eaton & Hawley Customs Brokers, Box 657, Gananoque (K7G 2V2)
*613/659-2252
International-Import Customs Brokers Inc., Box 160 (KOE 1LO)
*613/659-2271 — **066-3221
Mendelssohn Commercial Ltd., Box 160, Gananoque, Ont. K7G 2T7
*613/659-2393
Peace Bridge Brokerage Ltd., Box 70 (KOE 1LO)
*613/659-3200 — **066-36523

LEAMINGTON

W.J. Bondy Customs Brokers Ltd., Box 225 (N8H 3W2)
*519/326-8631

LISTOWEL

Russell A. Farrow Ltd., Box 52 (N4W 3H2)
*519/291-1602 — **069-5232

LONDON

Border Brokers Inc., Roxburgh Rd., Box 2513, Terminal A (N6A 4G9)
*519/681-4881 — **064-7234
Border Brokers Inc. (Airport), 750 Crumlin Side Rd. (N5V 3B6)
*519/453-0340 — **via London
International-Import Customs Brokers Inc., Roxburgh Rd., R.R. 4 (Box 473, Stn. B, N6A 4W8)
*519/681-6011 — **06-967854
KN Customs Brokers, 511 Commercial Cres. (N5V 1Z2)
*519/452-1690 — **064-7585
Link Customs Services Ltd., Roxburg Rd., Box 580, Lambeth, Ont. N0L 1S0
*519/681-4002 — **064-7562
London Brokerage Co., 195 Dufferin Ave., Box 425 (N6A 4W1)
*519/434-5705

MIDLAND

Binus & Garrett Ltd., 917 King St., Box 296 (L4R 4K8)
*705/526-8842 — **06-875528 (via Barrie)

MISSISSAUGA

Abacus Customs Brokers Ltd., Rm. 14, 5425 Dixie Rd. (L4W 1E6)
*416/625-5036 — **06-968690

Airspeed (see Border Brokers, Interport)
*416/625-0819

Airspeed (see Border Brokers, Air Cargo Term.)
*416/676-2520

Affiliated Customs Brokers Ltd., #15, 5425 Dixie Rd. (L4W 1E6)
*416/624-2858 — **06-23282

Associated Customs Air Clearance Co. Ltd., Box 129, Toronto AMF (L5P 1A8)
*416/677-2151 — **06-968665

Blaiklock Inc., #201, Air Cargo Bldg. B, Toronto AMF (L5P 1A2)
*416/676-2550 — **065-24318

Border Brokers Inc., Rm. 17, Air Cargo Terminal Box 100, Toronto AMF (L5P 1A7)
*416/676-3700 — **069-83656

Border Brokers Inc. (Interport), 5425 Dixie Rd. (L4W 1E6)
*416/625-1720 — **069-60361

Border Brokers Inc. (Toronto Transportation Services), Box 40, Malton Stn. (L4T 3B5)
*416/678-6700 — **069-68824

Delmar Customs Brokers Ltd., Box 13, Toronto AMF (L5P 1A2)
*416/676-3380 — **06-983625

Emery Customs Brokerage Ltd., Box 255, Toronto AMF (L5P 1B1)
*416/676-3940 — **06-968671

Russell A. Farrow Ltd., Cargo Bldg. E, Box 153, Toronto AMF (L5P 1P1)
*416/677-3362

General Customs Brokers Inc., 5425 Dixie Rd. (L4W 1E6)
*416/624-1895 — **06-961434

Hartwick, O'Shea & Cartwright Ltd., Box 155, Toronto AMF (L5P 1B1)
*416/676-3230

In 'N' Out Customs Brokers Inc., Box 277, Malton Stn. (L4T 3B6)

M & M Customs & Forwarding Services Inc., Box 4, Toronto AMF (L5P 1A2)
*416/678-1130

Metro Customs Brokers Ltd., Box 56, Toronto AMF (L5P 1A2)
*416/366-7605 — **06-219744

O.D.P. Custom Brokers Ltd., Box 22, Toronto AMF (L5P 1A2)
*416/676-3357

G.M. Patry Ltd., Genaire Bldg., Box 202, Toronto AMF (L5P 1B1)
*416/676-2735 — **06-968693

Peace Bridge Brokerage Ltd., Air Cargo Bldg., Block B, Box 130 (L5P 1A9)
*416/677-2740 — **06-968591

Roberts Customs & Traffic Service Ltd., #417, Cargo Bldg. B, Toronto Int'l. Airport (L5P 1A2)
*416/678-6475

Robinson & Heath Ltd., Box 183, Toronto AMF (L5P 1B1)
*416/676-3614 — **06-219896

F.S. Sellar (1976) Ltd., Box 156, Toronto AMF
*416/676-2760 — **06-968588

K.B. Slaven & Associates Inc., Box 171, Toronto AMF (L5P 1A2)
*416/657-1100 — **06-983632

Tudor Customs Brokers Ltd., 5425 Dixie Rd. (L4W 1E6)
*416/624-9654 — **06-960273

Union Transport of Canada Ltd., Box 14, Toronto AMF (L5P 1A2)
*416/677-0464 — **06-983622

NAPANEE

See Kingston, Ont.

NEWMARKET

Newmarket Customs Services, Box 292 (L3Y 4X1)
*416/895-5555

Robinson & Heath Ltd., Box 292 (L3Y 4X1)
*416/895-5555

Walch Customs Brokers, 477 Timothy St. (Box 32, L3Y 4W3)
*416/895-8162

NIAGARA FALLS

Border Brokers Inc., Box 448 (L2E 6T8)
*416/262-4214 — **via Niagara Whirlpool

Border Brokers Inc. (Whirlpool), Box 448 (L2E 6T8)
*416/354-1686 — **061-5186

Currier & Smith Ltd., 4451 River Rd., Box 205 (L2E 6T3)
*416/354-2761 — **02-21620

Russell A. Farrow Ltd., Lewiston/Queenston Bridge, Box 635 (L2E 6V5)
*416/262-4256 — **069-5232

Federated Customs Brokers Ltd., Box 265 (L2E 6T3)
*416/262-4646 — **061-5261

International-Import Customs Brokers Inc., 4451 River Rd. (Box 306, L2E 6T8)
*416/356-2671, 262-4252 — **06-967854

KN Customs Brokers, Queenston-Lewiston Truck Terminal, Unit 6 (L0S 1L0)
*416/262-4208

W.G. McKay Ltd., Box 453 (L2E 6V2)
*416/262-5121

J.A. Newport & Co. Ltd., 548 Clifton Ave., Box 327 (L2E 6T8)
*416/358-7181 — **021-5176

Peace Bridge Brokerage Ltd., Lewiston Queenston Bridge (L2E 6T3)
*416/262-4262 — **061-5277

Wm. L. Rutherford Ltd., Lewiston-Queenston Bridge, Box 542 (L2E 6V2)
*416/262-4803 — **061-5298

United Customs Brokers (Ontario) Ltd., 4425 River Rd. (L2E 3E8)
*416/364-4727 — **02-29047

Universal Customs Brokers Ltd., 4357 River Rd., Box 533 (L2E 6V2)
*416/356-6882

Wm. F. Willson Brokerage Ltd., Box 505 (L2E 6V2)
*416/354-4911

Henry Weiner Ltd., Box 2005 (L2E 6V2)
*416/262-4271

NORTH BAY

Charles F. Brown Limited, P.O. Drawer 777, 1399 Hammond St., Ste. 203 (P1B 8J8)
*705/474-2820

OAKVILLE

Border Brokers Inc., Box 443 (L6J 5A8)
*416/844-3249 — **via Toronto

W.G. Chamberlain Ltd., 1100 Invicta Dr., Unit 23 (L6H 2K9)
*416/845-9851

International-Import Customs Brokers Inc., 1045 North Service Rd., Ste. B (L6H 1A7)
*416/842-2710 — **06-967854

KN Customs Brokers, 1050 Grand Blvd. (L6J 5C1)
416/842-0231 — **06-22135

W.G. McKay Ltd., 1041 North Service Rd. E., #100 (L6H 1A6)
*416/844-1435 — **via Toronto

Thomas Meadows & Co. Canada Ltd., 1011 North Service Rd. E. (L6H 1A6)
*416/845-3601

Oakville Customs Brokerage, 1041 North Service Rd. E., Box 1088 (L6J 5E7)
*416/844-7070 — **06-982346

Robinson & Heath Ltd., 1011 North Service Rd. E., Box 37 (L6J 4Z5)
*416/845-3808 — **06-219896

ORANGEVILLE
Border Brokers Inc., Box 188 (L9W 2Z6)
*519/941-1564 — **via Toronto

ORILLIA
Binus & Garrett Ltd., 5 Peter St. S., Box 215 (L3V 6J3)
*705/325-2383

OSHAWA
Border Brokers Inc., Box 185 (L1H 7L1)
*416/723-4611 — **via Toronto
Ivan W. Davie, Whitby (R.R. 1, Ashburn, Ont. L0B 1A0)
*416/655-4352
International-Import Customs Brokers Inc., 205 Simcoe St. S. (Box 295, L1H 7L3)
*416/723-3461 — **06-967854
W.G. McKay Ltd., 115 Simcoe St. S., 2nd floor (L1H 4G7)
*416/579-4513
Thomas Meadows & Co. Canada Ltd., 25 King St. E. (L1H 1A3)
*416/723-3464
Mendelssohn-Commercial Ltd., Box 160 (L1H 7L2)
*416/728-7181

OTTAWA
Border Brokers Inc., 2473 Sheffield Rd., Box 9244 (K1G 3T9)
*613/741-4674 — **053-4543
Carleton Customs Services, R.R. 5, Hunt Club Rd. (K1G 3N3)
*613/737-5113
Lenore I. Glover, 43 Daly Ave. (K1N 6E1)
*613/232-8301 — **053-3765
Charles Higgerty Limited, 1673 Carling Ave. (K2A 1C4)
*613/728-1843 — **053-4142
International-Import Customs Brokers Inc., 2473 Sheffield Rd. (K1B 2V6)
*613/746-7859 — **053-4169
International-Import Customs Brokers Inc., Ottawa International Airport, Hunt Club Rd. (K1G 3N3)
*613/521-4751 — **053-4169
KN Customs Brokers, 130 Albert St., Ste. 908 (K1P 5G4)
*613/238-7510 — **053-3742
Mendelssohn-Commercial Ltd., 2473 Sheffield Rd. (K1B 3V6)
*613/745-9737
Peace Bridge Brokerage Ltd., 1673 Carling Ave., Ste. 104-A (K2A 1C4)
*613/729-5191 — **053-4471
Sidney A. Smith, 71 Bank St., Room 304 (K1P 5N2)
*613/235-6324

PEMBROKE
Ray R. Tardiff, 527 Pembroke St. W., Box 10 (K8A 6X1)
*613/732-8041

PERTH
Joan H. Wickware, 1 Sheldon Place (K7H 3C2)
*613/267-2064

PRESCOTT
R.A. Strader Customs House Brokerage, Bridge Plaza, Johnstown (Box 280, K0E 1T0)
*613/925-4271

ST. CATHARINES
International-Import Customs Brokers Inc., 244 Dunkirk Rd. (Box 935, L2R 6Z4)
*416/685-1316 — **06-15389
Peace Bridge Brokerage Ltd., 15 Church St., Box 301 (L2R 6T7)
*416/682-8318 —**061-5245

ST. THOMAS
Buckland Customs Brokers Ltd., 73 Gaylord Rd. (N5P 3R9)
*519/631-4944 — **064-73552

SARNIA
Border Brokers Inc., Box 429 (N7T 7J2)
*519/344-1184 — **064-76144
Russell A. Farrow Ltd., Box 233 (N7T 7H9)
*519/344-2473
S.M. Hewitt Ltd., Bldg. C, Blue Water Bridge, Box 606 (N7T 7J4)
*519/344-2108 — **064-76146
International-Import Customs Brokers Inc., Blue Water Bridge Plaza (Box 683, N7T 7J7)
*519/332-1270
Peace Bridge Brokerage Ltd., General Delivery (N7T 2M0)
*519/337-7501
Wm. F. Willson Brokerage Limited, Box 254 (N7T 7H9)
*519/344-3619 —**064-76196

SAULT STE. MARIE
Cole McCubbin Ltd., Box 236 (P6A 5L6)
*705/254-6448 —**06-777160

SCARBOROUGH
See Toronto

SIMCOE
Peace Bridge Brokerage Ltd., 56 Norfolk St., Box 331 (N3Y 4L5)
*519/426-0160 —**061-81222

SMITHS FALLS
Mrs. Doris H. Frey, Box 152 (K7A 4T1)
*613/283-2501

STONEY CREEK
See Hamilton

STRATFORD
Border Brokers Inc., Box 518 (N5A 6T7)
*519/271-7570 — **via Kitchener
Jack Rutherford Customs Brokers Ltd., 121 Ontario St.
*519/273-3592

SUDBURY
George A. Gray Customs Brokers Ltd., 1191 Lansing Ave., Box 2365, Stn. A (P3A 4S8)
*705/560-2400

THUNDER BAY
Border Brokers Inc., Box 3268, Stn. P (P7B 5J8)
*807/344-5797 — **073-4386
Cole McCubbin Ltd., Balmoral & Hewiston Sts., Box 134 (P7C 4V5)
*807/622-5861 — **07-34695

TIMMINS
Purves Customs Brokers Ltd., 23 Cedar Stn. N., Box 1091 (P4N 7H9)
*705/267-6266

TORONTO (See also Mississauga for airport)
Able Customs Brokers Ltd., Box 787, Terminal A (M8X 2N8)
*416/252-7321 — **06-967666
Active Customs Brokers Ltd., 32 Front St. W. (M5J 1C5)
*416/366-6227
Affiliated Customs Brokers Ltd., 159 Bay St., Room 501 (Box 239, Stn. A, M5W 1B7)
*416/364-9596 — **06-23282
also: #104, 1608 The Queensway (M8Z 1V6)
*416/255-5110 — **06-23282
Airspeed Brokers (1962) Ltd., 40 University Ave. (Box 5, Term. A, M5W 1A2)
*416/977-3344 —**via Border Brokers (065-24221)
Airspeed (see Border Brokers, Queensway)
*416/259-4601
Airspeed (see Border Brokers, Scarboro)
*416/293-6564
Wm. T. Bathgate Ltd., Ste. 340, 48 Yonge St. (M5E 1G6)
*416/368-8053
Bay Customs Brokers, 1608 The Queensway, #101 (M8Z 1V4)
*416/259-9269 — **06-983647
Bertram & Cumming Ltd., 159 Bay St., #812 (M5J 1J7)
*416/364-1441 — **06-22185 FEDCOMTOR

Blackpool Brokerage Ltd., 55 Bloor St. W., Ste. 220 (M4W 1A6)
*416/967-6700 — **05-25176
Blaiklock Inc., 11 King St. W., Ste. 1400 (M5H 3K8)
*416/364-7141 — **065-24318
Border Brokers Inc. (Corporate & Central), Box 4040, Terminal A (M5W 1L2)
*416/977-7777 — **065-24221
Border Brokers Inc. (Queensway), #223, 1608 The Queensway (M8Z 1W2)
*416/252-3384 — **069-67705
Border Brokers Inc. (Scarboro), 2055 Kennedy Rd. (Box 128, Agincourt, Ont. M1S 3B4)
*416/291-6201 — **via Toronto
Border Brokers Inc. (Toronto West), 2854 Dundas St. W. (M6P 1Y7)
*416/766-6451 — **via Toronto
Edward Callaghan Ltd., 212 King St. W., Ste. 207 (M5H 1K5)
*416/593-5588 —**065-24088
Carson Customs Brokers Ltd., 185 Bay St. (M5J 1K6)
*416/363-6421 —**06-217628
Century Customs Brokers Ltd., 155 University Ave., Ste. 201 (M5H 3B7), freight forwarding only
*416/869-0279 — **06-22619
W.G. Chamberlain Ltd., 55 Bloor St. W., Ste. 220 (M4W 1A6)
*416/967-6700
Clarke Transport International Inc., 20 Victoria St., #705 (M5C 2N8)
*416/868-1000 — **06-217632
Clear Custom Brokers Ltd., 159 Bay St., Room 401 (M5J 1J7)
*416/363-5025 —**06-22296
Collard Customs Brokers Ltd., 185 Bay St., Ste. 201 (M5J 1K6)
*416/364-3010 —**065-24682
Counselor Customs Brokers Ltd., 1608 The Queensway (M8Z 1W9)
*416/252-5861 — **06-984608
Crickmore, LeRoy & Davis Ltd., #217, 159 Bay St. (M5J 1J7)
*416/362-6791
Currier & Smith Ltd., 22 Front St. W., Ste. 725 (M5J 1N7)
*416/366-6421 — **065-24366
Dawson Customs Brokerage Co., 55 York St., Ste. 1610 (M5J 1R7)
*416/364-5251
Elmac World Transport Ltd., 34 King St. E. (M5C 1E5)
*416/368-3008 — **065-24311
Federated Customs Brokers Ltd., 22 Front St. W., #725 (M5J 1N6)
*416/363-9051 — **06-22185
M. Gurza Customs Brokers Ltd., 32 Front St. W. (M5J 1C5)
*416/368-2098
Hawkyard-Nolan Limited, 32 Front St. W. (M5J 1C5)
*416/362-7691 — **06-219887
Henderson Bros., #201, 8 King St. E. (M5C 1B5)
*416/364-0507
Highway Brokers Ltd., 1608 The Queensway, West Bldg. (M8Z 1V4)
*416/259-3758 — **06-217823
Imex Customs Brokers, Division of K-Con Holdings Ltd., 1608 The Queensway (M8Z 1V4)
*416/252-2524 — **06-967547
International-Import Customs Brokers Inc., 48 Yonge St., #230 (Box 5640, M5W 1P1)
*416/869-1340 — **06-219519
KN Customs Brokers, One Yonge St. (M5E 1N7)
*416/366-3981
A.W.W. Kyle Inc., 185 Bay St., Ste. 703 (M5J 1K6)
*416/364-6196 — **065-24051
Leimar Transportation Services Ltd., 159 Bay St. (M5J 1J7)
*416/364-1466
Lep International Inc., 44 Wellington St. E. (M5E 1B7)
*416/364-0421 — **06-22013
MacKinnon & McCaskill Ltd., 215 Mavety St. (M6P 2M1)
*416/766-2336 — **06-22509
Don G. McIntosh, Custom House, Broker & Consultant, 1 Yonge St., #2407 (M5E 1E5)
*416/363-7351
W.G. McKay Ltd., 40 University Ave., Main floor (M5J 1J9)
*416/593-1380 — **06-219785
Thomas Meadows & Co. Canada Ltd., 55 Yonge St. (M5E 1P1)
*416/366-9241 — **06-22252
Mendelssohn-Commercial Ltd., 8 Colborne St., 4th floor (M5E 1E1)
*416/868-1411 — **06-22659
Milne & Craighead, 60 Yonge St., #304 (M5E 1H9)
*416/364-7690 — **06-23288
Jas. C. Norris & Son, 1608 The Queensway, Rm. W101A (M8Z 1V6)
*416/252-7863
J.D. O'Hearn & Co. Ltd., 1608 The Queensway (M8Z 1W5)
*416/259-5076
Panalpina World Transport Ltd., 100 University Ave. (M5J 1V6)
*416/368-2912 — **06-219509
Peace Bridge Brokerage Ltd., 75 The East Mall (M8Z 2L9)
*416/259-2335 — **06-967875
also: 2055 Kennedy Rd., Scarboro, Ont. M1T 3G3
*416/298-0550 — **065-25349
Protran Limited, 159 Bay St., Ste. 1005 (M5J 1J7)
*416/360-1880 — **06-22997
Robinson & Heath Ltd., 32 Front St. W. (M5J 1C5)
*416/362-1371 — **06-219896
Wm. L. Rutherford Ltd., Room 219, 165 Queensway (M8Y 1H8)
*416/255-5591 — **06-22985
Gus Ryder, 1608 The Queensway (M8Z 1V5)
*416/259-2731
St. Arnaud & Bergevin Ltée, 55 Bloor St. W., Ste. 220 (M4W 1A6)
*416/967-6700
Schenker of Canada Ltd., 34 King St. E., 6th Floor (M5C 1E7)
*416/864-1740 — **06-219855
J.W. Smith Customs Brokers Ltd., 85 The East Mall (M8Z 5W4)
*416/252-4188 — **06-967553
David M. Stewart Ltd., 159 Bay St., #315 (M5J 2L8)
*416/364-7793 — **06-23579
Frank R. Stockwell Ltd., 1608 The Queensway (M8Z 1W9)
*416/255-7311
Sutherland International Despatch, 60 Yonge St. (M5E 1H5)
*416/363-4181 — **06-217814
Thompson, Ahern & Co., Ltd., Ste. 401, 220 Bay St. (M5J 1P4)
*416/366-2761 — **06-219796
J. MacD. Thomson Ltd., 48 Yonge St., Ste. 330 (M5E 1N8)
*416/362-7111 — **065-24308
Trans Commerce Brokerage Co. Ltd., 159 Bay St., Ste. 722 (M5J 1M5)
*416/363-3338 — **06-22842
United Customs Brokers (Ontario) Ltd., 159 Bay St., Ste. 801 (M5J 1M2)
*416/364-7431 — **065-24097
Universal Customs Brokers Ltd., 159 Bay St., Room 1030 (M5J 1C8)
*416/363-7511 — **06-219838
E.W. Unsworth Ltd., Ste. 410,11,12, 159 Bay St. (M5J 1K5)
*416/368-7604
Henry Weiner Ltd., 380 Wellington St. W. (M5V 1E3)
*416/869-1303 — *062-3125
Wm. F. Willson Brokerage Ltd., 1608 The Queensway, Ste. 228 (M8Z 1V7)
*416/252-4697 — **06-984635
X-M Brokers Limited, 1608 The Queensway (M8Z 1W7)

*416/255-7743 — **06-968742

TRENTON

Tilley Customs Brokers Ltd., Box 626 (K8V 5R7)
*613/392-3563

WALLACEBURG

Florence L. Borton, Minnie St., Box 243 (N8A 4L6)
*519/627-1020

WELLAND

International-Import Customs Brokers Inc., 268 Plymouth Rd. (Box 668, L3B 5B4)
*416/732-1321 — **06-15389

Peace Bridge Brokerage Ltd., Box 515 (L3B 5R3)
*416/735-2288 — **061-5274

WINDSOR

Blaiklock Inc., Box 1742, Stn. A (N9A 6Y1)
*519/253-0844 — **064-77661

Border Brokers Inc. (Bridge), 728 Church Rd. (Box 547, N9A 6M6)
*519/256-5457 — **064-77735

Border Brokers Inc. (Tunnel), #200, 310 Hanna St. E. (Box 547, N9A 6M6)
*519/256-2681 — **via Windsor Bridge

Wm. Egleston Ltd., 44 Wyandotte St. E. (N9H 3G6)
*519/252-7201

Russell A. Farrow Ltd., 747 Huron Church Rd., Box 333 (N9A 6L6)
*519/252-4415 — **064-77661

Federated Customs Brokers Ltd., 687 Huron Church Rd. (N9C 2K1)
*519/252-1101 — **064-77672

International-Import Customs Brokers Inc., 712 Huron Church Rd., Windsor-Ambassador Bridge (Box 516, N9A 6M6)
*519/258-6030 — **06-967854

Frederick W. Johnson Ltd., 310 Hanna St. E. (N8X 4W6)
*519/256-1847

KN Customs Brokers, 711 Huron Church Rd. (N9C 2K1)
*519/252-1195 — **064-77685

Mason's Brokerage Ltd., 48 Wyandotte St. E., Box 292 (N9A 6K7)
*519/254-2509 — **064-77777

W.G. McKay Ltd., 703 Huron Line (N9A 6J5)
*519/256-8451 — **064-77841

Mendelssohn Commercial Ltd., 48 Wyandotte St. E. (Box 292, N9A 5W5)
*519/254-2509

Peace Bridge Brokerage Ltd., Box 1149 (N9A 6P8)
*519/253-4455 — **064-77648

Robinson & Heath Ltd., 703 Huron Church Rd. (N9C 2K1)
*519/255-7220

Wm. L. Rutherford Ltd., 721 Huron Church Rd., Ste. 1 (N9A 6P2)
*519/254-4369

J. MacD. Thomson Ltd., Box 533 (N9C 2K2)
*519/254-5433 — **064-77652

United Customs Brokers (Ontario) Ltd., 310 Hanna St. E. (N8X 4W6)

Henry Weiner Ltd., 729 Huron Church Rd. (Box 7266, Sandwich Stn., N9C 3Z1)
*519/258-4632 — **064-77814

Wm. F. Willson Brokerage Ltd., Box 354 (N9C 6K7)
*519/256-4973 — **064-77787

X-M Brokers Ltd., 753 Huron Church Rd. (N9C 2K1)
*519/253-3570 — **06-477819

WOODSTOCK

Parkview Customs Brokerage Ltd., Box 694 (N4S 4L3)
*519/539-4461

Geo. L. Underhill, 653 Canterbury St., Box 184 (N4S 7W8)
*519/537-5661 — **064-74140

Quebec

ARMSTRONG

J.H. Kenneth Viens Inc., Box 188, Armstrong (via Liniere, Beauce Cty., P.Q. G0M 1J0)
*418/597-3333

BAIE COMEAU

Michel Simard Courtier en Douane Enr., 1181 Des Rochers, Hauterive, P.Q. G5C 1V2
*418/589-3930

BLACKPOOL/LACOLLE

See Lacolle

CHAMBORD

Lac St-Jean–Chibougamau Customs Brokerage Reg'd., Box 36 (G0W 1G0)
*418/342-6484 — **051-36157

CHICOUTIMI

Saguenay Customs Brokers Reg'd., Courtiers en douanes du Saguenay Enr., 343 Racine E., app 2, Box 533 (G7H 5C8)
*418/543-4771 — **051-36157

COWANSVILLE

R.S. Eastman Ltd., Box 33 (J2K 3H1)
*514/263-2838

DORVAL

Able Customs Brokers Ltd., Box 1, Stn. AMF (H4Y 1A2)
*514/631-7130

Affiliated Customs Brokers Ltd., Box 335, Room 125, Montreal AMF (H4Y 1A8)
*514/636-3926 — **05-821518
also: 10765 Côte de Liesse Rd., Ste. 482 (H9P 2R9)
*514/631-1839 — **05-25177

Blaiklock Inc., Air Cargo Bldg., Rm. 108, Montreal Int'l. Airport (H4Y 1X9)
*514/631-1843 — **via Montreal

Border Brokers Inc. (Truck Terminal), 10765 Côte de Liesse Rd. (H9P 2R9)
*514/631-8558 — **via Montreal

Border Brokers Inc., Box 36, Montreal AMF (H4Y 1A2)
*514/636-3930 — **058-21878

Emery Customs Brokerage Ltd., Box 171, AMF Cargo Bldg., Montreal Int'l. Airport (H4Y 1A5)
*514/636-3480

G.M. Patry Ltd., Air Cargo Bldg., Montreal Int'l. Airport (H4Y 1A9)
*514/636-3450 — **05-822596

G.M. Perrault Inc., Room 114, Air Cargo Bldg., Montreal AMF (H4Y 1A5)
*514/636-8591 — **05-822755

DRUMMONDVILLE

André Gallant Inc., 508 D Lindsay (Box 622, J2B 6W6)
*819/477-1302

GRANBY

J.A. Leveille & Sons Inc., 250 St. Urbain St. (J2G 8M8)
*514/378-8474 — **05-832597

HIGHWATER

Mrs. Edith McLean, R.R. 4, Mansonville, P.Q. J0E 1X0
*514/292-3339

HULL

See Ottawa, Ont.

HUNTINGDON

Affiliated Customs Brokers Ltd., 4C Bouchette St., Box 220 (JOS 1HO)
*514/264-6207 — **05-25177

JOLIETTE

Gaetan B. Davignon, Courtier en Douanes Ltée, C.P. 114 (J6E 3Z3)
*514/756-8271

LACOLLE

Affiliated Customs Brokers Ltd., Box 130 (J0J 1J0)
*514/246-3868 — **05-25177

Auburn & Tremblay Customs Brokers, Box 75 (J0J 1J0)
*514/246-3447

Blaiklock Inc., 338A Ridge Rd. (J0J 1J0)
*514/861-8116

Blackpool Brokerage Ltd., Box 100 (J0J 1J0)
*514/246-3828

Border Brokers Inc., Box 339 (J0J 1J0)
*514/246-3840 — **05-831501

Claude Dauphin Inc., 26 Beaulieu St. (Box 548, J0J 1J0)
*514/246-3271

Elmac World Transport Ltd., 1 rue Barrier St., St. Bernard de Lacolle, P.Q. J0J 1J0
*514/246-3790

International-Import Customs Brokers Inc., 337 Cheminguay (Box 700, J0J 1J0)
*514/861-0074, 246-2102 — **05-24220

Mendelssohn-Commercial Ltd., Box 99 (J0J 1J0)
*514/246-3022

Peace Bridge Brokerage Ltd., 330 Ridge Rd. (J0J 1J0)
*514/246-2313 — **05-831538

United Customs Brokers Ltd. (J0J 1J0)
*514/246-3438

LASALLE

Acme Customs Brokers Ltd., 7403 Newman Blvd. (H8N 1X5)
*514/366-3650 — **05-24692

Affiliated Customs Brokers Ltd., 7403 Newman Blvd., Ste. 201 (H8N 1X5)
*514/366-1704 — **05-25177

Alliance Customs Brokers Inc., 7403 Newman Blvd. (H8N 1X5)
*514/363-0035 — **05-836150

Auburn & Tremblay Customs Brokers Inc., 7403 Newman Blvd., Box 8 (H2N 1X5)
*514/366-7445

Border Brokers Inc., 7403 Newman Blvd. (H8N 1X5)
*514/366-6000 — **via Montreal

LEVIS

Yvon Dolbec Enr'g., 124 St. Pierre St., Box 94, Stn. B, Quebec, P.Q. G1K 7A1
*418/692-0450 — **051-3953

Frank M. O'Dowd Inc., 93 St. Peter St., Quebec, P.Q. G1K 7A1
*418/692-1755 — **051-3428

Robert L. Samson, 227 St. Joseph St., Lauzon, P.Q. G6V 1E2
*418/833-1023

A. Trepanier & Fils Ltée, 17 St. Jacques St., C.P. 70, Stn. B, Quebec, P.Q. G1K 7A3
*418/692-1040 — **051-2292

MARIEVILLE

Roger Lemaire & Associés Inc., 132 Grand Ruisseau (G0L 1G0)
*514/658-2195 — **05-830534

MIRABEL

Affiliated Customs Brokers Ltd., Cargo Bldg. D, Ste. 214 (J7N 1C2)
*514/476-2641 — **05-268853

Blaiklock Inc., #242, Brokers & Forwarders Bldg., Montreal Int'l. Airport (J7N 1C2)
*514/476-3783 — **05-267306

Border Brokers Inc., Room 236, Bldg. D, Montreal Int'l. Airport (J7N 1C2)
*514/476-3345 — **052-4319

Peace Bridge Brokerage Ltd., Cargo Bldg. A, Room A-124, Montreal Int'l. Airport (J7N 1B9)
*514/476-2780 — **05-25193

G.M. Perrault Inc., Edifice des Transitaires, Ste. 202 (J7N 1C2)
*514/476-3786 — **05-25434

MONTREAL (see also Dorval and Mirabel for airport, and LaSalle, which is listed separately)

Affiliated Customs Brokers Ltd., Box 100, Place d'Armes (H2Y 3G5)
*514/845-1211 — **05-25177

Allports Customs Brokers Ltd., 410 rue Saint Nicholas, Ste. 244 (H2Y 2P5)
*514/288-3225 — **05-24775

Apex Customs Brokers, Box 353, Place d'Armes (H2Y 3H1)
*514/849-4271

G. Bechard Ltée, 410 St. Nicholas St. (H2Y 2P5)
*514/282-0303 — **055-60803

Bensol Customs Brokers Ltd., 410 St. Nicholas St., Ste. 241 (H2Y 2P5)
*514/842-8036 — **055-60896

B.G.L. Brokerage Ltd., 300 St. Sacrement St. (H2Y 1X4)
*514/844-8636 — **055-61012

Blackpool Brokerage Ltd., 410 St. Nicholas St., Ste. 112 (H2Y 2P5)
*514/285-1500 — **05-25176

Blaiklock Inc., Ste. 520, 300 St. Sacrement St. (H2Y 1X4)
*514/842-5231 — **055-60969

Bolger Agency Inc., 411 DesRecollets St. (H2Y 1W3)
*514/842-2946

Border Brokers Inc., Place d'Armes, Box 1750 (H2Y 3L7)
*514/849-3751 — **055-60718

Arthur L. Brunette Ltée, 300 St. Sacrement, #2 (H2Y 1X4)
*514/844-1068

Cargo Expediters Ltd., 300 St. Sacrement St., Room 12 (H2Y 1X4)
*514/844-8486 — **055-60740

Carson Customs Brokers Ltd., 468 rue St-Jean (H2Y 2S1)
*514/288-7230

Century Customs Brokers Ltd., 407 McGill St., Ste. 605 (H2Y 2G3)
*514/288-0150 — **055-61118

Circle International Freight (Canada) Ltd., 410 Nicholas St., #101 (H2Y 2P5)
*514/844-2531 — **05-24764

Clarke International Inc., 1134 St. Catherine St. W., 3rd floor (H3B 1H4)
*514/876-8545 — **05-24476

Delmar Customs Brokers Ltd., Box 1416, Place d'Armes (H2Y 3K5)
*514/285-1301 — **055-60494

Delta Customs Brokers, 407 McGill St., Ste. 701 (H2Y 2G3)
*514/843-8864 — **05-268586

Edgar Doucet Limitée, 300 St. Sacrement St., Room 505 (H2Y 1X9)
*514/849-2463 — **05-268897

Elmac World Transport Ltd., 410 St. Nicholas St. (H2Y 2P8)
*514/842-5411 — **055-61056

Federated Customs Brokers Ltd., 240 St. Jacques St. W. (H2Y 1M5)
*514/849-5351 — **05-25672

J.A. Finlayson Inc., 300 St. Sacrement St. (H2Y 1X4)
*514/844-8881

General Customs Brokers Inc., 286 St. Paul St. W. (H2Y 2A4)
*514/286-9616

Globe Customs Brokers Inc., 751 Victoria Sq. (H2Y 2J6)
*514/288-2100

J. René Hebert Ltée, 300 St. Sacrement St. (H2Y 1X7)
*514/845-5191 — **055-61147

Impex Customs Services Ltd., 407 McGill St., Room 411 (H2Y 2G3)
*514/844-1714

Intercontinental Tariff Ltd., 468 rue St-Jean, #405 (H2Y 2S1)
*514/842-1493 — **05-27331

International-Import Customs Brokers Inc., #420, 276 St. James St. W. (H2Y 2G4)
*514/849-3611, 285-1883 — **05-24220

H. Kennedy Ltd., 410 St. Nicholas St., Ste. 602 (Box 1595, Place d'Armes, H2Y 3L2)
*514/849-1782 — **05-24562
Kerrin, Egan, Freeman Inc., #704, 407 McGill St. (H2Y 2G3)
*514/866-3044 — **05-268722
KN Customs Brokers, 612 St. James St. (H3H 3Y5)
*514/281-1644 — **05-267568
A.W.W. Kyle Inc., 353 St. Nicholas St. (H2Y 2P2)
*514/849-2161 — **055-61149
Leimar Transportation Service Ltd., 300 St. Sacrement St. (H2Y 1X4)
*514/842-9821 — **055-60545
Lep International Inc., 407 McGill St., #203 (H2Y 2G5)
*514/849-9321 — **05-25666
McAvoy & Levy Inc., 411 Des Recollets St. (H2Y 1W3)
*514/844-2604
Thomas Meadows & Co. Canada Ltd., 751 Victoria Sq. (H2Y 2J4)
*514/849-1243 — *05-25356
Mendelssohn-Commercial Ltd., 300 St. Sacrement St., #425 (H2Y 1X4)
*514/849-3651 — **055-61065
Merchant Customs Brokers Ltd., 353 St. Nicholas St. (H2Y 2P1)
*514/844-3421 — **055-60445
Milgram & Co., Ltd., 407 McGill St. (H2Y 2G7)
*514/288-2161 — **05-24692
J.O. Moquin Enrg., 353 St. Nicholas St. (H2Y 2P1)
*514/288-8915
Murray Agency, 112 McGill St. (H2Y 2E5)
*514/866-1737 — **055-61793
Omnitrans Customs Brokers Inc., #1005, 407 McGill St. (H2Y 2G3)
*514/288-3712 — **055-60216
Panalpina World Transport (Eastern) Ltd., 410 St. Nicholas St. (H2Y 2P7)
*514/849-5671 — **055-60767
Peace Bridge Brokerage Ltd., 300 St. Sacrement St. (H2Y 1X4)
*514/842-9891 — **05-25435
Gérard M. Perrault Inc., 360 ouest rue St-Jacques, #1906 (H2Y 1P5)
*514/842-9656
Precision Forwarders & Brokers Ltd., 407 McGill St. (H2Y 2G3)
*514/849-2115
C.E. Racine & Cie Ltée, 300 St. Sacrement St., Ste. 104 (H2Y 1X4)
*514/288-0271 — **055-61159
J.J. Robertson Ltée Ltd., 353 St. Nicholas St., Room 302 (H2Y 2P1)
*514/845-0293 — **055-61323
Robinson & Heath Ltd., 300 St. Sacrement St., Box 874, Place d'Armes (H2Y 3J4)
*514/288-2586 — **05-27194
William J. Ross Inc., 411 DesRecollets St. (H2Y 1W3)
*514/849-2565
J.P. St. Arnaud & Co. Ltd., 407 McGill St., #810 (H2Y 2G3)
*514/844-3341
St. Arnaud & Bergevin Ltd., Ste. 100, 410 St. Nicholas St., Box 578, Place d'Armes (H2Y 2P5)
*514/285-1500 — **05-25176
Schenker of Canada Ltd., 465 St. Jean St. (H2Y 2P3)
*514/284-1003 — **055-60653
Seamont Brokerage & Transport Ltd., 770 Mill St. (H3C 1Y3)
*514/931-0306 — **05-25777
United Customs Brokers Ltd., 407 McGill St. (H2Y 2G6)
*514/845-3171 — **055-61029

PHILIPSBURG

Affiliated Customs Brokers Ltd., Box 120 (JOJ 1NO)
*514/248-2773 — **05-25177
B.G.L. Brokerage Ltd., Box 209 (J0J 1N0)
*514/248-7768
Blackpool Brokerage Ltd., Highway 7 (Box 22, J0J 1N0)
*514/248-2553
United Customs Brokers Ltd. (J0J 1N0)
*514/861-8718

POINTE CLAIRE

Dolbec Mackenzie Ltd., 6600 Trans Canada, #330 (H9R 4S2)
*514/694-3480

QUEBEC

A.E. Bertrand, 1090 Brown Ave. (G1S 3A1)
*418/687-1450
Guy Côte Inc., 67 St. Pierre St. (G1K 7A1)
*418/692-1970 — **05-25176
Yvon Dolbec, Enr'g., Box 94, Stn. B (G1K 7A1)
*418/692-0450 — 051-3953
KN Customs Brokers, 126 rue St-Pierre (Box 1559, Stn. B, G1K 7A6)
*418/694-0121 — **051-3710
Frank M. O'Dowd Inc., 93 St. Pierre St., Box 6, Stn. B (G1K 7A1)
*418/692-1755 — **051-3428
St. Arnaud & Bergevin Ltée, Box 126 (G1K 4A2)
*418/692-1970
L. Robert Samson, 227 St. Joseph St., Lauzon, P.Q. G6V 1E2
*418/833-1023
A. Trepanier & Fils Ltée, 17 St. Jacques St., C.P. 70, Stn. B (G1K 7A3)
*418/692-1040 — **051-2292

RIVIERE-DU-LOUP

J.R. D'Amours, 31 rue St-Henri, Box 252 (G5R 1Z6)
*418/862-4160

ROCK ISLAND

Affiliated Customs Brokers Ltd., Box 310 (JOB 2KO)
*819/876-2753 — **05-25177
United Customs Brokers Ltd., 20 Notre Dame Blvd., Box 24 (JOB 2KO)
*819/876-2151 — **055-61029

ST-HYACINTHE

Roger Lemaire & Associes Inc., Box 291, 2285 Girouard St. (J2S 7B6)
*514/658-2195 — **05-830534
St-Hyacinthe Customs Brokers Reg'd., 7600 Duplessis (C.P. 668, J2S 7A9)
*514/773-9753 — **05-268709

ST-JEAN

Blackpool Brokerage Ltd., 109 Richelieu St., Box 155 (J3B 6X2)
*514/346-9767

ST-JEROME

J.R. Palardy Inc., 356 rue Labelle (Box 175, J7Z 5T7)
*514/432-4671

SEPT ILES

J. René Hebert Ltée, 700 Laure Blvd., #164 (G4R 1Y1)
*418/968-1075 — **051-84218
St-Arnaud & Bergevin Ltée, 685 Laure Blvd. (Box 250, G4R 1X8)
*418/962-6214 — **05-84183

SHAWINIGAN

Fernand Pelletier, 120 119th St., Box 662 (G9P 3H1)
*819/536-5911
A.G. Simard, Box 532, Grand'Mere, P.Q. G9T 5L3
*819/538-3114

SHERBROOKE

Alliance Customs Brokers Inc., 254 Marquette St. (J1H 1M1)
*819/563-9262 — **05-836131
H.H. Woollerton Ltd., 448 King St. W., Box 5 (J1H 5H5)
*819/569-9131 — **05-836146

SOREL
Mendelssohn-Commercial Ltd., Box 264 (J3P 5N7)
*514/742-5929 — **055-61687

STANHOPE
Affiliated Customs Brokers Ltd., Box 30, Coaticook, P.Q. J1A 2S8
*819/849-2794 — **05-25177
Alliance Customs Brokers Inc., Box 90 (J0B 3C0)
*819/849-4821 — **05-836150
United Customs Brokers Ltd. (JOB 3CO)
*819/849-4048

SUTTON
R.S. Eastman Ltd., Box 12 (JOE 2KO)
*514/538-2905

THETFORD MINES
R. Theberge Inc., Box 278 (G6G 5T1)
*418/335-7674

TROIS-RIVIERES
Chenevert Ltée, 825 Normand Blvd., Box 1147 (G9A 5K8)
*819/375-4931 — **05-837124

VALLEYFIELD
J. Deschenes Inc., 70 Champlain St., Box 99 (J6S 4V5)
*514/373-7616

VAL D'OR
Geo. H. Bouchard, Source Gabriel, Box 306 (J9P 4P4)
*819/824-4240

VICTORIAVILLE
L.R. Charron Inc., 47 est Notre Dame (Box 27, G6P 6S4)
*819/758-0511

New Brunswick

BATHURST
Customs Brokerage Ltd., 123 Main St. (Box 785)
*506/548-3349
M.E. & P.E. Samson, Box 420, 484 King Ave. (E2A 3Z3)
*506/548-8841

EDMUNDSTON
B. Fernand Nadeau, Box 383 (E3V 3L1)
*506/735-3692 — **014-45544

FREDERICTON
Border Brokers Inc., 659 Queen St., Box 1145, Stn. A (E3B 5C2)
*506/455-3213 — **014-46172
International-Import Customs Brokers Inc., 91 Regent (E3B 3W3)
*506/455-3139 — **014-47239

MONCTON
Border Brokers Inc., Box 749 (E1C 8M9)
*506/855-9730 — **014-2649
Frank Fales & Sons Ltd., 20 Mechanic St. (E1C 4V3)
*506/388-1163 — **014-2690

SAINT JOHN
Border Brokers Inc., Box 6056, Stn. A (E2L 4R5)
*506/693-1418 — **014-47410
Border Brokers Inc. (Truck Sufferance Warehouse), Box 3342, Stn. B (E2M 4X9)
*506/672-5524 — **via Saint John
Frank Fales & Sons Ltd., Box 6008, Stn. A (E2L 4R5)
*506/657-6800 — **014-47478
International-Import Customs Brokers Inc., 124 Prince William St. (E2L 4S4)
*506/693-1401 — **014-47239
Peace Bridge Brokerage Ltd., 133 Prince William St., Ste. 101 (Box 6728, Stn. A, E2L 4S2)
*506/657-1824 — **014-47386

ST. STEPHEN
Albert E. Horne & Son, 213 Milltown Blvd. (Box 430, E2L 2X3)
*506/466-1933

WOODSTOCK
Border Brokers Inc., Box 645, R.R. 3 (EOJ 2BO)
*506/328-2189 — **014-27529

Nova Scotia

HALIFAX
Affiliated Customs Brokers, Sackville Place 1, #202 (B3J 1K1)
*902/422-1256 — **019-22675
also: (airport) Box 1627, Stn. M (B3J 2Z1)
Border Brokers Inc., Box 752, Stn. M (B3J 2V3)
*902/429-4430 — **019-21661
Border Brokers Inc. (Airport), Box 754, Armdale Stn. (B3L 4K5)
*902/861-2238 — **019-22806
Border Brokers Inc. (Truck Sufferance Warehouse), Box 255, Armdale Stn. (B3L 4K1)
*902/867-2304 — **019-22806
Elmac World Transport Ltd., One Sackville Place, 5121 Sackville St., #204 (B3J 1K1)
*902/423-8324 — **019-21503
Federated Customs Brokers Ltd., 1657 Barrington St., #507 (B3J 2A1)
*902/422-6421 — **019-21786
General Customs Brokers (ATL) Inc., 1657 Barrington St., Ste. 224-5 (B3J 2A1)
*902/423-9381
International-Import Customs Brokers Inc., 1568 Hollis St. (Box 921, B3J 2V9)
*902/422-9666 — **01-921674
KN Customs Brokers, 5161 George St., #716 (Box 3350, B3J 1M7)
*902/425-6571 — **019-22843
Peace Bridge Brokerage Ltd., 1568 Hollis St., Box 144 (B3J 2M4)
*902/423-6131 — **019-21599

KENTVILLE
International-Import Customs Brokers Inc., 1079 Commercial St., Box 760, New Minas, N.S. B4N 3X9
*902/678-2102 — **01-921674

NEW GLASGOW
General Customs Brokers (Atlantic) Ltd., 200 Provost St. (Box 847, B2H 5K7)
*902/752-8200 — **019-36523

NORTH SYDNEY
R. Hickey & Co., 12 Archibald Ave., Box 669 (B2A 2W1)

SYDNEY
E. & M. Trading Co., 448 Prince St. (B1P 5L4)
*902/539-2019

TRURO
General Customs Brokers (Atlantic) Ltd., Box 1034 (B2N 5G9)
*902/893-9477 — **019-34502

YARMOUTH
Bluenose Customs Brokers Ltd., 4 Collins St., Box 176 (B5A 4B2)
*902/742-2511

Newfoundland

CORNER BROOK
J.P. Rogers, 2 St. Clair Ave. (A2H 5K7)
*709/634-4742

ST. JOHN'S
Avalon Customs Brokers Ltd., 67 Water St. (A1C 1C1)
*709/754-1200 — **016-4940
Geo. Canning, Box 5264 (A1C 5W1)
*709/754-0626
P.F. Collins, Customs Brokers Ltd., 162 Duckworth St., Box 5514 (A1C 5W4)

*709/726-7596 **016/4622

Yukon Territories

WHITEHORSE

Bailey Richardson Ins. Agencies Ltd., 208B Main St. (Y1A 2A9)
*403/667-4271 — **036-8-396

RAILWAY COMPANIES IN CANADA

With their equipment and principal officials, and name of express company operating over (or connecting with) their line.

ALGOMA CENTRAL RAILWAY

Box 7000, Sault Ste. Marie, Ont. P6A 5P6
(705) 949-2113
Express Co.—Algoma Central
322 miles. 28 locomotives. 1,687 cars.
President—L. N. Savoie, Sault Ste. Marie, Ont.
Vice-President & General Manager, Marine Division—P. R. Cresswell, Sault Ste. Marie, Ont.
Vice President, Rail—S. A. Black, Sault Ste. Marie, Ont.
Manager, Materials—W.C. Mersereau, Sault Ste. Marie, Ont.
Traffic Manager—C. H. Paul, Sault Ste. Marie, Ont.

B.C. HYDRO RAIL

970 Burrard St., Vancouver, B.C. V6Z 1Y3
(604) 663-2212
Express Co., none (Canadian National and Canadian Pacific Exp. connect)
104 miles. 22 locomotives. 228 cars.
Freight Traffic Manager—R.W. Newton, New Westminster
Manager Railway Operations—G.I. Stevenson, New Westminster, B.C.

BRITISH COLUMBIA RAILWAY

1095 W. Pender St., Vancouver B. C. V6E 2N6
(604) 681-3131
Express Co. none (Canadian National and Canadian Pacific Exp. Cos. connect)
1260.8 miles. 126 locomotives. 9,966 freight cars.
Owners—Government of British Columbia
President & Chief Executive Officer—M. C. Norris, Vancouver, B.C.
Vice President, Marketing & Sales—A. C. Sturgeon, Vancouver, B.C.

BURLINGTON NORTHERN INC.

176 E. 5th St., St. Paul, Minn. 55101
(612) 298-2120
22,988 miles (only 181 miles in Canada). 2,345 locomotives. 113,122 cars.
Chairman—L. W. Menk, St. Paul, Minn.
President & Chief Executive Officer—R.C. Greyson, St. Paul, Minn.
Senior Vice-President, Operations—W.F. Thompson, St. Paul, Minn.
Senior Vice-President—I. C. Ethington, St. Paul, Minn.
Vice-President, Purchasing & Material—J. Tierney, St. Paul, Minn.

BURLINGTON NORTHERN (MANITOBA) LTD.

963 Lindsay St., Winnipeg, Man. R3N 1X6
President—N.M. Lorentzsen, St. Paul, Minn.
Terminal Supt.—J.A. Lowry, Winnipeg

CANADA & GULF TERMINAL RAILWAY

Box 578, Mont Joli, P.Q. G5H 3L3
(418) 775-4373
30 miles. 1 locomotive.
General Manager—J. B. Quimper, Mont Joli, P.Q.

CANADIAN NATIONAL RAILWAYS

935 Lagauchetiere St. W., Box 8100, Montreal, P.Q. H3C 3N4
(514) 877-5430
Express Co.—Canadian National
23,992 miles including C. Vt. Ry. (364 miles) and D. W. and P. Ry. (170 miles). 1825 locomotives. 107,030 cars.
Chairman of the Board—J.A. Dextraze

Officers:

President & Chief Executive Officer—R.A. Bandeen
President, CN Holdings—C.F. Armstrong
President & Chief Executive Officer—CN Investment, T. Ceraschi
President & General Manager, CN Express Division—C. Perron
President, CN Rail—R.E. Lawless
President & General Manager, Newfoundland Transportation Division—R.G. Messenger
Corporate Vice President—J.M. LeClair
Corporate Vice President—K.E. Hunt
Senior Vice President—A.H. Hart, Q.C.
Vice President & Secretary of the Company—G.M. Cooper
Vice President & General Counsel—E.D. Pinsonnault, Q.C.
Vice President, Corporate Affairs—J. Gratwick
Vice President, Real Estate—R. Lagacé
Vice President, Marketing—J.H.D. Sturgess
Vice President, Labour Relations—S.T. Cooke
Vice President, Personnel—A.E. Deegan
Vice President, Purchases & Materials—W.H. Bailey
Vice President, Operations—J.L. Cann
Vice President, Atlantic Region (Moncton)—D.W. Blair
Vice President, St. Lawrence Region (Montreal)—Y.H. Masse
Vice President, Great Lakes Region (Toronto)—A.R. Williams
Vice President, Prairie Region (Winnipeg)—R.J. Hansen
Vice President, Mountain Region (Edmonton)—R.A. Walker
Assistant Secretary of the Company—P.A. Quesnel
Treasurer—G.C. Church
Corporate Comptroller—S.D.H. Thomas

Purchases & Materials - Managers:

P.J. MacKay, Moncton, N.B.; D.G. Parsons, Montreal; C.H. Rose, Toronto; P.W. Kirk, Transcona, Man.; P.W. Dawson, Edmonton, Alta.

Sales Managers - Freight:

E.R. Murphy, Atlantic Region, Moncton, N.B.
E.J. Hlusko, St. Lawrence Region, Montreal
A.L. Burns, Great Lakes Region, Toronto
A.C. Johnston, Prairie Region, Winnipeg
A.F. Heuman, Mountain Region, Edmonton

CANADIAN PACIFIC LIMITED

Box 6042, Stn. A, Montreal, P.Q. H3C 3E4
(514) 395-5151 Telex: 05-25857
Chairman & Chief Executive Officer—F.S. Burbidge
President—W.W. Stinson
Vice Presidents—J.C. Ames, J.C. Anderson, J.P.T. Clough, D.S. Maxwell, Q.C., J.A. McDonald, R.T. Riley, I.B. Scott

CP RAIL

Box 6042, Stn. A, Montreal, P.Q. H3C 3E4
(514) 395-5151 Telex: 055-61579
15,519.76 Miles. 1,284 Locomotives. 71,372 Cars.
Executive Vice President—R.S. Allison
Vice Presidents—G.E. Benoit, J.M. Bentham, R. Colosimo, R.C. Gilmore, C.R. Pike, D.C. Coleman, Toronto, Ont.; J.W. Malcolm, Winnipeg, Man.; J.D. Bromley, Vancouver, B.C.
Director of Purchasing—D. Fahey
Manager, Sales Administration—G.J. Askwith

Regional General Managers, Operation & Maintenance—J.B. Chabot, J.P. Kelsall, Toronto, Ont.; R.J. Shepp, Winnipeg, Man.; L.A. Hill, Vancouver, B.C.

CARTIER RAILWAY COMPANY

Port Cartier, P.Q. G5B 2H3
(418) 766-2208
Express Co.—None
276 miles. 54 locomotives. 1,789 cars.
President—G. Massobrio
Vice-President—J.M.R. Gagnon
Secretary-Treasurer—J. G. Chenevert
Director of Purchases—G. S. Peniston

CHESAPEAKE & OHIO RAILWAY

(Part of the Chessie System Railroads)
Terminal Tower, Cleveland, Ohio 44101
(216) 623-2200
(No Express on Canadian Lines)
(201 miles in Canada)
President—J.T. Collinson, Cleveland, Ohio.
Asst. Vice President, Purchases & Materials—J.S. Ketzner

CONRAIL (Consolidated Rail Corporation)

6 Penn Center Plaza, Philadelphia, Pa. 19104
(215) 977-4000
326 miles in Canada.
Chairman & Chief Executive Officer—L.S. Crane
President & Chief Operating Officer—S.M. Reed
Senior Vice President, Marketing & Sales—J.A. Hagen
Vice President, Marketing—R.H. Steiner
Vice President, Sales—A.A. Michaud
Director, Multi-Modal Sales—A. Buford Smith
Vice President, Materials & Purchasing—J.T. Whatmough

DEVCO RAILWAY

Box 2500, Sydney, N.S. B1P 6K9
(902) 562-5525
Express Co.—None (Canadian National Express connects)
88 miles. 16 locomotives. 1,223 cars
President—A.S. Rankin
Vice-President—B. R. MacDade
Transportation & Shipping Manager—E. C. Townsend
Manager, Purchasing—F. Heffernan
Traffic Supervisor—F. MacLennan

DOMINION ATLANTIC RAILWAY

Kentville, N.S. B4N 2N3
(902) 678-3223, 4
Express Co.—Canadian Pacific (ph: 678-7309; vehicle service ph: 678-7300)
277 miles. (equipment included with CP Rail)
Manager—E. W. Purssell
District Representative, Marketing & Sales—P.O. Tobiasson

ESQUIMALT & NANAIMO RAILWAY

#700, 200 Granville St., Vancouver, B.C. V6C 2R3
Express Co.—Canadian Pacific
195 miles. (equipment included with CP Rail)
Supt.—H.L. MacAulay, Vancouver

ESSEX TERMINAL RAILWAY

1070 University Ave. W., Windsor, Ont. N9A 5S4
(519) 253-5281 – Telex: 064-77767
(Freight only.)
22 miles. 6 locomotives. 5 cars.
President—C.S. Locke, Chicago, Ill.
Vice-President & General Manager—M. A. Elder, Windsor, Ont.
Car Acct.—T.R. Belchuk, Walkerville, Ont.

GRAND RIVER RAILWAY

101 King St. W., Cambridge, Ont. N3H 1B5
16 miles. (equipment included with CP Rail)
Manager—G.A. Nutkins, London, Ont.
District Manager, Marketing & Sales—A.V. Barna, Cambridge (519/653-3224)
Purchasing Agent—A.H. Ivey, Toronto, Ont.
Supt.—D.L. Condie, Cambridge (519/653-1700)

GREATER WINNIPEG WATER DISTRICT RAILWAY

598 Plinguet St., St. Boniface, Man. R2J 2W7
(204) 233-1456
Express Co.—None.
97 miles. 4 locomotives. 142 cars.
Railway Supervisor—J. Nielson, St. Boniface, Man.

LAKE ERIE & NORTHERN RAILWAY

101 King St. W., Cambridge, Ont. N3H 1B5
48 miles. (equipment included with CP Rail)
Manager—G.A. Nutkins, London, Ont.
District Manager, Marketing & Sales—A.V. Barna, Cambridge (519/653-3224)
Purchasing Agent—A.H. Ivey, Toronto, Ont.
Supt.—D.L. Condie, Cambridge (519/653-1700)

NAPIERVILLE JUNCTION RAILWAY

1117 Ste. Catherine St. W., Montreal, P.Q. H3B 1H9
(514) 842-7669
Express Co.—None
28 miles. 2 locomotives. 29 cars.
President—K.P. Shoemaker, Albany, N.Y.
Vice-President, Traffic—T.E. O'Brien, Albany, N.Y.
Traffic Manager—T. F. Winnett, Montreal, P.Q.
General Freight Agent—R.L. Deneault, Montreal, P.Q.

NORFOLK & WESTERN RAILWAY

Roanoke, Va. 24042
(No Express Co. in Canada, freight only)
7,554 miles (only 322 miles of leased line in Canada).
1,386 locomotives. 92,467 cars.
Chairman & Chief Executive Officer—J.P. Fishwick
President—R.B. Claytor
Senior Vice President, Merchandise Traffic—J.R. McMichael
Vice President, Material Management—R.A. Brogan
Director, Public Relations & Advertising—L.M. Phelps (703/981-4941)

NORTHERN ALBERTA RAILWAYS

Since January 1, 1981 is the Peace River Division of CNR.

ONTARIO NORTHLAND RAILWAY

195 Regina St., North Bay, Ont. P1B 8L3
(705) 472-4500
(Owned by Province of Ontario)
Express Co.—Ontario Northland
754 miles. 38 locomotives. 1,286 cars.
Chairman—J. Mathews
General Manager—R.O. Beatty
Director, Passenger Service, Tourism & Public Affairs—R.L. Moore
Director of Purchases—D.E. Innes

QUEBEC CENTRAL RAILWAY

165 Wellington St. N., Sherbrooke, P.Q. J1H 5C3
(819) 563-3220
Express Co.—Canadian Pacific
353 miles (equipment included with CP Rail)
Manager—J.V. Rivest
Manager, Marketing & Sales—G. S. McKeogh

QUEBEC NORTH SHORE & LABRADOR RAILWAY

#1650, 1245 Sherbrooke St. W., Montreal, P.Q. H3G 1G8
(514) 849-5636
Express Co.—None
357 miles. 81 locomotives. 4,728 cars.
President—M.B. Mulroney, Montreal, P.Q.

Manager—G.A. Dolliver, Sept Iles, P.Q.

ROBERVAL & SAGUENAY RAILWAY
Box 1277, Jonquiere (Arvida), P.Q. G7S 4K8
(418) 548-1121
Box 6090, Montreal, P.Q. H3C 2H8
Express Co.—None (Canadian National Express connects)
100 miles. 14 locomotives. 425 cars.
Vice-President—(tba), Jonquiere (Arvida), P.Q.
Head of Services Freight & Car Acctg. & Freight Claim Agent—Rita Boulianne, Jonquiere (Arvida), P.Q.

TORONTO, HAMILTON & BUFFALO RAILWAY
TH&B Station, Hunter St. E., Hamilton, Ont. L8N 1M1
(416) 522-9394
110 miles. 17 locomotives. 1,172 cars.
President—R.S. Allison, Toronto, Ont.
Vice-President—W.W. Stinson, Montreal, P.Q.
General Manager—J. A. Hill, Hamilton, Ont.
Purchasing Agent—S. A. Davis, Hamilton, Ont.

VIA RAIL CANADA INC.
1801 McGill College Ave., 13th floor, Box 8116, Montreal, P.Q. H3C 3N3
(514) 286-2311
(Passenger Services only)
President—J.F. Roberts
Vice President, Marketing—G.C. Campbell
Vice President, Operations—B.E. Horsman
Vice President, VIA Atlantic—A.W. Raftus
Vice President, VIA Quebec—J.L. Moisan
Vice President, VIA Ontario—A.R. Campbell
Vice President, VIA West—H.F. Murray
Vice President, Development & Planning—R. Béchamp
Vice President, Finance & Administration—J.A. Hanna
Director, Corporate Affairs—G. Dufault
Vice President, Human Resources—J.P. Laroche
Vice President, Law & Secretary—G. Fortin, Q.C.
Director, Public Relations—E. LeBlanc
Comptroller/Treasurer—A.R. Cave

WHITE PASS & YUKON ROUTE
Box 4070, Whitehorse, Y.T. Y1A 3T1
(403) 667-7611
Express Co.—None
110 miles. 19 locomotives. 450 cars.
President—J.F. Fraser

AIR LINE COMPANIES IN CANADA

Following are major airline companies operating in Canada. For a complete list, including local carriers, contact Canadian Government Publishing Centre, Supply & Services Canada, Ottawa, Ont. K1A 0S9.

AIR CANADA
(Air Canada is under the jurisdiction of the Ministry of Transport, Ottawa, Ont.)
General Sales Office—One Place Ville Marie, Montreal, P.Q. H3B 3P7 (514/874-4560) - Telex 06-217537
Chairman—Pierre Taschereau, Q.C.
President & Chief Executive Officer—Claude Taylor
Group Enterprises
includes Computer & Systems Services, and Subsidiary Companies
Executive Vice President & Chief—J.W. McGill
Airline Operations
includes Planning, Scheduling, Fleet Capacity Planning, Government & Industry Affairs, Passenger Planning & Marketing, and Cargo
Executive Vice President & Chief—P.J. Jeanniot
Airline Technical Operations
includes Maintenance, Flight Operations, Purchasing & Supply, Engineering, Properties & Facilities, Aircraft Technology, Petroleum Purchasing, and Safety
Group Vice President—L.M. Raverty
Airline Sales & Service
Group Vice President—R.W. Linder
Corporate Finance & Planning
Senior Vice President—D.J. Groom
Corporate & Legal Affairs
Senior Vice President—R.T. Vaughan
Corporate & Human Relations
includes Personnel, and Public Affairs
Senior Vice President—J.E. Whitelaw
Senior Vice President, Ontario—J.M. Callen

AIR FRANCE
Canadian Head Office—Place Ville Marie, Montreal, P.Q. H3B 3N4 (514/861-9861)
Cargo Manager for Canada—J.L. Le Bos, Montreal (476-3832)
Montreal Regional Cargo Manager—A. Ohayon (476-3832)
Montreal Airport Cargo Manager—A. Pinet (476-3833)
Toronto Cargo Manager—M. Buckley (416/676-2782)
Toronto Cargo Supervisor—J. Touchard (676-2782)

AIR JAMAICA LTD.
100 Front St. W., Toronto, Ont. M5J 1E3

AIRWEST AIRLINES LTD.
16th floor, 1055 W. Hastings St., Vancouver, B.C. V6E 2H2

ALITALIA
Canadian Head Office—2055 Peel St., Montreal, P.Q. H3A 1V8
General Manager for Canada—Italo Morgera
Commercial Manager for Canada—Martino Mainardi

AMERICAN AIRLINES
Canadian Sales Office—40 St. Clair Ave. W., Toronto, Ontario M4V 1M4 (416/925-4800)
General Manager, Canada—E.D. Moberly (416/961-9291)
Manager, Freight Sales Toronto—R.A. Macdonald (416/676-3823)

BRITISH AIRWAYS
Canadian Head Office—1 Dundas St. W., 25th floor, Toronto, Ont. M5G 2B2 (416/595-2600)
Manager for Canada—Andrew Makin
District Sales Manager (Toronto)—M. Curson
Montreal Office—Place Ville Marie (514/874-4040)
District Sales Manager (Montreal)—A.E. Sirsly

CP AIR
Executive Office—One Grant McConachie Way, Vancouver International Airport, B.C. V7B 1V1 (604/270-5211)
President & Chief Executive Officer—I. A. Gray
Executive Vice-President—J.K. Dakin
Senior Vice President, Administration & Public Affairs—H. D. Cameron
Senior Vice President, Finance & Accounting—C.F. O'Brien
Vice President, Administration—G.E. Manning
Vice President, Eastern Canada—E.W. Ogden
Vice President, Technical Services—G.A. Worden
Vice President, Flight Operations—Capt. W.G. Sinclair
Vice President, Marketing Services—D. Huisman
Vice President, Sales & Service—H.B. O'Toole
General Manager, Charter—F.E. Basiren

CZECHOSLOVAK AIRLINES
Canadian Head Office—1 Place Ville Marie, #2236, Montreal, P.Q. H3B 3M4

DELTA AIR LINES INC.
Canadian Head Office—3300 Cote Vertu W., #110, Montreal, P.Q. H4R 2B7 (514/337-1420)
Director, Canada—H.J. Canvin
Reservation Manager—F. Reeb
Station Manager—R.W. Vinet

EASTERN AIR LINES
District Sales Office—Westmount Sq., Montreal, P.Q. H3Z 2S7 (514/931-7594)
Manager, Passenger & Cargo Sales—J.-L. Garaud
Manager, Reservations—Guy Uddenberg
Manager, Ticket Office—K.T. Brown
Manager, Airport Services (Dorval Airport)—P.P. Benoit
Manager, Passenger Services (Ottawa Airport)—(tba)

EASTERN PACIFIC AVIATION LTD.
R.R. 1, Abbotsford Airport, Abbotsford, B.C. V2S 1M3 (604/859-3586)
President—Dr. W. Evans
Operations Manager, Chief Pilot—E.J. Samaras
Secretary—Dr. Ian Hadfield

EASTERN PROVINCIAL AIRWAYS
Head Office—Box 5001, Gander, Nfld. A1V 1W9 (709/256-3941)
Chairman—K.A. Miller
President & Chief Executive Officer—H.R. Steele
Vice President, Marketing—W.L. Verrier
Vice President, Operations & Maintenance—A.C. Walker
Vice President, Finance—I.J. Kilpatrick
Vice President, Administration & Planning—R.P. Rideout
Corporate Secretary—R. McCabe
Controller—N.J. Jackman
Manager, Data Processing—D. W. Moss
Director, Sales & Service—W.T. Reilly
Director, Public Affairs & Advertising—J.G. MacPherson

FINNAIR
Head Office, Canadian Division—8 King St. E., #1800, Toronto, Ont. M5C 1B5 (416/362-1511)
Manager, Canadian Division—I. Mitro

IRISH INTERNATIONAL AIRLINES
Canadian Office—1405 Peel St., #206, Montreal, P.Q. H3A 1S5

KLM ROYAL DUTCH AIRLINES
Canadian Head Office—1245 Sherbrooke St. W., Montreal, P.Q. H3G 1G2 (514/844-3041)
General Manager Canada—P. van Vliet
Marketing & Sales Manager, Canada—A. E. van Wettum
Cargo Manager, Canada—A.I. Masclé
Station Manager (Mirabel Airport)—L. G. Melling

"LOT" Polish Airlines
Canadian Office—1000 Sherbrooke St. W., #2107, Montreal, P.Q. H3A 2P2 (514/844-2674,5)
General Manager for Canada—J. Wyganowski
Asst. General Manager for Canada—M. Bielec
Cargo & Station Manager—J. Pietrzak
Toronto Direct Line—416/364-2035

LUFTHANSA GERMAN AIRLINES
Canadian Head Office—55 Yonge St., Toronto, Ont. M5E 1J4 (416/869-3215)
Manager, Canada—H. Kozel
Assistant Manager, Canada—H. Hundertmark
District Sales Promotion Manager—E. Skorski

MEXICANA AIRLINES (Aeronaves de Mexico)
Canadian Office—180 Bloor St. W., #508, Toronto, Ont. M5S 2V6 (416/961-2080)
District Sales Manager—Paul F. Nix

NORCANAIR
Head Office—Box 850, Prince Albert, Sask. S6V 5S4 (306/764-4271) - Telex 074-2876 Saskatoon
President—J. B. Lloyd
Manager, Traffic/Northern Operations—J.W. Klassen
Manager, Engineering—A. Malena
Manager, Maintenance—E. Beauliua
Manager, Flight Operations—G. Eikel
Comptroller—D.J. Wood

NORDAIR LTD.
Head Office—100 Alexis Nihon Blvd., 7th floor, St. Laurent, P.Q. H4M 2P4
President & Chief Executive Officer—A.F. Lizotte
Vice-President, Sales & Marketing—Ronald Patmore
Vice-President, Customer Services—Victor Pappalardo

NORTHWARD AIRLINES LTD.
Hangar 11, Municipal Airport, Edmonton, Alta. T5G 2Z3

NORTHERN THUNDERBIRD AIR
Box 1510, Prince George, B.C. V2L 4V5
(604) 963-9611
Executive Vice President & General Manager—Jack Stelfox

NORTHWEST TERRITORIAL AIRWAYS LTD.
Head Office—Yellowknife Airport, Postal Service 9000, Yellowknife, N.W.T. X1A 2R3 (403/873-8555)
President & Chairman of the Board—R.P. Engle
Vice President, Operations—John Robertson
Manager, Scheduled Services—Keith Johns
Traffic Manager, Charter Services—Norm Stannard

PACIFIC WESTERN AIRLINES LTD.
-not confirmed for 1982-
Head Office—Ste. 700, 700 2nd St. S.W., Calgary, Alta. T2P 2W1 (403/261-7760)
President & Chief Executive Operator—R. T. Eyton
Executive Vice President & Chief Operating Officer—H.D. Cope
Senior Vice President, Finance, & Secretary—D.F. Granger
Vice President, In-Flight Services & Catering—A.C. Campbell
Vice President, Western Region—G.J. Cooke
Vice President, Administration—A.W. Corbett
Vice President, Technical Services—W. Dobin
Vice President, Flight Operations—K. Fransbergen
Vice President, Central Region—K.E. Gray
Vice President, Public & Industry Affairs—D.R. Jacox
Vice President, Eastern Region—E. Caron
Vice President, Legal & Regulatory Affairs—M. Sigler
Treasurer—R.W. Benallick
Controller—J.V.R. Wark

QANTAS AIRWAYS LTD.
Western Office—Hotel Vancouver, 900 W. Georgia St., Vancouver, B.C. V6C 1P9 (604/684-1441)
Sales Manager, Western Canada—J.M. Watson
Eastern Office—#907, 80 Bloor St. W., Toronto, Ont. M5S 2V1 (416/922-3593)
Sales Manager, Eastern Canada—R. Haas

QUEBEC AVIATION LTEE
Executive Office—Hangar 2, Aéroport de Québec, Ste-Foy, P.Q. G2E 3M3 (418/872-1200) - Telex 051-3979
President—Léo Vanasse
General Manager—Marc Racicot
Chief Pilot—Richard DesRuisseaux
Chief Engineer—Roger Savard
Traffic Manager—Colin Simard
Controller—A. Labbé

QUEBECAIR
Head Office—Montreal International Airport, Box 490, Dorval, P.Q. H4Y 1B5 (514/636-3896)

SABENA Belgian World Airlines
Canadian Regional Office—#421, 131 Bloor St. W., Toronto, Ont. M5S 1R1 (416/961-1904)
District Sales Manager—L. Verroken (961-2075)
Cargo Co-ordinator—M. MacLaren (676-3337)
Ticket Office—961-1904

SCANDINAVIAN AIRLINES SYSTEM INC. (SAS)
Canadian Area Sales Office—1200 McGill College Ave., Ste. 1420, Montreal, P.Q. H3B 4G7 (514/861-8317)
Area Manager, Canada—Hans J. Dedekam
Sales—Eric Kuutti
District Sales Manager, Toronto—S. Tapson
District Sales Manager, Vancouver—R. Groves

SOUTH AFRICAN AIRWAYS
Canadian Office—Box 195, Commercial Union Tower, Toronto Dominion Centre, Toronto, Ont. M5K 1H6 (416/864-9100)
Sales Manager, Canada—P.G. Lanch
Resident Rep., Vancouver—S. Elmy

TAP - AIR PORTUGAL
Canadian Offices:
60 Bloor St. W., #206, Toronto, Ont. M4W 3B8 (416/964-7723)
1010 Sherbrooke St. W., #2005, Montreal, P.Q. H3A 2R7 (514/849-6163)

TRANS NORTH TURBO AIR LTD.
Box 4338, Whitehorse Airport, Whitehorse, Y.T. Y1A 3T6

TRANS PROVINCIAL AIRLINES
Head Office—Box 280, Prince Rupert, B.C. V8J 3P6 (604/627-1341)
General Manager—Gene Storey
Controller—William Bebington
Maintenance Manager—J.F. Hidber

UNITED AIR LINES INC.
c/o Box 66100, O'Hare Int'l. Airport, Chicago, Ill. 60666

US AIR
Canadian District Sales Office—Royal York Hotel, Toronto, Ont. M5J 1E3 (416/368-1913)
District Sales Manager—Lorne Kelsey
Airport Manager, Malton—Al Kelly
Airport Manager, Dorval—Wally Hume
District Sales Manager, Montreal—Carle Chadillon

WARDAIR INTERNATIONAL LTD.
Head Office—2201 Toronto Dominion Tower, Edmonton Centre, Edmonton, Alta. T5J 0K4
Toronto—6299 Airport Rd., Mississauga, Ont. L4V 1N3 (416/671-3100)
Chairman & President—Maxwell W. Ward
Senior Vice President—T.L. Spalding
Vice President, Operations—G.D. Curley
Vice President, Marketing—B. Walker
Secretary Treasurer—M.D. Ward
Director, Customer Relations & Consumer Affairs—J.L. Shaffer
Director, Legal Services—I.C. Wilkie

GOVERNMENT INFORMATION SOURCE & QUICK REFERENCE TABLE

EDITOR'S NOTE: Following are government sources of information listed alphabetically under topics of frequent need or interest. Where governments refer enquiries to Associations or Community Organizations the latter have been listed. Under each topic, Federal information sources are listed first. (Only head office addresses are given for Federal sources of information. Refer to the main government listings in this book for regional offices of the Federal government.) Provincial sources are listed second, and then municipal sources in major population areas if jurisdiction applies. A few of the "topics" following are more properly for use as QUICK REFERENCE guides to addresses of frequently contacted Departments, such as Justice, Solicitors General, etc.

If no Branch or Division is given, address enquiries to Information Services.

See GOVERNMENT, alphabetically following for the main source of information in each province and for the Federal Government telephone referral services.

Suggestions, corrections or additions to this table are welcome. Contact: Editor, 130 Harlandale Ave., Willowdale, Ont. M2N 1P3.

ABORTION
see Family Planning

ADOPTION
see Child Welfare

AGED, THE
see Old Age Assistance

ADULT EDUCATION
see Education

AGRICULTURE
Canada Employment & Immigration Commission (Labour Market Planning & Adjustment Branch), Ottawa, Ont. K1A OJ9 (819/994-3771) (agricultural employment programs and services)

Canadian Dairy Commission, 2197 Riverside Dr., Ottawa, Ont. K1A OZ2 (613/998-9490)

Canadian Grain Commission, 600, 303 Main St., Winnipeg, Man. R3C 3G8 (204/949-2770)

Dept. of Agriculture, Information Services, Sir John Carling Bldg., Ottawa, Ont. K1A OC7 (613/995-5222)

Dept. of Agriculture, Farm Improvement Loans Administration, Sir JohnCarling Bldg., Ottawa, Ont. K1A 0C5 (613/995-5880, ext. 519) (loans for farmers)

Dept. of Industry, Trade & Commerce, Agriculture, Fisheries & Food Products Branch, 235 Queen St., Ottawa, Ont. K1A OH5 (613/995-8107)

Dept. of Regional Economic Expansion, Prairie Farm Rehabilitation Admin., 1901 Victoria Ave., Regina, Sask. S4P OR5 (306/359-5070)

Farm Credit Corp. Canada, Box 2314, Stn. D, Ottawa, Ont. K1P 6J9 (613/996-6606) (agricultural mtge. loans)

Livestock Feed Board of Canada, Box 177, Snowdon Stn., Montreal, P.Q. H3X 3T4 (514/283-7505); 17655 57th Ave., #3, Surrey (Cloverdale), B.C. V3S 1H1 (604/576-8144)

National Farm Products Marketing Council, 300 Sparks St., 2nd floor, Place de Ville, Centre Bldg., Ottawa, Ont. K1R 7S3 (613/995-2297)

National Film Board, Box 6100, Montreal, P.Q. H3C 3H5 (514/333-3333)

Statistics Canada, Ottawa, Ont. K1A OT6 (613/995-4869)

Alta.: Dept. of Agriculture, Communications Division, 9718 107 St., Edmonton, Alta. T5K 2C8 (403/427-2127)

B.C.: Information Services, Ministry of Agriculture & Food, Parliament Bldgs., Victoria, B.C. V8W 2Z7 (604/387-5121)

Man.: Dept. of Agriculture, Distributions Centre, 411 York Ave., Winnipeg, Man. R3C 3M1 (204/944-3845)

N.B.: Information Officer, Dept. of Agriculture, Box 6000, Research Stn., Fredericton, N.B. E3B 5H1 (506/453-2666)

Nfld.: Dept. of Rural, Agricultural & Northern Development, Prov. Agriculture Bldg., Brookfield Rd., Mount Pearl, Nfld. (709/737-3840)

N.S.: Admin. Division, Dept. of Agriculture, Hollis Bldg., Box 190, Halifax, N.S. B3J 2M4 (902/424-3244)

Ont.: Information Branch, Ministry of Agriculture & Food, Queen's Park, Toronto, Ont. M7A 1A5 (416/965-1056)

P.E.I.: Information Section, Dept. of Agriculture & Forestry, Box 2000, Charlottetown, P.E.I. C1A 7N8 (902/892-4101)

Que.: Dept. of Agriculture, Fisheries & Food, Communications Division, 200A Chemin Ste-Foy, Quebec, P.Q. G1R 4X6 (418/643-2673)

Sask.: Public Information, Saskatchewan Agriculture, Walter Scott Bldg., Regina, Sask. S4S OB1 (306/565-5155)

AIR POLLUTION

see Environment

ALCOHOLISM

see Drugs

ALL-TERRAIN VEHICLES

see Leisure Craft

ANIMAL CONTROL

Animal Control is a municipal responsibility. Contact the City Clerk who will refer your request to the appropriate department and/or agency in the municipality. *See* "Municipalities" in the Index for addresses.

APPRENTICESHIP PROGRAMS

Alta.: Apprenticeship & Trade Certification Branch, Dept. of Advanced Education & Manpower, 11160 Jasper Ave., Edmonton, Alta. T5K OL1 (403/427-8765)

B.C.: Apprenticeship Training Programs, Ministry of Labour, 4946 Canada Way, Burnaby, B.C. V5G 4J6 (604/294-3878)

Man.: Dept. of Labour & Manpower, Training & Development Branch, 600 Norquay Bldg., Winnipeg, Man. R3C OP8 (204/944-3337)

N.B.: Manpower Operations, Dept. of Labour & Manpower, Box 6000, Fredericton, N.B. E3B 5H1 (506/453-2260)

Nfld.: Dept. of Labour & Manpower, Confederation Bldg., St. John's, Nfld. A1C 5T7 (709/737-2729)

N.S.: Dept. of Labour & Manpower, Box 697, Halifax, N.S. B3J 2T8 (902/424-5651)

Ont.: Apprenticeship Branch, Ministry of Colleges & Universities, Mowat Block, Queen's Park, Toronto, Ont. M7A 2B5 (416/965-4211)

P.E.I.: Apprenticeship Branch, Box 2000, Charlottetown, P.E.I. C1A 7N8 (902/892-3416)

Que.: Apprenticeship Service, Dept. of Labour & Manpower, 255 Cremazie est, Montreal, P.Q. H2M 1L5 (514/873-4646)

Sask.: Dept. of Labour, Apprenticeship & Standards Division, 1914 Hamilton St., Regina, Sask. S4P 4V4 (306/565-2440)

Dept. of Continuing Education, 1855 Victoria Ave., Regina, Sask. S4P 3V5 (306/565-5600)

Yukon: Dept. of Education & Vocational Training, Box 2703, Whitehorse, Y.T. Y1A 2C6 (403/667-5131)

ARBITRATION

see Labour

ARCHIVES

see History

ARCTIC

Arctic Transportation Division, Government, Industry & International Relations Branch, Dept. of Transport, Ottawa, Ont. K1A ON5 (613/992-4340)

Dept. of Energy, Mines & Resources Canada, Polar Continental Shelf Project, 880 Wellington St., Ottawa, Ont. K1A OE4 (613/996-3388)

Dept. of Indian Affairs & Northern Development, Ottawa, Ont. K1A OH4 (819/997-9920)

Dept. of National Defence, Information Services, Ottawa, Ont. K1A OK2 (613/996-2353)

Dept. of National Health & Welfare, Ottawa, Ont. K1A OK9 (613/996-4950)

Public Works Canada, Sir Charles Tupper Bldg., Ottawa, Ont. K1A OM2 (613/998-9560)

Scientific Information & Publications Branch, Dept. of Fisheries & Oceans, 240 Sparks St., Ottawa, Ont. K1A OH3 (613/993-2372) (arctic fishery)

The National Film Board, Box 6100, Montreal, P.Q. H3C 3H5 (514/333-3333)

National Museums of Canada, Ottawa, Ont. K1A OM8 (613/995-9832)

National Research Council of Canada, Ottawa, Ont. K1A OR6 (613/993-9101)

Public Archives of Canada, 395 Wellington St., Ottawa, Ont. K1A ON3 (613/992-2669)(arctic history)

N.W.T.: TravelArctic, Dept. of Economic Development & Tourism, Government of the N.W.T., Yellowknife, N.W.T. X1A 2L9 (403/873-7320)

ARTS

The Canada Council, 255 Albert St. (Box 1047), Ottawa, Ont. K1P 5V8 (613/237-3400)

Canadian Broadcasting Corp.–English Services Division, Box 500, Stn. A, Toronto, Ont. M5W 1E6 (416/925-3311); French Services Division, Box 6000, Montreal, P.Q. H3C 3A8 (514/285-3211)

Dept. of Communications, Arts & Culture Branch, Rm. 10F2, 15 Eddy St., Hull, P.Q. (Mailing: Ottawa, Ont. K1A 0C8) (819/994-2355)

Dept. of Indian Affairs & Northern Development, Ottawa, Ont. K1A OH4 (819/997-9920) (Indian & Eskimo art)

Public Relations & Information Services, Public Works Canada, Sir Charles Tupper Bldg., Ottawa, Ont. K1A OM2 (613/998-9560) (fine arts in federal bldgs.)

National Arts Centre, Confederation Sq., Box 1534, Stn. B, Ottawa, Ont. K1P 5W1 (613/996-5051)

National Film Board, Box 6100, Montreal, P.Q. H3C 3H5 (514/333-3333)

The National Gallery of Canada, Elgin St., Ottawa, Ont. K1A OM8 (613/992-4636)

National Museum of Man, Ottawa, Ont. K1A OM8 (613/992-3497)(Indian & Eskimo Art)

Alta.: Dept. of Culture, 10004 104 Ave., Edmonton, Alta. T5J OK5 (403/427-6530, pub. affairs)

Alberta Art Foundation, 4th floor, 10158 103 St., Edmonton, Alta. T5J 0X6 (403/427-9969)

B.C.: Cultural Services Branch, Ministry of Provincial Secretary & Government Services, Parliament Bldgs., Victoria, B.C. V8V 1X4 (604/387-5848)

Man.: Dept. of Cultural Affairs & Historic Resources, 3rd floor, 200 Vaughan St., Winnipeg, Man. R3C 1T5 (204/944-3980)

Manitoba Arts Council, Centennial Concert Hall, Room 123, 555 Main St., Winnipeg, Man. R3B 1C3 (204/944-2237)

N.B.: Dept. of Tourism, Box 12345, Fredericton, N.B. E3B 5C3 (506/453-2377)

Theatre New Brunswick, The Playhouse, Box 566, Fredericton, N.B. E3B 5A6 (506/455-3080)

Cultural Development, Dept. of Youth, Recreation & Cultural Resources, Box 6000, Fredericton, N.B. E3B 5H1 (506/453-2555)

Nfld.: Cultural Affairs Division, Dept. of Culture, Recreation & Youth, Arts & Culture Centre, Box 1854, St. John's, Nfld. A1C 5P9 (709/737-3650)

N.S.: Dept. of Culture, Recreation & Fitness, Cultural Affairs Division, (5151 Terminal Rd., 8th floor), Box 864, Halifax, N.S. B3J 2V2 (902/424-5929)

Art Gallery of Nova Scotia, (6152 Coburg Rd.), Box 2262, Halifax, N.S. B3J 3C8 (902/424-7542)

Ont.: Ontario Arts Council, 151 Bloor St. W., Toronto, Ont. M5S 1T6 (416/961-1660)

Ministry of Culture & Recreation, Arts, Heritage & Libraries Division, 2nd floor, 77 Bloor St. W., Toronto, Ont. M7A 2R9 (416/965-5665)

P.E.I.: Cultural Affairs Office, Dept. of Community Affairs, (11 Kent St.), Box 2000, Charlottetown, P.E.I. C1A 7N8 (902/892-0221)

P.E.I. Council of the Arts, (84 Great George St.), Box 2234, Charlottetown, P.E.I. C1A 8C3 (902/892-8788)

Que.: Dept. of Cultural Affairs, 225 Grande Allée, Quebec, P.Q. G1R 5G5 (418/643-2183)

Sask.: Saskatchewan Arts Board, 2550 Broad St., Regina, Sask. S4P 3V7 (306/565-4056) Toll free Sask. only 1-800-667-3533

Organization of Saskatchewan Arts Councils, Box 488, Estevan, Sask. S4A 2A5 (306/634-4724)

Calgary: Calgary Region Arts Foundation, #105, 305 25 Ave. S.W., Calgary, Alta. T2S OL3 (403/265-5102)

Hamilton: Hamilton & Region Arts Council, Box 2080, Stn. A, Hamilton, Ont. L8N 3Y7 (416/529-9485)

London: Advisory Committee on the Arts, City Hall, London, Ont. N6A 4L9 (519/679-4530)

Montreal: Conseil des Arts de la Communauté Urbaine de Montréal, 2, Complexe Desjardins, C.P. 129, Montréal, P.Q. H5B 1E6 (514/872-2074)

Activités Culturelles, 7400, boul. St-Michel, Montréal, P.Q. H2A 2Z8 (514/727-3711)

Oshawa: Oshawa & Dist. Council for the Arts, Box 414, Oshawa, Ont. L1H 7L5

Quebec City: Service des Loisirs et Parcs, Hôtel de Ville, Quebec, P.Q. G1R 4S9 (418/694-6284)

St. John's: Arts & Culture Centre, Prince Philip Dr., Box 1854, St. John's, Nfld. A1C 5P9 (709/737-3650)

Saskatoon: Saskatoon Gallery & Conservatory Corp., 950 Spadina Cres. E., Box 569, Saskatoon, Sask. S7K 3L6 (306/664-9610)

Toronto: Metropolitan Toronto Cultural Affairs, 5th floor, West Tower, City Hall, Toronto, Ont. M5H 2N1 (416/367-8674)

Vancouver: Community Arts Council, 315 W. Cordova St., Vancouver, B.C. V6B 1E5 (604/683-4358)

Victoria: Community Arts Council of Greater Victoria, 1162 Fort St., Victoria, B.C. V8V 3K8 (604/386-1814)

Windsor: Arts Council Windsor & Region, 360 Fairview Ave. W., Essex, Ont. N8M 1Y5 (519/776-6441)

ASSESSMENT

Alta.: Assessment Appeal Board, #1040, 10055 106 St., Edmonton, Alta. T5K 2Y2 (403/427-7658)

Dept. of Municipal Affairs, 9925 107 St., Edmonton, Alta. T5K 2H9 (403/427-8940)

B.C.: B.C. Assessment Authority, 1537 Hillside Ave., Victoria, B.C. V8T 4Y2 (604/595-6211)

Man.: Municipal Assessment, #1350, 405 Broadway, Winnipeg, Man. R3C 3L6 (204/944-2596)

N.B.: Assessment Branch, Dept. of Municipal Affairs, (231 Regent St.) Box 6000, Fredericton, N.B. E3B 5H1 (506/453-2546)

Nfld.: Dept. of Municipal Affairs, Assessment Division, Carnell Bldg., Pippy Place, St. John's, Nfld. A1C 5T7 (709/737-3701)

N.S.: Dept. of Municipal Affairs, Box 216, Halifax, N.S. B3J 2M4 (902/424-5671)

Ont.: Property Assessment Program, Ministry of Revenue, 77 Bloor St. W., Toronto, Ont. M7A 1X8 (416/965-2182) (regional offices in most major centres to deal with valuation & inquiries)

P.E.I.: Land Valuation & Assessment Division, Dept. of Finance, Box 2000, Charlottetown, P.E.I. C1A 7N8 (902/892-3595)

Que.: Dept. of Revenue, Operations Office, 3800 rue Marly, Ste-Foy, P.Q. G1X 4A5 (418/643-6150); *or* 3 Complexe Desjardins, C.P. 3000, Montreal, P.Q. H5B 1A4 (514/873-2611)

Sask.: Saskatchewan Assessment Authority, 2024 Albert St., Regina, Sask. S4P 3V7 (306/565-2666)

Yukon: Assessments Branch, Dept. of Municipal & Community Affairs, Box 2703, Whitehorse, YT Y1A 2C6 (403/667-5234)

Quebec Urban Community: Assessment Dept., 399 St-Joseph est, Quebec, P.Q. G1K 8E2 (418/529-8771)

ASTRONOMY

Astronomy Division, National Museum of Science & Technology, 1867 St. Laurent Blvd., Ottawa, Ont. K1A OM8 (613/998-9520)

Herzberg Institute of Astrophysics, National Research Council of Canada, Ottawa, Ont. K1A OR6 (613/593-6060)

ATHLETICS

see Recreation

ATMOSPHERE

Atmospheric Environment Service, 4905 Dufferin St., Downsview, Ont. M3H 5T4 (416/667-4551) (and regional offices in the provinces, see Index)

ATOMIC ENERGY

Atomic Energy of Canada Ltd., 275 Slater St., Ottawa, Ont. K1A OS4 (613/237-3270) (research & devel.)

Atomic Energy Control Board, Box 1046, Ottawa, Ont. K1P 5S9 (613/995-5894) (regulatory & control aspects)

Dept. of Energy, Mines & Resources, Energy Sector, 580 Booth St., Ottawa, Ont. K1A OE4 (613/995-9351)

National Film Board, Box 6100, Montreal, P.Q. H3C 3H5 (514/333-3333)

Alta.: Energy Resources Conservation Board, 640 5th Ave. S.W., Calgary, Alta. T2P 3G4 (403/261-8311)

N.B.: N.B. Electric Power Commission, Box 2000, Fredericton, N.B. E3B 4X1 (506/453-4215)

Nfld.: Dept. of Mines & Energy, Energy Branch, 95 Bonaventure Ave., Box 4750, St. John's, Nfld. A1C 1T7 (709/737-3159)

Ont.: Ontario Energy Board, 9th floor, 14 Carlton St., Toronto, Ont. M5B 1J2 (416/963-0812)

Ministry of Energy, 12th floor, 56 Wellesley St. W., Toronto, Ont. M7A 2B7 (416/965-2459)

Ontario Hydro, 700 University Ave., Toronto, Ont. M5G 1X6 (416/592-5111)

ATTORNEYS-GENERAL

see Justice

AUDITORS-GENERAL

Auditor General of Canada, 240 Sparks St., Ottawa, Ont. K1A OG6 (613/593-5094)

Alta.: Office of the Auditor General, #835, 9925 109 St., Edmonton, Alta. T5K 2J8 (403/427-4222)

B.C.: Office of the Auditor General, 8 Bastion Sq., Victoria, B.C. V8V 1X4 (604/387-6803)

Man.: Provincial Auditor, Legislative Bldg., Winnipeg, Man. R3C OV8 (204/944-3790)

N.B.: Office of the Auditor General, Box 758, Fredericton, N.B. E3B 5B4 (506/453-2243)

Nfld.: Dept. of the Auditor General, Confederation Bldg., St. John's, Nfld. A1C 5R8 (709/737-2700)

N.S.: Auditor General, Hollis Bldg. (Box 793), Halifax, N.S. B3J 2V2 (902/424-5855)

Ont.: Office of the Provincial Auditor, Queen's Park, Toronto, Ont. M7A 1A2 (416/965-1381)

P.E.I.: Office of the Auditor General, Box 2000, Charlottetown, P.E.I. C1A 7N8 (902/892-3516)

Que.: Office of the Auditor General, 900 d'Youville, Suite 301, Quebec, P.Q. G1R 3P7 (418/643-2781)

Sask.: Provincial Auditor, 1825 Lorne St., Regina, Sask. S4S 3V7 (306/565-6391)

AUTOMOBILE INSURANCE

Alta.: Auto Insurance Board, 8th floor, Capitol Sq., 10065 Jasper Ave., Edmonton, Alta. T5J 3B1 (403/427-5428)

B.C.: Insurance Corp. of B.C. (Autoplan), Box 11131, Royal Centre, 1055 W. Georgia St., Vancouver, B.C. V6E 3R4 (604/665-2800, 8 am - 5 pm) (public insurance corporation)

Man.: Manitoba Public Insurance Corp. (Autopac), Box 6300, 9th floor, 330 Graham Ave., Winnipeg, Man. R3C 4A4 (204/942-0331) (public insurance corporation)

N.B.: Board of Commissioners of Public Utilities, 110 Charlotte St., Saint John, N.B. E2L 2J4 (506/658-2502)

Nfld.: Supt. of Insurance, Elizabeth Towers, (Mailing: Confederation Bldg., St. John's, Nfld. A1C 5T7) (709/737-2594)

N.S.: Dept. of Attorney General, Box 7, Halifax, N.S. B3J 2L6 (902/424-7793)

Ont.: Ministry of Consumer & Commercial Relations:
Office of the Supt. of Insurance, 555 Yonge St., Toronto, Ont. M7A 2H6 (416/963-0471) (advisory)
Ontario Motor Vehicle Accident Claims Fund, 555 Yonge St., 7th floor, Toronto, Ont. M7A 2J4 (416/963-0532) (compensation to victims of uninsured motorists)

P.E.I.: Supt. of Insurance, Dept. of Justice, Box 2000, Charlottetown, P.E.I. C1A 7N8 (902/892-5411)

Que.: Dept. of Financial Institutions & Co-operatives, 800, Place d'Youville, Quebec, P.Q. G1R 4Y5 (418/643-1411)

Sask.: Saskatchewan Government Insurance, 2260 11th Ave., Regina, Sask. S4P 0J9 (306/565-1200)

AVIATION

Air Canada, Public Affairs, Place Ville Marie, Montreal, P.Q. H3B 3P7 (514/874-4571)

Air Transport Committee, Canadian Transport Commission, Ottawa, Ont. K1A 0N9 (819/997-6030) (Commercial Air Services)

Canada Map Office, Dept. of Energy, Mines & Resources, 615 Booth St., Ottawa, Ont. K1A 0E9 (613/998-9900)

Dept. of Industry, Trade & Commerce, Transportation Industries Branch, 235 Queen St., Ottawa, Ont. K1A 0H5 (613/995-3201)

Dept. of National Defence, Information Services, Ottawa, Ont. K1A 0K2 (613/996-2353)

Dept. of Supply & Services, Aerospace & Armament Products Centre, Ottawa, Ont. K1A 0S5 (819/997-5970)

Eldorado Aviation Ltd., #3 Hangar, Saskatoon Airport, Saskatoon, Sask.

Transport Canada, Director General, Civil Aeronautics, Ottawa, Ont. K1A 0N8 (613/992-3254)

National Aeronautical Establishment, National Research Council, Montreal Rd., Ottawa, Ont. K1A 0R6 (613/993-2427)

National Film Board, Box 6100, Montreal, P.Q. H3C 3H5 (514/333-3333)

National Museum of Science & Technology, Aviation & Space Division, 1867 St. Laurent Blvd., Ottawa, Ont. K1A 0M8 (613/998-3814)

Statistics Canada, Ottawa, Ont. K1A 0T6 (613/997-6942)

Alta.: Aviation Branch, Dept. of Transportation, 161 Transportation Bldg., 9630 106 St., Edmonton, Alta. T5K 2B8 (403/427-4830)

B.C.: B.C. Aviation Council, International Airport South, Box 23529, Vancouver AMF, B.C. V7B 1W2 (604/278-9330)

Man.: Transportation Division, Dept. of Highways & Transportation, 15th floor, 215 Garry St., Winnipeg, Man. R3C 3Z1 (204/944-2004)

Ont.: Ministry of Natural Resources, Aviation & Fire Management Centre, Box 310, Sault Ste. Marie, Ont. P6A 5L8 (705/942-1800)

P.E.I.: Dept. of Tourism, Industry & Energy, Box 2000, Charlottetown, P.E.I. C1A 7N8 (902/892-7411)

Que.: Government Air Service, Dept. of Transport, 700, boul. St-Cyrille est, Quebec, P.Q. G1R 5H1 (418/643-8975)

Sask.: Transportation Agency of Saskatchewan, Admin. Services Branch, 1914 Hamilton St., Regina, Sask. S4P 4V4 (306/565-5314)

BANKING

Bank of Canada, Ottawa, Ont. K1A 0G9 (613/563-8111)

Canada Deposit Insurance Corp., Box 2340, Stn. D, Ottawa, Ont. K1P 5W5 (613/996-2081)

Inspector-General of Banks, Dept. of Finance, Ottawa, Ont. K1A 0G5 (613/992-0377)

Statistics Canada, Ottawa, Ont. K1A 0T6 (613/995-9771)

Alta.: Alberta Securities Commission, 10th floor, 10065 Jasper Ave., Edmonton, Alta. T5J 3B1 (403/427-5201)
Alberta Treasury, Banking & Cash Management, Rm. 508, Terrace Bldg., Edmonton, Alta. T5K 2C3 (403/427-9766)

B.C.: Financial Operations, Ministry of Finance, Parliament Bldgs., Victoria, B.C. V8V 1X4 (604/387-5273)
Securities, Brokers, Insurance & Real Estate, Ministry of Consumer & Corporate Affairs, 1050 W. Pender St., 7th floor, Vancouver, B.C. V6E 3S7

Man.: Manitoba Development Corp., 600, 428 Portage Ave., Winnipeg, Man. R3C 0E4 (204/949-1844)
Manitoba Agricultural Credit Corp., 1500 Notre Dame Ave., Winnipeg, Man. R3E 0P9 (204/786-3401)
Dept. of Finance, 109 Legislative Bldg., Winnipeg, Man. R3C 0V8 (204/944-3754)

N.S.: Trusts & Debt Management Division, Dept. of Finance, Box 187, Halifax, N.S. B3J 2N3 (902/424-5555)

P.E.I.: Dept. of Justice, Corporations Division, Box 2000, Charlottetown, P.E.I. C1A 7N8 (902/892-5411)

Que.: Dept. of Financial Institutions & Co-operatives, 800, Place d'Youville, Quebec, P.Q. G1R 4Y5 (418/643-1411)

Sask.: Communications & Development, Dept. of Co-operation & Co-op. Development, 2055 Albert St., Regina, Sask. S4P 3V7 (306/565-5807) (information on Co-ops.)

BANKRUPTCY

Supt. of Bankruptcy, Dept. of Consumer & Corporate Affairs Canada, Place du Portage, Phase 2, Ottawa/Hull, K1A 0C9 (819/997-1059)

Statistics Canada, Ottawa, Ont. K1A 0T6 (613/995-9771)

Alta.: Registrar in Bankruptcy, Law Courts, 1-A Sir Winston Churchill Sq., Edmonton, Alta. T5J 0R2 (403/423-7110); or, Registrar in Bankruptcy, Courthouse, 611 4th St. S.W., Calgary, Alta. T2P 1T5

B.C.: Ministry of Consumer & Corporate Affairs, 940 Blanshard St., Victoria, B.C. V8W 3E6 (604/387-3531)

Man.: Master, Referee & Registrar in Bankruptcy, 232 Law Courts Bldgs., 411 Broadway Ave., Winnipeg, Man. R3C 0V8 (204/944-2083)

N.B.: Registrar, Court of Queen's Bench, Justice Bldg., Queen St., (Box 6000), Fredericton, N.B. E3B 5H1 (506/453-2452)

N.S.: Dept. of Consumer Affairs, Consumer Services Bureau, Debtor Assistance Section, Box 998, Halifax, N.S. B3J 2X3 (902/424-4690)

Que.: Ministère de la Justice, Faillites et Fraudes, 1200, route de l'Eglise, Ste-Foy, P.Q. G1V 4M1 (418/643-7172)

Sask.: Registrar in Bankruptcy, Court House, Regina, Sask. S4P 3V7 (306/565-5383)

BIBLIOGRAPHY (Bibliographic Services)

Canada Institute for Scientific & Technical Information, National Research Council of Canada, Montreal Rd., Ottawa, Ont. K1A 0S2 (613/993-1600)

Dept. of Indian Affairs & Northern Development, Ottawa, Ont. K1A 0H4 (819/997-9920) (Indians, Eskimos, The North)

Dept. of Labour, Ottawa, Ont. K1A OJ2 (819/997-3540) (collective bargaining, industrial relations, labour economics, standards & unions)
Dept. of National Defence Headquarters Library, 2nd floor, North Tower, 101 Colonel By Dr., Ottawa, Ont. K1A OK2 (613/996-0831)
Dept. of Regional Economic Expansion Library, Ottawa, Ont. K1A OM4 (819/997-6075)
National Gallery of Canada, Ottawa, Ont. K1A OM8 (613/995-6245) (post-mediaeval Western art books & periodicals)
National Library, Ottawa, Ont. K1A ON4 (613/996-3817) (referrals)
National Museums of Canada Library, Ottawa, Ont. K1A OM8 (613/998-3923) (museology)
Statistics Canada, Ottawa, Ont. K1A OT6 (613/995-9034)

Alta.: Provincial Archives, 12845 102 Ave., Edmonton, Alta. T5N OM6 (403/427-1750)
Legislature Library, 216 Legislature Bldg., Edmonton, Alta. T5K 2B6 (403/427-2473)
Library Services, Dept. of Culture, 16214 114 Ave., Edmonton, Alta. T5M 2Z5 (403/427-2556)
B.C.: Legislative Library, Parliament Bldgs., Victoria, B.C. V8V 1X4 (604/387-6500)
Library Services Branch, 1250 Quadra St., Victoria, B.C. V8V 1X4 (604/387-6517)
Man.: Legislative Library, 200 Vaughan St., Winnipeg, Man. R3C 0V8 (204/944-3784)
Public Library Services, 139 Hamelin St., Winnipeg, Man. R3T 4H4 (204/453-7549)
N.B.: N.B. Library Service, Box 6000, Fredericton, N.B. E3B 5H1 (506/453-2224)
N.B. Legislative Library, Box 6000, Fredericton, N.B. E3B 5H1 (506/453-2338)
Nfld.: Nfld. Provincial Reference Dept., Arts & Culture Centre, Allandale Rd., St. John's, Nfld. A1B 3A3 (709/737-3954, 55)
N.S.: N.S. Provincial Library, 5250 Spring Garden Rd., Halifax, N.S. B3J 1E8 (902/424-5450)
Ont.: Ontario Legislative Library, Research & Information Services, Legislative Bldg., Queen's Park, Toronto, Ont. M7A 1A2 (416/965-4545)
Libraries & Community Information Branch, 7th floor, 77 Bloor St. W., Toronto, Ont. M7A 2R9 (416/965-2696)
P.E.I.: Provincial Library, University Ave., Charlottetown, P.E.I. C1A 7N9 (902/892-3504, ext. 54)
Que.: Centre de Documentation, Ministère des Affaires Culturelles, 225 Grande-Allée est, Québec, P.Q. G1R 5G5 (418/643-6330)
Bibliothèque Nationale du Québec, 1700 rue Saint Denis, Montreal P.Q. H2X 3K6 (514/873-4553)
Archives nationales du Québec, Pavillon Casault, portes 1 et 2, 1210 ave du Séminaire, Ste-Foy, Quebec, P.Q. G1V 4N1 (418/643-2167)
Quebec Legislative Library, Edifice Pamphile Le May, Hôtel du Parlement, Quebec, P.Q. G1A 1A5 (418/643-2896)
Sask.: Legislative Library, Legislative Bldg., Regina, Sask. S4S OB3 (306/565-2277)
Provincial Library, 1352 Winnipeg St., Regina, Sask. S4P 3V7 (306/565-2972)

BILINGUALISM

Commr. of Official Languages, 66 Slater St., Ottawa, Ont. K1A OT8 (613/996-6368 or 995-7717)
Communications Branch, Secretary of State, Ottawa, Ont. K1A OM5 (819/997-0055)
Official Languages Branch, Treasury Board Secretariat, Ottawa, Ont. K1A OR5 (613/996-9086)

Alta.: Alberta Education, Communications Branch, 10th floor, 11160 Jasper Ave., Edmonton, Alta. T5K OL2 (403/427-2285)
B.C.: Modern Languages Services, Ministry of Education, #200, 7900 Alderbridge Way, Richmond, B.C. V6X 2A5 (604/273-9431)
Man.: Dept. of Cultural Affairs & Historical Resources, 390 York Ave., Winnipeg, Man. R3C 0P3 (204/944-3095)
N.B.: Cabinet Secretariat, Box 6000, Fredericton, N.B. E3B 5H1 (506/453-2141)
Ont.: Office of the Government Co-ordinator of French-language Services, 6th floor, Mowat Block, Queen's Park, Toronto, Ont. M7A 1B8 (416/965-3865; Renseignements-Ontario 1-800-268-7507)
Languages of Instruction Commission of Ontario, 25 Grosvenor St., Toronto, Ont. M4Y 1A9 (416/965-3155)
Sask.: No provincial agency.

BIRDS

see Wildlife

BIRTH CERTIFICATES

see Vital Statistics

BOATS

see Leisure Craft

BROADCASTING

Canadian Broadcasting Corp.: English Services Division, Box 500, Stn. A, Toronto, Ont. M5W 1E6 (416/925-3311); French Services Division, Box 6000, Montreal, P.Q. H3C 3A8 (514/285-3211)
Canadian Radio-television & Telecommunications Commission:
Mailing address: Ottawa, Ont. K1A ON2
Office location & shipping address: Centre Bldg., Terrasses de la Chaudiere, 1 Promenade du Portage, Hull, P.Q.
Public inquiries: (819) 997-0313
Phone numbers & staff inquiries: (819) 997-4704
Teleglobe Canada, 680 Sherbrooke St. W., Montreal, P.Q. H3A 2S4 (514/281-5217)

Que.: Radio-Quebec, Centre des Resources Documentaires, 655 Parthenais, Montreal, P.Q. (514/873-5243)

BUILDING CONSTRUCTION

see Construction

BURSARIES, STUDENT

see Student Aid

BUSINESS REGULATIONS

(See "Industry" for Business Services)

Dept. of Consumer & Corporate Affairs Canada, Place du Portage, Phase 2, Ottawa-Hull, K1A OC9 (819/997-1142)
Dept. of Industry, Trade & Commerce, Business Centre, 235 Queen St., Ottawa, Ont. K1A OH5 (613/995-5771)
Revenue Canada, Taxation, Information Services, 875 Heron Rd., Ottawa, Ont. K1A OL8 (613/995-2961)

Alta.: Dept. of Consumer & Corporate Affairs, Room 425, Legislative Bldg., Edmonton, Alta. T5K 2B6 (403/427-4081) (and regional offices throughout province)
Dept. of Tourism & Small Business, Box 2500, Edmonton, Alta. T5J 2Z4 (403/427-4321)
B.C.: Registrar of Companies, 940 Blanshard St., Waddington Bldg., Victoria, B.C. V8W 2H3 (604/387-3966)
Man.: Dept. of Economic Development & Tourism, Industrial & Trade Development, #701, 155 Carlton St., Winnipeg, Man. R3C 3H8 (204/944-2470)
Dept. of Consumer & Corporate Affairs & Environment, Office of the Deputy Minister, #351, Legislative Bldg., Winnipeg, Man. R3C OV8 (204/944-3742)
Consumers' Bureau, 307 Kennedy St., Winnipeg, Man. R3C 0V8 (204/956-2040)
Corporations & Business Names Registration Branch, 10th floor, Woodsworth Bldg., Winnipeg, Man. R3C 3L6 (204/944-2500)
N.B.: Consumer & Corporate Affairs Branch, Dept. of Justice, Box 6000, Fredericton, N.B. E3B 5H1 (506/453-2682)

Nfld.: Director of Corporate Affairs, Dept. of Justice, Confederation Bldg., St. John's, Nfld. A1C 5T7 (709/737-2594)

Ont.: Business Practices Division, (416/963-0321), and/or Companies Division, (963-0371), Ministry of Consumer & Commercial Relations, 555 Yonge St., Toronto, Ont. M7A 2H6

P.E.I.: Corporations Division, Dept. of Justice, Box 2000, Charlottetown, P.E.I. C1A 7N8 (902/892-5411)

Que.: Communications, Dept. of Industry, Trade & Tourism, 710 Place d'Youville, Quebec, P.Q. G1R 4Y4 (418/643-5070)

Dept. of Revenue, 3800, rue Marly, Ste-Foy, P.Q. G1X 4A5 (418/643-6677)

Sask.: Dept. of Consumer & Commercial Affairs, 1871 Smith St., Regina, Sask. S4P 3V7 (306/565-5550)

Yukon: Consumer & Corporate Affairs, Box 2703, Whitehorse, Y.T. Y1A 2C6 (403/667-5256)

Burlington: Licence Administrator, 1st floor, 426 Brant St., Burlington, Ont. L7R 2G2 (416/335-7700)

Calgary: City Licence Dept., Box 2100, Calgary, Alta. T2P 2M5 (403/268-5521)

Edmonton: Business Development Dept., 2410 Oxford Tower, 10235 101 St., Edmonton, Alta. T5J 3G1 (403/428-5464)

LaSalle: Finance Dept., City Hall, 13 Strathyre, LaSalle, P.Q. H8R 3P6 (514/366-7110)

Mississauga: Licensing Section, Building Dept., 3rd floor, City Hall, 1 City Centre Dr., Mississauga, Ont. L5B 1M2 (416/279-7600)

Montreal: Permits & Inspections, 810 est rue St-Antoine, Montreal, P.Q. H2Y 1A6 (514/872-3573)

Quebec: Service des Finances, Hôtel de Ville, Quebec, P.Q. G1R 4S9 (418/694-6028)

Regina: City License Dept., Box 1790, Regina, Sask. S4P 3C8 (306/569-7251)

Toronto: Metropolitan Licensing Commission, 20 Holly St., Toronto, Ont. M4S 3B1 (416/488-2221)

Vancouver: Director of Permits & Licenses, City Hall, Vancouver, B.C. V5Y 1V4 (604/873-7520)

CANADA PENSION PLAN

see Pensions

CAREER PLANNING

Occupational & Career Analysis & Development Branch, Canada Employment & Immigration Commission, Ottawa-Hull K1A OJ9 (819/994-3125)

Alta.: Guidance & Counselling Supervisor, Dept. of Education, 11160 Devonian Bldg., Edmonton, Alta. T5K OL2 (403/427-2899)

B.C.: Career/Technical Programs, Post-Secondary Dept., Dept. of Education, Parliament Bldgs., Victoria, B.C. V8V 1X4 (604/387-6060)

Man.: Dept. of Labour & Manpower, New Careers, 5th floor, 213 Notre Dame Ave., Winnipeg, Man. R3B 1N3 (204/944-2823)

Women's Bureau, 241 Vaughan St., Winnipeg, Man. R3C 1T6 (204/944-3476)

N.B.: Dept. of Education, Pupil Personnel Services Branch, Box 6000, Fredericton, N.B. E3B 5H1 (506/453-2242, Anglophone section; 453-2742, Francophone section)

Nfld.: Supervisor of Guidance Counselling, Dept. of Education, Box 2017, St. John's, Nfld. A1C 5R9

N.S.: Consultant (Guidance), Dept. of Education, Box 578, Trade Mart, Scotia Sq., Halifax, N.S. B3J 2S9 (902/424-5806)

Ont.: Ministry of Education, Program Division, 900 Bay St., Toronto, Ont. M7A 1L2: Teachers' Services Section, 416/965-6126; Senior & Continuing Education Branch, 965-3592

Ministry of Agriculture & Food, Education Research & Special Services Division, 801 Bay St., Toronto, Ont. M7A 1A3 (416/965-6695)

P.E.I.: Teaching & Instructional Support, Dept. of Education, Box 2000, Charlottetown, P.E.I. C1A 7N8 (902/892-3504)

Que.: Ministère de la Fonction Publique, Planification des carrières, 1052, Conroy, Québec, P.Q. G1R 4Z9 (418/643-2502)

Sask.: Guidance Consultant, Regional Services Division, Dept. of Education, 2220 College Ave., Regina, Sask. S4P 3V7 (306/565-6045)

CENSORSHIP (Film Classification)

Alta.: Board of Censors, Main floor, CN Tower, 10004 104 Ave., Edmonton, Alta. T5J OK5 (403/427-2006)

B.C.: Director of Film Classification, 140 E. 8th Ave., Vancouver, B.C. V5T 1R7 (604/879-6564)

Man.: Film Classification Board, Unit 6, 1313 Border St., Winnipeg, Man. R3H 0X4 (204/633-0547)

N.B.: N.B. Film Classification Board, Dept. of Youth, Recreation & Cultural Resources, Room G12, 110 Charlotte St., Saint John, N.B. E2L 2J4 (506/658-2436)

Nfld.: Accepts what is passed by New Brunswick

N.S.: Amusements Regulation Board, Box 607, Halifax, N.S. B3J 2R7 (902/424-4493)

Ont.: Theatres Branch, 1075 Millwood Rd., Toronto, Ont. M4G 1X6 (416/421-2462)

P.E.I.: Accepts what is passed by New Brunswick

Que.: Bureau de surveillance du cinéma, (Cinema Supervisory Board), 360 McGill, Montreal, P.Q. H2Y 2E9 (514/873-2371)

Sask.: Saskatchewan Film Classification Board, Dept. of Consumer & Commercial Affairs, 2425 Victoria Ave., Regina, Sask. S4P 3E4 (306/565-5883)

CHEMICALS

Dept. of Industry, Trade & Commerce, Chemicals Branch, 235 Queen St., Ottawa, Ont. K1A OH5 (613/593-7303)

Technical Information Service, National Research Council of Canada, Ottawa, Ont. K1A OS3 (613/993-1753)

Statistics Canada, Ottawa, Ont. K1A OT6 (613/996-3226)

Alta.: Industrial & Engineering Services Dept., Alberta Research Council, 4th floor, Terrace Plaza, 4445 Calgary Trail S., Edmonton, Alta. T6H 5R7 (403/438-0666)

B.C.: Technical Information Service, B.C. Research, 3650 Wesbrook Mall, Vancouver, B.C. V6S 2L2 (604/224-4331)

Man.: Business Development Branch, Dept. of Economic Development & Tourism, #701, 155 Carlton St., Winnipeg, Man. R3C 0V8 (204/944-2455)

N.S.: N.S. Research Foundation Corp., Box 790, Dartmouth, N.S. B2Y 3Z7 (902/424-8670)

Ont.: Ontario Research Foundation, Sheridan Park, Mississauga, Ont. L5K 1B3 (416/822-4111)

Sask.: Dept. of Industry & Commerce, Sask. Power Bldg., Regina, Sask. S4P 3V7 (306/565-2232)

CHILD WELFARE

National Film Board, Box 6100, Montreal, P.Q. H3C 3H5 (514/333-3333)

Alta.: Director of Child Welfare, Dept. of Social Services & Community Health, 10030 107 St., Edmonton, Alta. T5J 3E4 (403/427-6370)

B.C.: Family & Children's Services, Ministry of Human Resources, Parliament Bldgs., Victoria, B.C. V8V 1X4 (604/387-3211)

Man.: Child & Family Services, Dept. of Community Services & Corrections, 831 Portage Ave., Winnipeg, Man. R3G ON6 (204/775-9761) (Children's Aid Societies in Portage la Prairie, Brandon & Winnipeg)

N.B.: Child & Family Services, Dept. of Social Services, Box 6000, Fredericton, N.B. E3B 5H1 (506/453-2950) (Adoption and Child Services Programs in all area and branch offices)

Nfld.: Dept. of Social Services, Confederation Bldg., St. John's, Nfld. A1C 5T7 (709/737-2668) (Branch Offices in all cities & towns)

N.S.: Family & Children's Services, Dept. of Social Services, Box 696, Halifax, N.S. B3J 2T7 (902/424-3202) (child welfare services including adoption in all areas of the province)

Ont.: Operational Support Branch, Ministry of Community & Social Services, 2nd floor, 700 Bay St., Toronto, Ont. M7A 1E9 (416/965-4363) (Adoption: Children's Aid Societies in all regions of the Province)

P.E.I.: Child & Family Services Division, Dept. of Health & Social Services, Box 2000, Charlottetown, P.E.I. C1A 7N8 (902/892-5421)
(Adoptions–private Child Welfare Agencies): Catholic Family Services Bureau, Box 698, Pownal St., Charlottetown, P.E.I. C1A 7L3 (894-8591); Protestant Family Services Bureau, Box 592, Charlottetown, P.E.I. C1A 7L1 (892-2441); Prince County Family Service Bureau, Box 1648, Summerside, P.E.I. C1N 2V5 (436-9171)
Que.: Direction de la consultation et protection sociale, Ministère des Affaires Sociales, 1075, chemin Ste-Foy, Quebec, P.Q. G1S 2M1 (Adoption: District Offices throughout the province)
Sask.: Community Health Services Branch, Dept. of Health, 3475 Albert St., Regina, Sask. S4S 6X6 (306/565-7123)
(Adoption: REACH (Resources for Adoption of Children) Dept. of Social Services, 1920 Broad St., Regina, Sask. S4P 3V6 (565-3655) (Dist. Offices in all major cities)).
Yukon: Dept. of Health & Human Resources, Box 2703, Whitehorse, Y.T. Y1A 2C6 (403/667-5674)

Toronto: Children's Aid Society of Metro Toronto, 33 Charles St. E., Toronto, Ont. M4Y 1R9 (416/924-4646)
Catholic Children's Aid Society of Metro Toronto, 26 Maitland St., Toronto, Ont. M4Y 1C6 (416/925-6641)

CITIZENSHIP

Communications Branch, Dept. of Secretary of State, Ottawa, Ont. K1A OM5 (819/997-0055)
National Film Board, Box 6100, Montreal, P.Q. H3C 3H5 (514/333-3333)

Ont.: Newcomer Services Branch, Multiculturalism & Citizenship Division, Ministry of Culture & Recreation, 77 Bloor St. W., 5th floor, Toronto, Ont. M7A 2R9 (416/965-2285)
Que.: Ministère des Communautes Culturelles et de l'Immigration, 355, rue McGill, Montreal, P.Q. H2Y 2E8 (514/873-4136)

CIVIL DEFENCE

see Emergency Measures

CIVIL RIGHTS

see Citizenship; *see* Human Rights

CLIMATE

Climatic Information, Atmospheric Environment Service, 4905 Dufferin St., Downsview, Ont. M3H 5T4 (416/667-4614)

Alta.: Atmospheric Sciences Division, Alberta Research Council, Room 204, Campus Tower, 8625 112 St., Edmonton, Alta. T6G 1K8 (403/432-8125)
B.C.: Air Studies Branch, Ministry of Environment, Parliament Bldgs., Victoria, B.C. V8V 1X4 (604/387-1834)
Man.: Environmental Management Division, Dept. of Consumer & Corporate Affairs & Environment, Bldg. 2, 139 Tuxedo Blvd., Winnipeg, Man. R3N 0H6 (204/895-5337)
N.B.: Climatologist, Dept. of the Environment, Box 6000, Fredericton, N.B. E3B 5H1 (506/453-2626)
Nfld.: Dept. of Environment, Elizabeth Towers, 100 Elizabeth Ave., St. John's, Nfld. A1B 1R9 (709/737-2559)
N.S.: Dept. of Development, Box 519, Halifax, N.S. B3J 2R7 (902/429-8921)
Ont.: Ministry of Agriculture & Food, Economics Branch, Legislative Bldgs., Toronto, Ont. M7A 1B6 (416/965-1064)
P.E.I.: Agroclimatology Section, Dept. of Agriculture & Forestry, Box 1600, Charlottetown, P.E.I. C1A 7N3 (902/892-5465)
Que.: Ministère de l'Environnement, Service de la Météorologie, 194, Ave. St-Sacrement, Quebec, P.Q. G1N 4J5 (418/643-4588)
Sask.: Saskatchewan Research Council, Physics Division, 30 Campus Dr., Saskatoon, Sask. S7N OX1 (306/664-5417)

COAL

Dept. of Energy, Mines & Resources, Energy Sector, 580 Booth St., Ottawa, Ont. K1A OE4 (613/995-9351)
Dept. of Industry, Trade & Commerce, Resource Industries Branch, Industrial Minerals Division, 235 Queen St., Ottawa, Ont. K1A OH5 (613/992-1581)
National Film Board, Box 6100, Montreal, P.Q. H3C 3H5 (514/333-3333)
Statistics Canada, Ottawa, Ont. K1A OT6 (613/996-3139)

Alta.: Alberta Geological Survey, Alberta Research Council, 4445 Calgary Trail S., Edmonton, Alta. T6H 5R7 (403/438-0555)
Energy Resources Conservation Board, 640 5th Ave. S.W., Calgary, Alta. T2P 3G4 (403/261-8311)
B.C.: Ministry of Energy, Mines & Petroleum Resources, Parliament Bldgs., Victoria, B.C. V8V 1X4 (604/387-6588)
Man.: Mineral Resources Division, Dept. of Energy & Mines, 989 Century St., Winnipeg, Man. R3H OW4 (204/633-9543)
N.B.: Mineral Resources, Dept. of Natural Resources, Box 6000, Fredericton, N.B. E3B 5H1 (506/453-2206)
N.S.: Engineering & Inspection, Dept. of Mines & Energy, Box 1087, Halifax, N.S. B3J 2X1 (902/424-4049)
Ont.: No provincial agency.
Que.: Dept. of Energy & Resources, Energy Branch, 8 rue Cook, Quebec, P.Q. G1R 5H2 (418/643-3724)
Sask.: Administrative Services Branch, Dept. of Mineral Resources, 1914 Hamilton St., Regina, Sask. S4P 4V4 (306/565-2528)

COMBINES

Director of Investigation & Research, Dept. of Consumer & Corporate Affairs Canada, (Place du Portage, Phase 1, Hull) (Mailing: Ottawa, Ont. K1A 0C9) (819/997-3301)
Restrictive Trade Practices Commission, Box 336, Stn. A, Ottawa, Ont. K1N 8V3 (613/992-0217)

COMMUNICATIONS

Canadian Broadcasting Corp.: English Services Division, Box 500, Stn. A, Toronto, Ont. M5W 1E6 (416/925-3311); French Services Division, Box 6000, Montreal, P.Q. H3C 3A8 (514/285-3211)
Canadian Radio-television & Telecommunications Commission:
Mailing: Ottawa, Ont. K1A ON2
Office location & shipping address: Centre Bldg., Terrasses de la Chaudiere, 1 Promenade du Portage, Hull, P.Q.
Public inquiries: (819) 997-0313
Phone numbers & staff inquiries: (819) 997-4704
Dept. of Communications, Information Services, 300 Slater St., Ottawa, Ont. K1A OC8 (613/995-8185)
Dept. of Supply & Services, Ottawa, Ont. K1A 0S9 (819/997-5362)
National Film Board, Box 6100, Montreal, P.Q. H3C 3H5 (514/333-3333)
National Museums of Canada, Ottawa, Ont. K1A OM8 (613/995-9832)
Statistics Canada, Ottawa, Ont. K1A OT6 (613/996-9271)
Teleglobe Canada, 680 Sherbrooke St. W., Montreal, P.Q. H3A 2S4 (514/281-5215)
Telesat Canada, 333 River Rd., Ottawa, Ont. K1L 8B9 (613/746-5920)

Alta.: Public Relations Dept., Alberta Government Telephones, 10020 100 St., Edmonton, Alta. T5J 0N5 (403/425-4723)
B.C.: Ministry of Universities, Science & Communications, Parliament Bldgs., Victoria, B.C. V8V 1X4 (604/387-1417)
Man.: Man. Telephone System, 489 Empress St., Winnipeg, Man. R3C 3V6 (204/947-4111)
N.B.: Dept. of Transportation, Communications Policy Division, Box 6000, Fredericton, N.B. E3B 5H1 (506/453-2802)
Nfld.: Communications Division, Dept. of Intergovernmental Affairs, Confederation Bldg., St. John's, Nfld. A1C 5T7 (709/737-3296)
N.S.: Board of Commrs. of Public Utilities, Box 3058, Halifax South, Halifax, N.S. B3J 3G7 (902/424-4448)
Ont.: Ministry of Transportation & Communications, 1201 Wilson Ave., Downsview, Ont. M3M 1J8 (416/248-3711)

P.E.I.: Dept. of Highways & Public Works, Box 2000, Charlottetown, P.E.I. C1A 7N8 (902/892-7431)

Que.: Ministère des Communications, Direction des Communications, 1037 de la Chevrotière, Edifice G, Rez de chaussée, Bloc 4, Québec, P.Q. G1R 4Y7 (418/643-3162)

La Régie des services publics, 2875 boul. Laurier, Ste-Foy, P.Q. G1V 2M2 (418/643-5560)

Sask.: Saskatchewan Telecommunications, 2350 Albert St., Regina, Sask. S4P 2Y4 (306/347-3737)

COMMUNITY PLANNING

Canada Mtge. & Housing Corp., Montreal Rd., Ottawa, Ont. K1A OP7 (613/748-2693)

Dept. of Indian Affairs & Northern Development, Ottawa, Ont. K1A OH4 (819/997-9920) (Native communities)

Planning & Co-ordination Branch, Dept. of Regional Economic Expansion, Ottawa, Ont. K1A OM4 (819/997-1013)

Alta.: Planning Director, Dept. of Municipal Affairs, Jarvis Bldg., 9925 107th St., Edmonton, Alta. T5K 1G5 (403/427-2125)

B.C.: Planning Branch, Ministry of Municipal Affairs, Parliament Bldgs., Victoria, B.C. V8W 3E9 (604/387-5925)

Man.: Dept. of Municipal Affairs, Municipal Planning Branch, 14th floor, 405 Broadway, Winnipeg, Man. R3C OV8 (204/944-2150)

N.B.: Dept. of Municipal Affairs, Community Planning Branch, Centennial Bldg., Box 6000, Fredericton, N.B. E3B 5H1 (506/453-2171)

Nfld.: Provincial Planning Office, Dept. of Municipal Affairs, Confederation Bldg., St. John's, Nfld. A1C 5T7 (709/737-3090)

N.S.: Community Planning Division, Dept. of Municipal Affairs, Box 216, Halifax, N.S. B3J 2M4 (902/424-4091)

Ont.: Community Planning Advisory Branch, Ministry of Housing, 4th floor, 56 Wellesley St. W., Toronto, Ont. M7A 2K7 (416/965-3352)

P.E.I.: Dept. of Community Affairs, Planning Division, Box 2000, Charlottetown, P.E.I. C1A 7N8 (902/892-3561)

Que.: Dept. of Municipal Affairs, 1039, De La Chevrotière, Quebec, P.Q. G1R 4Z3 (418/643-7854)

Sask.: Community Planning Branch, Dept. of Urban Affairs, 1791 Rose St., Regina, Sask. S4P 3V7 (306/565-2881)

For Community Planning Officials in cities and towns contact The Planning Dept. *See* Index, 'Municipalities' for addresses.

COMMUNITY SERVICES

Citizenship Sector, Citizens' Participation, Secretary of State Dept., (15 Eddy St., Hull), Ottawa, Ont. K1A OM5 (819/994-2255)

Dept. of Indian Affairs & Northern Development, Ottawa, Ont. K1A OH4 (819/997-9920) (Native communications)

National Film Board, Box 6100, Montreal, P.Q. H3C 3H5 (514/333-3333)

Alta.: Dept. of Social Services & Community Health, 10030 107 St., Edmonton, Alta. T5J 3E4 (403/427-2734)

B.C.: Ministry of Human Resources, Parliament Bldgs., Victoria, B.C. V8V 1X4 (604/387-3016)

Man.: Recreation & Fitness Division, Dept. of Fitness, Recreation & Sport, #304, 379 Broadway, Winnipeg, Man. R3C 3N4 (204/944-3769)

N.B.: Municipal Services Branch, Dept. of Municipal Affairs, Box 6000, Fredericton, N.B. E3B 5H1 (506/453-2434)

Nfld.: Deputy Minister, Dept. of Social Services, Confederation Bldg., St. John's, Nfld. A1C 5T7 (709/737-3582)

N.S.: Dept. of Culture, Recreation & Fitness, Box 864, 5151 Terminal Rd., Halifax, N.S. B3J 2V2 (902/424-7512)

Ont.: Leadership Training & Intercultural Development, Citizenship Development Branch, 416/965-6621, and/or Community Information Services (funds Community Information Centres in Ontario), 965-0862, both branches of the Ministry of Culture & Recreation, 77 Bloor St. W., Toronto, Ont. M7A 2R9

P.E.I.: Dept. of Community Affairs, Box 2000, Charlottetown, P.E.I. C1A 7N8 (902/892-3561)

Que.: Dept. of Social Affairs, 1075, ch. Ste-Foy, 2nd floor, Quebec, P.Q. G1S 2M1 (418/643-6392)

Ministère des Communications, Direction des Communications, 1037 de la Chevrotière, Edifice G, Rez de chaussée, Bloc 4, Québec, P.Q. G1R 4Y7 (418/643-7167)

Sask.: Community Services Branch, Community & Personal Services Division, Dept. of Social Services, 1920 Broad St., Regina, Sask. S4P 3V6 (306/565-3632)

COMPENSATION

see Crime; *see* Workers'

CONSERVATION

Canadian Conservation Institute, National Museums of Canada, 1030 Innes Rd., Ottawa, Ont. K1A OM8 (613/998-3721) (Conservation of works of art and museum artifacts)

Dept. of Energy, Mines & Resources, Office of Energy Conservation, 580 Booth St., Ottawa, Ont. K1A OE4 (613/995-1801)

Environment Canada, Information Branch, Ottawa, Ont. K1A OH3 (613/997-2800)

Dept. of Regional Economic Expansion, Information Services, Ottawa, Ont. K1A OM4 (819/997-2096)

National Film Board, Box 6100, Montreal, P.Q. H3C 3H5 (514/333-3333)

National Museum of Natural Sciences, Ottawa, Ont. K1A OM8 (613/996-3102)

Alta.: Environment Council of Alberta, 2100 College Plaza Tower 3, 8215 112 St., Edmonton, Alta. T6G 2M4 (403/427-5792)

Energy Resources Conservation Board, 640 5th Ave. S.W., Calgary, Alta. T2P 3G4 (403/261-8311)

B.C.: Ministry of Environment, Information Services Branch, 810 Blanshard St., Victoria, B.C. V8W 3E1 (604/387-5162)

Man.: Dept. of Consumer & Corporate Affairs & Environment, Environmental Management Division, Box 7, 139 Tuxedo Ave., Winnipeg, Man. (204/895-5337)

N.B.: Forest Management Branch, Dept. of Natural Resources, Box 6000, Fredericton, N.B. E3B 5H1 (506/453-2432)

Nfld.: Wildlife Division, Dept. of Culture, Recreation & Youth, (Bldg. 810, Pleasantville), Box 4750, St. John's, Nfld. A1C 5T7 (709/737-2815)

N.S.: Program Planning, Dept. of Lands & Forests, Box 698, Halifax, N.S. B3J 2T9 (902/424-4103)

Ont.: Ministry of the Environment, 135 St. Clair Ave. W., Toronto, Ont. M4V 1P5 (416/965-1658)

Conservation Authorities & Water Management Branch, Ministry of Natural Resources, Rm. 5620, Whitney Block, Queen's Park, Toronto, Ont. M7A 1W3 (416/965-6287) *See Conservation Authorities below*

P.E.I.: Planning Division, Dept. of Highways & Public Works, Box 2000, Charlottetown, P.E.I. C1A 7N8 (902/892-7431)

Enersave Office, Dept. of Tourism, Industry & Energy, Box 2000, Charlottetown, P.E.I. C1A 7N8 (902/892-7411)

Que.: Information Service, Dept. of Recreation, Fish & Game, 150 est, boul. St-Cyrille, Québec, P.Q. G1R 4Y3 (418/643-3127)

Dept. of Environment, 2360, ch. Ste-Foy, Québec, P.Q. G1V 4H2 (418/643-2795)

Sask.: SaskTravel, Saskatchewan Tourism & Renewable Resources, 3211 Albert St., Regina, Sask. S4S 5W6 (306/565-2300)

ONTARIO CONSERVATION AUTHORITIES

Ausable Bayfield Conservation Authority, Box 459, Exeter, Ont. NOM 1S0 (519/235-2610)

Cataraqui Region Conservation Authority, R.R. 1, Glenburnie, Ont. KOH 1SO (613/546-9965)

Catfish Creek Conservation Authority, R.R. 5, Aylmer, Ont. N5H 2R4 (519/773-9605)

Central Lake Ontario Conservation Authority, 1650 Dundas St. E., Whitby, Ont. L1N 2K8 (416/579-0411)

Credit Valley Conservation Authority, Meadowvale, Ont. LOJ 1KO (416/451-1615)

Crowe Valley Conservation Authority, Box 416, Marmora, Ont. K0K 2M0 (613/472-3137)

Essex Region Conservation Authority, 360 Fairview Ave. W., Essex, Ont. N8M 1Y6 (519/776-5209)

Ganaraska Region Conservation Authority, Box 328, Port Hope, Ont. L1A 3W4 (416/885-6067)

Grand River Conservation Authority, Box 729, Cambridge, Ont. N1R 5W6 (519/621-2761)

Halton Region Conservation Authority, 310 Main St., Milton, Ont. L9T 1P4 (416/878-4131)

Hamilton Region Conservation Authority, Box 7099, Ancaster, Ont. L9G 3L3 (416/525-2181)

Kawartha Region Conservation Authority, R.R. 1, Cameron, Ont. K0M 1G0 (705/887-3309)

Kettle Creek Conservation Authority, R.R. 8, St. Thomas, Ont. N5P 3T3 (519/631-1270)

Lakehead Region Conservation Authority, Box 3476, Thunder Bay, Ont. P7B 5J9 (807/344-5857)

Long Point Region Conservation Authority, Box 525, Simcoe, Ont. N3Y 4N5 (519/426-4623)

Lower Thames Valley Conservation Authority, 100 Thames St., Chatham, Ont. N7L 2Y8 (519/354-7310)

Lower Trent Region Conservation Authority, 441 Front St., Trenton, Ont. K8V 6C1 (613/394-4829)

Maitland Valley Conservation Authority, Box 5, Wroxeter, Ont. NOG 2XO (519/335-3557)

Mattagami Region Conservation Authority, 167 Wilson Ave., Timmins, Ont. P4N 2T2 (705/264-5309)

Metro Toronto & Region Conservation Authority, 5 Shoreham Dr., Downsview, Ont. M3N 1S4 (416/661-6600)

Mississippi Valley Conservation Authority, Box 419, Carleton Place, Ont. K7C 3P5 (613/257-4272)

Moira River Conservation Authority, 217 N. Front St., Belleville, Ont. K8P 3C3 (613/968-3434)

Napanee Region Conservation Authority, 25 Ontario St. W., Napanee, Ont. K7R 3S6 (613/354-3312)

Niagara Peninsula Conservation Authority, Box 460, Fonthill, Ont. LOS 1EO (416/892-2621)

Nickel District Conservation Authority, 200 Brady St., Sudbury, Ont. P3E 5K3 (705/674-5249)

North Bay Mattawa Conservation Authority, Box 1215, North Bay, Ont. P1B 8K4 (705/474-5420)

North Grey Region Conservation Authority, Box 759, Owen Sound, Ont. N4K 5W9 (519/376-3076)

Nottawasaga Valley Conservation Authority, R.R. 1, Angus, Ont. LOM 1BO (705/424-1479)

Otonabee Region Conservation Authority, 727 Lansdowne St. W., Peterborough, Ont. K9J 1Z2 (705/745-5791)

Prince Edward Region Conservation Authority, Box 310, Picton, Ont. KOK 2TO (613/476-7408)

Raisin Region Conservation Authority, Box 10, Martintown, Ont. KOC 1SO (613/528-4584)

Rideau Valley Conservation Authority, Box 599, Manotick, Ont. KOA 2NO (613/692-3571)

St. Clair Region Conservation Authority, 205 Mill Pond Cres., Strathroy, Ont. N7G 3P9 (519/245-3710)

Sauble Valley Conservation Authority, Box 759, Owen Sound, Ont. N4K 5W9 (519/376-3076)

Saugeen Valley Conservation Authority, R.R. 1, Hanover, Ont. N4N 3B8 (519/364-1255)

Sault Ste. Marie Region Conservation Authority, 99 Foster Dr., Sault Ste. Marie, Ont. P6A 5X6 (705/949-9111)

South Lake Simcoe Conservation Authority, (120 Bayview Ave.), Box 282, Newmarket, Ont. L3Y 4X1 (416/895-1281)

South Nation River Conservation Authority, Berwick, Ont. KOC 1GO (613/984-2400)

Upper Thames River Conservation Authority, Fanshawe Dam, R.R. 6, (Mailing: Box 6278, Stn. D, London, Ont. N5W 5S1) (519/451-2800)

CONSTITUTION

National Library, 395 Wellington St., Ottawa, Ont. K1A ON4 (613/996-3842)

Privy Council Office, Langevin Block, 80 Wellington St., Ottawa, Ont. K1A OA3 (transcripts of federal-provincial constitutional conferences)

Public Archives of Canada, 395 Wellington St., Ottawa, Ont. K1A ON3 (613/992-2669)

Secretary of State, Communications Branch, Ottawa, Ont. K1A OM5 (819/997-0055)

All provinces, see Justice, except

Que.: Ministère des Affaires Intergouvernementales, 1225 Place Georges V, Direction générale des Affaires canadiennes, Edifice H, Québec, P.Q. G1R 4Z7 (418/643-4564)

B.C.: Deputy Minister, Intergovernmental Relations Ministry, Parliament Bldgs., Victoria, B.C. V8V 1X4 (604/387-3410)

Sask.: Dept. of Intergovernmental Affairs, Walter Scott Bldg., Regina, Sask. S4S OB1 (306/565-6355)

CONSTRUCTION

Canada Institute for Scientific & Technical Information (Technical Information Service), National Research Council of Canada, Ottawa, Ont. K1A OS2 (613/993-1753)

Canada Mtge. & Housing Corp., Montreal Rd., Ottawa, Ont. K1A OP7 (613/748-2263) (bldg. code standards)

Dept. of Indian Affairs & Northern Development, Ottawa, Ont. K1A OH4 (819/997-9920) (construction in the north)

Dept. of Industry, Trade & Commerce, Construction & Consulting Services Branch, 235 Queen St., Ottawa, Ont. K1A OH5 (613/992-0028)

Dept. of Veterans Affairs, Ottawa, Ont. K1A OP4 (613/992-4234)

National Film Board, Box 6100, Montreal, P.Q. H3C 3H5 (514/333-3333)

National Research Council of Canada, Division of Building Research, Montreal Rd., Ottawa, Ont. K1A OR6 (613/993-2607)

Public Works Canada, Public Relations & Information Services, Sir Charles Tupper Bldg., Ottawa, Ont. K1A OM2 (613/998-9560)

Transport Canada, Airports & Construction Services Directorate, Floor 19E, Place de Ville, Ottawa, Ont. K1A ON8 (613/992-0271)

Statistics Canada, Ottawa, Ont. K1A OT6 (613/995-4219)

Alta.: Research & Planning, Dept. of Labour, 5th floor, IBM Bldg., Edmonton, Alta. T5K OG5 (403/427-8531)

Alberta Bureau of Statistics, Alberta Treasury, 7th floor, 9811 109 St., Edmonton, Alta. T5J 0C8 (403/427-3058)

Alberta Dept. of Housing & Public Works, 3rd floor, 10050 112 St., Edmonton, Alta. T5K 2J1 (403/427-3917, Deputy Minister)

B.C.: Central Statistics Bureau, Ministry of Industry & Small Business Development, Parliament Bldgs., Victoria, B.C. V8V 1X4 (604/387-1502)

Ministry of Lands, Parks & Housing, Parliament Bldgs., Victoria, B.C. V8V 1X4 (604/387-5381)

Man.: Mechanical & Engineering Branch, Dept. of Labour & Manpower, 500 Norquay Bldg., 401 York Ave., Winnipeg, Man. R3C OP8 (204/944-3373) (inspection of public bldgs.)

N.B.: Professional Services Division, Dept. of Supply & Services, Box 6000, Fredericton, N.B. E3B 5H1 (506/453-2239)

Dept. of Transportation, Kings Place, Box 6000, Fredericton, N.B. E3B 5H1 (506/453-2549)

Nfld.: Dept. of Public Works & Services, Planning & Construction Division, Confederation Bldg., Box 4750, St. John's, Nfld. A1C 5T7 (709/737-3684)

N.S.: Dept. of Labour & Manpower, Box 697, Halifax, N.S. B3J 2T8 (902/424-4313)

N.S. Housing Commission, Royal Bank Bldg., Dartmouth, N.S. B2Y 3Z3 (902/424-4266)

Ont.: Construction Health & Safety Branch, Ministry of Labour, 8th floor, 400 University Ave., Toronto, Ont. M7A 1T7 (416/965-7161)

Ministry of Consumer & Commercial Relations, Technical Standards Division, Building Code Branch, 400 University Ave., Toronto, Ont. M7A 2J9 (416/965-5881)

P.E.I.: Director of Buildings Branch, Dept. of Highways & Public Works, Box 2000, Charlottetown, P.E.I. C1A 7N8 (902/892-7431)

Que.: Ministère du Travail et de la Main-d'oeuvre et de la Sécurité du Revenu, 425, St-Amable, Quebec, P.Q. G1R 4Z1 (418/643-8078)

Office de la Construction, 3530 Jean Talon St. W., Montreal, P.Q. H3R 2G3 (514/341-7740)

Régie des entreprises de construction du Québec, 1100, Crémazie boul. est, Montreal, P.Q. H2P 2X2 (admin.: 514/725-9321; info.: 725-6433)

CONSUMER PROTECTION

Director, Communications Service, Dept. of Consumer & Corporate Affairs Canada, Place du Portage, Phase 1, Ottawa/Hull, K1A OC9 (819/997-2938) (product safety, textile labelling, consumer complaints, consumer information, misleading advertising, combines investigation, bankruptcy, federal corporation laws, patents, copyright, trade marks, industrial designs, weights and measures, electricity and gas inspection, and inspection of meat, fish and food)

Statistics Canada, Ottawa, Ont. K1A OT6 (613/995-4078) (Price Indexes)

Alta.: Consumer Relations Division, Dept. of Consumer & Corporate Affairs, 9th floor, 10065 Jasper Ave., Edmonton, Alta. T5J 3B1 (403/427-2244)

B.C.: Ministry of Consumer & Corporate Affairs, 940 Blanshard St., Victoria, B.C. V8W 3E6 (604/387-6831)

Man.: Consumers' Bureau, 307 Kennedy St., Winnipeg, Man. R3C OV8 (204/956-2040)

N.B.: Consumer & Corporate Affairs Branch, Consumer Affairs Division, Dept. of Justice, Box 6000, Fredericton, N.B. E3B 5H1 (506/453-2659)

Nfld.: Dept. of Justice, Confederation Bldg., St. John's, Nfld. A1C 5T7 (709/737-2591)

N.S.: Consumer Services Bureau, (5151 Terminal Rd.), Box 998, Halifax, N.S. B3J 2X3 (902/424-4690)

Ont.: Consumer Services Bureau, Ministry of Consumer & Commercial Relations, 555 Yonge St., Toronto, Ont. M7A 2H6 (416/963-0321) See Ontario government listings for regional offices.

P.E.I.: Environmental & Consumer Services, Dept. of Community Affairs, Box 2000, Charlottetown, P.E.I. C1A 7N8 (902/892-5321)

Que.: Consumer Protection Bureau, 700 Boul. St-Cyrille est, 15th floor, Quebec, P.Q. G1R 5A9 (418/643-1467) (see Index for regional offices)

Sask.: Saskatchewan Consumer & Commercial Affairs, 1871 Smith St., Regina, Sask. S4P 3V7 (306/565-5550)

CONTINUING EDUCATION

see Education

CONVENTION FACILITIES

see Tourism

CO-OPERATIVES

Canada Mtge. & Housing Corp., Montreal Rd., Ottawa, Ont. K1A OP7 (613/748-2373)

Dept. of Agriculture, Co-operatives Unit, Food & Agriculture Marketing Branch, Sir John Carling Bldg., Ottawa, Ont. K1A OC5 (613/995-5880)

Director, Corporations Branch, Dept. of Consumer & Corporate Affairs Canada, Place du Portage, Phase 2, Ottawa/Hull, K1A OC9 (819/997-1058)

Dept. of Indian Affairs & Northern Development, Ottawa, Ont. K1A OH4 (819/997-9920) (Native communities)

Information Branch, Dept. of Insurance, Ottawa, Ont. K1A OH2 (613/996-8587)

National Film Board, Box 6100, Montreal, P.Q. H3C 3H5 (514/333-3333)

Alta.: Co-operatives Branch, Dept. of Consumer & Corporate Affairs, PO Bag 600, Provincial Bldg., Stettler, Alta. T0C 2L0 (403/742-4481)

B.C.: Registrar of Companies, 940 Blanshard St., Victoria, B.C. V8W 3E6 (604/387-5188)

Supt. of Co-operatives, 1050 W. Pender St., Vancouver, B.C. V6E 3S7 (604/682-7031)

Man.: Dept. of Co-operative Development, #900, 405 Broadway Ave., Winnipeg, Man. R3C 3L6 (204/944-3682)

N.B.: Agricultural Credit & Co-operative Branch, Dept. of Agriculture, Research Stn., Box 6000, Fredericton, N.B. E3B 5H1 (506/453-2315)

Nfld.: Dept. of Justice, Confederation Bldg., St. John's, Nfld. A2C 5T7 (709/737-2582)

N.S.: Registrar of Joint Stock Companies, Box 1529, Halifax, N.S. B3J 2Y4 (902/424-7770)

Ont.: Credit Unions & Co-operatives Services Branch, Financial Institutions Division, Ministry of Consumer & Commercial Relations, 555 Yonge St., Toronto, Ont. M7A 2H6 (416/963-0515)

Que.: Quebec Bureau of Statistics, Dept. of Industry, Trade & Tourism, 117 St-André, Quebec, P.Q. G1K 3Y3 (418/643-5116)

Dept. of Financial Institutions & Co-operatives, 800, place d'Youville, Quebec, P.Q. G1R 4Y5 (418/643-1411)

Sask.: Dept. of Co-operation & Co-operative Development, 2055 Albert St., Box 7121, Regina, Sask. S4P 3S1 (306/565-5807)

COPYRIGHT

see Patents

CORONERS

Alta.: Office of the Chief Medical Examiner, Alberta Attorney General, Calgary Health Sciences Centre, 3330 Hospital Dr. N.W., Calgary, Alta. T2N 4N1 (403/261-8123)

B.C.: Office of the Chief Coroner, 245 E. Columbia St., New Westminster, B.C. V3L 3W1 (604/521-6601)

Man.: Administrator, Fatality Inquiries Act, 4th floor, 405 Broadway, Winnipeg, Man. R3C 3L6 (204/944-2049)

N.B.: Dept. of Justice, Box 6000, Fredericton, N.B. E3B 5H1 (506/453-3604)

Nfld.: Dept. of Justice, Confederation Bldg., St. John's, Nfld. A1C 5T7 (709/737-2872)

Ont.: Chief Coroner, Ministry of the Solicitor General, 26 Grenville St., Toronto, Ont. M7A 2G9 (416/965-6678)

P.E.I.: Dept. of Justice, Box 2000, Charlottetown, P.E.I. C1A 7N8 (902/892-5411)

Que.: Bureau du coroner, Dept. of Justice, 1600, rue Semple, Quebec, P.Q. G1N 4B8 (418/643-3982)

Sask.: Dept. of the Attorney General, Chief Coroner, 2476 Victoria Ave., Regina, Sask. S4P 3V7 (306/565-5570)

Yukon: Dept. of Justice, Public Administrator & Chief Coroner, Box 2703, Whitehorse, Y.T. Y1A 2C6 (403/667-5317)

COURTS & JUDGES

see Justice

CREATIVE ARTS

see Handicrafts

CREDIT COUNSELLING

see Debtors' Assistance

CRIME COMPENSATION

Alta.: Dept. of the Attorney General, 4th floor, 9833 109 St., Edmonton, Alta. T5K 2E8 (403/427-5115)

B.C.: Ministry of Attorney General, Parliament Bldgs., Victoria, B.C. V8V 1X4 (604/384-4434)

Man.: The Criminal Injuries Compensation Board, 333 Maryland St., Winnipeg, Man. R3G 1M2 (204/775-7821)

N.B.: Dept. of Justice, Box 6000, Fredericton, N.B. E3B 5H1 (506/453-2721)

Nfld.: Dept. of Justice, Confederation Bldg., St. John's, Nfld. A1C 5T7 (709/737-2872)

Ont.: Criminal Injuries Compensation Board, Ministry of the Attorney General, 439 University Ave., 17th floor, Toronto, Ont. M5G 1Y8

Que.: Commission de la santé et de la sécurité du travail, Indemnisation des victimes d'actes criminels, Complexe Desjardins, Tour du Sud, 27e étage, C.P. 787, Succ Desjardins, Montreal, P.Q. H5B 1B9 (514/873-6029)

Sask.: Criminal Injuries Compensation Board, 122 3rd Ave. N., Saskatoon, Sask. S7K 2H6 (306/664-5153)

Yukon: Compensation to Victims of Criminal Injury, Supreme Court of Yukon, Box 2703, Whitehorse, Y.T. Y1A 2C6

CROWN LANDS

Alta.: Asst. Deputy Minister, Public Lands, Dept. of Energy & Natural Resources, 9915 108 St., South Tower, Petroleum Plaza, Edmonton, Alta. T5K 2E1 (403/427-3498)

B.C.: Asst. Deputy Minister, Lands & Housing Regional Operations Division, Ministry of Lands, Parks & Housing, Parliament Bldgs., Victoria, B.C. V8W 2Y9 (604/387-6269)

Man.: Crown Lands Branch, Dept. of Natural Resources, Box 2, 1495 St. James St., Winnipeg, Man. R3H OW9 (204/786-9268)

Asst. Director of Agricultural Crown Lands Section, Dept. of Agriculture, Box 30, 1495 St. James St., Winnipeg, Man. R3H OW9 (204/786-9274)

N.B.: Director of Lands, Dept. of Natural Resources, Box 6000, Fredericton, N.B. E3B 5H1 (506/453-2513)

Nfld.: Director of Crown Lands Admin., Dept. of Forestry Resources & Lands, Howley Bldg., Higgins Line, St. John's, Nfld. A1C 5T7 (709/754-0090)

N.S.: Director, Land Acquisition & Registry, Dept. of Lands & Forests, Dennis Bldg., 1740 Granville St., Halifax, N.S. B3J 2T9 (902/424-4267)

Ont.: Lands Management Branch, Lands & Waters, Ministry of Natural Resources, Queen's Park, Toronto, Ont. M7A 1W3 (416/965-4507)

P.E.I.: Dept. of Community Affairs, Building & Development Services, Box 2000, Charlottetown, P.E.I. C1A 7N8 (902/892-0221)

Que.: Ministère de l'Energie et des Ressources, Direction de la Gestion du territoire, 200B Chemin Ste-Foy, Quebec, P.Q. G1R 4X7 (418/643-7685)

Sask.: Director, Lands Branch, Dept. of Agriculture, Walter Scott Bldg., Regina, Sask. S4S OB1 (306/565-5200)

CULTURE

see Arts

CURRENCY

Bank of Canada, Ottawa, Ont. K1A OG9 (613/563-8111)

Royal Canadian Mint, Place Vanier, 355 River Rd., 6th floor, Vanier, Ont. K1A OG8 (613/993-2595)

CUSTOMS

Revenue Canada, Customs & Excise Division, Ottawa, Ont. K1A OL5 (613/593-6220)

DAIRYING

Dept. of Agriculture, Dairy, Fruit & Vegetable Division, 2255 Carling Ave., Ottawa, Ont. K1A 0Y9 (613/995-5433)

Dept. of Industry, Trade & Commerce, Livestock, Meat & Dairy Products Division, Agriculture, Fisheries & Food Products Branch, 235 Queen St., Ottawa, Ont. K1A OH5 (613/995-8107)

Food Research Institute, Research Branch, Agriculture Canada, Ottawa, Ont. K1A OC6 (613/995-3722)

National Film Board, Box 6100, Montreal, P.Q. H3C 3H5 (514/333-3333)

Statistics Canada, Ottawa, Ont. K1A OT6 (613/995-4853)

Alta.: Dairy Division, Dept. of Agriculture, and Alberta Dairy Control Board, both at Provincial Bldg., 50th Ave. & 52nd St., Wetaskiwin, Alta. T9A OS7 (403/352-9211)

B.C.: Dairy Branch, Ministry of Agriculture & Food, Parliament Bldgs., Victoria, B.C. V8W 2Z7 (604/387-5121)

Man.: Dept. of Agriculture, Animal Industry Branch, Agricultural Services Complex, Univ. of Manitoba Campus, Winnipeg, Man. R3T 2N2 (204/269-1220)

N.B.: Communications Section, N.B. Dept. of Agriculture & Rural Development, Box 6000, Fredericton, N.B. E3B 5H1 (506/453-2258)

Nfld.: Dept. of Rural, Agricultural & Northern Development, Prov. Agriculture Bldg., Brookfield Rd., Mount Pearl, Nfld. (709/737-3840)

N.S.: Provincial Dairy Supt., Dept. of Agriculture & Marketing, Box 550, Truro, N.S. B2N 5E3 (902/895-1571)

Ont.: Farm Products Quality Branch, Milk Industry Section, Ministry of Agriculture & Food, Legislative Bldgs., Toronto, Ont. M7A 1A7 (416/965-2411)

Milk Commission of Ontario, Farm Products Marketing Branch, Ministry of Agriculture & Food, Legislative Bldgs., Toronto, Ont. M7A 2B2 (416/965-2124)

P.E.I.: Dairy Division, Dept. of Agriculture & Forestry, Box 1600, Charlottetown, P.E.I. C1A 7N3 (902/892-5465)

P.E.I. Milk Commission, Box 335, Charlottetown, P.E.I. C1A 7K7 (902/892-5331)

Que.: Ministry of Agriculture, Fisheries & Food, Dairy Products Inspection Service, 200 A Chemin Ste-Foy, 11th floor, Quebec, P.Q. G1R 4X6 (418/643-2500)

Sask.: Dept. of Agriculture, Dairy Section, Animal Industry Branch, Walter Scott Bldg., Regina, Sask. S4S OB1 (306/565-4675)

DAY CARE SERVICES

National Day Care Information Centre, Dept. of National Health & Welfare, Ottawa, Ont. K1A 1B5 (613/995-0128)

Alta.: Dept. of Social Services & Community Health, Day Care Branch, 10030 107 St., Edmonton, Alta. T5J 3E4 (403/427-2734)

B.C.: Rehabilitation & Support Services, Ministry of Human Resources, Parliament Bldgs., Victoria, B.C. V8V 1X4 (604/387-3016)

Man.: Child Day Care Program, 3rd floor, 267 Edmonton St., Winnipeg, Man. R3C 1S3 (204/944-2197)

N.B.: Administrator, Day Care Services, Dept. of Social Services, (Lynch Bldg.) Box 6000, Fredericton, N.B. E3B 5H1 (506/453-2943)

Nfld.: Director of Day Care & Homemaker Services, Dept. of Social Services, Confederation Bldg., St. John's, Nfld. A1C 5T7 (709/737-3590)

N.S.: Director of Day Care Services, Family & Children's Services Division, Dept. of Social Services, Box 696, Halifax, N.S. B3J 2T7 (902/424-3204)

Ont.: Program Information, Ministry of Community & Social Services, Hepburn Block, 6th floor, Toronto, Ont. M7A 1E9 (416/965-4914)

P.E.I.: Co-ordinator, Early Childhood Development, Dept. of Health & Social Services, Box 2000, Charlottetown, P.E.I. C1A 7N8 (902/892-5471)

Que.: Office des services de garde à l'enfance, 201 place Charles-Lemoyne, 3e étage, Longueuil, P.Q. J4K 2T5

Sask.: Day Care Branch, Dept. of Social Services, 1920 Broad St., Regina, Sask. S4P 3V6 (306/565-3855)

N.W.T.: Co-ordinator, Special Services, Dept. of Health & Social Services, Government of the N.W.T., Yellowknife, N.W.T. X1A 2L9 (403/873-7160)

Yukon: Dept. of Health & Human Resources, Box 2703, Whitehorse, Y.T. (403/667-5746)

Calgary: Day Care Consultant, Social Services Dept., Box 2100, Calgary, Alta. T2P 2M5 (403/268-5111)

Toronto: Metropolitan Toronto Children's Services Division, Dept. of Community Services, City Hall, Toronto, Ont. M5H 2N2 (416/367-8128)

DEATH CERTIFICATES
see Vital Statistics

DEBTORS' ASSISTANCE
Alta.: Family Financial Counselling (Debtors' Assistance), Dept. of Consumer & Corporate Affairs, 10065 Jasper Ave., Edmonton, Alta. T5J OH4 (403/427-5210)
B.C.: Consumer Credit & Debtor Assistance Branch, Ministry of Consumer & Corporate Affairs, 940 Blanshard St., Victoria, B.C. V8W 3E6 (604/387-1747)
Man.: County Court of Winnipeg, Room 236, 405 Broadway, Winnipeg, Man. R3C 3L6 (204/944-3133)
N.S.: Dept. of Consumer Affairs, Consumer Services Bureau, Debtor Assistance Section, Box 998, Halifax, N.S. B3J 2X3 (902/424-4690)
Ont.: Referee of the Small Claims Courts, Judicial District of York, Ministry of Attorney General, #257, 444 Yonge St., Toronto, Ont. M5B 2H4 (416/965-5591)
see Toronto, below
P.E.I.: Consumer Services Division, Dept. of Justice, Box 2000, Charlottetown, P.E.I. C1A 7N8 (902/892-5411)
Que.: Greffier de la Cour des Petites Créances, Palais de Justice, 1 est, rue Notre Dame, Ch. 3.150, Montréal, P.Q. H2Y 1B6 (514/873-6873)
Sask.: Dept. of Consumer & Commercial Affairs, Provincial Mediation Board, 1871 Smith St., Regina, Sask. S4P 3V7 (306/565-5404)

Hamilton: Family Services of Hamilton-Wentworth Inc., 350 King St. E., Hamilton, Ont. L8N 3Y3 (416/523-5640)
The Catholic Social Services of Hamilton, 82 Stinson St., Hamilton, Ont. L8N 1S2 (527-3823)
Kitchener: Catholic Social Services (Kitchener-Waterloo Dist.), 74 Weber St. W., Kitchener, Ont. N2H 3Z3 (519/743-6333)
Oakville: Halton Consumer Credit Counselling Service, 168 Lakeshore Rd. E., Oakville, Ont. L6J 1H6 (416/842-1459)
Oshawa: Oshawa & Dist. Credit Counselling Service, 172 King St. E., Oshawa, Ont. L1H 1B6 (416/579-1951)
Ottawa: Credit Counselling Service of Ottawa, 187 Bay St., Ottawa, Ont. K1R 5Y7 (613/236-3637)
St. Catharines: Credit Counselling of Regional Niagara, 11 Bond St., St. Catharines, Ont. L2R 4Z4 (416/684-9401)
Toronto: Credit Counselling Service of Metro Toronto, #301, 100 Lombard St., Toronto, Ont. M5C 1M3 (416/366-5251)
Windsor: Credit Counselling Service of Metropolitan Windsor, 2260 University Ave. W., Windsor, Ont. N9B 1E5 (519/258-2030)

DEFENCE
Dept. of National Defence, Information Service, Ottawa, Ont. K1A OK2 (613/996-2353)
Dept. of External Affairs, Domestic Information Programs, Ottawa, Ont. K1A OG2 (613/593-7064)
Dept. of Industry, Trade & Commerce, Defence Programs Branch, 235 Queen St., Ottawa, Ont. K1A OH5 (613/992-8584)
National Film Board, Box 6100, Montreal, P.Q. H3C 3H5 (514/333-3333)

DELINQUENCY
Ministry of the Solicitor General, Consultation Centre, 340 Laurier Ave. W., Ottawa, Ont. K1A OP8
National Film Board, Box 6100, Montreal, P.Q. H3C 3H5 (514/333-3333)
Statistics Canada, Ottawa, Ont. K1A OT6 (613/995-0711)

Alta.: Dept. of Social Services & Community Health, 10030 107 St., Edmonton, Alta. T5J 3E4 (403/427-2734)
B.C.: Ministry of the Attorney General, Corrections Branch, 535 Yates St., Victoria, B.C. V8V 1X4 (604/387-6366)
Man.: Dept. of Community Services & Corrections, Legislative Bldg., Winnipeg, Man. R3C OV8 (204/944-3048)
N.B.: Dept. of Justice, Box 6000, Fredericton, N.B. E3B 5H1 (506/453-2462)
Nfld.: Dept. of Social Services, Confederation Bldg., St. John's, Nfld. A1C 5T7 (709/737-2492)
N.S.: Special Protection Services Section, Family & Children's Services Division, Dept. of Social Services, Box 696, Halifax, N.S. B3J 2T7 (902/424-4632)
Ont.: Juvenile Probation/Aftercare Correctional Programs, Children's Services Division, Ministry of Community & Social Services, 10th floor, 700 Bay St., Toronto, Ont. M7A 1E9 (416/965-8067)
P.E.I.: Probation & Family Court Services, Dept. of Justice, Box 2000, Charlottetown, P.E.I. C1A 7N8 (902/892-5411)
Que.: Dept. of Social Affairs, Delinquency Director, 1075 chemin Ste-Foy, Ste-Foy, P.Q. G1S 2M1
Sask.: Youth Services Unit, Dept. of Social Services, 1920 Broad St., Regina, Sask. S4P 3V6 (306/565-3610)
Yukon: Dept. of Health & Human Resources, Box 2703, Whitehorse, Y.T. Y1A 2C6 (403/667-5674)

DENTAL SERVICES
B.C.: Dental Care Plan of B.C., Box 1500, Victoria, B.C. V8W 8G8 (604/387-5241)
Man.: Dental Health Services, Dept. of Health, 3rd floor, 831 Portage Ave., Winnipeg, Man. R3G ON6 (204/775-9761)
Sask.: Sask. Dental Plan, 3475 Albert St., Regina, Sask. S4S 6X6 (306/565-4580)

DESIGN
Design Canada, Dept. of Industry, Trade & Commerce, Ottawa, Ont. K1A OH5 (613/992-0341)

Man.: Manitoba Design Institute, 155 Carlton St., 7th floor, Winnipeg, Man. R3C 3H8 (204/944-2468)

DISCRIMINATION (Employment)
Appeals & Investigations Branch, Public Service Commission, 5th floor, 300 Laurier Ave. W., Ottawa, Ont. K1A OM7 (613/996-4200)
Canadian Human Rights Commission, Ottawa, Ont. K1A 1E1 (613/995-1151)

Alta.: Alberta Human Rights Commission, 501, 10053 111 St., Edmonton, Alta. T5K 2H8 (403/427-7661)
B.C.: Director, Human Rights Branch, Ministry of Labour, 5th floor, 880 Douglas St., Victoria, B.C. V8W 2B7 (604/387-6861)
Man.: Man. Human Rights Commission, 200, 323 Portage Ave., Winnipeg, Man. R3B 2C1 (204/944-3007, 8)
N.B.: N.B. Human Rights Commission, Box 6000, Fredericton, N.B. E3B 5H1
Nfld.: Nfld. Human Rights Commission, Dept. of Justice, Gordonna Bldg., Kenmount Rd., Box 4750, St. John's, Nfld. A1C 5T7 (709/737-2709)
N.S.: N.S. Human Rights Commission, (Lord Nelson Arcade), Box 2221, Halifax, N.S. B3J 3C4 (902/424-4111)
Ont.: Human Rights Commission, 400 University Ave., Toronto, Ont. M7A 1T7 (416/965-6841)
P.E.I.: Human Rights Commission, Box 2000, Charlottetown, P.E.I. C1A 7N8 (902/894-7797)
Que.: Director, Dept. of Special Investigations, Dept. of Labour, 255 Cremazie St. E., Montreal, P.Q. H2M 1L5
Commission des droits de la Personne du Québec, 360, rue St-Jacques, Mezzanine, Montreal, P.Q. H2Y 1P5 (514/873-5146) Toll free in Quebec 1-800-361-6477. Quebec Office: 1279 boul. Charest ouest, 7e étage, Québec, P.Q. G1N 4K7 (418/643-1872)
Sask.: Saskatchewan Human Rights Commission, 8th floor, 224 4th Ave. S., Saskatoon, Sask. S7K 5M5 (306/664-5952)
N.W.T.: Fair Practices Officer, Dept. of Justice & Public Services, Government of N.W.T., Yellowknife, N.W.T. X1A 2L9 (403/873-7486)
Yukon: Dept. of Consumer & Corporate Affairs, Labour Standards, Box 2703, Whitehorse, Y.T. Y1A 2C6 (403/667-5312)

DIVORCE
Dept. of Justice, Ottawa, Ont. K1A OH8 (613/995-9308)
Statistics Canada, Ottawa, Ont. K1A OT6 (613/995-7808)

Alta.: granted in Court of Queen's Bench under federal law. (Court Services, Attorney General's Dept., 9833 109 St., Edmonton, Alta. T5K 2E8, 403/427-4992)

B.C.: Court Services (Law Courts), 850 Burdett St., Victoria, B.C. V8W 1B4 (604/387-1521)

Man.: Court of Queen's Bench, Room 224, Woodsworth Bldg., 405 Broadway, Winnipeg, Man. R3C 1L6 (204/944-3024) (also Court Houses at Brandon, Dauphin, Portage la Prairie, The Pas)

N.B.: Dept. of Justice, Box 6000, Fredericton, N.B. E3B 5H1 (506/453-2784)

Nfld.: Supreme Court Registry, Courthouse, Duckworth St., St. John's, Nfld. A1C 5M3 (709/726-4482)

Unified Family Court, 21 Kings Bridge Rd., St. John's, Nfld. A1C 3K4 (709/753-5873)

N.S.: Prothonotaries, Law Courts, 1815 Upper Water St., Halifax, N.S. B3J 3C8 (902/424-4900)

Ont.: Divorce cases heard by county courts. (Ministry of the Attorney General, 18 King St. E., Toronto, Ont. M5C 1C5, 416/965-5184)

P.E.I.: Prothonotary/Supreme Court, Box 2200, Charlottetown, P.E.I. C1A 8B9

Que.: Quebec divorces handled by Superior Court, Palais de Justice, Division des divorces, 12, rue St-Louis, Quebec, P.Q. G1R 4P6, 418/643-4010 (Ministère de la Justice, Direction des Communication, 1200 rte de l'Eglise, Ste-Foy, P.Q. G1V 4M1)

Sask.: Court Services, Dept. of Attorney General, 2476 Victoria Ave., Regina, Sask. S4P 3V7 (306/565-5352)

Yukon: Supreme Court of Yukon, Box 2703, Whitehorse, Y.T. Y1A 2C6 (403/667-4431)

DOG LICENCES & REGULATIONS

see Animal Control

DRIVER LICENCES

Alta.: Motor Vehicles Division, Dept. of the Solicitor General, Box 3140, Stn. A, Edmonton, Alta. T5J 2G7 (403/427-7013)

B.C.: Motor Vehicle Branch, Ministry of Transportation & Highways, 2631 Douglas St., Victoria, B.C. V8T 5A3 (604/387-3224)

Man.: Motor Vehicle Branch, Highway Services Bldg., 1075 Portage Ave., Winnipeg, Man. R3G OS1 (204/775-0281)

N.B.: Motor Vehicle Branch, Highway Safety Division, Dept. of Provincial Secretary, Box 6000, Fredericton, N.B. E3B 5H1 (506/453-2352)

Nfld.: Motor Registration Division, Dept. of Transportation, Viking Bldg., St. John's, Nfld. A1C 5T4

N.S.: Registry of Motor Vehicles, 6061 Young St., Box 1652, Halifax, N.S. B3J 2Z3 (902/424-5531)

Ont.: Driver Licensing & Control Office, Ministry of Transportation & Communications, East Bldg., 2680 Keele St., Downsview, Ont. M3M 3E6 (416/249-3303, 4)

P.E.I.: Highway Safety Division, Dept. of Highways & Public Works, Box 2000, Charlottetown, P.E.I. C1A 7N8 (902/892-5306)

Que.: Motor Vehicle Bureau, Dept. of Transport, Ste. 330, 880, chemin Ste-Foy, Quebec, P.Q. G1S 2K8

Sask.: Motor Vehicle Division, Saskatchewan Government Insurance, 2260 11th Ave., Regina, Sask. S4P 2N7 (306/565-1200)

N.W.T.: Vital Statistics, Dept. of Justice & Public Services, Box 1320, Yellowknife, N.W.T. X1A 2L9 (403/873-7401)

Yukon: Motor Vehicles Branch, Dept. of Consumer & Corporate Affairs, Box 2703, Whitehorse, Y.T. Y1A 2C6 (403/667-5315)

DRUGS (and Alcohol)

Dept. of National Health & Welfare (613/992-4575):

Health Protection Branch, Room 116, HPB Bldg., Tunney's Pasture, Ottawa, Ont. K1A OL2

Drugs Directorate, Room 126, HPB Bldg., Tunney's Pasture, Ottawa, Ont. K1A OL2 (613/996-6816)

Library, Health Services & Promotion Branch, Jeanne Mance Bldg., 5th floor, Tunney's Pasture, Ottawa, Ont. K1A 1B4 (613/996-4513)

National Film Board, Box 6100, Montreal, P.Q. H3C 3H5 (514/333-3333)

Statistics Canada, Ottawa, Ont. K1A OT6 (613/995-8201)

Alta.: Dept. of Social Services & Community Health, 10030 107 St., Edmonton, Alta. T5J 3E4 (403/427-2734)

Alta. Alcoholism & Drug Abuse Commission, 6th floor, 10909 Jasper Ave., Edmonton, Alta. T5J 3M9 (427-7301)

B.C.: B.C. Alcohol & Drug Programs, Box 50, 805 W. Broadway, Vancouver, B.C. V5Z 1K1 (604/873-0263)

Man.: Alcoholism Foundation of Manitoba, 1580 Dublin Ave., Winnipeg, Man. R3E OL4 (204/775-8601)

N.B.: Alcohol & Drug Dependency Commission, Box 6000, Fredericton, N.B. E3B 5H1 (506/453-2136)

Nfld.: Dept. of Health, Confederation Bldg., St. John's, Nfld. A1C 5T7 (709/737-3125)

Alcohol & Drug Addiction Foundation of Nfld. & Labrador, Box 4554, St. John's, Nfld. A1C 6C8 (579-4041)

N.S.: N.S. Commission on Drug Dependency, 5668 South St., Halifax, N.S. B3J 1A6 (902/424-4270)

Ont.: Ministry of Health, Health Information & Promotion Branch, 9th floor, Hepburn Block, Queen's Park, Toronto, Ont. M7A 1S2 (416/965-5167)

Alcoholism & Drug Addiction Research Fdn., 33 Russell St., Toronto, Ont. M5S 2S1 (416/595-6000)

P.E.I.: Addiction Services of P.E.I., Box 37, Charlottetown, P.E.I. C1A 7K2 (902/892-4265)

Que.: Service de Toxicomanie, Affaires Sociales, 1075, Chemin Ste-Foy, Quebec, P.Q. G1S 2M1 (418/643-9887)

Sask.: Alcoholism Commission of Saskatchewan, 3475 Albert St., Regina, Sask. S4S 6X6 (306/565-4085)

N.W.T.: Alcohol & Drug Program, Dept. of Social Services, Government of the N.W.T., Yellowknife, N.W.T. X1A 2L9 (403/873-7904)

Alcohol & Drug Co-ordinating Council, Box 1769, Yellowknife, N.W.T. XOE 1HO (403/873-7904)

Yukon: Alcohol & Drug Services, Box 2703, Whitehorse, Y.T. Y1A 2C6 (403/667-5777)

ECONOMIC PLANNING

Dept. of Finance, Ottawa, Ont. K1A OG5 (613/996-5225)

Dept. of Regional Economic Expansion, Ottawa, Ont. K1A OM4 (819/997-2670)

Economic Council of Canada, Box 527, Ottawa, Ont. K1P 5V6 (613/993-1052)

Alta.: Dept. of Economic Development, Strategic Planning Branch, 10th floor, 10909 Jasper Ave., Edmonton, Alta. T5J 3M8 (403/427-3627)

B.C.: Ministry of Industry & Small Business Development, Parliament Bldgs., Victoria, B.C. V8V 1X4 (604/387-6701)

Man.: Economic & Operations Research Branch, Dept. of Economic Development & Tourism, 6th floor, 155 Carlton St., Winnipeg, Man. R3C 3H8 (204/944-2394)

N.B.: Dept. of Commerce & Development, Box 6000, Fredericton, N.B. E3B 5H1 (506/453-2489)

Nfld.: Economic & Resource Policy, Cabinet Secretariat, Dept. of Executive Council, Confederation Bldg., St. John's, Nfld. A1C 5T7 (709/737-3255)

N.S.: Dept. of Development, Development Strategy Division, Box 519, 5151 George St., Halifax, N.S. B3J 2R7 (902/424-6624)

Ont.: Office of Economic Policy, Ministry of Treasury, 5th floor, Frost Bldg. N., Toronto, Ont. M7A 1Z1 (416/965-3184)

P.E.I.: Policy & Priorities Board, Box 2000, Charlottetown, P.E.I. C1A 7N8 (902/892-4211)

Que.: Dept. of Labour & Manpower, 425 St-Amable, Quebec, P.Q. G1R 4Z1 (418/643-3880)

Quebec Planning & Development Bureau, Complexe G, Bloc 2, 1060 rue Conroy, Quebec, P.Q. G1R 5E6 (418/643-3285)

Sask.: Dept. of Finance, Budget Bureau, Legislative Bldg., Regina, Sask. S4S OB3 (306/565-6780)

Yukon: Economic Research & Planning Unit, Box 2703, Whitehorse, Y.T. Y1A 2C6

Calgary: Dept. of Business Development, Natural Resources Bldg., Ste. 317, 205 9th Ave. S.E., Box 2100, Calgary, Alta. T2P 2M5 (403/268-2331)
Hamilton: Economic Development Dept., Regional Municipality of Hamilton Wentworth, Box 910, 115 King St. W., 15th floor, Hamilton, Ont. L8N 3V9 (416/526-4222)
LaSalle: Treasurer, City Hall, 13 Strathyre Ave., LaSalle, P.Q. H8R 3P6 (514/366-7110)
London: Dept. of Community Services, Planning Division, City Hall, 300 Dufferin Ave., (Box 5035, London, Ont. N6A 4L9) (519/679-4980)
Mississauga: Finance Dept., 9th floor, Univac Bldg., 55 City Centre Dr., Mississauga, Ont. L5B 1M2 (416/279-7600)
Montreal (Region): Economic Development Office, Montreal Urban Community, 800 Victoria Sq., Suite 4130, Box 55, Montreal, P.Q. H4Z 1A8 (514/872-6996)
Oshawa: Real Estate Division, Planning & Development Dept., City Hall, 50 Centre St. S., Oshawa, Ont. L1H 3Z7 (416/725-7351)
Planning Dept., Regional Municipality of Durham, 105 Consumers Dr., Whitby, Ont. L1N 1C4 (668-7731)
Quebec City: Service d'urbanisme, Hôtel de Ville, Quebec, P.Q. G1R 4S9 (418/694-6422)
Quebec City Metro Area: Industrial Promotion Dept., Quebec Urban Community, 399 St-Joseph est, Quebec, P.Q. G1K 8E2 (418/529-8771)
Regina: City Manager, City Hall, (2476 Victoria Ave.), Box 1790, Regina, Sask. S4P 3C8 (306/569-7311)
Toronto: Planning & Development Dept., City Hall, Toronto, Ont. M5H 2N2 (416/367-7182)

ECONOMIC & SOCIAL RESEARCH

Bank of Canada, Ottawa, Ont. K1A OG9 (613/563-8111)
Canada Mtge. & Housing Corp., Montreal Rd., Ottawa, Ont. K1A OP7 (613/748-2000)
Dept. of Finance, Economic Analysis Division, Place Bell Canada, Ottawa, Ont. K1A OG5 (613/992-9353)
Dept. of Indian Affairs & Northern Development, Ottawa, Ont. K1A OH4 (819/997-9920) (Native peoples)
Dept. of Labour, Employment Relations & Conditions of Work Branch, Ottawa, Ont. K1A OJ2 (613/997-2861)
Dept. of National Health & Welfare, Ottawa, Ont. K1A OK9 (613/996-4950)
Dept. of Regional Economic Expansion, Project Assessment & Evaluation Branch, Ottawa, Ont. K1A OM4 (819/997-3288)
Dept. of Secretary of State, Library, Ottawa, Ont. K1A OM5 (819/997-5391)
Economic Council of Canada, Box 527, Ottawa, Ont. K1P 5V6 (613/993-1052)
Public Archives of Canada, 395 Wellington St., Ottawa, Ont. K1A ON3 (613/992-2669)
Statistics Canada, Ottawa, Ont. K1A OT6 (613/995-0575)
Transportation Development Centre, 1000 Sherbrooke St. W., Montreal, P.Q. H3A 2R3 (514/283-4008)
Transport Canada, Strategic Planning, Ottawa, Ont. K1A 0N5 (613/593-5680)

Alta.: Northern Development Branch, Dept. of Tourism & Small Business, 2nd floor, Provincial Bldg., Bag 900-14, Peace River, Alta. TOH 2X0 (403/624-6274)
Alberta Native Secretariat, 2nd floor, South Tower, 10030 107 St., Edmonton, Alta. T5J 3E4 (403/427-8407)
B.C.: Economic Analysis & Research Bureau, Ministry of Industry & Small Business Development, Parliament Bldgs., Victoria, B.C. V8V 1X4 (604/387-3707)
Man.: Economics Branch, Dept. of Agriculture, 903 Norquay Bldg., 401 York Ave., Winnipeg, Man. R3C OV8 (204/944-3491)
Dept. of Economic Development & Tourism, Economic & Operations Research Branch, 6th floor, 155 Carlton St., Winnipeg, Man. R3C 3H8 (204/944-2394)
N.B.: Dept. of Finance, Box 6000, Fredericton, N.B. E3B 5H1 (506/453-2534)
Dept. of Social Services, Box 6000, Fredericton, N.B. E3B 5H1 (506/453-2955)
Nfld.: Refer to: Institute of Social & Economic Research, Memorial Univ., St. John's, Nfld. A1C 5S7 (709/737-8156)
N.S.: Dept. of Development, Planning & Economics Branch, Box 519, Halifax, N.S. B3J 2R7 (902/424-7532)
Dept. of Social Services, Box 696, Halifax, N.S. B3J 2T7 (902/424-4039)
Ont.: Alcoholism & Drug Addiction Research Foundation of Ont., 33 Russell St., Toronto, Ont. M5S 2S1 (416/595-6000)
Economics Branch, Ontario Ministry of Agriculture & Food, Legislative Bldgs., Toronto, Ont. M7A 1B6 (416/965-1064)
P.E.I.: Policy & Priorities Board, Box 2000, Charlottetown, P.E.I. C1A 7N8 (902/892-4211)
Que.: Press Secretary, Dept. of Industry, Trade & Tourism, 710, Place d'Youville, Quebec, P.Q. G1R 4Y4 (418/643-5086)
Dept. of Labour & Manpower, 425 St-Amable, Quebec, P.Q. G1R 4Z1 (418/643-3880)
Office of Planning & Development, Complexe G, Bloc 2, 3e étage, 1060 rue Conroy, Quebec, P.Q. G1R 5E6 (418/643-3285)
Sask.: Dept. of Co-operation & Co-operative Development, 5th floor, 2055 Albert St., Regina, Sask. S4P 3V7 (306/565-5807)

EDUCATION

Canadian Broadcasting Corp.: English Services Division, Box 500, Stn. A, Toronto, Ont. M5W 1E6 (416/925-3311); French Services Division, Box 6000, Montreal, P.Q. H3C 3A8 (514/285-3211)
Canada Mtge. & Housing Corp., Montreal Rd., Ottawa, Ont. K1A OP7 (613/748-2609)
Dept. of Indian Affairs & Northern Development, Ottawa, Ont. K1A OH4 (819/997-9920) (Native peoples)
Dept. of Employment & Immigration, Enquiries Officer, Public Affairs Division, Ottawa, Ont. K1A OJ9 (819/994-6313)
Dept. of Regional Economic Expansion, Ottawa, Ont. K1A OM4 (819/997-2096)
Statistics Canada, Ottawa, Ont. K1A OT6 (613/995-9694)
Dept. of Veterans Affairs, Public Affairs Directorate, Ottawa, Ont. K1A OP4 (613/992-4234)

Alta.: Alberta Education, Communications Branch, Devonian Bldg., 11160 Jasper Ave., Edmonton, Alta. T5K OL2 (403/427-2285)
Alberta Advanced Education & Manpower, Communications Branch, Devonian Bldg., East Tower, 11160 Jasper Ave., Edmonton, Alta. T5K OL1 (403/427-7160)
ACCESS (Alberta Educational Communications Corp.), 16930 114 Ave., Edmonton, Alta. T5M 3S2 (403/451-3160)
Alberta Educational Communications Authority, #502, 10053 111 St., Edmonton, Alta. T5K 2H8 (403/427-4918)
B.C.: Ministry of Education, Information Services (Rms. 327 & 330, St. Ann's Academy), Parliament Bldgs., Victoria, B.C. V8V 1X4 (604/387-5041)
Man.: Information Officer, Dept. of Education, Room 506, 1181 Portage Ave., Winnipeg, Man. R3G OT3 (204/786-0254)
N.B.: Dept. of Education, Box 6000, Fredericton, N.B. E3B 5H1 (506/453-3678)
Dept. of Continuing Education, Box 6000, Fredericton, N.B. E3B 5H1 (506/453-2597)
Nfld.: Supervisor of Information, Statistics & Publications, Dept. of Education, Confederation Bldg., Box 2017, St. John's, Nfld. A1C 5R9 (709/737-2990)
N.S.: Publication & Reference, Dept. of Education, Box 578, Trade Mart, Halifax, N.S. B3J 2S9 (902/424-5570)
Ont.: Government of Ontario Book Store, 880 Bay St., Toronto, Ont. M7A 1N8 (416/965-2054)
Ministry of Education, Communication Services Branch, Mowat Block, Queen's Park, Toronto, Ont. M7A 1L2 (416/965-6407)
P.E.I.: Dept. of Education, Box 2000, Charlottetown, P.E.I. C1A 7N8 (902/892-3504)
Que.: Information Officer, Dept. of Education, Bldg. G, 16th floor, Government Bldgs., Quebec, P.Q. G1R 5A5 (418/643-7095)
Sask.: Dept. of Education, 2220 College Ave., Regina, Sask. S4P 3V7 (306/565-6030)

Dept. of Continuing Education, 1855 Victoria Ave., Regina, Sask. S4P 3V5 (306/565-5600)

Yukon: Dept. of Education & Vocational Training, Box 2703, Whitehorse, Y.T. Y1A 2C6 (403/667-5126)

ELECTIONS (and Election Expenses)

Chief Electoral Officer, 440 Coventry Rd., Ottawa, Ont. K1A OM6 (613/993-2975)

National Library, Ottawa, Ont. K1A ON4 (613/995-9481)

Public Archives of Canada, 395 Wellington St., Ottawa, Ont. K1A ON3 (613/992-2669)

Alta.: Chief Electoral Officer, West Chambers Bldg., Main floor, 12220 Stony Plain Rd., Edmonton, Alta. T5N 3Y4 (403/427-7191)

B.C.: Chief Electoral Officer, 559 Michigan St., Victoria, B.C. V8V 1X4 (604/387-5305)

Man.: Chief Electoral Officer, 249 Legislative Bldg., Winnipeg, Man. R3C OV8 (204/944-3225)

N.B.: Chief Electoral Officer, Elections Branch, Dept. of Municipal Affairs (Hilton Rd.) Box 6000, Fredericton, N.B. E3B 5H1 (506/453-2218)

Nfld.: Chief Electoral Officer, 278 Lemarchant Rd., St. John's, Nfld. A1E 1P7 (709/579-0031)

N.S.: Chief Electoral Officer, 9th floor, Howe Bldg., Box 1116, Halifax, N.S. B3J 2X1 (902/424-8584)

Ont.: Chief Election Officer, 70 Lombard St., Toronto, Ont. M5C 1M3 (416/965-6831)

Commission on Election Contributions & Expenses, 8th floor, Britannica House, 151 Bloor St. W., Toronto, Ont. M5S 1S4 (416/965-0455)

P.E.I.: Chief Electoral Officer, Box 2000, Charlottetown, P.E.I. C1A 7N8 (902/892-5411)

Que.: Chief Electoral Officer, 3460, La Pérade, Ste-Foy, Quebec, P.Q. G1X 3Y5 (418/643-5380)

Directeur General du Bureau du Financement des Partis Politiques, 1 Complexe Desjardins, #2204, Tour du Sud, C.P. 187, Succ Desjardins, Montréal, P.Q. H5B 1B3 (514/873-7131)

Sask.: Chief Electoral Officer, Dept. of the Executive Council, 2349 Broad St., Regina, Sask. S4P 1Y9 (306/565-4000)

Brampton: City Clerk's Dept., 150 Central Park Dr., Brampton, Ont. L6T 2T9 (416/793-4110)

Burlington: Clerk's Dept., 2nd floor, 426 Brant St., Burlington, Ont. L7R 3Z6 (416/335-7708)

Calgary: City Clerk's Dept., Box 2100, Calgary, Alta. T2P 2M5 (403/268-5861)

Edmonton: Election Office & Census, 11611 105 Ave., Edmonton, Alta. T5H 0L9 (403/428-5311)

Halifax: City Clerk, City Hall, Box 1749, Halifax, N.S. B3J 3A5 (902/426-6538)

Hamilton: City Clerk's Office, City Hall, 71 Main St. W., Hamilton, Ont. L8N 3T4 (416/527-0241)

Kitchener: City Clerk's Office, 2nd floor, City Hall, 22 Frederick St., Box 1118, Kitchener, Ont. N2G 4G7 (519/885-7240)

LaSalle: City Clerk, City Hall, 13 Strathyre Ave., LaSalle, P.Q. H8R 3P6 (514/366-7110)

London: City Clerk's Dept., City Hall, 300 Dufferin Ave., London, Ont. N6A 4L9 (519/679-4530)

Mississauga: Clerk's Dept., 1 City Centre Dr., Mississauga, Ont. L5B 1M2 (416/279-7600)

Montreal: Secrétariat Municipal, 275 est Notre Dame, S. 120, Montreal, P.Q. H2Y 1C6 (514/872-3140)

Niagara Falls: City Clerk's Office, City Hall, 4310 Queen St., Niagara Falls, Ont. L2E 6X5 (416/356-7521)

Oshawa: City Clerk's Dept., City Hall, 50 Centre St. S., Oshawa, Ont. L1H 3Z7 (416/725-7351)

Quebec City: City Clerk's Office, City Hall, Quebec, P.Q. G1R 4S9 (418/694-6074)

Regina: City Clerk's Office, City Hall, 2476 Victoria Ave., Box 1790, Regina, Sask. S4P 3C8 (306/569-7262)

Saint John: Deputy Municipal Electoral Officer, 11th floor, 15 Market Sq., Saint John, N.B. E2L 1E8 (506/658-2432)

St. John's: City Clerk, City Hall, New Gower St., St. John's, Nfld. A1C 5M2 (709/726-8820)

Saskatoon: City Clerk, City Hall, Saskatoon, Sask. S7K OJ5 (306/664-9242)

Sudbury: City Clerk's Office, 200 Brady St., Sudbury, Ont. P3E 4S5 (705/674-3141)

Thunder Bay: City Clerk's Office, City Hall, Donald St., Thunder Bay, Ont. P7E 5V3 (807/623-2711, ext. 2233)

Toronto: City Clerk's Dept., City Hall, Toronto, Ont. M5H 2N2 (416/367-7036)

Vancouver: City Clerk, City Hall, 453 W. 12th Ave., Vancouver, B.C. V5Y 1V4 (604/873-7266)

Victoria: City Manager's Office, No. 1 Centennial Sq., Victoria, B.C. V8W 1P6 (604/385-5711)

Windsor: City Clerk, City Hall, Windsor, Ont. N9A 6S1 (519/255-6211)

Winnipeg: City Clerk, Civic Centre, Winnipeg, Man. R3B 1B9 (204/946-0436)

ELECTRIC POWER

Energy Policy Sector, Dept. of Energy, Mines & Resources, 580 Booth St., Ottawa, Ont. K1A OE4 (613/995-9351)

National Energy Board, Trebla Bldg., 473 Albert St., Ottawa, Ont. K1A OE5 (613/593-6936)

Northern Canada Power Commission, 7909 51 Ave., Box 5700, Stn. L, Edmonton, Alta. T6C 4J8 (403/465-3377) (information re generation & supply of electric power north of 60)

Statistics Canada, Ottawa, Ont. K1A OT6 (613/996-3139)

Alta.: Energy Resources Conservation Board, 640 5th Ave. S.W., Calgary, Alta. T2P 3G4 (403/261-8311)

B.C.: B.C. Hydro & Power Authority, 970 Burrard St., Vancouver, B.C. V6Z 1Y3 (604/663-2660)

Man.: Manitoba Hydro, Box 815, Winnipeg, Man. R3C 2P4 (204/474-3311)

Winnipeg Hydro, 5th floor, Admin. Bldg., Civic Centre, Winnipeg, Man. R3B 1C1 (204/946-1100)

N.B.: Information Services Dept., N.B. Electric Power Commission, Box 2000, Fredericton, N.B. E3B 4X1 (506/453-4215)

Nfld.: Nfld. & Labrador Hydro, Box 9100, St. John's, Nfld. A1A 2X8 (709/737-1400)

N.S.: Corporate Relations Dept., N.S. Power Corp., Box 910, Halifax, N.S. B3J 2W5 (902/424-5561)

Ont.: Ontario Hydro, 700 University Ave., Toronto, Ont. M5G 1X6 (416/592-5111)

P.E.I.: Public Utilities Commission, 134 Kent St., Box 577, Charlottetown, P.E.I. C1A 7L1 (902/892-3501)

Que.: Dept. of Energy & Resources, Energy Branch, 8 rue Cook, Quebec, P.Q. G1R 5H2 (418/643-3724)

Hydro-Quebec, 75 ouest Dorchester, Montreal, P.Q. H2Z 1A4 (514/289-2211)

Sask.: Saskatchewan Power Corp., 2025 Victoria Ave., Regina, Sask. S4P OS1 (306/525-7650)

EMERGENCY MEASURES

Emergency Planning Canada, Ottawa, Ont. K1A OW6 (613/992-3322)

Alta.: Alberta Disaster Services, 10320 146 St., Edmonton, Alta. T5N 3A2 (403/427-2772)

B.C.: Provincial Emergency Program, Parliament Bldgs., Victoria, B.C. V8V 1X4 (604/387-5956)

Man.: Manitoba Emergency Measures Org., 15th floor, 405 Broadway Ave., Winnipeg, Man. R3C 3L6 (204/284-2070)

N.B.: Emergency Measures Org., Province of N.B., (15 Carleton St.), Box 6000, Fredericton, N.B. E3B 5H1 (506/453-2133)

Nfld.: Emergency Measures Org., Plymouth Bldg., Fort William, St. John's, Nfld. A1C 1K5 (709/737-3703, 722-2107)

N.S.: Emergency Measures Org. (N.S.), Box 1502, Halifax, N.S. B3J 2Y3 (902/424-5620)

Ont.: Emergency Planning Office, Ministry of the Solicitor General, 25 Grosvenor St., Toronto, Ont. M7A 2H3 (416/965-6932)

P.E.I.: Emergency Measures Org., (Environment & Consumer Services Division, Dept. of Community Affairs, 3 Queen St.), Box 2000, Charlottetown, P.E.I. C1A 7N8 (902/892-9174)

Que.: Bureau de la Protection Civile du Québec, 1200, rte de l'-Eglise, 2e étage, C.P. 10,000, Ste-Foy, Quebec, P.Q. G1V 4M1 (418/643-3256)

Sask.: Saskatchewan Emergency Measures Org., 1791 Rose St., Regina, Sask. S4P 3V7 (306/525-8121)

N.W.T.: Emergency Measures Chief, Government of the N.W.T., Yellowknife, N.W.T. X1A 2L9 (403/873-7554)

Yukon: Yukon Emergency Measures Org., Box 2703, Whitehorse, Y.T. Y1A 2C6 (403/667-5220)

EMPLOYMENT

See Index "Employment Centres" for lists of Regional Centres in Canada.

Canada Dept. of Labour, Communication Services Directorate, Ottawa, Ont. K1A OJ2 (819/994-2238)

Dept. of Employment & Immigration, Enquiries Officer, Public Affairs Division, Ottawa, Ont. K1A OJ9 (819/994-6313)

National Film Board, Box 6100, Montreal, P.Q. H3C 3H5 (514/333-3333)

Public Service Commission of Canada, Ottawa, Ont. K1A OM7 (613/996-5010)

Statistics Canada, Ottawa, Ont. K1A OT6 (613/995-9404)

Alta.: Employment Development, Manpower Services Division, Dept. of Advanced Education & Manpower, 6th floor, Devonian Bldg. East, 11160 Jasper Ave., Edmonton, Alta. T5K OL1 (403/427-4630)

Alberta Dept. of Labour, Labour Research Services, 5th floor, IBM Bldg., 10808 99 Ave., Edmonton, Alta. T5K OG5 (403/427-8531)

B.C.: Ministry of Labour, Research & Planning Branch, Parliament Bldgs., Victoria, B.C. V8V 1X4 (604/387-3445)

Man.: Employment Standards Division, Dept. of Labour & Manpower, 607 Norquay Bldg., 401 York Ave., Winnipeg, Man. R3C OP8 (204/944-3352)

N.B.: Labour Market Services Branch, Dept. of Labour & Manpower, Box 6000, Fredericton, N.B. E3B 5H1 (506/453-2722)

Nfld.: Dept. of Labour & Manpower, Confederation Bldg., St. John's, Nfld. A1C 5T7 (709/737-2729)

N.S.: Dept. of Labour & Manpower, Box 697, Halifax, N.S. B3J 2T8 (902/424-4313)

Ont.: Employment Standards Branch, Ministry of Labour, 3rd floor, 400 University Ave., Toronto, Ont. M7A 1V2 (416/965-5152)

P.E.I.: Employment Standards, Dept. of Labour, Box 2000, Charlottetown, P.E.I. C1A 7N8 (902/892-3416)

Que.: Dept. of Labour & Manpower, 425 St-Amable, Quebec, P.Q. G1R 4Z1 (418/643-3880)

Sask.: Dept. of Labour, 1914 Hamilton St., Regina, Sask. S4P 4V4 (306/565-2412)

ENERGY

Atomic Energy of Canada Ltd., 275 Slater St., Ottawa, Ont. K1A OS4 (613/237-3270)

Dept. of Energy, Mines & Resources, Energy Sector, 580 Booth St., Ottawa, Ont. K1A OE4 (613/995-9351)

Technology Information Division, CANMET, 555 Booth St., Ottawa, Ont. K1A OG1 (613/995-4029, 996-1330)

Energy Supplies Allocation Board, 3rd floor, 588 Booth St., Ottawa, Ont. K1A OE4 (613/996-3559)

National Energy Board, Trebla Bldg., 473 Albert St., Ottawa, Ont. K1A OE5 (613/593-6936)

National Film Board, Box 6100, Montreal, P.Q. H3C 3H5 (514/333-3333)

National Research Council of Canada, Energy Inquiry Centre, Ottawa, Ont. K1A 0S2 (613/993-3861)

Petroleum Compensation Board, 580 Booth St., Ottawa, Ont. K1A 0E4 (613/996-2611)

Statistics Canada, Ottawa, Ont. K1A OT6 (613/996-3139)

Alta.: Energy Resources Conservation Board, 640 5th Ave. S.W., Calgary, Alta. T2P 3G4 (403/261-8311)

Resource Information Services, Dept. of Energy & Natural Resources, Petroleum Plaza South, 7th floor, 9915 108 St., Edmonton, Alta. T5K 2C9 (403/427-7003)

B.C.: B.C. Utilities Commission, 1177 W. Hastings St., Vancouver, B.C. V6E 2L7 (604/689-1831)

Man.: Dept. of Energy & Mines, 156 Legislative Bldg., Winnipeg, Man. R3C OV8 (204/944-4601)

N.B.: N.B. Electric Power Commission, (527 King St.), Box 2000, Fredericton, N.B. E3B 4X1 (506/453-4444)

Nfld.: Energy Branch, Dept. of Mines & Energy, 95 Bonaventure Ave., Box 4750, St. John's, Nfld. A1C 5T7 (709/737-3159)

N.S.: Industrial & Information Services, N.S. Research Foundation Corp., Box 790, Dartmouth, N.S. B2Y 3Z7 (902/424-8670)

Dept. of Mines & Energy, 1649 Hollis St., Box 668, Halifax, N.S. B3J 2T3 (902/424-7680)

Ont.: Ontario Energy Board, 9th floor, 14 Carlton St., Toronto, Ont. M5B 1J2 (416/963-0812)

P.E.I.: Industry Branch, Dept. of Tourism, Industry & Energy, Box 2000, Charlottetown, P.E.I. C1A 7N8 (902/892-7411)

Que.: Energy Admin., Dept. of Energy & Resources, 1305, Chemin Ste-Foy, Quebec, P.Q. G1S 4N5 (418/643-3724)

Sask.: Saskatchewan Research Council, 30 Campus Dr., Saskatoon, Sask. S7N OX1 (306/664-5400)

ENVIRONMENT (see also Conservation)

Atmospheric Environment Service, 4905 Dufferin St., Downsview, Ont. M3H 5T4 (416/667-4551)

Dept. of Indian Affairs & Northern Development, Ottawa, Ont. K1A OH4 (819/997-9920)

Enquiry Centre, Environment Canada, Ottawa, Ont. K1A OH3 (613/997-2800)

National Film Board, Box 6100, Montreal, P.Q. H3C 3H5 (514/333-3333)

Alta.: Alberta Environment, Communications Branch, 9820 106 St., Edmonton, Alta. T5K 2J6 (403/427-6267)

Environment Council of Alberta, 2100 College Plaza, Tower 3, 8215 112 St., Edmonton, Alta. T6G 2M4 (403/427-5792)

B.C.: Ministry of Environment, Information Services Branch, 810 Blanshard St., Victoria, B.C. V8W 3E1 (604/387-5162)

Man.: Environmental Management Division, Dept. of Consumer & Corporate Affairs & Environment, Box 7, 139 Tuxedo Blvd., Winnipeg, Man. R3N 0H6 (204/895-5337)

Manitoba Environmental Council, Box 139, 139 Tuxedo Blvd., Winnipeg, Man. R3N 0H6 (204/895-5317)

N.B.: Information Programs, Dept. of the Environment, Box 6000, Fredericton, N.B. E3B 5H1 (506/453-3700)

Nfld.: Dept. of Environment, Elizabeth Towers, 100 Elizabeth Ave., St. John's, Nfld. A1B 1R9 (709/737-2559)

N.S.: Dept. of the Environment, Box 2107, Halifax, N.S. B3J 3B7 (902/424-8600)

Ont.: Information Services Branch, Ministry of the Environment, 135 St. Clair Ave. W., Toronto, Ont. M4V 1P5 (416/965-1658)

The Conservation Council of Ontario, 6th floor, 45 Charles St. E., Toronto, Ont. M4Y 1S2

P.E.I.: Environmental & Consumer Services, Dept. of Community Affairs, Box 2000, Charlottetown, P.E.I. C1A 7N8 (902/892-9174)

Que.: Information Service, Dept. of Environment, 2360 Chemin Ste-Foy, Quebec, P.Q. G1V 4H2 (418/643-2795)

Sask.: Dept. of the Environment, 5th floor, 1855 Victoria Ave., Regina, Sask. S4P 3V5 (306/565-6113)

N.W.T.: Chief, Division of Environmental Services & Science, Dept. of Renewable Resources, Government of N.W.T., Yellowknife, N.W.T. X1A 2L9 (403/873-7554)

ESKIMOS

see Inuit

EXHIBITIONS (Agricultural & Industrial)

Dept of Agriculture Canada, Animal Production Division, Sir John Carling Bldg., Ottawa, Ont. K1A OC5 (613/995-5880)

Dept. of Industry, Trade & Commerce, Trade Commissioner Service & International Marketing, 235 Queen St., Ottawa, Ont. K1A OH5 (613/996-7065)

Dept. of Labour, A/V Section, Ottawa, Ont. K1A OJ2 (613/994-2238)

Dept. of National Defence, Directorate of Exhibitions & Displays, National Defence Headquarters, Ottawa, Ont. K1A OK2 (819/994-0095)

Canadian Government Expositions Centre, Dept. of Supply & Services, 440 Coventry Rd., Ottawa, Ont. K1A OT1 (613/993-9732)

National Aeronautical Collection, Ottawa, Ont. K1A OM8 (613/998-4566)

National Film Board, Box 6100, Montreal, P.Q. H3C 3H5 (514/333-3333)

National Museum of Science & Technology, Ottawa, Ont. K1A OM8 (613/998-4566)

Alta.: Edmonton Exhibition Association, Edmonton Northlands, (Box 1480) Edmonton, Alta. T5J 2N5 (403/471-7210)

Public Affairs Bureau, 9th floor, Petroleum Plaza, 9945 108 St., Edmonton, Alta. T5K 2G6 (403/427-2754)

B.C.: Ministry of Industry & Small Business Development, #315, 800 Hornby St., Vancouver, B.C. V6Z 2C5 (604/689-4411)

Ministry of Agriculture & Food, Parliament Bldgs., Victoria, B.C. V8W 2Z7 (604/387-5121)

Pacific National Exhibition, Exhibition Park, Vancouver, B.C. V5K 4W3 (604/253-2311)

Man.: Dept. of Agriculture, Production Division, Agricultural Training Branch, #810, 401 York Ave., Winnipeg, Man. R3C 0V8 (204/944-4521)

Promotion & Information Services Branch, Dept. of Economic Development & Tourism, 5th floor, 155 Carlton St., Winnipeg, Man. R3C 3H8 (204/944-2474)

N.B.: Dept. of Commerce & Development, Box 6000, Fredericton, N.B. E3B 5H1 (506/453-2965)

Promotion Branch, Dept. of Tourism, Box 12345, Fredericton, N.B. E3B 5C3 (506/453-2377)

N.B. Information Service, Box 6000, Fredericton, N.B. E3B 5H1 (506/453-2240)

Nfld.: Dept. of Rural, Agricultural & Northern Development, Prov. Agriculture Bldg., Brookfield Rd., Mount Pearl, Nfld. (709/737-3840)

Dept. of Development, Promotion & Development Division, Box 4750, St. John's, Nfld. A1C 5T7 (709/737-2781)

N.S.: Dept. of Agriculture & Marketing, Box 190, Halifax, N.S. B3J 2M4 (902/424-5719)

Information Division, Dept. of Government Services, Box 54, Halifax, N.S. B3J 2L4 (902/424-7540)

Ont.: Most Ministries organize exhibitions. For specific information contact Special Projects Officer, Property Management Branch, Ministry of Government Services, 8th floor, Ferguson Block, Queen's Park, Toronto, Ont. M7A 1N3 (416/965-2075)

Agricultural & Horticultural Societies Branch, Ministry of Agriculture & Food, 801 Bay St., Toronto, Ont. M7A 2B2 (416/965-1091) (fall fairs info.)

P.E.I.: Dept. of Agriculture & Forestry, Box 1600, Charlottetown, P.E.I. C1A 7N3 (902/892-5465)

Market Development Centre, Box 1510, Charlottetown, P.E.I. C1A 7N3 (902/892-4165)

Que.: Dept. of Agriculture, Fisheries & Food, Communications Division, 200A Chemin Ste-Foy, Quebec, P.Q. G1R 4X6 (418/643-2673)

Communications Division, Dept. of Industry, Trade & Tourism, 710, Place d'Youville, Quebec, P.Q. G1R 4Y4 (418/643-5070)

Sask.: Dept. of Agriculture, Communications, Walter Scott Bldg., Regina, Sask. S4S OB1 (306/565-5149)

Dept. of Industry & Commerce, 3rd floor, 2121 Saskatchewan Dr., Regina, Sask. S4P 3V7 (306/565-2232)

EXPLOSIVES

Dept. of Energy, Mines & Resources, Explosives Branch, 580 Booth St., Ottawa, Ont. K1A OE4 (613/593-7211)

EXPORTS

Dept. of Industry, Trade & Commerce, Business Centre, 235 Queen St., Ottawa, Ont. K1A OH5 (613/995-5771)

Export Development Corp., 110 O'Connor St., Box 655, Ottawa, Ont. K1P 5T9 (613/237-2570)

Statistics Canada, Ottawa, Ont. K1A OT6 (613/995-6305)

Alta.: Trade Development, Dept. of Economic Development, 11th floor, 10909 Jasper Ave., Edmonton, Alta. T5J 3M8 (403/427-4809)

International Marketing, Dept. of Agriculture, 9718 107 St., Edmonton, Alta. T5K 2C8 (403/427-4241)

B.C.: Ministry of Industry & Small Business Development, #315, 800 Hornby St., Vancouver, B.C. V6Z 2C5 (604/689-4411)

Man.: Dept. of Economic Development, Market Development, 155 Carlton St., #1 Lakeview Sq., Winnipeg, Man. R3C 3H8 (204/944-2466)

N.B.: Dept. of Commerce & Development, Box 6000, Fredericton, N.B. E3B 5H1 (506/453-2875)

N.S.: Dept. of Development, Market Development Centre, Box 519, Halifax, N.S. B3J 2R7 (902/424-8921)

Ont.: Ministry of Industry & Tourism, Trade Policy Branch, Hearst Block, 900 Bay St., Toronto, Ont. M7A 2E6 (416/965-4347)

P.E.I.: Market Development Centre, Box 1510, Charlottetown, P.E.I. C1A 7N3 (902/892-4165)

Que.: Dept. of Industry, Trade & Tourism, 1, Place Ville Marie, 23rd floor, Montreal, P.Q. H3B 3M6 (514/873-3548); International Services: Office québécoise du commerce extérieur (873-3515)

Sask.: Dept. of Industry & Commerce, 3rd floor, 2121 Saskatchewan Dr., Regina, Sask. S4P 3V7 (306/565-2232)

EXPROPRIATION

Dept. of Justice, Property & Commercial Law Section, Ottawa, Ont. K1A OH8 (613/996-1555)

Dept. of National Defence, Ottawa, Ont. K1A OK2 (613/996-2353)

Public Works Canada, Public Relations & Information Services, Sir Charles Tupper Bldg., Ottawa, Ont. K1A OM2 (613/998-9560)

Alta.: Surface Rights Board, 16th floor, Century Place, 9803 102A Ave., Edmonton, Alta. T5J 3A3 (403/427-2444); and 6th floor, Standard Life Bldg., 639 5th Ave. S.W., Calgary, Alta. T2P 0M9 (403/261-6467)

B.C.: Ministry of Attorney General, Parliament Bldgs., Victoria, B.C. V8V 1X4 (604/384-4434)

Man.: Land Acquisition Branch, 12th floor, Woodsworth Bldg., 405 Broadway, Winnipeg, Man. R3C 3L6 (204/944-2908)

N.B.: Dept. of Supply & Services, Box 6000, Fredericton, N.B. E3B 5H1 (506/453-2998)

Nfld.: Dept. of Public Works & Services, Expropriation Division, Confederation Bldg., Box 4750, St. John's, Nfld. A1C 5T7 (709/737-3356)

N.S.: Dept. of Attorney General, Box 7, Halifax, N.S. B3J 2L6 (902/424-4222)

Expropriations Compensation Board, Box 2071, Halifax, N.S. B3J 2Z1 (902/424-8982)

Ont.: Ontario Board of Negotiation, Ste. 1800, 439 University Ave., Toronto, Ont. M5G 1Y8 (416/965-2867)

Land Compensation Board, 3rd floor, 10 King St. E., Toronto, Ont. M5C 1C3 (416/965-1012)

P.E.I.: Dept. of Highways & Public Works, Box 2000, Charlottetown, P.E.I. C1A 7N8 (902/892-7431)

Que.: Direction générale de l'exploitation des immeubles, Ministère des Travaux publics et de l'Approvisionnement, (Public Works & Supply), 475, rue St-Amable, 5e étage, Québec, P.Q. G1R 4X9 (418/643-2259)

Sask.: Public & Private Rights Board, Room 501, 2240 Albert St., Regina, Sask. S4P 3V7 (306/565-4071)

Calgary: City of Calgary Law Dept., Box 2100, Calgary, Alta. T2P 2M5 (403/268-2441)

Halifax: Development Dept., City Hall, Box 1749, Halifax, N.S. B3J 3A5 (902/426-6533)

Hamilton: City Clerk's Dept., City Hall, 71 Main St. W., Hamilton, Ont. L8N 3T4 (416/527-0241)

LaSalle: City Clerk, 13 Strathyre Ave., LaSalle, P.Q. H8R 3P6 (514/366-7110)

London: Legal Dept., City Hall, 300 Dufferin Ave., Box 5035, London, Ont. N6A 4L9 (519/679-4940)

Mississauga: Property Section, City Clerk's Dept., 1 City Centre Dr., Mississauga, Ont. L5B 1M2 (416/279-7600)

Montreal: Service des Immeubles, 507 Place d'Armes, Ste. 300, Montreal, P.Q. H2Y 2W8 (514/872-3604)

Quebec City: Service des travaux publics, Hôtel de Ville, Quebec, P.Q. G1R 4S9 (418/694-6384)

Regina: City Manager, 2476 Victoria Ave., Regina, Sask. (306/569-7311)
City Solicitor, City Hall, Box 1790, Regina, Sask. S4P 3C8 (306/569-7472)

Saint John: Legal Dept., Box 1971/Market Sq., Saint John, N.B. E2L 4L1 (506/658-2860)

Saskatoon: Office of the City Solicitor, City Hall, Saskatoon, Sask. S7K OJ5 (306/644-9270)

Thunder Bay: Community Planning & Development Division, City Hall, Donald St., Thunder Bay, Ont. P7E 5V3 (807/623-2711)

Toronto (City): City Solicitor, City Legal Dept., City Hall, Toronto, Ont. M5H 2N2 (416/367-7341)

Toronto (Metro): Metropolitan Solicitor, City Hall, Toronto, Ont. M5H 2N1 (416/367-8040)

Vancouver: Director of Legal Services, City Hall, 453 W. 12th Ave., Vancouver, B.C. V5Y 1V4 (604/873-7011)

Victoria: City Solicitor, No. 1 Centennial Sq., Victoria, B.C. V8W 1P6 (604/385-5711)

Windsor: City Property Dept., 68 Chatham St. E., Windsor, Ont. N9A 6S1 (519/255-6400)

Winnipeg: Director of Land Surveys & Real Estate, 4th floor, 10 Fort St., Winnipeg, Man. R3C 1C4 (204/985-5241)
City Solicitor, Law Dept., Council Bldg., City Hall, Winnipeg, Man. R3B 1B9 (204/946-0285)

EXTERNAL AFFAIRS

Dept. of External Affairs, Domestic Information Programs Division, Sussex Dr., Ottawa, Ont. K1A OG2 (613/593-7064)

Canadian International Development Agency, Public Affairs Division, 200 Promenade du Portage, Hull (mailing: Ottawa, Ont. K1A 0G4) (819/997-6100)

Dept. of Labour, Policy Co-ordination & Liaison Branch, Ottawa, Ont. K1A OJ2 (819/997-1333)

Alta.: Dept. of Federal & Intergovernmental Affairs, 14th floor, South Tower, 10030 107 St., Edmonton, Alta. T5J 3E4 (403/427-2611)

Que.: Ministère des Affaires Intergouvernementales, Direction générale des Affaires Internationales, Edifice H, 1225, Place Georges V, Quebec, P.Q. G1R 4Z7 (418/643-7278)

FAMILY ALLOWANCES

Dept. of National Health & Welfare, Income Security Programs Branch, Brooke Claxton Bldg., Tunney's Pasture, Ottawa, Ont. K1A 0L4 (613/992-5865)

See "Welfare" this table, for provincial Depts. administering Family Benefits.

Que.: Régie des rentes du Québec, Direction des allocations familiales du Québec, Box 5200, Quebec, P.Q. G1K 7S9 (418/643-3430)

FAMILY COUNSELLING

see Matrimonial

FAMILY PLANNING

Family Planning Division, Health Services & Promotion Branch, Dept. of National Health & Welfare, Jeanne Mance Bldg., Tunney's Pasture, Ottawa, Ont. K1A 1B4 (613/992-3609)

Alta.: Family Planning Services, Dept. of Social Services & Community Health, 10030 107 St., Edmonton, Alta. T5J 3E4 (403/427-4579)

B.C.: Health Education, Ministry of Health, 1515 Blanshard St., Victoria, B.C. V8W 3C8 (604/387-5257)

Man.: Medical-Public Health Branch, Dept. of Health, 831 Portage Ave., Winnipeg, Man. R3G ON6 (204/775-9761)

N.B.: Refer to: Planned Parenthood N.B., Victoria Health Centre, 43 Brunswick St., Fredericton, N.B. E3B 1G5 (506/454-1808)

Nfld.: Refer to: Planned Parenthood Nfld./Labrador, 21 Factory Lane, St. John's, Nfld. A1C 3J8 (709/753-7333)

N.S.: Refer to: Planned Parenthood of N.S., 1815 Hollis St., Halifax, N.S. B3J 1W3 (902/423-2090)

Ont.: Family Health, Ministry of Health, 15 Overlea Blvd., 6th floor, Toronto, Ont. M4H 1A9 (416/963-1098)

P.E.I.: Dept. of Health & Social Services, Health Branch, Box 2000, Charlottetown, P.E.I. C1A 7P1 (902/892-5471)

Que.: Social Affairs Dept., Planification Division, 1075 Chemin Ste-Foy, 7th floor, Quebec, P.Q. G1S 2M1 (418/643-3313)

Sask.: Community Services, Dept. of Health, 3475 Albert St., Regina, Sask. S4S 6X6 (306/565-3086)

Brampton: Peel Regional Health Unit, Family Planning Clinic, 10 Peel Centre Dr., 2nd floor, Brampton, Ont. L6T 4B9 (416/791-0740)

Calgary: Family Planning Clinic (Local Board of Health), 237 7 Ave. S.E., Box 2100, Calgary, Alta. T2P 2M5 (403/268-2772)

Guelph: Family Planning Birth Control Centre, 21 Quebec St., Guelph, Ont. N1H 2T1 (519/821-0637)

Halifax: Refer to: Planned Parenthood of Halifax Dartmouth, 5239 Young St., Halifax, N.S. B3K 5L4 (902/455-9656)

Hamilton: Refer to: Planned Parenthood Centre, 2nd floor, 4 Catharine St. N., Hamilton, Ont. L8R 1H8 (416/528-3009, 528-7343)

London: Family & Children's Services of London & Middlesex, Box 848, Stn. B, London, Ont. N6A 4Z5 (519/434-8461)

Mississauga: Peel Regional Health Unit, Family Planning Clinic, 2444 Hunrontario St., 2nd floor, Mississauga, Ont. L5B 2V1 (416/270-0587, 270-0662)

Montreal: Refer to: L'Association pour le Planning des Naissances de Montréal, 336 Sherbrooke E., Montreal, P.Q. H2X 1E6 (514/844-3349)

Saskatoon: Catholic Family Services, 635 Main St., Saskatoon, Sask. S7H 0J8 (306/244-7773, or 244-7787)

Thunder Bay: Refer to: Family Planning & Birth Control, Northwestern Ont. Women's Centre, 316 Bay St., Thunder Bay, Ont. P7B 1S1 (807/345-7802)

Toronto: Dept. of Public Health, Family Planning Services, 37 Spadina Rd., Toronto, Ont. M5R 2S9 (416/961-8459)

Vancouver: City Health Dept., 1060 W. 8th Ave., Vancouver, B.C. V6H 1C4 (604/736-2033)

Windsor: Metro Windsor-Essex County Health Unit, 1550 Ouellette Ave., Windsor, Ont. N8X 1K7 (519/258-2146)

Winnipeg: Medical Health Officer, 280 William Ave., Winnipeg, Man. R3B 0R1 (204/946-0122)

FEDERAL-PROVINCIAL RELATIONS

Federal Provincial Relations Office, 59 Sparks St., Ottawa, Ont. K1A OA3 (613/996-8954)

Dept. of Agriculture, Regional Development & International Affairs Branch, Ottawa, Ont. K1A 0C5 (613/995-8195)

Dept. of Finance, Federal-Provincial Relations Division, Ottawa, Ont. K1A OG5 (613/996-1432)

Dept. of National Health & Welfare, Intergovernmental & International Affairs Branch, Ottawa, Ont. K1A 0K9 (613/593-5210)

Alta.: Federal & Intergovernmental Affairs, 14th floor, 10030 107th St., South Tower, Edmonton, Alta. T5J 3E4 (403/427-2611)

B.C.: Office of the Premier, Parliament Bldgs., Victoria, B.C. V8V 1X4 (604/387-6202)

Man.: Policy Co-ordination Group, Premier's Office, Room 138, 450 Broadway, Winnipeg, Man. R3C 0V8 (204/944-3931)

Federal Provincial Relations & Research Division, Dept. of Finance, Room 4, 450 Broadway, Winnipeg, Man. R3C OV8 (204/944-3757)

Cultural Development Branch, Dept. of Cultural Affairs & Historical Resources, 3rd floor, 200 Vaughan St., Winnipeg, Man. R3C 0V8 (204/944-3753)

N.B.: Deputy Secretary to the Cabinet for Policy & Priorities, Cabinet Secretariat, Box 6000, Fredericton, N.B. E3B 5H1 (506/453-2579)

Nfld.: Intergovernmental Affairs Secretariat, Confederation Bldg., St. John's, Nfld. A1C 5T7 (709/737-2848)

N.S.: Executive Director, Intergovernmental Affairs Office, 1690 Hollis St., Halifax, N.S. B3J 3J9 (902/424-4263)

Federal-Provincial Taxation & Fiscal Relations Division, Dept. of Finance, Box 187, Halifax, N.S. B3J 2N3 (902/424-4168)

Ont.: Federal-Provincial & Intergovernmental Affairs Secretariat, Ministry of Intergovernmental Affairs, 5th floor, Mowat Block, Queen's Park, Toronto, Ont. M7A 1C2 (416/965-2927)

P.E.I.: Asst. Secretary to the Cabinet (Intergovernmental Affairs), Executive Council, Box 2000, Charlottetown, P.E.I. C1A 7N8 (902/892-4296)

Que.: Ministère des Affaires intergouvernementales, Direction générale des Affaires canadiennes, Edifice H, 1225, place Georges V, Quebec, P.Q. G1R 4Z7 (418/643-4564)

Sask.: Intergovernmental Affairs Dept., Walter Scott Bldg., Regina, Sask. S4S OB1 (306/565-6355)

FIELD CROPS

Information Services, Agriculture Canada, Ottawa, Ont. K1A OC7 (613/995-8963)

Dept. of Industry, Trade & Commerce, Agriculture, Fisheries & Food Products Branch, Agricultural Products Division, 235 Queen St., Ottawa, Ont. K1A OH5 (613/995-8107)

Prairie Regional Laboratory, National Research Council of Canada, Saskatoon, Sask. S7N OW9 (306/665-5248)

Statistics Canada, Ottawa, Ont. K1A OT6 (613/995-4877)

Alta.: Field Crops Branch, Plant Industry Division, Alta. Dept. of Agriculture, Bag Service #47, 5718 56 Ave., Lacombe, Alta. TOC 1SO (403/423-4214, 782-4641)

B.C.: Field Crops Branch, Ministry of Agriculture, Parliament Bldgs., Victoria, B.C. V8W 2Z7 (604/387-5121) (for Horticultural crops refer to Horticultural Branch)

Man.: Crops Section, Soils & Crops Branch, Dept. of Agriculture, 908 Norquay Bldg., Winnipeg, Man. R3C OP8 (204/944-3820)

N.B.: Dept. of Agriculture & Rural Development, Box 6000, Fredericton, N.B. E3B 5H1 (506/453-2666)

Nfld.: Dept. of Rural, Agricultural & Northern Development, Prov. Agriculture Bldg., Brookfield Rd., Mount Pearl, Nfld. (709/737-3840)

N.S.: Soils & Crops Branch, N.S. Dept. of Agriculture & Marketing, Box 550, Truro, N.S. B2N 5E3 (902/895-1571)

Ont.: Soils & Crops Branch, Ont. Ministry of Agriculture & Food, Queen's Park, Toronto, Ont. M7A 2B2 (416/965-1081)

P.E.I.: Crops & Engineering Section, Field Services Branch, Dept. of Agriculture & Forestry, Box 1600, Charlottetown, P.E.I. C1A 7N3 (902/892-5465)

Que.: Productions vegetales, Dept. of Agriculture & Food, 200A Chemin Ste-Foy, Quebec, P.Q. G1R 4X6 (418/643-1371)

Sask.: Plant Industry Branch, Dept. of Agriculture, Walter Scott Bldg., Regina, Sask. S4S OB1 (306/565-4660)

FILM CLASSIFICATION

see Censorship

FILM LIBRARIES & FILM PRODUCTION

Canada Post Office, Confederation Heights, Ottawa, Ont. K1A OB1 (613/998-4463)

Canadian Broadcasting Corp.: English Services Division, Box 500, Stn. A, Toronto, Ont. M5W 1E6 (416/925-3311); French Services Division, Box 6000, Montreal, P.Q. H3C 3A8 (514/285-3211)

Canadian Centre for Films on Art, 75 Albert St., Ste. B-20, Ottawa, Ont. K1P 5E7 (613/232-2495)

Canadian Film Development Corp., C.P. 71, Tour de la bourse, #2220, Montreal, P.Q. H4Z 1A8 (514/283-6363); #602, 111 Avenue Rd., Toronto, Ont. M5R 3J8 (416/966-6436); #1500, 1176 W. Georgia St., Vancouver, B.C. V6E 4A2

Canadian Film Institute, 75 Albert St., Ste. 1105, Ottawa, Ont. K1P 5E7 (613/232-2495)

Canada Mtge. & Housing Corp., Montreal Rd., Ottawa, Ont. K1A OP7 (613/748-2604)

Dept. of Industry, Trade & Commerce, Public Information Directorate, 235 Queen St., Ottawa, Ont. K1A OH5 (613/995-7274)

Dept. of National Health & Welfare, Audio Visual Library, Ottawa, Ont. K1A OK9 (613/995-2934)

Dept. of Labour, Ottawa, Ont. K1A OJ2 (819/994-2238)

National Film Board, Box 6100, Montreal, P.Q. H3C 3H5 (514/333-3333)

National Film Library of Canada, 75 Albert St., Ste. B-20, Ottawa, Ont. K1P 5E7 (613/232-2495)

National Museum of Man, Media & Public Relations, Ottawa, Ont. K1A OM8 (613/993-0881)

National Science Film Library, Canadian Film Institute, 75 Albert St., Ste. B-20, Ottawa, Ont. K1P 5E7 (613/232-2495)

Statistics Canada, Ottawa, Ont. K1A OT6 (613/996-9301)

Alta.: Public Affairs Bureau, 11510 Kingsway Ave., Edmonton, Alta. T5G 2Y5 (403/427-4381)

B.C.: Special Services Branch, Ministry of Tourism, 1117 Wharf St., Victoria, B.C. V8W 2Z2 (604/387-6490)

Man.: Citizens' Inquiry Service, Room 511, 401 York Ave., Winnipeg, Man. R3C OP8 (204/944-3744) Toll free in Manitoba 1-800-282-8060

School Film Services, Room 214A, 1181 Portage Ave., Winnipeg, Man. R3G OT3 (204/786-0222)

Ont.: Ministry of Industry & Tourism Films, c/o City Films, 376 Wellington St. W., Toronto, Ont. M5V 1E3 (416/869-1633)

Que.: Ministère des Communications, Direction des Communications, 1037 de la Chevrotière, Edifice G, Rez de chaussée, Bloc 4, Québec, P.Q. G1R 4Y7 (418/643-3162)

Dept. of Cultural Affairs, 225 Grande Alleé est, Québec, P.Q. G1R 5G5 (418/643-2183)

Sask.: SASKMEDIA Corp., 1112 Winnipeg St., Box 7120, Regina, Sask. S4P 3S7 (306/565-5100)

Yukon: Audio-visual Services, Dept. of Library & Information Resources, Box 2703, Whitehorse, Y.T. Y1A 2C6 (403/667-5240)

FINANCE

Bank of Canada, Ottawa, Ont. K1A OG9 (613/563-8111)

Dept. of Finance, Economic Programs & Government Finance Branch, Place Bell Canada, Ottawa, Ont. K1A OG5 (613/992-1526)

Federal Business Development Bank, 901 Victoria Sq., Montreal, P.Q. H3C 3C3 (514/283-5904) (capital financing, equity financing & management services)

Treasury Board, Place Bell Canada, Ottawa, Ont. K1A OR5 (613/995-6141)

Statistics Canada, Ottawa, Ont. K1A OT6 (613/995-9771)

Alta.: Deputy Provincial Treasurer, 434 Terrace Bldg., Edmonton, Alta. T5K 2C3 (403/427-4106)

B.C.: Economics & Policy Division, Ministry of Finance, Parliament Bldgs., Victoria, B.C. V8V 1X4 (604/387-1471)

Man.: Dept. of Finance, 109 Legislative Bldg., Winnipeg, Man. R3C OV8 (204/944-3754)

N.B.: Dept. of Finance, Box 6000, Fredericton, N.B. E3B 5H1 (506/453-2534)

Nfld.: Director of Admin., Dept. of Finance, Confederation Bldg., St. John's, Nfld. A1C 5T7 (709/737-2924)

N.S.: Admin. Asst. to Deputy, Dept. of Finance, Box 187, Halifax, N.S. B3J 2N3 (902/424-5554)

Ont.: Taxation & Fiscal Policy Branch, Ministry of Treasury & Economics, Queen's Park, Toronto, Ont. M7A 1Y7 (416/965-5058)

P.E.I.: Dept. of Finance, Box 2000, Charlottetown, P.E.I. C1A 7N8 (902/894-8112)

Que.: Quebec Bureau of Statistics, Finance Service, Dept. of Industry, Trade & Tourism, 117 St-André, Quebec, P.Q. G1K 3Y3 (418/643-5020)
Dept. of Finance, Bldg. C, 1025 St-Augustin St., Quebec, P.Q. G1R 4Z6 (418/643-4426)
Sask.: Dept. of Finance, Budget Bureau, Legislative Bldgs., Regina, Sask. S4S 0B3 (306/565-6780)
Crown Investments Corp. of Saskatchewan, Ste. 300, 2400 College Ave., Regina, Sask. S4P 1C8 (306/565-6851)

FINE ARTS

see Arts

FIRE PREVENTION

Canadian Transport Commission, Railway Transport Committee, Ottawa, Ont. K1A 0N9 (819/997-7046)
Dept. of Public Works Canada, Dominion Fire Commr., Sir Charles Tupper Bldg., Riverside & Heron, Ottawa, Ont. K1A 0M2 (613/998-4617)
Canadian Forestry Service, Environment Canada, Ottawa, Ont. K1A 1G5 (613/997-2800)
National Film Board, Box 6100, Montreal, P.Q. H3C 3H5 (514/333-3333)
National Research Council of Canada, Division of Building Research, Montreal Rd., Ottawa, Ont. K1A 0R6 (613/993-2204)

Alta.: Fire Prevention Branch, Dept. of Labour, 701 IBM Bldg., 10808 99 Ave., Edmonton, Alta. T5K 0G2 (403/427-8392)
B.C.: Fire Commissioner's Office, #1, 2780 E. Broadway, Vancouver, B.C. V5M 1Y8 (604/251-3131)
Man.: Dept. of Natural Resources, Forest Branch, #300, 500 Kenaston Blvd., Winnipeg, Man. (204/477-4605)
Fire Commr.'s Office, Dept. of Labour & Manpower, 510 Norquay Bldg., 401 York Ave., Winnipeg, Man. R3C 0V8 (204/944-3322)
N.B.: N.B. Fire Marshal, Dept. of Labour & Manpower, Box 6000, Fredericton, N.B. E3B 5HI (506/453-2134)
Director, Forest Management Branch, Dept. of Natural Resources, 212 Queen St., Fredericton, N.B. E3B 1A8 (506/453-2530)
Nfld.: Fire Commr's. Office, Pleasantville Fire Stn., St. John's, Nfld. A1C 5T7 (709/726-1050)
Dept. of Forestry Resources & Lands, Director of Protection, Confederation Bldg., St. John's, Nfld. A1C 5T7 (709/737-3752)
N.S.: N.S. Provincial Fire Marshal, Box 697, Halifax, N.S. B3J 2T8 (902/424-5721)
Ont.: Office of the Fire Marshal, 590 Keele St., Toronto, Ont. M6N 4X2 (416/965-4871)
Aviation & Fire Management Centre, Ministry of Natural Resources, Box 310, (55 Church St.), Sault Ste. Marie, Ont. P6A 5L8 (705/942-1800)
P.E.I.: Office of Provincial Fire Marshal, Dept. of Community Affairs, Box 2000, Charlottetown, P.E.I. C1A 7N8 (902/892-3561)
Que.: Service de la Protection des Forets Contre le feu, Direction de la Conservation, Ministère de l'Energie et des Ressources, 175 St-Jean St., Quebec, P.Q. G1R 1N4 (418/643-7735)
Director General of Fire Prevention, Dept. of Municipal Affairs, 1279 Charest ouest, Quebec, P.Q. G1N 4K7 (418/643-2014)
Sask.: Forest Protection Branch, Dept. of Tourism & Renewable Resources, Box 3003, Prince Albert, Sask. S6V 6G1 (306/922-2298)
Fire Commr., Fire Safety Unit, Occupational Health & Safety Division, Dept. of Labour, 1150 Rose St., Regina, Sask. S4P 3V7 (306/565-4516)
Yukon: Fire Marshal, Dept. of Municipal & Community Affairs, Box 2703, Whitehorse, Y.T. Y1A 2C6 (403/667-5217)

Montreal: Fire Dept., 4040, ave du Parc, Montreal, P.Q. H2W 1S8 (514/872-3763)
Toronto: City of Toronto Fire Prevention Bureau, City Hall, Toronto, Ont. M5H 2N2 (416/367-7695)

FISH & GAME REGULATIONS

see Wildlife

FISHERIES

See also Oceanography
Dept. of Industry, Trade & Commerce, Agriculture, Fisheries & Food Products Branch, Fisheries & Fish Products Division, 235 Queen St., Ottawa, Ont. K1A 0H5 (613/995-8107)
Dept. of Fisheries & Oceans, Scientific Information & Publications Branch, 240 Sparks St., Ottawa, Ont. K1A 0E6 (613/996-2372)
International North Pacific Fisheries Commission, 6640 N.W. Marine Dr., Vancouver, B.C. V6T 1X2 (604/228-1128)
International Pacific Salmon Fisheries Commission, Box 30, New Westminster, B.C. V3L 4X9 (604/521-3771)
Freshwater Fish Marketing Corp., 1199 Plessis Rd., Winnipeg, Man. R2C 3L4 (204/222-7301)
National Film Board, Box 6100, Montreal, P.Q. H3C 3H5 (514/333-3333)
National Museum of Natural Sciences, Ottawa, Ont. K1A 0M8 (613/996-3102) (Fishes & General Aquatic Life)
Northwest Atlantic Fisheries Org., Box 638, Dartmouth, N.S. B2Y 3Y9 (902/469-9105)
Parks Canada, Information Division, Ottawa, Ont. K1A 1G2 (819/997-0088)
Statistics Canada, Ottawa, Ont. K1A 0T6 (613/992-8006)

Alta.: Fish & Wildlife Division, Dept. of Energy & Natural Resources, 8th floor, South Tower, Petroleum Plaza, 9915 108 St., Edmonton, Alta. T5K 2C9 (403/427-6729)
B.C.: Ministry of Environment, Parliament Bldgs., Victoria, B.C. V8V 1X5 (604/387-1961)
Man.: Fisheries Branch, Dept. of Natural Resources, Box 20, 1495 St. James St., Winnipeg, Man. R3H 0W9 (204/786-9543)
N.B.: Dept. of Fisheries, Box 6000, Fredericton, N.B. E3B 5H1 (506/453-2251)
Nfld.: Dept. of Fisheries, 5th floor, Atlantic Place, Water St., St. John's, Nfld. A1C 5T7 (709/737-3727)
N.S.: Dept. of Fisheries, Box 2223, Halifax, N.S. B3J 3C4 (902/424-4560)
Ont.: Fisheries Branch, Outdoor Recreation, Ministry of Natural Resources, Queen's Park, Toronto, Ont. M7A 1W3 (416/965-7883)
P.E.I.: Dept. of Fisheries, Box 2000, Charlottetown, P.E.I. C1A 7N8 (902/892-3493)
Que.: Dept. of Recreation, Fish & Game, 150 est, boul. St-Cyrille, Quebec, P.Q. G1R 4Y3 (418/643-2464)
Fisheries Branch, Dept. of Industry, Trade & Tourism, 1090, Raymond Casgrain, Quebec, P.Q. G1S 2E4 (418/643-1869)
Dept. of Agriculture, Fisheries & Food, 2, Pomeraye St., Gaspé, P.Q. G0C 1R0 (418/368-3480)
Sask.: Fisheries Branch, Dept. of Tourism & Renewable Resources, Room 202, Provincial Office Bldg., Prince Albert Sask. S6V 1B5 (306/764-1541)
Yukon: District Supervisor, Dept. of Fisheries & Oceans, 122 Industrial Rd., Whitehorse, Y.T. Y1A 2T9 (403/667-2235)
N.W.T.: Freshwater Institute, Dept. of Fisheries & Oceans, 501 University Cres., Winnipeg, Man. R3T 2N6

FITNESS

see Recreation

FOOD

(*see also* Nutrition)
Dept. of Agriculture Canada, Food Advisory Division, Sir John Carling Bldg., Ottawa, Ont. K1A 0C5 (613/995-5880) (buying, preparation and preservation of agricultural foods)
Consumer Products Branch, Bureau of Consumer Affairs, Dept. of Consumer & Corporate Affairs Canada, Place du Portage, Phase 1, Ottawa/Hull, K1A 0C9 (819/997-1591) (food labelling, packaging, advertising and grading)
Dept. of Fisheries & Oceans, Ottawa, Ont. K1A 0E6 (613/995-2041)

Dept. of Industry, Trade & Commerce, Agriculture, Fisheries & Food Branch, 235 Queen St., Ottawa, Ont. K1A OH5 (613/995-8107)

National Film Board, Box 6100, Montreal, P.Q. H3C 3H5 (514/333-3333)

FOREIGN AFFAIRS

see External Affairs

FOREIGN EXCHANGE

Bank of Canada, Ottawa, Ont. K1A OG9 (613/563-8111)

FOREST RESOURCES

Environment Canada, Information Branch, Ottawa, Ont. K1A OH3 (613/997-2800)

Regional Information Officers:

Nfld. Forest Research Centre, Box 6028, Bldg. 304, Pleasantville, St. John's, Nfld. A1C 5X8 (709/737-4672)

Maritimes Forest Research Centre, Box 4000, Fredericton, N.B. E3B 5P7 (506/452-3541)

Laurentian Forest Research Centre, 1080 du Vallon Rd., Ste-Foy, P.Q. G1V 4C7 (418/694-4428)

Great Lakes Forest Research Centre, Box 490, 1219 Queen St. E., Sault Ste. Marie, Ont. P6A 5M7 (705/949-9461)

Northern Forest Research Centre, 5320 122nd St., Edmonton, Alta. T6G 3S5 (403/435-7369)

Pacific Forest Research Centre, 506 W. Burnside Rd., Victoria, B.C. V8Z 1M5 (604/388-3811)

Dept. of Industry, Trade & Commerce, Resource Industries Branch, Forest Products Group, 235 Queen St., Ottawa, Ont. K1A OH5 (613/992-7128)

National Film Board, Box 6100, Montreal, P.Q. H3C 3H5 (514/333-3333)

Statistics Canada, Ottawa, Ont. K1A OT6 (613/992-2371)

Alta.: Public Affairs Officer, Dept. of Energy & Natural Resources, 7th floor, Petroleum Plaza South, 9915 108 St., Edmonton, Alta. T5K 2C9 (403/427-7003)

B.C.: Ministry of Forests, 1450 Government St., Victoria, B.C. V8W 3E7 (604/387-5985)

Man.: Forestry Branch, Dept. of Natural Resources, #300, 500 Kenaston Blvd., Winnipeg, Man. (204/477-4605)

N.B.: Forest Management Branch, Dept. of Natural Resources, Box 6000, Centennial Bldg., Fredericton, N.B. E3B 5H1 (506/453-2485)

Nfld.: Dept. of Forest Resources & Lands, 6th floor, Atlantic Place, Water St., St. John's, Nfld. A1C 5T7 (709/737-3245)

N.S.: Dept. of Lands & Forests, Box 68, Truro, N.S. B2N 5B8 (902/895-1591)

Ont.: Forest Resources Group, Forest Resources, Ministry of Natural Resources, Queen's Park, Toronto, Ont. M7A 1W3 (416/965-2785)

P.E.I.: Forestry Branch, Dept. of Agriculture & Forestry, Box 2000, Charlottetown, P.E.I. C1A 7N8 (902/892-0228)

Que.: Quebec Bureau of Statistics, Dept. of Industry, Trade & Tourism, 117 St-André, Quebec, P.Q. G1K 3Y3 (418/643-5116)

Dept. of Energy & Resources, Communications, 200 B Chemin Ste-Foy, Quebec, P.Q. G1R 4X7 (418/643-8060)

Sask.: Forestry Branch, Dept. of Tourism & Renewable Resources, Room 300, Provincial Government Bldg., Prince Albert, Sask. S6V 1B5 (306/922-3133)

FUEL

see Coal; Oil; Natural Gas; Electric Power; Nuclear Energy

FUR FARMING

Animal Production Division, Agriculture Canada, #469, Sir John Carling Bldg., Ottawa, Ont. K1A OC5 (613/995-5880) (information re all aspects of the fur industry)

Statistics Canada, Ottawa, Ont. K1A OT6 (613/995-4853)

Alta.: Dept. of Agriculture, Animal Health Division, 9718 107 St., Edmonton, Alta. T5K 2C8 (403/427-2306)

B.C.: No provincial agency.

Man.: Dept. of Agriculture, Veterinary Services Branch, Agricultural Services Complex, University of Manitoba, Winnipeg, Man. R3T 2N2 (204/269-1220)

N.S.: Dept. of Agriculture & Marketing, Livestock Services Branch, Hancock Bldg., Box 550, Truro, N.S. B2N 5E3 (902/895-1571)

Ont.: Supervisor of Fur Farms, Ministry of Agriculture & Food, Veterinary Services Branch, Legislative Bldgs., Toronto, Ont. M7A 1B3 (416/965-5841)

P.E.I.: P.E.I. Fish & Wildlife Division, Dept. of Community Affairs, Box 2000, Charlottetown, P.E.I. C1A 7N8 (902/892-9174)

Que.: Productions animales, Dept. of Agriculture & Food, 200 A Chemin Ste-Foy, 1er étage, Quebec, P.Q. G1R 4X6 (418/643-7597)

Sask.: Production & Marketing Division, Dept. of Agriculture, Provincial Veterinary Lab, 4840 Wascana Pkwy., Regina, Sask. S4S OB1 (306/565-6424)

Dept. of Tourism & Renewable Resources, Fur Unit, 49 12th St. E., Prince Albert, Sask.

Dept. of Northern Saskatchewan, Resources Branch, Wildlife Division, Box 3003, Prince Albert, Sask.

GARBAGE

Garbage disposal is a Municipal concern. Contact the City Clerk's Office (see Index, Municipalities) of each particular municipality for information re present garbage handling and future innovations.

GAS

see Oil

GEOGRAPHY

Dept. of Energy, Mines & Resources, Surveys & Mapping Branch, 615 Booth St., Ottawa, Ont. K1A OE9 (613/994-9872)

Environment Canada, Lands Directorate, Ottawa, Ont. K1A OE7 (819/997-2010)

National Film Board, Box 6100, Montreal, P.Q. H3C 3H5 (514/333-3333)

Public Archives of Canada, 395 Wellington St., Ottawa, Ont. K1A ON3 (613/992-2669)

Alta.: Alberta Historic Sites Board, Old St. Stephen's College, 8820 112 St., Edmonton, Alta. T6G 2P8 (403/427-2022)

B.C.: Ministry of Environment, Information Services Branch, 810 Blanshard St., Victoria, B.C. V8W 3E1 (604/387-5162)

Man.: Map Distribution & Remote Sensing, Surveys & Mapping Branch, 1007 Century St., Winnipeg, Man. R3H OW4 (204/632-8681)

N.S.: Surveys Division, Dept. of Lands & Forests, Dennis Bldg., 1740 Granville St., Halifax, N.S. B3J 2T9 (902/424-4102)

Que.: Centre d'études nordiques/Northern Studies Centre, Laval Univ., Ste-Foy, Quebec, P.Q. G1K 7P4 (418/656-3340)

Commission de toponymie, 220 Grande Allée est, #160, Québec, P.Q. G1R 2J1 (418/643-9705)

Sask.: Saskatchewan Tourism & Renewable Resources, Marketing & Promotions, 3211 Albert St., Regina, Sask. S4S 5W6 (306/565-2300)

GEOLOGY

Dept. of Energy, Mines & Resources, Geological Survey of Canada, 601 Booth St., Ottawa, Ont. K1A OE8 (613/995-4342)

Institute of Sedimentary & Petroleum Geology, 3303 33rd St. N.W., Calgary, Alta. T2L 2A7 (403/284-0110)

Alta.: Alberta Geological Survey, Alberta Research Council, 4445 Calgary Trail S., Edmonton, Alta. T6H 5R7 (204/438-0555)

B.C.: Ministry of Energy, Mines & Petroleum Resources, Parliament Bldgs., Victoria, B.C. V8V 1X4 (604/387-5975)

Man.: Dept. of Energy & Mines, Mineral Resources Division, 989 Century St., Winnipeg, Man. R3H OW4 (204/633-9543)

N.B.: Mineral Resources, Dept. of Natural Resources, Box 6000, Fredericton, N.B. E3B 5H1 (506/453-2206)

Nfld.: Dept. of Mines & Energy, 95 Bonaventure Ave., Box 4750, St. John's, Nfld. A1C 5T7 (709/737-3159)

N.S.: Mineral Resources Division, Dept. of Mines & Energy, Box 1087, Halifax, N.S. B3J 2X1 (902/424-4162)

Ont.: Ontario Geological Survey, Ministry of Natural Resources, 77 Grenville St., Toronto, Ont. M5S 1B3 (416/965-0190)

P.E.I.: Dept. of Tourism, Industry & Energy, Box 2000, Charlottetown, P.E.I. C1A 7N8 (902/892-7411)

Que.: Ministère de l'Energie et des Ressources, Exploration géologique et minérale, 1620, boul de l'Entente, Quebec, P.Q. G1S 4N6 (418/643-4617)

Sask.: Geological Survey Branch, Dept. of Mineral Resources, TD Bank Bldg., 1914 Hamilton St., Regina, Sask. S4P 4V4 (306/565-2560)

GOVERNMENT (GENERAL)

Government of Canada (Telephone Referral Services)

The Federal Government provides a telephone referral service to assist the public in locating the Government of Canada organizations most likely responsible for their concerns. The service in Manitoba is operated, on a contract basis, by the Manitoba Citizens' Enquiry Service. The Federal Government Department in charge is: Government of Canada Dept. of Communications, Information Services, 300 Slater St., Ottawa, Ont. K1A OC8 (613/995-8185)

Following are locations presently offering the referral service from 8 a.m. to 5 p.m. except where otherwise indicated:-

Halifax: (902) 426-3511 (8 a.m. to 5 p.m.) and 426-3414 (5 p.m. to 8 a.m.)

Moncton: (506) 858-2345 (24 hours)

Saint John, N.B.: (506) 658-4567 (24 hours)

Fredericton: (506) 452-3777 (24 hours)

St. John's, Nfld.: (709) 737-5454 (8 a.m. to 5 p.m.) and 722-6614 (5 p.m. to 8 a.m.)

Quebec City: (418) 694-3456

Montreal: (514) 283-5454 (8 a.m. to 5 p.m.) and 842-4101 (5 p.m. to 8 a.m.)

Sherbrooke: (819) 565-4850

Ottawa: (613) 996-8211 (24 hours)

Toronto: (416) 362-6211 (8 a.m. to 5 p.m.) and 923-1224 (5 p.m. to 8 a.m.)

Hamilton: (416) 525-1951

London: (519) 679-4000

Winnipeg: (204) 957-8920 (8 a.m. to 5 p.m. for Winnipeg callers only) and 1-800-292-8920 (toll free for those in Manitoba calling long distance)

Regina: (306) 569-5454

Saskatoon: (306) 665-5454

Calgary: (403) 231-5151

Edmonton: (403) 425-5151

Vancouver: (604) 666-3311

Victoria: (604) 388-3211

Information Services in the Federal Government

Agriculture: Information Services, Ottawa, Ont. K1A OC7 (613/995-5222)

Canada Council: Information Services, Ottawa, Ont. K1P 5V8 (613/237-3400)

Canadian Government Office of Tourism: Public Information, Ottawa, Ont. K1A 0H6 (613/995-0511)

Canadian Government Expositions Centre: Dept. of Supply & Services, 440 Coventry Rd., Ottawa, Ont. K1A OT1 (613/993-9732)

Canadian International Development Agency: Public Affairs Branch, 200 Promenade du Portage, Hull (mailing: Ottawa, Ont. K1A 0G4) (819/997-6100)

Canadian Radio-television Commission:
Mailing address: Ottawa, Ont. K1A ON2
Office location & shipping address: Centre Bldg., Terrasses de la Chaudiere, 1 Promenade du Portage, Hull, P.Q.
Public inquiries: (819) 997-0313
Phone numbers & staff inquiries: (819) 997-4704

Canadian Transport Commission: Information Services, Ottawa, Ont. K1A ON9 (819/997-0344)

Canada Mtge. & Housing Corp.: Information Services, Ottawa, Ont. K1A 0P7 (613/748-2609)

Communications: Information Services, Ottawa, Ont. K1A OC8 (613/995-8185)

Consumer & Corporate Affairs: Communications Service, Place du Portage Phase 1, 50 Victoria St., Hull/Ottawa K1A 0C9 (819/997-2938)

Employment & Immigration: Public Affairs Division, Ottawa, Ont. K1A OJ9 (819/994-6313)

Energy, Mines & Resources: Communications, Ottawa, Ont. K1A OE4 (613/995-3065)

Environment Canada: Information Branch, Ottawa, Ont. K1A 0H3 (613/997-2800)

External Affairs: Operations Centre, Ottawa, Ont. K1A OG2 (613/996-9134)

Finance: Information Division, Ottawa, Ont. K1A OG5 (613/992-1573)

Fisheries & Oceans Canada: Communications Branch, Ottawa, Ont. K1A OE6 (613/995-2041)

Indian Affairs & Northern Development: General Information & Library Services, Ottawa, Ont. K1A OH4 (819/997-0380)

Industry, Trade & Commerce: Business Centre, Ottawa, Ont. K1A OH5 (613/995-5771)

Justice: Information Services, Ottawa, Ont. K1A OH8 (613/995-2569)

Labour Canada: Communication Services Directorate, Ottawa, Ont. K1A OJ2 (819/994-2238)

Metric Commission Canada: Information Directorate, Box 4000, Ottawa, Ont. K1S 5G8 (613/996-4000)

National Capital Commission: Public Affairs Division, Ottawa, Ont. K1P 6J6 (613/992-4231)

National Defence: Information Services, Ottawa, Ont. K1A OK2 (613/996-2353)

National Film Board: Public Relations, Box 6100, Stn. A, Montreal, P.Q. H3C 3H5 (514/333-3333)
Ottawa Offices: 150 Kent St., Ottawa, Ont. K1A 0M9 (613/992-3615)

National Gallery of Canada: Media & Public Relations, Ottawa, Ont. K1A OM8 (613/996-8031)

National Health & Welfare: Information Directorate, Ottawa, Ont. K1A OK9 (613/996-4950)

National Library of Canada: Public Relations Division, Ottawa, Ont. K1A ON4 (613/996-9111)

National Museums of Canada: Information Services, Ottawa, Ont. K1A OM8 (613/593-4285)

National Museum of Man: Media & Public Relations, Ottawa, Ont. K1A OM8 (613/993-0881)

National Museum of Natural Sciences: Information Centre, Ottawa, Ont. K1A OM8 (613/996-3107)

National Museum of Science & Technology: Public Relations Office, Ottawa, Ont. K1A 0M8 (613/998-4566)

National Research Council: Public Information Branch, Ottawa, Ont. K1A OR6 (613/993-9101)

Post Office: Public Affairs Branch, Ottawa, Ont. K1A OB1 (613/998-8305)

Privy Council Office: Information Services, Ottawa, Ont. K1A OA3 (613/992-7608)

Public Archives of Canada: Information Services, Ottawa, Ont. K1A ON3 (613/996-1473)

Public Service Commission: Public Affairs Directorate, Ottawa, Ont. K1A OM7 (613/593-7691)

Public Works: Public Relations & Information Services, Ottawa, Ont. K1A OM2 (613/998-9560)

Regional Economic Expansion: Information Branch, Ottawa, Ont. K1A OM4 (819/997-2096)

Revenue Canada, Customs & Excise: Public Relations Branch, Ottawa, Ont. K1A OL5 (613/593-6220)

Revenue Canada, Taxation: Information Services Branch, Ottawa, Ont. K1A OL8 (613/995-2961)

Royal Canadian Mounted Police: Public Relations Branch, 1200 Alta Vista Dr., Ottawa, Ont. K1A OR2 (613/993-1085)

Science Council of Canada: Public Affairs, 100 Metcalfe St., Ottawa, Ont. K1P 5M1 (613/995-6954)

Science & Technology: Communications Division, 270 Albert St., Ottawa, Ont. K1A 1A1 (613/995-3093)

Secretary of State: Communications Branch, Ottawa, Ont. K1A OM5 (819/997-0231)

Social Sciences & Humanities Research Council: Information Division, 255 Albert St., Ottawa, Ont. K1P 6G4 (613/995-9330)
Solicitor General: Communications Division, Ottawa, Ont. K1A OP8 (613/995-1032)
Statistics Canada: Information Division, Ottawa, Ont. K1A OT6 (613/992-2959, 992-4734)
Supply & Services: Information Services, Ottawa, Ont. K1A OS5 (819/997-7363)
Transport: Public Affairs, Ottawa, Ont. K1A ON5 (613/996-5861)
Treasury Board Secretariat: Communications Division, Ottawa, Ont. K1A OR5 (613/995-6141)
Veterans Affairs: Public Affairs Directorate, Ottawa, Ont. K1A OP4 (613/992-4234)

Provincial Government Information Agencies

Alta.: Public Affairs Bureau, Petroleum Plaza, 9945 108th St., Edmonton, Alta. T5K 2G6 (403/427-2754)
B.C.: Government Information Services, Ministry of Provincial Secretary & Government Services, Room 102, Parliament Bldgs., Victoria, B.C. V8V 1X4 (604/387-1337)
Man.: Citizens' Inquiry Service, Room 511, 401 York Ave., Winnipeg, Man. R3C OP8 (204/944-3744) Toll free in Manitoba 1-800-282-8060
N.B.: N.B. Information Service, Box 6000, Fredericton, N.B. E3B 5H1 (506/453-2240)
Nfld.: Nfld. Information Service, Main floor, Confederation Bldg., St. John's, Nfld. A1C 5T7 (709/737-3612)
N.S.: Information Division, Dept. of Government Services, Box 54, Halifax, N.S. B3J 2L4 (902/424-6980)
Ont.: Citizens' Inquiry Bureau, Ministry of Culture & Recreation, 77 Bloor St. W., 6th floor, Queen's Park, Toronto, Ont. M7A 2R9 (416/965-3535) Local TTY 965-5130; Inwats TTY 1-800-268-7095
P.E.I.: Island Information Service, (102 Kent St.), Box 2000, Charlottetown, P.E.I. C1A 7N8 (902/892-3428)
Que.: Government Communications, Dept. of Communications, 1037 de la Chevrotière, Edifice G, Rez de Chaussée, Bloc 4, Quebec, P.Q. G1R 4Y7 (418/643-3162)
Sask.: Information Services Branch, Executive Council, Legislative Bldg., Regina, Sask. S4S OB3 (306/565-6281)
Provincial Inquiry Centre, 217 Walter Scott Bldg., Regina, Sask. S4S 0B1 (306/565-6291) Toll free in Saskatchewan 1-800-667-8755 except Lloydminster & Creighton ask Operator for Zenith 0-8599
N.W.T.: Dept. of Information, Government of the Northwest Territories, Yellowknife, N.W.T. X1A 2L9 (403/873-7251)
Yukon: Public Affairs Bureau, Box 2703, Whitehorse, Y.T. Y1A 2C6 (403/667-5170)

Information Sources in Major Canadian Cities

Brampton: City Clerk, 150 Central Park Dr., Brampton, Ont. L6T 2T9 (416/793-4110)
Burlington: Clerk's Dept., 2nd floor, 426 Brant St., Burlington, Ont. L7R 3Z6 (416/335-7708)
Calgary: City Clerk's Dept., Box 2100, Calgary, Alta. T2P 2M5 (403/268-5861)
Hamilton: City Clerk's Office, City Hall, 71 Main St. W., Hamilton, Ont. L8N 3T4 (416/527-0241)
Hull: Bureau du Greffier, Hôtel de Ville, 25 rue Laurier, C.P. 1970, Succ. A, Hull, P.Q. J8X 3Y9 (819/777-2781)
Kitchener: City Clerk's Dept., 2nd floor, City Hall, 22 Frederick St., Box 1118, Kitchener, Ont. N2G 4G7 (519/885-7240)
LaSalle: City Clerk, City Hall, 13 Strathyre Ave., LaSalle, P.Q. H8R 3P6 (514/366-7110)
London: City Clerk's Dept., City Hall, 300 Dufferin Ave., London, Ont. N6A 4L9 (519/679-4530)
Mississauga: Information & Public Relations Dept., 1 City Centre Dr., Mississauga, Ont. L5B 1M2 (416/279-7600)
Montreal: Secrétariat Administratif, 275 est Notre-Dame, S. 415, Montreal, P.Q. H2Y 1C6 (514/872-2941)
Niagara Falls: City Hall, 4310 Queen St., Niagara Falls, Ont. L2E 6X5 (416/356-7521)
Oshawa: City Clerk's Dept., City Hall, 50 Centre St. S., Oshawa, Ont. L1H 3Z7 (416/725-7351)
Quebec City: Gérance, Hôtel de Ville, Quebec, P.Q. G1R 4S9 (418/694-6373)
Regina: City Clerk's Office, City Hall, 2476 Victoria Ave., Box 1790, Regina, Sask. S4P 3C8 (306/569-7262)
Saint John: Common Clerk's Office, City Hall, Box 1971/Market Sq., Saint John, N.B. E2L 4L1 (506/658-2862)
Saskatoon: City Commr., City of Saskatoon, City Hall, Saskatoon, Sask. S7K OJ5 (306/664-9209)
Sudbury: City Clerk's Office, 200 Brady St., Box 1000, Sudbury, Ont. P3E 4S5 (705/674-3141)
Thunder Bay: City Clerk's Office, City Hall, Donald St., Thunder Bay, Ont. P7E 5V3 (807/623-2711, ext. 2230)
Toronto: City Clerk's Dept., Public Information & Communication Services, City Hall, Toronto, Ont. M5H 2N2 (416/367-7341)
Toronto (Metro): Metropolitan Toronto Clerk's Dept., 2nd floor, City Hall, Toronto, Ont. M5H 2N1 (367-8016)
Vancouver: City Clerk, City Hall, 453 W. 12th Ave., Vancouver, B.C. V5Y 1V4 (604/873-7266)
Victoria: City Manager's Office, No. 1 Centennial Sq., Victoria, B.C. V8W 1P6 (604/385-5711)
Windsor: City Hall, Windsor, Ont. N9A 6S1 (519/255-6500)
Winnipeg: City Clerk's Dept., Citizen Inquiry, Council Bldg., Civic Centre, 510 Main St., Winnipeg, Man. R3B 1B9 (204/946-0171)

GRANTS & SUBSIDIES

(See also Student Aid)

The Canada Council, 255 Albert St., Ottawa, Ont. K1P 5V8 (613/237-3400)
Canada Employment & Immigration Commission, Employment Development Branch, Ottawa, Ont. K1A OJ9
Local Employment Programs, 819/994-2396
Summer Canada, 819/994-2495
Community Development Projects, 819/994-3044
Canada Community Services Projects, 819/994-2399
New Technology Employment Program, 819/994-2711
Canada Mtge. & Housing Corp., Montreal Rd., Ottawa, Ont. K1A OP7 (613/748-2000)
Dept. of Agriculture, Agricultural Stabilization Board, Sir John Carling Bldg., Ottawa, Ont. K1A OC5 (613/995-5404) (agricultural commodity subsidies)
Dept. of Indian Affairs & Northern Development, Ottawa, Ont. K1A OH4 (613/994-9915) (Native peoples)
Dept. of Justice, Programs & Law Information Section, Justice Bldg., Ottawa, Ont. K1A 0H8 (613/992-5549)
(includes: Civil Law/Common Law Student Exchange Program; Consultation & Development Fund; Criminal Law Reform Fund; Duff-Rinfret Scholarship Program; Employment of Law Students by Dept. of Justice; Employment of Law Students by Police Forces; Fellowships in Legislative Drafting; Native Law Students Program; Special Projects - Legal Aid)
Dept. of National Health & Welfare (613/996-4950):
Health Services & Promotion Branch, Ottawa, Ont. K1A OK9 (Family Planning, New Horizons, National Welfare Grants)
National Health Research & Development Program, Health Services & Promotion Branch, Ottawa, Ont. K1A 0K9 (992-7116)
Health Promotion Contribution Program, Health Promotion Directorate, 5th floor, Jeanne Mance Bldg., Ottawa, Ont. K1A 1B4 (996-4533)
Welfare Grants Directorate, Ottawa, Ont. K1A 1B5 (992-7773)
Dept. of Regional Economic Expansion, Ottawa, Ont. K1A OM4 (819/997-2408) (industrial grants)
Dept. of Secretary of State, Ottawa/Hull K1A 0M5 (819/997-0055):
Citizenship Branch (819/994-1566)
Multiculturalism Program (819/994-3120)
Language Programs Branch (819/994-1917)
Fitness & Recreation Canada Directorate/Sport Canada, Fitness & Amateur Sport Branch, 365 Laurier Ave. W., Ottawa, Ont. K1A 0X6 (613/996-4510)

Medical Research Council, Ottawa, Ont. K1A OW9 (613/996-8170)
Grants program: 996-8172
Awards program: 996-8173

National Museums of Canada, Museum Assistance Programs, 300 L'Esplanade Laurier, Room 2000, Ottawa, Ont. K1A OM8; 613/996-8504

Alta.: Dept. of Municipal Affairs, 9925 107 St., Edmonton, Alta. T5K 2H9 (403/427-2732)

B.C.: Ministry of Provincial Secretary & Government Services, Parliament Bldgs., Victoria, B.C. V8V 1X4 (604/387-5823)

Man.: Citizens' Inquiry Service, 511 Norquay Bldg., 401 York Ave., Winnipeg, Man. R3C 0P8 (204/994-3744) Toll free in Manitoba 1-800-282-8060

N.B.: Grants Committee, Cabinet Secretariat, Box 6000, Fredericton, N.B. E3B 5H1 (506/453-2384)

N.S.: Provincial Grants Committee, c/o Management Board Offices, Box 1619, Halifax, N.S. B3J 2Y3 (902/424-7750)

Ont.: In Ontario almost all government Ministries have grants programs. For specific information inquire from Citizen's Inquiry Bureau, Ministry of Culture & Recreation, Queen's Park, Toronto, Ont. M7A 2R9 (416/965-3535)

P.E.I.: Treasury Board, Box 2000, Charlottetown, P.E.I. C1A 7N8 (902/892-9108)

Que.: Quebec Industrial Development Corp., Edifice Tour de la Bourse, C.P. 276, Bureau 4205, Montreal, P.Q. H4Z 1E8 (514/873-4375)

Sask.: Provincial Inquiry Centre, 217 Walter Scott Bldg., Regina, Sask. S4S 0B1 (306/565-6291). Elsewhere in Saskatchewan direct dial 1-800-667-8755 toll free.
Dept. of Rural Affairs, 2240 Albert St., Regina, Sask. S4P 3V7 (306/565-2727)
Dept. of Culture & Youth, Avord Tower, Regina, Sask. S4P 3V7 (306/565-5749)
Dept. of Urban Affairs, 1791 Rose St., Regina, Sask. S4P 3V7 (306/565-2635)
Saskatchewan Arts Board, 2550 Broad St., Regina, Sask. S4P 3V7 (306/565-4056)

Halifax: Tax Concession & Grants Committee, c/o City Treasurer's Office, Box 1749, Halifax, N.S. B3J 3A5 (902/426-6497)

Hamilton: City Clerk's Office, City Hall, 71 Main St. W., Hamilton, Ont. L8N 3T4 (416/527-0241)

LaSalle: General Manager, City Hall, 13 Strathyre Ave., LaSalle, P.Q. H8R 3P6 (514/366-7110)

London: Finance Dept., City Hall, 300 Dufferin Ave., Box 5035, London, Ont. N6A 4L9 (519/679-4960)

Mississauga: Treasury Dept., 9th floor, Univac Bldg., 55 City Centre Dr., Mississauga, Ont. L5B 1M3 (416/279-7600)

Niagara Falls: City Treasurer's Office, City Hall, 4310 Queen St., Niagara Falls, Ont. L2E 6X5 (416/356-7521)

Oshawa: Treasury & Finance Dept., City Hall, 50 Centre St. S., Oshawa, Ont. L1H 3Z7 (416/725-7351)

Quebec City: City Clerk's Office, City Hall, Quebec, P.Q. G1R 4S9 (418/694-6074)

Regina: City Manager, City Hall, (2476 Victoria Ave.), Box 1790, Regina, Sask. S4P 3C8 (306/569-7311)

Saint John: Commr. of Finance, City Hall, Saint John, N.B. E2L 4L1 (506/658-2922)

Saskatoon: City Council, c/o City Clerk, City Hall, Saskatoon, Sask. S7K OJ5 (306/664-9242)

Toronto: City of Toronto Neighbourhood Committee, City Hall, Toronto, Ont. M5H 2N2 (416/367-7039)

Vancouver: Director of Social Planning, City Hall, 453 W. 12th Ave., Vancouver, B.C. V5Y 1V4 (604/873-7480)

Victoria: City Manager's Office, No. 1 Centennial Sq., Victoria, B.C. V8W 1P6 (604/385-5711)

Windsor: City Clerk, City Hall, Windsor, Ont. N9A 6S1 (519/255-6211)

Winnipeg: City Clerk, Civic Centre, Winnipeg, Man. R3B 1B9 (204/946-0436)

GUARANTEED INCOME

(The Governments of Canada are in various stages of planning regarding income supplements. For the most recent developments in a particular province write to the Directors listed below).

Federal: Asst. Deputy Minister, Policy, Planning & Information, Dept. of National Health & Welfare, Brooke Claxton Bldg., Ottawa, Ont. K1A OK9 (613/995-7231)

Alta.: Director, Income Security Branch, Dept. of Social Services & Community Health, 10030 107 St., Edmonton, Alta. T5J 3E4 (403/427-6431)

B.C.: Manager of Human Resources, Ministry of Human Resources, Parliament Bldgs., Victoria, B.C. V8V 1X4 (604/387-1486)

Man.: Social Security Services Division, Dept. of Community Services & Corrections, 267 Edmonton St., Winnipeg, Man. R3C 1S2 (204/944-2696)

N.B.: Executive Director of Social Services, Dept. of Social Services, Box 6000, Fredericton, N.B. E3B 5H1 (506/453-3634)

Nfld.: Director, Planning & Research, Dept. of Social Services, Confederation Bldg., St. John's, Nfld. A1C 5T7 (709/737-3607)

N.S.: Director of Policy, Planning & Research, Dept. of Social Services, Box 696, Halifax, N.S. B3J 2T7 (902/424-4039)

Ont.: Ministry of Community & Social Services, Guaranteed Income (Disabled), Income Maintenance Unit, 7th floor, 2195 Yonge St., Toronto, Ont. M4S 2B2 (416/965-5142)
Ministry of Revenue, Guaranteed Income (Aged), Guaranteed Income & Tax Credit Branch, 10th floor, 77 Bloor St. W., Toronto, Ont. M7A 1X8 (416/965-0111)

P.E.I.: Director, Special Services, Health Branch, Dept. of Health & Social Services, Box 2000, Charlottetown, P.E.I. C1A 7N8 (902/892-5421)

Que.: Asst. Deputy Minister, Dept. of Labour, Manpower & Income Security, 425 St-Amable, Québec, P.Q. G1R 4Z1 (418/643-3935)

Sask.: Income Support Division, Saskatchewan Social Services, 1920 Broad St., Regina, Sask. S4P 3V6 (306/565-4130)

Yukon: Dept. of Health & Human Resources, Box 2703, Whitehorse, Y.T. Y1A 2C6 (403/667-5674)

N.W.T.: Deputy Minister, Depts. of Health & Social Services, Government of N.W.T., Yellowknife, N.W.T. X1A 2L9 (403/873-7119)

HEALTH

Dept. of National Health & Welfare, Ottawa, Ont. K1A OK9 (613/996-4950)

National Film Board, Box 6100, Montreal, P.Q. H3C 3H5 (514/333-3333)

Dept. of Veterans Affairs, Veterans Services, Dominion Bldg., Box 770, Charlottetown, P.E.I. C1A 8M9 (902/894-5072)

Statistics Canada, Ottawa, Ont. K1A OT6 (613/995-0780)

Alta.: Dept. of Social Services & Community Health, 10030 107 St., Edmonton, Alta. T5J 3E4 (403/427-2734)

B.C.: Ministry of Health, Parliament Bldgs., Victoria, B.C. V8V 1X4 (604/386-3166)

Man.: Dept. of Health, Community Health Directorate, 831 Portage Ave., Winnipeg, Man. R3G ON6 (204/775-9761)

N.B.: Dept. of Health, Box 6000, Fredericton, N.B. E3B 5H1 (506/453-2536)

Nfld.: Dept. of Health, Confederation Bldg., St. John's, Nfld. A1C 5T7 (709/737-3125)

N.S.: Dept. of Health, Box 488, Joseph Howe Bldg., Halifax, N.S. B3J 2R8 (902/424-4391)

Ont.: Ministry of Health, 10th floor, Hepburn Block, Queen's Park, Toronto, Ont. M7A 1R3 (416/965-5167)

P.E.I.: Dept. of Health & Social Services, Health Branch, Box 3000, Charlottetown, P.E.I. C1A 7P1 (902/892-5471)

Que.: Dept. of Social Affairs, 1075 Ste-Foy Rd., 2nd floor, Quebec, P.Q. G1S 2M1 (418/643-6392)

Sask.: Dept. of Health, 3475 Albert St., Regina, Sask. S4S 6X6 (306/565-3168)

Yukon: Health Services Branch, Dept. of Health & Human Resources, Box 2703, Whitehorse, Y.T. Y1A 2C6 (403/667-5367)

Calgary: Local Board of Health, Box 2100, Calgary, Alta. T2P 2M5 (403/269-8800)

Edmonton: Local Board of Health, 7th floor, CN Tower, Edmonton, Alta. T5J OK1 (403/428-3636)

Hamilton: Hamilton-Wentworth Regional Health Unit, 74 Hughson St. S., Box 897, Hamilton, Ont. L8N 3P6 (416/528-1441)

LaSalle: Dept. of Public Health, City Hall, 13 Strathyre Ave., LaSalle, P.Q. H8R 3P6 (514/366-7110)

London: Middlesex Dist. Health Unit, 346 South St., London, Ont. N6B 1B9 (519/673-0110)

Montreal: Social Affairs Dept., 1453 Beaubien E., #200, Montreal, P.Q. H2G 3C6 (514/872-4300)

North York: Dept. of Public Health, 5100 Yonge St., Willowdale, Ont. M2N 5V7 (416/224-6203)

Regina: City Health Dept., 1910 McIntyre St., Regina, Sask. S4P 2R3 (306/522-3621)

Saskatoon: Saskatoon Community Health Dept., 440 2nd Ave. N., Saskatoon, Sask. S7K 2C3 (306/664-9627)

Sudbury: Sudbury & Dist. Health Unit, 1300 Paris Cres., Sudbury, Ont. P3E 3A3 (705/522-9200)

Toronto: Dept. of Public Health, City Hall, Toronto, Ont. M5H 2N2 (416/367-7401)

Metro Area:

East York Health Unit, 550 Mortimer Ave., East York, Ont. M4J 2H2 (461-8136)

Etobicoke Health Dept., Civic Centre, Etobicoke, Ont. M9C 2Y2 (626-4532)

Scarborough Health Dept., 160 Borough Dr., Scarborough, Ont. M1P 4N8 (296-7454)

York Health Dept., 2700 Eglinton Ave. W., Toronto, Ont. M6M 1V1 (653-2700)

Vancouver: City Health Dept., 1060 W. 8th Ave., Vancouver, B.C. V6H 1C4 (604/736-2033)

Windsor: Metro Windsor-Essex County Health Unit, 1550 Ouellette Ave., Windsor, Ont. N8X 1K7 (519/258-2146)

Winnipeg: Director of Health Inspections, 280 William Ave., Winnipeg, Man. R3B 0R1 (204/946-0444)

HISTORY

Dept. of Veterans Affairs, Public Affairs Directorate, Ottawa, Ont. K1A OP4 (613/992-4234)

Directorate of History, National Defence Headquarters, Ottawa, Ont. K1A OK2; 613/992-6416 (history of Canadian Armed Forces)

National Film Board, Box 6100, Montreal, P.Q. H3C 3H5 (514/333-3333)

National Library, Ottawa, Ont. K1A ON4 (613/995-9481)

National Museum of Man, History Division, Ottawa, Ont. K1A OM8 (613/995-2981)

National Postal Museum, 180 Wellington St., Ottawa, Ont. K1A 1C6 (613/995-9904)

Public Archives of Canada, 395 Wellington St., Ottawa, Ont. K1A ON3 (613/992-2669)

Statistics Canada, Ottawa, Ont. K1A OT6 (613/995-9034)

Alta.: Provincial Archives, 12845 102 Ave., Edmonton, Alta. T5N OM6 (403/427-1750)

B.C.: Provincial Archives, Parliament Bldgs., Victoria, B.C. V8V 1X4 (604/387-5885)

Man.: Provincial Archives of Man., 200 Vaughan St., Winnipeg, Man. R3C OP8 (204/944-3971)

N.B.: Historical Resources Admin., Box 6000, Fredericton, N.B. E3B 5H1 (506/453-2324)

Nfld.: Provincial Archives, Colonial Bldg., St. John's, Nfld. A1C 2C9 (709/753-9380)

N.S.: Public Archives of Nova Scotia, 6016 University Ave., Halifax, N.S. B3H 1W4 (902/423-9115)

Ont.: Archives of Ontario, Ministry of Culture & Recreation, 77 Grenville St., Toronto, Ont. M7A 2R9 (416/965-4039)

P.E.I.: Public Archives of P.E.I., Box 1000, Charlottetown, P.E.I. C1A 7M4 (902/892-7949)

Que.: Legislative Library, Government Bldgs., Quebec, P.Q. G1A 1A5 (418/643-2896)

Archives nationales du Quebec, Pavillon Casault, portes 1 et 2, 1210 ave du Séminaire, Ste-Foy, Québec, P.Q. G1V 4N1 (418/643-2167)

Sask.: Saskatchewan Archives Board: Univ. of Regina, Regina, Sask. S4S OA2 (306/565-4068), Saskatoon Office: Univ. of Saskatchewan, Saskatoon, Sask. S7N OWO (306/664-5832)

Dept. of Culture & Youth, 11th floor, Avord Tower, Regina, Sask. S4P 3V7 (306/565-5749)

Yukon: Yukon Archives & Records Services, Dept. of Information Resources, 2071 Second Ave., Whitehorse, Yukon, Y1A 2C6 (403/667-5321)

N.W.T.: Prince of Wales Northern Heritage Centre, Government of the N.W.T., Yellowknife, N.W.T. X1A 2L9 (403/873-7551)

HORTICULTURE

Chief, Ornamental Section, Ottawa Research Station, Agriculture Canada, Central Experimental Farm, Bldg. 50, Ottawa, Ont. K1A OC6 (613/995-9827)

Statistics Canada, Ottawa, Ont. K1A OT6 (613/995-4877)

Alta.: Alberta Tree Nursery & Horticulture Centre, R.R. 6, Edmonton, Alta. T5B 4K3 (403/973-3351)

B.C.: Horticulture Branch, Ministry of Agriculture, Parliament Bldgs., Victoria, B.C. V8W 2Z7 (604/387-5121)

Man.: Horticultural Section, Soils & Crops Branch, 908 Norquay Bldg., 401 York Ave., Winnipeg, Man. R3C 0P8 (204/944-3830)

N.B.: Plant Industry Branch, N.B. Dept. of Agriculture & Rural Development, Box 6000, Fredericton, N.B. E3B 5H1 (506/453-2108)

Nfld.: Dept. of Rural, Agricultural & Northern Development, Atlantic Place, Water St., St. John's, Nfld. A1C 5T7 (709/737-3172)

N.S.: Horticulture & Biology Services Branch, Dept. of Agriculture & Marketing, Box 550, Truro, N.S. B2N 5E3 (902/895-1571)

Ont.: Soils & Crops Branch, Ministry of Agriculture & Food, Legislative Bldgs., Toronto, Ont. M7A 2B2 (416/965-1081)

P.E.I.: Crops & Engineering Section, Field Services Branch, Dept. of Agriculture & Forestry, Box 1600, Charlottetown, P.E.I. C1A 7N3 (902/892-5465)

Que.: Horticultural Branch, Dept. of Agriculture & Food, 200A chemin Ste-Foy, Quebec, P.Q. G1R 4X6 (418/643-1371)

Sask.: Plant Industry Branch, Dept. of Agriculture, Walter Scott Bldg., Regina, Sask. S4S OB1 (306/565-4660)

HOSPITAL INSURANCE & HOSPITALS

Dept. of Veterans Affairs, Rm. M143, National Defence Medical Centre, Alta Vista Dr., Ottawa, Ont. K1A 0K6 (613/998-3889) (veterans' hospitals)

Statistics Canada, Ottawa, Ont. K1A OT6 (613/995-0991)

See "Medical Insurance" this table.

See Index for Depts. of Health, & Hospitals

HOUSE OF COMMONS

see Parliament

HOUSING

Canadian Housing Design Council, Montreal Rd., Ottawa, Ont. K1A OP7 (613/748-2515, 6)

Canada Mtge. & Housing Corp., Canadian Housing Information Centre, Montreal Rd., Ottawa, Ont. K1A 0P7 (613/748-2367)

Statistics Canada, Ottawa, Ont. K1A OT6 (613/995-8213)

Alta.: Alberta Housing Corp., 9405 50 St., Edmonton, Alta. T6B 2T4 (403/468-3535)

B.C.: Ministry of Lands, Parks & Housing, Parliament Bldgs., Victoria, B.C. V8W 3E1 (604/387-5381)

Housing Management Commission, 515 W. 10th Ave., Vancouver, B.C. V5Z 4A8 (604/873-0313)

Man.: Manitoba Housing & Renewal Corp., 287 Broadway, Winnipeg, Man. R3C 0R9 (204/944-4748)

N.B.: N.B. Housing Corp., Box 611, Fredericton, N.B. E3B 5B2 (506/454-5563)

Nfld.: Nfld. & Labrador Housing Corp., Box 220, St. John's, Nfld. A1C 5J2 (709/722-3554)

N.S.: N.S. Housing Commission, Box 280, Bedford, N.S. B4N 2X2 (902/835-9995), and Box 815, Dartmouth, N.S. B2Y 3Z3 (902/424-4483)

Ont.: Ministry of Municipal Affairs & Housing, Queen's Park, Toronto, Ont. M7A 2K4 (416/965-9780)

Ontario Housing Corp., 101 Bloor St. W., Toronto, Ont. M5S 1P8 (416/965-9820)

P.E.I.: P.E.I. Housing Corp., Box 1388, Charlottetown, P.E.I. C1A 7N1 (902/892-0221)

Que.: Quebec Housing Corp., 1054 Conroy, Edifice G, bloc 2, 4e étage, Québec, P.Q. G1R 5E7 (418/643-3023)

Sask.: Saskatchewan Housing Corp., 2500 Victoria Ave., Regina, Sask. S4P 3V7 (306/565-4177)

Yukon: Yukon Housing Corp., 203A Main St., Whitehorse, Y.T. Y1A 2B2 (403/667-5759)

Calgary: Housing & Community Renewal Division, Planning Dept., Box 2100, Calgary, Alta. T2P 2M5 (403/268-4217)

Edmonton: City Real Estate & Housing Manager, Centennial Bldg., Edmonton, Alta. T5J 0H1 (403/428-5986)

Guelph: Wellington & Guelph Housing Authority, 214 Woolwich St., Guelph, Ont. N1H 3V7 (519/824-7822)

LaSalle: City Engineer's Dept., 13 Strathyre Ave., LaSalle, P.Q. H8R 3P6 (514/366-7110)

London: Housing Division, #607, City Hall, 300 Dufferin Ave., London, Ont. N6A 4L9 (519/679-5464)

Montreal: Restauration et Conservation du Patrimoine Résidential, Montreal, P.Q. H2Y 1H2 (514/872-3882)

Niagara Falls: East Niagara Housing Authority, 4483 Queen St., Niagara Falls, Ont. L2E 2L4 (416/354-1678)

Oshawa: Oshawa Housing Authority, City Hall, 50 Centre St. S., 5th floor, 'A' Wing, Oshawa, Ont. L1H 3Z7 (416/725-3552

Oshawa Housing Co. Ltd., c/o City Clerk's Dept., City Hall, 50 Centre St. S., Oshawa, Ont. L1H 3Z7 (416/725-7351)

Quebec City: Office Municipal d'Habitation de Québec, 575, rue du Roi, Quebec, P.Q. G1K 8A4 (418/694-6104)

Saint John: Dept. of Community Planning & Development, Housing & Renewal Services Branch, City Hall, Box 1971, Saint John, N.B. E2L 4L1 (506/658-2800)

Saskatoon: Saskatoon Housing Authority, 535 24 St. E., Saskatoon, Sask. S7K 4K5 (306/665-6330)

Sudbury: Sudbury Dist. Housing Authority, 96 Larch St., Ste. 302, Sudbury, Ont. P3E 1C1 (705/674-8323)

Thunder Bay: Thunder Bay Dist. Housing Authority, Inter City Plaza, 862 Fort William Rd., Thunder Bay, Ont. P7B 3A5 (807/345-3391)

Toronto (City): Dept. of Housing, 180 Dundas St. W., Ste. 1400, Toronto, Ont. M5G 1Z8 (416/367-7885)

Toronto (Metro): Metropolitan Toronto Housing Co. Ltd., 110 Eglinton Ave. E., Toronto, Ont. M4P 2Y1 (416/484-7101)

Vancouver: Greater Vancouver Housing Corp., 2215 W. 10th Ave., Vancouver, B.C. V6K 2J1 (604/731-1155)

Victoria: Planning Dept., City Hall, No. 1 Centennial Sq., Victoria, B.C. V8W 1P6 (604/385-5711, loc. 290)

Windsor: Windsor Housing Authority, 1400 Ouellette Ave., Windsor, Ont. N9A 6R3 (519/254-1681)

City of Windsor Housing Co. Ltd., 68 Chatham St. E., Windsor, Ont. N9A 6S1 (519/255-6405)

Winnipeg: Director of Environmental Planning, 100 Main St., Winnipeg, Man. R3C 1A5 (204/985-5155)

HUMAN RIGHTS

Canadian Human Rights Commission, Ottawa, Ont. K1A 1E1 (613/995-1151)

Federal Correctional Investigator, Box 950, Stn. B, Ottawa, Ont. K1P 5R1 (613/996-9771) (prisoners' ombudsman)

Alta.: Alberta Human Rights Commission, #501, 10053 111 St., Edmonton, Alta. T5K 2H8 (403/427-7661)

Office of the Ombudsman, #1630, 10020 101A Ave., Edmonton, Alta. T5J 3G2 (403/427-2756); – Calgary branch: #1080, 700 4 Ave. S.W., Calgary, Alta. T2P 3J4 (403/261-6185)

B.C.: Human Rights Commission, #2, 880 Douglas St., Victoria, B.C. V8W 2B7 (604/387-5024)

Man.: Human Rights Commission, 200, 323 Portage Ave., Winnipeg, Man. R3B 2C1 (204/944-3007)

Office of the Ombudsman, 509 491 Portage Ave., Winnipeg, Man. R3B 2E4 (204/774-4491)

N.B.: Human Rights Commission, Dept. of Labour & Manpower, Box 6000, Fredericton, N.B. E3B 5H1 (506/453-2301)

Office of the Ombudsman, Box 6000, Fredericton, N.B. E3B 5H1 (506/453-2789)

Nfld.: Nfld. Human Rights Commission, Dept. of Justice, (Gordonna Bldg., Kenmount Rd.), Box 4750, St. John's, Nfld. A1C 5T7 (709/737-2709)

Office of the Ombudsman, 49-55 Elizabeth Ave., St. John's, Nfld. A1C 5T7 (709/753-7730, 737-3704)

N.S.: N.S. Human Rights Commission, Lord Nelson Arcade, (Box 2221), Halifax, N.S. B3J 3C4 (902/424-4111)

Ombudsman for the Province of N.S., Box 2152, Halifax, N.S. B3J 3B7 (902/424-6780)

Ont.: Ontario Human Rights Commission, 12th floor, 400 University Ave., Toronto, Ont. M7A 1T7 (416/965-6841) (regional offices in twelve major centres)

Ombudsman for Ontario, 125 Queen's Park, Toronto, Ont. M5S 2C7 (416/596-3300) - regional offices in Thunder Bay and North Bay

P.E.I.: Human Rights Commission, Box 2000, Charlottetown, P.E.I. C1A 7N8 (902/894-7797)

Que.: Le Protecteur du Citoyen (ombudsman), 14, rue Haldimand, Quebec, P.Q. G1R 4N4 (418/643-2688)

Commission des droits de la Personne, 360 rue St-Jacques, Mezzanine, Montreal, P.Q. H2Y 1P5 (514/873-5146) Toll free in Quebec 1-800-361-6477; Quebec office: 1279 boul Charest ouest, 7e étage, Québec, P.Q. G1N 4K7 (418/643-1872)

Sask.: Human Rights Commission, 8th floor, Canterbury Towers, 224 4th Ave. S., Saskatoon, Sask. S7K 5M5 (306/664-5952); – Regina office: 1819 Cornwall St., S4P 3V7 (306/565-2530); – Prince Albert office: 5th floor, 800 Central Ave., S6V 4V1 (306/764-6846)

Ombudsman, 2310 Scarth St., Regina, Sask. S4P 2J7 (306/565-6211)

HYDRO

see Public Utilities; *see* Electric Power

IMMIGRATION

Dept. of Employment & Immigration, Public Affairs Division, Immigration & Demographic Policy, Ottawa, Ont. K1A OJ9 (819/994-4015)

Health & Welfare Canada, Medical Services Branch, Jeanne Mance Bldg., Tunney's Pasture, Ottawa, Ont. K1A OL3

Statistics Canada, Ottawa, Ont. K1A OT6 (613/996-5254)

Ont.: Selective Placement Services, Small Business Development Branch, Ministry of Industry & Tourism, 7th floor, Hearst Block, 900 Bay St., Toronto, Ont. M7A 2E1 (416/965-5331)

Que.: Dept. of Cultural Communities & Immigration, 355, rue McGill, Montreal, P.Q. H2Y 2E8 (514/873-4136)

IMMUNIZATION SERVICES

Dept. of National Health & Welfare, Quarantine & Regulatory, Medical Services Branch, Ottawa, Ont. K1A OL3

See "Health" this table, for provinces and cities.

IMPORTS

Office of Special Trade Relations, Dept. of Industry, Trade & Commerce, 235 Queen St., Ottawa, Ont. K1A OH5 (613/995-8356)

External Trade Division, Statistics Canada, Tunney's Pasture, Ottawa, Ont. K1A 0Z9 (613/995-6305)

Alta.: Process Industry Development, Dept. of Economic Development, 2nd floor, Pacific Plaza, 10909 Jasper Ave., Edmonton, Alta. T5J 3M8 (403/427-2269)

B.C.: Ministry of Industry & Small Business Development, #315, 800 Hornby St., Vancouver, B.C. V6Z 2C5 (604/689-4411)

Man.: Dept. of Economic Development, Market Development, 1 Lakeview Sq., 5th floor, 155 Carlton St., Winnipeg, Man. R3C 3H8 (204/944-2466)

N.B.: Dept. of Commerce & Development, Box 6000, Fredericton, N.B. E3B 5H1 (506/453-2965)

Ont.: Trade Policy Branch, Policy & Priorities Division, Ministry of Industry & Tourism, 900 Bay St., Toronto, Ont. M7A 2E6 (416/965-7119)

INCOME TAX

see Taxation

INCORPORATION OF COMPANIES & ASSOCIATIONS

Director, Corporations Branch, Dept. of Consumer & Corporate Affairs Canada, Place du Portage, Phase 2, Ottawa/Hull, K1A OC9 (819/997-1058)

Alta.: Registrar of Corporations, Alberta Consumer & Corporate Affairs, Century Place, 9803 102A Ave., Edmonton, Alta. T5J 3A3 (403/427-2311)

B.C.: Registrar of Companies, 940 Blanshard St., Waddington Bldg., Victoria, B.C. V8W 3E6 (604/387-1775)

Man.: Corporations & Business Names Registration Branch, Dept. of Consumer & Corporate Affairs & Environment, 10th floor, Woodsworth Bldg., 405 Broadway, Winnipeg, Man. R3C 3L6 (204/944-2500)

N.B.: Registrar of Companies, Consumer & Corporate Affairs Branch, Dept. of Justice, Box 6000, Fredericton, N.B. E3B 5H1 (506/453-2703)

Dept. of Commerce & Development, Box 6000, Fredericton, N.B. E3B 5H1 (506/453-2965)

Nfld.: Registry of Deeds, Companies & Securities, Dept. of Justice, Confederation Bldg., St. John's, Nfld. A1C 5T7 (709/737-3316)

N.S.: Registry of Joint Stock Companies, (1680 Granville St.), Box 1529, Halifax, N.S. B3J 2Y4 (902/424-7770)

Ont.: Companies Services Branch, Ministry of Consumer & Commercial Relations, 555 Yonge St., 2nd floor, Toronto, Ont. M7A 2H6 (416/963-0377)

P.E.I.: Dept. of Justice, Box 2000, Charlottetown, P.E.I. C1A 7N8 (902/892-5411)

Que.: Dept. of Financial Institutions & Co-operatives, Service des compagnies, 6th floor, 800, Place d'Youville, Quebec, P.Q. G1R 4Y5 (418/643-5253)

Sask.: Corporations Branch, Dept. of Consumer & Commercial Affairs, Room 308, 1919 Rose St., Regina, Sask. S4P 3V7 (306/565-2962)

Yukon: Dept. of Consumer & Corporate Affairs, Box 2703, Whitehorse, Y.T. Y1A 2C6 (403/667-5623)

INDIANS

see Inuit

INDUSTRIAL DESIGN

Industrial Design Office, Copyright & Industrial Design Branch, Dept. of Consumer & Corporate Affairs Canada, Place du Portage, Phase 1, Ottawa/Hull, K1A OC9 (819/997-1725)

National Design Council, 235 Queen St., Ottawa, Ont. K1A OH5 (613/992-0341)

Design Canada, Dept. of Industry, Trade & Commerce, 235 Queen St., Ottawa, Ont. K1A OH5 (613/992-0341)

Alta.: Dept. of Economic Development, Industry Development Branch, 9th floor, Pacific Plaza, 10909 Jasper Ave., Edmonton, Alta. T5J 3L9 (403/427-2005)

B.C.: Design Council of B.C., 4635 Clovelly Walk, West Vancouver, B.C. V7W 1H3

Man.: Industrial Design Director, Dept. of Economic Development & Tourism, #800, 155 Carlton St., Winnipeg, Man. R3C 3H8 (204/944-2468)

N.B.: Commerce & Industry Services Branch, Dept. of Commerce & Development, Box 6000, Fredericton, N.B. E3B 5H1 (506/453-2875)

Nfld.: Dept. of Development, Promotion & Development Division, Box 4750, St. John's, Nfld. A1C 5T7 (709/737-2781)

N.S.: N.S. Design Institute, Dept. of Development, Box 519, Halifax, N.S. B3J 2R7 (902/424-7715)

Ont.: Business Opportunities Section, Industrial Development Branch, Ministry of Industry & Tourism, 6th floor, Hearst Block, 900 Bay St., Toronto, Ont. M7A 2E1 (416/965-2085)

Que.: Dept. of Industry, Trade & Tourism, 710, place d'Youville, Quebec, P.Q. G1R 4Y4 (418/643-5070)

INDUSTRIAL RELATIONS

Communication Services Directorate, Canada Dept. of Labour, Ottawa, Ont. K1A OJ2 (819/994-2238)

See "Labour", this table, for provincial Depts.

INDUSTRIAL SAFETY

Occupational Safety & Health, Dept. of Labour, Ottawa, Ont. K1A OJ3 (819/997-3520)

Information Directorate, Dept. of National Health & Welfare, Ottawa, Ont. K1A OK9 (613/996-4950)

Alta.: Communications Director, Occupational Health & Safety Division, Alberta Workers' Health, Safety & Compensation, 5th floor, 10709 Jasper Ave., Edmonton, Alta. T5J 3N3 (403/427-5541)

B.C.: Elevating Devices Branch, #215, 4946 Canada Way, Burnaby, B.C. V5G 4J6 (604/291-6446)

Occupational Environment Branch, Ministry of Labour, #220, 4946 Canada Way, Burnaby, B.C. V5G 4J6 (604/291-9494)

Man.: Director of Mechanical & Engineering, Dept. of Labour & Manpower, 500 Norquay Bldg., 401 York Ave., Winnipeg, Man. R3C OP8 (204/944-3373)

N.B.: N.B. Occupational Health & Safety Commission, Box 6000, Fredericton, N.B. E3B 5H1 (506/453-2467)

Nfld.: Workers' Compensation Board, Box 9000, Stn. B, St. John's, Nfld. A1A 3B8 (709/754-2940)

N.S.: Dept. of Labour & Manpower, Occupational Safety Division, Box 697, Halifax, N.S. B3J 2T8 (902/424-7649)

Ont.: Industrial Health & Safety Branch, Ministry of Labour, 400 University Ave., 9th floor, Toronto, Ont. M7A 1T7 (416/965-4125)

P.E.I.: Worker's Compensation Board, Box 757, Charlottetown, P.E.I. C1A 7L7 (902/894-8555)

Dept. of Labour, Riverside Dr., Box 2000, Charlottetown, P.E.I. C1A 7N8 (902/892-3416)

Que.: Dept. of Labour, Manpower & Income Security, Electrical Installation Inspection Service, 425 St-Amable, Québec, P.Q. G1R 4Z1 (418/643-3935)

Sask.: Occupational Health & Safety Branch, Dept. of Labour, 1150 Rose St., Regina, Sask. S4P 3V7 (306/565-4481)

Yukon: Dept. of Consumer & Corporate Affairs, Occupational Health & Safety, Box 2703, Whitehorse, Y.T. Y1A 2C6 (403/667-5450)

INDUSTRY (including Business Services)

The Business Centre (Industry, Trade & Commerce Canada), 235 Queen St., Ottawa, Ont. K1A OH5 (613/995-5771). This centre was established to help businessmen reach the proper government branch or department; to set up appointments in advance of their visit to Ottawa, and give advice and guidance on government programs and services.

Federal Business Development Bank, 901 Victoria Sq., Montreal, P.Q. H2Z 1R1 (514/283-5904) (capital financing, equity financing, and management services of training, information and counselling)

Statistics Canada, Ottawa, Ont. K1A OT6 (613/992-2150)

Alta.: Industrial & Engineering Services Dept., Alberta Research Council, 4th floor, 4445 Calgary Trail S., Edmonton, Alta. T6H 5R7 (403/438-0666)
Dept. of Economic Development, Industry Development Branch, 9th floor, Pacific Plaza, 10909 Jasper Ave., Edmonton, Alta. T5J 3L9 (403/427-2005)
B.C.: Ministry of Industry & Small Business Development, Information Services, Parliament Bldgs., Victoria, B.C. V8V 1X4 (604/387-6701)
Man.: Dept. of Economic Development & Tourism, Program Development & Technical Services, 5th floor, 155 Carlton St., Winnipeg, Man. R3C 3H8 (204/944-2023)
N.B.: Dept. of Commerce & Development, Box 6000, Fredericton, N.B. E3B 5H1 (506/453-2965)
Nfld.: Dept. of Development, Promotion & Development Division, Box 4750, St. John's, Nfld. A1C 5T7 (709/737-2797)
N.S.: Dept. of Development, Box 519, Halifax, N.S. B3J 2R7 (902/424-8920)
Industrial Estates Ltd., Ste. 700, 5151 George St., Halifax, N.S. B3J 1M5 (902/425-6331)
N.S. Research Foundation Corp., Box 790, Dartmouth, N.S. B2Y 3Z7 (902/424-8670)
Ont.: Communications Division, Ministry of Industry & Tourism, 900 Bay St., Hearst Block, Queen's Park, Toronto, Ont. M7A 2E3 (416/965-7075)
Toronto Area Industrial Development Board, 11 King St. W., #1008, Toronto, Ont. M5H 1A3 (416/368-1616)
P.E.I.: Dept. of Tourism, Industry & Energy, Box 2000, Charlottetown, P.E.I. C1A 7N8 (902/892-7411)
Que.: Dept. of Industry, Trade & Tourism, 710, place d'Youville, Quebec, P.Q. G1R 4Y4 (418/643-5070)
Sask.: Dept. of Industry & Commerce, 3rd floor, 2121 Saskatchewan Dr., Regina, Sask. S4P 3V7 (306/565-2232) Telex: 071-2675

Brampton: Information Services, Region of Peel, 10 Peel Centre Dr., Brampton, Ont. L6T 4B9 (416/791-9400, ext. 318)
Burlington: Business Services Division, City Hall, 426 Brant St., Box 5013, Burlington, Ont. L7R 3Z6 (416/335-7711)
Calgary: Business Development Dept., Natural Resources Bldg., Ste. 317, 205 9th Ave. S.E., Box 2100, Calgary, Alta. T2P 2M5 (403/268-2331)
Dartmouth: Industrial Commission, City Hall, Box 817, Dartmouth, N.S. B2Y 3Z3 (902/469-9211)
Guelph: Industrial Commissioner, City Hall, Guelph, Ont. N1H 3A1 (519/822-1260, ext. 241)
LaSalle: City Engineer's Dept., 13 Strathyre Ave., LaSalle, P.Q. H8R 3P6 (514/366-7110)
Mississauga: See Brampton
Oshawa: Director of Development, Regional Municipality of Durham, 605 Rossland Rd., Whitby, Ont. L1N 6A3 (416/668-8000)
Quebec Urban Community: Industrial Development Board, 399 St-Joseph est, Québec, P.Q. G1K 8E2 (418/529-8771)
Saint John: Saint John Fundy Region Development Commission, Box 1971, Saint John, N.B. E2L 4L1 (506/658-2918)
Winnipeg: Winnipeg Business Development Corp., #400, 177 Lombard Ave., Winnipeg, Man. R3B OW7 (204/944-8686)

INSULATION & ENERGY SAVING (Grants & Information)

Canada Mtge. & Housing Corp., Montreal Rd., Ottawa, Ont. K1A 0P7 (613/748-2000)
Energy Conservation Branch, Energy, Mines & Resources Canada, 580 Booth St., Ottawa, Ont. K1A 0E4 (613/995-3065) Toll free 1-800-267-9563

Alta.:
B.C.: Communications, Ministry of Energy, Mines & Petroleum Resources, Parliament Bldgs., Victoria, B.C. V8V 1X4 (604/387-5178)
Man.: Energy Information Centre, Dept. of Energy & Mines, #203, 500 Portage Ave., Winnipeg, Man. R3C 0G1 (204/944-4154) Toll free in Manitoba 1-800-282-8069
COSP Information Office, 110 Osborne St., Winnipeg, Man. (204/949-4266)
N.B.: Minister of Finance, Energy Secretariat, Box 6000, Fredericton, N.B. E3B 5H1 (506/453-3684)
Nfld.: Public Information, Dept. of Mines & Energy, Box 4750, St. John's, Nfld. A1C 5T7 (709/737-2411)
N.S.: No provincial agency. Contact: Home Insulation Program, Canada Mtge. & Housing Corp., 7001 Mumford Rd., Halifax, N.S. B3L 4N8 (902/453-2421)
Ont.: Industrial Energy Conservation & Oil Substitution Incentive Program, Ministry of Industry & Tourism, 900 Bay St., Queen's Park, Toronto, Ont. M7A 2E3 (416/965-7075)
Ontario Development Corp., 1200 Bay St., Toronto, Ont. M7A 2E7 (416/956-4622) (assists in installation of energy conservation equipment)
Conservation & Renewable Energy Program, Ministry of Energy, 56 Wellesley St. W., Toronto, Ont. M7A 2B7 (416/965-3051)
P.E.I.: P.E.I. Enersave, Shaw Bldg., Box 2000, Charlottetown, P.E.I. C1A 7N8 (902/892-7411)
Que.:
Sask.: Office of Energy Conservation, Dept. of Mineral Resources, 1914 Hamilton St., Regina, Sask. S4P 4V4 (306/565-3031)
Saskatchewan Power Corp., Energy Conservation Office, 2025 Victoria Ave., Regina, Sask. S4P 0S1 (306/525-7474) Toll free in Saskatchewan 1-800-667-5621

INSURANCE (LIFE, FIRE)

See also Automobile Insurance; Dental Services; and Medical Insurance.

Dept. of Insurance, 140 O'Connor St., Ottawa, Ont. K1A OH2 (613/996-8587, information)
Statistics Canada, Ottawa, Ont. K1A OT6 (613/995-9771)

Alta.: Supt. of Insurance, Dept. of Consumer & Corporate Affairs, 10065 Jasper Ave., Edmonton, Alta. T5J 3B1 (403/427-2244)
B.C.: Office of the Supt. of Insurance, #800, 1050 W. Pender St., Vancouver, B.C. V6E 3S7 (604/682-7031)
Man.: Supt. of Insurance, Room 1142, 405 Broadway Ave., Winnipeg, Man. R3C 3L6 (204/944-2542)
N.B.: Supt. of Insurance, Dept. of Justice, 364 York St., Room 210, Box 6000, Fredericton, N.B. E3B 3P7 (506/453-2541)
Nfld.: Supt. of Insurance, Elizabeth Towers, St. John's, Nfld. A1C 5T7 (709/737-2594)
N.S.: Supt. of Insurance, Dept. of Attorney General, Box 7, Halifax, N.S. B3J 2L6 (902/424-7793)
Ont.: Office of the Supt. of Insurance, 6th floor, 555 Yonge St., Toronto, Ont. M7A 2H6 (416/963-0493)
P.E.I.: Supt. of Insurance, Dept. of Justice, Box 2000, Charlottetown, P.E.I. C1A 7N8 (902/892-5411)
Que.: Insurance Branch, Dept. of Financial Institutions & Co-operatives, Ste. 803, 800, Carré d'Youville, Quebec, P.Q. G1R 4Y5 (418/643-5783)
Sask.: Supt. of Insurance, Saskatchewan Consumer & Commercial Affairs, 1871 Smith St., Regina, Sask. S4P 3V7 (306/565-2957)

INTERNATIONAL AFFAIRS

see Exports; *see* External Affairs; *see* Trade

INUIT

Public Enquiries, Dept. of Indian Affairs & Northern Development, Ottawa, Ont. K1A OH4 (819/997-0380)
Medical Services, Dept. of Health & Welfare, Ottawa, Ont. K1A OL3
National Film Board, Box 6100, Montreal, P.Q. H3C 3H5 (514/333-3333)
National Museum of Man, Canadian Ethnology Service & Archaeological Survey of Canada, Ottawa, Ont. K1A 0M8 (613/996-4540, 996-5250)
Native Citizens' Directorate, Secretary of State, Ottawa, Ont. K1A 0M5 (819/994-3835)

Alta.: Alberta Executive Council/Native Secretariat, 2nd floor, South Tower, 10030 107 St., Edmonton, Alta. T5J 3E4 (403/427-8407)

B.C.: First Citizens' Fund Administration, Ministry of Provincial Secretary & Government Services, Parliament Bldgs., Victoria, B.C. V8V 1X4 (604/387-3206)

Que.: New Quebec Branch, Dept. of Energy & Resources, 1530 boul. de l'Entente, Quebec, P.Q. G1A 1P3 (418/643-8045)

Ont.: Native Community Branch, Ministry of Culture & Recreation, 77 Bloor St. W., 5th floor, Toronto, Ont. M7A 2R9 (416/965-5003)

Sask.: Dept. of Northern Sask., Box 5000, La Ronge, Sask. SOJ 1LO (306/425-4496)
and refer to: Federation of Saskatchewan Indians, 1114 Central Ave., Prince Albert, Sask. S6V 4V6 (306/764-3411)

INVESTMENT
(Corporate & Capital; Industrial & Commercial)
For land purchase, see Real Estate.

See also Incorporation of Companies, *and* Industry

Foreign Investment Review Agency, 240 Sparks St., Ottawa, Ont. (613/995-9449)

Statistics Canada, Ottawa, Ont. K1A OT6 (613/995-9013)

Alta.: Dept. of Economic Development, Industry Development Branch, 9th floor, Pacific Plaza, 10909 Jasper Ave., Edmonton, Alta. T5J 3L9 (403/427-2005)

B.C.: Ministry of Industry & Small Business Development, Information Services, Parliament Bldgs., Victoria, B.C. V8V 1X4 (604/387-6701)

Man.: Dept. of Economic Development & Tourism, Industrial Development Branch, 155 Carlton St., Winnipeg, Man. R3C 0V8 (204/944-2455)

N.B.: Dept. of Commerce & Development, Box 6000, Fredericton, N.B. E3B 5H1 (506/453-3649)

Nfld.: Dept. of Development, Promotion & Development Division, Box 4750, St. John's, Nfld. A1C 5T7 (709/737-2781)

N.S.: Dept. of Development, Development Services Division, Box 519, Halifax, N.S. B3J 2R7 (902/424-8921)

Ont.: Corporations Tax Branch, Ministry of Revenue, 77 Bloor St. W., Toronto, Ont. M7A 1Y1 (416/965-1165) – relocation to Oshawa planned for fall of 1982

P.E.I.: Dept. of Tourism, Industry & Energy, Box 2000, Charlottetown, P.E.I. C1A 7N8 (902/892-7411)

Que.: Dept. of Financial Institutions & Co-operatives, 800, Place d'Youville, Quebec, P.Q. G1R 4Y5 (418/643-1411)

Sask.: Dept. of Industry & Commerce, 3rd floor, 2121 Saskatchewan Dr., Regina, Sask. S4P 3V7 (306/565-2232) Telex: 071-2675

IRON & STEEL

Dept. of Energy, Mines & Resources, Mineral Policy Sector, 580 Booth St., Ottawa, Ont. K1A OE4 (613/995-9466)

Dept. of Industry, Trade & Commerce, Iron & Steel Division, 235 Queen St., Ottawa, Ont. K1A OH5 (613/992-0025)

National Film Board, Box 6100, Montreal, P.Q. H3C 3H5 (514/333-3333)

Statistics Canada, Ottawa, Ont. K1A OT6 (613/992-0388)

Alta.: Alberta Geological Survey, Alberta Research Council, 4445 Calgary Trail S., Edmonton, Alta. T6H 5R7 (403/438-0555)
Dept. of Economic Development, Industry Development Branch, 9th floor, Pacific Plaza, 10909 Jasper Ave., Edmonton, Alta. T5J 3L9 (403/427-2005)
Dept. of Energy & Natural Resources, 9915 108 St., Edmonton, Alta. T5K 2C9 (403/427-7003)

B.C.: Ministry of Energy, Mines & Petroleum Resources, Parliament Bldgs., Victoria, B.C. V8V 1X4 (604/387-3787)

Nfld.: Dept. of Mines & Energy, 95 Bonaventure Ave., Box 4750, St. John's, Nfld. A1C 5T7 (709/737-3159)

N.S.: Dept. of Mines & Energy, Box 1087, Halifax, N.S. B3J 2X1 (902/424-4161)
Sydney Steel Corp., Public Relations, Box 1450, Sydney, N.S. B1P 6K5 (902/564-5471)

Ont.: Industry Sector, Policy Branch, Policy & Priorities Division, Ministry of Industry & Tourism, 900 Bay St., Toronto, Ont. M7A 2E6 (416/965-7196)

Que.: Quebec Bureau of Statistics, Dept. of Industry, Trade & Tourism, 117 St-André, Quebec, P.Q. G1K 3Y3 (418/643-5116)

Sask.: Admin. Services Branch, Dept. of Mineral Resources, 1914 Hamilton St., Regina, Sask. S4P 4V4 (306/565-2528)

JUSTICE DEPARTMENTS, COURTS & JUDGES

Commr. for Federal Judicial Affairs, Lord Elgin Plaza, 66 Slater St., Ottawa, Ont. K1A 1E3 (613/992-9175)

Information Services, Dept. of Justice, Ottawa, Ont. K1A OH8 (613/995-2569)

Statistics Canada, Ottawa, Ont. K1A OT6 (613/995-0709)

Alta.: Dept. of the Attorney General, 9833 109 St., Edmonton, Alta. T5K 2E8 (403/427-2745)

B.C.: Ministry of Attorney General, Parliament Bldgs., Victoria, B.C. V8V 1X4 (604/384-4434)
Court Services (Law Courts), 6th floor, 850 Burdett St., Victoria, B.C. V8W 1B4 (604/387-1521)

Man.: Dept. of the Attorney General, 104 Legislative Bldg., 450 Broadway, Winnipeg, Man. R3C 0V8 (204/946-3728 & 3181)

N.B.: Dept. of Justice, Box 6000, Fredericton, N.B. E3B 5H1 (506/453-2208)
Court of Queen's Bench: 453-2821, and 453-2776
Provincial Court: 453-2120, and 453-2806
Family Court, 453-2015

Nfld.: Dept. of Justice, Confederation Bldg., St. John's, Nfld. A1C 5T7 (709/737-2872)

N.S.: Dept. of the Attorney General, Provincial Bldg., (Box 7) Halifax, N.S. B3J 2L6 (902/424-4222)

Ont.: Ministry of the Attorney General, 18 King St. E., 18th floor, Toronto, Ont. M5C 1C5 (416/965-5184)

P.E.I.: Dept. of Justice, Box 2000, Charlottetown, P.E.I. C1A 7N8 (902/892-5411)
The Prothonotary, Supreme Court, Box 2200, Charlottetown, P.E.I. C1A 8B9 (902/892-9131)

Que.: Dept. of Justice, Direction des Communications, 1200, rte de l'Eglise, 9e étage, Ste-Foy, P.Q. G1V 4M1 (418/643-5140)

Sask.: Executive Director of Court Services, Dept. of the Attorney General, 2476 Victoria Ave., Regina, Sask. S4P 3V7 (306/565-5385)

Yukon: Dept. of Justice, Box 2703, Whitehorse, Y.T. Y1A 2C6 (403/667-5446)

See Index for Courts, Judges, etc.

JUVENILES

see Youth Services

LABOUR

Canada Employment & Immigration Commission, Public Affairs Division, Ottawa, Ont. K1A OJ9 (819/994-6313)

Canada Labour Relations Board, 3rd floor, Tower D, 125 Sussex Dr., Ottawa, Ont. K1A OX8 (613/992-3541)

Communication Services Directorate, Canada Dept. of Labour, Ottawa, Ont. K1A OJ2 (819/994-2238)

National Film Board, Box 6100, Montreal, P.Q. H3C 3H5 (514/333-3333)

National Research Council of Canada, Employee Relations Branch, Ottawa, Ont. K1A OR6 (613/993-9391)

Statistics Canada, Ottawa, Ont. K1A OT6 (613/992-5613)

Alta.: Dept. of Labour, 10th floor, 10808 99th Ave., Edmonton, Alta. T5K OG5 (403/427-8387)

B.C.: Ministry of Labour, (880 Douglas St.), Parliament Bldgs., Victoria, B.C. V8V 1X4 (604/387-5071)

Man.: Dept. of Labour & Manpower, 604 Norquay Bldg., Kennedy & York, Winnipeg, Man. R3C OP8 (204/944-3334,5)

N.B.: Dept. of Labour & Manpower, Box 6000, Fredericton, N.B. E3B 5H1 (506/453-2320)

Nfld.: Dept. of Labour & Manpower, Confederation Bldg., St. John's, Nfld. A1C 5T7 (709/737-2711)

N.S.: Dept. of Labour & Manpower, Box 697, Halifax, N.S. B3J 2T8 (902/424-6647)

Ont.: Labour Relations Board, 4th floor, 400 University Ave., Toronto, Ont. M7A 1V4 (416/965-4151)

P.E.I.: Dept. of Labour, Riverside Dr., Box 2000, Charlottetown, P.E.I. C1A 7N8 (902/892-3416)

Que.: Dept. of Labour, Manpower & Income Security, 425, St-Amable, Quebec, P.Q. G1R 4Z1 (418/643-3880)

Sask.: Dept. of Labour, 1914 Hamilton St., Regina, Sask. S4P 4V4 (306/565-2401)

LANDLORD & TENANT REGULATIONS (& Rent Control)

Alta.: Consumer & Corporate Affairs, 9th floor, 10065 Jasper Ave., Edmonton, Alta. T5J 3B1 (403/427-2244)

B.C.: Office of the Rentalsman, #1000, 1050 W. Pender St., Vancouver, B.C. V6E 3Z4 (604/682-8741, 689-0811)

Man.: Office of the Rentalsman, Dept. of Consumer & Corporate Affairs & Environment, 307 Kennedy St., Winnipeg, Man. R3C 0V8; 204/956-1010 (Landlord & Tenant)

Manitoba Rent Review, Room 304, 379 Broadway, Winnipeg, Man. R3C 3N4 (204/944-2476)

N.B.: Dept. of Justice, Box 6000, Fredericton, N.B. E3B 5H1 (506/453-2589)

Nfld.: Dept. of Justice, Confederation Bldg., St. John's, Nfld. A1C 5T7 (709/737-2608)

N.S.: Chairman, Rent Review Commission, Dept. of Consumer Affairs, 5151 Terminal Rd., Halifax, N.S. B3J 2V2 (902/424-4690)

Ont.: Ministry of the Attorney General, 18 King St. E., Toronto, Ont. M5C 1C5 (416/965-5184)

Residential Tenancy Commission, 3rd floor, 77 Bloor St. W., Toronto, Ont. M5S 1S2 (416/964-7808)

P.E.I.: Office of the Rentalsman, Box 2000, Charlottetown, P.E.I. C1A 7N8 (902/894-8559)

Que.: Commission des loyers, 10 est rue St-Antoine, Ch. 11.65, Montreal, P.Q. H2Y 1B6 (514/873-4001)

Sask.: Dept. of Consumer & Commercial Affairs: Office of the Rentalsman, 1871 Smith St., Regina, Sask. S4P 3V7 (306/565-2699); 224 4th Ave. S., Saskatoon, Sask. S7K 5M5 (306/664-5680)

Rent Appeal Commission, 224 4th Ave. S., Saskatoon, Sask. S7K 5M5 (306/664-6120)

Yukon: Dept. of Consumer & Corporate Affairs, Consumer Services, Box 2703, Whitehorse, Y.T. Y1A 2C6 (403/667-5312)

Calgary: Landlord & Tenant Advisory Board, (205 8th Ave. S.E.), Box 2100, Calgary, Alta. T2P 2M5 (403/268-4656)

Edmonton: Landlord & Tenant Advisory Board, 10237 98th St., Musial Bldg., Edmonton, Alta. T5J 0M7 (403/426-4951)

Guelph: Guelph Information, 161 Waterloo Ave., Guelph, Ont. N1H 3H9 (519/821-0632)

Hamilton: Landlord & Tenant Advisory Bureau, City Hall, 71 Main St. W., Hamilton, Ont. L8P 1H4 (416/527-0241, ext. 330)

Kitchener: Regional Solicitor's Office, Regional Municipality of Waterloo, Marsland Centre, Waterloo, Ont. N2J 4G7 (416/885-9588)

London: Housing Division, 50 King St., London, Ont. N6A 1B9 (519/679-5464)

Mississauga: Landlord & Tenant Officer, 5170 Dixie Rd., #304, Mississauga, Ont. L4W 1E3 (416/625-4432)

Niagara Falls: Bureau contact: Information Niagara, 5017 Victoria Ave., Niagara Falls, Ont. L2E 4C9 (416/356-4636)

Oshawa: Durham Housing Registry, Regional Municipality of Durham, Dept. of Social Services, 50 McMillan Dr., Oshawa, Ont. L1G 3Z6 (416/579-0622)

Residential Tenancy Commission (Durham Region), 340 George St. N., Peterborough, Ont. K9H 7E8 (Zenith 9-6000)

St. Catharines: Information Niagara, 360 St. Paul St., St. Catharines, Ont. L2R 3N2 (416/682-6611)

Thunder Bay: Social Services Dept., 10 S. Algoma St., Thunder Bay, Ont. P7B 3A7 (807/623-2711, ext. 2-335)

Toronto: Metropolitan Toronto Landlord & Tenant Advisory Bureau, 67 Adelaide St. E., Toronto, Ont. M5C 1K8

Windsor: Landlords & Tenants Advisory Bureau, 68 Chatham St. E., Windsor, Ont. N9A 6S1 (519/255-6307)

LAND TITLES

Alta.: Attorney General's Dept., Land Titles Office, 100 St. & 102A Ave., Box 2380, Edmonton, Alta. T5J 2T3 (403/427-2742); – Land Titles Office, Box 7575, J.J. Bowlen Bldg., 620 7th Ave. S.W., Calgary, Alta. T2P 1T5 (403/261-6511)

B.C.: Attorney General's Ministry, Land Title Office, Director of Land Titles, #201, 1250 Quadra St., Victoria, B.C. V8W 2K7 (604/387-3055) (See Index for list of local offices)

Man.: Dept. of the Attorney General, Land Titles Office, Woodsworth Bldg., 405 Broadway, Winnipeg, Man. R3C 3L6 (204/944-2246)

N.B.: Dept. of Justice, Box 6000, Fredericton, N.B. E3B 5H1 (506/453-2817)

N.S.: Dept. of Attorney General, Box 7, Halifax, N.S. B3J 2L6 (902/424-4222)

Ont.: Ministry of Consumer & Commercial Relations, Director of Titles, 543 Yonge St., 3rd floor, Toronto, Ont. M7A 2J8 (416/963-0423)

P.E.I.: Charlottetown Registry Office, Properties & Surveys Division, Box 2000, Charlottetown, P.E.I. C1A 7N8 (902/892-7431)

Que.: Land Titles Office, Dept. of Energy & Resources, 200 B Chemin Ste-Foy, Quebec, P.Q. G1R 4X7 (418/643-4714)

Sask.: Land Titles Office, Dept. of the Attorney General, 2476 Victoria Ave., Regina, Sask. S4P 3V7 (306/565-5507)

Yukon: Dept. of Justice, Land Titles, Box 2703, Whitehorse, Y.T. Y1A 2C6 (403/667-5611)

LEGAL AID

Alta.: Legal Aid Society of Alberta, #401, Melton Bldg., 10310 Jasper Ave., Edmonton, Alta. T5J 2W4 (403/427-7575)

B.C.: Legal Services Society, Box 12120, #700-S, 555 W. Hastings St., Vancouver, B.C. V6B 4N6 (604/689-0741)

Man.: Legal Aid Society of Man., 325 Portage Ave., Winnipeg, Man. R3B 2B9 (204/947-6501)

N.B.: Legal Aid New Brunswick, Box 1144, Fredericton, N.B. E3B 5C2 (506/455-9976)

Nfld.: Nfld. Legal Aid Commission, 21 Church Hill, St. John's, Nfld. A1C 3Z8 (709/753-7860)

N.S.: N.S. Legal Aid Commission, 5212 Sackville St., Ste. 301, Halifax, N.S. B3J 1K6 (902/423-1291)

Ont.: Ontario Legal Aid Plan, 145 King St. W., Suite 1000, Toronto, Ont. M5H 3L7 (416/361-0766)

P.E.I.: Public Defender, 42 Water St., Box 2200, Charlottetown, P.E.I. C1A 8B9 (902/892-5409)

Que.: Commission des services juridiques (Legal Services Commission), 2 Complexe Desjardins, Tour de l'Est, Bur. 1404, Montreal, P.Q. H5B 1B3 (514/873-3562)

Sask.: Saskatchewan Community Legal Services Commission, 311 21st St. E., Saskatoon, Sask. S7K 0C1 (306/664-5300)

Yukon: Dept. of Justice, Legal Aid, Box 2703, Whitehorse, Y.T. Y1A 2C6 (403/667-5210)

LEISURE CRAFT REGULATIONS

Small Vessels:

Ship Safety Branch, Canadian Coast Guard, Transport Canada Bldg., Place de Ville, Ottawa, Ont. K1A 0N7 (613/992-8025)

Navigation Canals, Parks Canada, Information Division, Ottawa, Ont. K1A 1G2 (819/997-0088) (includes Trent–Severn and Rideau canal systems)

Small Craft Harbours Directorate, Fisheries & Oceans Canada, Ottawa, Ont. K1A 0E6 (613/995-2003)

Snowmobiles & All-terrain Vehicles:

Alta.: Motor Vehicles Division, 10001 Bellamy Hill, Edmonton, Alta. T5J 3B7 (403/427-7013)

B.C.: Ministry of Lands, Parks & Housing, Parliament Bldgs., Victoria, B.C. V8V 1X4 (604/387-5091)

Man.: Motor Vehicle Branch, Highway Safety Division, Dept. of Highways & Transportation, Box 15, 139 Tuxedo Blvd., Winnipeg, Man. R3N OH6 (204/895-5127)

N.B.: Motor Vehicle Division, Vehicle Registration Section, Dept. of Transportation, Box 6000, Fredericton, N.B. E3B 5H1 (506/453-2443)

Nfld.: Dept. of Transportation, Motor Registration Division, Viking Bldg., Crosbie Rd., St. John's, Nfld. A1B 3K3

N.S.: Registry of Motor Vehicles, 6061 Young St., Box 1652, Halifax, N.S. B3J 2Z3 (902/424-5531)

Ont.: Vehicle Licensing Office, Ministry of Transportation & Communications, 6th floor, Ferguson Block, Queen's Park, Toronto, Ont. M7A 2A2 (416/965-1226); Snowmobile Information: Box 201, Stn. Q, Toronto, Ont. M4T 1L0 (416/249-2677)

P.E.I.: Highway Safety Division, Dept. of Highways & Public Works, Box 2000, Charlottetown, P.E.I. C1A 7N8 (902/892-5306)

Que.: Ministère des Transports, Bureau des véhicules automobiles, Service du Contrôle du Permis de conduire, 880 Chemin Ste-Foy, No. 412, Quebec, P.Q. G1S 2K8

Sask.: Motor Vehicle & Driving Licensing Division, Highway Traffic Board, 2260 11th Ave., Regina, Sask. S4P 3V7 (306/565-4031)

LIBRARIES

see Bibliography

LIQUOR CONTROL

Statistics Canada, Ottawa, Ont. K1A OT6 (613/995-8201)

Alta.: Alberta Liquor Control Board, 12360 142 St., Edmonton, Alta. T5L 2H1 (403/454-6521)

B.C.: B.C. Liquor Control & Licensing Branch, Box 640, Victoria, B.C. V8W 2P8 (604/387-1254)

Man.: Liquor Control Commission, Box 1023, Winnipeg, Man. R3C 2X1 (204/284-2501)

N.B.: Liquor Corp., Box 20787, Fredericton, N.B. E3B 5B8 (506/454-1551)

N.B. Liquor Licensing Board, Box 20264, Fredericton, N.B. E3B 5V3 (506/453-3728)

Nfld.: Nfld. Liquor Corp., Box 8750, Kenmount Rd., St. John's, Nfld. A1B 3V1 (709/754-1100)

Nfld. Liquor Licensing Board, (Ashley Bldg., Peet St.), Box 8550, St. John's, Nfld. A1B 3P2 (709/753-7800)

N.S.: Liquor License Board, Ste. 401, 277 Pleasant St., Dartmouth, N.S. B2Y 4B7 (902/469-6160)

Ont.: Liquor Control Board of Ontario, 55 Lakeshore Blvd. E., Toronto, Ont. M5E 1A4 (416/965-4977)

P.E.I.: Liquor Control Commission, Box 967, Charlottetown, P.E.I. C1A 7M4 (902/892-8541)

Que.: Régie des permis d'alcool du Québec, 1 est, rue Notre-Dame, bur 9.200, Montreal, P.Q. H2Y 1B6 (514/873-3577); 125 rue Dalhousie, Quebec, P.Q. G1K 4C7 (418/643-4392)

Sask.: Liquor Licensing Commission, 1660 Park St., Regina, Sask. S4N 2G2 (306/565-4275) (licensed outlets)

Saskatchewan Liquor Board, Box 5054, Regina, Sask. S4P 3M3 (306/565-4213) (liquor control)

Yukon: Yukon Liquor Corp., #278, 9031 Quartz Rd., Whitehorse, Y.T. Y1A 4P9 (403/667-5245)

LIVESTOCK

Animal Production Division, Dept. of Agriculture, Sir John Carling Bldg., Ottawa, Ont. K1A OC5 (613/995-5880)

Animal Pathology Division, Food Production & Inspection Branch, Dept. of Agriculture, Box 11300, Stn. H, Ottawa, Ont. K2H 8P9 (613/998-9320)

Agriculture, Fisheries & Food Products Branch, Livestock, Meat & Dairy Products Division, Dept. of Industry, Trade & Commerce, 235 Queen St., Ottawa, Ont. K1A OH5 (613/995-8107)

National Film Board, Box 6100, Montreal, P.Q. H3C 3H5 (514/333-3333)

Statistics Canada, Ottawa, Ont. K1A OT6 (613/995-4853)

Alta.: Animal Industry Division, Alberta Agriculture, 9718 107 St., Edmonton, Alta. T5K 2C8 (403/427-5091)

B.C.: Livestock Branch, Ministry of Agriculture & Food, Parliament Bldgs., Victoria, B.C. V8W 2Z7 (604/387-5121)

Man.: Animal Industry Branch, Dept. of Agriculture, Agricultural Services Complex, Univ. of Man. Campus, Winnipeg, Man. R3T 2N2 (204/269-1220)

N.B.: Livestock & Poultry Branch, Dept. of Agriculture & Rural Development, Box 6000, Fredericton, N.B. E3B 5H1 (506/453-2457)

Nfld.: Dept. of Rural, Agricultural & Northern Development, Prov. Agriculture Bldg., Brookfield Rd., Mount Pearl, Nfld. (709/737-3840)

N.S.: Livestock Services, Dept. of Agriculture & Marketing, Box 550, Truro, N.S. B2N 5E3 (902/895-1571)

Ont.: Ministry of Agriculture & Food, Live Stock Branch, Legislative Bldgs., Toronto, Ont. M7A 1B4 (416/965-5971)

P.E.I.: Dept. of Agriculture & Forestry, Box 2000, Charlottetown, P.E.I. C1A 7N8 (902/892-4101)

Que.: Animal Production Service, Dept. of Agriculture & Food, 200 A, Ste-Foy Rd., 1st floor, Quebec, P.Q. G1R 4X6 (418/643-7597)

Sask.: Animal Industry Branch, Saskatchewan Agriculture, Walter Scott Bldg., 3085 Albert St., Regina, Sask. S4S OB1 (306/565-4675)

LOTTERIES

Interprovincial

Atlantic Loto, 860 Main St., Moncton, N.B. E1C 8W6 (506/854-5680)

Interprovincial Lottery Corp. (created through an agreement among all the provinces to jointly manage an Interprovincial Lottery marketing the Provincial/Super Loto), Ste. 2503, 2 Bloor St. W., Toronto, Ont. M4W 3H8 (416/968-7769)

Alta.: Attorney General's Dept., Gaming Control, Park Sq. Bldg., 20th floor, 10001 Bellamy Hill, Edmonton, Alta. T5J 3C1 (403/427-5052)

B.C.: Lotteries Branch, Ministry of Provincial Secretary & Government Services, 940 Blanshard St., Victoria, B.C. V8W 3E6 (604/387-5311)

Man.: Manitoba Lotteries & Gaming Licensing Board, Dept. of Co-operative Development, #301, 207 Donald St., Winnipeg, Man. R3C 1M5 (204/944-2670)

Manitoba Lotteries & Gaming Control Commission, #301, 207 Donald St., Winnipeg, Man. R3C 1M5 (204/944-3524)

N.B.: Dept. of Finance, Box 6000, Fredericton, N.B. E3B 5H1 (506/453-2097)

Nfld.: Dept. of Justice, Confederation Bldg., St. John's, Nfld. A1C 5T7 (709/737-2872) (lotteries illegal in Nfld.)

N.S.: N.S. Lottery Commission, Box 545, Dartmouth, N.S. B2Y 3Y8 (902/424-4520)

Ont.: Lotteries Branch, Ministry of Consumer & Commercial Relations, 555 Yonge St., Toronto, Ont. M4Y 1Y7; 416/963-0272 (regulations)

Ontario Lottery Corp., 2 Bloor St. W., Toronto, Ont. M4W 3H8 (416/961-6262) (operating Wintario; The Provincial; Lottario and Super Loto)

P.E.I.: Dept. of Justice, Box 2000, Charlottetown, P.E.I. C1A 7N8 (902/892-5411)

Que.: Société des loteries et courses du Québec (known as LOTO-QUEBEC and operating Mini-Loto, Inter-Loto, 6/36, La Quotidienne, Loto/Select and instant lotteries), 2000 Berri St., Montreal, P.Q. H2L 4N5 (514/282-8000, admin.; 873-5353, info.)

Régie des Loteries et Courses du Québec, 2055, Peel, suite 700, Montreal, P.Q. H3A 2K9 (514/873-5180)

MANPOWER CENTRES

see Employment

MANUFACTURING

Dept. of Industry, Trade & Commerce, Business Centre, 235 Queen St., Ottawa, Ont. K1A OH5 (613/995-5771)

National Film Board, Box 6100, Montreal, P.Q. H3C 3H5 (514/333-3333)
National Research Council of Canada, Manufacturing Technology Centre, Division of Mechanical Engineering, Ottawa, Ont. K1A OR6 (613/993-2436, 2471)
Technical Information Service, National Research Council of Canada, Ottawa, Ont. K1A 0S3 (613/993-1753)
Statistics Canada, Ottawa, Ont. K1A OT6 (613/992-3297)

Alta.: Alberta Bureau of Statistics, Alberta Treasury, 7th floor, 9811 109 St., Edmonton, Alta. T5J 0C8 (403/427-3058)
B.C.: Ministry of Industry & Small Business Development, #315, 800 Hornby St., Vancouver, B.C. V6Z 2C5 (604/689-4411)
Man.: Business Development Branch, Dept. of Economic Development & Tourism, #701, 155 Carlton St., Winnipeg, Man. R3C 0V8 (204/944-2455)
N.B.: Dept. of Commerce & Development, Box 6000, Fredericton, N.B. E3B 5H1 (506/453-2965)
Nfld.: Dept. of Development, Development & Promotion Division, Box 4750, St. John's, Nfld. A1C 5T7 (709/737-2781)
N.S.: Dept. of Development, Development Operations Division, Box 519, Halifax, N.S. B3J 2R7 (902/424-4243)
Industrial Estates Ltd., Ste. 700, Bank of Montreal Tower, 5151 George St., Halifax, N.S. B3J 1M5 (902/425-6331)
Ont.: Ministry of Industry & Tourism, Industrial Development Branch, 900 Bay St., Queen's Park, Toronto, Ont. M7A 2E4 (416/965-0157)
P.E.I.: Industry Branch, Dept. of Tourism, Industry & Energy, Box 2000, Charlottetown, P.E.I. C1A 7N8 (902/892-7411)
Que.: Quebec Bureau of Statistics, Dept. of Industry, Trade & Tourism, 117 St-André, Quebec, P.Q. G1K 3Y3 (418/643-5116)

MAPS & CHARTS & AERIAL PHOTOGRAPHS

see also "Tourism" for Road Maps

Dept. of Energy, Mines & Resources:
Canada Map Office, 615 Booth St., Ottawa, Ont. K1A OE9 (613/998-9900)
National Air Photo Library, 615 Booth St., Ottawa, Ont. K1A OE9 (995-4560)
Geological Survey of Canada, 601 Booth St., Ottawa, Ont. K1A OE8 (995-4342) (geological)
Earth Physics Branch, 1 Observatory Cres., Ottawa, Ont. K1A OY3 (613/995-5544) (gravity, seismology & geomagnetism)
Canada Centre for Remote Sensing, 2464 Sheffield Rd., Ottawa, Ont. K1A OY7 (613/995-1210) (Landsat imagery)
Mining Recorder, Map Office, Box 1500, Yellowknife, N.W.T. X1A 2R3 (403/920-8227)
Regional Geologist, 200 Range Rd., Whitehorse, Y.T. Y1A 3V1 (403/668-5151)
Maritime Resources Management Service, Box 310, 16 Station St., Amherst, N.S. B4H 3Z5 (902/667-7231)
Bureau Regional de Vente de Cartes, 1535 Chemin Ste-Foy, Quebec, P.Q. G1S 2P1 (418/694-3325)
Marine Chart & Publications Sales, Canadian Hydrographic Service, Fisheries & Oceans Canada, 1675 Russell Rd., Ottawa, Ont. K1G 3H6 (613/998-4931)
Public Archives of Canada, 395 Wellington St., Ottawa, Ont. K1A ON3 (613/995-1077)
Statistics Canada, Ottawa, Ont. K1A OT6 (613/996-5254)

Alta.: Map Distribution, Alberta Bureau of Surveying & Mapping, Energy & Natural Resources, 4949 94B Ave., Edmonton, Alta. T6B 2T5
Travel Alberta, 14th floor, 10065 Jasper Ave., Edmonton, Alta. T5J OH4 (403/427-4324)
Dept. of Energy & Natural Resources, Map & Air Photo Distribution Services, 2nd floor, Petroleum Plaza, North Tower, 9945 108 St., Edmonton, Alta. T5K 2G6 (Maps, 403/427-3520; Air Photos, 403/427-3519; Ref. Library, 403/427-7417)
B.C.: MAPS-B.C., Map Production, Ministry of Environment, Parliament Bldgs., Victoria, B.C. V8V 1X4 (604/387-3174, 5)
Man.: Map Distribution & Remote Sensing, Surveys & Mapping Branch, 1007 Century St., Winnipeg, Man. R3H 0W4 (204/632-8681)
Map Sales, Dept. of Natural Resources, 59 Elizabeth Dr., Thompson, Man. R8N 1X4 (204/778-4411)
Map Sales, Dept. of Natural Resources, Prov. Bldg., 3rd St. & Ross Ave., The Pas, Man. R9A 1M4 (204/623-6411)
N.B.: Lands Branch, Dept. of Natural Resources, Box 6000, Fredericton, N.B. E3B 5H1 (506/453-2513)
Nfld.: Director of Mapping, Dept. of Forestry Resources & Lands, Howley Bldg., Higgins Line, St. John's, Nfld. A1C 5T7 (709/737-3305)
N.S.: Dept. of Lands & Forests, Box 698, Halifax, N.S. B3J 2T9 (902/424-6696)
Ont.: Public Service Centre, Ministry of Natural Resources, Queen's Park, Toronto, Ont. M7A 1W3 (416/965-6511)
Ministry of Transportation & Communications, Record Services Office, East Bldg., 1201 Wilson Ave., Downsview, Ont. M3M 1J8 (416/248-3476) - County maps only
P.E.I.: Land Registration & Information Service, Surveys & Mapping Division, 120 Water St., Summerside, P.E.I. C1N 1A9 (902/436-2107)
Que.: Dept. of Energy & Resources, Cartography Service, 1995, boul. Charest ouest, Quebec, P.Q. G1N 4H9 (418/643-4522)
Dessin et Cartographie, 620, rue Godin, Vanier, P.Q. G1M 2K3 (418/643-5110)
Dept. of Agriculture, Fisheries & Food, Communications Division, 200 A Chemin Ste-Foy, Quebec, P.Q. G1R 4X6 (418/643-2673)
Sask.: Central Survey & Mapping Agency, Saskatchewan Highways & Transportation, 3211 Albert St., Regina, Sask. S4S 5W6 (306/565-2799)

MARINE SCIENCES

see Oceanography

MARRIAGE LICENCES

see Vital Statistics

MATRIMONIAL & FAMILY COUNSELLING

Alta.: Conciliation Counselling, Divorce Mediation, Edmonton Courts, 500 Century Place, 9803 102A Ave., Edmonton, Alta. T5J 3A6 (403/427-8329)
B.C.: Ministry of Human Resources, Parliament Bldgs., Victoria, B.C. V8V 1X4 (604/387-1544)
Man.: Dept. of Community Services & Corrections, Marriage Conciliation Service, Bldg. 30, 139 Tuxedo Ave., Winnipeg, Man. R3C 0V8 (204/895-5023)
N.B.: Child & Family Services, Dept. of Social Services, Box 6000, Fredericton, N.B. E3B 5H1 (506/453-2950)
P.E.I.: Dept. of Health & Social Services, Box 2000, Charlottetown, P.E.I. C1A 7N8 (902/892-5471)
Protestant Family Service Bureau, Box 592, Charlottetown, P.E.I. C1A 7L1 (902/892-2441)
Que.: Social Affairs Dept., Psycho-social Consultation Service, 1005 Chemin Ste-Foy, 6th floor, Quebec, P.Q. G1S 4N4 (418/643-6658)
Sask.: Dept. of Social Services, 1920 Broad St., Regina, Sask. S4P 3V6 (306/565-3605)
Regina Family Service Bureau, 1801 Toronto St., Regina, Sask. S4P 1M7 (306/527-6675)

MEDICAL INSURANCE

Health Insurance Division, Health Resources Directorate, Health Services & Promotion Branch, Dept. of National Health & Welfare, Ottawa, Ont. K1A 1B4 (613/995-6186)

Alta.: Alberta Hospitals & Medical Care, Health Care Insurance Plan: Edmonton – Groat Rd. & 118th Ave. (Box 1360) T5J 2N3 (403/427-1432); Calgary – 629B 7th Ave. S.W. T2P 0Y9 (403/261-6411)
Hospital Insurance, Alberta Hospitals & Medical Care, Centre West, 10035 108th St., Box 2222, Edmonton, Alta. T5J 3E1

B.C.: B.C. Medical Services Commission, (1515 Blanshard St.) Parliament Bldgs., Victoria, B.C. V8W 3C8 (604/387-3411) – Medical Services Plan of B.C., Box 1600, Victoria, B.C. V8W 2X9 (604/386-3166)
Hospital Programs, Ministry of Health, 1515 Blanshard St., Victoria, B.C. V8W 3C8 (604/387-1066)
Man.: Manitoba Health Services Commission, 599 Empress St., Winnipeg, Man. R3C 2T6 (204/786-7107, 786-7398)
N.B.: Hospital/Medicare New Brunswick, Insured Services Division, Dept. of Health, Box 5100, Fredericton, N.B. E3B 5G8 (506/453-2161)
Nfld.: Nfld. Medical Care Commission, Elizabeth Towers, Elizabeth Ave., St. John's, Nfld. A1C 5J3 (709/722-6980)
Hospital Services Division, Dept. of Health, Confederation Bldg., St. John's, Nfld. A1C 5T7
N.S.: N.S. Health Services & Insurance Commission, Box 760, Halifax, N.S. B3J 2V2 (902/424-8902)
Hospital Insurance, Dept. of Health, Box 488, Halifax, N.S. B3J 2R8
Ont.: Ontario Health Insurance Plan (OHIP), 7 Overlea Blvd., Toronto, Ont. M4H 1A9 (General inquiries: 416/482-1111)
P.E.I.: P.E.I. Health Services Commission, Box 4500, Charlottetown, P.E.I. C1A 7P4 (902/892-4281)
Hospital Services Commission of P.E.I., Box 4500, Charlottetown, P.E.I. C1A 7P4
Que.: Quebec Health Insurance Board, Box 6600, Quebec, P.Q. G1K 7T3 (418/643-9407)
Hospital Insurance, Dept. of Social Affairs, 1075 Ch. Ste-Foy, Québec, P.Q. G1A 1B9
Sask.: Saskatchewan Medical Care Insurance Commission, 3475 Albert St., Regina, Sask. S4S 6X6 (306/565-3475)
Saskatchewan Hospital Services Plan, 3475 Albert St., Regina, Sask. S4S 6X6 (306/565-3269)
N.W.T.: Medical/Hospital Insurance, N.W.T. Health Care Plan, Government of N.W.T., Yellowknife, N.W.T. X1A 2L9
Yukon: Yukon Health Care Insurance Plan, Box 2703, Whitehorse, Y.T. Y1A 2C6 (403/667-5367)
Yukon Hospital Insurance Services, Box 2703, Whitehorse, Y.T. Y1A 2C6

MENTAL HEALTH

see Health

MERCHANDISING

Dept. of Agriculture, Marketing & Economics Branch, Sir John Carling Bldg., Ottawa, Ont. K1A OC5 (613/995-5880)
Dept. of Consumer & Corporate Affairs Canada, Place du Portage, Phase 1, Ottawa-Hull, K1A OC9 (819/997-4109)
Dept. of Indian Affairs & Northern Development, Ottawa, Ont. K1A OH4 (819/997-9920) (Indian and Eskimo arts and crafts)
Dept. of Industry, Trade & Commerce, Business Centre, 235 Queen St., Ottawa, Ont. K1A OH5 (613/995-5771)
Statistics Canada, Ottawa, Ont. K1A OT6 (613/992-2478)
See "Trade" this table for Provincial Depts. of Trade & Commerce.

METALS

Dept. of Energy, Mines & Resources, Canada Centre for Mineral & Energy Technology, 555 Booth St., Ottawa, Ont. K1A OG1 (613/996-4807)
Technology Information Division, CANMET, 555 Booth St., Ottawa, Ont. K1A OG1 (996-4807, 995-4029)
Dept. of Industry, Trade & Commerce, Resource Industries Branch, Non-Ferrous Metals Division, 235 Queen St., Ottawa, Ont. K1A OH5 (613/992-0088)
National Film Board, Box 6100, Montreal, P.Q. H3C 3H5 (514/333-3333)
Statistics Canada, Ottawa, Ont. K1A OT6 (613/992-0388)

Alta.: Industrial & Engineering Services Dept., Alberta Research Council, 4th floor, 4445 Calgary Trail S., Edmonton, Alta. T6H 5R7 (403/432-8181)
B.C.: Ministry of Energy, Mines & Petroleum Resources, Parliament Bldgs., Victoria, B.C. V8V 1X4 (604/387-5975)
Man.: Mineral Resources Division, Dept. of Energy & Mines, 989 Century St., Winnipeg, Man. R3H OW4 (204/633-9543)
N.B.: Mineral Resources, Dept. of Natural Resources, Box 6000, Fredericton, N.B. E3B 5H1 (506/453-2206)
Nfld.: Dept. of Mines & Energy, 95 Bonaventure Ave., Box 4750, St. John's, Nfld. A1C 5T7 (709/737-3159)
N.S.: Mineral Resources, Dept. of Mines & Energy, Box 1087, Halifax, N.S. B3J 2X1 (902/424-4162)
Ont.: Mineral Resources Branch, Ministry of Natural Resources, Queen's Park, Toronto, Ont. M7A 1W3 (416/965-1311)
Que.: Dept. of Energy & Resources, Mines Branch, 1620, boul. de l'Entente, Quebec, P.Q. G1S 4N6 (418/643-8045)
Sask.: Admin. Services Branch, Dept. of Mineral Resources, 1914 Hamilton St., Regina, Sask. S4P 4V4 (306/565-2528)

METEOROLOGY

see Climate

METRIC CONVERSION

Metric Commission Canada, Information Directorate, Box 4000, Ottawa, Ont. K1S 5G8 (613/996-4000)

Alta.:
B.C.: Metric Conversion Committee, Ministry of Universities, Science & Communications, #300, 756 Fort St., Victoria, B.C. V8W 1L4 (604/387-6864)
Man.: Manitoba Research Council, Dept. of Economic Development & Tourism, #533 One Lakeview Sq., 155 Carlton St., Winnipeg, Man. R3C 3H8 (204/944-2031)
N.B.: Dept. of Municipal Affairs, Metric Information, Box 6000, Fredericton, N.B. E3B 5H1 (506/453-3690)
Nfld.: Metric Conversion & Standards Division, Consumer Affairs, 2nd floor, Elizabeth Towers, St. John's, Nfld. A1C 5T7 (709/737-2580)
N.S.: No provincial agency. Contact: Metric Commission Canada, Atlantic Region, #118, 1505 Barrington St., Halifax, N.S. B3J 3K5 (902/423-8134)
Ont.: Metric & Standards Secretariat, Ministry of Industry & Tourism, Hearst Block, 900 Bay St., Toronto, Ont. M7A 2E1 (416/965-6513)
P.E.I.: Metric Information, 102 Kent St., Box 2000, Charlottetown, P.E.I. C1A 7N8 (902/892-0333)
Que.: Le Program d'assistance pour la conversion au système international d'unités, Centre de recherche industrielle du Québec, Répondeur métrique, C.P. 9038, Ste-Foy, P.Q. G1V 4C7 (418/659-1558) Québec toll free 1-800-463-3390
Sask.: Metric Information Centre, Dept. of Revenue, Supply & Services, 14th floor, Avord Tower, 2002 Victoria Ave., Regina, Sask. S4P 3V7 (306/565-6992)

METRIC MEASUREMENT

see Weights & Measures

MILK PRODUCTION

see Dairying

MINIMUM WAGES

Dept. of Labour, Employment Relations & Conditions of Work, Ottawa, Ont. K1A OJ2 (613/997-3900)

Alta.: Dept. of Labour, Employment Standards Branch, 4th floor, 10339 124 St., Edmonton, Alta. T5N 3W1 (403/427-3731)
B.C.: Employment Standards Branch, Ministry of Labour, Parliament Bldgs., Victoria, B.C. V8V 1X4 (604/387-1381)
Man.: Employment Standards Division, Dept. of Labour & Manpower, 609 Norquay Bldg., 401 York Ave., Winnipeg, Man. R3C OP8 (204/944-3352,3)
N.B.: Dept. of Labour & Manpower, Manpower Operations Branch, Box 6000, Fredericton, N.B. E3B 5H1 (506/453-2725)
Nfld.: Labour Standards Division, Dept. of Labour & Manpower, (Beothuck Bldg.), Confederation Bldg., St. John's, Nfld. A1C 5T7 (709/737-2742)

N.S.: Dept. of Labour & Manpower, Labour Standards Division, Box 697, Halifax, N.S. B3J 2T8 (902/424-4311)
Ont.: Employment Standards Branch, Ministry of Labour, 3rd floor, 400 University Ave., Toronto, Ont. M7A 1T7 (416/965-5251) Ontario toll free number 1-800-268-9001 (several regional offices)
P.E.I.: Employment Standards Branch, Dept. of Labour, Box 2000, Charlottetown, P.E.I. C1A 7N8 (902/892-3416)
Que.: Commission des normes du travail, 750, Charest Blvd. E., Quebec, P.Q. G1K 7Z5 (418/643-1420)
Sask.: Apprenticeship & Standards Division, 1914 Hamilton St., Regina, Sask. S4P 4V4 (306/565-2438, 2486)
Yukon: Dept. of Consumer & Corporate Affairs, Labour Standards, Box 2703, Whitehorse, Y.T. Y1A 2C6 (403/667-5312)

MINING
Technology Information Division, CANMET, Dept. of Energy, Mines & Resources, 555 Booth St., Ottawa, Ont. K1A OG1 (613/995-4029, 995-4039)
National Film Board, Box 6100, Montreal, P.Q. H3C 3H5 (514/333-3333)
National Museum of Science & Technology, 1867 St. Laurent Blvd., Ottawa, Ont. K1A OM8 (613/998-4566)
Statistics Canada, Ottawa, Ont. K1A OT6 (613/996-3139)

Alta.: Energy Resources Conservation Board, 640 5th Ave. S.W., Calgary, Alta. T2P 3G4 (403/261-8311)
B.C.: Ministry of Energy, Mines & Petroleum Resources, Parliament Bldgs., Victoria, B.C. V8V 1X4 (604/387-3781)
Man.: Mineral Resources Division, Dept. of Energy & Mines, 989 Century St., Winnipeg, Man. R3H OW4 (204/633-9543)
N.B.: Mineral Resources, Dept. of Natural Resources, Box 6000, Fredericton, N.B. E3B 5H1 (506/453-2206)
Nfld.: Dept. of Mines & Energy, 95 Bonaventure Ave., Box 4750, St. John's, Nfld. A1C 5T7 (709/737-3159)
N.S.: Engineering & Inspection, Dept. of Mines & Energy, 1690 Hollis St., Halifax, N.S. B3J 2X1 (902/424-4161)
Ont.: Mines Library, Ministry of Natural Resources, Room 812, 77 Grenville St., Toronto, Ont. M5S 1B3 (416/965-1352)
Mining Health & Safety Branch, Ministry of Labour, 15th floor, 400 University Ave., Toronto, Ont. M7A 1T7 (416/965-1328)
P.E.I.: Industry Branch, Dept. of Tourism, Industry & Energy, Box 2000, Charlottetown, P.E.I. C1A 7N8 (902/892-7411)
Que.: Ministère de l'Energie et Ressources, Division des Mines, 1620, boul. de l'Entente, Quebec, P.Q. G1S 4N6 (418/643-8045)

MOTOR VEHICLES
see Driver Licenses;
see Transportation

MUNICIPAL AFFAIRS
Municipal Grants Division, Real Estate Services Directorate, Public Works Canada, Ottawa, Ont. K1A 0M2 (613/998-8587)
Public Finance Division, Statistics Canada, Ottawa, Ont. K1A OT6 (613/995-9897)

Alta.: Municipal Affairs Dept., Communications Branch, 4th floor, 9925 107 St., Edmonton, Alta. T5K 2H9 (403/427-8862,3)
B.C.: Ministry of Municipal Affairs, Parliament Bldgs., Victoria, B.C. V8V 1X4 (604/387-5925)
Man.: Dept. of Municipal Affairs, 14th floor, 405 Broadway, Winnipeg, Man. R3C 3L6 (204/944-4129)
N.B.: Dept. of Municipal Affairs, Box 6000, Fredericton, N.B. E3B 5H1 (506/453-2656)
Nfld.: Dept. of Municipal Affairs, Confederation Bldg., St. John's, Nfld. A1C 5T7 (709/737-3049)
N.S.: Dept. of Municipal Affairs, Box 216, Halifax, N.S. B3J 2M4 (902/424-4141)
Ont.: Ministry of Municipal Affairs & Housing, Asst. Deputy Minister's Office, 6th floor, Mowat Block, Queen's Park, Toronto, Ont. M7A 1C2 (416/965-0131)
P.E.I.: Dept. of Community Affairs, Box 2000, Charlottetown, P.E.I. C1A 7N8 (902/892-3561)
Que.: Ministère des Affaires municipales, Direction des communications, 1039 Chevrotière, Edifice G, 29e étage, Québec, P.Q. G1R 4Z3 (418/643-7854)
Sask.: Dept. of Urban Affairs, 1791 Rose St., Regina, Sask. S4P 3V7 (306/565-2635)
Yukon: Yukon Dept. of Municipal & Community Affairs, Box 2703, Whitehorse, Y.T. Y1A 2C6 (403/667-5742)

liaison with province
The City Clerk's Office is usually responsible for municipal-provincial liaison. See "Government" this section, for addresses of major cities, and see the Index for addresses of other municipalities.

MUSEUMS
National Museums of Canada, Information Services Division, Ottawa, Ont. K1A OM8 (613/593-4285) (Inquiries: 995-9832) (National Gallery of Canada; National Museum of Man; National Museum of Natural Sciences; National Museum of Science & Technology)
Statistics Canada, Ottawa, Ont. K1A OT6 (613/995-9688)

Alta.: Provincial Museum of Alta., 12845 102 Ave., Edmonton, Alta. T5N OM6 (403/427-1730)
B.C.: B.C. Provincial Museum, 601 Belleville St., Victoria, B.C. V8V 1X4 (604/387-3701)
Man.: Manitoba Museum of Man & Nature, 190 Rupert Ave., Winnipeg, Man. R3B ON2 (204/956-2830)
N.B.: N.B. Museum, 277 Douglas Ave., Saint John, N.B. E2K 1E5 (506/693-1196)
N.S.: N.S. Museum, 1747 Summer St., Halifax, N.S. B3H 3A6 (902/429-4610)
Ont.: Arts, Heritage & Libraries Division, Ministry of Culture & Recreation, 77 Bloor St. W., 7th floor, Toronto, Ont. M5S 1M2 (416/965-4021)
Royal Ontario Museum, 100 Queen's Park, Toronto, Ont. M5S 2C6 (416/978-3690)
Que.: Musée du Quebec, Parc des Champs de Bataille, 1 rue Wolfe, Québec, P.Q. G1R 5H3 (418/643-7134)
Musée de l'Assemblée nationale, Parliament Bldgs., Quebec, P.Q. G1A 1A3
Ministère des Affaires culturelles, 225 Grande Allée, Quebec, P.Q. G1R 5G5 (418/643-2183)
Sask.: Western Development Museum, Headquarters, 2610 Lorne Ave. S., Box 1910, Saskatoon, Sask. S7K 3S5 (306/652-1910)
Saskatchewan Museum of Natural History, Dept. of Culture & Youth, Wascana Park, Regina, Sask. S4P 3V7 (306/565-2815)

NARCOTICS
see Drugs

NATIONAL DEFENCE
see Defence

NATURAL GAS
see Oil

NATURAL RESOURCES
Dept. of Energy, Mines & Resources, Communications, 580 Booth St., Ottawa, Ont. K1A OE4 (613/995-3065)
Environment Canada, Ottawa, Ont. K1A OH3 (613/997-2800)
Statistics Canada, Ottawa, Ont. K1A OT6 (613/996-3139)

Alta.: Natural Resources Co-ordinating Council, 9820 106 St., Edmonton, Alta. T5K 2J6 (403/427-6236)
Dept. of the Environment, 9820 106 St., Edmonton, Alta. T5K 2J6 (403/427-6236)
Dept. of Energy & Natural Resources, Petroleum Plaza South, 9915 108 St., Edmonton, Alta. T5K 2C9 (403/427-7425)
B.C.: Ministry of Energy, Mines & Petroleum Resources, Parliament Bldgs., Victoria, B.C. V8V 1X4 (604/387-6242)
Ministry of Environment, Information Services Branch, 810 Blanshard St., Victoria, B.C. V8W 3E1 (604/387-5162)

Man.: Dept. of Natural Resources, 1495 St. James St., Winnipeg, Man. R3H OW9 (204/775-0221)

N.B.: Dept. of Natural Resources, Box 6000, Fredericton, N.B. E3B 5H1 (506/453-2501)

Nfld.: Dept. of Mines & Energy, 95 Bonaventure Ave., Box 4750, St. John's, Nfld. A1C 5T7 (709/737-3159)
Dept. of Forest Resources & Lands, 6th floor, Atlantic Place, Water St., St. John's, Nfld. A1C 5T7 (709/737-3228)

Ont.: Communication Services Branch, Ministry of Natural Resources, Queen's Park, Toronto, Ont. M7A 1W3 (416/965-2756)

P.E.I.: Dept. of Tourism, Industry & Energy, Box 2000, Charlottetown, P.E.I. C1A 7N8 (902/892-7411)

Que.: Information Services, Dept. of Energy & Resources, 200 Chemin Ste-Foy, Quebec, P.Q. G1R 4X7 (418/643-8060)

Sask.: Dept. of Tourism & Renewable Resources, Information Services, 3211 Albert St., Regina, Sask. S4S 5W6 (306/565-2304)
Admin. Services Branch, Dept. of Mineral Resources, 1914 Hamilton St., Regina, Sask. S4P 4V4 (306/565-2528)

NAVIGATION (Coastal & Inland)

Canadian Hydrographic Service, Fisheries & Oceans Canada, Ottawa, Ont. K1A OE6 (613/995-4437)

Canadian Transport Commission, Ottawa, Ont. K1A ON9 (819/997-1227)

National Harbours Board, 320 Queen St., Tower A, Place de Ville, Ottawa, Ont. K1A ON6 (613/992-0019)

St. Lawrence Seaway Authority, Place de Ville, Ottawa, Ont. K1R 5A3 (613/992-4108)

NUCLEAR ENERGY

Atomic Energy Control Board, Box 1046, Ottawa, Ont. K1P 5S9 (613/995-5894)

Eldorado Nuclear Ltd., Ste. 400, 255 Albert St., Ottawa, Ont. K1P 6A9 (613/238-5222)

Dept. of Energy, Mines & Resources, Energy Sector, 580 Booth St., Ottawa, Ont. K1A OE4 (613/995-9351)

Alta.: Energy Resources Conservation Board, 640 5th Ave. S.W., Calgary, Alta. T2P 3G4 (403/261-8311)

N.B.: N.B. Electric Power Commission, 527 King St., (Box 2000), Fredericton, N.B. E3B 4X1 (506/453-4444)

Nfld.: Dept. of Mines & Energy, 95 Bonaventure Ave., Box 4750, St. John's, Nfld. A1C 5T7 (709/737-3159)

N.S.: Dept. of Mines & Energy, Box 668, Halifax, N.S. B3J 2T3 (902/424-7680)

Ont.: Ontario Hydro, 700 University Ave., Toronto, Ont. M5G 1X6 (416/592-5111)

P.E.I.: Dept. of Tourism, Industry & Energy, Box 2000, Charlottetown, P.E.I. C1A 7N8 (902/892-7411)

NUTRITION

Bureau of Nutritional Sciences, Health Protection Branch, Dept. of National Health & Welfare, Tunney's Pasture, Ottawa, Ont. K1A OL2 (613/593-6091)

Alta.: Nutrition Services, Community Health Services, Alberta Social Services & Community Health, 10030 107 St., Edmonton, Alta. T5J 3E4 (403/427-2650)

B.C.: Division of Nutrition & Health Education, Health Promotion Programs, Ministry of Health, 1515 Blanshard St., Victoria, B.C. V8W 3C8 (604/387-1451)
B.C. Food Information, Ministry of Agriculture, 10344 E. Whalley Ring Rd., Surrey, B.C. V3T 4H4 (604/584-7691)

Man.: Nutritionist, Dept. of Health, 2nd floor, 880 Portage Ave., Winnipeg, Man. R3G OP1 (204/786-3436)

N.B.: Director, Nutrition Services, Public Health Services, Box 6000, Fredericton, N.B. E3B 5H1 (506/453-2380)

Nfld.: Nutrition Director, Dept. of Health, Box 4750, St. John's, Nfld. A1C 5T7 (709/737-2684)
Nutrition Consultant, Dept. of Social Services, Box 4040, Harvey Rd., St. John's, Nfld. A1C 5Y6 (709/737-3465)

N.S.: Nutrition Services, Dept. of Health, Box 488, Halifax, N.S. B3J 2R8 (902/424-4393)

Ont.: Nutrition, Public Health Resource Service, Public Health Branch, Ontario Ministry of Health, 5th floor, 15 Overlea Blvd., Toronto, Ont. M4H 1A9 (416/965-5884)

P.E.I.: Director, Division of Nursing, Box 3000, Charlottetown, P.E.I. C1A 7P1 (902/892-5471)
Nutrition Co-ordinator, Dept. of Health & Social Services, Box 2000, Charlottetown, P.E.I. C1A 7N8 (902/892-5471)

Que.: Nutrition Division, Dept. of Social Affairs, 1075 Ste-Foy Rd., Quebec, P.Q. G1S 2M1 (418/643-2884)

Sask.: Provincial Nutritionist, Health Promotion Division, Community Health Services Branch, 3475 Albert St., Regina, Sask. S4S 6X6 (306/565-3079)

OCCUPATIONAL TRAINING

Staff Development Branch, Public Service Commission, Ottawa, Ont. K1A OM7 (819/997-3690)

Dept. of Employment & Immigration, Public Affairs Division, Inquiries Officer, Ottawa, Ont. K1A OJ9 (819/994-6313) (See Index for list of Regional Centres in Canada.)

Alta.: Director of Manpower Training, (403/427-4630), and Director of Technical – Vocational Programs, (403/427-5614), both at Alberta Dept. of Advanced Education & Manpower, 6th floor, Devonian Bldg. East, 11160 Jasper Ave., Edmonton, Alta. T5K OL1

B.C.: Apprenticeship Training Programs, Ministry of Labour, 4946 Canada Way, Burnaby, B.C. V5G 4J6 (604/294-3878)

Man.: Dept. of Education, Community Colleges Division, 2055 Notre Dame Ave., Winnipeg, Man. R3H OJ9 (204/633-6183)

N.B.: Dept. of Continuing Education, 416 York St., Box 6000, Fredericton, N.B. E3B 5H1 (506/453-2597)

Nfld.: Division of Vocational Education, Box 4750, St. John's, Nfld. A1C 5T7 (709/737-3101)

N.S.: Adult Education, Dept. of Education, Box 578, Trade Mart, Halifax, N.S. B3J 2S9 (Admin.: 902/424-5974, 5960)

Ont.: Apprenticeship Branch, Ministry of Colleges & Universities, Mowat Block, Queen's Park, Toronto, Ont. M7A 2B5 (416/965-4201)

P.E.I.: Apprenticeship Branch, Dept. of Labour, Box 2000, Charlottetown, P.E.I. C1A 7N8 (902/892-3416)

Que.: General & Vocational Colleges Section, Dept. of Education, Bldg. G, 1035 De La Chevrotiere, Quebec, P.Q. G1R 5A5 (418/643-7450)
Dept. of Labour & Manpower, 425 St-Amable, Quebec, P.Q. G1R 4Z1 (418/643-3880)

Sask.: Dept. of Continuing Education, 1855 Victoria Ave., Regina, Sask. S4P 3V5 (306/565-5594)

OCEANOGRAPHY

see also Fisheries

Bedford Institute of Oceanography, Box 1006, Dartmouth, N.S. B2Y 4A2 (902/426-2626)

Defence Research Establishment Atlantic, Box 1012, Dartmouth, N.S. B2Y 3Z7 (902/426-3100)

Defence Research Establishment Pacific, Forces Mail Office, Victoria, B.C. VOS 1BO (604/388-1665)

Dept. of Energy, Mines & Resources, Ottawa, Ont. K1A OE4 (613/995-3065)
Atlantic Geoscience Centre, Box 1006, Dartmouth, N.S. B2Y 4A2 (902/426-2367)
Geological Survey of Canada, 601 Booth St., Ottawa, Ont. K1A OE8 (613/995-4342)
Polar Continental Shelf Project, Energy, Mines & Resources, 880 Wellington St., 4th floor, Ottawa, Ont. K1A OE4 (613/996-3388)

Dept. of Fisheries & Oceans Canada, 240 Sparks St., Ottawa, Ont. K1A 0E6
Arctic Biological Stn., Fisheries & Oceans, 555 St. Pierre Blvd., Ste Anne de Bellevue, P.Q. H9X 3R4 (514/457-3660, ext. 40)
Biological Stn., Fisheries & Oceans, St. Andrews, N.B. EOG 2XO (506/529-8854)
Canada Centre for Inland Waters, Ocean & Aquatic Sciences, Burlington, Ont. L7R 4A6 (416/637-4341)

Canadian Hydrographic Service, Ocean & Aquatic Sciences, 615 Booth St., Ottawa, Ont. K1A 0E6 (613/995-4437)
Canadian Journal of Fisheries & Aquatic Sciences, Ottawa, Ont. K1A 0E6 (613/996-1830)
Environmental Services, Maritime Command, FMO Halifax, N.S. B3K 2X0
Halifax Laboratory, Fisheries & Oceans, Box 550, Halifax, N.S. B3J 2S7 (902/426-6250)
Institute of Ocean Sciences, The Library, Box 6000, Sidney, B.C. V8L 4B2 (604/656-8392)
Marine Science & Information Directorate, 7th floor, 240 Sparks St., Ottawa, Ont. K1A 0E6 (613/995-2039)
Marine Division, Water Pollution Control Directorate, Environmental Protection Service, Ottawa, Ont. K1A 1C8 (819/997-1612)
Nfld. Region Librarian, Fisheries & Oceans, Box 5667, St. John's, Nfld. A1C 5X1 (709/737-2022)
Ocean Science Affairs Branch, 7th floor, 240 Sparks St., Ottawa, Ont. K1A 0E6 (613/995-2045)
Quebec Region Directorate, C.P. 15500, 901 Cap Diamant, Québec, P.Q. G1K 7Y7 (418/694-3010)
Pacific Biological Stn., Fisheries & Oceans, Nanaimo, B.C. V9R 5K6 (604/750-5202)
Scientific Information & Publications Branch, Fisheries & Oceans Canada, 240 Sparks St., Ottawa, Ont. K1A 0E6 (613/996-2372)
Technology Services Laboratory, Fisheries Management, Pacific Region, Fisheries & Oceans, 6640 N.W. Marine Dr., Vancouver, B.C. V6T 1X2 (604/224-1366)
West Vancouver Laboratory, Fisheries & Oceans, 4160 Marine Dr., West Vancouver, B.C. V7V 1N6 (604/926-4112)

National Film Board, Box 6100, Montreal, P.Q. H3C 3H5 (514/333-3333)
National Museum of Natural Sciences, Ottawa, Ont. K1A 0M8 (613/996-3102) – Botany and Zoology Divisions
National Research Council of Canada, Atlantic Research Laboratory, Halifax, N.S. B3H 3Z1 (902/426-8332)
National Research Council of Canada, Hydraulics Laboratory, Ottawa, Ont. K1A 0R6 (613/993-2417)

B.C.: B.C. Research, 3650 Wesbrook Mall, Vancouver, B.C. V6S 2L2 (604/224-4331)
Nfld.: Dept. of Environment, Elizabeth Towers, Elizabeth Ave., St. John's, Nfld. A1B 1R9 (709/737-2559)
NORDCO Limited, Box 8833, St. John's, Nfld. A1B 3T2 (709/754-2401)
N.S.: N.S. Research Foundation Corp., Box 790, Dartmouth, N.S. B2Y 3Z7 (902/424-8670)
Ont.: Royal Ontario Museum, Dept. of Ichthyology & Herpetology, 100 Queen's Park, Toronto, Ont. M5S 2C6 (416/978-4836)
P.E.I.: Dept. of Fisheries, Box 2000, Charlottetown, P.E.I. C1A 7N8 (902/892-3493)
Que.: Dept. of Agriculture & Food, Maritime Fisheries Research Branch, (Direction générale des Pêches maritimes), 2700, rue Einstein, Ste-Foy, P.Q. G1P 3W8 (418/643-8084)

OIL & NATURAL GAS

Dept. of Energy, Mines & Resources, Energy Sector, 580 Booth St., Ottawa, Ont. K1A OE4 (613/995-9351)
Dept. of Energy, Mines & Resources, Canadian Oil & Gas Lands Admin., 580 Booth St., Ottawa, Ont. K1A OE4 (613/993-3760) (offshore, federal lands)
Dept. of Indian Affairs & Northern Development, Ottawa, Ont. K1A OH4 (819/997-9920)
National Film Board, Box 6100, Montreal, P.Q. H3C 3H5 (514/333-3333)
Statistics Canada, Ottawa, Ont. K1A OT6 (613/996-3139)

Alta.: Energy Resources Conservation Board, 640 5th Ave. S.W., Calgary, Alta. T2P 3G4 (403/261-8311)
B.C.: Ministry of Energy, Mines & Petroleum Resources, Parliament Bldgs., Victoria, B.C. V8V 1X4 (604/387-3485)
Man.: Petroleum Branch, Dept. of Energy & Mines, 989 Century St., Winnipeg, Man. R3H OW4 (204/633-9543)
N.B.: Mineral Resources, Dept. of Natural Resources, Box 6000, Fredericton, N.B. E3B 5H1 (506/453-2206)
Nfld.: Dept. of Mines & Energy, 95 Bonaventure Ave., Box 4750, St. John's, Nfld. A1C 5T7 (709/737-2356)
N.S.: Dept. of Mines & Energy, Energy Resources, Box 1087, Halifax, N.S. B3J 2X1 (902/424-4576)
Ont.: Mineral Resources Branch, Petroleum Resources, Ministry of Natural Resources, 1106 Dearness Dr., London, Ont. N6E 1N9 (519/681-5350)
P.E.I.: Dept. of Tourism, Industry & Energy, Box 2000, Charlottetown, P.E.I. C1A 7N8 (902/892-7411)
Que.: Dept. of Energy & Resources, Energy Branch, 8 rue Cook, Québec, P.Q. G1R 5H2 (418/643-3724)
Sask.: Admin. Services Branch, Dept. of Mineral Resources, 1914 Hamilton St., Regina, Sask. S4P 4V4 (306/565-2528)

OLD AGE ASSISTANCE

Income Security Programs Branch, Dept. of National Health & Welfare, Brooke Claxton Bldg., Tunney's Pasture, Ottawa, Ont. K1A 0L4 (613/992-5865)

Alta.: Senior Citizen's Bureau, Dept. of Social Services & Community Health, 10030 107 St., Edmonton, Alta. T5J 3E4 (403/427-7876)
B.C.: GAIN for Seniors, Box 2500, Victoria, B.C. V8W 3A1 (604/387-6022)
Man.: Manitoba Supplement for Pensioners, Dept. of Community Services & Corrections, #301, 267 Edmonton St., Winnipeg, Man. R3C 1S2 (204/944-2686)
N.B.: Consultant on Community Based Services for Seniors, Dept. of Social Services, Box 6000, Fredericton, N.B. E3B 5H1 (506/453-2040)
Nfld.: Dept. of Social Services, Confederation Bldg., St. John's, Nfld. A1C 5T7 (709/737-3243)
N.S.: Senior Citizens Secretariat, Box 2065, Halifax, N.S. B3J 2Z1 (902/424-6322)
Director of Family Benefits, Dept. of Social Services, Box 696, Halifax, N.S. B3J 2T7 (902/424-4262)
Ont.: Ministry of Community & Social Services, Operational Support Branch, 700 Bay St., Toronto, Ont. M7A 1E9 (416/965-1818)
Guaranteed Income & Tax Credit Branch, Ministry of Revenue, Queen's Park, Toronto, Ont. M7A 2B3 (In Metro Toronto, 416/965-8470; toll-free numbers: Area Code 705, Zenith 8-2000; other Ontario residents, 1-800-268-7121)
P.E.I.: Director, Services for the Aging, Social Services Branch, Dept. of Health & Social Services, Box 2000, Charlottetown, P.E.I. C1A 7N8 (902/892-5471)
Que.: Dept. of Social Affairs, 1075, Ste-Foy Rd., Quebec, P.Q. G1S 2M1 (418/643-7167)
Sask.: Saskatchewan Income Plan (Senior Citizens Benefits Program), Income Support Division, Saskatchewan Social Services, 1920 Broad St., Regina, Sask. S4P 3V6 (306/565-4130)

OMBUDSMEN

see Human Rights

PARKS & RECREATION

Parks Canada, Information Division, Ottawa, Ont. K1A 1G2 (819/997-0088) (national parks)
National Film Board, Box 6100, Montreal, P.Q. H3C 3H5 (514/333-3333)

Alta.: Dept. of Recreation & Parks, 10363 108 St., Edmonton, Alta. T5J 1L7 (403/427-2008)
B.C.: Ministry of Lands, Parks & Housing, Parks & Outdoor Recreation Division, 1019 Wharf St., Victoria, B.C. V8W 2Y9 (604/387-1696)
Man.: Dept. of Natural Resources, Parks Branch, 200 Vaughan St., Winnipeg, Man. R3C 1T5 (204/944-3703)
N.B.: Field Operations, N.B. Dept. of Tourism, Box 12345, Fredericton, N.B. E3B 5C3 (506/453-2509)
Nfld.: Provincial Parks Division, Dept. of Culture, Recreation & Youth, Box 4750, St. John's, Nfld. A1C 5T7 (709/737-2430)

N.S.: Parks & Recreation Division, Dept. of Lands & Forests, R.R. 1, Belmont, Col. Co., N.S. BOM 1CO (902/662-3030)

Ont.: Ontario Provincial Parks & Recreational Areas, Outdoor Recreation, Ministry of Natural Resources, Queen's Park, Toronto, Ont. M7A 1W3 (416/965-3081)

P.E.I.: Dept. of Highways & Public Works, Box 2000, Charlottetown, P.E.I. C1A 7N8 (902/892-7431)

Que.: Parks Branch, Dept. of Leisure, Fish & Game, Place de la Capitale, 10th floor, 150 est, St-Cyrille, Quebec, P.Q. G1R 4Y1 (418/643-5349)

Sask.: Dept. of Tourism & Renewable Resources: Program Planning Branch, 306/565-2322; Park Development Branch, 306/565-2846; both at 3211 Albert St., Regina, Sask. S4S 5W6

Yukon: Parks & Historic Resources Branch, Dept. of Renewable Resources, Box 2703, Whitehorse, Y.T. Y1A 2C6 (403/667-5634)

PARLIAMENT (Protocol, Parliamentary Procedures, etc.)

The Clerk of the Senate and Clerk of Parliaments, Parliament Bldgs., Ottawa, Ont. K1A OA4 (613/992-2493)

Clerk of the House of Commons, Parliament Bldgs., Ottawa, Ont. K1A OA6 (613/593-5178)

Library of Parliament, Parliament Bldgs., Ottawa, Ont. K1A OA9 (613/992-3122)

Alta.: Clerk of Legislative Assembly, 313 Legislative Bldg., Edmonton, Alta. T5K 2B6 (403/427-2477)

B.C.: Clerk of Legislative Assembly, Parliament Bldgs., Victoria, B.C. V8V 1X4 (604/387-3785)

Man.: Clerk of the Executive Council, 204 Legislative Bldg., Winnipeg, Man. R3C OV8 (204/944-3717)

N.B.: Legislative Library, Legislative Bldg., Box 6000, Fredericton, N.B. E3B 5H1 (506/453-2338, reference; 506/453-2622, govt. publications)

Nfld.: Legislative Librarian, 3rd floor, Confederation Bldg., St. John's, Nfld. A1C 5T7

N.S.: Clerk of Legislative Assembly, Province House, Halifax, N.S. B3J 2P8 (902/424-5978)

Ont.: Clerk of the Legislative Assembly, Parliament Bldgs., Toronto, Ont. M7A 1A2 (416/965-1406)

P.E.I.: Clerk of the Legislative Assembly, Box 2000, Charlottetown, P.E.I. C1A 7N8 (902/892-4296)

Que.: Secretary General of the National Assembly, Parliament Bldgs., Quebec, P.Q. G1A 1A4 (418/643-2724)

Sask.: Legislative Assembly Office, 239 Legislative Bldg., Regina, Sask. S4S OB3 (306/565-2279)

PAROLE BOARDS

see also Prisons

National Parole Board, 340 Laurier Ave. W., Ottawa, Ont. K1A OR1 (613/992-2818)

Alta.: Correctional Services Branch, Dept. of the Solicitor General, 7th floor, Melton Bldg., 10310 Jasper Ave., Edmonton, Alta. T5J 2W4 (403/427-3440)

B.C.: B.C. Parole Board, Office of the Chairman, 411 Dunsmuir St., Vancouver, B.C. V6B 1X4 (604/668-2661)

Man.: No provincial parole system in Manitoba.

N.B.: Chairman, N.B. Parole Board, c/o University of N.B. Law School, Ludlow Hall, Fredericton, N.B. E3B 5A3 (506/453-4669)

Nfld.: No provincial parole system in Newfoundland.

N.S.: No provincial parole system in Nova Scotia.

Ont.: Ontario Board of Parole, 2195 Yonge St., 2nd floor, Toronto, Ont. M4S 2B2 (416/963-0368)

P.E.I.: No provincial parole system in P.E.I.

Que.: Probation & Houses of Detention Service, Dept. of Justice, 1200 rte de l'Eglise, Ste-Foy, P.Q. G1V 4M1 (418/643-4122)
Quebec Parole Board, above address, 418/643-7713

Sask.: Corrections Division, Saskatchewan Social Services, 1920 Broad St., Regina, Sask. S4P 3V6 (306/565-3490)

PASSPORTS

Passport Office, Dept. of External Affairs, L.B. Pearson Bldg., Sussex Dr., Ottawa, Ont. K1A OG3 (613/995-8481) (See Index for list of Regional Passport Offices)

PATENTS & COPYRIGHT

Bureau of Corporate Affairs, Dept. of Consumer & Corporate Affairs Canada, Place du Portage, Phase 1, Ottawa/Hull, K1A OC9
Patent Office:- 819/997-1936
Copyright Office:- 819/997-1725
Trade Mark Office:- 819/997-1061
Industrial Design Office:- 819/997-1725

PENSIONS

Canada Employment & Immigration Commission, Annuities Branch, Box 12000, Bathurst, N.B. E2A 4L8

Canadian Pension Commission, Veterans Affairs Bldg., Ottawa, Ont. K1A OP4 (613/992-2157) (Claims for veterans'disability & dependant pensions under the Pension Act, Civilian War Pensions & Allowances Act, Former Prisoner of War Compensation Act, RCMP Pension Continuation Act, RCMP Superannuation Act, Flying Accidents Compensation Regulations)

Dept. of National Health & Welfare, Income Security Programs Branch (CPP/FA/OAS), 333 River Rd., Vanier, Ont. K1A 0L1 (613/993-9760)

Dept. of Labour, Economic Analysis Branch, Ottawa, Ont. K1A OJ2 (819/997-3019)

Dept. of Supply & Services Canada, Superannuation Division, Box 5010, Moncton, N.B. E1C 8Z5 (506/388-6222)

Pension Review Board, (Pension Act), 473 Albert St., Ottawa, Ont. K1R 5B4 (613/995-7464)

Statistics Canada, Ottawa, Ont. K1A OT6 (613/995-6918) (Private plans)

Alta.: Alberta Government Pension Boards, Office of the Chairman, 9811 109 St., Edmonton, Alta. T5K 0C8 (403/427-7104)
Alberta Treasury, Office of the Controller, Pensions, 10035 108 St., Edmonton, Alta. T5J 3G5 (403/427-6981)

B.C.: Superannuation Branch, Parliament Bldgs., Victoria, B.C. V8V 4R5 (604/387-1002)

Man.: Manitoba Supplement for Pensioners, Dept. of Community Services & Corrections, Room 301, 267 Edmonton St., Winnipeg, Man. R3C 1S2 (204/944-2686)

N.B.: Director of Pensions, Dept. of Finance, Box 6000, Fredericton, N.B. E3B 5H1 (506/453-2296)

Nfld.: Director of Pensions, Dept. of Finance, Confederation Bldg., St. John's, Nfld. A1C 5T7 (709/737-3931)

N.S.: Dept. of Social Services, Box 696, Halifax, N.S. B3J 2T7 (902/424-4325)

Ont.: Pension Commission of Ont., Ministry of Consumer & Commercial Relations, 10 Wellesley St. E., Toronto, Ont. M7A 2K2 (416/963-0527)

Que.: Régie des rentes du Québec, Direction du Régime de rentes du Québec, et Direction des régimes supplémentaires de rentes, Box 5200, Québec, P.Q. G1K 7S9 (418/643-8309)

Sask.: Pension Benefits Branch, Dept. of Labour, 1914 Hamilton St., Regina, Sask. S4P 4V4 (306/565-2458)

PERFORMING ARTS

see Arts

PHOTOGRAPHIC MATERIAL

Canada Centre for Remote Sensing, 2464 Sheffield Rd., Ottawa, Ont. K1A OY7 (613/995-1210)

Canada Mtge. & Housing Corp., Montreal Rd., Ottawa, Ont. K1A OP7 (613/748-2604)

Dept. of Energy, Mines & Resources, National Air Photo Library, 615 Booth St., Ottawa, Ont. K1A OE9 (613/995-4560)

Dept. of National Health & Welfare, Audio-Visual Library, Ottawa, Ont. K1A OK9 (613/995-2934)

National Museums of Canada, Photographic Services, Ottawa, Ont. K1A 0M8 (613/995-7659)

Public Archives of Canada, 395 Wellington St., Ottawa, Ont. K1A ON3 (613/992-2669)

Alta.: Audio-Visual Services, Public Affairs Bureau, 11510 Kingsway Ave., Edmonton, Alta. T5G 2Y5 (403/427-4364)

B.C.: Special Services Branch, Ministry of Tourism, 1117 Wharf St., Victoria, B.C. V8W 2Z2 (604/387-6490)

Man.: Information Services Branch, Photographic Section #511, 401 York Ave., Winnipeg, Man. R3C OP8 (204/944-4114)

N.S.: Information Division, Dept. of Government Services, Box 54, Halifax, N.S. B3J 2L4 (902/424-4165)

Ont.: Photo Library, Ministry of Industry & Tourism, 900 Bay St., Toronto, Ont. M7A 2E1 (416/965-5411)

P.E.I.: Communications Division, Dept. of Tourism, Industry & Energy, Box 2000, Charlottetown, P.E.I. C1A 7N8 (902/892-7411)

Sask.: Photographic Art Services, #306, 3085 Albert St., Regina, Sask. S4S 0B1 (306/565-6300)

Write to Provincial government inquiry centres listed under "Government" this table for complete lists of government departments that will provide photographic material.

PLANNING

see Community Planning

POLLUTION

see Environment

POLICE

R.C.M.P., Public Relations Branch, 1200 Alta Vista Dr., Ottawa, Ont. K1A OR2 (613/993-1085)

Dept. of the Solicitor General, Ottawa, Ont. K1A OP8 (613/593-5105)

Statistics Canada, Ottawa, Ont. K1A OT6 (613/995-0709)

Alta.: Dept. of the Solicitor General, 10310 Jasper Ave., Edmonton, Alta. T5J 1Y8 (403/427-3457)

B.C.: R.C.M.P. "E" Division Headquarters, 2881 Nanaimo St., Victoria, B.C. V8T 4Z8 (604/388-3371)

Man.: Dept. of the Attorney General, #104, 450 Broadway, Winnipeg, Man. R3C 0V8 (204/944-3728 & 3181)

N.B.: Dept. of Justice, Box 6000, Fredericton, N.B. E3B 5H1 (506/453-3603)

Nfld.: Dept. of Justice, Confederation Bldg., St. John's, Nfld. A1C 5T7 (709/737-2872)

N.S.: Dept. of the Attorney General, Box 7, Halifax, N.S. B3J 2L6 (902/424-4222)

Ont.: Ontario Provincial Police, 90 Harbour St., Toronto, Ont. M7A 2S1 (416/965-5751)

P.E.I.: Dept. of Justice, Box 2000, Charlottetown, P.E.I. C1A 7N8 (902/892-5411)

Que.: Sûreté du Quebec, 1701, Parthenais, C.P. 1400, Succ. C, Montreal, P.Q. H2L 4K7 (514/395-4141)

Sask.: Dept. of the Attorney General, 2476 Victoria Ave., Regina, Sask. S4P 3V7 (306/565-5560)

Montreal: Service de Police de la Communauté Urbaine de Montreal, 750 rue Bonsecours, Montreal, P.Q. H2Y 3C7 (514/934-2121)

Toronto: Metropolitan Toronto Police, 590 Jarvis St., Toronto, Ont. M4Y 2J5 (416/967-2222)

POLITICAL SCIENCE

see Government (General)

POPULATION

Public Archives of Canada, 395 Wellington St., Ottawa, Ont. K1A ON3 (613/992-2669) (early figures)

Statistics Canada, Ottawa, Ont. K1A OT6 (613/996-5254)

Alta.: Alberta Bureau of Statistics, Alberta Treasury, 7th floor, 9811 109 St., Edmonton, Alta. T5J 0C8 (403/427-3058)

B.C.: Central Statistics Bureau, Ministry of Industry & Small Business Development, Parliament Bldgs., Victoria, B.C. V8V 1X4 (604/387-1502)

Man.: Manitoba Bureau of Statistics, Room 614, 155 Carlton St., Lakeview # 1, Winnipeg, Man. R3C 0V8 (204/944-2985)

N.B.: Economics & Statistics Branch, Dept. of Finance, Box 6000, Fredericton, N.B. E3B 5H1 (506/453-2484)

Nfld.: No Provincial Agency. Contact: Statistics Canada, Box 8556, St. John's, Nfld. A1B 3P2 (709/737-4646)

N.S.: Statistical Services Branch, Dept. of Development, 8th floor, Bank of Montreal Tower (Box 519), Halifax, N.S. B3J 2R7 (902/424-5691)

Ont.: Central Statistical Services, Ministry of Treasury & Economics, Frost Bldg. North, 3rd floor, Toronto, Ont. M7A 1Y7 (416/965-2217)

Que.: Quebec Bureau of Statistics, Dept. of Industry, Trade & Tourism, 117 St-André, Québec, P.Q. G1K 3Y3 (418/643-5116)

Sask.: Bureau of Statistics, Executive Council, 3475 Albert St., Regina, Sask. S4S 6X6 (306/565-6327)

POSTAL SERVICE

Director of Public Affairs, Canada Post Corp., Confederation Heights, Ottawa, Ont. K1A OB1 (613/998-8023)

POULTRY

Dept. of Agriculture:

- Livestock & Poultry Division, #500, 2255 Carling Ave., Ottawa, Ont. K1A 0Y9 (613/995-5433) (For general livestock and poultry information)
- Animal Pathology Division, Food Production & Inspection Branch, 801 Fallowfield Rd., Box 11300, Stn. H, Ottawa, Ont. K2H 8P9 (613/998-9320) (For poultry disease information)

Dept. of Industry, Trade & Commerce, Livestock, Meat & Dairy Products Division, 235 Queen St., Ottawa, Ont. K1A OH5 (613/995-8107)

Statistics Canada, Ottawa, Ont. K1A OT6 (613/995-4853)

Alta.: Poultry Branch, Animal Industry Division, 9718 107th St., Edmonton, Alta. T5K 2C8 (403/427-5090)

B.C.: Poultry Branch, 32916 Marshall Rd., Abbotsford, B.C. V2S 1K2 (604/859-8919)

Man.: Poultry Section, Agricultural Services Complex, University Cres., Winnipeg, Man. R3T 2N2 (204/269-1220)

N.B.: Livestock & Poultry Branch, Dept. of Agriculture & Rural Development, Box 6000, Fredericton, N.B. E3B 5H1 (506/453-2457)

Nfld.: Poultry Specialist, Dept. of Rural, Agricultural & Northern Development, Prov. Agriculture Bldg., Brookfield Rd., Mount Pearl, Nfld. (709/737-3840)

N.S.: Livestock Services Branch, Poultry Section, Dept. of Agriculture, Box 550, Truro, N.S. B2N 5E3 (902/895-1571)

Ont.: Dept. of Animal & Poultry Science, Ontario Agricultural College, Univ. of Guelph, Guelph, Ont. N1G 2W1 (519/824-4120)

P.E.I.: Livestock Section, Dept. of Agriculture & Forestry, Box 1600, Charlottetown, P.E.I. C1A 7N3 (902/892-5465)

Que.: Animal Production Service, Dept. of Agriculture & Food, 1er étage, 200 A Ste-Foy Rd., Quebec, P.Q. G1R 4X6 (418/643-7597)

Sask.: Poultry Specialist, Provincial Veterinary Lab, 4840 Wascana Pkwy., Regina, Sask. S4S OB1 (306/565-6424)

PRICES

Marketing Services Division, Dept. of Agriculture, #624, Sir John Carling Bldg., Ottawa, Ont. K1A OC5 (613/995-5880) (producer, wholesale & retail prices, volumes, stocks, storage & movement of Canadian agricultural products, imports & exports)

Marketing Services Branch, Dept. of Fisheries & Oceans, Ottawa, Ont. K1A OE6 (613/995-2177) (fish prices)

Statistics Canada, Ottawa, Ont. K1A OT6 (613/995-4078)

Alta.: Alberta Bureau of Statistics, Alberta Treasury, 7th floor, 9811 109 St., Edmonton, Alta. T5J 0C8 (403/427-3058)

B.C.: Central Statistics Bureau, Ministry of Industry & Small Business Development, Parliament Bldgs., Victoria, B.C. V8V 1X4 (604/387-1502)

Man.: Deputy Minister, Dept. of Consumer & Corporate Affairs & Environment, Legislative Bldg., Winnipeg, Man. R3C OV8 (204/944-3742)

Ont.: Central Statistical Services, Ministry of Treasury & Economics, Frost Bldg. North, 3rd floor, Toronto, Ont. M7A 1Y7 (416/965-7078)

P.E.I.: Marketing Branch, Dept. of Agriculture & Forestry, Box 2000, Charlottetown, P.E.I. C1A 7N8 (902/892-4101)

Que.: Quebec Bureau of Statistics, Dept. of Industry, Trade & Tourism, 117 St-André, Quebec, P.Q. G1K 3Y3 (418/643-5116)

Sask.: Dept. of Labour, Statistics, 1914 Hamilton St., Regina, Sask. S4P 4V4 (306/565-2419)

PRISONS

see also Parole Boards

Ministry of the Solicitor General, 340 Laurier Ave. W., Ottawa, Ont. K1A OP8 (613/995-1032) (Federal penitentiaries only)

Correctional Service of Canada, Ottawa, Ont. K1A OP9 (613/992-5891)

Statistics Canada, Ottawa, Ont. K1A OT6 (613/995-0711)

Alta.: Dept. of the Solicitor General, 7th floor, Melton Bldg., 10310 Jasper Ave., Edmonton, Alta. T5J 2W4 (403/427-3440)

B.C.: B.C. Corrections Branch, 535 Yates St., Victoria, B.C. V8V 1X4 (604/387-5948)

Man.: Commr. of Corrections, Dept. of Community Services & Corrections, Bldg. 21, 139 Tuxedo Ave., Winnipeg, Man. R3N OH6 (204/895-5349)

N.B.: Dept. of Justice, Box 6000, Fredericton, N.B. E3B 5H1 (506/453-2462)

Nfld.: Dept. of Justice, Adult Corrections Division, Box 6084, St. John's, Nfld. A1C 5X8 (709/753-8191)

N.S.: Dept. of the Attorney General, Box 7, Halifax, N.S. B3J 2L6 (902/424-4222)

Ont.: Communications Branch, Ministry of Correctional Services, 2001 Eglinton Ave. E., Scarborough, Ont. M1L 4P1 (416/750-3421)

P.E.I.: Director of Corrections, Dept. of Justice, Box 2000, Charlottetown, P.E.I. C1A 7N8 (902/892-5411)

Que.: Ministère de la Justice, Direction générale de la probation et des établissements de détention, 1200, route de l'Eglise, 7e étage, Ste-Foy, P.Q. G1V 4M1

Sask.: Dept. of Social Services, Corrections Services, 1920 Broad St., Regina, Sask. S4P 3V6 (306/565-3573)

Yukon: Corrections Branch, Dept. of Justice, Box 2703, Whitehorse, Y.T. Y1A 2C6 (403/667-5124)

See Index for list of Prisons.

PROPERTY

see Real Estate
see Crown Lands

PUBLIC COMMERCIAL VEHICLES ("For Hire" Carriers)

"For Hire" Carriers, i.e. motor vehicles used in the transportation, for compensation, of passengers or goods, must be provincially registered and licensed before being allowed to operate. For information relating to licensing requirements and other regulations contact the following:

Alta.: Motor Transport Board, Dept. of Transportation, Provincial Bldg., Box 5002, Red Deer, Alta. T4N 5Y5 (403/343-5430)

B.C.: Supt. of Motor Carriers, Motor Carrier Commission, Ministry of Transportation & Highways, 4240 Manor St., Burnaby, B.C. V5G 3X5 (604/438-5511)

Man.: The Highway Traffic & Highway Transport Board, Room 200, 301 Weston St., Winnipeg, Man. R3E 3H4 (204/786-6708)

N.B.: Motor Carrier Board, Provincial Bldg., 110 Charlotte St., Saint John, N.B. E2L 2J4 (506/658-2502)

Nfld.: Board of Commrs. of Public Utilities, Motor Carrier Division, 120 Torbay Rd., Box 9188, St. John's, Nfld. A1A 2X9 (709/726-6432)

N.S.: Board of Commrs. of Public Utilities, Box 3058 South, Halifax, N.S. B3J 3G7 (902/424-4448)

Ont.: Registrar of Motor Vehicles, 1201 Wilson Ave., Downsview, Ont. M3M 1J8

P.E.I.: Public Utilities Commission, (134 Kent St.), Box 577, Charlottetown, P.E.I. C1A 7L1 (902/892-3501)

Que.: Commission des transports du Québec, 585 est, boul. Charest, Québec, P.Q. G1K 7W5 (418/643-5694); Montreal Office: 505 est, rue Sherbrooke, Montréal, P.Q. H2L 1K2 (514/873-2006)

Sask.: Highway Traffic Board, 2260 11th Ave., Regina, Sask. S4P 3V7 (306/565-4271)

PUBLIC HEALTH

see Health

PUBLIC UTILITIES

Statistics Canada, Ottawa, Ont. K1A OT6 (613/996-3139)

Alta.: Public Utilities Board, 11th floor, 10055 106 St., Edmonton, Alta. T5J 2Y2 (403/427-4911)

B.C.: B.C. Utilities Commission, 21st floor, 1177 W. Hastings St., Vancouver, B.C. V6E 2L7 (604/689-1831)

Man.: Public Utilities Board, 1146-405 Broadway Ave., Winnipeg, Man. R3C 3L6 (204/944-2638)

N.B.: N.B. Board of Commrs. of Public Utilities, 110 Charlotte St., Saint John, N.B. E2L 2J4 (506/658-2504)

Nfld.: Board of Commrs. of Public Utilities, Box 9188, St. John's, Nfld. A1A 2X9 (709/726-6432)

N.S.: Board of Commrs. of Public Utilities, Box 3058, Halifax South, Halifax, N.S. B3J 3G7 (902/424-4448)

Ont.: Ontario Hydro, 700 University Ave., Toronto, Ont. M5G 1X6 (416/592-5111)

P.E.I.: Public Utilities Commission, (134 Kent St.), Box 577, Charlottetown, P.E.I. C1A 7L1 (902/892-3501)

Que.: Régie des services publics, 2875, boul. Laurier, #1200, Ste-Foy, Quebec, P.Q. G1V 2M2 (418/643-5560)

Sask.: Saskatchewan Power Corp., 2025 Victoria Ave., Regina, Sask. S4P OS1 (306/525-7650)
Saskatchewan Telecommunications, 2121 Saskatchewan Dr., Regina, Sask. S4P 3Y2 (306/347-3737)

PUBLIC WORKS

Public Works Canada, Sir Charles Tupper Bldg., Ottawa, Ont. K1A OM2 (613/998-9560)

Alta.: Alberta Housing & Public Works, College Plaza, 8215 112 St., Edmonton, Alta. T6G 5A9 (403/427-3921)

B.C.: B.C. Buildings Corp., #400, 910 Government St., Victoria, B.C. V8W 2T4 (604/387-1353)
Ministry of Provincial Secretary & Government Services, Parliament Bldgs., Victoria, B.C. V8V 1X4 (604/387-5723)

Man.: Dept. of Government Services, Woodsworth Bldg., Winnipeg, Man. R3C 3L6 (204/944-3940)

N.B.: Dept. of Supply & Services, Box 6000, Fredericton, N.B. E3B 5H1 (506/453-2998)

Nfld.: Dept. of Public Works & Services, Confederation Bldg., St. John's, Nfld. A1C 5T7 (709/737-3678)

N.S.: Dept. of Government Services, Box 54, Halifax, N.S. B3J 2L4 (902/424-4980)

Ont.: Information Services Section, Ministry of Government Services, 12th floor, Ferguson Block, Queen's Park, Toronto, Ont. M7A 1N3 (416/965-6683)

P.E.I.: Dept. of Highways & Public Works, (11 Kent St.), Box 2000, Charlottetown, P.E.I. C1A 7N8 (902/892-7431)

Que.: Dept. of Public Works & Supply, 475, St-Amable, Quebec, P.Q. G1R 4X9 (418/643-1259)

Sask.: Dept. of Government Services, 1942 Hamilton St., Regina, Sask. S4P 3V7 (306/565-6910)

Yukon: Dept. of Highways & Public Works, Box 2703, Whitehorse, Y.T. Y1A 2C6 (403/667-5144)

PUBLICATIONS

Canadian ISBN Agency, c/o National Library of Canada, 395 Wellington St., Ottawa, Ont. K1A ON4 (819/997-9565)

Canadian Government Publishing Centre, Supply & Services Canada, Ottawa, Ont. K1A OS9 (819/997-5362)

Statistics Canada, Ottawa, Ont. K1A OT6 (613/992-3151)

Alta.: Public Affairs Bureau, 11510 Kingsway Ave., Edmonton, Alta. T5G 2Y5 (403/427-4387)

B.C.: Queen's Printer, Parliament Bldgs., Victoria, B.C. V8V 4R6 (604/387-6692)

Man.: Office of the Queen's Printer, 200 Vaughan St., Winnipeg, Man. R3C 1T5 (204/944-3104)

N.B.: Queen's Printer, Box 6000, Fredericton, N.B. E3B 5H1 (506/453-2520)

Nfld.: Queen's Printer, Box 4750, St. John's, Nfld. A1C 5T7

N.S.: N.S. Government Bookstore, Box 637, Halifax, N.S. B3J 2T3 (902/424-7580)

Ont.: Ontario Government Bookstore, 880 Bay St., Toronto, Ont. M7A 1N8 (416/965-6015); and the Publications Centre (5th floor)

Que.: Quebec Official Publisher, 1283, boul. Charest ouest, Quebec, P.Q. G1N 2C9 (418/643-9810)

Sask.: Queen's Printer of Saskatchewan, Walter Scott Bldg., Regina, Sask. S4S OB1 (306/565-6892)

PURCHASING AGENTS

Federal Government

Supply & Services Canada, Ottawa, Ont. K1A 0S5 (819/997-7363)

Regional Supply Centres:

Atlantic Region Supply Centre, Burnside Industrial Park, Box 3000, Dartmouth, N.S. B2Y 4A8 (902/426-3881)

Quebec Regional Supply Centre, 800 Golf Rd., Nun's Island, Montreal, P.Q. H3E 1G9 (514/283-5791)

Ontario Regional Supply Centre, 295 The West Mall, Ste. 200, Etobicoke, Ont. M9C 5A4 (416/622-8111)

Manitoba Region Supply Centre, 266 Graham Ave., 7th floor, Winnipeg, Man. R3C 3W6 (204/949-6114)

Western Region Supply Centre, 2nd floor, 10255 100 Ave., Edmonton, Alta. T5J 1J9 (403/420-3720)

Pacific Region Supply Centre, 3551 Viking Way, Richmond, B.C. V5V 1W6 (604/544-6364)

Alta.: Purchasing Branch, Supply Division, Alberta Government Services, 19th floor, Park Sq., 10001 Bellamy Hill, Edmonton, Alta. T5J 3C1 (403/427-4111)

B.C.: Purchasing Commission, Parliament Bldgs., Victoria, B.C. V8V 1T8 (604/387-6522)

Man.: Purchasing Branch, Dept. of Government Services, 2nd floor, 530 Century St., Winnipeg, Man. R3C 0V8 (204/944-0070) Telex: 07-57652

N.B.: Central Purchasing Branch, Box 8000, Fredericton, N.B. E3B 5H6 (506/453-2245)

Nfld.: Government Purchasing Agency, 2nd floor, Ayre's Home Centre, Pippy Place, Box 4750, St. John's, Nfld. A1C 5T7 (709/737-3343); purchasing for all provincial government departments.

N.S.: N.S. Government Purchasing Agency, (10th floor, 45 Alderney Dr.), Box 787, Halifax, N.S. B3J 2V2 (902/424-5520)

Ont.: Central Purchasing Services, Ministry of Government Services, 1200 Bay St., Toronto, Ont. M7A 1N3 (416/965-6937)

Each Ministry also has its own Purchasing Agent:

Ministry of the Attorney General Purchasing Agent, 18 King St. E., Toronto, Ont. M5C 1C5 (416/965-2845)

Ministry of Community & Social Services Purchasing Agent, 7th floor, Hepburn Block, Queen's Park, Toronto, Ont. M7A 1E9 (416/965-0647)

Ministry of Consumer & Commercial Relations, Manager, Purchasing, 10 Wellesley St. E., Main floor, Toronto, Ont. M7A 2H8 (416/963-0342)

Ministry of Education Purchasing Agent, 7th floor, Mowat Block, Queen's Park, Toronto, Ont. M7A 1L2 (416/965-5990)

Ministry of the Environment Purchasing Agent, 135 St. Clair Ave. W., Toronto, Ont. M4V 1P5 (416/965-6637)

Ministry of Industry & Tourism Purchasing Agent, 900 Bay St., Toronto, Ont. M7A 2E2 (416/965-4311)

Ministry of Intergovernmental Affairs, see Ministry of Treasury & Economics

Ministry of Labour Purchasing Agent, 400 University Ave., Toronto, Ont. M7A 1T7 (416/965-6118)

Ministry of Municipal Affairs & Housing Purchasing Manager, Hearst Block, 4th floor, Queen's Park, Toronto, Ont. M7A 2K5 (416/965-9780)

Ministry of the Solicitor General Purchasing Agent, 12th floor, 25 Grosvenor St., Toronto, Ont. M7A 1Y6 (416/965-3360)

Ministry of Transportation & Communications, Supply & Services Branch, 1201 Wilson Ave., Central Bldg., Downsview, Ont. M3M 1J8 (416/248-3178)

Purchasing & Supply Office: Room 130, 248-3361
Materials & Operating Supplies: Room 139, 248-3241
Vehicles & Equipment: Room 143, 248-3841

Ministry of Treasury & Economics Purchasing Agent, Purchasing Section, 4th floor, 1075 Bay St., Toronto, Ont. M7A 1Y7 (416/965-4453)

Que.: The General Purchasing Service, 1155, rue Claire Fontaine, 4e étage, Québec, P.Q. G1R 4X8 (418/643-3395)

Sask.: Saskatchewan Government Purchasing Agency, Operations Division, Revenue, Supply & Services, Smith St. at 12th Ave., Regina, Sask. S4P 3V7 (306/565-6871)

Brampton: Purchasing Agent, Supply & Services Dept., 150 Central Park Dr., Brampton, Ont. L6T 2T9 (416/793-4110)

Burlington: Purchasing Division, 3rd floor, 426 Brant St., Burlington, Ont. L7R 3Z6 (416/335-7659)

Calgary: Purchasing Agent, City Hall, Box 2100, Calgary, Alta. T2P 2M5 (403/244-2123)

Halifax: Purchasing Manager, City Hall, Box 1749, Halifax, N.S. B3J 3A5 (902/426-6486)

Hamilton: Purchasing Dept., City Hall, 71 Main St. W., Hamilton, Ont. L8N 3T4 (416/527-0241, ext. 231)

Hull: Director, Purchasing Dept., City Hall, 100 Edmonton St., Hull, P.Q. (819/770-0280)

Kitchener: Director of Purchasing, City Hall, Box 1118, Kitchener, Ont. N2G 4G7 (519/885-7274)

London: Director of Purchasing, City Hall, 300 Dufferin Ave., London, Ont. N6A 4L9 (519/679-4900)

Mississauga: Director of Purchasing & Supply, City Hall, 1 City Centre Dr., Mississauga, Ont. L5B 1M2 (416/279-7600)

Montreal: Director, Supply & Services Dept., 9515 St-Hubert St., Montreal, P.Q. H2M 1Z4 (514/384-5380)

Niagara Falls: Purchasing Agent, City Hall, 4310 Queen St., Niagara Falls, Ont. L2E 6X5 (416/356-7521)

Oshawa: Director of Purchasing, City Hall, 50 Centre St. S., Oshawa, Ont. L1H 3Z7 (416/725-7351)

Quebec: Purchasing Agent, City Hall, Room 405, Quebec, P.Q. G1R 4S9 (418/694-6242)

Regina: Director of Purchasing, City Hall, (2476 Victoria Ave.), Box 1790, Regina, Sask. S4P 3C8 (306/569-7333)

Saint John: Purchasing Agent, City Hall, Box 1971, Saint John, N.B. E2L 4L1 (506/658-2930)

St. John's: Purchasing Agent, City Hall, New Gower St., St. John's, Nfld. A1C 5M2 (709/726-8820)

Saskatoon: Purchasing Manager, 88 24th St., Saskatoon, Sask. S7K 0K4 (306/664-9605)

Sudbury: Director of Purchasing, Civic Square, 200 Brady St., Sudbury, Ont. P3E 4S5 (705/674-3141)

Thunder Bay: Director, Administrative Services, City Hall, 500 Donald St. E., Thunder Bay, Ont. P7E 5V3 (807/623-2711, ext. 252)

Toronto: Commr. of Purchasing & Supply, City Hall, Toronto, Ont. M5H 2N2 (416/367-7311)

Vancouver: Purchasing Agent, City Hall, 2nd floor, Vancouver, B.C. V5Y 1V4 (604/873-7252)

Victoria: City Purchasing Agent, City Hall, #1 Centennial Sq., Victoria, B.C. V8W 1P6 (604/385-5711, loc. 242)

Windsor: Director of Purchasing, Rm. 100, City Hall, Box 1607, Windsor, Ont. N9A 6S1 (519/255-6309)

Winnipeg: Director, Purchasing Dept., Admin. Bldg., Civic Centre, Winnipeg, Man. R3B 1B9 (204/946-0451)

RADIO & TELEVISION

Canadian Broadcasting Corp., Box 8478, Ottawa, Ont. K1G 3J5 (613/731-3111)

Canadian Radio-Television & Telecommunications Commission, Ottawa, Ont. K1A 0N2 (819/997-4484)

Que.: Société de radio-télévision du Québec, Public Relations Officer, 800 rue Fullum, Montréal, P.Q. H2K 3L7 (514/873-5567)

La Régie des services publics, 2875, boul. Laurier, Ste-Foy, P.Q. G1V 2M2 (418/643-5560)

REAL ESTATE REGULATIONS

(*See also* Crown Lands)

Canada Mtge. & Housing Corp., Montreal Rd., Ottawa, Ont. K1A 0P7 (613/748-2000)

Chief of Registration, Office of the Registrar General of Canada, Dept. of Consumer & Corporate Affairs, Place du Portage, Phase 2, Hull (mailing: Ottawa, Ont. K1A 0C9) (819/997-1265)

Alta.: Supt. of Real Estate, Dept. of Consumer & Corporate Affairs, 9th floor, 10065 Jasper Ave., Edmonton, Alta. T5J 3B1 (403/427-2244)

B.C.: Supt. of Insurance, 1050 W. Pender St., Vancouver, B.C. V6E 3S7 (604/682-7031)

Man.: Manitoba Public Utilities Board, 11th floor, Woodsworth Bldg., 405 Broadway, Winnipeg, Man. R3C 3L6 (204/944-2640)

N.B.: Consumer & Corporate Affairs Branch, Dept. of Justice, Box 6000, Fredericton, N.B. E3B 5H1 (506/453-2659)

Nfld.: Real Estate Division, Dept. of Justice, Elizabeth Towers, St. John's, Nfld. A1C 5T7 (709/737-2596)

N.S.: Consumer Services Bureau, (5151 Terminal Rd.), Box 998, Halifax, N.S. B3J 2X3 (902/424-4690)

Ont.: Registrar of Real Estate Agents & Brokers, Business Practices Division, Ministry of Consumer & Commercial Relations, 555 Yonge St., 5th floor, Toronto, Ont. M7A 2H6 (416/963-0406)

Real Property Registration Branch, Ministry of Consumer & Commercial Relations, 543 Yonge St., 2nd floor, Toronto, Ont. M7A 2J8 (416/963-0462)

P.E.I.: Dept. of Justice, Box 2000, Charlottetown, P.E.I. C1A 7N8 (902/892-5411)

Dept. of Community Affairs, Building & Development Services, Box 2000, Charlottetown, P.E.I. C1A 7N8 (902/892-0221)

Que.: Service du courtage immobilier du Québec, Ministère des Institutions financières et Coopératives, 800, Place d'-Youville, 12e, Quebec, P.Q. G1R 4Y5 (418/643-4597)

Sask.: Insurance & Real Estate Branch, Dept. of Consumer & Commercial Affairs, 1871 Smith St., Regina, Sask. S4P 3V7 (306/565-2953)

Lands Branch, Dept. of Agriculture, Walter Scott Bldg., Regina, Sask. S4S 0B1 (306/565-5200)

Saskatchewan Farm Ownership Board, 3130 8th St. E., Saskatoon, Sask. S7H 0W2 (306/664-5105)

Calgary: Refer to: Calgary Real Estate Board, 503 7 St. S.W., Calgary, Alta. T2P 1Y9 (403/263-0530)

Edmonton: Real Estate & Housing, 9th floor, CN Tower, Edmonton, Alta. T5J 0K1 (403/428-5986)

Guelph: Refer to: Guelph & Dist. Real Estate Board, 400 Woolwich St., Guelph, Ont. N1H 3X1 (519/824-7270)

Hamilton: Real Estate Dept., City Hall, 71 Main St. W., Hamilton, Ont. L8N 3T4 (416/527-0241, ext. 376)

LaSalle: General Manager, City Hall, 13 Strathyre Ave., LaSalle, P.Q. H8R 3P6 (514/366-7110)

London: Refer to: London & St. Thomas Real Estate Board, 311 Oxford St. E., London, Ont. N6A 1V3 (519/434-6871)

Montreal: Refer to: Montreal Real Estate Board, 1080 Beaver Hall Hill, Montreal, P.Q. H2Z 1T3 (514/866-4711)

Niagara Falls: Refer to: Regional Real Estate Association, 4411 Portage Rd., Box 456, Niagara Falls, Ont. L2E 6V2 (416/356-7593)

Oshawa: Real Estate Division, Planning & Development Dept., City Hall, 50 Centre St. S., Oshawa, Ont. L1H 3Z7 (416/725-7351)

Quebec: Service de l'urbanisme, Hôtel de Ville, Quebec, P.Q. G1R 4S9 (418/694-6422)

Regina: Development & Public Relations Dept., City Hall, (2476 Victoria Ave.), Box 1790, Regina, Sask. S4P 3C8 (306/569-7499)

Saint John: Real Estate Dept., Box 1971, Saint John, N.B. E2L 4L1 (506/658-2800)

St. John's: City Hall, New Gower St., St. John's, Nfld. A1C 5M2 (709/726-8820)

Saskatoon: Refer to: Saskatoon Real Estate Board, 1149 8th St. E., Saskatoon, Sask. S7H 0S3 (306/244-4453)

Thunder Bay: Refer to: Thunder Bay Real Estate Board, 1135 Barton St., Thunder Bay, Ont. P7B 5N3 (807/623-8422)

Toronto: Refer to: Toronto Real Estate Board, 1883 Yonge St., Toronto, Ont. M4S 1Y7 (416/481-6151)

Vancouver: Refer to: Real Estate Board of Greater Vancouver, 1101 W. Broadway, Vancouver, B.C. V6H 1G2 (604/736-4551)

Windsor: Refer to: The Windsor-Essex County Real Estate Board, 515 Riverside Dr. W., Windsor, Ont. N9A 5K7 (519/258-1875)

Winnipeg: Director of Land Surveys & Real Estate, 4th floor, 10 Fort St., Winnipeg, Man. R3C 1C4 (204/985-5241)

RECREATION

(*See also* Parks; and Tourism)

Parks Canada, Information Division, Ottawa, Ont. K1A 1G2 (819/997-0088) (national parks, historic parks & sites, tourism in the North)

Dept. of Industry, Trade & Commerce, Office of Tourism, Ottawa, Ont. K1A 0H6 (613/996-4610)

Fitness & Amateur Sport Canada, Ottawa, Ont. K1A 0X6 (613/996-4510) (includes Sport Canada, Fitness Canada)

National Film Board, Box 6100, Montreal, P.Q. H3C 3H5 (514/333-3333)

Alta.: Recreation Development Division, Dept. of Recreation & Parks, 10363 108 St., Edmonton, Alta. T5J 1L8 (403/427-5721)

B.C.: Ministry of Provincial Secretary & Government Services, Recreation & Sport Branch, Parliament Bldgs., Victoria, B.C. V8V 1X4 (604/387-1931)

Man.: Dept. of Fitness, Recreation & Sport, #304, 379 Broadway, Winnipeg, Man. R3C 3N4 (204/944-3769)

N.B.: Field Operations, Dept. of Tourism, Box 12345, Fredericton, N.B. E3B 5C3 (506/453-2509)

Sports (506/453-2928), and Recreation (506/453-2312), both c/o Dept. of Youth, Box 6000, Fredericton, N.B. E3B 5H1

Nfld.: Recreation & Sport Services Division, Dept. of Culture, Recreation & Youth, c/o Workers' Comp. Bldg., Forest Rd., St. John's, Nfld. A1C 5T7 (709/737-2779)

N.S.: Director of Sport & Community Services, Dept. of Culture, Recreation & Fitness, Box 864, Halifax, N.S. B3J 2V2 (902/424-7586)

Consultant, Physical Education, Dept. of Education, Box 578, Halifax, N.S. B3J 2S9 (902/424-4139)

Ont.: Tourism Marketing Branch, Division of Tourism, Ministry of Industry & Tourism, 900 Bay St., Hearst Block, Toronto, Ont. M7A 2E5 (416/965-4008)

Ministry of Culture & Recreation, Arts, Heritage & Libraries Division, 77 Bloor St. W., Toronto, Ont. M7A 2R9 (416/965-5665)

P.E.I.: Youth, Fitness & Recreation, Dept. of Community Affairs, Box 2000, Charlottetown, P.E.I. C1A 7N8 (902/892-9174)

Que.: Tourisme Québec, C.P. 20,000, Quebec, P.Q. G1K 7X2 (418/643-2290)

High Commission for Youth, Recreation & Sports, Dept. of Recreation, Fish & Game, 150 est boul. St-Cyrille, Québec, P.Q. G1R 4Y3 (418/643-3127)

Sask.: SaskTravel, Saskatchewan Tourism & Renewable Resources, 3211 Albert St., Regina, Sask. S4S 5W6 (306/565-2300)

Dept. of Culture & Youth, 11th floor, Avord Tower, Regina, Sask. S4P 3V7 (306/565-5749)

Yukon: Recreation Branch, Dept. of Education, Box 2703, Whitehorse, Y.T. Y1A 2C6 (403/667-5254)

N.W.T.: Recreation Division, Dept. of Local Government, Government of the N.W.T., Yellowknife, N.W.T. X1A 2L9 (403/873-7245)

REGIONAL ECONOMIC EXPANSION

Information Division, Dept. of Regional Economic Expansion, Ottawa, Ont. K1A OM4 (819/997-2096) located at 200 Promenade du Portage, Hull

Regional Development & International Affairs Branch, Dept. of Agriculture, Ottawa, Ont. K1A 0C5 (613/995-8195)

REGISTRARS-GENERAL

Registration Division, Office of the Registrar General of Canada, Dept. of Consumer & Corporate Affairs, Place du Portage, Phase 2, Hull (mailing: Ottawa, Ont. K1A 0C9) (819/997-1265)

See also "Vital Statistics", this table.

P.E.I.: Dept. of Justice, Box 2000, Charlottetown, P.E.I. C1A 7N8 (902/892-5411)

Que.: Service des Archives Civiles, Dept. of Justice, 117 rue St-André, Québec, P.Q. G1K 3Y3 (418/643-6436)

Sask.: Dept. of Provincial Secretary, Room 308, 1919 Rose St., Regina, Sask. S4P 3V7 (306/565-2951)

REHABILITATION

Bureau on Rehabilitation, Dept. of National Health & Welfare, 6th floor, Brooke Claxton Bldg., Ottawa, Ont. K1A 1B5 (613/593-6247)

National Parole Board, 340 Laurier Ave. W., Ottawa, Ont. K1A OR1 (613/992-2818)

Alta.: Rehabilitation Services Division, Dept. of Social Services & Community Health, 11th floor, 10030 107 St., Edmonton, Alta. T5J 3E4 (403/427-2734)

B.C.: Income Assistance Division, Ministry of Human Resources, Parliament Bldgs., Victoria, B.C. V8V 1X4 (604/387-1486)

Man.: Vocational Rehabilitation Services, Dept. of Community Services & Corrections, Bldg. 15, 139 Tuxedo Ave., Winnipeg, Man. R3C OV8 (204/895-5134)

Nfld.: Provincial Director of Rehabilitation, Dept. of Social Services, Confederation Bldg., St. John's, Nfld. A1C 5T7 (709/737-3548)

N.S.: Rehabilitation & Community Services Division, Dept. of Social Services, Box 696, Halifax, N.S. B3J 2T7 (902/424-6762)

Ont.: Ministry of Community & Social Services, Policy Services & Program Evaluation Branch, 3rd floor, Hepburn Block, Queen's Park, Toronto, Ont. M7A 1E9 (416/965-5088)

Ministry of Correctional Services, 2001 Eglinton Ave. E., Scarborough, Ont. M1L 4P1 (416/750-3421)

P.E.I.: Director of Field Services, Social Services Branch, Dept. of Health & Social Services, Box 2000, Charlottetown, P.E.I. C1A 7N8 (902/892-5421)

Que.: Director of Social Rehabilitation Division, Que. Workers' Security & Health Commission, 524 Bourdages St., Quebec, P.Q. G1K 7E2 (418/643-5850)

Sask.: Director of Vocational Rehabilitation, Chateau Tower, 1920 Broad St., Regina, Sask. S4P 3V6 (306/565-3844)

Yukon: Rehabilitation Co-ordinator, Health Services Branch, Box 2703, Whitehorse, Y.T. Y1A 2C6 (403/667-5723)

RENT CONTROL

see Landlord & Tenant

RESEARCH

see Economic; and Science

RESOURCES DEVELOPMENT

Dept. of Energy, Mines & Resources, Energy Sector, and/or Mineral Policy Sector, 580 Booth St., Ottawa, Ont. K1A OE4 (613/995-9351)

Dept. of Fisheries & Oceans, Resource Allocation Branch, 240 Sparks St., Ottawa, Ont. K1A OE6 (613/995-2060)

Dept. of Indian Affairs & Northern Development, Ottawa, Ont. K1A OH4 (819/997-0799)

Dept. of Industry, Trade & Commerce, Resource Industries Branch, 235 Queen St., Ottawa, Ont. K1A OH5 (613/996-4963)

Dept. of Regional Economic Expansion, Ottawa, Ont. K1A 0M4 (819/997-2096)

National Film Board, Box 6100, Montreal, P.Q. H3C 3H5 (514/333-3333)

National Research Council of Canada, Ottawa, Ont. K1A OR6 (613/993-9101)

Alta.: Dept. of Economic Development, Strategic Planning Branch, 10th floor, 10909 Jasper Ave., Edmonton, Alta. T5J 3M8 (403/427-3627)

B.C.: Ministry of Industry & Small Business Development, Parliament Bldgs., Victoria, B.C. V8V 1X4 (604/387-6701)

Man.: Natural Resources Division, Dept. of Natural Resources, 302 Legislative Bldg., Winnipeg, Man. R3C 0V8 (204/944-3730; 786-9183)

Manitoba Hydro, 820 Taylor Ave., Winnipeg, Man. R3C 2P4 (204/474-3311)

N.B.: Dept. of Natural Resources, Mineral Resources, Box 6000, Fredericton, N.B. E3B 5H1 (506/453-2206)

Nfld.: Dept. of Environment, Elizabeth Towers, Elizabeth Ave., St. John's, Nfld. A1B 1R9 (709/737-2559)

N.S.: Dept. of Development, Box 519, 5151 George St., Halifax, N.S. B3J 2R7 (902/424-8920)

Ont.: Ontario Northland Transportation Commission, 195 Regina St., North Bay, Ont. P1B 8L3 (705/472-4500)

Ministry of Natural Resources, Queen's Park, Toronto, Ont. M7A 1W3 (Forest Resources: 416/965-4319; Mineral Resources: 416/965-4271)

Ministry of Northern Affairs, 10 Wellesley St. E., 9th floor, Toronto, Ont. M4Y 1G2 (416/965-7577)

P.E.I.: Industry Branch, Dept. of Tourism, Industry & Energy, Box 2000, Charlottetown, P.E.I. C1A 7N8 (902/892-7411)

Que.: Information Service, Dept. of Energy & Resources, 200 B Chemin Ste-Foy, Quebec, P.Q. G1R 4X7 (418/643-8060)

Sask.: Admin. Services Branch, Dept. of Mineral Resources, 1914 Hamilton St., Regina, Sask. S4P 4V4 (306/565-2528)

Saskatchewan Tourism & Renewable Resources, SaskTravel, 3211 Albert St., Regina, Sask. S4S 5W6 (306/565-2300)

SALES TAXES

Revenue Canada, Customs & Excise Division, Ottawa, Ont. K1A OL5 (613/995-2946)

Alta.: Alberta Treasury, Revenue Administration, 6th floor, 9811 109 St., Edmonton, Alta. T5K 0C8 (403/427-3044) (No consumer sales taxes in Alberta)

B.C.: Ministry of Finance (Social Services Tax), Parliament Bldgs., Victoria, B.C. V8V 2M1 (604/387-6440)

Man.: Retail Sales Tax Branch, 115 Norquay Bldg., 401 York Ave., Winnipeg, Man. R3C 0V8 (204/943-3561)

N.B.: Tax Admin. Branch, Dept. of Finance, Box 3000, Fredericton, N.B. E3B 5G5 (506/453-2401)

Nfld.: Taxation Division, Dept. of Finance, Confederation Bldg., St. John's, Nfld. A1C 5T7 (709/737-2933)

N.S.: Provincial Tax Commission, Box 755, Halifax, N.S. B3J 2V4 (902/424-4411)

Ont.: Retail Sales Tax Branch, Ministry of Revenue, 17th floor, 77 Bloor St. W., Toronto, Ont. M7A 1X9 (416/487-7161) (twelve district offices)

P.E.I.: Revenue Division, Dept. of Finance, Box 1330, Charlottetown, P.E.I. C1A 7N1 (902/892-8546)

Que.: Dept. of Revenue, 3800 rue Marly, Ste-Foy, P.Q. G1X 4A5 (418/643-6677)

Sask.: Revenue Division, Dept. of Revenue, Supply & Services, 3475 Albert St., Regina, Sask. S4S 6X6 (306/565-6645)

SCHOOL BOARDS

see Education

SCIENCE & SCIENTIFIC RESEARCH

Atomic Energy of Canada Ltd., 275 Slater St., Ottawa, Ont. K1A OS4 (613/237-3270)

Canadian Conservation Institute, National Museums of Canada, 1030 Innes Rd., Ottawa, Ont. K1A OM8 (613/998-3721)

Canadian Grain Commission, Grain Research Laboratory, Room 1404, 303 Main St., Winnipeg, Man. R3C 3G9 (204/949-2768)

Canadian Transport Commission, Ottawa, Ont. K1A ON9 (819/997-0677)

Canadian Wildlife Service, Environment Canada, Ottawa, Ont. K1A OE7 (613/997-1095)

Dept. of Agriculture, Food Production & Inspection Branch, Sir John Carling Bldg., Ottawa, Ont. K1A OC5 (613/995-5880)

Dept. of Agriculture, Research Branch, Central Experimental Farm, Ottawa, Ont. K1A OC6 (613/995-9071)

Dept. of Energy, Mines & Resources, Ottawa, Ont. K1A OE4:

Geological Survey of Canada, 601 Booth St., Ottawa, Ont. K1A 0E8 (613/995-4342) (geology & geophysics)

Canada Centre for Mineral & Energy Technology, 555 Booth St., Ottawa, Ont. K1A OG1 (613/995-4132) (mining, mineral processing, metallurgical and energy technology research)

Earth Physics Branch, 1 Observatory Cres., Ottawa, Ont. K1A OY3 (613/995-5544) (gravity, seismology & geomagnetism)

Polar Continental Shelf Project, 880 Wellington St., Ottawa, Ont. K1A OE4 (613/996-3388) (ice physics, hydrography)

Canada Centre for Remote Sensing, 2464 Sheffield Rd., Ottawa, Ont. K1A OY7 (613/993-0121)

Office of Energy Research & Development, 580 Booth St., Ottawa, Ont. K1A OE4 (613/992-9488)

Dept. of Fisheries & Oceans, Scientific Information & Publications Branch, Ottawa, Ont. K1A OE6 (613/996-1830)

Dept. of Indian Affairs & Northern Development, Ottawa, Ont. K1A OH4 (819/997-9920)

Dept. of Industry, Trade & Commerce, Technology Branch, 235 Queen St., Ottawa, Ont. K1A OH5 (613/995-7151)

Medical Research Council of Canada, Ottawa, Ont. K1A OW9 (613/996-8170)

Ministry of State for Science & Technology, 270 Albert St., Ottawa, Ont. K1A 1A1 (613/995-3093)

National Film Board, Box 6100, Montreal, P.Q. H3C 3H5 (514/333-3333)

National Gallery of Canada, Restoration & Conservation Laboratory, Lorne Bldg., Elgin St., Ottawa, Ont. K1A OM8 (613/996-8274)

National Museum of Man, Education & Cultural Affairs, Ottawa, Ont. K1A OM8 (613/993-0881)

National Museum of Natural Sciences, Ottawa, Ont. K1A OM8 (613/996-3102)

National Research Council of Canada, Canada Institute for Scientific & Technical Information, Ottawa, Ont. K1A OS2 (613/993-1600)

Science Council of Canada, 100 Metcalfe St., Ottawa, Ont. K1P 5M1 (613/996-1729)

Statistics Canada, Ottawa, Ont. K1A OT6 (613/995-3014)

Transport Development Centre Library, 1000 Sherbrooke St. W., Box 549, Montreal, P.Q. H3A 2R3 (514/283-4008)

Alta.: Alberta Research Council, 11315 87th Ave., Edmonton, Alta. T6G 2C2 (403/432-8181)

B.C.: Ministry of Universities, Science & Communications, Parliament Bldgs., Victoria, B.C. V8V 1X4 (604/387-6008)

B.C. Research, 3650 Wesbrook Mall, Vancouver, B.C. V6S 2L2 (604/224-4331)

Man.: Manitoba Research Council, Room 501, No. 1, Lakeview Sq., 155 Carlton St., Winnipeg, Man. R3C 3H8 (204/944-2031)

N.B.: Research & Productivity Council, Box 6000, Fredericton, N.B. E3B 5H1 (506/455-8994)

Nfld.: No provincial agency.

N.S.: N.S. Research Foundation Corp., Box 790, Dartmouth, N.S. B2Y 3Z7 (902/424-8670)

Ont.: Alcoholism & Drug Addiction Research Foundation, 33 Russell St., Toronto, Ont. M5S 2S1 (416/595-6000)

Ontario Geological Survey, 77 Grenville St., Toronto, Ont. M5S 1B3 (416/965-0190)

Ontario Hydro, 700 University Ave., Toronto, Ont. M5G 1X6 (416/592-5111)

Research Library, Ministry of Natural Resources, Maple, Ont. L0J 1E0 (416/832-2761)

Ontario Research Foundation, Sheridan Park, Mississauga, Ont. L5K 1B3 (416/822-4111)

P.E.I.: Refer to: University of P.E.I., Charlottetown, P.E.I. C1A 4P3 (902/892-4121)

Que.: Dept. of Energy & Resources, Mineral Research Centre (Centre de Recherches Minerales), 2700, rue Einstein, Ste-Foy, P.Q. G1P 3W8 (418/643-4540)

Dept. of Agriculture, Fisheries & Food, Research Directorate, 2700 rue Einstein, Ste-Foy, P.Q. G1P 3W8 (418/643-2459)

Sask.: Saskatchewan Research Council Library, 30 Campus Dr., Saskatoon, Sask. S7N OX1 (306/664-5454)

SENIOR CITIZENS

see Old Age Assistance

SNOWMOBILES

see Leisure Craft

SOCIAL RESEARCH

see Economic

SOCIAL SERVICES

Dept. of National Health & Welfare, Social Service Programs Branch, Social Services Division, 9th floor, Claxton Bldg., Tunney's Pasture, Ottawa, Ont. K1A 1B5 (613/996-8941)

Alta.: Dept. of Social Services & Community Health, 10030 107 St., Edmonton, Alta. T5J 3E4 (403/427-2734)

B.C.: Library, Ministry of Human Resources, 800 Cassiar St., Vancouver, B.C. V5K 4N6 (604/299-9131)

Man.: Dept. of Community Services & Corrections, Social Security Operations, 267 Edmonton St., Winnipeg, Man. R3C 1S2 (204/944-2696)

N.B.: Dept. of Social Services, Box 6000, Fredericton, N.B. E3B 5H1 (506/453-2590)

Nfld.: Dept. of Social Services, Confederation Bldg., St. John's, Nfld. A1C 5T7 (709/737-3243)

N.S.: Dept. of Social Services, J.W. Johnston Bldg., Box 696, Halifax, N.S. B3J 2T7 (902/424-4325)

Ont.: Ministry of Community & Social Services, Communications Branch, 7th floor, Hepburn Block, Queen's Park, Toronto, Ont. M7A 1E9 (416/965-7825)

P.E.I.: Dept. of Health & Social Services, Box 2000, Charlottetown, P.E.I. C1A 7N8 (902/892-5471)

Que.: Dept. of Social Affairs, 1075 chemin Ste-Foy, 2nd floor, Quebec, P.Q. G1A 1B9 (418/643-6392)

Sask.: Dept. of Social Services, 1920 Broad St., Regina, Sask. S4P 3V6 (306/565-3605)

Yukon: Dept. of Human Resources, Box 2703, Whitehorse, Y.T. Y1A 2C6 (403/667-5674)

Montreal: Social Affairs Dept., 435, rue du Champ-de-Mars, Montreal, P.Q. H2Y 1B3 (514/872-4262)

Toronto: Metropolitan Toronto Social Services Dept., 4th floor, East Tower, City Hall, Toronto, Ont. M5H 2N1 (416/367-8623)

SOLICITORS GENERAL

Dept. of the Solicitor General, 340 Laurier Ave. W., Ottawa, Ont. K1A OP8 (613/995-1032)

Alta.: Dept. of the Solicitor General, Legislative Bldgs., Edmonton, Alta. T5K 2B6 (403/427-2468)

B.C.: Ministry of Attorney General, Parliament Bldgs., Victoria, B.C. V8V 1X4 (604/384-4434)

N.B.: Dept. of Justice, Box 6000, Fredericton, N.B. E3B 5H1 (506/453-2583)

Nfld.: Dept. of Justice, Confederation Bldg., St. John's, Nfld. A1C 5T7 (709/737-2872)

Ont.: Ministry of the Solicitor General, 25 Grosvenor St., Toronto, Ont. M7A 1Y6 (416/965-2021)

P.E.I.: Dept. of Justice, Box 2000, Charlottetown, P.E.I. C1A 7N8 (902/892-5411)

Sask.: Dept. of the Attorney General, 2476 Victoria Ave., Regina, Sask. S4P 3V7 (306/565-5472)

SPACE

Dept. of Communications, Information Services, Ottawa, Ont. K1A 0C8 (613/995-8185)

Dept. of Energy, Mines & Resources, Canada Centre for Remote Sensing, 2464 Sheffield Rd., Ottawa, Ont. K1A OY7 (613/993-0121)

Dept. of National Defence, Information Services, Ottawa, Ont. K1A OK2 (613/996-2353)

National Research Council of Canada, Ottawa, Ont. K1A OR6 (613/993-9101)

SPORTS

see Recreation

STANDARDS

Canadian General Standards Board, Place du Portage III, Hull (819/997-5710) (Mailing: Ottawa, Ont. K1A 1G6)

Canada Mtge. & Housing Corp., Montreal Rd., Ottawa, Ont. K1A OP7 (613/748-2263)

Dept. of Energy, Mines & Resources, Explosives Branch, 580 Booth St., Ottawa, Ont. K1A OE4 (613/593-7211)

Dept. of Labour, Employment Relations & Conditions of Work, Ottawa, Ont. K1A OJ2 (613/997-3900)

Dept. of Public Works, Materials Standards Secretariat, Sir Charles Tupper Bldg., Ottawa, Ont. K1A OM2 (613/998-4866)

Metric Commission Canada, Box 4000, Ottawa, Ont. K1S 5G8 (613/996-4000)

National Defence Headquarters, Ottawa, Ont. K1A OK2 (military specifications & standards)

National Research Council of Canada, Division of Physics, Ottawa, Ont. K1A OS1 (613/993-9101)

Standards Council of Canada, 350 Sparks St., Ottawa, Ont. K1R 7S8 (613/238-3222)

Transport Canada:

The Canadian Air Transportation Administration, Ottawa, Ont. K1A 0N8, 613/992-2451

The Canadian Marine Transportation Administration, Ottawa, Ont. K1A 0N7, 613/995-3277

The Canadian Surface Transportation Administration, Ottawa, Ont. K1A 0N5, 613/996-5959

Transportation of Dangerous Goods, Ottawa, Ont. K1A 0N5, 613/992-4624

For Provincial Labour Standards see "Labour" this table

STATISTICS

Bank of Canada, Ottawa, Ont. K1A OG9 (613/563-8111)

Dept. of Employment & Immigration, Public Affairs Division, Enquiries Officer, Ottawa, Ont. K1A OJ9 (819/994-6313)

Canada Mtge. & Housing Corp., Montreal Rd., Ottawa, Ont. K1A OP7 (613/748-2000)

Dept. of Indian Affairs & Northern Development, Communications & Information Branch, Ottawa, Ont. K1A OH4 (819/997-9920)

Labour Canada, Communication Services Directorate, Ottawa, Ont. K1A OJ2 (819/994-2238)

Statistics Canada, Ottawa, Ont. K1A 0T6 (613/992-2959 or 992-4734) See Index for regional offices.

Alta.: Alberta Bureau of Statistics, Alberta Treasury, 7th floor, 9811 109 St., Edmonton, Alta. T5J 0C8 (403/427-3058)

B.C.: Central Statistics Bureau, Ministry of Industry & Small Business Development, Parliament Bldgs., Victoria, B.C. V8V 1X4 (604/387-1502)

Man.: Man. Bureau of Statistics, Room 614, 155 Carlton St., Lakeview # 1, Winnipeg, Man. R3C 0V8 (204/944-2985)

N.B.: Economics & Statistics Branch, Dept. of Finance, Box 6000, Fredericton, N.B. E3B 5H1 (506/453-2484)

Nfld.: Nfld. Statistics Agency, Cabinet Secretariat, 3rd floor, Confederation Bldg., Box 4750, St. John's, Nfld. A1C 5T7 (709/737-2913)

N.S.: Statistical Services Branch, Dept. of Development, Box 519, Halifax, N.S. B3J 2R7 (902/424-5691)

Ont.: Central Statistical Services, Frost Bldg. North, 3rd floor, Toronto, Ont. M7A 1Y7 (416/965-7078)

P.E.I.: Dept. of Finance, Box 2000, Charlottetown, P.E.I. C1A 7N8 (902/894-8112)

Que.: Quebec Bureau of Statistics, Dept. of Industry, Trade & Tourism, 117 St-André, Quebec, P.Q. G1K 3Y3 (418/643-5116)

Sask.: Planning Bureau, Executive Council, 218 Walter Scott Bldg., 3085 Albert St., Regina, Sask. S4S 0B1 (306/565-6305)

N.W.T.: Motor Vehicle & Vital Statistics Registry, Dept. of Public Services, Government of N.W.T., Yellowknife, N.W.T. X1A 2L9 (403/873-7401)

Yukon: Economic Research & Planning Unit, Box 2703, Whitehorse, Y.T. Y1A 2C6 (403/667-5470)

STEEL

see Iron

STUDENT AID

Dept. of Indian Affairs & Northern Development, Ottawa, Ont. K1A OH4 (819/997-9920) (Native students)

Alta.: Students Finance Board, 1100 Park Sq., 10001 Bellamy Hill Rd., Edmonton, Alta. T5J 3B6 (403/427-2740)

B.C.: Student Services Branch, Ministry of Education, 835 Humboldt St., Victoria, B.C. V8V 2M4 (604/387-5951,2)

Man.: Student Aid Branch, Dept. of Education, 693 Taylor Ave., Winnipeg, Man. R3M 3T9 (204/284-8230)

N.B.: Student Aid Branch, Dept. of Youth, Recreation & Cultural Resources, Box 6000, Fredericton, N.B. E3B 5H1 (506/453-2577)

Nfld.: Student Aid Division, Dept. of Education, Thomson Student Centre, Memorial University of Nfld., St. John's, Nfld. A1C 5S7 (709/737-2689)

N.S.: Student Aid Office, Dept. of Education, Box 578, 5614 Fenwick St., Halifax, N.S. B3J 2S9 (902/424-7737)

Ont.: Student Awards Branch, Ministry of Education, 8th floor, Mowat Block, Queen's Park, Toronto, Ont. M7A 2B4 (416/965-5241)

P.E.I.: Student Aid, Dept. of Education, Box 2000, Charlottetown, P.E.I. C1A 7N8 (902/892-3504)

Que.: Service des Prêts et Bourses, Dept. of Education, Bldg. G, 22nd floor, Quebec, P.Q. G1R 5A5 (418/643-3750)

Sask.: Student Services Branch, Dept. of Continuing Education, 1855 Victoria Ave., Regina, Sask. S4P 3N5 (306/565-5618)

Yukon: Post Secondary Grants & Loans, Dept. of Education, Box 2703, Whitehorse, Y.T. Y1A 2C6 (403/667-5141)

SUCCESSION DUTIES

Technical Application Section, Compliance Directorate, Revenue Canada Taxation, 875 Heron Rd., Ottawa, Ont. K1A OL8 (613/995-1965)

B.C.: Assessor & Collector of Probate & Succession Duties, Parliament Bldgs., Victoria, B.C. V8V 1X4 (604/387-3328)

N.B.: Treasury Officer, Room 344, Centennial Bldg., Fredericton, N.B. E3B 5H1 (506/453-2565)

Nfld.: Manager, Information Ruling Branch, Dept. of Finance, Confederation Bldg., St. John's, Nfld. A1C 5T7 (709/737-3831)

N.S.: Director, Revenue, Dept. of Finance, Box 187, Halifax, N.S. B3J 2N3 (902/424-8951)

Ont.: Director, Succession Duty & Land Taxes Branch, Ministry of Revenue, 77 Bloor St. W., 17th floor, Toronto, Ont. M7A 1Y2 (416/965-2971)

Que.: Dept. of Revenue, Succession Division, 3800 rue Marly, Ste-Foy, P.Q. G1X 4A5

TAXATION

(*see also* Sales Taxes)

Dept. of Finance, Ottawa, Ont. K1A 0G5 (613/992-1573)

Revenue Canada, Taxation, 875 Heron Rd., Ottawa, Ont. K1A 0L8 (613/995-2961)

Alta.: Alberta Treasury, 434 Terrace Bldg., Edmonton, Alta. T5K 2C3 (403/427-4106)

B.C.: Ministry of Finance, Parliament Bldgs., Victoria, B.C. V8V 1X4 (604/387-5321)

Man.: Dept. of Finance, Taxation Division, Norquay Bldg., Winnipeg, Man. R3C 0V8 (204/943-3561)

N.B.: Provincial Tax Commissioner, Dept. of Finance, Tax Administration Branch, Box 3000, Fredericton, N.B. E3B 5G5 (506/453-2401)

Nfld.: Dept. of Finance, Confederation Bldg., St. John's, Nfld. A1C 5T7 (709/737-3831)

N.S.: Provincial Tax Commr., Box 755, Halifax, N.S. B3J 2V4 (902/424-6717)

Ont.: Ministry of Revenue, Parliament Bldgs., Queen's Park, Toronto, Ont. M7A 1X8 (416/965-2099)

P.E.I.: Dept. of Finance, Box 2000, Charlottetown, P.E.I. C1A 7N8 (902/892-8546)

Que.: Dept. of Revenue, 3800 rue Marly, Ste-Foy, P.Q. G1X 4A5 (418/643-6677)

Sask.: Dept. of Revenue, Supply & Services, Revenue Division, 3475 Albert St., Regina, Sask. S4S 6X6 (306/565-6645)

Montreal: Service des Finances, Secteur du Revenu, Hôtel de Ville, 275 est Notre-Dame, S. 15, Montreal, P.Q. H2Y 1C6 (514/872-3160)

Toronto: Finance Dept., Tax Branch, 1st floor, City Hall, Toronto, Ont. M5H 2N2 (416/367-7115, tax info.)

TELEPHONES

see Communications

TELEVISION

see Radio

TOPOGRAPHY

see Maps & Charts

TOURISM & TOURIST INFORMATION (Convention Facilities)

Parks Canada, Information Division, Ottawa, Ont. K1A 1G2 (819/997-0088) (national parks & historic sites)

Dept. of Industry, Trade & Commerce, Canadian Government Office of Tourism, 235 Queen St., Ottawa, Ont. K1A 0H5 (613/996-4610)

Statistics Canada, Ottawa, Ont. K1A 0T6 (613/995-0847)

Alta.: Travel Alberta, Dept. of Tourism & Small Business, 14th floor, 10065 Jasper Ave., Edmonton, Alta. T5J 0H4 (403/427-4321)

B.C.: Tourism British Columbia, Ministry of Tourism, 1117 Wharf St., Victoria, B.C. V8W 2Z2 (604/387-6416)

Man.: Travel Manitoba, Dept. of Economic Development & Tourism, Dept. 2068, Legislative Bldg., Winnipeg, Man. R3C 0V8 (204/944-3777)

N.B.: Promotion Branch, Dept. of Tourism, Box 12345, Fredericton, N.B. E3B 5C3 (506/453-2377)

Nfld.: Tourist Services Division, Dept. of Development, (146-148 Forest Rd.), Box 2016, St. John's, Nfld. A1C 5R8 (709/737-2832)

N.S.: Convention Officer, Dept. of Tourism, (5151 Terminal Rd.), Box 456, Halifax, N.S. B3J 2R5 (902/424-7657)

Ont.: Ministry of Industry & Tourism, Tourism Marketing Branch, Parliament Bldgs., Toronto, Ont. M7A 2E5 (416/965-4008)

P.E.I.: Visitor Services Division, Dept. of Tourism, Industry & Energy, Box 940, Charlottetown, P.E.I. C1A 7M5 (902/892-2457)

Que.: Dept. of Recreation, Fish & Game, Place de la Capitale, 150 est, boul. St-Cyrille, 15th floor, Quebec, P.Q. G1R 4Y3 (418/643-2266)

Sask.: Saskatchewan Tourism & Renewable Resources, Marketing & Promotions, 3211 Albert St., Regina, Sask. S4S 5W6 (306/565-2300)

Yukon: Tourism Yukon, Box 2703, Whitehorse, Y.T. Y1A 2C6 (403/667-5340)

Calgary: Tourist & Convention Association, Hospitality Centre, 1300 6th Ave. S.W., Calgary, Alta. T3C 0H8 (403/263-8510)

Charlottetown: Chamber of Commerce, Box 67, Charlottetown, P.E.I. C1A 7K2 (902/892-3424)

P.E.I. Convention Bureau, Box 2077, Charlottetown, P.E.I. C1A 7N7 (902/892-5900)

Dartmouth: Tourist Bureau, Thistle St., Dartmouth, N.S. B2Y 3Z3 (902/466-2728)

Director of Tourism, City of Dartmouth, Box 817, Dartmouth, N.S. B2Y 3Z3 (902/469-9211)

Edmonton: Convention Bureau, #690, 10123 99 St., Edmonton, Alta. T5J 3H1 (403/426-4715)

Guelph: Chamber of Commerce, Trafalgar Sq., Guelph, Ont. N1H 6N6 (519/822-8081)

Halifax: Visitors & Convention Bureau, Ste. 508, Market Mall, Scotia Sq., Box 1749, Halifax, N.S. B3J 3A5 (902/426-8736)

Hamilton: Visitors & Convention Services, Region of Hamilton-Wentworth, 100 Main St. E., Box 910, Hamilton, Ont. L8N 3V9 (416/526-4222)

Kingston: Bureau of Tourism, 209 Ontario St., Box 486, Kingston, Ont. K7L 2Z1 (613/548-4415)

Kitchener: Kitchener Visitor & Convention Bureau, 67 King St. E., Box 2367, Stn. B, Kitchener, Ont. N2H 6M2 (519/576-5000)

London: Visitors & Convention Services, 300 Dufferin Ave., Box 5035, London, Ont. N6A 4L9 (519/672-1970)

Mississauga: Mississauga Board of Trade, 100 City Centre Dr., Mississauga, Ont. L5B 2C9 (416/276-4357)

Montreal: Commission d'initiative et de développement économiques de Montréal/Développement Touristique (CIDEM-Tourisme), #206, 155 est rue Notre-Dame, Montreal, P.Q. H2Y 1B5 (514/872-3561)

Convention & Visitors' Bureau, Mart F, 49 Frontenac, Box 889, Place Bonaventure, Montreal, P.Q. H5A 1E6 (514/871-1129)

Niagara Falls: Niagara Falls, Canada Visitor & Convention Bureau, 5433 Victoria Ave., Niagara Falls, Ont. L2G 3L1 (416/356-6061)

Oshawa: Oshawa Chamber of Commerce, (48 Simcoe St. S.), Box 2067, Oshawa, Ont. L1H 7N2 (416/728-1683)

Ottawa: Canada's Capital Visitors & Convention Bureau, 7th floor, Capitol Sq. Bldg., 222 Queen St., Ottawa, Ont. K1P 5V9 (613/237-5150)

Quebec: Tourism & Convention Dept. of the Quebec Urban Community, 60, rue d'Auteuil, Quebec, P.Q. G1R 4C4 (418/692-2471)

Regina: Regina Chamber of Commerce, 2145 Albert St., Regina, Sask. S4P 2V1 (306/527-4658)

Saint John: City Hall, Box 1971, Saint John, N.B. E2L 4L1 (506/658-2878)

St. John's: St. John's Tourist Commission, City Hall, Box 1567, St. John's, Nfld. A1C 5P3 (709/722-7080)

Saskatoon: Saskatoon Tourist & Convention Bureau, 601 Spadina Cres. E., Saskatoon, Sask. S7K 3G8 (306/242-1206)

Sudbury: Convention & Visitors Services of Sudbury, Civic Square, Box 1000, Sudbury, Ont. P3E 4S5 (705/674-3141)

Thunder Bay: Public Affairs, Visitors & Convention Dept., Paterson Park, 520 Leith St., Thunder Bay, Ont. P7C 1M9 (807/623-2711)

Toronto: Convention & Tourist Bureau of Metropolitan Toronto, Ste. 110, Box 510, Toronto Eaton Centre, 220 Yonge St., Toronto, Ont. M5B 2H1 (416/979-3133)

Vancouver: Greater Vancouver Convention & Visitors Bureau, 701 W. Georgia St., Pacific Centre, Box 10171, Vancouver, B.C. V7Y 1H5 (604/682-2222)

Victoria: Greater Victoria Visitor Information Centre, 812 Wharf St., Victoria, B.C. V8W 1T3 (604/382-2127)

Vancouver Island Publicity Bureau, 635 Humboldt St., Victoria, B.C. V8W 1A7 (604/382-3551)

Windsor: Tourist & Convention Bureau of Windsor & Essex County, Place Goyeau, 80 Chatham St. E., Windsor, Ont. N9A 2W1 (519/255-6530)

Winnipeg: Mayor's Office, Council Bldg., Civic Centre, Winnipeg, Man. R3B 1B9 (204/946-0196)

Winnipeg Convention Centre, 375 York Ave., Winnipeg, Man. R3C 3J3 (204/956-1720)

British Tourist Authority

Canadian Office: Box 504, Stn. F, Toronto, Ont. M4Y 2L8 (416/925-6326)

U.S. Travel Service

Executive Office: (416/364-0723)

Travel USA, 2 Carlton St., Toronto, Ont. M5B 1K4 (416/964-3094)

TRADE

Dept. of Finance, Ottawa, Ont. K1A OG5 (613/992-6985)

Dept. of Industry, Trade & Commerce, Business Centre, 235 Queen St., Ottawa, Ont. K1A OH5 (613/995-5771)

Export Development Corp., Box 655, Ottawa, Ont. K1P 5T9 (613/237-2570)

Statistics Canada, Ottawa, Ont. K1A OT6 (613/995-6305)

Alta.: Trade Development, Dept. of Economic Development, 11th floor, 10909 Jasper Ave., Edmonton, Alta. T5J 3M8 (403/427-4809)

B.C.: Ministry of Industry & Small Business Development, 800 Hornby St., Vancouver, B.C. V6Z 2C5 (604/689-4411)

Man.: Dept. of Economic Development, Market Development, No. 1, Lakeview Sq., 155 Carlton St., Winnipeg, Man. R3C 3H8 (204/944-2466)

N.B.: Dept. of Commerce & Development, Box 6000, Fredericton, N.B. E3B 5H1 (506/453-2975)

N.S.: Transportation Policy Branch & Market Development Centre, Box 519, Halifax, N.S. B3J 2R7 (902/424-4242)

Ont.: Trade Policy Branch, Policy & Priorities Division, Ministry of Industry & Tourism, 900 Bay St., Toronto, Ont. M7A 1S6 (416/965-7119)

P.E.I.: Dept. of Tourism, Industry & Energy, Box 2000, Charlottetown, P.E.I. C1A 7N8 (902/892-7411)

Que.: Dept. of Industry, Trade & Tourism, Commerce Section, 1, Place Ville Marie, 23rd floor, Montreal, P.Q. H3B 3M6 (514/873-3540)

Sask.: Dept. of Industry & Commerce, 3rd floor, 2121 Saskatchewan Dr., Regina, Sask. S4P 3V7 (306/565-2232); Telex: 071-2675

TRADE MARKS

see Patents

TRAINING

see Apprenticeship
see Occupational

TRANSLATIONS

Translation Bureau, Dept. of the Secretary of State, Ottawa, Ont. K1A 0M5 (819/997-3686) (translations for all federal Depts. & agencies)

N.B.: N.B. Translation Bureau, French & English Sections, 191 Prospect Place, 3rd floor, Fredericton, N.B. E3B 2T7 (506/453-2920)

Debate Section & Interpreters, 751 Brunswick St., Fredericton, N.B. E3B 5H1 (506/453-2648)

Que.: Direction de la traduction, Ministère des Communications, 5555 3rd Ave. W., Charlesbourg, P.Q. G1H 6R1 (418/643-9450)

Banque de terminologie du Québec, Service de la diffusion par terminal, 800, Square Victoria, Montreal, P.Q. H4Z 1G8 (514/873-7733) documentation and terminological data banks

TRANSPORTATION

see also Public Commercial Vehicles

Manager, Corporate Information, Air Canada, 38th floor, Place Ville Marie, Montreal, P.Q. H3B 3P7 (514/874-4889), and any local office

Canadian National Railways, System Headquarters, Montreal, P.Q. H3C 3N4 (514/877-5430)

Canadian Transport Commission, Ottawa, Ont. K1A ON9 (819/997-0677) (for list of District Offices, see Index)

Dept. of Indian Affairs & Northern Development, Ottawa, Ont. K1A OH4 (819/997-9920) (northern only)

Dept. of Industry, Trade & Commerce, Transportation Industries Branch, 235 Queen St., Ottawa, Ont. K1A OH5 (613/995-3201)

Dept. of Transport, Place de Ville, Ottawa, Ont. K1A ON5 (613/996-5861)

National Aeronautical Collection, Ottawa, Ont. K1A OM8 (613/998-4566)

National Aeronautical Establishment, National Research Council of Canada, Ottawa, Ont. K1A OR6 (613/993-2427)

National Film Board, Box 6100, Montreal, P.Q. H3C 3H5 (514/333-3333)

National Harbours Board, 320 Queen St., Ottawa, Ont. K1A ON6 (613/996-6400)

National Museum of Science & Technology, Ottawa, Ont. K1A OM8 (613/998-4566)

National Research Council of Canada, Division of Mechanical Engineering, Ottawa, Ont. K1A 0R6 (613/993-2424)

Northern Transportation Co. Ltd., 9945 108 St., Edmonton, Alta. T5K 2G9 (403/423-9201)

St. Lawrence Seaway Authority, Ottawa, Ont. K1R 5A3 (613/992-4108)

Statistics Canada, Ottawa, Ont. K1A OT6 (613/992-1461)

Transportation Development Centre, 1000 Sherbrooke St. W., Box 549, Montreal, P.Q. H3A 2R3 (514/283-7504)

Alta.: Alberta Transportation, Public Communications Office, #201, 9630 106 St., Edmonton, Alta. T5K 2B8 (403/427-7674)

Motor Transport Board, Provincial Bldg., Box 5002, Red Deer, Alta. T4N 5Y5 (403/343-5430)

Alberta Resources Railway Corp., Room 305, 9630 106 St., Edmonton, Alta. T5K 2B8 (403/427-3165)

B.C.: Ministry of Transportation & Highways, Parliament Bldgs., Victoria, B.C. V8V 1X4 (604/387-5657 transp.; 387-3183 hwys.)

Urban Transit Authority, (844 Courtney St.), Box 610, Victoria, B.C. V8W 2P3 (604/385-2551)

Man.: Transportation Division, Dept. of Highways & Transportation, 15th floor, 215 Garry St., Winnipeg, Man. R3C 3Z1 (204/944-2004, 944-3772)

N.B.: Dept. of Transportation, Admin. Director, Box 6000, Fredericton, N.B. E3B 5H1 (506/453-2237)

Nfld.: Dept. of Transportation, Atlantic Place, Water St., St. John's, Nfld. A1C 5T7 (709/737-3641)

Dept. of Public Works & Services, Confederation Bldg., St. John's, Nfld. A1C 5T7 (709/737-3678)

N.S.: Dept. of Transportation, Provincial Bldg., Hollis St., Box 186, Halifax, N.S. B3J 2N2 (902/424-4036)

Ont.: Ministry of Transportation & Communications, 1201 Wilson Ave., Downsview, Ont. M3M 1J8 (416/248-3591)

GO Transit, 3625 Dufferin St., Downsview, Ont. M3K 1Z2 (416/630-2635)

P.E.I.: Transportation Division, Dept. of Highways & Public Works, Box 2000, Charlottetown, P.E.I. C1A 7N8 (902/892-0291)

Que.: Quebec Transport Commission, La Fayette Bldg., 585 Charest Blvd. E., Quebec, P.Q. G1K 7W5, 418/643-5673 (Montreal branch: 505 Sherbrooke St. E., Place du Cercle, Montreal, P.Q. H2L 1K2, 514/873-6414)

Sask.: Highway Maps, Overweight & Over-Dimension Permits, Dept. of Highways & Transportation, 1855 Victoria Ave., Regina, Sask. S4P 3V5 (306/565-4800)

The Highway Traffic Board, Vehicle Registration, Driver Licencing & Highway Safety, 2260 11th Ave., Regina, Sask. S4P 3V7 (306/565-4271)

Transportation Agency of Saskatchewan, Admin. Services Branch, 1914 Hamilton St., Regina, Sask. S4P 4V4 (306/565-5314)

Calgary: Transportation Dept., Box 2100, Calgary, Alta. T2P 2M5 (403/268-2111)

Edmonton: Edmonton Transit, 10426 81 Ave., Edmonton, Alta. T6E 1X5 (403/428-5648)

Hamilton: Traffic Dept., City Hall, 71 Main St. W., Box 2040, Hamilton, Ont. L8N 3T4 (416/527-0241)

London: London Transit Commission, 450 Highbury Ave., London, Ont. N5W 5L2 (519/451-1340)

Mississauga: Mississauga Transit, 975 Gillian St., Mississauga, Ont. L5C 3B1 (416/279-5800)

Montreal: CTCUM, 159 St-Antoine St. W., Montreal, P.Q. H2Z 1H3 (514/877-6300)

Montreal (Urban): Metro Transit Bureau, 2 Complexe Desjardins, Box 129, Montreal, P.Q. H5B 1E6 (514/872-6811)

Quebec: Que. Urban Community Transit Commission, 720 des Rocailles, Quebec, P.Q. G2J 1A5 (418/627-2351)

Regina: Regina Transit System, 1157 Albert St., Regina, Sask. S4R 2R2 (306/569-7726)

St. John's: City Hall, New Gower St., St. John's, Nfld. A1C 5M2 (709/726-8820)

Saskatoon: Saskatoon Transit System, 315 Ave "C" N., Saskatoon, Sask. S7L 1J3 (306/652-6233)

Sudbury: Transportation Dept., 200 Brady St., Box 1000, Sudbury, Ont. P3E 4S5 (705/674-3141)

Toronto: Toronto Transit Commission, 1900 Yonge St., Toronto, Ont. M4S 1Z2 (416/481-4252)

Winnipeg: Commr. of Works & Operations, Civic Centre, Winnipeg, Man. R3B 1B9 (204/946-0378)

TRAPPING

see Wildlife

UNEMPLOYMENT INSURANCE

Public Affairs Division, Canada Employment & Immigration Commission, Ottawa, Ont. K1A 0J9 (819/994-6489)

Regional Offices:

199 Grafton St., Charlottetown, P.E.I. C1A 8K1

167 Kenmount Rd., St. John's, Nfld. A1B 3L8

1888 Brunswick St., Halifax, N.S. B3J 3E4

565 Priestman St., Fredericton, N.B. E3B 5V6

1441, rue St-Urbain, Montreal, P.Q. H2X 2M8

Regional Sub-headquarters: 494 Dundas St., Belleville, Ont. K8N 5C1

4900 Yonge St., Willowdale, Ont. M2N 6A8

167 Lombard Ave., Winnipeg, Man. R3B 0T6

2101 Scarth St., Regina, Sask. S4P 2H9

9925 109th St., Edmonton, Alta. T5K 2J8

1055 W. Georgia St., Vancouver, B.C. V6E 2P8

Statistics Canada, Ottawa, Ont. K1A 0T6 (613/995-8445)

URBAN RENEWAL, DESIGN & GROWTH

Canada Mtge. & Housing Corp., Canadian Housing Information Centre, Montreal Rd., Ottawa, Ont. K1A 0P7 (613/748-2367)

Alta.: Alberta Housing Corp., 9405 50 St., Edmonton, Alta. T6B 2T4 (403/468-3535)

Alberta Home Mtge. Corp., #205, 10050 112 St., Edmonton, Alta. T2K 2L7 (403/482-7151)

B.C.: Ministry of Municipal Affairs, Parliament Bldgs., Victoria, B.C. V8V 1X4 (604/387-5925)

Man.: Manitoba Housing & Renewal Corp., 287 Broadway, Winnipeg, Man. R3C 0R9 (204/944-4748)

N.B.: N.B. Housing Corp., Box 611, Fredericton, N.B. E3B 5B2 (506/454-5563)

Nfld.: Nfld. & Labrador Housing Corp., Box 220, Elizabeth Towers, St. John's, Nfld. A1C 5J2 (709/722-3554)

N.S.: No provincial agency.

Ont.: Ministry of Municipal Affairs & Housing, Community Renewal Branch, 56 Wellesley St. W., Toronto, Ont. M7A 2K4 (416/965-2826)

P.E.I.: P.E.I. Housing Corp., Box 1388, Charlottetown, P.E.I. C1A 7N1 (902/892-0221)

Que.: Quebec Housing Corp., 1054 Conroy, Edifice G, bloc 2, 4e étage, Québec, P.Q. G1R 5E7 (418/643-3023)

Sask.: Saskatchewan Housing Corp., 2500 Victoria Ave., Regina, Sask. S4P 3V7 (306/565-4177)

Calgary: Housing & Community Renewal Division, Box 2100, Calgary, Alta. T2P 2M5

Edmonton: Land Use Planning Branch, City Planning Dept., 12th floor, Phipps McKinnon Bldg., Edmonton, Alta. T5J 3G2 (403/428-3119)

Halifax: Development Dept., City Hall, Box 1749, Halifax, N.S. B3J 3A5 (902/426-6522)

Hamilton: Community Development, City Hall, 71 Main St. W., Hamilton, Ont. L8N 3T4 (416/527-0241)

Montreal: Service de l'Urbanisme, 85 est, rue Notre-Dame, Montreal, P.Q. H2Y 1B5

Quebec City: Service de l'Urbanisme, Hôtel de Ville, Quebec, P.Q. G1R 4S9 (418/694-6422)

Regina: City Planning Dept., City Hall, (2476 Victoria Ave.), Box 1790, Regina, Sask. S4P 3C8 (306/569-7551)

Saint John: Housing & Renewal Services Branch, Dept. of Community Planning & Development, 15 Market Sq., Box 1971, Saint John, N.B. E2L 4L1 (506/658-2856)

Saskatoon: Director of Planning & Development; or City Planning Officer, City Planning Dept., both at City Hall, Saskatoon, Sask. S7K 0J5 (306/644-9206)

Toronto: Planning & Development Dept., 19th floor, East Tower, City Hall, Toronto, Ont. M5H 2N2 (416/367-7185)

Vancouver: City Planning Dept., 453 W. 12th Ave., Vancouver, B.C. V5Y 1V4 (604/873-7344)

Windsor: Commr. of Planning, City Hall, Windsor, Ont. N9A 6S1 (519/255-6281)

Winnipeg: Director of Environmental Planning, 100 Main St., Winnipeg, Man. R3C 1A5 (204/985-5155)

VETERANS AFFAIRS

War Veterans Allowance Board, 6th floor, Dominion Bldg., Box 7700, Charlottetown, P.E.I. C1A 8M9 (902/894-5072)

Dept. of Veterans Affairs, Public Affairs Directorate, Ottawa, Ont. K1A 0P4 (613/992-4234) (See Index for list of District Offices)

VITAL STATISTICS

Dept. of Indian Affairs & Northern Development, Ottawa, Ont. K1A 0H4 (819/997-9920)

Statistics Canada, Main Bldg., Tunney's Pasture, Ottawa, Ont. K1A 0T6 (613/995-9593)

Alta.: Director of Vital Statistics, 400, 10405 100 Ave., Edmonton, Alta. T5J 0A6 (403/427-2681)

B.C.: Division of Vital Statistics, Ministry of Health, 1515 Blanshard St., Victoria, B.C. V8W 3C8 (604/386-3166, loc. 2410)

Man.: Office of Vital Statistics, 104 Norquay Bldg., 401 York Ave., Winnipeg, Man. R3C 0V8 (204/944-3701)

N.B.: Registrar General of Vital Statistics, Room G 72, Centennial Bldg., Box 6000, Fredericton, N.B. E3B 5H1 (506/453-2385)

Nfld.: Vital Statistics Division, Dept. of Health, Confederation Bldg., St. John's, Nfld. A1C 5T7 (709/737-3308)

N.S.: Vital Statistics, Dept. of Health, Provincial Bldg. (Box 157), Halifax, N.S. B3J 2M9 (902/424-4373)

Ont.: Registrar General, Ministry of Consumer & Commercial Relations, Room M-25, Macdonald Block, Queen's Park, Toronto, Ont. M7A 1Y5 (416/965-1687)

P.E.I.: Director of Vital Statistics, Dept. of Health & Social Services, Box 3000, Charlottetown, P.E.I. C1A 7P1 (902/892-5471)

Que.: Copies of birth and marriage certificates are issued by the Civil Archives of the judicial district where the event was registered. For list of offices contact: Registre de la population, 1279 boul Charest ouest, (3e), Québec, P.Q. G1N 2C9 (418/643-7433). Death certificates are issued by the central office at Ministère de la Justice, Registre de référence, 117 St-André, Québec, P.Q. G1K 3Y3 (418/643-6436)

Sask.: Division of Vital Statistics, Dept. of Health, 3475 Albert St., Regina, Sask. S4S 6X6 (306/565-3092)

Yukon: Vital Statistics, Dept. of Health & Human Resources, Box 2703, Whitehorse, Y.T. Y1A 2C6 (403/667-5207)

U.K. Certificates

England & Wales: General Register Office, St. Catherines House, 10 Kingsway, London, WC2B 6JP

Northern Ireland: Registrar General, Oxford House, 49/55 Chichester St., Belfast, BT1 4HL

Scotland: General Register Office, New Register House, Edinburgh, EH1 3YT

Irish Republic: Registrar General, Custom House, Dublin 1

WAGES

see Labour

WATER POLLUTION

see Environment

WATER RESOURCES

Inland Waters Directorate, Environmental Conservation Service, Environment Canada, Ottawa, Ont. K1A OH3 (613/997-6555)

National Film Board, Box 6100, Montreal, P.Q. H3C 3H5 (514/333-3333)

Alta.: Water Resources Administration Division, Dept. of the Environment, 7th floor, Oxbridge Place, 9820 106 St., Edmonton, Alta. T5K 2J6 (403/427-6168)

B.C.: Ministry of Environment, Information Services Branch, 810 Blanshard St., Victoria, B.C. V8W 3E1 (604/387-5162)

Man.: Water Resources Branch, 1577 Dublin Ave., Winnipeg, Man. R3E 3J5 (204/786-9423)

N.B.: Dept. of the Environment, Box 6000, Fredericton, N.B. E3B 5H1 (506/453-3700)

Nfld.: Dept. of Environment, Elizabeth Towers, Elizabeth Ave., St. John's, Nfld. A1B 1R9 (709/737-2563)

N.S.: Dept. of the Environment, Box 2107, Halifax, N.S. B3J 3B7 (902/424-8600)

Ont.: Public Lands Section, Land Management Branch, Ministry of Natural Resources, Room 6440, Whitney Block, Queen's Park, Toronto, Ont. M7A 1W3 (416/965-2741) (Crown land and water management and disposition programs)

Conservation Authorities & Water Management Branch, Ministry of Natural Resources, Room 5628, Whitney Block, Toronto, Ont. M7A 1W3 (416/965-6287) (Engineering design standards for flood control structures, and watershed planning)

Water Resources Branch, Ministry of the Environment, 135 St. Clair Ave. W., Toronto, Ont. M4V 1P5 (416/965-6141)

P.E.I.: Dept. of Community Affairs, Environmental & Consumer Services Division, (3 Queen St.), Box 2000, Charlottetown, P.E.I. C1A 7N8 (902/892-9174)

Que.: Dept. of Environment, Inventories & Research Branch, 2360 Ste-Foy Rd., Ste-Foy, P.Q. G1V 4H2 (418/643-2795)

Sask.: Dept. of the Environment, Water Management Service, 5th floor, 1855 Victoria Ave., Regina, Sask. S4P 3V5 (306/565-6141)

WEATHER

see Climate

WEIGHTS & MEASURES

Legal Metrology Branch, Consumer Affairs Bureau, Dept. of Consumer & Corporate Affairs Canada, Standards Bldg., Tunney's Pasture, Ottawa, Ont. K1A OC9 (613/992-3819)

Standards Council of Canada, 350 Sparks St., Ottawa, Ont. K1R 7S8 (613/238-3222)

National Film Board, Box 6100, Montreal, P.Q. H3C 3H5 (514/333-3333)

See also "Standards", this table

WELFARE

Dept. of National Health & Welfare, Ottawa, Ont. K1A OK9

Income Security Programs Branch (613/992-1865)

Social Service Programs Branch (992-2741)

Policy, Planning & Information Branch (995-7231)

National Council of Welfare, Ottawa, Ont. K1A OK9 (613/995-6265)

Statistics Canada, Ottawa, Ont. K1A OT6 (613/995-0657)

Alta.: Dept. of Social Services & Community Health, 10030 107 St., Edmonton, Alta. T5J 3E4 (403/427-2734)

B.C.: Income Assistance Division, Ministry of Human Resources, Parliament Bldgs., Victoria, B.C. V8V 1X4 (604/387-1486)

Man.: Dept. of Community Services & Corrections, Income Security, 267 Edmonton St., Winnipeg, Man. R3C 1S2 (204/944-2681)

N.B.: Communications & Federal/Provincial Relations Unit, Dept. of Social Services, Box 6000, Fredericton, N.B. E3B 5H1 (506/453-2953)

Nfld.: Dept. of Social Services, Confederation Bldg., St. John's, Nfld. A1C 5T7 (709/737-2478)

N.S.: Dept. of Social Services, Box 696, Halifax, N.S. B3J 2T7 (902/424-4325)

Ont.: Ministry of Community & Social Services, Communications Branch, 7th floor, Hepburn Block, Queen's Park, Toronto, Ont. M7A 1E9 (416/965-7825)

P.E.I.: Dept. of Health & Social Services, Box 2000, Charlottetown, P.E.I. C1A 7N8 (902/892-5471)

Que.: No provincial agency.

Sask.: Income Support Division, Saskatchewan Social Services, 1920 Broad St., Regina, Sask. S4P 3V6 (306/565-3520)

Yukon: Dept. of Human Resources, Box 2703, Whitehorse, Y.T. Y1A 2C6 (403/667-5674)

WILDLIFE (Fish & Game Regulations, Trapping)

Canadian Wildlife Service, Environment Canada, Ottawa, Ont. K1A OE7 (613/997-1095) Wildlife area regulations & migratory birds regulations.

National Film Board, Box 6100, Montreal, P.Q. H3C 3H5 (514/333-3333)

National Museum of Natural Sciences, Ottawa, Ont. K1A OM8 (613/996-3102)

Alta.: Fish & Wildlife Division, Dept. of Energy & Natural Resources, 8th floor, South Tower, Petroleum Plaza, 9915 108 St., Edmonton, Alta. T5K 2C9 (403/427-6729)

B.C.: Fish & Wildlife Branch, Ministry of Environment, Parliament Bldgs., Victoria, B.C. V8V 1X5 (604/387-1628)

Man.: Public Information Services, Dept. of Natural Resources, Box 22, 1495 St. James St., Winnipeg, Man. R3H OW9 (204/775-0221)

N.B.: Fish & Wildlife Branch, 349 King St., Box 6000, Fredericton, N.B. E3B 5H1 (506/453-2440)

Nfld.: Wildlife Division, Dept. of Culture, Recreation & Youth, (Bldg. 810, Pleasantville), Box 4750, St. John's, Nfld. A1C 5T7 (709/737-2815)

N.S.: Director of Wildlife, Dept. of Lands & Forests, Box 516, Kentville, N.S. B4N 3X3 (902/678-8921)

Ont.: Wildlife Branch, Outdoor Recreation, Ministry of Natural Resources, Queen's Park, Toronto, Ont. M7A 1W3 (416/965-4251)

P.E.I.: Fish & Wildlife Unit, Dept. of Community Affairs, Box 2000, Charlottetown, P.E.I. C1A 7N8 (902/892-9174)

Que.: Dept. of Recreation, Fish & Game, 150, est, boul. St-Cyrille, Quebec, P.Q. G1R 4Y3 (418/643-2266)

Sask.: Fisheries Branch, 306/565-2884, and Wildlife Branch, 306/565-2886, both at: Dept. of Tourism & Renewable Resources, 3211 Albert St., Regina, Sask. S4S 5W6

Yukon: Wildlife Branch, Box 2703, Whitehorse, Yukon, Y1A 2C6 (403/667-5221)

N.W.T.: Supt., Wildlife Service, N.W.T. Government, Yellowknife, N.W.T. X1A 2L9 (403/873-7411)

WOMEN'S RIGHTS

Affirmative Action, Canada Employment & Immigration Commission, Ottawa, Ont. K1A 0J9 (613/994-6588)

Office of the Co-ordinator, Status of Women Canada, 151 Sparks St., Ottawa, Ont. K1A 1C3 (613/995-9397)

Office of Equal Opportunities for Women, Public Service Commission, Ottawa, Ont. K1A 0M7 (613/996-4208)

Canadian Advisory Council on the Status of Women, Box 1541, Stn. B, Ottawa, Ont. K1P 5R5 (613/992-4975)

Native Women's Office, Dept. of Secretary of State, Ottawa, Ont. K1A 0M5 (819/994-3970)

Special Advisor, Status of Women, Health & Welfare Canada, Ottawa, Ont. K1A 0K9 (613/996-8820)

Women's Bureau, CMHC, Ottawa, Ont. K1A 0P7 (613/748-2212)

Women's Bureau, Labour Canada, Ottawa, Ont. K1A OJ2 (819/997-1550, 994-3779)

Women's Employment Division, Canada Employment & Immigration Commission, Ottawa, Ont. K1A 0J9 (613/994-6727)

Women's Program, Dept. of Secretary of State, Ottawa, Ont. K1A 0M5 (613/994-3190)

Alta.: Women's Bureau, Room 1402, 10015 103 Ave., Edmonton, Alta. T5J OH1 (403/427-2470)

B.C.: No provincial agency.

Man.: Women's Bureau, Dept. of Labour & Manpower, 241 Vaughan St., Winnipeg, Man. R3C 1T6 (204/944-3476)

N.B.: N.B. Advisory Council on the Status of Women, 386 St. George St., Moncton, N.B. E1C 1X2 (506/388-9660)

Nfld.: Dept. of Justice, Confederation Bldg., St. John's, Nfld. A1C 5T7 (709/737-2872)

N.S.: Advisory Council on Status of Women, Box 745, Halifax, N.S. B3J 2T3 (902/424-8662)

Ont.: Women's Bureau, Ministry of Labour, 15th floor, 400 University Ave., Toronto, Ont. M7A 1T7 (416/965-1537)

P.E.I.: Advisory Council on the Status of Women, Box 2000, Charlottetown, P.E.I. C1A 7N8 (902/894-8973)

Que.: Council on the Status of Women, 700, boul. St-Cyrille est, 16e étage, Quebec, P.Q. G1R 5A9 (418/643-4326, or 1-800-463-2851); Montreal Office: 1255, Carré Philippe, bur. 708, Montreal, P.Q. H3B 3G1 (514/873-8384)

Sask.: Women's Division, Dept. of Labour, 1914 Hamilton St., Regina, Sask. S4P 4V4 (306/565-2452)

Other Women's Information Sources:

Montreal: Centre d'Information et de Référence pour Femmes, 3585, rue Saint Urbain, Montreal, P.Q. H2X 2N6 (514/842-4781)

Toronto: YWCA Women's Development Centre, 15 Birch Ave., Toronto, Ont. M4V 1E1 (416/925-3137) (will give phone and address of Women's Centre in cities across Canada)

Women's Information & Referral Service (416/925-1154)

Vancouver: Vancouver Status of Women, 400A W. 5th Ave., Vancouver, B.C. V5Y 1J8 (604/873-1427)

WORKERS' COMPENSATION

Occupational Safety & Health Branch, Dept. of Labour, Ottawa, Ont. K1A OJ2 (819/997-3520) (for persons in federal employment)

Alta.: Workers' Compensation Board, 9912 107 St., Edmonton, Alta. T5J 2S5 (403/427-1100)

B.C.: Workers' Compensation Board, 5255 Heather St., Vancouver, B.C. V5Z 3L8 (604/266-0211)

Man.: Workers Compensation Board, 333 Maryland St., Winnipeg, Man. R3G 1M2 (204/786-5471)

N.B.: Workmen's Compensation Board, Box 160, Saint John, N.B. E2L 3X9 (506/652-2250, or 1-800-222-9775)

Nfld.: Workers' Compensation Board, Box 9000, Stn. B, St. John's, Nfld. A1A 3B8 (709/754-2940)

N.S.: Workers Compensation Board of N.S., 5668 South St. (Box 1150), Halifax, N.S. B3J 2Y2 (902/424-5758)

Ont.: Workmen's Compensation Board, 2 Bloor St. E., Toronto, Ont. M4W 3C3 (416/965-8851)

P.E.I.: Workers' Compensation Board, Box 757, Charlottetown, P.E.I. C1A 7L7 (902/894-8555)

Que.: Commission de la santé et de la sécurité du travail, 1199 rue Bleury, Montréal, P.Q. H3B 3J1 (514/873-7545)

Sask.: Workers' Compensation Board, 1840 Lorne St., Regina, Sask. S4P 2L8 (306/565-4370)

Yukon: Workers' Compensation Board, #300, 4110 4th Ave., Whitehorse, Y.T. Y1A 4N7 (403/667-5645)

YOUTH SERVICES

Social Service Programs Branch, Social Services Division, Dept. of National Health & Welfare, Ottawa, Ont. K1A 1B5 (613/995-1050)

Ministry of the Solicitor General, Human Resource Branch, 340 Laurier Ave. W., Ottawa, Ont. K1A OP8 (613/996-5576, 7)

Alta.: No provincial agency.

B.C.: Ministry of Human Resources, Family & Children's Services, Parliament Bldgs., Victoria, B.C. V8V 1X4 (604/387-3127)

Man.: Manitoba Youth Centre, 170 Doncaster St., Winnipeg, Man. R3N 1X9 (204/475-2010)

Child & Family Services, Dept. of Community Services & Corrections, 831 Portage Ave., Winnipeg, Man. R3G ON6 (204/775-9761)

N.B.: Dept. of Youth, Recreation & Cultural Resources, Box 6000, Fredericton, N.B. E3B 5H1 (506/453-2312)

Nfld.: Director of Youth Services, Dept. of Culture, Recreation & Youth, Box 2016, St. John's, Nfld. A1A 5R8 (709/753-4901)

N.S.: Dept. of Social Services, Family & Children's Services Division, Box 696, Halifax, N.S. B3J 2T7 (902/424-4279)

Ont.: Youth Secretariat, 700 Bay St., 2nd floor, Toronto, Ont. M5G 1Z6 (416/965-3540)

Que.: Office franco-québécois pour la jeunesse, 1214, rue de la Montagne, Montreal, P.Q. H3G 1Z1 (514/873-4255)

Sask.: Dept. of Culture & Youth, 11th floor, Avord Tower, Regina, Sask. S4P 3V7 (306/565-5749)

ZONING

Alta.: Planning Director, Dept. of Municipal Affairs, 7th floor, 9925 107 St., Edmonton, Alta. T5K 2H9 (403/427-2125)

B.C.: Ministry of Municipal Affairs, Parliament Bldgs., Victoria, B.C. V8V 1X4 (604/387-5925)

Man.: Municipal Planning Branch, Dept. of Municipal Affairs, 14th floor, 405 Broadway, Winnipeg, Man. R3C 3L6 (204/944-2150)

N.B.: Planning Branch, Dept. of Municipal Affairs, Box 6000, Fredericton, N.B. E3B 5H1 (506/453-2171)

Nfld.: Planning Division, Dept. of Municipal Affairs, Confederation Bldg., St. John's, Nfld. A1C 5T7 (709/737-3090)

N.S.: Community Planning Division, Dept. of Municipal Affairs, Box 216, Halifax, N.S. B3J 2M4 (902/424-4091)

Ont.: Community Planning Review Branch, Ministry of Housing, 56 Wellesley St. W., 8th floor, Toronto, Ont. M7A 2K4 (416/965-6418)

P.E.I.: Dept. of Community Affairs, Building & Development Services, Box 2000, Charlottetown, P.E.I. C1A 7N8 (902/892-0221)

Que.: Municipal Affairs Dept., Regional & Town Planning Division, Bldg. G, 1039 de la Chevrotière, Quebec, P.Q. G1R 4Z3 (418/643-2080)

Sask.: Community Planning Branch, Dept. of Urban Affairs, 1791 Rose St., Regina, Sask. S4P 3V7 (306/565-2881)

Montreal: Permits & Inspection Dept., 810 est rue St-Antoine, Ste. 100, Montreal, P.Q. H2Y 1A6 (514/872-3181)

Toronto: Dept. of Buildings, Buildings Information Section, 17th floor, East Tower, City Hall, Toronto, Ont. M5H 2N2 (416/367-7600)

DIPLOMATIC DIRECTORY

COMMONWEALTH OF NATIONS

The Commonwealth is a free association of 38 independent member countries. Their combined population is over 902 million, nearly one-quarter of the population of the world. Their combined area is over ten million square miles, nearly one-fifth of the world's land area.

For information pertaining to the Commonwealth write to: Information Division, Commonwealth Secretariat, Marlborough House, Pall Mall, London SW1Y 5HX, Eng.

Member States

(showing Capital, Population & Date of Membership - Dates for Australia, Canada & New Zealand are those on which Dominion Status was acquired):

Australia - Canberra; 13,485,900; Jan. 1, 1901
The Bahamas - Nassau; 200,000; July 10, 1973
Bangladesh - Dacca; 72,000,000; Apr. 18, 1972
Barbados - Bridgetown; 247,500; Nov. 30, 1966
Botswana - Gaborone; 675,000; Sept. 30, 1966
Britain - London; 55,836,300
Canada - Ottawa; 22,446,000; July 1, 1867
Cyprus - Nicosia; 640,000; Mar. 13, 1961
Dominica - Roseau; 80,000; Nov., 1978
Fiji - Suva; 600,000; Oct. 10, 1970
The Gambia - Banjul; 495,000; Feb. 18, 1965
Ghana - Accra; 9,200,000; Mar. 6, 1957
Grenada - St. George's; 110,000; Feb. 7, 1974
Guyana - Georgetown; 830,000; May 26, 1966
India - New Delhi; 604,000,000; Aug. 15, 1947
Jamaica - Kingston; 2,000,000; Aug. 6, 1962
Kenya - Nairobi; 12,000,000; Dec. 12, 1963
Lesotho - Maseru; 1,180,000; Oct. 4, 1966
Malawi - Lilongwe; 4,916,000; July 6, 1964
Malaysia - Kuala Lumpur; 11,900,000; Aug. 31, 1957
Malta - Valletta; 298,000; Sept. 21, 1964
Mauritius - Port Louis; 880,000; Mar. 12, 1968
Nauru - Nauru; 7,000; Jan. 31, 1968
New Zealand - Wellington; 3,100,000; Sept. 26, 1907
Nigeria - Lagos; 79,759,000; Oct. 1, 1960
Papua New Guinea - Port Moresby; 2,570,000; Sept. 16, 1975
Seychelles - Victoria; 58,000; June 28, 1976
Sierra Leone - Freetown; 3,000,000; Apr. 27, 1961
Singapore - Singapore; 2,220,000; Oct. 15, 1965
Solomon Islands - Honiara; 184,500; July 7, 1978
Sri Lanka - Colombo; 13,000,000; Feb. 4, 1948
Swaziland - Mbabane; 500,000; Sept. 6, 1968
Tanzania - Dar es Salaam; 14,500,000; Dec. 9, 1961
Tonga - Nuku'alofa; 90,000; June 4, 1970
Trinidad & Tobago - Port of Spain; 1,033,000; Aug. 31, 1962
Uganda - Kampala; 10,500,000; Oct. 9, 1962
Western Samoa - Apia; 151,000; Aug. 28, 1970
Zambia - Lusaka; 4,500,000; Oct. 24, 1964
Associated States: Antigua (Feb. 27, 1967); Dominica (Mar. 3, 1967); Nevis & Anguilla (Feb. 27, 1967); St. Lucia (Mar. 1, 1967); St. Vincent (Oct. 27, 1969)

THE QUEEN & ROYAL FAMILY

The House of Windsor

In 1917 the late King George V., by Proclamation, changed the House name of the Royal Family from Saxe-Coburg-Gotha to the House of Windsor.

THE QUEEN.–Elizabeth the Second, (Elizabeth Alexandra Mary, of Windsor) by the Grace of God, of the United Kingdom, Canada and Her other Realms and Territories Queen; Head of the Commonwealth, Defender of the Faith, Succeeded to the throne February 6th, 1952, and was crowned June 2nd, 1953, at Westminster Abbey. Her Majesty, the elder daughter of the late King George VI and Queen Elizabeth, The Queen Mother, was born at 17 Bruton St., London, W.1, on April 21st, 1926, married November 20th, 1947, H.R.H. The Prince Philip, Duke of Edinburgh, K.G., K.T., O.M., G.B.E.

THE CHILDREN of Queen Elizabeth and H.R.H. The Prince Philip, Duke of Edinburgh are:

H.R.H. Prince Charles Philip Arthur George, Prince of Wales and Earl of Chester, Duke of Cornwall and Duke of Rothesay, Earl of Carrick and Baron Renfrew, Lord of the Isles, and Great Steward of Scotland, K.G., K.T., G.C.B., A.D.C., born November 14th, 1948.

H.R.H. The Princess Anne, Mrs. Mark Phillips, G.C.V.O., born August 15th, 1950. Married November 14th, 1973 Captain Mark Anthony Peter Phillips, C.V.O., A.D.C.

H.R.H. The Prince Andrew Albert Christian Edward, born February 19th, 1960.

H.R.H. The Prince Edward Antony Richard Louis, born March 10th, 1964.

THE LATE GEORGE VI.–George VI succeeded to the Throne December 11th, 1936; and was crowned at Westminster Abbey, May 12th, 1937. Second son of King George V and Queen Mary, he was born at York Cottage, Sandringham, on December 14th, 1895, married, April 26, 1923, Lady Elizabeth Bowes-Lyon, daughter of the Earl and Countess of Strathmore and Kinghorne. As Heir Presumptive succeeded to the Throne on the abdication of Edward VIII.

QUEEN ELIZABETH, THE QUEEN MOTHER, born August 4th, 1900, daughter of the 14th Earl of Strathmore and Kinghorne; married, April 26th, 1923.

THE ISSUE of the late King George VI and Queen Elizabeth are:

The reigning Sovereign, Elizabeth the Second (elder daughter).

The Princess Margaret (Rose), C.I., G.C.V.O., born August 21st, 1930, married Antony Charles Robert Armstrong-Jones, G.C.V.O., (since created Earl of Snowdon) May 6th, 1960, and has issue, Viscount Linley, born November 3rd, 1961 and Lady Sarah Frances Elizabeth Armstrong-Jones, born May 1st, 1964. Marriage dissolved 1978.

SUCCESSION–The order stands:

The Prince of Wales
The Prince Andrew
The Prince Edward
The Princess Anne, Mrs. Mark Phillips
Peter Phillips
The Princess Margaret, Countess of Snowdon
The Viscount Linley
Lady Sarah Armstrong-Jones
The Duke of Gloucester
The Earl of Ulster
Lady Davina Windsor
Lady Rose Windsor
The Duke of Kent
The Earl of St. Andrews
Lord Nicholas Windsor
Lady Helen Windsor
Lord Frederick Windsor
Princess Alexandra, the Hon. Mrs. Angus Ogilvy
Mr. James Ogilvy
Miss Marina Ogilvy

Her Majesty's Household

Lord Chamberlain, The Lord Maclean, K.T., G.C.V.O., K.B.E.
Lord Steward of the Household, The Duke of Northumberland, K.G., T.D.
Master of the Horse, The Earl of Westmorland, K.C.V.O.
Private Secretary to the Queen, The Rt. Hon. Sir Philip Moore, K.C.V.O., C.M.G., K.C.B.
Keeper of the Privy Purse & Treasurer, Peter Miles
Master of the Household, Vice-Admiral Sir Peter Ashmore, K.C.B., K.C.V.O., D.S.C.
Crown Equerry, Lt.-Col. Sir John Miller, K.C.V.O., D.S.O., M.C.
Press Secretary, Michael Shea

The Lord Chamberlain has the general supervision of the Royal Household.

COMMONWEALTH & FOREIGN GOVERNMENT REPRESENTATIVES IN CANADA

Commonwealth countries are designated by 'High Commr.' Foreign countries are designated by 'Ambassador' (H.E. is His Excellency).

Embassy of the Democratic Republic of Afghanistan
2341 Wyoming Ave. N.W., Washington D.C. 20008, U.S.A.
(202) 234-3770
Ambassador, vacant
Chargé d'Affaires, Salem M. Spartak

Embassy of Algeria
435 Daly Ave., Ottawa, Ont. K1N 6H3
(613) 232-9453
Ambassador, H.E. Missoum Sbih

Embassy of Arab Republic of Egypt
454 Laurier Ave. E., Ottawa, Ont. K1N 6R3
(613) 234-4931
Ambassador, H.E. Hassan Fahmy A.M.(m)
Commercial Office of the Embassy, 85 Range Rd., #207 (238-6263)
Press Office of the Embassy, 85 Range Rd., #905 (563-1248)
Arab League Information Centre, 170 Laurier Ave. W., #709 (239-4594)

Embassy of Argentina
130 Slater St., 6th Floor, Ottawa, Ont. K1P 5H6
(613) 236-2351
Ambassador, H.E. Esteban Arpad Takacs

Australian High Commission
130 Slater St., Ottawa, Ont. K1P 5H6
(613) 236-0841
High Commr., H.E. B.G. Dexter
Deputy High Commr., J.S. Bailey
Commercial Counsellor, J.V. McMahon

Embassy of Austria
445 Wilbrod St., Ottawa, Ont. K1N 6M7
(613) 563-1444
Ambassador, H.E. Dr. August Tarter
Minister-Counsellor, Dr. Harald Miltner

High Commission of Bahamas
c/o Embassy of the Bahamas, 600 New Hampshire Ave. N.W., Ste. 865, Washington, D.C. 20037, U.S.A.
(202) 338-3940
High Commr., H.E. Reginald L. Weed
Counsellor, Dr. Patricia E.J. Rodgers

High Commission of Bangladesh
85 Range Rd., Apt. 402, Ottawa, Ont. K1N 8J6
(613) 236-0138/9
High Commr., tba
Second Secretary, Abdus Samad
Third Secretary, Najmul Husain Ansar

High Commission for Barbados
Suite 700, 151 Slater St., Ottawa, Ont. K1P 5H3
(613) 236-9517/8; 236-0014
High Commr., H.E. Stanley L. Taylor

Embassy of Belgium
85 Range Rd., Ottawa, Ont. K1N 8J6
(613) 236-7267
Ambassador, H.E. J.R. Vanden Broock
Counsellor, Vincent van der Mersch
First Secretary, J. Ballegeer

Embassy of People's Republic of Benin
58 Glebe Ave., Ottawa, Ont. K1S 2C3
(613) 237-7366
Ambassador, H.E. L.B. Ahouandogbo
Counsellor, Lawani Emmanuel Nourou

Embassy of Bolivia
85 Range Rd., Ste. 901, Ottawa, Ont. K1N 8J6
(613) 232-5396
Chargé d'affaires, Carlos Costa du Rels

High Commission of Botswana
c/o Embassy of the Republic of Botswana, Suite 404, Van Ness Center, 4301 Connecticut Ave. N.W., Washington, D.C. 20008, U.S.A.
(202) 244-4990/1

Embassy of Brazil
255 Albert St., Ste. 900, Ottawa, Ont. K1P 6A9
(613) 237-1090
Ambassador, H.E. Geraldo de Carvalho Silos

High Commission of Britain
80 Elgin St., Ottawa, Ont. K1P 5K7
(613) 237-1530
High Commr., H.E. The Lord Moran, K.C.M.G.
Deputy High Commr. & Head of Chancery, E.T. Davies
Counsellor (Economic & Commercial), J. Brasnett
Counsellor (Cultural Affairs), W.E. Brook

Embassy of Bulgaria
325 Stewart St., Ottawa, Ont. K1N 6K5
(613) 232-3215
Ambassador, H.E. Stefan Stanev

Embassy of Burma
c/o 2300 S St. N.W., Washington, D.C. 20008, U.S.A.
Ambassador, H.E. U. Kyau Khaing

Embassy of Burundi
151 Slater St., #800, Ottawa, Ont. K1P 5H3
(613) 236-8483
Ambassador, H.E. Jérôme Ntungumburanye

Embassy of Cameroon
170 Clemow Ave., Ottawa, Ont. K1S 2B4
(613) 236-1522
Ambassador, H.E. Lucas Zaa Nkweta

Embassy of Cape Verde Islands
c/o The Permanent Mission of the Republic of Guinea Bissau, 211 E. 43rd St., Rm. 604, New York, N.Y. 10017, U.S.A.

Embassy of Central African Empire
c/o 1618 22nd St. N.W., Washington, D.C. U.S.A. 20008
(202) 483-7800
Ambassador, H.E. J.T. Makombo

Embassy of Chad
c/o 1725 K St. N.W., #302, Washington, D.C. 20006, U.S.A.
(202) 331-7696

Embassy of Chile
56 Sparks St., Suite 801, Ottawa, Ont. K1P 5A9
(613) 235-4402 & 235-9940
Ambassador, H.E. Mario Silva-Concha

Embassy of the People's Republic of China
415 St. Andrew St., Ottawa, Ont. K1N 5H3
(613) 234-2706
Ambassador, H.E. Wang Tung

Embassy of Colombia
151 Sparks St., Ste. 406, Ottawa, Ont. K1P 5E3
(613) 235-9798
Ambassador, H.E. Jorge Perico Cardenas

Embassy of the Congo
c/o Permanent Mission of the Congo to the U.N., 14 E. 65th St., New York, N.Y. 10021, U.S.A.
(212) 744-7840, 1, 2
Ambassador, H.E. Nicolas Mondjo

Embassy of Costa Rica
46 Beaver Ridge, Ottawa, Ont. K2E 6E1
(613) 224-2461
Ambassador, H.E. Jose Rafael Echeverria Villafranca

Embassy of Cuba
388 Main St., Ottawa, Ont. K1S 1E3
(613) 563-0141
Ambassador, H.E. Dr. Carlos Amat Forés

High Commission of Cyprus
c/o Embassy of Cyprus, 2211 R St. N.W., Washington D.C. 20008, U.S.A.
(202) 462-5772
High Commr., H.E. A.J. Jacovides

Embassy of Czechoslovakia
50 Rideau Terrace, Ottawa, Ont. K1M 2A1
(613) 234-6581
Ambassador, H.E. Stefan Murin

Embassy of Denmark
85 Range Rd., Ottawa, Ont. K1N 8J6
(613) 234-0704
Ambassador, H.E. Vagn Korsbaek
Counsellor, Helmer Hetting
Counsellor (Agricultural Affairs), L. Ingerslev Madsen

Embassy of Ecuador
320 Queen St., Ste. 2226, Ottawa, Ont. K1R 5A3
(613) 238-5032
Ambassador, H.E. R.G. Velasco

Embassy of El Salvador
294 Albert St., #302, Ottawa, Ont. K1P 6E6
(613) 238-2939
Ambassador, vacant

High Commission of Fiji
c/o One United Nations Plaza, New York, N.Y. 10017, U.S.A.
(212) 355-7316/7/8
High Commr., H.E. Filipe Nagera Bole

Embassy of Finland
Suite 401, 222 Somerset St. W., Ottawa, Ont. K2P 2G3
(613) 236-2389
Ambassador, H.E. Ossi Sunell
First Secretary, Hannu Hamala

Embassy of France
42 Sussex Dr., Ottawa, Ont. K1M 2C9
(613) 232-1795
Ambassador, H.E. Jean Béliard
First Counsellor, René Ala

Embassy of Gabon
4 Range Rd., Ottawa, Ont. K1N 8J5
(613) 232-5301
Ambassador, H.E. Hubert Ondias-Souna

High Commission of The Gambia
c/o 1785 Massachusetts Ave. N.W., Washington, D.C. 20036, U.S.A.
(202) 265-3252
High Commissioner, H.E. Ousman Ahmadou Sallah

Embassy of the German Democratic Republic
1717 Massachusetts Ave. N.W., Washington, D.C. 20036, U.S.A.
(202) 232-3134
Ambassador, H.E. Dr. Horst Grunert

Embassy of the Federal Republic of Germany
1 Waverley St., Ottawa, Ont. K2P OT8
(613) 232-1101
Ambassador, H.E. Erich Straetling

High Commission of Ghana
Suite 810, 85 Range Rd., Ottawa, Ont. K1N 8J6
(613) 236-0871
High Commr., H.E. Alex N. Abankwa
Minister-Counsellor, I.Y. Andoh

Embassy of Greece
80 MacLaren St., Ottawa, Ont. K2P OK6
(613) 238-6271
Ambassador, H.E. Emmanuel Megalokonomos

Grenada High Commission
280 Albert St., #301, Ottawa, Ont. K1P 5G8
(613) 236-9581
High Commr., H.E. Jimmy Emmanuel

Embassy of Guatemala
294 Albert St., #500, Ottawa, Ont. K1P 6E6
(613) 237-3941
Ambassador, H.E. A. Arturo Rivera G.

Embassy of Guinea
112 Kent St., #208, Place de Ville, Tower B, Ottawa, Ont. K1P 5P2
(613) 232-1133
Ambassador, H.E. A. Doukouré

High Commission of Guyana
151 Slater St., Suite 309, Ottawa, Ont. K1P 5H3
(613) 235-7249
High Commr., H.E. Burnett A. Halder

Embassy of Haiti
Place de Ville, 112 Kent St., #1308, Ottawa, Ont. K1P 5P2
(613) 238-1628
Ambassador, H.E. Hervé Denis

Embassy of Holy See
Apostolic Nunciature, 724 Manor, Rockcliffe Park, Ottawa, Ont. K1M OE3
(613) 746-4914
The Apostolic Pro-Nuncio, H.E. the Most Rev. Angelo Palmas

Embassy of Honduras
350 Sparks St., Ste. 403, Ottawa, Ont. K1R 7S8
(613) 233-8900
Ambassador, H.E. Max Velasquez-Diaz

Embassy of the Hungarian People's Republic
7 Delaware Ave., Ottawa, Ont. K2P OZ2
(613) 232-1711 & 234-8316
Ambassador, tba

Embassy of Iceland
c/o Embassy of Iceland, 2022 Connecticut Ave. N.W., Washington D.C. 20008, U.S.A.
(202) 265-6653
Ambassador, H.E. Hans G. Andersen
Minister-Counsellor, Sverrir H. Gunnlaugsson

High Commission of India
10 Springfield Rd., Ottawa, Ont. K1M 1C9
(613) 744-3751
High Commr., H.E. Dr. G.S. Dhillon
Deputy High Commr., J. Jacob

Embassy of Indonesia
255 Albert St., Ste. 1010, Kent Sq., Bldg. C, Ottawa, Ont. – (new address as of early 1982 is: 287 MacLaren St., Ottawa, Ont. K2P 0M2)
Ambassador, H.E. Widodo Budidarmo
Head of the Consular Section, vacant

Embassy of the Islamic Republic of Iran
85 Range Rd., Ste. 308, Ottawa, Ont. K1N 8J6
(613) 236-9108/9
Ambassador, vacant
Chargé d'Affaires, S.M.H. Adeli

Embassy of the Republic of Iraq
215 McLeod St., Ottawa, Ont. K2P OZ8
(613) 236-0177/8
Ambassador, H.E. Abdo Ali Hamdan Al-Dairi

Embassy of Ireland
170 Metcalfe St., Ottawa, Ont. K2P 1P3
(613) 233-6281/2
Ambassador, H.E. Sean P. Kennan
First Secretary, Paul Murray

Embassy of Israel
410 Laurier Ave. W., Ste. 601, Ottawa, Ont. K1R 7T3
(613) 237-6450
Ambassador, H.E. Yeshayahu Anug

Embassy of Italy
275 Slater St., 11th floor, Ottawa, Ont. K1P 5H9
(613) 232-2401/2/3
Ambassador, H.E. Francesco Paolo Fulci
Minister, Sergio Silvio Balanzino
Counsellor (Social & Labour Affairs), Antonio Venturella
Commercial Counsellor, Giulio Terzi de Sant'Agata

Embassy of the Ivory Coast Republic
9 Marlborough Ave., Ottawa, Ont. K1N 8E6
(613) 236-9919
Ambassador, H.E. Louis Guirandou-N'Diaye

High Commission of Jamaica
85 Range Rd., Ste. 201, Ottawa, Ont. K1N 8J6
(613) 233-9311
High Commr., Leslie A. Wilson

Embassy of Japan
255 Sussex Dr., Ottawa, Ont. K1N 9E6
(613) 236-8541
Ambassador, H.E. M. Suma

Embassy of Jordan
100 Bronson Ave., Suite 701, Ottawa, Ont. K1R 6G8
(613) 238-8090
Ambassador, H.E. Talal Hikmat

High Commission of Kenya
141 Laurier Ave. W., Ste. 600, Ottawa, Ont. K1P 5J3
(613) 563-1773
High Commr., H.E. Mwabili Kisaka

Embassy of the Republic of Korea
151 Slater St., Ottawa, Ont. K1P 5H3
(613) 232-1715
Ambassador, H.E. Kyoo Hyun Lee

Embassy of Kuwait
c/o Embassy of Kuwait, 2940 Tilden St. N.W., Washington D.C. 20008, U.S.A.
(202) 966-0702
Ambassador, H.E. Shaikh Saud Nasir Al-Sabah

Embassy of the Lao People's Democratic Republic
c/o 2222 S St. N.W., Washington, D.C. 20008, U.S.A.
(202) 332-6416
Ambassador, (vacant)
Counsellor, Chargé d'affaires, a.i., Khamtan Ratanavong

Embassy of Lebanon
640 Lyon St., Ottawa, Ont. K1S 3Z5
(613) 236-5825
Ambassador, H.E. Soleiman Farah

High Commission of the Kingdom of Lesotho
350 Sparks St., Ste. 910, Ottawa, Ont. K1R 7S8
(613) 236-9449
High Commr., H.E. Mothusi Thamsanqa Mashologu

Embassy of Liberia
c/o 5201 16th St. N.W., Washington D.C. 20011, U.S.A.
(202) 723-0437
Ambassador, H.E. J.S. Guannu

Socialist People's Libyan Arab Jamahiriya
c/o Permanent Mission of the Socialist People's Libyan Arab Jamahiriya to the U.N., 866 United Nations Plaza, New York, N.Y. 10017, U.S.A.
(212) 752-5775/6/7
Ambassador, vacant

Liechtenstein
The Ambassador of Switzerland is in charge of the interests of Liechtenstein in Canada.

Embassy of Luxembourg
c/o Embassy of Luxembourg, 2200 Massachusetts Ave. N.W., Washington D.C. 20008, U.S.A.
(202) 265-4171
Ambassador, H.E. Adrien Meisch

Embassy of Madagascar
c/o Permanent Mission to the U.N., 801 Second Ave., Ste. 404, New York, N.Y. 10017, U.S.A.
(212) 986-9491/2
Ambassador, H.E. Blaise Rabetafika

Malawi High Commission
112 Kent St., Ste. 905, Ottawa, Ont. K1P 5P2
(613) 236-8931
High Commr., H.E. A.A. Upindi

High Commission of Malaysia
60 Boteler St., Ottawa, Ont. K1N 8Y7
(613) 237-5182
High Commr., H.E. Bakri Aiyub Chazali

Embassy of Mali
50 Goulburn Ave., Ottawa, Ont. K1N 8C8
(613) 232-1501
Ambassador, H.E. Zona Ousmane Dao

High Commission of Malta
c/o Embassy of Malta, 44 rue Jules Lejeune, 1060 Brussels, Belgium
(02) 343.01.95
High Commr., (vacant)
Acting, A.J.B. Soler

Embassy of Mauritania
c/o Permanent Mission to the U.N., 600 Third Ave., New York, N.Y. 10016, U.S.A.
(212) 697-2490
Ambassador, H.E. Mohamed Said Ould Hamody

High Commission of Mauritius
c/o Embassy of Mauritius, Suite 134, 4301 Connecticut Ave. N.W., Washington, D.C. 20008, U.S.A.
(202) 244-1491
High Commr., C. Jesseramsing (acting)

Embassy of Mexico
130 Albert St., Room 206, Ottawa, Ont. K1P 5G4
(613) 233-8988, 9272
Ambassador, H.E. Agustin Barrios Gomez

Embassy of Mongolia
c/o the Permanent Mission of The Mongolian Republic to the United Nations, 6 E. 77th St., New York, N.Y. 10021, U.S.A.
(212) 861-9460

Embassy of Morocco
38 Range Rd., Ottawa, Ont. K1N 8J4
(613) 236-7391
Ambassador, H.E. Nourreddine Hasnaoui

Embassy of Nepal
2131 Leroy Place N.W., Washington D.C. 20008, U.S.A.
(202) 667-4550
Ambassador, H.E. Bhekh B. Thapa

Netherlands Embassy
275 Slater St., Ottawa, Ont. K1P 5H9
(613) 237-5030
Ambassador, H.E. N. van Dijl

New Zealand High Commission
Ste. 801, 99 Bank St., Ottawa, Ont. K1P 6G3
(613) 238-5991
High Commr., H.E. Hon. Edward Latter
Deputy High Commr., Dr. L.A. Beath

Embassy of Nicaragua
c/o Ambassador's Residence, 100 Bronson Ave., Apt. 1204, Ottawa, Ont.
Ambassador, H.E. Francisco Navarro

Embassy of Niger
38 Blackburn Ave., Ottawa, Ont. K1N 8A3
(613) 232-4291
Ambassador, H.E. Lambert Messan

Nigeria High Commission
295 Metcalfe St., Ottawa, Ont. K2P 1R9
(613) 236-0521
High Commr., H.E. O. Akadiri

Embassy of Norway
140 Wellington St., Ottawa, Ont. K1P 5A2
(613) 238-6571
Ambassador, H.E. Petter Graver
First Secretary, Truls Hanevold

Embassy of the Sultanate of Oman
2342 Massachusetts Ave. N.W., Washington, D.C. 20008, U.S.A.
(202) 387-1980
Ambassador, tba

Embassy of Pakistan
170 Metcalfe St., Ottawa, Ont. K2P 1P3
(613) 238-7881
Ambassador, H.E. Altaf A. Shaikh

Embassy of Panama
c/o 2862 McGill Terr. N.W., Washington D.C. 20008, U.S.A.
(202) 483-1407
Ambassador, H.E. Juan José Amado III

High Commission of Papua New Guinea
c/o 1140 19th St. N.W., #503, Washington, D.C., 20036, U.S.A.
(202) 659-0856
High Commr., H.E. Kubulan Los

Embassy of Paraguay
c/o Permanent Mission of Paraguay to the O.A.S., 2400 Massachusetts Ave. N.W., Washington, D.C. 20008, U.S.A.
(202) 483-6960
Ambassador, H.E. Dr. Mario Lopez Escobar

Embassy of Peru
170 Laurier Ave. W., #1007, Ottawa, Ont. K1P 5V5
(613) 238-1777
Ambassador, H.E. Jorge Pablo Fernandini

Embassy of Philippines
130 Albert St., Ottawa, Ont. K1P 5G4
(613) 233-1121
Ambassador, H.E. Ramon Del Rosario

Embassy of Poland
443 Daly Ave., Ottawa, Ont. K1N 6H3
(613) 236-0468
Ambassador, H.E. Stanislaw Pawlak
Minister-Counsellor, Wladyslaw Rolski

Embassy of Portugal
645 Island Park Dr., Ottawa, Ont. K1Y OB8
(613) 729-0883
Ambassador, H.E. Luiz Gois Figueira

Embassy of the State of Qatar in Canada
c/o Permanent Mission to the U.N., 747 Third Ave., 22nd floor, New York, N.Y. 10017, U.S.A.
(212) 486-9335
Ambassador, H.E. Jasim Y. Jamal

Embassy of the Socialist Republic of Romania
655 Rideau St., Ottawa, Ont. K1N 6A3
(613) 232-5345
Ambassador, H.E. Barbu Popescu

Embassy of the Republic of Rwanda
350 Sparks St., #903, Ottawa, Ont. K1P 7S9
(613) 238-1603
Ambassador, H.E. Jean-Marie Sibomana

High Commission of St. Lucia
Place de Ville, Tower B, 112 Kent St., #1701, Ottawa, Ont. K1P 5P2
(613) 236-8952
High Commr., H.E. Lucius Mason

Embassy of Saudi Arabia
99 Bank St., Ste. 901, Ottawa, Ont. K1P 6B9
(613) 237-4100
Ambassador, tba
Chargé d'Affaires, a.i., Ahmed Mohammed Beyari

Embassy of Senegal
57 Marlborough Ave., Ottawa, Ont. K1N 8E8
(613) 238-6392
Ambassador, H.E. Saliou Diodj Faye

High Commission of Seychelles
c/o 2 Mill St., London, Eng. W1R 9TE

High Commission of the Republic of Sierra Leone
c/o Embassy of Sierra Leone, 1701 19th St. N.W., Washington, D.C. 20009, U.S.A.
(202) 265-7700
High Commr., vacant

High Commission of Singapore
c/o Permanent Mission of Singapore to the U.N., One United Nations Plaza, New York, N.Y. 10017, U.S.A.
(212) 826-0840
High Commr., H.E. T.T.B. Koh

High Commission of Solomon Islands
c/o Canadian High Commission, Honiara, Solomon Islands

Embassy of Somalia
112 Kent St., #918, Place de Ville, Tower B, Ottawa, Ont. K1P 5P2
(613) 563-4541
Ambassador, H.E. Abdinur Yusuf

Embassy of South Africa
15 Sussex Dr., Ottawa, Ont. K1M 1M8
(613) 744-0330
Ambassador, H.E. J.J. Becker

Embassy of Spain
350 Sparks St., Ste. 802, Ottawa, Ont. K1R 7S8
(613) 237-2193/4
Ambassador, H.E. Antonio Elias

High Commission of the Democratic Socialist Republic of Sri Lanka
85 Range Rd., Suites 102-104, Ottawa, Ont. K1N 8J6
(613) 233-8449
High Commr., H.E. R.C.A. Vandergert

Embassy of the Democratic Republic of the Sudan
85 Range Rd., #1010, Ottawa, Ont. K1N 8J6
(613) 236-8964
Ambassador, H.E. Dr. Francis Mading Deng

Embassy of Suriname
c/o Embassy of the Republic of Suriname, 2600 Virginia Ave. N.W., Ste.711, Washington, D.C. 20037, U.S.A.
(202) 338-6980
Ambassador, H.E. A.F. Heidweiller

High Commission of Swaziland
c/o Chancery of Swaziland, 441 Van Ness Centre, 4301 Connecticut Ave. N.W., Washington D.C. 20008, U.S.A.
(202) 362-6683
High Commr., tba

Embassy of Sweden
441 MacLaren St., Ottawa, Ont. K2P 2H3
(613) 236-8553
Ambassador, H.E. Kaj Bjork

Embassy of Switzerland
5 Marlborough Ave., Ottawa, Ont. K1N 8E6
(613) 235-1837
Ambassador, H.E. Olivier Exchaquet
Secretary of Embassy, Dr. Walter Fetscherin

Embassy of the Syrian Arab Republic
2215 Wyoming Ave. N.W., Washington, D.C. 20008, U.S.A.
(202) 232-6313
Ambassador, H.E. Dr. Rafic Jouejati

High Commission of the United Republic of Tanzania
50 Range Rd., Ottawa, Ont. K1N 8J4
(613) 232-1509
High Commr., H.E. Chief M. Lukumbuzya

Embassy of Thailand
Ste. 704, 85 Range Rd., Ottawa, Ont. K1N 8J6
(613) 237-1517
Ambassador, H.E. Chinda Attanan

Embassy of Togo
12 Range Rd., Ottawa, Ont. K1N 8J3
(613) 238-5916/3
Ambassador, H.E. Kokougan Agbéviadé Apaloo

High Commission for the Republic of Trinidad & Tobago
#508, 75 Albert St., Ottawa, Ont. K1P 5E7
(613) 232-2418/9
High Commr., H.E. J.R.P. Dumas

Embassy of Tunisia
515 O'Connor St., Ottawa, Ont. K1S 3P8
(613) 237-0330
Ambassador, H.E. Rafik Said

Embassy of Turkey
197 Wurtemburg St., Ottawa, Ont. K1N 8L9
(613) 232-1577
Ambassador, H.E. Turgut Sunalp

High Commission of Uganda
170 Laurier Ave. W., Suite 601, Ottawa, Ont. K1P 5V5
(613) 233-7797/8
High Commr., H.E. William W. Rwetsiba

Embassy of the Union of Soviet Socialist Republics
285 Charlotte St., Ottawa, Ont. K1N 8L5
(613) 235-4341
Ambassador, H.E. Dr. Alexander N. Yakovlev

Embassy of the United Arab Emirates
c/o 747 Third Ave., New York, N.Y. 10017, U.S.A.
(212) 371-0480
Ambassador, H.E. Fahim Sultan Al-Qasimi

Embassy of the United States of America
100 Wellington St., Ottawa, Ont. K1P 5T1
(613) 238-5335
Ambassador, H.E. Paul H. Robinson
Minister, the Hon. Richard J. Smith
Counsellor for Scientific & Technological Affairs, Dr. R.W. Getzinger
Counsellor for Economic Affairs, Peter W. Lande
Counsellor for Political Affairs, Dwight N. Mason
Counsellor for Public Affairs, Jack Shellenberger
Counsellor for Commercial Affairs, W.C. Lenahan
Counsellor for Consular Affairs, R.W. Seefeldt
Counsellor for Administrative Affairs, G.J. Krieger, Jr.

Embassy of Upper Volta
48 Range Rd., Ottawa, Ont. K1N 8J4
(613) 238-4796

Ambassador, H.E. Louis-Dominique Ouedraogo

Embassy of Uruguay
Box 682, Ottawa, Ont., K1P 5P8
(613) 234-4223
Ambassador, H.E. Raul Benavidez

Embassy of Venezuela
320 Queen St., Ste. 2000, Ottawa, Ont. K1R 5A3
(613) 235-5151
Ambassador, H.E. Francisco Paparoni
Counsellor, Domingo Llanos-Aldrey

High Commission of Western Samoa
300 E. 44th St., 3rd floor, New York, N.Y. 10017, U.S.A.
(212) 682-1482
High Commr., H.E. Iulai Toma

Embassy of Yemen Arab Republic
600 New Hampshire Ave. N.W., Ste. 860, Washington, D.C. 20037, U.S.A.
(202) 965-4760

Embassy of People's Democratic Republic of Yemen
c/o Permanent Mission to the U.N., 413 E. 51st St., New York, N.Y. 10022, U.S.A.
(212) 752-3066
Ambassador, H.E. Abdalla Saleh Ashtal

Embassy of the Socialist Federal Republic of Yugoslavia
17 Blackburn Ave., Ottawa, Ont. K1N 8A2
(613) 233-6289
Ambassador, H.E. Krsto Bulajic

Embassy of Zaire
18 Range Rd., Ottawa, Ont. K1N 8J3
(613) 236-7103, 4
Ambassador, H.E. Pongo Mavulu

High Commission of Zambia
130 Albert St., Ste. 1610, Ottawa, Ont. K1P 5G4
(613) 563-0712
High Commr., H.E. Lt. Gen. Benjamin Ndabila Mibenge

CONSULATES & TRADE COMMISSIONS IN CANADA

Arab Republic of Egypt
Elhamy Abbas Refaat, Consul General for Arab Republic of Egypt, 3754 Chemin Côte des Neiges, Montréal, P.Q. H3H 1V6 (514/937-7781)

Argentina
Luis Tomas Sanviti, Consul General for Argentina, 1010 St. Catherine St. W., #737, Montréal, P.Q. H3B 1G1 (514/866-3819)

Australia
J.R. Garran, Consul General for Australia, #2324, Commerce Court West, Box 69, Toronto, Ont. M5L 1B9 (416/367-0783)

P.B. Clare, Consul General for Australia, Box 12519, Oceanic Plaza, 1066 W. Hastings St., Vancouver, B.C. V6E 3X1 (604/684-1177)

Austria
H. Ockermueller, Hon. Consul for Austria, 1131 Kensington Rd. N.W., Calgary, Alta. T2N 3P4 (403/283-6526)

H.A. Hansen, Hon. Consul for Austria, 526 Young Ave., Halifax, N.S. B3H 2V3 (902/423-7593)

N.F. Loewenheim, Hon. Consul General for Austria, 1350 Sherbrooke St. W., Montréal, P.Q. H3G 1J1 (514/845-8661) – G. Canisius, Trade Commr., #1410, 1010 Sherbrooke St. W., 849-3709

F.A. Istl, Hon. Consul General for Austria, 1243 Islington Ave., #711, Toronto, Ont. M8X 1Y9 (416/239-0338) – G. Graf, Trade Commr., 2 Bloor St. E., #3330, 967-3348

J. Hecht, Hon. Consul General for Austria, 525 Seymour St., Vancouver, B.C. V6B 3H9 (604/683-7571) – H. Schneider, Trade Commr., #1220, 736 Granville St. (683-5808)

Dr. F. Eckhardt, Hon. Consul for Austria, 54 Harrow St., Winnipeg, Man. R3M 2Y7 (204/452-9750)

Bahrain
Dr. Adel Bukhowa, Consul for Bahrain, 1869 Dorchester Blvd. W., Montréal, P.Q. H3H 1R4 (514/931-7000)

Barbados
June Alleyne, Vice Consul for Barbados, 666 Sherbrooke St. W., #1105, Montréal, P.Q. H3A 1E7 (514/288-1200)

Stan Carter, Consul for Barbados, (George Branker, Orville Folkes, Vice Consuls), all at 11 King St. W., #1108, Toronto, Ont. M5H 1A3 (416/869-0600); George Brome, Vice Consul, 4900 Yonge St., Willowdale, Ont. M2N 6A8 (416/224-4671)

Belgium
J.E. Baugh, Hon. Consul for Belgium, #1930, 633 6th Ave. S.W., Calgary, Alta. T2P 2Y5 (403/233-2926)

W. Henning, Hon. Consul for Belgium, #1800, 10405 Jasper Ave., Edmonton, Alta. T5J 3N4 (403/423-8658)

J.E.A. de Belie, Hon. Consul for Belgium, 6126 Regina Terrace, Halifax, N.S. B3H 1N5 (902/425-6546)

F.E. Swinnen, Hon. Consul for Belgium, #400, 365 Richmond St., London, Ont. N6A 3C2 (519/672-8660)

Ernest Vanderlinden (M), Consul General for Belgium, #2222, 1 Place Ville Marie, Montréal, P.Q. H3B 3M4 (514/866-8678)

René Amyot, Hon. Consul for Belgium, 55 d'Auteuil, Box 879, Québec, P.Q. G1R 4T5 (418/692-3910)

G.E.R. Sneath, Hon. Consul for Belgium, 17th Floor, 1920 Broad St., Regina, Sask. S4P 3V2 (306/352-8761)

Anthony G. Ayre, O.B.E., Hon. Consul for Belgium, Box 6012 (340 Duckworth St.), St. John's, Nfld. A1C 5X4 (709/726-8948)

L. de Mey (M), Consul General for Belgium, #1901, 8 King St. E., Toronto, Ont. M5C 1B5 (416/364-5283)

X. Van Migem, Consul General for Belgium, #1560, 701 W. Georgia St., Box 10119, Pacific Centre, Vancouver, B.C. V7Y 1C6 (604/682-1878)

J. Boeckx, Hon. Consul for Belgium, #308, 1041 Beaverhill Blvd., Winnipeg, Man. R2J 3K2 (204/256-0117)

People's Republic of Benin
Mrs. Marie Archambault, Hon. Consul for Benin, 429 ave. Viger, Montréal, P.Q. H2L 2N9 (514/849-3695)

Bolivia
Carlos Pechtel, Hon. Consul for Bolivia, 11231 Jasper Ave., Edmonton, Alta. T5K 0L5 (403/488-1525) Telex: 037-2991

José Arto, Hon. Consul for Bolivia, 1212 Peel St., #201, Montreal, P.Q. H3B 2T6 (514/861-4802)

(Toronto) Ronald Arellano, Consul General for Bolivia, 104 Mill Rd., Etobicoke, Ont. M9C 1X8 (416/622-2080)

Dr. A.S. Andree, Consul for Bolivia, #504, 1033 Davie St., Vancouver, B.C. V6B 2G4 (604/685-8121)

Brazil
John M. Hutton, Hon. Consul for Brazil, 6464 Chebucto Rd., Halifax, N.S. B3L 1L4 (902/425-3284)

Aloysio Marés Dias Gomide, Consul General for Brazil, 1 Place Ville Marie, #1505, Montréal, P.Q. H3B 2B5 (514/866-3313)

J. Stanislaus Fowler, Hon. Consul for Brazil, Box 4246, Stn. A, St. John's, Nfld. A1B 3N9 (709/726-7702)

Alcindo C. Guanabara, Consul for Brazil, 130 Bloor St. W., #616, Toronto, Ont. M5S 1N5 (416/921-0709)

Britain

S.T. Baker, Hon. Consul for Britain, 333 7 Ave., Calgary, Alta. T2P 2Z1 (403/256-7379)

M.A. Holding, Consul General for Britain, #1404, Three McCauley Plaza, 10025 Jasper Ave., Edmonton, Alta. T5J 1S6 (403/428-0375)

M.B. Collins, M.B.E., Consul for Britain, 1645 Granville St., 10th Floor, Halifax, N.S. B3J 1X3 (902/422-7488)

A.M. Simons, Consul General for Britain, 635 Dorchester Blvd. W., #901, Montréal, P.Q. H3B 1R6 (514/866-5863)

R.E. Holloway, Consul General for Britain, 200 University Ave., 8th Floor, Toronto, Ont. M5H 3E3 (416/593-1290)

H.H. Tucker, O.B.E., Consul General for Britain, 602 W. Hastings St., 4th Floor, Vancouver, B.C. V6B 1P6 (604/683-4421)

Bulgaria

Strahil I. Tchervenkov, Consul General for Bulgaria, 100 Adelaide St. W., #1410, Toronto, Ont. M5H 1S3 (416/363-7307) – Atanas Vlahov, Consul & Trade Commr., Ste. 1405

Central African Republic

J.-F. Boisvert, Hon. Consul for Central African Republic, #1155, 500 Place d'Armes, Montréal, P.Q. H2Y 2W2 (514/849-8381)

Chile

Eduardo Clavijo, Consul General for Chile, 1010 St. Catherine St. W., #910, Montréal, P.Q. H3B 3R7 (514/861-5669)

Roberto Plaza Canas, Consul for Chile, 56 Sparks St., #802, Ottawa, Ont. K1P 5A9 (613/232-3877)

Pablo Cabrera, Consul for Chile, 330 Bay St., #1205, Toronto, Ont. M5H 2S8 (416/366-9570)

Joaquin Grubner, Hon. Consul for Chile, #305, 1124 Lonsdale Ave., North Vancouver, B.C. V7M 2H1 (604/965-6211)

China (People's Republic)

Zhu Yi, Consul General for People's Republic of China, 3380 Granville St., Vancouver, B.C. V6H 3K3 (604/736-6784)

Colombia

Mrs. Amparo Harper, Consul General for Colombia, 1500 Stanley St., Montréal, P.Q. H3A 1R3 (514/849-4852)

Mrs. Ligia de Bonitto, Consul General for Colombia, 67 Yonge St., Toronto, Ont. M5E 1J8 (416/366-5092)

Beatriz Hernandez de Horry, Hon. Consul for Colombia, 4202 Musqueam Dr., Salish Park, Vancouver, B.C. V6N 3R7 (604/261-8211)

Costa Rica

Frank Schnabel, Hon. Consul for Costa Rica, 1170 Peel St., #1172, Montréal, P.Q. H3B 2T4 (514/866-8159)

Mrs. Martha E. de Gallegos, Consul General for Costa Rica, 46 Beaver Ridge, Ottawa, Ont. K2E 6E1 (613/224-2461)

(Toronto) Mrs. Carmen Maria Pachecco, Hon. Consul for Costa Rica, 75 The Donway West, #507, Don Mills, Ont. M3C 2E9 (416/449-8333)

W.A. Dow, Hon. Consul for Costa Rica, (Miss M.J. Cooke, Hon. Vice Consul), #804, 1550 Alberni St., Vancouver, B.C. V6G 1A5 (604/682-3865)

Cuba

Consul General for Cuba, 1415 Pine Ave., Montréal, P.Q. H3G 1B2 (514/843-8897); Antonio Conejo-Mesa, Trade Commr., 845-0191

Severo Claudio Vigoa, Consul General for Cuba, 170 University Ave., Toronto, Ont. M5H 3B3 (416/362-3622)

Czechoslovakia

Josef Zabokrtsky, Consul General for Czechoslovakia, 1305 Pine Ave. W., Montréal, P.Q. H3G 1B2 (514/849-4495)

Miroslav Otta, Consul, Commercial, for Czechoslovakia, 1280 St. Mark St., Montréal, P.Q. H3H 2G1 (514/937-6331)

Denmark

K. Mortensen, Hon. Consul for Denmark, 1235 11 Ave. S.W., Calgary, Alta. T3C 0M5 (403/245-5755)

Donn Larsen, Hon. Consul for Denmark, 10244 105 St., Edmonton, Alta. T5J 3L5 (403/426-1457)

H. Mathers, Hon. Consul for Denmark, Box 3550 (South), Halifax, N.S. B3J 3J3 (902/429-5680)

J.F. Bruun, Consul General for Denmark, (Henning Stoffregen, Consul), 1245 Sherbrooke St. W., Montréal, P.Q. H3G 1G2 (514/849-5391/2/3)

Dr. R.B. McKenzie, Hon. Vice Consul for Denmark, 495 King George Hwy., Newcastle, N.B. E1V 1M6 (506/622-1199)

J.E. Fortier, Hon. Consul for Denmark, 880 Chemin Ste-Foy, Québec, P.Q. G1S 2L2 (418/681-0708)

G. Allen Rasmussen, Hon. Consul for Denmark, 1200 McIntyre St., Regina, Sask. S4R 2M6 (306/525-2537)

E.L. Teed, Hon. Consul for Denmark, 133 Prince William St., Saint John, N.B. E2L 4S1 (506/652-6320)

Peter N. Outerbridge, Hon. Consul for Denmark, 87 Water St., Box 5128, St. John's, Nfld. A1C 5V6 (709/726-8000)

T. Dithmer, Consul General for Denmark, (L. Haugsted, Consul, Commercial; O. Lipholdt Petersen, Consul, Consular Affairs), 151 Bloor St. W., Toronto, Ont. M5S 1S4 (416/962-5661/2)

F.K. Petersen, Hon. Consul for Denmark, #1101, 475 Howe St., Vancouver, B.C. V6C 2B3 (604/684-5171)

Vern Simonsen, Hon. Consul for Denmark, #903, 386 Broadway Ave., Winnipeg, Man. R3C 3R6 (204/956-1440)

Djibouti

André L. Chales, Hon. Consul for Djibouti, 1010 Sherbrooke St. W., #2107, Montréal, P.Q. H3A 2R7

Dominican Republic

Dr. Julio Mota Castellanos, Consul General for Dominican Republic, 3435 Drummond St., #5, Montréal, P.Q. H3G 1X8 (514/843-4540)

A.C. Douglas, Hon. Consul for Dominican Republic, 13313 Niagara River Pkwy., Niagara Falls, Ont. L2E 6S6 (416/382-3146)

Dr. A.J. Gravel, Hon. Vice Consul for Dominican Republic, 170 W. Grande Allée, Québec, P.Q. G1R 2G9 (418/694-9613)

John Driscoll, Hon. Consul for Dominican Republic, 59 Broad St., Saint John, N.B. E2L 1Y3

Dr. H.T. Renouf, Hon. Consul for Dominican Republic, 10 Forest Ave., St. John's, Nfld. A1C 3J9 (709/726-9158)

Cyrus H. McLean, Hon. Consul for Dominican Republic, #808, 1445 Marpole Ave., Vancouver, B.C. V6H 1S5 (604/738-1414)

Eastern Caribbean Commission

L.M. Mason, Ag. Commr. for Eastern Caribbean Commn., 112 Kent St., #1701, Ottawa, Ont. K1P 5P2 (613/236-8952)

Ecuador

Armando Duque Duque, Consul General for Ecuador, 1500 Stanley St., #226, Montréal, P.Q. H3A 1R3 (514/849-0200)

Carlos Izurieta, Consul for Ecuador, 4206 Bloor St. W., Toronto, Ont. M9C 1Z4 (416/622-1856)

J.J. Fedyk, Hon. Consul for Ecuador, 777 Cardero St., #609, Vancouver, B.C. V6G 2G4 (604/685-6818)

El Salvador

René-E.-M. Ascoli, Hon. Vice Consul for El Salvador, 370 boul. St-Joseph est, Montréal, P.Q. H2T 1J6 (514/842-7053)

Esmond Lando, Q.C., Hon. Consul for El Salvador, #606, 1200 Burrard St., Vancouver, B.C. V6Z 2C7 (604/681-1434)

Finland

Christian Graefe, C.M., K.H., Hon. Consul for Finland, Hotel Macdonald, Edmonton, Alta. T5J 0N6 (403/426-7865)

A.C. Huxtable, Hon. Consul for Finland, Box 2252, Halifax, N.S. B3J 3C8 (902/423-6055)

Antero Huhtala, Consul & Trade Commr. for Finland, #1101, 1010 St. Catherine St. W., Montréal, P.Q. H3B 3S2 (514/866-2202)
Thomas McGloan, Hon. Consul for Finland, Box 7174, Stn. A, (133 Prince William St.), Saint John, N.B. E2L 4S6 (506/693-7268)
M.O. Kaihla, Hon. Consul for Finland, Box 969, Sault Ste. Marie, Ont. P6A 5N5 (705/253-7724)
Kauko E. Maki, Q.C., Hon. Consul for Finland, Box 490, Sudbury, Ont. P3E 4P6 (705/675-7503)
A.A. Kajander, Q.C., Hon. Consul for Finland, Box 2870, Thunder Bay, Ont. P7B 5G3 (807/344-9161)
Gerard Evans, Q.C., Hon. Vice Consul for Finland, #131, 101 Mall, Pine St. N., Timmins, Ont. P4N 6K6 (705/264-1285)
Bengt V. Gestrin, Hon. Consul General for Finland, (M. Hasa, Consul), #602, 2221 Yonge St., Toronto, Ont. M4S 2B4 (416/486-1642); J. Numminen, Consul & Trade Commr. (482-4111)
K.H.W. Seppala, Hon. Consul for Finland, 12 E. 3rd Ave., Vancouver, B.C. V5T 1C3 (604/879-8671)
Robert Purves, Hon. Consul for Finland, #704, 167 Lombard Ave., (Inter Ocean Grain Co.), Winnipeg, Man. R3B 0V3 (204/942-7457)

France

Garnet T. Page, Hon. Vice Consul for France, 909 5th Ave. S.W., Calgary, Alta. T2P 0N8 (403/262-1544)
Patrick Berron, Trade Commr. for France, #902, 304 8th St. S.W., Calgary, Alta. T2P 1C2 (403/233-2061)
A. Cano, Hon. Consul for France, 1500 ave Roussel ouest, Chicoutimi, P.Q. G7G 1T4 (418/549-7515)
Claude Maynot, Consul General for France, 10240 124th St., Edmonton, Alta. T5N 3W6 (403/482-3636)
Paul Chavy, Hon. Vice Consul for France, 3170 Romans Ave., Halifax, N.S. B3L 3W9 (902/455-7035)
Eric Lem, Consul for France in the Atlantic Provinces, C.P. 1109, Moncton, N.B. E1C 8P6 (506/855-4303)
Jean Honnorat, Consul General for France, (Georges Hatton, Trade Counsellor), 2 Elysée, Place Bonaventure, C.P. 202, Montréal, P.Q. H5A 1B1 (514/878-4381)
Camille Goora, Hon. Consular Agent for France, 30 Blowers St., North Sydney, N.S. B2A 2Y5 (902/794-4800)
Henri Rethore, Consul General for France, 1110 ave des Laurentides, Québec, P.Q. G1S 3C3 (418/688-0430)
René Rottiers, Hon. Vice Consul for France, 1816 7th Ave. N., #17, Regina, Sask. S4R 0J2 (306/545-9912)
C.F. Whelly, Q.C., Hon. Consular Agent for France, 40 Charlotte St., Saint John, N.B. E2L 2H6 (506/693-1193)
Stephen French, Hon. Vice Consul for France, 10 Amherst Place, St. John's, Nfld. A1E 3J5 (709/579-2259)
Pierre Guerand, Consul General for France, 40 University Ave., #620, Toronto, Ont. M5J 1T1 (416/977-3131); Michel Paoletti, Trade Counsellor, 480 University Ave., #900 (977-1257)
Paul Bazin, Consul General for France, 736 Granville St., #1201, Vancouver, B.C. V6Z 1H9 (604/681-2301); Robert Jany, Trade Commr., 736 Granville St., #320 (684-1271)
Rolf Hougen, Hon. Consular Agent for France, 305 Main St., Whitehorse, Y.T. Y1A 2B4 (403/667-4222)
Louis Vannini, Consul for France, 40 Westgate, Winnipeg, Man. R3C 2E1 (204/774-4825)

Gabon

Bernard Dubois, Hon. Consul for Gabon, 4520 de Salaberry St., Montréal, P.Q. H4J 1H4 (514/334-4666)
Dr. Julius Kuhl, Hon. Consul for Gabon, 347 Bay St., #700, Toronto, Ont. M5H 2R7 (416/362-1288)

Gambia

Jochem Carton, O.C., Hon. Consul General for Gambia, 363 St. Francois Xavier St., #230, Montréal, P.Q. H2Y 3P9 (514/849-2885)

Germany, Federal Republic

Dr. Richard Achenbach, Consul General for Germany, #2500, 10004 104 Ave., Edmonton, Alta. T5J 0K1 (403/429-6421)
Frederick H. Howard, Hon. Consul for Germany, #900 Cogswell Tower, Scotia Sq., Halifax, N.S. B3J 3K1 (902/428-4350)
Peter D. Kruse, Hon. Consul for Germany, 289 Frederick St., Kitchener, Ont. N2H 6M1 (519/576-8650)
Mrs. Helene Schoettle, Consul General for Germany, 3455 rue de la Montagne, Montréal, P.Q. H3G 2A3 (514/286-1820)
Prof. Dr. Gunter Kocks, Hon. Consul for Germany, 2721 23rd Ave., Regina, Sask. S4S 1E5 (306/586-8762)
G.K. Sann, Hon. Consul for Germany, 22 Poplar Ave., St. John's, Nfld. A1B 1C8 (709/753-7777)
Dr. Ernst-Guenther Koch, Consul General for Germany, 77 Admiral Rd., Toronto, Ont. M5R 2L4 (416/925-2813)
Dr. Hasso Freiherr von Maltzahn, Consul General for Germany, #501, 325 Howe St., Vancouver, B.C. V6C 2A2 (604/684-8377)
Rudolf Thiele, Hon. Consul for Germany, 222 Oxford St., Box 876, Winnipeg, Man. R3C 2S1 (204/453-1001)

Greece

P. Anghelakis, Consul General for Greece, 2000 Peel St., #925, Montréal, P.Q. H3A 2W5 (514/845-2105)
John G. Thomoglou, Consul General for Greece, 100 University Ave., #1004, Toronto, Ont. M5G 1V6 (416/593-1636)
Ioannis Vavvas, Consul for Greece, #890, 1 Bentall Centre, 505 Burrard St., Vancouver, B.C. V7X 1M4 (604/681-1381)

Grenada

(Montreal) Miss Bridget Joseph, Hon. Consul for Grenada, 825 Pellerin St., Ville Brossard, P.Q. H4W 2L2 (514/671-2054)
W. Otway, Hon. Consul for Grenada, 143 Yonge St., #101, Toronto, Ont. M5C 1W7 (416/368-1332)
(Winnipeg) C. Shade, Hon. Consul for Grenada, 10 Rice Rd., Fort Richmond, Man. R3T 3N4 (204/269-7069)

Guatemala

J. Paul Becker, Hon. Consul for Guatemala, Box 401, Place Bonaventure, 39 Fundy F Floor, Montréal, P.Q. H5A 1B7 (514/861-5919); Mrs. Juana Chavez, Consul General; Juana Chavez, Trade Commr.
Paul Bouchard, Hon. Consul for Guatemala, 50 rue Aberdeen, Québec, P.Q. G1R 2C7 (418/523-0426)
(Toronto) Jose Alberto Bacardi, Hon. Consul for Guatemala, 1000 Steeles Ave. E. (Box 554), Brampton, Ont. L6V 2L3 (416/459-3727)
Dr. B.W. Hoeter, Hon. Consul for Guatemala, 736 Granville St., V6Z 1G7 (604/682-4831)

Guyana

C.R. Jones, Consul General for Guyana, 123 Edward St., Toronto, Ont. M5E 1E2 (416/977-5540 or 3326)

Haiti

J.-A. Auguste, Consul General for Haiti, 44 Fundy F, Place Bonaventure, C.P. 187, Montréal, P.Q. H5A 1A9 (514/871-8993)
(vacant) Consul General for Haiti, 8 Jardins de Merici, #106, Québec, P.Q. G1R 4N9 (418/681-0824)
Max Charles, Consul General for Haiti, 920 Yonge St., #808, Toronto, Ont. M4W 3C7 (416/923-7833)

Honduras

Mrs. Victoria Midence, Vice Consul for Honduras, 1225 St. Mark St., Apt. 101, Montréal, P.Q. H3H 2E7 (514/935-9708)
Ivan Romero, Counsellor & Consul for Honduras, 350 Sparks St., #403, Ottawa, Ont. K1R 7S8 (613/233-8900)
Mrs. Mercedes Bourqui, Hon. Consul for Honduras, 653 Village Pkwy. No. 36, Unionville, Ont. L3R 2R2 (416/964-6422)
Enrique Gonzalez Calvo, Hon. Consul for Honduras, #104, 535 W. Georgia St., Box 3654, Vancouver, B.C. V6B 3Y8 (604/685-7711)

Hong Kong

Peter Chen, Hong Kong Trade Development Council, #1100, 347 Bay St., Toronto, Ont. M5H 2R7 (416/366-3594)

Hungarian People's Republic

Ede Sziklai, Trade Commr. for Hungary, 1350 Sherbrooke St. W., #1510, Montréal, P.Q. H3G 1J1 (514/849-9261/2)

Lajos Schrok, Deputy Trade Commr. for Hungary, 102 Bloor St. W., 4th Floor, Toronto, Ont. M5S 1M8 (416/923-3596)

Iceland

Clifford A. Marteinsson, Hon. Vice Consul for Iceland, 158 Cornwallis Dr. N.W., Calgary, Alta. T2K 1V1 (403/289-7165)

Gudmundur A. Arnason, Hon. Consul for Iceland, 14434 McQueen Rd., Edmonton, Alta. T5N 3L6 (403/455-7946)

A.C. Huxtable, Hon. Consul for Iceland, 16th Floor, 1791 Barrington St., Box 2252, Halifax, N.S. B3J 3C8 (902/423-6055)

J.G. Gauvreau, Hon. Consul General for Iceland, Box 175, Place Bonaventure, Montréal, P.Q. H5A 1A7 (514/875-2071)

Mrs. M.E. Lahey, Hon. Consul General for Iceland, 198 Lisgar Rd., Rockcliffe Park, Ottawa, Ont. K1M 0E6 (613/741-4681)

A.M. Goodridge, Hon. Consul for Iceland, 57 Military Rd., St. John's, Nfld. A1C 2C5 (709/754-2292)

J. Ragnar Johnson, Q.C., Hon. Consul for Iceland, #1125, 65 Queen St. W., Toronto, Ont. M5H 1M7; Jon R. Johnson, Hon. Vice Consul

Harold S. Sigurdson, Hon. Consul for Iceland, #1804, 1055 Dunsmuir St., Vancouver, B.C. (604/688-5421)

Birgir Brynjolfsson, Hon. Consul General for Iceland, 1351 Clifton St., Winnipeg, Man. R3E 2V1 (204/786-6557)

India

P.N. Soni, Consul General for India, 2 Bloor St. E., Toronto, Ont. M4W 1A8 (416/960-0751)

B.K. Mitra, Consul General for India, 325 Howe St., Vancouver, B.C. V6C 1Z7 (604/681-0644)

Indonesia

Sidik Martohardjono, Hon. Consul for Indonesia, 470 Granville St., #930, Vancouver, B.C. V6C 1V5 (604/669-0574)

Iraq

B.K.M. Al-Dilaimi, Consul for Iraq, 3019 Chemin St. Sulpice, Montréal, P.Q. H3H 1B6 (514/937-9144)

Ireland

H.E. Kane, Hon. Consul for Ireland, 20 King St., Box 6489, Stn. A, Saint John, N.B. E2L 1G2 (506/657-3000)

Israel

Yitzchak Mayer, Consul General for Israel, 2085 Union St., #1675, Montréal, P.Q. H3A 2C3 (514/288-9277); Yair Ofek, Trade Commr.

David Ariel, Consul General for Israel, 102 Bloor St. W., Toronto, Ont. M5S 1M8 (416/961-1126); Baruch Barak, Minister for Economic Affairs (961-1242)

Italy

Arcangelo Martino, Hon. Vice Consul for Italy, #203, 50 Dalhousie St., Brantford, Ont. N3T 2H8 (519/753-0404)

Joseph C. De Paoli, Hon. Vice Consul for Italy, #205, 606 7th Ave. S.W., Calgary, Alta. T2P 0Y7 (403/264-0000)

Edmonton: vacant (Vice Consulate)

Luigi Ferraro, Hon. Vice Consul for Italy, 69 Wyndham St. N., #303, Guelph, Ont. N1H 4E7 (519/836-6820)

Halifax: vacant (Vice Consulate)

Arnaldo Bucciero, Vice Consul for Italy, 15 King St. W., Hamilton, Ont. L8P 1A4 (416/529-5030)

Diego L. Bastianutti, Hon. Vice Consul for Italy, 221 King St. E., Kingston, Ont. K7L 3A6 (613/549-3154)

Luigi Rossetti, Hon. Vice Consul for Italy, 344 Richmond St., London, Ont. N6A 2C3 (519/438-6740)

Francesco Capece Galeota, Consul General for Italy, 3489 Drummond Ave., Montréal, P.Q. H3G 1X6 (514/849-8351)

Alessandro Sorrentino, Sr. Trade Commr. for Italy, 1801 McGill College Ave., #1490, Montréal, P.Q. H3A 2N4 (514/284-0265)

Domenico Morabito, Hon. Vice Consul for Italy, 4904 Victoria Ave., Niagara Falls, Ont. L2E 4C6 (416/356-2231)

Gian M. Marogna, Hon. Consular Agent for Italy, #2, 222 3rd Ave. W., Box 640, Prince Rupert, B.C. V8J 3S1 (604/624-4328)

(Québec) Aldo Landini, Hon. Consul for Italy, 760 Place Philippe, #5, Ste-Foy, P.Q. G1V 2P7 (418/681-5237)

Mrs. Lucia Papini, Hon. Vice Consul for Italy, 82 Lowry Place, Regina, Sask. S4S 4P5 (306/586-6832)

Antonio Domenichini, Hon. Vice Consul for Italy, 785 Exmouth St., Sarnia, Ont. N7T 5P7 (519/336-0101)

R.C. Peres, Hon. Vice Consul for Italy, #201, 212 Queen St. E., Sault Ste. Marie, Ont. P6A 1M2 (705/949-9411)

Dr. Roberto Grosso, Hon. Vice Consul for Italy, 96 Larch St., Sudbury, Ont. P3E 1C1 (705/674-4922)

Giovanna Zovatto, Hon. Vice Consul for Italy, 419 Victoria Ave. E., 1st Floor, Thunder Bay, Ont. P7E 1A6 (807/622-9052)

Rino C. Bragagnolo, Hon. Vice Consul for Italy, #131, 101 Mall, 38 Pine St. N., Timmins, Ont. P4N 6K6 (705/264-1285)

Pier Luigi Conti, Consul General for Italy, 136 Beverley St., Toronto, Ont. M5T 1Y5 (416/977-1566)

Sandro Fermani, Trade Commr. for Italy, One First Canadian Place, Box 22, Toronto, Ont. M5X 1A9 (416/362-1036)

Mrs. Emily Tenisci, Hon. Consular Agent for Italy, 1190 2nd Ave., Trail, B.C. V1R 1L4 (604/368-9794)

Giuseppe Gaudiello, Consul General for Italy, #110, 736 Granville St., Vancouver, B.C. V6Z 1G4 (604/684-7288)

Dr. Piero Tosarelli, Trade Commr. for Italy, #624, 736 Granville St., Vancouver, B.C. V6Z 1H2 (604/685-8451)

Frank De Angelis, Hon. Vice Consul for Italy, 1291 Erie St. E., Windsor, Ont. N9A 3Z6 (519/256-0092)

Domenico Povoledo, Hon. Vice Consul for Italy, #318, 283 Portage Ave., Winnipeg, Man. R3B 2B5 (204/943-7637)

Ivory Coast

J.T.A. Wilson, Hon. Consul for Ivory Coast, 73 Wanless Cres., Toronto, Ont. M4N 1V7 (416/485-1514)

Jamaica

B. Cochran, Hon. Trade Commr. for Jamaica, Box 2065, Halifax, N.S. B3J 2Z1 (902/429-4370)

Danny Powel, Consul & Trade Commr. for Jamaica, 214 King St. W., #216, Toronto, Ont. M5H 1K4 (416/598-3393); Oswald Murray, Consul General (598-3008)

Japan

T. Sada, Consul General for Japan, #2600, 10020 100th St., Edmonton, Alta. T5J 0N4 (403/422-3752)

K. Omura, Consul General for Japan, #2701, 1155 Dorchester Blvd. W., Montréal, P.Q. H3B 2K9 (514/866-3429)

Dr. M.C. Shumiatcher, Hon. Consul General for Japan, 2100 Scarth St., Regina, Sask. S4P 2H6 (306/352-2651)

R. Mogi, Consul General for Japan, Box 10, Toronto Dominion Centre, Toronto, Ont. M5K 1A1 (416/363-7038)

S. Omori, Consul General for Japan, #1210, 1177 W. Hastings St., Vancouver, B.C. V6E 2K9 (604/684-5868)

M. Kitamura, Consul General for Japan, #730, 215 Garry St., Winnipeg, Man. R3C 3P3 (204/943-5554)

Korea

Chang Hoon Kim, Consul General for Korea, 1000 Sherbrooke St. W., #2205, Montréal, P.Q. H3A 2P2 (514/845-3243)

Sang Hoon Lee, Consul General for Korea, 439 University Ave., #700, Toronto, Ont. M5G 1Y8 (416/598-4608)

Dae Wan Kang, Consul General for Korea, #830, 1066 W. Hastings St., Vancouver, B.C. V6E 3X1 (604/681-9581)

Kuwait

Ernest W. Assaly, Hon. Consul for Kuwait, 160 MacLaren St., Ottawa, Ont. K2P 0K9 (613/235-7231)

Lebanon

Michael A. Awid, Hon. Consul for Lebanon, 10187 103 St., Edmonton, Alta. T5J 0Y6 (403/424-0485)

G. Arab, Hon. Consul for Lebanon, 227 Bedford Hwy., Halifax, N.S. B3M 2J9 (902/443-1666)

M. Hraibeh, Consul General for Lebanon, 40 ch. Côte Ste Catherine, Montréal, P.Q. H2V 2A2 (514/276-2638)

Liberia

L.M. Bloomfield, Hon. Consul General for Liberia, 1080 Beaver Hall Hill, #2020, Montréal, P.Q. H2Z 1S8 (514/871-9121)

G.F. Henderson, Hon. Consul General for Liberia, 160 Elgin St., Ottawa, Ont. K1N 8S3 (613/232-1781)

H.A.D. Oliver, Hon. Consul General for Liberia, 1030 W. Georgia St., #1011, Vancouver, B.C. V6E 3B5 (604/681-6418)

Liechtenstein

The Embassy of Switzerland is in charge of the interests of Liechtenstein in Canada.

Lithuania

Dr. J. Zmuidzinas, Hon. Consul General for Lithuania, 1 Trillium Terrace, Toronto, Ont. M8Y 1V9 (416/251-9090)

Luxembourg

Mrs. Marie-Claire Lefort, Hon. Consul General for Luxembourg, 3877 Draper Ave., Montréal, P.Q. H4A 2N9 (514/487-3387)

Madagascar

Léopold Bernier, Hon. Consul for Madagascar, 459 St-Sulpice St., Montréal, P.Q. H2Y 2V8 (514/844-4427)

James Morten Goodfellow, Hon. Consul for Madagascar, 335 Watson Ave., Oakville, Ont. L6J 3V5 (416/845-8914)

Malaysia

Wan A. Wahab, Consul & Trade Commr. for Malaysia, Box 172, Toronto Dominion Centre, Toronto, Ont. M5K 1H6 (416/869-3886)

David McClary Johnston, Hon. Consul for Malaysia, c/o Davis & Co., 14th Floor, 1030 W. Georgia St., Vancouver, B.C. V6E 3C2 (604/687-9444)

Malawi

Yvon Maloney, Hon. Consul for Malawi, 410 St-Nicolas St., #216, Montreal, P.Q. H2Y 2P8 (514/842-5411)

Mali

Charles C. Melville, Hon. Consul for Mali, 2290 Duncan Rd., Mount Royal, P.Q. H4P 1Z9 (514/342-0353)

Malta

John Pisani, Hon. Consul & Trade Commr. for Malta, 3323 Dundas St. W., Toronto, Ont. M6P 2A6 (416/767-4902)

Mexico

E.P.A. Carlberg, Hon. Consul for Mexico, 95 Bessemer Rd., London, Ont. N6E 1P9 (519/681-3331)

Daniel Galan Mendez, Consul General for Mexico, 1000 Sherbrooke St. W., #2170, Montréal, P.Q. H3A 1G6 (514/288-4916)

Mrs. Madeleine Charland Therrien, Hon. Consul for Mexico, 950 St-Louis Rd., Sillery, P.Q. G1S 1C7 (418/681-4482)

Zenaido Acosta, Consul General for Mexico, #1301, Box 255, Commerce Court E., Toronto, Ont. M5L 1E9 (416/368-5792); Jose Luis Atristain, Trade Commr., 2 Bloor St. E., #3520 (922-4481)

Renato Irigoyen, Consul General for Mexico, #310, 625 Howe St., Vancouver, B.C. V6C 2T6 (604/684-3547)

Monaco

Michel Pasquin, Hon. Consul General for Monaco, 612 St. James St., Montréal, P.Q. H3C 1E1 (514/844-0516)

F.A.W. Ziegler, Hon. Consul General for Monaco, 736 Granville St., Vancouver, B.C. V6Z 1G3 (604/684-0015)

Netherlands

J. Heersink, Hon. Vice Consul for Netherlands, 2201 Lakeshore Rd., Burlington, Ont. L7R 1A8 (416/634-7624)

G.H. Hollenbach, Hon. Vice Consul for Netherlands, 24 Gissing Dr. S.W., Calgary, Alta. T3E 4V7 (403/242-4170)

Dr. O.S. Akkerman, Hon. Vice Consul for Netherlands, 882 Charing Cross Rd., Chatham, Ont. N7M 5H2 (519/352-1250)

D'Arcy D. Duncan, Consul for Netherlands, #930, 10020 101A Ave., Edmonton, Alta. T5J 3G2 (403/428-7513)

J.H. Haylock, Hon. Consul for Netherlands, Box 673, Halifax, N.S. B3J 2T3 (902/423-4744)

Dr. H. Westenberg, Hon. Vice Consul for Netherlands, 115 Lower Union St., Kingston, Ont. K7L 2N9 (613/542-7095)

Dr. H. Heeneman, Hon. Vice Consul for Netherlands, 100 Waterloo St., London, Ont. N6B 2M5 (519/432-9973)

Baron Diederik H. Speyart, Consul General for Netherlands, 1 Place Ville Marie, #1736, Montréal, P.Q. H3B 2C1 (514/866-4875); J. van der Velden, Vice Consul

J.P. Boutin, Hon. Consul for Netherlands, 71 St. Pierre St., Québec, P.Q. G1K 7A8 (418/692-0660)

Ir. E.H. Grolle, Hon. Consul for Netherlands, 4114 18th Ave., Regina, Sask. S4S 0C4 (306/584-5466)

F.G. Elkin, Hon. Consul for Netherlands, 167 Prince William St., Saint John, N.B. E2L 4R8 (506/693-1403)

A.G. Ayre, O.B.E., Hon. Consul for Netherlands, 340 Duckworth St., Box 6012, St. John's, Nfld. A1C 5X4 (709/726-8948)

Dr. K.J. Postma, Hon. Vice Consul for Netherlands, 1106 CN Tower, #604, Saskatoon, Sask. S7K 1J5 (306/652-4751)

R.P. Welter, Hon. Vice Consul for Netherlands, 179 Algoma St., Thunder Bay, Ont. P7B 3C1 (807/344-5721)

Th. M.T.M. Kasteel, Consul General for Netherlands, 1 Dundas St. W., #2106, Box 2, Toronto, Ont. M5C 1Z3 (416/598-2520); T.C.A. Driessen, Vice Consul (Commercial); A.L. Rypkema, Vice Consul (Social Affairs)

Q.P.A. de Marees van Swinderen, Consul General for Netherlands, 475 Howe St., #721, Vancouver, B.C. V6C 2B3 (604/684-6448)

B.A. Van Ruiten, Hon. Consul for Netherlands, Box 219, Winnipeg, Man. R3C 2G9 (204/633-1771)

New Zealand

R.D. Sutherland, Consul General for New Zealand, 2 Bloor St. E., #2922, Toronto, Ont. M4W 1A8 (416/961-9797)

R.J. Graham, Consul for New Zealand, 701 W. Georgia St., #1160, Box 10071, Pacific Centre, Vancouver, B.C. V7Y 1B6 (604/684-7388)

Nicaragua

Mrs. Sonia Blanchard, Hon. Consul for Nicaragua, 69 Woodlawn Circle, Dollard-des-Ormeaux, P.Q. H9A 1Z1 (514/683-3404)

Niger

Pierre Thomas, Hon. Consul for Niger, 225 St. James St. W., Montréal, P.Q. H2Y 1M6 (514/845-6126)

Norway

Dorman R. Butt, Vice Consul for Norway, Box 310, Botwood, Nfld. A0H 1E0 (709/257-2421)

A. Jonassen, Consul for Norway, 513 8 Ave. S.W., #302, Calgary, Alta. T2P 1G3 (403/269-1193)

A.J. Johannessen, Consul for Norway, 6003 102 A Ave., Edmonton, Alta. T6A 0R5 (403/466-0478)

K. Karlsen, Consul for Norway, 2089 Upper Water St., Halifax, N.S. B3J 2X1 (902/423-7389)

I. Traa, Consul General for Norway, 407 rue McGill, #802, Montréal, P.Q. H2Y 2G3 (514/842-6883)

J.A. Ellis, Vice Consul for Norway, 5026 Argyle St., Box 490, Port Alberni, B.C. V9Y 7M9 (604/723-7373)

Gaetan Thivierge, Consul for Norway, 2 Nouvelle France, Québec, P.Q. G1K 7A2 (418/525-8171)

D.F. MacGowan, Consul for Norway, 40 Wellington Row, Box 6850, Stn. A, Saint John, N.B. E2L 4S3 (506/652-3800)

H. Collingwood, Consul for Norway, 58 Kenmount Rd., St. John's, Nfld. A1B 3P1 (709/722-6850)

Mrs. Elizabeth Anstensen, Consul for Norway, 846 University Dr., Saskatoon, Sask. S7N 0J7 (306/653-2055)

Mrs. J.E. Harriss, Vice Consul for Norway, 181 Charlotte St., Sydney, N.S. B1P 6G9 (902/539-4800)

J. Styffe, Vice Consul for Norway, 360 Wolseley St., Thunder Bay, Ont. P7A 3H4 (807/345-7083)

Erskine Carter, Hon. Consul for Norway, 250 University Ave., Toronto, Ont. M5H 3E9 (416/593-5511)

T. Ronneng, Consul General for Norway, 837 W. Hastings St., Vancouver, B.C. V6C 1B6 (604/682-2281)

C.P. Ridout, Consul for Norway, 850 Gordon St., Box 577, Victoria, B.C. V8W 2P5 (604/384-1174)

André Bouchard, Consul for Norway, 241 rue de la Fabrique, Ville de la Baie, P.Q. G7B 2S7 (418/544-2714)

M.E. Benum, Consul for Norway, 39 Brookhaven Bay, Winnipeg, Man. R2J 2S4 (204/885-1500)

Pakistan

Anwar Saifullah Khan, Consul General for Pakistan, 2100 Drummond St., #505, Montréal, P.Q. H3G 1X1 (514/845-2297)

Panama

Mrs. Maria De Solomon, Consul General for Panama, 1 Fanshawe Dr., Brampton, Ont. L6Z 1A7 (416/846-1855)

Mrs. Litz Guissel Stanziola De Rovelli, Hon. Consul for Panama, 10355 146th St., Edmonton, Alta. (403/482-2263)

Aida Torrijos, Consul General for Panama, 2351 Hingston Ave., Montreal, P.Q. H4A 2J3 (514/684-9014)

F.G. McGinley, Hon. Consul General for Panama, 1433 Beach Ave., #201, Vancouver, B.C. V6G 1Y5

Peru

Juan Garland, Consul General for Peru, Apt. 501, 2250 Guy St., Montréal, P.Q. H3H 2M3 (514/932-3692)

Stephen Zisman, Hon. Consul for Peru, 344 Bloor St. W., #303, Toronto, Ont. M5S 1W9 (416/967-0767)

Guillermo Crosby Pinillos, Hon. Consul General for Peru, 747 Cardero St., Vancouver, B.C. V6G 2G3 (604/669-1347)

V.L. Baird, Hon. Consul for Peru, 436 Main St., Winnipeg, Man. R3B 1B2 (204/947-0131)

Philippines

Honorio T. Cagampan, Consul General for Philippines, 111 Avenue Rd., #605, Toronto, Ont. M5R 3J8 (416/922-7181)

Vicente Romero, Consul General for Philippines, 470 Granville St., #301-8, Vancouver, B.C. V6B 1V5 (604/685-7645); Jose Zarate, Trade Commr.

Poland

Boguslaw Miernik, Consul General for Poland, 1500 Pine Ave. W., Montréal, P.Q. H3G 1B4 (514/937-9481)

K. Szwarc, Trade Commr. for Poland, 3501 ave du Musée, Montréal, P.Q. H3G 2C8 (514/282-1732)

Tadeusz Janicki, Consul General for Poland, 2603 Lakeshore Blvd. W., Toronto, Ont. M8V 1G5 (416/252-5471) – Trade Commr., W. Skrzypkowski

Portugal

A.R. Moreira, Hon. Consul for Portugal, Box 355, Halifax, N.S. B3J 2N7 (902/423-7211)

Carlos Maria de Barros e Sa David Calder, Consul General for Portugal, 4920 de Maisonneuve Blvd. W., #405, Montréal, P.Q. H3Z 1N1 (514/487-4322)

Armando Dias Godinho, Trade Commr. for Portugal, 1801 McGill College, #1150, Montréal, P.Q. H3A 2N4 (514/282-1264)

Fernao Mendonca Perestrelo, Hon. Consul for Portugal, 1105 Belvedere, #321, Québec, P.Q. G1S 3G5 (418/681-8650)

E.S. Martins, Hon. Vice Consul for Portugal, 154 Canada Dr., St. John's, Nfld. A1E 2M8 (709/368-1271)

Antonio Bettencourt Viana, Consul General for Portugal, 159 Bay St., #520, Toronto, Ont. M5J 1J7 (416/360-8260)

J.C.O. Valadas, Vice Consul for Portugal, Box 2068, Vancouver, B.C. V6B 3S3 (604/681-2425)

A. Gustavo Uriel da Rosa, Jr., Consul for Portugal, #902, 228 Notre Dame Ave., Winnipeg, Man. R3B 1N7 (204/943-8941)

Socialist Republic of Romania

Gheorghe Zamfirescu, Sr. Trade Commr. for Romania, 3664 Mountain St., Montréal, P.Q. H3G 2A8 (514/842-1770)

Rwanda

Pierre Valcour, Hon. Consul for Rwanda, 1151 Alexandre-Desève, Montréal, P.Q. H2L 2T7 (514/527-2859)

San Marino

Raymond Lette, Hon. Consul General for San Marino, 27 McNider Ave., Montréal, P.Q. H2V 3X4 (514/871-3838)

South Africa

A. Jaquet, Consul for South Africa, #1404, 800 Dorchester Blvd. W., Montréal, P.Q. H3B 1X9 (514/878-9217)

E.A. Erasmus, Consul (Commercial) for South Africa, Box 103, Commerce Court Stn., Toronto, Ont. M5L 1E2 (416/364-0314)

Spain

José Guasp, Hon. Vice Consul for Spain, 10437 124 St., Edmonton, Alta. T5N 1R7 (403/482-4859)

Louis Holmes, Hon. Vice Consul for Spain, 1525 Birmingham St., Box 3550 South, Halifax, N.S. B3J 3J3 (902/429-5680)

Rafael Rodriguez-Candela, Hon. Vice Consul for Spain, 123 Portledge Ave., Moncton, N.B. E1C 5S8 (506/855-0905)

Count Campo-Rey, Consul General for Spain, 1 Westmount Sq., #1456, Montréal, P.Q. H3Z 2P9 (514/935-5235); Commercial Affairs, Place Bonaventure (866-4914)

Pierre Villa, Hon. Vice Consul for Spain, 250 rue Lachance, Québec, P.Q. G1P 2H3 (418/683-2531)

Capt. José L. Arambarri, Hon. Vice Consul for Spain, 10 Topsail Rd., Box W2097, St. John's, Nfld. A1E 2A5 (709/726-1804)

Gerardo Miguel Otero, Consul (Commercial) for Spain, 55 Bloor St. W., #1204, Toronto, Ont. M4W 1A5 (416/967-0488)

Harold F. Fishleigh, Hon. Vice Consul for Spain, #506, 365 Bloor St. E., Toronto, Ont. M4W 3L4 (416/924-7424)

F.P. Bernard, Hon. Vice Consul for Spain, #1100, 700 W. Georgia St., Box 10025, Vancouver, B.C. V7Y 1A1 (604/688-9471)

Sweden

R. Zoumer, Consul for Sweden, 420 47th Ave. S.W., Calgary, Alta. T2S 1C4 (403/243-1093)

Lars Fahlstrom, Consul for Sweden, #1910, 10015 103 Ave., Edmonton, Alta. T5J 0H1 (403/423-5444)

G. Jennegren, Consul for Sweden, Box 2027, Halifax, N.S. B3J 2Z1 (902/429-5252)

C.E. Winberg, Consul General for Sweden, 1155 Dorchester Blvd. W., #800, Montréal, P.Q. H3B 2H7 (514/866-4019); Trade Office at Ste. 1020 (878-4462)

G. de Lery Demers, Q.C., Hon. Consul for Sweden, 425 boul. Charest est, Québec, P.Q. G1K 3H9 (418/529-9968)

Larry A. Kyle, Consul for Sweden, 1850 Cornwall St., Regina, Sask. S4P 2K3 (306/523-5681)

G. McGillivray, Consul for Sweden, Box 6340, Stn. A., (Hilyard Place, Bldg. A), Saint John, N.B. E2L 3Z5 (506/693-2613)

Peter N. Outerbridge, Hon. Consul for Sweden, Box 5128, St. John's, Nfld. A1C 5V6 (709/726-8000)

Larry A. Kyle, Consul for Sweden, 410 22nd St. E., #850, Saskatoon, Sask. S7K 5T6 (306/665-7844)

Leif Holmvall, Consul & Trade Commr. for Sweden, 920 Yonge St., #820, Toronto, Ont. M4W 3C7 (416/967-7172)

(Toronto) I. Soderstrom, Consul General for Sweden, 2201 Eglinton Ave. E., Scarborough, Ont. M1L 2N4 (416/751-6307)

K.A. Stahl, Consul General for Sweden, 207 W. Hastings St., #1105, Vancouver, B.C. V6B 1H7 (604/684-5971); Trade Office at 1177 W. Hastings St., #1106 (685-1288)

N.E. Carlson, Consul for Sweden, 1035 Mission St., Winnipeg, Man. R2J 0A4 (204/233-0671)

Switzerland

Dr. Pierre Monod, Hon. Vice Consul for Switzerland, 11723 Edinboro Rd., Edmonton, Alta. T6G 1Z9 (403/433-7946)

Theodor Dudli, Consul General for Switzerland, 1572 Ave. Dr. Penfield, Montréal, P.Q. H3G 1C4 (514/932-7181)

Jean-P. Beltrami, Hon. Consul for Switzerland, 2985 1er Ave., Québec, P.Q. G1L 3P2
Bernard Stofer, Consul General for Switzerland, 100 University Ave., #1000, Toronto, Ont. M5J 1V6 (416/593-5371)
Pierre Vigny, Consul General for Switzerland, 505 Burrard St., #1130, Vancouver, B.C. V7X 1M5 (604/684-2231)

Syria
Muhammad Fayez Al-Rifai, Hon. Consul for Syria, 324 Arlington Cres., Beaconsfield, P.Q. H9W 2K3 (514/695-3530)

Thailand
R.C. Meech, Q.C., Consul for Thailand, 8th Floor, 250 University Ave., Toronto, Ont. M5H 3E9 (416/593-5511)
Horst Gergen Koehler, C.M., Consul for Thailand, 736 Granville St., #106, Vancouver, B.C. V6Z 1H4 (604/687-1143)

Trinidad & Tobago
Rabindranath Permanand, Consul General for Trinidad, #1202, 365 Bloor St. E., Toronto, Ont. M4Y 2L8 (416/922-3175)

Turkey
W.H. Baxter, Hon. Consul General for Turkey, 100 Adelaide St. W., #1300, Toronto, Ont. M5H 1S3 (416/364-9344)

Union of Soviet Socialist Republics
Alexander S. Ereskovksy, Consul General for U.S.S.R., 3655 Museum Ave., Montréal, P.Q. H3G 2E1 (514/843-5901)
Igor A. Konovalov, Head of Trade Mission for U.S.S.R., 95 Wurtemburg St., Ottawa, Ont. K1N 8Z7 (613/235-9741)

United States of America
Richard L. Wilson, Consul General for U.S.A., 615 Macleod Trail S.E., Calgary, Alta. T2G 4T8 (403/266-8962)
Thomas F. Wilson, Consul General for U.S.A., Cogswell Tower, Scotia Sq., #910, Halifax, N.S. B3J 3K1 (902/429-2480)
Lloyd Michael Rives, Consul General for U.S.A., Box 65, Stn. Desjardins, Montréal, P.Q. H5B 1G1 (514/281-1886)
George W. Jaeger, Consul General for U.S.A., Box 939, (1 Ste-Genevieve), Québec, P.Q. G1R 4T9 (418/692-2095)
Frederick Smith, Jr., Consul General for U.S.A., 360 University Ave., Toronto, Ont. M5G 1S4 (416/595-1700)
Robert W. Moore, Consul General for U.S.A., 1199 W. Hastings St., Vancouver, B.C. V6E 2Y4 (604/685-4311)
Ms. Lillian Mullin, Consul General for U.S.A., 6 Donald St., Winnipeg, Man. R3L 0K7 (204/475-3348)

Upper Volta
Frederick Stinson, Hon. Consul for Upper Volta, 196 Adelaide St. W., Toronto, Ont. M5H 1W7 (416/977-1000)

Uruguay
Consul General for Uruguay, 1010 St. Catherine St. W., #347, Montréal, P.Q. H3B 3R7 (514/866-0217)
Carlos F. Reif, Hon. Consul for Uruguay, #2990, Toronto Dominion Bank Tower, Box 10069, Pacific Centre, Vancouver, B.C. V7Y 1B6 (604/682-0404)

Venezuela
Genaro Verde-Ortega, Consul General for Venezuela, 1410 Stanley St., #600, Montréal, P.Q. H3A 1P8 (514/842-3417)
C.A. Taylhardat, Consul General for Venezuela, 2 Carlton St., #703, Toronto, Ont. M5B 1J3
José Chacon-Delgado, Consul for Venezuela, 525 Seymour St., #716, Vancouver, B.C. V6B 3H7 (604/685-6104)

Yugoslavia
Naum Nacevski, Consul General for Yugoslavia, 377 Spadina Rd., Toronto, Ont. M5T 2V7 (416/481-7279)
Mauro Hencic, Consul General for Yugoslavia, 1237 Burrard St., Vancouver, B.C. V7X 1X1 (604/685-8391)

CANADIAN EMBASSIES & HIGH COMMISSIONS ABROAD

Afghanistan
(Embassy), c/o Box 1042, Islamabad, Pakistan

Algeria
(Established 1965): Cdn. Embassy, B.P. 225, Alger Gare Algiers, Algeria Tel: 60-66-11
Ambassador, L.A. Delvoie

Arab Republic of Egypt
(Established 1954): Cdn. Embassy, 6 Sharia Mohamed Fahmi el Sayed, Garden City. Postal Address: Kasr el Doubara Post Office, Garden City, Cairo, Arab Republic of Egypt Tel: 2-3110
Ambassador, R. Elliott

Argentina
(Established 1941): Cdn. Embassy, Brunetta Bldg., Suipacha & Santa Fé, Buenos Aires. Postal Address: Casilla de Correo 1598, Buenos Aires, Argentina Tel: 32-90-81
Ambassador, D.W. Fulford

Australia
(Established 1939): Cdn. High Commission, Commonwealth Ave., Canberra ACT 2600, Australia. Tel: 73-3844
High Commissioner, R.C. Anderson

Austria
(Established 1952): Cdn. Embassy, Luegerring 10, A-1010 Vienna, Austria. Tel: 63-36-91
Ambassador, M.D. Copithorne

Bahamas
(Established 1971): (High Commission), c/o Box 1500, Kingston 10, Jamaica

Bahrein
(Embassy), c/o Box 25281, Safat, Kuwait City, Kuwait

Bangladesh
Cdn. High Commission, House No. CWN 16A, Rd. 48, Gulshan. Postal Address: Box 569, General Post Office, Dacca-2, Bangladesh. Tel: 300181
High Commissioner, A.R. Wright

Barbados
Cdn. High Commission, Commonwealth Development Corp. Bldg., Culloden Rd., St. Michael. Postal Address: Box 404, Bridgetown, Barbados. Tel: 9-3550
High Commissioner, A.B. Roger

Belgium
(Established 1939): Cdn. Embassy, rue de Loxum, 6, B-1000, Brussels, Belgium. Tel: 513-79-40
Ambassador, D'I. Fortier

Belize
(High Commission), c/o Box 1500, Kingston 10, Jamaica

Benin, People's Republic
(Established 1962): (Embassy), c/o Box 1639, Accra, Ghana

Bermuda
(Commission), c/o Canadian Consulate General, 1251 Ave. of the Americas, New York, N.Y. 10020, U.S.A.

Bolivia
(Established 1961): (Embassy), c/o Casilla 1212, Lima, Peru

Botswana
(High Commission), c/o Box 26006, Arcadia, Pretoria, 0007 South Africa

Brazil
(Established 1941): Cdn. Embassy, Avenida das Nacoes, Number 16, Setor das Embaixadas Sul, Brasilia, Brazil. Postal address: Caixa Postal 07.0961, 70000, Brasilia D.F., Brazil. Tel: (61) 223-7515
Ambassador, R.S. MacLean

Britain
(Established 1880): Cdn. High Commission–Chancery: Sir John A. Macdonald Bldg., 1 Grosvenor Sq., London W1X OAB England. Tel: 01-629-9492; Canada House, Trafalgar Sq., Cockspur St., SW1Y 5BJ. Tel: 01-629-9492
High Commissioner, Mrs. J.C. Wadds

Brunei
(Commission): c/o Box 990, Kuala Lumpur, Malaysia

Bulgaria
(Established 1968): (Embassy), c/o Proléterskih Brigada 69, 11000 Belgrade, Yugoslavia

Burma
(Established 1958): (Embassy), c/o Box 569, Dacca, Bangladesh

Burundi
(Established 1971): (Embassy), c/o Box 8341, Kinshasa, Zaire

Cameroon
(Established 1962): Cdn. Embassy, Immeuble Soppo Priso, Rue Conrad Adenauer, Yaounde, Cameroon. Postal address: Box 572, Yaounde, Cameroon. Tel: 22-02-03
Ambassador, J.D.E. Denault

Cape Verde Islands, Republic of
(Embassy), c/o Box 3373, Dakar, Senegal

Central African Republic
(Established 1962): (Embassy), c/o Box 572, Yaounde, Cameroon

Chad
(Established 1962): (Embassy), c/o Box 572, Yaoude, Cameroon

Chile
(Established 1942): Cdn. Embassy, Ahumada 11, 10th floor, Santiago. Postal Address, Casilla 427, Santiago, Chile. Tel: 62256
Ambassador, G. Buick

China, People's Republic
(Established 1971): Cdn. Embassy, No. 10, San Li Tun Rd., Chao Yang District, Peking, China. Tel: 521475
Ambassador, M. Gauvin, O.C., C.V.O., D.S.O.

Colombia
(Established 1953): Cdn. Embassy, Calle 76, No. 11-52, Bogota. Postal addresses: (airmail) Apartado Aéreo 53531-Bogota 2, Colombia; (surface) Apartado Nacional 696 Bogota 2, Colombia. Tel: 235-5066
Ambassador, G.D. Valentine

Comores
(Embassy), c/o Box 1022, Dar-es-Salaam, Tanzania

Congo, People's Republic
(Established 1962): (Embassy), c/o Box 8341, Kinshasa, Republic of Zaire

Costa Rica
(Established 1961): Cdn. Embassy, Apartado Postal 10303, San José, Costa Rica. Tel: 23-04-46
Ambassador, R.D. Sirrs

Cuba
(Established 1945): Cdn. Embassy, Calle 30, No. 518, Esquina A7A, Miramar Havana, Cuba. Tel: 26421. Postal Address: Box 499 (HVA), Ottawa, Ont. K1N 8T7
Ambassador, G.R. Harman

Cyprus
(Established 1961): (High Commission), c/o Box 6410, Tel Aviv, Israel

Czechoslovakia
(Established 1943): Cdn. Embassy, Mickiewiczova 6, Prague 6, Czechoslovakia. Tel: 32-6941
Ambassador, P.A.E. Johnston

Denmark
(Established 1946): Cdn. Embassy, Kr. Bernikowsgadel, 1105 Copenhagen K, Denmark. Tel: (01) 12-22-99
Ambassador, M.A. Macpherson

Djibouti
(Embassy) c/o Box 1130, Addis Ababa, Ethiopia

Dominica
(High Commission), c/o Box 404, Bridgetown, Barbados

Dominican Republic
(Established 1954): (Embassy), c/o Apartado del Este, No. 62302, Caracas, Venezuela

Ecuador
(Established 1960): Cdn. Embassy, 146 Corea y Amazonas, 6th floor. Postal address: Sucursal 11 CCI, Quito, Ecuador
Ambassador, S.H. Nutting

El Salvador
(Established 1961): (Embassy), c/o Apartado Postal 10303, San José, Costa Rica

Ethiopia
(Established 1966): Cdn. Embassy, African Solidarity Insurance Bldg., Haile Selassie I Square, Addis Ababa, Ethiopia. Postal address: Box 1130, Addis Ababa, Ethiopia. Tel: 44-83-35
Ambassador, A.L. Morantz

Fiji
(Established 1971): (High Commission), c/o Box 12-049, Wellington North, New Zealand

Finland
(Established 1949): Cdn. Embassy, P. Esplanadi 25B, 00100 Helsinki, Finland. Postal address: Box 779, 00101 Helskinki 10, Finland. Tel: 17-11-41
Ambassador, A.W.J. Robertson

France
(Established 1928): Cdn. Embassy, 35, Ave. Montaigne, 75008 Paris, VIII, France. Tel: 225-99-55
Ambassador, Michel Dupuy

Gabon
(Established 1962): Cdn. Embassy, Box 4037, Libreville, Gabon. Tel: 72.41.54
Ambassador, J.D.E. Denault (resident in Abidjan)

Gambia
(Embassy), c/o Box 3373, Dakar, Senegal

German Democratic Republic
(Embassy), c/o Ulica Matejki 1/5, Warsaw, 00-481, Poland

Germany (Federal Republic)
(Established 1950): Cdn. Embassy, Friedrich-Wilhelm Strasse 18, 5300 Bonn 1, Germany. Tel: (228) 231061
Ambassador, K. Goldschlag

Ghana
(Established 1957): Cdn. Embassy, E115/3 Independence Ave., Accra, Ghana. Postal address: Box 1639, Accra, Ghana. Tel: 28555
High Commissioner, M. Faguy

Greece
(Established 1943): Cdn. Embassy, 4 Ioannou Ghennadiou St. & Ypsilantou, Athens 140, Greece. Tel: 739-511
Ambassador, J. Barker

Grenada
(Established 1974): (High Commission), c/o Box 404, Bridgetown, Barbados

Guatemala
(Established 1961): Cdn. Embassy, Galerias Espana, 6th floor, 7 Avenida 11-59, Zona 9. Postal Address: Box 400, Guatemala, C.A. Tel: 64955
Ambassador, C.T. Charland (resident in Mexico City)

Guinea
(Established 1962): (Embassy), c/o Box 3373, Dakar, Senegal

Guinea-Bissau
(Established 1975): (Embassy), c/o Box 3373, Dakar, Senegal

Guyana
(Established 1963): Cdn. High Commission, High & Young Sts. Postal Address: Box 660, Georgetown, Guyana. Tel: 72081
High Commissioner, J.W. Graham

Haiti
(Established 1954): Cdn. Embassy, Edifice Banque Nova Scotia, rte de Delmas. Postal Address: Box 826, Port-au-Prince, Haiti. Tel: 2-2358
Ambassador, H.B. Singleton

Holy See
(Established 1970): Cdn. Embassy, Via della Conciliazione 4/D, 00193, Rome, Italy. Tel: (06) 654-7316
Ambassador, Y. Beaulne

Honduras
(Established 1961): (Embassy), c/o Apartado Postal 10303, San José, Costa Rica

Hong Kong
Commission for Canada, 14/15 floors, Asian House, 1 Hennessy Rd., Hong Kong. Postal address: Box 20264, Hennessy Rd. Post Office, Hong Kong. Tel: 5-282222
Commissioner, W. Warden

Hungary
(Established 1965): Cdn. Embassy, Budakeszi, ut 55/DP/8, Budapest H-1021, Hungary. Tel: 365-728
Ambassador, Ms. D.J. Armstrong

Iceland
(Established 1949): (Embassy), c/o Postuttak, Oslo 1, Norway

India
(Established 1947): Cdn. High Commission, 7/8 Shantipath, Chanakyapuri, New Delhi 110021. Postal address: Box 5207, New Delhi, India. Tel: 61-9461
High Commissioner, J.G. Hadwen

Indonesia
(Established 1953): Cdn. Embassy, 5th floor, WISMA Metropolitan, JL. Jendral Sudirman. Postal address: Box 52/JKT, Indonesia. Tel: 584030
Ambassador, W.H. Montgomery

Iran
(Established 1958): (Embassy), c/o Royal Danish Embassy, Tehran, Iran

Iraq
(Established 1961): Cdn. Embassy, 47/1/7 Al Mansour. Postal address: C.P.O. Box 323, Baghdad, Iraq. Tel: 552-1459
Ambassador, W.M. Weynerowski

Ireland
(Established 1940): Cdn. Embassy, 65 St. Stephens Green, Dublin 2, Ireland. Tel: 781-988
Ambassador, tba

Israel
(Established 1954): Cdn. Embassy, 220 Hayarkon St., Tel Aviv. Postal address: Box 6410, Tel Aviv, Israel. Tel: 22-8122
Ambassador, J.S. Stanford

Italy
(Established 1947): Cdn. Embassy, Via G.B. de Rossi, 27, Rome 00161, Italy. Tel: 855-341
Ambassador, G.E.H. Hardy

Ivory Coast
(Established 1962): Cdn. Embassy, Immeuble "Le General", Ave. Botreau-Roussel, 4 eme et 5 eme etages, Abidjan. Postal Address: 01 C.P. 4104, Abidjan 01, Ivory Coast. Tel: 32-20-09
Ambassador, E. Hébert

Jamaica
(Established 1962): Cdn. High Commission, Royal Bank Bldg., 30-36 Knutsford Blvd., Kingston. Postal address: Box 1500, Kingston 5, Jamaica. Tel: 926-1500
High Commissioner, T.B. Sheehan

Japan
(Established 1929): Cdn. Embassy, 3-38 Akasaka 7-chome, Minato-ku, Tokyo 107, Japan. Tel: 408-2101
Ambassador, B.I. Rankin

Jordan
(Established 1965): (Embassy), c/o C.P. 2300, Beirut, Lebanon

Kenya
(Established 1962): Cdn. High Commission, Comcraft House, Hailé Selassie Ave., Nairobi. Postal address: Box 30481, Nairobi, Kenya. Tel: 334-033
High Commissioner, G.F. Bruce

Kiribati (Republic of)
(High Commission), c/o Box 12-049, Wellington North, New Zealand

Korea
(Established 1964): Cdn. Embassy, 10th floor, Kolon Bldg., 45 Mugyo-Dong, Jung-Ku. Postal Address: Box 6299, Seoul 100, Korea. Tel: 776-4062
Ambassador, tba

Kuwait
(Established 1965): Cdn. Embassy, No. 28, Quaraish St., Nuzha District, Kuwait City. Postal address: Box 25281, Safat, Kuwait City. Tel: 511451
Ambassador, H.S. Hay

Laos
(Embassy), c/o Box 2090, Bangkok, Thailand

Lebanon
(Established 1954): Cdn. Embassy, Immeuble Sabbagh, rue Hamra, C.P. 2300, Beirut, Lebanon. Tel: 350-660
Ambassador, T.J. Arcand

Lesotho
(High Commission), c/o Box 26006, Arcadia 0007, Pretoria, South Africa

Liberia
(Embassy), c/o Box 1639, Accra, Ghana

Libyan Arab Republic
(Embassy), c/o Kasr el Doubara Post Office, Cairo, Arab Republic of Egypt

Luxembourg
(Established 1945): (Embassy), c/o rue de Loxum, 6, 1000 Brussels, Belgium

Madagascar
(Established 1969): (Embassy), c/o Box 1022, Dar-es-Salaam, Tanzania

Malawi
(High Commission), c/o Box 1313, Lusaka, Zambia

Malaysia
(Established 1958): Cdn. High Commission, American International Assurance Bldg., Ampang Rd., Kuala Lumpur, Malaysia. Postal Address: Box 990, Kuala Lumpur, Malaysia. Tel: 89722
High Commissioner, J.R. Francis

Mali
(Embassy), c/o 01 Box 4104, Abidjan, Ivory Coast

Malta
(Established 1964): (High Commission), c/o Via G B de Rossi 27, Rome, Italy 00161

Mauritania
(Embassy), c/o Box 3373, Dakar, Senegal

Mauritius
(High Commission), c/o Box 1022, Dar-es-Salaam, United Republic of Tanzania

Mexico
(Established 1944): Cdn. Embassy, Melchor Ocampo 463-7, Mexico 5, D.F., Mexico. Tel: 533-06-10
Ambassador, C.T. Charland

Mongolia
(Embassy), c/o 23 Starokonyushenny Pereulok, Moscow, U.S.S.R.

Morocco
(Established 1962): Cdn. Embassy, 13 Bis, Rue Jaafar As-Sadik. Postal Address: B.P. 709, Rabat-Agdal, Maroc. Tel: 713-75
Ambassador, G. Duguay

Mozambique
(Embassy), c/o Box 1313, Lusaka, Zambia

Nepal
(Established 1965): (Embassy), c/o Box 5207, New Delhi, India

Netherlands
(Established 1939): Cdn. Embassy, Sophialaan 7, The Hague, Netherlands. Tel: 614111
Ambassador, G.-H. Blouin

New Zealand
(Established 1940): Cdn. High Commission, I.C.I. Bldg., Molesworth St. N.I., Wellington, New Zealand. Postal Address: Box 12-049, Wellington North, New Zealand. Tel: 739-577
High Commissioner, Mrs. I. Johnson

Nicaragua
(Established 1961): (Embassy), c/o Apartado Postal 10303, San José, Costa Rica

Niger
(Established 1962): (Embassy), c/o 01 Box 4104, Abidjan, Ivory Coast

Nigeria
(Established 1960): Cdn. High Commission, Niger House, Tinubu St., Lagos, Nigeria. Postal address: Box 851, Lagos, Nigeria. Tel: 660-130
High Commissioner, C.G. Bullis

Norway
(Established 1943): Cdn. Embassy, Oscars gate 20, Oslo 3, Norway. Postal address: Postuttak, Oslo 1, Norway. Tel: 46-69-55
Ambassador, A.G. Campbell

Oman
(Established 1974): (Embassy), c/o Box 5050, Jeddah, Saudi Arabia

Pakistan
(Established 1950): Cdn. Embassy, Diplomatic Enclave No. 5, Islamabad. Postal Address: Box 1042, G.P.O., Islamabad, Pakistan Tel: 21101
Ambassador, A.D. Small

Panama
(Established 1961): (Embassy), c/o Apartado Postal 10303, San José, Costa Rica

Papua New Guinea
(High Commission), c/o Commonwealth Ave., Canberra, Act 2600, Australia

Paraguay
(Established 1962): (Embassy), c/o Casilla de Correo 1598, Buenos Aires, Argentina

Peru
(Established 1944): Cdn. Embassy, 132 Calle Libertad, Miraflores, Lima. Postal Address: Casilla 1212, Lima, Peru. Tel: 46-38-90
Ambassador, J.-Y. Grenon

Philippines
Cdn. Embassy, 4th floor, PAL Bldg., Ayala Ave., Makati, Rizal. Postal address: Box 971, Commercial Centre, Makati, Rizal, Manila, Philippines. Tel: 87-65-36
Ambassador, E.L. Bobinski

Poland
(Established 1943): Cdn. Embassy, Ulica Matejki 1/5, Warsaw 00-481, Poland. Tel: 29-80-51
Ambassador, J.M. Fraser

Portugal
(Established 1952): Cdn. Embassy, Rua Rosa Araujo 2, 6th floor, Lisbon 2, Portugal. Tel: 56-25-47

Ambassador, Hon. L. Lamoureux

Qatar
(Established 1974): (Embassy), c/o Box 25281, Safat, Kuwait City, Kuwait

Romania
(Established 1968): Cdn. Embassy, 36 Nicolae Iorga, 71118 Bucharest. Postal address: Box 2966, Post Office No. 22, Bucharest, Romania. Tel: 50-65-80
Ambassador, P.M. Roberts

Rwanda
(Embassy), c/o Box 8341, Kinshasa, Zaire

St. Lucia
(High Commission), c/o Box 404, Bridgetown, Barbados

St. Vincent & the Grenadines
(High Commission), c/o Box 404, Bridgetown, Barbados

Sao Tome & Principe
(Embassy), c/o Box 572, Yaounde, Cameroon

Saudi Arabia
Cdn. Embassy, 6th floor, Office Tower, Commercial & Residential Centre, King Abdul Aziz St., Jeddah. Postal address: Box 5050, Jeddah, Saudi Arabia. Tel: 643-4900
Ambassador, W.J. Jenkins

Senegal
(Established 1962): Cdn. Embassy, 45 Ave. de la Republique, Dakar. Postal address: Box 3373, Dakar, Senegal. Tel: 210290
Ambassador, M. Perron

Seychelles
(Established 1976): (High Commission), c/o Box 1022, Dar-es-Salaam, Tanzania

Sierra Leone
(Established 1961): (High Commission), c/o Box 851, Lagos, Nigeria

Singapore
(Established 1966): Cdn. High Commission, Faber House, 7th-8th floors, 230 Orchard Rd., Singapore 9. Postal Address: Box 845, Singapore 1. Tel: 737-1322
High Commissioner, L.M. Berry

Solomon Islands
(High Commission), c/o Canadian High Commission to Australia, Commonwealth Ave., Canberra ACT 2600, Australia

Somali Democratic Republic
(Established 1968): (Embassy), c/o Box 5050, Jeddah, Saudi Arabia

South Africa (Republic of)
(Established 1940): Cdn. Embassy, Nedbank Plaza, Church & Beatrix Sts. Postal Address: Box 26006, Arcadia, Pretoria, South Africa. Tel: 28-7062
Ambassador, R.M. Middleton

Spain
(Established 1953): Cdn. Embassy, Edificio Goya, Calle Nunez de Balboa 35. Postal address: Apartado 587, Madrid, Spain. Tel: 225-9119
Ambassador, J.J.C. Dupuis

Sri Lanka
Cdn. High Commission, 6 Gregory's Rd., Cinnamon Gardens, Colombo. Postal address: Box 1006, Colombo, Sri Lanka. Tel: 95841

High Commissioner, R.W. Clark

Sudan
(Established 1961): (Embassy), c/o Kasr el Doubara Post Office, Cairo, Arab Republic of Egypt

Suriname, Republic
(Established 1975): (Embassy), c/o Box 660, Georgetown, Guyana

Swaziland
(High Commission), c/o Box 26006, Arcadia, Pretoria 0007, South Africa

Sweden
(Established 1947): Cdn. Embassy, Tegelbacken 4 (7th floor), Stockholm. Postal address: Box 16129, S-10323, Stockholm 16, Sweden. Tel: 23-79-20
Ambassador, tba

Switzerland
(Established 1947): Cdn. Embassy, 88 Kirchenfeldstrasse, 3005 Berne. Postal Address: Box 3000, Berne 6, Switzerland. Tel: (031) 44-63-81
Ambassador, P. Dumas

Syrian Arab Republic
(Established 1965): (Embassy) c/o C.P. 2300, Beirut, Lebanon

Tanzania, United Republic
(Established 1962): Cdn. High Commission, Pan African Insurance Bldg., Independence Ave., Dar-es-Salaam. Postal address: Box 1022, Dar-es-Salaam, Tanzania. Tel: 20651
High Commissioner, K. Johansen

Thailand
(Established 1961): Cdn. Embassy, 138 Silom Rd., Box 2090, Bangkok, Thailand. Tel: 234-1561
Ambassador, F. Bild

Togo
(Established 1962): (Embassy), c/o Box 1639, Accra, Ghana

Tonga
(Established 1971): (High Commission), c/o Box 12-049, Wellington North, New Zealand

Trinidad & Tobago
(Established 1962): Cdn. High Commission, 72 South Quay. Postal address: Box 1246, Port-of-Spain, Trinidad. Tel: 62-34787
High Commissioner, P.E. Laberge

Tunisia
(Established 1961): Cdn. Embassy, 2, Place Virgile, Notre Dame de Tunis. Postal address: B.P. 31, Belvedere, Tunis. Tel: 286-577
Ambassador, A.E. Blanchette

Turkey
(Established 1947): Cdn. Embassy, Nenehatun Caddesi No. 75, Gazioamanpasa, Ankara, Turkey. Tel: 27-58-03
Ambassador, M. Beaudoin

Tuvalu
(High Commission): c/o Box 12-049, Wellington, New Zealand

Uganda
(Established 1962): (High Commission), c/o Box 30481, Nairobi, Kenya

Union of Soviet Socialist Republics
(Established 1943): Cdn. Embassy, 23 Starokonyushenny Pereulok, Moscow, U.S.S.R. Tel: 241-9155
Ambassador, G.A.H. Pearson

United Arab Emirates
(Established 1974): (Embassy), c/o Box 2581 Safat, Kuwait City, Kuwait

United States of America
(Established 1927): Cdn. Embassy, 1746 Massachusetts Ave. N.W., Washington, D.C. 20036, U.S.A. Tel: (202) 785-1400. Telex: 0089664
Ambassador, P.M. Towe

Upper Volta
(Established 1962): (Embassy), c/o 01 Box 4104, Abidjan, Ivory Coast

Uruguay
(Established 1952): (Embassy), c/o Casilla de Correo, 1598 Buenos Aires, Argentina

Venezuela
(Established 1952): Cdn. Embassy, Avenida La Estancia 10, 16 piso Ciudad Commercial Tamanaco, Caracas. Postal address: Apartado del Este No. 62302, Caracas, Venezuela. Tel: 91-32-77
Ambassador, C.O.R. Rousseau

Viet-Nam-Hanoi, Socialist Republic
(Embassy), c/o Box 2090, Bangkok, Thailand

Western Samoa
(Established 1971): (High Commission), c/o Box 12-049, Wellington North, New Zealand

West Indies (Associated States)
(Established 1971): (Commission), c/o Box 404, Bridgetown, Barbados

Yemen Arab Republic
(Established 1975): (Embassy), c/o Box 5050, Jeddah, Saudi Arabia

Yemen, People's Democratic Republic
(Established 1976): (Embassy), c/o Box 5050, Jeddah, Saudi Arabia

Yugoslavia
(Established 1943): Cdn. Embassy, Proleterskih Brigada 69, 11000 Belgrade, Yugoslavia. Tel: 434-524
Ambassador, J.G. Harris

Zaire, Republic
(Established 1962): Cdn. Embassy, Edifice Shell, Coin Av. Wangata et boul du 30-juin, Kinshasa. Postal address: Box 8341, Kinshasa, Zaire. Tel: 227-06
Ambassador, R.A.J. Chrétien

Zambia, Republic
(Established 1966): Cdn. High Commission, Barclays Bank North End Branch, Cairo Rd. Postal Address: Box 31313, Lusaka, Zambia. Tel: 75187
High Commissioner, T.C. Bacon

Zimbabwe
Cdn. High Commission, 45 Bainef Ave. Postal Address: Box 1430, Salisbury, Zimbabwe
High Commissioner, R.W. McLaren

CANADIAN CONSULATES ABROAD

Australia
Melbourne, Victoria: B.A. Gagosz, Consul General, 17th floor, Princess Gate East Tower, 151 Flinders St., Melbourne, Victoria, Australia 3000. Tel: 63-8431
Sydney, New South Wales: M.B. Blackwood, Consul General, 8th floor, A.M.P. Centre, 50 Bridge St., Sydney 2000, N.S.W., Australia. Tel: 337-2707

Bahamas
Nassau: A.M. Duffield, Hon. Consul, Office Z1, Out Island Traders Bldg., Ernest St., Box SS6371, Nassau, Bahamas. Tel: 323-2123

Bolivia
La Paz: M. Woolgar, Hon. Consul, #508, 1420 J. De La Riva St. Postal Address: Consulado Del Canada, Casilla 20408. Tel: 370-5224

Brazil
Rio de Janeiro: W.B. Schumacher, Consul General, Edificio Metropole, Av. Presidente Wilson 165, 6 Andar, Rio de Janeiro, Brazil. Postal address: Caixa Postale 2164-Z-C-00. Tel: 240-9912
Sao Paulo: V.G. Lotto, Consul General, Edificio Top Center, Avenida Paulista 854, 5th floor, Sao Paulo. Postal address: Caixa Postale 22002, Sao Paulo. Tel: 287-2122

Britain
Birmingham: C.B. Danby, Consul, Bristol & West House, 2 St. Philip's Place, Birmingham B3 2QJ, England. Tel: (021) 233-2127
Glasgow: Miss H.O. Ring, Consul, Ashley House, 195 W. George St., Glasgow G2 2HS, Scotland. Tel: (041) 248-3026

Dominican Republic
Santo Domingo: J.A. Brache, Hon. Consul, Mahatma Gandhi 200, Corner Juan Sanchez Ramirez, Santo Domingo 1, Dominican Republic. Tel: (809) 689-0002

France
Bordeaux: C. Bédard, Consul General, Croix du mail, rue Claude-Bonnier, 33080 Bordeaux Cédex, France. Tel: 96-15-61
Marseille: A. Potvin, Consul General, 24 ave du Prado, 13006 Marseille, France. Tel: 37-19-37
St-Pierre: J.-P. Andrieux, Hon. Consul, Place Général de Gaulle, Box 297, St-Pierre, St-Pierre et Miquelon. Tel: (709) 4-12-426
Strasbourg: Ms. J. Loranger, Consul General, Le Kleber Center, 10 Place du Temple-neuf, 67007 Strasbourg, France. Postal address: B.P. 288/R7, 67007 Strasbourg Cedex. Tel: 32-65-96

Germany
Berlin: (Military Mission & Consulate), K. Goldshlag, Head of Mission, (resident in Bonn), Europa Center, 1 Berlin 30, Germany. Tel: 261-1161
Dusseldorf: J.M.T. Thomas, Consul General, 4 Dusseldorf, Immermannstrasse 3, Dusseldorf, Germany. Tel: 35-34-71
Hamburg: R.J.K. Berlet, Consul General, Esplanade 41-47, Hamburg, Germany. Tel: 35-18-05

Iceland
Reykjavik: J.H. Bergs, Hon. Consul General, Skulagata 20, Reykjavik, Iceland. Tel: 25355

Italy
Milan: C.J. Van Tighem, Consul General, Via Vittor Pisani 19, 20124 Milan, Italy. Tel: 652-600

Macao
(Consulate), c/o Commission for Canada, Box 20264, Hennessy Rd. Post Office, Hong Kong

Mexico

Acapulco: Mrs. M.C. Dubé de Sagaon, Hon. Vice Consul, Hotel El Mirador Plaza, La Quebrada 74, Acapulco, Gro., Mexico. Tel: 3-72-91

Guadalajara: E. Vigil, Ave. Vallarta No. 1373, Box 32-6, Guadalajara, Jalisco, Mexico. Tel: (36) 25-9932

Monaco

(Consulate General), c/o 24 ave du Prado, 13006 Marseille, France

Paraguay

Asuncion: Juan Neufeld, Hon. Consul, AZARA 532, Asuncion. Postal Address: Casilla de Correo 173, Asuncion, Paraguay. Tel: 43506

San Marino

(Consulate), c/o the Canadian Embassy, Via G.B. de Rossi 27, 00161 Rome, Italy

Spain

Malaga: J. Schwarzmann, Hon. Consul, No. 18 Plaza de Toros Vieja, 18A 4th Floor, Malaga, Spain. Tel: (952) 318-145

United States of America

Atlanta, Ga. 30303: R.W. Stewart, Consul General), 900 Coastal States Bldg., 260 Peachtree St. Tel: (404) 577-6810

Boston, Mass. 02116: J.-M.-G. Déry, Consul General), 500 Boylston St. Tel: (617) 262-3760

Buffalo, N.Y. 14203: W.R. Van, Consul & Sr. Trade Commr., 1 Marine Midland Centre. Tel: (716) 852-1247

Chicago, Ill. 60604: R.H. Gayner, Consul General, Suite 2000, 310 South Michigan Ave. Tel: (312) 427-1031

Cleveland, Ohio 44113: N.W. Boyd, Consul & Sr. Trade Commr., Illuminating Bldg., 55 Public Sq. Tel: (216) 771-0150

Dallas, Texas 75201: F.T. Jackman, Consul & Sr. Trade Commr., 2001 Bryan Tower, Ste. 1600. Tel: (214) 742-8031

Detroit, Mich. 48226: T.F. Harris, Consul & Sr. Trade Commr., 1920 First Federal Bldg., 1001 Woodward Ave. Tel: (313) 965-2811

Los Angeles, Calif. 90014: J.S. Nutt, Consul General, 510 West Sixth St. Tel: (213) 627-9511

Minneapolis, Min. 55402: G.E.B. Blackstock, Consul & Sr. Trade Commr., 15 South Fifth St. Tel: (612) 336-4641

New Orleans, La. 70130: A. Béchard, Consul General, Suite 2110, International Trade Mart, 2 Canal St. Tel: (504) 525-2136

New York, N.Y. 10020: K. Taylor, Consul General, 1251 Ave. of the Americas. Tel: (212) 586-2400

Philadelphia, Pa. 19102: W.G. Pybus, Consul & Sr. Trade Commr., Suite 1310, 3 Parkway Bldg. Tel: (215) 561-1750

San Francisco, Calif. 94111: H.J. Horne, Consul General, 1 Maritime Plaza, Golden Gate Way Center. Tel: (415) 981-2670

Seattle, Wash. 98101: J.R. Sharpe, Consul General, 412 Plaza 600, Sixth & Stewart. Tel: (206) 447-3804

CANADIAN PERMANENT MISSIONS & DELEGATIONS

TO THE UNITED NATIONS AT GENEVA, & TO THE CONFERENCE OF THE COMMITTEE ON DISARMAMENT: 10A ave. de Bude, 1202, Geneva, Switzerland.

TO THE UNITED NATIONS, NEW YORK: Suite 250, 866 United Nations Plaza, New York, N.Y.

TO THE UNITED NATIONS EDUCATIONAL, SCIENTIFIC & CULTURAL ORG.: 1, rue Miollis, Paris 75732, Paris Cédex 15, France

TO THE UNITED NATIONS ENVIRONMENT PROGRAM: Comcraft House, Hailé Sélassie Ave., (Box 30481), Nairobi, Kenya

TO THE UNITED NATIONS FOOD & AGRICULTURAL ORG.: Via G.B. de Rossi, 00161 Rome, Italy

TO THE NORTH ATLANTIC COUNCIL: Leopold III Blvd., 1110 Brussels, Belgium.

TO THE EUROPEAN COMMUNITIES: 5th floor, rue de Loxum 6, B-1000, Brussels, Belgium

TO THE ORG. FOR ECONOMIC CO-OPERATION & DEVELOPMENT: 19, rue de Franqueville, 75016 Paris, France

TO THE INTERNATIONAL ATOMIC ENERGY AGENCY, VIENNA: Luegerring 10, 1010 Vienna, Austria

TO THE UNITED NATIONS INDUSTRIAL DEVELOPMENT ORG., VIENNA: Luegerring 10, 1010 Vienna, Austria

TO THE MUTUAL & BALANCED FORCE REDUCTION TALKS: Luegerring 10, 1010 Vienna, Austria

TO THE SECRETARIAT OF THE GENERAL AGREEMENT ON TARIFFS & TRADE (GATT): 10A ave de Budé, 1202, Geneva, Switzerland

OBSERVER MISSION TO THE ORGANIZATION OF AMERICAN STATES: 2450 Massachusetts Ave. N.W., Washington, D.C. 20008, U.S.A.

PERMANENT JOINT BOARD ON DEFENCE (Canada–U.S.A.)–CANADIAN SECTION: c/o R.P. Cameron, Director General, Bureau of International Security, Policy & Arms Control Affairs, Dept. of External Affairs, Ottawa

CANADIAN HIGH COMMR. IN LONDON

Canadian High Commission, 1, Grosvenor Sq., London W.1

Telephone: 629-9492

and at Canada House, Trafalgar Sq., London S.W. 1

Canadian Government Departments with offices in London, in addition to the Department of External Affairs are: Industry, Trade & Commerce, Employment & Immigration, National Defence, National Film Board, National Health & Welfare, National Revenue (Customs & Excise), Public Archives, Public Works, Supply & Services, Transport, Wheat Board.

Public Affairs including art gallery, cinema, tourist office, veterans affairs, information and inquiry centre.

High Commr., H.E. Mrs. Jean Casselman Wadds

Deputy High Commr., C. Hardy

Minister (Commercial), M. Forsyth-Smith

CANADIAN AGENTS GENERAL IN LONDON

Alta.:- Alberta House, 1 Mount St., London W1, Agent General, J.H. McKibben (phone: 01-499-3061)

B.C.:- British Columbia House, 1 Regent St., London SW1Y 4NS, Agent General, A.H. Hart, Q.C. (phone: 01-930-6857)

Ont.:- Ontario House, Charles II St., London SW1Y 4QS, Agent General, W. Ross DeGeer (phone: 01-930-6404)

Que.:- Quebec House, 12 Upper Grosvenor St., London W1, Agent General, Gilles Loiselle (phone: 01-629-4155)

Sask.:- 14/16 Cockspur St., London SW1Y 5BL, Agent General, W.M. Johnson (phone: 01-930-7491)

FOREIGN TRADE SERVICE ABROAD

Afghanistan - c/o Pakistan

Algeria

J.L.N. Villeneuve, Commercial Counsellor, Canadian Embassy, C.P. 225, Alger Gare, Algiers, Algeria. Telex: 52036, Phone: 60-61-90 to 93

Arab Republic of Egypt

L.T. Dickenson, Commercial Counsellor, Canadian Embassy, Kasr el Doubara Post Office, 6 Mohamed Fahmy El Sayed St., Garden City, Cairo, Arab Republic of Egypt. Cable: CANADIAN, Phone: 23110

Argentina

M. Perrault, Commercial Counsellor, Canadian Embassy, Casilla de Correo 3898, Suipacha 1111, Buenos Aires, Argentina. Cable: CANADIAN, Phone: 32-9081, Telex: 121383 (121383 AR CANAD), Territory includes Falkland Islands.

Australia

A.C. Perron, Consul (Commercial), 8th Floor, 50 Bridge St., Sydney, N.S.W. 2000, Australia. Tel: 231-6522. Telex: 20600 (CAN GOVT AA 20600). Cable: Canadian Sydney. Territory includes Australian Capital Territory, New South Wales, Queensland, Northern Territory, Papua New Guinea, Solomon Islands.

Austria

R.R. Parlour, Commercial Counsellor, Commercial Division, Canadian Embassy, Dr. Karl Luegerring 10, 1010 Vienna, Austria. Cable: CANADIAN, Phone: 63-36-91, Telex: 75320 (DOMCAN A), Territory includes Albania.

Bahamas - c/o Jamaica

Bahrein - c/o Kuwait

Bangladesh - c/o Thailand

Barbados - c/o Trinidad & Tobago

Belgium

J.N.R. Ferland, Commercial Counsellor, Canadian Embassy, Rue Loxum 6, B-1000 Brussels, Belgium. Cable: CANADIAN, Phone 513.79.40, Telex: 21613 (DOMCAN BRU), Territory: Luxembourg.

Belize - c/o Jamaica

Benin - c/o Ivory Coast

Bermuda - c/o USA (New York)

Bolivia - c/o Peru

Brazil

(1) J.C. Bradford, Commercial Counsellor, Canadian Embassy, Caixa Postal 07-0961, SES-Edificio Venacio IV Cobertura, 70000 Brasilia DF, Brazil. Cable: CANADIAN, Phone: Brasilia 237515, Telex: 38061 1296 (CANADA BSB) Territory: Central West, Northeast & Amazon Basin, Minas Gerais. (2) M.G. Stinson, Consul & Trade Commr., Canadian Consulate, Caixa Postal 2164-ZC-00, Edificio Metropole, Avenida Presidente Wilson 165, 20000 Rio de Janeiro, Brazil. Cable: CANADIAN, Phone: 242-4140, Telex: 38021 22583, (ECAN BR)Territory: States of Rio de Janeiro, Espirito Santo, Bahia. (3) H. Sarafian, Consul & Trade Commr., Canadian Consulate, Caixa Postal 22002, Edificio Topcenter, Avenida Paulista, 854, 5° andar, Sao Paulo, Brazil. Cable: CANADIAN, Phone: 287-2234, Telex: 38011 (112323 CANADIAN BR), Territory: States of Sao Paulo, Parana, Santa Catarina, Rio Grande, do Sul, Mato Grosso. (Businessmen are advised to send only letters to this address. To ensure prompt arrival of parcels of any kind, the sender should consult the Sao Paulo office first about the best method to use.)

Britain

(1) M. Forsyth-Smith, Minister (Commercial), Canadian High Commission, One Grosvenor Sq., London, WIX OAB, Eng. Cable: SLEIGHING, London, Phone: 629-9492, (Area Code 01), Telex: 261592 (DOMINION LDN), Territory includes Gibraltar. (2) R. Banks, Commercial Officer, Ashley House, 195 W. George St., Glasgow, Scotland G22HS. Cable: CANTRACOM, Phone: 248-3026 (Area Code 041), Telex: 778650 (CANTRACOM GLW), Territory: Scotland, Northern Ireland.

Bulgaria - c/o Yugoslavia

Burma - c/o Thailand

Burundi - c/o Zaire

Cameroon

J.N. Guérin, Commercial Counsellor, Canadian Embassy, Immeuble Soppo Priso, Box 572, Yaoundé, Cameroon. Cable: DOMCAN Yaoundé, Telex 8209 (DOMCAN 8209KN), Phone 22-02-03

Cape Verde Islands - c/o Senegal

Central African Republic - c/o Zaire

Chad - c/o Zaire

Chile

J.M. Roy, Commercial Counsellor, Canadian Embassy, Casilla 771, Ahumada 11, 10th floor, Santiago, Chile. Cable: CANADIAN, Phone: 64189, Telex: 3520068 3520068 (DOMCAN).

China, People's Republic

A.A. Lomas, Minister (Commercial), Canadian Embassy, 10 San Li Tun, Peking, People's Republic of China. Phone: 521475

Colombia

P.D. Donohue, Commercial Counsellor, Canadian Embassy, Apartado Aereo 53531/2, Calle 58, No. 10-42, Bogota, Colombia. Cable: CANADIAN, Telex: 044568 (DOMCAN BOG), Phone: 355477

Comores - c/o Kenya

Congo - c/o Zaire

Costa Rica

R.R.M. Logie, Commercial Counsellor, Canadian Embassy, Apartado Postal 10303, 6th floor, Cronos Bldg., Calle 3 y Avda Central, San Jose, Costa Rica. Cable: DOMCAN SAN JOSE, Phone: 230588, Telex: 2179 (DOMCAN), Territory includes Canal Zone

Cuba

L.L. Samuel, Commercial Secretary, Commercial Division, Canadian Embassy, Gaveta 6125, Calle 30 No. 518 esquina 7a Avenida, Miramar, Havana, Cuba. Send all mail to: Commercial Division, Box 499 (HVA), Ottawa, Ont. K1N 8T7. Cable: CANADIAN HAVANA, Phone: 2-6421.

Cyprus - c/o Israel

Czechoslovakia

D.E.F. Taylor, Commercial Counsellor, Commercial Division, Canadian Embassy, Mickiewiczova 6, 125 33, Prague 6, Czechoslovakia. Phone: 326941, Telex: 121061 (DOMCAN PHA), Cable: DOMCAN PRAGUE

Denmark

E.C.H. Shelly, Commercial Counsellor, Canadian Embassy, Kr. Bernikowsgade 1, 1105 Copenhagen V, Denmark, Cable: CANADIAN, Phone: 01-21-36-22. Telex: 27036 (DMCNC DK), Territory: Greenland.

Djibouti - c/o Kenya

Dominica - c/o Trinidad & Tobago

Dominican Republic - c/o Venezuela

Ecuador

J.G. Kneale, Commercial Secretary, Canadian Embassy, Edificio Belmonte, Box 6512 CCI, Quito, Ecuador. Phone 458-016

El Salvador - c/o Guatemala

Ethiopia - c/o Kenya

Fiji - c/o New Zealand

European Communities

Mission of Canada to the European Communities, rue Loxum 6, B-1000 Brussels, Belgium, Cable: CANADIAN, Phone: 513.0600, Telex: 21613 (DOMCAN BRU). The Mission handles only those inquiries that relate to Community law, regulations and activities or that require liaison with the Commission of the European Communities.

Finland

C.P. McPherson, Commercial Counsellor, Canadian Embassy, P. Esplanadi 25B, Box 779, 00100 Helsinki 10, Finland. Cable: DOMCAN HELSINKI, Phone: 171141, Telex: 121363 (121363 DMCNH)

France

A. Blum, Minister-Counsellor (Commercial), Canadian Embassy, 35 Ave. Montaigne, 75008 Paris, France. Cable: CANADIAN PARIS, Phone: 225-99-55, Telex: 28806 (DOMCAN A PARIS), Territory: Andorré, Monaco.

Gabon - c/o Zaire

Gambia - c/o Senegal

German Democratic Republic - c/o Poland

Germany

W.J. Collett, Minister-Economic (Commercial), Canadian Embassy, Friedrich-Wilhelmstrasse 18, 53 Bonn, West Germany. Cable: CANADIAN, Phone: 231061, Telex: 886421 (DOMCA D), Territory: States of Baden-Wuerttenberg, Bavaria, Hesse, Rhineland-Palatinate, Saar. (2) J.G. Tardif, Consul, Canadian Consulate General, Immermannstrasse 3, 4 Duesseldorf, West Germany. Cable: CANADIAN, Phone: 353471, Telex: 8587144 (DMCN D), Territory: State of North Rhine-Westphalia. (3) O. Von Finckenstein, Consul, Canadian Consulate General, Esplanade 41-47, 2000 Hamburg 36, West Germany. Cable: CANADIAN, Phone: 351805, Telex: 215555 (DMCNH D), Territory: City States of Hamburg and Bremen, States of Lower Saxony & Schleswig-Holstein, West Berlin.

Ghana - c/o Nigeria

Greece

E.D.T. Wismer, Commercial Counsellor, Canadian Embassy, 4 Ioannou Ghennadiou St., Athens 140, Greece, Cable: CANADIAN ATHENS, Phone: 739-511, Telex: 5584 (215584 DOM GR).

Grenada - c/o Trinidad & Tobago

Guatemala

C.E. Rufelds, Consul, Canadian Embassy, 6th Floor, 7 Avenida 11-59, Zona 9, Box 400 Guatemala, C.A., Guatemala. Telex: 5206 (DOMCAN GU 5206), Cable: CANADIAN, Phone: 65-497

Guinea - c/o Senegal

Guinea Bissau - c/o Senegal

Guyana - c/o Trinidad & Tobago

Haiti - c/o Trinidad & Tobago

Honduras - c/o Guatemala

Hong Kong

D.I. Campbell, Canadian Govt. Trade Commission, 14/15 floors, Asian House, 1 Hennessy Rd., Box 20264, Hong Kong, Hong Kong. Cable: CANADIAN, Phone: 5-282224, 5-282423, Telex: 73391 (DOMCAN 73391), Territory: Macao.

Hungary

C.E. Butterworth, Commercial Secretary, Canadian Embassy, Budakeszi ut 55/d P/8, 1021 Budapest, Hungary, Phone: 365-728, 365-738, 165-858, Telex: 22-4588 (CANADA H)

Iceland - c/o Norway

India

D.H. Wright, Commercial Counsellor, Canadian High Commission, Box 5208, Shanti Path, Chanakyapuri, New Delhi 21, India. Cable: CANADIAN, Phone: 61-9461, Telex: 2346 (DOMCAN NDI 2346)

Indonesia

M.C. Spencer, Commercial Counsellor, Canadian Embassy, 5th floor, WISMA Metropolitan, JL. Jendral Sudirman, Box 52/JKT, Jakarta, Indonesia. Phone: 58.40.30. Telex: 011-44345 (DOMCAN DKT 44345).

Iran

c/o Royal Danish Embassy, Tehran

Iraq

L.R. MacKay, Commercial Counsellor, Commercial Division, Canadian Embassy, Box 323, Baghdad, Iraq. Cable: DOMCAN BAGHDAD, Phone: 5521459, Telex: 2486 (DOMCAN IK)

Ireland

J.J. McKennirey, Commercial Counsellor, Canadian Embassy, 65/68 St. Stephen's Green, Dublin 2, Ireland. Cable: DOMCAN, Phone: 781-988, Telex: 5488 (DMCN E1).

Israel

J.S.A. Sotvedt, Commercial Counsellor, Canadian Embassy, 220 Hayarkon St., Tel Aviv, Israel. Cable: CANADIAN, Phone: 228122, Telex: 341293

Italy

S.G. Harris, Minister (Economic/Commercial), Canadian Embassy, Via G.B. de Rossi 27, 00161 Rome, Italy. Cable: CANADIAN, Phone: 864-327, Telex: 61056 (DOMCAN ROME)

Ivory Coast

J. Filion, Commercial Counsellor, Canadian Embassy, Box 4104, Le General Bldg., Cor. Ave. du Commerce et Bottreau-Roussel Plateau, Abidjan, Ivory Coast. Cable: DOMCAN ABIDJAN, Phone: 32-20-09, Telex: 593 (DOMCAN Abidjan 593)

Jamaica

O.W. Bennett, Commercial Counsellor, Canadian High Commission, Box 1500, Knutsford Blvd., Kingston 10, Jamaica. Cable: CANADIAN, Phone: 92-61500, Telex: 2130 (BEAVER JA)

Japan

L.J. Taylor, Minister, (Economic/Commercial), Embassy of Canada, 3-38 Akasaka 7-Chome, Minato-ku, Tokyo 107, Japan. Cable: CANADIAN, Phone: 408-2101/8, Telex: TK 2218 (DOMCAN TK 2218)

Jordan - c/o Turkey

Kenya

R.E. Pedersen, Commercial Counsellor, Canadian High Commission, Box 43778, Nairobi, Kenya. Cable: DOMCAN NAIROBI, Phone: 334033, Telex: 22198 (DOMCAN NRB)

Korea

R.A. Fairweather, Commercial Counsellor, Canadian Embassy, 10th floor, 45 Mugyo-Dong, Jung-Ku. CPO Box 6299, Seoul 100, Republic of Korea) Telex: 27425, Phone: 776-4062. Cable: CANADA SEOUL

Kuwait

R. Lockhead, Commercial Counsellor, Canadian Embassy, Box 25281 Safat, Kuwait City, Kuwait. Tel: 511451. Telex: 3549 (MCAN KT). Cable CANAD Kuwait

Laos - c/o Thailand

Lebanon

J.S. Marrow, Commercial Officer, Canadian Embassy, Sabbag Centre, Hamra St., Beirut, Lebanon

Liberia - c/o Ivory Coast

Libyan Arab Republic - c/o Arab Republic of Egypt

Luxembourg - c/o Belgium

Madagascar - c/o Kenya

Malawi - c/o Zambia

Malaysia

R. Frenette, Commercial Counsellor, Canadian High Commission, Box 990, A.I.A. Bldg., Ampang Rd., Kuala Lumpur, Malaysia. Cable: DOMCAN, Phone: 89722. Telex: KL/30269 (DOMCAN MA 30269)

Mali - c/o Ivory Coast

Malta - c/o Italy

Mauritania - c/o Senegal

Mauritius - c/o Kenya

Mexico

D.J.S. Winfield, Minister-Counsellor (Economic/Commercial), Canadian Embassy, Apartado Postal 105-05, Mexico 5, D.F., Mexico. Cable: CANADIAN, Phone: 254-32-88, Telex: 17-71-191 (DOMCAN MEX).

Mongolia - c/o USSR

Morocco

S.F. Pattee, Commercial Counsellor, Commercial Division, Canadian Embassy, B.P. 709, Rabat-Agdal, Morocco. Phone: 713-75/76/77, 713-70, Telex: 31964 (CDA RABAT 31964)

Mozambique - c/o Zambia

Nepal - c/o India

Netherlands

J.D.R. Roy, Commercial Counsellor, Canadian Embassy, Sophialaan 7, The Hague, Netherlands, Cable: CANADIAN, Phone: 61-41-11, Telex: 31270 (DOMCAN HAGUE).

New Zealand

G.T. Keys, Commercial Counsellor, Canadian High Commission, Box 12-049, Wellington North, ICI Bldg., 3rd floor, Molesworth St., Wellington, New Zealand, Cable: DOMCAN WELLINGTON, Phone: 739577, Territory: Cook Islands, French Oceania, Gilbert Island, Tahiti, Tonga, Western Samoa, Fiji, New Caledonia, New Hebrides, Tokelau, Niue

Nicaragua - c/o Costa Rica

Niger - c/o Ivory Coast

Nigeria

R.F. Andrigo, Commercial Counsellor, Canadian High Commission, Box 851, Niger House, 1/5 Odunlami St., Lagos, Nigeria. Cable: CANADIAN, Phone: 53630, Telex: 21275 (DOMCAN LAGOS)

Norway

P. Belanger, Commercial Counsellor, Canadian Embassy, Postuttak, Oslo 1, Norway. Cable: CANADIAN, Phone: 46-69-55, Telex: Oslo 11880 (11880 DOMCAN)

Oman - c/o Kuwait

Pakistan

T.G. Cullen, Commercial Secretary, Canadian Embassy, Box 1042, Diplomatic Enclave, Ramna 5, Islamabad, Pakistan. Cable: CANADIAN, Phone: 21101-04, Telex: DOMCAN IBA 700

Panama - c/o Costa Rica

Papua New Guineau - c/o Australia

Paraguay - c/o Argentina

Peru

T. Parrott, Commercial Counsellor, Canadian Embassy, Libertad 130, Miraflores, Plaza Washington, Lima, Peru. Cable: CANADIAN, Phone: 463890, Telex: 25323 PU (DOMCAN 25323)

Philippines

C.S. Russel, Commercial Secretary, Commercial Division, Canadian Embassy, Box 971, Commercial Centre, Makati, Rizal, Philippines. Cable: CANADIAN, Phone: 87-65-36 or 87-78-46, Telex: 3676 (DOMCAN PN 3676).

Poland

H.J. Himmelsbach, Commercial Secretary, Canadian Embassy, Matejki 1/5 Srodmiescie, Warsaw, Poland. Cable: DOMCAN WARSAW, Phone: 29-80-51, Telex: 813424, (813424 CANAPL).

Portugal

R.J. Ledoux, Commercial Counsellor, Canadian Embassy, Rua Rosa Araujo, 2-7°, 7th floor, Lisbon 2, Portugal. Cable: CANADIAN, Phone: 56-25-49, Telex: 12377 (DOMCAN P), Territory: Azores, Madeira

Qatar - c/o Kuwait

Romania

E.A. Mallory, Commercial Secretary, Canadian Embassy, 36 Str. N. Iorga, Box 2966, P.O. No. 22, Bucharest, Romania. Phone: 11-87-91, Telex: 865-10690 (CANAD R)

Rwanda - c/o Zaire

St. Lucia - c/o Trinidad & Tobago

St. Vincent & The Grenadines - c/o Trinidad & Tobago

Sao Tome & Principe - c/o Zaire

Saudi Arabia

D.S. McCracken, Commercial Counsellor, Canadian Embassy, King Abdul Aziz St., Queen's Bldg., 6th floor, Box 5050, Jeddah, Saudi Arabia. Cable: DOMCAN JEDDAH, Phone: 34597/8, Telex: 40060 SJ DOMCAN

Senegal

R.B. Noble, Commercial Secretary, Canadian Embassy, Box 3373, Dakar, Senegal. Tel: 210290. Telex: 632 (632 DOMCAN SG). Cable: Domcan Dakar

Seychelles - c/o Kenya

Sierra Leone - c/o Nigeria

Singapore

J.J. Ganderton, Commercial Counsellor, Canadian High Commission, Box 845, Faber House, 7 & 8 floors, 230/236 Orchard Rd., Singapore 9, Singapore. Cable: CANADIAN, Phone: 37-1322, Telex: 277 (DOMCAN SPORE), Territory: Brunei.

Somali Democratic Republic - c/o Saudi Arabia

South Africa

B.B. Fraser, Commercial Officer, Box 26006, Arcadia, Pretoria 0007, South Africa. Tel: 48-7062. Telex: 53-720 SA (3-720 SA). Cable: Candom Pretoria

Spain

Z.W. Burianyk, Commercial Counsellor, Canadian Embassy, Apartado 117,35 Nunez de Balboa, Madrid, Spain. Cable: CANADIAN MADRID, Phone: 225-9119, Telex: 27347 (DOMCAN E), Territory: Equatorial Guinea, Provinces outside the Peninsula, Balearic Islands, Canary Islands

Sri Lanka - c/o India

Sudan - c/o Arab Republic of Egypt

Suriname - c/o Trinidad & Tobago

Sweden

S.B. McDowall, Commercial Counsellor, Canadian Embassy, Box 16129, S-103 23, Stockholm 16, Sweden. Cable: CANADIAN, Phone: 23-79-20, Telex: 10687 (10687 DOMCAN S)

Switzerland

B. Dussault, Commercial Counsellor, Canadian Embassy, Kirchenfeldstrasse 88, 3000 Berne, Switzerland. Cable: CANADIAN BERNE, Phone: 44-63-81, Telex: 32489 (DMCNB CH), Territory: Liechtenstein.

Syrian Arab Republic - c/o Turkey

Tanzania - c/o Kenya

Thailand

W. Roberts, Commercial Secretary & Consul, Canadian Embassy, Box 2090, 138 Silom Rd., Bangkok, Thailand. Phone: 234-1561/8, Telex: 2671 (DOMCAN TH2671)

Togo - c/o Ivory Coast

Tonga - c/o New Zealand

Trinidad & Tobago

M.W. McQuinn, Commercial Secretary, Canadian High Commission, Box 1246, Huggins Bldg., 72 South Quay, Port-of-Spain, Trinidad. Cable: DOMCAN PORT OF SPAIN, Phone: 62-34787, 62-37254-8, Telex: 226 (226 DOMCAN WG)

Tunisia

W.A. McKenzie, Commercial Counsellor, C.P. 31, Belvedere, Tunis, Tunisia. Tel: 286-577. Telex: 12-324 (DOMCAN 12324 TN). Cable: Domcan Tunis

Turkey

R.C. Brown, Commercial Counsellor, Canadian Embassy, Nenehatun Caddesi 75, Gaziosmanpasa, Ankara, Turkey. Cable: DOMCAN ANKARA, Phone: 27-58-03/04/05, Telex: 42369 (DOMCAN ANKARA).

Uganda - c/o Kenya

Union of Soviet Socialist Republics

M.R. Bell, Minister-Counsellor (Economic), Canadian Embassy, 23 Starokonyushenny Pereulok, Moscow, U.S.S.R. Cable: CANAD MOSCOW, Phone: 241-90-34, Telex: 7401 (DOMCAN MSK 401)

United Arab Emirates - c/o Kuwait

United States

(1) G.F. Mintenko, Minister-Counsellor (Commercial), Canadian Embassy, 1746 Massachusetts Ave. N.W., Washington, D.C. 20036. Cable: CANADIAN, Phone: (202) 785-1400 (Defence Production), Telex: 0089664 (DOMCANA WSH), Territory: U.S. Government and agencies; International organizations with headquarters in Washington. All other trade promotion inquiries relating to the Washington, D.C. area should be addressed to the Consulate in Philadelphia. (2) P.A. Théberge, Deputy Consul General (Commercial), Canadian Consulate General, 1251 Ave. of the Americas, New York, N.Y. 10020, Phone: 586-2400 (Area Code 212), Night Line: 586-2403, Telex: 0012642 (DOMCAN NYK), Territory: States of Connecticut, New Jersey (twelve northern counties), Southern New York. Other countries: Bermuda. (3) H.W. Guy, Consul & Senior Trade Commr., Canadian Consulate General, 900 Coastal States Bldg., 260 Peachtree St., Atlanta, Georgia 30303. Phone: 577-6810 (Area Code 404), Telex: 00542676, Territory: Alabama, Florida, Georgia, Mississippi, North & South Carolina, Tennessee. (4) R.D. Merner, Consul & Senior Trade Commr., Canadian Consulate General, 500 Boylston St., Boston, Mass. 02116. Phone: 263-3760 (Area Code 617), Telex: 00940625 (DOMCAN BSN), Territory: States of Maine, Massachusetts, New Hampshire, Rhode Island, Vermont. Other countries: St. Pierre & Miquelon. (5) R.D. Chan, Consul & Trade Commr., Canadian Consulate, One Marine Midland Center, Suite 3550, Buffalo, N.Y. 14203. Phone: 852-1247 (Area Code 716), Telex: 009-1329 (DOMCAN-BUF), Territory: Northern New York State. (6) J.A. Elliott, Consul & Senior Trade Commr., Canadian Consulate General, 310 South Michigan Ave., Suite 2000, Chicago, Ills. 60604, Phone: 427-1031 (Area Code 312), Telex: 00254171 (DOMCAN CGO), Territory: States of Illinois, Iowa, Missouri, Nebraska, Southern Wisconsin. (7) Mrs. P. Marsden-Dole, Consul & Trade Commr., Canadian Consulate, Illuminating Bldg., 55 Public Sq., Cleveland, Ohio 44113. Phone: 771-0150 (Area Code 216), Telex: 00985364 (DOMCAN CLV), Territory: States of Ohio, Kentucky, West Virginia, Western Pennsylvania. (8) G.A. MacLennan, Consul & Trade Commr., Canadian Consulate, 2001 Bryan Tower, Suite 1600, Dallas, Texas 75201. Phone: 742-8031 (Area Code 214), Telex: 00732637 (DOMCAN DAL), Territory: States of Texas, Arkansas, Kansas, Oklahoma, Louisiana. (9) W.G. Huxtable, Consul & Trade Commr., Canadian Consulate, 1920 First Federal Bldg., 1001 Woodward Ave., Detroit, Mich. 48226. Phone: 965-2811 (Area Code 313). Telex: 00230715 (DOMCAN DET), Territory: City of Toledo, Ohio; States of Michigan & Indiana. (10) A.D. McArthur, Consul & Senior Trade Commr., Canadian Consulate General, 510 West Sixth St., Los Angeles, Calif. 90014. Phone: 627-9511 (Area Code 213), Telex: 00674119 (DOMCAN LSA). Territory: States of Arizona, New Mexico, California (ten southern counties), Clark County in Nevada. (11) R.D.P. Lee, Consul & Trade Commr., Canadian Consulate, 15 South Fifth St., Minneapolis 55402, Minn. Phone: 336-4641 (Area Code 612) Telex: 00290229 (DOMCAN MPS), Territory: States of Minnesota, North & South Dakota, Montana (East of the Divide), Northern Wisconsin. (12) A.G. Virtue, Consul & Trade Commr., Canadian Consulate, 3 Parkway Bldg., Suite 1310, Philadelphia, Penna., 19102. Cable: CANADIAN, Phone: 561-1750 (Area Code 215), Telex: 00845266 (DOMCAN PHA), Territory: States of Delaware, Maryland, New Jersey (nine southern counties), Eastern Pennsylvania, Virginia, District of Columbia. (13) W.L. Clarke, Consul & Sr. Trade Commr., Canadian Consulate General, One Maritime Plaza, Golden Gate Center, San Francisco, Calif. 94111. Phone: 981-2670 (Area Code 415) Telex: 0034321 (DOMCAN SFO), Territory: States of California (except the ten southern counties), Colorado, Hawaii, Nevada (except Clark County), Utah, Wyoming. (14) J.F. Murray, Consul & Trade Commr., Canadian Consulate General, 412 Plaza 600, Sixth & Stewart, Seattle, Washington 98101, Phone: 447-3820 (Area Code 206), Telex: 00328762 (DOMCAN SEA), Territory: States of Alaska, Idaho, Montana (West of the Divide), Oregon, Washington.

Upper Volta - c/o Ivory Coast

Uruguay - c/o Argentina

Venezuela

L.D. Lederman, Commercial Counsellor, Canadian Embassy, Torre Europa, Avenida Francisco de Miranda, Caracas, Venezuela. Cable: CANADIAN, Phone: AC2-339776, Telex: 23377 (DOMCAN VE), Territory: Netherlands Antilles.

Viet-Nam - c/o Thailand

Western Samoa - c/o New Zealand

Yemen Arab Republic - c/o Saudi Arabia

Yemen (People's Democratic Republic) - c/o Saudi Arabia

Yugoslavia

R.C. Lee, Commercial Counsellor, Canadian Embassy, Proleterskih Brigada 69, 11000 Belgrade, Yugoslavia. Cable: DOMCAN BELGRADE, Phone: 434-524, Telex: 11137 (YU DOMCA).

Zaire, Republic

F.J. Laberge, Commercial Secretary, Canadian Embassy, Box 8341, Kinshasa, Republic of Zaire. Cable: DOMCAN KIN, Phone: 22706, Telex: 21303 (DOMCAN ZR)

Zambia - c/o Zimbabwe

Zimbabwe

H.H. McNairnay, Commercial Secretary, Canadian Embassy, 45 Baines Ave., Box 1430, Salisbury, Zimbabwe. Phone 793801, Telex 4465 (4466 RH)

UNITED NATIONS

Dept. of Public Information

The United Nations Department of Public Information is located in New York, N.Y., U.S.A. Publications issued for the public may be ordered through the Sales Section, United Nations, Room A-3315, New York, N.Y. 10017.

United Nations Association in Canada

63 Sparks St., #808, Ottawa, Ont. K1P 5A6

(613) 232-5751

Executive Director, Gregory Wirick

United Nations High Commr. for Refugees

Branch Office for Canada: #401, 280 Albert St., Ottawa, Ont. K1P 5G8

(613) 232-0909

Representative, Raymond Terrillon

Information Officer, Guy Ouellet

Canadian UNICEF Committee

443 Mount Pleasant Rd., Toronto, Ont. M4S 2L8

(416) 482-4444

Executive Director, Harry S. Black

Canadian Commission for Unesco

Box 1047, Ottawa, Ont. K1P 5V8

(613) 237-3408

Secretary General, Claude Lussier

Secrétaire général associé, J.-V. Morin

GOVERNMENT OF CANADA

All political authority in Canada is divided between the federal and provincial governments according to the provisions of the British North America Act. Local municipalities are a concern of the provinces, and derive their authority from Acts of provincial legislation.

The Parliament of Canada consists of the Queen (represented in Canada by the Governor General), an Upper House called the Senate, and an elected House of Commons.

The Senate

Senators are appointed by the Governor General on the recommendation of the Prime Minister of Canada. Senators appointed prior to 2nd June 1965 hold their positions for life, but those appointed after that date hold their positions only until they attain the age of seventy-five years. A Senator to be eligible for appointment must be a Canadian citizen or a British subject and at least thirty years of age. He must own real property worth a net of $4,000 in the province he represents and he must be worth at least $4,000 over and above all debts. He must be a resident of the province for which he was appointed or if he is appointed for Quebec, a resident of one of the electoral divisions of the former province of Lower Canada.

The Speaker of the Senate is appointed by the Governor General.

The Senate as originally constituted at Confederation consisted of 72 members. Through the addition of new provinces and the general growth of Canada it now has 104 members, the latest change in representation having been made June 19, 1975, by providing for one Senator from the Yukon Territory and one from the Northwest Territories. By provinces, representation is as follows: Nfld. 6, P.E.I. 4, N.S. 10, N.B. 10, Que. 24, Ont. 24, Man. 6, Sask. 6, Alta. 6, B.C. 6, Yukon 1, N.W.T. 1: Total 104.

The House of Commons

The members of the House of Commons are elected by the people. The ordinary legal limit of duration for each House is five years, sitting at least once a year. The Speaker is elected by the House.

By virtue of Section 51 of the British North America Acts, 1867 to 1975, after each decennial census the representation in the House of Commons is readjusted. Pursuant to the Electoral Boundaries Readjustment Act, and rules laid down therein, a representation order is prepared which redraws the constituency boundaries in each province.

The representation in the House of Commons for the 32nd Parliament is as follows: Alta. 21; B.C. 28; Man. 14; N.B. 10; Nfld. 7; N.S. 11; Ont. 95; P.E.I. 4; Que. 75; Sask. 14; N.W.T. 2; and the Yukon 1; making a total of 282.

GOVERNOR GENERAL & COMMANDER-IN-CHIEF

Government House, Rideau Hall, Ottawa, Ont. K1A 0A1
(613) 749-5933
His Excellency The Right Honourable Edward Schreyer, C.C., C.M.M., C.D.
GOVERNOR GENERAL'S HOUSEHOLD
Secretary to the Governor General & Secretary General of the Order of Canada, & Secretary General of the Order of Military Merit, Esmond U. Butler, C.V.O.
Deputy Secretary, Jacques Noiseux
Comptroller of the Household, D.C. McKinnon, C.V.O., C.D.
Director of the Chancellery of Canadian Orders & Decorations, Roger de C. Nantel, M.V.O., C.D.
Administrative Secretary, Edmond Joly de Lotbinière
Cultural Advisor, vacant
Press Secretary, René Chartier
Attaché, Miss Jeanne Marsolais
Asst. to the Secretary, & Travel Officer, Maj. Colin Sangster, C.D.
Aides-de-Camp, Captain D. John, Lt. (N) R. Mifflin, Capitaine B. Tremblay

Honorary Historian & Archivist, Dr. Robert H. Hubbard, O.C.

PRIVY COUNCIL OFFICE

Ottawa, Ont. K1A OA3
Clerk of the Privy Council & Secretary to the Cabinet, P. Michael Pitfield

PRIVY COUNCIL

Members of the Queen's Privy Council for Canada, According to Seniority Therein (NOTE: In this list the prefix "Rt. Hon." indicates membership in the British Privy Council or is in accordance with the Table of Titles.)
President of the Privy Council, Hon. Yvon Pinard

Member & Date when Sworn In:

Hon. William Earl Rowe, Aug. 30, 1935
Hon. Lionel Chevrier, Apr. 18, 1945
Hon. Paul Joseph James Martin, Apr. 18, 1945
Hon. Douglas Charles Abbott, Apr. 18, 1945
Hon. Hugues Lapointe, Aug. 25, 1949
Hon. Gabriel-Edouard Rinfret, Aug. 25, 1949
Hon. Walter Edward Harris, Jan. 18, 1950
Hon. James Sinclair, Oct. 15, 1952
Hon. John Whitney Pickersgill, June 12, 1953
Hon. Paul Theodore Hellyer, Apr. 26, 1957
Hon. Howard Charles Green, June 21, 1957
Hon. Donald Methuen Fleming, June 21, 1957
Hon. George Hees, June 21, 1957
Hon. Léon Balcer, June 21, 1957
Hon. George Randolph Pearkes, June 21, 1957
Hon. Gordon Churchill, June 21, 1957
Hon. Edmund Davie Fulton, June 21, 1957
Hon. Douglas Scott Harkness, June 21, 1957
Hon. Ellen Louks Fairclough, June 21, 1957
Hon. J. Angus MacLean, June 21, 1957
Hon. Michael Starr, June 21, 1957
Hon. William McLean Hamilton, June 21, 1957
Hon. William J. Browne, June 21, 1957
Hon. Jay Waldo Monteith, Aug. 22, 1957
Hon. Francis Alvin George Hamilton, Aug. 22, 1957
H.R.H. The Prince Philip, Duke of Edinburgh, Oct. 14, 1957
Hon. Henri Courtemanche, May 12, 1958
Hon. David James Walker, Aug. 20, 1959
Hon. Joseph-Pierre-Albert Sévigny, Aug. 20, 1959
Hon. Hugh John Flemming, Oct. 11, 1960
Hon. Walter Dinsdale, Oct. 11, 1960
Hon. Jacques Flynn, Dec. 28, 1961
Hon. Paul Martineau, Aug. 9, 1962
Hon. Richard Albert Bell, Aug. 9, 1962
Rt. Hon. Roland Michener, Oct. 15, 1962
Hon. Marcel-Joseph-Aimé Lambert, Feb. 12, 1963
Hon. Théogène Ricard, Mar. 18, 1963
Hon. Frank Charles McGee, Mar. 18, 1963
Hon. Martial Asselin, Mar. 18, 1963
Hon. Walter Lockhart Gordon, Apr. 22, 1963
Hon. Mitchell William Sharp, Apr. 22, 1963
Hon. Azellus Denis, Apr. 22, 1963
Hon. George James McIlraith, Apr. 22, 1963
Hon. William Moore Benidickson, Apr. 22, 1963
Hon. Maurice Lamontagne, Apr. 22, 1963
Hon. Lucien Cardin, Apr. 22, 1963
Hon. Allan Joseph MacEachen, Apr. 22, 1963
Hon. Jean-Paul Deschatelets, Apr. 22, 1963
Hon. Hédard Robichaud, Apr. 22, 1963
Hon. John Watson MacNaught, Apr. 22, 1963
Hon. Roger Teillet, Apr. 22, 1963
Hon. Charles Mills Drury, Apr. 22, 1963
Hon. John Robert Nicholson, Apr. 22, 1963
Hon. Harry Hays, Apr. 22, 1963
Hon. John Joseph Connolly, Feb. 3, 1964
Hon. Maurice Sauvé, Feb. 3, 1964
Hon. Yvon Dupuis, Feb. 3, 1964
Hon. E.J. Benson, June 29, 1964
Hon. Léo A.J. Cadieux, Feb. 15, 1965
Hon. Lawrence T. Pennell, July 7, 1965
Hon. Jean-Luc Pépin, July 7, 1965
Hon. Alan Aylesworth Macnaughton, Oct. 25, 1965
Hon. Jean Marchand, Dec. 18, 1965
Hon. Jean-Pierre Côté, Dec. 18, 1965
Hon. John Napier Turner, Dec. 18, 1965
Rt. Hon. Pierre Elliott Trudeau, Apr. 4, 1967
Hon. Joseph-Jacques-Jean Chretien, Apr. 4, 1967
Hon. Pauline Vanier, Apr. 11, 1967
Hon. John Parmenter Robarts, July 5, 1967
Hon. Louis J. Robichaud, July 5, 1967
Hon. Dufferin Roblin, July 5, 1967
Hon. Alexander B. Campbell, July 5, 1967
Hon. Ernest Charles Manning, July 5, 1967
Hon. Joseph Roberts Smallwood, July 5, 1967
Hon. Robert L. Stanfield, July 7, 1967
Hon. Charles Ronald McKay Granger, Sept. 25, 1967
Hon. Bryce Stuart Mackasey, Feb. 9, 1968
Hon. Donald Stovel Macdonald, Apr. 20, 1968
Hon. John Carr Munro, Apr. 20, 1968
Hon. Gérard Pelletier, Apr. 20, 1968
Hon. Jack Davis, Apr. 26, 1968
Hon. Horace Andrew Olson, July 6, 1968
Hon. Jean-Eudes Dubé, July 6, 1968
Hon. Stanley Ronald Basford, July 6, 1968
Hon. Donald Campbell Jamieson, July 6, 1968
Hon. Eric William Kierans, July 6, 1968
Hon. Robert Knight Andras, July 6, 1968
Hon. James Armstrong Richardson, July 6, 1968
Hon. Otto Emil Lang, July 6, 1968
Hon. Herbert E. Gray, Oct. 20, 1969
Hon. Robert Douglas George Stanbury, Oct. 20, 1969
Hon. Jean-Pierre Goyer, Dec. 22, 1970
Hon. Alastair William Gillespie, Aug. 12, 1971
Hon. Martin Patrick O'Connell, Aug. 12, 1971
Hon. Patrick Morgan Mahoney, Jan. 28, 1972
Hon. Stanley Haidasz, Nov. 27, 1972
Hon. Eugene F. Whelan, Nov. 27, 1972
Hon. Warren Allmand, Nov. 27, 1972
Hon. J. Hugh Faulkner, Nov. 27, 1972
Hon. André Ouellet, Nov. 27, 1972
Hon. Marc Lalonde, Nov. 27, 1972
Hon. Jeanne Sauvé, Nov. 27, 1972
Rt. Hon. Bora Laskin, Jan. 7, 1974
Hon. Lucien Lamoureux, June 10, 1974
Hon. Raymond Joseph Perrault, Aug. 8, 1974
Hon. Barnett Jerome Danson, Aug. 8, 1974
Hon. J. Judd Buchanan, Aug. 8, 1974
Hon. Roméo LeBlanc, Aug. 8, 1974
Hon. Muriel McQueen Fergusson, Nov. 7, 1974
Hon. Pierre Juneau, Aug. 29, 1975
Hon. Marcel Lessard, Sept. 26, 1975
Hon. Jack Sydney G. Cullen, Sept. 26, 1975
Hon. Leonard S. Marchand, Sept. 15, 1976
Hon. John Roberts, Sept. 15, 1976
Hon. Monique Bégin, Sept. 15, 1976
Hon. Jean-Jacques Blais, Sept. 15, 1976
Hon. Francis Fox, Sept. 15, 1976
Hon. Anthony C. Abbott, Sept. 15, 1976
Hon. Iona Campagnolo, Sept. 15, 1976
Hon. Joseph-Philippe Guay, Nov. 3, 1976
Hon. John Henry Horner, Apr. 21, 1977
Hon. Norman A. Cafik, Sept. 16, 1977
Hon. Gilles Lamontagne, Jan. 19, 1978
Hon. John M. Reid, Nov. 24, 1978
Hon. Pierre De Bané, Nov. 24, 1978
Rt. Hon. Charles Joseph Clark, June 4, 1979
Hon. Walter David Baker, June 4, 1979
Hon. Flora MacDonald, June 4, 1979
Hon. James A. McGrath, June 4, 1979
Hon. Erik H. Nielsen, June 4, 1979
Hon. Allan Frederick Lawrence, June 4, 1979
Hon. John C. Crosbie, June 4, 1979
Hon. David S.H. MacDonald, June 4, 1979
Hon. Lincoln Alexander, June 4, 1979

Hon. Roch LaSalle, June 4, 1979
Hon. Donald F. Mazankowski, June 4, 1979
Hon. Elmer M. MacKay, June 4, 1979
Hon. Arthur Jacob Epp, June 4, 1979
Hon. John Allen Fraser, June 4, 1979
Hon. William Jarvis, June 4, 1979
Hon. Allan McKinnon, June 4, 1979
Hon. Sinclair McKnight Stevens, June 4, 1979
Hon. John Wise, June 4, 1979
Hon. Ronald George Atkey, June 4, 1979
Hon. Ramon John Hnatyshyn, June 4, 1979
Hon. David Crombie, June 4, 1979
Hon. Robert D. de Cotret, June 4, 1979
Hon. William Heward Grafftey, June 4, 1979
Hon. Perrin Beatty, June 4, 1979
Hon. J. Robert Howie, June 4, 1979
Hon. Steven Eugene Paproski, June 4, 1979
Hon. Ronald Huntington, June 4, 1979
Hon. Michael H. Wilson, June 4, 1979
Hon. Renaude Lapointe, Nov. 30, 1979
Hon. Stanley Howard Knowles, Nov. 30, 1979
Hon. Hazen Robert Argue, Mar. 3, 1980
Hon. Gerald Regan, Mar. 3, 1980
Hon. Mark MacGuigan, Mar. 3, 1980
Hon. Robert Phillip Kaplan, Mar. 3, 1980
Hon. James Sydney Fleming, Mar. 3, 1980
Hon. William Rompkey, Mar. 3, 1980
Hon. Pierre Bussières, Mar. 3, 1980
Hon. Charles Lapointe, Mar. 3, 1980
Hon. Edward Lumley, Mar. 3, 1980
Hon. Yvon Pinard, Mar. 3, 1980
Hon. Donald Johnston, Mar. 3, 1980
Hon. Lloyd Axworthy, Mar. 3, 1980
Hon. Paul Cosgrove, Mar. 3, 1980
Hon. Judy Erola, Mar. 3, 1980
Hon. James A. Jerome, Feb. 16, 1981
Hon. Allister Grosart, Feb. 16, 1981
Hon. Jacob Austin, Sept. 22, 1981
Hon. Charles L. Caccia, Sept. 22, 1981
Hon. Serge Joyal, Sept. 22, 1981
Hon. W. Bennett Campbell, Sept. 22, 1981

SENATE OF CANADA

Senators are styled "Honourable". The list is according to Seniority.
Speaker, Hon. Jean Marchand
Senator's Indemnity, $43,800 per annum.
Senator's annual expenses allowance, $7,200.

Senators, with designation & P.O. Address:

S.A. Hayden, Toronto, Toronto, Ont.
John J. Connolly, Ottawa West, Ottawa, Ont.
Donald Cameron, Banff, Banff, Alta.
David Croll, Toronto-Spadina, Toronto, Ont.
Fred A. McGrand, Sunbury, Fredericton Jct., N.B.
Florence Elsie Inman, Murray Harbour, Montague, P.E.I.
Hartland de M. Molson, Alma, Montreal, P.Q.
Joseph A. Sullivan, North York, Toronto, Ont.
John M. Macdonald, Cape Breton, North Sydney, N.S.
Louis-P. Beaubien, Bedford, Montreal, P.Q.
Allister Grosart, Pickering, Toronto, Ont.
Edgar Fournier, Madawaska-Restigouche, Iroquois, N.B.
Jacques Flynn, Rougemont, Quebec, P.Q.
David J. Walker, Toronto, Toronto, Ont.
Rheal Belisle, Sudbury, Sudbury, Ont.
Paul Yuzyk, Fort Garry, Winnipeg, Man.
Orville H. Phillips, Prince, Alberton, P.E.I.
Azellus Denis, La Salle, Montreal, P.Q.
Eric Cook, Harbour Grace, St. John's, Nfld.
Daniel Aiken Lang, South York, Toronto, Ont.
William Moore Benidickson, Kenora-Rainy River, Kenora, Ont.
Earl Adam Hastings, Palliser-Foothills, Calgary, Alta.
Harry William Hays, Calgary, Calgary, Alta.
Charles Robert McElman, Nashwaak Valley, Fredericton, N.B.
Douglas Keith Davey, York, Toronto, Ont.
Jean-Paul Deschatelets, Lauzon, Montreal, P.Q.
Hazen Robert Argue, Regina, Kayville, Sask.
J.G. Leopold Langlois, Grandville, Quebec, P.Q.
Douglas Donald Everett, Fort Rouge, Winnipeg, Man.
Maurice Lamontagne, Inkerman, Aylmer, P.Q.
Andrew Ernest Thompson, Dovercourt, Kendal, Ont.
Keith Laird, Windsor, Windsor, Ont.
Herbert O. Sparrow, Saskatchewan, North Battleford, Sask.
Richard James Stanbury, York Centre, Toronto, Ont.
William John Petten, Bonavista, St. John's, Nfld.
Louis de G. Giguere, de la Durantaye, Montreal, P.Q.
Ernest C. Manning, Edmonton West, Edmonton, Alta.
Gildas L. Molgat, Ste. Rose, Winnipeg, Man.
Paul C. Lafond, Gulf, Hull, P.Q.
Ann Elizabeth Bell, Nanaimo-Malaspina, Nanaimo, B.C.
Edward M. Lawson, Vancouver, Vancouver, B.C.
H. Carl Goldenberg, Rigaud, Westmount, P.Q.
George C. van Roggen, Vancouver-Point Grey, Vancouver, B.C.
Sidney L. Buckwold, Saskatoon, Saskatoon, Sask.
Renaude Lapointe, Mille Isles, Montreal, P.Q.
Mark Lorne Bonnell, Murray River, Murray River, P.E.I.
Guy Williams, Richmond, Richmond, B.C.
Frederick William Rowe, Lewisporte, St. John's, Nfld.
George James McIlraith, Ottawa Valley, Ottawa, Ont.
Henry D. Hicks, The Annapolis Valley, Halifax, N.S.
Bernard Alasdair Graham, The Highlands, Sydney, N.S.
Martial Asselin, Stadacona, La Malbaie, P.Q.
Joan Neiman, Peel, Caledon East, Ont.
Raymond J. Perrault, North Shore-Burnaby, Vancouver, B.C.
John Morrow Godfrey, Rosedale, Toronto, Ont.
Maurice Riel, Shawinigan, Westmount, P.Q.
Louis-J. Robichaud, L'Acadie-Acadia, St-Antoine, N.B.
Daniel Riley, Saint John, Saint John West, N.B.
A. Irvine Barrow, Halifax-Dartmouth, Halifax, N.S.
Ernest G. Cottreau, South Western Nova, Yarmouth, N.S.
George Isaac Smith, Colchester, Truro, N.S.
Jack Austin, Vancouver South, Vancouver, B.C.
Paul Lucier, Yukon, Whitehorse, Yukon
Jean Marchand, de la Vallière, Quebec, P.Q.
David Gordon Steuart, Prince Albert-Duck Lake, Regina, Sask.
Pietro Rizzuto, Repentigny, Laval sur le Lac, P.Q.
Willie Adams, Northwest Territories, Rankin Inlet, N.W.T.
Horace Andrew (Bud) Olson, Alberta South, Iddesleigh, Alta.
Royce Frith, Lanark, Perth, Ont.
Peter Bosa, York-Caboto, Etobicoke, Ont.
Duff Roblin, Red River, Winnipeg, Man.
Joseph-Philippe Guay, St. Boniface, St. Boniface, Man.
Stanley Haidasz, Toronto-Parkdale, Toronto, Ont.
Florence Bayard Bird, Carleton, Ottawa, Ont.
Philip Derek Lewis, St. John's, St. John's, Nfld.
Jack Marshall, Humber-St. George's-St. Barbe, Corner Brook, Nfld.
Margaret Jean Anderson, Northumberland-Miramichi, Newcastle, N.B.
Robert Muir, Cape-Breton-The Sydneys, Sydney Mines, N.S.
L. Norbert Thériault, Baie du Vin, Baie Ste-Anne, N.B.
Dalia Wood, Montarville, Montreal, P.Q.
Fernand-E. Leblanc, Saurel, Montreal, P.Q.
Yvette B. Rousseau, de Salaberry, Hull, P.Q.
R.J. Balfour, Regina, Regina, Sask.
Lowell Murray, Grenville-Carleton, Ottawa, Ont.
R.A. Donahoe, Halifax, Halifax, N.S.
Martha P. Bielish, Lakeland, Warspite, Alta.
Guy Charbonneau, Kennebec, Montreal, P.Q.
Arthur Tremblay, Les Laurentides, Quebec, P.Q.
C. William Doody, Harbour Main-Bell Island, St. John's, Nfld.
Heath Macquarrie, Hillsborough, Victoria, P.E.I.
Nathan Nurgitz, Winnipeg North, Winnipeg, Man.
Cyril B. Sherwood, Royal, Norton, N.B.
Peter Stollery, Spadina, Toronto, Ont.

Government Leader, Hon. R.J. Perrault, P.C.
Opposition Leader, Hon. Jacques Flynn, P.C.

Officers of the Senate:

Clerk of the Senate & Clerk of the Parliaments, Robert Fortier, Q.C., LL.B.
First Clerk Asst., Richard G. Greene
Law Clerk & Parliamentary Counsel, Raymond L. du Plessis
Director of Committees, Flavien J. Belzile
Gentleman Usher of the Black Rod, Thomas G. Bowie
Director of Admin. & Personnel, J.W. Dean
Editor of Debates & Chief of Reporting Branch, T.S. Hubbard
Chief of English Minutes & Journals, Gary O'Brien
Chief of French Minutes & Journals, Monique Tomka

HOUSE OF COMMONS, CANADA

Thirty-second Parliament. Last General Election, Feb. 18, 1980. Legal duration, 5 years from the day of the return of the writs.
Clerk of the House, C.B. Koester
Political Parties, *Leaders,* Liberal, Rt. Hon. Pierre Elliott Trudeau; Progressive Conservative, Rt. Hon. Joseph Clark; New Democratic, Ed Broadbent
Party Standings, Lib. 147; P.C. 102; NDP 33; total 282

THE CANADIAN MINISTRY

(According to Precedence)
Prime Minister, Right Hon. Pierre Elliott Trudeau
Deputy Prime Minister, and Minister of Finance, Hon. Allan Joseph MacEachen
Minister of Transport, Hon. Jean-Luc Pepin
Minister of Justice & Attorney General, and Minister of State for Social Development, Hon. Jean Chrétien
Minister of Indian Affairs & Northern Development, Hon. John Carr Munro
Minister of State for Economic Development, Hon. Horace Andrew Olson
Minister of Industry, Trade & Commerce, Hon. Herbert Eser Gray
Minister of Agriculture, Hon. Eugene Francis Whelan
Minister of Consumer & Corporate Affairs, Hon. André Ouellet
Minister of Energy, Mines & Resources, Hon. Marc Lalonde
Leader of the Government in the Senate, Hon. Raymond Joseph Perrault
Minister of Fisheries & Oceans, Hon. Roméo LeBlanc
Minister of State for Science & Technology, and Minister of the Environment, Hon. John Roberts
Minister of National Health & Welfare, Hon. Monique Bégin
Minister of Supply & Services, Hon. Jean-Jacques Blais
Minister of Communications, Hon. Francis Fox
Minister of National Defence, Hon. Gilles Lamontagne
Minister of Regional Economic Expansion, Hon. Pierre De Bané
Minister of State (Canadian Wheat Board), Hon. Hazen Robert Argue
Secretary of State, Hon. Gerald Regan
Secretary of State for External Affairs, Hon. Mark MacGuigan
Solicitor General, Hon. Robert Phillip Kaplan
Minister of State (Multiculturalism), Hon. James Sydney Fleming
Minister of National Revenue, Hon. William Rompkey
Minister of State (Finance), Hon. Pierre Bussières
Minister of State (Small Businesses), Hon. Charles Lapointe
Minister of State (Trade), Hon. Edward Lumley
President of the Queen's Privy Council, Hon. Yvon Pinard
President of the Treasury Board, Hon. Donald Johnston
Minister of Employment & Immigration, Hon. Lloyd Axworthy
Minister of Public Works, Hon. Paul Cosgrove
Minister of State (Mines), Hon. Judy Erola
Minister of State, Hon. Jacob Austin
Minister of Labour, Hon. Charles L. Caccia
Minister of State, Hon. Serge Joyal
Minister of Veterans Affairs, Hon. W. Bennett Campbell

PARLIAMENTARY SECRETARIES

John Evans, to Deputy Prime Minister, and Minister of Finance
Robert Bockstael, to Minister of Transport
Ron Irwin, to Minister of Justice & Attorney General, and Minister of State for Social Development
Ray Chénier, to Minister of Indian Affairs & Northern Development
Gérald Laniel, to Minister of Industry, Trade & Commerce
Marcel Ostiguy, to Minister of Agriculture
Gary McCauley, to Minister of Consumer & Corporate Affairs
John Campbell, to Minister of Veterans Affairs
Roy MacLaren, to Minister of Energy, Mines & Resources
George Henderson, to Minister of Fisheries & Oceans
Roger Simmons, to Minister of State for Science & Technology, and Minister of the Environment
Doug Frith, to Minister of National Health & Welfare
Norm Kelly, to Minister of Supply & Services

Ursula Appolloni, to Minister of National Defence
Russell MacLellan, to Minister of Regional Economic Expansion
Gilbert Parent, to Minister of Labour
Louis Duclos, to Secretary of State for External Affairs
Céline Hervieux-Payette, to Solicitor General
Pierre Deniger, to Minister of State (Multiculturalism)
Claud Tessier, to Minister of National Revenue
Ralph Ferguson, to Minister of State (Small Business & Tourism)
Claude-André Lachance, to Minister of State (Trade)
David Collenette, to President of the Privy Council

Dennis Dawson, to Minister of Employment & Immigration
Raymond Savard, to Minister of Public Works
Jack Masters, to Minister of State (Mines)

Alphabetical list of Members of Parliament, party affiliation (Electoral District), Preferred address and Ottawa phone number:

Allmand, Hon. Warren., Lib. (Notre-Dame-de-Grâce), House of Commons, Ottawa, Ont. K1A 0A6, 995-2251
Althouse, Vic., NDP (Humboldt-Lake Centre), House of Commons, Ottawa, Ont. K1A 0A6, 995-8321
Andre, Harvie, PC (Calgary Centre), #104, 524 17th Ave. S.W., Calgary, Alta. T2S 0B2, 992-6124
Anguish, Doug, NDP (The Battlefords-Meadow Lake), House of Commons, Ottawa, Ont. K1A 0A6, 992-3257
Appolloni, Ursula, Lib. (York South-Weston), House of Commons, Ottawa, Ont. K1A 0A6, 992-3128
Axworthy, Hon. Lloyd, Lib. (Winnipeg-Fort Garry), House of Commons, Ottawa, Ont. K1A 0A6, 994-2482
Bachand, André, Lib. (Missisquoi), 329 rue Bruce, Cowansville, P.Q. J2K 3A7, 996-2578
Baker, George, Lib. (Gander-Twillingate), House of Commons, Ottawa, Ont. K1A 0A6, 996-1541
Baker, Hon. Walter, PC (Nepean-Carleton), 8 Commanche Dr., Nepean, Ont. K2E 6E9, 992-4394
Beatty, Hon. Perrin, PC (Wellington-Dufferin-Simcoe), 635 Perth St., Fergus, Ont. N1M 2S8, 995-1518
Beauchamp-Niquet, Suzanne, Lib. (Roberval), 2097 boul. Wallberg, Dolbeau, P.Q. G8L 1J8, 996-5321
Bégin, Hon. Monique, Lib. (Saint-Léonard-Anjou), #330, 5167 est rue Jean-Talon, Montréal, P.Q. H1S 1K8, 996-5461
Benjamin, L.G., NDP (Regina West), House of Commons, Ottawa, Ont. K1A 0A6, 992-6823
Berger, David, Lib. (Laurier), #1207, 100 ave Bronson, Ottawa, Ont. K1R 6G8, 996-7267
Blackburn, Derek, NDP (Brant), #607, 23 Lynwood Dr., Brantford, Ont. N3S 6S3, 996-7265
Blaikie, William, NDP (Winnipeg-Birds Hill), House of Commons, Ottawa, Ont. K1A 0A6, 995-6339
Blais, Hon. Jean-Jacques, Lib. (Nipissing), 200 ave Parsons, North Bay, Ont. P1A 1S7, 992-4784

Blaker, Rod, Lib. (Lachine), 157 MacKay St., Ottawa, Ont. K1M 2B5, 992-7685
Blenkarn, Don, PC (Mississauga South), House of Commons, Ottawa, Ont. K1A 0A6, 995-8554
Bloomfield, Garnet M., Lib. (London-Middlesex), House of Commons, Ottawa, Ont. K1A 0A6, 992-2936
Bockstael, Robert, Lib. (St. Boniface), House of Commons, Ottawa, Ont. K1A 0A6, 995-2772
Bosley, John, PC (Don Valley West), House of Commons, Ottawa, Ont. K1A 0A6, 992-0978
Bossy, Maurice, Lib. (Kent), House of Commons, Ottawa, Ont. K1A 0A6, 996-4971
Bradley, T.A., PC (Haldimand-Norfolk), House of Commons, Ottawa, Ont. K1A 0A6, 996-5789
Breau, Herbert, Lib. (Gloucester), C.P. 968, Tracadie, N.B. E0C 2B0, 996-2871
Broadbent, Edward, NDP (Oshawa), 450 Laurier Ave. E., Ottawa, Ont. K1N 6R3, 995-7224
Bujold, Rémi, Lib. (Bonaventure-Iles-de-la-Madeleine), House of Commons, Ottawa, Ont. K1A 0A6, 996-7046
Burghardt, Jack, Lib. (London West), House of Commons, Ottawa, Ont. K1A 0A6, 995-0231
Bussières, Hon. Pierre, Lib. (Charlesbourg), 705 Place de Charente, Charlesbourg, P.Q. G1G 2W6, 992-0777
Caccia, Hon. Charles L., Lib. (Davenport), 349 St. Clair Ave. E., Toronto, Ont. M4T 1P3, 992-2576
Campbell, Coline, Lib. (South West Nova), House of Commons, Ottawa, Ont. K1A 0A6, 995-6296
Campbell, John J., Lib. (LaSalle), 582 90th Ave., LaSalle, P.Q. H9R 2Z7, 992-0788
Campbell, Hon. W. Bennett, Lib. (Cardigan), House of Commons, Ottawa, Ont. K1A 0A6, 996-4649
Cardiff, J. Murray, PC (Huron-Bruce), #602, 100 Bronson Ave., Ottawa, Ont., 995-4465
Carney, Pat, PC (Vancouver Centre), House of Commons, Ottawa, Ont. K1A 0A6, 995-7691
Chénier, J. Raymond, Lib. (Timmins-Chapleau), House of Commons, Ottawa, Ont. K1A 0A6, 992-2798
Chrétien, Hon. Jean, Lib. (Saint-Maurice), 1 Bower Ave., Ottawa, Ont. K1S 0J9, 992-2200
Clark, Rt. Hon. Joseph, PC (Yellowhead), Rm 448-N, House of Commons, Ottawa, Ont. K1A 0A6, 996-5084
Clarke, Bill, PC (Vancouver Quadra), #702, 6060 Balsam St., Vancouver, B.C. V6M 4C1, 995-3611
Coates, Robert C., PC (Cumberland-Colchester), 46 Regent St., Amherst, N.S. B4H 3T1, 992-2072
Collenette, David M., Lib. (York East), 523 Soudan Ave., Toronto, Ont. M4S 1X1, 996-2955
Comtois, J.-Roland, Lib. (Terrebonne), 201 boul. Iberville, Repentigny, P.Q. J6A 1Z3, 593-7537
Cook, Chuck, PC (North Vancouver-Burnaby), House of Commons, Ottawa, Ont. K1A 0A6, 992-2839
Cooper, Albert, PC (Peace River), House of Commons, Ottawa, Ont. K1A 0A6, 992-0902
Corbett, R.A., PC (Fundy-Royal), Gagetown, N.B. E0A 1V0, 995-4995
Corbin, Eymard E., Lib. (Madawaska-Victoria), Rm. 439-C, House of Commons, Ottawa, Ont. K1A 0A6, 992-0648
Corriveau, Léopold, Lib. (Frontenac), 423 nord, rue Notre-Dame, Thetford Mines, P.Q. G6G 2S5, 992-6361
Cosgrove, Hon. Paul J., Lib. (York-Scarborough), House of Commons, Ottawa, Ont. K1A 0A6, 996-5132
Cossitt, Tom, PC (Leeds-Grenville), Box 97, Brockville, Ont. K6V 5T7, 992-8655
Côté, Eva, Lib. (Rimouski-Témiscouata), 30 Léonidas, Rimouski, P.Q. G5L 2S7, 996-0802
Cousineau, René, Lib. (Gatineau), 517, rue Craik, Gatineau, P.Q. J8P 5N8, 992-2722
Crombie, Hon. David, PC (Rosedale), 809 Eastbourne Ave., Ottawa, Ont. K1K 0H8, 995-5586
Crosbie, Hon. John, PC (St. John's West), House of Commons, Ottawa, Ont. K1A 0A6, 995-0702
Crosby, Howard E., PC (Halifax West), House of Commons, Ottawa, Ont. K1A 0A6, 995-5653
Crouse, Lloyd R., PC (South Shore), 4 Linden Ave., Lunenburg, N.S. B0J 2C0, 992-0927
Cullen, Hon. Bud, Lib. (Sarnia), 206 MacKenzie St. N., Sarnia, Ont. N7T 6K9, 996-4984
Cyr, Alexandre, Lib. (Gaspé), 165 est, rue Commerciale, Chandler, P.Q. G0C 1K0, 992-1161
Dantzer, Vincent M., PC (Okanagan North), House of Commons, Ottawa, Ont. K1A 0A6, 995-8042
Darling, Stan, PC (Parry Sound-Muskoka), Box 540, Ryerson Cres., Burks Falls, Ont. P0A 1C0, 996-3076
Daudlin, Robert, Lib. (Essex-Kent), 1297 Hwy. 18 E., Kingsville, Ont. N9Y 2N7, 992-2617
Dawson, Dennis, Lib. (Louis-Hébert), House of Commons, Ottawa, Ont. K1A 0A6, 593-7661
Deans, Ian, NDP (Hamilton Mountain), House of Commons, Ottawa, Ont. K1A 0A6, 995-2581
De Bané, Hon. Pierre, Lib. (Matapédia-Matane), House of Commons, Ottawa, Ont. K1A 0A6, 992-8289
de Corneille, Roland, Lib. (Eglinton-Lawrence), House of Commons, Ottawa, Ont. K1A 0A6, 992-7771
de Jong, Simon, NDP (Regina East), House of Commons, Ottawa, Ont. K1A 0A6, 992-4593
Demers, Yves, Lib. (Duvernay), 3155, Cap-à-l'Aigle, Duvernay, Laval, P.Q. H7E 1C8, 992-4284
Deniger, Pierre, Lib. (Laprairie), House of Commons, Ottawa, Ont. K1A 0A6, 995-0121
Desmarais, Louis R., Lib. (Dollard), House of Commons, Ottawa, Ont. K1A 0A6, 996-5376
Dick, Paul, PC (Lanark-Renfrew-Carleton), 17 Kingsford Cres., Kanata, Ont. K2K 1T5, 992-6580
Dingwall, David C., Lib. (Cape-Breton-East Richmond), Site 13, Box 2, R.R. 3, Sydney, N.S. B1P 6G5, 996-4743
Dinsdale, Hon. Walter G., PC (Brandon-Souris), 3205 Rosser Ave., Brandon, Man. R7B 0H1, 992-2352
Dion, Rolland, Lib. (Portneuf), House of Commons, Ottawa, Ont. K1A 0A6, 992-2659
Dionne, Marcel, Lib. (Chicoutimi), House of Commons, Ottawa, Ont. K1A 0A6, 995-0183
Dionne, Maurice A., Lib. (Northumberland-Miramichi), House of Commons, Ottawa, Ont. K1A 0A6, 992-5681
Domm, Bill, PC (Peterborough), 11 Parkview Ave., Peterborough, Ont. K9H 5M5, 995-6108
Dubois, Jean-Guy, Lib. (Lotbinière), 25 Daveluy, Victoriaville, P.Q. G6P 8S6, 996-4756
Duclos, Louis, Lib. (Montmorency), 88 ave Royale, Ste-Pétronille, Ile d'Orléans, P.Q. G0A 4C0, 995-8857
Dupont, Raymond, Lib. (Chambly), 5245 boul. Cousineau, #251, St-Hubert, P.Q. J3Y 6J8, 992-0049
Dupras, Maurice, Lib. (Labelle), La Marquise, Mont-Gabriel, P.Q. J0R 1R0, 995-5609
Duquet, Gérard, Lib. (Québec-Est), 720 19e rue, Québec, P.Q. G1J 1W5, 992-2745
Ellis, Jack, PC (Prince Edward-Hastings), 48 Selena Dr., Belleville, Ont. K8P 4C4, 996-9726
Elzinga, Peter, PC (Pembina), Sherwood Park, Alta. T8A 3K3, 992-2349
Epp, Hon. Jake, PC (Provencher), Box 2800, Steinbach, Man. R0A 2A0, 996-7239
Erola, Hon. Judy, Lib. (Nickel Belt), House of Commons, Ottawa, Ont. K1A 0A6, 996-4382
Ethier, Denis, Lib. (Glengarry-Prescott-Russell), C.P. 10, Glen Robertson, Ont. K0B 1H0, 992-2855
Evans, John, Lib. (Ottawa Centre), 17 Impala Cres., Ottawa, Ont. K1V 9B7, 995-1757
Fennell, Scott, PC (Ontario), House of Commons, Ottawa, Ont. K1A 0A6, 995-5381
Ferguson, Ralph, Lib. (Lambton-Middlesex), House of Commons, Ottawa, Ont. K1A 0A6, 996-4791
Fisher, Douglas, Lib. (Mississauga North), House of Commons, Ottawa, Ont. K1A 0A6, 995-0777
Fleming, Hon. Jim, Lib. (York West), 69 Ivy Cres., Ottawa, Ont., 997-9900
Flis, Jesse P., Lib. (Parkdale-High Park), House of Commons, Ottawa, Ont. K1A 0A6, 992-3213

Forestall, J. Michael, PC (Dartmouth-Halifax East), 49A Celtic Dr., Dartmouth, N.S. B2Y 3G5, 992-4133
Foster, Maurice, Lib. (Algoma), 3011 Linton Rd., Ottawa, Ont. K1Y 8H1, 995-2291
Fox, Hon. Francis, Lib. (Blainville-Deux-Montagnes), St-Eustache, P.Q. J7R 2L2, 997-4740
Francis, Lloyd, Lib. (Ottawa West), House of Commons, Ottawa, Ont. K1A 0A6, 995-0151
Fraser, Hon. John A., PC (Vancouver South), 147 Glebe Ave., Ottawa, Ont. K1S 2C4, 992-3026
Fretz, Girve, PC (Erie), 3318 Poplar Ave., Ridgeway, Ont. L0S 1N0, 992-8865
Friesen, Benno, PC (Surrey-White Rock-North Delta), 13387 13A Ave., Surrey, B.C. V4A L3C, 992-6582
Frith, Douglas C., Lib. (Sudbury), House of Commons, Ottawa, Ont. K1A 0A6, 996-3357
Fulton, Jim, NDP (Skeena), House of Commons, Ottawa, Ont. K1A 0A6, 995-1127
Gamble, John, PC (York North), 25 Rouge River Cres., Markham, Ont. L3P 3J2, 995-6403
Garant, Alain, Lib. (Bellechasse), 363 rue St-François, St-François-d'Orléans, P.Q. G0A 3A0, 996-2998
Gass, Mel, PC (Malpeque), House of Commons, Ottawa, Ont. K1A 0A6, 995-8913
Gauthier, Jean-R., Lib. (Ottawa-Vanier), 1741 Dorset Dr., Ottawa, Ont. K1H 5T7, 992-4766
Gendron, Rosaire, Lib. (Kamouraska-Rivière-du-Loup), 5 rue Amyot, Rivière-du-Loup, P.Q. G5R 3E6, 992-0983
Gilchrist, Gordon, PC (Scarborough East), House of Commons, Ottawa, Ont. K1A 0A6, 995-7485
Gimaiel, Pierre, Lib. (Lac-St-Jean), 385 Rang Des Iles, St-Gédéon, P.Q. G0W 2P0, 995-7052
Gingras, René, Lib. (Abitibi), 731 4e Ave. ouest, Amos, P.Q. J9T 1R2, 996-5535
Gourd, Robert, Lib. (Argenteuil), 10991 rang St-Etienne, St-Benoit, Mirabel, P.Q. J0N 1K0, 995-8231
Gourde, Gaston, Lib. (Lévis), Lévis, P.Q., 593-4355
Gray, Hon. Herb, Lib. (Windsor West), 1253 Victoria Ave., Windsor, Ont. N8X 1N8, 996-1880
Greenaway, Lorne, PC (Cariboo-Chilcotin), 735 Western Ave., Williams Lake, B.C., 593-7576
Guilbault, Jacques, Lib. (St-Jacques), 3748 Parc Lafontaine, Montréal, P.Q. H2L 3M4, 992-8052
Gurbin, Gary, PC (Bruce-Grey), House of Commons, Ottawa, Ont. K1A 0A6, 995-5711
Gustafson, Len, PC (Assiniboia), House of Commons, Ottawa, Ont. K1A 0A6, 995-9107
Halliday, Bruce, PC (Oxford), Box 518, 85 William St. N., Tavistock, Ont. N0B 2R0, 996-6674
Hamilton, Hon. Alvin, PC (Qu'Appelle-Moose Mountain), Box 486, R.R. 1, Manotick, Ont. K0A 2N0, 992-2115
Hamilton, Frank, PC (Swift Current-Maple Creek), #3, 767 3rd Ave. N.W., Swift Current, Sask. S9H 0T2, 992-2013
Hargrave, Bert, PC (Medicine Hat), Box 99, Walsh, Alta. T0J 3L0, 992-7434
Harquail, Maurice, Lib. (Restigouche), House of Commons, Ottawa, Ont. K1A 0A6, 992-9984
Hawkes, Jim, PC (Calgary West), House of Commons, Ottawa, Ont. K1A 0A6, 995-2901
Heaps, Rev. Daniel J.M., N.D.P. (Spadina), House of Commons, Ottawa, Ont. K1A 0A6, 593-4264
Hees, Hon. George, PC (Northumberland), 7 Coltrin Pl., Rockcliffe Park, Ottawa, Ont. K1M 0A5, 992-2251
Henderson, George R., Lib. (Egmont), House of Commons, Ottawa, Ont. K1A 0A6, 996-4714
Herbert, Hal, Lib. (Vaudreuil), 79 Hazelwood Ave., Hudson, P.Q. J0P 1H0, 992-8053
Hervieux-Payette, Céline, Lib. (Mercier), 1 rue des Erables, Répentigny, P.Q. J6A 3B8, 992-0004
Hnatyshyn, Hon. Ramon J., PC (Saskatoon West), 724 Saskatchewan Cres. E., Saskatoon, Sask. S7N 0L2, 993-0171
Hopkins, Leonard D., Lib. (Renfrew-Nipissing-Pembroke), 33 Sunset Cres., Petawawa, Ont. K8H 2L8, 992-7712
Hovdebo, Stan J., NDP (Prince Albert), House of Commons, Ottawa, Ont. K1A 0A6, 995-0590
Howie, Hon. J. Robert, PC (York-Sunbury), 678 Churchill Row, Fredericton, N.B. E3B 1P6, 996-6417
Hudecki, Stanley, Lib. (Hamilton West), House of Commons, Ottawa, Ont. K1A 0A6, 996-9681
Huntington, Hon. A. Ron, PC (Capilano), 1752 Ottawa Pl., West Vancouver, B.C. V7V 2T7, 995-4432
Irwin, Ron, Lib. (Sault Ste. Marie), House of Commons, Ottawa, Ont. K1A 0A6, 996-2907
Isabelle, Gaston, Lib. (Hull), 51 rue Port-Royal, Lucerne, Aylmer, P.Q. J9J 1C7, 992-5516
Ittinuar, Peter, NDP (Nunatsiaq), 151 Riverdale Ave., Ottawa, Ont., 992-2062
Jarvis, Hon. William, PC (Perth), 50 Cobourg St., Stratford, Ont. N5A 3E5, 992-3018
Jelinek, Otto, PC (Halton), House of Commons, Ottawa, Ont. K1A 0A6, 996-2358
Jewett, Pauline, NDP (New Westminister-Coquitlam), #303, 9303 Salish Court, Burnaby, B.C. V3J 7B7, 992-9105
Johnston, Hon. Donald J, Lib. (St-Henri-Westmount), House of Commons, Ottawa, Ont. K1A 0A6, 995-0284
Joyal, Hon. Serge, Lib. (Hochelaga-Maisonneuve), 166 rue King, Montréal, P.Q. H3C 2P3, 992-5261
Kaplan, Hon. Bob, Lib. (York Centre), House of Commons, Ottawa, Ont. K1A 0A6, 992-4323
Keeper, Cyril, NDP (Winnipeg-St. James), House of Commons, Ottawa, Ont. K1A 0A6, 995-1551
Kelly, Norm, Lib. (Scarborough Centre), House of Commons, Ottawa, Ont. K1A 0A6, 996-0877
Kempling, Bill, PC (Burlington), #209, 2160 Lakeshore Rd., Burlington, Ont. L7R 1A7, 992-4420
Kilgour, David, PC (Edmonton-Strathcona), House of Commons, Ottawa, Ont. K1A 0A6, 995-8695
Killens, Thérèse, Lib. (St-Michel), 9865 ave St-Charles, Montréal, P.Q. H2C 2L2, 992-2612
King, Fred, PC (Okanagan-Similkameen), House of Commons, Ottawa, Ont. K1A 0A6, 992-0423
Knowles, Hon. Stanley H., NDP (Winnipeg North Centre), 359 Elm St., Winnipeg, Man. R3M 3N6, 992-4618
Korchinski, Stanley J., PC (Mackenzie), Box 69, Rama, Sask. S0A 3H0, 992-0805
Kristiansen, Lyle, NDP (Kootenay West), House of Commons, Ottawa, Ont. K1A 0A6, 995-9511
Kushner, John, PC (Calgary East), House of Commons, Ottawa, Ont. K1A 0A6, 996-3429
Lachance, Claude-A., Lib. (Rosemont), House of Commons, Ottawa, Ont. K1A 0A6, 992-4587
Lajoie, Claude G., Lib. (Trois-Rivières), 66 rue Duplessis, Cap-de-la-Madeleine, P.Q. G8T 7T5, 996-7269
Lalonde, Hon. Marc, Lib. (Outremont), House of Commons, Ottawa, Ont. K1A 0A6, 593-5252
Lambert, Hon. Marcel, PC (Edmonton West), House of Commons, Ottawa, Ont. K1A 0A6, 992-2036
Lamontagne, Hon. J. Gilles, Lib. (Langelier), House of Commons, Ottawa, Ont. K1A 0A6, 996-4450
Landers, Mike, Lib. (Saint John), House of Commons, Ottawa, Ont. K1A 0A6, 996-0864
Lang, Peter, Lib. (Kitchener), House of Commons, Ottawa, Ont. K1A 0A6, 995-9705
Laniel, Gérald, Lib. (Beauharnois-Salaberry), 72 rue Mathias, Valleyfield, P.Q. J6T 3K9, 992-4573
Lapierre, Jean, Lib. (Shefford), House of Commons, Ottawa, Ont. K1A 0A6, 995-8886
Lapointe, Hon. Charles, Lib. (Charlevoix), C.P. 12, Tadoussac, P.Q. G0T 2A0, 995-1333
Lapointe, Normand, Lib. (Beauce), rue Principale, C.P. 61, St-Victor, Beauce, P.Q. G0H 2B0, 996-4974
La Salle, Hon. Roch, PC (Joliette), 92 15e rue, Crabtree, P.Q. J0K 1B0, 992-2639
Lawrence, Hon. Allan, PC (Durham-Northumberland), R.R. 1, Janetville, Ont. L0B 1K0, 992-8756
LeBlanc, Hon. Roméo, Lib. (Westmorland-Kent), House of Commons, Ottawa, Ont. K1A 0A6, 995-2211
Leduc, Jean-L., Lib. (Richelieu), House of Commons, Ottawa, Ont. K1A 0A6, 995-6411

Note: All phone numbers are Ottawa numbers.

Lefebvre, Thomas, Lib. (Pontiac-Gatineau-Labelle), Davidson, P.Q. J0X 1R0, 992-5373
Lewis, Douglas G., PC (Simcoe North), #903, 400 Slater St., Ottawa, Ont., 995-3532
Lewycky, Laverne M., NDP (Dauphin), House of Commons, Ottawa, Ont. K1A 0A6, 992-3394
Loiselle, Bernard, Lib. (Verchères), 130 rue St-Laurent, Beloeil, P.Q. J3G 2J3, 992-8514
Lonsdale, Bruce, Lib. (Timiskaming), House of Commons, Ottawa, Ont. K1A 0A6, 995-5577
Lumley, Hon. Edward C, Lib. (Stormont-Dundas), House of Commons, Ottawa, Ont. K1A 0A6, 995-9001
MacBain, Al, Lib. (Niagara Falls), House of Commons, Ottawa, Ont. K1A 0A6, 996-3374
MacDonald, Hon. Flora, PC (Kingston & the Islands), 82 Earl St., Kingston, Ont. K7L 2G7, 992-4883
MacEachen, Hon. Allan J., Lib. (Cape Breton Highlands-Canso), R.R. 1, Whycocomagh, Inverness Co., N.S. B0E 1N0, 992-9171
MacGuigan, Hon. Mark, Lib. (Windsor-Walkerville), 2020 Willistead Cres., Windsor, Ont. N8Y 1K5, 995-1851
Mackasey, Hon. Bryce, Lib. (Lincoln), House of Commons, Ottawa, Ont. K1A 0A6, 995-0153
MacKay, Hon. Elmer M., PC (Central Nova), Lorne, Pictou Co., N.S. B0K 1C0, 992-3590
MacLaren, Roy, Lib. (Etobicoke North), House of Commons, Ottawa, Ont. K1A 0A6, 995-7614
MacLellan, Russell, Lib. (Cape Breton-The Sydneys), House of Commons, Ottawa, Ont. K1A 0A6, 995-6459
Malépart, Jean-C., Lib. (Ste-Marie), House of Commons, Ottawa, Ont. K1A 0A6, 992-6779
Malone, Arnold, PC (Crowfoot), Camrose, Alta., 992-4460
Maltais, André, Lib. (Manicouagan), House of Commons, Ottawa, Ont. K1A 0A6, 996-1094
Manly, Jim, NDP (Cowichan-Malahat-The Islands), House of Commons, Ottawa, Ont. K1A 0A6, 996-4722
Marceau, Gilles, Lib. (Jonquière), 501 rue St-Bernard, Jonquière, P.Q. G7X 2T1, 992-3269
Massé, Paul-A., Lib. (St-Jean), House of Commons, Ottawa, Ont. K1A 0A6, 995-9141
Masters, Jack, Lib. (Thunder Bay-Nipigon), 153 Whalen St., Thunder Bay, Ont. P7A 7H9, 992-2406
Mayer, Charles, PC (Portage-Marquette), Box 640, Carberry, Man. R0K 0H0, 996-2508
Mazankowski, Hon. Don, PC (Vegreville), House of Commons, Ottawa, Ont. K1A 0A6, 995-1755
McCain, Fred, PC (Carleton-Charlotte), Box 37, Florenceville, N.B. E0J 1K0, 992-3061
McCauley, Gary F., Lib. (Moncton), House of Commons, Ottawa, Ont. K1A 0A6, 996-4476
McCuish, Lorne, PC (Prince George-Bulkley Valley), House of Commons, Ottawa, Ont. K1A 0A6, 996-7784
McDermid, John, PC (Brampton-Georgetown), House of Commons, Ottawa, Ont. K1A 0A6, 995-7321
McGrath, Hon. James A., PC (St. John's East), House of Commons, Ottawa, Ont. K1A 0A6, 998-1783
McKenzie, Dan, PC (Winnipeg-Assiniboine), House of Commons, Ottawa, Ont. K1A 0A6, 992-2143
McKinnon, Hon. Allan B., PC (Victoria), #504, 1420 Beach Dr., Victoria, B.C. V8S 2N8, 995-6255
McKnight, Bill, PC (Kindersley-Lloydminster), House of Commons, Ottawa, Ont. K1A 0A6, 995-8082
McLean, Walter, PC (Waterloo), House of Commons, Ottawa, Ont. K1A 0A6, 995-8281
McMillan, Thomas, PC (Hillsborough), House of Commons, Ottawa, Ont. K1A 0A6, 995-9537
McRae, Paul, Lib. (Thunder Bay-Atikokan), House of Commons, Ottawa, Ont. K1A 0A6, 992-6418
Miller, Ted, NDP (Nanaimo-Alberni), House of Commons, Ottawa, Ont. K1A 0A6, 995-0881
Mitchell, Margaret, NDP (Vancouver East), House of Commons, Ottawa, Ont. K1A 0A6, 992-6030
Mitges, Gus, PC (Grey-Simcoe), 579 10th St. E., Owen Sound, Ont. N4K 1S9, 992-2430
Munro, Donald W., PC (Esquimalt-Saanich), 5035 Lochside Dr., Cordova Bay, Victoria, B.C. V8Y 2G1, 996-3003
Munro, Hon. John C., Lib. (Hamilton East), House of Commons, Ottawa, Ont. K1A 0A6, 997-0002
Murphy, Rod, NDP (Churchill), House of Commons, Ottawa, Ont. K1A 0A6, 995-9732
Murta, Jack B., PC (Lisgar), Box 33, Graysville, Man. R0G 0T0, 992-4040
Neil, Douglas, PC (Moose Jaw), 1447 Grace St., Moose Jaw, Sask. S6H 3E1, 992-3178
Nicholson, Aideen, Lib. (Trinity), House of Commons, Ottawa, Ont. K1A 0A6, 992-8234
Nickerson, Dave, PC (Western Arctic), House of Commons, Ottawa, Ont. K1A 0A6, 995-9579
Nielsen, Hon. Erik, PC (Yukon), House of Commons, Ottawa, Ont. K1A 0A6, 992-3480
Nowlan, Patrick, PC (Annapolis Valley-Hants), House of Commons, Ottawa, Ont. K1A 0A6, 992-2815
Nystrom, Lorne E., NDP (Yorkton-Melville), House of Commons, Ottawa, Ont. K1A 0A6, 992-4473
Oberle, Frank, PC (Prince George-Peace River), House of Commons, Ottawa, Ont. K1A 0A6, 996-2316
Ogle, Bob, NDP (Saskatoon East), House of Commons, Ottawa, Ont. K1A 0A6, 996-4585
Olivier, Jacques, Lib. (Longueuil), House of Commons, Ottawa, Ont. K1A 0A6, 992-4633
Orlikow, David, NDP (Winnipeg North), 71 St. Cross St., Winnipeg, Man. R2W 3X9, 992-2289
Ostiguy, Marcel, Lib. (St-Hyacinthe), House of Commons, Ottawa, Ont. K1A 0A6, 995-0988
Ouellet, Hon. André, Lib. (Papineau), 2285 Virginia Dr., Ottawa, Ont. K1H 6R9, 995-8872
Paproski, Hon. Steven, PC (Edmonton North), House of Commons, Ottawa, Ont. K1A 0A6, 992-2503
Parent, Gilbert, Lib. (Welland), House of Commons, Ottawa, Ont. K1A 0A6, 992-2768
Parker, Sid, NDP (Kootenay East-Revelstoke), House of Commons, Ottawa, Ont. K1A 0A6, 992-3352
Patterson, Alex B., PC (Fraser Valley East), 33520 Marshall Rd., Abbotsford, B.C. V2S 1K9, 992-2940
Pelletier, Irénée, Lib. (Sherbrooke), 151 rue Ontario, Sherbrooke, P.Q. J1J 3P8, 992-8585
Penner, B. Keith, Lib. (Cochrane), House of Commons, Ottawa, Ont. K1A 0A6, 992-2919
Pepin, Hon. Jean-Luc, Lib. (Ottawa-Carleton), House of Commons, Ottawa, Ont. K1A 0A6, 996-7501
Peterson, Jim, Lib. (Willowdale), House of Commons, Ottawa, Ont. K1A 0A6, 995-5028
Pinard, Hon. Yvon, Lib. (Drummond), 10 Rogers Lane, Drummondville, P.Q. J2C 1H8, 995-5681
Portelance, Arthur, Lib. (Gamelin), #204, 6625 est rue Sherbrooke, Montreal, P.Q. H1N 1C7, 995-4014
Prud'homme, Marcel, Lib. (St-Denis), 428 est, rue Beaubien, Montréal, P.Q. H2S 1S3, 992-3560
Rae, Bob, NDP (Broadview-Greenwood), 5 Withrow Ave., Toronto, Ont. M4K 1C8, 995-0687
Regan, Hon. Gerald, Lib. (Halifax), House of Commons, Ottawa, Ont. K1A 0A6, 997-0622
Reid, Joe, PC (St. Catharines), House of Commons, Ottawa, Ont. K1A 0A6, 995-1013
Reid, Hon. John M., Lib.-Lab. (Kenora-Rainy River), Box 208, Kenora, Ont. P9N 3X3, 992-2772
Riis, Nelson A., NDP (Kamloops-Shuswap), House of Commons, Ottawa, Ont. K1A 0A6, 995-6931
Roberts, Hon. John, Lib. (St. Paul's), 641 St. Clair Ave. W., Toronto, Ont. M6C 1A7, 997-1441
Robinson, Svend J., NDP (Burnaby), House of Commons, Ottawa, Ont. K1A 0A6, 992-4026
Robinson, Wm. K., Lib. (Etobicoke-Lakeshore), 108 Riverwood Pkwy., Toronto, Ont. M8Y 4G1, 996-5597
Roche, Douglas, PC (Edmonton South), House of Commons, Ottawa, Ont. K1A 0A6, 992-2363
Rompkey, Hon. Wm., Lib. (Grand Falls-White Bay-Labrador), 4 Costello Ave., Ottawa, Ont. K2H 7C4, 996-4630

Rooney, David, Lib. (Bonavista-Trinity-Conception), House of Commons, Ottawa, Ont. K1A 0A6, 992-2291
Rose, Mark, NDP (Mission-Port Moody), House of Commons, Ottawa, Ont. K1A 0A6, 992-0511
Rossi, Carlo, Lib. (Bourassa), House of Commons, Ottawa, Ont. K1A 0A6, 996-0984
Roy, Marcel, Lib. (Laval), 66 ave Laval, Laval-des-Rapides, P.Q. H7N 3V4, 992-0657
Sargeant, Terry, NDP (Selkirk-Interlake), House of Commons, Ottawa, Ont. K1A 0A6, 992-9703
Sauvé, Hon. Jeanne, Lib. (Laval-des-Rapides), House of Commons, Ottawa, Ont. K1A 0A6, 992-5042
Savard, Raymond, Lib. (Verdun), 5555 boul. Champlain, Verdun, P.Q. H4H 1A2, 593-7556
Schellenberger, Stan, PC (Wetaskiwin), Box 2122, Spruce Grove, Alta. T0E 2C0, 996-3446
Schroder, Jim, Lib. (Guelph), 400 Slater St., Centre Town Plaza, Ottawa, Ont., 995-9241
Scott, Geoff, PC (Hamilton-Wentworth), House of Commons, Ottawa, Ont. K1A 0A6, 992-0611
Scott, Wm. C., PC (Victoria-Haliburton), Kinmount, Ont. K0M 2A0, 995-5822
Shields, Jack, PC (Athabasca), House of Commons, Ottawa, Ont. K1A 0A6, 995-9095
Siddon, Tom, PC (Richmond-South Delta), House of Commons, Ottawa, Ont. K1A 0A6, 995-4988
Simmons, Roger, Lib. (Burin-St. George's), House of Commons, Ottawa, Ont. K1A 0A6, 996-2084
Skelly, Raymond, NDP (Comox-Powell River), House of Commons, Ottawa, Ont. K1A 0A6, 995-0840
Smith, David, Lib. (Don Valley East), House of Commons, Ottawa, Ont. K1A 0A6, 995-2446
Speyer, Chris, PC (Cambridge), House of Commons, Ottawa, Ont. K1A 0A6, 995-8471
Stevens, Hon. Sinclair, PC (York-Peel), R.R. 3, King City, Ont. L0G 1K0, 992-3366
Stewart, Ronald, PC (Simcoe South), House of Commons, Ottawa, Ont. K1A 0A6, 995-3295
Tardif, Alain, Lib. (Richmond), House of Commons, Ottawa, Ont. K1A 0A6, 992-4501
Taylor, Gordon, PC (Bow River), House of Commons, Ottawa, Ont. K1A 0A6, 992-4964
Tessier, Claude, Lib. (Mégantic-Compton-Stanstead), 2946, rue Agnes, Lac Mégantic, P.Q. G6B 1K6, 992-2689
Thacker, Blaine A., PC (Lethbridge-Foothills), House of Commons, Ottawa, Ont. K1A 0A6, 995-4843
Thomson, John, PC (Calgary South), House of Commons, Ottawa, Ont. K1A 0A6, 992-4524
Tobin, Brian, Lib. (Humber-Port-au-Port-St. Barbe), House of Commons, Ottawa, Ont. K1A 0A6, 996-5509
Tousignant, Henri, Lib. (Témiscamingue), House of Commons, Ottawa, Ont. K1A 0A6, 995-1225
Towers, Gordon T., PC (Red Deer), 4134 35 St., Red Deer, Alta. T4N 0P8, 992-4171
Trudeau, Rt. Hon. Pierre Elliott, Lib. (Mount Royal), House of Commons, Ottawa, Ont. K1A 0A6, 992-4211
Turner, Charles, Lib. (London East), 290 Wellington Rd. S., London, Ont. N6C 4N9, 992-8070
Vankoughnet, Bill, PC (Hastings-Frontenac), 76 Robert St., Napanee, Ont. K7R 2M3, 992-4848
Veillette, Michel, Lib. (Champlain), #3, 105 rue Chapleau, Cap-de-la-Madeleine, P.Q. G8W 1B8, 995-9391
Waddell, Ian, NDP (Vancouver-Kingsway), House of Commons, Ottawa, Ont. K1A 0A6, 996-8036
Watson, Ian, Lib. (Châteauguay), 67 boul. d'Anjou, Châteauguay, P.Q. J6J 2R1, 992-0164
Weatherhead, David, Lib. (Scarborough West), House of Commons, Ottawa, Ont. K1A 0A6, 996-4758
Wenman, Robert L., PC (Fraser Valley West), 17081 4th Ave., Surrey, B.C., 992-1812
Whelan, Hon. Eugene F., Lib. (Essex-Windsor), 727 Front Rd. N., Amherstburg, Ont. N9V 2V6, 995-9133
Wilson, Hon. Michael H., PC (Etobicoke Centre), House of Commons, Ottawa, Ont. K1A 0A6, 995-7398
Wise, Hon. John, PC (Elgin), R.R. 4, St. Thomas, Ont. N5P 3S8, 992-2933
Wright, Bill, PC (Calgary North), House of Commons, Ottawa, Ont. K1A 0A6, 995-7813
Yanakis, Antonio, Lib. (Berthier-Maskinongé), 181 boul. Morin, Ville St-Gabriel, P.Q. J0K 2N0, 992-8072
Young, Neil, NDP (Beaches), House of Commons, Ottawa, Ont. K1A 0A6, 995-7246
Yurko, Wm. J., PC (Edmonton East), 12203 42 Ave., Edmonton, Alta. T6J 0X1, 593-5527

List of Electoral Districts, giving name of member. Refer to alphabetical list preceeding, for party affiliation, addresses and Ottawa phone numbers:

Abitibi PQ - René Gingras
Algoma Ont - Maurice Foster
Annapolis Valley-Hants NS - Patrick Nowlan
Argenteuil PQ - Robert Gourd
Assiniboia Sask - Len Gustafson
Athabasca Alta - Jack Shields
Beaches Ont - Neil Young
Beauce PQ - Normand Lapointe
Beauharnois-Salaberry PQ - Gérald Laniel
Bellechasse PQ - Alain Garant
Berthier-Maskinongé PQ - Antonio Yanakis
Blainville-Deux-Montagnes PQ - Francis Fox
Bonaventure-Iles-de-la-Madeleine PQ - Rémi Bujold
Bonavista-Trinity-Conception Nfld - David Rooney
Bourassa PQ - Carlo Rossi
Bow River Alta - Gordon Taylor
Brampton-Georgetown Ont - John McDermid
Brandon-Souris Man - Walter G. Dinsdale
Brant Ont - Derek Blackburn
Broadview-Greenwood Ont - Bob Rae
Bruce-Grey Ont - Gary Gurbin
Burin-St. George's Nfld - Roger Simmons
Burlington Ont - Bill Kempling
Burnaby BC - Svend J. Robinson
Calgary Centre Alta - Harvie Andre
Calgary East Alta - John Kushner
Calgary North Alta - Bill Wright
Calgary South Alta - John Thomson
Calgary West Alta - Jim Hawkes
Cambridge Ont - Chris Speyer
Cape Breton-East Richmond NS - David C. Dingwall
Cape Breton Highlands-Canso NS - Allan J. MacEachen
Cape Breton-The Sydneys NS - Russell MacLellan
Capilano BC - A. Ron Huntington
Cardigan PEI - W. Bennett Campbell
Cariboo-Chilcotin BC - Lorne Greenaway
Carleton-Charlotte NB - Fred McCain
Central Nova NS - Elmer M. MacKay
Chambly PQ - Raymond Dupont
Champlain PQ - Michel Veillette
Charlesbourg PQ - Pierre Bussières
Charlevoix PQ - Charles Lapointe
Châteauguay PQ - Ian Watson
Chicoutimi PQ - Marcel Dionne
Churchill Man - Rod Murphy
Cochrane Ont - B. Keith Penner
Comox-Powell River BC - Raymond Skelly
Cowichan-Malahat-The Islands BC - Jim Manly
Crowfoot Alta - Arnold Malone
Cumberland-Colchester NS - Robert C. Coates
Dartmouth-Halifax East NS - J. Michael Forrestall
Dauphin Man - Laverne M. Lewycky
Davenport Ont - Charles L. Caccia
Dollard PQ - Louis R. Desmarais
Don Valley East Ont - David Smith
Don Valley West Ont - John Bosley
Drummond PQ - Yvon Pinard
Durham-Northumberland Ont - Allan Lawrence
Duvernay PQ - Yves Demers

Note: All phone numbers are Ottawa numbers.

Edmonton East Alta - Wm. J. Yurko
Edmonton North Alta - Steven Paproski
Edmonton South Alta - Douglas Roche
Edmonton-Strathcona Alta - David Kilgour
Edmonton West Alta - Marcel Lambert
Eglinton-Lawrence Ont - Roland de Corneille
Egmont PEI - George R. Henderson
Elgin Ont - John Wise
Erie Ont - Girve Fretz
Esquimalt-Saanich BC - Donald W. Munro
Essex-Kent Ont - Robert Daudlin
Essex-Windsor Ont - Eugene F. Whelan
Etobicoke Centre Ont - Michael H. Wilson
Etobicoke-Lakeshore Ont - Wm. K. Robinson
Etobicoke North Ont - Roy MacLaren
Fraser Valley East BC - Alex B. Patterson
Fraser Valley West BC - Robert L. Wenman
Frontenac PQ - Léopold Corriveau
Fundy-Royal NB - R.A. Corbett
Gamelin PQ - Arthur Portelance
Gander-Twillingate Nfld - George Baker
Gaspé PQ - Alexandre Cyr
Gatineau PQ - René Cousineau
Glengarry-Prescott-Russell Ont - Denis Ethier
Gloucester NB - Herbert Breau
Grand Falls-White Bay-Labrador Nfld - Wm. Rompkey
Grey-Simcoe Ont - Gus Mitges
Guelph Ont - Jim Schroder
Haldimand-Norfolk Ont - T.A. Bradley
Halifax NS - Gerald Regan
Halifax West NS - Howard E. Crosby
Halton Ont - Otto Jelinek
Hamilton East Ont - John C. Munro
Hamilton Mountain Ont - Ian Deans
Hamilton-Wentworth Ont - Geoff Scott
Hamilton West Ont - Stanley Hudecki
Hastings-Frontenac Ont - Bill Vankoughnet
Hillsborough PEI - Thomas McMillan
Hochelaga-Maisonneuve PQ - Serge Joyal
Hull PQ - Gaston Isabelle
Humber-Port-au-Port-St. Barbe Nfld - Brian Tobin
Humboldt-Lake Centre Sask - Vic Althouse
Huron-Bruce Ont - J. Murray Cardiff
Joliette PQ - Roch La Salle
Jonquière PQ - Gilles Marceau
Kamloops-Shuswap BC - Nelson A. Riis
Kamouraska-Rivière-du-Loup PQ - Rosaire Gendron
Kenora-Rainy River Ont - John M. Reid
Kent Ont - Maurice Bossy
Kindersley-Lloydminster Sask - Bill McKnight
Kingston & the Islands Ont - Flora MacDonald
Kitchener Ont - Peter Lang
Kootenay East-Revelstoke BC - Sid Parker
Kootenay West BC - Lyle Kristiansen
Labelle PQ - Maurice Dupras
Lachine PQ - Rod Blaker
Lac-St-Jean PQ - Pierre Gimaiel
Lambton-Middlesex Ont - Ralph Ferguson
Lanark-Renfrew-Carleton Ont - Paul Dick
Langelier PQ - J. Gilles Lamontagne
Laprairie PQ - Pierre Deniger
LaSalle PQ - John J. Campbell
Laurier PQ - David Berger
Laval PQ - Marcel Roy
Laval-des-Rapides PQ - Jeanne Sauvé
Leeds-Grenville Ont - Tom Cossitt
Lethbridge-Foothills Alta - Blaine A. Thacker
Lévis PQ - Gaston Gourde
Lincoln Ont - Bryce Mackasey
Lisgar Man - Jack B. Murta
London East Ont - Charles Turner
London-Middlesex Ont - Garnet M. Bloomfield
London West Ont - Jack Burghardt
Longueuil PQ - Jacques Olivier
Lotbinière PQ - Jean-Guy Dubois
Louis-Hébert PQ - Dennis Dawson
Mackenzie Sask - Stanley J. Korchinski
Madawaska-Victoria NB - Eymard E. Corbin
Malpeque PEI - Mel Gass
Manicouagan PQ - André Maltais
Matapédia-Matane PQ - Pierre De Bané
Medicine Hat Alta - Bert Hargrave
Mégantic-Compton-Stanstead PQ - Claude Tessier
Mercier PQ - Céline Hervieux-Payette
Mission-Port Moody BC - Mark Rose
Missisquoi PQ - André Bachand
Mississauga North Ont - Douglas Fisher
Mississauga South Ont - Don Blenkarn
Moncton NB - Gary F. McCauley
Montmorency PQ - Louis Duclos
Moose Jaw, Sask - Douglas Neil
Mount Royal PQ - Pierre Elliott Trudeau
Nanaimo-Alberni BC - Ted Miller
Nepean-Carleton Ont - Walter Baker
New Westminster-Coquitlam BC - Pauline Jewett
Niagara Falls Ont - Al MacBain
Nickel Belt Ont - Judy Erola
Nipissing Ont - Jean-Jacques Blais
Northumberland Ont - George Hees
Northumberland-Miramichi NB - Maurice A. Dionne
North Vancouver-Burnaby BC - Chuck Cook
Notre-Dame-de-Grâce PQ - Warren Allmand
Nunatsiaq NWT - Peter Ittinuar
Okanagan North BC - Vincent M. Dantzer
Okanagan-Similkameen BC - Fred King
Ontario Ont - Scott Fennell
Oshawa Ont - Edward Broadbent
Ottawa-Carleton Ont - Jean-Luc Pepin
Ottawa Centre Ont - John Evans
Ottawa-Vanier Ont - Jean-R. Gauthier
Ottawa West Ont - Lloyd Francis
Outremont PQ - Marc Lalonde
Oxford Ont - Bruce Halliday
Papineau PQ - André Ouellet
Parkdale-High Park Ont - Jesse P. Flis
Parry Sound-Muskoka Ont - Stan Darling
Peace River Alta - Albert Cooper
Pembina Alta - Peter Elzinga
Perth Ont - Wm. Jarvis
Peterborough Ont - Bill Domm
Pontiac-Gatineau-Labelle PQ - Thomas Lefebvre
Portage-Marquette Man - Charles Mayer
Portneuf PQ - Rolland Dion
Prince Albert Sask - Stan J. Hovdebo
Prince Edward-Hastings Ont - Jack Ellis
Prince George-Bulkley Valley BC - Lorne McCuish
Prince George-Peace River BC - Frank Oberle
Provencher Man - Jake Epp
Qu'Appelle-Moose Mountain Sask - Alvin Hamilton
Québec-Est PQ - Gérard Duquet
Red Deer Alta - Gordon T. Towers
Regina East Sask - Simon de Jong
Regina West Sask - L.G. Benjamin
Renfrew-Nipissing-Pembroke Ont - Leonard D. Hopkins
Restigouche NB - Maurice Harquail
Richelieu PQ - Jean-Louis Leduc
Richmond PQ - Alain Tardif
Richmond-South Delta BC - Tom Siddon
Rimouski-Témiscouata PQ - Eva Côté
Roberval PQ - Suzanne Beauchamp-Niquet
Rosedale Ont - David Crombie
Rosemont PQ - Claude-A. Lachance
St-Denis PQ - Marcel Prud'homme
St-Henri-Westmount PQ - Donald J. Johnston
St-Hyacinthe PQ - Marcel Ostiguy
St-Jacques PQ - Jacques Guilbault
St-Jean PQ - Paul-André Massé
Saint John NB - Mike Landers
St-Léonard-Anjou PQ - Monique Bégin
Ste-Marie PQ - Jean-C. Malépart

St-Maurice PQ - Jean Chrétien
St-Michel PQ - Thérèse Killens
St. Boniface Man - Robert Bockstael
St. Catharines Ont - Joe Reid
St. John's East Nfld - James A. McGrath
St. John's West Nfld - John C. Crosbie
St. Paul's Ont - John Roberts
Sarnia Ont - Bud Cullen
Saskatoon East Sask - Bob Ogle
Saskatoon West Sask - Ramon Hnatyshyn
Sault Ste. Marie Ont - Ron Irwin
Scarborough Centre Ont - Norm Kelly
Scarborough East Ont - Gordon Gilchrist
Scarborough West Ont - David Weatherhead
Selkirk-Interlake Man - Terry Sargeant
Shefford PQ - Jean Lapierre
Sherbrooke PQ - Irénée Pelletier
Simcoe North Ont - Douglas G. Lewis
Simcoe South Ont - Ronald Stewart
Skeena BC - Jim Fulton
South Shore NS - Lloyd R. Crouse
South West Nova NS - Coline Campbell
Spadina Ont - Rev. Daniel Heaps
Stormont-Dundas Ont - Edward C. Lumley
Sudbury Ont - Douglas C. Frith
Surrey-White Rock-North Delta BC - Benno Friesen
Swift Current-Maple Creek Sask - Frank Hamilton
Témiscamingue PQ - Henri Tousignant
Terrebonne PQ - J.-R. Comtois
The Battlefords-Meadow Lake Sask - Doug Anguish
Thunder Bay-Atikokan Ont - Paul McRae
Thunder Bay-Nipigon Ont - Jack Masters
Timiskaming Ont - Bruce Lonsdale
Timmins-Chapleau Ont - J. Raymond Chénier
Trinity Ont - Aideen Nicholson
Trois-Rivières PQ - Claude G. Lajoie
Vancouver Centre BC - Pat Carney
Vancouver East BC - Margaret Mitchell
Vancouver Kingsway BC - Ian Waddell
Vancouver Quadra BC - Bill Clarke
Vancouver South BC - John A. Fraser
Vaudreuil PQ - Hal Herbert
Vegreville Alta - Don Mazankowski
Verchères PQ - Bernard Loiselle
Verdun PQ - Raymond Savard
Victoria BC - Allan B. McKinnon
Victoria-Haliburton Ont - Wm. C. Scott
Waterloo Ont - Walter McLean
Welland Ont - Gilbert Parent
Wellington-Dufferin-Simcoe Ont - Perrin Beatty
Western Arctic NWT - Dave Nickerson
Westmorland-Kent NB - Roméo LeBlanc
Wetaskiwin Alta - Stan Schellenberger
Willowdale Ont - Jim Peterson
Windsor-Walkerville Ont - Mark MacGuigan
Windsor West Ont - Herb Gray
Winnipeg-Assiniboine Man - Dan McKenzie
Winnipeg-Birds Hill Man - Wm. Blaikie
Winnipeg-Fort Garry Man - Lloyd Axworthy
Winnipeg North Man - David Orlikow
Winnipeg North Centre Man - Stanley H. Knowles
Winnipeg-St. James Man - Cyril Keeper
Yellowhead Alta - Joseph Clark
York Centre Ont - Bob Kaplan
York East Ont - David M. Collenette
York North Ont - John Gamble
York-Peel Ont - Sinclair Stevens
York-Scarborough Ont - Paul J. Cosgrove
York South-Weston Ont - Ursula Appolloni
York-Sudbury NB - J. Robert Howie
York West Ont - Jim Fleming
Yorkton-Melville Sask - Lorne E. Nystrom
Yukon (YT) - Erik Nielsen

SALARIES & ALLOWANCES

Members of the Senate receive a sessional allowance of $43,800 per annum. Members of the House of Commons receive $43,800. In addition, for each session of Parliament, they may be paid travelling expenses between their place of residence or constituency and Ottawa. Senators receive an annual expense allowance of $7,200, and members of the House of Commons an annual expense allowance of $14,700; which are paid quarterly and are not subject to income tax. *All payments enumerated below are in addition to the sessional and expense allowances and are per annum.* The Prime Minister: $50,000; a Cabinet Minister and the Leader of the Opposition in the House of Commons: $33,600; a Leader of a Party that has a recognized membership of twelve or more persons in the House of Commons: $20,200; the Chief Government Whip and the Chief Opposition Whip: $9,300; the Speaker of the House of Commons: $33,600; the Deputy Speaker of the House of Commons: $17,700

Office of the PRIME MINISTER

Langevin Block, Parliament Bldgs., Ottawa, Ont. K1A OA2
The Rt. Hon. Pierre Elliott Trudeau, 992-4211
Private Secretary, Cécile Viau, 996-1774
Executive Assistant, T. Johnson, 992-4211
Principal Secretary, T. Axworthy, 995-0312
Executive Assistant to Principal Secretary, Marie-Helene Fox, 992-7193
Legislative Assistant, Joyce Fairbairn, 996-1945
Press Secretary, P. Gossage, 992-7362
Nominations Secretary, Geoffrey O'Brian, 995-7861
Special Assistants, A. Burelle, J. Moore, R. Coleman
Correspondence Co-ordinator, Patrick McDonald, 996-4008

FEDERAL GOVERNMENT DEPARTMENTS & AGENCIES

DEPT. OF AGRICULTURE

Sir John Carling Bldg., 930 Carling Ave., Ottawa, Ont. K1A OC5
Information Contact, A.E. Caldwell, Director General, Information Services, Phone: (613) 995-8963

The Department conducts research, grades and inspects farm products, prevents and controls diseases and pests of crops and livestock, promotes high-quality seed and purebred livestock, and administers price stability and other policies to help solve production and marketing problems of agriculture in Canada. The results of work in these various fields and information on the policies of the Dept. are made available to the public.

Acts Administered

Advance Payments for Crops Act
Agricultural Products Board Act
Agricultural Products Co-operative Marketing Act
Agricultural Products Marketing Act
Agricultural Stabilization Act
Animal Disease & Protection Act
Canada Agricultural Products Standards Act
Canada Dairy Products Act
Canada Grain Act
Canadian Dairy Commission Act
Cheese & Cheese Factory Improvement Act
Cold Storage Act
Criminal Code, Sec. 188, Racetrack Supervision

Crop Insurance Act
Dept. of Agriculture Act
Experimental Farm Stns. Act
Farm Credit Act
Farm Improvement Loans Act
Farm Products Marketing Agencies Act
Farm Syndicates Credit Act
Feeds Act
Fertilizers Act
Foot & Mouth Disease, Control & Extirpation Act
Fruit, Vegetables & Honey Act
Grain Futures Act
Hay & Straw Inspection Act
Humane Slaughter of Food Animals Act
Inland Water Freight Rates Act
Inspection & Sale Act
Livestock & Livestock Products Act
Livestock Feed Assistance Act
Livestock Pedigree Act
Maple Products Industry Act
Meat & Canned Foods Act
Meat Inspection Act
Milk Test Act
Pest Control Products Act
Pesticide Residue Compensation Act
Plant Quarantine Act
Prairie Farm Assistance Act
Seeds Act
Wheat Co-operative Marketing Act

MINISTER, Hon. Eugene F. Whelan
Policy Advisor, P.W. Christensen
Admin. Asst., N. Morris
Res. Asst., M.A. Allen
Special Assts., L. Durnbeck; E. Di Emanuele
Parliamentary Secretary, Marcel Ostiguy
Deputy Minister, Gaétan Lussier, B.S.A., M.Sc., Hon. Ph.D.
Executive Asst., B. Howard
Departmental Secretary, D.F. Kirkland
Senior Secretariat Officer, F. Lemon
Director General, Management Accountability, W.B. Mountain, Ph.D.
Senior Asst. Deputy Minister (Policy Advisor), G.I. Trant, Ph.D.

Personnel Administration Branch

Director General, S.J. Whitney (Branch includes: Field Personnel Programs; Staffing & Development; Classification; Staff Relations; Official Languages)

Finance & Administration Branch

Asst. Deputy Minister, A.G. Ross, C.A. (Branch includes: Financial Admin.; Systems & Consulting; Admin.; Libraries; Internal Audit)

Strategic Planning & Evaluation Branch

Director General, J.E. Cox, Dip. T.P. (Nottm)

Information Services

Director General, A.E. Caldwell

Regional Development & International Affairs Branch

Asst. Deputy Minister, C.F. Brouillard
Director, Federal-Provincial Relations Directorate, W.H. Jarvis
Director General, International Affairs Directorate, J.R. McQueen
Director, Overseas Projects Division, J.P. Ferland
Director, International Liaison Service, A. Renaud, Ph.D.
Director General, Production Development Directorate, F. Payne, B.S.A.
Director, Animal Production Division, J.H. Cochran, B.Sc. (Agr.)
Director, Crop Production Division, S.W. Garland, B.S.A.
Director, Farm Development Division, W.A. McBride, Ph.D.
Director General, Regional Development Directorate, P.C.W. Caskey, B.A.
Director, Production Analysis Division, B.B. Perkins, Ph.D.
Director, Development Analysis & Co-ordination Division, G. Forrester
Regional Development Directors:
Newfoundland, T. Espie, Ph.D.
Prince Edward Island, J. Lowering, Ph.D.
Nova Scotia, D. Byers, Ph.D.
New Brunswick, L.P. Albert, M.A.
Quebec, G. Grammond, M.Sc. (Econ.)
Ontario, N. Ball
Manitoba, J. Wiens
Saskatchewan, G. Gorrell, B.S.A.
Alberta, W.J. Lockhart, M.Sc. (Ag. Econ.)
British Columbia, J. Berry, B.Sc. (Agr.)

Food Production & Inspection Branch

Asst. Deputy Minister, J.E. McGowan, D.V.M.
Director General, Veterinary Inspection (Operations), V.I. Reed, D.V.M.
Director General, Production & Inspection (Operations), R. Roy, M.Sc.
Director General, Health of Animals, C. L'Ecuyer, D.V.M.
Director, Animal Health Division, I.R. Reid, D.V.M.
Director, Animal Pathology Division, N.G. Willis, D.V.M.
Director General, Food Inspection, J.B. Morrissey, D.V.M.
Director, Meat Hygiene Division, M.G. Morissette, D.V.M.
Director, Livestock & Poultry Division, M.S. Mitchell, M.Sc.
Director, Dairy, Fruit & Vegetable Division, D.S. MacLachlan, Ph.D.
Director, Laboratory Services Division, G.D. Ritchie, M.S.
Director, Plant Products & Quarantine Division, R.E. Wight, M.S.A.
Director, Racetrack Division, B. Toews
Director, Finance & Admin. Division, K.P. Riley, B.Comm.
Director, Planning & Analysis Division, M.E. Doyle, B.A.
Director, Program Co-ordination Division, D. Harkin

Marketing & Economics Branch

Asst. Deputy Minister, Yvan Jacques
Director General, Market Development, P.W. Couse, B.S.A.
Director, Marketing Services Division, C.E. Hill
Director, Market Improvement Division, R. Stern
Director, Food Processing & Distribution Division, P. Sterne, M.B.A.
Director, Food & Nutrition Services, N.W. Tape, Ph.D.
Director General, Market Analysis & Trade Policy, S. Borland, Ph.D.
Director, Food Markets Analysis Division, H. Migie, M.A. (Econ.)
Director, Commodity Markets Analysis Division, D.D. Hedley, Ph.D.
Director, International Trade Policy Division, G.J. Dobson, Ph.D.

Research Branch

Asst. Deputy Minister, E.J. LeRoux, Ph.D.
Executive Asst., D.J.E. Demars, Ph.D.
Senior Advisor, International Research & Development, T.H. Anstey, Ph.D.
Director General, Atlantic Region, E.E. Lister, Ph.D.
Director General, Quebec Region, J.J. Jasmin, M.Sc.
Director General, Ontario Region, J.J. Cartier, Ph.D.
Director General, Western Region, A.A. Guitard, Ph.D.
Director General, Institutes & Program Co-ordination Directorate, J.W. Morrison, Ph.D.
Director, Finance & Admin. Division, J.E. Ryan, R.I.A.

Research Co-ordinators & Analysts

Animals, F.K. Kristjansson, Ph.D.
Crops, W.J. Saidak, Ph.D.
Food, R.R. Riel, Ph.D.
Production, C.J. Bishop, Ph.D.

Protection, R.M. Prentice, M.Sc.
Resources, R.L. Halstead, Ph.D., J. Nowland, Ph.D.
Program, J.C. St-Pierre, Ph.D.
Contracts, J.R. Aitken, Ph.D.

Special Advisors

Programs, L. Dessureaux, Ph.D.
Resources, W.B. Baier, M.Sc.

Directors, Research Centres, Institutes & Services:

Animal Research Centre, R.S. Gowe, Ph.D.
Chemistry & Biology Research Institute, I. de la Roche, Ph.D.
Biosystematics Research Institute, G.A. Mulligan, M.Sc.
Food Research Institute, J. Holme, Ph.D.
Land Resource Research Institute, J.S. Clark, Ph.D.
Research Centre, London, Ont., H.V. Morley, Ph.D.
Engineering & Statistical Research Institute, P.W. Voisey, F.I. Mech. E.
Research Program Service, R. Trottier, Ph.D.

Directors, Research Stations:

St. John's West, Nfld., H.W.R. Chancey, M.S.A.
Charlottetown, P.E.I., L.B. MacLeod, Ph.D.
Kentville, N.S., G.M. Weaver, Ph.D.
Fredericton, N.B., C.S. Bernard, Ph.D.
Ste-Foy, P.Q., S.J. Bourget, Ph.D.
Lennoxville, P.Q., Y. Martel, Ph.D.
St-Jean, P.Q., C.B. Aubé, Ph.D.
Delhi, Ont., vacant
Ottawa, Ont., T. Rajhathy, M.Sc.
Harrow, Ont., C.G. Marks, Ph.D.
Vineland Stn., Ont., vacant
Brandon, Man., B.H. Sonntag, Ph.D.
Morden, Man., D.K. McBeath, Ph.D.
Winnipeg, Man., D.G. Dorrell, Ph.D.
Melfort, Sask., S.E. Beacom, Ph.D.
Regina, Sask., vacant
Saskatoon, Sask., J.R. Hay, Ph.D.
Swift Current, Sask., W.L. Pelton, Ph.D.
Beaverlodge, Alta., L.P.S. Spangelo, Ph.D.
Lacombe, Alta., D.E. Waldern, Ph.D.
Lethbridge, Alta., J.E. Andrews, Ph.D.
Agassiz, B.C., J.E. Miltimore, Ph.D.
Kamloops, B.C., J.D. McElgunn, Ph.D.
Sidney, B.C., J.M. Molnar, Ph.D.
Summerland, B.C., G.C. Russell, Ph.D.
Vancouver, B.C., M. Weintraub, Ph.D.

Canadian Grain Commission

303 Main St., Winnipeg, Man. R3C 3G8
Chief Commr., H.D. Pound
Asst. Chief Commr., G.G. Leith
Commr., R.H. Harland
Executive Director, E.E. Baxter
Director, Inspection Division, V. Duke
Director, Grain Research Laboratory, Dr. K.H. Tipples
Director, Weighing Division, J.S.T. Swanson
Director, Economics & Statistics Division, D.N. Kennedy
Asst. Commrs.:
Man.: (vacant), Winnipeg
Sask.: J.H. Davidson, Regina; W.J. McHugh, Saskatoon
Alta.: G. Marshall, Calgary
Ont.: R. Clark, Harrow
Que.: L. Beaudoin, North Hatley

Marketing Agencies

National Farm Products Marketing Council
Place de Ville, Centre Bldg., 2nd floor, 300 Sparks St., Ottawa, Ont. K1R 7S3
(613) 995-2297
Chairman, J. Menzies
Canadian Egg Marketing Agency
116 Albert St., Ottawa, Ont. K1P 5G3
(613) 238-2514
General Manager, Jean Brassard
Canadian Turkey Marketing Agency
44 Peel Centre Dr., Brampton, Ont. L6T 4B5
(416) 792-3500
A/General Manager, M. Krowchuck
Canadian Chicken Marketing Agency
44 Peel Centre Dr., Brampton, Ont. L6T 4B5
(416) 792-6622
General Manager, R. LeBlanc

Agriculture Departmental & Agency Regional Offices:

FARM CREDIT CORP.
2255 Carling Ave., Ottawa, Ont. K2A 3W9
Regional Locations:
B.C.: 1451 Ellis St., Kelowna, B.C. V1Y 7N5
Alta.: 400 Chancery Hall, 3 Sir Winston Churchill Sq., Edmonton, Alta. T5J 2C5
Sask.: 500 South Broad Plaza, 2045 Broad St., Regina, Sask. S4P 2B7
Man.: 777 Portage Ave., Winnipeg, Man. R3G 3L1
Ont.: 105 Silvercreek Pkwy N., Guelph, Ont. N1H 7G7
Que.: 2700 Laurier Blvd., Ste-Foy, P.Q. G1V 4C7
Atlantic: 1133 St. George Blvd., Moncton, N.B. E1C 8N6

CANADIAN DAIRY COMMISSION
2197 Riverside Dr., Ottawa, Ont. K1A OZ2

CANADIAN GRAIN COMMISSION
303 Main St., Winnipeg, Man. R3C 3G8

AGRICULTURAL STABILIZATION BOARD
Sir John Carling Bldg., 930 Carling Ave., Ottawa, Ont. K1A OC5

AGRICULTURAL PRODUCTS BOARD
Sir John Carling Bldg., 930 Carling Ave., Ottawa, Ont. K1A OC5

CANADIAN LIVESTOCK FEED BOARD
5180 Queen Mary Rd., Montreal, P.Q. H3X 1T8
Branch Office:
17655 57th Ave., Surrey (Cloverdale), B.C. V3T 1H1

NATIONAL FARM PRODUCTS MARKETING COUNCIL
300 Sparks St., Ottawa, Ont. K1R 7S3

PERSONNEL ADMIN. BRANCH
Headquarters:
Sir John Carling Bldg., 930 Carling Ave., Ottawa, Ont. K1A OC5
Field Locations:
N.B.:
Atlantic Region Personnel Office, 1222 Main St., Moncton, N.B. E1C 8R2
Que.:
Que. Region Personnel Office, 200, 4221 St. Catherine St. W., Montreal, P.Q. H3Z 1P6
Ont.:
Ottawa-Hull Region Personnel Office, 580 Booth St., Ottawa, Ont. K1A OY9
Ont. Region Personnel Office, 4900 Yonge St., Willowdale, Ont. M2N 6B9
Man.:
Man.-Sask. Region Personnel Office, 401, 303 Main St., Winnipeg, Man. R3C 3G7
Sask.:
Sask. Dist. Personnel Office, 403 Financial Bldg., 230 22nd St. E., Saskatoon, Sask. S7K OE9
Alta.:
Alta.-B.C. Region Personnel Office, Box 2916, Stn. M, Calgary, Alta. T2P 3C3
B.C.:
B.C. Dist. Personnel Office, 350, 625 Howe St., Vancouver, B.C. V6C 2T6

FINANCE & ADMIN. BRANCH
Sir John Carling Bldg., 930 Carling Ave., Ottawa, Ont. K1A OC5

INFORMATION SERVICES
Sir John Carling Bldg., 930 Carling Ave., Ottawa, Ont. K1A OC7

REGIONAL DEVELOPMENT & INTERNATIONAL AFFAIRS BRANCH
Headquarters: Sir John Carling Bldg., 930 Carling Ave., Ottawa, Ont. K1A OC5
Regional Offices:
Nfld.: Box 7098, St. John's, Nfld. A1E 3Y3
P.E.I.: Box 1210, Charlottetown, P.E.I. C1A 7M8
N.S.: Box 698, Truro, N.S. B2N 5E5
N.B.: Box 20280, Fredericton, N.B. E3B 4Z7
Que.: 2815 boul. Laurier, Ste-Foy, P.Q. G1V 2L9
Ont.: 102 Bloor St. W., Toronto, Ont. M5S 1M8
Man.: 303 Main St., Winnipeg, Man. R3C 3H5
Sask.: 1955 Smith St., Regina, Sask. S4P 2N9
Alta.: 10621 100th Ave., Edmonton, Alta. T5J OB3
B.C.: 816 Government St., Victoria, B.C. V8W 1W9

FOOD PRODUCTION & INSPECTION BRANCH
Headquarters: Sir John Carling Bldg., 930 Carling Ave., Ottawa, Ont. K1A 0C5

Regional offices - Veterinary Inspection (Operations) Directorate:
Terminal Plaza Bldg., 1222 Main St., Moncton, N.B. E1C 8L4
685 Cathcart St., Montreal, P.Q. H3B 1M7
909 Jane St., Toronto, Ont. M6N 4C6
Federal Bldg., 269 Main St., Winnipeg, Man. R3C 1B2
Federal Bldg., 1975 Scarth St., Regina, Sask. S4P 2H3
Govt. of Canada Bldg., 220 4th Ave. S.E., Calgary, Alta. T2P 3C3
1001 W. Pender St., Vancouver, B.C. V6E 2M7

Regional offices - Production & Inspection (Operations) Directorate:
Sir Humphrey Gilbert Bldg., St. John's, Nfld. A1C 5W8
Terminal Plaza Bldg., 1222 Main St., Moncton, N.B. E1C 9A7
Sternthal Bldg., 1435 St. Alexandre St., Montreal, P.Q. H3A 2G4
Kinhurst Bldg., 160 Springhurst Ave., Toronto, Ont. M6K 1C3
Federal Bldg., 269 Main St., Winnipeg, Man. R3C 1B2
Motherwell Bldg., 1901 Victoria Ave., Regina, Sask. S4P 3W5
Federal Bldg., 9820 107 St., Edmonton, Alta. T5K 1E7
1001 W. Pender St., Vancouver, B.C. V6E 2M7

Regional offices - Racetrack Division:
6074 Hammond Rd., Halifax, N.S. B3K 2R7
8180 Devonshire Rd., Montreal, P.Q. H4P 2K3
6700 Finch Ave. W., Rexdale, Ont. M9W 5P5
1400 Merivale Rd., Ottawa, Ont. K2G 3N7
2747 E. Hastings St., Vancouver, B.C. V5K 1Z8

Regional establishments - Animal Pathology Division of Health of Animals Directorate:
Animal Diseases Research Institute (Eastern), 810 Fallowfield Rd., Ottawa, Ont. K2H 8P9
Animal Diseases Research Institute (Western), Box 640, Lethbridge, Alta. T1J 3Z4
Animal Pathology Laboratory (Atlantic Area), Box 1410, Sackville, N.B. E0A 3C0
Animal Pathology Laboratory, 3000 Sicotte St., St-Hyacinthe, P.Q. J2S 2L8
Animal Pathology Laboratory, 620 Gordon St., Guelph, Ont. N1G 1Y4
Animal Pathology Laboratory, 269 Main St., Winnipeg, Man. R3C 1B2
Animal Pathology Laboratory, 116 Veterinary Rd., Saskatoon, Sask. S7N 2R3
Animal Pathology Laboratory, 3802 W. 4th Ave., Vancouver, B.C. V6R 1P5

AUDITOR GENERAL'S OFFICE

240 Sparks St., Ottawa, Ont. K1A OG6
(613) 995-3766

The Auditor General is responsible for examining the accounts relating to government departments, Crown Corporations and other public instrumentalities. The Auditor General reports annually to the House of Commons the results of his examinations.

Auditor General, Kenneth M. Dye

Regional Offices
Ste. 301, 1888 Brunswick St., Halifax, N.S. B3J 3J8
Room 1005, 685 Cathcart St., Montreal, P.Q. H3B 1M7
4900 Yonge St., Willowdale, Ont. M2N 6A4
#1545, 155 Carlton St., Winnipeg, Man. R3C 3H8
Room 302, Financial Bldg., 2101 Scarth St., Regina, Sask. S4P 2H9
#420, 10909 Jasper Ave., Edmonton, Alta. T5J 3L9
550 Pacific Centre, 701 W. Georgia St., Vancouver, B.C. V7Y 1B6

CANADIAN HUMAN RIGHTS COMMISSION

257 Slater St., Ottawa, Ont. KIA 1E1
(613) 996-2558; visual ear # 996-5211
Information Officer, Sally Jackson

Regional Offices
Atlantic: (#212, 5675 Spring Garden Rd.), Box 3545 South, Halifax, N.S. B3J 3J2 (902/426-8380)
Quebec: 2021 Union Ave., #1115, Montréal, P.Q. H3A 2S9 (514/283-5218)
Ontario: 55 St. Clair Ave. E., #623, Toronto, Ont. M4T 1M2 (416/966-5527)
Prairie: 323 Portage Ave., #211, Winnipeg, Man. R3B 2C1 (204/949-2189; visual ear # 949-2882)
Alberta & N.W.T.: 10506 Jasper Ave., #416, Edmonton, Alta. T5J 2W9 (403/420-4040)
Western: 789 W. Pender St., #1002, Vancouver, B.C. V6C 1H2 (604/666-2251)

CANADIAN INTERNATIONAL DEVELOPMENT AGENCY

Place du Centre, 200 Promenade du Portage, Hull, P.Q. K1A 0G4
(819) 997-5456

The Agency administers Canada's international development programs.

President, Marcel Massé
Senior Vice President, W. McWhinney
Vice President, Policy, G. Shortliffe
Vice President, Multilateral Programs, D. Lindores
Vice President, Bilateral Programs, N. Power
Vice President, Comptroller, D. Aitchison
Vice President, Resources, P. Sicard
Vice President, Special Programs, L. Perinbam
Director General, Personnel & Administration, C. Bassett
Director General, Industrial Co-operation, G. Lambert
Director General, Public Affairs, Ann C. Jamieson
Director, Consultant & Industrial Relations, M.C. Sutherland-Brown

CANADIAN JUDICIAL COUNCIL

130 Albert St., Ottawa, Ont. K1A OW8
Phone: (613) 992-1944
Secretary, Pierre Chamberland

(The members of the Council are the Chief Justice of Canada, who is the Chairman, and the Chief Justices and Associate Chief Justices of each Superior Court or Branch or Division thereof).

CANADIAN RADIO-TELEVISION & TELECOMMUNICATIONS COMMISSION

Ottawa, Ont. K1A ON2
(819) 997-0313 (Information Services)

The Commission supervises and regulates broadcasting and telecommunications in Canada, and issues and renews licences to broadcasting stations.

Chairman, John Meisel, 997-3430
Vice Chairmen, John Lawrence, 997-3831; Réal Therrien, 997-3917
Commrs., J.-L. Gagnon, Rosalie Gower, John Grace, Paul Klingle, Jeanne LaSalle, James Robson
and the following part-time members chosen regionally:
Marianne Barrie, St. Thomas
Richard DeStafano, Sudbury

Marc Gervais, Sherbrooke
Edythe Goodridge, St. John's
Steve Patrick, Winnipeg
Marke K. Raines, Burnaby
Gilles Soucy, Campbellton
Executive Director, Corporate Management, Eric Boyd
Senior Executive Director, Operations, K.L. Wyman
Executive Director, Broadcasting, Lise Ouimet
Executive Director, Telecommunications, vacant
Secretary General, J.G. Patenaude (997-1027)
General Counsel, Avrum Cohen (act.)

CANADIAN TRANSPORT COMMISSION

Ottawa, Ont. K1A ON9
(819) 997-0677

Information concerning this Commission can be obtained from the Secretary, above address.

Western Division, Canadian Transport Commission

3rd floor, 350 3rd Ave. N., Saskatoon, Sask. S7K 6G7

Regional Offices, Railway Transport Committee, Canadian Transport Commission

60 Adelaide St. E., 4th floor, Toronto, Ont. M5C 1J8
#372, 220 4th Ave. S.E., Box 2917, Stn. M, Calgary, Alta. T2P 3C3
Box 11148, 1055 W. Georgia St., #1740, Vancouver, B.C. V6E 3P3
#301, 303 Main St., Winnipeg, Man. R3C 3G7
4th floor, Terminal Plaza Bldg., 1222 Main St., Moncton, N.B. E1C 1H6
Ste. 702, 685 Cathcart St., Montreal, P.Q. H3B 1M7
33 S. Court St., #323, Box 2174, Stn. P, Thunder Bay, Ont. P7B 2W6

DEPT. OF COMMUNICATIONS

300 Slater St., Ottawa, Ont. K1A OC8
Information Contact, John Davidson, Information Services, Phone, (613) 995-8185

The Department of Communications was set up to foster the orderly operation and development of communications services in Canada. The Department protects Canadian interests in international telecommunications matters, manages the radio frequency spectrum, encourages the development of new communication facilities and co-ordinates telecommunication services for departments of the Government of Canada.

The Communications Department also formulates and develops policies and programs for the achievement of national arts and cultural objectives and promotes effective inter-agency co-operation in this field.

Acts Administered in Whole or in Part by the Minister of Communications

Broadcasting Act
Canada Council Act
Canadian Film Development Corporation Act
Canadian Radio-television & Telecommunications Act, 1974-75-76, S.C., c. 49
Cultural Property Export & Import Act
Dept. of Communications Act
Laurier House Act
National Arts Centre Act
National Film Act
National Library Act
National Museums Act
National Transportation Act (concerning telegraphs & telephones)
Public Archives Act
Radio Act
Railway Act (concerning telegraphs & telephones)
Social Sciences & Humanities Research Council Act
Teleglobe Canada Act (RSC 1970, c. 11)
Telegraphs Act
Telesat Canada Act

MINISTER, Hon. Francis Fox
Deputy Minister, Pierre Juneau
Sr. Asst. Deputy Minister (Policy), Jean Fournier
Asst. Deputy Minister (Space Program), Alexander Curran
Asst. Deputy Minister (Research), D.F. Parkhill
Asst. Deputy Minister (Spectrum Management & Government Telecommunications), Ken Hepburn
Asst. Deputy Minister (Arts & Culture), Léo A. Dorais
Director General, International Telecommunications, Gaby Warren
Director General, National Telecommunications, Vince Hill
Director General, Telecommunication Regulatory Services, John de Mercado
Director General, Space Technology & Applications, Dr. B.C. Blevis
Director General, Federal Provincial Relations, Charles McGee
Director General, Space Programs, Dr. C.A. Franklin
Director, Space Programs Management, R.W. Breithaupt
Director General, Research Policy & Planning, Sydney Wagner
Director General, Information Technology Research & Development, vacant
Director General, Communications System Research & Development, A.R. Kaye
Director General, Radar & Communications Technology Research & Development, R.E. Barrington
Director General, Security & Communications Support Services, vacant
Director General, Communications Economics, Elisabeth Kriegler
A/Director General, Broadcasting & Social Policy, Elizabeth Kriegler
Director General, Personnel, J.A.F. Vieni
Director, Research & Statistics Directorate, John Thera
Director, Cultural Industries, Ian McLaren
Director, Performing & Visual Arts & Heritage Division, vacant
Director, Financial Analysis & Program Evaluation, Jim MacDonald
Director, Management Services, P.A. Forget

Governmental Bodies that Report Through Minister of Communications

Canada Council
Canadian Broadcasting Corporation
Canadian Cultural Property Export Review Board
Canadian Film Development Corporation
Canadian Radio-television & Telecommunications Commission
National Arts Centre
National Film Board
National Library
National Museums of Canada (National Gallery of Canada; National Museum of Natural Sciences; National Museum of Man; National Museum of Science & Technology)
Public Archives
Social Sciences & Humanities Research Council
Teleglobe Canada
Telesat Canada

Communications Regional Offices

325 Granville St., Vancouver, B.C. V6C 1S5
#200, 386 Broadway Ave., Winnipeg, Man. R3C 3Y9
55 St. Clair Ave. E., 9th floor, Toronto, Ont. M4T 1M2
2085 rue Union, Montreal, P.Q. H3A 2C3
1222 Main St., Moncton, N.B. E1C 8P9

DEPT. OF CONSUMER & CORPORATE AFFAIRS

Place du Portage, Hull, P.Q. K1A OC9
General Information, Communications Service, Consumer & Corporate Affairs Canada, Place du Portage, Hull, P.Q. K1A OC9 (phone: (819) 997-2938)

Acts Administered

Bankruptcy Act

Boards of Trade Act
Combines Investigation Act
Companies' Creditors Arrangement Act
Consumer & Corporate Affairs Canada Act
Consumer Packaging & Labelling Act
Co-operative Associations, Canada Act
Copyright Act
Corporations Act, Canada
Corporations, Canada Business Act
Electricity Inspection Act
Farmers' Creditors Arrangement Act
Gas Inspection Act
Government Companies Operation Act
Hazardous Products Act
Industrial Design Act
National Trade Mark & True Labelling Act
"Parliament Hill" use of expression Act
Patent Act
Pawnbrokers Act
Pension Fund Societies Act
Precious Metals Marking Act
Public Documents Act
Public Officers Act
Public Servants Inventions Act
Seals Act
Tax Rebate Discounting Act
Textile Labelling Act
Timber Marking Act
Trade Marks Act
Trade Unions Act
Weights & Measures Act

The Department also participates in the administration of the following statutes:
Agricultural Products Standards Canada Act
Bills of Exchange Act
Broadcasting Act
Canada Development Corporation Act
Co-operative Credit Associations Act
Corporations & Labour Unions Returns Act
Currency & Exchange Act
Dairy Products, Canada Act
Defence Production Act
Excise Act
Fish Inspection Act
Food & Drugs Act
Inspection & Sale Act
Insurance Companies, Canada & British, Act
Interest Act
Loan Companies Act
Maple Products Industry Act
National Energy Board Act
National Transportation Act
Publication of Statutes Act
Railway Act
St. Lawrence Seaway Authority Act
Shipping Conferences Exemption Act
Small Loans Act
Telesat Canada Act
Trust Companies Act
Wages Liability Act
Winding-up Act (Part 1)

MINISTER, Hon. André Ouellet
Deputy Minister, George Post
A/Asst. Deputy Minister, Corporate Affairs, J.H.A. Gariepy
Asst. Deputy Minister, Consumer Affairs, K. Francoeur Hendriks
Asst. Deputy Minister, Competition Policy, L.A.W. Hunter
A/Director General, Policy Co-ordination, Roger Gagnon
Departmental Secretary, J. Gariepy
Financial & Administrative Services, R. Murray
Personnel Branch, Director, J.G. Soulière
Legal Branch, A/Director, R. Kelly
Asst. Deputy Registrar General, David R. Taylor
Director, Standard of Conduct Advisory Group, G.J. Robert Boyle
A/Chief of Registration, D.D. Kirchmayer
Communications Service, A/Director, J. MacLeod
Bureau of Competition Policy, Director of Investigation & Research (Combines Investigation Act), L.A.W. Hunter
Senior Deputy Director, D.P. DeMelto
Manufacturing Branch, A/Director, G. Orr
A/Services Branch, Director, W.F. Lindsay
Resources Branch, Director, vacant
Bureau of Consumer Affairs, Asst. Deputy Minister, K. Francoeur Hendriks
Consumer Services Branch, Director, M. Wadsworth
Consumer Research Branch, Director, G. Hiscocks
Consumer Fraud Protection Branch, Director, R. McKay
Product Safety Branch, Director, J.W. Black
Legal Metrology & Lab. Services Branch, Director, J. Quigley
Bureau of Corporate Affairs, A/Asst. Deputy Minister, J.H.A. Gariepy
Research Branch, Director, F. Hay
Corporations Branch, Director, F.J. Sparling
Supt. of Bankruptcy, Jacques Brazeau
Commr. of Patents, J.H.A. Gariépy
Patents Operations, Director, W. Clare
Copyright & Industrial Design Service, A/Director, B. Bloor
A/Trade Marks Registrar, G. Partington
Atlantic Region, Director, Robert G. Moir
Que. Region, Director, R. Rusinek
Ont. Region, Director, R.G. Knapp
Prairie Region, Director, W.A. Empke
Pacific Region, Director, M.C. Monaghan

Consumer & Corporate Regional & District Offices:

Atlantic Region

6th floor, Montreal Tower, 5151 George St., Halifax, N.S. B3J 1M5
District Offices
503 Herald Tower, 4 Herald St., Corner Brook, Nfld. A2H 4B7
#1, 1000 Windmill Rd., Dartmouth, N.S. B3B 1L7
2nd floor, 633 Queen St., Fredericton, N.B. E3B 1C3
3rd floor, 1222 Main St., Moncton, N.B. E1C 1H6
245 Federal Bldg., Corner Dorchester & Charlotte, Sydney, N.S. B1P 5Z2
Room 4, Dominion Bldg., Charlottetown, P.E.I. C1A 4A9
295 Bayside Dr., Saint John, N.B. E2J 1B1
5th floor, 510 Sir Humphrey Gilbert Bldg., Duckworth St., St. John's, Nfld. A1C 1G4

Quebec Region

#1100, 1410 Stanley St., Montreal, P.Q. H3A 1P8
District Offices
940, rue Chabanel, Chicoutimi, P.Q. G7H 5W2
Edifice Banque de Montréal, 800 Carré d'Youville, pièce 1801, Quebec, P.Q. G1R 3P4
320 rue St-Germain, #403, Rimouski, P.Q. G5L 1C2
25 nord, rue Wellington, Chambre 500, Sherbrooke, P.Q. J1H 5B1
2nd floor, Edifice Trust Royal, 1300, Notre Dame St., Trois-Rivières, P.Q. G9A 4X3

Ontario Region

6th floor, 4900 Yonge St., Willowdale, Ont. M2N 6B8
District Offices
7th floor, 25 St. Clair Ave. E., Toronto, Ont. M4T 1M2
430 Waterloo St. S., Thunder Bay, Ont. P7E 6E4
1283 Sparks St., Sudbury, Ont. P3A 2C7
Union Gas Bldg., 3rd floor, 20 Hughson St. S., Hamilton, Ont. L8N 2A1
781 Richmond St., London, Ont. N6A 3H4
240 Bank St., Ottawa, Ont. K2P 1X2

Pacific Region

Box 10059, Pacific Centre Ltd., 700 W. Georgia St., Vancouver, B.C. V7Y 1C9
District Offices
478 Bernard Ave., 3rd floor, Kelowna, B.C. V1Y 6N7
#316, 295 Winnipeg St., Box 87, Penticton, B.C. V2A 5M2
7th floor, 299 Victoria St., Prince George, B.C. V2L 5B8
#401, 1230 Government St., Victoria, B.C. V8W 1Y3

Prairie Region

260 St. Mary Ave., Winnipeg, Man. R3C 0M6
District Offices
201, 260 rue St. Mary, Winnipeg, Man. R3C OM6
Barnett Bldg., 1008 7 Ave. S.W., Calgary, Alta. T2P 1A7
3421 8th St. E., Saskatoon, Sask. S7H 0W5
2212 Scarth St., Regina, Sask. S4P 2J6
Oliver Bldg., 10225 100 Ave., Edmonton, Alta. T5J OA1

OFFICE OF THE CORRECTIONAL INVESTIGATOR (prisoners' ombudsman)

Box 950, Stn. B, Ottawa, Ont. K1P 5R1
(613) 996-9771/2
Correctional Investigator, R.L. Stewart
Asst., D.C. Turnbull

CORRECTIONAL SERVICE CANADA

Headquarters: Ottawa, Ont. K1A OP9
Deputy Commissioner, Communications, John Braithwaite (613/995-0114)

Institutional Addresses:

Following are the names and addresses of the institutions, shown by province, the type of security and the name of the Director. (CCC is Community Correctional Centre)

Atlantic Region:

Regional Headquarters, 2nd floor, Terminal Plaza Bldg., 1222 Main St., Moncton, N.B. E1C 1H6: Regional Director General, R. Clark
Dorchester Penitentiary, Box A, Dorchester, N.B. EOA 1MO (Max) E. Niles (Int. Warden)
Westmorland Institution, Box 130, Dorchester, N.B. EOA 1MO (Min) R. Maguire
The Parr Town Centre, 19-25 Hazen Ave., Saint John, N.B. E2L 3G6 (CCC), R. H. Smith
Springhill Institution, Box 2140, Springhill, N.S. BOM 1XO (Med) A. Stevenson (Warden)
Carlton Centre, 5853 College St., Halifax, N.S. B3H 1X5 (CCC) R.T. Bentley
Shulie Lake Institution, Box 10, R.R. 3, Parrsboro, N.S. BOM 1SO (Min) F. Rushton

Quebec Region

Regional Headquarters, 1600 E. St. Martin Blvd., Tower A, Laval, P.Q. H7G 4R8; J.-P. Dugas, Regional Director General
Regional Reception Centre, Box 5550, St. Anne des Plaines, P.Q. JON 1HO (Max) R. Jourdain
Correctional Development Centre, Que., 1300 Montée St. François, St. Vincent de Paul, Ville de Laval, P.Q. H7C 1S6 (Max) P.G.L. Goulem
Cowansville Institution, Box 5000, Cowansville, P.Q. J2K 3N7 (Med) J.P. Lupien
Montée St. François Institution, 200 Montée St. François, St. Vincent de Paul, Ville de Laval, P.Q. H7C 1S6 (Min) J.P. Dallaire
Laval Institution, 180 Montée St. François, Ville de Laval, P.Q. H7C 1S6 (Max) Pierre Viau
Archambault Institution, Box 1210, Ste. Anne des Plaines, P.Q. JON 1HO (Max) A. LeMarier
Ste. Anne des Plaines Institution, Box 390, Ste. Anne des Plaines, P.Q. JON 1HO (Min) R. Benoit
Federal Training Centre, 6099 Blvd. Levesque, St. Vincent de Paul, Ville de Laval, P.Q. H7C 1P1 (Med) M.A. Lafleur
Leclerc Institution, 400 Montée St. François, Ville de Laval, P.Q. H7C 1S1 (Med) I. Kulik
Correctional Staff College, Que., 5500 Blvd. Levesque, St. Vincent de Paul, Ville de Laval, P.Q. H7C 1N7, R. Rabeau
La Macaza Institution, S.S. 200, L'Annonciation, Quebec, P.Q. J0T 1T0 (Med) M. Jacques
Pie IX, 8900 Pie IX Blvd., Montreal, P.Q. H1Z 3V1 (CCC) D. Roberge
Benoit XV, 2097 Benoit XV Blvd., Quebec, P.Q. G1L 2Z8 (CCC) C. Pelletier
Martineau, 10345 St. Laurent Blvd., Montreal, P.Q. H3L 2P1 (CCC) R. Martin
Ogilvy, 435 Ogilvy St., Montreal, P.Q. H3N 1M3 (CCC) D. Paulovic
Sherbrooke, 2190 Sherbrooke St. E., Montreal, P.Q. H2K 1C7 (CCC) G. Petit-Clair

Ontario Region

Regional Headquarters, Box 1174, 400 King St. W., Kingston, Ont. K7L 4Y8, A. Trono, Regional Director General
Regional Supply Centre, Box 1121, Kingston, Ont. K7L 4Y5
Regional Reception Centre, Box 22, Kingston, Ont. K7L 4V7 (Max) A. Graham (A/Warden)
Regional Psychiatric Centre, Box 2500, Kingston, Ont. K7L 4Z4 (Max) Dr. F.P. Stephens (A/Medical Director)
Warkworth Institution, Box 760, Campbellford, Ont. KOL 1L0 (Med) M. Dawson
Joyceville Institution, Box 880, Kingston, Ont. K7L 4X9 (Med) K.R. Payne
Pittsburg Institution, Box 4510, Kingston, Ont. K7L 5E5 (Min) J.R. Caird
Collins Bay Institution, Box 190, Kingston, Ont. K7L 4V9 (Med) H.C. Reynett
Frontenac Institution, Box 7500, Kingston, Ont. K7L 5E6 (Min) G. Downing
The Portsmouth Centre, 508 Portsmouth Ave., Kingston, Ont. K7M 1V8 (CCC) P. Grooms (A/Supt.)
Beaver Creek Correctional Camp, Box 1240, Gravenhurst, Ont. POC 1GO (Min) T. Van Petegem
Montgomery Centre, 2384 Yonge St., 2nd floor, Box 339, Stn. K, Toronto, Ont. M4P 2G7 (CCC) J. Currie
Millhaven Institution, Box 280, Bath, Ont. KOH 1GO (Max) J. Ryan
Bath Institution, Box 1500, Bath, Ont. KOH 1GO (Min) C. McQuade (A/Supt.)
Prison for Women, Box 515, Kingston, Ont. K7L 4W7 (Max) G. Caron (Warden)
Correctional Staff College, Ont., Box 260, Kingston, Ont. K7L 4V8 M.E. Millar

Prairie Region

Regional Headquarters, 2002 Quebec Ave., Box 9223, Saskatoon, Sask. S7K 3X5, J. Phelps, Regional Director General
Regional Psychiatric Centre, (2520 Central Ave.), Box 9243, Saskatoon, Sask. S7K 3X5 (Max) W. Davis (A/Medical Director)
Stony Mountain Institution, Box 4500, Winnipeg, Man. R0C 3W8 (Med) T. Sawatsky
Rockwood Institution, Box 72, Stony Mountain, Man. ROC 3AO (Min) J.W. Keane
The Osborne Centre, 45 Edmonton St., Winnipeg, Man. R3C 1P8 (CCC) J. Christian
Sask. Penitentiary, Box 160, Prince Albert, Sask. S6V 5R6 (Max) J. O'Sullivan
Sask. Farm Institution, Box 160, Prince Albert, Sask. S6V 5R6 (Min) L.K. Jacobson
Oskana Centre, 1300 11th Ave., Regina, Sask. S4P 0G7 (CCC) J. Friel (Supt.)
The Grierson Centre, 9542 101 Ave., Edmonton, Alta. T5J 2J6 (CCC) D. Clark
Portal Centre, 1916 11 Ave. S.W., Calgary, Alta. T3C 0N8 (CCC) R. Johnson
Drumheller Institution, Box 3000, Drumheller, Alta. TOJ OYO (Med) L. Simonsen
Correctional Staff College, Edmonton, Box 638, Edmonton, Alta. T5J 2K8, V. Alward, act.

Bowden Institution, Box 6000, Innisfail, Alta. TOM 1AO (Med) R. Desrochers
Edmonton Institution, Box 2290, Edmonton, Alta. T5J 3H7 (Max) R.L. Benner
Altadore Centre, 1941 42nd Ave. S.W., Calgary, Alta. T2T 2M6 (CCC) H. Parker

Pacific Region:

Regional Headquarters: Ste. 204, 2306 McCallum Rd., Abbotsford, B.C. V2S 3P4, J. Murphy, Regional Director General
Regional Psychiatric Centre, Box 3000, Abbotsford, B.C. V2S 4P4 (Max) Dr. C. Roy
William Head Institution, Box 4000, Stn. A, Victoria, B.C. V8X 4Y8 (Med) A. Bender
Mission Institution, Box 60, Slave Lake Rd., Mission City, B.C. V2V 4L8 (Med) J. Stonoski
Mountain Institution, Box 1200, Agassiz, B.C. V0M 1A0 (Med) W. Mort
Matsqui Institution, Box 2500, Abbotsford, B.C. V2S 4P3 (Med) D. Dhillon
Correctional Staff College, Pacific, 91 E. Columbia St., New Westminster, B.C. V3L 3V4, W.A. Hellyer, Director
Robson Centre, 1301 Robson St., Vancouver, B.C. V6E 1C6 (CCC) S. Dehoon
Ferndale Institution, Box 50, Mission, B.C. V2V 4L8 (Min) M. Van Der Veen
Elbow Lake Institution, Box 50, Harrison Mills, B.C. VOM 1LO (Min) S. Tschierschwitz
The Pandora Centre, 921 Pandora Ave., Victoria, B.C. V8V 3P4 (CCC) P.J. Zanichelli
Kent Institution, Box 1500, Agassiz, B.C. V0M 1A0 (Max) J. Dowsett
Matsqui Trailers Day Parole Centre, Box 248, Abbotsford, B.C. V2S 4N9 (CCC) J. White

National Parole Service

Headquarters: 340 Laurier Ave. W., Ottawa, Ont. K1A OP9

The National Parole Service is integrated with the Correctional Service of Canada. There are District Parole Offices or Sub District Offices in major centres across Canada. The National Parole Board is a separate entity listed alphabetically in this section of the Almanac.

OFFICE OF THE CHIEF ELECTORAL OFFICER

Ottawa, Ont. K1A OM6
Phone: (613) 993-2975

The office is responsible for the conduct of all federal elections and by-elections and elections in the Northwest Territories, and in addition, any votes taken under the Canada Temperance Act.

Chief Electoral Officer, Jean-Marc Hamel
Executive Asst., Mrs. A. Lortie
Asst. Chief Electoral Officer, R.A. Gould
Director, Election Financing, R.G. Dubé
Director of Operations, Louis Lavoie

EMERGENCY PLANNING CANADA

Ottawa, Ont. K1A OW6
(613) 992-3322

Emergency Planning Canada (EPC) co-ordinates federal government planning aimed at mitigating the effects of emergencies and peacetime disasters, and the federal planning for civil defence in time of war. Civil defence links are maintained with NATO countries and the United States.

A regional director in each provincial capital maintains contact with federal government departments and with provincial and municipal governments.

Chief Executive Officer, W.B. Snarr

DEPT. OF EMPLOYMENT & IMMIGRATION

140 Promenade du Portage, Hull, P.Q. (mailing: Ottawa, Ont. K1A 0J9)

Public Affairs: C. Jennings, Director General (phone: (819) 994-6013)

The Department was established in 1977 to provide services for the Canada Employment & Immigration Commission. It incorporates two divisions, The Strategic Policy & Planning Division, which is responsible for research and evaluation with regard to current and future plans and programs; and The Public Affairs Division, which is responsible for information activities to promote the Commission's objectives, and for liaison with Parliament.

The Immigration Appeal Board, and the Canada Employment & Immigration Advisory Council report to Parliament through the Minister.

MINISTER, Hon. Lloyd Axworthy
Executive Asst., Michael Quiggin
Chief, Administrative Services, J.R. Langlois
Deputy Minister/Chairman, J.D. Love
Assoc. Deputy Minister, M.A.J. Lafontaine
Asst. Deputy Minister, Strategic Policy & Planning, P.B. Fay
Director General, Public Affairs, C. Jennings

DEPT. OF ENERGY, MINES & RESOURCES

580 Booth St., Ottawa, Ont. K1A OE4
Information Contact, J.B. Kinsella, Executive Director, Communications (phone: (613) 995-3065)

The Minister of Energy is Responsible for the Administration of the Following Acts:

Alta.-B.C. Boundary Act, 1974
Atomic Energy Control Act
Canada Lands Surveys Act
Canadian Home Insulation Program Act
Dept. of Energy, Mines & Resources Act
Electoral Boundaries Readjustment Act
Energy Supplies Emergency Act
Explosives Act
Home Insulation (N.S. & P.E.I.) Program Act
National Energy Board Act
Nuclear Liability Act
Oil & Gas Production & Conservation Act
Oil Substitution & Conservation Act
Public Lands Grants Act
Representation Commr. Act, 1963
Resources & Technical Surveys Act
Arctic Waters Pollution Prevention Act (in part)
Territorial Lands Act
Petroleum Administration Act
Petro Canada Act
Petroleum Corporations Monitoring Act

MINISTER, Hon. Marc Lalonde, P.C., Q.C., LL.L., M.A.
Minister of State (Mines), Hon. Judy Erola
Deputy Minister, Marshall Cohen, B.A., LL.M.
Assoc. Deputy Minister, A.E. Collin, M.Sc., Ph.D.
Senior Asst. Deputy Minister, Energy, W.E. Clark, B.A., M.A., Ph.D.
Senior Asst. Deputy Minister, Mines, C.H. Smith, M.A., Ph.D.
Senior Asst. Deputy Minister, International Minerals, Jean-Paul Drolet, M.Sc., D.Sc.
Asst. Deputy Minister, Energy Policy Analysis, George Tough, B.A., M.A.
Asst. Deputy Minister, Conservation & Non-Petroleum, Reiner Hollbach, B.A., M.A., Ph.D.
Asst. Deputy Minister, Petroleum, Roland Priddle, M.A.
Asst. Deputy Minister, Canada Oil & Gas Lands Administration, H.L. Laframboise
Asst. Deputy Minister, Petroleum Prices & Compensation, A. Digby Hunt, B.Sc.
Asst. Deputy Minister, Research & Technology, Kenneth Whitham, M.A., Ph.D., F.R.S.C.
Asst. Deputy Minister, Earth Sciences, W.W. Hutchison, B.Sc., M.A., Ph.D.
Asst. Deputy Minister, Mineral Policy, C. George Miller, Ph.D.
Asst. Deputy Minister, Personnel & Management Practices, Irene Johnson, B.A., M.A.

Asst. Deputy Minister, Finance & Administration, Stuart Mensforth, C.A.
Asst. Deputy Minister, Administration, William McKim, B.Sc.
Director General, Communications, D.C. Hanright

Research & Technology Sector

The Research & Technology Sector is responsible for the development and management of research and development programs in energy and mineral technology and in remote sensing.

Canada Centre for Mineral & Energy Technology (CANMET)

Director General, W.G. Jeffery, B.Sc., M.Sc., Ph.D.
Deputy Director General, V.A. Haw, B.S., M.S.
Director, Energy Research, D.A. Reeve, B.Sc., Ph.D.
Division Directors:
Mineral Sciences Laboratories, W.A. Gow, B.A.Sc.
Physical Metallurgy Research Laboratories, W.H. Erickson, B.A., B.Sc., Ph.D.
Energy Research Laboratories, B.I. Parsons, B.Sc., Ph.D., D.Phil.
Mining Research Laboratories, T.S. Cochrane, B.A.Sc., M.Sc., P.Eng.
Chiefs of Divisions:
Technology Information, J.E. Kanasy, B.Sc., B.S., M.A., Ph.D.
Technical Services, E.K. Swimmings, B.Sc., P.Eng.

CANMET Western Research Laboratory (Energy), Box 3294, Sherwood Park, Alta. T8A 2A6
CANMET Elliot Lake Laboratory (Mining), Box 100, Elliot Lake, Ont. P5A 2J6
CANMET Western Office (Mining), 3303 33rd St. N.W., Calgary, Alta. T2L 2A7
CANMET Eastern Laboratory (Energy), Box 1042, Sydney, N.S. B1P 6J7

Canada Centre for Remote Sensing

Director General, E.A. Godby, B.Sc., M.Sc.
Data Acquisition Division, Ralph Baker, B.Eng., M.Sc.
Applications Division, W.M. Strome, B.Sc., M.A.Sc., Ph.D.
Data Processing Division, E. Shaw, B.Sc., Ph.D.
Program Planning & Evaluation, J.C. Henein, B.Eng., M.Sc.

Office of Energy Research & Development

Director, P.J. Dyne, B.A., Ph.D.

Explosives Branch

Chief Inspector of Explosives, B.P. McHugh, B.Sc.
Regional Inspectors:
#410, Sir John Thompson Bldg., 1256 Barrington St., Halifax, N.S. B3J 1Y6
Box 463, 1262 Maguire Ave., Sillery, P.Q. G1T 2R8
7th floor, 580 Booth St., Ottawa, Ont. K1A 0E4
Box 2868, Stn. M, 220 4th Ave. S.E., Calgary, Alta. T2P 3C2
7th floor, 100 W. Pender St., Vancouver, B.C. V6B 1R8

Earth Sciences Sector

The Earth Sciences Sector is responsible for providing the earth-science information needed for effective use and demarcation of the Canadian landmass.

Geological Survey of Canada

A/Director General, J.G. Fyles, B.A.Sc., M.A.Sc., Ph.D.
Chief Geologist, J.G. Fyles, B.A.Sc., M.A.Sc., Ph.D.
Division Directors:
Terrain Sciences, J.S. Scott, M.A.Sc., Ph.D.
Precambrian Geology, J.C. McGlynn, B.Sc., M.Sc., Ph.D.
Economic Geology, G.B. Leech, B.A.Sc., M.Sc., Ph.D.
Central Laboratories & Technical Services, J.A. Maxwell, B.Sc., M.Sc., Ph.D.
Resource Geophysics & Geochemistry, A.G. Darnley, B.A., M.A., Ph.D.
Geological Information, R.G. Blackadar, B.A., M.A., Ph.D.
Institute of Sedimentary & Petroleum Geology, W.W. Nassichuk, B.Sc., M.Sc., Ph.D., 3033 33 St. N.W., Calgary, Alta. T2L 2A7
Atlantic Geoscience Centre, M.J. Keen, B.A., Ph.D., Bedford Institute of Oceanography, Box 1006, Dartmouth, N.S. B2Y 4A2
Cordilleran Geology, R.B. Campbell, B.A.Sc., M.Sc., Ph.D., 100 W. Pender St., Vancouver, B.C. V6B 1R8
Pacific Geoscience Centre, Marine Geology Unit, Patricia Bay, C.J. Yorath, B.Sc., M.Sc., Ph.D., Box 6000, Sidney, B.C. V8L 4B2

Surveys & Mapping Branch

Director General, R.E. Moore, B.E., M.Sc., P.Eng.
Geodetic Survey Division, Dominion Geodesist & Director, L.J. O'Brien, B.Eng., M.Sc., P.Eng.
Topographical Survey Division, Director, J.M. Zarzycki, M.Sc., Ph.D., P.Eng.
Legal Surveys Division, Surveyor General & Director, W.V. Blackie, B.Sc., C.L.S., N.S.L.S.
Regional Surveyors:
Box 668, 8th floor, Bellanca Bldg., 50th St., Yellowknife, N.W.T. X1A 2N5
204 Range Rd., Whitehorse, Y.T. Y1A 3V1
Box 10062, 700 W. Georgia St., Vancouver, B.C. V7Y 1B6
108th St. Bldg., #1010, 9942 108 St., Edmonton, Alta. T5K 2J5
#409, Torwest Tower, 1853 Hamilton St., Regina, Sask. S4P 2C1
25 St. Clair Ave. E., #901, Toronto, Ont. M4T 1M2
#305, 275 Portage Ave., Winnipeg, Man. R3B 2B3
Plaza Level, 2750 ch. Ste-Foy, #104, Ste-Foy, P.Q. G1V 1V6
Box 368, 46 Havelock St., Amherst, N.S. B4H 3Z5
Geographical Services Directorate, Director, R. Groot, M.Sc., C.L.S.
Reproduction & Distribution Division, Director, J.A. McArthur
International Boundary Commission, Canadian Commr., A.C. McEwen, LL.B., LL.M., Ph.D., C.L.S., O.L.S., N.L.S.
Canadian Permanent Committee on Geographical Names, Chairman, Jean-Paul Drolet, M.Sc., D.Sc.

Earth Physics Branch

Director General, J.G. Tanner, B.Sc., Ph.D.
Division Directors:
Seismology & Geothermal Studies, M.J. Berry, B.Sc., M.A., Ph.D.
Geomagnetism, P.H. Serson, B.A., M.A., Ph.D.
Gravity & Geodynamics, M.R. Dence, B.Sc., F.R.C.S. (act.)

Polar Continental Shelf Project

Director, G.D. Hobson, B.Sc., M.Sc.

Mineral Policy Sector

The Mineral Policy Sector carries out broad economic and mineral commodity studies and gathers comprehensive domestic and world data on nonrenewable resources, for the use of government and industry. Based on these studies, the Sector develops policies for the development, processing and use of minerals and provides advice to industry and to governments.
Directors General:
Mineral Development Branch, R.D. Hutchinson, B.Sc., Ph.D.
Mineral Supply Branch, R.J. Shank, B.Eng.
Information Systems Division, Director, J.T. Brennan, B.A.

Energy Sector

The Energy Sector is responsible for the development of energy programs and policies; the direction of studies relating to energy sources and requirements and the co-ordination of policy advice. The Senior Assistant Deputy Minister serves as advisor on overall plans and policies relating to energy sources and requirements. The Sector administers and manages the federal interests in energy resources of all Canada lands offshore from the east and west coasts and in the Northwest Territories, Yukon and Arctic Islands as well as those federally owned mineral rights in the provinces that become available for disposition, and it makes policy recommendations on offshore resources.

Directors General:

Energy Policy Analysis, L.M. Good, B.A., M.A., Ph.D.
Energy Strategy, R.G. Blackburn, B.A., M.A.
International Energy Relations, D.W. Campbell
Conservation & Renewable Energy, I.E. Efford, B.Sc., Ph.D.
Petroleum Resources, J.P. Hea, B.A., Ph.D.
Petroleum Utilization, C.A. Landry, B.Eng.
Natural Gas, C.B. Marriott, M.A., M.Sc.
International Petroleum, K.A. LeMesurier, B.A., M.A.
Canada Oil & Gas Lands Administration, D.G. Crosby, B.A., B.Sc., M.S., Ph.D.
Energy Emergency Planning Group, B.A. Taylor, B.A.
Petroleum Incentives Program, R.C. Creech, F.C.G.A.
Pricing & Compensation Operations, vacant
Policy Rulings & Evaluation, R.S.G. Thompson, B.A., M.A., LL.M.
Financial & Fiscal Analysis, J.M. Banigan, M.B.A., B.Comm.
Canadianization, J.B. Carruthers, B.A.

Senior Advisors:

Energy Policy Co-ordination, R.B. Toombs, B.A.Sc., B.A. (Econ.), M.Sc.
Electrical Energy, A.R. Scott, B.Sc.
Coal Branch, J.H. Walsh, B.Eng., M.Eng., Sc.D.
Uranium & Nuclear Energy, R.W. Morrison, B.Eng.

Regional Offices:

Petroleum Incentives Program Office, #332, 220 4th Ave. S.E., Box 2907, Stn. M, Calgary, Alta. T2P 3L7
Coal Branch, 3303 33 St. N.W., Calgary, Alta. T2L 2A7
Canada Oil & Gas Lands Administration, Box 1006, Dartmouth, N.S. B2Y 4A2
Canada Oil & Gas Lands Administration, #408, 354 Water St., St. John's, Nfld. A1C 5H5

Departmental Information Offices/ Conservation & Renewable Energy Branch Offices

Atlantic Place 7th floor, Box 65, 215 Water St., St. John's, Nfld. A1C 6C9
#503, 5151 George St., Halifax, N.S. B3J 1M5
835 Champlain St., Dieppe, N.B. E1A 1P6
Waterfront Shopping Centre, 98 Water St., Summerside, P.E.I. C1N 4N6
605 Dorchester Blvd. W., Ground floor, Montreal, P.Q. H3B 1P4
2242 Lakeshore Blvd. W., Toronto, Ont. M8V 1A5
Main floor, 110-112 Osborne St. S., Winnipeg, Man. R3L 1Y5
#706, 119 4th Ave. S., Saskatoon, Sask. S7K 5X2
#200, 22 Sir Winston Churchill Ave., St. Albert, Alta. T8N 1B4
5021 Kingsway, 3rd floor, Burnaby, B.C. V5H 4A5
2078 2nd Ave., Whitehorse, Y.T. Y1A 1B1
4922 52nd St., Yellowknife, N.W.T. X0E 1H0

Communications Liaison Office: #622, 220 4th Ave., Calgary, Alta. T2G 4X3

Boards & Crown Corporations Reporting to Parliament Through the Minister

National Energy Board
Atomic Energy of Canada Ltd.
Eldorado Nuclear Ltd.
Eldorado Aviation Ltd.
Energy Supplies Allocation Board
Atomic Energy Control Board
Uranium Canada Ltd.
Petro Canada
Petroleum Compensation Board
Petroleum Monitoring Agency

ENERGY SUPPLIES ALLOCATION BOARD

588 Booth St., Ottawa, Ont. K1A 0E4

The Board is responsible for the allocation of crude oil to refiners and for the allocation of refined products to wholesale petroleum customers, and for devising a supplementary rationing program to reinforce the allocation programs, as required. It searches for alternate energy sources to alleviate demands on petroleum supplies, and monitors trends in petroleum supply and demand to evaluate the need to recommend introduction of a mandatory allocation program as provided by the Energy Supplies Emergency Act.

Chairman of the Board, H.F. Stevenson
Director General of Energy Emergency Planning Group, B.A. Taylor
Director, Planning, Evaluation & Systems, G.N. Currie
Director, Operations, Planning & Design, N.D. Morgan

ENVIRONMENT CANADA

Ottawa, Ont. K1A OH3

Information Directorate, Director General, François Pagé
Departmental Inquiry Centre, (613) 997-2800
Atmospheric Environment, Downsview, (416) 667-4723

Legislation Administered

Canada Water Act
Canada Wildlife Act
Clean Air Act
Environmental Contaminants Act
Fisheries Act
Forestry Development & Research Act
Historic Sites & Monuments Act
Migratory Birds Convention Act
National Battlefields at Quebec Act
National Parks Act
Ocean Dumping Control Act

MINISTER, Hon. John Roberts
Executive Asst., Ivan Fleischmann
Deputy Minister, J. Blair Seaborn
Senior Asst. Deputy Minister, J. Gérin
Policy, Director General, Dr. J.S. Maini
Intergovernmental Affairs, Director General, Dr. P.M. Bird
Planning & Evaluation, Director General, (vacant)
Asst. Deputy Minister, Finance & Admin., W.E. Armstrong
Asst. Deputy Minister, Canadian Forestry Service, F.L.C. Reed
Asst. Deputy Minister, Environmental Protection, R. Robinson
Asst. Deputy Minister, Atmospheric Environment, J.P. Bruce
Asst. Deputy Minister, Environmental Conservation, Dr. W.B. Mountain
Executive Chairman, Federal Environmental Assessment Review Office, E.R. Cotterill
Secretary, Environmental Advisory Council, Dr. E.F. Roots
Secretary, Forestry Advisory Council, Dr. D.R. Redmond
Legal Services, Senior Counsel, M. Prabhu
Science Advisor, Dr. E.F. Roots

Finance & Administration Service

Fontaine Bldg., Hull, P.Q. (mailing: Ottawa, Ont. K1A 1C7)

Asst. Deputy Minister, W.E. Armstrong
Director General (Finance), G.P. Vachon
Director General (Personnel & Organization), L.O. Pertus
Director General (Departmental Management Services), J.C. Richard
Director General, Computing & Applied Statistics, Dr. D.M. Brown
Director (Departmental Internal Financial Audit), J.A. Jackson
Departmental IMPAC Co-ordinator, J.J. Eatock

Environmental Conservation Service

Headquarters: Place Vincent Massey, Hull, P.Q. (mailing: Ottawa, Ont. K1A 1C7)

Asst. Deputy Minister, Dr. W.B. Mountain

Inland Waters Directorate

Director General, N.H. James
A/Director, Admin. Branch, A.M. Tippins

Director, Research Co-ordination & Program Evaluation, A. Lachance
Director, Water Planning & Management Branch, R.L. Pentland
Director, Water Quality Branch, W. Traversy
Director, Water Resources Branch, J.E. Slater
Senior Research Advisor, Dr. H.R. Eisenhauer

Canadian Wildlife Service

Director General, Bertrand Tétreault
Director, Management & Admin. Branch, D.K. Pollock
Director, Migratory Birds Branch, H.J. Boyd
Director, Wildlife Research & Interpretation Branch, J.A. Keith
Co-ordinators:
Ecological Assessment, Dr. V.E.F. Solman
Convention on International Trade in Endangered Species, J.B. Heppes
Scientific & Technical Publications, E.L. Kulin
Mammalogy & Wildlife Research, Dr. F.G. Cooch
Wildlife Pathology & Parisitology, Dr. L.P.E. Choquette
Wildlife Toxicology, Dr. D.B. Peakall
Regulations & Enforcement, J. Stoner
Biometrics, Dr. A.R. Sen

Lands Directorate

Director General, R.J. McCormack
A/Director, Land Data & Evaluation Branch, J. Thie
Director, Policy Research & Co-ordination Branch, L.C. Munn
Director, Office of Program Planning & Evaluation, J.W. Maxwell

Policy & Program Development Directorate

Director General, C.J. Stoll
Planning, J.C. Dumesnil
Director, Policy & Economics Branch, Y. Soucy
Director, Integration & Environmental Assessment Branch, V.V. Spence

Environmental Conservation Regional Offices

Inland Waters Directorate, 6009 Quinpool Rd., Box 365, Halifax, N.S. B3J 2P8, A/Director, D.L. Egar
Canadian Wildlife Service, Box 1590, Sackville, N.B. E0A 3C0, Director, J. Inder
Lands Directorate, Box 365, Halifax, N.S. B3J 2P8, Director, R. Beardmore
Inland Waters Directorate, Champlain Bldg., Place Laurier, Box 10,100, Ste-Foy, P.Q. G1V 4H5, Director, C. Triquet
Canadian Wildlife Service, Champlain Bldg., Place Laurier, Box 10,100, Ste-Foy, P.Q. G1V 4H5, Director, Dr. P. DesMeules
Lands Directorate, Champlain Bldg., Place Laurier, Box 10,100, Ste-Foy, P.Q. G1V 4H5, A/Director, J.-L. Belair
National Water Research Institute, Box 5050, Burlington, Ont. L7R 4A6, Director, Dr. G.K. Rogers
Inland Waters Directorate, Box 5050, 867 Lakeshore Rd., CCIW, Burlington, Ont. L7R 4A6, Director, E.T. Wagner
Canadian Wildlife Service, 1725 Woodward Dr., Ottawa, Ont. K1G 3Z7, Director, J.E. Bryant
Lands Directorate, 867 Lakeshore Rd., Box 5050, Burlington, Ont. L7R 4A6, Director, G. Bangay
Inland Waters Directorate, 1st floor, Motherwell Bldg., 1901 Victoria Ave., Regina, Sask. S4P 3K4, Director, D.A. Davis
Canadian Wildlife Service, Imperial Oil Bldg., 10th floor, 9942 108th St., Edmonton, Alta. T5K 2J5, Director, W. Stevens
Inland Waters Directorate, Room 502, 1001 W. Pender St., Vancouver, B.C. V6E 2M7, Director, E.M. Clark
Canadian Wildlife Service, Box 340, Delta, B.C. V4K 3Y3, Director, G.H. Staines
Lands Directorate, Room 904, 1001 W. Pender St., Vancouver, B.C. V6E 2M7, Director, Dr. D.S. Lacate

Canadian Forestry Service

Headquarters: Place Vincent Massey, Hull, P.Q. (mailing: Ottawa, Ont. K1A 1G5)

Asst. Deputy Minister, F.L.C. Reed
A/Director General, Research & Technical Services, J.H. Cayford
Director, Forest Insects & Disease Survey & Services, Dr. T.E. Sterner
Director, Forest Research & Development, Dr. L.W. Carlson
Chief, Scientific & Technical Editing, Mrs. J.C. Lalonde
Director General, Forestry Relations & Renewal, W.K. Fullerton
A/Director, Forestry Relations & Initiatives, H.N. LeBlanc
Chief, Forestry Subvention Program, R.J. Neale
Co-ordinator, Extractional Forestry, Dr. G.A. Steneker
A/Director General, Policy & Economics, Dr. T.C.M. Place
Forest Pest Management Institute, 1195 Queen St. E., Sault Ste. Marie, Ont. P6A 5M7, Director, Dr. G.W. Green
Petawawa National Forestry Institute, Chalk River, Ont. K0J 1J0, Director, Dr. R.M. Newnham

Canadian Forestry Service Regional Establishments

Nfld. Forest Research Centre, Box 6028, St. John's, Nfld. A1C 5X8, Director, Dr. W.J. Carroll
Maritimes Forest Research Centre, Box 4000, Fredericton, N.B. E3B 5P7, Director, Dr. M.M. Neilson
Laurentian Forest Research Centre, 1080 route du Vallon, Ste-Foy, P.Q. G1V 4C7, Director, Dr. C. Winget
Great Lakes Forest Research Centre, 1219 Queen St. E., Sault Ste. Marie, Ont. P6A 5M7, A/Director, R.A. Haig
Northern Forest Research Centre, 5320 122nd St., Edmonton, Alta. T6H 3S5, A/Director, D. Kiil
Pacific Forest Research Centre, Canadian Forestry Service, 506 W. Burnside Rd., Victoria, B.C. V8Z 1M5, Director, Dr. D.R. MacDonald

Atmospheric Environment Service

Headquarters: 4905 Dufferin St., Downsview, Ont. M3H 5T4

The Service issues weather warnings and forecasts. It provides information, consultation and advice on weather, climate, air quality, sea state and ice in navigable waters; on the impact of atmospheric, ice and sea state conditions on human activities, and the impact of human activities on the atmosphere. To support these programs, AES plans and operates the systems which collect, process and archive atmospheric, ice and sea state data, and conducts and promotes research in the atmospheric sciences.

Asst. Deputy Minister, J.P. Bruce
Central Services Directorate, Director General, D.K. Smith
Field Services Directorate, Director General, J.A.W. McCulloch
Atmospheric Research Directorate, Director General, Dr. W.L. Godson
Canadian Climate Centre, Director General, M.K. Thomas
Admin. Branch, Director, R. Lee
Program Devel. & Evaluation Branch, Director, G.M. Shimizu

Atmospheric Environment Regional Offices & Directors

Atlantic: R.H. O'Brien, (act.), 1496 Bedford Hwy., Bedford, N.S. B4A 1E5
Quebec: R.J. Fichaud, 100 Alexis Nihon Blvd., 3rd floor, Ville St-Laurent, P.Q. H4M 2N6
Ontario: G.A. McPherson, 25 St. Clair Ave. E., Toronto, Ont. M4T 1M2
Central: M.W. Balshaw, 266 Graham Ave., Room 1000, Winnipeg, Man. R3C 3V4
Western: B.M. Burns, Argyll Centre, 6325 103 St., Edmonton, Alta. T6H 5H6
Pacific: J.R. Mathieson, Ste. 700, 1200 W. 73rd Ave., Vancouver, B.C. V6P 6H9
Canadian Meteorological Centre: F.J. Lemire, 2121 N. Service Rd., Ste. 404, Trans Canada Hwy., Dorval, P.Q. H9P 1J3
For Climatological Information contact Canadian Climate Centre

Environmental Protection Service

Place Vincent Massey, Hull (mailing: Ottawa, Ont. K1A 1C8)

Asst. Deputy Minister, R.M. Robinson

Director General, Air Pollution Control Directorate, M. Rivers
A/Director, Abatement & Compliance Branch, P. Choquette
A/Director, Technology Development Branch, J.A. Vézina
Director, Air Pollution Programs Branch, Dr. D. Kelley
A/Director General, Water Pollution Control Directorate, Dr. J.D. Salloum
A/Director, Abatement & Compliance Branch, Dr. L. Buffa
A/Director, Technology Development Branch, R.J.P. Brouzes
A/Director, Water Pollution Programs Branch, G.A. Allard
Director General, Environmental Impact Control Directorate, Dr. S.O. Winthrop
Director, Environmental Contaminants Control Branch, Dr. J.E. Brydon
Director, Environmental Emergencies Branch, Dr. J.D. Kingham
Director, Waste Management Branch, V. Niemela
A/Director General, Policy, Planning & Assessment Directorate, G.M. Cornwall
Director, Finance & Admin. Branch, G.A. Coates

Environmental Protection Service Regional Offices

Atlantic: 5th floor, Queen's Square, 59 Alderney Dr., Dartmouth, N.S. B2Y 2N6
Quebec: 4th floor, 1550 Maisonneuve Blvd. W., Montreal, P.Q. H3G 1N2
Ontario: 25 St. Clair Ave. E., Toronto, Ont. M4T 1M2
Western & Northern: Room 804, 9942 108th St., Edmonton, Alta. T5K 2J5
Pacific & Yukon: Kapilano 100, Park Royal, West Vancouver, B.C. V7T 1A2

District Offices

N.W.T.: 9th floor, Bellanca Bldg., Box 370, Yellowknife, N.W.T. XOE 1HO
Yukon: Room 225, Federal Bldg., Whitehorse, Y.T. Y1A 3A4
Alberta: Room 804, 9942 108th St., Edmonton, Alta. T5K 2J5
Saskatchewan: 1901 Victoria Ave., Regina, Sask. S4P 2N9
Manitoba: 800 Kensington Bldg., 275 Portage Ave., Winnipeg, Man. R3B 2B3
New Brunswick: 364 Argyle St., Fredericton, N.B. E3B 1T9
Prince Edward Island: Box 115, Dominion Bldg., Queen St., Charlottetown, P.E.I. C1A 4A9
Newfoundland: Box 5037, St. John's, Nfld. A1C 5V3

Parks Canada

Les Terrasses de la Chaudière, Hull, P.Q. (mailing: Ottawa, Ont. K1A 1G2)

Asst. Deputy Minister, A.T. Davidson
Director General, G.A. Yeates
Director, National Parks Branch, S.F. Kun
Director, National Historic Parks & Sites Branch, H. Tetu

Parks Canada Regional Offices

Atlantic: Parks Canada, Historic Properties Bldg., Upper Water St., Halifax, N.S. B3J 1S9
Ontario: Parks Canada, 132 Second St. E. (Box 1359), Cornwall, Ont. K6H 5V4
Quebec: Parks Canada, 1141 rte de l'Eglise, Ste-Foy, P.Q. G1V 4H5
Western: Parks Canada, 220 4th Ave. S.E., Calgary, Alta. T2P 3H8
Prairie: Parks Canada, 391 York Ave., Winnipeg, Man. R3C 0P4

Canals Offices:

Ontario: Rideau Canal, 12 Maple Ave. N., Smiths Falls, Ont. K7A 1Z5; Trent-Severn Canal Office, Parks Canada, Ashburnham Dr., Box 567, Peterborough, Ont. K9J 6Z6
Quebec: Quebec Canals, 1369 Bourgogne St., Chambly, P.Q. J3L 1Y4

National Parks

Kluane: Mile 1019 Alaska Hwy., Haines Junction, Y.T. YOB 1LO
Nahanni: Postal Bag 300, Fort Simpson, N.W.T. X0E 0N0
Auyuittuq: Pangnirtung, N.W.T. XOA ORO
Pacific Rim: Box 280, Ucluelet, B.C. VOR 3AO
Mount Revelstoke: Box 350, Revelstoke, B.C. VOE 2SO
Glacier: Box 350, Revelstoke, B.C. V0E 2S0
Yoho: Box 99, Field, B.C. VOA 1GO
Kootenay: Box 220, Radium Hot Springs, B.C. VOA 1MO
Jasper: Box 10, Jasper, Alta. TOE 1EO
Banff: Box 900, Banff, Alta. TOL OCO
Wood Buffalo: Box 750, Fort Smith, N.W.T. XOE OPO
Elk Island: Site 4, R.R. 1, Fort Saskatchewan, Alta. T0B 1P0
Waterton Lakes: Waterton Park, Alta. TOK 2NO
Prince Albert: Box 100, Waskesiu Lake, Sask. SOJ 2YO
Riding Mountain: Wasagaming, Man. ROJ 2HO
Pukaskwa: Box 550, Marathon, Ont. POT 2EO
Point Pelee: R.R. 1, Leamington, Ont. N8H 3V4
Georgian Bay Islands: Box 28, Honey Harbour, Ont. POE 1EO
St. Lawrence Islands: Box 469, Mallorytown Landing, Ont. KOE 1RO
La Mauricie: Box 758, Shawinigan, P.Q. G9N 6V9
Forillon: Box 1220, Gaspé, P.Q. GOC 1RO
Kouchibouguac: Kouchibouguac, Kent. Co., N.B. EOA 2AO
Fundy: Box 40, Alma, N.B. EOA 1BO
Prince Edward Island: Box 487, Charlottetown, P.E.I. C1A 7L1
Kejimkujik: Box 36, Maitland Bridge, N.S. BOT 1NO
Cape Breton Highlands: Ingonish Beach, Cape Breton, N.S. BOC 1LO
Gros Morne: Box 130, Rocky Harbour, Bonne Bay, Nfld. AOK 4NO
Terra Nova: Glovertown, Nfld. AOG 2LO

National Historic Parks/Sites

Cape Spear: Box 5879, St. John's, Nfld. A1C 5X4
Signal Hill: Box 5879, St. John's, Nfld. A1C 5X4
Castle Hill: Box 5879, St. John's, Nfld. A1C 5X4
L'Anse aux Meadows: Box 70, St-Lunaire, Griquet, Nfld. A0K 4N0
Port aux Choix: Box 70, St-Lunaire, Griquet, Nfld. A0G 2X0
Fort Amherst: Box 487, Charlottetown, P.E.I. C1A 7L1
Province House: Box 487, Charlottetown, P.E.i. C1A 7L1
Fort Edward: Parks Canada, Annapolis Royal, N.S. B0S 1A0
Prince of Wales Martello Tower: Box 1480, Halifax North, N.S. B3K 5H7
York Redoubt: Box 1480, Halifax North, N.S. B3K 5H7
Halifax Citadel: Box 1480, Halifax North, N.S. B3K 5H7
Alexander Graham Bell National Historic Park: Box 159, Baddeck, N.S. BOE 1BO
Grand Pré: Parks Canada, Annapolis Royal, N.S. B0S 1A0
St. Peter's Canal: Box 8, St. Peter's, N.S. BOE 3BO
Fortress of Louisbourg: Box 160, Louisbourg, N.S. BOA 1MO
Fort Anne: Annapolis Royal, N.S. B0S 1A0
Port Royal: Annapolis Royal, N.S. B0S 1A0
Carleton Martello Tower: 454 Whipple St., Saint John, N.B. E2M 2R3
Fort Beauséjour: 454 Whipple St., Saint John, N.B. E2M 2R3
St. Andrews Blockhouse: 454 Whipple St., Saint John, N.B. E2M 2R3
Lachine Canal: 71369 Bourgogne St., Box 234, Chambly, P.Q.
Battle of Chateauguay: Box 886, Ormstown, P.Q. J0S 1K0
National Battlefields Park: 390, de Bernières Ave., Quebec, P.Q. G1R 2L7
Cartier-Brébeuf Park: 75 de l'Espinay St., Quebec, P.Q. G1L 4V8
Fortifications of Québec: 2 D'Auteuil St., Québec, P.Q. G1K 7R3
Artillery Park: 2 D'Auteuil St., Québec, P.Q. G1K 7R3
Fort Lennox: St-Paul-de-l'Ile-aux-Noix, P.Q. J0J 1G0
Fort Chambly: 2 Richelieu St., Chambly, P.Q. J3L 2B6
Coteau-du-Lac: Box 211, Coteau-du-Lac, P.Q. J0P 1B0
Les Forgues du Saint-Maurice: 10150 boul. des Forges, Trois-Rivières, P.Q. G9L 1B1
Maison Laurier: 12 Laurier Ave., Ville des Laurentides, P.Q. JOR 1CO
Fort Témiscamingue: Ville-Marie, P.Q. J0Z 3R0
Fort George: Box 787, Niagara-on-the-Lake, Ont. LOS 1JO
Queenston Heights & Brock's Monument: c/o Fort George National Historic Parks, Niagara-on-the-Lake, Ont. LOS 1JO
Bellevue House: 35 Centre St., Kingston, Ont. K7L 4E5

Kingston Martello Towers: 35 Centre St., Kingston, Ont. K7L 4E5
Fort Wellington: Box 479, Prescott, Ont. KOE 1TO
Fort St. Joseph: Box 188, Richards Landing, Ont. P0R 1J0
Fort Malden: Box 38, Amherstburg, Ont. N9V 2Z2
Bethune Memorial House: 235 John St., Gravenhurst, Ont. P0C 1G0
Woodside: 528 Wellington St. N., Kitchener, Ont. N2H 5L5
Lower Fort Garry: Box 7, Group 342, R.R. 3, Selkirk, Man. R1A 2A8
Fort Prince of Wales: Box 127, Churchill, Man. ROB OEO
York Factory: Box 157, Churchill, Man.
Riel House: 330 River Rd., St. Vital, Man. R2M 3Z8
Cypress Hills Massacre: Box 278, Maple Creek, Sask. S0N 1N0
Fort Espérance: c/o Lower Fort Garry, Box 7, Group 342, R.R. 3, Selkirk, Man. R1A 2A8
Fort Walsh: Box 278, Maple Creek, Sask. SON 1NO
Battleford: Battleford, Sask. SOM OEO
Batoche: Battleford, Sask. S0M 0E0
Rocky Mountain House: Box 2130, Rocky Mountain House, Alta. TOM 1TO
Fort Langley: Box 129, Fort Langley, B.C. VOX 1JO
Fort St. James: Box 1148, Fort St. James, B.C. VOJ 1PO
St. Roch: 1100 Chestnut St., Vancouver, B.C. V6J 1A3
Fort Rodd Hill: 604 Belmont St., Victoria, B.C. V9C 2W8
S.S. Klondike: 200 Range Rd., Whitehorse, Y.T. Y1A 3V1
Klondike National Historic Sites: Box 390, Dawson City, Yukon Y0B 1G0

DEPT. OF EXTERNAL AFFAIRS

Lester B. Pearson Bldg., 125 Sussex Dr., Ottawa, Ont. K1A OG2
General Enquiries, (613/996-9134)
Minister's Office, (613/995-1851)
Press Enquiries, (613/995-1874)
Passports, (613/995-8481)
Publications, (613/593-7064)
Personnel, (613/995-6474) (for names and addresses of Canadian personnel abroad)

The Department of External Affairs administers Canada's external relations in all spheres of activity.

The Secretary of State for External Affairs Administers The Following Statutes:

Diplomatic & Consular Privileges & Immunities Act
Dept. of External Affairs Act
Food & Agriculture Org. of the United Nations Act
Fort Falls Bridge Authority Act
Geneva Conventions Act
High Commissioner in the United Kingdom Act
International Boundary Waters Treaty Act
International Development Research Centre Act
Privileges & Immunities (International Organizations) Act
Privileges & Immunities (North Atlantic Treaty Org.) Act
Rainy Lake Watershed Emergency Control Act
Roosevelt Campobello International Park Commission Act
Territorial Sea & Fishing Zones Act
Treaties of Peace (Austria & Germany, Bulgaria, Italy, Romania, Hungary,Finland, Japan and Turkey)
United Nations Act

Other Responsibilities

In addition to the Department, the Secretary of State for External Affairs is responsible to Parliament for the following agencies, which are listed alphabetically elsewhere in the federal government listings of this book (see bold headings):
Canadian International Development Agency
International Joint Commission (Canadian Section)
International Boundary Commission (Canadian Section)
Permanent Joint Board on Defence
Roosevelt-Campobello International Park Commission
Foreign Claims Commission
International Development Research Centre

SECRETARY OF STATE FOR EXTERNAL AFFAIRS, Hon. Mark MacGuigan
Under-Secretary of State for External Affairs, A.E. Gotlieb
Associate Under-Secretary, De M. Marchand
Deputy Under Secretaries, M. de Goumois, D. Molgat, J.H. Taylor, E.P. Black, W.J. Jenkins
Asst. Under-Secretaries, J. Gignac, J.R. McKinney, L.A.H. Smith, M.Y. Catley-Carlson, W.T. Delworth, R.V. Gorham, E.G. Lee, M. Shenstone, J. Touchette

Passport Office

125 Sussex Dr., Ottawa, Ont. K1A OG3
Director, R.J. Sutherland

Regional Passport Offices:

220 4th Ave. S.E., Calgary, Alta. T2G 4X3, 403/231-5171, 2, 3
#500, 10117 Jasper Ave., Edmonton, Alta. T5J 1W8, 403/420-2622, 23
#601, 440 King St., Fredericton, N.B. E3B 5B9, 506/452-3900, 2
#1210, Barrington Tower, Scotia Sq., Halifax, N.S. B3J 1P3, 902/426-2770, 71
#1006, 20 Hughson St. S., Hamilton, Ont. L8N 2A1, 416/523-2831
#709, 451 Talbot St., London, Ont. N6A 5C9, 519/679-4366
Mezzanine floor, Commerce House, 1080 Beaver Hall Hill, Montreal, P.Q. H2Z 1S8, 514/283-2152
5th floor, Condominium 2535, 2535 Laurier Blvd. S., Ste-Foy, P.Q. J1V 4M3, 418/694-4990
4th floor, 354 Water St., St. John's, Nfld. A1C 1C4, 709/737-4616
6th floor, 101 22nd St. E., Saskatoon, Sask. S7K 0E1, 306/665-5106, 7
#1012, 10th floor, Royal Trust Tower, Box 304, Toronto Dominion Centre, Toronto, Ont. M5K 1K2, 416/369-3251
Sub office at 4900 Yonge St., Ground floor, Willowdale, Ont. M2N 6A6
#610, 800 W. Pender St., Vancouver, B.C. V6C 2V6, 604/666-1221
#228, 816 Government St., Victoria, B.C. V8W 1W8, 604/388-0213
#504, 100 Ouellette St., Windsor, Ont. N9A 6T3, 519/253-3507
#1310, Richardson Bldg., 1 Lombard Place, Winnipeg, Man. R3B 0X4, 204/949-2190

Passports

Canadian Passports are issued only to Canadian citizens. The total life of a Canadian passport is five years. The passport is a valuable document, the loss of which must be reported to the local police and either to the Passport Office, Ottawa, one of the regional offices listed above, or to the nearest Canadian diplomatic mission (Embassy, High Commissioner's Office) or Consular Office abroad.

Passport Requirements:

All applicants (including children whose names will appear in a parent's passport) must submit documentary proof of Canadian Citizenship: (a) applicants born in Canada–Certificate of Birth; or–Certificate of Canadian Citizenship (includes miniature certificate), large certificates issued after Feb. 14, 1977, are not acceptable; (b) applicants not born in Canada–Certificate of Canadian Citizenship, or–Certificate of Naturalization in Canada; or–Certificate of Registration of Birth Abroad; or Certificate of Retention of Canadian Citizenship.

Fee Schedule:

Canadian passport $20.00
Businessman's Canadian passport $22.00
Addition of a married name to a maiden name passport $5.00

Application for passport:

Application for a Passport should be mailed to reach the Passport Office, Dept. of External Affairs, Ottawa, at least two weeks plus mailing time before the passport is required. Alternatively, they may be presented in person at any of the regional offices listed above. *Regional offices do not accept mailed-in applications.* Canadian citizens residing abroad should apply to the Canadian mission in their country of residence.

Regulations and instructions for persons applying for Canadian passports in Canada are contained in "Passport Application Form A" for persons 16 and over, and "Passport Application Form B for a child under 16" which can be obtained from any post office in Canada, from the Passport Office, Ottawa, from the regional offices, or from travel agencies.

Every application for passport must be signed by a guarantor from one of the eligible categories listed on the form who must also certify the back of one of the applicant's photographs. In addition to being a member of one of the groups listed, the guarantor must be a Canadian Citizen who has known the applicant personally for at least two years. If there is no person available within the group of eligible guarantors who has known the applicant for the required two years appropriate instructions will be found in the application form.

Warning:

The attention of applicants and guarantors is drawn to Section 58(2) of the Criminal Code covering passport fraud whereby: "Every one who, while in or out of Canada, for the purpose of procuring a passport for himself or any other person, makes a written or oral statement that he knows is false or misleading is guilty of an indictable offence and is liable to imprisonment for two years."

Children:

The name of a child under 16 years of age may be included in the passport of either parent but may not be included in the passports of both parents at the same time. Separate passports for children under 16 years may be obtained by submitting application Form B. If a child's name is to be added to an existing passport or transferred from one parent's passport to the passport of the other parent, Form B-1 must be submitted.

Visas

A passport alone does not confer the right to enter any country. Travellers are advised to check with the embassy or consulate of the country they wish to visit to determine visa and entry/exit requirements, health certificates, customs, currency, etc., all of which are subject to change without notice.

Work Permits:

Most countries will not allow non-residents to accept gainful employment unless they have applied for and been granted work permits prior to their entry.

FEDERAL-PROVINCIAL RELATIONS OFFICE

59 Sparks St., Ottawa, Ont. K1A OA3
Secretary to the Cabinet, Michael J.L. Kirby
Executive Asst., Betty Yolkouskie (613/995-5188)

DEPT. OF FINANCE

Place Bell Canada, 160 Elgin St., Ottawa, Ont. K1A OG5
Information Contact, Ben Ward, Director, Information Division (phone: 613-992-1573)

The Department of Finance has a policy responsibility in connection with the following Acts:

Anti-Dumping Act
Bank Act
Bank of Canada Act
Bills of Exchange Act
Bretton Woods Agreements Act
Canada Deposit Insurance Corp. Act
Canada Development Corp. Act, 1971
Canadian & British Insurance Companies Act
Canadian Fishermen's Loan Act
Canadian National Railways Capital Revision Act
Canadian National Railways Financing & Guarantee Act
Canadian National Railways Refunding Act
Co-operative Credit Associations Act
Currency & Exchange Act
Customs Tariff
Dept. of Insurance Act
Diplomatic Service (Special) Superannuation Act
Excise Tax Act
Export Credits Insurance Act
Federal-Provincial Fiscal Arrangements and Established Programs Financing, 1977, Act
Financial Administration Act
Foreign Insurance Companies Act
Gold Export Act
Governor General's Retiring Annuity Act
Halifax Relief Commission Pension Continuation Act
Income Tax Act
International Development Association Act
Investment Companies Act
Loan Companies Act
Members of Parliament Retiring Allowances Act
Municipal Development & Loan Act
Municipal Grants Act
Newfoundland Additional Financial Assistance Act
Newfoundland Additional Grants Act
Oil Export Tax Act
Pension Benefits Standards Act
Prairie Grain Loans Act
Prairie Grain Producers Interim Financing Act
Prince Edward Island Subsidy Act
Provincial Subsidies Act
Quebec Savings Banks Act
Tariff Board Act
Tax Rental Agreements Act
Trust Companies Act
Winding Up Act

MINISTER, Hon. Allan J. MacEachen (992-9171)
Executive Asst., Colin MacDonald (996-7861)
Special Asst., M. Gillan (996-7861)
MINISTER OF STATE, Hon. Pierre Bussières (992-0777)
Executive Asst., Louis Alberti (996-3461)
Administration Branch, Director General, R.E. Crosby (995-8487)
Personnel, vacant
Director, Financial Services, D.D. Lusby (995-6264)
Inspector General of Banks, W.A. Kennett (992-0377)

Deputy Minister, I.A. Stewart (992-4925)
Assoc. Deputy Minister, B.J. Drabble (996-1963)
Senior Asst. Deputy Minister, A.S. Rubinoff (992-1630)
Fiscal Policy & Economic Analysis Branch, Asst. Deputy Minister, S.J. Handfield-Jones (995-6391)
General Director, J.H. Sargent (996-7389)
Director, Economic Analysis Division, D.C. Featherstone (992-9353)
Director, Long Range & Structural Analysis Division, C.S. Clark (996-5225)
Director, Capital Markets Division, G. King (992-5885)
Director, Fiscal Policy Division, vacant
Tax Policy & Legislation Branch, Asst. Deputy Minister, G. Jenkins (992-1630)
General Director, R.A. Short (992-1785)
Director, Tax Policy Legislation Division, vacant
Director, Tax Analysis & Commodity Tax Division, S.N. Poddar (996-8267)
Economic Programs & Government Finance Branch, Asst. Deputy Minister, M. Daniels (992-1526)
General Director, D. Levin (992-9885)
Director, Economic Development Division, F. Swift (996-0807)
Director, Energy & Resource Policy Division, H.G.P. Taylor (992-0782)
Director, Government Finance Division, M.B. Foster (996-9599)
Federal-Provicial Relations & Social Policy Branch, Asst. Deputy Minister, G. Veilleux (996-0735)
General Director, J.H. Lynn (996-5083)

Director, Federal Provincial Relations Division, C. Lemelin (996-1432)
Director, Social Policy Division, M. Chartier-Gauvin (996-0533)
International Trade & Finance Branch, Asst. Deputy Minister, R.K. Joyce (992-6985)
Director General, E.A. Oestreicher (996-6572)
Director, International Economic Relations Division, vacant
Director, Tariffs Division, L.M. Russell (996-6477)
Director, International Finance Division, M.G. Kelly (996-0314)
Director, International Programs Division, G. Proulx (996-6267)

Crown Corps., Etc. That Report Through Finance Minister:

Auditor General
Anti-Dumping Tribunal
Bank of Canada
Canadian Deposit Insurance Corp.
Dept. of Insurance
Inspector General of Banks
The Tariff Board

DEPT. OF FISHERIES & OCEANS

240 Sparks St., Ottawa, Ont. K1A OE6

Director, Communications Branch, Ian Hamilton (613/995-2201)

Acts Administered

Coastal Fisheries Protection Act
Fish Inspection Act
Fisheries Act
Fisheries Development Act
Fisheries Improvement Loans Act
Fisheries Prices Support Act
Fisheries & Oceans Research Advisory Council Act
Fishing & Recreational Harbours Act
Freshwater Fish Marketing Act
Great Lakes Fisheries Convention Act
North Pacific Fisheries Convention Act
Northern Pacific Halibut Fisheries Convention Act
Northwest Atlantic Fisheries Convention Act
Pacific Fur Seals Convention Act
Pacific Salmon Fisheries Convention Act
Saltfish Act
Whaling Convention Act

MINISTER, Hon. Roméo LeBlanc
Deputy Minister, D.D. Tansley

Assistant Deputy Ministers

Economic Development & Marketing, Gary C. Vernon (995-5148)
Pacific & Freshwater Fisheries, H. Doug Johnston (995-1343)
Atlantic Fisheries Service, Dr. Art W. May (995-2195)
Ocean Science & Surveys, Gerry N. Ewing (995-2197)

Pacific & Freshwater Fisheries

Director General, Pacific Region, C.W. Shinners (604/666-6097)
Director General, Western Region, Dr. Herb Lawler (204/269-7379, ext. 284)
Director General, Ontario Region, Dr. John Davis (416/637-4673)

Atlantic Fisheries Service

Director General, Atlantic Operations Directorate, L. Scott Parsons (995-2055)
Director General, Newfoundland Region, Eric Dunne (709/737-4417)
Director General, Scotia-Fundy Region, Dick Crouter (902/426-2581)
Director General, Gulf Region, Len J. Cowley (506/758-2510)

Ocean Science & Surveys

Dominion Hydrographer, Steve B. MacPhee (995-4405)
Director General, Pacific Region, Dr. Cedric Mann (604/656-8215)
Director General, Central Region, Tom D.W. McCulloch (416/637-4339)
Director General, Atlantic Region, Dr. Allan Longhurst (902/426-3492)

Other Services

Director General, Management Services Bureau, Tom Ford (902/995-4613)
Director General, Small Craft Harbours Directorate, Dr. Ken Brodersen (995-2003)

Associated Agencies

Freshwater Fish Marketing Corp.
Canadian Saltfish Corp.
Fisheries Prices Support Board

Fisheries & Oceans Regional Offices

Pacific Region: 1090 W. Pender St., Vancouver, B.C. V6E 2P1
Western Region: 501 University Cres., Winnipeg, Man. R3T 2N6
Ontario Region: 3050 Harvester Rd., Burlington, Ont. L7N 3J1
Scotia-Fundy Region: 1649 Hollis St. (Box 550, Halifax, N.S. B3J 2S7)
Gulf Region: Memramcook Institute, Box 270, St. Joseph, N.B. E0A 2Y0
Newfoundland Region: Box 5667, St. John's, Nfld. A1C 5X1

Ocean Science & Surveys

Institute of Ocean Sciences, 9860 W. Saanich Rd., Sidney, B.C. V8L 4B2
Canada Cente for Inland Waters, Box 5050, Burlington, Ont.
Bedford Institute of Oceanography, Box 1006, Dartmouth, N.S.

FISHERIES COMMISSIONS

INTERNATIONAL PACIFIC SALMON FISHERIES COMMISSION
Box 30, New Westminster, B.C. V3L 4X9
(604) 521-3771
Director, A.C. Cooper
Canadian Commrs., C.W. Shinners, A.W. Dixon, W.W. Forrest
INTERNATIONAL PACIFIC HALIBUT COMMISSION
Box 5009, Univ. of Washington, Seattle, Wash., U.S.A. 98105
(206) 634-1838
Director of Investigation, D.A. McCaughran
Canadian Commrs., P. Wallin, M. Hunter, D. McLeod
NORTHWEST ATLANTIC FISHERIES ORGANIZATION
Box 638, Dartmouth, N.S. B2Y 3Y9
(902) 469-9105
Executive Secretary, J.C.E. Cardoso
This organization is composed of three autonomous bodies:
General Council, Chairman, Dr. A.W. May (also President of the Organization)
Fisheries Commission, Chairman, J.B.P. Farnell
Scientific Council, Chairman, R.H. Letaconnoux
INTER-AMERICAN TROPICAL TUNA COMMISSION
c/o Scripps Institute of Oceanography, La Jolla, Calif. 92093
(714) 453-2820
Director of Investigation, Dr. James Joseph
Canadian Commrs., J.S. Beckett (one vacancy)
INTERNATIONAL NORTH PACIFIC FISHERIES COMMISSION
6640 N.W. Marine Dr., Vancouver, B.C. V6T 1X2
(604) 228-1128
Executive Director, K. Shima
Canadian Commrs., D.F. Miller, J. Garcia, M. Florian, H.D. Johnston
GREAT LAKES FISHERY COMMISSION
1451 Green Rd., Ann Arbor, Mich., U.S.A. 48105
(313) 662-3209
Executive Secretary, Carlos M. Fetterolf, Jr.
Canadian Commrs., Dr. H.A. Regier, H.D. Johnston, K.H. Loftus, Dr. M.G. Johnson

INTERNATIONAL WHALING COMMISSION
The Red House, Station Rd., Cambridge, Eng. CB4 4NP
(022) 023-3971
Secretary, Dr. R. Gambell
Canadian Commr., M.C. Mercer
NORTH PACIFIC FUR SEAL COMMISSION
U.S. National Marine Fisheries Service, Washington, D.C. 20235
Secretary, J.W. Gehringer
Canadian Commrs., M. Hunter; M. Bigg (alternate)
INTERNATIONAL COMMISSION FOR THE CONSERVATION OF ATLANTIC TUNAS
Madrid, Spain
Canadian Commrs., W. Fraser, J. Beckett, H. Trudeau
CANADA/NORWAY SEALING COMMISSION
c/o Dept. of Fisheries & Oceans, 240 Sparks St., Ottawa, Ont. K1A 0E6
Canadian Commrs., Dr. A.W. May, M. Short, J.W. Carroll (alternate)

HARBOUR COMMISSIONS

FRASER RIVER HARBOUR COMMISSION
#505, 713 Columbia St., New Westminster, B.C. V3M 1B2
(604) 524-6655

HAMILTON HARBOUR COMMISSION
605 James St. N., Hamilton, Ont. L8L 1J9
(416) 525-4330

LAKEHEAD HARBOUR COMMISSION
Box 2266, Thunder Bay, Ont. P7B 5E8
(807) 344-3594

NANAIMO HARBOUR COMMISSION
105 Front St., Box 131, Nanaimo, B.C. V9R 5R4
(604) 753-4146

NORTH FRASER HARBOUR COMMISSION
Oak St. Wharf, Foot Oak St. S., Vancouver, B.C. V6P 4B9
(604) 261-3161

OSHAWA HARBOUR COMMISSION
1050 Farewell St., Box 492, Oshawa, Ont. L1H 6N6
(416) 576-0400

PORT ALBERNI HARBOUR COMMISSION
2750 Harbour Rd., Box 99, Port Alberni, B.C. V9Y 7M6
(604) 723-5312

TORONTO HARBOUR COMMISSION
60 Harbour St., Toronto, Ont. M5J 1B7
(416) 863-2036

WINDSOR HARBOUR COMMISSION
500 Riverside Dr. W., Windsor, Ont. N9A 5K6
(519) 258-5741

HOUSE OF COMMONS STAFF

For List of Members etc., See Index
Speaker, Hon. Jeanne Sauvé

Procedural Services

Clerk of the House, C.B. Koester
Law Clerk & Parliamentary Counsel, J.P.J. Maingot
Clerk Asst., M. Pelletier
Second Clerk Asst., Alexander Small
Third Clerk Asst., Réginald-L. Boivin
Third Clerk Asst., Maxime Guitard

Heads of Branches:

Committees & Private Legislation, A. Mackenzie
Journals, C. Desrosiers
Parliamentary Relations Secretariat, I. Imrie
Table Research, M. Kirby

Building Services

Sergeant-at-Arms, Maj. Gen. M.G. Cloutier
Director of Restaurant & Cafeterias, W. Pentecost
Director of Members' Services, K. Martin
Director of Logistics, J.A. Spénard
Director of Security Services, R. Quintal

Administrative Services

The Administrator, A. Silverman
Comptroller, E.A. Riedel
Director General, Human Resources, R. Blain
Director of Support Services, R.J. Desramaux
Parliamentary Reporting Services, J. Sabourin
Director of Internal Audit, J.M. Sévigny

IMMIGRATION APPEAL BOARD

Ottawa, Ont. K1A OK1
(613) 995-6486
Chairman, Janet V. Scott
Vice Chairman, F. Glogowski
Senior Registrar, Mrs. M.J. Denis
Chief, Finance & Admin., T.R. Hickey
Legal Officer, Ms. P.M. Wall

DEPT. OF INDIAN AFFAIRS & NORTHERN DEVELOPMENT

Les Terrasses de la Chaudière, Ottawa, Ont. K1A OH4
Information Contact, P.J. Gibson, Director, Communications (Personnel) (phone: 819/997-9920)

The duties of the Minister of Indian Affairs & Northern Development include: a) the settlement of Indian and Inuit claims through the Office of Native Claims; b) administration of the Indian Act and development programs to benefit Canada's Indian and Inuit people; c) administration of federal statutes respecting the Northwest Territories and Yukon Territory and their resources and affairs; and d) federal responsibility for Northern Canada Power Commission.

Acts Administered:

Dept. of Indian Affairs & Northern Development Act
Indian Act
Canada Oil & Gas Production Act
Territorial Lands Act
Northern Inland Waters Act
Arctic Waters Pollution Prevention Act
Yukon Act
Northwest Territories Act
Yukon Placer Mining Act
Yukon Quartz Mining Act
Northern Power Commission Act
Dominion Water Power Act
Canada Land Surveys Part III
Indian Oil & Gas Act
James Bay & Northern Quebec Native Claims Settlement Act
Land Titles Act
Public Lands Grant Act
Various Appropriation Acts

MINISTER, Hon. J.C. Munro
Executive Asst., F. Viola
Deputy Minister, P.M. Tellier
Asst. Deputy Ministers:
Corporate Policy, J.C. Tait
Indian & Inuit Affairs, D.K. Goodwin
Northern Affairs, G.N. Faulkner
Finance & Professional Services, R.J. Fournier
Executive Director, Office of Native Claims, C. Demers
Director General, Personnel, J. Cyr (division includes: Audit; Employee Counselling; Staff Relations; & Human Resources)
Communications, Director, P.J. Gibson
Director General, Communications, R.H. Knox
Corporate Policy
Director, Policy Co-ordination Branch, A. Midgley
Director, Evaluation, A. Gratias
Director, Intergovernmental Affairs, I.B. Cowie
Director, Research, Dr. K.B. Cooke
Indian & Inuit Affairs Program

Director, Public Communications & Parliamentary Relations, R.K. Kelly
Director General, Program Planning & Policy Co-ordination, D.E. Goodleaf
Director General, Economic & Social Development, D. Chatain
Director General, Reserves & Trusts, J.D. Leask
A/Director General, Housing & Band Support, F. Jetté

Northern Affairs Program
Director, Public Communications & Parliamentary Relations, T. Keleher
Director General, Northern Policy & Programming, J. Hucker
A/Director General, Northern Environment, A.H. Jones
Director, Non-Renewable Resources, Dr. H.W. Woodward
Director, Northern Economic Planning, M. Klein
Director General, N.W.T. Federal Liaison Bureau, N.J. MacPherson

Finance & Professional Services
(includes: Engineering & Architecture; Operations; Departmental Audit; Information Systems; Data Processing; Management Consulting Services; Accounting; Resource Planning; Contracts & Services; Management Improvement Project)

Indian & Northern Affairs Regional Offices:

Indian & Inuit Affairs:

Alta.: 9942 108 St., Edmonton, Alta. T5K 2J5
B.C.: Box 10061, Pacific Centre, 700 W. Georgia St., Vancouver, B.C. V7Y 1C1
Man.: 275 Portage Ave., Rm. 1100, Winnipeg, Man. R3B 3A3
N.S.: (40 Havelock St.), Box 160, Amherst, N.S. B4H 3Z3
N.W.T.: 3rd floor, 5110A 50th Ave. (Box 2760), Yellowknife, N.W.T. XOE 1HO
Ont.: 5th floor, 55 St. Clair Ave. E., Toronto, Ont. M4T 2P8
Que.: 1141 Route de l'Eglise, (Box 8300), Ste-Foy, P.Q. G1V 4C7
Sask.: 2332 11th Ave., Regina, Sask. S4P 2G7
Yukon: Box 4100, Whitehorse, Y.T. Y1A 3S9

Northern Affairs:

N.W.T.: A/Director, A.G. Redshaw, Box 1500, Yellowknife, N.W.T. X1A 2R3
Yukon: Director, D. Watson, 200 Range Rd., Whitehorse, Y.T. Y1A 3V1

DEPT. OF INDUSTRY, TRADE & COMMERCE

235 Queen St., Ottawa, Ont. K1A OH5
Information Contact, Jean B. Chrétien, Manager, Public Affairs, Public Information Directorate (613/995-7137)

This Department is responsible for the establishment, growth and efficiency of manufacturing, processing and tourist industries in Canada and for the development of export trade and external policies.

The Minister is Responsible for the Following Statutes & Regulations:

Dept. of Industry, Trade & Commerce Act
Canadian Commercial Corp. Act
Export & Import Permits Act
Employment Support Act
Foreign Investment Review Act
Fruit, Vegetables & Honey Act
Industrial Research & Development Incentives Act
Export Development Act
Standards Council of Canada Act
Statistics Act
National Design Council Act
Corp. & Labour Unions Returns Act
Defence Supplies Act
Textile & Clothing Board Act
Employment Support Regulations
Industrial Research & Development Incentives Regulations
Automotive Adjustment Assistance Regulations
General Adjustment Assistance Regulations
Shipbuilding Temporary Assistance Regulations
Ship Const. Subsidy Regulations
Pharmaceutical Industry Development Assistance Regulations
United Nations Rhodesian Regulations

MINISTER, Hon. Herb Gray (996-1880)
Minister of State for Small Business & Tourism, Hon. Charles Lapointe (995-1333)
Minister of State for Trade, Hon. Ed Lumley (995-9001)
Deputy Minister, R. Johnstone (992-4292)
Assoc. Deputy Minister, W.R. Teschke (593-5805)
Director, Departmental Secretariat, vacant (995-1410)
Head of Protocol, Wm. Jones (996-3113)
A/Director General, Corporate Affairs Branch, H.A. Reynolds (992-1744)
Director, Public Information Directorate, D.E. Fyfe (995-7137)
Director General, Personnel Branch, P.L. Rainboth (996-5761)
A/Director, Office of Departmental Review, G.G. Hudson (996-2045)
Director, Legal Services, D. Lefebvre (995-3163)

Canadian Government Office of Tourism

Asst. Deputy Minister, Tourism, T.R.G. Fletcher (996-5651)
Director, Policy Planning Co-ordination, A.J. Moore (995-9256)
Director, Administrative Services, D.J. Molloy (992-1680)
Director General, Tourism Marketing, Gordon Ruston (992-3166)
Director, Marketing Communications, O.H. Tiessen (995-6052)
Director, Marketing Operations, U.S.A., R.E. Desjardins (995-6367)
Director, Marketing Operations, Canada, P. Turcotte (992-5753)
Director, Special Markets, P.W. Lennon (996-9631)
Director General, Tourism Development, tba (992-5256)
Secretary, Tourism Development East, Miss D. Trudel (995-8426)
Co-ordinator, Tourism Development West, R. Duncombe (995-8426)
Director, Industry, Evaluation & Improvement, B.F. Campbell (996-5653)

Finance

Asst. Deputy Minister, P.E. Quinn (995-1088)
A/Director General, Admin., Evaluation & Systems, M. Azam (593-7457)
COSTPRO - Canadian Organization for the Simplification of Trade Procedures, 151 Sparks St., #302, President, R.C. Milne (995-2814)
Director General, Corporate Analysis Branch, N.A. Fraser (593-6158)
A/Director, Financial Policy & Liaison Branch, W.A. Kilfoyle (593-7886)
Director General, Small Business Secretariat, K.G. Wilson (996-2695)
Business & Government Liaison, C. Plourde (995-6794)

Industry & Commerce Development

Asst. Deputy Minister, A.M. Guérin (995-6277)
Director General, Agriculture, Fisheries & Food Products Branch, C. Stuart (992-1289)
Director General, Chemicals Branch, A.E. LeNeveu (593-7303)
Design Canada 110 O'Connor St., Executive Director, P.C. Fredenburgh (992-0341)
Director General, Electrical & Electronics Branch, D.S. Loftus (593-4481)
Director, Energy Group, R.L. Borden (996-4448)
Director General, Grain Marketing Office, W.J. O'Connor (995-7127)
Director General, Machinery Branch, J.P. Reny (992-1129)
Director General, Resource Industries Branch, E.J. Ward (996-4963)
Director, Forest Products Group, R.W. Ross (992-7128)
Director, Metals & Minerals Group, G. Nash (992-5672)
Director General, Technology Branch, H.C. Douglas (995-7151)

Director General, Textiles & Consumer Products Branch, P. Marceau (992-4078)
Director General, Transportation Industries Branch, M. Brennan (996-4122)
Director, Vehicle Systems Directorate, I.R. Craig
Director, Aerospace Industries Directorate, R.G. Haack
Director, Marine & Rail Directorate, G.E. Hughes-Adams
Director General, Office of Service Industries, J.A. Dawson (593-7746)
Director General, Construction & Consulting Services Branch, J.A. Dawson (593-7746)
Director General, Transportation Services Branch, J.A. Dawson (593-7746)
(includes: Air Transport; Maritime Transport; Traffic Services)
Director General, Distribution Services Branch, J.A. Dawson (593-7746)
(includes: Wholesale & Retail Distribution; Merchandising Services)

Economic Policy & Analysis

A/Asst. Deputy Minister, C.J. Hindle (996-7951)
(includes: Micro Economic Analysis; Trade & Structural Analysis; Economic Intelligence)

Trade Commissioner Service & International Marketing

Asst. Deputy Minister, B.C. Steers (996-7065)
Head, International Marketing Policy Group, R.A. Kilpatrick (593-7815)
Director General, United States Bureau, D.H. Gilchrist (593-5467)
Director General, Trade Fairs & Missions Branch, D.J. Janigan (996-6153)
Director General, Defence Programs Branch, T.M. Chell (992-8584)
Director General, Office of Overseas Projects, F.R. Petrie (995-2888)
Director, Asia/Pacific & International Financing, G.T. Keys (995-3054)
Chief, Western Hemisphere/Europe Division, Mrs. J.C. McCloskey (996-5357)
Chief, Africa/Middle East Division, D.J. Browne (995-7752)
Chief, Special Projects Division, K.E. Hacker (593-4963)
Director General, Trade Commissioner Service & Canadian Regional Offices, A.T. Eyton (995-8337)

Canadian Regional Offices

Newfoundland Region: 127 Water St., Box 6148, St. John's, Nfld. A1C 5X8 – 709/737-5511 – Telex: 016-4749 – Regional Director General, B.W. Holmes
Nova Scotia Region: #1124, 5251 Duke St., Halifax, N.S. B3J 1N9 – 902/426-7540 – Telex: 019-21829 – Regional Director General, E.A. Coolen
P.E.I. Region: 97 Queen St., Box 2289, Charlottetown, P.E.I. C1A 8C1 – 902/892-1211 – Telex: 014-44129 – Regional Director General, T.A. Charles
New Brunswick Region: #642, 440 King St., Fredericton, N.B. E3B 5H8 – 506/452-3190 – Telex: 014-46140 – Regional Director General, J.B. McLaren
Quebec City: #620, 2 Place Québec, Québec, P.Q. G1R 2B4, 418/694-4726
Quebec Region: Box 1270, Stn. B, #600, 685 Cathcart St., Montreal, P.Q. H3B 3K9 – 514/283-6254 – Telex: 055-60768 – Regional Director General, J.R. Mercier
Ontario Region: One First Canadian Place, #4840, Box 98, Toronto, Ont. M5X 1B1 – 416/369-4951 – Telex: 065-24378 – Regional Director General, J.D. Blackwood
Manitoba Region: #507, 386 Broadway Ave., Winnipeg, Man. R3C 3R6 – 204/949-2381 – Telex: 075-7624 – Regional Director General, G. Rezek
Saskatchewan Region: #980, 2002 Victoria Ave., Regina, Sask. S4P 0R7 – 306/569-5020 – Telex: 071-2745 – Regional Director General, Geo. Hazen
Alberta & NWT Region: #500, 9939 Jasper Ave., Edmonton, Alta. T5J 2W8 – 403/420-2944 – Telex: 037-2762 – Regional Director General, D.H.M. Branion
B.C. & Yukon Region: #2743, Box 49178, Three Bentall Centre, 595 Burrard St., Vancouver, B.C. V7X 1K8 – 604/666-1434 – Telex: 04-51191 – Regional Director General, R.M. Dawson

International Trade Relations

Asst. Deputy Minister, R.E. Latimer (996-4176)
Co-ordinator, Country Profile Task Force, G.W. Green (593-5647)
Chairman, Automotive Task Force, C. Stuart (996-3361)
Director General, Office of General Relations, P.T. Eastham (995-7119)
Director General, Trade Policy Branch, G. Elliot (992-4100)
Director General, Office of Special Import Policy, C.D. Arthur (992-3386)
Director General, European Bureau, A.W.A. Lane (992-4815)
Director General, Bureau of Asian & Pacific Affairs, A.L. Halliday (995-2218)
Director General, Bureau of African & Middle Eastern Affairs, W. Lavoie (593-4824)
Director General, Western Hemisphere Bureau, A.R.A. Gherson (996-5533)

Foreign Investment Review Agency

240 Sparks St.
Commissioner, G. Howarth (995-9601)
Information & Inquiries, J. Brulé (995-9449)

Metric Commission Canada

240 Sparks St.
Chairman, D.R.B. McArthur (995-6457)
Executive Director, P.C. Boire (995-6458)

Boards & Advisory Committees

Export Development Corporation
110 O'Connor St. (Box 655, Ottawa, Ont. K1P 5T9)
237-2570
Enterprise Development Board
235 Queen St., Ottawa, Ont. K1A 0H5
Secretary, J.C. Clarke (995-7958)
Machinery & Equipment Advisory Board
235 Queen St., Ottawa, Ont. K1A 0H5
Secretary, H.L. Jones (992-1004)
National Design Council
110 O'Connor St., Ottawa, Ont.
A/Chairman, D. Daly (992-0341)
Standards Council of Canada
#1210, 350 Sparks St., Ottawa, Ont. K1R 7S8
Executive Director, R.L. Hennessy (238-3222)
Textile & Clothing Board
235 Queen St., Ottawa, Ont. K1A 0H5
Executive Director, J.M. MacKillop (593-6336)

DEPT. OF INSURANCE

140 O'Connor St., 15th & 16th floors, Ottawa, Ont. K1A 0H2

The Department of Insurance is charged with the administration of the federal laws pertaining to the operations of federally registered or licensed financial institutions and with the provision of actuarial services for government pension, insurance and social security programs.

The Department administers the following: Canadian & British Insurance Companies Act, Foreign Insurance Companies Act, Civil Service Insurance Act, Trust Companies Act, Loan Companies Act, Co-operative Credit Association Act, Pension Benefits Standards Act, Investment Companies Act, Part 1 of the Excise Tax Act.

Minister in Charge, Minister of Finance
Supt. of Insurance, R. Humphrys
Asst. Supt., R.M. Hammond
Chief Actuary, W. Riese

Branches: 155 University Ave., 14th floor, Toronto, Ont. M5H 3B7; 276 St. James St. W., Montreal, P.Q. H2Y 1N3; 169 Pioneer Ave., 6th floor, Winnipeg, Man. R3C OH2; 1713 Bedford Row, Room 609, Box 1505, Halifax, N.S. B3J 1T3; Toronto Dominion Tower, Pacific Centre, 700 W. Georgia St., Room 1140, Box 10063, Vancouver, B.C. V7Y 1B6

INTERNATIONAL BOUNDARY COMMISSION

Phone: (613) 995-4951

This Commission has jurisdiction over regulation and maintenance of the Canada-U.S. boundary in accordance with the Boundary Treaty of 1925, and the International Boundary Commission Act, R.S.C. 1970, c. I-19.

Canadian Section:

Commr., A.C. McEwen, LL.B., LL.M., Ph.D., C.L.S., O.L.S., 615 Booth St., Ottawa, Ont. K1A OE9

United States Section:

Commr., Frank A. Whetstone

INTERNATIONAL JOINT COMMISSION

Phone: Ottawa (613) 995-2984; Washington (202) 296 2142

This Commission has jurisdiction over questions arising between Canada and the United States, involving the use and regulation of waters forming or crossing the common boundary.

Canadian Section:

Chairman, vacant
Commrs., E.R. Olson, C.N. Bedard
Secretary, David G. Chance, 100 Metcalfe St., 18th floor, Ottawa, Ont. K1P 5M1 (613/995-2984)

United States Section:

Chairman, vacant
Commrs., Keith Bulen, D. Totten
Secretary, David A. Laroche, 1717 H St. N.W., Washington, D.C. 20440 (202/296-2142)

DEPT. OF JUSTICE

Ottawa, Ont. K1A OH8

The Department of Justice provides legal services to the government and the various government departments, and superintends the administration of justice not within the jurisdiction of the provinces.

Information from Information Services (phone: 613-995-2569)

The Department of Justice administers or has a special interest in the following Acts:

Alberta Criminal Procedure Act
Annulment of Marriages Act
Bills of Lading Act
Canada Evidence Act
Canada Prize Act
Canadian Bill of Rights
Canadian Human Rights Act
Criminal Code
Crown Liability Act
Dept. of Justice Act
Divorce Act
Emergency Powers Act
Escheats Act
Extradition Act
Federal Court Act
Food & Drugs Act
Foreign Enlistment Act
Fugitive Offenders Act
Interpretation Act
Judges Act
Law Reform Commission Act
Lord's Day Act
Maritime Code
Marriage Act
Narcotic Control Act
Official Secrets Act
Ontario Superior Courts Act
Permanent Court of International Justice Act
Postal Services Interruption Relief Act
Statute Revision Act
Statutory Instruments Act
Supreme Court Act
Tax Review Board Act
Territorial Supreme Courts Act
Tobacco Restraint Act
War Measures Act
Yukon Act

MINISTER, Hon. Jean Chrétien, P.C., Q.C.
Deputy Minister & Deputy Attorney General, Roger Tassé, Q.C.
Assoc. Deputy Minister, Civil Law, M.P. Ollivier, Q.C.
Assoc. Deputy Minister, Litigation, D.H. Christie, Q.C.
Asst. Deputy Ministers:
- Admin., W.C. MacIver
- Legislative Programing, H.A. McIntosh, Q.C.
- Public Law, B.L. Strayer, Q.C.
- Policy Planning & Development, P. Gravelle
- Departmental Legal Services, H. Calof, Q.C.
- Legal Services, S.J. Skelly

Asst. Deputy Attorneys General:
- Civil Litigation, T.B. Smith, Q.C.
- Criminal Law, D.J.A. Rutherford, Q.C.
- Taxation, A. Garon, Q.C.
- Property & Commercial Law, P.M. Troop, Q.C.

Chief Legislative Counsel, Gérard Bertrand, Q.C.
Assoc. Chief Legislative Counsel, Mary Dawson, Q.C.
Chief General Counsel, E.A. Bowie, Q.C.
General Counsel:
- Civil Law, P.R. Coderre, Q.C.
- Indian Claims, S.F. Sommerfeld, Q.C.
- Property Law, W.M. Weekes, Q.C.
- Legislation, P.E. Johnson
- Policy Planning & Criminal Law Amendments, D.C. Préfontaine
- Criminal Law, E.G. Ewaschuk, Q.C.
- Programs & Law Information Development, L.S. Fairbairn
- Legal Services, J.S. Milligan
- Corporate Planning, H.R. Johnson
- Criminal Code Review, E.A. Tollefson, Q.C.
- Privy Council, M.H. Pepper, Q.C.
- Constitutional & International Law, M.L. Jewett
- Advisory & Administrative Law, Alice Desjardins, Q.C.
- Information Law & Privacy Section, S.J. Skelly
- Public Law, F.J.E. Jordan, E.I. MacDonald, Q.C.
- Tax Litigation, W. Lefebvre
- Civil Litigation, vacant
- Criminal Prosecutions, W.H. Corbett
- Litigation, D.H. Aylen, Q.C., L.P. Chambers, Q.C., I.G. Whitehall, Q.C., J.R. Power, Q.C., W.I.C. Binnie, Q.C.

Senior Counsel:
- Administration (Legal), W.S. Regan
- Commercial Law, R.E. Williams, Q.C.
- Constitutional Law, G.F. Fitzgerald
- Civil Litigation, E. Mitchell-Thomas, Q.C.

Department of Justice Regional Offices

Halifax Regional Office

1791 Barrington St., 12th floor, Halifax, N.S. B3J 3L1
Director, J.M. Bentley, Q.C. (902/426-3164)

Montreal Regional Office

C.P. 938, Place d'Armes, Montreal, P.Q. H2Y 3J4
Director, R.F. Paul, Q.C. (514/283-4972)

Toronto Regional Office

Box 57, Toronto Dominion Centre, Toronto, Ont. M5K 1E7
Director, L.R. Olsson, Q.C. (416/369-3101)

Winnipeg Regional Office
301 Centennial House, 310 Broadway, Winnipeg, Man. R3C OS6
Director, D.G. Frayer (204/949-2252)

Saskatoon Regional Office
Room 301, 229 4th Ave. W., Saskatoon, Sask. S7K 4E4
Director, B.D. Collins, Q.C. (306/665-4756)

Edmonton Regional Office
Room 928, Royal Trust Tower, Edmonton Centre, Edmonton, Alta. T5J 2Z2
Director, Julius Isaac, Q.C. (403/420-2983)

Vancouver Regional Office
Royal Centre, 1900, 1055 W. Georgia St., Box 11118, Vancouver, B.C. V6G 3P9
Director, M.M. de Weerdt, Q.C. (604/544-3701)

Yellowknife Regional Office
City Hall, Box 8, Yellowknife, N.W.T. XOE 1HO
Director, G. Bickert (403/873-3551)

Whitehorse Crown Attorney's Office
Room 205, 3105 Third Ave., Box 1076, Whitehorse, Y.T. Y1A 1E5
Crown Attorney, P.G. Hodgkinson (403/667-4418)

DEPT. OF LABOUR
Ottawa, Ont. K1A OJ2
Information from, Communication Services Directorate (phone: 819-997-2617)

Acts Administered by Labour Canada
The Canada Labour Code
Dept. of Labour Act
Fair Wages & Hours of Labour Act
Government Employees Compensation Act
Merchant Seamen Compensation Act

MINISTER, Hon. Charles Caccia
Deputy Minister, Thomas M. Eberlee
Executive Asst. to Deputy Minister, D.K. Deyell
Asst. Deputy Minister, Policy Co-ordination & Liaison, R. Armstrong
Director, Legal Services, A.J. Roach
Director General, Regional Operations, C.D. Harper
Director, Women's Bureau, Ratna Ray
Asst. Deputy Minister, Federal Mediation & Conciliation Service, W.P. Kelly
Director, Federal Mediation & Conciliation Service, Guy de Merlis
Director, Program Planning & Technical Support, J.A. Fuchs
Chief, Arbitration Services, A.C. Sinclair
Asst. Deputy Minister, Program Development & Central Operations, A. Déom
Director, Occupational Safety & Health, J.W. McLellan
Director, Library & Legislative Analysis, J.P. Whitridge
Director, Employment Relations & Conditions of Work, G. Markle
Director, Labour Data, V. Johnston
Director, Economic Analysis Branch, M. Mueller
Director General, Administrative Policy & Services, N.P. Ewing
Director, Communications Services, W.T. Jack
(division includes Data Processing, Finance, and Operational Services)

Regions
Director, Atlantic Region, G. Blanchard
Director, St. Lawrence Region, C.E. Poirier
Director, Great Lakes Region, T. Beaton
Director, Central Region, R. Mattey
Director, Mountain Region, A.R. Gibbons

Boards that Report to Parliament through the Minister of Labour
Merchant Seamen Compensation Board
Canada Labour Relations Board

LAW REFORM COMMISSION OF CANADA
Varette Bldg., 130 Albert St., Ottawa, Ont. K1A OL6
(613) 996-7844
Chairman, Frank C. Muldoon
Members, Judge E.J. Houston, Réjean Paul, Louise Lemelin
Secretary, Jean Côté
Director of Operations, M.H.F. Webber

LIBRARY OF PARLIAMENT
Ottawa, Ont. K1A OA9

The Library of Parliament, established in Ottawa in 1867, is administered by the Parliamentary Librarian appointed by the Crown. From its basic collection of 550,000 books, documents, periodicals, microfilm, and video tapes, and a diversity of automated information retrieval services, its staff provides information, reference and research services to Parliament, its officers and staff, Parliamentary committees and Parliamentary associations.

Parliamentary Librarian, Erik J. Spicer
Assoc. Parliamentary Librarian, Richard Paré
Asst. Parliamentary Librarian, vacant
Director, Information & Reference Branch, Lloyd Heaslip
Director, Research Branch, P.A.C. Laundy
Director, Technical Services Branch, Florence B. Moore
Director, Admin. & Personnel, J.-J. Cardinal

DEPT. OF NATIONAL DEFENCE
101 Colonel By Dr., Ottawa, Ont. K1A OK2
Information Contact is the Press Liaison Officer (phone: 613-996-2353)

The Department is organized under the National Defence Act. The Minister has the control and management of the Canadian Forces and of all matters relating to national defence establishments and works for the defence of Canada except the procurement of military supplies which is a function of the Dept. of Supply & Services.

Legislation Administered
National Defence Act
Canadian Forces Superannuation Act
Defence Services Pension Continuation Act
Visiting Forces Act
Part of the Aeronautics Act

MINISTER, Hon. J. Gilles Lamontagne
Executive Asst., R.L. Lacroix
Deputy Minister, C.R. Nixon
Chief of the Defence Staff, General R.M. Withers, C.M.M., C.D.
Vice Chief of the Defence Staff, Lieut.-Gen. G.C. Theriault, C.M.M., C.D.
Asst. Deputy Minister (Policy), J.F. Anderson
Assoc/Asst. Deputy Minister (Policy), Maj.-Gen. C.J.W. Gauthier, C.D.
Asst. Deputy Minister (Personnel), Lieut.-Gen. H.A. Carswell, C.D.
Assoc/Asst. Deputy Minister (Personnel), W.R. Green
Asst. Deputy Minister (Finance), L.E. Davies
Asst. Deputy Minister (Materiel), L.G. Crutchlow
Assoc/Asst. Deputy Minister (Materiel), Maj-Gen. E.B. Creber, C.D.
Deputy Chief of the Defence Staff, Vice Admiral J. Allan, C.M.M., C.D.
Judge Advocate General, Brig.-Gen. J.P. Wolfe, C.D.
Director General Information, Brig.-Gen. J.M.L. Bourgeois, C.D.
President, Defence Const. (1951) Ltd., A.G. Bland

Commands
Maritime Command
Commander, Vice Admiral J.A. Fulton, C.M.M., C.D.

Commander (Pacific), Rear Admiral W.A. Hughes, C.D.
Mobile Command
Commander, Lieut.-Gen. C.H. Belzile, C.D.
Air Command
Commander, Lieut.-Gen. K.E. Lewis, C.M.M., C.D.
Training Systems Headquarters
Commander, Brig.-Gen. R.B. Button, C.D.
Northern Region
Commander, Brig.-Gen. B. Baile, C.D.
Canadian Forces Europe
Commander, Maj.-Gen. F.J. Richard, C.D.
Canadian Forces Communication Command
Commander, Brig.-Gen. D.P. Harrison, C.D.

Operations Groups

1 Combat Group, Calgary, Alta
Commander, Brig.-Gen. J.A. Cotter, C.D.
Special Service Force, Petawawa, Ont.
Commander, Brig.-Gen. G.H.J. Lessard, M.B., C.D.
Quarter General due 5e Groupement de Combat, Valcartier, P.Q.
Commander, Brig.-Gen. R.P. Beaudry, C.D.
The Canadian Airborne Regiment, Petawawa, Ont.
Commander, Col. K.R. Foster, C.D.
The Combat Training Centre, Gagetown, N.B.
Commander, Brig.-Gen. G.R. Cheriton, O.M.M., C.D.
4 Canadian Mechanized Battle Group, Canadian Forces Europe
Commander, Brig.-Gen. A.J. Dechastelain, C.D.
Headquarters 1 Canadian Air Group, Canadian Forces Europe
Commander, Brig.-Gen. B.R. Campbell, O.M.M., C.D.

Canadian Services Colleges

National Defence College, Kingston, Ont., Maj.-Gen. L.V. Johnson, C.D.
Canadian Forces College, Toronto, Ont., Cmdr. C. Cotaras, C.D.
Canadian Land Forces Command & Staff College, Kingston, Ont., Col. P.H. Carew, C.D.
Royal Military College, Kingston, Ont., Brig. Gen. J.A. Stewart, C.D.
Royal Roads Military College, Royal Roads, B.C., Col. G.L. Logan, C.D.
College Militaire Royal de St. Jean, St. Jean, P.Q., Col. C.E. Savard, O.M.M., C.D.

Regional Information Offices of National Defence

DND Office of Information, Maritime Region, FMO Halifax, N.S.
DND Office of Information, Que. Region, St. Hubert, P.Q.
DND Office of Information, Ont. Region, 1107 Avenue Rd., Toronto, Ont.
DND Office of Information, Man/Sask. Region, CFB Winnipeg, Westwin, Man.
DND Office of Information, Alta. Region, CFB Edmonton, Lancaster Park, Alta.
DND Office of Information, Pacific Region, FMO Victoria, B.C.

NATIONAL ENERGY BOARD

473 Albert St., Ottawa, Ont. K1A OE5
Phone: (613) 992-4370

The Board reports to Parliament through the Minister of Energy, Mines & Resources.

Chairman, C.G. Edge
Vice Chairman, R.F. Brooks
Assoc. Vice Chairmen, L.M. Thur, W.A. Scotland (designated officer, Northern Pipeline Agency), J. Farmer
Members, J.R. Hardie, J.L. Trudel, J.R. Jenkins, R.B. Horner, A.B. Gilmour
Secretary, G. Yorke-Slader

NATIONAL FILM BOARD

Box 6100, Montreal, P.Q. H3C 3H5
Phone: (514) 333-3333

The Board produces and distributes films and other audio-visual material designed to reflect the Canadian nation and identity, and produces films for government departments.

Government Film Commr., James de B. Domville
Deputy Film Commr., François N. Macerola
Asst. Film Commr. & Secretary of the Board, Reta Kilpatrick
Director of Admin., Marc Devlin
Director of Production, English, Peter Katadotis
Director of Production, French, Jean-Marc Garand
Director of Distribution, William Litwack
Director of Technical & Production Services, Marcel Carrière
Director of Public Relations, Mrs. Ann Garneau
Director of Personnel, Gilles Roy
Secretary of the Board, Reta Kilpatrick
Regional Managers:
Halifax, Terence Ryan
Montreal, Pierre Ducharme
Ottawa, Alan Palmer
Toronto, John Boundy
Winnipeg, Henri Moquin
Vancouver, Bruce Pilgrim

DEPT. OF NATIONAL HEALTH & WELFARE

Brooke Claxton Bldg., Ottawa, Ont. K1A OK9
Information Contact, P. Couture, Director, Information Directorate (phone: (613) 992-4575)

Acts Administered

Dept. of National Health & Welfare Act
Blind Persons Act
Canada Assistance Plan Act
Canada Pension Plan
Disabled Persons Act
Environment Contaminants Act
Excise Tax Act Sec. 45
Family Allowances Act
Food & Drugs Act
Hazardous Products Act, Sec. 9 & 10
Health Resources Fund Act
Hospital Insurance & Diagnostic Services Act
Immigration Act, Part III
Medical Care Act
Narcotic Control Act
Old Age Assistance Act
Old Age Security Act
Public Works Health Act
Quarantine Act
Radiation Emitting Devices Act
Unemployment Assistance Act
Vocational Rehabilitation of Disabled Persons Act

MINISTER, Hon. Monique Bégin, P.C., M.P.
Deputy Minister of National Health & Welfare, J.L. Fry
Principal Executive Officer, Carol Chauvin
Principal Nursing Officer, Dr. M.J. Flaherty
Director, National Council of Welfare Secretariat, K. Battle
Director General, Personnel Administration Branch, H.P. Hansen
Director, Internal Audit Directorate, K.F. McCarthy

Management Practices Branch

Asst. Deputy Minister, Admin., C.E. Caron
Financial Admin., Director General, D. Smith
Departmental Administrative Services, Director, B.I. Driscoll
Management Planning, Director, B. Bowen
Information Directorate, Director, P. Couture, M.A.

Regional Information Officers:

Alta.: Donald W. Carlson, Financial Bldg., Room 205, 10621 100 Ave., Edmonton, Alta. T5J OB3
Que.: Jean Martinet, 1 Complexe Desjardins, Ste. 1004, Box 94, Montreal, P.Q. H5B 1B2
Ont.: Nes Lubinsky, 9th floor, 789 Don Mills Rd., Toronto, Ont. M3C 1T5

B.C.: Tony Strachan, Room 105, 1525 W. 8th Ave., Vancouver, B.C. V6J 1T5
N.S.: Pat Brownlow, #740, Barrington Tower, Scotia Sq., Halifax, N.S. B3J 3J4

Health Services & Promotion Branch

Asst. Deputy Minister, Dr. M.M. Law, 992-6449
Executive Asst., Dr. Luc Goudreault, 996-7542
Consultant Pediatrician, Dr. P.G. Banister, 995-5671
Special Advisor, Dr. A. de Villiers, 995-1681
Director, Special Projects, G.B. Rosenfeld, 995-6883
Director, Program Evaluation, R. Pelletier, 995-6883
Planning & Management Services, A/Director, O. Marquardt, 593-5866
Branch Financial Management, A/Chief, H. Holtz, 992-5192
Branch Administration, Chief, A. Goulet, 992-0613
Health Services, A/Director General, F.D. Kealey, 992-7794
Senior Medical Consultant, Dr. R. Lennox, 996-2616
Institutional & Professional Services, Director, D.F. Moffatt, 996-6039
Mental Health, Director, B. Wattie, 995-0166
Family Planning, Director, S. Brazeau, 992-3609
Community Health, A/Director, O. Gareau, 995-9994
Extramural Research Programs, Director General, Dr. R.A. Heacock, 992-7116
Grants & Contributions, A/Director, G. Smith, 992-5291
Health Promotion, Director General, R. Draper, 995-5741
Programs, A/Director, Dr. D. Thornton, 996-4363
Program Resources, Director, Mrs. L. Pinder, 996-3134
Regional Services, Director, B. Roadhouse, 996-4533

Regional Offices

Regional Director, M. Keddy, Atlantic Region, 5409 Rainnie Dr., Halifax, N.S. B3J 1P8, 902/426-2700
Regional Director, P. Lamarche, Québec Region, 2001 Université, 17th floor, Montréal, P.Q. H3A 2A6, 514/283-4583
Regional Director, J. Hill, Ontario Region, #410, 102 Bloor St. W., Toronto, Ont. M5S 1M8, 966-6483
Regional Director, R. Wally, Prairies Region, #603, 213 Notre Dame Ave., Winnipeg, Man. R3B 1N3, 204/949-6574
A/Regional Director, M. Sanderson, Pacific Region, #202, 560 W. Broadway, Vancouver, B.C. V5Z 1E9, 604/666-6061
Health Resources, Director General, R. Lachaine, 593-6509
Health Economics & Data Analysis, Director, W. Mennie, 996-3211
Health Insurance, Director, Dr. D. Stewart, 995-6186
Health Manpower, Director, Dr. J.A. Dupont, 995-1681
Health Facilities Design, Director, T. Ogrodnik, 992-8471
Personnel Services, Manager, R. Ballantyne, 593-5986
Staffing & Human Resources, A/Senior Advisor, Joan Taylor, 992-4711
Classification & Organization, A/Senior Advisor, T. McNeil, 995-7251
Staff Relations Training & Compensation, Senior Advisor, T. Pearson, 992-4711

Medical Services Branch

(Ottawa, Ont. K1A OL3)
Asst. Deputy Minister, Dr. L.M. Black
Executive Asst. to ADM, M. Fillion
Special Advisor to the ADM, I.C. Inglis
Advisor to ADM, Native Affairs, C. Prince
Bilingualism Advisor, Official Languages, L.B. Abud-Lapierre
Director General, Operations, G.B. Campbell
Assoc. Director, East, Dr. B. Wheatley (act.)
Assoc. Director, West, vacant
Director, Native Health Services, Mrs. L. Davies
Consultant, Alcohol & Drug Abuse, Dr. J.D. Copping
Director, Environmental Contaminants Program, N. Campagna (act.)
Director, Health Advisory Services, P. Cochrane
Senior Consultant, Public Service Health, Dr. I.A. Marriott (act.)
Senior Consultant, Immigration Medical Services, Dr. B.S. Leslie
Senior Consultant, Quarantine & Regulatory, Dr. B.S. Leslie
Director, Emergency Services, Mrs. L. Davies
Director, Prosthetic Services, Dr. L. Kawula
Director, Administrative Services, J.M. Sabey
Director General, Policy, Planning & Evaluation, Dr. F.H. Hicks
Director, Policy, Planning & Evaluation, R. Cardillo
Director, Indian & Inuit Health Policy, Dr. V. Tookenay

Regional Directors

Atlantic: J. Sinclair, 439 Ralston Bldg., 1557 Hollis St., Halifax, N.S. B3J 1V6
Que.: M. Savoie, M.D., 300 Léo Pariseau St., 2nd floor, Montreal, P.Q. H2X 3P9
Ont.: J.E. Thorpe, 370 Catherine St., Ottawa, Ont. K1A OL3
Man.: Dr. A.I. Murdock, 500 Commissioners Bldg., 303 Main St., Winnipeg, Man. R3C OH4
Sask.: R. Avison, 500 Derrick Bldg., 2431 11th Ave., Regina, Sask. S4P OK3
Alta.: Dr. G.I. Lynch (act.), 401 Toronto Dominion Tower, Edmonton Centre, Edmonton, Alta. T5J 2Z1
Yukon Territory: M.D. Shellenberg, Yukon Manor, No. 2 Hospital Rd., Whitehorse, Y.T. Y1A 3H8
N.W.T.: Dr. J.D. Martin, Bag 7777, Yellowknife, N.W.T. X1A 2R3
Pacific: Dr. P.T. Presage, 4th floor, 814 Richards St., Vancouver, B.C. V6B 3A9
Overseas: Dr. B. Brett, 2nd floor, 301 Elgin St., Ottawa, Ont. K1A OL3

Hospitals (of twenty beds or more)

Ont.:
Sioux Lookout Zone Hospital, Sioux Lookout, Ont. POV 2TO
Moose Factory General Hospital, Moose Factory, Ont. POL 1WO
Man.:
Percy E. Moore Hospital, Hodgson, Man. ROC 1NO
Sask.:
Fort Qu'Appelle Indian Hospital, Fort Qu'Appelle, Sask. SOG 1SO
Alta.:
Blood Indian Hospital, Box 490, Cardston, Alta. TOK OKO
N.W.T.:
Frobisher Bay General Hospital, Box 580, Frobisher Bay, N.W.T. XOA OHO
Inuvik General Hospital, Inuvik, N.W.T. XOE OTO
Yukon:
Whitehorse General Hospital, 5 Hospital Rd., Whitehorse, Y.T. Y1A 3H7
Mayo General Hospital, Mayo, Y.T. YOB 1MO

Field Offices, Prosthetic Services

Field Admin. Operations:
General Manager, c/o Sunnybrook Medical Centre, 2075 Bayview Ave., Toronto, Ont. M4N 3M5

Factory:
Plant Manager, c/o Sunnybrook Medical Centre, 2075 Bayview Ave., Toronto, Ont. M4N 3M5

Prosthetic Services Centres:
Saint John, N.B.: Officer in Charge, c/o West Saint John Community Hospital, Box 3610, Stn. B, Saint John, N.B. E2N 4X3
Montreal, P.Q.: Officer in charge, c/o Centre Hospitalier Côte-des-Neiges, 4565 Queen Mary Rd., Montreal, P.Q. H3W 1W5
Ottawa, Ont.: Officer in charge, c/o Room G-117, D.N.D. Medical Centre, Alta Vista Dr., Ottawa, Ont. K1A OK6
Toronto, Ont.: Regional Supt., Central Region, c/o Sunnybrook Medical Centre, 2075 Bayview Ave., Toronto, Ont. M4N 3M5
London, Ont.: Officer in charge, c/o Victoria Hospital, Box 5471, Westminster Campus, London, Ont. N6A 4L6
Winnipeg, Man.: Regional Supt., Prairie Region, c/o Deer Lodge Hospital, 2109 Portage Ave., Winnipeg, Man. R3J OL3
Calgary, Alta.: Officer in Charge, c/o Col. Belcher Hospital, 1213 4th St. S.W., Calgary, Alta. T2A OX7
Edmonton, Alta.: Officer in Charge, c/o University Hospital, Mewburn Pavilion, Edmonton, Alta. T6G 2B7
Vancouver, B.C.: Regional Supt., Western Region, c/o Shaughnessy Hospital, 4500 Oak St., Vancouver, B.C. V6H 3N1

Victoria, B.C.: Supt., c/o Memorial Pavilion, 2355 Richmond Ave., Victoria, B.C. V8R 4S2

Health Protection Branch
(Ottawa, Ont. K1A OL2)
A/Asst. Deputy Minister, A.J. Liston
A/Director General, Drugs Directorate, D. Cook
Director General, Foods Directorate, Dr. I.C. Munro
Director General, Environmental Health Directorate, Dr. E. Somers
Director General, Laboratory Centre for Disease Control, Dr. A.J. Clayton
Director, Finance & Admin. Directorate, M.T. McElrone
Director General, Field Operations Directorate, J.R. Elliot

Regional Directors:
Halifax: Mrs. J. Hopkins, Ralston Bldg., 1557 Hollis St., Halifax, N.S. B3J 2R7
Montreal: P. Thisdèle, 1001 St. Laurent Blvd., Longueuil, P.Q. J4K 1C7
Toronto: Dr. C. Broughton, 2301 Midland Ave., Scarborough, Ont. M1P 4R7
Winnipeg: D.A. Gray, 310, 269 Main St., Winnipeg, Man. R3C 1B2
Vancouver: A.J. Sandbrook, 1001 W. Pender St., Vancouver, B.C. V6E 2M7

Policy Development
Special Advisor, John E. Osborne
Director, Program Evaluation, Don Ogston
Senior Advisor, Status of Women, Mrs. Freda Paltiel
Corporate Manager, Access to Information Project, Guy Demers

Income Security Programs
Asst. Deputy Minister, D.M. Lyngseth
Director General, Planning, Evaluation & Liaison, R.J. Allen
Asst. Director General, Planning & Liaison, P. Fortier
Director, Special Projects Team, R.F. Kemp
Director, Finance Admin., D.H. Stewart
Director, Admin., W.A. McDonald

Canada Pension Plan Family Allowances & Old Age Security Programs
Director General, Programs Operations, John Soar
Deputy Director General, Programs Operations, R.K. Stuart
Director, Regional Programs Operations, D. Jones
Director, Legislation Application & Appeals Division, R.A. Johnson
Director, Planning & Development, G. Dubé
Director, International Operations, Guy Gauthier
Director, Disability Determination, Dr. A. Moineau
Director, Claims & Benefits, L. Thibault-Allen

Regional Offices:
Western Area:
British Columbia Regional Office: 436 Federal Bldg., 1230 Government St., Victoria, B.C. V8W 2P1
Alberta Regional Office: Manulife House, 10055 106th St., Edmonton, Alta. T5J 2Z6
Saskatchewan Regional Office: 1975 Scarth St., Regina, Sask. S4P 3K4
Manitoba Regional Office: Bestlands Bldg., 191 Pioneer Ave., Winnipeg, Man. R3C 3P4
Ontario Area: 789 Don Mills Rd., Don Mills, Ont. M3C 1T5
Quebec Area: 15 rue Henderson, Quebec, P.Q. G1K 7L5
Atlantic Area:
New Brunswick Regional Office: 633 Queen St., Fredericton, N.B. E3B 4Z6
Nova Scotia Regional Office: Ste. 1400, Barrington Tower, Scotia Sq., Halifax, N.S. B3J 3J4
Prince Edward Island Regional Office: 97 Queen St., Box 1238, Charlottetown, P.E.I. C1A 7M9
Newfoundland Regional Office: 310 Pleasantville, Box 9430, St. John's, Nfld. A1A 2Y5

Policy, Planning & Information Branch
Asst. Deputy Minister, E.M. Murphy
Executive Director, R.W. Christensen
Director, Science Policy Liaison Unit, B. Bélovic
Director, Constituency Liaison & Survey Research, M. Badour
Director General, Policy Resources, G.R. Traversy
Director General, Information Systems, J.N. Kent

Social Service Programs Branch
(Ottawa, Ont. K1A 1B5)
Asst. Deputy Minister, B.J. Iverson
Director, Planning & Evaluation, B. Long
Director General, Canada Assistance Plan, D.J. Byrne
A/Director, Welfare Services & Work Activity, H. Clifford
Director, Asst. & Vocational Rehab. Services Admin., N.N. Papove
Director, Field Operations, G. Amyotte
A/Director, Social Services, R. Yzerman
Director, National Welfare Grant, L.M.W. Pisapio
Director, New Horizons, G.H. Aubut
Director, Bureau on Rehabilitation, A. LeBlanc

Regional Representatives (New Horizons):
Nfld.: Harold House, #602, 165 Duckworth St., St. John's, Nfld. A1C 5W4
N.S.: Pat Young, 5670 Spring Garden Rd., Halifax, N.S. B3J 1H6
N.B.: Blair Bourgeois, 1222 Main St., Moncton, N.B. E1C 1H6
P.E.I.: Blair Bourgeois, #101, 3 Harbour Side, Charlottetown, P.E.I. C1A 7M9
Que.: Charles Douville, Box 93, Desjardins Stn., Montreal, P.Q. H5B 1B2
Ont.: Fernand Lozier, Ste. 1104, 2300 Yonge St., Toronto, Ont. M4P 1E4
Man.: Cal Zacharias, 191 Pioneer Ave., Winnipeg, Man. R3C 3N7
Sask.: Norma Wallace, 1975 Scarth St., 4th floor, Regina, Sask. S4P 3K4
Alta.: Don Mayne, 10621 100th Ave., Room 203, Edmonton, Alta. T5J OB4
B.C.: Mrs. Patricia Fulton, 1525 W. 8th Ave., Vancouver, B.C. V6J 1T5

Intergovernmental & International Affairs
Asst. Deputy Minister, N. Préfontaine
Senior Advisor, Program Support, R. Rouleau
Director, Federal-Provincial & Interdepartmental Liaison, P. Jodoin
A/Director, International Affairs, M. Careau

NATIONAL JOINT COUNCIL OF THE PUBLIC SERVICE OF CANADA

This council provides a forum for consultation on labour issues between the Government of Canada and the bargaining agents for its employees.

Chairman of the National Joint Council & Official Side, Fred Drummie, Deputy Secretary, Personnel Policy Branch, Treasury Board, 19th floor, Place Bell Canada, Ottawa, Ont. K1A OR5
Co-Chairman, G. Myers, Business Manager, International Brotherhood of Electrical Workers, Local 2228, 1335 Carling Ave., Ottawa, Ont. K1Z 6A9
General Secretary, D. Davidge, 140 O'Connor St., East Tower, 4th floor, Room 411, Box 1525, Stn. B, Ottawa, Ont. K1P 5V2

NATIONAL LIBRARY OF CANADA BIBLIOTHEQUE NATIONALE DU CANADA
395 Wellington St., Ottawa, Ont. K1A ON4

The National Library receives by law two copies of each book and periodical published in Canada; publishes the national bibliography, *Canadiana*; maintains a union catalogue showing what books are held by some 350 Canadian libraries; offers an interlibrary loan service and reference, advisory and consultative services to researchers. Collection strengths are in Canadiana, Canadian newspapers and periodicals, Canadian government documents, and Canadian music.

NATIONAL PAROLE BOARD

340 Laurier Ave. W., Ottawa, Ont. K1A OR1
Chairman, Wm. R. Outerbridge (613/995-1308)
Vice Chairman, R. Labelle
Members (headquarters), J.H. Hollies, E. Hobbs, R.L. Hutson, P. Young, R. Evans, G. Clermont
Executive Director, L. McCafferty

Regions

Atlantic

Box 1370, Moncton, N.B. E1C 8T6
Senior Member, M. Casey
Member, M. Gallant
Regional Executive Officer, E. Williams (506/388-6345)

Quebec

505 Sherbrooke St. E., 2nd floor, Montreal, P.Q. H2L 4N3
Senior Member, J.P. Gilbert
Members, P. Boulanger, M. Lecorre, R. Beaupré
Regional Executive Officer, G. Parry (514/283-4584)

Ontario

Box 620, Kingston, Ont. K7L 4X1
Senior Member, M. Benson
Members, M. Stienburg, A.E. Beaupré, L.F. Taylor
Regional Executive Officer, J. Nugent (613/549-3890)

Prairie

Financial Bldg., No. 505, Saskatoon, Sask. S7K OE9
Senior Member, R. Gillies
Members, K. Howland, D. Chisholm, D. Betz
Regional Executive Officer, N. Fagnou (306/665-4228)

Pacific

4664 Lougheed Hwy., Room 230, Burnaby, B.C. V5C 5T5
Senior Member, K. Louis
Members, N. Harrison, S. Holt
Regional Executive Officer, W.D. MacGregor (604/666-2121)

BUREAU DU COMMISSAIRE AUX LANGUES OFFICIELLES OFFICE OF THE COMMISSIONER OF OFFICIAL LANGUAGES

-Not confirmed for 1982-
Ottawa, Ont. K1A OT8
Commissaire/Commr., Maxwell Yalden
Sous-commissaire/Deputy Commr., Gilles Lalande
Directeur des plaintes/Director of Complaints Branch, Robin Skuce
Directeur des études spéciales/Director of Special Studies Branch, Maurice Héroux
Directeur, Politique et Liaison/Director of Policy & Liaison Branch, Stuart C. Beaty
Directeur de l'information/Director of Information Branch, Christine Sirois

PUBLIC ARCHIVES OF CANADA

395 Wellington St., Ottawa, Ont. K1A ON3
(613) 996-1473

The Public Archives of Canada is a research institution responsible for acquiring archival material "of every kind, nature and description" concerning all aspects of Canadian life and the development of the country. It provides suitable research services and facilities to make this material available to the public. In addition, as part of the federal government administration, it has broad responsibilities with regard to the promotion of efficiency and economy in the management of government records. The Public Archives includes private papers, public records, machine readable archives, maps, paintings, photographs, films, sound recordings and books on Canadian history and related subject fields.

Dominion Archivist, Dr. W.I. Smith (992-2473)
Archives Branch, Director General, M. Swift (996-1569)
Departmental Admin., Executive Director, A.C. Taylor (992-5524)
Communication Services, Director, Mrs. Y. Iler (995-7611)
Federal Records Division, A/Director, J. O'Brien (996-8507)
Library, Director, N. St. Pierre (996-3051)
National Film Archives, Director, S. Kula (996-6009)
Manuscript Division, Director, R.S. Gordon (996-8498)
National Map Collection, Director, Mrs. B. Kidd (992-0468)
Picture Division, Director, G. Delisle (996-6011)
National Photography Collection, Director, A. Birrell (992-2761)
Machine Readable Archives, Director, H. Naugler (997-2764)
Records Management Branch, Records Centre Bldg., Tunney's Pasture, Director General, J. Atherton (992-1624)
National Personnel Records Centre, Director, J. Paveling (995-6161)
Federal Records Centres, Director, J.R. St-Jean (993-4729)
Records Management Services, Director, W.O. Potter (996-5904)

Regional Offices

Halifax Federal Records Centre, Morris Dr. & Akerley Blvd., Dartmouth, N.S.: Chief, W. Shea (902/426-5940)
Montreal Federal Records Centre, 665 Montée de Liesse, Ville St-Laurent, P.Q.: Chief, G. Pommainville (514/341-4114)
Toronto Federal Records Centre, 190 Carrier Rd., Rexdale, Ont.: Chief, H. Hrushowy (416/667-4534)
Micrographic Advisory Section, 220 Lesmill Rd., Don Mills, Ont.: Chief, H. Rivnie (966-5539)
Winnipeg Federal Records Centre, 201 Weston St., Winnipeg, Man.: Chief, R. Weinholdt (204/786-8647)
Edmonton Federal Records Centre, 8707 51 Ave., Edmonton, Alta.: Chief, P.K. Smoth (403/420-3120)
Vancouver Federal Records Centre, 3103 Thunderbird Cres., Lake City Industrial Park, Burnaby, B.C.: Chief, H. Chapin (604/939-4488)

PUBLIC SERVICE COMMISSION OF CANADA

Ottawa, Ont. K1A OM7
Phone: (613) 593-7691

The Commission is in charge of staffing the public service according to the merit principle. It can delegate its authority wherever practical, though not its responsibility to Parliament.

It provides training and development services, including language training, for public servants. It hears appeals on appointments, demotion or release, and investigates complaints of discrimination in public service employment.

Commrs., Edgar Gallant (Chairman), Anita Szlazak, John Edwards
Director General, Staffing Branch, A.J. Neilson
Director General, Appeals & Investigation Branch, T.G. Morry
Director General, Audit Branch, P. Smith
Director General, Language Training Branch, R. Lapointe
Director General, Staff Development Branch, J.A. St-Aubin
Director General, Corporate Systems & Services Branch, J.F. Ferguson
Director General, Senior Executive Programs Branch, J.Y. Ranger
Director, Secretariat Services, W. Wells

Regional & District Staffing Offices:

Room 300, 10355 Jasper Ave., Edmonton, Alta. T5J 1Y6 (403/420-3138)
4th floor, 5161 George St., Halifax, N.S. B3J 1M8 (902/426-2171)
860 Main St., #603, Moncton, N.B. E1C 8M1 (506/388-6622)

Ste. 300, 685 Cathcart St., Montreal, P.Q. H3B 2R1 (514/283-6315)
3rd floor, 400 Cooper St., Ottawa, Ont. K1A OM7 (613/996-9676)
Rm. 205, 1126 Chemin St-Louis, Sillery, P.Q. G1S 1E5 (418/694-3230)
Room 1110, 1867 Hamilton St., Regina, Sask. S4P 2C2 (306/569-5720)
Ste. 1100, 180 Dundas St. W., Toronto, Ont. M5G 2A8 (416/369-3131)
#313, 1575 W. Georgia St., Vancouver, B.C. V6G 3A6 (604/666-1696)
Ste. 302, 4114 4th Ave., Whitehorse, Yukon Y1A 4N7 (403/668-4487)
Room 500, 286 Smith St., Winnipeg, Man. R3C OK6 (204/949-2166)
9th floor, 4922 52nd St., Yellowknife, N.W.T. XOE 1HO (403/873-3525)

PUBLIC SERVICE STAFF RELATIONS BOARD

140 O'Connor St., Box 1525, Stn. B, Ottawa, Ont. K1P 5V2
Phone: (613) 992-5012
Minister through whom PSSRB reports to Parliament: Hon. Yvon Pinard, President of the Privy Council.

The Board consists of a full time Chairman, Vice Chairman and not less than three Deputy Chairmen who hold office for periods not exceeding ten years and six full time members who hold office for periods not exceeding seven years. All appointments are made by the Governor in Council and are during good behaviour.

Chairman, J.H. Brown, Q.C.
Vice Chairman, J.-M. Cantin, Q.C.
Deputy Chairmen, L. Mitchell, Q.C.; Mrs. Michelle Falardeau-Ramsay; D.H. Kates
Members: D.G. Pyle; J. Mayes; S. Frankel; R. Steward; C. Edwards; J. Galipeault
Senior Officers:
Director of Mediation Services, Ken Strike
Secretary Registrar, G.E. Plant
Director, Legal Services, J.E. McCormick
Director of Admin., J.M. Weldon
Director General, Pay Research Bureau, R.C. DesLauriers

DEPT. OF PUBLIC WORKS

Sir Charles Tupper Bldg., Confederation Heights, Ottawa, Ont. K1A OM2
Information Contact, Director of Public Relations & Information Services, Sir Charles Tupper Bldg. (phone: 613 998-9560)

Acts Administered

The Public Works Act

MINISTER, Hon. Paul Cosgrove
Deputy Minister, J.A.H. Mackay
Asst. Deputy Minister, Realty, A.J. Perrier
Asst. Deputy Minister, Design & Construction, Guy Desbarats
Asst. Deputy Minister, Finance & Admin., Ralph McGougan
Asst. Deputy Minister, Operations, A.D. Wilson
Asst. Deputy Minister, Revenue Dependency, Frank Currie
Executive Secretary, R.A. Fonberg
Director, Public Relations & Information Services, A. Normand
Director, Official Languages, J.H. Davison
Dominion Fire Commissioner, G.A. Hope
Director, Policy Development & Analysis, D.A. Carter
Director, Strategic Planning Processes & Systems, M.E. Plouffe
Director General, Personnel, E.J. Fitzpatrick
Director General, Real Estate Services, J. Roy
Director General, Property Administration, A.H. Fallis
Executive Director, Energy Management, W.N. Thomas
Director, Headquarters Operational Services, A.B. Mundy
Director, Contract Policy & Administration, S.C. Ings
Director General, Design & Construction Services, M.W. Paul
A/Director General, Design & Construction Technology, N.M. Hoyt
Director, Special Services, N.G. Norris
Director, Solar Projects, F. Snape
Director General, Finance, R.J. Giroux
Director, Management Information Services, A.R. Durston
Asst. Secretary, & Director of Admin., B.P. Armstrong
Director, Emergency Preparedness, K.G. Farrell
Regional Directors General:
Atlantic, J.M. Dunphy
Ont., E.D. Manchul
Pacific, R.B. Angus
Que., Guy Wolfe
Western, J.A. Brown
National Capital, H.D. McFarland

Public Works Regional Offices

Atlantic Region: Box 2247, 1190 Barrington St., Halifax, N.S. B3J 3C9
Field Offices:
Nfld.: Box 4600, Bldg. 301, Pleasantville, St. John's, Nfld.
N.B.: Box 7350, 189 Prince William St., Saint John, N.B.
P.E.I.: Box 1268, Dominion Bldg., Charlottetown, P.E.I.
Que. Region: 2001 University St., Montreal, P.Q. H3A 1K3
Field Offices:
Quebec: Champlain Harbour Stn., Wolfe's Cove, Quebec, P.Q. G1K 4K2
Rimouski: 180 de la Cathédrale St., Rimouski, P.Q. G5L 7C7
Ont. Region: 4900 Yonge St., Willowdale, Ont. M2N 6A6
Field Offices:
London: 457 Richmond St. (Box 668), London, Ont. N6A 4Y4
Sault Ste. Marie: 107 East St., Sault Ste. Marie, Ont. P6A 3C7
Thunder Bay: 540 W. Arthur St., Thunder Bay, Ont. P7E 5R7
National Capital Region: L'Esplanade Laurier, 140 O'Connor St., Ottawa, Ont. K1A OM3
Western Region: Box 488, 10th floor, 9925 109th St., Edmonton, Alta. T5K 2J8
Field Offices:
Alta: 205 9th Ave. S.E., Calgary, Alta. T2G OR3
Man. (Fort Churchill): Box 1000, Fort Churchill, Man. ROB OEO
Man. (Winnipeg): 269 Main St., Winnipeg, Man. R3C 1B2
Sask. (Regina): 2101 Scarth St., Regina, Sask. S4P 2H9
Sask. (Saskatoon): Hanselman Court, McNab Park, Saskatoon, Sask.
Pacific Region: 1166 Alberni St., Vancouver, B.C. V6E 3Z3
Field Office:
Yukon: 201 Range Rd., Takhini, Whitehorse, Y.T. Y1A 3A4

DEPT. OF REGIONAL ECONOMIC EXPANSION

The Department is designed to improve, or where necessary, create the conditions needed to foster sustained economic growth in specific areas across Canada which lag economically behind the country's major growth centres.

The aim is to narrow the economic gaps between regions and provide all Canadians more equitable economic opportunities. DREE's activities are divided into three major areas: General Development Agreements, signed with each of the provinces; industrial incentives; and other programs to meet specific needs in certain regions.

Information: Public Information Branch, Dept. of Regional Economic Expansion, 200 Promenade du Portage, Hull, P.Q. Mailing: Ottawa, Ont. K1A OM4 (phone: 819/997-2913)

Acts Administered

Regional Economic Expansion Act
Regional Development Incentives Act
Agricultural & Rural Development Act
Prairie Farm Rehabilitation Act
Cape Breton Development Corp. Act

MINISTER, Hon. Pierre de Bané
Deputy Minister, R.C. Montreuil
Asst. Deputy Minister, Finance & Admin., J. MacNaught
Asst. Deputy Minister, Planning & Co-ordination, T.E. Reid
Asst. Deputy Minister, Atlantic, R.H. McGee

Asst. Deputy Minister, Que., C. Huot
Asst. Deputy Minister, Ont., R. Marshall
Asst. Deputy Minister, Western, J.D. Collinson
Director, Personnel, L. Bradet
Director General, Financial Services, H. Frederiksen
Director, Legal Services, P. Sorokan
Director, Information, Carol Racine
Director General, Analysis & Liaison, R.D. Glass
Director General, Project Assessment & Evaluation, C.J. Hindle
Director General, Industrial Incentives, J. Wansbrough

Atlantic Development Council

The council provides an advisory service to the Dept. of Regional Economic Expansion. The Council consists of 11 members appointed by the federal Government in consultation with the governments of the Atlantic Provinces. It advises the Minister on plans and programs for social and economic development and their impact on the region.

Executive Director, J.L. Miller, Bldg. 102, Churchill Ave., 2nd floor, Pleasantville, St. John's, Nfld. A1A 1N1

DREE Offices

Applications for DREE development incentives and loan guarantees are processed at the following offices of the Dept. of Regional Economic Expansion, in the province where the project is to be located:

Regional Offices

Atlantic: 14th floor, 770 Main St. (Box 1210, Moncton, N.B. E1C 8P9)
Que.: Ste. 4328, 800 Victoria Square (Box 247, Montreal, P.Q. H4Z 1E8)
Ont.: 6th floor, 1300 Yonge St., Toronto, Ont. M4T 1X3
Western: 601 Spadina Cres., Saskatoon, Sask. S7K 3G8

Provincial Offices

90 O'Leary Ave., Box 8950, St. John's, Nfld. A1B 3R9
134 Kent St., Box 1115, Charlottetown, P.E.I. C1A 7M8
11th floor, 45 Alderney Dr., Box 1320, Dartmouth, N.S. B2Y 4B9
Armstrong Bldg., 590 Brunswick St., Box 578, Fredericton, N.B. E3B 5A6
Claridge Bldg., 220 Grande Allée E., Quebec, P.Q. G1R 2J1
Court Holding Bldg., 233 Court St. S., Thunder Bay, Ont. P7B 2X9
#400, 3 Lakeview Bldg., Box 981, Winnipeg, Man. R3C 2V2
1102 8th Ave., 3rd floor, Regina, Sask. S4R 1C9
401 Motherwell Bldg., 1901 Victoria Ave., Regina, Sask. S4P OR5 (PFRA)
Financial Bldg., 10621 100th Ave., 8th floor, Edmonton, Alta. T5J OB3
Bank of Commerce Bldg., 1175 Douglas St., Victoria, B.C. V8W 2E1

Branch Offices

Box 730, Stn. A, Goose Bay Airport, Goose Bay, Labrador, Nfld. AOP 1SO
Keystone Place, 270 Douglas Ave., Box 700, Bathurst, N.B. E2A 3Z6
320 St. Germain St. E., 4th floor, Rimouski, P.Q. G5L 1C2
Plaza III, 690 Sacré Coeur ouest, Alma, P.Q. G8B 6V4
1335 King St. W., #401, Sherbrooke, P.Q. J1J 2B8
Place de Québec, 888 3rd Ave., Val d'Or, P.Q. J9P 5E6
Royal Bank Tower, 128 Larch St., Ste. 603, Sudbury, Ont. P3E 5J8
74 Caribou Rd., Thompson, Man. R3N 0L3
Box 2407, Prince Albert, Sask. S6V 7G3
#706, 299 Victoria St., Prince George, B.C. V2L 5B8
#301, 108 Lambert St., Whitehorse, Y.T. Y1A 1Z2
Precambrian Bldg., 10th floor, P.O. Bag 6100, Yellowknife, N.W.T. X1A 1CO

RESTRICTIVE TRADE PRACTICES COMMISSION

Box 336, Stn. A, Ottawa, Ont. K1N 8V3
Phone: (613) 992-0217

In the case of specified trade practices such as exclusive dealing the Commission on application by the Director of Investigation & Research, after holding a hearing, may issue an order prohibiting such practice if the situation comes within the criteria specified. It is also responsible for appraising evidence relating to combines and other restrictive business practices submitted to it by the Director and the parties under investigation, holding hearings and making reports to the Minister of Consumer & Corporate Affairs.

Chairman, O.G. Stoner
Vice Chairman, L.-A. Couture, Q.C.
Members, R.S. MacLellan, Q.C., F. Roseman
Secretary, G.M. Payette
Petroleum Industry Inquiry
Executive Director, J.S. Church
Secretary of the Inquiry, J.A. Judd

REVENUE CANADA–CUSTOMS & EXCISE

Public Relations Branch, Ottawa, Ont. K1A OL5 (phone: 613-593-6220)

Acts Administered in Whole by Customs & Excise:

Dept. of National Revenue Act
Anti-Dumping Act
Customs Act
Customs Tariff Act
Excise Act
Excise Tax Act

In addition, Customs & Excise administers parts of many Acts that are the main responsibility of other Departments. Inquire from Public Relations, above, for list.

MINISTER, Hon. William Rompkey
Executive Asst., Robert Ward
Deputy Minister (Customs & Excise), J.P. Connell
Executive Asst., J. Guèvremont
Asst. Deputy Minister, Customs Programs, T.C. Greig
Director General, Special Assessment Programs, K.H. McCammon
Director General, International Traffic Programs, E.D. Warren
Director General, Tariff Programs, A.T. Wickham
Asst. Deputy Minister, Field Operations, A. Morin
Director General, Field Support, M.A. Gallup
Asst. Deputy Minister, Excise, A.E. Hannah
Director General, Exise Operations, M.P. Bourgeois
Director General, Excise Programs, R.F. Fulford
Asst. Deputy Minister, Finance & Admin., J.G. Threader
Director General, Planning & Consulting Services, T.R. Young
Director General, Personnel Admin., R.K. Cox
Director, Public Relations Branch, J. Laurin
Director General, Audit & Evaluation, C.T. Clark
Director, Legal Services, T.W. Sommerville

Regional Offices, Customs & Excise

Address: The Regional Collector of Customs, Revenue Canada, Customs & Excise, at
Halifax, Quebec, Montreal, Ottawa, Hamilton, London, Toronto, Windsor (Ont.), Winnipeg, Regina, Calgary, and Vancouver.

REVENUE CANADA–TAXATION

Director of Information Services, L.M. Smith, 123 Slater St., Ottawa, Ont. K1A OL8 (phone: 613 995-2287)

Acts Administered by Taxation

The Income Tax Acts of Canada and nine provinces
Canada Pension Plan Act, Part I
Unemployment Insurance Act, Part IV

Deputy Minister (Taxation), Bruce A. MacDonald
Asst. Deputy Minister, Policy & Systems Branch, H.E. Garland
Director General, Verification & Collections, D.S. Brooks
Director General, Compliance, J.L. Gourlay
Director General, Systems, M. Lagasse
Director General, Decentralization Co-ordination Directorate, L.A. Rondeau
Asst. Deputy Minister, Legislation Branch, D.L.H. Davidson
Director General, Non-Corporate Rulings & Publications, C.W. Mavor
Director General, Corporate Rulings, J.R. Robertson
Asst. Deputy Ministers, Regional Operations:
Atlantic, W.J. Skinner
Quebec, T.E. Weldon
Ontario, J.A. Morrison
Western, H.G. Ladd
Asst. Deputy Minister, Management Services, R.C. Blackwell
Director General, Appeals Branch, R.M. Beith
Director, Information Services, L.M. Smith
Director, Management Audit Branch, W. Clarke
Director, Legal Services, C. McNab
Director, Management Controls, P.E. Langlois

District Taxation Offices

Nfld.:
165 Duckworth St., St. John's, Nfld. A1C 5X6
P.E.I.:
97 Queen St., Charlottetown, P.E.I. C1A 7N1
N.S.:
1557 Hollis St., Halifax, N.S. B3J 2T5
Dorchester St., Box 1300, Sydney, N.S. B1P 6K3
N.B.:
65 Canterbury St., Saint John, N.B. E2L 4H9
Que.:
165 Dorchester St. S., Quebec, P.Q. G1K 7L3
50 Couture St., Sherbrooke, P.Q. J1H 4G9
305 Dorchester Blvd. W., Montreal, P.Q. H2Z 1A6
11 Terminus St. E., Rouyn, P.Q. J9X 3B5
Ont.:
360 Lisgar St., Ottawa, Ont. K1A OL9
385/387 Princess St., Kingston, Ont. K7L 1C1
11 Station St., Belleville, Ont. K8N 2S3
36 Adelaide St. E., Toronto, Ont. M5C 1J7
150 Main St. W., Hamilton, Ont. L8N 3E1
166 Frederick St., Kitchener, Ont. N2H 2M4
32-46 Church St., St. Catharines, Ont. L2R 3B9
451 Talbot St., London, Ont. N6A 5C9
185 Ouellette Ave., Windsor, Ont.
19 Lisgar St. S., Sudbury, Ont. P3E 3L5
201 North May St., Thunder Bay, Ont. P7C 3P5
Man.:
391 York Ave., Winnipeg, Man. R3C OP5
Sask.:
1955 Smith St., Regina, Sask. S4P 2N9
201, 21st St. E., Saskatoon, Sask. S7K OA8
Alta.:
220 4th Ave. S.E., Calgary, Alta. T2G 4X3
9820 107th St., Edmonton, Alta. T5K 1E8
B.C.:
277 Winnipeg St., Penticton, B.C. V2A 1N6
1166 W. Pender St., Vancouver, B.C. V6E 3H8
1415 Vancouver St., Victoria, B.C. V8V 3W4

ROOSEVELT CAMPOBELLO INTERNATIONAL PARK COMMISSION

The Commission administers an international park on Campobello Island, N.B. as a memorial to the late F.D. Roosevelt. Phone: (506) 752-2922

Canadian Section:

Vice Chairman, Hon. Hedard Robichaud
Commrs., D. Walker, R.A. Tweedie

United States Section:

Chairman, Hon. Edmund S. Muskie
Commr., Curtis Hutchins
Plus Three alternate Commrs. appointed by each of the two governments
A/Executive Secretary, Henry W. Stevens, Lubec, Maine
Supt., Henry W. Stevens

ROYAL CANADIAN MOUNTED POLICE

Honorary Commr., Her Majesty Queen Elizabeth II
Ottawa, Ont. K1A OR2
Information Contact, Supt. J.R. Bentham, Officer i/c Public Relations Branch (phone: 613-993-1085)

In 1873 the North West Mounted Police was constituted to provide Police protection in the unsettled portions of the North West. In 1904 the title "Royal" was given to the Force. In 1920 The Dominion Police was amalgamated with this Force and the name changed to "Royal Canadian Mounted Police." The headquarters was moved from Regina to Ottawa and the Force may now be called upon to perform duties in any portion of the Dominion. In 1928 the R.C.M.P. absorbed the Sask. Provincial Police and in 1932 the Provincial Police Forces of Alta., Man., N.B., N.S. & P.E.I. were absorbed in like manner. During the year 1932, the Force also assumed the administration of the Preventive Service Branch of the Dept. of National Revenue. On August 1, 1950, the duties of the Nfld. Rangers and certain members of the Nfld. Constabulary were taken over by the R.C.M.P., and on the 15th of the same month the B.C. Provincial Police were similarly absorbed. These arrangements were made by agreements between the respective Provincial Governments concerned and the Federal Government. The term of engagement in the R.C.M.P. is five years. Recruits are trained at Regina, Sask.

Commr., R.H. Simmonds
Deputy Commr. (Admin.), D.J. Beiersdorfer
Deputy Commr. (Canadian Police Service), J.N.G.R. Marcoux
Deputy Commr. (Criminal Operations), H. Jensen

Division & Commanding Officer

"A" Division:
400 Cooper St., Ottawa, Ont. K1A OR4
C/Supt. R.M. Shorey, Commanding Officer
"B" Division:
Box 4300, Pleasantville, St. John's, Nfld. A1C 5S8
C/Supt. W. Schramm, Commanding Officer
"C" Division:
4225 Dorchester Blvd. W., Westmount, P.Q. H3Z 2T4
A/Commr. J.L.P. Mantha, Commanding Officer
"D" Division:
1091 Portage Ave., (Box 922), Winnipeg, Man. R3C 2T4
A/Commr. A.T. McHaffie, Commanding Officer
"E" Division:
1061 Fort St., Victoria, B.C. V8V 3K7
Deputy Commr. T.S. Venner, Commanding Officer
"E-1" District:
1200 W. 73rd Ave., Vancouver, B.C. V6P 6G6
A/Commr. D.K. Wilson, Commanding Officer
"E-2" District:
1061 Fort St., Victoria, B.C. V6P 6G6
C/Supt. T.A. Farr, Commanding Officer
"F" Division:
Box 2500, Derrick Bldg., Regina, Sask. S4P 3E1
A/Commr., W.J. Neil, Commanding Officer
"G" Division:
Bag 5000, Yellowknife, N.W.T. XOE 1HO
Chief Supt. H.A. Feagan, Commanding Officer
"H" Division:
Box 2286, 1741 Hollis St., Halifax, N.S. B3J 3E1
Chief Supt. C.J. Reid, Commanding Officer
"J" Division:
Box 310, Woodstock Rd., Fredericton, N.B. E3B 4Z8
Chief Supt. W.J. Hunter, Commanding Officer
"K" Division:
Box 1320, 11140 109 St., Edmonton, Alta. T5J 2N1
A/Commr., D.A. Whyte, Commanding Officer

"L" Division:
Box 1360, 450 University Ave., Charlottetown, P.E.I. C1A 7N1
Chief Supt. R.M. Culligan, Commanding Officer
"M" Division:
Whitehorse, Yukon Y1A 1H5
Supt. H.T. Nixon, Commanding Officer
"N" Division:
Box 8900, Ottawa, Ont. K1A OR2
Chief Supt. G.M. Allen, Commanding Officer
"O" Division:
Box 519 Adelaide P.O., 225 Jarvis St., Toronto, Ont. M5C 2M3
Asst. Commr. M.S. Sexsmith, Commanding Officer
"HQ" Division:
1200 Alta Vista Dr., Ottawa, Ont. K1A OR2
Chief Supt. J.E.J. Julien, Commanding Officer
"Depot" Division:
Box 6500, Regina, Sask. S4P 3J7
Chief Supt. G.C. Caldick, Commanding Officer

MINISTRY OF STATE FOR SCIENCE & TECHNOLOGY

270 Albert St., Ottawa, Ont. K1A 1A1
Information Contact, Chief, Communications Services (phone: 613 996-3501)

The Ministry of State for Science & Technology is responsible for encouraging the development and use of science and technology in support of national goals and public policy.

MINISTER OF STATE, Hon. John Roberts
Executive Asst., Herb Metcalfe
Principal Officers:
Secretary of the Ministry, L. Denis Hudon
A/Asst. Secretary (Government), D. Maasland
Asst. Secretary (Industry), D.C. Thom
Asst. Secretary (University), Dr. D.I.R. Low
Director (Corporate Services), J.P. McLaughlin

Agencies reporting to Minister

Science Council of Canada
National Research Council
Natural Sciences & Engineering Research Council
Inter-Council Co-ordinating Committee

DEPT. OF THE SECRETARY OF STATE

Ottawa, Ont. K1A OM5
Information from, Communications Branch (15 Eddy St., Hull), Mailing: Ottawa, Ont. K1A OM5 (phone: 819/997-0055)

The responsibilities of the department are:

(a) to encourage the acquisition and use of the two official languages in Canadian society, thereby re-enforcing the equality of status;

(b) to advise on matters of state protocol and to manage state ceremonies and events;

(c) to ensure the co-ordinated development, formulation, implementation, and review of federal education policies and programs in support of national objectives;

(d) to provide translation and interpretation services in all languages in accordance with the needs of Parliament, the government and its agencies;

(e) to promote effective Canadian citizenship, and to co-ordinate the formulation and development of national policies affecting citizenship;

(f) to provide facilities to grant and to give proof of Canadian citizenship and to encourage and assist eligible persons to acquire and value such citizenship.

Acts Administered in whole or in part by the Secretary of State Department

Canada Student Loans Act
Canada Temperance Act
Citizenship Act
Department of State Act
Federal-Provincial Fiscal Arrangements Act, 1967, Part II
Public Service Employment Act
Translation Bureau Act

SECRETARY OF STATE, Hon. Gerald Regan (997-4740)
MINISTER OF STATE, MULTICULTURALISM, Hon. James Fleming (997-9900)

Under Secretary of State, Huguette Labelle (994-1132)
National Co-ordinator of Citizenship Judges, Judge A.K. McKeown, 150 Kent St. (992-0396)
Senior Asst. Under Secretary of State, G.T. Rayner (994-1130)
Director General, Education Support Programs Branch, vacant (994-2284)
Director, Language Programs, Lise Brisson-Noreau (994-3577)
Director, Internal Audit Directorate, Jean Hurst (997-2953)
Asst. Under Secretary of State, Administration & Central Services, Paul-E. Larose (994-3046)
Director General, Personnel Admin. Branch, Marc Senécal (997-1873)
Director General, Information Branch, C.F. Hobbs (997-0641)
Director General, Finance Branch, A. Belliveau (997-1923)
Director General, Communications Branch, Richard Dicerni, act. (997-0376)
Director, State Ceremonial Directorate, Georges Bernier (994-3200)
Director, Administrative Services Directorate, G.W. Rowbotham (997-2576)
Head, Translation Services, F.R. Leroux (997-3877)
Asst. Under Secretary of State, Citizenship & Official Languages, Jean-Paul Lefebvre (994-1112)
Director General, Co-ordination & Analysis Branch, Jean Trudeau (994-1115)
Director General, Regional Operations, Marc Rochon (994-1162)
Director General, Citizens Participation Directorate, Brian Gilhuly,act. (994-1313)
Citizenship inquiries outside National Capital Region (994-1566)
National Capital Region Court of Canadian Citizenship, 150 Kent St., Judge Yvon Kerr (992-4485)
Director, Promotion of Official Languages, Denis Roberge (994-1966)
Director, Human Rights, Guy Voisin (994-2226)
Director, Voluntary Action, Art New (994-2258)
Director, Open House Canada, Brian Gilhuly (994-1313)
Registrar of Canadian Citizenship, Dr. Jean James, act. (994-2869)
Director, Development & Services, Mike Andrassy (994-2602)
Director, Women's Program Directorate, Nancy Lawand (994-3190)
Director, Multiculturalism Directorate, Orest Kruhlak (994-3120)
Director, Official Language Minority Groups, Marcel Saint-Onge (994-4003)
Director, Native Citizens Directorate, R. Saunders (994-3835)
Asst. Under Secretary of State, Translation, P. Le Quellec (997-1026)
Translation Bureau, Information: 997-3686

Regional Offices, Secretary of State

5281 Duke St., Halifax, N.S. B3J 3M1
#504, 860 Main St., Moncton, N.B. E1C 1G2
1080 Beaver Hall Hill, Room 2102, Montreal, P.Q. H2Z 1S8
#200, 25 St. Clair Ave. E., Toronto, Ont. M4T 1M2
#201, 303 Main St., Winnipeg, Man. R3C 3G7
2101 Scarth St., #200, Regina, Sask. S4P 2H9
#310, 9828 104th Ave., Edmonton, Alta. T5J 0J9
1525 W. 8th Ave., Room 207, Vancouver, B.C. V6J 1T5

Courts of Canadian Citizenship

Atlantic
Sir Humphrey Gilbert Bldg., Duckworth St., Box E5368, St. John's, Nfld. A1C 5W2–(709) 737 5566
5281 Duke St., Halifax, N.S. B3J 3M1–(902) 426 2148

Ste. 503, 860 Main St., Moncton, N.B. E1C 1G2–(506) 388-7050

Quebec

Room 2100, 1080 Beaver Hall Hill, Montreal, P.Q. H2Z 1S8–(514) 283 5656

5167 Jean Talon St. E., Montreal, P.Q. H1S 1K8–(514) 283-6817

6420 St-Denis, Montreal, P.Q. H2S 2R7–(514) 283 6835

Ste. 730, 900 Place d'Youville, Quebec, P.Q. G1R 3P7 – (418) 694-3831

Ontario

9th floor, 150 Kent St., Ottawa, Ont. K1A OM5–(613) 992 4485

Ste. 814, 55 St. Clair Ave. E., Toronto, Ont. M4T 1M2–(416) 966 6424

Dufferin Mall, #221, 900 Dufferin St., Toronto, Ont. M6H 4B1 –(416) 966 6433

2nd floor, 44 Collier St., Barrie, Ont. L4M 1GO–(705) 726 4534

Ste. 101, George Sq., 37 George St. N., Brampton, Ont. L6X 1R5–(416) 459 1215

Bond Towers, Upper Concourse, 44 Bond St. W., Oshawa, Ont. L1G 6R2–(416) 723 1216

Room 412, 150 Main St. W., Hamilton, Ont. L8P 1H8–(416) 523 2361

#601, 43 Church St., St. Catharines, Ont. L2R 7E1–(416) 684 8501

70 King St. N., Waterloo, Ont. N2J 2X1–(519) 886 3120

Room 326, 19 Lisgar St., Sudbury, Ont. P3E 3L4–(705) 673 1121

Ste. 207, 33 S. Court St., Thunder Bay, Ont. P7B 2W6–(807) 345 2316

Main floor, Government of Canada Bldg., 451 Talbot St., London, Ont. N6A 5C9–(519) 679 4334

#906, 100 Ouellette Ave., Windsor, Ont. N9A 6T3–(519) 252 4238

Prairies

#200, 303 Main St., Winnipeg, Man. R3C 3G7–(204) 949 3792

2nd floor, 2101 Scarth St., Regina, Sask. S4P 2H9–(306) 569 5535

#505, 230 22nd St. E., Saskatoon, Sask. S7K OE9–(306) 665 4115

Room 310, Sir Alexander Mackenzie Bldg., 9828 104th Ave., Edmonton, Alta. T5J OJ9–(403) 420 3355

Box 2498, #254, 220 4th Ave. S.E., Calgary, Alta. T2P 3C1–(403) 231 5539

Pacific

1075 W. Georgia St., Vancouver, B.C. V6E 3C9–(604) 666-3971

#105, 816 Government St., Victoria, B.C. V8W 1W9–(604) 388-3464

#102, 1433 St. Paul St., Kelowna, B.C. V1Y 2E4–(604) 763 5322

Ste. 210, Royal Bank Bldg., 550 Victoria St., Prince George, B.C. V2L 2K1–(604) 564 2311

King George Centre, 10022 King George Hwy., Surrey, B.C. V3T 2W4–(604) 581 2249

MINISTRY OF THE SOLICITOR GENERAL

340 Laurier Ave. W., Ottawa, Ont. K1A OP8

Information Contact, Paschal O'Toole, Director, Communication Division, (phone: 613 593-5105)

The duties, powers and functions of the Solicitor General of Canada extend to and include all matters over which the Parliament of Canada has jurisdiction, not by law assigned to any other department, branch or agency of the Government of Canada, relating to (a) reformatories, prisons and penitentiaries; (b) parole and remissions; and (c) The Royal Canadian Mounted Police.

Acts Administered by the Solicitor General

Criminal Records Act
Parole Act
Penitentiary Act
Royal Canadian Mounted Police Act
Royal Canadian Mounted Police Pension Continuation Act
Royal Canadian Mounted Police Superannuation Act
Prisons & Reformatories Act

SOLICITOR GENERAL, Hon. Bob Kaplan
Executive Asst., Steve Le Drew
Deputy Solicitor General of Canada, A. Bissonnette

Royal Canadian Mounted Police

Commr., R.H. Simmonds

Correctional Service of Canada

Commr., Donald R. Yeomans

National Parole Board

Chairman, Wm. R. Outerbridge

Ministry Regional Offices

Atlantic: Consultation Centre, 1075 Main St., Moncton, N.B. E1C 1H2 (506/388-6368)

Quebec: Consultation Centre, 666 Sherbrooke St. W., Montreal, P.Q. H3A 1E7 (514/283-7362)

Ontario: Consultation Centre, 2 St. Clair Ave. W., Toronto, Ont. M4V 1L5 (416/966-8107)

Prairies: Consultation Centre, 1501 8th St. E., Saskatoon, Sask. S7H 5J6 (306/665-4262)

B.C.: Consultation Centre, 700 W. Georgia St., Vancouver, B.C. V7Y 1E8 (604/666-6079)

Addresses for RCMP, Correctional Service and National Parole Board are listed elsewhere. See Index.

STANDARDS COUNCIL OF CANADA

350 Sparks St., #1205, Ottawa, Ont. K1R 7S8
(613) 238-3222
Standards Information Service, 1-800-267-8220

STATISTICS CANADA

Ottawa, Ont. K1A OT6

Information Contact, Central Inquiries, User Services, Statistics Canada (phone: 613 992-2959 or 992-4734)

The function of Statistics Canada is to compile, analyze and publish statistical information on the economic and social life of Canada, to conduct statistical surveys as necessary for this purpose, and to conduct censuses of population, housing, merchandising and agriculture.

Chief Statistician of Canada, Martin Wilk

Asst. Chief Statistician (Corporate Management), G. Labossière
  Director General, Systems & Data Processing, J.P. Trudel

Asst. Chief Statistician (Regional Operations & Marketing), D.A. Worton
  Director, Information Division, D. Davidson
  Director, User Services Division, R.E. Drover
  Director, Regional Operations, C.J. Konzuc
  Chief Librarian, Mrs. G. Ellis

Asst. Chief Statistician (Economic Statistics), G. Leclerc
  Director General, System of National Accounts & Analysis, J.S. Wells
  Director General, Operations, J.B. Salley
  (includes Gross National Product Division, Industry Product Division, Financial Flows & Multinational Enterprises Division, Balance of Payments Division, Standards Division, Business Register Division, Manufacturing & Primary Industries Division, External Trade Division, Prices Division, Merchandising & Services Division, Business Finance Division, Labour Division, Transportation & Communications Division, Construction Division, Input-Output Division, Business Survey Methods Division)

Asst. Chief Statistician (Social Statistics), I.P. Fellegi
  Director General, Census & Household Statistics, Miss J.R. Podoluk (includes Consumer Income & Expenditure Division, Demography Division)
  Asst. Chief Statistician (Institutions & Agriculture Statistics), L.E. Rowebottom (includes Agriculture, Public Finance, Health, Education, Science, and Culture)

Director General, Operations, B. Petrie (includes Census Operations Division, Census & Household Survey Methods)

Data Access & Use, Regional Offices

Alta.: Statistics Canada, #215, 11010 101 St., Edmonton, Alta. T5H 4C5
B.C.: Statistics Canada, Alvin Bldg., 1145 Robson St., Vancouver, B.C. V6E 3W8
Man.: Statistics Canada, #602, General Post Office, 266 Graham Ave., Winnipeg, Man. R3C OK4
Nfld.: Statistics Canada, 2nd floor, Viking Bldg., Crosbie Rd., St. John's, Nfld. A1B 3P2
N.S.: Statistics Canada, Box 244, 213 Sir John Thompson Bldg., 1256 Barrington St., Halifax, N.S. B3J 1Y6
Ont.: Statistics Canada, Arthur Meighen Bldg., 25 St. Clair Ave. E., Toronto, Ont. M4T 1M4
Que.: Statistics Canada, 1500 Atwater Ave., Alexis Nihon Plaza, Montreal, P.Q. H3Z 1Y2
Sask.: Statistics Canada, 530 Midtown Centre, 1783 Hamilton St., Regina, Sask. S4P 2B6

DEPT. OF SUPPLY & SERVICES

11 Laurier St., Hull, P.Q. (Mailing, Ottawa, Ont. K1A OS5)
Information Contact, Nicole Fontaine, Chief, External Communications & Media Relations (phone: 819/997-7363)

The Dept. of Supply & Services serves as the purchasing and accounting arm of the federal Government. It provides a number of major common services in the areas of procurement, supply and printing and in the areas of accounting, payment, audit and management advisory services.

The Minister of Supply & Services is the Receiver General for Canada and is also responsible for Statistics Canada.

Acts Administered by Supply & Services:

Dept. of Supply & Services Act
Defence Production Act
Royal Canadian Mint Act
Surplus Crown Assets Act

MINISTER, Hon. Jean-Jacques Blais

Supply Administration

Deputy Minister & Queen's Printer, Guy D'Avignon
Asst. Deputy Minister, Science & Engineering Procurement, A.W. Allan
Asst. Deputy Minister, Corporate Management, A.R. Bailey
Asst. Deputy Minister, Commercial Supply, G.A. Berger
Director General, Program Evaluation & Audit Sector, D.A. Myhill
Director General, Systems, C. Guruprasad
Director General, Canadian Government Printing Office, Ed Roberts
Director General, Supply Operations, J.N. Courtney
Director General, Science Centre, Dr. G. Ste-Marie
Director General, Canadian Government Publishing Centre, P.J. Leroux
Director General, Electronics & Data Processing Products Centre, J.G. Ford
Director General, Aerospace & Armament Products Centre, S.R. Kerr
Director General, Marine & Industrial Machinery Products Centre, J.P. Charbonneau
Director General, Regional Operations, H.H. Floyd
Executive Secretary, Supply Administration, G. Lafrenière
Executive Director, Canadian General Standards Board, B.H.E. Maynard

Services Administration

Deputy Minister & Deputy Receiver General for Canada, David Kirkwood
Asst. Deputy Minister, Management Services, David J. Steele
Asst. Deputy Minister, Operational Services, G.C. Capello
Asst. Deputy Minister, Planning & Finance, W. Davis
Director General, Audit Services Bureau, G.J. Brown
Director General, Bureau of Management Consulting, J.R.R. Thivierge
Director General, Advisory Bureau for Computing, E.S. Zenowski
Director General, Payments & Compensation Services, Bryan Crossfield
Director General, Government of Canada Banking & Accounting, A.G. Irvine
Director General, Operations, P.A. Fournier
Director General, Data Processing, Dr. W. Pajor
Director General, Departmental Administrative & Advisory Services, G.F. Davis
Director, Task Force on Service to the Public, Roger August

Joint Administration

Director General, Personnel, Marcel Caron
Director, Legal Services, R.L. Evans
Director, Information Services Branch, Claude Grégoire
Parliamentary Returns, Pierre Groulx

Crown Corporations, Boards, Commissions, reporting through the Minister of Supply & Services:

Royal Canadian Mint
Crown Assets Disposal Corp.
Canadian Arsenals Ltd.

Services Administration Regional Offices

Eastern Region
- Regional: Place Sillery, 1126 chemin St-Louis, 5e étage, Sillery, P.Q. G1S 1E5
- Halifax: Box 1659, Halifax, N.S. B3J 2Z9
- Charlottetown: Box 5000, Charlottetown, P.E.I. C1A 7V6
- Fredericton: Box 5000, Fredericton, N.B. E3B 5G6
- St. John's: Box 1314, St. John's, Nfld. A1C 5N5

Montreal: #1600, 1010 Lagauchetière St. W., Montreal, P.Q. H3B 2R5
Quebec: Box 5000, Québec, P.Q. G1K 7S7
Superannuation: Box 5010, Moncton, N.B. E1C 8Z5
Central Region
- Regional: 400 Cumberland St., Ottawa, Ont. K1A 0S5
- Ottawa South: 8th floor, 2323 Riverside Dr., Ottawa, Ont. K1A 0S5
- House of Commons: 150 Wellington St., Ottawa, Ont. K1A 0S5
- Hull: 1C2, Phase III, Place du Portage, Hull, P.Q. K1A 0S5
- National Capital Region Pay Operations: 17th floor, Jeanne Mance Bldg., Tunney's Pasture, Ottawa, Ont. K1A 0G7
- CGPB: Sacred Heart Blvd., Hull, P.Q. K1A 0S5
- Ottawa East: 400 Cumberland St., Ottawa, Ont. K1A 0S5
- RCMP: 1200 Alta Vista Dr., Ottawa, Ont. K1A 0S5
- Ottawa Centre: 2nd floor, 122 Bank St., Ottawa, Ont. K1A 0S5
- Securities Deposit: 234 Wellington St., Ottawa, Ont. K1A 0X1

Toronto: 24 Ferrand Dr., Don Mills, Ont. M3C 2Y5
- London: Box 5303, London, Ont. N6A 4K8

Western Region
- Regional: 8th floor, 10179 105 St., Edmonton, Alta. T5J 3N1
- Winnipeg: 344 Edmonton St., Winnipeg, Man. R3B 2Y1
- Saskatoon: #602, 101 22nd St. E., Saskatoon, Sask. S7K 0E5
- Regina: 11th floor, 1867 Hamilton St., Regina, Sask. S4P 2C2
- Edmonton: 9820 107 St., Edmonton, Alta. T5J 1E9
- Vancouver: 325 Granville St., Vancouver, B.C. V6C 1S6
- Victoria: Box 5000, Victoria, B.C. V8W 2Z4

Overseas Office
- CGSO Headquarters: Canadian Forces Europe, CFPO 5000, Belleville, Ont. K0K 3R0, or CGSO Headquarters: Canadian Forces Europe, 763 LAHR/SCHU, Germany

Supply Administration Regional Offices

Pacific Region: 3551 Viking Way, Richmond, B.C. V6V 1W6
Western Region: 10225 100 Ave., Edmonton, Alta. T5J 1J9

Man. Region: #710, 266 Graham Ave., Winnipeg, Man. R3C 3W6
Ont. Region: 295 West Mall, Ste. 200, Etobicoke, Ont. M9C 5A4
Capital Region: 1010 Somerset St. W., Ottawa, Ont. K1A OT4
Que. Region: 800 Golf Rd., Nun's Island, Montreal, P.Q. H3E 1G9
Atlantic Region: Box 3000, Main PO, Dartmouth, N.S. B2Y 4A8
Overseas Offices
London, Eng.: MacDonald House, No. 1, Grosvenor Sq., London, W1X OAB, Eng.
Koblenz, Germany: 5400 Koblenz, Mainzer Strasse 39, Postfach 566, Germany

Canadian Government Publications

Approximately 145 commercial and university bookstores in Canada are designated as special authorized agents to sell Government publications.

TARIFF BOARD

365 Laurier Ave. W., Journal Bldg. South, 21st floor, Ottawa, Ont. K1A OG7
Phone: (613) 996-8541
Chairman, John A. MacDonald
First Vice Chairman, G. Deachman
Second Vice Chairman, G.J. Gorman, Q.C.
Members, A.C. Kilbank, K.C. Martin, J. Bertrand, R.K. Matthie
Secretary, J.E. Lafrance

TAX REVIEW BOARD

381 Kent St., Ottawa, Ont. K1A OM1
Phone: (613) 995-9045
Chairman, Hon. L. Cardin, P.C., Q.C.
Asst. Chairman, F.J. Dubrule, Q.C.
Members, Roland St-Onge, Q.C., D.E. Taylor, Guy Tremblay, M.J. Bonner, J.B. Goetz, Q.C.
Registrar, tba

DEPT. OF TRANSPORT

Transport Canada Bldg., Place de Ville, Ottawa, Ont. K1A ON5
Information Contact, Ian Macdonald, Director General, Public Affairs (phone: 613 996-5861)

The Minister of Transport is responsible for the regulation and administration of federal transportation policies and programs in Canada.

The department is a corporate structure including groups responsible for operations, review co-ordination, planning and development, as well as Crown agencies with varying degrees of autonomy.

The operational sector consists of the Air, Marine and Surface Administrations, which regulate and provide certain services for aeronautical, marine and surface transportation. The other groups provide guidance in such areas as research, intergovernmental liaison, Arctic transportation and the transport of dangerous goods, as well as planning in all aspects of transportation.

The activities of six Crown corporations are co-ordinated by the Marine Administration: the National Harbours Board; St. Lawrence Seaway Authority; and the Atlantic, Laurentian, Great Lakes and Pacific Pilotage Authorities.

Acts Administered

Aeronautics Act
Arctic Waters Pollution Prevention Act
Canada Shipping Act
Dept. of Transport Act
Government Harbours & Piers Act
Government Railways Act
Hamilton Harbour Commissioners Act
Harbour Commissions Act
Intercolonial Railway and P.E.I. Railway Employees' Provident Fund Act
Marine & Aviation War Risks Act
Maritime Code Act
Motor Vehicle Safety Act
Motor Vehicle Tire Safety Act
National Energy Board Act
National Transportation Act
Navigable Waters Protection Act
Ontario Harbours Agreement Act
Passenger Tickets Act
Pilotage Act
Railway Act
Toronto Harbour Commissioners Act
Transport Act
Trenton Harbour Act

Dept. of Transport Responsible for, but does not Administer

Air Canada Act
Atlantic Region Freight Assistance Act
Bills of Lading Act
Canadian National Montreal Terminals Act
Canadian National Railways Act
Canadian National Railways Capital Revision Act
Canadian National Railways Financing & Guarantee Act, 1970
Canadian National Railways Financing & Guarantee Act, 1973
Canadian National Railways Refunding Act, 1955
Canadian National Steamship Act, 1927
Canadian National Toronto Terminals Act
Carriage by Air Act
Carriage of Goods by Water Act
Crows Nest Pass Agreement
Ferries Act
Freight Rates Reduction Act
Government Vessels Discipline Act
International Rapids Power Development Act
Maritime Freight Rates Act
Motor Vehicle Transport Act
National Harbours Board Act
National Transcontinental Railway Act
Railway Relocation & Crossing Act
St. Lawrence Seaway Authority Act
Shipping Conferences Exemption Act
Winnipeg Terminals Act

Some Transport Implications

Bridges Act
Excise Tax Act, c. E-13, Part II
Government Property Traffic Act
National Energy Board Act
United States Wreckers Act

Minister of Transport Responsible for

Canada Grains Act
Canadian Wheat Board Act
Prairie Grain Advance Payments Act
Prairie Grain Provision Payments Act
Two Price Wheat Act
Western Grain Stabilization Act

MINISTER, Hon. Jean-Luc Pepin
Deputy Minister, Arthur Kroeger
Senior Asst. Deputy Minister, T.J. Wilkins

Asst. Deputy Minister, Finance, N. van Duyvendyk
(includes: Administrative Services; Budgets & Financial Services; Financial Planning & Policy; Financial Audit & Review; Computer Services; and Materiel Management)
Asst. Deputy Minister, Personnel, L.R. Huneault
(includes: Personnel; Transport Canada Training Institute; Official Languages; Employee Relations and Departmental Security)
Director General, Public Affairs, I. MacDonald
Departmental General Counsel, D. Lefebvre
Asst. Deputy Minister, Strategic Planning, N.G. Mulder
(includes: Strategic Studies; General Systems Planning; Economic & Regional Analysis; Principles, Pricing & Financing; and Research & Development)
Asst. Deputy Minister, Co-ordination, J.L. Charron

(includes: Government, Industry & International Relations; Policy Advice; Arctic Transportation; Telecommunications & Electronics; Transport of Dangerous Goods; Departmental Secretariat; and Transport Canada Ombudsman)

Director General, Review, V.N. Malizia

(includes: Programming Branch; Evaluation Branch; and Financial Audit)

Administrator, Canadian Air Transportation Administration, W.M. McLeish

Deputy Administrator, R.P. St John

Director General, Civil Aeronautics, P.E. Arpin

(includes: Bilingual Instrument Flight Rules; Telecommunication & Electronics; Flight Services; Air Traffic Services; Aviation Safety Bureau; Aeronautical Licensing & Inspection; Aeronautical Standards & Legislation; Management Advisory Services; Policy Co-ordination; Planning & Development)

Director General, Policy Planning & Programming, Air, L.G. Potvin

Director, Personnel, Air, J. Gauthier

Director General, Airports & Construction Services, J.Y. Sebastyan

Director, Operations Review, Janet Shrieves

Director General, Finance, Air, F. Mousseau

Administrator, Canadian Marine Transportation Administration, G.M. Sinclair

Deputy Administrator, Planning, M. Brennan

Director, Programming & Finance, A. Gagnon

Commr., Canadian Coast Guard, A.L. Collier

Deputy Commr., R.A. Quail

(includes: Coast Guard Pilotage, Fleet Systems, Ship Safety, Aids & Waterways, Planning & Co-ordination, Telecommunications & Electronics)

Administrator, Canadian Surface Transportation Administration, J.R. Giroux

Deputy Administrator, R.J. Marsham

Director General, Highway Transportation, G.G. Belec

(includes: Road & Motor Vehicle Traffic Safety; Highways; Motor Carriers)

Director General, Railway Transportation, K.A. Henderson

(includes: Grain Transportation; Freight Development; Railway Passenger Development; Railway Planning)

Director General, Surface Planning & Co-ordination, Dennis Pratt

(includes: Surface Finance & Administration; Surface Policy & Urban Transportation Assistance; Urban Transportation Research; Surface Program Planning & Co-ordination)

Director General, Water Transportation Assistance, W.G. George

Canadian Air Transportation Regional Offices

Atlantic Region: Box 42, Moncton, N.B. E1C 8K6

Quebec Region: Box 5000, Montreal International Airport, Dorval, P.Q. H4Y 1B9

Ontario Region: 4900 Yonge St., Ste. 300, Willowdale, Ont. M2N 6A5

Central Region: Box 8550, Winnipeg, Man. R3C OP6

Western Region: Federal Bldg., 9820 107th St., Edmonton, Alta. T5K 1G3

Pacific Region: 739 W. Hastings St., Vancouver, B.C. V6C 1A2

Canadian Coast Guard Regional Offices

Maritimes Region: Box 1013, Dartmouth, N.S. B2Y 3Z7

Nfld. Region: Box 1300, St. John's, Nfld. A1C 5N5

Central Region: One Yonge St., 20th floor, Toronto, Ont. M5E 1E5

Laurentian Region: 2 Place Québec, Room 212, Québec, P.Q. G1R 2B5

Western Region: Box 10060, Pacific Centre, 700 W. Georgia St., Vancouver, B.C. V7Y 1E1

Crown Corporations reporting to Parliament through the Minister

Canadian National
VIA Rail Canada
Air Canada
Northern Transportation Co. Ltd.

Crown Corporations Reporting to the Administrator of the Canadian Marine Transportation Administration

St. Lawrence Seaway Authority
National Harbours Board
Atlantic Pilotage Authority
Laurentian Pilotage Authority
Great Lakes Pilotage Authority
Pacific Pilotage Authority

Autonomous Agencies Reporting to Parliament through the Minister

Canadian Transport Commission

TREASURY BOARD

160 Elgin St., Ottawa, Ont. K1A OR5

Information Contact, Yvan P. Roy, Director, Communications Division (phone: 613-995-6053)

The Treasury Board is a separate portfolio of government with its own minister, the President of the Treasury Board

The committee constituting the Treasury Board includes, in addition to the President, the Minister of Finance and four other ministers appointed by Governor-in-Council. The major functions of the Treasury Board are to advise the Cabinet on the optimum allocation of public funds among government programs and to permit the efficient and effective use of the government's manpower and material resources.

The Treasury Board derives its authority from the Financial Administration Act.

PRESIDENT, Hon. Donald J. Johnston
Secretary, John Manion
Deputy Secretary (Program Branch), R.L. Richardson
Deputy Secretary (Personnel Policy Branch), F.R. Drummie
Deputy Secretary (Administrative Policy Branch), P. Meyboom
Deputy Secretary (Official Languages Branch), E. Aquilina
Comptroller General, Harry Rogers

DEPT. OF VETERANS AFFAIRS

Veterans Affairs Bldg., Lyon & Wellington Sts., Ottawa, Ont. K1A OP4

Information Contact, Director of Public Affairs (phone: 613-992-4234)

Acts Administered by Veterans Affairs:

Allied Veterans Benefits Act
Children of War Dead (Education Assistance) Act
Civilian War Pensions & Allowances Act (Part XI)
Dept. of Veterans Affairs Act
Fire Fighters War Service Benefits Act
Returned Soldiers' Insurance Act
Soldier Settlement Act
Supervisors War Service Benefits Act
Veterans Benefit Act, 1954
Veterans Insurance Act
Veterans' Land Act
Veterans Rehabilitation Act
War Service Grants Act
War Veterans Allowance Act
Women's Royal Naval Services & the South African Military Nursing Service (Benefits) Act

By the Canadian Pension Commission

Pension Act
Civilian War Pensions & Allowances Act (Parts I to X)
Compensation for Former Prisoners of War Act
Halifax Relief Commission Pension Continuation Act

By the Pension Review Board
Pension Act (Secs. 75 to 81)

By the War Veterans Allowance Board
War Veterans Allowance Act
Civilian War Pensions & Allowances Act (Part XI)

By the Bureau of Pensions Advocates
Pension Act (Part II)

MINISTER, Hon. W. Bennett Campbell
Deputy Minister, W.B. Brittain, D.F.C., B.Sc. (Econ.)
Asst. Deputy Minister (Finance, Personnel, Admin.), A. DeGagné
Asst. Deputy Minister (Veterans Services), J.C. Smith
Director General, Veterans' Land Admin., D.E. Keen
Director, Legal Services, H.E. Robertshaw
Director, Public Affairs, B.R. Cormier

Veterans Affairs and Bureau of Pensions Advocates District Offices
St. John's, Nfld.: Box 5068, Sir Humphrey Gilbert Bldg., Duckworth St. E. (A1C 5V4)
Corner Brook, Nfld.: 2nd floor, Herald Towers, Millbrook Shopping Centre, Box 1156 (A2H 6T2)
Charlottetown, P.E.I.: 134 Kent St., Box 1300 (C1A 7M8)
Halifax, N.S.: Box 576, 1780 Summer St. (B3J 2R7) (Bureau of Pensions Advocates Office: 6009 Quinpool Rd., B3K 5J7)
Campbellton, N.B.: #501, 157 Water St. (E3N 3G7)
Saint John, N.B.: 600 Main St., Rocca Bldg. "C", Box 1406 (E2L 4J7) (Bureau of Pensions Advocates Office: Room 222, 189 Prince William St., Box 220, E2L 4J7)
Gatineau, P.Q.: 358-B Maloney Blvd. W. (J8P 1E4)
Quebec, P.Q.: Place Laurier, Edifice Champlain, Ste. 6010, 2700 boul. Laurier, Ste-Foy (G1V 4K5)
Montreal, P.Q.: 4545 Queen Mary Rd. (H3W 1W4)
Sherbrooke, P.Q.: 31 King St. W., #441 (J1H 1N5)
Ottawa, Ont.: 10th floor, 2323 Riverside Dr. (K1A OP5)
Kingston, Ont.: New Federal Bldg., Box 7 (K7L 4B7)
Toronto, Ont.: 4900 Yonge St., Willowdale, M2N 6B2
Hamilton, Ont.: National Revenue Bldg., Main & Caroline Sts., Box 490 (L8N 3J9)
London, Ont.: Victoria Hospital, 777 Baseline Rd. E., Box 5837, Term. A (N6A 4N9)
Bureau of Pensions Advocates Office: 451 Talbot St., Box 5337 (N6A 5C9)
North Bay, Ont.: Federal Bldg., Worthington & Ferguson Ave., Box 540 (P1B 8J4)
Brampton, Ont.: #302, 37 George St. N. (L6X 1R5)
Peterborough, Ont.: 201 Charlotte St., Box 1867 (K9J 7X7)
Thunder Bay, Ont.: Room 303, 33 S. Court St. (P7B 2W6)
Brandon, Man.: 153 11th St., #242 (R7A 4J5)
Winnipeg, Man.: 169 Pioneer Ave. (R3C OH3)
Regina, Sask.: 2nd floor, 1901 Victoria Ave. (S4P 3R4)
Saskatoon, Sask.: 506 Federal Bldg., 1st Ave. & 22nd St. E. (S7K OE6)
Calgary, Alta.: #305, 510 12th Ave. S.W. (T2R 0X5)
Edmonton, Alta.: Baker Centre, 8th floor, 10025 106th St. (T5J 1G7)
Vancouver, B.C.: 3rd floor, 1155 Robson St. (V6E 1B9)
Victoria, B.C.: Room 232, 816 Government St. (V8W 3B3)
Penticton, B.C.: #201, 246 Martin St. (V2A 5K3)
Prince George, B.C.: #408, 550 Victoria St. (V2L 2K1)
London, England: Canadian High Commission, Veterans Affairs Division, Canada House, Trafalgar Sq., London, SW1Y 59J

Departmental Institutions
Veterans' Home, Saskatoon, Sask.
Deer Lodge Hospital, Winnipeg, Man.
Rideau Veterans' Home, Ottawa, Ont.
Ste. Anne's Hospital, Ste. Anne de Bellevue, P.Q.

Senior Treatment Medical Offices
St. John's Nfld.: Veterans Pavilion, General Hospital, Box 5068 (A1C 5V4)
Cornerbrook, Nfld.: Box 1156 (A2H 6T2)
Charlottetown, P.E.I.: 134 Kent St., Box 1300 (C1A 7M8)
Halifax, N.S.: King Medical Clinic, Pleasant St., Dartmouth
Sydney, N.S.: 230 Charlotte St., Box 1594 (B1P 6R8)
Saint John, N.B.: Chesley Place, Box 1406 (E2L 4J7)
Campbellton, N.B.: 157 Water St., Box 310 (E3N 3G7)
Québec, P.Q.: 2700 Laurier Blvd., Ste-Foy (G1V 4K5)
Montreal, P.Q.: 4545 Queen Mary Rd. (H3W 1W4)
Sherbrooke, P.Q.: 31 King St. W. (G1N 1N5)
Gatineau, P.Q.: 358-B Maloney Blvd. E. (J8P 1E4)
Ottawa, Ont.: 2323 Riverside Dr., Box 8476, New Term PO (K1G 3H9)
Kingston, Ont.: Federal Bldg., Box 7 (K7L 1X4)
Toronto, Ont. (North): Sunnybrook Medical Centre, Box 750, Stn. K (M4P 2H3)
Toronto, Ont. (South): 11 Front St. (M5J 1A4)
Hamilton, Ont.: Ntl. Revenue Bldg., Main & Caroline, Box 490 (L8N 3J9)
London, Ont.: Victoria Hospital, 777 Baseline Rd., Box 5337 (N6A 4N9)
Windsor, Ont.: 880 Ouellette Ave. (N9A 4H7)
North Bay, Ont.: Federal Bldg., Box 540 (P1B 8J4)
Thunder Bay, Ont.: 33 S. Court St. (P7B 2W6)
Peterborough, Ont.: 201 Charlotte St. (K9J 2T7)
Brampton, Ont.: 37 George St. (L6X 1R5)
Winnipeg, Man.: 1200 Portage Ave. (R3G 0T5)
Brandon, Man.: 153 11th St. (R7A 4J5)
Regina, Sask.: 1901 Victoria Ave. (S4P 3R4)
Saskatoon, Sask.: Federal Bldg., 1st Ave. & 22nd St. E. (S7K 0E6)
Calgary, Alta.: 510 12th Ave. S.W. (T2R 0X5)
Edmonton, Alta.: Baker Centre, 10025 106 St. (T5J 1G7)
Vancouver, B.C.: Shaughnessy Hospital, 4500 Oak St. (V6H 3N1)
Victoria, B.C.: Memorial Pavilion, 2355 Richmond Rd. (V8R 4S2)

Canadian Pension Commission
Veterans Affairs Bldg., Ottawa
Chairman, A.O. Solomon, Q.C., C.D., B.A., LL.B., B.P.A.
Deputy Chairman, H.J. Clarke
Chief Medical Advisor, J. Mutch, M.D. (act.)
Secretary, J. Nickerson
District Offices of the Commission: Representatives of the Commission, known as Senior Pension Medical Examiners, are located in principal cities across Canada.

Pension Review Board
Trebla Bldg., Ottawa, Ont. K1R 5B4
Chairman, R.N. Jutras, B.A., B.Ed.
Deputy Chairman, W.P. Power, B.A., B.C.L.
Registrar, P.M. Godin

War Veterans Allowance Board
Dominion Bldg., Charlottetown, P.E.I. C1A 8M9
Chairman, D.M. Thompson
Deputy Chairman, D.T. McFarlane

Bureau of Pensions Advocates
Veterans Affairs Bldg., Ottawa
Chief Pensions Advocate, L.T. Aiken
Deputy Chief Pensions Advocate, L.M. Hanway
District Offices for the Bureau are the same as District Offices for the Department, with two or three exceptions. See List above.

The Commonwealth War Graves Commission
Veterans Affairs Bldg., Ottawa
Secretary-General, P.V.B. Grieve
Asst.-Secretary-General, S.M. Newell

FEDERAL CROWN CORPORATIONS

AGRICULTURAL STABILIZATION BOARD

Sir John Carling Bldg., 930 Carling Ave., Ottawa, Ont. K1A OC5
(613) 995-5404, 995-5423 (exec. office)
Chairman, Dr. G.I. Trant
Secretary Manager, A.E. Proulx
Processing office: (613) 994-1610

AIR CANADA

Place Ville Marie, Montreal, P.Q. H3B 3P7
(514) 874-4560
Cable: Aircanada
Telex: 06-217537

Air Canada is a publicly owned air transportation service with a route network throughout Canada, to the United States, Bermuda and the Caribbean, and to the United Kingdom and Europe.

President & Chief Executive Officer, Claude I. Taylor

ATLANTIC PILOTAGE AUTHORITY

Suite 1203, Bank of Montreal Tower, Halifax, N.S. B3J 1M5
(902) 426-2550

The Authority operates a pilotage service within the Atlantic Region which includes all the compulsory pilotage waters of the four Atlantic provinces.

Chairman, A.D. Latter
Members, G.E. Simmons, Halifax; D.R. Bell, Halifax; R.J. Kane, Saint John; W.R. Anderson, Newcastle; T.H. Goodyear, St. John's; R. Ching, Souris

ATOMIC ENERGY OF CANADA LTD.

275 Slater St., Ottawa, Ont. K1A OS4
(613) 237-3270

The operations of the Co. include 1) the development of economic nuclear power, 2) scientific research and development in the atomic energy field, 3) the marketing of nuclear reactors, and 4) the production and sale of radioactive isotopes and associated equipment.

Chairman of the Board, Robert Després
President, James Donnelly

ATOMIC ENERGY CONTROL BOARD

Box 1046, Ottawa, Ont. K1P 5S9
(613) 995-5894

The Atomic Energy Control Board derives its authority from the Atomic Energy Control Act and is responsible for regulatory control of the health, safety and security aspects of atomic energy materials, equipment and facilities and the security of atomic energy information.

President, J.H. Jennekens
Members, Miss Sylvia O. Fedoruk, Sask. Cancer Commission, Univ. Hospital, Saskatoon, Sask.; Prof. P. Marmet, Université Laval, Québec; J.L. Olsen, President & Chief Executive Officer, Phillips Cables Ltd., Brockville, Ont.; Ex officio member, President, National Research Council.
Legal Advisor, P.J. Barker
Secretary, R.W. Blackburn
Director General, Reactor Regulation Directorate, Z. Domaratzki
Director General, Fuel Cycle & Materials Regulation Directorate, W.D. Smythe
Director General, Regulatory Research Directorate, P.E. Hamel
Director, Planning & Admin. Branch, J.G. McManus
Chief, Office of Public Information, H.J.M. Spence

BANK OF CANADA

Ottawa, Ont. K1A OG9
(613) 563-8111

The Bank is responsible for regulating "credit and currency in the best interests of the economic life of the nation".

The Bank acts as fiscal agent for the Government of Canada in respect of the management of the public debt of Canada and the Exchange Fund Account. The sole right to issue paper money for circulation in Canada is vested in the Bank of Canada.

Governor, G.K. Bouey
Senior Deputy Governor, R.W. Lawson
Deputy Governors, G.E. Freeman; A. Jubinville; B.J. Drabble; D.J.R. Humphreys
Advisors, J.N.R. Wilson; J. Bussières; W.A. McKay; J.W. Crow; G.G. Thiessen; S. Vachon
Secretary, J.S. Roberts
Chief, Securities Dept., D.G.M. Bennett
Chief, Research Dept., W.R. White
Chief, Dept. of Monetary & Financial Analysis, C. Freedman
Chief, International Dept., J. Conder
Chief, Dept. of Banking Operations, R.E.A. Robertson
Chief, Public Debt Dept., J.M. Andrews
Secretary, J.S. Roberts
Chief, Computer Services Dept., Edith M. Whyte
Chief, Personnel Admin. Dept., R.L. Flett
Chief, Administrative Services Dept., R.H. Osborne
Comptroller & Chief Accountant, A.C. Lamb
Auditor, J.M.E. Morin

THE CANADA COUNCIL

Box 1047, Ottawa, Ont. K1P 5V8
(613) 237-3400

The Council makes grants and offers services to individuals and organizations in the arts.

Chairman, Mavor Moore
Director, Charles Lussier
Assoc. Director, Timothy Porteous

CANADA DEPOSIT INSURANCE CORP.

Box 2340, Stn. D, Ottawa, Ont. K1P 5W5
(613) 996-2081

This Corporation was established in 1967 to provide, for the benefit of persons having deposits with member institutions, insurance against the loss of such deposits because of the insolvency of the member institution. The maximum deposit insurance is $20,000 for each person in each member institution. Membership in the Corporation is restricted to banks, trust companies and mortgage loan companies.

Chairman, John F. Close
Secretary Treasurer, T.J. Davis

CANADA EMPLOYMENT & IMMIGRATION COMMISSION

140 Promenade du Portage, Hull, P.Q. (mailing: Ottawa, Ont. K1A OJ9)
Public Affairs: C. Jennings, Director General (819/994-6013)

Acts Administered

Immigration Act, 1976
Unemployment Insurance Act, 1971
Unemployment & Immigration Reorganization Act
Part I, Employment & Immigration Dept./Commission Act
Part II, Canada Employment & Immigration Advisory Council Act
Adult Occupational Training Act
Emergency Gold Mining Assistance Act (jointly with Energy, Mines & Resources)
Regional Development Incentives Act
Reinstatement in Civil Employment Act
Employment Tax Credit Act

Regulations

Immigration Regulations, 1978
Unemployment Insurance Regulations
National Employment Service Regulations
Labour Mobility & Assessment Incentives Regulations
Manpower Mobility Regulations
Adult Occupational Training Regulations

Employment Tax Credit Program Regulations

CHAIRMAN, J.D. Love
Executive Asst., K. Sigurdson
VICE CHAIRMAN, M.A.J. Lafontaine
Executive Asst., G. Laporte
Commrs., W.E. McBride, J.M. Nicholson
Executive Secretary, A.J. Banerd
Personnel Division, Executive Director, D.J. Lindley
Finance & Admin. Division, Executive Director, F. Godbout
Benefit Programs Division, Executive Director, J.C.V. Charlebois
National Systems & Services Division, Executive Director, B.K. Dertinger
Labour Market Policy Division, Executive Director, D.R. Campbell
Immigration & Demographic Policy Division, Executive Director, J.C. Best
Director General, Foreign Service, J. Bissett

Canada Immigration Offices

There are Immigration Offices in the Canadian Embassies and Consulates abroad. See the Diplomatic Section of the Almanac for addresses etc., and contact the "Immigration Section".

The Commission has Immigration Offices at most ports of entry and customs offices in Canada. For specific addresses and other information contact the Public Affairs Branch of the Commission.

Regional Offices of the Canada Employment & Immigration Commission:

Regional Headquarters with Executive Directors/Directors General

Nfld.: G. Everard, Director General, (167 Kenmount Rd.), Box 12051, St. John's, Nfld. A1B 3Z4
N.S.: J.P. Leblanc, Director General, (5161 George St.), Box 2463, Halifax, N.S. B3J 2M4
P.E.I.: D.G. Wallace, Director General, (199 Grafton St.), Box 8000, Charlottetown, P.E.I. C1A 8K1
N.B.: D. Demers, Director General, (565 Priestman St.), Box 2600, Fredericton, N.B. E3B 5V6
Que.: G. Béland, Executive Director, (1441 St-Urbain St.), Box 7500, Montreal, P.Q. H2X 2M9
Ont.: J.D. Boyd, Executive Director, 4900 Yonge St., Willowdale, Ont. M2N 6A8
Man.: J. Van der Loo, Director General, Grain Exchange Bldg., 167 Lombard Ave., Winnipeg, Man. R3B OT6
Sask.: W.G. Johnson, Director General, 2101 Scarth St., Room 600, Regina, Sask. S4P 2H9
Alta.: R. Gates, Director General, Manulife House, 5th floor, 9925 109th St., Edmonton, Alta. T5K 2J8
B.C.: I. Thomson, Director General, Royal Centre, 1055 W. Georgia St., (Box 11145), Vancouver, B.C. V6E 2P8

Canada Employment Centres

Centres are located at the following places in Canada. In addition there are Centres on Campus at all Universities and most Colleges in Canada. See the Education section of the Almanac and contact "The Canada Employment Centre on Campus".

CEC: Canada Employment Centre; CMC: Canada Manpower Centre; UIC: Unemployment Insurance Office; It: Itinerant.

Abbotsford, B.C. (CEC): 2111 McCallum Rd., V2S 3N7, 604/853-1112
Acton Vale, P.Q. (CMC): 1185 boul. St-André, J0H 1A0, 514/546-2794
Ajax, Ont. (CEC): 174 Harwood Ave. S., L1S 2H7, 416/942-1273
Alberton, P.E.I. (It): Erskine Clark Bldg., C0B 1B0, 902/853-2610
Alma, P.Q. (CEC): 1055 sud, av du Pont, G8B 2V7, 418/668-3301
Amherst, N.S. (CEC): (98 Victoria St.), Box 248, B4H 3Z2, 902/667-5163
Amos, P.Q. (CEC): 22 ouest 1ère Av, J9T 1T8, 819/732-3231
Amqui, P.Q. (It): 12 av du Parc, G0J 1B0, 418/692-2140
Annapolis Royal, N.S. (It): Legion Social Centre, B0S 1A0, 902/532-5196
Antigonish, N.S. (CEC): (Federal Bldg.), Box 730, B2G 2C3, 902/863-1352
Arichat, N.S. (It): Court House Bldg., B0E 1A0, 902/226-3479
Arnprior, Ont. (CEC): 68 Daniel St. N., K7S 2K5, 613/623-3173
Asbestos, P.Q. (CMC): 280 1ère Av, J1T 3N1, 819/879-5491
Ashcroft, B.C. (CEC): (402 Brinks St.), Box 460, V0K 1A0, 604/453-2221
Atikokan, Ont. (CEC): Main & Burns Sts., P0T 1C0, 807/597-6374
Aylmer, Ont. (CEC): 52 Talbot St. E., N5H 1H4
Baddeck, N.S. (CEC): Govt. of Canada Bldg., Chebucto & Queen, B0E 1B0, 902/295-2623
Baie Comeau, P.Q. (CEC): 166 boul. Lasalle, G4Z 1S5, 418/296-4851
Banff, Alta. (CEC): (Federal Bldg.), Box 1899, T0L 0C0, 403/762-4200
Barrie, Ont. (CEC): (48 Owen St.), Box 2500, L4M 3H1, 705/728-2468
Barrington Passage, N.S. (It): Victoria Hotel, B0W 1G0, 902/637-2188
Bathurst, N.B. (CEC): (Harbourview Blvd.), Box 4000, E2A 1R6, 506/548-7951
Beauharnois, P.Q. (CMC): 35 rue St-Laurent, J6N 1V1, 514/429-4693
Bécancour, P.Q. (CMC): 1000 7ième rue, pièce 104, G0X 1B0, 819/294-2536
Bedford, P.Q. (CMC): 71 rue Principale, J0J 1A0, 514/248-7284
Bedford, N.S. (CEC): (Bedford Place), Box 217, B4A 2X2, 902/835-3328
Bell Island, Nfld. (It): Federal Bldg., A0A 1H0, 709/488-2827
Belleville, Ont. (CEC): (228 Dundas St. E.), Box 4800, K8N 5E2, 613/968-4561
Beloeil, P.Q. (CEC): 597 boul. Laurier, J3G 4J1, 514/467-9314
Berthierville, P.Q. (CEC): (584 rue Montcalm), C.P. 1230, J0K 1A0, 514/836-3793
Blairmore, Alta. (CEC): Federal Bldg., 20th Ave. & 27th St., T0K 0E0, 403/562-8118
Blind River, Ont. (CEC): Municipal Bldg., P0R 1B0, 705/356-9865
Bracebridge, Ont. (CEC): 98 Manitoba St., P0B 1C0, 705/645-2204
Brampton, Ont. (CMC): 41 George St. S., L6Y 2E1, 416/451-1240
Brampton, Ont. (UIC): 20 Nelson St. W., L6X 2M5, 416/457-1577
Brandon, Man. (CEC): Box 1178, R7A 6A2, 204/727-0583
Brantford, Ont. (CEC): (58 Dalhousie St.), Box 1570, N3T 5V6, 519/756-6101
Bridgetown, N.S. (It): Federal Bldg., Granville St. W., B0S 1C0
Bridgewater, N.S. (CEC): (Pleasant St.), Box 3100, B4V 2W6, 902/543-7184
Brockville, Ont. (CEC): 52 King St. E., K6V 1B1, 613/342-4487
Brooks, Alta. (CEC): 120 1st Ave. W., T0J 0J0, 403/362-3488
Brossard, P.Q. (CEC): 100 Place Charles Lemoyne, #200, Longueuil, P.Q. J4K 2T4
Buckingham, P.Q. (CEC): 101 est rue MacLaren, J8L 1J9, 819/986-3383
Buctouche, N.B. (It): (Municipal Bldg.), Box 370, E0A 1G0, 506/743-2700
Burlington, Ont. (CEC): (440 Elizabeth St.), Box 5007, L7R 4C3, 416/637-3851
Burnaby, B.C. (CEC): #411, 5021 Kingsway, V5H 4C1, 604/437-3761
Burns Lake, B.C. (It): c/o Box 1460, Vanderhoof, B.C. V0J 3A0, 604/692-3215
Cabano, P.Q. (CEC): 149 rue Commerciale, G0L 1E0, 418/854-3937
Caledonia, N.S. (It): North Queens Electric Bldg., B0T 1B0, 902/242-2800
Calgary, Alta. (CEC) Temporary Emp.: 1415 1st St. S.E., T2G 2J3, 403/231-4936
Calgary Metro, Alta. (CEC): (220 4th Ave. S.E.), Box 2530, T2P 2T7, 403/231-4020
Calgary Northeast, Alta. (CEC): (727 33rd St. N.E.), Box 20, Stn. J, T2A 6M3, 403/231-5840
Calgary South, Alta. (CEC): (7015 Macleod Trail S.W.), Box 5175, Stn. A, T2H 1X3, 403/231-4810

Cambridge, Ont. (CEC): (35 Dickson St.), Box 250, N1R 5T8, 519/621-7150
Campbell River, B.C. (CEC): 940 Alder St., V9W 2P8, 604/286-6212
Campbell's Bay, P.Q. (CMC): (rue Front), C.P. 399, J0X 1K0, 819/648-2146
Campbellford, Ont. (CEC): 36 Front St.
Campbellton, N.B. (CEC): (37 Roseberry St.), Bag 5002, E3N 3L3, 506/753-3323
Campobello, N.B. (lt): Roosevelt-Campobello Internat. Park Commn., Welshpool, N.B. E0G 3H0
Camrose, Alta. (CEC): 4901 50th Ave., #207, T4V 0S2, 403/672-5597
Canso, N.S. (lt): Town Hall, B0H 1H0
Cap-aux-Meules, P.Q. (CEC): Edifice Boudreau, rue Principale, Iles-de-la-Madeleine, P.Q. G0B 1B0, 418/986-4622
Caraquet, N.B. (CEC): (10 Portage St.), Box 730, E0B 1K0, 506/727-3407
Carleton Place, Ont. (CEC): (42 Bridge St.), Box 1420, K0A 1J0, 613/257-3344
Castlegar, B.C. (lt): 105 Maple St., V1N 2A8, 604/365-7235
Causapscal, P.Q. (CEC): 6 nord, rue St-Jacques, G0J 1J0, 418/756-3421
Chambly, P.Q. (CEC): 1465 boul. Industriel, J3L 4C4, 514/658-0643
Chandler, P.Q. (CEC): 109 ouest rue Commerciale, G0C 1K0, 418/689-3381
Chapleau, Ont. (CEC): Federal Bldg., Lorne & Birch St., P0M 1K0, 705/864-1622
Charlottetown, P.E.I. (CEC): (193 Grafton St.), Box 8000, C1A 8K1, 902/892-0171
Chateauguay, P.Q. (CEC): 12 Place Valencia, J6K 4N4, 514/691-4350
Chatham, Ont. (CEC): (10 Centre St.), Box 2019, N7M 5L9, 519/352-2800
Chatham, N.B. (CMC): Federal Bldg., Duke St., E1N 3A4, 506/773-5847
Chelmsford, Ont. (CEC): (Bayside Balfour Mall), Box 1660, P0M 1L0, 705/855-9037
Chester, N.S. (CEC): 22 Union St., B0J 1J0, 902/275-4404
Cheticamp, N.S. (lt): Main St., B0E 1H0, 902/224-2017
Chibougamau, P.Q. (CEC): 462 ième rue, G8P 1N7, 819/748-6464
Chicoutimi, P.Q. (CEC): 267 est, rue Racine, G7H 1S5, 418/549-8233
Chilliwack, B.C. (CEC): (115 Yale Rd. E.), Box 367, V2P 2P4, 604/792-1371
Churchill, Man. (lt): Federal Bldg.
Clarenville, Nfld. (CEC): Box 940, A0L 1J0, 709/466-7920
Coaticook, P.Q. (CMC): 57 est, rue Principale, J1A 1N1, 819/849-2757
Cobourg, P.Q. (CEC): 281 McGill St., K9A 3P8, 416/372-3326
Cochrane, Ont. (CEC): 146 6th St., P0L 1C0, 705/272-5229
Collingwood, Ont. (CEC): 5 Hurontario St., L9Y 3Z3, 705/445-1010
Contrecoeur, P.Q. (lt): (5217 rue Marie-Victorin), C.P. 219, J0L 1C0, 514/587-2039
Corner Brook, Nfld. (CEC): (4 Herald Ave.), Box 2004, A2H 6J6, 709/639-9271
Cornwall, Ont. (CMC): 132 Second St. E., K6H 5R3, 613/933-4260
Cornwall, Ont. (UIC): 340 Pitt St., K6J 5B2, 613/933-7641
Courcelette, P.Q. (CMC): Edifice 500, Base des Forces Canadiennes, Valcartier, P.Q. G0A 1B0
Courtenay, B.C. (CEC): 576 England Ave., V9N 5M7, 604/334-3151
Cowansville, P.Q. (CEC): 224 rue Sud, J2K 2X4, 514/263-0505
Cranbrook, B.C. (CEC): 101 10th Ave. S., V1C 2N1, 604/489-4101
Creighton, Sask. (CEC): Box 520, S0P 0A0, 306/687-7441
Creston, B.C. (CEC): (223B 10th Ave. N.), Box 748, V0B 1G0, 604/428-5366
Dalhousie, N.B. (CMC): (520 Adelaide St.), Box 1720, E0K 1B0, 506/684-3367
Dartmouth, N.S. (CEC): (46 Portland St.), Box 9, B2Y 3Y2, 902/426-2995
Dartmouth, N.S. (lt): Adult Voc. Training, 10 Acadia St., B2Y 2W1, 902/463-6470
Dartmouth East, N.S. (CEC): (73 Tacoma Dr.), Box 2400, B2W 4A5, 902/426-5996
Dartmouth North, N.S. (CEC): 1000 Windmill Rd., B3B 1L7, 902/426-3199
Dauphin, Man. (CEC): 135 2nd Ave. N.E., R7N 0Z6, 204/638-3711
Dawson Creek, B.C. (CEC): 10401 10th St., Rm. 203, V1G 3T8, 604/782-5877
Delhi, Ont. (CMC): Federal Bldg., Church St.
Digby, N.S. (CEC): (Evangeline Mall), Box 879, B0V 1A0, 902/245-4781
Disraeli, P.Q. (CMC): 212 rue St-Joseph, G0N 1E0, 418/449-3728
Doaktown, N.B. (lt): Naple Bldg., Main St., E0C 1G0, 506/365-7775
Dolbeau, P.Q. (CEC): 1500 rue des Erables, G8L 2W7, 418/276-0633
Dominion, N.S. (lt): Duggan St., B0A 1E0, 902/849-6504
Don Mills, Ont. (CEC): See Toronto
Dorion, P.Q. (CEC): 35 rue St-Charles, J7V 7K8, 514/455-5717
Downsview, Ont. (CEC): 1315 Finch Ave. W., 5th Fl., M3J 2G6, 416/638-5115
Drumheller, Alta. (CEC): (196 3rd Ave. W.), Box 550, T0J 0Y0, 403/823-3365
Drummondville, P.Q. (CEC): 150, rue Marchand, J2C 4N1, 819/477-4150
Dryden, Ont. (CEC): 34 Princess St., P8N 1C6, 807/233-2331
Duncan, B.C. (CEC): 20 Coronation Ave., V9L 2S7, 604/748-5231
Dunnville, Ont. (CEC): 201 Broad St. E., N1A 1G1, 416/774-7501
East Angus, P.Q. (CMC): 61 rue Laurier, J0B 1R0, 819/832-2443
Edmonton, Alta. (CMC) Casual Labour: 10615 101st St., T5H 2S2, 403/425-5090
Edmonton Metro, Alta. (CEC): 10210 107th St., T5J 0G2, 403/420-2202
Edmonton North, Alta. (CEC): 8907 118th Ave., T5B 0T5, 403/420-2040
Edmonton North, Alta. (UIC): 10210 107th St., T5J 0G2, 403/425-5869
Edmonton South, Alta. (CEC): 10452 82nd Ave., T6E 2A2, 403/420-2447
Edmonton West, Alta. (CEC): 10158 156th St., T5P 2P9, 403/420-2047
Edmundston, N.B. (CMC): 22 Emerson St., E3V 1R7, 506/735-3358
Edmundston, N.B. (UIC): (10 Court St.), Box 460, E3V 3L1, 506/735-4721
Edson, Alta. (CEC): 5005 5th Ave., T0E 0P0, 403/723-3326
Elliot Lake, Ont. (CEC): 10 Elizabeth Walk, P5A 1Z3, 705/848-2231
Espanola, Ont. (CEC): (200 Espanola Mall), Box 2210, P0P 1C0, 705/869-4552
Estevan, Sask. (CEC): 1302 3rd St., S4A 0S2, 306/634-3624
Exeter, Ont. (CEC): 35 Main St. S., N0M 1S0, 519/235-0471
Farnham, Ont. (CEC): 360 est, rue Principale, J2N 1L7, 514/293-3683
Fernie, B.C. (CEC): (461 3rd Ave.), Box 760, V0B 1M0, 604/423-6806
Flin Flon, Man. (CEC): (54 Main St.), Box 730, R8A 1N5, 204/687-8231
Florenceville, N.B. (CEC): McCain Bldg., Main St., E0J 1K0, 506/392-5537
Forestville, P.Q. (CMC): 51 2ième Ave., G0T 1E0, 418/587-2288
Fort Erie, Ont. (CEC): 55 Jarvis St., L2A 5M5, 416/871-3932
Fort Frances, Ont. (CEC): 210 1st St. E., P9A 1K5, 807/274-5307
Fort McMurray, Alta. (CEC): 10010 Franklin Ave., T9H 2K6, 403/743-2258
Fort Nelson, B.C. (CEC): (Federal Bldg.), Box 596, V0C 1R0, 604/774-2727
Fort Qu'Appelle, Sask. (CEC): (Main St.), Box 37, S0G 1S0

Fort Simpson, N.W.T. (CEC): (Federal Bldg.), Box 380, X0E 0N0, 403/695-2238
Fort Smith, N.W.T. (CEC): (Pinecrest Bldg., McDougal Rd.), Box 1018, X0E 0P0, 403/872-2747
Fort St. James, B.C. (lt): c/o Box 1460, Vanderhoof, B.C. V0J 3A0, 604/966-7073
Fort St. John, B.C. (CEC): 10139 101st Ave., V1J 2B4, 604/785-6166
Fredericton, N.B. (CEC): (440 King St.), Box 12000, E3B 5G4, 506/452-3600
Frobisher Bay, N.W.T. (CEC): (Royal Bank Bldg.), Box 639, X0E 0H0, 819/979-5315
Gananoque, Ont. (CEC): 5 Charles St. S., K7G 1V9, 613/382-2124
Gander, Nfld. (CEC): (Fraser Shopping Mall), Box 347, A1V 1W7, 709/651-3256
Gaspé, P.Q. (CEC): Place Jacques-Cartier, rue de la Reine, G0C 1R0, 418/368-3331
Gatineau, P.Q. (CEC): (89 rue Maple), C.P. 1080, J8P 7E3, 819/663-1115
Georgetown, Ont. (CEC): 7 James St., L7G 2H2, 416/877-6915
Geraldton, Ont. (CEC): 414 Main St., P0T 1M0, 807/854-0902
Gimli, Man. (CEC): (80 6th Ave.), Box 1770, R0C 1B0, 204/642-5193
Glace Bay, N.S. (CEC): (59 Main St.), Box 310, B1A 5V4, 902/849-8650
Goderich, Ont. (CEC): 35 East St., N7A 1N2, 519/524-8342
Golden, B.C. (lt): 412 6th Ave. E., #7A, V0A 1H0, 604/344-6411
Granby, P.Q. (CEC): 615 rue Principale, J2G 2Y1, 514/378-8722
Grand Falls, Nfld. (CEC): (24 High St.), Box 709, A2A 2K2, 709/489-6671
Grand Falls, N.B. (CEC): Grand Falls Mall, E0J 1M0, 506/473-1873
Grand Forks, B.C. (CEC): Box 1409, V0H 1H0, 604/442-2132
Grand Manan, N.B. (lt): Federal Bldg., North Head
Grand-Mère, P.Q. (CEC): (570 6ième Av), C.P. 428, G9T 2H2, 819/538-3384
Grande Cache, Alta. (CEC): (Shoppers' Mall), Box 1050, T0E 0Y0, 403/827-2027
Grande Centre, Alta. (CEC): (5002 51st St.), Box 1109, T0A 1T0, 403/594-4475
Grande Prairie, Alta. (CEC): 10118 101st Ave., T8V 0Y2, 403/532-4411
Guelph, Ont. (CEC): 147 Wyndham St. N., N1H 4E9, 519/822-3150
Guysborough, N.S. (CEC): (Municipal Bldg.), Box 230, B0H 1N0, 902/533-2119
Halifax, N.S. (CEC): 16 Dentith Rd., B3R 2H9, 902/426-2670
Halifax Metro, N.S. (CEC): (7001 Mumford Rd.), Box 2990, Armdale PO, B3L 4N5, 902/426-7250
Halifax North, N.S. (CEC): 2089 Gottingen St., B3K 3B2, 902/426-3468
Halifax South, N.S. (CEC): (5670 Spring Garden Rd.), Box 219, B3J 2N5, 902/426-2950
Halifax South, N.S. (CEC) Adm., Prof. & Tech.: (5670 Spring Garden Rd.), Box 219, B3J 2N5, 902/426-2580
Halifax West, N.S. (CEC): (7001 Mumford Rd.), Box 2990, Armdale PO, B3L 4N5, 902/426-7250
Hamilton, Ont. (CEC): 11 Rebecca St., 4th Fl., L8N 2A2, 416/523-2365
Hamilton East, Ont. (CMC): 199 Parkdale Ave. N., L8H 5X4, 416/545-7123
Hamilton Mtn., Ont. (CEC): (845 Upper James St.), Box 2070, Stn. A, L8N 3R5, 416/389-9525
Happy Valley, Nfld. (CEC): (Hamilton River Rd.), Box 3010, A0P 1E0, 709/896-3323
Harbour Grace, Nfld. (CEC): Box 1900, A0A 2M0, 709/596-7141
Hawkesbury, Ont. (CEC): 212 Main St. E., K6A 1A5, 613/632-2759
Hay River, N.W.T. (CEC): (202 Federal Bldg.), Box 1065, X0E 0R0, 403/874-6739
Hearst, Ont. (CEC): (9 Prince St.), Box 2200, P0L 1N0, 705/362-4207
High Level, Alta. (CEC): (Fahlman Bldg.), Gen. Delivery, T0H 1Z0, 403/926-3777
High Prairie, Alta. (CEC): (5203 49th St.), Box 360, T0G 1E0, 403/523-3331
Hillsborough, N.B. (lt): Post Office Bldg., E0A 1X0, 506/734-2203
Hope, B.C. (CEC): Box 69, V0X 1L0, 604/869-9901
Houston, B.C. (CEC): Box 1269, V0G 1Z0, 604/845-2602
Hull, P.Q. (CEC): 200 boul. Sacré-Coeur, J8X 1E1, 819/770-1510
Humboldt, Sask. (CEC): (537 Main St.), Box 2198, S0K 2A0, 306/682-5414
Huntingdon, P.Q. (CMC): 27 rue du Prince, J0S 1H0, 514/264-3031
Ingersoll, Ont. (CEC): 36 Charles St. W., N5C 2L6, 519/485-0990
Ingonish, N.S. (lt): Legion Hall, B0C 1K0
Inuvik, N.W.T. (CEC): (Kingmingya Rd.), Box 1678, X0E 0T0, 403/979-2122
Inverness, N.S. (CEC): (Federal Bldg.), Box 41, B0E 1N0, 902/258-2995
Isle Madame, N.S. (lt): Arichat & Petit de Grat, B0E 2L0
Jasper, Alta. (CEC): (621 Patricia St.), Box 1388, T0E 1E0, 403/852-4418
Joliette, P.Q. (CEC): (389 rue Notre Dame), C.P. 420, J6E 3H5, 514/756-1094
Jonquière, P.Q. (CEC): (177 rue Ste-Dominique), C.P. 160, G7X 6K4, 418/542-4555
Kamloops, B.C. (CEC): 345 3rd Ave., V2C 3M5, 604/372-2515
Kapuskasing, Ont. (CEC): 8 Queen St., P5N 1G7, 705/335-2337
Kedgwick, N.B. (CEC): Provincial Bldg., E0K 1C0
Kelowna, B.C. (Support Centre): 471 Queensway Ave., V1Y 6S6, 604/763-9253
Kelowna, B.C. (CEC): 471 Queensway Ave., V1Y 6S6, 604/762-3018
Kenora, Ont. (CEC): (326 2nd St. S.), Box 5170, P9N 3X9, 807/468-3101
Kentville, N.S. (CEC): (325 Main St.), Box 150, B4N 3W5, 902/678-7391
Kimberley, B.C. (lt): c/o 250 Howard St., V1A 2Y7, 604/427-4831
Kingston, Ont. (CEC): (791 Princess St.), Box 210, K7L 4V8, 613/546-3541
Kingston West, Ont. (CEC): 675 Bath Rd., K7M 4X2, 613/389-8742
Kirkland Lake, Ont. (CEC): (15 Government Rd. E.), Box 576, P2N 3J8, 705/567-9205
Kitchener, Ont. (CEC): 141 Ontario St. N., 6th Fl., N2G 4L6, 519/742-4421
Kitimat, B.C. (CEC): 311 Federal Bldg., V8C 1T6, 604/632-4691
L'Annonciation, P.Q. (lt): 16 nord rue Principale, J0T 1T0, 819/275-3155
L'Ardoise, N.S. (lt): Community Centre, B0E 1S0
L'Assomption, P.Q. (CEC): (178 rue Notre Dame), C.P. 799, J0K 1G0, 514/589-5751
La Baie, P.Q. (CEC): 831 boul. de la Grande Baie, G7B 1C3, 418/544-2871
La Malbaie, P.Q. (CEC): 21 rue St-André, G0T 1J0, 418/665-3784
La Pocatière, P.Q. (CEC): 201 9ième Av., G0R 1Z0, 418/856-2041
La Ronge, Sask. (CEC): (La Ronge Ave.), Box 324, S0J 1L0, 306/425-2229
La Sarre, P.Q. (CMC): 223 rue Principale, J9Z 1Y5, 819/333-5444
La Tuque, P.Q. (CEC): (375 rue St-Joseph), C.P. 338, G9X 1L5, 819/523-2781
Labrador City, Nfld. (CEC): (Carol Lake Shop. Centre), Box 452, A2V 2K7, 709/944-3655
Lac Mégantic, P.Q. (CMC): 5227 rue Frontenac, G6B 1H2, 819/583-2200
Lachine, P.Q. (lt): 2920 rue Notre Dame, H8S 2H1, 514/634-7131
Lachute, P.Q. (CEC): 505 rue Béthanie, J8H 4A6, 514/562-3791
Langley, B.C. (CEC): #204, 20218 Fraser Hwy., V3A 4E6, 604/533-1201
Leamington, Ont. (CEC): 74 Talbot St. W., N8H 1M4, 519/326-6141
Lethbridge, Alta. (CMC): 419 7th St. S., T1J 2G5, 403/327-8535

Lethbridge, Alta. (UIC): 417 Mayor Magrath Dr., T1J 4C6, 403/329-6522
Levis, P.Q. (CMC): 164 rue Commerciale, G6V 3P5, 418/694-3978
Levis, P.Q. (UIC/CAC): 2 rte 2, G6V 6X8, 418/694-4081
Lindsay, Ont. (CEC): 34 Cambridge St. S., K9V 3B8, 705/324-3562
Listowel, Ont. (CEC): 210 Main St. E., N4W 2B7, 519/291-2920
Liverpool, N.S. (CEC): 164 Main St., B0T 1K0, 902/354-3471
Lloydminster, Sask. (CEC): 4618 49th Ave., S9V 0T2, 403/825-6291
Lockeport, N.S. (It): Federal Bldg., B0T 1L0, 902/656-2512
London, Ont. (CMC): (120 Queen's Ave.), Box 5711, N6A 4S7, 519/679-4444
London, Ont. (UIC): (451 Talbot St.), Box 5711, Stn. A, N6A 4S7, 519/679-4351
Longueuil, P.Q. (CEC): 371 rue St-Jean, J4H 2X9, 514/677-9157
Louisbourg, N.S. (It): Federal Bldg., B0A 1M0, 902/733-2115
Louiseville, P.Q. (CEC): (50 rue St-André), C.P. 10, J5V 2L6, 819/228-2761
Lunenburg, N.S. (CEC): (121 Pelham St.), Box 849, B0J 2C0, 902/634-8807
Lynn Lake, Man. (CMC): Federal Bldg., R0B 0W0, 204/356-8300
Mackenzie, B.C. (CEC): (Federal Bldg.), Box 1870, V0J 2C0, 604/997-6615
Magog, P.Q. (CEC): (67 est rue Principale), C.P. 189, J1X 3W8, 819/843-3361
Manitoulin Island, Ont. (It): c/o Hospital Bldg., Mindemoya, Ont. P0P 1S0, 705/377-5722
Maniwaki, P.Q. (CEC): 116 rue King, J9E 2L3, 819/449-4444
Maple Ridge, B.C. (CEC): 22335 Lougheed Hwy., V2X 2T3, 604/467-5515
Marystown, Nfld. (CEC): (Ville Marie Dr.), Box 1111, A0E 2M0, 709/279-1900
Matane, P.Q. (CEC): 750 ouest av du Parc, G4W 3W8, 418/562-2876
McAdam, N.B. (CEC): Federal Bldg., E0H 1K0
Meadow Lake, Sask. (CEC): 101 1st St. E., S0M 1V0, 306/236-5668
Medicine Hat, Alta. (CEC): 406 2nd St. S.E., T1A 0C3, 403/526-2825
Melfort, Sask. (CEC): (104 McLeod St. E.), Box 1060, S0E 1A0, 306/752-5731
Melville, Sask. (CEC): 317 Main St., S0A 2P0, 306/728-5483
Merritt, B.C. (CEC): 2090 Coultee Ave., V0K 2B0, 604/378-5151
Meteghan, N.S. (It): Meteghan Fire Hall, B0W 2J0, 902/645-2311
Middle Musquodoboit, N.S. (It): Land & Forest Office, B0N 1X0
Middleton, N.S. (CEC): (11 Commercial St.), Box 100, B0S 1P0, 902/825-4675
Midland, Ont. (CEC): 525 Dominion Ave., L4R 1P7, 705/526-2224
Milton, Ont. (CMC): 310 Main St., L9T 1P4, 416/878-8418
Minto, N.B. (CEC): (Main St.), Box 370, E0E 1J0, 506/327-3339
Mission, B.C. (CEC): #209, 33123 1st Ave., V2V 1G5, 604/826-1204
Mississauga, Ont. (CEC): 165 Dundas St. W., L5A 3M3, 416/275-1900
Moncton, N.B. (CEC): (77 Vaughan Harvey Blvd.), Box 5003, E1C 8R5, 506/388-6717
Mont-Joli, P.Q. (CEC): 1498 boul. Jacques Cartier, G5H 2V4, 418/775-4727
Mont-Laurier, P.Q. (CEC): 530 boul. Paquette, J9L 3N5, 514/623-5811
Montague, P.E.I. (CEC): (Southern Kings Regional Service Centre), Box 1500, C0A 1R0, 902/838-2831
Montmagny, P.Q. (CEC): 115 av de la Gare, G5V 2T2, 418/248-1102
Montmorency, P.Q. (CEC): 4096, boul. Ste-Anne, G1C 2J4, 418/694-3282
Montreal, P.Q. (CEC) Adm., Prof. & Tech.: (800 Place Victoria), C.P. 64, Succ. Tour de la Bourse, H4Z 1B1, 514/238-4555
Montreal, P.Q. (CEC) Placement des Immigrants: 1500 rue Atwater, Place Alexis-Nihon, H3Z 2W9, 514/283-5429
Montreal Centre-Ouest, P.Q. (CEC): 4205 rue St-Denis, H2J 2K9, 514/283-4525
Montreal Centre-Est, P.Q. (CEC): (5800 rue St-Denis), C.P. 700, Stn. A, H2S 3L7, 514/273-3311
Montreal Centre-Sud, P.Q. (CEC): 2085 rue Union, H3A 2C5, 514/283-4444
Montreal Nord, P.Q. (CMC): 9310 boul. St-Laurent, H2N 1N5, 514/333-2820
Montreal Nord-Est, P.Q. (CMC): 3730 est boul. Crémazie, H2A 1B5, 514/374-3900
Montreal Nord-Ouest, P.Q. (CEC): 5250 rue Ferrier, H4P 1L4, 514/735-4781
Montreal Nord-Ouest, P.Q. (UIC/CAC): 9275, rue Clark, H2N 2H3, 514/384-3580
Montreal Ouest, P.Q. (CEC): 4060 ouest rue Ste-Catherine, H3Z 2V6, 514/283-6655
Montreal Sud-Est, P.Q. (CEC): 3450 est rue Ontario, H1W 1R3, 514/283-4515
Montreal Est, P.Q. (CEC): 6850 est rue Sherbrooke, H1N 3L9, 514/254-9949
Moose Jaw, Sask. (CEC): 61 Ross St. W., S0E 1A0, 306/693-0555
Moosonee, Ont. (CEC): Post Office Bldg., P0L 1Y0, 705/336-2278
Morden, Man. (CEC): (11th & Stephen Sts.), Box 1418, R0G 1J0, 204/822-4491
Mount Pearl, Nfld. (CEC): c/o (36B Bannister St., St. John's West), Box 2510, A1N 2Z9
Mulgrave, N.S. (CEC): (MacLeod St.), Box 220, B0E 2G0, 902/747-2562
Murdochville, P.Q. (CMC): (600 2ième rue), C.P. 910, G0E 1W0, 418/784-2838
Nackawic, N.B. (CEC): Town Hall, E0H 1P0, 506/575-2241
Nanaimo, B.C. (CEC): 155 Skinner St., V9R 5E8, 604/753-4181
Napanee, Ont. (CEC): #207, 120 Centre St., K0K 2R0, 613/354-3367
Neepawa, Man. (CEC): (405 1st Ave.), Box 598, R0J 1H0, 204/476-2841
Neguac, N.B. (It): Village Hall, Main Rd., E0C 1S0, 506/776-8812
Nelson, B.C. (CEC): 514 Vernon St., V1L 4E7, 604/352-3155
New Glasgow, N.S. (CEC): 35 Donald St., B2H 4T9, 902/752-0500
New Liskeard, Ont. (CEC): 83 Whitewood Ave., P0J 1P0, 705/647-6741
New Richmond, P.Q. (CEC): 128 ouest boul. Perron, G0C 2B0, 418/392-5031
New Sudbury, Ont. (CMC): 1349 Lasalle Blvd., P3A 1Z2, 705/566-0555
New Waterford, N.S. (CEC): 3400 Plummer Ave., B1H 1Y9, 902/863-2405
New Westminster, B.C. (CEC): 29 6th St., V3L 2Y9, 604/526-4511
Newcastle, N.B. (CEC): (155 Pleasant St.), Box 1030, E1V 3V5, 506/622-3421
Newmarket, Ont. (CMC): 462 Park Ave., L3Y 1W1, 416/895-5135
Newmarket, Ont. (UIC): (713 Davis Dr.), Box 2001, L3Y 2R3, 705/895-1621
Niagara Falls, Ont. (CEC): 4500 Queen St., L2E 2L5, 416/356-7261
Noelville, Ont. (CEC): 35 Notre Dame Ave., P0M 2N0, 705/898-2860
North Battleford, Sask. (CEC): 1254 100th St., S9A 0V7, 306/445-9481
North Bay, Ont. (CMC): 101 Worthington St. E., P1B 1G5, 705/472-3700
North Bay, Ont. (UIC): 579 Fraser St., P1B 3X3, 705/474-8420
North Sydney, Ont. (CEC): 59 Prince St., B2A 1J8, 902/794-4794
North Vancouver, B.C. (CEC): 1221 Lonsdale Ave., V7M 2H5, 604/988-1151
O'Leary, P.E.I. (CEC): (West Prince Services Centre), Box 8, C0B 1V0, 902/859-2400
Oakville, Ont. (CEC): 130 George St., L6J 3C1, 416/845-3891

100 Mile House, B.C. (CEC): Box 1240, V0K 2E0, 604/395-4013
Orangeville, Ont. (CEC): 22 Mill St., L9W 3R2, 519/941-0371
Orillia, Ont. (CEC): 17 Peter St. N., L3V 4Y8, 705/326-7336
Oshawa, Ont. (CEC): 44 Bond St. W., L1H 4H8, 416/579-9402
Ottawa, Ont. (CEC): 3rd Fl., Tower B, 300 Laurier Ave. W., K1A 0J6, 613/235-1851
Ottawa East, Ont. (CEC): Place Vanier, Tower C, 25 McArthur Rd., K1L 6R3, 613/993-9810
Ottawa South, Ont. (CEC): (1335 Bank St.), Box 9777, K1G 4A5, 613/523-6930
Ottawa West, Ont. (CEC): 1400 Merivale Rd.
Owen Sound, Ont. (CEC): 901 3rd St. E., N4K 1P1, 519/376-4280
Oxford, N.S. (It): Town Hall, B0M 1P0, 902/447-2170
Parrsboro, N.S. (It): Town Hall, B0M 1S0, 902/254-2187
Parry Sound, Ont. (CEC): 74 James St., P2A 1T8, 705/746-9374
Paspébiac, P.Q. (It): (Edifice Federal), C.P. 819, G0C 2K0, 418/752-3496
Peace River, Alta. (CEC): 10015 98th St., T0H 2X0, 403/624-4485
Pembroke, Ont. (CEC): 178 Pembroke St. E., K8A 3J7, 613/735-0681
Penticton, B.C. (CEC): 305 Main St., #203, V2A 6N5, 604/492-3848
Perth, Ont. (CEC): (13 Herriott St.), Box 336, K7H 3E4, 613/267-1921
Perth-Andover, N.B. (It): Office of Provincial Labour Dept., Main St., E0J 1V0, 506/273-2871
Peterborough, Ont. (CEC): Box 1120, K9J 7H4, 705/743-1952
Petitcodiac, N.B. (It): Legion Bldg., E0A 2H0, 506/756-2171
Picton, Ont. (CEC): 205 Main St., K0K 2T0, 613/476-3227
Pictou, N.S. (CEC): 31 Front St., B0K 1H0, 902/485-4366
Pierreville, P.Q. (It): 78 rue Georges, J0G 1J0, 514/568-2017
Placentia, Nfld. (CEC): Box 399, A0B 2Y0, 709/227-3753
Plaster Rock, N.B. (It): Pugh Bldg., Main St., E0J 1W0, 506/356-2680
Plessisville, P.Q. (CEC): 1800 rue St-Calixte, G6L 1R6, 819/362-3271
Pointe-Claire, P.Q. (CEC): 189 boul. Hymus, H9R 1E9, 514/695-9311
Port Alberni, B.C. (CEC): 4835 Argyle St., V9Y 1V9, 604/724-0151
Port aux Basques, Nfld. (CEC): (Sheaves Bldg.), Box 849, A0M 1C0, 709/695-3091
Port Cartier, P.Q. (CMC): 2 rue Elie Rochefort, G5B 1M9, 418/766-5935
Port Colborne, Ont. (CEC): 184 Elm St., L3K 4N8, 416/834-3629
Port Coquitlam, B.C. (CEC): #300, 2540 Shaughnessy St., V3C 3Y6, 604/941-8221
Port Hardy, B.C. (CEC): (Market St.), Box 700, V0N 2P0, 604/949-7474
Port Hawkesbury, N.S. (CEC): Box 699, B0E 2V0, 902/625-2500
Port Hope, Ont. (CEC): 67 John St., L1A 2Z4, 416/885-6323
Portage La Prairie, Man. (CEC): (211 Saskatchewan Ave. E.), Box 1117, R1N 3C5, 204/857-8731
Powell River, B.C. (CEC): 4812 Joyce Ave., V8A 3B8, 604/485-2721
Prescott, Ont. (CEC): (292 Centre St.), K0E 1T0, 613/925-2808
Prince Albert, Sask. (CEC): #204, 10 13th St. E., S6V 1C6, 306/763-2613
Prince George, B.C. (North Central Support Centre): 550 Victoria St., #304, V2L 3M9, 604/564-4111
Prince George, B.C. (CEC): 1395 6th Ave., V2L 3M9, 604/562-4181
Prince Rupert, B.C. (CEC): #420, 309 2nd Ave. W., V8J 3T1, 604/624-9671
Princeton, B.C. (CEC): 185 Bridge St., V0X 1W0, 604/295-6951
Pugwash, N.S. (It): Pugwash Co-op., B0K 1L0, 902/243-2109
Québec, P.Q. (CEC) Beauport: 190 sud, boul. Dorchester, G1K 5Y9, 418/529-8781
Québec, P.Q. (CEC) Charlesbourg: 137 ouest Des Chênes, G1L 1K6, 418/627-4414
Québec, P.Q. (CEC) Portneuf: 1285 ouest boul. Charest, G1N 2C9, 418/694-4800
Québec, P.Q. (CEC) Ste-Foy: 930 chemin Ste-Foy, G1S 2L4, 418/694-4722
Quesnel, B.C. (CEC): 346 Reid St., V2J 2M4, 604/992-5538
Rankin Inlet, N.W.T. (CEC): Gen. Delivery, X0E 0G0, 403/645-2853
Red Deer, Alta. (CEC): #206, 4909 50th St., T4N 1X0, 403/342-1168
Regina, Sask. (CEC): 2045 Broad St., S4P 2N6, 306/569-6130
Renfrew, Ont. (CEC): 251 Raglan St. S., K7V 1R3, 613/432-4878
Repentigny, P.Q. (CEC): 155 rue Notre Dame, J6A 5L3, 514/585-2044
Revelstoke, B.C. (CEC): (313 3rd St. W.), Box 2580, V0E 2S0, 604/837-5106
Richibucto, N.B. (CEC): (Main St.), Box 518, E0A 2M0, 506/523-4437
Richmond, B.C. (CMC): 5633 No. 3 Rd., V6X 2C7, 604/273-6431
Richmond, B.C. (UIC): 3871 No. 3 Rd., V6X 2V9, 604/273-7128
Richmond, P.Q. (CMC): 109 rue Coiteux, J0B 2H0, 819/826-3729
Rimouski, P.Q. (CEC): 70 est rue St-Germain, G5L 7J9, 418/723-2257
Rivière-du-Loup, P.Q. (CEC): 298 boul. Thériault, G5R 1L8, 418/862-9510
Roberval, P.Q. (CEC): (721 boul. St-Joseph), C.P. 67, G8H 2L3, 418/275-0361
Rocky Harbour, Nfld. (CEC): (Main Rd.), Box 100, A0K 4N0, 709/458-2624
Rouyn, P.Q. (CEC): 40 ave du Lac, J9X 4N3, 819/764-6711
Sackville, N.B. (CMC): (84 Main St.), Box 568, E0A 3C0, 506/536-0753
Sacré-Coeur, P.Q. (CMC): 144 nord rue Principale, G0T 1Y0, 418/236-4628
Ste-Agathe-des-Monts, P.Q. (CEC): 38 rue Principale, J8C 1J4, 819/326-4300
Ste-Anne-des-Monts, P.Q. (CEC): 119 ouest 3ième av., G0E 2G0, 418/763-3305
St. Anthony, Nfld. (CEC): (Barney Bldg.), Box 99, A0K 4S0, 709/454-8388
St. Boniface, Man. (CEC): 170 Marion St., R2H 0T4, 204/949-2511
St. Catharines, Ont. (CEC): 43 Church St., L2R 5C7, 416/688-5670
St. Eustache, P.Q. (CEC): 367 boul. Sauvé, J7P 2B1, 514/473-1220
Ste-Foy, P.Q. (CMC): 2700 boul. Laurier, G1V 2L8, 418/659-2972
Ste-Foy, P.Q. (CSSQ/CMC): (2700 boul. Laurier), C.P. 9008, G1V 4K5, 418/694-4800
St-Gabriel de Brandon, P.Q. (It): (108 rue Deguoy), C.P. 99, J0K 2N0, 514/835-2828
St-George, N.B. (It): Federal Bldg., E0G 2Y0
St-Hyacinthe, P.Q. (CEC): 775 rue St-Dominique, J2S 5M8, 514/773-7481
St-Jean, P.Q. (CEC): 49 rue St-Charles, J3B 7J7, 514/346-2111
St-Jérôme, P.Q. (CEC): 225 rue du Palais, J7Z 1X7, 514/436-4930
Saint John, N.B. (CEC): (400 Main St.), Box 7000, E2L 4V4, 506/658-4919
St. John's Centre, Nfld. (CEC): (Viking Bldg.), Box 8548, Stn. A, A1B 2X3, 709/737-5252
St. John's East, Nfld. (CEC): (Bldg. 223, Pleasantville), Box 4800, A1C 5T8, 709/737-4700
St. John's Metro, Nfld. (CEC): (Bldg. 223, Pleasantville), Box 4800, A1C 5T8, 709/737-5303
St-Laurent, P.Q. (UIC/CAC): 790 boul. Laurentien, H4M 2M6, 514/748-8189
St-Léonard, P.Q. (UIC/CAC): (7510 boul. Viau), C.P. 1500, Succ. Jean-Talon, H1S 2P3, 514/374-2750
Ste-Marie-Beauce, P.Q. (CMC): 287 Marguerite-Bourgeois, G0S 2Y0, 418/387-2916
St. Paul, Alta. (CEC): (5105 50th Ave.), Box 309, T0A 3A0, 403/645-4428
St. Peter's, N.S. (It): Provincial Bldg., Main St., B0E 3B0, 902/535-2022

St-Quentin, N.B. (CMC): (193 Canada St.), Box 549, E0K 1J0, 506/235-2615
Ste-Scholastique, P.Q. (It): (10150 rue St-Vincent), C.P. 234, J0N 1S0, 514/258-2411
St-Stephen, N.B. (CEC): (93 Milltown Blvd.), Box 5004, E3L 3B4, 506/466-4507
Ste-Thérèse, P.Q. (CEC): 212 boul. Curé-Labelle, J7E 1X2, 514/430-2800
St. Thomas, Ont. (CEC): 403 Talbot St., #215, N5P 1B7, 519/631-5470
Salmon Arm, B.C. (CEC): (333 Hudson St.), Box 1510, V0E 2T0, 604/832-8083
Sarnia, Ont. (CEC): (112 Christina St. N.), Box 936, N7V 5T6, 519/336-7680
Saskatoon, Sask. (CEC): 101 22nd St. E., S7K 0E2, 306/665-4515
Saskatoon, Sask. (CEC) Casual Labour: 326 1st Ave. S., S7K 1K4, 306/665-4986
Sault Ste. Marie, Ont. (CEC): (390 Bay St.), Box 2400, P6A 5N9, 705/254-5101
Sault Ste. Marie, Ont. (CEC): 1416 Wellington St.
Scarborough, Ont. (CEC): 2472 Eglinton Ave. E., M1K 2R2, 416/264-2111
Scarborough, Ont. (It): 2500 Lawrence Ave. E., M1P 2R7, 416/751-9520
Scarborough, Ont. (It): 1610 Midland Ave., M1P 3C5, 416/751-9520
Sechelt, B.C. (CEC): (1192 Cowrie St.), Box 1520, V0N 3A0, 604/885-2722
Selkirk, Man. (CEC): #12, 366 Main St., R1A 1T6, 204/482-3323
Senneterre, P.Q. (CMC): (273 ouest 3ième rue), C.P. 218, J0Y 2M0, 819/737-2377
Sept-Iles, P.Q. (CEC): 701 boul. Laure, G4R 1X8, 418/962-5501
Shawinigan, P.Q. (CMC): (395 av de la Station), C.P. 218, G9N 6T9, 819/536-5633
Shawinigan, P.Q. (UIC/CAC): 695 av de la Station, G9N 7J7, 819/537-8851
Shediac, N.B. (CEC): 1172 Main St., E0A 3G0, 506/532-6633
Sheet Harbour, N.S. (It): Fire Hall, B0J 3B0, 902/885-2377
Shelburne, N.S. (CEC): (Water & John Sts.), Box 819, B0T 1W0, 902/875-2452
Sherbrooke, P.Q. (CMC): 437 est rue King, J1G 1B7, 819/565-4943
Sherbrooke, P.Q. (UIC/CAC): 299 rue Olivier, J1H 1X4, 819/565-4733
Sherbrooke, N.S. (It): Municipal Bldg., B0J 3C0, 902/522-2854
Shippegan, N.B. (It): Au Moderna Bldg., E0B 2P0, 506/336-8409
Shubenacadie, N.S. (It): Federal Bldg., B0N 2H0
Simcoe, Ont. (CEC): 122 Norfolk St. N., N3Y 3N8, 519/426-5270
Slave Lake, Alta. (CEC): (106 1st St. N.E.), Box 724, T0G 2A0, 403/849-4153
Smithers, B.C. (CEC): (1090 Main St.), Box 1028, V0J 2N0, 604/847-3248
Smiths Falls, Ont. (CEC): 17 Church St. E., K7A 1H1, 613/283-4790
Snow Lake, Man. (It): Council Bldg., R0B 1M0
Sorel, P.Q. (CMC): (60 rue Elizabeth), C.P. 395, J3P 5N8, 514/743-7916
Sorel, P.Q. (UIC/CAC): (13A rue Georges), C.P. 500, J3P 1B7, 514/743-4841
Souris, P.E.I. (CEC) Eastern Kings Reg. Service Centre: Box 550, C0A 2B0, 902/687-3022
Springdale, Nfld. (CEC): (Main St.), Box 670, A0J 1T0, 709/673-3841
Springhill, N.S. (CEC): (68 Main St.), Box 2050, B0M 1X0, 902/597-3791
Springhill, N.S. (CEC): (Springhill Medium Security Institution), Box 2140, B0M 1X0, 902/597-3755, loc. 251
Squamish, B.C. (CEC): 38043 Cleveland St., V0N 3G0, 604/892-9012
Steinbach, Man. (CEC): (302 Main St.), Box 1149, R0A 2A0, 204/326-6475
Stephenville, Nfld. (CEC): (Govt. of Canada Bldg.), Box 690, A2N 3B5, 709/643-2104
Stettler, Alta. (CEC): 5104 50th Ave., T0C 2L0, 403/742-4421
Stoney Creek, Ont. (CMC): 174 Hwy. 8, L8G 1C3, 416/664-4496
Stratford, Ont. (CEC): 100 Albert St., N5A 6S7, 519/271-4120
Strathroy, Ont. (CEC): 25 Centre St., N7G 2R3, 519/245-3900
Streetsville, Ont. (It): 167 Queen St. S., L5M 1L2, 416/279-1821
Sturgeon Falls, Ont. (CEC): 48 William St., P0H 2G0, 705/753-1106
Sudbury, Ont. (CEC): 880 LaSalle Blvd., P3A 1X6, 705/566-4521
Sudbury, Ont. (CEC): 144 Pine St., P3C 1X3, 705/675-2211
Sudbury, Ont. (CEC) Youth Employment Centre: 144 Pine St., P3C 1X3, 705/675-5234
Sudbury, Ont. (CEC) Administration: 880 LaSalle Blvd., P3E 1X6
Summerside, P.E.I. (CEC): (120 Water St.), Box 100, C1A 4T6, 902/436-2104
Surrey, B.C. (CEC): 10524 King George Hwy., V3T 3X2, 604/588-5981
Sussex, N.B. (CEC): (48 Maple Ave.), Box 1670, E0E 1P0, 506/433-3400
Swan River, Man. (CEC): 203 5th Ave. N., E0E 1P0, 204/734-4438
Swift Current, Sask. (CEC): 50 Herbert St. E., S9H 1M2, 306/773-8324
Sydney, N.S. (CEC): (49 Dorchester St.), Box 850, B1P 6J3, 902/539-3510
Sydney, N.S. (CEC): (308 George St.), Box 850, B1P 6J7
Sydney Mines, N.S. (CEC): 105 Main St., B1V 2L3, 902/736-6231
Terrace, B.C. (CEC): 4630 Lazelle Ave., V8G 1S6, 604/635-7134
Terrebonne, P.Q. (CEC): 878 boul. des Seigneurs, J6W 1V1, 514/471-3722
The Pas, Man. (CEC): (151 Fischer Ave.), Box 660, R9A 1K7, 204/623-3453
Thetford Mines, P.Q. (CEC): 222 sud boul. Smith, G6G 5T3, 418/335-2972
Thompson Man. (CEC): 83 Churchill Dr., R8N 0L6, 204/778-4471
Thunder Bay North, Ont. (CEC): 33 Court St. S., P7B 5E6, 807/344-6601
Thunder Bay South, Ont. (CEC): 130 S. Syndicate Ave., 2nd Fl., P7E 1C7, 807/623-2731
Tillsonburg, Ont. (CEC): 4 Ridout St. E., N4G 2C5, 519/842-5907
Timmins, Ont. (CEC): 38 Pine St. N., P4N 7J9, 705/267-6271
Toronto, Ont. (CEC) Metro Training Centre: (25 St. Clair Ave. E.), Box 420, Stn. Q, M4T 2M9, 416/966-6125
Toronto, Ont. (CEC) Etobicoke: 1243 Islington Ave., 4th Fl., M8X 1Y9, 416/236-1931
Toronto, Ont. (CEC) Long Branch: 3253 Lakeshore Blvd. W., M8V 1M3, 416/236-1931
Toronto, Ont. (CEC) Dundas East: 3rd Fl., 200 Dundas St. E., M5B 1A4, 416/363-5931
Toronto, Ont. (CEC): (75 The Donway W.), Box 3600, Don Mills, Ont. M3C 2T9, 416/449-8359
Toronto, Ont. (CEC) Danforth East: 1985A Danforth Ave., M4C 1J7, 416/694-0280
Toronto, Ont. (CEC) Danforth West: (745 Danforth Ave.), Box 625, Stn. J, M4J 4Z3, 416/461-5449
Toronto, Ont. (CEC) High Park: 2968 Dundas St. W., M6P 1Y8, 416/766-3211
Toronto, Ont. (CEC) Bloor-Islington: (883 Bloor St. W.), Box 2000, Stn. E, M6H 4E4, 416/537-2072
Toronto, Ont. (CEC) St. Clair: 1384 St. Clair Ave. W., M6E 1E6, 416/654-8662
Toronto, Ont. (CEC) Toronto Centre: 20 Eglinton Ave. W., 21st Fl., M4R 2G2, 416/484-5702, emp.; 484-1711, ins.
Toronto, Ont. (CEC): 180 Wellington St. W., 9th Fl., M5J 1J1, 416/369-3424
Toronto, Ont. (CEC) North York: (4900 Yonge St.), Box 1400, Stn. A, Willowdale, Ont. M2N 6A4, 416/224-3777
Tracadie, N.B. (CEC): (Pharmacy Roussel Bldg.), Box 1000, E0C 2B0, 506/395-3309
Trail, B.C. (CEC): 835 Spokane St., V1R 3W4, 604/368-5566
Trenton, Ont. (CEC): 72 Front St., K8V 4N4, 613/392-6531

Trois-Rivières, P.Q. (CMC): (950 rue Royale), C.P. 1750, G9A 4H8, 819/379-6440
Trois-Rivières, P.Q. (UIC/CAC): 140 rue St-Antoine, G9A 4J5, 819/379-3900
Truro, N.S. (CEC): 15 Arlington Place, B2N 3T8, 902/895-1647
Uranium City, Sask. (CEC): (152 2nd St. N.), Box 398, S0J 2W0, 306/489-3100
Val D'Or, P.Q. (CEC): 550 3e Av., J9P 1S4, 819/825-5640
Valleyfield, P.Q. (CEC): 157 rue Victoria, J6T 1A5, 514/373-6220
Vancouver, B.C. (CEC): 1110 W. Georgia St., V6E 3H7, 604/681-8253
Vancouver, B.C. (Metro Support Centre): 750 Cambie St., #400, V6B 4V5, 604/666-1056
Vancouver, B.C. (CEC): 125 10th Ave. E., V5T 1Z3, 604/872-7431
Vancouver, B.C. (CEC) Prof. & Tech.: #1400, 789 W. Pender St., V6C 1J6, 604/666-2351
Vancouver, B.C. (CMC) Immigration Reception: 622 Seymour St., V6B 3K5, 604/666-2181
Vancouver, B.C. (CMC) Temporary: 6 2nd Ave. E., V5T 1B1, 604/879-7154
Vancouver East, B.C. (CEC): 1747 E. Hastings St., V5L 1T1, 604/251-2421
Vancouver South, B.C. (CEC): 5550 Fraser St., V5W 3W1, 604/666-1021
Vancouver West, B.C. (CEC): 2902 W. Broadway, V6K 2G8, 604/732-1311
Vanderhoof, B.C. (CEC): (1809 Stewart St.), Box 1460, V0J 3A0, 604/567-4795
Verdun, B.C. (CEC): 1055 rue Galt, H4G 2R1, 514/769-3774
Vernon, B.C. (CEC): 3202 31st St., V1T 5J1, 604/545-2125
Victoria, B.C. (Vancouver Island Support Centre): 1111 Blanshard St., V8V 3A9, 604/388-3113
Victoria, B.C. (CEC): 810 Fort St., V8W 3A9, 604/388-3481
Victoriaville, P.Q. (CEC): 108 rue Olivier, G6P 6V6, 819/758-0551
Ville de Laval, P.Q. (CEC): 3 Place Laval, H7N 1A3, 514/663-5910
Ville-Marie, P.Q. (CMC): 18 rue Notre Dame de Lourdes, J0Z 3W0, 819/629-2757
Ville St-Georges, P.Q. (CMC): 12435 est 1ière av., G5Y 2E3, 418/228-8806
Ville St-Georges, P.Q. (UIC/CAC): 11780 est 1ière av., G5Y 2C8, 418/228-5508
Wabush, Nfld. (CMC): Sir Wilfred Grenfell Hotel, A0R 1B0
Wainright, Alta. (CEC): (1006 4th Ave.), Box 460, T0B 4P0, 403/842-3389
Walkerton, Ont. (CEC): 100 Scott St., N0G 2V0, 519/881-2010
Wallaceburg, Ont. (CEC): 602 Wellington St., N8A 2Y5, 519/627-3348
Waterloo, Ont. (CEC): 232 King St. N., N2J 2Y7, 519/579-1550
Waterloo, P.Q. (CMC): 5376 rue Foster, J0E 2N0, 514/539-2838
Welland, Ont. (CEC): 225 Main St. E., L3B 3W7, 416/735-5323
Wellington, P.E.I. (CEC): (Medical Arts Centre), Box 27, C0B 2E0, 902/854-2516
Weston, Ont. (CEC) Administration: 1646 Jane St., M9N 2R9
Weston, Ont. (CEC): 1747 Jane St., M9N 2S5, 416/247-8261
Wetaskiwin, Alta. (CEC): 4811 51st St., T9A 1L1, 403/352-6081
Weyburn, Sask. (CEC): 140 1st St., S4H 0T2, 306/842-5424
Whitby, Ont. (CEC): 132 Dundas St. W., L1N 2L9
Whitehorse, Y.T. (CEC): 101 Federal Bldg., Y1A 2B5, 403/667-5050
Williams Lake, B.C. (CMC): 99 2nd Ave. N., V2G 1Z3, 604/392-4184
Williams Lake, B.C. (UIC): 197 2nd Ave. N., #310, V2G 1Z5, 604/392-6528
Willowdale, Ont.: See Toronto
Windsor, N.S. (CEC): 58 Gerrish St., B0N 2T0, 902/798-4726
Windsor, Ont. (CEC): 467 University Ave. W., N9A 5R2, 519/254-1611
Winnipeg, Man. (CEC) Stony Mountain Inst.: Box 4500, R3C 3W8, 204/453-5541
Winnipeg, Man. (CMC) Temporary: 104 Arthur St., R3H 1H3, 204/949-5398
Winnipeg, Man. (CMC) Prof. & Exec.: #400, 209 Notre Dame Ave., R3B 2V7, 204/949-6518
Winnipeg, Man. (CMC) Job Info.: 393 Portage Ave., R3B 2C5, 204/949-2281
Winnipeg Metro, Man. (CEC): 344 Edmonton St., R3B 2X7, 204/949-6378
Winnipeg Centre, Man. (CEC): 344 Edmonton St., R3B 2X7, 204/949-5326
Winnipeg East, Man. (CEC): 220 Hespeler Ave., R2L 2C4, 204/666-6820
Winnipeg North, Man. (CMC): 1354 Main St., R2W 3T8, 204/582-4677
Winnipeg North, Man. (UIC): 1070 Main St., R2W 5J3, 204/949-3242
Winnipeg South, Man. (CEC): 1048 Pembina Hwy., R3T 1Z8, 204/452-9466
Winnipeg West, Man. (CEC): 1822 Portage Ave., R3J 0G5, 204/783-8132
Woodstock, Ont. (CEC): 35 Metcalfe St., N4S 3E6, 519/537-2385
Woodstock, N.B. (CEC): (Regent St.), Box 2001, E0J 2B0, 506/328-2398
Yarmouth, N.S. (CMC): (Yarmouth Mall), Box 520, B5A 4B6, 902/742-7883
Yarmouth, N.S. (UIC): (15 Willow St.), Box 249, B5A 4B2, 902/742-7102
Yellowknife, N.W.T. (CEC): (4916 49th St.), Box 1170, X0E 1H0, 403/873-2746
Yorkton, Sask. (CEC): 18 Broadway St. E., S3N 0K3, 306/783-9421

CANADA MORTAGE & HOUSING CORPORATION

Montreal Rd., Ottawa, Ont. K1A OP7
(613) 746-4611

This Corporation administers the National Housing Act. It is primarily responsible for delivering federal housing assistance programs designed to facilitate the supply of housing, particularly for those of low and moderate income and to insure loans made by approved lenders on the open market and to make direct loans in areas not served by these lenders.

Special programs are available to provincial and municipal governments including a residential rehabilitation assistance program, a land assembly assistance program and a community services program.

President, R.V. Hession
General Counsel, Vice President, (vacant)
Program Policy & Research, Vice President, R.T. Adamson
Program Operations, Vice President, R.J. Boivin
Finance, Vice President, D.W. Knight
Organization Development, Vice President, N.E. Hallendy

CMHC Regional Offices:

B.C.: Ste. 800, 1500 W. Georgia St., Vancouver, B.C. V6G 3A1 (604/666-2516)
Prairie: 111 2nd Ave. S. (Box 1107, Saskatoon, Sask. S7K 1K6) (306/665-4900)
Ont.: Atria North, Phase 1, 2255 Sheppard Ave. E., Willowdale, Ont. M2J 1W7 (416/498-7300)
Que.: Place du Canada, Ste. 900, Montreal, P.Q. H3B 2N2 (514/283-4464)
Atlantic: Ste. 1400, 44 Prince William St. (Box 7320, Stn. A, Saint John, N.B. E2L 4S7) (506/658-4460)

CANADA POST CORP.

Confederation Heights, Ottawa, Ont. K1A 0B1
(613) 998-8305

Canada Post is in charge of postal service in Canada.

President, Michael Warren

Regional Public Affairs Offices

Atlantic: Box 1689, Halifax, N.S. B3J 2B1 (902/426-2246)
Saint John: 506/658-4754
St. John's: 709/737-5209

Quebec: 1550 boul. de Maisonneuve ouest, 7th floor, Montréal, P.Q. H3G 2R0 (514/283-4435)

Ontario: 21 Front St. W., #552, Toronto, Ont. M5J 1A1 (416/369-3155)
London: 519/679-5050
Ottawa: 613/996-6164
North Bay: 705/474-3480

Western: Box 10064, Pacific Centre, 700 W. Georgia St., Vancouver, B.C. V7Y 1C2 (604/666-3997)
Edmonton: 403/420-3052
Calgary: 403/231-5502
Saskatoon: 306/665-4713
Regina: 306/359-6441
Winnipeg: 204/949-2228

CANADIAN ARSENALS LTD.

5 Montée des Arsenaux, Le Gardeur, P.Q. J5Z 2P4

In co-operation with the private sector and the armed forces, Canadian Arsenals Ltd. maintains a state of readiness for the production of required ammunitions and other related products required by the National Defence for the protection of Canada. The Corporation reports to Parliament through the Minister of Supply & Services.

President & Chief Executive Officer, L.A. Bergeron
Senior Vice President, J.R. Greene
Vice President, Procurement, Jacky Malka
Vice President, Marketing, Gen. R.A. Reid
Vice President, Research & Development, Léo Tardif
Vice President, Administration, Richard Monette

CANADIAN BROADCASTING CORPORATION

Box 8478, Ottawa, Ont. K1G 3J5
(613) 731-3111

The CBC provides the national broadcasting service in Canada.

President, A.W. Johnson
Executive Vice President, Pierre DesRoches
Vice President & General Manager, English Services, Peter Herrndorf
Vice President & General Manager, French Services, R. David

CANADIAN COMMERCIAL CORPORATION

112 Kent St., 17th floor, Ottawa, Ont. K1A 1E9
(613) 996-0034

EXPORT SUPPLY CENTRE
Ottawa, Ont. K1A 0S6
(819) 997-5714

CCC serves as procurement agent for foreign governments and international agencies using the facilities of the Dept. of Supply & Services to identify and contract on behalf of Canadian sources of supply. It also works to expand capital project exports by serving as a prime contractor when this arrangement will put Canadian suppliers in a better competitive position. CCC complements the role of EDC, CIDA and the Dept. of Industry, Trade & Commerce.

President, R.L. Gillen
Director, Export Supply Centre, O.I. Matthews

CANADIAN DAIRY COMMISSION

4th floor, 2197 Riverside Dr., Ottawa, Ont. K1A OZ2
(613) 998-9490
Chairman, Gilles Choquette
Vice Chairman, E.G. Hodgins
Commr., Cliff McIsaac

CANADIAN FILM DEVELOPMENT CORPORATION

C.P. 71, Tour de la Bourse, Suite 2220, Montreal, P.Q. H4Z 1A8
(514) 283-6363

The Corporation supports and develops the feature film industry in Canada by investing in productions, and making loans to producers.

Chairman, David P. Silcox
Executive Director, André Lamy

CANADIAN NATIONAL RAILWAYS

Box 8100, Montreal, P.Q. H3C 3N4
(514) 877-5430

The Company was incorporated to operate and maintain a national railway system including the Canadian Northern Railway System, the Canadian Government Railways and, subject to approval of the Governor-in-Council, other lines in Canada.

Chairman of the Board, J.A. Dextraze
President & Chief Executive Officer, Dr. R.A. Bandeen
Senior Vice President, A.H. Hart
Corporate Vice President, Finance, Dr. M. LeClair
Corporate Vice President, Admin., K.E. Hunt
Vice President & Senior Executive Officer, CN Rail, R.E. Lawless

CANADIAN PATENTS & DEVELOPMENT LTD.

275 Slater St., Ottawa, Ont. K1A OR3
Chairman of the Board, P.R. Gendron, 996-5736
Vice President & Chief Executive Officer, W.D. Gordon, 996-5736
Secretary, W.D. Gordon, 996-5530
Treasurer, Miss L. Lipke, 996-5736
Marketing & Licensing Chief, K.F. Crowe, 996-5530
Patent Branch Chief, J.R. Hughes, 996-4670

CANADIAN SALTFISH CORPORATION

139 Water St., Box 6088, St. John's, Nfld. A1C 5X8
(709) 722-7500

This Corporation was established to improve the earnings of primary producers of cured saltfish in participating provinces.

Chairman, L.J. Cowley
President & General Manager, Kjell Henriksen
Comptroller, W.R. Moyse, C.G.A.

CANADIAN WHEAT BOARD

423 Main St., Winnipeg, Man. R3C 2P5
(204) 949-3416

The Board is the sole marketing agency for western Canadian wheat, oats and barley moving into export channels and also the only source of supply for those same grains to the domestic market for human consumption.

Chief Commr., W.E. Jarvis
Asst. Chief Commr., R.L. Kristjanson
Commrs., C.W. Gibbings, J.L. Leibfried, F.M. Hetland
Treasurer/Comptroller, Peebles Kelly
Senior Advisor/Marketing, F.T. Rowan
Solicitor, H.B. Monk
Executive Director, Marketing, G.P. Machej
Executive Director, Planning, H.F. Bjarnason
Executive Director, Admin., J.E. McLaughlin
Secretary to the Board & Asst. Executive Director, Admin., M. Hunter

CAPE BRETON DEVELOPMENT CORPORATION

Box 1330, Sydney, N.S. B1P 6K3
(902) 539-5910

This Corporation has two divisions–the Coal Division and the Industrial Development Division. The responsibility of the Coal Division is to conduct coal mining and related operations in the Sydney coal fields on the Island of Cape Breton. The responsibility of the Industrial Development Division is (a) to promote and assist in the financing and development of industry on the

Island of Cape Breton, and (b) to provide employment to broaden the base of the economy of the Island.
President, D.S. Rankin

CROWN ASSETS DISPOSAL CORPORATION

450 Rideau St., Box 8451, Ottawa, Ont. K1G 3J8
(613) 995-3237

This Corporation is the agency responsible for the sale of all materials and equipment surplus to the needs of Federal government Departments and certain Crown agencies. It also acts as agent for the U.S., British and other governments in the sale of their surplus assets located in Canada.
General Manager, R.B. Vaillant

DEFENCE CONSTRUCTION (1951) LTD.

SBI Bldg., Billings Bridge Plaza, 2323 Riverside Dr., Ottawa, Ont. K1A OK3
(613) 998-9548

The Crown company that administers the major construction and building repair and maintenance programs and contracts for engineering consultant and architectural services for the Dept. of National Defence. In addition, upon request, provides technical advice and assistance to other Government Departments and agencies.
President & General Manager, A.G. Bland, P.Eng.
Vice President, Planning, J.H. Stitt, P.Eng.
Vice President, Construction, J.D. McIlveen, P. Eng.
Treasurer, T.D. Heavens
Secretary, W.J. Mulock

ECONOMIC COUNCIL OF CANADA

Box 527, Ottawa, Ont. K1P 5V6
(613) 993-1052

A council to recommend measures that will achieve the highest possible levels of employment and efficient production in Canada, to ensure that a consistent rate of economic growth is maintained and that all citizens share in the proceeds of that growth; and to publish an annual review of medium and long-term economic prospects and problems.
Secretary, William Haviland

ELDORADO AVIATION LTD.

Wholly owned subsidiary of Eldorado Nuclear Ltd.
President, N.M. Ediger
Operations Office: Airport, Hangar No. 3, Saskatoon, Sask. S7L 5P4
General Manager, W.H.R. Field

ELDORADO NUCLEAR LTD.

A company to mine and refine uranium and to produce nuclear fuels in Canada.
Head Office, 255 Albert St., Ste. 400, Ottawa, Ont. K1P 6A9
(613) 238-5222
President, N.M. Ediger
Executive Vice President, M.J. Moreau
Vice President, Finance, T.J. Gorman
Vice President, Refining, R.G. Dakers
Vice President, Mining, K. Haapanen
Vice President, Marketing, George Boyce
Secretary, S. Mackay-Smith
Treasurer, G.A. Frost

Refinery Operations

215 John St., Port Hope, Ont. L1A 3A1
(416) 885-4511

Beaverlodge Operations

Box 7010, Eldorado, Sask. SOJ OTO

EXPORT DEVELOPMENT CORPORATION

110 O'Connor St., Ottawa, Ont. (Mailing: Box 655, Ottawa, Ont. K1P 5T9)
(613) 237-2570; Telex: 053-4136; Cable: EXCREDCORP

EDC provides insurance and bank guarantee services to Canadian exporters and arranges credit for foreign buyers in order to facilitate and develop export trade. The facilities include: 1) insurance of Canadian firms against non-payment when Canadian goods and services are sold abroad; 2) insurance for Canadian firms against wrongful calls on performance securities, and guarantees for banks providing securities related to performance or bids; 3) insurance and guarantees to financial institutions against losses incurred in financing either the Canadian supplier or the foreign buyer in an export transaction; 4) medium-term supplier financing through the purchase of promissory notes issued to an exporter by a foreign buyer (forfaiting); 5) long-term financing in the form of direct buyer credits, and allocations under lines of credit to foreign purchasers of Canadian capital equipment and services; 6) insurance against loss of Canadian investments abroad by reason of political actions.
Chairman of the Board & President, Sylvain Cloutier
Vice President, Loans Group, J. Arès
Vice President, Insurance Group, D.A. Keill
Vice President, Marketing & Communications, J.R. Hegan

Eastern Region: Box 124, Tour de la Bourse, Montreal, P.Q. H4Z 1C3
A.O. Werlen, Asst. Vice President
Atlantic Office: 1791 Barrington St., #1401, Halifax, N.S. B3J 3L1
C.T. Wood, Atlantic Representative
Ontario Region: Box 64, 1 First Canadian Place, Toronto, Ont. M5X 1B1
G.R. Hammond, Asst. Vice President
Western Region: #1030, One Bentall Centre, 505 Burrard St., Vancouver, B.C. V7X 1M5
R.G. Hunt, Asst. Vice President

FARM CREDIT CORPORATION CANADA

434 Queen St., Ottawa, Ont. K1P 6J9
(613) 996-6606
Chairman, Rolland P. Poirier
Vice Chairman, Paul Babey
Secretary, W.R. deGruchy

FEDERAL BUSINESS DEVELOPMENT BANK

901 Victoria Sq., Montreal, P.Q. H2Z 1R1
(514) 283-5904

The Federal Business Development Bank promotes and assists in the establishment and development of business enterprises in Canada by providing, in the manner and to the extent authorized by its Act of Incorporation, financial assistance, management counselling, management training, information and advice and such other services as are ancillary or incidental to the foregoing.
President, G.A. Lavigueur, Montreal
Executive Vice President, E.C. Scott, Montreal

FBDB Regional Offices:

Atlantic: 1400 Cogswell Tower, Scotia Sq., Halifax, N.S. B3J 2Z7
Quebec: 800 Victoria Sq., #4600, Montreal, P.Q. H4Z 1C8
Ontario: 250 University Ave., Toronto, Ont. M5H 3E5
Prairie & Northern: 161 Portage Ave., Winnipeg, Man. R3B OY4
B.C. & Yukon: 900 W. Hastings St., Vancouver, B.C. V6C 1E7

FISHERIES PRICES SUPPORT BOARD

Ottawa, Ont. K1A OE6
(613) 996-0459

The Board, subject to approval of the Governor-in-Council, is empowered to purchase fishery products at prescribed prices or to pay deficiency payments to producers of fishery products equal to the difference between a prescribed price and the average price at which such products were sold.
Chairman, A.J. Maloney
Executive Director, J.J. LeVert

FRESHWATER FISH MARKETING CORPORATION

1199 Plessis Rd., Winnipeg, Man. R2C 3L4
(204) 222-7301

This Corporation is empowered to market and trade in lake fish, and fish by-products in Canada and abroad.

President, J.T. Dunn
Vice President, Marketing, Al Mackenzie

GREAT LAKES PILOTAGE AUTHORITY, LTD.

Box 95, Cornwall, Ont. K6H 5R9
(613) 933-2995

The Authority provides pilotage services in Canadian waters of the St. Lawrence River commencing at the northern entrance of St. Lambert Lock, the Great Lakes area and the Port of Churchill, Manitoba.

President, R.G. Armstrong
Vice President, L.E. Beland
Secretary Treasurer, R.M. Childerhose
General Manager, B.N. Gravelle
Western Region Office, 345 Lakeshore Blvd., St. Catharines, Ont. (phone: 416-934-2921)
Eastern Region Office, 132 Second St. E., Cornwall, Ont. (phone: 613-933-2991)

HARBOURFRONT

Head Office: 417 Queen's Quay W., Toronto, Ont. M5V 1A2 (416/364-7127)
Programming: 235 Queen's Quay W., Toronto, Ont. (416/364-5665)

Harbourfront is a 92 acre lakefront revitalization project in downtown Toronto, aimed at creating a mixed use area blending living accommodation, offices and entertainment areas. The Corporation acts under the guidance of a Board of Directors appointed by the Federal Minister of Public Works, which board includes representation from the City of Toronto and Metro.

General Manager, Howard Cohen
Director of Programming, Ann Tindal
Director of Development, Frank Mills
Director of Property & Finance, Tom Falus
Director of Communications, Fiona McCall

LAURENTIAN PILOTAGE AUTHORITY

1080 Beaver Hall Hill, Room 1804, Montreal, P.Q. H2Z 1S8
(514) 283-6320

The Authority provides pilotage services in the province of Quebec, north of St. Lambert Lock.

Chairman, Paul Bailly
Vice Chairman, Yvon Matte
Director of Operations, Guy LaHaye
Secretary, Wilfrid Menard
Treasurer, Bernard Meunier

LIVESTOCK FEED BOARD OF CANADA

(5180 Queen Mary Rd., #400), Box 177 Snowdon Stn., Montreal, P.Q. H3X 3T4
(514) 283-7505

Chairman, Dr. Roger Perreault
Vice Chairman, Gus Sonneveld
Members, A.S. Mair, W. Everett
Secretary to the Board, A.D. Mutch

MEDICAL RESEARCH COUNCIL OF CANADA

Ottawa, Ont. K1A OW9
(613) 996-8170

The Medical Research Council does not maintain laboratories of its own. Its primary function is to assist and promote basic, applied and clinical research in Canada in the health sciences. Research in faculties of medicine and their affiliated institutions and hospitals, in faculties of dentistry and pharmacy, and research in other faculties which is highly relevant to health, is supported chiefly through an extensive program of grants-in-aid designed to defray the normal direct costs of approved projects. Personnel support is provided by means of studentships and fellowships for research training at the pre- and post-doctoral level, and through scholarships and career investigator awards for the support of a limited number of fully-trained investigators working in Canadian universities.

President, Dr. Pierre Bois
Director, Grants Program, Dr. J.M. Roxburgh
Director, Special Programs, Dr. F.S. Rolleston
Director, Communications, Dr. P.A. Costin
Director, Special Studies, Dr. K.J. Paynter
Manager, Awards Programs, M. O'Brecht
Secretary, Miss D.J. Wright

NATIONAL ARTS CENTRE CORPORATION

Box 1534, Stn. B, Ottawa, Ont. K1P 5W1
(613) 996-5051

The Corporation is charged with encouraging the performing arts in the national capital region, and with supporting the efforts of the Canada Council to promote the arts throughout the country.

Chairman, Arthur Gelber, O.C.
Director General, Donald MacSween
Secretary, Donald Stephenson

THE NATIONAL BATTLEFIELDS COMMISSION

390 de Bernières Ave., Quebec, P.Q. G1R 2L7
(418) 694-3506

This Commission was established to preserve and administer the historic Battlefields at Quebec City.

Chairman, Fernand Tremblay, Archit.
Secretary, Leon Taschereau

NATIONAL CAPITAL COMMISSION

161 Laurier Ave. W., Ottawa-Hull, K1P 6J6
(613) 992-4231

This Commission is responsible for the planning and development of the National Capital Region.

Chairman, Hon. C.M. Drury
General Manager, Ian Dewar
Secretary General, B. Turner-Davis
Executive Director, Planning, J. Schouten (act.)
Executive Director, Property, E.H. Braun
Executive Director, Development, J.A. MacNiven
Executive Director, Public Activities, A. Bonin
Executive Director, Finance & Admin., J. Van Essen

NATIONAL HARBOURS BOARD

Tower A, Place de Ville, 320 Queen St., Ottawa, Ont. K1A ON6
(613) 996-6400

The Board is responsible under the direction of the Minister of Transport for the administration of certain Canadian Ports and Grain Elevators under its jurisdiction.

Chairman, Pierre A.H. Franche
Vice President, Corporate Affairs, Jacques Auger
Member, Dr. S.H. Weyman
Member, Marian Robson
Vice President, Law & Corporate Secretary, F.B. Ellam
Director of Technical Services, F. MacNaughton
Vice President, Finance, J. Hanna
Vice President, Operations, D.N. Morrison
Director General of Police & Security, D.N. Cassidy
Director of Policy, Planning & Development, Y. Gagnon

Port General Managers:

Halifax, N.S., R. Beck
Saint John & Belledune, N.B., G.C. Mouland
St. John's, Nfld., D. Fox
Sept-Iles, P.Q., S. Tremblay
Quebec, P.Q., H. Allard
Chicoutimi & Baie des Ha! Ha! Y.A. Hébert
Trois-Rivières, P.Q., P. Alain

Montreal, P.Q., N. Beshwaty
Churchill, Man., D. Figursky
Vancouver, B.C., F. Spoke
Prince Rupert, B.C., K.R. Krauter

Elevator Managers:
Port Colborne, R.R. Fisher
Prescott, R.E. Bailey

NATIONAL MUSEUMS OF CANADA

Ottawa, Ont. K1A OM8
(613) 995-9832

The National Museums of Canada, located in Ottawa, include the National Gallery of Canada, the National Museum of Man (including the Canadian War Museum), the National Museum of Natural Sciences, and the National Museum of Science & Technology (including the National Aeronautical Collection). As well, the National Museums of Canada administers a series of national programs: the Canadian Conservation Institute, the National Inventory Program, the Mobile Exhibits Program, the International Program, and the Museum Assistance Programs.

Chairman, Board of Trustees, Dr. Sean B. Murphy
Vice Chairman, Board of Trustees, Judge René J. Marin
Secretary General, Ian Christie Clark
Asst. Secretary General, Programs, R.W. Nichols
Comptroller, Jacques Coulombe

NATIONAL RESEARCH COUNCIL OF CANADA

Montreal Rd., Ottawa, Ont. K1A OR6
(613) 993-9101

The National Research Council of Canada has the mandate of supporting scientific and industrial research in Canada. The NRC Act assigns but does not limit NRC to the following functions: utilization of Canada's natural resources; improvement of technical methods and processes used in Canadian industry; maintenance and improvement of the primary physical standards of measurement for Canada; setting standards of the quality of material used in public works; standardization of scientific and technical apparatus used in Canadian industry and government; fostering the carrying out of scientific and industrial research, including long term problems such as energy, food, construction and transportation.

In addition to its "in-house" research activity, NRC is also closely allied with Canadian industry through competitive programs of research and development and through programs of direct financial assistance.

President, Dr. Larkin Kerwin, B.Sc., M.Sc., D.Sc., LL.D., F.R.S.C.
Vice President (Industry), K. Glegg, B.Eng., M.Sc.
Senior Vice President, W.A. Cumming, B.Sc., P. Eng.
Vice President (Personnel & Administrative Services), P.J. Choquette, B. Comm.
Vice President (External Relations), B.A. Gingras, B.Sc., M.Sc., Ph.D., D.Phil.
Executive Secretary, B.D. Leddy, B.A., B.Comm.
Executive Director, Interlaboratory Programs, J.K. Pulfer, B.Sc., M.Sc.
Atlantic Region Director, R.F. Pottie, B.Sc., Ph.D.
Division of Biological Sciences: Director, C.T. Bishop, B.Sc., B.A., Ph.D., F.R.S.C.
Division of Bldg. Research: Director, C.B. Crawford, B.Sc., M.Sc., D.I.C.
Division of Chemistry: Director, D.M. Wiles, B.Sc., M.Sc., Ph.D.
Division of Mechanical Engineering: Director, E.H. Dudgeon, B.A.Sc., M.A.Sc.
National Aeronautical Establishment: Director, G.M. Lindberg, B.Sc., Ph.D.
Division of Physics: Director, P.A. Redhead, B.A., M.A., Ph.D., F.R.S.C., F.I.E.E.E., F.A.P.S.
Herzberg Institute of Astrophysics: Director, J.L. Locke, B.A., M.A., Ph.D., F.R.S.C.
Division of Electrical Engineering: Director, J.Y. Wong, B.Sc., M.Sc., Ph.D.
Prairie Regional Laboratory, Saskatoon, Sask.: Director, B.M. Craig, B.S.A., M.Sc., Ph.D.
Atlantic Regional Laboratory, Halifax, N.S.: Director, F.J. Simpson, B.Sc., M.Sc., Ph.D.
Space Research Facilities Branch: Chief, J.F. Aitken, B.Sc.

NATURAL SCIENCES & ENGINEERING RESEARCH COUNCIL

Montreal Rd., Ottawa, Ont. K1A 0R6
(613) 993-3659

The functions of NSERC are to promote and assist research in the natural sciences and engineering other than the health sciences and to advise the Minister of State for Science & Technology. NSERC carries out its functions through a program of scholarships and grants in aid of research, intended primarily for university researchers and students.

President, Dr. G.M. MacNabb
Executive Director, Dr. Gilles Julien
Finance & Administration Director & Treasurer, J.-L. Meunier
Programs Director, Dr. T.R. Ingraham
Secretary of the Council, Dr. M. Brochu

NORTHERN CANADA POWER COMMISSION

7909 51st Ave., Box 5700, Stn. L, Edmonton, Alta. T6C 4J8
(403) 465-3377

The Commission is concerned with the planning, construction and management of public utilities, primarily electrical, on a commercial basis. It is empowered to survey utility requirements, construct utility plants and distribution systems, and operate public utility plants in the N.W.T., the Yukon and, subject to the approval of the Governor-in-Council, elsewhere in Canada.

General Manager, J. Long
Comptroller, R. Phillips
Asst. General Manager, Corporate & Public Affairs, B.G. Christie
Asst. General Manager, Engineering & Operations, J.D. Allan

NORTHERN TRANSPORTATION CO. LTD.

Head Office: 9945 108 St., Edmonton, Alta. T5K 2G9
(403) 423-9201

NTCL provides marine transportation services throughout the Mackenzie River Watershed, the Western Arctic Coast and islands and along the Western Coast of Hudson Bay.

Chairman, S.D. Cameron
President & Chief Executive Officer, L.R. Montpetit
Executive Vice President, D.J. Burnett
Vice President, Operations, J.A.D. van Weelderen
Vice President, Finance, & Treasurer, J.G. Anderson
Corporate Secretary, R. Gélinas

PACIFIC PILOTAGE AUTHORITY

605 1200 W. Pender St., Vancouver, B.C. V6E 2T9
(604) 666-6771

The Authority operates pilotage services in Canadian Waters in and around British Columbia.

Chairman, R.A. Hubber-Richard
Secretary, Mrs. E.M. Hall
Chief Accountant, A.O. Kornman
Supt. of Operations, Capt. V.D. Fry

PETRO-CANADA

Box 2844, Calgary, Alta. T2P 2M7
(403) 232-8000
350 Sparks St., Ste. 306, Ottawa, Ont. K1R 7S8
(613) 238-8951

Petro-Canada is involved in southern basin exploration, production, research and development, refining and marketing as well as northern exploration, oil sands development and the examination of possible northern gas transmission systems. Through Petro Canada Exploration Inc., the Corporation is involved in production and exploration of oil and natural gas in

Alberta, Saskatchewan and northeastern British Columbia. It also owns 45 per cent. of Panarctic Oils Ltd., 17 per cent. of Syncrude Canada Ltd., 16 per cent. in the proposed Alsands oil sands plant, 50 per cent. in the proposed Canstar oil sands plant, and is a participant in the Polar Gas Project. Petro-Canada's mandate emphasizes certain goals: to increase the supply of energy available to Canadians; to assist the Government in the formulation of its national energy policy; to increase the Canadian presence in the petroleum industry.
Chairman of the Board & Chief Executive Officer, Wilbert H. Hopper
President & Chief Operating Officer, Andrew Janisch
Executive Vice President, J.I. Bell
Senior Vice President, Sam Stewart
Group Vice President, Marketing & Manufacturing, V.G. Sundstrom
Group Vice President, Exploration, R.A. Meneley
Group Vice President, Production, J.M. Stanford
Vice President, Human Resources & Corporate Admin., James Scurr
Vice President, Environment & Social Affairs, D. Bowie
Vice President, Information & Systems, D. McKay
Vice President, Downstream Development, R.S. Vincent
Vice President, Corporate Planning, R. Campbell
Vice President, Coal, K.G. Donald
Senior Vice President, General Counsel & Secretary, D.P. O'Brien
Vice President & Treasurer, F.B. Grant
Vice President & Controller, W. Morrow

ROYAL CANADIAN MINT
Ottawa, Ont. K1A OG8

The RCM has three plants located in Ottawa, Hull and Winnipeg. These plants manufacture all subsidiary coins required for Canada and also tender for foreign circulating and numismatic contracts. Most of the newly mined Canadian gold is refined in the Ottawa plant.
President, Yvon Gariépy
Vice President, Marketing, Robert Huot (phone: 613-993-2248)

SCIENCE COUNCIL OF CANADA
100 Metcalfe St., Ottawa, Ont. K1P 5M1
Phone (General Reception): (613) 996-1729

The duties of the Council are to assess Canada's scientific and technological resources, requirements and potential and to increase public awareness of these issues.
Chairman, Dr. Claude Fortier
Vice Chairman, tba
Executive Director, Dr. Maurice L'Abbé
Deputy Executive Director, Jorge Miedzinski
Director of Research, Dr. James M. Gilmour
Secretary, E.V. Nyberg (996-2822)

ST. LAWRENCE SEAWAY AUTHORITY
Place de Ville, 320 Queen St., Ottawa, Ont. K1R 5A3
(613) 992-4108

The Authority has control of construction, maintenance and operation of the Seaway.
President, W.A. O'Neil
Vice President, M.M. Bienvenu
Member, W.F. Blair
Secretary, L.E. Beland
Eastern Region, Box 97, St. Lambert, P.Q. J4P 3N7:
Vice President, E.J. Rossi
Western Region, 508 Glendale Ave., St. Catharines, Ont. L2R 6V8:
Vice President, M.S. Campbell

SEAWAY INTERNATIONAL BRIDGE CO.
c/o St. Lawrence Seaway Authority

SOCIAL SCIENCES & HUMANITIES RESEARCH COUNCIL
255 Albert St., Ottawa, Ont. K1P 6G4
(613) 995-9330

The objective of the Council is to promote and assist excellence in Canadian research and scholarship in the social sciences and humanities.
President, André Fortier
Vice President, T.H.B. Symons
Director, Information, Aurèle Ouimet
Executive Director, J.G. Nicholson

TELEGLOBE CANADA
680 Sherbrooke St. W., Montreal, P.Q. H3A 2S4
(514) 281-7981

Teleglobe Canada was created as a Crown Corporation in 1950 to establish, maintain and operate Canada's external telecommunications services and to co-ordinate their use with the services of other countries.
President & Chief Executive Officer, J.-C. Delorme
Vice President, Secretary & General Counsel, D.J. Lévesque
Executive Vice President, Operations, N.T. Byrne
Executive Vice President, Corporate Affairs, A. Lapointe
Vice President, Marketing, A.G. Wallace
Vice President, Operations, G.F. Foley
Vice President, Finance, J. Lévesque
Vice President, International Affairs, R. Seguin
Vice President, Engineering & System Development, M. Fournier
Vice President, Personnel & Admin., J.S. Crispin
Director General, Policy & Planning, C. Gutkin
Director General, Public Relations, T.L. Babinski
Director General, Management Information Systems, F. Urbanski

TELESAT CANADA
333 River Rd., Vanier, Ont. K1L 8B9
(613) 746-5920

The Corporation is responsible for Canada's domestic communications satellites.
President, E.D. Thompson
Chairman of the Board of Directors, D.A. Golden
Vice President, Planning & Admin., Jean Baby
Vice President, Business Development, R.M. Lester
Vice President, Engineering, John Almond
Vice President, Operations, J.W. Crawford
Vice President & Treasurer, Ronald Turta
Secretary & General Counsel, Ronald Wieleba (act.)

URANIUM CANADA LTD.
580 Booth St., Ottawa, Ont. K1A 0E4

Reports through the Minister of Energy, Mines & Resources.
President, G.M. MacNabb (613/993-0029)

VIA RAIL CANADA INC.
1801 McGill College Ave., Ste. 1300 (Box 8116, Montreal, P.Q. H3C 3N3)
(514) 286-2417

The corporation is totally responsible for those passenger rail services previously operated by CN and CP Rail.
Chairman & President, J.F. Roberts
Vice President, Marketing, G.C. Campbell
Vice President, Development & Planning, R. Béchamp
Vice President, Operations, B.E. Hursman
Vice President, Finance & Administration, J.A. Hanna
Asst. to President, G. Dufault
Vice President, Human Resources, J.P. Laroche
Vice President, Law, & Secretary, G. Fortin
Director, Public Relations, E. LeBlanc
Comptroller/Treasurer, A.R. Cave

Vice President, VIA Atlantic (Moncton, N.B.), A.W. Raftus
Vice President, VIA Québec (Montreal, P.Q.), J.L. Moisan
Vice President, VIA Ontario (Toronto, Ont.), A.R. Campbell

Vice President, VIA West (Winnipeg, Man.), H.F. Murray

PROVINCE OF ALBERTA

Entered Confederation September 1, 1905.
Area, 246,422 sq. miles
Population, Bureau of Statistics, July 1, 1981: 2,178,425
Seat of Government: Legislative Bldg., Edmonton
Lieutenant-Governor: The Hon. Frank Lynch-Staunton
Secretary: Miss Patricia Halligan

EXECUTIVE COUNCIL

Premier, President of Executive Council, Hon. Peter Lougheed (Rm. 307; 427-2251)
Provincial Treasurer, Hon. Louis D. Hyndman (Rm. 323; 427-8809)
Minister of Energy & Natural Resources, Hon. C. Mervin Leitch (Rm. 407; 427-3740)
Attorney General & Government House Leader, Hon. Neil Crawford (Rm. 227; 427-2339)
Minister of Hospitals & Medical Care, Hon. David J. Russell (Rm. 420; 427-3665)
Minister of Municipal Affairs, Hon. Marvin E. Moore (Rm. 423; 427-3744)
Minister of Agriculture, Hon. Dallas W. Schmidt (Rm. 228; 427-2137)
Minister of Federal & Intergovernmental Affairs, Hon. Dick Johnston (Rm. 127; 427-2585)
Minister of Labour, Hon. Leslie G. Young (Rm. 404; 427-3664)
Minister of Education, Hon. David King (Rm. 319; 427-2025)
Minister of Advanced Education & Manpower, Hon. James D. Horsman (Rm. 130; 427-2291)
Minister of Consumer & Corporate Affairs, Hon. Julian G.J. Koziak (Rm. 224; 427-2305)
Minister of Social Services & Community Health, Hon. R.J. (Bob) Bogle (Rm. 424; 427-2607)
Solicitor General, Hon. Graham L. Harle (Rm. 425; 427-2468)
Minister of Housing & Public Works, Hon. T.W. (Tom) Chambers (Rm. 207; 427-3666)
Minister of Environment, Hon. John W. Cookson (Rm. 222; 427-2391)
Minister of Economic Development, Hon. Hugh L. Planche (Rm. 320; 427-2134)
Minister of Transportation, Hon. Henry Kroeger (Rm. 419; 427-2080)
Minister of Government Services, Hon. Stewart A. McCrae (Rm. 131; 427-3667)
Minister of Utilities & Telephones, Hon. Larry R. Shaben (Rm. 403; 427-3016)
Minister of Tourism & Small Business, Hon. J. Allen Adair (Rm. 104; 427-3162)
Minister of Recreation & Parks, Hon. Peter Trynchy (Rm. 107; 427-3672)
Minister of State for Economic Development, International Trade, Hon. Horst A. Schmid (Rm. 324; 427-2535)
Associate Minister of Public Lands & Wildlife, Hon. James E. Miller (Rm. 409; 427-3674)
Associate Minister of Telephones, Hon. Dr. P. Neil Webber (Rm. 132; 427-2272)
Minister responsible for Native Affairs, Hon. Dr. Donald J. McCrimmon (Rm. 229; 427-3675)
Minister responsible for Culture, Hon. Mary J. LeMessurier (Rm. 402; 427-4928)
Minister responsible for Workers' Health, Safety & Compensation, Hon. Bill W. Diachuk (Rm. 203; 427-2331)
Minister responsible for Personnel Administration, Hon. Greg P. Stevens (Rm. 126; 427-0158)
Deputy Minister of Executive Council, & Secretary of Cabinet, Harry B. Hobbs (Rm. 305; 427-2251)

LEGISLATIVE ASSEMBLY

Nineteenth Legislature, Last Election, March 14, 1979. Maximum Duration, 5 Years
Party Standings: Progressive Conservative (P.C.), 73; Social Credit (S.C.), 4; New Democratic Party (N.D.P.), 1; Independent (Ind.) 1; Total 79.
Leader of the Opposition: Robert Clark
Indemnities & Allowances: Members' Sessional Indemnity (including expense allowance): $27,176
Salaries: Speaker, $19,600; Deputy Speaker, $7,300; Leader of Opposition, $32,000; Premier, $39,300; Members of Executive Council, $32,000 (with portfolio); $22,700 (without portfolio)
Officers: Clerk of Assembly, Bohdan J.D. Stefaniuk (phone 403/427-2477); Clerk Asst., D.J. Blain; Law Clerk, M.W.J. Clegg
Speaker: Hon. G. Amerongen

Members

Following is constituency: Member, Address & Phone:
Athabasca: F.P. Appleby, P.C., Box 930, Athabasca, Alta. TOG OBO (675-2002)
Banff/Cochrane: Greg P. Stevens, P.C., 126 Legislative Bldg., Edmonton (427-0158)
Barrhead: K.R. Kowalski, P.C., 51 Bellevue Cres., St. Albert, Alta. T8N 0A5 (458-2502)
Bonnyville: E.D. Isley, P.C., Box 2136, Bonnyville, Alta. TOA OLO (826-5658)
Bow Valley: Fred Mandeville, S.C., Box 1387, Brooks, Alta. TOJ OJO (362-2762)
Calgary-Bow: Dr. Neil Webber, P.C., 132 Legislative Bldg., Edmonton (427-2272)
Calgary-Buffalo: T.L. Sindlinger, Ind., 1411 27 St. S.W., Calgary, Alta. T3C 1L4 (246-8758)
Calgary-Currie: Dennis L. Anderson, P.C., 2839 29 St. S.W., Calgary, Alta. T3E 2K7 (246-2339)
Calgary-Egmont: C.M. Leitch, P.C., 407 Legislative Bldg., Edmonton (427-3740)
Calgary-Elbow: D.J. Russell, P.C., 420 Legislative Bldg., Edmonton (427-3665)
Calgary-Fish Creek: W.E. Payne, P.C., 111 Lake Placid Dr. S.E., Calgary, Alta. T2J 5R6 (271-6378)
Calgary-Foothills: Stewart A. McCrae, P.C., 131 Legislative Bldg., Edmonton (427-3667)
Calgary-Forest Lawn: J.B. Zaozirny, P.C., 4012 17 Ave. S.E., Calgary, Alta. T2A 0S7 (273-4433)
Calgary-Glenmore: Hugh Planche, P.C., 320 Legislative Bldg., Edmonton (427-2134)
Calgary-McCall: Andrew Little, P.C., 1111 15 St. N.W., Calgary, Alta. T2N 2B5 (284-2844)
Calgary-McKnight: Eric Musgreave, P.C., 80 Rosevale Dr. N.W., Calgary, Alta. T2K 1N5 (289-1889)
Calgary-Millican: David J. Carter, P.C., #111, 2885 80 Ave. S.E., Calgary, Alta. T2C 0H9 (252-0079)
Calgary-Mountain View: Stanley Kushner, P.C., Box 112, Site 2, R.R. 7, Calgary, Alta. T2P 2G7 (248-6599)
Calgary-North Hill: E.A. Oman, P.C., 3311 Copithorne Rd. N.W., Calgary, Alta. T2L OL2 (282-4680)
Calgary-Northwest: Mrs. Sheila Embury, P.C., 1204 Varsity Est Rd. N.W., Calgary, Alta. T3B 2X2 (288-4868)
Calgary-West: Peter Lougheed, P.C., 307 Legislative Bldg., Edmonton (427-2251)
Camrose: Gordon Stromberg, P.C., 513 Legislative Bldg., Edmonton, Alta. T5K 2B6 (855-3953)
Cardston: John Thompson, P.C., Spring Coulee, Alta. TOK 2CO (758-6672)
Chinook: Henry Kroeger, P.C., 419 Legislative Bldg., Edmonton (427-2080)
Clover Bar: Dr. W.A. Buck, S.C., Box 3330, Fort Saskatchewan, Alta. T8L 2T3 (998-1234)
Cypress: A.W. Hyland, P.C., Box 117, Bow Island, Alta. TOK OGO (545-2122)
Drayton Valley: Mrs. Shirley Cripps, P.C., R.R. 1, Westerose, Alta. TOC 2VO (682-2105)

Drumheller: L.M. Clark, P.C., Box 601, East Coulee, Alta. TOJ 1BO (787-3996)
Edmonton Avonmore: H.A. Schmid, P.C., 324 Legislative Bldg., Edmonton (427-2535)
Edmonton Belmont: Wm. Mack, P.C., 7850 Jasper Ave., Edmonton, Alta. T5K 3R9 (424-9597)
Edmonton Beverly: B.W. Diachuk, P.C., 203 Legislative Bldg., Edmonton (427-2331)
Edmonton Calder: T.W. Chambers, P.C., 207 Legislative Bldg., Edmonton (427-3666)
Edmonton Centre: Mary J. LeMessurier, P.C., 402 Legislative Bldg., Edmonton (427-4928)
Edmonton Glengarry: R.D.B. Cook, P.C., 513 Legislative Bldg., Edmonton (427-1811)
Edmonton Glenora: L.D. Hyndman, P.C., 323 Legislative Bldg., Edmonton (427-8809)
Edmonton Gold Bar: A.P. Hiebert, P.C., 6312 93 Ave., Edmonton, Alta. T6B OW4 (469-6104)
Edmonton Highlands: David King, P.C., 319 Legislative Bldg., Edmonton (427-2025)
Edmonton Jasper Place: Leslie Young, P.C., 404 Legislative Bldg., Edmonton (427-3664)
Edmonton Kingsway: Dr. Ken Paproski, P.C., 211 Westridge Rd., Edmonton, Alta. T5T 1B8 (487-0170)
Edmonton Meadowlark: Gerard Amerongen, P.C., 10236 Connaught Dr., Edmonton, Alta. T5N 3J2 (452-7213)
Edmonton Mill Woods: M.G. Pahl, P.C., 323 Lee Ridge Rd., Edmonton, Alta. T6K 0N5 (463-0271)
Edmonton Norwood: Mrs. Catherine Chichak, P.C., 10224 129 St., Edmonton, Alta. T5N 1W7 (452-5080)
Edmonton Parkallen: Neil S. Crawford, P.C., 227 Legislative Bldg., Edmonton (427-2339)
Edmonton Strathcona: J.G.J. Koziak, P.C., 224 Legislative Bldg., Edmonton (427-2305)
Edmonton Whitemud: Peter Knaak, P.C., 15108 53A Ave., Edmonton, Alta. T6H 4Z6 (435-5989)
Edson: Dr. Ian C. Reid, Box 2327, Hinton, Alta. TOE 1CO (865-3107)
Grande Prairie: Elmer E. Borstad, P.C., 9017 101 St., Grande Prairie, Alta. T8V 2P2 (532-2544)
Highwood: George K. Wolstenholme, P.C., Box 105, Nanton, Alta. TOL 1RO (486-2337)
Innisfail: N.I. Pengelly, P.C., Box 243, Delburne, Alta. TOM OVO (749-2039)
Lac La Biche/Fort McMuray: N.A. Weiss, P.C., 92 Hill Dr., Fort McMurray, Alta. T9H 2A4 (743-2333)
Lacombe: J.W. Cookson, P.C., 222 Legislative Bldg., Edmonton (427-2391)
Lesser Slave Lake: Larry Shaben, P.C., 403 Legislative Bldg., Edmonton (427-3016)
Lethbridge East: Dick Johnston, P.C., 127 Legislative Bldg., Edmonton (427-2585)
Lethbridge West: John Gogo, P.C., 1635 Scenic Heights, Lethbridge, Alta. T1K 1N4 (329-4646)
Little Bow: R.A. Speaker, S.C., Box 3032, Enchant, Alta. TOK OVO (739-3919)
Lloydminster: James Miller, P.C., 400 Legislative Bldg., Edmonton (427-3674)
Macleod: E.L. Fjordbotten, P.C., Box 71, Granum, Alta. TOL 1AO (687-2129)
Medicine Hat: James D. Horsman, P.C., 130 Legislative Bldg., Edmonton (427-2291)
Olds/Didsbury: R.C. Clark, S.C., Box 533, Carstairs, Alta. TOM ONO (337-3168)
Peace River: J.A. Adair, P.C., 104 Legislative Bldg., Edmonton (427-3162)
Pincher Creek/Crowsnest: F.D. Bradley, P.C., Box 390, Blairmore, Alta. TOK OEO (562-2702)
Ponoka: Dr. Don McCrimmon, P.C., 229 Legislative Bldg., Edmonton (427-3675)
Red Deer: N.F. Magee, P.C., #301, 4326 Michener Dr., Red Deer, Alta. T4N 2B1 (343-0561)
Redwater/Andrew: George Topolnisky, P.C., Box 300, Andrew, Alta. TOB OLO (365-3606)
Rocky Mountain House: Jack M. Campbell, P.C., Box 43, Caroline, Alta. TOM OMO (722-3033)
St. Albert: Mrs. Myrna Fyfe, P.C., 33 Glenmore Cres., St. Albert, Alta. T8N OS6 (459-3966)
St. Paul: Dr. Charles E. Anderson, P.C., Box 1840, St. Paul, Alta. TOA 3AO (645-3127)
Sherwood Park: Henry Woo, P.C., 1019 Adamson Cres., Sherwood Park, Alta. T8A 1E4 (467-4348)
Smoky River: M.E. Moore, P.C., 423 Legislative Bldg., Edmonton (427-3744)
Spirit River/Fairview: W.G. Notley, N.D.P., Box 69, Fairview, Alta. TOM 1LO (835-2917)
Stettler: G.L. Harle, P.C., 425 Legislative Bldg., Edmonton (427-2468)
Stony Plain: W.F. Purdy, P.C., Box 38, Wabamun, Alta. TOE 2KO (892-2125)
Taber-Warner: Robert J. Bogle, P.C., 424 Legislative Bldg., Edmonton (427-2606)
Three Hills: Mrs. Constance Osterman, P.C., R.R. 1, Carstairs, Alta. TOM ONO (337-3434)
Vegreville: J.S. Batiuk, P.C., Box 146, Mundare, Alta. TOB 3HO (764-3975)
Vermilion/Viking: T.F. Lysons, P.C., Box 270, Vermilion, Alta. TOB 4MO (853-5265)
Wainwright: Charles Stewart, P.C., Box 519, Wainwright, Alta. TOB 4PO (842-3035)
Wetaskiwin/Leduc: Dallas Schmidt, P.C., 228 Legislative Bldg., Edmonton (427-2137)
Whitecourt: Peter Trynchy, P.C., 107 Legislative Bldg., Edmonton (427-3672)

OFFICE OF THE PREMIER

307 Legislature Bldg., Edmonton, Alta. T5K 2B7
(403) 427-2251
Deputy Minister of Executive Council, Harry B. Hobbs
Executive Director, Bob Giffin
Special Secretary, Pat Lobregt
News Secretary, Ron Liepert
Executive Secretary to Premier, Joseph M. Dutton
Director of the Southern Alberta Premier's Office, Lee S. Richardson

GOVERNMENT DEPARTMENTS

DEPT. OF ADVANCED EDUCATION & MANPOWER

11160 Jasper Ave., Edmonton, Alta. T5K OL1
Information from: Communications Services (phone: 403-427-2781)

Acts Administered

Alberta Educational Communications Act (administered jointly with the Dept. of Education)
Banff Centre Act
Colleges Act
Dept. of Advanced Education & Manpower Act
Education of Service Men's Children Act
Employment Agencies Act
Manpower Development Act
Private Vocational Schools Act
Students Finance Act
Students Loan Guarantee Act
Universities Act

MINISTER, Hon. J.D. Horsman
Deputy Minister, Dr. H. Kolesar
Co-ordinator, Personnel Services, R.C. Carson
Executive Director, Planning Secretariat, T.N. Pollard

Administrative Services

Asst. Deputy Minister, Dr. R.A. Bosetti

Director, Colleges & Univs., Dr. S. Hameed
Director, Legislative Services, K.A. MacIver
Director, Finance Operations, W.G. Edmonds
Director, Financial Planning, A.S. Dobbins
Director, Campus Development, Dr. M.R. Fenske
Director, Communications, Mrs. B. Deters

Program Services
Asst. Deputy Minister, Dr. D.E. Berghofer
Director, College Programs, Dr. N.W.J. Clarke
Director, Degree Programs & Research, Dr. F.B. Ogilvie
Director, Further Education, H.R.D. Beckman
Director, Learning Systems, Dr. D.G. Crawford
Director, Health & Social Service Programs, Dr. M.G. Massey-Hicks
A/Director, Tech/Voc. Programs, L.S. Villett

Field Services
Asst. Deputy Minister, H.E.R. Ottley
Director, Operations, J.L. Booth
Director, Student & Instructional Services, Dr. A.M. Hendry
Personnel Manager, K.D. Forth

Manpower Services
Asst. Deputy Minister, Dr. E.A. Mansfield
Director, Apprenticeship, R.H. Watson
Executive Director, Career Development, D.J. Chabillon
Director, Career Counselling, J.G. Anderson
Director, Career Resources, J.B. Day
Director, Special Manpower Programs, D.R. Cantera
Executive Director, Employment Development, J.A. Corneil
Director, Manpower Mobility, J.C. Dowie
Director, Job Identification, B.R. Mathews
Director, Manpower Training, E.W. Emerson

Students Finance Administration
Chief Executive Officer, F.T. Hemingway (#1100, 10001 Bellamy Hill Rd., Edmonton, Alta. T5J 3B6)
Co-ordinator, Southern Alta., A. Bussoli (3rd floor, Guido Bldg., 805 9 St. S.W., Calgary, Alta. T2P 2Y6)

Students Finance Board
Chairman, R.A. Wiznura (#1100, 10001 Bellamy Hill Rd., Edmonton, Alta. T5J 3B6)

DEPT. OF AGRICULTURE
9718 107th St., Edmonton, Alta. T5K 2C8 (unless otherwise shown)
Information (phone: 403-427-2727)

Acts Administered
Agricultural Development Act
Agricultural Pests Act
Agricultural Relief Advances Act
Agricultural Service Board Act
Agricultural Societies Act
Agrologists Act
Alta. Agricultural Research Trust Act
Artificial Insemination of Domestic Animals Act
Bee Act
Beet Lien Act
Brand Act
Crop Liens Priorities Act
Crop Payments Act
Crop Payments (Irrigated Land Sales) Act
Dairy Board Act
Dairymen's Act
Dept. of Agriculture Act
Farm Home Improvements Act
Farm Implements Act
Federal-Provincial Farm Assistance Act
Feeder Assns. Guarantee Act
Frozen Food Act
Fur Farms Act
Grain Buyers Licensing Act
Grain Charges Limitation Act
Hail & Crop Insurance Act
Harvesting Liens Act
Horned Cattle Purchases Act
Irrigation Land Manager Act
Line Fence Act
Livery Stables Keepers Act
Livestock & Livestock Products Act
Livestock Brand Inspection Act
Livestock Diseases Act, 1971
Livestock Injury Act
Margarine Act
Marketing of Agricultural Products Act
Meat Inspection Act
Names of Homes Act
Seed Control Areas Act
Seed Dealers Act
Seed Grain Purchases Act
Soil Conservation Act
Stray Animals Act
Surface Rights Act
Threshers Lien Act
Vegetable Sales (Alta.) Act
Veterinary Surgeons Act
Weed Control Act
Wheat Board Money Trust Act

MINISTER, Hon. Dallas W. Schmidt
A/Deputy Minister, H.M. Douglas
  Personnel Branch, Manager, C. Davidson
  Planning & Research Secretariat, Chairman, N.S. Thomson
Asst. Deputy Minister, Research & Operations, Dr. A.O. Olson
  Communications Division, J.R. Andrew
  Departmental Services, T.A. Champion
  Financial Services, D.J. Yakabuski
Asst. Deputy Minister, Development, C.J. McAndrews
  Irrigation Division, Director, J.C. Purnell
  Extension Division, Director, J. Calpas
  Engineering & Rural Services Division, Director, D. Janzic
  Home Economics & 4H Division, Director, Irene Leavitt
  Irrigation Council Secretariat, Manager, R.F. Smith
Asst. Deputy Minister, Economic & Marketing Services, J.H. Hanna
  Marketing Services, Director, D. Glover
  Economic Services, Director, Melvin Cameron
  Rural Development, Executive Director, Dr. J.E. Wiebe
Asst. Deputy Minister, International Marketing, B. Mehr
  Trade Directors, L. Normand, D. Clarke
Asst. Deputy Minister, Production, H.M. Douglas
  Animal Industry Division, Director, J.S. Lore (includes Beef Cattle & Sheep Branch, Poultry Commr., Horse Industry Branch, and Pork Industry Branch)
  Dairy Division, Commr., F.R. Hutchings (Box 6120, Wetaskiwin)
  Plant Industry Division, Director, W.V. Dent (includes Crop Protection, Pest Control, Field Crops, Horticulture, Soils, and Weed Control)
  Animal Health Division, Director, Dr. R.G. Christian

Boards & Commissions
Surface Rights Board, 16th floor, Century Place, 9803 102A Ave., Edmonton, Alta. T5J 3A3 (403/427-2444)
  Chairman, C.H.R. Nielsen
Alta. Grain Commission, 9718 107 St., Edmonton, Alta. T5K 2C8 (403/427-7329)
  Chairman, J.W. Channon
Alta. Dairy Control Board, Box 6120, Wetaskiwin, Alta. T9A 0S7 (403/352-9211)
  Chairman, J.R. Gylander
Alta. Hail & Crop Insurance Corp., Bag Service #16, 5718 56 St., Lacombe, Alta. T0C 1S0 (403/782-4661)
  General Manager, E.A. Patching
Agricultural Development Corp., 4910 52nd St., Camrose, Alta. T4V 2V4

General Manager, Admin., E.G. Suarez
General Manager, Lending, D. Kavanagh

Regional Agricultural Offices

Region 1 - Southern (Lethbridge): Regional Director, C.S. Clark, Agriculture Center, Lethbridge, Alta. T1J 4C7
Region 2 - Southwest (Airdrie): Regional Director, A. Reimer, Bag Service #1, Airdrie, Alta. TOM OBO
Region 3 - Central (Red Deer): Regional Director, A.D. MacKenzie, 4747 Ross St., Box 5002, Red Deer, Alta. T4N 5Y5
Region 4 - Northwest (Vermilion): Regional Director, R.F. Berkan, Box 330, Vermilion, Alta. TOB 4MO
Region 5 - Northwest (Barrhead): Regional Director, J.B. Tackaberry, Box 1540, Barrhead, Alta. TOG OEO
Region 6 - Peace (Fairview): Regional Director, E. Horton, Box 777, Fairview, Alta. TOH 1LO

Agricultural Products Marketing Council

11th floor, 9718 107 St., Edmonton, Alta. T5K 2C8
(403) 427-2164
Secretary, Tom Sydness
PRODUCER MARKETING BDS. & COMMNS.:
Alta. Broiler Growers' Marketing Board
Don Potter, Secretary Manager, 11826 100 Ave., Edmonton, Alta. T5K OK3 (488-2125)
Alta. Turkey Growers' Marketing Board
Don Potter, Secretary Manager, 11826 100 Ave., Edmonton, Alta. T5K OK3 (488-2281)
Alta. Egg & Fowl Marketing Board
D.A. Guichon, General Manager, #150, 515 17 Ave. S.W., Calgary, Alta. T2S OA9 (264-6185)
Alta. Pork Producers' Marketing Board
Ed Schultz, General Manager, 11826 100 Ave., Edmonton, Alta. T5K 0K3
Alta. Vegetable Growers Marketing Board
Arthur Anderson, Secretary, Box 2273, Taber, Alta. TOK 2GO (223-4242)
Alta. Potato Commission
R.E. Marfleet, Secretary Manager, 220F 12A St. N., Lethbridge, Alta. T1H 2J1 (328-7018)
Alta. Cattle Commission
Stockman's Centre, #241, 2116 27 Ave. N.E., Calgary, Alta. T2E 7A6 (230-2161)
Alta. Fresh Vegetable Marketing Board
c/o Secretary Manager, 220F 12A St. N., Lethbridge, Alta. T1H 2J1 (328-7018)
Alta. Sheep & Wool Commission
R.W. Shopland, Secretary, 12821 52 St., Edmonton, Alta. T5A 3P8 (476-4213)

ALCOHOLISM & DRUG ABUSE COMMISSION

6th floor, Pacific Plaza Bldg., 10909 Jasper Ave., Edmonton, Alta. T5J 3M9
(403) 427-7301
Public Affairs Director, E.J. Sear

ALBERTA ART FOUNDATION

4th floor, 10158 103 St., Edmonton, Alta. T5J 0X6
(403) 427-9968
Chairman, Dale M. Simmons
Secretary, W.H. Kaasa

ATTORNEY GENERAL'S DEPT.

9833 109 St., Edmonton, Alta. T5K 2E8
Information 403/427-2745

Acts Administered

Admin. of Estates Act
Administrative Procedures Act
Age of Majority Act
Alberta Evidence Act
Alberta Lord's Day Act
Alimony Orders Enforcement Act
Animal Protection Act
Arbitration Act
Assignments of Book Debts Act
Bills of Sale Act
Blind Persons' White Cane Act
Builders Lien Act
Bulk Sales Act
Chattel Security Registries Act
Commrs. for Oaths Act
Common Parties Contracts & Conveyances Act
Conditional Sales Act
Constitutional Questions Act
Contributory Negligence Act
Court Forms Act
Court of Appeal Act
Court of Queen's Bench Act
Criminal Injuries Compensation Act
Dangerous Dogs Act
Daylight Saving Time Act
Defamation Act
Defence of Common Employment Act
Demise of the Crown Act
Dept. of the Attorney General Act
Devolution of Real Property Act
Domestic Relations Act
Dower Act

Execution Creditors Act
Exemptions Act
Expropriation Act
Extra-curial Orders Act
Extra-Provincial Enforcement of Custody Orders Act
Factors Act
Family Court Act
Family Relief Act
Fatal Accidents Act
Fatality Inquiries Act
Federal Courts Jurisdiction Act
Fraudulent Preferences Act
Frustrated Contracts Act
Garagemen's Lien Act
Gas Utilities Act
Guarantees Acknowledgment Act
Infants Act
Innkeepers Act
Interpretation Act
Intestate Succession Act
Judicature Act
Jury Act
Justices of the Peace Act
Juvenile Court Act
Land Surveyors Act
Land Titles Act
Land Titles Act Clarification Act
Landlord's Rights on Bankruptcy Act
Legal Profession Act
Legitimacy Act
Limitation of Actions Act

Maintenance Order Act
Married Women's Act
Masters & Servants Act
Matrimonial Property Act
Mechanical Recording of Evidence Act
Mentally Incapacitated Persons Act
Motor Vehicle Accident Claims Act
National Housing Loans Act (Alta.)
Notaries Public Act
Oaths of Office Act
Occupiers Liability Act
Partition & Sale Act
Partnership Act
Perpetuities Act
Petty Trespass Act
Police Act, 1973
Possessory Liens Act

Private Streets Act
Proceedings Against the Crown Act
Provincial Court Act
Public Inquiries Act
Public Trustee Act
Public Utilities Board Act
Queen's Counsel Act
Reciprocal Enforcement of Judgments Act
Reciprocal Enforcement of Maintenance Orders Act
Regulations Act
Reports of Judicial Proceedings Act
Revised Statutes Act
Road Building Machinery Equipment Act
Sale of Goods Act
Seduction Act
Seizures Act
Service of Documents during Postal Interruptions Act
Sex Disqualification Removal Act
Small Claims Act
Statutes Act
Summary Convictions Act
Surrogate Courts Act
Survival of Actions Act
Survivorship Act
Tort-Feasors Act
Transfer & Descent of Land Act
Trustee Act
Ultimate Heir Act
Unconscionable Transactions Act
Uniformity of Legislation Act
Warehouse Receipts Act
Warehousemen's Liens Act
Wills Act
Women's Institute Act
Woodmen's Lien Act

ATTORNEY GENERAL, GOVERNMENT HOUSE LEADER & PROVINCIAL SECRETARY, Hon. Neil Crawford, Q.C.
Deputy Attorney General, Deputy Provincial Secretary, Queen's Proctor, and Inspector of Legal Offices, R.W. Paisley, Q.C.
Asst. Deputy Minister (Constitutional & Energy Law), W. Henkel, Q.C.
A/Asst. Deputy Minister (Civil), D. Rae
A/Director of Civil Law, J.E. Klinck
Public Trustee, L.W. Gardiner, Q.C.
Director, Legal Research & Analysis, E.F. Gamache
Asst. Deputy Minister (Administration), C.R. Shank
Executive Manager, Court Services, Bob Dunster
A/Asst. Deputy Minister (Criminal), B. Fraser
Director, Criminal Justice, Y. Roslak, Q.C.
Provincial Agent, Special Prosecutions, H.B. Casson, Q.C.
Chief Legislative Counsel, P.J. Pagano
Inspector of Land Titles, D. Lamont
Chief Medical Examiner, Dr. J.C. Butt, Calgary

Associated Agencies
Alberta Law Foundation
#315, 131 9th Ave. S.W., Calgary, Alta.
(403) 264-7401
Chairman, C.G. Virtue, Q.C.
Board of Review
c/o Ms. Lorraine Green, Administrator, Board of Review, Alberta Hospital, Box 307, Edmonton, Alta. (403/973-2233)
Crimes Compensation Board
4th floor, 9833 109 St., Edmonton, Alta. T5K 2E8
(403) 427-7217
Chairman, Ernest Watkins, Q.C.
Fatality Review Board
#611, 3330 Hospital Hill Dr. N.W., Calgary, Alta. T2N 4N1
(403) 261-8123
Chairman, Edward MacCallum
Alberta Gaming Commission
10th floor, 10109 106 St., Edmonton, Alta.
(403) 427-9796
Chairman, D. Gardner
Land Compensation Board
#202, 909 5th Ave. S.W., Calgary, Alta. T2P 0N8
(403) 261-6141
Chairman, K.J. Boyd
Public Utilities Board
11th floor, Manulife House, 10055 106 St., Edmonton, Alta. T5J 2Y2
(403) 427-4901
Chairman, W.R. Horton
Calgary Office: 10th floor, 640 5 Ave. S.W., Calgary, Alta. T2P 3G4 (261-6306)

AUDITOR GENERAL
#835, 9925 109 St., Edmonton, Alta. T5K 2J8
(403) 427-4220
Auditor General, D.W. Rogers

PROVINCIAL CANCER HOSPITALS BOARD
11560 University Ave., Edmonton, Alta. T6G 1Z2
Executive Director, B.C. Lentle
Clinics & Hospitals Operated by The Provincial Cancer Hospitals Bd:
Edmonton:
Cross Cancer Institute, 11560 University Ave., T6G 1Z2
Phone: (403) 432-8771
Director, Dr. R.N. MacDonald
Calgary:
Southern Alberta Cancer Centre, 2104 2nd St. S.W., T2S 1S5
Phone: (403) 263-0770
Director, Dr. M. Jerry
Administrator, W.A. Foster
Lethbridge:
Lethbridge Cancer Clinic, Municipal Hospital, T1J 1W5
Phone: (403) 327-4531
Director, Dr. D.A. Rice

CENSOR BOARD
Main floor, CN Tower, 10004 104 Ave., Edmonton, Alta. T5J 0K5
(403) 427-2006
Chairman, O.G. Hooper

DEPT. OF CONSUMER & CORPORATE AFFAIRS
Room 224, Legislative Bldg., Edmonton, Alta. T5K 2B6
Information Contact, Communications, 1100 Capitol Sq., 10065 Jasper Ave., Edmonton, Alta. T5J 3B1 (phone: 403/427-9883)

Acts Administered
Alberta Insurance Act
Cemeteries Act
Cemetery Companies Act
Collection Practices Act
Companies Act
Condominium Property Act
Co-operative Associations Act
Co-operative Marketing Associations Act
Credit & Loan Agreements Act
Credit Union Act
Credit Union Federation of Alta. Ltd. Act
Debtors' Assistance Act
Dept. of Consumer & Corporate Affairs Act
Deposits Regulation Act
Direct Sales Cancellation Act
Franchises Act
Fuel Oil Licensing Act
Insurance Corporations Tax Act
Investment Contracts Act
Landlord & Tenant Act
Licensing of Trades & Businesses Act
Mortgage Brokers Regulation Act
Native Co-operative Guarantee Act
Prearranged Funeral Services Act

Public Contributions Act
Real Estate Agents' Licensing Act
Religious Societies' Lands Act
Sale of Chattels by Public Auction Act
Securities Act
Societies Act
Trust Companies Act
Unfair Trade Practices Act
Wage Assignments Act

MINISTER, Hon. Julian Koziak
Deputy Minister, J. Barry Martin
Asst. Deputy Minister, Program Development, D.E.L. Keown
Executive Director, Program Development, S.T. Saleh
Asst. Deputy Minister, Program Support, J.O. Darwish
Executive Director, Program Support, V.W. Stephens
Asst. Deputy Minister, Regional Delivery, H.J. Thomas
Executive Director, Regional Delivery, George Blochert
Director, Consumer Credit Program, D.A. Bence
Director, Trust Companies Program, T. Dansereau
Director, Credit Unions Program, H. Eklund
Director, Consumer Education & Information, K.W. Shields
Director, Standards Development Program, R.H. Turner
Director, Licensing Program, K.E. Unterschultz
Supt. of Real Estate, Roy Nolan
Supt. of Insurance, Ron Kaiser
Director, Co-operatives, R. Moore
Registrar, Corporate Registry, W.W. Proskiw
A/Chairman, Alberta Securities Commission, W.T. Pidruchney
Secretary, Automobile Insurance Board, E. Collins

DEPT. OF CULTURE

CN Tower, 10004 104 Ave., Edmonton, Alta. T5J OK5, unless otherwise noted
Information from Communications Director (403/427-6530)
MINISTER, Hon. Mary J. LeMessurier
Deputy Minister, J. O'Neil
International Development, Executive Officer, R. Verge
Communications Director, M. Layman

Finance & Administration

Executive Director, G.R. Batra

Cultural Development

Asst. Deputy Minister, W.H. Kaasa
Director, Visual Arts, L. Graff
Director, Performing Arts, R. Cook
Director, Film & Literary Arts, J.P. Gillese
Director, Library Services, J. Forsyth
Director, Cultural Heritage, B. Bryant
Director, Board of Censors, O.G. Hooper
Manager, Northern Alta. Jubilee Auditorium, R.V. Wigmore
Manager, Southern Alta. Jubilee Auditorium, B. Burke
A/Director, Cultural Facilities Development, J. Kokotilo

Historical Resources

Asst. Deputy Minister, Dr. W. Byrne
Director, Provincial Museum, Dr. J. Lunn
Director, Provincial Archives, A. Ridge
Director, Historic Sites Service, Dr. F. Pannekoek
Director, Archaeological Survey, Dr. W.J. Byrne

ALBERTA DISASTER SERVICES

10320 146 St., Edmonton, Alta. T5N 3A2
(403) 427-2772
Executive Director, E. Tyler
Director, Dangerous Goods Project Office, E. Tyler
Deputy Executive Director, S.R. Langman
Director, Admin., M.G.H. Sterr
Director, Finance, G.P. Rezansoff
Director, Plans & Operations, V.L. Kunce
Director, Training, S.K. Bricker
Director, Municipal Services, B.J. McNally
Public Affairs Officer, W.G. Bissett

DEPT. OF ECONOMIC DEVELOPMENT

12th floor, Pacific Plaza, 10909 Jasper Ave., Edmonton, Alta. T5J 3M8
Information Contact, Mary Ricard, Communications Director (phone: 403 427-0669)

Acts Administered

Dept. of Economic Development Act

MINISTER, Hon. Hugh Planche
MINISTER OF STATE FOR ECONOMIC DEVELOPMENT, INTERNATIONAL TRADE, Hon. Horst A. Schmid
Deputy Minister, Development & Trade, Dallas J. Gendall, 427-0662
Deputy Minister, Planning & Services, C.J. Roth, 427-2083
Asst. Deputy Minister, Development & Trade, K.H.G. Broadfoot, 427-2297
Asst. Deputy Minister, Planning & Services, Dr. B.E. Sullivan, 427-0665
Asst. Deputy Minister, Admin., H.S. Young, 427-0667
Asst. Deputy Minister, Trade Development Branch, E.R.W. Lack, 427-4809
Executive Director, Industry Development Branch, Dr. Alan Vanterpool, 427-2005
Executive Director, Process Industry Branch, C.L. Dmytruk, 427-2269
Executive Director, Transportation Services Branch, W.A. Danzinger, 427-5232
Executive Director, Strategic Planning Branch, E.G. Shaske, 427-3627

Foreign Offices

London: Alberta House, 1 Mount St., London, W1, Eng., Director, Paul King
Los Angeles: Ste. 703, 510 W. 6 St., Los Angeles, Calif 90014
Houston: #1425, 5444 Westheimer, Houston, Texas 77056, Director, Rob Scott

DEPT. OF EDUCATION

Devonian Bldg., 11160 Jasper Ave., Edmonton, Alta. T5K OL2
Information from, Communications Branch, Devonian Bldg. (phone: 403-427-2286)

Acts Administered

Alta. School Act
Dept. of Education Act
School Elections Act
School Bldgs. Act
Teaching Profession Act

MINISTER, Hon. David King
Deputy Minister, vacant
Assoc. Deputy Minister (Instruction), Dr. J.S.T. Hrabi
Assoc. Deputy Minister (Support Services), Dr. S.N. Odynak
Director of Communications, Ms. L.L. Lomax
Director of Field Services, Dr. E.A. Torgunrud
Director of Special Education Services, Dr. H.J. McLeod
Supervisor, Special Education, K. McKie
Supervisor, Guidance & Counselling, Dr. T. Mott
Supt., Alberta School for the Deaf, K. Boesen
Director of School Bldgs., Dr. J.W. Kulba
Director of Planning & Research, Dr. M.R. Fenske
Director of Curriculum, Dr. G.H. Bevan
Assoc. Directors of Curriculum, F. Crowther (Social Studies), G. Popowich, M.Ed. (Mathematics, Science), M. Adamson, M.Ed. (Learning Resources), J. Harder, Ph.D. (Industrial Education), M. Thornton, Ph.D. (Language & Fine Arts)
Director of Early Childhood Services, Dr. H.I. Hastings
Co-ordinator of Program Approval, Dr. D. Jeffares
Co-ordinator of Program Development, M. McLeod
Director of Student Records & Computer Services, Dr. J.E. Reid
Director, Language Services, Dr. P.A. Lamoureux
Registrar, Dr. L. Rappel
Director, Alta. Correspondence School, Mrs. A. Turnbull
Manager, School Book Branch, M. Fedorak
Director of Finance, Statistics & Legislation, Dr. W.R. Duke
Director, Personnel Services, D.B. Pinckston

Co-ordinator, Educational Opportunities Fund, D. Ewasiuk
Co-ordinator, Educational Exchange/Special Projects, N.J. Chamchuk
Director, Student Evaluation, Dr. L.E. Symyrozum
Administrator, Library Services, Mrs. H. Skirrow

Associated Agencies

ACCESS–Alta. Educational Communications Corp., 16930 114 Ave., Edmonton, Alta. T5M 3S2 (403/451-3160)
Alta. Educational Communications Authority, #502, 10053 111 St., Edmonton, Alta. T5K 2H8 (403/427-4918); H.G. Kratz

DEPT. OF ENERGY & NATURAL RESOURCES

Petroleum Plaza, South Tower, 9915 108 St., Edmonton, Alta. T5K 2C9
Information Contact, J.I. Pringle, Resource Information Co-ordinator (phone: 403/427-4003)

Acts Administered

Aerial Photographic Survey Act
Agricultural & Recreational Land Ownership Act
Alta. Energy Co. Act
Alta. Gas Trunk Line Company Act
Alta. Natural Resources Act
Alta. Natural Resources Act (1962)
Arbitration Amendment Act
Builders' Lien Act
Canada Shipping Act
Clay & Marl Act
Clay & Marl Crown Leases Act, 1965
Crown Cultivation Leases Act
Dept. of Energy & Natural Resources Act
Fish Inspection Act
Fish Marketing Act
Fisheries Act
Fisheries Development Act
Forest Development Research Trust Fund Act
Forest & Prairie Protection Act
Forest Reserves Act
Forests Act, 1971
Freehold Mineral Taxation Act, 1972
Homestead Lease Loan Act
Landmen Licensing Act
Mineral Declaratory Act
Mineral Taxation Act
Mineral Titles Clarification Act
Mineral Titles Redemption Act
Mines & Minerals Act
Mines & Minerals Amendment Act
Natural Gas Price Admin. Act
Natural Gas Pricing Agreement Act
Natural Gas Pricing Agreement Amendment Act
Oil Sands Technology & Research Authority Act
Petroleum Marketing Act
Public Lands Act
Public Lands Amendment Act, 1979
Public Lands & Wildlife Statutes Amendment Act, 1979
Recreation, Parks & Wildlife Act
Sand & Gravel Act
Wildlife Act
Willmore Wilderness Park Act

MINISTER, Hon. C. Mervin Leitch
ASSOC. MINISTER, Hon. J.E. Miller (responsible for Public Lands & Wildlife)
Deputy Minister, Energy Resources, Dr. G.B. Mellon
Deputy Minister, Renewable Resources, F.W. McDougall
Assoc. Deputy Minister, Finance & Admin., M.F. Kanik
Asst. Deputy Minister, Alberta Forest Service, J.A. Brennan
Asst. Deputy Minister, Public Lands, vacant
Asst. Deputy Minister, Policy Analysis & Planning, vacant
Asst. Deputy Minister, Fish & Wildlife, vacant (Fish & Wildlife Division: 10015 103 Ave., Edmonton, Alta. T5J OH1, 427-0326)
Asst. Deputy Minister, Minerals Disposition, M.J. Day
Asst. Deputy Minister, Mineral Revenues, A. Graff
Executive Director, Administrative Services, G.A. Ford
Executive Director, Resource Evaluation & Planning, L.J. Cooke
Executive Director, Economic - Financial Services, R.H. Cook
Director, Resource Information Services, D.W. Annesley
Director, Foreign Ownership of Land Admin., F.D. Coombs

Associated Agencies

Alta. Oil Sands Equity
1131 Petroleum Plaza, 9945 108 St., Edmonton, Alta. T5K 2G6
403/427-2492
Alta. Petroleum Marketing Commission
#1000, 205 5 Ave. S.W., Calgary, Alta. T2P 2V7
403/262-8808
Alta. Oil Sands Technology & Research Authority
#500, 10010 106 St., Edmonton, Alta. T5J 3L8
403/427-7623
and 10th floor, 640 5 Ave. S.W., Calgary, Alta. T2P 0M6 (403/261-3380)
Chairman, C.W. Bowman
Information & Records Officer, L.G. Benzer

ENERGY RESOURCES CONSERVATION BOARD

640 5th Ave. S.W., Calgary, Alta. T2P 3G4
(403) 261-8311
Chairman, V. Millard

DEPT. OF THE ENVIRONMENT

Oxbridge Plaza, 9820 106 St., Edmonton, Alta. T5K 2J6
Information: phone 403/427-2738

Acts Administered

Agricultural Chemicals Act
Alta. Environmental Research Trust Act
Beverage Container Act
Clean Air Act
Clean Water Act
Drainage Dists. Act
Dept. of the Environment Act
Environment Council Act
Ground Water Control Act
Hazardous Chemicals Act
Land Surface Conservation & Reclamation Act
Litter Act
Water Resources Act

MINISTER, Hon. J.W. Cookson
Deputy Minister, W. Solodzuk
Asst. Deputy Ministers:
Environmental Protection Services, E.E. Kupchanko
Water Resources Management Services, P.G. Melynchuck
Environmental Co-ordination Services, H.W. Thiessen
Finance & Administration Services, Wm. Simon
Executive Director:
Alberta Environmental Centre, Vegreville, Dr. R.S. Weaver
Directors:
Pollution Control Division, R.N. Briggs
Standards & Approvals Division, J. Defir
Earth Sciences Division, L.D. Sadler
Technical Services Division, R.K. Deeprose
Design & Construction Division, J.W. Thiessen
Water Resources Management Division, A.R. Strome
Operation & Maintenance Division, F.G. Primus
Research Management Division, Dr. Jay Shah
Environmental Assessment Division, K.R. Smith
Planning Division, C.L. Primus
Land Assembly Division, J.M. King
Land Reclamation Division, D.G. Harrington
Special Projects, R.E. Bailey
Personnel & Organization Development Division, M. Wartenbe
Financial Planning Division, J.A. Kolar
Financial Operations Division, E. Luczak, act.
Systems & Computing Division, D.K. Lougheed, act.

Public Communications Division, J. Champion, act.

Associated Agencies

Alta. Environmental Research Trust
8th floor, 620 7 Ave. S.W., Calgary, Alta. T2P 0Y8
(403) 261-2360
Administrative Secretary, John Russell
Environment Council of Alta.
2100 College Plaza, Tower 3, Edmonton, Alta. T6G 2M4
(403) 427-5792
Chief Executive Officer, A. Crerar

DEPT. OF FEDERAL & INTERGOVERNMENTAL AFFAIRS

14th floor, Seventh Street Plaza, South Tower, Edmonton, Alta. T5J 3E4
Information Contact, Anita Duncan, Library Technician (403-427-2611)

MINISTER, Hon. D. Johnston
Executive Asst., N. Betkowski
Deputy Minister, Dr. J. Peter Meekison
Executive Director, Research & Planning, Oryssia Lennie
Executive Director of Resources & Industrial Development, Ron Thumblert
Executive Director of Social & Cultural Affairs, Richard Dalon
Executive Director of International Affairs, Wayne Clifford

ALBERTA GENERAL INSURANCE CO.

10221 104 St., Edmonton, Alta. T5J 1B7
Phone: (403) 422-2197
Chairman, J.E. Hart
General Manager, H.J. Simmons

DEPT. OF GOVERNMENT SERVICES

18th floor, Park Sq., 10001 Bellamy Hill, Edmonton, Alta. T5J 3C1
(403) 427-7988
MINISTER, Hon. Stewart A. McCrae
Deputy Minister, J.T. Kyle
Asst. Deputy Minister, Computing & Systems Division, R.A. Gehmlich
Asst. Deputy Minister, Admin. Services Division, G.H. Hill
Asst. Deputy Minister, Operating & Maintenance Division, W.S. Davies
Asst. Deputy Minister, Supply Division, S.A. Pepper
Managing Director, Public Affairs Bureau, F. Calder
Director, Metric Conversion Branch, J.P. Markovich

ALBERTA HISTORIC SITES BOARD (Responsible for Geographical Names)

Chairman, Mrs. Mary Lobay, 3219 118 St., Edmonton, Alta.
Secretary, the Director, Historic Sites Service, 8820 112 St., Edmonton, Alta. T6G 2P8 (phone: 403-427-2022)

DEPT. OF HOSPITALS & MEDICAL CARE

Information: 403/427-1432
MINISTER, Hon. Dave Russell (420 Legislative Bldg., 427-3665)
Executive Asst., Terry Roberts
Deputy Minister, Dr. Lloyd Grisdale (11010 101 St., Box 2222, Edmonton, Alta. T5J 3E1; 427-7164)
Executive Asst., Miss P.J. Kohut
Asst. Deputy Minister, Finance & Admin., G.R. Beck, 427-7010
Asst. Deputy Minister, Hospital Services, K.G. Moore, 427-8596
Asst. Deputy Minister, Policy Development, C.A. Meilicke, 427-8599

Health Care Insurance Plan

118 Ave. & Groat Rd., (Box 1360, Edmonton, Alta. T5J 2N3)
(403) 427-1558
Asst. Deputy Minister, vacant

DEPT. OF HOUSING & PUBLIC WORKS

See addresses, below.

Information Contact, Wm. J.E. Rees, Director, Public Relations (403/427-6518)

Acts Administered

Dept. of Housing & Public Works Act
Alta. Home Mortgage Corp. Act
Alta. Housing Act
Architects Act
Public Works Act
Senior Citizens Housing Act

MINISTER, Hon. Tom Chambers, 207 Legislature Bldg., Edmonton, Alta. T5K 2B6, 427-3666

Deputy Minister of Housing, M.D. Rasmusson
3rd floor, 10050 112 St., Edmonton, Alta. T5K 2J1
(403) 427-3917
Director, Finance & Admin., R. Reshke
President, ALTA. HOUSING CORP., K. Paholko
President, ALTA. HOME MTGE. CORP., J.M. Engelman

Deputy Minister of Public Works, N. Fleming
20th floor, 8215 112 St., Edmonton, Alta. T6G 5A9
(403) 427-3921
Asst. Deputy Minister, Project Management Division, Tony Hargreaves
Asst. Deputy Minister, Design & Construction Management, Ed McLellan
Asst. Deputy Minister, Development Services, H.H. Neelands
Asst. Deputy Minister, Realty Division, Del Jackson
Director, Finance & Admin., R. Reshke

DEPT. OF LABOUR

IBM Bldg., 10808 99 Ave., Edmonton, Alta. T5K OG2
Information Contact, Anji Husain, Communications Director (phone: 403 427 5585)

Acts Administered

Alta. Labour Act, 1973
Alta. Uniform Building Standards Act
Boilers & Pressure Vessels Act, 1975
Dept. of Labour Act
Electrical Protection Act
Elevators & Fixed Conveyances Act
Firefighters & Policemen Labour Relations Act
Fire Prevention Act
Gas Protection Act
Individual's Rights Protection Act
Industrial Wages Security Act
Lightning Rod Act
Pension Benefits Act
Plumbing & Drainage Act
Shared Responsibility: Amusements Act

404 Legislative Bldg., Edmonton, Alta.:
MINISTER, Hon. Leslie G. Young
Asst. to the Minister, Don Goodale

IBM Bldg., 10808 99 Ave., Edmonton, Alta.:
Deputy Minister, D.I. Gardner
Executive Director, Admin. Services, J.L. Myroon
Communications Director, A. Husain
Personnel Manager, L.H. Martin

Board of Industrial Relations

Chairman, A. Dubensky, Q.C.
Members, Calgary: A.K. Aldridge, L. Chikinda, O.N. Demco, Angus MacDonald, J. Nichols, Mike Tamton, Bryan Van Rassel; Edmonton: Ray Drisdelle, Jack Dyck, Mrs. D.M. Gares, F. Kuzemski, Clinton Mellors, D.B. Mitchell, E.S. Sunley

Labour Division

Asst. Deputy Minister, G. Meier
Divisional Admin., Director, vacant
Labour Standards Branch, Director, E.C. Krogh, act.
Conciliation & Mediation, Director, H.J.H. Libke
Labour Management Services, Director, J. Fricke, act.

Labour Research, Director, G.H. Wright
Pension Benefits Branch, Supt., A.H. Wakefield

General Safety Services Division

Asst. Deputy Minister, D.J. Morrison
Executive Co-ordinator, vacant
Divisional Admin., Director, V.E. Feguenne
Boilers & Pressure Vessels, Chief Inspector, J.L. Smith
Bldg. Standards Branch, Director, Dave Monsen
Electrical Protection Branch, Chief Inspector, K.N. Fennessey
Elevators & Fixed Conveyances, Chief Inspector, V.M. Petersen
Fire Prevention Branch, Fire Commr., W.D. MacKay
Gas Protection Branch, Chief Inspector, J.T. Mercer
Plumbing Inspection Branch, Chief Inspector, W.A. Milligan

Human Rights Commission

501 Edwards Professional Bldg., Edmonton, Alta. T5J 2S5
Chairman, R. Lundrigan
Director, R.S. Meldrum

LIFE OF ALBERTA DIVISION (Toronto Mutual Life Insurance Co.)

Ste. 408, 11456 Jasper Ave., Edmonton, Alta. T5K OM1
(403) 488-0136
Manager, Admin., Joan C. Gourlay

LIVESTOCK DISASTER COMMITTEE

6909 116 St., Box 8070, Sub PO 'F', Edmonton, Alta. T6H 4P2
(403) 436-9340
Chairman, Dr. G.W. Summers

DEPT. OF MUNICIPAL AFFAIRS

9925 107 St., Edmonton, Alta. T5K 2H9
Information Contact, A. Parsons, Director of Public Affairs (phone: 403 427 8863)

Acts Administered

Alberta Property Tax Reduction Act
Assessment Appeal Board Act
County Act
Dept. of Municipal Affairs Act
Electric Power & Pipeline Act
Improvement Districts Act
Lloydminster Municipal Amalgamation Act
Local Authorities Board Act
Local Tax Arrears Consolidation Act
Municipalities Assessment & Equalization Act
Municipal & Provincial Valuation Act
Municipal & School Administration Act
Municipal Election Act
Municipal Government Act
Municipal Tax Exemption Act
Municipal Taxation Act
New Towns Act
Northwest Alberta Regional Commission Act
Planning Act, 1977
Special Areas Act
Tax Recovery Act

MINISTER, Hon. Marvin E. Moore
Deputy Minister, A.R. Grover
Director, Personnel Admin. Branch, O. Milner
Director Public Affairs Branch, A. Parsons
Solicitor, W.J. Nugent
Director, Urban Advisory Group & Special Projects Branch, F. Marlyn
Asst. Deputy Minister, Municipal Admin. Services Division, T. Forgrave
Director, Municipal Inspection & Advisory Services Branch, J.M. Fleming
Director, Tax Recovery Branch, K.W. Metcalfe
Director, Grants & Subsidies Branch, D. Gingara
Asst. Deputy Minister, Improvement Districts Operations Division, R. Ford (includes: Land Tenure Secretariat, Metis Development Branch, I.D. Field Operations, and I.D. Finance & Admin.)
Asst. Deputy Minister, Planning Services Division, J.G. Thomas (includes: Inter-Agency Planning, Planning Services, Planning Support Services, and Planning Research)
Asst. Deputy Minister, Assessment Services Division, R.G. Gagne (includes: Operations, Research & Systems, Inspection & Advisory Services, and Training Branch)
Executive Director, Finance & Admin. Division, vacant (includes: Accounts, Central Services, and Property Taxation)

Associated Agencies

Local Authorities Board, 10909 Jasper Ave., Edmonton, Alta. T5J 3L9 (427-4278)
Chairman, C.I. Shelley
Assessment Appeal Board, 1040 Manulife House, 10055 106 St., Edmonton, Alta. T5K 2Y2 (427-7658)
Chairman, P. Klompas
Assessment Equalization Board, 9925 107 St., Edmonton, Alta. T5K 2H9 (427-8965)
Chairman, R.G. Gagne
Alta. Planning Board, 9th floor, 9925 107 St., Edmonton, Alta. T5K 2H9 (427-4864)
Director of Admin., A.J. Suelzle
Special Areas Board, Provincial Bldg., Box 820, Hanna, Alta. TOJ 1PO (854-4451)
A/Chairman, A.G. Grover
Northeast Alberta Region Commission, #609, 8215 112 St., Edmonton, Alta. T6G 2C7 (427-6888)
Commr., R.V. Henning

NATIVE AFFAIRS OFFICE

229 Legislative Bldg., Edmonton, Alta. T5K 2B6
(403) 427-3675
Executive Asst., Gloria Wittrup

Native Secretariat

2nd floor, South Tower, 10030 107 St., Edmonton, Alta. T5J 3E4

The Native Secretariat assists in the co-ordination of policies relating to Native people in the Province. It does not provide programs or services, but works with existing program departments to ensure that the necessary services are provided. The Native Secretariat supports a number of Native organizations with grants in aid toward self help and development programs throughout the Province.

Executive Director, Bill Donahue

OFFICE OF THE OMBUDSMAN

#1630, 10020 101A Ave., Edmonton, Alta. T5J 3G2
(403) 427-2756
Ombudsman, Dr. Randall Ivany
Solicitor to the Ombudsman, Alex B. Weir
Calgary Branch: #1080, 700 4 Ave. S.W., Calgary, Alta. T2P 3J4; Ralph Toews, in charge (phone: 403-261-6185)

ALBERTA GOVERNMENT PENSION BOARDS

Office of the Chairman: 9811 109 St., Edmonton, Alta.

Acts Administered

Local Authorities Pension Act
M.L.A. Pension Act
Public Service Management Pension Act
Public Service Pension Act
Special Forces Pension Act
Universities Academic Pension Act

Chairman of the Boards, J.E. Faries

ALBERTA PERSONNEL ADMINISTRATION

Floors 10-13, Jarvis Bldg., 9925 107 St., Edmonton, Alta. T5K 2H9

Acts Administered

The Public Service Act

MINISTER, Hon. Greg P. Stevens, 126 Legislative Bldg., 427-0158
Public Service Commissioner, J.E. Dixon, 12th floor, Jarvis Bldg., 427-8116

DEPT. OF RECREATION & PARKS
10363 108 St., Edmonton, Alta. T5J 1L8
Information from, Communications Office (403/427-2008)

Acts Administered
Recreation & Parks Act
Recreation Development Act
Provincial Parks Act
Wilderness Areas Act

MINISTER, Hon. P. Trynchy
Executive Asst., Terry Archer
Deputy Minister, E.B. Mitchelson
ADMINISTRATIVE SERVICES: Sun Bldg., 10363 108 St., Edmonton
Executive Director, Dave Rehill
Public Relations Manager, Ken Williams
RECREATION DEVELOPMENT:
Asst. Deputy Minister, Julian Nowicki
PROVINCIAL PARKS: Sun Bldg., 10363 108 St., Edmonton
Asst. Deputy Minister, James Potton
Director, Operations & Construction, J.P. Acton
Director, Parks Planning Branch, D.E. Cline

ALBERTA RESEARCH COUNCIL
11315 87 Ave., Edmonton, Alta. T6G 2C2
Information from: Mrs. D.M. Hollands, Secretary of the Council (403/438-1777)

President, Dr. G.G. Cloutier
Director, Policy Development & Program Evaluation, Dr. R. Green
Secretary of Council, Mrs. D.M. Hollands
Energy Resources Division, Director, Dr. J.G. Douglas (includes: Oil Sands Research, and Coal Research)
Frontier Sciences Division, Director, Dr. D.J. Currie (includes: Chemistry Dept., and Biology Group)
Natural Resources Division, Director, Dr. E.A. Babcock (includes: Geological Survey, Soils Dept., Groundwater Dept., Atmospheric Sciences Dept., and Drafting)
Industrial & Engineering Division, Director, Dr. D.L. Mitchell (includes: Industrial & Engineering Services Dept., Transportation & Surface Water Engineering Dept., Solar & Wind Energy Program, Electricity Research Program, Chemical Processing Group, Forest Products Research Program, Gasoline & Oil Testing Lab., and Instrumentation & Machine Shop)
Administration Division, Director, W.J. Cherpeta (includes: editing services, library services, purchasing, financial services, safety unit, materials management services, occupational health services, and personnel)

ALBERTA RESOURCES RAILWAY CORP.
A provincially owned Corporation leased to the CNR.
Chairman of the Board, Hon. Henry Kroeger, 419 Legislative Bldg., Edmonton, Alta. T5K 2B6
Vice Chairman, Hon. L.D. Hyndman
Managing Director, Charles Anderson, 3rd floor, Transportation Bldg., Edmonton, Alta. T5K 2B8 (phone: 403 427-3165)
Secretary Treasurer, A.F. Collins, 434 Terrace Bldg., Edmonton, Alta. T5K 2C3

DEPT. OF SOCIAL SERVICES & COMMUNITY HEALTH
Seventh St. Plaza, 10030 107 St., Edmonton, Alta. T5J 3E4
Information: Director, Communications (phone: 403 427-4801)

Acts Administered
Alcoholism & Drug Abuse Act
Alcoholism & Drug Abuse Fundation Act
Assured Income for the Severely Handicapped Act
Blind Persons Act
Blind Persons Guide Dog Act
Cemeteries Act
Change of Name Act
Chartered Physiotherapists Act
Child Welfare Act
Chiropractic Profession Act
Dental Association Act
Dental Auxiliaries Act
Dental Mechanics Act
Dental Technicians Act
Dept. of Social Services & Community Health Act
Dependent Adults Act
Disabled Persons Act
Disabled Persons Pension Act
Emergency Medical Aid Act
Health Unit Act
Human Tissue Gift Act
Maintenance & Recovery Act
Marriage Act
Medical Profession Act
Medical Services Research Fdn. Act
Mental Health Act, 1972
Metis Betterment Act
Naturopathy Act
Nursing Assistants Registration Act
Nursing Services Act
Ophthalmic Dispensers Act
Optometry Act
Pharmaceutical Association Act
Podiatry Act
Preventive Social Services Act
Psychiatric Nurses Association Act
Psychiatric Nursing Training Act
Psychologists Act
Public Health Act
Radiological Technicians Act (except Part 2)
Registered Dieticians Association Act
Registered Nurses Act
Senior Citizens Benefits Act, 1973
Social Care Facilities Licensing Act
Social Care Facilities Review Committee Act
Social Development Act
Social Workers Act
Supplementary Allowances Act
Treatment Services Act
Tuberculosis Act
Venereal Diseases Prevention Act
Vital Statistics Act

MINISTER, Hon. R.J. Bogle
Chief Deputy Minister, Stanley H. Mansbridge
Deputy Minister, Health Services, Dr. Sheila Durkin
Deputy Minister, Social Services, Dave Stolee

Associated Agencies
Alta. Alcoholism & Drug Abuse Commission

Vital Statistics
Director, H. Hersom, Division of Vital Statistics, Dept. of Social Services & Community Health, 10405 100 Ave., 4th floor, Edmonton, Alta. T5J OA6 (Gen. office phone: 403/427-2681)
Fee for Birth Certificate: $3.00
Fee for Death Certificate: $3.00

DEPT. OF THE SOLICITOR GENERAL
Melton Bldg., 6th & 7th floors, 10310 Jasper Ave., Edmonton, Alta. T5J 1Y8
Information Contact, Victoria Hadden, Communications, Solicitor General, 5th floor, Melton Bldg. (phone: 403 427-7245, 427-4882)

Acts Administered
Corrections Act

Dept. of the Solicitor General Act
Highway Traffic Act (with Transportation)
Liquor Control Act
Liquor Licensing Act
Liquor Plebiscites Act (with Attorney General)
Motor Vehicle Accident Claims Act
Motor Vehicle Administration Act
Off-Highway Vehicle Act (with Transportation)
Police Act (with Attorney General)
Private Investigators & Security Guards Act
Racing Commission Act

MINISTER, Hon. Graham Harle
Deputy Minister, Rheal J. LeBlanc
Asst. Deputy Minister (Corrections), Robert J. King
Regional Directors, Corrections, Edmonton, H.A. O'Handley; Calgary, B.J. Doyle; North/South, R.H. Bricker
Director of Law Enforcement, Ed Witherden
Director of Finance & Admin., Peter Schmidt
Director of Personnel, Harvey Geddes
Director of Staff Training & Development, J.W. Johnson
Asst. Deputy Minister, Motor Vehicle Admin., George Pedersen
Chairman, Driver Control Board, Jack Routledge
Director of Research & Planning, Oskar Anderson

Boards
Alta. Liquor Control Board
12360 142 St., Edmonton, Alta. T5L 2H1 (403/454-6521)
Chairman, W.M. Skoreyko
Alta. Racing Commission
507 Sloane Sq., 5920 1A St. S.W., Calgary, Alta. T2H OG3 (403/261-6551)
Chairman, Roy Farran

SUCCESSION DUTY OFFICE
200 Chancery Hall, 3 Sir Winston Churchill Sq., Edmonton, Alta. T5J 2C4
Phone: (403) 427-2744
Solicitor for Collector of Succession Duties, M.W. Howey, Q.C.

ALBERTA GOVERNMENT TELEPHONES
10020 100 St., Edmonton, Alta. T5J ON5
Information Contact, N.G. Sarofen, General Public Relations Manager (phone: 403/425-4723)

ASSOC. MINISTER OF TELEPHONES, Hon. Dr. P.N. Webber
President, J.A. Barnes
Vice President, Operations, J.C.D. Mallet-Paret
Vice President, Finance, H.M. Neldner
Vice President, Administration, J.R. McDonald
Vice President, Corporate Planning & Network Development, J. Szaszkiewicz
Vice President, Customer Sales & Services, D.F. Baillie

DEPT. OF TOURISM & SMALL BUSINESS
16th floor, Capitol Square Bldg., 10065 Jasper Ave., Edmonton, Alta. T5J OH4 (403/427-2280)
Information Contact: Communications Director (403/427-2858)

Acts Administered
Dept. of Tourism & Small Business Act
Alberta Opportunity Fund Act
Northern Alberta Development Council Act

MINISTER, Hon. J.A. "Boomer" Adair
Deputy Minister, A.G. McDonald (427-4368)
Asst. Deputy Minister, Tourism Division (Travel Alberta), D.A. Hayes (427-4324)
Executive Director, Marketing, J.L. Engel (427-4336)
Director, Development Branch, W.W. Warren (427-3761)
Asst. Deputy Minister, Small Business Development, R.H. Blake (427-3685)
Executive Director, Small Business Assistance Branch, P. Shragge (427-3685)
Executive Director, Regional Business Development Branch, C.E. Whyte (427-5267)
Executive Director, Northern Development, R.M. Finnerty (624-6274)
Administrative Division
Director, P.C. Crerar (427-1946)
Manager, Personnel, G. Halbersma (427-8780)
Manager, Finance, E.R. Halberg (427-4837)
Director, Communications, vacant (427-2858)

Associated Agencies
Alberta Opportunity Co.
Box 1860, Ponoka, Alta. TOC 2HO
(403) 783-4481
Managing Director, R.W. Parker
Northern Alberta Development Council
#206, 9621 96 Ave., PO Bag 900-14, Peace River, Alta. TOH 2X0
(403) 624-6274

DEPT. OF TRANSPORTATION
Transportation Bldg., 9630 106 St., Edmonton, Alta. T5K 2B8
Information Contact, J. Tansowny, Executive Asst., 310 Transportation Bldg. (phone: 403 427-2081)

Acts Administered
Highway Traffic Act
Dept. of Transportation Act
Motor Transport Act
Public Highways Development Act
Off-Highway Vehicle Act

MINISTER, Hon. Henry Kroeger
Executive Asst., D. West
Chief Deputy Minister, R.G. McFarlane
Executive Asst., J. Tansowny
Deputy Minister, Engineering, R.H. Cronkhite
Asst. Deputy Minister, Engineering, M.A. Kehr
Asst. Deputy Minister, Admin., D.A. McGeachy
Asst. Deputy Minister, Program Planning, L. Root
Deputy Minister, Regional Transportation, H.M. Alton
Asst. Deputy Minister, Regional Transportation, N. Chorney

Associated Agency
Motor Transport Board
Provincial Bldg., 4920 51 St., Box 5002, Red Deer, Alta. T4N 5Y5 (343-5430)
Chairman, H.H. Hendrickson

ALBERTA TREASURY
434 Terrace Bldg., 9515 107 St., Edmonton, Alta. T5K 2C3
Information Contact, D.J. Barr, Manager, Communications, (403/427-4786)

Acts Administered
Alta. Corporate Income Tax Act
Alta. Heritage Savings Trust Fund Act
Alta. Income Tax Act
Alta. Loan Act
Alta. Municipal Financing Corp. Act
Amusements Act
Appropriation Act
Chartered Accountants Act
Civil Service Garnishee Act
Crown Property Municipal Grants Act
Estate Tax Rebate Act
Financial Admin. Act
Fuel Oil Administration Act
Fuel Oil Tax Act
Government Emergency Guarantee Act
Government Land Purchases Act
Local Authorities Pension Act
MLA Pension Act
Municipal Debentures Act

Municipal Land Loans Act
Pension Fund Act
Public Service Administrative Transfer Act
Public Service Management Pension Act
Public Service Pension Act
Special Forces Pension Act
Statistics Bureau Act
Tobacco Tax Act
Treasury Branch Deposits Guarantee Act
Treasury Branches Act
Universities Academic Pension Act
Utility Companies Income Tax Rebates Act

PROVINCIAL TREASURER, Hon. Lou Hyndman
Deputy Provincial Treasurer, A.F. Collins
Controller, A.D. O'Brien
Assoc. Deputy Provincial Treasurer, Finance, A.J. McPherson
Asst. Deputy Provincial Treasurer, Budget & Management, C.A. MacKenzie
Asst. Deputy Provincial Treasurer, Revenue & Admin., A.H. Kalke
Asst. Deputy Provincial Treasurer, Finance Programs, J.M. Drinkwater
Asst. Deputy Provincial Treasurer, Fiscal Policy & Economics, G.L. Duncan
Supt., Treasury Branches of Alberta, F. Sparrow, 9925 109 St., 427-2721

Associated Agency

Alta. Municipal Financing Corp., H.H. Strohbach, General Manager, 434 Terrace Bldg., Edmonton, Alta. T5K 2C3 (403/427-3052)

ALBERTA WOMEN'S BUREAU

Room 1402, 10015 103 Ave., Edmonton, Alta. T5J OH1
(403) 427-2470
Director, E. Phyllis Ellis

WORKERS' COMPENSATION BOARD

9912 107 St., Edmonton, Alta. T5J 2S5
(403) 427-1100
Chairman, Roy H. Jamha
Members, P. Kolba, A.E. Hohol
Secretary, T.P. Griffin, F.C.I.S., A.M.B.I.M.
Executive Director, Admin., T.P. Griffin, F.C.I.S., A.M.B.I.M.
Executive Director, Claims Services, J. Wisocky
Executive Director, Finance, J.R. Thomson
Senior Solicitor & Counsel to the Board, J.D. Carr, B.A., L.L.B.

Rehabilitation Centre

7123 119 St., Edmonton, Alta. T5J 2LB (Phone: 434-3441)
Administrative Director, W.L. Jarman, M.C.P.A., C.H.A.

ALBERTA WORKERS' HEALTH, SAFETY & COMPENSATION

Occupational Health & Safety Division

Information from: Communications Director, 5th floor, 10709 Jasper Ave., Edmonton, Alta. T5J 3N3 (403/427-5541)

MINISTER, Hon. Bill W. Diachuk, 203 Leg. Bldg.

The Division administers certain regulations under The Occupational Health & Safety Act.

PROVINCE OF BRITISH COLUMBIA

Entered Confederation July 20, 1871.
Area: 366,255 sq. miles
Population: 2,636,500 (est. 1980)
Seat of Government: Parliament Bldgs., Victoria, B.C.
Lieutenant-Governor: The Hon. Henry P. Bell-Irving, D.S.O., O.B.E., E.D.
Secretary: J.M. Roberts

EXECUTIVE COUNCIL

Premier, and President of the Council, Hon. William Richards Bennett
Deputy Premier, and Minister of Human Resources, Hon. Grace McCarthy
Provincial Secretary, and Minister of Government Services, Hon. Evan M. Wolfe
Attorney General, Hon. L. Allan Williams
Minister of Finance, Hon. Hugh A. Curtis
Minister of Agriculture, Hon. James J. Hewitt
Minister of Education, Hon. Brian R.D. Smith
Minister of Labour, Hon. John H. Heinrich
Minister of Municipal Affairs, Hon. William N. Vander Zalm
Minister of Transportation & Highways, Hon. Alexander V. Fraser
Minister of Energy, Mines & Petroleum Resources, Hon. Robert H. McClelland
Minister of Health, Hon. J.A. Nielsen
Minister of Industry & Small Business Development, Hon. Donald M. Phillips
Minister of Forests, Hon. Thomas M. Waterland
Minister of Environment, Hon. C. Stephen Rogers
Minister of Lands, Parks & Housing, Hon. James R. Chabot
Minister of Consumer & Corporate Affairs, Hon. Hon. Peter Hyndman
Minister of Universities, Science & Communications, Hon. Patrick L. McGeer
Minister of Intergovernmental Relations, Hon. Garde B. Gardom
Minister of Tourism, Hon. Patricia J. Jordan

LEGISLATIVE ASSEMBLY

Thirty-second Legislature. Last Election, May 10, 1979. Maximum Duration, 5 Years.
Party Standings: Social Credit (S.C.) 31; New Democratic Party (N.D.P.-C.C.F.) 26; Total 57.
Leader of the Opposition: David Barrett
Indemnities & Allowances: Each member of the Executive Council and the Legislative Assembly receives an annual allowance of $26,200 and $13,100 for expenses. In addition, the Premier receives a salary of $35,800 and each member of the Executive Council with Portfolio $30,700 (without Portfolio $23,200). The Leader of the Opposition has a special allowance of $24,300, the Speaker receives a special allowance of $24,300 and the Deputy Speaker or Leader of a recognized political party an allowance of $10,850.
Officers: Speaker, Hon. Harvey W. Schroeder; Clerk of Assembly, Ian M. Horne, Q.C. (phone: 604/387-3785); Auditor General, Mrs. Erma Morrison; Sergeant-at-Arms, A.M. Hutchinson

Members

Following is constituency (population): member, address:

Alberni (28,024): R.E. Skelly, N.D.P., 4957 Argyle St., Port Alberni, B.C. V9Y 1V6 (387-6003)
Atlin (3,158): Alan L. Passarell, N.D.P., Parliament Bldgs., Victoria, B.C. V8V 1X4 (382-5207)
Boundary-Similkameen (29,733): James J. Hewitt, S.C., No. 107, 309 Martin St., Penticton, B.C. V2A 5K4 (387-3656)
Burnaby-Edmonds (26,760): Ms. Rosemary Brown, N.D.P., Parliament Bldgs., Victoria, B.C. V8V 1X4 (387-6082)
Burnaby-North (34,840): Eileen E. Dailly, N.D.P., 541 Appian Way, Coquitlam, B.C. (387-6097)

Burnaby-Willingdon (33,009): James G. Lorimer, N.D.P., Parliament Bldgs., Victoria, B.C. V8V 1X4 (387-3798)
Cariboo (31,531): Alex V. Fraser, S.C., Parliament Bldgs., Victoria, B.C. V8V 1X4 (387-3180)
Central Fraser Valley ( ): W.S. Ritchie, S.C., Parliament Bldgs., Victoria, B.C. V8V 1X4 (387-3441)
Chilliwack (35,635): H.W. Schroeder, S.C., Parliament Bldgs., Victoria, B.C. V8V 1X4 (387-3952)
Columbia River (6,608): James R. Chabot, S.C., Parliament Bldgs., Victoria, B.C. V8V 1X4 (387-1221)
Comox (36,983): Ms. Karen Sanford, N.D.P., R.R. 2, Courtenay, B.C. V9N 5M9 (387-3652)
Coquitlam-Moody ( ): Stuart M. Leggatt, N.D.P., Parliament Bldgs., Victoria, B.C. V8V 1X4 (387-1491)
Cowichan-Malahat (28,347): Mrs. Barbara B. Wallace, N.D.P., Parliament Bldgs., Victoria, B.C. V8V 1X4 (387-6094)
Delta (67,259): Walter Davidson, S.C., Parliament Bldgs., Victoria, B.C. V8V 1X4 (387-3729)
Dewdney (33,493): George Mussallem, S.C., 22289 Lougheed Hwy., Maple Ridge, B.C. V2X 2W1 (387-6983)
Esquimalt-Port Renfrew ( ): Frank J. Mitchell, N.D.P., Parliament Bldgs., Victoria, B.C. V8V 1X4 (387-5426)
Kamloops (44,855): Claude H. Richmond, S.C., Parliament Bldgs., Victoria, B.C. V8V 1X4 (387-3595)
Kootenay (22,219): Terence P. Segarty, S.C., #108, 117 10th Ave. S., Cranbrook, B.C. V1C 2N1 (387-6349)
Langley (46,876): R.H. McClelland, S.C., Parliament Bldgs., Victoria, B.C. V8V 1X4 (387-5295)
Mackenzie (23,439): D.F. Lockstead, N.D.P., 3222 Cariboo Ave., Powell River, B.C. V8A 1A2 (387-6774)
Maillardville-Coquitlam ( ): Norman Levi, N.D.P., Parliament Bldgs., Victoria, B.C. V8V 1X4 (387-6076)
Nanaimo (32,006): D.D. Stupich, N.D.P., 11495 Dunsmuir St., Nanaimo, B.C. V9R 2V2 (387-6004)
Nelson-Creston (19,205): L. Nicolson, N.D.P., R.R. 1, Nelson, B.C. V1L 5P4 (387-6063)
New Westminster (30,781): D.G. Cocke, N.D.P., Parliament Bldgs., Victoria, B.C. V8V 1X4 (387-6064)
North Island ( ): Colin S. Gabelnann, N.D.P., Parliament Bldgs., Victoria, B.C. V8V 1X4 (387-5527)
North Peace River (11,604): Anthony J. Brummett, S.C., Parliament Bldgs., Victoria, B.C. V8V 1X4 (387-5677)
North Vancouver-Capilano (27,777): Angus Ree, S.C., 6712 Dufferin Ave., West Vancouver, B.C. V7W 2K2 (387-6847)
North Vancouver-Seymour (38,749): Jack Davis, S.C., Parliament Bldgs., Vancouver, B.C. V8V 1X4 (387-6277)
Oak Bay-Gordon Head ( ): Brian R.D. Smith, S.C., 2041 Cadboro Bay Rd., Victoria, B.C. V8R 5G4 (387-5891)
Okanagan North (24,756): Mrs. Pat Jordan, S.C., Parliament Bldgs., Victoria, B.C. V8V 1X4 (387-1201)
Okanagan South (42,558): W.R. Bennett, S.C., Parliament Bldgs., Victoria, B.C. V8V 1X4 (387-6200)
Omineca (13,116): J.J. Kempf, S.C., Parliament Bldgs., Victoria, B.C. V8V 1X4 (387-3038)
Prince George North ( ): J.H. Heinrich, S.C., #1, 1598 Sixth Ave., Prince George, B.C. V2L 5B5 (387-1986)
Prince George South ( ): W.B. Strachan, S.C., 1445 W. Central St., Prince George, B.C. V2N 1P6 (387-5133)
Prince Rupert (13,107): G.R. Lea, N.D.P., Parliament Bldgs., Victoria, B.C. V8V 1X4 (387-6065)
Richmond (47,403): James A. Nielsen, S.C., 11420 Seabrook Cres., Richmond, B.C. V7A 3H3 (387-6480)
Rossland-Trail (19,949): C.A.C. D'Arcy, N.D.P., #2, 860 Eldorado St., Trail, B.C. V1R 3V4 (387-3287)
Saanich & the Islands (36,481): H.A. Curtis, S.C., Parliament Bldgs., Victoria, B.C. V8V 1X4 (387-3751)
Shuswap-Revelstoke ( ): W.S. King, N.D.P., Parliament Bldgs., Victoria, B.C. V8V 1X4 (387-3964)
Skeena (20,090): Frank Howard, N.D.P., Parliament Bldgs., Victoria, B.C. V8V 1X4 (387-1492)
South Peace River (11,261): D. McG. Phillips, S.C., Parliament Bldgs., Victoria, B.C. V8V 1X4 (387-3093)
Surrey ( ): W.N. Vander Zalm, S.C., Parliament Bldgs., Victoria, B.C. V8V 1X4 (387-3602)
Ernest Hall, N.D.P., Parliament Bldgs., Victoria, B.C. V8V 1X4 (387-1491)
Vancouver Centre (49,500): E.O. Barnes, N.D.P., Parliament Bldgs., Victoria, B.C. V8V 1X4 (387-6002)
G.V. Lauk, N.D.P., Parliament Bldgs., Victoria, B.C. V8V 1X4 (387-3546)
Vancouver East (46,426): David Barrett, N.D.P., Parliament Bldgs., Victoria, B.C. V8V 1X4 (387-6770)
A.B. Macdonald, Q.C., N.D.P., Parliament Bldgs., Victoria, B.C. V8V 1X4 (387-6283)
Vancouver-Little Mountain (46,730): Grace M. McCarthy, S.C., Parliament Bldgs., Victoria, B.C. V8V 1X4 (387-6600)
Evan M. Wolfe, S.C., Parliament Bldgs., Victoria, B.C. V8V 1X4 (387-1241)
Vancouver-Point Grey (52,576): Garde B. Gardom, Q.C., S.C., Parliament Bldgs., Victoria, B.C. V8V 1X4 (387-5845)
Dr. Patrick L. McGeer, S.C., Parliament Bldgs., Victoria, B.C. V8V 1X4 (387-6580)
Vancouver South (54,929): C.S. Rogers, S.C., 6391 Fraser St., Vancouver, B.C. V5W 3A3 (387-3769)
Peter S. Hyndman, S.C., 6391 Fraser St., Vancouver, B.C. V5W 3A3 (387-3302)
Victoria (52,226): Charles Barber, N.D.P., Parliament Bldgs., Victoria, B.C. V8V 1X4 (387-3079)
Gordon Hanson, N.D.P., Parliament Bldgs., Victoria, B.C. V8V 1X4 (387-3797)
West Vancouver-Howe Sound (36,327): L. Allan Williams, S.C., Parliament Bldgs., Victoria, B.C. V8V 1X4 (387-1866)
Yale-Lillooet (17,279): Thomas M. Waterland, S.C., Parliament Bldgs., Victoria, B.C. V8V 1X4 (387-6240)

OFFICE OF THE PREMIER

Legislative Bldgs., Victoria, B.C. V8V 1X4
(604) 387-1715
Premier, Hon. W.R. Bennett
Executive Director, W.A.R. Tozer
Deputy Minister, P. Kinsella
Press Secretary, H. Leiren

GOVERNMENT DEPARTMENTS

PROVINCIAL AGRICULTURAL LAND COMMISSION

#133, 4940 Canada Way, Burnaby, B.C. V5G 4K6
(604) 294-5211
Chairman, Dr. M.F. Clarke
General Manager, R. Murdoch

MINISTRY OF AGRICULTURE & FOOD

Parliament Bldgs., Victoria, B.C. V8W 2Z7
Information Contact, Ron Sera, Director, Information Services Branch (phone: 604/387-5121, Local 260)

Acts Administered

Agricultural Credit Act
Agricultural Land Commission Act
Agricultural Land Development Act
Agricultural Produce Grading Act
Agricultural & Rural Development (B.C.) Act
Agrologists Act
Bee Act
Cattle Horn Act
Farm Distress Act
Farm Income Insurance Act
Farm Products Industry Improvement Act
Farmers' & Womens' Institutes Act
Fur Farm Act
Grasshopper Control Act
Insurance for Crops Act
Livestock Act

Livestock Brand Act
Livestock Disease Control Act
Livestock Industry Act
Livestock Protection Act
Livestock Public Sale Act
Margarine Act
Meat Inspection Act
Milk Industry Act
Ministry of Agriculture & Food Act
Natural Products Marketing (B.C.) Act
Pharmacists Act
Plant Protection Act
Seed Grower Act
Seed Potato Act
Soil Conservation Act
Veterinary Laboratory Act
Veterinary Medical Act
Weed Control Act

MINISTER, Hon. James J. Hewitt
Deputy Minister, S.B. Peterson
Executive Director, Policy Development & Planning, D.M. Matviw
Executive Director, Finance & Admin., J.F. Newman
Executive Officer, P.H. Pettyfer
Director, Information Services, R.A. Sera
Asst. Deputy Minister, Field Operations, E.M. King
Executive Director, Specialist & Regulatory Services, R.J. Miller
Director, Dairy, D.J. Blair
Director, Engineering, T.A. Windt, Abbotsford
Director, Crop Protection, J.C. Arrand
Director, Soils, R.S. Bertrand, Cloverdale
Director, Veterinary, Dr. R.J. Avery
Recorder of Brands, W.M. McConnell
Director, Youth Development, D.E. Freed, Summerland
Executive Director, Production Services, M.G. Oswell
Director, Apiculture, J. Corner, Vernon
Director, Farmland Resources, J.D. Anderson
Director, Field Crops, J.V. Zacharias
Director, Horticulture, A.C. Carter
Director, Livestock, J.A. Pelter
Director, Poultry, Dr. H.C. Carlson
Regional Director, South Coastal, W.E.A. Wickens, Abbotsford
Regional Director, Okanagan-Kootenay, B.A. Hodge, Summerland
Regional Director, Thompson-Cariboo, A.N. Isfeld, Kamloops
Regional Director, Central, R.N. Kohlert, Prince George
Regional Director, Peace River, B.E. Baehr, Dawson Creek
Asst. Deputy Minister, Financial Assistance Programs, I.C. Carne
Director, ARDA, J.R. Steele
Co-ordinator, Farm Finance Programs, B.A. Hackett
Director, Agricultural Credit, M.K. Thompson
Director, Crop Insurance, P. Humphry-Baker, Kelowna
Director, Farm Income Insurance, vacant
Director, Farm Products Finance, J.B. Phillips
Director, Property Management, B.R. Richardson, Langley
Asst. Deputy Minister, Economics & Marketing Services, Dr. G.A. MacEachern
Director, Economics, vacant
Director, Marketing, D.A. Rugg

Associated Agencies

Agricultural Land Commission
#133, 4940 Canada Way, Burnaby, B.C. V5G 4K6
(604) 294-5211
Chairman, Dr. M.F. Clarke
Milk Board
800 S. Cassiar St., Vancouver, B.C. V5K 4N6
(604) 299-9131
Chairman, E.D. Daum
B.C. Marketing Board
Parliament Bldgs., Victoria, B.C. V8W 2Z7
(604) 387-5121
Secretary, A.J. Helmersen

Agricultural Commodity Marketing Boards

B.C. Chicken Marketing Board, Ste. 203, 5752 176th St., Surrey, B.C. V3S 4C8, 576-2855. Manager, R.A. Stafford
B.C. Cranberry Marketing Board, 2851 No. 8 Rd., Richmond, B.C. V6V 1S2, 278-6271. Secretary, Heinz Knoedler
B.C. Egg Marketing Board, Box 310, Abbotsford, B.C. V2S 4N9, 853-3348. General Manager, J. Campbell
B.C. Grape Marketing Board, Box 1060, Kelowna, B.C. V1Y 7P7, 762-4652. Secretary, Mrs. C. Bielert
B.C. Hog Marketing Commission, 2564 Montrose Ave., Abbotsford, B.C. V2S 3T3, 853-9461. Chairman, Jack Reams
B.C. Mushroom Marketing Board, #9770, 199A St., R.R. 5, Langley, B.C. V3A 4P8, 888-2811. Secretary, W. Blomme
B.C. Oyster Marketing Board, Box 970, Ladysmith, B.C. VOR 2EO, 245-2939. Secretary, P. Irvine
B.C. Sheep & Wool Commission, c/o Secretary Treasurer, Hildred Finch, R.R. 1, Cawston, B.C. V0X 1C0, 499-5717
B.C. Tree Fruit Marketing Board, 1473 Water St., Kelowna, B.C. V1Y 1J6, 762-2604. Secretary, J. Bell
B.C. Turkey Marketing Board, #218, 17704 56 Ave., Surrey, B.C. V3S 1C7, 574-7447. Secretary, Colyn Welsh
B.C. Vegetable Marketing Commission, #212, 17704 56th Ave., Surrey, B.C. V3S 1C7, 576-8291. Secretary Manager, E.B. Pratt
Council of Marketing Bds. of B.C., 846 Broughton St., Victoria, B.C. V8W 1E4, 383-7171. Secretary, J.L. Wessel

ALCOHOL & DRUG PROGRAMS

See Ministry of Health

ASSESSMENT AUTHORITY

1537 Hillside Ave., Victoria, B.C. V8T 4Y2

An independent Authority to maintain the real property assessment rolls for all real property throughout the province. This responsibility includes the valuation of real property for assessment purposes.

Commr., J.T. Gwartney (604/595-6211)

ATTORNEY GENERAL'S MINISTRY

Parliament Bldgs., Victoria, B.C. V8V 4S6

Information Contacts, Secretary to the Attorney General (phone: 387-1866), or L.E. Sawyer, Director, Information Services (phone: 384-4434)

Acts Administered

Accountants (Certified General) Act
Accountants (Chartered) Act
Accountants (Management) Act
Age of Majority Act
Arbitration Act
Architects (Landscape) Act
Attorney General Act
Barristers & Solicitors Act
Bonding Act
Book Accounts Assignment Act
Builders Lien Act
Chattel Mortgage Act
Commercial Tenancy Act
Community Regulation Act
Company Act
Condominium Act
Constitutional Question Act
Coroners Act
Correction Act
County Boundary Act
County Court Act
Court Agent Act
Court of Appeal Act
Court Order Enforcement Act
Court Order Interest Act
Court Rules Act

Creditor Assistance Act
Criminal Injury Compensation Act
Crown Franchise Act
Crown Proceeding Act
Curfew Act
Disciplinary Authority Protection Act
Escheat Act
Estate Administration Act
Estates of Missing Persons Act
Evidence Act
Expropriation Act
Family Compensation Act
Family Relations Act
Federal Courts Jurisdiction Act
Fire Services Act
Fireworks Act
Fort Nelson Indian Reserve Minerals Revenue Sharing Act
Fraudulent Conveyance Act
Fraudulent Preference Act
Frustrated Contract Act
Good Samaritan Act
Holiday Shopping Act
Homestead Act
Horse Racing Act
Hotel Guest Registration Act
Hotel Keepers Act
Infants Act
Interpretation Act
Judicial Review Procedure Act
Jury Act
Justice Administration Act
Land (Settled Estates) Act
Land (Wife Protection) Act
Land Title Act
Land Title Inquiry Act
Land Transfer Form Act
Law & Equity Act
Law Reform Commission Act
Legal Services Society Act
Legitimacy Act
Libel & Slander Act
Limitation Act
Married Woman's Property Act
Motion Picture Act
Municipal Act
National Cablevision Ltd. Transfer of Jurisdiction Act
Negligence Act
Notaries Act
Occupiers Liability Act
Offence Act
Ombudsman Act
Partition of Property Act
Patients Property Act
Pension Society Act
Perpetuity Act
Police Act
Power of Appointment Act
Powers of Attorney Act
Prevention of Cruelty to Animals Act
Private Investigators & Security Agencies Act
Probate Recognition Act
Property Law Act
Provincial Court Act
Public Service Bonding Act
Public Trustee Act
Queen's Counsel Act
Recognizances Act
Recovery of Goods Act
Regulation Act
Rent Distress Act
Repairers Lien Act
Sale of Goods Act
Sale of Goods in Bulk Act
Sale of Goods on Condition Act
Sales on Consignment Act
Securities (Forged Transfer) Act
Sheriff Act
Small Claim Act
Statute of Frauds Act
Statute Revision Act
Statute Uniformity Act
Subpoena (Interprovincial) Act
Supreme Court Act
Survivorship & Presumption of Death Act
Traffic Victims Indemnity Fund, 1961 Act
Trust Variation Act
Trustee Act
Tug Boat Worker Lien Act
Warehouse Lien Act
Warehouse Receipt Act
Wills Act
Wills Variation Act
Woodworker Lien Act

ATTORNEY GENERAL, Hon. L. Allan Williams, Q.C.
Deputy Attorney General, Richard H. Vogel
Assoc. Deputy Attorney General, (Statute Revision), Gilbert D. Kennedy, Q.C.
Asst. Deputy Minister (Courts), David Warren
Asst. Deputy Attorney General (Policy & Planning), R.D. Adamson
Asst. Deputy Attorney General (Criminal Law), A.E. Filmer
Legal Services to Government, Ian L. Jessiman, Q.C.
Asst. Deputy Minister (Police Services), Robin Bourne
Fire Commr., Gordon R. Anderson
Public Trustee, Clinton W. Foote
Director, Co-ordinated Law Enforcement Unit, Robert Simson
Consultant, Sheriff Services, Tom Fox
Chief Coroner, Robert Galbraith
Director, Justice Development Commission, R.H. Vogel
Director, Land Titles, H.T. Kennedy, #201, 1250 Quadra St., Victoria, B.C. V8W 2K7

Land Title Offices (& Registrar)

Victoria: R.E. Hooper, Law Courts, 850 Burdett Ave. (V8W 1B4) 387-3303
Vancouver: D.H. Sturch, 800 Hornby St. (V6Z 2C5) 521-9641
New Westminster: S.A.P. Birchfield, Queen's Court, 625 Agnes St. (V3M 1G9) 521-9641
Kamloops: J.C. Groves, Court House, 7 W. Seymour St. (V2C 1E6)
Nelson: Mrs. A.M. Marion, Box 290 (V1L 5P9) 352-2211, loc. 301
Prince George: E.J. Raven, Box 1840 (V2L 4V8) 563-0501
Prince Rupert: W.G. Gandy, 730 Second Ave. W. (V8J 1H3) 624-2121

Associated Agencies

Judicial Council, Pacific Centre, 700 W. Georgia St., Vancouver, B.C. V7Y 1B6 (604/668-2864)
Law Reform Commission, 1055 W. Hastings St., Vancouver, V6E 2E9 (604/668-2366)
Legal Services Society, Box 12120, #700-S, 555 W. Hastings St., Vancouver, B.C. V6B 4N6 (604/689-0741)
Parole Board of B.C., #203, 10334 152A St., Surrey, B.C. V3R 7P6 (604/581-4414); Chairman, John Konrad
B.C. Police Commission, No. 1550, 409 Granville St., Vancouver, V6C 1T2 (604/668-2385)
B.C. Racing Commission, 210, 4259 Canada Way, Burnaby, V5G 1H1 (604/438-6555)
Rules Commission, Provincial Court, Courthouse, 800 Smithe St., Vancouver, B.C. (604/668-2864)

OFFICE OF THE AUDITOR GENERAL

8 Bastion Sq., Victoria, B.C. V8V 1X4
Auditor General, Mrs. Erma Morrison
Deputy Auditor General, Robert J. Hayward

B.C. BUILDINGS CORP. (A Crown Corp.)

#400, 910 Government St., Victoria, B.C. V8W 2T4

(604) 387-1353

The Corporation provides land and buildings for the accommodation of all departments of the Government and manages these properties.

President & Chief Executive Officer, Peter Dolezal
Vice President, Administration Group, & Chief Financial Officer, Dennis Truss
Vice President, Planning & Client Services Group, Ron MacKenzie
Vice President, Development Group, John Davies
Vice President, Property Management Group, Al Kemp
Corporate Secretary, Ashley Bernadine
Manager, Human Resources & Corporate Affairs, Bill Heschuk

B.C. CANCER FOUNDATION

601 W. 10th Ave., Vancouver, B.C. V5Z 1L3
(604) 873-8401
President, R.K. Lester
Hon. Secretary, W.W. Bennett
Hon. Treasurer, J.E. Larsen

B.C. CELLULOSE CO. (A Crown Corp.)

2659 Douglas St., Victoria, B.C. V8T 4M3
(604) 386-8794

MINISTRY OF CONSUMER & CORPORATE AFFAIRS

940 Blanshard St., Victoria, B.C. V8W 3E6 (except where otherwise indicated)
Information from Information & Education (phone: 604 387-1251)

Acts Administered

Bankruptcy Act (Federal, Part X, Orderly Payment of Debts)
Blind Persons Rights Act
Book Accounts Assignment Act
Cemetery Act
Cemetery Company Act
Cemetery (Municipal) Act
Chattel Mortgage Act
Commercial Tenancy Act
Company Act
Company Clauses Act
Commodity Contract Act
Condominium Act
Consumer Protection Act, 1967
Consumer Protection Act
Co-operative Association Act
Credit Reporting Act
Credit Union Act
Creditor Assistance Act
Cremation Act
Debt Collection Act
Debtor Assistance Act
Funeral Plan Act
Hotel Guest Registration Act
Hotel Keepers Act
Insurance Act
Insurance (Marine) Act
Investment Contract Act
Liquor Control & Licensing Act
Liquor Distribution Act
Ministry of Consumer & Corporate Affairs Act
Mortgage Brokers Act
Motor Dealer Act
Mutual Fire Insurance Companies Act - Not Consolidated
Partnership Act
Pawnbrokers Act
Pyramid Distribution Act
Real Estate Act
Rent Distress Act
Repairers Lien Act
Residential Tenancy Act
Sale of Goods Act
Sale of Goods on Closing Out Act
Sale of Goods on Consignment Act
Sales of Goods on Condition Act
Savings & Loan Associations Act - Not Consolidated
Securities Act (excluding S. 140)
Securities (Forged Transfer Act)
Society Act
Trade Practice Act
Trading Stamp Act
Travel Agents Act
Trust Company Act
Tugboat Worker Lien Act
Vancouver Stock Exchange Act
Warehouse Lien Act
Warehouse Receipt Act
Woodworker Lien Act

MINISTER, Hon. Peter S. Hyndman (387-1541)
Policy Co-ordination, Ken Chamberlain, Vancouver (668-2911)
Special Asst., Tom Walters (387-1541)
A/Deputy Minister, E.T. Cantell, Q.C. (387-1269)
Asst. Deputy Minister, Consumer Affairs, Stewart Goodings (387-1789)
A/Asst. Deputy Minister, Corporate Affairs, M. Jorre de St. Jorre (387-3942)

Liquor Control & Licensing Branch

General Manager, Allan Gould (387-1254)

Liquor Distribution Branch

3200 E. Broadway, Vancouver, B.C. V5M 1Z6
General Manager, R.A. Wallace (254-5711)
Communications Manager, Joyce Courtney (254-5711)

Rentalsman

1050 W. Pender St., Vancouver, B.C. V6E 3Z4
Rentalsman, J.D. Patterson (689-0811)
Deputy Rentalsmen, Peter Smith, Chris Green
Condominium Officer, Elaine McAndrew (387-3319)

Policy, Legislation & Program Planning Branch

Director, Chris Lovelace, act. (387-1721)

Legal Services

Director, David Edgar (387-1749)
Solicitor, David Morris

Administration & Personnel

Executive Director of Finance & Admin., Bill Stewart (387-3609)
Director of Finance, Bill MacMunn (387-1288)
Director of Personnel, vacant (387-1247)

Consumer Affairs

Director, Consumer Education & Information Branch, John Usher (387-1251)
Trade Liaison Chief, Arch Snow (387-1251)
A/Director, Operations Branch, Bruce McCulloch (387-1271)
Registrar of Motor Dealers, Norm Manning (387-1271)
Registrar of Travel Agents, Bill Rourke (1050 W. Pender, Vancouver, B.C. V6E 3S7, 668-3029)
Consumer Centres
1130 W. Pender St., Vancouver, B.C. V6E 4A4, Manager, Eileen Wershler (668-2911)
940 Blanshard St., Victoria, B.C. V8W 3E6, Manager, David Nicholls (387-6831)
521 Seymour St., Kamloops, B.C. V2C 2G8, Manager, Margaret Spina (374-5676)
280 Victoria St., Prince George, B.C. V2L 4X3, Manager, Rick Clements (562-9331)
Director, Consumer Credit & Debtor Assistance Branch, Harry Atkinson, Victoria, V8W 3E6 (387-1747)

Branch at: 1130 W. Pender St., Vancouver, B.C. V6E 4A4
Debt Counsellors at all Consumer Centres plus: Nanaimo, #25, 1150 Terminal Ave. N., V9S 5L6 (753-7151)
Director, Investigation Branch, Michael Hanson (387-3548)

Corporate Affairs

Registrar of Companies, Maurice Jorre de St. Jorre (387-3966)
Supervisor, Central Registry, Bill Collier (387-3229)
Supt., Brokers, Real Estate & Insurance, R.L. Bullock, 8th floor, 1050 W. Pender St., Vancouver, B.C. V6E 3S7 (682-7031)
Supt., Credit Unions, Co-operatives & Trust Companies, J. Henry Thomas, 7th floor, 1050 W. Pender St., Vancouver, B.C. V6E 3S7 (668-2947)

Agencies, Boards & Commissions

Auditors Certification Board
Contact: Rupert Bullock (Supt. of Brokers, Insurance & Real Estate), 1050 W. Pender St., Vancouver, B.C. V6E 3S7 (682-7031)
Corporate & Financial Services Commission
#204, 1148 Hornby St., Vancouver, B.C. V6Z 1V8
Chairman, W.H.K. Edmonds, Q.C. (668-2987)
Travel Assurance Board
Chairman, Gustav Kroll (682-4704)
c/o Registrar of Travel Services, #600, 1130 W. Pender St., Vancouver, B.C. V6E 4A4
Credit Union Reserve Board
#430, 2609 Granville St., Vancouver, B.C. V6H 3H8
Chairman, J.T. Edwards (736-6611)
General Manager, J.R. Montgomery (736-6611)

Associated Councils

Insurance Council of B.C., #405, 325 Howe St., Vancouver, B.C. V6C 2A3 (683-8471)
Real Estate Council, #608, 626 W. Pender St., Vancouver, B.C. V6B 1V9 (683-9664)

MINISTRY OF EDUCATION

Parliament Bldgs., Victoria, B.C. V8V 1X4
Information Contact, Information Services (phone: 604 387-5041)

Acts Administered

Schools Act (and Regulations)
Colleges & Provincial Institutes Act
B.C. Educational Institutes Capital Financing Authority Act (and Regulations)
B.C. School Districts Capital Financing Authority Act
Independent Schools Support Act
Institute of Technology (B.C.) Act
Registered Music Teachers' Act
School District Housing Enabling Act

MINISTER, Hon. Brian Smith (387-5891)
Deputy Minister, R.J. Carter (387-5191)
Asst. Deputy Minister, Educational Finance Dept., J.R. Fleming (387-5191)
Ministry Comptroller, G.E. Wilcox (387-6336)
Schools Finance & Facilities Division, Executive Director, J.L. Doyle (387-5227)
Post-Secondary Finance & Facilities Division, Executive Director, Hector McIntyre (387-5351)
Asst. Deputy Minister, Management Operations Dept., Carl Daneliuk (387-5191)
Operations & Management Services Division, Executive Director, Bryan Stoodley (387-1309)
Policy & Legislative Services Division, Executive Director, John Walsh (387-5204)
Data & Information Services Division, Executive Director, Dr. Nancy Greer (387-6925)
Asst. Deputy Minister, Schools Dept., Glenn Wall (387-5191)
Programs Division, Executive Director, Dr. Jerry Mussio (387-6925)
Operations & Services Division, Executive Director, Dr. A.J.H. Newberry (387-6934)
Special Education Division, Executive Director, Wayne Desharnais (387-1842)
Institutional Affairs Division, Executive Director, W.L.B. Hawker (387-6934)
Asst. Deputy Minister, Post-Secondary Dept., Dr. G.L. Fisher (387-5191)
Continuing Education Division, Executive Director, Dr. Ron Faris (387-1411)
Management Services Division, Executive Director, Dr. J.F. Newberry (387-3032)
Program Services Division, Executive Director, Lorne Thompson (387-5712)

Associated Agencies

Academic Council, 209 Burns House, 26 Bastion Sq., Victoria, B.C. V8W 1H9 (387-6095), Executive Director, Don Couch
Management Advisory Council, 7671 Alderbridge Way, Richmond, B.C. V6X 1Z9 (273-1118), Executive Director, Robert Harris
Occupational Training Council, 7671 Alderbridge Way, Richmond, B.C. V6X 1Z9 (273-2891), Executive Director, Jack Cooper
Joint Board of Teacher Education, #207, 26 Bastion Sq., Victoria, B.C. V8W 1H9 (387-3530), Chairman, Dr. R.J. Leskiw
Knowledge Network of the West (KNOW), Box 3200, Victoria, B.C. V8W 3H4 (721-5669), Co-ordinator, Network Field Services, Glen Mitchell

PROVINCIAL EMERGENCY PROGRAM

Parliament Bldgs., Victoria, B.C. V8V 1X4
(604) 387-5956
Provincial Emergency Program Director, R.E. Neale

B.C. ENERGY COMMISSION

21st floor, 1177 W. Hastings St., Vancouver, B.C. V6E 2L7
(604) 689-1831
Chairman, Marie Taylor
Commrs., Donald Kilpatrick, J.D.V. Newlands, Barry Sullivan

MINISTRY OF ENERGY, MINES & PETROLEUM RESOURCES

Parliament Bldgs., Victoria, B.C. V8V 1X4
Information Contact, P. Hrushowy (phone: 604 387-5200)

Acts Administered

B.C. Utilities Commission Act
Coal Act
Copper Industry Incentive Act
Geothermal Resource Act
Indian Reserve Mineral Resource Act
Mineral Act
Mineral Land Tax Act
Mineral Processing Act
Mineral Prospectors Act
Mineral Resource Tax Act
Mines Act
Mining (Placer) Act
Ministry of Energy, Mines & Petroleum Resources Act
Petroleum & Natural Gas Act
Petroleum Underground Storage Act

MINISTER, Hon. R.H. McClelland
Deputy Minister, R. Illing
Asst. Deputy Minister, Finance & Admin., John Lewis
Asst. Deputy Minister, Energy Resources, E.R. Macgregor
Asst. Deputy Minister, Mineral Resources, Andrew Freyman
Asst. Deputy Minister, Petroleum Resources, R.W. Durie

MINISTRY OF ENVIRONMENT

810 Blanshard St., Victoria, B.C. (Mailing: Parliament Bldgs., Victoria, B.C. V8V 1X5)
Information Contact, Information Officer (phone: (604) 387 5162)

Major Legislation Administered
Agricultural Land Commission Act
All Terrain Vehicles Act and Snowmobile Regulations
Creston Valley Wildlife Management Area Act
Dept. of the Environment Act
Ditches & Watercourses Act
Domestic Animal Protection Act
Drainage Dyking & Development Act
Drainage & Dyking Adjustment & Repeal Act
Dykes Maintenance Act
Dyking Assessment Adjustment Act
Ecological Reserves Act
Environment & Land Use Act
Fisheries Act of B.C.
Fish Inspection Act
Firearms Act
Fur Farm Act
Libby Dam Storage Reservoir Act
Litter Act
Okanagan Flood Control Act
Okanagan River Boundaries Settlement
Pesticide Control Act
Pollution Control Act
River-bank Protection Act
Water Act
Water Utilities Act
Weather Modification Activity Act
Wildlife Act

Federal Statutes
Fisheries Act, B.C. Fishery Regulations
Game Export Act
Migratory Birds Convention Act (and Regulations)
(Canada) Wildlife Act

MINISTER, Hon. Stephen Rogers
Deputy Minister, B.E. Marr
Asst. Deputy Minister, Environmental Management, A. Murray
Director, Water Management Branch, P.M. Brady
Inspector of Dykes, K.J. Chisholm
Director, Terrestrial Studies Branch, W.A. Benson
Director, Surveys & Mapping Branch, E.R. McMinn
Director, Fish & Wildlife Branch, D. Robinson
Director, Marine Resources Branch, T.G. Halsey
Director, Waste Management Branch, R.H. Ferguson
Director, Environmental Laboratory, Dr. R. Swingle
Director, Pesticide Control Branch, R. Kobylnyk
Director, Provincial Emergency Program, R.E. Neale
Chairman, Pollution Control Board, C.J.G. MacKenzie
Chairman, Pesticide Control Appeal Board, F.A. Hillier
Asst. Deputy Minister, Assessment & Planning Division, W.N. Venables
Director, Planning Branch, Dr. J. O'Riordan
Director, Assessment Branch, Dr. A.N. Boydell
Director, Aquatic Studies, Dr. R.J. Buchanan
Director, Air Studies Branch, Dr. R. Wilson
Director, Information Services Branch, R. Cameron
Public Information Officer, T.C. Jones

B.C. FERRY CORP.
818 Broughton St., Victoria, B.C. V8W 1E4
(604) 387-1401
General Manager & Chief Executive Officer, C. Gallagher

MINISTRY OF FINANCE
Parliament Bldgs., Victoria, B.C. V8V 1X4
Information from Information Services (phone: 604-387-1557)

Acts Administered
Assessment Act
Assessment Authority Act
Auditor General Act
Bonding Act
B.C. Corporation Income Tax Act
B.C. Electric Company Acquisition Act
B.C. Railway Company Share Capital Purchase Act, 1972
B.C. Railway Finance Act
Business Licence Act
Capital Commission Act
Commonwealth Trust Matching Financial Assistance Act
Corporation Capital Tax Act
Deficit Repayment Act
Educational Institution Capital Finance Act
Esquimalt & Nanaimo Railway Belt Tax Act
Financial Control Act
Financial Administration Act
Financial Information Act
Funds Control Act
Gasoline (Coloured) Tax Act
Gasoline Tax Act
Gasoline Tax Act, 1958
Horse Racing Tax Act
Hospital District Finance Act
Hotel Room Tax Act
Income Control Act
Inflation Tax Act
Inscribed Stock Act
Insurance Premium Tax Act
Land Tax Deferment Act
Law Stamp Act
Loan Authorization Cancellation Act
Logging Tax Act
Mining Tax Act
Motive Fuel Tax Act
Municipal Aid Act
Obsolete Statutes Repeal Act, 1980
Pacific North Coast Native Co-operative Act
Petroleum Sales Act
Power Development Act
Probate Fee Act
Public Service Bonding Act
Purchasing Commission Act
Revenue Act
Social Service Tax Act
Special Assistance in the Cost of Education Act
Special Funds Act
Special Purpose Appropriation Act, 1980
Supply Act - annual
System Act
Taxation (Rural Area) Act
Tobacco Tax Act
Toll Removal Act
Toll Removal Act, 1964
Trade Licence Act
Transmission Line (Underground) Act
Unclaimed Money Act
Universities Real Estate Development Corp. Act

MINISTER, Hon. Hugh A. Curtis
Deputy Minister, L.I. Bell
Asst. Deputy Minister (Treasury & Admin.), H.G. Ferguson
Asst. Deputy Minister (Economics & Policy), D.L. Emerson
Asst. Deputy Minister (Revenue), K.M. Lightbody
Comptroller General, D.R. Alexander
Deputy Secretary, Treasury Board, K.O. Saddlemyer
Ministry Controller, W.E. Evans
Director, Data Processing, P.W. Wilkinson
Director, Treasury, P.M. O'Neill
Director, Government Agencies, George Brodie
Director, Personnel & Payroll, T.F. Cuthbert
Director, Financial Policy & Analysis, Alan Eastwood
Director, Tax & Fiscal Policy, P.J. Adams
Director, Economics & Statistics, Larry Blain
Director, Consumer Taxation, E.J. Turner
Director, Revenue Admin. & Collections, Norm Mogensen
Director, Income Taxation, Keith Prowse
A/Surveyor of Taxes, C.E. Holder
Director, Natural Resources & Economic Development, P. Halkett
Director, Justice & Regulatory Services, W.D. Mitchell
Director, Services to Government, E.L. Munro

Associated Agencies

B.C. Regional Hospital Dists. Financing Authority (Chairman, Hon. H.A. Curtis)
Assessment Appeal Board (Chairman, W.M. Anderson)
B.C. Assessment Authority (Chairman, J.T. Gwartney)
B.C. Systems Corp. (Chairman, C.R. Mallory Smith)
Treasury Board (Chairman, Hon. H.A. Curtis)
B.C. Educational Institutions Capital Financing Authority (Chairman, Hon. H.A. Curtis)
B.C. School District Capital Financing Authority (Chairman, Hon. H.A. Curtis)
Provincial Capital Commission (Chairman, M.D.W. Young)
Purchasing Commission (Chairman, A.W. Charlton)
The address for each of the above is Parliament Bldgs., Victoria, B.C. V8V 1X4

MINISTRY OF FORESTS

Parliament Bldgs., Victoria, B.C. V8V 1X4
Information Contact, Information Services Branch (phone: (604) 387 5985); Ministry Offices: 1450 Government St.

Acts Administered

Boom Chain Brands Act
Forest Act
Ministry of Forests Act
Range Act

MINISTER, Hon. Thomas Waterland
Deputy Minister, T.M. Apsey
Asst. Deputy Minister, Operations, R. Robbins
Regional Managers:
Vancouver, D.T. Grant
Prince Rupert (located in Smithers), J.A. Biickert
Prince George, J.R. Cuthbert
Cariboo (located in Williams Lake), J.A.D. McDonald
Kamloops, A.B. Robinson
Nelson, M.G. Isenor
Asst. Deputy Minister, Forestry Division (Chief Forester), W. Young
(includes Planning, Inventory, Research, Silviculture, and Protection)
Asst. Deputy Minister (Timber, Range & Recreation Division), A.C. MacPherson
(includes Range Management, Timber Management, Recreation Management, Valuation, and Engineering)
Asst. Deputy Minister (Finance & Admin.), R.J. Cullen
(includes Personnel, Training Services, Comptroller, Systems, Legal & Administrative Services, and Technical Services)

MINISTRY OF HEALTH

Parliament Bldgs., Victoria, B.C. V8V 1X4
Information from: Support Services Centre, 836 Roderick St., Admin. Officer, C.M.L. Buchanan (604/387-6631)

Acts Administered

Adoption Act (certain sections)
Alcohol & Drug Commission Act
Ambulance Act
Anatomy Act
Chiropractors Act
Community Care Facility Act
Community Resource Board Act (certain sections)
Constitution Act (certain sections)
Dental Technicians Act (certain sections)
Dentists Act
Forensic Psychiatry Act
Good Samaritan Act (certain sections)
Health Act
Health Emergency Act
Health Science Centre (UBC) Act
Hearing Aid Act
Heroin Treatment Act
Hospital Act
Hospital (Auxiliary) Act
Hospital District Finance Act (certain sections)
Hospital Districts Act
Hospital Insurance Act
Human Tissue Gift Act
Marriage Act
Medical Practitioners Act
Medical Service Act
Mental Health Act
Ministry of Health Act
Name Act
Naturopaths Act
Nurses (Registered) Act
Nurses (Psychiatric) Act
Nurses (Practical) Act
Optometrists Act
Pharmacists Act (certain sections)
Physiotherapists Act
Podiatrists Act
Psychologists Act
Public Toilet Act
Tuberculosis Institution Act
Venereal Disease Act
Vital Statistics Act
Wills Act (part II)

MINISTER, Hon. J.A. Nielsen
Deputy Minister, Dr. Chapin Key, 387-5494

Ministry Support Services

Asst. Deputy Minister, J. Bainbridge, 387-5401
Management Services, Director, J.P.B. Langran, 387-5811
Support Services Centre, 836 Roderick St., Admin. Officer, C.M.L. Buchanan, 387-6631
Financial Services Division, Sr. Director, R.A. Munro, 387-6655
Health Personnel, Director, W. Locker, 387-5161

Planning & Development

Executive Director, C. Buckley, 387-6776
Vital Statistics, Director of Division, W.D. Burrowes (387-6463)
For a certificate of a registration or record (including search fee covering one 3-year period): $5.00 per copy
For a certified copy, photostatic copy or photographic print of a registration (including fee for search covering one 3-year period): $5.00 per copy
For each search for one registration or record for each three-year period or fraction thereof over which the search is conducted: $2.00
Management Information Services, Director, Dr. W. Dietiker, 387-5741

Health Promotion & Information

Executive Director, M.L. Chazottes, 387-5257
Director, Nutrition & Health Education, P. Wolczuk, 387-1451
Audio Visual Centre: Program Manager, G. White, 387-5881

Community Health Services

Senior Asst. Deputy Minister, Dr. G.H. Bonham, 387-6540
Vancouver Bureau, Asst. Deputy Minister, Dr. J. Smith, 874-2331
Care Services, Asst. Deputy Minister, Mrs. I. Kelly, 387-1301
Long Term & Home Care, Director, vacant, 387-1205
Mental Health, Director, Dr. John Gray, 387-3339
Preventive Services, Asst. Deputy Minister, Dr. H.M. Richards, 387-6224
Director, Dental Health Services, Dr. A. Gray, 387-1461
Director, Epidemiology, Dr. R. White, 387-1349
Director, Public Health Nursing, L. Crane, 387-3771
Director, Public Health Inspection, A. Hindley, 387-1484
Director, Speech & Hearing, D. Zink, 387-1571

Professional & Institutional Services

Senior Asst. Deputy Minister, R. McDermit, 387-6401
Institutional Services, Asst. Deputy Minister, R. Thomson, 387-6545

Hospital Consultation & Inspection Division, Director, H.R. McGann, 387-1534
Research Division, Director, R. Goodacre, 387-3795
Medical Consultation Division, Senior Medical Consultant, Dr. C.F. Ballam, 387-3755
Hospital Construction & Planning Division, Director, G.R. Fisher, 387-3027
Finance Division, Director, A.C. Laugharne, 387-6547
Hospital Claims, Supervisor, V.A.J. Richards, 387-6551
Administrative Services Division, Director, J.D. Herbert, 387-6543
Medical Services Commission, Chairman, Dr. D.M. Bolton, 387-3411
Claims Division, Manager, W.H. Thorpe, 387-3533
Doctor Registration, C.A. Dahl, 387-5821

Alcohol & Drug Programs
Box 50, 805 W. Broadway, Vancouver, B.C. V5X 1K1
(604) 873-0263
Executive Director, J.S. Russell

Emergency Health Services Commission
Executive Director, Dr. P. Ransford, 387-6891

Dental Care Plan of B.C.
Box 1500, Victoria, B.C. V8W 8G8
Director, vacant, 387-5241

Medical Services Plan of B.C.
Box 1600, Victoria, B.C. V8W 2X9
(604) 386-3166

MINISTRY OF HUMAN RESOURCES
Parliament Bldgs., Victoria, B.C. V8V 1X4
Information Contact, T. MacDonald, Manager, Division Office Supply & Services (phone: (604) 387-3125)

Acts Administered
Adoption Act
Child Paternity & Support Act
Community Resources Bds. Act
Family & Child Service Act
Guaranteed Available Income for Need Act
Human Resources Facility Act

MINISTER, Hon. Grace M. McCarthy
Deputy Minister, John Noble
Asst. Deputy Minister, E.L. Northup
Executive Directors, T.D. Bingham, R.K. Butler, R.F. Cronin, H.E. Saville, S.G. Travers
Manager, Income Assistance Division, R.M. Willems
Manager, Health Care Division, Walter Camozzi, 800 Cassiar St., Vancouver, V5K 4N6
Manager, Family & Children's Services, Mrs. M. Dahl
Manager, Tranquille, Tranquille, B.C., T. Prysiazniuk
Manager, Woodlands, New Westminster, B.C., Dr. A.P. Hughes

HUMAN RIGHTS COMMISSION
880 Douglas St., 2nd floor, Victoria, B.C., V8W 2B7
(604) 387-5024
A/Chief Executive Officer, Ms. Hanne Jensen

B.C. HYDRO & POWER AUTHORITY
970 Burrard St., Vancouver, B.C. V6Z 1Y3
(604) 663-2212
President, J. Novman Olsen
Executive Vice President, Operations, E.H. Martin
Executive Vice President, Administration, J.P. Sheehan
Secretary, Wm. D. Mitchell

MINISTRY OF INDUSTRY & SMALL BUSINESS DEVELOPMENT
Parliament Bldgs., Victoria, B.C. V8V 1X4
Information Contact, George Baker, Information Services (604/387-6701)

Acts Administered
Ministry of Industry & Small Business Development Act
Development Corporation of B.C. Act
Statistics Act

MINISTER, Hon. Don Phillips
Deputy Minister, A.L. (Sandy) Peel
Asst. Deputy Minister, Trade & Industry, J. McKeown
Asst. Deputy Minister, Program Implementation & Co-ordination, R.A. Food
Director, Administration, B.E. Warburton

Associated Agencies
B.C. Development Corp.
272 Granville Sq., 200 Granville St., Vancouver, B.C. V6C 1S4
(604) 689-8411
B.C. Railway
1095 W. Pender St., Vancouver, B.C. V6E 2N6
(604) 681-3131
B.C. Harbours Board
#1200, 1177 W. Hastings St., Vancouver, B.C. V6E 2K3
(604) 689-8571
Executive Secretary, J.D. King

INSURANCE CORP. OF B.C. (AUTOPLAN)
Box 11131, Royal Centre, 1055 W. Georgia St., Vancouver, B.C. V6E 3R4
(604) 665-2800

MINISTRY OF INTERGOVERNMENTAL RELATIONS
Parliament Bldgs., Victoria, B.C. V8V 1X4
MINISTER, Hon. Garde B. Gardom, 387-5845
Deputy Minister, J.G. Matkin, 387-1796
Deputy Minister (Constitutional Affairs), Melvin H. Smith, 387-1796
Asst. Deputy Minister, Mark Krasnick, 387-1796
Intergovernmental Relations Officers: Rm. 276D, 387-1796, 387-6958

MINISTRY OF LABOUR
Parliament Bldgs., Victoria, B.C. V8V 1X4
Information Contact, Jack Ross, A/Director, Information Services (phone: 604 387-6575)

Acts Administered
Apprenticeship Act
Boiler & Pressure Vessel Act
Electrical Energy Inspection Act
Employment Standards Act
Essential Services Disputes Act
Factory Act
Gas Act
Human Rights Code
Labour Code
Ministry of Labour Act
Wage (Public Construction) Act
Refugee Settlement Act
Workers' Compensation Act

Other Statutes Affecting Labour
Barbers Act
Builders Lien Act
Coal Mine Regulation Act
Fire Department Act
Hairdressers Act
Labour Regulation Act
Mining Regulation Act
Public Service Labour Relations Act
Repairers Lien Act
Woodworkers Lien Act

MINISTER, Hon. Jack Heinrich, 387-1986
Executive Asst., Richard Butler, 387-3336
Deputy Minister, Douglas Cameron, 387-3282
Administrative Asst., Michael Taylor, 387-5495
Asst. Deputy Minister, Finance & Administration, Human Rights, and Employment Standards, Stephen Stackhouse, 387-5611
Program Services Branch, A/Director, Claude Heywood, 387-5141
Finance & Administration, Director, Heinz Schwarz, 387-1615
Personnel, A/Director, Tony Raymond, 387-1564
Information Services, A/Director, Jack Ross, 387-6575
Human Rights, A/Director, Hanne Jensen, 387-6861
Policy, Arbitration & Special Services, Director, Alan Portigal, 387-1281
Employment Standards, Director, Ralph Sollis, 387-3284
Asst. Deputy Minister, Manpower, Robert Gray, (Vancouver, 291-6122)
Apprenticeship, Director, Blair Anderson, (Vancouver, 294-3878)
Employment Training, Director, Virginia Greene, 387-1131
Trade Schools, Director, Ossie Sylvester, (Vancouver, 291-7591)
Consultative Services, Director, Ranjit Azad, (Vancouver, 291-6116)
Refugee Settlement & Immigration, Director, Wayne Mullins, (Vancouver, 291-8222)
Asst. Deputy Minister, Labour Relations & Safety Services, Douglas Cameron (act.), (Vancouver, 291-7351)
Mediation Services, A/Director, Clark Gilmour, (Vancouver, 291-0681)
Labour Education, Director, Ron Tweedie, (Vancouver, 291-6126)
Compensation Advisory Services, Employees, W. Flesher, (Vancouver, 291-9448)
Compensation Advisory Services, Employers, B. Bucher, (Vancouver, 291-0401)
Occupational Environment, Director, Ken Martin, (Vancouver, 291-9494)
Executive Director, Safety Engineering Services, Wilf Lawson, (Vancouver, 879-7531)
Electrical Safety, Director, Al Luck
Gas Safety, Director, W. Montgomery
Elevating Devices, Director, Alf Moser
Boiler & Pressure Vessel Safety, Director, Brian Cole
Legal Services, M. Crimp, 387-5142

Boards & Commissions

Employment Standards Board
880 Douglas St., Victoria, B.C. V8W 2B7
(604) 387-6801
Chairman, J.R. Edgett

Labour Relations Board of B.C.
1275 W. 6th Ave., Vancouver, B.C. V6H 1A6
(604) 736-2421
Chairman, vacant

Human Rights Commission
880 Douglas St., Victoria, B.C. V8W 2B7
(604) 387-5024
A/Executive Director, Ms. Hanne Jensen

Workers' Compensation Board
5255 Heather St., Vancouver, B.C. V5Z 3L8
(604) 266-0211
Chairman, vacant

Workers' Compensation Boards of Review
4946 Canada Way, Burnaby, B.C. V5G 4J6
(604) 291-7511
Administrative Chairman, Paul Devine

Essential Services Advisory Agency
659 Leg-in-Boot Sq., False Creek, Vancouver, B.C. V5Z 1B2
(604) 879-6881
Chairman, Clive McKee

Provincial Apprenticeship Board
880 Douglas St., Victoria, B.C. V8W 2B7
(604) 387-5141
Chairman, Claude Heywood

MINISTRY OF LANDS, PARKS & HOUSING

Parliament Bldgs., Victoria, B.C. V8V 1X4
Information from: Public Relations Director, 1019 Wharf St., 604/387-3502

Acts Administered

Ecological Reserves Act
Greenbelt Act
Home Conversion & Leasehold Loan Act
Home Purchase Assistance Act
Housing Construction (Elderly Citizens) Act
Land Act
Ministry of Lands, Parks & Housing Act
Mobile Home Act
Motor Vehicle (All Terrain) Act
Park Act
Park (Regional) Act
Provincial Home Acquisition Act
Recreational Land Greenbelt Encouragement Act
University Endowment Lands Administration Act
West Coast National Park Act

Regulations Administered

Air Space Titles Act (Survey Regs.)
Canada Shipping Act (Boating Regs.)
Coal Act (Survey Regs.)
Land Registry Act (Survey Regs.)
Mineral Act (Survey Regs.)
Official Surveys Act (Survey Regs.)
Petroleum & Natural Gas Act (Survey Regs.)
Strata Titles Act (Survey Regs.)

MINISTER, Hon. James R. Chabot, 387-1221
Deputy Minister, J.C. Johnston, 1019 Wharf St., 387-3397
Asst. Deputy Minister, Lands Division, Robert Ahrens, 1019 Wharf St., 387-5710
Director, Public Relations, Sybil Ainscough, 1019 Wharf St., 387-3502
Asst. Deputy Minister, Parks & Outdoor Recreation Division, Christopher Gray, 1019 Wharf St., 387-3322
Public Information Officer, John Walters, 1019 Wharf St., 387-1696
Asst. Deputy Minister, Lands & Housing Regional Operations Division, T.E. Lee, 1019 Wharf St., 387-6269
Asst. Deputy Minister, Housing Division, Andrew Armitage, 1019 Wharf St., 387-6054
Manager, Home Purchase Assistance, Harry Rounds, 838 Fort St., 387-5381
Manager, Mobile Home Registry, Marion Price, 838 Fort St., 387-5381
Surveyor General, vacant, 345 Quebec St., 387-3240

B.C. Housing Management Commission

515 W. 10th St., Vancouver, B.C. V5Z 4A8
(604) 873-0313
General Manager, Keith Davis
Chairman, Mary Kerr

MINISTRY OF MUNICIPAL AFFAIRS

747 Fort St., Victoria, B.C. (Mailing address: Parliament Bldgs., Victoria, B.C. V8V 1X4)
Information Contact, Joan Stephens, Education & Information Officer (phone: 604/387-5925)

Acts Administered

Municipal Act
Municipalities Enabling & Validating Act
Local Services Act
Municipal Finance Authority of B.C. Act
Mobile Home Tax Act

Urban Transit Authority Act
Sewerage Facilities Assistance Act
Resort Municipality of Whistler Act
Revenue Sharing Act
Provincial Transit Service Act
Islands Trust Act

MINISTER, Hon. W.N. Vander Zalm
Deputy Minister, J.P. Taylor
Inspector of Municipalities, C.H.L. Woodward, F.C.I.S.
Asst. Deputy Minister, G.C. Harkness
Asst. Deputy Minister & Deputy Inspector of Municipalities, T.F. Moore, F.C.I.S.
Executive Officer, G.E. Whelen, F.C.I.S.
Executive Director, Admin., J.G. Callan, A.C.I.S.
Executive Director, Planning, E. Karlsen
Executive Director, Finance, H.G. Topham, C.A.
Director, Research Branch, K. McLeod
Director, Building Standards Branch, J. Currie
Director, Engineering Branch, A. McTaggart

Associated Agencies
Islands Trust
Urban Transit Authority

B.C. PETROLEUM CORP.
600 1199 W. Hastings St., Vancouver, B.C. V6E 3T5
(604) 685-0411
Chairman, Hon. Robert H. McClelland
Directors, P. McGeer, L. Mulholland, D. Rawlyk
Secretary, Bruna Martinuzzi
Comptroller, Gordon S. Thomas
Manager, Gas Supply & Special Projects, S.T. Akers
General Manager & Manager, Natural Gas Division, D.W. Rawlyk

MINISTRY OF PROVINCIAL SECRETARY & GOVERNMENT SERVICES
Room 247, Main Parliament Bldgs., Victoria, B.C. V8V 1X4
Information Contact, P.A. Battisson, Administrative Officer (phone: 604-387-6604)

Acts Administered
Blind Persons Contribution Act
B.C. Buildings Corporation Act
British Columbia Day Act
Constitution Act
Document Disposal Act
Dogwood, Rhododendron & Trillium Act
Douglas Day Act
Election Act
Emblem & Tartan Act
Financial Disclosure Act
Heritage Conservation Act
Indian Advisory Act
Inquiry Act
Klondike National Historic Park Act
Legislative Assembly Allowances & Pension Act
Legislative Assembly Privilege Act
Legislative Library Act
Legislative Procedure Review Act
Library Act
Lottery Act
Ministry of the Provincial Secretary & Government Services Act
Museum Act
Pacific National Exhibition Incorporation Act
Pension Agreement Act
Pension (College) Act
Pension (Municipal) Act
Pension (Public Service) Act
Pension Society Act
Pension (Teachers) Act
Public Service Act
Public Service Benefit Plan Act
Public Service Labour Relations Act
Queen's Printer Act
Recreational Facilities Act
Scholarship Act
Transpo 86 Corporation Act

PROVINCIAL SECRETARY & MINISTER OF GOVERNMENT SERVICES, Hon. E. Wolfe
Deputy Provincial Secretary, I.L. Thomson
Asst. Deputy Minister, Information Programs, Douglas Heal
Asst. Deputy Ministers, Jerry Woytack, Barry Kelsey, Allan Turner
Chief, Protocol & Special Services, David Harris
Director, Library Services, P. Martin
Director, Cultural Services, Tom Fielding
Director, Heritage Conservation, R. Irvine
Director, Recreation & Fitness, Dr. C. Campbell
Chairman, Government Employees Relations Bureau, Mike Davison
Chief Electoral Officer, H. Goldberg
Secretary, Government House, Victoria, J.M. Roberts
Director, Postal Branch, L.E. Hall
Public Service Commission, Chairman, R.W. Long
Queen's Printer, H. Britt
Superannuation Commr., J.D. Reid
Central Microfilm Services, Director, H.B. Bennett
Legislative Librarian, J.G. Mitchell
Provincial Archivist, John Bovey
First Citizens' Fund Administration, Director, R. Modeste
Provincial Museum, Director, Yorke Edwards
B.C. Lottery, Director, Jim Taylor
Tour Guides, Co-ordinator, Lynn McCaughey

PUBLIC SERVICE COMMISSION
544 Michigan, Victoria, B.C. V8V 1S3
Chairman, R.W. Long (387-5263)
Commrs., W.N. Venables, Marie Taylor

Division Directors
Executive Director, Staffing, K.M. Hanson, 387-5263
Executive Director, Staff Development & Safety Programs, W.R. Tremaine, 387-1561

B.C. RESEARCH
3650 Wesbrook Mall, Vancouver, B.C. V6S 2L2
(604) 224-4331
Executive Director, V.A. Mode, Ph.D.

B.C. STEAMSHIP CO. (1975) LTD. (A Crown Corp.)
254 Belleville St., Victoria, B.C.
(604) 388-7397

MINISTRY OF TOURISM
1117 Wharf St., Victoria, B.C. V8W 2Z2
Information from: Ben J. Pires, (604/387-5498)

Acts Administered
Ministry of Tourism Act
B.C. Government Travel Bureau Act

MINISTER, Hon. Pat J. Jordan
Deputy Minister, Dr. J.R. Rae, Victoria, 387-1906
Asst. Deputy Minister, Marketing, J.G. Plul
Vancouver Office: 800 Hornby St., Vancouver, B.C. V6Z 2C5, 668-2861
Victoria: 387-6929
Asst. Deputy Minister, Operations, J.F. Currie, Victoria, 387-6929

Beautiful British Columbia Magazine
Editorial Office: 1117 Wharf St., 387-6487
Subscription Office: 200 Esquimalt Rd., Victoria, B.C. V9A 7B4, 387-3692/3651

MINISTRY OF TRANSPORTATION & HIGHWAYS

940 Blanshard St., Victoria, B.C. V8W 3E6 (Highways)
2631 Douglas St., Victoria, B.C. V8T 4X7 (Transportation)
Information Contact: R.J. Baines, Senior Information Officer (604/387-3182)

Acts Administered

Highway Act
Engineering Profession Act
Commercial Transport Act
Motor Vehicle Act
Motor Carrier Act
Highways Scenic Improvement Act
Ferry Act
Pipe Line Act
Railway Act
Riverbank Protection Act
Ministry of Transportation & Highways Act
Motor Vehicle Transportation Act (Canada)
Highway (Industrial) Act

MINISTER, Hon. Alex V. Fraser
Deputy Minister, R.G. Harvey, P.Eng.
Asst. Deputy Minister, Admin., A.E. Rhodes (387-3185) - includes Personnel Services, Financial Services, Information Services, Air Services, Property Services
Asst. Deputy Minister, Operations, T.R. Johnson, P.Eng. (387-3260) - includes Engineering (highway design & surveys, geotechnical & materials engineering, bridge engineering, traffic engineering, planning, highway safety engineering), Construction (highway construction & paving), Operations Services (highway maintenance & equipment services)
Asst. Deputy Minister, Transport Policy, D.A. Kasianchuk, Ph.D. (387-3362)
Chief Inspection Engineer, F. Christensen (4299 Canada Way, Burnaby)
Supt. of Motor Vehicles, R.G. Whitlock
Director, Weigh Scales, J. McDicken
Chairman, Motor Carrier Commission, Judge G. Ross Sutherland (#203, 535 Thurlow St., Vancouver) 668-2903
Supt. of Motor Carriers, A.R. Fitch (4240 Manor St., Burnaby)

TREASURY BOARD

Parliament Bldgs., Victoria, B.C. V8V 1X4
(604) 387-5801
Chairman, Hon. Hugh A. Curtis
Members, Hon. W.R. Bennett, Hon. G.B. Gardom, Hon. B. Smith, Hon. R.H. McClelland, Hon. E.M. Wolfe
Secretary, L.I. Bell
Chairman, Government Employee Relations Bureau, M. Davison

MINISTRY OF UNIVERSITIES, SCIENCE & COMMUNICATIONS

Parliament Bldgs., Victoria, B.C. V8V 1X4
Information from: Finance & Administration (604/387-3690)

Acts Administered

Educational Institution Capital Finance Act
Science Council Act
Special Purpose Appropriation Act, 1980, ss. 1 (g), (h), (i)
Telephone (Rural) Act
University Act

MINISTER, Hon. Dr. Pat McGeer, 387-6580
Deputy Minister, Dr. Robert Stewart, 387-6008
Asst. Deputy Minister, Universities, A.E. Soles
Asst. Deputy Minister, Communications, H.J. Page, 387-1417
Director, Finance & Admin., N.N. Aleksenko, 387-3690
Communications
Director, Systems Development & Regulation Branch, T.A. Prentice, 387-5446
Director, Telecommunications Services Branch, R. Mussenden, 387-5411

Asst. Director, Common Carrier Systems, G.H. Stock, 387-6967
Metric Conversion, Executive Director, E. Gosh, 387-6864

WORKERS' COMPENSATION BOARD

5255 Heather St., Vancouver, B.C. V5Z 3L8
(604) 266-0211
Chairman, vacant
Commrs., J. Miazowa, M. Parr
Executive Director, Admin. & Finance, J. Taylor
Executive Director, Compensation Services, A. Mullan
Executive Director, Prevention Services, C. Calhoun
Executive Director, Legal, I. Tufts
Executive Director, Medical Services, Dr. J. Gibbings

PROVINCE OF MANITOBA

Entered Confederation July 15, 1870.
Area: 251,000 Sq. Miles.
Population: 1979, 1,098,904
Seat of Government: Legislative Bldg., Winnipeg, Man.
Lieutenant-Governor: The Hon. Pearl McGonigal
Official Secretary: Mrs. K. Brown

EXECUTIVE COUNCIL (1981)

Premier, President of the Council, and Minister of Dominion Provincial Relations, Hon. Sterling Lyon, Q.C., Rm. 204, 944-3714
Minister of Energy & Mines, and Deputy Premier, Hon. Donald William Craik, Rm. 156, 944-4601
Minister without Portfolio, Hon. Edward Robert McGill, Rm. 172, 944-4219
Minister of Government Services, Hon. Warner H. Jorgenson, Rm. 141, 944-2979
Minister of Health, Hon. Louis Ralph Sherman, Rm. 301, 944-3731
Minister of Economic Development & Tourism, Hon. John Franklin Johnston, Rm. 358, 944-3903
Minister of Agriculture, Hon. James Erwin Downey, Rm. 165, 944-3722
Minister of Education, Hon. Keith Alan Cosens, Rm. 168, 944-3720
Attorney General, and Minister for Urban Affairs, Hon. Gerald Wayne J. Mercier, Rm. 104, 944-3728
Minister of Fitness, Recreation & Sport, and Minister of Co-operative Development, Hon. Robert David Banman, Rm. 333, 944-3719
Minister of Cultural Affairs & Historical Resources, Hon. Norma Lorraine Price, Rm. 343, 944-3729
Minister of Labour & Manpower, Hon. Ken MacMaster, Rm. 227, 944-3741
Minister of Finance, Hon. Alan Brian Ransom, Rm. 103, 944-3952
Minister of Natural Resources, Hon. Harry J. Enns, Rm. 302, 944-3730
Minister of Community Services & Corrections, Hon. George Clement Minaker, Rm. 314, 944-3048
Minister of Municipal Affairs, and Minister of Northern Affairs, Hon. Douglas Macleod Gourlay, Rm. 330, 944-3788
Minister of Highways & Transportation, Hon. Donald Warder Orchard, Rm. 203, 944-3723
Minister of Consumer & Corporate Affairs & Environment, Hon. Gary Filmon, Rm. 357, 944-3725

Clerk of Executive Council, D.R.C. Bedson, Rm. 204, 944-3717

LEGISLATIVE ASSEMBLY

Thirty-first Legislature. Last Election October 11, 1977. Legal Duration, 5 Years.

Party Standings: Progressive Conservative (P.C.) 32; New Democratic Party (N.D.P.) 20; Liberal (Lib.) 1; Progressive Party of Manitoba (Prog.) 3; Vacant 1; Total 57.
Leader of the Opposition, Howard Pawley, Q.C.
Indemnities & Allowances: Members' Sessional Indemnity, $17,966.26, plus an Expense Allowance of $8,983.13 and a Constituency Allowance of $1,500. In addition to the Sessional Indemnity, the Premier receives $26,600. Other Ministers receive $20,600. (Manitoba has a cost of living indexing system as prescribed by Sec. 59(3) of The Legislative Assembly Act).
Officers: Speaker, Hon. Harry E. Graham; Law Officers, R.H. Tallin; A.C. Balkaran; Clerk of Assembly, Jack R. Reeves (phone 944-3707); Clerk's Asst., Gordon Mackintosh; Sergeant-at-Arms, Edward Laing

Members of the Legislative Assembly

Following is constituency (number of registered voters in brackets): member, party affiliation and business phone number: NOTE:- Address for all is Legislative Bldg., Winnipeg, Man. R3C OV8

Arthur (8,563): Jim Downey, P.C., 944-3722
Assiniboia (17,105): Norma Price, P.C., 944-3729
Birtle-Russell (7,952): Harry E. Graham, P.C., 944-3706
Brandon East (11,052): Leonard S. Evans, N.D.P., 944-3710
Brandon West (15,200): Edward McGill, P.C., 944-3727
Burrows (9,295): Ben Hanuschak, Prog., 944-4807
Charleswood (20,763): Sterling Lyon, Q.C., P.C., 944-3713
Churchill (9,501): Jay Cowan, N.D.P., 944-3710
Crescentwood (11,588): Warren Steen, P.C., 944-3709
Dauphin (10,516): Jim Galbraith, P.C., 944-3709
Elmwood (11,195): Russell J. Doerr N.D.P., 944-3710
Emerson (8,646): Albert Dreidger 4-3709
Flin Flon (7,679): Thomas Barro 944-3710
Fort Garry (21,742): L.R. (Bud) P.C., 944-3731
Fort Rouge (14,272): June W b., 944-2962
Gimli (9,849): Keith Cosens -3720
Gladstone (9,948): James on, P.C., 944-3709
Inkster (12,836): Sidney C., Prog., 944-4012
Kildonan (14,390): Pet D.P., 944-3710
Lac Du Bonnet (11,7? skiw, N.D.P., 944-3710
Lakeside (9,414): H ns, P.C., 944-3730
La Verendrye (11 Banman, P.C., 944-3719
Logan (7,760): V nkins, N.D.P., 944-3710
Minnedosa (9 d Blake, P.C., 944-3709
Morris (8,95 H. Jorgenson, P.C., 944-2979
Osborne (1 erry Mercier, Q.C., P.C., 944-3728
Pembina onald Orchard, P.C., 944-3723
Point Du 93): Donald Malinowski, N.D.P., 944-3710
Portage la Pr e (9,665): Lloyd G. Hyde, P.C., 944-3709

SEE ADDENDA

Radisson (11,841): Abe Kovnats, P.C., 944-3709
Rhineland (10,217): Arnold Brown, P.C., 944-3709
Riel (24,817): Donald W. Craik, P.C., 944-4601
River Heights (10,459): Gary Filmon, P.C., 944-3725
Roblin (7,570): J. Wally McKenzie, P.C., 944-3709
Rock Lake (8,409): Henry J. Einarson, P.C., 944-3709
Rossmere (22,189): Vic Schroeder, N.D.P., 944-3710
Rupertsland (6,809): Harvey Bostrom, N.D.P., 944-3710
St. Boniface (11,024): Laurent L. Desjardins, N.D.P., 944-3710
St. George (7,813): Bill Uruski, N.D.P., 944-3710
St. James (11,327): George Minaker, P.C., 944-3048
St. Johns (9,442): Saul Cherniack, Q.C., N.D.P., 944-3710
St. Matthews (9,327): Len Domino, P.C., 944-3709
St. Vital (11,154): D.J. Walding, N.D.P., 944-3710
Ste. Rose (8,218): A.R. (Pete) Adam, N.D.P., 944-3710
Selkirk (12,299): Howard Pawley, Q.C., N.D.P., 944-3712
Seven Oaks (19,813): Saul A. Miller, N.D.P., 944-3710
Souris Killarney (9,568): Brian Ransom, P.C., 944-3952
Springfield (12,952): Bob Anderson, P.C., 944-3709
Sturgeon Creek (15,702): J. Frank Johnston, P.C., 944-3724
Swan River (9,102): Douglas Gourlay, P.C., 944-3788
The Pas (8,909): Ron McBryde, N.D.P., 944-3710
Thompson (10,786): Ken MacMaster, P.C., 944-3741
Transcona (15,408): Wilson Parasiuk, N.D.P., 944-3710
Virden (7,836): Morris McGregor, P.C., 944-3709
Wellington (8,650): Brian Corrin, N.D.P., 944-3710
Winnipeg Centre (7,843): J.R. (Bud) Boyce, Prog., 944-4806
Wolseley (9,167): vacant

OFFICE OF THE PREMIER

204 Legislative Bldg., Winnipeg, Man. R3C OV8
Premier, Hon. Sterling Lyon, Q.C. (204/944-3714)
Clerk of the Executive Council, D.R.C. Bedson (944-3717)
Executive Asst. to the Premier, Mrs. Olive MacPhail (944-3715)
Special Asst. to the Premier, W.R. McCance (944-3716)
Private Secretary, Mrs. Shirley Goerzen (944-3714)

GOVERNMENT DEPARTMENTS

DEPT. OF AGRICULTURE

Legislative Bldg., Winnipeg, Man. R3C OV8
Information Contact, R.L. Baseraba, Director, Administrative & Accounting Services, 809 Norquay Bldg., 401 York Ave., Winnipeg, Man. R3C 0V8 (phone: 204/944-3433)

Acts Administered

Agricultural Credit Corp. Act
Agricultural Lands Protection Act
Agricultural Productivity Council Act
Agricultural Societies Act
Dept. of Agriculture Act
Animal Diseases Act
Animal Husbandry Act (except Parts I, II & IV)
Bee Act
Bee Keepers Act
Cattle Producers Association Act
Coarse Grain Marketing Control Act
Community Seed Cleaning Plant Loans Act
Crop Insurance Act
Crown Lands Act (only concerning the issue of leases and permits of occupation, or use and related administration of primarily agricultural lands or having a secondary agricultural use)
Dairy Act
Farm Machinery & Equipment Act
Fruit & Vegetable Sales Act
Horned Cattle Purchases Act
Horse Racing Regulation Act
Horticultural Society Act
Land Rehabilitation Act
Livestock & Livestock Products Act
Margarine Act
Milk Prices Review Act
Natural Products Marketing Act
Noxious Weeds Act
Pesticides & Fertilizers Control Act
Plant Pests & Diseases Act
Poultry Breeders Act
Seed & Fodder Relief Act
Veterinary Medical Act
Veterinary Science Scholarship Fund Act
Veterinary Services Act
Water Services Board Act
Women's Institutes Act

MINISTER, Hon. James E. Downey
Deputy Minister, R.C. Bailey
Management Services Division, Asst. Deputy Minister, G.J. Lacomy
(Division includes Internal Audit & Systems, Administrative & Accounting Services, Financial Administration, Computer Services Unit, Personnel Services, Program Analysis)
Production Division, Asst. Deputy Minister, T.L. Pringle
Director, Agricultural Training Branch, R.M. Deveson

Director, Animal Industry Branch, C.H. McNaughton, Agric. Services Complex, Univ. of Manitoba Campus, 269-1220
Director, Communications Branch, V.E. McNair
Director, Technical Services Branch, E.T. Oatway
Director, Soils & Crops Branch, C.C. Cranston
Director, Veterinary Services Branch, Dr. J.A. McPhedran, Agric. Services Complex, Univ. of Manitoba Campus, 269-1220
Principal, Agricultural Extension Centre, K. Smith, 1129 Queen's Ave., Brandon, 728-5724

Director, Central Region, G.A. Arnott, 25 Tupper St. N., Portage la Prairie, Man. R1N 3K1, 857-9711
Director, Eastern Region, F.J. Slevinsky, Box 50, 250 1st St., Beausejour, Man. R0E 0C0, 268-1411
Director, Interlake Region, D. Webster, Box 2000, 317 River Rd., Arborg, Man. R0C 0A0, 376-5212
Director, Northwest Region, G. Arnal, 302 Main St. S., Dauphin, Man. R7N 1K7, 638-9711
Director, Southwest Region, J. Neabel, Agricultural Extension Centre, 1129 Queen's Ave., Brandon, Man. R7A 1L9, 728-5724

Marketing & Development Division, Asst. Deputy Minister, M.B. Kraut
Director, Economics Branch, W.I.R. Johnson
Director, Marketing Branch, A.E. Gascoigne
Land & Water Development Division, Assoc. Deputy Minister, E.P. Hudek
Director, Agri-Water, W.E. Griffin, 2022 Currie Blvd., Brandon, 725-0912
Head, Agricultural Land Utilization Branch, J.R.D. Partridge
Head, Agri-Land, G. Crawford Jenkins
Asst. Director, Agricultural Crown Lands Section, G.T. Somers, 1495 St. James St., Winnipeg, 786-9274

Associated Agencies

Farm Machinery Board, 9th floor, Norquay Bldg., Winnipeg, Man. R3C 0P8 (944-3854), Secretary Manager, R.B. Chinn
Manitoba Agricultural Credit Corp., 1500 Notre Dame Ave., Winnipeg, Man. R3E 0P9 (786-3401), General Manager, N. Potter
Manitoba Agricultural Lands Protection Board, c/o Dept., Executive Director, J.F. Muirhead
Manitoba Crop Insurance Corp., 25 Tupper St. N., Portage la Prairie, Man. R1N 3K1 (857-9711), Manager, H.E. Tolton
Manitoba Natural Products Marketing Council, #901, 401 York Ave., Winnipeg, Man. R3C 0P8 (944-4495), Secretary, R. Kapilik
Manitoba Water Services Board, Imperial Sq. Bus. Park, 2022 Currie Blvd., Brandon, Man. R7A 5Y6 (727-5358), General Manager, vacant
Milk Prices Review Commission, #202, 379 Broadway, Winnipeg, Man. R3C 0V3 (944-4607), Executive Secretary (Economist), D. Tully

Agricultural Marketing Boards

Man. Chicken Broiler Producers' Marketing Board: E. Kitchen, General Manager, 1200 King Edward St., Winnipeg, Man. R3H OR5 (633-6617)
Man. Egg Producers' Marketing Board: H. Pauls, Secretary Manager, 1200 King Edward St., Winnipeg, Man. R3H OR5 (633-9122)
Man. Hog Producers' Marketing Board: W.B. Munro, Manager, 750 Marion St., Winnipeg, Man. R2J OK4 (233-4991)
Man. Honey Producers' Marketing Board: G. Kreutzer, Secretary, 2004 Crescent Rd. W., Portage la Prairie, Man. R1N 1A3 (857-3041)
Man. Milk Producers' Marketing Board: R. Scott, Secretary Manager, #104, 1580 Dublin Ave., Winnipeg, Man. R3E 0L4 (786-6063)
Man. Root Crop Producers' Marketing Board: D. Ring, General Manager, 1200 King Edward St., Winnipeg, Man. R3H OR5 (633-7926)
Man. Turkey Producers' Marketing Board: E. Kitchen, General Manager, 1200 King Edward St., Winnipeg, Man. R3H OR5 (633-6615)
Man. Vegetable Producers' Marketing Board: D. Ring, General Manager, 1200 King Edward St., Winnipeg, Man. R3H OR5 (633-7926)

PROVINCIAL ARCHIVES

200 Vaughan St., Winnipeg, Man. R3C 0V8
(204) 944-3971
Provincial Archivist, Peter Bower

ATTORNEY GENERAL'S DEPT.

5th floor, Woodsworth Bldg., 405 Broadway, Winnipeg, Man. R3C 3L6
For Information phone: (204) 944-2878

Acts Administered

Attorney General's Act
Condominium Act
Constitutional Questions Act
Corrections on Certain Certificates of Title Act
Corrections Act, Part II
Court of Appeal Act
County Court Judges' Criminal Courts Act
County Courts Act
Court of Queen's Bench Act
Criminal Injuries Compensation Act
Crown Attorney's Act
Escheats Act
Executive Government Org. Act (Sec. 12 (2) only, as Keeper of the Great Seal)
Expropriation Act
Extra Provincial Custody Orders Enforcement Act
Fatality Inquiries Act
Hudson's Bay Co. Land Register Act
Human Rights Act
Interprovincial Subpoena Act
Intoxicated Persons Detention Act
Reciprocal Enforcement of Judgments Act
Jury Act
Law Fees Act
Law Reform Commission Act
Legal Aid Services Society of Man. Act
Liquor Control Act
Lotteries Act (Sec. 12 only)
Reciprocal Enforcement of Maintenance Orders Act
Man. Volunteer Reserve Act
Mental Health Act, Part IV
Personal Property Security Act
Privacy Act
Private Investigators' & Security Guards' Act
Proceedings Against the Crown Act
Provincial Judges Act
Provincial Police Act
Public Trustee Act
Real Property Act
Registry Act
Regulations Act
Sheriffs Act
Special Surveys Act
Suitor's Moneys Act
Summary Convictions Act
Surrogate Courts Act
Surveys Act, Part I
Uniformity of Legislation Act, Commissioners on
Unsatisfied Judgment Fund Act (where reference is made to Attorney General)
Vacant Property Act

ATTORNEY GENERAL, Hon. Gerry W.J. Mercier, Q.C. (944-3728)
Deputy Minister, G.E. Pilkey, Q.C. (944-3739)
Director of Criminal Prosecutions, J.P. Guy (944-2873)
Director of Civil Litigation, D.W. Moylan, Q.C. (944-2847)

Legislative Counsel, R.H. Tallin (944-3708)
Public Trustee, J.D. Raichura (944-2703)
Administrator of Court Services, M. Bruce (944-2049)
Registrar of Personal Property, D. Crockatt (944-2656)
Trusts & Estates Division, 944-2710

Land Titles Districts & Registrars

Registrar-General of Manitoba, M.M. Colquhoun, 405 Broadway, Winnipeg (944-2243)
Deputy Registrar-General, C.A. Evans (944-2242)
District Registrars
Winnipeg: C.A. Evans (944-2242)
Portage la Prairie: J. Kushniruk
Brandon: E.J. Finch
Morden: R.M. Wilson
Boissevain: J. Grewal
Neepawa: Vipin Patel
Dauphin: W.A. Finch

Manitoba Liquor Control Commission

1555 Buffalo Place, Winnipeg, Man. R3T 1L9
Phone: (204) 284-2501
A/Chairman, A.B. Tevendale
Chief Inspector, Liquor Law Enforcement, D. Kirkpatrick

Criminal Injuries Compensation Board

333 Maryland St., Winnipeg, Man. R3G 1M2
(204) 775-7821

Human Rights Commission

#200, 323 Portage Ave, Winnipeg, Man. R3B 2C1
(204) 944-3007
Executive Director, vacant
Chief Human Rights Officer, J.A.K. McCuaig

Manitoba Police Commission

5th floor, 405 Broadway, Winnipeg, Man. R3C 3L6
(204) 944-2825
Executive Director, M. Mulder

OFFICE OF THE PROVINCIAL AUDITOR

Legislative Bldg., Winnipeg, Man. R3C 0V8
(204) 944-3790
Provincial Auditor, W.K. Ziprick, C.A.
Asst. Provincial Auditor, Fred H. Jackson, C.A.

DEPT. OF COMMUNITY SERVICES & CORRECTIONS

Information Contact: K. Gray, Director, Operational Support Services, 3rd floor, 210 Osborne St. N., Winnipeg, Man. R3C 0V8 (204/944-3267)

Acts Administered

Change of Name Act
Child Welfare Act
Corrections Act (except Part II)
Family Maintenance Act
Marriage Act
Parents' Maintenance Act, Sec. 10
Social Allowance Act
Social Service Administration Act
Vital Statistics Act

MINISTER, Hon. George Minaker, 944-3048
Deputy Minister, Ronald D. Johnstone, 944-3099
Executive Director, Administrative Services Division, vacant, 944-3038
Director, Vital Statistics Branch, Lou Gorski, #104, 401 York Ave., Winnipeg, 944-4168
Fee for each copy of a birth, marriage or death certificate is $5.

External Agencies & Residential Care Services Division
Executive Director, Office of Residential Care, L. Dewalt, 944-3584
Executive Director, Agency Relations, S.P. Cels, 944-3243
Community Health & Social Services Division
831 Portage Ave. – 775-9761
Director of Child Welfare, R.J. Ross
Executive Director, Rehabilitative Services, R.J. Burns
A/Director (Mentally & Physically Handicapped), D. Heslip, 895-5136
Director (Mental Retardation), Dr. G. Lowther, 775-9761
Director (Employment Services), M. Pedlow, 728-7000
Social Security Services Division
Provincial Director, Income Security Services (#301, 267 Edmonton St.), R. Freedman, 944-2696
Child Day Care Branch, Director, M. Humphrey, 944-2668
Corrections Division
Commissioner of Corrections, H.J. Schnieder, 895-5349
Director, Probation Services, 172 Doncaster St., Dr. J. Dragan, 895-5090
Director, Adult Corrections, D.H. Lawrence, 895-5370
Director, Juvenile Corrections, J. Bock, 895-5353

Associated Agency

Social Services Advisory Committee
#202, 323 Portage Ave., Winnipeg, Man. R3B 2C1 (944-3003)
Chairman, Betty Ireton
Secretary, D. Picken

DEPT. OF CONSUMER & CORPORATE AFFAIRS & ENVIRONMENT

Legislative Bldg., Winnipeg, Man. R3C 0V8
Information Contacts, Consumer Affairs: Director, Consumers Bureau, 307 Kennedy St., Winnipeg, Man. R3B 2M7 (phone: 204/956-2040); Government policies & programs: N.R. Donogh, Director, Information Services, Room 29, Legislative Bldg., Winnipeg (phone: 944-3746)

Acts Administered

Public Utilities Board Act
Mtge. Brokers & Mtge. Dealers Act
Securities Act
Business Names & Registration Act
Landlord & Tenant Act
Embalmers & Funeral Directors Act
Real Estate Brokers Act
Prearranged Funeral Services Act
Gas Pipe Line Act
Corporations Act
Consumer Protection Act
Personal Investigations Act
Insurance Act
Insurance Corporations Tax Act
Clean Environment Act
Certain regulations under The Public Health Act

MINISTER, Hon. Gary A. Filmon
Deputy Minister, J.E. Mason
Asst. Deputy Minister of Environmental Management Division, Dr. W.G. Bowen
Director of Consumers' Bureau, Paul Cavenagh
Rentalsman, Joseph Locke, 307 Kennedy St. (956-1010)
Director of Arbitration (Tenancy Arbitration Bureau), Gary Julius
Director of Corporations & Business Names Registration Branch, H. Khan
Director of Information Services Branch, N.R. Donogh
Supt. of Insurance, Miss Emily Stamp

Associated Agencies

The Public Utilities Board, No. 1146, 405 Broadway, Winnipeg, Man. R3C 3L6 (204/944-2638); Chairman, Lance Partridge
Man. Housing & Renewal Corp., 287 Broadway, Winnipeg, Man. R3C 0R9 (204/944-4748)
The Man. Securities Commission, No. 1128, 405 Broadway, Winnipeg, Man. R3C 3L6 (204/944-2548, Telex: 07-587528); Chairman, D.M. Peden, Q.C.

The Clean Environment Commission, 139 Tuxedo Blvd., Winnipeg, Man. R3N 0H6 (204/895-5333); Chairman, Stan Eagleton

Tenancy Arbitration Bureau, 10th floor, 405 Broadway Ave., Winnipeg, Man. R3C 3L6 (204/944-2476)

DEPT. OF CO-OPERATIVE DEVELOPMENT

#900, 405 Broadway, Winnipeg, Man. R3C 3L6

Information Contact, R.P. Pozernick, #302, 379 Broadway Ave., Winnipeg, Man. R3C 3N4 (phone: 204/944-4015)

Acts Administered

Co-operatives Act
Co-operative Association Loans & Loans Guarantee Act
Credit Unions Act
Credit Unions & Caisses Populaires Act
Lotteries & Gaming Control Act
Wheat Board Money Trust Act

MINISTER, Hon. Bob Banman
Deputy Minister, R.M. Brighty, 327 Leg. Bldg.
Director of Admin., R.P. Pozernick
Director of Research & Planning, W. Hadikin
Director of Co-operative & Credit Union Development, V. Hryshko
Director of Co-operative & Credit Union Regulation, H. Johnstone

Boards, Commissions & Agencies

Co-operative Loans & Loans Guarantee Board, Chairman, R. Brighty, 327 Legislative Bldg., Winnipeg, Man. R3C 0V8 (944-3748)

Co-operative Promotion Board, Chairman, R. Brighty, 405 Broadway, Winnipeg, Man. R3C 3L6 (944-3682)

Credit Union Stabilization Fund, Box 9900, 215 Garry St., Winnipeg, Man. R3C 3E2 (942-6331), Chief Executive Officer, C.P. Hansen

Le Fonds de Securité des Caisses Populaires, 390F Provencher Blvd., Winnipeg, Man. R2H 0H1 (233-6352), General Manager, Robert Balcaen

Lotteries & Gaming Licensing Board, 3rd floor, 207 Donald St., Winnipeg, Man. R3C 1M5 (944-3047), General Manager, G. Manness

Manitoba Lotteries & Gaming Control Commission, 3rd floor, 207 Donald St., Winnipeg, Man. R3C 1M5 (944-3047), General Manager, G. Manness

DEPT. OF CULTURAL AFFAIRS & HISTORICAL RESOURCES

Legislative Bldg., Winnipeg, Man. R3C 0V8

Information Contact, G.W. Gessell, Director, Finance & Administration, 3rd floor, 200 Vaughan St., Winnipeg, Man. R3C 1T5 (204/944-4080)

Acts Administered

Amusements Act, Part III
Arts Council Act
Centennial Centre Corporation Act
Le Centre Culturel Franco-Manitobain Act
Heritage Manitoba Act
Historic Sites & Objects Act
Legislative Library Act
Museums & Miscellaneous Grants Act
The Museum of Man & Nature Act
Public Libraries Act

MINISTER, Hon. Norma L. Price
Deputy Minister, J. Rene Prefontaine
Director of Finance & Administration, G.W. Gessell
Director of Cultural Development, C.W. Semchyshyn
Director of Public Library Services, K. Adams
Legislative Librarian, Mrs. Joyce Irvine
Provincial Archivist, P. Bower
Director of Historic Resources, J.D. McFarland
Director of Translation Services, A. Martin

Associated Agencies

Film Classification Board (and Film Classification Appeal Board), #6, 1313 Border St., Winnipeg, Man. R3H 0X4 (633-0547)

Manitoba Arts Council, #123, 555 Main St., Winnipeg, Man. R3B 1C3 (944-2239)

Historic Sites Advisory Board, 200 Vaughan St., Winnipeg, Man. R3C 0V8 (944-4389)

Manitoba Centennial Centre Corporation, #101, 555 Main St., Winnipeg, Man. R3B 1C3 (956-1360)

Le Centre Culturel Franco-Manitobain, 340 boul. Provencher, St. Boniface, Man. R2H 0G7 (233-8972)

Museum of Man & Nature, 190 Rupert Ave., Winnipeg, Man. R3B 0N2 (956-2830)

Heritage Manitoba Board, 3rd floor, 200 Vaughan St., Winnipeg, Man. R3C 0V8 (944-3844)

Public Library Services, 139 Hamelin St., Winnipeg, Man. R3T 4H4 (453-7549)

DOMINION-PROVINCIAL RELATIONS

The Premier's Office is responsible for Dominion-Provincial Relations. Write to Office of the Premier, Winnipeg, Man. R3C 0V8 for up-to-date information.

DEPT. OF ECONOMIC DEVELOPMENT & TOURISM

358 Legislative Bldg., Winnipeg, Man. R3C 0V8

Information from: Administrative & Internal Services (204/944-2036)

Acts Administered

Convention Centre Corporation Act
Design Institute Act
Dept. of Industry & Commerce Act
Horse Racing Commission Act
International Peace Garden Act
Manitoba Trading Corporation Act
Research Council Act
Statistics Act
Tourism & Recreation Act

MINISTER, Hon. J. Frank Johnston (944-3724)
- Special Advisor, Norm Bergman, 944-4043

Deputy Minister, R.S. Thompson, 944-3751
Special Projects Co-ordinator, R.M. Armstrong, 944-2432
Administrative & Internal Services
- Administration, W.A. Mialkowski, 944-2066
- Manitoba Bureau of Statistics (155 Carlton St.), W. Falk, 944-2988
- (Services also include: Business Library, Economics & Operations Research, Central Registry, Word Processing)

Program Development & Technical Services, Asst. Deputy Minister, I.H. Blicq, 944-2023
- Enterprise Manitoba – Industrial Development Agreement, Manager, H.G. Eliasson, 944-2465
- Program Development, Director, J.O. Allison, 944-2018
- Industrial Infrastructure, Director, S.T. Webb, 944-2415
- Human Resource Management, Director, J.D. Feindel, 944-2425
- Industrial Design, Director, J.G. Norget, 944-2468
- Technology, Director, Dr. G.S. Trick, 944-2030
- **Manitoba Research Council,** 5th floor, 155 Carlton St., Winnipeg, Man. R3C 3H8 (944-2030), Executive Director, Dr. G.S. Trick
- **Industrial Technology Centre,** 1329 Niakwa Rd., Winnipeg, Man. R3C 3H8 (255-9625), A/Director, B.G. Dodds
- **Canadian Food Products Development Centre,** Box 1240, Portage la Prairie, Man. R1N 3J9 (857-7861), Director, T.J. McEwen
- **Health Industry Development Centre,** 1329 Niakwa Rd., Winnipeg, Man. R3C 3G5 (255-9627), Director, B.G. Dodds
- **Manitoba Design Institute,** 155 Carlton St., 8th floor, Winnipeg, Man. R3C 3H8 (944-2468), Executive Director, J.G. Norget

Small Enterprise Development, General Director, L.H. Tough, 944-2015
Rural Small Enterprise Incentives, Project Manager, T.T. Dupley, 944-2019
Small Enterprise Development, Director, B.N. Docking, 944-2008
Community Commercial Development, Director, S.T. Webb, 944-2415

Enterprise Development Centres

Winnipeg Enterprise Development Centre, 1329 Niakwa Rd., Winnipeg, Man. R3C 3G5 (255-9640/41), Manager, M.B. Levy
Small Business Centre, Manager, Suzanne Mireault, 255-9624
Dauphin Enterprise Development Centre, Keays St. & Industrial Rd., Box 601, Dauphin, Man. R7N 7A5 (638-3602), Manager, Steve Davidge
Brandon Enterprise Development Centre, #320, 340 9th St., Brandon, Man. R7A 6C2 (728-3372), Manager, H.O. Bergman

Industry & Trade Development, Asst. Deputy Minister, G.E. Hayes, 944-2455
Industrial Benefits, Special Projects, D. Sprange, 944-2464
Communications & Creative Services, J.G. Norget, 944-2468
Aerospace Projects, H. Grant, 944-2432

Travel Manitoba, Asst. Deputy Minister, R.W. Yuel, 944-2229
Development, W. Barbaza, 944-2307
Marketing, R. Bridge, 944-4204
Travel Information Services, 944-4025

Associated Agencies

Manitoba Trading Corporation
5th floor, 155 Carlton St., Winnipeg, Man. R3C 3H8
(204) 944-2466
Chairman, R.S. Thompson

Manitoba Horse Racing Commission
c/o Assiniboia Downs, 3975 Portage Ave., Winnipeg, Man. R3K 1W5
(204) 837-2247
Chairman, G.S. Halter, Q.C.
Executive Secretary, D.R. Bond

DEPT. OF EDUCATION

1181 Portage Ave., Winnipeg, Man. R3G OT3
Information, Eileen Pruden, Information Officer, Room 506 (phone: 204-786-0254)

Acts Administered

Blind Persons' & Deaf Persons' Maintenance & Education Act
Education Dept. Act
Licensed Practical Nurses Act, Ss. 14,15
Public Schools Act
Public Schools Finance Board Act
School Attendance Act
Teachers Pensions Act
Universities Establishment Act
Universities Grants Commission Act
University of Manitoba Act

MINISTER, Hon. Keith A. Cosens
Deputy Minister, R.A. MacIntosh, 162 Leg. Bldg.

Administration & Finance Division

Asst. Deputy Minister, B.E. Besteck
Departmental Administrative Support Services, Director, L.A. Floyde
Board of Reference, Secretary, C. Bridle
Finance, Director, D.G. Bell
Man. Text Book Bureau, 277 Hutchings St., Manager, W.B. Woolston
Teacher Certification & Records, Director, Dr. R. Constant
Education Data Services, Dr. R. Constant

Bureau de l'Education Française

Sous-ministre adjoint, R.J. Duhamel

Program Development & Support Services Division

Assoc. Deputy Minister, G.M. Davies
Program Development Directorate, Director, S.A.I. Bullock
Curriculum Services Branch, Co-ordinator, A. Janzen
Native Education Branch, Director, Flora Zaharia
Support Services Directorate, Director, John Dyck
Child Development & Support Services, Co-ordinator, N. Cenerini
Correspondence Branch, Principal, D. Eirikson
Student Aid Branch, 693 Taylor Ave., Director, F.R. Kleiman
Research, Director, M.P. Yakimishyn
Post Secondary Career Development Branch, Director, P. Ferris
Special Mature Student Program, Director, C. Sigurdson

Community Colleges Division

2055 Notre Dame Ave., Winnipeg
Asst. Deputy Minister, Peter F. Penner
Director of Admin., J.W. Heuvel
Director of Programs, E.A. Ramsay
Communications Officer, T. K. Morgan (633-6183)
Canada Manpower Office, Officer in Charge, J. Purse

Boards & Commissions

Board of Reference, 511 1181 Portage Ave., Winnipeg, Man. R3G OT3 (786-0340)
The Advisory Board, 511 1181 Portage Ave., Winnipeg, Man. R3G OT3 (786-0340)
The Board of Teacher Education & Certification, 312 1181 Portage Ave., Winnipeg, Man. R3G OT3 (786-0331)
Collective Agreement Board, #162, Legislative Bldg., Winnipeg, Man. R3C 0V8 (944-3752)
Public Schools Finance Board, #502, 1181 Portage Ave., Winnipeg, Man. R3G OT3 (786-0480)
Teachers' Retirement Allowances Fund Board, 308 1181 Portage Ave., Winnipeg, Man. R3G OT3 (786-0242)
Universities Grants Commission, #226, 530 Century St., Winnipeg, Man.

EMERGENCY MEASURES ORG.

405 Broadway Ave., Winnipeg, Man. R3C 3L6
Phone: (204) 284-2070 - 24 hr. response

DEPT. OF ENERGY & MINES

Information Contact, R.D. Bettner (204/944-3674)

Acts Administered

Energy Authority Act
Energy Council Act
Gas Pipeline Act
Gas Storage & Allocation Act
Greater Winnipeg Distribution Act
Industrial Minerals Drilling Act
Mineral Exploration Assistance Act
Mines Act
Mines & Natural Resources Department Act (as it applies to Mines)
Mining Royalty Tax Act (secs. 20-25)
Mining & Metallurgy Compensation Act
Pipe Line Act

MINISTER, Hon. Donald W. Craik
Deputy Minister, M.G. Anderson, 156 Leg. Bldg., R3C 0V8, 944-3130
Mineral Resources Division, 993 Century St., R3H 0W4, Asst. Deputy Minister, Dr. I. Haugh, 633-9543, ext. 280
Energy Division, 2nd floor, 500 Portage Ave., R3C 0E9, Asst. Deputy Minister, L.P. Haberman, 944-2122
Administrative Services Branch, 2nd floor, 500 Portage Ave., R3C 0E9, Director, R.D. Bettner, 944-3674

Associated Agencies

Manitoba Mineral Resources Ltd.
Mining Board

Oil & Natural Gas Conservation Board
Manitoba Energy Authority
Manitoba Energy Council

DEPT. OF FINANCE

Room 109, Legislative Bldg., Winnipeg, Man. R3C OV8
Information from Deputy Minister of Finance (phone: 204 944-3754)

Acts Administered

Canada Pension Plan Act
Corporation Capital Tax Act
Energy Rate Stabilization Act
Farmers Emergency Grants Act
Financial Administration Act
Fire Insurance Reserve Fund Act
Gasoline Tax Act
Gift Tax Act (Man.)
Homeowners Tax & Insulation Assistance Act
Hospital Capital Financing Authority Act
Hospital Debentures Guarantee Act, 1960
Income Tax Act (Man.)
Man. Telephone System Debt Adjustments Act, 1955
Metallic Minerals Royalty Act
Mineral Acreage Tax Act
Mineral Taxation Act
Mining Royalty & Tax Act (except Sec. 20-25)
Motive Fuel Tax Act
Pari-Mutuel Tax Act
Provincial-Municipal Tax Sharing Act
Public Officers Act
Retail Sales Tax Act
Revenue Act, 1964
School Capital Financing Authority Act
School Dists. Debenture Interest Guarantee Act
Sewage Disposal & Water Supply Systems Debenture Interest Guarantee Act
Special Employment Program Act, 1977
Special Municipal Loan & General Emergency Fund Act
Succession Duty Act (Man.)
Suitors' Moneys Act
Taxation Agreement Act, 1957
Tobacco Tax Act
Treasury Branches Act
Unsatisfied Judgment Fund Act (in part)

MINISTER OF FINANCE, Hon. A. Brian Ransom
Deputy Minister of Finance, Charles E. Curtis
Asst. Deputy Ministers of Finance
(Treasury), Neil S. Benditt
(Federal-Provincial Relations & Research), James R. Eldridge
(Taxation), Charles A. Perry
(Comptroller) W.C. Fraser

Associated Agencies

Man. Hospital Capital Financing Authority, Room 9, Legislative Bldg., Winnipeg R3C OV8 (944-3756)
Man. School Capital Financing Authority, Room 9, Legislative Bldg., Winnipeg R3C OV8 (944-3756)

DEPT. OF FITNESS, RECREATION & SPORT

#302, 379 Broadway Ave., Winnipeg, Man. R3C 3N4
Information Contact: R.P. Pozernick, Director of Administration (204/944-3765)

Acts Administered

Boxing & Wrestling Commission Act
Fitness & Amateur Sport Act

MINISTER, Hon. Bob Banman
Deputy Minister, Alan R. Miller, 327 Leg. Bldg., 944-3764
Director of Research & Planning, W. Hadikin, 9th floor, 405 Broadway, 944-2782
Director of Admin., R.P. Pozernick, 944-3765
Director of Sport, D. Stone, 944-3526
Director of Recreation & Fitness, G. Maurice, 944-4397
Manitoba Boxing & Wrestling Commission
#302, 379 Broadway Ave., Winnipeg, Man. R3C 3N4
(204) 944-3535
Chairman, J. Trifunov

DEPT. OF GOVERNMENT SERVICES

15th floor, Woodsworth Bldg., 405 Broadway, Winnipeg, Man. R3C OV8
Information from: J.K. Wilkins, Co-ordinator, Policy Research & Development (204/944-4102)

Acts Administered

Emergency Measures Act
Government House Act
Government Purchases Act
Land Acquisition Act
Public Printing Act
Dept. of Public Works Act

MINISTER, Hon. W.H. Jorgenson (944-2979)
Deputy Minister, Boris R. Hryhorczuk (944-4414)
Executive Director, Central Admin., D.F. Coyle (944-3940)
(includes: Administration, Budgets & Internal Audit, Personnel Services, Operational Support Services)
Co-ordinator, Emergency Measures Org., H. Eckert (944-4789)
Executive Director, Supply & Services, C.R. McIntyre (944-0070)
Director, Central Vehicle Services, R. Glover (944-3680)
Director, Purchasing, E. Baranet (944-0070)
Director, Supply Services, J. Smith (944-0070)
Queen's Printer, B. Hudson (944-3105)
Executive Director, Project Services, N.T. Osler (888-3280)
(includes: Land Acquisition, Design Services, and Project Management)
Executive Director, Field Services, S.K. McMillan (888-3280)
(includes: Physical Plant, Support Services, and Construction Services) *and*
Gimli Industrial Park, Manager, J. Dunlop (642-8465)
Energy Management & Technical Services, Manager, S. Ursel (888-3280)

DEPT. OF HEALTH

Information Contact, Scott Bennett, Program Co-ordinator to Deputy Minister, Rm. 309, Legislative Bldg., Winnipeg, Man. R3C 0V8 (204/944-4072/3771)

Acts Administered

Alcoholism Foundation Act
Anatomy Act
Cancer Treatment & Research Foundation Act
Dental Association Act
Dental Health Workers Act
Dental Health Services Act
Dental Mechanics Act
Elderly & Infirm Persons' Housing Act (with respect only to personal care homes and hostels as defined in the Act)
Dept. of Health Act
District Health & Social Services Act
Health Sciences Centre Act
Health Services Act
Health Services Insurance Act
Hearing Aid Act
Hospital Aid Act
Hospitals Act
Human Tissue Act
Medical Act
Mental Health Act (except Parts III & IV)
Narcotic Drug Addicts Act
Pharmaceutical Act
Licensed Practical Nurses Act (except Secs. 14 & 15)
Prescription Drugs Cost Assistance Act
Private Hospitals Act
Psychiatric Nurses Training Act
Public Health Act (except. Reg. P 210 - R5, Div. IV)
Registered Psychiatric Nurses Act

Registered Nurses Act
Sanatorium Board of Manitoba Act
Tuberculosis Control Act

MINISTER, Hon. L.R. Sherman
Deputy Minister, Dr. George Johnson, act. (944-3731
Operational Facilities & Support Services
- Codham Provincial Laboratory, 750 William Ave., Director, Dr. J.C. Witt, 944-0270
- Brandon Mental Health Centre, Box 420, Director, Dr. A.H. Moyes, 728-7110
- Selkirk Mental Health Centre, Box 9600, Director, Dr. M.C. Kovacs, 477-1860
- Medical Supplies & Home Care Equipment, Director, C. Jacyk, 222-3278

Community Mental Health Services
- Asst. Deputy Minister (Institutional Services) & Chief Provincial Psychiatrist, Dr. R.H. Tavener, 944-3767
- Forensic Services, 75 Emily St., Director, Dr. R.G. Bankier, 787-3887

Community Health Services
- Asst. Deputy Minister, D.F. McLean, 944-3750
- Medical Public Health Directorate, Executive Director, Dr. W.G. French, 775-9761
- Division also includes Clinical Health Services, Hearing Program, Epidemiological Services, Venereal Disease Control, Public Health Nursing Services, Maternal & Child Care Services, Home Care, Services to Well Elderly, Research, Home Economics Directorate, Health Education & Library, Dental Health Services, Community Mental Health Services

Associated Agencies

Alcoholism Foundation of Manitoba
- #201, 1580 Dublin Ave., Winnipeg, Man. R3E 0L4 (775-8601)
- Chairman, G.L. Miles
- Executive Director, David Cruickshank

Board of Health
- 831 Portage Ave., Winnipeg, Man. R3G 0N6
- Secretary, H. Schmidt, 775-9761

Manitoba Cancer Treatment & Research Foundation
- 100 Olivia St., Winnipeg, Man. R3E 0V9
- Executive Director, L.G. Israels, M.D., 787-2241

Dental Mechanics Act Committee
- 3rd floor, 831 Portage Ave., Winnipeg, Man. R3G 0N6
- Secretary, P. Todman, 775-9761

Manitoba Dental Health Workers Board
- 831 Portage Ave., Winnipeg, Man. R3G 0N6
- Secretary Registrar, M. Balcaen, 775-9761

Drug Standards/Therapeutics Committee - Paramedical Services
- 4th floor, 831 Portage Ave., Winnipeg, Man. R3G 0N6
- Secretary, Ken Brown, 775-9761

The Hearing Aid Board
- 307 Kennedy St., Winnipeg, Man. R3C 0V8
- Secretary, P. Cavenagh, 956-2040

Manitoba Mental Health Research Foundation
- 700 William Ave., Winnipeg, Man. R3E 0Z3
- Chairman, Dr. J.D. Adamson, 787-3865

Sanatorium Board of Manitoba
- 629 McDermot Ave., Winnipeg, Man. R3A 1P6
- Chairman, J. Argue, 774-5501
- Executive Director, R.F. Marks, C.A.

Manitoba Health Services Commission

599 Empress St., Box 925, Winnipeg, Man. R3C 2T6
Chairman, G. Pollock, Q.C., 942-0501
Executive Director, T.R. Edwards, 786-7176
Secretary, D.B. Nelson, 786-7192
Asst. Executive Director, Insured Benefits & Administration, G.W. McCaffrey, 786-7231
Asst. Executive Director, Facilities, F. DeCock, 786-7285
Director, Administration Division, F.S. Anderson, 786-7372

DEPT. OF HIGHWAYS & TRANSPORTATION

Legislative Bldg., Winnipeg, Man. R3C 0V8
Information Services, Room 29, Legislative Bldg., Winnipeg, Man. R3C 0V8 (phone: 204-946-7175)

Acts Administered

Government Air Services Act
Highways Dept. Act
Highways Protection Act
Highway Traffic Act (except those portions having to do with insurance and registration which are specifically delegated to the Man. Public Insurance Corp.)
Manitoba Data Services Act
Manitoba Telephone Act
Snowmobile Act
Taxicab Act
Trans-Canada Highway Act
Unsatisfied Judgment Fund Act (in part)

MINISTER, Hon. Donald W. Orchard
Deputy Minister, J.W.E. Brako

Transportation Division

15th floor, 215 Garry St., Winnipeg, Man. R3C 3Z1
Director, J.C. Rea, 944-2005
Manager, Transportation Programs Branch, J. Wallace
Manager, Freight Policy Branch, D. Schaefer
Manager, Passenger Policy Branch, W. Graham
Manager, Research & Planning Branch, S. Bhattacharyya

Highways Branch

Highways Services Bldg., 215 Garry St., Winnipeg
Asst. Deputy Minister, J. Peacock
Director of Admin., W. Dyck
Director of Operations, S. Goodbrandson
Director of Planning & Design, B.K. Johnston
Chief Land Surveyor, T.R. Miller

Highways Garages

10 Midland St., Winnipeg
Mechanical Supt., Jack Yellowlees

Motor Vehicle Branch

1075 Portage Ave., Winnipeg, Man.
Registrar of Motor Vehicles, P. Dygala
Deputy Registrar, Highway Safety, C. Prociuk
Deputy Registrar, Driver Licensing, B. Hewitt
Driver Testing, W.E. Kurz
Driver Education, D. Carlson

Associated Agencies

Driver License Suspension Appeal Board, 1075 Portage Ave., Winnipeg, Man. R3G 0S1
Highway Traffic Board, Room 200, 301 Weston St., Winnipeg, Man. R3E 3H4 (786-6708)
Highway Transport Board, Room 200, 301 Weston St., Winnipeg, Man. R3E 3H4 (786-8703)
Taxicab Board, Room 200, 301 Weston St., Winnipeg, Man. R3E 3H4 (774-4402)

MANITOBA HYDRO

Box 815, Winnipeg, Man. R3C 2P4
(204) 474-3311
President & Chief Executive Officer, L.D. Blachford
General Manager, Corporate Operations, J.J. Arnason
General Manager, Corporate Resources, R.M. Fraser
General Manager, Engineering & Construction, D.S. Duncan
General Counsel, J.F. Funnell
Asst. General Manager, Finance, A.K. McKean
Asst. General Manager, Customer Service, H.L. Dahl
Asst. General Manager, Corporate Relations, C.E. Birston
Asst. General Manager, Human Resources, R.F. Manning
Asst. General Manager, Engineering & Construction, G.C. March

A/Asst. General Manager, System Planning & Operations, W.J. Tishinski
Director, Public Affairs, Verne Prior

DEPT. OF LABOUR & MANPOWER

604 Norquay Bldg., 401 York Ave., Winnipeg, Man. R3C 0V8
Information Contact, D. Meakin, Communications (phone: 204/944-2497)

Acts Administered

Amusements Act (Part II)
Apprenticeship & Tradesmen's Qualifications Act
The Barbers Act
Buildings & Mobile Homes Act
Construction Industry Wages Act
Electricians' Licence Act
Elevator Act
Employment Services Act
Employment Standards Act
Fire Depts. Arbitration Act
Fires Prevention Act (Part II)
Gas & Oil Burner Act
Hairdressers Act
Labour Relations Act
Operating Engineers & Fireman Act
Payment of Wages Act
Pension Benefits Act
Power Engineers Act
Remembrance Day Act
Steam & Pressure Plants Act
Vacation with Pay Act
Workplace Health & Safety Act

MINISTER, Hon. Ken MacMaster, 944-3741
Executive Asst., M. Conway, 944-4184
Deputy Minister, M.C. Eyolfson, 944-3782
Asst. to Deputy Minister, E. Smith, 944-4039

Special Consultant to the Minister on the Status of Women, E. Holtmann, 693 Taylor Ave., 284-8240

Asst. Deputy Minister, Labour, G. Boucher, 944-3335
Asst. Deputy Minister, Manpower, O. Buffie, 944-3333
Director of Administration, R. Gorchynski, 944-3411
Special Projects Officer, A. Jasen, 944-3413

Labour Division

Director, Employment Standards Branch, R. Moggey, 944-3352
Fire Commissioner, A. Thorimbert, 944-3322
Director, Conciliation Services, N. Pound, 944-3367
Director, Mechanical & Engineering Branch, L.A. O'Morrow, 944-3373
Registrar, Manitoba Labour Board, J. Korpesho, 944-4311
Supt., Pension Commission, A.J. O'Brien, 944-2740
Director, Workplace Safety & Health Branch, J.E. Reimer, 944-3605

Manpower Division

Director, Research, J. Nykoluk, 944-2295
Director, Immigration & Settlement, E. Carriere, 944-2802
Director, Training & Development Branch, D. McCulloch, 944-3337
Director, Employment & Youth Services, T. Mindell, 693 Taylor Ave., 284-8240
Director, Federal Provincial Training Agreements, A. Berg, 693 Taylor Ave., 284-8240
Director, Manpower Development, M. Geller, 213 Notre Dame Ave., 944-3161
Director, Career Resources Centres, M. Cornell, 944-3399

Women's Bureau, S. Bradshaw, Director, 241 Vaughan St., 944-3476

LEGISLATIVE LIBRARY

200 Vaughan St., Winnipeg, Man. R3C 0V8
(204) 944-3784
Legislative Librarian, Mrs. Joyce Irvine

The Legislative Library is open to the public for reference and research.

DEPT. OF MUNICIPAL AFFAIRS

14th floor, 405 Broadway, Winnipeg, Man. R3C 3L6
Information Contact, Kenneth Cameron (phone: 204 944-2200)

Acts Administered

Municipal Act
Local Authorities Election Act
Soldiers' Taxation Relief Act
Planning Act
Local Government Dists. Act
Municipal Assessment Act
Dept. of Municipal Affairs Act
Municipal Board Act

MINISTER, Hon. Douglas Gourlay
Deputy Minister, G.D. Forrest (312 Legislative Bldg.)
Asst. Deputy Minister, D.M. Sanders (944-4278)
Director of Admin., Kenneth Cameron (944-2200)
Director, Municipal Assessment, J. Reimer (944-2596)
Director, Municipal Budget & Finance, R. Dennis (944-2564)
Director, Municipal Planning, J.N. Whiting (944-2150)
Director, Municipal Services, L.R.J. Fulsher (944-2572)
Provincial Planning Branch, David Johns (944-2591)

The Municipal Board

No. 1234, 405 Broadway, Winnipeg, Man. R3C 3L6
(204) 944-2941
Chairman, John Acthim

DEPT. OF NATURAL RESOURCES

Information from: Office of the Deputy Minister, Rm. 310, Legislative Bldg., Winnipeg, Man. R3C 0V8 (204/944-3785)

Acts Administered

Conservation Districts Act
Crown Lands Act
Dutch Elm Disease Act
Dyking Authority Act
Ecological Reserves Act
Fires Prevention Act (Part I)
Fisheries Act
Fishermen's Assistance & Polluters' Liability Act
Forest Act
Ground Water & Water Well Act
Lake of the Woods Control Board Act
Manitoba Natural Resources Act
Manitoba Natural Resources Development Act
Manitoba Natural Resources Agreement Amendment Act
Provincial Park Lands Act
Predator Control Act
Rivers & Streams Act
Surveys Act (Part II)
Water Commission Act
Water Resources Administration Act
Water Power Act
Water Rights Act
Water Supply Districts Act
Wildlife Act
and
Manitoba Fishery Regulations (sec. 34 of The Fisheries Act, Canada)

MINISTER, Hon. Harry J. Enns
Deputy Minister, J.D. McNairnay, 944-3785
Asst. Deputy Minister, D.C. Surrendi, 346 Leg. Bldg., 944-4477
Asst. Deputy Minister, D. Doyle
Director, Crown Lands Branch, J.A. Barr, Box 2, 1495 St. James St., 786-9540
Director, Fisheries Branch, W. Hayden, Box 20, 1495 St. James St., 786-9543
Director, Wildlife Branch, R.C. Goulden, Box 24, 1495 St. James St., 786-9483

Director, Forest Branch, H.P. Laws, #300, 500 Kenaston Blvd., 477-4605

A/Director, Parks Branch, E. Wong, #3, 200 Vaughan St., 944-4413

Director, Water Resources Branch, T.E. Weber, 1577 Dublin Ave., 786-9424

Executive Director, Administrative Services Division, W.J. Podolsky, #5, 191 Broadway, 944-4056

Associated Agencies

Conservation Districts Authority

Conservation Districts Commission

Lake of the Woods Control Board

Lower Red River Valley Water Commission

Manitoba-NWT Boundary Commission

Manitoba-Ontario Boundary Commission

Manitoba-Saskatchewan Boundary Commission

Manitoba Water Commission

Prairie Provinces Water Board

Souris River Water Commission

DEPT. OF NORTHERN AFFAIRS

59 Elizabeth Dr., Thompson, Man. R8N 1X4

(204) 778-4411

MINISTER, Hon. D.M. Gourlay, 314 Leg. Bldg., Winnipeg

Deputy Minister, Dale F. Stewart, 151 Leg. Bldg., Winnipeg, 944-4172

Local Government Development, Director, W.K. Boehm, Box 31, Elizabeth Dr., 778-4411

Administrative Support Division, Director, Mrs. I. Dube, Box 37, Elizabeth Dr., 778-4411

Agreements Management Division, Director, M.C. McKay, #920, 405 Broadway, Winnipeg, 944-2507

OFFICE OF THE OMBUDSMAN

#509, 491 Portage Ave., Winnipeg, Man. R3B 2E4

(204) 774-4491

Provincial Ombudsman, G.W. Maltby

MANITOBA PUBLIC INSURANCE CORP.

Box 6300, 9th floor, 330 Graham Ave., Winnipeg, Man. R3C 4A4

(204) 942-0331

The Corporation administers Manitoba's Public Automobile Insurance Service, and also sells general insurance on a competitive basis.

MANITOBA TELEPHONE SYSTEM

489 Empress St., Winnipeg, Man. R3C 3V6

(204) 947-4111

MTS is a wholly owned Crown Corporation enacted by Provincial legislation, the policy of which is formulated by the Board of Commissioners of the System.

Chairman, W.J.A. Bulman

Vice Chairman & Asst. General Manager, S.G. Anderson

General Manager, G.W. Holland

Director of Finance, R.C. Vannevel

Corporate Secretary, J.K. Beatty

DEPT. OF URBAN AFFAIRS

For information contact the office of the Minister, Hon. G.W.J. Mercier, Rm. 104, Legislative Bldg., Winnipeg, Man. R3C 0V8

Deputy Minister, G.D. Forrest

Asst. Deputy Minister, D.M. Sanders

Executive Asst., T.J. Clarke

PROVINCE OF NEW BRUNSWICK

Entered Confederation July 1, 1867

Area: 27,985 sq. miles

Population: 707,100 (1980 est.)

Seat of Government: Legislative Bldg., Fredericton

Lieutenant-Governor: The Hon. Hedard Robichaud

Official Secretary: Mrs. Paulette Violette

Aides-de-Camp: Major Ronald LeBlanc; Inspector Kenneth Kerr, RCMP; Captain Boyd Ring, C.D., RNB Regiment; Lieutenant Susan Knight; Lt. (N) William O'Connell; Captain S.D. Christensen

EXECUTIVE COUNCIL

Premier, Hon. Richard B. Hatfield

Minister of Agriculture & Rural Development, Hon. Malcolm N. MacLeod

Minister of Commerce & Development, Hon. Gerald S. Merrithew

Minister of Education, Hon. Charles G. Gallagher

Minister of the Environment, Hon. Eric J. Kipping

Minister of Finance, Hon. Fernand G. Dubé, Q.C.

Minister of Fisheries, Hon. Jean Gauvin

Minister of Health, Hon. Brenda M. Robertson

Minister of Justice, Hon. Rodman E. Logan, Q.C.

Minister of Labour & Manpower, Hon. Mabel M. DeWare

Minister of Municipal Affairs, Hon. Horace B. Smith

Minister of Natural Resources, Hon. J.W. Bird

Chairman, N.B. Electric Power Commission, Hon. G.W.N. Cockburn, Q.C.

Minister of Social Services, Hon. Leslie I. Hull

Minister of Supply & Services, Hon. Harold N. Fanjoy

Minister of Tourism, Hon. Leland McGaw

Minister of Transportation, Hon. Wilfred G. Bishop

Minister of Youth, Recreation & Cultural Resources, Hon. Jean-Pierre Ouellet

Chairman, Treasury Board, Hon. J.-M. Simard

Clerk of the Executive Council, Harry A. Nason (506/453-2384)

LEGISLATIVE ASSEMBLY

--not confirmed for 1982--

Forty-ninth Legislature. Last General Election, October 23, 1978. Maximum Duration, 5 years.

Party Standings: Progressive Conservative (P.C.) 30; Liberal (Lib.) 28; Total 58

Leader of the Opposition: Joseph Daigle

Indemnities & Allowances: Members' Sessional Indemnity $20,000. In addition to the Sessional Indemnity, the Premier receives $30,000; Other ministers $20,000; Ministers without portfolio $10,000; Leader of the Opposition $20,000.

Officers: Speaker, Robert B. McCready; Chaplain, Canon Peter Cowland; Clerk of Assembly, David L.E. Peterson; Asst. Clerk, Harold W. Brown; Sergeant-at-Arms, Leo F. McNulty; Official Reporter, Miss Phyllis A. LeBlanc; Official Translator, Alban Haché

Members

Following is constituency (number of registered voters): member, address and phone number:

Albert (5,651): Malcolm N. MacLeod, P.C., 92 Fairway Blvd., Riverview, N.B. E1B 1T3 (453-2448)

Bathurst (9,846): Paul Kenny, Lib., R.R. 5, Bathurst, N.B. E2A 3Y8 (546-6206)

Bay du Vin (5,124): Reginald MacDonald, Lib., R.R. 2, Black River Bridge, N.B. E0C 1B0

Campbellton (7,706): Fernand G. Dubé, P.C., 811 George St., Fredericton, N.B. E3B 1K8 (453-2451)

Caraquet (8,323): Onil Doiron, Lib., C.P. 95, Caraquet, N.B. EOB 1KO (727-2404)

Carleton Centre (4,945): Richard B. Hatfield, P.C., 7 Elmcroft Place, Fredericton, N.B. E3B 1Y8 (453-2144)

Carleton North (5,364): Charles G. Gallagher, P.C., Box 128, Centreville, N.B. EOJ 1HO (453-2523)

Carleton South (5,700): P. Steven Porter, P.C., Houlton Rd., Woodstock, N.B. EOJ 2BO (323-3907)
Charlotte Centre (3,531): Sheldon Lee, Lib., R.R. 3, St. George, N.B. EOG 2YO (755-2213)
Charlotte-Fundy (4,527): James N. Tucker, P.C., Box 74, Back Bay, Charlotte Co., N.B. EOG 1BO (755-2664)
Charlotte West (4,265): Leland W. McGaw, P.C., Moores Mills, R.R. 1, Charlotte Co., N.B. EOG 2LO (453-2428)
Chatham (6,730): Frank E. Kane, Lib., 12 Park Dr., Chatham, N.B. E1N 2Y9 (773-4289)
Dalhousie (6,537): Allan Maher, Lib., 413 Victoria St., Dalhousie, N.B. EOK 1BO (684-2390)
Edmundston (7,506): Jean-Maurice Simard, P.C., 64 Forty-eighth Ave., Edmundston, N.B. E3V 3C9 (453-2574)
Fredericton North (13,851): Edwin G. Allen, P.C., 330 Sunset Ave., Fredericton, N.B. E3A 1B2 (472-2297)
Fredericton South (15,069): J.W. Bird, P.C., 7 Simcoe Court, Fredericton, N.B. E3B 2W9 (453-2510)
Grand Falls (4,522): Everard Daigle, Lib., Box 250, Grand Falls, N.B. EOJ 1MO (473-3550)
Kent Centre (4,804): Alan R. Graham, Lib., Box 5, Rexton, N.B. EOA 2LO (523-6627)
Kent North (5,511): Joseph Z. Daigle, Q.C., Lib., Box 520, Richibucto, N.B. E0A 2M0 (453-2598)
Kent South (7,766): Bertin LeBlanc, Lib., Ste-Marie-de-Kent, N.B. EOA 3AO (755-3041)
Kings Centre (8,848): Harold Fanjoy, P.C., Box 150, Grand Bay, N.B. EOG 1WO (453-2591)
Kings East (8,364): Hazen Myers, P.C., 497 Main St., Sussex, N.B. EOE 1PO (433-4393)
Kings West (11,894): J.B.M. Baxter, Q.C., P.C., 143 Green Rd., Kingshurst, Saint John, N.B. E2H 1T2 (897-8538)
Madawaska Centre (4,723): Gerald H. Clavette, Lib., Rivière Verte, Madawaska Co., N.B. EOL 1EO (263-5687)
Madawaska-les-Lacs (6,008): Jean-Pierre Ouellet, P.C., Box 65, Baker Brook, Madawaska Co., N.B. EOL 1AO (453-2412)
Madawaska South (5,027): Heliodore Côté, Grand Falls, N.B. EOJ 1MO (473-1880)
Memramcook (8,706): William Malenfant, Lib., 114 Champlain St., Dieppe, N.B. E1A 1N7 (382-8571)
Miramichi Bay (6,587): B. Edgar LeGresley, Lib., Box 119, Neguac, N.B. EOC 1SO (776-8891)
Miramichi-Newcastle (7,767): John McKay, Lib., 541 Old King George Hwy., Newcastle, N.B. E1V 1J8 (622-1163)
Southwest Miramichi (6,579): Morris Green, Lib., Box 204, Doaktown, N.B. EOC 1GO (365-4648)
Moncton East (10,347): J. Raymond Frenette, Lib., 30 Vista Dr., Moncton, N.B. E1A 4L5 (855-3719)
Moncton North (11,263): Michael McKee, Lib., 37 McSweeney Ave., Apt. 2, Moncton, N.B. E1C 7C6 (855-3000)
Moncton West (10,017): Mrs. Mabel DeWare, P.C., 234 Highfield St., Moncton, N.B. E1C 5R1 (453-2342)
Nepisiguit-Chaleur (6,220): Frank R. Branch, Lib., Box 1, Site 9, Bathurst, R.R. 5, N.B. E2A 3Z2 (546-4323)
Nigadoo-Chaleur (8,109): Pierre Godin, Lib., Petit Rocher, N.B. EOB 2EO (783-3080)
Oromocto (7,737): LeRoy J. Washburn, Lib., 402 Covert St., Oromocto, N.B. E2V 1E7 (455-3337, loc. 23)
Petitcodiac (13,784): C. William Harmer, P.C., Box 328, Petitcodiac, R.R. 2, N.B. EOA 2HO (756-3567)
Queens North (3,683): Wilfred G. Bishop, P.C., Chipman, R.R. 1, N.B. EOE 1CO (453-2559)
Queens South (3,895): Robert McCready, Lib., Youngs Cove Road, N.B. EOE 1SO (362-2186)
Restigouche East (4,878): Rayburn D. Doucett, Lib., Jacquet River, N.B. EOB 1TO (237-2080)
Restigouche West (6,646): J. Alfred Roussel, Lib., Box 204, St. Quentin, N.B. EOK 1JO (235-2082)
Riverview (8,538): Brenda M. Robertson, P.C., 22 Grindstone Dr., Riverview, N.B. E1B 3N9 (453-2581)
East Saint John (11,629): Gerald S. Merrithew, P.C., 3 Kennington St., East Saint John, N.B. E2J 2Z1 (453-2472)
Saint John-Fundy (7,494): B.J. Harrison, P.C., Box 688, Rothesay, N.B. EOG 2WO (847-4413)
Saint John Harbour (6,506): Louis Murphy, Lib., 134 Milford Rd. W., Saint John, N.B. E2M 4R5 (672-4073)
Saint John North (6,655): Eric Kipping, P.C., 52 Meadowbank Ave., Saint John, N.B. E2L 1R1 (453-2639)
Saint John-Park (7,019): Mrs. Shirley Dysart, Lib., 914 Kennebecasis Dr., Saint John, N.B. E2L 3W2 (657-6365)
Saint John South (6,655): Miss Nancy Clark, P.C., 11 Canterbury St., Saint John, N.B. E2L 2C3 (847-4614)
Saint John West (11,089): R.E. Logan, Q.C., P.C., 37 Buena Vista Ave., West Saint John, N.B. E2M 2S7 (453-2583)
St. Stephen-Milltown (4,583): G.W.N. Cockburn, P.C., 40 Hawthorne St., Box 157, St. Stephen, N.B. E3L 1W6 (453-4444)
Shediac-Cap Pelé (9,980): Azor LeBlanc, Lib., Box 1000, Shediac, N.B. EOA 3GO (532-2795)
Shippegan-les-Iles (8,304): Jean Gauvin, P.C., Shippegan, N.B. EOB 2PO (453-2662)
Sunbury (7,040): Horace B. Smith, P.C., Hoyt, N.B. EOG 2BO (453-2558)
Tantramar (7,186): Lloyd Folkins, P.C., Box 389, Sackville, N.B. EOA 3CO (536-2932)
Tracadie (9,253): Douglas Young, Lib., Tracadie, N.B. EOC 2BO (395-3387)
Victoria-Tobique (7,257): J. Douglas Moore, P.C., Box 668, Perth-Andover, N.B. EOJ 1VO (273-3621)
York North (10,178): David Bishop, P.C., McLaren Cres., Box 62, Nackawic, N.B. EOH 1PO (575-2115)
York South (10,529): Leslie I. Hull, P.C., 36 Westwood Dr., Box 35, Silverwood, N.B. E3B 4X7 (453-2313)

OFFICE OF THE PREMIER

Centennial Bldg., Box 6000, Fredericton, N.B. E3B 5H1
(506) 453-2144
Executive Asst., Ross McKean
Appointments Secretary, Carolyn Atkinson
Office Manager, George Robinson
Personal Secretary, Isabel Caverhill
Correspondence Secretary, Mona Bowes
Executive Secretary, Jeannette Cogswell
Director of N.B. Information Service, Fernand Lévesque (453-2240)

GOVERNMENT DEPARTMENTS

DEPT. OF AGRICULTURE & RURAL DEVELOPMENT

Box 6000, Fredericton, N.B. E3B 5H1
Information Contact, Ellsworth DeMerchant, Communications Section (phone: 506 453-2258)

Acts Administered

Agricultural Associations Act
Agricultural Rehabilitation & Development Act
Agricultural Schools Act
Apiary Inspection Act
Artificial Insemination Act
Branding Act
Community Auction Sales Act
Co-operative Assns. Act
Credit Unions Act
Credit Unions Federations Act
Crop Insurance Act
Dairy Industry Act
Dairy Products Act
Disease of Animals Act
Drainage of Farmlands Act
Encouragement of Seed Growing Act
Farm Adjustment Act
Farm Credit Corp. Assist. Act
Farm Improvement Assistance Loans Act
Farm Income Assurance Act
Farm Loans Act

Farm Machinery Loans Act
Farm Products Boards & Marketing Agencies Act
Farm Products Marketing Act
Fences Act
Forest Products Act
Grain Act
Imitation Dairy Products Act
Injurious Insect & Pest Act
Livestock Incentives Act
Marshland Reclamation Act
Natural Products Grades Act
Oleomargarine Act
Plant Diseases Act
Potato Disease Eradication Act
Potato Warehouse Assistance Act
Poultry Health Protection Act
Pounds Act
Regional Savings & Loan Societies Act
Sheep Protection Act
Tile Drainage Loans Act
Warble Fly Free Area Act
Weed Control Act
Women's Institute Act

MINISTER, Hon. Malcolm N. MacLeod (453-2448)
Deputy Minister, H.R. Scovil, B.Sc.(Agr.), M.S. (453-2450)
Asst. Deputy Minister, David MacMinn (453-2366)
Asst. Deputy Minister, D.R. Boudreau (453-2449)
Directors of Branches:
Plant Industry, E.T. Pratt (453-3870)
Potato Division, C.E. Smith, B.Sc. (Agr.), Ph.D. (453-2759)
Communications Section, Ellsworth DeMerchant (453-2258)
Extension & Economics, Dewitt Lister (453-2333)
Livestock & Poultry, F. Johnson, B.Sc.(Agr.) (453-2457)
Veterinary, Dr. C.S. Rammage (453-2219)
Marketing Division, Elliott Keizer (453-2315)
Credit Unions & Co-operatives, W.W. Church (453-2315)
Market Development Branch, D.N. Cressman (453-2214)
Market Organization & Inspection Branch, Wayne Buffett (453-2186)
Home Economics, Mrs. Nancy Cook, B.H.Sc., M.Sc.A. (453-2428)
Agricultural Engineering, Earle Gilchrist, B.Sc. (Agr.) (453-2691)
General Admin., C.R. Chase (453-2521)
Planning & Development Division, Executive Director, Peter C. Schousboe (453-2406)

Associated Agencies

Farm Products Marketing Commission: R.D. Gilbert, Chairman; Wayne J. Buffett, Secretary, N.B. Dept. of Agriculture (453-2186)
Farm Adjustment Board: Manager, J.C. Snyder, N.B. Dept. of Agriculture (453-2524); Chairman, Earle Gilchrist, B.Sc. (Agr.)
Livestock Incentives Act, and Farm Machinery Loans Act: Administrator, Brian DuPlessis (453-2457)
Dairy Products Commission: Chairman, H.H. Hicks; Secretary-Administrator, Eugene Morris (453-2427)
Address for each of the above is Box 6000, Fredericton, N.B. E3B 5H1

Marketing Boards

N.B. Apple Marketing Board, R.R. #6, Fredericton, N.B. E3B 4X7 (454-9636); Secretary-Manager, Roger A. King
N.B. Chicken Marketing Board, R.R. 6, Fredericton, N.B. E3B 4X7 (454-9636); Secretary-Manager, Roger A. King
N.B. Cream Marketing Board, Box 490, Sussex, N.B. EOE 1PO (433-1775); Secretary, Ms. Ella Walker
N.B. Egg Marketing Board, Chestnut Complex, 476 York St., Fredericton, N.B. E3B 2T9 (455-7605); Secretary-Manager, Richard Gorham
N.B. Greenhouse Products Marketing Board, R.R. 6, Fredericton, N.B. E3B 4X7 (454-9636); Secretary Manager, Roger A. King
N.B. Hog Marketing Board, Co-op Atlantic, Box 750, Moncton, N.B. E1C 8N5 (858-6324); Secretary-Manager, Watson Cudmore
N.B. Milk Marketing Board, Box 490, Sussex, N.B. EOE 1PO (433-1775); Chairman, Wm. Sherwood
N.B. Turkey Marketing Board, R.R. #6, Fredericton, N.B. E3B 4X7 (454-9642); Secretary-Manager, Roger A. King
N.B. Potato Agency, Box 238, Florenceville, N.B. EOJ 1KO (392-6156); Co-Chairmen, R.J. Keenan, L. Poitras

OFFICE OF THE AUDITOR GENERAL

Box 758, Fredericton, N.B. E3B 5B4
(506) 453-2243
Auditor General, W.D. Cumberland

DEPT. OF COMMERCE & DEVELOPMENT

Box 6000, Fredericton, N.B. E3B 5H1
Information Contact, Valerie Robinson, Information Officer (phone: (506) 453-3984)

Acts Administered

Commerce & Development Act

MINISTER, Hon. Gerald S. Merrithew
Deputy Minister, J.P. Blanchard
Asst. Deputy Minister, Planning & Admin., G.A. Levesque
Asst. Deputy Minister, Commerce & Industry Services, D.G. Skaling
Asst. Deputy Minister, Industrial Development, W.H. Bryden

Associated Agencies

N.B. Industrial Development Board, Box 6000, Fredericton, N.B. E3B 5H1 (506/453-2474)
Provincial Holdings Ltd., Box 6000, Fredericton, N.B. E3B 5H1 (506/453-2474)
N.B. Research & Productivity Council, College Hill Rd., Fredericton, N.B. E3B 5H1 (506/455-8994)

COMMUNITY IMPROVEMENT CORP.

377 York St., Box 428, Fredericton, N.B. E3B 5R4
(506) 454-5533
General Manager, F.J. Arsenault
Treasurer/Comptroller, W.C. Mallory
Director of Program Co-ordination, R.E. Crighton

CRIMES COMPENSATION

For information contact Dept. of Justice, Centennial Bldg., Fredericton, N.B. E3B 5H1

DEPT. OF CONTINUING EDUCATION

416 York St., Box 6000, Fredericton, N.B. E3B 5H1
(506) 453-2597

Acts Administered

N.B. Community College Act
Trade Schools Act

MINISTER, Hon. Charles C. Gallagher
Deputy Minister, P.J.H. Malmberg
Deputy Minister, A.A. Saintonge
Executive Director, Administrative Services, L.J. Arsenault
Co-ordinator, Professional Development, Josephine Lynam
Director, Curriculum Services (Anglophone), Peter Kilburn
Director, Curriculum Services (Francophone), Wilfred Savoie
Director, Extension Services, Claude Boucher
Co-ordinator, Women's Training, Ellen King

DEPT. OF EDUCATION

Box 6000, Fredericton, N.B. E3B 5H1
Information Contact, Bob Steeves (phone: 506-453-2085)

Acts Administered

Auxiliary Classes Act
Education of the Aurally or Visually Handicapped Persons Act
Schools Act

MINISTER, Hon. Charles G. Gallagher
Deputy Minister, Armand Saintonge
Deputy Minister, P.J.H. Malmberg

Educational Services Division (French)
Asst. Deputy Minister, A.A. Pinet
Director of Program Development & Implementation, N. Bérubé
Director of Pupil Personnel Services, J.L. Guérette
Director of Evaluation, Sylvio Chenard
Director of Special Education, Pierre Dumas
Director of Professional Development, R. Chouinard

Educational Services Division (English)
Asst. Deputy Minister, G.E.M. MacLeod
Director of Program Development & Implementation, Lester Bartlett
Director of Pupil Personnel Services, Richard Harvey
Director of Evaluation, Ronald Elliott
Director of Special Education, Elizabeth J. Owens
Director of Professional Development, G.C. Keilty

Finance & Administration
Asst. Deputy Minister, Derek A. Bone
Director of Admin., R.G. Cornell
Director of Buildings, Paul Leger
Director of Teacher Certification, Richard O. Gauvin
Director of Personnel, D.B. Estabrooks
Director of District Financial Services, James Galvin
Director of Planning & Development, R.C. Manore

EMERGENCY MEASURES ORG.
Dept. of Municipal Affairs, (15 Carleton St.), Box 6000, Fredericton, N.B. E3B 5H1
Director, Henry G. Irwin (phone: 506-453-2656)

DEPT. OF THE ENVIRONMENT
Box 6000, Fredericton, N.B. E3B 5H1
Information Contact, G.N. Hill, Co-ordinator of Information Programs (506/453-3700)

Acts Administered
Beverage Containers Act
Clean Environment Act
Pesticides Control Act
Unsightly Premises Act

MINISTER, Hon. Eric Kipping
Deputy Minister, Brian B. Barnes
Director, Pollution Control Branch, D.R. Silliphant
Director, Water Resources Branch, W. Franklin Cardy
Director, Environmental Services, Dr. D.I. Besner
Administrative Officer, J.M. McMahon

Associated Agency
N.B. Environmental Council, Box 6000, Fredericton, N.B. E3B 5H1 (506) 453-2861
Chairman, John Henderson

DEPT. OF FINANCE
Centennial Bldg., Fredericton, N.B. E3B 5H1
Information Contact, G.E. Kitchen, Director of Administration (phone: 506/453-2511)

Acts Administered
Appropriation Act
Business Grant Act
Canada Pension Plan Agreement Act
Financial Admin. Act
Gasoline & Motive Fuel Tax Act
Guarantee Act
Income Tax Act
Loan Act
Lotteries Act
Members' Superannuation Act
Provincial Loans Act
Public Service Superannuation Act
Real Property Tax Act
Social Services & Education Tax Act
Teachers' Pension Act
Theatres, Cinematographs & Amusements Act
Tobacco Tax Act

MINISTER, Hon. Fernand G. Dubé, Q.C.
Deputy Minister, Ian MacBain
Asst. Deputy Minister and Director of Treasury & Debt Management, I.D. Cameron
Comptroller, John Astle, C.A.
Director of Admin., G.E. Kitchen
Director of Pensions, A.D. Haley
Provincial Tax Commissioner, D.V. Bamford
Director of Taxation & Fiscal Policy, Robert Kelly
Director, Economics & Statistics Branch, Clifford Marks
Co-ordinator of Field Services, David Morrison

Legislative Assembly
Auditor General, W.D. Cumberland, C.A.
Ombudsman, Joseph E. Bérubé

Office of the Queen's Printer
Queen's Printer, Patrick Lynch

Provincial Archives
Provincial Archivist, Mrs. Marion Beyea

N.B. Electric Power Commission
Box 2000, Fredericton, N.B. E3B 4X1
Chairman, Hon. G.W.N. Cockburn
Secretary, P.S. Creaghan
General Manager, A.J. O'Connor

Civil Service Commission
Chairman, Jean Paul LeBlanc

OFFICE OF THE FIRE MARSHAL
Provincial Fire Marshal, G.R. Elliott, Box 6000, Fredericton, N.B. E3B 5H1
Phone: (506) 453-2430

DEPT. OF FISHERIES
Kings Place, Fredericton, N.B. E3B 5H1
Information from, N.B. Information Service, Box 6000, Fredericton, N.B. E3B 5H1 (phone: 506-453-2240)

Acts Administered
Fisheries Development Act
Fish Inspection Act
Irish Moss Act

MINISTER, Hon. Jean Gauvin
Deputy Minister, Tim Andrew
Special Advisor, Clarence Duguay
Director General, Operations & Services, Denis Haché
Director, Finance & Administration, Alfred Losier
Director, Resource Policy & Planning, Henri Legaré
Director, Technical Services, Nihat Ozerdem
Director, Fisheries Training & Marketing Services, Joe Gallant
Director, School of Fisheries, Gérard Saint-Cyr

Associated Agency
N.B. Fisheries Development Board, Dept. of Fisheries, Box 6000, Fredericton, N.B.; Chairman & Chief Executive Officer, J.B.R. Savoie; Secretary, Rosaire LeBlanc (453-2302)

DEPT. OF HEALTH
Box 6000, Fredericton, N.B. E3B 5H1
Information from Office of the Deputy Minister (phone: 506-453-2542)

Acts Administered

Advanced Life Support Services Act
Alcoholism & Drug Dependency Commission of N.B. Act
Anatomy Act
Cemetery Companies Act
Change of Name Act
Health Act
Health Services Advisory Council Act
Health Services Act
Hospital Protection Act
Hospital Schools Act
Hospital Services Act
Human Tissue Act
Infirm Persons Act
Marriage Act
Medical Consent of Minors Act
Medical Services Payment Act
Mental Health Act
Mentally Retarded Children Act
Prescription Drug Payment Act
Public Hospitals Act
Treatment of Intoxicated Persons Act
Venereal Diseases Prevention Act
White Cane Act

MINISTER, Hon. Brenda Robertson
Deputy Minister, William K. Morrissey (453-2542)
Director, Admin. Division, R.D. Kirkley (453-2775)
Asst. Deputy Minister, Insured Services Division, William Alwood (453-2055)
Director, Hospital Services, Dr. D. Ingraham (453-2283)
Medical Director, Dr. G. St. Pierre (453-2715)
Director, Medicare, R. Saunders (453-2191)
Director, Planning & Evaluation Division, J.H. Carter (453-2582)
Asst. Deputy Minister, Personal Health Services Division, Dr. H.W. Wyile (453-2321)
Dental Health Director, Dr. John Blackmer (453-2933)
Mental Health Director, J.A. Wolstenholme (453-2235)
Director, Nursing Homes, Mrs. Claire Morris (453-3821)
Public Health Services Director, Dr. C. Devadason (453-2321)
Public Health Inspection Director, R.A. Hicks (453-2397)
Public Health Nursing Director, L. Bourque (453-2360)

Vital Statistics

Registrar General, Marianne Wiezel (453-2311)
For Birth, Marriage and Death Certificates remit $3 for each copy required. The fee for each wallet size certificate is $3. A search only is $2, and a genealogical search is $10.

Associated Agencies

Health Services Advisory Council, c/o Dept., Secretary, Faith Fairweather (453-2008)
Alcoholism & Drug Dependency Commission, Chairman, Dr. G.E. Chalmers (453-2136)

HISTORICAL RESOURCES ADMIN.

Box 6000, Fredericton, N.B. E3B 5H1

Acts Administered

Archives Act
Historic Sites Protection Act
Kings Landing Corp. Act
N.B. Museum Act
MINISTER in Charge, Hon. Charles Gallagher
Deputy Head, George MacBeath (453-2896)
Asst. Deputy Head, T. Michael O'Rourke (453-2324)
Provincial Archivist, Marion Beyea (453-2637)
Kings Landing Corp., General Manager, Douglas Cole (363-3081)
N.B. Museum, Director, David Ross (693-1196)
Legislative Library, Director, Jocelyne LeBel (453-2338)
Village Historique Acadien, Director, Jean-Yves Theriault (727-3467)
Historic Sites, Director, Ralph Whitehead (453-2324)
Archaeology, Dr. Christopher Turnball (453-2324)
Administrative Management Director, R.A. MacDiarmid (453-2636)

N.B. HOUSING CORP.

Box 611, Fredericton, N.B. E3B 5B2
(506) 454-5563
President, K.C. Scott

DEPT. OF JUSTICE

Room 216, Centennial Bldg., Fredericton, N.B. E3B 5H1
Information Contact, Administrative Services Director, Room 216, Centennial Bldg. (phone: 506-453-2589)

Acts Administered

Absconding Debtors Act
Age of Majority Act
Arrest & Examinations Act
Assignment of Book Debts Act
Assignments & Preferences Act
Auctioneers License Act
Bills of Sale Act
Bulk Sales Act
Children of Unmarried Parents Act
Collection Agencies Act
Commrs. for Taking Affidavits Act
Companies Act
Compensation for Victims of Crime Act
Conditional Sales Act
Constables Act
Consumer Bureau Act
Contributory Negligence Act
Controverted Elections Act
Coroners Act
Corporations Act
Corrections Act
Corrupt Practices Inquiries Act
Cost of Credit Disclosure Act
County Court Act
Court Reporters Act
Creditors Relief Act
Criminal Prosecution Expenses Act
Crown Debts Act
Crown Prosecutors Act
Dangerous Buildings Removal Act
Defamation Act
Demise of the Crown Act
Deposit Insurance Act
Deserted Wives & Children Maintenance Act
Devolution of Estates Act
Direct Sellers Act
Divorce Court Act
Dower Act
Easements Act
Escheats & Forfeitures Act
Evidence Act
Executors & Trustees Act
Expropriation Act
Factors & Agents Act
Fatal Accidents Act
Federal Courts Jurisdiction Act
Fines & Forfeitures Act
Fisherman's Union Act
Foreign Judgments Act
Foreign Residents Corporation Act
Frustrated Contracts Act
Garnishee Act
Great Seal Act
Guardianship of Children Act
Habeas Corpus Act
Infirm Persons Act
Innkeepers Act
Inquiries Act
Insurance Act
Interpretation Act

Intoxicated Persons Detention Act
Judges Disqualification Removal Act
Judicature Act
Jury Act
Juvenile Courts Act
Landlord & Tenant Act
Legal Aid Act
Legitimation Act
Liens on Goods & Chattels Act
Limitation of Actions Act
Limited Partnership Act (Provincial Secretary)
Lord's Day Act
Married Woman's Property Act
Mechanics Lien Act
Memorials' Executions Act
N.B. Liquor Corp. Act
Notaries Public Act
N.S. Grants Act
Official Languages of N.B. Act
Parents' Maintenance Act
Partnership Act
Partnerships Registration Act
Parole Act
Pre-arranged Funeral Services Act
Premium Tax Act
Presumption of Death Act
Private Investigators & Security Guards Act
Probate Courts Act
Proceedings Against the Crown Act
Property Act
Protection of Persons Acting Under Statute Act
Provincial Courts Act
Public Records Act
Queen's Counsel & Precedence Act
Quieting of Titles Act
Real Estate Agents Licensing Act
Reciprocal Enforcement of Judgments Act
Reciprocal Enforcement of Maintenance Orders Act
Recording of Evidence by Sound Recording Machine Act
Registry Act
Regulations Act
Residential Rent Review Act
Residential Tenancies Act
Sale of Goods Act
Sale of Lands Publication Act
Salvage Dealers Licensing Act
Sheriffs Act
Statute of Frauds
Summary Convictions Act
Surety Bonds Act
Survival of Actions Act
Survivorship Act
Testators Family Maintenance Act
Tortfeasors Act
Training School Act
Trust, Building & Loan Companies Licensing Act
Trust Companies Act
Trustees Act
Unconscionable Transactions Relief Act
Wage-Earners Protection Act
Warehouse Receipts Act
Warehouseman's Lien Act
Wills Act
Winding-up Act

MINISTER OF JUSTICE, Hon. R.E. Logan, Q.C.
Deputy Minister of Justice, G.F. Gregory, Q.C.
Executive Director, Program Admin., R.L. Scammell
Director of Administrative Services, Carolyn Lovely
Director of Policing, Barry Athey
Director of Consumer & Corporate Services, Karl Dore
Correctional Services Director, W.B. Connor
Director of Law Reform, vacant
Director of Legal Services, D. Norman, Q.C.
Supt. of Insurance, T.O.C. Makin
Chief Registrar of Deeds, R.J. Flemming
Chief Sheriff, Coroner, G. Garneau
Director, Public Prosecutions, H. Hazen Strange, Q.C.

Associated Agencies

Expropriations Advisory Board, Ste. 300, 774 Main St., Moncton, N.B. E1C 1E8 (858-2528)
Real Estate Council, Box 6000, Fredericton, N.B. E3B 5H1 (455-9733)

DEPT. OF LABOUR & MANPOWER

Box 6000, Fredericton, N.B. E3B 5H1
Information Contact, M.W. McGuigan, Director, Administrative Services (phone: 506 453-2303)

Acts Administered

Boiler & Pressure Vessel Act
Electrical Installation & Inspection Act
Elevators & Lifts Act
Employment Standards Advisory Board Act
Fair Wages & Hours of Labour Act
Fire Prevention Act
Human Rights Act
Industrial Relations Act
Industrial Standards Act
Industrial Training & Certification Act
Minimum Employment Standards Act
Minimum Wage Act
Mobile Homes Act
Occupational Safety Act
Pension Plan Registration Act
Plumbing Installation & Inspection Act
Silicosis Compensation Act
Vacation Pay Act
Workmen's Compensation Act

MINISTER, Hon. Mabel DeWare
Deputy Minister, vacant
Asst. Deputy Minister, C.A. Dean
Administrative Services Director, M.W. McGuigan
Engineering Services Executive Director, P. Fitzpatrick
  Engineering Standards Director, C. Kimball
  Technical Inspection Director, D. Ross
  Office of the Fire Marshal, G. Elliott
  Program Development & Planning Director, J.J.M. Boucher
Industrial Relations Service Executive Director, J. Roushorne
  Industrial Relations Branch, Assoc. Director, J.A. Thomas
Manpower & Labour Market Services Executive Director, C.A. Dean
  Manpower Operations Director, J.S. Harris
  Labour Market Services Director, H. North

Associated Agencies

N.B. Human Rights Commission, Box 6000, Fredericton, N.B. E3B 5H1 (453-2301); Chairman, Dr. Noel Kinsella; Director, J.M. O'Brien
N.B. Industrial Relations Board, Box 908, Fredericton, N.B. E3B 1BO (453-2881); Chairman, Weldon Graser; Vice Chairman, Wallace Turnbull; Executive Officer, R. Boyd
Occupational Health & Safety Commission, Box 6000, Fredericton, N.B. E3B 5H1 (453-2467), Chairman, Bryan Walker; Executive Director, R.W.A. Yeates
Workmen's Compensation Board, Box 160, Saint John, N.B. E2L 3X9 (652-2250); Chairman, R.C. Jones; Vice Chairman, R.C. Boudreau; Commr., M.P. Fisher

N.B. LIQUOR CORP.

Box 20787, Fredericton, N.B. E3B 5B8
(506) 454-1551
Chairman, B.L. Kinney
Asst. General Manager, M.C. Lewis
Controller, L.W. Hughes
Secretary, Elizabeth Vroom

DEPT. OF MUNICIPAL AFFAIRS

Centennial Bldg., Fredericton, N.B. E3B 5H1
Information Contact, H.G. Irwin (phone: 506-453-2656)

Acts Administered

Assessment Act
Closing of Retail Establishments Act
Community Planning Act
Condominium Property Act, Sec. 7(11)
Control of Municipalities Act
Controverted Elections Act
Elections Act (Provincial)
Emergency Measures Act
Flood & Storm Damage Act
Legislative Assembly Act, Secs. 23 & 24
Metric Conversion Act
Municipal Assistance Act
Municipal Capital Borrowing Act
Municipal Debenture Act
Municipal Elections Act
Municipal Heritage Preservation Act
Municipal Thoroughfare Easements Act
Municipalities Act
Real Property Tax Act, as it pertains to Assessment
Registry Act, as it pertains to Affidavits
Residential Property Tax Relief Act

MINISTER, Hon. H.B. Smith
Deputy Minister, R.L. Bishop
Asst. Deputy Minister & Director of Admin., H.G. Irwin
Assessment Branch, Director, E.A. Cronk (231 Regent St.)
Community Planning Branch, Director, T. Jellinek, M.T.P.I.C.
Emergency Measures Org., Director, H.G. Irwin
Engineering & Technical Services Branch, Director, R.G. Stuart
Municipal Services Branch, Director, G.B. Hawkins
Electoral Officer, Lloyd Nickerson

Assessment Appeals Tribunal

Chairman, Louis A. Robichaud
Secretary, Lionel Soucy

Municipal Capital Borrowing Board

Chairman, R.L. Bishop
Secretary, C.E. Fisher

Provincial Planning Committee

Chairman, Ronald Hicks

DEPT. OF NATURAL RESOURCES

Box 6000, Fredericton, N.B. E3B 5H1
Information, (506/453-2614)

Acts Administered

Abandoned Lands Act
Bituminous Shale Act
Crown Lands Act
Crown Lands & Forests Act
Dams & Sluiceways Act
Ecological Reserves Act
Endangered Species Act
Fisheries Act
Forest Fires Act
Forest Products Act
Forest Service Act
Game Act
Grand Lake Development Act
Grand Lake Development Corp. Act
Mining Act
Mining Income Tax Act
Oil & Natural Gas Act
Ownership of Minerals Act
Oyster Fisheries Act
Quarriable Substances Act
Reserved Roads Act
Scalers Act
Surveys Act
Territorial Division Act
Trespass to Lands & Lumber Act
Underground Storage Act

MINISTER, Hon. J.W. Bird
Executive Asst., J.M. Connely
Deputy Minister, R.E. Hanusiak
Special Asst., T.E. Sifton
Asst. Deputy Minister, Forest Resources, Dr. G.L. Baskerville
Asst. Deputy Minister, Regional Operations, E.T. Owens
Asst. Deputy Minister, Mineral Resources, Dr. R.R. Potter
Director of Crown Lands, R.H. Young
Director of Departmental Resources, W.A. Pert
Director of Fish & Wildlife, H. Haswell
Director of Forest Extension, J. Hermelin
Director of Forest Management, R.E. Redmond
Director of Forest Utilization, B.B. Meadows
Director of Mineral Exploration, J.B. Hamilton
Director of Policy & Planning, R.S. Watson
Regional Resource Managers at Bathurst, Edmundston, Fredericton, Hampton, Newcastle

Associated Agencies

Forest Protection Ltd., Box 1030, Fredericton, N.B. E3B 5C3 (357-3366)
Forest Products Commission, Box 6000, Fredericton, N.B. E3B 5H1 (453-2196)

OFFICE OF THE OMBUDSMAN

Box 6000, Fredericton, N.B. E3B 5H1
Phone: (506) 453-2789
Ombudsman, J.E. Bérubé
Administrative Asst. to the Ombudsman, Mrs. Magella St-Pierre
Solicitor, Charles Ferris
Secretary to the Ombudsman, Mrs. Doris Palmer

N.B. POLICE COMMISSION

98 Prospect St. W., Fredericton, N.B. E3B 2T8
(506) 453-2069

The Commission administers the Police Act and promotes effective, efficient police services, and the prevention of crime.
Deputy Head, Commr. & Acting Chairman, C.J.H. Kilburn

DEPT. OF SOCIAL SERVICES

Box 6000, Fredericton, N.B. E3B 5H1
Information Contact, Information & Publications Unit, phone: (506) 453-2001

Acts Administered

Social Welfare Act
Adoption Act
Blind Persons Allowance Act
Child & Family Services & Family Relations Act
Child Welfare Act
Children of Unmarried Parents Act
Day Care Act
Deserted Wives & Children Maintenance Act
Disabled Persons Allowance Act
Hospital Schools Act
Jordan Memorial Sanatorium Act
Mentally Retarded Children Act
The Miramichi Auxiliary Home Act
Senior Citizens' Shelter Assistance Act
Special Care Homes Act

MINISTER, Hon. Leslie Hull
Deputy Minister, Georgio Gaudet

Associated Agencies

Social Welfare Appeals Board
Citizens Advisory Councils
Miramichi Rehabilitation Centre Advisory Board

DEPT. OF SUPPLY & SERVICES

Room 471, Centennial Bldg., (Box 6000), Fredericton, N.B. E3B 5H1
Information Contact, D. Richford, phone: 506/453-2998

Acts Administered

Public Works Act
Public Purchasing Act
Queen's Printer Act

MINISTER, Hon. Harold N. Fanjoy
Deputy Minister, Glendon C. Graham
Executive Director, Bi-Centennial Commission, D.J. Lee
Executive Director, Finance & Admin., D. Richford
Executive Director, Buildings Division, R.P. Lynch
Executive Director, Printing & Translation, J.C. Hache
Queen's Printer, P. Lynch
Executive Director, Supply & Buildings Operation, J.H. Fowler
Manager, General Services, S. McDonald
Director, Supply, F.G. McLeod
Director, Maintenance, F.W. Boone
Executive Director, Data Processing, J.G. Scott

DEPT. OF TOURISM

Box 12345, Fredericton, N.B. E3B 5C3
Information from P.E. Thériault, Communications Supervisor, phone: 506/453-2377 –Toll free Tourism Information 1-800-561-0123

Acts Administered

Parks Act
Tourism Development Act

MINISTER, Hon. Leland McGaw
Deputy Minister, R.S. MacLaggan
Asst. Deputy Minister, J.K. McKay
Director, Administrative Services, A.P. Peterson
Director, Marketing, W.A. Broad
Director, Promotion, H.T. Gorman
Director, Technical Services, T.E. Kearney
Executive Director, Operations, D.J. Archibald
Director, Planning & Development, J.A. Syroid

DEPT. OF TRANSPORTATION

Box 6000, Fredericton, N.B. E3B 5H1
Information Contact, M.V. MacFadyen, 2nd floor, Kings Place, Fredericton, N.B. (phone: 506-453-2230)

Acts Administered

Corporation Securities Registration Act
Highway Act
Motor Carrier Act
Motor Vehicle Act
Motorized Snow Vehicles Act
Public Utilities Act
Securities Act
Security Frauds Prevention Act
N.B. Transportation Act

MINISTER, Hon. W.G. Bishop
Deputy Minister, G.D. Reeleder
Deputy Minister, Motor Vehicles Admin. & Public Safety, H.H.D. Cochrane
Asst. Deputy Minister (of Operations) & Chief Highway Engineer, L.W. Smith
Asst. Deputy Minister (of Policy, Planning & Communications), D.L. Seheult
Director of Structures, J.C. Fraser
Director of Technical Services, D.F. Hallett
Director of Design, G.A. Rushton
Director of Engineering Admin., M.V. MacFadyen
Director of Traffic, J.M. Veness
Director of Planning, P.E. Rouse
Director of Administrative Services, D. Stillwell
Director of Right of Way, M. McInnis
Director of Construction, F.V. Maddox
Director of Transportation & Communications, R.D. Macintosh
Motor Vehicle Director, & Registrar of Motor Vehicles, J.E. Ferris
License Suspension Appeal Board, 453-2016
Motor Vehicle Dealer Licensing Board, 453-2215
Tax Administration Director & Provincial Tax Commr., D.V. Bamford

Associated Agencies

N.B. Motor Carrier Board
110 Charlotte St., Saint John, N.B. E2L 2J4
(506) 658-2502
Secretary, W.P. MacMurray
Board of Commissioners of Public Utilities
110 Charlotte St., Saint John, N.B. E2L 2J4
(506) 658-2502
Chairman, A.J. Robichaud (act.)
Secretary, W.P. MacMurray

DEPT. OF YOUTH, RECREATION & CULTURAL RESOURCES

Centennial Bldg., Fredericton, N.B. E3B 5H1
Information Contact, E.H. Bringloe (phone: 506-453-2414)

Acts Administered

Libraries Act
Theatres, Cinematographs & Amusements Act
Youth Assistance Act

MINISTER, Hon. Jean-Pierre Ouellet
Deputy Minister, Normand Martin
Director, Administrative Services, E.H. Bringloe
Director, Recreation & Regional Development, J. Zauhar
Director, Student Aid, Mrs. E.L. Briggs
Director, Amateur Sports, R.J. McLenahan
Director, Cultural Affairs, John Saunders
Director, Handcrafts, George Fry
Director, N.B. Library Services, A. Hall

Associated Agency

N.B. Film Classification Board

PROVINCE OF NEWFOUNDLAND

Entered Confederation March 31, 1949
Area: 156,185 sq. miles
Population: 579,900 (1980 est.)
Seat of Government: Confederation Bldg., St. John's
Lieutenant-Governor: Hon. W. Anthony Paddon, C.M., M.D.
Private Secretary: Major Donald Barter

EXECUTIVE COUNCIL

Premier, and Minister for Intergovernmental Affairs, and Minister responsible for Communications, Hon. A.B. Peckford
President of the Council, Hon. Wm. W. Marshall, Q.C.
Minister of Finance, and President of the Treasury Board, Hon. Dr. J.F. Collins
Minister of Justice, Hon. G.R. Ottenheimer
Minister of Mines & Energy, Hon. Leo D. Barry
Minister of Development, Hon. H.N. Windsor
Minister of Health, Hon. H.W. House
Minister of Fisheries, Hon. James C. Morgan
Minister of Forest Resources & Lands, Hon. Charles J. Power
Minister of Rural, Agricultural & Northern Development, Hon. D.J. Goudie
Minister of Labour & Manpower, Hon. J.W. Dinn
Minister of Transportation, Hon. Ron Dawe
Minister of Social Services, Hon. T.V. Hickey
Minister of Culture, Recreation & Youth, and Minister of Environment, Hon. H.D. Andrews

Minister of Public Works & Services, Hon. D.H. Young
Minister of Municipal Affairs, Hon. Hazel R. Newhook
Minister of Education, Hon. Lynn Verge

Clerk of the Executive Council, David A. Vardy, 737-2844
Deputy Clerk of the Executive Council, R.J. Jenkins

HOUSE OF ASSEMBLY

Thirty-eighth General Assembly. Last Election, June 18th, 1979. Maximum Duration, 5 years.
Party Standings: Progressive Conservative (P.C.) 34; Liberal (Lib.) 17; Vacant 1; Total 52
Leader of the Opposition: Leonard Stirling
Indemnities: Sessional Indemnity, $19,000. In addition the Premier receives $28,455; other Ministers, $17,315; Leader of the Opposition, $17,315; Govt. Whip, $3,090; Opposition Whip, $3,090; Chairman of Committees (Deputy Speaker), $10,000; Speaker, $17,315; a Minister without Portforlio, $8,657; the Opposition House Leader, $10,000.
Officers: Speaker, Hon. Leonard Simms; Clerk of House of Assembly, Miss Bettie Duff; Law Clerk, John Noel; Sergeant-at-Arms, Cyril Kirby

Members

Following is constituency (population): member, and office phone number (address all mail to Confederation Bldg., St. John's, Nfld. A1C 5T7):

Baie Verte–White Bay (13,075): Tom Rideout, P.C., 737-3400
Bay of Islands (12,762): Luke Woodrow, P.C., 737-3400
Bellevue (13,453): Donald C. Jamieson, Lib., 737-3391
Bonavista North (11,101): Len Stirling, Lib., 737-3393
Bonavista South (8,662): James Morgan, P.C., 737-3226
Burgeo–Bay d'Espoir (8,788): Hal Andrews, P.C., 737-3400
Burin–Placentia West (12,996): Don Hollett, Lib., 737-3393
Carbonear (10,977): Rod Moores, Lib., 737-3392
Conception Bay South (16,552): John Butt, P.C., 737-3424
Eagle River (4,979): Ronald E. Hiscock, Lib., 737-3816
Exploits (13,759): Dr. Hugh Twomey, P.C., 737-3400
Ferryland (7,522): Charles Power, P.C., 737-2810
Fogo (9,692): Beaton Tulk, Lib., 737-3393
Fortune–Hermitage (9,540): Don Stewart, P.C., 737-3400
Gander (11,242): Hazel Newhook, P.C., 737-2574
Grand Bank (12,331): Leslie Thoms, Lib., 737-3393
Grand Falls (8,729): Leonard Simms, P.C., 737-3403
Green Bay (10,768): Brian Peckford, P.C., 737-3570
Harbour Grace (9,059): Haig Young, P.C., 737-3678
Harbour Main–Bell Island (11,890): Norman E. Doyle, P.C., 737-3400
Humber East (10,233): Lynn Verge, P.C., 737-3024
Humber Valley (12,658): Wallace House, P.C., 737-3124
Humber West (10,677): Raymond Baird, P.C., 737-3400
Kilbride (15,327): Robert J. Aylward, P.C., 737-3400
LaPoile (10,780): Stephen A. Neary, Lib., 737-3392
Lewisporte (13,241): Freeman White, Lib., 737-3393
Menihek (15,799): Peter J. Walsh, P.C., 737-3400
Mount Pearl (12,687): Neil Windsor, P.C., 737-3048
Mount Scio (10,824): Leo Barry, P.C., 737-2767
Naskaupi (10,110): Joe Goudie, P.C., 737-3200
Placentia (8,859): Bill Patterson, P.C., 737-3400
Pleasantville (16,664): Jerry Dinn, P.C., 737-2722
Port au Port (9,230): Jim Hodder, Lib., 737-3393
Port de Grave (11,004): Randy M. Collins, P.C., 737-3400
St. Barbe (11,516): Trevor Bennett, Lib., 737-3393
St. George's (10,328): Ronald G. Dawe, P.C., 737-3400
St. John's Centre (7,120): Dr. Patrick J. McNicholas, P.C., 737-3400
St. John's East (10,034): William Marshall, P.C., 722-7584
St. John's East Extern (12,344): Tom Hickey, P.C., 737-3580
St. John's North (9,231): John Carter, P.C., 737-3400
St. John's South (8,921): Dr. John Collins, P.C., 737-2942
St. John's West (8,249): Harold Barrett, P.C., 737-3400
St. Mary's–The Capes (8,311): Derek Hancock, Lib., 737-3816
Stephenville (10,624): Fred R. Stagg, P.C., 737-3400
Straits of Belle Isle (12,448): Edward Roberts, Lib., 737-3397
Terra Nova (9,842): Tom Lush, Lib., 737-3393
Torngat Mountains ( ): Garfield Warren, Lib., 737-3393
Trinity–Bay de Verde (9,116): vacant
Trinity North (10,644): Charles Brett, P.C., 737-3641
Twillingate (8,412): Wm. N. Rowe, Lib., 737-3393
Waterford–Kenmount (14,322): Gerry Ottenheimer, P.C., 737-2869
Windsor–Buchans (10,294): Graham Flight, Lib., 737-3816

OFFICE OF THE PREMIER

8th floor, Confederation Bldg., St. John's, Nfld. A1C 5T7
Parliamentary Asst., Norman Doyle, M.H.A.
Press Secretary, Frank Petten (737-3564)
Chief of Staff, Alvin Hewlett
Executive Asst., Des Sullivan
Executive Asst., Ms. Luanne Leamon
Senior Policy Advisor, Cabot Martin
Special Asst., Grand Falls, Jean Shea
Special Asst., Corner Brook, Mrs. Neta Allen

GOVERNMENT DEPARTMENTS

AGRICULTURE

See Rural Development

ALCOHOL & DRUG ADDICTION FOUNDATION

Box 4554, St. John's, Nfld. A1C 6C8
(709) 579-4041/2
Executive Director, George W.N. Skinner

OFFICE OF THE AUDITOR GENERAL

Confederation Bldg., St. John's, Nfld. A1C 5T7
(709) 737-2700
Auditor General, J.F. McGrath, C.A.
Deputy Auditor General, J.E. Richards, B.Comm.

NEWFOUNDLAND CANCER TREATMENT & RESEARCH FOUNDATION

25 Kenmount Rd., St. John's, Nfld. A1B 1W1
(709) 753-2599
Administrator, H.C. King

NEWFOUNDLAND CRIMES COMPENSATION BOARD

319 Duckworth St. (Box 5955, St. John's, Nfld. A1C 5X4)
(709) 726-3524

DEPT. OF CULTURE, RECREATION & YOUTH

146-148 Forest Rd. (Mailing: Confederation Bldg., St. John's, Nfld. A1C 5T7)
Information Contact, David Doyle, Public Information Officer (709/737-2922)

Acts Administered

Armistice Day Act
Arts Council Act
Canada Games Park Commission Act
Books (Preservation of Copies) Act
Commemoration Day Act
Exhibition of Advertisements Act
Floral Emblem Act
Historic Objects, Sites & Records Act
Labrador Act
Lands Transfer Act
National Flag Act
National Parks (Lands) Act
Nfld. Coat of Arms Act
Nfld. & Labrador Amateur Sports Federation Act
Nfld. Standard Time Act
Newspapers & Books Act
Provincial Parks Act

Public Libraries Act
Reindeer Agreement Act, 1937
Trout Hatcheries & Nurseries Act
Wild Life Act
Wilderness, Ecological, Reserves Act

MINISTER, Hon. Hal Andrews, 737-2810
Deputy Minister, S.F. Manuel, 737-2812
Asst. Deputy Minister, Cultural Affairs & Historic Resources, W.B. Frost, 737-3609
Asst. Deputy Minister, Parks & Youth Recreation, D.S. Johnson, 737-3556
Director of Administration, L.G. Christopher
Director, Wildlife Division, D.G. Pike
Director, Historic Resources Division, M. Bowe
Director, Provincial Parks Division, D. Hustins
Director, Cultural Affairs Division, J.C. Perlin
Director, Recreation & Sport Services, R. Hillier
Director, Youth Services, W. Wilson

DEPT. OF DEVELOPMENT

Ste. 504, Atlantic Place, St. John's, Nfld. (Mailing: Box 4750, St. John's, Nfld. A1C 5T7)
Information, phone: 709/737-2781

Acts Administered

Dept. of Development Act
Animal & Poultry Feed Mill Act
Industrial Development (Incentives) Act
Industries Act
Innkeepers Act
Nfld. Research Council Act
Tourist Establishments Act
and
Corner Brook Housing Corporation Act
Housing Act
Nfld. & Labrador Housing Corporation Act
St. John's Housing Corporation Act
St. John's Housing Corporation (Lands) Act
and
Thirteen Local, Personal and Private Statutes and/or Agreements (Acts).

MINISTER, Hon. Neil Windsor, 737-2791
Deputy Minister, H.M. Clarke, 737-2787
Asst. Deputy Minister, P.J. Duggan, 737-2788
Director, Tourist Services Division, M.L. Joy

Associated Agencies

Nfld. & Labrador Development Corp.
Box 9548, St. John's, Nfld. A1A 2Y4
(709) 753-3560
St. John's Housing Corp.
Elizabeth Towers, St. John's, Nfld. A1B 1R9
(709) 754-2640
Chairman, P. Withers
Nfld. & Labrador Housing Corp.
Box 220, St. John's, Nfld. A1C 5J2
(709) 722-3554
Chairman, P.G. Withers
Corner Brook Housing Corp.
c/o Confederation Bldg., St. John's, Nfld. A1C 5T7
Chairman, G. Easton

DEPT. OF EDUCATION

Confederation Bldg., St. John's, Nfld. A1C 5R9
Information from Supervisor of Information & Statistics (phone: 709 737-2990)

Acts Administered

College of Fisheries Act, 1964
College of Trades & Tech. Act, 1969
Dept. of Education Act, 1968
Education Apportionment Act, 1970
Education (Public Examinations) Act, 1956
Education (Teachers' Pensions) Act, 1962
Education (Teacher Training) Act, 1968
Local School Tax Act, 1970
Memorial Univ. Act, 1952
Regulation of Trades Schools Act, 1960
School Attendance Act, 1962
Teachers' Loan Act, 1957
Schools Act, 1970
Technical & Vocational Training Act, 1960
Vocational Education Act, 1952

MINISTER, Hon. L. Verge
Deputy Minister, C. Roebothan, M.Ed., 737-3027
Asst. Deputy Minister (Academic), Cyril McCormick, 737-3026
Asst. Deputy Minister (Financial), Donald Sansome, 737-3025
Asst. Deputy Minister (Elementary & Secondary Education), Lorne Wheeler, 737-3025
DIVISION OF ADMIN., Director, Aubrey Halfyard
Supervisor of Grants, R. Beaufield
Admin. Officer, J. Bennett
Supervisor of Student Aid, Norm Snelgrove
Registrar, Teachers' Certification, Bruce Caravan
DIVISION OF INSTRUCTION, Director, C.K. Brown, Ph.D.
Curriculum Section, Asst. Director, O.R. Lawrence, M.Ed.
Consultants:
English, E. Jones
Home Economics, vacant
Social Studies, Melvin Regular
Music, vacant
Vocational Education, S. Marshall
Art, vacant
Science, Harold Elliott
Physical Education, James Saunders, B.P.E., B.Ed.
Instructional Materials Section, Asst. Director, N. Harris
Testing Section, Asst. Director, Clifford Penney
DIVISION OF SCHOOL SERVICES, Boyce Fradsham
Supervisor of Educational Planning, Harold Press
Supervisor of Information, Robert Parsons
DIVISION OF SPECIAL SERVICES, Michael Steer
DIVISION OF TECHNICAL & VOCATIONAL EDUCATION, Director, A. Van Kesteren
DIVISION OF ADULT & CONTINUING EDUCATION, Director, Wm. Shallow
DENOMINATIONAL COMMITTEES:
Denominational Education Com., Integrated Education Com., Executive Secretary, M. Riggs
Roman Catholic Education Com., Executive Secretary, J.K. Tracey, Ph.D.
Pentecostal Education Com., Executive Secretary, Pastor A.E. Batstone

EMERGENCY MEASURES ORG.

c/o Dept. of Justice, Confederation Bldg., St. John's, Nfld. A1C 5T7 (709) 737-3703
Director, John Greer

DEPT. OF ENVIRONMENT

Elizabeth Towers (Mailing: Confederation Bldg., St. John's, Nfld. A1C 5T7)
Information from Information Services, Confederation Bldg.

Acts Administered

Dept. of Environment Act
Environmental Assessment Act
Pesticides Control Act
Waste Material (Disposal) Act
Waters Protection Act

MINISTER, Hon. H. Andrews
Deputy Minister, A. Kinsman
Asst. Deputy Minister, D.G. Jeans
Director of Admin., R.J. Learning

DEPT. OF FINANCE

Confederation Bldg., St. John's, Nfld. A1C 5T7

Information: Inquiries should be made to the Directors of the various divisions.

Acts Administered

Civil Service Act
Civil Service (Transferred Employees) Act
Conflict of Interest Act
Constabulary Pensions Act
Forest Land (Management & Taxation) Act
Gasoline Tax Act
Horse Racing (Regulation & Tax) Act
Increase of Pensions Act
Insurance Companies Tax Act
Insurance Premiums Tax Act
Members House of Assembly Pensions Act
Mining Tax Act
Public Service Pension Act
Retail Sales Tax Act
Tobacco Tax Act

MINISTER, Hon. Dr. John F. Collins, F.R.C.P.(E)
Deputy Minister, D.G. Norris, 737-2946
Asst. Deputy Minister (Revenue), Robert Clarke, 737-2955
Asst. Deputy Minister (Loan & Debt), Gilbert Gill, C.A., 737-2949
Comptroller of Finance, B.G. Carew, C.A.
Director of Admin., Mary Mansfield
Director of Debt Management, Anne Perry, C.A.
Director of Pensions & Payrolls, J.R. Bennett
Director of Government Accounts, Ian Cowan, C.A.
Director of Taxation, Robert Clarke
Director of Internal Audit, Eric Wells, C.A.
Director of Fiscal Policy, Brian Bursey

Associated Agencies

Nfld. Liquor Corp., Kenmount Rd., Box 8750, St. John's, Nfld. A1B 3V1 (709/754-1100); President, D.M. Chafe
Nfld. Municipal Financing Corp., Dept. of Finance, Confederation Bldg., St. John's, Nfld. A1C 5T7 (709/737-2926)

DEPT. OF FISHERIES

5th floor, Atlantic Place, St. John's, Nfld. A1C 5T7
Information from the Deputy Minister's Office

Acts Administered

Coasting Vessels (Bounties) Act
Fish Inspection Act
Fisheries Loan Act
Fishery Salt (Sale & Distribution) Act
Fishing Ships (Bounties) Act
Fishing & Coasting Vessels Rebuilding & Repairs (Bounties) Act, 1958
Salt Fish Marketing Act

MINISTER, Hon. Jim Morgan (737-3705)
Deputy Minister, G. Slade (737-3707)
Asst. Deputy Minister (Fisheries Development), Leslie Dean (737-3710)
Asst. Deputy Minister (Facilities), H.W. Goudie (737-3711)
Asst. Deputy Minister (Planning & Administration), R.A. Andrews (737-2754)
Director of Field Services, L. Shirley (737-3732)
Director of Admin., J. Dunphy (737-3708)
Chairman, Nfld. Fisheries Loan Board, Fred Pike (737-3692)
Chairman, Fishing Industry Advisory Board, Frank Dopplinger, Box 8010, Stn. A, St. John's, Nfld. A1B 3M7 (737-3695)

DEPT. OF FOREST RESOURCES & LANDS

6th Floor, Atlantic Place (Mailing: Box 4750, St. John's, Nfld. A1C 5T7)
Information from: R. Sparkes, Public Information Officer (709/737-3245)

Acts Administered

Abandoned Lands Act
Administration & Control of the Lands of the Crown (Transfer)
Anglo Newfoundland Development Co. Act
Alexis Watershed (Timber Operations) Act
Bowaters Act
Crown Lands Act
Development Areas (Lands) Act
Dept. of Forestry & Agriculture Act
Forest Fires Act
Forest (Exchange & Acquisition) Act
Forest Land Management & Taxation Act
Forest Management Clarification Act
Logging Camps Act
Labrador Lands Reservations Act
Newfoundland Geographical Names Board Act
Reservation of Land to the Crown Act
Sawmills Act
Transportation of Timber Act
Timber Licence (Reversion to the Crown)
Timber Scalers Act
Unimproved Lands (Redistribution Act)
Veterans Land Settlement Act

MINISTER, Hon. Charles Power, 737-3226
Deputy Minister, H.H. Stanley, 737-3228
Asst. Deputy Minister, Forestry, Dr. M. Nazir, 737-2704
Asst. Deputy Minister, Lands, K. Beanlands, 737-3236
Asst. Deputy Minister, Regional Services & Operations, S.W. Hoddinott, 737-3234
Director of Admin., Hollis Oates
Forestry Directors:
Director of Protection, J.A. Doyle
Director of Forest Management & Inventory, R. Mercer
Director of Forest Products Development, R. Pelley
Land Directors:
Director of Crown Lands Admin., John Power
Director of Surveying, Neil MacNaughton
Director of Mapping, R. Crutcher
Director of Land Management, R. Warren
Director of Research, G. Thomas
Regional Services Directors:
Eastern Region Director, R. Winsor, Bldg. T851, Pleasantville, Nfld. A1C 5T7 (737-2641)
Central Region Director, R.M. Carroll, 30 Airport Blvd., Gander, Nfld. A1V 1T5 (256-7131)
Western Region Director, I. Downton, Box 1017, Corner Brook, Nfld. A2H 6J3 (639-9111)
Labrador Region Director, A. King, Box 370, Goose Bay, Lab. A0P 1C0, 896-3405

HARMON CORP.

277 Oregon Ave., Box 328, Stephenville, Nfld. A2N 2Z5
Phone: (709) 643-3771
General Manager, Walter H. MacKay
Chairman, J.G. Cochrane, Box 328, Stephenville, Nfld. A2N 2Z5 (643-2363)

DEPT. OF HEALTH

Confederation Bldg., St. John's, Nfld. A1C 5T7
Information Contact, C. Templeman, Director of Admin. (phone: 709 737-3106)

Acts Administered

Children's Hospital (Management) Act
Communicable Diseases Act
Dental Act
Dept. of Health Act
Embalmers & Funeral Directors Act
Exhumation Act
Food & Drugs Act
General Hospital (Management) Act
Grand Falls Hospital (Management) Act
Health & Public Welfare Act
Homes for Special Care Act, 1973
Hospital Insurance (Agreement) Act
Mentally Incompetent Persons Estate Act
Midwifery Act

Nfld. Dietitians Act
Nfld. Hospital Association Act
Nfld. Medical Care Insurance Act
Nfld. Registered Nurses Act
Optometry Act
Pharmaceutical Act
Physiotherapy Act
Private Homes for Special Care (Allowances) Act, 1973
Registration (Vital Statistics) Act
Solemnization of Marriage Act, 1974 (to be proclaimed)
St. Clare's Mercy Hospital (Incorporation) Act
Venereal Disease Prevention Act
Welfare Institutions Licensing Act
Western Memorial Hospital Corporation Act

Cancer Treatment & Research Foundation Act, 1971
Human Tissue Act, 1971
Mental Health Act, 1971
Hospitals Act, 1971
Medical Act, 1974

MINISTER, Hon. H.W. House
Deputy Minister, A.M. Hearn, B.Comm., D.H.A., 737-3127
Asst. Deputy Minister, D. Howell, 737-3130

A/Director of Planning & Development, G. Gover
Director of Admin., C.E. Templeman
Director of Health Policy, Gerald White, B.Comm.
Director, Government Hospitals & Medical Services, Cyril Galway
Chief Medical Health Officer, David Severs, B.M., Bch.
Director, Hospital Services Division, A.N. Ludlow, B.Comm.
Director of Mental Health Services, Howard Strong, M.D.
Director of Tuberculosis Control, E. Knowling, M.D.
Director, Public Health Inspection Services Division, D.A. Strong, C.S.I. (C)
Director of the Nfld. Public Health Laboratories, Ralph Butler, Ph.D., Dip. Bact.
Director, Public Health Nursing Division, Miss J. Lewis, S.R.N.
Registrar of Vital Statistics, Harvey J. Dewey
(Fee for each Birth, Marriage, or Death Certificate issued: $5.)

Associated Agencies

Nfld. Medical Care Commission
Elizabeth Towers, Elizabeth Ave., St. John's, Nfld. A1C 5J3
(709) 722-6980
Executive Director, Robert Peddigrew
Medical Director, Gregory Russell, M.D.

NEWFOUNDLAND & LABRADOR HYDRO

Philip Place, (Box 9100, St. John's, Nfld. A1A 2X8)
(709) 753-8990
Chairman & Chief Executive, V.L. Young
Vice President, Corporate Planning, D.W. Mercer
Vice President, Legal, C.J. Greene, Q.C.
Vice President, Operations, J.P. Henderson
Director, Public Relations, C.W. Bursey
Director, Industrial Relations, S. Dicks
Vice President, Engineering & Construction, L.J. Cole
Vice President, Finance, John Baxter
Director, Construction, E.W. Rendell
Director, Engineering, G. Sturge

INTERGOVERNMENTAL AFFAIRS SECRETARIAT

(Executive Council)
Confederation Bldg., St. John's, Nfld. A1C 5T7
(709) 737-2848
Information from: G. Korbai, Director of Support Services, 709/737-3670
Minister, Hon. A. Brian Peckford
Deputy Minister, Cyril J. Abery

DEPT. OF JUSTICE

Confederation Bldg., St. John's, Nfld. A1C 5T7
Information Contact, G.W. Smith, Asst. Deputy Minister, Administration & Planning (phone: 709 737-2890)

Acts Administered

Accident & Sickness Insurance Act, 1971
Assignment of Book Debts Act
Attachment of Wages Act
Automobile Dealers Act
Automobile Insurance Act
Bills of Sale Act
Bulk Sales Act
Certified Public Accountants Act
Change of Name Act, 1978
Chartered Accountants Act
Chartered Accountants & Certified Public Accountants Merger Act
Chattels Real Act
Collection Agencies Act
Companies (Guarantees) Act
Commissioner for Oaths Act
Companies Act
Conditional Sales Act
Constabulary Act
Conveyancing Act
Co-operative Societies Act
Credit Reporting Agencies Act
Criminal Injuries Compensation Act
Detention of Intoxicated Persons Act
Direct Sellers Act
District Court Act, 1976
Election Act
Electoral Boundaries Delimitation Act, 1973
Emergency Measures Act
Exhumation Act
Evidence Act
Family Courts Act
Fatal Accidents Act
Fire Insurance Act
Fire Prevention Act
Hawkers & Pedlars Act
Human Rights Anti-Discrimination Act
Income Tax Discounters Act
Industrial Accidents Inquiries Act
Industrial Accountants Act
Industrial & Provident Societies Act
Inspection of Legal Offices Act
Insurance Adjusters Act
Insurance Companies Act
Insurance Contracts Act
Investment Contracts Act
Judgment Recovery (Nfld.) Ltd. Act
Judicature Act
Justices Act
Landlord Tenant (Residential Tenancies) Act
Legal Aid Act
Life & Accident Insurance Agents (Licensing) Act
Life Insurance Act
Limited Partnership Act
Loan Companies & Finance Companies (Licensing) Act
Lodgers' Goods Protection Act
Maintenance Orders (Enforcement) Act
Maritime Hospital Service Association Re-Incorporation Act, 1949
Matrimonial Properties Act
Mechanics' Lien Act
Mortgage Brokers Act
Motor Carrier Act
Nfld. Architects Act
Nfld. Company of Rangers Act
Nfld. Consumer Protection Act
Nfld. Engineering Profession Act
Nfld. Family Guidance Association Act, 1972
Nfld. Hairdressers' Association Act
Nfld. Human Rights Code

Nfld. Law Reform Commission Act, 1971
Act 1, Geo. V, Cap. 5 (concerning the Nfld. Marine Insurance Co. Ltd. of Nfld.)
Notaries Public Act
Oaths Act
Parliamentary Commissioner (Ombudsman) Act
Partnership Act
Partners & Joint Debtors (Compromises) Act
Pension Plans (Designation of Beneficiaries) Act
Perpetuities & Accumulations Act
Pesticides Control Act
Petty Trespass Act
Prisons Act
Private Investigators & Security Guards Act
Proceedings Against the Crown Act
Provincial Court Act, 1974
Public Accountancy Act
Public Enquiries Act
Public Utilities Act
Public Utilities (Acquisition of Lands) Act
Real Estate Trading Act
Registration of Deeds Act
Sale of Goods Act
Salvage Dealers Licensing Act
Securities Act
Small Claims Act
St. John's Fire Department Act, 1972
Summary Proceedings Act
Tenements (Recovery of Possession) Act
Trade Practices Act
Trustee Act
Trust & Loan Companies (Licensing) Act
Unconscionable Transactions Relief Act
Unified Family Court Act
Unsolicited Goods & Credit Cards Act
Warehousemen's Lien Act
Warehouse Receipts Act
Weights & Measures Act

MINISTER OF JUSTICE & ATTORNEY GENERAL, Hon. Gerald R. Ottenheimer
Deputy Minister of Justice & Deputy Attorney General, R.G. Penney, 737-2872
Associate Deputy Minister of Justice, Miss M. Cameron, 737-2880
Associate Deputy Attorney General, C.J. Goodyear, 737-2868
Asst. Deputy Minister, Admin. & Planning, G.W. Smith
Asst. Deputy Minister, Consumer Affairs, R. Barter
Office of the Legislative Counsel
Senior Legislative Counsel, A.J. Noel
Legislative Counsel, L. Black, C. Lake
Chief Crown Prosecutor, J. Byrne
Criminal Law Division, R. Hyslop, R. Richards, M. Roche, S. O'-Regan, J. Embree, Ruth Peters, R. Simmonds, E. Cardwell
Civil Law Division, J.A. Nesbitt, Q.C., F. McLoughlin, Mary E. Noonan, I.A. Grey, M. Cameron, H. Buckingham, J. Cummings, A. Battcock, G. Lang, Q.C., R. Cole, J. Ashley, J. Thistle
Chief of Police, R.J. Roche, Royal Newfoundland Constabulary
Chief of St. John's Fire Dept., A. Gosse
Fire Commissioner, J. Cardoulis
Director of Adult Corrections, M. McNutt
Supt., H.M. Penitentiary, A. Yetman
Director, Provincial Firearms Admin., H. Vivian
Director, Emergency Measures Org., J. Greer
Chief Accountant, G. Mouland
Inspector of Legal Offices, F. Squires
Chief Supt., R.C.M.P., W. Schramm
Registrar of Deeds, Companies & Securities, Gerald Tessier, Q.C.
Chief Electoral Officer, D. Whelan
Human Rights Commission: Commr., Mrs. G. Keough
Registrar of Bills & Sales, Mrs. D. Driscoll
Director of Consumer Affairs, Mrs. B. Lane
Director of Corporate Affairs, and Supt. of Insurance, G. French
Director of Landlord Tenant Relations, C. Bradbury
Registrar of Co-operatives, S. Kean

Associated Agencies

Board of Commrs. of Public Utilities
The Nfld. Crimes Compensation Board
The Nfld. Family Guidance Association
Nfld. Law Reform Commission
Nfld. Legal Aid Commission
NOTE:- Address for each of the above is c/o Dept. of Justice, Confederation Bldg., St. John's, Nfld. A1C 5T7

DEPT. OF LABOUR & MANPOWER

Confederation Bldg., St. John's, Nfld. A1C 5T7
Information from the Deputy Minister's Office

Acts Administered

Dept. of Labour & Manpower Act
Apprenticeship Act
Barbers & Hairdressers Shop Closing Act
Blind Workmen's Compensation Act
Boiler & Pressure Vessel Act
Building Contractors (Licensing) Act
Elevators Act
Emergency Compensation of Employees Act
Employers' Liability Act
Fishing Industry (Collective Bargaining) Act, 1971
Industrial Standards Act
Industrial Statistics Act
Labour Relations Act
Labour Standards Act
Nfld. Teacher (Collective Bargaining) Act
Occupational Health & Safety Act
Public Service (Collective Bargaining) Act
Radiation Health & Safety Act
Shops Closing Act
Workmen's Compensation Act

MINISTER, Hon. J.W. Dinn
Deputy Minister, T.A. Blanchard, 737-2723
Asst. Deputy Minister of Labour, A. Bannister, 737-2715
Asst. Deputy Minister of Manpower, R.K. Langdon, 737-2721
Executive Director, Occupational Health & Safety, Dr. A.L. Colohan
Director of Admin., R.C. Williams
Director of Industrial Relations, H. Noseworthy
Director of Manpower, C.J. Carter
Director of Labour Standards, G.H.D. Jackman
Director of Engineering & Technical Services, A.W. Diamond
Industrial Standards Officer, W.J. Dwyer

Associated Agencies

Labour Relations Board, Confederation Bldg., St. John's, Nfld. A1C 5T7 (737-2707); Chairman, G.G. Easton; Chief Executive Officer, J.M. Noel
Labour Standards Board, Confederation Bldg., St. John's, Nfld. A1C 5T7 (737-2742); Chairman, D. Dooley
Manpower Training & Certification Board, Confederation Bldg., St. John's, Nfld. A1C 5T7; Chairman, K.F. Duggan, P. Eng.
Workers' Compensation Board, #146, 148 Forest Rd., Box 9000, St. John's, Nfld. A1A 3B8 (754-2940); Chairman, E. Maynard

LAW REFORM COMMISSION

c/o Justice Dept., Confederation Bldg., St. John's, Nfld. A1C 5T7 (709/737-2880)

DEPT. OF MINES & ENERGY

Box 4750, St. John's, Nfld. A1C 5T7
Information Contact, Kevin Whelan, Director of Admin. (phone: (709) 737-3660)

Acts Administered

Dept. of Mines & Energy Act
Electrical Power Control Act

Labrador Lands (Reservation) Act
Mineral Act, 1976
Mineral Lands, Certain, Act
Mineral Vesting in the Crown Act
Nfld. & Labrador Hydro Act
Nfld. & Labrador Hydro (Water Power) Act
Nfld. & Labrador Rural Electricity Act
Petroleum & Natural Gas Act
Quarry Materials Act, 1976
Regulation of Mines Act
Rescission of Reservation Act
Rural Electrification Act
Undeveloped Mineral Areas Act

MINISTER, Hon. Leo Barry, 737-2767
Deputy Minister, John H. McKillop, 737-2766
Asst. Deputy Minister, Mines, John M. Fleming, 737-2768
Asst. Deputy Minister, Energy, Edward Power, 737-2764
Director of Admin., Kevin Whelan, 737-3660
Director of Energy Policy, Douglas Inkster, 737-2765
Director of Mineral Development, Bryan Greene, 737-2763
Director of Mineral Lands & Mines, Norman Kipnis, P.Eng., 737-2773
Director of Mines & Quarries, William J. Walsh, 737-2773
Accountant, Felix Croke, 737-3660
Administrator of Field Surveys, Wayne Ryder, 737-2301
Registrar, Miss Eileen Cody, 737-3660

Associated Agencies
Nfld. & Labrador Hydro, Philip Place, St. John's, Nfld.
Offshore Petroleum Directorate, Atlantic Place, St. John's, Nfld.
Rural Electricity Authority, Philip Place, St. John's, Nfld.

DEPT. OF MUNICIPAL AFFAIRS
Confederation Bldg., St. John's, Nfld. A1C 5T7
Information from Office of the Deputy Minister (phone: 709 737-3049)

Acts Administered
Assessment Act
Assessment (Validation) Act, 1959
Botwood Water Corp. Act, 1952
Carbonear Fire Brigade Act
Carbonear Water Co. Acts
City of Corner Brook Act
City of St. John's Acts
Crown Corporations (Local Taxation) Act
Development Areas (Lands) Act
Harbour Grace Water Co. Acts
(Town of) Jerseyside Boundaries Act
Larkin's Pond Reservoir Act
Municipal Grants Act
Municipalities Act
Nuisances & Municipal Regulations Act
Rural District of Placentia (Amendment) Act, 1953
St. John's Municipal Elections Act
St. John's Metropolitan Area Act
St. John's Municipal Loans Acts
Town Council Bond Guarantee Act, 1951
Urban & Rural Planning Act
Water & Sewerage Corp. of Greater Corner Brook Act, 1951

MINISTER, Hon. Hazel Newhook
Deputy Minister, C. Randell, 737-3049
Asst. Deputy Minister (Technical Services), W. Haynes, 737-3050
Asst. Deputy Minister (Local Govt. Services), R.E. Corbett, 737-3051
Director of Local Government Admin., A.W. Brown
Director of Assessments, N. Mullett
Director of Municipal Engineering Services, E.W. Mercer
Local Government Engineer, S.G. Dyke
Director of Urban & Rural Planning, J.T. Allston
Director of Admin., W.O. Hiscock
Director of Municipal Finance, C. Goodland
Director of Development Control, D.J. Ryan

OMBUDSMAN
49 - 55 Elizabeth Ave., St. John's, Nfld. A1C 5T7
Phone: (709) 753-7730
Parliamentary Commr. (Ombudsman), Ambrose H. Peddle

BOARD OF COMMRS. OF PUBLIC UTILITIES
120 Torbay Rd., St. John's, Nfld. A1A 2X9
(709) 726-6432
Chairman, J.A.G. MacDonald, P.Eng.
Vice Chairmen, R.E. Good, C.W. Earle, C.A.
Commr., G.F. Lawrence
Clerk, Carol Horwood
Executive Director, E.H. Hodder

DEPT. OF PUBLIC WORKS & SERVICES
Confederation Bldg., Box 4750, St. John's, Nfld. A1C 5T7
Information Contact, D.C. Peckham, Asst. Deputy Minister, Admin. (phone: 709/737-3374)

Acts Administered
Civil Service Act
Public Service (Pensions) Amendment Act
Public Service Commission Act
Expropriations Act
Family Home Expropriation Act
Financial Administration Act
Public Works Act
Public Tender Act
Polytechnical Institute Act
Pippy Park Commission Act

MINISTER, Hon. H. Young
Deputy Minister, V. Hollett, 737-3676
Asst. Deputy Minister, Admin., D.C. Peckham, 737-3374
Assoc. Deputy Minister, Technical, T.E. Bursey, 737-3377
Director, Finance & Admin., W. Delaney
Director, Tendering & Contracts, B. Hillyard
Director, Property Management, E. White
Registrar, J. Kelsey
Director, Planning & Construction, R. Brophy
Administrator, Accommodations, L. Newhook
Director, Printing Services, D. Dawe
Director, Newfoundland Information Services, R. Callahan
Director, Government Purchasing Agency, E.E. Rowe
Director, Fleet Management, N. Payne
Director, Design Division, E. Snook
Director, Expropriations, K. Brocklehurst

Public Service Commission
(16 Forest Rd., St. John's, A1C 2B9)
(709) 737-2751
Chairman, A.J. Goss
Vice Chairman, V.J. Rossiter
Commrs., J.G. Weeks, D. Whitten

C.A. Pippy Park Commission
(Box 12, 79 Nagle's Hill)
Executive Director, A.M. Cochrane

DEPT. OF RURAL, AGRICULTURAL & NORTHERN DEVELOPMENT
Confederation Bldg., St. John's, Nfld. A1C 5T7
Information Contact, Irvine Mullett, Information Specialist (709/737-3172)

Acts Administered
Dept. of Rural, Agricultural & Northern Development Act
Agricultural Societies Act
Dog Act
Farm Development Loan Act
Fur Farms Act
Livestock Act
Livestock (Community Sales) Act
Livestock (Health) Act

Livestock (Insurance) Act
Meat Inspection Act
Natural Products Marketing Act
Newfoundland Crop Insurance Act
Newfoundland Farm Products Corp. Act
Newfoundland Veterinary Medical Act
Plant Protection Act
Poultry & Poultry Products Act
Protection of Animals Act
Vegetable (Grading) Act

MINISTER, Hon. Joseph Goudie
Deputy Minister, G.J. O'Reilly, 737-3202
Asst. Deputy Minister, Rural Development, Terence Healey, 737-3201
Asst. Deputy Minister, Agriculture, W.C. Parkinson, 737-3787
Asst. Deputy Minister, Northern Development, John McGrath, 896-8646, Goose Bay

Boards & Commissions

Rural Development Authority, Manager, D. Stone
Community Development Board, Chairman, Neville Squire
Rural Incentives Board, Chairman, F. Cook
Federal/Provincial Craft Board, Chairman, F. Cook

Agricultural Agencies & Marketing Boards

Agricultural Products Marketing Board
Provincial Agriculture Bldg., Box 4750, St. John's, Nfld. A1C 5T7
(709) 737-3799
Chairman, George Cross

Nfld. Farm Development Loan Board
Provincial Agriculture Bldg., Box 4750, St. John's, Nfld. A1C 5T7
(709) 737-3799
Manager, D. Stone

Nfld. Farm Products Corp.
Bldg. 902, Box 9311, Stn. B, St. John's, Nfld. A1A 2Y3
(709) 722-3751
President, J. McDonald

Nfld. Egg Marketing Board
Box 9396, St. John's, Nfld. A1A 2Y3
(709) 722-2953
Manager, M.F. Dicks

Nfld. Chicken Marketing Board
Prudential Bldg., Box 9251, St. John's, Nfld. A1A 2X9
(709) 722-7490
Manager, A.J. Hutchings

DEPT. OF SOCIAL SERVICES

Confederation Bldg., St. John's, Nfld. A1C 5T7
Information Contact, Ms. Lynn Churchill, Information Officer (709/737-2656)

Acts Administered

Adoption of Children Act
Blind Persons Allowances Act
Child Welfare Act
Children of Unmarried Parents Act
Disabled Persons Act
Social Assistance Act
Welfare of Children Act
Alcohol Education Research Foundation Act
Limited Administration of Estates (Members of Services) Act
Welfare Institutions Licensing Act
Day Care & Homemaker Act
Neglected Adults Act
Social Workers Registration Act
Rehabilitation Act
Private Homes for Special Care (Allowances) Act

MINISTER, Hon. T.V. Hickey
Deputy Minister, G. Pike, 737-3582
Asst. Deputy Minister, Income Support & Family Services, G. Pope, 737-3585
Asst. Deputy Minister, Rehabilitation & Community Resource Development, F. Compton, 737-3594
Director of Admin., E. Johnson
Director of Social Assistance, M.J. Vincent
Director of Child Welfare, F.J. Simms
Director of Juvenile Corrections, R. Rowsell
Director of Rehabilitation, W. Davis
Director of Mental Retardation Services, Noel Browne
Nutritional Consultant, Ms. M. Coombes
Director of Regional Services, R. Tiller
Director of Employment Opportunities, A. Vaughan
Director of Day Care & Homemaker Services, & Director of Staff Development, Mrs. V. Hoyles
Director of Services to Senior Citizens, R. Gabriel
Director of Planning & Research, R. Day
Director of Enquiries, Mrs. Mary Codner

Associated Agencies

Address: Confederation Bldg., St. John's
The Social Assistance Appeal Board
The Child Welfare Board
The Youth Guidance Authority
Day Care & Homemaker Services Licensing Board

SUCCESSION DUTY OFFICE

For information, write to Dept. of Finance, Confederation Bldg., St. John's, Nfld. A1C 5T7

DEPT. OF TRANSPORTATION

6th floor, Atlantic Place, Water St., St. John's, Nfld. A1C 6C9
Information from Administrative Officer (phone: 709 737-2300)

MINISTER, Hon. Ron Dawe
Deputy Minister, A.L. White, P. Eng., 737-3643
Asst. Deputy Minister, Administrative Services, M.J. Fewer, 737-3639
Asst. Deputy Minister, Technical Services, J. O'Reilly, P.Eng., 737-3640
Director of Admin., E.J. Browne
Registrar of Motor Vehicles, Michael Haire, Viking Bldg., St. John's
Director of Transportation, E.J. O'Brien
Air Services Co-ordinator, William Brown

TREASURY BOARD

Confederation Bldg., St. John's, Nfld. A1C 5T7
(709) 737-2467 (Asst. Secretary, Management)
President, Hon. Dr. John Collins, 737-2942
Secretary, Peter Kennedy, 737-3359
Asst. Secretary (Financial), D.K. Roberts, 737-2646
Asst. Secretary (Personnel), W.D.L. Powell, 737-2633
Director, Organization & Management, A.B. Peckford, 737-2840
Director, Budgeting, E.P. Kent, 737-2473
Director, Collective Bargaining, Allan Andrews, 737-2471
Director, Classification & Pay, Raymond Finn, 737-3383
Director, Insurance Division, Gerald Winsor, 737-2310
Director, Treasury Board Staff, Noreen Holden, 737-2467

COUNCIL OF MARITIME PREMIERS

Box 2044, Halifax, N.S. B3J 2Z1
(902) 424-7590

Activities of the Council include the fostering of policy co-ordination and program co-operation between the three Maritime Provinces (New Brunswick, Nova Scotia, Prince Edward Island) in such fields as Regional Economic Development; Transportation; Communications; Energy; Education; Offshore Resources......

The Council of Maritime Premiers has four agencies:

Maritime Provinces Higher Education Commission: an advisory body to government and a co-ordinator and advisor to post-secondary institutions of higher education.

Land Registration & Information Service: a mapping and survey group charged with establishing a reformed land registry system.

Maritime Resource Management Service: provides special services to the region in cartography, planning, aerial photography and resource management and planning.

Maritime Municipal Training & Development Board: is dedicated to the improvement of municipal administrative capabilities.

The Council Secretariat provides continuity and administration for the Council's activities. A Regional Treasury Board provides overall budgetary, administrative and personnel supervision.

ATLANTIC PROVINCES ECONOMIC COUNCIL

One Sackville Place, #500, Halifax, N.S. B3J 1K1
(902) 422-6516
Executive Vice President, vacant
and
181 Westmorland St., Fredericton, N.B. E3B 3L6 (506/455-6689)
and
136 Crosbie Rd., St. John's, Nfld. A1B 3K3 (709/722-5830)

PROVINCE OF NOVA SCOTIA

Entered Confederation July 1, 1867
Area: 21,425 sq. miles
Population: 852,500 (1980 est.)
Seat of Government: Province House, Halifax
Lieutenant Governor: The Hon. J.E. Shaffner

EXECUTIVE COUNCIL

Premier, President of the Executive Council, and Chairman of the Policy Board, Hon. John M. Buchanan, Q.C.
Minister of Development, Hon. Roland J. Thornhill
Minister of Lands & Forests, Hon. George Henley
Minister of Health, Hon. Gerald Sheehy
Attorney General, and Provincial Secretary, Hon. Harry How, Q.C.
Minister of Mines & Energy, Hon. Ronald Barkhouse
Minister of Agriculture & Marketing, Hon. Roger Bacon
Minister of Tourism, Hon. Bruce Cochran
Minister of Municipal Affairs, Hon. John MacIsaac
Minister of Labour & Manpower, Hon. Kenneth Streatch
Chairman of Management Board, Hon. Ronald Giffin
Minister of Education, Hon. Terence Donahoe
Minister of Transportation, Hon. Thomas J. McInnis
Minister of Finance, Hon. Joel Matheson, Q.C.
Minister of Social Services, Hon. Laird Stirling
Minister of Government Services, Hon. Gerald Lawrence
Minister of Fisheries, and Minister of Intergovernmental Affairs, Hon. Edmund Morris
Minister of Consumer Affairs, Hon. Ronald S. Russell
Minister of Environment, Hon. R. Fisher Hudson, Q.C.
Minister of Culture, Recreation & Fitness, Hon. J. Greg Kerr
Secretary to the Executive Council, Joseph H. Clarke, 902/424-6611
Clerk of the Executive Council, Harold F.G. Stevens, 902/424-5970

HOUSE OF ASSEMBLY

Fifty third Assembly. Last Election, October 6, 1981. Maximum Duration, 5 years.
Party Standings: Progressive Conservative (P.C.) 37; Liberal (Lib.) 13; New Democratic Party (N.D.P.) 1; Independent (Ind.) 1; Total, 52.
Leader of the Opposition, A.M. (Sandy) Cameron
Indemnities & Allowances (1982): Members' Sessional Indemnity, $16,400 & $8,200 Expenses Allowance. In addition to the Sessional Indemnity and Expense Allowance the Premier receives $32,000; Other Ministers $25,000; Leader of the Opposition $25,000; Speaker $15,000; Deputy Speaker, $7,500.
Officers: Speaker, Hon. Arthur Donahoe; Clerk of Assembly, H.F. Muggah (phone: 902/424-5978); Asst. Clerk, R.K. MacArthur; Legislative Counsel, Graham Walker; Sergeant-at-Arms, Harold Long.

Members (preliminary list)

Following is constituency: member, address and phone:

Annapolis East: Gerald Sheehy, D.V.M., P.C., Box 787, Middleton, BOS 1PO (825-4637)
Annapolis West: J. Greg Kerr, P.C., R.R. 1, Granville Ferry, BOS 1KO (532-5426)
Antigonish: Dr. J. William Gillis, Lib., R.R. 4, Lanark, B2G 2L2 (863-3242)
Argyle: Hugh Tinkham, Lib., R.R. 5, Dayton, B5A 4A9 (742-2957)
Bedford–Musquodoboit Valley: Kenneth Streatch, P.C., Elderbank, BON 1KO (384-2096)
Cape Breton Centre: Dr. M. Laffin, P.C., 3430 Duggan Ave., New Waterford, B1H 1P5
Cape Breton East: Don MacLeod, P.C., 25 Forrest St., Glace Bay, B1A 1G8
Cape Breton North: Brian Young, P.C., 81 Meech Ave. N., Sydney, B2A 3M4
Cape Breton Nova: Paul MacEwan, Ind., Box 1, Whitney Pier, B1N 3B1 (539-6146)
Cape Breton South: Vincent MacLean, Lib., 62 Milton St., Sydney, B1P 4L8 (539-6659)
Cape Breton The Lakes: Osborne Fraser, Lib., 151 Monteith Ave., Westmount, B1R 1K9 (539-5353)
Cape Breton West: Donald MacLeod, P.C., R.R. 2, Marion Bridge, B0A 1P0
Clare: Chester Melanson, Lib., Box 35, Church Point, B0W 1M0
Colchester North: Ed Lorraine, Lib., R.R. 5, Truro, B2N 5B3
Colchester South: Dr. R. Colin Stewart, P.C., Box 190, Stewiacke, BON 2JO (378-2214)
Cole Harbour: Dave Nantes, P.C., 80 AspenWay, Dartmouth, B2V 1H8 (434-5821)
Cumberland Centre: Guy Brown, Lib., Box 1049, Springhill, BOM 1XO (597-3863)
Cumberland East: Roger Bacon, P.C., R.R. 6, Amherst, B4H 3Y4 (667-8674)
Cumberland West: George Henley, P.C., Box 261, Oxford, BOM 1PO (447-2662)
Dartmouth East: Richard Weldon, P.C., 25 Raymoor Dr., Dartmouth, B2X 1G6 (434-5236)

Dartmouth North: Laird Stirling, P.C., 96 Chappell St., Dartmouth, B3A 3P8 (466-5711)
Dartmouth South: Roland Thornhill, P.C., 299 Portland St., Dartmouth, B2Y 1K3 (469-2309)
Digby: Joseph Casey, Lib., R.R. 2, Granville Ferry, BOS 1KO (532-5015)
Guysborough: A.M. (Sandy) Cameron, Lib., Box 70, Sherbrooke, BOJ 3CO (522-2020)
Halifax Atlantic: John Buchanan, Q.C., P.C., 3 Leiblin Dr., Halifax, B3R 1N2 (477-2648)
Halifax Bedford Basin: Joel R. Matheson, Q.C., P.C., 30 Robert Allen Dr., Halifax, B3M 3G8 (443-1616)
Halifax Chebucto: Alexa McDonough, N.D.P., 1581 Conrose Ave., Halifax, B3H 4C4
Halifax Citadel: Arthur R. Donahoe, P.C., 2190 Armcrescent E., Halifax, B3L 3C7 (429-5670)
Halifax Cornwallis: Terry Donahoe, P.C., 1641 Walnut St., Halifax, B3H 3S3 (423-3385)
Halifax Eastern Shore: Thomas McInnis, P.C., Box 158, Musquodoboit Harbour, B0J 2L0 (889-3444)
Halifax Needham: Edmund Morris, P.C., 15 Fleming Dr., Halifax, B3P 1A8 (477-5017)
Halifax St. Margaret's: Jerry Lawrence, P.C., 8 Kingfisher Cres., Halifax, B3M 3B2 (443-5266)
Hants East: Jack Hawkins, Lib., Enfield, Hants County, B0N 1N0
Hants West: Ron Russell, P.C., R.R. 1, Falmouth, BOP 1LO (798-8528)
Inverness North: John Archie MacKenzie, Lib., Belle Cote, BOE 1CO (235-2233)
Inverness South: B.J. MacLean, P.C., 25 Philpott St., Port Hawkesbury, B0E 2V0
Kings North: Edd Twohig, P.C., Box 877, Kentville, B4N 2A9 (678-1211)
Kings South: Harry W. How, P.C., 5 Bay St., Wolfville, BOP 1XO (542-3019)
Kings West: George Moody, P.C., R.R. 1, Waterville, BOP 1VO (538-3094)
Lunenburg Centre: Bruce Cochran, P.C., Box 440, Mahone Bay, BOJ 2EO (624-9095)
Lunenburg East: Ron Barkhouse, P.C., New Ross, BOJ 2MO (389-2029)
Lunenburg West: M.C. (Mel) Pickings, P.C., R.R. 3, Bridgewater, B4V 2W2 (543-4269)
Pictou Centre: Jack MacIsaac, P.C., 204 Almont Ave., New Glasgow, B2H 3G9 (752-8087)
Pictou East: Donald Cameron, P.C., R.R. 3, Merigomish, BOK 1GO (926-2889)
Pictou West: Donald P. McInnes, P.C., R.R. 2, Pictou, BOK 1HO (485-6864)
Queens: John Leefe, P.C., 38 Barss St., Liverpool, BOT 1KO (354-5553)
Richmond: Greg MacIsaac, P.C., Box 961, Port Hawkesbury, B0E 2V0
Sackville: Malcolm A. MacKay, P.C., 158 Stokil Dr., Lower Sackville, B4C 2G6 (865-0405)
Shelburne: Harold M. Huskilson, Lib., Box 298, Shelburne, BOT 1WO (875-2822)
Truro–Bible Hill: Ron Giffin, P.C., 34 Broad St., Truro, B2N 3G2 (895-5600)
Victoria: R. Fisher Hudson, P.C., Box 153, Baddeck, BOE 1BO (295-3462)
Yarmouth: J. Fraser Mooney, Lib., 60 Porter St., Yarmouth, B5A 2Y9 (742-9146)

OFFICE OF THE PREMIER

Province House, Halifax, N.S. B3J 2T3
(902) 424-6600
Principal Asst. to the Premier, Fred J. Dickson, 424-4135
Executive Asst. to the Premier, Lawrence O'Neil, 424-6602
Administrative Asst., Mrs. Phyllis Jeffrey, 424-6603
Private Secretary, Miss Norma Marriott, 424-6604
Press Secretary, John O'Brien, 424-3995

GOVERNMENT DEPARTMENTS

DEPT. OF AGRICULTURE & MARKETING

Box 190, Halifax, N.S. B3J 2M4
Information Contact, D.C. Bishop, Co-ordinator of Admin. & Exhibitions (phone: 902 424-5719)

Acts Administered

Agriculture & Marketing Act
Agriculture & Rural Credit Act
Agrologists Act
Baby Chick Protection Act
Brucellosis Control Act
Cold Storage Plants Loan Act
Control of Cattle Pests (an Act Respecting)
Co-operative Assns. Act
Crop & Livestock Insurance Act
Fences & Detention of Stray Livestock (an Act to Provide for)
Fences & Impounding of Animals Act
Imitation Dairy Products Act
Livestock Brands Act
Livestock Health Services Act
Livestock Loans Guarantee Act
Margarine Act
Marshland Reclamation Act
Natural Products Marketing Act
Pest Control Products (An Act Respecting)
Potato Industry Act
Poultry Health Protection Act
Provincial Grain Commission Act
Sheep Protection & Dog Regulation Act
Stray Animals Act
Veterinary Assistance Act
Weed Control Act

MINISTER, Hon. Roger S. Bacon
Deputy Minister, W.V. Grant
Chief Director of Operations, R.E. Morehouse
Director of Accounting, R.F. McEwan, Truro
Branch Directors
Agriculture Development & Credit Services, A.A. Rovers, Truro
Soils & Crops Services, J.D. Johnson, Truro
Livestock Services, S.F. Allaby, Truro
Extension Services, R.J. Huggard, Truro
Horticulture & Biology Services, C.G. Embree, Truro
Marketing & Economics, G.B. Kinsman, Truro
N.S. Agricultural College, Dr. H.F. MacRae, Principal, Truro

Agricultural Marketing Boards

N.S. Marketing Board; Chairman, J.H. Haylock; Secretary, R.E. Morehouse, Box 190, Halifax, N.S. B3J 2M4 (424-3245)
Pork Producers Marketing Board of N.S.; Secretary, James Shand, Box 1341, Truro, N.S. B2N 5E8 (895-0581)
N.S. Winter Grain Marketing Board, Chairman, J.E. Peill, Box 130, Canning, N.S. BOP 1HO (582-3347)
N.S. Wool Marketing Board; Secretary, Roy MacKenzie, Box 550, Truro, N.S. B2N 5E3 (895-1571)
N.S. Chicken Marketing Board; Secretary, Lloyd Robinson, Box 129, Port Williams, N.S. BOP 1TO (542-5971)
N.S. Egg & Pullet Producers Marketing Board; Secretary, James Bragg, Box 1096, Truro, N.S. B2N 5G9 (895-6341)
N.S. Turkey Marketing Board; Secretary, John McManus, Box 130, Kentville, N.S. B4N 3W4 (678-5836)
N.S. Flue Cured Tobacco Growers Marketing Board; Secretary, E.B. Pridham, Box 154, Kentville, N.S. B4N 3W4 (678-7365)
N.S. Processing Pea Marketing Board; Secretary, Earl Kidston, Box 156, Port Williams, N.S. B0P 1T0 (542-3921)

Associated Agencies

Weed Control Chief Inspector, G.D. Palfrey, (act.), Truro, N.S. B2N 5E3 (895-1571)
N.S. Crop & Livestock Insurance Commission, Manager, Don MacNeil, Box 1092, Truro, N.S. B2N 5G9 (895-4431)
Provincial Chemistry Lab., Supervisor, Ben Harnish, Truro

Provincial Grain Commission, Box 785, Kentville, N.S. B4N 3X9 (678-4840) Secretary, Robert Dechman

Atlantic Pesticide Residue Detection Lab., Chemist, Michael Shreve, Kentville, N.S. B4N 1J5

DEPT. OF THE ATTORNEY GENERAL

Box 7, Halifax, N.S. B3J 2L6

Information from Office of the Deputy Attorney General (phone: 902-424-4223)

Acts Administered

Accountants General of the Supreme Court Act
Companies Act
Companies Winding Up Act
Corporations Registration Act
Costs & Fees Act
County Court Act
County Court Clerks Act
County Court Judges' Criminal Courts Act
Court & Penal Institutions Act
Expropriation Act
Fatality Inquiries Act
Female Prisoners' Maintenance Act
Fire Prevention Act
Insurance Act
Insurance Premium Tax Act
Interest on Judgements Act
Judicature Act
Juries Act
Justices' Courts Act
Justices' & Magistrates' Protection Act
Justices of the Peace Act
Law Reform Act
Night Courts Act
Notaries & Commissioners Act
Maintenance Orders Enforcement Act
Partnerships & Business Names Registration Act
Police Services Act
Private Investigators & Private Guards Act
Prothonotaries & Clerks of the Crown Act
Prosecuting Officers Act
Public Officers Act
Public Trustee Act
Reciprocal Enforcement of Custody Orders Act
Reciprocal Enforcement of Judgements Act
Registry Act
Regulations Act
Securities Act
Sheriffs Act
Societies Act

ATTORNEY GENERAL, Hon. Harry How, Q.C.
Deputy Attorney General, Gordon F. Coles, Q.C.
Director (Civil), R.G. Conrad, Q.C.
Director (Criminal), Gordon S. Gale, Q.C.
Director (Correctional Services), J.L. Crane
Director (Programs & Administration), R.A. MacDonald
Asst. Director (Criminal), Martin Herschorn
Asst. Director (Civil), Bruce Davidson
Asst. Director (Civil), Reinhold Endres
Departmental Solicitors: William Wilson, Douglas Keefe, Gregory Evans, Mollie Dunsmuir, Dana Giovannetti, David Giovannetti, Linda Garber, Kenneth Fiske, Robert Lutes, Elizabeth Cuddihy, Marion Tyson, Gordon Gillis, Joanne McKeough, J.M. Burgess, Noella Fisher, Wayne Cochrane, James Spurr

N.S. Law Reform Advisory Commission

Chairman, L. Smith
Secretary & Executive Director, G.D. Walker
Legal Research Officer, Gordon Johnson

Expropriations Compensation Board

Box 2071, 9th floor, 1690 Hollis St., Halifax, N.S. B3J 2L6
(902) 424-8982
Chairman, vacant
Vice Chairman, J.A. Turner

OFFICE OF THE AUDITOR GENERAL

Box 793, Halifax, N.S. B3J 2V2
Phone: (902) 424-5907
Auditor General, A.W. Sarty, C.A.

CIVIL SERVICE COMMISSION

Box 943, Halifax, N.S. B3J 2V9
Phone: (902) 424-4131
Commr., Hugh R. Macdonald
Administration Director, R.A. Falconer
Staffing Director, E.W. Pace
Staff Relations Director, G.L. Hall
Managerial Compensation & Research Director, B.B. MacCharles
Office Services, Supervisor, Mrs. B. Slaunwhite

DEPT. OF CONSUMER AFFAIRS

Box 998, Halifax, N.S. B3J 2X3

Information Contact, Bob Fowler, Director, Finance & Planning (phone: 902/424-4690)

Acts Administered

Collection Agencies Act
Consumer Protection Act
Consumer Reporting Act
Consumer Services Act
Credit Union Act
Direct Sellers' Licensing & Regulation Act
Embalmers & Funeral Directors Act
Instalment Payment Contracts Act
Loan Companies Inspection Act
Prearranged Funeral Services Act
Real Estate Brokers' Licensing Act
Rent Review Act
Residential Tenancies Act
Theatres & Amusements Act
Part X of the Bankruptcy Act–Orderly Payment of Debts

MINISTER, Hon. Ronald Russell
Deputy Minister, Mrs. Cathy MacNutt

Divisions

Amusements Regulation Board, Box 607, Halifax, N.S. B3J 2R7 (424-4493)
Consumer Services Bureau, Box 998, Halifax, N.S. B3J 2X3 (424-4690)
Credit Union Inspection, 1740 Granville St., Halifax, N.S. B3J 2X3 (424-4317)
Residential Tenancies Board, Box 998, Halifax, N.S. B3J 2X3 (424-4690)
Rent Review Commission, Box 820, Halifax, N.S. B3J 2V2 (424-4690), Chairman, R.R. Duplak

DEPT. OF CULTURE, RECREATION & FITNESS

(8th floor, 5151 Terminal Rd.), Box 864, Halifax, N.S. B3J 2V2
(902) 424-7512

Act Administered

Recreation Act, 1973 (and Amendment 1979)
and
Lottery Regulations

MINISTER, Hon. Greg Kerr
Deputy Minister, Louis Stephen
Director of Sport & Community Services, David McNamara
Director of Cultural Affairs, Allison Bishop
Curator, Art Gallery of Nova Scotia, Bernie Riordon

DEPT. OF DEVELOPMENT

Box 519, Halifax, N.S. B3J 2R7

Information from Development Services (Development Dept.) (phone: 902-424-8920, Telex: 019 22548)

Acts Administered
Voluntary Planning Act
Resources Development Board Act
Research Foundation Corp. Act
Industrial Loan Act
Industrial Development Act
Industrial Estates Ltd. Act
Louisburg District Planning & Development Commission Act
Sydney Steel Corp. Act
Industrial Property Act
Industry Closing Act
Statistics Act
Planning Act

MINISTER, Hon. Roland Thornhill
Deputy Minister, A. Pinard (act.)
Agent General for Nova Scotia in England, Donald Smith
Telex: 51-915867
Operations Division, Managing Director, C.M. Yeates
Market Development Centre, Director, F. Were
Business Development Centre, Director, J. Chaisson
Projects Division, Executive Director, D. MacKinnon (act.)
Strategy Division, Executive Director, A.F. Pinard
Planning & Economics Branch, Director, D. MacKinnon
Statistical Services Branch, Director, C. Conrad
Federal/Provincial Development Agreements Branch, Director, B. Gallivan
Voluntary Planning, Director, D.M. Macdonald
Resources Development Board, Manager, C. Arthur
Personnel Manager, John Despault

Associated Agencies
Industrial Estates Ltd.
Ste. 700, 5151 George St., Halifax, N.S. B3J 1M5
(902) 425-6331; Telex: 091-22517
President, W. Leslie Single
Waterfront Development Corp. Ltd.
5077 George St., Halifax, N.S. B3J 1M3
(902) 422-6591
President, H.P. Bonner
Controller & Treasurer, D.L. Moss
Halifax International Containers Ltd. (Halicon)
Ste. 900, Cogswell Tower, Scotia Sq., Halifax, N.S. B3J 3K1
(902) 429-4350
President, F.H. Howard

N.S. COMMISSION ON DRUG DEPENDENCY
4th floor, 5668 South St., Halifax, N.S. B3J 1A6
(902) 424-4270
Executive Director, Marvin M. Burke, R.S.W.

DEPT. OF EDUCATION
Box 578, Halifax, N.S. B3J 2S9
Information Contact, Supervisor, Education Reference Service (phone: 902-424-5570)

Acts Administered
Education Act
Education Assistance Act
Teachers Pension Act
N.S. Student Aid Act

MINISTER, Hon. T.R.B. Donahoe
Deputy Minister, G.J. McCarthy

Higher Education
Financial Analyst, A.C. Carras
Co-ordinator, Student Aid, G.E. Knickle

Public School Operations
Chief Director of Education, M.J. Woodford
Director, Curriculum Development, vacant
Director, Inspection Services, S.A. Sheffield
Director, School Planning & Conveyance, A.N. Higdon

Education Programs
Chief Director of Education, B.J. Nicholson
Director, Adult Education, T.M. Jones
Director, Teacher Education, R.P. Carter
Director, Education Resource Services, J.L. Martin
Administrative Asst., N.S. Museums (1747 Summer St., Halifax), Marilyn Covey
Provincial Librarian, Carin A. Somers, 5250 Spring Garden Rd., Halifax
Co-ordinator, Ethnic Services, P.A. Johnstone
Director, Publication & Reference Service, Fay P. Lee

Finance & Budgeting Program
Chief Director of Education, J.R. Levangie
Director, Financial Management, N.N. Graham
Supervisor, School Book Bureau, M.A. Reinhardt
Co-ordinator, Teachers' Pensions, F.J. Laba
Director, Public Education Grants & Financing, W.H. Vincent

EMERGENCY MEASURES
Dept. of Environment, 1690 Hollis St., Box 1502, Halifax, N.S. B3J 2Y3
(902) 424-5620
Director, J.A. Gray

ENERGY COUNCIL
Dept. of Mines & Energy, 1640 Hollis St. (Box 668), Halifax, N.S. B3J 2T3
Chairman, John C. Smith
Director, John French

DEPT. OF THE ENVIRONMENT
Box 2107, Halifax, N.S. B3J 3B7
Information from: Co-ordinator, Environmental Reports & Enquiries (phone: 902-424-8627)

Acts Administered
Beverage Containers Act
Environmental Protection Act
Water Act
Well Drilling Act

MINISTER, Hon. R. Fisher Hudson, Q.C.
Deputy Minister, C.D. Carter, P.Eng.
Chief Director of Operations, A.L Carroll
Director, Admin. & Accounting, J.G. Shea
Director, Inspection & Monitoring, A.J. Crouse
Director, Water Planning & Management, J.F. Jones
Director, Environmental Assessment, vacant
Director, Utilities, J.A. Turner
Director, Emergency Measures, J.A. Gray

Associated Agencies
Environmental Control Council
23 LaPlanche St. (Box 279, Amherst, N.S. B4H 3Z2)
(902) 667-7214
Executive Secretary, Morris Haugg

DEPT. OF FINANCE
Box 187, Halifax, N.S. B3J 2N3
Information from Office of the Deputy Minister (phone: 902-424-5554)

Acts Administered
Corporations Tax Act

MINISTER, Hon. Joel R. Matheson, Q.C.
Deputy Minister, R.S. Brookfield, C.A.
Admin. Asst., Jack Q. Stuewe
Controller, A.G. Manuel, C.A.
Trusts & Debt Management, Director, H.W.V. Matthews
Provincial Tax Commr., S.L. Wile, C.A., Box 187, Halifax, N.S. B3J 2N3
Financial Counsel, Noella Fisher, L.L.B.

A/Director of Federal-Provincial Fiscal Relations, Marlyn Marvin
Director of Accounting, C.P. Hubley
Director of Pensions & Payroll Services, P.J. Fleet
Director, Revenue, Ivan Richardson
Director of Internal Audit, C.H. Loveless, C.A.
Supt. of Pension Registration, P.J. Fleet

DEPT. OF FISHERIES

Box 2223, Halifax, N.S. B3J 3C4 (10th floor, Maritime Centre, 1505 Barrington St., Halifax, N.S.)
Information Contact, George R. Richard, Director of Planning & Finance (phone: 902/424-4560)

Acts Administered

Fisheries Development Act
N.S. Fisheries Act
Sea Plants Harvesting Act
Irish Moss Act

MINISTER, Hon. Edmund L. Morris
Deputy Minister, D.A. MacLean
Director of Planning & Finance, G.R. Richard
Resource Education Officer, K.R. Weston
Marketing Development Officer, Mrs. Janis Raymond
Supervisor of Administrative Services, C.G. Allen
Supervisor, Socio-Economic Support, D.C. Thomas
Director of Marine Resources, A.A. Longard
Director of Estuarine & Inland Fisheries, L.L. MacLeod
Supervisor, Product Development & Marketing, M.A. Drebot
Director of Industrial Development, J.A. Marsters
Chief Loan Officer, E.A. MacIntosh
Supervisor, Vessels & Gear, Olafur Egilsson
Director of Training & Field Services, James J. McLevey
Supervisor of Field Services, Clarrie F. MacKinnon
Supervisor of Fishermen's Training, D.F. Robertson, Fisheries Training Centre, Box 700, Pictou, N.S. BOK 1HO (902/485-4525)

DEPT. OF GOVERNMENT SERVICES

1505 Barrington St., Box 54, Halifax, N.S. B3J 2L4 (902/424-4980)

MINISTER, Hon. Jerry Lawrence
Administrative Asst., Dagmar Worthington
Deputy Minister, D.J. Power
Administrative Asst., R.J. Forhan
Executive Director, Policy & Planning Division, C.J. Fear
Executive Director, Construction & Accommodation Services Division, M.T. Zareski
A/Executive Director, Information Services Division, A.C. Crouch
Executive Director, Systems & Computer Services Division, D.G. Beaulieu
Executive Director, Finance & Administration Services Division, D.T. Tobin

DEPT. OF HEALTH

8th floor, Joseph Howe Bldg., Hollis St., (Box 488, Halifax, N.S. B3J 2R8)
Information from Health Educator (phone: 902-424-4391)

Acts Administered

Anatomy Act
Chiropractic Act
Dental Act
Dental Technicians Act
Denturist Act
Dispensing Opticians Act
Drug Dependency Act
Hairdressers Act
Halifax Infirmary Act
Health Act
Health Councils Act
Health Services & Insurance Act
Hospital Services Planning Commission Act
Hospitals Act
Human Tissue Gift Act
Medical Act
Medical Radiological Technicians Act
Municipal Hospitals Loan Act
N.S. Hospital Act
N.S. Sanatorium Act
Nursing Assts. Act
Occupational Therapists Act
Optometry Act
Pharmacy Act
Physiotherapy Act
Professional Dietitians Act
Psychologists Act
Registered Nurses Association Act
Solemnization of Marriage Act
Veterinary Medical Act
Victoria General Hospital Act
Vital Statistics Act

MINISTER, Hon. Gerald Sheehy
Deputy Minister, Dr. J.E.H. Miller
Administrative Asst. to Deputy Minister, W. Grady
Administrative Asst. to Deputy Minister, G.A. Reno
Administrator, Community Health Services, Dr. W.H. Sullivan
Administrator, Health Care Institutions, Dr. A.D. Thomson
Administrator, Psychiatric Mental Health Services, Dr. F.R. Townsend
Administrator, Environmental Health, C.E. Tupper
Administrator, Finance, A.V. Rowland
Director, Administration, S.R. Kenny
Administrator, Program Development & Evaluation, D.R. Keats
Deputy Registrar General & Director, Registration Services, D.F. Arthur (424-4373)
(Births, Marriages & Deaths) For information address inquiries to: Deputy Registrar General, Dept. of Health, Provincial Bldg., Halifax. Fee: for each certificate $5.
Departmental Legal Counsel, W. Cochrane

HEALTH SERVICES & INSURANCE COMMISSION

Box 760, Halifax, N.S. B3J 2V2
(902) 424-8902
Chairman, Dr. M. Laffin
Vice Chairman, C.E. Larsen
Executive Director, J.G. Hare, C.A.
Executive Secretary, D.H. Waller
General Manager, Maritime Medical Care Inc. (Medical Services Insurance), S.P. Brannan

HOUSING COMMISSION

Box 815, Dartmouth, N.S. B2Y 3Z3
(902) 424-4483
Executive Director, A.F. Pinard

HUMAN RIGHTS COMMISSION

3rd floor, Lord Nelson Arcade, Spring Garden Rd., Box 2221, Halifax, N.S. B3J 3C4
(902) 424-4111
Director, G.F. McCurdy
Chief Human Rights Officer, K. Jega Nathan

INTERGOVERNMENTAL AFFAIRS

1690 Hollis St., Halifax, N.S. B3J 3J9
Minister, Hon. Edmund Morris

DEPT. OF LABOUR & MANPOWER

Box 697, Halifax, N.S. B3J 2T8
Information Contact, Brian Condran, Information Officer (phone: 902 424-4680)

Acts Administered

Amusement Devices Safety Act (and Regulations)

Apprenticeship & Tradesmen's Qualifications Act (and Regulations)
Construction Safety Act (and Regulations)
Electrical Installation Act
Elevators & Lifts Act
Fire Prevention Act
Industrial Safety Act (and Regulations)
Labour Standards Code (Regulations, Orders and Schedules)
Lightning Rod Act
Stationary Engineers Act (and Regulations)
Steam Boiler & Pressure Vessel Act
Trade Union Act (and Regulations)

MINISTER, Hon. Kenneth Streatch
Deputy Minister, R.E. Anderson
Asst. to Deputy Minister, P.F. Langlois
Fire Marshal, Charles Findlay
Executive Director of Manpower, Graham Langley
Director of Apprenticeship, vacant
Director of Labour Research, Jean Dobson
Director of Labour Standards, Ross Mitchell
Director of Occupation Safety, Grant Hitton
Director of Admin. & Accounting, Peter Horne
Director of Conciliation Services, S.E. Farris

Associated Agencies
Workers' Compensation Board
Box 1150, Halifax, N.S. B3J 2Y2 (424-8081)
Chairman, John Lynk
Executive Director, J.H. Cottenden
Labour Relations Board (N.S.)
Box 697, Halifax, N.S. B3J 2T8 (424-6730)
Chairman, Judge R.J. McCleave
Chief Executive Officer, K.H. Horne
Construction Industry Panel
Box 697, Halifax, N.S. B3J 2T8 (424-6730)
Chairman, Judge R.J. McCleave
Chief Executive Officer, K.H. Horne
Provincial Apprenticeship Board
Box 697, Halifax, N.S. B3J 2T8 (424-5651)
Chairman, Mark Cleary
Stationary Engineers Act, Board of Examiners
Box 697, Halifax, N.S. B3J 2T8 (424-5567)
Chairman, J.D. Fraser, P.Eng.
Minimum Wage Board
Box 697, Halifax, N.S. B3J 2T8 (424-4311)
Chairman, John MacIntyre
Labour Standards Tribunal
13 Valleyfield Rd., Dartmouth, N.S. B2W 1M9 (434-7383)
Chairman, D.G. Ruck
Provincial Manpower Board
Box 697, Halifax, N.S. B3J 2T8
Chairman, Struan Robertson

DEPT. OF LANDS & FORESTS
Toronto Dominion Bldg., Barrington St., Box 698, Halifax, N.S. B3J 2T9
Information Contact, Deputy Minister, Lands & Forests (phone: 902/424-4121)

Acts Administered
Lands & Forests Act: Part I: Crown Lands; Part II: Forests; Part III: Game
Forest Improvement Act
Pulpwood Marketing Act
Scott Maritimes Pulp Ltd. Agreement Act
N.S. Pulp Ltd. Agreement Act
Land Holdings Disclosure Act
Land Titles Clarification Act
Beaches & Foreshores Act
Beaches Preservation & Protection Act
Provincial Parks Act
Parks Development Act
Scalers' Act

MINISTER, Hon. D.L. Geo. Henley (424-4037)
Deputy Minister, D.L. Eldridge (424-4121)
Senior Director, Admin., Gary E. Rix (424-6694)
Senior Director, Program Planning, J.D. Smith (424-4103)
Director, Reforestation & Silviculture, Ed Bailey, Truro (895-1591)
Director, Forest Resources Planning & Mensuration, Fred Wellings, Truro (895-1591)
Director of Parks & Recreation, Barry Diamond, Debert (662-3030)
Director of Wildlife, Merrill Prime, Kentville (678-8921)
Senior Director of Land Services, H. Burt Robertson (424-5481)
Director of Surveys, K.P. Aucoin (424-4102)
Director of Land Acquisition & Registry, J.D. Bancroft (424-4267)
Senior Director of Operations, R.G. MacGregor (424-5826)
Director of Forest Management, Private Lands, W.L. Johnson (424-5703)
Co-ordinator, Air Services, L.D. Crocker, Shubenacadie (758-3438)
Manager, Forest Protection (Fire), vacant, Shubenacadie (758-2232)

N.S. LIQUOR COMMISSION
6176 Young St., Halifax, N.S. B3K 5M4
(902) 454-5841
Chief Commr., J.D. Thompson
General Manager, D.W. Pulsifer

N.S. LIQUOR LICENSE BOARD
Ste. 401, 277 Pleasant St., Dartmouth, N.S. B2Y 4B7
(902) 469-6160
Chairman, C. William Singer

MANAGEMENT BOARD
10th floor, Joseph Howe Bldg. (Box 1619, Halifax, N.S. B3J 2Y3)
(902) 424-7750
Chairman, Hon. R.C. Giffin
Deputy Minister, B.D. Anthony

DEPT. OF MINES & ENERGY
1690 Hollis St. (Box 1087), Halifax, N.S. B3J 2X1
Information Contact, Mrs. Valerie Brisco, Library Research Asst. (phone: 902-424-4161)

Acts Administered
Mineral Resources Act
Metalliferous Mines & Quarries Regulation Act
Coal Mines Regulation Act
Petroleum & Natural Gas Act
Gypsum Mining Income Tax Act
Underground Gas Storage Act
Bituminous Shale Conservation Act

MINISTER, Hon. Ronald Barkhouse
Deputy Minister, Energy Policy, J.J. Laffin
Director, Admin., C. James
Supervisor of Mineral Rights, R. Slater
Director, Mineral Resources, J.A. Garnett
Head, Energy Minerals, W. Potter
Head, Geological Services, P. Giles
Head, Mineral Deposits, D. Murray
Regional Geologist, Stellarton, J. Bingley
Director, Engineering Division, J. Amirault
Supervisor, Mine Inspection, C.F. MacDonald
Operations Manager, Drilling, D.E. Polley

Associated Agencies
Novaco, Box 147, Sydney Mines, N.S. B1V 1Y3 (736-6268); Chairman, J.P. Shannon; Chief Executive Officer, J.C. Smith

DEPT. OF MUNICIPAL AFFAIRS
Box 216, Halifax, N.S. B3J 2M4
Information Contact, W.R. McKee, Manager, Administrative Services (phone: 902-424-5666)

Acts Administered

Assessment Act
Bonus Act
Building Code Act
Ditches & Water Courses Act
Fences & Impounding of Animals Act
Industrial Commns. Act
Municipal Act
Municipal Affairs Act
Municipal Elections Act
Municipal Boundaries & Representation Act
Municipal Finance Corporation Act
Municipal Grants Act
Municipal Housing Corporations Act
Municipal Land Transfer Tax Act
Municipal Loan & Bldg. Fund Act
Municipal Taxation Time Extension Act
Planning Act
Regional Transit Authority Act
Rural Fire Dist. Act
Sheep Protection & Dog Regulation Act
Stray Animals Act
Towns Act
Village Services Act

MINISTER, Hon. Jack MacIsaac
Deputy Minister, John Mullally
Director of Assessment, Bob Warren
Director of Community Planning, Ron Simpson
Director of Finance & Administration, Ed Cramm
Director of Municipal Advisory Services, A.A. Cameron
Director of Policy Development & Research, Gerrie Masters
Departmental Solicitors, Mrs. J.W. Willwerth, LL.B., Mrs. F. Robertson, LL.B.

OMBUDSMAN

Ombudsman, Dr. Harry D. Smith, Box 2152, Royal Bank Bldg., Halifax, N.S. B3J 3B7 (phone: 902 424-6780)

N.S. POWER CORP.

Scotia Sq., Box 910, Halifax, N.S. B3J 2W5
(902) 424-6230
President & Chief Executive Officer, Dr. L.F. Kirkpatrick

PUBLIC ARCHIVES OF N.S.

6016 University Ave., Halifax, N.S. B3H 1W4
Provincial Archivist, Hugh A. Taylor

BOARD OF COMMRS. OF PUBLIC UTILITIES

1526 Dresden Row, Box 3058, South Halifax, N.S. B3J 3G7
(902) 424-4448
Chairman, J.S. Drury, Q.C.

This Board exercises authority over all public utilities in N.S., including water, electricity, telephone, and transportation. Acts administered are:

Rural Telephone Act
Municipal Boundaries & Representation Act
Bonus Act
Motor Carrier Act
Motor Vehicle Transport Act
Gasoline & Fuel Oil Licensing Act
Salvage Yards Act

N.S. RESEARCH FOUNDATION CORP.

100 Fenwick St., (Box 790, Dartmouth, N.S. B2Y 3Z7)
(902) 424-8670
President, Dr. J.E. Blanchard

DEPT. OF SOCIAL SERVICES

Box 696, Halifax, N.S. B3J 2T7
Information Contact, J.A.A. MacKinnon (phone: 902-424-4326)

Acts Administered

Social Assistance & Family Benefits Act
Homes for Special Care Act
Social Services Councils Act
Acts dealing with Family & Child Welfare:
Children's Services Act
Family Maintenance Act
Day Care Services Act
Infant Custody Act
Family Court Act

MINISTER, Hon. Laird Stirling
Deputy Minister, J.A. MacKenzie
Chief Administrator, Miss Gwen Pickering
Administrative Asst. to Deputy Minister, J.A.A. MacKinnon
Administrator, Rehabilitation & Community Services, J.A. MacIsaac
Administrator, Family & Children's Services, W.D. Greatorex
Director of Social Research & Planning, Miss Bessie Harris
Regional Administrator North Shore Area with headquarters in New Glasgow, R.C. Purdy
Regional Administrator Western Area with headquarters in Yarmouth, D.G. Raymond
Regional Administrator Halifax Area, Mrs. J.M. MacKinnon
Regional Administrator Cape Breton Area with headquarters in Sydney, Cyril Reddy
Regional Administrator Central Area with Headquarters in Kentville, D.M. Penney
N.S. School for Boys, Shelburne, H. Muinonen, Supt.
N.S. Youth Training Centre, Truro, J.A. Walker, Supt.
N.S. School for Girls, Truro, William MacLeod, Supt.

SYDNEY STEEL CORP. (A Crown Corp.)

Box 1450, Sydney, N.S. B1P 6K5
(902) 564-5471

DEPT. OF TOURISM

Box 456, Halifax, N.S. B3J 2R5
Information Contact, D. Brennan (phone: (902) 424-5959)

Acts Administered

Camping Establishments Act & Regulations
Hotel Regulations Act & Regulations

MINISTER, Hon. Bruce Cochran
Deputy Minister, K.M. Mounce
Special Asst., J.B. Bugden
Director of Marketing, Daniel Brennan
Director of Planning, Bernard LeBlanc
Field Marketing Representative, Montreal, Therese Papillon (514/843-5160)
Field Marketing Representative, Portland, Maine, Mary Martin (207/772-0017)

Tourist Information

Toll free - U.S. (except Hawaii, Alaska & Maine), 1 (800) 341-6096
Toll free - Maine, 1 (800) 492-0643
Toll free - Ontario (area codes 613, 416, 519, 705), 1 (800) 565-7140
Toll free - Quebec & Nfld. (area codes 418, 514, 819, 709), 1 (800) 565-7180

DEPT. OF TRANSPORTATION

6th floor, Provincial Bldg., Hollis St., Halifax, N.S. B3J 2N2
Information Contact, Office of the Deputy Minister

Acts Administered

Public Highways Act
Motor Vehicle Act

MINISTER, Hon. Thomas J. McInnis
Deputy Minister, W.P. Kerr
Chief Engineer, B.J. Hamm
Chief Engineer, Operations, W.W. Piggott
Director of Claims, C.E. Caines
Director of Traffic Engineering, F.C.S. Lee

Registrar of Motor Vehicles, J.J. Thibault

WORKERS' COMPENSATION BOARD

See Dept. of Labour & Manpower

PROVINCE OF ONTARIO

Entered Confederation July 1, 1867
Area: 412,582 sq. miles
Population: 8,570,400 (1980 est.)
Seat of Government: Parliament Bldgs., Toronto
Lieutenant Governor: The Hon. John Black Aird
Executive Officer: Mrs. E. Harvey

EXECUTIVE COUNCIL

Premier, and President of the Council, Hon. William G. Davis, Q.C.
Deputy Premier, and Minister of Energy, Hon. Robert Welch, Q.C.
Minister of Intergovernmental Affairs, Hon. Thomas L. Wells
Minister of Northern Affairs, Hon. Leo Bernier
Minister of Transportation & Communications, Hon. James W. Snow
Provincial Secretary for Social Development, Hon. Margaret Birch
Minister of Municipal Affairs & Housing, Hon. Claude Bennett
Treasurer of Ontario, and Minister of Economics, Hon. Frank S. Miller
Minister of Health, Hon. Dennis R. Timbrell
Minister of Education, and Minister of Colleges & Universities, Hon. Bette M. Stephenson, M.D.
Attorney General, and Solicitor General, Hon. Roy McMurtry, Q.C.
Minister of Agriculture & Food, Hon. Lorne C. Henderson
Minister of the Environment, Hon. Keith C. Norton, Q.C.
Minister of Community & Social Services, Hon. Frank Drea
Minister of Industry & Tourism, Hon. Larry Grossman, Q.C.
Chairman of Management Board of Cabinet, and Chairman of Cabinet, Hon. George McCague
Minister of Culture & Recreation, Hon. Reuben Baetz
Minister of Government Services, Hon. Douglas J. Wiseman
Minister of Labour, Hon. Robert G. Elgie, M.D.
Provincial Secretary for Justice, and Minister of Consumer & Commercial Relations, Hon. Gordon W. Walker, Q.C.
Minister without Portfolio, Hon. Bud Gregory
Minister of Natural Resources, Hon. Alan W. Pope, Q.C.
Minister of Correctional Services, Hon. Nicholas G. Leluk
Minister of Revenue, Hon. George L. Ashe
Provincial Secretary for Resources Development, Hon. Russell H. Ramsay
Minister without Portfolio, Hon. R. Bruce McCaffrey
Minister without Portfolio, Hon. Norman W. Sterling, Q.C.

Secretary of the Cabinet, and Clerk of the Executive Council, Edward Stewart

GOVERNMENT OF ONTARIO ADMINISTRATIVE DIVISIONS

Justice Policy Field (includes: Attorney General; Consumer & Commercial Relations; Correctional Services; Solicitor General; Northern Affairs)
Resources Development Policy Field (includes: Agriculture & Food; Energy; Environment; Municipal Affairs & Housing; Industry & Tourism; Labour; Natural Resources; Northern Affairs; Transportation & Communications)
Social Development Policy Field (includes: Colleges & Univs.; Community & Social Services; Education; Health; Culture & Recreation; Northern Affairs)
Other Ministries:
Treasury & Economics
Intergovernmental Affairs
Government Services
Revenue

LEGISLATIVE ASSEMBLY

Thirty-second Parliament. Last election, March 19, 1981. Maximum duration, 5 Years.
Party Standings: Progressive Conservative (P.C.) 70; Liberal (L.) 34 (including 1 Liberal-Labour); New Democratic (N.D.P.) 21; Total 125
Leader of the Opposition, Dr. Stuart L. Smith
Indemnities & Allowances: Sessional Indemnity, $30,000 per annum; and expense allowance of $10,000 for Members. In addition to his indemnity and allowance as a Member of the Legislative Assembly the Premier receives a salary of $33,200 per annum and a Leader's Allowance of $6,000; similarly, each Minister with portfolio receives a salary of $23,300 per annum. Ministers without portfolio receive salaries of $11,700 per annum. The Leader of the Opposition receives an additional indemnity of $23,300 as well as a Leader's Allowance of $4,000. The Leader of the Third Party receives an additional indemnity of $11,700 as well as a Leader's Allowance of $2,000.
Officers & Clerks: Speaker, Hon. John M. Turner; Clerk of the House & Chief Election Officer, Roderick Lewis, Q.C.; Sergeant-at-Arms, Thomas Stelling; Senior Legislative Counsel, A.N. Stone, Q.C.; Postmaster, J.D. Campbell; Ministry of Government Services, Legislative Services Branch, A. Cameron, Director

Members

Following is alphabetical list of members, with Party affiliation, constituency in brackets, and Toronto phone: Mailing address for all is Parliament Bldgs., Toronto, Ont. M7A 1A2

Andrewes, Philip, *P.C.* (Lincoln) 965-7147
Ashe, George, *P.C.* (Durham West) 965-2901
Baetz, Reuben, *P.C.* (Ottawa West) 965-8098
Barlow, Bill, *P.C.* (Cambridge) 965-6736
Bennett, Claude, *P.C.* (Ottawa South) 965-6456
Bernier, Leo, *P.C.* (Kenora) 965-3707
Birch, Margaret, *P.C.* (Scarborough East) 965-6502
Boudria, Don, *L.* (Prescott & Russell) 965-5806
Bradley, James, *L.* (St. Catharines) 965-5684
Brandt, Andy, *P.C.* (Sarnia) 965-6838
Breaugh, Michael J., *N.D.P.* (Oshawa) 965-3215
Breithaupt, James R., *L.* (Kitchener) 965-1646
Bryden, Marion, *N.D.P.* (Beaches-Woodbine) 965-4726
Cassidy, Michael, *N.D.P.* (Ottawa Centre) 965-1764
Charlton, Brian, *N.D.P.* (Hamilton Mountain) 965-7024
Conway, Sean G., *L.* (Renfrew North) 965-4043
Cooke, Dave, *N.D.P.* (Windsor-Riverside) 965-6286
Copps, Sheila, *L.* (Hamilton Centre) 965-5677
Cousens, Don, *P.C.* (York Centre) 965-8420
Cunningham, Eric G., *L.* (Wentworth North) 965-5681
Cureatz, Sam L., *P.C.* (Durham East) 965-4186
Davis, William G., *P.C.* (Brampton) 965-1941
Dean, Gordon, *P.C.* (Wentworth) 965-7517
Di Santo, Odoardo, *N.D.P.* (Downsview) 965-1349
Drea, Frank, *P.C.* (Scarborough Centre) 965-2341
Eakins, John, *L.* (Victoria-Haliburton) 965-9681
Eaton, Robert G., *P.C.* (Middlesex) 965-7254
Edighoffer, Hugh, *L.* (Perth) 965-5682
Elgie, Robert, *P.C.* (York East) 965-4101
Elston, Murray, *L.* (Huron Bruce) 965-5688
Epp, Herbert, *L.* (Waterloo North) 965-5941
Eves, Ernie, *P.C.* (Parry Sound) 965-4837
Fish, Susan, *P.C.* (St. George) 965-5631
Foulds, Jim, *N.D.P.* (Port Arthur) 965-1965
Gillies, Phil, *P.C.* (Brantford) 965-5487
Gordon, Jim, *P.C.* (Sudbury) 965-5800
Grande, Tony, *N.D.P.* (Oakwood) 965-9071
Gregory, Bud, *P.C.* (Mississauga East) 965-2337
Grossman, Larry, *P.C.* (St. Andrew-St. Patrick) 965-1617
Haggerty, Ray, *L.* (Erie) 965-2551

Harris, Michael, *P.C.* (Nipissing) 965-5365
Havrot, Ed, *P.C.* (Timiskaming) 965-4959
Henderson, Lorne C., *P.C.* (Lambton) 965-1041
Hennessy, Mickey, *P.C.* (Fort William) 965-4130
Hodgson, William, *P.C.* (York North) 965-4813
Johnson, Jack, *P.C.* (Wellington-Dufferin-Peel) 965-4828
Johnston, Richard F., *N.D.P.* (Scarborough West) 965-7771
Jones, Terry, *P.C.* (Mississauga North) 965-4849
Kells, Morley, *P.C.* (Humber) 965-5366
Kennedy, R. Douglas, *P.C.* (Mississauga South) 965-4819
Kerr, George A., *P.C.* (Burlington South) 965-4646
Kerrio, Vince, *L.* (Niagara Falls) 965-7903
Kolyn, Al, *P.C.* (Lakeshore) 965-5445
Lane, John, *P.C.* (Algoma-Manitoulin) 965-6659
Laughren, Floyd, *N.D.P.* (Nickel Belt) 965-9357
Leluk, Nicholas G., *P.C.* (York West) 965-5952
Lupusella, Tony, *N.D.P.* (Dovercourt) 965-5644
MacDonald, Donald C., *N.D.P.* (York South) 965-5948
Mackenzie, Bob, *N.D.P.* (Hamilton East) 965-2694
MacQuarrie, Bob, *P.C.* (Carleton East) 965-4422
Mancini, Remo, *L.* (Essex South) 965-5678
Martel, Elie W., *N.D.P.* (Sudbury East) 965-2692
McCaffrey, Bruce, *P.C.* (Armourdale) 965-3578
McCague, George, *P.C.* (Dufferin-Simcoe) 965-6795
McClellan, Ross, *N.D.P.* (Bellwoods) 965-0622
McEwen, J. Earl, *L.* (Frontenac-Addington) 965-7940
McGuigan, James, *L.* (Kent-Elgin) 965-5676
McKessock, Bob, *L.* (Grey) 965-4360
McLean, Allan, *P.C.* (Simcoe East) 965-4974
McMurtry, Roy, *P.C.* (Eglinton) 965-1664
McNeil, Ronald K., *P.C.* (Elgin) 965-4848
Miller, Frank S., *P.C.* (Muskoka) 965-6361
Miller, Gordon, *L.* (Haldimand-Norfolk) 965-0393
Mitchell, Robert C., *P.C.* (Carleton) 965-3645
Newman, Bernard, *L.* (Windsor-Walkerville) 965-5683
Nixon, Robert F., *L.* (Brant-Oxford-Norfolk) 965-3726
Norton, Keith, *P.C.* (Kingston & The Islands) 965-1611
O'Neil, Hugh P., *L.* (Quinte) 965-7957
Peterson, David, *L.* (London Centre) 965-4320
Philip, Ed, *N.D.P.* (Etobicoke) 965-0894
Piché, Rene, *P.C.* (Cochrane North) 965-4811
Pollock, Jim, *P.C.* (Hastings-Peterborough) 965-4812
Pope, Alan, *P.C.* (Cochrane South) 965-1301
Ramsay, Russ, *P.C.* (Sault Ste. Marie) 965-7721
Reed, Julian, *L.* (Halton-Burlington) 965-7896
Reid, T. Patrick, *L.-Lab.* (Rainy River) 965-5869
Renwick, James A., *N.D.P.* (Riverdale) 965-5928
Riddell, Jack, *L.* (Huron-Middlesex) 965-1080
Robinson, Alan M., *P.C.* (Scarborough-Ellesmere) 965-4825
Rotenberg, David, *P.C.* (Wilson Heights) 965-3586
Roy, Albert, *L.* (Ottawa East) 965-6731
Runciman, Robert W., *P.C.* (Leeds) 965-9436
Ruprecht, Tony, *L.* (Parkdale) 965-1122
Ruston, Richard F., *L.* (Essex North) 965-4298
Samis, George R., *N.D.P.* (Cornwall) 965-9579
Sargent, Edward, *L.* (Grey-Bruce) 965-5505
Scrivener, Margaret, *P.C.* (St. David) 965-0605
Sheppard, Howard, *P.C.* (Northumberland) 965-6200
Shymko, Yuri, *P.C.* (High Park-Swansea) 965-7516
Smith, Stuart L., *L.* (Hamilton West) 965-1676
Snow, James W., *P.C.* (Oakville) 965-2101
Spensieri, Mike, *L.* (Yorkview) 965-7920
Stephenson, Bette, *P.C.* (York Mills) 965-5277
Sterling, Norman, *P.C.* (Carleton-Grenville) 965-9499
Stevenson, Ross, *P.C.* (Durham York) 965-4843
Stokes, John E., *N.D.P.* (Lake Nipigon) 965-9581
Swart, Mel, *N.D.P.* (Welland-Thorold) 965-7714
Sweeney, John, *L.* (Kitchener-Wilmot) 965-9611
Taylor, George, *P.C.* (Simcoe Centre) 965-6454
Taylor, James A., *P.C.* (Prince Edward-Lennox) 965-2492
Timbrell, Dennis R., *P.C.* (Don Mills) 965-2421
Treleaven, Richard L., *P.C.* (Oxford) 965-4440
Turner, John M., *P.C.* (Peterborough) 965-2331
Van Horne, Ronald G., *L.* (London North) 965-7757
Villeneuve, Osie F., *P.C.* (Stormont, Dundas & Glengarry) 965-4836
Walker, Gordon, *P.C.* (London South) 963-0311
Watson, Andy, *P.C.* (Chatham-Kent) 965-4385
Welch, Robert, *P.C.* (Brock) 965-2041
Wells, Thomas L., *P.C.* (Scarborough North) 965-3606
Wildman, Bud, *N.D.P.* (Algoma) 965-6224
Williams, John, *P.C.* (Oriole) 965-6931
Wiseman, Douglas, *P.C.* (Lanark) 965-1101
Worton, Harry, *L.* (Wellington South) 965-5978
Wrye, Bill, *L.* (Windsor-Sandwich) 965-6584
Yakabuski, Paul J., *P.C.* (Renfrew South) 965-4800

Alphabetical List of Constituencies

(Number of Registered Voters in Brackets):

Algoma (18,386): Bud Wildman
Algoma-Manitoulin (20,212): John Lane
Brampton (59,187): William G. Davis
Brantford (44,311): Phil Gillies
Brant-Oxford-Norfolk (38,328): Robert F. Nixon
Brock (35,346): Robert Welch
Burlington South (56,545): George A. Kerr
Cambridge (46,081): Bill Barlow
Carleton (50,946): Robert C. Mitchell
Carleton East (56,496): Bob MacQuarrie
Carleton-Grenville (37,263): Norman Sterling
Chatham-Kent (39,222): Andy Watson
Cochrane North (25,509): Rene Piché
Cochrane South (35,133): Alan Pope
Cornwall (34,029): George R. Samis
Dufferin-Simcoe (48,888): George McCague
Durham East (47,393): Sam L. Cureatz
Durham-York (41,693): Ross Stevenson
Durham West (46,823): George Ashe
Elgin (38,858): Ronald K. McNeil
Erie (31,564): Ray Haggerty
Essex North (33,938): Richard F. Ruston
Essex South (36,073): Remo Mancini
Fort William (40,247): Mickey Hennessy
Frontenac-Addington (35,040): J. Earl McEwen
Grey (36,455): Bob McKessock
Grey-Bruce (35,539): Edward Sargent
Haldimand-Norfolk (44,142): Gordon I. Miller
Halton-Burlington (43,337): Julian Reed
Hamilton Centre (38,003): Sheila Copps
Hamilton East (48,620): Bob MacKenzie
Hamilton Mountain (46,192): Brian Charlton
Hamilton West (41,056): Dr. Stuart L. Smith
Hastings-Peterborough (33,310): Jim Pollock
Huron-Bruce (35,985): Murray Elston
Huron-Middlesex (30,130): Jack Riddell
Kenora (28,413): Leo Bernier
Kent-Elgin (33,007): James McGuigan
Kingston & The Islands (38,217): Keith Norton
Kitchener (46,835): James R. Breithaupt
Kitchener-Wilmot (42,181): John Sweeney
Lake Nipigon (19,744): Jack Stokes
Lambton (31,379): Lorne C. Henderson
Lanark (29,668): Douglas J. Wiseman
Leeds (35,406): Robert Runciman
Lincoln (31,387): Philip Andrewes
London Centre (47,683): David Peterson
London North (48,617): Ronald G. Van Horne
London South (59,614): Gordon Walker
Middlesex (32,446): Robert G. Eaton
Mississauga East (44,089): Bud Gregory
Mississauga North (55,251): Terry Jones
Mississauga South (42,511): R. Douglas Kennedy
Muskoka (24,759): Frank S. Miller
Niagara Falls (45,208): Vince Kerrio
Nickel Belt (24,359): Floyd Laughren
Nipissing (42,247): Michael Harris
Northumberland (42,909): Howard Sheppard
Oakville (40,194): James W. Snow

Oshawa (41,124): Michael J. Breaugh
Ottawa Centre (45,324): Michael Cassidy
Ottawa East (45,497): Albert Roy
Ottawa South (50,647): Claude Bennett
Ottawa West (52,139): Reuben Baetz
Oxford (50,501): Richard Treleaven
Parry Sound (28,474): Ernie Eves
Perth (43,680): Hugh Edighoffer
Peterborough (58,901): John Turner
Port Arthur (39,207): Jim Foulds
Prescott & Russell (39,111): Don Boudria
Prince Edward-Lennox (30,525): James A. Taylor
Quinte (44,996): Hugh P. O'Neil
Rainy River (18,320): T. Patrick Reid
Renfrew North (28,248): Sean G. Conway
Renfrew South (35,133): Paul J. Yakabuski
St. Catharines (52,660): James Bradley
Sarnia (46,807): Andy Brandt
Sault Ste. Marie (50,240): Russ Ramsay
Simcoe Centre (52,644): George Taylor
Simcoe East (44,578): Allan McLean
Stormont, Dundas & Glengarry (31,522): Osie F. Villeneuve
Sudbury (43,133): Jim Gordon
Sudbury East (45,527): Elie W. Martel
Timiskaming (28,892): Ed. Havrot
Victoria-Haliburton (38,132): John Eakins
Waterloo North (44,263): Herbert Epp
Welland-Thorold (39,712): Mel Swart
Wellington-Dufferin-Peel (46,325): Jack Johnson
Wellington South (47,868): Harry Worton
Wentworth (39,420): Gordon Dean
Wentworth North (47,903): Eric G. Cunningham
Windsor-Riverside (47,174): Dave Cooke
Windsor-Sandwich (37,419): Bill Wrye
Windsor-Walkerville (37,698): Bernard Newman
York Centre (58,784): Don Cousens
York North (50,833): William Hodgson

METROPOLITAN TORONTO

Armourdale (48,794): Bruce McCaffrey
Beaches-Woodbine (38,432): Marion Bryden
Bellwoods (20,962): Ross McClellan
Don Mills (50,717): Dennis R. Timbrell
Dovercourt (23,822): Tony Lupusella
Downsview (35,039): Odoardo Di Santo
Eglinton (47,471): Roy McMurtry
Etobicoke (39,606): Ed Philip
High Park-Swansea (38,708): Yuri Shymko
Humber (56,864): Morley Kells
Lakeshore (43,035): Al Kolyn
Oakwood (33,027): Tony Grande
Oriole (50,052): John Williams
Parkdale (28,178): Tony Ruprecht
Riverdale (30,954): James A. Renwick
St. Andrew-St. Patrick (35,383): Larry Grossman
St. David (39,026): Margaret Scrivener
St. George (45,833): Susan Fish
Scarborough Centre (40,661): Frank Drea
Scarborough East (46,332): Margaret Birch
Scarborough-Ellesmere (41,290): Alan M. Robinson
Scarborough North (65,593): Thomas L. Wells
Scarborough West (38,994): Richard F. Johnston
Wilson Heights (43,771): David Rotenberg
York East (45,058): Dr. Robert Elgie
York Mills (56,308): Bette Stephenson, M.D.
York South (43,060): Donald C. MacDonald
York West (52,976): Nicholas G. Leluk
Yorkview (44,057): Mike Spensieri

OFFICE OF THE PREMIER

Parliament Bldgs., Toronto, Ont. M7A 1A1
Phone: 965-1941
Deputy Minister, Dr. E.E. Stewart
Private Secretary, Miss H. Anderson
Executive Director, C.H. Westcott
Press Officer, Sally Barnes

GOVERNMENT DEPARTMENTS

MINISTRY OF AGRICULTURE & FOOD

801 Bay St., Toronto (Mailing address: Queen's Park, Parliament Bldgs., Toronto, Ont. M7A 1A3)
Information Contact, Director, Information Branch, 801 Bay St. (M7A 1A5) (phone: 416-965-1056)

Acts Administered

Abandoned Orchards Act
Agricultural Assns. Act
Agricultural Committees Act
Agricultural Rehabilitation & Development Act (Ont.)
Agricultural Representatives Act
Agricultural Research Institute of Ont. Act
Agricultural Societies Act
Agricultural Tile Drainage Installation Act, 1972
Animals for Research Act
Artificial Insemination of Livestock Act
Beef Cattle Marketing Act
Bees Act
Brucellosis Act
Bull Owners' Liability Act
Commodity Board Members Act, 1976
Commodity Boards & Marketing Agencies Act
Co-operative Loans Act
Crop Insurance Act (Ont.)
Dead Animal Disposal Act
Dog Licensing & Live Stock & Poultry Protection Act
Drainage Act
Edible Oil Products Act
Farm Income Stabilization Act, 1976
Farm Products Containers Act
Farm Products Grades & Sales Act
Farm Products Marketing Act
Farm Products Payments Act
Fruits & Vegetables Produce for Processing Act
Fur Farms Act, 1971
Grain Elevator Storage Act
Horticultural Societies Act
Hunter Damage Compensation Act
Junior Farmer Establishment Act
Live Stock & Live Stock Products Act
Live Stock Branding Act
Live Stock Community Sales Act
Live Stock Medicines Act, 1973
Meat Inspection Act (Ont.)
Milk Act
Ministry of Agriculture & Food Act
Non-Resident Agricultural Interests Registration Act, 1980
Oleomargarine Act
Ont. Agricultural Museum Act
Ont. Food Terminal Act
Plant Diseases Act
Pounds Act
Provincial Auctioneers Act
Riding Horse Establishments Act, 1972
Seed Potatoes Act
Stock Yards Act
Tile Drainage Act, 1971
Topsoil Preservation Act
Weed Control Act
Wool Marketing Act, 1974

MINISTER, Hon. Lorne C. Henderson
Executive Asst. to Minister, Morris Huff
Deputy Minister, Duncan M. Allan
Executive Director, Marketing Division, W.V. Doyle
Executive Director (Production & Rural Development), vacant

Executive Director (Agricultural Education & Research), Dr. J.C. Rennie
Executive Director (Finance & Admin. Division), R. Sewell
Director, Accounts Branch, D. Broome
Director, Administrative Services Branch, C. Russell
Director, Agricultural & Horticultural Societies Branch, R.T. McMahon
Director, Rural Development Branch, N. Watson
Director, Audit Services Branch, M. Chang
Director, Economics Branch, Dr. E.A. Haslett
Director, Extension Branch, A.G. Bennett
Director, Farm Products Quality Branch, D.E. Williams
Director, Farm Products Marketing Branch, J.H. Krauter
Director, Home Economics Branch, Ms. M. McGhee
Director, Information Branch, R.R. Snell
Director, Legal Branch, F.F. Gallant, Q.C.
Librarian, K. Sunquist
Commr., Live Stock, H.E. McGill
Director, Market Development Branch, A. Cooper
Chairman, Farm Products Appeal Tribunal, K.A. McEwen
Director, Personnel Branch, R.J. Johnston
Director, Program Co-ordination Secretariat, D.B. George
Director, Soils & Crops Branch, G. Driver
Director, Veterinary Services Branch, Dr. K.A. McDermid
Director, Horticultural Research Institute of Ont., Vineland Stn., Dr. G. Collin
Principal, Centralia College of Agricultural Tech., Huron Park, J.D. Jamieson
Principal, Kemptville College of Agricultural Tech., Kemptville, J.D. Curtis
Principal, New Liskeard College of Agricultural Tech., New Liskeard, D.W. Taylor
Director, Provincial Pesticide Residue Testing Laboratory, Guelph, Dr. R. Frank
Principal, Ridgetown College of Agricultural Tech., Ridgetown, J.A. MacDonald
Principal, Alfred College of Agricultural Tech., Alfred, M. Paulhus

Agricultural Representatives

County/Dist.: Name, Address:
Algoma: A.G. Mitchell, 1496 Wellington St. E., Sault Ste Marie, P6A 2R1
Brant: D.N. Graham, 207 Greenwich St., Brantford, N3S 2X7
Bruce: M.R. Bolton, Box 1330, Walkerton, NOG 2VO
Carleton: W.D. Black, 26 Thorncliff Place, Nepean, K2H 6L2
Cochrane North: N.R. Tarlton, Experimental Farm, Kapuskasing, P5N 2X9
Cochrane South: P. Sabourin, Box 608, Matheson, POK 1NO
Dufferin: T.P. Sullivan, R.R. 4, Orangeville, L9W 2Z1
Dundas: R.A. Humphries, Box 488, Winchester, KOC 2KO
Durham: A.O. Dalrymple, 234 King St. E., Bowmanville, L1C 1P5
Elgin: J.A. Anderson, 594 Talbot St., St. Thomas, N5P 1C7
Essex: L.M. Weber, 46 Fox St., Essex, N8M 2S2
Frontenac: E.R. Jennings, 1055 Princess St., Kingston, K7L 1H3
Glengarry: G.J. Smith, Box 579, Alexandria, KOC 1AO
Grenville: J.D. Lambie, Box 2004, Kemptville, KOG 1JO
Grey: B.H. Bolton, 181 Toronto St. S., Markdale, NOC 1HO
Haldimand: H.U. Bentley, Box 129, Cayuga, NOA 1EO
Halton: H.J. Stanley, 17 Wilson Dr., Milton, L9T 3J7
Hastings: W.D. Tipper, Box 340, Stirling, KOK 3EO
Huron: D.S. Pullen, Box 159, Clinton, NOM 1LO
Kenora: E.H. Lick, Ont. Govt. Bldg., Box 3000, Dryden, P8N 3B3
Kent: B.G. Fraser, 435 Grand Ave. W., Chatham, N7M 5L1
Lambton: W.T. Abraham, Box 730, Petrolia, NON 1RO
Lanark: R.C. Bradford, 10 Sunset Blvd., Perth, K7H 2Y2
Leeds: C.A. Tanner, Box 635, Brockville, K6V 5V8
Lennox & Addington: G.M. Mills, 41 Dundas St. W., Napanee, K7R 1Z5
Manitoulin: H.R. Hodder, Box 328, Gore Bay, POP 1HO
Middlesex: R.A. Forsyth, 195 Dufferin Ave., London, N6A 1K7
Muskoka and Parry Sound: S. MacDonald, Box 130, Huntsville, POA 1KO
Niagara North: N.W. Hoag, Vineland Stn., LOR 2EO
Niagara South: C.K. Clay, 574 S. Pelham St., Welland, L3C 3C6
Nipissing: A. Pommainville, 222 McIntyre St. W., North Bay, P1B 2Y8
Norfolk: J.R. Richards, Box 587, Simcoe, N3Y 4N5
Northumberland: D.F. Young, Box 820, Brighton, KOK 1HO
Ontario: H.I. Bell, Box 309, Uxbridge, LOC 1KO
Oxford: C.B. Matthews, Box 666, Woodstock, N4S 7Z5
Peel: R.E. Bell, 3 Elizabeth St. S., Brampton, L6Y 1P7
Perth: A.W. Scott, Box 398, 413 Hibernia St., Stratford, N5A 5W2
Peterborough: J.R. Cockburn, 55 George St. N., Peterborough, K9J 3G2
Prescott: R.L. Farmer, Box 110, Plantagenet, KOB 1LO
Prince Edward: L.W. Matheson, Box 470, Picton, KOK 2TO
Rainy River: J.G. Young, Front St., Emo, POW 1EO
Renfrew: W.C.D. Little, 315 Raglan St. S., Renfrew, K7V 1R6
Russell: A. Beauchesne, Box 540, 666 rue Notre Dame, Embrun, KOA 1WO
Simcoe North: C.J. Nesbitt, Box 340, Elmvale, LOL 1PO
Simcoe South: J.K. McRuer, Box 370, Alliston, LOM 1AO
Stormont: D.C. Miller, 109 Eleventh St. W., Cornwall, K6H 5T3
Sudbury: A.J. Lemay, 1414 LaSalle Blvd, Sudbury, P3A 1ZO
Thunder Bay: W.R. Broadworth, Ont. Govt. Bldg., 435 James St. S., Thunder Bay, P7E 6E3
Timiskaming: N.R. Tarlton, Box G, New Liskeard, POJ 1PO
Victoria: C.L. Hamilton, 322 Kent St. W., Lindsay, K9V 2Z9
Waterloo: G.H. Thompson, 279 Weber St. N., Waterloo, N2J 3H8
Wellington: M.T. Chamberlain, Box 159, Fergus, N1M 2W7
Wentworth: W.D. Keys, R.R. 1, Ancaster, L9G 3K9
York: A.A. Wall, Newmarket Plaza, Newmarket, L3Y 2N1

Agriculture Boards & Commissions

Agricultural Research Institute of Ont.; Director, J.C. Rennie, Ministry of Agriculture, 801 Bay St., Toronto, Ont. M7A 1A3 (965-6695)
Crop Insurance Commission of Ontario, 5th floor, 801 Bay St., Toronto, Ont. M7A 1B7 (965-1811); General Manager, H. Ediger
Farm Income Stabilization Commission, 5th floor, 801 Bay St., Toronto, Ont. M7A 1B7 (965-1811)
Farm Machinery Advisory Board; Chairman, Clayton Cargess, R.R. 2, Denfield, Ont.
Farm Products Appeal Tribunal, 12th floor, 801 Bay St., Toronto, Ont. M7A 2B2 (965-5844)
The Milk Commission of Ontario; Chairman, J.H. Krauter, Farm Products Marketing Branch, Ministry of Agriculture & Food, Parliament Bldgs., Toronto, Ont. M7A 2B2 (416/965-2124)
Ont. Food Terminal Board; Chairman, Doug E. Williams, 165 The Queensway, Toronto, Ont. M8Y 1H8 (416/259-5479)
Ont. Stock Yards Board; Chairman, D. Matheson, 590 Keele St., Toronto, Ont. M6N 3E3 (767-1163)

Agricultural Marketing Boards

FARM PRODUCTS MARKETING BOARD, Farm Products Marketing Branch, Parliament Bldgs., Toronto, Ont. M7A 2B2
(416) 965-2124
Chairman, John H. Krauter
- Apple Marketing Commission, Manager, W.A. Wheatstone, Ste. 123, 1454 Dundas St. E., Mississauga, Ont. L4X 1L4 (416/275-4525)
- Asparagus Growers' Marketing Board, Secretary Manager, David Lapos, 504 Newbold St., London, Ont. N6E 1K6 (519/681-6010)
- Bean Producers' Marketing Board, Manager & Marketing Agent, C. Broadwell, 1112 Dearness Dr., London, Ont. N6E 1N9 (519/681-1720)
- Berry Growers' Marketing Board (Strawberries & Raspberries for Processing), Chairman, J.A. Steel, R.R. 1, Waterford, Ont. N0E 1Y0 (519/443-7280)
- Burley Tobacco Growers Marketing Board, Secretary, Brad Caughy, 180 Keil Dr. S., Chatham, Ont. N7M 5Y6 (519/352-6710)

Chicken Producers' Marketing Board, Secretary, John E. Janzen, Unit 15, 3525 Mainway, Burlington, Ont. L7R 3Y8 (416/335-4496)
Cream Producers' Marketing Board, Secretary Manager, J. Bilyea, 50 Maitland St., Toronto, Ont. M4Y 1C7 (416/920-2700)
Egg Producers' Marketing Board, General Manager, B. Ellsworth, 5799 Yonge St., 10th floor, Willowdale, Ont. M2M 3V3 (416/223-5330)
Flue-Cured Tobacco Growers' Marketing Board, Secretary, J.A. Leathong, Box 70, Tillsonburg, Ont. N4G 4H4 (519/842-3661)
Fresh Grape Growers' Marketing Board, Secretary Treasurer, A. Huisman, Box 100, Vineland Stn., Ont. LOR 2EO (416/688-0990)
Fresh Potato Growers' Marketing Board, Secretary Manager, L. Armstrong, 1463 Ontario St., Burlington, Ont. L7S 1G6 (416/637-5609)
Grape Growers' Marketing Board, Secretary, J.R. Rainforth, Box 100, Vineland Station, Ont. LOR 2EO (416/688-0990)
Greenhouse Vegetable Producers' Marketing Board, Secretary, Keith Malott, Box 417, Leamington, Ont. N8H 3W5 (519/326-2604)
Milk Marketing Board, Secretary, H. Parker, 50 Maitland St., Toronto, Ont. M4Y 1C7 (416/920-2700)
Pork Producers' Marketing Board, Secretary, R.J. Bluhm, 4198 Dundas St. W., Box 1103, Toronto, Ont. M8X 1Y6 (416/239-2921, 239-2939)
Potato Growers Marketing Board, Secretary Manager, L. Armstrong, 1463 Ontario St., Burlington, Ont. L7S 1G6 (416/637-5609)
Processing Tomato Seedling Plant Growers Marketing Board, Secretary, D. Moore, Box 417, Leamington, Ont. N8H 3W5 (519/326-2604, 326-4481)
Rutabaga Producers' Marketing Board, Secretary Treasurer, Ms. D. Milton, Box 328, Lucan, Ont. N0M 2J0 (519/326-2604)
Seed Corn Growers' Marketing Board, Secretary, Brad Caughy, 180 Keil Dr. S., Chatham, Ont. N7M 5Y6 (519/352-6710)
Soya Bean Growers' Marketing Board, Secretary Manager, Otis McGregor, Box 1199, Chatham, Ont. N7M 5L8 (519/352-7730)
Tender Fruit Producers' Marketing Board, Secretary Manager, J. Rainforth, Box 100, Vineland Station, Ont. LOR 2EO (416/688-0990)
Turkey Producers' Marketing Board, General Manager, Ken Crawford, 1400 Bishop St., Cambridge (G), Ont. N1R 6J1 (519/621-2110)
Vegetable Growers' Marketing Board, Secretary Manager, John Mumford, 502 Newbold St., London, Ont. N6E 1K6 (519/681-1875)
Wheat Producers' Marketing Board (Ont. Winter Wheat), General Manager, R. Addeman, 880 Richmond St., Chatham, Ont. N7M 5K8 (519/354-4430)

ALCOHOLISM & DRUG ADDICTION RESEARCH FOUNDATION

33 Russell St., Toronto, Ont. M5S 2S1
(416) 595-6000

The Addiction Research Foundation is an agency of the province of Ontario responsible for conducting programs of research, clinical investigation, professional training and information in the alcohol and drug dependence field.

Chairman, Dr. John B. Macdonald
President & Chief Executive Officer, Dr. Joan Marshman
Director, Clinical Institute Hospital, Dr. E.M. Sellers
Director, Education Resources Division, H.J. Schankula
Director, Division of Social & Biological Studies, R.E. Popham
Director, School for Addiction Studies, Dr. D.E. Meeks
Director, Regional Programs Division, J.C. LaRocque
Director, Administrative & Support Services Division, A.P. Charles
Library, 595-6144; Marketing, 595-6056

There are regional centres in Belleville, Chatham, Cornwall, Hamilton, Kapuskasing, Kenora, Kingston, Kitchener, London, Mississauga, North Bay, Oakville, Orillia, Oshawa, Ottawa, Owen Sound, Pembroke, Peterborough, Sarnia, Sault Ste. Marie, Simcoe, South Porcupine, Sudbury, Thunder Bay, Timmins, Toronto, Welland and Windsor

MINISTRY OF THE ATTORNEY GENERAL

18 King St. E., Toronto, Ont. M5C 1C5
Information from Miss C. Williams (phone: 416/965-7503)

Acts Administered

Absconding Debtors Act
Absentees Act
Accidental Fires Act
Accumulations Act
Admin. of Justice Act
Age of Majority & Accountability Act
Aliens' Real Property Act
Arbitrations Act
Architects Act
Assessment Review Court Act
Assignments & Preferences Act
Bail Act
Barristers Act
Blind Persons' Rights Act
Bulk Sales Act
Business Records Protection Act
Change of Name Act
Charitable Gifts Act
Charities Accounting Act
Children's Law Reform Act
Commrs. for Taking Affidavits Act
Compensation for Victims of Crime Act
Constitutional Questions Act
Conveyancing & Law of Property Act
Costs of Distress Act
County Court Judges' Criminal Courts Act
County Courts Act
County Judges Act
Creditors' Relief Act
Crown Admin. of Estates Act
Crown Agency Act
Crown Attorneys Act
Crown Witnesses Act
Disorderly Houses Act
Dog Owners' Liability Act
Dominion Courts Act
Escheats Act
Estates Administration Act
Estreats Act
Evidence Act
Execution Act
Expropriations Act
Extra-Judicial Services Act
Factors Act
Family Law Reform Act
Fines & Forfeitures Act
Fraudulent Conveyances Act
Fraudulent Debtors Arrest Act
Frustrated Contracts Act
Gaming Act
General Sessions Act
Habeas Corpus Act
Hospitals & Charitable Institutions Inquiries Act
Hotel Registration of Guests Act
Innkeepers Act
Interpretation Act
Judges' Orders Enforcement Act
Judicature Act
Judicial Review Procedure Act
Juries Act
Justices of the Peace Act
Landlord & Tenant Act

Law Society Act
Legal Aid Act
Libel & Slander Act
Limitations Act
Lord's Day (Ont.) Act
Master & Servant Act
Matrimonial Causes Act
Mechanics' Lien Act
Mental Incompetency Act
Mercantile Law Amendment Act
Ministry of the Attorney General Act
Minors Act
Minors' Protection Act
Mortgages Act
Negligence Act
Notaries Act
Occupiers' Liability Act
Ont. Law Reform Commission Act
Ont. Municipal Board Act
Partition Act
Pawnbrokers Act
Perpetuities Act
Powers of Attorney Act
Proceedings Against the Crown Act
Professional Engineers Act
Property & Civil Rights Act
Provincial Court (Civil Division) Project Act
Provincial Courts Act
Provincial Offences Act
Public Accounting Act
Public Authorities Protection Act
Public Halls Act
Public Inquiries Act
Public Institutions Inspection Act
Public Officers Act
Public Officers' Fees Act
Public Trustee Act
Quieting Titles Act
Reciprocal Enforcement of Judgments Act
Reciprocal Enforcement of Maintenance Orders Act
Regulations Act
Religious Organizations' Lands Act
Replevin Act
Sale of Goods Act
Settled Estates Act
Sheriffs Act
Short Forms of Conveyances Act
Short Forms of Leases Act
Short Forms of Mortgages Act
Small Claims Courts Act
Solicitors Act
Statute of Frauds
Statutes Act
Statutory Powers Procedure Act
Succession Law Reform Act
Surrogate Courts Act
Ticket Speculation Act
Time Act
Trespass to Property Act
Trustee Act
Unconscionable Transactions Relief Act
Unified Family Court Act
Univ. Expropriation Powers Act
Variation of Trusts Act
Vendors & Purchasers Act
Vexatious Proceedings Act
Wages Act
Warehousemen's Lien Act
Warehouse Receipts Act

ATTORNEY GENERAL, Hon. Roy McMurtry, Q.C.
Deputy Attorney General, A. Rendall Dick, Q.C.
Executive Counsel, Simon Chester

Legislative Counsel
Legislative Bldg., Queen's Park
Senior Legislative Counsel, A.N. Stone, Q.C.
Legislative Counsel, J.A. Fader
Registrar of Regulations, W.R. Anderson, Q.C.
Counsel, D.E. Phillips, D.L. Revell, A.S. Tucker, F.N. Williams, R. Yurkow
Legislative Editor, J. Cannon

Courts Administration
Asst. Deputy Attorney General & Director of Courts Admin., B.W. McLoughlin
Inspector of Legal Offices & Deputy Director of Courts Admin., M.S. Fitzpatrick, Q.C.

Criminal Law Division
Asst. Deputy Attorney General & Director of Criminal Law, R.M. McLeod, Q.C.
Deputy Director of Criminal Law & Director of Crown Attorneys, J.D. Takach, Q.C.
Deputy Director of Crown Attorneys, W.H. Langdon, Q.C.
Senior Crown Counsel, Criminal Law, J.D. Watt
Crown Law Office, Criminal,
Director, H.F. Morton, Q.C.
Deputy Director, H.G. Black
Counsel, D. Doherty, D. Hunt, E.G. Hachborn, R.A. Cormack, Q.C., R. Lundy, Q.C., A.R. Taylor, E.F. Then, J. Casey, I. Koziebrocki, B. Wein, J. Blacklock, M. Segal, C. Hill, I. MacDonnell, M.A. MacDonald, L.H. Cecchetto, J.C. Pearson, B.T. Evans, H. Campbell, P. Lindsay, R. Macdonald, D. Frost, S. Ficek, M. Bernstein, D. Ewart

Civil Law Division
Asst. Deputy Attorney General, Civil Law, B. Wright, Q.C.
Director of Crown Law Office, Civil, J. Polika, Q.C.
Counsel, M. Bader, D.W. Brown, Q.C., D. Dukelow, V. Freidin, B. Johnston, T.W. Lane, Q.C., T. Lederer, T. Marshall, Q.C., S. McAuley, Q.C., T. McCabe, J. Minor, T.H. Wickett, P. Lockett, P. Jacobsen, J. Zarudny, R. Kay, L. Hunter, B. Fox, H. Paisley, M. Fleishman, M. Smith
Director of Constitutional Law, J. Cararzan, Q.C.
Counsel, C. Creighton, E. Goldberg, L.E. Weinrib
Director of Common Legal Services, J.B. Gleason
Official Guardian, L.W. Perry, Q.C.
Deputy Official Guardian, J.E.C. Beatty
Counsel, G.W. Glass, G.R. Hodgson, E.H. Kasdan, E.H. Levenspil, E.C. Purvis, S.J. Sinica, R.L. Stephenson, J. Coons, H. Atwood, J.C.C. Beatty, Q.C., E. Freedman, E.M. Henry, Q.C., A. Ingram, Y. Lazor, G.C. Puver
Child Representation, A. Wolfish

ASST. DEPUTY ATTORNEY GENERAL, POLICY, PLANNING & INTERGOVERNMENTAL AFFAIRS, vacant

Policy Development Division
Counsel, S.V. Fram, K. Weiler, C. Perkins, A.Q. Shipley, J.D. Ewart, S. McCann

Programs & Administration Division
General Manager, G.H. Carter
Director, Finance & Services, H.A. Gibbs
Director, Audit Services, J. Solymos
Director, Personnel Management, vacant
Co-ordinator, Planning & Evaluation, D. Mueller
Director, Information & Computer Systems, D.H.S. Thornton

Ontario Law Reform Commission
18 King St. E., 16th floor, Toronto, Ont. M5C 1C5
(416) 965-4761
Chairman, Dr. D. Mendes da Costa, Q.C., LL.D.
Vice Chairman, Hon. G.A. Gale, C.C., Q.C., LL.D.
Members, Hon. R.A. Bell, P.C., Q.C., W.R. Poole, Q.C., Hon. J.C. McRuer, O.C., LL.D., D.C.L., B.A. Percival, Q.C.
Counsel, Ms. M. Patricia Richardson

Administrative Tribunals

Assessment Review Court

80 Bloor St. W., Ste. 705, Toronto, Ont. M5S 1L9
965-7574
Chairman, B.H.B. Bowlby, Q.C.
Vice Chairmen, S.R.R. McNeil, G.C. Hewson
Provincial Registrar, T.G. Murphy

Board of Negotiation

Ste. 1800, 439 University Ave., Toronto, Ont. M5G 1Y8
965-2867
Chairman, W.C. Dymond

Criminal Injuries Compensation Board

17th floor, 439 University Ave., Toronto, Ont. M5G 1Y8
965-4755
Chairman, Allan Grossman
Registrar, D.D. Graham

Ont. Municipal Board

180 Dundas St. W., Toronto, Ont. M5G 1E5
965-1912
Chairman, H.E. Stewart
Vice Chairmen, A.H. Arrell, Q.C., A.L. McCrae, W.T. Shrives, W.H.J. Thompson, Q.C., D.S. Colbourne, D.D. Diplock, Q.C., P.M. Brooks, H.H. Lancaster
Members, A.B. Ball, C.G. Ebers, Q.C., H.W. Kelly, Q.C., J.A. Wheler, E.A. Seaborn, A.J.L. Chapman, Q.C., W.E. Dyer, Q.C., C.G. Charron, Q.C., K.D. Bindhardt, D.H. McRobb, P.G. Wilkes, J.E. Hendy, V.M. Singer, Q.C., M.D. Henderson, D.M. Rogers, Q.C., D.L. Santo, T.F. Baines, Q.C.

Land Compensation Board

10 King St. E., Toronto, Ont. M5C 1C3
965-1012
Chairman, vacant
Vice Chairmen, James Worrall, Q.C., S.R. Cole
Members, G.M. Hobart, D.W. Middleton, Grant Campbell, Q.C., G.T.J. Dobbs
Registrar, C.E. Warner

OFFICE OF THE PROVINCIAL AUDITOR

Queen's Park, Toronto, Ont. M7A 1A2
Phone: (416) 965-1381
Provincial Auditor, F.N. Scott
Asst. Provincial Auditor, D.F. Archer

BOARD OF DIRECTORS OF CHIROPRACTIC

Suite 15D, 20 Prince Arthur Ave., Toronto, Ont. M5R 1B1
(416) 922-6355
Chairman, S.E. West, D.C., 66 March St., Sault Ste. Marie, Ont. P6A 2Z2
Vice-Chairman, F.N. Barnes, D.C., 3293 Lakeshore Blvd. W., Toronto, Ont. M8W 1M8
Secretary-Treasurer, K.S. Wood, D.C.

CIVIL SERVICE COMMISSION

Frost Bldg. S., Queen's Park (3rd floor), Toronto, Ont. M7A 1Z5
Minister to whom The Commission Reports, Chairman of The Management Board of Cabinet
Chairman, Civil Service Commission, G.H. Waldrum
Commrs., Mrs. E.M. McLellan, D. Sinclair; Mrs. Anne Kemp; T.E. Armstrong, Q.C.; R.J. Butler; H.F. Gilbert
Secretary, R.A. Whitelaw (phone: 965-3364)

Civil Service Commission Staff

Executive Director, Staff Relations Division, J.R. Scott
Compensation Division
Executive Director, Compensation Division, J.A. Jackson
Director, Benefits Policy Branch, Miss E. Aboud
Director, Classification Branch, H.D. Burt
Director, Pay Policy Branch, K.W. Skelton
Staffing Division
Director, Recruitment Branch, L. Tobias
Director, Staff Development Branch, T.A. Dawes
Director, Administrative Services Branch, I.H. Jennings
Director, Personnel Audit Branch, P.G. Schwindt
Executive Secretary, Senior Appointments & Compensation, J. Hansen

Public Service Grievance Board

180 Dundas St. W., 20th floor, Toronto, Ont. M5G 1Z8
Chairman, Professor C. Gordon Simmonds
Secretary, H.F. Goss

Public Service Classification Rating Committee

180 Dundas St. W., 20th floor, Toronto, Ont. M5G 1Z8
Chairman, Professor C. Gordon Simmonds
Secretary, H.F. Goss

Grievance Settlement Board

180 Dundas St. W., 21st floor, Toronto, Ont. M5G 1Z8
Chairman, J.F.W. Weatherill
Registrar, H.F. Goss

Ontario Public Service Labour Relations Tribunal

180 Dundas St. W., 21st floor, Toronto, Ont. M5G 1Z8
Chairman, Owen B. Shime, Q.C.
Registrar, H.F. Goss

MINISTRY OF COLLEGES & UNIVERSITIES

(See Ministry of Education)

MINISTRY OF COMMUNITY & SOCIAL SERVICES

Hepburn Block, Queen's Park, Toronto, Ont. M7A 1E9 (unless otherwise noted below)
Information Contact, M. Sellors, Communications Branch, 1st floor, Macdonald Block (phone: 416/965-7825)

Acts Administered

Charitable Institutions Act
Child Welfare Act
Children's Institutions Act
Children's Mental Health Centres Act
Children's Probation Act (Bill 95)
Children's Residential Services Act
Day Nurseries Act
Developmental Services Act
District Welfare Administration Bds. Act
Elderly Persons' Centres Act
Family Benefits Act
General Welfare Assistance Act
Homemakers & Nurses Services Act
Homes for the Aged & Rest Homes Act
Homes for Retarded Persons Act
Ministry of Community & Social Services Act
Provincial Courts Act (part)
Training Schools Act
Unified Family Court Act (part)
Vocational Rehabilitation Services Act

MINISTER, Hon. Frank Drea
Deputy Minister, Robert D. Carman
Federal-Provincial Relations Office, Executive Co-ordinator, G. Heagle, 965-1673
Communications, Director, D.M. Rennie, 965-7252
Operational Review & Audit Branch, Director, Dr. G. Mazuryk, 965-5214
Legal Services, Director, Douglas Rutherford, 965-5147
French Language Services, Co-ordinator, A.L. Allan, 965-2341
Social Assistance Review Board, Rm. M1-56, Macdonald Block, Executive Secretary, F. Mulrooney, 965-4787
Training Schools Advisory Board, 2nd floor, 700 Bay St., Chairman, Barry Lowes, 965-1871
Children's Services Review Board, Box 251, Toronto Dominion Centre, Chairman, J.E. Ford, 965-1632

Finance & Administration, Asst. Deputy Minister, O.M. Berg, 965-0996

(division includes: Capital & Admin. Services, Systems Management, Personnel, Federal-Provincial Cost Sharing, Management Improvement, Finance, Financial Planning & Corporate Analysis, Accounts)

Children's & Adults'

Assoc. Deputy Minister, Policy & Program, Judge George Thomson, 965-4914

Asst. Deputy Minister, Operations, Peter Barnes, 965-7683

Executive Co-ordinator, Institutions, Dr. R.A. Farmer, 965-5395

Director, Operational Support, D. Alfieri, 965-4363

Ministry Regional Offices are located at Sault Ste. Marie, Toronto, London and Kingston

MINISTRY OF CONSUMER & COMMERCIAL RELATIONS

Information from Consumer Information Centre, Main floor, 555 Yonge St., Toronto, Ont. M7A 2H6 (416/963-1111); For Departmental inquiries contact Director, Communications Services, S. Paul (963-0339)

Acts Administered

Apportionment Act
Assignments & Preferences Act
Athletics Control Act
Bailiffs Act
Bills of Sale Act
Boilers & Pressure Vessels Act
Boundaries Act
Bread Sales Act
Building Code Act, 1974
Business Corps. Act
Business Practices Act
Cemeteries Act
Certification of Titles Act
Collection Agencies Act
Commodity Futures Act
Compulsory Automobile Insurance Act
Condominium Act
Consumer Protection Act
Consumer Protection Bureau Act
Consumer Reporting Act
Co-operative Corps. Act
Co-operative Health Services of Ontario Assets Protection Act, 1981
Corporation Securities Registration Act
Corporations Act
Corporations Information Act
Credit Unions & Caisses Populaires Act
Debt Collectors Act
Deposits Regulation Act
Discriminatory Business Practices Act
Egress from Public Buildings Act
Elevating Devices Act
Energy Act
Factors Act
Gasoline Handling Act
Guarantee Companies Securities Act
Insurance Act
Investment Contracts Act
Land Titles Act
Limited Partnerships Act
Liquor Control Act
Liquor Licence Act
Loan & Trust Corps. Act
Marine Insurance Act
Marriage Act
Ministry of Consumer & Commercial Relations Act
Mortgage Brokers Act
Mortmain & Charitable Uses Act
Motor Vehicle Accident Claims Act
Motor Vehicle Dealers Act
Ont. Credit Union League Ltd. Act, 1972
Ont. Deposit Insurance Corp. Act
Ont. New Home Warranties Plan Act
Operating Engineers Act
Paperback & Periodical Distributors Act
Partnership Act
Partnerships Registration Act
Pension Benefits Act
Personal Property Security Act
Petroleum Products Price Freeze Act
Prearranged Funeral Services Act
Prepaid Hospital & Medical Services Act
Racing Commission Act
Real Estate & Business Brokers Act
Registered Insurance Brokers Act
Registry Act
Residential Premises Rent Review Act
Residential Tenancies Act
Securities Act
Theatres Act
Toronto Stock Exchange Act
Travel Industry Act
Unclaimed Articles Act
Upholstered & Stuffed Articles Act
Vital Statistics Act
Wine Content Act
also:
Lotteries (authority to licence)

MINISTER, Hon. Gordon W. Walker
Deputy Minister, D.A. Crosbie
Director, Legal Services, E. Ciemiega, Q.C.

Consumer Services Bureau

Main floor, 555 Yonge St., Main floor, Toronto, Ont. M7A 2H6
(416) 963-1111
Asst. Director, B.A. Tyson
Regional Offices:
143 Main St. E., #206, Hamilton, Ont. L8N 1G4, 416/529-8177
80 Dundas St. E., London, Ont. N6H 1B4, 519/679-7150
1673 Carling Ave., #102, Ottawa, Ont. K2A 1C4, 613/725-1489
139 George St. N., Peterborough, Ont. K9J 3G6, 705/743-8728
199 Larch St., 5th floor, Sudbury, Ont. P3E 5P9, 705/675-4378
435 James St. S., Thunder Bay, Ont. P7E 6E3, 807/475-1641
250 Windsor Ave., 6th floor, Windsor, Ont. N9A 6V9, 519/254-6413

Ontario Securities Commission

10 Wellesley St. E., Toronto, Ont. M7A 2H7
(416) 963-0223
Chairman, H.J. Knowles, Q.C.
Vice Chairman, H.S. Bray, Q.C.
Director, C.R.B. Salter, Q.C.

Pension Commission of Ontario

2nd floor, 10 Wellesley St. E., Toronto, Ont.
(416) 963-0527
Chairman, Donna Jane Haley, Q.C.
Supt. of Pensions, J.W. Bentley

Ontario Racing Commission

3rd floor, 10 Wellesley St. E., Toronto, Ont.
(416) 963-0520
Chairman, N.E. Hardy
Director, W.R. McDonnell

Commercial Registration Appeal Tribunal

10th floor, 1 St. Clair Ave. W., Toronto, Ont. M4T 1L6
(416) 965-7798
Chairman, J. Yaremko, Q.C.
Registrar, A. Verge

Business Practices Division

Executive Director, R.A. Simpson
Director, Consumer Advisory Services Branch, D.I. Radford
Registrar of Motor Vehicle Dealers, A.W. Abrams

Registrar of Bailiffs, Collection Agencies, Mtge. Brokers, Consumer Reporting & Paperback & Periodical Distributors, A. Binstock
Manager, Central Registration, vacant
Commercial Liaison Officer, A.R. Walker
Consumer Liaison Officer, Mrs. E.A. Rowan
Director, Consumer Advisory Service, D.I. Radford
Director, Investigation & Enforcement, D.L. Mitchell
Director, Commercial Registration, vacant

Financial Institutions
Executive Director, M.A. Thompson, Q.C.
Director, Insurance Services, R.G. Cooper
Director, Financial Examinations Services, H.R. Terhune
Director, Credit Unions & Co-operative Services, J.M. Best
Registrar, Agents, Brokers & Adjusters, W.G. Stride
Co-ordinator, Automobile Casualty Insurance, W.B. Laur
Director, Motor Vehicle Accident Claims, E.H. Miles

Property Rights Division
3rd floor, 543 Yonge St., Toronto, Ont.
Provincial Property Registrar, D.M. Peacock
Director of Real Property Registration, V.S. McCutcheon
Director, Legal & Survey Standards, R.E. Priddle
Director of Personal Property Registration, T.M. Rundle

Office of the Registrar General
Mailing: Macdonald Block, Queen's Park, Toronto, Ont. M7A 1Y5
Public Counter: Macdonald Block, 2nd floor, Room M2-25
Deputy Registrar General, E. Pike
Fee for each Birth, Death, or Marriage Certificate: $3.

Technical Standards Division
400 University Ave., Toronto, Ont.
Executive Director, H.Y. Yoneyama
Director, Pressure Vessels Safety Branch, H.J. Wright
Director & Chief Inspector of Elevating Devices, T. Gordon Smith
Director, Fuels Safety Branch, H.T. Jones
Director of Building Code, G. Adams
Registrar of Upholstered & Stuffed Articles, J.D. MacDougall

Companies Division
Executive Director, B.C. Howard
Director, Company Services, H.H. Ozolins

Theatres Branch
Director, M. Brown

Lotteries Branch
Director, E.C. Fisher

Liquor Licence Board
55 Lakeshore Blvd. E., Toronto, Ont. M5E 1A4
(416) 965-4651
Chairman, W.L. Blair
Executive Director, R.W. Cooper

Liquor Control Board
55 Lakeshore Blvd. E., Toronto, Ont. M5E 1A4
Chairman, W.J. Bosworth (965-4901)
General Manager, F.A. MacInnis (965-4911)

Liquor Licence Appeal Tribunal
10th floor, 1 St. Clair Ave. W., Toronto, Ont. M4V 1K6
(416) 965-7798
Chairman, J. Yaremko, Q.C.

Residential Tenancy Commission
3rd floor, 77 Bloor St. W., Toronto, Ont. M5S 1M2
(416) 964-7808
Chief Tenancy Commissioner, P.C. Williams

Building Code Commission
400 University Ave., Toronto, Ont. M7A 2J9
(416) 965-5881

Building Materials Evaluation Commission
400 University Ave., Toronto, Ont. M7A 2J9
(416) 965-5881

Land Registrars
Provincial Property Registrar, D.M. Peacock
*Combined Registry & Land Titles Systems Office:

*Algoma: P.H. George, Box 550, Sault Ste. Marie, Ont. P6A 5M8
Brant: P. Gale (act.), Court House, 80 Wellington St., Brantford, Ont. N3T 2L9
*Bruce: J.A. MacDonald, Box 1690, Walkerton, Ont. NOG 2VO
Carleton: J.W.G. Armstrong, Court House, 67 Nicholas St., Ottawa, Ont. K1N 7B9
*Cochrane: G.W. Ash, Box 580, Cochrane, Ont. POL 1CO
Dufferin: A.T. Woodland, 75 First St., Orangeville, Ont. L9W 2E7
Dundas: P.T. Miedema, 5th St., Morrisburg, Ont. KOC 1XO
*Durham: G.F. Mackay, 400 Centre St. S., Whitby, Ont. L1N 4W2
*Elgin: R.H. Davis, Box 4, St. Thomas, Ont. N5P 3T5
*Essex: W.C. Bear, 250 Windsor Ave., Windsor, Ont. N9A 6P8
Frontenac: W.D. Robertson, Court House, Kingston, Ont. K7L 2N4
Glengarry: R.H. Gregoire, Box 668, Alexandria, Ont. KOC 1AO
Grenville: L.A. Cross, Box 1660, Prescott, Ont. KOE 1TO
Grey North: W.I. McArthur, Court House, 596 9th Ave. E., Owen Sound, Ont. N4K 3E3
Grey South: W.I. McArthur, Box 10, Durham, Ont. NOG 1RO
Haldimand: S. Vander Schelde, Box 310, Cayuga, Ont. NOA 1EO
Haliburton: Mrs. J.A. Jackson, Box 270, Minden, Ont. KOM 2KO
*Halton: Heinz Stolch, County Admin. Bldg., 491 Steeles Ave. E., Milton, Ont. L9T 1Y7
*Hastings: S.C. Geneja, 280 Pinnacle St., Belleville, Ont. K8N 3A9
Huron: D.G. Hill, Box 216, Goderich, Ont. N7A 3Z2
*Kenora: R. Edmonds, 220 Main St. S., Kenora, Ont. PN9 3X7
Kent: D.R. Craven, 40 William St. N., Chatham, Ont. N7M 5L8
Lambton: Kenneth Doan, Box 3021, Sarnia, Ont. N7T 7N5
Lanark North: J.C. Smithson, Box 1180, Almonte, Ont. KOA 1AO
Lanark South: Dale T. Wilson, 10 Sunset Blvd., Box 278, Perth, Ont. K7H 3E4
Leeds: L.A. Cross, Box 633, Brockville, Ont. K6V 5V2
Lennox: B.M. Drew, Box 307, Napanee, Ont. KOK 2RO
*Manitoulin: J.A. Graham, Box 265, Gore Bay, Ont. POP 1HO
Middlesex East: J.B. Sorensen, New Court House, 80 Dundas St., (Box 5600), London, Ont. N6A 2P3
*Middlesex West: W. Newman, Drawer 9, Glencoe, Ont. NOL 1MO
*Muskoka: R.C. Stewart, Box 720, Bracebridge, Ont. POB 1CO
*Newcastle: G.F. MacKay, Box 178, Bowmanville, Ont. L1C 3K9
*Niagara North: D.W. Baird, Box 126, St. Catharines, Ont. L2R 6R4
*Niagara South: S. Vander Schelde, 20 Cross St. N., Welland, Ont. L3B 3G1
*Nipissing: S.S. Mercer, 514 Main St. W., North Bay, Ont. P1B 2V4
Norfolk: Ron Logan, Court House, No. 3 Hwy. West, Box 9, Simcoe, Ont. N3Y 4K8
Northumberland East: Mrs. F.I. McDonald, Box 339, Colborne, Ont. KOK 1SO
Northumberland West: S.C. Geneja, 860 William St., Box 668, Cobourg, Ont. K9A 4K8
Ottawa: J.H. Hall, Court House, 2 Daly Ave., Ottawa, Ont. K1N 6E2
*Oxford: R.K. Thomson, Box 246, Woodstock, Ont. N4S 7W8
*Parry Sound: J. Boyer, Box 276, Parry Sound, Ont. P2A 2X4
*Peel: D.O. Cannon, 7765 Hurontario St., Box 1200, Brampton, Ont. L6V 2L8
Perth: J. Menard, Box 902, Stratford, Ont. N5A 6T1

*Peterborough: W.E. Giles, Court House, 470 Water St., Peterborough, Ont. K9H 3M3
*Port Hope: G.F. MacKay, 17 Mill St. N., Box 122, Port Hope, Ont. L1A 3W3
*Prescott: A. Bénard, Box 302, L'Orignal, Ont. KOB 1KO
Prince Edward: R.G. Rowe, Box 1310, Picton, Ont. KOK 2TO
*Rainy River: L.G. Leblanc, Box 398, Fort Frances, Ont. P9A 3M7
Renfrew: B.L. O'Brien, Box 760, Pembroke, Ont. K8A 6X1
*Russell: W.M. Stanley, Box 10, Russell, Ont. KOA 3BO
*Simcoe: A.G. Kneeshaw, Court House, 114 Worsley St., Barrie, Ont. L4M 1M1
Stormont: Mrs. V.A. McDonald, Box 1268, Cornwall, Ont. K6H 5V3
*Sudbury: W. Zaverucha, 199 Larch St., 3rd fl., Sudbury, Ont. P3E 5P9
*Thunder Bay: J.M. Donnelly, 29 Royston Court, Thunder Bay, Ont. P7A 4Y7
*Timiskaming: H.C. Thib, Box 159, Haileybury, Ont. POJ 1PO
Toronto (City) (Reg.): J. Haughey, 100 Queen St. W., Toronto, Ont. M5H 2N1
Toronto Boroughs & York South (Reg.): T.C. Blacklock, 100 Queen St. W., Toronto, Ont. M5H 2N1
Toronto & York Land Titles: B. Cowley, 100 Queen St. W., Toronto, Ont. M5H 2N1
Victoria: E.A. Legacy, act., 28 Francis St., Lindsay, Ont. K9V 3R9
Waterloo North: D.R. McKnight, 200 Frederick St., Kitchener, Ont. N2G 3W9
Waterloo South: Madeleine Goldstein, 150 Main St., Cambridge, Ont. N1R 1W4
Wellington North: R.S. Budge, Box 389, Arthur, Ont. NOG 1AO
Wellington South: K.M. McCrea, Box 905, Guelph, Ont. N1H 6M6
*Wentworth: V. Mattuzzi, 50 Main St. E., Hamilton, Ont. L8N 1E9
*York North: J. Small, 50 Eagle St. W., Newmarket, Ont. L3Y 6B1

MINISTRY OF CORRECTIONAL SERVICES

2001 Eglinton Ave. E., Scarborough, Ont. M1L 4P1
Information Contact, Communications Branch (phone: 416/750-3421); or General Inquiry (750-3333)

Acts Administered

Ministry of Correctional Services Act

MINISTER, Hon. Nicholas G. Leluk
Chairman, Minister's Advisory Council for the Treatment of the Offender, W.J. Eastaugh
Chairman, Ontario Board of Parole, Ms. D.M. Clark (2195 Yonge St.), 963-0368
Deputy Minister, A. Campbell
Administrative Asst. to the Deputy Minister, Mrs. M. Grey
Director, Inspection & Investigation Branch, S. Teggart

Executive Director, Institutional Programs, M.J. Duggan
Regional Director, Central Region, J.L. Main
Regional Director, Western Region, T. McCarron
Regional Director, Eastern Region, S. Shoom
Regional Director, Northern Region, G.F. Tegman
Director, Institutional Staff Training, J. de Domenico
Director, Institutional Program Support Services, Dr. J.J. Hug
Manager, Inmate Classification & Transfer, G. Simpson
Manager, Industrial Programs, J. Pahapill
Chief Education Officer, W. Tilden
Chief, Library Services, T.J.B. Anderson
Senior Medical Consultant, Dr. P.W. Humphries
Professional Consultants:
Chaplaincy, Rev. D. Janzen
Dentistry, Dr. C.H.M. Williams
Food Services & Nutrition, Mrs. I.E. Beal
Executive Director, Community Programs, A.F. Daniels
Director, Support Services, D.G. Evans
Director, Community Resource Centres, A.S. Nuttall
Director, Probation & Parole Services, D.E. Taylor
Executive Director, Planning & Support Services, M.J. Algar
(includes: Communications, Internal Audit, Legal Services, Management Data Services, Planning & Research, Supply & Services, Accounting, Budgeting, Analysis & Evaluation, Policy Planning)
Director, Human Resources Management, V.J. Crew (inc.: Women's Advisor; Compensation & Staff Relations; Staffing & Human Resources Planning; and Personnel Services)

Institutions (with Supts.)

Western Region:

Brantford Jail, I.H. Wright
Burtch Correctional Centre, Brantford, J. Moclair
Chatham Jail, J. Pinder
Elgin-Middlesex Detention Centre, London, J.T. O'Brien
Guelph Correctional Centre, W.J. Taylor
Ontario Correctional Institute, Brampton, L. Nelmes
Owen Sound Jail, W.A. Hoey
Sarnia Jail, J. Whitely
Stratford Jail, J.M. Sinclair
Vanier Centre for Women, Brampton, Miss S. Nicholls
Walkerton Jail, B. Parker
Waterloo Detention Centre, Cambridge, R.H. Nash
Wellington Detention Centre, Guelph, J. Cassidy
Windsor Jail, M.V. Villeneuve

Central Region:

Barrie Jail, D. McFarlane
Hamilton-Wentworth Detention Centre, Hamilton, R.D. Phillipson
Maplehurst Correctional Centre/Adult Training Centre, Milton, A.J. Roberts
Metro Toronto East Detention Centre, A.J. Dunbar
Metro Toronto West Detention Centre, R.P.G. Barrett
Mimico Correctional Centre, C. De Grandis
Niagara Detention Centre, Thorold, J.G. Hildebrandt
Toronto Jail, I.D. Starkie

Eastern Region:

Brockville Jail, L. Hudson
Cobourg Jail, H.J. Yorke
Cornwall Jail, R. Dagenais
Lindsay Jail, P. Campbell
L'Orignal Jail, L. Migneault
Millbrook Correctional Centre, J.A. Rundle
Ottawa-Carleton Detention Centre, Ottawa, J.J. Duncan
Pembroke Jail, T.R. Chambers
Perth Jail, C.R. Stewart
Peterborough Jail, L. Wiles
Quinte Detention Centre, Napanee, W.F. Schneider (act.)
Rideau Correctional Centre, Burritt's Rapids, G.R.D. Fisher
Whitby Jail, F.R. Gill

Northern Region:

Fort Frances Jail, C.M. Gillespie
Haileybury Jail, W.J. Martin
Kenora Jail, L.W. Goss
Monteith Correctional Centre, W.E. Peters
Monteith Jail, W.E. Peters
North Bay Jail, R.S. Doan
Parry Sound Jail, T.M. Wight
Sault Ste. Marie Jail, E.D. Lock
Sudbury Jail, A. Hooson
Thunder Bay Correctional Centre, J.R. Keddie
Thunder Bay Jail, A.D. Abbott

ONTARIO CRIPPLED CHILDREN'S CENTRE

350 Rumsey Rd., Toronto, Ont. M4G 1R8
(416) 425-6220
Executive Director, D.H. Martin
Medical Director, D.A. Gibson

MINISTRY OF CULTURE & RECREATION

Queen's Park, Toronto, Ont. M7A 1A2

Information from: Communications Branch, 77 Bloor St. W., 6th floor (phone: 416-965-0615)

Acts Administered

Archives Act
Art Gallery of Ontario Act
Arts Council Act
Centennial Centre of Science & Technology Act
Community Recreation Centres Act
Historical Parks Act
John Graves Simcoe Memorial Foundation Act
Ministry of Culture & Recreation Act, 1974
Ministry of Culture & Recreation Amendment Act, 1975
McMichael Canadian Collection Act
Ont. Educational Communications Authority Act
Ont. Heritage Act, 1974
Ont. Heritage Amendment Act, 1975
Ont. Lottery Corp. Act
Public Libraries Act
Royal Botanical Gardens Act
Royal Ontario Museum Act

MINISTER, Hon. Reuben C. Baetz
Deputy Minister, Ward Cornell
Provincial Archivist, Wm. G. Ormsby
Asst. Deputy Minister, ARTS, HERITAGE & LIBRARIES DIVISION, J.D. McCullough
Director, Cultural Industries Branch, D. Spence
Director, Arts Services Branch, N.A. Best
Director, Cultural Industries Branch, D. Spence
Director, Heritage Admin. Branch, R.G. Bowes
Director, Historical Planning & Research Branch, R.B. Apted
Director, Heritage Trust, L.T. Ryan
Manager, Old Fort William, W.E. Lee
General Manager, Huronia Historical Parks, P. Deault
Executive Co-ordinator, Libraries & Community Information Branch, Brian Shannon (Acting Director, Mrs. Grace Buller)
Executive Director, CITIZENSHIP DIVISION, George Bancroft
Director, Citizenship Services Branch, Ms. W.E. Steinkrauss
Director, Newcomer Services Branch, Kay Eastham
Co-ordinator, Ontario Welcome House, Miss E. Ellman
Director, Native Community Branch, Fred Boden
Manager, Translation Bureau, Louise Beaugrand-Champagne
Asst. Deputy Minister, SPORTS, RECREATION & FIELD SERVICES, Robert Secord
Director, Sports & Recreation Branch, J.A. Halstead
Supervisor, Recreation & Fitness Service Section, R.R. Wittenberg
Director, Communications Branch, Robert Cohen
Co-ordinator, Citizens' Inquiry Bureau, Mrs. M. Snitman
Executive Director, FINANCE & ADMIN. DIVISION, B. Webber (includes: Auditing, Finance Branch, Personnel Branch, Capital Support Unit, Administrative Services)

Associated Agencies

The following ministerial agencies, boards and commissions report to the Ont. Legislature through the Minister of Culture & Recreation:

Archives of Ontario, 77 Grenville St., Toronto, Ont. M7A 2R9 (416/965-4039)
Art Gallery of Ontario, 317 Dundas St. W., Toronto, Ont. M5T 1G4 (416/977-0414)
Royal Ontario Museum, 100 Queen's Park, Toronto, Ont. M5S 2C6 (416/978-3690)
Royal Botanical Gardens, Box 399, Hamilton, Ont. L8N 3H8 (416/527-1158)
The McMichael Canadian Collection, Islington Ave., Kleinburg, Ont. L0J 1C0 (416/893-1121)
Ontario Educational Communications Authority (TVOntario), 2180 Yonge St., Toronto, Ont. M4S 2C1 (416/484-2600)
Ontario Arts Council, Ste. 500, 151 Bloor St. W., Toronto, Ont. M5S 1T6 (416/961-1660)
Ontario Lottery Corp., 24th floor, 2 Bloor St. W., Toronto, Ont. M4W 1A1 (416/961-6262)
Ontario Science Centre, 770 Don Mills Rd., Don Mills, Ont. M3C 1T3 (416/429-4100)
CJRT/FM Radio Station, 297 Victoria St., Toronto, Ont. M5B 1W1 (416/595-0404)
Council for Franco Ontarian Affairs, 10th floor, 1200 Bay St., Toronto, Ont. M7A 2R9 (416/965-0599)
John Graves Simcoe Memorial Foundation, 8 York St., Toronto, Ont. M5J 1R2 (416/965-2673)
Ontario Heritage Foundation, 7th floor, 77 Bloor St. W., Toronto, Ont. M7A 2R9 (416/965-9504)
Ontario Advisory Council on Multiculturalism & Citizenship, 1200 Bay St., 10th floor, Toronto, Ont. M7A 2R9 (416/965-6889)
Huronia Historical Development Council, Box 160, Midland, Ont. L4R 4K8 (705/526-7838)
Conservation Review Board, c/o Dept. (416/965-1432)

BOARD OF DIRECTORS OF DRUGLESS THERAPY (Naturopathy)

135 Coldwater Rd. W., Orillia, Ont. L3V 3L5
Chairman, J.G. LaPlante, N.D.
Vice Chairman, W.W. Morris, N.D.
Secretary Treasurer, R.B. Farquharson, N.D.

ONTARIO ECONOMIC COUNCIL

81 Wellesley St. E., Toronto, Ont. M4Y 1H6
(416) 965-4315
Chairman, Thos. E. Kierans
Research Director & Executive Secretary, Lorie Tarshis

MINISTRY OF EDUCATION, & MINISTRY OF COLLEGES & UNIVERSITIES

Mowat Block, Queen's Park, Toronto, Ont. M7A 1L2
(unless otherwise noted)
Information Contact, General Inquiry (phone: 416-965-6407)

Acts Administered

The Education Act, 1974
Ministry of Colleges & Universities Act
School Bds. & Teachers Collective Negotiations Act, 1975
Teachers' Superannuation Act
Teaching Profession Act
Ont. School Trustees' Council Act

Apprenticeship & Tradesmen's Qualification Act
Colleges Collective Bargaining Act
Private Vocational Schools Act

various University, Institutional and College Acts

MINISTER, Hon. Bette M. Stephenson, M.D.
Executive Asst., R.N. Donaldson (965-3708)
Deputy Minister, Dr. H.K. Fisher, 965-2605
Executive Asst., George DeMetra, 965-2334
Asst. Deputy Minister, Council for Franco-Ontarian Education, B. Kipp, 965-2190

Colleges & Universities

Asst. Deputy Minister, B.A. Wilson, 965-6865
Teacher Education, Director, D.H.M. Dunn, 965-5477
University Relations, Director, vacant, 965-2827
College Affairs, Director, John Humber, 965-5375
Student Awards, Director, William Clarkson, 965-7191
Manpower Training, Asst. Deputy Minister, Kenneth Hunter, 965-5342
Manpower Training, Director, E.L. Kerridge, 965-6161
Apprenticeship, Director, H.T. Beggs, 965-4201

Education

Administration & Planning, Asst. Deputy Minister, T.P. Adams, 965-5342
Planning & Policy Analysis, Executive Director, D.A. Penny, 965-3620

(includes: Research, Policy Analysis & Legislation, Management Information Systems, Grants Policy)
Operations, Executive Director, F.J. Kidd, 965-1375
(includes: Office Services, Financial Services, Management Review, Communication Services, Personnel)
Education Programs, Asst. Deputy Minister, G. Podrebarac, 965-4232
Executive Director, Curriculum Development, R. Thomas, 965-5624
Director, Special Education, G. Bergman, 965-2663
Director, Special Projects, Pat Fleck, 965-5620
Director, Elementary Education, L. Maki, 965-5982
Director, Senior & Continuing Education, vacant, 965-2666
Executive Director, Regional Services, R.G. Rist, 965-5606
Director, Provincial Schools Branch, J. Rees, 965-4587
Northwestern Ontario Region, Box 5000, 435 James St. S., Thunder Bay, Ont. P7E 5G6, 807/475-1581, Regional Director, Miss F. Poleschuk
Midnorthern Ontario Region, 199 Larch St., Sudbury, Ont P3E 5P9, 705/675-4401, Regional Director, C.E. Butcher
Northeastern Ontario Region, Box 3020, 477 McKeown Ave., North Bay, Ont. P1B 8K7, 705/474-7210, Regional Director, J.J. Sullivan
Western Ontario Region, 759 Hyde Park Rd., London, Ont. N6H 3S6, 519/472-1440, Regional Director, D. Kinchlea
Central Ontario Region, Ste. 3201, 2025 Sheppard Ave. E., Willowdale, Ont. M2J 1W4, 416/491-0330, Regional Director, J. Storey
Eastern Ontario Region, Merivale Shopping Fair, 1580 Merivale Rd., Ottawa, Ont. K2B 4B5, 613/225-9210, Regional Director, Ray Doyle

Agencies, Boards & Commissions

College Relations Commission
111 Avenue Rd., #400, Toronto, Ont. M5R 3J8
(416) 922-7679
Chairman, Dr. B.M. Downie
Chief Executive Officer, R.H. Field
Languages of Instruction Commission of Ontario
17th floor, 25 Grosvenor St., Toronto, Ont. M4Y 1A9
(416) 965-3155
Chairman, Ryan Paquette
Executive Secretary, G.C. Filion
Education Relations Commission
111 Avenue Rd., Ste. 400, Toronto, Ont. M5R 3J8
(416) 922-7679
Chairman, Dr. Bryan M. Downie
Chief Executive Officer, R.H. Field
Ontario Council on University Affairs
700 Bay St., 7th floor, Toronto, Ont. M5H 2T8
Chairman, Dr. W.C. Winegard, 965-5233
Council of Regents for Colleges of Applied Arts & Technology
10th floor, Mowat Block, 900 Bay St., Toronto, Ont. M7A 1L2
(416) 965-4234
Chairman, Norman E. Williams
Executive Secretary, Mrs. D. Murdoch
Ontario Educational Services Corp.
3rd floor, 120 Bloor St. W., Toronto, Ont. M3C 3E9
(416) 965-1923
Chairman, D.C. McGeachy (London, Ont.)
Secretary Treasurer, I.G. McHaffie, Toronto
Teachers' Superannuation Commission
190 Finch Ave. W., Willowdale, Ont. M2R 1M4
(416) 226-2700
Chairman, J.R. Thomson
Director, J.R. Causley

EMERGENCY MEASURES

Planning for emergencies in Ontario is carried on by several Ministries as an extension of their normal responsibilities. Individual municipalities may also operate Emergency Programs at their own expense.

MINISTRY OF ENERGY

12th floor, 56 Wellesley St. W., Toronto, Ont. M7A 2B7
Information Contact, Tom Coleman, Manager, Information Services (phone: 416-965-2459)

Acts Administered

Ministry of Energy Act
Ont. Energy Board Act
Ont. Energy Corp. Act
Power Corp. Act

MINISTER, Hon. Robert Welch, Q.C.
Deputy Minister, Glenn Thompson
Special Asst., Catherine Paterson
Administrative Officer, Paul Cunningham
Director, Communications, Michael Van Dusen
Executive Co-ordinator, Conventional Energy, Bruce MacOdrum
Policy Co-ordinator, Electric Power, Richard Lundeen
Asst. Deputy Minister, Conservation & Renewable Energy, vacant
Director, Renewable Energy, Dr. Roger Higgin
Director, Energy Conservation, Douglas Carl
Executive Co-ordinator, Strategic Planning & Analysis, Dr. William Stevenson

Associated Agencies

Ontario Energy Board, 9th floor, 14 Carlton St., Toronto, Ont. M5B 1J2 (416/963-0821)
Ontario Hydro, 700 University Ave., Toronto, Ont. M5G 1X6 (416/592-5111)
Ontario Energy Corp., 5th floor, 101 Bloor St. W., Toronto, Ont. M5S 1P8, 416/965-2441 (Executive Vice President, Peter Lamb)

MINISTRY OF THE ENVIRONMENT

135 St. Clair Ave. W., Toronto, Ont. M4V 1P5
Information Contact, R.J. Frewin, Director, Information Services Branch (phone: 416-965-1658)

Acts Administered

Ont. Water Resources Act
Environmental Assessment Act
Environmental Protection Act
Pesticides Act

MINISTER, Hon. Keith C. Norton, Q.C.
Deputy Minister, Gerard Raymond
Executive Director, Financial & Administrative Services Division, G.E. Higham
Asst. Deputy Ministers
Environmental Assessment & Planning, J.W. Giles
Executive Director, Resources Division, W.B. Drowley
Regional & Laboratories Operations, W.D. Bidell

Associated Boards

Environmental Assessment Board
1 St. Clair Ave. W., 5th floor, Toronto, Ont. M4V 1K7
(416) 965-2531
Chairman, B.E. Smith
Environmental Appeal Board
1 St. Clair Ave. W., 5th floor, Toronto, Ont. M4V 1K7
(416) 965-2531
Chairman, Mrs. L.C. DeGroot
Waste Management Advisory Board
1 St. Clair Ave. W., 6th floor, Toronto, Ont. M4V 1K6
(416) 965-3007

Associated Committees

Farm Pollution Advisory Committee
Pesticides Advisory Committee

Associated Commissions/Corporations

Royal Commission on the Northern Environment
215 Red River Rd., #201, Thunder Bay, Ont. P7B 1A5

(807) 345-3658
Ontario Waste Management Corp.
60 Bloor St. W., Toronto, Ont. M4W 1A5
(416) 963-1162

ONTARIO GEOGRAPHIC NAMES BOARD

Ministry of Natural Resources, Room 2542, Whitney Block, Queen's Park, Toronto, Ont. M7A 1W3
(416) 965-6515
Executive Secretary & Manager, Nomenclature Section, Michael B. Smart

MINISTRY OF GOVERNMENT SERVICES

Queen's Park, Toronto, Ont. M7A 1N3
Information from Information Section, 12th floor, Ferguson Block, Queen's Park, Toronto, Ont. (phone: 416-965-6683)

MINISTER, Hon. D.J. Wiseman
Deputy Minister, Alan Gordon
Director, Management Planning, J.W. Filby
Asst. Deputy Minister, Accommodation, L. Pencak
Executive Director, Admin., J. Silver
A/Executive Director, Communications & Computer Services, J.G. O'Neill
Executive Director, Marketed Services, J.J.M. Kelly
Executive Director, General Services, E.F.H. Strauss

Branch Directors

Administrative Services, J.A. Vanner
Audit, C.D. Bacher
Central Purchasing Services, B.V. Cooke
Computer Support Services, J.G. O'Neill (act.)
Design Services, D. Dastur
Downsview Computing Centre, G. Cuculick
Employee Benefits, R.H. Westmore
Employee Data Services, Mrs. R. Kazan
Employee Health Services, Dr. H. Chambers
Finance, V. Chaves
Government Payments, H.T.B. Hurson
Leaside Data Centre, H. Sauer (act.)
Legal Branch, R. Stupart
Legislative Services, A.L. Cameron
Personnel, A.G. Marshall
Program Management, A. Henein
Property Management, G.A. Mann
Queen's Park Computing Centre, D. McGeown
Realty Services, W.A. Gray
Special Services, G. Browne
Telecommunication Services, B. Robertson

Ontario Government Bookstore

880 Bay St., Toronto, Ont. M5S 1Z8
Phone: (416) 965-2054

Associated Boards

Public Service Superannuation Board, 13th floor, Drew Bldg., Queen's Park, Toronto, Ont. M7A 1R1
(416) 965-1709
Secretary, J.D. Macdonald

MINISTRY OF HEALTH

Hepburn Block, Queen's Park, Toronto, Ont. M7A 1S2
Information: Direct Inquiries to Health Information & Promotion Branch, Ministry of Health (416 965-3101)

Acts Administered

*Alcoholism & Drug Addiction Research Foundation Act
Ambulance Act
*Cancer Act
*Cancer Remedies Act
*Chiropody Act
*Dental Technicians Act
Denture Therapists Act, 1974
*Drugless Practitioners Act
Fluoridation Act
*Funeral Services Act, 1976
Health Disciplines Act, 1974
Health Insurance Act, 1972
Homes for Special Care Act
Ministry of Health Act, 1972
Municipal Health Services Act
Nursing Homes Act, 1972
*Ophthalmic Dispensers Act
Private Hospitals Act
*Psychologists Registration Act
Public Health Act
Public Hospitals Act
*Radiological Technicians Act
Sanatoria for Consumptives Act
Venereal Diseases Prevention Act
War Veterans Burial Act

Mental Health Legislation

Community Psychiatric Hospitals Act
Hypnosis Act
Mental Health Act
Mental Hospitals Act
*Ont. Mental Health Foundation Act
Private Sanitaria Act

** administered by Associated Bodies*

MINISTER OF HEALTH, Hon. Dennis R. Timbrell
Deputy Minister of Health, G. Scott
Legal Branch Director, D. Bernstein, Q.C.
Policy Development Branch Director, D. Bogart
Strategic Research & Manpower Planning Director, A.F. LeBlanc
Health Information & Promotion Branch Director, P. Jackman

Management Development

Co-ordinator, A.I. Rands

Admin. & Health Insurance

Asst. Deputy Minister, R.A. LeNeveu
Director, Human Resources Branch, R. Oss
Director, Audit Branch (7 Overlea Blvd., M4H 1A8), G.L. Woods
Executive Director, Information Systems Division (15 Overlea Blvd.), J.A. Sarjeant
Director, Data Development & Evaluation Branch (15 Overlea Blvd.), H.I. MacKillop
Director, Management Systems Branch (15 Overlea Blvd.), D. Harry
General Manager, Health Insurance Division (7 Overlea Blvd., M4H 1A8), M.H. Gibson
District Offices:
25 Main St. W., Hamilton, Ont. L8P 4P9
1055 Princess St., Kingston, Ont. K7L 5A9
227 Queen's Ave., London, Ont. N6A 1J8
75 Albert St., Ottawa, Ont. K1P 5Y9
2195 Yonge St., Toronto, Ont. M5W 1G9
295 Bond St., Sudbury, Ont. P3S 2J8
435 James St. S., Box 5000, Thunder Bay, Ont. P7E 6E3
44 Bond St. W., Oshawa, Ont. L1H 7R1
55 City Centre Dr., Mississauga, Ont. L5B 2T4

Finance & Administration Division

Executive Director, S. Dreezer
Director, Fiscal Resources Branch, R.H. Reid
Director, Finance & Accounts Branch (7 Overlea Blvd.), K.C. Khosla
Director, Supply & Services Branch, R.L. Brethour
Health Boards Secretariat, Executive Secretary, D. McKay

Community Health Services

Asst. Deputy Minister, Dr. B. Suttie
District Health Council Program, Executive Director, D.W. Corder
Executive Director, Health Programs Division, Dr. G.K. Martin
Director, Public Health Branch, Dr. B.J. Blake

Director, Program Advisory Branch, Dr. G. Gold
Director, Program Development Branch, R.G. Berry

Institutional Health Services

Asst. Deputy Minister, Dr. A.E. Dyer
Executive Co-ordinator, Mental Health Policy & Planning, Dr. G. Heseltine
Director, Psychiatric Hospitals Branch, G.D. Cardiff
Executive Co-ordinator, Emergency Health Services Group, vacant
Director, Ambulance Services Branch (7 Overlea Blvd., M4H 1A9), G.J. Ventura
Executive Director, Institutional Division (15 Overlea Blvd.), W. Bain
Director, Laboratory Services Branch (Resources Rd., Islington), Dr. D. S. Willoughby
Director, Institutional Planning Branch, J.R. Hagerman
Director, Institutional Operations Branch, A. Boehm

Associated Agencies

Ont. Council of Health, 14th floor, 700 Bay St., Toronto, M5G 1Z6; (965-5031); Chairman, Dr. R.B. Holmes
Alcoholism & Drug Addiction Research Foundation, 33 Russell St., Toronto, M5S 2S1 (595-6048); President, Dr. Joan Marshman
Denture Therapists Appeal Board, Rm. SW 1175, 11th floor, Hepburn Block, Queen's Park, Toronto, Ont. M7A 1R3 (965-7285); Chairman, E.A. Pickering
Funeral Services Review Board, Rm. SW 1175, 11th floor, Hepburn Block, Queen's Park, Toronto, Ont. M7A 1R3 (965-7285); Chairman, Dr. S.E. Rosenberg
Health Disciplines Board, Room SW 1175, 11th floor, Hepburn Block, Queen's Park, Toronto, Ont. M7A 1R3, 965-7285; Chairman, E.A. Pickering
Health Facilities Appeal Board, Room SW 1175, 11th floor, Hepburn Block, Queen's Park, Toronto, Ont. M7A 1R3, 965-7285; Chairman, P.Z. Magda
Health Services Appeal Board, Room SW 1175, 11th floor, Hepburn Block, Queen's Park, Toronto, Ont. M7A 1R3, 965-7285; Chairman, S.P. Ryan, Q.C.
Hospital Appeal Board, Room SW 1175, 11th floor, Hepburn Block, Queen's Park, Toronto, Ont. M7A 1R3, 965-7285; Chairman, P.B. Tobias
Laboratory Review Board, Room SW 1175, 11th floor, Hepburn Block, Queen's Park, Toronto, Ont. M7A 1R3, 965-7285; Chairman, P.Z. Magda
Mental Health Advisory Review Board, Rm. SW 1175, 11th floor, Hepburn Block, Queen's Park, Toronto, Ont. M7A 1R3 (965-7285); Chairman, Hon. Mr. Justice E.L. Haines
Nursing Homes Review Board, Room SW 1175, 11th floor, Hepburn Block, Queen's Park, Toronto, Ont. M7A 1R3, 965-7285; Chairman, P.Z. Magda
Ont. Mental Health Foundation, 365 Bloor St. E., #1708, Toronto, M4V 1K9 (920-7721); Chairman, Mrs. P. Creighton
Ont. Cancer Treatment & Research Foundation, 7 Overlea Blvd., Toronto, M4H 1A8, 423-4240; Chairman, G.R. Cunningham
Ont. Cancer Institute, 500 Sherbourne St., Toronto, M4X 1K9, 924-0671; Director, R. Bush, M.D., F.R.C.P.(C)

ONTARIO HYDRO

700 University Ave., Toronto, Ont. M5G 1X6
(416) 592-5111
Chairman, Hugh L. Macaulay, B.A.
Vice Chairman, A.J. Bowker
President, Milan Nastich
Directors, J.C. Lavigne; P. Lind; A.B. Cousins; W.A. Stewart; Sister Mary Zimmerman; J.A.G. Bell; A.G. Hearn; Dr. O.J.C. Runnalls; L.N. Savoie
General Counsel & Secretary, W.E. Raney, Q.C.
Executive Vice Presidents:
P.G. Campbell, Operations
A. Niitenberg, Planning & Admin.
Vice Presidents:
L.A. Coles, Distribution & Marketing
F.W. Gomer, Human Resources
H.A. Jackson, Design & Construction
S.G. Horton, Supply & Services
L.G. McConnell, Production & Transmission
J.G. Matthew, Power System Program
D.B. MacCarthy, Corporate Relations
E.H. Burdette, Finance
Treasurer, D. Peper

MINISTRY OF INDUSTRY & TOURISM

900 Bay St., Hearst Block, Queen's Park, Toronto, Ont. M7A 1T2
Information Contact, Jerry Gautreau, Media Relations Branch (phone: 416/965-7075)

Acts Administered

Ministry of Industry & Tourism Act
Act Respecting Development Corps. in Ont.
Ontario Place Corp. Act
Ont. Research Foundation Act
Sheridan Park Corp. Act
Tourism Act

MINISTER, Hon. Larry Grossman, Q.C.
Deputy Minister, Bernard Ostry
Asst. Deputy Minister, Industry, D.B. Tully
Asst. Deputy Minister, Tourism, J.G. Laschinger
Executive Director, Admin. Division, A.S. Bronskill
Executive Director, Communications Branch, P. Jacobsen

Industry Division

Director, Small Business Development, M.J. Baker
Director, Industrial Development, J.B. Blanchard
Director, Evaluation & Assessment, A.D. Croll
Director, Trade Development, Ms. J. Rush

Industry Operations Branch

Executive Director, J.R. Ardagh
Director, Central East Area, C.T. Dyment, 5 Fairview Mall Dr., 4th floor, Suite 480, Willowdale, Ont. M2J 2Z1, 416/491-7680
Director, Western Area, D.C. Watson, 195 Dufferin St., 6th floor, Suite 607, London, Ont. N6A 1K7, 519/433-8105
Director, Northern Area, K.A. Croswell, 767 Barrydowne Rd., Sudbury, Ont. P3A 3T6, 705/675-4330
Director, Central West Area, D.M. Grant, 305 King St. W., Kitchener, Ont. N2G 1B9, 519/744-6391
Director, Eastern Area, T.A. Lillico, 56 Sparks St., #404, Ottawa, Ont. K1P 5A9, 613/566-3703

International Offices

Agent General, W.R. DeGeer, Ontario House, Charles II St., London, SW1Y 4OS, Eng.
Manager, Business Development Section, C.B. MacConnell
Manager, Selective Placement Section, B. Monette
Manager, Tourism Development Section, vacant
Manager, J.V. Wessinger, Bockenheimer Landstr. 51/53, 6000 Frankfurt/Main Germany
Manager, W.A. Fowler, World Trade Center Bldg., Room 1219, 4-1 Hamamatsu-cho, 2-chome, Minato-ku, Tokyo 105, Japan
Manager, P. Lavelle, 19 Ave. Montaigne, Paris, 75008, France
Manager, B.B. Williams, 208 South Lasalle St., #1816, Chicago, Ill. 60604
Manager, F.J. Hall, 700 South Flower St., #1420, Los Angeles, Calif. 90017
Manager, D.M. Rogers, 1251 Ave. of the Americas, Suite 1080, New York, N.Y. 10020
Manager, J.B. Donoghue, Peachtree Centre, 233 Peachtree St., Atlanta, Ga. 30303
Manager, S.S. Chen, Admiralty Centre Tower II, #1303, Harcourt Rd., Hong Kong

Division of Tourism

Director, Tourism Development, R.L. Brock

Director, Tourism Marketing, T.H. Gibson
Director, Tourism Operations, P.M. Sharpe

Ministry Agencies

Ontario Development Corp.
1200 Bay St., Queen's Park, Toronto, Ont. M7A 2E7
(416) 965-4622
Chairman, James H. Joyce
Executive Director & Chief Executive Officer, J.D. Girvin
5 Fairview Mall Dr., Ste. 480, Willowdale, Ont. M2J 2Z1
(416) 491-7996
195 Dufferin Ave., Ste. 607, London, Ont. N6A 1K7
(519) 433-2871
73 Mississaga St. E., Box 746, Orillia, Ont. L3V 6K7
(705) 325-5553
20 Hughson St. S., Ste. 601, Hamilton, Ont. L8N 2A1
(416) 527-3010
305 King St. W., Ste. 507, Kitchener, Ont. N2G 1B9
(519) 794-1991
201 City Centre Dr., #608, Mississauga, Ont. L5B 2T4
(416) 279-9150
Northern Ontario Development Corp.
6th floor, 1200 Bay St., Queen's Park, Toronto, Ont. M7A 2E7
(416) 965-4622
Chairman, Peter H. Harrower
Executive Director & Chief Executive Officer, J.D. Girvin
435 James St. S., Thunder Bay, Ont. P7C 5G6
(807) 475-1671
273 Third Ave., Timmins, Ont. P4N 1E2
(705) 264-1323
Ont. Govt. Bldg., 4th floor, 199 Larch St., Sudbury, Ont. P3E 5P9
(705) 675-4333
Eastern Ontario Development Corp.
1200 Bay St., Queen's Park, Toronto, Ont. M7A 2E7
(416) 965-4622
Chairman, Norman Carson
Executive Director & Chief Executive Officer, J.D. Girvin
56 Sparks St., Ottawa, Ont. K1P 5A9
(613) 566-3707
1055 Princess St., Kingston, Ont. K7L 5T3
(613) 547-2251
Ontario Place Corp.
955 Lakeshore Blvd. W., Toronto, Ont. M6K 3B9
(416) 965-7917
Chairman, William P. Cooper
General Manager, B.H. Longhurst
Ontario Research Foundation
Sheridan Park, Mississauga, Ont. L5K 1B3
(416) 822-4111
Chairman, J.S. Dewar
Minaki Lodge Resort Ltd.
55 Bloor St. W., Ste. 817, Toronto, Ont.
President & Chief Executive Officer, F.J. Boyer

MINISTRY OF INTERGOVERNMENTAL AFFAIRS

6th floor, Mowat Block, Queen's Park, Toronto, Ont. M7A 1B8
Information Contact, Marjorie Rebane, Information Services, 6th floor, Mowat Block, Toronto (416/965-5514, 4706)

Acts Administered

Ministry of Intergovernmental Affairs Act, 1978

MINISTER, Hon. Thomas L. Wells
Executive Asst., Larry Kent
Director, Information Services, D. Massicotte
Deputy Minister, D.W. Stevenson
Co-ordinator of French Language Services, D.W. Stevenson, 965-1020
Ministry Planning & Co-ordination, Executive Co-ordinator, S.J. Clasky, 965-7039
Office of Intergovernmental Affairs, Executive Director, E.D. Greathed, 965-1710

Associated Agencies

Advisory Committee on Confederation, 5th floor, Mowat Block, Queen's Park, Toronto, Ont. M7A 1C2 (965-2927)
Ontario-Quebec Permanent Commission, 5th floor, Mowat Block, Queen's Park, Toronto, Ont. M7A 1C2 (965-2927)

MINISTRY OF LABOUR

400 University Ave., Toronto, Ont. M7A 1T7
Information Contact, J. Bilyk, Senior Media Relations Officer, Information Services Branch (phone: 416 965-7941)

Acts Administered

Blind Workmen's Compensation Act
Employment Agencies Act
Employment Standards Act
Government Contracts Hours & Wages Act
Hospital Labour Disputes Arbitration Act
Industrial Standards Act
Labour Relations Act
Labour Relations Amendment Act (Bill 25)
Occupational Health & Safety Act (Bill 70)
One Day's Rest In Seven Act
Ontario Human Rights Code
Rights of Labour Act
Workmen's Compensation Act
Workmen's Compensation Insurance Act

MINISTER, Hon. Robert G. Elgie, M.D.
Deputy Minister, T.E. Armstrong, Q.C.
Admin. Division, Executive Director, D.J. Morgan
Information Services Director, J.W. Preiner
Employment Standards Branch, Director, J.R. Scott
Industrial Relations Division, Asst. Deputy Minister, L.V. Pathe
Director of Conciliation & Mediation Services, J. Speranzini
Occupational Health & Safety Division, Asst. Deputy Minister, Dr. Ann E. Robinson
Director of Construction Health & Safety Branch, R.K. Cleverdon
Director of Industrial Health & Safety Branch, J. McNair
Director of Mining Health & Safety Branch, P.B. McCrodan
Director of Occupational Health Branch, H. Nelson
Director of Special Studies & Services Branch, Dr. M. Fitch
Director of Standards & Programs Branch, A. Heath
Ont. Human Rights Commission (965-6841), Chairman, Dr. Dorothea Crittenden
Executive Director, G.A. Brown
Ont. Labour Relations Board (965-4151), Chairman, G.W. Adams
Registrar, D. Aynsley
Solicitor, R. McDowell
Program Analysis & Implementation, Asst. Deputy Minister, Nicholas Ignatieff
Director of Legal Services, P. Hess, Q.C.
Women's Programs
Director of Women's Bureau, Marnie Clarke (965-1537)
Director of Women Crown Employees' Office, Rita Burak

Associated Agencies

Advisory Council on Occupational Health & Safety, c/o Dept. (965-2448)
Office of Arbitration, c/o Dept. (965-5669)
Ontario Manpower Commission, c/o Dept. (965-9017)
The Workmen's Compensation Board, 2 Bloor St. E., Toronto, Ont. M4W 3E7–Chairman, Lincoln M. Alexander – 965-8880

MANAGEMENT BOARD

7th floor, Frost Bldg. S., Queen's Park, Toronto, Ont. M7A 1Y7
Chairman, Hon. George McCague
Secretary of Management Board, R.J. Butler
Asst. Secretary of Management Board, J.W. Keenan
Director, Resources Development, Ms. L. McCordic
Director, Education & Social Services, E.V. Margetts
Director, Expenditure Policy & Divisional Services, P.A. Gelinas
Director, Justice & General Government, R. Norberg

Director, Administrative Policy, L.F. Pitura
Director, Organization Policy, D.S. Campbell
Director, Management Technology, B. Cook
Director, Management Standards Project, J. Hay

MINISTRY OF MUNICIPAL AFFAIRS & HOUSING

Hearst Block, 4th floor, Queen's Park, Toronto, Ont. M7A 2K5 (unless otherwise noted)
Information Contact, Communications Branch, 56 Wellesley St. W., 2nd floor, Toronto, Ont. M7A 2K4 (phone: 416/965-9780)

Acts Administered

Brantford-Brant Annexation Act, 1980
City of Cornwall Annexation Act, 1974
City of Gloucester Act, 1980
City of Hamilton Act, 1975
City of Hazeldean-March Act, 1978
City of Nepean Act, 1978
City of Port Colborne Act, 1974
City of Sudbury Hydro-Electric Service Act, 1980
City of Thorold Act, 1975
City of Thunder Bay Act, 1968-69
City of Timmins-Porcupine Act, 1972
City of Toronto Act, 1980
County of Oxford Act
District Municipality of Muskoka Act
District of Parry Sound Local Government Act, 1979
Durham Municipal Hydro-Electric Service Act, 1979
Elderly Persons' Housing Aid Act
Haliburton Act
Halton Municipal Hydro-Electric Service Act, 1979
Hamilton-Wentworth Municipal Hydro-Electric Service Act, 1980
Housing Development Act
Line Fences Act
Local Improvement Act
Ministry of Municipal Affairs & Housing Act, 1981
Moosonee Development Area Board Act
Municipal Act
Municipal Affairs Act
Municipal Arbitrations Act
Municipal Conflict of Interest Act
Municipal Corporations Quieting Orders Act
Municipal Elderly Residents' Assistance Act
Municipal Elections Act
Municipal Franchises Act
Municipal Subsidies Adjustment Repeal Act, 1976
Municipal Tax Assistance Act
Municipal Unemployment Relief Act
Municipal Works Assistance Act
Municipality of Metropolitan Toronto Act
Municipality of Shuniah Act, 1936
North Pickering Development Corporation Act, 1974
Ontario Housing Corporation Act
Ontario Land Corporation Act
Ontario Planning & Development Act
Ontario Student Housing Corporation Act, 1978
Ontario Unconditional Grants Act
Ontario Youth Employment Act
Ottawa-Carleton Amalgamations & Elections Act, 1973
Ottawa-Carleton Municipal Hydro-Electric Service Act, 1980
Oxford Municipal Hydro-Electric Service Act, 1977
Parkway Belt Planning & Development Act
Peel Municipal Hydro-Electric Service Act, 1977
Planning Act
Police Village of St. George Act, 1980
Provincial Parks Municipal Tax Assistance Act
Public Parks Act
Public Utilities Act
Public Utilities Corporations Act
Regional Municipality of Durham Act
Regional Municipality of Haldimand-Norfolk Act
Regional Municipality of Halton Act
Regional Municipality of Hamilton-Wentworth Act
Regional Municipality of Niagara Act
Regional Municipality of Ottawa-Carleton Act
Regional Municipality of Ottawa-Carleton Land Acquisition Act, 1980
Regional Municipality of Peel Act
Regional Municipality of Sudbury Act
Regional Municipality of Waterloo Act
Regional Municipality of York Act
Road Access Act
Shoreline Property Assistance Act
Snow Roads & Fences Act
Statute Labour Act
Tax Sales Confirmation Act, 1974
Territorial Division Act
Tom Longboat Act, 1980
Toronto District Heating Corporation Act, 1980
Toronto Islands Act, 1980
Town of Wasaga Beach Act, 1973
Township of North Plantagenet Act, 1976
Village of Point Edward Act, 1979
Waterloo Electrical Service Areas Act, 1977
Wharfs & Harbours Act
York Municipal Hydro-Electric Service Act, 1978

MINISTER, Hon. Claude F. Bennett
Executive Asst., Larry Malloy
Deputy Minister, Richard M. Dillon
Manager, Ministry Office Operations, R.G. Brown
Director, Audit Operations, Mrs. M.M. Janes (60 Bloor W.)
Director, Communications Branch, R.A.C. Adams (56 Wellesley W.)
Director, Legal Services, Paul McIntyre (101 Bloor W.)
Executive Co-ordinator, Policy & Program Development Secretariat, John Burkus
Manager, Affirmative Action Program, Marilyn Fitzgerald (101 Bloor W.)
Executive Director, Finance & Admin. Division, B.S. Crowley (60 Bloor W.) (includes Finance, Personnel, Supply & Services, and Management Systems)
Corporate Secretary, E.J. Whaley (101 Bloor W.)

Community Development

(101 Bloor St. W.)
Asst. Deputy Minister, R.M. McDonald
Executive Director, Technical Services Division, D.G. Wells
Executive Director, Community Housing Division, D.A.M. Wilson

Community Planning

(56 Wellesley St. W.)
Asst. Deputy Minister, W. Wronski
Executive Director, Plans Administration Division, M. Farrow (includes Community Planning, Review, and Operations Control)

Land Development

Asst. Deputy Minister, R.W. Riggs (60 Bloor W.)
Director, Townsend New Community Branch, G.H. Tonking (60 Bloor W.)
Director, Marketing & Long Term Planning Branch, R. Grant

Ontario Housing Corp.

101 Bloor St. W., Toronto, Ont. M5S 1P8
(416) 965-9820
Chairman of the Board, A.R. Moses
General Manager, D.J. Beesley
Director, Operations Branch (Ont.), Fred Peters

Ontario Mortgage Corp.

60 Bloor St. W., Toronto, Ont. M4W 3K7
(416) 965-9135
Chairman of the Board, H.W. Hignett
General Manager, D. Haley

Ontario Land Corp.
10th floor, 60 Bloor St. W., Toronto, Ont. M4W 3K7
(416) 965-2512

Municipal Affairs
Asst. Deputy Minister, E.M. Fleming (6th floor, Mowat Block)
Director, Local Government Organization Branch, R.M. Farrow (4th floor, Mowat Block)
Executive Director, Municipal Operations Division, J.G. Church (6th floor, Mowat Block)

MINISTRY OF NATURAL RESOURCES
Whitney Block, 99 Wellesley St. W., Toronto, Ont. M7A 1W3
Information Contact, Ken Robertson, Supervisor, Information Services Section, Communications Services Branch (phone: 416 965-2756)

Acts Administered
Algonquin Forestry Authority Act, 1974
Algonquin Provincial Park Extension Act
Beach Protection Act
Beds of Navigable Waters Act
Canada Company's Land Act
Conservation Authorities Act
Crown Timber Act
Endangered Species Act
Fish Inspection Act
Fisheries Loans Act
Forest Fires Prevention Act
Forest Tree Pest Control Act
Forestry Act
Freshwater Fish Marketing Act
Game & Fish Act
Gananoque Lands Act, 1961-67
Gas & Oil Leases Act
Historical Parks Act
Industrial & Mining Lands Compensation Act
Lac Seul Conservation Act, 1928
Lake of the Woods Control Board Act, 1922, c. 21
Lakes & Rivers Improvement Act
Migratory Birds Convention Act
Mineral Emblem Act, 1975
Mining Act
Mining Tax Act
Ministry of Natural Resources Act, 1972
National Radio Observatory Act, 1962-63, c. 90
Niagara Parks Act
North Georgian Bay Recreational Reserve Act, 1962-63, c. 8
Ont. Geographic Names Board Act
Ont. Harbours Agreement Act, 1962-63, c. 95
Ottawa River Water Powers Act, 1943, c. 21
Parks Assistance Act
Petroleum Resources Act
Pits & Quarries Control Act, 1971, c. 96
Provincial Parks Act
Public Lands Act
Seine River Diversion Act, 1952, c. 98
Settlers' Pulpwood Protection Act
Spruce Pulpwood Exportation Act
St. Clair Parkway Commission Act, 1966, c. 146
St. Lawrence Parks Commission Act
Surveyors Act
Surveys Act
Trees Act
Wild Rice Harvesting Act
Wilderness Areas Act
Wolf Damage to Live Stock Compensation Act, 1972
Woodlands Improvement Act
Woodmen's Employment Act
Woodmen's Lien for Wages Act

MINISTER, Hon. Alan W. Pope
Executive Asst., Francine Levesque
Administrative Asst., P.O. Coghill
Deputy Minister of Natural Resources, W.T. Foster
Asst. Deputy Minister, Northern Ont., G.A. McCormack
Asst. Deputy Minister, Southern Ont., J.R. Sloan
Asst. Deputy Minister, Admin., Mary Mogford
Policy Co-ordination Secretariat, M. Fordyce

Resources
Executive Co-ordinator, A.H. Peacock
Forest Resources Branch, Director, Dr. R. Bourchier
Timber Sales Branch, Director, E. Markus

Mineral Resources
Executive Co-ordinator, G.A. Jewett
Mineral Resources Branch, Director, Dr. T.P. Mohide
Ont. Geological Survey, Director, Dr. E.G. Pye

Outdoor Recreation
Executive Co-ordinator, L.H. Eckel
Provincial Parks Branch, Director, N. Richards
Fisheries Branch, Director, A.S. Holder
Wildlife Branch, Director, J.D. Roseborough

Lands & Waters
Executive Co-ordinator, H.A. Clarke
Conservation Authorities & Water Management Branch, A/Director, J. Anderson
Land Management Branch, Director, E.F. Anderson
Land Use Co-ordination Branch, Director, R.A. Riley
Office of Indian Resources Policy, Director, E.G. Wilson
Surveys & Mapping Branch, Director, R.G. Code

Administration Division
Administrative Services Branch, Director, J.A. Queen
Communications Services Branch, Director, F. Moritsugu
Legal Services Branch, Director, J. Shantora
Personnel Services Branch, Director, J. Shantora

Finance, Planning & Evaluation Group
Executive Co-ordinator, G.D. Spry
Budget & Program Analysis Branch, Director, M.W. Cox
Financial Services Branch, Director, A.C. Goddard
Internal Audit Services Branch, Director, A.A. Ward

Field Offices–Northern Ontario
Northwestern Regional Director, Box 5160, 808 Robertson St., Kenora, Ont. P9N 3X7
North Central Regional Director, 435 James St. S., Box 5000, Thunder Bay, Ont. P7C 5G6
Northern Regional Director, Box 3000, 140 Fourth Ave., Cochrane, Ont. POL 1CO
Northeastern Regional Director, 174 Douglas St. W., Sudbury, Ont. P3E 1G1

Field Offices–Southern Ontario
Algonquin Regional Director, Brendale Sq., Box 9000, Huntsville, Ont. POA 1KO
Eastern Regional Director, Provincial Government Bldg., South Boundary Rd., Kemptville, Ont. KOG 1JO
Central Regional Director, 10,670 Yonge St., Richmond Hill, Ont. L4C 3C9
Southwestern Regional Director, 1106 Dearness Drive, London, Ont. N6E 1N9

Ministerial Agencies
Algonquin Forestry Authority
11 Main St. W., Box 1198, Huntsville, Ont. P0A 1K0 (705/789-9647)
General Manager, I.D. Bird
Mining & Lands Commissioner
R569 Mowat Block, Queen's Park, Toronto, M7A 1A2; G.H. Ferguson, Q.C. (416/965-1824)
The Niagara Parks Commission
General Manager, D.R. Wilson, Admin. Bldg., Box 150, Niagara Falls, Ont. L2E 6T2 (416/356-2241)

Provincial Parks Council
c/o Provincial Parks Branch, Dept. of Natural Resources (416/965-3981)
The St. Lawrence Parks Commission
General Manager, R.A. Cook, Morrisburg, Ont. KOC 1XO (613/543-2951)
St. Clair Parkway Commission
General Manager, R.F. Harrison, Box 700, Corunna, Ont. NON 1GO (519/862-2291)

NIAGARA ESCARPMENT COMMISSION

232 Guelph St., Georgetown, Ont. L7G 4B1
(416) 877-5191

NIAGARA FALLS BRIDGE COMMISSION

Box 395, Niagara Falls, Ont. L2E 6T8
(416) 354-5641
General Manager & Secretary Treasurer, Donald K. Misener, St. Catharines, Ont.

MINISTRY OF NORTHERN AFFAIRS

10 Wellesley St. E., 10th floor, Toronto, Ont. M4Y 1G2
General Inquiry: (416) 965-7577

MINISTER, Hon. Leo Bernier (965-3707)
Deputy Minister, Art Herridge (965-8941)
Planning & Admin. Division, Executive Director, W.D. Tieman (965-5692)

Northeastern Region

421 Bay St., Sault Ste. Marie, Ont. P6A 1X3
Asst. Deputy Minister, H.J. Aiken (705/942-0100)
Offices are located at:
Blind River, Chapleau, Cochrane, Elliot Lake, Espanola, Hearst, Iroquois Falls, Kapuskasing, Kirkland Lake, Mindemoya, Moosonee, New Liskeard, North Bay, Sault Ste. Marie, Sturgeon Falls, Sudbury, Timmins, Wawa

Northwestern Region

12 Main St. S., Kenora, Ont. P9N 1S7
Asst. Deputy Minister, Wm. Charlton (807/468-3135)
Offices are located at:
Atikokan, Dryden, Fort Frances, Geraldton, Ignace, Kenora, Marathon, Rainy River, Red Lake, Sioux Lookout, Thunder Bay

Ontario Northland Transportation Commission

195 Regina St., North Bay, Ont. P1B 2J6
(705) 472-4500

OFFICE OF THE OMBUDSMAN

125 Queen's Park, Toronto, Ont. M5S 2C7
(416) 596-3300
Ombudsman, Donald R. Morand
Executive Director, F.E. McArdle
Executive Asst., Mark Nantais
Counsel & Special Advisor to the Ombudsman, Brian Goodman
Director of Legal Services & Complaint Policy, Michael Zacks
Director of General Investigations, Linda Bohnen
Director of Special Services, Ellen Adams
Director of Correctional & Psychiatric Services, Bob Macerollo
Controller, Allan Mills
Legislative Relations, Rm. 157, Legislative Bldg., 869-4163
Regional Offices: 591 Main St. E., #203, North Bay, Ont. P1B 1B7; Director, Gilles Morin (705/476-5800)
1265 E. Arthur St., Ste. 701, Thunder Bay, Ont. P7E 6E7; Area Manager, Michael Dunnill (807/623-5058)

Ontario Adv. Council on the PHYSICALLY HANDICAPPED

3rd floor, 700 Bay St., Toronto, Ont. M5G 1Z6
(416) 965-9537

BOARD OF DIRECTORS OF PHYSIOTHERAPY

124 Merton St., Toronto, Ont. M4S 2Z2
(416) 481-1554
Chairman, S. Joan Mesley
Secretary Treasurer, Colin Bell
Registrar, Shirley Read

ONTARIO RESEARCH FOUNDATION

Sheridan Park, Mississauga, Ont. L5K 1B3
Information from T.E. Kingry, Manager, Marketing Services (phone: 416-822-4111)
President, W.R. Stadelman
Secretary, J.N. Matthews
Treasurer, L.J. van Monsjou

MINISTRY OF REVENUE

Queen's Park, Toronto, Ont. M7A 1X8
Information Contact, D.M. Stones, Communications Advisor, (phone: 416 965-2099)

Acts Administered

Agricultural Development Act
Assessment Act
Corporations Tax Act, 1972
Gasoline Tax Act, 1973
Income Tax Act
Land Transfer Tax Act, 1974
Ministry of Revenue Act
Motor Vehicle Fuel Tax Act
Ont. Guaranteed Annual Income Act, 1974
Ont. Pensioners Property Tax Assistance Act, 1980
Provincial Land Tax Act
Race Track Tax Act
Retail Sales Tax Act
Small Business Development Corporations Act, 1979
Tobacco Tax Act

MINISTER OF REVENUE, Hon. George Ashe
Deputy Minister, T.M. Russell
Director, Audit Services Branch, F.I. Stephens
Director, Legal Services Branch, G. Stoodley, Q.C.
Director, Finance & Priorities Planning Branch, J.S. Purdon
Director, Province of Ontario Savings Office, C.S. Costanza

Tax Revenue Program

Asst. Deputy Minister, R.J. Weiers
Director, Corporations Tax Branch, C.H. Townsend
Director, Guaranteed Income & Tax Credit Branch, P.L. Weingarden
Director, Motor Fuels & Tobacco Tax Branch, D.W. Rowsell
Director, Retail Sales Tax Branch, J.J. Wilbee
Director, Special Investigations Branch, S.D. O'Hara
Director, Tax Appeals Branch, M.N. Gomes
Executive Director, Tax Operations & Design Division, L. Leonard
Director, Revenue & Operations Research Branch, E.M. Todres
Director, Taxation Data Centre Branch, R.I. Rea
Director, Taxpayer Services Branch, J.L. Allen

Property Assessment Program

Asst. Deputy Minister, W.J. Lettner
Director, Policies & Priorities Branch, R.G. Trbovich
Director, Data Services & Development Branch, W.J. Baxter
Director, Field Operations Branch, W. Donohue
Director, Special Properties Branch, C.E. Winter

Support Services Division

Executive Director, vacant
Director, Administrative & Financial Services Branch, F.G. Cholmondeley
Director, Management Systems Branch, D.A. Dickson
Director, Personnel Services Branch, E.C. Farragher
Communications Advisor, D.M. Stones

Ont. Adv. Council on SENIOR CITIZENS
2nd floor, 700 Bay St., Toronto, Ont. M5G 1Z6
(416) 965-2324

SOLDIERS' AID COMMISSION
7th floor, 2195 Yonge St., Toronto, Ont. M4S 2B2
(416) 965-4891

MINISTRY OF THE SOLICITOR GENERAL
George Drew Bldg., 11th floor, 25 Grosvenor St., Toronto, Ont. M7A 1Y6
Information Contact, Sidney Allinson, Communications Policy Advisor (phone: 416 965-2048)

Acts Administered
Ministry of the Solicitor General Act, 1972
Anatomy Act
Coroners Act, 1972
Egress from Public Buildings Act
Fire Accidents Act
Fire Depts. Act
Fire Fighters' Exemption Act
Fire Marshals Act
Hotel Fire Safety Act, 1971
Human Tissue Gift Act, 1971
Lightning Rods Act
Police Act
Private Investigators & Security Guards Act
Public Works Protection Act
Retail Business Holidays Act, 1975
Ont. Society for the Prevention of Cruelty to Animals Act, 1955

MINISTER, Hon. R. Roy McMurtry, Q.C.
Deputy Minister, J.D. Hilton, Q.C.
Executive Asst. to Deputy Minister, Miss J. Allen
Director of Legal Services, J.M. Ritchie
Executive Director, Admin., P.F.L. Gow
Communications Policy Advisor, S. Allinson
Systems Management & Policy Development, R.N. Rintoul
Police Liaison Co-ordinator, R. Kendrick

Public Safety Division
Asst. Deputy Minister, F.L. Wilson, Q.C.

Centre of Forensic Sciences
2nd floor, 25 Grosvenor St. (M7A 2G8)
(416) 965-2561
Director, D.M. Lucas

Office of the Fire Marshal
590 Keele St. (M6N 4X2)
(416) 965-4844
Fire Marshal, J.R. Bateman

Chief Coroner's Office
26 Grenville St., 2nd floor (M7A 2G9)
(416) 965-6678
Chief Coroner, H.B. Cotnam, M.D.
Deputy Chief Coroner, R.C. Bennett, M.D.
Executive Officer, J. Ebbs

Forensic Pathology
26 Grenville St., Basement (M7A 2G9)
(416) 965-1555
Provincial Forensic Pathologist, J. Hillsdon Smith, M.D.

Ontario Fire College
Box 850, Gravenhurst, Ont. POC 1GO
(705) 687-2294
Director, S. Gragg

Ontario Police Commission
25 Grosvenor St., 9th floor (M7A 2H3)
(416) 965-6071
Chairman, S. MacGrath
Members, N.T. McGrenere, Q.C., Dr. T.A. Hockin

Ontario Police College
Box 1190, Aylmer, Ont. N5H 2T2
(519) 773-5361
Director, W. Swanton

Ontario Police Arbitration Commission
25 Grosvenor St., 1st floor (M7A 2H3)
(416) 965-3348
Chairman, R. Egan

Ontario Provincial Police
90 Harbour St. (M7A 2S1)
(416) 965-4401
Commr., H.H. Graham
Deputy Commr., Operations, J.L. Erskine
Deputy Commr., Services, K.W. Grice
Information Section, Insp. P.M. Caney

Associated Agencies
Animal Care Review Board, 4th floor, Hearst Block, 900 Bay St., Toronto, Ont.

ONTARIO STATUS OF WOMEN COUNCIL
3rd floor, 700 Bay St., Toronto, Ont. M5G 1Z6
(416) 965-1111

MINISTRY OF TRANSPORTATION & COMMUNICATIONS
1201 Wilson Ave., West Tower, Downsview, Ont. M3M 1J8
Information Contact, Mrs. Aileen M. McEachern, Public & Safety Information Branch (phone: 416-248-3501)

Acts Administered
Airports Act
Bridges Act
Commuter Services Act
Ferries Act
Highway Traffic Act
Local Roads Bds. Act
Ministry of Transportation & Communications Act
Ministry of Transportation & Communications Creditors' Payment Act, 1975
Motorized Snow Vehicles Act
Municipal Electric Railways Act, RSO 1950, c. 248
Ont. Highway Transport Board Act
Ont. Telephone Development Corp. Act
Ont. Transportation Development Corp. Act
Public Commercial Vehicles Act
Public Service Works on Highways Act
Public Transportation & Highway Improvement Act
Public Vehicles Act
Railways Act, RSO 1950, c. 331
Telephone Act
Toll Bridges Act
Toronto Area Transit Operating Authority Act

MINISTER, Hon. James Snow
Executive Assts., J.D. McConaghy; F. Patterson; R. Brannen
Deputy Minister, H.F. Gilbert
Executive Asst., Mrs. E. Giansante
Manager, Affirmative Action Program, E. Rowed
Executive Director, Strategic Policy Secretariat, W.A. Rathbun
Director, Public & Safety Information Branch, J.F. Cederberg
A/Manager, Management Improvement Branch, H. Stone
Executive Director, Communications Division, D.R. Peebles
Asst. Deputy Minister, Provincial/Municipal Transportation, D.G. Hobbs
Asst. Deputy Minister, Operations, L.R. Eadie

Asst. Deputy Minister, Safety & Regulation, M.H. Larratt-Smith
Asst. Deputy Minister, Finance & Administration, J.R. Barr

Ontario Highway Transport Board
151 Bloor St. W., 10th floor, Toronto, Ont. M5S 2T5
(416) 965-1843
Chairman, B.B. Alexander
Secretary, Mrs. C. Davila, 965-1845

Ontario Telephone Service Commission
3625 Dufferin St., Downsview, Ont. M3K 1Z2
(416) 248-3831
Chairman, W. Bielski, Q.C.
Operations Executive, W.D. Phillips
Secretary Registrar, P.G. Schofield

Finance & Administration
Director, Office of Legal Services, C.J. McCombe
Executive Director, Services Division, B.D. Riddell
(inc: Computer Systems, and Supply & Services)
Director, Internal Audit Branch, A.C. Lennox
Director, Personnel Branch, I.J. Cowan
Director, Financial Planning & Administration, F.E. Wood
Executive Secretary, Management Employee Group, J. Gray

Safety & Regulation
Executive Director, Enforcement Division, C.R. Wilmot
Co-ordinator, Truck Transportation Office, R.G. Summerley
Executive Director, Transportation Regulation Division, J.L. Forster
Director, Licensing & Control Branch, H.F. Kivi
Director, Transportation Regulation Development Branch, A. Gaudet
Director, Vehicle Registration System Project, G.M. Thompson

Provincial/Municipal Transportation
Executive Director, Transportation Operations Division, J.B. Wilkes
Manager, Municipal Roads Office, J. Moffat
Manager, Transit Office, L.R. Kidman
Co-ordinator, Rail Office, M.R. Quinton
Co-ordinator, Marine & Pipeline Office, M. Kelch
Manager, Air Office, D.P. Garner
Executive Director, Policy Planning & Research Development Division, I.C. Campbell
Director, Research & Development Branch, P. Smith
Manager, Transportation Outlooks, M.R. Ernesaks
Co-ordinator, Transportation Energy Management, Dr. K.O. Sharrat

Operations
Director, Highway Program Development Branch, P.J. Harvey
Claims Engineer, Engineering Claims Office, J.H. Peer
Manager, Estimating Office, B.J. Giroux
Executive Director, Highway Engineering Division, F.G. Allen
Director, Highway Operations Branch, A.E. Argue
Manager, Structural Office, R.A. Dorton
Manager, Engineering Materials Office, A.G. Stermac
Manager, Surveys & Plans Office, J.E. Heffernan
(District Engineers are located at Bancroft, Chatham, Cochrane, Hamilton, Huntsville, Kenora, Kingston, London, New Liskeard, North Bay, Ottawa, Owen Sound, Port Hope, Sault Ste. Marie, Stratford, Sudbury, Thunder Bay, Toronto)

Regional Directors
Central: T.G. Smith
Southwestern: E.J. McCabe
Eastern: W.G. Wigle
Northern: G.F. Wetherall
Northwestern: W.D. Neilipovitz

Associated Agencies
Licence Suspension Appeal Board
1201 Wilson Ave., East Bldg., Downsview, Ont. M3M 1J8
248-3845
Secretary, Ann Ogiltree
Toronto Area Transit Operating Authority
(GO Transit)
3625 Dufferin St., Downsview, Ont. M3K 1Z2
630-2635
Chairman, L.H. Parsons
Managing Director, A.F. Leach

MINISTRY OF TREASURY & ECONOMICS
Queen's Park, Toronto, Ont. M7A 1Y7
Information Contact, Heather Walker, A/Manager, Communications Group, 5th floor, Frost Bldg. S., Toronto (416/965-7171)

Acts Administered
Audit Act, 1977
Farm Loans Act
Farm Loans Adjustment Act
Financial Administration Act
Gold Clauses Act
Ministry of Treasury & Economics Act, 1978
Ontario Economic Council Act
Ontario Education Capital Aid Corporation Act
Ontario Guaranteed Annual Income Act, 1974
Ontario Loan Act
Ontario Municipal Employees Retirement System Act
Ontario Municipal Improvement Corporation Act
Ontario Universities Capital Aid Corporation Act
Statistics Act
Supply Act

TREASURER OF ONTARIO & MINISTER OF ECONOMICS, Hon. Frank S. Miller
Executive Asst., Lyn Munro
Deputy Minister, Tom Campbell
Asst. Deputy Minister, Office of the Treasury, G. McIntyre, 965-1703
Asst. Deputy Minister, Office of the Budget & Intergovernmental Finance Policy, B. Jones, 965-4746
Asst. Deputy Minister, Office of Economic Policy, B.P. Davies, 965-3184
Asst. Deputy Minister, Support Services, C.P. Honey, 965-6616
Executive Director, Administration Services, D.W. Maskens, 965-5420
Executive Director, Central Statistical Services, vacant, 965-6566

Associated Agencies
Ontario Economic Council, 81 Wellesley St. E., Toronto, M4Y 1H8 (965-4315)
Ontario Education Capital Aid Corp., c/o Ministry (965-2451)
Ontario Municipal Employees Retirement Board, 2 Bloor St. W., Toronto, M4W 1E2 (967-0637)
Ontario Municipal Improvement Corp., c/o Ministry (965-2451)
Ontario Universities Capital Aid Corp., c/o Ministry (965-2451)

WORKMEN'S COMPENSATION BOARD
See Ministry of Labour

ONTARIO YOUTH SECRETARIAT
2nd floor, 700 Bay St., Toronto, Ont. M5G 1Z6
(416) 965-3540

PROVINCE OF PRINCE EDWARD ISLAND

Entered Confederation July 1, 1873
Area: 2,184 sq. miles
Population: 124,300 (est. 1980)
Seat of Government: Province House, Charlottetown
Lieutenant-Governor: The Hon. J.A. Doiron

EXECUTIVE COUNCIL

Premier, and President of the Council, Hon. J. Angus MacLean (892-3535)
Minister of Fisheries, and Minister of Labour, Hon. L.F. Rossiter (894-3144; 892-3416)
Minister of Finance, Hon. Lloyd G. MacPhail (894-4738)
Minister of Health & Social Services, Hon. James M. Lee (894-4567)
Minister of Highways & Public Works, Hon. George R. McMahon, Q.C. (894-8025)
Minister of Community Affairs, Hon. Patrick G. Binns (892-2659)
Minister of Justice & Attorney General, Hon. Horace B. Carver, Q.C. (892-5411)
Minister of Agriculture & Forestry, Hon. Prowse G. Chappell (892-4101)
Minister of Education, Hon. Frederick L. Driscoll (892-3504)
Minister of Tourism, Industry & Energy, Hon. Barry R. Clark (894-4821)

Clerk of the Executive Council and Secretary to the Cabinet, Douglas Boylan (892-4296)

LEGISLATIVE ASSEMBLY

Fifty-Fifth General Assembly. Last Election, Apr. 23, 1979. Legal Duration, 5 Years.
Party Standings: Progressive Conservative (P.C.) 22; Liberal (Lib.) 10; Total 32
Leader of the Opposition,
Indemnities & Allowances: Members' Sessional Indemnity, $12,000 plus Expense & Travelling Allowance of $6,000 (tax free). In addition to the Sessional Indemnity, the Premier receives $32,000, all other Ministers, $22,000.
Officers: Speaker, Daniel Compton; Clerk of Assembly, W.W. Reid; Sergeant-at-Arms, Keith Johnston

Members

Prince Edward Island elects two types of members to the House–Councillors and Assemblymen–a system unaltered since the Legislative Council was merged with the Assembly in 1893. Each of the 16 constituencies elects one of each. Each elector is qualified to vote for one councillor and one assemblyman.

Following is Dist.: Councillor, home address (sessional mailing address for all is Box 2000, Charlottetown, P.E.I. C1A 7N8):

Prince County
First: Robert E. Campbell, Lib., Alberton (853-2289)
Second: Allison Ellis, Lib., O'Leary, R.R. (859-2065)
Third: Edward Clark, Lib., Lot 16, Belmont (436-7157)
Fourth: Prowse Chappell, P.C., Summerside, R.R. (436-7130)
Fifth: Peter Pope, P.C., 340 Lefurgey Ave., Summerside (436-5361)

Queens County
First: Leone Bagnall, P.C., Hunter River (964-2639)
Second: Lloyd G. MacPhail, P.C., New Haven, Cornwall, R.R. 3 (675-2005)
Third: Fred Driscoll, P.C., 33 Hillside Dr., Sherwood (894-9714)
Fourth: Dan Compton, P.C., Belle River P.O. (962-2081)
Fifth: Wilfred MacDonald, P.C., 15 Beasley Ave., Parkdale (894-9598)
Sixth: Jim Larkin, P.C., 3 Maplewood Cres., Charlottetown (892-7604)

Kings County
First: Albert Fogarty, P.C., Souris West (687-2962)
Second: Leo F. Rossiter, P.C., Morell (967-2231)
Third: A.E. (Bud) Ings, Lib., Montague (838-2276)
Fourth: Gilbert Clements, Lib., Montague (838-2606)
Fifth: Lowell Johnston, P.C., Montague, R.R. 4 (962-2747)

Following is Dist.: Assemblyman, home address (mailing address for all is Box 2000, Charlottetown, P.E.I. C1A 7N8):

Prince County
First: Russell Perry, Lib., Tignish (882-2278)
Second: Keith Milligan, Lib., Tyne Valley (831-2105)
Third: Leonce Bernard, Lib., Wellington (854-2730)
Fourth: William MacDougall, P.C., North Bedeque (887-2590)
Fifth: George McMahon, P.C., Summerside (436-3921)

Queens County
First: Marion Reid, P.C., Hope River (964-2054)
Second: Gordon Lank, P.C., North Wiltshire (964-2319)
Third: Horace Carver, P.C., 55 Goodwill Ave., Charlottetown (892-8319)
Fourth: J. Angus MacLean, P.C., Belle River, R.R. 3 (962-2235)
Fifth: James M. Lee, P.C., 42 Centennial Dr., Sherwood (892-6653)
Sixth: Barry Clark, P.C., 14 Queen Elizabeth Dr., Charlottetown (892-6382)

Kings County
First: Ross Young, Lib., Souris R.R. (357-2711)
Second: Roddy Pratt, P.C., St. Peters Bay (961-2765)
Third: A.A. (Joey) Fraser, P.C., 109 Main St. N., Montague (838-4237)
Fourth: Patrick G. Binns, Murray River, R.R. 4 (962-2196)
Fifth: A.J. MacDonald, Lib., Little Pond, Souris R.R. 4 (538-2040)

OFFICE OF THE PREMIER

Province Bldg., (Box 2000, Charlottetown, P.E.I. C1A 7N8)
(902) 892-3535
Premier, Hon. J. Angus MacLean
Principal Secretary, David Weale
Executive Asst., Leo Walsh
Executive Secretary, Ms. Rosemary Trainor

GOVERNMENT DEPARTMENTS

DEPT. OF AGRICULTURE & FORESTRY

Box 2000, Charlottetown, P.E.I. C1A 7N8
Information Contact, Lynne Sherren, Information Director (phone: 902-892-4101)

Acts Administered

Agricultural Chemicals Act
Agricultural Encouragement Act
Agricultural Products Marketing Act
Agricultural Rehabilitation & Development Act (P.E.I.)
Agrologists Act
Apiary Inspection Act
Artificial Insemination (Act respecting)
Bangs Disease Eradication Act
P.E.I. Crop Insurance Act
P.E.I. Dairy Products Act
Division Fence Act
Dog Act
Domestic Animals Act
Farm Implement Act
Field Root Seeds Zoning Act
Forestry Act
Grain Elevators Act
Horned Cattle Purchases Act
Land Development Corp. Act
Livestock Branding & Tatooing Act
Livestock Community Auction Sales Act
Margarine Act
Marketing Act

Milk Act
Mink Protection Act
P.E.I. Natural Products Mktg. Act
Plant Disease Eradication Act
Potato Crop Mtge. Act
Potato Production Act
Poultry & Poultry Products Act
Racehorse Inspection Act
Standards of Agricultural Products, An Act respecting
Veterinary Assist. Act
Veterinary Profession Act
Weed Control Act
Women's Institute Act

MINISTER, Hon. Prowse Chappell
Deputy Minister, A.W. Humphrey
Management Services Director, Lloyd Palmer
Director of Forest Services, Frank Matheson
Director, Field Services, David Rogers
Director, Veterinary Services, vacant
Director, Technical Services, Dr. Awni Raad

Associated Agencies

Land Development Corp., Box 1390, Charlottetown, P.E.I. C1A 7N1, 902/892-4137; General Manager, W. Stanhope Moore, P.Ag.
Crop Insurance Agency, Box 2000, Charlottetown, P.E.I. C1A 7N8, 902/892-4101; Manager, Ron McInnis
P.E.I. Milk Commission, Farm Centre, Box 335, Charlottetown, P.E.I. C1A 7K7 (902/892-5331)

Agricultural Marketing Boards

P.E.I. Egg Commodity Marketing Board
Farm Centre, 420 University Ave., Charlottetown, P.E.I. C1A 4N6 (892-8401)
Manager, Alvin MacDonald
P.E.I. Hog Commodity Marketing Board
Farm Centre, 420 University Ave., Charlottetown, P.E.I. C1A 7Z5 (892-4201)
Manager, Don Mutch
P.E.I. Marketing Council
Box 2000, Charlottetown, P.E.I. C1A 7N8 (892-4101)
General Manager, John Sandham
P.E.I. Milk Market Sharing Quota Boards
Farm Centre, Box 878, Charlottetown, P.E.I. C1A 7N9(892-6422)
Secretary Manager, Arthur MacRae
P.E.I. Pedigreed Seed Commodity Marketing Board
R.R. 3, Vernon, P.E.I. C0A 2E0 (651-2742)
Secretary, Ronald McInnis
P.E.I. Potato Marketing Board
Farm Centre, 420 University Ave., Charlottetown, P.E.I. C1A 7Z5 (892-6551)
Manager, Don Anderson
P.E.I. Tobacco Commodity Marketing Board
Farm Centre, 420 University Ave., Charlottetown, P.E.I. C1A 4N6 (894-4215)
Secretary, Casey Lamers
P.E.I. Poultry Meat Commodity Board
c/o Raynor's Poultry Farm, Charlottetown R.R. 5, P.E.I. C1A 7J8
Secretary Treasurer, Wilfred Lentz
P.E.I. Vegetable Commodity Marketing Board
Box 2000, Charlottetown, P.E.I. C1A 7N8 (892-4101)
A/Secretary, J.M. Sandham

PUBLIC ARCHIVES

Box 1000, Charlottetown, P.E.I. C1A 7M4
(902) 892-7949

OFFICE OF THE AUDITOR GENERAL

Box 2000, Charlottetown, P.E.I. C1A 7N8
(902) 892-3516
Auditor General, T. Kaptein, C.A.

CIVIL SERVICE COMMISSION

Box 2000, Charlottetown, P.E.I. C1A 7N8
(902) 892-4134
Chairman, Don MacCormac

DEPT. OF COMMUNITY AFFAIRS

Jones Bldg., 11 Kent St. (Box 2000, Charlottetown, P.E.I. C1A 7N8)
Information from: Management Services Unit, 902/892-3561

Acts Administered

Auctioneers Act
Automobile Junkyards Act
Bills of Sale Act
Business Practices Act
Cemeteries Act
Charities Act
Collecting Agencies Act
Community Improvement Act
Conditional Sales Act
Consumer Protection Act
Consumer Reporting Act
Direct Sellers Act
Electrical Inspection Act
Elevator & Lifts Act
Emergency Measures Act
Environmental Protection Act
Fire Prevention Act
Fish & Game Protection Act
Highway Advertisements Act
Housing & Rentals Act
Landlord & Tenant Act
Lightning Rod Act
Mobile Homes Act
Municipalities Extension Act
Planning Act
Provincial Building Code Act
Provincial Civil Defence Act
Real Estate Trading Act
Recreation Development Act Regulations
Rural Fire Companies Act
Sale of Goods Act
Town Act
Town & Village Debenture Guarantee Act
Unsightly Premises Act
Unsightly Property Act
Village Service Act
Well Drillers Act

MINISTER, Hon. Patrick G. Binns
Deputy Minister, Harry O'Connell, 892-3561
Executive Director, Youth, Fitness & Recreation Unit, Dr. David Boswell, 892-3561
Executive Director, Management Services Unit, Errol Andrews, 892-3561
Executive Director, Planning Services Unit, Ginger Breedon, 892-3561

Environmental & Consumer Services Division

(3 Queen St.)
Director, Fish & Wildlife Unit, John Bain, 892-0221
Director, Water Resources Unit, Bernard Dousse, 892-0221
Director, Environmental & Technical Services Unit, Don Champion, 892-0221
Director, Building & Development Services Unit, Stan Bishop, 892-0221 (Fire Marshal, Ron Kennedy; Electrical & Plumbing Inspection Chief, Ed Power)
Director, Consumer Services Unit, Eric Goodwin, 892-5321
Director, Emergency Measures Unit, Lou Pantry, 892-0221

Community Resources Division

(Jones Bldg.)
General Manager, Michael Kelly, 892-3561
Director, Community Resource Unit, vacant, 892-3561

DEPT. OF EDUCATION

Box 2000, Charlottetown, P.E.I. C1A 7N8
Information Contact, Linda Trenton, Data & Information Officer (phone: 902 892-3504)

Acts Administered

School Act
An Act to Establish the University of P.E.I.
An Act to Establish Holland College of Applied Arts & Technology
Teachers' Superannuation Act
Maritime Provinces Higher Education Commission Act

MINISTER, Hon. Fred Driscoll
Deputy Minister, Lorne R. Moase
Chief Director of Programs & Services, vacant
Chief Director of Administrative Services, Wayne McMillan
Director of Planning, Charles Campbell
Director of Curriculum, Sterling Stratton
Director of Teaching & Instructional Support, Ronald F. Rice
Director of Finance, Garfield Andrew
Manager of Personnel, Dave MacPherson
Student Aid Administrator, David MacPherson
Manager of Transportation, Donald Curry
Provincial Librarian, Donald Scott

Associated Commission

Teachers' Superannuation Commission, c/o Ronald F. Rice, Dept. of Education

P.E.I. ENERGY CORPORATION

3 Queen St. (Box 2000, Charlottetown, P.E.I. C1A 7N8
(902) 892-1051
General Manager, Arthur Hiscock

DEPT. OF FINANCE

Box 2000, Charlottetown, P.E.I. C1A 7N8
Information Contact, Lois Thompson, Administrative Asst., 902/894-8112

Acts Administered

Appropriation Act
Audit Act
Canada Pension Plan Agreement & Loans Act
Civil Service Superannuation Act
Deposit Receipt Act
Development Borrowing Act
Entertainments Act
Financial Administration Act
Gasoline Tax Act
Health Tax Act
Income Tax Act
Legislative Assembly Retirement Allowances Act
Lotteries Act
Municipal Loans (Guarantee) Act
P.E.I. Loans Act
Public Accounting & Auditing Act
Real Property Assessment Act
Real Property Tax Act
Act to Relieve Non-Residents from certain Licenses & Taxes of Municipalities
Revenue Tax Act

MINISTER OF FINANCE, Hon. Lloyd G. MacPhail
Deputy Minister, G.D. Dennis, C.A.
Comptroller, W.B. White, C.A.
Economists, J. Palmer, M. Woodyard

DEPT. OF FISHERIES

Box 2000, Charlottetown, P.E.I. C1A 7N8
Information Contact, Administrator (phone: 902 892-3493)

Act Administered

Fish Inspection Act

MINISTER, Hon. Leo F. Rossiter
Deputy Minister, Louis D. Johnston
Administrator, O. MacKinnon
Development Branch, Director, B. Lewis (act.)
Resource Harvesting Division, Program Manager, B. Lewis
Processing & Quality Control Division, Program Manager, B. Lewis (act.)
Services Branch, Director, D. Judson
Extension Division, Program Manager, L. Creed
Product Handling Division, Program Manager, F. Herring
Economics & Statistics Division, Program Manager, D. Younker
Aquaculture Branch, Director, I. Judson

DEPT. OF HEALTH & SOCIAL SERVICES

Box 3000, Charlottetown, P.E.I. C1A 7P1
Information Contact, Ms. Jean MacKay (phone: 902-892-5471)

Acts Administered

Addiction Foundation of P.E.I. Act
Change of Name Act
Chiropractic Act
Cornea Transplant Act
Dental Profession Act
Dental Student Loan & Dental Practice Establishment Loan Act
Dispensing Opticians Act
Health Services Payment Act
Hillsborough Hospital Act
Hospitals Act
Hospital & Diagnostic Services Insurance Act
Human Tissue Gift Act
Licensed Nursing Assts.' Act
Marriage Act
Medical Act
Mental Health Act
New General Hospital Act
Nurses Act
Optometry Act
Pharmacy Act
Act Respecting the Practice of Physiotherapy
Premarital Health Examination Act
Act to Incorporate P.E.I. Pharmaceutical Services Inc.
Provincial Sanatorium Act
Public Health Act
Registered Occupational Therapists Act
Venereal Disease Prevention Act
Vital Statistics Act
White Cane Act

MINISTER, Hon. James M. Lee
Deputy Minister, Keith Wornell
Chief Health Officer, W.R. Stewart, 892-7331
Executive Asst., Richard O'Brien
Director of Community Health, vacant
Director of Cancer Control, W.T. Hooper, M.D.
Director of Dental Division, R.G. Romcke, D.D.S., D.D.P.H.
Director of Laboratories, John Craig, M.B., Ch.B.
Director of Mental Health, S.A. Malcolmson, M.D., C.R.C.P. (C)
Director of Community Mental Health, Eugene MacDonald, M.S.W.
Director of Pharmacy Division, L.R. Montigny, B.Sc.
Director of Nursing Services, Miss Ella MacLeod, M.S.
Director of Community Hygiene, Richard Davies
Director of Research, Planning & Evaluation Unit, Robert Thomson
Director of Human Resources, Rick Callaghan
Director of Special Care & Sanatorium Complex, R. Stewart, M.D., C.M.
Director of Vital Statistics, Donald Deacon
For each copy of a Birth, Marriage or Death Certificate, the fee is $3.

Associated Agencies

Health Services Commission of P.E.I., Box 4500, Charlottetown, P.E.I. C1A 7P4, 902/892-4281; Chairman, Mrs. Lucille Hogg

Hospital Services Commission of P.E.I., Box 4500, Charlottetown, P.E.I. C1A 7P4 (902/892-4281); Chairman, J. Brendon McGinn

P.E.I. Laboratory Council, Box 3000, Charlottetown, P.E.I. C1A 7P1, 902/892-3571

Addiction Services of P.E.I., Box 37, Charlottetown, P.E.I. C1A 7K2, 902/892-4265; Executive Director, Dr. Mark Triantafillou

Social Services Branch

Box 2000, Charlottetown, P.E.I. C1A 7N8

Information Contact, R.G. Dumont, Director of Administration (902/892-5421)

Acts Administered

Adoption Act
Blind Persons' Act
Child Care Facilities Act
Children's Act
Children's Protection Act
Disabled Persons (An Act Respecting Allowances for)
P.E.I. General Welfare Assistance Act
Rehabilitation of Disabled Persons (An Act to Provide for)

Director of Field Services, J.E. Kiley
Director of Services to the Aging, L.G. MacNevin
Director of Special Services, vacant
Director of Administration, R.G. Dumont

P.E.I. HERITAGE FOUNDATION

Box 922, Charlottetown, P.E.I. C1A 7L9
(902) 892-9127
Executive Director, Catherine Hennessey

DEPT. OF HIGHWAYS & PUBLIC WORKS

Box 2000, Charlottetown, P.E.I. C1A 7N8

Information Contact, P.J. Murphy (phone: 902 894-4111)

Acts Administered

Access to Public Buildings Act
Architects Act
Crown Building Corporation Act
Engineering Profession Act
Expropriation Act
Highway Traffic Act
Judgement Recovery (P.E.I.) Ltd., An Act to Incorporate
Land Survey Act, 1971 (& 1951)
Land Surveyors Act
Off-Highway Vehicle Act
Public Works Act
Queens Printer Act
Recreation Development Act
Roads Act
Vehicle Dealers & Salesmen Act
Winter Works Projects Act

MINISTER, Hon. George R. McMahon, Q.C.
Deputy Minister, B.J. Scott
Asst. Deputy Minister, John Gilmore
Director of Admin., P.J. Murphy
Chief Engineer, T.W. Walker
Director of Planning, Glen Beaton
Director of Services, Douglas Murray
Director of Buildings & Parks, Neil Walker
Director of Highway Safety, Irwin Jenkins
Director of Highway Maintenance, George Trainor
Director of Island Information Service, Chris Brittain
Supt. of Mechanical Branch, Joseph Caswell
Queens Printer, G.W. Auld

P.E.I. HOUSING CORP.

Box 1388, Charlottetown, P.E.I. C1A 7N1
(902) 892-0221
General Manager, Dale Turner

HUMAN RIGHTS COMMISSION

180 Richmond St. (Box 2000, Charlottetown, P.E.I. C1A 7N8)
(902) 894-7797
Executive Director, Tom Klewin

DEPT. OF JUSTICE & ATTORNEY GENERAL

Box 2000, Charlottetown, P.E.I. C1A 7N8

Information Contact, M.H. Wigginton, Director of Admin. (phone: 902 892-5411)

Acts Administered

Affidavits Act
Age of Majority Act
Ancient Burial Grounds Act
Appeals Act
Apportionment Act
Arbitration Act
Assignment of Book Debts Act
Bailable Proceedings Act
Bulk Sales Act
Charities Act
Companies Act
Commorientes Act
Condominium Act
Contributory Negligence Act
Controverted Elections Act (Provincial)
Co-operative Associations Act
Coroners Act
Corporation Securities Registration Act
Court Stenographers Act
Credit Union Act
Crown Proceedings Act
Death Inquiries Act, 1965
Defamation Act
Dependents of a Deceased Person Relief Act
Designation of Beneficiaries Act
Election Act
Escheats Act
Evidence Act
Extra-Provincial Custody Orders Enforcement Act
Factors Act
Family Law Reform Act
Fatal Accidents Act
Fishermen's Unions Act
Frauds on Creditors Act
Frustrated Contracts Act
Garage Keeper's Lien Act
Garnishee Act
Habeas Corpus & Certiorari Act
Human Rights Act
Insurance Act
Interpretation Act
Investigation of Titles Act
Jails Act
Judgment & Execution Act
Judicature Act
Junk Dealers Act
Jury Act
Land Titles Act
Law Reform Commission Act
Law Society & Legal Profession Act
Legal Aid Act
Liquor Control Act
Licensing or Registration of Certain Corporations & Persons Act
Lord's Day (P.E.I.) Act
Mechanics' Lien Act
Motor Carrier Act
National Park Act
Official Trustee Act
Parole Act
Partnership Act
Perpetuities Act
Police Act
Premium Tax Act
Probate Act

Probation Act
Provincial Administrator of Estates Act
Provincial Court Act
Provincial Guardian (Transfer of Funds) Act
Public Utilities Commission Act
Quieting Titles Act
Racing & Sports Commission Act
Real Estate Trading Act
Real Property Act
Reciprocal Enforcement of Judgments Act
Reciprocal Enforcement of Maintenance Orders Act
Registry Act
Revised Statutes Confirmation & Amendment Act, 1974
Securities Act
Sheriffs' Act
Statute of Frauds
Statute of Limitations
Statute Revision Act
Statute Law Revision Act
Store Hours Act
Summary Proceedings Act
Summary Trespass Act
Surety & Guarantee Companies Act
Act to Enable Survival of Actions
Time in Public Offices Act
Trustee Act
Unclaimed Articles Act
Unconscionable Transactions Relief Act
Uniformity Commrs. Act
Variation of Trusts Act
Warehousemen's Lien Act
Water & Sewerage Act
Winding Up Act

MINISTER OF JUSTICE & ATTORNEY-GENERAL, Hon. H.B. Carver
Deputy Minister of Justice & Deputy Attorney-General, A.J. Currie
Director of Legal Services, Ian W.H. Bailey
Department Solicitor, R.C. Thompson
Director of Prosecutions, R.B. Hubley
Crown Counsel, D.E. Coombs, R.B. Hubley, David O'Brien
Legislative Counsel, Raymond Moore
Director of Admin., M.H. Wigginton
Director of Probation, J.P. Arbing
Director of Corrections, L.P. Lynch

DEPT. OF LABOUR

Box 2000, Charlottetown, P.E.I. C1A 7N8
Information Contact, L.W. Brammer, Deputy Minister (phone: 902 892-3416)

Acts Administered

Apprenticeship & Tradesmen Qualifications Act
Blind Workers Compensation Act
P.E.I. Labour Act
Minimum Age of Employment Act
Power Engineers Act
Steam Boiler Act
Trades School Act
Truck Operators Remuneration Act
Workers Compensation Act

MINISTER, Hon. Leo F. Rossiter
Deputy Minister, L.W. Brammer
Administrative Officer, Glenda F. Stewart
Chief Boiler Inspector, W.A. Miller West
Chief Labour Standards Inspector, Roy J. Doucette
Director of Manpower Resources, Peter McGonnell
Manager of Apprenticeship, Louis Dalton

Workers' Compensation Board

Box 757, Charlottetown, P.E.I. C1A 7L7
Chairman, M.E. Campbell (902/894-8555)
Secretary, C.E. Ready

Labour Relations Board

Box 2000, Charlottetown, P.E.I. C1A 7N8
Chairman, J.J. Revell (902/892-3418)
Chief Executive Officer, W.S. MacKinnon

Employment Standards Advisory Board

Box 2000, Charlottetown, P.E.I. C1A 7N8 (892-3416)
Chairman, Michael F. Hennessey
Secretary, Roy J. Doucette

Power Engineers Examining Board

Box 2000, Charlottetown, P.E.I. C1A 7N8 (892-3416)
Chairman, Miller West

LIQUOR CONTROL COMMISSION

Box 967, Charlottetown, P.E.I. C1A 7M4
(902) 892-8541
Chairman, Blake Wood

MALPEQUE OYSTER CULTURES INC.

Ellerslie R.R., P.E.I. COB 1JO
(902) 831-2575
General Manager, Elmer Hutchinson

POLICY & PRIORITIES BOARD

Box 2000, Charlottetown, P.E.I. C1A 7N8
(902) 892-4211
Secretary, H.E. Phillips

PUBLIC UTILITIES COMMISSION

Confederation Court Mall (Box 577, Charlottetown, P.E.I. C1A 7L1)
(902) 892-3501
Chairman, W.R. Brennan

Acts Administered

Public Utilies Commission Act
Electric Power & Telephone Act
Petroleum Products Act
Motor Carrier Act
Water & Sewerage Act

OFFICE OF THE RENTALSMAN

11 Kent St. (Box 2000, Charlottetown, P.E.I. C1A 7N8)
(902) 894-8559
Rentalsman, John Comeau

DEPT. OF TOURISM, INDUSTRY & ENERGY

Box 2000, Charlottetown, P.E.I. C1A 7N8
(902) 892-7411

Acts Administered

Innkeepers Act
Oil, Natural Gas & Minerals Act
Lending Authority Act
Market Development Act
Industrial Enterprises Act
Industrial Enterprises Inc. Loans Act
Area Industrial Commission Act
Georgetown Shipyard Inc. (An Act to incorporate)

MINISTER, Hon. Barry Clark
Deputy Minister, vacant
Director of Tourism, Garth Staples
Administrator, W.G. Bustard

Associated Agencies

Market Development Centre
  Box 1510, Charlottetown, P.E.I. C1A 7N3
  (902) 892-4165
  General Manager, Don Baker
Industrial Enterprises Inc.
  West Royalty Industrial Park, Charlottetown, P.E.I. C1E 1B0
  (902) 892-3551
  General Manager, Ivan MacKenzie

P.E.I. Lending Authority
134 Kent St., Charlottetown, P.E.I. C1A 7N1
(902) 892-4247
General Manager, William Jay

TREASURY BOARD
Box 2000, Charlottetown, P.E.I. C1A 7N8
(902) 892-9108
Chairman, Hon. Lloyd G. MacPhail
Secretary to Treasury Board, Philip MacDougall

PROVINCE OF QUEBEC
Entered Confederation July 1, 1867
Area: 594,860 sq. miles
Population: 6,303,400 (1980 est.)
Seat of Government: Government Bldgs., Québec City
Lieutenant-Governor: The Hon. Jean-Pierre Côté
Executive Asst. & Senior Aide-de-Camp, Lt.-Col. Michel Giguère, C.D., A.D.C.

EXECUTIVE COUNCIL
Prime Minister, and President of the Executive Council, René Lévesque
Deputy Prime Minister, and Minister of State for Cultural & Scientific Development, Jacques-Yvan Morin
Minister of Municipal Affairs, Jacques Léonard
Minister of Education, Camille Laurin
Minister of State for Economic Development, Bernard Landry
Minister of Labour, Manpower & Income Security, Pierre Marois
Minister-Delegate for Parliamentary Affairs, and Government House Leader, Claude Charron
Minister of Intergovernmental Affairs, Claude Morin
Minister-Delegate of Housing & Consumer Protection, Guy Tardif
Minister of State for Social Development, Denis Lazure
Minister of Agriculture, Fisheries & Food, Jean Garon
Minister of Administration, and Chairman of Treasury Board, Yves Bérubé
Minister of the Environment, Marcel Léger
Minister of Finance, and Minister of Financial Institutions & Cooperatives, Jacques Parizeau
Minister of State (Management), François Gendron
Minister of Energy & Resources, Yves Duhaime
Minister of Justice, and Minister of State for Electoral Reform, Marc-André Bédard
Minister of Recreation, Fish & Game, Lucien Lessard
Minister of Transport, Michel Clair
Minister of Social Affairs, Pierre-Marc Johnson
Minister of Cultural Affairs, Clement Richard
Minister of Cultural Communities & Immigration, Gerald Godin
Minister of Communications, Jean-François Bertrand
Minister of State for the Status of Women, Pauline Marois
Minister of the Civil Service, Denise Leblanc-Bantey
Minister of Industry, Trade & Tourism, Rodrigue Biron
Minister of Revenue, Raynald Fréchette
Minister of Public Works & Supply, Alain Marcoux

NATIONAL ASSEMBLY
Thirty-second Legislature. Last Election, April 13, 1981. Maximum Duration, 5 Years.
Party Standings: Parti Quebecois (P.Q.) 80; Liberal (Lib.) 42; Total 122
Leader of the Opposition, Claude Ryan
Indemnities & Allowances: Members' Annual Indemnity, $33,110 plus $7,500 entertainment expenses. In addition to the Annual Indemnity the Prime Minister receives $43,043; other Ministers, $30,580; Speaker, $30,580; Leader of the Opposition, $30,580.

Officers: Speaker, Claude Vaillancourt; Deputy Speakers, J.-P. Jolivet, Rèal Rancourt; Secretary General of National Assembly, René Blondin (phone: 418/643-2724); Asst. Secretaries, Jacques Lessard, Pierre Duchesne; Sergeant-at-Arms, René Jalbert, Clerk of the Agenda Paper, Constance Pinault; Law Clerk of the Legislature, Michel Leclerc; Secretary of Legislation Committee, Gilles Paradis; Clerk of Votes & Proceedings, Gustave Gervais; Librarian, Jacques Prémont.

Members
Constituency: Member, Party Affiliation (NOTE:- address for all is Hôtel du Gouvernement, Quebec, P.Q.):

Abitibi-Est: Jean-Paul Bordeleau, P.Q.
Abitibi-Ouest: François Gendron, P.Q.
Anjou: Pierre-Marc Johnson, P.Q.
Argenteuil: Claude Ryan, Lib.
Arthabaska: Jacques Baril, P.Q.
Beauce-Nord: Adrien Ouellet, P.Q.
Beauce-Sud: Herman Mathieu, Lib.
Beauharnois: Laurent Lavigne, P.Q.
Bellechasse: Claude Lachance, P.Q.
Berthier: Albert Houde, Lib.
Bertrand: Denis Lazure, P.Q.
Bonaventure: Gérard-D. Levesque, Lib.
Bourassa: Patrice Laplante, P.Q.
Bourget: Camille Laurin, P.Q.
Brôme-Missisquoi: Pierre Paradis, Lib.
Chambly: Luc Tremblay, P.Q.
Champlain: Marcel Gagnon, P.Q.
Chapleau: John J. Kehoe, Lib.
Charlesbourg: Denis de Belleval, P.Q.
Charlevoix: Raymond Mailloux, Lib.
Châteauguay: Roland Dussault, P.Q.
Chauveau: Raymond Brouillet, P.Q.
Chicoutimi: Marc-André Bédard, P.Q.
Chomedey: Lise Bacon, Lib.
Crémazie: Guy Tardif, P.Q.
D'Arcy McGee: Herbert Marx, Lib.
Deux-Montagnes: Pierre de Bellefeuille, P.Q.
Dorion: Huguette Lachapelle, P.Q.
Drummond: Michel Clair, P.Q.
Dubuc: Hubert Desbiens, P.Q.
Duplessis: Denis Perron, P.Q.
Fabre: Michel Leduc, P.Q.
Frontenac: Gilles Grégoire, P.Q.
Gaspé: Henri Le May, P.Q.
Gatineau: Michel Gratton, Lib.
Gouin: Jacques Rochefort, P.Q.
Groulx: Elie Fallu, P.Q.
Hull: Gilles Rocheleau, Lib.
Huntingdon: Claude Dubois, Lib.
Iberville: Jacques Beauséjour, P.Q.
Iles-de-la-Madeleine: Denise LeBlanc, P.Q.
Jacques-Cartier: Joan Dougherty, Lib.
Jeanne-Mance: Michel Bissonnet, Lib.
Jean-Talon: Jean-Claude Rivest, Lib.
Johnson: Carmen Juneau, P.Q.
Joliette: Guy Chevrette, P.Q.
Jonquière: Claude Vaillancourt, P.Q.
Kamouraska-Témiscouata: Léonard Lévesque, P.Q.
Labelle: Jacques Léonard, P.Q.
L'Acadie: Thérèse Lavoie-Roux, Lib.
Lac-Saint-Jean: Jacques Brassard, P.Q.
Lafontaine: Marcel Léger, P.Q.
La Peltrie: Pauline Marois, P.Q.
Laporte: André Bourbeau, Lib.
Laprairie: Jean-Pierre Saintonge, Lib.
L'Assomption: Jacques Parizeau, P.Q.
Laurier: Christos Sirros, Lib.
Laval-des-Rapides: Bernard Landry, P.Q.
Laviolette: Jean-Pierre Jolivet, P.Q.
Lévis: Jean Garon, P.Q.
Limoilou: Raymond Gravel, P.Q.
Lotbinière: Rodrigue Biron, P.Q.

Louis-Hébert: Claude Morin, P.Q.
Maisonneuve: Louise Harel, P.Q.
Marguerite-Bourgeoys: Fernand Lalonde, Lib.
Marie-Victorin: Pierre Marois, P.Q.
Marquette: Claude Dauphin, Lib.
Maskinongé: Yvon Picotte, Lib.
Matane: Yves Bérubé, P.Q.
Matapédia: Léopold Marquis, P.Q.
Mégantic-Compton: Fabien Bélanger, Lib.
Mercier: Gérald Godin, P.Q.
Mille-Iles: Jean-Paul Champagne, P.Q.
Montmagny-L'Islet: Jacques LeBlanc, P.Q.
Montmorency: Clément Richard, P.Q.
Mont-Royal: John Ciaccia, Lib.
Nelligan: Clifford Lincoln, Lib.
Nicolet: Yves Beaumier, P.Q.
Notre-Dame-de-Grâce: Reed Scowen, Lib.
Orford: Georges Vaillancourt, Lib.
Outremont: Pierre C. Fortier, Lib.
Papineau: Mark Assad, Lib.
Pontiac: Robert Middlemiss, Lib.
Portneuf: Michel Pagé, Lib.
Prévost: Robert Dean, P.Q.
Richelieu: Maurice Martel, P.Q.
Richmond: Yvon Vallières, Lib.
Rimouski: Allain Marcoux, P.Q.
Rivière-du-Loup: Jules Boucher, P.Q.
Robert Baldwin: John O'Gallagher, Lib.
Roberval: Michel Gauthier, P.Q.
Rosemont: Gilbert Paquette, P.Q.
Rousseau: René Blouin, P.Q.
Rouyn-Noranda-Témiscamingue: Gilles Baril, P.Q.
Saguenay: Lucien Lessard, P.Q.
Sainte-Anne: Maximilien Polak, Lib.
Saint-François: Réal Rancourt, P.Q.
Saint-Henri: Roma Hains, Lib.
Saint-Hyacinthe: Maurice Dupré, P.Q.
Saint-Jacques: Claude Charron, P.Q.
Saint-Jean: Jerome Proulx, P.Q.
Saint-Laurent: Claude Forget, Lib.
Saint-Louis: Harry Blank, Lib.
Sainte-Marie: Guy Bisaillon, P.Q.
Saint-Maurice: Yves Duhaime, P.Q.
Sauvé: Jacques-Yvan Morin, P.Q.
Shefford: Roger Paré, P.Q.
Sherbrooke: Raynald Fréchette, P.Q.
Taillon: René Levesque, P.Q.
Taschereau: Richard Guay, P.Q.
Terrebonne: Yves Blais, P.Q.
Trois-Rivières: Denis Vaugeois, P.Q.
Ungava: Marcel (Jim) Lafrenière, P.Q.
Vachon: David Payne, P.Q.
Vanier: Jean-François Bertrand, P.Q.
Vaudreuil-Soulanges: Daniel Johnson, Lib.
Verchères: Jean-Pierre Charbonneau, P.Q.
Verdun: Lucien Caron, Lib.
Viau: William Cusano, Lib.
Viger: Cosmo Maciocia, Lib.
Vimont: Jean-Guy Rodrigue, P.Q.
Westmount: Richard French, Lib.

OFFICE OF THE PRIME MINISTER

885 Grande Allée est, Edifice J, 3e étage, Québec, P.Q. G1A 1A2
(418) 643-5321
Executive Asst., Jean-Roch Boivin
Deputy Executive Asst., Michel Carpentier
Executive Secretary, Claude Malette
Press Secretary, Gratia O'Leary
Administrative Asst., Gilles R. Tremblay
Director of Communications, Jean-F. Cloutier

GOVERNMENT DEPARTMENTS

DEPT. OF AGRICULTURE, FISHERIES & FOOD

200A Chemin Ste-Foy, Québec City, P.Q. G1R 4X6
Information Contact, Marcel Thivièrge, Director, Communications Dept. (phone: 418-643-2673)

Acts Administered

Act to constitute the Société Québécoise d'initiatives Agro-Alimentaires
Act to preserve agricultural land
Act to promote long term farm credit by private institutions
Act to promote special credit to agricultural producers during critical periods
Agricultural Abuses Act
Agricultural Exploitations (An act to promote the development of), 1967
Agricultural Marketing Act
Agricultural Merit Act
Agricultural Products & Food Act
Agricultural Societies Act
Agriculture Dept. Act
Animal Protection Act
Bees Act
Butter & Cheese Societies Act
Colonization Land Acquisition Act
Colonization Land Sales Act
Colonization Societies Act
Crop Insurance Act, 1967
Dairies (An Act to promote the development & modernization of regional), 1967
Dairy & Agricultural Schools Act
Dairy Products & Dairy Products Substitutes Act, 1969
Farm Credit Act
Farm Improvement Act
Farm Income Stabilization Insurance (Act respecting)
Farm Loan Act
Farm Producers Act, 1972
Farm Producers (Acts to promote credit to), 1972
Farmers' Clubs Act
Farmers' & Dairymens' Association Act
Horticultural Societies Act
Pioneering Merit Act
Plant Protection Act
Real Estate Assessment Act
Settlers Protection Act
Stock-breeding Syndicates Act
Thoroughbred Cattle Act

MINISTER, Jean Garon
Deputy Minister, Ferdinand Ouellet, B.S.A., M.Sc.
Asst. Deputy Ministers, L.J. Marquis; J. Guy Charbonneau; Raymond Moore; Marcel Pelletier; Ronald Carré
Director of Regional Agricultural Offices & Laboratories, H. Melanson, L.S.A.
Veterinary Service Director, André Gravel
Artificial Insemination & Livestock Improvement Director, Claude Hayes
Personnel Service Director, Gaston Gaudreau (Int.)
Accounting Service Director, André Guimond
Legal Branch Director, Me Paul-André Gagné
Communications Dept., Director, Marcel Thivièrge
Agricultural Hydraulics Service Director, Denys Vinet
Marketing Branch Director, Jean Desjardins
Food Inspection, Director, Claude Bergeron
Industrial Development Service, Director, Yves Proulx
Agricultural Education Service, Director, Ludger Dufour
Vegetable Products Service, Director, Lionel Lachance
Animal Products Service, Director, Conrad Bernier

Associated Agencies

Agricultural Marketing Board,

President, Dr. Benoit Lavigne, B.S.A., M.Sc., Ph.D., 201 est, boul. Crémazie, Montreal, P.Q. H2M 1L3 (514/873-4024); 1020, route de l'Eglise, Ste-Foy, P.Q. G1V 3V9 (418/643-2640)
Farm Credit Bureau (Office du crédit agricole)
President, Me Camille Moreau, B.A., LL.L., #500, 1020 route de l'Eglise, Ste-Foy, P.Q. G1V 4P2
Agricultural Insurance Board
President, Jacques Brulotte, 352, boul. St-Sacrement, Quebec, P.Q. G1N 3Y2 (418/643-7331)
Quebec Sugar Refinery
Mont-Saint-Hilaire (Rouville), P.Q. J3H 4G6
Director General, André Marier
Agricultural Research Council
Secretary, Marcel Belzile, 200A ch. Ste-Foy, Québec, P.Q.

Agricultural Marketing Boards

Fédération des producteurs de lait du Québec (Dairy Producers)
515, ave. Viger, Montréal, P.Q. H2L 2P2
(514) 288-6141
Secretaire, Henri Dorval
Fédération des producteurs de lait industriel du Québec (Industrial Dairy Producers)
Ste. 201, 515, ave. Viger, Montréal, P.Q. H2L 2P2
(514) 288-6141
Secretaire, Roch Morin
Fédération des producteurs de volailles du Québec (Que. Poultry Producers Federation)
515, ave. Viger, Montréal, P.Q. H2L 2P2
(514) 288-6141
Secretaire, Serge Deschamps
Fédération des producteurs d'oeufs de consommation du Québec (Egg Producers)
1355, boul. Graham Bell, Boucherville, P.Q. J4B 6A1
(514) 655-6410
Secretaire, Bertrand Cloutier
Office des producteurs de bleuets du Saguenay-Lac-St-Jean (Saguenay-Lac-St-Jean Blueberry Producers)
422 rue Racine, Chicoutimi, P.Q. G7H 1T3
(418) 549-7353
Secretaire, René-C. Bergeron
Office des producteurs de tabac à cigare et à pipe du Québec (Cigar & Pipe Tobacco Producers)
60, rue Venne, Saint-Jacques (Montcalm), P.Q. JOK 2RO
(514) 839-3641
Secretaire, Réjean Bédard
Federation des producteurs de fruits et legumes du Québec (Fruit & Bean)
515, ave. Viger, Montréal, P.Q. H2L 2P2
(514) 288-6141
Secretaire, Gerald Tetreault
Office des producteurs de sucre et sirop d'érable de Québec-sud (Southern Que. Sugar & Maple Syrup Producers)
318, 27ième rue, Saint-Georges est (Beauce), P.Q. G5Y 5C7
(418) 228-5588
Secretaire, Marcel Gaulin
Québec Flue-Cured Tobacco Board
1800 rg. St-Albert, St-Thomas CTE, Joliette, P.Q. JOK 3Z0
(514) 759-0916
Secretaire, Mme J.P. Corriveau

OFFICE OF THE AUDITOR-GENERAL

900 Place d'Youville, Suite 301, Québec City, P.Q. G1R 3P7
(418) 643-2781
Auditor General, Rhéal Chatelain

CIVIL SERVICE DEPT.

Bldg. G, Cité parlementaire, Québec, P.Q. G1R 4Z9
Information Contact, François Lamarre, Executive Secretary
MINISTER, Denise Leblanc Bantey (418/643-3833)
Deputy Minister, vacant (643-4432)
Asst. Deputy Ministers, Raymond Conti, J.-M. Lalande, Marc Carrier
Director General, Labour Relations, Gaetan Langlois, 643-1793
Director General, Development of Human Resources, Jacques Nadon (643-1793)
Director General, Systems, Roland Vandal (643-7777)

DEPT. OF COMMUNICATIONS

Cité parlementaire, Edifice G (tour), Québec City, P.Q. G1R 4Y7
Information Contact, Adélard Guillemette, Directeur du Service des communications (phone: 418 643-1529)

Acts Administered

Cinema Supervision Bureau Act
Communications Dept. Act
Que. Broadcasting Bureau Act
Public Service Board Act

MINISTER, Jean-François Bertrand
Deputy Minister, Pierre A. Deschênes
Asst. Deputy Minister, Jean-Lucien Caron
Asst. Deputy Minister, Operations, Bertrand Croteau
Asst. Deputy Minister, Information, Jean Laurin
Communications, Adélard Guillemette
Director General, Admin., Mme Claire Monette
Director General, Publications, Jacques Brunelle
Executive Secretary, Council of Directors of Communications, Mme Raymonde Saint-Germain

Associated Agencies

Editeur official du Qué./Que. Official Publisher, 1283, Charest Boul. W., Québec, P.Q. G1N 2C9–Editor, Chs.-H. Dubé (418/643-9810)
Régie des services publics (Public Service Board), 2875, boul. Laurier, Ste-Foy, Québec, P.Q. G1V 2M2–Juge Yvon Côté (418/643-8958)
La Société de radio-télédiffusion du Québec (Quebec Broadcasting Bureau–Radio-Quebec), 800, rue Fullum, Montreal, P.Q. H2K 3L7–Gérard Barbin, President & General Manager (514/873-4611)

DEPT. OF CULTURAL AFFAIRS

225, Grande Allée est, Quebec, P.Q. G1R 5G5
Information Contact, Director of Communications (phone: 418 643-2183)

Acts Administered

Cultural Affairs Department Act
Publishers Loss Insurance Act
Public Libraries Act
Artistic, Literary & Scientific Competitions Act
Music & Dramatic Art Institute Act
Provincial Museums Act
Handicraft Council Act
Place des Arts Act
Booksellers Accreditation Act
Quebec National Library Act
Grand Theatre de Quebec Act
Cultural Property Act
Act to preserve agricultural land
Montreal Museum of Fine Arts Act
Act to incorporate the Société québécoise de développement des industries culturelles
An act respecting the guarantee of certain loans to publishers and booksellers and to amend the Quebec Industrial Development Assistance Act
Act to again amend the cities and towns Act and the Municipal Code
Act to amend the code of Civil Procedure in respect of the exemption from seizure of foreign cultural property
Photographic Proof of Documents Act

MINISTER, Clément Richard
Deputy Minister, Roland Arpin
Assoc. Deputy Ministers, Nicole Martin, Bruno Grégoire, J.-J. Chagnon

Co-ordinator, Intergovt. Relations, Monique Levasseur-Bouchard
Co-ordinator, Inuit & Indian Affairs, Michel Noel
Director, Planning & Programming, André Garon
Director General, Administration, R.P. Morin
Director General, Arts & Letters, Georges Cartier
(includes: Artists' Aid, Book Division, Visual Environment Division, Performing Arts Division)
Director General, Québec Heritage, Bernard Ouimet
(includes: Historic Sites & Archaeology, and Ethnology Division)
Museums Director General, André Juneau
Director General, Quebec Museum (1 rue Wolfe), Pierre Lachapelle
Chief Conservator, André Marchand
Director, Contemporary Art Museum (Cité du Havre, Montreal), Louise Letocha
Director, Private Museums & Exhibit Centres, Jean Rivet
National Archives, Conservator, Robert Garon (1210 ave du Séminaire, Ste-Foy, G1V 4N1)
National Library, Chief Conservator, J.R. Brault (1700 St-Denis, Montreal)
Director General, Conservatories of Music and of Dramatic Art, Pierre Genest

Regional Offices

Director, Roger Ricard (int.)
Regional offices are located at Chicoutimi, Hauterive, Hull, Montreal, Noranda, Quebec, Rimouski, Sherbrooke, Trois-Rivières

Associated Agency

Cinema Supervisory Board
360 McGill, Montreal, P.Q. H2Y 2E9
(514) 873-2371
President, André Guérin

DEPT. OF CULTURAL COMMUNITIES & IMMIGRATION

355 McGill St., Montreal, P.Q. H2Y 2E8
Information Contact: Enrico Riggi, Communications Director (phone: 514/873-4546)

Acts Administered

Dept. of Immigration Act, 1968 (and Amendments)

MINISTER, Gérald Godin
Deputy Minister, Juliette Barcelo
Asst. Deputy Ministers, Régis Vigneau, Roger Prud'homme
Secretary, vacant

DEPT. OF EDUCATION

Bldg. G, Cité parlementaire, Québec City, P.Q. G1R 5A5
Information from Yves Bernard, Director of the Inquiries Service (phone: 418-643-7095)

Acts Administered

Education Dept. Act
Superior Council of Education Act
Professional Matriculation Act
Private Education Act
Specialized Schools Act
Dairy & Agricultural Schools Act
Fine Arts Schools Act
School Bds. Grants Act
Univ. of Que. Act
Council of Univs. Act
Univ. Assistance Act
Univ. Investments Act
Student Loans & Scholarships Act
Teachers Scholarships Act
Scholastic Merit Act

MINISTER, Camille Laurin
Deputy-Minister, Jacques Girard
Assoc. Deputy Minister (Catholic Faith), Richard Brosseau
Assoc. Deputy Minister (Protestant Faith), Ernest Spiller
Asst. Deputy Minister (Nursery, Elementary & Secondary Schools), André Rousseau
Asst. Deputy Minister (Inter-related Services), André Beaudoin
Asst. Deputy Minister (Administration), Jean Pronovost
Asst. Deputy Minister (Planning), Pierre Lucier
Ministry Secretariat, Robert Trempe
Director, Internal Audit, J.-M. Verreault
Director, Catholic Education, Michel Stein
Director, Accounting, Pierre Beauchamp
Director, Legal Service, M.-A. Patoine
Director, Protestant Education, Raymond Jensen
Director General, Management, Jacques Cardinal
Co-ordinator, Women's Programs, Diane Gagnon
Co-ordinator, Indian & Inuit Activities, Jacqueline Dorman
Director General, Teacher Development, Roger Thériault
Director General, College Education, Nicole Brodeur
Director General, University Education & Research, Léo Paré
Director General, Student Financial Aid, Paul Boudreau
Director General, Adult Education, Robert Diamant
Director, Private Education, Denis Olivier

Associated Agencies

Superior Council of Education
President, Claude Benjamin, 2050 St-Cyrille ouest, Québec, P.Q. G1V 2K8
Council of (Que.) Universities
Presidente, Mme Paule Leduc, 2700, boul. Laurier, Ste-Foy, P.Q.
Private Education Advisory Com.
President, Jean-Yves Drolet, Education Faculty, Laval Univ., Ste-Foy, P.Q.

EMERGENCY MEASURES (Bureau de la protection civile du Québec)

1200, route de l'Eglise, 2e étage, Ste-Foy, P.Q. G1V 4M1
(418) 643-4776

DEPT. OF ENERGY & RESOURCES

200 Chemin Ste-Foy, Québec, P.Q. G1R 4X7
Information Contact, J.-C. de LaDurantaye, Director, Communication Service (418/643-8060)

Acts Administered

Lands & Forests Act
An Act to Amend the Lands & Forests Act
Forest Resources Utilization Act
Farmers & Settlers Pulpwood Sales Price Act
Tree Protection Act
Timber-Driving Companies Act
Cullers Act
Forestry School & Research Act
Forestry Merit Act
Geographical Commission Act
Cadastre Act
Certain Electoral Districts Land Titles Act
Québec Wood Salvage, Logging & Forest Development Co. Act
An Act respecting the Acquisition of Certain Forest Land
An Act to Assure the Protection of the Forest Resources of the Province
Charter of the Québec Cartography Co.
An Act respecting Ecological Reserves
Forestry Credit Act
Natural Resources Dept. Act
Energy & Electricity Act
Mining Act
Mining Duties Act
Petroleum Products Commerce Act
Raw Metal Sales Act

MINISTER, Yves L. Duhaime
Deputy Minister, Jean-Noel Poulin

Assoc. Deputy Minister (Energy), Richard Pouliot, 1050 St-Augustin (643-3724)
Assoc. Deputy Minister (Lands & Forests), J. Claude Mercier (643-5032)
Assoc. Deputy Minister (Mines), Charles E. Beaulieu (643-4617)
Asst. Deputy Ministers:
(Forests), P.-P. Légaré, 643-7048
(Territorial Domaine), Maurice Duval, 643-4685
(Energy Saving & New Energy Development), Renaud Lapierre, 643-3724
(Mineral & Geological Research), A.F. Laurin, 643-4617
(Mines Exploration & Development), André Dorr, 643-7760
Director General, Administration, André Lachance
Director General, Territorial Domaine, Maurice Duval
Technical Surveys, Michel Paradis
Legal Surveys, Paul Nadeau
Lands Management, Germain Girard
Director General, Forests, P.-P. Légaré
Director General, Regional Operations, Jacques Caron

Associated Agencies

Ecological Reserve Advisory Board
2700 rue Einstein, Québec, P.Q. G1P 3W8
(418) 643-7606
Secretary, Gilles Gagnon
Electricity & Gas Board
2100 Drummond, Montréal, P.Q. H3G 1X1
(514) 873-2452
Secretary, M.B. Boissonnault
Rexfor
1195 ave de La Vigerie, Ste-Foy, P.Q. G1V 4N3
(418) 659-4530
President, Michel Duchesneau
SDBJ (Société de developpement de la Baie James)
800 boul. de Maisonneuve est, #2300, Montréal, P.Q. H2L 4M6
(514) 284-0270
President, Charles Boulva
Director, Information & Public Relations, Jacques Gauthier
Société du Cartographie (Que. Cartography Co.)
1995 ouest boul. Charest, Ste-Foy, P.Q. G1N 4H9
(418) 773-8426
Director, Grégoire Girard
SOQUEM (Société québécoise d'exploration minière)
3108 Chemin Ste-Foy, Ste-Foy, P.Q. G1X 1P8
(418) 658-5400
President, P.J. Bourassa
Société National de l'amiante (Asbestos Office): 850 Ouellet Blvd. ouest, Thetford Mines, P.Q. G6G 7A5, President, Daniel Perlstein
SOQUIP (Société québécoise d'initiatives pétrolières)
3340 de la Pérade, Ste-Foy, P.Q. G1X 2L7
(418) 651-9543
President, Pierre Martin

DEPT. OF ENVIRONMENT

2360 chemin Ste-Foy, Québec, P.Q. G1V 4H2
Information Contact, Suzanne Beaulieu, Direction des communications et de l'education (418/643-6071)

MINISTER, Marcel Léger
Deputy Minister, André Caillé, 643-7860
Asst. Deputy Minister, Administration, J.-Y. Babin
Asst. Deputy Minister, Central Operations, B. Harvey
Asst. Deputy Minister, Regional Operations, G. Théberge
Environmental Protection, Guy Audet, 643-7456
Ecological Reserves, Léopold Gaudreau, 1640 boul. de l'Entente, 643-5397
Water Quality Improvement, Gaston Couillard, 643-4630
(includes services for urban, agricultural, industrial, lakes & rivers, hydraulic locks, public works)
Air & Lands Quality Improvement, Jean-A. Roy, 643-4336
(includes air improvement, dangerous wastes, land management, industrial hygiene)

Conseil consultatif de l'environnement

(Environment Advisory Council)
1020 rue St-Augustin, Québec, P.Q. G1R 4Z4
President, Réal L'Heureux, 643-3818

DEPT. OF FINANCE

1025, St-Augustin, Québec, P.Q. G1R 4Z6
Information Contact, Director, Communications (phone: 418-643-4426)

Acts Administered

Financial Admin. Act
Charter of the Qué. Deposit & Investment Fund
Public Curatorship Act
Lotteries & Races Act (Division IV)
Deposit Act

MINISTER, Jacques Parizeau
Deputy Minister, Michel Caron
Asst. Deputy Minister, Finance, Gilles Tremblay
Asst. Deputy Minister, Fiscal Policy, Michel Grignon
Asst. Deputy Minister, Research, Denis Bédard
Asst. Deputy Minister, Special Projects, Michel Labonté
Asst. Deputy Minister, (Comptroller), Guy Langlois
Public Curator, Rémi Lussier, Tour de la bourse, C.P. 51, Montreal, P.Q. H4Z 1J6 (873-4074)
Administration, Director, André Montminy

Treasury Board

President, Yves Bérubé
Secretary, Robert Tessier

Associated Agencies

Caisse de dépôt et placement du Qué. (Que. Deposit & Investment Fund), 1200, Tour de la bourse, Montreal, P.Q. H4Z 1B4 (514/873-2460)
Société des loteries et courses du Qué., 1 Parc Samuel Holland, Ste. 145, Quebec, P.Q. G1S 4M6 (418/643-8996); and, 2000, rue Berri, Montreal, P.Q. H2L 4N5

DEPT. OF FINANCIAL INSTITUTIONS & CO-OPERATIVES

800, place d'Youville, Québec, P.Q. G1R 4Y5
(also, 800 place Victoria, Montréal, P.Q.)
Information Contact, T.-L. Simard, Director, Communication Service (phone: 418/643-8695)

Acts Administered

Automobile Insurance Board Act
Automobile Insurance Act
"Caisses d'Entraide économique" (An Act respecting the)
Cemetery Companies Act
Church Incorporation Act
Collection Agents Act
Companies Act
Companies Information Act
Co-operative Agricultural Associations Act
Co-operative Associations Act
Co-operative Development Society Act
Co-operative Syndicates Act
Extra-Provincial Companies Act
Fabrique Act
Fish & Game Clubs Act
Gas, Water & Electricity Companies Act
Guarantee Companies Act
Insurance Act
Insurance Brokers Act
Loan & Investment Societies Act
Mineral Exploration Partnerships Act
Mining Companies Act
Mortmain Act
National Benefit Societies Act
Professional Syndicates Act
Quebec Deposit Insurance Act

Real Estate Brokerage Act
Religious Corporations Act
Roman Catholic Cemetery Corporations Act
Roman Catholic Bishops Act
Savings & Credit Unions Act
Securities Act
Special Corporate Powers Act
Telegraph & Telephone Companies Act
Trust Companies Act

MINISTER, Jacques Parizeau
Deputy Minister, Jean-Marie Bouchard
Assoc. Deputy Minister, Adrien Rioux
Asst. Deputy Ministers, Victor P. Guerci, Jacques Roy, André Delisle
Co-operative Associations Service, Marc Jean
Insurance Service, Jacques Roy
Deposit Insurance Board, President, J.-M. Bouchard
Savings & Credit Unions Service, Roger Lequy
Quebec Securities Commission, Chairman, Gérald Lacoste
Companies Service, Hubert Gaudry
Trust & Finance Companies Service, Alfred Vaillancourt
Real Estate Brokerage Service, Paul Guy
Central File of Business Enterprises, vacant, 643-6847
Management Service, Gilles Beaulieu
Communication Service, T.-L. Simard
Inspection Service, G.-A. Prenovost

QUEBEC HEALTH INSURANCE BOARD

1125, chemin Saint-Louis, Sillery (C.P. 6600, Quebec, P.Q. G1K 7T3)
President & Director General, Dr. Martin Laberge
Secretary, Paul-Emile Lafrance
Director, Communications, Jacques Duguay (643-9401)

QUEBEC HEALTH RESEARCH FOUNDATION (Fonds de la recherche en santé du Québec)

1851 est, rue Sherbrooke, #1101, Montreal, P.Q. H2K 4L5
(514) 873-2114
Président, Louis Poirier, M.D.
Scientific Secretary, Gilles Leboeuf, M.D.
Executive Secretary, Yvon Poirier

DEPT. OF HOUSING & CONSUMER PROTECTION

1045 de la Chevrotière, 7e étage (Tour), Québec, P.Q. G1R 5E9
(418) 643-3360
MINISTER, Guy Tardif

Agencies

Consumer Protection Bureau
6 rue de l'Université, Québec, P.Q. G1R 5G8
(418) 643-1557
Director, P.B. Meunier

Quebec Rental Board (Régie du logement)
1, rue Notre Dame est, bur. 1180, Montréal, P.Q. H5B 1A4
(514) 873-6575
Chairman, Claude Chapdelaine

Quebec Housing Corp. (Société d'habitation du Québec)
3 place Desjardins, Tour nord, 25e étage, Montréal, P.Q. H2Y 1B6
(514) 873-8278
Chairman, Jean-Marie Couture

HYDRO-QUEBEC

75 Dorchester Blvd. W., Montreal, P.Q. H2Z 1A4
(514) 289-2211
President & Chief Executive Officer, R.A. Boyd, Eng.
Subsidiaries:
Hydro-Québec International, 870 de Maisonneuve Blvd. E., Montreal, P.Q. H2L 4S8, President & Chief Executive Officer, Guy Monty, Eng.
Société d'énergie de la Baie James (SEBJ), 800 de Maisonneuve Blvd. E., Montreal, P.Q. H2L 4M8, 514/844-3741; President & Chief Executive Officer, Claude Laliberté, Eng.

DEPT. OF INDUSTRY, TRADE & TOURISM

1, Place Ville-Marie, 23rd floor, Montréal, P.Q. H3B 3M6
710, Place d'Youville, Québec, P.Q. G1R 4Y4
Information Contact, Director, Communications, Québec (phone: 418/643-5084)

Acts Administered

Industry, Trade & Tourism Act, 1979
Bureau of Statistics Act
Industrial Development Assistance Act
An Act respecting the Centre de recherche industrielle du Québec
An Act respecting the Société des alcools du Québec
An Act respecting the establishment of an integrated steel complex by Sidbec
An Act respecting the Société du parc industriel du centre du Québec
An Act respecting the Société du parc industriel et commercial aéroportuaire de Mirabel
An Act respecting the Société générale de financement du Québec
An Act respecting the Société Inter-Port de Québec
An Act to establish the Institut national de productivité
Industrial Funds Act
An Act respecting corporations for the development of Québec business firms
An Act respecting fiscal incentives to industrial development
An Act respecting assistance for tourist development
Hotels Act
Commercial Establishments Business Hours Act
An Act respecting stuffing & upholstered & stuffed articles

MINISTER, Rodrigue Biron
Executive Asst., Adrien Ouellet
Deputy Minister, Claude Descoteaux
Asst. Deputy Ministers, Michel Audet, Marcel Bergeron, Patrick Hyndman, Maurice Turgeon, Ronald Clark, Christian Latortue, Michel Archambault

Regional Delegates

Regional Offices are located at Rimouski, New Carlisle, Jonquière, Québec, Montmagny, St-Georges-de-Beauce, Trois-Rivières, Victoriaville, Sherbrooke, St-Jérôme, Longueuil, Montréal, Hull, Noranda, Hauterive, Laval

Economic Counsellors

Edmonton, Alta.: Bureau du Québec, 10010 106 St., 10th floor, Edmonton, Alta. T5J 3L8. Economic Counsellor, Gaston Provencher (403/423-6651) Telex: 03742811
Toronto, Ont.: Bureau du Québec, 20th floor, Commerce Court North, Box 391, Commerce Court Postal Stn., Toronto, Ont. M5L 1G3. Economic Counsellor, Guy Leblanc (416/868-1754), Telex: 0622071
Atlanta, Ga., U.S.A.: Délégation du Québec, Peachtree Center Tower, Ste. 1501, 230 Peachtree St. N.W., Atlanta, Ga. 30303. Economic Counsellor, Albert Brull (404/581-0488), Telex: 0054-2689
Boston, Mass., U.S.A.: Délégation du Québec, 100 Franklin St., 4th floor, Boston, Mass. 02116. Economic Counsellor, Bertin Tremblay (617/426-2660), Telex: 00940683
Chicago, Ill., U.S.A.: Délégation du Québec, 35 E. Wacker St., Ste. 2052, Chicago, Ill. 60601. Economic Counsellor, Serge Bouchard (312/726-0681), Telex: 00254339
Dallas, Tex., U.S.A.: Délégation du Québec, 900 Adolphus Tower, 1412 Main St., Dallas, Tex. 75202. Economic Counsellor, Jacques Wanner (214/742-6095), Telex: 00730055
Los Angeles, Ca., U.S.A.: Délégation du Québec, 700 South Flower St., Ste. 1520, Los Angeles, Cal. 90014. Economic Counsellor, Robert Jones (213/689-4861), Telex: 00677620
New York, N.Y., U.S.A.: Délégation générale du Québec, 17 W. 50th St., Rockefeller Center, New York, N.Y. 10020. Economic Counsellor, Louis Granger (212/397-0200), Telex: 00126405
Brussels, Belgium: Délégation générale du Québec, ave des Arts 46, 7e étage, 1040 Brussels, Belgium. Economic Counsellor, Gilles Dault (011-32-2) 512.00.36), Telex: 46.25276

Caracas, Venezuela: Délégation du Québec, Edificio ABA, piso, App 2736, Calle Vera Cruz, Las Mercedes, Caracas 1010A, Venezuela. Economic Counsellor, Camil Côté (011-58-2) 913.831, Telex: 23491

Dusseldorf, Germany: Délégation du Québec, Konigsallee 30, Ko-Center, 4000 Dusseldorf 1, Germany. Economic Counsellor, Norbert Arsenault (011-49-211) (32.08.16), Telex: 41.8587659

London, Eng.: Délégation générale du Québec, 12 Upper Grosvenor St., London W1X 9PA, Eng. Economic Counsellor, Michel Gélinas (629.4155), Telex: 51.261618

Milan, Italy: Délégation du Québec, Via Piccinni no. 2, 4 Piano, 20131 Milan, Italy. Economic Counsellor, Yves Cousineau (011-39-2) 208.204, Telex: 43.334163

Paris, France: Délégation générale du Québec, 66, rue Pergolèse, 75116 Paris, France. Economic Counsellor, Richard Tremblay (011.33-1) (502.1410), Telex: 42.620401

Tokyo, Japan: Délégation du Québec, Ste. 501, Sanno Grand Bldg., 14-2 Nagata-cho, 2-Chome, Chiyoda-Ku, Tokyo 100, Japan. Economic Counsellor, Paul Trahan (011-81-3) (581.4618), Telex: 722.3842

Mexico: Délégation du Québec, Taine #411, Colonia Polanco, Mexico D.F. Economic Counsellor, Reinhard Neubauer (905/250-8222), Telex: 22.170976

Agencies Responsible to Minister of Industry & Commerce

Centre de recherche industrielle du Québec (Industrial Research Centre)
C.P. 9038, Ste-Foy, P.Q. G1V 4C7
(418) 659-1550
245, Hymus Blvd., Pointe-Claire, P.Q. H9R 4S6
(514) 694-3330
President & General Manager, Guy Bertrand

Société de développement industriel du Québec (Que. Industrial Development Corp.)
1126 Chemin St-Louis, Ste. 700, Place Sillery, Quebec, P.Q. G1S 1E5
(418) 643-5172
Tour de la Bourse, 800 Place Victoria, Ste. 4205, Montréal, P.Q. H4Z 1E8
(514) 873-4375
President & General Manager, François Lebrun

Le Groupe SGF (Société générale de financement) (General Investment Corp.)
680 Sherbrooke ouest, Ste. 800, Montréal, P.Q. H3A 2M7
(514) 288-5764
President & General Manager, Guy Coulombe

Sidbec
507, Place d'Armes, Montreal, P.Q. H2Y 2W8
(514) 392-7771
Chairman of the Board, President & Chief Executive Officer, Robert De Coster
Sidbec-Dosco: 507, Place d'Armes, Montreal, P.Q. H2Y 2W8, 514/392-7771, Chairman of the Board & Chief Executive Officer, Robert De Coster; President & Chief Operating Officer, Gilles Charette, 392-6532
Sidbec-Normines: 440, Dorchester Blvd. W., Ste. 1401, Montreal, P.Q. H2Z 1V7, 514/875-2533, President, Cyrille Dufresne

La Société des alcools du Québec (SAQ) (Que. Liquor Corp.)
905 de Lorimier, Montréal, P.Q. H2K 3V9
(514) 873-3816
President & General Manager, Daniel Wermenlinger
and 2900 rue Einstein, Ste-Foy, P.Q. G1K 7N3 (418/643-4321)

La Société du parc industriel et commercial aéroportuaire de Mirabel (SPICAM)
1200 McGill College, Ste. 2120, Montréal, P.Q. H3B 4G7
(514) 878-1110
Vice President, Jacques Rostenne

La Société Inter-Port de Québec
17, St-Louis, Québec, P.Q. G1R 3Y8
(418) 643-8713
General Manager, Ghislain Girard

Société du parc industriel du centre du Québec (SPICQ) (Central Que. Industrial Park Corp.)
1000 7e rue, Bécancour, P.Q. G0X 1B0
(809) 294-6656
Managing Director, Roland Leclerc

Institut national de productivité
1 Complexe Desjardins, C.P. 157, bur 1509, Tour sud, Montréal, P.Q. H5B 1B3
(514) 873-7601
General Manager, Fernand Gauthier

Conseil du Tourisme
614 Grande Allée est, Québec, P.Q. G1R 2K5
(418) 643-4468
Secretary General, André Paquette

DEPT. OF INTERGOVERNMENTAL AFFAIRS

1225, Place Georges V, Québec City, P.Q. G1R 4Z7
Information Contact, Director of Communications (phone: 418-643-3044)

Acts Administered

Intergovernmental Affairs Dept. Act
Agents General & Delegates General Act

MINISTER, Claude Morin
Deputy Minister, Robert Normand
Asst. Deputy Minister for International Affairs, Jean Chapdelaine
Director of Admin., Gilbert L'Heureux

Offices in Canada, U.S. and Abroad

Abidjan: Raymond Bégin, Bureau du Québec, a/s Ambassade du Canada, 01-B.P. 4104, Abidjan 01, Côte d'Ivoire. Tél: 32-20-09, Télex: 983593 (DOMCAN ABIDJAN)

Atlanta: Jean-Marc Roy, Délégation du Québec, Peachtree Center, #1501, 230 Peachtree St. N.W., Atlanta, Georgia 30303, U.S.A. Tél: (404) 581-0488, Télex: 54-26-89

Boston: Jacques Vallée, Délégation du Québec, 100 Franklin St., 4th floor, Boston, Mass. 02109, U.S.A. Tél: (617) 426-2660, Télex: 00940683 (Québec BSN)

Bruxelles: Jean-Marc Léger, Délégation générale du Québec, Avenue des Arts 46, 1040 Bruxelles, Belgique. Tél: (9-011-32-2) 512-0036, Télex: 4625276 (QUEBRU B)

Buenos Aires: Service d'immigration du Québec, a/s Ambassade du Canada, Casilla de Correo 1598, Buenos Aires, Argentine. Tél: (01-329081) (82 à 88), Télex: 3321383 (AR CANAD)

Caracas: Gérard Frigon, Délégation du Québec, Edificio ABA, 4e étage, Apartado 2736, Caracas 1010A, Venezuela. Tél: 011582 - 913831. Télex: (31) 23491 (ORIVECA)

Chicago: Gérard Vézina, Délégation du Québec, 35 E. Wacker Dr., #2052, Chicago, Ill. 60601, U.S.A. Tél: (312) 726-0681. Télex: 00254339 (QUEBEC GOV. CGO)

Dallas: Délégation du Québec, Adolphus Tower #900, 1412 Main St., Dallas, Texas 75202, U.S.A. Tél: (214) 742-6095, Télex: 00730112 (WU TELTEX DAL)

Dusseldorf: Albert Jessop, Délégation du Québec, Donigsallee 30, Ko-Center, 4 Dusseldorf, Allemagne. Tél: 0211-32-08-16, Télex: 418587659 (QUED D)

Edmonton: Bureau du Québec, 10010 106th St., 10th floor, Edmonton, Alta. T5J 3L8. Tél: (403) 423-6651, Télex: 03742811 (GOVTQUE EDM)

Hong Kong: Bureau d'immigration du Québec, a/s Commission for Canada, 14th floor, Asian House, 1 Hennessy Rd., B.P. 20264, Hennessy Road PO, Hong Kong. Tél: 283-861, Télex: 73391 (DOMCAN)

Lafayette: Marc Boucher, Délégation du Québec, Box 4011, 303 ouest rue Vermilion, Lafayette, Louisiane 70502, U.S.A. Tél: (318) 232-8080, Télex: 00586684 (QUEBEC GOV LFY)

Lisbonne: Service d'immigration du Québec, a/s Ambassade du Canada, 14-5 Praça Marquiz de Pombal, Lisbonne 1298, Portugal. Tél: 53-70-38, Télex: 12377 (DOMCAN)

Londres: Gilles Loiselle, Délégation générale du Québec, 12 Upper Grosvenor St., Londres W.1, England. Tél: 629-4155, Télex: 51261618 (QUELON LDN)

Los Angeles: Yves Labonté, Délégation du Québec, 700 South Flower St., #1520, Los Angeles, Calif. 90017, U.S.A. Tél: (213) 689-4861, Télex: 00677620 (QUELA LSA)
Mexico: Henri Dorion, Délégation générale du Québec, Taine 411, Polanco, Mexico 5 D.F., Mexico. Tél: 250-8208
Milan: Jean Martucci, Délégation du Québec, Via Piccinni no 2, 20131 Milano, Italie. Tél: (02) 208-204, Télex: 26163 (QUELANO)
Moncton: C.-H. Dubé, Bureau du Québec, Place l'Assomption Comp. 6009, 770 Main St., Moncton, N.B. E1C 1E7. Tél: (506) 382-7851, Télex: 0142168 (GOUVQUE MCTN)
New York: Richard Pouliot, Délégation générale du Québec, 17 W. 50th St., Rockefeller Center, New York, N.Y. 10020, U.S.A. Tel: (212) 397-0200, Télex: 00126405 (QUEBEC GOVT NYK)
Paris: Yves Michaud, Délégation générale du Québec, 66 rue Pergolèse, Paris 75116, France. Tél: 502-1410, Télex: 4262401 (DELEBEC PARIS)
Port-au-Prince: Délégation du Québec, B.P. 2243, Port-au-Prince, Haiti, W.1. Tél: 5-3102, Télex: 2033490280 (DELG-PAP)
Rome: Service d'immigration du Québec, a/s Ambassade du Canada, Bureau des visas, 30 via Zara, Rome, Italie. Tél: 844-0158, Télex: 4361056 (DOMCAN)
Tokyo: Paul Trahan, Délégation du Québec, Sanno Grand Bldg., #501, 14-2 Nagata-cho-2-chome, Chiyoda-ku, Tokyo, Japon. Tél: 581-4618, Télex: J23842 (TOKEBEC)
Toronto: Jean-Marc Blondeau, Bureau du Québec, Commerce Court North, 20th floor, Box 391, Toronto, Ont. M5L 1G3. Tél: (416) 868-1754, Télex: 0622071 (GOVTQUE TOR)
Washington: Louis B. Parent, Bureau du tourisme du Québec, 2033 Main St. N.W., 4th floor, Washington, D.C. 20036, U.S.A. Tél: (202) 659-8990, Télex: 00892731 (QUEBEC WSH)

DEPT. OF JUSTICE

1200 rte de l'Eglise, 9e étage, Ste-Foy, P.Q. G1V 4M1
Information Contact, Mme Micheline Bouzigon, Directrice des Communications (phone: 418-643-5140)

Acts Administered

Access to Justice (Act to promote)
Advisory Council on Justice Act
Attorney General's Prosecutors Act
Bailiffs Act
Change of Name Act
Civil Marriage (An Act Respecting)
Civil Protection Act
Civil Status Registers Reconstitution Act
Collecting Agents Act
Conciliation between Lessees & Property Owners Act
Coroners Act
Courts of Justice Act
Crime Victims Compensation Act
Criminal Cases Recognizance Act
Crown Witnesses Payment Act
Declaratory Judgments of Death (An Act Respecting)
Detective or Security Agencies Act
Disorderly Houses Act
Excessive Increases of Rent in 1973 (An Act to Prevent)
Explosives (An Act Concerning)
Expo 67 Public Security Maintenance Act
Expropriation Act
Fines Payment Act
Fire Investigations Act
Highway Code
Insurance Act
Interpretation Act
Jury Act
Justice Dept. Act
Lease of Things (An Act Respecting)
Legal Aid Act
Liquor Permit Control Commission Act
Lotteries & Races Act
Magistrates' Privileges Act
Matrimonial Regimes (An Act Respecting)
Municipal Courts Act
Officers of Justice Salary Act
Penal Actions Act
Police Act
Probation & Houses of Detention Act
Publications & Public Morals Act
Que. Liquor Corp. Act
Que. Police Force Syndical Plan (An Act Respecting The)
Reciprocal Enforcement of Maintenance Orders Act
Registry Office Act
Sheriff's Act
Stamps Act
Stenographers' Act
Summary Convictions Act
Tear Bomb Act
Theatrical Performances Act
Transport Act
Youth Protection Act

MINISTER, Marc-André Bédard
Deputy Minister, Daniel Jacoby, 643-4090
Assoc. Deputy Ministers, P.-A. Gendreau, Rémy Bouchard, Germain Halley, A.-F. Bisson, Clément Ménard, Me Jacques Lachapelle, Pierre Verdon
Director, Civil Law, vacant, 643-8405

Death certificates ($2) are available from Ministère de la Justice, Registre de référence, 117 rue St-André, Québec, P.Q. G1K 373, 418/643-6436. Birth and marriage certificates are issued by the Civil Archives of the Judicial District where the event was registered. Also $2. Contact the Central Office at 117 rue St-André for a list of the 32 offices in Quebec.

Associated Agencies

Que. Police Commission
2050, St-Cyrille ouest, Ste-Foy, P.Q. G1V 2K8
(418) 643-7897
President, Juge Roger Gosselin
Liquor Permit Board (Régie des permis d'alcool du Québec)
1 est Notre Dame, Ste. 9.200, Montreal, P.Q. H2Y 1B6
(514) 873-3577
Legal Services Commission (Commission des services juridiques)
2 Complexe Desjardins, Tour de l'Est, Bur. 1404, Montreal, P.Q. H5B 1B3
(514) 873-3562
President, Yves Lafontaine
Secretary, Jacques Lemaitre-Auger
Youth Protection Committee (Comité de la protection de la jeunesse)
505 boul. Dorchester ouest, Montreal, P.Q. H2Z 1A8
(514) 873-5428
President, Jacques Tellier
Justice Advisory Council
President, Henri Grondin, 1 Parc Samuel Holland, bur. 2340, Québec, P.Q. G1S 4P2 (418/687-3233)
Bureau du Code Civil
10 rue St-Antoine, bur. 635, Montréal, P.Q. H2Y 1A2
(514) 873-2375
Juge Gérard Trudel, responsable
Commission des droits de la personne
360 rue St-Jacques, bur. 611, Montréal, P.Q. H2Y 1P5
(514) 873-5146
Société québécoise d'information juridique
1 rue Notre-Dame est, bur. 1200, Montréal, P.Q. H2Y 1B6
(514) 873-8206
President, Claude Tellier
Sûreté du Québec
1701 rue Parthenais, bur. 701, Montréal, P.Q. H2K 3S7
(514) 395-4161
Director General, Jacques Beaudoin
Institut de police de Nicolet
350 rue d'Youville, Nicolet, P.Q. J0G 1E0
(819) 293-4545

Director, Marcel Vermette
Institut de médicine et de police scientifique (forensic science)
1701 rue Parthenais, 5e étage, Montréal, P.Q. H2K 3S7
(514) 873-2718
Director, Bernard Péclet
Bureau de la protection civile du Québec
1200 rte de l'Eglise, 2e étage, Ste-Foy, P.Q. G1V 4M1
(418) 643-2387
P.-A. Brown, responsable
Tribunal de la jeunesse
1281 boul. Charest ouest, Québec, P.Q. G1M 2C9
(418) 643-4295
Juge en chef, Jean Rouillard
Commission de refonte des lois et des réglements (Law Reform)
1200 rte de l'Eglise, Ste-Foy, P.Q. G1V 4M1
(418) 643-4808
President, Roch Rioux
Commission de la Representation
3460 rue La Pérade, Ste-Foy, P.Q. G1X 3Y5
(418) 643-9870

LABOUR, MANPOWER & INCOME SECURITY DEPT.

425 St-Amable, Québec, P.Q. G1R 4Z1
255, Crémazie Blvd. E., Montreal, P.Q. H2M 1L5
Information Contact, Director, Communications (phone: 418/643-8078)

Acts Administered

Admin. & Consultation
Labour & Manpower Dept. Act
Advisory Council on Labour & Manpower Act (Council)
Working Conditions
Labour Code
An Act respecting labour standards (CNT)
Construction Industry Labour Relations Act
Collective Agreement Decrees Act
National Holiday Act
Public Safety & Wage Security
Industrial & Commercial Establishments Act
Public Buildings Safety Act
Workmen's Compensation Act (WCC)
An Act respecting indemnities for victims of asbestosis and silicosis in mines and quarries (WCC)
Pressure Vessels Act
Scaffolding Inspection Act
Lightning Rods Act
Vocational Training & Control
Manpower Vocational Training & Qualification Act
Electricians & Electrical Installations Act
Master Electricians Act
Pipe-Mechanics Act
Master Pipe-Mechanics Act
Placement
Employment Bureaus Act

MINISTER, Pierre Marois
Deputy Minister, J.T. Boudreau
Assoc. Deputy Minister, A. Ouellet
Asst. Deputy Ministers, Yvan Blain; Réjean Parent; P.-Y. Vachon; Guy Lapointe
Labour Commissioner General, Robert Levac
Labour Relations, Director, Raymond Désilets
Conciliation & Arbitration, Micheline Maheux
Labour Standards, Director, Louis J. Lemieux
Manpower, Director, Roger Pelletier (int.)
Inspection, Director, Gérard Pedneault
Consulting Engineers, Eugène Arrelle
Plans Approval Service, Pierre Masson
Electrical Installations Inspection Service, Roger Morin
Plumbing Inspection Service, Rémi Sauvé
Public Buildings Inspection Service, Georges-A. Paquet
Research Centre, Director, Réjean Parent
Personnel, Director, Marc A. Laliberté
Communications, Director, Denis Tanguay (a.i.)

Labour Related Bodies

Labour Standards Commission
(Commission des normes du travail (CNT))
750, Charest Blvd. E., Québec, P.Q. G1K 7Z5
(418) 643-4936
President, vacant
Advisory Council on Labour & Manpower
255, Crémazie Blvd. E., Montreal, P.Q. H2M 1L5
(514) 873-5114
Secretary, Romuald Dufour
and 425 St-Amable, Québec, P.Q. G1R 4Z1 (418/643-9193), President, Raymond Parent
Construction Office (Office de la Construction du Qué.)
3530 Jean Talon St. W., Montreal, P.Q. H3R 2G3
Chairman, Jean-Yves Gagnon (514/341-7740)
Branches at: 825 Ste-Thérèse St., Quebec, P.Q. G1N 1S6; and, 4850, Metropolitain blvd., Montreal, P.Q. H1S 2Z7
Régie des Entreprises de Construction du Que.
1100 Cremazie Blvd. E., Montreal, P.Q. H2P 2X2
(514) 725-9321
President, Gaétan Dufour
Commission de formation professionnelle
1010 rue Borne, Québec, P.Q. G1N 1L9
(418) 687-3540
President, Gaston Clermont

OFFICE DE LA LANGUE FRANCAISE

700, boul. St-Cyrille est, 2e étage, Québec, P.Q. G1R 5G7 (418/643-1908)
800, square Victoria, 16e étage, Montreal, P.Q. H4Z 1G8 (514 873-6565)
Président, Raymond Gosselin (Montreal)
Vice président, Jean-G. Lavigne (Montreal)
Président de la Commission de toponymie (Geographical Commission), François Beaudin (Quebec)
Secrétaire, P.-A. Chouinard (Montreal)
Directeur de la Banque de terminologie, J.-M. Fortin (Quebec)

DEPT. OF MUNICIPAL AFFAIRS

Bldg. G, 1039 Chevrotière, Québec City, P.Q. G1R 4Z3
Information Contact, Director, Communications, 1275 boul. Charest ouest (phone: 418-643-3955)

Acts Administered

An Act to enable municipalities to tax certain educational establishments
An Act to enable municipalities to tax hospital centres and reception centres
Act to Grant Special Subsidies to municipalities of 10,000 inhabitants and over
Act respecting the vicinity of the new international airport
Cities & Towns Act
Dept. of Municipal Affairs Act
Destitution of Municipal Officers Act
Family Housing Act
Fire Prevention Act
Industrial Funds Act
Interdiction of Municipal Subsidies Act
Intermunicipal Fire Prevention Act
Mining Towns Act
Mining Villages Act
Mont Sainte Anne Park Vicinity Act
Municipal Code
Municipal Commission Act
Municipal Concessions Act
Municipal Fraud & Corruption Act
Municipal Justice Courts Act
Municipal & School Debentures & Borrowing Act
Municipal & School Tax Payment Act
Municipal Services Sales Act
Municipal Tax Exemption Act
Municipal Winter Works Act

Municipal Works Act
Municipality of the North Shore of the Gulf of St. Lawrence Act
New Que. International Airport Development Act
Organization of Certain Areas into Municipalities Act
Peddlers Act
Public Libraries Act
Public Street Act
Que. Housing Corp. Act
Real Property Assessment Act
Regroupment of Municipalities Act
Road Construction Assistance Act

MINISTER, Jacques Léonard
Deputy Minister, Patrick Kenniff
Asst. Deputy Ministers, J.-L. Lapointe; Paul Laliberté; Michel Lucier
Communications Service, Director, P.-R. Chantelois

Associated Agencies

Quebec Municipal Commission
1039 de la Chevrotière, Edifice G, 29e étage, Québec, P.Q. G1R 4Z3
(418) 643-2046
President, Juge Richard Beaulieu
Outaouais Management Board
768 boul. St-Joseph, Hull, P.Q. J8X 3Y5
(819) 770-1500
President, Robert Blais
Office for the Settlement of Disputed Claims (Révision de l'évaluation)
3 Complexe Desjardins, 27e étage, C.P. 125, Montréal, P.Q. H5B 1A4
(514) 873-4083
President, Yvon Genest
and 800 place d'Youville, 9e étage, Québec, P.Q. G1R 3P4
National Management Commission
150 St-Cyrille est, place de la Capitale, 8e étage, Québec, P.Q. G1R 2B1
(418) 643-8358
President, Jean-Marc Rivest

OUTAOUAIS DEVELOPMENT CORP. (Société d'aménagement de l'Outaouais)

Maison du Citoyen, 25 rue Laurier (C.P. 1666, Hull, P.Q. J8X 3Y5)
(819) 770-1500
Chairman & General Manager, Roger Blais
Secretary, Guy Gagnon
Director, Admin. & Finance, Richard Roussel
Director, Industrial & Commercial Expansion, Normand Bégin
Director, Marketing & Tourism, vacant
Director, Operations, Louis Tourville
Director, Engineering & Construction, Léon Martin

QUEBEC PLANNING & DEVELOPMENT BUREAU

Complexe G, Bloc 2, 1er étage, 1060 rue Conroy, Québec, P.Q. G1R 5E6
President & Director General, Hugues Morrissette (418/643-3285)
Director, Finance, Paul Fecteau (643-5367)

PUBLIC PROTECTOR (Le Protecteur du Citoyen)

14, rue Haldimand, Québec City, P.Q. G1R 4N4 (phone: 418-643-2688)
5199 rue Sherbrooke est, #2931, Montréal, P.Q. H1T 3X2 (phone: 514-253-1944)
Public Protector, Mme Luce Patenaude

PUBLIC SERVICE COMMISSION (Office du recrutement et de la sélection du personnel de la fonction publique du Québec)

1050, rue Conroy, Québec, P.Q. G1R 4Z8
Président, Claude Bélanger
Members, Mrs. Lyne Fournier, Jean Mercier
Secretary, Jean-Marc Ducharme (418/643-9932)

DEPT. OF PUBLIC WORKS & SUPPLY

475, St-Amable, Québec City, P.Q. G1R 4X9
Information Contact, Information Service (phone: 418-643-6430)

Acts Administered

Government Supply Branch Act
Public Works & Supply Dept. Act
Public Works Act
Que. Real Estate Development Corp. Act

MINISTER, Alain Marcoux
Deputy Minister, Pierre Sarault
Asst. Deputy Ministers, Jean-Claude Careau; Jean Taillon; Lorain Groleau
Law Officer, Gerald Roiter
Accountant, Etienne Genest

Associated Agencies

Que. Real Estate Development Corp./Société de Développement immobilier du Québec (SODEVIQ)
475, St-Amable, Quebec, P.Q. G1R 4X9
(418) 643-1259
President, Jean-Claude Careau

QUEBEC OFFICIAL PUBLISHER

1283, boul. Charest ouest, Québec, P.Q. G1N 2C9
(418) 643-5150
Publisher, Pierre A. Deschênes

DEPT. OF RECREATION, FISH & GAME

150 est, boul. St-Cyrille, Québec, P.Q. G1R 4Y3
Information: (418) 643-3127

Acts Administered

Recreation, Fish & Game Act
Wildlife Conservation Act
Provincial Parks Act
Fish & Game Clubs Act
Migratory Birds Convention Act

MINISTER, Lucien Lessard
Deputy Minister, Pierre Le François, 643-2207
Asst. Deputy Minister, Administration, J.-G. Houde, 643-8452
Asst. Deputy Minister, Equipment, Jacques Lefebvre, 643-2205
Asst. Deputy Minister, Recreation, Pierre Bernier, 643-3250
Asst. Deputy Minister, Regional Operations, Michel Noel De Tilly, 643-2465
Asst. Deputy Minister, Parks, Pierre Boucher, 643-2207
Director, Planning, Pierre Lefebvre, 643-8766
Director, Communications, Benoit Roy, 643-2984
Director General, Equipment, L.P. Déry, 643-5633
Director, Wildlife Research, Raymond Sarrazin, 643-2227
Director, Wildlife Conservation, André Magny, 643-7674
Director General, Parks & Recreation, Gilles Barras, 643-5518 (includes Sports, Cultural & Social Activities)

Associated Agency

Wildlife Council
1 Place Ville Marie, #2433, Montreal, P.Q. H3B 3M9
(514) 873-7157
Secretary, S.-J. Vincent

DEPT. OF REVENUE

3800 rue Marly, Ste-Foy, P.Q. G1X 4A5
3, Complexe Desjardins, C.P. 3000, Montréal, P.Q. H5B 1A4
Information Contact, René A. Roy (phone: 418 643-6092)

Acts Administered

Revenue Dept. Act
Taxation Act

Act respecting the application of the Taxation Act
Act respecting fiscal incentives to industrial development
Succession Duties Act
Retail Sales Tax Act
Tobacco Tax Act
Meals & Hotels Tax Act
Fuel Tax Act
Telecommunications Tax Act
License Act
Que. Pension Plan (contributions)
Health Insurance Board Act (Bill 19, 1978)
Broadcast Advertising Tax Act
Land Transfer Duties Act
Real Estate Tax Refund Act
Self-employed Workers (An Act to authorize payment of allowances to certain) RSQ 1977 c p 1

MINISTER, Raynald Fréchette
Deputy Minister, Alban D'Amours
Asst. Deputy Ministers, Alain Dompierre; Paul-E. Moreau; Denis Rheault; Jean Laurin
Legal Branch, Director, Vincent-W. Kooiman
Management Control Branch, Director, Louis Morissette
Personnel Admin. Branch, Director General, Michel Vaillancourt
Public Relations Service, Director, René-A. Roy
Legislation Branch, Director General, vacant
Planning, Research & Development Branch, A/Director General, Denis Rheault
Operations Branch, Director General, Alain Dompierre (Immediate Assessment, Collection, Tax Rolls, Computer Operations, Returns, Monthly Remittances, Refunds)
Operations Office–Quebec, Director, Paul-E. Guay
Operations Office–Montreal, Director, Jean-Paul Chartier
Audit Branch, Director General, Paul-E. Moreau (Income Tax & Sales Tax Audit, Special Investigations, Succession Duties)
Co-ordination Office, Director, vacant
Audit Office, Quebec, Director, J.-M. Boudreau
Chief Assessor, Income Tax, Quebec, vacant
Chief Assessor, Sales Tax, Quebec, Florent Castonguay
Audit Office, Montreal, Director, Roger Couillard
Chief Assessor, Income Tax, Montreal, Gaston Courchesne
Chief Assessor, Sales Tax, Montreal, Sylvain Boyer
Special Investigations–Quebec, Director, Yves Morissette
Special Investigations–Montreal, Director, Roger Delage

Associated Agency
Régie des loteries et courses du Québec
2055, rue Peel, bur. 700, Montréal, P.Q. H3A 2K9
(514) 873-5180
President & Director General, Pierre Langevin

DEPT. OF SOCIAL AFFAIRS
1075 Ste-Foy Rd., Québec City, P.Q. G1S 2M1
Information Contact, Roger Ladouceur, Executive Asst. to Deputy Minister (418 643-6451)

MINISTER, Pierre Marc Johnson
Deputy Minister, Jean-Claude Deschênes
Asst. Deputy Minister, Admin., Richard Dufour
Asst. Deputy Minister, Health Programs, Réjean Cantin
Asst. Deputy Minister, Professional Relations, 2050, boul. St-Cyrille W., Ste-Foy, Jean Meloche
Asst. Deputy Minister, Social Welfare, Luc Malo
Chairman, Family & Social Affairs Council, Madeleine Blanchet, 1126, chemin St-Louis, Sillery, P.Q. G1S 1E5

Associated Agency
Régie de l'assurance-maladie
1125 chemin St-Louis, Québec, P.Q. G1K 7T3
(418) 643-3445
President, Martin Laberge

QUEBEC BUREAU OF STATISTICS
Centre d'information et de documentation, 117 rue St-André, Québec, P.Q. G1K 3Y3

TRANSLATION SERVICE
Dept. of Communications, 5555 3e ave ouest, Charlesbourg, P.Q. G1H 6R1
(418) 643-9450
Director, Luc Dufour

DEPT. OF TRANSPORT
700, boul. Saint-Cyrille est, Québec City, P.Q. G1R 5H1
Information from Director, Communications (418/643-6860); Montreal Information, 255, boul. Crémazie est, 514/873-3444

MINISTER, Michel Clair, 643-6980
Deputy Minister, Pierre Michaud, 643-6740
Asst. Deputy Ministers:
Planning & Development, René Vincent, 643-7346
Engineering, J.-L. Charland, 643-3576
Operations, René Blais, 643-6902
Budget, Ghislain Leblond, 643-6993
Personnel & Administration, Marcel-G. Baril, 643-2378
Director, Accounting, Lucien Létourneau, 643-6705
Director, Legal Dept., Michel Crevier, 643-6937
Interdepartmental Relations, J.-F. Bouchard (int.), 643-5177
Transport Laws & Regulations, Office, 1601 boul. Hamel, Edifice G, Québec, P.Q. G1N 3Y7, 643-3176
Government Air Service, Benoît Ste-Marie, Aéroport de Ste-Foy, Ste-Foy, P.Q. G2E 3L9, 872-0100

Associated Agencies
Quebec Transport Commission
585, boul. Charest est, Quebec, P.Q. G1K 7W5
(418) 643-2359
505, rue Sherbrooke est, Montreal, P.Q. H2L 1K2
(514) 873-5481
President, Judge Adolphe Prévost
Conseil des transports de la région de Montreal
1410, rue Stanley, Montreal, P.Q. H3A 1P9
(514) 873-5467
President, Paul Lussier
Quebec Autoroutes Authority (Office des autoroutes du Québec)
255, boul. Crémazie est, Montreal, P.Q. H2M 1L5
(514) 388-9201
President, Georges Tremblay
Quebec Ferry Co.
109, rue Dalhousie, Quebec, P.Q. G1K 7A1
(418) 643-2019
President & General Manager, Marcel Latouche
Société du port ferrovière Baie-Comeau-Hauterive
28, Place La Salle, Baie-Comeau, P.Q. G4Z 1K4
(418) 296-6785
President, H. Léonard
Transport Advisory Council
700 boul. St-Cyrille est, Québec, P.Q. G1R 5H1
(418) 643-7604
Régie de l'assurance automobile du Québec
1134 ch. St-Louis, Sillery, P.Q. G1S 1E5
(418) 643-7620
Présidente & Directrice générale, Claudine Sotiau
Société des traversiers du Québec (Ferries)
109 rue Dalhousie, C.P. 36, Stn. B, Québec, P.Q. G1K 7A1
President & Director General, J. Clermont (643-2019)

WORKERS HEALTH & SECURITY COMMISSION (Commission de la Santé et de la Sécurité du Travail)
1199 de Bleury, C.P. 6056, Succ A, Montréal, P.Q. H3C 4E1
(514) 873-3503
and 524 Bourdages, Box 1200, Québec, P.Q. G1K 7E2
(418) 643-5850
President, Robert Sauvé

Vice President (Admin.), J.-G. Massé
Vice President (Inspection), Gilles Néron
Vice President (Prevention), Me J.-L. Bertrand
Vice President (Restitution), Me Lionel Bernier (Réparation)
Director, Crime Victims Compensation, J.-M. Bertrand
Director, Communications, Alain Pontaut (514/873-7545)

PROVINCE OF SASKATCHEWAN

Entered Confederation September 1, 1905
Area: 251,700 sq. miles
Population: 969,200 (1980 est.)
Seat of Government: Legislative Bldg., Regina
Lieutenant-Governor: The Hon. Irwin McIntosh
Secretary: Mrs. Laura Champ

EXECUTIVE COUNCIL

Premier, and President of the Council, Hon. Allan Blakeney
Attorney General, and Minister of Intergovernmental Affairs, Hon. Roy Romanow
Minister of Finance, Hon. E. Tchorzewski
Minister of Labour, Hon. Gordon Snyder
Minister of Northern Saskatchewan, Hon. J. Hammersmith
Minister of the Environment, Hon. G.R. (Ted) Bowerman
Minister of Urban Affairs, Hon. W. Smishek
Minister of Rural Affairs, Hon. E.E. Kaeding
Minister of Highways & Transportation, Hon. B. Long
Provincial Secretary, and Minister of Mineral Resources, Hon. Elwood Cowley
Minister of Health, Hon. H. Rolfes
Minister of Revenue, Supply & Services, Hon. W.A. Robbins
Minister of Agriculture, Hon. G. MacMurchy
Minister of Tourism & Renewable Resources, and Minister of Government Services, Hon. R. Gross
Minister of Social Services, Hon. D. Lingenfelter
Minister of Culture & Youth, Hon. C. White
Minister of Education, and Minister of Continuing Education, Hon. D. McArthur
Minister of Industry & Commerce, Hon. Norman Vickar
Minister of Co-operatives, and Minister of Telephones, Hon. Don Cody
Minister of Consumer Affairs, Hon. M. Koskie
Cabinet Secretary, Florence Wilkie
Clerk of Executive Council, Bob Weese (phone: 306/565-6340)

LEGISLATIVE ASSEMBLY

Nineteenth Legislature. Last Election, October 18, 1978. Maximum Duration 5 Years.
Party Standings: New Democratic Party (N.D.P.) 44; Progressive Conservative (PC) 15; Unionest (U.N.) 2; Total 61
Leader of the Opposition, E.A. Berntson
Indemnities & Allowances: Members' Indemnity (including expense allowance), $26,533; Members of Athabasca, and Cumberland, $28,278; In addition to the Sessional Indemnity, the Premier receives $32,136; other Ministers, $24,175; Leader of the Opposition, $24,175 and office allowance of $58,965 per annum; Speaker, $9,434; Deputy Speaker, $5,601.
Officers: Speaker, Hon. John Brockelbank; Deputy Speaker, W.J.G. Allen; Clerk of Assembly, G.L. Barnhart, M.A.; Sergeant-at-Arms, A.R. Ponto; Law Clerk, Merrilee Charowsky; Legislative Librarian, Miss C. MacDonald

Members

Following is Constituency: Member: (address for all is Legislative Bldg., Regina, Sask. S4S OB3):

Arm River: Gerry Muirhead, PC (734-2830)
Assiniboia-Gravelbourg: Allen Engel, NDP (472-5980)
Athabasca: F. Thompson, NDP (235-4222)
The Battlefords: David Miner, NDP (565-7396)
Bengough-Milestone: Robert Pickering, PC (436-2250)
Biggar: E.L. Cowley, NDP (565-2506)
Canora: A.S. Matsalla, NDP (563-5794)
Cumberland: N.H. MacAuley, NDP (425-2486)
Cut Knife-Lloydminster: Robert Long, NDP (387-6373)
Estevan: Jack Chapman, NDP (634-2037)
Humboldt: E.L. Tchorzewski, NDP (565-6060)
Indian Head-Wolseley: Graham Taylor, PC (698-2788)
Kelsey-Tisdale: Neil Hardy, PC (865-2431)
Kelvington-Wadena: N.E. Byers, NDP (586-6069)
Kindersley: Robert Andrew, PC (463-4247)
Kinistino: Donald Cody, NDP (565-5625)
Last Mountain-Touchwood: G. MacMurchy, NDP (565-5886)
Maple Creek: Joan Duncan, PC (667-2332)
Meadow Lake: George McLeod, PC (236-6137)
Melfort: N. Vickar, NDP (565-6450)
Melville: J.R. Kowalchuk, NDP (876-2048)
Moose Jaw North: J.L. Skoberg, NDP (693-4981)
Moose Jaw South: G.T. Snyder, NDP (565-2396)
Moosomin: L.W. Birkbeck, PC (565-5302)
Morse: R.J. Gross, NDP (565-2833)
Nipawin: R.L. Collver, UN (585-1339)
Pelly: N. Lusney, NDP (542-3280)
Prince Albert: M. Feschuk, NDP (763-3044)
Prince Albert-Duck Lake: Jerry Hammersmith, NDP (565-2901)
Qu'Appelle: Gary Lane, PC (569-3097)
Quill Lakes: M. Koskie, NDP (565-5895)
Redberry: D. Banda, NDP (226-4216)
Regina Centre: N. Shillington, NDP (527-3482)
Regina Elphinstone: A.E. Blakeney, NDP (565-6271)
Regina Lakeview: Douglas McArthur, NDP (565-7363)
Regina North-East: W.E. Smishek, NDP (565-6774)
Regina North-West: J. Solomon, NDP (565-7394)
Regina Rosemont: B. Allen, NDP (545-7486)
Regina South: Paul Rousseau, PC (586-2894)
Regina Victoria: H.H.P. Baker, NDP (522-2981)
Regina Wascana: Clint White, NDP (565-7778)
Rosetown-Elrose: Herbert Swan, PC (859-4407)
Rosthern: R. Katzman, PC (661-2468)
Saltcoats: E. Kaeding, NDP (565-2260)
Saskatoon Buena Vista: H.H. Rolfes, NDP (565-7345)
Saskatoon Centre: P.P. Mostoway, NDP (373-2061)
Saskatoon Eastview: Bernard Poniatowski, NDP (374-8890)
Saskatoon Mayfair: B.M. Dyck, NDP (244-4377)
Saskatoon Nutana: W.A. Robbins, NDP (565-5832)
Saskatoon Riversdale: R. Romanow, NDP (565-5353)
Saskatoon-Sutherland: Peter Prebble, NDP (652-5664)
Saskatoon Westmount: J.E. Brockelbank, NDP (565-2282)
Shaunavon: Dwain Lingenfelter, NDP (565-3661)
Shellbrook: G.R. Bowerman, NDP (565-6100)
Souris-Cannington: E. Berntson, PC (928-2021)
Swift Current: D. Ham, UN (525-5077)
Thunder Creek: W.C. Thatcher, PC (692-2995)
Turtleford: L.E. Johnson, NDP (883-2702)
Weyburn: J.A. Pepper, NDP (842-2030)
Wilkie: James Garner, PC (843-3393)
Yorkton: R. Nelson, NDP (783-4766)

OFFICE OF THE PREMIER

Legislative Bldg., Regina, Sask. S4S OB3
Deputy Minister to the Premier, J.E. Sinclair (306/565-6276)
Asst. to the Deputy Minister, Becky Taylor (565-7448)
Principal Secretary to the Premier, Bill Knight (565-6515)
Executive Director, Premier's Secretariat, Valorie Preston (565-6324)
Cabinet Press Officer, Greg Gertz (565-6256)

GOVERNMENT DEPARTMENTS

DEPT. OF AGRICULTURE

Walter Scott Bldg., 3085 Albert St., Regina, Sask. S4S OB1

Information Contact, Henry Zilm, Statistics & Public Information Branch (306/565-5165)

Acts Administered

Agricultural Aids Act
Agricultural Development & Adjustment Act
Agricultural Implements Act
Agricultural Incentives Act
Agricultural Leaseholds Act
Agricultural Products Market Development Fund Act
Agricultural Research Foundation Act
Agricultural Research Funding Act
Agricultural Societies Act
Agrologists Act
Animal Identification Act
Animal Products Act
Animal Protection Act
Apiaries Act
Artificial Insemination (Animals) Act
Beef Stabilization Act
Cattle Marketing Voluntary Deductions Act
Conservation & Development Act
Crop Payments Act
Dept. of Agriculture Act
Diseases of Animals Act
Drainage Act
Expropriation Act
Expropriation (Rehabilitation Proj.) Act
Family Farm Improvement Act
Farm Security Act
Farming Communities Land Act
Grain & Fodder Conservation Act
Hog Marketing Deductions Act
Horned Cattle Purchases Act
Horse Racing Regulation Act
Horticultural Societies Act
Irrigation Districts Act
Land Bank Act
Line Fence Act
Live Stock Loans Guarantee Act
Live Stock Purchase & Sale Act
Milk Control Act
Natural Products Marketing Act
Noxious Weeds Act
Pest Control Act
Pest Control Products (Sask.) Act
Pollution (by Live Stock) Control Act
Prairie Agricultural Machinery Institute Act
Private Ditches Act
Provincial Lands Act
Sale or Lease of Certain Lands Act
Sask. Agricultural Returns Stabilization Act
Sask. Crop Insurance Act
Sask. Farm Ownership Act
Sask. 4-H Foundation Act
Sask. Grain Car Corporation Act
Sask. Grain Marketing Control Act
Seed Control Areas Act
Seed Dealers Act
Seed Grain Advances Act
Sheep Protection & Dog Licensing Act
Soil Drifting Control Act
South Sask. River Irrigation Act
Stray Animals Act
Vegetable & Honey Sales Act
Veterinarians Act
Veterinary Services Act
Watershed Assns. Act
Water Users Act

MINISTER, Hon. Gordon MacMurchy
Deputy Minister, Dr. G.J. Gartner
Assoc. Deputy Minister, M. Benson
Asst. Deputy Minister, Stuart Kramer
Director, Administrative Services, R.P. Knoll
Director, Communications, Roger C. Fry
Director, Personnel & Training, C. Folk
Director, Statistics, Henry Zilm
Director, Public Information, Lorraine Johnson
General Manager, Agricultural Development Corp. of Sask., G. Wells
Director, Family Farm Improvement Branch, P.O. Moen
Director, Irrigation Extension Branch (Box 9, Outlook), H.A. Fjeld
Co-ordinator, Staff Training & Program Content, J.F. Hickie
Co-ordinator, North West Region, H.R. Kingdon, Provincial Office Bldg., North Battleford, Sask. S9A 3G7
Co-ordinator, South West Region, R.E. Middleton, 850 Cheadle St. W., Swift Current, Sask. S9H 4G3
Co-ordinator, North East Region, A.W. Sereda, Box 1480, Tisdale, Sask. SOE 1TO
Co-ordinator, East Central Region, M.W. Oxman, Provincial Bldg., Yorkton, Sask. S3N 2Y4
Co-ordinator, West Central Region, C.G. Casswell, Box 1690, Main St., Kindersley, Sask. SOL 1SO
Co-ordinator, South East Region, N.L. White, 110 Souris Ave., Weyburn, Sask. S4H 2Z9
Director, Conservation & Development Branch, J.F. Danyluk
Director, Lands Branch, J. Hoffort

Production Division

Director, Animal Industry Branch, R.W. May
Director, Marketing & Economics Division, G. Pearson
Director, Plant Industry Branch, J.A. Buchan
Director, Veterinary Services Branch, Dr. W.C. Weir

Associated Agencies & Marketing Bds.

Sask. Land Bank Commission, Rm. 142, 3211 Albert St., Regina, Sask. S4S 5W6 (565-5321); Chairman, G.H. Wesson
Crop Insurance Board, 2240 Albert St., Regina, Sask. S4P 2J3 (565-5055); General Manager, J. Campbell
Milk Control Board, 620 2045 Broad St., Regina, Sask. S4P 1Y4 (565-5319); Chairman, S.H. Barber
FarmStart (Corp.), 3085 Albert St., Regina, Sask. S4S OB1 (565-6460); General Manager, G.D.L. Hetland
Sask. Hog Marketing Commission, 1402 Quebec N., Saskatoon, Sask. S7K 1V5 (653-3014); Chairman, D. MacKay
Agricultural Development Corp. of Sask., 11th floor, 2500 Victoria Ave., Regina, Sask. S4P 3X2 (565-5035)
Sheep & Wool Marketing Commission, 1402 Quebec Ave. N., Saskatoon, Sask. S7K 1V5 (664-5200)
Sask. Farm Ownership Board, 3130 8th St. E., Saskatoon, Sask. S7H OW2 (664-5105); Director, Ed Rasmussen
Agricultural Implements Board, Rm. 522, 3211 Albert St., Regina, Sask. S4S 5W6 (565-5291); Director, D.G. Lehman
Prairie Agricultural Machinery Institute, Box 1900, Humboldt, Sask. SOK 2AO (682-2555)
Sask. Chicken Marketing Board, Box 1637, 1601 McAra St., Regina, Sask. S4P 3C4 (527-1425)
Sask. Commercial Egg Producers Marketing Board, Box 1637, 1601 McAra St., Regina, Sask. S4P 3C4 (525-2115)
Sask. Turkey Producers Marketing Board, Box 1637, 1601 McAra St., Regina, Sask. S4P 3C4 (522-2855)

SASKATCHEWAN ARCHIVES BOARD

Offices: Univ. of Regina, Regina, Sask. S4S OA2 (phone: (306) 565-4068); Murray Memorial Library, Univ. of Sask., Saskatoon, Sask. S7N OWO (phone: (306) 664-5832)
Chairman, Hon. D. McArthur
Provincial Archivist, Ian E. Wilson
Asst. Provincial Archivist, D.H. Bocking

SASKATCHEWAN ARTS BOARD

2550 Broad St., Regina, Sask. S4P 3V7
(306) 565-4056; toll free in Sask.: 1-800-667-3533
Executive Director, Joy Cohnstaedt
Visual Arts Consultant, Patrick Close
Performing Arts Consultant, Rita Deverell
Literary Arts Consultant, Judy Krause

DEPT. OF ATTORNEY GENERAL

2476 Victoria Ave., Regina, Sask. S4P 3V7
Information Contact, Gary Brandt, Director of Administrative Services (phone: 306 565-5472)

Acts Administered

Absconding Debtors Act
Absentee Act
Admin. of Estates of Mentally Disordered Persons Act
Age of Majority Act
Agreements of Sale Cancellation Act
Arbitration Act
Assignment of Wages Act
Attachment of Debts Act
Attorney General's Act
Bulk Sales Act
Children of Unmarried Parents Act
Choses in Action Act
Closing-out Sales Act
Commissioners for Oaths Act
Community Cablecasters Act
Community Legal Services (Sask.) Act
Constitutional Questions Act
Contributory Negligence Act
Coroners Act
Court of Appeal Act
Court Officials Act
Creditors' Relief Act
Criminal Injuries Compensation Act
Crown Admin. of Estates Act
Crown Suits (Costs) Act
Demise of the Crown Act
Dept. of Intergovernmental Affairs Act
Dependants' Relief Act
Deserted Wives' & Children's Maintenance Act
Devolution of Real Property Act
Distress Act
Doukhobors of Canada C.C.U.B. Trust Fund Act
Escheats Act
Executions Act
Exemptions Act
Expropriation Procedure Act
Extra-Provincial Custody Orders Enforcement Act
Factors Act
Fatal Accidents Act
Federal Courts Act
Foreign Judgments Act
Fraudulent Preferences Act
Garage Keepers Act
Homesteads Act
Hotel Keepers Act
Improvements under Mistake of Title Act
Infants Act
Interpretation Act
Interprovincial Subpoena Act
Intestate Succession Act
Judges' Orders Enforcement Act
Judgments Extension Act
Jury Act
Justices of the Peace Act
Land Contracts (Actions) Act
Land Titles Act
Law Reform Commission Act
Laws Declaratory Act
Legal Profession Act
Legitimacy Act
Libel & Slander Act
Limitation of Actions Act
Limitation of Civil Rights Act
Lord's Day (Sask.) Act
Marriage Settlement Act
Married Persons Property Act
Matrimonial Property Act
Mechanics' Lien Act
Meewasin Valley Authority Act
Members of the Legislative Assembly Conflict of Interest Act
Mentally Disordered Persons Act
Minors Tobacco Act
Notaries Public Act
Parents' Maintenance Act
Penalties & Forfeitures Act
Personal Property Security Act
Police Act
Police Pension (Saskatoon) Funding Act
Potash Corporation of Saskatchewan Act
Potash Development Act
Privacy Act
Private Investigators & Security Guards Act
Proceedings against the Crown Act
Provincial Court Act
Public Inquiries Act
Public Officers' Protection Act
Public Utilities Easements Act
Public Works Creditor's Payment Act
Queen's Bench Act
Queen's Counsel Act
Reciprocal Enforcement of Judgments Act
Reciprocal Enforcement of Maintenance Orders Act
Recording of Evidence by Sound Recording Machine Act
Recovery of Possession of Land Act
Regulations Act
Revised Statutes Act, 1974
Sale of Goods Act
Sales on Consignment Act
Sask. Evidence Act
Sask. Human Rights Code
Seduction Act
Slot Machine Act
Small Claims Enforcement Act
Statute Law Amendment Act
Statutes Act
Summary Offences Procedure Act
Surface Rights Acquisition & Compensation Act
Surrogate Court Act
Survivorship Act
Tabling of Documents (Postponement) Act
Thresher Employees Act
Threshers' Lien Act
Trading Stamp Act
Traffic Safety Court of Saskatchewan Act
Trustee Act
Unconscionable Transactions Relief Act
Unified Family Court Act
Variation of Trusts Act
Warehousemen's Lien Act
Wills Act
Woodmen's Lien Act

ATTORNEY GENERAL, Hon. Roy Romanow, Q.C.
Executive Assts., J. Stocks, P. Godfrey, C. Wolburn
Deputy Attorney General, Dr. R. Gosse, Q.C.
Special Asst., R. Hewitt
Asst. Deputy Minister (Admin.), J. Benning
Assoc. Deputy Minister (Criminal Law), S. Kujawa, Q.C.
Co-ordinator, Policy & Legislative Programs, J. Scratch
Director of Administrative Services, G. Brandt
Director of Personnel & Training, B. Sockett
Director of Civil Law, H.M. Ketcheson, Q.C.
Executive Director of Court Services, P.T. Guttormsson
Administrative Director, Provincial Court, G.C. McNutt
Director of Policing, W.G. Logan
Executive Director of Property Management, P. McPhie
Master of Titles, G. Jackson
Chief Surveyor, Land Titles, R. Pankiw
Administrator of Estates, D. Spicer
Official Guardian, J.G.L. Jamieson
Director of Public Prosecutions, D. Perras, Q.C.
Chief Coroner, Dr. J.S. McMillan

Solicitors, L. Anderson, B.J. Bauer, D. Bogdasavich, A. Brent, L. Brierley, D. Britton, D.M. Brown, T.D.R. Caldwell, J.D.S. Connelly, C. Crane, E. Crosbie, F.W. Dehm, S. Eisner, J. Falle, J.W. Field, E. Gunn, J.W. Hagemeister, R. Hart, R. Hewitt, T. Hinz, G. Holtzman, B. Hornsberger, P.A. Hryorchuk, J.A. Johnson, A. Johnston, R. Kirkham, J.M. Kulyk, W. Lawton, T.J. Matchett, K. MacKay, J.C. MacPherson, D. McKillop, G. Peacock, J. Plemel, M. Popescul, B. Pottruff, C.R. Quinney, K. Rondeau, J. Sather, C. Snell, L.T.K. Sullivan, J.T.V. Taylor, G. Tegart, D.L. Tennent, W.K. Tucker, W.A. Wall, M.S. Woods
Constitutional Law Branch, Director, J.D. Whyte
Co-ordinator, Constitutional Law, James MacPherson
Crown Solicitor, G.V. Peacock

Associated Agencies

Communications Secretariat, 3rd floor, 3085 Albert St., Regina, Sask. S4S 0B1 (565-2048); Director, R.J. Simpson
Sask. Criminal Injuries Compensation Board, 10th floor, 122 3rd Ave. N., Saskatoon, Sask. S7K 2H6 (664-5153); Chairman, D. Windels
The Law Reform Commission of Sask., 122 3rd Ave. N., Saskatoon, Sask. S7K 2H6 (664-6127); Chairman, R.C.C. Cuming
*The Public & Private Rights Board, Room 501, 2240 Albert St., Regina, Sask. S4P 3V7 (565-4071); Chairman, M. Kuziak
Sask. Community Legal Services Commission, 311 21st St. E., Saskatoon, Sask. S7K 0C1 (664-5300); Chairman, I.J. Wilson
The Sask. Human Rights Commission, 8th floor, 224 4th Ave. S., Saskatoon, Sask. S7K 5M5 (664-5952); Executive Director, S. Day
Sask. Police Commission, 4th floor, 1855 Victoria Ave., Regina, Sask. S4P 3V5 (565-6518); Executive Director, H. Joudrey
*The Surface Rights Arbitration Board, 2024 Albert St., Regina, Sask. S4P 3V7 (565-3941); Chairman, R.A. Bews
*These Boards report to the Attorney General but not through the department.

PROVINCIAL AUDITOR

5th floor, 1825 Lorne St., Regina, Sask. S4P 3V7
(306) 565-6360
Provincial Auditor, W.G. Lutz, F.C.A.
Deputy Provincial Auditors, W.G. Bucknall, C.A.; G.F. Wendel, C.A.; G.S. Erickson, C.A.; J.A. Hunt, C.A.

DEPT. OF CONSUMER & COMMERCIAL AFFAIRS

1871 Smith St., Regina, Sask. S4P 3V7
Information Contact, A. Gill (phone: 306-565-5577)

Acts Fully Administered

Auctioneers Act
Business Corporations Act
Business Names Registration Act
Canadian Institute of Management (Sask. Division) Act
Cemeteries Act
Collection Agents Act
Companies Act
Companies Winding Up Act
Condominium Property Act
Consumer Product Warranties Act
Cost of Credit Disclosure Act
Credit Reporting Agencies Act
Dept. of Consumer & Commercial Affairs Act
Direct Sellers Act
Guarantee Companies Securities Act
Insurance Premiums Tax Act
Investment Contracts Act
Landlord & Tenant Act
Loan Companies Act
Mining Associations Act
Mortgage Brokers Act
Motor Dealers Act
Municipal Hail Insurance Act
Names of Homes Act
Non-profit Corporations Act
Partnership Act
Plumbing Contractors Licensing Act
Provincial Mediation Board Act
Pyramid Franchises Act
Real Estate Brokers Act
Religious Societies Land Act
Residential Tenancies Act
Sale of Training Courses Act
Saskatchewan Insurance Act
Securities Act
Societies Act
Theatres & Cinematographs Act
Trust & Loan Companies Licensing Act
Trust Companies Act
Unsolicited Goods & Credit Cards Act

MINISTER, Hon. Murray J. Koskie
Deputy Minister, Vee Lynne Pearson

Associated Agency

Sask. Securities Commission
1919 Rose St., Regina, Sask. S4P 3V7
(306) 565-5645
Chairman, R.K. Stevenson
Registrar, W.C. Costiuk

DEPT. OF CONTINUING EDUCATION

1855 Victoria Ave., Regina, Sask. S4P 3V5
Telex: 071 2446
Information Contact, Admin. Services (phone: 306-525-5600)

Acts Administered

Dept. of Continuing Education Act
Community College Act
Nurses' Education Act
Private Vocational Schools Regulation Act
Student Assistance & Student Aid Fund Act
Univ. of Regina Act
Univ. of Sask. Act
Universities Commission Act

MINISTER, Hon. D. McArthur
Deputy Minister, Dr. Wil Toombs
Assoc. Deputy Minister, L.A. Riederer
Administrative & Financial Services Division, Executive Director, F.C. May
Institutional Division, Executive Director, Lorne Sparling
Occupational Training Division, Executive Director, Paul Dudgeon
Policy & Planning Division, Executive Director, Sarah Landy
Student Services Branch, Director, Morris Campbell

DEPT. OF CO-OPERATION & CO-OPERATIVE DEVELOPMENT

2055 Albert St., Box 7121, Regina, Sask. S4P 3S1
Information Contact, Art G. Nogue, Director of Communications & Development (phone: 306 565-5789)

Acts Administered

Dept. of Co-operation Act
Co-operative Assns. Act
Co-operative Marketing Assns. Act
Credit Union Act
Family Farm Credit Act
Production Act

MINISTER, Hon. Don Cody
Deputy Minister, J.E. Reed
Director of Admin. & Research, A. Munholland
Director of Operations, L. Warkentin
Asst. Director of Associations, C.W. Norman
Asst. Director of Credit Unions, G. Robinson

Associated Bds.

Co-op Guarantee Board

Co-op Securities Board
Mutual Aid Board

CROWN INVESTMENTS CORP.
(A Crown Corp.)

Ste. 300, 2400 College Ave., Regina, Sask. S4P 1C8
(306) 565-6851
President, G.H. Beatty

DEPT. OF CULTURE & YOUTH

11th floor, Avord Tower, Regina, Sask. S4P 3V7
Inquiry, 306/565-5739

Acts Administered

Dept. of Culture & Youth Act
Heritage Property Act
Recreation & Cultural Facilities Capital Grants Act
Sask. Multicultural Act
Western Development Museum Act
Sask. Centre of the Arts Act
Arts Board Act

MINISTER, Hon. Clint White
Deputy Minister, Liz Dowdeswell
A/Executive Director, Central Services Branch, Ron Borden
Executive Director, Sport & Recreation Branch, Barb Zimmer
Executive Director, Cultural Activities Branch, Dick Clarke
Director of Youth Employment Services, Ron Borden
Director of Budget & Grants, Ron Borden
Director of Regional Services, W.R. Ellis
Director of Communications, Gillian McCreary
Director of Museums Branch, Dr. John Storer

Associated Agencies

Sask. Arts Board
Sask. Centre of the Arts Board
Sask. Heritage Advisory Board
Sask. Heritage Property Review Board
Sask. Multicultural Advisory Board
Western Development Museum Board

ECONOMIC DEVELOPMENT CORP.
(A Crown Corp.)

1106 Winnipeg St., Regina, Sask. S4R 6N9
(306) 565-7200
Chairman, Hon. Norman Vickar
President, Neil Overend

DEPT. OF EDUCATION

2220 College Ave., Parkview Place, Regina, Sask. S4P 3V7, except where otherwise indicated.
Information from Office of the Director, Information Bureau (phone: 306 565-6030)

Acts Administered

Education Act, 1978
Teachers' Life Insurance (Government Contributory) Act
Teachers' Superannuation Act, 1970
Teachers' Federation Act
School Business Officials Association of Sask. Act
Education of Soldiers' Dependent Children Act
Regulations under the Education Act

MINISTER, Hon. Doug McArthur
Deputy Minister, R.C. Clayton
Asst. Deputy Minister, John Hurnard
Official Minority Language Office, Executive Director, Lou Julé
Education Consultant, Robert Cousin
Director, Information Bureau, Ron Ware
Correspondence School, Principal, Steve Senyk
School for the Deaf, Cumberland Ave., Saskatoon, Principal, John Anderson

Administrative Services Division

Executive Director, Gil Dumelie
Manager, Book Bureau, Joe Braun, 1330 Winnipeg St.
Director, Financial Management, John Moneo
Director, Management Information Systems, Ron Cox
Director, Personnel, Shirley Murray

Policy, Planning & Special Projects Division

Executive Director, Garry Wouters
Director, Special Projects, Joanne Bonneville
Director, Community Education, Adrian Gibbons
Director, Policy, Planning & Research, Ken Horsman
Consultant, Bob Arkell

Development Division

Executive Director, Phil Schalm
Program Development, Director, Al Schell
Instructional Resources, Assoc. Director, vacant
  Consultant, School Libraries, Art Forgay
  Consultant, Audio-Visual, Ann Davidson
  Consultant, Radio-Tape, Delee Cameron
  Resource Centre Librarian, Jane Naisbitt
Teacher Services, Assoc. Director, Jack Struthers
  Consultant, Marg Stevenson
Student Services, Assoc. Director, Fred Nakonechny

Regional Services Division

Executive Director, Peter Dyck
Assoc. Executive Director, Jack Lloyd
Educational Administration, Director, Ken Kirby
  Chief, School Admin. & Negotiations Unit, Ivan McKay
  Chief, School Grant Admin., Les Barrett
Consultative Services
  Consultant, Guidance, Mike Homenuk
  Consultant, Driver Education, Gordon McGregor
  Consultant, Industrial Arts, John Edwards
  Physical Education, Chief, John Campbell
  Alcohol & Drug Education Liaison Program, Chief, Gerald Kleisinger
Special Education, Director, Bob Livingston
  Consultant, Communication Handicaps, Susan Alexander
  Consultant, Visually Impaired, Larry Carlson
  Consultant, Severely Handicapped, Jim Seiferling
  Consultants, Special Education, Vic Andreas, Dale Bellin, Elmer Richert, Alan Phillips, Harry Dahl, Peter Waldbillig, Wayne Adair

Associated Commission

Teachers' Superannuation Commission, 1914 Hamilton St., Regina, S4P 4V4
  Executive Secretary, Wally Sawchuk

EMERGENCY MEASURES ORG.

1791 Rose St., Regina, Sask. S4P 3V7
(306) 525-8121
Director, J.T. Eaton

DEPT. OF THE ENVIRONMENT

5th floor, 1855 Victoria Ave., Regina, Sask. S4P 3V5
Information Contact, George Reamsbottom, Director, Public Information & Education Branch (phone: 306 565-6128)

Acts Administered

Dept. of the Environment Act
Environmental Assessment Act
Litter Control Act
Air Pollution Control Act
Drainage Control Act
Water Resources Management Act
Water Power Act
Water Rights Act
Ecological Reserves Act
Ground Water Conservation Act

MINISTER, Hon. Ted Bowerman
Deputy Minister, R.L. Carter

Director, Admin. Branch, vacant
Executive Director, Water Management Service, S.R. Blackwell
Executive Director, Environmental Protection Service, G.W. Howard
Director, Public Information & Education Branch, G.M. Reamsbottom
Director, Policy, Planning & Research Branch, H.S. Maliepaard
Executive Director, Environmental Assessment Secretariat, R.L. Kellow

DEPT. OF FINANCE

Room 115, Legislative Bldg., Regina, Sask. S4S OB3
Information Contact, K. Mackrill (phone: 306 565-6765)

Acts Administered

Accredited Public Accountants Act
Canadian Farm Loan Priority Act
Certified General Accountants Act
Certified Public Accountants Act
Chartered Accountants Act
Corporation Income Tax Collection Agreement Act
Deferred Charges Act
Estate Tax Rebate Act, 1969
Estate Tax Rebates Reciprocal Arrangements Act, 1970
Federal Provincial Agreements Act
Heritage Fund (Saskatchewan) Act
Income Tax Act
Industrial Accountants Act
Interprovincial Steel & Pipe Corp. Ltd. Assistance Act, 1966
Loans (Special Powers) Act
Municipal Financing Corporation Act
Prince Albert Pulp Co. Ltd. Assistance Act, 1968
Public Officials Security Act
Public Service Act
Purchase of Lands Act
Railway Taxation Act
Reconstruction & Rehabilitation Fund Act
Relief Act
Sask. Corp. Income Tax Act, 1947 (and 1949)
Sask. Diamond Jubilee Act, 1978
Sask. Economic Development Corp. Foreign Exchange Reserve Act, 1973
Sask. Loans Act
Sask. Water Supply Board Deficit Act, 1973
Taxation Agreement Act
Tax Rental Agreement Act, 1957

MINISTER OF FINANCE, Hon. E. Tchorzewski
Deputy Minister, R. Douglas
Asst. to Deputy Minister, B. McKenzie
Asst. Deputy Minister, M. Costello
Senior Treasury Consultant, D. Clarke
Director of Admin., K. Mackrill
Director of Budget Bureau, L. McFarlane
Director of Taxation & Fiscal Policy Branch, D. Rowlatt
Director of Bureau of Management Improvement, R. Clarke
Comptroller, G. Kraus
Director of Investment & Financial Services Branch, M.I. Meiklejohn

Associated Agencies

Municipal Financing Corp. of Sask., 2400 College Ave., Regina, Sask. S4P 1C8 (565-5910)
Sask. Public Service Commission, 3211 Albert St., Regina, Sask. S4S 5W6 (565-7500); Chairman, D.A. Bock

SASKATCHEWAN FOREST PRODUCTS CORP. (A Crown Corp.)

550 First Ave. E., Prince Albert, Sask. S6V 2A5
(306) 764-4266
General Manager, N.S. Denmark
Manager of Industrial Relations & Personnel, W. McFadzean

FUR MARKETING SERVICE (A Crown Corp.)

1100 Broad St., Regina, Sask. S4R 1X8
(306) 525-1000; 527-5656
Manager, A.J. Cooke

DEPT. OF GOVERNMENT SERVICES

1942 Hamilton St., Regina, Sask. S4P 3V7
Information Branch: Director, Doug Archer, 306/565-6910

Acts Administered

Dept. of Government Services Act
Public Works Act
Architects Act

MINISTER, Hon. Reg Gross
Deputy Minister, D.E. Foley
Executive Director of Operations, I.G. Laidlaw
Director, Property & Planning Branch, Don Nevill (565-6945)
Director, Architecture & Engineering Branch, Allan Smith (565-6977)
Director, Regina Operations, Dan Morin (565-2027)
Director, Northern Operations, Tom Gallagher (565-2029)
Director, Southern Operations, Jonathan Bingham (565-2033)
Director, Public Works Branch, Pat Brown (664-5180)
Director, Administrative Services Branch, Doug Archer (565-6910)
Director, Personnel & Training Branch, W.A. Longley (565-6913)

DEPT. OF HEALTH

3475 Albert St., Regina, Sask. S4S 6X6
Information Contact, K.S. MacDonald, Director, Personnel & Training Branch (phone: 306-565-3070)

Acts Administered

Abandoned Refrigerator Act, 1967
Anatomy Act
Cancer Control Act
Change of Name Act
Dental Care Act, 1974
Dept. of Health Act, 1974
Health Services Act
Hearing Aid Act, 1973
Hospital Revenue Act, 1966
Hospital Standards Act

Acts in which the Department has a Direct Interest

Alcoholism Commission of Sask. Act, 1968
Dental Profession Act, 1978
Denturists Act, 1977
Emergency Medical Aid Act, 1976
Human Tissue Gift Act, 1974
Medical Care Insurance Supplementary Provisions Act, 1968
Ophthalmic Dispensers Act, 1977
Registered Nurses Act, 1978
Sask. Medical Care Insurance Act
Sask. Psychiatric Nurses Act, 1977
South Sask. Hospital Centre Act
Tuberculosis Sanatoria & Hospitals Act
University Hospital Act

MINISTER OF HEALTH, Hon. Herman H. Rolfes
Deputy Minister, K.J. Fyke
Assoc. Deputy Ministers, Dr. P.A.R. Glynn, D.S. Kelly
Director of Negotiations, B. Topp
Solicitor, R.G. Ellis, Q.C.
Director, Administrative Services, L. Krahn
Director, Personnel & Training, K.S. Macdonald
Director, Professional Training & Staff Development, E.L. Breese
Director, Medical Services Division, M. Lyseiko
Director, Provincial Laboratories, Dr. H.E. Robertson
Director, Policy Research & Management Services, W.F. Roger

Director, Vital Statistics, V. Cloarec
Fee for each copy of a birth, marriage, or death certificate: $5.
Provincial Epidemiologist, Dr. R. West
Executive Director, Prescription Drug Plan, J.C. Reid
Director, Health Promotion, E. Scott
Director, Sask. Aids to Independent Living, R. Wallace
Director, Psychiatric Services, J. Yarske

Community Health Services Branch

Director, Community Health Services Branch, Dr. H. Walker
Director, Child Health Division, Dr. H.C. Grocott
Director, Communicable & Venereal Disease Control Division, Dr. H. Grocott (act.)
Director, Nutrition Division, L. Harasym
Executive Director, Sask. Hospital Services Plan, G. Loewen
Executive Director, Sask. Dental Plan, Dr. Michael Lewis

Sask. Anti-Tuberculosis League

Medical Director & General Supt., Dr. G.D. Barnett, Sanatorium, Fort Qu'Appelle
Asst. Administrator, Saskatoon Sanatorium, M. Sucey

Associated Agencies

Sask. Medical Care Insurance Commission
3475 Albert St., Regina, Sask. S4S 6X6 (565-3423)
Executive Director, G.C. Patchett
Alcoholism Commission of Sask.
3475 Albert St., Regina, Sask. S4S 6X6 (565-4085)
Executive Director, B. Kearns, act.

HIGHWAY TRAFFIC BOARD

11th floor, 2260 11th Ave., Regina, Sask. S4P 3V7
(306) 565-4047
Chairman, W.A. Sheard
Director, Motor Carrier Branch, D.T. Pollock, 565-4039
Director, Vehicle Regulation, P.R. Landry, 565-4031
Director, Driver Licensing Branch, L.A. Henbury, 565-4027
Director, Traffic Safety Branch, A.C. Shiels, 565-5318
Director, Policy & Planning Branch, W.R. McLaren, 565-4030
Director, Admin. & Personnel, G.W. Russell, 565-4022

DEPT. OF HIGHWAYS & TRANSPORTATION

1855 Victoria Ave., Regina, Sask. S4P 3V5
Information from G.M. Hansen, Director of Communications (phone: 306/565-4804)

Act Administered

Highways Act

MINISTER, Hon. R.G. (Bob) Long
Deputy Minister, T.B. Gentles (565-4949)
Assoc. Deputy Minister (Operations), J.R. Sutherland (565-4906)
Director of Support Services, J.A. Schwartz (565-4908)
Chief Engineer, M.F. Clark (565-4907)
Director, Planning Branch, R.P. Couturier (565-4758)
Director, Traffic Safety Engineering Branch, A.J. Popoff (565-4750)
Director, Works Branch, D.A. Belliveau (565-4866)
Operations Engineer, M.J. Herasymuik (565-4809) (there are district engineers at North Battleford, Prince Albert, Regina, Saskatoon, Swift Current and Yorkton)
Road Design Engineer, G.T. Stanger (565-4832)
Senior Geotechnical Engineer, R.A. Lidgren (565-4858)
Materials Testing Engineer, H.A. Eley, 1610 Park St., Regina (565-4916)
Research Engineer, R.W. Culley, 1610 Park St., Regina (565-4918)
Surfacing Engineer, G. Heiman (565-4846)
Maintenance Engineer, B. Martin (565-4859)
Director, Equipment Branch, W.R. Tuer (565-4835)
Director, Financial Services Branch, P. Fitzel (565-4734)
Director, Management Services Branch, A.I. Massier (565-4723)
Director, Personnel Branch, R.M. Reavley (565-4757)
Director, Public Communications Branch, G.M. Hansen (565-4804)
Director, Surveys Branch, John Turnbull (565-4900)
Director, Central Survey & Mapping Agency, John Turnbull (565-4900)

DEPT. OF INDUSTRY & COMMERCE

3rd floor, 2121 Saskatchewan Dr., Regina, Sask. S4P 3V7
Information Contact, Director, Communications Branch, Bill Scott, 306 565-2226

Acts Administered

Dept. of Industry & Commerce Act, 1965
Industry Incentives Act, 1970
Industry & Commerce Development Act, 1972
Scrap Vehicles Act, 1973

MINISTER, Hon. Norman Vickar
Deputy Minister, Jeff Bugera (565-2171)
Director, Communications Branch, W.G. Scott (565-2226)
Executive Director, Support Services Division, R.K. McNabb (565-4593)
(includes: Program Management, Personnel & Admin., and Planning)
Executive Director, Business Services Division, Bryce Baron (565-2208)
Director, Regional Services Branch, Lyle Pederson (565-2212)
Director, Development Services Branch, Bart Drope (565-2243)
Executive Director, Trade & Industry Promotion Division, Wayne Lorch (565-2218)
Director, Trade Branch, vacant
Director, Industry Promotion Branch, Don Jesse (565-2204)

GOVERNMENT INFORMATION SERVICES

Room 7, Legislative Bldg., Regina, Sask. S4S OB3
(306) 565-6281

The central information arm of the government, acting as the co-ordinating unit for the information sections of the departments.

Director, Mel Hinds

SASKATCHEWAN GOVERNMENT INSURANCE (A Crown Corp.)

2260 11th Ave., Regina, Sask. S4P OJ9
Phone: (306) 565-1200
General Manager, J. Green, Q.C.

DEPT. OF LABOUR

1914 Hamilton St., Regina, Sask. S4P 4V4
Information from Administrative Services (phone: 306 565-2410)

Acts Administered

Apprenticeship & Tradesmen's Qualification Act
Boiler & Pressure Vessel Act
Building Trades Protection Act
Construction Industry Labour Relations Act
Dept. of Labour Act
Electrical Inspection & Licensing Act
Employment Agencies Act
Fire Departments Platoon Act
Fire Prevention Act
Gas Inspection & Licensing Act
Labour Standards Act
Occupational Health & Safety Act
Passenger & Freight Elevator Act
Pension Benefits Act
Radiation Health & Safety Act
Theatres & Cinematographs Act, Sec. 19
Trade Union Act
Wages Recovery Act
Workers' Compensation Act, 1979

Workmen's Compensation Board Superannuation Act

MINISTER, Hon. Gordon T. Snyder
Deputy Minister, D.G. McMillan
Assoc. Deputy Minister, R. Sass
Industrial Relations Branch, Executive Director, S. Walter (includes: Industrial Relations, Labour Relations, Workers' Advocates)
LABOUR RELATIONS BOARD, Chairman, N.W. Sherstobitoff, Q.C., 1070 Avord Towers, Saskatoon, Sask. S7K 1H1
MINIMUM WAGE BOARD, Chairman, Mary Rocan
Labour Development Branch, Executive Director, C.W. Dotson
Senior Manpower Planning Officer, vacant
Administrative Services Division, Director, P.J. More
Policy Planning & Research Division, Director, D. Goss
Labour Library, Librarian, Fraser Russell, 6th floor, 1914 Hamilton St., Regina
Apprenticeship & Standards Division, Director, vacant
Women's Division, Director, M. Twigg
Pension Benefits Branch, Executive Director, G. Ford
Occupational Health & Safety, 1150 Rose St., Regina, Sask. S4P 3V7, Director, R. Sass
Health & Safety Standards, Senior Occupational Health Officer, W. Nelson
Occupational Hygiene Unit, Senior Occupational Hygienist, G. Scattergood
Mines Safety Inspection Unit, Chief Inspector of Mines, J. Alderman
Radiation Health Physicist, Dr. D. Brown
Safety Services, Director, P.J. Sheasby
Boilers, Pressure Vessels, Chief Inspector, R.V. Curry
Electrical & Elevator, Chief Inspector, J.T. Kokotailo
Gas Safety, Chief Inspector, H.A. Lines
Fire Safety, Fire Commr., Murray Fisher
Education & Research, Director, J. Smythe

Workers' Compensation Board
1840 Lorne St., Regina, Sask. S4P 2L8 (565-4370)
Chairman, Brian King
Members, H.S. Elkin, M.G. Bourne

LEGISLATIVE LIBRARY
Legislative Bldg., Regina, Sask. S4S 0B3
(306) 565-2277
Legislative Librarian, Miss Christine MacDonald

PROVINCIAL LIBRARY
Sedco Bldg., 1352 Winnipeg St., Regina, Sask. S4P 3V7
(306) 565-2976

The Provincial Library acts as the co-ordinating agency for public library services and programs throughout the province. The Professional Services Branch provides collection services, as well as bibliographic, interlibrary loan, reference and circulation services. Technical Services Branch offers centralized cataloguing services to all public libraries. The Support Services Branch is responsible for all administration and policy and research activities within the Provincial Library.

A/Provincial Librarian, Merry D. Harbottle
Director of Professional Services, Leah Siebold
Director of Technical Services, Shirley Sefton
Director of Support Services, Sheila Page

LIQUOR BOARD
Box 5054, Regina, Sask. S4P 3M3
(306) 565-4211
Chairman, D. Earle MacRae

LIQUOR LICENSING COMMISSION
1660 Park St., Regina, Sask. S4N 2G2
(306) 565-4275
Chairman & Secretary, E. Dale Tilling
Vice Chairman, R.L. Sabine

DEPT. OF MINERAL RESOURCES
1914 Hamilton St., Box 5114, Regina, Sask. S4P 4V4
Information Contact, Publications Office (306/565-2526)

Acts Administered
Coal Conservation Act
Dept. of Mineral Resources Act
Mineral Resources Act
Mineral Taxation Act
Natural Gas Development & Conservation Board Act
Oil & Gas Conservation Act
Oil & Gas Conservation, Stabilization & Development Act, 1973
Oilwell Income Tax Act
Pipe Lines Act
Public Utilities Cos. Act
Road Allowance Crown Oil Act
Sand & Gravel Act

MINISTER, Hon. E. Cowley
Deputy Minister, Don P. Moroz
Assoc. Deputy Minister, K. Laxdal
Director, Personnel & Admin., Janis M. Rathwell
Director, Petroleum & Natural Gas Branch, D.R. Gillard
Director, Geology & Mines Branch, Dr. L.S. Beck
Director, Data & Statistics, vacant
Administrator, Mineral Titles Transfer, C. Dumba
Director, Mineral Revenues, Steve Zurawski
Director, Office of Energy Conservation, Fred Heal
Director, Policy Planning & Research, Ron Sully
Director, Communications, Ralph Smith

DEPT. OF NORTHERN SASKATCHEWAN
Box 5000, La Ronge, Sask. S0J 1L0
Information Contact, Bev Hamm, Executive Asst. to Deputy Minister (phone: 306 425-4200)

Acts Administered
Dept. of Northern Sask. Act
Northern Admin. Act
Northern Sask. Economic Development Act

The department is responsible for the administration of most provincial government programs within the Northern Administration District.

MINISTER, Hon. J. Hammersmith
Deputy Minister, R.L. Purdie
Executive Assts. to Deputy Minister, A. Roy Morin (La Ronge); N. Murray (Regina)
Asst. Deputy Minister, Project Management, D. Murphy
Asst. Deputy Minister, Resources & Economic Development, Cliff Superrault
Asst. Deputy Minister, Academic Education, Health Services & Social Services, B. Hill
Director, Manpower Secretariat, Mike Mercredi
Admin. Branch, Director, J. Morris

SASKATCHEWAN OIL & GAS CORP. (A Crown Corp.)
#1500, 1920 Broad St., Box 1550, Regina, Sask. S4P 3C4
(306) 565-7000

Saskoil Resources Inc.
#1435, 300 5th Ave. S.W., Calgary, Alta. T2P 3C4
(403) 265-4032
a wholly-owned subsidiary

Chairman of the Board, Hon. E.L. Cowley
Secretary, E. Kassian
President, J.R. Sadler
Vice President, Exploration, W.J. Douglas
Vice President, Finance & Corporate Services, J.P. Landry
Vice President, Resource Development, D.M. Christensen
General Manager, Oil & Gas Division, P.M. Greenwood
General Manager, Heavy Oil Division, G.B. Armstrong

OMBUDSMAN
2310 Scarth St., Regina, Sask. S4P 3V7
(306) 565-6211
Ombudsman, David A. Tickell
Saskatoon Sub-office: 206 4th Ave. S.: Asst. to Ombudsman, G.R. Thomson

SASKATCHEWAN POWER CORP. (A Crown Corp.)
2025 Victoria Ave., Regina, Sask. S4P 0S1
(306) 527-7611
President, R.H. Moncur

GOVERNMENT PRINTING CO. (A Crown Corp.)
2005 8th Ave., Regina, Sask. S4R 7B2
(306) 525-3557
General Manager, D.B. Breher

DEPT. OF PROVINCIAL SECRETARY
308, 1919 Rose St., Regina, Sask. S4P 3P1
Information (306) 565-2951

Acts Administered
Bird Emblem Act
Floral Emblem Act
Provincial Arms Act
Provincial Secretary's Act

MINISTER, Hon. Elwood Cowley

SASKATCHEWAN PUBLIC SERVICE COMMISSION
3211 Albert St., Regina, Sask. S4S 5W6
Chairman, David Bock
Director, Administration Branch, Russ Moore, 565-7507
Director, Communications Branch, Pat Bugera, 565-7657
Director, Compensation Research Branch, Rick McKillop, 565-7625
A/Executive Director, Departmental Services Branch, David Babiuk, 565-7560
Director, Personnel Services Branch, Jim Penrod, 565-7520
Director, Staff Relations Branch, Tor Veltheim, 565-7606
Director, Staff Training & Development Branch, Bill Duncan, 565-7590

SASKATCHEWAN RESEARCH COUNCIL
30 Campus Dr., Saskatoon, Sask. S7N OX1
(306) 664-5400
Executive Director, Dr. T.P. Pepper, Univ. Campus (Saskatoon)
Secretary, D.N. Murray, 2839 Angus St., Regina
Administrative Officer, R.E. Melvin
Chemistry & Biology Division, Dr. E.C. Coxworth
Engineering Division, Dr. W.H.W. Husband
Geology Division, Dr. R.G. Arnold
Industrial Services Division, A. Scharf
Physics Division, Dr. J. Maybank

DEPT. OF REVENUE, SUPPLY & SERVICES
Avord Tower, 2002 Victoria Ave., Regina, Sask. S4P 3V7 (except where otherwise indicated)
Information Contact, Brian Leibel, Manager, Support Services Division (phone: 306/565-6532)

Acts Administered
Dept. of Revenue, Supply & Services Act
Education & Health Tax Act
Queen's Printer Act
Purchasing Act
Tobacco Tax Act
Farm Cost Reduction Act
Insurance Premiums Tax Act
Fuel Petroleum Products Act
Liquor Consumption Tax Act

MINISTER, Hon. W.A. Robbins
Deputy Minister, C.A. Carr, 565-6520
Executive Director, Revenue Division, vacant
Executive Director, Operations Division, John Law
Executive Director, Support Services Division, K. Brehm
Executive Director, Systems Division, K. Taylor
A/Director, Central Vehicle Agency, L. Benson
Director, Purchasing Agency, H.C. Abells
Director, Mail & Telecommunications, E. Bereti
Director, Office Services Agency, Leo Hoffman
Director, Metric Information Centre, K. Beesley
Queen's Printer, R.S. Reid
Supervisor, Provincial Inquiry Centre, Robert Leonard, 565-6291

DEPT. OF RURAL AFFAIRS
2240 Albert St., Regina, Sask. S4P 3V7
Information Contact, Wes Mazer, Director, Administrative Services (306/565-2727)

Acts Administered
Controverted Municipal Elections Act
Dept. of Rural Affairs Act
Municipal Employees Superannuation Act
Municipal Expropriation Act
Municipal Revenue Sharing Act
Municipal Tax Sharing (Potash) Act
Municipal Unit & County Act
Planning & Development Act
Rural Municipality Act
Rural Municipal Secretary Treasurers Act
Tax Enforcement Act
Tax Sharing (Pipelines) Act
Time Act

MINISTER, Hon. Edgar Kaeding, 565-2260
Deputy Minister, A.J. Webster, 565-2630
Special Asst. to Deputy Minister, M.A. Czornobay, 565-2632
Assoc. Deputy Minister of Road Services, H.A. Clampitt, 565-2630
Executive Director, D.V. Gilewich, 565-2701
Chief Municipal Engineer, G. Grass, 565-2716
Administrative Services Branch, W. Mazer, 565-2727
Municipal Management & Financial Advisory Services Branch, N.J. Bichel, 565-2656
Community Planning Branch, L. Talbot, 565-2732
Assessment Branch (Dual for Urban & Rural Affairs Depts.), N. Rudrick, 565-2666
Municipal Employees' Superannuation, S. Wowk, 565-2684
Bridge Branch, E. Anderson, 565-2706
Planning & Research Branch, W. Antonio, 565-2720

SASKCOMP (A Crown Corp.)
(Saskatchewan Computer Utility Corp.)
2161 Scarth St., Regina, Sask. S4P 2H8
(306) 565-3951

SASKMEDIA (A Crown Corp.)
(The Saskatchewan Educational Communications Corp.)
1112 Winnipeg St., Box 7120, Regina, Sask. S4P 3S7
(306) 565-5100
Chairman, Board of Directors, Dr. Murray P. Scharf
General Manager, Lloyd J. McDonald

DEPT. OF SOCIAL SERVICES
1920 Broad St., Regina, Sask. S4P 3V6
Information Contact, Jim Oxman, Director, Public Relations Branch (phone: 306 565-3665)
General Inquiries: 565-3494

Acts Administered
Dept. of Social Services Act
Blind Persons' Allowances Act
Children of Unmarried Parents Act

Community Services Act
Corrections Act
Disabled Persons' Allowance Act
Family Services Act
Housing & Special-care Homes Act
Rehabilitation Act
Sask. Assistance Act, 1966

MINISTER, Hon. D. Lingenfelter, 565-3661
Deputy Minister, Duane Adams, 565-3491
Operations Division, A/Executive Director, Steven Pillar, 565-4909
Income Support Division, A/Executive Director, Art Urhen, 565-3641
Community & Personal Services Division, Executive Director, Don Schurman, 565-3644
Core Services Branch, Director, Dick Baxter, 693-5131
Day Care Branch, Director, Shirley McKendry, 565-3855
Community & Employment Services Branch, Director, Mel Gill, 565-3632
Regional Services Division, Executive Director, Nola Seymoar, 565-7357
Family & Youth Services Branch, Director, Vic Wiebe, 565-3647
Continuing Care Division, Executive Director, Steve Petz, 565-3629
Home Care Branch, Director, Helene Donahue, 565-5010
Residential Care Branch, Director, Wayne McKendrick, 565-7854

SASKATCHEWAN TELECOMMUNICATIONS (SASK TEL) (A Crown Corp.)

2121 Saskatchewan Dr., Regina, Sask. S4P 3Y2
Information Contact, F.P. Petruic, Manager, Public Affairs (phone: 306/347-2000)
President, A.L.M. Nelson
Vice President, Customer Services, F.A. Degenstein
Vice President, Network Services, P. Van Vliet
Vice President, Administration, R.E. Bason
Vice President, Operations Development, S.F. Lee
Vice President, Personnel & Public Affairs, J. Houston
Vice President, General Counsel, T.A. Howe

DEPT. OF TELEPHONES

2121 Saskatchewan Dr., Regina, Sask. S4P 3Y2
Minister, Hon. D. Cody
Deputy Minister, A.L.M. Nelson (347-2200)
Rural Admin. Manager, H.G. Booth (347-2603)

DEPT. OF TOURISM & RENEWABLE RESOURCES

3211 Albert St., Regina, Sask. S4S 5W6 except where otherwise shown
Information Contact, SaskTravel (phone: 306/565-2300)

Acts Administered

Dept. of Tourism & Renewable Resources Act
Fisheries Act
Fur Act
Game Act
Game Export Act
Litter Control Act
Migratory Birds Convention Act
Pollution of Certain Waters Act
Payment of Wolf & Coyote Bounties Act
Summary Offences Procedure Act
Forest Act
Prairie & Forest Fires Act
Provincial Lands Act
Provincial Parks, Protected Areas etc. Act
Regional Parks Act

MINISTER, Hon. Reg Gross
Deputy Minister, F.J. Bogdasavich (565-2930)
Asst. Deputy Minister, Ron Stengler (565-2380)
Fisheries, Director, G.E. Couldwell (565-2884)
Wildlife, Director, R. MacLennan (565-2886)
Firearm Safety Supervisors, Don Pryce, Regina (565-2314); G. Hamilton, Prov. Office Bldg., Prince Albert, Sask. S6V 1B5 (764-6433)
Forestry Branch, Provincial Office Bldg., Prince Albert, Sask. S6V 1B5
Director, W.S. Bailey (763-6434)
Policy Planning, Director, Frank Hart (565-2322)
Tourism Development, Director, Roger Franklin (565-2330)
Assistance Programs, Director, G. Rathwell (565-2897)
Supervisor of Lands, T. Wagner (565-2796)
Marketing & Promotions, Director, Leona Gorr (565-4069)
Supervisor, Public Information Services, N. Matthies (565-2306)
Supervisor, Design & Publications, J. Glasser (565-2316)
Park Development, Director, Curtis Miles (565-2846)
Visitor Services, A/Director, Albert Dubé (565-2936)
Operations, Director, B. Tether (565-2323)
Program Planning, Director, vacant (565-2322)
Administrative Services, Director, Mae Boa (565-2880)

SASKATCHEWAN TRANSPORTATION AGENCY

4th floor, T.D. Bank Bldg., 1914 Hamilton St., Regina, Sask. S4P 4V4
(306) 565-7814

SASKATCHEWAN TRANSPORTATION CO. (A Crown Corp.)

2041 Hamilton St., Regina, Sask. S4P 2E2
(306) 565-3347
General Manager, R.M. Suggitt

DEPT. OF URBAN AFFAIRS

1791 Rose St. (Box 7110, Regina, Sask. S4P 3V7)
Information Contact, Irene Rau, Information Officer, 306/565-2686

Acts Administered

Border Areas Act
Carlyle Lake Resort Act
Civil Defence Act
Community Capital Fund Act, 1980
Community Planning Profession Act
Controverted Municipal Elections Act
Cut Knife Reference Act
Flin Flon Extension of Boundaries Act, 1952
Gas & Electrical Rates (Public Corporations) Act
House Building Assistance Act, 1974
Industrial Towns Act
Jackfish-Murray Lake Resort Municipality Act, 1974
Lloydminster Municipal Amalgamation Act, 1930
Local Government Board Act
Local Government Board (Special Powers) Act
Local Government Board (Temporary Special Powers) Act
Local Improvements Act
Management Accountants Act
Municipal Corporation of Uranium City & Dist. Act, 1956
Municipal Debentures Repayment Act
Municipal Development & Loan (Sask.) Act
Municipal Expropriation Act
Municipal Improvements Assistance (Sask.) Act
Municipal Industrial Development Corporations Act
Municipal Public Works Act
Municipal Revenue Sharing Act
Municipal Water Assistance Act
Planning & Development Act
Property Improvement Grant Act
Renters Property Tax Rebate Act
Saskatchewan Assessment Act
Senior Citizens Home Repair Assistance Act
Senior Citizens School Tax Rebate Act

Sewage Drainage Inquiry Act
Tax Enforcement Act
Time Act
Urban Municipal Administrators' Act
Urban Municipal Elections Act
Urban Municipality Act
Wakamow Valley Authority Act
Wascana Centre Act
Water Pollution Control Assistance Act

MINISTER, Hon. Walter E. Smishek
Deputy Minister, Don Moroz, 565-2660
Assoc. Deputy Minister, David Innes, 565-2733
Administrative Services, Don Bennett, 565-2831
Municipal Management & Finance Division, Kevin Hayes, 565-2674
Advisory Services Branch, John Marusiak, 565-2642
Municipal Grants Branch, Donald Koop, 565-2675
Property Tax Rebates Branch, Henry Kutarna, 565-2683
Regional Planning Branch, Henry McCutcheon, 565-2268
Community Planning Branch, Garry Parker, 565-2687
Urban Development Branch, Keith Schneider, 565-2647
Emergency Measures Org., Jim Eaton, 525-8121
Sask. Assessment Authority, Executive Director, N.M. Rudrick, 565-2666

Associated Agencies
Board of Examiners
1791 Rose St., Regina, Sask. S4P 3V7 (565-2831)
Secretary, vacant
Municipal Water Assistance Board
1791 Rose St., Regina, Sask. S4P 3V7 (565-2663)
Secretary, vacant
Provincial Planning Appeals Board
1791 Rose St., Regina, Sask. S4P 3V7 (565-2687)
Secretary, G. Parker
Sask. Assessment Appeal Board
1791 Rose St., Regina, Sask. S4P 3V7 (565-2658)
Secretary, K.E. Mackie
Local Government Board
1920 Broad St., Regina, Sask. S4P 3V6 (565-6221)
Secretary, J.F. Chaney
Sask. Housing Corp.
#800, 2500 Victoria, Regina, Sask. S4P 3V7 (565-4177)
Manager, S. Willox
Municipal Employees Superannuation Commission
2240 Albert St., Regina, Sask. S4P 2V7 (565-2684)
Executive Secretary, S.E. Wowk

WORKERS' COMPENSATION BOARD
See Dept. of Labour

NORTHWEST TERRITORIES
Reconstituted 1st September, 1905.
Area: 1,304,903 sq. miles
Population: 46,063 (Dec. 1979)
Seat of Government: Yellowknife, N.W.T.

The Northwest Territories comprises all that part of Canada north of the Sixtieth Parallel of North Latitude, except the portions thereof within the Yukon Territory and the Provinces of Quebec, Newfoundland, Ontario and Manitoba. The Northwest Territories Act, Chapter 331, R.S.C., 1952 as amended to 1974 provides for the Government of the Northwest Territories by a Commissioner under instructions given from time to time by the Governor in Council or the Minister of the Department of Indian Affairs and Northern Development. The Act also provides for a Council consisting of twenty-two elected members, representing constituencies in the Northwest Territories. Members serve for four year terms. Legislative powers are exercised by the Commissioner in Council on such matters as direct taxation within the Territories, maintenance of municipal institutions, licenses, solemnization of marriages, property and civil rights, administration of justice, education, public health and generally all matters of a local nature. The administration of the Territories under the Northwest Territories Act and the Ordinances passed by the Commissioner in Council is carried on by the Public Service of the Northwest Territories. Development of resources and certain programs involving Dene and Inuit are carried on by the Dept. of Indian Affairs & Northern Development.

COMMISSIONER & COUNCIL OF THE NORTHWEST TERRITORIES
Commr., J.H. Parker
Council:
Baffin Central:
Baffin South: Joe Arlooktoo
Central Arctic: Kane Tologanak
Foxe Basin: Mark Evaluarjuk
Frobisher Bay: Dennis Patterson
Great Slave East: Robert Sayine
Hay River: Don Stewart
High Arctic: Ludy Pudluk
Hudson Bay: Moses Appaqiq
Inuvik: Tom Butters
Keewatin North: William Noah
Keewatin South: Tagak Curley
Mackenzie Delta: Richard Nerysoo
Mackenzie Great Bear: Peter Fraser
Mackenzie Liard: Nick Sibbeston
Pine Point: Bruce McLaughlin
Rae-Lac-la-Martre: James Wah-Shee
Slave River: Arnold J. McCallum
Western Arctic: Nellie Cournoyea
Yellowknife Centre: Bob MacQuarrie
Yellowknife North: George Braden
Yellowknife South: Lynda Sorensen
Clerk of the Council, W.H. Remnant

TERRITORIAL OFFICIALS
Deputy Commr., Bob Pilot
Director of Information, A. Sorensen
Deputy Ministers:
Economic Development & Tourism, Rod Morrison
Local Government, L. Elkin
Public Works, P. Moody
Social Services, Ron Crossley
Health, Ron Crossley
Public Services, Stein Lal
Renewable Resources, Ted Bowyer
Finance, E. Nielsen
Education, B. Lewis
Government Services, John Quirke
Director of Personnel, Jim Blewett

FEDERAL OFFICIALS
Director, Northern Co-ordination & Social Development Branch, Ottawa, F.B. Fingland
Chief, Territorial Relations Branch, Ottawa, R.L. Kennedy
Regional Director, Dept. of Indian Affairs & Northern Development, Yellowknife, Hiram Beaubier

LEGAL SERVICES
Director, Dept. of Public Services (Admin. of Justice), Stein Lal
Chief of Legal Services, Stein Lal
Legal Counsel, J.G. Gilmour, S. Johnson, Joel Fournier
Legislative Counsel, Dare Pearce
Public Trustee, Elsie Bagan
Registrar of Land Titles, Garry MacDougall
Registrar of Motor Vehicles, A. Maksymowich
Registrar of Vital Statistics, A.P. Matheson
(Fee for certificates of Birth, Marriage or Death, $5. per certificate).

YUKON TERRITORY

-not confirmed for 1982-
Organized June 13th, 1898
Population: (Aug., 1980) 24,569
Area: 536,223 sq. kilometres
Seat of Government: Whitehorse

Yukon was created as a separate territory in June, 1898. Provision is made for a locally elected government selected from among an elected Legislative Assembly of 16 members with a four year tenure of office. A federally appointed Commissioner oversees federal interests in the territory, but the day-to-day operation of the Government of Yukon rests with the wholly elected Executive Council or Cabinet.

The Executive Council consists of the Government Leader as chairman and four members nominated by the Government Leader in the Assembly and appointed by the Commissioner.

The territorial legislature has power to make ordinances on generally all matters of a local nature in the territory, including the imposition of local taxes, property and civil rights and the administration of justice, education and welfare.

Legislative powers vested in the provinces but not available to the territory include control of unoccupied Crown land, renewable and non-renewable resources (except wildlife), public debt through the issuing of bonds and the power to amend the Yukon Act, a federal statute.

MEMBERS OF LEGISLATIVE ASSEMBLY

Campbell: Bob Flemming, Ind.
Faro: M. Byblow, Ind.
Hootalinqua: L. Falle, P.C.
Klondike: Meg McCall, P.C.
Kluane: Alice McGuire, Lib.
Mayo: Swede Hanson, P.C.
Old Crow: Grafton Njootli, P.C.
Tatchun: Howard Tracey, P.C.
Watson Lake: D.E. Taylor, P.C.
Whitehorse North Centre: Geoff Lattin, P.C.
Whitehorse Porter Creek East: D. Lang, P.C.
Whitehorse Porter Creek West: Doug Graham, P.C.
Whitehorse Riverdale North: Chris Pearson, P.C.
Whitehorse Riverdale South: Iain MacKay, Lib.
Whitehorse South Centre: Roger Kimmerly, N.D.P.
Whitehorse West: Tony Penikett, N.D.P.
Clerk of Assembly, Pat Michael

EXECUTIVE COUNCIL MEMBERS

Government Leader, and Minister responsible for land claims, pipelines, Finance, Executive Council Office, Public Service Commission, Chris Pearson
Minister of Tourism & Economic Development, and Renewable Resources, Dan Lang
Minister of Justice, Education, Consumer & Corporate Affairs, Government Services, and Information Resources, Doug Graham
Minister of Highways & Public Works, Municipal & Community Affairs, Yukon Housing Corp., and Yukon Liquor Corp., Geoff Lattin
Minister of Health & Human Resources, and Workers' Compensation Board, Meg McCall
Executive Council Office, Linda J. Adams, Deputy Minister

DEPUTY MINISTERS

Finance, Any Johnston
Education, Terry Weninger
Consumer & Corporate Affairs, Doug Spray
Government Services, Andy Vantell
Health & Human Resources, Jim Davie
Highways & Public Works, L.W. Blackman
Information Resources, Garth Graham
Intergovernmental Affairs, Harry Murphy
Justice, Padraig O'Donoghue
Municipal & Community Affairs, Grant Livingston
Public Service Commission, Paul Roddick
Renewable Resources, Lynn Chambers
Tourism & Economic Development, Peter Kent
Workers' Compensation Board, Brian Booth, Executive Secretary
Yukon Housing Corporation, Larry Turner, General Manager
Yukon Liquor Corporation, Rolly Thibault, General Manager

OTHER GOVERNMENT OFFICIALS

Administrator, Corporate Affairs, John Lawson
Administrator, Consumer Affairs, Ron Wilson
Deputy Registrar of Motor Vehicles, Paul Labrash
Asst. Supt. of Education, Dave Pritchard
A/Director, Revenue & Taxation, Lynda Gunderson
Director, Supply Services, Derm O'Donovan
Chief, Alcohol & Drug Services, Charles McLaughlin
Deputy Registrar, Vital Statistics, Arlene Kovac
Asst. Director, Highways & Public Works, Kurt Koken
Asst. Director, Human Resources, Ross Findlater
Territorial Librarian, Jean Dirksen
Territorial Archivist, Miriam McTiernan
Solicitor, Legal Services, Sid Horton
Registrar of Land Titles, Wayne Macara
Public Administrator, Joan Vienott
Supt., Corrections Services, Gary Snow
Land Claims Administrator, Gordon Steele
Chief, Municipal Services, Len Imrie
Lands Administrator, Bob Friesen
Chief Territorial Assessor, Mel Smith
Director, Pipeline Branch, John Ferbey
Director, Parks & Historic Resources, Don Hutton
Director, Tourism Marketing, George Sinfield

DEPT. OF JUSTICE

Director of Justice, P. O'Donoghue, Q.C.
Judicial Administrator, B.L. Stubbins
Administrative Officer, Mrs. C. Zatorski

COURTS & JUDGES, FEDERAL

SUPREME COURT OF CANADA

Supreme Court Bldg., Wellington St., Ottawa, Ont. K1A OJ1

The Supreme Court of Canada, first established in 1875 by the Supreme and Exchequer Court Act, is now governed by the Supreme Court Act (R.S.C. 1970, c. S-19, as amended by R.S.C. (1st supp.), c. 44, 1974-75-76, c. 18).

The Supreme Court sits at Ottawa and exercises general appellate jurisdiction throughout Canada in civil and criminal cases. The judgment of the Court is final and conclusive. The Court is also required to advise on questions referred to it by the Governor in Council. Under section 55 of the Supreme Court Act, important questions concerning the interpretation of the British North America Act, the constitutionality or interpretation of any federal or provincial law, the powers of Parliament or of the provincial legislatures or of both levels of government, among other matters, may be referred by the Government to the Supreme Court for consideration.

In civil cases, appeals may be brought from any final judgment of the highest court of last resort in a province by obtaining leave to do so from that court or from the Supreme Court itself. The Supreme Court will grant permission to appeal if it is of the opinion that a question of public importance is involved, one that transcends the immediate concerns of the parties to the litigation.

In criminal cases, the Court will hear appeals concerning indictable offences where an acquittal has been set aside or where there has been a dissenting judgment on a point of law in a provincial court of appeal. The Supreme Court may, in addition, hear appeals on questions of law concerning both summary convictions and indictable offences if permission to appeal is first granted by the Court.

There are normally three sessions of the Court each year, beginning on the fourth Tuesday in January, the fourth Tuesday in April and the first Tuesday in October.

The Court consists of a Chief Justice, who is called the Chief Jutice of Canada, and eight puisne judges. They are appointed by the Governor in Council and hold office during good behaviour but are removable by the Governor General on address of the Senate and the House of Commons. They cease to hold office on attaining the age of 75 years.

The Court is responsible for its own administration and budgeting. Its estimates are submitted to Parliament by the Minister of Justice. The Registrar has the rank of Deputy Head and, subject to the direction of the Chief Justice, is responsible for the Registry, the Library, the Supreme Court Reports as well as personnel.

Chief Justice of Canada, Rt. Hon. Bora Laskin, P.C.

Puisne Judges, Hon. Ronald Martland, Hon. Ronald A. Ritchie, Hon. R.G.B. Dickson, Hon. Jean Beetz, Hon. Willard Z. Estey, Hon. W.R. McIntyre, Hon. Julien Chouinard, Hon. Antonio Lamer

Registrar, Bernard C. Hofley, Q.C.

Deputy Registrar, Mills Shipley

Chief Librarian, Peter Freeman

Asst. Librarians, Mary Jane T. Sinclair, Johane Thibodeau

Asst. Registrar (Process), Réginald P. Boudreau

Clerk of Process, E.J. Bisson

THE FEDERAL COURT OF CANADA

Supreme Court of Canada Bldg., Kent & Wellington Sts., Ottawa, Ont. K1A OH9

The Federal Court of Appeal has jurisdiction on appeals from the Trial Division, appeals from Federal Tribunals, review of decisions of Federal Boards and Commissions, appeals from Tribunals and reviews under section 28 of the Federal Court Act, and references by Federal Boards and Commissions.

The Trial Division of the Federal Court of Canada has jurisdiction in claims against the Crown, claims by the Crown, miscellaneous cases involving the Crown, claims against or concerning Crown Officers and Servants, relief against Federal Boards, Commissions and other Tribunals, Inter-Provincial and Federal-Provincial disputes, industrial, industrial property matters, admiralty, income tax and estate tax appeals, citizenship appeals, aeronautics, Inter-Provincial works and undertakings, residuary jurisdiction for relief if there is no other Canadian court that has such jurisdiction, jurisdiction in specific matters conferred by Federal Statutes.

Chief Justice, The Hon. Arthur Louis Thurlow

Judicial Administrator (Appeal Division), Huguette R. Narum

Assoc. Chief Justice, The Hon. James A. Jerome

Judicial Administrator (Trial Division), Pauline C. Bratt

Court of Appeal Judges, Hon. Louis Pratte; Hon. Darrel Verner Heald; Hon. John J. Urie; Hon. William F. Ryan; Hon. Gerald E. LeDain

Trial Division Judges, (The Hon. Mr. Justice): A. Alex. Cattanach; Hugh F. Gibson; Allison Arthur Mariotti Walsh; Frank U. Collier; George A. Addy; Patrick M. Mahoney, P.C.; Raymond G. Decary; Jean-Eudes Dubé, P.C.; Louis Marceau

Administrator of the Court, Robert Biljan (act.)

Registry of the Court

Principal Office, Ottawa, Ont.

Asst. Administrator, Appeal Division, vacant

Clerk of Process, Appeal Division, J.P. Briand

Clerk of Process, Trial Division, J.F.D. Cousineau

Clerk of Process & Manual Co-ordinator, P.F. Scott

Clerk of Process & Court Registrar Co-ordinator, J. Strader

Local Offices

Montreal: Palais de Justice, 11th floor, 1 Notre Dame St. E., Montreal, P.Q. H2Y 1B6 (514/283-4936), Dist. Administrator, Joseph L. Daoust

Toronto: Canada Life Bldg., 8th floor, 330 Universiy Ave., Toronto, Ont. M5G 1R7 (416/369-3356), Dist. Administrator, J. Alfred Preston

Vancouver: The Pacific Centre, Box 10065, 700 W. Georgia St., Vancouver, B.C. V7Y 1B6 (604/666-3232), Dist. Administrator, P.R. Gaudet

Halifax: 154 Anchorage House, Historic Properties, 1869 Upper Water St., Halifax, N.S. B3J 1S9 (902/426-3282), Dist. Administrator, R.C. Howell

Winnipeg: 224 Woodsworth Bldg., 405 Broadway, Winnipeg, Man. R3C 3L6 (204/949-2509), Dist. Administrator, A. Rouse

Saskatoon: The Court House, 520 Spadina Cres. E., Saskatoon, Sask. (306/665-4509), Dist. Administrator, Miss Margaret Petersen

Regina: The Court House, 2425 Victoria Ave., Regina, Sask. S4P 3E4 (306/359-5268), Dist. Administrator, F.C. Newis

Calgary: The Court House, 611 4th St. S.W., Calgary, Alta. T2P 1T5 (403/231-5920), Dist. Administrator, James M. McLaughlin

Edmonton: The Law Court Bldg., 1A Sir Winston Churchill Sq., Edmonton, Alta. (403/423-7110), Dist. Administrator, D.S. Huff

Quebec City: The Superior Court, Palais de Justice, Room C-22, 12 St-Louis St., Quebec, P.Q. G1R 4P6 (418/694-4920), Dist. Administrator, Maurice Gobeil

St. John's: The Court House, Duckworth St., Box 937, St. John's, Nfld. A1C 5M3 (709/722-6524), Dist. Administrator, Henry J. Thorne

Saint John: Provincial Bldg., 4th floor, Room 427, 110 Charlotte St., Saint John, N.B. (506/648-4990), Dist. Administrator, B.R. Guss

Fredericton: Justice Bldg., Supreme Court of New Brunswick, Queen St., Room 202, Box 6000, Fredericton, N.B. E3B 5H1 (506/452-3016), Dist. Administrator, Murray F. Cain, Q.C.

Charlottetown: Sir Henry Louis Davies Courthouse, 42 Water St., Box 2200, Charlottetown, P.E.I. C1A 8B9 (902/892-9900), Dist. Administrator, George E. MacMillan

Whitehorse: Federal Bldg., 308 Main St., Room 259, Whitehorse, Y.T. Y1A 2B5 (403/668-4314), Dist. Administrator, A.A. Schmidt

Yellowknife: Court House, Box 550, Yellowknife, N.W.T. XOE 1HO (403/873-2044), Dist. Administrator, Alexander Stewart

THE COURT MARTIAL APPEAL COURT OF CANADA

Supreme Court of Canada Bldg., Kent & Wellington Sts., Ottawa, Ont. K1A OH9

President, Hon. Mr. Justice H.F. Gibson

Judicial Administrator, Miss R.C. Poirier

Puisne Judges, (The Honourable) Arthur L. Thurlow; Yves Bernier; Angus Alexander Cattanach; Allison A.M. Walsh; Louis Pratte; Darrel V. Heald; Frank U. Collier; David R. Verchere; Arthur R. Jessup; David M. Dickson; Gordon C. Hall; Gordon L.S. Hart; William R. Sinclair; John J. Urie; George A. Addy; Patrick M. Mahoney, P.C.; Raymond G. Decary; William F. Ryan; Lawrence T. Pennell; Ignace J. Deslauriers; Alphonse Barbeau; James K. Hugessen; Yves Forest; Murdoch A. MacPherson; Jean-Eudes Dubé, P.C.; Gerald E. Le Dain; G. Arthur Martin; Louis Marceau; Benjamin Hewak; Alexander M. MacIntosh; William J. Trainor; Robert C. Rutherford; Charles C. Locke; Lloyd G. McKenzie; Hugh P. Legg; James A. Jerome; Lawrence A. Poitras; John Watson Brooke; James Creighton Cavanagh

Administrator of the Court, Robert Biljan (act.)

Registry of the Court

Asst. Administrator, vacant

Clerk of Process, J.P. Briand

OFFICE OF THE COMMISSIONER FOR FEDERAL JUDICIAL AFFAIRS

Ottawa, Ont. K1A 1E3

(613) 992-9175

The Office oversees administrative matters respecting the Federal Court of Canada, the Canadian Judicial Council and all federally appointed judges other than those of the Supreme Court of Canada.

Commr., S. Samuels, Q.C.

Deputy Commr., A. Laframboise
Chief, Judges Administration, Mrs. L. Fox
Editor, Federal Court Law Reports, Mrs. F. Rosenfeld

COURTS, JUDGES, ETC., ALBERTA

COURT OF APPEAL

Court House, 611 4th St. S.W., Calgary
Chief Justice of Alberta, Hon. W.A. McGillivray, Calgary
Justices of Appeal, Hon. N.D. McDermid, Calgary; Hon. C.W. Clement, Edmonton; Hon. Samuel S. Lieberman, Edmonton; Hon. D.C. Prowse, Calgary; Hon. A.F. Moir, Edmonton; Hon. W.J. Haddad, Edmonton; Hon. James H. Laycraft, Calgary; Hon. A.M. Harradence, Calgary; Hon. W.A. Stevenson, Edmonton; Hon. J.W. McClung, Edmonton; Hon. R.H. Belzil, Edmonton; Hon. R.P. Kerans, Calgary

COURT OF QUEEN'S BENCH

Chief Justice, Hon. W.R. Sinclair, Edmonton
Justices, Hon. W.K. Moore, Calgary; Hon. P. Greschuk, Edmonton; Hon. W.J.C. Kirby, Calgary; Hon. A.M. Dechene, Edmonton; Hon. M.B. O'Byrne, Edmonton; Hon. H.J. MacDonald, Calgary; Hon. D.H. Bowen, Edmonton; Hon. J.C. Cavanagh, Edmonton; Hon. M.E. Shannon, Calgary; Hon. D.C. McDonald, Edmonton; Hon. F.H. Quigley, Calgary; Hon. W.R. Brennan, Calgary; Hon. V.P. Moshansky, Calgary; Hon. T.H. Miller, Edmonton; Hon. J.M. Hope, Edmonton; Hon. J.H. Waite, Calgary; Hon. L.D. MacLean, Lethbridge; Hon. G.R. Forsyth, Calgary; Hon. J.N. Decore, Edmonton; Hon. H.S. Patterson, Calgary; Hon. J.S. Cormack, Edmonton; Hon. S.V. Legg, Edmonton; Hon. J.G. Kidd, Calgary; Hon. C.G. Yanosik, Lethbridge; Hon. H.S. Rowbotham, Calgary; Hon. J.B. Feehan, Edmonton; Hon. A.W. Crossley, Edmonton; Hon. D.H. Medhurst, Calgary; Hon. A.H. Wachowich, Edmonton; Hon. J.D. Bracco, Edmonton; Hon. Elizabeth A. McFadyen, Edmonton; Hon. J.K. Holmes, Calgary; Hon. J.B. Dea, Edmonton; Hon. Mary M. Hetherington, Calgary; Hon. R.P. Foisy, Edmonton; Hon. R.A. Cawsey, Edmonton; Hon. H.S. Prowse, Calgary; Hon. W.G. Egbert, Calgary; Hon. P.C.G. Power, Edmonton; Hon. S.S. Purvis, Edmonton; Hon. J.A. Agrios, Edmonton; Hon. J.S. Kryczka, Calgary; Hon. J.J. Stratton, Edmonton; Hon. R.A. Dixon, Calgary; Hon. F.R. MacNaughten, Edmonton; Hon. V.W. Smith, Edmonton; Hon. M.E. Lomas, Calgary; Hon. W.J. Girgulis, Edmonton; Hon. J.B. Veit, Edmonton

Bankruptcy

Court of Queen's Bench Judges have jurisdiction in bankruptcy.
Registrar in Bankruptcy, M.B. Funduk, Law Courts, 1A Sir Winston Churchill Sq., Edmonton, Alta. T5J 0R2
Registrar in Bankruptcy, W.H. Dagleish, Q.C., Courthouse, 611 4th St. S.W., Calgary, Alta. T2P 1T5

Registration of Instruments

The Personal Property Registration Branch encompasses Vehicle and Central Registry functions of registration and searches. Central Registry, located on the 16th floor, A.E. LePage Bldg., 10130 103 St., Edmonton, Alta., registers personal property other than itinerant machines; such as partnerships, trade names, limited partnerships and mobile homes. Vehicle Registry, at the same address as Central Registry, registers personal property defined as itinerant machines such as motor vehicles, aircraft, trailers, oilwell drilling equipment, rolling railway stock, mobile homes, farm machinery, and farm or industrial tractors.

SURROGATE COURT

Chief Justice, Hon. W.R. Sinclair, Edmonton
Justices, (Same as Court of Queen's Bench)

JUDICIAL DISTRICTS

Calgary

Regional Manager, J. McLaughlin, act.
Sheriff, W. Moore
Regional Agent, South, P.S. Chrumka, Q.C.
Agents of the Attorney General & Crown Counsel, Rocky Mountain Plaza, Calgary: B.R. Fraser; T.A. Beattie; G.J. Belecki; M.A. Brown; J.P. Brunnen; R.H. Davie; M. Delong; B.W. Duncan; L. England; I. Goldman; L. Greive; S.A. Jackson; I.F. Kirkpatrick; P.J. Knoll; M. Krotter; S.M. Manolescu; P.W. Martin; D.M. McDonald; B. Newton; S.K. O'Ferral; R.K. Sood; L. Stein; M. Stober; R. Synenko; E.G. Wilson

Drumheller

District Administrator & Sheriff, J. Gretzan, Drumheller
Agent of the Attorney General & Crown Counsel, Drumheller: J.T. McBride

Edmonton

Regional Manager & Sheriff, D. Huff, Edmonton
Regional Agent, North, D.C. Abbott, Q.C.
Regional Manager, North (Court Services), P.J. Zyla
Senior Agent, J.S. Koval
Agents of the Attorney General & Crown Counsel, Century Place, Edmonton: M.G. Allen; M. Braun; B. Brown; J.K. Conley; M.C. Elton; W.M. Ferries; D.L. Gibson; A.P. Hazell; J.W. Jackie; K.J. Leathem; G.J. Lepine; E. McKall; R.G. McCuaig; J.E. Mos; E.M. Nash; B. Peterson; H.E. Pickard; W.G. Pinckney; A.E.Piragoff; B. Rosborough; S.M. Sanderman; P.R. Solotki; R.S. Stelmaczonek; W.R. Stephen; J.M. Stewart; R.F. Taylor; K.E. Tjosvold; G. Tomljanovic; J. Watson; L. Wenden; K.T. Woroby; I. Yaverbaum; J.J. Yusep
Provincial Agent, Special Prosecutions, H.B. Casson, Q.C.
Agents of the Attorney General & Crown Counsel, 9833 109 St., Edmonton: W. Dunfield; Y. Roslak, Q.C.; J. Connors, Q.C.; M.N. McCrank; L.Z. Mozeson; D. Nelson-Zutter; B.S. Pannu; D.D.G. Reynolds; V.V. Stefaniuk; P.V. Teasdale

Fort McMurray

Agents of the Attorney General & Crown Counsel, Fort McMurray: D.G. Algie; D.J. McNab

Grande Prairie

District Administrator, J.R. Bachinski, Grande Prairie
Agents of the Attorney General & Crown Counsel, Grande Prairie: K. Staples; T.M. Hawkesworth; W.A. Skinner

Hanna

District Administrator & Sheriff, J. Gretzan, Hanna

High Prairie

Agent of the Attorney General & Crown Counsel, High Prairie: L.A. Kurata

Hinton

Agent of the Attorney General & Crown Counsel, Hinton: M. Watson

Lethbridge

District Administrator, W. Hewko, Lethbridge
Regional Manager, South (Court Services), E. Kisel
Agents of the Attorney General & Crown Counsel, Lethbridge: D.V. Hartigan, Q.C.; N.H. Clair; R.B. Coleman; E.J. Coughlan; G.K. Falconer; J.H. Langston; C.E. Musk, Q.C.; P.A. Scott

Lloydminster

Agent of the Attorney General & Crown Counsel, Lloydminster; B. Fraser

Fort Macleod

District Administrator, E.D. Horon, Fort Macleod

Medicine Hat

District Administrator & Sheriff, D. Friesen, Medicine Hat
Agents of the Attorney General & Crown Counsel, Medicine Hat: D.J. Greaves; W.W. Cocks; D.J. Carter

Peace River

District Administrator & Sheriff, T.B. Neary, Peace River
Agents of the Attorney General & Crown Counsel, Peace River: L.A. Kurata; J. McPherson; R. Smith; E.H. Wahl

Red Deer

District Administrator & Sheriff, O.D. Lowe, Red Deer

Agents of the Attorney General & Crown Counsel, Red Deer: N.P. Riebeek; L.E. Goddard; M.L. Graham; J.R. Saunders; P. Yelle

St. Paul

Agents of the Attorney General & Crown Counsel, St. Paul: D. Demetrick; W. Summerlus

Vegreville

District Administrator & Sheriff, S.C. Girvan, Vegreville

Senior Agent of Attorney General: P.V. Teasdale

Sheriff, S.C. Girvan

Wetaskiwin

District Administrator & Sheriff, E. Rurka, Wetaskiwin

Agents of the Attorney General & Crown Counsel, Wetaskiwin: D. Plosz; J.B. Hill; O. Yereniuk; R. Dann

LAND REGISTRATION DISTRICTS

North Alta.: All that part of the Province of Alberta which lies north of Township 34 up to the Alberta / Northwest Territories

Inspector, Land Titles, D. Lamont, Calgary

Asst. Inspector, K.B. Payne

South Alta.: All that part of the Province of Alberta from the Alberta / U.S. border up to and including Township 34 (just south of Innisfail)

PROVINCIAL JUDGES

The Provincial Court includes The Family & Juvenile Division, The Small Claims Division and The Criminal Division.

Chief Provincial Judge, Hon. C.A. Kosowan

Asst. Chief Judges, Hon. C.L. Liden, Edmonton; Hon. A.G. Lynch-Staunton, Lethbridge; Hon. J.H. MacKenzie, Red Deer; Hon. H.G. Oliver, Calgary; Hon. D.E. Patterson, Grande Prairie; Hon. C.H. Rolf, Edmonton; Hon. W.G.W. White, Edmonton; Hon. J.S. Woods, Calgary

Judges of the Provincial Court: District & Name:

Banff, Hon. A.W. Aunger

Calgary: Hon. E.P. Adolphe; Hon. H.A. Allard; Hon. W.J. Anderson; Hon. I.A. Blackstone; Hon. G.G. Cioni; Hon. E.L. Collins; Hon. A.P. Demong; Hon. R.S. Dinkel; Hon. D.F. Fitch; Hon. J.C. Gorman; Hon. W.J. Harvie; Hon. L.A. Justason; Hon. N.P. Leveque; Hon. H. Litsky; Hon. N.A. Mackie; Hon. D.M. McDonald; Hon. T.B. McMeekin; Hon. R.B. Nelles; Hon. J.J. O'Connor; Hon. J.D. Reilly; Hon. G.R. Rennie; Hon. B.C. Stevenson; Hon. F.A. Thurgood

Camrose: Hon. J.A. Murray

Drumheller: Hon. G.W. Clozza

Edmonton: Hon. G.E. Beaudry; Hon. A.P. Blakey; Hon. M.M. Bowker; Hon. J.G. Bradburn; Hon. J. Campbell; Hon. A.P. Catonio; Hon. H.R. Chisholm; Hon. A.G. Chrumka; Hon. K.L. Crockett; Hon. K.A. Cush; Hon. J.H. Day; Hon. J. Dimos; Hon. G. Forbes; Hon. S.A. Friedman; Hon. N.G. Hewitt; Hon. E.G. Hughson; Hon. R.E. Hyde; Hon. L.L. Jones; Hon. J.Z. Koshuta; Hon. H.G. Langton; Hon. P.C.C. Marshall; Hon. M.F. McInerney; Hon. W.F. McLean; Hon. K.J. Plomp; Hon. J.B. Ritchie; Hon. D. Saks; Hon. A. Shamchuk; Hon. R.B. Spevakow; Hon. E.D. Stack; Hon. R. Thomas; Hon. M.G. Tomyn; Hon. H.F. Wilson; Hon. D.R. Wong

Fort Macleod: Hon. T.R. Jervis; Hon. L.B. Levine

Fort McMurray: Hon. H.H. Aime; Hon. M. Horrocks

Grande Prairie: Hon. E.H. Gerhart

High Prairie: Hon. B.O. Barker

Hinton: Hon. M.H. Porter

Lethbridge: Hon. F.T. Byrne; Hon. F.W. Coward; Hon. M. Hoyt; Hon. L.W. Hudson; Hon. R.A. Jacobson

Medicine Hat: Hon. D. Brand; Hon. J.P. Wambolt

Nanton: Hon. J.M. Robbins

Peace River: Hon. T. Janakas; Hon. A.W. Ludwig

Red Deer: Hon. D.L. Crowe; Hon. D.R. McCormick; Hon. R.D. McIntosh; Hon. T.G. Schollie; Hon. W.A. Shaw

Sherwood Park: Hon. A.H. Elford

St. Paul: Hon. M.W. Hopkins

Vermilion: Hon. R.L. Tibbitt

Wetaskiwin: Hon. N.A. Rolf

COURTS, JUDGES, ETC., BRITISH COLUMBIA

-not confirmed for 1982-

COURT OF APPEAL

Law Courts, 800 Smithe St., Vancouver, B.C. V6Z 2E1

Chief Justice of B.C., Hon. N.T. Nemetz, Vancouver

Justices of Appeal, Hons.: M.M. McFarlane, J.D. Taggart, P.D. Seaton, A.B.B. Carrothers, E.E. Hinkson, W.A. Craig, J.S. Aikins, J.D. Lambert, J.A. Macdonald, G.J.F. Baker, V. Meredith all of Vancouver

Supernumerary Judge, Hon. E.B. Bull, Vancouver

Registrars, T.J. Halbert, Victoria; P.J. Abel, Vancouver

SUPREME COURT

Law Courts, 800 Smithe St., Vancouver, B.C. V6Z 2E1

Chief Justice of Supreme Court, Hon. A. McEachern, Vancouver

Justices, Hons. F.C. Munroe, J.G. Gould, W.K. Smith, A.B. Macfarlane, H.C. McKay, R.P. Anderson, T.R. Berger, D.E. Andrews, Kenneth E. Meredith, A.A. Mackoff, E.D. Fulton, J.C. Bouck, S.M. Toy, H.E. Hutcheon, L.G. McKenzie, G.L. Murray, H.P. Legg, W.J. Trainor, P.M. Proudfoot, K.S. Fawcus, H.A. Callaghan, A.G. MacKinnon, M.R. Taylor, C.R. Locke, W.A. Esson, all of Vancouver

Supernumerary Judges, Hons. J.G. Ruttan, D.R. Verchere, V.L. Dryer, G.G.S. Rae, W.J. Wallace, P.D. Dohm, R.M.P. Paris all of Vancouver

Registrar, T.J. Halbert

Bankruptcy

Supreme Court Judges have jurisdiction in bankruptcy.

Registrars in Bankruptcy

T.J. Halbert, 850 Burdett Ave., Victoria, B.C. V8W 1B4 (387-5211)

John P. Abel, 800 Smithe St., Vancouver, B.C. V6Z 2E1 (668-2809)

K.G. Grahame, 1420 Water St., Kelowna, B.C. V1Y 1J2 (763-6430)

Mrs. L.E. Beaulac, 320 Ward St., Nelson, B.C. V1L 1S6 (352-2211)

G.R. Fulton, 653 Clarkson St., New Westminster, B.C. V3M 1C9 (521-9641)

Mrs. S. Smith, 3001 27th St., Vernon, B.C. V1T 4W5 (545-2278)

G.F.S. Goddard, 1600 3rd Ave., Prince George, B.C. V2L 3G6 (562-8131)

Mrs. C. Adams, 100 Market Place, Prince Rupert, B.C. V8J 1B7 (624-2121)

COUNTY COURT JUDGES

County: Address (Judge/s)

Cariboo: Court House, 1600 3rd Ave., Prince George, B.C. V2L 3G6 (D.M. MacDonald, F.S. Perry, C.R. Lander, S.J. Hardinge)

Chilliwack: Court House, 77 College St., Chilliwack, B.C. V2P 4L7 (F.K. Grimmett)

East Kootenay: Court House, 102 11th Ave. S., Cranbrook, B.C. V1C 2P8 (M. Provenzano)

Nanaimo: Court House, 35 Front St., Nanaimo, B.C. V9R 5J1 (L.F. Cashman, F.A. Melvin)

Nelson: Court House, 320 Ward St., Nelson, B.C. V1L 1S6 (K.D. Houghton)

Prince Rupert: Court House, 100 Market Place, Prince Rupert, B.C. V8J 1B8 (Richard T. Low)

Vancouver: Court House, 800 Smithe St., Vancouver, B.C. V6Z 2E1 (G.B. Ladner, A.W. McClellan, T.G. Darling, H.L. Skipp, D.B. MacKinnon, David H. Campbell, R.M.P. Paris, J.E. Spencer, A.A.W. MacDonnell, M.I. Catliff, D.T. Wetmore, John J. Anderson, T.K. Fisher, J.C. Cowan, P.J. van der Hoop)

Victoria: Law Courts, 850 Burdett Ave., Victoria, B.C. V8W 1B4 (M.L. Tyrwhitt-Drake, E.J.C. Stewart, P.J. Millward)

West Kootenay: Court House, 102 11th Ave. S., Cranbrook, B.C. V1C 2P3 (L.S. Gansner, Supern.)
Westminster: Court House, 653 Clarkson St., New Westminster, B.C. V3M 1C9 (L.M. McDonald, D.E. McTaggart, A. Stewart McMorran, D.B. Hinds, C. Murray Hyde, W.H. Davies)
Williams Lake: Court House, 540 Borland St., Williams Lake, B.C. V2G 1R8 (W.D. Ferry)
Yale: Court House, 1165 Battle St., Kamloops, B.C. V2C 2N4 (D.R. Andrews, D.M. MacDonald)
Yale: Court House, 100 Main St., Penticton, B.C. V2A 5A5 (A.D.C. Washington)
Yale: Court House, 3001 27th St., Vernon, B.C. V1T 4W5 (K.F. Arkell)

PROVINCIAL COURT JUDGES

His Hon. Lawrence S. Goulet, Chief Judge of the Provincial Court, Box 32, Court House, 800 Smithe St., Vancouver, B.C. V6Z 2E1
His Hon. Alfred Watts, Assoc. Chief Judge of the Provincial Court (Supernumerary)

Names of Judges with addresses:

Alder, Harold E., 101, 850 Burdett Ave., Victoria, B.C. V8W 1B4
Allan, Robert B., 101, 850 Burdett Ave., Victoria, B.C. V8W 1B4
Anderson, Ernest L., 4914 222nd St., Langley, B.C. V3A 2P4
Barnett, Charles C., #107, 540 Borland St., Williams Lake, B.C. V2G 1R8
Behncke, Jurgen P.W., Court House, 3001 27th St., Vernon, B.C. V1T 4W5
Beirnes, Arthur D., 222 Main St., Vancouver, B.C. V6A 2S8
Bendrodt, Erik H., 222 Main St., Vancouver, B.C. V6A 2S8
Bowen-Colthurst, T.G., Administrative Judge, Court House, Front St., Nanaimo, B.C., V9R 5J1
Boyle, Harry D., 2625 Yale St., Vancouver, B.C. V5K 1C2
Brahan, Lawrence C., 2020 Cameron St., Victoria, B.C. V8T 3N5
Byrne, B. Patricia, 6263 Gilpin St., Burnaby, B.C. V5G 3Z8
Campbell, Douglas R., Administrative Judge, 2625 Yale St., Vancouver, B.C. V5K 1C2
Campbell, Wm. E., 6900 Minoru Blvd., Richmond, B.C. V6Y 1Y1
Carmichael, Andrew J., 814 Richards St., Vancouver, B.C. V6B 3A7
Clare, L.P., 3002 Christmas Way, Coquitlam, B.C. V3C 2M3
Collings, P. D'A., 10475 138 St., Surrey, B.C. V3T 4K4
Collins, Darrall S., Q.C., Administrative Judge, 110, 4506 Lakelse Ave., Terrace, B.C. V8G 1P4
Collingwood, Norman, 6900 Minoru Blvd., Richmond, B.C. V6Y 1Y1
Collver, Ross D., 6263 Gilpin St., Burnaby, B.C. V5G 3Z8
Cook, A.S.K., #2, 7104 Ash Cres., Langara Gdns., Vancouver, B.C. V6P 3K7
Coultas, Gerald R., 222 Main St., Vancouver, B.C. V6A 2S8
Craig, Wallace G., 222 Main St., Vancouver, B.C. V6A 2S8
Cronin, Edmond J., 222 Main St., Vancouver, B.C. V6A 2S8
Cullinane, Thomas R., 115, 350 Barlow Ave., Quesnel, B.C. V2J 2C1
D'Andrea, Richard O., Court House, Box 639, Rossland, B.C.
Davies, John L., 222 Main St., Vancouver, B.C. V6A 2S8
Denroche, George S., Administrative Judge, Court House, 1456 St. Paul St., Kelowna, B.C. V1Y 1J2
Diebolt, Wm. J., Courthouse, 800 Smithe St., Vancouver, B.C. V6Z 2E1
Drysdale, John A.W., #302, 2890 Point Grey Rd., Vancouver, B.C. V6K 1A9
Ellis, H.M., 1456 St. Paul St., Kelowna, B.C. V1Y 1J2
Friesen, Nick, 32203 S. Fraser Way, Abbotsford, B.C. V2T 1W6
Giles, F.C., 238 Government St., Duncan, B.C. V9L 1A5
Gilmour, Gordon H., 1165 Battle St., Kamloops, B.C. V2G 1R8
Gordon, James P., 1165 Battle St., Kamloops, B.C. V2C 2N4
Govan, Philip R., 6900 Minoru Blvd., Richmond, B.C. V6Y 1Y3
Graham, Robert C.S., Room 200, Courthouse, Prince Rupert, B.C. V8J 1B7
Grandison, Reg. D., 1330 Marine Dr., West Vancouver, B.C. V7T 3J2
Green, F.S., 101, 850 Burdett St., Victoria, B.C. V8W 1B4
Greer, D.M., 35 Front St., Nanaimo, B.C. V9R 5J1
Greig, Robert W., 4465 Clarence Taylor Cres., Delta, B.C. V4K 3C9
Groberman, Joel R., 7826 Ash St., Vancouver, B.C. V6P 3L6
Hamilton, Claude E., 814 Richards St., Vancouver, B.C. V6B 3A7
Heard, Lance, 238 Government St., Duncan, B.C. V9L 1A5
Hogg, Gilbert P., Q.C., #202, 1170 Rockland Ave., Victoria, B.C. V8V 3H7 (Supernumerary)
Holmes, Delores R., 6263 Gilpin St., Burnaby, B.C. V5G 3Z8
Hume, Douglas D., 222 Main St., Vancouver, B.C. V6A 2S8
Husband, Kimball J., 62 Courtenay Cres., New Westminster, B.C. V3L 4M2
Jensen, Robert C., 511 Royal Ave., New Westminster, B.C. V3L 1H9
Johnson, Gordon H., 222 Main St., Vancouver, B.C. V6A 2S8
Johnson, J.S.P., 103, 6953 Alberni St., Powell River, B.C. V8A 2B8
Jones, Darrell D., Administrative Judge, 222 Main St., Vancouver, B.C. V6A 2S8
Josephson, Ian B., Court House, 605 Columbia Ave., Castlegar, B.C.
Keffer, Leonard J., Box 730, Nelson, B.C. V1L 5R4
Kenney, James H., 975 Brunswick St., Prince George, B.C. V2L 2C3
Klinger, Wilfred W., Courthouse, 100 Main St., Penticton, B.C. V2A 5A5
Lamperson, George W., Administrative Judge, 1165 Battle St., Kamloops, B.C. V2C 2N4
Layton, John D., 814 Richards St., Vancouver, B.C. V6B 3A7
Levis, David M., Administrative Judge, 1201, 103rd Ave., Dawson Creek, B.C. V1G 3T9
Lewis, Cecil J., 222 Main St., Vancouver, B.C. V6A 2S8
Libby, Keith J., 222 Main St., Vancouver, B.C. V6Z 2S8
Lundeen, Marvin A., Q.C., Court House, Salmon Arm, B.C. V0E 2T0
Lunn, David J., Administrative Judge, Court House, Cranbrook, B.C. V1C 2P2
McAdam, Duncan K., #101, 850 Burdett St., Victoria, B.C. V8W 1B4
MacAlpine, Milton I., 32203 S. Fraser Way, Abbotsford, B.C. V2T 1W6
MacArthur, Clifford B., 975 Brunswick St., Prince George, B.C. V2L 2C3
McCarthy, John L., 222 Main St., Vancouver, B.C. V6A 2S8
Macdonald, Malcolm A., Family Division, 2625 Yale St., Vancouver, B.C. V5K 1C2
McGillivray, J.B., 100 Main St., Penticton, B.C. V2A 5A5
McGivern, Hugh J., 222 Main St., Vancouver, B.C. V6A 2S8
McQueen, Roy S., leave of absence
MacIntyre, John L., 222 Main St., Vancouver, B.C. V6A 2S8
MacLeod, Wm. E., 4110 6th Ave., Port Alberni, B.C. V9Y 4M9
Meagher, Thomas. W., 77 College St., Chilliwack, B.C. V2P 4L7
Metzger, R.W., 420 Cumberland Rd., Courtenay, B.C. V9N 5M6
Millar, Perry S., #211, 420 Cumberland Rd., Courtenay, B.C. V9N 5M6
Moffett, David, 222 Main St., Vancouver, B.C. V6A 2S8
Morrison, Nancy E., 235 E. 23rd St., North Vancouver, B.C. V7L 3E4
Munro, Ronald S., Box 2, 1600 Third Ave., Prince George, B.C. V2L 3G6
Nimsick, Leo A., Court House, Cranbrook, B.C. V1C 2P2
O'Donnell, Edward, Administrative Judge, 814 Richards St., Vancouver, B.C. V6B 3A7
Ostler, Wm. L., Administrative Judge, 850 Burdett St., Victoria, B.C. V8W 1B4 (Supernumerary)
Overend, Dennis B., Courthouse, 3001 27th St., Vernon, B.C. V1T 4W5
Page, Kenneth D., 245 E. 23rd St., North Vancouver, B.C. V7L 3E4
Paradis, J.B., 245 E. 23rd St., North Vancouver, B.C. V7L 3E4
Pearce, Lorne A., Administrative Judge, 850 Burdett Ave., Victoria, B.C. V8W 1B4
Poole, Reginald, 2625 Yale St., Vancouver, B.C. V5K 1C2
Reed, Douglas C., Administrative Judge, 5642 176A St., Surrey, B.C. V3S 4G9

Romilly, Selwyn R., 6263 Gilpin St., Burnaby, B.C. V5G 3Z8
Sarich, Anthony, 908 'C' Alder St., Campbell River, B.C. V9W 2P6
Sather, Eugene A., 5642 176A St., Surrey, B.C. V3S 4G9
Scarlett, Edward P., 5642 176A St., Surrey, B.C. V3S 4G9
Scherling, Ken, Box 3610, Smithers, B.C. VOJ 2NO
Scow, Alfred J., 3002 Christmas Way, Coquitlam, B.C. V3C 2M3
Sedgwick, Harvey J., 222 Main St., Vancouver, B.C. V6A 2S8 (Supernumerary)
Selbie, Wm. S., Administrative Judge, 511 Royal Ave., New Westminster, B.C. V3L 1H9
Shaw, James K., 522 7th St., New Westminster, B.C. V3M 5T5
Shupe, Terry W., 1165 Battle St., Kamloops, B.C. V2C 2N4
Simpson, D. Ross, 1165 Battle St., Kamloops, B.C. V2C 2N4
Skelhorne, Roger G., 10600 100 St., Fort St. John, B.C. V1J 4L6
Smith, K.A.P.D., 222 Main St., Vancouver, B.C. V6A 2S8
Stewart, George O., Administrative Judge, 975 Brunswick St., Prince George, B.C. V2L 2C3
Sutherland, George R., leave of absence
Thomas, Harry F., 1165 Battle St., Kamloops, B.C. V2C 2N4
Vamplew, Darragh M., 77 College St., Chilliwack, B.C. V2P 4L7
Varcoe, John B., 22460 Dewdney Trunk Rd., Maple Ridge, B.C. V2X 3J6
Walker, Carl I., Box 381, Squamish, B.C. VON 3GO
Ward, D.W.S., R.R. 1, Eaglecrest, Qualicum Beach, B.C. VOR 2TO
Wardill, S.H., Courthouse, Front St., Nanaimo, B.C. V9R 5J1
Wong, R.B.S.K., 222 Main St., Vancouver, B.C. V6A 2S8
Woodliffe, C.J., 800 Smithe St., Vancouver, B.C. V6Z 2E1

OFFICIAL ADMINISTRATORS

Official Administrator, Address; Corporate Name (Dist.)

(vacant), Court House, Atlin; County of Prince Rupert (Atlin)
J.A. Baker, Room 100, 420 Cumberland Rd., Courtenay; County of Vancouver Island (Courtenay)
W.L. Draper, Court House, Room 147, 102 11th Ave. S., Cranbrook; County of Kootenay (Cranbrook)
M.M. Karen, Ste. 201, Court House, 1136, 103rd Ave., Dawson Creek; County of Cariboo (Dawson Creek)
F.R. Carmichael, Court House, Box 340, 404 4th Ave., Fernie; County of Kootenay (Fernie)
J.W. Olson, Court House, Box 39, Golden; County of Kootenay (Golden)
S. Matsuo, Court House, Box 850, Central Ave., Grand Forks; Counties of Yale & Kootenay (Grand Forks)
C.W. Foote, Court House, 800 Hornby St., Vancouver; County of Vancouver (Kamloops)
R.E. Manson, Court House, 1420 Water St., Kelowna; County of Yale (Kelowna)
M. Sakakibara, Court House, Main St., Box 70, Lillooet; County of Cariboo (Lillooet)
L.P. Lean, Box 339, Merritt; Counties of Yale & Westminster (Merritt)
D.P. Ramsay, Box 129, Nanaimo V9R 5K7; County of Vancouver Island (Nanaimo)
C.W. Foote, Court House, 800 Hornby St., Vancouver; County of Kootenay (Nelson)
R.J. Westaway, Box 2260, 607 Columbia St., New Westminster; County of Westminster (New Westminster)
Edgar Dewdney, Box 129, Penticton V2A 6K2; County of Yale (Penticton)
W.G. Mundell, 4515 Elizabeth St., Port Alberni; County of Vancouver Island (Port Alberni)
J.V. Gaspard, 6243 Walnut St., Powell River; County of Vancouver (Powell River)
J.T. Coleman, 900, 550 Victoria St., Prince George; County of Cariboo (Prince George)
C.W. Foote, 800 Hornby St., Vancouver; County of Prince Rupert (Prince Rupert)
W.L. Marshall, Court House, 151 Vermilion Ave., Box 9, Princeton; County of Yale (Princeton)
S.W. Minifie, 102, 350 Barlow Ave., Quesnel; County of Cariboo (Quesnel)
D.G.B. Roberts, Box 380, Revelstoke; County of Yale (Revelstoke)
D.R. Blatchford, Box 100, Salmon Arm; County of Yale (Salmon Arm)
A.W. Milton, Box 340, Smithers; County of Prince Rupert (Smithers)
A.D. Sherwood, Box 910, Rossland VOG 1YO; County of South West Kootenay (Rossland)
C.W. Foote, 800 Hornby St., Vancouver; County of Vancouver (Vancouver)
N.A. Nelson, Court House, 3001 27th St., Vernon; County of Yale (Vernon)
Ian M. Horne, Q.C., 302 Royal Trust Bldg., 612 View St., Victoria; County of Vancouver Island (Victoria)
A.E. Vandenburgh, 123 Borland St., Williams Lake; County of Cariboo (Williams Lake)

DISTRICT REGISTRARS OF THE SUPREME COURT & REGISTRARS OF THE COUNTY COURT

Registry: Registrar (County), Address:

Ashcroft: S.W. Henswold (Cariboo), Courthouse, Sixth St. & Railroad Ave., Ashcroft (Postal address: Box 639, Ashcroft)
Campbell River: K.H. Scott (Vancouver Island), 908 C Alder St., Campbell River
Chase: W. Fader (Cariboo), Box 581, Chase
Chilliwack: E. Hornby (Westminster), Courthouse, 77 College St., Chilliwack
Clearwater: Ms. B. Mills (Cariboo), Courthouse, Clearwater
Clinton: C. Jolly (Cariboo), Courthouse, Clinton
Courtenay: R. Krayenhoff (Vancouver Island), Courthouse, 420 Cumberland Rd., Box 3014, Courtenay
Cranbrook: vacant (Kootenay), Courthouse, 102 11th Ave. S., Cranbrook
Creston: R.J. Grout (Kootenay), Courthouse, Box 1790, Creston
Dawson Creek: G.W. Schmidt (Cariboo), 1201 103 Ave., Dawson Creek
Duncan: Ms. L. Pellet (Vancouver Island), Courthouse, 238 Government St., Duncan
Fernie: R. Girvin (Kootenay), Courthouse, Fourth Ave., Box 1800, Fernie
Fort St. John: Muriel Lythall (Cariboo), Courthouse, 1060 100 Ave., Box 4000, Fort St. John
Fort Nelson: Adine Wong (Cariboo), Box 190, Fort Nelson
Golden: B. Scardifield (Kootenay), Courthouse, Tenth Ave. & Sixth St., Golden (postal address: Box 1500, Golden)
Grand Forks: G.J. Redding (Kootenay), Courthouse, Central Ave., Box 1059, Grand Forks
Kamloops: T.W. Knight (Yale), Courthouse, 1165 Battle St., Kamloops
Kelowna: K.G. Grahame (Yale), Courthouse, 1420 Water St., Kelowna
Kitimat: Mary Milmine (Prince Rupert), 1101 Kingfisher Ave., Kitimat
Lillooet: D.K. Johnson (Cariboo), Court House, Main St., Box 96, Lillooet
Lytton: R. Shand (Cariboo), Courthouse, Lytton
Merritt: Elaine Ohata (Yale), Courthouse, 1840 Nicola Ave., Box 880, Merritt
Nanaimo: L. Varipati (Vancouver Island), Courthouse, 35 Front St., Nanaimo
Nelson: Elaine Baulac (Deputy) (Kootenay), Courthouse, 320 Ward St., Nelson
New Westminster: G. Rupert Fulton (Westminster), Courthouse, 653 Clarkson St., New Westminster
Oliver: Mrs. Alice Wiebe (Yale), Box 1350, Courthouse, Oliver
100 Mile House: Ms. Bonita Conway (Cariboo), Box 805, 100 Mile House
Penticton: E.L. Millington (Yale), Courthouse, 100 Main St., Penticton
Port Alberni: Peter Whitton (Vancouver Island), 4110 6th Ave. N., Port Alberni
Powell River: Otto Bigalke (Vancouver), Room 103, 6953 Alberni St., Powell River

Prince George: G.F. Goddard (Cariboo), Provincial Govt. Bldg., 1600 Third Ave., Box 28, Prince George
Prince Rupert: Charlotte Adams (Prince Rupert), Room 200, Courthouse, Market St., Prince Rupert
Princeton: Agnes Marshall (Yale), Courthouse, 151 Vermilion Ave., Box 1210, Princeton
Quesnel: Stanley Wilson (Cariboo), Courthouse, 350 Barlow Ave., Quesnel (postal address: Box 5000, Quesnel)
Revelstoke: G.R. Evans (Yale), Box 2130, Revelstoke
Richmond: D.K. Stevenson (Vancouver), 6931 Granville Ave., Richmond
Rossland: K.R. Burton (Kootenay), Courthouse, 2288 Columbia Ave., Box 639, Rossland
Salmon Arm: Margaret Man (Yale), Courthouse, 3715 Hudson St., Salmon Arm (postal address: Box 1990, Salmon Arm)
Smithers: Greg Ozeroff (Prince Rupert), Courthouse, 1 Fifth Ave., Smithers (postal address: Box 2239, Smithers)
Surrey: Yvonne Jensen (Westminster), 10475 138th St., Surrey
Terrace: A.J. Glover (Prince Rupert), Courthouse, 4506 Lakelse Ave., Terrace
Valemont: T. Gould (Cariboo), Courthouse, Cariboo
Vancouver: John P. Abel (Vancouver), Court House, 800 Smithe St., Vancouver
Vanderhoof: Olga Smith (Cariboo), Courthouse, Church Ave. & Victoria St., Box 1220, Vanderhoof
Vernon: Stan Smith (Yale), Courthouse, 3001 27th St., Vernon
Victoria: T.J. Halbert (Vancouver Island), Law Courts, 850 Burdett Ave., Victoria
Williams Lake: Mary Swift (Cariboo), Courthouse, 540 Borland St., Williams Lake (postal address: Box 130, Williams Lake)

COURTS, JUDGES, ETC., MANITOBA

COURT OF APPEAL

Winnipeg
Chief Justice of Manitoba, Hon. Samuel Freedman
Judges of Appeal, The Hon. Alfred Maurice Monnin; The Hon. G.C. Hall; The Hon. P. Matas; The Hon. J.F. O'Sullivan, The Hon. C. Huband
Registrar, B.T. Cadger (944-2647)

COURT OF QUEEN'S BENCH

224 Woodsworth Bldg., Winnipeg (944-3024)
Chief Justice of the Court of Queen's Bench, The Hon. A.S. Dewar
Puisne Judges of the Court of Queen's Bench, Hon. L. Deniset; Hon. J.E. Wilson; Hon. J.M. Hunt; Hon. J.R. Solomon; Hon. A.C. Hamilton; Hon. W.S. Wright; Hon. P.S. Morse; Hon. B. Hewak; Hon. G. Kroft; Hon. J.A. Scollin
Masters, Referees & Registrars in Bankruptcy, G. Richardson, R. Cantlie
Prothonotary & Registrar, A. Rouse, 944-3026

Bankruptcy

Queen's Bench Judges in the Province have jurisdiction in bankruptcy.

Registrar in Bankruptcy, Grey Richardson, Law Courts Bldg., Winnipeg (944-2083)

COUNTY COURTS

General Office, 944-3125

WINNIPEG

Chief Judge, A.R. Philp
Senior Judge, C.I. Keith
Judges, J.W.M. Thompson; B.R. Coleman; G.J. Barkman; P.D. Ferg; G.O. Jewers; G.H. Lockwood; D.P. Kennedy; R. Krindle
Chief County Court Clerk, A. Rouse, 944-3026

BRANDON – W.J.D.

Judge, L.P. Ferg
Clerk of the Court, P. Goshulak, 727-0597

DAUPHIN – D.J.D.

Judge, W.M. Darichuk
Clerk of the Court, P. Chomiak, 638-9111

PORTAGE LA PRAIRIE – C.J.D.

Judge, A.C. Miller
Clerk of the Court, T.H. Simmons, 857-5821

THE PAS – N.J.D.

Judge, W.M. Darichuk
Clerk of the Court, C. Martin, 623-3491

COUNTY COURT & SURROGATE COURT – ST. BONIFACE

Judge, A. Dureault
County Court Clerk, G. Vrigon, 233-7061

SURROGATE COURT OF WINNIPEG

Court Registrar, Miss R. Costello
General Office, 944-3184

Registration of Instruments

Bills of Sale and Chattel Mortgages must be registered with the Clerk of the County Court of the Judicial Division in which the goods or chattels are situate.

Registration of Conditional Sales is not required.

PROVINCIAL JUDGES COURT

373 Broadway, Winnipeg, Man. R3C 0T9
Chief Judge, H. ff Gyles, Q.C.
Chief Clerk, A. Ziemianski, 944-4504

PROVINCIAL JUDGES COURT (CRIMINAL DIVISION)

Senior Judge, I.V. Dubienski
Provincial Judges, *Winnipeg*, F. Allen; M. Baryluk; H. Collerman; A.J. Conner; J.J. Enns; R.L. Kopstein; T.J. Lismer; W.R. Martin; S. Minuk; L.R. Mitchell; G.B. McTavish; W.E. Norton; C.N. Rubin; R.E. Trudel
Clerks of Court, S. Harrison (944-3454); D. Dowbenko (944-2457)

Brandon W.J.D., Judge A. James; Judge R. Mykle
Clerk of Court, P. Goshulak, 727-0597
Portage la Prairie C.J.D., Judge B.P. McDonald
Clerk of Court, T.H. Simmons, 857-5821
Thompson N.J.D., Judge C.K. Newcombe
Clerk of Court, L. Rowan, 778-4411
The Pas N.J.D., Judge K.F. Stefanson
Clerk of Court, Claire Martin, 623-3491
Dauphin D.J.D., Judge R.M.B. Toews
Clerk of Court, P. Chomiak, 638-9111

PROVINCIAL JUDGES COURT (FAMILY DIVISION)

Senior Judge, E.C. Kimelman
Provincial Judges, *Winnipeg*, P.L. Ashdown; R.J.B. Cramer; M. Garfinkel; R.H. Harris; B. Helper; R.A. Johnston; R.J. Meyers; R.J. Morlock; W.H. Swail
Clerk of Court, E. Sharkey, 895-5007

Brandon W.J.D., Judge B.D. Giesbrecht
Clerk of Court, Mrs. Anna B. Wall, 728-7000

PROVINCIAL JUDGES COURT (TRAFFIC DIVISION)

General Office, 944-3156

SHERIFF'S & BAILIFF'S OFFICE

General Office, 944-2107
Chief Sheriff & Bailiff, A. Nielsen

COURT REPORTERS

Chief Court Reporter, G. McGregor
Court Reporters – 944-2097

ADMINISTRATION

Administrator, M. Bruce, 944-2049
Deputy Administrator, W. Flattery, 944-2087

COURTS, JUDGES, ETC., NEW BRUNSWICK

-not confirmed for 1982-

COURT OF APPEAL

Chief Justice of New Brunswick, Hon. C.J.A. Hughes, Fredericton

Judges: Hons. R.V. Limerick, Fredericton; J.N. Bugold, Fredericton; H.E. Ryan, Saint John; G.A. Richard, Fredericton

Registrar, Murray F. Cain, Q.C., Fredericton (453-2452)

Deputy Registrars, A.M. DiGiacinto, Fredericton; Leopold Dubé, Fredericton

COURT OF QUEEN'S BENCH

Chief Justice, Court of Queen's Bench, Hon. A.J. Cormier, Moncton

Judges, Trial Division: Hons. D.M. Dickson, Fredericton; J. Paul Barry, Saint John; C.I.L. Leger, Moncton; R.C. Stevenson, Fredericton; S.G. Stratton, Saint John; B.A. Jean, Caraquet; H.E. Montgomery, Fredericton; R.L. Miller, Moncton; W.L.M. Creaghan, Fredericton; E.T. Caughey, St. Andrews; J.C. Abbis, Edmundston; W.W. Meldrum, Moncton; R.J. Higgins, Saint John; J.C. Angers, Campbellton

Judges, Family Division: Hon. H.E. Montgomery, Fredericton

Bankruptcy

Court of Queen's Bench of New Brunswick has jurisdiction in bankruptcy.

Registrars in Bankruptcy, A.M. DiGiacinto, Murray F. Cain, Q.C., Box 6000, Fredericton, N.B. E3B 5H1 (454-2452)

Court of Divorce & Matrimonial Causes

All judges of the Court of Queen's Bench have jurisdiction.

Registrar, Murray F. Cain, Q.C., Fredericton

Deputy Registrars, A.M. DiGiacinto, Léopol Dubé

Registration of Instruments

Bills of Sale, Chattel Mortgages, Conditional Sales and Hire Receipts must be registered within 30 days of execution.

Land transfer governed by priority of registration with no time limit.

Clerks of the Court of Queen's Bench:

Judicial District of:

Fredericton: A. Mehta
Saint John: B. Cosman
Moncton: C. Gillespie, Q.C.
Newcastle: G. Martin
Bathurst: G. Boudreau
Campbellton: M. Larlee
Edmundston: G. Theriault
Woodstock: M. Holmes

JUVENILE COURTS & JUDGES

Albert, Ian P. Mackin, Moncton
Carleton, James F.H. Crocco, Woodstock
Charlotte, Thomas Bell, St. Stephen
Gloucester, G.S. Bertrand, Bathurst
Kent, Jacques Sirois, Richibucto
Kings, Thomas Bell
Madawaska, Charles A. Dionne, Edmundston
Northumberland, John R. Kelly, Newcastle
Queens, Brian G. Savage, Oromocto
Restigouche, L.C. Ayles, Campbellton
Saint John, Thomas M. Bell, Saint John
Sunbury, Brian G. Savage, Oromocto
Victoria, T.W. Tomlinson, Grand Falls
Westmorland, Ian P. MacKin, Moncton
York, vacant, Fredericton

SHERIFFS

Sheriff (County), Address:

Chief Sheriff, A.M. Hughes, Fredericton
J.R. Wolfe (Albert), Moncton
R.C. Dickinson (Carleton), Woodstock
Roland Levesque (Gloucester), Bathurst
J.R. Wolfe (Kent), Moncton
Desmond Legassick (Kings), Saint John
George E. Daigle (Madawaska), Edmundston
C.A. McCoombs (Northumberland), Newcastle
Peter Dickens (Queens), Fredericton
Walter R. Thompson (Restigouche), Campbellton
Desmond Legassick (Saint John), Saint John
Peter Dickens (Sunbury), Fredericton
R.C. Dickinson (Victoria), Woodstock
J.R. Wolfe (Westmorland), Moncton
Peter Dickens (York), Fredericton
Roland Wasson (Charlotte), Saint John

JUDGES OF PROVINCIAL COURTS

County: Address (Judge/s):

Albert: 700 Main St., Moncton, N.B. E1C 1E4 (Hon. Percy C. Brian)

Carleton: Box 1329, Woodstock, N.B. E0J 2B0 (Hon. J.F.H. Crocco)

Charlotte: 41 King St., St-Stephen, N.B. E3L 2C1 (Hon. D.E. Rice)

Gloucester: Box 5001, Bathurst, N.B. E2A 3Z9 (Hon. G.S. Bertrand, Hon. Frederic Arsenault)

Kent: Box 5001, Moncton, N.B. E1C 8R3 (Hon. J.A. Sirois)

Kings: Court House, Hampton, N.B. E2L 3W9 (Hon. N.J. George)

Madawaska: Family Ct., 45 Church St., Edmundston, N.B. E3V 1J4 (Hon. C.A. Dionne); Prov. Ct., Box 233, Edmundston, N.B. E3V 3K8 (Hon. J.A. Robichaud, Hon. George Perusse)

Northumberland: 599 King George Hwy., Newcastle, N.B. E1V 1N6 (Hon. J.R. Kelly, Hon. A.P. Tracy-Gould)

Restigouche: Box 127, Campbellton, N.B. E3N 3G1 (Hon. Lewis C. Ayles)

Saint John: Prov. Ct., 15 Market Sq., Saint John, N.B. E2L 1E8 (Hon. A.G. Harrigan, Chief Judge; Hon. F.S. Taylor, Hon. James McNamee); Family Ct., Box 6398, Stn. A, Saint John, N.B. E2L 4R8 (Hon. T.M. Bell)

Sunbury: Box 94, Oromocto, N.B. E2V 2G4 (Hon. B.G. Savage)

Victoria: Grand Falls, N.B. E0J 1M0 (Hon. T.W. Tomlinson)

Westmorland: Box 5001, Moncton, N.B. E1C 8R3 (Prov. Ct.: Hon. H.J. Murphy, Hon. P.C. Brian; Fam. Ct.: Hon. I.P. Mackin)

York: Justice Bldg., Fredericton, N.B. E3B 5H1 (Hon. J.D. Harper, Hon. C. Blake Lynch)

COURTS, JUDGES, ETC., NEWFOUNDLAND

SUPREME COURT

St. John's

Court of Appeal:

Chief Justice, Hon. A.S. Mifflin

Judges, Hon. H.B. Morgan, Hon. J.R. Gushue

Trial Division:

Chief Justice, Hon. T.A. Hickman

Judges, Hon. Nathaniel S. Noel; Hon. J.W. Mahoney; Hon. N.H. Goodridge

Registrar of the Supreme Court, Edward Neary, Q.C.

Deputy Registrar, H. Thorne

Sheriff of Nfld., S. Carew

NOTE:- Address for each of the above is Court House, Duckworth St., St. John's, Nfld. A1C 5V5

Bankruptcy

The Supreme Court has jurisdiction in Bankruptcy.

Registrars in Bankruptcy, H.J. Thorne, Torbay Rd., St. John's; E.J. Hunt, 5 Devine Place, St. John's

UNIFIED FAMILY COURT

21 King's Bridge Rd., St. John's, Nfld. A1C 3K4

(709) 753-5873

Judge, Hon. R. Fagan

Administrator, Mrs. C. O'Brien

DISTRICT COURT OF NEWFOUNDLAND

Judicial Centre: Judges

St. John's: G.L. Steele (Chief Judge); Judges: V.P. McCarthy, W. Adams (355 Duckworth St., A1C 1H6)

Gander: Kevin Barry (Box 40, A1V 2E1)

Grand Falls: S. Inder (Provincial Bldg., A2A 1W9)

Corner Brook: P.L. Soper (Box 2006, A2H 6J8)

Brigus: R. Bartlett (Box 100, AOA 1KO)

Grand Bank: H.H. Cummings (Box 910, AOE 1WO)

PROVINCIAL COURT, ST. JOHN'S

Court House, Duckworth St., St. John's, Nfld. A1C 5V5

Chief Judge & Clerk of the Peace, C.P. Scott

Assoc. Chief Judge, E. Langdon

Judges, J.P. Trahey, W. Baker, G. Seabright

JUVENILE COURT, ST. JOHN'S

Court House, Duckworth St., St. John's, Nfld. A1C 5V5

Judge of the Juvenile Court, Charles L. Roberts

TRAFFIC COURT

Fort Townshend, St. John's, Nfld. A1C 6A7

Judge, Jack A. White

PROVINCIAL COURT JUDGES OUTSIDE ST. JOHN'S

Dist. & Judge, Address:

Bell Island: vacant, Bell Island, AOA 4HO

Bonavista: vacant, Bonavista, AOC 1BO

Bonne Bay: R. Jenkins, Woody Point, AOK 1PO

Channel: D. Peddle, Channel, AOM 1CO

Clarenville: Lloyd W. Wicks, Clarenville, AOE 1JO

Corner Brook: D.S. Luther, Corner Brook, A2H 6C3

Gander: J. Woodrow, Gander, A1V 1W7

Gander: O. Kennedy, Gander, A1V 1W7

Goose Bay: J.J. Igloliorte, Goose Bay, AOP 1GO

Grand Bank: Alan G. Anstey, Grand Bank, AOE 1WO

Grand Falls: I.N. Davis, Grand Falls, A2A 1W9

Harbour Grace: J. LeClair, Harbour Grace, AOA 2MO

Holyrood: J.G. Horan, Holyrood, AOA 2RO

Placentia: Terrence J. Corbett, Placentia, AOB 2YO

St. Anthony: vacant, St. Anthony, AOK 4SO

St. George's: vacant, St. George's, AON 1ZO

Springdale: W.A. Oldford, Springdale, AOJ 1TO

Stephenville: R. Culton, Stephenville, A2N 2Z4

Wabush: R.J. Whiffen, Wabush, AOR 1BO

COURTS, JUDGES, ETC., NOVA SCOTIA

SUPREME COURT

Appeal Division (ex officio members of Trial Division)

Chief Justice, The Hon. Mr. Justice Ian MacKeigan, Law Courts

Members, The Hon. Mr. Justice: A. Gordon Cooper; Thomas H. Coffin; Angus L. MacDonald; Malachi C. Jones; Leonard L. Pace; Gordon L.S. Hart

Trial Division (ex officio members of Appeal Division)

Chief Justice, The Hon. Gordon Stewart Cowan

Members, The Hon. Mr. (Madame) Justice: Vincent Morrison; A.M. MacIntosh; J. Doane Hallett; William J. Grant; Constance R. Glube; K.P. Richard; C. Denne Burchell, R. McLeod Rogers, Lorne O. Clarke

Prothonotary & Clerk of the Crown, Daniel B. Morrison, Q.C.

COURT FOR DIVORCE & MATRIMONIAL CAUSES

All Judges of the Trial Division of the Supreme Court and all Judges of the County Court except the County Court Judge for District Number One.

Registrar, Daniel B. Morrison, Q.C.

FAMILY COURT JUDGES

Name & address of judge (area served shown in parenthesis)

His Hon. Judge Louis B. Edwards, Box 345, Sydney, N.S. (Cape Breton & Victoria Counties)

His Hon. Judge Robert F. Ferguson, Box 785, Sydney, N.S. (Cape Breton & Victoria Counties)

His Hon. Judge Welsford G. Phillips, Box 488, New Glasgow, N.S. (Pictou & Cumberland Counties)

His Hon. Judge Raymond Bartlett, 2660 Agricola St., Halifax, N.S. (Halifax & Colchester Counties)

His Hon. Judge Murray A. North, 2660 Agricola St., Halifax, N.S. (Halifax County)

His Hon. Judge W. Marshall Black, Provincial Bldg., Kentville, N.S. (Kings & Halifax Counties)

His Hon. Judge Vincent J. LeBlanc, Provincial Bldg., Box 460, Yarmouth, N.S. (Queens, Shelburne, Yarmouth, Digby, & Annapolis Counties)

His Hon. Judge T. Daniel Tramble, Box 1390, Antigonish, N.S. (Antigonish, Guysborough, Inverness & Richmond Counties)

His Hon. Judge Paul Neidmayer, 2660 Agricola St., Halifax, N.S. (Halifax County)

His Hon. Judge Louis E. Moir, 2660 Agricola St., Halifax, N.S. (Halifax & Queens Counties)

His Hon. Judge Robert Butler, 2660 Agricola St., Halifax, N.S. (Halifax & Queens Counties)

His Hon. Tim Daley, 2660 Agricola St., Halifax, N.S. (Halifax County)

Bankruptcy

Supreme Court Judges have jurisdiction in bankruptcy.

Official Receiver under the Bankruptcy Act, R.B. Twohig, Dept. of Consumer & Corporate Affairs, Bankruptcy, 5151 George St., 6th floor, Halifax, N.S. B3J 1M5 (426-6080)

Registrars in Bankruptcy:

D.B. Morrison, Halifax
Wayne Canam, Pictou
Alex. D. Muggah, Sydney
J.D. Trefry, Yarmouth & Digby

Registration of Bills of Sale & Chattel Mortgages

In the Registry of Deeds for the registration district in which the chattels are situate. If they are in more than one district the Bill of Sale or Mortgage with affidavits, is filed in one district and a duplicate original, or a copy certified by the Registrar of that district, is filed in each other district. Filing must be completed within 30 days from execution.

SHERIFFS

Sheriff (County), Address:
T. MacNeil (Annapolis), Annapolis Royal
Gerald MacDonald (Antigonish), Antigonish
Wayne Magee (Cape Breton North), Sydney
Wayne Magee (Cape Breton South), Sydney
Ronald Conrad (Colchester), Truro
Aubrey Chapman (Cumberland), Amherst
J.R. McIntyre (Digby), Digby
H.E. Morrow (Guysborough), Guysborough
Garth Burbridge (Halifax), Halifax
J.G. Muir (Hants), Windsor
Melvin MacDonald (Inverness), Port Hood
Donald C. Keith (King's), Kentville
Michael Surette (Lunenburg), Bridgewater
W. Treby (Pictou), Pictou
Cyril M. Page (Queen's), Liverpool
J. Richard MacKay (Richmond), Arichat
Kendall Stoddard (Shelburne), Shelburne
Winston Cameron (Victoria), Baddeck
Louis Grant (Yarmouth), Yarmouth

COUNTY COURT JUDGES

Hons. P.J. O'Hearn; N.R. Anderson (Dist. No. 1); P.M. Nicholson (Dist. No. 2); Hanson Taylor Dowell (Dist. No. 3); Robert F. McLellan (Dist. No. 4); A.R. Lusby (Dist. No. 5); H.J. MacPherson (Dist. No. 6); Allan E. Sullivan (Dist. No. 7); Lester L. Clements (Dist. No. 2 & all other districts)

Clerks of County Courts

Clerk (Dist.), Place where Courts are held:
D.B. Morrison (No. 1), Halifax
Cyril Page; D. Bolivar; Carol Lynn Strang (No. 2), Lunenburg, Bridgewater, Liverpool, Shelburne, Barrington
Mrs. Barbara Wells; James R. MacIntyre (No. 3), Annapolis, Middleton, Little Brook, Yarmouth
Donald C. Keith; J. Grant Muir (No. 4), Kentville, Windsor, Truro
Wayne Canam; Kenneth Spicer (No. 5), Pictou, New Glasgow, Amherst
Mrs. Mary T. MacDonald; H. Morrow (No. 6), Port Hood, Antigonish, Guysborough, Sherbrooke
Dorothy Bezanson (No. 7), Sydney, Baddeck, Arichat, St. Peters

JUDGES OF THE PROVINCIAL MAGISTRATES COURT

His Honour Judge: Address to Provincial Magistrate's Court, ...
Amherst (Box 326, Amherst, N.S. B4H 3Z5, 667-2256) David Cole
Antigonish (Box 1506, Antigonish, N.S. B2G 2L8, 863-3676) H.A. Veniot, R.A. MacDonald
Bridgewater (84 Pleasant St., Bridgewater, N.S. B4V 1N1, 543-7143) Hiram Carver, J.P. Kennedy
Dartmouth (#200, 277 Pleasant St., Dartmouth, N.S. B2Y 3S2, 463-5341) M.D. Haley, R.B. Kimball, E.J. MacDonald
Digby (Box 1230, Digby, N.S. B0V 1A0, 245-4567) Kenneth Crowell, J.R. Nichols
Halifax (1815 Upper Water St., Halifax, N.S. B3J 1S7, 425-5880) Nathan Green (Chief Judge); W.J.C. Atton, R.J. McCleave, Sandra E. Oxner, Hughes Randall
Kentville (Box 457, Kentville, N.S. B4N 3X3, 678-6416) R.E. (Bud) Kimball, J.A. MacLellan
New Glasgow (114 Provost St., New Glasgow, N.S. B2H 2P4, 752-5106) H. Russell MacEwan
Port Hawkesbury (Box 404, Port Hawkesbury, N.S. B0E 2V0, 625-2605) D. Lewis Matheson
Sydney (Box 114, Sydney, N.S. B1P 6G9, 564-8246) G.R. LeVatte, Charles O'Connell, S.D. Campbell
Truro (Box 67, Truro, N.S. B2N 5B6, 895-4806) C.W. Archibald
Yarmouth (Main St., Yarmouth, N.S. B5A 1G3, 742-5075) P.R. Woolaver

REGISTRARS OF PROBATE

Listed alphabetically by location:
Amherst: Wm. Fairbanks, Box 103, B4H 3Y6 (667-8062)
Annapolis Royal: Barbara Wells, Box 275, BOS 1AO (532-5462)
Antigonish: Allisdair MacDonald, Box 1332, B2G 2L7 (863-2677)
Arichat: A.A. Bowen, Box 231, BOE 1AO (226-2818)
Baddeck: Anne Marie Campbell, Box 353, BOE 1BO (295-3234)
Barrington: Mrs. Marjorie Weeks, Box 100, BOW 1EO (637-2227)
Digby: Mrs. Lynn Durkee, Box 463, BOV 1AO (245-4203)
Guysborough: Mrs. W. MacDonald, BOH 1NO (533-4001)
Halifax: V.P. Allen, Q.C., 1815 Upper Water St., B3J 1S7 (425-5880)
Kentville: K.N. James, 37 Cornwallis St., B4N 2E2 (678-4679)
Liverpool: Miss Gloria Pentz, Box 727, BOT 1KO (354-4411)
Lunenburg: Arthur Hebb, Box 760, BOJ 2CO (634-8885)
Pictou: Mrs. Dorothy Robinson, Box 1199, BOK 1HO (485-4351)
Port Hood: Alex MacPhee, Box 178, BOE 2WO (787-2281)
Shelburne: Robert Robertson, Box 421, BOT 1WO (875-3409)
Sherbrooke: Mrs. Margaret MacIntosh, Box 166, BOJ 3CO (522-2600)
Sydney: J.A. Ross, Room 111, County Court House, B1S 2Z8 (564-6233)
Truro: Kenneth Starratt, Church St., B2N 3Z5 (895-8027)
Windsor: R.E. Meuse, Box 177, BON 2TO (798-3017)
Yarmouth: Rupert White, Court House, B5A 1G3 (742-5469)

COURTS, JUDGES, ETC., ONTARIO

SUPREME COURT OF ONTARIO

The Supreme Court consists of two branches: The Court of Appeal, 130 Queen St. W., Toronto, and The High Court of Justice, 130 Queen St. W., Toronto.

Appeals may be taken from The High Court of Justice, and, in certain cases, from The Court of Appeal to The Supreme Court of Canada.

Bankruptcy

Supreme Court Judges have jurisdiction.

Registrars in Bankruptcy, A.F. Rodger, Q.C.; J.M. Ferron, Q.C.; D.D. MacRae; W.C. McBride; G.C. Saunders; G.W. Dunn; H. Garfield; D.H. Sandler; S.D. Cork; H.F.H. Sedgewick; J.R. Donkin; B.S. Sischy, Q.C.; D.F. Burt, Q.C.

Matrimonial Causes

Actions for divorce are brought in the Supreme Court of Ontario, and are conducted according to rules passed by the Rules Committee and by the Judges of the High Court of Justice from time to time. Actions for divorce are heard by Judges of the Supreme Court of Ontario and Judges of the County and District Courts sitting as local judges of the High Court. The Court has power to grant divorce, annul marriage, grant alimony and provide for custody and maintenance of the children of the marriage.

Court of Appeal

The Court of Appeal hears appeals from the decisions of The High Court and of the lower courts.
Chief Justice of Ontario, Hon. W.G.C. Howland
Assoc. Chief Justice, Hon. B.J. MacKinnon
Justices, (The Honourable Mr. Justice): *A.R. Jessup, J.W. Brooke, *J.D. Arnup, C.L. Dubin, G.A. Martin, M.N. Lacourciere, L.W. Houlden, T.G. Zuber, D.G. Blair, The Honourable Madam Justice B. Wilson, F.S. Weatherston, J.W. Morden, D.S. Thorson, A. Goodman, P. de C. Cory

*Supernumerary Judge of the Court of Appeal

High Court of Justice

The High Court of Justice hears various cases, criminal and civil, and has a wider jurisdiction than the lower courts. A trial judge sits several times each year in the various counties and judicial districts.
Chief Justice of the High Court, Hon. G.T. Evans
Assoc. Chief Justice, Hon. W.D. Parker
Justices, (The Honourable Mr. Justice): *S.H.S. Hughes, *E.L. Haines, E.P. Hartt, *D.A. Keith, L.T. Pennell, J.H. Osler, P.T. Galligan, T.P. Callon, J.D. Cromarty, J.G.J. O'Driscoll, The Honourable Madam Justice M.M. Van Camp, R.E. Holland, D.F. O'Leary, D.H.W. Henry, R.F. Reid, S.G.M. Grange, J.M. Labrosse, J.B.S. Southey, A.W. Maloney, W.D. Griffiths, H. Krever, S.L. Robins, R.C. Rutherford, D.R. Steele, M.A. Craig, J.C. Holland, The Honourable Madam Justice J.L. Boland, R.S. Montgomery, D.H. Carruthers, W.J. Anderson, E. Saunders, W.R. DuPont, A.H. Hollingworth, J.E. Eberle, A.M. Linden, G.T. Walsh, C.A. Osborne, F.W. Callaghan, R.G. Trainor, W.G. Gray, E.E. Smith, J.W. O'Brien, M.A. Catzman

*Supernumerary Judges of the Supreme Court

Administrator, S.C.O., W.J. Dunlop

Officers of the Supreme Court

Registrar, R.B. Peterson
Executive Officer to the Chief Justices, B. Krivy, Q.C.
Registrar, Court of Appeal & Senior Deputy Registrar, S.C.O., W.F. Shaughnessy
Registrar, Divisional Court & Deputy Registrar, S.C.O., A.P. Bridges
Asst. Deputy Registrar, S.C.O., L.P. Burton
Local Registrar of the Judicial District of York, M.R. Elliott
Deputy Local Registrars, A.E. Chapman, J.E. Munroe, M.E. Dayton, A.C. Fernandes
Registrar in Bankruptcy, J.M. Ferron, Q.C.
Asst. Registrar in Bankruptcy, M.A. Driscoll
Senior Master, A.F. Rodger, Q.C.
Masters, G.C. Saunders, D.D. MacRae, W.C. McBride, G.W. Dunn, J.M. Ferron, Q.C., H. Garfield, D.H. Sandler, S.D. Cork, H.F.H. Sedgewick, W.R. Donkin, B.S. Sischy, Q.C., D.F. Burt, Q.C. – also D.T. Elliott (Ottawa) and A.D. From (Windsor)
Taxing Officer, W.C. McBride
Part-time Master & Taxing Officer, S.M. McBride, Q.C.
Part-time Taxing Officer, B.B. Osler, Q.C.
Special Examiners, Toronto: J.W. Pond, P.W. McHugh, A.C. Devenport, P.W. Rosenberger; Hamilton: M.J. Nimigan; Ottawa: L.A. Gillespie; St. Catharines: R. Penfound; Windsor: B. MacMillan; Timmins: E. Paquette
Ex-Officio Special Examiners, The Registrar, every Local Registrar, Deputy Registrar and Clerk of the County Court
Official Guardian, L.W. Perry, Q.C.
Deputy Official Guardian, J.E.C. Beatty, Q.C.
Accountant of the Supreme Court, E.J. McGann
Director of Courts Admin. & Inspector of Legal Offices, Brian W. McLoughlin – Address, 18 King St. E., Toronto.
Chief Reporter, R. Cuthbert (act.), Suite 716, 500 University Ave., Toronto
Official Referees (ex-officio)

Judges of County & District Courts, The Master of the Supreme Court of Ontario, Local Masters, The Registrar of the Supreme Court of Ontario, Deputy Registrars, Local Registrars, Deputy Local Registrars.

Surrogate Courts

Surrogate Courts have jurisdiction in the matters of wills, and estates of deceased persons.

There is a Surrogate Judge in every County Court.
Surrogate Clerk for Ontario, R.J. Geddes

Registration of Bills of Sale, etc.

Under the Bills of Sale Act, bills of sale must be registered in the office of the branch registrar of personal property security in the county or district in which the goods sold are situate at the time of execution thereof. In the case of a county, it should be registered within five days from the execution thereof. In the case of the Provisional County of Haliburton or of a district, a bill of sale must be registered within ten days from the date of execution. A registration is valid for three years.

Effective April 1, 1976, chattel mortgages, conditional sales and assignment of book debts came within the purview of The Personal Property Security Act, under which registration must be effected within 30 days from the date of execution of the security agreement. Registration period is three years. A central registry has been established for searches.

The Personal Property Security Act provides that where collateral is or includes fixtures or goods that may become fixtures, or crops, or oil, gas or other minerals to be extracted, or timber to be cut, a Notice of Security Interest may be registered in the proper land registry office.

COUNTY COURT JUDICIAL DISTRICTS

1) Essex, Kent, Lambton, Elgin, Middlesex, Oxford, Perth, Huron, Bruce
2) Brant, Haldimand, Niagara North, Niagara South, Norfolk, Hamilton-Wentworth
3) Halton, Waterloo, Wellington, Peel, Grey, Dufferin, Simcoe
4) York, York Region
5) Durham, Northumberland, Victoria, Hastings, Prince Edward, Lennox & Addington, Peterborough, Frontenac
6) Ottawa-Carleton, Prescott & Russell, Stormont, Dundas & Glengarry, Renfrew, Lanark, Leeds & Grenville
7) Kenora, Rainy River, Thunder Bay
8) Algoma, Cochrane, Manitoulin, Nipissing, Sudbury, Temiskaming, Parry Sound, Muskoka

COUNTY JUDGES & JUDICIAL OFFICERS, ONTARIO

Admin. of County, District & Small Claims Courts, Suite 1803, 400 University Ave., Toronto:—*Chief Judge*, W. E. C. Colter; *Associate Chief Judge*, W. D. Lyon.

COUNTY & JUDICIAL DISTRICT IN WHICH SITUATED	LOCAL MASTER SUPREME COURT	LOCAL REGISTRAR SUPREME COURT	REGISTRAR OF SURROGATE COURT & COUNTY OR DISTRICT COURT CLERK	CLERK'S PHONE
Algoma Dist.	8 I. A. Vannini	E. Longarini	E. Longarini	(705) 254-6911
Brant	2 E. O. Fanjoy	J. N. Bragg	J. N. Bragg	(519) 752-7828
Bruce	1 P. S. MacKenzie	J. W. Ellis	J. W. Ellis	(519) 881-0211
Cochrane Dist.	8 R. E. Maranger	A. A. Mainville	A. A. Mainville	(705) 272-4186
Dufferin	3 J. B. Webber	S. T. Collyer	S. T. Collyer	(519) 941-4744
Durham	1 J. P. Kelly	S. C. Roblin	S. C. Roblin	(416) 668-8845
Elgin	1 D. R. McDermid	S. G. Eggleston	S. G. Eggleston	(519) 633-1720
Essex	1 A. D. From, Q.C.	A. Eperon	A. Eperon	(519) 254-1159
Frontenac	5 A. R. Campbell	M. Evans	M. Evans	(613) 547-2283
Grey	3 S. Forslund	S. Forslund	S. Forslund	(519) 376-1461

COUNTY & JUDICIAL DISTRICT IN WHICH SITUATED	LOCAL MASTER SUPREME COURT	LOCAL REGISTRAR SUPREME COURT	REGISTRAR OF SURROGATE COURT & COUNTY OR DISTRICT COURT CLERK	CLERK'S PHONE
HALDIMAND	2 W. W. Leach	H. R. Bassindale	H. R. Bassindale	(416) 772-5352
HALTON	3 J. D. Carnwath	D. G. Westlake	D. G. Westlake	(416) 878-7281
HAMILTON-WENTWORTH	2 G. J. Sullivan	H. M. Guild	H. M. Guild	(416) 528-6708
HASTINGS	5 R. C. Honey	R. C. Bailey	R. C. Bailey	(613) 962-9106
HURON	1 F. G. Carter	F. W. Jewell	F. W. Jewell	(519) 524-2519
KENORA DIST.	7 G. F. Kinsman	P. Spalton	P. Spalton	(807) 468-6270
KENT	1 G. B. Clements	R. V. Page	R. V. Page	(519) 354-4450
LAMBTON	1 M. R. Meehan	M. Joan Nicholson	M. Joan Nicholson	(519) 337-3265
LANARK	6 J. R. Matheson	K. E. R. Fournier	K. E. R. Fournier	(613) 267-2021
LEEDS & GRENVILLE	6 C. J. Newton	Douglas Van Allen	Douglas Van Allen	(613) 342-2288
LENNOX & ADDINGTON	5 B. W. Hurley	W. D. Blakely	W. D. Blakely	(613) 354-3845
MANITOULIN DIST.	1 C. T. Murphy	J. A. Graham	J. A. Graham	(705) 282-2461 (Loc. Master's)
MIDDLESEX	8 G. P. Killeen	Robert Hawken	Robert Hawken	(519) 679-7161
MUSKOKA DIST.	8 S. B. Hogg	Sybil E. J. Jackson	Sybil E. J. Jackson	(705) 645-8793
NIAGARA NORTH	2 D. H. Scott	K. C. McGowan	K. C. McGowan	(416) 685-4284
NIAGARA SOUTH	2 G. G. Nicholls	Iris Head	Iris Head	(416) 735-0010
NIPISSING DIST.	2 F. L. Gratton	N. J. Prisco	N. J. Prisco	(705) 472-7911
NORFOLK	2 J. A. Pringle	K. C. Bannister	K. C. Bannister	(519) 426-6550
NORTHUMBERLAND	5 R. H. Carley	Edna V. Pennycook	Edna V. Pennycook	(416) 372-3751
OTTAWA-CARLETON	6 D. T. Elliot	G. Roscoe	G. Roscoe	(613) 566-3751
OXFORD	8 C. C. Misener	R. S. Beaudoin	R. S. Beaudoin	(519) 539-6187
PARRY SOUND DIST.	3 E. Loukidelis	W. H. Cardy	W. H. Cardy	(705) 746-5864
PEEL	3 B. B. Shapiro	R. D. Kohler	R. D. Kohler	(416) 457-5040
PERTH	5 J. A. Mullen	G. T. Roe	G. T. Roe	(519) 271-2572
PETERBOROUGH	6 G. L. Murdoch	S. A. McBride	S. A. McBride	(705) 745-0583
PRESCOTT & RUSSELL	6 R. J. Cusson	M. Théoret	M. Théoret	(613) 675-4567
PRINCE EDWARD	5 J. D. O'Flynn	J. K. Maddox	J. K. Maddox	(613) 476-6236
RAINY RIVER DIST.	6 B. B. Trembley	J. E. Bradley	J. E. Bradley	(807) 274-5961
RENFREW	3 F. E. Dunlap	I. E. Schimmens	I. E. Schimmens	(613) 732-8581
SIMCOE	3 A. M. Carter	B. C. Dunn	B. C. Dunn	(705) 728-1221
STORMONT, DUNDAS & GLENGARRY	6 G. A. Stiles	J. A. R. Lamoureux	J. A. R. Lamoureux	(613) 932-1290
SUDBURY DIST.	8 S. D. Loukidelis	J. A. O. Seaton	J. A. O. Seaton	(705) 675-4162
TEMISKAMING DIST.	8 J. D. Bernstein	R. J. MacArthur	R. J. MacArthur	(705) 672-3321
THUNDER BAY DIST.	7 P. S. FitzGerald	J. Stakiw	J. Stakiw	(807) 475-1575
VICTORIA & HALIBURTON	5 L. A. Woods	J. E. Boyd	J. E. Boyd	(705) 324-2542
WATERLOO	3 F. Costello (Sr. Judge)	Mary Allcroft	Mary Allcroft	(519) 745-9373
WELLINGTON	3 E. G. McNeely	G. A. Goldrich	G. A. Goldrich	(519) 824-4100
YORK	4 A. F. Rodger, Q.C.	R. Peterson Registrar S.C.O.	R. J. Geddes (Reg. of Surrogate Ct.) E. Thompson (Clerk)	(416) 965-7316 (416) 965-7351
YORK REGION	4 D. R. Shearer	T. B. Cyr	T. B. Cyr	(416) 898-5441

COUNTY & JUDICIAL DISTRICT IN WHICH SITUATED	COUNTY TOWN (ADDRESS TO COUNTY COURT HOUSE)	COUNTY AND SURROGATE JUDGE "His Honour"	SHERIFF	CLERK OF THE PEACE AND CROWN ATTORNEY
ALGOMA DIST.	8 Sault Ste. Marie, P6A 5M8	I. A. Vannini R. B. Warren R. Stortini	P. R. Upper	N. S. Douglas Assts.: W. S. Johnson, Jr., P. Gavrel, G. Wasyliniuk
BRANT	2 Brantford, N3T 2L9	E. O. Fanjoy	J. N. Bragg	Chas. Borda, Q.C. Asst.: K. A. Swanson, Q.C.
BRUCE	1 Walkerton, N0G 2V0	P. S. MacKenzie	A. I. Minard	R. J. Houlahan
COCHRANE DIST.	8 Cochrane, P0L 1C0	R. E. Maranger	R. Lamarche	Coch. N.: R. N. Fournier Coch. S.: L. A. Lizzi, Q.C. Asst. H. Connolly
DUFFERIN	3 Orangeville, (51 Zina St., L9W 1E5)	J. B. Webber	S. T. Collyer	E. C. A. Williams
DURHAM	5 Whitby, L1N 5S4	J. P. Kelly (Sr. Judge) D. M. Lawson W. B. Lane H. M. O'Connell	M. Bain	J. E. Howell, Q.C. Assts.: E. Bradley S. Welch, D. H. Brown E. S. Kingston
ELGIN	1 St. Thomas, N5P 3T9	D. R. McDermid	S. G. Eggleston	J. N. Buchanan, Q.C.
ESSEX	1 Windsor, N9A 6N4	C. Zalev (Sr. Judge) P. I. B. Staniszewski J. P. McMahon W. Hollinger R. J. Huneault K. G. Ouellette	W. W. Bradley	B. McIntyre Assts.: J. S. Dietrich, Q.C. D. Harrison D. Macintyre R. Guthrie R. Morris A. Bradie G. Demarco
FRONTENAC	5 Kingston, K7L 2N4	A. R. Campbell	A. J. Woodman	J. E. Sampson, Q.C. Assts.: J. McKenna J. H. R. Bett

COUNTY & JUDICIAL DISTRICT IN WHICH SITUATED	COUNTY TOWN (ADDRESS TO COUNTY COURT HOUSE)	COUNTY AND SURROGATE JUDGE "His Honour"	SHERIFF	CLERK OF THE PEACE AND CROWN ATTORNEY
GREY	3 Owen Sound, N4K 3E3	E. A. Robson	C. M. Simpson	K. A. Rae, Q.C.
HALDIMAND	2 Cayuga, N0A 1E0	W. W. Leach	H. R. Bassindale	V. B. Collins, Q.C.
HALTON	3 Milton, L9T 1Y7	J. K. Blair T. E. Quinlan J. D. Carnwath	R. M. Sprowl	J. A. Treleaven, Q.C. Assts.: J. D. Ayre, A. A. Vale P. D. Stunt B. R. Calhoun
HAMILTON-WENTWORTH	2 Hamilton, L8N 1E9	C. S. Lazier W. T. Stayshyn G. J. Sullivan (Sr. Judge) J. C. Scime W. K. Warrender G. E. McTurk J. E. Van Duzer R. T. P. Gravely D. M. Steinberg P. W. Perras D. E. Cooper	J. E. Betzner	A. Zuraw, Q.C. Assts.: J. A. Lambier D. G. McLean, Q.C., R. LeDressay C. H. Gage, Q.C. D. Paquette G. M. Read L. J. Urban D. G. Carr F. Campling J. R. Manishen R. Nuttall
HASTINGS	5 Belleville, (235 Pinnacle St., K8N 3A9)	R. C. Honey	R. C. Bailey	G. A. Deline, Q.C. Asst.: J. J. Woods
HURON	1 Goderich, N7A 1M2	F. G. Carter	F. W. Jewell	R. G. E. Hunter
KENORA DIST.	7 Kenora, P9N 1S4	G. F. Kinsman	P. Spalton	E. C. Burton, Q.C. Assts.: R. D. Cummine J. D. Hay
KENT	1 Chatham, N7M 4K1	G. B. Clements	G. D. B. Sulman	S. A. B. Ward, Q.C. Asst. W. R. Wolski
LAMBTON	1 Sarnia, N7T 7N5	M. R. Meehan W. J. Luchak	B. Fraser	D. V. H. Vale Asst.: E. Hibberd
LANARK	6 Perth, K7H 3E2	J. R. Matheson	K. E. R. Fournier	J. D. Waugh
LEEDS & GRENVILLE	6 Brockville, K6V 5T7	C. J. Newton	Douglas Van Allen	J. L. K. Vamplew, Q.C. Asst. C. D. Mackintosh
LENNOX & ADDINGTON	5 Napanee, K0K 2R0	B. W. Hurley	W. D. Blakely	J. R. Morgan
MANITOULIN	8 Gore Bay, P0P 1H0	C. T. Murphy	J. A. Graham	H. Sauve, Q.C.
MIDDLESEX	1 London, N6A 1E7	J. A. Winter R. S. Macnab J. F. McCart G. P. Killeen (Sr. Judge) T. G. Street R. J. Flinn		M. E. Martin, Q.C. Assts.: J. J. Douglas J. A. Sutherland G. A. Guthrie I. A. MacDonald K. McGowan B. Farmer
MUSKOKA DIST.	8 Bracebridge, P0B 1C0	S. B. Hogg	Sybil E. J. Jackson	W. A. Newell, Q.C.
NIAGARA NORTH (JUDICIAL DIST. OF)	12 St. Catharines, (Box 277, L2R 6T7)	D. H. Scott F. J. Z. Kovacs D. L. McWilliam H. P. Cavers	J. B. Marlow	F. J. Keenan, Q.C. Assts.: R. E. Pringle, Q.C., A. Bell
NIAGARA SOUTH (JUDICIAL DIST. OF)	2 Welland, L3B 3W6	G. G. Nicholls F. M. Griffiths T. J. Jacob	L. E. Taylor	A. H. Root, Q.C. Assts.: D. S. McGarry, Q.C., R. J. Ely M. J. Quinn
NIPISSING DIST.	8 North Bay, P1B 4G1	F. L. Gratton	Nestor Prisco	D. W. Fenton Asst.: N. Neima
NORFOLK	2 Simcoe, N3Y 4L2	J. A. Pringle	K. C. Bannister	W. D. Drinkwalter, Q.C.
NORTHUMBERLAND	5 Cobourg, (Box 517, K9A 4L3)	R. H. Carley J. C. N. Currelly (Supern.)	K. C. Gorman	B. W. Long Asst.: C. R. Harris
OTTAWA-CARLETON (JUDICIAL DIST. OF)	6 Ottawa, K1N 6E2	K. A. Flanigan C. F. Doyle K. H. Fogarty R. J. Marin F. H. Poulin H. Soubliere P. U. C. Rouleau	R. B. Hamilton	J. Cassells, Q.C. Assts.: M. A. Lindsay, Q.C., B. Lennox G. Dzioba A. Berzins E. D. Gulliver R. G. Mosley D. Macdougall J. M. Stewart L. V. Charron
OXFORD	1 Woodstock, N4S 7W5	C. C. Misener	R. S. Beaudoin	F. J. Porter
PARRY SOUND DIST.	8 89 James St., Box 99, P2A 2X2	E. Loukidelis	T. J. Healey	E. C. Gerhart, Q.C.
PEEL	3 Brampton, (Box 8000, L6V 2M7)	B. B. Shapiro W. A. Maedel E. F. West E. R. Lovekin M. T. Morrissey J. G. Roberts M. G. Bolan H. J. Keenan	M. Hesp	L. J. McGuigan, Q.C. Assts.: J. D. Scott D. Quick S. E. Sherriff L. W. McConnery P. M. Taylor W. B. Trafford A. E. Bonkalu D. A. Fairgrieve E. F. Hung

COUNTY & JUDICIAL DISTRICT IN WHICH SITUATED	COUNTY TOWN (ADDRESS TO COUNTY COURT HOUSE)	COUNTY AND SURROGATE JUDGE "His Honour"	SHERIFF	CLERK OF THE PEACE AND CROWN ATTORNEY
PERTH	1 Stratford, (Box 726, N5A 6V6)	J. A. Mullen	G. T. Roe	D. G. Page, Q.C.
PETERBOROUGH	5 Peterborough, K9H 3M9	G. L. Murdoch	S. A. McBride	W. H. Carleton, Q.C. Assts.: B. W. Gilkinson J. C. Marsland
PRESCOTT & RUSSELL	6 L'Orignal, K0B 1K0	R. J. Cusson	M. Théoret	R. G. Masse
PRINCE EDWARD	5 Picton, K0K 2T0	J. D. O'Flynn	J. K. Maddox	R. D. Sheehy, Q.C.
RAINY RIVER DIST.	7 Fort Frances, P9A 3M7	B. Trembley	J. E. Bradley	W. M. Saranchuk
RENFREW	6 Pembroke, K8A 3K2	F. E. Dunlap	I. E. Schimmens	Peter Barnes Asst.: J. N. Pepper
SIMCOE	3 Barrie, L4M 1M1	J. A. Clare A. M. Carter D. G. E. Thompson H. D. P. Logan	E. G. Bowles	J. E. Murphy, Q.C. Assts.: J. H. Madden, Q.C. J. S. Alexander, Q.C.
STORMONT, DUNDAS & GLENGARRY	6 Cornwall, (26 Pitt St., K6J 3P2)	G. A. Stiles	J. A. R. Lamoureux	D. W. Johnson, Q.C. Assts.: A. H. Ain S. H. Rutwind
SUDBURY DIST.	8 Sudbury, P3C 1T9	S. D. Loukidelis J. A. Forget G. B. Smith	F. Lebrun	J. H. Sauvé, Q.C. Assts.: D. W. Upton Diana Fuller M. N. Rauf D. M. Retterath
TEMISKAMING DIST.	8 Haileybury, P0J 1K0	J. D. Bernstein J. B. Robinson	R. J. MacArthur	F. J. Arthur, Q.C.
THUNDER BAY DIST.	7 Thunder Bay, P7A 4B3	P. S. FitzGerald S. R. Kurisko W. J. Shea	G. H. Burns	C. B. Devlin, Q.C. Assts.: R. W. Courtis L. A. Nicol A. Hardiejowski D. M. Mitchell
VICTORIA & HALIBURTON	5 Box 484, K9V 4S5	L. A. Woods	J. E. Boyd	C. J. Meinhardt, Q.C. Assts.: J. Woron, Q.C. Linda C. Price
WATERLOO	3 Kitchener, N2H 1C3	D. F. Mossop F. Costello R. E. Salhany F. J. McDonald	A. G. Schmitt	W. J. Morrison, Q.C. Assts.: P. Speyer W. W. Johnston J. W. Robb B. J. Frazer D. M. Russell D. W. Wilson
WELLINGTON	3 Guelph, N1H 6J9	E. G. McNeely W. F. Higgins	G. A. Goldrich	R. F. Chaloner, Q.C. Assts.: J. Meagher O. Haw
YORK	4 Toronto, (361 University Ave., M5G 1Y1)	N. D. Coo (Senior Judge)	Philip J. Ambrose	J. P. Rickaby, Q.C., (18 King St. E., M5C 1C5)
YORK REGION	4 Newmarket (50 Eagle St. W., L3Y 6B1)	D. R. Shearer	G. A. Taggart	L. H. Owen Assts: D. Bellamy T. Dier

York County
Surrogate Judges

G. H. F. Moore	E. J. Houston
H. Waisberg	J. B. Trotter
W. F. B. Rogers	H. R. Locke
C. J. Henry	J. D. Hudson
R. G. Phelan	W. J. Rapson
E. F. Wren	G. Ferguson
B. W. Grossberg	J. D. Sheard
L. K. Graburn	B. C. Hawkins
H. S. Honsberger	R. G. Conant
H. M. O'Connell	R. I. Cartwright
F. J. Cornish	S. P. Webb
S. B. Hogg	F. J. Greenwood
H. W. Allen	A. Mandel
N. D. Coo	J. Gilbert
S. Dymond	P. R. German
	A. C. Whealy

York County
Asst. Crown Attorneys

Toronto Central (361 University Ave.): Deputy Crown Attorney, R. B. McGee, Q.C. (965-7338); Assts.: T. L. Archibald, R. N. Ash, W. J. Babe, Q.C., D. J. Bellehumeur, R. M. Bennett, S. D. Berger, B. Cavion, N. M. Chorney, Q.C., P. I. Chumak, A. D. Cooper, P. W. Culver, P. V. DeJulio, Ms. S. G. Dobney, J. J. Donohue, M. Engel, K. Evans, Ms. B. A. Ferns, E. W. Geller, Ms. M. Goebbels, C. F. Graham, P. D. Griffiths, Ms. M. J. Hall, F. M. Hoffman, Q.C., S. P. Howarth, R. M. Innes, Q.C., G. S. Lapkin, F. R. Moskoff, Q.C., W. G. Orr, Ms. P. J. Peters, U. M. Priwes, C. J. Punter, J. Ramsay, F. H. Rowell, J. K. Stewart, J. F. Wiley, B. J. Young.

Etobicoke (80 The East Mall): Deputy Crown Attorney, N. G. Matusiak, Q.C.; Assts.: Ms. M. F. Browne, L. M. Budzinsky, G. W. Croft, H. S. Goody, Ms. S. Hallett, B. W. Hill, M. G. Morten, W. D. Nesmith.

North York (1000 Finch Ave. W.): Deputy Crown Attorney, S. G. Leggett, Q.C.; Assts.: D. F. Angevine, L. J. Applegath, Q.C., F. E. Armstrong, Q.C., N. L. Kozloff, T. R. Lipson, E. B. Minden, K. D. Murray, C. H. Rutherford, Ms. B. Wexler Kogan.

Scarborough (1911 Eglinton Ave. E.): Deputy Crown Attorney, M. M. Lynch, Q.C.; Assts.: K. V. Anthony, W. B. Donaldson, Q.C., T. D. Kirby, B. E. Scott, G. Vordemberge, R. D. Warren, W. K. Wijesinha, Q.C.

SMALL CLAIMS COURTS & CLERKS, ONTARIO

Inspector of Legal Offices, M.S. Fitzpatrick, 18th floor, 18 King St. E., Toronto, Ont.

Director, Small Claims Courts, Ron McFarland

NOTE: Address Clerk of ..... (Giving number of Court) at ..... (Giving Address).

ALGOMA DIST.

1. H.M. Douglas, Court House, Sault Ste. Marie, Ont.
3. Mrs. T. Hoyle, 140 Main St., Thessalon, Ont. P0R 1L0 (705/842-3544)
4. J.C. Myers, Box 756, Wawa, Ont. POS 1KO (705/856-2872)

7 & 8. Mrs. S. Portelance, 10 W. Cul de Sac, Elliot Lake, Ont. P5A 1B2 (705/848-2383)

BRANT COUNTY

1. Mrs. Jean Harwood, 34 Market St., Brantford, Ont. N3T 2Z5 (519/753-0451)

BRUCE COUNTY

1. J.W. Ellis, Box 430, Walkerton, Ont. NOG 2VO (519/881-0211)
5. David Ellis, Box 1621, Port Elgin, Ont. NOH 2CO (519/832-2253)
8. C.V.J. Limpert, Box 514, Wiarton, Ont. NOH 2TO (519/534-1714)

COCHRANE DIST.

1. A.J. Filion, Box 1360, Cochrane, Ont. POL 1CO (705/272-4151)
2. S.W. Marciniwe, 47 Pine St. S., Timmins, Ont. P4N 2J9
4. A.R. Lauzon, Box 182, Kapuskasing, Ont. P5N 2Y6 (705/335-6383)
6. Adrien Cyr, (885 Centennial St.), Box 369, Iroquois Falls A, Ont. POK 1GO (705/232-4374)

DUFFERIN COUNTY

1. P.C. McNair, 21 First St., Orangeville, Ont. L9W 2C8 (519/941-1392)
2. Miss M.E. Hecker, R.R. 1, Shelburne, Ont. L0N 1S0 (519/925-5040)

DURHAM DIST.

1. Mrs. Sheila Camplin, Box 386, Whitby, Ont. L1N 5S4 (416/668-3624)
3. Mrs. Lynda Holstock, Box 340, Uxbridge, Ont. LOC 1KO (416/852-7113)
8. C.R. Halliday, 249 King St. W., Oshawa, Ont. L1J 2J7 (416/723-9332)

ELGIN COUNTY

1. J.L. Jones, 2 Wellington St., St. Thomas, Ont. N5P 3T9 (519/631-1241)

ESSEX COUNTY

2. R.F. McKim, 1389 Front Rd. S., Amherstburg, Ont. N9V 2M5
3. W.W. Sanford, 24 Thorncrest St., Kingsville, Ont. N9Y 1B7 (519/733-2633)
7. M.A. Kelly, 744 Ouellette Ave., Windsor, Ont. N9A 1C3 (519/258-8751)

FRONTENAC COUNTY

1. C.E. Morrison, Court House, Kingston, Ont. K7L 4X6 (613/548-8248)
6. Mrs. Audrey McWilliams, Sharbot Lake, Ont. KOH 2PO (613/279-2607)

GREY COUNTY

1. Geo. A. Wakeford, 880 2nd Ave. E., Owen Sound, Ont. N4K 4M5
2. Lambert Maxted, R.R. 3, Durham, Ont. NOG 1RO (519/369-3505)
3. Mrs. Marion V. Chapple, Box 632, Meaford, Ont. NOH 1YO (519/538-1014)

HALDIMAND JUDICIAL DIST.

3. R.S. Ash, 205 Cross St. W., Dunnville, Ont. N1A 1N4 (416/774-5859)

HALIBURTON PROVISIONAL COUNTY

2. Miss Betty H. Hodgson, Box 209, Haliburton, Ont. KOM 1SO (705/457-1732)

HALTON COUNTY

1. Bruce C. MacNab, 491 Steeles Ave., Milton, Ont. L9T 1Y7 (416/878-6771)
2. Mrs. E. Bunce, 225 Church St., Oakville, Ont. L6J 1N4 (416/845-7941)
6. Mrs. Ruth Morris, Box 384, Burlington, Ont. L7R 3Y3 (416/632-0680)

HAMILTON-WENTWORTH DIST.

1. Robt. A. Stone, 25 Hughson St. S., Hamilton, Ont. L8N 3M6 (416/522-9063)

HASTINGS COUNTY

1. J.A. Geen, 117 Front St., Belleville, Ont. K8P 2Y6
6. H. Price, Box 158, 108 Forsyth St., Marmora, Ont. KOK 2MO (613/472-2501)
9. E.F. Jackson, 80 Division St., Trenton, Ont. K8V 4NO (613/392-1655)
12. Mrs. Marjorie Towle, Box 36, Bancroft, Ont. KOL 1CO (613/332-3237)

HURON COUNTY

1. M. Cranston, Box 1, Goderich, Ont. N7A 3Y5 (519/524-7112)
5. Mrs. G. Farquhar, Box 399, Exeter, Ont. NOM 1SO (519/235-2058)
8. Mrs. S.G. Foxton, Box 1, Wingham, Ont. NOG 2WO (519/357-1196)

KENORA DIST.

1. Philip Spalton, Court House, 216 Water St., Kenora, Ont. P9N 1S4

3 & 4. R.S. Dawes, Box 636, Dryden, Ont. P8N 2Z4 (807/223-2613)

5. Mrs. O.M. English, Box 226, Red Lake, Ont. POV 2MO (807/727-2767)

KENT COUNTY

1. S. Blake Roszell, 1st floor, 21 Seventh St., Chatham, Ont. N7M 4K1 (519/354-0210)
5. R.W. Robinson, 437 James St., Wallaceburg, Ont. N8A 2N8 (519/627-1174)

LAMBTON COUNTY

1. Mrs. R. Albinson, 180 1/2 N. Christina St., Sarnia, Ont. N7T 5T9 (519/337-6651)
5. Mrs. Sharon L. Spence, Box 719, Forest, Ont. NON 1JO

LANARK COUNTY

1. K.E. Fournier, Box 40, Perth, Ont. K7H 3E2 (613/267-2021)
3. A.R. Thorpe, 165 George St., Carleton Place, Ont. K7C 1Z4 (613/257-2406)
4. E.H. Stansel, Box 331, Smiths Falls, Ont. K7A 4T2 (613/283-4420)

LEEDS & GRENVILLE COUNTIES

1. Eric Jensen, 27 King St. E., Brockville, Ont. K6V 1K7 (613/342-2833)
2. B.F. Gill, Box 1270, Prescott, Ont. KOE 1TO (613/925-4633)

LENNOX & ADDINGTON COUNTY

1. J.F. Russell, Box 51, Napanee, Ont. K7R 3L4 (613/354-5243)
8. Mrs. F. Boomhour, Box 51, Kaladar, Ont. KOH 1ZO (613/336-8952)

MANITOULIN DIST.

1. J.A. Graham, Court House, Gore Bay, Ont. POP 1HO (705/282-2461)
2. Mrs. Mary E. McHarg, Box 363, Little Current, Ont. POP 1KO (705/368-2277)

MIDDLESEX COUNTY

1. Roy Edgecombe, 80 Dundas St., London, Ont. N6A 1E7 (519/679-7017)
2. Mrs. Helen Romphf, 289 Anna St., Parkhill, Ont. NOM 2KO (519/294-6511)
6. Mrs. Marjorie Moffatt, 52 Frank St., Strathroy, Ont. N7G 2R4 (519/245-1477)

MUSKOKA DIST.

1. E. Owen McQuillen, Court House, Box 1821, Bracebridge, Ont. POB 1CO (705/645-2682)
3. G. McCallum, Box 2592, Huntsville, Ont. POA 1KO (705/789-5630)

NIAGARA NORTH DIST.

2. P.W. Snyder, 39 Queen St., St. Catharines, Ont.
5. K.D. McAlpine, 15 Main St. E., Box 293, Grimsby, Ont. L3M 4G5 (416/945-2756)

NIAGARA SOUTH DIST.

1. Mrs. T. Blackwell, Box 612, Welland, Ont. L3B 5R4 (416/734-7417)
4. H.A. Swain, #4, 5415 Victoria Ave., Niagara Falls, Ont. L2G 3L1 (416/356-3404)

NIPISSING DIST.
1. A.A. Turcotte, Box 238, Sturgeon Falls, Ont. POH 2GO (705/753-1090)
3. Mrs. Teresa Loyst, 390 Plouffe St., North Bay, Ont. P1B 4G1 (705/472-5860)

NORFOLK DIST.
1. D.G. Johnson, Court House, Box 605, Simcoe, Ont. N3Y 4N4 (519/426-3447)

NORTHUMBERLAND COUNTY
1. J. Hughes, 3 Jane St., Box 216, Port Hope, Ont. L1A 2E4
2. Geo. A. Mitchell, Box 546, Cobourg, Ont. K9A 4L3 (416/372-7153)
3. G.E. Coling, Box 97, Brighton, Ont. KOK 1HO (613/475-0961)

OTTAWA-CARLETON REG. MUN.
7. A.R. Merritt, 56 Sparks St., Box 1566, Stn. B, Ottawa, Ont. K1P 5Z4 (613/232-5408)

OXFORD COUNTY
1. Mrs. E.P. Taylor, 461 Dundas St., Woodstock, Ont. N4S 1C2 (519/537-8511)

PARRY SOUND DIST.
1. Mrs. E. Nichol, 89 James St., Parry Sound, Ont. P2A 1T7 (705/746-5464)
7. L.G. Gough, Box 239, South River, Ont. POA 1XO (705/386-2560)

PEEL DIST.
1. H. Rutherford, 5 Moore Cres., Brampton, Ont. L6W 1W8 (416/451-0121)
2. Mrs. Dorothy Turvill, 470 Hensall Circle, Mississauga, Ont. L5A 3V5 (416/277-1583)

PERTH COUNTY
1. A.N. Todd, 77 Downie St., Stratford, Ont. N5A 1W8
6. Mrs. Aileen Mutter, 595 Inkerman St. E., Listowel, Ont. N4W 2N8 (519/291-1423)

PETERBOROUGH COUNTY
1. H.R. McNabb, Court House, Peterborough, Ont. K9H 3M3 (705/745-0583, ext. 58)

PRESCOTT & RUSSELL COUNTIES
7. O. Gratton, 151 Main St., Room 35, Hawkesbury, Ont. K6A 1A1 (613/632-4282)
10. F.J. Pilon, Box 250, Rockland, Ont. KOA 3AO (613/446-4781)

PRINCE EDWARD COUNTY
1. D. Beaumont, Box 155, Picton, Ont. KOK 2TO (613/476-2390)

RAINY RIVER DIST.
1. J.E. Bradley, Box 8, Fort Frances, Ont. P9A 3M5 (807/274-5961)
4. J.E. Bradley, c/o Box 8, Fort Frances, Ont. P9A 3M5 (807/274-5961)

RENFREW COUNTY
1. I.E. Schimmens, Court House, Pembroke, Ont. K8A 5S2
3. Mrs. E. Desilets, 259 Raglan St., Box 386, Renfrew, Ont. K7V 1R3 (613/432-3193)
4. Mrs. C. Forsyth, 45 Hugh St. S., Arnprior, Ont. K7S 2V5 (613/623-2873)
7. J.J. Harrington, Killaloe Station, Ont. KOJ 2AO (613/757-2050)

SIMCOE COUNTY
1. Ruth Workman, Court House, Worsley St., Barrie, Ont. L4M 3P2 (705/728-4181)
4. R.C. McAllister, 649 Hurontario St., Collingwood, Ont. L9Y 2N6 (705/445-4240)
6. C.J. Bennett, 104 Borland St. E., Box 293, Orillia, Ont. L3V 2B7 (705/326-4251)
8. J.H. Malloy, 46 Centre St. S., Box 706, Alliston, Ont. LOM 1AO (705/435-9645)

STORMONT, DUNDAS & GLENGARRY COUNTIES
2. J.C. Cormier, 26 Bishop St., Box 1551, Alexandria, Ont. KOC 1AO (613/525-1872)
3. Mrs. Heather Menard, Box 1294, Cornwall, Ont. K6H 5V4 (613/932-1224)
6. Mrs. M.R. Sweeney, 167 Davis Dr., Iroquois, Ont. KOE 1KO (613/652-4521)
10. R.D. Wylie, Box 13, Winchester, Ont. KOC 2KO (613/774-3374)

SUDBURY DIST.
1. Mrs. G. Vannier, 38 Larch St., Sudbury, Ont. P3E 5M7 (705/675-4164)
3. Miss M.T. Arthurs, Town Hall, Espanola, Ont. POP 1CO (705/869-1150)
5. Mrs. Marian Pellow, Box 584, Chapleau, Ont. POM 1KO

TEMISKAMING DIST.
1. G. Kallunki, Court House, Haileybury, Ont. POJ 1KO (705/672-3606)
3. Mrs. E. Pearson, Box 147, Englehart, Ont. POJ 1HO (705/544-8185)
4. G.T. Hurd, Box 217, Kirkland Lake, Ont. P2N 3H7 (705/567-7060)

THUNDER BAY DIST.
2. Mrs. Edna Aubut, Box 309, Nipigon, Ont. POT 2JO (807/887-3829)
3. L. Danis, 277 Camelot St., Thunder Bay, Ont. P7A 4B3 (807/344-5801)
4. Mrs. E.A. Harness, Box 234, Schreiber, Ont. POT 2SO (807/824-2495)
5. Mrs. L. Payeur, Box 39, Geraldton, Ont. POT 1MO
6. J.D. McDonald, Box 224, Marathon, Ont. POT 2EO
7. Nicole M. Holmes, Box 90, Beardmore, Ont. POT 1GO (807/875-2176)

VICTORIA COUNTY
5. Mrs. M. Pepper, 59 Victoria Ave. N., Lindsay, Ont. K9V 4G4 (705/324-4251)

WATERLOO DIST.
1. S.E. Belyea, 58 Scott St., Kitchener, Ont. N2H 2R1 (519/745-8063)
3. Ian H. Dudgeon, 120 Main St., Cambridge, Ont. N1R 1V7 (519/623-0170)

WELLINGTON COUNTY
1. Mrs. D.G. Will, 25 Douglas St., Guelph, Ont. N1H 2S7 (519/822-0131)
4. Mrs. M. Ward, 230 Queen St. W., Fergus, Ont. N1M 1S8 (519/843-1644)
8. F. McEachern, 344 Smith St., Arthur, Ont. NOG 1AO (519/848-2205)
11. R.W. Hiller, Mount Forest, Ont. NOG 2LO (519/323-4358)

YORK JUDICIAL DIST.

Toronto Small Claims Court: Miss J. Cardwell, 444 Yonge St., 2nd Floor, Toronto, Ont. M5B 2H7 (416/598-2842)

Etobicoke Small Claims Court: R.A. Soderberg, 2265 Keele St., #209, Toronto, Ont. M6M 5B8 (416/249-8251)

Scarborough Small Claims Court: Mrs. M. White, 2130 Lawrence Ave. E., #306, Scarborough, Ont. M1R 5B9 (416/755-5228, 755-5229)

North York Small Claims Court: G.R. Beeby, 47 Sheppard Ave. E., 3rd Floor, Willowdale, Ont. M2N 5X5 (416/225-4846)

YORK REGION
1. C.J. Chapman, Court House, 50 Eagle St. W., 4th Floor, Newmarket, Ont. L3Y 6B1 (416/895-4291)
2. Mrs. Barbara Munro, Box 7, Sutton West, Ont. L0E 1R0 (416/722-5118)
3. J.A. Farrow, 550 Markham Rd., Richmond Hill, Ont. L4C 4X7 (416/884-3833)

PROVINCIAL JUDGES (Criminal Division)

Admin. of Provincial Courts (Criminal Division), 60 Queen St. W., Toronto, Ont. M5H 2M4 (416/965-7200)

Chief Judge, F.C. Hayes

County or Dist., with Judge (His Hon.), Address and Telephone:

Algoma J.D.: C.E. Boyd, J.D. Greco, Court House, Sault Ste. Marie, Ont. P6A 5M8 (705-254-6897); W.W. Cohen, Box 187, Bruce Mines, Ont. POR 1CO (705-785-3767), and 45 Hillside Dr. N., Elliot Lake, Ont. P5A 1X5 (705-848-2500)

Brant: W.A. MacDonald, 102 Wellington Sq., Brantford, Ont. N3T 2M2 (519-753-3121)

Bruce: F.W. Olmstead, Box 39, 215 Cayley St., Walkerton, Ont. N0G 2V0 (519-881-2333)

Cochrane J.D.: J.H. Caldbick, H.W. Gauthier, Ste. 125, 38 Pine St. N., Timmins, Ont. P4N 6K6 (705-264-2376); Gerard E. Cloutier, Court House, Box 2069, Cochrane, Ont. POL 1CO (705-272-4358)
Dufferin: W.D. August, Senior Judge, 75 First St., 2nd floor, Orangeville, Ont. L9W 2E7 (519-941-5802)
Durham J. Mun.: D.B. Dodds, N.H. Edmondson, 8th floor, 50 Centre St. S., Oshawa, Ont. L1H 3Z8 (416-723-5251)
Elgin: G.A. Phillips, Box 267, 30 St. Catherine St., St. Thomas, Ont. N5P 3T9 (519-633-1230)
Essex: G.R. Stewart, Sr. Judge, L.A. Henriksen, H. Momotiuk, S. Nosanchuk, Box 607, Windsor, Ont. N9A 6N4 (519-254-3741)
Frontenac: P.E.D. Baker, Senior Judge, P.H. Megginson, Box 400, 181 Barrie St., Kingston, Ont. K7L 4W2 (613-547-2286)
Grey: M.C. Hay, Box 233, 1133 Second Ave. E., Owen Sound, Ont. N4K 5P3 (519-376-0185)
Haldimand: M.J. Girard, Box 399, Munsee St., Cayuga, Ont. NOA 1EO (416-772-3818)
Halton Reg. Mun.: D.V. Latimer, W.S. Sharpe, 491 Steeles Ave. E., Milton, Ont. L9T 1Y7 (416-878-4161); J.E.C. Robinson, 760 Brant St., Burlington, Ont. L7R 4B7 (416-632-8811)
Hamilton-Wentworth Reg. Mun.: A.J. Marck, W.R. Morrison, Sr. Judge, E.A. Fairbanks, R.T. Bennett, P.R. Mitchell, C.J. Stiles, Box 2014, 125 Main St. E., Hamilton, Ont. L8N 3S1 (416-525-1840)
Hastings: J.L. Clendenning, 15 Victoria Ave., Belleville, Ont. K8N 1Z5 (613-962-3468)
Huron: W.G. Cochrane, 1 Court House Sq., Goderich, Ont. N7A 1M2 (519-524-9342)
Kenora J.D.: R.E. Bogusky, Box 3000, Dryden, Ont. P8N 3B3 (807-223-2348); D.A. McKenzie, W.W. Bradley, Court House, Kenora, Ont. P9N 1S4 (807-468-6132)
Kent: C.E. Perkins, 2nd floor, 21 Seventh St., Chatham, Ont. N7M 4J9 (519-352-9070)
Lambton: A. Fowler, A.M. Lang, Box 2017, 700 N. Christina St., Sarnia, Ont. N7T 7L1 (519-336-8830)
Lanark: D.C. Smith, Box 31, Smiths Falls, Ont. K7A 4S9 (613-283-1906)
Leeds & Grenville: J.A. Deacon, 75 Water St. W., Box 1360, Brockville, Ont. K6V 5Y6 (613-342-5003)
Lennox & Addington: R.C. Jackson, J.P. Coulson, #386, 41 Dundas St. W., Napanee, Ont. K7R 3P5 (613-354-5450)
Manitoulin J.D.: G.E. Michel, Sr. Judge, District Court House, Box 314, Gore Bay, Ont. POP 1HO (705-282-2531)
Middlesex: A.J. Baker, Sr. Judge, G.G. Marshman, J.M. Seneshen, J.L. Menzies, W.E. Bell, 80 Dundas St. E., Box 5600, Stn. A, London, Ont. N6A 1B4 (519-679-7070)
Muskoka J.D.: D.G. Bice, Box 1110, Dominion St., Bracebridge, Ont. POB 1CO (705-645-4422)
Niagara North J.D.: T.R. BeGora, H.W. Edmondstone, 68 Church St., Box 1537, St. Catharines, Ont. L2R 7J9 (416-685-4856)
Niagara South J.D.: J.L. Roberts, Sr. Judge, D.J. Wallace, Box 627, 4300 Queen St., Niagara Falls, Ont. L2E 6V5 (416-354-2780); J.M. Gardner, M.J. Girard, Box 236, 40 Division St., Welland, Ont. L3B 3Z6 (416-732-2493)
Nipissing J.D.: J.L. Lunney, 621 Main St. W., North Bay, Ont. P1B 2V6 (705-472-8120)
Norfolk J.D.: W.E. Ross, Box 605, Simcoe, Ont. N3Y 4N4 (519-426-8330)
Northumberland: J.D. Bark, S.H. Murphy, 1011 William St., Box 910, Cobourg, Ont. K9A 4K7 (416-372-0193)
Ottawa-Carleton Reg. Mun.: R.B. Hutton, Sr. Judge, L.A. Sherwood, P.D. White, J.P. Beaulne, B.T. Ryan, J.M. Bordeleau, P.R. Belanger, J. Nadelle, J.A. Archambault, 4th floor, 1 Nicholas St., Ottawa, Ont. K1N 7B7 (613-566-3901)
Oxford: R.G. Groom, Court House, Hunter St., Box 910, Woodstock, Ont. N4S 4G6 (519-537-2369)
Parry Sound D.: L.S. Geiger, Box 455, Parry Sound, Ont. P2A 2X5 (705-746-4271)
Peel Reg. Mun.: W.D. August, Senior Judge, G.L. Young, J.D. Ord, K.A. Langdon, W.G. Richards, 141 Clarence St., Brampton, Ont. L6W 3E6 (416-451-7551)
Perth: W.A. Ehgoetz, 17 George St. W., Stratford, Ont. N5A 1A6 (519-271-9252)
Peterborough: R.B. Batten, L.T.G. Collins, City Hall, 500 George St. N., Peterborough, Ont. K9H 3R9 (705-745-0583)
Prescott & Russell: J.F.R. Levesque, Court House, Box 272, L'-Orignal, Ont. KOB 1KO (613-675-4625)
Prince Edward: P. Coulson, Box 640, Picton, Ont. KOK 2TO (613-476-2606)
Rainy River J.D.: A.D. McLennan, Box 336, Fort Frances, Ont. P9A 3M7 (807-274-9832)
Renfrew: C.R. Merredew, 415 Pembroke St. W., Pembroke, Ont. K8A 6X3 (613-735-6886)
Simcoe: D.R. Inch, J.W.P. Anjo, N.J. Nadeau, 30 Poyntz St., Barrie, Ont. L4M 3P2 (705-728-1221); L.T. Montgomery, 19 Front St. N., Orillia, Ont. L3V 6J3 (705-326-2671)
Stormont, Dundas & Glengarry: M.J. Fitzpatrick, Box 998, 340 Pitt St., Cornwall, Ont. K6H 5R9 (613-933-7500), and Box 699, Alexandria, Ont. KOC 1AO (613-525-3173); H.B. Hunter, Box 858, Morrisburg, Ont. KOC 1XO (613-543-2193)
Sudbury J.D.: G.E. Michel, Sr. Judge, G.R. Matte, A. Falzetta, W.F. FitzGerald, Court House, 155 Elm St. W., Sudbury, Ont. P3C 1V1 (705-674-3151) and Town Hall, 100 Tudhope St., Espanola, Ont. POP 1CO (705-869-4334)
Temiskaming J.D.: E.W. Kenrick, Court House, Box 1208, Haileybury, Ont. POJ 1KO (705-672-3395)
Thunder Bay J.D.: R.B. Mitchell, Sr. Judge, R.D. Clarke, F.A. Sargent, R.J. Walneck, 2nd floor, 1805 E. Arthur St., Thunder Bay, Ont. P7E 5N7 (807-475-1335)
Victoria & Haliburton: G.W. Inrig, Box 82, 440 Kent St. W., Lindsay, Ont. K9V 4R8 (705-324-5302)
Waterloo J.D.: G.H. McConnell, Sr. Judge, J.R.H. Kirkpatrick, J.F. McCormick, D.J. MacMillan, R.D. Reilly, Ste. 1000, 200 Frederick St., Kitchener, Ont. N2H 6P1 (519-745-5633)
Wellington: H.R. Howitt, 36 Wyndham St. S., Guelph, Ont. N1H 7J5 (519-836-2501)
York Region: 50 Eagle St. W., 2nd floor, Newmarket, Ont. L3Y 6B1 (416/895-6600)
York J.D.:
- York North: C.P. Opper, Sr. Judge, C. Drukarsh, C.J. Morrison, J. Crossland, 1000 Finch Ave. W., Downsview, Ont. M3J 2C7
- York East: S.G. Tinker, Sr. Judge, A.W. Davidson, W.J. Camblin, C.E. Purvis, 1911 Eglinton Ave. E., Scarboro, Ont. M1L 4P4 (416/757-3686)
- York West: S.R. Roebuck, Sr. Judge, G.W. Gardhouse, R.J. Graham, C.J. Cannon, J.J. Belobradic, 80 The East Mall, Etobicoke, Ont. M8Z 5W3 (416/252-7885)
- Metro: F.C. Hayes, Chief Judge, H.A. Rice, Assoc. Chief Judge, D.F. Granam, H.D. Foster, J.L. Addison, M.J. Cloney, A.K. Meen, G.E. Carter, R.B. Knieper, P.J. Wilch, D. Vanek, C. Waisberg, L.E. Dicecco, B.M. Kelly, D. Draper, M.A. Charles, F.J. McMahon, P.B. Parker, C.H. Paris, S.W. Long, S.M. Harris, H.E. Zimmerman, J.S. Climans, W.P. Hryciuk, T.J. Graham, W.P. Ross, J. Bernhard, C.J. Horwitz, A.E. Charlton, R.D. Osborne, D.G. Scott, Old City Hall, 60 Queen St. W., Toronto, Ont. M5H 2M4 (416/965-7227)
- College Park: A. Brown, C. Scullion, M.A. Cadsby, C.E. Lewis, J. Murphy, P.B. Pickett, R. Scott, T. Mercer, 444 Yonge St., Toronto, Ont. M5B 2H4 (416/965-7504)

PROVINCIAL JUDGES (Family Division)

Admin. of Provincial Courts (Family Division), #2306, 700 Bay St., Toronto, Ont. M5G 1Z6 (416/965-3214)
Chief Judge, H.T.G. Andrews
Associate Chief Judge, R.J.K. Walmsley

In the Province of Ontario the Juvenile Delinquents Act, 1908 (Canada) has been proclaimed in the following areas:

County or Dist. with Judge, Address and Telephone (J.D. is Judicial Dist.)

Algoma J.D.: G.D. Holder, 473 Queen St. E., #100, Sault Ste. Marie, Ont. P6A 1Z7 (705-253-3288)
Brant: R.J. Hamilton, City Hall, 100 Wellington Sq., Brantford, Ont. N3T 2M2 (519-752-6559)

Bruce: J.M. Gammell, Box 578, Walkerton, Ont. NOG 2VO (519-881-0613)

Cochrane North D.: Gerard E. Cloutier, Court House, Box 2069, Cochrane, Ont. POL 1CO (705-272-4358)

Cochrane South D.: H.W. Gauthier, J. Caldbick, 38 Pine St. N., Timmins, Ont. P4N 6K6 (705-264-5228)

Dufferin: H.J. Slater, 75 First St., 2nd floor, Orangeville, Ont. L9W 2E7 (519-941-5802)

Durham J.D.: Richard H. Donald, J.B. Allen, 44 Bond St. W., 2nd floor, Box 2216, Oshawa, Ont. L1H 7V5 (416-728-1623)

Elgin: A.R. Webster, Box 327, 145 Curtis St., St. Thomas, Ont. N5P 3T9 (519-633-2160)

Essex: T.L. Docherty, F.H. Nowak, 4th floor, 250 Windsor Ave., Box 1508, Windsor, Ont. N9A 6R5 (519-254-2871)

Frontenac: K.E. Pedlar, W.J. Pickett, 469 Montreal St., Box 981, Kingston, Ont. K7L 4X8 (613-547-2223)

Grey: J.M. Gammell, 347 8th St. E., Box 206, Owen Sound, Ont. N4K 5P3 (519-371-1313)

Haldimand J.D.: R.J. Hamilton, Munsee St., Box 399, Cayuga, Ont. NOA 1EO (416-772-3818)

Halton J.D.: A.J. Fuller, 491 Steeles Ave. E., Milton, Ont. L9T 1Y7 (416-878-7268)

Hamilton-Wentworth J.D.: (Unified Family Court) J.E. Van Duzer, D.M. Steinberg, R.T.P. Gravely, D.E. Cooper, 100 James St. S., Hamilton, Ont. L8P 2Z3 (416-525-1550)

Hastings: D.K. Kirkland, Century Place, Ste. 402, Box 906, Belleville, Ont. K8N 5B6 (613-968-6759)

Huron: J.M. Gammell, 1 Court House Sq., Goderich, Ont. N7A 1M2 (519-524-6742)

Kenora D.: W.W. Bradley, Court House, Water St., Kenora, Ont. P9N 1S4 (807-468-3353); R.E. Bogusky, Box 3000, Dryden, Ont. P8N 3B3 (807-223-2348)

Kent: L.G. DeKoning, 1st floor, 21 Seventh St., Chatham, Ont. N7M 4K1 (519-354-0622)

Lambton: David F. Kent, 700 N. Christina St., Box 3021, Sarnia, Ont. N7T 7N5 (519-337-8713)

Lanark: D.C. Smith, Chambers St., Box 31, Smiths Falls, Ont. K7A 4S9 (613-283-1907)

Leeds & Grenville: J.A. Deacon, 75 Water St. W., Box 1360, Brockville, Ont. K6V 5Y6 (613-342-5003)

Lennox & Addington: D.K. Kirkland, 41 Dundas St. W., Box 386, Napanee, Ont. K7R 3P5 (613-354-3850)

Manitoulin J.D.: J.T. Robson, R.T. Runciman, District Court House, Box 314, Gore Bay, Ont. POP 1HO (705-282-2531)

Middlesex: M.H. Genest, H.A. Vogelsang, 80 Dundas St. E., Box 5600, Stn. A, London, Ont. N6A 2P3 (519-679-7090)

Muskoka J.D.: Wm. F. Golden, Dominion St., Box 159, Bracebridge, Ont. POB 1CO (705-645-2831)

Niagara North J.D.: J.W. Scott, 210 King St., Box 536, St. Catharines, Ont. L2R 6V9 (416-685-7142)

Niagara South J.D.: R.L. Budgell, 3 Cross St., Box 383, Welland, Ont. L3B 5P7 (416-734-7451)

Nipissing D.: J.J. Evans, 500 Main St. W., North Bay, Ont. P1B 2V4 (705-472-2680)

Norfolk J.D.: R.J. Hamilton, Box 605, Simcoe, Ont. N3Y 4N4 (519-426-8450)

Northumberland: B.C. Thompson, 55 King St. W., 1st floor, Cobourg, Ont. K9A 2M2 (416-372-0126)

Ottawa-Carleton J.D.: P.D. Hamlyn, J.P. Michel, G. Goulard, G. Guzzo, A.D. Sheffield, 1145 Bronson Place, Ottawa, Ont. K1S 4H4 (613-566-3834)

Oxford: J.F. Bennett, Court House, Hunter St., Woodstock, Ont. N4S 4G6 (519-537-2377)

Parry Sound D.: L.S. Geiger, 88 James St., Parry Sound, Ont. P2A 1T9 (705-746-8163)

Peel J.D.: W.L. Durham, R.E. Stauth, Box 220, Brampton, Ont. L6V 2L1 (416-457-5020)

Perth: J.F. Bennett, 17 George St. W., Stratford, Ont. N5A 1A6 (519-271-2640)

Peterborough: Her Hon. M.C. Maloney, B.C. Thompson, Court House, Warden's Walk, Peterborough, Ont. K9H 3M3 (705-745-0583)

Prescott & Russell: R. Lalande, Court St., Box 272, L'Orignal, Ont. KOB 1KO (613-675-4695)

Prince Edward: D.K. Kirkland, 332 Main St., Box 640, Picton, Ont. KOK 2TO (613-476-2606)

Rainy River J.D.: A.D. McLennan, 333 Church St., Box 336, Fort Frances, Ont. P9A 3M7 (807-274-9832)

Renfrew: L.P. Foran, 415 Pembroke St. W., Pembroke, Ont. K8A 6X3 (613-735-0697)

Simcoe: W.F. Golden, M.D. Morton, Box 184, Court House, 30 Poyntz St., Barrie, Ont. L4M 4T2 (705-728-1221, ext. 35)

Stormont, Dundas & Glengarry J.D.: Roch Lalande, 340 Pitt St., Box 56, Cornwall, Ont. K6H 5R9 (613-933-7500)

Sudbury J.D.: J.T. Robson, R.T. Runciman, 40 Larch St., Sudbury, Ont. P3E 5M7 (705-675-4231)

Sudbury (Espanola): R.T. Runciman, J.T. Robson, Town Hall, 100 Tudhope St., Box 126, Espanola, Ont. POP 1CO (705-869-4334)

Temiskaming D.: E.W. Kenrick, 4 Kirkland St. W., Box 253, Kirkland Lake, Ont. P2N 3H7 (705-567-9381)

Thunder Bay J.D.: P.S. Glowacki (Sr. Judge), G.R. Kunnas, 1805 E. Arthur St., 1st floor, Thunder Bay, Ont. P7E 5N7 (807-475-1365)

Toronto (Metro): See York

Victoria & Haliburton: Her Hon. M.C. Maloney, 440 Kent St. W., Box 82, Lindsay, Ont. K9V 4R8 (705-324-2425)

Waterloo J.D.: R.H. Fair, D.A. Bean, H.J. Slater, 2nd floor, Prov. Court House, 200 Frederick St., Kitchener, Ont. N2H 6N9 (519-576-9110)

Wellington: H.J. Slater, 36 Wyndham St. S., Box 244, Guelph, Ont. N1H 6J9 (519-822-7961)

York Region J.D.: T.M. Moore, J.P. Nevins, 50 Eagle St. W., Newmarket, Ont. L3Y 6B1 (416-364-6838)

York J.D.: K. Wang, L.A. Beaulieu (Sr. Judge), N. Weisman, J.D. Karswick, D.R. Main, R. Abella, J.C.M. James, W.E. MacLatchy, M.H. Caney, 311 Jarvis St., Toronto, Ont. M5B 2C4 (416-963-0684)

J.P. Felstiner, H. Douglas Wilkins, 47 Sheppard Ave. E., Willowdale, Ont. M2N 5X5 (416-224-7647)

F. Stewart Fisher, A.P. Nasmith, 160 Silverhill Dr., Islington, Ont. M9B 3W7 (416-236-2553)

C.R. Ball, D.F. Morrison, 1911 Eglinton Ave. E., Scarborough, Ont. M1L 2L6 (416-755-9209)

ASSESSMENT REVIEW COURTS & Regional Offices

Provincial Registrar, T.G. Murphy, 80 Bloor St. W., Ste. 705, Toronto, Ont. M5S 1L9 (416/965-7574)

Eastern Area: Regional Registrar, J.E. Crawford, 2378 Holly Lane, Room 208, Ottawa, Ont. K1V 7P1 (613/731-7166)

Metro Toronto Area: Regional Registrar, vacant, 80 Bloor St. W., Toronto, Ont. M5S 1L9 (416/965-6826)

Central Area: Regional Registrar, J.L.M. Harbinson, 713 Davis Dr., Ste. 303, Newmarket, Ont. L3Y 2R3 (416/895-1274)

Central Area Branch Office: Asst. Registrar, Mrs. C.M. Harris, 277 George St. N., #207, Peterborough, Ont. K9J 3G9

Grand River Niagara Area: Regional Registrar, R.E. Michor, 678 Main St. E., Ste. 303, Hamilton, Ont. L8M 1K2 (416/549-4173)

Southwestern Area: Regional Registrar, A.H. Johnson, 426 Third St., 1st floor, London, Ont. N5W 4W6 (519/453-6660)

Northern Area: Regional Resistrar, J.F. Boyd, Northgate Shopping Centre, #300, North Bay, Ont. P1B 2H3 (705/474-1612)

Northern Area Branch Office: Asst. Registrar, Mrs. D.C. Archambault, 85 Great Northern Rd., Sault Ste. Marie, Ont. P6B 4Y8 (705/949-5280)

COURTS, JUDGES, ETC., P.E.I.

SUPREME COURT

Judges, Hon. John P. Nicholson, Chief Justice; Hon. Frederic A. Large; Hon. C.R. McQuaid; Hon. M.J. McQuaid; Hon. Kenneth R. MacDonald; Hon. A.B. Campbell; Hon. G.G. Mitchell
Clerk of the Court & Prothonotary, George E. MacMillan
Deputy Prothonotaries, Terence L. Fitzgerald, Queens Co.; F.W. Lilly, Prince Co.; H.N. Kerwin, Kings Co.

Bankruptcy

Supreme Court Judges have jurisdiction in bankruptcy.
Registrar, George E. MacMillan, Box 2200, Charlottetown, C1A 8B9 (892-9131)

Estates Division

Registrar, Mrs. A. Ayers
General Division, Registrar, Hazel Thompson
Family Division, Registrar, Deborah Proud

Sheriffs

Kings Co., John Daly, Montague
Queens Co., Eric Mooreside, Charlottetown
Prince Co., Layton Schurman, Summerside

Court of Appeal

The Court of Appeal of P.E.I. is, except in special circumstances, composed of three or more Judges of the Supreme Court of P.E.I.

Registration of Instruments

Registration of Land Titles is with Registrar of Deeds. Registration of Chattel Mortgages, Lien Notes, Conditional Sales, and other Transfers of personal property is with Prothonotary or Deputy Prothonotary in the County affected.

Provincial Court Judges

Queens & Kings Counties, G.L. FitzGerald; B.R. Plamondon
Prince County, Norman H. Carruthers (Chief Provincial Court Judge)

COURTS, JUDGES, ETC., QUEBEC

JUGES DE LA COUR D'APPEL JUDGES OF THE COURT OF APPEAL

Montreal (10 est, St-Antoine, H2Y 1A2): Juge en chef, Hon. Marcel Crête; Juges: Hon. Marc Beauregard, Hon. Laurent Bélanger, Hon. Claude Bisson, Hon. Fred Kaufman, Hon. Albert H. Malouf, Hon. Albert Mayrand, Hon. Gerald McCarthy, Hon. Amédée Monet, Hon. Georges H. Montgomery, Hon. John A. Nolan, Hon. George R.W. Owen, Hon. Rodolphe Paré
Quebec (12, rue St-Louis, G1R 4P6): Juges: Hon. Yves Bernier, Hon. André Dubé, Hon. François Lajoie, Hon. Mme Claire L'-Heureux-Dubé, Hon. Maurice Jacques, Hon. Jean Turgeon

JUGES DE LA COUR SUPERIEURE/JUDGES OF SUPERIOR COURT

Address of Courts:
Montreal: 1 est, Notre Dame, Montreal, P.Q. H2Y 1B6 (514/873-6381)
Quebec: 12, rue St-Louis, Quebec, P.Q. G1R 4P6 (418/643-4046)
Amos: 891, 3e ave est, Amos, P.Q. J9T 2T4
Sherbrooke: 191, rue du Palais, Sherbrooke, P.Q. J1H 4R1
Rouyn: 2, ave. du Palais, Rouyn, P.Q. J9X 2N9
Hull: 17 rue Laurier, Hull, P.Q. J8X 4C1
Chicoutimi: 202, rue Jacques-Cartier, Chicoutimi, P.Q. G7H 5C5
Shawinigan: 791, 5e rue, Shawinigan, P.Q. G9N 6V9
Trois-Rivières: 250, rue Laviolette, Trois-Rivières, P.Q. G9A 1T9
Granby: 77 Principale, Granby, P.Q. J2G 9B3

Juge en Chef/Chief Justice, Hon. Jules Deschenes, Montreal
Juge en Chef associé/Senior Assoc. Chief Justice, Hon. Gabrielle Vallée, Quebec
Juge en Chef adjoint/Assoc. Chief Justice, Hon. James K. Hugessen, Montreal

Les Honorables: Maurice Archambault, Mtl., Harry L. Aronovitch, Mtl., François Auclair, Mtl., Alphonse Barbeau, Mtl., C.-Noel Barbes, Amos, Samuel S. Bard, Mtl., J.-Robert Beaudoin, Que., Jules Beauregard, Mtl., Jean-Jacques Bedard, Que., Marcel Belleville, Mtl., Claude Benoit, Mtl., Anthime Bergeron, Mtl., Camille L. Bergeron, Rouyn, Jean-Paul Bergeron, Mtl., Paul-Etienne Bernier, Que., Jean Bienvenue, Que., André G. Biron, Mtl., Ivan Bisaillon, Mtl., Jules Blanchet, Mtl., Jean-Guy Boilard, Mtl., Gérald Boisvert, Que., Jacques Boucher, Hull, Pierre Boudreault, Mtl., Bernard de L. Bourgeois, Mtl., Jean-Marie Brassard, Mtl., François Chevalier, Hull, Roger Chouinard, Chicoutimi, Vital Cliche, Val d'Or, Réjane L. Colas, Mtl., Gérard Corriveau, Que., Pierre Cote, Que., Maurice Cousineau, Mtl., Guy-Merril Desaulniers, Mtl., Gaston Desjardins, Que., Gérard Deslandes, Mtl., Ignace-J. Deslauriers, Mtl., André Deslongchamps, Mtl., Gaston Desmarais, Sherbrooke, André Desmeules, Que., René-W. Dionne, Que., Louis Doiron, Que., Jacques Dufour, Que., Denis Durocher, Mtl., Jacques Dugas, Mtl., Bernard Flynn, Mtl., Yves Forest, Mtl., Carrier Fortin, Sherbrooke,Orville Frenette, Hull, Gilles Gauthier, Shawinigan, André Gervais, Que., Paul M. Gervais, Sherbrooke, Charles D. Gonthier, Mtl., Bernard Gratton, Mtl., Benjamin J. Greenberg, Mtl., Claude Guérin, Mtl., René Hamel, Shawinigan, J.R. Hannan, Mtl., Gaston Harvey, Alma, René Hurtubise, Mtl., Yvon Jasmin, Mtl., W. Austin Johnson, Mtl., Claire Barrette Joncas, Mtl., Jacques Lacoursiere, Trois-Rivières, Ovide Laflamme, Que., R.-B. Lafrenière, Que., Maurice E. Lagace, Mtl., Ruston B. Lamb, Mtl., Ls.-Ph. Landry, Hull, Raymond Landry, Mtl., Roger Laroche, Trois-Rivières, Claude Larouche, Amos, Henri Larue, Rimouski, Albert Leblanc, Valleyfield, Guy Lebrun, Trois-Rivières, Yves Leduc, Mtl., Fernand Legault, Mtl., Lyse Lemieux, Mtl., Anatole Lesyk, Mtl., René Letarte, Que., Denis Levesque, Mtl., Yvan A. Macerola, Mtl., Kenneth C. MacKay, Mtl., Charles B. Major, Hull, Louise Mailhot, Mtl., Jean Marquis, Mtl., Edouard Martel, Mtl., Paul A. Martineau, Mtl., Vincent Masson, Que., Guy Mathieu, Mtl., Toussaint McNicoll, Que., Victor Melancon, Mtl., Maurice Mercure, Mtl., Perry Meyer, Mtl., Ivan Mignault, Que., Wm. Mitchell, Sherbrooke, Jean Moisan, Que., André Nadeau, Mtl., Marcel Nichols, Mtl., Jean-Claude Nolin, Mtl., J. Brendan O'Connor, Mtl., Roger Ouimet, Mtl., Louis Paradis, Mtl., Georges Pelletier, Que., Jean-Louis Peloquin, Sherbrooke, Châteauguay Perrault, Mtl., Charles-A. Phelan, Mtl., Jacques Philippon, Que., Pierre Pinard, Mtl., Lawrence A. Poitras, Mtl., Jean Provost, Mtl., Paul Reeves, Mtl., Gilles-Y. Renaud, Mtl., Jean-Guy Riopel, Mtl., Claude Rioux, Que., Gabriel Roberge, Que., Melvin L. Rothman, Mtl., Gerald J. Ryan, Mtl., André Savoie, Mtl., Georges Savoie, Sherbrooke, Gilles St-Hilaire, Que., Thomas Toth, Sherbrooke, Paul Trepanier, Mtl., André Trotier, Que., Gérard Turmel, Mtl., Jacques Vaillancourt, Mtl., Claude R. Vallerand, Mtl., Hubert Walters, Que., Jeanne L. Warren, Mtl.

Bankruptcy

Judges of the Superior Court have jurisdiction.

Registrars in Bankruptcy

Dist: Registrar, Address:

Abitibi: Simon Marcotte, 891, 3e rue ouest, Amos, P.Q. J9T 2T4 (819/732-6577)
Arthabaska: Pierre Sanche, 800, boul. Bois-Franc sud, Arthabaska, P.Q. G6P 5W5 (819/357-2054)
Beauce: J.-Claude Morin, 795, ave. du Palais, C.P. 820, St-Joseph (Beauce), P.Q. GOS 2VO (418/397-5251)
Bedford: Paul-E. Belisle, 920, rue Principale, Cowansville, P.Q. J2K 1K2 (514/263-3520); and Antonin Bourassa, 35, rue Dufferin, Granby, P.Q. J2G 4W5 (514/372-6635)

Bonaventure: Jean-Ls. Langlois, Palais de Justice, rue Principale, C.P. 517, New Carlisle, P.Q. GOC 1ZO (418/752-3105)
Chicoutimi: André-Gaétan Corneau, 202, rue Jacques Cartier est, Chicoutimi, P.Q. G7H 5C5 (418/543-2708)
Drummond: Daniel Kimpton, 1680, boul. St-Joseph, Drummondville, P.Q. J2C 2G3 (819/478-2513)
Frontenac: Luc Hinse, 693, rue St-Alphonse ouest, C.P. 579, Thetford Mines, P.Q. G6G 5T6 (418/338-2118)
Hauterive: Jacques Villeneuve, 71, rue Mance, Baie Comeau, P.Q. G4Z 1N2 (418/296-5534); and Louis-A. Vigneault, adj., 425, boul. Laure, Sept-Iles, P.Q. G4R 1X6 (418/962-2154)
Hull: Me Yves Daoust, 17, rue Laurier, Hull, P.Q. J8X 4C1 (819/771-3296)
Iberville: André Beauchamp, 109, rue St-Charles, Saint-Jean, P.Q. J3B 2C2 (514/347-3715)
Joliette: Jean Lemieux, 450, rue Saint-Louis, Joliette, P.Q. J6E 2Y8 (514/756-0544)
Kamouraska: Ubald Savard, 33, rue de la Cour, Rivière-du-Loup, P.Q. G5R 1J1 (418/862-3579)
Mingan: L.-A. Vignault, 425 rue Laure, Sept-Iles, P.Q. G4R 1X6
Montreal: Henri Massue-Monat, Ch. 1.95, 1, est Notre-Dame, Montreal, P.Q. H2Y 1B6 (514/873-3164)
Québec: Raymond Hains, 39, rue Saint-Louis, #520, Quebec, P.Q. G1R 4P6 (418/643-4258)
Rimouski: Ghislain Boulanger, 183, rue de la Cathédrale, Rimouski, P.Q. G5L 5J1 (418/722-3531)
Roberval: Mme Lucile Brassard, 750, boul. Saint-Joseph, Roberval, P.Q. G8H 2L5 (418/275-3666)
Rouyn-Noranda-Témiscamingue: Nelson McLean, 2, ave. du Palais, Rouyn, P.Q. J9X 2N9 (819/764-6709)
Saguenay: André-Gaétan Corneau, 202 est, Jacques Cartier, Chicoutimi, P.Q. G7H 5C5 (418/543-2708)
St-François: Gérard Besette, 191, ave. du Palais, Sherbrooke, P.Q. J1H 4R1 (819/562-2101)
Terrebonne: Jean Lemieux, 400, rue Laviolette, St-Jérôme, P.Q. J7Y 2T6 (514/436-7721)
Trois-Rivières: Me Daniel Kimpton et Me Jean-Paul Cossette, 250, rue Laviolette, Trois-Rivières, P.Q. G9A 1T9 (819/375-9668)

JUGES DE LA COUR PROVINCIALE/JUDGES OF PROVINCIAL COURT

(Address Juge de la Cour Provinciale, Palais de Justice, street address, unless otherwise indicated)

Juge en chef, Allan B. Gold, Montreal
Juge en chef adjoint, Gaston Rondeau, Montreal
Juges co-ordonnateurs, Jean-Guy Blanchette, Sherbrooke; Lucien Thinel, St-Jérôme
Juge en chef associé, Georges Chasse, Québec
Juges co-ordonnateurs, Jean Beaulieu, Val d'Or; André Gauthier, Chicoutimi; Roland Legendre, Québec

Alma (95 ave St-Joseph sud, G8B 3E5): Lucien Larouche
Amos (891 3e ave ouest, J9T 2T4): Claude Bigue, Gaston Labrèche
Arthabaska (800 boul. Bois Francs sud, G6P 5W5): Claude Pinard
Baie Comeau (71 rue Mance, G4Z 1N2): Sarto Cloutier
Chicoutimi (202 Jacques-Cartier, G7H 5C5): Claude Gagnon, Edmond Savard, Jean Simard, Lucien Tremblay
Cowansville (a/s 77 Principale, Granby, J2G 9B3): Guy Genest
Drummondville (1680 boul. St-Joseph, J2C 2G3): Jacques Biron
Granby (77 Principale, J2G 9B3): Bernard Légaré, Claude Léveillé
Hull (17 rue Laurier, J8X 4C1): Edgar Allard, Jules Barrière, Gérard Charron, Bernard Dagenais, Louis-Guy Robichaud, Jérôme F. Somers
Joliette (450 St-Louis, J6E 2Y9): Jean-Pierre Bourduas, Maurice Majeau
Longueuil (201 Place Charles Lemoyne, J4K 2T5): Pierre-Paul Langis
Matane (382 St-Jérôme, G4W 3B3): Charles B. Quimper
Montmagny (25 du Palais, G5V 1P6): Yvon Mercier
Montreal (1 est Notre-Dame, H2Y 1B6): Paul Beaudry, Gilles Bélanger, Rodolphe Bilodeau, Roland Bourret, Jacques Bousquet, Claire Kirkland Casgrain, Marc E. Cordeau, Léonce Côté, Alfred Crowe, Michael J.P. Cuddihy, Jacques Décary, Pierre Décary (supernum.), Bernard Desjarlais, Denys Dionne, Claude-René Dumais, Pierre Durand, Roy Fournier, Jean Fillion, Gilles Fillion, André P. Forget, Louis-Philippe Gagnon (supernum.), Dimitrios A. Hadjis, Ronald Halpin, Robert Hamel, Robert Hodge, J. Richard Hyde, Marc Lacoste, Gérard P. Laganière, Harold B. Lande (supernum.), Yves Laurier, Jean-Paul Lavallée, Bernard Lesage, Paul Mailloux, Huguette Marleau, Jean-Paul Noel, Raymond Pagé, Conrad Prénoveau, Adolphe Prévost, Léandre Prévost, Roland Robillard, Paul Robitaille, Pierre Roger, Jacques Tisseur, Réginald D. Tormey, Gérard Trudel (supernum.), Gilles Trudel, Robert Turgeon, Louis Vaillancourt, Pierre M. Verdy, François Wilhelmy
New Carlisle (rue Principale, G0C 1Z0): Rock Roy
Percé (rue Principale, G0C 2L0): Jean-Marc Roy
Québec (12 rue St-Louis, G1R 4P6): Roland Angers, Alexandre Bastien, Raymond Beaudet, Jean Bérubé, Gérald Bossé, Louis-Philippe Bouchard, Raymond Boucher, Charles Cimon, André Desjardins, Louis Dussault, Gill Fortier, Denis Gobeil, Roger Gosselin, Jean-Marie Houle, André Marceau, Joseph Marineau, Gaston Michaud, Rémi Paul, Guy Pinsonnault, Maurice Tessier, André Verge
Québec (585 boul. Charest est, G1K 3J2): Pierre Choquette
Rimouski (183 de la Cathédrale, G5L 5J1): Mark Dubé, Gilles Gagnon
Rivière-du-Loup (33 de la Cour, G5R 1J1): Michel Lemieux
Roberval (750 boul. St-Joseph, G8H 2L5): Bertrand Gagnon
Rouyn-Noranda (2 rue du Palais, J9X 2N9): Paul J. Bélanger, Jean-Charles Coutu
St-Hyacinthe (1550 Dessaulles, J2S 2S8): Denis Robert, Michel Dumaine
St-Jean (109 St-Charles, J3B 2C2): Jean Frédérick, Georges H. Long
St-Jérôme (400A Laviolette, J7Y 2T5): Jean-Louis Baillargeon, Jacques Duquette, André Surprenant
St-Joseph-de-Beauce (795 du Palais, G0S 2V0): Marcel Blais
Shawinigan (791 5e rue, G9N 1G2): Rosaire Lajoie
Sherbrooke (191 du Palais, J1H 4R1): Louis-Denis Bouchard, Jacques Pagé, Yvon Roberge
Sorel (46 Charlotte, J3P 1G3): Roger Gagné
Thetford Mines (693 St-Alphonse ouest, G6G 3X3): W. James Johnson
Trois-Rivières (250 Laviolette, G9A 1T9): Jean-Marie Châteauneuf, Yves Gabias, Ludovic Laperrière, Pierre Trudel
Val d'Or (900 7e rue, J9P 3P8): Miville St-Pierre
Valleyfield (180 Salaberry, J6T 2J2): Raphael Barrette, Pierre Brassard, Maurice Perron
Commn. des accidents de travail, 524 Bourdages, Québec, G1K 7E2: Robert Sauvé, prés.
Commn. des Affaires sociales, 440 boul. Dorchester ouest, Montréal, H2Z 1V7: Gilles Poirier, prés.
Commn. municipale du Qué., 680 St-Amable, Québec, G1R 4Z2: Richard Beaulieu
Commn. de police du Qué., 2050 boul. St-Cyrille ouest, Québec, G1V 2K8: Guy Tremblay
Commn. des transports, 505 rue Sherbrooke est, Montréal, H2L 1K2: vacancy
Régie de l'électricité et du gaz, 2100 Drummond, Montréal, H3G 1X1: Jacques Vadboncoeur
Régie des services publics, 2875 boul. Laurier, Québec, G1V 2M2: Yvon Côté, prés., Jean-Marc Tremblay
Tribunal de l'expropriation, 930 ch. Ste-Foy, Québec, G1S 2L4: Guy Dorion, pres., Jean-Marie Dussault; 1 est Notre-Dame, Montréal, H2Y 1B6: Yvette Dussault-Mailloux, Léon Nichols
Tribunal des mines, 250 Grande Allée ouest, Québec, G1R 2H4: Robert Langevin, prés.
Tribunal des Transports, 1 est Notre-Dame, Montréal, H2Y 1B6: Alexandre Lesage; 930 ch. Ste-Foy, Québec, G1S 2L4: Bernard Pinard, prés.

Tribunal du Travail, 39 St-Louis, Québec, G1R 3Z2: Denys Aubé, Robert Auclair, Louis Morin; 255 boul. Crémazie est, Montréal, H2M 1L5: René Beaudry, Marc Brière, Robert Burns, Jean-Paul Geoffroy (juge en chef), Jean-F. Girouard, Bernard Lesage, Bernard Prud'homme, Claude Saint-Arnaud

JUGES DE LA COUR DES SESSIONS DE LA PAIX/JUDGES OF SESSIONS OF THE PEACE

Juge en chef, Yves Mayrand, Montreal
Juge en chef adjoint, Rhéal Brunet, Montreal
Juges co-ordonnateurs, Roger Lagarde, St-Jérôme; Paul-A. Bélanger, Longueuil
Juge en chef associé, François Tremblay, Québec
Juges co-ordonnateurs, Marc Choquette, Marc-André Drouin, Maurice Langlois, Trois-Rivières

Joliette (450 St-Louis, J6E 2Y9): André Daviault, André Joly, Georges Sylvestre
Montréal (1 est Notre-Dame, H2Y 1B6): Maurice Allard, John d'Arcy Asselin, Marcel J. Beauchemin, Raymond Bernier, Bernard Bilodeau, André Chaloux, Roger Craig, Jean-Paul Dansereau, Monique P. Dubreuil, André Duranleau, Patrick Falardeau, Gérard Girouard, Jean Goulet, Bernard Grenier, Guy Guérin, Maurice Johnson, Claude Joncas, Marc Lamarre, Denis R. Lanctôt, Gabriel Lassonde, Jacques Lessard, Jean Longtin, Albert Ouellette, Paul Papineau, Maurice Rousseau, Hughes St-Germain, Benjamin Schecter, Joseph Tarasofsky, Luc Trudel, Roger Vincent
Montreal (Commn. de Police, 1 est Notre-Dame): Bruno Cyr
Montreal (CECO, 1701 rue Parthenais, H2K 3S7): Gilbert Morier
Montreal (Trib. de l'expropriation, 1 est Notre-Dame): Roger Savard
Québec (39 rue St-Louis, G1R 3Z2): André Bilodeau, Gilles Carle, Louis Carrier, Anatole Corriveau, Marcel Dionne, Jean Drouin, Jean Dutil, Louis Fortin, Paul E. Fortin, Jean Grenier, Gilles La Haye, Roch Lefrançois, Cyrille Potvin, Yvon Sirois
Rivière-du-Loup (33 de la Cour, G5R 1J1): Jean-Paul Bérubé
St-Jérôme (400 Laviolette, J7Y 2T5): François Beaudoin, Jacques Coderre, Stephen R. Cuddihy, Claude Lamoureux
St-Joseph-de-Beauce (795 du Palais, G0S 2V0): Charles Cliche
Sherbrooke (191 du Palais, J1H 4R1): Laurent Dubé, Benoît Turmel
Sorel (46 Charlotte, J3P 6N5): Paul-A. Peloquin
Trois-Rivières (250 Laviolette, G9A 5H2): René Crochetière

JUGES DU TRIBUNAL DE LA JEUNESSE/ JUDGES OF YOUTH COURT (District in Brackets)

M. Jean Rouillard, (Montreal) Juge en chef, 410 est, rue Bellechasse, Montréal H2S 1X3
M. Jean-Paul Boutet (Québec, Hauterive, Saguenay & Mingan) Juge coordonnateur, 1281, boul. Charest ouest, Québec G1N 2C9
M. Jean Arsenault, (Bonaventure & Gaspé) C.P. 637, New Carlisle G0C 1Z0
M. Claude R. Baillargeon, (Abitibi) 900, 7e rue, Val d'Or J9P 3P8
M. Rolland Beauchemin, (Montreal) 410 est, rue Bellechasse, Montréal H2S 1X3
M. Adelstan Bouchard, (St-Hyacinthe, Drummond & Richelieu) 1150 Ste-Anne, St-Hyacinthe J2S 5G9
M. René Boudreault, (Chicoutimi & Roberval) 250, rue Racine est, C.P. 517, Chicoutimi G7H 5C8
M. Barrie H. Brown, (Montréal) 16847 boul. Hymus, Kirkland H9H 3L4
M. Maurice Chevalier, (Hull, Labelle & Pontiac) 17 Laurier, Hull J8X 4C1
M. Henri Choinière (Montréal), 3901, rue Bannantyne, Montréal H4G 1C2
M. René L. Cousineau, (Montreal) 410 est, rue Bellechasse, Montréal H2S 1X3
M. Claude Crête, (Montreal & Beauharnois & Iberville) 410, rue Bellechasse est, Montreal H2S 1X3
M. Basil Danchyshyn, (Montreal) 410 est, rue Bellechasse, Montréal H2S 1X3
Mme Elaine Demers, (Montreal) 410 est, rue Bellechasse, Montréal H2S 1X3
M. Pierre G. Dorion, (Montreal) 410, est, rue Bellechasse, Montreal H2S 1X3
M. André Fauteux, (Montreal) 410 est, rue Bellechasse, Montréal H2S 1X3
Madame Louise Galipeault-Moisan, (Quebec) 1281, boul. Charest ouest, Quebec G1N 2C9
M. Albert Gobeil, (St-François & Bedford) 234 Dufferin, Sherbrooke J1H 4M2
M. Claude Edouard Hétu, (Joliette) 435 Baby, Joliette J6E 2W3
M. Gabriel Houde, (Montreal) 410 est, rue Bellechasse, Montréal H2S 1X3
M. Pierre Houde, (Trois-Rivières) C.P. 726, Trois-Rivières G9A 5N6
M. Michel Jasmin, (Montreal) 410 est, rue Bellechasse, Montréal H2S 1X3
M. Jacques Lamarche, (Montreal) 410 est, Bellechasse, Montreal H2S 1X3
M. Bertrand Laforest, (Montmagny, Kamouraska & Rimouski) 176 Lafontaine, C.P. 218, Rivière-du-Loup G5R 3A5
M. Pierre Lavery, (Montreal) 410 est, rue Bellechasse, Montréal H2S 1X3
M. Guy Le Chasseur, (Terrebonne) 85 ouest, de Martiny, St-Jérôme J7Y 3R8
M. Lionel Mougeot, (Labelle, Pontiac & Hull) 17 Laurier, Hull J8X 4C1
M. Gilles L. Ouellet (Abitibi) 900, 7e rue, Val d'Or J9P 3P8
M. Robert Perron, (Québec) 1281 ouest, boul. Charest, Québec G1N 2C9
Mme. Marguerite Choquette-Power, (Québec) 1281 ouest, boul. Charest, Québec G1N 2C9
M. Michele Rivet, (Montreal) 410 est, rue Bellechasse, Montréal H2S 1X3
M. Maurice E. Roy, (Chicoutimi & Roberval) 250 est, Racine, C.P. 517, Chicoutimi G7H 5C8
M. Rodolphe Roy, (Québec) 1281 ouest, boul. Charest, Quebec G1N 2C9
M. André Saint-Cyr, (Montreal) 410 est, rue Bellechasse, Montreal H2S 1X3
M. Jean-Paul St-Louis, (Montreal) 410 est, rue Bellechasse, Montreal H2S 1X3
M. André Sirois, (Québec) 1281 ouest, boul. Charest, Québec G1N 2C9
M. Gilles Therriault (Bedford & St-François) 234 Dufferin, Sherbrooke J1H 4M2
M. Marcel Trahan, (Montreal) 410 est, rue Bellechasse, Montréal H2S 1X3

LISTE DES COURS MUNICIPALES DE LA PROVINCE

Siège de la cour/Municipal Seat, Titulaire/Chief of Court

Acton Vale, Louis-B. Grignon
Alma, Jean-Paul Aubin
Ancienne-Lorette, Me. Robert Truchon
D'Anjou, André Tessier
Asbestos, J. Gilles Geoffroy
Aylmer, Pierre Taché
Baie St-Paul, vacant
Barkmere, Gavin Wyllie
Beaconsfield, Duncan Kisilenko
Beauceville-Est, Paul Laflamme
Beauharnois, Gaston Gamache
Beauport, François Veilleux, Pierre Gaudreau
Beaupré, Michael E. Hickson
Bedford, Jean Goyette
Bélair, Lucien Morneau
Bellefeuille, René Boismenu
Beloeil, Luc Alarie
Berthierville, J. H. Denis Gagnon
Bishopton, vacant
Blainville, Claude Paquette

Bois Brillant, Jean Guérin
Boucherville, Michel Jetté
Bromptonville, Gerald Lafrance
Brossard, Jacques P. Dansereau
Buckingham, Jacques Sauve
Candiac, Jean-Pierre Dépelteau
Cap-de-la-Madeleine, Richard Rioux
Chambly, Luc Geoffroy
Chapais, Robert Côté
Charlesbourg, Napoléon Beaudet
Châteauguay, Paul-Emile Lécuyer
Château-Richer, Maxime Langlois
Chibougamau, Robert Côté
Chicoutimi, René Lambert
Chicoutimi-Nord, André Morin
Coaticook, Gérald Lafrance
Côte St-Luc, Joseph Mendelson
Cowansville, Jean Goyette
Delson, Gérard Corbeil
Desbiens, vacant
Deux-Montagnes, Richard Lacharite
Dolbeau, Gilles Boivin
Dollard-des-Ormeaux, Rosaire Desbiens
Donnacona, Claude Fournier
Dorion, Jean-Guy Clement
Dorval, Georges E. Laurin
Drummondville, Maurice Laplante
Duberger, Napoléon Beaudet
East Angus, Roland Lamoureux
Esterel (ville d'), Maurice Mercure
Farnham, Gilles Mercure
Gatineau, Jean R. Dagenais
Giffard, François Veilleux
Granby, Gilles Mercure
Grand'Mère, Jean-Marc Champagne
Hampstead, J. Irving Halperin
Hauterive, vacant
Hudson, Robert La Haye
Hull, Raymond Séguin
Iberville, Adélard Forget
Ile Perrot, Jean Guy Clément
Joliette, Louis Laporte
Jonquière, Jean-Jacques Turcotte
La Baie, Adrien Morin
Lachine, Louis Legault
Lachute, Jean-Claude Paquin
Lac Mégantic, Michel Aubut
La Pocatière, Robert Daveluy
Laprairie, André Demers
Lasalle, Denis Laberge
L'Assomption, Gilles Thouin
Lauzon, Gilles Charest
Laval, Jean-Paul Grégoire, Pierre Lalande, Henri S. Beaulieu
Lennoxville, Roland Lamoureux
Lévis, Paul-Eugène Robitaille
Loretteville, Gilles Charest
Louiseville, Richard Rioux
Lucerne, Pierre Taché
Magog, Louis-Philippe Galipeault
Marieville, Louis-B. Grignon
Mascouche,
Mistassini, Jacquelin Légaré
Montmagny, Robert Daveluy
Montréal-Est, André Tessier
Montréal-Nord, Jean Chalifoux
Montréal-Ouest, Raymond Boyer
Mont-Royal, Jérôme C. Smyth
Mont-St-Hilaire, Stephen Clerk
Outremont, Adrien Paquette
Pierrefonds, Rosaire Desbiens
Pincourt, Robert La Haye
Plessisville, Jules Bellavance
Pointe-aux-Trembles, André Tessier, Gilles Pariseau
Pointe-Claire, Pierre Mondor
Pointe-Gatineau, Jean R. Dagenais
Repentigny, Gilles Thouin
Richmond, vacant
Rigaud, Jean-Guy Clément
Rimouski, J. Claude Gagnon
Roberval, Michel Lapointe
Rock-Island, Léonard Bergeron
Rosemère, Bernard Gardner
Roxboro, Ronald J. Montcalm
St-Adèle, Michel Bergevin
Ste-Agathe-des-Monts, Guy Godard
Ste-Anne-de-Bellevue, Yvan Poliquin
St-Antoine (cté Terrebonne), René Boismenu
St-Basile-le-Grand, Marc Boisvert
St-Bruno-de-Montarville, Guy Houle
Ste-Catherine, Gérard Corbeil
St-Césaire, Louis B. Grignon
St-Constant, Pierre Delorme
St-Eustache, René Boismenu
St-Félicien, Robert Côté
Ste-Foy, Marc Jessop
St-Gabriel-de-Brandon, J.H. Denis Gagnon
St-Georges, Thérèse Lemay-Lavoie
St-Hyacinthe, Gérald Locas
St-Jean, Robert Lanteigne
St-Jérôme, Jean Guérin
St-Lambert, Marc Gravel
St-Laurent, Paul Buisson, Pierre Mondor
St-Léonard-de-Port-Maurice, Arthur Boivin
St-Luc (district de St-Jean) Denis Boudrias
Ste-Marthe sur le Lac, Pierre Delorme
St-Pierre, Pierre Gaston
St-Raymond, Jean R. Côté
St-Rémi-de-Napierville, Pascal Pillarella
Ste-Thérèse, Claude Paquette
St-Tite, Jean L. Sanschagrain
Salaberry de Valleyfield, Jean-Guy Clément
Senneville, Pierre Mondor
Sept-Iles, Jean Dionne
Shawinigan, Claude Trudel
Shawinigan-Sud, Claude Trudel
Sherbrooke, Gérald E. Desmarais
Sillery, René Paquet
Sorel, Gaston Gauthier
Terrebonne, Michel Paquin
Tracy, Paul-Emile Ally
Trois-Rivières, Richard Rioux
Trois-Rivières-Ouest, Yvan Godin
Val Bélair, Lucien Morneau
Val d'Or, Raoul Grégoire
Valleyfield, Jean-Guy Clément
Vanier, Pierre Nadeau
Vaudreuil, Jean-Guy Clément
Verdun, Gilles Cadieux
Victoriaville, Jean-Louis Provencher
Waterloo, Michel Brun
Westmount, Georges Gould
Windsor, Gérard G. Boudreau
Québec, Laurent Cossette (en chef); Marcel Letourneau
Montréal, Bernard Tellier (en chef); Marcel Marier; Gérard Tourangeau; Herman Primeau; Claude Melançon; Guy Robert; Roger Pigeon; Alexander McTavish Stalker; Maurice Bourassa; André Massé; Lomer Rivard; René Déry; Louis-Jacques Léger; Luc Mercier

REGISTRATEURS
REGISTRARS

Division/Dist. Judiciaire: Registrateur, Chef-Lieu

Abitibi/Abitibi: Arthur Aylwin, 891 3e rue ouest, Amos J9T 2T4
Argenteuil/Térrebonne: Jacqueline Beaudry, 505, rue Bethanie, C.P. 337, Lachute J8H 3X5
Arthabaska/Arthabaska: Pierre Poirier, 800, boul. des Bois, Francs sud, Arthabaska G6P 5W5
Bagot/St-Hyacinthe: Mlle Raymonde Lajoie (Deputy), rue Lemonde, St-Liboire J0H 1R0

Beauce/Beauce: Claude Archambault, 111 7e rue, Beauceville-est G0S 1A0
Beauharnois/Beauharnois: Gérald Bernier, 150, chemin St-Louis, C.P. 37, Beauharnois J6N 3C1
Bellechasse/Montmagny: Raymond Remillard, 23, av. Chanoine-Audet, St-Raphael G0R 4C0
Berthier/Joliette: Gilles Harvey, 180, rue Champlain, Berthierville J0K 1A0
Bonaventure (Division no. 1)/Bonaventure: André Dumais, Palais de Justice, C.P. 250, New Carlisle G0C 1Z0
Bonaventure (Division no. 2)/Bonaventure: Hermel Gagnon, 10 rue Tracadiache, Carleton G0C 1J0
Brome/Bedford: Jean Brunelle, chemin St-Paul, Knowlton J0E 1V0
Chambly/Montréal: Roger Michon, Edifice Montval, 201, rue Charles-Lemoyne, C.P. 8, Succursale A, Longueuil J4K 2T5
Champlain/Trois Rivières: Georges Desnoyers, 181 Principale, Ste-Geneviève-de-Batiscan G0X 2R0
Charlevoix (Division no. 1)/Saguenay: Mme. Simone Chamberland, Palais de Justice, C.P. 638, La Malbaie G0T 1J0
Charlevoix (Division no. 2)/Saguenay: Denis Desgagne, 4 rue St-Jean Baptiste, Baie-St-Paul G0A 1B0
Chateauguay/Beauharnois: Maurice Demers, 164, rue St-Joseph, Ste-Martine J0S 1V0
Chicoutimi/Chicoutimi: Marcel Dufour, 326 rue des Saguenéens, Chicoutimi G7H 3A4
Coaticook/St-François: Mme Madeleine Morel, Hôtel de ville, 150 rue Child, Coaticook J1A 2B3
Compton/St-François: Paul Maheux, 89 rue du Parc, C.P. 459, Cookshire J0B 1M0
Deux-Montagnes/Térrebonne: André Péloquin, 140, rue St-Eustache, St-Eustache J7R 2K9
Dorchester/Beauce: Robert Genesse, 115 rue Langevin, Ste-Hénédine G0S 2R0
Drummond/Drummond: vacant, Palais de Justice, 1680, rue St-Joseph, Drummondville J2C 3G3
Frontenac/Beauce et St-François: Mlle. Jeannette Thibault, 5527, rue Frontenac, Lac Mégantic G6B 1H6
Gaspé: Owen Bouchard, Palais de Justice, C.P. 128, Percé G0C 2L0
Gatineau/Labelle: André Lanthier, 266, rue Notre-Dame, Maniwaki J9E 2J8
Hull/Hull: Me. René Janelle, 170, rue de l'Hôtel de Ville, Hull J8X 3X5
Huntingdon/Beauharnois: Gaétan Lalumière, 25, rue King, Huntingdon J0S 1H0
Iberville/Iberville: Gilles Carmel, 380 4e ave., Iberville J2X 1W9
Iles-de-la-Madeleine/Gaspé: (vacant), Palais de Justice, C.P. 97, Hâvre-Aubert G0B 1J0
Ile d'Orléans/Québec: Mlle. Christiane Vaillancourt, d.r., 1286, rue Royale, St-Laurent, I.O. G0A 3Z0
Joliette/Joliette: Jean-Guy Alie, 577, rue Notre-Dame, Joliette J6E 3H8
Kamouraska/Kamouraska: Louis-Henri Gagnon, 395, rue Chapleau, St-Pascal G0L 3Y0
Labelle/Labelle: Gilbert Paquette, 440, boul. Paquette, Mont-Laurier J9L 1K6
Lac St-Jean Est/Roberval: Raymond Richard, Hôtel de ville, 353, rue Turgeon, C.P. 98, Hébertville G0W 1S0
Lac St-Jean Ouest/Roberval: Réal Dupré, Palais de Justice, 742, boul. St-Joseph, Roberval G8H 2L5
Laprairie/Montréal: Jacques Mongeau, 214, rue St-Ignace, Laprairie J5R 1E5
L'Assomption/Joliette: Gaétan Giguère, 300, rue Dorval, L'Assomption J0K 1G0
La Tuque/St-Maurice: Richard Arsenault, 582, rue Commerciale, La Tuque G9X 3A9
Laval/Montréal: François Groulx, 155, rue Je-Me-Souviens, Ville de Laval, Ste-Rose H7L 1V6
Lévis/Québec: André Croteau, 6, route Trans-Canada, C.P. 1218, Lévis G6V 6R8
L'Islet/Montmagny: Julien Bélanger, C.P. 578, St-Jean, Port-Joli G0R 3G0
Lotbinière/Québec: Gaston D'Anjou, 6296, rue Principale, Ste-Croix G0S 2H0
Maskinongé/Trois-Rivières: Gilles Harvey, 51, rue St-Marc, Louiseville J5V 2E4
Matane/Rimouski: Louise Bédard, 750 rue du Phare ouest, Matane G4W 3W8
Matapédia/Rimouski: Anne de Billy, 29, boul. St-Benoît, C.P. 1508, Amqui G0J 1B0
Mégantic/Mégantic: vacant, C.P. 99, Inverness G0S 1K0
Missisquoi/Bedford: Guy Déry, 1, rue Principale, C.P. 300, Bedford J0J 1A0
Montcalm/Joliette et Labelle: François Larose, 1532, rue Albert, C.P. 190, Ste-Julienne J0K 2T0
Montmagny/Montmagny: Raymond Rémillard, 25 boul. Taché ouest, Montmagny G5V 2Z9
Montmorency/Québec: Mme Constance Rancourt (Deputy), 8032, rue Royale, Château-Richer G0A 1N0
Montréal/Montréal: Claude Desmarais, Palais de Justice, 1 est, rue Notre-Dame, Chambre 2175, Montréal H2Y 1B6
Napierville/Iberville: Maurice Demers, 361, rue St-Jacques, Napierville J0J 1L0
Nicolet (Division no. 1)/Trois-Rivières: Charles Gagnon, 3050, ave. Nicolas-Perreault, Bécancour G0X 1B0
Nicolet (Division no. 2)/Trois-Rivières: vacant, Palais de Justice, C.P. 70, Nicolet J0G 1E0
Papineau/Hull: Charles-Auguste Leduc, 228 rue Duquette, C.P. 28, Papineauville J0V 1R0
Percé/Gaspé: Owen Bouchard, Palais de Justice, C.P. 128, Percé G0C 2L0
Pontiac/Pontiac: Pierre Lavigne, Palais de Justice, C.P. 310, Campbell's Bay J0X 1K0
Portneuf/Québec: Jean Poirier, 300 Rte Nationale, Cap-Santé G0A 1L0
Québec/Québec: Réal Côté, 116, rue St-Pierre, C.P. 278, Québec G1K 7B1
Richelieu/Richelieu: Louis Talbot, Maison du Québec, 46, rue Charlotte, Sorel J3P 6N5
Richmond/St-François: Richard Thibault, Hôtel de ville, 746 nord, rue Principale, Richmond J0B 2H0
Rimouski/Rimouski: Me. André Michaud, 320, est, rue St-Germain, Rimouski G5L 1C2
Rouville/St-Hyacinthe: Jules-Henri Robert, 1601, rue Edmond-Guillet, C.P. 1080, Marieville J0L 1J0
Rouyn-Noranda/Rouyn-Noranda: Mme. Laurette Veilleux, 2, rue du Palais de Justice, Rouyn J9X 2N9
Saguenay/Hauterive: Me Romain Desrosiers, Palais de Justice, 71, ave. Mance, Baie-Comeau G4Z 1N2
Ste-Anne-des-Monts/Gaspé: Louis Bouchard, Palais de Justice, C.P. 517, Ste-Anne-des Monts G0E 2G0
St-Hyacinthe/St-Hyacinthe: Yvan Leclair, Ste. 101, 3100, boul. Laframboise, Saint-Hyacinthe J2S 4Z4
St-Jean/Iberville: Jean-Guy Hould, 320, boul. du Séminaire, St-Jean J3B 5K9
Sept-Iles/Hauterive: Réjean Lavoie, 425 rue Laure, Sept-Iles G4R 1X6
Shawinigan/St-Maurice: Léo Dupéré, Palais de Justice, 795, 5è rue, C.P. 608, Shawinigan G9N 6V6
Shefford/Bedford: Claude Gonthier, 77 rue Principale, Granby J2G 9B3
Sherbrooke/St-François: Jean Boucher, 174, rue du Palais de Justice, C.P. 634, Sherbrooke J1H 5K5
Soulanges/Montréal: Michel Brouillette, 199, rue Principale, C.P. 120, Coteau-Landing J0P 1C0
Stanstead/St-François: Mlle. Claire Cournoyer, 100, chemin Dufferin, C.P. 240, Stanstead Plain J0B 3E0
Témiscamingue/Témiscamingue: J.-Gilles Labranche, 8, rue St-Gabriel nord, C.P. 757, Ville Marie J0Z 3W0
Témiscouata/Kamouraska: Roger Ouellet, 65-A, rue Iberville, C.P. 578, Rivière-du-Loup G5R 3Z1
Térrebonne/Térrebonne: Guy Latour, 85, De Martigny ouest, bur. 103, St-Jérôme J7Y 3R8
Thetford/Mégantic: Germain Argouin, Palais de Justice, 693 ouest, rue St-Alphonse, Thetford Mines G6G 3X3
Trois-Rivières/Trois Rivières: Me. Marcel Laforce, 878, rue de Tonnancourt, Trois-Rivières G9A 4P8
Vaudreuil/Montréal et Beauharnois: René Chagnon, 420, boul. Roche, Vaudreuil J7V 2N1

Verchères/Richelieu: Gilles Côté, 461 blvd St-Joseph, Ste-Julie J0L 2C0
Wolfe/St-François: Mlle. Madeleine Lamoureux, rue Principale, C.P. 6, Ham-Sud J0B 3J0
Yamaska/Richelieu: Yves Beausoleil, 400 rue Notre-Dame, C.P. 29, St-François-du-Lac J0G 1M0

PROTONOTAIRES ET SHERIFFS PROTHONOTARIES & SHERIFFS

District: (Address)

Abitibi: (891 3e rue ouest, Amos J9T 2T4)
Prothonotary, Me Simon Marcotte
Sheriff, Jean Grenier
Arthabaska: (800 boul Bois-Franc sud, Arthabaska G6P 5W5)
Prothonotary, Me Pierre Sanche
Sheriff, J. Villeneuve
Beauce: (795 ave du Palais, St-Joseph G0S 2V0)
Prothonotary, Me Jean-Claude Morin
Sheriff, A. Gagné
Beauharnois: (180 Salaberry, Valleyfield J6T 2J2)
Prothonotary, Me Paul Brodeur
Sheriff, Danielle Corbeil
Bedford: (920 rue Principale, Cowansville J2K 1K2)
Prothonotaries & Sheriffs, Paul-Eugène Belisle, Antonin Bourassa
Bonaventure: (rue Principale, C.P. 517, New Carlisle G0C 1Z0)
Prothonotary & Sheriff, Me Jean-Louis Langlois
Chicoutimi: (202 Jacques-Cartier est, Chicoutimi G7H 5C5)
Prothonotary & Sheriff, Me André-G. Corneau
Drummond: (1680 boul St-Joseph, Drummondville J2C 2G3)
Prothonotary, Me Jacques Villeneuve
Sheriff, Steve Dolan
Frontenac: (693 St-Alphonse ouest, Thetford Mines G6G 5T6)
Prothonotary & Sheriff, Me Luc Hinse
Gaspé: (rue Principale, C.P. 188, Percé G0C 2L0)
Prothonotary, Jean Bourget
Sheriff, L. Cormier
Hauterive: (71 ave Mance, Baie-Comeau G4Z 1N2)
Prothonotary, vacant
Sheriffs, Yvon Corriveau, Mariette Bourassa
Hull: (17 rue Laurier, Hull J8X 4C1)
Prothonotary, Roger Rozon (int)
Sheriff, Lise Leblanc
Iberville: (109 St-Charles, St-Jean J3B 6Z5)
Prothonotary, André Beauchamp
Sheriff, Claude Audet
Joliette: (450 rue St-Louis, Joliette J6E 2Y9)
Prothonotary, Me Jean Lemieux
Sheriff, Jeanne Matte
Kamouraska: (33 de la Cour, Rivière-du-Loup G5R 3Y8)
Prothonotary, Ubald Savard
Sheriff, Maurice Morin
Labelle: (645 de la Madone, C.P. 116, Mont-Laurier J9L 3G9)
Prothonotary & Sheriff, J.-C. Ladouceur
Mingan: (425 boul Laure, Sept-Iles G4R 1X6)
Prothonotary & Sheriff, L.-A. Vignault
Montmagny: (25 rue du Palais, Montmagny G5V 1P5)
Prothonotary, Gilles Lamontagne
Sheriff, Gemma Nicole
Montreal: (1 rue Notre Dame est, Montreal H2Y 1B6)
Prothonotary, Me Jacques Dufour
Sheriffs, Guy Vaugeois, W. Lefebvre
Pontiac: (159 ave John, Campbell's Bay J0X 1K0)
Prothonotary, Me Gilles Pelletier
Sheriff, P.-Y. Lefebvre
Québec: (12 rue St-Louis, Québec G1R 4P6)
Prothonotaries, Serge Carrier, Me Pierre Côté
Sheriffs, Réal Campeau, J.R. Renaud
Richelieu: (46 rue Charlotte, Sorel J3P 6N5)
Prothonotary, Me André Ménard
Sheriffs, François Gélinas, Alain Larocque
Rimouski: (183 de la Cathédrale, Rimouski G5L 5J1)
Prothonotary & Sheriff, Ghislain Boulanger
Roberval: (750 boul St-Joseph, Roberval G8H 2L5)
Prothonotaries, Lucille Brassard, Marcel Fortin
Sheriff, L.-M. Lavoie
Rouyn-Noranda: (2 ave du Palais, Rouyn J9X 2N9)
Prothonotary & Sheriff, Me Nelson McLean
Saguenay: (30 chemin de la Vallée, La Malbaie G0T 1J0)
Prothonotary & Sheriff, Me Pierre Gaudreault
St-François: (191 ave du Palais, Sherbrooke J1H 4R1)
Prothonotaries & Sheriffs, Me Benoît Bachand, Gérard Bessette
St-Hyacinthe: (1550 rue Dessaulles, St-Hyacinthe J2S 2S8)
Prothonotary, Alain Larocque
Sheriff, J. Letourneau
St-Maurice: (791 5e rue, Shawinigan G9N 6V9)
Prothonotaries & Sheriffs, Lionel Fortin, Me Michel-M. Tremblay
Témiscamingue: (8 St-Gabriel, Ville-Marie J0Z 3W0)
Prothonotary & Sheriff, Guy Chenier
Terrebonne: (400 Laviolette, St-Jérôme J7Y 2T6)
Prothonotary, Me Jean Lemieux (int.)
Sheriff, André Dion
Trois-Rivières: (250 Laviolette, Trois-Rivières G9A 1T9)
Prothonotaries & Sheriffs, Me Daniel Kimpton, Me Paul-E. Marchand

COURTS, JUDGES, ETC., SASKATCHEWAN

COURT OF APPEAL

Court House, 2425 Victoria Ave., Regina, Sask. S4P 3V7
Chief Justice of Saskatchewan, Hon. E.D. Bayda
Judges of Appeal, Hon. M.J. Woods; Hon. R.N. Hall; Hon. R.L. Brownridge; Hon. R.A. MacDonald
Registrar, F.C. Newis, Regina

COURT OF QUEEN'S BENCH

Registrar of Courts, F.C. Newis, Court House, Regina, Sask. S4P 3V7
Regina: (Court House, 2425 Victoria Ave., Regina, Sask. S4P 3V7) Hons.: F.W. Johnson (Chief Justice); M.A. MacPherson, K.R. MacLeod, K.R. Halvorson, S. Cameron, G.M. Forbes, E.C. Malone, R.A. Cruickshank, J.G. McIntyre, R.H. McClelland
Local Registrar, G. Ullman (act.)
Sheriff, L. Dittrick
Saskatoon: (Court House, 520 Spadina Cres. E., Saskatoon, Sask. S7K 3G7) Hons.: G.E. Noble, A.L. Sirois, Madame M.J. Batten, C.L.B. Estey, J.H. Maher, D.H. Wright, S.J. Walker, F. Gerein
Local Registrar, M. Petersen
Sheriff, R. Stevens
Saskatoon Unified Family Court: (224 4th Ave. S., Saskatoon, Sask. S7K 3G7) Hons.: F.G. Dickson, Madame M.Y. Carter, J.S. Gagné
Local Registrar, M. Herauf
Battleford: (Court House, S0M 0E0) Hon. C.R. Wimmer
Local Registrar & Sheriff, D.I. Dament
Estevan: (Court House, S4A 0W5) Hon. F.A. Rutherford
Local Registrar & Sheriff, D.W. Henneberg
Assiniboia: (S0H 0B0) Local Registrar & Sheriff, J.W. Kessler
Gravelbourg: (Court House, S0H 1X0) Local Registrar & Sheriff, J.W. Kessler
Humboldt: (Court House, S0K 2A0) Hon. P.J. Dielschneider
Local Registrar & Sheriff, W. Siemens
Kerrobert: (Court House, S0L 1R0) Local Registrar & Sheriff, R. Stevens
Melfort: (Court House, S0E 1A0) Local Registrar & Sheriff, V.J. Johansen
Melville: (Provincial Bldg., S0A 2P0) Hon. T.L. Geatros
Local Registrar & Sheriff, S. Urbanoski

Moose Jaw: (Court House, S6H 4P1) Hon. R.A. MacLean
Local Registrar & Sheriff, D. Paquin
Moosomin: (Court House, S0G 3N0) Local Registrar & Sheriff, W.E. Dammann
Prince Albert: (Court House, S6V 4W7) Hons.: J. Milliken, I. Grotsky
Local Registrar & Sheriff, I.W. Dillabaugh
Shaunavon: (Court House, S0N 2M0) Local Registrar & Sheriff, M. Koski
Swift Current: (Court House, S9H 0J4) Hon. B. Moore
Local Registrar & Sheriff, M. Koski
Weyburn: (Court House, S4H 0L4) Local Registrar & Sheriff, W.E. Dammann
Wynyard: (Court House, S0A 4T0) Local Registrar & Sheriff, W. Siemens
Yorkton: (Court House, S3N 0C2) Hon. A.M. Kindred
Local Registrar & Sheriff, S. Urbanoski

Bankruptcy

Queen's Bench Justices have jurisdiction in bankruptcy.
Registrar, F.C. Newis, Court House, Regina, S4P 3V7

Registration of Instruments

Personal Property Security Agreements, Sale of Goods Act, S. 26.1; Factors Act, S. 9.1; Garage Keepers Liens; Writs of Execution, must be registered with the Registrar, Personal Property Registry, Box 7128, Regina, Sask. S4P 3S5.

OFFICIAL ADMINISTRATORS

Assiniboia: Co-operative Trust Co. of Canada, Regina
Battleford: Montreal Trust Co., Regina
Estevan: Montreal Trust Co., Regina
Gravelbourg: Co-operative Trust Co. of Canada, Regina
Humboldt: Co-operative Trust Co. of Canada, Saskatoon & Regina
Kerrobert: Montreal Trust Co., Regina
Melfort: Co-operative Trust Co. of Canada, Saskatoon
Melville: Guaranty Trust Co. of Canada, Regina
Moose Jaw: Co-operative Trust Co. of Canada, Regina
Moosomin: Guaranty Trust Co. of Canada, Regina
Prince Albert: Co-operative Trust Co. of Canada, Saskatoon
Regina: Guaranty Trust Co. of Canada, Regina
Saskatoon: Guaranty Trust Co. of Canada, Regina
Shaunavon: Guaranty Trust Co. of Canada, Regina
Swift Current: Montreal Trust Co., Regina
Weyburn: Co-operative Trust Co. of Canada, Regina
Wynyard: Co-operative Trust Co. of Canada, Saskatoon & Regina
Yorkton: Guaranty Trust Co. of Canada, Regina

AGENTS OF THE ATTORNEY-GENERAL

Judicial Circuit, Agent (Points Covered):

Estevan: Dennis Ball, (Ball, Klassen, etc), Drawer 609, Estevan, Sask. S4A 2A5; 306/634-2673; (Estevan)
Estevan: E.A. Komarnicki, Drawer 725, Estevan, Sask. S4A 2A4; 634-2616; (Carnduff, Oxbow)
Kamsack: Orest Rosowsky, Drawer 399, Kamsack, Sask. SOA 1SO; 306/542-2646; (farm out for Yorkton)
Melfort: Grant Carson, Drawer 1600, Melfort, Sask. S9E 1AO; 306/752-5781; (Wadena, Wynyard, Kinistino, Melfort, Nipawin, Tisdale, Hudson Bay, Rose Valley, Kelvington, Watson)
Melville: Jack Hillson, Box 2200, Melville, Sask. SOA 2PO; 306/728-4444; (Foam Lake, Melville, Esterhazy, Balcarres)
Melville: Leslie Matsalla, Box 2620, Melville, Sask. SOA 2PO; 306/728-5151; (Punnichy, Ituna)
Moose Jaw: Walter Wall, James Johnson, (Prosecution Unit), 110 Ominica St., Moose Jaw, Sask. S6H 6V2; 306/693-6116; (Moose Jaw, Craik, Mossbank, Assiniboia, Avonlea)
North Battleford: Terrence Matchett, Randy Kirkham, James Taylor, (Prosecution Unit), 1381 101st St., North Battleford, Sask. S9A OZ9; 306/445-6281; (North Battleford, Battleford, Wilkie, Onion Lake, Lloydminster)
North Battleford: Reginald Cawood, Harvey Walker, (Walker & Cawood), Box 905, North Battleford, Sask. S9A 2Z3; 306/445-6177; (Cutknife, Maidstone)
North Battleford: Horst Dahlem, Box 795, North Battleford, Sask. S9A 2Z3; 306/445-4497; (Meadow Lake, Pierceland, Goodsoil, Loon Lake, Green Lake, St. Walburg, Turtleford, Glaslyn)
North Battleford: Dennis Maher, (Maher & Lindgren), 1126 100th St., North Battleford, Sask. S9A OV5; 306/445-2422; (Unity)
North Battleford: Norman Miller, 1641 100th St., North Battleford, Sask. S9A OW5; 306/445-9487; (Spiritwood, Wilhelm)
North Battleford: Richard Gibbons, Box 820, Shellbrook, Sask. S0J 2E0
Prince Albert: Joseph Kulyk, John Field, Peter Hryhorchuk, James Plemel, Martel Popescul, Bruce Bauer, (Prosecution Unit), 800 Central Ave., Prince Albert, Sask. S6V 6Z2; 306/922-2204; (Prince Albert, Big River, Debden, Shellbrook, Waskesiu, Montreal Lake, Smeaton, Wakaw, Birch Hills, Pelican Narrows, Sandy Bay, Creighton, Sturgeon Landing, Cumberland House)
Prince Albert: Lloyd Balicki, (Dutchak & Balicki), 201, 46 12th St. E., Prince Albert, Sask. S6V 1B2; 306/764-2227; (farm out for Prince Albert)
Prince Albert: Irwin Carson, (Carson & Siwak), 1109 Central Ave., Prince Albert, Sask. S6V 4V7; 306/763-7467; (LaRonge, LaLoche, Buffalo Narrows, Ile a la Crosse, Uranium City, Fond du Lac, Stony Rapids)
Prince Albert: Leo Pinel, (Cherkewich & Pinel), 1105 Central Ave., Prince Albert, Sask. S6V 4V4; 306/764-1537; (farm out for Prince Albert)
Regina: Delmar Perras, Q.C., Kenneth MacKay, Richard Quinney, Murray Brown, 2476 Victoria Ave., 15th floor, Regina, Sask. S4P 3V7; 306/565-5490; (Administration)
Regina: Special Prosecutions, A.S. Brent, 2476 Victoria Ave., 15th floor, Regina, Sask. S4P 3V7 (306/565-5490)
Regina: Douglas Britton, Steven Connelly, Ellen Gunn, Al Johnston, Judith Falle, (Prosecution Unit), Court House, 2476 Victoria Ave., 12th floor, Regina, Sask. S4P 3E4; 306/565-5444; (Regina, Strasbourg, Southey, Fort Qu'Appelle, Indian Head, Lumsden, Weyburn, Milestone, Kipling, Bengough, Radville, Fillmore)
Regina: Ted Zarzeczny, Terry Graf, Roger Linka (Graf, Zarzeczny & Linka), 2132 Broad St., Regina, Sask. S4P 1Y5; 306/525-8180; (Broadview, Moosomin)
Regina: Gerald Kraus, (Toews, Kaufman, Kraus, etc.), 2042 Cornwall St., Regina, Sask. S4P 2K5; 306/525-2191; (farm out for Regina)
Regina: Louise Simard, 2343 Broad St., Regina, Sask. S4P 1Y9; 306/569-0808; (farm out for Regina)
Regina: Ronald G. Gates (Gates & Herle), 452 Albert St. N., Regina, Sask. S4P 3V2; 306/949-5544
Regina: Wilfrid Meagher, Frits Luberti, William Tymchyshym, John Stoesser, David Orr (Regina Prosecutors Office), 1770 Halifax St., Regina, Sask. S4P 1T1; 306/569-7509; (none, City Prosecutors)
Rosthern: Robert Simpson, Q.C., Rosthern, Sask. SOK 3RO; 306/232-4331; (Rosthern)
Saskatoon: T.D.R. Caldwell, Q.C., Terry Hinz, Frederick Dehm, Leslie Sullivan, (Prosecution Unit), 224 4th Ave. S., 9th floor, Saskatoon, Sask. S7K 5M5; 306/664-5149; (Saskatoon)
Saskatoon: Special Prosecutions, Wilfrid Tucker, 224 4th Ave. S., 9th floor, Saskatoon, Sask. S7K 5M5; 306/664-6940
Saskatoon: Mel Annand, (Dokken, Eberle etc.) #100, 241 2nd Ave. S., Saskatoon, Sask. S7K 1K8; 306/244-6117; (Carrot River, Porcupine Plain, Naicam)
Saskatoon: Peter Foley, (Gauley, Dierker & Dahlem), Box 638, Saskatoon, Sask. S7K 3L7; 306/653-1212; (farm out for Saskatoon)
Saskatoon: Irving Goldenberg, (Stevenson, Prosser & Goldenberg), 308, 220 3rd Ave. S., Saskatoon, Sask. S7K 1M1; 306/244-1347; (farm out for Saskatoon)
Saskatoon: Albert Lavoie, (Jamieson, Lavoie, etc.), 243 3rd Ave. S., Saskatoon, Sask. S7K 1M4; 306/653-5410; (Outlook, and farm out for Saskatoon)

Saskatoon: Dennis Loewen, (Henderson, Donlevy, Campbell), 239 20th St. E., Saskatoon, Sask. S7K OA5; 306/652-1234; (farm out for Saskatoon)

Saskatoon: Denis Quon, #207, 115 2nd Ave. N., Saskatoon, Sask. S7K 2B1; 306/665-8828; (Eston, Kindersley, Kerrobert, Radisson, Hafford, Blaine Lake)

Saskatoon: Nick Sherstobitoff, (Sherstobitoff, Stromberg & Young), 1070 Avord Tower, Saskatoon, Sask. S7K 3H1; 306/652-7575; (farm out for Saskatoon)

Saskatoon: George Taylor, Q.C., Ian Buckwold, (Goldenberg, Taylor, Randal, etc.), #301, 402 21st St. E., Saskatoon, Sask. S7K 1M2; 306/242-0235; (Hanley, Davidson, Humboldt, Vonda, Colonsay, Lanigan, Watrous, Imperial, Elbow)

Saskatoon: Robert Walker, Steven Carter, (Walker, Kaiser & Walker), Box 3007, Saskatoon, Sask. S7K 3S9; 306/653-0466; (Rosetown, Biggar)

Saskatoon: Benjamin Wolff, Barrie Stricker, Sonja Hansen, Lee Ayres (Saskatoon Prosecutors Office), 140 4th Ave. N., Saskatoon, Sask. S7K 3R6; 306/665-2100; (none, City Prosecutors)

Shaunavon: Jim Benison, Drawer 280, Shaunavon, Sask. SON 2MO; 306/297-2633; (Shaunavon, Ponteix, Gravelbourg)

Shellbrook: Brock Folkerson, Box 820, Shellbrook, Sask. SOG 2EO; 306/747-2641; (farm out for Prince Albert)

Swift Current: Jack Hagemeister, 121 Lorne St. N., Swift Current, Sask. S9H 0J4; 306/773-9836; (Swift Current, Morse, Maple Creek)

Swift Current: Donald Krueger, (Krueger, McLaughlin & Quon), Box 100, Swift Current, Sask. S9H OA8; 306/773-7205; (Kyle, Cabril, Gull Lake, Leader)

Swift Current: Morris A. Froslee (Anderson, Nimegeers etc.), Box 619, Swift Current, Sask. S9H 3W4; 306/773-2891

Swift Current: Jakob Wiebe (Wilson, MacBean etc.), Box 550, Swift Current, Sask. S9H 3W4; 306/773-9343

Weyburn: Donna Stinson, (Stinson & Assoc.), Box 1060, Weyburn, Sask. S4H 2L3; 306/842-2657; (Weyburn R.C.M.P., Carlyle)

Yorkton: David Tennent, Q.C., (Prosecution Unit), 32 Broadway St. E., Yorkton, Sask. S3N OK4; 306/783-3651; (Yorkton, Preeceville, Canora, Kamsack, Pelly)

Yorkton: Rosemary Weisgerber, 180-A Broadway W., Yorkton, Sask. S3N 2V6; 306/782-3131; (farm out for Yorkton)

JUDGES OF PROVINCIAL COURT

Judges of the Provincial Courts are addressed as His Hon. Judge

Estevan (Court House, S4A 0W5): R.E. Lee

Kerrobert (Court House, S0L 1R0): W.B. Tennant

La Ronge (Court House, S0J 1L0): C.R. Fafard, G.R. Moxley

Meadow Lake (Court House, S0M 1V0): G.T. Seniuk

Melfort (Court House, S0E 1A0): E.C. Diehl, E.R. Gosselin

Moose Jaw (Court House, S6H 1Y9): G.C. King, A.J. Muir

North Battleford (Court House, S9A 1K4): L.P. Deshaye, E.E. MacKay, D.M. Arnot

Prince Albert (Court House, S6V 6Z2): W.R. Bonnycastle, H.W. Goliath, T.W. Ferris, R.H. Allan

Regina (Court House, S4P 3V7): E.C. Boychuk (Chief Judge), L.F. Bence, J.J. Flynn, H.J. Boyce, H.D. Parker, E.A. Lewchuk, S.E. McLean, A.R. Andreychuk, K.E. Bellerose, D.E. Fenwick, B.D. Henning, L.J. Smith

Saskatoon (Court House, S7K 3G7): R.N. Conroy, Mrs. Tillie Taylor, R.H. King, A.C. McMurdo, M.A. Wedge, J.R.H. Tucker, C. Peet, R.J. Kucey, J.B.J. Nutting

Swift Current (Court House, S9H 0J4): G.K. Fielding, G.B. Shaner

Weyburn (Court House, S4H 0L4): R.J. Neville

Wynyard (Court House, S0A 4T0): A.R. Chorneyko

Yorkton (Court House, S3N 0C2): K. Andrychuk, E.S. Bobowski

On leave to Govt. of Canada: J.R.O. Archambault

LAND REGISTRATION DISTRICTS

The Land Titles Act provides for registration of title according to the Torrens System

The Regina Land Registration Dist.

Master of Titles, G.R. Jackson, Regina S4P 3V7

Registrar, K.H. Swallow, Regina S4P 3V6

Deputy Registrars, A.J. MacPherson, I.M. Jesse

Moose Jaw Land Registration Dist.

Registrar, H.A. Boyce, Moose Jaw S6H 4P1

Deputy Registrars, A.J. Rollie; F.J. Helm

Battleford Land Registration Dist.

Registrar, E.C. Fuchs, Battleford SOM OEO

Deputy Registrars, T.R. Scott; Peter Foth

Prince Albert Land Registration Dist.

Registrar, J.L.W. MacKenzie, Prince Albert S6V 1B3

Deputy Registrars, Mrs. I.M. Logue; R.A. Reiser

The Yorkton Land Registration Dist.

Registrar, S.A. King, Yorkton S3N 2Y4

Deputy Registrars, P.G. Larson; M.C. Scott

The Saskatoon Land Registration Dist.

Registrar, A. Goertzen, Saskatoon S7K 3G7

Deputy Registrars, T.H. Cook, N.B. Kortko

Humboldt Land Registration Dist.

Registrar, W.R. Hoffman, Humboldt SOK 2AO

Deputy Registrars, S.R. McNabb; R.J. Karpinski

Swift Current Land Registration Dist.

Registrar, G.F. Hartley, Swift Current S9H 4G3

Deputy Registrars, J.J. Sykes, R.W. Heebner

COURTS, JUDGES, ETC., NORTHWEST TERRITORIES

COURT OF APPEAL

Court House, Box 550, Yellowknife, N.W.T. X0E 1H0

Note:- The Court of Appeal is composed of the Judges of the Court of Appeal of Alberta with the addition of the ex officio judge of the Supreme Court of the Northwest Territories.

Chief Justice, The Hon. William A. McGillivray

Judges, Hons.: N.D. McDermid, C.F. Tallis, C.W. Clement, J.H. Laycraft, S.L. Lieberman, A.M. Harradence, D.C. Prowse, R.P. Kerans, A.F. Moir, W.A. Stevenson, W.J. Haddad, J.W. McClung, H.C.B. Maddison, R.H. Belzil

Registrar, A. Stewart, Yellowknife

Deputy Registrar, X.F. Mercredi, Yellowknife

SUPREME COURT

Judges, The Hon. Calvin F. Tallis, Yellowknife, The Hon. H.C.B. Maddison, Whitehorse (ex-officio)

Deputy Judges, Hons.: A.M. Dechene, Edmonton; Peter Greschuk, Edmonton; J.C. Cavanagh, Edmonton; D.H. Bowen, Edmonton; D. McDonald, Edmonton; J. Ducros, Ottawa; J.K. Hugessen, Montreal; M.L. Rothman, Montreal; T.H. Miller, Edmonton; N. Primrose, Edmonton; J.D. Bracco, Edmonton; Jean-Guy Boilard, Montreal; K.H. Fogarty, Ottawa

Chief of Court Services, P. Schauerte

Clerk, A. Stewart, Yellowknife

Sheriff, R.E. Moore, Yellowknife

Bankruptcy

Registrar, A. Stewart, Yellowknife

TERRITORIAL COURT

(Juvenile, Family & Citizenship)

Chief Judge, J.R. Slaven

Judges, R. Halifax, P. Ayotte

Clerk, A.C. Milton, Yellowknife

Justices of the Peace

T. Akerolik, Rankin Inlet; Peter Akikkungark, Gjoa Haven; O. Alakannuaq, Pelly Bay; W.J. Alexie, Fort McPherson; E. Anoee, Eskimo Point; Simon Awa, Frobisher Bay; J. Ayaligak, Coppermine

Peter Baril, Frobisher Bay; Miss C.M. Barnabe, Yellowknife; J.A. Black, Yellowknife; P. Bobinski, Hay River; A.L. Bourque, Frobisher Bay; Brent Burton, Hay River

R.A. Carman, Pine Point; A. Carpenter, Sachs Harbour; G. Carter, Yellowknife; C. Chapman, Watson Lake; D. Cichelly, Inuvik; A. Clifford, Baker Lake; W. Cormier, Cape Dorset; J. Cumming, Yellowknife

R. Dewar, Sanikiluaq; T. Dialla, Pangnirtung

C. Edgi, Fort Good Hope; T. Enuaraq, Clyde River; M. Evaloakjuk, Igloolik; E. Erkloo, Pond Inlet

A. Galvin, Resolute Bay; M. Gardlund, Aklavik; F. Greenland, Aklavik

L. Hardy, Norman Wells; A. Harvey, Pine Point; F. Hasey, Hay River; F. Heeley, Coppermine; A.D. Hemeyer, Hay River; L. Heron, Fort Smith; J. Herring, Fort Simpson; Patricia Horner, Fort Resolution

D. Jenkins, Fort Providence; R.L. James, Yellowknife

P. Kamingoak, Coppermine; E. Kakudluk, Broughton Is.; I. Kingwatsiak, Cape Dorset; S. Klause, Hay River; M. Kolola, Lake Harbour; L. Kooneeliusie, Broughton Is.; R. Kuptana, Holman Island

A. Larocque, Hay River; B.R.L. Ledoux, Inuvik; E. Lyall, Spence Bay

B. MacNeil, Hay River; C. Mains, Hay River; J. Maksagak, Cambridge Bay; A. Manning, Spence Bay; P. Marlow, Snowdrift; R. Mayers, Cambridge Bay; E. Melnychuk, Tuktoyaktuk; M. Mendo, Fort Norman; R. Mercer, Rankin Inlet; G. Mercredi, Fort Smith; R. Milligan, Yellowknife; A.C. Milton, Yellowknife; L. Moran, Fort McPherson; G. Morgan, Frobisher Bay; C. Murray, Cambridge Bay

S.E. Neyando, Fort McPherson; J. Niego, Baker Lake

J. Paton, Frobisher Bay; G. Porter, Gjoa Haven; L. Pudluk, Resolute Bay

A.J. Reynolds, Cape Dorset; M. Rispin, Yellowknife; S. Rodriguez, Yellowknife; T. Rose, Ft. Franklin; D. Ruben, Paulatuk; G. Ruben, Paulatuk; T. Ryan, Cape Dorset

A. Semmler, Inuvik; D. Sibbald, Yellowknife; M. Solomon, Coral Harbour; V. Steen, Tuktoyaktuk; M. Strusinski, Hall Beach;

A. Takolik, Spence Bay; C. Tinashlu, Repulse Bay; A. Totakik, Spence Bay; A. Tunraluk, Frobisher Bay

A. Ullikatar, Arctic Bay; Dorothe Unka, Ft. Resolution

M. Vaydik, Rankin Inlet

G. Wainman, Inuvik; Katherine Walterhouse, Ft. Smith; P. Watson, Tungsten; J. West, Pine Point; A. Whitford, Yellowknife; F. Wittlinger, Pangnirtung

COURTS, JUDGES, ETC., YUKON TERRITORY

COURT OF APPEAL

Hon. H.C.B. Maddison, Whitehorse; Hon. C.F. Tallis, Yellowknife; Hons. N.T. Nemetz, C.J., J.D. Taggart, P.D. Seaton, A.B.B. Carrothers, E.E. Hinkson, W.A. Craig, M.M. McFarlane, J.D. Lambert, J.A. Macdonald, R.P. Anderson, all of Vancouver

Registrar of the Court of Appeal, A.A. Schmidt, Whitehorse

SUPREME COURT

Mr. Justice H.C.B. Maddison, Whitehorse

Ex-officio: Mr. Justice Calvin F. Tallis, Yellowknife

Deputy Judges of the Supreme Court: Hons. J.G. Ruttan, V.L. Dryer, K.E. Meredith (all of British Columbia); Hons. R.P. Kerans, T.H. Miller, J.W. McClung, J.B. Feehan, A.H. Wachowich, J.D. Bracco, W.A. Stevenson (all of Alberta)

Clerk of the Supreme Court, A.A. Schmidt, Whitehorse

Deputy Clerk, N.L. Farkvam, Whitehorse

Sheriff's Office

Sheriff, A. Adams

Deputy Sheriffs, J. Lindsay, P. Cowan

TERRITORIAL COURT OF YUKON

Chief Judge, Barry D. Stuart

Second Judge, vacant

Judges are vested with civil jurisdiction in suits not exceeding $1,500.

Clerk, J.R. Simpson

Deputy Clerks, Miss P. MacNeil, Miss P. Munro, Mrs. E. Touet

Juvenile Court Judges

Chief Judge, Second Judge, and all Deputy Judges, plus Mary McCulloch, Justice of the Peace, Watson Lake, Y.T.

Small Claims Court

Mrs. A. Brandt, Whitehorse; J.R. Simpson, Whitehorse; F.J. O'Connell, Carmacks; Mrs. M. McCulloch, Watson Lake

Justices of the Peace

Beaver Creek, Beat Ledergerber

Carcross, Ms. Muriel Dobson, Eldon Bjerke

Carmacks, Odiel Vandenberghe, Frank O'Connell, Gary Felker, Paul Nugent

Dawson, P.E. Foth, Bryson Leary, Frank Lidstone, J.S. Bilton, James Reilly

Destruction Bay, Pieter Van Der Veen

Elsa, William Bennett

Faro, Robert Gault, Gordon Frey

Haines Junction, Gordon MacDonald, Wolfgang Riedl

Mayo, Simon Mason-Wood, Emery Shilleto

Old Crow, Mrs. Edith Josie

Pelly Crossing, Mrs. Kathleen Thorpe

Ross River, Ms. Margaret Thomson, Mrs. C.G. MacDonald

Teslin, Ross Regan, Cliff Weiers, Robert Studds

Watson Lake, Mrs. Marion Bjorkman, Mrs. Mary McCulloch, Gordon Toole

Whitehorse, Blake Baxter, J.A. McCormick, C.E. Hannah, Mrs. S.D. Jones, Gerald Vander Wolf, Miss M.A. MacNeil, David Gairns, Mrs. Margaret Tanner, J.R. Simpson, William Thomson, Mrs. Anne Brandt, Steve Smyth, H.M. Scholl, Ms. S.A. Copeland, Ms. Patricia Cummings, Mrs. Margaret Joe, Miss Patricia Munro, Mrs. Liz Touet, Ms. Carol Friesen

Bankruptcy

Registrar, A.A. Schmidt, Whitehorse

OFFICIAL RECEIVERS UNDER THE BANKRUPTCY ACT

Superintendent of Bankruptcy—Jacques B. Braseau, C.A., Place du Portage, Hull, P.Q. K1A 0C9

DIVISION AND JURISDICTION	RECEIVER AND ADDRESS
Alberta	
Division No. 1	
Edmonton Red Deer Wetaskiwin Camrose (sub-district) Stettler Peace River Grande Prairie (sub-district)	(vacant), Dept. of Consumer & Corporate Affairs, Bankruptcy, 10225 100 Ave., Edmonton, Alta.
Division No. 2	
Calgary Medicine Hat Lethbridge Taber (sub-district) Bassano (sub-district) Hanna MacLeod	S. Faber, Dept. of Consumer & Corporate Affairs, 1008 7th Ave. S.W., Calgary
British Columbia	
Division No. 1	
Prince Rupert	E.H. Henderson, C.A., Dept. of Consumer & Corporate Affairs, Bankruptcy, Box 10066, Pacific Centre, 700 W. Georgia St., Vancouver
Division No. 2	
Victoria Nanaimo	Same as Division No. 1
Division No. 3	
Vancouver New Westminster	Same as Division No. 1
Division No. 4	
Yale Cariboo	Same as Division No. 1
Division No. 5	
West Kootenay East Kootenay	Same as Division No. 1
Division No. 6	
Parts of Yale and Cariboo north of 52nd parallel	Same as Division No. 1
Manitoba	
(No Divisions)	G.L. Gibson, Dept. of Consumer & Corporate Affairs, 203, 260 St. Mary Ave., Winnipeg
New Brunswick	
Division No. 1	
Saint John Queens Kings Charlotte	R. B. Twohig, Dept. of Consumer & Corporate Affairs, Bankruptcy, 5151 George St., Halifax, N.S.
Division No. 2	
York Sunbury Carleton Victoria Madawaska	Same as Division No. 1
Division No. 3	
Gloucester Northumberland Restigouche	Same as Division No. 1
Division No. 4	
Westmorland Kent Albert	Same as Division No. 1

DIVISION AND JURISDICTION	RECEIVER AND ADDRESS
Newfoundland	
(No Divisions)	R. B. Twohig, Dept. of Consumer & Corporate Affairs, Bankruptcy, 5151 George St., Halifax, N.S.
Nova Scotia	
Division No. 1	
Halifax Hants Lunenburg Queens Annapolis Kings	R. B. Twohig, Dept. of Consumer & Corporate Affairs, Bankruptcy, 5151 George St., Halifax, N.S.
Division No. 2	
Pictou Guysborough Cumberland Colchester Antigonish	Same as Division No. 1
Division No. 3	
Cape Breton Inverness Richmond Victoria	Same as Division No. 1
Division No. 4	
Digby Yarmouth Shelburne	Same as Division No. 1
Ontario	
Division No. 1	
Thunder Bay Kenora Rainy River	G.L. Gibson, Dept. of Consumer & Corporate Affairs, 203, 260 St. Mary Ave., Winnipeg, Man.
Division No. 2	
Sudbury Algoma Manitoulin	R. Fontaine, Dept. of Consumer & Corporate Affairs, 767 Barrydowne Rd., Sudbury, Ont.
Division No. 3	
Simcoe Muskoka	C. Versnel, Dept. of Consumer & Corporate Affairs, 7th floor, 25 St. Clair Ave. E., Toronto, Ont.
Division No. 4	
Grey Bruce Dufferin	Same as Division No. 3
Division No. 5	
Middlesex Huron Perth Oxford Elgin	R. Kaplan, Dept. of Consumer & Corporate Affairs, 217 York St., London
Division No. 6	
Essex Lambton Kent	Same as Division No. 5
Division No. 7	
Wentworth Norfolk Haldimand Welland Brant Lincoln Halton	S. E. MacPherson, Dept. of Consumer & Corporate Affairs, Bankruptcy, 20 Hughson St. S., Hamilton, Ont.
Division No. 8	
Waterloo Wellington	Same as Division No. 7

DIVISION AND JURISDICTION	RECEIVER AND ADDRESS
Division No. 9	
York	Same as Division No. 3
Peel	
Ontario	
Division No. 10	
Peterborough	Same as Division No. 3
Northumberland and Durham	
Victoria and Haliburton	
Division No. 11	
Frontenac	R. Cyr, Dept. of Consumer & Corporate Affairs, Bankruptcy, 240 Bank St., Ottawa, Ont.
Lennox and Addington	
Hastings	
Prince Edward	
Division No. 12	
Carleton	Same as Division No. 11
Renfrew	
Lanark	
Russell and Prescott	
Stormont, Dundas and Glengarry	
Leeds and Grenville	
Division No. 13	
Nipissing	Same as Division No. 2
Division No. 14	
Parry Sound	Same as Division No. 2
Division No. 15	
Temiskaming	Same as Division No. 2
Division No. 16	
Cochrane	Same as Division No. 2

Prince Edward Island

(No Divisions)	R. B. Twohig, Dept. of Consumer & Corporate Affairs, Bankruptcy, 5151 George St., Halifax, N.S.

Quebec

Division No. 1	
Montreal	M. Fortin, Dept. of Consumer & Corporate Affairs, 10 Notre Dame St. E., Montreal
Richelieu	
St. Hyacinthe	
Beauharnois	
Division No. 2	
Quebec	J.C. Bresse, Dept. of Consumer & Corporate Affairs, 800 Youville Sq., Quebec
Montmagny	
(Anticosti)	
Division No. 3	
Rimouski	Same as Division No. 2
Division No. 4	
St. Francois	(vacant) Dept. of Consumer & Corporate Affairs, Bankruptcy, 25 Wellington St. N., Sherbrooke, P.Q.
Division No. 5	
Trois-Rivières	Same as Division No. 1
St. Maurice	
Division No. 6	
Hull	R. Cyr, Dept. of Consumer & Corporate Affairs, Bankruptcy, 240 Bank St., Ottawa, Ont.
Pontiac	
Division No. 7	
Chicoutimi	Same as Division No. 2
Saguenay	
Division No. 8	
Joliette	Same as Division No. 1
Division No. 9	
Roberval	Same as Division No. 2
Division No. 10	
Kamouraska	Same as Division No. 2
Division No. 11	
Gaspé, Bonaventure	Same as Division No. 2
Division No. 12	
Abitibi	Same as Division No. 1
Division No. 13	
Beauce	Same as Division No. 2
Division No. 14	
Iles de la Madeleine	Same as Division No. 2
Division No. 15	
Arthabaska	Same as Division No. 4
Division No. 16	
Rouyn-Noranda-Temiscamingue	Same as Division No. 1
Division No. 17	
Megantic	Same as Division No. 4
Division No. 18	
Terrebonne	Same as Division No. 1
Labelle	
Division No. 19	
Iberville	Same as Division No. 1
Division No. 20	
Bedford	Same as Division No. 4
Division No. 21	
Drummond	Same as Division No. 4
Division No. 22	
Hauterive	Same as Division No. 2
Mingan	

Saskatchewan

Divisions No. 1 & 3	
Regina	L.A. Krieger, Dept. of Consumer & Corporate Affairs, Bankruptcy, 3421 8th St. E., Saskatoon, Sask.
Division No. 2	
Saskatoon	Same as Division No. 1

Yukon Territory

A. R. Gillon, Dept. of Consumer & Corporate Affairs, Bankruptcy, Vancouver

Northwest Territories

(vacant), Dept. of Consumer & Corporate Affairs, 10225 100 Ave., Edmonton, Alta.

Registrars in Bankruptcy

(See "Bankruptcy" in the Courts & Judges section of each Provincial Government listing.)

JURISDICTION IN COURTS IN BANKRUPTCY

a) Alberta, British Columbia, Nova Scotia, Ontario, Newfoundland and Prince Edward Island—The Supreme Court of Province.
b) Manitoba and Saskatchewan—Court of Queen's Bench of Province.
c) New Brunswick—Court of Queen's Bench of Province.
d) Quebec—Superior Court of Province.
e) Yukon Territory—Territorial Court of the Territory.
f) Northwest Territories—a Stipendiary Magistrate.

MUNICIPAL GOVERNMENT

EDITOR'S NOTE:- This Municipal Section of the Almanac is in three parts. *Part 1* is a complete list of local municipalities in Canada, listed by provinces, and including population and electoral districts. Each provincial list is preceded by notes about local municipal organization and elections. *Part 2* includes major cities and towns in Canada, listed alphabetically. British Columbia has several municipalities called Districts which have the required population for inclusion in this list. *Part 3* includes regional governments in large population areas.

Part 1
(Cities, Towns, Villages, etc., with Officials, listed by Province)

ALBERTA

Alberta legislation concerning municipal government includes: The Municipal Government Act, The County Act, The Improvement District Act, The Special Areas Act, and The New Towns Act.

Municipal government in Alberta is either rural or urban. Rural municipal governments are organized into Counties and Municipal Districts with elected councils responsible for all municipal functions and the levying of taxes. Two other rural categories are Improvement Districts and Special Areas. These are geographically large, sparsely populated areas for which the provincial government levies and collects all taxes and provides services.

Urban municipalities include Summer Villages, Villages, Towns, New Towns and Cities. These are fully autonomous municipal units, each with an elected council. They are responsible for providing all municipal services within their corporate limits and for levying taxes and rates.

Requirements for Incorporation

The property owners of a summer resort may petition for incorporation as a Summer Village if the area contains 50 separate buildings each of which has been occupied as a dwelling any time during the six month period preceding the receipt of the petition.

An area for incorporation as a Village, must have 75 separate dwellings continuously occupied for the prior six months.

A Village may be formed into a Town if it contains over 1,000 inhabitants and the council requests the change in status.

A Town may be formed into a City if it contains over 10,000 inhabitants and the council requests the change in status.

Incorporations and changes in status are determined by the Lieutenant Governor in Council (Provincial Cabinet) on the recommendation of the Minister of Municipal Affairs. It is not necessary to change status by reason of population change.

Cities in CAPITALS; Towns marked †; Counties marked ‡; Municipal Districts marked *; Balance are villages or summer villages (SV).

Area Code for Alberta is 403

MUNICIPALITY	POP.	FEDERAL ELECTORAL DISTRICT	PROVINCIAL ELECTORAL DISTRICT	CLERK OR SECRETARY WITH ADDRESS & PHONE
Acadia No. 34*	651			M.R. Peers, Mun. Dist. Sec., Box 30, Acadia Valley, Alta. TOJ OAO (972-3808)
Acme	411	Bow River	Three Hills	Mrs. M. Malaka, Mun. Adm., Box 299, Acme, Alta. TOM OAO (546-3783)
Airdrie†	5,897	Bow River	Three Hills	D. Nichol, Mun. Adm., Box 1238, Airdrie, Alta. TOM OBO (948-5907)
Alberta Beach, SV	474	Yellowhead	Stony Plain	Mrs. B. Lehman, Mun. Adm., Box 278, Alberta Beach, Alta. TOE OAO (924-3181)
Alix	874	Crowfoot	Lacombe	Mrs. E.E. Keates, Village Sec., Box 87, Alix, Alta. TOC OBO (747-2495)
Alliance	228	Crowfoot	Sedgewick-Coronation	E.A. Trann, Village Sec., Box 149, Alliance, Alta. TOB OAO (879-3911)
Athabasca†	1,846	Athabasca	Athabasca	C.M. Sawatzky, Town Sec., Box 450, Athabasca, Alta. TOG OBO (675-2063)
Athabasca No. 12‡	5,406			S.L. Bemount, County Sec. Treas., Box 540, Athabasca, Alta. TOG OBO (675-2273)
Amisk	185	Crowfoot	Wainwright	Mrs. J. Debord, Mun. Adm., Amisk, Alta. TOB OBO (856-3980)
Andrew	565	Vegreville	Redwater-Andrew	A. Holubowich, Mun. Adm., Box 180, Andrew, Alta. TOB OCO (365-3687)
Argentia Beach SV	2	Wetaskiwin	Wetaskiwin-Leduc	S.A. Long, Argentia Beach Village Sec., R.R. 1, Westerose, Alta. TOC 2VO (586-2052)
Arrowwood	164	Bow River	Little Bow	Mrs. M. McKeague, Village Sec. Treas., Arrowwood, Alta. TOL OBO (534-3821)
Barnwell	351			Ms. S. Clements, Village Adm., Box 159, Barnwell, Alta. TOK 0B0 (223-4018)
Barons	285	Bow River	Little Bow	Mrs. C.E.J. Ragan, Village Adm., Box 129, Barons, Alta. TOL OJO (757-3633)
Barrhead†	3,519	Yellowhead	Barrhead	W. Romanchuk, Mun. Sec., Box 189, Barrhead, Alta. TOG OEO (674-3301)

Cities in CAPITALS; Towns marked †; Counties marked ‡; Municipal Districts marked *; Balance are villages or summer villages (SV).
Area Code for Alberta is 403

MUNICIPALITY	POP.	FEDERAL ELECTORAL DISTRICT	PROVINCIAL ELECTORAL DISTRICT	CLERK OR SECRETARY WITH ADDRESS & PHONE
Barrhead No. 11‡	5,148			A.W. Charles, County Sec. Treas., Box 820, Barrhead, Alta. TOG OEO (674-3331)
Bashaw†	885	Crowfoot	Camrose	K. Moore, Town Mgr., Box 510, Bashaw, Alta. TOB OHO (372-3911)
Bassano†	1,148	Medicine Hat	Bow Valley	D.G. Neighbour, Mun. Adm., Box 645, Bassano, Alta. TOJ OBO (472-3815)
Bawlf	298	Crowfoot	Camrose	Mrs. R.E. Halverson, Mun. Adm., Box 25, Bawlf, Alta. TOB OJO (373-3797)
Beaumont†	2,144	Wetaskiwin	Wetaskiwin-Leduc	Mrs. I. Royer, Town Sec., Box 120, Beaumont, Alta. TOC OHO (988-8782)
Beaver No. 9‡	4,950			A.R. Cross, County Sec., Box 140, Ryley, Alta. TOB 4AO (663-3730)
Beaverlodge†	1,847	Peace River	Grande Prairie	I.L. Hegland, Town Sec., Box 30, Beaverlodge, Alta. TOH OCO (354-2201)
Beiseker	508	Bow River	Three Hills	Mrs. P. Whitnack, Mun. Adm., Box 349, Beiseker, Alta. TOM OGO (547-3774)
Bentley	828	Wetaskiwin	Lacombe	Mrs. L. Stevenson, Mun. Adm., Bentley, Alta. TOC OJO (748-4044)
Berwyn	534	Peace River	Spirit River-Fairview	Mrs. S. Sandboe, Village Sec., Berwyn, Alta. TOC OEO (338-3922)
Betula Beach SV	4	Yellowhead	Stony Plain	R.C. Sheldon, Betula Beach Sec., c/o Box 8272, Stn. F, Edmonton, Alta. T6H 4W6 (434-8826)
Big Valley	344	Crowfoot	Stettler	Mrs. A. Swainston, Village Sec., Box 236, Big Valley, Alta. TOJ OGO (876-2269)
Birchcliff SV	41		Rocky Mountain House	H.A. Raymond, Birchcliff Sec., Box 667, Sylvan Lake, Alta. TOM 1ZO (887-2543)
Bittern Lake	140	Wetaskiwin	Wetaskiwin-Leduc	Ms. A. Hoyme, Village Sec., Bittern Lake, Alta. TOC OLO (672-7373)
Black Diamond†	1,465	Bow River	Highwood	Mrs. D. Kreh, Town Sec., Box 10, Black Diamond, Alta. TOL OHO (933-4124)
Blackfalds†	1,325	Wetaskiwin	Lacombe	J. Rogers, Mun. Adm., Box 220, Blackfalds, Alta. TOM OJO (885-4677)
Blackie	329	Bow River	Little Bow	Mrs. N. Parker, Village Sec., Box 132, Blackie, Alta. TOL OJO (684-3688)
Bon Accord†	1,220	Pembina	St. Albert	Ms. L.M. Davies, Town Sec., Box 100, Bon Accord, Alta. TOA OKO (921-3550)
Bonnyville No. 87*	9,916			R.A. Doonanco, Mun. Dist. Sec., Box 278, Bonnyville, Alta. TOA OLO (826-3171)
Bonnyville†	4,256	Athabasca	Bonnyville	Mrs. O. Cross, Mun. Adm., Box 308, Bonnyville, Alta. TOA OLO (826-3496)
Bonnyville Beach SV	45	Athabasca	Bonnyville	D.L. Demers, Village Sec. Treas., Box 1527, Bonnyville, Alta. TOA OLO (826-3611)
Botha	160	Crowfoot	Stettler	Mrs. P. Ganshirt, Village Sec., Box 160, Botha, Alta. TOC ONO (742-5079)
Bowden	963	Red Deer	Innisfail	Mrs. M.W. Chamney, Village Sec., Box 338, Bowden, Alta. TOM OKO (224-3395)
Bow Island†	1,398	Medicine Hat	Cypress	V.O. Foss, Town Sec., Bow Island, Alta. TOK OGO (545-2292)
Boyle	651	Athabasca	Athabasca	D.C. Baillie, Mun. Adm., Boyle, Alta. TOA OMO (689-3643)
Breton	566		Drayton Valley	Mrs. C. Strand, Village Sec., Box 480, Breton, Alta. TOC OPO (696-3636)
Brooks†	8,873	Medicine Hat	Bow Valley	R. Jenkins, Mun. Adm., Box 880, Brooks, Alta. TOJ OJO (362-3333)
Bruderheim†	1,014	Pembina	Clover Bar	Ms. L.B. Struth, Town Sec., Box 280, Bruderheim, Alta. TOB OSO (428-0961)
Burdett	223	Medicine Hat	Cypress	J.C. Kreeft, Village Sec., Box 40, Burdett, Alta. TOK OJO (833-3836)
CALGARY	560,618	Calgary Centre; Cal. E.; Cal. N.; Cal. S.; Cal. W.	Cal. Bow; Cal. Buffalo; Cal. Currie; Cal. Egmont; Cal. Elbow; Cal. Foothills; Cal. Glenmore; Cal. McCall; Cal. McKnight; Cal. Millican; Cal. Mountain View; Cal. North Hill; Cal. W.	Mrs. J.E. Woodward, Clerk, City Hall, Box 2100, Calgary, Alta. T2P 2M5 (268-5861)

Cities in CAPITALS; Towns marked †; Counties marked ‡; Municipal Districts marked *; Balance are villages or summer villages (SV).

Area Code for Alberta is 403

MUNICIPALITY	POP.	FEDERAL ELECTORAL DISTRICT	PROVINCIAL ELECTORAL DISTRICT	CLERK OR SECRETARY WITH ADDRESS & PHONE
Calmar†	990	Wetaskiwin	Wetaskiwin-Leduc	R. Park, Mun. Adm., Box 472, Calmar, Alta. TOC OVO (958-3604)
CAMROSE	11,898	Crowfoot	Camrose	R.A. Mackwood, Clerk, City Hall, Camrose, Alta. T4V OS8 (672-4426)
Camrose No. 22‡	7,367			W.R. Gartner, County Sec. Treas., 5402 48A Ave., Camrose, Alta. T4V OL3 (672-4446)
Canmore†	3,166	Bow River	Banff	F.J. Kosa, Town Mgr., Box 460, Canmore, Alta. TOL OMO (678-5593)
Carbon	453	Bow River	Drumheller	Ms. W.J. Sowerby, Mun. Adm., Box 249, Carbon, Alta. TOM OLO (572-3244)
Cardston†	3,043	Lethbridge-Foothills	Cardston	K.D. Bevans, Town Sec., Box 280, Cardston, Alta. TOK OKO (653-3366)
Cardston No. 6*	4,443			R.W. Legge, Mun. Dist. Sec., Box 580, Cardston, Alta. TOK OKO (653-4244)
Carmangay	280	Bow River	Little Bow	Mrs. L. Teskey, Village Sec., Box 130, Carmangay, Alta. TOL ONO (643-3595)
Caroline	402	Red Deer	Rocky Mountain House	R. Como, Mun. Adm., Box 148, Caroline, Alta. TOM OMO (722-3781)
Carstairs†	1,474	Red Deer	Olds-Didsbury	M.A. Moojelsky, Mun. Adm., Box 370, Carstairs, Alta. TOM ONO (337-3341)
Castle Island SV	4		Stony Plain	Mrs. B. Lehman, Castle Island Sec., Box 371, Onoway, Alta. TOE 1VO (924-3181)
Castor†	1,207	Crowfoot	Stettler	M. Yakielashek, Town Adm., Castor, Alta. TOC OXO (882-3215)
Cayley	173	Bow River	Highwood	Mrs. S. Tetachuk, Village Sec., Box 28, Cayley, Alta. TOL OPO (395-3731)
Cereal	231	Crowfoot	Hanna-Oyen	J.H. Halpenny, Village Sec., Cereal, Alta. TOJ ONO (326-3818)
Champion	371	Bow River	Little Bow	Mrs. M. Robinson, Village Sec., Box 367, Champion, Alta. TOL ORO (897-3833)
Chauvin	331	Vegreville	Wainwright	Mrs. B. Swanson, Mun. Adm., Box 160, Chauvin, Alta. TOB OVO (858-3881)
Chestermere Lake SV	424			Mrs. B. Berg, Chestermere Lake Sec. Treas., Box 54, Site 2, R.R. 7, Calgary, Alta. T2P 2G7 (272-9744)
Chipman	324	Vegreville	Vegreville	Ms. L. Olausen, Village Sec. Treas., Chipman, Alta. TOB OWO (363-3982)
Claresholm†	3,425	Bow River	Macleod	L. Flexhaug, Town Sec., Box 1000, Claresholm, Alta. TOL OTO (625-3381)
Clive	338	Wetaskiwin	Lacombe	Mrs. H. Orange, Village Sec., Box 82, Clive, Alta. TOC OYO (784-3366)
Cluny	105	Bow River	Drumheller	Mrs. S. Papp, Village Sec., Cluny, Alta. TOJ OPO (734-3753)
Clyde	400	Pembina	Redwater-Andrew	Ms. L.C. McCullough, Village Sec., Box 190, Clyde, Alta. TOG OPO (348-5356)
Coaldale†	4,391	Lethbridge-Foothills	Taber-Warner	E. McIlroy, Mun. Adm., Box 970, Coaldale, Alta. TOK OLO (345-4417)
Coalhurst	801	Lethbridge-Foothills	Cardston	Ed. Ferguson, Village Adm., Box 890, Coalhurst, Alta. TOL OVO (320-1333)
Cochrane†	2,948	Bow River	Banff	M.J. Schmitke, Town Adm., Cochrane, Alta. TOL OWO (932-2075)
Cold Lake†	1,642	Athabasca	Bonnyville	M.J. Goyan, Mun. Adm., Box 98, Cold Lake, Alta. TOA OVO (639-3112)
Consort	609	Crowfoot	Sedgewick-Coronation	J.P. Trieber, Village Sec., Consort, Alta. TOC 1BO (577-3623)
Coronation†	1,421	Crowfoot	Sedgewick-Coronation	K.J. Hollinger, Town Sec., Coronation, Alta. TOC 1CO (578-3679)
Coutts	407	Medicine Hat	Taber-Warner	Ms. S.A. Heather, Village Sec., Box 236, Coutts, Alta. TOK ONO (344-3848)
Cowley	333	Lethbridge-Foothills	Pincher Creek-Crowsnest	W.T. Smith, Village Sec., Box 40, Cowley, Alta. TOK OPO (628-3808)
Cremona	334	Red Deer	Olds-Didsbury	Mrs. C.J. Haggerty, Village Sec., Box 164, Cremona, Alta. TOM ORO (637-3762)
Crossfield†	1,055	Bow River	Olds-Didsbury	C.K. Crockett, Town Sec. Mgr., Crossfield, Alta. TOM OSO (946-5565)
Crowsnest Pass (Mun. of)†	7,340	Lethbridge-Foothills	Pincher Creek-Crowsnest	J. Kapalka, Mun. Adm., c/o Box 370, Coleman, Alta. TOK OMO (562-8836)

Cities in CAPITALS; Towns marked †; Counties marked ‡; Municipal Districts marked *; Balance are villages or summer villages (SV).

Area Code for Alberta is 403

MUNICIPALITY	POP.	FEDERAL ELECTORAL DISTRICT	PROVINCIAL ELECTORAL DISTRICT	CLERK OR SECRETARY WITH ADDRESS & PHONE
Crystal Springs SV	34	Wetaskiwin	Wetaskiwin-Leduc	Mrs. C.G. McElroy, Crystal Springs Sec., #100, 11025 82 Ave., Edmonton, Alta. T6G OT1 (433-5017)
Czar	190	Crowfoot	Wainwright	Ms. T. Peterson, Village Sec., Box 30, Czar, Alta. TOB OZO
Daysland†	666	Crowfoot	Camrose	Mrs. A. Crossley, Town Sec., Daysland, Alta. TOB 1AO (374-3767)
Delburne	555	Red Deer	Innisfail	Mrs. E. Smart, Mun. Adm., Box 341, Delburne, Alta. TOM OVO (749-3606)
Delia	232	Crowfoot	Hanna-Oyen	Ms. E. Battle, Village Sec., Delia, Alta. TOJ OWO (364-3787)
Derwent	147	Vegreville	Lloydminster	J.R. Bober, Village Sec., Box 46, Derwent, Alta. TOB 1CO (741-2155)
Devon†	3,669	Wetaskiwin	Wetaskiwin-Leduc	G.G. Beach, Town Sec., Devon, Alta. TOC 1EO (987-3334)
Dewberry	164	Vegreville	Lloydminster	Mrs. O.A. Rewuski, Village Sec., Dewberry, Alta. TOB 1GO (847-3053)
Didsbury†	2,866	Red Deer	Olds-Didsbury	A.A. Wray, Town Sec., Box 928, Didsbury, Alta. TOM OWO (335-3391)
Donalda	278	Crowfoot	Camrose	Ms. G.E. Froebel, Village Sec. Treas., Box 40, Donalda, Alta. TOB 1HO (883-2345)
Donnelly	340	Peace River	Smoky River	D.J. Maisonneuve, Village Sec., Donnelly, Alta. TOH 1GO (925-3835)
Drayton Valley†	5,076	Yellowhead	Drayton Valley	K.J.P. Pugh, Town Sec. Treas., Box 837, Drayton Valley, Alta. TOE OMO (542-5327)
DRUMHELLER	6,380	Bow River	Drumheller	D.A. Guidolin, City Clerk, Box 430, Drumheller, Alta. TOJ OYO (823-6300)
Duchess	420	Medicine Hat	Bow Valley	Mrs. H. Kraus, Village Sec., Box 90, Duchess, Alta. TOJ OZO (378-4452)
Eaglesham	229	Peace River	Smoky River	Ms. L. Alberg, Village Sec. Treas., Box 209, Eaglesham, Alta. TOH 1HO (359-3895)
Eckville†	828	Red Deer	Rocky Mountain House	Mrs. M.K. Schofer, Mun. Adm., 5023 51 Ave. W., Box 587, Eckville, Alta. TOM OXO (746-2171)
Edberg	140	Crowfoot	Camrose	Mrs. B.J. Ledene, Mun. Adm., Box 82, Edberg, Alta. TOB 1JO (877-3997)
Edgerton	363	Vegreville	Wainwright	R.S. Groves, Village Sec., Box 57, Edgerton, Alta. TOB 1KO (755-3933)
EDMONTON	505,773	Edmonton East; Ed. N.; Ed. S.; Ed. Strathcona; Ed. W.	Edmonton Avonmore; Ed. Belmont; Ed. Beverly; Ed. Calder; Ed. Centre; Ed. Glengarry; Ed. Glenora; Ed. Gold Bar; Ed. Highlands; Ed. Jasper Place; Ed. Kingsway; Ed. Meadowlark; Ed. Mill Woods; Ed. Norwood; Ed. Parkallen; Ed. Sherwood Park; Ed. Strathcona; Ed. Whitemud	C.J. McGonigle, Clerk, City Hall, Edmonton, Alta. T5J 2R7 (428-5448)
Edmonton Beach SV	300	Yellowhead	Stony Plain	K. Waters, Mun. Adm. for Edmonton Beach, Box 1428, Stony Plain, Alta. TOE 2GO (963-4211)
Edson†	5,671	Yellowhead	Edson	G.R. Kurceba, Town Sec. Treas., Box 1388, Edson, Alta. TOE OPO (723-4401)
Elk Point†	1,041	Vegreville	St. Paul	P. Vincent, Mun. Adm., Box 448, Elk Point, Alta. TOA 1AO (724-3894)
Elnora	241	Red Deer	Innisfail	Mrs. G.W. Renouf, Village Sec. Treas., Box 629, Elnora, Alta. TOM OYO (773-3922)
Empress	238	Medicine Hat	Bow Valley	G.J. Turner, Village Sec., Box 159, Empress, Alta. TOJ 1EO (565-3938)
Entwistle	499	Yellowhead	Whitecourt	Mrs. A. Burke, Village Sec. Treas., Box 270, Entwistle, Alta. TOE OSO (727-3652)
Evansburg	801	Yellowhead	Whitecourt	Mrs. J. Halpin, Village Sec., Box 39, Evansburg, Alta. TOE OTO (727-3551)
Fairview No. 136*	1,799			L.C. French, Mun. Dist. Sec., Box 189, Fairview, Alta. TOH 1LO (835-4903)

Cities in CAPITALS; Towns marked †; Counties marked ‡; Municipal Districts marked *; Balance are villages or summer villages (SV).

Area Code for Alberta is 403

MUNICIPALITY	POP.	FEDERAL ELECTORAL DISTRICT	PROVINCIAL ELECTORAL DISTRICT	CLERK OR SECRETARY WITH ADDRESS & PHONE
Fairview†	3,027	Peace River	Spirit River-Fairview	L. Chorney, Town Mgr., Box 730, Fairview, Alta. TOH 1LO (835-2033)
Falher†	1,162	Peace River	Smoky River	G.A. Nicolet, Mun. Adm., Box 155, Falher, Alta. TOH 1MO (837-2183)
Ferintosh	166	Crowfoot	Camrose	Mrs. M. Fankhanel, Mun. Adm., Ferintosh, Alta. TOB 1MO (877-3767)
Flagstaff No. 29‡	4,653			O.W. Likness, County Sec. Treas., County Offices, Sedgewick, Alta. TOB 4CO (384-3537)
Foothills No. 31*	9,069			T.J. Motil, Mun. Dist. Sec. Treas., Box 160, High River, Alta. TOL 1BO (652-2341)
Foremost	572	Medicine Hat	Cypress	Mrs. C.I. Burton, Mun. Adm., Box 159, Foremost, Alta. TOK OXO (867-3733)
Forestburg	963	Crowfoot	Camrose	C.T. Farvolden, Village Sec., Box 210, Forestburg, Alta. TOB 1WO (582-3560)
Fort Assiniboine	194	Yellowhead	Barrhead	Mrs. L. Davison, Village Sec. Treas., Box 150, Fort Assiniboine, Alta. TOG 1AO (584-3922)
Fort Macleod†	3,123	Lethbridge	Macleod	M. Wevers, Mun. Co-ord., Box 1420, Fort Macleod, Alta. TOL OZO (553-4425)
FORT McMURRAY	27,784	Athabasca	Lac la Biche-McMurray	G.E. Bussieres, City Clerk, 42 Riedel St., Fort McMurray, Alta. T9H 3E1 (743-1000)
Fort Saskatchewan†	11,482	Pembina	Clover Bar	The Town Sec. Treas., 10005 102 St., Fort Saskatchewan, Alta. T8L 2C5 (998-2266)
Forty Mile No. 8‡	3,518			G.B. Nicoll, County Mun. Adm., Box 160, Foremost, Alta. TOK OXO (867-3530)
Fox Creek†	1,905	Yellowhead	Whitecourt	N. Ozoroff, Town Sec. Mgr., Box 149, Fox Creek, Alta. TOH 1PO (622-3896)
Gadsby	48	Crowfoot	Stettler	J. Craig, Village Sec., Box 74, Gadsby, Alta. TOC 1KO (574-3765)
Galahad	184	Crowfoot	Sedgewick-Coronation	Ms. D. Herle, Village Sec., Galahad, Alta. TOB 1RO (583-3741)
Ghost Lake SV	42	Bow River	Banff	E.H. Janzen, Ghost Lake Village Sec., Box 23, Site 12, R.R. 5, Calgary, Alta. T2P 2G6 (268-5783)
Gibbons†	1,785	Pembina	St. Albert	Mrs. M. Metrunec, Town Sec., Box 68, Gibbons, Alta.TOA 1NO (923-3331)
Girouxville	315	Peace River	Smoky River	A.A. Gagnon, Village Sec., Box 26, Girouxville, Alta. TOH 1SO (323-4270)
Gleichen†	339	Bow River	Drumheller	Mrs. I. Whitwell, Mun. Adm., Box 159, Gleichen, Alta. TOJ 1NO (734-3732)
Glendon	454	Athabasca	Bonnyville	Mrs. H. Runzer, Village Sec., Glendon, Alta. TOA 1PO (635-3807)
Glenwood	251	Lethbridge-Foothills	Cardston	Mrs. J. Lybbert, Village Sec. Treas., Box 1068, Glenwood, Alta. TOK 2RO (626-3233)
Golden Days SV	23	Wetaskiwin	Wetaskiwin-Leduc	Mrs. E. Toth, Golden Days Village Sec., R.R. 1, Site 5, Thorsby, Alta. TOC 2PO (389-2428)
Grand Centre†	3,107		Bonnyville	A.J. Baer, Town Sec., Box 70, Grand Centre, Alta. TOA 1TO (594-4494)
Grande Cache†	4,423	Yellowhead	Edson	D. Dukart, Mun. Adm., Box 300, Grande Cache, Alta. TOE OYO (827-3362)
GRANDE PRAIRIE	22,718	Peace River	Grande Prairie	Mrs. L.M. Saunders, Clerk, City Hall, Grande Prairie, Alta. T8V 2P5 (532-4471)
Grande Prairie No. 1‡	11,269			J. McGowan, County Mgr., 8611 108 St., Grande Prairie, Alta. T8V 4C5 (532-9722)
Grandview SV	30	Wetaskiwin	Wetaskiwin-Leduc	Ms. G. Trudel, Grandview Village Adm., c/o 5307 95 Ave., Edmonton, Alta. T6B 1A2 (462-0944)
Granum†	424	Lethbridge-Foothills	Macleod	N. Webster, Town Sec. Treas., Box 88, Granum, Alta. TOL 1AO (687-3822)
Grassy Lake	170	Medicine Hat	Cypress	Ms. M.F. Turnbull, Village Sec. Treas., Box 629, Grassy Lake, Alta. TOK OZO (655-2377)
Grimshaw†	2,209	Peace River	Peace River	R.A. Rondeau, Town Adm., Box 377, Grimshaw, Alta. TOH 1WO (332-4626)

Cities in CAPITALS; Towns marked †; Counties marked ‡; Municipal Districts marked *; Balance are villages or summer villages (SV).
Area Code for Alberta is 403

MUNICIPALITY	POP.	FEDERAL ELECTORAL DISTRICT	PROVINCIAL ELECTORAL DISTRICT	CLERK OR SECRETARY WITH ADDRESS & PHONE
Gull Lake SV	92	Wetaskiwin	Lacombe	J.H.A. Trottier, Gull Lake Village Sec. Treas., 35 McFarlane Ave., Red Deer, Alta. T4N 5S9 (346-3934)
Hairy Hill	96	Vegreville	Vegreville	S. Bidulock, Village Sec., Box 59, Hairy Hill, Alta. TOB 1SO (768-3861)
Half Moon Bay SV	40	Pembina		H.A. Raymond, Half Moon Bay Mun. Adm., Box 667, Sylvan Lake, Alta. TOM 1ZO (887-2543)
Halkirk	152	Crowfoot	Stettler	Mrs. H.J. Anderson, Village Sec., Box 126, Halkirk, Alta. TOC 1MO (884-2464)
Hanna†	2,764	Crowfoot	Hanna-Oyen	R. Wemyss, Mun. Adm., Box 430, Hanna, Alta. TOJ 1PO (854-4433)
Hardisty†	671	Crowfoot	Sedgewick-Coronation	W.S. Pedlar, Town Sec., Town Offices, Hardisty, Alta. TOB 1YO (888-3623)
Hay Lakes	287	Wetaskiwin	Clover Bar	Ms. S. Perkin, Village Sec., Box 40, Hay Lakes, Alta. TOB 1WO (878-3200)
Heisler	215	Crowfoot	Camrose	Mrs. R.E. Halverson, Mun. Adm., Box 25, Heisler, Alta. TOB 2AO (889-3774)
High Level†	2,134	Peace River	Peace River	C. Svendsen, Mun. Adm., Box 485, High Level, Alta. TOH 1ZO (926-2201)
High Prairie†	2,281	Athabasca	Lesser Slave Lake	B.S.D. Walt, Town Mgr., Box 179, High Prairie, Alta. TOG 1EO (523-3388)
High River†	4,281	Bow River	Highwood	J. Crisp, Mun. Adm., Box 1870, High River, Alta. TOB 1BO (652-2307)
Hill Spring	192	Lethbridge-Foothills	Cardston	K.L. Tolman, Village Sec., Hill Spring, Alta. TOK 1EO (626-3876)
Hines Creek	527	Peace River	Spirit River-Fairview	Ms. H. Dow, Mun. Adm., Hines Creek, Alta. TOH 2AO (494-3690)
Hinton†	8,018	Yellowhead	Edson	Mrs. A.C. Baisley, Town Sec., Box 818, Hinton, Alta. TOE 1BO (865-2217)
Holden	393	Vegreville	Vegreville	Mrs. C.B. MacKay, Village Sec. Treas., Box 357, Holden, Alta. TOB 2CO (688-3928)
Hughenden	265	Crowfoot	Wainwright	Ms. J. Ruud, Village Sec., Box 64, Hughenden, Alta. TOB 2EO (856-3830)
Hussar	182	Bow River	Drumheller	G.G. Montgomery, Village Sec., Box 100, Hussar, Alta. TOJ 1SO (787-3766)
Hythe	680	Peace River	Grande Prairie	Mrs. P. Belaire, Village Sec., Box 219, Hythe, Alta. TOH 2CO (356-3888)
Innisfail†	4,831	Red Deer	Innisfail	D.W. Bartley, Town Mgr., Box 220, Innisfail, Alta. TOM 1AO (227-3376)
Innisfree	267	Vegreville	Vermilion-Viking	Mrs. A.M. Stepanik, Village Sec., Box 69, Innisfree, Alta. TOB 2GO (592-3886)
Irma	500	Vegreville	Wainwright	D.D. Creasy, Mun. Adm., Box 419, Irma, Alta. TOB 2HO (754-3665)
Irricana	461	Bow River	Three Hills	Ms. S. Silbernagel, Mun. Adm., Box 100, Irricana, Alta. TOM 1BO (935-4672)
Irvine†	366	Medicine Hat	Cypress	Margaret Toole, Town Adm., Box 90, Irvine, Alta. TOJ 1VO (834-3923)
Island Lake SV	37	Athabasca	Athabasca	H.M. Olyan, Island Lake Village Sec., #280, 10149 109 St., Edmonton, Alta. T5J 1M8 (426-6868)
Itaska Beach SV	5		Wetaskiwin-Leduc	R.C. Sheldon, Itaska Beach Village Sec., Box 8272, Stn. F, Edmonton, Alta. T6H 4W6 (434-8826)
Kapasiwin SV	2		Stony Plain	Mrs. J. Drever, Kapasiwin Village Sec., 115 Hillcrest Pl., Edmonton, Alta. T5R 5X6 (484-3666)
Killam†	1,005	Crowfoot	Sedgewick-Coronation	Mrs. V.L. Engel, Mun. Adm., Box 189, Killam, Alta. TOB 2LO (385-3977)
Kinuso	305	Athabasca	Lesser Slave Lake	Miss J. Roe, Village Sec., Box 57, Kinuso, Alta. TOG 1KO (775-3570)
Kitscoty	520	Vegreville	Lloydminster	Mrs. J.E. Buha, Village Sec., Box 53, Kitscoty, Alta. TOB 2PO (846-2221)
Kneehill No. 48*	5,974			J.C. Jeffery, Mun. Adm., Box 400, Three Hills, Alta. TOM 2AO (443-5541)
Lac la Biche†	2,035	Athabasca	La la Biche-McMurray	R.B. Persson, Town Sec., Box 387, Lac la Biche, Alta. TOA 2CO (623-4323)

Cities in CAPITALS; Towns marked †; Counties marked ‡; Municipal Districts marked *; Balance are villages or summer villages (SV).
Area Code for Alberta is 403

MUNICIPALITY	POP.	FEDERAL ELECTORAL DISTRICT	PROVINCIAL ELECTORAL DISTRICT	CLERK OR SECRETARY WITH ADDRESS & PHONE
Lacombe†	5,218	Wetaskiwin	Lacombe	F.W. Lacey, Mun. Mgr., Box 310, Lacombe, Alta. TOC 1SO (782-6666)
Lacombe No. 14‡	8,399			E.E. Koberstein, County Sec., Box 1330, Lacombe, Alta. TOC 1SO (782-6601)
Lac Ste. Anne No. 28‡	6,586			A.R. Koberstein, County Sec., Box 219, Sangudo, Alta. TOE 2AO (785-2359)
Lakeview SV	9		Stony Plain	Mrs. J. Killips, Lakeview Village Sec., 56 Lancaster Cres., St. Albert, Alta. T8N 2N8 (458-6213)
Lamont No. 30‡	4,625			W.J. Leskiw, County Sec., Box 150, Lamont, Alta. TOB 2RO (424-6541)
Lamont†	1,371	Vegreville	Clover Bar	Mrs. M.M. Fedun, Town Sec., Box 207, Lamont, Alta. TOB 2RO (895-2010)
Lavoy	124	Vegreville	Vegreville	Ms. E. Grykuliak, Village Sec., Box 141, Lavoy, Alta. TOB 2SO (658-3788)
Leduc†	11,603	Wetaskiwin	Wetaskiwin-Leduc	M.D. Littman, Village Sec., Box 187, Leduc, Alta. TOC 1VO (986-2261)
Leduc No. 25‡	10,949			F.A. Rolof, County Sec., 4301 50 St., Leduc, Alta. T9E 2X3 (986-2251)
Legal	1,032	Pembina	St. Albert	Mrs. A. Montpetit, Village Sec., Legal, Alta. TOG 1LO (961-3773)
LETHBRIDGE	53,135	Lethbridge-Foothills	Lethbridge East; Lethbridge West	J. Gerla, Clerk, City Hall, Lethbridge, Alta. T1J OP6 (328-2341)
Lethbridge No. 26‡	9,243			F.D. Clark, County Mgr., 905 4 Ave. S., Lethbridge, Alta. T1J 4E4 (328-5525)
Linden	401	Red Deer	Three Hills	F. Sillito, Village Sec., Box 206, Linden, Alta. TOM 1JO (546-3888)
LLOYDMINSTER	14,093	Vegreville	Lloydminster	D. Newlin, Clerk, City Hall, Lloydminster, Alta. S9V OT8 (825-6184)
Lomond	193	Bow River	Little Bow	Ms. L. Braun, Village Sec., Box 213, Lomond, Alta. TOL 1GO (792-3611)
Longview	281	Bow River	Highwood	Mrs. M.L. Bailey, Village Sec., Box 221, Longview, Alta. TOL 1HO (558-3922)
Lougheed	227	Crowfoot	Sedgewick-Coronation	S.M. Towers, Village Sec., Box 155, Lougheed, Alta. TOB 2VO (386-3970)
Magrath†	1,464	Medicine Hat	Cardston	R.H. Bly, Mun. Adm., Box 520, Magrath, Alta. TOK 1JO (758-6333)
Ma-Me-O-Beach SV	87	Wetaskiwin	Wetaskiwin-Leduc	Mrs. M.L. Helgren, Mun. Adm. for Ma-Me-O-Beach, c/o R.R. 2, Westerose, Alta. T0C 2V0 (586-2251)
Manning†	1,166	Peace River	Peace River	Mrs. L. Lovlin, Town Sec. Treas., Box 125, Manning, Alta. TOH 2MO (836-3606)
Mannville	812	Vegreville	Vermilion-Viking	Mrs. D.J. Johnson, Mun. Adm., Box 158, Mannville, Alta. TOB 2WO (763-3500)
Marwayne	450	Vegreville	Lloydminster	G.T. Horton, Village Sec., Box 39, Marwayne, Alta. TOB 2XO (847-3962)
Mayerthorpe†	1,502	Yellowhead	Whitecourt	E. Mitchell, Town Sec., Mayerthorpe, Alta. TOE 1NO (786-2330)
McLennan†	1,212	Peace River	Smoky River	L.J. Lamoureux, Mun. Adm., Box 356, McLennan, Alta. TOH 2LO (324-3065)
MEDICINE HAT	37,684	Medicine Hat	Medicine Hat-Redcliff	L.P. Godin, Clerk, City Hall, Medicine Hat, Alta. T1A OC7 (526-5971)
Mewatha Beach SV	15			Ms. D.L. Milke, Mewatha Beach Village Sec., 31 Bernard Dr., St. Albert, Alta. T8N OB3 (459-5976)
Milk River†	814	Medicine Hat	Taber-Warner	The Town Adm., Milk River, Alta. TOK 1MO (647-3773)
Millet	965	Wetaskiwin	Wetaskiwin-Leduc	P. Benedetto, Village Mgr., Box 143, Millet, Alta. TOC 1ZO (423-3775)
Milo	100	Bow River	Little Bow	Mrs. B. Peterson, Village Sec., Milo, Alta. TOL 1LO (599-3883)
Minburn No. 27‡	4,609			L.E. Powley, County Mgr., Box 550, Vegreville, Alta. TOB 4LO (632-2082)
Minburn	143	Vegreville	Vermilion-Viking	Ms. L. Hodge, Village Sec. Treas., Minburn, Alta. TOB 3BO (763-3509)
Mirror	479	Crowfoot	Lacombe	Mrs. L.L. Schultz, Mun. Adm., Box 130, Mirror, Alta. TOB 3CO (788-3011)

Note: Lloydminster pop. is Sask./Alta. combined.

Cities in CAPITALS; Towns marked †; Counties marked ‡; Municipal Districts marked *; Balance are villages or summer villages (SV).
Area Code for Alberta is 403

MUNICIPALITY	POP.	FEDERAL ELECTORAL DISTRICT	PROVINCIAL ELECTORAL DISTRICT	CLERK OR SECRETARY WITH ADDRESS & PHONE
Morinville†	4,207	Pembina	St. Albert	Ms. A.M. Gibeault, Town Mgr., Box 420, Morinville, Alta. TOG 1PO (939-4361)
Morrin	230	Crowfoot	Drumheller	Ms. M. Trentham, Village Sec., Box 149, Morrin, Alta. TOJ 2BO (772-3870)
Mountain View No. 17‡	8,695			F.J. Dawley, County Adm., Box 100, Didsbury, Alta. TOM OWO (335-3311)
Mundare†	668	Vegreville	Vegreville	Mrs. L. Fundytus, Town Sec., Mundare, Alta. TOB 3HO (764-3929)
Munson	125	Crowfoot	Drumheller	Ms. L. Straughan, Village Adm., Munson, Alta. TOJ OYO (823-6987)
Myrnam	411	Vegreville	Lloydminster	Mrs. A.L. Bettcher, Village Sec., Myrnam, Alta. TOB 3KO (366-3910)
Nakamun Park SV	13		Barrhead	Mrs. C.G. McElroy, Nakamun Park Village Sec., #100, 11025 82 Ave., Edmonton, Alta. T6G OT1 (433-5017)
Nampa	352	Peace River	Smoky River	Miss M. Bykewich, Village Sec. Box 174, Nampa, Alta. TOH 2RO (322-3851)
Nanton†	1,527	Bow River	Highwood	Mrs. D.L. Todd, Town Sec. Treas., Box 609, Nanton, Alta. TOL 1RO (486-2029)
Newell No. 4‡	5,977			D.N. James, County Adm., Box 130, Brooks, Alta. TOJ OJO (362-3266)
New Norway	269	Crowfoot	Camrose	Mrs. O.R. Wigglesworth, Mun. Adm., Box 60, New Norway, Alta. TOB 3LO (855-3915)
New Sarepta	366	Wetaskiwin	Clover Bar	Mrs. L. Hickman, Village Sec., Box 134, New Sarepta, Alta. TOB 3MO (941-3929)
Nobleford	551	Lethbridge-Foothills	Macleod	Ms. N.R. Howe, Village Adm., Box 67, Nobleford, Alta. TOL 1SO (824-3555)
Norglenwold SV	94	Red Deer	Rocky Mountain House	H.A. Raymond, Norglenwold Village Sec., Box 667, Sylvan Lake, Alta. TOM 1ZO (887-2543)
Okotoks†	2,967	Bow River	Highwood	J.A. Barrie, Town Adm., Box 220, Okotoks, Alta. TOL 1TO (938-4404)
Olds†	4,488	Red Deer	Olds-Didsbury	R. Hilton, Town Mgr. Treas., Box 189, Olds, Alta. TOM 1PO (556-6981)
Onoway	500	Yellowhead	Stony Plain	Mrs. R.M. Vaughan, Village Sec., Box 10, Onoway, Alta. TOE 1VO (967-5338)
Oyen†	1,011	Crowfoot	Hanna-Oyen	J.B. Lijdsman, Town Sec., Box 360, Oyen, Alta. TOJ 2JO (664-3511)
Paintearth No. 18‡	2,603			T. Hager, County Sec. Treas., Castor, Alta. TOC OXO (882-3211)
Paradise Valley	191	Vegreville	Lloydminster	Mrs. B. Ellis, Village Sec. Treas., Box 24, Paradise Valley, Alta. TOB 3RO (745-2287)
Parkland No. 31‡	23,703			D.E. Konelsky, County Sec., Mun. Offices, Stony Plain, Alta. TOE 2GO (963-2231)
Peace No. 135*	1,583			L.D. Goodhope, Mun. Adm., Box 34, Berwyn, Alta. TOH OEO (338-3845)
Peace River†	5,754	Peace River	Peace River	G.G. Paul, Town Sec. Treas., Box 125, Peace River, Alta. TOH 2XO (624-2574)
Pelican Narrows SV	25	Athabasca	Bonnyville	D.L. Demers, Pelican Narrows Village Sec., c/o Box 1527, Bonnyville, Alta. TOA OLO (826-3611)
Penhold†	1,242	Red Deer	Innisfail	Mrs. G. Robinson, Mun. Adm., Box 14, Penhold, Alta. TOM 1RO (886-4039)
Picture Butte†	1,329	Lethbridge-Foothills	Macleod	P.P. Ries, Mun. Adm., 120 4th St., Picture Butte, Alta. TOV 1KO (732-4555)
Pincher Creek†	3,825	Lethbridge-Foothills	Pincher Creek-Crowsnest	T.D. Lyon, Town Mgr., Box 159, Pincher Creek, Alta. TOK 1WO (627-3156)
Pincher Creek No. 9*	2,879			K.E. Phillips, Mun. Dist. Sec., Box 279, Pincher Creek, Alta. TOK 1WO (627-3130)
Plamondon	236	Athabasca	La la Biche-McMurray	Ms. J.M. Bourassa, Village Sec., Box 98, Plamondon, Alta. TOA 2TO (798-3883)
Point Alison SV	8		Stony Plain	Mrs. C. Tenove, Point Alison Village Sec., c/o 11708 83 Ave., Edmonton, Alta. T6G OV3 (433-5664)
Ponoka No. 3‡	7,223			G.J. Vold, County Sec. Treas., Box 1830, Ponoka, Alta. TOC 2HO (783-3333)

Cities in CAPITALS; Towns marked †; Counties marked ‡; Municipal Districts marked *; Balance are villages or summer villages (SV).
Area Code for Alberta is 403

MUNICIPALITY	POP.	FEDERAL ELECTORAL DISTRICT	PROVINCIAL ELECTORAL DISTRICT	CLERK OR SECRETARY WITH ADDRESS & PHONE
Ponoka†	4,873	Wetaskiwin	Ponoka	J.L. West, Mun. Mgr., Box 1029, Ponoka, Alta. TOC 2HO (783-4431)
Poplar Bay SV	22	Wetaskiwin	Wetaskiwin-Leduc	Mrs. G. Trudel, Poplar Bay Village Sec., 5307 95 Ave., Edmonton, Alta. T6B 1A2 (469-0944)
Provost†	1,627	Crowfoot	Wainwright	L.H. Komaransky, Mun. Adm., 4904 51 Ave., Provost, Alta. TOB 3SO (753-2261)
Provost No. 52*	2,665			Mrs. L.L. McDonald, Mun. Dist. Sec., 4504 53 Ave., Provost, Alta. TOB 3SO (753-2434)
Radway	218	Pembina	Redwater-Andrew	A.J. Styra, Village Sec., Box 280, Radway, Alta. TOA 2VO (736-3574)
Rainbow Lake†	813	Peace River	Peace River	Mrs. D. Bello, Town Sec., Box 149, Rainbow Lake, Alta. TOH 2YO (956-3934)
Raymond†	2,673	Medicine Hat	Cardston	B.M. Watson, Mun. Adm., Box 629, Raymond, Alta. TOK 1YO (752-3322)
Redcliff†	3,641	Medicine Hat	Medicine Hat-Redcliff	H.W. Beach, Town Sec., 2 3rd St. N.E., Redcliff, Alta. TOJ 2PO (548-3618)
RED DEER	41,371	Red Deer	Red Deer	R. Stollings, Clerk, City Hall, Box 5008, Red Deer, Alta. T4N 3T4 (347-4421)
Red Deer No. 23‡	13,575			R.J. Stonehouse, County Sec. Treas., Box 920, Red Deer, Alta. T4N 5H3 (347-3364)
Redwater†	1,856	Pembina	Redwater-Andrew	K. Miller, Town Adm., Redwater, Alta. TOA 2WO (735-3519)
Rimbey†	1,858	Wetaskiwin	Ponoka	R. Spelrem, Town Sec., Box 350, Rimbey, Alta. TOC 2JO (843-2113)
Rochon Sands SV	44		Stettler	Ms. N. Smith, Rochon Sands Village Sec., c/o Box 1746, Stettler, Alta. TOC 2LO (742-3579)
Rockyford	321	Bow River	Drumheller	R.W. Munchrath, Village Sec., Rockyford, Alta. TOJ 2RO (533-3950)
Rocky Mountain House†	4,467	Red Deer	Rocky Mountain House	P.D. Lyster, Town Mgr., Box 1509, Rocky Mountain House, Alta. TOM 1TO (845-2866)
Rocky View No. 44*	16,863			W.M. Ryder, Mun. Dist. 44 Adm., Box 3009, Stn. B, Calgary, Alta. T2M 4L6 (230-1401)
Rosalind	186	Crowfoot	Camrose	Mrs. R.E. Halverson, Mun. Adm., Box 25, Rosalind, Alta. TOB 3YO (375-3996)
Rosemary	273	Medicine Hat	Bow Valley	Mrs. H. Retzlaff, Village Sec., Box 4, Rosemary, Alta. TOJ 2WO (378-4508)
Ross Haven SV	52		Stony Plain	M. Anker, Ross Haven Village Sec., 14403 110A Ave., Edmonton, Alta. T5N 1J7 (454-9414)
Rumsey	97	Crowfoot	Drumheller	Ms. V.P. Foesier, Village Sec. Treas., Box 72, Rumsey, Alta. TOJ 2YO (368-3949)
Rycroft	538	Peace River	Spirit River-Fairview	Mrs. M. Barbarich, Village Sec. Treas., Box 360, Rycroft, Alta. TOH 3AO (765-3652)
Ryley	551	Vegreville	Vegreville	Ms. S.J. Fitt, Village Sec., Box 230, Ryley, Alta. TOB 4AO (663-3653)
ST. ALBERT	29,512	Pembina	St. Albert	Mrs. F. Daniel, City Clerk, 30 Sir Winston Churchill Blvd., St. Albert, Alta. T8N 3A3 (459-6601)
St. Paul No. 19‡	5,973			A. Roy, County Sec., County Offices, St. Paul, Alta. TOA 3AO (645-3301)
St. Paul†	5,066	Vegreville	St. Paul	W.C. Horner, Mun. Adm., Box 1480, St. Paul, Alta. TOA 3AO (645-4481)
Sandy Beach SV	65		Stony Plain	D.M. Banks, Sandy Beach Village Adm., c/o Box 4233, Edmonton, Alta. T6E 4T2 (455-2050)
Sangudo	422	Yellowhead	Whitecourt	Mrs. L. Clark, Village Sec., Box 190, Sangudo, Alta. TOE 2AO (785-2258)
Seba Beach SV	126	Yellowhead	Stony Plain	Mrs. S.A. Ryan, Village Sec., Box 124, Seba Beach, Alta. TOE 2BO (797-3863)
Sedgewick†	848	Crowfoot	Sedgewick-Coronation	L.A. Kneeland, Town Sec., Box 129, Sedgewick, Alta. TOB 4CO (384-3504)
Sexsmith†	1,141	Peace River	Grande Prairie	A.J. Algar, Mun. Adm., Box 420, Sexsmith, Alta. TOH 3CO (568-3681)

Cities in CAPITALS; Towns marked †; Counties marked ‡; Municipal Districts marked *; Balance are villages or summer villages (SV).
Area Code for Alberta is 403

MUNICIPALITY	POP.	FEDERAL ELECTORAL DISTRICT	PROVINCIAL ELECTORAL DISTRICT	CLERK OR SECRETARY WITH ADDRESS & PHONE
Silver Beach SV	26	Wetaskiwin	Wetaskiwin-Leduc	Mrs. C.G. McElroy, Silver Beach Village Sec., c/o #100, 11025 82 Ave., Edmonton, Alta. T6G OT1 (433-5017)
Silver Sands SV	63		Stony Plain	Mrs. P. Jarvie, Silver Sands Village Sec., c/o 12407 95A St., Edmonton, Alta. T5G 1S6 (477-3697)
Slave Lake†	4,328	Athabasca	Lesser Slave Lake	F. Abbott, Town Sec., Box 563, Slave Lake, Alta. TOG 2AO (849-3606)
Smoky Lake†	1,121	Vegreville	Redwater-Andrew	E. Oshann, Town Sec. Treas., Box 460, Smoky Lake, Alta. TOA 3CO (656-3674)
Smoky Lake No. 13‡	3,154			C. Smigerowsky, County Mgr., Box 310, Smoky Lake, Alta. TOA 3CO (656-3730)
Smoky River No. 130*	2,990			L. Turcotte, Mun. Dist. Adm., Box 210, Falher, Alta. TOH 1MO (837-2221)
South View SV	36		Stony Plain	O. Monsson, South View Village Sec., c/o 8320 166 St., Edmonton, Alta. T5R 2S8 (484-4173)
Spirit River No. 133*	857			Mrs. R.E. Giles, Mun. Dist. Sec., Box 389, Spirit River, Alta. TOH 3GO (864-3500)
Spirit River†	1,107	Peace River	Spirit River-Fairview	Mrs. E.S. Reid, Town Sec., Box 130, Spirit River, Alta. TOH 3GO (864-3998)
Spruce Grove†	9,074	Yellowhead	Stony Plain	Gwynn Alcorn, Town Sec., Box 130, Spruce Grove, Alta. TOE 2CO (962-2611)
Standard	349	Bow River	Drumheller	Ms. E.M. Larsen, Mun. Adm., Box 58, Standard, Alta. TOJ 3GO (644-3968)
Starland No. 47*	2,223			J.V. Simpson, Mun. Adm., Box 249, Morrin, Alta. TOJ 2BO (772-3793)
Stavely†	516	Bow River	Macleod	Ms. F. Miller, Town Adm., Stavely, Alta. TOL 1ZO (549-3761)
Stettler†	5,035	Crowfoot	Stettler	C.W. Dunford, Town Adm., Box 280, Stettler, Alta. TOC 2LO (742-2305)
Stettler No. 6‡	4,924			N.C. Fakas, County Adm., Box 1270, Stettler, Alta. TOC 2LO (742-4441)
Stirling	664	Medicine Hat	Cardston	Norma Millar, Mun. Adm., Box 325, Stirling, Alta. TOK 2EO (756-3379)
Stony Plain†	4,442	Yellowhead	Stony Plain	J. Van Doesburg, Town Sec., Box 810, Stony Plain, Alta. TOE 2GO (963-2151)
Strathcona No. 20‡	46,057			E.J. Briscoe, County Sec. Treas., 2001 Sherwood Dr., Sherwood Park, Alta. T8A 3W7 (464-8111)
Strathmore†	2,724	Bow River	Drumheller	Mrs. K. Corner, Town Sec., Box 359, Strathmore, Alta. TOJ 3HO (934-3133)
Strome	299	Crowfoot	Camrose	Mrs. A. Pooler, Village Sec., Box 51, Strome, Alta. TOB 4HO (376-3558)
Sturgeon No. 90*	15,880			G.J. Boddez, Mun. Dist. Sec., 9601 100 St., Morinville, Alta. TOG 1PO (939-4321)
Sundance Beach SV	18	Wetaskiwin	Wetaskiwin-Leduc	K.D. Armstrong, Sundance Beach Mun. Adm., 9322 73 Ave., Edmonton, Alta. T6E 1A7 (433-4969)
Sundre†	1,604	Red Deer	Olds-Didsbury	H. Doering, Mun. Adm., Box 420, Sundre, Alta. TOM 1XO (638-3551)
Sunset Beach SV	21			G.R. Hawthorne, Sunset Beach Mun. Adm., 12147 59 St., Edmonton, Alta. T5W 3Y4 (471-5512)
Sunset Point SV	60		Stony Plain	Mrs. M. Hervieux, Sunset Plain Village Sec., 11441 125 St., Edmonton, Alta. T5M ON1 (454-3406)
Swan Hills†	2,553	Yellowhead	Barrhead	L. Stocking, Town Sec., Box 149, Swan Hills, Alta. TOG 2CO (333-4477)
Sylvan Lake†	3,650	Red Deer	Rocky Mountain House	P.J. Grimson, Town Sec., Box 70, Sylvan Lake, Alta. TOM 1ZO (887-2141)
Taber†	5,708	Medicine Hat	Taber-Warner	J.E. Maddison, Town Mgr., Box 2229, Taber, Alta. TOK 2GO (223-3515)
Taber No. 14*	6,134			D. Francis, Mun. Dist. Sec., Box 2230, Taber, Alta. TOK 2GO (223-3541)
Thorhild No. 7‡	3,324			P. Goruk, County Sec. Treas., Box 519, Thorhild, Alta. TOA 3JO (398-3741)

Cities in CAPITALS; Towns marked †; Counties marked ‡; Municipal Districts marked *; Balance are villages or summer villages (SV).
Area Code for Alberta is 403

MUNICIPALITY	POP.	FEDERAL ELECTORAL DISTRICT	PROVINCIAL ELECTORAL DISTRICT	CLERK OR SECRETARY WITH ADDRESS & PHONE
Thorhild	547	Pembina	Redwater-Andrew	Ms. R.J. Malysh, Village Sec., Box 313, Thorhild, Alta. TOA 3JO (398-3688)
Thorsby	701	Wetaskiwin	Wetaskiwin-Leduc	Ms. B. Senio, Village Sec. Treas., Thorsby, Alta. TOC 2PO (788-3935)
Three Hills†	1,868	Red Deer	Three Hills	R.C. Thomson, Mun. Adm., Box 610, Three Hills, Alta. TOM 2AO (443-5822)
Tilley	370	Medicine Hat	Bow Valley	Mrs. J. Alcock, Village Sec. Treas., Box 155, Tilley, Alta. TOJ 3KO (377-2203)
Tofield†	1,440	Vegreville	Clover Bar	J.N. Brodie, Mun. Adm., Tofield, Alta. TOB 4JO (662-3269)
Torrington	279	Red Deer	Three Hills	Ms. I.H. Wilson, Village Sec., Torrington, Alta. TOM 2BO (631-3866)
Trochu†	854	Red Deer	Three Hills	W.T. Peterson, Mun. Adm., Box 340, Trochu, Alta. TOM 2CO (442-3085)
Turner Valley†	1,207	Bow River	Highwood	Ms. S. Kuprowsky, Mun. Adm., Box 595, Turner Valley, Alta. TOL 2AO (933-7737)
Two Hills†	1,302	Vegreville	Vegreville	M.D. Pawliuk, Town Adm., Two Hills, Alta. TOB 4KO (657-3395)
Two Hills No. 21‡	3,636			G. Popowich, County Sec., Box 490, Two Hills, Alta. TOB 4KO (657-2929)
Valleyview†	2,066	Red Deer	Smoky River	W.D. Broadhurst, Mun. Adm., Box 270, Valleyview, Alta. TOH 3NO (524-3924)
Val Quentin SV	98		Stony Plain	Mrs. M. Hervieux, Val Quentin Mun. Adm., c/o 11441 125 St., Edmonton, Alta. T5M ON1 (454-3406)
Vauxhall†	1,075	Medicine Hat	Little Bow	Mrs. A.A. Seierstad, Town Sec., Box 312, Vauxhall, Alta. TOK 2KO (654-2488)
Vegreville†	4,809	Vegreville	Vegreville	G.J. Burnstad, Mun. Adm., Vegreville, Alta. TOB 4LO (632-2606)
Vermilion†	3,455	Vegreville	Vermilion-Viking	C.D. Magnusson, Town Sec. Mgr., Box 328, Vermilion, Alta. TOB 4MO (853-5358)
Vermilion River No. 24‡	6,967			J. Scott, County Sec., Kitscoty, Alta.TOB 2PO (846-2244)
Veteran	301	Crowfoot	Sedgewick-Coronation	Mrs. L. Schetzsle, Mun. Adm., Box 560, Veteran, Alta. TOC 2SO (575-3954)
Viking†	1,227	Vegreville	Vermilion-Viking	Ms. L. Hanson, Mun. Adm., Box 369, Viking, Alta. TOB 4NO (336-3466)
Vilna	372	Vegreville	St. Paul	Mrs. L. Sorochan, Village Sec., Vilna, Alta. TOA 3LO (636-3620)
Vulcan No. 2‡	3,873	Bow River	Little Bow	D.J. Stanford, County Adm., Box 180, Vulcan, Alta. TOL 2BO (485-2241)
Vulcan†	1,520	Bow River	Little Bow	H.K. Wallace, Mun. Adm., Vulcan, Alta. TOL 2BO (485-2417)
Wabamun	637			Mrs. M. Ivan, Village Sec., Box 152, Wabamun, Alta. TOE 2K0 (892-2699)
Wainwright No. 61*	3,839			H.A. McDonogh, Mun. Dist. Adm., Box 670, Wainwright, Alta. TOB 4PO (842-4454)
Wainwright†	4,115	Vegreville	Wainwright	E.N. Bouchard, Mun. Adm., Box 160, Wainwright, Alta. TOB 4PO (842-3381)
Wanham	233	Peace River	Spirit River-Fairview	Ms. J. Manzulenko, Village Sec., Wanham, Alta. TOH 3PO (694-3946)
Warburg	507	Wetaskiwin	Drayton Valley	Mrs. L. Bredin, Village Sec., Box 29, Warburg, Alta. TOC 2TO (848-2252)
Warner	468		Taber-Warner	Mrs. P. Hedberg, Village Sec., Box 88, Warner, Alta. TOK 2LO (642-3877)
Warner No. 5‡	3,574			J.K. Duncan, County Sec., Warner, Alta. TOK 2LO (642-3635)
Warspite	92	Vegreville	Redwater-Andrew	Mrs. J. Cymbaluk, Village Sec. Treas., Box 65, Warspite, Alta. TOA 3PO (383-3826)
Waskatenau	295	Vegreville	Redwater-Andrew	Mrs. P. Wirun, Mun. Adm., Box 99, Waskatenau, Alta. TOA 3PO (358-2208)
Wembley†	1,119	Peace River	Grande Prairie	Mrs. K. Steinke, Town Sec., Box 89, Wembley, Alta. TOH 3SO (766-2269)
West Cove SV	37		Stony Plain	K.D. Armstrong, West Cove Village Sec., c/o 9322 73 Ave., Edmonton, Alta. T6E 1A7 (433-4969)
Westlock No. 92*	6,720			W.J. Elliott, Mun. Dist. Sec., Box 219, Westlock, Alta. TOG 2LO (429-1135)

Cities in CAPITALS; Towns marked †; Counties marked ‡; Municipal Districts marked *; Balance are villages or summer villages (SV).
Area Code for Alberta is 403

MUNICIPALITY	POP.	FEDERAL ELECTORAL DISTRICT	PROVINCIAL ELECTORAL DISTRICT	CLERK OR SECRETARY WITH ADDRESS & PHONE
Westlock†	3,824	Pembina	Athabasca	S.J. Hewson, Town Sec., Box 2220, Westlock, Alta. TOG 2LO (349-4444)
WETASKIWIN	9,167	Wetaskiwin	Wetaskiwin-Leduc	Mrs. A.M. Hopfe, City Clerk, Box 6266, Wetaskiwin, Alta. T9A 1L2 (352-3344)
Wetaskiwin No. 10‡	8,475			J. McGowan, County Sec. Treas., 5109 51 St., Wetaskiwin, Alta. T9A 2A5 (352-3321)
Wheatland No. 16‡	4,944			J. Montgomery, County Sec., Box 90, Strathmore, Alta. TOJ 3HO (934-3321)
Whitecourt†	5,153	Yellowhead	Whitecourt	W.L. Winger, Mun. Adm., Box 509, Whitecourt, Alta. TOE 2LO (778-2273)
Whitesands SV	5			R.J. Krejci, White Sands Sec., c/o Box 460, Stettler, Alta. TOC 2L0 (742-4431)
Wildwood	445	Yellowhead	Whitecourt	Mrs. G. Engley, Village Sec., Box 216, Wildwood, Alta. TOE 2MO (325-3790)
Willingdon	354	Vegreville	Redwater-Andrew	G. Bidniak, Village Sec., Box 210, Willingdon, Alta. TOB 4RO (367-2337)
Willow Creek No. 26*	4,422			R.R. Hartfelder, Mun. Dist. Sec., Box 550, Claresholm, Alta. TOL OTO (625-3351)
Yellowstone SV	68		Stony Plain	Mrs. M. Hervieux, Yellowstone Village Sec., c/o 11441 125 St., Edmonton, Alta. T5M ON1 (454-3406)
Youngstown	308	Crowfoot	Hanna-Oyen	Mrs. I. Bowman, Mun. Adm., Youngstown, Alta. TOJ 3PO (779-3873)

Administrators, Alberta Improvement Districts

Dist. 1: L. Perschon, Room 307, Prov. Admin., 770 6 St. S.W., Medicine Hat, Alta. T1A 4J6 (529-3565)
Dists. 4, 6, 8, 9: L. Perschon (act.), 8th floor, Alberta Place, 1520 4 St. S.W., Calgary, Alta. T2R 1H5 (261-6124)
Dist. 7: G.R. Dompnier, Box 1588, Drumheller, Alta. TOJ OYO (823-5740)
Dist. 10: W. Willows, Box 550, Rocky Mountain House, Alta. TOM 1TO (845-3394)
Dists. 12, 14: R.H. Hanson, Box 1240, Edson, Alta. TOE OPO (723-3343)
Dist. 15: A.T. Robson, Box 1496, Whitecourt, Alta. TOE 2LO (778-4844)
Dist. 16: P. Adamson, Box 1079, Valleyview, Alta. TOH 3NO (524-3193)
Dist. 17: R. Campbell, Box 898, Westlock, Alta. TOG 2LO (349-3788)
Dist. 17: L. Kruger, Box 239, High Prairie, Alta. TOG 1EO (523-4561)
Dists. 18, 24 (Fort Chip): J.P. Leskiw, Box 23, Lac la Biche, Alta. T0A 2C0 (623-4474)
Dists. 19, 20: B. Irmen, Box 69, Spirit River, Alta. T0H 3G0 (864-3760)
Dist. 22: C.J. Curr, Bag 900, Peace River, Alta. T0H 2X0 (624-6121)
Dist. 23: G. Snelgrove, Box 66, High Level, Alta. T0H 1Z0 (926-3802)

BRITISH COLUMBIA

In British Columbia there are 28 regional district governments which provide local government to unorganized areas and co-ordinate activities involving the incorporated municipalities within their boundaries. These incorporated municipalities include villages, towns, cities, and districts, which municipalities are distinguished generally by size and minor differences in provincial regulation.

Municipal elections in all municipalities are held on the third Saturday of November, except Vancouver, where they are on the third Wednesday of November of every even-numbered year. Terms of office are two years. Until recently it has been the practice to elect half the Council annually but some municipalities have changed to electing all their officials at the same election every two years.

Legislation: The Municipal Act, excluding the City of Vancouver, which is regulated under the provisions of the Vancouver Charter.

Cities in CAPITALS; District municipality marked†; Towns marked ‡; Balance are villages.
Area Code for British Columbia is 604

MUNICIPALITY	POP.	FEDERAL ELECTORAL DISTRICT	PROVINCIAL ELECTORAL DISTRICT	CLERK WITH WITH ADDRESS & PHONE
Abbotsford†	9,507	Fraser Valley East	Central Fraser Valley	D.S. Donald, Dist. Mun. Clerk, 33914 Essendene Ave., Abbotsford, B.C. V2S 2H8 (853-1155)
Alert Bay	605	Comox-Powell River	North Island	J. Rowell, Village Clerk, Box 28, Alert Bay, B.C. VON 1AO (974-5213)
ARMSTRONG	2,260	Okanagan North	Shuswap-Revelstoke	R.W. Fitzsimmons, City Clerk, Box 40, Armstrong, B.C. VOE 1BO (546-3023)
Ashcroft	2,032	Cariboo-Chilcotin	Yale-Lillooet	R. Grivel, Village Clerk, Box 129, Ashcroft, B.C. VOK 1AO (453-9161)

Cities in CAPITALS; District municipality marked†; Towns marked ‡; Balance are villages.
Area Code for British Columbia is 604

MUNICIPALITY	POP.	FEDERAL ELECTORAL DISTRICT	PROVINCIAL ELECTORAL DISTRICT	CLERK WITH WITH ADDRESS & PHONE
Belcarra		Mission Port Moody	Coquitlam-Moody	G. Holland, Village Clerk, Box 27, R.R. 1, Belcarra, B.C. V3H 3C8 (939-4411)
Burnaby†	131,599	Burnaby; North Vancouver-Burnaby	Burnaby-Edmonds; Burnaby North; Burnaby-Willingdon	J. Hudson, Dist. Mun. Clerk, 4949 Canada Way, Burnaby, B.C. V5G 1M2 (294-7944)
Burns Lake	1,433	Prince George-Bulkley Valley	Omineca	J.G. Pierce, Village Clerk, Box 570, Burns Lake, B.C. VOJ 1EO (692-7224)
Cache Creek	1,050	Cariboo-Chilcotin	Yale-Lillooet	Mrs. J. Gibbons, Village Clerk, Box 7, Cache Creek, B.C. VOK 1HO (457-6237)
Campbell River†	12,072	Comox-Powell River	North Island	W.T. Halstead, Dist. Mun. Clerk, 301 St. Anns Rd., Campbell River, B.C. V9W 4C7 (287-2121)
CASTLEGAR	6,255	Kootenay West	Rossland-Trail	Ron Skillings, City Clerk, 460 Columbia Ave., Castlegar, B.C. V1N 1G7 (365-7227)
Central Saanich†	7,413	Esquimalt-Saanich	Saanich & the Islands	F.B. Durrand, Saanichton Dist. Mun. Clerk, Box 26, Saanichton, B.C. VOS 1MO (652-4444)
Chase	1,425	Kamloops-Shuswap	Shuswap-Revelstoke	Mrs. S. Timpany, Village Clerk, Box 440, Chase, B.C. VOE 1MO (679-8914)
Chetwynd	1,487	Prince George-Peace River	South Peace River	J.A. Teslyk, Village Clerk, Box 357, Chetwynd, B.C. VOC 1JO (788-2281)
Chilliwack†	28,421	Fraser Valley East	Chilliwack	Miss C. Waugh, Dist. Mun. Clerk, 8550 Young Rd. S., Chilliwack, B.C. V2P 4P1 (792-9311)
Clinton	808	Cariboo-Chilcotin	Cariboo	D.R. Long, Village Clerk, Box 309, Clinton, B.C. VOK 1KO (459-2514)
Coldstream†	4,995	Okanagan North	Okanagan North	D.G. Morris, Coldstream Dist. Mun. Clerk, 9901 Kalamalka Rd., Vernon, B.C. V1B 1L6 (545-5304)
Comox‡	5,359	Comox-Powell River	Comox	R.G. Kew, Town Clerk, 1809 Beaufort Ave., Comox, B.C. V9N 4B8 (339-2202)
Coquitlam†	62,000	Mission-Port Moody; New Westminster-Coquitlam	Coquitlam-Moody; Maillardville-Coquitlam	T. Klassen, Dist. Mun. Clerk, 1111 Brunette Ave., Coquitlam, B.C. V3K 1E9 (526-3611)
COURTENAY	7,733	Comox-Powell River	Comox	D. Ratcliffe, City Clerk, 750 Cliffe Ave., Courtenay, B.C. V9N 2J7 (334-4441)
CRANBROOK	13,510	Kootenay East-Revelstoke	Kootenay	J.C. Haves, City Clerk, 40 Tenth Ave. S., Cranbrook, B.C. V1C 2M8 (426-4211)
Creston‡	3,552	Kootenay East-Revelstoke	Nelson-Creston	B. Olszamowski, Town Clerk, 904 Vancouver St., Creston, B.C. VOB 1GO (428-2214)
Cumberland	1,697	Comox-Powell River	Comox	J.E. Wilson, Village Clerk, Box 340, Cumberland, B.C. VOR 1SO (336-2291)
DAWSON CREEK	10,528	Prince George-Peace River	South Peace River	H. Hansen, City Clerk, Box 150, Dawson Creek, B.C. V1G 4G4 (782-3351)
Delta†	64,492	Richmond-South Delta; Surrey-White Rock-North Delta	Delta	P.J. Gairns, Dist. Mun. Clerk, 4450 Clarence Taylor Cres., Delta, B.C. V4K 3E2 (946-4141)
DUNCAN	4,106	Cowichan-Malahat-The Islands	Cowichan-Malahat	P.E. Douville, City Clerk, Box 820, 200 Craig St., Duncan, B.C. V9L 3Y2 (746-6126)
Elkford	1,873	Kootenay East-Revelstoke	Kootenay	R. Miles, Village Clerk, Box 340, Elkford, B.C. VOB 1HO (865-2241)
ENDERBY	1,482	Okanagan North	Shuswap-Revelstoke	S. Woldringh, City Clerk, Box 68, Enderby, B.C. VOE 1VO (838-7230)
Esquimalt†	15,053	Esquimalt-Saanich	Esquimalt-Port Renfrew	G. Merz, Dist. Mun. Clerk, 1229 Esquimalt Rd., Victoria, B.C. V9A 3P1 (385-2461)
FERNIE	4,608	Kootenay East-Revelstoke	Kootenay	Ian Turner, City Clerk/Adm., Box 190, Fernie, B.C. VOB 1MO (423-6817)
Fort Nelson	2,916	Prince George-Peace River	North Peace River	C.J. Griffith, Village Clerk, Fort Nelson, B.C. VOC 1RO (774-2541)
Fort St. James	2,110	Prince George-Bulkley Valley	Omineca	G. Williams, Village Clerk, Box 640, Fort St. James, B.C. VOJ 1PO (996-8233)
FORT ST. JOHN	8,947	Prince George-Peace River	North Peace River	S.E. Kary, City Clerk, 10631 100th St., Fort St. John, B.C. V1J 3Z5 (785-4443)
Fraser Lake	1,430	Prince George-Bulkley Valley	Omineca	H. Ellens, Village Clerk, Box 430, Fraser Lake, B.C. VOJ 1SO (699-6257)

Cities in CAPITALS; District municipality marked†; Towns marked ‡; Balance are villages.
Area Code for British Columbia is 604

MUNICIPALITY	POP.	FEDERAL ELECTORAL DISTRICT	PROVINCIAL ELECTORAL DISTRICT	CLERK WITH WITH ADDRESS & PHONE
Fruitvale	1,481	Kootenay West	Rossland-Trail	R.W. Maddison, Village Clerk, Box 370, Fruitvale, B.C. VOG 1LO (367-9522)
Gibsons	2,074	Comox-Powell River	Mackenzie	J.W. Copland, Village Clerk, Box 340, Gibsons, B.C. VON 1VO (886-2274)
Golden‡	3,282	Kootenay East-Revelstoke	Columbia River	J.D. Ukryn, Town Clerk, Box 350, Golden, B.C. VOA 1HO (344-2271)
Gold River	1,942	Nanaimo-Alberni	North Island	N.H. Paulson, Village Clerk, Box 610, Gold River, B.C. VOP 1GO (283-2202)
GRAND FORKS	3,096	Okanagan-Similkameen	Boundary-Similkameen	W.M. Slater, City Clerk, Box 220, Grand Forks, B.C. V0H 1H0 (442-8266)
Granisle	1,210	Prince George-Bulkley Valley	Omineca	Ms. C. Otting, Village Clerk, Box 128, Granisle, B.C. VOV 1WO (697-2248)
GREENWOOD	931	Okanagan-Similkameen	Boundary-Similkameen	K. Hamanishi, City Clerk, Box 129, Greenwood, B.C. VOH 1JO (445-6644)
Harrison Hot Springs	572	Fraser Valley East	Chilliwack	D. Brown, Village Clerk, Box 28, Harrison Hot Springs, B.C. VOM 1KO (796-2171)
Hazelton	371	Skeena	Skeena	D. Aberley, Village Clerk, Box 40, Hazelton, B.C. VOJ 1YO (842-5991)
Hope‡	2,963	Fraser Valley East	Yale-Lillooet	R. DeSorcy, Town Clerk, Box 609, Hope, B.C. VOX 1LO (869-5671)
Houston†	2,673	Prince George-Bulkley Valley	Omineca	R. Haggstrom, Dist. Mun. Clerk, Box 370, Houston, B.C. VOJ 1ZO (845-2238)
Hudson Hope†	1,330	Prince George-Peace River	North Peace River	Mrs. F.E. Lavallee, Dist. Mun. Clerk, Box 330, Hudson Hope, B.C. VOC 1VO (783-9911)
Invermere	1,194	Kootenay East-Revelstoke	Columbia River	A.R. Miller, Village Clerk, Box 339, Invermere, B.C. VOA 1KO (342-9281)
KAMLOOPS	58,311	Kamloops-Shuswap	Kamloops	W.K. Thiessen, City Clerk, 7 Victoria St. W., Kamloops, B.C. V2C 1A2 (374-3311)
Kaslo	756	Kootenay West	Nelson-Creston	J. McAulay, Village Clerk, Box 576, Kaslo, B.C. VOG 1MO (353-2311)
KELOWNA	51,955	Okanagan North	Okanagan South	R. Beauchamp, City Clerk, 1435 Water St., Kelowna, B.C. V1Y 1J4 (763-6011)
Kent†	2,924	Fraser Valley East	Chilliwack	R.M. Conlin, Kent Dist. Mun. Clerk, Box 70, Agassiz, B.C. VOM 1AO (796-2235)
Keremeos	702	Okanagan-Similkameen	Boundary-Similkameen	D.H. DeGagne, Village Clerk, Box 160, Keremeos, B.C. VOX 1NO (499-2711)
KIMBERLEY	7,111	Kootenay East-Revelstoke	Columbia River	B. Bennett, City Clerk, 340 Spokane St., Kimberley, B.C. V1A 2E8 (427-5311)
Kitimat†	11,956	Skeena	Skeena	A. Jones, Dist. Mun. Clerk, 270 City Centre, Box 3000, Kitimat, B.C. V8C 1T2 (632-2161)
Ladysmith‡	4,004	Cowichan-Malahat-The Islands	Nanaimo	J.W. Runciman, Town Clerk, Box 220, Ladysmith, B.C. VOR 2EO (245-2218)
Lake Cowichan	2,369	Cowichan-Malahat-The Islands	Cowichan-Malahat	Mrs. P. Akerley, Village Clerk, Box 860, Lake Cowichan, B.C. VOR 2GO (749-6681)
LANGLEY	10,123	Fraser Valley West	Langley	R. Wilson, City Clerk, 5549 204 St., Langley, B.C. V3A 1Z4 (530-3131)
Langley†	36,659	Fraser Valley West	Langley	D.J. Doubleday, Dist. Mun. Clerk, 4914 221st St., Langley, B.C. V3A 3Z8 (534-3211)
Lillooet	2,218	Cariboo-Chilcotin	Yale-Lillooet	S. Stearn, Village Clerk, Box 610, Lillooet, B.C. VOK 1VO (256-4289)
Lions Bay	785	Capilano	West Vancouver-Howe Sound	Mrs. O.B. Pullen, Village Clerk, Box 141, Lions Bay, B.C. VON 2EO (921-9333)
Logan Lake	1,388	Kamloops-Shuswap	Yale-Lillooet	J. Noble, Village Clerk, Box 190, Logan Lake, B.C. VOK 1WO (523-6225)
Lumby	1,081	Okanagan North	Okanagan North	L.W. Anderson, Village Clerk, Box 430, Lumby, B.C. VOE 2GO (547-2171)
Lytton	468	Cariboo-Chilcotin	Yale-Lillooet	J. Drake, Village Clerk, Box 100, Lytton, B.C. VOK 1ZO (455-2355)
Mackenzie†	5,338	Prince George-Peace River	Prince George North	V. Ciccone, Dist. Mun. Clerk, Box 340, Mackenzie, B.C. VOJ 2CO (997-3221)
Maple Ridge†	29,462	Mission-Port Moody	Dewdney	F.B. Magee, Dist. Mun. Clerk, 11890 224th St., Maple Ridge, B.C. V2X 6A9 (463-7811)

Cities in CAPITALS; District municipality marked†; Towns marked ‡; Balance are villages.
Area Code for British Columbia is 604

MUNICIPALITY	POP.	FEDERAL ELECTORAL DISTRICT	PROVINCIAL ELECTORAL DISTRICT	CLERK WITH WITH ADDRESS & PHONE
Masset	1,563	Skeena	Prince Rupert	A. Brockley, Village Clerk, Masset, B.C. VOT 1MO (626-3995)
Matsqui†	31,178	Fraser Valley East; Fraser Valley West	Central Fraser Valley	Mrs. H. Cochran, Matsqui Dist. Mun. Clerk, 32383 S. Fraser Way, Clearbrook, B.C. V2T 1W7 (853-2281)
McBride	619	Prince George-Bulkley Valley	Prince George South	E.R. Leiske, Village Clerk, Box 519, Mc-Bride, B.C. VOJ 2EO (569-2292)
MERRITT	5,680	Okanagan-Similkameen	Yale-Lillooet	L. den Boer, City Clerk, Box 189, Merritt, B.C. VOR 2BO (378-4224)
Midway	589	Okanagan-Similkameen	Boundary-Similkameen	R.J. Hatton, Village Clerk, Box 160, Midway, B.C. VOH 1MO (449-2222)
Mission†	14,997	Mission-Port Moody	Dewdney	D.F. West, Dist. Mun. Clerk, Box 20, Mission, B.C. V2V 4L9 (826-6271)
Montrose	1,197	Kootenay West	Rossland-Trail	J.G. Pontius, Village Clerk, Box 103, Montrose, B.C. VOG 1PO (367-7234)
Nakusp	1,416	Kootenay West	Nelson-Creston	J.M. Gould, Village Clerk, Box 280, Nakusp, B.C. VOG 1RO (265-3689)
NANAIMO	40,336	Nanaimo-Alberni	Nanaimo	S. Gray, Acting City Clerk, 455 Wallace St., Nanaimo, B.C. V9R 5J6 (754-4251)
NELSON	9,235	Kootenay West	Nelson-Creston	D.P. Ormond, City Clerk, 502 Vernon St., Nelson, B.C. V1L 4E8 (352-5511)
New Denver	668	Kootenay West	Nelson-Creston	J.S. Hildebrand, Village Clerk, Box 40, New Denver, B.C. VOG 1SO (358-2316)
New Hazelton†	693	Skeena	Skeena	W. Sturgeon, Dist. Mun. Clerk, Box 340, New Hazelton, B.C. V0J 2J0 (842-6607)
NEW WESTMINSTER	38,393	New Westminster-Coquitlam	New Westminster	P.J. Larkin, City Clerk, 511 Royal Ave., New Westminster, B.C. V3L 1H9 (521-3711)
North Cowichan†	15,956	Cowichan-Malahat-The Islands	Cowichan-Malahat	Mrs. J. MacLeod, North Cowichan Dist. Mun. Clerk, Box 278, Duncan, B.C. V9L 3X4 (746-7101)
North Saanich†	4,697	Esquimalt-Saanich	Saanich & the Islands	E.F. Fairs, North Saanich Dist. Mun. Clerk, Box 2027, Sidney, B.C. V8L 3S3 (656-3918)
North Vancouver†	63,471	Capilano; North Vancouver-Burnaby	North Vancouver-Capilano; North Vancouver-Seymour	Mrs. H.W. Egleston, Dist. Mun. Clerk, 355 W. Queens Rd., North Vancouver, B.C. V7N 2K6 (987-7131)
NORTH VANCOUVER	31,934	Capilano; North Vancouver-Burnaby	North Vancouver-Capilano; North Vancouver-Seymour	R.W. Watson, City Clerk, 141 W. 14th St., North Vancouver, B.C. V7M 1H9 (985-7761)
Oak Bay†	17,658	Victoria	Oak Bay-Gordon Head	L. Pollock, Oak Bay Dist. Mun. Clerk, 2167 Oak Bay Ave., Victoria, B.C. V8R 1G2 (598-3311)
Oliver	1,641	Okanagan-Similkameen	Boundary-Similkameen	R. Martineau, Village Clerk, Box 638, Oliver, B.C. VOH 1TO (498-3405)
100 Mile House	1,584	Cariboo-Chilcotin	Cariboo	T. Wood, Village Clerk, Box 340, 100 Mile House, B.C. VOK 2EO (395-2434)
Osoyoos	2,100	Okanagan-Similkameen	Boundary-Similkameen	L. Miles, Village Clerk, Box 301, Osoyoos, B.C. VOH 1VO (495-6515)
Parksville‡	3,187	Nanaimo-Alberni	Comox	B.R. Kirk, Town Clerk, Box 1390, Parksville, B.C. VOR 2SO (248-6144)
Peachland†	2,286	Okanagan-Similkameen	Okanagan South	H.O. Lever, Dist. Mun. Clerk, Box 390, Peachland, B.C. VOH 1XO (767-2647)
Pemberton	254	Cariboo-Chilcotin	West Vancouver-Howe Sound	T.W. Wood, Village Clerk, Pemberton, B.C. VON 2LO (894-6246)
PENTICTON	21,344	Okanagan-Similkameen	Boundary-Similkameen	G.A. Paul, City Clerk, 171 Main St., Penticton, B.C. V2A 5A9 (492-3043)
Pitt Meadows†	4,689	Mission-Port Moody	Dewdney	J.J. Antalek, Dist. Mun. Clerk, 12007 Harris Rd., Pitt Meadows, B.C. VOM 1PO (465-5454)
PORT ALBERNI	19,585	Nanaimo-Alberni	Alberni	G.A. Wiley, City Clerk, 4850 Argyle St., Port Alberni, B.C. V9Y 1V8 (723-2146)
Port Alice	1,497	Comox-Powell River	North Island	Mrs. L. Rydberg, Village Clerk, Box 130,Port Alice, B.C. VON 2NO (284-3391)
Port Clements	409	Skeena	Prince Rupert	B. Barnewall, Village Clerk, Box 198, Port Clements, B.C. VOT 1RO (557-4295)
PORT COQUITLAM	23,926	Mission-Port Moody	Coquitlam-Moody	R.A. Freeman, City Clerk, 2272 McAllister Ave., Port Coquitlam, B.C. V3C 2A8 (941-5411)

Cities in CAPITALS; District municipality marked†; Towns marked ‡; Balance are villages.
Area Code for British Columbia is 604

MUNICIPALITY	POP.	FEDERAL ELECTORAL DISTRICT	PROVINCIAL ELECTORAL DISTRICT	CLERK WITH WITH ADDRESS & PHONE
Port Edward	1,189	Skeena	Prince Rupert	G. Weir, Village Clerk, Port Edward, B.C. VOV 1GO (628-3667)
Port Hardy†	3,653	Comox-Powell River	North Island	J. Gustafson, Dist. Mun. Clerk, Box 68, Port Hardy, B.C. VON 2PO (949-6665)
Port McNeill	1,480	Comox-Powell River	North Island	R.J. Smith, Village Clerk, Box 728, Port McNeill, B.C. VON 2RO (956-3308)
PORT MOODY	11,649	Mission-Port Moody	Coquitlam-Moody	J.I. Brovold, City Clerk, 2425 St. John's St., Port Moody, B.C. V3H 2B2 (936-7211)
Pouce Coupé	776	Prince George-Peace River	South Peace River	Ms. J. Wonnacott, Village Clerk, Box 190, Pouce Coupé, B.C. VOC 2CO (786-5794)
Powell River†	13,694	Comox-Powell River	Mackenzie	D. Back, Dist. Mun. Clerk, 6910 Duncan St., Powell River, B.C. V8A 1V4 (483-3231)
PRINCE GEORGE	59,929	Prince George-Bulkley Valley; Prince George-Peace River	Prince George North; Prince George South	W. Buchanan, City Clerk, 1100 Patricia Blvd., Prince George, B.C. V2L 3V9 (564-5151)
PRINCE RUPERT	14,754	Skeena	Prince Rupert	J.C. Ewart, City Clerk, 424 W. Third Ave., Prince Rupert, B.C. V8J 1L7 (627-1781)
Princeton‡	3,132	Okanagan-Similkameen	Yale-Lillooet	W.G. Sanderson, Town Clerk, Box 670, Princeton, B.C. VOX 1WO (295-6144)
Qualicum Beach	1,724	Nanaimo-Alberni	Comox	L. Klees, Village Clerk, Box 130, Qualicum Beach, B.C. VOR 2TO (752-6921)
QUESNEL	7,637	Cariboo-Chilcotin	Cariboo	City Clerk, 405 Barlow Ave., Quesnel, B.C. V2J 2C3 (992-2111)
REVELSTOKE	4,615	Kootenay East-Revelstoke	Shuswap-Revelstoke	G.H. Sawada, City Clerk, Box 170, Revelstoke, B.C. VOE 2SO (837-2161)
Richmond†	102,000	Richmond-South Delta	Richmond	G. Morris, Dist. Mun. Clerk, 6911 No. 3 Rd., Richmond, B.C. V6Y 2C1 (278-5511)
ROSSLAND	3,716	Kootenay West	Rossland-Trail	W.H. Vickers, City Clerk, Box 1179, Rossland, B.C. VOG 1YO (362-7396)
Saanich†	81,200	Esquimalt-Saanich; Victoria	Oak Bay-Gordon Head; Saanich & the Islands; Victoria	R.M. Sharp, Saanich Dist. Mun. Clerk, 770 Vernon Ave., Victoria, B.C. V8X 2W7 (386-2241)
Salmo	1,089	Kootenay West	Nelson-Creston	H.E. Russill, Village Clerk, Box 250, Salmo, B.C. VOG 1ZO (357-9433)
Salmon Arm†	9,391	Kamloops-Shuswap	Shuswap-Revelstoke	F.W. Spence, Dist. Mun. Clerk, Box 40, Salmon Arm, B.C. VOE 2TO (832-6021)
Sayward	465	Comox-Powell River	North Island	Mrs. J. Phye, Acting Village Clerk, Box 29, Sayward, B.C. VOP 1RO (282-3328)
Sechelt	822	Comox-Powell River	Mackenzie	J.M.A. Shanks, Village Clerk, Box 129, Sechelt, B.C. VON 3AO (885-2043)
Sidney‡	6,732	Esquimalt-Saanich	Saanich & the Islands	G. Logan, Town Clerk, 2440 Sidney Ave., Sidney, B.C. V8L 1Y7 (656-1184)
Silverton	253	Kootenay West	Nelson-Creston	Mrs. M.J. Welch, Village Clerk, Box 14, Silverton, B.C. VOG 2BO (358-2472)
Slocan	351	Kootenay West	Nelson-Creston	Mrs. V. Hamilton, Village Clerk, Box 50, Slocan, B.C. VOG 2CO (355-2277)
Smithers‡	3,783	Skeena	Skeena	R.A. Carter, Town Clerk/Adm., Box 879, Smithers, B.C. VOJ 2NO (847-3251)
Spallumcheen†	3,378	Okanagan North	Shuswap-Revelstoke	R.G. Graham, Spallumcheen Dist. Mun. Clerk, 3570 Bridge St., Armstrong, B.C. VOE 1BO (546-3013)
Sparwood†	4,050	Kootenay East-Revelstoke	Kootenay	Miss L. Montemurro, Dist. Mun. Clerk, Box 520, Sparwood, B.C. VOB 2GO (425-6271)
Squamish†	8,368	Cariboo-Chilcotin	West Vancouver-Howe Sound	C.C. Schattenkirk, Dist. Mun. Clerk/Adm., Box 310, Squamish, B.C. VON 3GO (892-5217)
Stewart†	1,382	Skeena	Atlin	J. Parnum, Dist. Mun. Clerk, Box 460, Stewart, B.C. VOT 1WO (636-2251)
Summerland†	6,724	Okanagan-Similkameen	Boundary-Similkameen	G. Redlich, Dist. Mun. Clerk, Box 159, Summerland, B.C. VOH 1ZO (494-6451)
Surrey†	116,497	Fraser Valley West; Surrey-White Rock-North Delta	Surrey	W. Vollrath, Dist. Mun. Clerk, 14245 56th Ave., Surrey, B.C. V3W 1J2 (591-4011)
Tahsis	2,050	Comox-Powell River	North Island	V. Allen, Village Clerk, Box 519, Tahsis, B.C. VOP 1XO (934-6344)

Cities in CAPITALS; District municipality marked†; Towns marked ‡; Balance are villages.
Area Code for British Columbia is 604

MUNICIPALITY	POP.	FEDERAL ELECTORAL DISTRICT	PROVINCIAL ELECTORAL DISTRICT	CLERK WITH WITH ADDRESS & PHONE
Taylor	649	Prince George-Peace River	North Peace River	Mrs. M. Mitchell, Village Clerk, Box 300, Taylor, B.C. VOC 2KO (789-3392)
Telkwa	691	Prince George-Bulkley Valley	Omineca	Mrs. P. Krenz, Village Clerk, Box 220, Telkwa, B.C. VOJ 2XO (846-5212)
Terrace†	10,251	Skeena	Skeena	R. Hallsor, Dist. Mun. Clerk, 3215 Eby St., Terrace, B.C. V8G 2X6 (635-6311)
Tofino	612	Nanaimo-Alberni	Alberni	Mrs. J. Hansen, Village Clerk, Box 9, Tofino, B.C. VOR 2ZO (725-3229)
TRAIL	9,976	Kootenay West	Rossland-Trail	A.R. Mitchell, City Clerk, 1394 Pine Ave., Trail, B.C. V1R 4E6 (364-1262)
Tumbler Ridge†	5	Prince George-Peace River	South Peace River	P.D. Walsh, Tumbler Ridge Dist. Mun. Clerk, c/o #132, 800 Hornby St., Vancouver, B.C. V6Z 2C5 (668-2439)
Ucluelet	1,180	Nanaimo-Alberni	Alberni	J.F.M. Henderson, Village Clerk, Box 9, Ucluelet, B.C. VOR 3AO (726-7744)
Valemount	878	Prince George-Bulkley Valley	Prince George South	Ms. M. Torgerson, Village Clerk, Box 168, Valemount, B.C. VOE 2ZO (566-4435)
VANCOUVER	410,188	Vancouver Centre; Vanc. E.; Vanc. Kingsway; Vanc. Quadra; Vanc. S.	Vancouver Centre; Vanc. E.; Vanc. Little Mountain; Vanc. Point Grey; Vanc. S.	R. Henry, City Clerk, 453 W. 12th Ave., Vancouver, B.C. V5Y 1V4 (873-7011)
Vanderhoof	1,990	Prince George-Bulkley Valley	Omineca	B. Ritchie, Village Clerk, Box 97, Vanderhoof, B.C. VOJ 3AO (567-4711)
VERNON	17,546	Okanagan North	Okanagan North	G.R. Moore, City Clerk, 3400 30th St., Vernon, B.C. V1T 5E6 (545-1361)
VICTORIA	62,551	Victoria	Victoria	C. Crisp, City Clerk, 1 Centennial Sq., Victoria, B.C. V8W 1P6 (385-5711)
Warfield	1,957	Kootenay West	Rossland-Trail	W.F. Kirk, Warfield Village Clerk, 555 Schofield Hwy., Trail, B.C. V1R 2G7 (368-8202)
West Vancouver†	37,144	Capilano	West Vancouver-Howe Sound	J.D. Allan, Dist. Mun. Clerk, 750 17th St., West Vancouver, B.C. V7V 3T3 (922-1211)
Whistler†	1,200	Cariboo-Chilcotin	West Vancouver-Howe Sound	Mrs. K. Robinson, Dist. Mun. Clerk, Box 35, Whistler, B.C. VON 1BO (932-5535)
WHITE ROCK	12,497	Surrey-White Rock-North Delta	Surrey	A.T. Russell, City Clerk/Adm., City Hall, Box 188, White Rock, B.C. V4B 5C6 (531-9111)
Williams Lake‡	6,199	Cariboo-Chilcotin	Cariboo	R.J. Mitchell, Town Clerk, 450 Mart St., Williams Lake, B.C. V2G 1N3 (392-2311)
Zeballos	337	Comox-Powell River	North Island	Ms. J. Kirk, Village Clerk-Treas., Box 29, Zeballos, B.C. VOP 2AO (ph. 229)

British Columbia Regional Districts with Principal Appointed Officers

Area Code for British Columbia is 604

Alberni-Clayoquot: A. Kilpatrick, 4586 Victoria Quay, Port Alberni, B.C. V9Y 8G3 (723-2401)
Bulkley-Nechako: C.R. Sinclair, Box 820, Burns Lake, B.C. VOJ 1EO (692-3195)
Capital: D.A. Young, Drawer 1000, 524 Yates St., Victoria, B.C. V8W 2S6 (388-4421)
Cariboo: G. Laubenstein, #301, 172 N. 2nd Ave., Williams Lake, B.C. V2G 1Z6 (392-3351)
Central Coast: Mrs. L. Sissons, Box 10, Hagensborg, B.C. VOT 1HO (982-2433)
Central Fraser Valley: H. Porter, Box 490, Aldergrove, B.C. VOX 1AO (856-7704)
Central Kootenay: B. Baldigara, 601 Vernon St., Nelson, B.C. V1L 4E9 (352-6665)
Central Okanagan: A.T. Harrison, 540 Groves Ave., Kelowna, B.C. V1Y 4Y7 (763-4918)
Columbia-Shuswap: E.L. Lalonde, Box 978, Salmon Arm, B.C. VOE 2TO (832-8194)
Comox-Strathcona: W. d'Easum, 4795 Headquarters Rd., Courtenay, B.C. V9N 5W3 (334-4452)
Cowichan Valley: R. Keir, 137 Evans St., Duncan, B.C. V9L 1P5 (746-4485)
Dewdney-Alouette: N.A. Cook, 32386 Fletcher Ave., Mission, B.C. V2V 5T1 (826-1291)
East Kootenay: W. McNamar, 19 24th Ave. S., Cranbrook, B.C. V1C 3H8 (489-2791)
Fraser-Cheam: J.D. Orr, 46208 Airport Rd., Chilliwack, B.C. V2P 1A5 (792-0061)
Fraser-Fort George: K. Ball, Suite 311, 1717 Third Ave., Prince George, B.C. V2L 3G7 (563-9225)
Greater Vancouver: G.W. Carlisle, 2294 W. Tenth Ave., Vancouver, B.C. V6K 2H9 (731-1155)
Kitimat-Stikine: J. Pousette, #9, 4644 Lazelle Terrace, Terrace, B.C. V8G 1S6 (635-7251)
Kootenay-Boundary: L.J. Robinson, 1159 Pine Ave., Trail, B.C. V1R 4E2 (368-9148)
Mount Waddington: D. Caldwell, Box 729, Port McNeill, B.C. VON 2RO (956-3301)
Nanaimo: W. Ilott, Box 40, Lantzville, B.C. VOR 2HO (390-4111)
North Okanagan: P. Mackiewich, 2903 35th Ave., Vernon, B.C. V1T 2S7 (545-5368)
Okanagan-Similkameen: J. Rheume, 1101 Main St., Penticton, B.C. V2A 5E6 (492-0237)

Peace River-Liard: M. Stewart, Box 810, Dawson Creek, B.C. V1G 4H7 (782-5891)
Powell River: G.A. Calvert, Sec., 5776 Marine Ave., Powell River, B.C. V8A 4K4 (483-3231)
Skeena-Queen Charlotte: D. Smith, #4, 214 Third Ave., Prince Rupert, B.C. V8J 1L1 (624-2002)
Squamish-Lillooet: I.R. Knowles, Box 219, Pemberton, B.C. VON 2LO (894-6371)
Sunshine Coast: L.D. Jardine, Box 800, Sechelt, B.C. VON 3AO (885-2261)
Thompson-Nicola: E. Shishido, 2079 Falcon Rd., Kamloops, B.C. V2C 4J2 (372-9336)

MANITOBA

All municipalities in Manitoba (except Winnipeg) are governed by the Manitoba Municipal Act. Winnipeg is governed by the City of Winnipeg Act.

In Manitoba there are no counties or regional governments. There are incorporated cities, towns, villages, and rural municipalities. Requirement for incorporation is by population and assessment. In order to incorporate into a village, a community requires 750 people and a tax base of $750,000. For a town the requirement is 1,500 people and $1,500,000 assessment. For a city it is 10,000 population.

All municipal elections are held every three years. The next election is in October, 1983.

Cities in CAPITALS; Towns marked †; Villages marked ‡; Balance are rural municipalities.
Area Code for Manitoba is 204

MUNICIPALITY	POP.	FEDERAL ELECTORAL DISTRICT	PROVINCIAL ELECTORAL DISTRICT	SECRETARY-TREASURER WITH ADDRESS & PHONE
Albert RM	727	Brandon-Souris	Arthur	Rick Branston, Sec., Box 70, Tilston, Man. ROM 2BO (686-2271)
Altona†	2,480	Lisgar	Rhineland	J. Sawatzky, Town Sec., Box 1630, Altona, Man. ROG OBO (324-6468)
Arborg‡	861	Selkirk-Interlake	Interlake	C.C. Fulsher, Village Sec., Box 159, Arborg, Man. ROC OAO (376-2647)
Archie RM	670	Portage-Marquette	Virden	A.W. Cole, Sec., McAuley, Man. ROM 1HO (722-2053)
Argyle RM	1,561	Lisgar	Turtle Mountain	Mrs. Anna Nordman, Sec., Box 40, Baldur, Man. ROK OBO (535-2176)
Arthur RM	862	Brandon-Souris	Arthur	R. Laing, Sec., Melita, Man. ROM 1LO (522-3263)
Beauséjour†	2,422	Provencher	Lac du Bonnet	H.P. Colmer, Town Sec., Box 1028, Beauséjour, Man. ROE OCO (268-2008)
Benito‡	507	Dauphin	Swan River	Deanna Taillefer, Village Sec., Benito, Man. ROL OCO (539-2634)
Bifrost RM	1,873	Selkirk-Interlake	Interlake	G. Thorsteinson, Sec., Arborg, Man. ROC OAO (376-2391)
Binscarth‡	430	Portage-Marquette	Russell	Mrs. Barbara Murray, Village Sec., Box 264, Binscarth, Man. ROJ OGO (532-2223)
Birtle RM	1,212	Portage-Marquette	Virden	F.R. Stevenson, Sec., Box 70, Birtle, Man. ROM OCO (842-3403)
Birtle†	821	Portage-Marquette	Virden	K.W. Wilson, Town Sec., Box 57, Birtle, Man. ROM OCO (842-3234)
Blanshard RM	924	Portage-Marquette	Minnedosa	L.E. Strachan, Sec., Box 179, Oak River, Man. ROK 1TO (566-2146)
Boissevain†	1,584	Brandon-Souris	Turtle Mountain	G.A. May, Town Sec., Box 490, Boissevain, Man. ROK OEO (534-2433)
Boulton RM	565	Dauphin	Russell	Raymond Bomback, Sec., Inglis, Man. ROJ OXO (564-2581)
Bowsman‡	483	Dauphin	Swan River	B.M. Shinn, Village Sec., Bowsman, Man. ROL OHO (238-4351)
BRANDON	34,901	Brandon-Souris	Brandon East; Brandon West	I.L. Thomson, City Clerk, City Hall, Box 960, Brandon, Man. R7A 6A2 (728-2278)
Brenda RM	976	Brandon-Souris	Arthur	B.G. Griffith, Sec., Waskada, Man. ROM 2EO (673-2401)
Brokenhead RM	2,898	Provencher	Lac du Bonnet	Wayne Omichinski, Sec., Box 490, Beau-séjour, Man. ROE OCO (268-1624)
Cameron RM	730	Brandon-Souris	Arthur	J.F. Archer, Sec., Box 399, Hartney, Man. ROM OXO (858-2590)
Carberry†	1,423	Portage-Marquette	Gladstone	E.J.W. McCallum, Town Sec., Box 130, Carberry, Man. ROK OHO (834-2195)
Carman†	2,272	Lisgar	Pembina	Bruce Lyle, Town Sec., Box 160, Carman, Man. ROG OJO (745-2443)
Cartier RM	2,896	Lisgar	Lakeside	A.C. Carriere, Sec., Box 117, Elie, Man. ROH OHO (353-2214)
Cartwright‡	361	Lisgar	Turtle Mountain	Mrs. B.M. Thompson, Village Sec., Cart-wright, Man. ROK OLO (529-2454)
Clanwilliam RM	577	Portage-Marquette	Minnedosa	Mrs. Janet Nylen, Sec., Box 40, Erickson, Man. ROJ OPO (636-2431)

Cities in CAPITALS; Towns marked †; Villages marked ‡; Balance are rural municipalities.
Area Code for Manitoba is 204

MUNICIPALITY	POP.	FEDERAL ELECTORAL DISTRICT	PROVINCIAL ELECTORAL DISTRICT	SECRETARY-TREASURER WITH ADDRESS & PHONE
Coldwell RM	1,582	Selkirk-Interlake	Lakeside	Thor Hjartarson, Sec., Box 90, Lundar, Man. ROC 1YO (762-5421)
Cornwallis RM	3,760	Brandon-Souris	Arthur; Minnedosa	Mrs. C.E. McDougall, Sec., Box 338, Brandon, Man. R7A 5Z2 (727-2436)
Crystal City‡	513	Lisgar	Pembina	C.S. Fallis, Village Sec., Box 310, Crystal City, Man. ROK ONO (873-2591)
Daly RM	1,820	Portage-Marquette	Minnedosa	J.K. Archibald, Sec., Box 538, Rivers, Man. ROK 1XO (328-7410)
Dauphin RM	2,931	Dauphin	Dauphin	W.C. Wallwin, Sec., Box 539, Dauphin, Man. R7N 2V3 (638-4531)
Dauphin†	9,265	Dauphin	Dauphin	E.C. Day, Town Sec., 21 2nd Ave. N.W., Dauphin, Man. R7N 1H1 (638-3938)
Deloraine†	1,019	Brandon-Souris	Arthur	R.H. Amey, Town Sec., Box 510, Deloraine, Man. ROM OMO (747-2655)
De Salaberry RM	2,670	Provencher	Emerson	T.F. Tetreault, Sec., Box 40, St. Pierre, Man. ROA 1VO (433-7406)
Dufferin RM	2,592	Lisgar	Pembina; Morris	G.C. Rothwell, Sec., Carman, Man. ROG OJO (745-2301)
Dunnottar‡	219	Selkirk-Interlake	Gimli	Mrs. Mary Wayne, Dunnottar Village Sec., #210, 1839 Main St., Winnipeg, Man. R2V 2A4 (334-2175)
East St. Paul RM	3,369	Provencher	Springfield	Maynard Olson, Sec., 3021 Birds Hill Rd., Birds Hill, Man. ROE OHO (668-8112)
Edward RM	973	Brandon-Souris	Arthur	Robert Trott, Sec., Box 100, Pierson, Man. ROM 1SO (634-2231)
Elkhorn‡	527	Brandon-Souris	Virden	D.S. Whiteford, Village Sec., Box 280, Elkhorn, Man. ROM ONO (845-2161)
Ellice RM	537	Portage-Marquette	Virden	Claude Chartier, Sec., St. Lazare, Man. ROM 1YO (683-2241)
Elton RM	1,505	Portage-Marquette	Minnedosa	Mrs. J.I. Taylor, Sec., Forrest, Man. ROK OWO (728-7834)
Emerson†	756	Provencher	Emerson	Mrs. M.M. Sigurdson, Town Sec., Box 340, Emerson, Man. ROA OLO (373-2002)
Erickson‡	558	Portage-Marquette	Minnedosa	Mrs. Janet Nylen, Village Sec., Box 40, Erickson, Man. ROJ OPO (636-2431)
Eriksdale RM	1,012	Selkirk-Interlake	Interlake	H.K. Rutherford, Sec., Eriksdale, Man. ROC OWO (739-2666)
Ethelbert RM	882	Dauphin	Dauphin	D.J. Dohan, Sec., Ethelbert, Man. ROL OTO (742-3212)
Ethelbert‡	493	Dauphin	Dauphin	Mrs. E. Kuzyk, Village Sec., Box 115, Ethelbert, Man. ROL OTO (742-3301)
FLIN FLON	8,152 (Man.)	Churchill	Flin Flon	E.K. Watson, City Clerk, Box 100, Flin Flon, Man. R8A 1M6 (687-7511)
Franklin RM	2,168	Provencher	Emerson	A. Hudyma, Sec., Dominion City, Man. ROA OHO (427-2557)
Garson‡	290	Provencher	Lac du Bonnet	Mrs. G.V. Leiman, Village Sec., Box 24, Garson, Man. ROE ORO (268-2382)
Gilbert Plains RM	1,491	Dauphin	Russell	F. Drebnisky, Sec., Gilbert Plains, Man. ROL OXO (548-2326)
Gilbert Plains‡	847	Dauphin	Russell	E.J. Mouck, Village Sec., Box 39, Gilbert Plains, Man. ROL OXO (548-2761)
Gimli RM	2,290	Selkirk-Interlake	Gimli	E. Berezowski, Sec., Box 1246, Gimli, Man. ROC 1BO (642-5065)
Gimli†	1,659	Selkirk-Interlake	Gimli	Mrs. D. Lloyd, Town Sec., Box 88, Gimli, Man. ROC 1BO (642-5210)
Gladstone†	976	Portage-Marquette	Gladstone	Mrs. Helen Tefs, Town Sec., Box 25, Gladstone, Man. ROJ OTO (385-2332)
Glenboro‡	720	Lisgar	Gladstone	D.E. Foster, Village Sec., Box 190, Glenboro, Man. ROK OXO (827-2083)
Glenella RM	788	Dauphin	Ste. Rose	Mrs. Shirley Heintz, Sec., Glenella, Man. ROJ OVO (352-4281)
Glenwood RM	839	Brandon-Souris	Arthur	L.E. Dane, Sec., Box 518, Souris, Man. ROK 2CO (483-2169)
Grandview RM	1,356	Dauphin	Russell	D.L. McIntyre, Sec., Grandview, Man. ROL OYO (546-2564)
Grandview†	1,013	Dauphin	Russell	J.W. Wilson, Town Sec., Box 219, Grandview, Man. ROL OYO (546-2792)
Gretna‡	510	Lisgar	Rhineland	Ms. Mary Harder, Village Sec., Box 159, Gretna, Man. ROG OVO (327-5578)

Cities in CAPITALS; Towns marked †; Villages marked ‡; Balance are rural municipalities.
Area Code for Manitoba is 204

MUNICIPALITY	POP.	FEDERAL ELECTORAL DISTRICT	PROVINCIAL ELECTORAL DISTRICT	SECRETARY-TREASURER WITH ADDRESS & PHONE
Grey RM	2,409	Lisgar	Morris	R.D. Hayward, Sec., Elm Creek, Man. ROG ONO (436-2014)
Hamiota RM	809	Portage-Marquette	Virden	L.L. Brown, Sec., Box 100, Hamiota, Man. ROM OTO (764-2779)
Hamiota‡	765	Portage-Marquette	Virden	L.L. Brown, Village Sec., Box 100, Hamiota, Man. ROM OTO (764-2779)
Hanover RM	6,931	Provencher	Emerson; La Verendrye	C. Teetaert, Sec., Box 1720, Steinbach, Man. ROA 2AO (326-2331)
Harrison RM	1,202	Portage-Marquette	Minnedosa	Mrs. W. Franks, Sec., Box 220, Newdale, Man. ROJ 1JO (849-2107)
Hartney†	484	Brandon-Souris	Arthur	A. Hicks, Town Sec., Box 339, Hartney, Man. ROM OXO (858-2429)
Hillsburg RM	753	Dauphin	Russell	Charles Filewich, Sec., Box 998, Roblin, Man. ROL 1PO (937-2155)
Killarney†	2,371	Brandon-Souris	Turtle Mountain	G.D. Macaulay, Town Sec., Killarney, Man. ROK 1GO (523-7247)
La Broquerie RM	1,523	Provencher	Emerson; La Verendrye	Laurent Tetrault, Sec., Box 130, La Broquerie, Man. ROA OWO (424-5251)
Lac du Bonnet RM	2,365	Provencher	Lac du Bonnet	Ms. B. Neisteter, Sec., Box 100, Lac du Bonnet, Man. ROE 1AO (345-2619)
Lac du Bonnet‡	971	Provencher	Lac du Bonnet	W.D. Besel, Village Sec., Box 339, Lac du Bonnet, Man. ROE 1AO (345-2579)
Lakeview RM	598	Dauphin	Gladstone	Mrs. V. Wild, Sec., Box 100, Langruth, Man. ROH ONO (445-2243)
Langford RM	740	Lisgar	Ste. Rose	Mrs. D. Brown, Sec., Box 280, Neepawa, Man. ROJ 1HO (476-5775)
Lansdowne RM	1,150	Dauphin	Ste. Rose	W.W. Boughton, Sec., Box 141, Arden, Man. ROJ OBO (368-2202)
Lawrence RM	958	Dauphin	Ste. Rose	D. MacLure, Sec., Rorketon, Man. ROL 1RO (732-2333)
Leaf Rapids†	2,067	Churchill	Churchill	M.P. Riddell, Town Mgr., Box 220, Leaf Rapids, Man. ROB 1WO (473-2436)
Lorne RM	2,596	Lisgar	Turtle Mountain	Mrs. M. Lussier, Sec., Somerset, Man. ROG 2LO (744-2133)
Louise RM	1,343	Lisgar	Pembina	C.S. Fallis, Sec., Crystal City, Man. ROK ONO (873-2591)
Macdonald RM	3,247	Lisgar	Morris	L.F. Erb, Sec., Box 100, Sanford, Man. ROG 2JO (736-2255)
MacGregor‡	789	Portage-Marquette	Gladstone	R.C. Locke, Village Sec., Box 190, MacGregor, Man. ROH ORO (685-2211)
Manitou‡	883	Lisgar	Pembina	W.E. Sampson, Village Sec., Box 280, Manitou, Man. ROG 1GO (242-2515)
McCreary RM	832	Dauphin	Ste. Rose	Mrs. Nellie McLeod, Sec., McCreary, Man. ROJ 1BO (835-2309)
McCreary‡	614	Dauphin	Ste. Rose	Ms. Vinetta Hannaburg, Village Sec., Box 267, McCreary, Man. ROJ 1BO (835-2341)
Melita†	1,169	Brandon-Souris	Arthur	C.E. Hicks, Town Sec., Box 364, Melita, Man. ROM 1LO (522-3413)
Miniota RM	1,181	Portage-Marquette	Virden	Mrs. S.D. Richardson, Sec., Miniota, Man. ROM 1MO (567-3683)
Minitonas RM	1,513	Dauphin	Swan River	Norman Bruce, Sec., Box 9, Minitonas, Man. ROL 1GO (525-4461)
Minitonas‡	605	Dauphin	Swan River	Norman Bruce, Village Sec., Box 9, Minitonas, Man. ROL 1GO (525-4461)
Minnedosa†	2,718	Portage-Marquette	Minnedosa	J.K. Wishart, Town Sec./T., Box 426, Minnedosa, Man. ROJ 1EO (867-2727)
Minto RM	732	Portage-Marquette	Minnedosa	Miss A.A. Gowing, Sec., Minnedosa, Man. ROJ 1EO (867-3865)
Montcalm RM	1,794	Lisgar	Rhineland	Yves Sabourin, Sec., Box 300, Letellier, Man. ROG 1CO (737-2271)
Morden†	3,942	Lisgar	Pembina	Abe Bergman, Town Sec., Box 2440, Morden, Man. ROG 1JO (822-4434)
Morris RM	3,148	Lisgar	Morris; Emerson	Mrs. Alice Loving, Sec., Box 518, Morris, Man. ROG 1KO (746-2642)
Morris†	1,572	Lisgar	Morris	Mrs. M.L. Devlin, Town Sec., Box 28, Morris, Man. ROG 1KO (746-2531)
Morton RM	1,177	Brandon-Souris	Turtle Mountain	G.A. May, Sec., Box 490, Boissevain, Man. ROK OEO (534-2433)

Cities in CAPITALS; Towns marked †; Villages marked ‡; Balance are rural municipalities.
Area Code for Manitoba is 204

MUNICIPALITY	POP.	FEDERAL ELECTORAL DISTRICT	PROVINCIAL ELECTORAL DISTRICT	SECRETARY-TREASURER WITH ADDRESS & PHONE
Mossey River RM	1,202	Dauphin	Dauphin	J.E. Pascal, Sec., Box 80, Fork River, Man. ROL OVO (657-2331)
Napinka‡	151	Brandon-Souris	Arthur	C.M. Richardson, Village Sec., Napinka, Man. ROM 1NO (665-2378)
Neepawa†	3,508	Portage-Marquette	Ste. Rose	D. Lyle, Town Sec., Box 339, Neepawa, Man. ROJ 1HO (476-2317)
Niverville‡	1,251	Provencher	Emerson	E. Enns, Village Sec., Box 267, Niverville, Man. ROA 1EO (388-4600)
North Cypress RM	2,049	Portage-Marquette	Gladstone	E.J.W. McCallum, Sec., Box 130, Carberry, Man. ROK OHO (834-2195)
North Norfolk RM	2,974	Portage-Marquette	Gladstone	R.C. Locke, Sec., Box 190, MacGregor, Man. ROH ORO (685-2211)
Notre Dame de Lourdes‡	651	Lisgar	Turtle Mountain	R. Fouasse, Village Sec., Notre Dame de Lourdes, Man. ROG 1MO (248-2348)
Oak Lake†	367	Brandon-Souris	Arthur	Donna Garland, Town Sec., Box 100, Oak Lake, Man. ROM 1PO (855-2423)
Oakland RM	958	Brandon-Souris	Arthur	Doug Boake, Sec., Nesbitt, Man. ROK 1PO (824-2374)
Ochre River RM	1,085	Dauphin	Dauphin	Mrs. I. Mayne, Sec., Box 40, Ochre River, Man. ROL 1KO (733-2423)
Odanah RM	612	Portage-Marquette	Minnedosa	Mrs A.A. Gowing, Sec., Minnedosa, Man. ROJ 1EO (867-3282)
Pembina RM	2,213	Lisgar	Pembina	R.J. Moore, Sec., Box 189, Manitou, Man. ROG 1GO (242-2838)
Pilot Mound‡	730	Lisgar	Pembina	George Fraser, Village Sec., Box 39, Pilot Mound, Man. ROG 1PO (825-2587)
Pipestone RM	2,138	Brandon-Souris	Arthur	Wm. Busby, Sec., Reston, Man. ROM 1XO (877-3327)
Plum Coulee‡	477	Lisgar	Rhineland	R.W. Wiebe, Village Sec., Box 36, Plum Coulee, Man. ROG 1RO (829-3419)
Portage la Prairie RM	7,177	Portage-Marquette	Portage la Prairie; Morris	W.M. McMillan, Sec., 35 Tupper St. S., Portage la Prairie, Man. R1N 1W7 (857-3821)
PORTAGE LA PRAIRIE	12,571	Portage-Marquette	Portage la Prairie	Wayne Woodman, City Clerk, Box 490, Portage la Prairie, Man. R1N 3C1 (857-9781)
Powerview‡	668	Provencher	Lac du Bonnet	L.A. Holm, Village Sec., Box 235, Powerview, Man. ROE 1PO (367-8483)
Rapid City†	412	Portage-Marquette	Minnedosa	Mrs. R.B. Grist, Town Sec., Box 146, Rapid City, Man. ROK 1WO (826-2679)
Rhineland RM	4,550	Lisgar	Rhineland	J. Bergen, Clerk, Box 270, Altona, Man. ROG OBO (324-5357)
Richot RM	3,768	Provencher	Emerson	J. Brodeur, Sec., Box 70, St. Adolphe, Man. ROA 1SO (883-2293)
Rivers†	1,185	Portage-Marquette	Minnedosa	D.L. Harris, Town Sec., Box 520, Rivers, Man ROK 1XO (328-5250)
Riverside RM	1,081	Brandon-Souris	Turtle Mountain	W.A. Bradford, Sec., Dunrea, Man. ROK OSO (776-2113)
Riverton‡	685	Selkirk-Interlake	Interlake	T. Bjarnason, Village Sec., Box 250, Riverton, Man. ROC 2RO (378-2281)
Roblin RM	1,030	Lisgar	Turtle Mountain	H.A. Lamb, Sec., Box 9, Cartwright, Man. ROK OLO (529-2363)
Roblin†	1,971	Dauphin	Russell	Miss K.P. Black, Town Sec., Box 730, Roblin, Man. ROL 1PO (937-2552)
Rockwood RM	5,962	Selkirk-Interlake	Gimli; Lakeside	Albert Dellebuur, Sec., Box 902, Stonewall, Man. ROC 2ZO (467-2272)
Roland RM	1,032	Lisgar	Pembina	Mrs. Joan Harrison, Sec., Box 119, Roland, Man. ROG 1TO (343-2061)
Rosedale RM	2,050	Portage-Marquette	Ste. Rose	Harold McConnell, Sec., Box 100, Neepawa, Man. ROJ 1HO (476-5414)
Rossburn RM	890	Portage-Marquette	Russell	Ernie Antonow, Sec., Box 100, Rossburn, Man. ROJ 1VO (859-2779)
Rossburn‡	652	Portage-Marquette	Russell	Len Mackedenski, Village Sec., Box 70, Rossburn, Man. ROJ 1VO (859-2762)
Rosser RM	1,269	Selkirk-Interlake	Lakeside	Mrs. E.B. Lindsay, Sec., Rosser, Man. ROH 1EO (467-5711)
Russell RM	710	Portage-Marquette	Russell	Mrs. Margaret Cooper, Sec., Box 220, Russell, Man. ROJ 1WO (773-2294)

Cities in CAPITALS; Towns marked †; Villages marked ‡; Balance are rural municipalities.
Area Code for Manitoba is 204

MUNICIPALITY	POP.	FEDERAL ELECTORAL DISTRICT	PROVINCIAL ELECTORAL DISTRICT	SECRETARY-TREASURER WITH ADDRESS & PHONE
Russell†	1,524	Portage-Marquette	Russell	G.W. Brad, Town Sec., Box 10, Russell, Man. ROJ 1WO (773-2253)
St. Andrews RM	6,831	Selkirk-Interlake	Selkirk; Gimli	Leslie Price, Sec., Clandeboye, Man. ROC OPO (738-2264)
Ste. Anne‡	1,350	Provencher	La Verendrye	J.G. Levesque, Village Sec., Box 220, Ste. Anne, Man. ROA 1RO (422-5293)
Ste. Anne RM	2,876	Provencher	La Verendrye	Jonas Goossen, Sec., Ste. Anne, Man. ROA 1RO (422-5929)
St. Claude‡	612	Lisgar	Morris	Mrs. G. Magne, Village Sec., St. Claude, Man. ROG 1ZO (379-2382)
St. Clements RM	5,724	Selkirk-Interlake	Gimli	W. Sokolowski, Sec., R.R. 1, East Selkirk, Man. ROE OMO (482-3387)
St. Francois Xavier RM	692	Selkirk-Interlake	Lakeside	John Schellenberg, Sec., Box 100, St-François-Xavier, Man. R0H 1J0 (864-2092)
St. Laurent RM	1,272	Selkirk-Interlake	Lakeside	Mrs. W.V. Johnson, Sec., St. Laurent, Man. ROC 2SO (646-2259)
St. Lazare‡	476	Portage-Marquette	Virden	Claude Chartier, Village Sec., St. Lazare, Man. ROM 1YO (683-2241)
St. Pierre-Jolys‡	906	Provencher	Emerson	Mrs. C. Bourgeois, Village Sec., St. Pierre, Man. ROA 1VO (433-7832)
Ste. Rose RM	1,117	Dauphin	Ste. Rose	Mrs. J. Rosenkranz, Sec., Box 30, Ste. Rose du Lac, Man. ROL 1SO (447-2633)
Ste. Rose du Lac‡	1,038	Dauphin	Ste. Rose	Ms. M. Coles, Village Sec., Box 445, Ste. Rose du Lac, Man. ROL 1SO (447-2229)
Saskatchewan RM	867	Portage-Marquette	Minnedosa	Thelma Anderson, Sec., Rapid City, Man. ROK 1WO (826-2515)
Selkirk†	9,862	Selkirk-Interlake	Selkirk	K.R. Conrad, Town Sec., 200 Eaton Ave., Selkirk, Man. R1A OW6 (482-4321)
Shellmouth RM	958	Dauphin	Russell	C.M. Nicholson, Sec., Box 62, Inglis, Man. ROJ OXO (564-2589)
Shell River RM	1,274	Dauphin	Russell	Charles Filewich, Sec., Box 998, Roblin, Man. ROL 1PO (937-4430)
Shoal Lake‡	865	Portage-Marquette	Virden	Walter Swereda, Village Sec., Box 342, Shoal Lake, Man. ROJ 1ZO (759-2270)
Shoal Lake RM	945	Portage-Marquette	Virden	Mrs. T. Chegwin, Sec., Box 278, Shoal Lake, Man. ROJ 1ZO (759-2565)
Sifton RM	917	Brandon-Souris	Arthur	Donna Garland, Sec., Box 100, Oak Lake, Man. ROM 1PO (855-2423)
Siglunes RM	1,626	Selkirk-Interlake	Interlake	Mel Bullerwell, Sec., Box 8, Ashern, Man. ROC OEO (768-2641)
Silver Creek RM	808	Portage-Marquette	Russell	A. Chaytor, Sec., Angusville, Man. ROJ OAO (773-2449)
Snow Lake†	1,645	Churchill	Flin Flon	John Janeson, Town Sec., Box 40, Snow Lake, Man. ROB 1MO (358-2551)
Somerset‡	625	Lisgar	Turtle Mountain	W. Raine, Village Sec., Somerset, Man. ROG 2LO (744-2171)
Souris†	1,712	Brandon-Souris	Arthur	L.E. Dane, Town Sec., Box 518, Souris, Man. ROK 2CO (483-2169)
South Cypress RM	854	Portage-Marquette	Gladstone	E. Plaetinck, Sec., Box 219, Glenboro, Man. ROK OXO (827-2252)
South Norfolk RM	1,414	Lisgar	Gladstone	G. Rodger, Sec., Box 30, Treherne, Man. ROG 2VO (723-2044)
Springfield RM	6,944	Provencher	Springfield	Eric Towler, Sec., Oakbank, Man. ROE 1JO (477-1736)
Stanley RM	4,098	Lisgar	Pembina	M.W. Foussard, Sec., Box 1327, Morden, Man. ROG 1JO (822-6251)
Steinbach†	5,979	Provencher	La Verendrye	Jack Kehler, Town Sec., Box 1090, Steinbach, Man. ROA 2AO (326-9877)
Stonewall†	1,826	Selkirk-Interlake	Lakeside	Jerome Mauws, Town Sec., Box 250, Stonewall, Man. ROC 2ZO (467-5597)
Strathclair RM	1,380	Portage-Marquette	Virden	Mrs. J. McKerchar, Sec., Box 160, Strathclair, Man. ROJ 2CO (365-2196)
Strathcona RM	1,125	Lisgar	Turtle Mountain	Garry Hanna, Sec., Box 100, Belmont, Man. ROK OCO (537-2241)
Swan River†	3,742	Dauphin	Swan River	Harry Showdra, Town Sec., Swan River, Man. ROL 1ZO (734-4586)
Swan River RM	3,443	Dauphin	Swan River	Miss W.E. Pico, Sec., Box 610, Swan River, Man. ROL 1ZO (734-3344)

Cities in CAPITALS; Towns marked †; Villages marked ‡; Balance are rural municipalities.
Area Code for Manitoba is 204

MUNICIPALITY	POP.	FEDERAL ELECTORAL DISTRICT	PROVINCIAL ELECTORAL DISTRICT	SECRETARY-TREASURER WITH ADDRESS & PHONE
Taché RM	4,436	Provencher	Springfield	E.J. Laurin, Sec., Box 100, Lorette, Man. ROA OYO (878-3321)
Teulon‡	873	Selkirk-Interlake	Gimli	Don Rybachuk, Village Sec., Box 69, Teulon, Man. ROC 3BO (886-2314)
The Pas†	6,602	Churchill	The Pas	A. Moule, Town Adm., Box 870, The Pas, Man. R9A 1K8 (623-6481)
Thompson RM	1,390	Lisgar	Pembina	J.G. Murray, Sec., Box 190, Miami, Man. ROG 1HO (435-2114)
THOMPSON	17,291	Churchill	Thompson	City Clerk, Box 2260, Thompson, Man. R8N 1S6 (778-7033)
Treherne‡	706	Lisgar	Gladstone	G. Rodger, Village Clerk, Box 30, Treherne, Man. ROG 2VO (723-2044)
Turtle Mountain RM	1,458	Brandon-Souris	Turtle Mountain	G.D. Macaulay, Sec., Box 160, Killarney, Man. ROK 1GO (523-7058)
Victoria RM	1,467	Lisgar	Gladstone	W. Rutherford, Sec., Holland, Man. ROG OXO (526-2423)
Victoria Beach RM	195	Selkirk-Interlake	Lac du Bonnet	Mrs. Edith Davidson, Mun. Sec., #304, 283 Portage Ave., Winnipeg, Man. R3B 2B5 (943-1070)
Virden†	2,865	Brandon-Souris	Virden	D.A. Reid, Town Sec., Box 310, Virden, Man. ROM 2CO (748-2440)
Wallace RM	2,052	Brandon-Souris	Virden	D.A. Reid, Sec., Box 310, Virden, Man. ROM 2CO (748-2440)
Waskada‡	257	Brandon-Souris	Arthur	B.G. Griffith, Village Sec., Waskada, Man. ROM 2EO (673-2401)
Wawanesa‡	1,487	Brandon-Souris	Arthur	Mrs. B. Roney, Village Sec., Box 278, Wawanesa, Man. ROK 2GO (824-2244)
Westbourne RM	2,170	Portage-Marquette	Gladstone	June Stewart, Sec., Box 150, Gladstone, Man. ROJ OTO (385-2388)
West St. Paul RM	2,570	Selkirk-Interlake	Selkirk	M.E. Didyk, Sec., 3550 Main St., R.R. 1, Winnipeg, Man. R3C 2E4 (338-0306)
Whitehead RM	1,291	Brandon-Souris	Arthur; Minnedosa	W.J. Dane, Sec., Box 107, Alexander, Man. ROK OAO (752-2261)
Whitemouth RM	1,903	Provencher	Springfield	Mrs. Edna Kozyra, Sec., Whitemouth, Man. ROE 2GO (348-2221)
Whitewater RM	885	Brandon-Souris	Turtle Mountain	J.D. Stilwell, Sec., Box 53, Minto, Man. ROK 1MO (776-2172)
Winchester RM	946	Brandon-Souris	Arthur	I.A. Morton, Sec., Deloraine, Man. ROM OMO (747-2572)
Winkler†	4,167	Lisgar	Rhineland	H. Fast, Town Sec., Box 1055, Winkler, Man. ROG 2XO (325-8211)
WINNIPEG	610,000	Winnipeg-Assiniboine; Winnipeg-Birds Hill; Winnipeg-Fort Garry; Winnipeg North; Winnipeg North Centre; Winnipeg-St. James	Assiniboia; Burrows; Charleswood; Concordia; Ellice; Elmwood; Fort Garry; Fort Rouge; Inkster; Kildonan; Kirkfield Park; Logan; Niakwa; Osborne; Radisson; Riel; River East; River Heights; Rossmere; St. Boniface; St. James; St. Johns; St. Norbert; St. Vital; Seven Oaks; Sturgeon Creek; Transcona; Tuxedo; Wolseley	R.J. Fergusson, City Clerk, Civic Centre, Winnipeg, Man. R3B 1B9 (946-0196)
Winnipeg Beach†	582	Selkirk-Interlake	Gimli	Ernest Buhler, Town Sec., Box 160, Winnipeg Beach, Man. ROC 3GO (389-2698)
Winnipegosis‡	893	Dauphin	Dauphin	E. Fosty, Village Sec., Box 370, Winnipegosis, Man. ROL 2GO (656-4791)
Woodlands RM	2,558	Selkirk-Interlake	Lakeside	Mrs. Irene Johnson, Sec., Woodlands, Man. ROC 3HO (383-5679)
Woodworth RM	1,275	Brandon-Souris	Virden	E.R. Routledge, Sec., Kenton, Man. ROM OZO (838-2317)

Manitoba Local Government Districts

Incorporated under "The Local Government Districts Act," January 1st, 1945; J.L. Fulsher, Director, Municipal Services & Research, 1344, 405 Broadway, Winnipeg, Man. R3C 3L6

Local Government District with Resident Administrator

Area Code for Manitoba is 204

Alexander: R.A. Bouvier, St. George, Man. R0E 1M0 (367-2235)
Alonsa: Max. Hryciuk, Alonsa, Man. R0H 0A0 (767-2054)
Armstrong: A.B. Martin, Inwood, Man. R0C 1P0 (278-3377)
Churchill: Mrs. Elsie Forrest, Box 459, Churchill, Man. R0B 0E0 (675-8871)
Consol: William Hildebrand, Box 578, The Pas, Man. R9A 1K6 (623-2931)
Fisher: Mrs. Mabel White, Box 280, Fisher Branch, Man. R0C 0Z0 (372-6393)
Gillam: J.E. Bartlett, Box 100, Gillam, Man. R0B 0L0 (652-2121)
Grahamdale: Mrs. Ardene Franz, Box 160, Moosehorn, Man. R0C 2E0 (768-2858)
Grand Rapids: Mrs. Lillian M. Turner, Grand Rapids, Man. R0C 1E0 (639-2260)
Lynn Lake: A.H. Enns, Box 100, Lynn Lake, Man. R0B 0W0 (356-2418)
Mountain: W. Kuby, Box 389, Swan River, Man. R0L 1Z0 (734-3124)
Mystery Lake: R.G. Thompson, Box 730, Thompson, Man. R8N 1N5 (677-4075)
Park: S. Yakielashek, Box 310, Russell, Man. R0J 1W0 (773-2822)
Pinawa: R.A. Dale, Box 100, Pinawa, Man. R0E 1L0 (753-2331)
Piney: R. Preteau, Box 48, Vassar, Man. R0A 2J0 (437-2284)
Reynolds: Richard Andries, Hadashville, Man. R0E 0X0 (426-5305)
Stuartburn: Mrs. Judy Reimer, Box 59, Vita, Man. R0A 2K0 (425-3218)

NEW BRUNSWICK

The provincial government of New Brunswick provides all services of a municipal nature for the rural area of the province. An advisory committee is elected at public meetings biennially to assist and advise the Minister. Acts of the legislature governing municipalities are the Municipalities Act, the Municipal Assistance Act, the Community Planning Act, the Assessment Act, the Municipal Capital Borrowing Act, the Municipal Elections Act, and the Control of Municipalities Act.

Population requirements for incorporation of municipalities are 10,000 for cities and 1,000 for towns. There are no specified requirements for villages.

Municipal elections are held every three years on the second Monday in May. The next election will be in May, 1983.

Cities in CAPITALS; Towns marked †; Balance are villages.
Area Code for New Brunswick is 506

MUNICIPALITY	POP.	COUNTY	FEDERAL ELECTORAL DISTRICT	PROVINCIAL ELECTORAL DISTRICT	CLERK WITH ADDRESS & PHONE
Alma	334	Albert	Fundy-Royal	Albert	Mrs. Elsie O'Regan, Village Clerk, Alma, N.B. E0A 1B0 (887-2646)
Aroostook	464	Victoria	Madawaska-Victoria	Victoria-Tobique	Village Clerk, Aroostook, N.B. E0J 1B0 (273-2545)
Atholville	1,862	Restigouche	Restigouche	Dalhousie	Mrs. Jeannette Gould, Village Clerk, Atholville, N.B. E0K 1A0 (753-3221)
Baker Brook	499	Madawaska	Madawaska-Victoria	Madawaska-les-Lacs	Gilla Ouelette, Village Clerk, Baker Brook, N.B. E0L 1A0 (258-3250)
Balmoral	1,722	Restigouche	Restigouche	Dalhousie	J.-G. Mercier, Village Clerk, Balmoral, N.B. E0B 1C0 (826-2826)
Bas-Caraquet	1,728	Gloucester	Gloucester	Caraquet	Théophane Noel, Village Clerk, Bas-Caraquet, N.B. E0B 1E0 (727-4411)
Bath	882	Carleton	Carleton-Charlotte	Carleton North	Mrs. S. Cook, Village Clerk, Bath, N.B. E0J 1E0 (278-3227)
BATHURST	16,301	Gloucester	Gloucester	Bathurst	Louise C. Wafer, City Clerk, PO Drawer D, Bathurst, N.B. E2A 3Z1 (546-6651)
Belledune	747	Gloucester	Restigouche	Nigadoo-Chaleur	Tom Luczanko, Village Clerk, Belledune, N.B. E0B 1G0 (522-5613)
Beresford	3,199	Gloucester		Nigadoo-Chaleur	N. Godin, Village Clerk, Beresford, N.B. E0B 1H0 (783-3463)
Bertrand	1,203	Gloucester	Gloucester		M.J.L. Theriault, Village Clerk, Bertrand, N.B. E0B 1J0 (727-2239)
Blacks Harbour	1,619	Charlotte	Carleton-Charlotte	Charlotte-Fundy	E. Armstrong, Village Clerk, Blacks Harbour, N.B. E0G 1H0 (456-3683, res.; 456-3324, bus.)

Cities in CAPITALS; Towns marked †; Balance are villages.
Area Code for New Brunswick is 506

MUNICIPALITY	POP.	COUNTY	FEDERAL ELECTORAL DISTRICT	PROVINCIAL ELECTORAL DISTRICT	CLERK WITH ADDRESS & PHONE
Blackville	924	Northumberland	Northumberland-Miramichi	Southwest-Miramichi	J.J. Sturgeon, Village Clerk, Blackville, N.B. EOC 1CO (843-6337)
Bristol	860	Carleton	Carleton-Charlotte	Carleton North	L. McLean, Village Clerk, Bristol, N.B. EOJ 1GO (392-6182)
Buctouche	2,556	Kent	Westmorland-Kent	Kent South	Mlle T. Langis, Village Clerk, Buctouche, N.B. EOA 1GO (743-6988)
Cambridge-Narrows	406	Queens	Fundy-Royal	Queens North	Mrs. S. Knight, Village Clerk, Cambridge-Narrows, N.B. EOE 1EO (488-2154)
CAMPBELLTON	10,110	Restigouche	Restigouche	Campbellton	J.E. Woods, City Clerk, Box 100, Campbellton, N.B. E3N 3G1 (753-7767)
Canterbury	501	York	Carleton-Charlotte	York South	L.J. Donovan, Village Clerk, Canterbury, N.B. EOH 1CO (279-2044)
Cap Pelé	2,287	Westmorland	Westmorland-Kent	Shediac-Cap Pelé	E. Fougère, Village Clerk, Box 159, Cap-Pelé, N.B. E0A 1J0 (577-4157)
Caraquet†	3,950	Gloucester	Gloucester	Caraquet	Lucien Sonier, Town Clerk, Box 420, Caraquet, N.B. EOB 1KO (727-3423)
Centreville	606	Carleton	Carleton-Charlotte	Carleton Centre	Mrs. B. McHatten, Village Clerk, Centreville, N.B. EOJ 1HO (276-4437)
Charlo	1,302	Restigouche	Restigouche	Dalhousie	Mrs. D. Giroux, Village Clerk, Charlo, N.B. EOB 1MO (684-3597)
Chatham†	7,601	Northumberland	Northumberland-Miramichi	Chatham	J.F. Lamkey, Town Clerk, Box 309, Chatham, N.B. E1N 3A7 (773-5891)
Chipman	1,999	Queens	Fundy-Royal	Queens North	Miss Brenda Barton, Village Clerk, Chipman, N.B. EOE 1CO (339-6835)
Clair	792	Madawaska	Madawaska-Victoria	Madawaska-les-Lacs	Mrs. Nicole Michaud, Village Clerk, Clair, N.B. EOL 1BO (992-2181)
Dalhousie†	5,640	Restigouche	Restigouche	Dalhousie	A.A. Upton, Town Clerk, Box 70, Dalhousie, N.B. EOK 1BO (684-5554)
Darlington	624	Restigouche	Restigouche	Dalhousie	Mrs. A. Letourneau, Village Clerk, Darlington, N.B. EOK 1BO (684-3800)
Dieppe†	7,460	Westmorland	Moncton	Petitcodiac	Town Clerk, Champlain Place, Dieppe, N.B. E1A 4X6 (854-9080)
Doaktown	1,022	Northumberland	Northumberland-Miramichi	Southwestern Miramichi	Herbert Lyons, Village Clerk, Doaktown, N.B. EOC 1GO (365-7970)
Dorchester	1,125	Westmorland	Westmorland-Kent	Tantramar	Mrs. Anela Greenberg, Village Clerk, Dorchester, N.B. EOA 1MO (379-2582)
Douglastown	1,032	Northumberland	Northumberland-Miramichi	Miramichi-Newcastle	Mrs. Anne B. Comeau, Village Clerk, Douglastown, N.B. EOC 1HO (773-5127)
Drummond	675	Victoria	Madawaska-Victoria	Grand Falls	Gerald Levesque, Village Clerk, R.R. 2, Drummond, N.B. EOJ 1MO (473-3601)
East Riverside-Kingshurst	1,042	Kings	Fundy-Royal	Kings West	Joan Fitzgerald, Village Clerk, c/o 2055 Rothesay Rd., Renforth, N.B. E2H 2K2 (847-2288)
EDMUNDSTON	12,710	Madawaska	Madawaska-Victoria	Edmundston	L. Hebert, City Clerk, 7 Canada Rd., Edmundston, N.B. E3V 1T7 (735-8491)

Cities in CAPITALS; Towns marked †; Balance are villages.
Area Code for New Brunswick is 506

MUNICIPALITY	POP.	COUNTY	FEDERAL ELECTORAL DISTRICT	PROVINCIAL ELECTORAL DISTRICT	CLERK WITH ADDRESS & PHONE
Eel River Crossing	811	Restigouche	Restigouche	Dalhousie	Mrs. Bessie Savoie, Village Clerk, Eel River Crossing, N.B. EOB 1PO (826-2490)
Fairvale	3,258	Kings	Fundy-Royal	Kings West	Mrs. Sandra Shields, Fairvale Village Clerk, Box 538, Rothesay, N.B. EOG 2WO (847-4758)
Florenceville	768	Carleton	Carleton-Charlotte	Carleton North	Wayne Thomas, Village Clerk, Florenceville, N.B. EOJ 1KO (392-6347)
FREDERICTON	45,248	York	York-Sunbury	Fredericton North; Fredericton South	S. Thorburn, City Clerk, Box 130, Fredericton, N.B. E3B 4Y7 (455-9426)
Fredericton Junction	33	Sunbury	Carleton-Charlotte	Sunbury	Mrs. Lena Bunker, Village Clerk, Fredericton Junction, N.B. EOG 1TO (368-2656)
Gagetown	655	Queens	Fundy-Royal	Oromocto	Leslie Knight, Village Clerk, Gagetown, N.B. EOC 1VO (488-2178)
Gondola Point	1,846	Kings	Fundy-Royal		Mrs. Jane Hutton, Village Clerk, Box 579, Gondola Point, N.B. EOG 2WO (849-2588)
Grande-Anse	765	Gloucester	Gloucester	Caraquet	Pierre Laforest, Mun. Adm., Grande Anse, N.B. EOB 1RO (732-5411)
Grand Bay	2,947	Kings	Fundy-Royal	Kings Centre	Mrs. Mildred Crawford, Village Clerk, Grand Bay, N.B. EOG 1WO (738-8039)
Grand Falls†	6,223	Victoria	Madawaska-Victoria	Grand Falls	J.L. Côté, Town Clerk, Box 800, Grand Falls, N.B. EOJ 1MO (473-3175)
Grand Harbour	31	Charlotte	Carleton-Charlotte	Charlotte-Fundy	Mrs. A. Ingalls, Village Clerk, Grand Harbour, N.B. EOG 2CO (662-8109)
Hampton	2,641	Kings	Fundy-Royal	Kings West	Mrs. E. Bowland, Village Clerk, Hampton, N.B. EOG 1ZO (832-7661)
Hartland†	974	Carleton	Carleton-Charlotte	Carleton Centre	Mrs. D. Hill, Town Clerk, Box 58, Hartland, N.B. EOJ 1NO (375-4357)
Harvey	376	York	Fundy-Royal	Albert	Bernie McCann, Village Clerk, Harvey, N.B. EOH 1HO (366-2166)
Hillsborough	1,153	Albert	Fundy-Royal	Albert	Robert Tingley, Village Clerk, Hillsborough, N.B. EOA 1XO (734-2657)
Jacquet River	735	Restigouche	Restigouche	Dalhousie	A.C. Hickey, Village Clerk, Jacquet River, N.B. EOB 1TO (237-2839)
Kedgwick	1,271	Restigouche	Restigouche	Restigouche West	Eudore Dubé, Village Clerk, Kedgwick, N.B. EOK 1CO (284-2160)
Lac Baker	325	Madawaska	Madawaska-Victoria	Madawaska-les-Lacs	Miss R. Pelletier, Village Clerk, Lac Baker, N.B. EOL 1CO (992-2531)
Lamèque	973	Gloucester	Gloucester	Shippegan-les-Iles	H.P. Guignard, Village Clerk, Lamèque, N.B. EOB 1VO (334-2246)
Loggieville	784	Northumberland	Northumberland-Miramichi	Chatham	J.H. Ross, Village Clerk, Loggieville, N.B. EOC 1LO (773-3140)
McAdam	1,985	York	Carleton-Charlotte	York South	Mrs. Marjorie O'Keefe, Village Clerk, McAdam, N.B. EOH 1KO (784-2293)
Meductic	170	York	Carleton-Charlotte	York South	Clair Estey, Village Clerk, Meductic, N.B. EOH 1LO (328-8861)

Cities in CAPITALS; Towns marked †; Balance are villages.
Area Code for New Brunswick is 506

MUNICIPALITY	POP.	COUNTY	FEDERAL ELECTORAL DISTRICT	PROVINCIAL ELECTORAL DISTRICT	CLERK WITH ADDRESS & PHONE
Millville	308	York	York-Sunbury	York North	Mrs. M. Hull, Village Clerk, Millville, N.B. EOH 1MO (463-2625)
Minto	3,714	Sunbury-Queens	Fundy-Royal	Queens North	Mrs. Rose Collette, Village Clerk, Minto, N.B. EOE 1JO (327-3383)
MONCTON	55,934	Westmorland	Moncton	Moncton E.; Monc. N.; Monc. W.; Petitcodiac	J.A. Clark, City Clerk, 774 Main St., Moncton, N.B. E1C 1E8 (854-3333)
Nackawic†	1,341	York	York-Sunbury	York North	Mrs. Anne Porter, Town Clerk, Nackawic, N.B. EOH 1PO (575-8439)
Neguac	1,733	Northumberland	Northumberland-Miramichi	Miramichi Bay	G.R. Savoie, Village Clerk, Neguac, N.B. EOC 1SO (776-8806)
Nelson-Miramichi	1,543	Northumberland	Northumberland-Miramichi	Miramichi-Newcastle	Miss Doreen Lynch, Village Clerk, Nelson-Miramichi, N.B. EOC 1TO (622-1126)
Newcastle†	6,423	Northumberland	Northumberland-Miramichi	Miramichi-Newcastle	W.R. Dickison, Town Clerk, Box 332, Newcastle, N.B. E1V 3M4 (622-2195)
Nigadoo	799	Gloucester	Restigouche	Nigadoo-Chaleur	D.W. Pelletier, Village Clerk, Nigadoo, N.B. EOB 2AO (783-2488)
North Head	647	Charlotte	Carleton-Charlotte	Charlotte-Fundy	Mrs. H. Cronk, Village Clerk, North Head, N.B. EOG 2MO (662-8335)
Norton	1,285	Kings	Fundy-Royal	Kings Centre	Mrs. S.E. Keirstead, Village Clerk, Norton, N.B. EOG 2NO (839-2373)
Oromocto†	10,276	Sunbury	York-Sunbury	Oromocto	T.L. Winter, Town Clerk, 137 MacDonald Ave., Oromocto, N.B. E2V 1A6 (357-8487)
Paquetville	601	Gloucester	Gloucester	Caraquet	Mrs. M. Gallien, Village Clerk, Paquetville, N.B. EOB 2BO (764-2789)
Perth-Andover	1,973	Victoria	Madawaska-Victoria	Victoria-Tobique	Murray Watters, Village Clerk, Perth-Andover, N.B. EOJ 1VO (273-2871)
Petitcodiac	1,472	Westmorland	Moncton	Petitcodiac	Mrs. Ralph Stiles, Village Clerk, Petitcodiac, N.B. EOA 2HO (756-2179)
Petit-Rocher	1,790	Gloucester	Restigouche	Nigadoo-Chaleur	Guy Clavette, Village Clerk, Petit-Rocher, N.B. EOB 2EO (783-3688)
Plaster Rock	1,368	Victoria	Madawaska-Victoria	Victoria-Tobique	Ken Harding, Village Clerk, Plaster Rock, N.B. EOJ 1WO (356-2196)
Pointe-Verte	617	Gloucester	Restigouche	Nigadoo-Chaleur	Normand Doiron, Village Clerk, Pointe-Verte, N.B. EOB 2HO (783-3559)
Port Elgin	492	Westmorland	Westmorland-Kent	Tantramar	Miss M. Smart, Village Clerk, Port Elgin, N.B. EOA 2KO (538-2221)
Quispamsis	4,968	Kings	Fundy-Royal	Kings West	D.G. Scott, Village Clerk, Quispamsis, N.B. (847-8889)
Renforth	1,572	Kings	Fundy-Royal	Kings West	Miss Joan Fitzgerald, Village Clerk, 2055 Rothesay Rd., Renforth, N.B. E2H 2K2 (847-2288)
Rexton	872	Kent	Westmorland-Kent	Kent North	Peter Kavanagh, Village Clerk, Rexton, N.B. EOA 2LO (523-6921)
Richibucto	1,909	Kent	Westmorland-Kent	Kent North	R.J. Belliveau, Village Clerk, Richibucto, N.B. EOA 2MO (523-4813)

Cities in CAPITALS; Towns marked †; Balance are villages.
Area Code for New Brunswick is 506

MUNICIPALITY	POP.	COUNTY	FEDERAL ELECTORAL DISTRICT	PROVINCIAL ELECTORAL DISTRICT	CLERK WITH ADDRESS & PHONE
Riverside-Albert	467	Albert	Fundy-Royal		Mrs. Betty Betts, Village Clerk, Riverside-Albert, N.B. EOA 2RO (882-2314)
Riverview†	14,177	Albert	Moncton		G.E. Hamilton, Town Clerk, 30 Honour House Ct., Riverview, N.B. E1B 3Y9 (386-8874)
Rivière-Verte		Madawaska	Madawaska-Victoria	Madawaska-les-Lacs	Mrs. E. Therrien, Village Clerk, Rivière-Verte, N.B. EOL 1EO (263-8641)
Rogersville	1,138	Northumberland	Northumberland-Miramichi	Kent North	Gerald Fournier, Village Clerk, Rogersville, N.B. EOA 2TO (775-2518)
Rothesay	1,283	Kings	Fundy-Royal	Kings East	H.E. Smith, Village Clerk, Box 301, Rothesay, N.B. EOG 2WO (847-8889)
Sackville†	5,755	Westmorland	Westmorland-Kent	Tantramar	Mrs. M. Andrews, Town Clerk, Box 660, Sackville, N.B. EOA 3CO (536-0590)
Saint Andrews†	1,711	Charlotte	Carleton-Charlotte	Charlotte West	R.C. Bartlett, Town Clerk, Box 160, Saint Andrews, N.B. EOG 2XO (529-3145)
Ste-Anne-de-Madawaska	1,341	Madawaska	Madawaska-Victoria	Madawaska South	Mrs. Pierrette Boutôt, Village Clerk, Ste-Anne-de-Madawaska, N.B. EOL 1GO (445-2449)
Saint André	310	Madawaska	Madawaska-Victoria	Madawaska South	Claude Doiron, Village Clerk, Saint André, N.B. EOG 2XO (473-3112)
Saint-Antoine	1,062	Kent	Westmorland-Kent	Kent South	Mrs. Monette Leger, Saint-Antoine, N.B. EOA 2XO (525-2212)
Saint-Basile	3,072	Madawaska	Madawaska-Victoria	Madawaska Centre	Miss D. Michaud, Village Clerk, Saint-Basile, N.B. EOL 1HO (263-8513)
Saint-François-de-Madawaska	650	Madawaska	Madawaska-Victoria	Madawaska-les-Lacs	Mrs. Colette Lévesque, Village Clerk, Saint-François-de-Madawaska, N.B. EOL 1JO (992-2186)
Saint George†	1,148	Charlotte	Carleton-Charlotte	Charlotte Centre	V. Meating, Town Clerk, Box 148, Saint George, N.B. EOG 2YO (755-3721)
Saint Hilaire	168	Madawaska	Madawaska-Victoria	Madawaska-les-Lacs	Mrs. J. Ouellette, Village Clerk, Saint Hilaire, N.B. E3V 3K3 (735-8491)
Saint-Jacques	1,374	Madawaska	Madawaska-Victoria	Madawaska Centre	Mrs. Bella Bérubé, Village Clerk, Saint-Jacques, N.B. EOL 1KO (735-8976)
SAINT JOHN	85,956	Saint John	Carleton-Charlotte; Fundy-Royal; Saint John	East Saint John; St. J.-Fundy; St. J. Harbour; St. J. North; St. J.-Park; St. J. South; St. J. West	D.H. Garey, City Clerk, Box 1971, Market Sq., Saint John, N.B. E2L 4L1 (658-2800)
Saint-Joseph	741	Westmorland	Westmorland-Kent	Madawaska Centre	P.E. Gaudet, Village Clerk, Saint-Joseph, N.B. EOA 2YO (758-2078)
Saint-Léolin	770	Gloucester	Gloucester		G. Battah, Village Clerk, Saint-Léolin, N.B. EOB 2MO (732-5367)
St. Leonard†	1,593	Madawaska	Madawaska-Victoria	Madawaska South	Mrs. S. Cassista, Town Clerk, Box 390, St. Leonard, N.B. EOL 1MO (423-6381)
Saint-Louis-de-Kent	1,278	Kent	Westmorland-Kent	Kent South	Kenneth Johnson, Village Clerk, Saint-Louis-de-Kent, N.B. EOA 2ZO (876-2441)
St. Martins	544	Saint John	Fundy-Royal	Saint John-Fundy	Mrs. S. Roy, Village Clerk, St. Martins, N.B. EOG 2ZO (833-4363)

Cities in CAPITALS; Towns marked †; Balance are villages.
Area Code for New Brunswick is 506

MUNICIPALITY	POP.	COUNTY	FEDERAL ELECTORAL DISTRICT	PROVINCIAL ELECTORAL DISTRICT	CLERK WITH ADDRESS & PHONE
Saint-Quentin	2,300	Restigouche	Restigouche	Restigouche West	Don Ouellet, Village Clerk, Box 489, Saint-Quentin, N.B. EOK 1JO (235-2425)
St. Stephen†	5,264	Charlotte	Carleton-Charlotte	St. Stephen-Milltown	T. Moore, Town Clerk, 34 Milltown Blvd., St. Stephen, N.B. E3L 1G3 (466-1566)
Salisbury	1,410	Westmorland	Moncton	Petitcodiac	Mrs. I.R. McWilliam, Village Clerk, Salisbury, N.B. EOA 3EO (372-5011)
Seal Cove	526	Charlotte	Carleton-Charlotte	Charlotte-Fundy	Mrs. B. Brown, Village Clerk, Seal Cove, N.B. EOG 3BO (662-3533)
Shediac†	4,216	Westmorland	Westmorland-Kent	Shediac-Cap Pelé	Roger Leblanc, Town Clerk, Shediac, N.B. EOA 3GO (532-2421)
Sheila	885	Gloucester	Gloucester	Tracadie	Miss C. Rousselle, Village Clerk, Sheila, N.B. EOC 1ZO (395-5759)
Shippegan†	2,344	Gloucester	Gloucester	Shippegan-les-Iles	F.J. Robichaud, Town Clerk, Box 280, Shippegan, N.B. EOB 2PO (336-2310)
Stanley	435	York	York-Sunbury	York North	Mrs. Shirley Samson, Village Clerk, Stanley, N.B. EOH 1TO (367-2685)
Sussex†	3,938	Kings	Fundy-Royal	Kings Centre	E.G. Perry, Town Clerk, Box 1057, Sussex, N.B. EOE 1PO (433-3973)
Sussex Corner	864	Kings	Fundy-Royal	Kings East	Mrs. R.M. Lambe, Village Clerk, Sussex Corner, N.B. EOE 1RO (433-2146)
Tide Head	897	Restigouche	Restigouche	Dalhousie	H.M. Wirtanen, Village Clerk, Tide Head, N.B. EOK 1KO (753-7492)
Tracadie†	2,591	Gloucester	Gloucester	Tracadie	Zoel Arseneau, Town Clerk, Box 720, Tracadie, N.B. EOC 2BO (395-2689)
Tracy	662	Sunbury	Carleton-Charlotte	Sunbury	Mrs. Edrie Golding, Village Clerk, Tracy, N.B. EOG 3CO (368-2882)
Verret	244	Madawaska	Madawaska-Victoria		Mme D. Ouellette, Village Clerk, Verret, N.B. (739-9065)
Westfield	1,048	Kings	Fundy-Royal	Kings Centre	W. Warwick, Village Clerk, Westfield, N.B. EOJ 3JO (757-2258)
Woodstock†	4,869	Carleton	Carleton-Charlotte	Carleton South	E.L. Dickinson, Town Clerk, Box 1059, Woodstock, N.B. EOJ 2BO (328-3307)

NEWFOUNDLAND

The provincial government of Newfoundland exercises control over the activities of all municipalities in accordance with the Department of Municipal Affairs and Housing Act. Under the provisions of the Municipalities Act, 1980, the Department exercises a certain degree of financial and administrative control over all municipalities excepting the Cities of St. John's and Corner Brook. The towns and communities do not require ministerial approval of their annual budgets, but the Department employs inspectors to oversee municipal activities. The province assumes responsibility for public health, welfare and law enforcement which are elsewhere generally considered to be municipal functions.

The cities, towns and communities incorporated in Newfoundland are authorized to levy taxes and to provide public works, fire protection, recreation and make local by-laws. Towns and communities have virtually the same powers, the sole exception being that the community councils have a more simplified election procedure.

City and town councils in Newfoundland are elected every four years on the second Tuesday in November. Community councils are elected at every second annual meeting held between January 1 and March 1, or at such later date as the Minister may approve. A quorum for an annual meeting is ten per cent. of the taxpayers.

Cities in CAPITALS; Towns marked †; Communities marked‡.
Area Code for Newfoundland is 709

MUNICIPALITY	POP.	FEDERAL ELECTORAL DISTRICT	PROVINCIAL ELECTORAL DISTRICT	CLERK WITH ADDRESS & PHONE
Admirals Beach‡	370	St. John's West	St. Mary's-The Capes	Mrs. E. Dalton, Community Clerk, Box 276, Admirals Beach, Nfld. AOA 3AO (521-2671)
Anchor Point‡	329	Humber-Port au Port-St. Barbe	Strait of Belle Isle	Mrs. L. Genge, Community Clerk, Anchor Point, Nfld. AOK 1AO (456-2777)
Appleton†	342	Gander-Twillingate	Gander	Mrs. M. Goulding, Town Clerk, Box 31, Site 4, R.R. 1, Appleton, Nfld. A0G 2K0 (679-2289)
Aquaforte‡	172	St. John's West	Ferryland	Ronald Coady, Community Clerk, Aquaforte, Nfld. AOA 1AO (363-2260)
Arnold's Cove†	1,160	St. John's West	Bellevue	Clyde Guy, Town Clerk, Box 70, Arnold's Cove, Nfld. AOB 1AO (463-2323)
Avondale†	937	St. John's East	Harbour Main-Bell Island	Mrs. C. Kelly, Town Clerk, Box 59, Avondale, Nfld. AOA 1BO (229-4201)
Badger†	1,160	Grand Falls-White Bay-Labrador	Windsor-Buchans	Mrs. V. Roberts, Town Clerk, Box 130, Badger, Nfld. AOH 1AO (539-2406)
Badger's Quay†	1,468	Gander-Twillingate	Bonavista North	Harry Harding, Town Clerk, Box 64, Badger's Quay, Nfld. AOG 1BO (536-2010)
Baie Verte†	2,528	Grand Falls-White Bay-Labrador	Baie Verte-White Bay	William Rowe, Town Clerk, Box 218, Baie Verte, Nfld. AOK 1BO (532-8222)
Baine Harbour‡	204	Burin-St. George's	Burin-Placentia West	Ed. Whittle, Community Clerk, Baine Harbour, Nfld. AOE 1AO (443-2177)
Bay de Verde†	749	Bonavista-Trinity-Conception	Trinity-Bay de Verde	Mrs. M. Walsh, Town Clerk, Box 10, Bay de Verde, Nfld. AOA 1EO (587-2260)
Bay L'Argent†	474	Burin-St. George's	Fortune-Hermitage	Keith Osbourne, Town Clerk, Box 29, Bay L'Argent, Nfld. AOE 1BO (461-2606)
Bay Roberts†	4,072	Bonavista-Trinity-Conception	Port de Grave	Cyril Mercer, Town Mgr., Box 114, Bay Roberts, Nfld. AOA 1GO (786-2126)
Bayview†	385	Gander-Twillingate	Twillingate	Ms. M. Gillard, Town Clerk, Site 9, Box 10, Bayview, Nfld. A0G 4M0 (884-2640)
Bellburns‡	148	Humber-Port au Port-St. Barbe	St. Barbe	Mrs. Miriam Hulan, Community Clerk, Bellburns, Nfld. AOK 1HO (898-2302)
Belleoram†	536	Burin-St. George's	Fortune-Hermitage	Mrs. H. Gould, Town Clerk, Belleoram, Nfld. AOH 1BO (881-6161)
Berry Head‡	923	Humber-Port au Port-St. Barbe	Port au Port	Ms. T. Hann, Berry Head Community Clerk, Box 39, Port au Port East, Nfld. AON 1TO (648-2731)
Bide Arm‡	305	Grand Falls-White Bay-Labrador	Baie Verte-White Bay	Mrs. J. Randell, Community Clerk, Bide Arm, Nfld. AOK 1JO (457-2378)
Birchy Bay†	646	Gander-Twillingate	Lewisporte	Mrs. P. Budden, Town Clerk, Box 40, Birchy Bay, Nfld. AOG 1EO (659-3221)
Bird Cove‡	395	Humber-Port au Port-St. Barbe	St. Barbe	Mark Kennedy, Community Clerk, Bird Cove, Nfld. AOK 1LO (247-5116)
Biscay Bay‡	88	St. John's West	St. Mary's-The Capes	Fred White, Community Sec., Biscay Bay, Nfld. AOA 4BO (438-2425)
Bishop's Cove‡	366	Bonavista-Trinity-Conception	Harbour Grace	Miss S. Lynch, Bishop's Cove Clerk, Box 148, R.R. 1, Spaniards Bay, Nfld. AOA 3XO (589-2204)
Bishop's Falls†	4,504	Gander-Twillingate	Exploits	Ms. J.M. Budgell, Town Clerk, Box 310, Bishop's Falls, Nfld. AOH 1CO (258-6581)
Bonavista†	4,299	Bonavista-Trinity-Conception	Bonavista South	David Hiscock, Town Clerk, Box 279, Bonavista, Nfld. AOC 1BO (468-7816)
Botwood†	4,554	Gander-Twillingate	Exploits	Mrs. A. Rowsell, Town Clerk, Box 490, Botwood, Nfld. AOH 1EO (257-2839)
Branch‡	452	St. John's West	St. Mary's-The Capes	Augustine Power, Community Clerk, Branch, Nfld. AOB 1EO (338-2920)
Brent's Cove‡	379	Grand Falls-White Bay-Labrador	Baie Verte-White Bay	Mrs. M. Matthews, Community Clerk, Brent's Cove, Nfld. AOK 1RO (661-7131)
Brigus†	912	Bonavista-Trinity-Conception	Port de Grave	Mrs. A. Whelan, Town Clerk, Box 200, Brigus, Nfld. AOA 1KO (528-4588)
Bryants Cove‡	354	Bonavista-Trinity-Conception	Harbour Grace	Mrs. L. Noseworthy, Bryants Cove Clerk, c/o Box 2, Site 5, Riverhead, Nfld. A0A 3P0 (596-2291)
Buchans†	512	Grand Falls-White Bay-Labrador	Windsor-Buchans	Mrs. M. Hamilton, Town Clerk, Box 190, Buchans, Nfld. AOH 1GO (672-3972)
Burgeo†	2,474	Burin-St. George's	Burgeo-Bay d'Espoir	George Ball, Jr., Town Clerk, Box 220, Burgeo, Nfld. AOM 1AO (886-2250)

Cities in CAPITALS; Towns marked †; Communities marked‡.
Area Code for Newfoundland is 709

MUNICIPALITY	POP.	FEDERAL ELECTORAL DISTRICT	PROVINCIAL ELECTORAL DISTRICT	CLERK WITH ADDRESS & PHONE
Burin†	2,892	Burin-St. George's	Burin-Placentia West	Ms. H. Fizzard, Town Clerk, Box 370, Burin, Nfld. AOE 1EO (891-1760)
Burlington‡	381	Grand Falls-White Bay-Labrador	Baie Verte-White Bay	Mrs. J. Morris, Community Clerk, Burlington, Nfld. AOK 1SO (252-2607)
Burnt Islands†	914	Burin-St. George's	La Poile	Mrs. E. Keeping, Town Clerk, Box 39, Burnt Islands, Nfld. AOM 1BO (698-3512)
Campbellton†	757	Gander-Twillingate	Lewisporte	Miss J. Harnett, Town Clerk, Box 70, Campbellton, Nfld. AOG 1LO (261-2300)
Cape St. George etc.‡	1,426	Humber-Port au Port-St. Barbe	Port au Port	Mrs. Joyce Felix, Community Clerk, Cape St. George, Nfld. AON 1EO (644-2290)
Carbonear†	5,026	Bonavista-Trinity-Conception	Carbonear	J.L. Walsh, Town Clerk, Box 999, Carbonear, Nfld. AOA 1TO (596-2701)
Carmanville†	911	Gander-Twillingate	Fogo	Mrs. M. Robbins, Town Clerk, Box 145, Carmanville, Nfld. AOG 1NO (534-2814)
Cartwright‡	675	Grand Falls-White Bay-Labrador	Eagle River	Mrs. S. Mullins, Community Clerk, Box 129, Cartwright, (Lab.), Nfld. AOK 1VO (938-7259)
Catalina†	1,129	Bonavista-Trinity-Conception	Trinity North	Mrs. D. Freake, Town Clerk, Box 2, Catalina, Nfld. AOC 1JO (469-2615)
Centreville†	683	Gander-Twillingate	Bonavista North	Mrs. G. Brown, Town Clerk, Box 41, Centreville, Nfld. AOG 4PO (678-2840)
Chance Cove†	487	Bonavista-Trinity-Conception	Bellevue	Mrs. E. Rowe, Town Clerk, Chance Cove, Nfld. AOB 1KO (460-4151)
Change Islands†	535	Gander-Twillingate	Lewisporte	Mrs. S. Edwards, Town Clerk, Change Islands, Nfld. AOG 1RO (621-4181)
Channel-Port aux Basques†	6,187	Burin-St. George's	La Poile	Mrs. M. Kettle, Town Clerk, Box 70, Channel-Port aux Basques, Nfld. AOM 1CO (695-2214)
Chapel Arm†	712	Bonavista-Trinity-Conception	Bellevue	Mrs. A. Power, Town Clerk, Chapel Arm, Nfld. AOB 1LO (592-2720)
Clarenville†	2,807	Bonavista-Trinity-Conception	Trinity North	Mrs. E. Blackmore, Town Clerk, Box 66, Clarenville, Nfld. AOE 1JO (466-7937)
Clarke's Beach†	997	Bonavista-Trinity-Conception	Port de Grave	Mrs. M. Boone, Town Clerk, Box 159, Clarke's Beach, Nfld. AOA 1WO (786-3993)
Coachman's Cove‡	293	Grand Falls-White Bay-Labrador	Baie Verte-White Bay	David Philpott, Community Clerk, Coachman's Cove, Nfld. AOK 1XO (253-5161)
Colinet‡	246	St. John's West	St. Mary's-The Capes	Mrs. J. Goodyear, Community Clerk, Colinet, Nfld. AOB 1MO (521-2300)
Colliers†	840	Bonavista-Trinity-Conception	Harbour Main-Bell Island	Mrs. G.M. Whelan, Town Clerk, Box 84, Colliers, Nfld. AOA 1YO (229-4333)
Come By Chance†	380	St. John's West	Bellevue	Mrs. P. Smith, Town Clerk, Box 89, Come By Chance, Nfld. AOB 1NO (542-3240)
Comfort Cove-Newstead‡	734	Gander-Twillingate	Lewisporte	Gerald Head, Community Clerk, Box 10, Comfort Cove-Newstead, Nfld. AOG 3KO (244-4121)
Conception Bay South†	9,743	St. John's East	Conception Bay South	G.W. Martin, Town Clerk, Box 280, Conception Bay South, Nfld. AOA 2YO (834-2151)
Conception Harbour†	910	St. John's East	Harbour Main-Bell Island	Mrs. A.M. Poole, Town Clerk, Conception Harbour, Nfld. AOA 1ZO (229-4781)
Conche‡	431	Grand Falls-White Bay-Labrador	Strait of Belle Isle	Mrs. M. Hunt, Community Clerk, Box 25, Conche, Nfld. AOK 1YO (622-3346)
Conne River†	531	Burin-St. George's	Burgeo-Bay d'Espoir	M. McDonald, Town Clerk, Conne River, Nfld. A0H 1J0 (882-2470)
Cook's Harbour†	326	Humber-Port-au-Port-St. Barbe	Strait of Belle Isle	Ms. L. Pittman, Town Clerk, Cook's Harbour, Nfld. A0K 1Z0 (249-3111)
Cormack‡	672	Humber-Port au Port-St. Barbe	Humber Valley	Mrs. Z. Muise, Community Clerk, Box 4, Site 4, Cormack, Nfld. AOK 2EO (635-5351)
CORNER BROOK	25,198	Humber-Port au Port-St. Barbe	Bay of Islands; Humber East; Humber West	Ms. K. Furlong, City Clerk, City Hall, Corner Brook, Nfld. A2H 6E1 (634-8291)
Cottlesville†	404	Gander-Twillingate	Twillingate	Mrs. D. Philpott, Town Clerk, Box 10, Cottlesville, Nfld. A0H 1S0 (629-3505)
Cow Head†	650	Humber-Port au Port-St. Barbe	St. Barbe	M. Gilley, Town Clerk, Box 40, Cow Head, Nfld. AOK 2AO (243-2446)
Cox's Cove‡	1,004	Humber-Port au Port-St. Barbe	Bay of Islands	Ms. E.L. Robinson, Community Clerk, Box 100, Cox's Cove, Nfld. AOL 1CO (688-2900)

Cities in CAPITALS; Towns marked †; Communities marked‡.
Area Code for Newfoundland is 709

MUNICIPALITY	POP.	FEDERAL ELECTORAL DISTRICT	PROVINCIAL ELECTORAL DISTRICT	CLERK WITH ADDRESS & PHONE
Crow Head‡	277	Gander-Twillingate	Twillingate	Miss H. Locke, Community Clerk, Box 250, Crow Head, Nfld. AOG 4MO (884-5651)
Cupids†	750	Bonavista-Trinity-Conception	Port de Grave	L. Martin, Town Clerk, Box 99, Cupids, Nfld. AOA 3BO (528-4428)
Daniel's Harbour‡	579	Humber-Port au Port-St. Barbe	St. Barbe	Mrs. J.C. O'Brien, Community Clerk, Box 68, Daniel's Harbour, Nfld. AOK 2CO (898-2300)
Davis Inlet‡	274	Grand Falls-White Bay-Labrador	Eagle River	Phil Jeddor, Community Clerk, Davis Inlet, (Lab.) Nfld. AOP 1AO (478-0843)
Deer Lake†	4,546	Humber-Port au Port-St. Barbe	Humber Valley	W. Dominie, Town Clerk, Box 940, Deer Lake, Nfld. AOK 2EO (635-3222)
Dover†	960	Gander-Twillingate	Bonavista North	Newman Willis, Town Clerk, Dover, Nfld. AOG 1XO (537-2139)
Duntara†	138	Bonavista-Trinity-Conception	Bonavista South	Ms. D. Power, Town Clerk, Duntara, Nfld. AOC 1MO (447-3190)
Dunville†	1,909	St. John's West	Placentia	Mrs. G. Foote, Town Clerk, Box 190, Dunville, Nfld. AOB 1SO (227-2811)
Durrell†	1,137	Gander-Twillingate	Twillingate	D.H. Burton, Town Clerk, Durrell, Nfld. AOG 1YO (884-5496)
Eastport†	567	Gander-Twillingate	Terra Nova	Ida Babstock, Town Clerk, Box 119, Eastport, Nfld. AOG 1ZO (677-2161)
Elliston†	540	Bonavista-Trinity-Conception	Bonavista South	Mrs. M.M. Clouter, Town Clerk, Box 115, Elliston, Nfld. AOC 1NO (468-2647)
Embree†	855	Gander-Twillingate	Lewisporte	Mrs. M. Lane, Town Clerk, Embree, Nfld. AOG 2AO (535-8712)
Englee†	989	Grand Falls-White Bay-Labrador	Baie Verte-White Bay	Edith Randell, Town Clerk, Box 69, Englee, Nfld. AOK 2JO (866-2711)
English Harbour East‡	278	Burin-St. George's	Fortune-Hermitage	Mrs. Mary Kearley, Community Clerk, English Harbour East, Nfld. AOE 1MO (245-4291)
Fermeuse‡	531	St. John's West	Ferryland	Patrick Walsh, Community Clerk, Fermeuse, Nfld. AOA 2GO (363-2400)
Ferryland‡	780	St. John's West	Ferryland	Mrs. R. Walsh, Community Clerk, Ferryland, Nfld. AOA 2HO (432-2415)
Flatrock†	743	St. John's East	St. John's East Extern	Frank Maynard, Flatrock Town Clerk, c/o Site 10, Box 20, R.R. 1, Torbay, Nfld. AOA 3ZO (437-6312)
Fleur de Lys†	694	Grand Falls-White Bay-Labrador	Baie Verte-White Bay	Mrs. J. Traverse, Town Clerk, Fleur de Lys, Nfld. A0K 2M0 (253-3131)
Flower's Cove†	436	Humber-Port au Port-St. Barbe	Strait of Belle Isle	W. Rose, Town Clerk, Box 149, Flower's Cove, Nfld. AOK 2NO (456-2124)
Fogo†	1,103	Gander-Twillingate	Fogo	B. Pomeroy, Town Clerk, Box 57, Fogo, Nfld. AOG 2BO (266-2237)
Forteau‡	465	Grand Falls-White Bay-Labrador	Strait of Belle Isle	G. Buckle, Community Clerk, Forteau, Nfld. AOK 2PO (931-2241)
Fortune†	2,406	Burin-St. George's	Grand Bank	H. Lake, Town Mgr., Box 159, Fortune, Nfld. AOE 1PO (832-2810)
Fox Cove†	469	Burin-St. George's	Burin-Placentia West	Mrs. R. Scott, Fox Cove Clerk, c/o Box 17, Site 25, R.R. 1, Burin, Nfld. AOE 1EO (891-1884)
Fox Harbour‡	627	St. John's West	Placentia	Mrs. F. Spurvey, Community Clerk, Box 64, Fox Harbour, Nfld. AOB 1VO (227-2271)
Frenchman's Cove‡	307	Burin-St. George's	Grand Bank	Mrs. M. Power, Community Clerk, Frenchman's Cove, Nfld. AOE 1RO (826-2383)
Freshwater†	1,426	St. John's West	Placentia	F. Smith, Town Clerk, Box 190, Freshwater, Nfld. AOB 1WO (227-2421)
Gallants‡	101	Humber-Port au Port-St. Barbe	St. George's	Ronald Samms, Community Clerk, Gallants, Nfld. AOL 1GO (646-2639)
Gambo†	2,994	Gander-Twillingate	Bonavista North	Mrs. E. Barkhouse, Town Clerk, Box 250, Gambo, Nfld. A0G 1T0 (674-4476)
Gander†	9,301	Gander-Twillingate	Gander	J. Fox, Town Clerk, Box 280, Gander, Nfld. A1V 1W6 (651-2930)
Garnish†	678	Burin-St. George's	Grand Bank	Ms. L. Balsam, Town Clerk, Box 70, Garnish, Nfld. AOE 1TO (826-2330)
Gaskiers-Point La Haye‡	633	St. John's West	St. Mary's-The Capes	Gertrude Kielly, Gaskiers Community Clerk, c/o Box 122, R.R. 1, St. Mary's, Nfld. AOB 3BO (525-2253)

Cities in CAPITALS; Towns marked †; Communities marked‡.
Area Code for Newfoundland is 709

MUNICIPALITY	POP.	FEDERAL ELECTORAL DISTRICT	PROVINCIAL ELECTORAL DISTRICT	CLERK WITH ADDRESS & PHONE
Gaultois†	558	Burin-St. George's	Fortune-Hermitage	Miss B. MacDonald, Town Clerk, Box 101, Gaultois, Nfld. AOH 1NO (841-6131)
Gayside‡	353	Gander-Twillingate	Lewisporte	Mrs. L. Budden, Community Clerk, Gayside, Nfld. AOG 2JO (659-6101)
Gillams‡	491	Humber-Port au Port-St. Barbe	Bay of Islands	Mrs. S. Blanchard, Gillams Community Clerk, c/o Box 14, Site 5, R.R. 2, Corner Brook, Nfld. A2H 6B9 (783-2800)
Glenburnie-Birchy Head-Shoal Harbour‡	443	Humber-Port au Port-St. Barbe	St. Barbe	Ms. I. Stickland, Glenburnie Community Clerk, c/o Box 87, Woody Point, Bonne Bay, Nfld. AOK 1PO (453-7220)
Glenwood†	1,128	Gander-Twillingate	Gander	A.B. Thistle, Town Clerk, Box 130, Glenwood, Nfld. AOG 2KO (679-2159)
Glovertown†	2,350	Gander-Twillingate	Terra Nova	N.A. Sparkes, Town Clerk, Box 224, Glovertown, Nfld. AOG 2LO (533-2351)
Goose Cove East‡	339	Grand Falls-White Bay-Labrador	Strait of Belle Isle	Tony Sexton, Community Clerk, Goose Cove East, Nfld. AOK 4SO (454-2783)
Goulds†	3,317	St. John's West	Kilbride	Mrs. June Pike, Town Clerk, Box 130, Goulds, Nfld. AOA 2KO (368-7431)
Grand Bank†	3,802	Burin-St. George's	Grand Bank	A.S. White, Town Clerk, Box 640, Grand Bank, Nfld. AOE 1WO (832-1600)
Grand Falls†	8,729	Grand Falls-White Bay-Labrador	Grand Falls	D. Shapleigh, Town Clerk, Box 439, Grand Falls, Nfld. A2A 2J8 (489-4240)
Grand Le Pierre‡	368	Burin-St. George's	Fortune-Hermitage	Mrs. B. Fizzard, Community Clerk, Grand Le Pierre, Nfld. AOE 1YO (662-4151)
Great Harbour Deep‡	303	Grand Falls-White Bay-Labrador	Baie Verte-White Bay	Mrs. D. Cassell, Community Clerk, Great Harbour Deep, Nfld. AOK 2ZO (843-3241)
Greenspond†	382	Gander-Twillingate	Bonavista North	Mrs. H. Harding, Town Clerk, Box 44, Greenspond, Nfld. AOG 2NO (269-3111)
Halfway Point†	2,144	Humber-Port au Port-St. Barbe	Bay of Islands	Miss K. Parsons, Town Clerk, Halfway Point-Benoits Cove, Nfld. AOL 1AO (789-2981)
Hampden‡	780	Grand Falls-White Bay-Labrador	Humber Valley	Ms. L. Osmond, Community Clerk, Hampden, Nfld. AOK 2YO (455-5106)
Hant's Harbour†	507	Bonavista-Trinity-Conception	Trinity-Bay de Verde	David Bown, Town Clerk, Hant's Harbour, Nfld. A0B 1Y0 (586-2330)
Happy Adventure‡	387	Gander-Twillingate	Terra Nova	Mrs. D. Turner, Happy Adventure Clerk, c/o Box 106, Eastport, Nfld. A0G 1Z0 (677-2593)
Happy Valley-Goose Bay†	8,075	Grand Falls-White Bay-Labrador	Naskaupi	Al Durno, Town Clerk, Box 40, Happy Valley-Goose Bay, Nfld. AOP 1EO (896-3321)
Harbour Breton†	2,317	Burin-St. George's	Fortune-Hermitage	Ms. Marie Cribb, Town Clerk, Box 130, Harbour Breton, Nfld. AOH 1PO (885-2354)
Harbour Grace†	2,937	Bonavista-Trinity-Conception	Harbour Grace	J.P. Yetman, Town Clerk, Box 399, Harbour Grace, Nfld. AOA 2NO (596-3631)
Harbour Grace South‡	393	Bonavista-Trinity-Conception	Harbour Grace	Mrs. T. Newman, Community Clerk, Harbour Grace South, Nfld. AOA 2NO (596-2572)
Harbour Main†	1,313	St. John's East	Harbour Main-Bell Island	Mrs. J.R. Ezekiel, Town Clerk, Box 40, Harbour Main, Nfld. AOA 2PO (229-3722)
Hare Bay†	1,598	Gander-Twillingate	Bonavista North	R. Fifield, Town Clerk, Box 130, Hare Bay, Nfld. AOG 2PO (537-2187)
Hawkes Bay†	489	Humber-Port au Port-St. Barbe	St. Barbe	Mrs. Y. House, Town Clerk, Box 24, Hawkes Bay, Nfld. AOX 3BO (248-6366)
Heart's Content†	634	Bonavista-Trinity-Conception	Trinity-Bay de Verde	Mrs. A. Cumby, Town Clerk, Box 31, Heart's Content, Nfld. AOB 1ZO (583-2491)
Heart's Delight†	842	Bonavista-Trinity-Conception	Trinity-Bay de Verde	Mrs. G.E. Sooley, Town Clerk, Heart's Delight, Nfld. AOB 2AO (588-2708)
Heart's Desire†	380	Bonavista-Trinity-Conception	Trinity-Bay de Verde	Mrs. P. St. George, Town Clerk, Heart's Desire, Nfld. AOB 2BO (588-2280)
Hermitage-Sandyville‡	830	Burin-St. George's	Fortune-Hermitage	Guy Herritt, Community Clerk, Box 126, Hermitage-Sandyville, Nfld. AOH 1SO (883-2343)
Hogan's Pond†	110	St. John's East	Mount Scio	c/o J.G. Whalen, Central Supply, Bldg. 801, Pleasantville, St. John's, Nfld. A1A 1B8
Holyrood†	1,610	St. John's East	Harbour Main-Bell Island	Mrs. E. Devereaux, Town Clerk, Box 100, Holyrood, Nfld. AOA 2RO (229-3252)
Hopedale‡	447	Grand Falls-White Bay-Labrador	Eagle River	Sam Pyogge, Community Clerk, Hopedale, Nfld. AOP 1GO (933-0864)

Cities in CAPITALS; Towns marked †; Communities marked‡.
Area Code for Newfoundland is 709

MUNICIPALITY	POP.	FEDERAL ELECTORAL DISTRICT	PROVINCIAL ELECTORAL DISTRICT	CLERK WITH ADDRESS & PHONE
Howley†	404	Humber-Port-au-Port-St. Barbe	Humber Valley	Mrs. B. Gilley, Town Clerk, Howley, Nfld. A0K 3E0 (635-2231)
Hughes Brook‡	114	Humber-Port au Port-St. Barbe	Bay of Islands	Miss D.A. Lidstone, Hughes Brook Community Clerk, c/o Box 36, Site 17, R.R. 2, Corner Brook, Nfld. A2H 6B9 (783-2876)
Indian Bay‡	198	Gander-Twillingate	Bonavista North	Mrs. M. Cook, Community Clerk, Indian Bay, Nfld. AOG 2VO (678-2727)
Irishtown‡	707	Humber-Port au Port-St. Barbe	Bay of Islands	Ms. M. White, Community Clerk, Irishtown, c/o Box 21, Site 16, R.R. 2, Corner Brook, Nfld. A2H 6B9 (783-2413)
Isle aux Morts†	1,270	Burin-St. George's	La Poile	Miss F. Barnes, Town Clerk, Box 176, Isle aux Morts, Nfld. AOM 1JO (698-3441)
Jacques Fontaine‡	197	Burin-St. George's	Fortune-Hermitage	L. Harris, Community Clerk, Box 51, Jacques Fontaine, Nfld. AOE 2TO (461-2712)
Jerseyside†	1,027	St. John's West	Placentia	D.P. O'Keefe, Town Clerk, Box 70, Jersey-side, Nfld. AOB 2GO (227-2086)
Joe Batt's Arm†	1,023	Gander-Twillingate	Fogo	A.J. Coffin, Town Clerk, Box 28, Joe Batt's Arm, Nfld. AOG 2XO (658-3490)
Keels‡	142	Bonavista-Trinity-Conception	Bonavista South	A. Turner, Community Clerk, Keels, Nfld. AOC 1RO (447-3171)
King's Cove‡	231	Bonavista-Trinity-Conception	Bonavista South	T.M. Maddox, Community Clerk, King's Cove, Nfld. AOC 1SO
King's Point‡	770	Grand Falls-White Bay-Labrador	Green Bay	Miss N. Richards, Community Clerk, King's Point, Nfld. AOJ 1HO (268-3830)
Kippens†	1,267	Humber-Port-au-Port-St. Barbe	Port au Port	Mrs. P. Sweet, Town Clerk, 253 Kippens Rd., Kippens, Nfld. A2N 1B8 (643-2352)
Labrador City†	12,012	Grand Falls-White Bay-Labrador	Menihek	E.J. Snow, Town Clerk, Box 280, Labrador City, Nfld. A2V 2K5 (944-2621)
Lamaline†	543	Burin-St. George's	Grand Bank	Mrs. B. King, Town Clerk, Box 40, Lamaline, Nfld. AOE 2CO (857-2341)
L'Anse au Clair‡	249	Grand Falls-White Bay-Labrador	Strait of Belle Isle	G. Chubbs, Community Clerk, L'Anse au Clair, (Lab.) Nfld. AOK 3KO (931-2481)
L'Anse au Loup‡	536	Grand Falls-White Bay-Labrador	Strait of Belle Isle	G.W. Linstead, Community Clerk, L'Anse au Loup, Nfld. AOK 3LO (927-5573)
Lark Harbour‡	771	Humber-Port au Port-St. Barbe	Bay of Islands	Miss S. Sheppard, Community Clerk, Box 40, Lark Harbour, Nfld. AOL 1HO (681-2270)
La Scie†	1,256	Grand Falls-White Bay-Labrador	Baie Verte-White Bay	Mrs. V. Short, Town Clerk, Box 130, La Scie, Nfld. AOK 3MO (657-2266)
Lawn†	1,025	Burin-St. George's	Grand Bank	Mrs. R.M. Bennet, Town Clerk, Box 29, Lawn, Nfld. AOE 2EO (873-2439)
Lawrence Pond†	11	St. John's East	Conception Bay South	Tom Walters, Lawrence Pond Clerk, c/o Box 4432, St. John's, Nfld. A1C 5Y2 (579-7631)
Leading Tickles West‡	594	Gander-Twillingate	Exploits	Mrs. L. Luscombe, Community Clerk, Box 39, Leading Tickles West, Nfld. AOH 1TO (483-2180)
Lewin's Cove‡	470	Burin-St. George's	Burin-Placentia West	Ms. L. Inkpen, Community Clerk, Lewin's Cove, Nfld. AOE 2GO (891-2180)
Lewisporte†	3,782	Gander-Twillingate	Lewisporte	R. Lush, Town Clerk, Box 219, Lewisporte, Nfld. AOG 3AO (535-2737)
Little Bay‡	375	Grand Falls-White Bay-Labrador	Green Bay	E. Pitts, Community Clerk, Little Bay, Nfld. AOE 2HO (267-3281)
Little Bay East‡	213	Burin-St. George's	Fortune-Hermitage	Mrs. S. Myles, Community Clerk, Box 52, Little Bay East, Nfld. A0E 2J0 (461-2538)
Little Bay Islands‡	422	Grand Falls-White Bay-Labrador	Green Bay	Ms. C. Wiseman, Community Clerk, Box 64, Little Bay Islands, Nfld. AOJ 1KO (626-3511)
Little Burnt Bay†	524	Gander-Twillingate	Lewisporte	Mrs. D. Randell, Town Clerk, Box 40, Little Burnt Bay, Nfld. AOG 3BO (535-6415)
Little Catalina†	736	Bonavista-Trinity-Conception	Bonavista South	Ms. J. Stagg, Town Clerk, Box 59, Little Catalina, Nfld. AOC 1WO (469-2795)
Long Harbour†	675	St. John's West	Placentia	Ms. C. Bruce, Town Clerk, Box 40, Long Harbour, Nfld. AOB 2JO (228-2920)
Lord's Cove‡	409	Burin-St. George's	Grand Bank	Mrs. L. Slaney, Community Clerk, Lord's Cove, Nfld. AOE 2CO (857-2575)

Cities in CAPITALS; Towns marked †; Communities marked‡.
Area Code for Newfoundland is 709

MUNICIPALITY	POP.	FEDERAL ELECTORAL DISTRICT	PROVINCIAL ELECTORAL DISTRICT	CLERK WITH ADDRESS & PHONE
Lourdes‡	987	Humber-Port au Port-St. Barbe	Port au Port	Ms. R. Le Coure, Community Clerk, Box 29, Lourdes, Nfld. AON 1RO (642-5812)
Lumsden†	597	Gander-Twillingate	Fogo	Mrs. I. Gibbons, Town Clerk, Box 100, Lumsden, Nfld. AOG 3EO (530-2309)
Lushes Bight-Beaumont‡	470	Gander-Twillingate	Green Bay	Mrs. B. Burton, Community Clerk, Lushes Bight-Beaumont, Nfld. AOJ 1AO (264-3271)
Main Brook†	551	Grand Falls-White Bay-Labrador	Strait of Belle Isle	Ms. E.R. Pilgrim, Town Clerk, Main Brook, Nfld. AOK 3NO (865-6561)
Makkovik‡	307	Grand Falls-White Bay-Labrador	Eagle River	Miss S. Mitchell, Community Clerk, Makkovik, Nfld. AOP 1JO (933-2222)
Mary's Harbour‡	366	Grand Falls-White Bay-Labrador	Eagle River	F. Rumbolt, Community Clerk, Mary's Harbour, Nfld. AOK 3PO (921-6281)
Marystown†	5,915	Burin-St. George's	Burin-Placentia W.	H. Cluett, Town Clerk, Box 1118, Marystown, Nfld. AOE 2MO (279-1661)
Massey Drive†	381	Humber-Port-au-Port-St. Barbe	Humber East	Ms. E. Crewe, Massey Drive Town Clerk, c/o Box 74, Corner Brook, Nfld. A2H 6C3
McIvers‡	389	Humber-Port au Port-St. Barbe	Bay of Islands	Ms. B. Parsons, McIvers Community Clerk, c/o Box 30, Site 2, R.R. 2, Corner Brook, Nfld. A2H 6B9 (688-9997)
Meadows‡	642	Humber-Port au Port-St. Barbe	Bay of Islands	L. Anderson, Meadows Community Clerk, c/o Box 13, Site 8, R.R. 2, Corner Brook, Nfld. A2H 6B9 (783-2510)
Melrose‡	389	Bonavista-Trinity-Conception	Trinity North	Ms. M. Peters, Community Clerk, Melrose, Nfld. AOC 1YO (469-3401)
Middle Arm‡	555	Grand Falls-White Bay-Labrador	Baie Verte-White Bay	Ms. R. Smith, Community Clerk, Box 51, Middle Arm, Nfld. AOK 3RO (252-6421)
Miles Cove‡	168	Gander-Twillingate	Green Bay	Mrs. N. Reid, Community Clerk, Miles Cove, Nfld. AOJ 1LO (652-3505)
Millertown‡	273	Grand Falls-White Bay-Labrador	Windsor-Buchans	Ms. A. Gale, Community Clerk, Box 56, Millertown, Nfld. AOH 1VO (852-6216)
Milltown†	1,325	Burin-St. George's	Burgeo-Bay D'Espoir	C. Sutton, Town Clerk, Box 70, Milltown, Nfld. AOH 1WO (882-2232)
Ming's Bight‡	412	Grand Falls-White Bay-Labrador	Baie Verte-White Bay	Ms. B. Best, Ming's Bight, Nfld. AOK 3SO (254-6516)
Morrisville‡	217	Burin-St. George's	Burgeo-Bay D'Espoir	J. Taylor, Community Clerk, Morrisville, Nfld. AOH 1WO (882-2257)
Mount Carmel†	675	St. John's West	St. Mary's-The Capes	Mrs. T. McDonald, Town Clerk, Mount Carmel, Nfld. AOB 2MO (521-2040)
Mount Pearl†	10,193	St. John's West	Mount Pearl	Mrs. C. McCarthy, Town Clerk, Box 130, Mount Pearl, Nfld. A1N 2C2 (368-3149)
Musgrave Harbour†	1,530	Gander-Twillingate	Fogo	Mrs. R. Goodyear, Town Clerk, Box 159, Musgrave Harbour, Nfld. AOG 3JO (655-2119)
Musgravetown†	641	Bonavista-Trinity-Conception	Terra Nova	E. Gulliford, Town Clerk, Box 4, Musgravetown, Nfld. AOC 1ZO (467-2726)
Nain‡	812	Grand Falls-White Bay-Labrador	Eagle River	D. White, Community Clerk, Box 59, Nain, (Lab.) Nfld. AOP 1LO (922-2842)
New Perlican†	325	Bonavista-Trinity-Conception	Trinity-Bay de Verde	Mrs. R. Bailey, Town Clerk, New Perlican, Nfld. AOB 2SO (583-2500)
Newtown†	490	Gander-Twillingate	Bonavista North	G. Tulk, Town Clerk, Newtown, Nfld. AOG 3LO (536-2374)
Nippers Harbour‡	260	Grand Falls-White Bay-Labrador	Baie Verte-White Bay	Mrs. B. Prole, Community Clerk, Box 10, Nippers Harbour, Nfld. AOK 3TO (255-3151)
Norman's Cove†	1,155	Bonavista-Trinity-Conception	Bellevue	Mrs. A. Smith, Town Clerk, Box 70, Norman's Cove, Nfld. AOB 2JO (592-2490)
Norris Arm†	1,342	Gander-Twillingate	Lewisporte	Mrs. B. Saunders, Town Mgr., Box 70, Norris Arm, Nfld. AOG 3MO (653-2519)
Norris Point‡	1,065	Humber-Port au Port-St. Barbe	St. Barbe	Mrs. R. Organ, Community Clerk, Box 119, Norris Point, Nfld. AOK 3VO (458-2207)
Northern Arm†	332	Gander-Twillingate	Exploits	Mrs. D. Jewen, Northern Arm Town Clerk, c/o Box 1073, Botwood, Nfld. A0H 1E0 (257-3482)
North River‡	253	Bonavista-Trinity-Conception	Port de Grave	Mrs. F. Cummings, Community Clerk, North River, Nfld. AOA 3CO (786-6958)

Cities in CAPITALS; Towns marked †; Communities marked‡.
Area Code for Newfoundland is 709

MUNICIPALITY	POP.	FEDERAL ELECTORAL DISTRICT	PROVINCIAL ELECTORAL DISTRICT	CLERK WITH ADDRESS & PHONE
North West River†	1,022	Grand Falls-White Bay-Labrador	Naskaupi	A. McLean, Town Clerk, Box 100, North West River, (Lab.) Nfld. AOP 1MO (497-8533)
Old Perlican†	626	Bonavista-Trinity-Conception	Trinity-Bay de Verde	Mrs. J. Barter, Town Clerk, Box 13, Old Perlican, Nfld. AOA 3GO (587-2266)
Pacquet‡	427	Grand Falls-White Bay-Labrador	Baie Verte-White Bay	Miss S. Gillingham, Community Clerk, Pacquet, Nfld. AOK 3XO (251-4231)
Paradise†	2,131	St. John's East	Conception Bay South	A. Walsh, Town Clerk, Box 100, Paradise, Nfld. AOA 2EO (368-6661)
Parkers Cove‡	381	Burin-St. George's	Burin-Placentia West	Mrs. H. Synard, Community Clerk, Parkers Cove, Nfld. AOE 1HO (443-2292)
Parson's Pond‡	544	Humber-Port au Port-St. Barbe	St. Barbe	Mrs. D. Payne, Community Sec., Box 39, Parson's Pond, Nfld. AOK 3ZO (243-2564)
Pasadena†	1,850	Humber-Port au Port-St. Barbe	Humber Valley	Mrs. E. Fisher, Town Clerk, Box 149, Pasadena, Nfld. AOL 1KO (686-2800)
Peterview†	1,099	Gander-Twillingate	Exploits	Mrs. V. Samson, Town Clerk, Peterview, Nfld. A0H 1Y0 (257-2926)
Petty Harbour†	930	St. John's West	Ferryland; Kilbride	Mrs. G. Walsh, Town Clerk, Box 52, Petty Harbour, Nfld. AOA 3HO (368-3959)
Pilley's Island‡	544	Gander-Twillingate	Green Bay	Mrs. B. Traverse, Community Clerk, Pilley's Island, Nfld. AOJ 1MO
Pinware‡	167	Grand Falls-White Bay-Labrador	Eagle River	P. Pike, Community Clerk, Pinware, (Lab.) Nfld. A0K 5S0 (927-5829)
Placentia†	2,209	St. John's West	Placentia	J.M. Kelly, Town Clerk, Box 99, Placentia, Nfld. AOB 2YO (227-2151)
Plate Cove East‡	164	Bonavista-Trinity-Conception	Bonavista South	Mrs. J. Philpott, Community Clerk, Plate Cove East, Nfld. AOC 2CO (545-2239)
Plate Cove West‡	284	Bonavista-Trinity-Conception	Bonavista South	W.P. Walsh, Community Clerk, Plate Cove West, Nfld. AOC 2EO (545-2362)
Point au Gaul‡	148	Burin-St. George's	Grand Bank	P.M. Lockyer, Community Clerk, Site 8, Box 20, R.R. 1, Point au Gaul, Nfld. AOE 2CO (857-2514)
Point Lance‡	135	St. John's West	St. Mary's-The Capes	D. McGrath, Community Sec., Point Lance, Nfld. AOB 1EO (338-2164)
Point Leamington†	882	Gander-Twillingate	Exploits	Mrs. P. Earle, Town Clerk, Box 39, Point Leamington, Nfld. AOH 1ZO (484-3421)
Point May‡	372	Burin-St. George's	Grand Bank	Mrs. B. Fleming, Point May Community Sec., c/o Box 5, Site 4, R.R. 1, Grand Bank, Nfld. AOE 2CO (857-2643)
Point of Bay‡	243	Gander-Twillingate	Exploits	Mrs. S. Anstey, Community Clerk, Point of Bay, Nfld. AOH 2AO (257-2138)
Pool's Cove‡	242	Burin-St. George's	Fortune-Hermitage	Mrs. C. Williams, Community Clerk, Pool's Cove, Nfld. AOH 2BO (665-3511)
Port Anson‡	137	Gander-Twillingate	Green Bay	Miss D. Hewlett, Community Clerk, Port Anson, Nfld. AOJ 1NO (652-3652)
Port au Bras‡	395	Burin-St. George's	Burin-Placentia W.	Mrs. G. Brenton, Port au Bras Community Clerk, c/o Box 17, Site 20, R.R. 1, Burin, Nfld. AOE 1EO (891-1202)
Port aux Choix†	1,375	Humber-Port au Port-St. Barbe	St. Barbe	Miss Ann Marie Skinner, Town Clerk, Box 89, Port aux Choix, Nfld. AOK 4CO (861-3409)
Port-au-Port-West†	1,012	Humber-Port au Port-St. Barbe	Port au Port	D. McCann, Town Clerk, Box 89, Port au Port West, Nfld. AON 1AO
Port Blandford†	815	Bonavista-Trinity-Conception	Terra Nova	Mrs. R. Greening, Town Clerk, Box 76, Port Blandford, Nfld. A0C 2G0 (543-2170)
Port Hope Simpson‡	548	Grand Falls-White Bay-Labrador	Eagle River	M. Burden, Community Clerk, Port Hope Simpson, (Lab.) Nfld. AOK 4EO
Port Kirwan‡	140	St. John's West	Ferryland	Mrs. H. Brothers, Port Kirwan Community Clerk, c/o Site 2, Box 9, Fermeuse, Nfld. A0A 2G0 (363-2285)
Port Rexton‡	463	Bonavista-Trinity-Conception	Trinity North	Ms. L. Long, Community Clerk, Box 55, Port Rexton, Nfld. AOC 2HO (464-2006)
Port Saunders†	691	Humber-Port au Port-St. Barbe	St. Barbe	Ms. J. Plowman, Town Clerk, Box 39, Port Saunders, Nfld. AOK 4HO (861-3105)
Portugal Cove†	1,527	St. John's East	Mount Scio; St. John's East Extern	Mrs. S. Critch, Town Clerk, Portugal Cove, Nfld. AOA 3KO (895-2601)
Portugal Cove South‡	354	St. John's West	St. Mary's-The Capes	C. Molloy, Community Clerk, Box 8, Site 11, Portugal Cove South, AOA 4BO

Cities in CAPITALS; Towns marked †; Communities marked‡.
Area Code for Newfoundland is 709

MUNICIPALITY	POP.	FEDERAL ELECTORAL DISTRICT	PROVINCIAL ELECTORAL DISTRICT	CLERK WITH ADDRESS & PHONE
Port Union†	678	Bonavista-Trinity-Conception	Trinity North	T. Sutton, Town Clerk, Box 91, Port Union, Nfld. AOC 2JO (469-2571)
Postville‡	164	Grand Falls-White Bay-Labrador	Eagle River	Mrs. D. Fudge, Community Clerk, Postville, Nfld. AOP 1NO (479-0830)
Pouch Cove†	1,543	St. John's East	St. John's East Extern	Mrs. A. Walsh, Town Clerk, Box 59, Pouch Cove, Nfld. AOA 3LO (335-2848)
Raleigh‡	333	Grand Falls-White Bay-Labrador	Strait of Belle Isle	A. Elliott, Community Clerk, Raleigh, Nfld. AOK 4JO (452-3281)
Ramea†	1,226	Burin-St. George's	Burgeo-Bay d'Espoir	W. Cutler, Jr., Town Clerk, Box 69, Ramea, Nfld. AOM 1NO (625-2280)
Red Bay‡	301	Grand Falls-White Bay-Labrador	Strait of Belle Isle	H. Moores, Community Clerk, Red Bay (Lab.) Nfld. AOK 4KO (920-0013)
Red Harbour‡	206	Burin-St. George's	Burin-Placentia West	R. Masters, Community Clerk, Red Harbour, Nfld. AOE 2RO
Reidville‡	402	Humber-Port au Port-St. Barbe	Humber Valley	Mrs. G. King, Reidville Community Clerk, c/o Box 5, Site 12, R.R. 2, Deer Lake, Nfld. AOK 2EO (635-5232)
Rencontre East‡	214	Burin-St. George's	Fortune-Hermitage	P. Mullins, Community Sec., Rencontre East, Nfld. AOH 2CO (848-3186)
Renews-Cappahayden‡	528	St. John's West	Ferryland	W.C. Hynes, Community Clerk, Box 40, Renews, Nfld. AOA 3NO (363-2365)
Rigolet‡	238	Grand Falls-White Bay-Labrador	Eagle River	Ms. S.M. Flowers, Community Sec., Rigolet (Lab.) Nfld. AOP 1PO (947-0082)
Riverhead‡	426	St. John's West	St. Mary's-The Capes	Ms. B. Corcoran, Community Clerk, Box 247, Riverhead, Nfld. AOB 3BO (525-2880)
River of Ponds‡	290	Humber-Port au Port-St. Barbe	St. Barbe	Ms. D. Maher, Community Clerk, River of Ponds, Nfld. AOK 4MO (225-3161)
Roberts Arm†	1,064	Gander-Twillingate	Green Bay	Mrs. J. Paddock, Town Clerk, Box 10, Roberts Arm, Nfld. AOJ 1RO (652-3331)
Rocky Harbour‡	1,267	Humber-Port au Port-St. Barbe	St. Barbe	Miss C. Shears, Community Clerk, Rocky Harbour, Nfld. AOK 4NO (458-2376)
Roddickton†	1,234	Grand Falls-White Bay-Labrador	Baie Verte-White Bay	Miss P. Decker, Town Clerk, Box 10, Roddickton, Nfld. AOK 4PO (457-2413)
Rose Blanche†	984	Burin-St. George's	La Poile	Mrs. L. Fudge, Town Clerk, Box 159, Rose Blanche, Nfld. A0M 1P0 (956-2067)
Rushoon‡	504	Burin-St. George's	Burin-Placentia West	Ms. J. Hann, Community Clerk, Rushoon, Nfld. AOE 2SO (443-2572)
St. Alban's†	2,040	Burin-St. George's	Burgeo-Bay d'Espoir	Mrs. C. Willcott, Town Clerk, Box 10, St. Alban's, Nfld. AOH 2EO (538-3132)
St. Anthony†	2,987	Grand Falls-White Bay-Labrador	Strait of Belle Isle	W. Biles, Town Mgr., Box 128, St. Anthony, Nfld. AOK 4SO (454-2583)
St. Bernard's‡	611	Burin-St. George's	Fortune-Hermitage	Mrs. D. Hodder, Community Clerk, Box 70, St. Bernard's, Nfld. AOE 2TO (461-2532)
St. Brendan's‡	528	Gander-Twillingate	Terra Nova	B. Bridgeman, Community Clerk, St. Brendan's, Nfld. AOG 3VO (669-3333)
St. Bride's‡	573	St. John's West	St. Mary's-The Capes	Mrs. M.A. Lundrigan, Community Clerk, St. Bride's, Nfld. AOB 2ZO (337-2160)
St. George's†	1,976	Burin-St. George's	St. George's	Mrs. N. Chubb, Town Clerk, Box 250, St. George's, Nfld. AON 1ZO (647-3283)
St. Jacques†	1,061	Burin-St. George's	Fortune-Hermitage	Mrs. M. Snook, Town Clerk, St. Jacques, Nfld. A0H 1K0 (888-3211)
ST. JOHN'S	86,576	St. John's East; St. John's West	Kilbride; Mount Scio; Pleasantville; St. J. Centre; St. J. East; St. J. North; St. J. West; Waterford-Kenmount	R. Greene, City Clerk, City Hall, St. John's, Nfld. A1C 5M2 (726-8820)
St. Joseph's‡	294	St. John's West	St. Mary's-The Capes	A. Healey, Community Clerk, Box 3, R.R. 1, St. Joseph's, Nfld. AOB 3AO (521-2695)
St. Lawrence†	2,258	Burin-St. George's	Grand Bank	G. Quirke, Town Clerk, Box 128, St. Lawrence, Nfld. AOE 2VO (873-2222)
St. Lunaire-Griquet‡	921	Grand Falls-White Bay-Labrador	Strait of Belle Isle	Miss C. Earles, Community Clerk, Box 9, St. Lunaire-Griquet, Nfld. AOK 2XO (623-2222)
St. Mary's‡	485	St. John's West	St. Mary's-The Capes	P. Fagan, Community Sec., Box 15, St. Mary's, Nfld. AOB 3BO (525-2160)
St. Paul's‡	456	Humber-Port au Port-St. Barbe	St. Barbe	J. Legge, Community Clerk, St. Paul's, Nfld. AOK 4YO (243-2279)

Cities in CAPITALS; Towns marked †; Communities marked‡.
Area Code for Newfoundland is 709

MUNICIPALITY	POP.	FEDERAL ELECTORAL DISTRICT	PROVINCIAL ELECTORAL DISTRICT	CLERK WITH ADDRESS & PHONE
St. Phillips†	807	St. John's East	Mount Scio; Conception Bay South	Ms. E. Picco, St. Phillips Town Clerk, c/o Box 21, Site 5, R.R. 1, Paradise, Nfld. AOA 2EO (895-2151)
St. Shotts‡	221	St. John's West	St. Mary's-The Capes	R. Molloy, Community Sec., St. Shotts, Nfld. AOA 3RO (438-2454)
St. Thomas†	461	St. John's East	Conception Bay South	Mrs. R.G. Wheeler, Town Clerk, Box 7, Site 22, St. Thomas, Nfld. A0A 2E0 (895-2576)
St. Vincent's†	850	St. John's West	St. Mary's-The Capes	H. White, Town Clerk, Box 31, St. Vincent's, Nfld. AOB 3CO (525-2753)
Sally's Cove‡	188	Humber-Port au Port-St. Barbe	St. Barbe	C. Laing, Community Sec., Sally's Cove, Nfld. AOK 4ZO
Salmon Cove†	733	Bonavista-Trinity-Conception	Carbonear	Miss Jacqueline Penney, Town Clerk, Salmon Cove, Nfld. AOA 3SO (596-6218)
Salvage†	242	Gander-Twillingate	Terra Nova	Mrs. C. Burden, Town Clerk, Salvage, Nfld. A0G 3X0 (677-3535)
Sandringham‡	260	Gander-Twillingate	Terra Nova	C. Rodgers, Community Clerk, Sandringham, Nfld. AOG 3YO (677-2286)
Sandy Cove‡	168	Gander-Twillingate	Terra Nova	Mrs. E. Brown, Sandy Cove Community Clerk, c/o Box 22, Site 8, Eastport, Nfld. AOG 1ZO (677-2544)
Seal Cove‡	510	Burin-St. George's	Fortune-Hermitage	Mrs. S. Forsey, Community Clerk, Seal Cove, Nfld. AOH 2GO (666-4431)
Seldom-Little Seldom	522	Gander-Twillingate	Fogo	Mrs. I. Harnett, Town Clerk, Box 100, Seldom, Nfld. AOG 3ZO (627-3401)
Shoal Harbour†	1,009	Bonavista-Trinity-Conception	Trinity North	Mrs. I. Thistle, Town Clerk, Box 179, Shoal Harbour, Nfld. AOC 2LO (466-2970)
Small Point†	684	Bonavista-Trinity-Conception	Carbonear	Ms. L. Diamond, Small Point Town Clerk, c/o Site 6, Box 24, Adams Cove, Nfld. AOA 1TO (598-2610)
South Brook (Hall's Bay)†	828	Gander-Twillingate	Green Bay	Mrs. H. Rowsell, Town Clerk, Box 63, South Brook, Nfld. AOJ 1SO (657-2206)
South Brook (Humber Valley)‡	446	Humber-Port au Port-St. Barbe	Humber Valley	J. Turner, South Brook Community Sec., c/o Box 186, Pasadena, Nfld. AOL 1KO (686-2867)
Southern Harbour†	759	St. John's West	Placentia	Mrs. L. Ryan, Town Clerk, Box 10, Southern Harbour, Nfld. AOB 3HO (463-2329)
South River†	598	Bonavista-Trinity-Conception	Port de Grave	Mrs. E. Crane, Town Clerk, Box 40, South River, Nfld. AOA 3WO (786-6761)
Spaniard's Bay†	1,568	Bonavista-Trinity-Conception	Harbour Grace	L.R. Gosse, Town Clerk, Box 190, Spaniard's Bay, Nfld. AOA 3XO (786-3568)
Springdale†	3,513	Grand Falls-White Bay-Labrador	Green Bay	E. Taylor, Town Mgr., Box 57, Springdale, Nfld. AOJ 1TO (673-3439)
Steady Brook‡	292	Humber-Port au Port-St. Barbe	Humber Valley	Mrs. M. Hillier, Steady Brook Comty. Clerk, c/o Box 1, Site 4, R.R. 1, Corner Brook, Nfld. A2H 2N2 (634-7601)
Stephenville†	10,280	Humber-Port au Port-St. Barbe	Stephenville	J.E.E. Warren, Town Clerk, Box 420, Stephenville, Nfld. A2N 2Z5 (643-2803)
Stephenville Crossing†	2,207	Humber-Port au Port-St. Barbe	St. George's	N. Dallard, Town Clerk, Box 68, Stephenville Crossing, Nfld. AON 2CO (646-2600)
Summerford†	1,099	Gander-Twillingate	Twillingate	Mrs. L. Wheeler, Town Clerk, Box 59, Summerford, Nfld. AOG 4EO (629-3419)
Summerside‡	830	Humber-Port au Port-St. Barbe	Bay of Islands	Ms. B. Wellman, Summerside Community Clerk, c/o Box 63, Site 12, R.R. 2, Corner Brook, Nfld. A2H 6B9 (783-2722)
Sunnyside†	726	Bonavista-Trinity-Conception	Bellevue	Mrs. M. Smith, Town Clerk, Box 89, Sunnyside, Nfld. AOB 3JO (542-3506)
Terra Nova‡	88	Gander-Twillingate	Terra Nova	R. Galloway, Community Sec., Terra Nova, Nfld. AOC 1LO (265-6221)
Terrenceville†	764	Burin-St. George's	Fortune-Hermitage	Mrs. L. Hickey, Town Clerk, Box 54, Terrenceville, Nfld. AOE 2XO (662-3376)
Tilt Cove‡	69	Grand Falls-White Bay-Labrador	Baie Verte-White Bay	Mrs. A. Snooks, Community Clerk, Box 16, Tilt Cove, Nfld. AOK 3MO (675-2640)
Tilting‡	377	Gander-Twillingate	Fogo	Mrs. M.M. O'Keefe, Community Clerk, Box 75, Tilting, Nfld. AOG 4HO (658-3525)
Tilton†	581	Bonavista-Trinity-Conception	Harbour Grace	N. Young, Town Clerk, Box 309, R.R. 1, Tilton, Nfld. A0A 3X0 (786-7273)

Cities in CAPITALS; Towns marked †; Communities marked‡.
Area Code for Newfoundland is 709

MUNICIPALITY	POP.	FEDERAL ELECTORAL DISTRICT	PROVINCIAL ELECTORAL DISTRICT	CLERK WITH ADDRESS & PHONE
Torbay†	2,908	St. John's East	St. John's East Extern	Mrs. M. Thorne, Town Clerk, Box 190, Torbay, Nfld. AOA 3ZO (437-6532)
Traytown‡	367	Gander-Twillingate	Terra Nova	W. Patey, Community Clerk, Traytown, Nfld. AOG 4KO (533-2565)
Trepassey†	1,427	St. John's West	St. Mary's-The Capes	Ms. R. Boland, Town Clerk, Box 129, Trepassey, Nfld. AOA 4BO (438-2641)
Trinity†	559	Gander-Twillingate	Bonavista North	Mrs. S. Brown, Town Clerk, Box 82, Trinity, Nfld. A0G 4L0 (678-2551)
Trinity‡	367	Bonavista-Trinity-Conception	Trinity North	Mrs. B. Vokey, Community Clerk, Box 42, Trinity, Nfld. AOC 2SO (464-3435)
Triton†	1,091	Gander-Twillingate	Green Bay	Ms. V. Fudge, Town Clerk, Box 10, Triton, Nfld. AOJ 1VO (263-2264)
Trout River‡	784	Humber-Port au Port-St. Barbe	St. Barbe	N. Sheppard, Community Clerk, Box 89, Trout River, Nfld. AOK 5PO (451-5376)
Twillingate†	1,404	Gander-Twillingate	Twillingate	W.R. Hull, Town Mgr., Box 220, Twillingate, Nfld. AOG 4MO (884-2438)
Upper Island Cove†	1,851	Bonavista-Trinity-Conception	Harbour Grace	Mrs. D. Mercer, Town Clerk, Box 149, Upper Island Cove, Nfld. AOA 4EO (589-2503)
Victoria†	1,767	Bonavista-Trinity-Conception	Carbonear	C. White, Town Clerk, Box 130, Victoria, Nfld. AOA 4GO (596-3783)
Wabana†	4,824	St. John's East	Harbour Main-Bell Island	Mrs. D. Butler, Town Clerk, Box 1229, Wabana, Nfld. AOA 4HO (488-2990)
Wabush†	3,769	Grand Falls-White Bay-Labrador	Menihek	A. Rodkowski, Town Clerk, Box 190, Wabush, (Lab.) Nfld. A0R 1B0 (282-6953)
Wareham†	505	Gander-Twillingate	Bonavista North	F. Hunt, Town Clerk, Box 40, Wareham, Nfld. A0G 4P0 (678-2529)
Wedgewood Park†	1,236	St. John's East	St. John's East Extern	Mrs. J. Murphy, Town Clerk, 12 Gleneyre St., #306, Wedgewood Park, Nfld. A1A 2M7 (753-6626)
Wesleyville†	1,167	Gander-Twillingate	Bonavista North	L. Davis, Town Mgr., Box 143, Wesleyville, Nfld. AOG 4RO (536-2412)
Westport‡	464	Grand Falls-White Bay-Labrador	Baie Verte-White Bay	Mrs. S. Jacobs, Community Clerk, Westport, Nfld. AOK 5RO (224-5346)
West St. Modeste‡	277	Grand Falls-White Bay-Labrador	Strait of Belle Isle	F. Marshall, Community Clerk, West St. Modeste, Nfld. AOK 5SO (927-5583)
Whitbourne†	1,268	Bonavista-Trinity-Conception	Bellevue	Ms. W. Lynch, Town Clerk, Box 119, Whitbourne, Nfld. AOB 3KO (759-2780)
Whiteway‡	260	Bonavista-Trinity-Conception	Trinity-Bay de Verde	Don Harwin, Community Clerk, Whiteway, Nfld. AOB 3LO (588-2897)
Wild Bight‡	285	Grand Falls-White Bay-Labrador	Green Bay	Mrs. J. Verge, Wild Bight Community Clerk, c/o R.R. 1, Springdale, Nfld. AOJ 1TO (267-4351)
Windsor†	6,349	Grand Falls-White Bay-Labrador	Windsor-Buchans	Miss K. Antle, Town Clerk, Box 220, Windsor, Nfld. AOH 2HO (489-2277)
Winterland‡	184	Burin-St. George's	Burin-Placentia West	Ms. D. Marshall, Community Clerk, Winterland, Nfld. AOE 2YO (279-3701)
Winterton†	796	Bonavista-Trinity-Conception	Trinity-Bay de Verde	M. Pinhorn, Town Clerk, Box 59, Winterton, Nfld. AOB 3MO (583-2010)
Woodstock‡	334	Grand Falls-White Bay-Labrador	Baie Verte-White Bay	V.R. Bussey, Community Clerk, Woodstock, Nfld. AOK 5XO (251-3176)
Woody Point‡	529	Humber-Port au Port-St. Barbe	St. Barbe	Mrs. S. Butt, Community Clerk, Woody Point, Nfld. AOK 1PO (453-2273)
York Harbour‡	330	Humber-Port au Port-St. Barbe	Bay of Islands	Mrs. V. Robinson, Community Clerk, York Harbour, Nfld. AOL 1LO (681-2280)

NOVA SCOTIA

Nova Scotia is geographically divided into 18 counties. Twelve of these constitute separate municipalities. The remaining six are each divided into two districts, and each of these constitutes a separate municipality. Thus there are 24 rural municipalities. Within these areas are autonomous incorporated towns (39) and cities (3), (the cities have their own charters), and other local organizations with limited jurisdiction, including school boards, boards of school trustees, village commissions, local service commissions, rural fire districts, and other special purpose forms.

Requirements for incorporation of a new town are 1,500 population in an area of less than 640 acres.

The organization of towns is specified in the Towns Act, and that of rural municipalities in the Municipal Act. Villages are governed by the Village Service Act. Additional regulation is provided by the Municipal Affairs Act, the Municipal Boundaries & Representation Act, the Municipal Finance Corporation Act, and the Planning Act.

All general and special municipal elections, including elections for school board members, are governed by the Municipal Elections Act, 1980.

The term of office for mayors, councillors, aldermen, and elective school board members is three years. Elections take place on the third Saturday in October, every third year, beginning in 1979. This eliminates overlapping terms in towns and the Cities of Dartmouth and Sydney. Transitional arrangements permitted the councillors elected in 1977 to retain office until 1980 when their replacements were elected for two-year terms. Thus, the full system, with all council and school board members being elected on the same day will only be fully operational in the elections in 1982.

Cities in CAPITALS; Towns marked †; Villages marked‡; Balance are Rural Municipalities.
Area Code for Nova Scotia 902

MUNICIPALITY	POP.	COUNTY	FEDERAL ELECTORAL DISTRICT	PROVINCIAL ELECTORAL DISTRICT	CLERK OR SECRETARY WITH ADDRESS & PHONE
Amherst†	10,263	Cumberland	Cumberland-Colchester	Cumberland East	V.M. Parrett, Town Clerk, Box 516, Amherst, N.S. B4H 4A1 (667-3352)
Annapolis RM	19,610	Annapolis	South West Nova	Annapolis East; Annapolis West	Ronald Grant, Mun. Clerk, Box 100, Annapolis Royal, N.S. BOS 1AO (532-2331)
Annapolis Royal†	738	Annapolis	South West Nova	Annapolis West	Lt. Col. D.W. Souchen, Town Clerk, Box 310, Annapolis Royal, N.S. BOS 1AO (532-2043)
Antigonish†	5,442	Antigonish	Cape Breton Highlands-Canso	Antigonish	S.L. MacLellan, Town Clerk, 274 Main St., Antigonish, N.S. B2G 2C4 (863-1312)
Antigonish RM	11,996	Antigonish	Cape Breton Highlands-Canso	Antigonish	Mrs. D. Flikke, Mun. Clerk, Box 598, Antigonish, N.S. BOH 1BO (863-1117)
Argyle RM	8,618	Yarmouth	South West Nova	Argyle	J.P. Doucet, Mun. Clerk, Box 10, Tusket, N.S. BOW 3MO (648-2311)
Aylesford‡	687	Kings	Annapolis Valley-Hants	Kings West	P.H. Nichols, Village Clerk, Aylesford, N.S. BOP 1CO
Baddeck‡	943	Victoria	Cape Breton Highlands-Canso	Victoria	Mabel MacEachern, Village Clerk, Baddeck, N.S. BOE 1BO (295-3231)
Barrington RM	7,258	Shelburne	South Shore	Shelburne	J.R. Fry, Mun. Clerk, Box 100, Barrington, N.S. BOW 1EO (637-2015)
Bedford†	7,589	Halifax	Halifax West	Bedford-Musquodoboit Valley	D. English, Town Clerk, #400, 1496 Bedford Hwy., Bedford, N.S. B4A 1E5 (835-9936)
Berwick†	1,701	Kings	Annapolis Valley-Hants	Kings West	H.E. Jones, Town Clerk, Box 130, Berwick, N.S. BOP 1EO (538-3657)
Bible Hill‡	4,266	Colchester	Cumberland-Colchester	Truro-Bible Hill	H.D. Boyce, Village Clerk, Bible Hill, N.S. B2N 2R9
Bridgetown†	1,037	Annapolis	South West Nova	Annapolis West	W. Hamilton, Town Clerk, Box 309, Bridgetown, N.S. BOS 1CO (665-4637)
Bridgewater†	6,010	Lunenburg	South Shore	Lunenburg West	W.E. Hebb, Town Clerk, Box 9, Bridgewater, N.S. B4V 2W7 (543-4651)
Brooklyn‡	1,179	Queens	South Shore	Queens	J.M. Kral, Village Clerk, Box 236, Brooklyn, N.S. BOJ 1HO
Canning‡	789	Kings	Annapolis Valley-Hants	Kings North	H.L. Gates, Village Clerk, Box 9, Canning, N.S. BOP 1HO
Canso†	1,173	Guysborough	Cape Breton Highlands-Canso	Guysborough	Miss M. MacDougall, Town Clerk, Box 189, Canso, N.S. BOH 1HO (366-2525)
Cape Breton RM	42,969	Cape Breton	Cape Br.-E. Richmond; Cape Br. Highlands-Canso; Cape Br.-The Sydneys	Cape Breton-The Lakes; Cape Br. West; Victoria	J. MacEachern, Mun. Clerk, Court House, Sydney, N.S. B1S 2Z7 (564-5541)
Chester‡	1,121	Lunenburg	South Shore	Lunenburg East	I. Mitchell, Village Clerk, Box 535, Chester, N.S. BOJ 1JO
Chester RM	9,955	Lunenburg	South Shore	Lunenburg East	L.R. Feader, Mun. Clerk, Box 396, Chester, N.S. BOJ 1JO (275-3554)
Clare RM	9,149	Digby	South West Nova	Clare	D.J. Comeau, Mun. Clerk, Box 458, Little Brook, N.S. BOW 1ZO (769-2031)

Cities in CAPITALS; Towns marked †; Villages marked‡; Balance are Rural Municipalities.
Area Code for Nova Scotia 902

MUNICIPALITY	POP.	COUNTY	FEDERAL ELECTORAL DISTRICT	PROVINCIAL ELECTORAL DISTRICT	CLERK OR SECRETARY WITH ADDRESS & PHONE
Clark's Harbour†	1,077	Shelburne	South Shore	Shelburne	Mrs. H. Nickerson, Town Clerk, Box 160, Clark's Harbour, N.S. BOW 1PO (745-2390)
Colchester RM	27,524	Colchester	Cumberland-Colchester	Colchester North; Colchester South	H.G. Creelman, Mun. Clerk, Box 697, Truro, N.S. B2N 5E7 (895-1501)
Cornwallis Square‡		Kings	Annapolis Valley-Hants	Kings West	Mrs. L. Toole, Village Clerk, Waterville, N.S. B0P 1V0
Cumberland RM	17,076	Cumberland	Cumberland-Colchester	Cumberland West	F.A. Harrison, Mun. Clerk, Box 126, Amherst, N.S. B4H 4Y6 (667-2313)
DARTMOUTH	65,341		Dartmouth-Halifax East	Dartmouth East; Dartmouth North; Dartmouth South	Bruce Smith, City Clerk, Box 817, Dartmouth, N.S. B2Y 3Z3 (466-7401)
Digby†	2,542	Digby	South West Nova	Digby	J. Wheelhouse, Town Clerk, Box 579, Digby, N.S. BOV 1AO (245-4262)
Digby RM	9,202	Digby	South West Nova	Digby	W. McMillan, Mun. Clerk, Box 429, Digby, N.S. BOV 1AO (245-4777)
Dominion†	2,938	Cape Breton	Cape Breton-East Richmond	Cape Breton Centre	B. Clark, Town Clerk, Commercial St., Dominion, N.S. BOA 1EO (849-6556)
Dover‡		Halifax	Halifax West	Halifax-St. Margarets	Village Clerk, Dover, N.S.B0H 1V0
Freeport‡	474	Digby	South West Nova	Digby	Heather Titus, Village Clerk, Freeport, N.S. BOV 1BO (839-2154)
Glace Bay†	21,836	Cape Breton	Cape Breton-East Richmond	Cape Breton East	B. Sterns, Town Clerk, McKeen St., Glace Bay, N.S. B1A 5B9 (849-5541)
Greenwood‡	134	Kings	Annapolis Valley-Hants	Kings West	Mrs. L. Gertridge, Village Clerk, Box 1068, Greenwood, N.S. BOP 1NO
Guysborough RM	7,340	Guysborough	Cape Breton Highlands-Canso; Central Nova	Guysborough	Ms. C. Tynski, Mun. Clerk, Box 79, Guysborough, N.S. BOH 1NO (533-3705)
HALIFAX	117,882		Halifax; Halifax West	Halifax Atlantic; Hal. Bedford Basin; Hal. Chebucto; Hal. Citadel; Hal. Cornwallis; Hal. Needham	Mrs. G. Blennerhassett, City Clerk, Box 1749, Halifax, N.S. B3J 3A5 (426-6430)
Halifax RM	95,289	Halifax	Dartmouth-Hal. East; Hal. West	Hal. Atlantic; Hal. Eastern Shore; Hal.-St. Margarets	G.J. Kelly, Mun. Clerk, 2750 Dutch Village Rd., Halifax, N.S. B3L 4K3 (477-5641)
Hants East RM	14,042	Hants	Annapolis Valley-Hants	Hants East	N.D. Glover, Mun. Clerk, Box 190, Shubenacadie, N.S. BON 2HO (758-2299)
Hants West RM	12,642	Hants	Annapolis Valley-Hants	Hants West	R. Haley, Mun. Clerk, Box 344, Windsor, N.S. BON 2TO (798-8391)
Hantsport†	1,423	Hants	Annapolis Valley-Hants	Kings South	J.D. McGinn, Town Clerk, Box 399, Hantsport, N.S. BOP 1PO (684-3211)
Havre Boucher‡	544	Antigonish	Cape Breton Highlands-Canso	Antigonish	C. Corbett, Village Clerk, Box 12, Havre Boucher, N.S. BOH 1PO
Hebbville‡	481	Lunenburg	South Shore	Lunenburg West	Village Clerk, Hebbville, N.S.B0J 2C0
Inverness RM	17,367	Inverness	Cape Breton Highlands-Canso	Inverness North; Inverness South	A.A. Murray, Mun. Clerk, Box 179, Port Hood, N.S. BOE 2WO (787-2274)
Kentville†	5,056	Kings	Annapolis Valley-Hants	Kings North	D.P. Hardy, Town Clerk, Box 218, Kentville, N.S. B4N 3W4 (678-2107)

Cities in CAPITALS; Towns marked †; Villages marked‡; Balance are Rural Municipalities.
Area Code for Nova Scotia 902

MUNICIPALITY	POP.	COUNTY	FEDERAL ELECTORAL DISTRICT	PROVINCIAL ELECTORAL DISTRICT	CLERK OR SECRETARY WITH ADDRESS & PHONE
Kings RM	38,091	Kings	Annapolis Valley-Hants	Kings North; Kings South; Kings West	R. Ramsey, Mun. Clerk, Box 100, Kentville, N.S. B4N 3W3 (678-6141)
Kingston‡	1,562	Kings	Annapolis Valley-Hants	Kings West	Mrs. A. Williamson, Village Clerk, Box 254, Kingston, N.S. BOP 1RO
Lawrencetown‡	627	Annapolis	South West Nova	Annapolis East	Mrs. C. Lowe, Village Clerk, Box 38, Lawrencetown, N.S. BOS 1AO
Liverpool†	3,336	Queens	South Shore	Queens	D. Clattenburg, Town Clerk, Box 550, Liverpool, N.S. BOT 1KO (354-5701)
Lockeport†	1,030	Shelburne	South Shore	Shelburne	H. Chymist, Town Clerk, Box 189, Lockeport, N.S. BOT 1LO (656-2216)
Louisbourg†	1,519	Cape Breton	Cape Breton-East Richmond	Cape Breton West	Miss E. MacPherson, Town Clerk, Box 88, Louisbourg, N.S. BOA 1MO (733-2014)
Lunenburg†	3,024	Lunenburg	South Shore	Lunenburg Centre	J.A. Wentzell, Town Clerk, Box 129, Lunenburg, N.S. BOJ 2CO (634-4410)
Lunenburg RM	22,160	Lunenburg	South Shore	Lunenburg Centre; Lunenburg East; Lunenburg West	D.E. Steele, Mun. Clerk, Box 200, Bridgewater, N.S. B4V 2W8 (543-8181)
Mahone Bay†	1,236	Lunenburg	South Shore	Lunenburg Centre	G. Brimicombe, Town Clerk, Box 239, Mahone Bay, N.S. BOJ 2EO (624-8327)
Middleton†	1,823	Annapolis	South West Nova	Annapolis East	E. Bennett, Town Clerk, Box 340, Middleton, N.S. BOS 1PO (825-4841)
Milton‡	1,918	Queens	South Shore	Queens	J.S. Chute, Village Clerk, Milton, N.S. BOT 1PO
Mulgrave†	1,206	Guysborough	Cape Breton Highlands-Canso	Guysborough	Harry MacFarlane, Town Clerk, Box 129, Mulgrave, N.S. BOE 2GO (747-2243)
New Glasgow†	10,672	Pictou	Central Nova	Pictou Centre	H.E. Aikens, Town Clerk, Box 7, New Glasgow, N.S. B2H 5E1 (752-4278)
New Minas‡	2,873	Kings	Annapolis-Valley-Hants	Kings South	A.P. Dakin, Village Clerk, New Minas, N.S. B4N 3G1
New Waterford†	9,223	Cape Breton	Cape Breton-East Richmond	Cape Breton Centre	Jerry Ryan, Town Clerk, 3371 Plummer Ave., New Waterford, N.S. B1H 1Y8 (862-6401)
North Sydney†	8,319	Cape Breton	Cape Breton-The Sydneys	Cape Breton North	E. Snow, Town Clerk, Box 370, North Sydney, N.S. B2A 3M4 (794-7213)
Oxford†	1,498	Cumberland	Cumberland-Colchester	Cumberland West	H.M. McCormack, Town Clerk, Box 338, Oxford, N.S. BOM 1PO (447-2170)
Parrsboro†	1,857	Cumberland	Cumberland-Colchester	Cumberland West	Ashley Brown, Town Clerk, Box 400, Parrsboro, N.S. BOM 1SO (254-2036)
Pictou RM	20,792	Pictou	Central Nova	Pictou East; Pictou West	J.W. Clattenburg, Mun. Clerk, Box 910, Pictou, N.S. BOK 1HO (485-4311)
Pictou†	4,588	Pictou	Central Nova	Pictou West	D.L. Steele, Town Clerk, Box 640, Pictou, N.S. BOK 1HO (485-4372)
Port Hawkesbury†	4,008	Inverness	Cape Breton Highlands-Canso	Inverness South	C.J. MacDonald, Town Clerk, Box 10, Port Hawkesbury, N.S. BOE 2VO (625-2746)
Port Williams‡	993	Kings	Annapolis Valley-Hants	Kings North	Mrs. B.L. Gates, Village Clerk, Box 153, Port Williams, N.S. BOP 1TO
Pugwash‡	746	Cumberland	Cumberland-Colchester	Cumberland East	Mrs. M. Baker, Village Clerk, Pugwash, N.S. BOK 1LO

Cities in CAPITALS; Towns marked †; Villages marked‡; Balance are Rural Municipalities.
Area Code for Nova Scotia 902

MUNICIPALITY	POP.	COUNTY	FEDERAL ELECTORAL DISTRICT	PROVINCIAL ELECTORAL DISTRICT	CLERK OR SECRETARY WITH ADDRESS & PHONE
Queens RM	9,586	Queens	South Shore	Queens	L.D. Robertson, Mun. Clerk, Box 1264, Liverpool, N.S. BOT 1KO (354-3453)
Richmond RM	12,281	Richmond	Cape Br.-E. Richmond; Cape Br. Highlands-Canso	Richmond	L. Digout, Mun. Clerk, Box 120, Arichat, N.S. BOE 1AO (226-2400)
River Hebert‡	861	Cumberland	Cumberland-Colchester	Cumberland Centre	Mrs. L. Sawatsky, Village Clerk, River Hebert, N.S. BOL 1GO
St. Mary's RM	3,106	Guysborough	Central Nova	Guysborough	Miss M. Pushie, Mun. Clerk, Box 276, Sherbrooke, N.S. B0T 3C0 (522-2049)
St. Peter's‡	705	Richmond	Cape Breton Highlands-Canso	Richmond	L. Digout, Village Clerk, St. Peter's, N.S. BOE 1AO
Shelburne RM	5,094	Shelburne	South Shore	Shelburne	J.P. MacDonald, Mun. Clerk, Box 280, Shelburne, N.S. BOT 1WO (875-3083)
Shelburne†	2,511	Shelburne	South Shore	Shelburne	H.C. Blades, Town Clerk, Box 670, Shelburne, N.S. BOT 1WO (875-2991)
Springhill†	5,220	Cumberland	Cumberland-Colchester	Cumberland Centre	D. Maddison, Town Clerk, Box 1000, Springhill, N.S. BOM 1XO (597-3751)
Stellarton†	5,366	Pictou	Central Nova	Pictou Centre	A.A. Pearson, Town Sec., Box 2200, Stellarton, N.S. BOK 1SO (752-2114)
Stewiacke†	1,174	Colchester	Cumberland-Colchester	Colchester South	Ioan Astle, Town Clerk, Box 8, Stewiacke, N.S. BON 2JO (378-2231)
SYDNEY	30,645	Cape Breton	Cape Breton-The Sydneys	Cape Breton South	Paul Roach, City Clerk, Box 730, Sydney, N.S. B1P 6H7 (539-0940)
Sydney Mines†	8,965	Cape Breton	Cape Breton-The Sydneys	Cape Breton North	Mrs. L. Gordon, Town Clerk, Box 100, Sydney Mines, N.S. B1V 2L5 (736-6226)
Tatamagouche‡	636	Colchester	Cumberland-Colchester	Colchester North	Mrs. S. Crawford, Village Clerk, Box 14, Tatamagouche, N.S. BOK 1VO
Tiverton‡	315	Digby	South West Nova	Digby	Ms. M. Cossaboon, Village Clerk, Box 16, Tiverton, N.S. BOV 1GO
Trenton†	3,224	Pictou	Central Nova	Pictou Centre	C.R. Campbell, Town Clerk, Box 328, Trenton, N.S. BOK 1XO (752-5311)
Truro†	12,840	Colchester	Cumberland-Colchester	Truro-Bible Hill	D.G. Gilroy, Town Clerk, Box 427, Truro, N.S. B2N 5C5 (895-4484)
Uplands Park‡	336	Halifax	Halifax West	Halifax-St. Margarets	M. Stenton, Village Clerk, Uplands Park, N.S. B4B 1E8
Victoria RM	8,156	Victoria	Cape Breton Highlands-Canso	Victoria	Mabel MacEachern, Mun. Clerk, Box 370, Baddeck, N.S. BOE 1BO (295-3231)
Westport‡	341	Digby	South West Nova	Digby	Caroline Norwood, Village Clerk, Box 1192, Westport, N.S. BOV 1HO
Westville†	4,251	Pictou	Central Nova	Pictou Centre	C. Purvis, Town Clerk, Box 923, Westville, N.S. BOK 2AO (396-5144)
Weymouth‡	483	Digby	South West Nova	Digby	C.W. Mullen, Village Clerk, Box 84, Weymouth, N.S. BOW 3TO
Windsor†	3,702	Hants	Annapolis Valley-Hants	Hants West	L.A. Armstrong, Town Clerk, Box 158, Windsor, N.S. BON 2TO (798-2275)
Wolfville†	3,073	Kings	Annapolis Valley-Hants	Kings South	R. Thomson, Town Clerk, Box 418, Wolfville, N.S. BOP 1XO (542-3037)

Cities in CAPITALS; Towns marked †; Villages marked‡; Balance are Rural Municipalities.
Area Code for Nova Scotia 902

MUNICIPALITY	POP.	COUNTY	FEDERAL ELECTORAL DISTRICT	PROVINCIAL ELECTORAL DISTRICT	CLERK OR SECRETARY WITH ADDRESS & PHONE
Yarmouth†	7,801	Yarmouth	South West Nova	Yarmouth	Miss K.J. Moses, Town Clerk, Court House, 403 Main St., Yarmouth, N.S. B5A 1G3 (742-2521)
Yarmouth RM	8,767	Yarmouth	South West Nova	Yarmouth	Wm. Scott, Mun. Clerk, Box 15, Yarmouth, N.S. B5A 4B1 (742-7159)

ONTARIO

LOCAL MUNICIPALITIES

(List does not include upper-tier municipalities)

Cities (2 in Metro Toronto, 5 in Niagara region, 3 in Waterloo region, 5 in Ottawa-Carleton region and 2 in Peel region, 1 each in Durham, Haldimand-Norfolk, Halton, Hamilton-Wentworth and Sudbury regions, 19 in counties, 4 in districts)....45

Boroughs (all in Metro Toronto area)....4

Towns (5 in Niagara region, 6 in Sudbury region, 7 in York region, 4 in Durham region, 3 each in Haldimand-Norfolk, Halton and Hamilton-Wentworth regions, 3 in Muskoka district municipality, 2 in Oxford restructured county, 1 in Peel, 70 in counties, 35 in districts)....143

Villages (1 in Ottawa-Carleton, 110 in counties, 8 in districts)....119

Townships (5 in Ottawa-Carleton, 4 in Waterloo, 3 in Durham region, 3 in Muskoka district municipality, 2 each in Haldimand-Norfolk, Hamilton-Wentworth, Niagara and York regions, 331 in counties, 124 in districts)....478

Improvement districts (1 in counties, 8 in districts)....9

TOTAL 798

Notes:-

Source: 1981 Municipal Directory, Ministry of Municipal Affairs & Housing.

Besides organized villages, there were 82 police villages as of Aug. 1, 1981. These are run by boards of trustees elected by residents. Such boards cannot levy taxes or pass by-laws for the borrowing of money. Instead, the police village requisitions the township, of which it is a part, for financing.

Counties united for administrative purposes are: Leeds and Grenville; Prescott and Russell; Stormont, Dundas and Glengarry.

Towns include those separated for municipal purposes.

The southern part of Ontario is divided into upper-tier municipal units which are the counties, and the restructured areas, including the Regional Municipalities, the District Municipality of Muskoka, the Municipality of Metro Toronto and the Restructured County of Oxford.

The cities and separated towns located within the counties do not come within the jurisdiction of the upper tier councils. The cities within the restructured areas function as full partners in the upper tier system.

County councils consist of the reeves of all the local municipalities and in the cases of larger communities, the deputy reeves. Restructured upper tier councils more closely reflect representation by population.

Restructured units which contain about two-thirds of the Provincial population generally have fewer and larger local municipalities within them than do the counties and the functions of the upper tier councils of restructured areas are more extensive than those of the counties (i.e. water supply, sewage treatment, broad planning, social services, long term financing and appointment of police commissioners).

Northern Ontario consists of 1 regional municipality (Sudbury) within which the local municipalities are not incorporated within a two-tier municipal system. The north is divided into 10 administrative districts which have no municipal significance.

MUNICIPAL ELECTIONS

Under The Municipal Elections Act, 1977, local government elections in Ontario are held on the second Monday in November. A standard two-year term of office is provided for all municipal councils, school boards and other local boards.

The preliminary list of electors is based on information obtained through annual enumeration by the assessment commissioner during the month of September.

A mandatory advance poll is held by all municipalities on the Saturday, nine days before polling day. Additional advance polls may be held as provided by a by-law passed by the council of a municipality before Nomination Day.

A person may be nominated by filing the required papers in the municipal clerk's office from 9 a.m. until 5 p.m. on the Official Nomination Day. Nomination papers may also be filed in the week preceding Nomination Day during the normal office hours of the clerk. In the event insufficient nominations for any office are received on the Nomination Day, additional nominations may be received on the immediately succeeding Wednesday. Nomination papers must be signed by at least ten electors entitled to vote and must be certified by the clerk. The names of candidates and the offices for which they are nominated are posted after certification.

Cities in CAPITALS; Towns marked †; Boroughs marked *; Villages marked •; Townships (Twp); ‡ means separated for municipal purposes from county; balance are either small places or unincorporated places (which have been named but not organized)

MUNICIPALITY	POP.	COUNTY OR DISTRICT	FEDERAL ELECTORAL DISTRICT	PROVINCIAL ELECTORAL DISTRICT	CLERK WITH ADDRESS AND PHONE
Actinolite	80	Hastings	Hastings-Frontenac	Hastings-Peterborough	
Acton		Halton Reg. Mun.	Halton	Halton-Burlington	Part of Halton Hills
Addison	98	Leeds & Grenville	Leeds-Grenville	Leeds	

Cities in CAPITALS; Towns marked †; Boroughs marked *; Villages marked •; Townships (Twp); ‡ means separated for municipal purposes from county; balance are either small places or unincorporated places (which have been named but not organized)

MUNICIPALITY	POP.	COUNTY OR DISTRICT	FEDERAL ELECTORAL DISTRICT	PROVINCIAL ELECTORAL DISTRICT	CLERK WITH ADDRESS AND PHONE
Adelaide Twp	2,185	Middlesex		Huron-Middlesex	F. Gare, Clerk, R.R. 3, Kerwood, Ont. NOM 2BO (519/247-3626)
Adjala Twp	3,614	Simcoe	Wellington-Dufferin-Simcoe	Dufferin-Simcoe	A. McKenna, Clerk, Box 2, Loretto, Ont. LOG 1LO (416/729-2330)
Admaston Twp	1,394	Renfrew		Renfrew South	Mrs. B. Briscoe, Clerk, R.R. 2, Renfrew, Ont. K7V 3Z5 (613/432-2885)
Adolphustown Twp	750	Lennox & Addington		Prince Edward-Lennox	Mrs. B.M. Miller, Clerk, R.R. 1, Bath, Ont. KOH 1GO (613/373-2859)
Ahmic Harbour	61	Parry Sound D.	Parry Sound-Muskoka	Parry Sound	
Ailsa Craig•	780	Middlesex	Lambton-Middlesex	Huron-Middlesex	Mrs. J. Coursey, Village Clerk, Box 29, Ailsa Craig, Ont. NOM 1AO (519/293-3401)
Airy Twp	938	Nipissing D.	Renfrew-Nipissing-Pembroke	Renfrew North	H. Luckasavitch, Clerk, Box 217, Whitney, Ont. KOJ 2MO (705/637-2650)
Ajax†	24,380	Durham Reg. Mun.	Ontario	Durham West	A.T. Hodges, Town Clerk, 65 Harwood Ave. S., Ajax, Ont. L1S 2H9 (416/683-4550)
Alban	351	Sudbury D.	Nickel Belt	Sudbury East	
Albemarle Twp	898	Bruce		Grey-Bruce	G.W. Hotham, Clerk, R.R. 6, Wiarton, Ont. NOH 2TO (519/534-2668)
Alberton Twp	740	Rainy River D.	Kenora-Rainy River	Rainy River	Mrs. B. Kempf, Clerk, Box 759, Fort Frances, Ont. P9A 3N1 (807/274-6053)
Alcona Beach	861	Simcoe	Simcoe South	Simcoe Centre	Part of Innisfil Twp.
Aldborough Twp	3,040	Elgin	Elgin	Kent-Elgin	C.I. Black, Clerk, Box 490, Rodney, Ont. NOL 2CO (519/785-0560)
Aldershot		Hamilton-Wentworth Reg. Mun.	Burlington	Burlington South	Part of Burlington
Alexandria†	3,341	Stormont, Dundas & Glengarry	Glengarry-Prescott-Russell	Stormont, Dundas & Glengarry	D.O. Collin, Town Clerk, Box 700, Alexandria, Ont. KOC 1AO (613/525-1110)
Alfred•	1,100	Prescott & Russell	Glengarry-Prescott-Russell	Prescott & Russell	P.E. Desforges, Village Clerk, C.P. 70, Alfred, Ont. KOB 1AO (613/679-2292)
Alfred Twp	1,911	Prescott & Russell	Glengarry-Prescott-Russell	Prescott & Russell	J.Y. Cadieux, Clerk, Box 30, Lefaivre, Ont. KOB 1JO (613/679-2750)
Algoma Mills	336	Algoma D.	Algoma	Algoma-Manitoulin	
Algonquin	117	Leeds & Grenville	Leeds-Grenville	Carleton-Grenville	
Alice	58	Renfrew	Renfrew-Nipissing-Pembroke	Renfrew North	
Alice & Fraser Twp	3,193	Renfrew	Renfrew-Nipissing-Pembroke	Renfrew North	A. Donohue, Clerk, R.R. 4, Pembroke, Ont. K8A 6W5 (613/735-6291)
Allanburg	230	Niagara Reg. Mun.	Welland	Welland	
Allandale		Simcoe	Simcoe South	Simcoe Centre	Part of Barrie
Allenford	250	Bruce	Bruce-Grey	Grey-Bruce	Police Village
Alliston†	4,619	Simcoe	Wellington-Dufferin-Simcoe	Dufferin-Simcoe	B.A. Gauley, Town Clerk, Box 910, Alliston, Ont. LOM 1AO (705/435-6219)
Alma	271	Wellington	Wellington-Dufferin-Simcoe	Wellington-Dufferin-Peel	
Almonte†	3,821	Lanark	Lanark-Renfrew-Carleton	Lanark	R.J. France, Town Clerk, 14 Bridge St., Box 400, Almonte, Ont. KOA 1AO (613/256-1685)

Cities in CAPITALS; Towns marked †; Boroughs marked *; Villages marked •; Townships (Twp); ‡ means separated for municipal purposes from county; balance are either small places or unincorporated places (which have been named but not organized)

MUNICIPALITY	POP.	COUNTY OR DISTRICT	FEDERAL ELECTORAL DISTRICT	PROVINCIAL ELECTORAL DISTRICT	CLERK WITH ADDRESS AND PHONE
Alnwick Twp	798	Northumberland		Northumberland	Ms. I. Sherwin, Clerk, Box 34, Roseneath, Ont. KOK 2XO (416/352-2841)
Alton	438	Peel Reg. Mun.	York-Peel	Wellington-Dufferin-Peel	
Altona	85	Durham Reg. Mun.	Bruce-Grey	Durham York	
Alvinston•	708	Lambton	Lambton-Middlesex	Lambton	Mrs. B. Walker, Village Clerk, 517 River St., Alvinston, Ont. NON 1AO (519/898-2173)
Amabel Twp	2,830	Bruce	Bruce-Grey	Grey-Bruce	W.E. Johnston, Clerk, R.R. 2, Hepworth, Ont. NOH 1PO (519/422-1551)
Amaranth Twp	2,470	Dufferin		Wellington-Dufferin-Peel	W. Bospoort, Clerk, R.R. 1, Laurel, Ont. LON 1LO (519/941-1007)
Ameliasburgh Twp	4,843	Prince Edward	Prince Edward-Hastings	Prince Edward-Lennox	J. Plamondon, Clerk, Ameliasburgh, Ont. KOK 1AO (613/962-2782)
Amherstburg†	5,836	Essex	Essex-Windsor	Essex South	Tom Kilgallin, Town Clerk, 271 Sandwich St. W., Amherstburg, Ont. N9V 2A5 (519/736-5401)
Amherst Is. Twp	388	Lennox & Addington	Kingston & the Islands	Kingston & the Islands	Mrs. D. Pearce, Clerk, Stella, Ont. KOH 2SO (613/389-3393)
Amherst View	5,295	Frontenac	Hastings-Frontenac	Prince Edward-Lennox	
Ancaster†	14,073	Hamilton-Wentworth Reg. Mun.	Hamilton-Wentworth	Wentworth North	L.V. Hayden, Town Clerk, 300 Wilson St. E., Ancaster, Ont. L9G 2B9 (416/648-4401)
Anderdon Twp	5,005	Essex	Essex-Windsor	Essex South	L.E. Mailloux, Clerk, R.R. 4, Amherstburg, Ont. N9V 2Y9 (519/736-5051)
Angus	3,494	Simcoe	Simcoe South	Dufferin-Simcoe	Police Village
Anson, Hindon & Minden Twp	2,387	Haliburton	Victoria-Haliburton	Victoria-Haliburton	Mrs. E. Burke, Clerk, Box 98, Minden, Ont. KOM 2KO (705/286-1260)
Ansonville		Cochrane D.	Timmins-Chapleau	Cochrane South	Part of Iroquois Falls
Antrim	37	Ottawa-Carleton Reg. Mun.	Lanark-Renfrew-Carleton	Renfrew South	
Appin	205	Middlesex	Lambton-Middlesex	Middlesex	
Apple Hill	271	Stormont, Dundas & Glengarry	Glengarry-Prescott-Russell	Stormont, Dundas & Glengarry	Police Village
Appleton	141	Lanark	Lanark-Renfrew-Carleton	Lanark	
Apsley	281	Peterborough	Victoria-Haliburton	Hastings-Peterborough	
The Archipelago Twp	553	Parry Sound D.		Parry Sound	Wm. J. Mosley, Clerk, 9 James St., Parry Sound, Ont. P2A 1T6 (705/746-4243)
Ardbeg	38	Parry Sound D.	Parry Sound-Muskoka	Parry Sound	
Arden	137	Frontenac	Hastings-Frontenac	Frontenac-Addington	
Arkona•	428	Lambton	Lambton-Middlesex	Lambton	R. Jefferson, Village Clerk, Box 95, Arkona, Ont. NOM 1BO (519/828-3490)
Armour Twp	769	Parry Sound D.		Parry Sound	Mrs. E. Rayner, Clerk, Box 533, Burk's Falls, Ont. POA 1CO (705/382-3332)
Armstrong Twp	1,450	Timiskaming D.	Timiskaming	Timiskaming	G. Gauthier, Clerk, Box 218, Earlton, Ont. POJ 1EO (705/563-2375)
Armstrong Station	323	Thunder Bay D.	Thunder Bay-Nipigon	Lake Nipigon	
Arnprior†	5,911	Renfrew	Lanark-Renfrew-Carleton	Renfrew South	G.M. Buffam, Town Clerk, Box 130, Arnprior, Ont. K7S 3H4 (613/623-4231)

Cities in CAPITALS; Towns marked †; Boroughs marked *; Villages marked •; Townships (Twp); ‡ means separated for municipal purposes from county; balance are either small places or unincorporated places (which have been named but not organized)

MUNICIPALITY	POP.	COUNTY OR DISTRICT	FEDERAL ELECTORAL DISTRICT	PROVINCIAL ELECTORAL DISTRICT	CLERK WITH ADDRESS AND PHONE
Arnstein	90	Parry Sound D.	Parry Sound-Muskoka	Parry Sound	
Arran Twp	1,559	Bruce	Bruce-Grey	Grey-Bruce	A. Sim, Clerk, R.R. 2, Tara, Ont. NOH 2NO (519/934-2051)
Artemesia Twp	1,988	Grey		Grey	H.M. Johnson, Clerk, Box 219, Flesherton, Ont. NOC 1EO (519/924-2208)
Arthur Twp	2,006	Wellington	Wellington-Dufferin-Simcoe	Wellington-Dufferin-Peel	Mrs. D. McCallum, Clerk, R.R. 4, Kenilworth, Ont. NOG 2EO (519/848-3620)
Arthur•	1,669	Wellington	Wellington-Dufferin-Simcoe	Wellington-Dufferin-Peel	W.H. MacDonald, Village Clerk, Box 490, Arthur, Ont. NOG 1AO (519/848-2120)
Arva	147	Middlesex	London-Middlesex	Middlesex	
Ashburn	114	Durham Reg. Mun.	Ontario	Durham West	
Ashfield Twp	1,863	Huron		Huron-Bruce	D.M. Simpson, Clerk, R.R. 3, Goderich, Ont. N7A 3X9 (519/395-2753)
Ashton	142	Ottawa-Carleton Reg. Mun.	Lanark-Renfrew-Carleton	Carleton-Grenville	
Asphodel Twp	1,703	Peterborough	Peterborough	Hastings-Peterborough	R. Hendricks, Clerk, R.R. 3, Hastings, Ont. KOL 1YO (705/696-2161)
Assiginack Twp	860	Manitoulin D.	Algoma	Algoma-Manitoulin	Mrs. S. Keys, Clerk, Box 238, Manitouwaning, Ont. POP 1NO (705/859-3196)
Athens•	998	Leeds & Grenville	Leeds-Grenville	Leeds	Mrs. B.A. Hayes, Village Clerk, Box 159, Athens, Ont. KOE 1BO (613/924-2044)
Atherley	367	Simcoe	Simcoe North	Simcoe East	
Athol Twp	1,187	Prince Edward	Prince Edward-Hastings	Prince Edward-Lennox	Aleita Moore, Clerk, R.R. 3, Picton, Ont. KOK 2TO (613/476-2003)
Atikokan Twp	5,733	Rainy River D.		Rainy River	Mrs. E.J. Gavin, Clerk, Box 1330, Atikokan, Ont. POT 1CO (807/597-2738)
Attercliffe	56	Haldimand-Norfolk Reg. Mun.	Erie	Haldimand-Norfolk	
Atwood	720	Perth	Perth	Perth	
Atwood Twp	320	Rainy River D.	Kenora-Rainy River	Rainy River	P.W. Giles, Clerk, Box 27, Rainy River, Ont. POW 1LO (807/852-3529)
Auburn	222	Huron	Huron-Bruce	Huron-Bruce	
Auden	90	Thunder Bay D.	Thunder Bay-Nipigon	Lake Nipigon	
Augusta Twp	6,392	Leeds & Grenville	Leeds-Grenville	Carleton-Grenville	R. Gilmour, Clerk, R.R. 2, Prescott, Ont. KOE 1TO (613/925-4231)
Aurora†	15,001	York Reg. Mun.	York-Peel	York North	K.B. Rodger, Town Clerk/Adm., 50 Wellington St. W., Aurora, Ont. L4G 3L8 (416/727-1375; Toronto line: 889-3109)
Avening	64	Simcoe	Grey-Simcoe	Dufferin-Simcoe	
Avonmore	300	Stormont, Dundas & Glengarry	Stormont-Dundas	Stormont, Dundas & Glengarry	Police Village
Aylmer†	5,156	Elgin	Elgin	Elgin	C. Knapp, Town Clerk, 46 Talbot St. W., Aylmer, Ont. N5H 1J7 (519/773-3164)
Ayr	1,331	Waterloo Reg. Mun.	Cambridge	Cambridge	Part of North Dumfries Twp.
Ayton	450	Grey	Bruce-Grey	Grey	Police Village
Azilda		Sudbury D.	Nickel Belt	Nickel Belt	Part of Rayside-Balfour
Baden	824	Waterloo Reg. Mun.	Waterloo	Kitchener-Waterloo	

Cities in CAPITALS; Towns marked †; Boroughs marked *; Villages marked •; Townships (Twp); ‡ means separated for municipal purposes from county; balance are either small places or unincorporated places (which have been named but not organized)

MUNICIPALITY	POP.	COUNTY OR DISTRICT	FEDERAL ELECTORAL DISTRICT	PROVINCIAL ELECTORAL DISTRICT	CLERK WITH ADDRESS AND PHONE
Bagot & Blythfield Twp	1,074	Renfrew		Renfrew South	J.B. Valiquette, Clerk, Hwy. 508, Calabogie, Ont. KOJ 1HO (613/752-2222)
Bailieboro	172	Peterborough	Durham-Northumberland	Peterborough	
Bainsville	27	Stormont, Dundas & Glengarry	Glengarry-Prescott-Russell	Stormont, Dundas & Glengarry	
Bala	536	Muskoka Dist. Mun.	Parry Sound-Muskoka	Muskoka	Part of Muskoka Lakes Twp.
Baldwin Twp	682	Sudbury D.	Algoma	Nickel Belt	J. Cochrane, Clerk, Mc-Kerrow, Ont. POP 1MO (705/869-4220)
Ballantrae	165	York Reg. Mun.	York-Peel	York North	
Ballinafad		Wellington	Wellington-Dufferin-Simcoe	Wellington-Dufferin-Peel	Part of Halton Hills
Balm Beach	412	Simcoe	Simcoe North	Simcoe Centre	
Balmertown	1,918	Kenora D.	Kenora-Rainy River	Kenora	Improvement Dist., c/o I.C. Trow, Box 190, Balmertown, Ont. P0V 1C0
Baltimore	142	Northumberland	Northumberland	Northumberland	
Bancroft•	2,346	Hastings	Hastings-Frontenac	Hastings-Peterborough	D. Paterson, Village Clerk, Box 790, Bancroft, Ont. KOL 1CO (613/332-3332)
Bangor, Wicklow & McClure Twp	891	Hastings	Hastings-Frontenac	Hastings-Peterborough	D.C. Bloom, Clerk, Box 130, Maynooth, Ont. KOL 2SO (613/338-2811)
Bannockburn	134	Hastings	Hastings-Frontenac	Hastings-Peterborough	
Baptiste	111	Hastings	Hastings-Frontenac	Hastings-Peterborough	
Barclay Twp	1,084	Kenora	Kenora-Rainy River	Rainy River	Mrs. B. Beddome, Clerk, 37 King St., Dryden, Ont. P8N 1B4 (807/223-5509)
Barrie Twp	609	Frontenac		Frontenac-Addington	Miss N.J. Cannon, Clerk, Box 28, Cloyne, Ont. KOH 1KO (613/336-8633)
BARRIE	36,566	Simcoe	Simcoe South	Simcoe Centre	B.R.J. Straughan, City Clerk, 84 Collier St., Barrie, Ont. L4M 4T5 (705/726-4242)
Barrie Is. Twp	103	Manitoulin D.		Algoma-Manitoulin	J. Lane, Clerk, R.R. 2, Gore Bay, Ont. POP 1HO (705/282-2762)
Bar River	42	Algoma D.	Algoma	Algoma	
Barry's Bay•	1,310	Renfrew	Renfrew-Nipissing-Pembroke	Renfrew South	V. Shulist, Village Clerk, Box 940, Barry's Bay, Ont. KOJ 1BO (613/756-2747)
Barwick	60	Rainy River D.	Kenora-Rainy River	Rainy River	
Bastard & S. Burgess Twp	2,324	Leeds & Grenville		Leeds	Mrs. S. Bryden, Clerk, Box 500, Delta, Ont. KOE 1GO (613/928-2251)
Batawa	484	Hastings	Northumberland	Quinte	
Bath•	1,016	Lennox & Addington	Hastings-Frontenac	Prince Edward-Lennox	Mrs. J.Y. Carruthers, Village Clerk, Box 100, Bath, Ont. KOH 1GO (613/352-3361)
Bathurst Twp	2,416	Lanark	Lanark-Renfrew-Carleton	Lanark	D.R. Somerville, Clerk, R.R. 4, Perth, Ont. K7H 3C6 (613/267-5353)
Baxter	154	Simcoe	Simcoe South	Dufferin-Simcoe	
Bayfield•	611	Huron	Huron-Bruce	Huron-Middlesex	P.M. Graham, Village Clerk, Box 99, Bayfield, Ont. NOM 1GO (519/565-2455)
Bayham Twp	4,085	Elgin	Elgin	Elgin	J.A. Petrie, Clerk, Box 160, Straffordville, Ont. NOJ 1YO (519/866-5521)
Bayside	3,356	Hastings	Northumberland		

Cities in CAPITALS; Towns marked †; Boroughs marked *; Villages marked •; Townships (Twp); ‡ means separated for municipal purposes from county; balance are either small places or unincorporated places (which have been named but not organized)

MUNICIPALITY	POP.	COUNTY OR DISTRICT	FEDERAL ELECTORAL DISTRICT	PROVINCIAL ELECTORAL DISTRICT	CLERK WITH ADDRESS AND PHONE
Beachburg•	673	Renfrew	Renfrew-Nipissing-Pembroke	Renfrew South	Mrs. P. McLeese, Village Clerk, Box 100, Beachburg, Ont. KOJ 1CO (613/582-3625)
Beamsville		Niagara Reg. Mun.	Lincoln	Lincoln	Part of Lincoln
Beardmore Twp	588	Thunder Bay D.	Cochrane	Cochrane North	R. Nylund, Clerk, Box 239, Beardmore, Ont. POT 1GO (807/875-2639)
Beaverton	1,737	Durham Reg. Mun.	Victoria-Haliburton	Durham York	Part of Brock Twp.
Beckwith Twp	2,611	Lanark		Lanark	A. Hawkins, Clerk, R.R. 2, Carleton Place, Ont. K7C 3P2 (613/257-1539)
Bedell	43	Leeds & Grenville		Carleton-Grenville	
Bedford Twp	731	Frontenac	Hastings-Frontenac	Frontenac-Addington	L. Bresee, Clerk, R.R. 2, Westport, Ont. KOG 1XO (613/273-3264)
Beeton•	1,658	Simcoe	Simcoe South	Dufferin-Simcoe	S.E. Knapp, Village Clerk, Box 130, Beeton, Ont. LOG 1AO (416/729-2278)
Belgrave	204	Huron	Huron-Bruce	Huron-Bruce	
Belle River†	3,432	Essex	Essex-Windsor	Essex North	A.H. Sipila, Town Clerk, 499 Notre Dame, Box 250, Belle River, Ont. NOR 1AO (519/728-2700)
BELLEVILLE	35,102	Hastings	Prince Edward-Hastings	Quinte	E.M. Dafoe, City Clerk, City Hall, Belleville, Ont. K8N 2Y8 (613/968-6481)
Bell Ewart	409	Simcoe	Simcoe South	Simcoe Centre	
Bells Corners		Ottawa-Carleton Reg. Mun.	Nepean-Carleton	Carleton	PO of Ottawa
Belmont•	744	Elgin	Elgin	Elgin	Ms. K. Barons, Village Clerk, 186 Washburn St., Belmont, Ont. NOL 1BO (519/644-1071)
Belmont & Methuen Twp	2,131	Peterborough		Hastings-Peterborough	Meryl Martin, Clerk, Box 10, Havelock, Ont. KOL 1ZO (705/778-2308)
Belwood	166	Wellington	Wellington-Dufferin-Simcoe	Wellington-Dufferin-Peel	Police Village
Bentinck Twp	2,979	Grey	Bruce-Grey	Grey	L. Klages, Clerk, R.R. 1, Elmwood, Ont. NOG 1SO (519/364-1909)
Berkeley	132	Grey	Bruce-Grey	Grey	
Berwick	113	Stormont, Dundas & Glengarry	Stormont-Dundas	Stormont, Dundas & Glengarry	
Bethany	314	Victoria	Durham-Northumberland	Victoria-Haliburton	
Bewdley	475	Northumberland	Northumberland	Northumberland	Police Village
Bexley Twp	765	Victoria	Victoria-Haliburton	Victoria-Haliburton	Mrs. H.A. Russell, Clerk, Box 5, Coboconk, Ont. KOM 1KO (705/454-3322)
Bicroft	670	Haliburton		Victoria-Haliburton	Improvement District, c/o Ms. S. McColl, Mun. Office, Cardiff, Ont. KOL 1M0
Biddulph Twp	2,235	Middlesex	London-Middlesex	Huron-Middlesex	A. Hodgins, Clerk, R.R. 1, Lucan, Ont. NOM 2JO (519/227-4269)
Big Island	226	Prince Edward	Prince Edward-Hastings		
Billings Twp	387	Manitoulin D.		Algoma-Manitoulin	Mrs. J. Acheson, Clerk, Kagawong, Ont. POP 1JO (705/282-2611)
Binbrook	465	Hamilton-Wentworth Reg. Mun.	Hamilton-Wentworth	Wentworth	Part of Glanbrook Twp.
Biscotasing	45	Sudbury D.	Timmins-Chapleau	Nickel Belt	

Cities in CAPITALS; Towns marked †; Boroughs marked *; Villages marked •; Townships (Twp); ‡ means separated for municipal purposes from county; balance are either small places or unincorporated places (which have been named but not organized)

MUNICIPALITY	POP.	COUNTY OR DISTRICT	FEDERAL ELECTORAL DISTRICT	PROVINCIAL ELECTORAL DISTRICT	CLERK WITH ADDRESS AND PHONE
Bishop's Mills	97	Leeds & Grenville	Leeds-Grenville	Carleton-Grenville	
Black River-Matheson Twp	3,567	Cochrane D.	Timiskaming	Cochrane South	T.E. Monahan, Clerk, Box 601, Matheson, Ont. POK 1NO (705/273-2313)
Blackstock	265	Durham Reg. Mun.	Durham-Northumberland	Durham York	
Blackwater	80	Durham Reg. Mun.	Victoria-Haliburton	Durham York	
Blair	360	Waterloo Reg. Mun.	Waterloo	Cambridge	
Blandford-Blenheim Twp	6,806	Oxford	Oxford	Brant-Oxford-Norfolk	K. Reibling, Clerk, Box 100, Drumbo, Ont. NOJ 1G9 (613/463-5347)
Blanshard Twp	2,012	Perth	Perth	Perth	N. Webb, Clerk, R.R. 6, St. Mary's, Ont. NOM 2VO (519/229-8707)
Blenheim†	3,999	Kent	Essex-Kent	Kent-Elgin	C. Gault, Town Clerk, Box 399, Blenheim, Ont. NOP 1AO (519/676-5405)
Blind River†	3,174	Algoma D.	Algoma	Algoma	K.G. Corbiere, Town Clerk, Box 640, Blind River, Ont. POR 1BO (705/356-2251, 2)
Bloomfield•	727	Prince Edward	Prince Edward-Hastings	Prince Edward-Lennox	Mrs. S. Vincent, Village Clerk, Box 190, Bloomfield, Ont. KOK 1GO (613/393-2838)
Bloomingdale	313	Waterloo Reg. Mun.	Waterloo	Waterloo North	
Bloomsburg	67	Haldimand-Norfolk Reg. Mun.	Haldimand-Norfolk	Brant-Oxford-Norfolk	
Blue Twp	113	Rainy River D.	Kenora-Rainy River	Rainy River	J.F. Trenchard, Clerk, Box 34, Sleeman, Ont. POW 1MO (807/852-3907)
Bluevale	204	Huron	Huron-Bruce	Huron-Bruce	
Blyth•	890	Huron	Huron-Bruce	Huron-Bruce	L.B. Walsh, Village Clerk, Box 239, Blyth, Ont. NOM 1HO (519/523-4545)
Blytheswood	183	Essex	Essex-Kent	Essex South	
Bobcaygeon•	1,629	Victoria	Victoria-Haliburton	Victoria-Haliburton	Ms. L.C. Hamilton, Village Clerk, 21 Canal St., Bobcaygeon, Ont. KOM 1AO (705/738-2363)
Bogart	26	Hastings	Prince Edward-Hastings	Hastings-Peterborough	
Bolton		Peel Reg. Mun.	York-Peel	Wellington-Dufferin-Peel	Part of Caledon
Bond Head	562	Simcoe	Simcoe South	Simcoe Centre	
Bonfield Twp	1,718	Nipissing D.	Nipissing	Parry Sound	R.A. Vaillancourt, Clerk, 514 Yonge St., Bonfield, Ont. POH 1EO (705/776-2641)
Borden		Simcoe	Simcoe South	Dufferin-Simcoe	
Bosanquet Twp	4,039	Lambton	Lambton-Middlesex	Lambton	R.F. McCordic, Clerk, Box 269, Thedford, Ont. NOM 2NO (519/296-4953)
Bothwell†	922	Kent	Kent	Kent-Elgin	R. Menzies, Town Clerk, Box 400, Bothwell, Ont. NOP 1CO (519/695-2722)
Bourget	949	Prescott & Russell	Glengarry-Prescott-Russell	Prescott & Russell	Police Village
Bourkes	51	Timiskaming D.	Timiskaming	Cochrane South	
Bowmanville		Durham Reg. Mun.	Durham-Northumberland	Durham East	Part of Newcastle
Bracebridge†	8,485	Muskoka Dist. Mun.	Parry Sound-Muskoka	Muskoka	K.C. Veitch, Town Clerk, 23 Dominion St., Bracebridge, Ont. POB 1CO (705/645-5264)
Bradford†	6,789	Simcoe	Simcoe South	Simcoe Centre	R. Mullen, Town Clerk, Box 160, Bradford, Ont. LOG 1CO (705/775-5303)

Cities in CAPITALS; Towns marked †; Boroughs marked *; Villages marked •; Townships (Twp); ‡ means separated for municipal purposes from county; balance are either small places or unincorporated places (which have been named but not organized)

MUNICIPALITY	POP.	COUNTY OR DISTRICT	FEDERAL ELECTORAL DISTRICT	PROVINCIAL ELECTORAL DISTRICT	CLERK WITH ADDRESS AND PHONE
Braeside•	505	Renfrew	Lanark-Renfrew-Carleton	Renfrew South	J. Burns, Village Clerk, Box 40, Braeside, Ont. KOA 1GO (613/623-5433)
BRAMPTON	140,649	Peel Reg. Mun.	Brampton-Georgetown	Brampton	R.A. Everett, City Clerk, 150 Central Park Dr., Brampton, Ont. L6T 2T9 (416/793-4110)
Brant Twp	3,330	Bruce	Bruce-Grey	Grey-Bruce	G. Napper, Clerk, R.R. 1, Elmwood, Ont. NOG 1SO (519/881-0188)
Brantford Twp	9,309	Brant	Brant	Brant-Oxford-Norfolk	c/o The Clerk, 73 Charlotte St., Box 1295, Brantford, Ont. N3T 5T6 (519/756-7470)
BRANTFORD	73,055	Brant	Brant	Brantford	W. Coulson, City Clerk, 100 Wellington Sq., Brantford, Ont. N3T 2M3 (519/759-4150)
Brechin	255	Simcoe	Simcoe North	Simcoe East	Police Village
Brent	27	Nipissing D.	Renfrew-Nipissing-Pembroke	Renfrew North	
Breslau	715	Waterloo Reg. Mun.	Waterloo	Waterloo North	
Brethour Twp	191	Timiskaming D.	Timiskaming	Timiskaming	R. Lachapelle, Clerk, Belle Vallée, Ont. POJ 1AO (705/647-7632)
Bridgenorth	1,368	Peterborough	Peterborough	Peterborough	
Brigden	548	Lambton	Sarnia	Lambton	Police Village
Bright	324	Oxford	Oxford	Brant-Oxford-Norfolk	
Brighton Twp	3,125	Northumberland	Northumberland	Northumberland	Mrs. E. Cameron, Clerk, R.R. 7, Brighton, Ont. KOK 1HO (613/475-2894)
Brighton†	3,554	Northumberland	Northumberland	Northumberland	Mrs. S.M. Patterson, Village Clerk, Box 189, Brighton, Ont. KOK 1HO (613/475-0670)
Britt	468	Parry Sound D.	Parry Sound-Muskoka	Parry Sound	
Brock Twp	9,109	Durham Reg. Mun.	Victoria-Haliburton	Durham York	G.S. Graham, Clerk, Box 10, Cannington, Ont. LOE 1EO (705/432-2681)
BROCKVILLE	19,967	Leeds & Grenville	Leeds-Grenville	Leeds	A.J. Miles, City Clerk, Victoria Hall, Brockville, Ont. K6V 3P5 (613/342-8772)
Brodhagen	165	Perth	Perth	Perth	
Bromley Twp	1,201	Renfrew		Renfrew South	M. Rice, Clerk, R.R. 1, Douglas, Ont. KOJ 1SO (613/649-2342)
Bronte	2,027	Halton Reg. Mun.	Halton	Oakville	Part of Oakville
Brooke	31	Lanark	Lanark-Renfrew-Carleton		
Brooke Twp	2,003	Lambton	Lambton-Middlesex	Lambton	J. Myre, Clerk, R.R. 7, Alvinston, Ont. NON 1AO (519/898-5566)
Brooklin	1,679	Durham Reg. Mun.	Ontario	Durham West	
Brougham	312	Durham Reg. Mun.	Ontario	Durham York	
Brougham Twp	173	Renfrew	Renfrew-Nipissing-Pembroke	Renfrew South	M. Hanes, Clerk, Dacre, Ont. KOJ 1NO (613/649-2379)
Brown Hill	82	York Reg. Mun.		Durham York	
Brownsville	310	Oxford	Oxford	Oxford	
Bruce Twp	1,905	Bruce		Huron-Bruce	C.J. Ellis, Clerk, R.R. 3, Tiverton, Ont. NOG 2TO (519/368-7066)
Brucefield	189	Huron	Huron-Bruce	Huron-Middlesex	
Bruce Mines†	569	Algoma D.	Algoma	Algoma	N.A. Kilian, Town Clerk, Box 220, Bruce Mines, Ont. POR 1CO (705/785-3340)

Cities in CAPITALS; Towns marked †; Boroughs marked *; Villages marked •; Townships (Twp); ‡ means separated for municipal purposes from county; balance are either small places or unincorporated places (which have been named but not organized)

MUNICIPALITY	POP.	COUNTY OR DISTRICT	FEDERAL ELECTORAL DISTRICT	PROVINCIAL ELECTORAL DISTRICT	CLERK WITH ADDRESS AND PHONE
Brudenell & Lyndoch Twp	828	Renfrew	Renfrew-Nipissing-Pembroke	Renfrew South	V. Jahn, Clerk, Box 91, Quadeville, Ont. KOJ 2GO (613/758-2651)
Brunetville		Cochrane D.	Cochrane	Cochrane North	PO of Kapuskasing
Brussels•	993	Huron	Huron-Bruce	Huron-Bruce	W.H. King, Village Clerk, Box 119, Brussels, Ont. NOG 1HO (519/887-6572)
Bryanston	138	Middlesex	London-Middlesex	Middlesex	
Buckhorn	168	Peterborough	Victoria-Haliburton	Hastings-Peterborough	
Bullocks Corners	171	Hamilton-Wentworth Reg. Mun.	Hamilton-Wentworth	Wentworth North	
Burford Twp	5,576	Brant		Brant-Oxford-Norfolk	P.H. Dearling, Clerk, 6 King St. E., Box 249, Burford, Ont. NOE 1AO (519/449-2434)
Burgessville	289	Oxford	Oxford	Oxford	
Burk's Falls•	841	Parry Sound D.	Parry Sound-Muskoka	Parry Sound	C.F. Neal, Village Clerk, Box 160, Burk's Falls, Ont. POA 1CO (705/382-3138)
Burleigh & Anstruther Twp	1,150	Peterborough	Victoria-Haliburton	Hastings-Peterborough	Mrs. H. Lambe, Clerk, Box 128, Apsley, Ont. KOL 1AO (705/656-4445)
Burleigh Falls	62	Peterborough	Victoria-Haliburton	Hastings-Peterborough	
BURLINGTON	112,722	Halton Reg. Mun.	Burlington	Burlington North; Burlington South	D. Briault, City Clerk, 426 Brant St., Burlington, Ont. L7R 3Z6 (416/335-7777)
Burnstown	76	Renfrew	Lanark-Renfrew-Carleton	Renfrew South	
Burnt River	218	Victoria	Victoria-Haliburton	Victoria-Haliburton	
Burpee Twp	183	Manitoulin D.		Algoma-Manitoulin	R. Morrell, Clerk, R.R. 1, Evansville, Ont. POP 1EO (705/282-2820)
Burritts Rapids	156	Leeds & Grenville	Leeds-Grenville	Carleton-Grenville	
Burtch	114	Brant		Brant-Oxford-Norfolk	
Burwash	616	Sudbury D.	Nickel Belt	Sudbury East	
Buttonville	102	York Reg. Mun.	York North	York Centre	
Buxton	91	Kent	Essex-Kent	Kent-Elgin	
Byng	140	Haldimand-Norfolk Reg. Mun.	Haldimand-Norfolk	Haldimand-Norfolk	
Byng Inlet	136	Parry Sound D.	Parry Sound-Muskoka	Parry Sound	
Cache Bay†	689	Nipissing D.	Nipissing	Nipissing	Mrs. C. Lisk, Town Clerk, 55 Cache St., Cache Bay, Ont. POH 1GO (705/753-1220)
Caesarea	547	Durham Reg. Mun.	Durham-Northumberland	Durham York	
Cainsville	196	Brant		Brant-Oxford-Norfolk	
Caintown	40	Leeds & Grenville	Leeds-Grenville	Leeds	
Caistorville	72	Niagara Reg. Mun.	Erie	Lincoln	Part of West Lincoln Twp.
Calabogie	289	Renfrew	Lanark-Renfrew-Carleton	Renfrew South	
Caldwell Twp	1,804	Nipissing D.	Timiskaming	Nipissing	M. Tellier, Clerk, 2 Verchere St., Verner, Ont. POH 2MO (705/594-2318)
Caledon†	25,797	Peel Reg. Mun.	York-Peel	Wellington-Dufferin-Peel	C. Patterson, Town Clerk, Box 10, Caledon East, Ont. LON 1EO (416/584-2273)
Caledon East					PO of Caledon
Caledonia		Haldimand-Norfolk Reg. Mun.	Haldimand-Norfolk	Haldimand-Norfolk	Part of Haldimand
Caledonia Twp	1,396	Prescott & Russell	Glengarry-Prescott-Russell	Prescott & Russell	Mrs. G. Levac, Clerk, St. Bernardin, Ont. KOB 1NO (613/678-6840)
Callander	1,058	Parry Sound D.	Parry Sound-Muskoka	Parry Sound	

Cities in CAPITALS; Towns marked †; Boroughs marked *; Villages marked •; Townships (Twp); ‡ means separated for municipal purposes from county; balance are either small places or unincorporated places (which have been named but not organized)

MUNICIPALITY	POP.	COUNTY OR DISTRICT	FEDERAL ELECTORAL DISTRICT	PROVINCIAL ELECTORAL DISTRICT	CLERK WITH ADDRESS AND PHONE
Calstock	84	Cochrane D.	Cochrane	Cochrane North	
Calvin Twp	524	Nipissing D.	Nipissing	Parry Sound	Mrs. K. Moore, Clerk, R.R. 2, Mattawa, Ont. POH 1VO (705/744-2700)
Camborne	50	Northumberland	Northumberland	Northumberland	
Cambray	216	Victoria	Victoria-Haliburton	Victoria-Haliburton	Police Village
Cambridge Twp	4,282	Prescott & Russell		Prescott & Russell	A. Ouimet, Clerk, Box 86, St. Albert, Ont. KOA 3CO (613/764-5444)
CAMBRIDGE	74,435	Waterloo Reg. Mun.	Cambridge	Cambridge	City Clerk, 46 Dickson St., Box 669, Cambridge G, Ont. N1R 5W8 (519/623-1340)
Camden Twp	2,600	Kent	Kent	Kent-Elgin	C. McFadden, Clerk, 199 Queen St. E., Dresden, Ont. NOP 1MO (519/683-4921)
Camden East Twp	3,807	Lennox & Addington	Hastings-Frontenac	Frontenac-Addington	L. Keech, Clerk, Centreville, Ont. KOK 1NO (613/378-2475)
Cameron	145	Nipissing D.		Renfrew North	Improvement Dist., c/o Mrs. B. Diggle, R.R. 1, Mattawa, Ont. P0H 1V0
Cameron	193	Victoria	Victoria-Haliburton	Victoria-Haliburton	
Cameron Falls	123	Thunder Bay D.	Cochrane	Lake Nipigon	
Camlachie	221	Lambton	Lambton-Middlesex	Lambton	
Campbellford†	3,329	Northumberland	Northumberland	Northumberland	M.W. Stillman, Town Clerk, 36 Front St. S., Box 1056, Campbellford, Ont. KOL 1LO (705/653-1900)
Campbellville	144	Halton Reg. Mun.	Halton	Halton-Burlington	Part of Milton
Cannifton	387	Hastings	Prince Edward-Hastings	Hastings-Peterborough	
Cannington	1,419	Durham Reg. Mun.	Victoria-Haliburton	Durham York	Part of Brock Twp.
Capreol†	3,918	Sudbury Reg. Mun.	Nickel Belt	Sudbury East	E. Bérubé, Town Clerk, 9 Morin St., Capreol, Ont. POM 1HO (705/858-1212)
Caradoc Twp	5,653	Middlesex	Lambton-Middlesex	Middlesex	Mrs. Marion Loker, Clerk, Box 190, Mt. Brydges, Ont. NOL 1WO (519/264-1001)
Caramat	382	Thunder Bay D.	Cochrane	Lake Nipigon	
Carden Twp	500	Victoria		Victoria-Haliburton	Mrs. B.M. Dewell, Clerk, R.R. 1, Sebright, Ont. LOK 1WO (705/833-2811)
Cardiff Twp	528	Haliburton		Victoria-Haliburton	Gayle Billings, Clerk, Mun. Office, R.R. 3, Bancroft, Ont. KOL 1CO (613/339-2323)
Cardinal•	1,720	Leeds & Grenville	Leeds-Grenville	Carleton-Grenville	W. Baldwin, Village Clerk, 152 Water St., Cardinal, Ont. KOE 1EO (613/657-3266)
Cardinal Heights		Ottawa-Carleton Reg. Mun.		Carleton East	
Cargill	233	Bruce	Bruce-Grey		
Carleton Place†	5,574	Lanark	Lanark-Renfrew-Carleton	Lanark	W.K. Morris, Town Clerk, 175 Bridge St., Carleton Place, Ont. K7C 2V8 (613/257-3101)
Carling Twp	732	Parry Sound D.		Parry Sound	D. White, Clerk, R.R. 1, Nobel, Ont. POG 1GO (705/342-5856)
Carlisle	565	Hamilton-Wentworth Reg. Mun.	Hamilton-Wentworth	Wentworth North	
Carlow Twp	421	Hastings	Hastings-Frontenac	Hastings-Peterborough	Mrs. T. Hass, Clerk, Boulter, Ont. KOL 1GO (613/332-1760)

Cities in CAPITALS; Towns marked †; Boroughs marked *; Villages marked •; Townships (Twp); ‡ means separated for municipal purposes from county; balance are either small places or unincorporated places (which have been named but not organized)

MUNICIPALITY	POP.	COUNTY OR DISTRICT	FEDERAL ELECTORAL DISTRICT	PROVINCIAL ELECTORAL DISTRICT	CLERK WITH ADDRESS AND PHONE
Carlsbad Springs	478	Ottawa-Carleton Reg. Mun.	Ottawa-Carleton	Carleton East	
Carnarvon Twp	988	Manitoulin D.	Algoma	Algoma-Manitoulin	Mrs. M. McCutcheon, Clerk, Box 187, Mindemoya, Ont. POP 1SO (705/377-5726)
Carp	691	Ottawa-Carleton Reg. Mun.	Lanark-Renfrew-Carleton	Renfrew South	
Carrick Twp	2,463	Bruce	Huron-Bruce	Huron-Bruce	G.S. Pennington, Clerk, R.R. 2, Mildmay, Ont. NOG 2JO (519/367-5330)
Carrying Place	183	Prince Edward	Prince Edward-Hastings	Prince Edward-Lennox	
Cartier	673	Sudbury D.	Nickel Belt	Nickel Belt	
Casey Twp	483	Timiskaming D.	Timiskaming	Timiskaming	D. Ramsay, Clerk, Box 460, Belle Vallée, Ont. POJ 1AO (705/647-7257)
Casimir, Jennings & Appleby Twp	1,264	Sudbury D.		Sudbury East	Mrs. D. Roy, Clerk, Box 70, St. Charles, Ont. POM 2WO (705/867-2032)
Casselman•	1,585	Prescott & Russell	Glengarry-Prescott-Russell	Prescott & Russell	G. Lortie, Village Clerk, Box 180, Casselman, Ont. KOA 1MO (613/764-2944)
Castleford	76	Renfrew	Renfrew-Nipissing-Pembroke	Renfrew South	
Castleton	326	Northumberland	Northumberland	Northumberland	
Cataraqui		Frontenac	Kingston & the Islands	Frontenac-Addington	PO of Kingston
Cavan Twp	3,782	Peterborough	Peterborough	Peterborough	Mrs. J.M. Wismer, Clerk, Box 189, Millbrook, Ont. LOA 1GO (705/932-2929)
Cayuga		Haldimand-Norfolk Reg. Mun.	Haldimand-Norfolk	Haldimand-Norfolk	Part of Haldimand
Cedar Springs	281	Kent	Essex-Kent	Kent-Elgin	
Cedar Valley	92	York Reg. Mun.	York-Peel		
Centralia	207	Huron	Huron-Bruce	Huron-Middlesex	
Central Patricia	145	Kenora D.	Kenora-Rainy River	Lake Nipigon	
Centreville	58	Lennox & Addington	Hastings-Frontenac	Frontenac-Addington	
Ceylon	50	Grey	Grey-Simcoe	Grey	
Chalk River•	1,022	Renfrew	Renfrew-Nipissing-Pembroke	Renfrew North	Mrs. P. Rantz, Village Clerk, 15 Main St., Chalk River, Ont. KOJ 1JO (613/589-2985)
Chamberlain Twp	365	Timiskaming D.	Timiskaming	Timiskaming	Mrs. A. Jackson, Clerk, R.R. 3, Englehart, Ont. POJ 1HO (705/544-8088)
Chambers Corner	62	Niagara Reg. Mun.	Erie	Erie	
Chandos Twp	520	Peterborough		Hastings-Peterborough	Mrs. G. Roberts, Clerk, R.R. 1, Apsley, Ont. KOL 1AO (705/656-4936)
Chapleau Twp	3,276	Sudbury D.		Nickel Belt	J.G. Maddox, Clerk, Box 129, Chapleau, Ont. POM 1KO (705/864-1330)
Chapman Twp	396	Parry Sound D.		Parry Sound	Mrs. M. Osborne, Clerk, Box 70, Magnetawan, Ont. POA 1PO (705/387-3947)
Chapple Twp	919	Rainy River D.	Kenora-Rainy River	Rainy River	Mrs. D.I. Dyson, Clerk, Box 4, Barwick, Ont. POW 1AO (807/487-2354)
Chaput-Hughes		Timiskaming D.	Timiskaming	Timiskaming	Part of Kirkland Lake
Charing Cross	441	Kent	Essex-Kent	Kent-Elgin	
Charlottenburgh Twp	6,312	Stormont, Dundas & Glengarry	Stormont-Dundas	Stormont, Dundas & Glengarry	M.J. Lapierre, Clerk, Box 40, Williamstown, Ont. KOC 2JO (613/347-2444)
Charlton†	194	Timiskaming D.	Timiskaming	Timiskaming	Mrs. M.C. Brownlee, Town Clerk, Box 226, Englehart, Ont. POJ 1HO (705/544-2579)

Cities in CAPITALS; Towns marked †; Boroughs marked *; Villages marked •; Townships (Twp); ‡ means separated for municipal purposes from county; balance are either small places or unincorporated places (which have been named but not organized)

MUNICIPALITY	POP.	COUNTY OR DISTRICT	FEDERAL ELECTORAL DISTRICT	PROVINCIAL ELECTORAL DISTRICT	CLERK WITH ADDRESS AND PHONE
Chatham Twp	7,019	Kent	Kent	Chatham-Kent	F. Ewing, Clerk, 2 Lowe St., Chatham, Ont. N7L 1J5 (519/352-8260)
CHATHAM	40,928	Kent	Kent	Chatham-Kent	M.M. Miller, City Clerk, 315 King St. W., Box 640, Chatham, Ont. N7M 5K8 (519/352-4500)
Chatsworth•	384	Grey	Bruce-Grey	Grey	Mrs. D.M. Hillis, Village Clerk, Box 76, Chatsworth, Ont. NOH 1GO (519/794-2802)
Cheapside		Haldimand-Norfolk Reg. Mun.	Haldimand-Norfolk	Haldimand-Norfolk	Part of Nanticoke
Chelmsford	89	Sudbury Reg. Mun.	Nickel Belt	Nickel Belt	Part of Rayside-Balfour
Cheltenham		Peel Reg. Mun.	York-Peel	Wellington-Dufferin-Peel	Part of Caledon
Cheminis	178	Timiskaming D.	Timiskaming	Timiskaming	
Chemung Park	500	Peterborough	Peterborough	Peterborough	
Chenaux	53	Renfrew	Renfrew-Nipissing-Pembroke	Renfrew South	
Cheney	73	Prescott & Russell	Glengarry-Prescott-Russell	Prescott & Russell	
Chepstow	225	Bruce	Bruce-Grey	Huron-Bruce	
Cherry Valley	273	Prince Edward	Prince Edward-Hastings	Prince Edward-Lennox	
Cherrywood		Durham Reg. Mun.	Ontario	Durham West	Part of Pickering
Chesley†	1,859	Bruce	Bruce-Grey	Grey-Bruce	R. Small, Town Clerk, Box 70, Chesley, Ont. NOG 1LO (519/363-2524)
Chesterville•	1,423	Stormont, Dundas & Glengarry	Stormont-Dundas	Stormont, Dundas & Glengarry	G.P. Thompson, Village Clerk, 1 Mill St., Chesterville, Ont. KOC 1HO (613/448-2342)
Chisholm Twp	1,015	Nipissing D.	Nipissing	Parry Sound	E. Boehme, Clerk, R.R. 1, Powassan, Ont. POH 1ZO (705/724-3526)
Christie Twp	444	Parry Sound D.	Parry Sound-Muskoka	Parry Sound	Mrs. M.J. Van Duzen, Clerk, R.R. 3, Parry Sound, Ont. P2A 2W9 (705/732-4601)
Churchill	196	Simcoe	Simcoe South	Simcoe Centre	
Chute à Blondeau	350	Prescott & Russell	Glengarry-Prescott-Russell	Prescott & Russell	
Clandeboye	125	Middlesex	Ontario	Durham York	
Clarence Twp	6,381	Prescott & Russell	Glengarry-Prescott-Russell	Prescott & Russell	R. Lalonde, Clerk, Box 70, Clarence Creek, Ont. KOA 1NO (613/488-2570)
Clarence Creek	395	Prescott & Russell	Glengarry-Prescott-Russell	Prescott & Russell	
Clarendon & Miller Twp	426	Frontenac	Hastings-Frontenac	Frontenac-Addington	Mrs. D. Mika, Clerk, Plevna, Ont. KOH 2MO (613/479-2231)
Clarksburg	481	Grey	Grey-Simcoe	Grey	
Clarkson		Peel Reg. Mun.	Mississauga South	Mississauga South	Part of Mississauga
Clear Creek	78	Haldimand-Norfolk Reg. Mun.	Haldimand-Norfolk	Haldimand-Norfolk	
Clifford•	613	Wellington	Wellington-Dufferin-Simcoe	Grey	Mrs. D. Epworth, Village Clerk, Box 29, Clifford, Ont. NOG 1MO (519/327-8141)
Clinton†	3,107	Huron	Huron-Bruce	Huron-Middlesex	C.C. Proctor, Town Clerk, 23 Albert St., Clinton, Ont. NOM 1LO (519/482-3997)
Cobalt†	1,777	Timiskaming D.	Timiskaming	Timiskaming	R.D. Scott, Town Clerk, Box 189, Cobalt, Ont. POJ 1CO (705/679-8877)

Cities in CAPITALS; Towns marked †; Boroughs marked *; Villages marked •; Townships (Twp); ‡ means separated for municipal purposes from county; balance are either small places or unincorporated places (which have been named but not organized)

MUNICIPALITY	POP.	COUNTY OR DISTRICT	FEDERAL ELECTORAL DISTRICT	PROVINCIAL ELECTORAL DISTRICT	CLERK WITH ADDRESS AND PHONE
Cobden•	1,050	Renfrew	Renfrew-Nipissing-Pembroke	Renfrew South	R. Schilling, Village Clerk, Box 40, Cobden, Ont. KOJ 1KO (613/646-2282)
Cobourg†	11,264	Northumberland	Durham-Northumberland	Northumberland	B.W. Baxter, Town Clerk/ Adm., 55 King St. W., Cobourg, Ont. K9A 2M2 (416/372-2288)
Cochenour	624	Kenora D.	Kenora-Rainy River	Kenora	
Cochrane†	4,725	Cochrane D.	Cochrane	Cochrane North	L.J. Adshead, Town Clerk, Box 490, Cochrane, Ont. POL 1CO (705/272-4361)
Cockburn Is. Twp	2	Manitoulin D.	Algoma	Algoma-Manitoulin	A. Clipperton, Clerk, Box 489, Massey, Ont. POP 1PO (705/865-2920)
Coe Hill	162	Hastings	Hastings-Frontenac	Hastings-Peterborough	
Colborne Twp	1,710	Huron	Huron-Bruce	Huron-Bruce	H. Milburn, Clerk, R.R. 5, Goderich, Ont. N7A 3Y2 (519/524-4669)
Colborne•	1,790	Northumberland	Northumberland	Northumberland	A. Learmonth, Village Clerk, Box 357, Colborne, Ont. KOK 1SO (416/355-2821)
Colchester North Twp	3,679	Essex		Essex South	M. Girard, Clerk, R.R. 2, Essex, Ont. N8M 2X6 (519/776-6476)
Colchester South Twp	4,977	Essex		Essex South	T.H. Lowe, Clerk, 44 King St., Harrow, Ont. NOR 1GO (519/738-2282)
Coldwater•	774	Simcoe	Simcoe North	Simcoe East	Nancy Barron, Village Clerk, Box 490, Coldwater, Ont. LOK 1EO (705/686-3606)
Coldwell	98	Thunder Bay D.	Cochrane	Lake Nipigon	
Coleman Twp	628	Timiskaming D.	Timiskaming	Timiskaming	E.W. Tresidder, Clerk, Box 472, Cobalt, Ont. POJ 1CO (705/679-8833)
Colgan	188	Simcoe	Wellington-Dufferin-Simcoe	Dufferin-Simcoe	
Collingwood Twp	2,578	Grey		Grey	W.C. Knott, Clerk, Box 40, Clarksburg, Ont. NOH 1JO (519/599-3031)
Collingwood†	11,550	Simcoe	Grey-Simcoe	Dufferin-Simcoe	C.K. Morrison, Town Clerk, Box 157, Collngwood, Ont. L9Y 3Z5 (705/445-1030)
Collins	102	Thunder Bay D.	Thunder Bay-Nipigon	Lake Nipigon	
Collins Bay	6,897	Frontenac	Kingston & the Islands	Frontenac-Addington	
Colwell	128	Simcoe	Simcoe South	Dufferin-Simcoe	
Comber	649	Essex	Essex-Windsor	Essex North	
Combermere	214	Renfrew	Renfrew-Nipissing-Pembroke	Renfrew South	
Concord		York Reg. Mun.	York North	York North	
Conestogo	548	Waterloo Reg. Mun.	Waterloo	Waterloo North	
Coniston		Sudbury Reg. Mun.	Nickel Belt	Sudbury East	Part of Nickel Centre
Conmee Twp	529	Thunder Bay D.	Thunder Bay-Nipigon	Port Arthur	Mrs. F.M. Pajamaki, Clerk, R.R. 1, Kakabeka Falls, Ont. POT 1WO (807/577-9392)
Connaught		Cochrane D.	Timmins-Chapleau	Cochrane South	Part of Timmins
Consecon	363	Prince Edward	Prince Edward-Hastings	Prince Edward-Lennox	
Cooks Mills	1,010	Nipissing D.	Nipissing	Nipissing	
Cookstown•	836	Simcoe	Simcoe South	Simcoe Centre	Mrs. V. Webb, Village Clerk, 19 Queen St., Cookstown, Ont. LOL 1LO (705/458-4329)
Cooksville		Peel Reg. Mun.	Mississauga North	Mississauga East; Mississauga North	Part of Mississauga

Cities in CAPITALS; Towns marked †; Boroughs marked *; Villages marked •; Townships (Twp); ‡ means separated for municipal purposes from county; balance are either small places or unincorporated places (which have been named but not organized)

MUNICIPALITY	POP.	COUNTY OR DISTRICT	FEDERAL ELECTORAL DISTRICT	PROVINCIAL ELECTORAL DISTRICT	CLERK WITH ADDRESS AND PHONE
Copetown	147	Hamilton-Wentworth Reg. Mun.	Hamilton-Wentworth	Wentworth North	
Coppell	77	Cochrane D.	Cochrane	Cochrane North	
Corbeil	79	Nipissing D.	Nipissing	Parry Sound	
Corbetton	90	Dufferin	Wellington-Dufferin-Simcoe	Grey	
Corinth	114	Elgin	Elgin	Elgin	
Cornell	110	Oxford		Oxford	
CORNWALL	46,152	Stormont, Dundas & Glengarry	Stormont-Dundas	Cornwall	R. Allaire, City Clerk, 360 Pitt St., Cornwall, Ont. K6J 3P9 (613/932-6252)
Cornwall Twp	5,022	Stormont, Dundas & Glengarry	Stormont-Dundas	Cornwall	B.J. Chisholm, Clerk, R.R. 1, Long Sault, Ont. KOC 1PO (613/933-1162)
Corunna	3,723	Lambton	Sarnia	Lambton	
Corwhin	60	Wellington	Guelph	Wellington South	
Cosby, Mason & Martland Twp	1,602	Sudbury D		Sudbury East	R. Vaillancourt, Clerk, Box 156, Noelville, Ont. POM 2NO (705/898-2294)
Cottam	514	Essex	Essex-Kent	Essex North	
Courtice		Durham Reg. Mun.	Durham-Northumberland	Durham East	Part of Newcastle
Courtland	602	Haldimand-Norfolk Reg. Mun.	Haldimand-Norfolk	Brant-Oxford-Norfolk	
Craighurst	90	Simcoe	Simcoe North		
Craigleith	131	Grey	Grey-Simcoe	Grey	
Cramahe Twp	2,478	Northumberland		Northumberland	Ms. R. Rutledge, Clerk, Box 39, Castleton, Ont. KOK 1MO (416/344-7352)
Crediton	439	Huron	Huron-Bruce	Huron-Middlesex	
Creemore•	1,104	Simcoe	Grey-Simcoe	Dufferin-Simcoe	E.J. Underwood, Village Clerk, Box 40, Creemore, Ont. LOM 1GO (705/466-2242)
Creighton		Sudbury Reg. Mun.	Nickel Belt	Nickel Belt	Part of Walden
Crown Hill	167	Simcoe	Simcoe North	Simcoe East	
Crumlin	228	Middlesex	London-Middlesex	Middlesex	
Crysler	490	Stormont, Dundas & Glengarry	Stormont-Dundas	Stormont, Dundas & Glengarry	
Culross Twp	1,727	Bruce	Huron-Bruce	Huron-Bruce	R. Cronin, Clerk, Box 10, Teeswater, Ont. NOG 2SO (519/392-6623)
Cultus	145	Haldimand-Norfolk Reg. Mun.	Haldimand-Norfolk	Haldimand-Norfolk	
Cumberland Twp	15,643	Ottawa-Carleton Reg. Mun.	Glengarry-Prescott-Russell	Prescott & Russell	H.E. Saulnier, Clerk, R.R. 3, Box 15, Navan, Ont. KOA 2SO (613/835-2526)
Curran	214	Prescott & Russell	Glengarry-Prescott-Russell	Prescott & Russell	
Cutler	175	Algoma D.	Algoma	Algoma-Manitoulin	
Dack Twp	435	Timiskaming D.	Timiskaming	Timiskaming	Mrs. L. Williams, Clerk, R.R. 2, Englehart, Ont. POJ 1HO (705/544-7525)
Dalkeith	141	Stormont, Dundas & Glengarry	Glengarry-Prescott-Russell	Stormont, Dundas & Glengarry	
Dalston	34	Simcoe	Simcoe North	Simcoe Centre	
Dalton	28	Algoma D.	Timmins-Chapleau	Algoma	
Dalton Twp	315	Victoria		Victoria-Haliburton	Mrs. B.M. Dewell, Clerk, R.R. 1, Sebright, Ont. LOK 1WO (705/833-2996)
Darling Twp	309	Lanark		Lanark	Mrs. D. Ranger, Clerk, R.R. 4, Lanark, Ont. KOG 1KO (613/259-5263)

Cities in CAPITALS; Towns marked †; Boroughs marked *; Villages marked •; Townships (Twp); ‡ means separated for municipal purposes from county; balance are either small places or unincorporated places (which have been named but not organized)

MUNICIPALITY	POP.	COUNTY OR DISTRICT	FEDERAL ELECTORAL DISTRICT	PROVINCIAL ELECTORAL DISTRICT	CLERK WITH ADDRESS AND PHONE
Dashwood	434	Huron	Huron-Bruce	Huron-Middlesex	
Dawn Twp	1,823	Lambton	Lambton-Middlesex	Lambton	Mrs. J. Langstaff, Clerk, R.R. 4, Dresden, Ont. NOP 1MO (519/692-5148)
Day & Bright Add'l. Twp	252	Algoma D.	Algoma	Algoma	Mrs. G.M. Mosher, Clerk, R.R. 2, Iron Bridge, Ont. POR 1HO (705/842-5102)
Deep River†	5,306	Renfrew	Renfrew-Nipissing-Pembroke	Renfrew North	R. Adam, Town Clerk, Box 400, Deep River, Ont. KOJ 1PO (613/584-3672)
Delaware Twp	2,229	Middlesex		Middlesex	Mrs. J. Patrick, Clerk, Box 70, Delaware, Ont. NOL 1EO (519/652-5441)
Delhi Twp	14,931	Haldimand-Norfolk Reg. Mun.	Haldimand-Norfolk	Brant-Oxford-Norfolk; Haldimand-Norfolk	R.K. Granger, Clerk, 183 Main St., Delhi, Ont. N4B 2W9 (519/582-2100)
Deloro•	242	Hastings	Hastings-Frontenac	Hastings-Peterborough	Mrs. B. Young, Deloro Village Clerk, c/o Box 78, R.R. 2, Marmora, Ont. KOK 2MO (613/472-2172)
Delta	310	Leeds & Grenville	Leeds-Grenville	Leeds	
Denbigh, Abinger & Ashby Twp	681	Lennox & Addington		Frontenac-Addington	J. Pauhl, Clerk, Denbigh, Ont. KOH 1LO (613/333-2736)
Departure Lake	200	Cochrane D.	Cochrane	Cochrane North	
Depot Harbour	457	Parry Sound D.	Parry Sound-Muskoka	Parry Sound	
Derby Twp	2,481	Grey	Bruce-Grey	Grey-Bruce	A.W. Wilkinson, Clerk, R.R. 3, Owen Sound, Ont. N4K 5N5 (519/376-2672)
Desbarats	252	Algoma D.	Algoma	Algoma	
Desboro	170	Grey	Bruce-Grey	Grey	
Deseronto†	1,751	Hastings	Prince Edward-Hastings	Hastings-Peterborough	C.J. Milligan, Town Clerk, 331 Main St., Deseronto, Ont. KOK 1XO (613/396-2440)
Devlin	93	Rainy River D.	Kenora-Rainy River	Rainy River	
Dilke Twp	227	Rainy River D.	Kenora-Rainy River	Rainy River	Mrs. M. Cunningham, Clerk, Box 40, Pinewood, Ont. POW 1KO (807/483-5480)
Dobbinton	74	Bruce	Bruce-Grey	Grey-Bruce	
Domville	37	Leeds & Grenville	Leeds-Grenville	Carleton-Grenville	
Dorion Twp	460	Thunder Bay D.	Thunder Bay-Nipigon	Lake Nipigon	Helena Osala, Clerk, R.R. 1, Dorion, Ont. POT 1KO (807/857-2289)
Dorking	66	Perth		Perth	
Dorset		Haliburton	Victoria-Haliburton	Victoria-Haliburton	
Douglas	291	Renfrew	Renfrew-Nipissing-Pembroke	Renfrew South	
Douro Twp	3,349	Peterborough		Peterborough	C. Sullivan, Clerk, Douro, Ont. KOL 1SO (705/652-3374)
Dover Twp	4,351	Kent	Kent	Chatham-Kent	Mrs. M. Van Horne, Clerk, 515 Grand Ave. W., Box 217, Chatham, Ont. N7M 5K3 (519/354-3350)
Downie Twp	2,400	Perth	Perth	Perth	Mrs. M. King, Clerk, St. Pauls Station, Ont. NOK 1VO (519/271-0619)
Downsview			York Centre	Downsview	Part of Metro Toronto
Drayton•	767	Wellington	Wellington-Dufferin-Simcoe	Wellington-Dufferin-Peel	Mrs. J. Campbell, Village Clerk, Box 160, Drayton, Ont. NOG 1PO (519/638-3097)
Dresden†	2,430	Kent	Kent	Kent-Elgin	J.L. Babcock, Town Clerk, 485 St. George St., Box 730, Dresden, Ont. NOP 1MO (519/683-4306)
Drumbo	397	Oxford	Oxford	Brant-Oxford-Norfolk	
Drummond Twp	1,984	Lanark	Lanark-Renfrew-Carleton	Lanark	J.M. McFarlane, Clerk, R.R. 6, Perth, Ont. K7H 3C8 (613/267-5444)

Cities in CAPITALS; Towns marked †; Boroughs marked *; Villages marked •; Townships (Twp); ‡ means separated for municipal purposes from county; balance are either small places or unincorporated places (which have been named but not organized)

MUNICIPALITY	POP.	COUNTY OR DISTRICT	FEDERAL ELECTORAL DISTRICT	PROVINCIAL ELECTORAL DISTRICT	CLERK WITH ADDRESS AND PHONE
Dryden†	6,482	Kenora D.	Kenora-Rainy River	Kenora	W.M. Wake, Town Clerk, 30 Van Horne Ave., Dryden, Ont. P8N 2A7 (807/223-2225)
Duart	127	Kent	Kent	Kent-Elgin	
Dublin	282	Perth	Perth	Perth	
Dubreuilville	895	Algoma D.	Cochrane	Algoma	Improvement Dist., c/o J. Trottier, Box 149, Dubreuilville, Ont. P0S 1B0
Dugwal		Cochrane D.	Timmins-Chapleau	Cochrane South	Part of Timmins
Dummer Twp	2,038	Peterborough	Peterborough	Hastings-Peterborough	D. Clifford, Clerk, Warsaw, Ont. K0L 3A0 (705/652-8392)
Dunchurch	150	Parry Sound D.	Parry Sound-Muskoka	Parry Sound	
Dundalk•	1,168	Grey	Grey-Simcoe	Grey	Mrs. A.L. Clarke, Village Clerk, 80 Main St. E., Dundalk, Ont. N0C 1B0 (519/923-2144)
Dundas†	19,266	Hamilton-Wentworth Reg. Mun.	Hamilton-Wentworth	Wentworth North	L.J. Mikulich, Town Clerk/ Adm., Town Hall, 60 Main St., Dundas, Ont. L9H 2P8 (416/628-6327)
Dungannon Twp	1,081	Hastings	Hastings-Frontenac	Hastings-Peterborough	E. Rupnow, Clerk, L'Amable, Ont. K0L 2L0 (613/332-1328)
Dungannon	208	Huron	Huron-Bruce	Huron-Bruce	Near Goderich
Dunnville†	11,470	Haldimand-Norfolk Reg. Mun.	Haldimand-Norfolk	Haldimand-Norfolk	F. Scholfield, Town Clerk/ Adm., Mun. Bldg., Box 187, Dunnville, Ont. N1A 2X5 (416/774-7595)
Dunsford	125	Victoria	Victoria-Haliburton	Victoria-Haliburton	
Duntroon	109	Simcoe	Grey-Simcoe	Dufferin-Simcoe	
Dunvegan	77	Stormont, Dundas & Glengarry	Glengarry-Prescott-Russell	Stormont, Dundas & Glengarry	
Dunwich Twp	2,293	Elgin		Kent-Elgin	K. Loveland, Clerk, 156 Main St., Dutton, Ont. N0L 1J0 (519/762-2204)
Durham†	2,467	Grey	Bruce-Grey	Grey	W.R. McDonald, Town Clerk, Box 639, Durham, Ont. N0G 1R0 (519/369-2200)
Dutton•	1,043	Elgin	Elgin	Kent-Elgin	D. Moran, Village Clerk, Box 59, Dutton, Ont. N0L 1J0 (519/762-2736)
Dymond Twp	1,134	Timiskaming D.	Timiskaming	Timiskaming	F.W. Shepherdson, Clerk, R.R. 2, Box 1, Unit 30, New Liskeard, Ont. P0J 1P0 (705/647-6044)
Dysart et al Twp	3,379	Haliburton	Victoria-Haliburton	Victoria-Haliburton	W.B. Wood, Clerk, Box 389, Haliburton, Ont. K0M 1S0 (705/457-1740)
Eady		Simcoe	Simcoe North	Simcoe East	
Eagle River	146	Kenora D.	Kenora-Rainy River	Kenora	
Ear Falls Twp	2,036	Kenora D.		Kenora	V. Aultman, Clerk, Box 309, Ear Falls, Ont. P0V 1T0 (807/222-3624)
Earlton	1,008	Timiskaming D.	Timiskaming	Timiskaming	
East Ferris Twp	3,090	Nipissing D.	Nipissing	Parry Sound	F.B. Claridge, Clerk, R.R. 1, Corbeil, Ont. P0H 1K0 (705/752-2740)
East Garafraxa Twp	1,633	Dufferin		Wellington-Dufferin-Peel	J.C. Woods, Clerk, R.R. 3, Orton, Ont. L0N 1N0 (519/928-5298)
East Gwillimbury†	11,773	York Reg. Mun.	York-Peel	Durham York	J.F. Hopkins, Town Clerk, 18066 Leslie St., Sharon, Ont. L0G 1V0 (416/478-4291)

Cities in CAPITALS; Towns marked †; Boroughs marked *; Villages marked •; Townships (Twp); ‡ means separated for municipal purposes from county; balance are either small places or unincorporated places (which have been named but not organized)

MUNICIPALITY	POP.	COUNTY OR DISTRICT	FEDERAL ELECTORAL DISTRICT	PROVINCIAL ELECTORAL DISTRICT	CLERK WITH ADDRESS AND PHONE
East Hawkesbury Twp	2,927	Prescott & Russell	Glengarry-Prescott-Russell	Prescott & Russell	Mrs. R. Clermont, Clerk, Box 340, St. Eugène, Ont. KOB 1PO (613/674-2170)
East Luther Twp	886	Dufferin	Wellington-Dufferin-Simcoe	Wellington-Dufferin-Peel	F. Newson, Clerk, Box 400, Grand Valley, Ont. LON 1GO (519/928-5784)
Eastnor Twp	1,029	Bruce		Grey-Bruce	M. Cameron, Clerk, Box 40, Lion's Head, Ont. NOH 1WO (519/793-3227)
Eastons Corners	107	Leeds & Grenville	Leeds-Grenville	Carleton-Grenville	
East Wawanosh Twp	1,156	Huron	Huron-Bruce	Huron-Bruce	Mrs. W. Thompson, Clerk, Belgrave, Ont., NOG 1EO (519/357-2880)
East Williams Twp	1,249	Middlesex		Huron-Middlesex	Mrs. D. McLachlan, Clerk, Box 99, Ailsa Craig, Ont. NOM 1AO (519/232-4506)
East York*	100,858	Metro	Broadview; Don Valley West; Rosedale; York East	Don Mills; York East	W. Alexander, Borough Clerk, 550 Mortimer Ave., (East York), Toronto, Ont. M4J 2H2 (416/461-9451)
East Zorra-Tavistock Twp	7,146	Oxford	Oxford	Oxford	J.V. Killing, Clerk, Hickson, Ont. NOJ 1LO (519/462-2697)
Eberts	31	Kent		Chatham-Kent	
Echo Bay	745	Algoma D.	Algoma	Algoma	
Eden	214	Elgin	Elgin	Elgin	
Edwardsburgh Twp	4,393	Leeds & Grenville	Leeds-Grenville	Carleton-Grenville	R. Austin, Clerk, Box 84, Spencerville, Ont. KOE 1XO (613/658-3055)
Eganville•	1,307	Renfrew	Renfrew-Nipissing-Pembroke	Renfrew South	D.H. Washington, Village Clerk, Box 249, Eganville, Ont. KOJ 1TO (613/628-3101)
Egremont Twp	2,049	Grey		Grey	Mrs. V. Watson, Clerk, Box 183, Mount Forest, Ont. NOG 2LO (519/334-3480)
Eilber & Devitt Twp	1,228	Cochrane D.	Cochrane	Cochrane North	Y. Brousseau, Clerk, Box 129, Mattice, Ont. POL 1TO (705/362-8000)
Ekfrid Twp	2,138	Middlesex	Lambton-Middlesex	Middlesex	Mrs. J. Newitt, Clerk, Box 276, Appin, Ont. NOL 1AO (519/289-2016)
Elderslie Twp	1,242	Bruce	Bruce-Grey	Grey-Bruce	R. Wagner, Clerk, Box 57, Chesley, Ont. NOG 1LO (519/363-3039)
Eldon Twp	1,890	Victoria		Victoria-Haliburton	D.A. Grant, Clerk, Kirkfield, Ont. KOM 2BO (705/438-3132)
Eldorado	78	Hastings	Hastings-Frontenac	Hastings-Peterborough	
Elgin	292	Leeds & Grenville	Leeds-Grenville	Leeds	
Elginburg	243	Frontenac	Kingston & the Islands	Frontenac-Addington	
Elizabethtown Twp	7,182	Leeds & Grenville	Leeds-Grenville	Leeds	D. Stewart, Clerk, R.R. 2, Addison, Ont. KOE 1AO (613/345-1223)
Elizabethville	33	Northumberland	Durham-Northumberland		
Elk Lake	564	Timiskaming D.	Timiskaming	Timiskaming	
Ellice Twp	3,062	Perth	Perth	Perth	A. Siroen, Clerk, Rostock, Ont. NOK 1TO (519/393-6237)
Elliot Lake†	12,893	Algoma D.	Algoma	Algoma-Manitoulin	J.S. Bloom, Town Clerk, 45 Hillside Dr. N., Elliot Lake, Ont. P5A 1X5 (705/848-2287)
Elma Twp	3,916	Perth		Perth	G.S. Tucker, Clerk, Atwood, Ont. NOG 1BO (519/356-2231)
Elmhurst Beach	87	York Reg. Mun.	Victoria-Haliburton	Durham York	

Cities in CAPITALS; Towns marked †; Boroughs marked *; Villages marked •; Townships (Twp); ‡ means separated for municipal purposes from county; balance are either small places or unincorporated places (which have been named but not organized)

MUNICIPALITY	POP.	COUNTY OR DISTRICT	FEDERAL ELECTORAL DISTRICT	PROVINCIAL ELECTORAL DISTRICT	CLERK WITH ADDRESS AND PHONE
Elmira		Waterloo Reg. Mun.		Waterloo North	Part of Woolwich Twp.
Elmvale•	1,162	Simcoe	Simcoe South	Simcoe Centre	Mrs. F. Townes, Village Clerk, 55 Queen St. W., Elmvale, Ont. LOL 1PO (705/322-2122)
Elora•	2,476	Wellington	Wellington-Dufferin-Simcoe	Wellington-Dufferin-Peel	F.E. Moynihan, Village Clerk, Box 508, Elora, Ont. NOB 1SO (519/846-9691)
Elzevir & Grimsthorpe Twp	661	Hastings	Hastings-Frontenac	Hastings-Peterborough	Mrs. J. Holmes, Clerk, Box 63, R.R. 3, Tweed, Ont. KOK 3J0 (613/478-5818)
Embrun	1,763	Prescott & Russell	Glengarry-Prescott-Russell	Prescott & Russell	
Emily Twp	4,374	Victoria		Victoria-Haliburton	Mrs. L. O'Neill, Clerk, Mun. Office, R.R. 4, Omemee, Ont. KOL 2WO (705/799-6010)
Emo Twp	1,035	Rainy River D.	Kenora-Rainy River	Rainy River	M.G. McComb, Clerk, Box 358, Emo, Ont. POW 1EO (807/482-2378)
Emsdale	110	Parry Sound D.	Parry Sound-Muskoka	Parry Sound	
Englehart†	1,689	Timiskaming D.	Timiskaming	Timiskaming	D.J. Paterson, Town Clerk, Box 399, Englehart, Ont. POJ 1HO (705/544-2244)
Enniskillen Twp	3,440	Lambton	Lambton-Middlesex	Lambton	R.C. White, Clerk, Box 1000, Petrolia, Ont. NON 1RO (519/882-2490)
Ennismore Twp	3,092	Peterborough		Peterborough	N.K. Kyle, Clerk, 801 Tara Rd., Ennismore, Ont. KOL 1TO (705/292-9892)
Enterprise	295	Lennox & Addington	Hastings-Frontenac	Frontenac-Addington	
Eramosa Twp	4,269	Wellington		Wellington-Dufferin-Peel	L.T. Hindley, Clerk, R.R. 1, Rockwood, Ont. NOB 2KO (519/856-9951)
Erieau•	470	Kent	Essex-Kent	Kent-Elgin	V.M. Burke, Village Clerk, Box 121, Erieau, Ont. NOP 1NO (519/676-3681)
Erie Beach	392	Niagara Reg. Mun.	Erie	Erie	
Erie Beach•	256	Kent	Essex-Kent	Kent-Elgin	Dena De Gelas, Erie Beach Village Clerk, c/o Box 100, Erieau, Ont. NOP 1NO (519/676-3681)
Erin•	2,175	Wellington	Wellington-Dufferin-Simcoe	Wellington-Dufferin-Peel	Ms. P. McDermott, Village Clerk, Box 149, Erin, Ont. NOB 1TO (519/883-2604)
Erin Twp	5,799	Wellington		Wellington-Dufferin-Peel	D.R. Emmons, Clerk, Box 250, Hillsburgh, Ont. NOB 1ZO (519/855-4407)
Erinsville	89	Lennox & Addington	Hastings-Frontenac	Frontenac-Addington	
Ernestown Twp	11,128	Lennox & Addington	Hastings-Frontenac	Prince Edward-Lennox	R. Blakely, Clerk, Box 57, Odessa, Ont. KOH 2HO (613/386-7351)
Escott Twp (Front of)	1,078	Leeds & Grenville	Leeds-Grenville	Leeds	Mrs. J.R. Williams, Escott Twp Clerk, Box 210, Lansdowne, Ont. KOE 1LO (613/659-3455)
Espanola†	5,888	Sudbury D.	Algoma	Algoma-Manitoulin	J.R. Walsworth, Town Clerk, Box 638, Espanola, Ont. POP 1CO (705/869-1540)
Essa Twp	15,078	Simcoe	Simcoe South	Dufferin-Simcoe	A. Roth, Clerk, Box 10, Angus, Ont. LOM 1BO (705/424-9770)
Essex†	6,240	Essex	Essex-Windsor	Essex South	Kay Rupert, Town Clerk, 33 Talbot St. S., Essex, Ont. N8M 1A8 (519/776-7336)

Cities in CAPITALS; Towns marked †; Boroughs marked *; Villages marked •; Townships (Twp); ‡ means separated for municipal purposes from county; balance are either small places or unincorporated places (which have been named but not organized)

MUNICIPALITY	POP.	COUNTY OR DISTRICT	FEDERAL ELECTORAL DISTRICT	PROVINCIAL ELECTORAL DISTRICT	CLERK WITH ADDRESS AND PHONE
Etobicoke*	292,045	Metro	Etobicoke Centre; Etobicoke Lakeshore; Etobicoke North	Etobicoke; Humber; Lakeshore; York West	R.F. Cloutier, Borough Clerk, Civic Centre, Etobicoke, Ont. M9C 2Y2 (416/626-4270)
Euphemia Twp	1,300	Lambton		Lambton	Mrs. J. Webber, Clerk, R.R. 2, Bothwell, Ont. NOP 1CO (519/695-2312)
Euphrasia Twp	1,405	Grey		Grey	Mrs. G.H. Falls, R.R. 2, Meaford, Ont. NOH 1YO (519/538-2030)
Evanturel Twp	595	Timiskaming D.	Timiskaming	Timiskaming	S.D. Leonard, Clerk, Box 37, Englehart, Ont. POJ 1HO (705/544-7462)
Everett	438	Simcoe	Wellington-Dufferin-Simcoe	Dufferin-Simcoe	
Everton	170	Wellington	Guelph	Wellington-Dufferin-Peel	
Exeter†	3,532	Huron	Huron-Bruce	Huron-Middlesex	Ms. E. Bell, Town Clerk, 406 Main St., Box 759, Exeter, Ont. NOM 1SO (519/235-0310)
Fairport	581	Durham Reg. Mun.	Ontario	Durham West	
Fanshawe	59	Middlesex	London-Middlesex	Middlesex	
Faraday Twp	1,476	Hastings	Hastings-Frontenac	Hastings-Peterborough	Mrs. E. Mackey, Clerk, Box 929, Bancroft, Ont. KOL 1CO (613/332-3638)
Fargo	75	Kent		Kent-Elgin	
Farlane	33	Kenora D.	Kenora-Rainy River	Kenora	
Fauquier Twp	1,403	Cochrane D.	Cochrane	Cochrane North	A. Filion, Clerk, 53 St. Aubin Ave., Moonbeam, Ont. POL 1VO (705/367-2244)
Fenelon Twp	4,247	Victoria	Victoria-Haliburton	Victoria-Haliburton	Mrs. R. Woodcock, Clerk, Cameron, Ont. KOM 1GO (705/359-1346)
Fenelon Falls•	1,627	Victoria	Victoria-Haliburton	Victoria-Haliburton	Mrs. M. Baker, Village Clerk, Box 179, Fenelon Falls, Ont. KOM 1NO (705/887-3133)
Fergus†	5,981	Wellington	Wellington-Dufferin-Simcoe	Wellington-Dufferin-Peel	G.B. Woods, Town Clerk, 198 St. Andrew St. W., Fergus, Ont. N1M 2W7 (519/843-3250)
Fesserton	195	Simcoe	Simcoe North	Simcoe East	
Feversham	185	Grey	Grey-Simcoe	Grey	
Field Twp	741	Nipissing D.	Timiskaming	Nipissing	R. Lafond, Clerk, 110 rue Morin, Field, Ont. POH 1MO (705/758-6659)
Finch Twp	2,305	Stormont, Dundas & Glengarry	Stormont-Dundas	Stormont, Dundas & Glengarry	A.V. Empey, Clerk, Box 99, Berwick, Ont. KOC 1GO (613/984-2821)
Finch•	377	Stormont, Dundas & Glengarry	Stormont-Dundas	Stormont, Dundas & Glengarry	M.A. Boyer, Village Clerk, Box 200, Finch, Ont. KOC 1KO (613/984-2525)
Fingal	345	Elgin	Elgin	Elgin	
Fisherville		Haldimand-Norfolk Reg. Mun.	Haldimand-Norfolk	Haldimand-Norfolk	Part of Haldimand
Fitzroy Harbour	431	Ottawa-Carleton Reg. Mun.	Lanark-Renfrew-Carleton	Renfrew South	Part of West Carleton Twp.
Flamborough Twp	24,018	Hamilton-Wentworth Reg. Mun.	Hamilton-Wentworth	Wentworth North	J.A. Smith, Clerk, Box 50, Waterdown, Ont. LOR 2HO (416/689-7351)
Flesherton•	597	Grey	Grey-Simcoe	Grey	W. Littlejohns, Village Clerk, 4 Elizabeth St., Flesherton, Ont. NOC 1EO (519/924-2609)
Fletcher	78	Kent	Essex-Kent	Kent-Elgin	

Cities in CAPITALS; Towns marked †; Boroughs marked *; Villages marked •; Townships (Twp); ‡ means separated for municipal purposes from county; balance are either small places or unincorporated places (which have been named but not organized)

MUNICIPALITY	POP.	COUNTY OR DISTRICT	FEDERAL ELECTORAL DISTRICT	PROVINCIAL ELECTORAL DISTRICT	CLERK WITH ADDRESS AND PHONE
Flinton	204	Lennox & Addington	Hastings-Frontenac	Frontenac-Addington	
Florence	199	Lambton	Lambton-Middlesex	Lambton	
Flos Twp	2,419	Simcoe		Simcoe Centre	Mrs. M. Berry, Clerk, 14 Queen St. E., Elmvale, Ont. LOL 1PO (705/322-2033)
Flower Station	50	Lanark	Lanark-Renfrew-Carleton	Lanark	
Foley Twp	1,070	Parry Sound D.	Parry Sound-Muskoka	Parry Sound	Mrs. M. Kendrick, Clerk, R.R. 2, Parry Sound, Ont. P2A 2W8 (705/378-2211)
Foleyet	538	Sudbury D.	Timmins-Chapleau	Nickel Belt	
Fordwich	412	Huron	Huron-Bruce	Huron-Bruce	
Forest†	2,679	Lambton	Lambton-Middlesex	Lambton	John Byrne, Town Clerk, Box 610, Forest, Ont. NON 1JO (519/873-2335)
Foresters Falls	148	Renfrew	Renfrew-Nipissing-Pembroke	Renfrew South	
Forfar	88	Leeds & Grenville	Leeds-Grenville	Leeds	
Formosa	395	Bruce	Bruce-Grey	Huron-Bruce	
Fort Erie†	23,808	Niagara Reg. Mun.	Erie	Erie	J.A. Sauer, Town Clerk, 200 Jarvis St., Fort Erie, Ont. L2A 2S6 (416/871-1600)
Fort Frances†	9,088	Rainy River D.	Kenora-Rainy River	Rainy River	N.S. Kingerski, Town Clerk, Box 38, Fort Frances, Ont. P9A 3M5 (807/274-5323)
Fournier	225	Prescott & Russell	Glengarry-Prescott-Russell	Prescott & Russell	
Foxboro	319	Hastings	Prince Edward-Hastings	Hastings-Peterborough	
Frankford•	1,872	Hastings	Northumberland	Quinte	W. Tod, Village Clerk, Box 388, Frankford, Ont. K8V 4NO (613/398-6200)
Franktown	135	Lanark	Lanark-Renfrew-Carleton	Lanark	
Frankville	176	Leeds & Grenville	Leeds-Grenville	Leeds	
Franz	39	Algoma D.	Cochrane	Algoma	
Fraserdale	385	Cochrane D.	Timiskaming	Cochrane North	
Frazerville	118	Peterborough	Peterborough	Northumberland	
Freelton	310	Hamilton-Wentworth Reg. Mun.	Hamilton-Wentworth	Wentworth North	
French River	126	Parry Sound D.	Parry Sound-Muskoka	Parry Sound	
Front of ...					see name, Front of
Frood Mine	129	Sudbury Reg. Mun.	Sudbury		Part of City of Sudbury
Fullarton Twp	1,605	Perth	Perth	Perth	W. MacDougald, Clerk, R.R. 1, Fullarton, Ont. NOK 1HO (519/229-8828)
Gads Hill Station	109	Perth	Perth	Perth	
Gagnon	67	Prescott & Russell	Glengarry-Prescott-Russell	Prescott & Russell	
Galetta	155	Ottawa-Carleton Reg. Mun.	Lanark-Renfrew-Carleton	Renfrew South	
Galt		Waterloo Reg. Mun.	Cambridge	Cambridge	Part of Cambridge
Gamebridge	153	Simcoe	Victoria-Haliburton	Simcoe East	
Galway & Cavendish Twp	342	Peterborough		Hastings-Peterborough	Mrs. J. McCausland, Clerk, Kinmount, Ont. KOM 2AO (705/488-2981)
Gananoque†‡	4,907	Leeds & Grenville	Leeds-Grenville	Leeds	G.W. Drysdale, Town Clerk/Adm., Box 100, Gananoque, Ont. KOH 1RO (613/382-2149)
Garden River	186	Algoma D.	Algoma	Algoma	
Garson		Sudbury D.	Nickel Belt	Sudbury East	Part of Nickel Centre
Gateway	5,500	Nipissing D.	Nipissing	Nipissing	

Cities in CAPITALS; Towns marked †; Boroughs marked *; Villages marked •; Townships (Twp); ‡ means separated for municipal purposes from county; balance are either small places or unincorporated places (which have been named but not organized)

MUNICIPALITY	POP.	COUNTY OR DISTRICT	FEDERAL ELECTORAL DISTRICT	PROVINCIAL ELECTORAL DISTRICT	CLERK WITH ADDRESS AND PHONE
Gauthier	151	Timiskaming D.	Timiskaming	Timiskaming	Improvement Dist., c/o Mrs. V. Hudson, 139 McKay St., Dobie, Ont. P0K 1B0
Geco	275	Thunder Bay D.		Lake Nipigon	
Gelert		Haliburton	Victoria-Haliburton	Victoria-Haliburton	
Georgetown		Halton Reg Mun.	Brampton-Georgetown	Halton-Burlington	Part of Halton Hills
Georgian Bay Twp	1,944	Muskoka Dist. Mun.	Parry Sound-Muskoka	Muskoka	Mrs. M.C. Leduc, Clerk, R.R. 1, Port Severn, Ont. L0K 1S0 (705/538-2337)
Georgina Twp	18,969	York Reg. Mun.	Victoria-Haliburton	Durham York	Mrs. M. Wilkinson, Clerk, R.R. 2, Keswick, Ont. L4P 3E9 (416/476-4301)
Geraldton†	3,010	Thunder Bay D.	Cochrane	Lake Nipigon	D.J. Horne, Town Clerk, Box 70, Geraldton, Ont. P0T 1M0 (807/854-1100)
Gilford	127	Simcoe	Simcoe South	Simcoe Centre	
Gillies	39	Timiskaming D.	Timiskaming	Timiskaming	
Gillies Twp	408	Thunder Bay D.		Fort William	Mrs. E. Forrest, Clerk, South Gillies, Ont. P0T 2V0 (807/939-6594)
Gilmour	85	Hastings	Hastings-Frontenac	Hastings-Peterborough	
Glackmeyer Twp	1,137	Cochrane D.		Cochrane North	I. Thomas, Clerk, Box 1867, Cochrane, Ont. P0L 1C0 (705/272-4313)
Glammis	56	Bruce	Bruce-Grey	Huron-Bruce	
Glamorgan Twp	527	Haliburton	Victoria-Haliburton	Victoria-Haliburton	Mrs. E.V. Bates, Clerk, Box 70, Gooderham, Ont. K0M 1R0 (613/447-2410)
Glanbrook Twp	9,945	Hamilton-Wentworth Reg. Mun.	Hamilton-Wentworth	Wentworth	C. Switzer, Clerk, Box 130, Mount Hope, Ont. L0R 1W0 (416/679-4121)
Glanworth	123	Middlesex	Middlesex East	Middlesex	
Glencoe•	1,743	Middlesex	Lambton-Middlesex	Middlesex	Wm. Black, Village Clerk, Box 218, Glencoe, Ont. N0L 1M0 (519/287-2015)
Glenelg Twp	1,416	Grey		Grey	J.S. Black, Clerk, R.R. 1, Markdale, Ont. N0C 1H0 (519/986-2785)
Glen Huron	95	Simcoe	Grey-Simcoe	Dufferin-Simcoe	
Glen Miller	605	Hastings	Northumberland	Quinte	
Glen Robertson	312	Stormont, Dundas & Glengarry	Glengarry-Prescott-Russell	Stormont, Dundas & Glengarry	
Glen Tay	120	Lanark	Lanark-Renfrew-Carleton	Lanark	
Glen Williams		Halton Reg. Mun.	Brampton-Georgetown	Halton-Burlington	Part of Halton Hills
Glenwood Park	90	York Reg. Mun.		Durham York	
GLOUCESTER	71,276	Ottawa-Carleton Reg. Mun.	Ottawa-Carleton	Carleton East	F. Meldrum, Gloucester City Clerk, 4550 Bank St., Box 8333, Ottawa, Ont. K1G 3V5 (613/822-7880)
Goderich Twp	2,365	Huron		Huron-Middlesex	R.E. Thompson, Clerk, R.R. 2, Clinton, Ont. N0M 1L0 (519/482-9225)
Goderich†	7,298	Huron	Huron-Bruce	Huron-Middlesex	L. McCabe, Town Clerk, 57 West St., Goderich, Ont. N7A 2K5 (519/524-8344)
Gogama	702	Sudbury D.	Timmins-Chapleau	Nickel Belt	
Golden Lake	229	Renfrew	Renfrew-Nipissing-Pembroke	Renfrew South	
Gooderham	182	Haliburton	Victoria-Haliburton	Victoria-Haliburton	
Goodwood	303	Durham Reg. Mun.	Bruce-Grey	Durham York	
Gordon & Allan Twp	409	Manitoulin D.	Algoma	Algoma-Manitoulin	Mrs. D. Field, Clerk, R.R. 2, Gore Bay, Ont. P0P 1H0 (705/282-2702)

Cities in CAPITALS; Towns marked †; Boroughs marked *; Villages marked •; Townships (Twp); ‡ means separated for municipal purposes from county; balance are either small places or unincorporated places (which have been named but not organized)

MUNICIPALITY	POP.	COUNTY OR DISTRICT	FEDERAL ELECTORAL DISTRICT	PROVINCIAL ELECTORAL DISTRICT	CLERK WITH ADDRESS AND PHONE
Gore Bay†	783	Manitoulin D.	Algoma	Algoma-Manitoulin	Mrs. J. Foster, Town Clerk, Box 298, Gore Bay, Ont. POP 1HO (705/282-2420)
Gormley	178	York Reg. Mun.	York-Peel	York North	
Gorrie	424	Huron	Huron-Bruce	Huron-Bruce	
Gosfield North Twp	3,705	Essex	Essex-Kent	Essex North	B. Weaver, Clerk, Box 130, Cottam, Ont. NOR 1BO (519/839-4844)
Gosfield South Twp	7,260	Essex	Essex-Kent	Essex South	M.E. Boose, Clerk, 504 Division Rd. N., Kingsville, Ont. N9Y 2Y9 (519/733-2305)
Goudreau	135	Algoma D.	Cochrane	Algoma	
Goulbourn Twp	9,327	Ottawa-Carleton Reg. Mun.	Nepean-Carleton	Carleton-Grenville	R.C. Gagne, Clerk, Box 189, Stittsville, Ont. KOA 3GO (613/836-4864)
Goward	144	Nipissing D.	Timiskaming	Timiskaming	
Gowganda	108	Timiskaming D.	Timiskaming	Timiskaming	
Grafton	402	Northumberland	Northumberland	Northumberland	
Graham	60	Thunder Bay D.	Thunder Bay-Nipigon	Lake Nipigon	
Grand Bend•	759	Lambton	Lambton-Middlesex	Lambton	Mrs. L. Clipperton, Village Clerk, Box 340, Grand Bend, Ont. NOM 1TO (519/238-8461)
Grand Valley•	1,160	Dufferin	Wellington-Dufferin-Simcoe	Wellington-Dufferin-Peel	L.M. Canivet, Village Clerk, Box 249, Grand Valley, Ont. LON 1GO (519/928-5652)
Granton	313	Middlesex	London-Middlesex	Huron-Middlesex	
Grattan Twp	1,284	Renfrew	Renfrew-Nipissing-Pembroke	Renfrew South	J.A. O'Grady, Clerk, Box 663, Eganville, Ont. KOJ 1TO (613/628-2547)
Gravenhurst†	8,298	Muskoka Dist. Mun.	Parry Sound-Muskoka	Muskoka	J.R. McColl, Town Clerk/Adm., Box 1360, Gravenhurst, Ont. POC 1GO (705/687-3412)
Greenbank	237	Durham Reg. Mun.	Durham-Northumberland	Durham York	
Greenfield	89	Stormont, Dundas & Glengarry	Glengarry-Prescott-Russell	Stormont, Dundas & Glengarry	
Green Lane	57	Prescott & Russell	Glengarry-Prescott-Russell	Prescott & Russell	
Greenock Twp	1,953	Bruce	Bruce-Grey	Huron-Bruce	G.A. Woelfle, Clerk, R.R. 1, Cargill, Ont. NOG 1JO (519/366-2226)
Greensville	204	Hamilton-Wentworth Reg. Mun.	Hamilton-Wentworth	Wentworth North	
Green Valley	478	Stormont, Dundas & Glengarry	Glengarry-Prescott-Russell	Stormont, Dundas & Glengarry	
Greenwood		Durham Reg. Mun.	Ontario	Durham York	Part of Pickering
Gregoires Mill	169	Cochrane D.	Cochrane	Cochrane North	
Grey Twp	2,036	Huron	Huron-Bruce	Huron-Bruce	Mrs. J. Badley, Clerk, R.R. 3, Brussels, Ont. NOG 1HO (519/887-6268)
Griffith & Matawatchan Twp	337	Renfrew	Renfrew-Nipissing-Pembroke	Cochrane North	Audrey Youmans, Clerk, R.R. 3, Dacre, Ont. KOJ 1NO (613/333-2770)
Grimsby†	15,403	Niagara Reg. Mun.	Lincoln	Lincoln	R.C. Bracher, Town Clerk/Adm., 160 Livingston Ave., Box 159, Grimsby, Ont. L3M 4G3 (416/945-9634)
Grimsthorpe	95	Manitoulin D.	Algoma	Algoma-Manitoulin	
GUELPH	71,408	Wellington	Guelph	Wellington South	W.G. Hall, City Clerk, 59 Carden St., Guelph, Ont. N1H 3A1 (519/822-1260)

Cities in CAPITALS; Towns marked †; Boroughs marked *; Villages marked •; Townships (Twp); ‡ means separated for municipal purposes from county; balance are either small places or unincorporated places (which have been named but not organized)

MUNICIPALITY	POP.	COUNTY OR DISTRICT	FEDERAL ELECTORAL DISTRICT	PROVINCIAL ELECTORAL DISTRICT	CLERK WITH ADDRESS AND PHONE
Guelph Twp	2,918	Wellington		Wellington South	G. Mitchell, Clerk, R.R. 5, Guelph, Ont. N1H 6J2 (519/822-4661)
Guilletville		Sudbury Reg. Mun.	Nickel Belt	Sudbury East	Part of Valley East
Gunne	55	Kenora D.	Kenora-Rainy River	Kenora	
Hagar Twp	1,081	Sudbury D.	Nickel Belt	Sudbury East	P. McDonald, Clerk, Box 79, Markstay, Ont. POM 2GO (705/853-4536)
Hagarty & Richards Twp	1,417	Renfrew	Renfrew-Nipissing-Pembroke	Renfrew South	Z. Bloskie, Clerk, Wilno, Ont. KOJ 2NO (613/757-2344)
Hagerman Twp	410	Parry Sound D.	Parry Sound-Muskoka	Parry Sound	V. Misener, Clerk, Dunchurch, Ont. POA 1GO (705/389-2466)
Haileybury†	4,997	Timiskaming D.	Timiskaming	Timiskaming	Mrs. M. Rajala, Town Clerk, Box 219, Haileybury, Ont. POJ 1KO (705/672-3363)
Haldimand†	16,428	Haldimand-Norfolk Reg. Mun.	Haldimand-Norfolk	Haldimand-Norfolk	Ms. S.R. Trowbridge, Town Clerk, Box 400, Cayuga, Ont. NOA 1EO (416/772-3324)
Haldimand Twp	3,364	Northumberland		Northumberland	Ms. I. Mitchell, Clerk, Box 70, Grafton, Ont. KOK 2GO (416/349-2822)
Haley	163	Renfrew	Renfrew-Nipissing-Pembroke	Renfrew South	
Haliburton	1,124	Haliburton	Victoria-Haliburton	Victoria-Haliburton	
Hallowell Twp	4,444	Prince Edward		Prince Edward-Lennox	M.G. MacDonald, Clerk, R.R. 1, Picton, Ont. KOK 2TO (613/393-2011)
Halton Hills†	34,051	Halton Reg. Mun.	Brampton-Georgetown	Halton-Burlington	K. Richardson, Halton Hills Town Clerk, 36 Main St. S., Georgetown, Ont. L7G 4X1 (416/877-5185)
HAMILTON	306,538	Hamilton-Wentworth Reg. Mun.	Hamilton East; Ham. Mountain; Ham.-Wentworth; Ham. West; Lincoln	Ham. Centre; Ham. East; Ham. West; Wentworth; Wentworth North	E.A. Simpson, City Clerk, City Hall, 71 Main St. W., Hamilton, Ont. L8N 3T4 (416/527-0241)
Hamilton Twp	8,740	Northumberland	Durham-Northumberland	Northumberland	S.W. Zeran, Clerk, R.R. 6, Cobourg, Ont. K9A 4J9 (416/342-2811)
Hammond	226	Prescott & Russell	Glengarry-Prescott-Russell	Prescott & Russell	
Hampton		Durham Reg. Mun.	Durham-Northumberland	Durham East	Part of Newcastle
Hanover†	5,786	Grey	Bruce-Grey	Grey	G.B. Kueneman, Town Clerk, 451 10th Ave., Hanover, Ont. N4N 2P1 (519/364-2780)
Harcourt	141	Haliburton	Victoria-Haliburton	Victoria-Haliburton	
Harley	73	Brant	Brant	Brant-Oxford-Norfolk	near Burford
Harley Twp	593	Timiskaming D.	Timiskaming	Timiskaming	James Goddard, Clerk, R.R. 2, New Liskeard, Ont. POJ 1PO (705/647-5439)
Harrington West	93	Oxford	Oxford	Oxford	
Harris Twp	510	Timiskaming D.	Timiskaming	Timiskaming	Mrs. W. Gibson, Clerk, Box 129, New Liskeard, Ont. POJ 1PO (705/647-5094)
Harriston†	1,954	Wellington	Wellington-Dufferin-Simcoe	Grey	Mrs. E. Gordon, Town Clerk, Box 10, Harriston, Ont. NOG 1ZO (519/338-3444)
Harrow†	2,039	Essex	Essex-Kent	Essex South	B.E. Baltzer, Town Clerk, 44 King St. E., Harrow, Ont. NOR 1GO (519/738-2523)
Harrowsmith	533	Frontenac	Hastings-Frontenac	Frontenac-Addington	
Hartington	158	Frontenac	Hastings-Frontenac	Frontenac-Addington	
Harvey Twp	1,754	Peterborough	Victoria-Haliburton	Hastings-Peterborough	J.W. Millage, Clerk, Buckhorn, Ont. KOL 1JO (70/657-8883)

Cities in CAPITALS; Towns marked †; Boroughs marked *; Villages marked •; Townships (Twp); ‡ means separated for municipal purposes from county; balance are either small places or unincorporated places (which have been named but not organized)

MUNICIPALITY	POP.	COUNTY OR DISTRICT	FEDERAL ELECTORAL DISTRICT	PROVINCIAL ELECTORAL DISTRICT	CLERK WITH ADDRESS AND PHONE
Harwich Twp	6,554	Kent	Kent-Essex	Kent-Elgin	W.M. Phipps, Clerk, 117 McGregor St., Blenheim, Ont. NOP 1AO (519/676-5491)
Harwood	262	Northumberland	Northumberland	Northumberland	
Hastings•	951	Northumberland	Northumberland	Northumberland	I. Williams, Village Clerk, Box 250, Hastings, Ont. KOL 1YO (705/696-2351)
Hatchley	62	Brant	Brant	Brant-Oxford-Norfolk	
Havelock•	1,236	Peterborough	Peterborough	Hastings-Peterborough	D. Kelloway, Village Clerk, Box 190, Havelock, Ont. KOL 1ZO (705/778-2282)
Hawkesbury†	9,804	Prescott & Russell	Glengarry-Prescott-Russell	Prescott & Russell	J.B. Cuillerier, Town Clerk, 600 Higginson St., Hawkesbury, Ont. K6A 1H1 (613/632-4171)
Hawkestone	309	Simcoe	Simcoe North	Simcoe East	
Hawkesville	164	Waterloo Reg. Mun.	Waterloo	Waterloo North	
Hawk Junction	363	Algoma D.	Timmins-Chapleau	Algoma	
Hawk Lake	12	Kenora D.	Kenora-Rainy River	Kenora	
Hay Twp	1,992	Huron	Huron-Bruce	Huron-Middlesex	Ms. J. Ducharme, Clerk, Box 250, Zurich, Ont. NOM 2TO (519/236-4351)
Hayesland	53	Hamilton-Wentworth Reg. Mun.	Hamilton-Wentworth	Wentworth North	
Haysville	82	Waterloo Reg. Mun.	Waterloo	Kitchener-Wilmot	
Head, Clara & Maria Twp	406	Renfrew	Renfrew-Nipissing-Pembroke	Renfrew South	Mrs. S. Senack, Clerk, Bissett Creek, Ont. KOJ 1EO (613/586-2323)
Hearst†	5,212	Cochrane D.	Cochrane	Cochrane North	L. Corbeil, Town Clerk, Bag 5000, Hearst, Ont. POL 1NO (705/362-4341)
Heaslip	27	Timiskaming D.	Timiskaming	Timiskaming	
Heathcote	101	Grey	Grey-Simcoe	Grey	
Heidelberg	363	Waterloo Reg. Mun.	Waterloo	Waterloo North	
Hensall•	1,005	Huron	Huron-Bruce	Huron-Middlesex	Elizabeth Oke, Village Clerk, 108 King St., Hensall, Ont. NOM 1XO (519/262-2812)
Hepworth•	391	Bruce	Bruce-Grey	Grey-Bruce	J.B. Downs, Village Clerk, Box 40, Hepworth, Ont. NOH 1PO (519/935-2911)
Hermon	46	Hastings	Hastings-Frontenac	Hastings-Peterborough	
Heron Bay North	121	Thunder Bay D.	Cochrane	Lake Nipigon	
Herschel Twp	885	Hastings	Hastings-Frontenac	Hastings-Peterborough	Mrs. E. Dafoe, Clerk, R.R. 2, Bancroft, Ont. KOL 1CO (613/332-3757)
Hespeler		Waterloo Reg. Mun.	Cambridge	Cambridge	Part of Cambridge
Hesson	108	Perth	Perth	Perth	
Hibbert Twp	1,449	Perth	Perth	Perth	C. Friend, Clerk, Dublin, Ont. NOK 1EO (519/345-2931)
Hickson	228	Oxford	Oxford	Oxford	
Highgate•	417	Kent	Kent	Kent-Elgin	H. Schram, Village Clerk, Box 109, Highgate, Ont. NOP 1TO (519/678-3936)
Highland Grove	83	Haliburton	Victoria-Haliburton	Victoria-Haliburton	
Hilliard Twp	318	Timiskaming D.	Timiskaming	Timiskaming	Mrs. B. Iles, Clerk, Hilliardton, Ont. P0J 1L0
Hillier Twp	1,531	Prince Edward	Prince Edward-Hastings	Prince Edward-Lennox	S.J. Wellein, Clerk, Hillier, Ont. KOK 2JO (613/399-3377)
Hillsburgh	819	Wellington	Wellington-Dufferin-Simcoe	Wellington-Dufferin-Peel	
Hilton	43	Northumberland	Northumberland	Northumberland	near Brighton

Cities in CAPITALS; Towns marked †; Boroughs marked *; Villages marked •; Townships (Twp); ‡ means separated for municipal purposes from county; balance are either small places or unincorporated places (which have been named but not organized)

MUNICIPALITY	POP.	COUNTY OR DISTRICT	FEDERAL ELECTORAL DISTRICT	PROVINCIAL ELECTORAL DISTRICT	CLERK WITH ADDRESS AND PHONE
Hilton Twp	129	Algoma D.		Algoma	Mrs. A. Langer, Clerk, Box 4, Hilton Beach, Ont. POR 1GO (705/246-2472)
Hilton Beach•	217	Algoma D.	Algoma	Algoma	Mrs. M. Betournay, Village Clerk, Box 25, Hilton Beach, Ont. POR 1GO (705/246-2242)
Himsworth North Twp	2,345	Parry Sound D.		Parry Sound	Isla Rochette, Clerk, Box 100, Callander, Ont. P0H 1H0 (705/752-1410)
Himsworth South Twp	1,370	Parry Sound D.	Parry Sound-Muskoka	Parry Sound	A.F. Everest, Clerk, Box 159, Powassan, Ont. P0H 1Z0 (705/724-2740)
Hinchinbrooke Twp	1,147	Frontenac	Hastings-Frontenac	Frontenac-Addington	Mrs. M. Howes, Clerk, R.R. 1, Parham, Ont. KOH 2KO (613/374-2619)
Holland Twp	2,278	Grey		Grey	A. Rosenburg, Clerk, Box 197, Holland Centre, Ont. NOH 1RO (519/794-2307)
Holland Centre	202	Grey	Bruce-Grey	Grey	
Holland Landing	1,782	York Reg. Mun.	York-Peel	Durham York	Part of East Gwillimbury
Holstein	218	Grey	Bruce-Grey	Grey	
Holtyre	424	Cochrane D.	Timiskaming	Cochrane South	
Honeywood	133	Dufferin	Wellington-Dufferin-Simcoe	Dufferin-Simcoe	
Hope Twp	3,413	Northumberland	Durham-Northumberland	Northumberland	Ms. F. Aird, Clerk, Box 85, Port Hope, Ont. L1A 3V9 (416/885-4431)
Hornby		Halton Reg. Mun.	Halton	Halton-Burlington	Part of Halton Hills
Hornepayne	1,694	Algoma D.	Cochrane	Algoma	
Horning's Mills	159	Dufferin	Wellington-Dufferin-Simcoe	Grey	
Horton Twp	1,961	Renfrew	Renfrew-Nipissing-Pembroke	Renfrew South	W.L. Humphries, Clerk, R.R. 5, Renfrew, Ont. K7V 3Z8 (613/432-6271)
Howard Twp	2,592	Kent		Kent-Elgin	J.A. Trudgen, Clerk, Box 369, Ridgetown, Ont. NOP 2CO (519/674-3315)
Howe Is. Twp	218	Frontenac		Kingston & the Islands	Mrs. M. MacPherson, Clerk, R.R. 4, Gananoque, Ont. (613/544-6348)
Howick Twp	3,080	Huron	Huron-Bruce	Huron-Bruce	W.R. Ball, Clerk, Gorrie, Ont. NOG 1XO (519/335-3208)
Howland Twp	884	Manitoulin D.	Algoma	Algoma-Manitoulin	A.B. Heise, Clerk, Sheguiandah, Ont. POP 1WO (705/368-2009)
Hoyle		Cochrane D.	Timmins-Chapleau	Cochrane South	Part of Timmins
Hudson	565	Kenora D.	Kenora-Rainy River	Kenora	
Hudson Twp	442	Timiskaming D.	Timiskaming	Timiskaming	L. Gray, Clerk, R.R. 1, New Liskeard, Ont. POJ 1PO (705/647-5568)
Hughes	112	Hastings		Hastings-Peterborough	
Hullett Twp	1,854	Huron		Huron-Bruce	Harry Lear, Clerk, Box 226, Londesboro, Ont. NOM 2HO (519/523-4340)
Humber Grove		Peel Reg. Mun.		Wellington-Dufferin-Peel	Part of Caledon
Humphrey Twp	684	Parry Sound D.		Parry Sound	Mrs. J.M. Fraser, Clerk, R.R. 2, Parry Sound, Ont. P2A 2W8 (705/732-4300)
Hungerford Twp	2,515	Hastings	Prince Edward-Hastings	Hastings-Peterborough	Mrs. B. Jones, Clerk, Box 568, Tweed, Ont. KOK 3JO (613/478-3035)
Huntingdon Twp	1,750	Hastings	Prince Edward-Hastings	Hastings-Peterborough	Mrs. L. Danford, Clerk, R.R. 5, Madoc, Ont. KOK 2KO (613/473-2119)

Cities in CAPITALS; Towns marked †; Boroughs marked *; Villages marked •; Townships (Twp); ‡ means separated for municipal purposes from county; balance are either small places or unincorporated places (which have been named but not organized)

MUNICIPALITY	POP.	COUNTY OR DISTRICT	FEDERAL ELECTORAL DISTRICT	PROVINCIAL ELECTORAL DISTRICT	CLERK WITH ADDRESS AND PHONE
Huntsville†	11,031	Muskoka Dist. Mun.	Parry Sound-Muskoka	Muskoka	E.H. Hares, Town Clerk, Box 2700, Huntsville, Ont. POA 1KO (705/789-5575)
Hurkett	35	Thunder Bay D.	Thunder Bay-Nipigon	Lake Nipigon	
Huron Twp	2,533	Bruce		Huron-Bruce	Ms. M. Colling, Clerk, Box 2, Ripley, Ont. NOG 2RO (519/395-2935)
Huttonville		Peel Reg. Mun.	Brampton-Georgetown	Brampton	Part of Brampton
Hyde Park	149	Middlesex	London-Middlesex	Middlesex	
Ignace Twp	2,131	Kenora D.	Kenora-Rainy River	Rainy River	D. Hatch, Clerk, Box 248, Ignace, Ont. POT 1TO (807/934-2202)
Ilderton	330	Middlesex	London-Middlesex	Middlesex	
Indian River	69	Peterborough	Peterborough	Peterborough	
Ingersoll†	8,252	Oxford	Oxford	Oxford	G.R. Staples, Town Clerk, 118 Oxford St., Box 340, Ingersoll, Ont. N5C 3K5 (613/485-0120)
Ingleside	1,106	Stormont, Dundas & Glengarry	Stormont-Dundas	Stormont, Dundas & Glengarry	
Inglewood		Peel Reg. Mun.	York-Peel	Wellington-Dufferin-Peel	Part of Caledon
Ingoldsby	84	Haliburton	Victoria-Haliburton	Victoria-Haliburton	
Inkerman	107	Stormont, Dundas & Glengarry	Stormont-Dundas	Stormont, Dundas & Glengarry	
Innerkip	655	Oxford	Oxford	Oxford	
Innisfil Twp	16,052	Simcoe	Simcoe South	Simcoe Centre	R.I. Groh, Clerk, Stroud, Ont. LOL 2MO (705/436-3710)
Inverary	252	Frontenac	Hastings-Frontenac	Frontenac-Addington	
Invermay	125	Bruce	Bruce-Grey	Grey-Bruce	
Inwood	243	Lambton	Lambton-Middlesex	Lambton	
Iona	120	Elgin	Elgin	Kent-Elgin	
Iron Bridge•	803	Algoma D.	Algoma	Algoma	N. Forest, Village Clerk, Box 460, Iron Bridge, Ont. POR 1HO (705/843-2033)
Iroquois•	1,241	Stormont, Dundas & Glengarry	Stormont-Dundas	Stormont, Dundas & Glengarry	Betty Marlin, Village Clerk, Civic Bldg., Dundas St., Iroquois, Ont. KOE 1KO (613/652-4422)
Iroquois Falls†	6,307	Cochrane D.	Timmins-Chapleau	Cochrane South	J.J. Buchan, Town Clerk, Box 230, Iroquois Falls, Ont. POK 1GO (705/232-6357)
Island Falls	98	Cochrane D.	Timiskaming	Cochrane North	
Island Grove	294	York Reg. Mun.	Victoria-Haliburton	Durham York	
Jack Fish	4	Thunder Bay D.		Lake Nipigon	
Jaffray & Melick Twp	3,483	Kenora D.	Kenora-Rainy River	Kenora	G.R. Meads, Clerk, R.R. 2, Kenora, Ont. P9N 3W8 (807/548-4234)
James Twp	603	Timiskaming D.	Timiskaming	Timiskaming	Mrs. V. McFarlane, Clerk, Box 158, Elk Lake, Ont. POJ 1GO (705/678-2237)
Janetville	296	Victoria	Durham-Northumberland	Victoria-Haliburton	
Jasper	374	Leeds & Grenville	Leeds-Grenville	Leeds	
Jellicoe	163	Thunder Bay D.	Cochrane	Lake Nipigon	
Jerseyville		Hamilton-Wentworth Reg. Mun.	Hamilton-Wentworth	Wentworth North	Part of Ancaster
Jocelyn Twp	131	Algoma D.		Algoma	Mrs. K. Young, Clerk, Richards Landing, Ont. POR 1JO (705/246-2752)
Jogues	180	Cochrane D.	Cochrane	Cochrane North	
Johnson Twp	703	Algoma D.	Algoma	Algoma	Mrs. M. McEwen, Clerk, Box 160, Desbarats, Ont. POR 1EO (705/782-6601)
Johnstown	560	Leeds & Grenville	Leeds-Grenville	Quinte	

Cities in CAPITALS; Towns marked †; Boroughs marked *; Villages marked •; Townships (Twp); ‡ means separated for municipal purposes from county; balance are either small places or unincorporated places (which have been named but not organized)

MUNICIPALITY	POP.	COUNTY OR DISTRICT	FEDERAL ELECTORAL DISTRICT	PROVINCIAL ELECTORAL DISTRICT	CLERK WITH ADDRESS AND PHONE
Joly Twp	135	Parry Sound D.	Parry Sound-Muskoka	Parry Sound	Susan Webster, Clerk, Box 519, Sundridge, Ont. POA 1ZO (705/384-5428)
Jordan	447	Niagara Reg. Mun.	Lincoln	Lincoln	
Jumbo Gardens	1,222	Thunder Bay D.	Thunder Bay-Nipigon	Port Arthur	
Kagawong	141	Manitoulin D.	Algoma	Algoma-Manitoulin	
Kakabeka Falls	367	Thunder Bay D.	Thunder Bay-Nipigon	Port Arthur	
Kaladar, Anglesea & Effingham Twp	1,277	Lennox & Addington		Frontenac-Addington	C. Hasler, Clerk, R.R. 1, Flinton, Ont. KOH 1PO (613/336-2286)
KANATA	20,000	Ottawa-Carleton Reg. Mun.	Lanark-Renfrew-Carleton	Carleton; Carleton-Grenville	B.C. Switzer, City Clerk, City Hall, Kanata, Ont. K2L 2N3 (613/592-4281)
Kapuskasing†	12,178	Cochrane D.	Cochrane	Cochrane North	Lucille Wilson, Town Adm., 88 Riverside Dr., Kapuskasing, Ont. P5N 1B3 (705/335-2341)
Kashabowie	71	Thunder Bay D.	Thunder Bay-Atikokan	Lake Nipigon	
Katrine	182	Parry Sound D.	Parry Sound-Muskoka	Parry Sound	
Kearney†	583	Parry Sound D.	Parry Sound-Muskoka	Parry Sound	D.S. MacLean, Town Clerk, Box 38, Kearney, Ont. POA 1MO (705/636-7752)
Kearns	403	Timiskaming D.	Timiskaming	Timiskaming	
Keene	275	Peterborough	Peterborough	Peterborough	
Keewatin†	1,832	Kenora D.	Kenora-Rainy River	Kenora	E.A. Sherred, Town Clerk, 102 10th St., Keewatin, Ont. POX 1CO (807/547-2881)
Kemptville†	2,415	Leeds & Grenville	Leeds-Grenville	Carleton-Grenville	M.R. McIntyre, Town Clerk, Box 130, Kemptville, Ont. KOG 1JO (613/258-3483)
Kendal		Durham Reg. Mun.	Durham-Northumberland	Durham East	Part of Newcastle
Kenilworth	105	Wellington	Wellington-Dufferin-Simcoe	Wellington-Dufferin-Peel	
Kenmore	242	Ottawa-Carleton Reg. Mun.	Nepean-Carleton	Carleton-Grenville	
Kennebec Twp	737	Frontenac		Frontenac-Addington	Mrs. B. Tryan, Clerk, Box 70, Arden, Ont. KOH 1BO (613/335-2000)
Kenora†	9,992	Kenora D.	Kenora-Rainy River	Kenora	J.C. Callan, Town Clerk, Box 1110, Kenora, Ont. P9N 3X7 (807/468-8906)
Kent Bridge	116	Kent	Kent	Chatham-Kent	
Kenyon Twp	2,794	Stormont, Dundas & Glengarry	Glengarry-Prescott-Russell	Stormont, Dundas & Glengarry	J. Steel, Clerk, R.R. 5, Alexandria, Ont. KOC 1AO (613/527-2090)
Keppel Twp	2,687	Grey	Bruce-Grey	Grey-Bruce	J. Taylor, Clerk, R.R. 1, Kemble, Ont. NOH 1SO (519/376-5861)
Kerns Twp	477	Timiskaming D.	Timiskaming	Timiskaming	L. Gray, Clerk, R.R. 1, New Liskeard, Ont. POJ 1PO (705/647-5568)
Kerwood	126	Middlesex	Lambton-Middlesex	Huron-Middlesex	
Keswick	1,217	York Reg. Mun.	Victoria-Haliburton	Durham York	
Key Harbour	61	Parry Sound D.		Parry Sound	
Killaloe Station•	716	Renfrew	Renfrew-Nipissing-Pembroke	Renfrew South	Miss W. Lepine, Village Clerk, Box 159, Killaloe Station, Ont. KOJ 2AO (613/757-2300)
Killarney	445	Manitoulin D.	Nickel Belt	Algoma-Manitoulin	
Kimberley	98	Grey	Grey-Simcoe	Grey	
Kinburn	177	Ottawa-Carleton Reg. Mun.	Lanark-Renfrew-Carleton	Renfrew South	
Kincardine†	5,343	Bruce	Bruce-Grey	Huron-Bruce	C.R. Merritt, Town Clerk, 707 Queen St., Box 329, Kincardine, Ont. NOG 2GO (519/396-3468)

Cities in CAPITALS; Towns marked †; Boroughs marked *; Villages marked •; Townships (Twp); ‡ means separated for municipal purposes from county; balance are either small places or unincorporated places (which have been named but not organized)

MUNICIPALITY	POP.	COUNTY OR DISTRICT	FEDERAL ELECTORAL DISTRICT	PROVINCIAL ELECTORAL DISTRICT	CLERK WITH ADDRESS AND PHONE
Kincardine Twp	3,147	Bruce		Huron-Bruce	Mrs. M. Eskrick, Clerk, R.R. 5, Box 14, Kincardine, Ont. NOG 2GO (519/396-7685)
King Twp	14,671	York Reg. Mun.	York-Peel	York North	C.H. Duncan, Clerk, R.R. 2, King City, Ont. LOG 1KO (416/833-5321)
King City	2,182	York Reg. Mun.	York-Peel	York North	
King Kirkland	355	Timiskaming D.	Timiskaming	Timiskaming	
Kingsford	64	Rainy River D.		Rainy River	Improvement Dist., c/o L.N. Hoskins, R.R. 2, Emo, Ont. POW 1E0
Kingsmill	35	Elgin	Elgin	Elgin	
Kingston Twp	25,820	Frontenac		Frontenac-Addington	D.A. Gordon, Clerk, PO Bag 3400, Kingston, Ont. K7L 1XO (613/384-1770)
KINGSTON	61,088	Frontenac	Kingston & the Islands	Kingston & the Islands	R.J. Hamilton, Chief Adm. Officer, City Hall, 216 Ontario St., Kingston, Ont. K2L 2Z3 (613/546-4291)
Kingsville†	5,134	Essex	Essex-Kent	Essex South	H. Kreling, Town Clerk, 41 Division St. S., Kingsville, Ont. N9Y 1P4 (519/733-2315)
Kinloss Twp	1,284	Bruce	Huron-Bruce	Huron-Bruce	W.F. Hawthorne, Clerk, R.R. 5, Holyrood, Ont. NOG 2BO (519/395-3575)
Kinmount	270	Victoria	Victoria-Haliburton	Victoria-Haliburton	
Kiosk	254	Nipissing D.	Parry Sound-Muskoka	Parry Sound	
Kippen	43	Huron	Huron-Bruce	Huron-Middlesex	
Kirkfield	200	Victoria	Victoria-Haliburton	Victoria-Haliburton	
Kirkland Lake†	12,768	Timiskaming D.	Timiskaming	Timiskaming	R.J. McDonald, Town Clerk, Box 757, Kirkland Lake, Ont. P2N 2V2 (705/567-9361)
KITCHENER	138,271	Waterloo Reg. Mun.	Kitchener; Waterloo	Kitchener; Kitchener-Wilmot	R.W. Pritchard, City Clerk, 22 Frederick St., Box 1118, Kitchener, Ont. N2G 4G7 (519/885-7100)
Kitley Twp	1,842	Leeds & Grenville	Leeds-Grenville	Leeds	C. Johnston, Clerk, Frankville, Ont. KOE 1HO (613/275-2277)
Kleinburg	227	York Reg. Mun.	York North	York North	
Komoka	812	Middlesex	Lambton-Middlesex	Middlesex	
Kormak	102	Sudbury D.	Timmins-Chapleau	Nickel Belt	
Kowkash	64	Thunder Bay D.		Lake Nipigon	
Laclu	128	Kenora D.	Kenora-Rainy River	Kenora	
Lac Seul	65	Kenora D.	Kenora-Rainy River	Kenora	
Lafontaine	230	Simcoe	Simcoe North	Simcoe Centre	
Laird Twp	802	Algoma D.	Algoma	Algoma	Ms. P. McKay, Clerk, R.R. 4, Echo Bay, Ont. POS 1CO (705/248-2395)
Lakefield•	2,266	Peterborough	Peterborough	Peterborough	Mrs. B. Dunford, Village Clerk, Box 400, Lakefield, Ont. KOL 2HO (705/652-3381)
Lake of Bays Twp	2,046	Muskoka Dist. Mun.	Parry Sound-Muskoka	Muskoka	E.R. Bryant, Clerk, Dwight, Ont. POA 1HO (705/635-2272)
Lakeport	130	Northumberland	Northumberland	Northumberland	
L'Amable	88	Hastings	Hastings-Frontenac	Hastings-Peterborough	
Lambeth	2,876	Middlesex	London-Middlesex	Middlesex	
Lanark•	759	Lanark	Lanark-Renfrew-Carleton	Lanark	Mrs. J. Dugdale, Town Clerk, Box 20, Lanark, Ont. KOG 1KO (613/259-2398)
Lanark Twp	967	Lanark	Lanark-Renfrew-Carleton	Lanark	Mrs. R.J. Mather, Clerk, R.R. 2, Lanark, Ont. KOG 1KO (613/259-5686)

Cities in CAPITALS; Towns marked †; Boroughs marked *; Villages marked •; Townships (Twp); ‡ means separated for municipal purposes from county; balance are either small places or unincorporated places (which have been named but not organized)

MUNICIPALITY	POP.	COUNTY OR DISTRICT	FEDERAL ELECTORAL DISTRICT	PROVINCIAL ELECTORAL DISTRICT	CLERK WITH ADDRESS AND PHONE
Lancaster Twp	3,092	Stormont, Dundas & Glengarry		Stormont, Dundas & Glengarry	M.J. Samson, Clerk, North Lancaster, Ont. KOC 1ZO (613/347-3231)
Lancaster•	587	Stormont, Dundas & Glengarry	Glengarry-Prescott-Russell	Stormont, Dundas & Glengarry	J. MacDonald, Village Clerk, Box 220, Lancaster, Ont. KOC 1NO (613/347-2023)
Lang	103	Peterborough	Peterborough	Peterborough	
Langstaff	1,095	York Reg. Mun.	York North	York Centre	
Langton	421	Haldimand-Norfolk Reg. Mun.	Haldimand-Norfolk	Haldimand-Norfolk	
Lansdowne	542	Leeds & Grenville	Leeds-Grenville	Leeds	
La Passe	120	Renfrew	Renfrew-Nipissing-Pembroke	Renfrew South	
Larchwood		Sudbury Reg. Mun.	Nickel Belt	Nickel Belt	Part of Rayside-Balfour
Larder Lake Twp	1,173	Timiskaming D.	Timiskaming	Timiskaming	R.E. Emmell, Clerk, Box 40, Larder Lake, Ont. POK 1LO (705/643-2158)
La Salette	148	Haldimand-Norfolk Reg. Mun.	Haldimand-Norfolk	Brant-Oxford-Norfolk	
La Salle	2,703	Essex	Essex-Windsor	Essex North	Part of Sandwich West Twp.
Latchford†	456	Timiskaming D.	Timiskaming	Timiskaming	Mrs. L. Godden, Town Clerk, Drawer 10, Latchford, Ont. POJ 1NO (705/676-2416)
Laurel	99	Dufferin	Wellington-Dufferin-Simcoe	Wellington-Dufferin-Peel	
La Vallée Twp	930	Rainy River D.	Kenora-Rainy River	Rainy River	Mrs. I.A. Elliott, Clerk, Box 99, Devlin, Ont. POW 1CO (807/486-3452)
Lavant, Dalhousie & N. Sherbrooke Twp	1,048	Lanark	Lanark-Renfrew-Carleton	Lanark	Mrs. M. Kirkham, Clerk, McDonald's Corners, Ont. KOG 1MO (613/278-2694)
Laxton, Digby & Longford Twp	664	Victoria	Victoria-Haliburton	Victoria-Haliburton	F.V. Le Craw, Clerk, Norland, Ont. KOM 2LO (705/454-3418)
Leamington†	11,539	Essex	Essex-Kent	Essex South	J.A. Simon, Town Clerk, 38 Erie St. N., Leamington, Ont. N8H 2Z3 (519/326-5761)
Leaskdale	167	Durham Reg. Mun.	Ontario	Durham York	
Leeds & Lansdowne Twp, Front of	4,049	Leeds & Grenville	Leeds-Grenville	Leeds	R.A. Wood, (Front) Leeds & Lansdowne Twp Clerk, Box 129, Lansdowne, Ont. KOE 1LO (613/659-2415)
Leeds & Lansdowne Twp, Rear of	2,391	Leeds & Grenville	Leeds-Grenville	Leeds	Mrs. A.M. Landon, (Rear) Leeds & Lansdowne Twp Clerk, Box 160, Lyndhurst, Ont. KOH 1NO (613/928-2423)
efaivre	216	Prescott & Russell	Glengarry-Prescott-Russell	Prescott & Russell	
efroy	534	Simcoe	Simcoe South	Simcoe Centre	
eonard	59	Ottawa-Carleton Reg. Mun.	Glengarry-Prescott-Russell	Prescott & Russell	
epage	51	Cochrane D.	Cochrane	Cochrane North	
imehouse		Halton Reg. Mun.	Halton	Halton-Burlington	Part of Halton Hills
imerick Twp	290	Hastings		Hastings-Peterborough	Mrs. I. Phillips, Clerk, Box 154, Gilmour, Ont. KOL 1WO (613/337-5500)
moges	616	Prescott & Russell	Glengarry-Prescott-Russell	Prescott & Russell	
ncoln†	14,296	Niagara Reg. Mun.	Lincoln	Lincoln	M.F. Duc, Town Clerk, Box 1030, Beamsville, Ont. LOR 1BO (416/563-8205)

Cities in CAPITALS; Towns marked †; Boroughs marked *; Villages marked •; Townships (Twp); ‡ means separated for municipal purposes from county; balance are either small places or unincorporated places (which have been named but not organized)

MUNICIPALITY	POP.	COUNTY OR DISTRICT	FEDERAL ELECTORAL DISTRICT	PROVINCIAL ELECTORAL DISTRICT	CLERK WITH ADDRESS AND PHONE
Lindsay Twp	353	Bruce		Grey-Bruce	Mrs. K. MacLeod, Clerk, R.R. 2, Lion's Head, Ont. NOH 1WO (519/793-3522)
Lindsay†	13,755	Victoria	Victoria-Haliburton	Victoria-Haliburton	W.B. Bates, Town Clerk, 180 Kent St. W., Lindsay, Ont. K9V 2Y6 (705/324-6171)
Linwood	455	Waterloo Reg. Mun.	Waterloo	Waterloo North	
Lion's Head•	475	Bruce	Bruce-Grey	Grey-Bruce	Mrs. J. Ashcroft, Village Clerk, Box 208, Lion's Head, Ont. NOH 1WO (519/793-3731)
Lisle	258	Simcoe	Wellington-Dufferin-Simcoe	Dufferin-Simcoe	
Listowel†	4,972	Perth	Perth	Perth	H.A. Fischer, Town Clerk, 330 Wallace Ave. N., Listowel, Ont. N4W 1L3 (519/291-2950)
Little Britain	359	Victoria	Victoria-Haliburton	Victoria-Haliburton	
Little Current†	1,517	Manitoulin D.	Algoma	Algoma-Manitoulin	Jim McGee, Town Clerk, 50 Meredith St., Little Current, Ont. POP 1KO (705/368-2277)
Lloydtown	36	York Reg. Mun.	York-Peel	York North	
Lobo Twp	4,763	Middlesex		Middlesex	R. Lewis, Clerk, R.R. 2, Ilderton, Ont. NOM 2AO (519/666-0190)
Lochalsh	64	Algoma D.	Cochrane	Algoma	
Lochiel Twp	3,194	Stormont, Dundas & Glengarry		Stormont, Dundas & Glengarry	E.C. McNaughton, Clerk, Box 56, Dalkeith, Ont. KOB 1EO(613/525-3283)
Locust Hill	89	York Reg. Mun.	York North	York Centre	
Logan Twp	2,232	Perth	Perth	Perth	M. Scherbarth, Clerk, R.R. 1, Bornholm, Ont. NOK 1AO (519/345-2339)
Londesborough	176	Huron	Huron-Bruce	Huron-Bruce	
London Twp	5,889	Middlesex	London-Middlesex	Huron-Middlesex; Middlesex	A.F. Bannister, Clerk, 15 Church St. E., Arva, Ont. NOM 1CO (519/438-2191)
LONDON	256,789	Middlesex	London East; London-Middlesex; London West	London Centre; London North; London South	C. McNorgan, City Clerk, 300 Dufferin Ave., Box 5035, London, Ont. N6A 4L9 (519/679-4500)
Longford	43	Simcoe	Simcoe North	Simcoe East	
Longlac Twp	2,189	Thunder Bay D.	Cochrane	Lake Nipigon	L.H. Simons, Clerk, Box 366, Longlac, Ont. POT 2AO (807/876-2316)
Long Point (Beach)	217	Haldimand-Norfolk Reg. Mun.	Haldimand-Norfolk	Haldimand-Norfolk	
Long Sault	1,096	Stormont, Dundas & Glengarry	Stormont-Dundas	Cornwall	
Longueuil Twp	1,106	Prescott & Russell	Glengarry-Prescott-Russell	Prescott & Russell	Ms. J. Charlebois, Clerk, R.R. 2, L'Orignal, Ont. KOB 1KO (613/675-4727)
Longwood	60	Middlesex		Middlesex	
Lonsdale	64	Hastings	Prince Edward-Hastings	Hastings-Peterborough	
Loon Lake	30	Thunder Bay D.	Thunder Bay-Nipigon	Port Arthur	
L'Orignal•	1,453	Prescott & Russell	Glengarry-Prescott-Russell	Prescott & Russell	A. Bénard, Village Clerk, Box 271, L'Orignal, Ont. KOB 1KO (613/675-2294)
Lorneville	51	Victoria	Victoria-Haliburton	Victoria-Haliburton	
Loughborough Twp	3,278	Frontenac		Frontenac-Addington	Mrs. B.L. Peters, Clerk, Box 100, Sydenham, Ont. KOH 2TO (613/376-3027)
Lovering	89	Simcoe	Simcoe North	Simcoe East	
Low Bush River	52	Cochrane D.		Cochrane North	

Cities in CAPITALS; Towns marked †; Boroughs marked *; Villages marked •; Townships (Twp); ‡ means separated for municipal purposes from county; balance are either small places or unincorporated places (which have been named but not organized)

MUNICIPALITY	POP.	COUNTY OR DISTRICT	FEDERAL ELECTORAL DISTRICT	PROVINCIAL ELECTORAL DISTRICT	CLERK WITH ADDRESS AND PHONE
Lowther	18	Cochrane D.	Cochrane	Kenora	
Lucan•	1,547	Middlesex	London-Middlesex	Huron-Middlesex	E.J. Melanson, Village Clerk, Box 231, Lucan, Ont. NOM 2YO (519/227-4253)
Lucknow•	1,155	Bruce	Huron-Bruce	Huron-Bruce	A.E. Herbert, Village Clerk, Box 40, Lucknow, Ont. NOG 2HO (519/528-3539)
Lunenberg	115	Stormont, Dundas & Glengarry	Stormont-Dundas	Stormont, Dundas & Glengarry	
Lutterworth Twp	554	Haliburton	Victoria-Haliburton	Victoria-Haliburton	W. Hughes, Clerk, Box 176, Minden, Ont. KOM 2KO (705/286-1541)
Lyn	562	Leeds & Grenville	Leeds-Grenville	Leeds	
Lynden	457	Hamilton-Wentworth Reg. Mun.	Hamilton-Wentworth	Wentworth North	
Lyndhurst	213	Leeds & Grenville	Leeds-Grenville	Leeds	
Lynedoch	191	Haldimand-Norfolk Reg. Mun.	Haldimand-Norfolk	Haldimand-Norfolk	
Maberly	118	Lanark	Lanark-Renfrew-Carleton	Lanark	
Macdiarmid	444	Thunder Bay D.	Cochrane	Lake Nipigon	
Macdonald, Meredith & Aberdeen Twp	1,428	Algoma D.	Algoma	Algoma	Mrs. J. Robbins, Clerk, Box 10, Echo Bay, Ont. POS 1CO (705/248-2441)
Machar Twp	570	Parry Sound D.		Parry Sound	Mrs. C.A. Ardiel, Clerk, Box 70, South River, Ont. POA 1XO (705/386-7741)
Machin Twp	1,134	Kenora D.	Kenora-Rainy River	Cochrane North	Mrs. M. Wiebe, Clerk, Box 249, Vermilion Bay, Ont. POV 2VO (807/227-2633)
Mackenzie	25	Thunder Bay D.	Thunder Bay-Nipigon	Port Arthur	
MacTier	690	Muskoka Dist. Mun.	Parry Sound-Muskoka	Muskoka	
Macton	56	Wellington		Wellington-Dufferin-Peel	
Madawaska	288	Nipissing D.	Renfrew-Nipissing-Pembroke	Renfrew North	
Madoc Twp	1,579	Hastings	Hastings-Frontenac	Hastings-Peterborough	Mrs. E. Brownson, Clerk, Box 503, Madoc, Ont. KOK 2KO (613/473-2677)
Madoc•	1,240	Hastings	Hastings-Frontenac	Hastings-Peterborough	D. Parks, Village Clerk, Box 310, Madoc, Ont. KOK 2KO (613/473-4123)
Madsen	391	Kenora D.	Kenora-Rainy River	Kenora	
Magnetawan•	217	Parry Sound D.	Parry Sound-Muskoka	Parry Sound	Mrs. M. Osborne, Village Clerk, Box 70, Magnetawan, Ont. POA 1PO (705/387-3947)
Maidstone Twp	8,248	Essex	Essex-Windsor	Essex North	L. St. Pierre, Clerk, R.R. 3, Essex, Ont. NOR 1EO (519/727-5191)
Maitland	584	Leeds & Grenville	Leeds-Grenville	Carleton-Grenville	
Malahide Twp	5,132	Elgin		Elgin	R.R. Millard, Clerk, 87 John St. S., Aylmer, Ont. N5H 2C3 (519/773-5344)
Malden Twp	5,078	Essex	Essex-Windsor	Essex South	C.F. Daigle, Clerk, R.R. 2, Amherstburg, Ont. N9V 2Y8 (519/736-3141)
Mallorytown	290	Leeds & Grenville	Leeds-Grenville	Leeds	
Malton		Peel Reg. Mun.	Mississauga North	Mississauga North	Part of Mississauga
Manilla	224	Victoria	Victoria-Haliburton	Victoria-Haliburton	
Manitouwadge Twp	2,979	Thunder Bay D.	Cochrane	Lake Nipigon	Loraine Latimer, Clerk, Manitou Rd., Manitouwadge, Ont. POT 2CO (807/826-3227)
Manitowaning	378	Manitoulin D.	Algoma	Algoma-Manitoulin	

Cities in CAPITALS; Towns marked †; Boroughs marked *; Villages marked •; Townships (Twp); ‡ means separated for municipal purposes from county; balance are either small places or unincorporated places (which have been named but not organized)

MUNICIPALITY	POP.	COUNTY OR DISTRICT	FEDERAL ELECTORAL DISTRICT	PROVINCIAL ELECTORAL DISTRICT	CLERK WITH ADDRESS AND PHONE
Manotick	1,410	Ottawa-Carleton Reg. Mun.	Nepean-Carleton	Carleton-Grenville	
Manvers Twp	3,323	Victoria	Durham-Northumberland	Victoria-Haliburton	R. Davidson, Clerk, Bethany, Ont. LOA 1AO (705/277-2321)
Maple	2,026	York Reg. Mun.	York North	York North	
Mara Twp	3,647	Simcoe	Simcoe North	Simcoe East	A. Newman, Clerk, Box 130, Brechin, Ont. LOK 1BO (705/484-5374)
Marathon Twp	2,365	Thunder Bay D.		Cochrane North	R. Mitchell, Clerk, Box 190, Marathon, Ont. POT 2EO (807/229-1340)
Mariposa Twp	4,804	Victoria		Victoria-Haliburton	J.W. Doble, Clerk, Box 70, Oakwood, Ont. KOM 2MO (705/953-9900)
Markdale•	1,337	Grey	Grey-Simcoe	Grey	Mrs. B. Rouse, Village Clerk, 50 Lorne St., Markdale, Ont. NOC 1HO (519/986-2831)
Markham†	73,063	York Reg. Mun.	York North	York Centre	G.F. Roseblade, Town Clerk, 8911 Woodbine Ave., Markham, Ont. L3R 1A1 (416/297-1900)
Markstay	521	Sudbury D.	Nickel Belt	Sudbury East	
Marlbank	227	Hastings	Prince Edward-Hastings	Hastings-Peterborough	
Marmora•	1,293	Hastings	Hastings-Frontenac	Hastings-Peterborough	W.A. Shannon, Village Clerk, Box 417, Marmora, Ont. KOK 2MO (613/472-2533)
Marmora & Lake Twp	1,538	Hastings	Hastings-Frontenac	Hastings-Peterborough	Ms. M.E. Gawley, Clerk, Hwy. 7 West, Marmora, Ont. KOK 2MO (613/472-2629)
Martintown	366	Stormont, Dundas & Glengarry	Stormont-Dundas	Stormont, Dundas & Glengarry	
Maryborough Twp	2,287	Wellington	Wellington-Dufferin-Simcoe	Wellington-Dufferin-Peel	R. Skeoch, Clerk, Box 39, Moorefield, Ont. NOG 2KO (519/638-2831)
Massey†	1,351	Sudbury D.	Algoma	Algoma-Manitoulin	B. St. Denis, Town Clerk, Box 490, Massey, Ont. POP 1PO (705/865-2181)
Matachewan	538	Timiskaming D.	Timiskaming	Timiskaming	Improvement Dist., c/o Mrs. R. Hagan, Box 177, Matachewan, Ont. P0K 1M0
Matawatchan	107	Renfrew	Renfrew-Nipissing-Pembroke	Renfrew South	
Matchedash Twp	507	Simcoe	Simcoe North	Simcoe East	Mrs. J.G. Flemming, Clerk, R.R. 1, Coldwater, Ont. LOK 1EO (705/686-7994)
Matilda Twp	3,155	Stormont, Dundas & Glengarry	Stormont-Dundas	Stormont, Dundas & Glengarry	W.E. Horner, Clerk, Brinston, Ont. KOE 1CO (613/652-4403)
Mattagami Heights		Cochrane D.	Timmins-Chapleau	Nickel Belt	Part of Timmins
Mattawa†	2,697	Nipissing D.	Renfrew-Nipissing-Pembroke	Parry Sound	Ms. L. Villeneuve, Town Clerk, Box 390, Mattawa, Ont. POH 1VO (705/744-5611)
Mattawan Twp	81	Nipissing D.		Parry Sound	I.J. Burke, Clerk, Box 313, Mattawa, Ont. POH 1VO (705/744-5737)
Mattice	816	Cochrane D.	Cochrane	Cochrane North	
Maxville•	831	Stormont, Dundas & Glengarry	Glengarry-Prescott-Russell	Stormont, Dundas & Glengarry	R. Charbonneau, Village Clerk, Box 277, Maxville, Ont. KOC 1TO (613/527-2705)
Maynooth	281	Hastings	Hastings-Frontenac	Hastings-Peterborough	

Cities in CAPITALS; Towns marked †; Boroughs marked *; Villages marked •; Townships (Twp); ‡ means separated for municipal purposes from county; balance are either small places or unincorporated places (which have been named but not organized)

MUNICIPALITY	POP.	COUNTY OR DISTRICT	FEDERAL ELECTORAL DISTRICT	PROVINCIAL ELECTORAL DISTRICT	CLERK WITH ADDRESS AND PHONE
Mayo Twp	396	Hastings		Hastings-Peterborough	Mrs. V. McMunn, Clerk, R.R. 4, Bancroft, Ont. KOL 1CO (613/332-2637)
McCrosson & Tovell Twp	224	Rainy River D.	Kenora-Rainy River	Rainy River	P. Huntley, Clerk, R.R. 1, Pinewood, Ont. POW 1KO (807/488-5704)
McDougall Twp	2,517	Parry Sound D.		Parry Sound	D.P. Willett, Clerk, R.R. 3, Parry Sound, Ont. P2A 2W9 (705/342-5252)
McGarry Twp	1,435	Timiskaming D.		Timiskaming	Mrs. J.E. Lamb, Clerk, 27 Webster St., Virginiatown, Ont. POK 1XO (705/634-2145)
McGillivray Twp	1,854	Middlesex	Lambton-Middlesex	Huron-Middlesex	W.J. Amos, Clerk, 171 King St., Parkhill, Ont. NOM 2KO (519/294-6871)
McGregor	810	Essex	Essex-Windsor	Essex South	
McKellar Twp	587	Parry Sound D.	Parry Sound-Muskoka	Parry Sound	Mrs. R.M. Hurd, Clerk, Box 69, McKellar, Ont. POG 1CO (705/389-2842)
McKenzie Island	144	Kenora D.	Kenora-Rainy River	Kenora	
McKerrow	323	Sudbury D.	Algoma	Nickel Belt	
McKillop Twp	1,494	Huron	Huron-Bruce	Huron-Bruce	Mrs. M. McClure, Clerk, R.R. 1, Seaforth, Ont. NOK 1WO (519/527-1916)
McMurrich Twp	409	Parry Sound D.	Parry Sound-Muskoka	Parry Sound	R.E. Gibb, Clerk, Box 70, Sprucedale, Ont. POA 1YO (705/685-7901)
McNab Twp	4,107	Renfrew	Lanark-Renfrew-Carleton	Renfrew South	M. Yantha, Clerk, R.R. 2, Arnprior, Ont. K7S 3G8 (613/623-5756)
Meaford†	4,091	Grey	Grey-Simcoe	Grey	H.L. Floto, Town Clerk, Box 758, Meaford, Ont. NOH 1YO (519/538-1060)
Meath	55	Renfrew	Renfrew-Nipissing-Pembroke	Renfrew South	
Medonte Twp	4,077	Simcoe	Simcoe North	Simcoe East	G. Cunnington, Clerk, Moonstone, Ont. LOK 1NO (705/835-2003)
Melancthon Twp	2,126	Dufferin	Wellington-Dufferin-Simcoe	Grey	Mrs. M. Hunter, Clerk, R.R. 6, Shelburne, Ont. LON 1SO (519/925-5525)
Melbourne	339	Middlesex	Lambton-Middlesex	Middlesex	
Merlin	722	Kent	Essex-Kent	Kent-Elgin	
Merrickville•	934	Leeds & Grenville	Leeds-Grenville	Carleton-Grenville	E. Stille, Village Clerk, Box 340, Merrickville, Ont. KOG 1NO (613/269-4471)
Mersea Twp	8,821	Essex	Essex-Kent	Essex South	L. Foster, Clerk, Mun. Bldg., 38 Erie St. N., Leamington, Ont. N8H 2Z3 (519/326-5725)
Metcalfe Twp	889	Middlesex		Middlesex	R. Wilson, Clerk, R.R. 2, Kerwood, Ont. NOM 2BO (519/247-3868)
Metcalfe	681	Ottawa-Carleton Reg. Mun.	Nepean-Carleton	Carleton-Grenville	
Michipicoten Twp	4,595	Algoma D.	Timmins-Chapleau	Algoma	K.P. Zurby, Clerk, 40 Broadway Ave., Wawa, Ont. POS 1KO (705/856-2244)
Middlemiss	81	Middlesex	Lambton-Middlesex	Middlesex	
Middleville	110	Lanark	Lanark-Renfrew-Carleton	Lanark	
Midhurst	626	Simcoe	Simcoe South	Simcoe Centre	
Midland†	11,726	Simcoe	Simcoe North	Simcoe East	M.T. Owen, Town Clerk, 575 Dominion Ave., Midland, Ont. L4R 1R2 (705/526-4275)
Midlothian	27	Parry Sound D.		Parry Sound	

Cities in CAPITALS; Towns marked †; Boroughs marked *; Villages marked •; Townships (Twp); ‡ means separated for municipal purposes from county; balance are either small places or unincorporated places (which have been named but not organized)

MUNICIPALITY	POP.	COUNTY OR DISTRICT	FEDERAL ELECTORAL DISTRICT	PROVINCIAL ELECTORAL DISTRICT	CLERK WITH ADDRESS AND PHONE
Mildmay•	981	Bruce	Bruce-Grey	Huron-Bruce	D.H. Johnston, Village Clerk, Box 128, Mildmay, Ont. NOG 2JO (519/367-2617)
Millbank	383	Perth	Perth	Perth	
Millbridge	58	Hastings	Hastings-Frontenac	Hastings-Peterborough	
Millbrook•	903	Peterborough	Durham-Northumberland	Peterborough	Mrs. F. Fox, Village Clerk, Box 58, Millbrook, Ont. LOA 1GO (705/932-2780)
Milton†	24,163	Halton Reg. Mun.	Halton	Halton-Burlington	R. Main, Town Clerk, 251 Main St. E., Milton, Ont. L9T 1P1 (416/878-7211)
Milverton•	1,469	Perth	Perth	Perth	A.J. Brubacher, Village Clerk, 25 Mill St. E., Milverton, Ont. NOK 1MO (519/595-8321)
Minaki	191	Kenora D.	Kenora-Rainy River	Kenora	
Minden	590	Haliburton	Victoria-Haliburton	Victoria-Haliburton	
Mine Centre	88	Rainy River D.	Rainy River		
Minesing	256	Simcoe	Simcoe South	Simcoe Centre	
Minet Point	315	Simcoe	Simcoe South	Simcoe Centre	
Minett	50	Muskoka Dist. Mun.	Parry Sound-Muskoka	Muskoka	
Minnitaki	53	Kenora D.	Kenora-Rainy River	Kenora	
Minto Twp	2,105	Wellington	Wellington-Dufferin-Simcoe	Grey	D.M. Aitchison, Clerk, Box 160, Harriston, Ont. NOG 1ZO (519/338-2511)
Missanabie	242	Algoma D.	Cochrane	Algoma	
MISSISSAUGA	298,045	Peel Reg. Mun.	Mississauga North; Mississauga South	Mississauga East; Mississauga North; Mississauga South	T.L. Julian, City Clerk, 1 City Centre Dr., Mississauga, Ont. L5B 1M2 (416/279-7600)
Mitchell†	2,706	Perth	Perth	Perth	D.J. Eplett, Town Clerk, 169 St. David St., Mitchell, Ont. NOK 1NO (519/348-8429)
Moffat		Halton Reg. Mun.	Halton	Halton-Burlington	Part of Milton
Monckland	165	Stormont, Dundas & Glengarry	Stormont-Dundas	Stormont, Dundas & Glengarry	
Monkton	550	Perth	Perth	Perth	
Monmouth Twp	710	Haliburton	Victoria-Haliburton	Victoria-Haliburton	Mrs. S. Hunter, Clerk, Box 10, Wilberforce, Ont. KOL 3CO (705/448-2981)
Mono Twp	3,964	Dufferin		Dufferin-Simcoe	K. McNenly, Clerk, R.R. 1, Orangeville, Ont. L9W 2Y8 (519/941-3599)
Mono Mills		Peel Reg. Mun.	York-Peel	Wellington-Dufferin-Peel	Part of Caledon
Montague Twp	3,951	Lanark	Lanark-Renfrew-Carleton	Lanark	B. Czaharynski, Clerk, Box 755, Smiths Falls, Ont. K7A 4W6 (613/283-7478)
Monteagle Twp	1,131	Hastings	Hastings-Frontenac	Hastings-Peterborough	G. Davis, Clerk, R.R. 1, Maple Leaf, Ont. KOL 2RO (613/338-5536)
Monteith	183	Cochrane D.	Timmins-Chapleau	Cochrane South	
Montrock	784	Cochrane D.	Timmins-Chapleau	Cochrane South	
Moonbeam	925	Cochrane D.	Cochrane	Cochrane North	
Moore Twp	9,591	Lambton	Sarnia	Lambton	R. Whitman, Clerk, Box 40, Brigden, Ont. NON 1BO (519/864-1155)
Moorefield	304	Wellington	Wellington-Dufferin-Simcoe	Wellington-Dufferin-Peel	
Mooretown	250	Lambton	Sarnia	Lambton	
Moose Creek	382	Stormont, Dundas & Glengarry	Stormont-Dundas	Stormont, Dundas & Glengarry	
Moose Factory	554	Cochrane D.	Timiskaming	Cochrane North	
Moosonee	1,301	Cochrane D.	Timiskaming	Cochrane North	Devel. Area Bd.

Cities in CAPITALS; Towns marked †; Boroughs marked *; Villages marked •; Townships (Twp); ‡ means separated for municipal purposes from county; balance are either small places or unincorporated places (which have been named but not organized)

MUNICIPALITY	POP.	COUNTY OR DISTRICT	FEDERAL ELECTORAL DISTRICT	PROVINCIAL ELECTORAL DISTRICT	CLERK WITH ADDRESS AND PHONE
Morewood	254	Stormont, Dundas & Glengarry	Stormont-Dundas	Stormont, Dundas & Glengarry	
Morley Twp	565	Rainy River D.		Rainy River	Mrs. E.M. Stutvoet, Clerk, Box 40, Stratton, Ont. POW 1NO (807/483-5455)
Mornington Twp	2,974	Perth	Perth	Perth	E. Bancroft, Clerk, R.R. 1, Newton, Ont. NOK 1RO (519/595-8917)
Morpeth	305	Kent	Kent	Kent-Elgin	
Morris Twp	1,716	Huron		Huron-Bruce	Nancy Michie, Clerk, R.R. 4, Brussels, Ont. NOG 1HO (519/887-6472)
Morrisburg•	2,301	Stormont, Dundas & Glengarry	Stormont-Dundas	Stormont, Dundas & Glengarry	L.D. Barkley, Village Clerk, Box 737, Morrisburg, Ont. KOC 1XO (613/543-2504)
Morriston	251	Wellington	Guelph	Wellington South	
Morson Twp	159	Rainy River D.	Kenora-Rainy River	Rainy River	P.W. Giles, Clerk, Box 27, Rainy River, Ont. POW 1LO (807/852-3529)
Morton	76	Leeds & Grenville	Leeds-Grenville	Leeds	
Mosa Twp	1,333	Middlesex		Middlesex	Ms. B.A. McKinnon, Clerk, Box 458, Glencoe, Ont. NOL 1MO (519/693-4660)
Moscow	71	Lennox & Addington	Hastings-Frontenac	Frontenac-Addington	
Mountain Twp	2,851	Stormont, Dundas & Glengarry	Stormont-Dundas	Stormont, Dundas & Glengarry	Mrs. J. Maxwell, Clerk, Box 9, Mountain, Ont. KOE 1SO (613/989-2915)
Mountain Grove	126	Frontenac	Hastings-Frontenac	Frontenac-Addington	
Mount Albert	909	York Reg. Mun.	York-Peel	Durham York	
Mount Brydges	1,573	Middlesex	Lambton-Middlesex	Middlesex	
Mount Elgin	289	Oxford	Oxford	Oxford	
Mount Forest†	3,402	Wellington	Wellington-Dufferin-Simcoe	Wellington-Dufferin-Peel	A. Brubacher, Town Clerk, 102 Main St., Mount Forest, Ont. NOG 2LO (519/323-2150)
Mount Hope	687	Hamilton-Wentworth Reg. Mun.	Hamilton-Wentworth	Wentworth	
Mount Pleasant	545	Brant	Brant	Brant-Oxford-Norfolk	near Brantford
Mount Pleasant	169	Peterborough	Durham-Northumberland	Peterborough	Part of Cavan Twp
Muirkirk	48	Kent	Kent	Kent-Elgin	
Mull	45	Kent	Kent	Kent-Elgin	
Mulmur Twp	1,804	Dufferin		Dufferin-Simcoe	T. Horner, Clerk, R.R. 2, Lisle, Ont. LOM 1MO (705/466-3341)
Muncey	27	Middlesex	Lambton-Middlesex	Middlesex	
Murillo	210	Thunder Bay D.	Thunder Bay-Nipigon	Port Arthur	
Murray Twp	5,848	Northumberland	Northumberland	Northumberland	C.K. Rose, Clerk, R.R. 1, Trenton, Ont. K8V 5P4 (613/392-4435)
Muskoka Lakes Twp	4,605	Muskoka Dist. Mun.	Parry Sound-Muskoka	Muskoka	W.J. Dodd, Clerk, Box 129, Port Carling, Ont. POB 1JO (705/765-3156)
Myrtle	134	Durham Reg. Mun.	Ontario	Durham West	
Nairn Twp	547	Sudbury D.	Algoma	Nickel Belt	Mrs. L.M. Ritchie, Clerk, Nairn Centre, Ont. POM 2L0 (705/869-4232)
Nairn Centre	457	Sudbury D.	Algoma	Nickel Belt	
Nakina Twp	902	Thunder Bay D.	Cochrane	Lake Nipigon	Nicole Harel, Clerk, Box 89, Nakina, Ont. POT 2HO (807/329-5916)
NANTICOKE	19,104	Haldimand-Norfolk Reg. Mun.	Haldimand-Norfolk	Brant-Oxford-Norfolk; Haldimand-Norfolk	D.M. Kilpatrick, Nanticoke City Clerk, 230 Main St., Port Dover, Ont. NOA 1NO (519/583-0890)

Cities in CAPITALS; Towns marked †; Boroughs marked *; Villages marked •; Townships (Twp); ‡ means separated for municipal purposes from county; balance are either small places or unincorporated places (which have been named but not organized)

MUNICIPALITY	POP.	COUNTY OR DISTRICT	FEDERAL ELECTORAL DISTRICT	PROVINCIAL ELECTORAL DISTRICT	CLERK WITH ADDRESS AND PHONE
Napanee†	4,848	Lennox & Addington	Hastings-Frontenac	Prince Edward-Lennox	J.C. McNamee, Town Clerk, Box 97, Napanee, Ont. K7R 3M1 (613/354-3351)
Nashville	137	York Reg. Mun.	York North	York North	
Naughton		Sudbury Reg. Mun.	Nickel Belt	Nickel Belt	Part of Walden
Navan	407	Ottawa-Carleton Reg. Mun.	Glengarry-Prescott-Russell	Prescott & Russell	
Neebing Twp	608	Thunder Bay D.		Fort William	Mrs. L. Hammond, Clerk, R.R. 3, Stn. F, Thunder Bay, Ont. P7C 4V2 (807/964-2092)
Nelles Corners		Haldimand-Norfolk Reg. Mun.	Haldimand-Norfolk	Haldimand-Norfolk	Part of Haldimand
NEPEAN	83,374	Ottawa-Carleton Reg. Mun.	Nepean-Carleton	Carleton	D.E. Hobbs, City Clerk, 3825 Richmond Rd., Nepean, Ont. K2H 5C2 (613/829-1510)
Nephton	86	Peterborough	Peterborough	Hastings-Peterborough	
Nestleton Station	137	Durham Reg. Mun.	Durham-Northumberland	Durham York	
Nestorville	70	Algoma D.	Algoma	Algoma	Part of Thessalon Twp.
Neustadt•	498	Grey	Bruce-Grey	Grey	Mrs. A. Helwig, Village Clerk, Box 66, Neustadt, Ont. NOG 2MO (519/799-5758)
Newboro'•	244	Leeds & Grenville	Leeds-Grenville	Leeds	Mrs. R.M. Taylor, Village Clerk, Newboro', Ont. KOG 1PO (613/272-2265)
Newburgh•	629	Lennox & Addington	Hastings-Frontenac	Frontenac-Addington	Mrs. M. Roantree, Village Clerk, Box 8, Newburgh, Ont. KOK 2SO (613/378-6617)
Newbury•	422	Middlesex	Lambton-Middlesex	Middlesex	T. Ritchie, Village Clerk, 37 Hagerty St., Newbury, Ont. NOL 1ZO (519/693-4941)
Newcastle†	32,006	Durham Reg. Mun.	Durham-Northumberland	Durham East	David Oakes, Newcastle Town Clerk, 40 Temperance St., Bowmanville, Ont. L1C 3A6 (416/623-3379)
New Dundee	741	Waterloo Reg. Mun.	Waterloo	Kitchener-Wilmot	
New Hamburg	3,628	Waterloo Reg. Mun.	Waterloo	Kitchener-Wilmot	Part of Wilmot Twp.
Newington	278	Stormont, Dundas & Glengarry	Stormont-Dundas	Stormont, Dundas & Glengarry	
New Liskeard†	5,496	Timiskaming D.	Timiskaming	Timiskaming	W.F. Chatwin, Town Clerk, Box 730, New Liskeard, Ont. POJ 1PO (705/647-4367)
New Lowell	257	Simcoe	Grey-Simcoe	Dufferin-Simcoe	
Newmarket†	28,234	York Reg. Mun.	Grey-Simcoe	Dufferin-Simcoe	G.M. Blight, Town Clerk, Box 328, Newmarket, Ont. L3Y 4X7 (416/895-5193)
Newton	158	Perth	Perth	Perth	
Newton Robinson	50	Simcoe	Simcoe South	Dufferin-Simcoe	
NIAGARA FALLS	70,771	Niagara Reg. Mun.	Niagara Falls	Niagara Falls	J.L. Collinson, City Clerk, City Hall, 4310 Queen St., Niagara Falls, Ont. L2E 6X5 (416/356-7521)
Niagara-on-the-Lake†	12,307	Niagara Reg. Mun.	Niagara Falls	Brock	J.Y. Fleming, Niagara-on-the-Lake Town Clerk, Box 100, Virgil, Ont. LOS 1TO (416/468-3266)

Cities in CAPITALS; Towns marked †; Boroughs marked *; Villages marked •; Townships (Twp); ‡ means separated for municipal purposes from county; balance are either small places or unincorporated places (which have been named but not organized)

MUNICIPALITY	POP.	COUNTY OR DISTRICT	FEDERAL ELECTORAL DISTRICT	PROVINCIAL ELECTORAL DISTRICT	CLERK WITH ADDRESS AND PHONE
Nichol Twp	3,462	Wellington		Wellington-Dufferin-Peel	P.H. Cheney, Clerk, R.R. 1, Wellington Place, Fergus, Ont. N1M 2W3 (519/846-5317)
Nickel Centre†	12,281	Sudbury Reg. Mun.	Nickel Belt	Sudbury East	P.G. Olivier, Town Clerk, 190 Church St., Garson, Ont. POM 1VO (705/693-2771)
Nipigon Twp	2,510	Thunder Bay D.	Thunder Bay-Nipigon	Lake Nipigon	F.G. Wheeler, Clerk, Box 160, Nipigon, Ont. POT 2JO (807/887-3135)
Nipissing Twp	1,086	Parry Sound D.	Parry Sound-Muskoka	Parry Sound	C.H. Barton, Clerk, Nipissing, Ont. POH 1WO (705/724-2144)
Nipissing Junction	38	Nipissing D.	Nipissing	Nipissing	
Nixon	90	Haldimand-Norfolk Reg. Mun.	Haldimand-Norfolk	Brant-Oxford-Norfolk	
Nobel	291	Parry Sound D.	Parry Sound-Muskoka	Parry Sound	
Nobleton	1,537	York Reg. Mun.	York-Peel	York North	
Noelville	665	Sudbury D.	Nickel Belt	Sudbury East	
Norembega	94	Cochrane D.	Timiskaming	Cochrane North	
Norfolk Twp	10,980	Haldimand-Norfolk Reg. Mun.	Haldimand-Norfolk	Brant-Oxford-Norfolk; Haldimand-Norfolk	R. Loncke, Clerk, Box 128, Langton, Ont. NOE 1GO (519/875-4485)
Normanby Twp	2,576	Grey	Bruce-Grey	Grey	W.L. Brusso, Clerk, Ayton, Ont. NOG 1CO (519/665-7550)
Normandale	138	Haldimand-Norfolk Reg. Mun.	Haldimand-Norfolk	Haldimand-Norfolk	
North Algona Twp	549	Renfrew	Renfrew-Nipissing-Pembroke	Renfrew South	Mrs. E. Frew, Clerk, Box 99, Golden Lake, Ont. KOJ 1XO (613/625-2561)
NORTH BAY	50,417	Nipissing D.	Nipissing	Nipissing	R.F. Barton, City Clerk, 200 McIntyre St. E., Box 360, North Bay, Ont. P1B 8H8 (705/474-0400)
North Burgess Twp	618	Lanark		Lanark	Mrs. N. Bell, Clerk, R.R. 3, Perth, Ont. K7H 3C5 (613/267-4035)
North Buxton	122	Kent	Essex-Kent	Kent-Elgin	
North Cobalt	1,133	Timiskaming D.	Timiskaming	Timiskaming	
North Crosby Twp	674	Leeds & Grenville		Leeds	Mrs. B. Botting, Clerk, Box 8, Westport, Ont. KOG 1XO (613/273-2097)
North Dorchester Twp	6,690	Middlesex		Middlesex	P.J. Sidebottom, Clerk, Box 209, Dorchester, Ont. NOL 1GO (519/268-7334)
North Dumfries Twp	4,869	Waterloo Reg. Mun.	Cambridge	Cambridge	H. Griffin, Clerk, R.R. 4, Cambridge G, Ont. N1R 5S5 (519/621-0340)
North Easthope Twp	2,168	Perth	Perth	Perth	W.R. Hoffard, Clerk, R.R. 1, Stratford, Ont. N5A 6S2 (519/625-8726)
North Elmsley Twp	2,003	Lanark		Lanark	M.C. McEwen, Clerk, R.R. 5, Perth, Ont. K7H 3C7 (613/267-3371)
North Fredericksburgh Twp	2,671	Lennox & Addington		Prince Edward-Lennox	Mrs. H. O'Neil, Clerk, R.R. 2, Napanee, Ont. K7R 3K7 (613/354-2351)
North Gower	625	Ottawa-Carleton Reg. Mun.	Nepean-Carleton	Carleton-Grenville	
North Lancaster	174	Stormont, Dundas & Glengarry	Glengarry-Prescott-Russell	Stormont, Dundas & Glengarry	
North Marysburgh Twp	1,067	Prince Edward		Prince Edward-Lennox	J. Wells, Clerk, R.R. 4, Picton, Ont. KOK 2TO (613/476-4436)

Cities in CAPITALS; Towns marked †; Boroughs marked *; Villages marked •; Townships (Twp); ‡ means separated for municipal purposes from county; balance are either small places or unincorporated places (which have been named but not organized)

MUNICIPALITY	POP.	COUNTY OR DISTRICT	FEDERAL ELECTORAL DISTRICT	PROVINCIAL ELECTORAL DISTRICT	CLERK WITH ADDRESS AND PHONE
North Monaghan Twp	1,167	Peterborough	Peterborough	Peterborough	Mrs. I.C. Richardson, Clerk, R.R. 3, Peterborough, Ont. K9J 6X4 (705/743-4341)
North Plantagenet Twp	2,597	Prescott & Russell		Prescott & Russell	N. Dicaire, Clerk, Box 70, Curran, Ont. KOB 1CO (613/673-4797)
North Ridge	112	Essex	Essex-Kent	Essex North	
The North Shore Twp	2,030	Algoma D.		Algoma-Manitoulin	Mrs. L. Doggett, Clerk, Box 70, Spanish, Ont. POP 2AO (705/844-2300)
North Spirit Lake	166	Kenora D.	Kenora-Rainy River		
North Woodslee	131	Essex	Essex-Windsor	Essex North	
NORTH YORK	560,280	Metro	Don Valley East; Don Valley West; Eglinton-Lawrence; Willowdale; York Centre; York East; York Scarborough; York South-Weston; York West	Armourdale; Don Mills; Downsview; Etobicoke; Oriole; Wilson Heights; York Mills; York South; Yorkview	E. Roberts, City Clerk, 5100 Yonge St., Willowdale PO, North York, Ont. M2N 5V7 (416/224-6411)
Norval		Halton Reg. Mun.	Halton	Halton-Burlington	Part of Halton Hills
Norwich Twp	9,795	Oxford	Oxford	Oxford	R.C. Watkins, Clerk, Box 100, Otterville, Ont. NOJ 1RO (519/863-2709)
Norwood•	1,288	Peterborough	Peterborough	Hastings-Peterborough	R. Althouse, Village Clerk, 78 Colborne St., Norwood, Ont. KOL 2VO (705/639-5343)
Nottawasaga Twp	4,508	Simcoe		Dufferin-Simcoe	R. Campbell, Clerk, Duntroon, Ont. LOM 1HO (705/445-0199)
Novar	176	Parry Sound D.	Parry Sound-Muskoka	Parry Sound	
Oakland	34	Essex	Essex-Kent	Essex South	near Leamington
Oakland Twp	1,296	Brant		Brant-Oxford-Norfolk	Ms. B. Cadman, Clerk, Oakland, Ont. NOE 1LO (519/446-2924)
Oakville†	69,881	Halton Reg. Mun.	Halton	Oakville	D.W. Brown, Town Clerk, 1225 Trafalgar Rd., Box 310, Oakville, Ont. L6J 5A6 (416/845-6601)
Oakwood	382	Victoria	Victoria-Haliburton	Victoria-Haliburton	
Oba	60	Algoma D.	Cochrane	Algoma	
O'Connor Twp	565	Thunder Bay D.	Thunder Bay-Atikokan	Fort William	Mrs. R. Delyea, Clerk, R.R. 1, Kakabeka Falls, Ont. POT 1WO (807/475-4761)
Odessa	877	Lennox & Addington	Hastings-Frontenac	Prince Edward-Lennox	
Oil City	209	Lambton	Lambton-Middlesex	Lambton	
Oil Springs•	675	Lambton	Lambton-Middlesex	Lambton	F.W. Baines, Village Clerk, Box 22, Oil Springs, Ont. NON 1PO (519/834-2939)
Olden Twp	755	Frontenac		Frontenac-Addington	Mrs. M. Scott, Clerk, Box 74, Mountain Grove, Ont. KOH 2EO (613/335-5539)
Oliver Twp	2,113	Thunder Bay D.	Thunder Bay-Nipigon	Port Arthur	Ms. J.C. Ross, Clerk, Murillo, Ont. POT 2GO (807/935-2613)
Omemee•	813	Victoria	Victoria-Haliburton	Victoria-Haliburton	Mrs. H.A. Villeneuve, Village Clerk, Mun. Office, King St., Omemee, Ont. KOL 2WO (705/799-5032)
Ompah	89	Frontenac	Hastings-Frontenac	Frontenac-Addington	
Onaping Falls†	6,227	Sudbury Reg. Mun.	Nickel Belt	Nickel Belt	R. Demers, Onaping Falls Town Clerk, Box 250, Levack, Ont. POM 2CO (705/966-3431)
Onondaga Twp	1,383	Brant	Brant	Brant-Oxford-Norfolk	Mrs. V. Whytock, Clerk, R.R. 7, Brantford, Ont. N3T 5L9 (519/759-8572)

Cities in CAPITALS; Towns marked †; Boroughs marked *; Villages marked •; Townships (Twp); ‡ means separated for municipal purposes from county; balance are either small places or unincorporated places (which have been named but not organized)

MUNICIPALITY	POP.	COUNTY OR DISTRICT	FEDERAL ELECTORAL DISTRICT	PROVINCIAL ELECTORAL DISTRICT	CLERK WITH ADDRESS AND PHONE
Opasatika Twp	688	Cochrane D.	Cochrane	Cochrane North	B. Sigouin, Clerk, Box 100, Opasatika, Ont. P0L 1Z0 (705/335-8280)
Ops Twp	3,226	Victoria	Victoria-Haliburton	Victoria-Haliburton	M. Musgrave, Clerk, Box 337, R.R. 5, Lindsay, Ont. K9V 4R5 (705/324-5132)
Orangeville†	13,034	Dufferin	Wellington-Dufferin-Simcoe	Dufferin-Simcoe	R.B. Lackey, Town Clerk, 87 Broadway St., Orangeville, Ont. L9W 1K1 (519/941-0440)
Orchard Beach	82	York Reg. Mun.	Victoria-Haliburton	Durham York	
Orford Twp	1,524	Kent	Kent	Kent-Elgin	A. Glassford, Clerk, Box 49, Highgate, Ont. N0P 1T0 (519/678-3961)
Orillia Twp	6,595	Simcoe	Simcoe North	Simcoe East	J.B. Mather, Clerk, Box 159, Orillia, Ont. L3V 6J3 (705/325-2316)
ORILLIA	23,698	Simcoe	Simcoe North	Simcoe East	B.D. Bayne, City Clerk, 35 West St. N., Box 340, Orillia, Ont. L3V 6J6 (705/325-1311)
Oro Twp	6,485	Simcoe	Simcoe North	Simcoe East	H. Neufeld, Clerk, R.R. 2, Oro Station, Ont. L0L 2E0 (705/487-2016)
Orono		Durham Reg. Mun.	Durham-Northumberland	Durham East	
Orr Lake	249	Simcoe	Simcoe North	Simcoe East	
Orrs Lake	218	Waterloo Reg. Mun.	Cambridge	Cambridge	
Orrville	109	Parry Sound D.	Parry Sound-Muskoka	Parry Sound	
Orton	42	Dufferin	Wellington-Dufferin-Simcoe	Wellington-Dufferin-Peel	
Osgoode Twp	9,259	Ottawa-Carleton Reg. Mun.	Nepean-Carleton	Carleton-Grenville	F. Wilson, Clerk, Box 130, Metcalfe, Ont. K0A 2P0 (613/821-1107)
OSHAWA	115,197	Durham Reg. Mun.	Oshawa	Durham East; Oshawa	R.A. Henderson, City Clerk, 50 Centre St. S., Oshawa, Ont. L1H 3Z7 (416/725-7351)
Osnabruck Twp	4,056	Stormont, Dundas & Glengarry		Stormont, Dundas & Glengarry	Mrs. L. Smith, Clerk, Box 340, R.R. 3, Ingleside, Ont. K0C 1M0 (613/537-2362)
Oso Twp	1,215	Frontenac		Frontenac-Addington	Miss S. Donnelly, Clerk, Box 89, Sharbot Lake, Ont. K0H 2P0 (613/279-2935)
Osprey Twp	1,815	Grey	Grey-Simcoe	Grey	Mrs. M. Smith, Clerk, Maxwell, Ont. N0C 1J0 (519/922-2551)
Ostrander	84	Oxford	Oxford	Oxford	
Otonabee Twp	4,618	Peterborough	Peterborough	Peterborough	D.A. Crossley, Clerk, Box 70, Keene, Ont. K0L 2G0 (705/295-6852)
OTTAWA	301,567	Ottawa-Carleton Reg. Mun.	Nepean-Carleton; Ottawa-Carleton; Ottawa Centre; Ottawa-Vanier; Ottawa West	Carleton; Carleton East; Ottawa Centre; Ottawa East; Ottawa South; Ottawa West	Mrs. E. Cooper, City Clerk, City Hall, 111 Sussex Dr., Ottawa, Ont. K1N 5A1 (613/563-3111)
Otterville	785	Oxford	Oxford	Oxford	
OWEN SOUND	19,697	Grey	Grey-Simcoe	Grey-Bruce	W.H. Clark, City Clerk, City Hall, 808 2nd Ave. E., Owen Sound, Ont. N4K 2H4 (519/376-1440)
Owens, Williamson & Idington Twp	1,410	Cochrane D.	Cochrane	Cochrane North	R.J. Hein, Clerk, Box 100, Val Rita, Ont. P0L 2G0 (705/335-6146)
Oxdrift	60	Kenora D.	Kenora-Rainy River	Kenora	
Oxford Mills	135	Leeds & Grenville	Leeds-Grenville	Carleton-Grenville	

Cities in CAPITALS; Towns marked †; Boroughs marked *; Villages marked •; Townships (Twp); ‡ means separated for municipal purposes from county; balance are either small places or unincorporated places (which have been named but not organized)

MUNICIPALITY	POP.	COUNTY OR DISTRICT	FEDERAL ELECTORAL DISTRICT	PROVINCIAL ELECTORAL DISTRICT	CLERK WITH ADDRESS AND PHONE
Oxford on Rideau Twp	3,812	Leeds & Grenville	Leeds-Grenville	Carleton-Grenville	G.R. Paterson, Clerk, Twp. Hall, Oxford Mills, Ont. KOG 1SO (613/258-3995)
Pagwa River	35	Cochrane D.	Cochrane	Cochrane North	
Paincourt	403	Kent	Kent	Chatham-Kent	
Paipoonge Twp	2,597	Thunder Bay D.		Fort William	A.J. Wellington, Clerk, R.R. 6, Thunder Bay, Ont. P7C 5N5 (807/939-1543)
Paisley•	1,067	Bruce	Bruce-Grey	Grey-Bruce	R. Brown, Village Clerk, Box 460, Paisley, Ont. NOG 2NO (519/353-5609)
Pakenham Twp	1,359	Lanark		Lanark	H. Brodmann, Clerk, Box 59, Pakenham, Ont. KOA 2XO (613/624-5430)
Palermo	269	Halton Reg. Mun.	Halton	Oakville	
Palgrave		Peel Reg. Mun.	York-Peel	Wellington-Dufferin-Peel	Part of Caledon
Palmerston†	1,987	Wellington	Wellington-Dufferin-Simcoe	Grey	A. Guiler, Town Clek, Box 190, Palmerston, Ont. NOG 2PO (519/343-2340)
Palmerston & N. & S. Canonto Twp	337	Frontenac		Frontenac-Addington	Mrs. D. Sargeant, Clerk, Snow Road Stn., Ont. KOH 2RO (613/479-5595)
Pamour		Cochrane D.	Timmins-Chapleau	Cochrane South	Part of Timmins
Papineau Twp	646	Nipissing D.		Parry Sound	Mrs. N. Mackey, Clerk, Box 630, Mattawa, Ont. POH 1VO (705/744-5610)
Paris†	7,048	Brant	Brant	Brant-Oxford-Norfolk	J.G. Fairlie, Town Clerk, 59 Grand River St. N., Paris, Ont. N3L 2M3 (519/442-6324)
Park Head	53	Bruce	Bruce-Grey	Grey-Bruce	
Parkhill†	1,274	Middlesex	Lambton-Middlesex	Huron-Middlesex	Wm. Norris, Town Clerk, 229 Main St., Box 9, Parkhill, Ont. NOM 2KO (519/294-6363)
Parry Sound†	6,078	Parry Sound D.	Parry Sound-Muskoka	Parry Sound	W. Ed. Ewing, Town Clerk, 52 Seguin St., Parry Sound, Ont. P2A 1B4 (705/746-2101)
Peel Twp	3,856	Wellington		Wellington-Dufferin-Peel	Mrs. C. Oosterveld, Clerk, Box 119, Drayton, Ont. NOG 1PO (519/638-3314)
Pefferlaw	750	York Reg. Mun.	Victoria-Haliburton	Durham York	
Pelee Twp‡	263	Essex	Essex-Kent	Essex South	D. McTavish, Clerk, Pelee Island, Ont. NOR 1MO (519/724-2931)
Pelee Island		Essex	Essex-Kent	Essex South	
Pelham†	10,849	Niagara Reg. Mun.	Erie	Lincoln	M. Hackett, Town Clerk, Pelham Town Square, Box 400, Fonthill, Ont. LOS 1EO (416/892-2607)
PEMBROKE	14,249	Renfrew	Renfrew-Nipissing-Pembroke	Renfrew North	Mrs. K. June Nighbor, City Clerk/Adm., 1 Pembroke St. E., Pembroke, Ont. K8A 6X3 (613/735-6821)
Pembroke Twp	1,277	Renfrew	Renfrew-Nipissing-Pembroke	Renfrew North	Daryl Ryan, Clerk, R.R. 4, Pembroke, Ont. K8A 6W5 (613/735-5962)
Pendleton	82	Prescott & Russell	Glengarry-Prescott-Russell	Prescott & Russell	
Penetanguishene†	5,388	Simcoe	Simcoe North	Simcoe Centre	Y.A. Gagné, Town Clerk, 10 Robert St. W., Penetanguishene, Ont. LOK 1PO (705/549-7453)
Percy Twp	2,433	Northumberland	Northumberland	Northumberland	Mrs. W. Platt, Clerk, Box 129, Warkworth, Ont. KOK 3KO (705/924-2931)
Perkinsfield	342	Simcoe	Simcoe North	Simcoe Centre	

Cities in CAPITALS; Towns marked †; Boroughs marked *; Villages marked •; Townships (Twp); ‡ means separated for municipal purposes from county; balance are either small places or unincorporated places (which have been named but not organized)

MUNICIPALITY	POP.	COUNTY OR DISTRICT	FEDERAL ELECTORAL DISTRICT	PROVINCIAL ELECTORAL DISTRICT	CLERK WITH ADDRESS AND PHONE
Perry Twp	1,191	Parry Sound D.		Parry Sound	Mrs. D. Marshall, Clerk, Box 70, Emsdale, Ont. POA 1JO (705/636-5941)
Perry Station	45	Niagara Reg. Mun.	Erie		
Perth†	5,776	Lanark	Lanark-Renfrew-Carleton	Lanark	T.G. Kent, Town Clerk, 80 Gore St. E., Perth, Ont. K7H 1H9 (613/267-3311)
Petawawa•	5,565	Renfrew	Renfrew-Nipissing-Pembroke	Renfrew North	R. Rantz, Village Clerk, Box 69, Petawawa, Ont. K8H 2X1 (613/687-5536)
Petawawa Twp	7,400	Renfrew	Renfrew-Nipissing-Pembroke	Renfrew North	D.W. Brumm, Clerk, 680 Hwy. 17 W., Pembroke, Ont. K8A 7H5 (613/735-6551)
PETERBOROUGH	61,241	Peterborough	Peterborough	Peterborough	S. Hendry, City Clerk, 500 George St. N., Peterborough, Ont. K9H 3R9 (705/742-7771)
Petersburg	315	Waterloo Reg. Mun.	Waterloo	Kitchener-Wilmot	
Petrolia†	4,315	Lambton	London-Middlesex	Lambton	H.G. Kerby, Town Clerk, Box 1270, Petrolia, Ont. NON 1RO (519/882-2350)
Phelpston	176	Simcoe	Simcoe South	Simcoe Centre	
Phillipsburg	117	Waterloo Reg. Mun.	Waterloo	Kitchener-Wilmot	
Pickerel	115	Parry Sound D.	Parry Sound-Muskoka	Parry Sound	
Pickering†	35,872	Durham Reg. Mun.	Ontario	Durham West; Durham York	B. Taylor, Town Clerk, 1710 Kingston Rd., Pickering, Ont. L1V 1C7 (416/683-2760)
Pickering Beach		Durham Reg. Mun.	Ontario	Durham West	Part of Ajax
Pickle Lake Twp	1,029	Kenora D.	Kenora-Rainy River	Kenora	R.A. Lake, Clerk, Box 98, Pickle Lake, Ont. P0V 3A0 (807/928-2034)
Picton†	4,353	Prince Edward	Prince Edward-Hastings	Prince Edward-Lennox	G. Lodge, Town Clerk, Box 1670, Picton, Ont. KOK 2TO (613/476-5966)
Pike Bay	29	Bruce	Bruce-Grey	Grey-Bruce	
Pilkington Twp	1,845	Wellington	Guelph	Wellington-Dufferin-Peel	L. Day, Clerk, R.R. 2, Elora, Ont. NOB 1SO (519/846-9801)
Pine Grove	729	York Reg. Mun.	York North	York North	
Pine Orchard	72	York Reg. Mun.	York-Peel	York North	
Pinewood	92	Rainy River D.	Kenora-Rainy River	Rainy River	
Pinkerton	86	Bruce	Bruce-Grey	Huron-Bruce	
Pittsburgh Twp	9,702	Frontenac	Hastings-Frontenac; Kingston & the Islands	Frontenac-Addington; Kingston & the Islands	Mrs. B. Webb, Clerk, Box 966, Kingston, Ont. K7L 4X8 (613/546-3283)
Plantagenet•	949	Prescott & Russell	Glengarry-Prescott & Russell	Prescott & Russell	R. Séguin, Village Clerk, 720 Concession St., Plantagenet, Ont. KOB 1LO (613/673-4859)
Plattsville	498	Oxford	Oxford	Brant-Oxford-Norfolk	
Plummer, Add'l Twp	549	Algoma D.	Algoma	Algoma	Mrs. B. Mills, Clerk, R.R. 1, Bruce Mines, Ont. POR 1CO (705/785-3479)
Plympton Twp	5,032	Lambton	Lambton-Middlesex	Lambton	A. McKinlay, Clerk, Box 400, Wyoming, Ont. NON 1TO (519/845-3939)
Pointe-aux-Roches	240	Essex	Essex-Windsor	Essex North	
Point Edward•	2,417	Lambton	Sarnia	Sarnia	J. Langner, Village Clerk, 36 St. Clair St., Point Edward, Ont. N7V 4G8 (519/337-3021)
Pontypool	497	Victoria	Durham-Northumberland	Victoria-Haliburton	
Porcupine		Cochrane D.	Timmins-Chapleau	Cochrane South	Part of Timmins

Cities in CAPITALS; Towns marked †; Boroughs marked *; Villages marked •; Townships (Twp); ‡ means separated for municipal purposes from county; balance are either small places or unincorporated places (which have been named but not organized)

MUNICIPALITY	POP.	COUNTY OR DISTRICT	FEDERAL ELECTORAL DISTRICT	PROVINCIAL ELECTORAL DISTRICT	CLERK WITH ADDRESS AND PHONE
Porquis Junction	237	Cochrane D.	Timmins-Chapleau	Cochrane South	
Port Burwell•	661	Elgin	Elgin	Elgin	The Village Clerk, Box 299, Port Burwell, Ont. NOJ 1LO (519/874-4343)
PORT COLBORNE	19,449	Niagara Reg. Mun.	Erie	Erie	L.C. Hunt, City Clerk, 239 King St., Port Colborne, Ont. L3K 4G8 (416/835-2900)
Port Credit		Peel Reg. Mun.	Mississauga South	Mississauga South	Part of Mississauga
Port Elgin†	5,840	Bruce	Bruce-Grey	Huron-Bruce	W.J. Coulter, Town Clerk, Box 550, Port Elgin, Ont. NOH 2CO (519/832-2008)
Port Hope†	9,992	Northumberland	Durham-Northumberland	Northumberland	F.N. Wakely, Town Clerk, Box 117, 56 Queen St., Port Hope, Ont. L1A 3V9 (416/885-4544)
Port Lambton	716	Lambton	Lambton-Middlesex	Lambton	
Portland	282	Leeds & Grenville	Leeds-Grenville	Leeds	
Portland Twp	4,112	Frontenac	Hastings-Frontenac	Frontenac-Addington	H. Watson, Clerk, Hartington, Ont. KOH 1WO (613/372-2743)
Port Maitland		Haldimand-Norfolk Reg. Mun.	Haldimand-Norfolk	Haldimand-Norfolk	Part of Dunnville
Port McNicoll•	1,950	Simcoe	Simcoe North	Simcoe East	A.J. Hancox, Village Clerk, Box 160, Port McNicoll, Ont. LOK 1RO (705/534-7281)
Port Nelson	1,619	Halton Reg. Mun.	Burlington		
Port Robinson		Niagara Reg. Mun.	Welland	Welland	
Port Ryerse		Haldimand-Norfolk Reg. Mun.	Haldimand-Norfolk	Haldimand-Norfolk	Part of Nanticoke
Port Stanley•	1,902	Elgin	Elgin	Elgin	D.J. Lacroix, Village Clerk, Bridge St., Box 70, Port Stanley, Ont. NOL 2AO (519/782-3383)
Powassan†	1,215	Parry Sound D.	Parry Sound-Muskoka	Parry Sound	Mrs. J. Croteau, Town Clerk, Box 250, Powassan, Ont. POH 1ZO (705/724-2813)
Prescott†‡	4,803	Leeds & Grenville	Leeds-Grenville	Carleton-Grenville	K.D. Boal, Town Clerk, Box 160, Prescott, Ont. KOE 1TO (613/925-4275)
Preston		Waterloo Reg. Mun.	Cambridge	Cambridge	Part of Cambridge
Priceville	158	Grey	Grey-Simcoe	Grey	
Prince Twp	734	Algoma D.		Algoma	Mrs. L. Konkin, Clerk, Box 726, Sault Ste. Marie, Ont. P6A 5N3 (705/253-6303)
Prince Albert		Durham Reg. Mun.	Durham-Northumberland	Durham York	Part of Port Perry
Proton Twp	1,636	Grey		Grey	Mrs. Jane Roth, Clerk, R.R. 1, Dundalk, Ont. NOC 1BO (519/923-2160)
Proton Station	75	Grey	Grey-Simcoe	Grey	
Providence Bay	172	Manitoulin D.	Algoma	Algoma-Manitoulin	
Puslinch Twp	4,480	Wellington	Guelph	Wellington South	Mrs. Brenda Beatson, Clerk, 2 Quebec St., Guelph, Ont. N1H 2T3 (519/822-6499)
Putnam	77	Middlesex	London-Middlesex	Middlesex	
Queenston	434	Niagara Reg. Mun.	Niagara Falls	Brock	
Queensville	327	York Reg. Mun.	York-Peel	Durham York	
Radcliffe Twp	846	Renfrew	Renfrew-Nipissing-Pembroke	Renfrew South	R. Norlock, Clerk, Box 70, Combermere, Ont. KOJ 1LO (613/756-3704)
Raglan Twp	801	Renfrew	Renfrew-Nipissing-Pembroke	Renfrew South	Ms. E. Krieger, Clerk, Palmer Rapids, Ont. KOJ 2EO (613/758-2061)

Cities in CAPITALS; Towns marked †; Boroughs marked *; Villages marked •; Townships (Twp); ‡ means separated for municipal purposes from county; balance are either small places or unincorporated places (which have been named but not organized)

MUNICIPALITY	POP.	COUNTY OR DISTRICT	FEDERAL ELECTORAL DISTRICT	PROVINCIAL ELECTORAL DISTRICT	CLERK WITH ADDRESS AND PHONE
Rainy River†	1,048	Rainy River D.	Kenora-Rainy River	Rainy River	H.A. Solomonian, Town Clerk, 404 Atwood Ave., Rainy River, Ont. POW 1LO (807/852-3244)
Raith	85	Thunder Bay D.	Thunder Bay-Nipigon	Lake Nipigon	
Raleigh Twp	6,394	Kent	Essex-Kent	Kent-Elgin	B.D. Johnston, Clerk, R.R. 5, Merlin, Ont. NOP 1WO (519/689-4360)
Rama Twp	1,295	Simcoe	Simcoe North	Simcoe East	L.E. Cotton, Clerk, Box 83, Washago, Ont. LOK 2BO (705/689-2261)
Ramsay Twp	2,328	Lanark		Lanark	R. Brydges, Clerk, R.R. 2, Almonte, Ont. KOA 1AO (613/256-2064)
Ratter & Dunnet Twp	1,595	Sudbury D.	Nickel Belt	Sudbury East	Mrs. E.M. Wilson, Clerk, Box 250, Warren, Ont. POH 2NO (705/967-2174)
Rawdon Twp	2,369	Hastings		Hastings-Peterborough	Mrs. K. Reid, Clerk, Springbrook, Ont. KOK 3CO (613/395-3962)
Rayside-Balfour†	15,369	Sudbury Reg. Mun.	Nickel Belt	Nickel Belt	R.J. Leclair, Rayside-Balfour Town Clerk, Box 639, Chelmsford, Ont. POM 1LO (705/855-9061)
Rear of ...					see Name, Rear of
Red Lake Twp	2,179	Kenora D.	Kenora-Rainy River	Kenora	Mrs. C.G. Achurch, Clerk, Box 308, Red Lake, Ont. POV 2MO (807/727-2311)
Red Rock Twp.	1,563	Thunder Bay D.	Thunder Bay-Nipigon	Lake Nipigon	B. Howarth, Clerk, Box 447, Red Rock, Ont. P0T 2P0 (807/886-2245)
Regan	150	Thunder Bay D.		Lake Nipigon	
Renfrew†	8,490	Renfrew	Renfrew-Nipissing-Pembroke	Renfrew South	R.G. Howse, Town Clerk, 128 Raglan St. S., Box 187, Renfrew, Ont. K7V 1P9 (613/432-4848)
Rexdale		Etobicoke North		Part of Metro Toronto	
Richards Landing	313	Algoma D.	Algoma	Algoma	
Richmond Twp	3,503	Lennox & Addington	Hastings-Frontenac	Prince Edward-Lennox	J.M. Kimmett, Clerk, Selby, Ont. KOK 2ZO (613/388-2603)
Richmond Hill†	36,599	York Reg. Mun.	York North	York Centre	C.D. Weldon, Town Clerk, 10266 Yonge St., Richmond Hill, Ont. L4C 4Y5 (416/884-8101)
Richvale	3,392	York Reg. Mun.		York Centre	
Rideau Twp	8,860	Ottawa-Carleton Reg. Mun.	Nepean-Carleton	Carleton-Grenville	Mrs. G.K. Heggart, Clerk, Box 310, North Gower, Ont. KOA 2TO (613/489-3314)
Ridgetown†	3,214	Kent	Kent	Kent-Elgin	R.G. Wilkinson, Town Clerk, 45 Main St. E., Ridgetown, Ont. NOP 2CO (519/674-5583)
Ridgeway	1,978	Niagara Reg. Mun.	Erie	Erie	
Ringwood	124	York Reg. Mun.	York-Peel	York North	
Ripley•	626	Bruce	Huron-Bruce	Huron-Bruce	W. McCreath, Village Clerk, Box 130, Ripley, Ont. NOG 2RO (519/395-2969)
Roblin	84	Lennox & Addington	Hastings-Frontenac	Prince Edward-Lennox	
Roche's Point	145	Simcoe	Victoria-Haliburton	Durham York	
Rochester Twp	4,310	Essex	Essex-Windsor	Essex North	D. Perdu, Clerk, Box 70, St. Joachim, Ont. NOR 1SO (519/728-2213)
Rockcliffe Park•	2,364	Ottawa-Carleton Reg. Mun.	Ottawa-Carleton	Carleton East	J.N. Ramsay, Village Clerk, 350 Springfield Rd., Ottawa, Ont. K1M OK7 (613/749-9791)

Cities in CAPITALS; Towns marked †; Boroughs marked *; Villages marked •; Townships (Twp); ‡ means separated for municipal purposes from county; balance are either small places or unincorporated places (which have been named but not organized)

MUNICIPALITY	POP.	COUNTY OR DISTRICT	FEDERAL ELECTORAL DISTRICT	PROVINCIAL ELECTORAL DISTRICT	CLERK WITH ADDRESS AND PHONE
Rockland†	4,040	Prescott & Russell	Glengarry-Prescott-Russell	Prescott & Russell	J.P. Pitre, Town Clerk, Box 909, Rockland, Ont. KOA 3AO (613/446-5142)
Rocklyn	75	Grey	Grey-Simcoe	Grey	
Rockwood	959	Wellington	Guelph	Wellington-Dufferin-Peel	
Rodney•	1,017	Elgin	Eglin	Kent-Elgin	Mrs. J. Dwyer, Village Clerk, Box 460, Rodney, Ont. NOL 2CO (519/785-0456)
Rolph, Buchanan, Wylie & McKay Twp	2,079	Renfrew	Renfrew-Nipissing-Pembroke	Renfrew North	Mrs. E. Millward, Clerk, R.R. 1, Deep River, Ont. KOJ 1PO (613/584-2714)
Romney Twp	1,794	Kent		Kent-Elgin	S. Brophey, Clerk, Box 610, Wheatley, Ont. NOP 2PO (519/825-4711)
Roseland	1,185	Essex		Essex North	
Roseneath	1,400	Northumberland	Northumberland	Northumberland	
Ross Twp	1,619	Renfrew	Renfrew-Nipissing-Pembroke	Renfrew South	Mrs. H.E. Wood, Clerk, Foresters Falls, Ont. KOJ 1VO (613/646-7428)
Rosseau•	214	Parry Sound D.	Parry Sound-Muskoka	Parry Sound	Mrs. E. Wood, Village Clerk, Box 8, Rosseau, Ont. POC 1JO (705/732-4231)
Rosslyn Village	320	Thunder Bay D.	Thunder Bay-Atikokan	Fort William	
Rossport	96	Thunder Bay D.	Cochrane	Lake Nipigon	
Roxborough Twp	2,994	Stormont, Dundas & Glengarry	Stormont-Dundas	Stormont, Dundas & Glengarry	W.E. Wright, Clerk, Box 189, Moose Creek, Ont. KOC 1WO (613/538-2531)
Ruscomb	91	Essex	Essex-Windsor	Essex North	
Russell Twp	5,380	Prescott & Russell		Prescott & Russell	J.G. Bourdeau, Clerk, Box 570, Embrun, Ont. KOA 1WO (613/443-3066)
Rutherford & George Is. Twp	475	Manitoulin D.	Nickel Belt	Algoma-Manitoulin	Mrs. J. Roque, Clerk, 31 Commissioner St., Killarney, Ont. POM 2AO (705/287-2424)
Rutherglen	85	Nipissing D.	Nipissing	Parry Sound	
Ruthven	384	Essex	Essex-Kent	Essex South	
Rydal Bank	51	Algoma D.	Algoma	Algoma	
Ryerson Twp	393	Parry Sound D.		Parry Sound	Mrs. M.E. Johnston, Clerk, Box 89, Burk's Falls, Ont. POA 1CO (705/382-3232)
St. Albert	222	Prescott & Russell	Glengarry-Prescott-Russell	Prescott & Russell	
Ste-Anne de Prescott	137	Prescott & Russell	Glengarry-Prescott-Russell	Prescott & Russell	
St. Anns	75	Niagara Reg. Mun.	Erie	Lincoln	
ST. CATHARINES	123,956	Niagara Reg. Mun.	St. Catharines; Welland	Brock; St. Catharines	T.R. Hollick, City Clerk, City Hall, Church St., Box 3012, St. Catharines, Ont. L2R 7C2 (416/688-5600)
St. Clair Beach•	2,359	Essex	Windsor-Walkerville	Essex North	A.M. Barrette, St. Clair Beach Village Clerk, 13803 Riverside Dr., Windsor, Ont. N8N 1B5 (519/735-6261)
St. Davids	480	Niagara Reg. Mun.	Niagara Falls	Brock	
St. Edmunds Twp	704	Bruce	Bruce-Grey	Grey-Bruce	Mrs. C. Wyonch, Clerk, Box 70, Tobermory, Ont. NOH 2RO (519/596-2430)
St. Eugène	493	Prescott & Russell	Glengarry-Prescott-Russell	Prescott & Russell	
St. George	930	Brant	Brant	Brant-Oxford-Norfolk	
St. Isidore de Prescott•	743	Prescott & Russell	Glengarry-Prescott-Russell	Prescott & Russell	N. Bonneville, Village Clerk, C.P. 58, St. Isidore de Prescott, Ont. KOC 2BO (613/524-2155)

Cities in CAPITALS; Towns marked †; Boroughs marked *; Villages marked •; Townships (Twp); ‡ means separated for municipal purposes from county; balance are either small places or unincorporated places (which have been named but not organized)

MUNICIPALITY	POP.	COUNTY OR DISTRICT	FEDERAL ELECTORAL DISTRICT	PROVINCIAL ELECTORAL DISTRICT	CLERK WITH ADDRESS AND PHONE
St. Jacobs	852	Waterloo Reg. Mun.	Waterloo	Waterloo North	
St. Joachim	137	Essex	Essex-Windsor	Essex North	
St. Joseph Twp	970	Algoma D.	Algoma	Algoma	M. Jagger, Clerk, Box 9, Richards Landing, Ont. POR 1JO (705/246-2625)
St. Marys†‡	4,709	Perth	Perth	Perth	K.G. Storey, Town Clerk, 175 Queen St. E., Box 998, St. Mary's, Ont. NOM 2VO (519/284-2340)
ST. THOMAS	27,059	Elgin	Elgin	Elgin	R.A. Barrett, City Clerk, City Hall, Box 520, St. Thomas, Ont. N5P 3V7 (519/631-1680)
St. Vincent Twp	1,853	Grey	Grey-Simcoe	Grey	J. Foster, Clerk, R.R. 1, Meaford, Ont. NOH 1YO (519/538-2421)
St. Williams	458	Haldimand-Norfolk Reg. Mun.	Haldimand-Norfolk	Haldimand-Norfolk	
Salem	743	Wellington		Wellington South	
Salford	153	Oxford	Oxford	Oxford	
Sandfield Twp	173	Manitoulin D.		Algoma-Manitoulin	Mrs. L.L. Case, Clerk, R.R. 3, Tehkummah, Ont. POP 2CO (705/859-3880)
Sand Point	86	Renfrew	Lanark-Renfrew-Carleton	Renfrew South	
Sandwich South Twp	4,952	Essex	Essex-Windsor	Essex North	Mrs. E. Oliver, Clerk, 3455 North Talbot Rd., Oldcastle, Ont. NOR 1LO (519/737-6971)
Sandwich West Twp	13,989	Essex	Essex-Windsor	Essex North	R.W. Dalgleish, Clerk, 5950 Malden Rd., Windsor, Ont. N9H 1S4 (519/969-7770)
Sarawak Twp	2,229	Grey	Grey-Simcoe	Grey-Bruce	G. Cameron, Clerk, R.R. 2, Owen Sound, Ont. N4K 5N4 (519/376-1469)
Sarnia Twp	19,322	Lambton	Sarnia	Sarnia	Mrs. E.A. Jolly, Clerk, 2109 London Rd., Sarnia, Ont. N7T 7H2 (519/542-5581)
SARNIA	50,252	Lambton	Sarnia	Sarnia	G.A.M. Thomas, City Clerk, 255 N. Christina St., Sarnia, Ont. N7T 7N2 (519/332-0330)
Sarsfield	290	Ottawa-Carleton Reg. Mun.	Glengarry-Prescott-Russell	Prescott & Russell	
Saugeen Twp	1,664	Bruce		Huron-Bruce	B. Murray, Clerk, Box 249, Port Elgin, Ont. NOH 2CO (519/832-5550)
SAULT STE. MARIE	80,548	Algoma D.	Sault Ste. Marie	Sault Ste. Marie	W.G. Lindsay, City Clerk, Civic Centre, Box 580, Sault Ste. Marie, Ont. P6A 5N1 (705/949-9111)
Scarborough*	427,503	Metro	Scarborough Centre; Scarborough East; Scarborough West; York-Scarborough	Scarborough Centre; Scarborough East; Scarborough-Ellesmere; Scarborough North; Scarborough West	J.J. Poots, Borough Clerk, 150 Borough Dr., Scarborough, Ont. M1P 4N7 (416/296-7111)
Schomberg	782	York Reg. Mun.	York-Peel	York North	
Schreiber Twp	1,986	Thunder Bay D.	Cochrane	Lake Nipigon	A.J. Gauthier, Clerk, 302 Scotia St., Schreiber, Ont. POT 2SO (807/824-2711)
Schumacher		Cochrane D.	Timmins-Chapleau	Cochrane South	Part of Timmins
Scotia	26	Parry Sound D.	Parry Sound-Muskoka	Parry Sound	
Scotland	687	Brant	Brant	Brant-Oxford-Norfolk	
Scudder	200	Essex	Essex-Kent	Essex South	

Cities in CAPITALS; Towns marked †; Boroughs marked *; Villages marked •; Townships (Twp); ‡ means separated for municipal purposes from county; balance are either small places or unincorporated places (which have been named but not organized)

MUNICIPALITY	POP.	COUNTY OR DISTRICT	FEDERAL ELECTORAL DISTRICT	PROVINCIAL ELECTORAL DISTRICT	CLERK WITH ADDRESS AND PHONE
Scugog Twp	12,373	Durham Reg. Mun.		Durham York	E.S. Cuddie, Clerk, Box 209, Port Perry, Ont. LOB 1NO (416/985-7346)
Seacliffe	420	Essex		Essex South	
Seaforth†	2,029	Huron	Huron-Bruce	Huron-Middlesex	J. Crocker, Town Clerk, 72 Main St. S., Seaforth, Ont. NOK 1WO (519/527-0160)
Seagram		Thunder Bay D.	Cochrane	Lake Nipigon	
Searchmont	390	Algoma D.	Algoma	Algoma	
Sebastopol Twp	523	Renfrew	Renfrew-Nipissing-Pembroke	Renfrew South	Mrs. V. Stevens, Clerk, Mun. Hall, Foymount, Ont. KOJ 1WO (613/754-2825)
Sebringville	534	Perth	Perth	Perth	
Seeleys Bay	452	Leeds & Grenville	Leeds-Grenville	Leeds	
Selkirk		Haldimand-Norfolk Reg. Mun.	Haldimand-Norfolk	Haldimand-Norfolk	Part of Nanticoke
Severn Bridge	95	Muskoka Dist. Mun.	Simcoe North	Simcoe East	
Seymour Twp	3,189	Northumberland		Northumberland	M. Smith, Clerk, Box 722, Campbellford, Ont. KOL 1LO (705/653-2330)
Shackleton & Machin Twp	914	Cochrane D.		Cochrane North	R. Deslandes, Clerk, Box 40, Fauquier, Ont. POL 1GO (705/339-2521)
Shakespeare	606	Perth	Perth	Perth	
Shallow Lake•	419	Grey	Bruce-Grey	Grey-Bruce	J. Shaw, Village Clerk, 266 Princess St., Shallow Lake, Ont. NOH 2KO (519/935-2248)
Shannonville	299	Hastings	Prince Edward-Hastings	Hastings-Peterborough	
Sharbot Lake	296	Frontenac	Hastings-Frontenac	Frontenac-Addington	
Shawanaga	67	Parry Sound D.	Parry Sound-Muskoka	Parry Sound	
Shedden	346	Elgin	Elgin	Elgin	
Sheffield	257	Hamilton-Wentworth Reg. Mun.	Hamilton-Wentworth	Wentworth North	near Cambridge
Sheffield Twp	1,204	Lennox & Addington		Frontenac-Addington	Mrs. P. Richmond, Clerk, Box 3, Tamworth, Ont. KOK 3GO (613/379-2923)
Shelburne†	3,001	Dufferin	Wellington-Dufferin-Simcoe	Wellington-Dufferin-Peel	W.A. Rintoul, Town Clerk, 203 Main St. E., Shelburne, Ont. LON 1SO (519/925-2600)
Sherborne, McClintock & Livingstone Twp	444	Haliburton	Victoria-Haliburton	Victoria-Haliburton	Mrs. D. Griffin, Clerk, Box 99, Dorset, Ont. POA 1EO (705/766-2211)
Sherwood, Jones & Burns Twp	1,860	Renfrew	Renfrew-Nipissing-Pembroke	Renfrew South	Mrs. U.A. Burchat, Clerk, Box 520, Barry's Bay, Ont. KOJ 1BO (613/756-2741)
Shillington	56	Cochrane D.	Timiskaming	Cochrane South	
Shuniah Twp	1,641	Thunder Bay D.		Port Arthur	Mrs. B. Clark, Clerk, 420 Leslie Ave., Thunder Bay, Ont. P7A 1X8 (807/683-3611)
Sidney Twp	15,821	Hastings	Hastings-Frontenac	Quinte	E.H. Lyons, Clerk, R.R. 5, Belleville, Ont. K8N 4Z5 (613/966-8330)
Simcoe†	14,149	Haldimand-Norfolk Reg. Mun.	Haldimand-Norfolk	Haldimand-Norfolk	C.R. Campbell, Town Clerk, 50 Colborne St. S., Box 545, Simcoe, Ont. N3Y 4N5 (519/426-5870)
Singhampton	238	Simcoe	Grey-Simcoe	Dufferin-Simcoe	
Sioux Lookout†	3,006	Kenora D.	Kenora-Rainy River	Kenora	P.E. Salem, Town Clerk-Tr., Box 158, Sioux Lookout, Ont. POV 2T2 (807/737-2700)

Cities in CAPITALS; Towns marked †; Boroughs marked *; Villages marked •; Townships (Twp); ‡ means separated for municipal purposes from county; balance are either small places or unincorporated places (which have been named but not organized)

MUNICIPALITY	POP.	COUNTY OR DISTRICT	FEDERAL ELECTORAL DISTRICT	PROVINCIAL ELECTORAL DISTRICT	CLERK WITH ADDRESS AND PHONE
Sioux Narrows	408	Kenora D.	Kenora-Rainy River	Kenora	Improvement Dist., c/o Mrs. M. Mysk, Box 417, Sioux Narrows, Ont. P0X 1N0
Skead		Sudbury D.	Nickel Belt	Nickel Belt	Part of Nickel Centre
Smith Twp	7,602	Peterborough		Peterborough	D.A. Holyoake, Clerk, 706 Carnegie St., Peterborough, Ont. K9L 1N1 (705/745-1389)
Smiths Falls†‡	9,016	Lanark	Lanark-Renfrew-Carleton	Lanark	W.M. Metcalfe, Town Clerk, Box 695, Smiths Falls, Ont. K7A 4T6 (613/283-4124)
Smithville	1,737	Niagara Reg. Mun.	Erie	Lincoln	
Smooth Rock Falls†	2,373	Cochrane D.	Cochrane	Cochrane North	D.R. Emmons, Town Clerk, Box 249, Smooth Rock Falls, Ont. POL 2BO (705/338-2717)
Snowdon Twp	573	Halburton	Victoria-Haliburton	Victoria-Haliburton	G. Wynne, Clerk, R.R. 1, Minden, Ont. KOM 2KO (705/286-2657)
Snow Road	33	Frontenac	Hastings-Frontenac	Frontenac-Addington	
Sombra Twp	4,258	Lambton	Lambton-Middlesex	Lambton	M.D. Burke, Clerk, Box 40, Sombra, Ont. NOP 2HO (519/892-3637)
Somerville Twp	1,464	Victoria	Victoria-Haliburton	Victoria-Haliburton	Mrs. M.J. McBride, Clerk, Box 59, Kinmount, Ont. KOM 2AO (705/488-2571)
Sonya	51	Durham Reg. Mun.	Victoria-Haliburton	Durham York	
Sophiasburgh Twp	1,906	Prince Edward		Prince Edward-Lennox	G.A. Way, Clerk, R.R. 8, Picton, Ont. KOK 2TO (613/476-2538)
South Algona Twp	304	Renfrew	Renfrew-Nipissing-Pembroke	Renfrew South	Martina Dwyer, Clerk, R.R. 4, Killaloe Station, Ont. KOJ 2AO (613/625-2499)
Southampton†	2,748	Bruce	Bruce-Grey	Huron-Bruce	W.R. Smith, Clerk, Box 340, Southampton, Ont. NOH 2LO (519/797-2015)
South Crosby Twp	1,480	Leeds & Grenville	Leeds-Grenville	Leeds	Mrs. M. Baxter, Clerk, Elgin, Ont. KOG 1EO (613/359-5830)
South Dorchester Twp	1,796	Elgin	Elgin	Elgin	Mrs. M. Wilson, Clerk, R.R. 2, Springfield, Ont. NOL 2JO (519/773-2186)
South Dumfries Twp	3,954	Brant	Brant	Brant-Oxford-Norfolk	G. Silverthorn, Clerk, Box 40, St. George, Ont. NOE 1NO (519/448-1432)
South Easthope Twp	1,918	Perth		Perth	C.J. Gingerich, Clerk, R.R. 1, Shakespeare, Ont. NOB 2PO (519/625-8738)
South Elmsley Twp	2,273	Leeds & Grenville	Leeds-Grenville	Leeds	D. Fergusson, Clerk, Lombardy, Ont. KOG 1LO (613/283-5427)
South Fredericksburgh Twp	1,129	Lennox & Addington		Prince Edward-Lennox	Mrs. P. Culhane, Clerk, R.R. 2, Napanee, Ont. K7R 3K7 (613/354-2420)
South Gower Twp	1,119	Leeds & Grenville		Carleton-Grenville	H. Sheppard, Clerk, R.R. 1, Kemptville, Ont. KOG 1JO (613/258-2781)
South Marysburgh Twp	909	Prince Edward	Prince Edward-Hastings	Prince Edward-Lennox	C. Walker, Clerk, R.R. 3, Picton, Ont. KOK 2TO (613/476-6771)
South Monaghan Twp	941	Peterborough	Peterborough	Peterborough	Ms. K. Alexander, Clerk, R.R. 1, Bailieboro, Ont. KOL 1BO (705/939-6079)
South Mountain	202	Stormont, Dundas & Glengarry	Stormont-Dundas	Stormont, Dundas & Glengarry	

Cities in CAPITALS; Towns marked †; Boroughs marked *; Villages marked •; Townships (Twp); ‡ means separated for municipal purposes from county; balance are either small places or unincorporated places (which have been named but not organized)

MUNICIPALITY	POP.	COUNTY OR DISTRICT	FEDERAL ELECTORAL DISTRICT	PROVINCIAL ELECTORAL DISTRICT	CLERK WITH ADDRESS AND PHONE
South Plantagenet Twp	1,599	Prescott & Russell		Prescott & Russell	Mrs. C. Nicholas, Clerk, Box 10, Fournier, Ont. KOB 1GO (613/524-2932)
South River•	1,115	Parry Sound D.	Parry Sound-Muskoka	Parry Sound	G.A. Hall, Village Clerk, 209 Ottawa Ave., South River, Ont. POA 1XO (705/386-2573)
South Sherbrooke Twp	557	Lanark	Lanark-Renfrew-Carleton	Lanark	Mrs. J. Warwick, Clerk, Maberly, Ont. KOH 2BO (613/268-2194)
South West Oxford Twp	8,338	Oxford		Oxford	Mrs. H. Prouse, Clerk, R.R. 1, Mount Elgin, Ont. NOJ 1NO (519/485-0477)
Southwold Twp	4,513	Elgin		Elgin	R.A. Pow, Clerk, Fingal, Ont. NOL 1KO (519/769-2010)
South Woodslee	241	Essex	Essex-Windsor	Essex North	
Spanish	1,082	Algoma D.	Algoma	Algoma-Manitoulin	
The Spanish River Twp	19,193	Sudbury D.	Algoma	Algoma-Manitoulin	A. Clipperton, Clerk, Box 489, Massey, Ont. POP 1PO (705/865-2646)
Sparta	229	Elgin	Elgin	Elgin	
Spencerville	434	Leeds & Grenville	Leeds-Grenville	Carleton-Grenville	
Springer Twp	2,111	Nipissing D.	Nipissing; Timiskaming	Nipssing	A. Sauve, Clerk, Box 1390, Sturgeon Falls, Ont. POH 2GO (705/753-0570)
Springfield•	528	Elgin	Elgin	Elgin	Mrs. C. Bearss, Clerk, Box 29, Springfield, Ont. NOL 2JO (519/773-8555)
Springford	279	Oxford	Oxford	Oxford	
Sprucedale	214	Parry Sound D.	Parry Sound-Muskoka	Parry Sound	
Staffa	67	Perth	Perth	Perth	
Stafford Twp	3,460	Renfrew		Renfrew North	D. Ryan, Clerk, R.R. 4, Pembroke, Ont. K8A 6W5 (613/735-6934)
Stanhope Twp	909	Haliburton	Victoria-Haliburton	Victoria-Haliburton	G.C. Bain, Clerk, R.R. 1, Haliburton, Ont. KOM 1SO (705/489-2379)
Stanley Twp	1,553	Huron	Huron-Bruce	Huron-Middlesex	M. Graham, Clerk, R.R. 1, Brucefield, Ont. NOM 1JO (519/482-9908)
Stanley	107	Thunder Bay D.	Thunder Bay-Atikokan	Fort William	
Stayner†	2,526	Simcoe	Grey-Simcoe	Dufferin-Simcoe	W.P. Spellman, Town Clerk, Box 200, Stayner, Ont. LOM 1SO (705/428-3210)
Steep Rock Lake	80	Rainy River D.	Thunder Bay-Atikokan	Rainy River	
Stella	83	Lennox & Addington	Kingston & the Islands	Kingston & the Islands	
Stephen Twp	4,171	Huron	Huron-Bruce	Huron-Middlesex	W.D. Wein, Clerk, Box 100, Crediton, Ont. NOM 1MO (519/234-6331)
Stevens	233	Thunder Bay D.	Cochrane	Lake Nipigon	
Stevensville	640	Niagara Reg. Mun.	Erie	Erie	
Stewarttown		Halton Reg. Mun.	Halton	Halton-Burlington	Part of Halton Hills
Stirling•	1,556	Hastings	Northumberland	Hastings-Peterborough	M.A. Rodgers, Village Clerk, Box 40, Stirling, Ont. KOK 3EO (613/395-3380)
Stockdale	107	Northumberland	Northumberland	Northumberland	
Stoco	128	Hastings	Prince Edward-Hastings	Hastings-Peterborough	
Stokes Bay	123	Bruce	Bruce-Grey	Grey-Bruce	
Stoney Creek†	32,628	Hamilton-Wentworth Reg. Mun.	Lincoln	Wentworth	J.A. Brezina, Stoney Creek Town Clerk, 777 Hwy. 8, Fruitland, Ont. LOR 1LO (416/643-1261)
Stoney Point	1,041	Essex	Essex-Windsor	Essex North	
Storrington Twp	2,931	Frontenac	Hastings-Frontenac	Frontenac-Addington	S.G. Silver, Clerk, R.R. 1, Battersea, Ont. KOH 1HO (613/353-2222)

Cities in CAPITALS; Towns marked †; Boroughs marked *; Villages marked •; Townships (Twp); ‡ means separated for municipal purposes from county; balance are either small places or unincorporated places (which have been named but not organized)

MUNICIPALITY	POP.	COUNTY OR DISTRICT	FEDERAL ELECTORAL DISTRICT	PROVINCIAL ELECTORAL DISTRICT	CLERK WITH ADDRESS AND PHONE
Stouffville					see Whitchurch-Stouffville
Straffordville	759	Elgin	Elgin	Elgin	
STRATFORD	26,517	Perth	Perth	Perth	R. Schulthies, City Clerk, 1 Wellington St., Stratford, Ont. N5A 2L1 (519/271-0250)
Strathcona	105	Lennox & Addington	Hastings-Frontenac	Frontenac-Addington	
Strathroy†	8,286	Middlesex	Lambton-Middlesex	Middlesex	T. Derreck, Town Clerk, 52 Frank St., Strathroy, Ont. N7G 2R4 (519/245-1070)
Stratton	100	Rainy River D.	Kenora-Rainy River	Rainy River	
Streetsville		Peel Reg. Mun.	Mississauga North	Mississauga North	Part of Mississauga
Strong Twp	1,196	Parry Sound D.	Parry Sound-Muskoka	Parry Sound	G. Russell, Clerk, Box 47, Sundridge, Ont. POA 1ZO (705/384-5819)
Stroud	892	Simcoe	Simcoe South	Simcoe Centre	
Sturgeon Bay	77	Simcoe	Simcoe North	Simcoe East	
Sturgeon Falls†	6,289	Nipissing D.	Nipissing	Nipissing	G. Savage, Town Clerk, Box 270, Sturgeon Falls, Ont. POH 2GO (705/753-2250)
Sturgeon Point•	45	Victoria	Victoria-Haliburton	Victoria-Haliburton	Mary Michie, Village Clerk, R.R. 3, Fenelon Falls, Ont. KOM 1NO (705/887-5616)
SUDBURY	92,350	Sudbury Reg. Mun.	Nickel Belt; Sudbury	Sudbury; Sudbury East	Mrs. E. Kerr, City Clerk, 200 Brady St., Box 1000, Sudbury, Ont. P3E 4S5 (705/674-3141)
Sullivan Twp	2,172	Grey	Bruce-Grey	Grey	G. Scott, Clerk, Desboro, Ont. N0H 1K0 (519/794-3024)
Sulphide	90	Hastings	Prince Edward-Hastings	Hastings-Peterborough	
Sultan	274	Sudbury D.	Timmins-Chapleau	Nickel Belt	
Summerstown	175	Stormont, Dundas & Glengarry	Stormont-Dundas	Stormont, Dundas & Glengarry	
Sundridge•	702	Parry Sound D.	Parry Sound-Muskoka	Parry Sound	Mrs. L. Fowler, Village Clerk, Box 129, Sundridge, Ont. POA 1ZO (705/384-5316)
Sunnidale Twp	2,220	Simcoe		Dufferin-Simcoe	E.M. Hannan, Clerk, R.R. 1, New Lowell, Ont. LOM 1NO (705/424-1941)
Sutton	3,655	York Reg. Mun.	Victoria-Haliburton	Durham York	Part of Georgina Twp.
Swastika		Timiskaming D.	Timiskaming	Timiskaming	Part of Kirkland Lake
Sydenham	528	Frontenac	Hastings-Frontenac	Frontenac-Addington	
Sydenham Twp	2,604	Grey	Grey-Simcoe	Grey	Mrs. E. Flood, Clerk, Mun. Office, R.R. 8, Owen Sound, Ont. N4K 5W4 (519/376-8487)
Tamworth	350	Lennox & Addington	Hastings-Frontenac	Frontenac-Addington	
Tara•	702	Bruce	Bruce-Grey	Grey-Bruce	Mrs. L.M. Hill, Village Clerk, 39 Yonge St., Tara, Ont. NOH 2NO (519/934-2544)
Tarbutt & Tarbutt Add'l Twp	309	Algoma D.		Algoma	J. Wiederkehr, Clerk, R.R. 1, Desbarats, Ont. POR 1EO (705/782-6776)
Tay Twp	6,002	Simcoe	Simcoe North	Simcoe East	B. Hopkins, Clerk, Box 100, Victoria Harbour, Ont. LOK 2AO (705/534-7248)
Tecumseh†	5,768	Essex	Windsor-Walkerville	Essex North	L.A. Lessad, Town Clerk, 917 Lesperance Rd., Windsor, Ont. N8N 1W9 (519/735-2184)
Tecumseth Twp	6,112	Simcoe		Dufferin-Simcoe	Ms. L. Duczak, Clerk, Box 220, Beeton, Ont. LOG 1AO (416/729-2231)

Cities in CAPITALS; Towns marked †; Boroughs marked *; Villages marked •; Townships (Twp); ‡ means separated for municipal purposes from county; balance are either small places or unincorporated places (which have been named but not organized)

MUNICIPALITY	POP.	COUNTY OR DISTRICT	FEDERAL ELECTORAL DISTRICT	PROVINCIAL ELECTORAL DISTRICT	CLERK WITH ADDRESS AND PHONE
Teeswater•	1,008	Bruce	Bruce-Grey	Huron-Bruce	R.D. Stevenson, Village Clerk, Box 369, Teeswater, Ont. NOG 2SO (519/392-6818)
Tehkummah Twp	416	Manitoulin D.	Algoma	Algoma-Manitoulin	Mrs. S.M. Pyette, Clerk, Tehkummah, Ont. POP 2CO (705/859-3293)
Temagami Twp	1,255	Nipissing D.	Timiskaming	Timiskaming	L. McAnulty, Clerk, Box 218, Temagami, Ont. POH 2HO (705/569-3421)
Temperanceville	183	York Reg. Mun.	York North	York Centre	
Terrace Bay Twp	2,114	Thunder Bay D.	Cochrane	Lake Nipigon	W.J. Hanley, Clerk, Box 40, Terrace Bay, Ont. POT 2WO (807/825-3315)
Thamesford	1,872	Oxford	Oxford	Lambton	
Thamesville•	980	Kent	Kent	Kent-Elgin	Mrs. V.R. Harry, Village Clerk, Box 280, Thamesville, Ont. NOP 2KO (519/692-3991)
Thedford•	696	Lambton	Lambton-Middlesex	Lambton	W. Earnshaw, Village Clerk, Box 189, Thedford, Ont. NOM 2NO (519/296-4980)
Thessalon†	1,652	Algoma D.	Algoma	Algoma	J.H. Stewart, Town Clerk, Box 220, Thessalon, Ont. POR 1LO (705/842-2217)
Thessalon Twp	750	Algoma D.	Algoma	Algoma	J. MacLean, Clerk, R.R. 1, Thessalon, Ont. POR 1LO (705/842-3800)
Thompson Twp	71	Algoma D.		Algoma	P.L. Eckman, Clerk, Box 278, Iron Bridge, Ont. POR 1HO (705/356-7393)
Thornbury†	1,460	Grey	Grey-Simcoe	Grey	L.H. Stuck, Town Clerk, Box 310, Thornbury, Ont. NOH 2PO (519/599-3250)
Thorndale	476	Middlesex	London-Middlesex	Middlesex	
Thornhill	1,135	York Reg. Mun.	York North	York Centre	
Thornloe•	161	Timiskaming D.	Timiskaming	Timiskaming	C.H. Edwards, Village Clerk, Thornloe, Ont. POJ 1SO (705/563-2256)
THOROLD	15,150	Niagara Reg. Mun.	Welland	Welland	R.M. Corbett, City Clerk, Box 1044, Thorold, Ont. L2V 4A7 (416/227-6613)
THUNDER BAY	112,053	Thunder Bay D.	Thunder Bay-Atikokan; Thunder Bay-Nipigon	Fort William; Lake Nipigon; Port Arthur	H.T. Kirk, City Clerk, 500 E. Donald St., Thunder Bay, Ont. P7E 5V3 (807/623-2711)
Thurlow Twp	6,312	Hastings	Prince Edward-Hastings	Hastings-Peterborough	W. Bouma, Clerk, Box 128, Cannifton, Ont. KOK 1KO (613/968-5553)
Tichborne	168	Frontenac	Hastings-Frontenac	Frontenac-Addington	
Tilbury†	4,350	Kent	Essex-Kent	Kent-Elgin	F.R. Reycraft, Town Clerk, Box 1299, Tilbury, Ont. NOP 2LO (519/682-2583)
Tilbury East Twp	2,767	Kent	Essex-Kent	Kent-Elgin	L.R. Smith, Clerk, R.R. 1, Merlin, Ont. NOP 1WO (519/682-0803)
Tilbury North Twp	3,201	Essex		Essex North	R. Levesque, Clerk, Box 70, Stoney Point, Ont. NOR 1NO (519/798-3115)
Tilbury West Twp	1,627	Essex		Essex North	D.H. McMillan, Clerk, Box 158, Comber, Ont. NOP 1JO (519/687-2240)
Tillsonburg†	9,774	Oxford	Oxford	Oxford	K.E. Holland, Town Clerk, 200 Broadway, Tillsonburg, Ont. N4G 5A7 (519/842-6428)
TIMMINS	44,251	Cochrane D.	Timmins-Chapleau	Cochrane South	G.B. Chevrette, City Clerk, 220 Algonquin Blvd. E., Timmins, Ont. P4N 1B3 (705/264-1331)

Cities in CAPITALS; Towns marked †; Boroughs marked *; Villages marked •; Townships (Twp); ‡ means separated for municipal purposes from county; balance are either small places or unincorporated places (which have been named but not organized)

MUNICIPALITY	POP.	COUNTY OR DISTRICT	FEDERAL ELECTORAL DISTRICT	PROVINCIAL ELECTORAL DISTRICT	CLERK WITH ADDRESS AND PHONE
Tiny Twp	6,844	Simcoe	Simcoe North	Simcoe Centre	G.L. Maurice, Clerk, Perkinsfield, Ont. LOL 2JO (705/526-4204)
Tiverton•	879	Bruce	Bruce-Grey	Huron-Bruce	Mrs. J. Whelen, Village Clerk, Box 92, Tiverton, Ont. NOG 2TO (519/368-7860)
Toledo	176	Leeds & Grenville	Leeds-Grenville	Leeds	
TORONTO	630,487	Metro	Beaches; Broadview-Greenwood; Davenport; Don Valley West; Eglinton-Lawrence; Parkdale High Park; Rosedale; St. Pauls; Spadina; Trinity; York South-Weston	Armourdale; Beaches-Woodbine; Bellwoods; Dovercourt; Eglinton; High Park-Swansea; Parkdale; Riverdale; St. Andrew-St. Patrick; St. David; St. George	R.V. Henderson, City Clerk, City Hall, Toronto, Ont. M5H 2N2 (416/367-7020)
Torrance	210	Muskoka Dist. Mun.	Parry Sound-Muskoka	Muskoka	
Tory Hill	41	Haliburton	Victoria-Haliburton	Victoria-Haliburton	
Tosorontio Twp	3,296	Simcoe	Wellington-Dufferin-Simcoe	Dufferin-Simcoe	G. McCracken, Clerk, R.R. 3, Everett, Ont. LOM 1JO (705/435-5957)
Tottenham•	2,866	Simcoe	Simcoe South	Dufferin-Simcoe	D.W. Fleck, Village Clerk, 18 Queen St. N., Box 310, Tottenham, Ont. LOG 1WO (416/936-4208)
TRENTON	14,784	Hastings	Northumberland	Quinte	A. Sharp, City Clerk, Box 490, Trenton, Ont. K8V 5R6 (613/392-2841)
Trout Creek†	628	Parry Sound D.	Parry Sound-Muskoka	Parry Sound	Mrs. B. Young, Town Clerk, Main St. W., Trout Creek, Ont. POH 2LO (705/723-5253)
Tuckersmith Twp	3,189	Huron	Huron-Bruce	Huron-Middlesex	J. McLachlan, Clerk, R.R. 5, Clinton, Ont. NOM 1LO (519/482-9523)
Tudor & Cashel Twp	522	Hastings		Hastings-Peterborough	B. Baker, Clerk, R.R. 1, Gilmour, Ont. KOL 1WO (613/474-2927)
Tupperville	178	Kent	Kent	Chatham-Kent	
Turbine		Sudbury Reg. Mun.	Nickel Belt	Nickel Belt	Part of Walden
Turkey Point	369	Haldimand-Norfolk Reg. Mun.	Haldimand-Norfolk	Haldimand-Norfolk	
Turnberry Twp	1,497	Huron		Huron-Bruce	Mrs. D. Kelly, Clerk, Bluevale, Ont. NOG 1GO (519/335-3665)
Tweed•	1,632	Hastings	Prince Edward-Hastings	Hastings-Peterborough	H.J. Jones, Village Clerk, 25 Spring St. W., Tweed, Ont. KOK 3JO (613/478-2535)
Twin City	71	Thunder Bay D.	Thunder Bay-Atikokan	Fort William	
Tyendinaga Twp	2,522	Hastings	Prince Edward-Hastings	Hastings-Peterborough	W.J. Walsh, Clerk, R.R. 1, Marysville, Ont. KOK 2NO (613/968-5445)
Tyrone		Durham Reg. Mun.	Durham-Northumberland	Durham East	Part of Newcastle
Udney	43	Simcoe	Simcoe North	Simcoe East	
Umfreville	37	Kenora-Rainy River	Kenora		
Uno Park		Timiskaming D.	Timiskaming	Timiskaming	
Upsala	254	Thunder Bay D.	Thunder Bay-Nipigon	Lake Nipigon	
Usborne Twp	1,684	Huron	Huron-Bruce	Huron-Middlesex	H.H.G. Strang, Clerk, R.R. 3, Exeter, Ont. NOM 1SO (519/235-2228)
Utterson	184	Muskoka Dist. Mun.	Parry Sound-Muskoka	Muskoka	

Cities in CAPITALS; Towns marked †; Boroughs marked *; Villages marked •; Townships (Twp); ‡ means separated for municipal purposes from county; balance are either small places or unincorporated places (which have been named but not organized)

MUNICIPALITY	POP.	COUNTY OR DISTRICT	FEDERAL ELECTORAL DISTRICT	PROVINCIAL ELECTORAL DISTRICT	CLERK WITH ADDRESS AND PHONE
Uxbridge Twp	11,173	Durham Reg. Mun.		Durham York	W.E. Taylor, Clerk, 20 Bascom St., Uxbridge, Ont. LOC 1KO (416/852-3301)
Val Albert	2,018	Cochrane D.	Cochrane	Cochrane North	Part of Kapuskasing
Val Caron		Sudbury Reg. Mun.	Nickel Belt	Sudbury East	Part of Valley East
Val Gagné	316	Cochrane D.	Timiskaming	Cochrane South	
Valley East†	20,825	Sudbury Reg. Mun.	Nickel Belt	Sudbury East	E. Lelièvre, Valley East Town Clerk, 1679 Regional Rd. 15, Val Caron, Ont. POM 3AO (705/897-4938)
Val Rita	728	Cochrane D.	Cochrane	Cochrane North	
Vanessa	139	Haldimand-Norfolk Reg. Mun.	Haldimand-Norfolk	Brant-Oxford-Norfolk	
VANIER	18,510	Ottawa-Carleton Reg. Mun.	Ottawa-Vanier	Ottawa East	Ted Proulx, City Clerk, 297 Dupuis St., Vanier, Ont. K1L 7H8 (613/746-8105)
Vankleek Hill†	1,634	Prescott & Russell	Glengarry-Prescott-Russell	Prescott & Russell	G. Sauvé, Town Clerk, 11 Queen St., Vankleek Hill, Ont. KOB 1RO (613/678-2206)
Varna	70	Huron	Huron-Bruce	Huron-Middlesex	
Varney	87	Grey	Bruce-Grey	Grey	
Vars	564	Ottawa-Carleton Reg. Mun.	Glengarry-Prescott-Russell	Prescott & Russell	
Vaughan†	25,041	York Reg. Mun.	York North	York Centre; York North	F.G. Jackman, Vaughan Town Clerk, 2141 Major MacKenzie Dr., Maple, Ont. LOJ 1EO (416/832-2281)
Verner	1,055	Nipissing D.	Timiskaming	Nipissing	
Vernon	305	Ottawa-Carleton Reg. Mun.	Nepean-Carleton	Carleton-Grenville	
Verona	991	Frontenac	Hastings-Frontenac	Frontenac-Addington	
Verulam Twp	2,317	Victoria	Victoria-Haliburton	Victoria-Haliburton	Mrs. B. Meacham, Clerk, 21 Canal St. E., Bobcaygeon, Ont. KOM 1AO (705/738-2431)
Vespra Twp	5,607	Simcoe	Simcoe South	Simcoe Centre	J. Tofts, Clerk, Midhurst, Ont. LOL 1XO (705/728-4784)
Vickers Heights	963	Thunder Bay D.	Thunder Bay-Atikokan	Fort William	
Victoria		Peel Reg. Mun.	York-Peel	Wellington-Dufferin-Peel	Part of Caledon
Victoria Harbour•	1,146	Simcoe	Simcoe North	Simcoe East	Mrs. D. Thatcher, Village Clerk, Box 40, Victoria Harbour, Ont. LOK 2AO (705/534-3443)
Vienna•	380	Elgin	Elgin	Elgin	Mrs. V. Van Belois, Village Clerk, Box 160, Straffordville, Ont. NOJ 1YO (519/866-5521)
Vineland Station	1,082	Niagara Reg. Mun.	Lincoln	Lincoln	
Vinemount		Hamilton-Wentworth Reg. Mun.	Lincoln	Wentworth	Part of Stoney Creek
Virgil	574	Niagara Reg. Mun.	Niagara Falls	Brock	
Virginiatown	1,189	Timiskaming D.	Timiskaming	Timiskaming	
Vittoria	425	Haldimand-Norfolk Reg. Mun.	Haldimand-Norfolk	Haldimand-Norfolk	
Wabigoon	362	Kenora D.	Kenora-Rainy River	Rainy River	
Wahnapitae		Sudbury Reg. Mun.	Nickel Belt	Sudbury East	Part of Nickel Centre
Wainfleet Twp	6,054	Niagara Reg. Mun.	Erie	Erie	R.J. Heil, Clerk, Box 38, Wainfleet, Ont. LOS 1VO (416/899-3463)

Cities in CAPITALS; Towns marked †; Boroughs marked *; Villages marked •; Townships (Twp); ‡ means separated for municipal purposes from county; balance are either small places or unincorporated places (which have been named but not organized)

MUNICIPALITY	POP.	COUNTY OR DISTRICT	FEDERAL ELECTORAL DISTRICT	PROVINCIAL ELECTORAL DISTRICT	CLERK WITH ADDRESS AND PHONE
Waldemar	171	Dufferin	Wellington-Dufferin-Simcoe	Wellington-Dufferin-Peel	
Walden†	10,289	Sudbury Reg. Mun.	Nickel Belt	Nickel Belt	A.J. Sedunow, Walden Town Clerk, Box 910, Lively, Ont. POM 2EO (705/692-3613)
Waldhof	55	Kenora D.	Kenora-Rainy River	Kenora	
Walford Station	153	Algoma D.	Algoma	Algoma-Manitoulin	
Walkerton†	4,498	Bruce	Bruce-Grey	Grey-Bruce	B. Martin, Town Clerk, Box 68, Walkerton, Ont. NOG 2VO (519/881-2223)
Walkerville		Essex	Windsor-Walkerville	Windsor-Walkerville	Part of Windsor
Wallace Twp	2,425	Perth		Perth	M. Burns, Clerk, Gowanstown, Ont. NOG 1YO (519/291-2760)
Wallaceburg†	11,143	Kent	Kent	Chatham-Kent	S.W. Parsons, Town Clerk, 786 Dufferin Ave., Wallaceburg, Ont. N8A 2V3 (519/627-1603)
Wallenstein	116	Wellington		Wellington-Dufferin-Peel	
Walsh	121	Haldimand-Norfolk Reg. Mun.	Haldimand-Norfolk	Haldimand-Norfolk	
Walters Falls	157	Grey	Bruce-Grey	Grey	
Walton	108	Huron	Huron-Bruce	Huron-Bruce	
Wanapitei		Sudbury Reg. Mun.	Nickel Belt	Sudbury East	Part of Nickel Centre
Wanup	94	Sudbury D.	Nickel Belt	Sudbury East	
Wardsville•	428	Middlesex	Lambton-Middlesex	Middlesex	H.V. Turton, Village Clerk, Box 64, Wardsville, Ont. NOL 2NO (519/693-4962)
Warkworth	552	Northumberland	Northumberland	Northumberland	
Warren	612	Sudbury D.	Nickel Belt	Sudbury East	
Warsaw	245	Peterborough	Peterborough	Hastings-Peterborough	
Warwick Twp	2,528	Lambton	Lambton-Middlesex	Lambton	G.S. Herbert, Clerk, R.R. 6, Forest Ont. NON 1JO (519/873-5867)
Wasaga Beach†	4,519	Simcoe	Grey-Simcoe	Dufferin-Simcoe	E.R. Raynor, Town Clerk, Box 110, Wasaga Beach, Ont. LOL 2PO (705/429-3844)
Washago	442	Simcoe	Simcoe North	Simcoe East	
Waterford		Haldimand-Norfolk Reg. Mun.	Haldimand-Norfolk	Brant-Oxford-Norfolk	Part of Nanticoke
WATERLOO	54,157	Waterloo Reg. Mun.	Waterloo	Waterloo North	R.C. Keeling, City Clerk, City Hall, 20 Erb St. W., Waterloo, Ont. N2J 4A8 (519/886-1550)
Watford•	1,413	Lambton	Lambton-Middlesex	Lambton	L. Barnes, Village Clerk, 318 Main St., Watford, Ont. NOM 2SO (519/876-2913)
Waubamik	35	Parry Sound D.	Parry Sound-Muskoka	Parry Sound	
Waubaushene	820	Simcoe	Simcoe North	Simcoe East	
Wawa	4,272	Algoma D.	Timmins-Chapleau	Algoma	
Webbwood†	511	Sudbury D.	Algoma	Algoma-Manitoulin	Mrs. J. Van Norman, Town Clerk, Box 9, Webbwood, Ont. POP 2GO (705/869-3861)
WELLAND	45,261	Niagara Reg. Mun.	Welland	Welland	D.G. Barrett, City Clerk, City Hall, 411 Main St. E., Welland, Ont. L3B 3X4 (416/735-1700)
Wellandport	209	Niagara Reg. Mun.	Erie	Lincoln	
Weller Park	862	Niagara Reg. Mun.	St. Catharines		

Cities in CAPITALS; Towns marked †; Boroughs marked *; Villages marked •; Townships (Twp); ‡ means separated for municipal purposes from county; balance are either small places or unincorporated places (which have been named but not organized)

MUNICIPALITY	POP.	COUNTY OR DISTRICT	FEDERAL ELECTORAL DISTRICT	PROVINCIAL ELECTORAL DISTRICT	CLERK WITH ADDRESS AND PHONE
Wellesley Twp	6,531	Waterloo Reg. Mun.	Waterloo	Waterloo North	S. Ludington, Clerk, Box 40, Linwood, Ont. NOB 2AO (519/699-4611)
Wellington•	1,055	Prince Edward	Prince Edward-Hastings	Prince Edward-Lennox	D. Marvin, Village Clerk, 261 Main St., Wellington, Ont. KOK 3LO (613/399-3424)
Wendover	362	Prescott & Russell	Glengarry-Prescott-Russell	Prescott & Russell	
West Carleton Twp	9,541	Ottawa-Carleton Reg. Mun.	Lanark-Renfrew-Carleton	Renfrew South	M.J. McLaren, Clerk, Box 410, Carp, Ont. KOA 1LO (613/832-3050)
West Garafraxa Twp	2,256	Wellington	Wellington-Dufferin-Simcoe	Wellington-Dufferin-Peel	Mrs. D.C. Rooney, Clerk, Belwood, Ont. NOB 1JO (519/843-2259)
West Gwillimbury Twp	4,055	Simcoe		Simcoe Centre	D.G.J. Wood, Clerk, Box 69, Bradford, Ont. LOG 1CO (416/775-2372)
West Hawkesbury Twp	2,528	Prescott & Russell	Glengarry-Prescott-Russell	Prescott & Russell	G. Lepage, Clerk, Box 39, Vankleek Hill, Ont. KOB 1RO (613/678-3003)
West Lincoln Twp	9,708	Niagara Reg. Mun.	Erie	Lincoln	J.G. Killins, Clerk, Box 400, Smithville, Ont. LOR 2AO (416/957-3346)
West Lorne•	1,256	Elgin	Elgin	Kent-Elgin	H.C.H. Ouwehand, Village Clerk, 168 Main St., Box 309, West Lorne, Ont. NOL 2PO (519/768-1234)
West Luther Twp	1,040	Wellington		Wellington-Dufferin-Peel	G.H. Duncan, Clerk, R.R. 4, Kenilworth, Ont. NOG 2EO (519/848-3497)
Westmeath Twp	1,994	Renfrew	Renfrew-Nipissing-Pembroke	Renfrew South	D.A. Hill, Clerk, R.R. 3, Cobden, Ont. KOJ 1KO (613/646-7861)
Westminster Twp	6,267	Middlesex	London-Middlesex	Middlesex	R.M. Malpass, Clerk, 765 Exeter Rd. London, Ont. N6E 1L3 (519/681-1300)
West Nissouri Twp	3,396	Middlesex	London-Middlesex	Middlesex	B. Parsons, Clerk, 184 King St., Thorndale, Ont. NOM 2PO (519/461-0750)
Westport•	686	Leeds & Grenville	Leeds-Grenville	Leeds	R.B. Kane, Village Clerk, Box 68, Westport, Ont. KOG 1XO (613/273-2191)
Westree	92	Sudbury D.	Timmins-Chapleau	Nickel Belt	
West Wawanosh Twp	1,366	Huron	Huron-Bruce	Huron-Bruce	Mrs. J.C. Armstrong, Clerk, R.R. 2, Lucknow, Ont. NOG 2HO (519/528-2903)
West Williams Twp	963	Middlesex	Lambton-Middlesex	Huron-Middlesex	J.A. Duncan, Clerk, R.R. 2, Parkhill, Ont. NOM 2KO (519/294-0001)
Wheatley•	1,600	Kent	Essex-Kent	Essex South	T. Jackson, Village Clerk, 171 Erie St. N., Box 530, Wheatley, Ont. NOP 2PO (519/825-4819)
Whitby†	35,359	Durham Reg. Mun.	Ontario	Durham West	D. McKay, Town Clerk, 575 Rossland Rd. E., Whitby, Ont. L1N 2M8 (416/668-5803)
Whitchurch-Stouffville†	13,415	York Reg. Mun.	York-Peel	York North	Mrs. P. Muir, Town Clerk, Box 419, Stouffville, Ont. LOH 1LO (416/640-1900)
Whitechurch	134	Bruce	Huron-Bruce	Huron-Bruce	
White Fish		Sudbury Reg. Mun.	Nickel Belt	Nickel Belt	Part of Walden
Whitefish Falls	161	Sudbury D.	Algoma	Algoma-Manitoulin	
White Lake	191	Renfrew	Lanark-Renfrew-Carleton	Renfrew South	
White River Twp.	1,077	Algoma D.	Cochrane	Algoma	L. Peebles, Clerk, Box 307, White River, Ont. P0M 3G0 (807/822-2450)

Cities in CAPITALS; Towns marked †; Boroughs marked *; Villages marked •; Townships (Twp); ‡ means separated for municipal purposes from county; balance are either small places or unincorporated places (which have been named but not organized)

MUNICIPALITY	POP.	COUNTY OR DISTRICT	FEDERAL ELECTORAL DISTRICT	PROVINCIAL ELECTORAL DISTRICT	CLERK WITH ADDRESS AND PHONE
Whitney	767	Nipissing D.	Renfrew-Nipissing-Pembroke	Renfrew North	
Wiarton†	2,060	Bruce	Bruce-Grey	Grey-Bruce	R.J. Kastner, Town Clerk, 542 Berford St., Box 310, Wiarton, Ont. NOH 2TO (519/534-1400)
Wicksteed Twp	1,619	Algoma D.	Cochrane	Algoma	B. Brouillard, Clerk, 68 Front St., Hornepayne, Ont. POM 1ZO (807/868-2020)
Wilberforce Twp	1,424	Renfrew	Renfrew-Nipissing-Pembroke	Renfrew South	Mrs. B. Thur, Clerk, R.R. 1, Golden Lake, Ont. KOJ 1XO (613/628-3084)
Wilberforce	266	Haliburton	Victoria-Haliburton	Victoria-Haliburton	
Wilcox Lake	1,377	York Reg. Mun.	York-Peel		
Williamsburg Twp	3,063	Stormont, Dundas & Glengarry	Stormont-Dundas	Stormont, Dundas & Glengarry	K. Schell, Clerk, Box 83, Williamsburg, Ont. KOC 2HO (613/535-2673)
Williamsford	264	Grey	Bruce-Grey	Grey	
Williamstown	336	Stormont, Dundas & Glengarry	Stormont-Dundas	Stormont, Dundas & Glengarry	
Willisville	107	Sudbury D.	Algoma	Algoma-Manitoulin	
Willow Beach	385	York Reg. Mun.	Victoria-Haliburton	Durham York	
Willow Cove	224	Hamilton-Wentworth Reg. Mun.	Burlington	Burlington South	
Willowdale		Metro	Willowdale		Part of Metro Toronto
Wilmot Twp	10,731	Waterloo Reg. Mun.		Kitchener-Wilmot	G. Swartzentruber, Clerk, 121 Huron St., New Hamburg, Ont. NOB 2GO (519/662-1613)
Wilno	164	Renfrew	Renfrew-Nipissing-Pembroke	Renfrew South	
Wilsonville		Haldimand-Norfolk Reg. Mun.	Haldimand-Norfolk	Brant-Oxford-Norfolk	Part of Nanticoke
Winchester Twp	2,958	Stormont, Dundas & Glengarry	Stormont-Dundas	Stormont, Dundas & Glengarry	G. MacGregor, Clerk, Box 40, Morewood, Ont. KOA 2RO (613/448-2772)
Winchester•	1,866	Stormont, Dundas & Glengarry	Stormont-Dundas	Stormont, Dundas & Glengarry	R.W. Annable, Village Clerk, 547 St. Lawrence St., Winchester, Ont. KOC 2KO (613/774-2105)
Windham Centre	130	Haldimand-Norfolk Reg. Mun.	Haldimand-Norfolk	Brant-Oxford-Norfolk	
WINDSOR	198,722	Essex	Essex-Windsor; Windsor-Walkerville; Windsor West	Windsor Riverside; Windsor Sandwich; Windsor-Walkerville	J.B. Adamac, City Clerk, 205 University Ave. E., Windsor, Ont. N9A 6S1 (519/255-6215)
Wingham†	2,891	Huron	Huron-Bruce	Huron-Bruce	J.B. Adams, Town Clerk, 274 Josephine St., Box 90, Wingham, Ont. NOG 2WO (519/357-3550)
Winona		Hamilton-Wentworth Reg. Mun.	Lincoln	Wentworth	Part of Stoney Creek
Winterbourne	322	Waterloo Reg. Mun.	Waterloo	Waterloo North	
Wolfe Is. Twp	1,075	Frontenac	Kingston & the Islands	Kingston & the Islands	Mrs. M. Bennett, Clerk, Box 130, Wolfe Island, Ont. KOH 2YO (613/385-2216)
Wolford Twp	1,225	Leeds & Grenville		Carleton-Grenville	Mrs. M.R. Bates, Clerk, Box 1, R.R. 3, Jasper, Ont. K0G 1G0 (613/283-8683)
Wollaston Twp	636	Hastings	Hastings-Frontenac	Hastings-Peterborough	Mrs. B. Wilson, Clerk, Box 99, Coe Hill, Ont. KOL 1PO (613/337-5731)
Wolverton	102	Oxford	Oxford	Brant-Oxford-Norfolk	

Cities in CAPITALS; Towns marked †; Boroughs marked *; Villages marked •; Townships (Twp); ‡ means separated for municipal purposes from county; balance are either small places or unincorporated places (which have been named but not organized)

MUNICIPALITY	POP.	COUNTY OR DISTRICT	FEDERAL ELECTORAL DISTRICT	PROVINCIAL ELECTORAL DISTRICT	CLERK WITH ADDRESS AND PHONE
Woodbridge		York Reg. Mun.	York North	York North	Part of Vaughan
Woodham	100	Perth	Perth	Perth	
Woodslee	233	Essex	Essex-Windsor	Essex North	
WOODSTOCK	26,363	Oxford	Oxford	Oxford	K. Miller, City Clerk, 500 Dundas St., Box 40, Woodstock, Ont. N4S 1C4 (519/539-1291)
Woodville•	569	Victoria	Victoria-Haliburton	Victoria-Haliburton	Mrs. K. Archer, Village Clerk, Box 9, Woodville, Ont. KOM 2TO (705/439-2505)
Wooler	190	Northumberland	Northumberland	Northumberland	
Woolwich Twp	16,197	Waterloo Reg. Mun.		Waterloo North	J. Current, Clerk, 69 Arthur St. S., Elmira, Ont. N3B 2M8 (519/669-5193)
Worthington Twp	194	Rainy River D.	Kenora-Rainy River	Rainy River	J.F. Trenchard, Clerk, Box 34, Sleeman, Ont. POW 1MO (807/852-3907)
Worthington		Sudbury Reg. Mun.	Nickel Belt	Nickel Belt	Part of Walden
Wroxeter	287	Huron	Huron-Bruce	Huron-Bruce	Part of Howick Twp.
Wyebridge	184	Simcoe	Simcoe North	Simcoe Centre	
Wyevale	257	Simcoe	Simcoe North	Simcoe Centre	
Wyoming•	1,549	Lambton	Lambton-Middlesex	Lambton	Mrs. C. De Schutter, Village Clerk, 623 Broadway St., Wyoming, Ont. NON 1TO (519/845-3351)
Yarker	365	Lennox & Addington	Hastings-Frontenac	Frontenac-Addington	
Yarmouth Twp	8,612	Elgin		Elgin	K.G. Sloan, Clerk, 1229 Talbot St., St. Thomas, Ont. N5P 1G8 (519/631-4860)
Yarmouth Centre	47	Elgin	Elgin	Elgin	
Ycliff	9	Kenora D.	Kenora-Rainy River	Kenora	
Yonge Twp, Front of	1,842	Leeds & Grenville	Leeds-Grenville	Leeds	Mrs. W. Ormiston, Clerk, Box 130, Mallorytown, Ont. KOE 1RO (613/923-5091)
Yonge & Escott Twp, Rear of	1,215	Leeds & Grenville		Leeds	Mrs. E. Carley, Clerk, Box 189, Athens, Ont. KOE 1BO (613/924-9049)
York*	132,915	Metro	Eglinton-Lawrence; York South-Weston; York West	Oakwood; York South	C. Rodrigo, Borough Clerk, 2700 Eglinton Ave. W., (York), Toronto, Ont. M6M 1V1 (416/653-2700)
Zephyr	201	Durham Reg. Mun.	Ontario	Durham York	
Zone Twp	1,190	Kent		Kent-Elgin	W. Revell, Clerk, R.R. 3, Bothwell, Ont. NOP 1CO (519/695-2307)
Zorra Twp	8,408	Oxford	Oxford	Oxford	W. Johnson, Clerk, Box 306, Ingersoll, Ont. N5C 3K5 (519/485-2490)
Zurich•	779	Huron	Huron-Bruce	Huron-Middlesex	Sharon Baker, Village Clerk, Box 280, Zurich, Ont. NOM 2TO (519/236-4974)

COUNTY & REGIONAL DISTRICT CLERKS, ONTARIO

County or District: Clerk and address (District Town):

Algoma D.: Sault Ste. Marie
Brant County: Dan Ciona, Clerk, Court House, Brantford, Ont. N3T 2L9 (519/752-1153)
Bruce County: C.F. Buckingham, Clerk, 215 Cayley St., Box 70, Walkerton, Ont. NOG 2VO (519/881-1291)
Cochrane D.: Cochrane
Dufferin County: H.W. Baker, Clerk, 51 Zina St., Orangeville, Ont. L9W 1E5 (519/941-2816)
Durham Reg. Mun.: C.W. Lundy, Clerk, 605 Rossland Rd. E., Whitby, Ont. L1N 6A3 (416/668-7711)
Elgin County: G. Leverton, Clerk, 9 Gladstone Ave., St. Thomas, Ont. N5R 2L3 (519/631-1460)
Essex County: P. Cramp, Clerk, 360 Fairview Ave. W., Essex, Ont. N8M 1Y6 (519/776-6441)
Frontenac County: J.E. Taylor, Clerk, Court House, Kingston, Ont. K7L 2N4 (613/548-4202)
Grey County: Mrs. M. Henderson, County Bldg., 595 9th Ave. E., Owen Sound, Ont. N4K 3E3 (519/376-2205)
Haldimand-Norfolk Reg. Mun.: Mrs. M.L. Johnston, Clerk, County Bldg., Box 2002, Cayuga, Ont. NOA 1EO (416/772-3337)

Haliburton County: Mrs. W. Lahay, Clerk, Box 399, Minden, Ont. KOM 2KO (705/286-1111)
Halton Reg. Mun.: G. Brown, Clerk, 1151 Bronte Rd., Box 7000, Oakville, Ont. L6J 6E1 (416/827-2151)
Hamilton-Wentworth Reg. Mun.: Mrs. J. Gallipeau, Clerk, 100 Main St. E., Box 910, Hamilton, Ont. L8N 3V9 (416/526-4154)
Hastings County: C.E. Bateman, Clerk, County Bldg., Pinnacle St., Belleville, Ont. K8N 3A9 (613/966-1311)
Huron County: B.G. Hanly, Clerk, Court House, Goderich, Ont. N7A 1M2 (519/524-8394)
Kenora D.: Kenora
Kent County: R.H. Foulds, Clerk, 435 Grand Ave. W., Box 1230, Chatham, Ont. N7M 5L8 (519/351-1010)
Lambton County: W.C. McRorie, Clerk, Box 3000, Wyoming, Ont. N0N 1T0 (519/845-3303)
Lanark County: K.I. Coulthart, Clerk, 43 Drummond St. E., Perth, Ont. K7H 1G1 (613/267-4011)
Leeds & Grenville County: G. Brown, Clerk, Box 729, Brockville, Ont. K6V 5V8 (613/342-3840)
Lennox & Addington County: D.J. Perry, Clerk, 97 Thomas St. E., Box 160, Napanee, Ont. K7R 3M3 (613/354-4883)
Manitoulin D.: Gore Bay
Middlesex County: R.E. Eddy, Clerk, 399 Ridout St. N., London, Ont. N6A 2P1 (519/434-7321)
Muskoka Dist. Mun.: G.G. Williams, Clerk, Box 1720, Bracebridge, Ont. POB 1CO (705/645-2231)
Niagara Reg. Mun.: W.J. Dawson, Clerk, 150 Berryman St., Box 3025, St. Catharines, Ont. L2R 7E9 (416/685-1571)
Nipissing D.: North Bay
Northumberland County: K.J. Symons, Clerk, 860 William St., Cobourg, Ont. K9A 3A9 (416/372-5322)
Ottawa-Carleton Reg. Mun.: W.H. Brunette, Clerk, 222 Queen St., Ottawa, Ont. K1P 5Z3 (613/563-2622)
Oxford County: J.H. Walls, Clerk, Court House, Box 397, Woodstock, Ont. N4S 7Y3 (519/539-5688)
Parry Sound D.: Parry Sound
Peel Reg. Mun.: L.E. Button, Clerk, 10 Peel Centre Dr., Brampton, Ont. L6T 4B9 (416/457-9400)
Perth County: J.A. Bell, Clerk, Court House, 1 Huron St., Stratford, Ont. N5A 5S4 (519/271-0531)
Peterborough County: W.D. Armstrong, Clerk, County Court House, Peterborough, Ont. K9H 3M3 (705/743-0380)
Prescott & Russell County: R. Ouimet, Clerk, Box 304, L'Orignal, Ont. KOB 1KO (613/675-4661)
Prince Edward County: T.S. Walker, Clerk, 332 Main St., Picton, Ont. KOK 2TO (613/476-2148)
Rainy River D.: Fort Frances
Renfrew County: E.M. Fraser, Clerk, 169 William St., Pembroke, Ont. K8A 1N7 (613/735-0128)
Simcoe County: A. Pelletier, Clerk, Admin. Centre, Midhurst, Ont. LOL 1XO (705/726-9300)
Stormont, Dundas & Glengarry County: R.J. Lapointe, Clerk, 20 Pitt St., Box 698, Cornwall, Ont. K6H 5T5 (613/932-4302)
Sudbury Reg. Mun.: P. Philion, Clerk, 200 Brady St., Box 370, Sudbury, Ont. P3E 4P2 (705/673-2171)
Sudbury D.: Espanola
Thunder Bay D.: Thunder Bay
Timiskaming D.: Haileybury
Mun. of Metropolitan Toronto: W.J. Lotto, Clerk, City Hall, Toronto, Ont. M5H 2N1 (416/367-9111)
Victoria County: C. McKay, Clerk, Court House, Box 419, Lindsay, Ont. K9V 3R9 (705/324-9411)
Waterloo Reg. Mun.: Mrs. E. Luhowy, Clerk, 8th floor, 20 Erb St. W., Waterloo, Ont. N2J 4A8 (519/885-9400)
Wellington County: Mrs. V.B. Myers, Clerk, 74 Woolwich St., Guelph, Ont. N1H 3T9 (519/822-1041)
York Reg. Mun.: R.N. Vernon, Clerk, 62 Bayview Ave., Box 147, Newmarket, Ont. L3Y 3W3 (416/895-1231; Toronto line: 382-2464)

PRINCE EDWARD ISLAND

Enabling legislation in P.E.I. includes: the City of Charlottetown Incorporation Act, the Town of Summerside Incorporation Act, the Town Act, the Village Service Act, and the Community Improvement Act. There are no population considerations for incorporation of a municipality, except that a village must have a minimum of 100 persons.

Dates of Municipal Elections:
Charlottetown: 1st Monday in November every second year.
Summerside: Last Tuesday in February, every year (term of office 2 years).
Towns: 1st Monday of November every second year.
Villages: Elections are held at the annual residents' meeting in February of each year (term of office 3 years).

Cities in CAPITALS; Towns marked †; Balance are Villages.
Area Code for Prince Edward Island is 902

MUNICIPALITY	POP.	FEDERAL ELECTORAL DISTRICT	PROVINCIAL ELECTORAL DISTRICT	CLERK WITH ADDRESS & PHONE
Abram's Village	317	Egmont		D. Arsenault, Abram's Village Clerk, Wellington Station R.R. 3, P.E.I. COB 2EO (854-2501)
Alberton†	1,065	Egmont	Prince First	Miss M.A. Forsyth, Town Clerk, Alberton, P.E.I. COB 1BO (853-2720)
Bedeque	148	Malpeque	Prince Fourth	Clara Lockhart, Village Clerk, Bedeque, P.E.I. COB 1CO (887-2244)
Borden†	589	Malpeque	Prince Fourth	F. Leard, Town Clerk, Box 22, Borden, P.E.I. COB 1XO (855-2225)
Bunbury	980	Cardigan	Queen's Third	Doris McDearmid, Bunbury Village Clerk, Box 1117, Charlottetown, P.E.I. C1A 7M8 (569-4217)
Cardigan	290	Cardigan	Kings Third	Kay Gardiner, Village Clerk, Cardigan, P.E.I. COA 1GO (583-2198)
Central Bedeque	193	Malpeque	Prince Fourth	Ms. Joan Linkletter, Central Bedeque Village Clerk, Summerside R.R. 3, P.E.I. C1N 4J9 (887-2978)

Cities in CAPITALS; Towns marked †; Balance are Villages.
Area Code for Prince Edward Island is 902

MUNICIPALITY	POP.	FEDERAL ELECTORAL DISTRICT	PROVINCIAL ELECTORAL DISTRICT	CLERK WITH ADDRESS & PHONE
CHARLOTTETOWN	17,063	Hillsborough	Queens Sixth	J.J. Butler, City Adm., Box 98, Charlottetown, P.E.I. C1A 7K2 (894-5552)
Cornwall	1,745	Malpeque	Queens Second	Richard Montigny, Village Clerk, Box 183, Cornwall, P.E.I. COA 1HO (675-2354)
Crapaud	321	Malpeque	Queens First	G.C. McLure, Village Clerk, Crapaud, P.E.I. COA 1JO (658-2188)
East Royalty	1,850	Hillsborough		Ms. Nadine Robb, East Royalty Village Clerk, Box 1786, Charlottetown, P.E.I. C1A 7N4 (892-4767)
Georgetown†	767	Cardigan	Kings Fifth	A.E. Hobbs, Town Clerk, Box 89, Georgetown, P.E.I. COA 1LO (652-2924)
Hillsborough Park	1,075			Mrs. N.B. Coughlin, Hillsborough Park Village Clerk, c/o Box 788, Charlottetown, P.E.I. C1A 7L9 (892-8628)
Hunter River	331	Malpeque	Queens Second	D. Nantes, Village Clerk, Hunter River, P.E.I. COA 1NO (964-2417)
Kensington†	1,150	Malpeque	Prince Fourth	Mrs. T.J. Stewart, Town Clerk, Box 315, Kensington, P.E.I. (836-3781)
Kinkora	327	Malpeque	Prince Fourth	D. Kirby, Village Clerk, Box 38, Kinkora, P.E.I. COB 1NO (887-2800)
Miminegash	417	Egmont	Prince First	Betty Gallant, Village Clerk, Miminegash, P.E.I. COB 1SO (882-2181)
Miscouche	792	Egmont	Prince Third	Mrs. M. Gallant, Village Clerk, Box 111, Miscouche, P.E.I. COB 1TO (436-9670)
Montague†	1,827	Cardigan	Kings Fourth	Mrs. M. Johnston, Town Clerk, Box 324, Montague, P.E.I. COA 1RO (838-2528)
Morell	350	Cardigan	Kings Second	F. MacKinnon, Village Clerk, Box 72, Morell, P.E.I. COA 1SO (961-2267)
Mount Stewart	368	Cardigan	Queens Third	Mrs. M.M. Affleck, Village Clerk, Box 143, Mount Stewart, P.E.I. COA 1TO (676-2536)
Murray Harbour	419	Cardigan	Kings Fourth	Mrs. S. Reynolds, Village Clerk, Box 34, Murray Harbour, P.E.I. COA 1VO (962-2615)
Murray River	523	Cardigan	Kings Fourth	Mrs. D. White, Village Clerk, Murray River, P.E.I. COA 1WO (962-2633)
North Rustico	705	Malpeque	Queens Second	Mrs. B. Gallant, Village Clerk, Box 38, North Rustico, P.E.I. COA 1XO (963-2414)
O'Leary	805	Egmont	Prince First	Beverley Coughlin, Village Clerk, Box 130, O'Leary, P.E.I. COB 1VO (859-3311)
Parkdale†	2,172	Hillsborough		A. Llewellyn, Parkdale Town Manager, 20 Linden Ave., Charlottetown, P.E.I. C1A 5Y8 (894-8755)
St. Eleanors	2,495	Egmont	Prince Fourth	Mrs. Betty Pinkham, St. Eleanors Village Clerk, 1 West Dr., Summerside, P.E.I. C1N 4E5 (436-2782)
St. Louis	166	Egmont	Prince First	Mrs. H. McKenna, Village Clerk, St. Louis, P.E.I. COB 1ZO (882-2411)
St. Peters Bay	370	Cardigan		Mrs. Ruth McKenzie, Village Clerk, Box 63, St. Peters Bay, P.E.I. COA 2AO (961-2307)
Sherwood	5,602	Hillsborough		J. Paquet, Sherwood Village Administrator, 31 Gordon Dr., Charlottetown, P.E.I. C1A 6B8 (894-5041)
Souris†	1,468	Cardigan	Kings First	Mrs. M. Ehler, Town Clerk, 75 Main St., Souris, P.E.I. COA 2BO (687-2157)
Southport	1,268	Cardigan	Queens Third	Carol Lowther, Southport Village Clerk, 5 Glendale Cres., Charlottetown R.R. 1, P.E.I. C1A 7J6
Summerside†	8,532	Egmont	Prince Third	N.G. Johnston, Town Clerk, Box 1510, Summerside, P.E.I. C1N 4K4 (436-4222)
Tignish	1,077	Egmont	Prince First	Mrs. K. Buote, Village Clerk, Box 57, Tignish, P.E.I. COB 2BO (882-2600)
Tyne Valley	164	Egmont	Prince Second	Marie Barlow, Village Clerk, Tyne Valley, P.E.I. COB 2CO (831-2938)
Victoria	210	Malpeque	Queens First	Mrs. K. MacVittie, Village Clerk, Victoria, P.E.I. COA 2GO (658-2085)
Wellington	359	Egmont	Prince Third	Diane Arsenault, Village Clerk, Wellington Station, P.E.I. COB 2EO (854-2849)

Cities in CAPITALS; Towns marked †; Balance are Villages.
Area Code for Prince Edward Island is 902

MUNICIPALITY	POP.	FEDERAL ELECTORAL DISTRICT	PROVINCIAL ELECTORAL DISTRICT	CLERK WITH ADDRESS & PHONE
West Royalty				Bob Hamilton, West Royalty Village Clerk, c/o Box 365, Charlottetown, P.E.I. C1A 7K7
Wilmot	1,637	Malpeque	Kings Fourth	E. Huestis, Wilmot Village Clerk, c/o Box 154, Summerside, P.E.I. C1N 4P6

MUNICIPALITIES IN QUEBEC

(Source: in part, the 1980 Municipal Directory, Bureau de la Statistique du Quebec).

The following notes are intended to help the reader to understand the concepts regarding municipal and territorial groupings in the Province of Quebec.

A. Municipality

definition: The word municipality indicates an organized territory. In referring to a group of residents of an organized territory, the law uses the word "Corporation". The two words "municipality" and "corporation" have been used since 1840.

Quebec municipalities are governed by a special charter, or by the Cities & Towns Act, or by the Municipal Code. By virtue of the B.N.A. Act all the power of each municipality depends on the Government of the Province.

Each municipality is administered by a board including a Mayor and generally six councillors who are elected every two or three years in the small municipalities ruled by the Municipal Code, and every four years in the cities and towns.

Types of municipalities in Quebec are Metropolitan Regions, Cities, Towns, Villages, Parishes, Districts, United Districts, Not Designated, and Indian Reserves. There are also over 100 unorganized areas, and Mining towns and villages. In general, organized municipalities in Quebec are defined by permanent population on a scale as follows: Metropolitan Region: 100,000 or more in a built-up area; Agglomeration: 2,000 to 100,000 in a built-up area; Cities: 6,000 or more; Towns: 2,000 or more.

B. County Municipalities

The County municipality has a board of directors and looks after the general interest of the whole municipal county. The municipal county includes all the municipalities administered under the Municipal Code and the unorganized territories within the area.

Members of the Board of Directors include the Mayors of all the local municipalities ruled by the Municipal Code. The President is elected by the members. The County municipalities can impose taxes directly.

C. Urban and Regional Communities

Since 1969 there has been a new type of decentralized administration: the urban and regional community. To the present time, only part of the Province is so governed and there are three areas in full operation.

Cities in CAPITALS (Ville); Towns/Villes marked (Ville); Villages marked (Village); Townships/Cantons (marked Canton); United townships/Cantons unis (marked Cantons*); Parishes marked (Paroisse); undesignated municipalities/sans designation marked (Mun.).

MUNICIPALITY	POP.	COUNTY	FEDERAL ELECTORAL DISTRICT	PROVINCIAL ELECTORAL DISTRICT	CLERK/GREFFIER OR SECRETARY-TREASURER (SEC) WITH ADDRESS & PHONE
Abercorn (Village)	320	Brome	Missisquoi	Brome-Missisquoi	C. Daignault, Sec., C.P. 29, Abercorn, P.Q. JOE 1BO (514/538-2046)
Acton Vale (Ville)	4,234	Bagot	St-Hyacinthe	Johnson	F. Ménard, Sec., C.P. 640, Acton Vale, P.Q. JOH 1AO (514/546-2704)
Adamsville (Mun.)	1,596	Brome	Missisquoi	Brome-Missisquoi	J. Giroux, Sec., a/s 281 ave des Erables, Brigham, P.Q. JOE 1CO (514/263-5942)
Aguanish (Mun.)	532	Saguenay	Manicouagan	Duplessis	Mme C. Blais, Sec., Aguanish, P.Q. GOG 1AO (418/533-2323)
Albanel (Canton)	1,065	Lac-St-Jean-Ouest	Roberval	Roberval	C. Marcil, Sec., C.P. 69, Albanel, P.Q. GOW 1AO (418/279-5250)
Albanel (Village)	892	Lac-St-Jean-Ouest	Roberval	Roberval	J. Plourde, Sec., Albanel, P.Q. GOW 1AO (418/279-5551)
Alleyn & Cawood (Cantons)*	148	Pontiac		Gatineau	Mrs. L. Hodgins, Sec., Danford Lake, P.Q. JOX 1PO (819/467-5343)
ALMA (Ville)	25,700	Lac-St-Jean-Est	Lac-St-Jean	Lac-St-Jean	R. Fortin, Greffier, Hôtel de Ville, 140 St-Joseph-Sud, Alma, P.Q. G8B 3R1 (418/662-6501)
Amherst (Canton)	566	Papineau		Papineau	Mme H. Lévesque, Sec., St-Rémi-d'Amherst PO, P.Q. JOT 2LO (819/687-3355)
Amos (Ville)	9,213	Abitibi	Abitibi	Abitibi Ouest	J.-G. Racicot, Greffier, Hôtel de ville, 182 1re rue est, Amos, P.Q. J9T 2G1 (819/732-5218)

Cities in CAPITALS (Ville); Towns/Villes marked (Ville); Villages marked (Village); Townships/Cantons (marked Canton); United townships/Cantons unis (marked Cantons*); Parishes marked (Paroisse); undesignated municipalities/sans designation marked (Mun.).

MUNICIPALITY	POP.	COUNTY	FEDERAL ELECTORAL DISTRICT	PROVINCIAL ELECTORAL DISTRICT	CLERK/GREFFIER OR SECRETARY-TREASURER (SEC) WITH ADDRESS & PHONE
Amos-Est (Mun.)	2,610	Abitibi	Abitibi	Abitibi Ouest	G. Lecours, Sec., 414 3e Ave. est, Amos-Est, P.Q. J9T 2G1 (819/732-8304)
Amqui (Ville)	3,949	Matapédia	Matapédia-Matane	Matapédia	F. Duranleau, Sec., C.P. 784, Amqui, P.Q. GOJ 1BO (418/629-4242)
Ancienne-Lorrette (Ville)	14,500	Québec	Louis-Hébert	La Peltrie	A. Bouchard, Greffier, C.P. 158, Ancienne-Lorette, P.Q. G2E 3J5 (418/872-9811)
Andréville (Village)	395	Kamouraska	Kamouraska-Rivière-du-Loup	Kamouraska-Témiscouata	Lise Desjardins, Sec., a/s St-André-de-Kamouraska, P.Q. GOL 2HO (418/493-2085)
Ange-Gardien (Village)	502	Rouville	Shefford	Iberville	J.-M. Marchand, Sec., C.P. 120, Ange-Gardien-de-Rouville, P.Q. JOE 1EO (514/293-7575)
Angliers (Village)	293	Témicamingue	Témiscamingue	Rouyn-Noranda-Témiscamingue	B. Peluso, Sec., C.P. 9, Angliers, P.Q. JOZ 1AO (819/949-4351)
Anjou (Ville)	36,500	Ile-de-Montréal	St-Léonard-Anjou	Anjou	L. Maltais, Greffier, 7701 Louis-H. Lafontaine, Anjou, P.Q. H1K 4B9 (514/352-4440)
Annaville (Village)	598	Nicolet	Richelieu	Nicolet	C. St. Bouchard, Sec., a/s St-Célestin, P.Q. JOC 1GO (819/229-3642)
Armagh (Village)	973	Bellechasse	Bellechasse	Bellechasse	G. Roy, Sec., Armagh, P.Q. GOR 1AO (418/466-2844)
Arntfield (Mun.)				Rouyn-Noranda-Témiscamingue	
Arthabaska (Ville)	6,300	Arthabaska	Lotbinière	Arthabaska	C. Aubert, Greffier, 841 boul. Bois-Francs sud, Arthabaska, P.Q. G6P 5W3 (819/357-2346)
Arundel (Canton)	495	Argenteuil		Argenteuil	Bernice Graham, Sec., C.P. 40, Arundel, P.Q. JOT 1AO (819/687-3991)
Asbestos (Ville)	8,600	Richmond	Richmond	Richmond	Serge Charland, Greffier, C.P. 88, Asbestos, P.Q. J1T 3M9 (819/879-7171)
Ascot (Canton)	8,100	Sherbrooke		St-François	A. Drouin, Sec., C.P. 268, Lennoxville, P.Q. J1M 1Z5 (819/563-3993)
Ascot Corner (Mun.)	1,939	Sherbrooke	Mégantic-Compton-Stanstead	St-François	Mme S. Jacques, Sec., C.P. 29, Ascot Corner, P.Q. JOB 1AO (819/569-6515)
Aston-Jonction (Village)	253	Nicolet	Lotbinière	Nicolet	Th. Leblanc, Sec., C.P. 27, Aston-Jonction, P.Q. GOZ 1AO (819/226-3302)
Aubert-Gallion (Mun.)	982	Beauce		Beauce-Sud	R. Poulin, Sec., a/s 820 20e rue, St-Georges-Ouest, P.Q. G5Y 4S3 (418/228-4665)
Auclair (Mun.)	591	Témiscouata	Rimouski	Kamouraska-Témiscouata	Lise Duchesne, Sec., (St-Emile D') Auclair, P.Q. GOL 1AO (418/899-6621)
Audet (Mun.)	680	Frontenac	Mégantic-Compton-Stanstead	Mégantic-Compton	J.-L. Boucher, Sec., Audet, P.Q. GOY 1AO (819/583-1596)
Aumond (Canton)	499	Gatineau		Gatineau	Benoit David, Sec., R.R. 1, Maniwaki, P.Q. J9E 3A8 (819/449-2895)
Austin (Mun.)	791	Brome	Missisquoi	Brome-Missisquoi	A.B. Lee, Sec., Austin (Brome), P.Q. JOB 1BO (819/843-2388)

Cities in CAPITALS (Ville); Towns/Villes marked (Ville); Villages marked (Village); Townships/Cantons (marked Canton); United townships/Cantons unis (marked Cantons*); Parishes marked (Paroisse); undesignated municipalities/sans designation marked (Mun.).

MUNICIPALITY	POP.	COUNTY	FEDERAL ELECTORAL DISTRICT	PROVINCIAL ELECTORAL DISTRICT	CLERK/GREFFIER OR SECRETARY-TREASURER (SEC) WITH ADDRESS & PHONE
Authier (Mun.)	450	Abitibi	Témiscamingue	Abitibi Ouest	Louise Lambert, Sec., Rang 10, Authier, P.Q. J0Z 1C0 (819/782-2256)
Ayer's Cliff (Village)	873	Stanstead	Mégantic-Compton-Stanstead	Orford	Mme G.S. Gauvin, Sec., C.P. 36, Ayer's Cliff, P.Q. J0B 1C0 (819/838-5006)
AYLMER (Ville)	29,000	Gatineau	Hull	Pontiac	H.B. Lavigne, Greffier, Hôtel de ville, 120 Principale, Aylmer, P.Q. J9H 3M3 (819/684-5372)
Baie-Comeau (Ville)	11,800	Saguenay	Manicouagan	Saguenay	Yvon Lemay, Greffier, 19 av. Marquette, Baie-Comeau, P.Q. G4Z 1K5 (418/296-4931)
Baie-de-Shawinigan (Village)	596	St-Maurice	St-Maurice	St-Maurice	Jos. Boisvert, Sec., Hôtel de ville, Baie-de-Shawinigan, P.Q. G9N 1Z3 (819/536-2217)
Baie-des-Sables (Mun.)	889	Matane	Matapédia-Matane	Matane	R. Pelletier, Sec., C.P. 39, Baie-des-Sables, P.Q. G0J 1C0 (418/772-6218)
Baie-d'Urfé (Ville)	3,955	Ile-de-Montréal	Vaudreuil	Nelligan	Mrs. A. Hopgood, Sec., 20410 Lakeshore Rd., Baie d'Urfé, P.Q. H9X 1P7 (514/457-5324)
Baie-James	10,000	Terr. du Nouveau-Québec		Abitibi Est; Abitibi Ouest; Ungava	c/o R. Champagne, Admin., 800 boul. de Maisonneuve est, Montréal, P.Q. H2L 4M6 (514/284-0270)
Baie-Johan-Beetz (Mun.)	157	Saguenay	Manicouagan	Duplessis	Mme Th. Tanguay, Sec., Baie-Johan-Beetz, P.Q. G0G 1B0 (418/539-0125)
Baie-St-Paul (Paroisse)	1,869	Charlevoix-Ouest	Charlevoix	Charlevoix	R. Lepage, Sec., 3 route de Lequerre, Baie-St-Paul, P.Q. G0A 1B0 (418/435-3125)
Baie-St-Paul (Ville)	4,062	Charlevoix-Ouest	Charlevoix	Charlevoix	J. Otis, Sec., C.P. 127, Baie-St-Paul, P.Q. G0A 1B0 (418/435-2205)
Baie-Trinité (Village)	794	Saguenay	Manicouagan	Saguenay	Mme M.C. Chouinard, Sec., C.P. 100, Baie-Trinité, P.Q. G0H 1A0 (418/939-2231)
Baieville (Village)	435	Yamaska	Richelieu	Nicolet	P.-H. Jutras, Sec., C.P. 70, Baieville, P.Q. J0G 1A0 (514/783-6695)
Barford (Canton)	631	Stanstead		Mégantic-Compton	S. Roussel, Sec., 509 rue Child, Coaticook, P.Q. J1A 2B9 (819/849-4715)
Barkmere (Ville)	48	Argenteuil	Argenteuil	Argenteuil	S. Notar, Sec., C.P. 1702, Succ. St-Laurent, St-Laurent PO, Barkmere, P.Q. H4L 4Z2 (514/748-6779)
Barnston (Canton)	1,322	Stanstead		Orford	S. Tremblay, Sec., R.R. 6, Coaticook, P.Q. J1A 2S5 (819/849-3952)
Barnston-Ouest (Mun.)	573	Stanstead		Orford	Mrs. W. Rozynska, Sec., a/s Way's Mills R.R. 1, Ayer's Cliff, P.Q. J0B 1C0 (819/838-4321)
Barraute (Village)	1,321	Abitibi	Abitibi	Abitibi-Est	R. Nantel, Sec., C.P. 279, Barraute, P.Q. J0Y 1A0 (819/734-2574)
BEACONSFIELD (Ville)	19,500	Ile-de-Montréal	Lachine	Nelligan	J. Rioux, Greffier, 303 boul. Beaconsfield, Beaconsfield, P.Q. H9W 4A7 (514/697-4660)

Cities in CAPITALS (Ville); Towns/Villes marked (Ville); Villages marked (Village); Townships/Cantons (marked Canton); United townships/Cantons unis (marked Cantons*); Parishes marked (Paroisse); undesignated municipalities/sans designation marked (Mun.).

MUNICIPALITY	POP.	COUNTY	FEDERAL ELECTORAL DISTRICT	PROVINCIAL ELECTORAL DISTRICT	CLERK/GREFFIER OR SECRETARY-TREASURER (SEC) WITH ADDRESS & PHONE
Beauceville (Ville)	4,276	Beauce	Beauce	Beauce-Nord	H. Turmel, Sec., C.P. 579, Beauceville, P.Q. GOS 1AO (418/774-9137)
Beaudry (Mun.)	643	Témiscamingue	Témiscamingue	Rouyn-Noranda-Témiscamingue	Mme C. Jalbert, Sec., Beaudry, P.Q. JOZ 1JO (819/764-9146)
BEAUHARNOIS (Ville)	7,500	Beauharnois	Beauharnois-Salaberry	Beauharnois	Me M. Beaumont, Greffier, 103 St-Laurent, Beauharnois, P.Q. J6N 1V8 (514/429-3546)
Beaulac (Village)	477	Wolfe	Richmond	Richmond	C. Jacques, Sec., a/s C.P. 40, Garthby, P.Q. GOY 1BO (418/458-2375)
Beaulieu (Village)	822	Montmorency 2	Montmorency	Montmorency	G. Lebel, Sec., a/s 3 chemin de l'Eglise, Ste-Pétronille, P.Q. GOA 4CO (418/828-2270)
BEAUPORT (Ville)	56,700	Québec	Montmorency	Montmorency; Limoilou	J. Simoneau, Greffier, C.P. 5187, Beauport, P.Q. G1E 6P4 (418/667-8554)
Beaupré (Ville)	2,821	Montmorency 1	Montmorency	Charlevoix	J.-P. Paré, Sec., C.P. 88, Beaupré, P.Q. GOA 1EO (418/827-4541)
Bécancour (Ville)	9,300	Nicolet	Richelieu	Nicolet	J.D. Poisson, Greffier, 10485 boul. Bécancour, Bécancour, P.Q. GOX 1BO (819/222-5601)
Bedford (Ville)	3,088	Missisquoi	Missisquoi	Brome-Missisquoi	B. Déry, Sec., 3 rue Principale, Bedford, P.Q. JOJ 1AO (514/248-2440)
Bedford (Canton)	703	Missisquoi		Brome-Missisquoi	Th. Lanctôt, Sec., C.P. 544, Bedford, P.Q. JOJ 1AO (514/248-7315)
Beebe Plain (Village)	1,148	Stanstead	Mégantic-Compton-Stanstead	Orford	A.F. Young, Sec., C.P. 254, Beebe, P.Q. JOB 1EO (819/876-2107)
Bégin (Mun.)	1,001	Chicoutimi	Lac-St-Jean	Dubuc	N. Brassard, Sec., Canton-Bégin, P.Q. GOV 1BO (418/672-4270)
Belcourt (Mun.)	377	Abitibi	Abitibi	Abitibi-Est	Mme. J. Goulet, Sec., a/s R.R. 2, Senneterre, P.Q. JOY 2MO (819/737-4422)
Belleau		St-Maurice	Lévis	Maskinongé	L.P. Bélanger, Admin., Min. of Municipal Affairs, 680 St-Amable, Québec, P.Q. G1R 4Z3 (418/643-7082)
Bellecombe (Mun.)	701	Témiscamingue	Témiscamingue	Rouyn-Noranda-Témiscamingue	Mme M. Bélanger, Sec., Rang 5, C.P. 32, Bellecombe, P.Q. JOZ 1KO (819/764-3143)
Bellefeuille (Paroisse)	3,522	Terrebonne	Labelle	Prévost	Fr. Morin, Sec., 964 boul La Salette, Bellefeuille, P.Q. JOR 1AO (514/436-7447)
Belleterre (Ville)	530	Témiscamingue	Témiscamingue	Rouyn-Noranda-Témiscamingue	B. Thibeault, Sec., C.P. 130, Belleterre, P.Q. JOZ 1LO (819/722-2122)
Beloeil (Ville)	16,800	Verchères	Verchères	Verchères	Le Greffier, C.P. 210, Beloeil, P.Q. J3G 4S9 (514/467-2835)
Bergeronnes (Canton)	246	Saguenay		Saguenay	H. Simard, Sec., a/s Grandes-Bergeronnes, P.Q. GOT 1GO (418/232-6326)
Bernières (Mun.)	4,350	Lévis	Lévis	Lévis	R. Noel, Sec., 1250 de la Coopérative, Bernières, P.Q. GOS 1CO (418/831-2877)

Cities in CAPITALS (Ville); Towns/Villes marked (Ville); Villages marked (Village); Townships/Cantons (marked Canton); United townships/Cantons unis (marked Cantons*); Parishes marked (Paroisse); undesignated municipalities/sans designation marked (Mun.).

MUNICIPALITY	POP.	COUNTY	FEDERAL ELECTORAL DISTRICT	PROVINCIAL ELECTORAL DISTRICT	CLERK/GREFFIER OR SECRETARY-TREASURER (SEC) WITH ADDRESS & PHONE
Bernierville (Village)	2,182	Mégantic	Frontenac	Frontenac	Mme R. Marchand, Sec., a/s C.P. 185, St-Ferdinand PO, P.Q. GOB 1NO (418/428-3890)
Berthier-sur-Mer (Paroisse)	1,070	Montmagny	Bellechasse	Montmagny-L'Islet	L. Lapointe-Roy, Sec., 2 Beau-Site, Berthier-sur-Mer, P.Q. GOR 1EO (418/259-7343)
Berthierville (Ville)	4,339	Berthier	Berthier-Maskinongé	Berthier	René Bayeur, Sec., C.P. 269, Berthierville, P.Q. JOK 1AO (514/836-3786)
Béthanie (Mun.)	391	Shefford	Shefford	Johnson	Rita Demers, Sec., a/s R.R. 3, Valcourt, P.Q. JOE 2LO (514/548-2126)
Bic (Mun.)	2,757	Rimouski	Rimouski	Rimouski	Camille Roussel, Sec., C.P. 99, Bic, P.Q. GOL 1BO (418/736-5833)
Biencourt (Mun.)	801	Rimouski	Rimouski	Rimouski	L. Létourneau, Sec., C.P. 70, Biencourt, P.Q. GOK 1TO (418/499-2423)
Bishopton (Village)	333	Wolfe	Richmond	Mégantic-Compton	M.-M. Lessard, Sec., C.P. 31, Bishopton, P.Q. JOB 1BO (819/884-5448)
Black Lake (Ville)	5,000	Mégantic	Frontenac	Frontenac	M. Réjean, Trés., C.P. 310, Black Lake, P.Q. GON 1AO (418/423-2773)
Blainville (Ville)	12,500	Terrebonne	Blainville-Deux Montagnes	Groulx	R. Blouin, Greffier, 1000 rue de la Mairie, Blainville, P.Q. J7C 3B5 (514/430-2442)
Blue Sea (Mun.)	472	Gatineau		Gatineau	G. Gauthier, Sec., C.P. 99, Blue Sea Lake PO, P.Q. JOX 1CO (819/463-5261)
Boisbriand (Ville)	12,000	Terrebonne	Blainville-Deux Montagnes	Groulx	M. Parthenais, Greffier, 940 Grande-Allée, Boisbriand, P.Q. J7G 2J7 (514/435-1954)
Bois-des-Fillion (Village)	4,451	Terrebonne	Terrebonne	Groulx	J.L. Laflamme, Sec., 60 36e Ave., Bois-des-Fillion, P.Q. J6Z 2G6 (514/621-1460)
Bois-Franc (Mun.)	353	Gatineau	Pontiac-Gatineau-Labelle	Gatineau	Mme F. Lafontaine, Sec., a/s R.R. 2, Maniwaki, P.Q. J9E 3A9 (819/449-3247)
Bolton-Est (Mun.)	448	Brome	Missisquoi	Brome-Missisquoi	Mrs. A.M. Côté, Sec., a/s C.P. 94, South Bolton, P.Q. JOE 2HO (514/292-5259)
Bolton-Ouest (Mun.)	534	Brome		Brome-Missisquoi	S. Quilliams, Sec., a/s R.R. 3, Foster, P.Q. JOE 1RO (514/539-0256)
Bonaventure (Mun.)	2,880	Bonaventure	Bonaventure-Iles-de-la-Madeleine	Bonaventure	Yvon Côté, Sec., C.P. 428, Bonaventure, P.Q. GOC 1EO (418/534-2313)
Bonsecours (Mun.)	513	Shefford	Shefford	Brome-Missisquoi	Mme S. Tessier, Sec., 300 de l'Eglise, Bonsecours, P.Q. JOE 1HO (514/532-4663)
Boucher (Mun.)	637	Champlain		Laviolette	M. Naud, Sec., a/s 1033 Principale, St-Joseph-de-Mékinac, P.Q. GOK 2EO (819/646-5686)
Boucherville (Ville)	28,000	Chambly	Verchères	Bertrand	C. Caron, Greffier, 500 Rivière aux Pins, Boucherville, P.Q. J4B 2Z7 (514/655-3131)
Bouchette (Canton)	509	Gatineau	Pontiac-Gatineau-Labelle	Gatineau	V. Guillot, Sec., Bouchette, P.Q. JOX 1EO (819/465-2003)

Cities in CAPITALS (Ville); Towns/Villes marked (Ville); Villages marked (Village); Townships/Cantons (marked Canton); United townships/Cantons unis (marked Cantons*); Parishes marked (Paroisse); undesignated municipalities/sans designation marked (Mun.).

MUNICIPALITY	POP.	COUNTY	FEDERAL ELECTORAL DISTRICT	PROVINCIAL ELECTORAL DISTRICT	CLERK/GREFFIER OR SECRETARY-TREASURER (SEC) WITH ADDRESS & PHONE
Bourget (Canton)	735	Chicoutimi		Dubuc	C. Côté-Bergeron, Sec., a/s 482 B Rang 2, St-Charles-Borromée, P.Q. GOV 1GO (418/672-2624)
Bowman (Mun.)	280	Papineau		Papineau	J. Larocque, Sec., a/s C.P. 29, R.R. 1, Val-des-Bois, P.Q. JOX 3CO (819/454-5000)
Brébeuf (Paroisse)	442	Terrebonne	Labelle	Labelle	G. Turcotte, Sec., Brébeuf, P.Q. JOT 1BO (819/425-5636)
Bristol (Canton)	1,073	Pontiac		Pontiac	K.R. Emmerson, Sec., a/s R.R. 4, Shawville, P.Q. JOX 2YO (819/647-5517)
Brome (Village)	277	Brome	Missisquoi	Brome-Missisquoi	Pauline Morin, Sec., C.P. 2, Brome, P.Q. JOE 1KO (514/243-0178)
Bromont (Ville)	5,007	Brome	Missisquoi	Brome-Missisquoi	Mireille Copeland, Greffier, 110 boul. Bromont, Bromont, P.Q. JOE 1LO (514/534-2021)
Brompton (Canton)	1,174	Richmond		Johnson	J.-M. Auger, Sec., C.P. 222, R.R. 1, Bromptonville, P.Q. JOB 1HO (819/846-3256)
Brompton Gore (Mun.)	308	Richmond		Johnson	L.-F. Ferland, Sec., a/s Racine PO, P.Q. JOE 1YO (514/532-2876)
Bromptonville (Ville)	3,100	Richmond	Richmond	Johnson	Aimé Benoît, Sec., C.P. 610, Bromptonville, P.Q. JOB 1HO (819/846-2788)
Brossard (Ville)	41,700	Laprairie	Laprairie	Laprairie	M.P. Daoust, Greffier, 3275 Lapinière, Brossard, P.Q. J4Z 2B4 (514/676-0201)
Brownsburg (Village)	3,077	Argenteuil	Argenteuil	Argenteuil	V. Charbonneau, Sec., C.P. 40, Brownsburg, P.Q. JOV 1AO (514/533-6687)
Bryson (Village)	836	Pontiac	Pontiac-Gatineau-Labelle	Pontiac	J.G. Lallemand, Sec., C.P. 119, Bryson, P.Q. JOX 1HO (819/648-5940)
BUCKINGHAM (Ville)	14,500	Papineau	Gatineau	Papineau	P. Hayes, Greffier, 515 rue Charles, Buckingham, P.Q. J8L 2K4 (819/986-3351)
Bury (Mun.)	1,065	Compton	Mégantic-Compton-Stanstead	Mégantic-Compton	Marie-A. Paré, Sec., C.P. 179, Bury, P.Q. JOB 1JO (819/872-3692)
Cabano (Ville)	3,254	Témiscouata	Rimouski	Kamouraska-Témiscouata	J.-L. Ouellet, Sec., 79 Commerciale, C.P. 188, Cabano, P.Q. GOL 1EO (418/854-2116)
Cadillac (Ville)	817	Abitibi	Abitibi	Abitibi-Est	Ovide Bourassa, Trés., C.P. 185, Cadillac, P.Q. JOY 1CO (819/759-3300)
Calixa-Lavalée (Paroisse)	393	Verchères	Verchères	Verchères	G.P. Chagnon, Sec., Calixa-Lavallée, P.Q. JOL 1AO (514/583-3296)
Calumet (Village)	705	Argenteuil	Argenteuil	Argenteuil	B. Rochmon, Sec., C.P. 10, Calumet, P.Q. JOV 1BO (819/242-6745)
Campbell's Bay (Village)	1,061	Pontiac	Pontiac-Gatineau-Labelle	Pontiac	Miss M. Lawn, Sec., C.P. 157, Campbell's Bay, P.Q. JOX 1KO (819/648-5511)
Candiac (Ville)	8,100	Laprairie	Laprairie	Laprairie	H. Santenne, Sec., 9 boul. Montcalm, bur. 730, Candiac, P.Q. J5R 3L5 (514/659-9677)
Caniapiscou				Laprairie	
Cap-à-l'Aigle (Village)	710	Charlevoix-Est	Charlevoix	Charlevoix	N. Dufour, Sec., C.P. 10, Cap-à-l'Aigle, P.Q. GOT 1BO (418/665-2795)

Cities in CAPITALS (Ville); Towns/Villes marked (Ville); Villages marked (Village); Townships/Cantons (marked Canton); United townships/Cantons unis (marked Cantons*); Parishes marked (Paroisse); undesignated municipalities/sans designation marked (Mun.).

MUNICIPALITY	POP.	COUNTY	FEDERAL ELECTORAL DISTRICT	PROVINCIAL ELECTORAL DISTRICT	CLERK/GREFFIER OR SECRETARY-TREASURER (SEC) WITH ADDRESS & PHONE
Cap-aux-Meules (Village)	1,352	Iles-de-la-Madeleine	Bonaventure-Iles-de-la-Madeleine	Iles-de-la-Madeleine	H. Poirier, Sec., Cap-aux-Meules, P.Q. GOB 1BO (418/986-2460)
Cap-Chat (Ville)	3,617	Gaspé-Ouest	Gaspé	Matane	B. St-Pierre, Trés., C.P. 388, Cap-Chat, P.Q. GOJ 1EO (418/786-5537)
CAP-DE-LA-MADELEINE (Ville)	33,900	Champlain	Champlain	Champlain	M. Thellend, Greffier, C.P. 220, Cap-de-la-Madeleine, P.Q. G8T 7W2 (819/375-1661)
Caplan (Mun.)	1,925	Bonaventure	Bonaventure-Iles-de-la-Madeleine	Bonaventure	A. Garant, Sec., C.P. 37, Caplan, P.Q. GOC 1HO (418/388-2075)
Cap-St-Ignace (Mun.)	3,140	Montmagny	Bellechasse	Montmagny-L'Islet	Paul Fortin, Sec., 72 du Manoir est, Cap-St-Ignace, P.Q. GOR 1HO (418/246-5820)
Cap-Santé (Mun.)	2,076	Portneuf	Portneuf	Portneuf	V. Frenette, Sec., Cap-Santé, P.Q. GOA 1LO (418/285-1207)
Capucins (Mun.)	439	Matane	Matapédia-Matane	Matane	J.-C. St-Pierre, Sec., Capucins, P.Q. GOJ 1HO (418/786-5904)
Carignan (Ville)	3,585	Chambly	Chambly	Chambly	L. Monty, Sec., a/s 670 St-Pierre, Chambly, P.Q. J3L 1L9 (514/658-1066)
Carillon (Village)	211	Argenteuil	Argenteuil	Argenteuil	A. Lafleur, Sec., Carillon, P.Q. JOV 1CO (514/537-3879)
Carleton (Ville)	2,538	Bonaventure	Bonaventure-Iles-de-la-Madeleine	Bonaventure	A. Allard, Sec., C.P. 237, Carleton, P.Q. GOC 1JO (418/364-7434)
Causapscal (Ville)	2,728	Matapédia	Bonaventure-Iles-de-la-Madeleine	Matapédia	H. Dubé, Greffier, C.P. 280, Causapscal, P.Q. GOJ 1JO (418/756-5588)
CHAMBLY (Ville)	11,900	Chambly	Chambly	Chambly	M. Mongrain, Greffier, C.P. 60, Chambly, P.Q. J3L 4B2 (514/658-8788)
Chambord (Mun.)	1,755	Lac-St-Jean-Ouest	Roberval	Roberval	J.P. Tremblay, Sec., 104 Principale, Chambord, P.Q. GOW 1GO (418/342-6274)
Champlain (Village)	538	Champlain	Champlain	Champlain	P. Trudel, Sec., 886 Notre-Dame, Champlain, P.Q. GOX 1CO (819/295-3892)
Champneuf (Mun.)	270	Abitibi	Abitibi	Abitibi-Ouest	A. Marchand, Sec., a/s Landrienne, P.Q. JOY 1EO (819/754-2003)
Chandler (Ville)	4,100	Gaspé-Est	Gaspé	Gaspé	J.-A. Arsenault, Sec., C.P. 459, Chandler, P.Q. GOG 1KO (418/689-2221)
Chapais (Ville)	3,147	Terr. du Nouveau-Québec	Abitibi	Ungava	R. Couture, Sec., C.P. 380, Chapais, P.Q. GOW 1HO (819/775-2511)
Chapeau (Village)	482	Pontiac	Pontiac-Gatineau-Labelle	Pontiac	Katie McMahon, Sec., Box 100, Chapeau Village, P.Q. JOX 1MO (819/689-2266)
Charette (Paroisse)	918	St-Maurice	Berthier-Maskinongé	Maskinongé	Mme C. Samson, Sec., C.P. 10, Charette, P.Q. GOX 1EO (819/221-2095)
Charlemagne (Ville)	4,050	L'Assomption	Terrebonne	L'Assomption	L.-M. Lepage, Sec., 82 Sacré-Coeur, Charlemagne, P.Q. J5Z 1W8 (514/581-2541)
CHARLESBOURG (Ville)	68,000	Québec	Charlesbourg	Charlesbourg; Chauveau	R. Godbout, Greffier, 7575 boul. Henri-Bourassa, Charlesbourg, P.Q. G1H 3E7 (418/628-7241)
Charny (Ville)	7,200	Lévis	Lévis	Lévis	T. Langlois, Greffier, 333 20ième rue, Charny, P.Q. G6W 5R6 (418/832-4695)

Cities in CAPITALS (Ville); Towns/Villes marked (Ville); Villages marked (Village); Townships/Cantons (marked Canton); United townships/Cantons unis (marked Cantons*); Parishes marked (Paroisse); undesignated municipalities/sans designation marked (Mun.).

MUNICIPALITY	POP.	COUNTY	FEDERAL ELECTORAL DISTRICT	PROVINCIAL ELECTORAL DISTRICT	CLERK/GREFFIER OR SECRETARY-TREASURER (SEC) WITH ADDRESS & PHONE
Chartierville (Mun.)	291	Compton	Mégantic-Compton-Stanstead	Mégantic-Compton	Mich. Fortier, Sec., Chartierville, P.Q. JOB 1KO (819/656-2323)
CHATEAUGUAY (Ville)	38,000	Châteauguay	Châteauguay	Châteauguay	L. Legault, Greffier, 5 boul. d'Youville, Châteauguay, P.Q. J6J 2P8 (514/692-6701)
Château-Richer (Ville)	3,101	Montmorency 1	Montmorency	Montmorency	F. Gravel, Sec., 8006 av. Royale, Château-Richer, P.Q. GOA 1NO (418/824-4411)
Chatham (Canton)	3,402	Argenteuil		Argenteuil	R. Cadieux, Sec., a/s C.P. 51, St-Philippe-d'Argenteuil, P.Q. JOV 2AO (514/562-9121)
Chénéville (Village)	700	Papineau	Argenteuil	Papineau	Jos. Lyrette, Sec., C.P.70, Chénéville, P.Q. JOV 1EO (819/428-3583)
Chénier (Mun.)	1,072	Arthabaska	Pontiac-Gatineau-Labelle	Richmond	Mme L. Nault, Sec., a/s C.P. 58, Tingwick, P.Q. JOA 1LO (819/359-2311)
Chertsey (Canton)	1,250	Montcalm		Rousseau	A. Levesque, Sec., C.P. 120, St-Théodore-de-Chertsey, P.Q. JOK 3KO (514/882-2920)
Chester-Est (Canton)	289	Arthabaska		Richmond	J.-L. Guillemette, Sec., R.R. 1, C.P. 587, Ste-Hélène-de-Chester, P.Q. GOP 1HO (819/382-2650)
Chester-Nord (Mun.)	193	Arthabaska		Arthabaska	R. Gardner, Sec., 67 Landry, Norbertville, P.Q. GOP 1BO (819/369-9277)
Chester-Ouest (Canton)	468	Arthabaska		Arthabaska	M. Gagnon, Sec., St-Paul-de-Chester, P.Q. GOP 1JO (819/382-2010)
Chesterville (Village)	248	Arthabaska	Richmond	Arthabaska	M. Lafontaine, Sec., a/s St-Paul-de-Chester PO, P.Q. GOP 1JO (819/382-2163)
Chibougamau (Ville)	10,500	Terr. du Nouveau-Québec	Abitibi	Ungava	G. Savard, Sec., 650 3e rue, Chibougamau, P.Q. G8P 1P1 (819/276-2688)
Chichester (Canton)	557	Pontiac		Pontiac	W. McDonald, Sec., C.P. 158, Chapeau, P.Q. JOX 1MO (819/689-2019)
CHICOUTIMI (Ville)	59,900	Chicoutimi	Chicoutimi	Chicoutimi	J.Y. Fortin, Greffier, 201 Racine est, C.P. 129, Chicoutimi, P.Q. G7H 5B8 (418/545-9550)
Chute-aux-Outardes (Village)	2,160	Saguenay	Charlevoix	Saguenay	G. Lavoie, Sec., C.P. 219, Chute-aux-Outardes, P.Q. GOH 1CO (418/567-2144)
Chute-St-Philippe (Mun.)	470	Labelle	Pontiac-Gatineau-Labelle	Labelle	M.-A. Bouchard, Sec., Chute-St-Philippe, P.Q. JOW 1AO (819/585-3397)
Clarenceville (Village)	296	Missisquoi	Missisquoi	Iberville	P.C. Selfe, Sec., C.P. 1, Clarenceville, P.Q. JOJ 1BO (514/294-2811)
Clarendon (Canton)	1,650	Pontiac		Pontiac	Lorna Younge, Sec., C.P. 777, Shawville, P.Q. JOX 2YO (819/647-3862)
Clermont (Ville)	3,518	Charlevoix-Est	Charlevoix	Charlevoix	G.-R. Savard, Sec., C.P. 760, Clermont, P.Q. GOT 1CO (418/439-3931)
Clermont (Canton)	437	Abitibi		Abitibi-Ouest	G. Miron, Sec., St-Vital-de-Clermont, P.Q. JOZ 3MO (819/333-6129)

Cities in CAPITALS (Ville); Towns/Villes marked (Ville); Villages marked (Village); Townships/Cantons (marked Canton); United townships/Cantons unis (marked Cantons*); Parishes marked (Paroisse); undesignated municipalities/sans designation marked (Mun.).

MUNICIPALITY	POP.	COUNTY	FEDERAL ELECTORAL DISTRICT	PROVINCIAL ELECTORAL DISTRICT	CLERK/GREFFIER OR SECRETARY-TREASURER (SEC) WITH ADDRESS & PHONE
Clerval (Mun.)	356	Abitibi	Témiscamingue	Abitibi-Ouest	Mme Y. Gervais, Sec., Clerval, P.Q. JOZ 1RO (819/783-2632)
Cleveland (Canton)	1,575	Richmond		Richmond	J. Saint-Jean, Sec., C.P. 328, Richmond, P.Q. JOB 2HO (819/826-3546)
Clifton, est (Canton)	371	Compton		Mégantic-Compton	Mrs. C. Bellam, Sec., Sawyerville, P.Q. JOB 3AO (418/889-2706)
Cloridorme (Canton)	1,369	Gaspé-Est		Gaspé	Th. Huet, Sec., C.P. 100, Cloridorme, P.Q. GOE 1GO (418/395-2808)
Cloutier (Mun.)	498	Témiscamingue	Témiscamingue	Rouyn-Noranda-Témiscamingue	Mme G. Gagné, Sec., C.P. 105, Cloutier, P.Q. JOZ 1SO (819/764-9237)
Coaticook (Ville)	6,300	Stanstead	Mégantic-Compton-Stanstead	Orford	Roma Fluet, Greffier, C.P. 85, Coaticook, P.Q. J1A 2S8 (819/849-2721)
Colombier (Mun.)	1,224	Saguenay		Saguenay	N. Beaulieu, Sec., a/s C.P. 69, Rivière Colombier, P.Q. GOH 1PO (418/565-3343)
Colombourg (Mun.)	644	Abitibi	Témiscamingue	Abitibi-Ouest	J.-D. Bélanger, Sec., Colombourg, P.Q. JOZ 1TO (819/333-4423)
Compton (Village)	591	Compton	Mégantic-Compton-Stanstead	St-François	A. Gagnon, Sec., C.P. 120, Compton, P.Q. JOB 1LO (819/835-5436)
Compton (Canton)	900	Compton	Mégantic-Compton-Stanstead	St-François	A. Gagnon, Sec., C.P. 120, Compton, P.Q. JOB 1LO (819/835-5436)
Compton Station (Mun.)	783	Compton	Mégantic-Compton-Stanstead	St-François	A. Legrand, Sec., R.R. 1, Compton, P.Q. JOB 1LO (819/835-5585)
Contrecoeur (Mun.)	4,823	Verchères	Verchères	Verchères	R. Choquet, Sec., 440 rue Ducharme, Contrecoeur, P.Q. JOL 1CO (514/786-2200)
Cookshire (Ville)	1,463	Compton	Mégantic-Compton-Stanstead	Mégantic-Compton	A. Croisetière, Trés., C.P. 430, Cookshire, P.Q. JOB 1MO (819/875-3165)
Coteau-du-Lac (Village)	1,345	Soulanges	Vaudreuil	Vaudreuil-Soulanges	Mme Nicole Lavoie, Sec., 4A Principale, Coteau-du-Lac, P.Q. JOP 1BO (514/763-5861)
Coteau-Landing (Village)	1,171	Soulanges	Vaudreuil	Vaudreuil-Soulanges	B. Masse, Sec., C.P. 150, Coteau-Landing, P.Q. JOP 1CO (514/267-9553)
Côte-Nord-du-Golfe-St-Laurent (Mun.)	4,755	Saguenay		Duplessis	a/s M. Richmond, Admin., Min. des Affaires Municipales, Bldg. G, 28e é tage, Québec, P.Q. G1R 4Z3 (418/643-2244)
COTE-ST-LUC (Ville)	25,700	Ile-de-Montréal	Mount Royal	D'Arcy McGee	Mme J. Habra, Greffier, 5490 av. Westminster nord, Côte-St-Luc, P.Q. H4X 2A6 (514/489-9771)
Courcelles (Paroisse)	1,072	Frontenac	Frontenac	Beauce-Sud	Mme N. Roy, Sec., Courcelles, P.Q. GOM 1CO (418/483-5540)
Cowansville (Ville)	11,900	Missisquoi	Missisquoi	Brome-Missisquoi	F. Blanchet, Greffier, 220 place Municipale, Cowansville, P.Q. J2K 1T4 (514/263-0141)
Crabtree (Village)	1,950	Joliette	Joliette	Joliette	J.-D. Payette, Sec., 199 2e Ave., Crabtree, P.Q. JOK 1BO (514/754-2402)
D'Alembert (Mun.)				Rouyn-Noranda-Témiscamingue	

Cities in CAPITALS (Ville); Towns/Villes marked (Ville); Villages marked (Village); Townships/Cantons (marked Canton); United townships/Cantons unis (marked Cantons*); Parishes marked (Paroisse); undesignated municipalities/sans designation marked (Mun.).

MUNICIPALITY	POP.	COUNTY	FEDERAL ELECTORAL DISTRICT	PROVINCIAL ELECTORAL DISTRICT	CLERK/GREFFIER OR SECRETARY-TREASURER (SEC) WITH ADDRESS & PHONE
Danville (Ville)	2,367	Richmond	Richmond	Richmond	M. Champagne, Sec., C.P. 428, Danville, P.Q. JOA 1AO (819/839-2966)
Daveluyville (Village)	1,271	Arthabaska	Lotbinière	Nicolet	G. Gagnon, Sec., C.P. 187, Daveluyville, P.Q. GOZ 1CO (819/367-2855)
Deauville (Village)	864	Sherbrooke	Shefford	Orford	Royer Emile, Sec., C.P. 60, Deauville, P.Q. JOB 1NO (819/864-4088)
Dégelis (Ville)	3,391	Témiscouata	Rimouski	Kamouraska-Témiscouata	Cécile Dumont, Sec., C.P. 130, Ville Dégelis, P.Q. GOL 1HO (418/853-2332)
De Grasse (Ville)	550	Saguenay	Manicouagan	Duplessis	Suzanne Mignault, Sec., a/s 1085 rue Lamothe, Moisie, P.Q. GOG 2XO (418/643-7082)
Deléage (Mun.)	1,431	Gatineau	Pontiac-Gatineau-Labelle	Gatineau	Mme A. Tremblay, Sec., a/s 199 boul. Deléage, Maniwaki, P.Q. J9E 2W8 (819/449-1979)
Delisle (Mun.)	2,058	Lac-St-Jean-Est		Lac-St-Jean	F. Côté, Sec., 96 rue St-Joseph, BP Delisle, P.Q. GOW 1LO (418/347-3720)
Delson (Ville)	4,504	Laprairie	Châteauguay	Châteauguay	R. Champigny, Sec., 50 Ste-Thérèse, Delson, P.Q. JOL 1GO (514/632-1050)
Denholm (Canton)	179	Gatineau		Gatineau	Mme I. Lasalle, Sec., a/s R.R. 1, Poltimore, P.Q. JOX 2SO (819/457-2992)
Desbiens (Ville)	1,673	Lac-St-Jean-Est	Roberval	Lac-St-Jean	F. Lapointe, Sec., C.P. 9, Desbiens, P.Q. GOW 1NO (418/346-5571)
Deschaillons (Village)	293	Lotbinière	Lotbinière	Lotbinière	R. Grimard, Sec., Deschaillons, P.Q. GOS 1GO (819/292-2512)
Deschaillons-sur-St-Laurent (Village)	1,073	Lotbinière	Lotbinière	Lotbinière	G. Lemay, Sec., C.P. 176, Deschaillons, P.Q. GOS 1GO (819/292-2085)
Deschambault (Village)	1,018	Portneuf	Portneuf	Portneuf	G. Groleau, Sec., 106 De La Salle, Deschambault, P.Q. GOA 1SO (418/286-3585)
Des Ruisseaux (Mun.)	2,618	Labelle		Labelle	J. Sigouin, Sec., a/s R.R. 4, C.P. 211, Mont-Laurier, P.Q. J9L 3G6 (819/623-5451)
DEUX-MONTAGNES (Ville)	9,500	Deux-Montagnes	Blainville-Deux-Montagnes	Deux-Montagnes	J.M. Racine, Greffier, C.P. 55, Deux-Montagnes, P.Q. J7R 4K1 (514/473-2796)
Disraeli (Paroisse)	778	Wolfe	Richmond	Frontenac	Mme F. Couture, Sec., C.P. 760, Disraeli, P.Q. GON 1EO (418/449-5329)
Disraeli (Ville)	3,327	Wolfe	Richmond	Frontenac	Joc. Turcotte, Sec., C.P. 370, Disraeli, P.Q. GON 1EO (418/449-2771)
Ditton (Canton)	368	Compton		Mégantic-Compton	R. Jetté, Sec., La Patrie PO, P.Q. JOB 1YO (819/888-2363)
Dixville (Village)	534	Stanstead	Mégantic-Compton-Stanstead	Mégantic-Compton	Guy Laprise, Sec., C.P. 45, Dixville, P.Q. JOB 1PO (819/849-3121)
Dolbeau (Ville)	8,800	Lac-St-Jean-Ouest	Roberval	Roberval	G. Blouin, Greffier, 1100 boul. Walberg, Dolbeau, P.Q. G8L 1G7 (418/276-0160)
Dollard-des-Ormeaux (Ville)	38,300	Ile-de-Montréal	Dollard	Nelligan; Robert Baldwin	Mme H. Plouffe, Greffier, 12001 boul. de Salaberry, Dollard-des-Ormeaux, P.Q. H9B 2A7 (514/684-1010)

Cities in CAPITALS (Ville); Towns/Villes marked (Ville); Villages marked (Village); Townships/Cantons (marked Canton); United townships/Cantons unis (marked Cantons*); Parishes marked (Paroisse); undesignated municipalities/sans designation marked (Mun.).

MUNICIPALITY	POP.	COUNTY	FEDERAL ELECTORAL DISTRICT	PROVINCIAL ELECTORAL DISTRICT	CLERK/GREFFIER OR SECRETARY-TREASURER **(SEC)** WITH ADDRESS & PHONE
Donnacona (Ville)	5,700	Portneuf	Portneuf	Portneuf	D. Roy, Trés., Hôtel de ville, Donnacona, P.Q. GOA 1TO (418/285-0110)
Dorion (Canton)	388	Pontiac		Gatineau	Ovila Ethier, Sec., a/s Lac-Cayamant PO, P.Q. JOX 1YO (819/463-5694)
Dorion (Ville)	5,700	Vaudreuil	Vaudreuil	Vaudreuil-Soulanges	A. Chartrand, Sec., C.P. 70, Dorion, P.Q. J7V 5V8 (514/455-3365)
DORVAL (Ville)	18,400	Ile-de-Montréal	Lachine-Lakeshore	Jacques Cartier	M. Guérin, Greffier, 60 av. Martin, Dorval, P.Q. H9S 3R4 (514/636-4040)
DRUMMOND-VILLE (Ville)	28,300	Drummond	Drummond	Drummond	L. Bernier, Greffier, 415 Lindsay, C.P. 398, Drummondville, P.Q. J2B 1G8 (819/478-4111)
Drummondville-Sud (Ville)	9,800	Drummond	Drummond	Drummond	P.-E. Bordeleau, Sec., 1015 Jogues, Drummondville-Sud, P.Q. J2B 4X7 (819/478-4637)
Dudswell (Canton)	669	Wolfe		Mégantic-Compton	E. Dawson, Sec., R.R. 2, St-Adolphe-de-Dudswell, P.Q. JOB 2LO (819/887-6607)
Duhamel (Mun.)	281	Papineau	Argenteuil	Papineau	Mme C. Lévesque, Sec., C.P. 117, Duhamel, P.Q. JOV 1GO (819/525-7921)
Duhamel-Ouest (Mun.)	492	Témiscamingue		Rouyn-Noranda-Témiscamingue	J.G. Trépanier, Sec., a/s C.P. 786, Ville-Marie, P.Q. JOZ 3WO (819/629-2829)
Dundee (Canton)	411	Huntingdon		Huntingdon	R.R. Allen, Sec., Ste-Agnès-de-Dundee, P.Q. JOS 1LO (514/264-4674)
Dunham (Ville)	2,590	Missisquoi	Missisquoi	Brome-Missisquoi	C. Choinière, Sec., C.P. 70, Dunham, P.Q. JOE 1MO (514/295-2418)
Duparquet (Ville)	670	Abitibi	Témiscamingue	Abitibi-Ouest	A. Cloutier, Sec., C.P. 190, Duparquet, P.Q. JOZ 1WO (819/948-2266)
Durham-Sud (Mun.)	1,040	Drummond	Richmond	Johnson	Monique L. Manseau, Sec., C.P. 70, Durham-Sud, P.Q. JOH 2CO (819/858-2044)
East Angus (Ville)	4,232	Compton	Mégantic-Compton-Stanstead	Mégantic-Compton	M. Roy, Sec., C.P. 400, East Angus, P.Q. JOB 1RO (819/832-2868)
East Broughton (Mun.)	1,383	Beauce	Frontenac	Frontenac	M.-L. Lessard, Sec., C.P. 37, East Broughton, P.Q. GON 1GO (418/427-3414)
East Broughton Station (Village)	1,126	Beauce	Frontenac	Frontenac	R. Trachy, Sec., C.P. 98, East Broughton Station, P.Q. GON 1HO (418/427-2608)
East Farnham (Village)	412	Brome	Missisquoi	Brome-Missisquoi	Mrs. G. Barrand, Sec., East Farnham, P.Q. JOE 1NO (514/263-0186)
Eastman (Village)	575	Brome	Missisquoi	Brome-Missisquoi	M. Brassard, Sec., C.P. 150, Eastman, P.Q. JOE 1PO (514/297-2114)
Eaton (Canton)	1,615	Compton		Mégantic-Compton	J. Hivert, Sec., R.R. 1, Cookshire, P.Q. JOB 1MO (819/875-3554)
Egan-Sud (Mun.)	451	Gatineau		Gatineau	Mrs. S. McKenzie, Sec., a/s 402 boul. Desjardins, Maniwaki, P.Q. J9E 2G1 (819/449-2845)
Elgin (Canton)	417	Huntingdon		Huntingdon	R.W. Antaya, Sec., R.R. 2, Huntingdon, P.Q. JOS 1HO (514/264-4291)

Cities in CAPITALS (Ville); Towns/Villes marked (Ville); Villages marked (Village); Townships/Cantons (marked Canton); United townships/Cantons unis (marked Cantons*); Parishes marked (Paroisse); undesignated municipalities/sans designation marked (Mun.).

MUNICIPALITY	POP.	COUNTY	FEDERAL ELECTORAL DISTRICT	PROVINCIAL ELECTORAL DISTRICT	CLERK/GREFFIER OR SECRETARY-TREASURER (SEC) WITH ADDRESS & PHONE
Entrelacs (Mun.)	466	Montcalm	Joliette	Rousseau	Mme Lise Bernier, Sec., 2411 boul. Entrelacs, Entrelacs, P.Q. JOT 2EO (514/228-2813)
Escoumins (Mun.)	2,330	Saguenay	Charlevoix	Saguenay	A. Caron, Sec., C.P. 160, Les Escoumins, P.Q. GOT 1KO (418/233-2766)
Escuminac (Mun.)	671	Bonaventure	Bonaventure-Iles-de-la-Madeleine	Bonaventure	Mrs. J. Cavanagh, Sec., Pointe à la Garde, Escuminac, P.Q. GOC 2MO (418/788-5644)
Esprit-Saint (Mun.)	540	Rimouski	Rimouski	Rimouski	M.A. Charron, Sec., a/s 1039 De La Chevrotière, Québec, P.Q. G1R 4Z3 (418/779-2273)
Estérel (Ville)	47	Terrebonne	Joliette	Rousseau	J.-G. Coupal, Sec., C.P. 8, Estérel, P.Q. JOT 1EO (514/228-2501)
Evain (Mun.)	2,416	Témiscamingue	Témiscamingue	Rouyn-Noranda-Témiscamingue	Mme M. Morel, Sec., C.P. 100, Evain, P.Q. JOZ 1YO (819/769-5918)
FARNHAM (Ville)	6,500	Missisquoi	Missisquoi	Iberville	J.-B. Luneau, Sec., 477 Hôtel de ville, Farnham, P.Q. J2N 2H3 (514/293-4460)
Fassett (Mun.)	503	Papineau	Argenteuil	Papineau	Luc Boucher, Sec., Fassett, P.Q. JOV 1HO (819/423-6943)
Fatima (Mun.)	2,786	Iles-de-la-Madeleine	Bonaventure-Iles-de-la-Madeleine	Iles-de-la-Madeleine	G. Poirier, Sec., C.P. 59, Fatima, P.Q. GOB 1GO (418/986-3341)
Ferland et Boileau (Mun.)			Lac-St-Jean	Dubuc	L. Simard, Sec., 466 Route 381, Ferland, P.Q. GOV 1HO (418/676-2282)
Ferme-Neuve (Paroisse)	826	Labelle	Pontiac-Gatineau-Labelle	Labelle	F. Lévesque, Sec., a/s R.R. 2, Mont-Laurier, P.Q. J9L 3G4 (819/587-4115)
Ferme-Neuve (Village)	2,113	Labelle	Pontiac-Gatineau-Labelle	Labelle	C. Campeau, Sec., C.P. 179, Ferme-Neuve, P.Q. JOW 1CO (819/587-3400)
Fermont (Ville)	3,534	Saguenay	Manicouagan	Duplessis	Jeannine Bellesort, Greffier, C.P. 520, Fermont, P.Q. GOG 1JO (418/287-5411)
Fiedmont et Barraute (Mun.)	936	Abitibi		Abitibi-Est	J.-L. Rompré, Sec., a/s C.P. 27, Barraute, P.Q. JOY 1AO (819/734-2451)
Fleuriault (Mun.)	645	Rimouski	Rimouski	Matapédia	A.-A. Caron, Sec., a/s St-Gabriel, P.Q. GOK 1MO (418/798-4443)
Fleurimont (Mun.)	7,100	Sherbrooke	Mégantic-Compton-Stanstead	St-François	R. Caron, Sec., 1735 ch. Galvin, Fleurimont, P.Q. J1G 3E7 (819/565-9954)
Fontainebleau (Mun.)	155	Wolfe	Richmond	Mégantic-Compton	Mme J. Lacroix, Sec., C.P. 89, Fontainebleau, P.Q. JOB 3JO (819/877-2778)
Forestville (Ville)	1,860	Saguenay	Charlevoix	Saguenay	R. Joncas, Sec., C.P. 70, Forestville, P.Q. GOT 1EO (418/587-2284)
Fort Coulonge (Village)	1,697	Pontiac	Pontiac-Gatineau-Labelle	Pontiac	Ken Rose, Sec., C.P. 640, Fort Coulonge, P.Q. JOX 1VO (819/683-2259)
Fortierville (Village)	427	Lotbinière	Lotbinière	Lotbinière	F.N. Dussault, Sec., Fortierville, P.Q. GOS 1J (418/287-5922)
Fossambault-sur-le-Lac (Village)	337	Portneuf	Portneuf	Chauveau	M. Marchand, Sec., C.P. 38, Fossambault-sur-le-Lac, P.Q. GOA 3MO (418/875-3133)

Cities in CAPITALS (Ville); Towns/Villes marked (Ville); Villages marked (Village); Townships/Cantons (marked Canton); United townships/Cantons unis (marked Cantons*); Parishes marked (Paroisse); undesignated municipalities/sans designation marked (Mun.).

MUNICIPALITY	POP.	COUNTY	FEDERAL ELECTORAL DISTRICT	PROVINCIAL ELECTORAL DISTRICT	CLERK/GREFFIER OR SECRETARY-TREASURER (SEC) WITH ADDRESS & PHONE
Franklin (Mun.)	1,552	Huntingdon		Huntingdon	Guy Frappier, Sec., C.P. 84, Franklin Centre, P.Q. JOS 1EO (514/827-2755)
Franquelin (Mun.)				Saguenay	
Frelighsburg (Paroisse)	670	Missisquoi	Missisquoi	Brome-Missisquoi	Mme L. Spracklin, Sec., C.P. 69, Frelighsburg, P.Q. JOJ 1CO (514/298-5133)
Frelighsburg (Village)	344	Missisquoi	Missisquoi	Brome-Missisquoi	Mme G. Benoît, Sec., C.P. 75, Frelighsburg, P.Q. JOJ 1CO (514/298-5497)
Frontenac (Mun.)	1,036	Frontenac		Mégantic-Compton	A. Grondin, Sec., a/s R.R. 1, Lac Mégantic, P.Q. G6B 2S1 (819/583-3295)
Fugèreville (Mun.)	461	Témiscamingue	Témiscamingue	Rouyn-Noranda-Témiscamingue	R. Lafrenière, Sec., Fugèreville, P.Q. JOZ 2AO (819/748-3241)
Gagnon (Ville)	3,386	Saguenay	Manicouagan	Duplessis	Mme S. Deschenes, Greffier, C.P. 370, Gagnon, P.Q. GOG 1KO (418/532-6303)
Gallix (Mun.)	700	Saguenay	Manicouagan	Duplessis	M. Gagnon, Sec., a/s 456 Arnaud, bur. 236, Sept-Iles, P.Q. GOG 1LO (418/583-2761)
Garthby (Canton)	353	Wolfe		Richmond	M. Bilodeau, Sec., R.R. 2, Garthby Station, P.Q. GOY 1BO (418/458-2363)
GASPE (Ville)	16,800	Gaspé-Est	Gaspé	Gaspé	R. Samuel, Greffier, C.P. 618, Gaspé, P.Q. GOC 1RO (418/368-2104)
GATINEAU (Ville)	76,500	Hull	Gatineau	Gatineau; Chapleau	J.-C. Laurin, Greffier, 280 boul. Maloney est, Gatineau, P.Q. J8P 1C6 (819/663-9261)
Gayhurst, sud-est (Canton)	189	Frontenac		Beauce-Sud	Y. Roy, Sec., a/s R.R. 2, St-Ludger, P.Q. GOM 1WO (819/548-5145)
Girardville (Mun.)	1,514	Lac-St-Jean-Ouest	Roberval	Roberval	A. Thibeault, Sec., C.P. 8, Girardville, P.Q. GOW 1RO (418/258-3293)
Godbout (Village)	593	Saguenay	Manicouagan	Saguenay	C. Vallée, Sec., C.P. 24, Godbout, P.Q. GOH 1GO (418/568-7581)
Godmanchester (Canton)	1,732	Huntingdon		Huntingdon	A. Hunter, Sec., C.P. 765, Godmanchester, P.Q. JOS 1HO (514/264-4116)
Gore (Canton)	420	Argenteuil		Argenteuil	C.A. Marcotte, Sec., a/s R.R. 1, Lakefield, P.Q. JOV 1KO (514/562-2025)
Gracefield (Village)	913	Gatineau	Pontiac-Gatineau-Labelle	Gatineau	P. Rondeau, Sec., C.P. 329, Gracefield, P.Q. JOX 1WO (819/463-3458)
GRANBY (Ville)	37,300	Shefford	Shefford	Shefford	R. Duval, Gérant, 87 Principale, Granby, P.Q. J2G 2T8 (514/372-6671)
Granby (Canton)	4,519	Shefford		Shefford	R. Paré, Sec., C.P. 579, Granby, P.Q. J2G 8C9 (514/372-3442)
Grand-Calumet (Canton)	911	Pontiac		Pontiac	J.M. Meloche, Sec., C.P. 130, Ile-du-Grand-Calumet, P.Q. JOX 1JO (819/648-5965)
Grande-Cascapédia (Mun.)	338	Bonaventure	Bonaventure-Iles-de-la-Madeleine	Bonaventure	C.R. Nadeau, Sec., C.P. 6, Grande-Cascapédia, P.Q. GOC 1TO (418/392-4745)
Grande-Entrée (Mun.)	1,001	Iles-de-la-Madeleine	Bonaventure-Iles-de-la-Madeleine	Iles-de-la-Madeleine	R. Bénard, Sec., C.P. 58, Grande-Entrée, P.Q. GOB 1HO (418/985-2277)

Cities in CAPITALS (Ville); Towns/Villes marked (Ville); Villages marked (Village); Townships/Cantons (marked Canton); United townships/Cantons unis (marked Cantons*); Parishes marked (Paroisse); undesignated municipalities/sans designation marked (Mun.).

MUNICIPALITY	POP.	COUNTY	FEDERAL ELECTORAL DISTRICT	PROVINCIAL ELECTORAL DISTRICT	CLERK/GREFFIER OR SECRETARY-TREASURER (SEC) WITH ADDRESS & PHONE
Grande-Ile (Mun.)	2,580	Beauharnois		Beauharnois	J.-C. Dupuis, Sec., 244 boul. Mgr Langois, Grande-Ile, P.Q. J6S 1B9 (514/373-8860)
Grande-Rivière (Ville)	4,475	Gaspé-Est	Gaspé	Gaspé	J. Carbery, Sec., C.P. 188, Grande-Rivière, P.Q. GOC 1VO (418/385-2282)
Grandes-Bergeronnes (Village)	784	Saguenay	Charlevoix	Saguenay	J. Girard, Sec., C.P. 158, Grandes-Bergeronnes, P.Q. GOT 1GO (418/232-6435)
Grandes-Piles (Paroisse)	437	Champlain	Champlain	Laviolette	G. Massicotte, Sec., 620 5e Ave., Grandes-Piles, P.Q. GOX 1HO (819/538-7866)
Grande-Vallée (Mun.)	1,525	Gaspé-Est	Gaspé	Gaspé	C.-E. Minville, Sec., Grande-Vallée, P.Q. GOE 1KO (418/393-2161)
GRAND-MERE (Ville)	15,600	Champlain	St-Maurice	Laviolette	J. Trussart, Greffier, 333 5e Ave., C.P. 350, Grand-Mère, P.Q. G9T 5L1 (819/538-9543)
Grand-Métis (Mun.)	340	Matane	Matapédia-Matane	Matane	Mme B.C. Lévesque, Sec., Grand-Métis, P.Q. GOJ 1ZO (418/775-4010)
Grand-Remous (Canton)	1,050	Gatineau		Gatineau	B.M. Bruyere, Sec., C.P. 96, Grand-Remous, P.Q. JOW 1EO (819/438-2877)
Grand-St-Esprit (Mun.)	548	Nicolet	Richelieu	Nicolet	C. Pinard, Sec., 5300 Grand St-Esprit, Grand-St-Esprit, P.Q. JOG 1BO (819/289-2971)
Grantham-Ouest (Mun.)	3,445	Drummond		Drummond	G. Raiche, Sec., 1425 boul. Lemire, Drummondville, P.Q. J2C 2B2 (819/477-5322)
Greenfield Park (Ville)	18,500	Chambly	Laprairie	Laporte	M. Girard, Trés., 156 boul. Churchill, Greenfield Park, P.Q. J4V 2M3 (514/671-5955)
Grenville (Canton)	1,822	Argenteuil		Argenteuil	R.W. Lemay, Sec., C.P. 148, R.R. 1, Grenville, P.Q. JOV 1JO (819/242-8762)
Grenville (Village)	1,517	Argenteuil	Argenteuil	Argenteuil	R. Dupuis, Sec., C.P. 220, Grenville, P.Q. JOV 1JO (819/242-2146)
Grosse-Ile (Mun.)	506	Iles-de-la-Madeleine	Bonaventure-Iles-de-la-Madeleine	Iles-de-la-Madeleine	Jeannot Gagnon, Sec., a/s Leslie PO, P.Q. GOB 1MO (418/985-2510)
Grosse-Roches (Mun.)	599	Matane	Matapédia-Matane	Matane	Mme G. Tremblay, Sec., Grosse-Roches, P.Q. GOJ 1KO (418/733-4961)
Guérin (Canton)	360	Témiscamingue		Rouyn-Noranda-Témiscamingue	P. Lavigne, Sec., Guérin, P.Q. JOZ 2EO (819/784-3557)
Halifax-Nord (Canton)	480	Mégantic		Frontenac	R. Gosselin, Sec., a/s Ste-Sophie-de-Mégantic, P.Q. GOP 1LO (819/362-3465)
Halifax-Sud (Canton)	630	Mégantic		Frontenac	L. Pinette, Sec., a/s 164 des Prés-Fleuris, St-Ferdinand, P.Q. GON 1NO (418/428-3306)
Halifax-Sud, partie sud-ouest (Canton)	220	Mégantic		Frontenac	C. Marcoux, Sec., a/s R.R. 1, boite 12, St-Ferdinand, P.Q. GON 1NO (819/428-3461)
Ham-Nord (Canton)	906	Wolfe		Richmond	D. Caron, Sec., 110 1ère av., Ham-Nord, P.Q. GOP 1AO (819/344-2424)

Cities in CAPITALS (Ville); Towns/Villes marked (Ville); Villages marked (Village); Townships/Cantons (marked Canton); United townships/Cantons unis (marked Cantons*); Parishes marked (Paroisse); undesignated municipalities/sans designation marked (Mun.).

MUNICIPALITY	POP.	COUNTY	FEDERAL ELECTORAL DISTRICT	PROVINCIAL ELECTORAL DISTRICT	CLERK/GREFFIER OR SECRETARY-TREASURER (SEC) WITH ADDRESS & PHONE
Hampden (Canton)	122	Compton		Mégantic-Compton	J. Macaulay, Sec., C.P. 212, Scotstown, P.Q. JOB 3BO (819/657-4930)
Hampstead (Ville)	7,800	Ile-de-Montréal	Mount Royal	D'Arcy McGee	M. Guay, Greffier, 5569 Ch. Queen Mary, Hampstead, P.Q. H3X 1W5 (514/487-1441)
Harrington (Canton)	679	Argenteuil		Argenteuil	A. Batty, Sec., a/s R.R. 2, boite 125, Arundel, P.Q. JOT 1AO (819/687-3802)
Hatley (Village)	182	Stanstead	Mégantic-Compton-Stanstead	Orford	N. Johnson, Sec., a/s R.R. 3, Ayer's Cliff, P.Q. JOB 1CO (819/838-4630)
Hatley (Canton)	541	Stanstead		Orford	Mrs. E.M. Woodward, Sec., C.P. 570, North Hatley, P.Q. JOB 2CO (819/842-2977)
Hatley, ouest (Canton)	374	Stanstead		Orford	J.G. Barratt, Sec., C.P. 360, Ayer's Cliff, P.Q. JOB 1CO (819/838-5877)
Haute-Mauricie (Mun.)	2,100	Champlain		Laviolette	Denis Tousignant, Sec., 1544 boul. Ducharme, B.G. 20, Haute-Mauricie, P.Q. G9X 3N8
Hauterive (Ville)	14,600	Saguenay	Charlevoix	Saguenay	G.Y. Gagnon, Greffier, 1000 Mingan, Hauterive, P.Q. G5C 1C5 (418/589-2071)
Havelock (Canton)	761	Huntingdon		Huntingdon	Mme G. Slater, Sec., Covey Hill Rd., Hemmingford, P.Q. JOS 1RO
Havre-aux-Maisons (Mun.)	2,000	Iles-de-la-Madeleine	Bonaventure-Iles-de-la-Madeleine	Iles-de-la-Madeleine	M.-A. Boudreau, Sec., C.P. 128, Havre-aux-Maisons, P.Q. GOB 1KO (418/969-2222)
Havre-St-Pierre (Mun.)	3,253	Saguenay	Manicouagan	Duplessis	R. Jomphe, Sec., 1081 De La Digue, Havre-St-Pierre, P.Q. GOG 1PO (418/538-2717)
Hébertville (Mun.)	2,547	Lac-St-Jean-Est	Lac-St-Jean	Lac-St-Jean	Guy Gagnon, Sec., C.P. 10, Hébertville, P.Q. GOW 1SO (418/344-1302)
Hébertville Station (Village)	1,365	Lac-St-Jean-Est	Lac-St-Jean	Lac-St-Jean	Y. Baril, Sec., C.P. 37, Hébertville Station, P.Q. GOW 1TO (418/343-3961)
Hemmingford (Canton)	1,725	Huntingdon		Huntingdon	R.L. Bouchard, Sec., C.P. 54, Hemmingford, P.Q. JOL 1HO (514/247-2050)
Hemmingford (Village)	754	Huntingdon	St-Jean	Huntingdon	D. Lawrence, Sec., C.P. 54, Hemmingford, P.Q. JOL 1HO (514/247-3310)
Henryville (Village)	581	Iberville	Missisquoi	Iberville	Y.G. Racine, Sec., C.P. 120, Henryville, P.Q. JOJ 1EO (514/347-7370)
Henryville (Mun.)	796	Iberville	Missisquoi	Iberville	R. Clouâtre, Sec., 133 St-Georges, Henryville, P.Q. JOJ 1EO (514/299-2655)
Hereford (Canton)	423	Compton		Mégantic-Compton	C. Boutin, Sec., a/s East Hereford, P.Q. JOB 1SO (819/844-2335)
Hinchinbrook (Canton)	1,475	Huntingdon		Huntingdon	L.J. Graham, Sec., a/s Athelstan, P.Q. JOS 1AO (514/264-2896)
Honfleur (Mun.)	864	Bellechasse	Bellechasse	Bellechasse	P. Fournier, Sec., 219 rue de l'Eglise, Honfleur, P.Q. GOR 1NO (418/885-4967)
Hope (Canton)	840	Bonaventure		Bonaventure	R. Chapados, Sec., C.P. 729, Paspébiac, P.Q. GOC 2KO (418/752-3526)

Cities in CAPITALS (Ville); Towns/Villes marked (Ville); Villages marked (Village); Townships/Cantons (marked Canton); United townships/Cantons unis (marked Cantons*); Parishes marked (Paroisse); undesignated municipalities/sans designation marked (Mun.).

MUNICIPALITY	POP.	COUNTY	FEDERAL ELECTORAL DISTRICT	PROVINCIAL ELECTORAL DISTRICT	CLERK/GREFFIER OR SECRETARY-TREASURER (SEC) WITH ADDRESS & PHONE
Hope Town (Mun.)	355	Bonaventure	Bonaventure-Iles-de-la-Madeleine	Bonaventure	H.E. Hayes, Sec., a/s R.R. 1, boite 45, St-Godefroy, P.Q. GOC 3CO (418/752-2087)
Howick (Village)	657	Châteauguay	Beauharnois-Salaberry	Huntingdon	G. Primeau, Sec., C.P. 126, Howick, P.Q. JOS 1GO (514/825-2032)
Huberdeau (Mun.)		Argenteuil	Argenteuil	Argenteuil	Mona St-Georges, Sec., C.P. 72, Huberdeau, P.Q. JOT 1GO (819/687-9188)
Hudson (Ville)	4,556	Vaudreuil	Vaudreuil	Vaudreuil-Soulanges	Louise L. Villandré, Greffier, C.P. 550, Hudson, P.Q. JOP 1HO (514/458-5349)
HULL (Ville)	60,100	Hull	Hull	Hull	R. Lesage, Greffier, C.P. 1970, Stn. B, Hull, P.Q. J8X 3Y9 (819/777-2781)
Hull, ouest (Canton)	3,200	Gatineau		Gatineau	G.A. Dupont, Sec., a/s Old Chelsea, P.Q. JOX 2NO (819/827-1124)
Hunterstown (Canton)	198	Maskinongé		Maskinongé	R.U. Guimond, Sec., 2810 Bergeron, St-Paulin, P.Q. JOK 3GO (819/268-2026)
Huntingdon (Ville)	3,100	Huntingdon	Beauharnois-Salaberry	Huntingdon	R. Alary, Sec., C.P. 89, Huntingdon, P.Q. JOS 1HO (514/264-5389)
Iberville (Ville)	8,700	Iberville	St-Jean	Iberville	A.L. Fréchette, Greffier, 855 1ère rue, Iberville, P.Q. J2X 3C7 (514/347-2318)
Ile-Cadieux (Ville)	82	Vaudreuil	Vaudreuil	Vaudreuil-Soulanges	Mrs. E.S. Cowan, Sec., Hôtel de ville, Ile-Cadieux, P.Q. J7V 5V5 (514/455-4640)
Ile-d'Anticosti				Duplessis	
Ile-d'Entrée (Village)	223	Iles-de-la-Madeleine	Bonaventure-Iles-de-la-Madeleine	Iles-de-la-Madeleine	C. Welsh, Sec., Ile-d'Entrée, P.Q. GOB 1CO (418/986-4709)
Ile Dorval (Ville)	8	Ile-de-Montréal	Lachine	Jacques-Cartier	Mrs. J. Saunderson, Trés., C.P. 2266, Dorval, P.Q. H9S 5J4 (514/695-5905)
Ile-du-Havre-Aubert (Mun.)	2,808	Iles-de-la-Madeleine		Iles-de-la-Madeleine	L. Reid, Sec., a/s C.P. 36, Havre-Aubert, P.Q. GOB 1JO (418/937-5205)
Ile-Perrot (Ville)	6,200	Vaudreuil	Vaudreuil	Vaudreuil-Soulanges	A. Portelance, Sec., 110 boul. Perrot, Ile-Perrot, P.Q. J7V 3G1 (514/453-1751)
Inverness (Village)	367	Mégantic	Frontenac	Lotbinière	R. Bergeron, Sec., 1845 Duflin, Inverness, P.Q. GOS 1KO (418/453-7790)
Inverness (Canton)	660	Mégantic		Lotbinière	M.P. Gagné, Sec., C.P. 99, Inverness, P.Q. GOS 1KO (418/453-7713)
Ireland (Mun.)	1,820	Mégantic		Frontenac	A. Grenier, Sec., C.P. 98, St-Ferdinand, P.Q. GON 1NO (418/428-3368)
Ireland, nord (Canton)	495	Mégantic	Frontenac	Frontenac	Mme Rolande L. Gouin, Sec., R.R. 1, B.P. 133A, St-Adrien d'Irlande, P.Q. GON 1MO (418/423-4600)
Isle-aux-Allumettes, est (Canton)	400	Pontiac		Pontiac	D. Czmielewski, Sec., R.R. 4, Chapeau, P.Q. JOX 1MO (819/689-2586)
Isle-des-Allumettes (Canton)				Pontiac	
Ivry-sur-le-Lac (Mun.)	220	Terrebonne		Labelle	L. Pellerin, Sec., 24 Albert, Ste-Agathe-des-Monts, P.Q. J8C 1Z5 (819/326-2381)

Cities in CAPITALS (Ville); Towns/Villes marked (Ville); Villages marked (Village); Townships/Cantons (marked Canton); United townships/Cantons unis (marked Cantons*); Parishes marked (Paroisse); undesignated municipalities/sans designation marked (Mun.).

MUNICIPALITY	POP.	COUNTY	FEDERAL ELECTORAL DISTRICT	PROVINCIAL ELECTORAL DISTRICT	CLERK/GREFFIER OR SECRETARY-TREASURER (SEC) WITH ADDRESS & PHONE
JOLIETTE (Ville)	17,200	Joliette	Joliette	Joliette	J.-A. Desormiers, Sec., 614 boul. Manseau, Joliette, P.Q. J6E 6J3 (514/756-8055)
JONQUIERE (Ville)	60,700	Chicoutimi	Jonquière	Jonquière	R. Perron, Greffier, C.P. 548, Secteur Arvida, Jonquière, P.Q. G7S 4K8 (418/548-7101)
Kamouraska (Village)	478	Kamouraska	Kamouraska-Rivière-du-Loup	Kamouraska-Témiscouata	C. Michaud, Sec., C.P. 127, Kamouraska, P.Q. GOL 1MO (418/492-5021)
Kazabazua (Mun.)	577	Gatineau	Pontiac-Gatineau-Labelle	Gatineau	E. Wilson, Sec., C.P. 10, Kazabazua, P.Q. JOX 1XO (819/467-2852)
Kénogami (Canton)				Jonquière	
Kiamika (Canton)	563	Labelle	Pontiac-Gatineau-Labelle	Labelle	J. Lacasse, Sec., Kiamika, P.Q. JOW 1GO (819/585-3225)
Kingsbury (Village)	223	Richmond	Richmond	Johnson	Y.B. Fontaine, Sec., Kingsbury, P.Q. JOB 1XO (819/826-3646)
Kingsey (Canton)	1,325	Drummond		Richmond	N. Provencher, Sec., C.P. 29, St-Felix-de-Kingsey, P.Q. JOB 2TO (819/848-2321)
Kingsey Falls (Village)	587	Drummond	Richmond	Richmond	L. Couture, Sec., C.P. 270, Kingsey Falls, P.Q. JOA 1BO (819/363-2623)
Kingsey Falls (Mun.)	395	Drummond	Richmond	Richmond	A. Bolduc, Sec., C.P. 120, Kingsey Falls, P.Q. JOA 1BO (819/363-2261)
Kirkland (Ville)	7,900	Ile-de-Montréal	Vaudreuil	Nelligan	R. Labrèche, Greffier, 17000 Hymus Blvd., Kirkland, P.Q. H9J 2W2 (514/694-4100)
LA BAIE (Ville)	20,100	Chicoutimi	Chicoutimi	Dubuc	R. Poitras, Greffier, 200 rue Victoria, C.P. 1006, La Baie, P.Q. G7B 3N4 (418/544-6851)
La Baleine (Mun.)	256	Charlevoix-Ouest	Charlevoix	Charlevoix	C.-E. Perron, Sec., 128 Principale, La Baleine, P.Q. GOA 2AO (418/438-2878)
Labelle (Mun.)	2,007	Labelle	Labelle	Labelle	C. Charbonneau, Sec., C.P. 390, Labelle, P.Q. JOT 1HO (819/686-2144)
Labrecque (Mun.)	1,050	Chicoutimi		Lac-St-Jean	G. Fleury, Sec., 223 Ambroise, St-Léon, P.Q. GOW 2SO (418/481-2022)
L'Acadie (Mun.)	2,566	St-Jean	St-Jean	St-Jean	D. L'Heureux, Sec., 246 ch. du Clocher, L'Acadie, P.Q. JOJ 1HO (514/347-8221)
Lac-à-la-Croix (Mun.)	1,022	Lac-St-Jean-Est	Roberval	Lac-St-Jean	H. Poirier, Sec., 372 St-Jean, Lac-Ste-Croix, P.Q. GOW 1WO (418/349-2033)
Lac-au-Saumon (Village)	1,306	Matapédia	Matapédia-Matane	Matapédia	J.-C. Dumoulin, Sec., C.P. 98, Lac-au-Saumon, P.Q. GOJ 1MO (418/778-3378)
Lac-Bouchette (Mun.)	1,704	Lac-St-Jean-Ouest	Roberval	Roberval	A. Gagnon, Sec., C.P. 40, Lac-Bouchette, P.Q. GOW 1VO (418/348-6338)
Lac-Brome (Ville)	4,200	Brome	Missisquoi	Brome-Missisquoi	R. Poitras, Greffier, C.P. 60, Knowlton, P.Q. JOE 1VO (514/243-6111)
Lac-Carré (Village)	652	Terrebonne	Labelle	Labelle	D. Serres, Sec., C.P. 270, Lac-Carré, P.Q. JOT 1JO (819/688-3104)

Cities in CAPITALS (Ville); Towns/Villes marked (Ville); Villages marked (Village); Townships/Cantons (marked Canton); United townships/Cantons unis (marked Cantons*); Parishes marked (Paroisse); undesignated municipalities/sans designation marked (Mun.).

MUNICIPALITY	POP.	COUNTY	FEDERAL ELECTORAL DISTRICT	PROVINCIAL ELECTORAL DISTRICT	CLERK/GREFFIER OR SECRETARY-TREASURER (SEC) WITH ADDRESS & PHONE
Lac-Delage (Ville)	194	Québec	Charlesbourg	Chauveau	R. Simoneau, Sec., Manoir Lac-Delage, Stoneham, P.Q. GOA 4PO (418/848-2417)
Lac-des-Aigles (Paroisse)	761	Rimouski	Rimouski	Rimouski	Mme F. Dubé, Sec., C.P. 70, Lac-des-Aigles, P.Q. GOK 1VO (418/779-2964)
Lac-des-Ecorces (Village)	638	Labelle	Pontiac-Gatineau-Labelle	Labelle	Guy Legault, Sec., Lac-des-Ecorces, P.Q. JOW 1HO (819/585-2555)
Lac-des-Ecorces (Mun.)	678	Labelle		Labelle	G. Legault, Sec., 111 rue du Boulevard, Lac-des-Ecorces, P.Q. JOW 1HO (819/585-2555)
Lac-des-Plages (Mun.)	286	Papineau	Argenteuil	Papineau	Mme S. Bernard, Sec., Lac-des-Plages, P.Q. JOT 1KO (819/426-2391)
Lac-des-Seize-Iles (Mun.)	194	Argenteuil	Argenteuil	Argenteuil	R. Cossette, Sec., C.P. 91, Lac-des-Seize-Iles, P.Q. JOT 2MO (514/226-5380)
Lac-Drolet (Mun.)	1,016	Frontenac	Lotbinière	Mégantic-Compton	R. Leclerc, Sec., 100 Principale, Lac-Drolet, P.Q. GOY 1CO (819/549-2332)
Lac-du-Cerf (Mun.)	385	Labelle	Pontiac-Gatineau-Labelle	Labelle	G. Ouimet, Sec., Lac-du-Cerf, P.Q. JOW 1SO (819/597-2424)
Lac-Edouard (Mun.)	315	Québec	Champlain	Laviolette	F. Matte, Sec., Lac-Edouard, P.Q. GOA 2GO (819/664-2210)
Lac-Etchemin (Ville)	2,768	Dorchester	Bellechasse	Bellechasse	Y. Létourneau, Greffier, C.P. 370, Lac-Etchemin, P.Q. GOR 1SO (418/625-4521)
Lac-Frontière (Mun.)	249	Montmagny	Bellechasse	Montmagny-L'Islet	Mme J.-M. Bolduc, Sec., Lac-Frontière, P.Q. GOR 1TO (418/245-3331)
Lachenaie (Ville)	7,700	L'Assomption	Terrebonne	Terrebonne	Luc Amireault, Greffier, 3341 Notre-Dame, Lachenaie, P.Q. J6W 3T8 (514/471-2424)
LACHINE (Ville)	40,900	Ile-de-Montréal	Lachine	Jacques-Cartier; Marquette	P. Rémillard, Greffier, 1800 boul. St-Joseph, Lachine, P.Q. H8S 2N4 (514/637-4411)
LACHUTE (Ville)	11,900	Argenteuil	Argenteuil	Argenteuil	R. Hébert, Sec., 380 Principale, Lachute, P.Q. J8H 1Y2 (514/562-5252)
Lac-Mégantic (Ville)	6,300	Frontenac	Mégantic-Compton-Stanstead	Mégantic-Compton	P. Fecteau, Greffier, 5527 Frontenac, bur. 200, Lac-Mégantic, P.Q. G6B 1H6 (819/583-2441)
Lac-Nominingue (Mun.)	1,350	Labelle		Labelle	Hélène L. Khushf, Sec., C.P. 9, Lac-Nominingue, P.Q. JOW 1RO (819/278-3611)
Lacolle (Village)	1,193	St-Jean	St-Jean	St-Jean	F. Desrochers, Sec., C.P. 400, Lacolle, P.Q. JOJ 1JO (514/246-3201)
La Conception (Mun.)	540	Labelle	Labelle	Labelle	Clarisse Bédard, Sec., La Conception, P.Q. JOT 1MO (819/686-3016)
La Corne (Mun.)	545	Abitibi	Abitibi	Abitibi-Ouest	V. Omer, Sec., La Corne, P.Q JOY 1RO (418/732-6527)
Lac-Paré (Paroisse)	75	Montcalm	Joliette	Rousseau	M. Rodier, Sec., 1336 Sherbrooke est, Montréal, P.Q. H2L 1M2 (514/526-8541)
Lac-Poulin (Village)	12	Beauce		Beauce-Sud	P. Poulin, Sec., C.P. 186, St-Georges, P.Q. G5Y 5C7 (418/228-6115)

Cities in CAPITALS (Ville); Towns/Villes marked (Ville); Villages marked (Village); Townships/Cantons (marked Canton); United townships/Cantons unis (marked Cantons*); Parishes marked (Paroisse); undesignated municipalities/sans designation marked (Mun.).

MUNICIPALITY	POP.	COUNTY	FEDERAL ELECTORAL DISTRICT	PROVINCIAL ELECTORAL DISTRICT	CLERK/GREFFIER OR SECRETARY-TREASURER (SEC) WITH ADDRESS & PHONE
Lac-St-Charles (Mun.)	3,502	Québec	Charlesbourg	Chauveau	R. Brassard, Sec., C.P. 8, Lac-St-Charles, P.Q. GOA 2HO (418/849-2811)
Lac-St-Joseph (Ville)	31	Portneuf	Portneuf	Chauveau	A. Létourneau, Sec., 4417 des Lierres, Orsainville, P.Q. G1G 1S2 (418/626-1745)
Lac-Ste-Marie (Mun.)	364	Gatineau	Pontiac-Gatineau-Labelle	Gatineau	A. Roy, Sec., C.P. 97, Lac-Ste-Marie, P.Q. JOX 1ZO (819/467-5437)
Lac-St-Paul (Mun.)	282	Labelle	Pontiac-Gatineau-Labelle	Labelle	A. Meilleur, Sec., Lac-St-Paul, P.Q. JOW 1KO (819/587-4283)
Lac-Sergent (Ville)	93	Portneuf	Portneuf	Portneuf	R. Gosselin, Trés., 1624, Zone E, Lac-Sergent, P.Q. GOA 2JO (418/875-2646)
Lac-Simon (Mun.)	376	Papineau	Argenteuil	Papineau	Mme G. Périard, Sec., C.P. 40, R.R. 1, Chénéville, P.Q. JOV 1EO (819/428-3367)
Lac-Supérieur (Mun.)	400	Terrebonne	Labelle	Labelle	L. Rehel, Sec., Lac-Carré, P.Q. JOT 1JO (819/688-2208)
Lac-Tremblant-Nord (Mun.)	6	Labelle	Labelle	Labelle	G. Vassilios, Sec., a/s 6256 av Terrebonne, Montréal, P.Q. H4D 1A6 (514/288-0685)
La Durantaye (Paroisse)	771	Bellechasse	Bellechasse	Bellechasse	Y. Delagrave, Sec., C.P. 99, La Durantaye, P.Q. GOR 1WO (418/884-3465)
Lafontaine (Village)	4,503	Terrebonne	Labelle	Prévost	F. Campbell, Sec., 70 106e av., Lafontaine, P.Q. J7Y 1G5 (514/438-2264)
Laforce (Mun.)	286	Témiscamingue	Témiscamingue	Rouyn-Noranda-Témiscamingue	B. Pichette, Sec., Rang 5, C.P. 35, Laforce, P.Q. JOZ 2JO (819/722-2550)
La Guadeloupe (Village)	1,797	Frontenac	Frontenac	Beauce-Sud	A. Beilleux, Sec., C.P. 279, La Guadeloupe, P.Q. GOM 1GO (418/457-3469)
La Macaza (Mun.)	553	Labelle	Labelle	Labelle	A. Ozell, Sec., C.P. 28, La Macaza, P.Q. JOT 1RO (819/275-2077)
La Malbaie (Ville)	4,120	Charlevoix-Est	Charlevoix	Charlevoix	R. Arpin, Sec., C.P. 518, La Malbaie, P.Q. GOT 1JO (418/665-3747)
Lamarche (Mun.)	566	Chicoutimi	Lac-St-Jean	Lac-St-Jean	W. Lessard, Sec., rue Principale, Lamarche PO, P.Q. GOW 1XO (418/481-2861)
La Martre (Mun.)	406	Gaspé-Ouest		Matane	M.C. Gagnon, Sec., La Martre, P.Q. GOE 2HO (418/288-5881)
Lambton (Mun.)	1,547	Frontenac	Mégantic-Compton-Stanstead	Mégantic-Compton	W. Turcotte, Sec., C.P. 206, Lambton, P.Q. GOM 1HO (418/486-7131)
La Minerve (Canton)	668	Labelle		Labelle	R. Bellefleur, Sec., La Minerve, P.Q. JOT 1SO (819/274-2364)
La Motte (Mun.)	424	Abitibi	Abitibi	Abitibi-Ouest	G. Robitaille, Sec., C.P. 55, La Motte, P.Q. JOY 1TO (819/498-3236)
Landrienne (Canton)	809	Abitibi		Abitibi-Ouest	J. Perron, Sec., Landrienne, P.Q. JOY 1VO (819/732-3847)
L'Ange-Gardien (Mun.)				Papineau	
L'Ange-Gardien (Paroisse)	2,354	Montmorency 1	Montmorency	Montmorency	R. Gariépy, Sec., C.P. 9, L'Ange-Gardien, P.Q. GOA 2KO (418/822-1555)

Cities in CAPITALS (Ville); Towns/Villes marked (Ville); Villages marked (Village); Townships/Cantons (marked Canton); United townships/Cantons unis (marked Cantons*); Parishes marked (Paroisse); undesignated municipalities/sans designation marked (Mun.).

MUNICIPALITY	POP.	COUNTY	FEDERAL ELECTORAL DISTRICT	PROVINCIAL ELECTORAL DISTRICT	CLERK/GREFFIER OR SECRETARY-TREASURER (SEC) WITH ADDRESS & PHONE
Langelier (Canton)	465	Champlain		Laviolette	C. Gagnon, Sec., La Croche, P.Q. GOX 1RO (819/523-2061)
L'Annonciation (Village)	2,180	Labelle	Labelle	Labelle	Lise Cadieux, Sec., C.P. 398, L'Annonciation, P.Q. JOT 1TO (819/275-2929)
Lanoraie-d'Autray (Mun.)	1,364	Berthier		Berthier	J.-P. Delorme, Sec., C.P. 308, Lanoraie, P.Q. JOK 1EO (514/887-2201)
Lantier (Mun.)	477	Terrebonne	Joliette	Labelle	Mme M. Quévillon, Sec., C.P. 39, Lantier, P.Q. JOT 1VO (819/326-2674)
La Patrie (Village)	455	Compton	Mégantic-Compton-Stanstead	Mégantic-Compton	Mme G. Charron, Sec., C.P. 29, La Patrie, P.Q. JOB 1YO (819/888-2514)
La Pêche (Mun.)	4,800	Gatineau		Gatineau	Ella Matte, Sec., C.P. 70, Ste-Cécile-de-Masham, P.Q. JOX 2WO (819/456-2161)
La Pérade (Village)	1,025	Champlain	Portneuf	Champlain	G. Marchand, Sec., C.P. 39, La Pérade, P.Q. GOX 2JO (418/325-2662)
La Plaine (Paroisse)	2,929	L'Assomption	Terrebonne	Terrebonne	M. Ouimet, Sec., 675 de l'Eglise, La Plaine, P.Q. JON 1BO (514/478-2555)
La Pocatière (Ville)	4,379	Kamouraska	Kamouraska-Rivière-du-Loup	Kamouraska-Témiscouata	C. Crête, Greffier, 410 9e rue, C.P. 668, La Pocatière, P.Q. GOR 1ZO (418/856-3394)
La Prairie (Ville)	9,500	Laprairie	Laprairie	Laprairie	G. Dupre, Trés., 600 boul. Ste-Elizabeth, La Prairie, P.Q. J5R 1V1 (514/659-1947)
La Présentation (Paroisse)	1,419	St-Hyacinthe	St-Hyacinthe	Verchères	J.-J. Giasson, Sec., 468 de l'Eglise, La Présentation, P.Q. JOH 1BO (514/796-3264)
La Rédemption (Paroisse)	788	Matapédia	Matapédia-Matane	Matapédia	L. Dubé, Sec., C.P. 39, La Rédemption, P.Q. GOJ 1PO (418/776-2925)
La Reine (Village)	390	Abitibi	Témiscamingue	Abitibi-Ouest	J.-M. Lefebvre, Sec., La Reine, P.Q. JOZ 2LO (819/769-7196)
La Reine (Mun.)	217	Abitibi	Témiscamingue	Abitibi-Ouest	Mme A. Gauthier, Sec., R.R. 1, La Reine, P.Q. JOZ 2LO (819/333-6131)
Larouche (Paroisse)	777	Chicoutimi	Jonquière	Lac-St-Jean	P.-H. Munger, Sec., 107 rue Gauthier, Larouche, P.Q. GOW 1VO (418/542-4863)
LaSALLE (Ville)	76,737	Ile-de-Montréal	LaSalle	Marguerite-Bourgeoys; Marquette; Verdun	Jacq. G. Boyer, Greffier, 13 Strathyre, LaSalle, P.Q. H8R 3P6 (514/366-7110)
La Sarre (Ville)	5,000	Abitibi	Témiscamingue	Abitibi-Ouest	M. Gagnon, Greffier, 4 Ave. est, La Sarre, P.Q. J9Z 1J9 (819/333-2282)
La Sarre (Canton)	3,497	Abitibi		Abitibi-Ouest	Me M. Lambert, Greffier, 10 Lapierre, La Sarre, P.Q. J9Z 2Y4 (819/333-5587)
L'Ascension (Paroisse)	498	Labelle	Labelle	Labelle	J. Légault, Sec., C.P. 30, L'Ascension, P.Q. JOT 1WO (819/275-3027)
L'Ascension-de-Notre-Seigneur (Paroisse)	1,535	Lac-St-Jean-Est		Lac-St-Jean	R. Boily, Sec., 45 Ave est, Langlais, P.Q. GOW 1YO (418/347-3482)
L'Ascension-de-Patapédia (Mun.)	411	Bonaventure	Bonaventure-Iles-de-la-Madeleine	Bonaventure	Mme L. Gallant, Sec., L'Ascension-de-Patapédia, P.Q. GOJ 1RO (418/299-2252)

Cities in CAPITALS (Ville); Towns/Villes marked (Ville); Villages marked (Village); Townships/Cantons (marked Canton); United townships/Cantons unis (marked Cantons*); Parishes marked (Paroisse); undesignated municipalities/sans designation marked (Mun.).

MUNICIPALITY	POP.	COUNTY	FEDERAL ELECTORAL DISTRICT	PROVINCIAL ELECTORAL DISTRICT	CLERK/GREFFIER OR SECRETARY-TREASURER (SEC) WITH ADDRESS & PHONE
L'Assomption (Paroisse)	2,664	L'Assomption	Joliette	L'Assomption	Mme D. Henri, Sec., 430 rg. du Golf, L'Assomption, P.Q. JOK 1GO (514/589-5565)
L'Assomption (Ville)	4,832	L'Assomption	Joliette	L'Assomption	M. Savoie, Greffier, 200 Ste-Anne, L'Assomption, P.Q. JOK 1GO (514/589-5671)
La Station-du-Coteau (Village)	863	Soulanges	Vaudreuil	Vaudreuil-Soulanges	B.H. Walker, Sec., 97 Lippée, Coteau-Station, P.Q. JOP 1EO (514/267-3683)
Laterrière (Village)	656	Chicoutimi	Jonquière	Dubuc	C. Potvin, Sec., C.P. 100, Laterrière, P.Q. GOV 1KO (418/678-2204)
Latulipe et Gaboury (Cantons)*	508	Témiscamingue		Rouyn-Noranda-Témiscamingue	R. Breton, Sec., Latulipe, P.Q. JOZ 2NO (819/747-4281)
La Tuque (Ville)	11,900	Champlain	Champlain	Laviolette	Noel Fillion, Greffier, C.P. 580, La Tuque, P.Q. G9X 3P4 (819/523-3677)
Launay (Canton)	383	Abitibi		Abitibi-Ouest	D. Chaput, Sec., Launay, P.Q. JOY 1WO (819/796-2561)
Laurentides (Ville)	1,800	L'Assomption	Terrebonne	Rousseau	R. Hogue, Sec., C.P. 128, Laurentides, P.Q. JOR 1CO (514/439-2539)
Laurier Station (Village)	1,350	Lotbinière	Lotbinière	Lotbinière	R. Tousignant, Sec., 137 de la Station, Laurier Station, P.Q. GOS 1NO (418/728-3852)
Laurierville (Village)	865	Mégantic	Frontenac	Lotbinière	G. Mercier, Sec., C.P. 133, Laurierville, P.Q. GOS 1PO (819/365-4317)
LAUZON (Ville)	12,500	Lévis	Lévis	Lévis	M. Fortin, Greffier, 35 rue Bargoné, Lauzon, P.Q. G6V 2G3 (418/837-5801)
LAVAL (Ville)	265,000	Ile-Jésus	Duvernay; Laval	Chomedey; Fabre; Laval-des-Rapides; Mille-Iles; Vimont	R. Bourcier, Greffier, 1 place du Souvenir, (Chomedey), Laval, P.Q. H7V 1W7 (514/688-6221)
Lavaltrie (Village)	1,532	Berthier	Berthier-Maskinongé	Berthier	R. Nantais, Sec., C.P. 330, Lavaltrie, P.Q. JOK 1HO (514/586-1366)
L'Avenir (Mun.)	1,022	Drummond	Richmond	Johnson	N. Raîche, Sec., 518 Principale, L'Avenir, P.Q. JOC 1BO (819/394-2481)
Laverlochère (Paroisse)	829	Témiscamingue	Témiscamingue	Rouyn-Noranda-Témiscamingue	Neven Noella, Sec., C.P. 159, Laverlochère, P.Q. JOZ 2PO (819/765-5111)
La Visitation-de-Champlain (Paroisse)	887	Champlain		Champlain	R.-A. Toupin, Sec., 819 Notre-Dame, Champlain, P.Q. GOX 1CO (819/295-3222)
La Visitation de la Bienheureuse-Vierge Marie (Paroisse)	391	Yamaska		Nicolet	J. Maillette, Sec., La Visitation, P.Q. JOG 1VO (514/564-5724)
Lawrenceville (Village)	529	Shefford	Shefford	Brome-Missisquoi	A. Mercier, Sec., C.P. 60, Lawrenceville, P.Q. JOE 1WO (514/535-6361)
Lebel-sur-Quévillon (Ville)	3,591	Terr. du Nouveau-Québec	Abitibi	Abitibi-Est	G. Boulet, Greffier, C.P. 430, Lebel-sur-Quévillon, P.Q. JOY 1XO (819/755-4826)
Leclercville (Village)	390	Lotbinière	Lotbinière	Lotbinière	Y. Boucher, Sec., Leclercville, P.Q. GOS 1RO (819/292-2273)
Leeds (Canton)	332	Mégantic		Frontenac	L. Trépanier, Sec., a/s R.R. 2, Pontbriand, P.Q. GON 1KO (418/424-3702)

Cities in CAPITALS (Ville); Towns/Villes marked (Ville); Villages marked (Village); Townships/Cantons (marked Canton); United townships/Cantons unis (marked Cantons*); Parishes marked (Paroisse); undesignated municipalities/sans designation marked (Mun.).

MUNICIPALITY	POP.	COUNTY	FEDERAL ELECTORAL DISTRICT	PROVINCIAL ELECTORAL DISTRICT	CLERK/GREFFIER OR SECRETARY-TREASURER (SEC) WITH ADDRESS & PHONE
Lefebvre (Mun.)	481	Drummond	Drummond	Johnson	France Noel, Sec., a/s R.R. 5, Durham-Sud, P.Q. JOH 2CO (819/394-2816)
Le Gardeur (Ville)	6,800	L'Assomption		L'Assomption	D. Jacques, Greffier, l'Montée des Arsenaux, Le Gardeur, P.Q. J5X 2C1 (514/585-1140)
Lemieux (Mun.)	324	Nicolet	Lotbinière	Lotbinière	France Hénault-Thibault, Sec., R.R. 2, Lemieux, P.Q. GOX 1SO (819/283-2506)
Lemoyne (Ville)	6,800	Chambly	Laprairie	Laporte	J. Comtois, Sec., 2205 St-Georges, Lemoyne, P.Q. J4R 1V7 (514/671-5948)
L'Enfant-Jésus (Paroisse)	607	Beauce	Beauce	Beauce-Nord	R.M. Doyon, Sec., Vallée-Jonction, P.Q. GOS 3JO (418/253-5571)
Lennoxville (Ville)	3,656	Sherbrooke	Sherbrooke	St-François	J. Gervais, Sec., 150 Queen, Lennoxville, P.Q. J1M 1J6 (819/569-9388)
L'Epiphanie (Paroisse)	2,059	L'Assomption		L'Assomption	G. Payette, Sec., 1027 Haut l'Achigan sud, L'Epiphanie, P.Q. JOK 1JO (514/588-2876)
L'Epiphanie (Ville)	2,941	L'Assomption	Joliette	L'Assomption	R. Livernoche, Sec., 66 Notre-Dame, C.P. 190, L'Epiphanie, P.Q. JOK 1JO (514/588-2425)
Léry (Ville)	1,850	Châteauguey	Châteauguay	Beauharnois	A. Girard, Sec., 1 Hôtel de ville, Léry, P.Q. J6N 1E8 (514/692-6861)
Les Becquets (Village)	587	Nicolet	Lotbinière	Lotbinière	G. Lemay, Sec., 131 av. Beauchemin, Les Becquets, P.Q. GOX 2ZO (819/263-2231)
Les Boules (Mun.)	525	Matane	Matapédia-Matane	Matane	Mme J. Marcheterre, Sec., Route 132, Les Boules, P.Q. GOJ 1SO (418/936-3479)
Les Cèdres (Village)	423	Soulanges	Vaudreuil	Vaudreuil-Soulanges	C.I. Pilon, Sec., C.P. 210, Les Cèdres, P.Q. JOP 1LO (514/452-4340)
Les Eboulements (Mun.)	1,185	Charlevoix-Ouest	Charlevoix	Charlevoix	A. Girard, Sec., C.P. 130, Les Eboulements, P.Q. GOA 2MO (418/635-2755)
Leslie, Clapham et Huddersfield (Cantons)*	960	Pontiac		Pontiac	J. Leclaire, Sec., C.P. 70, Otter Lake, P.Q. JOX 2PO (819/453-2591)
Les Méchins (Mun.)	1,466	Matane	Matapédia-Matane	Matane	Mme F. Verreault, Sec., C.P. 41, Les Méchins, P.Q. GOJ 1TO (418/729-3285)
Les Sept-Cantons-Unis-du-Saguenay*	439	Saguenay		Saguenay	a/s J. Thibault, Admin., Min. des Affaires Municipale, Bldg. G, 680 St-Amable, Québec, P.Q. G1R 4Z3 (418/643-7082)
Letang (Mun.)				Rouyn-Noranda-Témiscamingue	
L'Etang-du-Nord (Mun.)	2,605	Iles-de-la-Madeleine	Bonaventure-Iles-de-la-Madeleine	Iles-de-la-Madeleine	E. Leblanc, Sec., C.P. 29, Etang-du-Nord, P.Q. GOB 1EO (418/986-3321)
Letellier (Canton)	244	Saguenay		Duplessis	a/s C. Gagnon, Admin., Min. des Affaires Municipale, C.P. 714, Sept-Iles, P.Q. (418/968-2851)
LEVIS (Ville)	18,300	Lévis	Lévis	Lévis	R. Gendreau, Greffier, C.P. 1186, Lévis, P.Q. G6V 6R8 (418/833-3261)

Cities in CAPITALS (Ville); Towns/Villes marked (Ville); Villages marked (Village); Townships/Cantons (marked Canton); United townships/Cantons unis (marked Cantons*); Parishes marked (Paroisse); undesignated municipalities/sans designation marked (Mun.).

MUNICIPALITY	POP.	COUNTY	FEDERAL ELECTORAL DISTRICT	PROVINCIAL ELECTORAL DISTRICT	CLERK/GREFFIER OR SECRETARY-TREASURER (SEC) WITH ADDRESS & PHONE
Lingwick (Canton)	491	Compton		Mégantic-Compton	L. Rousseau, Sec., Ste-Marguerite PO, P.Q. JOB 2ZO (819/877-3311)
Linière (Village)	1,180	Beauce	Beauce	Beauce-Sud	J.-P. Champagne, Sec., C.P. 219, Linière, P.Q. GOM 1JO (418/685-3825)
L'Islet (Ville)	1,109	L'Islet	Bellechasse	Montmagny-L'Islet	J.-M. Gagnon, Sec., 92 7e rue, C.P. 68, L'Islet, P.Q. GOR 2CO (418/247-5345)
L'Islet-sur-Mer (Village)	817	L'Islet	Bellechasse	Montmagny-L'Islet	M. Rancourt, Sec., C.P. 99, L'Islet-sur-Mer, P.Q. GOR 2BO (418/247-3507)
L'Isle-Verte (Village)	1,177	Rivière-du-Loup	Kamouraska-Rivière-du-Loup	Rivière-du-Loup	R. Ouellet, Sec., C.P. 128, Isle-Verte, P.Q. GOL 1KO (418/898-2812)
Litchfield (Canton)	650	Pontiac		Pontiac	C. Robillard, Sec., C.P. 340, Campbell's Bay, P.Q. JOX 1KO (819/648-5511)
Lochaber (Canton)	517	Papineau		Papineau	F. Lafleur, Sec., C.P. 218, Thurso, P.Q. JOX 3BO (819/985-2169)
Lochaber, ouest (Canton)	420	Papineau		Papineau	F. Clement, Sec., C.P. 881, Thurso, P.Q. JOX 3BO (819/985-3283)
Longue-Pointe (Mun.)	568	Saguenay	Manicouagan	Duplessis	Mlle L. Ward, Sec., C.P. 68, Longue-Pointe-de-Mingan, P.Q. GOG 1VO (418/949-2053)
LONGUEUIL (Ville)	131,900	Chambly	Longueuil	Laporte; Marie-Victorin; Taillon	C. Gauthier, Greffier, 300 St-Charles ouest, Longueuil, P.Q. J4K 4Y7 (514/670-2220)
LORETTEVILLE (Ville)	14,700	Québec	Charlesbourg	Chauveau	G. Martel, Greffier, 305 Racine, Loretteville, P.Q. G2B 1E7 (418/842-1921)
Lorraine (Ville)	6,300	Terrebonne	Blainville-Deux-Montagnes	Groulx	N.B. Chalifour, Greffier, 100 Grande-Côte, Lorraine, P.Q. J6Z 1L9 (514/621-8550)
Lorrainville (Village)	986	Témiscamingue	Témiscamingue	Rouyn-Noranda-Témiscamingue	J. Damphousse, Sec., C.P. 218, Lorrainville, P.Q. JOZ 2RO (819/625-2167)
Lotbinière (Mun.)	1,199	Lotbinière	Lotbinière	Lotbinière	D. Blanchette, Sec., C.P. 70, Lotbinière, P.Q. GOS 1SO (418/796-2103)
Louiseville (Ville)	3,943	Maskinongé	Berthier-Maskinongé	Maskinongé	Luc Levasseur, Greffier, 105 St-Laurent, C.P. 38, Louiseville, P.Q. J5V 1J6 (819/228-5115)
Low (Canton)	881	Gatineau		Gatineau	J. Brady, Sec., C.P. 100, Low, P.Q. JOX 2CO (819/422-3879)
Luceville (Village)	1,500	Rimouski	Rimouski	Rimouski	J. Tremblay, Sec., C.P. 310, Luceville, P.Q. GOK 1EO (418/739-3566)
Lyster (Mun.)	2,009	Mégantic	Frontenac	Lotbinière	Denise Fournier, Sec., 114 Isabelle, Ste-Anasthasie, P.Q. GOS 2BO (819/389-5787)
Lytton (Canton)	247	Gatineau		Gatineau	G. O'Connor, Sec., R.R. 1, Montcerf, P.Q. JOW 1NO (819/449-4512)
Macamic (Ville)	1,758	Abitibi	Témiscamingue	Abitibi-Ouest	G. Carrier, Sec., C.P. 128, Macamic, P.Q. JOZ 2SO (819/782-4206)
Macamic (Paroisse)	786	Abitibi	Témiscamingue	Abitibi-Ouest	G. Champagne, Sec., C.P. 226, Macamic, P.Q. JOZ 2SO (819/782-2188)

Cities in CAPITALS (Ville); Towns/Villes marked (Ville); Villages marked (Village); Townships/Cantons (marked Canton); United townships/Cantons unis (marked Cantons*); Parishes marked (Paroisse); undesignated municipalities/sans designation marked (Mun.).

MUNICIPALITY	POP.	COUNTY	FEDERAL ELECTORAL DISTRICT	PROVINCIAL ELECTORAL DISTRICT	CLERK/GREFFIER OR SECRETARY-TREASURER (SEC) WITH ADDRESS & PHONE
Maddington (Canton)	321	Arthabaska		Nicolet	R. Benoît, Sec., 120 rue Principale, Maddington Falls, P.Q. GOZ 1CO (819/367-2289)
MAGOG (Ville)	13,300	Stanstead	Missisquoi	Orford	J.-P. Lange, Sec., 7 Principale est, C.P. 249, Magog, P.Q. J1X 1Y4 (819/843-6501)
Magog (Canton)	2,300	Stanstead		Orford	J.-P. Asselin, Sec., C.P. 400, R.R. 2, Magog, P.Q. J1X 3X7 (819/843-3286)
Malartic (Ville)	5,000	Abitibi	Abitibi	Abitibi-Est	M. Chagnon, Trés., C.P. 3090, Malartic, P.Q. JOY 1ZO (819/757-3611)
Maniwaki (Ville)	5,700	Gatineau	Pontiac-Gatineau-Labelle	Gatineau	R. Riel, Greffier, 266 Notre Dame, #335, Maniwaki, P.Q. J9E 2J8 (819/449-2800)
Manseau (Village)	643	Nicolet	Lotbinière	Lotbinière	Pauline Savoie, Sec., C.P. 67, Manseau, P.Q. GOX 1VO (819/356-2450)
Mansfield et Pontefract (Cantons)*	2,062	Pontiac		Pontiac	D. Marion, Sec., C.P. 479, Fort-Coulonges, P.Q. JOX 1RO (819/683-2944)
Maple Grove (Ville)	1,880	Beauharnois	Beauharnois-Salaberry	Beauharnois	M. LeBlanc, Sec., 149 St-Laurent, Maple Grove, P.Q. J6N 1K2 (514/429-5061)
Marbleton (Village)	544	Wolfe	Richmond	Mégantic-Compton	L.-E. Beauregard, Sec., St-Adolphe-de-Dudswell, P.Q. JOB 2LO (819/887-6874)
Marchand (Canton)	975	Labelle		Labelle	M.-P. Fortin, Sec., C.P. 695, L'Annonciation, P.Q. JOT 1TO (819/275-3202)
Maria (Mun.)	2,072	Bonaventure	Bonaventure-Iles-de-la-Madeleine	Bonaventure	J.-M. Dugas, Sec., C.P. 218, Maria, P.Q. GOC 1YO (418/759-3883)
Maricourt (Mun.)	585	Shefford	Abitibi	Johnson	R. Paquette, Sec., R.R. 1, Racine, P.Q. JOE 1YO (514/532-2243)
Marieville (Ville)	4,853	Rouville	Chambly	Iberville	Y. Vincent, Sec., 682 St-Charles, C.P. 519, Marieville, P.Q. JOL 1JO (514/658-8081)
Marsoui (Village)	532	Gaspé-Ouest	Gaspé	Matane	J.G. Hébert, Sec., C.P. 130, Marsoui, P.Q. GOE 1SO (418/288-5552)
Marston (Canton)	287	Frontenac		Mégantic-Compton	C. Larouche, Sec., 3550 Carignan, Lac-Mégantic, P.Q. G6B 1S3 (819/583-2337)
Martinville (Mun.)	408	Compton	Mégantic-Compton-Stanstead	Mégantic-Compton	D. Roy, Sec., Martinville, P.Q. JOB 2AO (819/835-5700)
Mascouche (Ville)	16,800	L'Assomption	Terrebonne	Terrebonne	Colette Marion, Greffier, 3034 boul. Ste-Marie, Mascouche, P.Q. JON 1CO (514/474-4133)
Maskinongé (Village)	1,013	Maskinongé	Berthier-Maskinongé	Maskinongé	Mme C.D. Fréchette, Sec., 36B St-Dennis, Maskinongé, P.Q. JOK 1NO (819/227-2515)
Masson (Ville)				Papineau	
Massueville (Village)	583	Richelieu	Richelieu	Richelieu	B. Choquette, Sec., 834 rue Royale, Massueville, P.Q. JOG 1KO (514/788-2966)
Matagami (Ville)	4,038	Terr. du Nouveau-Québec	Abitibi	Ungava	L.-J. Laflamme, Greffier, C.P. 160, Matagami, P.Q. JOY 2AO (819/739-2541)

Cities in CAPITALS (Ville); Towns/Villes marked (Ville); Villages marked (Village); Townships/Cantons (marked Canton); United townships/Cantons unis (marked Cantons*); Parishes marked (Paroisse); undesignated municipalities/sans designation marked (Mun.).

MUNICIPALITY	POP.	COUNTY	FEDERAL ELECTORAL DISTRICT	PROVINCIAL ELECTORAL DISTRICT	CLERK/GREFFIER OR SECRETARY-TREASURER (SEC) WITH ADDRESS & PHONE
Matane (Ville)	12,700	Matane	Matapédia-Matane	Matane	A. Lavoie, Sec., 230 ave St-Jérôme, Matane, P.Q. G4W 3A2 (418/562-2333)
Matapédia (Paroisse)	861	Bonaventure	Bonaventure-Iles-de-la-Madeleine	Bonaventure	A. Firth, Sec., C.P. 207, Matapédia, P.Q. GOJ 1VO (418/865-2917)
Mayo (Mun.)	185	Papineau	Gatineau	Papineau	Mrs. N. Somers, Sec., R.R. 1, Thurso, P.Q. JOX 3BO (819/986-5554)
McMasterville (Village)	3,280	Verchères	Verchères	Verchères	M. Lalande, Sec., 300 Caron, McMasterville, P.Q. J3G 1S5 (514/467-3580)
Melbourne (Canton)	985	Richmond		Johnson	T.E. Gilchrist, Sec., R.R. 2, boite 4, Melbourne, P.Q. JOB 2BO (819/826-3555)
Melbourne (Village)	461	Richmond	Richmond	Johnson	G.H. McKeage, Sec., C.P. 70, Melbourne, P.Q. JOB 2BO (819/826-2417)
Melocheville (Village)	1,700	Beauharnois	Beauharnois-Salaberry	Beauharnois	N. Charette, Sec., C.P. 60, Melocheville, P.Q. JOS 1JO (514/429-5385)
Mercier (Ville)	5,800	Châteauguay	Châteauguay	Châteauguay	R. Bergevin, Sec., C.P. 389, Mercier, P.Q. JOL 1KO (514/691-6090)
Messines (Mun.)	999	Gatineau	Pontiac-Gatineau-Labelle	Gatineau	P. Beaudoin, Sec., C.P. 69, Messines, P.Q. JOX 2JO (819/465-2407)
Métabetchouan (Ville)	3,365	Lac-St-Jean-Est	Roberval	Lac-St-Jean	J. Gagné, Greffier, 81 rue St-André, Métabetchouan, P.Q. GOW 2AO (418/349-2060)
Métis-sur-Mer (Village)	174	Matane	Matapédia-Matane	Matane	Mrs. A.J. Astle, Sec., C.P. 44, Métis Beach, P.Q. GOJ 1WO (418/936-3420)
Milan (Mun.)	225	Frontenac	Mégantic-Compton-Stanstead	Mégantic-Compton	D. Nicholson, Sec., Milan, P.Q. GOY 1EO (819/657-4551)
Mille-Isles (Mun.)	437	Argenteuil	Argenteuil	Argenteuil	W.M. Swimdells, Sec., R.R. 1, Bellefeuille PO, P.Q. JOR 1AO (514/438-2958)
MIRABEL (Ville)	13,100	Deux-Montagnes	Argenteuil	Argenteuil	C. Bélisle, Greffier, 14111 rue St-Jean, Ste-Monique, P.Q. JON 1RO (514/430-1622)
Mistassini (Village)	6,000	Lac-St-Jean-Ouest	Roberval	Roberval	La Sécrétaire, 173 boul. St-Michel, Mistassini, P.Q. GOW 2CO (418/276-3685)
Moffet (Mun.)	354	Témiscamingue	Témiscamingue	Rouyn-Noranda-Témiscamingue	A. Marcotte, Sec., C.P. 89, Moffet, P.Q. JOZ 2WO (819/747-5421)
Moisie (Mun.)	1,000	Saguenay	Manicouagan	Duplessis	S. Migneault, Sec., C.P. 33, Moisie, P.Q. GOG 2BO (418/927-2122)
Montbeillard (Mun.)				Rouyn-Noranda-Témiscamingue	
Montcalm (Canton)	214	Argenteuil		Argenteuil	H. Williams, Sec., C.P. 144, Weir, P.Q. JOT 2VO (819/687-2836)
Mont-Carmel (Mun.)	1,567	Kamouraska	Kamouraska-Rivière-du-Loup	Kamouraska-Temiscouata	M. Lévesque, Sec., C.P 17, Mont-Carmel, P.Q. GOL 1WO (418/498-2050)
Montcerf (Mun.)	540	Gatineau	Pontiac-Gatineau-Labelle	Gatineau	M.-P. Gosselin, Sec., Montcerf, P.Q. JOW 1NO (819/449-4578)
Montebello (Village)	1,286	Papineau	Argenteuil	Papineau	C.G. Beauchamp, Sec., 101 Notre Dame, Montebello, P.Q. JOV 1LO (819/423-5123)

Cities in CAPITALS (Ville); Towns/Villes marked (Ville); Villages marked (Village); Townships/Cantons (marked Canton); United townships/Cantons unis (marked Cantons*); Parishes marked (Paroisse); undesignated municipalities/sans designation marked (Mun.).

MUNICIPALITY	POP.	COUNTY	FEDERAL ELECTORAL DISTRICT	PROVINCIAL ELECTORAL DISTRICT	CLERK/GREFFIER OR SECRETARY-TREASURER (SEC) WITH ADDRESS & PHONE
Mont-Gabriel (Ville)	35	Terrebonne	Labelle	Prevost	L. Pellerin, Sec., 24 rue Albert, Ste-Agathe-des-Monts, P.Q. J8C 1Z5 (819/326-2381)
Mont-Joli (Ville)	6,300	Rimouski	Matapédia-Matane	Matapédia	G. Thibault, Sec., 40 Hôtel de ville, Mont-Joli, P.Q. G5H 1W8 (418/775-7285)
Mont-Laurier (Ville)	8,600	Labelle	Pontiac-Gatineau-Labelle	Labelle	C. Lauzon, Greffier, 450 Mercier, Mont-Laurier, P.Q. J9L 2W1 (819/623-1221)
Mont-Lebel (Mun.)	329	Rimouski	Rimouski	Rimouski	J.-A. Boudreault, Sec., R.R. 1, Ste-Blandine, P.Q. GOK 1JO (418/735-2952)
MONTMAGNY (Ville)	12,300	Montmagny	Bellechasse	Montmagny-L'Islet	J. Pelletier, Greffier, C.P. 40, Montmagny, P.Q. G5V 3S3 (418/248-3361)
Montminy (Canton)	1,206	Montmagny		Montmagny-L'Islet	R. Gagné, Sec., St-Paul-de-Montminy, P.Q. GOR 3YO (418/469-3120)
Montpellier (Mun.)	481	Papineau	Argenteuil	Papineau	M. Vaillant, Sec., C.P. 40, Montpellier, P.Q. JOV 1MO (819/428-3663)
MONTREAL (Ville)	1,069,700	Ile-de-Montréal	Bourassa; Dollard; Gamelin; Hochelaga-Maisonneuve; Lachine; LaSalle; Laurier; Mercier; Mont-Royal; Notre-Dame de Grâce; Outremont; Papineau; Rosemont; St-Denis; St-Henri-Westmount; St-Jacques; St-Léonard-Anjou; Ste-Marie; St-Michel; Verdun	Anjou; Bourassa; Bourget; Cremazie; D'Arcy McGee; Dorion; Gouin; Jeanne-Mance; L'Acadie; Lafontaine; Laurier; Maisonneuve; Mercier; Mont-Royal; Notre-Dame de Grâce; Outremont; Rosemont; Ste-Anne; St-Henri; St-Jacques; St-Laurent; St-Louis; Ste-Marie; Viau; Viger; Westmount	Marc Boyer, Greffier, 275 rue Notre Dame est, Montréal, P.Q. H2Y 1C6 (514/872-3140)
Montréal-Est (Ville)	4,186	Ile-de-Montréal	Mercier	Lafontaine	Véronique Geminari, Greffier, 11370 Notre Dame est, Montréal-Est, P.Q. H1B 2W6 (514/645-7431)
MONTREAL-NORD (Ville)	96,400	Ile-de-Montréal	Bourassa	Bourassa; Sauvé	Aline Ouimet, Greffier, 4242 Hôtel de ville, Montréal-Nord, P.Q. H1H 1S5 (514/322-6271)
Montréal-Ouest (Ville)	5,800	Ile-de-Montréal	Notre Dame de Grâce	Notre Dame de Grâce	H.M. McLaughlin, Sec., 50 Westminster sud, Montréal-Ouest, P.Q. H4X 1Y7 (514/481-8125)
Mont-Rolland (Mun.)	2,147	Terrebonne	Labelle	Rousseau	P. Dionne, Sec., 245 rue Morin, Mont-Rolland, P.Q. JOR 1GO (514/229-2200)
Mont-Royal (Ville)	20,100	Ile-de-Montréal	Mont-Royal	Mont-Royal	Margaret Quinlan, Greffier, 90 Roosevelt Ave., Mont-Royal, P.Q. H3R 1Z5 (514/737-1141)
Mont-St-Grégoire (Village)	656	Iberville	St-Jean	Iberville	J. Plourde, Sec., C.P. 149, Mont-St-Grégoire, P.Q. JOJ 1KO (514/347-3588)
Mont-St-Hilaire (Ville)	8,600	Rouville	Verchères	Verchères	L. Olivier, Greffier, 100 Centre Civique, Mont-St-Hilaire, P.Q. J3H 3M8 (514/467-2854)

Cities in CAPITALS (Ville); Towns/Villes marked (Ville); Villages marked (Village); Townships/Cantons (marked Canton); United townships/Cantons unis (marked Cantons*); Parishes marked (Paroisse); undesignated municipalities/sans designation marked (Mun.).

MUNICIPALITY	POP.	COUNTY	FEDERAL ELECTORAL DISTRICT	PROVINCIAL ELECTORAL DISTRICT	CLERK/GREFFIER OR SECRETARY-TREASURER (SEC) WITH ADDRESS & PHONE
Mont-St-Michel (Mun.)	672	Labelle	Pontiac-Gatineau-Labelle	Labelle	L. Gagnon, Sec., Mont-St-Michel, P.Q. JOW 1PO (819/587-3093)
Mont-St-Pierre (Village)	369	Gaspé-Ouest	Gaspé	Gaspé	Mme R. Ouellet, Sec., Mont-St-Pierre, P.Q. GOE 1VO (418/797-2898)
Mont-Tremblant (Mun.)	607	Terrebonne	Labelle	Labelle	G.R. Therrien, Sec., C.P. 179, Mont-Tremblant, P.Q. JOT 1ZO (819/425-3305)
Morin-Heights (Mun.)	1,388	Argenteuil	Argenteuil	Argenteuil	A. Basier, Sec., Morin-Heights, P.Q. JOR 1HO (514/226-3232)
Mulgrave et Derry (Cantons)*	201	Papineau		Papineau	Guy Carrière, Sec., 133 Judge, Buckingham, P.Q. J8L 1A9 (819/986-5401)
Murdochville (Ville)	3,909	Gaspé-Ouest	Gaspé	Gaspé	M. Jalbert, Trés., C.P. 1120, Murdochville, P.Q. GOE 1WO (418/784-2536)
Namur (Mun.)	520	Papineau	Argenteuil	Papineau	L. Leggett, Sec., Namur, P.Q. JOV 1NO (819/426-2155)
Nantes (Mun.)	1,000	Frontenac	Mégantic-Compton-Stanstead	Mégantic-Compton	R. Busque, Sec., C.P. 60, Nantes, P.Q. GOY 1GO (819/547-3655)
Napierville (Village)	2,160	Napierville	St-Jean	St-Jean	Y. Dupont, Sec., 361 St-Jacques, Napierville, P.Q. JOJ 1LO (514/245-3634)
Natashquan (Canton)	429	Saguenay		Duplessis	L. Landry, Sec., Natashquan, P.Q. GOG 2EO (418/726-3362)
Nédelec (Canton)	606	Témiscamingue		Rouyn-Noranda-Témiscamingue	R. Dessureault, Sec., Nédelec, P.Q. JOZ 2ZO (819/784-3311)
Nelson (Canton)	190	Mégantic		Lotbinière	J.-A. Côté, Sec., Ste-Agathe-de-Lotbinière, P.Q. GOS 2AO (418/599-2207)
Neuville (Village)	952	Portneuf	Portneuf	Portneuf	G. Côté, Sec., Neuville, P.Q. GOA 2RO (418/876-2280)
New Carlisle (Mun.)	1,782	Bonaventure	Bonaventure-Iles-de-la-Madeleine	Bonaventure	D. Smollet, Sec., C.P. 40, New Carlisle, P.Q. GOC 1ZO (418/752-3141)
New Glasgow (Village)	144	Terrebonne	Terrebonne	Rousseau	G. Beaudet, Sec., C.P. 35, New Glasgow, P.Q. JOR 1JO (514/436-2894)
Newport (Mun.)	2,429	Gaspé-Est	Gaspé	Gaspé	N. Wafer, Sec., C.P. 7, Newport, P.Q. GOC 2AO (418/777-2281)
Newport (Canton)	703	Compton		Mégantic-Compton	L. Macleod, Sec., C.P. 52, R.R. 1, Cookshire, P.Q. JOB 1MO (819/875-3520)
New Richmond (Ville)	4,300	Bonaventure	Bonaventure-Iles-de-la-Madeleine	Bonaventure	Denis Gagnon, Sec., C.P. 338, New Richmond, P.Q. GOC 2BO (418/392-5035)
Nicolet (Ville)	4,868	Nicolet	Richelieu	Nicolet	F. Vallée, Trés., C.P. 670, Nicolet, P.Q. JOG 1EO (819/293-4401)
Nicolet-Sud (Mun.)	410	Nicolet	Richelieu	Nicolet	Mme J. Fréchette, Sec., C.P. 265, Nicolet, P.Q. JOG 1EO (819/293-4525)
NORANDA (Ville)	9,809	Témiscamingue	Témiscamingue	Rouyn-Noranda-Témiscamingue	A. Beauséjour, Sec., C.P. 188, Noranda, P.Q. J9X 5A6 (819/762-7748)
Norbertville (Village)	280	Arthabaska	Lotbinière	Arthabaska	G. Gauvreau, Sec., R.R. 1, Norbertville, P.Q. GOP 1BO (819/369-9245)
Normandin (Village)	3,840	Lac-St-Jean-Ouest	Roberval	Roberval	F. Girard, Greffier, C.P. 127, Normandin, P.Q. GOW 2EO (418/274-2004)

Cities in CAPITALS (Ville); Towns/Villes marked (Ville); Villages marked (Village); Townships/Cantons (marked Canton); United townships/Cantons unis (marked Cantons*); Parishes marked (Paroisse); undesignated municipalities/sans designation marked (Mun.).

MUNICIPALITY	POP.	COUNTY	FEDERAL ELECTORAL DISTRICT	PROVINCIAL ELECTORAL DISTRICT	CLERK/GREFFIER OR SECRETARY-TREASURER (SEC) WITH ADDRESS & PHONE
Normétal (Mun.)	1,423	Abitibi	Témiscamingue	Abitibi-Ouest	Mme D. Mercier, Sec., C.P. 308, Normétal, P.Q. JOZ 3AO (819/788-2550)
Northfield (Mun.)	473	Gatineau		Gatineau	J.-M. Carpentier, Sec., C.P. 301, Gracefield, P.Q. JOX 1WO (819/463-2182)
North Hatley (Village)	771	Stanstead	Mégantic-Compton-Stanstead	Orford	Mrs. E.M. Woodward, Sec., C.P. 30, North Hatley, P.Q. JOB 2CO (819/842-2754)
Notre-Dame-Auxiliatrice-de-Buckland (Paroisse)	800	Bellechasse		Bellechasse	C. Métivier, Sec., C.P. 69, Buckland, P.Q. GOR 1GO (418/789-2851)
Notre-Dame-de-Bon-Secours (Paroisse)	1,138	Rouville		Chambly	Diane Bourdeau, Sec., 405 ch. Marieville, Richelieu, P.Q. J3L 4A7 (514/658-2662)
Notre-Dame-de-Bon-Secours-de-L'Islet (Paroisse)	1,175	L'Islet		Montmagny-L'Islet	B. Couillard, Sec., C.P. 480, L'Islet, P.Q. GOR 2BO (418/247-5795)
Notre-Dame-de-Bon-Secours, nord (Paroisse)	216	Papineau		Papineau	G. Gignac, Sec., 140 Principale, Montebello, P.Q. JOV 1LO (819/423-5550)
Notre-Dame-de-la-Doré (Paroisse)	1,902	Lac-St-Jean-Ouest	Roberval	Roberval	L. Dallaire, Sec., C.P. 100, Rivière-au-Doré, P.Q. GOW 2JO (418/256-3545)
Notre-Dame-de-la-Merci (Mun.)	359	Montcalm	Joliette	Rousseau	F. Viau, Sec., Notre-Dame-de-la-Merci, P.Q. JOT 2AO (819/424-2113)
Notre-Dame-de-la-Paix (Paroisse)	627	Papineau	Argenteuil	Papineau	H. Servant, Sec., C.P. 10, Notre-Dame-de-la-Paix, P.Q. JOV 1PO (819/522-6502)
Notre-Dame-de-Laterrière (Paroisse)	2,175	Chicoutimi		Dubuc	N. Girard, Sec., C.P. 69, Laterrière, P.Q. GOV 1KO (418/678-2647)
Notre-Dame-de-l'Ile-Perrot (Paroisse)	2,598	Vaudreuil		Vaudreuil-Soulanges	S. Jolin, Sec., 21 de l'Eglise, Ile-Perrot-Sud, P.Q. J7V 5V6 (514/453-4128)
Notre-Dame-de-Lorette (Mun.)	347	Lac-St-Jean-Ouest	Roberval	Roberval	Mme M.-M. Mercier, Sec., R.R. 2, Notre-Dame-de-Lorette, P.Q. GOW 1BO (418/276-1934)
Notre-Dame-de-Lourdes (Paroisse)	722	Mégantic		Lotbinière	Mme G. Côté, Sec., Lourdes PO, P.Q. GOS 1TO (819/385-4315)
Notre-Dame-de-Lourdes (Paroisse)	1,116	Joliette		Joliette	F. Hétu, Sec., 3971 Principale, Lourdes-de-Joliette, P.Q. JOK 1KO (514/753-7255)
Notre-Dame-de-Lourdes-de-Ham (Mun.)	301	Wolfe		Richmond	Mme L. Fréchette, Sec., Notre-Dame-de-Ham, P.Q. GOP 1CO (819/344-2788)
Notre-Dame-de-Lourdes-de-Lorrainville (Paroisse)	421	Témiscamingue		Rouyn-Noranda-Témiscamingue	Mme L. Perron, Sec., C.P. 399, Lorrainville, P.Q. JOZ 2RO (819/625-2166)
Notre-Dame-de-Montauban (Mun.)	887	Portneuf		Portneuf	T.D. Cauchon, Sec., C.P. 69, Montauban, P.Q. GOX 1WO (418/336-2020)
Notre-Dame-de-Pierreville (Paroisse)	739	Yamaska	Richelieu	Nicolet	M. Bénard, Sec., 336 Chenal-Tardif, Notre-Dame-de-Pierreville, P.Q. JOG 1GO (514/568-2462)

Cities in CAPITALS (Ville); Towns/Villes marked (Ville); Villages marked (Village); Townships/Cantons (marked Canton); United townships/Cantons unis (marked Cantons*); Parishes marked (Paroisse); undesignated municipalities/sans designation marked (Mun.).

MUNICIPALITY	POP.	COUNTY	FEDERAL ELECTORAL DISTRICT	PROVINCIAL ELECTORAL DISTRICT	CLERK/GREFFIER OR SECRETARY-TREASURER (SEC) WITH ADDRESS & PHONE
Notre-Dame-de-Pontmain (Mun.)	445	Labelle	Pontiac-Gatineau-Labelle	Gatineau; Labelle	J.P. Grenier, Sec., Notre-Dame-de-Pontmain, P.Q. JOW 1SO (819/597-2585)
Notre-Dame-de-Portneuf (Paroisse)	1,915	Portneuf		Portneuf	L. Morissette, Sec., Portneuf Station, P.Q. GOA 2ZO (418/286-6562)
Notre-Dame-de-St-Hyacinthe (Paroisse)	779	St-Hyacinthe		St-Hyacinthe	J.L. Giard, Sec., 1515 rg St-François, St-François R.R. 2, P.Q. J2S 7A9 (514/773-3720)
Notre-Dame-des-Bois (Mun.)	458	Frontenac	Mégantic-Compton-Stanstead	Mégantic-Compton	Gisèle Lambert, Sec., rue Principale, Notre-Dame-des-Bois, P.Q. JOB 2EO (819/888-2503)
Notre-Dame-des-Monts (Mun.)	875	Charlevoix-Est	Charlevoix	Charlevoix	F. Gaudreault, Sec., 15 rue Principale, Notre-Dame-des-Monts, P.Q. GOT 1LO (418/439-3891)
Notre-Dame-des-Neiges (Paroisse)	1,120	Rivière-du-Loup		Rivière-du-Loup	H. Belzile, Sec., C.P. 729, Trois-Pistoles, P.Q. GOL 4KO (418/851-3009)
Notre-Dame-des-Pins (Paroisse)	643	Beauce		Beauce-Sud	C. Thibault, Sec., Notre-Dame-des-Pins, P.Q. GOM 1KO (418/774-9514)
Notre-Dame-des-Prairies (Paroisse)	6,100	Joliette	Joliette	Joliette	R. Perreault, Sec., 225 boul. Antonio Barrette, Notre-Dame-des-Prairies, P.Q. J6E 1E7 (514/753-4279)
Notre-Dame-des-Sept-Douleurs (Paroisse)	111	Rivière-du-Loup		Rivière-du-Loup	A. Fraser, Sec., a/s Notre-Dame-de-L'Isle-Verte, P.Q. GOL 1KO (418/898-6036)
Notre-Dame-de-Stanbridge (Paroisse)	850	Missisquoi	Missisquoi	Brome-Missisquoi	Mme M. Fournier, Sec., Notre-Dame-de-Stanbridge, P.Q. JOJ 1MO (514/296-4410)
Notre-Dame-du-Bon-Conseil (Village)	1,029	Drummond	Drummond	Drummond	T. Shooner, Sec., 670 rue Notre Dame, Notre-Dame-du-Bon-Conseil, P.Q. JOC 1AO (819/336-2744)
Notre-Dame-du-Bon-Conseil (Paroisse)	952	Drummond	Drummond	Drummond	H. Bergeron, Sec., 68 10e rg de Simpson, Bon Conseil, P.Q. JOC 1AO (819/336-5374)
Notre-Dame-du-Lac (Ville)	2,185	Témiscouata	Rimouski	Kamouraska-Témiscouata	C.-A. Bélanger, Trés., C.P. 158, Notre-Dame-du-Lac, P.Q. GOL 1XO (418/899-6743)
Notre-Dame-du-Laus (Mun.)	1,117	Labelle	Gatineau	Papineau	Y. Larocque, Sec., C.P. 10, Notre-Dame-du-Laus, P.Q. JOX 2MO (819/767-2247)
Notre-Dame-du-Mont-Carmel (Paroisse)	2,615	Champlain		St-Maurice	C. Côté, Sec., 3860 Hôtel de ville, (Mont-Carmel), Valmont, P.Q. GOX 3JO (819/375-9856)
Notre-Dame-du-Mont-Carmel (Paroisse)	968	St-Jean		St-Jean	J.-G. Boudreau, Sec., R.R. 1, Lacolle, P.Q. JOJ 1JO (514/246-2692)
Notre-Dame-du-Nord (Mun.)	1,253	Témiscamingue	Témiscamingue	Rouyn-Noranda-Témiscamingue	L. Beauregard, Sec., C.P. 160, Notre-Dame-du-Nord, P.Q. JOZ 3BO (819/723-2294)
Notre-Dame-du-Portage (Paroisse)	877	Rivière-du-Loup	Kamouraska-Rivière-du-Loup	Rivière-du-Loup	J.-H. Normand, Sec., Notre-Dame-du-Portage, P.Q. GOL 1YO (418/862-2712)

Cities in CAPITALS (Ville); Towns/Villes marked (Ville); Villages marked (Village); Townships/Cantons (marked Canton); United townships/Cantons unis (marked Cantons*); Parishes marked (Paroisse); undesignated municipalities/sans designation marked (Mun.).

MUNICIPALITY	POP.	COUNTY	FEDERAL ELECTORAL DISTRICT	PROVINCIAL ELECTORAL DISTRICT	CLERK/GREFFIER OR SECRETARY-TREASURER (SEC) WITH ADDRESS & PHONE
Notre-Dame-du-Rosaire (Mun.)	550	Montmagny	Lac-St-Jean	Montmagny-L'Islet	R. Langevin, Sec., 252 rue Jolicoeur, Notre-Dame-du-Rosaire, P.Q. GOR 2HO (418/469-2802)
Notre-Dame-du-Sacré-Coeur-d'Issoudun (Paroisse)	633	Lotbinière		Lotbinière	S.T. Croteau, Sec., Issoudin PO, P.Q. GOS 1LO (418/728-2006)
Nouvelle (Mun.)	2,270	Bonaventure	Bonaventure-Iles-de-la-Madeleine	Bonaventure	E. Sleigher, Sec., C.P. 68, Nouvelle, P.Q. GOC 2EO (418/794-2253)
Noyan (Mun.)	646	Missisquoi	Missisquoi	Iberville	W. Pearson, Sec., C.P. 8, Noyan, P.Q. JOJ 1BO (514/294-2689)
Ogden (Mun.)	788	Stanstead		Orford	Mrs. F. Dustin, Sec., R.R. 3, Stanstead, P.Q. JOB 3EO (819/876-2953)
Oka (Paroisse)	984	Deux-Montagnes	Argenteuil	Deux-Montagnes	P. Quévillon, Sec., C.P. 38, Oka, P.Q. JON 1EO (514/479-8202)
Oka (Mun.)	1,405	Deux-Montagnes	Argenteuil	Deux-Montagnes	P. Lalonde, Sec., 183 des Anges, Oka, P.Q. JON 1EO (514/479-8388)
Omerville (Village)	1,308	Stanstead	Missisquoi	Orford	J.-P. Asselin, Sec., C.P. 39, Omerville, P.Q. J1X 4H4 (819/843-3286)
Orford (Canton)	550	Sherbrooke		Orford	G. Archambault, Sec., Ch. de Jouvence, Bonsecours, P.Q. JOE 1HO (514/532-4623)
Ormstown (Village)	1,516	Châteauguay	Beauharnois-Salaberry	Huntingdon	J.-C. Marcil, Sec., C.P. 279, Ormstown, P.Q. JOS 1KO (514/829-2625)
Otis (Canton)	602	Chicoutimi		Dubuc	B. Boudreault, Sec., C.P. 38, St-Félix-d'Otis, P.Q. GOV 1MO (418/544-5543)
Otterburn Park (Ville)	4,335	Rouville	Verchères	Verchères	J.M. Pouliot, Sec., 472 Prince Edward, Otterburn Park, P.Q. J3H 1W4 (514/467-0203)
OUTREMONT (Ville)	26,500	Ile-de-Montréal	Outremont	Outremont	J. Perreault, Greffier, 510 av. Davaar, Outremont, P.Q. H2V 2B9 (514/274-9451)
Pabos (Mun.)	1,009	Gaspé-Est	Gaspé	Gaspé	D.-A. Duguay, Sec., C.P. 39, Pabos, P.Q. GOC 2HO (418/689-2171)
Pabos-Mills (Mun.)	1,512	Gaspé-Est	Gaspé	Gaspé	L. Gadbois, Sec., C.P. 1432, Chandler, P.Q. GOC 1KO (418/689-3523)
Packington (Paroisse)	674	Témiscouata	Rimouski	Kamouraska-Témiscouata	Mme C.D. Dumont, Sec., Packington, P.Q. GOL 1ZO (418/853-5024)
Palmarolle (Mun.)	1,278	Abitibi	Témiscamingue	Abitibi-Ouest	Y. Ayotte, Sec., C.P. 100, Palmarolle, P.Q. JOZ 3CO (819/787-2303)
Papineauville (Village)	1,551	Papineau	Argenteuil	Papineau	M. Bergeron, Sec., C.P. 248, Papineauville, P.Q. JOV 1RO (819/427-5511)
Parent (Village)	384	Champlain	Champlain	Laviolette	E. Parent, Sec., C.P. 8, Parent, P.Q. GOA 2VO (819/667-2323)
Paspébiac (Mun.)	3,250	Bonaventure	Bonaventure-Iles-de-la-Madeleine	Bonaventure	A. Gignac, Sec., C.P. 130, Paspébiac, P.Q. GOC 2KO (418/752-2277)
Paspébiac-Ouest (Mun.)	766	Bonaventure	Bonaventure-Iles-de-la-Madeleine	Bonaventure	C. Berthelot, Sec., C.P. 99, Paspébiac-Ouest, P.Q. GOC 2KO (418/752-3011)

Cities in CAPITALS (Ville); Towns/Villes marked (Ville); Villages marked (Village); Townships/Cantons (marked Canton); United townships/Cantons unis (marked Cantons*); Parishes marked (Paroisse); undesignated municipalities/sans designation marked (Mun.).

MUNICIPALITY	POP.	COUNTY	FEDERAL ELECTORAL DISTRICT	PROVINCIAL ELECTORAL DISTRICT	CLERK/GREFFIER OR SECRETARY-TREASURER (SEC) WITH ADDRESS & PHONE
PERCE (Ville)	5,000	Gaspé-Est	Gaspé	Gaspé	B. Cloutier, Sec., C.P. 99, Percé, P.Q. GOC 2LO (418/782-2933)
Péribonka (Mun.)	611	Lac-St-Jean-Ouest	Roberval	Roberval	G. Savard, Sec., 312 boul. Niquet, Péribonka, P.Q. GOW 2GO (418/374-2967)
Petite-Matane (Mun.)	1,176	Matane	Matapédia-Matane	Matane	Lise Gagnon, Sec., Petite-Matane, P.Q. GOJ 1YO (418/566-2135)
Petite-Vallée (Mun.)	343	Gaspé-Est	Gaspé	Gaspé	A. Brousseau, Sec., Petite-Matane, P.Q. GOE 1YO (418/393-2552)
Philipsburg (Village)	329	Missisquoi	Missisquoi	Brome-Missisquoi	G. Bélisle, Sec., C.P. 83, Philipsburg, P.Q. JOJ 1NO (514/248-2124)
Piedmont (Mun.)	1,044	Terrebonne	Labelle	Prevost	G. Aubin, Sec., C.P. 120, Piedmont, P.Q. JOR 1KO (514/227-3137)
PIERREFONDS (Ville)	37,800	Ile-de-Montréal	Dollard; Vaudreuil	Nelligan; Robert Baldwin	Emile Nelligan, Greffier, 11072 boul. Gouin ouest, Pierrefonds, P.Q. H8Y 1X5 (514/684-4480)
Pierreville (Village)	1,296	Yamaska	Richelieu	Nicolet	R. Shooner, Sec., C.P. 162, Pierreville, P.Q. JOG 1JO (514/568-2139)
Pincourt (Ville)	8,200	Vaudreuil	Vaudreuil	Vaudreuil-Soulanges	G.A. Paquette, Sec., 919 boul. Duhamel, Pincourt, P.Q. J7V 4G8 (514/453-8981)
Piopolis (Mun.)	310	Frontenac	Mégantic-Compton-Stanstead	Mégantic-Compton	Gaby Richard, Sec., Piopolis, P.Q. GOY 1HO (819/583-3953)
Plaisance (Mun.)	927	Papineau	Argenteuil	Papineau	G. Lalande, Sec., C.P. 59, Plaisance, P.Q. JOV 1SO (819/427-5363)
Plessisville (Ville)	7,400	Mégantic	Frontenac	Arthabaska	B. Laliberté, Sec., 1700 St-Calixte, Plessisville, P.Q. G6L 1R3 (819/362-3284)
Plessisville (Paroisse)	2,350	Mégantic	Frontenac	Arthabaska	Jacques Leclerc, Sec., (1810 St-Laurent), C.P. 245, Plessisville, P.Q. G6L 2Y7 (819/362-2720)
Pohénégamook (Ville)	3,600	Kamouraska		Kamouraska-Témiscouata	G. Comeau, Sec., C.P. 159, Estcourt, Pohénégamook, P.Q. GOL 1JO (418/859-2533)
Pointe-à-la-Croix (Mun.)	1,546	Bonaventure		Bonaventure	J.P. Page, Sec., C.P. 147, Pointe-à-la-Croix, P.Q. GOC 1LO (418/788-2011)
Pointe-au-Pic (Village)	1,044	Charlevoix-Est	Charlevoix	Charlevoix	R. Tremblay, Sec., C.P. 307, Pointe-au-Pic, P.Q. GOT 1MO (418/665-2306)
Pointe-aux-Outardes (Village)	1,006	Saguenay	Charlevoix	Saguenay	Rose Caron, Sec., R.R. 1, boite 70, Chute-aux-Outardes, P.Q. GOH 1CO (418/567-2707)
Pointe-aux-Trembles (Paroisse)	1,091	Portneuf		Portneuf	Y. Raymond, Sec., 670 Rte. Nationale, Neuville PO, P.Q. GOA 2RO (418/876-2233)
POINTE-AUX-TREMBLES (Ville)	35,600	Ile-de-Montréal	Mercier	Lafontaine	Guy Vanier, Greffier, 11953 Notre-Dame est, Pointe-aux-Trembles, P.Q. H1B 2Y6 (514/645-5381)
Pointe-Calumet (Village)	2,544	Deux-Montagnes	Blaïnville-Deux-Montagnes	Deux-Montagnes	M.E.C. Dubuc, Sec., 861 boul. Lachapelle, Pointe-Calumet, P.Q. JON 1GO (514/473-7626)

Cities in CAPITALS (Ville); Towns/Villes marked (Ville); Villages marked (Village); Townships/Cantons (marked Canton); United townships/Cantons unis (marked Cantons*); Parishes marked (Paroisse); undesignated municipalities/sans designation marked (Mun.).

MUNICIPALITY	POP.	COUNTY	FEDERAL ELECTORAL DISTRICT	PROVINCIAL ELECTORAL DISTRICT	CLERK/GREFFIER OR SECRETARY-TREASURER (SEC) WITH ADDRESS & PHONE
POINTE-CLAIRE (Ville)	25,400	Ile-de-Montréal	Lachine	Jacques-Cartier	Mme M. Trudeau, Greffier, 451 boul. St-Jean, Pointe-Claire, P.Q. H9R 3J3 (514/697-0770)
Pointe-des-Cascades (Village)	730	Soulanges	Vaudreuil	Vaudreuil-Soulanges	M. Sauvé, Sec., C.P. 89, Pointe-des-Cascades, P.Q. JOP 1MO (514/455-3414)
Pointe-du-Lac (Mun.)	5,000	St-Maurice	Trois-Rivières	Maskinongé	J.-B. Pothier, Sec., 1597 Ch. Ste-Marguerite, Pointe-du-Lac, P.Q. GOX 1ZO (819/377-1121)
Pointe-du-Moulin (Ville)	231	Vaudreuil	Vaudreuil	Vaudreuil-Soulanges	J. Perrault, Sec., 1961 boul. Perrot, Ile-Perrot, P.Q. J7V 5V6 (514/453-4522)
Pointe-Fortune (Village)	379	Vaudreuil	Vaudreuil	Vaudreuil-Soulanges	Diane Ménard, Sec., C.P. 119, Pointe-Fortune, P.Q. JOP 1NO (514/451-5178)
Pointe-Lebel (Village)	1,426	Saguenay	Charlevoix	Saguenay	Y. Tremblay Sec., 365 rue Grenier, Pointe-Lebel, P.Q. GOH 1NO (418/589-8073)
Ponsonby (Canton)	164	Papineau		Papineau	P. Bennett, Sec., R.R. 1, Namur, P.Q. JOV 1NO (819/687-3649)
Pontiac (Mun.)	3,365	Pontiac		Pontiac	J. Ledoux, Sec., a/s R.R. 1, Luskville, P.Q. JOX 2GO (819/455-2401)
Pont-Rouge (Village)	3,392	Portneuf	Portneuf	Portneuf	Yves Laroche, Sec., C.P. 339, Pont-Rouge, P.Q. GOA 2XO (418/873-4481)
Portage-du-Fort (Village)	384	Pontiac	Pontiac-Gatineau-Labelle	Pontiac	C. Robillard, Sec., Portage-du-Fort, P.Q. JOX 1GO (819/648-5689)
Port-Cartier (Ville)	9,100	Saguenay	Manicouagan	Duplessis	V. Couture, Greffier, C.P. 387, Port-Cartier Ouest, P.Q. G5B 2G5 (418/766-2343)
Port Daniel est (Canton)	959	Bonaventure	Bonaventure-Iles-de-la-Madeleine	Bonaventure	B. Grenier, Sec., C.P. 116, Port-Daniel Est, P.Q. GOC 2NO (418/396-5225)
Port-Daniel ouest (Canton)	1,156	Bonaventure	Bonaventure-Iles-de-la-Madeleine	Bonaventure	J.A. Jones, Sec., C.P. 130, Port-Daniel Centre, P.Q. GOC 2NO (418/396-2773)
Portneuf (Ville)	1,328	Portneuf	Portneuf	Portneuf	M.A. Trudel, Sec., C.P. 100, Portneuf, P.Q. GOA 2YO (418/286-3844)
Potton (Canton)	1,671	Brome		Brome-Missisquoi	J.-Eddy Lessard, Sec., C.P. 143, Mansonville, P.Q. JOE 1XO (514/292-5555)
Poularies (Mun.)	876	Abitibi	Témiscamingue	Abitibi-Ouest	M. Pépin, Sec., C.P. 5, Poularies, P.Q. JOZ 3EO (819/782-2159)
Preissac (Mun.)				Abitibi-Ouest	
Prévost (Mun.)	3,400	Terrebonne	Labelle	Prevost	G. Charette, Sec., C.P. 190, Prévost, P.Q. JOR 1TO (514/224-2645)
Price (Village)	2,450	Matane	Matapédia-Matane	Matane	L. Pineau, Sec., 18 Fournier, Price, P.Q. GOJ 1ZO (418/775-2144)
Princeville (Paroisse)	1,590	Arthabaska		Arthabaska	Hervé Boudreau, Sec., (166 St-Jean Baptiste sud), C.P. 75, Princeville, P.Q. GOP 1EO (819/364-5430)
Princeville (Ville)	3,892	Arthabaska	Lotbinière	Arthabaska	F. Poiré, Sec., C.P. 279, Princeville, P.Q. GOP 1EO (819/364-5179)
Privat (Canton)	729	Abitibi		Abitibi-Ouest	D. Saillant, Sec., C.P. 224, Taschereau, P.Q. JOZ 3NO (819/796-2558)

Cities in CAPITALS (Ville); Towns/Villes marked (Ville); Villages marked (Village); Townships/Cantons (marked Canton); United townships/Cantons unis (marked Cantons*); Parishes marked (Paroisse); undesignated municipalities/sans designation marked (Mun.).

MUNICIPALITY	POP.	COUNTY	FEDERAL ELECTORAL DISTRICT	PROVINCIAL ELECTORAL DISTRICT	CLERK/GREFFIER OR SECRETARY-TREASURER (SEC) WITH ADDRESS & PHONE
QUEBEC (Ville)	177,000	Québec	Langelier; Louis-Hébert; Québec-Est	Chauveau; Jean-Talon; La Peltrie; Limoilou; Taschereau; Vanier	Antoine Carrier, Greffier, Hôtel de ville, C.P. 700, Québec, P.Q. G1R 4S9 (418/694-6074)
Racine (Mun.)	539	Shefford		Johnson	F. Ferland, Sec., 122 de la Rivière, Racine, P.Q. JOE 1YO (514/532-2826)
Ragueneau (Paroisse)	1,973	Saguenay	Charlevoix	Saguenay	G. Desmeules, Sec., 507 rte 138, Ragueneau, P.Q. GOH 1SO (418/567-2345)
Rainville (Mun.)	1,529	Missisquoi		Iberville	G.-H. Demers, Sec., 1810 Principale est, (Rainville), Farnham, P.Q. J2N 1N4 (514/293-3326)
Rapides-des-Joachims (Mun.)	203	Pontiac	Pontiac-Gatineau-Labelle	Pontiac	B. Boulianne, Sec., Rapides-des-Joachims, P.Q. KOJ 2HO (613/586-2328)
Rawdon (Village)	2,853	Montcalm	Joliette	Rousseau	T. Bélisle, Sec., C.P. 550, Rawdon, P.Q. JOK 1SO (514/834-2596)
Rawdon (Canton)	1,936	Montcalm		Rousseau	G. Bertrand, Sec., C.P. 730, Rawdon, P.Q. JOK 1SO (514/834-2589)
Remigny (Mun.)	505	Rouyn-Noranda	Témiscamingue	Rouyn-Noranda-Témiscamingue	P. Roy, Sec., Remigny, P.Q. JOZ 3HO (819/761-2421)
Repentigny (Ville)	30,000	L'Assomption	Terrebonne	L'Assomption	Jean Fafard, Greffier, 435 boul. Iberville, Repentigny, P.Q. J6A 2B6 (514/585-2660)
Richelieu (Ville)	1,720	Rouville	Chambly	Chambly	Mme Claire Côté, Sec., 1030 2e rue, Richelieu, P.Q. J3L 3Y1 (514/658-1157)
Richmond (Ville)	4,021	Richmond	Richmond	Richmond	G. Ducharme, Sec., 745 Gouin, Richmond, P.Q. JOB 2HO (819/826-3789)
Rigaud (Ville)	2,240	Vaudreuil	Vaudreuil	Vaudreuil-Soulanges	Marielle D'Aoust, Greffier, C.P. 460, Rigaud, P.Q. JOP 1PO (514/451-5342)
RIMOUSKI (Ville)	29,313	Rimouski	Rimouski	Rimouski	Hubert Dubé, Greffier, Hôtel de ville, C.P. 710, Rimouski, P.Q. G5L 7C7 (418/723-3313)
Rimouski-Est (Village)	2,352	Rimouski	Rimouski	Rimouski	Hervé Lavoie, Sec., 540 St-Germain est, Rimouski-Est, P.Q. G5L 1E9 (418/723-8388)
Ripon (Canton)	460	Papineau		Papineau	C. Beauchamp, Sec., R.R. 2, C.P. 40, Ripon, P.Q. JOV 1VO (819/983-7933)
Ripon (Village)	590	Papineau	Argenteuil	Papineau	René Lafontaine, Sec., C.P. 100, Ripon, P.Q. JOV 1VO (819/983-6685)
Risborough et Marlow, partie (Cantons)*	940	Frontenac		Beauce-Sud	Pierrette Morin, Sec., 203 Principale, St-Ludger, P.Q. GOM 1WO (819/548-5306)
Ristigouche (Canton)	307	Bonaventure		Bonaventure	B. Beaulieu, Sec., St-André-de-Ristigouche, P.Q. GOJ 2GO (418/865-2234)
Ristigouche, sud-est (Canton)	190	Bonaventure		Bonaventure	E. Gregoire, Sec., R.R. 2, Matapédia, P.Q. GOJ 1VO (418/788-5419)
Rivière-à-Claude (Mun.)	301	Gaspé-Ouest	Gaspé	Matane	C. Auclair, Sec., C.P. 10, Rivière-à-Claude, P.Q. GOE 1ZO (418/797-2828)

Cities in CAPITALS (Ville); Towns/Villes marked (Ville); Villages marked (Village); Townships/Cantons (marked Canton); United townships/Cantons unis (marked Cantons*); Parishes marked (Paroisse); undesignated municipalities/sans designation marked (Mun.).

MUNICIPALITY	POP.	COUNTY	FEDERAL ELECTORAL DISTRICT	PROVINCIAL ELECTORAL DISTRICT	CLERK/GREFFIER OR SECRETARY-TREASURER (SEC) WITH ADDRESS & PHONE
Rivière-à-Pierre (Mun.)	643	Portneuf	Portneuf	Portneuf	M.-A. Voyer, Sec., 810 rue Principale, Portneuf, P.Q. GOA 3AO (418/323-2112)
Rivière-au-Tonnerre (Mun.)	594	Saguenay	Manicouagan	Duplessis	Léona Noel, Sec., C.P. 129, Rivière-au-Tonnerre, P.Q. GOG 2LO (418/465-2255)
Rivière-Beaudette (Village)	235	Soulanges	Vaudreuil	Vaudreuil-Soulanges	P. Madore, Sec., 663 Ch. Frontière, Rivière-Beaudette, P.Q. JOP 1RO (514/269-2931)
Rivière-Blanche (Mun.)	984	Mégantic	Matapédia-Matane	Frontenac	G. Couture, Sec., 1096 Johnson, Thetford Mines, P.Q. G6G 5R6 (418/335-7048)
Rivière-Bleue (Mun.)	1,900	Témiscouata	Rimouski	Kamouraska-Témiscouata	F. Cassistat, Sec., 76 des Pins est, Rivière-Bleue, P.Q. GOL 2BO (418/893-2107)
Rivière-du-Gouffre (Mun.)	874	Rivière-du-Loup		Charlevoix	A. Lavoie, Sec., C.P. 373, Baie-St-Paul, P.Q. GOA 1BO (418/435-5113)
RIVIERE-DU-LOUP (Ville)	13,100	Rivière-du-Loup	Kamouraska-Rivière-du-Loup	Rivière-du-Loup	Raoul Savard, Greffier, Hôtel de ville, C.P. 37, Rivière-du-Loup, P.Q. G5R 3A6 (418/862-9810)
Rivière-Eternité (Mun.)	700	Chicoutimi	Chicoutimi	Dubuc	E. Bergeron, Sec., 1B rue Ste-Thérèse, Rivière-Eternité, P.Q. GOV 1PO (418/272-2860)
Rivière-Malbaie (Mun.)	1,877	Charlevoix-Est		Charlevoix	L. Bergeron, Sec., 400 ch de la Vallée, La Malbaie, P.Q. GOT 1JO (418/665-3218)
Rivière-Ouelle (Mun.)	1,382	Kamouraska	Kamouraska-Rivière-du-Loup	Kamouraska-Témiscouata	J.-P. Laboissonnière, Sec., Rivière-Ouelle, P.Q. GOL 2CO (418/856-1086)
Rivière-Pentecôte (Mun.)	927	Saguenay	Manicouagan	Duplessis	C. Gagnon, Sec., C.P. 39, Rivière-Pentecôte, P.Q. GOH 1RO (418/799-2262)
Rivière-Pigou (Mun.)		Saguenay		Duplessis	C. Gagnon, Sec., a/s 456 rue Arnaud, bur. 236, Sept-Iles, P.Q. G4R 3B1 (418/968-2851)
Rivière-St-Jean (Mun.)	530	Saguenay	Manicouagan	Duplessis	Marie Chambers, Sec., (Magpie), Rivière-St-Jean, P.Q. GOG 2NO (418/949-2304)
Robertsonville (Village)	1,687	Mégantic	Frontenac	Frontenac	J.-M. Talbot, Sec., 8a Notre Dame sud, Robertsonville, P.Q. GON 1LO (418/338-4377)
ROBERVAL (Ville)	10,500	Lac-St-Jean-Ouest	Roberval	Roberval	B. Harvey, Greffier, 851 blvd. St-Joseph, Roberval, P.Q. G8H 2L6 (418/275-0202)
Rock Forest (Mun.)	9,800	Sherbrooke	Shefford	Orford	
Rock Island (Ville)	1,221	Stanstead	Mégantic-Compton-Stanstead	Orford	Mme M. Massé, Sec., Hôtel de ville, Rock Island, P.Q. JOB 2KO (819/876-5631)
Rollet (Mun.)	571	Témiscamingue	Témiscamingue	Rouyn-Noranda-Témiscamingue	Mme J. Roch, Sec., Rollet, P.Q. JOZ 3JO
Roquemaure (Mun.)	652	Abitibi	Témiscamingue	Abitibi-Ouest	A. Lacasse, Sec., Roquemaure, P.Q. JOZ 3KO (819/787-2520)
Rosemère (Ville)	7,300	Terrebonne	Blainville-Deux-Montagnes	Groulx	J. Lafleur, Greffier, 100 Charbonneau, Rosemère, P.Q. J7A 3W1 (514/621-3500)
Rougemont (Village)	959	Rouville	St-Hyacinthe	Iberville	Jean Chabot, Sec., C.P. 100, Rougemont, P.Q. JOL 1MO (514/469-3484)

Cities in CAPITALS (Ville); Towns/Villes marked (Ville); Villages marked (Village); Townships/Cantons (marked Canton); United townships/Cantons unis (marked Cantons*); Parishes marked (Paroisse); undesignated municipalities/sans designation marked (Mun.).

MUNICIPALITY	POP.	COUNTY	FEDERAL ELECTORAL DISTRICT	PROVINCIAL ELECTORAL DISTRICT	CLERK/GREFFIER OR SECRETARY-TREASURER (SEC) WITH ADDRESS & PHONE
ROUYN (Ville)	17,600	Témiscamingue	Témiscamingue	Rouyn-Noranda-Témiscamingue	G. Marinovitch, Trés., Hôtel de ville, C.P. 220, Rouyn, P.Q. J9X 5C3 (819/762-1721)
Roxboro (Ville)	6,900	Ile-de-Montréal	Dollard	Robert-Baldwin	V.P. Gray, Sec., 13 Centre Commercial, Roxboro, P.Q. H8Y 2N9 (514/684-0555)
Roxton (Canton)	1,027	Shefford		Johnson	Thérèse Mongeau, Sec., C.P. 278, Roxton Falls, P.Q. JOH 1EO (514/548-2500)
Roxton Falls (Village)	1,204	Shefford	Shefford	Johnson	G. Sicotte, Sec., 189 Notre-Dame, Roxton Falls, P.Q. JOH 1EO (514/548-5790)
Sacré-Coeur (Mun.)	2,075	Saguenay	Rimouski	Saguenay	G. Lemieux, Sec., C.P. 159, Sacré-Coeur, P.Q. GOT 1YO (418/236-4621)
Sacré-Coeur-de-Jésus (Paroisse)	665	Beauce		Frontenac	L. Faucher, Sec., Rang 8, East Broughton, P.Q. GON 1GO (418/427-5513)
Sacré-Coeur-de-Jésus (Paroisse)	800	Joliette		Joliette	J.-D. Payette, Sec., 199 2e Ave., Crabtree, P.Q. JOK 1BO (514/754-2402)
Sacré-Coeur-de-Marie, sud (Paroisse)	714	Mégantic	Frontenac	Frontenac	V. Routhier, Sec., 201 Rang 8 sud, Sacré-Coeur-de-Marie, P.Q. GON 1WO (418/335-3968)
Saguay (Mun.)	264	Labelle		Labelle	M. Duval, Sec., Lac Saguay PO, P.Q. JOW 1LO (819/278-3972)
St-Adalbert (Mun.)	911	L'Islet	Bellechasse	Montmagny-L'Islet	D. Bourgault, Sec., St-Adalbert, P.Q. GOR 2MO (418/356-3991)
Ste-Adèle (Ville)	4,306	Terrebonne	Labelle	Rousseau	Claudette Pion, Greffier, C.P. 1108, Ste-Adèle-en-Bas, P.Q. JOR 1LO (514/229-2921)
St-Adelme (Paroisse)	618	Matane	Matapédia-Matane	Matane	Rita Ross, Sec., St-Adelme, P.Q. GOJ 2BO (418/733-4613)
St-Adelphe (Paroisse)	1,225	Champlain	Portneuf	Laviolette	Diane Lamy, Sec., 150 Baillargeon, St-Adelphe, P.Q. GOX 2GO (819/572-1000)
St-Adolphe-d'Howard (Mun.)	1,370	Argenteuil	Argenteuil	Argenteuil	Lise Villeneuve, Sec., 1881 chemin du village, St-Adophe-d'Howard, P.Q. JOT 2BO (819/327-2044)
St-Adrien (Mun.)	615	Wolfe	Richmond	Richmond	Léo Larivée, Sec., St-Adrien, P.Q. JOA 1CO (819/828-2929)
St-Agapit (Mun.)	2,762	Lotbinière		Lotbinière	P. Croteau, Sec., 100 rue du Centenaire, St-Agapit, P.Q. GOS 1ZO (418/888-4620)
Ste-Agathe (Paroisse)	423	Lotbinière	Frontenac	Lotbinière	J.A. Côté, Sec., Ste-Agathe-de-Lotbinière, P.Q. GOS 2AO (418/599-2207)
Ste-Agathe (Village)	699	Lotbinière	Frontenac	Lotbinière	Mme R. Viger, Sec., C.P. 125, Ste-Agathe, P.Q. GOS 2AO (418/599-2548)
Ste-Agathe (Paroisse)	921	Terrebonne		Labelle	E. Lanthier, Sec., C.P. 126, Ste-Agathe-des-Monts, P.Q. J8C 2AO (819/326-3187)
Ste-Agathe-des-Monts (Ville)	5,400	Terrebonne	Labelle	Labelle	M. Pellerin, Greffier, 50 St-Joseph, Ste-Agathe-des-Monts, P.Q. J8C 1M9 (819/326-4595)

Cities in CAPITALS (Ville); Towns/Villes marked (Ville); Villages marked (Village); Townships/Cantons (marked Canton); United townships/Cantons unis (marked Cantons*); Parishes marked (Paroisse); undesignated municipalities/sans designation marked (Mun.).

MUNICIPALITY	POP.	COUNTY	FEDERAL ELECTORAL DISTRICT	PROVINCIAL ELECTORAL DISTRICT	CLERK/GREFFIER OR SECRETARY-TREASURER (SEC) WITH ADDRESS & PHONE
Ste-Agathe-Sud (Village)	1,101	Terrebonne	Labelle	Labelle	D. Bellerive, Sec., 1700 Principale est, Ste-Agathe-des-Monts, P.Q. J8C 1M2 (819/326-3920)
Ste-Agnès (Paroisse)	550	Charlevoix-Est	Charlevoix	Charlevoix	D. Perron, Sec., 29 rue Principale, Ste-Agnès, P.Q. GOT 1RO (418/439-4188)
St-Aimé (Paroisse)	614	Richelieu	Richelieu	Richelieu	Mme J.F. Brouillard, Sec., 539 Rang Bord-de-l'eau, St-Aimé, P.Q. JOG 1KO (514/788-2737)
St-Aimé-des-Lacs (Mun.)	820	Charlevoix-Est	Charlevoix	Charlevoix	Jacques Dufour, Sec., 52 Principale, St-Aimé-des-Lacs, P.Q. GOT 1SO (418/439-2560)
St-Aimé-du-Lac-des-Iles (Mun.)	585	Labelle		Labelle	G. Roberge, Sec., Lac-des-Iles, P.Q. JOW 1JO (819/597-2584)
St-Alban (Paroisse)	536	Portneuf	Portneuf	Portneuf	Myriam Falardeau, Sec., C.P. 100, St-Alban, P.Q. GOA 2BO (418/268-8562)
St-Alban (Village)	725	Portneuf	Portneuf	Portneuf	R. Douville, Sec., C.P. 157, St-Alban, P.Q. GOA 3BO (418/268-3814)
St-Albert-de-Warwick (Paroisse)	1,026	Arthabaska		Richmond	L.G. Lacharité, Greffier, St-Albert, P.Q. JOA 1EO (819/353-2249)
St-Alexandre (Paroisse)	1,860	Kamouraska	Kamouraska	Kamouraska-Témiscouata	L. Chouinard, Sec., C.P. 14, St-Alexandre, P.Q. GOL 2GO (418/495-2440)
St-Alexandre (Paroisse)	1,454	Iberville	St-Jean	Iberville	Jeannine Brault, Sec., 104 rue Pavillon, C.P. 53, St-Alexandre-d'Iberville, P.Q. JOJ 1SO (514/347-3168)
St-Alexandre (Village)	402	Iberville		Iberville	Voir St-Alexandre (Paroisse)
St-Alexandre-des-Lacs (Paroisse)	287	Matapédia	Matapédia-Matane	Matapédia	Mme M. Poirier, Sec., St-Alexandre-des-Lacs, P.Q. GOJ 2CO (418/778-3532)
St-Alexis (Paroisse)	2,400	Maskinongé	Berthier-Maskinongé	Maskinongé	B. Gélinas, Sec., C.P. 96, St-Alexis-des-Monts, P.Q. JOK 1VO (819/265-2046)
St-Alexis (Village)	481	Montcalm	Joliette	Joliette	Suzanne Landry, Sec., 232 Principale, St-Alexis, P.Q. JOK 1TO (514/839-3455)
St-Alexis (Paroisse)	725	Montcalm	Joliette	Joliette	R. Lanoue, Sec., 232 Principale, St-Alexis (Cte Montcalm), P.Q. JOK 1TO (514/839-3455)
St-Alexis-de-Matapédia (Paroisse)	1,017	Bonaventure	Bonaventure-Iles-de-la-Madeleine	Bonaventure	R.J. Lévésque, Sec., St-Alexis-de-Matapédia, P.Q. GOJ 2EO (418/299-2030)
St-Alfred (Mun.)	387	Beauce	Beauce	Beauce-Nord	
St-Alphonse (Mun.)	1,015	Bonaventure	Bonaventure-Iles-de-la-Madeleine	Bonaventure	P. Bujold, Sec., St-Alphonse-de-Caplan, P.Q. GOC 2VO (418/388-5214)
St-Alphonse (Paroisse)	885	Shefford	Shefford	Brome-Missisquoi	G. Sauvage, Sec., 320 rue Principale, St-Alphonse-de-Granby, P.Q. JOE 2AO (514/378-0898)
St-Alphonse-de-Rodriguez (Paroisse)	1,071	Joliette	Berthier-Maskinongé	Berthier	R. Baillargeon, Sec., 101 ave Plage, St-Alphonse, P.Q. JOK 1WO (514/883-5188)

Cities in CAPITALS (Ville); Towns/Villes marked (Ville); Villages marked (Village); Townships/Cantons (marked Canton); United townships/Cantons unis (marked Cantons*); Parishes marked (Paroisse); undesignated municipalities/sans designation marked (Mun.).

MUNICIPALITY	POP.	COUNTY	FEDERAL ELECTORAL DISTRICT	PROVINCIAL ELECTORAL DISTRICT	CLERK/GREFFIER OR SECRETARY-TREASURER (SEC) WITH ADDRESS & PHONE
St-Amable (Paroisse)	3,311	Verchères	Verchères	Bertrand	E. Martel, Sec., C.P. 308, St-Amable, P.Q. JOL 1NO (514/649-3555)
St-Ambroise (Village)	3,200	Chicoutimi	Lac-St-Jean	Dubuc	J.-R. Claveau, Sec., 330 Simard, St-Ambroise-de-Chicoutimi, P.Q. GOV 1RO (418/672-4601)
St-Ambroise-de-Kildare (Paroisse)	2,060	Joliette	Berthier-Maskinongé	Joliette	Y. Ducharme, Sec., C.P. 57, Kildare, P.Q. JOK 1CO (514/756-4685)
St-Anaclet-de-Lessard (Paroisse)	1,923	Rimouski	Rimouski	Rimouski	J. Leclerc, Sec., C.P. 99, St-Anaclet, P.Q. GOK 1HO (418/723-2816)
St-André (Paroisse)	398	Kamouraska	Kamouraska-Rivière-du-Loup	Kamouraska-Témiscouata	J.-R. Lavoie, Sec., St-André-de-Kamouraska, P.Q. GOL 2HO (418/493-2294)
St-André-Avellin (Paroisse)	1,083	Papineau	Argenteuil	Papineau	J.G. Richer, Sec., C.P. 60, St-André-Avellin, P.Q. JOV 1WO (819/983-7767)
St-André-Avellin (Village)	1,154	Papineau	Argenteuil	Papineau	J.-G. Richer, Sec., C.P. 60, St-André-Avellin, P.Q. JOV 1WO (819/983-7767)
St-André-d'Acton (Paroisse)	1,507	Bagot		Johnson	M. Gauthier, Sec., C.P. 309, Acton Vale, P.Q. JOH 1AO (514/546-7070)
St-André-d'Argenteuil (Paroisse)	814	Argenteuil		Argenteuil	Mme T. Fournier, Sec., C.P. 179, St-André-Est, P.Q. JOV 1XO (514/537-3676)
Ste-André-du-Lac-St-Jean (Village)	565	Lac-St-Jean-Ouest	Roberval	Lac-St-Jean	M. Lapointe, Sec., 11 rue du College, St-André-du-Lac-St-Jean, P.Q. GOW 2KO (418/349-2571)
St-André-Est (Village)	1,220	Argenteuil	Argenteuil	Argenteuil	Y. Paré, Sec., C.P. 149, St-André-Est, P.Q. JOV 1XO (514/537-3527)
St-Ange-Gardien (Paroisse)	1,120	Rouville		Iberville	J.-M. Marchand, Sec., C.P. 120, Ange-Gardien-de-Rouville, P.Q. JOE 1EO (514/293-7575)
Ste-Angèle (Paroisse)	581	Maskinongé		Maskinongé	G. Gerbeau, Sec., 2451 Camirand, Ste-Angèle-de-Prémont, P.Q. JOK 1RO (819/268-5526)
Ste-Angèle-de-Mérici (Village)	602	Rimouski	Matapédia-Matane	Matapédia	B. Plante, Sec., C.P. 38, Ste-Angèle-de-Mérici, P.Q. GOJ 2HO (418/775-7333)
Ste-Angèle-de-Mérici (Paroisse)	721	Rimouski	Matapédia-Matane	Matapédia	Francine Heppell, Sec., C.P. 10, Ste-Angèle-de-Mérici, P.Q. GOJ 2HO (418/775-2940)
Ste-Angèle-de-Monnoir (Paroisse)	1,189	Rouville	St-Hyacinthe	Iberville	J. Deslauriers, Sec., Ste-Angèle-de-Monnoir, P.Q. JOL 1PO (514/466-7838)
Ste-Angélique (Paroisse)	526	Papineau		Papineau	Florence Gauthier, Sec., C.P. 279, Papineauville, P.Q. JOV 1RO (819/427-5221)
Saints-Anges (Paroisse)	679	Beauce		Beauce-Nord	Mme R.G. Tardif, Sec., Saints-Anges, P.Q. GOS 3EO (418/253-5991)
St-Anicet (Paroisse)	1,875	Huntingdon	Beauharnois-Salaberry	Huntingdon	C.G. Leblanc, Sec., 335 av. Jules Léger, St-Anicet, P.Q. JOS 1MO (514/264-2555)
Ste-Anne-de-Beaupré (Ville)	3,284	Montmorency 1	Montmorency	Charlevoix	J. Michel, Sec., C.P. 100, Ste-Anne-de-Beaupré, P.Q. GOA 3CO (418/827-3191)

Cities in CAPITALS (Ville); Towns/Villes marked (Ville); Villages marked (Village); Townships/Cantons (marked Canton); United townships/Cantons unis (marked Cantons*); Parishes marked (Paroisse); undesignated municipalities/sans designation marked (Mun.).

MUNICIPALITY	POP.	COUNTY	FEDERAL ELECTORAL DISTRICT	PROVINCIAL ELECTORAL DISTRICT	CLERK/GREFFIER OR SECRETARY-TREASURER (SEC) WITH ADDRESS & PHONE
Ste-Anne-de-Bellevue (Ville)	3,528	Ile-de-Montréal	Vaudreuil	Nelligan	Guy Lafrenière, Greffier, C.P. 40, Ste-Anne-de-Bellevue, P.Q. H9X 3L4 (514/457-5531)
Ste-Anne-de-la-Pérade (Paroisse)	1,487	Champlain	Portneuf	Champlain	R. Roy, Sec., 200 Principale, Ste-Anne-de-la-Pérade, P.Q. GOX 2JO (418/325-2841)
Ste-Anne-de-la-Pocatière (Paroisse)	1,145	Kamouraska	Kamouraska-Rivière-du-Loup	Kamouraska-Témiscouata	R. Pelletier, Sec., Rg. du Sable, Ste-Anne-de-la-Pocatière, P.Q. GOL 1WO (418/856-2798)
Ste-Anne-de-la-Pointe-au-Père (Paroisse)	2,084	Rimouski		Rimouski	Ginette Bouillon, Sec., 345 Terrase-Bon-Air, Pointe-au-Père, P.Q. GOK 1GO (418/724-7723)
Ste-Anne-de-La-Rochelle (Mun.)	544	Shefford	Shefford	Brome-Missisquoi	Thérèse Roberge, Sec., Ste-Anne-de-La-Rochelle, P.Q. JOE 2BO (514/539-1654)
Ste-Anne-de-Portneuf (Mun.)	1,300	Saguenay		Saguenay	G. Tremblay, Sec., C.P. 98, Rivière-Portneuf, P.Q. GOT 1PO (418/238-2642)
Ste-Anne-de-Sabrevois (Paroisse)	1,300	Iberville		Iberville	G. Lefort, Sec., C.P. 21, Sabrevois, P.Q. JOJ 2GO (514/347-6966)
Ste-Anne-des-Lacs (Paroisse)	735	Terrebonne		Prevost	Jeannine Genest, Sec., Lac-Guindon, P.Q. JOR 1BO (514/224-2675)
Ste-Anne-des-Monts (Ville)	6,100	Gaspé-Ouest	Gaspé	Matane	J.L. Lavoie, Sec., C.P. 458, Ste-Anne-des-Monts, P.Q. GOE 2GO (418/763-5511)
Ste-Anne-de-Sorel (Paroisse)	2,268	Richelieu	Richelieu	Richelieu	P.S. White, Sec., 748 Chenal du Moine, Ste-Anne-de-Sorel, P.Q. J3P 5N3 (514/742-1616)
Ste-Anne-des-Plaines (Paroisse)	6,100	Terrebonne	Terrebonne	Rousseau	G. Alary, Sec., 144A boul. Ste-Anne, Ste-Anne-des-Plaines, P.Q. JON 1HO (514/478-0211)
Ste-Anne-du-Lac (Village)	31	Mégantic		Frontenac	R. Samson, Sec., C.P. 112, Thetford Mines, P.Q. G6G 5R9 (418/338-0467)
Ste-Anne-du-Lac (Mun.)	674	Labelle	Pontiac-Gatineau-Labelle	Labelle	Denise Beaudry, Sec., Ste-Anne-du-Lac, P.Q. JOW 1VO (819/586-2110)
Ste-Anne-du-Sault (Paroisse)	886	Arthabaska		Nicolet	R. Désaulniers, Sec., C.P. 339, Daveluyville, P.Q. GOZ 1CO (819/367-2818)
Ste-Anne-d'Yamachiche (Paroisse)	1,217	St-Maurice		Maskinongé	P. Desaulniers, Sec., C.P. 338, Yamachiche, P.Q. GOX 3LO (819/296-3330)
St-Anselme (Paroisse)	1,233	Dorchester	Lévis	Bellechasse	M. Morin, Sec., St-Anselme, P.Q. GOR 2NO (418/885-4790)
St-Anselme (Village)	1,735	Dorchester	Lévis	Bellechasse	R. Royer, Sec., C.P. 40, St-Anselme, P.Q. GOR 2NO (418/885-4977)
St-Antoine (Ville)	6,900	Terrebonne		Prevost	Serge Forget, Greffier, 854 boul. St-Antoine, St-Antoine-des-Laurentides, P.Q. J7Z 3C5 (514/436-1762)
St-Antoine-de-la-Baie-du-Febvre (Paroisse)	568	Yamaska		Nicolet	J.-L. Provencher, Sec., C.P. 12, Baieville, P.Q. JOG 1AO (514/783-6911)

Cities in CAPITALS (Ville); Towns/Villes marked (Ville); Villages marked (Village); Townships/Cantons (marked Canton); United townships/Cantons unis (marked Cantons*); Parishes marked (Paroisse); undesignated municipalities/sans designation marked (Mun.).

MUNICIPALITY	POP.	COUNTY	FEDERAL ELECTORAL DISTRICT	PROVINCIAL ELECTORAL DISTRICT	CLERK/GREFFIER OR SECRETARY-TREASURER (SEC) WITH ADDRESS & PHONE
St-Antoine-de-la-Rivière-du-Loup (Paroisse)	4,165	Maskinongé		Maskinongé	Catherine McMurray, Sec., C.P. 67, St-Antoine-de-la-Rivière-du-Loup, P.Q. J5V 2L6 (819/228-5331)
St-Antoine-de-Lavaltrie (Paroisse)	1,686			Berthier	R. Nantais, Sec., C.P. 300, Lavaltrie, P.Q. JOK 1HO (514/586-1331)
St-Antoine-de-l'Isle-aux-Grues (Paroisse)	206	Montmagny		Montmagny-L'Islet	J.-E. Lavoie, Sec., Isle-aux-Grues, P.Q. GOR 1PO (418/248-6963)
St-Antoine-de-Padoue (Paroisse)	558	Verchères		Verchères	Gisèle Colette, Sec., C.P. 30, St-Antoine-sur-Richelieu, P.Q. JOL 1RO (514/787-3497)
St-Antoine-de-Padoue-de-Kempt (Paroisse)	415	Matapédia		Matane	M.-A. Lavoie, Sec., a/s R.R. 1, Padoue, P.Q. GOJ 1XO (418/775-5486)
St-Antoine-de-Pontbriand (Paroisse)	889	Mégantic		Frontenac	A. Pomerleau, 1160 de l'Eglise, Pontbriand, P.Q. GON 1KO (418/335-2639)
St-Antoine-de-Tilly (Paroisse)	1,138	Lotbinière	Lotbinière	Lotbinière	Mme C. Lambert, Sec., 3868 Ch. de Tilly, St-Antoine-de-Tilly, P.Q. GOS 2CO (418/477-2441)
St-Antoine-sur-Richelieu (Mun.)	822	Verchères	Verchères	Verchères	J.J. Dansereau, Sec., 35 Place des Pres, St-Antoine-sur-Richelieu, P.Q. JOL 1RO (514/787-3494)
St-Antonin (Paroisse)	2,885	Rivière-du-Loup	Kamouraska-Rivière-du-Loup	Rivière-du-Loup	Daniel Pelletier, Sec., C.P. 340, St-Antonin, P.Q. GOL 2JO (418/862-1056)
St-Apollinaire (Mun.)	2,400	Lotbinière	Lotbinière	Lotbinière	Y. Demers, Sec., 94 rue Principale, St-Apollinaire, P.Q. GOS 2EO (418/767-3996)
Ste-Apolline-de-Patton (Paroisse)	817	Montmagny	Bellechasse	Montmagny-L'Islet	R. Bernard, Sec., Ste-Apolline-de-Patton, P.Q. GOR 2PO (418/469-2287)
St-Armand-Ouest (Paroisse)	1,028	Missisquoi	Missisquoi	Brome-Missisquoi	Lucie Ménard, Sec., St-Armand Station, P.Q. JOJ 1TO (514/248-2344)
St-Arsène (Paroisse)	1,165	Rivière-du-Loup	Kamouraska-Rivière-du-Loup	Rivière-du-Loup	R. Bérubé, Sec., St-Arsène, P.Q. GOL 2KO (418/862-3789)
St-Athanase (Mun.)	311	Kamouraska	Kamouraska-Rivière-du-Loup	Kamouraska-Témiscouata	Francine Bélanger, Sec., St-Athanase, P.Q. GOL 2LO (418/859-2575)
St-Athanase (Paroisse)	3,900	Iberville	St-Jean	Iberville	G. Racine, Sec., C.P. 55, Iberville, P.Q. J2X 4J5 (514/347-1916)
St-Aubert (Mun.)	1,358	L'Islet	Bellechasse	Montmagny-L'Islet	L. Bois, Sec., C.P. 160, St-Aubert, P.Q. GOR 2RO (418/247-3256)
St-Augustin (Paroisse)	617	Lac-St-Jean-Ouest	Roberval	Roberval	Mme L. Lavoie, Sec., 712 rue Principale, St-Augustin, P.Q. GOW 1KO (418/374-2147)
St-Augustin-de-Desmaures (Paroisse)	5,700	Portneuf	Portneuf	La Peltrie	J.P. Theriault, Sec., C.P. 10, St-Augustin, P.Q. GOA 3EO (418/878-2955)
St-Augustin-de-Woburn (Paroisse)	775	Frontenac	Mégantic-Compton-Stanstead	Mégantic-Compton	A. Bouchard, Sec., C.P. 120, Woburn, P.Q. GOY 1RO (819/544-4211)

Cities in CAPITALS (Ville); Towns/Villes marked (Ville); Villages marked (Village); Townships/Cantons (marked Canton); United townships/Cantons unis (marked Cantons*); Parishes marked (Paroisse); undesignated municipalities/sans designation marked (Mun.).

MUNICIPALITY	POP.	COUNTY	FEDERAL ELECTORAL DISTRICT	PROVINCIAL ELECTORAL DISTRICT	CLERK/GREFFIER OR SECRETARY-TREASURER (SEC) WITH ADDRESS & PHONE
Ste-Aurélie (Mun.)	1,097	Beauce	Beauce	Beauce-Sud	T. Allen, Sec., 180 Ch. des Bois-Francs, Ste-Aurélie, P.Q. GOM 1MO (418/593-3021)
Ste-Barbe (Paroisse)	997	Huntingdon	Beauharnois-Salaberry	Huntingdon	Lucille Daigneault, Sec., 475 Ch. de L'Eglise, Ste-Barbe, P.Q. JOS 1PO (514/371-2504)
St-Barnabé (Paroisse)	1,269	St-Maurice	Trois-Rivières	Maskinongé	F. Milot, Sec., C.P. 100, St-Barnabé-Nord, P.Q. GOX 2KO (819/264-2085)
St-Barnabé (Paroisse)	934	St-Hyacinthe		St-Hyacinthe	D. Bélanger, Sec., 416 Rg. St-Amable, St-Barnabé-Sud, P.Q. JOH 1GO (514/792-3030)
St-Barthélémi (Paroisse)	1,991	Berthier	Berthier-Maskinongé	Berthier	A. Gervais, Sec., 1880 rue Bonin, St-Barthélémi, P.Q. JOK 1XO (514/885-3511)
St-Basile (Paroisse)	728	Portneuf	Portneuf	Portneuf	M. Jobin, Sec., C.P. 368, St-Basile-de-Portneuf, P.Q. GOA 3GO (418/329-2969)
St-Basile-le-Grand (Ville)	6,600	Chambly	Verchères	Chambly	J. Pierre Chabot, ing., Gérant, C.P. 400, St-Basile-le-Grand, P.Q. JOL 1SO (514/653-4261)
St-Basile-Sud (Village)	1,650	Portneuf	Portneuf	Portneuf	R. Pagé, Sec., C.P. 267, St-Basile-de-Portneuf, P.Q. GOA 3GO (418/329-2204)
Ste-Béatrix (Paroisse)	925	Joliette	Berthier-Maskinongé	Berthier	M. Loyer, Sec., 801 de l'Eglise, Ste-Béatrix, P.Q. JOK 1YO (514/883-8832)
St-Benjamin (Mun.)	1,073	Dorchester	Beauce	Beauce-Sud	Françoise Boulet, Sec., C.P. 100, St-Benjamin, P.Q. GOM 1NO (418/594-2156)
St-Benoît-du-Lac (Mun.)				Brome-Missisquoi	
St-Benoît-Joseph-Labre (Paroisse)	1,798	Matapédia	Bonaventure-Iles-de-la-Madeleine	Matapédia	Mme T. Gagné, Sec., a/s C.P. 1148, Amqui, P.Q. GOJ 1BO (418/629-4542)
St-Benoît-Labre (Paroisse)	1,406	Beauce	Beauce	Beauce-Sud	G. Vallée, Sec., C.P. 70, St-Benoît-Labre, P.Q. GOM 1PO (418/228-9250)
St-Bernard (Paroisse)	1,244	Dorchester	Lévis	Beauce-Nord	M. Nadeau, Sec., C.P. 70, St-Bernard, P.Q. GOS 2GO (418/475-6623)
St-Bernard (Village)	520	Dorchester	Lévis	Beauce-Nord	Madeleine Nadeau, Sec., C.P. 70, St-Bernard, P.Q. GOS 2GO (418/475-6623)
St-Bernard-de-Lacolle (Paroisse)	1,484	St-Jean	St-Jean	St-Jean	W. Houle, Sec., 158 St. Claude, St-Bernard-de-Lacolle, P.Q. JOJ 1VO (514/246-3348)
St-Bernard-de-l'Ile-aux-Coudres (Mun.)	695	Charlevoix-Ouest	Charlevoix	Charlevoix	F. Boudreault, Sec., 35 Royale est, St-Bernard-sur-Mer, P.Q. GOA 3JO (418/438-2379)
St-Bernard, sud (Paroisse)	533	St-Hyacinthe	St-Hyacinthe	Richelieu	Mme M. Lamoureux, Sec., St-Bernard (Michaudville), P.Q. JOH 1CO (514/792-3666)
St-Blaise (Paroisse)	1,484	St-Jean	St-Jean	St-Jean	Janette Chabot, Sec., 737 Principale, St-Blaise, P.Q. JOJ 1WO (514/291-5944)
Ste-Blandine (Paroisse)	1,375	Rimouski	Rimouski	Rimouski	Y. Brisson, Sec., C.P. 105, Ste-Blandine, P.Q. GOK 1JO (418/735-2752)

Cities in CAPITALS (Ville); Towns/Villes marked (Ville); Villages marked (Village); Townships/Cantons (marked Canton); United townships/Cantons unis (marked Cantons*); Parishes marked (Paroisse); undesignated municipalities/sans designation marked (Mun.).

MUNICIPALITY	POP.	COUNTY	FEDERAL ELECTORAL DISTRICT	PROVINCIAL ELECTORAL DISTRICT	CLERK/GREFFIER OR SECRETARY-TREASURER (SEC) WITH ADDRESS & PHONE
St-Bonaventure (Paroisse)	929	Yamaska	Drummond	Nicolet	R. Paul-Hus, Sec., 772 rte I43 nord, St-Bonaventure, P.Q. JOC 1CO (819/396-2335)
St-Boniface-de-Shawinigan (Village)	2,752	St-Maurice	St-Maurice	St-Maurice	R. Racine, Sec., 945 Principale, St-Boniface-de-Shawinigan, P.Q. GOX 2LO (819/535-3227)
Ste-Brigide-d'Iberville (Mun.)	1,250	Iberville	St-Jean	Iberville	Paul Beauregard, Sec., C.P. 9, Ste-Brigide, P.Q. JOJ 1XO (514/293-4683)
Ste-Brigitte-de-Laval (Paroisse)	1,883	Montmorency 1	Montmorency	Montmorency	J. Vallée, Sec., 357 Ste-Brigitte, Ste-Brigitte-de-Laval, P.Q. GOA 3KO (418/825-2515)
Ste-Brigitte-des-Saults (Paroisse)	728	Nicolet	Drummond	Nicolet	A. Allard, Sec., Ste-Brigitte-des-Saults, P.Q. JOC 1EO (819/334-2235)
St-Bruno (Mun.)	2,299	Lac-St-Jean-Est	Lac-St-Jean	Lac-St-Jean	R. Ouellet, Sec., C.P. 39, St-Bruno, P.Q. GOW 2LO (418/343-2303)
St-Bruno-de-Guigues (Paroisse)	1,124	Témiscamingue	Témiscamingue	Rouyn-Noranda-Témiscamingue	H. Drolet, Sec., C.P. 130, Guigues, P.Q. JOZ 2GO (819/728-2186)
St-Bruno-de-Montarville (Ville)	22,500	Chambly	Chambly	Chambly	Danielle Joyal, Greffier, 1585 Montarville, St-Bruno-de-Montarville, P.Q. J3V 3T8 (514/653-2443)
St-Cajétan-d'Armagh (Paroisse)	880	Bellechasse	Bellechasse	Bellechasse	G. Roy, Sec., Armagh, P.Q. GOR 1AO (418/466-2844)
St-Calixte (Mun.)	1,766	Montcalm	Joliette	Rousseau	J. Charette, Sec., 6230 rue Hôtel de ville, St-Calixte, P.Q. JOK 1ZO (514/222-2782)
St-Camille (Canton)	485	Wolfe	Richmond	Richmond	C. Proulx, Sec., St-Camille, P.Q. JOA 1GO (819/828-3222)
St-Camille-de-Lellis (Paroisse)	1,228	Bellechasse	Bellechasse	Bellechasse	Mme A. Vermette, Sec., C.P. 130, St-Camille-de-Bellechasse, P.Q. GOR 2SO (418/595-2233)
St-Casimir (Paroisse)	466	Portneuf	Portneuf	Portneuf	G. Beaudoin, Sec., St-Casimir, P.Q. GOA 3LO (418/339-2409)
St-Casimir (Village)	1,186	Portneuf	Portneuf	Portneuf	N. Tessier, Sec., 220 boul de la Montagne, St-Casimir, P.Q. GOA 3LO (418/339-2543)
St-Casimir-Est (Village)	385	Portneuf	Portneuf	Portneuf	Mme C. Foley, Sec., C.P. 276, St-Casimir, P.Q. GOA 3LO (418/339-2170)
Ste-Catherine (Paroisse)	2,947	Portneuf	Portneuf	Chauveau	M. Grenier, Sec., C.P. 250, Ste-Catherine, P.Q. GOA 3MO (418/875-2211)
Ste-Catherine (Ville)	6,000	Laprairie		Châteauguay	G. Derome, Greffier, 202 boul. Marie-Victorin, Ste-Catherine, P.Q. JOL 1EO (514/632-0590)
Ste-Catherine-de-Hatley (Mun.)	1,150	Stanstead	Mégantic-Compton-Stanstead	Orford	La Sécrétaire, C.P. 30, Katevale, P.Q. JOB 1WO (819/843-1935)
Ste-Cécile-de-Lévrard (Paroisse)	513	Nicolet	Lotbinière	Lotbinière	J.-P. Lehouillier, Sec., 234 Principale, Ste-Cécile-de-Lévrard, P.Q. GOX 2MO (819/263-2958)

Cities in CAPITALS (Ville); Towns/Villes marked (Ville); Villages marked (Village); Townships/Cantons (marked Canton); United townships/Cantons unis (marked Cantons*); Parishes marked (Paroisse); undesignated municipalities/sans designation marked (Mun.).

MUNICIPALITY	POP.	COUNTY	FEDERAL ELECTORAL DISTRICT	PROVINCIAL ELECTORAL DISTRICT	CLERK/GREFFIER OR SECRETARY-TREASURER (SEC) WITH ADDRESS & PHONE
Ste-Cécile-de-Milton (Canton)	1,315	Shefford	Shefford	Shefford	Germaine Bernier, Sec., 273 Principale, Ste-Cécile-de-Milton, P.Q. JOE 2CO (514/378-1942)
Ste-Cécile-de-Whitton (Mun.)	775	Frontenac	Mégantic-Compton-Stanstead	Mégantic-Compton	F. Gosselin, Sec., C.P. 39, Ste-Cécile-de-Whitton, P.Q. GOY 1JO (819/583-0770)
St-Célestin (Mun.)	716	Nicolet	Richelieu	Nicolet	G. Proulx, Sec., 155 rue Noel, St-Célestin, P.Q. JOC 1GO (819/229-3627)
St-Césaire (Paroisse)	1,600	Rouville	Shefford	Iberville	L. Benoît, Sec., C.P. 930, St-Césaire, P.Q. JOL 1TO (514/469-3897)
St-Césaire (Ville)	2,436	Rouville	Shefford	Iberville	P. Despars, Sec., C.P. 570, St-Césaire, P.Q. JOL 1TO (514/469-3108)
St-Charles (Village)	1,049	Bellechasse	Lévis	Bellechasse	D. Labbe, Sec., C.P. 147, St-Charles-de-Bellechasse, P.Q. GOR 2TO (418/887-6600)
St-Charles (Paroisse)	826	St-Hyacinthe	Verchères	Verchères	D. Labbe, Sec., C.P. 38, St-Charles-sur-Richelieu, P.Q. JOH 2GO (514/584-2984)
St-Charles-Boromé (Paroisse)	1,118	Bellechasse		Bellechasse	D. Labbe, Sec., 8 rue St-Louis, St-Charles-de-Bellechasse, P.Q. GOR 2TO (418/887-6600)
St-Charles-Borromée (Paroisse)	6,200	Joliette	Lac-St-Jean	Joliette	L. Grypinich, Sec., 525 Visitation, St-Charles-Borromée, P.Q. J6P 4P2 (514/756-1881)
St-Charles-de-Mandeville (Mun.)	1,255	Berthier	Berthier-Maskinongé	Berthier	R. Therrien, Sec., 148 boul. Desjardins, St-Charles-de-Mandeville, P.Q. JOK 1LO (514/835-2055)
St-Charles-des-Grondines (Village)	350	Portneuf	Portneuf	Portneuf	A. Portelance, Sec., 320 Principale, Grondines, P.Q. GOA 1WO (418/268-8661)
St-Charles-des-Grondines (Paroisse)	346	Portneuf	Portneuf	Portneuf	P. Paquette, Sec., 130 2e rang est, Grondines, P.Q. GOA 1WO (418/268-8583)
St-Charles-Garnier (Paroisse)	529	Rimouski	Rimouski	Matapédia	G. Beaulieu-Côté, Sec., C.P. 39, St-Charles-Garnier, P.Q. GOK 1KO (418/798-4769)
St-Charles-sur-Richelieu (Village)	360	St-Hyacinthe	Verchères	Verchères	L. Meunier, Sec., 52 Richelieu, St-Charles-sur-Richelieu, P.Q. JOH 2GO (514/584-2267)
Ste-Christine (Paroisse)	330	Portneuf	Portneuf	Portneuf	Mme G. Langlois, Sec., 55 Principale, Auvergne, P.Q. GOA 1AO (418/329-2256)
Ste-Christine (Paroisse)	485	Bagot	St-Hyacinthe	Johnson	Mme F. Bisaillon, Sec., Ste-Christine, P.Q. JOH 1HO (819/858-2500)
St-Christophe-d'Arthabaska (Paroisse)	1,030	Arthabaska		Arthabaska	B.C. Verville, Sec., R.R. 1, Arthabaska, P.Q. G6P 6S1 (819/357-2195)
St-Chrysostome (Village)	1,065	Châteauguay	Beauharnois-Salaberry	Huntingdon	Mme G. Huet, Sec., C.P. 98, St-Chrysostome, P.Q. JOS 1RO (514/826-3237)
Ste-Claire (Mun.)	2,670	Dorchester	Bellechasse	Bellechasse	S. Gagnon, Sec., C.P. 189, Ste-Claire, P.Q. GOR 2VO (418/883-3314)

Cities in CAPITALS (Ville); Towns/Villes marked (Ville); Villages marked (Village); Townships/Cantons (marked Canton); United townships/Cantons unis (marked Cantons*); Parishes marked (Paroisse); undesignated municipalities/sans designation marked (Mun.).

MUNICIPALITY	POP.	COUNTY	FEDERAL ELECTORAL DISTRICT	PROVINCIAL ELECTORAL DISTRICT	CLERK/GREFFIER OR SECRETARY-TREASURER (SEC) WITH ADDRESS & PHONE
St-Claude (Mun.)	803	Richmond	Richmond	Richmond	J.-C. Richard, Sec., R.R. 2, Windsor, P.Q. J1S 2L5 (819/845-2045)
St-Clément (Paroisse)	692	Rivière-du-Loup	Kamouraska-Rivière-du-Loup	Rivière-du-Loup	Rose-E. Santerre, Sec., St-Clément, P.Q. GOL 2NO (418/963-2421)
St-Cléophas (Paroisse)	411	Matapédia	Matapédia-Matane	Matapédia	G. Gagnon, Sec., R.R. 3, boite 4, Sayabec, P.Q. GOJ 3KO (418/536-3202)
St-Cléophas (Paroisse)	255	Joliette	Berthier-Maskinongé	Berthier	L. Bellerose, Sec., 750 Principale, St-Cléophas, P.Q. JOK 3AO (514/889-2489)
St-Clet (Mun.)	1,097	Soulanges	Vaudreuil	Vaudreuil-Soulanges	L. Sabourin, Sec., 4 du Moulin, St-Clet, P.Q. JOP 1SO (514/456-3363)
Ste-Clothilde (Paroisse)	496	Beauce		Beauce-Sud	M. Pomerleau, Sec., Corriveau, P.Q. GON 1CO (418/427-2637)
Ste-Clothilde (Paroisse)	1,225	Châteauguay	Châteauguay	Huntingdon	L. Rousse, Sec., 2452 ch. de l'Eglise, Ste-Clothilde, P.Q. JOL 1WO (514/826-3098)
Ste-Clothilde-de-Horton (Village)	373	Arthabaska	Drummond	Richmond	J.-R. Bédard, Sec., Ste-Clothilde, P.Q. JOA 1HO (819/336-2033)
Ste-Clothilde-de-Horton (Paroisse)	657	Arthabaska	Drummond	Richmond	J. Chabot, Sec., R.R. 2, Ste-Clothilde-Horton, P.Q. JOA 1HO (819/336-5420)
St-Colomban (Paroisse)	1,804	Deux-Montagnes	Argenteuil	Argenteuil	Mme M. Shewchuk, Sec., 325 Montée de l'Eglise, St-Colomban, P.Q. JOR 1NO (514/436-1453)
St-Côme (Paroisse)	1,380	Joliette	Berthier-Maskinongé	Berthier	B. Riopel, Sec., 1673 55e rue, St-Côme, P.Q. JOK 2BO (514/883-2726)
St-Côme-de-Kennebec (Paroisse)	1,402	Beauce	Beauce	Beauce-Sud	J.-P. Champagne, Sec., C.P. 219, Linière, P.Q. GOM 1JO (418/685-3825)
St-Constant (Ville)	9,200	Laprairie	Châteauguay	Châteauguay	G. Brisson, Sec., 147 St-Pierre, St-Constant, P.Q. JOL 1XO (514/632-8084)
Ste-Croix (Village)	1,751	Lotbinière	Lotbinière	Lotbinière	B. Lepage, Sec., 6310 Principale, Ste-Croix, P.Q. GOS 2HO (418/926-3494)
Ste-Croix (Paroisse)	823	Lotbinière	Lotbinière	Lotbinière	J.-P. Lemay, Sec., C.P. 100, Ste-Croix, P.Q. GOS 2HO (418/926-3982)
St-Cuthbert (Paroisse)		Berthier	Berthier-Maskinongé	Berthier	M. Sylvestre, Sec., C.P. 100, St-Cuthbert, P.Q. JOK 2CO (514/856-4852)
St-Cyprien (Mun.)	1,280	Rivière-du-Loup	Kamouraska-Rivière-du-Loup	Rivière-du-Loup	Mme B. Rousseau, Sec., C.P. 9, St-Cyprien, P.Q. GOL 2PO (418/963-2730)
St-Cyprien (Paroisse)	759	Dorchester	Bellechasse	Bellechasse	R. Fortier, Sec., Barré PO, P.Q. GOR 1BO (418/383-3230)
St-Cyprien (Paroisse)	980	Napierville	St-Jean	St-Jean	Y. Dupont, Sec., 361 St-Jacques, Napierville, P.Q. JOJ 1LO (514/245-3658)
St-Cyrille (Village)	1,057	Drummond	Drummond	Drummond	G. Gagnon, Sec., 575 Principale, St-Cyrille-de-Wendover, P.Q. JOC 1HO (819/397-4226)
St-Cyrille-de-Lessard (Paroisse)	946	L'Islet	Bellechasse	Montmagny-L'Islet	Aimé Lord, Sec., C.P. 87, St-Cyrille-de-L'Islet, P.Q. GOR 2WO (418/247-5186)

Cities in CAPITALS (Ville); Towns/Villes marked (Ville); Villages marked (Village); Townships/Cantons (marked Canton); United townships/Cantons unis (marked Cantons*); Parishes marked (Paroisse); undesignated municipalities/sans designation marked (Mun.).

MUNICIPALITY	POP.	COUNTY	FEDERAL ELECTORAL DISTRICT	PROVINCIAL ELECTORAL DISTRICT	CLERK/GREFFIER OR SECRETARY-TREASURER (SEC) WITH ADDRESS & PHONE
St-Damase (Paroisse)	512	Matapédia	Matapédia-Matane	Matapédia	Mme J.-B. Dumont, Sec., St-Damase, P.Q. GOJ 2JO (418/776-5386)
St-Damase (Paroisse)	1,174	St-Hyacinthe	St-Hyacinthe	St-Hyacinthe	Y. Tétreault, Sec., C.P. 8, St-Damase, P.Q. JOH 1JO (514/797-2285)
St-Damase (Village)	1,097	St-Hyacinthe	St-Hyacinthe	St-Hyacinthe	Y. Tétreault, Sec., C.P. 8, St-Damase, P.Q. JOH 1JO (514/797-2285)
St-Damase-de-L'Islet (Mun.)	710	L'Islet	Bellechasse	Montmagny-L'Islet	L. Lapointe, Sec., St-Damase-des-Aulnaies, P.Q. GOR 2XO (418/598-3474)
St-Damien (Paroisse)	1,123	Berthier	Berthier-Maskinongé	Berthier	Lise Bergevin, Sec., 6850 rte 347, St-Damase-de-Brandon PO, P.Q. JOK 2EO (514/835-7448)
St-Damien-de-Buckland (Paroisse)	2,024	Bellechasse	Bellechasse	Bellechasse	Jacques Thibault, Sec., C.P. 40, St-Damien-de-Buckland, P.Q. GOR 2YO (418/789-2526)
St-David (Paroisse)	1,023	Yamaska	Richelieu	Nicolet	L. Thibault, Sec., St-David-d'Yamaska, P.Q. JOG 1LO (514/789-2288)
St-David-de-Falardeau (Mun.)	1,691	Chicoutimi	Lac-St-Jean	Dubuc	C. Lavoie, Sec., C.P. 8, St-David-de-Falardeau, P.Q. GOV 1CO (418/673-4646)
St-David-de-l'Auberivière (Ville)	4,500	Lévis	Lévis	Lévis	G. Lavoie, Greffier, 784 Commerciale, St-David, P.Q. G6W 1E9 (418/837-9284)
St-Denis (Paroisse)	547	Kamouraska	Kamouraska-Rivière-du-Loup	Kamouraska-Témiscouata	P. Pelletier, Sec., St-Denis, P.Q. GOL 2RO (418/498-2648)
St-Denis (Paroisse)	981	St-Hyacinthe	Verchères	Verchères	P. Pétrin, Sec., 275 Nelson, St-Denis-sur-Richelieu, P.Q. JOH 1KO (514/787-2244)
St-Denis (Village)	892	St-Hyacinthe	Verchères	Verchères	Voir St-Denis (Paroisse)
St-Denis-de-Brompton (Paroisse)	1,196	Richmond	Richmond	Johnson	R. Carrier, Sec., C.P. 120, St-Denis-de-Brompton, P.Q. JOB 2PO (819/846-4612)
St-Didace (Paroisse)	478	Maskinongé	Berthier-Maskinongé	Berthier	Edouardina Lambert, Sec., 480 Principale, St-Didace, P.Q. JOK 2GO (514/835-4184)
St-Dominique (Mun.)	1,801	Bagot	St-Hyacinthe	St-Hyacinthe	R. Dubreuil, Sec., St-Dominique, P.Q. JOH 1LO (514/773-3200)
St-Dominique-du-Rosaire (Mun.)			Abitibi	Abitibi-Ouest	Suzanne Roy, Sec., St-Dominique-du-Rosaire, P.Q. JOY 2KO (819/732-3834)
St-Donat (Paroisse)	748	Rimouski	Rimouski	Matapédia	P.-Y. Desjardins, Sec., St-Donat, P.Q. GOK 1LO (418/739-4634)
St-Donat (Mun.)	2,562	Montcalm	Joliette	Rousseau	J. St-Georges, Sec., C.P. 28, St-Donat, P.Q. JOT 2CO (819/424-2383)
St-Dunstan-du-Lac-Beauport (Paroisse)	2,254	Québec	Charlesbourg	Chauveau	H.G. Zicat, Sec., 65 ch. le Tour-du-Lac, Lac-Beauport, P.Q. GOA 2CO (418/849-7141)
St-Edmond (Mun.)	232	Matapédia	Matapédia-Matane	Matapédia	P. Lavigne, Sec., Rg. 4, Lac-au-Saumon, P.Q. GOJ 1MO (418/778-3478)

Cities in CAPITALS (Ville); Towns/Villes marked (Ville); Villages marked (Village); Townships/Cantons (marked Canton); United townships/Cantons unis (marked Cantons*); Parishes marked (Paroisse); undesignated municipalities/sans designation marked (Mun.).

MUNICIPALITY	POP.	COUNTY	FEDERAL ELECTORAL DISTRICT	PROVINCIAL ELECTORAL DISTRICT	CLERK/GREFFIER OR SECRETARY-TREASURER (SEC) WITH ADDRESS & PHONE
St-Edmond (Mun.)	575	Lac-St-Jean-Ouest	Roberval	Roberval	A. Simard, Sec., 116 ch. Principal, St-Edmond-les-Plaines, P.Q. GOW 2MO (418/274-5085)
St-Edmond-de-Grantham (Paroisse)	520	Drummond	Drummond	Drummond	H. Lafleur, Sec., St-Edmond-de-Grantham, P.Q. JOC 1KO (819/395-4204)
St-Edouard (Mun.)	740	Maskinongé	Berthier-Maskinongé	Maskinongé	G. Gerbeau, Sec., 3621 Notre Dame, St-Edouard-de-Maskinongé, P.Q. JOK 2HO (819/268-2833)
St-Edouard (Paroisse)	1,113	Napierville	St-Jean	Huntingdon	D. Brosseau, Sec., St-Edouard-de-Napierville, P.Q. JOL 1YO (514/454-2576)
St-Edouard-de-Fabre (Paroisse)	710	Témiscamingue	Témiscamingue	Rouyn-Noranda-Témiscamingue	Anita Pelchat, Sec., C.P. 8, Fabre, P.Q. JOZ 1ZO (819/724-4441)
St-Edouard-de-Frampton (Paroisse)	1,406	Dorchester	Beauce	Beauce-Nord	M. Drouin, Sec., C.P. 40, Frampton, P.Q. GOR 1MO (418/479-5363)
St-Edouard-de-Lotbinière (Paroisse)	1,392	Lotbinière	Lotbinière	Lotbinière	G. Lemay, Sec., Rivière-Bois-Clair, P.Q. GOS 1YO (418/796-2158)
Ste-Edwidge-de-Clifton (Canton)	607	Compton	Mégantic-Compton-Stanstead	Mégantic-Compton	R. Favreau, Sec., Ste-Edwidge, P.Q. JOB 2RO (819/849-3372)
St-Elie (Paroisse)	963	St-Maurice	St-Maurice	Maskinongé	M.L. Samson, Sec., 87 Principale, St-Elie, P.Q. GOX 2NO (819/221-2839)
St-Elie-d'Orford (Paroisse)	2,684	Sherbrooke	Shefford	Orford	P. Auger, Sec., 2193 Hôtel de ville, St-Elie-d'Orford, P.Q. JOB 2SO (819/562-8666)
Ste-Elisabeth (Paroisse)	1,627	Joliette	Berthier-Maskinongé	Berthier	Pauline Ladouceur, Sec., 70 rue Pelland, Ste-Elisabeth, P.Q. JOK 2JO (514/759-2875)
Ste-Elisabeth-de-Warwick (Paroisse)	409	Arthabaska	Lotbinière	Richmond	F.K. Morin, Sec., R.R. 1, Warwick, P.Q. JOA 1MO (819/358-2761)
St-Eloi (Paroisse)	486	Rivière-du-Loup	Kamouraska-Rivière-du-Loup	Rivière-du-Loup	C. Ladrie, Sec., St-Eloi, P.Q. GOL 2VO (418/898-3083)
St-Elphège (Paroisse)	338	Yamaska	Richelieu	Nicolet	J. Coll, Sec., R.R. 1, Pierreville, P.Q. JOG 1JO (514/568-5570)
St-Elzéar (Mun.)	608	Bonaventure	Bonaventure-Iles-de-la-Madeleine	Bonaventure	Francine Ferlatte, Sec., C.P. 40, St-Elzéar-de-Bonaventure, P.Q. GOC 2WO (418/534-2611)
St-Elzéar (Mun.)	398	Témiscouata	Rimouski	Kamouraska-Témiscouata	Rosa Lavoie, Sec., St-Elzéar-de-Témiscouata, P.Q. GOL 2WO (418/854-5401)
St-Elzéar (Village)	650	Beauce	Beauce	Beauce-Nord	Mme C. Gilbert, Sec., C.P. 69, St-Elzéar (Beauce), P.Q. GOS 2JO (418/387-2534)
St-Elzéar-de-Beauce (Mun.)	506	Beauce	Beauce	Beauce-Nord	R. Larochelle, Sec., Rg. Bas-St-Jacques, St-Elzéar (Beauce), P.Q. GOS 2JO (418/387-2486)
Ste-Emélie-de-l'Energie (Paroisse)	1,073	Joliette	Berthier-Maskinongé	Berthier	Mme D. Lepine, Sec., C.P. 88, Ste-Emélie-de-L'Energie, P.Q. JOK 2KO (514/886-2458)
St-Emile (Village)	5,000	Québec	Charlesbourg	Chauveau	D. Leclerc, Sec., C.P. 9, St-Emile, P.Q. GOA 3NO (418/842-8466)

Cities in CAPITALS (Ville); Towns/Villes marked (Ville); Villages marked (Village); Townships/Cantons (marked Canton); United townships/Cantons unis (marked Cantons*); Parishes marked (Paroisse); undesignated municipalities/sans designation marked (Mun.).

MUNICIPALITY	POP.	COUNTY	FEDERAL ELECTORAL DISTRICT	PROVINCIAL ELECTORAL DISTRICT	CLERK/GREFFIER OR SECRETARY-TREASURER (SEC) WITH ADDRESS & PHONE
Ste-Emmélie (Paroisse)	367	Lotbinière	Lotbinière	Lotbinière	Hilaire Pressé, Sec., C.P. 32, Leclercville, P.Q. GOS 1RO (819/292-2005)
St-Ephrem-de-Beauce (Paroisse)	1,073	Beauce	Beauce	Beauce-Sud	G. Bolduc, Sec., C.P. 235, St-Ephrem, P.Q. GOM 1RO (418/484-2893)
St-Ephrem-de-Tring (Village)	875	Beauce	Beauce	Beauce-Sud	Mme T.G. Bolduc, Sec., C.P. 87, St-Ephrem-de-Tring, P.Q. GOM 1RO (418/484-2114)
St-Ephrem-d'Upton (Paroisse)	685	Bagot		Johnson	Y.H. Côté, Sec., C.P. 302, Upton, P.Q. JOH 2EO (514/549-4361)
St-Epiphane (Paroisse)	1,097	Rivière-du-Loup	Kamouraska-Rivière-du-Loup	Rivière-du-Loup	Thérèse Lebel, Sec., C.P. 68, St-Epiphane, P.Q. GOL 2XO (418/862-8800)
St-Esprit (Paroisse)	1,757	Montcalm	Joliette	Rousseau	R. Beaudoin, Sec., 21 Principale, St-Esprit, P.Q. JOK 2LO (514/839-3868)
St-Etienne (Mun.)	2,369	Lévis	Lévis	Beauce-Nord	G. Dubois, Sec., 1 place Chamberland, St-Etienne-de-Lauzon, P.Q. GOS 2LO (418/832-4023)
St-Etienne-de-Beauharnois (Mun.)	811	Beauharnois	Beauharnois-Salaberry	Beauharnois	Christiane Legault, Sec., 360 ch. St-Louis, St-Etienne--de-Beauharnois, P.Q. JOS 1SO (514/429-4167)
St-Etienne-de-Beaumont (Paroisse)	1,507	Bellechasse		Bellechasse	J.E. Walsh, Sec., 6 boul. Mercier, Beaumont, P.Q. GOR 1CO (418/833-3369)
St-Etienne-de-Bolton (Mun.)	277	Brome	Missisquoi	Brome-Missisquoi	G. Lacasse, Sec., St-Etienne-de-Bolton, P.Q. JOE 2EO (514/297-6361)
St-Etienne-des-Grès (Paroisse)	2,262	St-Maurice	St-Maurice	Maskinongé	G. Gauthier, Sec., 1211 Principale, St-Etienne-des-Grès, P.Q. GOX 2PO (819/535-3113)
St-Eugène (Paroisse)	1,361	L'Islet		Montmagny-L'Islet	A.M. Normand, Sec., Lamartine, P.Q. GOR 1XO (418/247-5340)
St-Eugène (Mun.)	934	Drummond	Drummond	Johnson	T. Dugre, Sec., 441 Rg. 13, St-Eugène, P.Q. JOC 1JO (819/396-5589)
St-Eugène (Mun.)	660	Lac-St-Jean-Ouest	Roberval	Roberval	R. Bruneau, Sec., C.P. 70, Argentenay, P.Q. GOW 1BO (418/276-1787)
St-Eugène-de-Guigues (Mun.)	495	Témiscamingue	Témiscamingue	Rouyn-Noranda-Témiscamingue	J. Rioux, Sec., St-Eugène-de-Guigues, P.Q. JOZ 3LO (819/785-2301)
St-Eugène-de-Ladrière (Paroisse)	593	Rimouski	Rimouski	Rimouski	Z. Cloutier, Sec., Ladrière, P.Q. GOL 1PO (418/869-2666)
Ste-Eulalie (Mun.)	848	Nicolet	Lotbinière	Nicolet	L. Champagne, Sec., C.P. 70, St-Eulalie, P.Q. GOZ 1EO (819/225-4404)
Ste-Euphémie-sur-Rivière-du-Sud (Mun.)	490	Montmagny	Bellechasse	Montmagny-L'Islet	D. Giroux, Sec., Ste-Euphémie, P.Q. GOR 2ZO (418/469-2869)
St-Eusèbe (Paroisse)	669	Témiscouata	Rimouski	Kamouraska-Témiscouata	S. Deschamps, Sec., St-Eusèbe, P.Q. GOL 2YO (418/899-2762)
St-Eustache (Ville)	23,300	Deux-Montagnes	Blainville-Deux-Montagnes	Deux-Montagnes	Guy Prud'Homme, Greffier, 235 rue St-Eustache, St-Eustache, P.Q. J7R 2L8 (514/472-4440)
St-Evariste-de-Forsyth (Mun.)	758	Frontenac	Frontenac	Beauce-Sud	R. Bureau, Sec., St-Evariste, P.Q. GOM 1SO (418/459-3349)

Cities in CAPITALS (Ville); Towns/Villes marked (Ville); Villages marked (Village); Townships/Cantons (marked Canton); United townships/Cantons unis (marked Cantons*); Parishes marked (Paroisse); undesignated municipalities/sans designation marked (Mun.).

MUNICIPALITY	POP.	COUNTY	FEDERAL ELECTORAL DISTRICT	PROVINCIAL ELECTORAL DISTRICT	CLERK/GREFFIER OR SECRETARY-TREASURER (SEC) WITH ADDRESS & PHONE
St-Fabien (Paroisse)	2,089	Rimouski	Rimouski	Rimouski	R. Roy, Sec., C.P. 127, St-Fabien, P.Q. GOL 2ZO (418/869-2950)
St-Fabien-de-Panet (Paroisse)	1,054	Montmagny	Bellechasse	Montmagny-L'Islet	Beatrice Gonthier, Sec., C.P. 9, Panet, P.Q. GOR 2JO (418/249-4471)
Ste-Famille (I.O.) (Paroisse)	1,080	Montmorency 2	Montmorency	Montmorency	Lise L. Létourneau, Sec., 3387 av. Royale, Ste-Famille (I.O.), P.Q. GOA 3PO (418/829-2565)
St-Faustin (Mun.)	864	Terrebonne	Labelle	Labelle	A. Gougeon, Sec., C.P. 120, St-Faustin, P.Q. JOT 2GO (819/688-2161)
St-Félicien (Ville)	8,200	Lac-St-Jean-Ouest	Roberval	Roberval	Gisèle Moreau, Greffier, 1058 boul. Sacré-Coeur, St-Félicien, P.Q. GOW 2NO (418/679-0251)
Ste-Félicité (Paroisse)	731	Matane	Matapédia-Matane	Matane	Denise Otis, Sec., C.P. 45, Ste-Félicité, P.Q. GOJ 2KO (418/733-4234)
Ste-Félicité (Village)	759	Matane	Matapédia-Matane	Matane	G. Pelletier, Sec., C.P. 9, Ste-Félicité, P.Q. GOJ 2KO (418/733-4628)
Ste-Félicité (Mun.)	621	L'Islet	Bellechasse	Montmagny-L'Islet	C.-A. Bourgault, Sec., Ste-Félicité, P.Q. GOR 3ZO (418/359-2018)
St-Félix-de-Dalquier (Mun.)	823	Abitibi	Abitibi	Abitibi-Ouest	J.-B. Carignan, Sec., St-Félix-de-Dalquier, P.Q. JOY 1GO (819/732-3891)
St-Félix-de-Valois (Village)	1,482	Joliette	Berthier-Maskinongé	Berthier	P.-A. Brosseau, Sec., C.P. 67, St-Félix-de-Valois, P.Q. JOK 2MO (514/889-5931)
St-Félix-de-Valois (Paroisse)	2,490	Joliette	Berthier-Maskinongé	Berthier	G. Charette, Sec., C.P. 220, St-Félix-de-Valois, P.Q. JOK 2MO (514/889-4161)
St-Félix-du-Cap-Rouge (Paroisse)	8,500	Québec		La Peltrie	L.-A. Bombardier, Sec., 4473 St-Félix, Cap-Rouge, P.Q. GOA 1KO (418/651-1225)
St-Féréol-les-Neiges (Mun.)	1,676	Montmorency 1	Charlevoix	Charlevoix	J. Pichette, Sec., 3453 av. Royale, St-Féréol-les-Neiges, P.Q. GOA 3RO (418/827-2584)
St-Fidèle-de-Mont-Murray (Paroisse)	1,006	Charlevoix-Est	Charlevoix	Charlevoix	G. Desbiens, Sec., 235 Principale, St-Fidèle, P.Q. GOT 1TO (418/434-2447)
St-Fidèle-de-Ristigouche (Mun.)	15	Bonaventure	Bonaventure-Iles-de-la-Madeleine	Bonaventure	a/s Min. des Affaires Municipales, 1039 De La Chevrotière, Quebec, P.Q. G1R 4Z3 (418/643-7082)
St-Firmin (Mun.)	485	Saguenay	Charlevoix	Charlevoix	Mme C.G. Dufour, Sec., Baie-Ste-Catherine, P.Q. GOT 1AO (418/237-4354)
Ste-Flavie (Paroisse)	792	Rimouski	Matapédia-Matane	Matapédia	V. Pelletier, Sec., 35 1e rg. est, Ste-Flavie, P.Q. GOJ 2LO (418/775-7050)
St-Flavien (Village)	703	Lotbinière	Lotbinière	Lotbinière	J.-F. Desrochers, Sec., St-Flavien, P.Q. GOS 2MO (418/728-2197)
St-Flavien (Paroisse)	635	Lotbinière	Lotbinière	Lotbinière	B. Demers, Sec., 1094 Rg. St-Joseph, St-Flavien, P.Q. GOS 2MO (418/728-2326)
Ste-Florence (Mun.)	646	Matapédia	Bonaventure-Iles-de-la-Madeleine	Matapédia	G. Thibault, Sec., C.P. 9, Ste-Florence, P.Q. GOJ 2MO (418/756-3904)
St-Fortunat (Mun.)	343	Wolfe	Richmond	Richmond	A. Bédard, Sec., St-Fortunat, P.Q. GOP 1GO (819/344-2798)

Cities in CAPITALS (Ville); Towns/Villes marked (Ville); Villages marked (Village); Townships/Cantons (marked Canton); United townships/Cantons unis (marked Cantons*); Parishes marked (Paroisse); undesignated municipalities/sans designation marked (Mun.).

MUNICIPALITY	POP.	COUNTY	FEDERAL ELECTORAL DISTRICT	PROVINCIAL ELECTORAL DISTRICT	CLERK/GREFFIER OR SECRETARY-TREASURER (SEC) WITH ADDRESS & PHONE
STE-FOY (Ville)	74,500	Québec	Louis-Hébert	Jean-Talon; La Peltrie; Louis-Hébert	Noel Perron, Greffier, 1000 rte de l'Eglise, Ste-Foy, P.Q. G1V 4E1 (418/657-4021)
St-François-d'Assise (Paroisse)	962	Bonaventure	Bonaventure-Iles-de-la-Madeleine	Bonaventure	J. Martin, Sec., C.P. 39, St-François-d'Assise, P.Q. GOJ 2NO (418/299-2066)
St-François-de-Beauce (Mun.)	935	Beauce	Beauce	Beauce-Nord	M. Rodrigue, Sec., 122 7e rue, Beauceville-Est, P.Q. GOS 1AO (418/774-6653)
St-François-de-Pabos (Mun.)	844	Gaspé-Est	Gaspé	Gaspé	G. Defraiche, Sec., C.P. 23, Pabos, P.Q. GOC 2HO (418/689-2990)
St-François-de-Sales (Mun.)	804	Lac-St-Jean-Ouest	Roberval	Roberval	Marie Blanchette, Sec., 541 Principale, St-François-de-Sales, P.Q. GOW 1MO (418/348-6736)
St-François-de-Sales-de-la-Rivière-du-Sud (Paroisse)	1,850	Montmagny	Bellechasse	Montmagny-L'Islet	G. Lamonde, Sec., 418 boul. St-François, St-François, P.Q. GOR 3AO (418/259-7228)
St-François-du-Lac (Paroisse)	847	Yamaska	Richelieu	Nicolet	Elaine Nadeau, Sec., C.P. 149, St-François-du-Lac, P.Q. JOG 1MO (514/568-5640)
St-François-du-Lac (Village)	971	Yamaska	Richelieu	Nicolet	Mme Etiennette Bélisle, Sec., C.P. 60, St-François-du-Lac, P.Q. JOG 1MO (514/568-3728)
Ste-Françoise (Paroisse)	626	Rivière-du-Loup	Kamouraska-Rivière-du-Loup	Rivière-du-Loup	R. Michaud, Sec., C.P. 39, Ste-Françoise, P.Q. GOL 3BO (418/851-1502)
Ste-Françoise (Mun.)	514	Lotbinière	Lotbinière	Lotbinière	Mme E. Boisvert, Sec., Ste-Françoise, P.Q. GOS 2NO (819/287-5755)
St-François (I.O.) (Paroisse)	455	Montmorency 2	Montmorency	Montmorency	R. Gosselin, Sec., 437 av. Royale, St-François (I.O.), P.Q. GOA 3SO (418/829-3100)
St-François-Ouest (Mun.)	661	Beauce	Beauce	Beauce-Nord	H. Rodrigue, Sec., 277 av. Lambert, Beauceville-Ouest, P.Q. GOM 1AO (418/774-9007)
St-François-Xavier-de-Batiscan (Paroisse)	970	Champlain	Champlain	Champlain	J. Bellefeuille, Sec., 395 Principale, Batiscan, P.Q. GOX 1AO (418/362-2162)
St-François-Xavier-de-Brompton (Paroisse)	1,470	Richmond	Richmond	Johnson	C. Frappier, Sec., C.P. 10, St-François-Xavier-de-Brompton, P.Q. JOV 2VO (819/845-3954)
St-François-Xavier-de-la-Petite-Rivière (Paroisse)	952	Charlevoix-Ouest	Charlevoix	Charlevoix	Clémentine Bouchard, Sec., C.P. 10, La-Petite-Rivière-St-François, P.Q. GOA 2LO (418/632-5721)
St-François-Xavier-des-Hauteurs (Paroisse)	931	Rimouski	Rimouski	Matapédia	C. Dupont, Sec., Les-Hauteurs-de-Rimouski, P.Q. GOR 1CO (418/798-8266)
St-François-Xavier-de-Viger (Mun.)	442	Rivière-du-Loup	Kamouraska-Rivière-du-Loup	Rivière-du-Loup	Mme L. Boucher, Sec., St-François-Xavier-de-Viger, P.Q. GOL 3CO (418/497-3784)
St-Frédéric (Paroisse)	902	Beauce	Beauce	Beauce-Nord	Ange-A. Nadeau, Sec., St-Frédéric, P.Q. GON 1PO (418/426-2571)
St-Fulgence (Mun.)	1,764	Chicoutimi	Lac-St-Jean	Dubuc	G. Tremblay, Sec., C.P. 70, St-Fulgence, P.Q. GOV 1SO (418/674-2588)

Cities in CAPITALS (Ville); Towns/Villes marked (Ville); Villages marked (Village); Townships/Cantons (marked Canton); United townships/Cantons unis (marked Cantons*); Parishes marked (Paroisse); undesignated municipalities/sans designation marked (Mun.).

MUNICIPALITY	POP.	COUNTY	FEDERAL ELECTORAL DISTRICT	PROVINCIAL ELECTORAL DISTRICT	CLERK/GREFFIER OR SECRETARY-TREASURER (SEC) WITH ADDRESS & PHONE
St-Gabriel (Paroisse)	812	Rimouski	Rimouski	Matapédia	M.-P. Leblanc, Sec., 10 rue Harvey, St-Gabriel-de-Rimouski, P.Q. GOK 1MO (418/798-4938)
St-Gabriel (Ville)	3,283	Berthier	Berthier-Maskinongé	Berthier	R. Gagnon, Sec., C.P. 750, St-Gabriel-de-Brandon, P.Q. JOK 2NO (514/835-2212)
St-Gabriel-de-Brandon (Paroisse)	1,449	Berthier	Berthier-Maskinongé	Berthier	C. Coutu, Sec., C.P. 929, St-Gabriel-de-Brandon, P.Q. JOK 2NO (514/835-5600)
St-Gabriel-de-Valcartier (Mun.)	2,080	Québec	Charlesbourg	Chauveau	B. Hicks, Sec., 1625 boul. Valcartier, Valcartier Village, P.Q. GOA 4SO (418/844-2332)
St-Gabriel-Lallemant (Mun.)	1,094	Kamouraska	Kamouraska-Rivière-du-Loup	Kamouraska-Témiscouata	Gina Lévesque, Sec., St-Gabriel-de-Kamouraska, P.Q. GOL 3EO (418/852-2801)
St-Gabriel-Ouest (Mun.)	134	Québec	Charlesbourg	Chauveau	J. Monaghan, Sec., a/s R.R. 1, Valcartier Village, P.Q. GOA 4SO (418/844-2105)
St-Gédéon (Village)	1,327	Frontenac	Beauce	Beauce-Sud	P.A. Pelchat, Sec., 102 1re ave sud, St-Gédéon-de-Beauce, P.Q. GOM 1TO (418/582-3341)
St-Gédéon (Paroisse)	658	Frontenac	Beauce	Beauce-Sud	H. Bégin, Sec., C.P. 187, St-Gédéon-de-Beauce, P.Q. GOM 1TO (418/582-3535)
St-Gédéon (Mun.)	1,660	Lac-St-Jean-Est	Lac-St-Jean	Lac-St-Jean	J. Audet, Sec., C.P. 99, St-Gédéon Village, P.Q. GOW 2PO (418/345-2273)
Ste-Geneviève (Ville)	2,904	Ile-de-Montréal	Vaudreuil	Nelligan	J. Lamoureux, Sec., 13 rue Chauret, Ste-Geneviève, P.Q. H9H 1G4 (514/626-2535)
Ste-Geneviève-de-Batiscan (Paroisse)	1,150	Champlain	Champlain	Champlain	J. Joubert, Sec., C.P. 70, Ste-Geneviève-de-Batiscan, P.Q. GOX 2RO (418/362-2078)
Ste-Geneviève-de-Berthier (Paroisse)	1,824	Berthier	Berthier-Maskinongé	Berthier	C. Joyal, Sec., C.P. 750, Berthierville, P.Q. JOK 1AO (514/836-3796)
St-Georges (Ville)	8,900	Beauce	Beauce	Beauce-Sud	E. Gendron, Greffier, 11700 boul. Lacroix, St-Georges-de-Beauce, P.Q. G5Y 1L3 (418/228-5555)
St-Georges (Village)	2,868	Champlain	St-Maurice	Laviolette	I. Pelletier, Sec., 400 106e Ave., St-Georges-de-Champlain, P.Q. G9T 3K1 (819/538-2435)
St-Georges-de-Cacouna (Village)	1,092	Rivière-du-Loup	Kamouraska-Rivière-du-Loup	Rivière-du-Loup	G. Guay, Sec., C.P. 40, Cacouna, P.Q. GOL 1GO (418/862-3708)
St-Georges-de-Cacouna (Paroisse)	621	Rivière-du-Loup	Kamouraska-Rivière-du-Loup	Rivière-du-Loup	Voir St-Georges-de-Cacouna (Village)
St-Georges-de-Clarenceville (Mun.)	495	Missisquoi	Missisquoi	Iberville	C.F. Adams, Sec., C.P. 7, Clarenceville, P.Q. JOJ 1BO (514/294-5564)
St-Georges-de-Windsor (Canton)	558	Richmond	Richmond	Richmond	Mme D. Clément, Sec., St-Georges-de-Windsor, P.Q. JOA 1JO (819/828-2676)

Cities in CAPITALS (Ville); Towns/Villes marked (Ville); Villages marked (Village); Townships/Cantons (marked Canton); United townships/Cantons unis (marked Cantons*); Parishes marked (Paroisse); undesignated municipalities/sans designation marked (Mun.).

MUNICIPALITY	POP.	COUNTY	FEDERAL ELECTORAL DISTRICT	PROVINCIAL ELECTORAL DISTRICT	CLERK/GREFFIER OR SECRETARY-TREASURER (SEC) WITH ADDRESS & PHONE
St-Georges-de-Windsor (Village)	280	Richmond	Richmond	Richmond	J.-G. Côté, Sec., St-Georges-de-Windsor, P.Q. JOA 1JO (819/828-2182)
St-Georges-Est (Paroisse)	1,526	Beauce	Beauce	Beauce-Sud	Y. Gilbert, Sec., 11785 1re Ave., St-Georges-Est, P.Q. G5Y 2C7 (418/228-2925)
St-Georges-Ouest (Ville)	6,500	Beauce	Beauce	Beauce-Sud	L. Nadeau, Greffier, 1500 6eme Ave., St-Georges-Ouest, P.Q. G5Y 3W1 (418/228-6132)
St-Gérard (Village)	513	Wolfe	Richmond	Mégantic-Compton	S. Tanguay, Sec., C.P. 59, St-Gérard, P.Q. GOY 1KO (819/877-2329)
St-Gérard-des-Laurentides (Paroisse)	1,629	St-Maurice	St-Maurice	St-Maurice	A. Martin, Sec., 431 des Frênes, B.G. 430, St-Gérard-des-Laurentides, P.Q. G9N 6T6 (819/539-9121)
St-Gérard-Magella (Paroisse)	1,615	L'Assomption	Joliette	L'Assomption	F. Ricard, Sec., 2501 Rang sud, Vaucluse PO, P.Q. JOK 3PO (514/588-5601)
St-Gérard-Majella (Paroisse)	357	Yamaska	Richelieu	Nicolet	R. Proulx, Sec., 370 Rg. Ste-Catherine, Yamaska-Est, P.Q. JOG 1XO (514/789-5240)
St-Germain (Paroisse)	375	Kamouraska	Kamouraska-Rivière-du-Loup	Kamouraska-Témiscouata	J.-L. Beaulieu, Sec., St-Germain, P.Q. GOL 3GO (418/492-7052)
St-Germain-de-Grantham (Village)	1,325	Drummond	Drummond	Drummond	Mme R. Bécotte, Sec., C.P. 187, St-Germain-de-Grantham, P.Q. JOC 1KO (819/395-4445)
St-Germain-de-Grantham (Paroisse)	1,413	Drummond	Drummond	Drummond	A. Béliveau, Sec., C.P. 40, St-Germain-de-Grantham, P.Q. JOC 1KO (819/395-4439)
Ste-Germaine-Boulé (Mun.)	1,100	Abitibi	Témiscamingue	Abitibi-Ouest	B. Jobin, Sec., C.P. 5, Boulé, P.Q. JOZ 1MO (819/787-2221)
Ste-Germaine-de-l'Anse-aux-Gascons (Paroisse)	1,567	Bonaventure	Bonaventure-Iles-de-la-Madeleine	Bonaventure	G. Huard, Sec., Gascon-Ouest, P.Q. GOC 1PO (418/396-5400)
Ste-Germaine-du-Lac-Etchemin (Paroisse)	1,456	Dorchester	Bellechasse	Bellechasse	E. Poulin, Sec., 218 3e Av., Lac-Etchemin, P.Q. GOR 1SO (418/625-2291)
Saints-Gervais et Protais (Paroisse)	1,835	Bellechasse	Bellechasse	Bellechasse	G. Breton, Sec., C.P. 69, St-Gervais, P.Q. GOR 3CO (418/887-6116)
St-Gilbert (Paroisse)	277	Portneuf	Portneuf	Portneuf	R. Marcotte, Sec., 91 Principale, St-Gilbert, P.Q. GOA 3TO (418/268-3439)
St-Gilles (Paroisse)	1,536	Lotbinière	Lévis	Lotbinière	N. Bolduc, Sec., C.P. 36, St-Gilles, P.Q. GOS 2PO (418/888-3198)
St-Godard-de-Lejeune (Mun.)	450	Témiscouata	Rimouski	Kamouraska-Témiscouata	E. Vézina, Sec., Lejeune PO, P.Q. GOL 1SO (418/855-2377)
St-Godefroy (Canton)	710	Bonaventure	Bonaventure-Iles-de-la-Madeleine	Bonaventure	Jocelyne Joseph, Sec., C.P. 157, St-Godefroy, P.Q. GOC 3CO (418/752-3427)
St-Grégoire-de-Greenlay (Village)	613	Richmond	Richmond	Johnson	R. Sundborg, Sec., 34 Greenland sud, Greenlay, P.Q. J1S 2J8 (819/845-4475)
St-Grégoire-le-Grand (Paroisse)	1,532	Iberville	St-Jean	Iberville	R. Meunier, Sec., Mont-St-Grégoire PO, P.Q. JOJ 1KO (514/347-3847)

Cities in CAPITALS (Ville); Towns/Villes marked (Ville); Villages marked (Village); Townships/Cantons (marked Canton); United townships/Cantons unis (marked Cantons*); Parishes marked (Paroisse); undesignated municipalities/sans designation marked (Mun.).

MUNICIPALITY	POP.	COUNTY	FEDERAL ELECTORAL DISTRICT	PROVINCIAL ELECTORAL DISTRICT	CLERK/GREFFIER OR SECRETARY-TREASURER (SEC) WITH ADDRESS & PHONE
St-Guillaume (Paroisse)	920	Yamaska	Drummond	Nicolet	G.-E. Amyot, Sec., C.P. 295, St-Guillaume, P.Q. J0C 1L0 (819/396-2403)
St-Guillaume (Village)	770	Yamaska		Nicolet	Voir St-Guillaume (Paroisse)
St-Guillaume-de-Granada (Mun.)				Rouyn-Noranda-Témiscamingue	C. Falardeau, Sec., Edifice Lessard, Granada, P.Q. J0Z 2C0 (819/764-6278)
St-Guy (Mun.)	173	Rimouski	Rimouski	Rimouski	M.A. Rioux, Sec., St-Guy, P.Q. G0K 1W0 (418/963-6738)
Ste-Hedwidge (Paroisse)	1,050	Lac-St-Jean-Ouest	Roberval	Roberval	Serge Desgagné, Sec., 200 Principale, Ste-Hedwidge-de-Roberval, P.Q. G0W 2R0 (418/275-3020)
Ste-Hélène (Paroisse)	1,221	Kamouraska	Kamouraska-Rivière-du-Loup	Kamouraska-Témiscouata	G. Dumont, Sec., C.P. 216, Ste-Hélène-de-Kamouraska, P.Q. G0L 3J0 (418/492-6830)
Ste-Hélène-de-Bagot (Mun.)	1,282	Bagot	St-Hyacinthe	Johnson	F. Nicaise, Sec., 379 7e Ave., Ste-Hélène-de-Bagot, P.Q. J0H 1M0 (514/791-2455)
Ste-Hélène-de-Breakeyville (Paroisse)	1,550	Lévis	Lévis	Beauce-Nord	J.-G. Brassard, Sec., 67 Ste-Hélène, Breakeyville, P.Q. G0S 1E0 (418/832-0356)
Ste-Hélène-de-Mancebourg (Paroisse)	450	Abitibi	Témiscamingue	Abitibi-Ouest	G. Veillette, Sec., Mancebourg, P.Q. J0Z 2T0 (819/333-6120)
Ste-Hénédine (Paroisse)	1,205	Dorchester	Lévis	Beauce-Nord	Yolande Pomerleau, Sec., C.P. 6, Ste-Hénédine, P.Q. G0S 2R0 (418/935-3628)
St-Henri (Mun.)	3,803	Lévis	Lévis	Beauce-Nord	R. Couture, Sec., 109 rue Allen, St-Henri-de-Lévis, P.Q. G0R 3E0 (418/882-2401)
St-Henri-de-Taillon (Mun.)	630	Lac-St-Jean-Est	Roberval	Lac-St-Jean	J.-P. Côté, Sec., 401 Hôtel de ville, Taillon PO, P.Q. G0W 2X0 (418/347-3243)
St-Herménégilde (Village)	156	Stanstead	Mégantic-Compton-Stanstead	Mégantic-Compton	Mme R. Lavigne, Sec., St-Herménégilde, P.Q. J0B 2W0 (819/849-2049)
St-Herménégilde (Mun.)	386	Stanstead	Mégantic-Compton-Stanstead	Mégantic-Compton	L. Dolbec, Sec., St-Herménégilde, P.Q. J0B 2W0 (819/849-3876)
St-Hilaire-de-Dorset (Paroisse)	169	Frontenac	Beauce	Beauce-Sud	R. Lamontagne, Sec., St-Hilaire-de-Dorset, P.Q. G0M 1G0 (418/459-6779)
St-Hilarion (Paroisse)	1,089	Charlevoix-Ouest	Charlevoix	Charlevoix	J. Rochefort, Sec., 53 Principale ouest, St-Hilarion, P.Q. G0A 3V0 (418/457-3463)
St-Hippolyte (Paroisse)	2,500	Terrebonne	Joliette	Rousseau	R. Sénécal, Sec., 2274 boul. Les Hauteurs, St-Hippolyte, P.Q. J0R 1P0 (514/563-2505)
St-Honoré (Mun.)	981	Témiscouata	Rimouski	Kamouraska-Témiscouata	Mme T. Landry, Sec., C.P. 70, St-Honoré-de-Témiscouata, P.Q. G0L 3K0 (418/497-3963)
St-Honoré (Paroisse)	897	Beauce	Beauce	Beauce-Sud	S. Poulin, Sec., St-Honoré-de-Shenley, P.Q. G0M 1V0 (418/485-6387)
St-Honoré (Mun.)	2,724	Chicoutimi	Lac-St-Jean	Dubuc	H. Blackburn, Sec., 690 de l'Hôtel de ville, St-Honoré-de-Chicoutimi, P.Q. G0V 1L0 (418/673-4843)

Cities in CAPITALS (Ville); Towns/Villes marked (Ville); Villages marked (Village); Townships/Cantons (marked Canton); United townships/Cantons unis (marked Cantons*); Parishes marked (Paroisse); undesignated municipalities/sans designation marked (Mun.).

MUNICIPALITY	POP.	COUNTY	FEDERAL ELECTORAL DISTRICT	PROVINCIAL ELECTORAL DISTRICT	CLERK/GREFFIER OR SECRETARY-TREASURER (SEC) WITH ADDRESS & PHONE
St-Hubert (Paroisse)	1,482	Rivière-du-Loup	Kamouraska-Rivière-du-Loup	Rivière-du-Loup	Mme F. Thériault, Sec., St-Hubert-de-Témiscouata, P.Q. GOL 3LO (418/497-3394)
ST-HUBERT (Ville)	55,400	Chambly	Chambly	Vachon	B. Houle, Greffier, 5900 boul. Cousineau, St-Hubert, P.Q. J3Y 7K8 (514/676-7744)
St-Hugues (Village)	433	Bagot	St-Hyacinthe	Johnson	W. Beaudry, Sec., 201 rue Palardy, St-Hugues, P.Q. JOH 1NO (514/794-2030)
St-Hugues (Paroisse)	805			Johnson	Voir St-Hugues (Village)
ST-HYACINTHE (Ville)	37,500	St-Hyacinthe	St-Hyacinthe	St-Hyacinthe	R. Bousquet, Greffier, 700 de l'Hôtel de ville, C.P. 10, St-Hyacinthe, P.Q. J2S 5B2 (514/773-2507)
St-Hyacinthe-le-Confesseur (Paroisse)	704	St-Hyacinthe	St-Hyacinthe	St-Hyacinthe	B. Lemay, Sec., 98 ch. St-Dominique, St-Hyacinthe, P.Q. JOH 1LO (514/774-7282)
St-Ignace-de-Loyola (Paroisse)	1,641	Berthier	Berthier-Maskinongé	Berthier	P.-A. Valois, Sec., 449 St-Joseph, St-Ignace-de-Loyola, P.Q. JOK 2PO (514/836-3376)
St-Ignace-de-Stanbridge (Paroisse)	808	Missisquoi	Missisquoi	Brome-Missisquoi	A. Galipeau, Sec., C.P. 39, St-Ignace-de-Stanbridge, P.Q. JOJ 1YO (514/296-4620)
St-Ignace-du-Coteau-du-Lac (Paroisse)	1,407	Soulanges	Vaudreuil	Vaudreuil-Soulanges	A. Sabourin, Sec., C.P. 59, Coteau-du-Lac, P.Q. JOP 1BO (514/763-5822)
Ste-Irène (Paroisse)	369	Matapédia	Matapédia-Matane	Matapédia	C. Simard, Sec., Ste-Irène-de-Matapédia, P.Q. GOJ 2PO (418/629-3874)
St-Irénée (Paroisse)	790	Charlevoix-Est	Charlevoix	Charlevoix	Mme L.T. Bhérer, Sec., 182 Ste-Irénée, St-Irénée, P.Q. GOT 1VO (418/452-3231)
St-Isidore (Village)	784	Dorchester	Lévis	Beauce-Nord	B. Parent, Sec., St-Isidore, P.Q. GOS 2SO (418/646-5670)
St-Isidore (Paroisse)	1,394	Dorchester	Lévis	Beauce-Nord	D. Turgeon, Sec., St-Isidore, P.Q. GOS 2SO (418/646-5902)
St-Isidore (Paroisse)	2,004	Laprairie	Châteauguay	Huntingdon	J.-B. Laberge, Sec., 636 St-Régis, St-Isidore, P.Q. JOL 2AO (514/454-9082)
St-Isidore-d'Auckland (Mun.)	756	Compton	Mégantic-Compton-Stanstead	Mégantic-Compton	L. Perron, Sec., St-Isidore-d'Auckland, P.Q. JOB 2XO (819/658-3637)
St-Jacques (Village)	2,073	Montcalm	Joliette	Joliette	G. Sincerny, Sec., 16 Maréchal, St-Jacques, P.Q. JOK 2RO (514/839-3671)
St-Jacques (Paroisse)	1,442	Montcalm	Joliette	Joliette	Voir St-Jacques (Village)
St-Jacques-de-Dupuy (Mun.)	1,041	Abitibi	Témiscamingue	Abitibi-Ouest	Léona Rochette, Sec., C.P. 10, Dupuy, P.Q. JOZ 1XO (819/783-2595)
St-Jacques-de-Horton (Mun.)	226	Arthabaska	Drummond	Richmond	J.-P. Fleurant, Sec., St-Clothilde, P.Q. JOA 1HO (819/336-5402)
St-Jacques-de-Leeds (Mun.)	797	Mégantic	Frontenac	Frontenac	G. Ouellette, Sec., C.P. 9, Leeds Village, P.Q. GON 1JO (418/424-3818)
St-Jacques-de-Parisville (Paroisse)	579	Lotbinière	Lotbinière	Lotbinière	Mme G. Lafond, Sec., Parisville, P,Q. GOS 1XO (819/292-2974)

Cities in CAPITALS (Ville); Towns/Villes marked (Ville); Villages marked (Village); Townships/Cantons (marked Canton); United townships/Cantons unis (marked Cantons*); Parishes marked (Paroisse); undesignated municipalities/sans designation marked (Mun.).

MUNICIPALITY	POP.	COUNTY	FEDERAL ELECTORAL DISTRICT	PROVINCIAL ELECTORAL DISTRICT	CLERK/GREFFIER OR SECRETARY-TREASURER (SEC) WITH ADDRESS & PHONE
St-Jacques-le-Majeur-de-Causapscal (Paroisse)	741	Matapédia	Bonaventure-Iles-de-la-Madeleine	Matapédia	A. Morissette, Sec., C.P. 775, Causapscal, P.Q. GOJ 1JO (418/756-5160)
St-Jacques-le-Majeur-de-Wolfestown (Paroisse)	167	Wolfe	Richmond	Frontenac	Dolorès Houde, Sec., R.R. 3, Disraeli, P.Q. GON 1EO (418/449-5321)
St-Jacques-le-Mineur (Paroisse)	1,107	Laprairie	St-Jean	St-Jean	F. Rémillard, Sec., 40 Principale, St-Jacques-le-Mineur, P.Q. JOJ 1ZO (514/347-5446)
St-Janvier (Paroisse)	355	Abitibi	Argenteuil	Abitibi-Ouest	Mme A.T. Bouchard, Sec., Chazel, P.Q. JOZ 1NO (819/333-6020)
St-Janvier-de-Joly (Mun.)	954	Lotbinière	Lotbinière	Lotbinière	R. Lambert, Sec., C.P. 278, Joly PO, P.Q. GOS 1MO (418/728-2611)
St-Jean (Canton)	1,452	Chicoutimi		Dubuc	F.X. Boudreault, Sec., 3 du Couvent, Anse St-Jean, P.Q. GOV 1JO (418/272-2633)
St-Jean-Baptiste (Mun.)	947	Rimouski	Matapédia-Matane	Matapédia	J.-C. Beaudet, Sec., (131A rue Doucet), C.P. 6, Mont-Joli, P.Q. G5H 3K8 (418/775-3296)
St-Jean-Baptiste (Paroisse)	2,350	Rouville	St-Hyacinthe	Iberville	G. Desautels, Sec., C.P. 300, St-Jean-Baptiste, P.Q. JOL 2BO (514/467-3456)
St-Jean-Baptiste-de-l'Isle-Verte (Mun.)	790	Rivière-du-Loup	Kamouraska-Rivière-du-Loup	Rivière-du-Loup	L. Dion, Sec., C.P. 175, Isle-Verte, P.Q. GOL 1KO (418/898-2256)
St-Jean-Baptiste-de-Nicolet (Paroisse)	1,777	Nicolet	Richelieu	Nicolet	H. Beauchemin, Sec., 725 boul. Louis-Frechette, Nicolet, P.Q. JOG 1EO (819/293-5117)
St-Jean-Baptiste-Vianney (Paroisse)	625	Matapédia	Matapédia-Matane	Matane	A. Beaupré, Sec., C.P. 39, St-Vianney, P.Q. GOJ 3JO (418/629-4082)
St-Jean-Chrysostome (Ville)	3,989	Lévis	Lévis	Beauce-Nord	C. Alain, Greffier, 1005 rue de l'Hôtel de ville, C.P. 1, St-Jean-Chrysostome-de-Lévis, P.Q. GOS 2TO (418/839-9417)
St-Jean-Chrysostome (Paroisse)	1,420	Châteauguay	Beauharnois-Salaberry	Huntingdon	H. Lemyre, Sec., 30 rue St-Antoine, St-Chrysostome, P.Q. JOS 1RO (514/826-3111)
St-Jean-de-Boischatel (Village)	2,424	Montmorency 1	Montmorency	Montmorency	M. Lefebvre, Sec., C.P. 158, Boischatel, P.Q. GOA 1HO (418/822-0721)
St-Jean-de-Brébeuf (Mun.)	437	Mégantic	Frontenac	Lotbinière	R. Pomerleau, Sec., R.R. 1, boite 4, Thetford Mines, P.Q. G6G 5R5 (418/453-2877)
St-Jean-de-Cherbourg (Paroisse)	210	Matane	Matapédia-Matane	Matane	Mme T. Imbeault, Sec., R.R. 1, St-Jean-de-Cherbourg, P.Q. GOJ 2RO (418/733-4716)
St-Jean-de-Dieu (Mun.)	2,099	Rivière-du-Loup	Kamouraska-Rivière-du-Loup	Rivière-du-Loup	Mme L. Rousseau, Sec., St-Jean-de-Dieu, P.Q. GOL 3MO (418/963-3026)
St-Jean-de-la-Lande (Mun.)	409	Témiscouata	Rimouski	Kamouraska-Temiscouata	A. Dubé, Sec., St-Jean-de-la-Lande, P.Q. GOL 3NO (418/853-2094)
St-Jean-de-la-Lande (Paroisse)	709	Beauce	Beauce	Beauce-Sud	L. Rodrigue, Sec., a/s Hamel PO, P.Q. GOM 1EO (418/228-9359)

Cities in CAPITALS (Ville); Towns/Villes marked (Ville); Villages marked (Village); Townships/Cantons (marked Canton); United townships/Cantons unis (marked Cantons*); Parishes marked (Paroisse); undesignated municipalities/sans designation marked (Mun.).

MUNICIPALITY	POP.	COUNTY	FEDERAL ELECTORAL DISTRICT	PROVINCIAL ELECTORAL DISTRICT	CLERK/GREFFIER OR SECRETARY-TREASURER (SEC) WITH ADDRESS & PHONE
St-Jean-de-Matha (Paroisse)	2,031	Joliette	Berthier-Maskinongé	Berthier	J.-M. Gadoury, Sec., C.P. 60, St-Jean-de-Matha, P.Q. JOK 2SO (514/886-3861)
St-Jean-des-Piles (Mun.)	496	Champlain	St-Maurice	Laviolette	Denise Trudel, Sec., 1594 Principale, St-Jean-des-Piles, P.Q. GOX 2VO (819/538-3829)
St-Jean (I.O.) (Paroisse)	815	Montmorency 2	Montmorency	Montmorency	Pauline Chabot, Sec., 2338 av. Royale, St-Jean-d'Orleans, P.Q. GOA 3WO (418/829-2206)
Ste-Jeanne-d'Arc (Paroisse)	506	Matapédia	Matapédia-Matane	Matapédia	L. Lavoie, Sec., C.P. 40, Ste-Jeanne-d'Arc-de-Matane, P.Q. GOJ 2TO (418/776-5660)
Ste-Jeanne-d'Arc (Village)	941	Lac-St-Jean-Ouest	Roberval	Roberval	Mme M. Chiasson, Sec., 170 Principale, Boulanger, P.Q. GOW 1EO (418/276-3166)
Ste-Jeanne-de-Pont-Rouge (Mun.)	1,074	Portneuf	Portneuf	Portneuf	Mme L. Marchand, Sec., C.P. 339, Pont-Rouge, P.Q. GOA 2XO (418/873-4243)
St-Jean-Port-Joli (Mun.)	3,290	L'Islet	Bellechasse	Montmagny-L'Islet	F. Heppell, Sec., C.P. 488, St-Jean-Port-Joli, P.Q. GOR 3GO (418/598-6473)
ST-JEAN-SUR-RICHELIEU (Ville)	35,200	St-Jean	St-Jean	St-Jean	Charlotte Morais, Greffier, Hôtel de ville, C.P. 1025, St-Jean-sur-Richelieu, P.Q. J3B 7B2 (514/347-5351)
ST-JEROME (Ville)	24,700	Terrebonne	Labelle	Prevost	Jacques Foucher, Greffier, 280 rue Labelle, St-Jérôme, P.Q. J7Z 5L1 (514/436-1511)
St-Jérôme-de-Matane (Paroisse)	890	Matane		Matane	Mme L. de G. Fortin, Sec., 378 av. St-Jérôme, Matane, P.Q. G4W 3B2 (418/562-3244)
St-Joachim (Paroisse)	1,409	Montmorency 1	Montmorency	Charlevoix	A. Gauthier, Sec., 172 l'Eglise, St-Joachim, P.Q. GOA 3XO (418/827-2987)
St-Joachim-de-Courval (Paroisse)	447	Yamaska	Drummond	Nicolet	A. Grondin, Sec., 115 Principale, St-Joachim-de-Courval, P.Q. JOC 1HO (819/397-4626)
St-Joachim-de-Shefford (Paroisse)	949	Shefford	Shefford	Shefford	R.L. Beauregard, Sec., a/s R.R. 3, Waterloo, P.Q. JOE 2NO (514/539-3201)
St-Joachim-de-Tourelle (Paroisse)	1,689	Gaspé-Ouest	Gaspé	Matane	V. Saint-Laurent, Sec., C.P. 39, Tourelle, P.Q. GOE 2JO (418/763-2629)
St-Joseph-de-Beauce (Ville)	3,227	Beauce	Beauce	Beauce-Nord	J. Giguère, Sec., C.P. 88, St-Joseph-de-Beauce, P.Q. GOS 2VO (418/397-5326)
St-Joseph-de-Beauce (Paroisse)	896	Beauce	Beauce	Beauce-Nord	J.-L. Lessard, Sec., R.R. 1, St-Joseph-de-Beauce, P.Q. GOS 2VO (418/397-5858)
St-Joseph-de-Blandford (Paroisse)	534	Nicolet	Lotbinière	Lotbinière	Pauline Savoie, Sec., C.P. 67, Manseau, P.Q. GOX 1VO (819/356-3450)
St-Joseph-de-Clericy (Mun.)				Rouyn-Noranda-Témiscamingue	C. Arcand, Sec., Clericy, P.Q. JOZ 1PO (819/637-2041)
St-Joseph-de-Coleraine (Mun.)	1,928	Mégantic		Frontenac	E. Gravel, Sec., C.P. 40, Coleraine, P.Q. GON 1BO (418/423-4000)
St-Joseph-de-Deschambault (Paroisse)	351	Portneuf	Portneuf	Portneuf	L. Trottier, Sec., R.R. 2, Deschambault, P.Q. GOA 1SO (418/286-3439)

Cities in CAPITALS (Ville); Towns/Villes marked (Ville); Villages marked (Village); Townships/Cantons (marked Canton); United townships/Cantons unis (marked Cantons*); Parishes marked (Paroisse); undesignated municipalities/sans designation marked (Mun.).

MUNICIPALITY	POP.	COUNTY	FEDERAL ELECTORAL DISTRICT	PROVINCIAL ELECTORAL DISTRICT	CLERK/GREFFIER OR SECRETARY-TREASURER (SEC) WITH ADDRESS & PHONE
St-Joseph-de-Ham-Sud (Paroisse)	222	Wolfe	Richmond	Richmond	Madeleine Lamoureux, Sec., C.P. 1, Ham-Sud, P.Q. JOB 3JO (819/877-2522)
St-Joseph-de-Kamouraska (Paroisse)	465	Kamouraska	Kamouraska-Rivière-du-Loup	Kamouraska-Témiscouata	G. Ouellet, Sec., St-Joseph-de-Kamouraska, P.Q. GOL 3PO (418/493-2350)
St-Joseph-de-la-Baie-du-Febvre (Mun.)	356	Yamaska	Richelieu	Nicolet	B. Caya, Sec., 258 Marie-Victorin, Baieville, P.Q. JOG 1AO (514/783-6509)
St-Joseph-de-Lanoraie (Paroisse)	1,281	Berthier	Berthier-Maskinongé	Berthier	J.P. Delorme, Sec., C.P. 308, Lanoraie, P.Q. JOK 1EO (514/887-2201)
St-Joseph-de-la-Pointe-de-Lévy (Paroisse)	545	Lévis	Lévis	Lévis	M. Blais, Sec., 910 Mgr Bourget, St-Joseph-de-Lévis, P.Q. G6V 6N4 (418/833-3882)
St-Joseph-de-la-Rive (Village)	254	Charlevoix-Ouest	Charlevoix	Charlevoix	Marthe Lafrance, Sec., 270 Ch. de L'Eglise, St-Joseph-de-la-Rive, P.Q. GOA 3YO (418/635-2742)
St-Joseph-de-Lepage (Paroisse)	399	Rimouski	Matapédia-Matane	Matapédia	A.-A. Dionne, Sec., 44 de la Rivière, Mont-Joli, P.Q. G5H 3N8 (418/775-7331)
St-Joseph-de-Maskinongé (Paroisse)	1,163	Maskinongé	Berthier-Maskinongé	Maskinongé	J. Lafrenière, Sec., 309 Petit Bois, Maskinongé, P.Q. JOK 1NO (819/227-4613)
St-Joseph-des-Erables (Mun.)	411	Beauce	Beauce	Beauce-Nord	E. Tardif, Sec., R.R. 3, St-Joseph-de-Beauce, P.Q. GOS 2VO (418/397-5339)
St-Joseph-de-Sorel (Ville)	2,744	Richelieu	Richelieu	Richelieu	J.-G. Trépanier, Sec., 700 Montcalm, St-Joseph-de-Sorel, P.Q. J3R 1C9 (514/742-3744)
St-Joseph-de-Soulanges (Paroisse)	2,049	Soulanges	Vaudreuil	Vaudreuil-Soulanges	N. Meilleur, Sec.,C.P. 240, Les Cèdres, P.Q. JOP 1LO (514/452-4651)
St-Joseph-du-Lac (Paroisse)	2,002	Deux-Montagnes	Blainville-Deux-Montagnes	Deux-Montagnes	Carole Giroux, Sec., 1110 Principale, St-Joseph-du-Lac, P.Q. JON 1MO (514/473-1619)
St-Jovite (Paroisse)	860	Terrebonne	Labelle	Labelle	F. Perreault, Sec., C.P. 668, St-Jovite, P.Q. JOT 2HO (819/425-3260)
St-Jovite (Village)	3,728	Terrebonne	Labelle	Labelle	J. Dupras, Sec., C.P. 159, St-Jovite, P.Q. JOT 2HO (819/425-2723)
St-Jude (Paroisse)	1,030	St-Hyacinthe	Verchères	Richelieu	Diane Bélanger, Sec., 870 St-Edouard, St-Jude, P.Q. JOH 1PO (514/792-3855)
St-Jules (Mun.)	472	Bonaventure	Bonaventure-Iles-de-la-Madeleine	Bonaventure	Mme J. Saint-Onge, Sec., R.R. 1, boite 34, Grande-Cascapédia, P.Q. GOC 1TO (418/759-3329)
St-Jules (Paroisse)	650	Beauce	Beauce	Beauce-Nord	V. Grondin, Sec., St-Jules, P.Q. GON 1RO (418/397-5444)
Ste-Julie (Mun.)	773	Mégantic	Frontenac	Lotbinière	Mme Danielle B. Bilodeau, Sec., 813 St-Pierre, Laurierville, P.Q. GOS 1PO (819/365-4200)
Ste-Julie (Ville)	10,200	Verchères	Verchères	Bertrand	Mme D. Blain, Greffier, C.P. 60, Ste-Julie, P.Q. JOL 2CO (514/649-1561)
St-Julien (Paroisse)	315	Wolfe	Richmond	Frontenac	L. Henri, Sec., St-Julien, P.Q. GON 1BO (418/423-4457)

Cities in CAPITALS (Ville); Towns/Villes marked (Ville); Villages marked (Village); Townships/Cantons (marked Canton); United townships/Cantons unis (marked Cantons*); Parishes marked (Paroisse); undesignated municipalities/sans designation marked (Mun.).

MUNICIPALITY	POP.	COUNTY	FEDERAL ELECTORAL DISTRICT	PROVINCIAL ELECTORAL DISTRICT	CLERK/GREFFIER OR SECRETARY-TREASURER (SEC) WITH ADDRESS & PHONE
Ste-Julienne (Paroisse)	3,523	Montcalm	Joliette	Rousseau	Ginette Marsolais, Sec., C.P. 250, Ste-Julienne, P.Q. JOK 2TO (514/831-2688)
St-Juste-de-Bretenières (Mun.)	1,010	Montmagny	Bellechasse	Montmagny-L'Islet	Diane Roy, Sec., C.P. 40, St-Juste-de-Bretenières, P.Q. GOR 3HO (418/244-6631)
St-Juste-du-Lac (Mun.)	781	Témiscouata	Rimouski	Kamouraska-Témiscouata	Nicole D. Chouinard, Sec., St-Juste-du-Lac, P.Q. GOL 3RO (418/899-2855)
St-Justin (Paroisse)	1,248	Maskinongé	Berthier-Maskinongé	Maskinongé	P.-E. Masson, Sec., 70 rue Guerin, St-Justin, P.Q. JOK 2VO (819/227-4554)
Ste-Justine (Paroisse)	1,985	Dorchester	Bellechasse	Bellechasse	G. Fournier, Sec., C.P. 70, Langevin, P.Q. GOR 1YO (418/383-3908)
Ste-Justine-de-Newton (Paroisse)	893	Vaudreuil	Vaudreuil	Vaudreuil-Soulanges	Monique Théoret, Sec., C.P. 28, Ste-Justine-de-Newton, P.Q. JOP 1TO (514/764-3353)
ST-LAMBERT (Ville)	20,300	Chambly	Laprairie	Laporte	Marie Ste-Marie, Greffier, 55 Argyle, St-Lambert, P.Q. J4P 2H3 (514/672-4444)
St-Lambert (Paroisse)	445	Abitibi	Témiscamingue	Abitibi-Ouest	Nicole Garant, Sec., Desmeloizes, P.Q. JOZ 1VO (819/788-2657)
St-Lambert-de-Lauzon (Paroisse)	2,390	Lévis	Lévis	Beauce-Nord	C. Girard, Sec., 1198 Du Pont, St-Lambert-de-Lévis, P.Q. GOS 2WO (418/889-9912)
ST-LAURENT (Ville)	63,178	Ile-de-Montréal	Dollard	L'Acadie; St-Laurent	Jacq. Leduc, Greffier, 777 boul. Laurentien, St-Laurent, P.Q. H4M 2M7 (514/744-6411)
St-Laurent (Mun.)	440	Abitibi	Témiscamingue	Abitibi-Ouest	J. Châteauvert, Sec., R.R. 1, C.P. 123, Gallichan, P.Q. JOZ 2BO (819/787-2380)
St-Laurent (I.O.) (Paroisse)	1,380	Montmorency 2	Montmorency	Montmorency	Claudette Pouliot, Sec., 1312 av. Royale, St-Laurent, (I.O.), P.Q. GOA 3ZO (418/828-2322)
St-Lazare (Paroisse)	1,224	Bellechasse	Bellechasse	Bellechasse	Adrienne Gosselin, Sec., C.P. 98, St-Lazare, P.Q. GOR 3JO (418/883-3841)
St-Lazare (Paroisse)	3,095	Vaudreuil	Vaudreuil	Vaudreuil-Soulanges	G. Prevost, Sec., C.P. 58, St-Lazare-de-Vaudreuil, P.Q. JOP 1VO (514/455-3075)
St-Léandre (Paroisse)	523	Matane	Matapédia-Matane	Matane	Mme D. Fortin, Sec., St-Léandre, P.Q. G3J 2V9 (418/737-4973)
St-Léonard (Mun.)	1,162	Nicolet	Drummond	Nicolet	L. Simard, Sec., C.P. 280, St-Léonard-d'Aston, P.Q. JOC 1MO (819/399-2117)
ST-LEONARD (Ville)	82,200	Ile-de-Montréal	St-Léonard	Jeanne-Mance; Viger	G. Larivée, Greffier, 8400 boul. Lacordaire, St-Léonard, P.Q. H1R 3B1 (514/321-7630)
St-Léonard-d'Aston (Village)	1,049	Nicolet	Drummond	Nicolet	L. Simard, Sec., C.P. 205, St-Léonard-d'Aston, P.Q. JOC 1MO (819/399-2596)
St-Léonard-de-Portneuf (Mun.)	1,047	Portneuf	Portneuf	Portneuf	E. Lesage, Sec., 509 Principale, St-Léonard-de-Portneuf, P.Q. GOA 4AO (418/337-6741)
St-Léon-de-Standon (Paroisse)	1,468	Dorchester	Bellechasse	Bellechasse	Mme S. Brousseau, Sec., 16 rue Roy, St-Léonard-de-Standon, P.Q. GOR 4LO (418/642-5633)

Cities in CAPITALS (Ville); Towns/Villes marked (Ville); Villages marked (Village); Townships/Cantons (marked Canton); United townships/Cantons unis (marked Cantons*); Parishes marked (Paroisse); undesignated municipalities/sans designation marked (Mun.).

MUNICIPALITY	POP.	COUNTY	FEDERAL ELECTORAL DISTRICT	PROVINCIAL ELECTORAL DISTRICT	CLERK/GREFFIER OR SECRETARY-TREASURER (SEC) WITH ADDRESS & PHONE
St-Léon-le-Grand (Paroisse)	1,290	Matapédia	Abitibi	Matapédia	R. Bérubé, Sec., C.P. 173, St-Léon-le-Grand, P.Q. GOJ 2WO (418/743-2914)
St-Léon-le-Grand (Paroisse)	1,061	Maskinongé		Maskinongé	Murielle Lessard, Sec., 170 Rang des Ambroises, St-Léon, P.Q. JOK 2WO (819/228-3236)
St-Liboire (Paroisse)	979	Bagot	St-Hyacinthe	St-Hyacinthe	J.-N. Lemonde, Sec., rue Lemonde, St-Liboire, P.Q. JOH 1RO (514/793-2811)
St-Liboire (Village)	652				Voir St-Liboire (Paroisse)
St-Liguori (Paroisse)	1,085	Montcalm	Joliette	Joliette	J. Charland, Sec., 850 Richard, St-Liguori, P.Q. JOK 2XO (514/753-3570)
St-Lin (Paroisse)	3,829	L'Assomption		Rousseau	L. Lortie, Sec., C.P. 220, St-Lin-des-Laurentides, P.Q. JOR 1CO (514/439-2941)
St-Louis (Paroisse)	695	Richelieu	Richelieu	Richelieu	Odette Larin, Sec., St-Louis-de-Richelieu, P.Q. JOG 1KO (514/788-2631)
St-Louis-de-Blandford (Paroisse)	729	Arthabaska		Lotbinière	Rock Martel, Sec., St-Louis-de-Blandford, P.Q. GOZ 1BO (819/364-2976)
St-Louis-de-France (Paroisse)	3,356	Champlain	Champlain	Champlain	G. Toupin, Sec., 805 boul. St-Jean ouest, St-Louis-de-France, P.Q. G8T 1A2 (819/374-6550)
St-Louis-de-Gonzague (Mun.)	570	Dorchester	Bellechasse	Bellechasse	Mme C. Bilodeau, Sec., Ravignan PO, P.Q. GOR 2LO (418/267-5931)
St-Louis-de-Gonzague (Paroisse)	1,324	Beauharnois	Beauharnois-Salaberry	Beauharnois	Micheline Carrière, Sec., St-Louis-de-Gonzague, P.Q. JOS 1TO (514/371-0523)
St-Louis-de-Kamouraska (Paroisse)	341	Kamouraska	Kamouraska-Rivière-du-Loup	Kamouraska-Témiscouata	Annette Raymond, Sec., C.P. 99, Kamouraska, P.Q. GOL 1MO (418/492-3144)
St-Louis-de-l'Isle-aux-Coudres (Paroisse)	559	Charlevoix-Ouest		Charlevoix	F. Dufour, Sec., C.P. 14, R.R. 1, St-Louis-de-l'Isle-aux-Coudres, P.Q. GOA 1XO (418/438-2742)
St-Louis-de-Pintendre (Paroisse)	2,701	Lévis	Lévis	Beauce-Nord	G. Dumont, Sec., 320 3e ave., Pintendre, P.Q. GOR 2KO (418/833-1300)
St-Louis-de-Terrebonne (Paroisse)	10,000	Terrebonne	Terrebonne	Terrebonne	P. Vermette, Sec., 4800 boul. des Seigneurs, St-Louis-de-Terrebonne, P.Q. JON 1NO (514/471-2888)
St-Louis-du-Ha!-Ha! (Paroisse)	1,483	Témiscouata	Rimouski	Kamouraska-Témiscouata	Mme P. Bérubé, Sec., 95 rue St-Charles, St-Louis-du-Ha!-Ha!, P.Q. GOL 3SO (418/854-2007)
Ste-Louise (Paroisse)	850	L'Islet	Kamouraska-Rivière-du-Loup	Kamouraska-Témiscouata	Françoise Pelletier, Sec., Ste-Louise, P.Q. GOR 3KO (418/354-2509)
St-Luc (Paroisse)	863	Matane	Matapédia-Matane	Matane	Mme A. Murray, Sec., 3 rue Noel, St-Luc-de-Matane, P.Q. GOJ 2XO (418/562-3074)
St-Luc (Paroisse)	616	Dorchester	Bellechasse	Bellechasse	Mme L. Jolin, Sec., Dijon PO, P.Q. GOR 1LO (418/636-2421)

Cities in CAPITALS (Ville); Towns/Villes marked (Ville); Villages marked (Village); Townships/Cantons (marked Canton); United townships/Cantons unis (marked Cantons*); Parishes marked (Paroisse); undesignated municipalities/sans designation marked (Mun.).

MUNICIPALITY	POP.	COUNTY	FEDERAL ELECTORAL DISTRICT	PROVINCIAL ELECTORAL DISTRICT	CLERK/GREFFIER OR SECRETARY-TREASURER (SEC) WITH ADDRESS & PHONE
St-Luc (Paroisse)	625	Champlain		Champlain	Rita Cossette, Sec., 600 de l'Eglise, St-Luc-de-Vincennes, P.Q. GOX 3KO (819/295-3217)
St-Luc (Ville)	7,800	St-Jean	St-Jean	St-Jean	J. Galipeau, Greffier, 347 boul. St-Luc, C.P. 90, St-Luc, P.Q. JOJ 2AO (514/348-7348)
Ste-Luce (Paroisse)	1,500	Rimouski	Rimouski	Rimouski	Gaétan Ross, Sec., 1 rue Langlois, C.P. 132, Ste-Luce, P.Q. GOK 1PO (418/739-4317)
Ste-Lucie-de-Beauregard (Mun.)	437	Montmagny	Bellechasse	Montagny-L'Islet	Y. Leclerc, Sec., Ste-Lucie-de-Beauregard, P.Q. GOR 3LO (418/223-3761)
Ste-Lucie-des-Laurentides (Mun.)	525	Terrebonne	Joliette	Labelle	D. Paquin, Sec., Ste-Lucie-de-Doncaster, P.Q. JOT 2JO (819/326-3198)
St-Lucien (Paroisse)	658	Drummond	Drummond	Richmond	R. Larochelle, Sec., St-Lucien, P.Q. JOC 1NO (819/397-4217)
St-Ludger (Village)	267	Frontenac	Beauce	Beauce-Sud	Mme G. Poulin-Duquette, Sec., C.P. 24, St-Ludger, P.Q. GOM 1WO (819/548-5843)
St-Ludger-de-Milot (Mun.)	763	Lac-St-Jean-Ouest	Roberval	Lac-St-Jean	Anne-M. Malenfant, Sec., C.P. 68, Milot, P.Q. GOW 2BO (418/373-2266)
Ste-Madeleine (Village)	1,222	St-Hyacinthe	St-Hyacinthe	Verchères	Mme J. Borduas, Sec., 850 St-Simon, Ste-Madeleine, P.Q. JOH 1SO (514/795-3822)
Ste-Madeleine-de-la-Rivière-Madeleine (Mun.)	782	Gaspé-Ouest	Gaspé	Gaspé	M. Fournier, Sec., Madeleine Centre, P.Q. GOE 1PO (418/393-2428)
Ste-Madeleine-de-Rigaud (Paroisse)	2,250	Vaudreuil	Vaudreuil	Vaudreuil-Soulanges	J.-D. Séguin, Sec., C.P. 580, Rigaud, P.Q. JOP 1PO (514/451-5673)
St-Magloire-de-Bellechasse (Mun.)	1,065	Bellechasse	Bellechasse	Bellechasse	I. Mercier, Sec., St-Magloire, P.Q. GOR 3MO (418/257-4421)
St-Majorique-de-Grantham (Paroisse)	780	Drummond	Drummond	Drummond	Germaine Fréchette, Sec., R.R. 4, Drummondville, P.Q. J2B 6V4 (819/478-7058)
St-Malachie (Paroisse)	1,170	Dorchester	Bellechasse	Bellechasse	Mme M. O'Farrell, Sec., 630 7ième rue, St-Malachie, P.Q. GOR 3NO (418/642-2102)
St-Malachie-d'Ormstown (Paroisse)	2,205	Châteauguay	Beauharnois-Salaberry	Huntingdon	J.-C. Marcil, Sec., C.P. 279, Ormstown, P.Q. JOS 1KO (514/829-2625)
St-Malo (Mun.)	446	Compton	Mégantic-Compton-Stanstead	Mégantic-Compton	J.-P. Roy, Sec., St-Malo, P.Q. JOB 2YO (819/658-3556)
St-Marc (Paroisse)	1,219	Verchères	Verchères	Verchères	J. Hébert, Sec., 220 Richelieu, St-Marc, P.Q. JOL 2EO (514/584-2258)
St-Marc-de-Figuery (Paroisse)	450	Abitibi	Abitibi	Abitibi-Ouest	R. McNeil, Sec., Figuery PO, P.Q. JOY 1JO (819/732-8501)
St-Marc-des-Carrières (Village)	2,648	Portneuf	Portneuf	Portneuf	J.-P. Julien, Sec., 965 ave. Bona Dussault, St-Marc-des-Carrières, P.Q. GOA 4BO (418/268-3862)
St-Marc-du-Lac-Long (Paroisse)	657	Témiscouata	Rimouski	Kamouraska-Témiscouata	C. Beaulieu, Sec., Les Etroits, P.Q. GOL 1TO (418/893-2643)

Cities in CAPITALS (Ville); Towns/Villes marked (Ville); Villages marked (Village); Townships/Cantons (marked Canton); United townships/Cantons unis (marked Cantons*); Parishes marked (Paroisse); undesignated municipalities/sans designation marked (Mun.).

MUNICIPALITY	POP.	COUNTY	FEDERAL ELECTORAL DISTRICT	PROVINCIAL ELECTORAL DISTRICT	CLERK/GREFFIER OR SECRETARY-TREASURER (SEC) WITH ADDRESS & PHONE
St-Marcel (Mun.)	673	L'Islet	Bellechasse	Montmagny-L'Islet	L. Caron, Sec., C.P. 10, 37 rte, St-Marcel-de-L'Islet, P.Q. GOR 3RO (418/356-2391)
St-Marcel (Paroisse)	590	Richelieu	St-Hyacinthe	Nicolet	S. Jutras, Sec., St-Marcel, P.Q. JOH 1TO (514/794-2794)
St-Marcellin (Paroisse)	300	Rimouski	Rimouski	Rimouski	B. Couturier, Sec., St-Marcellin, P.Q. GOK 1RO (418/798-4583)
Ste-Marcelline-de-Kildare (Mun.)	657	Joliette	Berthier-Maskinongé	Joliette	G. Fredette, Sec., 250 pièd de la Montagne, Ste-Marcelline, P.Q. JOK 2YO (514/883-8518)
Ste-Marguerite (Mun.)	372	Matapédia		Matapédia	Odette Corbin, Sec., Ste-Marguerite-Marie, P.Q. GOJ 2YO (418/756-3364)
Ste-Marguerite (Paroisse)	978	Dorchester	Beauce	Beauce-Nord	Jacqueline Giroux, Sec., Ste-Marguerite-de-Dorchester, P.Q. GOS 2XO (418/935-3825)
Ste-Marguerite-du-Lac-Masson (Paroisse)	1,610	Terrebonne	Joliette	Rousseau	M. Juneau, Sec., 472 des Pins, Lac Masson, P.Q. JOT 1LO (514/228-2543)
Ste-Marie (Ville)	8,000	Beauce	Beauce	Beauce-Nord	B. Fecteau, Greffier, C.P. 1750, Ste-Marie, P.Q. GOS 2YO (418/387-2301)
Ste-Marie-de-Blandford (Mun.)	397	Nicolet	Lotbinière	Lotbinière	Mme C. Deshaies, Sec., Ste-Marie-de-Blandford, P.Q. GOX 2WO (819/283-2203)
Ste-Marie-de-Monnoir (Paroisse)	1,713	Rouville	Chambly	Iberville	F. Guertin, Sec., C.P. 1396, Marieville, P.Q. JOL 1JO (514/460-2251)
Ste-Marie-de-Sayabec (Paroisse)	432	Matapédia	Matapédia-Matane	Matapédia	Cécile Fortin, Sec., C.P. 1, Sayabec, P.Q. GOJ 3KO (418/536-3501)
Ste-Marie-Madeleine (Paroisse)	963	St-Hyacinthe	St-Hyacinthe	Verchères	Carmen Masse, Sec., Rang St-Simon, Ste-Madeleine, P.Q. JOH 1SO (514/795-3222)
Ste-Marie-Salomé (Paroisse)	994	Montcalm	Joliette	Joliette	G. Martin, Sec., 860 des Près, Ste-Marie-Salomé, P.Q. JOK 2ZO (514/754-4264)
Ste-Marthe (Village)	192	Vaudreuil	Vaudreuil	Vaudreuil-Soulanges	Y. Massé, Sec., 555 Principale, Ste-Marthe, P.Q. JOP 2WO (514/459-4410)
Ste-Marthe (Paroisse)	864				Voir Ste-Marthe (Village)
Ste-Marthe-du-Cap-de-la-Madeleine (Mun.)	3,521	Champlain	Champlain	Champlain	A. Toupin, Sec., C.P. 158, Ste-Marthe-du-Cap-de-la-Madeleine, P.Q. G8T 8B2 (819/378-5949)
Ste-Marthe-sur-le-Lac (Village)	6,000	Deux-Montagnes	Blainville-Deux-Montagnes	Deux-Montagnes	E. McClish, Sec., 3000 ch. Oka, Ste-Marthe-sur-le-Lac, P.Q. JON 1PO (514/472-7310)
St-Martin (Paroisse)	2,385	Beauce	Beauce	Beauce-Sud	Carmelle Veilleux, Sec., 131 1re ave. est, St-Martin-de-Beauce, P.Q. GOM 1BO (418/382-5035)
Ste-Martine (Paroisse)	1,983	Châteauguay	Châteauguay	Huntingdon	G. Dubuc, Sec., C.P. 430, Ste-Martine, P.Q. JOS 1VO (514/427-3050)
Saints-Martyrs-Canadiens (Paroisse)	167	Wolfe	Richmond	Richmond	E. Leblanc, Sec., Saints-Martyrs, P.Q. GOY 1BO (418/458-2997)

Cities in CAPITALS (Ville); Towns/Villes marked (Ville); Villages marked (Village); Townships/Cantons (marked Canton); United townships/Cantons unis (marked Cantons*); Parishes marked (Paroisse); undesignated municipalities/sans designation marked (Mun.).

MUNICIPALITY	POP.	COUNTY	FEDERAL ELECTORAL DISTRICT	PROVINCIAL ELECTORAL DISTRICT	CLERK/GREFFIER OR SECRETARY-TREASURER (SEC) WITH ADDRESS & PHONE
St-Mathias (Paroisse)	2,053	Rouville	Chambly	Chambly	Mme N. Vigeant, Sec., C.P. 39, St-Mathias, P.Q. JOL 2GO (514/658-2841)
St-Mathieu (Paroisse)	673	St-Maurice	Rimouski	St-Maurice	Jacqueline Dubé, Sec., 561 ch. Deziel, St-Mathieu, P.Q. GOX 1NO (819/532-2205)
St-Mathieu (Mun.)	1,341	Laprairie	Châteauguay	Châteauguay	Guy Derome, Sec., 359 St-Edouard, St-Mathieu, P.Q. JOL 2HO (514/632-3637)
St-Mathieu (Paroisse)	490	Abitibi	Abitibi	Abitibi-Ouest	France Niveu, Sec., Harricanaw-Ouest, P.Q. JOY 1MO (819/732-8077)
St-Mathieu-de-Beloeil (Paroisse)	847	Verchères		Verchères	Marthe Tétrault, Sec., 2570 rue Bernard-Pilon, St-Mathieu-de-Beloeil, P.Q. J3G 4S5 (514/467-7490)
St-Mathieu-de-Dixville (Mun.)	329	Stanstead	Mégantic-Compton-Stanstead	Mégantic-Compton	Marguerite Loubier, Sec., R.R. 1, C.P. 119, Dixville, P.Q. JOB 1PO (819/849-3933)
St-Mathieu-de-Rioux (Paroisse)	700	Rimouski		Rimouski	R. Ouellet, Sec., St-Mathieu, P.Q. GOL 3TO (418/738-2953)
St-Maurice (Paroisse)	1,791	Champlain	Champlain	Champlain	R. Guilbert, Sec., C.P. 9, St-Maurice, P.Q. GOX 2XO (819/374-4525)
St-Maxime-du-Mont-Louis (Mun.)	1,690	Gaspé-Ouest	Gaspé	Gaspé	J.-G. Lemieux, Sec., C.P. 130, Mont-Louis, P.Q. GOE 1TO (418/797-2060)
St-Médard (Mun.)	386	Rimouski	Rimouski	Rimouski	L.P. Gagnon, Sec., C.P. 9, St-Médard, P.Q. GOL 3VO (418/963-5803)
Ste-Mélanie (Paroisse)	1,099	Joliette	Berthier-Maskinongé	Berthier	D. Lépine, Sec., 850 Principale, Ste-Mélanie, P.Q. JOK 3AO (514/889-5871)
St-Méthode (Mun.)	1,055	Lac-St-Jean-Ouest	Roberval	Roberval	Mme S. Girard, Sec., C.P. 9, Ticouape, St-Méthode, P.Q. GOW 2YO (418/679-1387)
St-Méthode-de-Frontenac (Mun.)	1,632	Frontenac	Frontenac	Frontenac	B. Haman, Sec., St-Méthode-de-Frontenac, P.Q. GON 1SO (418/487-2135)
St-Michel (Paroisse)	1,703	Bellechasse	Bellechasse	Bellechasse	J.-C. Gagnon, Sec., C.P. 100, St-Michel-de-Bellechasse, P.Q. GOR 3SO (418/884-2865)
St-Michel (Paroisse)	1,604	Napierville	Châteauguay	Huntingdon	P. Lemay, Sec., 654 Grand-Rang, St-Michel-de-Napierville, P.Q. JOL 2JO (514/454-2265)
St-Michel-de-Rougement (Paroisse)	988	Rouville	St-Hyacinthe	Iberville	Marielle Guertin, Sec., 980 rue Principale, Rougement, P.Q. JOL 1MO (514/469-3790)
St-Michel-des-Saints (Mun.)	2,059	Berthier	Berthier-Maskinongé	Berthier	V. Laforest, Sec., C.P. 160, St-Michel-des-Saints, P.Q. JOK 3BO (514/833-6941)
St-Michel-du-Squattec (Paroisse)	1,414	Témiscouata	Rimouski	Kamouraska-Témiscouata	G. Morin, Sec., C.P. 117, Squattec, P.Q. GOL 4HO (418/855-2185)
St-Michel-d'Yamaska (Paroisse)	900	Yamaska	Richelieu	Richelieu	Mme A. Salvas, Sec., 103 Bord-de-l'Eau, St-Michel-de-Yamaska, P.Q. JOG 1WO (514/789-2489)

Cities in CAPITALS (Ville); Towns/Villes marked (Ville); Villages marked (Village); Townships/Cantons (marked Canton); United townships/Cantons unis (marked Cantons*); Parishes marked (Paroisse); undesignated municipalities/sans designation marked (Mun.).

MUNICIPALITY	POP.	COUNTY	FEDERAL ELECTORAL DISTRICT	PROVINCIAL ELECTORAL DISTRICT	CLERK/GREFFIER OR SECRETARY-TREASURER (SEC) WITH ADDRESS & PHONE
St-Modeste (Paroisse)	607	Rivière-du-Loup	Kamouraska-Rivière-du-Loup	Rivière-du-Loup	Mme Liliane Castonguay, Sec., St-Modeste, P.Q. GOL 3WO (418/862-5525)
St-Moise (Paroisse)	625	Matapédia	Matapédia-Matane	Matapédia	Lucille Girard, Sec., C.P. 8, St-Moise, P.Q. GOJ 2ZO (418/776-2833)
Ste-Monique (Village)	224	Nicolet	Richelieu	Nicolet	M. Boisvert, Sec., Ste-Monique-de-Nicolet, P.Q. JOG 1NO (819/289-5303)
Ste-Monique (Paroisse)	485	Nicolet	Richelieu	Nicolet	Nicole Larochelle, Sec., 401 Petit-Esprit, Grand-St-Esprit, P.Q. JOG 1NO (819/289-2617)
Ste-Monique (Mun.)	817	Lac-St-Jean-Est	Roberval	Lac-St-Jean	J.C. Duchesne, Sec., C.P. 9, Ste-Monique, P.Q. GOW 2TO (418/347-3592)
St-Narcisse (Paroisse)	1,969	Champlain	Champlain	Champlain	R. Pinard, Sec., 353 Notre-Dame, St-Narcisse, P.Q. GOX 2YO (418/328-3170)
St-Narcisse-de-Beaurivage (Paroisse)	937	Lotbinière	Lévis	Lotbinière	A. Bélanger, Sec., Neubois PO, P.Q. GOS 1WO (418/475-6686)
St-Narcisse-de-Rimouski (Paroisse)	893	Rimouski	Rimouski	Rimouski	C. Proulx, Sec., 3 rue Pavillon, St-Narcisse PO, P.Q. GOK 1SO (418/735-2638)
St-Nazaire-d'Acton (Paroisse)	869	Bagot	St-Hyacinthe	Johnson	A. Gendron, Sec., 135 13e Rang, St-Nazaire, P.Q. JOH 1VO (819/398-2648)
St-Nazaire-de-Dorchester (Paroisse)	362	Dorchester	Bellechasse	Bellechasse	C. Fillion, Sec., 131 boul. Emile Lachance, St-Nazaire-de-Buckland, P.Q. GOR 3TO (418/642-5442)
St-Nérée (Paroisse)	942	Bellechasse	Bellechasse	Bellechasse	L. Lamontagne, Sec., 2171 Principale, St-Nérée, P.Q. GOR 3VO (418/243-2489)
St-Nicéphore (Mun.)	3,784	Drummond	Drummond	Drummond	Claire Fortin, Sec., C.P. 335, St-Nicéphore, P.Q. J2B 6W3 (819/477-5144)
St-Nicolas (Ville)	4,100	Lévis	Lévis	Lévis	Guy Godreau, Sec., 1365 rte Marie-Victorin, St-Nicolas, P.Q. GOS 2ZO (418/831-2034)
St-Nil (Mun.)		Matane	Matapédia-Matane	Matane	P. Picard, Admin., Min. des Affaires municipales, 1039 De La Chevrotière, Quebec, P.Q. G1Z 4Z3 (418/643-7082)
St-Noel (Village)	759	Matapédia	Matapédia-Matane	Matapédia	E. Doucet, Sec., C.P. 100, St-Noel, P.Q. GOJ 3AO (418/776-2936)
St-Norbert (Paroisse)	945	Berthier	Berthier-Maskinongé	Berthier	Ubaldine Dauphin, Sec., 1551 rg. sud, St-Norbert, P.Q. JOK 3CO (514/836-4700)
St-Norbert-d'Arthabaska (Paroisse)	266	Arthabaska	Lotbinière	Arthabaska	R. Lapierre, Sec., R.R. 1, Norbertville, P.Q. GOP 1BO (819/369-9639)
St-Norbert-de-Mont-Brun (Mun.)				Rouyn-Noranda-Témiscamingue	Diane Fournier, Sec., Mont-Brun, P.Q. GOZ 2YO (819/637-2001)
St-Octave-de-Dosquet (Paroisse)	951	Lotbinière	Lotbinière	Lotbinière	E. Demers, Sec., Dosquet, P.Q. GOS 1HO (418/728-3653)
St-Octave-de-Métis (Paroisse)	719	Matane	Matapédia-Matane	Matane	Mme M. Dufour, Sec., C.P. 57, St-Octave-de-Métis, P.Q. GOJ 3BO (418/775-2996)

Cities in CAPITALS (Ville); Towns/Villes marked (Ville); Villages marked (Village); Townships/Cantons (marked Canton); United townships/Cantons unis (marked Cantons*); Parishes marked (Paroisse); undesignated municipalities/sans designation marked (Mun.).

MUNICIPALITY	POP.	COUNTY	FEDERAL ELECTORAL DISTRICT	PROVINCIAL ELECTORAL DISTRICT	CLERK/GREFFIER OR SECRETARY-TREASURER (SEC) WITH ADDRESS & PHONE
Ste-Odile-sur-Rimouski (Paroisse)	554	Rimouski		Rimouski	R. Lepage, Sec., C.P. 595, Ste-Odile-sur-Rimouski, P.Q. G5L 7B5 (418/724-2210)
St-Odilon-de-Cranbourne (Paroisse)	1,532	Dorchester	Beauce	Beauce-Nord	A. Fecteau, Sec., C.P. 100, St-Odilon, P.Q. GOS 3AO (418/464-4801)
St-Omer (Paroisse)	1,201	Bonaventure	Bonaventure-Iles-de-la-Madeleine	Bonaventure	Mme T. Pichette, Sec., C.P. 157, St-Omer, P.Q. GOC 2ZO (418/364-3682)
St-Omer (Mun.)	480	L'Islet	Bellechasse	Montmagny-L'Islet	J.E. Morin, Sec., R.R. 1, St-Pamphile, P.Q. GOR 3XO (418/356-3625)
St-Onésime-d'Ixworth (Paroisse)	623	Kamouraska	Kamouraska-Rivière-du-Loup	Kamouraska-Témiscouata	R. Lemieux, Sec., St-Onésime, P.Q. GOR 3WO (418/856-3018)
St-Ours (Paroisse)	1,003				Voir St-Ours (Ville)
St-Ours (Ville)	731	Richelieu	Richelieu	Richelieu	Luc Allaire, Sec., C.P. 129, St-Ours, P.Q. JOG 1PO (514/785-2203)
St-Pacôme (Paroisse)	680	Kamouraska	Kamouraska-Rivière-du-Loup	Kamouraska-Témiscouata	L. Drapeau, Sec., St-Pacôme, P.Q. GOL 3XO (418/852-2079)
St-Pacôme (Village)	1,160	Kamouraska	Kamouraska-Rivière-du-Loup	Kamouraska-Témiscouata	Y. Lévesque, Sec., C.P. 3, St-Pacôme, P.Q. GOL 3XO (418/852-2731)
St-Pamphile (Ville)	3,460	L'Islet	Kamouraska-Rivière-du-Loup	Montmagny-L'Islet	R. Pelletier, Sec., C.P. 638, St-Pamphile, P.Q. GOR 3XO (418/356-5192)
St-Pascal (Mun.)	1,263	Kamouraska	Kamouraska-Rivière-du-Loup	Kamouraska-Témiscouata	R. Pelletier, Sec., C.P. 691, St-Pascal, P.Q. GOL 3YO (418/492-3312)
St-Pascal (Ville)	2,552	Kamouraska	Kamouraska-Rivière-du-Loup	Kamouraska-Té miscouata	S. Lévesque, Sec., C.P. 250, St-Pascal, P.Q. GOL 3YO (418/492-2312)
St-Patrice-de-Beaurivage (Village)	479	Lotbinière	Lévis	Lotbinière	J.-C. Mercier, Sec., C.P. 67, Beaurivage, P.Q. GOS 1BO (418/596-2383)
St-Patrice-de-Beaurivage (Paroisse)	489	Lotbinière	Lévis	Lotbinière	J.G. Chabot, Sec., Beaurivage, P.Q. GOS 1BO (418/596-2478)
St-Patrice-de-la-Rivière-du-Loup (Paroisse)	2,132	Rivière-du-Loup	Kamouraska-Rivière-du-Loup	Rivière-du-Loup	A. Sénéchal, Sec., 252 rue Fraser, Rivière-du-Loup, P.Q. G5R 3Y4 (418/862-8722)
St-Patrice-de-Sherrington (Paroisse)	1,905	Napierville	St-Jean	Huntingdon	P. Circé, Sec., 89 rue St-Patrice, Sherrington, P.Q. JOL 2NO (514/454-9053)
St-Paul (Mun.)	2,932	Joliette	Joliette	Joliette	Bella Perreault, Sec., 18 Brassard, St-Paul-d'Industrie, P.Q. JOK 3EO (514/759-4040)
St-Paul-d'Abbotsford (Paroisse)	2,314	Rouville		Iberville	Mme R. Tétreault, Sec., 926 Principale, St-Paul-d'Abbotsford, P.Q. JOE 1AO (514/379-5408)
St-Paul-de-Châteauguay (Mun.)	992	Châteauguay	Châteauguay	Huntingdon	F. Primeau, Sec., C.P. 126, Ste-Martine, P.Q. JOS 1VO (514/427-2022)
St-Paul-de-la-Croix (Paroisse)	549	Rivière-du-Loup	Kamouraska-Rivière-du-Loup	Rivière-du-Loup	Aline Boucher, Sec., St-Paul-de-la-Croix, P.Q. GOL 3ZO (418/898-2031)
St-Paul-de-l'Ile-aux-Noix (Paroisse)	1,095	St-Jean	St-Jean	St-Jean	M.-L. Lenoir, Sec., C.P. 60, Ile-aux-Noix, P.Q. JOJ 1GO (514/424-3166)
St-Paul-du-Nord (Mun.)	910	Saguenay	Charlevoix	Saguenay	Marguerite Dubé, Sec., C.P. 39, St-Paul-du-Nord, P.Q. GOT 1WO (418/231-2344)

Cities in CAPITALS (Ville); Towns/Villes marked (Ville); Villages marked (Village); Townships/Cantons (marked Canton); United townships/Cantons unis (marked Cantons*); Parishes marked (Paroisse); undesignated municipalities/sans designation marked (Mun.).

MUNICIPALITY	POP.	COUNTY	FEDERAL ELECTORAL DISTRICT	PROVINCIAL ELECTORAL DISTRICT	CLERK/GREFFIER OR SECRETARY-TREASURER (SEC) WITH ADDRESS & PHONE
Ste-Paule (Mun.)	141	Matane	Matapédia-Matane	Matane	G. Desjardins, Sec., Ste-Paule, P.Q. GOJ 3CO (418/536-3176)
St-Paulin (Village)	722	Maskinongé	Berthier-Maskinongé	Maskinongé	R.U. Guimond, Sec., 2875 Laflèche, St-Paulin, P.Q. JOK 3GO (819/268-2026)
St-Paulin (Paroisse)	731	Maskinongé	Berthier-Maskinongé	Maskinongé	J. Bellemare, Sec., C.P. 119, St-Paulin, P.Q. JOK 3GO (819/268-2890)
St-Paulin-Dalibaire (Paroisse)			Matapédia-Matane	Matane	a/s Min. des Affaires municipales, 1039 De La Chevrotière, Quebec, P.Q. G1Z 4Z3 (418/643-7082)
Ste-Perpétue (Mun.)	2,305	L'Islet	Bellechasse	Montmagny-L'Islet	M. Bernier, Sec., C.P. 308, Ste-Perpétue-de-l'Islet, P.Q. GOR 3ZO (418/359-2966)
Ste-Perpétue (Paroisse)	995	Nicolet		Nicolet	R. Lemaire, Sec., C.P. 14, Ste-Perpétue, P.Q. JOC 1RO (819/393-2740)
St-Philémon (Paroisse)	875	Bellechasse	Bellechasse	Bellechasse	Gabrielle Rouillard, Sec., C.P. 10, St-Philémon, P.Q. GOR 4AO (418/469-2890)
St-Philibert (Mun.)	395	Beauce	Beauce	Beauce-Sud	L. Paquet, Sec., St-Philibert, P.Q. GOM 1XO (418/228-6002)
St-Philippe (Paroisse)	2,445	Laprairie	St-Jean	Laprairie	A. Trudeau, Sec., C.P. 30, St-Philippe, P.Q. JOL 2KO (514/659-8742)
St-Philippe-de-Néri (Paroisse)	1,004	Kamouraska	Kamouraska-Rivière-du-Loup	Kamouraska-Témiscouata	E. Bérubé, Sec., C.P. 70, St-Philippe-de-Néri, P.Q. GOL 4AO (418/498-2872)
Ste-Philomène-de-Fortierville (Paroisse)	357	Lotbinière	Lotbinière	Lotbinière	R. Beaudet, Sec., Fortierville, P.Q. GOS 1JO (819/287-4406)
St-Pie (Paroisse)	1,782	Bagot	St-Hyacinthe	Iberville	Cécile Charron, Sec., C.P. 519, St-Pie-de-Bagot, P.Q. JOH 1WO (514/772-2002)
St-Pie (Village)	1,729	Bagot	St-Hyacinthe	Iberville	Jeanne Leduc, Sec., C.P. 9, St-Pie-de-Bagot, P.Q. JOH 1WO (514/772-2233)
St-Pie-de-Guire (Paroisse)	528	Yamaska	Richelieu	Nicolet	M. Gonzalez, Sec., St-Pie-de-Guire, P.Q. JOG 1RO (514/784-2488)
St-Pierre (Village)	341	Joliette	Joliette	Joliette	I. Coderre, Sec., 53 Sir Mathias Tellier, Joliette, P.Q. J6E 6C8 (514/756-4719)
St-Pierre (Ville)	5,800	Ile-de-Montréal	Notre-Dame-de-Grâce	Marquette	G. Goyette, Sec., 69 5e Ave., Ville St-Pierre, P.Q. H8R 1P1 (514/364-5153)
St-Pierre-Baptiste (Paroisse)	545	Mégantic	Frontenac	Lotbinière	P.-P. Desjardins, Sec., St-Pierre-Baptiste, P.Q. GOP 1KO (418/453-2610)
St-Pierre-de-Broughton (Mun.)	1,068	Beauce	Frontenac	Frontenac	E. Landry, Sec., 9 des Pins, St-Pierre-de-Broughton, P.Q. GON 1TO (418/424-3489)
St-Pierre-de-Lamy (Mun.)		Témiscouata	Rimouski	Kamouraska-Témiscouata	C. Ouellet, Admin., Min. des Affaires municipales, 1039 De La Chevrotière, Québec, P.Q. G1Z 4Z3 (418/497-2447)
St-Pierre-de-la-Rivière-du-Sud (Paroisse)	1,160	Montmagny	Bellechasse	Montmagny-L'Islet	G. Baillargeon, Sec., 785 Principale, St-Pierre-de-Montmagny, P.Q. GOR 4BO (418/248-3084)

Cities in CAPITALS (Ville); Towns/Villes marked (Ville); Villages marked (Village); Townships/Cantons (marked Canton); United townships/Cantons unis (marked Cantons*); Parishes marked (Paroisse); undesignated municipalities/sans designation marked (Mun.).

MUNICIPALITY	POP.	COUNTY	FEDERAL ELECTORAL DISTRICT	PROVINCIAL ELECTORAL DISTRICT	CLERK/GREFFIER OR SECRETARY-TREASURER (SEC) WITH ADDRESS & PHONE
St-Pierre-de-Sorel (Paroisse)	4,035	Richelieu	Richelieu	Richelieu	R. Fortier, Sec., 1275 ch. St-Ours, St-Pierre-de-Sorel, P.Q. J3P 2N4 (514/742-9961)
St-Pierre-de-Véronne (Mun.)	618	Missisquoi	Missisquoi	Brome-Missisquoi	C. Desranleau, Sec., C.P. 55, Pike River PO, P.Q. JOJ 1PO (514/248-3156)
St-Pierre-du-Lac (Paroisse)	480	Matapédia	Matapédia-Matane	Matapédia	J.-J. Bélanger, Sec., C.P. 216, Val-Brillant, P.Q. GOJ 3LO (418/742-3420)
St-Pierre (I.O.) (Paroisse)	1,450	Montmorency 2	Montmorency	Montmorency	R. Méthot, Sec., 1052 ch. Royale, St-Pierre, P.Q. GOA 4EO (418/828-2855)
St-Pierre-les-Becquets (Paroisse)	643	Nicolet	Lotbinière	Lotbinière	G. Lemay, Sec., C.P. 69, St-Pierre-les-Becquets, P.Q. GOX 2ZO (819/263-2231)
St-Placide (Paroisse)	700	Deux-Montagnes		Deux-Montagnes	P.E. Lefebvre, Sec., 1703 boul. St-Placide, St-Placide, P.Q. JOV 2BO (514/258-2305)
St-Placide (Village)	257				Voir St-Placide (Paroisse)
St-Placide-de-Béarn (Mun.)	907	Témiscamingue		Rouyn-Noranda-Témiscamingue	M. Mathieu, Sec., C.P. 69, Béarn, P.Q. JOZ 1GO (819/726-4121)
St-Polycarpe (Village)	548	Soulanges	Vaudreuil	Vaudreuil-Soulanges	J.-C. Aubry, Sec., 84 rue Elie Auclair, St-Polycarpe, P.Q. JOP 1XO (514/265-3612)
St-Polycarpe (Paroisse)	868				Voir St-Polycarpe (Village)
Ste-Praxède (Paroisse)	328	Wolfe		Frontenac	C. Proteau, Sec., R.R. 2, Ste-Praxède, P.Q. GON 1EO (418/449-5278)
St-Prime (Mun.)	2,273	Lac-St-Jean-Ouest	Roberval	Roberval	D. Taillon, Sec., 599 Principale, St-Prime, P.Q. GOW 2WO (418/251-2116)
St-Prosper (Mun.)	3,354	Dorchester	Beauce	Beauce-Sud	Bruno Reny, Sec., 7110 rue de La Salle, St-Prosper, P.Q. GOM 1YO (418/594-8135)
St-Prosper (Paroisse)	788	Champlain		Champlain	L. Gravel, Sec., 375 St-Joseph, St-Prosper, P.Q. GOX 3AO (418/328-8449)
Ste-Pudentienne (Village)	800	Shefford	Shefford	Shefford	R. Loignon, Sec., C.P. 160, Roxton Pond, P.Q. JOE 1ZO (514/372-6875)
Ste-Pudentienne (Paroisse)	1,621				Voir Ste-Pudentienne (Village)
St-Raphael (Village)	1,328	Bellechasse	Bellechasse	Bellechasse	A. Picard, Sec., C.P. 159, St-Raphael, P.Q. GOR 4CO (418/243-2853)
St-Raphael (Paroisse)	883	Bellechasse	Bellechasse	Bellechasse	R. Asselin, Sec., 20 rte. 281, St-Raphael, P.Q. GOR 4CO (418/243-2951)
St-Raphael-d'Albertville (Paroisse)	439	Matapédia	Bonaventure-Iles-de-la-Madeleine	Matapédia	G. Berger, Sec., Albertville, P.Q. GOJ 1AO (418/756-3289)
St-Raphael-de-l'Ile-Bizard (Paroisse)	6,250	Ile-de-Montréal		Nelligan	G. Ladouceur, Sec., 350 Montée de l'Eglise, Ile-Bizard, P.Q. H9C 1G9 (514/626-5005)
St-Raphael sud (Paroisse)	240	Nicolet	Lotbinière	Nicolet	Rita Martin, Sec., Aston-Jonction, P.Q. GOZ 1AO (819/226-3354)
St-Raymond (Ville)	3,599	Portneuf	Portneuf	Portneuf	L. Tremblay, Sec., C.P. 728, St-Raymond, P.Q. GOA 4GO (418/337-2202)

Cities in CAPITALS (Ville); Towns/Villes marked (Ville); Villages marked (Village); Townships/Cantons (marked Canton); United townships/Cantons unis (marked Cantons*); Parishes marked (Paroisse); undesignated municipalities/sans designation marked (Mun.).

MUNICIPALITY	POP.	COUNTY	FEDERAL ELECTORAL DISTRICT	PROVINCIAL ELECTORAL DISTRICT	CLERK/GREFFIER OR SECRETARY-TREASURER (SEC) WITH ADDRESS & PHONE
St-Raymond (Paroisse)	3,305	Portneuf	Portneuf	Portneuf	Guy Alain, Sec., C.P. 1448, St-Raymond, P.Q. GOA 4GO (418/337-7698)
St-Rédempteur (Village)	3,343	Lévis	Lévis	Lévis	H.-L. Beaudoin, Sec., 65 rue du Cap, St-Rédempteur, P.Q. GOS 3BO (418/831-4488)
St-Rémi (Paroisse)	1,392	Portneuf	Portneuf	Portneuf	Guy Gingras, Sec., C.P. 27, Lac-aux-Sables, P.Q. GOX 1MO (418/336-2331)
St-Rémi (Ville)	4,866	Napierville		Huntingdon	F. Wells, Greffier, C.P. 578, St-Rémi, P.Q. JOL 2LO (514/454-3993)
St-Rémi-de-Tingwick (Paroisse)	503	Arthabaska	Richmond	Richmond	Lucile Crête, Sec., St-Rémi-de-Tingwick, P.Q. JOA 1KO (819/359-2459)
St-René (Paroisse)	465	Beauce	Beauce	Beauce-Sud	M. Drouin, Sec., St-René, P.Q. GOM 1MO (418/382-5461)
St-René-de-Matane (Paroisse)	1,056	Matane	Matapédia-Matane	Matane	Mme M. Richard, Sec., C.P. 58, St-René-de-Matane, P.Q. GOJ 3EO (418/224-3768)
Ste-Rita (Mun.)	549	Rivière-du-Loup	Kamouraska-Rivière-du-Loup	Rivière-du-Loup	Mme V. Beaulieu, Sec., Ste-Rita, P.Q. GOL 4GO (418/963-6702)
St-Robert (Paroisse)	1,630	Richelieu	Richelieu	Richelieu	E. Lemoine, Sec., 474 Rang Picoudie, St-Robert, P.Q. JOG 1SO (514/782-2844)
St-Robert-Bellarmin (Mun.)	679	Frontenac	Beauce	Beauce-Sud	E. Lachance, Sec., Bellarmin, P.Q. GOM 1TO (418/582-3542)
St-Roche-de-l'Achigan (Paroisse)	3,100	L'Assomption	Terrebonne	Rousseau	Philippe Riopelle, Sec., 30 rue Dr. W. Locat, St-Roche-de-l'Achigan, P.Q. JOK 3HO (514/588-2326)
St-Roch-de-Mékinac (Paroisse)	335	Champlain	Champlain	Laviolette	C. Cossette, Sec., Rivière-Mékinac PO, P.Q. GOX 2EO (819/646-5603)
St-Roch-de-Richelieu (Paroisse)	1,500	Richelieu	Verchères	Verchères	Mme L. St-Laurent, Sec., 770 Principale, St-Roch-de-Richelieu, P.Q. JOL 2MO (514/785-2755)
St-Roch-des-Aulnaies (Mun.)	1,010	L'Islet	Kamouraska-Rivière-du-Loup	Kamouraska-Témiscouata	L. Castonguay, Sec., St-Roch-des-Aulnaies, P.Q. GOR 4EO (418/354-2975)
St-Roch-Ouest (Mun.)	381	L'Assomption	Terrebonne	Rousseau	M.H. Duval, Sec., 770 Riv-Nord, St-Roch-de-l'Achigan, P.Q. JOK 3HO (514/588-5095)
St-Romain (Mun.)	640	Frontenac	Mégantic-Compton-Stanstead	Mégantic-Compton	H. Hallie, Sec., C.P. 90, St-Romain, P.Q. GOY 1LO (418/486-7374)
ST-ROMUALD-D'ETCHEMIN (Ville)	9,500	Lévis	Lévis	Lévis	J.-G. Paquet, Greffier, (1245 Commerciale) C.P. 2007, St-Romuald, P.Q. G6W 5M3 (418/839-4141)
St-Rosaire (Paroisse)	650	Arthabaska	Lotbinière	Arthabaska	Ulysse Pratte, Sec., St-Rosaire, P.Q. GOZ 1CO (819/752-9491)
Ste-Rosalie (Village)	2,715	Bagot	St-Hyacinthe	St-Hyacinthe	Diane Martin, Sec., C.P. 30, Ste-Rosalie, P.Q. JOH 1XO (514/799-4141)
Ste-Rosalie (Paroisse)	1,179	Bagot	St-Hyacinthe	St-Hyacinthe	J. Girard, Sec., Ste-Rosalie, P.Q. JOH 1XO (514/799-3707)

Cities in CAPITALS (Ville); Towns/Villes marked (Ville); Villages marked (Village); Townships/Cantons (marked Canton); United townships/Cantons unis (marked Cantons*); Parishes marked (Paroisse); undesignated municipalities/sans designation marked (Mun.).

MUNICIPALITY	POP.	COUNTY	FEDERAL ELECTORAL DISTRICT	PROVINCIAL ELECTORAL DISTRICT	CLERK/GREFFIER OR SECRETARY-TREASURER (SEC) WITH ADDRESS & PHONE
Ste-Rose-de-Watford (Mun.)	974	Dorchester	Bellechasse	Bellechasse	C. Jacques, Sec., C.P. 39, Ste-Rose-de-Watford, P.Q. GOR 4GO (418/267-5451)
Ste-Rose-du-Nord (Paroisse)	500	Chicoutimi	Lac-St-Jean	Dubuc	Louise Condé, Sec., 126 Descente Des Femmes, Ste-Rose-du-Nord, P.Q. GOV 1TO (418/675-2250)
Ste-Sabine (Paroisse)	589	Bellechasse	Bellechasse	Bellechasse	Mme L.L. Lemieux, Sec., Ste-Sabine-de-Bellechasse, P.Q. GOR 4HO (418/383-3191)
Ste-Sabine (Paroisse)	712	Missisquoi	Missisquoi	Brome-Missisquoi	Rita Choquette, Sec., Ste-Sabine, P.Q. JOJ 2BO (514/293-5101)
St-Samuel (Paroisse)	486	Nicolet	Lotbinière	Richmond	P.-E. Bergeron, Sec., St-Samuel-de-Horton, P.Q. GOZ 1GO (819/353-2206)
St-Sauveur (Paroisse)	1,106	Terrebonne	Labelle	Prevost	M. Rainville, Sec., 195 Principale, St-Sauveur-des-Monts, P.Q. JOR 1RO (514/227-3608)
St-Sauveur-des-Monts (Village)	2,000	Terrebonne	Labelle	Prevost	Roger Brunette, Sec., C.P. 130, St-Sauveur-des-Monts, P.Q. JOR 1RO (514/227-2668)
St-Sébastien (Mun.)	789	Frontenac	Mégantic-Compton-Stanstead	Mégantic-Compton	C. Dion, Sec., St-Sébastien-de-Beauce, P.Q. GOY 1MO (819/652-2727)
St-Sébastien (Paroisse)	804	Iberville	Missisquoi	Iberville	C. Lafrance, Sec., St-Sébastien, P.Q. JOJ 2CO (514/244-3223)
Ste-Séraphine (Paroisse)	320	Arthabaska	Drummond	Richmond	Mme F.D. Pagé, Sec., Ste-Séraphine, P.Q. JOA 1EO (819/336-5510)
St-Sévère (Paroisse)	408	St-Maurice	Trois-Rivières	Maskinongé	P.-E. Gélinas, Sec., 66 Principale, St-Sévère, P.Q. GOX 3BO (819/264-5725)
St-Séverin (Paroisse)	318	Beauce	Beauce	Beauce-Nord	L.-P. Lachance, Sec., St-Séverin, P.Q. GON 1VO (418/426-2484)
St-Séverin (Paroisse)	1,080	Champlain		Laviolette	Ginette Hamelin, Sec., C.P. 120, St-Séverin, P.Q. GOX 2BO (418/365-5844)
St-Siméon (Paroisse)	1,416	Bonaventure	Bonaventure-Iles-de-la-Madeleine	Bonaventure	G. Bujold, Sec., C.P. 39, St-Siméon-de-Bonaventure, P.Q. GOC 3AO (418/534-2155)
St-Siméon (Village)	1,171	Charlevoix-Est	Charlevoix	Charlevoix	J.-G. Savard, Sec., 502 St-Laurent, St-Siméon, P.Q. GOT 1XO (418/638-3691)
St-Siméon (Paroisse)	625	Charlevoix-Est	Charlevoix	Charlevoix	J.-G. Savard, Sec., 372 Bergeron, St-Siméon, P.Q. GOT 1XO (418/638-2909)
St-Simon (Paroisse)	664	Rimouski	Rimouski	Rimouski	Chantal Lechasseur, Sec., St-Simon-de-Rimouski, P.Q. GOL 4CO (418/738-2896)
St-Simon (Paroisse)	1,115	Bagot	St-Hyacinthe	St-Hyacinthe	A.-E. St-Laurent, Sec., St-Simon-de-Bagot, P.Q. JOH 1YO (514/798-2158)
St-Simon-les-Mines (Mun.)	360	Beauce	Beauce	Beauce-Sud	Mme M. Rodrigue, Sec., St-Simon-les-Mines, P.Q. GOM 1KO (418/774-6966)
St-Sixte (Mun.)				Papineau	
Ste-Sophie (Mun.)	266	Mégantic	Frontenac	Frontenac	H. Béliveau, Sec., Ste-Sophie, P.Q. GOP 1LO (819/362-2466)

Cities in CAPITALS (Ville); Towns/Villes marked (Ville); Villages marked (Village); Townships/Cantons (marked Canton); United townships/Cantons unis (marked Cantons*); Parishes marked (Paroisse); undesignated municipalities/sans designation marked (Mun.).

MUNICIPALITY	POP.	COUNTY	FEDERAL ELECTORAL DISTRICT	PROVINCIAL ELECTORAL DISTRICT	CLERK/GREFFIER OR SECRETARY-TREASURER (SEC) WITH ADDRESS & PHONE
Ste-Sophie (Mun.)	5,100	Terrebonne	Terrebonne	Rousseau	Y. Desrosiers, Sec., 2212 boul. Ste-Sophie, Ste-Sophie, P.Q. JOR 1SO (514/438-7784)
Ste-Sophie-de-Lévrard (Paroisse)	926	Nicolet	Lotbinière	Lotbinière	Simonne Verville, Sec., 204 St-Antoine, Ste-Sophie-de-Lévrard, P.Q. GOX 3CO (819/288-5804)
St-Stanislas (Mun.)	1,421	Champlain	Champlain	Champlain	R. Cossette, Sec., 29 rue du Moulin, St-Stanislas, P.Q. GOX 3EO (418/328-3245)
St-Stanislas (Mun.)	398	Lac-St-Jean-Ouest	Roberval	Roberval	M.A. Girard, Sec., R.R. 3, Mistassini, P.Q. GOW 2CO (418/276-4476)
St-Stanislas-de-Kostka (Paroisse)	1,200	Beauharnois	Beauharnois-Salaberry	Beauharnois	R. Vaudrin, Sec., C.P. 14, St-Stanislas-de-Kostka, P.Q. JOS 1WO (514/373-1172)
St-Sulpice (Paroisse)	1,592	L'Assomption	Joliette	L'Assomption	Mme H. Ouellet, Sec., 1089 Notre-Dame, St-Sulpice, P.Q. JOK 3JO (514/589-4450)
St-Sylvère (Mun.)	1,007	Nicolet	Lotbinière	Nicolet	C. Desruisseaux, Sec., 213 rue de l'Ecole, St-Sylvère, P.Q. GOZ 1HO (819/285-2909)
St-Sylvestre (Village)	392	Lotbinière	Frontenac	Lotbinière	R. Jacques, Sec., St-Sylvestre, P.Q. GOS 3CO (418/596-2174)
St-Télésphore (Paroisse)	792	Soulanges	Vaudreuil	Vaudreuil-Soulanges	M. Descent, Sec., 1495 rte. 340, St-Télésphore, P.Q. JOP 1YO (514/269-2858)
St-Tharcisius (Paroisse)	728	Matapédia	Matapédia-Matane	Matapédia	Rita Rioux, Sec., St-Tharcisius, P.Q. GOJ 3GO (418/629-3947)
Ste-Thècle (Village)	1,761	Champlain	Champlain	Laviolette	A. Thiffeault, Sec., C.P. 195, Ste-Thècle, P.Q. GOX 3GO (418/289-2070)
Ste-Thècle (Paroisse)	1,070				Voir Ste-Thècle (Village)
St-Théodore-d'Acton (Paroisse)	1,343	Bagot	St-Hyacinthe	Johnson	F. Gauthier, Sec., 355 des Erables, St-Théodore-d'Acton, P.Q. JOH 1ZO (514/546-7187)
St-Théophile (Mun.)	1,030	Beauce	Beauce	Beauce-Sud	J. McCollough, Sec., St-Théophile, P.Q. GOZ 4AO (418/597-3998)
St-Théophile (Paroisse)	2,011	Champlain	St-Maurice	St-Maurice	Lilianne Garceau, Sec., 1082 37e Ave., Lac-à-la-Tortue, P.Q. GOX 1LO (819/538-5882)
STE-THERESE (Ville)	18,700	Terrebonne	Blainville-Deux-Montagnes	Groulx	C.-E. Desjardins, Greffier, (34 Blainville Ouest) C.P. 100, Ste-Thérèse, P.Q. J7E 4H7 (514/435-9521)
Ste-Thérèse-de-Gaspé (Mun.)	1,233	Gaspé-Est	Gaspé	Gaspé	E. Lelièvre, Sec., C.P. 99, Ste-Thérèse-de-Gaspé, P.Q. GOC 3BO (418/385-3281)
Ste-Thérèse-de-la-Gatineau (Mun.)	432	Gatineau	Pontiac-Gatineau-Labelle	Gatineau	Mme A.M. Paul, Sec., Ste-Thérèse-de-la-Gatineau, P.Q. JOX 2XO (819/449-4134)
St-Thomas (Paroisse)	2,261	Joliette	Joliette	Joliette	W. Roy, Sec., 941 Principale, St-Thomas-de-Joliette, P.Q. JOK 3LO (514/759-3405)

Cities in CAPITALS (Ville); Towns/Villes marked (Ville); Villages marked (Village); Townships/Cantons (marked Canton); United townships/Cantons unis (marked Cantons*); Parishes marked (Paroisse); undesignated municipalities/sans designation marked (Mun.).

MUNICIPALITY	POP.	COUNTY	FEDERAL ELECTORAL DISTRICT	PROVINCIAL ELECTORAL DISTRICT	CLERK/GREFFIER OR SECRETARY-TREASURER (SEC) WITH ADDRESS & PHONE
St-Thomas-d'Aquin (Paroisse)	2,248	St-Hyacinthe	St-Hyacinthe	St-Hyacinthe	Murielle Archambault, Sec., 105 Prévert, St-Thomas-d'Aquin, P.Q. JOH 2AO (514/796-5885)
St-Thomas-de-Cherbourg (Paroisse)				Matane	P. Picard, Admin., Min. des Affaires municipales, 1039 De La Chevrotière, Québec, P.Q. G1Z 4Z3 (418/643-7082)
St-Thomas-de-Pierreville (Paroisse)	659	Yamaska	Richelieu	Nicolet	F. Belletête, Sec., Pierreville, P.Q. JOG 1JO (514/568-6492)
St-Thomas-Didyme (Mun.)	990	Lac-St-Jean-Ouest	Roberval	Roberval	N. Darveau, Sec., 2 rue Gorget, Didyme, P.Q. GOW 1PO (418/274-3638)
St-Thuribe (Paroisse)	459	Portneuf	Portneuf	Portneuf	P. Julien, Sec., 330 rue Principale, St-Thuribe, P.Q. GOA 4HO (418/339-2413)
St-Timothée (Paroisse)	1,020	Champlain	Champlain	Laviolette	Y. Trudel, Sec., 1171 rue St-Pierre, Hérouxville, P.Q. GOX 1JO (418/365-7135)
St-Timothée (Village)	1,983	Beauharnois	Beauharnois-Salaberry	Beauharnois	J.-L. Sicotte, Sec., C.P. 69, St-Timothée, P.Q. JOS 1XO (514/371-4044)
St-Timothée (Paroisse)	4,400	Beauharnois	Beauharnois-Salaberry	Beauharnois	A. Hallé, Sec., C.P. 219, St-Timothée, P.Q. JOS 1XO (514/371-4013)
St-Tite (Ville)	3,161	Champlain	Champlain	Laviolette	P.-A. Desaulniers, Sec., 540 Notre-Dame, St-Tite, P.Q. GOX 3HO (418/365-5143)
St-Tite (Paroisse)	1,298	Champlain	Champlain	Laviolette	B. Cadotte, Sec., 540 Notre Dame, St-Tite, P.Q. GOX 3HO (418/365-5093)
St-Tite-des-Caps (Mun.)	1,667	Montmorency 1	Charlevoix	Charlevoix	R. Morency, Sec., 3 Leclerc, St-Tite-des-Caps, P.Q. GOA 4JO (418/823-2232)
St-Ubalde (Mun.)	1,530	Portneuf	Portneuf	Portneuf	Mme M. Paré, Sec., 427B Chabot, St-Ubalde, P.Q. GOA 4LO (418/277-2124)
St-Ulric (Village)	786	Matane	Matapédia-Matane	Matane	Mme T. Paquet, Sec., 2 De La Fabrique, St-Ulric, P.Q. GOJ 3HO (418/737-4763)
St-Ulric-de-Matane (Paroisse)	640	Matane	Matapédia-Matane	Matane	Mme D. Beaulieu, Sec., R.R. 2, St-Ulric, P.Q. GOJ 3HO (418/737-4573)
St-Urbain (Paroisse)	1,770	Charlevoix-Ouest	Charlevoix	Charlevoix	Guy Bouchard, Sec., C.P. 90, St-Urbain, P.Q. GOA 4KO (418/639-2467)
St-Urbain-Premier (Paroisse)	1,107	Châteauguay	Châteauguay	Huntingdon	O. Marcil, Sec., 199 Principale, St-Urbain-Premier, P.Q. JOS 1YO (514/427-2742)
Ste-Ursule (Paroisse)	1,250	Maskinongé	Berthier-Maskinongé	Maskinongé	J.P. Baril, Sec., 1700 St-François, Ste-Ursule, P.Q. JOK 3MO (819/228-4345)
St-Valentin (Paroisse)	575	St-Jean	St-Jean	St-Jean	R. Langlois, Sec., St-Valentin, P.Q. JOJ 2EO (514/291-5419)
St-Valère (Mun.)	1,092	Arthabaska	Lotbinière	Arthabaska	S. Jutras, Sec., 1617 11E Rang, St-Valère, P.Q. GOP 1MO (819/353-2219)
St-Valérien (Paroisse)	725	Rimouski	Rimouski	Rimouski	Bernadette Landry, Sec., C.P. 9, St-Valerien-de-Rimouski, P.Q. GOL 4EO (418/736-5887)

Cities in CAPITALS (Ville); Towns/Villes marked (Ville); Villages marked (Village); Townships/Cantons (marked Canton); United townships/Cantons unis (marked Cantons*); Parishes marked (Paroisse); undesignated municipalities/sans designation marked (Mun.).

MUNICIPALITY	POP.	COUNTY	FEDERAL ELECTORAL DISTRICT	PROVINCIAL ELECTORAL DISTRICT	CLERK/GREFFIER OR SECRETARY-TREASURER (SEC) WITH ADDRESS & PHONE
St-Valérien-de-Milton (Canton)	1,350	Shefford		Johnson	Lucie Paquette, Sec., C.P. 69, St-Valérien, P.Q. J0H 2B0 (514/549-2463)
St-Vallier (Village)	486	Bellechasse	Bellechasse	Bellechasse	Mme R. Tanguay, Sec., 347 De La Fabrique, St-Vallier Village, P.Q. G0R 4J0 (418/884-3451)
St-Vallier (Paroisse)	752	Bellechasse	Bellechasse	Bellechasse	G. Laliberté, Sec., 35 Montée de la Station, St-Vallier, P.Q. G0R 4J0 (418/884-2559)
St-Venant-de-Hereford (Paroisse)	155	Compton	Mégantic-Compton-Stanstead	Mégantic-Compton	P. Gendreau, Sec., R.R. 2, Paquetville, East Hereford, P.Q. J0B 1S0 (819/658-3503)
St-Viateur (Paroisse)	243	Berthier		Berthier	R. Laferrière, Sec., 1811 Rang York, St-Viateur, P.Q. J0K 1X0 (514/885-3252)
Ste-Victoire-d'Arthabaska (Paroisse)	3,460	Arthabaska	Lotbinière	Arthabaska	A. Allard, Sec., Parc de l'Expo, Victoriaville, P.Q. G6P 4K1 (819/752-9727)
Ste-Victoire-de-Sorel (Paroisse)	1,861	Richelieu	Richelieu	Richelieu	O. Bardier, Sec., 520 ch. Ste-Victoire, Ste-Victoire, P.Q. J0G 1T0 (514/782-3111)
St-Victor (Village)	1,062	Beauce	Beauce	Beauce-Sud	Richard Giguere, Sec., C.P. 40, St-Victor-de-Beauce, P.Q. G0M 2B0 (418/588-6854)
St-Victor-de-Tring (Mun.)	1,166				Voir St-Victor (Village)
St-Wenceslas (Village)	360	Nicolet	Drummond	Nicolet	F. Parre, Sec., 1135 rue Lessard, St-Wenceslas, P.Q. G0Z 1J0 (819/224-7524)
St-Wenceslas (Mun.)	781	Nicolet	Drummond	Nicolet	M. Constant, Sec., 1140 rue Hébert, St-Wenceslas, P.Q. G0Z 1J0 (819/224-7700)
St-Zacharie (Village)	1,296	Beauce	Beauce	Beauce-Sud	R. Lebreux, Sec., C.P. 222, St-Zacharie, P.Q. G0M 2C0 (418/593-4021)
St-Zacharie (Mun.)	1,145	Beauce	Beauce	Beauce-Sud	G. Faucher, Sec., St-Zacharie, P.Q. G0M 2C0 (418/593-2491)
St-Zénon (Paroisse)	775	Berthier	Berthier-Maskinongé	Berthier	J. Marcil, Sec., 6191 Principale, St-Zénon, P.Q. J0K 3N0 (514/884-5437)
St-Zénon-du-Lac-Humqui (Paroisse)	551	Matapédia	Matapédia-Matane	Matapédia	Jeannine Dechamplain, Sec., Lac-Humqui, P.Q. G0J 1N0 (418/743-2171)
St-Zéphirin-de-Courval (Paroisse)	889	Yamaska	Richelieu	Nicolet	J. Biron, Sec., St-Zéphirin, P.Q. J0G 1V0 (514/564-2070)
St-Zotique (Village)	1,577	Soulanges	Vaudreuil	Vaudreuil-Soulanges	Louise Viau, Sec., C.P. 150, St-Zotique, P.Q. J0P 1Z0 (514/267-9335)
SALABERRY-DE-VALLEYFIELD (Ville)	29,500	Beauharnois	Frontenac	Beauharnois	Léon Laberge, Greffier, (61 Ste-Cécile) C.P. 188, Salaberry-de-Valleyfield, P.Q. J6T 1L8 (514/373-2030)
Sault-au-Mouton (Village)	914	Saguenay	Charlevoix	Saguenay	M.D. Tremblay, Sec., C.P. 99, Sault-au-Mouton, P.Q. G0T 1Z0 (418/231-2170)
Sawyerville (Village)	891	Compton	Mégantic-Compton-Stanstead	Mégantic-Compton	Fernande Belhumeur, Sec., C.P. 186, Sawyerville, P.Q. J0B 3A0 (819/889-2252)

Cities in CAPITALS (Ville); Towns/Villes marked (Ville); Villages marked (Village); Townships/Cantons (marked Canton); United townships/Cantons unis (marked Cantons*); Parishes marked (Paroisse); undesignated municipalities/sans designation marked (Mun.).

MUNICIPALITY	POP.	COUNTY	FEDERAL ELECTORAL DISTRICT	PROVINCIAL ELECTORAL DISTRICT	CLERK/GREFFIER OR SECRETARY-TREASURER (SEC) WITH ADDRESS & PHONE
Sayabec (Village)	1,844	Matapédia	Matapédia-Matane	Matapédia	J.-P. Paquet, Sec., C.P. 117, Sayabec, P.Q. GOJ 3KO (418/536-5440)
Schefferville (Ville)	3,649	Terr. du Nouveau Québec	Manicouagan	Duplessis	J.-Y. Truchon, Sec., C.P. 1600, Schefferville, P.Q. GOG 2TO (418/585-2471)
Scotstown (Ville)	818	Compton	Mégantic-Compton-Stanstead	Mégantic-Compton	A. Charest, Trés., C.P. 129, Scotstown, P.Q. JOB 3BO (819/657-4965)
Scott (Village)	580	Dorchester	Lévis	Beauce-Nord	D. Drouin, Sec., 32 rue Bellerive, Scott-Jonction, P.Q. GOS 3GO (418/387-2037)
Senneterre (Ville)	4,289	Abitibi	Abitibi	Abitibi-Est	M. Courchesne, Sec., C.P. 789, Senneterre, P.Q. JOY 2MO (819/737-2296)
Senneterre (Paroisse)	700	Abitibi		Abitibi-Est	Georgette Dumont, Sec., C.P. 700, Senneterre, P.Q. JOY 2MO (819/737-4695)
Senneville (Village)	1,331	Ile-de-Montréal	Vaudreuil	Nelligan	Léo Viau, Sec., 35 ch. Senneville, Senneville, P.Q. H9X 1B8 (514/457-6020)
SEPT-ILES (Ville)	30,400	Saguenay	Manicouagan	Duplessis	G. Bélanger, Greffier, 546 Dequen, Sept-Iles, P.Q. G4R 2R4 (418/962-2525)
Shannon (Mun.)	3,484	Portneuf	Portneuf	Chauveau	J.A. Griffin, Sec., 154 Gosford nord, Shannon, P.Q. GOA 4NO (418/844-3638)
SHAWINIGAN (Ville)	24,100	St-Maurice	St-Maurice	St-Maurice	Yvon Boisvert, Greffier, Hôtel de ville, C.P. 400, Shawinigan, P.Q. G9N 6V3 (819/537-6626)
Shawinigan-Sud (Ville)	11,000	Champlain	St-Maurice	St-Maurice	G. Pinel, Sec., 1550 118e rue, Shawinigan-Sud, P.Q. G9P 3G8 (819/536-5671)
Shawville (Village)	1,705	Pontiac	Pontiac-Gatineau-Labelle	Pontiac	Mrs. E.F. Dale, Sec., C.P. 339, Shawville, P.Q. JOX 2YO (819/647-2979)
Sheen, Esher, Aberdeen & Malakoff (Cantons)*	139	Pontiac	Pontiac-Gatineau-Labelle	Pontiac	E. Jennings, Sec., Sheenboro PO, P.Q. JOX 2ZO (819/689-2751)
Shefford (Canton)	2,157	Shefford		Shefford	M.G. Campbell, Sec., C.P. 425, Waterloo, P.Q. JOE 2NO (514/539-2258)
Shenley (Canton)	1,002	Beauce		Beauce-Sud	R. Leblond, Sec., C.P. 128, St-Honoré, P.Q. GOM 1VO (418/485-6738)
SHERBROOKE (Ville)	75,300	Sherbrooke	Sherbrooke	St-François; Sherbrooke	R.L. Bélisle, Greffier, 145 Wellington nord, Sherbrooke, P.Q. J1H 5C1 (819/565-3054)
Shigawake (Mun.)	473	Bonaventure	Bonaventure-Iles-de-la-Madeleine	Bonaventure	W.T. Sullivan, Sec., R.R. 1, Box 70, Shigawake, P.Q. GOC 3EO (418/752-2587)
Shipshaw (Mun.)	1,397	Chicoutimi	Jonquière	Dubuc	S. Roy, Sec., 3760 St-Léonard, Shipshaw, P.Q. GOV 1VO (418/542-5021)
Shipton (Canton)	3,005	Richmond		Richmond	R. Allaire, Sec., C.P. 209, Danville, P.Q. JOA 1AO (819/839-2337)
SILLERY (Ville)	13,400	Québec	Louis-Hébert	Jean Talon; Louis-Hébert	G. Gravel, Greffier, C.P. 215, Sillery, P.Q. G1T 2R3 (418/527-3404)

Cities in CAPITALS (Ville); Towns/Villes marked (Ville); Villages marked (Village); Townships/Cantons (marked Canton); United townships/Cantons unis (marked Cantons*); Parishes marked (Paroisse); undesignated municipalities/sans designation marked (Mun.).

MUNICIPALITY	POP.	COUNTY	FEDERAL ELECTORAL DISTRICT	PROVINCIAL ELECTORAL DISTRICT	CLERK/GREFFIER OR SECRETARY-TREASURER (SEC) WITH ADDRESS & PHONE
SOREL (Ville)	19,900	Richelieu	Richelieu	Richelieu	J. Charbonneau, Greffier, Hôtel de ville, C.P. 97, Sorel, P.Q. J3P 5N6 (514/742-4583)
Stanbridge (Canton)	919	Missisquoi		Brome-Missisquoi	Mrs. C. Wescott, Sec., C.P. 240, Stanbridge Est, P.Q. JOJ 2HO (514/248-3188)
Stanbridge-Station (Mun.)	417	Missisquoi	Missisquoi	Brome-Missisquoi	C. Plouffe, Sec., Stanbridge-Station, P.Q. JOJ 2JO (514/248-2125)
Stanstead (Canton)	690	Stanstead		Orford	L. Poitras, Sec., R.R. 1, Georgeville, P.Q. JOB 1TO (819/876-2907)
Stanstead-Est (Mun.)	713	Stanstead		Orford	W. Gaulin, Sec., R.R. 2, Stanstead, P.Q. JOB 3EO (819/876-2430)
Stanstead Plain (Village)	1,171	Stanstead	Mégantic-Compton-Stanstead	Orford	Mrs. T. Winter, Sec., 23 Hackett, Stanstead, P.Q. JOB 3EO (819/876-2771)
Stoke (Canton)	1,817	Richmond		Johnson	M. Camirand, Sec., Stoke, P.Q. JOB 3GO (819/878-3790)
Stoneham et Tewkesbury (Cantons)*	2,549	Québec		Chauveau	Mme I. Johnston, Sec., 545 1e Ave., Stoneham, P.Q. GOA 4PO (418/848-2381)
Stornoway (Mun.)	577	Frontenac	Mégantic-Compton-Stanstead	Mégantic-Compton	R. Breton, Sec., C.P. 114, Stornoway, P.Q. GOY 1NO (819/652-2800)
Stratford (Canton)	850	Wolfe		Mégantic-Compton	J.-M. Picard, Sec., 115 Elgin, Stratford Centre, P.Q. GOY 1PO (418/443-2307)
Stukely-Sud (Village)	380	Shefford	Shefford	Brome-Missisquoi	Monique Beaudry, Sec., C.P. 30, Stukely-Sud, P.Q. JOE 2JO (514/297-3407)
Stukely-Sud (Mun.)	435	Shefford	Shefford	Brome-Missisquoi	Gisèle Lussier, Sec., a/s C.P. 270, Eastman, P.Q. J0E 1P0 (514/297-3440)
Suffolk et Addington (Cantons)*	440	Papineau		Papineau	Mme S. Blais, Sec., St-Emile-de-Suffolk, P.Q. JOV 1YO (819/426-2987)
Sullivan (Mun.)	1,978	Abitibi	Abitibi	Abitibi-Est	A. Simard, Sec., C.P. 40, Sullivan, P.Q. JOY 1NO (819/825-4596)
Sutton (Canton)	1,218	Brome		Brome-Missisquoi	Mary Moodey, Sec., C.P. 8, Sutton, P.Q. JOE 2KO (514/538-2290)
Sutton (Ville)	1,668	Brome	Missisquoi	Brome-Missisquoi	Suzanne Gilbert, Sec., C.P. 8, Sutton, P.Q. JOE 2KO (514/538-2090)
Taché (Canton)	1,828	Chicoutimi		Lac-St-Jean	R. Bouchard, Sec., C.P. 130, St-Nazaire-de-Chicoutimi, P.Q. GOW 2VO (418/662-4154)
Tadoussac (Ville)	1,016	Saguenay	Charlevoix	Saguenay	M. Côté, Sec., 251 rue Caron, Tadoussac, P.Q. GOT 2AO (418/235-4446)
Taschereau (Mun.)	502	Abitibi	Témiscamingue	Abitibi-Ouest	Majella Cloutier, Sec., Taschereau, P.Q. JOZ 3NO (819/796-2288)
Taschereau-Fortier (Mun.)	642	Dorchester		Beauce-Nord	Mme J. Vallières, Sec., a/s Scott-Jonction, P.Q. GOS 3GO (418/387-2142)
Témiscaming (Ville)	2,135	Témiscamingue	Témiscamingue	Rouyn-Noranda-Témiscamingue	R. Shank, Greffier, 31 Windsor, Témiscaming, P.Q. JOZ 3RO (819/627-3273)
Terrasse-Vaudreuil (Mun.)	1,863	Vaudreuil		Vaudreuil-Soulanges	R. Frenette, Sec., 74 7e Ave., Terrasse-Vaudreuil, P.Q. J7V 3M9 (514/453-8120)

Cities in CAPITALS (Ville); Towns/Villes marked (Ville); Villages marked (Village); Townships/Cantons (marked Canton); United townships/Cantons unis (marked Cantons*); Parishes marked (Paroisse); undesignated municipalities/sans designation marked (Mun.).

MUNICIPALITY	POP.	COUNTY	FEDERAL ELECTORAL DISTRICT	PROVINCIAL ELECTORAL DISTRICT	CLERK/GREFFIER OR SECRETARY-TREASURER (SEC) WITH ADDRESS & PHONE
Terrebonne (Ville)	11,800	Terrebonne	Terrebonne	Terrebonne	R. Barbe, Greffier, 86 St-André, Terrebonne, P.Q. J6W 3C3 (514/471-4192)
THETFORD MINES (Ville)	20,300	Mégantic	Frontenac	Frontenac	Y. Lamothe, Greffier, Hôtel de ville, C.P. 489, Thetford Mines, P.Q. G6G 5T3 (418/335-2981)
Thetford, sud (Canton)	2,325	Mégantic		Frontenac	A. Bourret, Sec., 477 St-Alphonse est, Thetford Mines, P.Q. G6G 3W1 (418/335-2268)
Thorne (Canton)	340	Pontiac		Pontiac	M. Bretzlaff, Sec., Ladysmith, P.Q. JOX 2AO (819/647-2356)
Thurso (Ville)	3,066	Papineau	Gatineau	Papineau	E. Boulerice, Sec., 161 Galipeau, Thurso, P.Q. JOX 3BO (819/985-2701)
Tingwick (Mun.)	332	Arthabaska	Richmond	Richmond	Lucienne Neault, Sec., 50 St-Joseph, Tingwick, P.Q. JOA 1LO (819/359-2311)
Tourville (Mun.)	1,106	L'Islet	Bellechasse	Montmagny-L'Islet	Mireille Jean, Sec., C.P. 206, Tourville, P.Q. GOR 4MO (418/359-3460)
Tracy (Ville)	12,500	Richelieu	Richelieu	Richelieu	L. Tardif, Greffier, 3025 boul. de la Mairie, Tracy, P.Q. J3R 1C2 (514/742-5671)
Trécesson (Canton)	810	Abitibi		Abitibi-Ouest	L. Poliquin, Sec., Villemontel, P.Q. JOY 2SO (819/732-8524)
Tremblay (Canton)	2,040	Chicoutimi		Dubuc	J.M. Claveau, Sec., 121 Martel, Chicoutimi-Nord, P.Q. G7H 5B2 (418/543-6875)
Très-St-Rédempteur (Paroisse)	425	Vaudreuil		Vaudreuil-Soulanges	H.-P. Thauvette, Sec., 1299 Principale, Très-St-Rédempteur, P.Q. JOP 1PO (514/451-5822)
Très-St-Sacrement (Paroisse)	1,386	Châteauguay		Huntingdon	G. Primeau, Sec., C.P. 126, Howick, P.Q. JOS 1GO (514/825-2032)
Tring-Jonction (Ville)	1,255	Beauce	Beauce	Beauce-Nord	M. Poulin, Sec., C.P. 10, Tring-Jonction, P.Q. GON 1XO (418/426-2497)
Trinité-des-Monts (Paroisse)	558	Rimouski		Rimouski	D. Michaud, Sec., La-Trinité-des-Monts, P.Q. GOK 1BO (418/779-2873)
Trois-Lacs (Mun.)	502	Arthabaska	Richmond	Richmond	B. Hinse, Sec., C.P. 51, Asbestos, P.Q. J1T 3M9 (819/879-4723)
Trois-Pistoles (Ville)	4,554	Rivière-du-Loup	Kamouraska-Rivière-du-Loup	Rivière-du-Loup	Gabriel Desjardins, Sec., 5 Notre-Dame est, Trois-Pistoles, P.Q. GOL 4KO (418/851-1995)
TROIS-RIVIERES (Ville)	51,200	St-Maurice	Trois-Rivières	Trois-Rivières	J. Lamy, Greffier, Hôtel de ville, C.P. 368, Trois-Rivières, P.Q. G9A 5H3 (819/374-3521)
Trois-Rivières-Ouest (Ville)	13,000	St-Maurice	Trois-Rivières	Maskinongé	C. Touzin, Greffier, 500 côte Richelieu, Trois-Rivières-Ouest, P.Q. G9A 2Z1 (819/375-7731)
Turgeon (Canton)	767	Labelle		Labelle	G. Conan, Sec., C.P. 150, Ste-Véronique, P.Q. JOW 1XO (819/275-3256)
Ulverton (Mun.)	309	Drummond	Richmond	Johnson	R.W. Simpson, Sec., R.R. 1, Melbourne, P.Q. JOB 2BO (819/826-2315)

Cities in CAPITALS (Ville); Towns/Villes marked (Ville); Villages marked (Village); Townships/Cantons (marked Canton); United townships/Cantons unis (marked Cantons*); Parishes marked (Paroisse); undesignated municipalities/sans designation marked (Mun.).

MUNICIPALITY	POP.	COUNTY	FEDERAL ELECTORAL DISTRICT	PROVINCIAL ELECTORAL DISTRICT	CLERK/GREFFIER OR SECRETARY-TREASURER (SEC) WITH ADDRESS & PHONE
Upton (Village)	832	Bagot	St-Hyacinthe	Johnson	Mme Y.H. Côté, Sec., C.P. 302, Upton, P.Q. JOH 2EO (514/549-4361)
Val-Alain (Mun.)	979	Lotbinière	Lotbinière	Lotbinière	D. Charbonneau, Sec., Val-Alain, P.Q. GOS 3HO (819/744-3222)
Val-Barrette (Village)	530	Labelle	Pontiac-Gatineau-Labelle	Labelle	C. Meilleur, Sec., C.P. 60, Val-Barrette, P.Q. JOW 1YO (819/585-3131)
Val-Bélair (Ville)	11,900	Québec	Portneuf	Chauveau	S. Mainguy, Sec., 1105 av. de l'Eglise nord, Val-Bélair, P.Q. GOA 1GO (418/842-1837)
Val-Brillant (Village)	683	Matapédia	Matapédia-Matane	Matapédia	Mme J. Saintonge, Sec., C.P. 215, Val-Brillant, P.Q. GOJ 3LO (418/742-3529)
Valcourt (Ville)	2,625	Shefford	Shefford	Johnson	P.-A. Giguère, Sec., C.P. 340, Valcourt, P.Q. JOE 2LO (514/532-3313)
Valcourt (Canton)	1,062	Shefford	Shefford	Johnson	C. Bombardier, Sec., R.R. 2, C.P. 219, Valcourt, P.Q. JOE 2LO (514/532-2688)
Val-David (Village)	2,150	Terrebonne	Labelle	Labelle	H. Auger, Sec., C.P. 220, Val-David, P.Q. JOT 2NO (819/322-2900)
Val-des-Bois (Mun.)	377	Papineau	Gatineau	Papineau	R. Bisson, Sec., Val-des-Bois, P.Q. JOX 3CO (819/454-2280)
Val-des-Lacs (Mun.)	419	Montcalm	Labelle	Labelle	Suzanne Valiquette, Sec., Val-des-Lacs, P.Q. JOT 2PO (819/326-5624)
Val-des-Monts (Mun.)	3,551	Papineau		Papineau	M. Emond, Sec., Val-des-Monts, P.Q. JOX 2RO (819/663-7759)
Val-d'Or (Ville)	20,000	Abitibi	Abitibi	Abitibi-Est	J.-A. Chouinard, Greffier, C.P. 400, Val-d'Or, P.Q. J9P 4P4 (819/824-9613)
Vallée-Jonction (Ville)	1,300	Beauce	Beauce	Beauce-Nord	G. Boily, Sec., C.P. 218, Vallée-Jonction, P.Q. GOS 3JO (418/253-5515)
Val-Morin (Mun.)	1,112	Terrebonne	Labelle	Labelle	M. Hews, Sec., C.P. 210, Val-Morin, P.Q. JOT 2RO (819/322-3635)
Val-Racine (Paroisse)	120	Frontenac	Mégantic-Compton-Stanstead	Mégantic-Compton	V. Dubé, Sec., R.R. 1, boite 13, Milan, P.Q. GOY 1EO (819/657-4730)
Val Senneville (Mun.)	820	Abitibi	Abitibi	Abitibi-Est	M. Thibault, Sec., C.P. 7, Senneville, P.Q. J0Y 2P0 (819/824-8356)
Val-St-Gilles (Mun.)	265	Abitibi	Témiscamingue	Abitibi-Ouest	R.-A. Richard, Sec., Val-St-Gilles, P.Q. JOZ 3TO (819/333-2158)
Vanier (Ville)	10,900	Québec	Québec-Est	Vanier	R. Gauvin, Greffier, 313 Bélanger, Vanier, P.Q. G1M 1V9 (418/687-3530)
VARENNES (Ville)	6,700	Verchères	Verchères	Bertrand	J.-G. Champoux, Sec., (175 Ste-Anne) C.P. 800, Varennes, P.Q. JOL 2PO (514/652-9888)
Vassan (Mun.)	1,100		Abitibi	Abitibi-Est	A. Boucher, Sec., Vassan, P.Q. JOY 2RO (819/824-8183)
Vaudreuil (Ville)	5,600	Vaudreuil	Vaudreuil	Vaudreuil-Soulanges	L. Lemire, Greffier, 2 rue Dutrisac, Vaudreuil, P.Q. J7V 7E6 (514/455-3371)
Vaudreuil-sur-le-Lac (Village)	450	Vaudreuil	Vaudreuil	Vaudreuil-Soulanges	R. Laberge, Sec., 420 boul. Roche, Vaudreuil, P.Q. J7V 5V5 (514/455-1133)

Cities in CAPITALS (Ville); Towns/Villes marked (Ville); Villages marked (Village); Townships/Cantons (marked Canton); United townships/Cantons unis (marked Cantons*); Parishes marked (Paroisse); undesignated municipalities/sans designation marked (Mun.).

MUNICIPALITY	POP.	COUNTY	FEDERAL ELECTORAL DISTRICT	PROVINCIAL ELECTORAL DISTRICT	CLERK/GREFFIER OR SECRETARY-TREASURER (SEC) WITH ADDRESS & PHONE
Venise-en-Québec (Mun.)	660	Missisquoi		Iberville	C. Desranleau, Sec., C.P. 111, Venise-en-Québec, P.Q. JOJ 2KO (514/244-5353)
Verchères (Ville)	3,586	Verchères	Verchères	Verchères	P. Colette, Sec., 581 Marie-Victorin, Verchères, P.Q. JOL 2RO (514/583-3077)
VERDUN (Ville)	68,000	Ile-de-Montréal	Verdun	Ste-Anne; Verdun	J.-N. Lefebvre, Greffier, 4555 av. Verdun, Verdun, P.Q. H4G 1M4 (514/769-2701)
Victoriaville (Ville)	21,100	Arthabaska	Lotbinière	Arthabaska	G.-H. Boisvert, Greffier, Hôtel de ville, C.P. 370, Victoriaville, P.Q. G6P 6T2 (819/758-8291)
Ville-Marie (Ville)	2,294	Témiscamingue	Témiscamingue	Rouyn-Noranda-Témiscamingue	G. Bernier, Sec., C.P. 70, Ville-Marie, P.Q. JOZ 3WO (819/629-2881)
Villeroy (Mun.)	535	Lotbinière	Lotbinière	Lotbinière	Laurette Paradis, Sec., Villeroy, P.Q. GOS 3HO (819/385-4605)
Vinoy (Mun.)	77	Papineau		Papineau	Mme C. Proulx, Sec., R.R. 1, Chénéville, P.Q. JOV 1EO (819/428-3713)
Waltham et Bryson (Cantons)*	466	Pontiac		Pontiac	G.-A. Labelle, Sec., C.P. 29, Waltham Station, P.Q. JOX 3HO (819/689-2342)
Warden (Village)	418	Shefford	Shefford	Shefford	R. Roy, Sec., C.P. 90, Warden, P.Q. JOE 2MO (514/539-1109)
Warwick (Canton)	1,728	Arthabaska		Arthabaska	J.-G. Laroche, Sec., C.P. 160, Warwick, P.Q. JOA 1MO (819/358-6017)
WARWICK (Ville)	2,900	Arthabaska	Lotbinière	Arthabaska	R. Bellefeuille, Greffier, C.P. 70, Warwick, P.Q. JOA 1MO (819/358-2323)
Waswanipi (Village)		Terr. Nouveau Québec	Abitibi	Ungava	La Sécretaire du Village, Waswanipi, P.Q.
Waterloo (Ville)	4,759	Shefford	Shefford	Shefford	R. Bellefeuille, Greffier, C.P. 50, Waterloo, P.Q. JOE 2NO (514/539-2282)
Waterville (Ville)	1,476	Compton	Mégantic-Compton-Stanstead	St-François	G. Boisvert, Sec., C.P. 40, Waterville, P.Q. JOB 3HO (819/837-2456)
Weedon (Canton)	563				Voir Weedon-Centre (Village)
Weedon-Centre (Village)	1,244	Wolfe	Richmond	Mégantic-Compton	R. Tardif, Sec., 450 2e Ave., Weedon-Centre, P.Q. JOB 3JO (819/877-2727)
Wendover et Simpson (Cantons)*	5,200	Drummond		Drummond	M.-A. Joyal, Sec., 1250 rue Proulx, St-Charles, Drummondville-Nord, P.Q. J2C 5A2 (819/397-4226)
Wentworth (Canton)	210	Argenteuil		Argenteuil	Mrs. J. Seale, Sec., R.R. 6, Lachute, P.Q. J8H 3W8 (514/533-6567)
Wentworth-Nord (Mun.)	460	Argenteuil		Argenteuil	Mme J. Strecko, Sec., C.P. 38, Laurel, (Montfort) P.Q. JOT 1YO (514/226-2416)
Westbury (Canton)	778	Compton		Mégantic-Compton	Pauline Paré, Sec., C.P. 40, East Angus, P.Q. JOB 1RO (819/832-3966)
WESTMOUNT (Ville)	21,600	Ile-de-Montréal	St-Henri-Westmount	Westmount	P. Patenaude, Greffier, 4333 Sherbrooke ouest, Westmount, P.Q. H3Z 1E2 (514/935-8531)
Wickham (Mun.)	1,720	Drummond	Drummond	Johnson	R. Dulmaine, Sec., C.P. 9, Wickham, P.Q. JOC 1SO (819/398-6340)

Cities in CAPITALS (Ville); Towns/Villes marked (Ville); Villages marked (Village); Townships/Cantons (marked Canton); United townships/Cantons unis (marked Cantons*); Parishes marked (Paroisse); undesignated municipalities/sans designation marked (Mun.).

MUNICIPALITY	POP.	COUNTY	FEDERAL ELECTORAL DISTRICT	PROVINCIAL ELECTORAL DISTRICT	CLERK/GREFFIER OR SECRETARY-TREASURER (SEC) WITH ADDRESS & PHONE
Windsor (Ville)	5,500	Richmond	Richmond	Johnson	J. Plante, Greffier, C.P. 1400, Windsor, P.Q. J1S 1J3 (819/845-2252)
Windsor (Canton)	1,522	Richmond		Johnson	Mme Moreau, Sec., C.P. 5, Windsor, P.Q. J1S 2L7 (819/845-2761)
Woodbridge (Canton)	668	Kamouraska		Kamouraska-Témiscouata	Suzanne Dionne, Sec., C.P. 57, Bruno-de-Kamouraska, P.Q. GOL 2MO (418/492-2612)
Wotton (Canton)	826	Wolfe		Richmond	B. Dion, Sec., C.P. 120, Wotton, P.Q. JOA 1NO (819/828-2144)
Wottonville (Village)	705	Wolfe	Richmond	Richmond	B. Nault, Sec., C.P. 60, Wotton, P.Q. JOA 1NO (819/828-2112)
Wright (Canton)	893	Gatineau		Gatineau	P. Monette, Sec., R.R. 3, Gracefield, P.Q. JOX 1WO (819/463-2143)
Yamachiche (Village)	1,186	St-Maurice	Trois-Rivières	Maskinongé	L. Desaulniers, Sec., C.P. 338, Yamachiche, P.Q. GOX 3LO (819/296-3330)
Yamaska (Village)	404	Yamaska	Richelieu	Richelieu	C. Villard, Sec., 85 Principale, Yamaska, P.Q. JOG 1WO (514/789-2333)
Yamaska-Est (Village)	322	Yamaska	Richelieu	Nicolet	D. Desmarais, Sec., 43 Guilbault, Yamaska-Est, P.Q. JOG 1XO (514/789-2175)

COUNTY MUNICIPALITIES, QUEBEC

County (County Town) Secretary-Treasurer and address:

Abitibi (Amos) P.E. Bégin, Comté Sec., C.P. 214, Amos, P.Q. J9T 3A6 (819/732-3503)
Argenteuil (Lachute) R. Desormeaux, Comté Sec., 430 Grace, C.P. 188, Lachute, P.Q. J8H 3X3 (514/562-4959)
Arthabaska (Arthabaska) C. Aubert, Comté Sec., 702 boul. Bois-Francs-Sud, Arthabaska, P.Q. G6P 5W3 (819/357-8266)
Bagot (St-Liboire) J.-N. Lemonde, Comté Sec., C.P. 120, St-Liboire, P.Q. JOH 1RO (514/793-2811)
Beauce (Beauceville) H. Rodrigue, Comté Sec., 277 ave. Lambert, Beauceville-Ouest, P.Q. GOM 1AO (418/774-9007)
Beauharnois (Beauharnois) R. Lupien, Comté Sec., 39 Jacques-Cartier, Valleyfield, P.Q. J6T 4R1 (514/373-4777)
Bellechasse (St-Raphael) Gabrielle Lantagne, Comté Sec., C.P. 129, St-Raphael, P.Q. GOR 4CO (418/243-6515)
Berthier (Berthierville) C. Joyal, Comté Sec., C.P. 750, Berthierville, P.Q. JOK 1AO (514/836-3748)
Bonaventure (New Carlisle) D. Smollett, Comté Sec., New Carlisle, P.Q. GOC 1ZO (418/752-3141)
Brome (Knowlton) J. Brunelle, Comté Sec., C.P. 810, Knowlton, P.Q. J0E 1V0 (514/243-6769)
Champlain (Ste-Geneviève-de-Batiscan) R. Bouchard, Comté Sec., C.P. 70, Batiscan, P.Q. GOX 1AO (418/362-2448)
Charlevoix-Est (La Malbaie) L. Bergeron, Comté Sec., 222 ch. de la Vallée, Rivière-Malbaie, P.Q. GOT 1JO (418/665-6321)
Charlevoix-Ouest (Baie-St-Paul) A. Lavoie, Comté Sec., C.P. 373, Baie-St-Paul, P.Q. GOA 1BO (418/435-2639)
Châteauguay (Ste-Martine) G. Primeau, Comté Sec., 164 St-Joseph, Ste-Martine, P.Q. JOS 1VO (514/825-2032)
Chicoutimi (Chicoutimi) J.-R. Turcotte, Comté Sec., C.P. 130, St-Fulgence, P.Q. GOV 1GO (418/674-2651)
Compton (Cookshire) J. Hivert, Comté Sec., C.P. 250, Cookshire, P.Q. JOB 1MO (819/875-3966)
Deux-Montagnes (Mirabel) Yvon Bélair, Comté Sec., 910 Principale, St-Joseph-du-Lac, P.Q. JON 1MO (514/473-2532)
Dorchester (Ste-Hénédine) C. Gagné, Comté Sec., Ste-Hénédine, P.Q. GOS 2RO (418/935-3795)
Drummond (Drummondville) R. Malouin, Comté Sec., 436 rue Lindsay, #102, Drummondville, P.Q. J2B 1G6 (819/477-2230)
Frontenac (Lac-Mégantic) L.-L. Bourque, Comté Sec., 5335 rue Frontenac, Lac Mégantic, P.Q. G6B 1H4 (819/583-3676)
Gaspé-Est (Percé) Owen Bouchard, Comté Sec., C.P. 9, Percé, P.Q. GOC 2LO (418/782-2061)
Gaspé-Ouest (Ste-Anne-des-Monts) J.-G. Lemieux, Comté Sec., C.P. 130, Mont-Louis, P.Q. GOE 1TO (418/797-2310)
Gatineau (Maniwaki) H. Kelly, Comté Sec., C.P. 307, Gracefield, P.Q. JOX 1WO (819/463-5445)
Huntingdon (Huntingdon) Ross Antaya, Comté Sec., C.P. 808, Huntingdon, P.Q. JOS 1HO (514/264-5411)
Iberville (Iberville) B. Larocque, Comté Sec., 55 5e Ave., Iberville, P.Q. J2X 1T1 (514/346-3636)
Iles-de-la-Madeleine (Ile-du-Havre-Aubert) Lise Chevrier, Comté Sec., C.P. 111, Iles-de-la-Madeleine, P.Q. GOB 1KO (418/986-4251)
Joliette (Joliette) L. Grypinich, Comté Sec., 90 rue Bernard, St-Charles-Borromée, P.Q. J6E 2C3 (514/756-1881)
Kamouraska (St-Pascal) Guy Lavoie, Comté Sec., C.P. 6, St-André, P.Q. GOL 2HO (418/493-2130)
Labelle (Mont-Laurier) Yvan Deslauriers, Comté Sec., 515 boul. Paquette, Mont Laurier, P.Q. J9L 1K9 (819/623-3485)
Lac-St-Jean-Est (Alma) G. Gagnon, Comté Sec., 351 rue Turgeon, Hébertville, Lac-St-Jean, P.Q. GOW 1SO (418/344-1302)
Lac-St-Jean-Ouest (Roberval) G. Boivin, Comté Sec., C.P. 417, Normandin, P.Q. GOW 2EO (418/274-2023)
Laprairie (La Prairie) G. Péladeau, Comté Sec., 210 St-Jacques, La Prairie, P.Q. J5R 1G3 (514/659-1975)
L'Assomption (L'Assomption) G. Giguère, Comté Sec., 255 St-Etienne, Ville de l'Assomption, P.Q. JOK 1GO (514/589-4491)
Lévis (St-Romuald-d'Etchemin) R. Noel, Comté Sec., 1000 rue St-Joseph, Bernières, P.Q. GOS 1CO (418/831-8877)
L'Islet (St-Jean-Port-Joli) B. Lévesque, Comté Sec., C.P. 457, St-Jean-Port-Joli, P.Q. GOR 3GO (418/598-6274)

Lotbinière (Ste-Croix) M. Lafleur, Comté Sec., 6310 Principale, Ste-Croix, P.Q. GOS 2HO (418/926-3015)
Maskinongé (Louiseville) G. Béland, Comté Sec., 151 St-Laurent, C.P. 56, Louiseville, P.Q. J5V 2L7 (819/228-4757)
Matane (Matane) R. Otis, Comté Sec., C.P. 187, Matane, P.Q. G4W 3B3 (418/562-2813)
Matapédia (Amqui) G. Paquet, Comté Sec., 27 boul. St-Benoît, Amqui, P.Q. GOJ 1BO (418/629-4248)
Mégantic (Inverness) V.R. Tremblay, Comté Sec., a/s R.R. 2, Thetford Mines, P.Q. G6G 5R6 (418/453-2470)
Missisquoi (Bedford) Y. Fortin, Comté Sec., C.P. 440, Bedford, P.Q. JOJ 1AO (514/248-2468)
Montcalm (Ste-Julienne) M. Sirois, Comté Sec., C.P. 187, Ste-Julienne, P.Q. JOK 2PO (514/831-2182)
Montmagny (Montmagny) B. Létourneau, Comté Sec., C.P. 325, Montmagny, P.Q. G5V 3S6 (418/248-2016)
Montmorency 1 (Château-Richer) D. Picard, Comté Sec., 8260 boul. Ste-Anne, Château-Richer, P.Q. GOA 1NO (418/824-4242)
Montmorency 2 (St-Famille, I.O.) J. Prémont, Comté Sec., 3893 ch. Royal, Ste-Famille, I.O., P.Q. GOA 3PO (418/829-2289)
Napierville (Napierville) Y. Dupont, Comté Sec., 361 St-Jacques, Napierville, P.Q. JOJ 1LO (514/245-3658)
Nicolet (Bécancour) A. Villeneuve, Comté Sec., 3723 St-Joseph, Gentilly, Bécancour, P.Q. GOX 1GO (514/222-5601)
Papineau (Papineauville) H. Servant, Comté Sec., C.P. 278, Papineauville, P.Q. JOV 1RO (819/427-6223)
Pontiac (Campbell's Bay) C. Robillard, Comté Sec., C.P. 340, Campbell's Bay, P.Q. JOX 1KO (819/648-5689)
Portneuf (Cap-Santé) F. Vauquelin, Comté Sec., 15 Vieux Chemin, Cap-Santé, P.Q. GOA 1LO (418/285-1207)
Québec (Loretteville) R. L'Heureux, Comté Sec., 102 Racine, Loretteville, P.Q. G2B 1C7 (418/842-1928)
Richelieu (Sorel) O. Bardier, Comté Sec., 520 Ch. Ste-Victoire, Ste-Victoire-de-Sorel, P.Q. JOG 1TO (514/782-2130)
Richmond (Richmond) A. Marier, Comté Sec., 11 Valiquette, Greenlay, P.Q. (819/845-2616)
Rimouski (Rimouski) R. Gagnon, Comté Sec., C.P. 387, Rimouski, P.Q. G5L 7C3 (418/723-5983)
Rivière-du-Loup (Rivière-du-Loup) Jeanne-d'Arc Ouellet, Comté Sec., C.P. 100, Ste-Epiphane, P.Q. GOL 2XO (418/862-3214)
Rouville (Marieville) Mrs. R. Rondeau, Comté Sec., 274 Ruisseau, Barré, Marieville, P.Q. JOL 1JO (514/466-7807)
Saguenay (Tadoussac) P. Bouchard, Comté Sec., 202 Thibault, Grandes-Bergeronnes, P.Q. GOT 1GO (418/232-6242)
St-Hyacinthe (St-Hyacinthe) M. Gaudet, Comté Sec., 308 rue St-Denis, St-Denis-sur-Richelieu, P.Q. JOH 1KO (514/787-2255)
St-Jean (St-Jean) A. O'Cain, Comté Sec., C.P. 281, St-Jean, P.Q. J3B 4L8 (514/348-6235)
St-Maurice (Yamachiche) J.-A. Pellerin, Comté Sec., 631 Ste-Anne, Yamachiche, P.Q. GOX 3LO (819/296-3330)
Shefford (Waterloo) B. Ledoux, Comté Sec., 398 rue Principale, Granby, P.Q. J2G 2W6 (514/378-6228)
Sherbrooke (Sherbrooke) G. Moreau, Comté Sec., C.P. 120, Rock Forest, P.Q. JOB 2JO (819/567-6482)
Soulanges (Coteau Landing) G. Thibault, Comté Sec., 173 Principale, Coteau Landing, P.Q. JOP 1CO (514/267-3204)
Stanstead (Ayer's Cliff) J.-P. Asselin, Comté Sec., C.P. 400, Magog, P.Q. J1X 3X7 (819/843-3286)
Témiscamingue (Ville-Marie) Denis Clermont, Comté Sec., C.P. 548, Ville-Marie, P.Q. JOZ 3WO (819/629-2829)
Témiscouata (Notre-Dame-du-Lac) Mrs. R.B. Charest, Comté Sec., C.P. 1, Sully, P.Q. GOL 4JO (418/859-2450)
Terrebonne (St-Jérôme) A. Tassé, Comté Sec., 236 ave. du Palais, ste. 206, St-Jérôme, P.Q. J7Z 1X8 (514/455-5611)
Vaudreuil (Vaudreuil) F.-E. Belliveau, Comté Sec., 420 boul. Roche, Vaudreuil, P.Q. J7V 2N1 (514/455-3691)
Verchères (Verchères) C. Geoffrion, Comté Sec., 611 Marie Victorin, C.P. 100, Verchères, P.Q. JOL 2RO (514/583-3535)
Wolfe (Ham-Sud) M. Lamoureux, Comté Sec., Ham-Sud, P.Q. JOB 3JO (819/877-2522)
Yamaska (St-François-du-Lac) R. Tessier, Comté Sec., C.P. 127, St-François-du-Lac, P.Q. JOG 1MO (514/568-3144)

Quebec Urban Communities (Regional Governments):

Communauté urbaine de Montréal (Montréal) G. Duhamel, Sec., 2 Complexe Desjardins, C.P. 129, Montréal, P.Q. H5B 1E6 (514/872-5246)
Communauté urbaine de Québec (Québec) Yvan Dallaire, Sec., 930 Chemin Ste-Foy, Québec, P.Q. G1S 2K9 (418/681-9611)
Communauté régionale de l'Outaouais (Hull) J.-G. Gariépy, Sec., 92 boul. St-Raymond, C.P. 210, Succ. A, Hull, P.Q. J8Y 1S7 (819/770-1380)

SASKATCHEWAN

Acts governing the municipal system in Saskatchewan are The Urban Municipality Act, and The Rural Municipality Act. There is also an Act called the Municipal Unit and County Act providing enabling legislation to create Counties if Rural and Urban municipalities so desire. The Act is based on voluntary consent. So far, no counties have been created in Saskatchewan. In the province there are the following types of incorporated municipalities: Organized Hamlets, Rural Municipalities, Villages, Towns and Cities. Subject to the critria outlined below, the incorporation of these municipalities is voluntary. Thus, a Village that qualifies to be named a Town, can remain a Village if the population so wishes.

Hamlets:- defined "organized" or "unorganized". They are not defined according to population, but are subdivisions of land divided into lots, blocks, or parcels for the purpose of a townsite plan and must be registered in the Land Titles Office of the District in which they are located. The Minister of Municipal Affairs is the sole authority for declaring a subdivision as a "hamlet". *Unorganized Hamlets* are defined as urban communities located in Rural Municipalities. They have *no* local representatives and are administered by the council of the Rural Municipality in which they are located. *Organized Hamlets* are declared after two-thirds of resident voters in an unorganized hamlet agree through the ballot box to organize. The Minister approves the decision to incorporate. Once "organized", the eligible electorate of the hamlet are entitled to annually elect three people from their number to form a Hamlet Board who strike a budget and submit it to the Rural Municipal Council in which the Hamlet is situated. The Rural Municipal Council administers the budget retaining at least twenty five per cent. of the same for administration overhead.

Villages:- are defined as communities with not less than 100 permanent residents and a taxable assessment of $200,000. The Village is represented by a Mayor and two to four councillors. The Mayor is elected by the eligible electorate every two years, the councillors every four.

Towns:- are defined as communities with not less than 500 permanent residents. They are represented by a Mayor and six councillors elected at large by the eligible electorate; the Mayor every two years, the councillors every four.

Cities:- are defined as communities with not less than 5,000 residents. They are represented by a Mayor and Aldermen (the number varies according to the number of Wards within municipal boundaries). Elections for all are every three years.

Rural Municipalities:- are declared and divided into Divisions according to a population/area formula. They are represented by a Reeve elected at large every two years. Councillors are also elected every two years but in 'staggered' sequence.

Municipal nominations are held Fourth Monday in October and elections on Wednesday of the following week for Rural Municipalities. Nominations are held in Urban Municipalities on the second Wednesday in October and elections on the fourth Wednesday in October.

Cities in CAPITALS; Towns marked †; Villages marked ‡; Balance are Rural Municipalities.
Area Code for Saskatchewan is 306

MUNICIPALITY	POP.	FEDERAL ELECTORAL DISTRICT	PROVINCIAL ELECTORAL DISTRICT	ADM. OR SECRETARY WITH ADDRESS & PHONE
Abbey‡	259	Swift Current-Maple Creek	Maple Creek	R.B. Sylvestre, Village Sec., Abbey, Sask. SON OAO (689-2281)
Aberdeen‡	445	Humboldt-Lake Centre	Kinistino	Ms. C. Unger, Village Sec., Aberdeen, Sask. SOK OAO (253-4311)
Aberdeen RM No. 373	771			G. Schmidt, Sec., Box 40, Aberdeen, Sask. SOK OAO (253-4312)
Abernethy RM No. 186	714			E.G. Behrns, Sec., Box 219, Abernethy, Sask. SOA OAO (333-2044)
Abernethy‡	305	Qu'Appelle-Moose Mountain	Melville	Mrs. J. Legaarden, Village Sec., Abernethy, Sask. SOA OAO (333-2271)
Adanac‡	29	Kindersley-Lloydminster	Wilkie	Mrs. V. Ralston, Village Sec., Adanac, Sask. SOK 4LO (228-2037)
Admiral‡	66	Swift Current-Maple Creek	Shaunavon	Mrs. Madeleine Spetz, Village Sec., Admiral, Sask. SON OBO (297-6356)
Alameda†	319	Qu'Appelle-Moose Mountain	Morse	Diane Truscot, Town Adm., Alameda, Sask. SOC OAO (489-2077)
Alida‡	171	Qu'Appelle-Moose Mountain	Souris-Cannington	Rod Heise, Village Sec., Alida, Sask. SOC OBO (443-2212)
Allan†	720	Humboldt-Lake Centre	Rosthern	S. Olszewski, Town Adm., Allan, Sask. SOK OCO (257-3272)
Alsask‡	288	Kindersley-Lloydminster	Kindersley	Mrs. R. Anderson, Village Sec., Alsask, Sask. SOL OAO (968-2394)
Alvena‡	114	Humboldt-Lake Centre	Kinistino	Wm. Magus, Village Sec., Alvena, Sask. SOK OEO (943-2101)
Aneroid‡	153	Swift Current-Maple Creek	Shaunavon	Mrs. I. Kemp, Village Sec., Aneroid, Sask. SON OCO (588-2300)
Annaheim‡	221	Humboldt-Lake Centre	Melfort	J. Verhelst, Village Sec., Annaheim, Sask. SOK OGO (598-2122)
Antelope Park RM No. 322	294			E. Murray, Sec., Box 70, Marengo, Sask. SOL 2KO (968-2759)
Antler‡	111	Qu'Appelle-Moose Mountain	Souris-Cannington	K. Dyon, Village Sec., Antler, Sask. S0L 0L0 (452-6155)
Antler RM No. 61	900			J.R. Robins, Sec., Box 70, Redvers, Sask. SOC 2HO (452-3263)
Arborfield†	463	Mackenzie	Nipawin	E.P. Sawchyn, Town Adm., Arborfield, Sask. SOE OAO (769-8533)
Arborfield RM No. 456	790			c/o Arborfield Town Clerk
Archerwill‡	313	Mackenzie	Kelsey-Tisdale	Mrs. B.J. Thuen, Village Sec., Archerwill, Sask. SOE OBO (323-2161)
Arcola†	547	Qu'Appelle-Moose Mountain	Souris-Cannington	C.W. Kellington, Town Adm., Arcola, Sask. SOC OGO (455-2212)
Arelee‡	69	Saskatoon West	Biggar	Ray Gaudet, Village Sec., Arelee, Sask. SOK OHO (237-4424)
Argyle RM No. 1	445			B.N. Brown, Sec., Gainsborough, Sask. SOC OZO (685-2010)
Arlington RM No. 79	459			J.R. Ballentine, Sec., Box 1115, Shaunavon, Sask. SON 2MO (297-2108)
Arm River RM No. 252	414			M.C. Boyle, Sec., Box 250, Davidson, Sask. SOG 1AO (567-3103)
Arran‡	110	Yorkton-Melville	Pelly	Mike Burtnack, Village Sec., Arran, Sask. SOA OBO (595-4521)
Asquith†	511	Saskatoon West	Biggar	Mrs. A. Raycraft, Town Adm., Asquith, Sask. SOK OJO (329-4341)
Assiniboia†	2,973	Assiniboia	Assiniboia-Gravelbourg	K. Bridges, Town Adm., Assiniboia, Sask. SOH OBO (642-4424)
Atwater‡	80	Qu'Appelle-Moose Mountain	Saltcoats	Mrs. G. Knezacek, Village Sec., Atwater, Sask. SOA OCO (745-2772)
Auvergne RM No. 76	606			George Faucher, Sec., Box 60, Ponteix, Sask. SON 1ZO (625-3210)
Avonlea‡	458	Assiniboia	Bengough-Milestone	Tim Forer, Village Sec., Avonlea, Sask. SOH OCO (868-2221)
Aylesbury‡	80	Moose Jaw	Arm River	Dorothy Thomas, Village Sec., Aylesbury, Sask. SOG OBO (734-2930)
Aylsham‡	153	Mackenzie	Nipawin	Mrs. L. MacFarlane, Village Sec., Aylsham, Sask. SOE OCO (862-9415)
Baildon RM No. 131	750			D. McCallum, Sec., Box 52, Sub #1, Moose Jaw, Sask. S6H 5VO (693-2166)

Cities in CAPITALS; Towns marked †; Villages marked ‡; Balance are Rural Municipalities .
Area Code for Saskatchewan is 306

MUNICIPALITY	POP.	FEDERAL ELECTORAL DISTRICT	PROVINCIAL ELECTORAL DISTRICT	ADM. OR SECRETARY WITH ADDRESS & PHONE
Balcarres†	729	Qu'Appelle-Moose Mountain	Melville	P. Boivin, Town Adm., Balcarres, Sask. SOG OCO (334-2566)
Balgonie†	715	Regina East	Qu'Appelle	Mrs. B. Marcia, Town Adm., Balgonie, Sask. SOG OEO (637-2284)
Bangor‡	77	Qu'Appelle-Moose Mountain	Saltcoats	Mrs. J. Bomberak, Village Sec., Bangor, Sask. SOA OEO (728-4084)
Barrier Valley RM No. 397	831			Mrs. Fern Lucas, Sec., McKague, Sask. SOE OZO (873-5604)
Battleford†	3,212	The Battlefords-Meadow Lake	The Battlefords	Gary Gelech, Town Adm., Battleford, Sask. SOM OEO (937-2653)
Battle River RM No. 438	733			Mrs. V. Ireland, Sec., Box 148, Battleford, Sask. SOM OEO (937-2235)
Bayne RM No. 371	1,454			Mrs. B.M. Hassen, Sec., Box 130, Bruno, Sask. SOK OSO (369-2511)
Beatty‡	110	Prince Albert	Melfort	James Mason, Village Sec., Beatty, Sask. SOJ OCO (752-3980)
Beaver River RM No. 622	1,288			C. Johnson, Sec., Box 129, Pierceland, Sask. SOM 2KO (839-2060)
Beechy‡	344	Kindersley-Lloydminster	Rosetown-Elrose	Mrs. M. Pearson, Village Sec., Box 153, Beechy, Sask. SOL OCO (859-2205)
Belle Plaine‡	68	Moose Jaw	Thunder Creek	Reg McKee, Village Sec., Belle Plaine, Sask. SOG OGO
Bengough†	603	Assiniboia	Bengough-Milestone	Ms. A. Reitenbach, Town Adm., Bengough, Sask. SOC OKO (268-2927)
Bengough RM No. 40	637			D.L. Leflar, Sec., Box 329, Bengough, Sask. SOC OKO (268-2055)
Benson‡	82	Assiniboia	Estevan	Mrs. D. Hawaleska, Village Sec., Benson, Sask. SOC OLO (634-7591)
Benson RM No. 35	668			Loris Shauf, Sec., Box 69, Benson, Sask. SOC OLO (634-6323)
Bethune‡	317	Moose Jaw	Thunder Creek	Mrs. J. Riche, Village Sec., Bethune, Sask. SOG OHO (638-3188)
Bienfait†	816	Assiniboia	Estevan	Elaine Konkin, Town Adm., Bienfait, Sask. SOC OMO (388-2344)
Big Arm RM No. 251	441	Moose Jaw	Arm River	W. Krawchuk, Sec., Box 10, Stalwart, Sask. SOG 4RO (963-2402)
Biggar†	2,511	Kindersley-Lloydminster	Biggar	R.G. Tyler, Town Adm., Box 489, Biggar, Sask. SOK OMO (948-3317)
Biggar RM No. 347	1,190			Mrs. Jane Morrow, Sec., Box 280, Biggar, Sask. SOK OMO (948-2422)
Big Quill RM No. 308	1,053			Wm. Krochak, Sec., Box 898, Wynyard, Sask. SOA 4TO (554-2533)
Big River†	838	The Battlefords-Meadow Lake	Turtleford	Tim Leurer, Town Adm., Big River, Sask. SOJ OEO (469-2112)
Big River RM No. 555	767			Mrs. Ivy Johnson, Sec., Box 219, Big River, Sask. SOJ OEO (469-2323)
Big Stick RM No. 141	286			Ms. O. Blohm, Sec., Box 9, Golden Prairie, Sask. SON OYO (667-3400)
Birch Hills†	926	Prince Albert	Kinistino	C.S. Friesen, Town Adm., Birch Hills, Sask. SOJ OGO (749-2232)
Birch Hills RM No. 460	962			Mrs. A. Crawford, Sec., Box 369, Birch Hills, Sask. SOJ OGO (749-2233)
Birsay‡	109	Kindersley-Lloydminster	Rosetown-Elrose	E.J. Whiteside, Village Sec., Birsay, Sask. SOL OGO (573-2011)
Bjorkdale‡	248	Mackenzie	Kelsey-Tisdale	Ms. J. Kehrig, Village Sec., Bjorkdale, Sask. SOE OEO (886-2167)
Bjorkdale RM No. 426	1,510			J.G. Kozakavich, Sec., Box 10, Crooked River, Sask. SOE ORO (873-5586)
Bladworth‡	112	Moose Jaw	Arm River	L.M. McCreary, Village Sec., Box 69, Bladworth, Sask. SOG OJO (567-5526)
Blaine Lake†	631	Prince Albert	Redberry	Eleanora Boyko, Town Adm., Blaine Lake, Sask. SOJ OJO (497-2531)
Blaine Lake RM No. 434	626			J. Burak, Sec., Box 38, Blaine Lake, Sask. SOJ OJO (497-2282)
Blucher RM No. 343	957			M.T. Elash, Sec., Box 100, Bradwell, Sask. SOK OPO (257-3344)
Bone Creek RM No. 108	601			E.K. Olson, Sec., 332 Center St., Shaunavon, Sask. SON 2MO (297-2570)

Cities in CAPITALS; Towns marked †; Villages marked ‡; Balance are Rural Municipalities .
Area Code for Saskatchewan is 306

MUNICIPALITY	POP.	FEDERAL ELECTORAL DISTRICT	PROVINCIAL ELECTORAL DISTRICT	ADM. OR SECRETARY WITH ADDRESS & PHONE
Borden‡	207	The Battlefords-Meadow Lake	Redberry	Mrs. S. Jonca, Village Sec., Borden, Sask. SOK ONO (997-2134)
Bounty‡	44	Kindersley-Lloydminster	Rosetown-Elrose	Mrs. K. Logan, Village Sec., Bounty, Sask. SOL OLO (856-4825)
Bracken‡	60	Swift Current-Maple Creek	Shaunavon	Mrs. D. Peakman, Village Sec., Bracken, Sask. SON OGO (293-2945)
Bradwell‡	153	Humboldt-Lake Centre	Rosthern	M.T. Elash, Village Sec., Bradwell, Sask. SOK OPO (257-3344)
Bratt's Lake RM No. 129	550			Kevin Ritchie, Sec., Box 130, Wilcox, Sask. SOG 5EO (732-2030)
Bredenbury†	441	Yorkton-Melville	Saltcoats	Mrs. O. Mosiman, Town Adm., Bredenbury, Sask. SOA OHO (898-2055)
Briercrest‡	139	Moose Jaw	Thunder Creek	Mrs. R. Johnston, Village Sec., Briercrest, Sask. SOH OKO (799-2005)
Britannia RM No. 502	1,245			E.A. Henning, Sec.,Box 661, Lloydminster, Sask. S9V OY7 (825-2610)
Broadview†	861	Qu'Appelle-Moose Mountain	Indian Head-Wolseley	L.J. Norton, Town Adm., Broadview, Sask. SOG OKO (696-2533)
Brock‡	183	Kindersley-Lloydminster	Kindersley	Mrs. J. Anderson, Village Sec., Brock, Sask. SOL OHO (379-2021)
Brock RM No. 64	457			J.A. Jackson, Sec., Kisbey, Sask. SOC 1LO (462-2010)
Broderick‡	135	Moose Jaw	Arm River	Mrs. J. Pederson, Village Sec., Broderick, Sask. SOH OLO (867-8916)
Brokenshell RM No. 68	489			H.J. Riviere, Sec., Box 60, Trossachs, Sask. SOC 2NO (842-5820)
Browning RM No. 34	801			R.J. Kirkpatrick, Sec., Box 40, Lampman, Sask. SOC 1NO (487-2444)
Brownlee‡	92	Moose Jaw	Thunder Creek	Mrs. E. Butler, Village Sec., Brownlee, Sask. SOH OMO (759-2302)
Bruno†	828	Humboldt-Lake Centre	Humboldt	A.R. Meyer, Town Adm., Bruno, Sask. SOK OSO (369-2514)
B-Say-Tah‡	92	Regina East	Qu'Appelle	F.J. Taylor, B-Say-Tah Village Sec., c/o Box 908, Fort Qu'Appelle, Sask. (332-4405)
Buchanan‡	434	Yorkton-Melville	Canora	M.C. Brezinski, Village Sec., Buchanan, Sask. SOA OJO (592-2144)
Buchanan RM No. 304	986			K. Statchuk, Sec., Box 10, Buchanan, Sask. SOA OJO (592-2055)
Buckland RM No. 491	3,087			C.L. Marshall, Sec., 99 River St. E., Prince Albert, Sask. S6V OA1 (763-2585)
Buena Vista‡	90	Moose Jaw	Qu'Appelle	Mrs. M.J. Radosh, Village Sec., Buena Vista, Sask. S0G 4C0 (938-4385)
Buffalo RM No. 409	669			Ed Hoffart, Sec., Box 100, Wilkie, Sask. SOK 4WO (843-2301)
Bulyea‡	122	Humboldt-Lake Centre	Last Mountain-Touchwood	Mrs. M. Flotre, Village Sec., Bulyea, Sask. SOG OLO (725-4936)
Burstall†	575	Swift Current-Maple Creek	Maple Creek	Mrs. S.G. Schmidt, Town Adm., Burstall, Sask. SON OHO (679-2000)
Cabri†	631	Swift Current-Maple Creek	Morse	L.L. Larson, Town Adm., Cabri, Sask. SON OJO (587-2500)
Cadillac‡	203	Swift Current-Maple Creek	Shaunavon	Mrs. V.F. Kendall, Village Sec., Cadillac, Sask. SON OKO (785-2100)
Calder‡	160	Yorkton-Melville	Pelly	Mrs. H. Tkachuk, Village Sec., Calder, Sask. SOA OKO (742-2158)
Calder RM No. 241	917			J.L. Mihalicz, Sec., Box 10, Wroxton, Sask. SOA 4SO (742-4233)
Caledonia RM No. 99	578			E.P. Audette, Sec., Box 328, Milestone, Sask. SOG 3LO (436-2050)
Cambria RM No. 6	482			D.E. Shauf, Sec., Drawer 210, Torquay, Sask. SOC 2LO (923-2000)
Cana RM No. 214	1,273			J.B. Chesney, Sec., Box 550, Melville, Sask. SOA 2PO (728-5645)
Canaan RM No. 225	320			A. Holbird, Sec., Box 99, Lucky Lake, Sask. SOL 1ZO (858-2234)
Candle Lake‡	196	Prince Albert	Shellbrook	Ms. S. Doodchenko, Village Sec., Box 119 (Meath Park), Candle Lake, Sask. SOJ 1TO (929-2236)
Cando‡	148	Kindersley-Lloydminster	Biggar	Lloyd Dallas, Village Sec., Cando, Sask. SOK OVO (937-3611)

Cities in CAPITALS; Towns marked †; Villages marked ‡; Balance are Rural Municipalities .
Area Code for Saskatchewan is 306

MUNICIPALITY	POP.	FEDERAL ELECTORAL DISTRICT	PROVINCIAL ELECTORAL DISTRICT	ADM. OR SECRETARY WITH ADDRESS & PHONE
Canora†	2,790	Yorkton-Melville	Canora	M.G. Kozoriz, Town Adm., Canora, Sask. SOA OLO (563-5773)
Canwood‡	338	Prince Albert	Shellbrook	Mrs. M. Tuttroen, Village Sec., Canwood, Sask. SOJ OKO (468-2016)
Canwood RM No. 494	2,272			A.E. Moar, Sec., Box 10, Canwood, Sask. SOJ OKO(468-2014)
Carievale‡	269	Qu'Appelle-Moose Mountain	Souris-Cannington	Mrs. R. Cameron, Village Sec., Carievale, Sask. SOC OPO (928-2033)
Carlyle†	1,134	Qu'Appelle-Moose Mountain	Souris-Cannington	D. Miller, Town Adm., Carlyle, Sask. SOC ORO (453-2363)
Carmichael‡	13	Swift Current-Maple Creek	Maple Creek	E. Zubot, Village Sec., Carmichael, Sask. SON 1AO (672-3501)
Carmichael RM No. 109	541			E. Zubot, Sec., Box 548, Gull Lake, Sask. SON 1AO (672-3501)
Carnduff†	1,071	Qu'Appelle-Moose Mountain	Souris-Cannington	D.H. Preston, Town Adm., Carnduff, Sask. SOC OSO (482-3300)
Caron RM No. 162	923			Mrs. S. Sparkes, Sec., Caron, Sask. SOH ORO (756-2353)
Carragana‡	106	Mackenzie	Kelsey-Tisdale	Mrs. Vera Campbell, Village Sec., Carragana, Sask. SOE OKO (278-2782)
Carrot River†	1,196	Mackenzie	Nipawin	Duril Touet, Town Adm., Carrot River, Sask. SOE OLO (768-2515)
Central Butte†	518	Moose Jaw	Thunder Creek	Jerry Fizell, Town Adm., Central Butte, Sask. SOH OTO (796-2288)
Ceylon‡	259	Assiniboia	Bengough-Milestone	V.B. McClarty, Village Sec., Ceylon, Sask. SOC OTO (454-2202)
Chamberlain‡	133	Moose Jaw	Arm River	Gladys Gottselig, Village Sec., Chamberlain, Sask. SOG OBO (638-6235)
Chaplin‡	382	Moose Jaw	Thunder Creek	Mrs. C. Plonka, Village Sec., Chaplin, Sask. SOH OVO (395-2221)
Chaplin RM No. 164	356			Mrs. Doris Bauck, Sec., Box 60, Chaplin, Sask. SOH OVO (395-2244)
Chester RM No. 125	837			Wilfred Geber, Sec., Box 180, Glenavon, Sask. SOG 1YO (429-2110)
Chesterfield RM No. 261	711			Ms. B.A. Dahl, Sec., Box 70, Eatonia, Sask. SOL OYO (967-2222)
Chitek Lake‡	172	The Battlefords-Meadow Lake	Turtleford	I. Leona Henry, Village Sec., Chitek Lake, Sask. SOJ OLO (984-4431)
Choiceland†	535	Mackenzie	Shellbrook	Mrs. K. Vandine, Town Adm., Choiceland, Sask. SOJ OMO (428-2070)
Churchbridge†	979	Yorkton-Melville	Saltcoats	W.M. Whitmarsh, Town Adm., Churchbridge, Sask. SOA OMO (896-2240)
Churchbridge RM No. 211	1,234			C.P. Chyz, Sec., Box 211, Churchbridge, Sask. SOA OMO (896-2522)
Clavet‡	195	Humboldt-Lake Centre	Rosthern	M. Hutmacher, Village Sec., Clavet, Sask. SOK OYO (373-8992)
Clayton RM No. 333	1,495			Doug Ferder, Sec., Box 220, Hyas, Sask. SOA 1KO (594-2832)
Climax‡	297	Swift Current-Maple Creek	Shaunavon	R.J. Johnson, Village Sec., Box 30, Climax, Sask. SON ONO (293-2124)
Clinworth RM No. 230	497			Mrs. R.A. Eckert, Sec., Box 120, Sceptre, Sask. SON 2HO (623-4229)
Coalfields RM No. 4	549			H. Kostuik, Sec., Bienfait, Sask. SOC OMO (388-2323)
Coderre‡	115	Moose Jaw	Thunder Creek	Mrs. Faye Johnstone, Village Sec., Coderre, Sask. SOH OXO (394-2070)
Codette‡	253	Mackenzie	Nipawin	Mrs. Anne Broda, Village Sec., Codette, Sask. SOE OPO (862-9391)
Coleville‡	398	Kindersley-Lloydminster	Kindersley	W. Bruce, Village Sec., Coleville, Sask. SOL OKO (965-2281)
Colgate‡	63	Assiniboia	Bengough-Milestone	Mrs. R. Underwood, Village Sec., Colgate, Sask. SOC OVO (456-2495)
Colonsay†	604	Humboldt-Lake Centre	Humboldt	Mrs. B. Crench, Town Adm., Colonsay, Sask. SOK OZO (255-2313)
Colonsay RM No. 342	457			Walter Yablonski, Sec., Box 130, Colonsay, Sask. SOK OZO (255-2233)
Connaught RM No. 457	1,146			R.J. McPherson, Sec., Box 25, Tisdale, Sask. SOE 1TO (873-2657)

Cities in CAPITALS; Towns marked †; Villages marked ‡; Balance are Rural Municipalities .
Area Code for Saskatchewan is 306

MUNICIPALITY	POP.	FEDERAL ELECTORAL DISTRICT	PROVINCIAL ELECTORAL DISTRICT	ADM. OR SECRETARY WITH ADDRESS & PHONE
Conquest‡	265	Kindersley-Lloydminster	Rosetown-Elrose	Ms. M. Latimer, Village Sec., Conquest, Sask. SOL OLO (856-2114)
Consul‡	160	Swift Current-Maple Creek	Shaunavon	Leif Helmerson, Village Sec., Consul, Sask. SON OPO (299-2030)
Corman Park RM No. 344	5,625			F.J. Sutter, Sec., 414 20th St. E., Saskatoon, Sask. S7K OB1 (664-3149)
Coronach†	936	Assiniboia	Assiniboia-Gravelbourg	A.M. Thompson, Town Adm., Coronach, Sask. SOH OZO (267-2150)
Cote RM No. 271	950			L.L. Konkin, Sec., Box 669, Kamsack, Sask. SOA 1SO (542-2121)
Coteau RM No. 255	651			G. Reed, Sec., Birsay, Sask. SOL OGO (573-2047)
Coulee RM No. 136	783			Mrs. M. Weinbender, Sec., 1680 Chaplin St. E., Swift Current, Sask. S9H 1K8 (773-5420)
Craik†	565	Moose Jaw	Arm River	Mrs. Peggy Johnson, Town Adm., Craik, Sask. SOG OVO (734-2250)
Craik RM No. 222	472			J.A. Tallon, Sec., Box 420, Craik, Sask. SOG OVO (734-2242)
Craven‡	180	Moose Jaw	Qu'Appelle	M.A. Parker, Village Sec., Craven, Sask. SOG OWO (485-3452)
Creelman‡	190	Assiniboia	Weyburn	Mrs. D. Allan, Village Sec., Creelman, Sask. SOG OXO (433-2011)
Creighton†	1,746	Mackenzie	Cumberland	D.J. Gibson, Town Adm., Creighton, Sask. SOP OAO (204/687-4162)
Cudworth†	907	Humboldt-Lake Centre	Kinistino	J.W. Haines, Town Adm., Cudworth, Sask. SOK 1BO (256-3492)
Cupar†	611	Humboldt-Lake Centre	Last Mountain-Touchwood	Mrs. K.M. Brown, Town Adm., Cupar, Sask. SOG OYO (723-4324)
Cupar RM No. 218	870			B.M. Sali, Sec., Markinch, Sask. SOG 3JO (726-2063)
Cut Knife†	530	Kindersley-Lloydminster	Cutknife-Lloydminster	Richard Emanuel, Town Adm., Box 338, Cut Knife, Sask. SOM ONO (398-2363)
Cut Knife RM No. 439	546			H.W. Riekman, Sec., Box 70, Cutknife, Sask. SOM ONO (398-2353)
Cymri RM No. 36	696			G.A.H. Molberg, Sec., Box 238, Midale, Sask. SOC 1SO (458-2244)
Dafoe‡	37	Humboldt-Lake Centre	Quill Lakes	Mrs. R. Jordan, Village Sec., Dafoe, Sask. SOK 1CO (554-3240)
Dalmeny‡	843	Saskatoon West	Rosthern	C.W. Giesbrecht, Village Sec., Dalmeny, Sask. SOK 1EO (254-2133)
Davidson†	1,092	Moose Jaw	Arm River	L.E. Larson, Town Adm., Davidson, Sask. SOG 1AO (567-2040)
Debden‡	385	Prince Albert	Turtleford	Suzanne Grimard, Village Sec., Debden, Sask. SOJ OSO (724-2040)
Deer Forks RM No. 232	389			W.P. Rolick, Sec., Box 250, Burstall, Sask. SON OHO (679-2000)
Delisle†	932	Saskatoon West	Biggar	J.D. Arntsen, Town Adm., Delisle, Sask. SOL OPO (493-2242)
Denholm‡	81	The Battlefords-Meadow Lake	Redbury	Mrs. J.E. Voigt, Village Sec., Denholm, Sask. SOM ORO
Denzil‡	215	Kindersley-Lloydminster	Wilkie	Roxanne Junkin, Village Sec., Denzil, Sask. SOL OSO (358-2118)
Dilke‡	112	Moose Jaw	Arm River	Mrs. C.R. Duesing, Village Sec., Dilke, Sask. SOG 1CO (488-4866)
Dinsmore‡	411	Kindersley-Lloydminster	Rosetown-Elrose	Mrs. D. McPherson, Village Sec., Dinsmore, Sask. SOL OTO (846-2220)
Disley‡	46	Moose Jaw	Qu'Appelle	Ms. M.L. McClure, Village Sec., Disley, Sask. SOG 3CO (485-3283)
Dodsland‡	312	Kindersley-Lloydminster	Kindersley	Margaret McConnell, Village Sec., Dodsland, Sask. SOL OVO (356-2055)
Dollard‡	71	Swift Current-Maple Creek	Shaunavon	J.R. Ballentine, Village Sec., Dollard, Sask. SON 2MO (297-2108)
Domremy‡	188	Prince Albert	Kinistino	Mrs. L. Cousin, Village Sec., Domremy, Sask. SOK 1GO (423-5244)
Douglas RM No. 436	724			H. Nowoselski, Sec., Speers, Sask. SOM 2VO (246-2171)
Drake‡	251	Humboldt-Lake Centre	Quill Lakes	Mrs. E. Schroder, Village Sec., Drake, Sask. SOK 2MO (363-2109)

Cities in CAPITALS; Towns marked †; Villages marked ‡; Balance are Rural Municipalities .
Area Code for Saskatchewan is 306

MUNICIPALITY	POP.	FEDERAL ELECTORAL DISTRICT	PROVINCIAL ELECTORAL DISTRICT	ADM. OR SECRETARY WITH ADDRESS & PHONE
Drinkwater‡	108	Moose Jaw	Thunder Creek	Mrs. P. Fessler, Village Sec., Drinkwater, Sask. SOH 1GO (693-5093)
Dubuc‡	146	Qu'Appelle-Moose Mountain	Saltcoats	Mrs. Edith Aldred, Village Sec., Box 126, Dubuc, Sask. SOA ORO (877-2022)
Duck Lake†	683	Prince Albert	Prince Albert-Duck Lake	L.C. Perret, Town Adm., Duck Lake, Sask. SOK 1JO (467-2011)
Duck Lake RM No. 463	919			L.C. Perret, Sec., Box 250, Duck Lake, Sask. SOK 1JO (467-2011)
Duff‡	87	Yorkton-Melville	Melville	Reta Schick, Village Sec., Duff, Sask. SOA OSO (728-3592)
Dufferin RM No. 190	631			Richard Hicks, Sec., Box 67, Bethune, Sask. SOG OHO (638-3112)
Dundurn†	540	Humboldt-Lake Centre	Arm River	Mrs. L.M. Freeden, Town Adm., Dundurn, Sask. SOK 1KO (492-2202)
Dundurn RM No. 314	598			Irene Starling, Sec., Box 159, Dundurn, Sask. SOK 1KO (492-2132)
Duval‡	132	Humboldt-Lake Centre	Last Mountain-Touchwood	G. Schultz, Village Sec., Duval, Sask. SOG 1GO (725-4062)
Dysart‡	254	Humboldt-Lake Centre	Last Mountain-Touchwood	Mrs. H. Glass, Village Sec., Dysart, Sask. SOG 1HO (432-2100)
Eagle Creek RM No. 376	741			Ray Gaudet, Sec., Box 100, Arelee, Sask. SOK OHO (237-4424)
Earl Grey‡	292	Humboldt-Lake Centre	Last Mountain-Touchwood	Ms. E. Eggleton, Village Sec., Earl Grey, Sask. SOG 1JO (939-2062)
Eastend†	771	Swift Current-Maple Creek	Shaunavon	Mrs. L. Osinski, Town Adm., Eastend, Sask. SON OTO (295-3322)
Eatonia†	553	Kindersley-Lloydminster	Kindersley	Ms. B.A. Dahl, Town Adm., Eatonia, Sask. SOL OYO (967-2251)
Ebenezer‡	165	Yorkton-Melville	Canora	Norman Zayshley, Village Sec., Ebenezer, Sask. SOA OTO (782-7434)
Edam‡	352	The Battlefords-Meadow Lake	Turtleford	Mrs. T. McMurphy, Village Sec., Edam, Sask. SOM OVO (397-2223)
Edenwold‡	134	Regina East	Qu'Appelle	Mrs. E.N. Mang, Village Sec., Edenwold, Sask. SOG 1KO (637-4121)
Edenwold RM No. 158	1,475			B.G. MacNamee, Sec., Box 10, Balgonie, Sask. SOG OEO (637-2522)
Elbow‡	301	Moose Jaw	Arm River	Mrs. E.A. Wilson, Village Sec., Elbow, Sask. SOH 1JO (854-2277)
Elcapo RM No. 154	976			Thelma Wright, Sec., Box 178, Broadview, Sask. SOG OKO (696-2474)
Eldon RM No. 471	919			Joseph Stakiw, Sec., Box 130, Maidstone, Sask. SOM 1MO (893-2391)
Elfros‡	213	Humboldt-Lake Centre	Kelvington-Wadena	Mrs. M. Corby, Village Sec., Box 40, Elfros, Sask. SOA OVO (328-2123)
Elfros RM No. 307	846			c/o Elfros Village Sec. (328-2011)
Elmsthorpe RM No. 100	593			Lawrence Harty, Sec., Box 240, Avonlea, Sask. SOH OCO (868-2011)
Elrose†	656	Kindersley-Lloydminster	Rosetown-Elrose	G. Searight, Town Adm., Elrose, Sask. SOL OZO (378-2202)
Elstow‡	146	Humboldt-Lake Centre	Rosthern	Mrs. V. Angelstad, Village Sec., Elstow, Sask. SOK 1MO (257-3889)
Emerald RM No. 277	1,115			D.A. Moleski, Sec., Box 160, Wishart, Sask. SOA 4RO (576-2002)
Endeavour‡	220	Yorkton-Melville	Canora	Isabel Schur, Village Sec., Endeavour, Sask. SOA OWO (547-4236)
Enfield RM No. 194	572			N.A. Krislock, Sec., Central Butte, Sask. SOH OTO (796-2025)
Englefeld‡	274	Humboldt-Lake Centre	Quill Lakes	Henry Boer, Village Sec., Englefeld, Sask. SOK 1NO (287-3151)
Enniskillen RM No. 3	686			Wm. Ringguth, Sec., Box 179, Oxbow, Sask. SOC 2BO (483-2277)
Enterprise RM No. 142	447			I. Solie, Sec., Box 150, Richmound, Sask. SON 2EO (669-2000)
Ernfold‡	92	Swift Current-Maple Creek	Morse	R.W. Drennan, Village Sec., Ernfold, Sask. SOH 1KO (629-3866)
Esterhazy†	3,019	Qu'Appelle-Moose Mountain	Saltcoats	Peter Woznesenski, Town Adm., Esterhazy, Sask. SOA OXO (745-3942)
ESTEVAN	9,012	Assiniboia	Estevan	M. Hoste, City Clerk, City Hall, 1102 4th St., Estevan, Sask. S4A OW7 (634-3676)

Cities in CAPITALS; Towns marked †; Villages marked ‡; Balance are Rural Municipalities .
Area Code for Saskatchewan is 306

MUNICIPALITY	POP.	FEDERAL ELECTORAL DISTRICT	PROVINCIAL ELECTORAL DISTRICT	ADM. OR SECRETARY WITH ADDRESS & PHONE
Estevan RM No. 5	1,149			J.D. Jenkins, Sec., 1329 4th St., Estevan, Sask. S4A OX1 (634-2222)
Eston†	1,512	Kindersley-Lloydminster	Kindersley	Bruno Kossmann, Town Adm., Eston, Sask. SOL 1AO (962-4444)
Etters Beach‡	5	Moose Jaw	Arm River	H. Waugh, Village Sec., Etters Beach, Sask. SOG 2JO (963-2220)
Evesham‡	53	Kindersley-Lloydminster	Wilkie	Marg Wells, Village Sec., Evesham, Sask. SOL 1BO (753-2614)
Excel RM No. 71	975			Mervin Guillemin, Sec., Box 190, Viceroy, Sask. SOH 4HO (268-4555)
Excelsior RM No. 166	1,242			Kenneth Merrills, Sec., Box 180, Rush Lake, Sask. SOH 3SO (784-3121)
Eyebrow‡	198	Moose Jaw	Thunder Creek	Mrs. Joy Harms, Village Sec., Eyebrow, Sask. SOH 1LO (759-2167)
Eyebrow RM No. 193	447			John Speir, Sec., Box 99, Eyebrow, Sask. SOH 1LO (759-2101)
Eye Hill RM No. 382	877			Vern Gintant, Sec., Box 69, Macklin, Sask. SOL 2CO (753-2075)
Fairlight‡	84	Qu'Appelle-Moose Mountain	Moosomin	J.F. Cawood, Village Sec., Fairlight, Sask. SOG 1MO (646-4536)
Fenwood‡	91	Yorkton-Melville	Melville	Miss M. Sedlovitch, Sec., Fenwood, Sask. SOA OYO (728-4069)
Ferland‡	73	Swift Current-Maple Creek	Shaunavon	R.A. Fournier, Village Sec., Ferland, Sask. SOH 1MO (478-2410)
Fertile Belt RM No. 183	1,364			J.V. Jacob, Sec., Box 190, Stockholm, Sask. SOA 3YO (793-2061)
Fertile Valley RM No. 285	743			Doug McAulay, Sec., Box 70, Conquest, Sask. SOL OLO (856-2037)
Fife Lake‡	89	Assiniboia	Assiniboia-Gravelbourg	Mildred Quarrie, Village Sec., Fife Lake, Sask. SOH 1NO (476-2608)
Fillmore‡	403	Assiniboia	Weyburn	Mrs. K. Levesque, Village Sec., Box 185, Fillmore, Sask. SOG 1NO (722-3330)
Fillmore RM No. 96	579			David Desautels, Sec., Box 130, Fillmore, Sask. SOG 1NO (722-3251)
Findlater‡	85	Moose Jaw	Thunder Creek	Mrs. N. Young, Village Sec., Findlater, Sask. SOG 1PO (638-4905)
Fish Creek RM No. 402	591			Wm. Kindrachuk, Sec., Box 160, Wakaw, Sask. SOK 4PO (233-4412)
Flaxcombe‡	100	Kindersley-Lloydminster	Kindersley	Mrs. M. Thompson, Village Sec., Flaxcombe, Sask. SOL 1EO (463-3439)
Fleming†	164	Qu'Appelle-Moose Mountain	Moosomin	Mrs. W.L. Russell, Town Adm., Fleming, Sask. SOG 1RO (435-4244)
Flett's Springs RM No. 429	1,125			C.W. Tetarenko, Sec., Box 69, Pathlow, Sask. SOK 3BO (752-360)
FLIN FLON	408 (Sask.)	Mackenzie		See Manitoba
Foam Lake†	1,501	Yorkton-Melville	Kelvington-Wadena	Mrs. G.E. Kreuger, Town Adm., Foam Lake, Sask. SOA 1AO (272-3244)
Foam Lake RM No. 276	1,231			D.W. Popowich, Sec., Box 490, Foam Lake, Sask. SOA 1AO (272-3334)
Forget‡	74	Qu'Appelle-Moose Mountain	Weyburn	Mrs. C. Taillon, Village Sec., Forget, Sask. SOC OXO (457-2730)
Fort Qu'Appelle†	1,764	Regina East	Qu'Appelle	H.J. Taylor, Town Adm., Fort Qu'Appelle, Sask. SOG 1SO (332-5266)
Fosston‡	104	Mackenzie	Kelvington-Wadena	D. Griller, Village Sec., Fosston, Sask. SOE OVO (322-4507)
Fox Valley‡	429	Swift Current-Maple Creek	Maple Creek	Mrs. Ann Ganert, Village Sec., Fox Valley, Sask. SON OVO (666-3020)
Fox Valley RM No. 171	626			Daniel Buye, Sec., Box 190, Fox Valley, Sask. SON OVO (666-2055)
Francis†	170	Assiniboia	Indian Head-Wolseley	C.A. Caron, Town Adm., Francis, Sask. SOG 1VO (245-3256)
Francis RM No. 127	961			See Town of Francis
Frenchman Butte RM No. 501	1,408			W.S. Howes, Sec., Box 180, Paradise Hill, Sask. SOM 2GO (344-2034)
Frobisher‡	187	Qu'Appelle-Moose Mountain	Souris-Cannington	Mrs. B. Johnstone, Village Sec., Frobisher, Sask. SOC OYO (486-2140)
Frontier‡	444	Swift Current-Maple Creek	Shaunavon	R.J. Dube, Village Sec., Box 30, Frontier, Sask. SON OWO (296-2030)
Frontier RM No. 19	412			c/o Frontier Village Sec.

Cities in CAPITALS; Towns marked †; Villages marked ‡; Balance are Rural Municipalities.
Area Code for Saskatchewan is 306

MUNICIPALITY	POP.	FEDERAL ELECTORAL DISTRICT	PROVINCIAL ELECTORAL DISTRICT	ADM. OR SECRETARY WITH ADDRESS & PHONE
Gainsborough‡	334	Qu'Appelle-Moose Mountain	Souris-Cannington	B.N. Brown, Village Sec., Gainsborough, Sask. SOC OZO (685-2010)
Garden River RM No. 490	822			Terry Huidston, Sec., Box 70, Meath Park, Sask. SOJ 1TO (929-2020)
Garry RM No. 245	929			J.T. Kuziak, Sec., Box 10, Jedburgh, Sask. SOA 1RO (647-2450)
Gerald‡	192	Qu'Appelle-Moose Mountain	Saltcoats	Mrs. K. Assailly, Village Sec., Gerald, Sask. SOA 1BO (745-2378)
Girvin‡	80	Moose Jaw	Arm River	B. MacPherson, Village Sec., Girvin, Sask. SOG 1XO (567-4268)
Gladmar‡	74	Assiniboia	Bengough-Milestone	Mrs. D. Petterson, Village Sec., Gladmar, Sask. SOC 1AO (969-4837)
Glaslyn‡	415	The Battlefords-Meadow Lake	Turtleford	P.G. Chorney, Village Sec., Glaslyn, Sask. SOM OYO (342-2144)
Glenavon‡	295	Qu'Appelle-Moose Mountain	Indian Head-Wolseley	Mrs. A. Shiplack, Village Sec., Glenavon, Sask. SOG 1YO (429-2011)
Glen Bain RM No. 105	616			M. Linton, Sec., Box 39, Glen Bain, Sask. SON OXO (264-3607)
Glen Ewen‡	143	Qu'Appelle-Moose Mountain	Souris-Cannington	Mrs. D. Carefoot, Village Sec., Glen Ewen, Sask. SOC 1CO (925-2211)
Glen McPherson RM No. 46	267			N. Ellis, Sec., Box 193, Mankota, Sask. SOH 2WO (478-2221)
Glenside‡	97	Moose Jaw	Arm River	Mrs. D. Rosa, Village Sec., Glenside, Sask. SOH 1TO (867-8932)
Glenside RM No. 377	530			R.E. Holt, Sec., Box 1084, Biggar, Sask. SOK OMO (948-3681)
Glentworth‡	103	Assiniboia	Shaunavon	E.P. Gasper, Village Sec., Glentworth, Sask. SOH 1VO (266-4920)
Glidden‡	57	Kindersley-Lloydminster	Kindersley	D.H. Maddocks, Village Sec., Glidden, Sask. SOL 1HO (463-3338)
Golden Prairie‡	100	Swift Current-Maple Creek	Maple Creek	Olive Blohm, Village Sec., Golden Prairie, Sask. SON OYO (667-3400)
Golden West RM No. 95	644			Miss B. Klatt, Sec., Box 70, Corning, Sask. SOG OTO (224-4456)
Goodeve‡	134	Yorkton-Melville	Melville	Mrs. M. Schurko, Village Sec., Goodeve, Sask. SOA 1CO (876-2041)
Good Lake RM No. 274	930			G.J. Predy, Sec., Box 896, Canora, Sask. SOA OLO (563-5244)
Goodsoil‡	235	The Battlefords-Meadow Lake	Meadow Lake	Cheryl Churko, Village Sec., Goodsoil, Sask. SOM 1AO (238-2094)
Goodwater‡	61	Assiniboia	Bengough-Milestone	Mrs. F.M. Johnston, Village Sec., Goodwater, Sask. SOC 1EO (456-2572)
Govan†	437	Humboldt-Lake Centre	Last Mountain-Touchwood	N. Sagen, Town Adm., Govan, Sask. SOG 1ZO (484-2011)
Grandview‡		Moose Jaw	Arm River	B. MacNeill, Grandview Village Sec., c/o 6038 Dewdney Ave. Regina, Sask. (565-4500)
Grandview RM No. 349	519			C.J. Weese, Sec., Kelfield, Sask. SOK 2CO (932-4911)
Grant RM No. 372	616			D. Dmytruk, Sec., Box 190, Vonda, Sask. SOK 4NO (258-2022)
Grass Lake RM No. 381	800			R.W. Toews, Sec., Reward, Sask. SOK 3NO (228-2988)
Grassy Creek RM No. 78	514			L.M. Meloche, Sec., Box 400, Shaunavon, Sask. SON 2MO (297-2520)
Gravelbourg†	1,464	Assiniboia	Assiniboia-Gravelbourg	E. Karlson, Town Adm., Box 510, Gravelbourg, Sask. SOH 1XO (648-3301)
Gravelbourg RM No. 104	699			c/o Gravelbourg Town Clerk (648-2412)
Grayson‡	280	Qu'Appelle-Moose Mountain	Melville	A. Marshall, Village Sec., Box 69, Grayson, Sask. SOA 1EO (794-2044)
Grayson RM No. 184	1,023			c/o Grayson Village Sec.
Great Bend RM No. 405	664			Ken Tanchak, Sec., Box 150, Borden, Sask. SOK ONO (997-2101)
Greenfield RM No. 529	378			G. Rempel, Sec., Turtleford, Sask. SOM 2YO (845-2045)
Grenfell†	1,363	Qu'Appelle-Moose Mountain	Indian Head-Wolseley	Jim Lowe, Town Adm., Grenfell, Sask. SOG 2BO (697-2815)

Cities in CAPITALS; Towns marked †; Villages marked ‡; Balance are Rural Municipalities.
Area Code for Saskatchewan is 306

MUNICIPALITY	POP.	FEDERAL ELECTORAL DISTRICT	PROVINCIAL ELECTORAL DISTRICT	ADM. OR SECRETARY WITH ADDRESS & PHONE
Griffin RM No. 66	696			R. Thurmeier, Sec., Box 70, Griffin, Sask. SOC 1GO (842-6298)
Guernsey‡	222	Humboldt-Lake Centre	Humboldt	Mrs. D. Dunne, Village Sec., Guernsey, Sask. SOK 1WO (365-4356)
Gull Lake†	1,114	Swift Current-Maple Creek	Maple Creek	A.W. Sweeting, Town Adm., Gull Lake, Sask. SON 1AO (672-3361)
Gull Lake RM No. 139	359			W.A. Bowes, Sec., Box 58, Gull Lake, Sask. SON 1AO (672-4430)
Hafford‡	558	The Battlefords-Meadow Lake	Redberry	R.A. Tanchak, Village Sec., Box 220, Hafford, Sask. SOJ 1AO (549-2331)
Hague‡	662	Saskatoon West	Rosthern	P.P. Unger, Village Sec., Hague, Sask. SOK 1XO (225-2155)
Halbrite‡	132	Assiniboia	Estevan	Mrs. A. Trombley, Village Sec., Halbrite, Sask. SOC 1HO (458-2556)
Handel‡	69	Kindersley-Lloydminster	Biggar	Steve Frukstuk, Village Sec., Handel, Sask. SOK 1YO (658-4738)
Hanley†	473	Moose Jaw	Arm River	W.G. Resch, Town Adm., Hanley, Sask. SOG 2EO (544-2202)
Happyland RM No. 231	654			J. Ries, Sec., Box 339, Leader, Sask. SON 1HO (628-3800)
Happy Valley RM No. 10	315			Mrs. L.A. Brown, Sec., Big Beaver, Sask. SOH OGO (267-4540)
Hardy‡	36	Assiniboia	Bengough-Milestone	Mrs. I. Rudland, Village Sec., Hardy, Sask. SOC 1JO (454-2705)
Harris‡	255	Saskatoon West	Biggar	Mrs. P. Garner, Village Sec., Harris, Sask. SOL 1KO (656-2122)
Harris RM No. 316	436			Jim Angus, Sec., Box 146, Harris, Sask. SOL 1KO (656-2072)
Hart Butte RM No. 11	501			V.R. Palmer, Sec., Box 210, Coronach, Sask. SOH OZO (267-2005)
Hawarden‡	141	Moose Jaw	Arm River	Mrs. F.B. Smith, Village Sec., Hawarden, Sask. SOH 1YO (855-2020)
Hazel Dell RM No. 335	1,254			U. McLaughlin, Sec., Box 87, Okla, Sask. SOA 2XO (325-4315)
Hazelwood RM No. 94	546			Mrs. F. Latimer, Sec., Box 270, Kipling, Sask. SOG 2SO (736-8121)
Hazenmore‡	119	Swift Current-Maple Creek	Shaunavon	R. McKeith, Village Sec., Hazenmore, Sask. SON 1CO (264-3417)
Hazlet‡	120	Swift Current-Maple Creek	Maple Creek	P. Buchanan, Village Sec., Hazlet, Sask. SON 1EO (678-2131)
Heart's Hill RM No. 352	642			W.R. Loveday, Sec., Box 458, Luseland, Sask. SOL 2AO (372-4224)
Hepburn‡	405	Saskatoon West	Rosthern	Mrs. V.M. Gossen, Village Sec., Hepburn, Sask. SOK 1ZO (947-2170)
Herbert†	1,043	Swift Current-Maple Creek	Morse	Ms. G. Wilson, Town Adm., Herbert, Sask. SOH 2AO (784-2400)
Herschel‡	108	Kindersley-Lloydminster	Rosetown-Elrose	Mrs. S. Cruickshank, Village Sec., Box 160, Herschel, Sask. SOL 1LO (377-2014)
Heward‡	69	Qu'Appelle-Moose Mountain	Weyburn	Mrs. D. Mitchall, Village Sec., Heward, Sask. SOG 2GO (457-2852)
Hillsborough RM No. 132	177			W.L. Burbank, Sec., 48 High St. W., Moose Jaw, Sask. S6H 1S3 (693-1329)
Hillsdale RM No. 440	718			D.M. Bryden, Sec., Box 280, Neilburg, Sask. SOM 2CO (823-4321)
Hodgeville‡	333	Swift Current-Maple Creek	Morse	L.A. Haubrich, Village Sec., Hodgeville, Sask. SOH 2BO (677-2223)
Holdfast‡	312	Moose Jaw	Arm River	H. Hemingway, Village Sec., Holdfast, Sask. SOG 2HO (488-2033)
Hoodoo RM No. 401	926			Lloyd Wedewer, Sec., Box 250, Cudworth, Sask. SOK 1BO (256-3281)
Hubbard‡	90	Yorkton-Melville	Melville	J. Paslawski, Village Sec., Hubbard, Sask. SOA 1JO (795-2880)
Hudson Bay†	2,404	Mackenzie	Kelsey-Tisdale	D. Guy, Town Adm., Hudson Bay, Sask. SOE OYO (865-2261)
Hudson Bay RM No. 394	2,260			R. Dolezar, Sec., Box 520, Hudson Bay, Sask. SOE OYO (865-2691)
Humboldt†	4,651	Humboldt-Lake Centre	Humboldt	W.L. Herman, Town Adm., Humboldt, Sask. SOK 2AO (682-2525)

Cities in CAPITALS; Towns marked †; Villages marked ‡; Balance are Rural Municipalities .
Area Code for Saskatchewan is 306

MUNICIPALITY	POP.	FEDERAL ELECTORAL DISTRICT	PROVINCIAL ELECTORAL DISTRICT	ADM. OR SECRETARY WITH ADDRESS & PHONE
Humboldt RM No. 370	1,357			F.W. Saliken, Sec., Box 420, Humboldt, Sask. SOK 2AO (682-2242)
Huron RM No. 223	344			D. Sloan, Sec., Box 159, Tugaske, Sask. SOH 4BO (759-2211)
Hyas‡	190	Yorkton-Melville	Pelly	R.W. Newman, Village Sec., Hyas, Sask. SOA 1KO (594-2817)
Imperial†	502	Moose Jaw	Arm River	Mrs. B.R. Babyak, Town Adm., Box 90, Imperial, Sask. SOG 2JO (963-2220)
Indian Head†	1,813	Qu'Appelle-Moose Mountain	Indian Head-Wolseley	L. Natyshak, Town Adm., Indian Head, Sask. SOG 2KO (695-3344)
Indian Head RM No. 156	649			J.Q. Hallett, Sec., Box 39, Indian Head, Sask. SOG 2KO (695-3464)
Insinger‡	56	Yorkton-Melville	Canora	Mrs. B. Thompson, Village Sec., Box 179, Insinger, Sask. SOA 1LO (647-2422)
Insinger RM No. 275	904			c/o Insinger Village Sec.
Invergordon RM No. 430	1,113			D. Dunlop, Sec., Box 40, Crystal Springs, Sask. SOK 1AO (749-2852)
Invermay‡	397	Yorkton-Melville	Kelvington-Wadena	Ms. V. Wolski, Village Sec., Invermay, Sask. SOA 1MO (593-2242)
Invermay RM No. 305	861			G.C. Wolkowski, Sec., Box 130, Invermay, Sask. SOA 1MO (593-2152)
Ituna†	910	Yorkton-Melville	Melville	E. Kutzul, Town Adm., Ituna, Sask. SOA 1NO (795-2272)
Ituna Bon Accord RM No. 246	973			Mrs. D. Olech, Sec., Box 190, Ituna, Sask. SOA 1NO (795-2202)
Jansen‡	232	Humboldt-Lake Centre	Quill Lakes	Mrs. E. Kral, Village Sec., Jansen, Sask. SOK 2BO (364-2148)
Jedburgh‡	47	Yorkton-Melville	Canora	J.T. Kuziak, Village Sec., Jedburgh, Sask. SOA 1RO (647-2450)
Kamsack†	2,766	Yorkton-Melville	Pelly	R.E. Murdock, Town Adm., Kamsack, Sask. SOA 1SO (542-2155)
Kannata Valley‡	46	Humboldt-Lake Centre	Last Mountain-Touchwood	Ms. D.C. Collins, Kannata Valley Village Sec., c/o Box 86, Silton, Sask. S0G 4L0 (938-2561)
Katepwa Beach‡	34	Qu'Appelle-Moose Mountain	Melville	W. Eurich, Katepwa Beach Village Sec., c/o Box 143, Lemburg, Sask. (335-2244)
Keeler‡	44	Moose Jaw	Thunder Creek	Mrs. L.B. Garry, Village Sec., Keeler, Sask. SOH 2EO (788-4424)
Kelfield‡	20	Kindersley-Lloydminster	Biggar	C.J. Weese, Village Sec., Kelfield, Sask. SOK 2CO (932-4911)
Kelliher‡	412	Humboldt-Lake Centre	Kelvington-Wadena	Mrs. J. Budd, Village Sec., Kelliher, Sask. SOA 1VO (675-2226)
Kellross RM No. 247	1,007			M.J. Wowk, Sec., Box 10, Leross, Sask. SOA 2CO (675-4423)
Kelvington†	1,053	Mackenzie	Kelvington-Wadena	A. Biletsky, Town Adm., Kelvington, Sask. SOA 1WO (327-4482)
Kelvington RM No. 366	1,032			B.C. McNamee, Sec., Box 519, Kelvington, Sask. SOA 1WO (327-4222)
Kenaston‡	375	Moose Jaw	Arm River	F. Poulin, Village Sec., Kenaston, Sask. SOG 2NO (252-2240)
Kendal‡	77	Assiniboia	Indian Head-Wolseley	Mrs. G. Mayer, Village Sec., Kendal, Sask. SOG 2PO
Kennedy‡	273	Qu'Appelle-Moose Mountain	Moosomin	Helen Gurski, Village Sec., Kennedy, Sask. SOG 2RO (538-2194)
Kenosee‡	86			J. Moyles, Village Sec., Kenosee, Sask. S0C 2S0 (577-2139)
Kerrobert†	1,100	Kindersley-Lloydminster	Wilkie	H.C. Edmonds, Town Adm., Kerrobert, Sask. SOL 1RO (834-2361)
Keys RM No. 303	702			G.L. Dranchuk, Sec., Box 899, Canora, Sask. SOA OLO (563-5331)
Key West RM No. 70	800			C. Lozinsky, Sec., Box 159, Ogema, Sask. SOC 1YO (459-2262)
Khedive‡	76	Assiniboia	Bengough-Milestone	Mrs. Annie Colbow, Village Sec., Khedive, Sask. SOC 1KO (442-4422)
Killaly‡	137	Qu'Appelle-Moose Mountain	Melville	Frank Malach, Village Sec., Killaly, Sask. SOA 1XO (748-2605)
Kincaid‡	245	Swift Current-Maple Creek	Shaunavon	Mrs. E.B. Harper, Village Sec., Kincaid, Sask. SOH 2JO (264-3366)

Cities in CAPITALS; Towns marked †; Villages marked ‡; Balance are Rural Municipalities .
Area Code for Saskatchewan is 306

MUNICIPALITY	POP.	FEDERAL ELECTORAL DISTRICT	PROVINCIAL ELECTORAL DISTRICT	ADM. OR SECRETARY WITH ADDRESS & PHONE
Kindersley†	3,709	Kindersley-Lloydminster	Kindersley	David Grout, Town Adm., Kindersley, Sask. SOL 1SO (463-2675)
Kindersley RM No. 290	1,252			D.C. Empey, Sec., Box 1210, Kindersley, Sask. SOL 1SO (463-2524)
King George RM No. 256	418			D.S. Clark, Sec., Box 100, Dinsmore, Sask. SOL OTO (846-2022)
Kingsley RM No. 124	805			D.D. Chambers, Sec., Box 239, Kipling, Sask. SOG 2SO (736-2272)
Kinistino†	763	Prince Albert	Kinistino	R.H. Wingfield, Town Adm., Kinistino, Sask. SOJ 1HO (864-2461)
Kinistino RM No. 459	1,323			L.W. Edeen, Sec., Box 310, Welding, Sask. SOJ 1HO (864-2474)
Kinley‡	65	Saskatoon West	Biggar	Mrs. M. Fowler, Village Sec., Kinley, Sask. SOK 2EO (237-4865)
Kipling†	1,024	Qu'Appelle-Moose Mountain	Moosomin	Gordon Hubbard, Town Adm., Kipling, Sask. SOG 2SO (736-2515)
Kisbey‡	252	Qu'Appelle-Moose Mountain	Souris-Cannington	Margaret Jackson, Village Sec., Kisbey, Sask. SOC 1LO (462-2212)
Krydor‡	93	The Battlefords-Meadow Lake	Redberry	Wm. Grewa, Village Sec., Krydor, Sask. SOJ 1KO (497-3516)
Kutawa RM No. 278	540			Mrs. F. Hall, Sec., Box 40, Punnichy, Sask. SOA 3CO (835-2030)
Kyle†	540	Kindersley-Lloydminster	Rosetown-Elrose	A.H. Fogg, Town Adm., Kyle, Sask. SOL 1TO (375-2525)
Lacadena RM No. 228	1,123			H.W. Hammell, Sec., Box 39, Lacadena, Sask. SOL 1VO (574-4753)
Lac Pelletier RM No. 107	670			H. Otterson, Sec., Box 70, Neville, Sask. SON 1TO (627-3226)
Lafleche†	639	Assiniboia	Assiniboia-Gravelbourg	W. Baran, Town Adm., Lafleche, Sask. SOH 2KO (472-5292)
Laird‡	214	Prince Albert	Rosthern	Oscar Klaassen, Village Sec., Laird, Sask. SOK 2HO (223-4343)
Laird RM No. 404	1,249			L.A. Ratzlaff, Sec., Box 160, Waldheim, Sask. SOK 4RO (945-2133)
Lajord RM No. 128	993			B. Ehnis, Sec., Lajord, Sask. SOG 2VO (568-2744)
Lake Alma‡	116	Assiniboia	Bengough-Milestone	Mrs. D. Lund, Village Sec., Lake Alma, Sask. SOC 1MO (447-2002)
Lake Alma RM No. 8	472			Mrs. M. Wick, Sec., Box 100, Lake Alma, Sask. SOC 1MO (447-2022)
Lake Johnston RM No. 102	330			H.S. Edgerton, Sec., Box 160, Mossbank, Sask. SOH 3GO (354-2414)
Lakeland RM No. 521	502			H. Paterson, Sec., Box 27, Christopher Lake, Sask. SOJ ONO (982-2010)
Lake Lenore‡	385	Humboldt-Lake Centre	Melfort	B.D. Lewis, Village Sec., Lake Lenore, Sask. SOK 2JO (368-2286)
Lake Lenore RM No. 399	732			L. Bernard, Sec., Box 280, St. Brieux, Sask. SOK 3VO (275-2066)
Lake of the Rivers RM No. 72	583			C.S. Lindsay, Sec., Box 610, Assiniboia, Sask. SOH OBO (642-3533)
Lakeside RM No. 338	697			D.S. Camp, Sec., Box 9, Quill Lake, Sask. SOA 3EO (383-2261)
Lakeview RM No. 337	975			M. Kreptul, Sec., Box 220, Wadena, Sask. SOA 4JO (338-2341)
Lampman†	720	Qu'Appelle-Moose Mountain	Estevan	Mrs. S.E. Fleck, Town Adm., Lampman, Sask. SOC 1NO (487-2462)
Lancer‡	170	Swift Current-Maple Creek	Maple Creek	Mrs. B. Hopfauf, Village Sec., Box 3, Lancer, Sask. SON 1GO (689-2925)
Landis‡	285	Kindersley-Lloydminster	Wilkie	Mrs. Agnes Small, Village Sec., Box 153, Landis, Sask. SOK 2KO (658-2155)
Lang‡	227	Assiniboia	Bengough-Milestone	Mrs. F. Hockley, Village Sec., Lang, Sask. SOG 2WO (464-2024)
Langenburg†	1,288	Qu'Appelle-Moose Mountain	Saltcoats	Dave Petz, Town Adm., Langenburg, Sask. SOA 2AO (743-2432)
Langenburg RM No. 181	1,063			Wm. Erhardt, Sec., Box 489, Langenburg, Sask. SOA 2AO (743-2341)
Langham†	1,034	Saskatoon West	Rosthern	G. Gray, Town Adm., Langham, Sask. SOK 2LO (283-4842)

Cities in CAPITALS; Towns marked †; Villages marked ‡; Balance are Rural Municipalities .
Area Code for Saskatchewan is 306

MUNICIPALITY	POP.	FEDERAL ELECTORAL DISTRICT	PROVINCIAL ELECTORAL DISTRICT	ADM. OR SECRETARY WITH ADDRESS & PHONE
Lanigan†	1,650	Humboldt-Lake Centre	Quill Lakes	W.R. Maier, Town Adm., Box 280, Lanigan, Sask. SOK 2MO (365-2809)
La Ronge†	1,714	Mackenzie	Cumberland	Bert Senft, Town Adm., La Ronge, Sask. SOJ 1LO (425-2066)
Lashburn†	703	Kindersley-Lloydminster	Cutknife-Lloydminster	Merle Tindall, Town Adm., Lashburn, Sask. SOM 1HO (285-3533)
Last Mountain Valley RM No. 250	624			N. Sagen, Sec., Box 160, Govan, Sask. SOG 1ZO (484-2011)
Laurier RM No. 38	679			G.L. Young, Sec., Box 219, Radville, Sask. SOC 2GO (869-2255)
Lawson‡	26	Moose Jaw	Thunder Creek	H.W. Folliott, Village Sec., Box 550, Lawson, Sask. SOH 2NO (796-4421)
Lawtonia RM No. 135	639			Art Thompson, Sec., Box 10, Hodgeville, Sask. SOH 2BO (677-2266)
Leader†	1,160	Swift Current-Maple Creek	Maple Creek	Ms. L.M. Grout, Town Adm., Box 39, Leader, Sask. SON 1HO (638-3333)
Leask‡	457	Prince Albert	Redberry	R. Poole, Village Sec., Leask, Sask. SOJ 1MO (466-2229)
Leask RM No. 464	1,168			c/o Leask Village Sec.
Lebret‡	268	Regina East	Melville	W.J. Baker, Village Sec., Lebret, Sask. SOG 2YO (332-6545)
Leipzig‡	44	Kindersley-Lloydminster	Wilkie	Mrs. A. Kappel, Village Sec., Leipzig, Sask. SOK 2NO (658-4445)
Lemberg†	426	Qu'Appelle-Moose Mountain	Melville	W. Eurich, Town Adm., Lemberg, Sask. SOA 2BO (335-2244)
Leoville‡	410	The Battlefords-Meadow Lake	Turtleford	Mrs. T. Krushelniski, Village Sec., Leoville, Sask. SOJ 1NO (984-2140)
Leross‡	91	Humboldt-Lake Centre	Last Mountain-Touchwood	Oscar Metz, Village Sec., Leross, Sask. SOA 2CO (675-4405)
Leroy†	436	Humboldt-Lake Centre	Quill Lakes	Mrs. E. Wiens, Town Adm., Leroy, Sask. SOK 2PO (286-3288)
Leroy RM No. 339	1,155			J. Psovsky, Sec., Box 100, Leroy, Sask. SOK 2PO (286-3261)
Leslie‡	71	Humboldt-Lake Centre	Kelvington-Wadena	Mrs. F.M. Casement, Village Sec., Leslie, Sask. SOA 2EO (272-3975)
Lestock‡	420	Humboldt-Lake Centre	Last Mountain-Touchwood	Mrs. B. Link, Village Sec., Box 209, Lestock, Sask. SOA 2GO (274-2277)
Liberty‡	127	Moose Jaw	Arm River	Mrs. M. Wolff, Village Sec., Liberty, Sask. SOG 3AO (847-2033)
Limerick‡	166	Assiniboia	Assiniboia-Gravelbourg	Fred Auser, Village Sec., Limerick, Sask. SOH 2PO (263-2020)
Lintlaw‡	225	Yorkton-Melville	Canora	Sharon Kowaski, Village Sec., Lintlaw, Sask. SOA 2HO (325-2006)
Lipton‡	353	Humboldt-Lake Centre	Last Mountain-Touchwood	Mrs. O. Huber, Village Sec., Lipton, Sask. SOG 3BO (336-2505)
Lipton RM No. 217	790			G.A. Thompson, Sec., Box 40, Lipton, Sask. SOG 3BO (336-2244)
Livingston RM No. 331	800			Mike Burtnack, Sec., Box 40, Arran, Sask. SOA OBO (595-4521)
LLOYDMINSTER	14,093	Kindersley-Lloydminster	Cutknife-Lloydminster	E.D. Newlin, City Clerk, City Hall, 5011 49th Ave., Lloydminster, Sask. S9V OT8 (403/825-6184)
Lockwood‡	52	Humboldt-Lake Centre	Quill Lakes	Mrs. E. Hurley, Village Sec., Lockwood, Sask. SOK 2RO (528-4430)
Lomond RM No. 37	521			Mrs. F.M. Johnston, Sec., Box 39, Goodwater, Sask. SOC 1EO (456-2566)
Lone Tree RM No. 18	299			R.J. Johnson, Sec., Box 30, Climax, Sask. SON ONO (293-2124)
Longlaketon RM No. 219	1,102			Ms. E. Eggleton, Sec., Box 100, Earl Grey, Sask. SOG 1JO (939-2144)
Loon Lake‡	365	The Battlefords-Meadow Lake	Meadow Lake	L.G. Williamson, Village Sec., Loon Lake, Sask. SOM 1LO (837-2090)
Loon Lake RM No. 561	1,105			Mrs. E. Suek, Sec., Box 40, Loon Lake, Sask. SOM 1LO (837-2076)
Loreburn‡	218	Moose Jaw	Arm River	Ms. M.A. Stronski, Village Sec., Loreburn, Sask. SOH 2SO (644-2097)
Loreburn RM No. 254	696			J.A. Forrest, Sec., Box 40, Loreburn, Sask. SOH 2SO (644-2022)

Note: Lloydminster pop. is Sask./Alta. combined

Cities in CAPITALS; Towns marked †; Villages marked ‡; Balance are Rural Municipalities .
Area Code for Saskatchewan is 306

MUNICIPALITY	POP.	FEDERAL ELECTORAL DISTRICT	PROVINCIAL ELECTORAL DISTRICT	ADM. OR SECRETARY WITH ADDRESS & PHONE
Lost River RM No. 313	463			S. Olszewski, Sec., Allan, Sask. SOK OCO (257-3272)
Love‡	125	Mackenzie	Nipawin	Mrs. V. Lambert, Village Sec., Box 94, Love, Sask. SOJ 1PO (276-2525)
Loverna‡	56	Kindersley-Lloydminster	Kindersley	Evelyn Murray, Village Sec., Loverna, Sask. SOL 2KO (968-2741)
Lucky Lake‡	375	Kindersley-Lloydminster	Rosetown-Elrose	A. Holbird, Village Sec., Lucky Lake, Sask. SOL 1ZO (858-2234)
Lumsden†	1,304	Moose Jaw	Qu'Appelle	Ms. C. Klempp, Town Adm., Lumsden, Sask. SOG 3CO (485-2404)
Lumsden RM No. 189	1,088			J.E. Spicer, Sec., Box 160, Lumsden, Sask. SOG 3CO (485-2231)
Lumsden Beach‡	1	Moose Jaw	Qu'Appelle	A.J.T. Boyd, Lumsden Beach Village Sec., c/o 2913 College Ave., Regina, Sask. (522-0708)
Luseland†	696	Kindersley-Lloydminster	Wilkie	Mrs. D. Gerrard, Town Adm., Luseland, Sask. SOL 2AO (372-4322)
Macklin†	884	Kindersley-Lloydminster	Wilkie	Vern Gintant, Town Adm., Macklin, Sask. SOL 2CO (753-2075)
MacNutt‡	142	Yorkton-Melville	Saltcoats	Mrs. J. Kramer, Village Sec., MacNutt, Sask. SOA 2KO (742-4391)
Macoun‡	192	Assiniboia	Estevan	Mrs. B. Mohns, Village Sec., Macoun, Sask. SOC 1PO (634-7497)
Macrorie‡	130	Kindersley-Lloydminster	Rosetown-Elrose	G.A. Prentice, Village Sec., Macrorie, Sask. SOL 2EO (243-2010)
Madison‡	35	Kindersley-Lloydminster	Kindersley	Miss L. Ewert, Village Sec., Madison, Sask. SOL 2GO (962-3888)
Maidstone†	994	Kindersley-Lloydminster	Cutknife-Lloydminster	A.L. Larson, Town Adm., Maidstone, Sask. SOM 1MO (893-2373)
Major‡	125	Kindersley-Lloydminster	Kindersley	Ms. L. Kollman, Village Sec., Major, Sask. SOL 2HO (834-5147)
Makwa‡	107	The Battlefords-Meadow Lake	Meadow Lake	Mrs. P. Barker, Village Sec., Makwa, Sask. SOM 1NO (236-5901)
Manitou Beach‡	136	Humboldt-Lake Centre	Humboldt	Thora Lewis, Manitou Beach Village Sec., c/o Box 1, R.R. 1, Watrous, Sask. (946-2102)
Manitou Lake RM No. 442	691			R.E. Doupe, Sec., Box 69, Marsden, Sask. SOM 1PO (826-5215)
Mankota‡	406	Swift Current-Maple Creek	Shaunavon	N. Ellis, Village Sec., Mankota, Sask. SOH 2WO (478-2331)
Mankota RM No. 45	554			G.W. McIvor, Sec., Mankota, Sask. SOH 2WO (478-2323)
Manor‡	373	Qu'Appelle-Moose Mountain	Souris-Cannington	D. Ingram, Village Sec., Manor, Sask. SOC 1RO (448-2130)
Mantario‡	34	Kindersley-Lloydminster	Kindersley	Ms. B. Dahl, Village Sec., Mantario, Sask. SOL 2JO (967-2222)
Maple Bush RM No. 224	295			W.T. Wowk, Sec., Box 160, Riverhurst, Sask. SOH 3PO (796-4402)
Maple Creek†	2,466	Swift Current-Maple Creek	Maple Creek	J.D. Connor, Town Adm., Box 428, Maple Creek, Sask. SON 1NO (667-2244)
Maple Creek RM No. 111	1,376			W.R. Coward, Sec., Box 188, Maple Creek, Sask. SON 1NO (667-2300)
Marcelin‡	273	Prince Albert	Redberry	Mrs. G. Desjardins, Village Sec., Marcelin, Sask. SOJ 1RO (226-2168)
Marengo‡	120	Kindersley-Lloydminster	Kindersley	Mrs. E. Murray, Village Sec., Marengo, Sask. SOL 2KO (968-2741)
Margo‡	178	Yorkton-Melville	Kelvington-Wadena	Mrs. V. Benson, Village Sec., Margo, Sask. SOA 2MO (324-2134)
Mariposa RM No. 350	468			F.A. Lang, Sec., Broadacres, Sask. SOK 4HO (834-5037)
Markinch‡	88	Humboldt-Lake Centre	Last Mountain-Touchwood	B.M. Sali, Village Sec., Markinch, Sask. SOG 3JO (726-2063)
Marquis‡	119	Moose Jaw	Thunder Creek	R.J. Gasper, Village Sec., Box 40, Marquis, Sask. SOH 2XO (788-2022)
Marquis RM No. 191	522			c/o Marquis Village Sec.
Marriott RM No. 317	642			O.O. Taylor, Sec., Box 366, Rosetown, Sask. SOL 2VO (882-3203)

Cities in CAPITALS; Towns marked †; Villages marked ‡; Balance are Rural Municipalities.
Area Code for Saskatchewan is 306

MUNICIPALITY	POP.	FEDERAL ELECTORAL DISTRICT	PROVINCIAL ELECTORAL DISTRICT	ADM. OR SECRETARY WITH ADDRESS & PHONE
Marsden‡	211	Kindersley-Lloydminster	Cutknife-Lloydminster	R. Doupe, Village Sec., Marsden, Sask. SOM 1PO (826-5215)
Marshall‡	435	Kindersley-Lloydminster	Cutknife-Lloydminster	Mrs. N. Eger, Village Sec., Marshall, Sask. SOM 1RO (387-6240)
Martensville†	1,823	Saskatoon West	Rosthern	C. Shaw, Town Adm., Box 250, Martensville, Sask. SOK 2TO (661-2166)
Martin RM No. 122	574			Ken Engel, Sec., Box 99, Wapella, Sask. SOG 4ZO (532-4332)
Maryfield‡	408	Qu'Appelle-Moose Mountain	Moosomin	W.D. Frazer, Village Sec., Maryfield, Sask. SOG 3KO (646-2143)
Maryfield RM No. 91	734			Mrs. D.C. Jurkovic, Sec., Box 70, Maryfield, Sask. SOG 3KO (646-2033)
Mayfield RM No. 406	608			Laurie Dubois, Sec., Box 100, Maymont, Sask. SOM 1TO (389-2112)
Maymont‡	215	The Battlefords-Meadow Lake	Redberry	Louis Karpan, Village Sec., Maymont, Sask. SOM 1TO (389-2051)
Mazenod‡	70	Assiniboia	Assiniboia-Gravelbourg	Mrs. J. Kesslar, Village Sec., Mazenod, Sask. SOH 2YO (354-7723)
McCraney RM No. 282	622			F. Poulin, Sec., Box 129, Kenaston, Sask. SOG 2NO (252-2240)
McKillop RM No. 220	614			W.D. Hunter, Sec., Box 369, Strasbourg, Sask. S0G 4V0 (725-3230)
McLean‡	192	Regina East	Qu'Appelle	Mrs. E.B. Ebenal, Village Sec., McLean, Sask. SOG 3EO (699-7279)
McLeod RM No. 185	952			M.J. Hanowski, Sec., Box 130, Neudorf, Sask. SOA 2TO (748-2233)
McTaggart‡	99	Assiniboia	Weyburn	N. Lynch, Village Sec., McTaggart, Sask. SOG 3GO (842-5911)
Meacham‡	184	Humboldt-Lake Centre	Humboldt	Elizabeth Saretzky, Village Sec., Meacham, Sask. SOK 2VO (376-2003)
Meadow Lake†	3,959	The Battlefords-Meadow Lake	Meadow Lake	Mrs. N. Docken, Town Adm., Meadow Lake, Sask. SOM 1VO (236-3622)
Meadow Lake RM No. 588	2,306			Harold Widdup, Sec., Box 668, Meadow Lake, Sask. SOM 1VO (236-5651)
Meath Park‡	301	Prince Albert	Shellbrook	Mrs. A. Mackonka, Village Sec., Meath Park, Sask. SOJ 1TO (929-2112)
Medstead‡	188	The Battlefords-Meadow Lake	Turtleford	Brian Evans, Village Sec., Medstead, Sask. SOM 1WO (342-4609)
Medstead RM No. 497	853			c/o Medstead Village Sec.
MELFORT	5,883	Mackenzie	Melfort	K. Dobson, City Clerk, Box 218, Melfort, Sask. SOE 1AO (752-2765)
MELVILLE	5,149	Yorkton-Melville	Melville	John Sedlovitch, City Clerk, City Hall, Box 1240, Melville, Sask. SOA 2PO (728-4545)
Mendham‡	118	Swift Current-Maple Creek	Maple Creek	Mrs. D. Moser, Village Sec., Mendham, Sask. SON 1PO (628-3936)
Meota‡	248	The Battlefords-Meadow Lake	Redberry	D.J. Wilkinson, Village Sec., Meota, Sask. SOM 1XO (892-2061)
Meota RM No. 468	1,047			c/o Meota Village Sec.
Mervin‡	174	The Battlefords-Meadow Lake	Turtleford	Mrs. K. MacNab, Village Sec., Mervin, Sask. SOM 1YO (845-2784)
Mervin RM No. 499	923			G. Rempel, Sec., Turtleford, Sask. SOM 2YO (845-2045)
Metinota‡	5	The Battlefords-Meadow Lake	Redberry	G. Griffith, Metinota Village Sec., c/o Box 47, Meota, Sask. S0M 1X0 (892-2183)
Meeting Lake RM No. 466	832			G. Lepage, Sec., Box 26, Mayfair, Sask. SOM 1SO (246-4228)
Meyronne‡	98	Swift Current-Maple Creek	Shaunavon	Delores Wright, Village Sec., Meyronne, Sask. SOH 3AO (264-3756)
Midale†	572	Assiniboia	Estevan	D.G. Tisdale, Town Adm., Midale, Sask. SOC 1SO (458-2400)
Middle Lake‡	270	Humboldt-Lake Centre	Kinistino	Mrs. C. Winkel, Village Sec., Middle Lake, Sask. SOK 2XO (367-2149)
Milden‡	249	Kindersley-Lloydminster	Rosetown-Elrose	Mrs. D. Linklater, Village Sec., Milden, Sask. SOL 2LO (935-2032)
Milden RM No. 286	512			J.F.H. Penner, Sec., Box 160, Milden, Sask. SOL 2LO (935-2181)
Milestone†	609	Assiniboia	Bengough-Milestone	E.P. Audette, Town Adm., Milestone, Sask. SOG 3LO (436-2130)

Cities in CAPITALS; Towns marked †; Villages marked ‡; Balance are Rural Municipalities .
Area Code for Saskatchewan is 306

MUNICIPALITY	POP.	FEDERAL ELECTORAL DISTRICT	PROVINCIAL ELECTORAL DISTRICT	ADM. OR SECRETARY WITH ADDRESS & PHONE
Milton RM No. 292	333			H.S. Murray, Sec., Box 70, Marengo, Sask. SOL 2KO (968-2741)
Minton‡	159	Assiniboia	Bengough-Milestone	D. Malmgren, Village Sec., Minton, Sask. SOC 1TO (969-2144)
Miry Creek RM No. 229	573			R.B. Sylvestre, Sec., Box 210, Abbey, Sask. SON OAO (689-2281)
Mistatim‡	139	Mackenzie	Kelsey-Tisdale	Mrs. L.J. Legare, Village Sec., Mistatim, Sask. SOE 1BO (889-2022)
Mistusinne‡	309			C. Desjardins, Mistusinne Village Sec., c/o 64 Tibbits Rd., Regina, Sask. S4S 2Z1 (586-5498)
Monet RM No. 257	864			P.J. Pylatuk, Sec., Box 370, Elrose, Sask. SOL OZO (378-2212)
Montmartre‡	552	Assiniboia	Indian Head-Wolseley	W.A. Laturnus, Village Sec., Box 120, Montmartre, Sask. SOG 3MO (424-2040)
Montmartre RM No. 126	1,027			c/o Montmartre Village Sec.
Montrose RM No. 315	606			N. French, Sec., Box 7, Donavon, Sask. SOL OWO (493-2694)
Moose Creek RM No. 33	595			W.M. Bennett, Sec., Box 10, Alameda, Sask. SOC OAO (489-2044)
MOOSE JAW	33,441	Moose Jaw	Moose Jaw North; Moose Jaw South	G. Stratton, City Clerk, City Hall, 228 Main St. N., Moose Jaw, Sask. S6H 3J8 (693-3621)
Moose Jaw RM No. 161	2,248			J. Nichols, Sec., 170 Fairford St. W., Moose Jaw, Sask. S6H 1V3 (692-3446)
Moose Mountain RM No. 63	768			Mrs. Rita Gauthier, Sec., Box 445, Carlyle, Sask. SOC ORO (453-6175)
Moosomin†	2,525	Qu'Appelle-Moose Mountain	Moosomin	Bob Wilson, Town Adm., Moosomin, Sask. SOG 3NO (435-2988)
Moosomin RM No. 121	641			Ken Engel, Sec., Box 1109, Moosomin, Sask. SOG 3NO (435-3113)
Moose Range RM No. 486	1,703			Mrs. M. McDonald, Sec., Box 699, Carrot River, Sask. SOE OLO (768-2212)
Morris RM No. 312	629			L. Stangland, Sec., Box 130, Young, Sask. SOK 4YO (259-2211)
Morse†	435	Swift Current-Maple Creek	Morse	Mrs. E. Lepp, Town Adm., Morse, Sask. SOH 3CO (629-3300)
Morse RM No. 165	830			J.A. Whyte, Sec., Box 340, Morse, Sask. SOH 3CO (629-3282)
Mortlach‡	317	Moose Jaw	Thunder Creek	Mrs. M. Grajczyk, Village Clerk, Mortlach, Sask. SOH 3EO (355-2239)
Mossbank†	444	Assiniboia	Assiniboia-Gravelbourg	Mrs. D. Tremblay, Town Adm., Mossbank, Sask. SOH 3GO (354-2414)
Mountain View RM No. 318	581			Mrs. S. Clayton, Sec., Box 130, Herschel, Sask. SOL 1LO (377-2144)
Mount Hope RM No. 279	886			Jim Down, Sec., Box 190, Semans, Sask. SOA 3SO (524-2055)
Mount Pleasant RM No. 2	524			B.R. Miller, Sec., Box 278, Carnduff, Sask. SOC OSO (482-3313)
Muenster‡	383	Humboldt-Lake Centre	Quill Lakes	L.P. Mitzel, Village Sec., Muenster, Sask. SOK 2YO (682-2794)
Naicam†	859	Humboldt-Lake Centre	Melfort	Ruby Lindsay, Town Adm., Naicam, Sask. SOK 2ZO (874-2280)
Neilburg‡	369	Kindersley-Lloydminster	Cutknife-Lloydminster	Dale Bryden, Village Sec., Neilburg, Sask. SOM 2CO (823-4321)
Netherhill‡	83	Kindersley-Lloydminster	Kindersley	Mrs. J. Shaver, Village Sec., Netherhill, Sask. SOL 2MO (463-3562)
Neudorf‡	437	Qu'Appelle-Moose Mountain	Melville	Mrs. S. Waldbauer, Village Sec., Neudorf, Sask. SOA 2TO (748-2551)
Neville‡	129	Swift Current-Maple Creek	Morse	Mrs. G. Porter, Village Sec., Neville, Sask. SON 1TO (627-3255)
Newcombe RM No. 260	633			D.H. Maddocks, Sec., Box 40, Glidden, Sask. SOL 1HO (463-3338)
Nipawin†	4,352	Mackenzie	Nipawin	J.S. Pass, Town Adm., Nipawin, Sask. SOE 1EO (862-4666)
Nipawin RM No. 487	1,360			Mrs. L.L. Drobot, Sec., Box 250, Codette, Sask. SOE OPO (862-5032)

Cities in CAPITALS; Towns marked †; Villages marked ‡; Balance are Rural Municipalities .
Area Code for Saskatchewan is 306

MUNICIPALITY	POP.	FEDERAL ELECTORAL DISTRICT	PROVINCIAL ELECTORAL DISTRICT	ADM. OR SECRETARY WITH ADDRESS & PHONE
Nokomis†	535	Humboldt-Lake Centre	Last Mountain-Touchwood	Steve Hryniuk, Town Adm., Nokomis, Sask. SOG 3RO (528-2010)
Norquay†	538	Yorkton-Melville	Pelly	R. Johnson, Town Adm., Norquay, Sask. SOA 2VO (594-2101)
NORTH BATTLEFORD	13,884	The Battlefords-Meadow Lake	The Battlefords	J.B. Jansen, City Clerk, City Hall, 1291 101 St., Box 460, North Battleford, Sask. S9A 2Y6 (445-9431)
North Battleford RM No. 437	874			B.W. Kosolofski, Sec., 1131 100 St., North Battleford, Sask. S9A OV3 (445-3604)
North Qu'Appelle RM No. 187	965			R. Patterson, Sec., Box 99, Fort Qu'Appelle, Sask. SOG 1SO (332-5202)
North Portal‡	157	Qu'Appelle-Moose Mountain	Estevan	C.J. Mitchell, Village Sec., North Portal, Sask. SOC 1WO (927-2865)
Norton RM No. 69	529			W. Lozinsky, Sec., Box 189, Pangman, Sask. SOC 2CO (442-2131)
Oakdale RM No. 320	529			W.S. Bruce, Sec., Box 249, Coleville, Sask. SOL OKO (965-2281)
Odessa‡	219	Assiniboia	Indian Head-Wolseley	Mrs. Y. Schatz, Village Sec., Odessa, Sask. SOG 3SO (957-2020)
Ogema†	436	Assiniboia	Bengough-Milestone	C. Lozinsky, Town Adm., Ogema, Sask. SOC 1YO (459-2230)
Old Post RM No. 43	905			E.P. Gasper, Sec., Box 70, Glentworth, Sask. S0H 1V0 (266-2002)
Orkney RM No. 244	2,578			J. Gazdewich, Sec., 26 5th Ave. N., Yorkton, Sask. S3N OY8 (782-2333)
Osage‡	58	Assiniboia	Weyburn	Mrs. H. Glover, Village Sec., Osage, Sask. SOG 3TO (722-3706)
Osler‡	437	Saskatoon West	Rosthern	Mrs. S. Peters, Village Sec., Osler, Sask. SOK 3AO (239-2155)
Outlook†	1,916	Moose Jaw	Arm River	L.W. Zarubiak, Town Adm., Outlook, Sask. SOL 2NO (867-8663)
Oxbow†	1,225	Qu'Appelle-Moose Mountain	Souris-Cannington	J.D. Haigh, Town Adm., Oxbow, Sask. SOC 2BO (483-2300)
Paddockwood‡	220	Prince Albert	Shellbrook	Mrs. K. McCalmon, Village Sec., Paddock-wood, Sask. SOJ 1ZO (989-2033)
Paddockwood RM No. 520	1,267			H.A. Stobbs, Sec., Box 120, Paddockwood, Sask. SOJ 1ZO (989-2124)
Palmer‡	58	Assiniboia	Assiniboia-Gravelbourg	W. Torgerson, Village Sec., Palmer, Sask. SOH 3JO (648-2838)
Pangman‡	245	Assiniboia	Bengough-Milestone	W. Lozinsky, Village Sec., Pangman, Sask. SOC 2CO (442-2131)
Paradise Hill‡	392	The Battlefords-Meadow Lake	Meadow Lake	Mrs. L. Marchadour, Village Sec., Paradise Hill, Sask. SOM 2GO (344-2066)
Parkdale RM No. 498	978			Mrs. C.W.J. Carnegie, Sec., Box 310, Glaslyn, Sask. SOM OYO (342-2015)
Parkside‡	100	Prince Albert	Redberry	A.P. Broten, Village Sec., Parkside, Sask. SOJ 2AO (747-2772)
Paynton‡	186	Kindersley-Lloydminster	Cutknife-Lloydminster	J.A. Wilson, Village Sec., Paynton, Sask. SOM 2JO (895-2020)
Paynton RM No. 470	334			c/o Paynton Village Sec.
Pelly‡	386	Yorkton-Melville	Pelly	Max Temrick, Village Sec., Pelly, Sask. SOA 2ZO (595-2124)
Pennant‡	216	Swift Current-Maple Creek	Morse	Mrs. V. Olson, Village Sec., Pennant, Sask. SON 1XO (626-3316)
Pense‡	457	Moose Jaw	Thunder Creek	L. Morrison, Village Sec., Pense, Sask. SOG 3WO (345-2332)
Pense RM No. 160	588			Ms. J. Foster, Sec., Box 190, Pense, Alta. SOG 3WO (345-2303)
Penzance‡	78	Moose Jaw	Arm River	Mrs. C. Strachan, Village Sec., Penzance, Sask. SOG 2XO (488-4802)
Perdue‡	454	Saskatoon West	Biggar	L.K. Foster, Village Sec., Box 208, Perdue, Sask. SOK 3CO (237-4337)
Perdue RM No. 346	530			See Perdue Village Sec. (237-4202)
Piapot‡	123	Swift Current-Maple Creek	Maple Creek	S.C. McGillivray, Village Sec., Box 100, Piapot, Sask. SON 1YO (262-2011)
Piapot RM No. 110	532			c/o Piapot Village Sec.
Pierceland‡	358	The Battlefords-Meadow Lake	Meadow Lake	Ms. D. Johnson, Village Sec., Pierceland, Sask. SOM 2KO (839-2015)

Cities in CAPITALS; Towns marked †; Villages marked ‡; Balance are Rural Municipalities .
Area Code for Saskatchewan is 306

MUNICIPALITY	POP.	FEDERAL ELECTORAL DISTRICT	PROVINCIAL ELECTORAL DISTRICT	ADM. OR SECRETARY WITH ADDRESS & PHONE
Pilger‡	147	Humboldt-Lake Centre	Kinistino	Mrs. L. Bregenser, Village Sec., Pilger, Sask. SOK 3GO (367-4927)
Pilot Butte†	1,089	Regina East	Qu'Appelle	Mrs. P. Leibel, Town Adm., Pilot Butte, Sask. SOG 3ZO (561-2247)
Pinto Creek RM No. 75	365			Mrs. H.J. Lott, Sec., Box 239, Kincaid, Sask. SOH 2JO (264-3277)
Pittville RM No. 169	436			P. Buchanan, Sec., Box 150, Hazlet, Sask. SON 1EO (678-2131)
Plato‡	48	Kindersley-Lloydminster	Kindersley	G.H. Redhead, Village Sec., Plato, Sask. SOL 2PO (574-2134)
Pleasantdale RM No. 398	1,063			A. Loyns, Sec., Pleasantdale, Sask. SOK 3HO (874-5732)
Pleasant Valley RM No. 288	505			Ms. S.L. Reynolds, Sec., Box 36, McGee, Sask. SOL 2BO (882-3394)
Plenty‡	204	Kindersley-Lloydminster	Kindersley	Mrs. L. Doering, Village Sec., Plenty, Sask. SOL 2RO (932-2045)
Plunkett‡	162	Humboldt-Lake Centre	Humboldt	Mrs. E. Shoemaker, Village Sec., Plunkett, Sask. SOK 3JO (944-4514)
Ponass Lake RM No. 367	1,240			Freda Lysyshin, Sec., Box 98, Rose Valley, Sask. SOE 1MO (322-2162)
Ponteix†	760	Swift Current-Maple Creek	Shaunavon	Mrs. L. Roberge, Town Adm., Ponteix, Sask. SON 1ZO (625-3222)
Poplar Valley RM No. 12	420			L. Kimball, Sec., Box 190, Rockglen, Sask. SOH 3RO (476-2062)
Porcupine RM No. 395	1,938			Ed Poniatowski, Sec., Box 190, Porcupine Plain, Sask. SOE 1HO (278-2368)
Porcupine Plain†	953	Mackenzie	Kelsey-Tisdale	A.F. Kaeding, Town Adm., Porcupine Plain, Sask. SOE 1HO (278-2262)
Prairie RM No. 408	698			F.A. Klotz, Sec., 201 21st St., Battleford, Sask. SOM OEO (937-2321)
Prairiedale RM No. 321	503			W.C. Hofmann, Sec., Box 90, Smiley, Sask. SOL 2ZO (964-2020)
Prairie Rose RM No. 309	584			D.C. McBurney, Sec., Box 89, Jansen, Sask. SOK 2BO (364-2013)
Preeceville†	1,253	Yorkton-Melville	Canora	I.K. Britton, Town Adm., Preeceville, Sask. SOA 3BO (547-2810)
Preeceville RM No. 334	1,697			P. Predy, Sec., Box 439, Preeceville, Sask. SOA 3BO (547-2029)
Prelate‡	337	Swift Current-Maple Creek	Maple Creek	W.J. Kosolofski, Village Sec., Prelate, Sask. SON 2BO (673-2340)
Primate‡	56	Kindersley-Lloydminster	Wilkie	H.R. Ostrosky, Village Sec., Primate, Sask. SOL 2SO (753-2875)
PRINCE ALBERT	30,121	Prince Albert	Prince Albert; Prince Albert-Duck Lake	T.M. Topping, City Clerk, City Hall, 1521 6th Ave. W., Prince Albert, Sask. S6V 5K2 (764-5251)
Prince Albert RM No. 461	3,169			P.G. Brown, Sec., 99 River St. E., Prince Albert, Sask. S6V OA1 (763-2469)
Progress RM No. 351	586			Mrs. D. Gerrard, Sec., Box 130, Luseland, Sask. SOL 2AO (372-4322)
Prud'homme‡	239	Humboldt-Lake Centre	Kinistino	Lucille Miskolczi, Village Sec., Prud'-homme, Sask. SOK 3KO (654-2165)
Punnichy‡	400	Humboldt-Lake Centre	Last Mountain-Touchwood	Mrs. G. Thibault, Village Sec., Punnichy, Sask. SOA 3CO (835-2135)
Qu'Appelle†	551	Regina East	Qu'Appelle	D. Ramsay, Town Adm., Qu'Appelle, Sask. SOG 4AO (699-2279)
Quill Lake‡	534	Humboldt-Lake Centre	Quill Lakes	Don Camp, Village Sec., Quill Lake, Sask. SOA 3EO (385-2592)
Quinton‡	189	Humboldt-Lake Centre	Last Mountain-Touchwood	H.M. Brockman, Village Sec., Quinton, Sask. SOA 3GO (835-2515)
Rabbit Lake‡	166	The Battlefords-Meadow Lake	Redberry	Ian McLennan, Village Sec., Rabbit Lake, Sask. SOM 2LO (824-2044)
Radisson†	444	The Battlefords-Meadow Lake	Redberry	P. Matyshyn, Town Adm., Radisson, Sask. SOK 3LO (827-2218)
Radville†	1,026	Assiniboia	Bengough-Milestone	L.R. Fisher, Town Adm., Radville, Sask. SOC 2GO (869-2477)
Rama‡	163	Yorkton-Melville	Canora	M. Brazinski, Village Sec., Rama, Sask. SOA 3HO (593-6065)
Raymore†	596	Humboldt-Lake Centre	Last Mountain-Touchwood	Arnold Maki, Town Adm., Raymore, Sask. SOA 3JO (746-2100)

Cities in CAPITALS; Towns marked †; Villages marked ‡; Balance are Rural Municipalities .
Area Code for Saskatchewan is 306

MUNICIPALITY	POP.	FEDERAL ELECTORAL DISTRICT	PROVINCIAL ELECTORAL DISTRICT	ADM. OR SECRETARY WITH ADDRESS & PHONE
Reciprocity RM No. 32	619			Rod Heise, Sec., Box 70, Alida, Sask. SOC OBO (443-2212)
Redberry RM No. 435	820			A.J. Tanchak, Sec., Box 160, Hafford, Sask. SOJ 1AO (549-2333)
Redburn RM No. 130	395			G.S. Drysdale, Sec., Box 250, Rouleau, Sask. SOG 4HO (776-2270)
Redvers†	910	Qu'Appelle-Moose Mountain	Souris-Cannington	E. Sigmeth, Town Adm., Redvers, Sask. SOC 2HO (452-3533)
Reford RM No. 379	605			K.E. Reiter, Sec., Box 689, Wilkie, Sask. SOK 4WO (843-2342)
REGINA	153,848	Regina East; Regina West	Qu'Appelle; Regina Centre; Reg. Elphinstone; Reg. Lakeview; Reg. North East; Reg. North West; Reg. Rosemont; Reg. South; Reg. Victoria; Reg. Wascana	Dean Power, City Clerk, City Hall, Box 1790, Regina, Sask. S4P 3C8 (569-7262)
Regina Beach†	632	Moose Jaw	Qu'Appelle	Annette Bower, Town Adm., Regina Beach, Sask. SOG 4CO (938-2202)
Reno RM No. 51	711			W.T. Manley, Sec., Box 90, Consul, Sask. SON OPO (299-2133)
Rhein‡	284	Yorkton-Melville	Pelly	H.P. Mengering, Village Sec., Rhein, Sask. SOA 3KO (273-2155)
Richard‡	25	The Battlefords-Meadow Lake	Redberry	E.A. Sargent, Village Sec., Richard, Sask. SOM 2VO (246-2171)
Richmound‡	186	Swift Current-Maple Creek	Maple Creek	Louis Franz, Village Sec., Richmound, Sask. SON 2EO (669-2166)
Ridgedale‡	147	Mackenzie	Nipawin	Mrs. E. Campbell, Village Sec., Ridgedale, Sask. SOE 1LO (277-2002)
Riverhurst‡	182	Moose Jaw	Thunder Creek	Mrs. A. Olson, Village Sec., Riverhurst, Sask. SOH 3PO (353-2220)
Riverside RM No. 168	703			A. Dionne, Sec., Box 129, Pennant, Sask. SON 1XO (626-3255)
Robsart‡	44	Swift Current-Maple Creek	Shaunavon	W.D. Olmsted, Village Sec., Robsart, Sask. SON 2GO (299-4400)
Rocanville†	927	Qu'Appelle-Moose Mountain	Moosomin	E. Neufeld, Town Adm., Rocanville, Sask. SOA 3LO (645-2022)
Rocanville RM No. 151	852			G.D. Giegle, Sec., Box 298, Rocanville, Sask. SOA 3LO (645-2055)
Roche Percée‡	129	Assiniboia	Estevan	Mrs. B. Thompson, Village Sec., Roche Percée, Sask. SOC OMO (634-4659)
Rockglen†	540	Assiniboia	Assiniboia-Gravelbourg	Mrs. L.M. Lawrick, Town Adm., Rockglen, Sask. SOH 3RO (476-2144)
Rockhaven‡	47	Kindersley-Lloydminster	Cutknife-Lloydminster	Mrs. S. Smith, Village Sec., Rockhaven, Sask. SOM 2RO (398-2744)
Rodgers RM No. 133	381			Roy Lucas, Sec., Box 70, Courval, Sask. SOH 1AO (394-4925)
Rosedale RM No. 283	608			W. Resch, Sec., Box 150, Hanley, Sask. SOG 2EO (544-2202)
Rosemount RM No. 378	323			P.B. Berezowski, Sec., Box 184, Landis, Sask. SOK 4JO (658-2034)
Rosetown†	2,720	Kindersley-Lloydminster	Rosetown-Elrose	K.S. Green, Town Adm., Rosetown, Sask. SOL 2VO (882-2214)
Rose Valley†	534	Mackenzie	Kelvington-Wadena	M.H. Holm, Town Adm., Rose Valley, Sask. SOE 1MO (322-2232)
Rosthern†	1,530	Prince Albert	Rosthern	Erryl Roth, Town Adm., Rosthern, Sask. SOK 3RO (232-4313)
Rosthern RM No. 403	1,986			K.W. Burnham, Sec., Box 126, Rosthern, Sask. SOK 3RO (232-4393)
Rouleau†	449	Moose Jaw	Thunder Creek	G.S. Drysdale, Town Adm., Rouleau, Sask. SOG 4HO (776-2270)
Round Hill RM No. 467	519			Ian McLennan, Sec., Box 9, Rabbit Lake, Sask. SOM 2LO (824-2044)
Round Valley RM No. 410	654			Garry Ritsco, Sec., Box 538, Unity, Sask. SOK 4LO (228-2248)
Ruddell‡	25	The Battlefords-Meadow Lake	Redberry	W.T. Buttrey, Village Sec., Ruddell, Sask. SOM 2SO (389-4813)
Rudy RM No. 284	572			Lois Haug, Sec., Box 1010, Outlook, Sask. S0L 2N0 (867-9349)

Cities in CAPITALS; Towns marked †; Villages marked ‡; Balance are Rural Municipalities.
Area Code for Saskatchewan is 306

MUNICIPALITY	POP.	FEDERAL ELECTORAL DISTRICT	PROVINCIAL ELECTORAL DISTRICT	ADM. OR SECRETARY WITH ADDRESS & PHONE
Rush Lake‡	121	Swift Current-Maple Creek	Morse	F. Steinley, Village Sec., Rush Lake, Sask. SOH 3SO (784-3381)
Ruthilda‡	46	Kindersley-Lloydminster	Biggar	Mrs. Pat Richards, Village Sec., Ruthilda, Sask. SOK 3SO (932-4426)
St. Andrews RM No. 287	666			M.S. Dyck, Sec., Box 488, Rosetown, Sask. SOL 2VO (882-2314)
St. Benedict‡	164	Humboldt-Lake Centre	Kinistino	Mrs. J. Martin, Village Sec., St. Benedict, Sask. SOK 3TO (289-2140)
St. Brieux‡	362	Humboldt-Lake Centre	Melfort	L. Bernard, Village Sec., St. Brieux, Sask. SOK 3VO (275-2066)
St. Gregor‡	144	Humboldt-Lake Centre	Quill Lakes	F. Raab, Village Sec., St. Gregor, Sask. SOK 3XO (366-2135)
St. Louis‡	441	Prince Albert	Kinistino	Mrs. Rita Ferland, Village Sec., St. Louis, Sask. SOJ 2CO (422-8471)
St. Louis RM No. 431	1,504			L.G. Gareau, Sec., Hoey, Sask. SOJ 1EO (423-6170)
St. Peter RM No. 369	1,487			J. Verhelst, Sec., Annaheim, Sask. SOK OGO (598-2122)
St. Philips RM No. 301	636			J. Vanin, Sec., Box 220, Pelly, Sask. SOA 2ZO (595-2050)
St. Victor‡	81	Assiniboia	Assiniboia-Gravelbourg	L. Collin, Village Sec., St. Victor, Sask. SOH 3TO (642-3218)
St. Walburg†	718	The Battlefords-Meadow Lake	Meadow Lake	Ms. M. Rosser-Swift, Town Adm., St. Walburg, Sask. SOM 2TO (248-3232)
Saltcoats†	512	Yorkton-Melville	Saltcoats	S. Spokes, Town Adm., Saltcoats, Sask. SOA 3RO (744-2212)
Saltcoats RM No. 213	1,047			E.M. Kitsch, Sec., Box 150, Saltcoats, Sask. SOA 3RO (744-2202)
Salvador‡	52	Kindersley-Lloydminster	Wilkie	Mrs. D. May, Village Sec., Salvador, Sask. SOL 2WO (372-4578)
Sandy Beach‡	5			R.A. Cairns, Village Sec., Sandy Beach, Sask. S0G 2Y0
Sarnia RM No. 221	483			H. Hemingway, Sec., Box 160, Holdfast, Sask. SOG 2HO (488-2033)
Saskatchewan Beach‡	61	Humboldt-Lake Centre	Last Mountain-Touchwood	Mrs. D. MacDonald, Saskatchewan Beach Village Sec., Box 98, Silton, Sask. S0G 4L0 (935-2932)
Saskatchewan Landing RM No. 167	566	Swift Current-Maple Creek	Morse	W.L. Kreuger, Sec., Box 40, Stewart Valley, Sask. SON 2PO (773-9115)
SASKATOON	144,269	Saskatoon East; Saskatoon West	S'toon Buena Vista; S'toon Centre; S'toon Eastview; S'toon Mayfair; S'toon Nutana; S'toon Riversdale; S'toon Sutherland; S'toon Westmount	J. Kolynchuk, City Clerk, City Hall, Saskatoon, Sask. S7K OJ5 (644-9240)
Sasman RM No. 336	1,594			S.J. Little, Sec., Box 130, Kuroki, Sask. SOA 1YO (338-2097)
Sceptre‡	204	Swift Current-Maple Creek	Maple Creek	Ms. Mina Anderson, Village Sec., Sceptre, Sask. SON 2HO (623-4244)
Scott†	209	Kindersley-Lloydminster	Wilkie	Mrs. L.F. Nielsen, Town Clerk, Scott, Sask. SOK 4AO (247-2100)
Scott RM No. 98	503			P.P. Thiele, Sec., Box 210, Yellow Grass, Sask. SOG 5JO (465-2512)
Sedley‡	367	Assiniboia	Indian Head-Wolseley	Mrs. C.S. Ferguson, Village Sec., Sedley, Sask. SOG 1VO (885-2133)
Semans‡	377	Humboldt-Lake Centre	Last Mountain-Touchwood	Mrs. Sharon Church, Village Sec., Box 113, Semans, Sask. SOA 3SO (524-2144)
Senlac‡	107	Kindersley-Lloydminster	Wilkie	Calvin Giggs, Village Sec., Box 130, Senlac, Sask. SOL 2YO (228-3339)
Senlac RM No. 411	364			c/o Senlac Village Sec.
Shackleton‡	38	Swift Current-Maple Creek	Maple Creek	Mrs. M.J. Heron, Village Sec., Shackleton, Sask. SON 2LO (587-2960)
Shamrock‡	78	Moose Jaw	Thunder Creek	Mrs. R.M. Drake, Village Sec., Shamrock, Sask. SOH 3WO (648-2915)
Shamrock RM No. 134	437			E.A. Henry, Sec., Box 40, Shamrock, Sask. SOH 3WO (648-3594)
Shaunavon†	2,183	Swift Current-Maple Creek	Shaunavon	Mrs. I. Houston, Town Adm., Box 820, Shaunavon, Sask. SON 2MO (297-2605)

Cities in CAPITALS; Towns marked †; Villages marked ‡; Balance are Rural Municipalities .
Area Code for Saskatchewan is 306

MUNICIPALITY	POP.	FEDERAL ELECTORAL DISTRICT	PROVINCIAL ELECTORAL DISTRICT	ADM. OR SECRETARY WITH ADDRESS & PHONE
Sheho‡	313	Yorkton-Melville	Kelvington-Wadena	F.W. Korpatnicki, Village Sec., Sheho, Sask. SOA 3TO (849-2044)
Shellbrook†	1,171	Prince Albert	Shellbrook	Kenneth Danger, Town Adm., Box 40, Shellbrook, Sask. SOJ 2EO (747-2262)
Shellbrook RM No. 493	1,805			c/o Shellbrook Village Sec.
Shell Lake‡	245	Prince Albert	Turtleford	E.W. Dallman, Village Sec., Shell Lake, Sask. SOJ 2GO (427-2272)
Sherwood RM No. 159	1,598			M.P. Schneider, Sec., 1840 Cornwall St., Regina, Sask. S4P 2K2 (525-5237)
Shields‡	459			G. Schmidt, Shields Village Sec., c/o 258 Anderson Cres., Saskatoon, Sask. S7H 4C2 (374-7936)
Silton‡	66	Humboldt-Lake Centre	Last Mountain-Touchwood	F. Thompson, Village Sec., Silton, Sask. SOG 4LO (485-2908)
Silverwood RM No. 123	897			M.P. Demofsky, Sec., Whitewood, Sask. SOG 5CO (735-2500)
Simpson‡	223	Moose Jaw	Arm River	Don Bergsveinson, Village Sec., Simpson, Sask. SOG 4MO (836-2020)
Sintaluta†	213	Qu'Appelle-Moose Mountain	Indian Head-Wolseley	Mrs. Ann Dolter, Town Adm., Sintaluta, Sask. SOG 4NO (727-2100)
Sliding Hills RM No. 273	1,189			A.S. Matsalla, Sec., Box 70, Mikado, Sask. SOA 2RO (563-5083)
Smeaton‡	275	Prince Albert	Shellbrook	Mrs. A. Falloon, Village Sec., Smeaton, Sask. SOJ 2JO (426-2044)
Smiley‡	111	Kindersley-Lloydminster	Kindersley	W.C. Hofmann, Village Sec., Smiley, Sask. SOL 2ZO (964-2020)
Snipe Lake RM No. 259	1,012			K.J. Fitzmaurice, Sec., Box 786, Eston, Sask. SOL 1AO (962-3214)
Southey†	704	Humboldt-Lake Centre	Last Mountain-Touchwood	Eric Schneider, Town Adm., Southey, Sask. SOG 4PO (726-2202)
South Qu'Appelle RM No. 157	1,213			D.R. McLeod, Sec., Box 66, Qu'Appelle, Sask. SOG 4AO (699-2257)
Souris Valley RM No. 7	585			Mrs. Jo Ann Wanner, Sec., Box 40, Oungre, Sask. SOC 1ZO (456-2676)
Sovereign‡	68	Kindersley-Lloydminster	Rosetown-Elrose	Mrs. A.M. Elliott, Village Sec., Sovereign, Sask. SOL 3AO (882-3743)
Spalding‡	357	Humboldt-Lake Centre	Melfort	Arlene Grunsky, Village Sec., Spalding, Sask. SOK 4CO (872-2276)
Spalding RM No. 368	1,096			I.W. Bonter, Sec., Box 10, Spalding, Sask. SOK 4CO (872-2166)
Speers‡	135	The Battlefords-Meadow Lake	Redberry	H.R. Nowoselski, Village Sec., Speers, Sask. SOM 2VO (246-2171)
Spiritwood†	901	The Battlefords-Meadow Lake	Turtleford	Mervin Vey, Town Adm., Spiritwood, Sask. SOJ 2MO (883-2161)
Spiritwood RM No. 496	1,944			R. Chambers, Sec., Spiritwood, Sask. SOJ 2MO (883-2034)
Springside‡	513	Yorkton-Melville	Canora	Mrs. C. Merriman, Village Sec., Springside, Sask. SOA 3VO (792-2022)
Spring Valley‡	44	Assiniboia	Bengough-Milestone	J.J. Thiele, Village Sec., Spring Valley, Sask. SOH 3XO (475-2803)
Springwater‡	79	Kindersley-Lloydminster	Biggar	Mrs. J. Heimbecker, Village Sec., Springwater, Sask. SOK 4EO (948-2327)
Spruce Lake‡	94	The Battlefords-Meadow Lake	Turtleford	Miss L.M. McKee, Village Sec., Spruce Lake, Sask. SOM 2WO (845-2291)
Spy Hill‡	352	Qu'Appelle-Moose Mountain	Saltcoats	Mrs. H. Plewes, Village Sec., Spy Hill, Sask. SOA 3WO (534-2255)
Spy Hill RM No. 152	684			A. Faul, Sec., Box 129, Spy Hill, Sask. SOA 3WO (534-2022)
Stanley RM No. 215	1,136			E.M. Kitsch, Sec., Box 70, Melville, Sask. SOA 2PO (728-2818)
Star City†	541	Mackenzie	Melfort	Mrs. J.B. Jacklin, Town Adm., Star City, Sask. SOE 1PO (863-2282)
Star City RM No. 428	1,182			Mrs. A. Campbell, Sec., Box 370, Star City, Sask. SOE 1PO (863-2522)
Stenen‡	182	Yorkton-Melville	Pelly	Mrs. V.S. Tanton, Village Sec., Stenen, Sask. SOA 3XO (548-4941)
Stewart Valley‡	126	Swift Current-Maple Creek	Morse	Mrs. D.E. Kreuger, Village Sec., Stewart Valley, Sask. SON 2PO (773-9115)

Cities in CAPITALS; Towns marked †; Villages marked ‡; Balance are Rural Municipalities .
Area Code for Saskatchewan is 306

MUNICIPALITY	POP.	FEDERAL ELECTORAL DISTRICT	PROVINCIAL ELECTORAL DISTRICT	ADM. OR SECRETARY WITH ADDRESS & PHONE
Stockholm‡	387	Qu'Appelle-Moose Mountain	Saltcoats	Mona Jacobs, Village Sec., Stockholm, Sask. SOA 3YO (793-2151)
Stonehenge RM No. 73	795			Fred Auser, Sec., Limerick, Sask. SOH 2PO (263-2020)
Stornoway‡	32	Yorkton-Melville	Pelly	P. Mandzuik, Village Sec., Stornoway, Sask. SOA 3ZO (273-4738)
Storthoaks‡	152	Qu'Appelle-Moose Mountain	Souris-Cannington	Mrs. I. Kirkpatrick, Village Sec., Box 40, Storthoaks, Sask. SOC 2KO (449-2210)
Storthoaks RM No. 31	695			c/o Storthoaks Village Sec.
Stoughton†	705	Qu'Appelle-Moose Mountain	Weyburn	G.W. Figler, Town Adm., Stoughton, Sask. SOG 4TO (457-2413)
Strasbourg†	862	Humboldt-Lake Centre	Last Mountain-Touchwood	Wm. Hunter, Town Adm., Strasbourg, Sask. SOG 4VO (725-3230)
Strongfield‡	101	Moose Jaw	Arm River	Mrs. D. Kennedy, Village Sec., Strongfield, Sask. SOH 3ZO (857-2150)
Sturgis†	786	Yorkton-Melville	Canora	Mrs. Y. Rongve, Town Adm., Sturgis, Sask. SOA 4AO (548-2108)
Success‡	82	Swift Current-Maple Creek	Morse	Mrs. S. Froese, Village Sec., Success, Sask. SON 2RO (773-9132)
Surprise Valley RM No. 9	426			D. Malmgren, Sec., Box 52, Minton, Sask. SOC 1TO (969-2144)
Sutton RM No. 103	544			H.S. Edgerton, Sec., Box 100, Mossbank, Sask. S0H 3G0 (354-2414)
SWIFT CURRENT	14,358	Swift Current-Maple Creek	Swift Current	Mrs. L. Thompson, City Clerk, City Hall, Box 340, 198 1st Ave. N.E., Swift Current, Sask. S9H 3W1 (773-2841)
Swift Current RM No. 137	1,863			J.C. Clark, Sec., Box 1210, Swift Current, Sask. S9H 3X4 (773-7314)
Tantallon‡	186	Qu'Appelle-Moose Mountain	Saltcoats	Mrs. J. Howie, Village Sec., Tantallon, Sask. SOA 4BO (643-2112)
Tecumseh RM No. 65	574			L.R. Cross, Sec., Box 300, Stoughton, Sask. SOG 4TO (457-2277)
Terrell RM No. 101	554			J.J. Thiele, Sec., Box 60, Spring Valley, Sask. SOH 3XO (475-2803)
Tessier‡	54	Saskatoon West	Biggar	Mrs. Ila Major, Village Sec., Tessier, Sask. SOL 3GO (656-4532)
The Gap RM No. 39	453			V.B. McClarty, Sec., Ceylon, Sask. SOC OTO (454-2202)
Theodore‡	463	Yorkton-Melville	Canora	Murray Bilokreli, Village Sec., Theodore, Sask. SOA 4CO (647-2315)
Thode‡	258			Mrs. E. Neudorf, Thode Village Sec., Box 202, Dundurn, Sask. S0K 1K0 (492-4680)
Three Lakes RM No. 400	1,145			Orest Lisitza, Sec., Box 100, Middle Lake, Sask. SOK 2XO (367-2172)
Tisdale†	3,070	Mackenzie	Kelsey-Tisdale	K.E. Smith, Town Adm., Tisdale, Sask. SOE 1TO (873-2681)
Tisdale RM No. 427	1,342			Miss B.L. Humel, Sec., Box 128, Tisdale, Sask. SOE 1TO (873-2334)
Tobin Lake‡	19			Vern Gabriel, Tobin Lake Village Sec., c/o Box 935, Nipawin, Sask. S0E 1E0 (862-5530)
Togo‡	197	Yorkton-Melville	Pelly	D.G. Hackney, Village Sec., Togo, Sask. SOA 4EO (597-2191)
Tompkins‡	274	Swift Current-Maple Creek	Maple Creek	A.L. Forsyth, Village Sec., Tompkins, Sask. SON 2SO (622-2020)
Torch River RM No. 488	2,554			Helen Garinger, Sec., Box 40, White Fox, Sask. SOJ 3BO (276-2066)
Torquay‡	344	Assiniboia	Estevan	I.T. Bonoskoski, Village Sec., Torquay, Sask. SOC 2LO (923-2172)
Touchwood RM No. 248	685			Mrs. P.M. Luthi, Sec., Box 160, Punnichy, Sask. SOA 3CO (835-2110)
Tramping Lake‡	200	Kindersley-Lloydminster	Wilkie	Mrs. E. Reiter, Village Sec., Tramping Lake, Sask. SOK 4HO (755-2002)
Tramping Lake RM No. 380	459			John Savostianik, Sec., Box 129, Scott, Sask. SOK 4AO (247-2033)
Tribune‡	78	Assiniboia	Bengough-Milestone	Mrs. K.M. Seghers, Village Sec., Tribune, Sask. SOC 2MO (456-2213)

Cities in CAPITALS; Towns marked †; Villages marked ‡; Balance are Rural Municipalities .
Area Code for Saskatchewan is 306

MUNICIPALITY	POP.	FEDERAL ELECTORAL DISTRICT	PROVINCIAL ELECTORAL DISTRICT	ADM. OR SECRETARY WITH ADDRESS & PHONE
Tugaske‡	179	Moose Jaw	Thunder Creek	Miss Nell Black, Village Sec., Tugaske, Sask. SOH 4BO (759-2243)
Tullymet RM No. 216	554			Mrs. D. McKinnon, Sec., Box 190, Balcarres, Sask. SOG OCO (334-2366)
Turtleford‡	442	The Battlefords-Meadow Lake	Turtleford	Ms. M.R. Conacher, Village Sec., Turtleford, Sask. SOM 2YO (845-2156)
Turtle River RM No. 469	485			Joe McMurphy, Sec., Box 128, Edam, Sask. SOM OVO (397-2311)
Tuxford‡	116	Moose Jaw	Thunder Creek	Maud Grand, Village Sec., Tuxford, Sask. SOH 4CO (693-2744)
Unity†	2,358	Kindersley-Lloydminster	Wilkie	Mrs. E. Sword, Town Adm., Box 1030, Unity, Sask. SOK 4LO (228-2661)
Uranium (Mun. Corp)	2,028	The Battlefords-Meadow Lake	Athabasca	W. Seaman, Mun. Corp. Clerk, Uranium, Sask. SOJ 2WO (498-3441)
Usborne RM No. 310	687			E.E. Weninger, Sec., Box 310, Lanigan, Sask. SOK 2MO (365-2924)
Val Marie‡	260	Swift Current-Maple Creek	Shaunavon	Mrs. L. Carlier, Village Sec., Val Marie, Ont. SON 2TO (298-2022)
Val Marie RM No. 17	722			B.W. Dixon, Sec., Box 59, Val Marie, Sask. SON 2TO (298-2009)
Valparaiso‡	58	Mackenzie	Melfort	Ms. J. Gervan, Village Sec., Valparaiso, Sask. SOE 1TO (873-2681)
Vanguard‡	286	Swift Current-Maple Creek	Morse	R.W. Kehoe, Village Sec., Vanguard, Sask. SON 2VO (582-2010)
Vanscoy‡	276	Saskatoon West	Biggar	Mrs. B. Thomas, Village Sec., Vanscoy, Sask. SOL 3JO (668-2008)
Vanscoy RM No. 345	1,376			W.R. Keeler, Sec., Vanscoy, Sask. SOL 3JO (668-2060)
Vawn‡	83	The Battlefords-Meadow Lake	Turtleford	Mrs. N. Johnson, Village Sec., Box 22, Vawn, Sask. SOM 2ZO (397-2526)
Veregin‡	164	Yorkton-Melville	Pelly	Mrs. Eva Moskal, Village Sec., Veregin, Sask. SOA 4HO (542-3420)
Vibank‡	384	Assiniboia	Indian Head-Wolseley	Mrs. M. Ecarnot, Village Sec., Vibank, Sask. SOG 4YO (762-2166)
Viceroy‡	109	Assiniboia	Assiniboia-Gravelbourg	Mrs. H. Dahl, Village Sec., Box 95, Viceroy, Sask. SOH 4HO (268-4543)
Victory RM No. 226	555			Mrs. R. Fraser, Sec., Box 100, Beechy, Sask. SOL OCO (859-2270)
Viscount‡	395	Humboldt-Lake Centre	Humboldt	Lloyd Wilkie, Village Sec., Box 100, Viscount, Sask. SOK 4MO (944-2199)
Viscount RM No. 341	767			M.H. Setrum, Sec., Box 100, Viscount, Sask. SOK 4MO (944-2044)
Vonda†	328	Humboldt-Lake Centre	Rosthern	Mrs. B. Ulmer, Town Adm., Vonda, Sask. SOK 4NO (258-2035)
Wadena†	1,509	Humboldt-Lake Centre	Kelvington-Wadena	L. Stanley, Town Adm., Wadena, Sask. SOA 4JO (338-2145)
Wakaw†	1,067	Prince Albert	Kinistino	Vic Chicoine, Town Adm., Wakaw, Sask. SOK 4PO (233-4223)
Wakaw Lake‡	16			R.L. Kindrachuk, Village Sec., Box 160, Wakaw, Sask. SOK 4PO (233-4412)
Waldeck‡	280	Swift Current-Maple Creek	Morse	Mrs. Kathy Lang, Village Sec., Waldeck, Sask. SOH 4JO (773-6275)
Waldheim†	706	Prince Albert	Rosthern	P. Ratzlaff, Town Adm., Waldheim, Sask. SOK 4RO (945-2161)
Waldron‡	61	Qu'Appelle-Moose Mountain	Saltcoats	Mrs. E.L. Smith, Village Sec., Waldron, Sask. SOA 4KO (728-5395)
Wallace RM No. 243	1,169			John Gazdewich, Sec., 26 5th Ave. N., Yorkton, Sask. S3N OY8 (782-2333)
Walpole RM No. 92	806			Carl Anderson, Sec., Box 90, Wawota, Sask. SOG 5AO (739-2545)
Wapella†	453	Qu'Appelle-Moose Mountain	Moosomin	Mrs. J. Ewasiuk, Town Clerk, Wapella, Sask. SOG 4ZO (532-4343)
Warman†	1,726	Saskatoon	Rosthern	P. Cannon, Town Adm., Warman, Sask. SOK 4SO (662-2133)
Waseca‡	84	Kindersley-Lloydminster	Cutknife-Lloydminster	Vera MacKay, Village Sec., Waseca, Sask. SOM 3AO (893-2900)
Watrous†	1,683	Humboldt-Lake Centre	Humboldt	C. Skrupski, Town Adm., Watrous, Sask. SOK 4TO (946-3369)

Cities in CAPITALS; Towns marked †; Villages marked ‡; Balance are Rural Municipalities .
Area Code for Saskatchewan is 306

MUNICIPALITY	POP.	FEDERAL ELECTORAL DISTRICT	PROVINCIAL ELECTORAL DISTRICT	ADM. OR SECRETARY WITH ADDRESS & PHONE
Watson†	944	Humboldt-Lake Centre	Quill Lakes	L. Negraeff, Town Adm., Watson, Sask. SOK 4VO (287-3224)
Waverley RM No. 44	523			E.P. Gasper, Sec., Box 70, Glentworth, Sask. SOH 1VO (266-4920)
Wawken RM No. 93	787			c/o Wawota Town Adm. (739-2332)
Wawota†	622	Qu'Appelle-Moose Mountain	Moosomin	C.W. Corkish, Town Adm., Box 90, Wawota, Sask. SOG 5AO (739-2216)
Webb‡	84	Swift Current-Maple Creek	Morse	D.R. Haley, Village Sec., Box 100, Webb, Sask. SON 2XO (674-2230)
Webb RM No. 138	556			c/o Webb Village Sec.
Weekes‡	127	Mackenzie	Kelsey-Tisdale	Mrs. P. Petterson, Village Sec., Weekes, Sask. SOE 1VO (278-2800)
Weirdale‡	160	Prince Albert	Shellbrook	Mrs. R. Krawec, Village Sec., Weirdale, Sask. SOJ 2ZO (929-4851)
Weldon‡	300	Prince Albert	Kinistino	F. Lima, Village Sec., Weldon, Sask. SOJ 3AO (887-2070)
Wellington RM No. 97	636			Miss J. Heffley, Sec., Box 2, Cedoux, Sask. SOG OPO (842-5606)
Welwyn‡	193	Qu'Appelle-Moose Mountain	Moosomin	Mrs. B. Cuthill, Village Sec., Welwyn, Sask. SOA 4LO (733-2077)
West Bend‡	25	Yorkton-Melville	Kelvington-Wadena	A. Woitas, Village Sec., West Bend, Sask. SOA 4MO (272-4644)
WEYBURN	9,243	Assiniboia	Weyburn	J.J. Norman, City Clerk, City Hall, Box 370, Weyburn, Sask. S4H 2K3 (842-5429)
Weyburn RM No. 67	1,223			L.E. Muma, Sec., 23 6th St. N.E., Weyburn, Sask. S4H 1A1 (842-2314)
Wheatlands RM No. 163	367			J.G. Gillis, Sec., Box 129, Mortlach, Sask. SOH 3EO (355-2233)
Whiska Creek RM No. 106	589			Kathleen Countryman, Sec., Vanguard, Sask. SON 2VO (582-2133)
White City‡	564	Regina East	Qu'Appelle	C. Woloshyn, Village Sec., Box 220, White City, Sask. SOG 5BO (568-2355)
White Fox‡	369	Mackenzie	Nipawin	Mrs. B. Dalziel, Village Sec., Box 38, White Fox, Sask. SOJ 3BO (276-2106)
White Valley RM No. 49	830			E.R. Greve, Sec., Box 520, Eastend, Sask. SON OTO (295-3322)
Whitewood†	1,072	Qu'Appelle-Moose Mountain	Moosomin	Town Adm., Whitewood, Sask. SOG 5CO (735-2210)
Wilcox‡	175	Assiniboia	Qu'Appelle	K. Ritchie, Village Sec., Wilcox, Sask. SOG 5EO (732-2030)
Wilkie†	1,604	Kindersley-Lloydminster	Wilkie	D. Topinka, Town Adm., Wilkie, Sask. SOK 4WO (843-2692)
Willner RM No. 253	477			M.C. Boyle, Sec., Box 250, Davidson, Sask. SOG 1AO (567-3103)
Willow Brook‡	72	Yorkton-Melville	Canora	M.J. Kowal, Village Sec., Willowbrook, Sask. SOA 4PO (783-6751)
Willow Bunch†	523	Assiniboia	Assiniboia-Gravelbourg	Jean Philippon, Town Adm., Willow Bunch, Sask. SOH 4KO (473-2450)
Willow Bunch RM No. 42	736			P.B. Swan, Sec., Willow Bunch, Sask. SOH 4KO (473-2302)
Willow Creek RM No. 458	1,367			B. Ross, Sec., Box 67, Brooksby, Sask. SOE OHO (863-4143)
Willowdale RM No. 153	723			Ms. C.M. Tebbutt, Sec., Box 58, White-wood, Sask. SOG 5CO (735-2344)
Wilton RM No. 472	1,606			M.L. Bates, Sec., Box 40, Marshall, Sask. SOM 1RO (387-6244)
Windthorst‡	215	Qu'Appelle-Moose Mountain	Indian Head-Wolseley	Martha Hassler, Village Sec., Windthorst, Sask. SOG 5GO (224-2033)
Winslow RM No. 319	579			W.D. Bentley, Sec., Box 310, Dodsland, Sask. SOL OVO (356-2106)
Wise Creek RM No. 77	391			L.M. Meloche, Sec., Box 400, Shaunavon, Sask. SON 2MO (297-2520)
Wiseton‡	201	Kindersley-Lloydminster	Rosetown-Elrose	Mrs. S.E. Elliott, Village Sec., Wiseton, Sask. SOL 3MO (357-2022)
Wishart‡	238	Humboldt-Lake Centre	Kelvington-Wadena	D.A. Moleski, Village Sec., Wishart, Sask. SOA 4RO (576-2002)
Wolseley†	883	Qu'Appelle-Moose Mountain	Indian Head-Wolseley	N.R. Hicks, Town Adm., Box 310, Wolseley, Sask. SOG 5HO (698-2477)

Cities in CAPITALS; Towns marked †; Villages marked ‡; Balance are Rural Municipalities .
Area Code for Saskatchewan is 306

MUNICIPALITY	POP.	FEDERAL ELECTORAL DISTRICT	PROVINCIAL ELECTORAL DISTRICT	ADM. OR SECRETARY WITH ADDRESS & PHONE
Wolseley RM No. 155	758			M. Wilton, Sec., Box 370, Wolseley, Sask. SOG 5HO (698-2522)
Wolverine RM No. 340	879			F.C. Saretsky, Sec., Burr, Sask. SOK OTO (682-3640)
Wood Creek RM No. 281	510			Don Bergsveinson, Sec., Box 10, Simpson, Sask. SOG 4MO (836-2020)
Wood Mountain‡	65	Assiniboia	Assiniboia-Gravelbourg	E.P. Gasper, Village Sec., Wood Mountain, Sask. SOH 4LO (266-2002)
Wood River RM No. 74	560			A. Baran Jr., Sec., Box 250, Lafleche, Sask. SOH 2KO (472-5235)
Woodrow‡	85	Assiniboia	Shaunavon	S. Calimente, Village Sec., Woodrow, Sask. SOH 4MO (472-3742)
Wreford RM No. 280	395			J.C. Fenton, Sec., Box 99, Nokomis, Sask. SOG 3RO (528-2202)
Wroxton‡	81	Yorkton-Melville	Pelly	Linda Napady, Village Sec., Wroxton, Sask. SOA 4SO (742-4557)
Wynyard†	2,121	Humboldt-Lake Centre	Quill Lakes	R. Bunko, Town Adm., Wynyard, Sask. SOA 4TO (554-2123)
Yarbo‡	139	Qu'Appelle-Moose Mountain	Saltcoats	Mrs. Irene Placatka, Village Sec., Yarbo, Sask. SOA 4VO (745-2474)
Yellow Creek‡	166	Prince Albert	Kinistino	Ms. S. Kwasnycia, Village Sec., Yellow Creek, Sask. SOK 4XO (279-2191)
Yellow Grass†	488	Assiniboia	Bengough-Milestone	J.A. Hill, Town Adm., Yellow Grass, Sask. SOG 5JO (465-2400)
YORKTON	15,077	Yorkton-Melville	Yorkton	City Clerk, City Hall, Box 400, Yorkton, Sask. S3N 2W3 (783-3614)
Young‡	495	Humboldt-Lake Centre	Humboldt	L. Stangland, Village Sec., Young, Sask. SOK 4YO (259-2211)
Zealandia†	150	Kindersley-Lloydminster	Rosetown-Elrose	Mrs. N. Hoffman, Town Clerk, Zealandia, Sask. SOL 3NO (882-3052)
Zelma‡	73	Humboldt-Lake Centre	Humboldt	Mrs. A.L. Fischer, Village Sec., Zelma, Sask. SOK 4ZO (257-3994)
Zenon Park‡	313	Mackenzie	Nipawin	Mrs. L. Campbell, Village Sec., Zenon Park, Sask. SOE 1WO (767-2233)

MUNICIPALITIES IN NORTHWEST TERRITORIES

LEGISLATION: The Municipal Ordinance of the Northwest Territories.

Requirements for incorporation in the Northwest Territories is by population and land assessment. In order to incorporate into a village, a hamlet requires 500 people and is raising or is about to raise revenue by taxing the assessment value of land. For a town the requirement is 1,000 people and $2,500 land assessment. For a city it is 6,000 people and $3,000 land assessment.

Municipal elections in all municipalities are held in the first week of December of every year. The mayor's term of office is two years from the first day of January next following his election. The four councillors receiving the highest number of votes in the election hold office for two years from the 31st day of December next following their election and the other councillors hold office for a term of one year from the 31st day of December next following their election.

Cities in CAPITALS; Towns marked †; Balance are Villages.
Area Code for Northwest Territories is 403

MUNICIPALITY	POP.	FEDERAL ELECTORAL DISTRICT	TERRITORIAL ELECTORAL DISTRICT	SEC.-TREAS. WITH ADDRESS & PHONE
Fort Simpson	1,000	Western Arctic	Mackenzie Liard	Ralph Rae, Sec., Fort Simpson, NWT X0E 0N0 (695-2253)
Fort Smith†	2,347	Western Arctic	Slave Lake	J. Haining, Sec., Fort Smith, NWT X0E 0P0 (872-2014)
Frobisher Bay	2,693	Eastern Arctic	South Baffin	J. Rizzotto, Sec., Frobisher Bay, NWT X0E 0H0 (819) 979-5381
Hay River†	3,500	Western Arctic	Hay River	Mrs. J. Hamilton, Sec., Hay River, NWT X0E 0R0 (874-6522)
Inuvik†	2,938	Western Arctic	Inuvik	Don Cave, Sec., Inuvik, NWT X0E 0T0 (979-2607)
Pine Point†	2,000	Western Arctic	Slave River	Doug Lagore, Sec., Pine Point, NWT X0E 0W0 (393-2800)
YELLOWKNIFE	9,981	Western Arctic	Great Slave Lake; Yellowknife South; Yellowknife North	Hugh Stevenson, Sec., Yellowknife, NWT X0E 1H0 (873-2671)

MUNICIPALITIES IN YUKON

Cities in CAPITALS; Balance as Shown.
Area Code for Yukon is 403

MUNICIPALITY	POP.	FEDERAL ELECTORAL DISTRICT	TERRITORIAL ELECTORAL DISTRICT	CLERK/SEC. WITH ADDRESS
Carmacks	420	Yukon	Tatchun	Cora Lyslo, Sec.T., Carmacks L.I.D., Carmacks, YT
Dawson	838	Yukon	Klondike	Karen Mason, Sec., Box 308, Dawson City, YT
Destruction Bay	80	Yukon	Kluane	S. Van der Veen, Pres., Community Club, Destruction Bay, YT
Haines Junction	268	Yukon	Kluane	Linda Eland, Sec.T., Haines Junction L.I.D., YT
Keno Hill	70	Yukon	Mayo	Brian Foote, Pres., Community Club, Keno, YT
Old Crow	224	Yukon	Old Crow	P. Seeker, Old Crow Co-op., Old Crow, YT
Pelly Crossing	100	Yukon	Tatchun	Danny Joe, Chief, Selkirk Indian Band, Pelly Crossing, YT
Ross River	350	Yukon	Campbell	Nancy Dieckmann, Pres., Community Club, Ross River, YT
Swift River		Yukon	Campbell	E. Chubay, Pres., Community Club, Swift River, YT
Teslin	241	Yukon	Campbell	Sherry Geddes, Sec.T., Teslin L.I.D., Teslin, YT
Upper Liard	100	Yukon	Campbell	Dixon Lutz, Chief, Indian Band, Upper Liard, YT
WHITEHORSE	15,500	Yukon	Whitehorse:- North Centre; Porter Creek East; Porter Creek West; Riverdale North; Riverdale South; South Centre; West	G. Van der Wolf, City Clerk, 2121 2nd Ave., Whitehorse, YT Y1A 1C2

MUNICIPAL GOVERNMENT Part 2 (Alphabetical List of Major Cities, including Council and Senior Administrative Officials)

BEAUPORT

C.P. 5187, Beauport, P.Q. G1E 6P4
Incorporated: (Fusionnée en 1976)
Area: 90.4 sq. km.
Population: 62,760 (1980)
Information: Directeur des communications, Maurice Parent (418/667-8554)

Conseil

Maire, Michel Rivard
Conseillers et districts: 1) Charles Deblois, 2) Jean-Marie Parent, 3) Alexis Bérubé, 4) Jean-Luc Duclos, 5) André Proulx, 6) Jean-Paul Michaud, 7) Rosaire Bédard, 8) Denis Robert, 9) Raymond Vézina, 10) Viateur Devost, 11) Réjean Garneau, 12) Jean-Roch Ferland, 13) Denis Boivin
Next election: November 1, 1984

Administration

Gérant, André Letendre (Manager)
Greffier, Jacques Simoneau (Clerk)
Directeur des services techniques, Roger Robert (Operations)
Asst. Directeur aux travaux publics, Jean Vézina (Public Works)
Urbaniste, Paul Giroux (Housing)
Trésorier, Paul Lepage, c.a.
Directeur du personnel, Louis-Philippe Hébert
Directeur de police, Emile Turgeon
Asst. Directeur aux incendies, Gaston Prémont (Fire)
Directeur du contentieux, Jean-Charles Lord (Solicitor)
Directeur des loisirs et parcs, Paul-André Lavigne (Recreation & Parks)
Responsable des achats, Claude Parent (Purchasing)

BRAMPTON

150 Central Park Dr., Brampton, Ont. L6T 2T9
Incorporated: January 1, 1974
Population: 130,000
Area: 98 sq. miles
Phone: (416) 793-4110

Council

Mayor, James E. Archdekin
Aldermen: Frank W. Andrews, Ward 1; Keith A. Coutlee, Ward 2; Robert V. Callahan, Ward 3; R. Frank Russell, Ward 4; Chris Gibson, Ward 5; Fred Kee, Ward 6; Eric Carter, Ward 7; Harry Chadwick, Ward 8; Rosemary Miller, Ward 9; Terry Piane, Ward 10; Bob Crowley, Ward 11
Next Election: November 1982

Administration

Chief Administrative Officer, Jack Galway
City Clerk, R.A. Everett
Treasurer, A. Salski
Commr., Planning & Development, F.R. Dalzell
Commr. of Parks & Recreation, Donald Gordon
Commr. of Building & By-Law Enforcement, L. Koehle
Fire Chief, J.R. Brunne
Transit Manager, C. Prentice
City Solicitor, J. Metras
Commr. of Public Works, J. Curran
Commr., Admin. & Finance, A. Solski

BRANDON

410 9th St., Brandon, Man. R7A 6A2
Incorporated: May 30, 1882
Population: 38,000
Area: 25.88 sq. miles
Phone: (204) 728-2278

Council
Mayor, Ken Burgess
Aldermen: Mike Melnyk (Ward 1); Margaret Workman (Ward 2); Gene Guentert (Ward 3); Richard Borotsik (Ward 4); Frederick Anderson (Ward 5); Wayne G. McLeod (Ward 6); Daniel Munroe (Ward 7); Audrey Martin (Ward 8); Ross Martin (Ward 9); Richard Dyck (Ward 10)
Next Election: October 1983 (three year term)

Administration
Executive Director & City Clerk, I.L. Thomson
Director of Finance & City Treasurer, F.G. Woodmass
Director of Operations & City Engineer, J.R. Slevinsky
Director of Services & Works, D. Wallace
Executive Secretary, C.R. Arvisais
Police Chief, Chief Constable K. Elliott
Fire Chief, E.C. Polnick
Airport Supervisor, R. Isleifson
E.M.O. & Safety Co-ordinator, J. Horn
Parks Dept. Supt., H. Stevenson
Purchasing Supervisor, S. McIntosh
Transit Supt., A. Arbour
Water Treatment Plant Supt., H. Irving
Welfare Supervisor, Mrs. F. Duncan

BRANTFORD
City Hall, 100 Wellington Sq., Brantford, Ont. N3T 2M3
Incorporated: May 31, 1877
Area: 13,061 acres
Population: 73,055 (1981)
Phone: (519) 759-4150

Council
Mayor, David E. Neumann
Aldermen: Mrs. Jo Brennan, John Starkey, Art Stanbridge, R.L. Lancaster, Max Sherman, Bob Mroz, Charles Ward, Larry Kings, Mary Welsh, Chuck McPhail, P.R. Hexamer
Next Election: November 1982 (two year terms)

Administration
Chief Administrative Officer, G. Wilson
City Clerk, W. Coulson
Treasurer, G. Westbrook
  Purchasing Officer, G. Sturgeon
Director of Planning, P.J. Beavis
City Engineer, R.S. Middleton
  Chief Building Official, R.D. McNicol
  Works Supt., Harry Gehue
Personnel Officer, J. Flood
Administrator, Board of Park Management/Recreation Commission, Hans Loewig
  Director of Recreation, Eric Finkelstein
  Supt. of Parks, L.W. Shipp
Manager, Civic Centre, Mrs. T. Learn
Development Commr., Lloyd Berryman

BURLINGTON
City Hall, 426 Brant St., Box 5013, Burlington, Ont. L7R 3Z6
Incorporated: January 1, 1974
Area: 72.65 sq. miles
Population: 112,722 (1980)
Phone: (416) 335-7777

Council
Mayor, Roly Bird
Aldermen, Ward 1: Walter Mulkewich, Jack Cowman; Ward 2: Joan Little, Tony Whitworth; Ward 3: Ted MacDonald, Linda Pugsley; Ward 4: David LaCombe, Barry Quinn; Ward 5: Yvonne Roach, Vern Connell; Ward 6: Stephen Toth, Tony Bedini; Ward 7: James Grieve, Bob Brechin; Ward 8: Patrick A. McLaughlin, William O'Connell
Next Election: November, 1982 (two year terms)

Administration
Chief Administrative Officer, Michael H. Boggs
City Clerk, Donald Briault
Director of Public Works, Mathieu Koevoets
Building Commr., William Hewitson
Director of Planning, Gary Goodman
Treasurer, Robert J. Rooks
Director of Personnel, David C. Murray
Director of Recreation Services, Laurie G. Branch
Chief, Fire Dept., Warren Corp
Manager, Business Services Division, Mary Dillon
Solicitor & Corporation Counsel, Douglas Brown

DISTRICT OF BURNABY
4949 Canada Way, Burnaby, B.C. V5G 1M2
Incorporated: September 22, 1892
Area: 10,681.9 hectares
Population: 142,000 (1981 est.)
Phone: (604) 294-7944

Council
Mayor, W.A. Lewarne
Aldermen, D.N. Brown, T.W. Constable, D.P. Drummond, A.H. Emmott, Doreen A. Lawson, G.H.F. McLean, E. Nikolai, V.V. Stusiak
Next Election: November 19, 1983 (two year terms)

Administration
Municipal Manager, Melvin J. Shelley
Municipal Clerk, James Hudson
Municipal Solicitor, William L. Stirling
Municipal Treasurer, Howard B. Karras
Director of Planning, Antony L. Parr
Personnel Director, Don F. Hicks
Parks & Recreation Administrator, Dennis Gaunt
Municipal Engineer, Ernie E. Olson
Chief Building Inspector, Mike J. Jones
Medical Health Officer, Dr. Sally L. Hemming
Director, Fire Services, Tom G. Nairn

CALGARY
Box 2100, Calgary, Alta. T2P 2M5
Incorporated: January 1, 1894
Area: 419.578 sq. km. (162 sq. miles)
Population: 591,857 (Apr. 1981)
Phone: (403) 268-2111

Council
Mayor, Ralph Klein
Aldermen, Ward 1: Pat Donnelly; Ward 2: Bob McCombie; Ward 3: Bob Hawkesworth; Ward 4: Don Hartman; Ward 5: Stan Nelson; Ward 6: Brian Lee; Ward 7: Elaine Husband; Ward 8: Barbara Scott; Ward 9: Jack Long; Ward 10: Gordon Shrake; Ward 11: Craig Reid; Ward 12: Larry Gilchrist; Ward 13: Jim Bell; Ward 14: Suzanne Higgins
Next Election: October, 1983

Administration
Chief Commr., G.H. Cornish
Commr. of Finance & Admin., A.F. Womack
Commr. of Operations, R.A. Welin
Commr. of Planning, W.C. Kuyt
City Clerk, Joyce E. Woodward
Data Processing Services, R. Barnes, Director
Electric System, E.C. Rowsell, General Manager
Engineering Dept., R.L. Ward, City Engineer
Finance Dept., P.A. Dawson, Director
Fire Dept., F. Archer, Fire Chief
Medical Officer of Health, Dr. J.Z. Garson
Business Development Dept., B.A. McDonald, Director
Land Dept., B.R. Musgrove, Director
Law Dept., D.O. Kvemshagen, City Solicitor
Parks/Recreation, F. McHenry, Director
Planning Dept., G. Steber, Jr., Director

Police Service, Brian Sawyer, Chief of Police
Social Service Dept., S.E. Blakley, Director
Transportation Dept., vacant, Director

CAMBRIDGE

City Hall, 46 Dickson St., Cambridge, Ont. N1R 5W8
Incorporated: January 1973
Area: 44.5 sq. miles
Population: 76,250
Phone: (519) 623-1340

Council

Mayor, C. Millar
Aldermen: J. Brewer, G. Bush, R. Dickson, J. Florence, C. Harrington, R. Jeffery, F. Kent, M. Love, P. Maher, H. Mazmanian, P. Nagge, S. Nelson, W. Struck, S. Takacs
Next Election: November 1982 (two year terms)

Administration

Chief Administrative Officer, B.C. Rennick
City Clerk, vacant
City Treasurer, J. McIntyre
Commr. of Planning & Development, S. Thorsen
Commr. of Engineering & Public Works, G. James
Commr. of Community Services, W. Taylor
Fire Chief, D. Pollington

CHARLESBOURG

7575 boul. Henri-Bourassa, Charlesbourg, P.Q. G1H 3E7
Population: 72,000
Phone: (418) 628-7241

Conseil

Maire, Me Pierre Bernier
Conseillers: Maurice Lortie, Michel Renauld, Marcel Dion, Jean Bégin, Jacques Caron, Roger Lefebvre, Jean-Marc Jacob, Francine Boutet, André Gignac, Claude Hamel, Joscelyn Roy, Jacques Roy, Léonard Lamy, Lawrence Pageau, Pierre Marier, Jean-Pierre Bouchard
Next Election: November 1984

Comite Executif

Président, Jean-Marc Jacob
Membres: Pierre Bernier, Jacques Caron, Jacques Roy, Lawrence Pageau, et gérant et gérant adj. de la Ville

Administration

Gérant, Michel Tremblay, ing. (Manager)
Greffier, Rosaire Godbout (Clerk)
Trésorier, Robert Légaré
Travaux publics, Gilbert Leclerc, surintendant (Public Works)
Service juridique, Me Yves Dussault, avocat (Legal Dept.)
Service de circulation, Raymond Paquin, ing. (Traffic)
Protection publique, Ghislain Fortin (Police)
Incendie, Serge Daigle (Fire)
Service du personnel, Jean-Marc Guay
Service des loisirs, François Borgia (Recreation)
Services techniques, Pierre Blais, ing. (Operations)
Service Urbanisme & Construction, Jean-Claude Bergeron (Housing)

CHARLOTTETOWN

Box 98, Charlottetown, P.E.I. C1A 7K2
Incorporated: 1855 (founded in 1763)
Area: 1732 sq. acres
Population: 17,063 (1976)
Phone: (902) 894-5552

Council

Mayor, Francis J. Moran
Aldermen, Ward 1: P.A. Murnaghan; Ward 2: J. Bruce MacIssac; Ward 3: Edward Rice; Ward 4: Wilson Ross, Russell Stewart; Ward 5: J. Patrick Gaudet, John D. Squarebriggs, Jr., Peter E. Kays; Ward 6: George MacDonald, John E. Ready
Elections every three years (November, 1983, 1986, 1989)

Administration

City Administrator, John J. Butler
Office Manager, Carl Bradley
Administrative Asst., Harry Gaudet
City Engineer, Edwin C. Smith, P.Eng.
Building Inspector, Foster W. MacKinnon
Fire Chief, Gordon F. Stewart
Fire Inspector, Wm. G. Hogan
Recreation Director, Charles E. Ryan
Chief of Police, Charles A. Ready
City Solicitor, N. Douglas Ross
Health Officer, Dr. Stewart MacDonald
Water Supply: Commrs. of Sewer & Water Supply, 10 Kirkwood Dr.

CHICOUTIMI

201 rue Racine est, Chicoutimi, P.Q. G7J 5B8
Incorporated: January 1, 1976
Population: 62,280
Phone: (418) 545-9550

Council

Mayor, Ulrec Blackburn
Wards & Councillors: 1) S.-J. Fillion, 2) G. Fillion, 3) D. Chiasson, 4) H. Lalancette, 5) Claudine Bouchard-Hudon, 6) J.-P. Régis, 7) P.-A. Hayes, 8) C. Gaudreault, 9) R. Girard, 10) C. Garon, 11) A. Hervé, 12) R. Hellé
Next Election: November, 1985

Administration

Directeur général, Jean-Jacques Simard
Directeur des services financiers et trésorier, Jean-Guy Boucher
Directeur des services à la population, et directeur général adjoint, Marcel Demers
Directeur du personnel, Roger Gonthier
Directeur des services planification et entretien, Robert Bouchard
Greffier, Jean-Yves Fortin
Directeur du service de sécurité publique, Gérard Giroux
Coordonnateur des projets, Benoit Simard

DISTRICT OF COQUITLAM

1111 Brunette Ave., Coquitlam, B.C. V3K 1E9
Incorporated: November 1, 1971
Area: 59 sq. miles
Population: 55,464
Information Contact: Municipal Clerk (phone: (604) 526-3611)

Council

Mayor, James L. Tonn (Nov. 30, 1983)
Aldermen, L.A. Bewley (Nov. 30, 1982); L. Garrison (Nov. 30, 1983); Wm. E. Henke (Nov. 30, 1983); Gloria Levi (Nov. 30, 1983); B.T.H. Robinson (Nov. 30, 1982); L. Sekora (Nov. 30, 1982)
Next Election: November 20, 1982 (overlapping terms)

Administration

Municipal Manager, R.A. LeClair
Municipal Clerk, T. Klassen
Municipal Engineer, A. Phillips
Municipal Planner, D. Buchanan
Municipal Solicitor, H. Castillou
Municipal Treasurer, V.A. Dong
Parks & Recreation Director, D.L. Cunnings
Personnel Director, F. Klewchuk
Fire Chief, A. Owens

CORNER BROOK

Box 1080, Corner Brook, Nfld. A2H 6E1
Incorporated: 1955
Area: 60.05 sq. miles
Population: 30,000
Phone: (709) 634-8291

Council

Mayor, George Hutchings
Councillors, Max Fillatre, Doyle Mills, Pat Griffin, Priscilla Boutcher, Frank Colbourne, Fred Basha
Next Election: November, 1985

Administration

City Manager, C.W. Keeping
City Clerk, K. Furlong
City Treasurer, G.S. Batt
Director of Development Control, D. Brown
Director of Parks & Recreation, B. Butler
Fire Chief, E. Clarke
City Planner, A. McMillan
Personnel Officer, H. March
Director of Economic Development, J. Parsons
City Engineer, J. Kennedy

DARTMOUTH

City Hall, Box 817, Dartmouth, N.S. B2Y 3Z3
Incorporated: November 13, 1961
Population: 65,341 (1976)
Area: 25 sq. miles
Phone: (902) 469-9211

Council

Mayor, Daniel P. Brownlow
Deputy Mayor, W.J. Grant Brennan
Aldermen, George Ibsen, C.J. Sarto, John Cunningham, Guy Williams, W.J.G. Brennan, Norman Crawford, Don Valardo, W.T. Withers, Barbara Hart, Leo Greenwood, Jack Greenough, Ralph Hawley, C.D. Ritchie, L.M. Fredericks
Next Election: October, 1982 (two year terms)

Administration

City Administrator, C.A. Moir
City Clerk-Treasurer, B.S. Smith
City Engineer, R.J. Fougere
Assessor, Donald Horne
Director of Planning & Development, D.A. Bayer
Building Inspector, Hawley Turner
Director of Social Services, W.G. McNeil
Director of Recreation, D.A. Lynch
City Solicitor, Suzanne Hood
Police Chief, Donald Trider (act.)
Fire Chief, Robert Patterson
Purchasing Agent, W.M. Whitman

CORPORATION OF DELTA

4450 Clarence Taylor Cres., Delta, B.C. V4K 3E2
Incorporated: November 10, 1879
Area: Land 181 sq. km; water 207 sq. km
Population: 76,000 (1980)
Phone: (604) 946-4141

Council

Mayor, E. Burnett, C.A.
Aldermen, D.J. Husband, Beth Johnson, P.A. Swenson, N. Lortie, K. Moser, S. Wilbee
Next Election: November 19, 1983 (two year terms)

Administration

Administrator, M.W.E. Allen
Clerk, P.J. Gairns
Controller-Treasurer, J.P. Good
Director of Engineering Services, J. Hamilton
Director of Inspections, S.T. Gertsman
Director of Planning Services, T.S. Dennison
Director of Leisure Services, J.O. Evans
Director of Personnel Services, J.C. Lambie
Fire Chief, J. Tapio
Chief Constable (Municipal Police), D.G. MacLeod

EDMONTON

City Hall, Edmonton, Alta. T5J 2R7
Incorporated: 1904
Area: 127.86 sq. miles
Population: 521,205
Information Contact: C.J. McGonigle, City Clerk (phone: 403-428-5448)

Council

Mayor, C.J. Purves
Aldermen: Ward 1: K.G. Newman, Olivia Butti; Ward 2: Ron Hayter, Jan Reimer; Ward 3: June Cavanagh, Ed Ewasiuk; Ward 4: Paul Norris, Gerry Wright; Ward 5: Percy Wickman, Lois Campbell; Ward 6: Bettie Hewes, Ed Leger
Next Election: October, 1983

Administration

Airport (Edmonton Municipal Airport), Kingsway Ave., L.W. Marchant, Manager
Assessor's Dept., 8th floor, Century Place
 City Assessor, S.M. Scott
Auditor General, E.J. Powell (Centennial Bldg.)
Business Development Dept., 1328 Imperial Oil Bldg., 10025 Jasper Ave., A. Bleiken, General Manager
By-law Enforcement Dept. (Centennial Bldg.), General Manager, J. Boddington
Central Supply & Service, (Centennial Bldg.), R. Littke, General Manager
City Clerk's Dept., 3rd floor, City Hall, C.J. McGonigle, City Clerk
Commrs.
 D.F. Burrows, Chief Commr.
 P.H. Walker, Commr. of Utilities & Engineering
 T.E. Adams, Commr. of Economic Affairs
Computer Systems Development & Services Dept., 18th floor, Phipps-McKinnon Bldg., D.S. Ausman, General Manager
Corporate Policy Planning Dept., 7th floor, City Hall, D.T. Campbell, Chief Corporate Planning Officer
Edmonton Parks & Recreation Dept., 10th floor, CN Tower, H. Monroe, General Manager
Edmonton Power, 6th-9th floor, Continental Bank Bldg., E. Kyte, General Manager
'Edmonton Telephones' (Mercantile Bldg.), G.K. Foster, General Manager
Edmonton Transit, 10426 81 Ave., E.V. Miller, General Manager
Edmonton Utilities Services, Main floor, City Hall, H.B. Fraser, General Manager
Executive Services Dept., 3rd floor, City Hall, George Earl, General Manager
Engineering Dept., 11th floor, Century Place, 9803 102A Ave., R.H. David, City Engineer & General Manager
Financial Dept., 5th floor, City Hall
Fire Dept., 10221 107 St.
 Fire Chief, L.C. Day
 Fire Prevention Branch, R.A. Kostash, Fire Marshal
 Fire Investigation Branch, J.H.P. Spencer, Chief
Law Dept., 8th floor, City Hall, Tony Konye, City Solicitor
Local Board of Health, 7th floor, CN Tower, Dr. J.M. Howell, Medical Officer of Health
Management Studies, Systems & Budget Dept., City Hall, S.W. Sadler, General Manager
Personnel Dept., 26th floor, CN Tower, W. Luyendyk, General Manager
Planning Dept., vacant, General Manager (Dept. includes Urban Design, and Zoning)
Police Dept., 4 Sir Winston Churchill Sq., R.F. Lunney, Chief of Police
Public Relations, 8th floor, City Hall, P.S. Brown, General Manager

Real Estate & Housing, (Centennial Bldg.), R. Scotnicki, General Manager
Social Service Dept., 6th floor, CN Tower, A.I. Dorosh, General Manager
Transportation Systems Design Dept., 10th floor, Century Place, R.A. Heise, General Manager
Water & Sanitation, (12220 Stony Plain Rd.), A.C. Beaulieu, General Manager

FREDERICTON

Box 130, Fredericton, N.B. E3B 4Y7
Incorporated: 1848
Area: 53 sq. miles
Population: 45,248 (1976)
Phone: (506) 455-9426

Council

Mayor, Elbridge C. Wilkins
Councillors, Ward 1: B.S. Woodside; Ward 2: R.W. Turnbull; Ward 3: H.S. Dixon; Ward 4: P.B. Snowball; Ward 5: N.H. Allen; Ward 6: Mrs. S.E. Washburn; Ward 7: G.R. Yeomans; Ward 8: A.M. DiGiacinto; Ward 9: I.M. Beattie; Ward 10: H.L. McFee; Ward 11: W.W. Thorpe; Ward 12: D.J. Wilson
Next Election: May, 1983 (triennial)

Administration

City Administrator, John C. Robison
City Solicitor, Charles S. Shannon
City Engineer, E. John Bliss
City Treasurer, Winston G. Hunter
City Clerk, Stanley R. Thorburn
Director of Administrative Services, Ronald Steeves
Tourist & Convention Officer, Albert E. King
Fire Chief, Thomas L. Powell
Police Chief, G.M. Carlisle
Recreation Director, Robert A. Mabie
Chief Building Inspector, Arthur F. Wade
Planning Director, Richard Danziger
Zoning Control Officer, David McQuade
Transit Manager, L.P. MacNeill

GATINEAU

Hôtel de Ville, 280 boul. Maloney, Gatineau, P.Q. J8P 1C6
Incorporated: 1946
Area: 103.40 sq. miles
Population: 75,800 (1978)

Counsel

Mayor, John R. Luck
Counsellors, L.-S. Joanisse, Richard Trottier, Conrad Bouffard, H.A. Leroux, Honoré Séguin, Gaétan Cousineau, M.N. Séguin, Raymond Gosselin, J.-R. Monette, Daniel Lauzon, G.Y. Langlois, Claude Bérard
Next Election: November, 1983

Administration

Gérant, Normand Racicot (Manager)
Greffier, J.-C. Laurin (City Clerk)
Directeur des Finances, Robert Bélair
Directeur des Services Techniques, Maurice Beauclair
Directeur de la Sûreté Municipale, Léopold Prévost (Police)
Directeur des Loisirs et Culture, Paul Morin (Recreation & Culture)
Directeur du Service du Personnel, Jean Gervais
Responsable du Service des Communications, Jacques Robert
Directeur Service des Incendies, James O'Farrell (Fire)
Directeur du Service d'Urbanisme, Claude Doucet (Housing)
Directeur Travaux Publics, Georges Raymond (Public Works)
Directeur du Service des Achats, Gilles Bourbonnais (Purchasing)

GUELPH

59 Carden St., Guelph, Ont. N1H 3A1
Incorporated: 1879
Area: 26 sq. miles
Population: 73,165 (Nov. 1980)
Phone: (519) 822-1260

Council

Mayor, Norman Jary
Aldermen: (elected at large): Paul Armstrong, Mel Cochrane, Rick Ferraro, Anne Godfrey, Carl Hamilton, Kenneth Hammill, David Kendrick, Margaret MacKinnon, Clara Marett, D.M. Valeriote, Jim Whitechurch
Next Election: November, 1982 (two year terms)

Administration

City Administrator, F.M. Woods
City Treasurer, M.R. Sather
City Clerk, W.G. Hall
City Engineer, R.D. Funnell
Director, Planning & Development, Kenneth L. Perry
Director, Recreation & Parks, Gus Stahlmann
Personnel Director, J.D. Kentner
Industrial Commr., Bruce Murray
City Solicitor, J.A. Runions
Fire Chief, Arnold Quillman
Police Chief, Lorne Halls
Electric-Guelph, Hydro, Gordon Stacey
Social Services (County & City), D. McLennan
Transportation, J. Quarrie
Medical Officer of Health (County & City), Dr. Robert Aldis

HALIFAX

Box 1749, Halifax, N.S. B3J 3A5
Incorporated: April 10, 1841
Area: 24.4 sq. miles
Population: 118,000
Information Contact: City Clerk (phone: 902-426-6431)

Council

Mayor, Ron Wallace
Aldermen: Ward 1, Doris Maley; Ward 2, Ronald Cromwell; Ward 3, Graham Downey; Ward 4, N.P. Meagher; Ward 5, Gerald O'Malley; Ward 6, Daniel Clarke; Ward 7, Nancy Wooden; Ward 8, Ronald Hanson; Ward 9, Thomas Jeffrey; Ward 10, Donald LeBlanc; Ward 11, Arthur Flynn; Ward 12, Alfred Hamshaw
Next Election: October, 1982

Administration

City Manager, Paul Calda, P. Eng.
City Clerk, Mrs. G.I. Blennerhassett, M.P.A.
City Treasurer & Director of Finance, B. Smith, C.A.
Director of Engineering & Works, Peter Connell, P. Eng.
City Solicitor, D.F. Murphy, Q.C.
Director of Development & Urban Renewal, R.B. Grant
Director of Planning, R.J. Matthews
Director of Employee Relations, Mildred Royer
Social Planner, H.D. Crowell
Director of Education, K.W. Perry
Director, Visitors & Convention Bureau, Bob Chisholm
Chief of Police, Fitzgerald F. Fry
Chief of Fire Dept., R. Horrocks
Executive Director, Halifax-Dartmouth Port Commission, Gary Blaikie
Manager, Public Service Commission, J.D. Kline
Internal Auditor, C.W. Smith
Chief Accountant, R. Ridgley
City Collector, R. O'Shaughnessy
Purchasing Agent, P. Messenger

HAMILTON

City Hall, Hamilton, Ont. L8N 3T4
Incorporated: 1846
Area: 54.38 sq. miles
Population: 306,640
Information Contact: City Clerk's Office, (416) 527-0241

Council
Mayor, W. Powell
Aldermen, Ward 1: P.J. Peterson, P. Drage; Ward 2: V.J. Agro; W.M. McCulloch; Ward 3: P.O. Valeriano, B. Hinkley; Ward 4: D. Gray, D.T. Lawrence; Ward 5: F.A. Lombardo, R. Wheeler; Ward 6: I. Stout, P. Cowell; Ward 7: H. Merling, J.A. Bethune; Ward 8: K.M. Edge, J. MacDonald
Next Election: November, 1982 (two year terms)

Administration
Airport, S.S. Mitchell, Manager
Building Commr., Paul Kuppe
City Architect, A.K. German, B.Arch.
City Clerk, E.A. Simpson
City Engineer, W.L. Phillips
City Solicitor, K.A. Rouff, B.A.
Community Development, E. Kowalski, Director
Culture & Recreation Dept., Miss A. Schimmel, Director
Fire Dept., L.G. Saltmarsh, Chief
Hamilton-Wentworth Regional Police Dept., G.V. Torrance, Chief
Parking Authority, D. Goldberg, Chairman
Planning Dept., V. Abraham, Director of Local Planning
Public Works Dept., R. Morden, Director
Cemetery Division, C. Orzel
Parks Division, R. Nutley
Real Estate Dept., D. Vyce, Director

HULL
25 Laurier St. (Box 1970, Stn. B, Hull, P.Q. J8X 3Y9)
Incorporated: 1875
Area: 11.76 sq. miles
Population: 61,700 (1981)
Information Contact: André Lacroix, Information & Public Relations Director (phone: (819) 777-2781)

Council
Mayor, Michel J. Légère
Aldermen, Ward 1: Claude Lemay; Ward 2: André Careau; Ward 3: Paul-Emile Poulin; Ward 4: Fernand Nadon; Ward 5: Jean-Yves Gougeon; Ward 6: Paul Brunet; Ward 7: G.A. Carrier; Ward 8: Pierre Cholette
Next Election: November, 1982

Administration
City Manager, J.-Aimé Desjardins, eng.
Asst. Manager, Jean-Guy St-Arnaud, o.m.a., c.g.a.
Asst. Manager & Planning Dept. Director, Gérald McMartin, eng.
City Clerk, Robert LeSage, o.m.a.
Arenas Dept., Yvon Sabourin, Director
Convention & Tourist Services, Rock Lapointe, Director
Data Processing Dept. Director, Jean-Pierre Bélanger
Engineering Dept., Murad Matin, Asst. Director
Finance Dept., Jacques Filiatrault, o.m.a., c.g.a., Director
Fire Dept., Roger Poitras, Director
Library Dept., Denis Boyer, Director
Personnel Dept., Jacques H. Labelle, Director
Planning Dept., J.-P. Chabot, Asst. Director
Police Dept., Rolland Morin, Director
Property Dept., H. Robert Danis, e.a., e.c., Director
Public Works Dept., Paul Lamarche, eng., Director
Purchasing Dept., Hector Bisson, Director
Recreation Dept., Jean A. Cadieux, Director

JONQUIERE
Hôtel de Ville (C.P. 2000, Jonquière, P.Q. G7X 7W7)
Incorporated: Jan. 1, 1975
Area/Superficie: 87,645 sq. m.
Population: 63,700
Information: Marcel Fortin (418) 548-7101

Conseil
Maire, Francis Dufour
Conseillers & Districts: 1) Rénald Laforte, 2) Henri Carrier, 3) Eugène Bugeaud, 4) Paulin Tremblay, 5) Gérard Pelletier, 6) Lionel Salesse, 7) Edouard Lapierre, 8) Gilles Paquet, 9) Mme Angéline D. Girard, 10) Normand Barette, 11) Yvon Dubé, 12) Yvon Fortin, 13) André Fay, 14) Elmer Proulx
Next Election: November 1983

Administration
Directeur général, Jean-Marc Gagnon
Directeur général adj. à l'administration, Pierre Quintal
Directeur général adj. aux services à la population, Errol Guérin
Directeur du contentieux, Mme Jocelyne T. Brown (Solicitor)
Trésorier, Yvan Nadeau
Greffier, René Perron (Clerk)
Directeur adj. à l'aménagement du territoire, R.-M. Fournier (Planning)
Directeur des services techniques, Raymond Gilbert (Operations)
Directeur des travaux publics, Roger Lavoie (Public Works)
Directeur du service de la protection publique, L.-M. Tremblay (Police)
Directeur du service des incendies, Ernest Boivin (Fire)
Directeur du service des achats, Paul Raymond (Purchasing)
Directeur du service des loisirs, Gérard Leroux (Recreation)
Chef de division - inspection et permis, Alain Jean (Building & Permits)
Chef de division - immeubles et parcs, Ernest Lapointe (Real Estate & Parks)
Chef de division - aqueduc et égouts, Henri Pedneault (Aqueducts & Sewers)
Chef de division - voies publiques, Maurice Bouchard (Roads)
Chef de division - imposition, Louis de la Sablonnière (Assessment)
Chef de division - atelier mécanique, Lionel Débigaré (Works Dept.)
Coordonnateur municipal, Patrick Tremblay

KAMLOOPS
7 Victoria St. W., Kamloops, B.C. V2C 1A2
Incorporated: July 1, 1893
Area: 113.22 sq. miles
Population: 65,000
Phone: (604) 374-3311

Council
Mayor, R.M. Latta
Aldermen, C.G. Branchflower, Kenna Cartwright, R.T. Chalmers, Howard D. Dack, Diane M. Kerr, Helen Kerr, G.A. Rye, Patricia A. Wallace
Next Election: November 20, 1982 (two year terms)

Administration
Administrator, G.R. Hayward
Director of Finance & Treasurer, W. Ridgway
Director of Planning, A.C. Backmeyer
Director of Engineering, J.P. Anderson
Director of Administrative Services, R.D. Kask
Director of Parks & Recreation, G.R. Kenny
Director of Personnel, vacant
City Clerk, W. Thiessen
City Solicitor, W.P. Turlock
Fire Chief, M. Smith
Police, RCMP City Detachment

KELOWNA
City Hall, 1435 Water St., Kelowna, B.C. V1Y 1J4
Incorporated: May 4, 1905
Area: 87.7 sq. miles
Population: 51,955 (1976)
Phone: (604) 763-6011

Council
Mayor, G. Dale Hammill

Aldermen, Mrs. J.E. Clark, Al Horning, B.W. Lee, F. Macklin, Mrs. Mary H. Serwa, T.W.P. Smithwick, J.H. Stuart, W.A.M. Stewart

Next Election: November 20, 1982 (two year terms)

Administration

City Administrator, W.S. Fleming
Deputy Administrator/Land Agent, R.A. Born
Airport Manager, Roger Sellick
Assessor (#218, 1626 Richter St.), P.F. Steeves
Chief of Inspection Services, K. Skinner
City Clerk, R.A. Beauchamp
Director of Civic Properties & Recreation Services, H. Markgraf
Director of Public Operations, H. Markgraf
Electrical Supt., R. McAndrew
Director of Engineering Services, W.S. Lakevold
Director of Finance, H.K. Hall
Fire Chief, J.E. Roberts
Personnel Manager, R. Bozzer
Director of Engineering Services & Pollution Control, W.S. Lakevold
Director of Planning Services, L.B. Kleyn
Police (350 Doyle Ave.) RCMP City Detachment

KINGSTON

City Hall, 216 Ontario St., Kingston, Ont. K2L 2Z3
Incorporated: 1846
Area: 11.69 sq. miles
Population: 60,902 (Dec. 1976)
Phone: (613) 546-4291

Council

Mayor, John P. Gerretsen
Aldermen, Sydenham Ward 1: Helen C. Cooper, William Knapp; Ontario Ward 2: John Clements, Gordon Travers; St. Lawrence Ward 3: Claude Clement, George L. Webb; Cataraqui Ward 4: William Jamieson, Neil McArthur; Frontenac Ward 5: Joe Hawkins, Herbert G. Hunter; Rideau Ward 6: Alex Lampropoulos, Grant Timmins; Victoria Ward 7: Patricia Hodge, Yuri Tarnowecky

Next Election: November, 1982 (two year terms)

Administration

Chief Administrative Officer, Robert J. Hamilton
City Clerk, M.C. Healy
Chief Bldg. Inspector, R. Ruttan
Fire Chief, K.A. Cowdy
Neighbourhood Improvement Program Co-ordinator, Gordon K. Ball
Parks & Recreation Commr., D. Fluhrer
Personnel Director, K.S. Ready
Planning & Urban Renewal Director, Rupert Dobbin
Police Chief, G.S. Rice
Public Utilities Commission, J.K. Fee
Public Works Commr., J.D. Graham
Director of Purchasing, Richard Plumley
Social Services Administrator, S. Routbard
City Solicitor, Norman C. Jackson
Traffic & Streets Administrator, K.G. Linseman
City Treasurer & Deputy Chief Administrative Officer, B.G. Cousens

KITCHENER

City Hall, 22 Frederick St., Box 1118, Kitchener, Ont. N2G 4G7
Incorporated: June 10, 1912
Area: 32,998.827 acres
Population: 138,271 (1981)
Information Contact: R.W. Pritchard, City Clerk, City Hall, 22 Frederick St., Kitchener (phone: 519 885-7242)

Council

Mayor, Morley A. Rosenberg, Q.C.
Aldermen, Centre Ward: Richard Christy; Rockway-St. Mary's Ward: W.A. Ferguson; Victoria Park Ward: Judy Balmer; Bridgeport-North Ward: Grace Stoner; Stanley Park Ward: G.L. Leadston; Chicopee Ward: D.V.P. Cardillo; Fairview Ward: James Ziegler; South Ward: A.D. Barron; Forest Ward; Donald Travers; West Ward: Brian Strickland

Next Election: November, 1982 (two year terms)

Administration

City Clerk, Robert W. Pritchard
City Co-ordinator, James R. Darrah
Finance Commr., Robert V. Eby
Fire Chief, Edward Johnston
City Solicitor, James Wallace
Parks & Recreation Commr., Frederick S. Graham
Commr. of Administrative Services, Roger A. Freeborn
Planning & Development Commr., Samuel Klapman
Public Works Commr., Hugh W. Flood

LASALLE

13 Strathyre Ave., LaSalle, P.Q. H8R 3P6
Incorporated: 1912
Area: 4,789 arpents
Population: 76,737
Phone: (514) 366-7110

Council

Mayor, Gerald Raymond
Councillors, L.-M. Gagnon, John Campbell, Gilles Beauchamp, Dominique Izzi, Robert Lefebvre, Robert Cordner

Next Election: November, 1983

Administration

General Manager, Robert Barbeau, Eng.
City Clerk, Jacqueline Giguère-Boyer
Treasurer, Roger Valade
Chief Engineer, Conrad Cormier, Eng.
Director of Public Health, Jean-Guy Bonnier, m.d.
Fire Director, Pierre Aquin
Recreation Manager, André Larose
Library Director, Anna Rovira
Personnel Manager, André St-Louis

LAVAL

City Hall, 1 Place du Souvenir, Chomedey, Laval, P.Q. H7V 1W7
Incorporated: August 5, 1965
Area: 93.6 sq. miles/242.41 sq. km
Population: 268,754 (December 1980)
Information: phone: (514) 688-6221

Council

Mayor, Claude Lefebvre
Councillors, R. Bussey, G. Ricard, Mrs. M. Courchesne, A. Corbo, A. Gervais, M. Clermont, Mrs. M. Gauthier, Y. Gauthier, G. Gagné, M. Lemay, S. Lacombe, R. Fortin, G. Vaillancourt, R. Legris, I. Bigman, R. Goyer, A. Brodeur, Y. Lambert, R. Gagnon, A. Boileau, Dr. R. Hebert, D. Goulet, Y. Tremblay, M. Bousquet

Next Election: November, 1985 (Four year terms)

Executive Committee

Dr. Lucien Paiment, Pierre Aubry, Raymond Fortin, J.-L. Lambert, Gilles Vaillancourt

Administration

City Manager, Marc Perron
City Clerk, Ronald Bourcier
City Engineer, Jean-Claude Lafond
Treasurer, Bernard Langevin
Police Director, Gaétan Belisle
Fire Chief, Robert Courteau

LETHBRIDGE

910 4th Ave. S., Lethbridge, Alta. T1J OP6

Incorporated: 1906
Area: 23 sq. miles

Population: 54,624
Phone: (403) 320-3000

Council
Mayor, A.C. Anderson
Aldermen, D.B. Carpenter, James Dunstan, Mrs. Elizabeth Hall, W.L. Kergan, D.M. LeBaron, Ed J. Martin, Frank N. Merkl, R.D. Tarleck
Next Election: October, 1983 (every three years)

Administration
City Manager, R.M. Bartlett
Engineering Director, S.H. Hamilton
Utility Director, O.P. Erdos (1003 4 Ave. S.)
Director of Community Services, T.B. Hudson (1020 20 St. S.)
Director of Economic Development, D.S. O'Connell
Finance Director, R.S. Vickers
City Clerk, John Gerla
City Solicitor, vacant
City Assessor, E.J. Dawson
Development Officer, F. Michna
Personnel Supt., G. Hopman
Chief Constable, R.D. Michelson (Police Stn.)
Fire Chief, E. Holberton (No. 1 Fire Hall)
License Inspector, W.E. Leishman
Purchasing Agent, R. Masson (280 5 St. N.)
Electric Distribution Supt., vacant (280 5 St. N.)
Transit Supt., E. Granger (4th Ave. N.)
Medical Health Officer, Dr. B.A. Lacey (542 7th St. S.)

LONDON
300 Dufferin Ave., Box 5035, London, Ont. N6A 4L9
Incorporated: 1855
Area: 68.24 sq. miles
Population: 256,789 (1980)
Information Contact: City Clerk (phone: 519/679-4530)

Council
Mayor, M.A. Gleeson
Controllers, Orlando Zamprogna, A.D. Cartier, Judith R. White, J. Bigelow
Aldermen, Ward 1: J.M. DeZorzi, J.W.T. Judson; Ward 2: E. Joan Smith, F.H. Flitton; Ward 3: J.F. Fontana, B. MacDonald; Ward 4: Andrew Grant, B.T. Martin; Ward 5: J.F. Tiller, G.E. Williams; Ward 6: T.C. Gosnell, J. McEwen; Ward 7: G.E. Avola, G. Jorgenson
Next Election: November, 1982 (two year terms)

Administration
City Administrator, M.C. Engels
City Clerk, P.C. McNorgan
City Treasurer, S.F. Readings
City Engineer, D.B. Dutton
Director of Planning & Development, K.L. Perry
City Solicitor, R.A. Blackwell
Director & Medical Officer of Health, Dr. D.A. Hutchison
Director of Planning, L.E. Draho
Personnel Director, G.B. Hyde
Director of Social Admin. & Development, H.G. Howlett
Fire Chief, E. Fenwick (act.)
Chief of Police, W.T. Johnson
Chief Building Official, R. Cerminara
Director of Purchasing, L. Snider
Traffic Director, J. Morgan
Housing & Area Rehabilitation Admin., H. Pulver
Director of Systems & Data Processing, K. Drysdale (act.)
Development Commr., D.J. Heron
Manager, Visitors & Convention Services of Greater London, A.F. Mandy

LONGUEUIL
C.P. 5000, Longueuil, P.Q. J4K 4Y7
Incorporated: 1874
Area: 19.5 sq. miles
Population: 132,860
Information Contact: Nicole Primeau (phone: (514) 651-4100)

Council
Mayor, Marcel Robidas
Councillors and Districts: 1) Jacques Bouchard; 2) Georges Touten; 3) Léonard Boulet; 4) Roger Ferland; 5) René Leblanc; 6) Lorenzo Defoy; 7) P.-A. Briand; 8) Gilles Déry; 9) Pierre Nantel; 10) Jacques Finet; 11) Serge Sévigny; 12) J.-P. Vermette; 13) Mme Jeannine Lavoie; 14) P.-E. Paquin; 15) Jacques Laplante; 16) Benoit Danault; 17) André Létourneau
Next Election: November 14, 1982

Administration
Directeur général, Fernand Poiré
Directeur général adj. et p.d.g. de l'Office de développement économique de Longueuil, Jean-G. Curzi
Directeur général adj. et directeur des Finances, Yves Després
Greffier, Claude Gauthier (Clerk)
Directeur du Personnel, Raymond Patry
Directeur de la Rénovation Urbaine, Roméo Paré (Urban Renewal)
Directeur du Génie et des Travaux publics, Jean Verdy (Engineering & Public Works)
Conseiller juridique, Me Claude Séguin
Chef de la Division des Usines de Traitement des Eaux, Jean-L. Bergeron (Water Works)
Urbaniste, Claude Doyon (Planning)
Trésorier, Jacques Paquin
Directeur de l'Informatique, Claude Chapleau
Chef de la Division des Achats, Robert Chabot (Purchasing)
Directeur de l'Evaluation, Rosaire Cayer (Assessment)
Directeur du Zonage et Permis, Maurice Comeau
Directeur de la Police, Pierre Robidoux
Directeur de la Prévention des Incendies, Léon Daigneault (Fire Prevention)
Directeur du Loisir, Gabriel Ducharme (Recreation)

TOWN OF MARKHAM
8911 Woodbine Ave., Markham, Ont. L3R 1A1
Incorporated: January 1, 1971
Area: 52,890 acres
Population: 73,063
Phone: (416) 477-7000

Council
Mayor, A. (Tony) Roman
Councillors, Ward 1: Doreen Quirk; Ward 2: Bob Sherwood; Ward 3: Dave Wilson; Ward 4: A.B. (Bud) Bonner; Ward 5: Gordon K. Landon; Ward 6: Elson Miles; Ward 7: Tom Gove
Next Election: November, 1982 (two year terms)

Administration
Chief Administrative Officer, N.J. Pickard
Town Clerk, Gary F. Roseblade
Town Solicitor, R.R. King
Town Treasurer, E.A. Barton
Director of Parks & Recreation, B. Wrigglesworth
Director of Planning, T.M. Januszewski
Building Director, W.C. Walker
Director of Engineering, D. Mukherjee
Fire Chief, M. Smith

MISSISSAUGA
1 City Centre Drive, Mississauga, Ont. L5B 1M2
Incorporated: January 1, 1974
Area: 111 sq. miles
Population: 298,045 (1980)
Phone: (416) 279-7600

Information Contact: James Kaakee, Director of Information & Public Relations

Council
Mayor, Hazel McCallion
Councillors, Ward 1: H.E. Kennedy; Ward 2: M. Marland; Ward 3: R. Skjarum; Ward 4: L. Taylor; Ward 5: F.J. McKechnie; Ward 6: D. Culham; Ward 7: D. Cook; Ward 8: S. Mahoney; Ward 9: T. Southorn
Next Election: November, 1982 (two year terms)

Administration
City Manager, Edward Halliday
City Clerk, Terence L. Julian
Deputy Clerk, Len McGillivary
City Treasurer, W. Munden
Commr. of Engineering & Works, Wm. Taylor
Commr. of Building & Zoning, Keith Cowan
Commr. of Planning, R. Edmunds
Commr. of Recreation & Parks, L. Love
Business Development Officer, Gordon Johnstone
Commr. of Finance, Don Ogilvie
City Solicitor, Len Stewart

MONCTON
City Hall, 774 Main St., Moncton, N.B. E1C 1E8
Incorporated: City - 1890
Area: 58.06 sq. miles
Population: 61,113 (1976)
Information Contact: City Clerk (phone: 506/854-3333)

Council
Mayor, D.H. Cochrane
Councillors: L.F. Belliveau (Deputy Mayor); L.I. McLaughlin (at large); N.H. Crossman, R.M. Jaillet (Ward 1); G.S. Rideout, S.J. McGrath (Ward 2); A.L. Galbraith, G.R. Carson (Ward 3); Y.J. Goguen, G.G. Bell (Ward 4)
Next Election: May, 1983 (triennial)

Administration
City Manager, M.E. MacLean
City Engineer, W.M. Steeves
City Clerk, M.B. Sullivan
City Treasurer, D.M. Moore
City Solicitor, J.F.E. White
Community Services Director, A.H. Buck
Town Planning Commr., W.A.G. Snook
Purchasing Director, D.W. Cormier
Police Chief, G.D.J. Cohoon
Fire Chief, J.H. Piers
General Manager, Moncton Industrial Development, Paul Daigle

MONTREAL
City Clerk's Office (Greffier de la Ville), Hôtel de Ville, Montreal, P.Q. H2Y 1C6: City Clerk, Marc Boyer
Incorporated: 1832
Area: 68.5 sq. miles
Population: 1,069,700 (1980)
Information Contact: Information Division (phone: 514 872-6010)

Council
Mayor, Jean Drapeau
Councillors and Districts:
1): Carmen Millette; 2): Fernand Desjardins; 3): Luc Larivee; 4): Claude Varin; 5): Jacques Martineau; 6): Michel Morin; 7): Normand Lussier; 8): André Roy; 9): Pierre Lorange; 10): Paul Beauchemin; 11): Jean Trottier; 12): Jean-K. Malouf; 13): C. René Paris; 14): Rocco A. Luccisano; 15): Marc Beaudoin; 16): Ernest Roussille; 17): Raymond Rail; 18): Fernand Joubert; 19): Claude Freniere; 20): Michel Hamelin; 21): Roger Sigouin; 22): Germain Roy; 23): Jean V. Arpin; 24): Réal Laramee; 25): Demetrius Manolakos; 26): George Savoidakis; 27): Nicole Gagnon-Larocque; 28): Jocelyne Ménard; 29): Arthur Gagnon; 30): Jean La Roche; 31): André Desjardins; 32): André Roussel; 33): Roger Larivee; 34): Sid Stevens; 35): Aimé Y. Charron; 36): Claude Provost; 37): Serge Belanger; 38): Sammy Forcillo; 39): Richard-G. Godin; 40): Joffre Laporte; 41): Nick Auf Der Maur; 42): Yves Magnan; 43): Germain Pregent; 44): Yvon Lamarre; 45): Angelo Anfossi; 46): Jean Lapostolle; 47): John N. Parker; 48): Michael Fainstat; 49): Justine Sentenne; 50): Gerry Snyder; 51): Lucien Gagne; 52): Manuel Feldman; 53): Edmond Synnott; 54): Abraham Cohen
Next Election: November, 1982

Executive Committee
Président, Yvon Lamarre
Vice Président, Pierre Lorange
Members, Justine Sentenne, Fernand Desjardins, Ernest Roussille, Gerry Snyder

Administration
Secrétariat Administratif de la Ville, Hôtel de Ville
Secrétaire administratif de la Ville, Jean-Louis Sauvé
Contentieux, Hôtel de Ville
Avocat en chef, Me Jean Péloquin (Solicitor)
Secretariat Municipal, Hôtel de Ville
Greffier de la Ville, Marc Boyer (Clerk)
Controleur général de la Ville, 330 est rue St-Paul
Controleur général, Roger Galipeau, c.a.
Finances, Hôtel de Ville
Directeur des Finances, Fernand Denis, c.a.
Bureau du Vérificateur, 276 ouest, rue St-Jacques, suite 615
Vérificateur, Guy-A. Trudel, c.a. (Auditor)
Travaux Publics, 700 est, rue St-Antoine (Public Works)
Directeur, Richard Vanier, ing.
Incendie, 4040, ave du Parc (Fire)
Directeur, Jean-Paul Moineau
Affaires Sociales, 435, rue du Champ-de-Mars
Directeur, Jean Séguin
Approvisionnement, 9515, rue St-Hubert (Purchasing & Supply)
Directeur, Yves Roy
Commission d'Initiative et de Dévelopement Economique de Montreal (CIDEM), 155 rue Notre-Dame est
Directeur et Commissaire-général, Pierre Shooner
Commission de la Fonction Publique, 1453 rue Beaubien est, #300
President, P.R. Belisle
Circulation, 7501, rue François-Perrault (Traffic Control)
Directeur, Yves Pellerin, ing.
Permis et Inspections, 810 est, rue St-Antoine
Directeur, Camille Chouinard, ing.
Personnel, Hôtel de Ville
Directeur, Gérard Perron
Gestion Immobilière, 507, Place d'Armes, suite 300 (Real Estate)
Directeur, Guy Lacoste, notaire
Restauration des Logements, 330 rue St-Paul est (Urban Renewal)
Directeur, Guy-R. Legault
Sports et Loisirs, 7400, boul. St-Michel (Recreation)
Directeur, Jean Emond
Activités culturelles, 7400 boul. St-Michel, Directeur, Yves Desmarais, Ph.D.
Urbanisme, 85 est, rue Notre Dame (Housing)
Directeur, Aimé Desautels

MOOSE JAW
228 Main St. N., Moose Jaw, Sask. S6H 3J8
Incorporated: November 20, 1903
Population: 33,441
Area: 17.25 sq. miles
Phone: (306) 693-3621

Council
Mayor, Herb E. Taylor
Aldermen, J.D. Armstrong, C.A. Cave, K.R. Chow, E. Chura, R.A. Dickinson, J. Freidin, G. Hunchuk, P. Norys, Jean A. Roe, M.E. Tolley
Next Election: Fall of 1982

Administration
City Commr., Wallace L. Johnson
City Clerk, George E.R. Stratton
Director of Finance, Darrell J. Metka
Manager, Assessment & Licensing, W.J. Rintoul
Economic Development Executive Director, Douglas G. Marr
City Social Services Director, S.M.S. (Sheila) Phillips
City Engineer, A.J. Schwinghamer
Director, Parks & Recreation, Andre R. Gate
City Planner, David Smith
Transit Manager, T.R. Moerkerk
Fire Chief, E.R. Belsey
Police Chief, Ron Riley
Personnel Director, C.N. Renwick

NEPEAN
3825 Richmond Rd., Nepean, Ont. K2H 5C2
Incorporated: 1850
Area: 80 sq. miles/51,374 acres
Population: 83,374
Phone: (613) 829-1510

Council
Mayor, Ben Franklin
Aldermen, Margaret Rywak, Beryl Gaffney, Gord Hunter, Al Brown, Hugh McDonald, Frank Reid
Next Election: November 1982 (two year terms)

Administration
Chief Administrative Officer, C.M. Beckstead
City Clerk, D.E. Hobbs
Commr. of Planning, W.T. Leathem
Commr. of Finance, Wm. Rice
Commr. of Works, A.C. Bellinger
Commr. of Parks & Recreation, R.J. Sulpher
Director of Personnel, G. Armstrong
Fire Chief, K. Davidson
Police Chief, E.G. Wersch
Information Officer, A. Bertram

NIAGARA FALLS
City Hall, 4310 Queen St., Niagara Falls, Ont. L2E 6X5
Incorporated: January 1, 1904
Area: 80.92 sq. miles
Population: 70,775
Information Contact: J.L. Collinson, City Clerk (phone: 416 356-7521)

Council
Mayor, S. Wayne Thomson
Aldermen: Norm Baker, Charles Cheesman, Patrick Cummings, Donald Dilts, Anthony Fera, Paisley Janvary, Vince Kerrio, Jr., Brian Merrett, Judy Orr, Norman Puttick, Harry Schisler, Thomas G. Somerville
Next Election: November, 1982 (two year terms)

Administration
City Manager, S.R. Price
Director of Municipal Works, R.W. Rodman
City Clerk, J.L. Collinson
City Treasurer, G.E. Farrell
City Solicitor, H.R. Young
Personnel Officer, A.L. Jobey
Police Chief, Donald Harris, Niagara Regional Police Dept., 68 Church St., St. Catharines
Fire Chief, David Kemp, Fire Hall, 5815 Morrison St., Niagara Falls

NORTH BAY
City Hall, Box 360, North Bay, Ont. P1B 8H8
Incorporated: 1925
Area: 128.9 sq. miles
Population: 50,205
Phone: (705) 474-0400

Council
Mayor, Dr. J. Smylie
Aldermen, D.E. King, Don Grassi, B.J. Goulet, Rosemary Zelinka, G.T. Valin, R.S. Lucenti, Daphne Mayne, Peter Baker, A.R. Hub Fedeli, Ed Deibel
Next Election: November, 1982 (two year terms)

Administration
Administrator, C.E. Armstrong
City Clerk, R.F. Barton
Director, Economic Development Dept., T. McGuire
City Engineer, D.C. Robinson
Fire Chief, A. Wharram (Victoria St. W.)
City Solicitor, M.B. Burke
Medical Officer of Health, Dr. P. DesGrosbois
Manager, Parking Authority, E. Simms (180 Worthington St. W.)
Director, Parks & Recreation, M. Shave
Arenas Manager, T. Talentino
Personnel Officer, R.A. Young
Director of Planning & Works, M.L. Daiter
Chief Bldg. Inspector, R. Vassbotn
Chief of Police, W. Wotherspoon
Director, Public Works Dept., D. Mills
Purchasing Agent, W.J. Gigg
Social Services Dept., Welfare Administrator, G. Cardinal
Treasurer, J. Ford
Water Commr., W.W. Walton

DISTRICT OF NORTH VANCOUVER
Box 86218, North Vancouver, B.C. V7L 4K1
Incorporated: August 6, 1891
Area: land, 40,121 acres; water, 3,910 acres
Population: 63,900 (1980)
Phone: (604) 987-7131

Council
Mayor, D.H. Bell (Nov. 82)
Aldermen, Marilyn Baker (Nov. 83); J.R. Ball (Nov. 82); E.F. Crist (Nov. 83); J.R. Lakes (Nov. 83); P.C. Powell (Nov. 82); Mary A. Segal (Nov. 82)
Next Election: November 20, 1982 (overlapping terms)

Administration
Municipal Manager, D.A. Welsh
Treasurer/Collector, E.M. Palmer
Municipal Clerk, Mrs. H.W. Egleston
Personnel Director, R.L. Willett
Municipal Engineer, E.J. Bremner
Director of Development, J.F. Sigurjonsson
Chief Bldg. Inspector, H.E. Carr
Purchasing Agent, D.M. Laing
Land Agent, G.A. Williams
Data Processing Co-ordinator, R. Waterberg
Medical Health Officer, Dr. W.E. MacBean
Fire Chief, R.G. McDonald
Chief Public Health Inspector, C.E. Young
Municipal Solicitor, R.J. Orr

NORTH YORK
5100 Yonge St., Willowdale, Ont. M2N 5V7
Incorporated as a City: February 14, 1979
Area: 69.44 sq. miles
Population: 563,000 (1980)
Information Contact: Anna Di Ruscio, Director of Information Services, 416/224-6083

Council
Mayor, Mel Lastman.
Controllers, Esther Shiner, Robert Yuill, Norman Gardner, Bill Sutherland
Wards & Aldermen: 1) Mario Sergio; 2) Mario Gentile; 3) Ms. Pat O'Neill; 4) Howard Moscoe; 5) Michael Foster; 6) Milton Berger; 7) Irv Chapley; 8) Andy Borins; 9) R.J. Summers; 10) Marie Labatte; 11) Peter Clarke; 12) Barry N. Burton; 13) Elinor Caplan; 14) Mrs. Betty Sutherland
Next Election: November, 1982 (two year terms)

Administration
Building Dept., Commr., E.Y. Uzumeri
Clerk's Dept., City Clerk, Earl Roberts; Director of Information Services, Anna Di Ruscio, APR
Dept. of Planning & Development, Commr., A. Bruce Davidson
Dept. of Public Health, Medical Officer of Health, Dr. A.M. Archibald
Dept. of Public Works, Commr., Brian Ruddy, P.Eng.
Fire Dept., Chief, Jos. H. Gibson
Legal Dept., City Solicitor, Charles E. Onley, Q.C.
Municipal Building Services, Commr., George Hardy
Parks & Recreation, Commr., Douglas W. Snow
Personnel Dept., Commr. of Personnel, Thos. Murphy
Traffic Dept., Commr., Sydney R. Cole
Treasury Dept., Commr. of Finance & Treasurer, Robert H. Davie
Emergency Measures Association: 489-2111

TOWN OF OAKVILLE
1225 Trafalgar Rd., Box 310, Oakville, Ont. L6J 5A6
Incorporated: May 27, 1857
Area: 55 sq. miles
Population: 73,603
Phone: (416) 845-6601

Council
Mayor, B.H. Barrett
Councillors and (Wards)
Ward 2 Local Councillors, Norm Connolly, Jackie Cutmore
Ward 2 Regional Councillors, Terry Mannell, Gord Reade
Ward 3 Local Councillors, Paul Farley, Liz Behrens
Ward 3 Regional Councillors, Ann Mulvale, Fred Oliver
Ward 4 Local Councillors, Bruce Attenborough, Gerry Smith
Ward 4 Regional Councillors, Carol Gooding, Keith Bird
Next Election: November, 1982 (two year terms)

Administration
Town Administrator, K.C. Needham
Town Clerk, D.W. Brown
Town Solicitor, C.R. Demaray
By-law Enforcement Officer & License Commr., G. Derrick
Director of Parks & Recreation, D.H. Rigg
Director of Personnel, A.A. Bishop
Director of Planning, R. Foy
Purchasing Agent, J.H. Rees
Treasurer, H.E. Henderson
Director of Buildings, J.H. Kelley
Chief, Fire Dept., J.W. Miller
Director of Public Works, O.H. Ellis, P. Eng.
Director of Planning & Design, L.D. McLeod
Town Surveyor & Land Purchase Officer, T.W. Connolly

OSHAWA
City Hall, 50 Centre St. S., Oshawa, Ont. L1H 3Z7
Incorporated: March 8, 1924
Area: 56.05 sq. miles
Population: 115,486 (1980)
Phone: (416) 725-7351

Council
Mayor, Allan C. Pilkey
Aldermen, John Aker, Michael Armstrong, Pauline Beal, J.E. DeHart, C. Elsey, John Howden, E. Kolodzie, Michael Lisko, C.J. Mason, B.D. McArthur, J.D. McLaughlin, Margaret Shaw, J.W. Wiley, D.W. Wilson
Next Election: November, 1982 (two year terms)

Administration
City Clerk, R.A. Henderson
Deputy City Clerk, B.C. Suter
Treasurer & Director of Finance, C.W. Keil
Director of Purchasing, W.J. Crompton
Tax/Revenue Officer, vacant
Director of Planning & Development, R.G. Madziya
Manager, Real Estate Branch, P.G. McDaniel
Manager, Buildings Branch, G.N. Bilous
Commr. of Works, F.E. Crome
Director of Operations, D.M. Robertson
Director of Engineering, A. Myklebost
Director of Administrative Services, vacant
Director of Community Services, A.G. Nelson
Director of Civic Auditorium & Arenas, W. Kurelo
Director of Parks & Property, P.J. Kennedy
Director of Recreation, C.C. Pell
Fire Dept., Chief, E.R. Stacey
Director of Personnel, T.E. Neill
City Solicitor, H.J. Couch

OTTAWA
City Hall, 111 Sussex Dr., Ottawa, Ont. K1N 5A1
Phone: (613) 563-3111
Incorporated: December 18, 1854
Area: 47.6 sq. miles
Population: 301,567 (1980)
Information: (phone: 613 563-3371)

Council
Mayor, Marion Dewar
Aldermen, Alta Vista Ward: Gregory MacDougall; Billings Ward: Brian Bourns; Britannia Ward: Marlene Catterall; By-Rideau Ward: Marc Laviolette; Canterbury Ward: Darrel Kent; Capital Ward: Howard Smith; Carleton Ward: Toddy Kehoe; Dalhousie Ward: Rolf Hasenack; Elmdale Ward: Graham Bird; Overbrook-Forbes Ward: Rhéal Robert; Queensboro Ward: Terry Denison; Richmond Ward: Don Reid; Riverside Ward: Jim Durrell; St. Georges Ward: Nancy Smith; Wellington Ward: Joe Cassey
Next Election: November, 1982 (two year terms)

Administration
Municipal Auditors, Clarkson, Gordon & Co.
Canada's Capital Visitors & Convention Bureau Inc., 222 Queen St., 7th floor
Executive Vice-President, Les McIlroy
Information Centre: Foyer, National Arts Centre
City Clerk, E.H. Cooper
Civic Complaints Bureau, 6th floor, 1355 Bank St.
Commercial & Industrial Development Corp. of Greater Ottawa, President & General Manager, W.A. Marshall
Community Development Dept.
Commr., R. Bailey
Planning Branch, 5th floor, City Hall, Director, J. Thoms
Urban Policy & Research, 5th floor, City Hall, Head, R. Roberts
Recreation, 6th floor, City Hall, Director, D. Gamble
Emergency Measures Org. of Ottawa-Carleton
Co-ordinator, H.T. Tremblay, 495 Richmond Rd. (725-3337)
Finance Dept., Commr. of Finance, S. Baldwin (includes Accounting, Collection, Taxation, Budgeting, Audit Division, Purchasing Branch, Equipment & Material Management)
Fire Dept., Chief, W. Chatterton
Health Dept., 1827 Woodward Dr. (Ottawa-Carleton Regional Area Health Unit), Director & Medical Officer of Health, Dr. S. Corber
Legal Dept., 4th floor, City Hall, City Solicitor, F. Askwith

Non-Profit Housing (City Living), 214 Hopewell Ave., General Manager, R. Kolbus
Ottawa Housing Authority, 220 Laurier St. W., K1P 5J8
Ottawa-Carleton Regional Transit Commission, 1500 St. Laurent Blvd., General Manager, J. Bonsall
Personnel Dept., 5th floor, City Hall
Commr. of Personnel Services, J.R. Cyr
Director, Labour Relations, S. Keith
Physical Environment Dept., 1355 Bank St., Commr., C. Sim (includes Operations, Admin. Branch, Engineering & Surveys Branch, Property Branch, Buildings & Equipment Branch, and Lansdowne Park)
Police Dept., Chief of Police, T.E. Welsh
Recreation, see Community Development
Social Services Dept. (Regional), 495 Richmond Rd., Commr., A. Pope
Water Supply Division (Regional), Director, J.N. Pritchard

PETERBOROUGH

500 George St. N., Peterborough, Ont. K9H 3R9
Incorporated: 1905
Area: 45.68 sq. kilometers
Population: 59,981
Phone: (705) 742-7771

Council

Mayor, Bob Barker
Aldermen: Ashburnham Ward: Paul Ayotte, Mike Donnelly; Monaghan Ward: Andy Clements, Jack Doris; Northcrest Ward: Gerry O'Connor, Roy Wood; Otonabee Ward: Gordon Holnbeck, Glenn J. Pagett; Town Ward: John Harris, Ann White
Next Election: November, 1982 (two year terms)

Administration

City Administrator, D.L. Hall
City Clerk, S. Hendry
City Engineer, J.G. Hooper
City Treasurer, C. Wills
Planning Director, J.W. Wood
Social & Family Services Director, G.W. Turner
Police Chief, W.J. Shrubb
Fire Chief, W. Manoll
Development Director, F.D. Biss

PORTAGE LA PRAIRIE

Box 490, Portage la Prairie, Man. R1N 3C1
Population: 13,000
Phone: (204) 857-9781
Incorporated: 1907

Council

Mayor, Elmer Greenslade
Aldermen: Wesley Chen, John Harrison, Jack McLean, Jack Shindleman, Ross Smith, Norman Tilley
Next Election: October, 1983

Administration

Secretary Treasurer, W.R. Woodman
Personnel Officer, M. Panchyshyn
City Engineer, B. Bowes
Supt. of Public Works, R. Rose
Supt. of Waterworks, M. Yablonski
Fire Chief, A. MacDonald
Recreation Director, W. Luchik

PRINCE GEORGE

City Hall, 1100 Patricia Blvd., Prince George, B.C. V2L 3V9
Incorporated: 1915
Area: 123 sq. miles
Population: 70,000
Information Contact: W. Buchanan, City Clerk (phone: (604) 564-5151)

Council

Mayor, Elmer W. Mercier (Nov. 82)
Aldermen, R.W. Godfrey (Nov. 82); S.C. Ross (Nov. 82); J.M. Sieb (Nov. 82); John Backhouse (Nov. 82); George McKnight (Nov. 82); Ed Bodner (Nov. 83); A.R. Greenwell (Nov. 83); H. Taal (Nov. 83); S. Sintich (Nov. 83); B. Brownridge (Nov. 83)
Next Election: November 20, 1982 (overlapping terms)

Administration

City Manager, Chester A. Jeffery
City Clerk, Wayne Buchanan
City Engineer, C.E. Obst
City Comptroller & Treasurer, W.D. Kennedy
Civic Properties & Recreation Commission, Manager, W. Woycik
Chief Bldg. Inspector, A.E. Everall
City Planner, M.B. Stagg
Fire Chief, H. Dornbierer (1111 7th Ave.)
Supt., Public Works, J. Welte (693 4th Ave.)
Police, 999 Brunswick St. (RCMP City Detachment)

QUEBEC

C.P. 700, Hôtel de Ville, Quebec, P.Q. G1R 4S9
Incorporated: June 5, 1832
Area: 35.53 sq. miles
Population: 177,082 (1976)
Information Contact: City Clerk (phone: 418 694-6082)

Council

Mayor, Jean Pelletier
Wards & Councillors: 1) J. Boudreau, 2) E. Loupret, 3) A. Forgues, 4) C. Lemieux, 5) R. Garon, 6) G. Theriault, 7) J.-G. Drolet, 8) A. Tremblay, 9) G. Marcotte, 10) A. Langlois, 11) Y. Vezina, 12) P. Mainguy, 13) L. Cimon, 14) R. Clermont, 15) T. Genest, 16) J.-P. Morency, 17) G. Barber, 18) G. Bisson, 19) G. Gilbert, 20) G. Gagnon, 21) L. Bouchard
Next Election: November, 1985 (four year terms)

Administration

Manager, Jacques Perreault, ing.
City Clerk, Me Antoine Carrier
Treasurer, Benoît Couture (int.)
Public Works, Roger Guay, ing.
Water Works, Yves Marchand
Legal Dept., Me Jean-Charles Brochu
Traffic Dept., Marcel Laliberté, ing.
Town Planning, Jean Rousseau
Police, Robert Vézina
Fire, M.C. Mainguy
Health, Jacques Roussel, m.d.
Personnel, Hervé Brosseau
Parks, Recreation, Laurent Bélanger
Auditor, Roger Lachance, c.a.
Public Roads, Roger Gagnon
Methods & Data Processing, André Boucher

REGINA

Box 1790, Regina, Sask. S4P 3C8
Incorporated: June 19, 1903
Area: 42.7 sq. km
Population: 161,142
Information Contact: City Clerk (phone: 306 569-7262)

Council

Mayor, Larry P. Schneider
Aldermen, G.J. Kleisinger, T. Cholod, T. Embury, A.J. Selinger, Ms. W.R. Staff, H. Van Mulligen, W.J. McKeown, E. Strass, Ms. V.A. McGregor, S.E. Oxelgren
Next Election: October, 1982

Administration

City Clerk, F.E. Howard
City Manager, W.K. Mann
Director of Assessment, F. Robb

Licence Inspector, W. Kuntz
Director of Development & Public Relations, J.S. Walker
Director of Bldgs. & Civic Properties, L. Hladun (act.)
Director of Personnel, N. Shrubb
Director of Planning, G.C. Burns (act.)
City Solicitor, L. Shaw
City Treasurer, D. Fisher
Medical Health Officer, Dr. T.Y. Chiao
City Comptroller, D. Power
Director of Public Works & Engineering, D. Schnell
Fire Chief, L. Yanko
Director of Purchasing, L. Katchuk
General Manager of Transit, G.H. McAdoo
Director of Emergency Measures Org., G.W.F. Harding
Director of Parks & Recreation, vacant

TOWNSHIP OF RICHMOND

6911 No. 3 Rd., Richmond, B.C. V6Y 2C1
Incorporated: 1879
Area: 41,529 acres
Population: 105,000 (1981, est.)
Phone: (604) 278-5511

Council

Mayor, G.J. Blair
Aldermen, G. Halsey-Brandt, K. Kumagai, H. Mawby, R.A. McMath, E.T. Novakowski, Mrs. C. Percival-Smith, H. Steves, T.M. Youngberg
Next Election: November 19, 1983 (two year terms)

Administration

Administrator, J.E. Brooks
Treasurer-Collector, A. Inglis
Director of Planning, W. Kerr
Municipal Engineer, B.E. Doughton
Municipal Solicitor, T. Nicholls
Municipal Clerk, G. Morris
Medical Health Officer, Dr. J.D. Garry
Chief Bldg. Inspector, R. Switzer
Personnel Director, A.L. Reed
Director of Leisure Services, D.G. Harwood
Purchasing Agent, W.T. McDonald
Chief License Inspector, R.W. Taylor
RCMP Supt., F. Schmidt
Fire Chief, T. Lorenz

DISTRICT OF SAANICH

770 Vernon Ave., Victoria, B.C. V8X 2W7
Incorporated: March 1, 1906
Area: 41.42 sq. miles
Population: 80,000 (1981 est.)
Phone: (604) 386-2241

Council

Mayor, M.B. Couvelier (Nov. 83)
Aldermen, Irene Block (Nov. 82); Mary Casilio (Nov. 82); Pat Crofton (Nov. 82); H. Knight (Nov. 83); John Mika (Nov. 82); A. Peterson (Nov. 83); H.F. Sturrock (Nov. 83); G.A. Vantreight (Nov. 83)
Next Election: November 20, 1982 (overlapping terms)

Administration

Administrator, William Tremayne
Municipal Clerk, T. Kirk
Controller-Treasurer, R. Broughton
Municipal Engineer, C.T. Warren
Municipal Planner, Gil Laurenson
Police Chief, R. Peterson
Fire Chief, A. Fryer
Parks & Recreation Director, W. Young

ST. CATHARINES

City Hall, Box 3012, St. Catharines, Ont. L2R 7C2
Incorporated: 1876
Area: 38.38 sq. miles
Population: 123,617
Information Contact: City Clerk (phone: 416 688-5600)

Council

Mayor, T. Roy Adams
Aldermen: John Bart, Joe McCaffery, Joseph Kushner, Joseph LaPlante, John Washuta, Barbara Black, Bill Stevenson, Jean Johnston, Stan Brickell, Denise Taylor, Bill Luey, Fred Lindal
Next Election: November, 1982 (two year terms)

Administration

City Administrator, Hugh J. Cook
City Clerk, Thomas R. Hollick, A.M.C.T.
City Treasurer, Lawrence A. Tufford, C.A.
City Engineer, John Warren, P. Eng.
Solicitor, Thomas A. Richardson, B.A., LL.B.
Personnel Director, F. Ainsley Barley
Director of Planning, William A. White
Director of Business Development, Ken Burke
Director of Parks & Recreation, Frank W. Anderson
Director of Supplies & Services, Ken Burke
Chief of Fire Dept., Joseph FitzGibbon
Purchasing Agent, A. Slingerland
Bldg. Inspector, Walter Bradley

SAINT JOHN

City Hall, (Box 1971), Saint John, N.B. E2L 4L1
Incorporated: May 18, 1785
Area: 121.69 sq. miles
Population: 118,700 (1979 est.)
Phone: (506) 658-2862

Common Council

Mayor, Robert Lockhart
Councillors: M.A. Vincent (Deputy Mayor), C.J. Denton, G.F. Elliot, K.R. Gould, H.G. Green, D.R. Knibb, Ralph Landers, J.D. MacCallum, Albert Vincent, Elsie Wayne
Next Election: May, 1983

Administration

Common Clerk, D.H. Garey
Commr. of Finance, R. Park
City Manager, Arthur McDermott
Commr. of Engineering & Works, J.C. MacKinnon
Deputy Commr. of Engineering, S. Armstrong
Deputy Commr. of Works, J.C. Gabriel
Purchasing Agent, M. Hanlon
General Manager, Power Commission, J.J. Donahue
Fire Chief, P. Clark
Police Chief, F. Ross

ST. JOHN'S

City Hall, St. John's, Nfld. A1C 5M2
Incorporated: 1888
Area: 13.422 sq. miles
Population: 88,000
Information Contact: R.J. Greene, City Clerk (phone: 709 726-8820)

Council

Mayor, John Murphy
Councillors at large: David Barrett, James Fagan, Suzanne Duff, Ronald Humphrey
Councillors in Wards: 1) Andy Wells, 2) John Teffier, 3) Bruce Tilley, 4) Thomas Osborne
Next Election: November, 1985 (every four years)

Administration

City Manager, Neil C. Cohoon
Director of Administrative Services & City Clerk, R.J. Greene
Director of Engineering & Works, J.J. Finn, P.Eng.
City Solicitor, Paul Stapleton, LL.B.
Director of Finance & Treasurer, J.B. Edgar, C.A.

Director of Planning, T. de Jong
Director, Personnel & Labour Relations, David Rahal
Director of Buildings, Wayne Purchase
Office Manager, Accounts Dept., Charles Stevenson
Tax Supervisor, Randell Penney
Chief Appraiser, H.G. Taylor
Streets Supt., Fred Cahill
Purchasing Agent, Melvin Rowe
Real Estate Officer, Ron Furlong
Taxi Inspector, William Grouchy
Traffic Engineer, Percy Rideout
Electrical Inspector, James Walsh
Plumbing Inspector, Albert Spurrell
Mechanical Supt., Oliver Tucker

SAINT-LAURENT

777, boul. Laurentien, Saint-Laurent, P.Q. H4M 2M7
Incorporated: February 27, 1893
Area: 16.6 sq. miles
Population: 63,178 (1979)
Phone: (514) 744-6411

Council

Mayor, Marcel Laurin
Councillors:
Saint-Louis: siège 1, Jerry M. Gold; siège 2, Irving Grundman
Beaudet: siège 1, Rodolphe Rousseau; siège 2, Aimé Caron
Decelles: siége 1, Magella Robichaud; siège 2, Georges Bourbonnière
Laval: siège 1, Norman Hartenstein; siège 2, Leonard Painter
Leduc: siège 1, Jean L. Cousineau, siège 2, Gilles Lauriault
Next Election: November, 1982

Administration

Directeur général, Guy Jasmin, c.g.a.
Directeur général adjoint, Administration, Pierre Lebeau, c.g.a.
Directeur général adjoint, Services Publics, Michel Desbiens, ing.
Directeur général adjoint, Développement, Charles Robitaille
Directeur général adjoint, Planification, François Guignard
Trésorier, Jean Kahalé, c.g.a.
Chefs de Service
Achats & Magasins, Lionel Achim (Purchasing & Supply)
Développement Economique et Commissaire Industriel, Simon Vauclair
Génie, G.V. Bourbonnais, ing. (Engineering)
Greffier, Me Jacqueline Leduc (Clerk)
Informatique, Jean-P. Bassellier
Permis & Inspections, André Hamel, e.a.
Personnel, Pierre-A. Lalonde
Prévention des incendies, Nelson David (Fire control)
Activités Sportives, Guy Bourgon
Activités Culturelles, Jean Camerlain
Service Communautaire, Thérèse Rousseau, M.D.
Voirie et Parcs, Jacques Pétrin (Recreation & Parks)
Urbanisme, Claude Charette
Recherches, Jean-Guy Côté, r.i.a.
Entretien de l'équipement, J.H. Bastien, ing. (Equipment Maintenance)

ST-LEONARD

8400 boul. Lacordaire, Saint-Léonard, P.Q. H1R 3B1
Population: 83,000 (est.)
Phone: (514) 321-7630

Council

Mayor, Antonio Di Ciocco
Councillors and Districts:
1): Jacques Di Blasio; 2): Tommaso Nanci; 3): Robert Benoît; 4): Joseph Andreoni; 5): Raymond Renaud; 6): Eduardo Di Bennardo; 7): Louis Turmel; 8): Rosario Ortona; 9): André Chrétien; 10): Jules Lauzon; 11): Jacques Proulx; 12): Jean A. Desjardins
Next Election: November, 1982

Administration

Gérant municipal, Robert Morin (City Manager)
Greffier, Georges Larivee (Clerk)
Directeur, Génie, Pierre Santamaria (Engineering)
Trésorier, Marcel Bouthillier
Directeur, travaux publics, Vilis Preiss (Public Works)
Directeur, Personnel, Jean-C. Durand
Directeur, prévention des incendies, Robert Desjardins (Fire Control)
Directeur, Service Communautaire, Gerard Soulard
Directeur, Aménagement, Gérard Gagnon
Directeur, Service Approvisionnement, André Latulippe (Supply)

SARNIA

255 N. Christina St., Sarnia, Ont. N7T 7N2
Incorporated: May 7, 1914
Area: 11, 672 acres
Population: 49,764 (1980)
Phone: (519) 332-0330

Council

Mayor, Marceil G. Saddy
Aldermen, Marcella Brown, John Kowalyshyn, Wills Rawana, Patrick O'Brien, Bernice Rade, Robert Gray, Doug Bain, June Lasenby
Next Election: November, 1982 (every two years)

Administration

City Manager, J.C. Robertson
City Clerk, G.A.M. Thomas
Director of Social Services, Louise Geres
Co-ordinator, Emergency Measures Org., Ron Larsen
Fire Chief, G.C. Hansen
Director of Parks & Recreation, Wm. Skerrett
Director of Personnel, J.A. Barker
Director of Community Planning & Renewal, R.M. Draker
Purchasing Agent, A.S. Parsons
City Solicitor, G.F. Gillespie
City Treasurer, Ron Brooks
Commr. of Works, D.W. Silliman
Police Chief, R.F. Cook
Transit Manager, C.S. Jones

SASKATOON

City Hall, Saskatoon, Sask. S7K OJ5
Incorporated: May 26, 1906
Area: 50.48 sq. miles
Population: 150,150 (1980 est.)
Information Contact: City Clerk (phone: 306/664-9242)

Council

Mayor, C. Wright
Aldermen, M.T. Cherneskey, H. Dayday, M. Hawthorne, O. Mann, Mrs. P. Lorje, G. Penner, G. Taylor, Q.C., Mrs. K. Waygood, D. Whalley, O. Wilson
Next Election: October, 1982

Administration

Arena Manager, E.B. Kobussen
City Assessor, F.B. Garland
Building Dept. Manager, B.T. Arling
City Clerk, J. Kolynchuk
City Commr., S.H. Dietze
City Comptroller, B. Veltkamp
Data Processing Manager, B.A. Penney
Electrical Engineer, W. Bunn
City Engineer, B. Brown
Finance Director, A.P. Gilewicz
Fire Chief, J. Sebestyen
A/Medical Health Officer, V.L. Matthews, M.D.
Industrial Development Manager, D. Fairlie
Commercial Light & Water Manager, S. Clewes
Parks & Recreation Manager, E.H. Smith

Parks Supt., D.A. Scott
Personnel Director, J.B. Morgan
Planning & Development Director, H.E. Wellman
Police Chief, J. Gibbons
Purchasing Manager, L.P. Ollenberger
City Solicitor, M.D. Irwin
Manager, Tax & License Dept., D. Traill
Transit Supt., J.A. Ross
City Treasurer, G. Nygaard
Director of Works & Utilities, J.A. Beveridge
Manager, Waterworks & Pollution Control, D. Kelly

SAULT STE. MARIE

Civic Centre, Box 580, Sault Ste. Marie, Ont. P6A 5N1
Incorporated: 1912
Area: 92 sq. miles
Population: 81,355
Information Contact: City Clerk (phone: 705/949-9111, ext. 303)

Council

Mayor, Don Macgregor
Aldermen: Ward 1: Stephen Butland, Charles Swift; Ward 2: Marsh Barsanti, Thomas Angus; Ward 3: William J. Syms, Walter Borowicz; Ward 4: Fred Dovigi, Michael Sanzosti; Ward 5: Arthur E. Gualazzi, Walter Chisholm; Ward 6: Joe Fratesi, Frank J. Manzo
Next Election: November, 1982 (two year terms)

Administration

City Administrator, Allan A. Jackson
City Clerk, William G. Lindsay
City Treasurer, Frederick Konkin, C.G.A.
City Engineer, Donald C. Redmond
City Solicitor, Lorie Bottos
Personnel Director, C. Roy Bernardi
Planning Director, John M. Bain
Director of Development, Gerard E. Duffy
Commr. of Parks & Recreation, Harold A. Brain
Supervisor of Building Services, Gerry Byrne
Fire Chief, John F. Ryan
Purchasing Agent, John I. Nash
Chief Building Inspector, Joseph D. LaRue
Tax Collector, Garry B. Mason
Economic Development Commr., D.L. Leighton

SHERBROOKE

145, rue Wellington nord, Sherbrooke, P.Q. J1H 5C1
Area: 22 sq. miles
Population: 87,000
Information: (819) 565-2828 (Communication Sherbrooke)

Council

Mayor, Jacques O'Bready
Councillors:
North Ward: Gaston Goulet, Jean-Guy Archambault, Camille Fortier
East Ward: Gérard Déziel, Claude Dallaire, Robert Boisvert
West Ward: Antonio Pinard, Roger Gingues, Réginald St-Laurent
Center Ward: Roméo Bergeron, ing.
Next Election: November, 1982

Administration

Directeur général, Roch Letourneau
Greffier, Robert Bélisle (Clerk)
Trésorier, Charles Martel
Contentieux, Me Pierre Huard (Solicitor)
Directeur, Relations publiques, André Collard
Directeur, Ressources humaines, Claude Lessard
Secrétaire administratif, Charles-A. Beaudoin
Directeur, Services techniques, Frank Mascolo (Operations)
Directeur, Travaux publics, Raymond Gagnon (Public Works)
Directeur, Hydro, Jean Bourassa
Directeur, Police, Jean-P. Pelletier
Directeur, Incendies, Francis Boudreau (Fire)
Directeur, Loisirs, Alvin Doucet (Recreation)
Directeur, Personnel, Claude Lessard
Directeur, Commissariat industriel, Daniel Migneault
Chef du Division, Evaluation, Claude Dupont (Assessment)

SUDBURY

City Hall, 200 Brady St., Sudbury, Ont. P3E 4S5
Incorporated: 1930
Area: 113 sq. miles
Population: 92,406 (1981)
Information Contact: Mrs. Ellen Kerr (phone: 705 674-3141)

Council

Mayor, Maurice Lamoureux
Aldermen and (Wards), 1: Andy Roy; 2: Diane Marleau; 3: Gary Peck; 4: S. Campbell; 5: R. Bartolucci; 6: B. Sutton; 7: R. de la Riva; 8: Ronald Symington; 9: R. Fera
Next Election: November, 1982 (two year terms)

Administration

City Clerk, Mrs. Ellen Kerr
Administrative & Community Services
  Director, G.D. Polano
  Director of Recreation, D. Waddell
  Director of Parks, L. Bigger
  Arena Manager, R. King
  Fire Chief, J. Barr
  Director of Data Processing, R. Philion
City Treasurer, D. Chmara
City Solicitor, F. Dean
Personnel Director, A.V. Bennett
City Engineer, P. Wong
Chief Transportation Engineer, T. Rukholm

SUMMERSIDE

Box 1510, Summerside, P.E.I. C1N 4K4
Incorporated: April 18, 1877
Population: 8,498
Phone: (902) 436-4222

Administration

Town Manager, Nelson Johnston
Police Chief, W.J.R. Macdonald
Fire Chief, James Peters
Recreation Director, Wm. Schurman

DISTRICT OF SURREY

14245 56 Ave., Surrey, B.C. V3W 1J2
Incorporated: November 10, 1879
Area: 132 sq. miles
Population: 125,000 (est.)
Phone: (604) 591-4132

Council

Mayor, D.A. Ross (Dec. 83)
Aldermen, Bonnie Schrenk (Dec. 82); M.G. Watkins (Dec. 82); R.J. Bose (Dec. 82); C.J. Campbell (Dec. 83); R.W. Jacobs (Dec. 83); W.A. Fomich (Dec. 83); Jack Wittacker (Dec. 82); P. Easton (Dec. 83)
Next Election: November 20, 1982 (overlapping terms)

Administration

Municipal Manager, D.J. Closkey
Engineer, M. Jones
Treasurer, D. Atkinson
Municipal Clerk, W. Vollrath
Solicitor, G. Hanrahan
Chief Inspector, D. Magnusson
Collector, K. Greenwood
Parks & Recreation, W.R. Green
Director of Economic Development, F.W. Wiles
Planner, G. Sixta
Fire Chief, A. Cleaver

Data Centre Director, R. Wiens
Personnel, W. Eccleston
Land Agent, L. Jefferson
Purchasing Director, R. Campbell

SYDNEY

Civic Centre, Box 730, Sydney, N.S. B1P 1A7
Incorporated: 1904
Area: 6.5 sq. miles
Population: 33,000
Phone: (902) 539-0940

Council

Mayor, Manning Macdonald
Aldermen: Ward 1: Vincent MacNeil, Alex MacInnis; Ward 2: Charles Palmer, Earl MacDonald; Ward 3: Angus Currie, Ross O'Handley; Ward 4: John Nardocchio, Archie MacRury; Ward 5: Dan Yakimchuk, Frank Starzomski; Ward 6: Duncan MacKay, John Kennedy
Next Election: October, 1982

Administration

City Manager, Dan R. MacLeod
City Treasurer, D.R. Farmer
City Solicitor, M.G. Whalley, Q.C.
City Clerk, Paul J. Roach
City Engineer, Frank MacDonald
Development Officer, Bernard Reppa
Manager, Water Commission, Alex MacDonald
Director of Recreation, John Fraser
Comptroller, Robert Halloran
Director, Social Services, James MacCormack
Chief of Police, John MacIntyre
Fire Chief, Donald Johnston
Deputy Treasurer & Purchasing Agent, A.V. MacKinnon

THUNDER BAY

City Hall, Donald St., Thunder Bay, Ont. P7E 5V3
Incorporated: January 1, 1970
Area: 156 sq. miles
Population: 111,476
Information Contact: City Clerk (phone: 807 623-2711, ext. 233)

Council

Mayor, Walter M. Assef
Aldermen, Current River Ward: C. Johnston, D. Waddington; McIntyre Ward: J. Vander Wees; McKellar Ward: L. Timko, Shirley Trotter; Neebing Ward: Don Smith; Northwood Ward: K. Boshcoff, Dale Willoughby; Red River Ward: J.P. Packota, Rita Ubriaco; Westfort Ward: Sterling Lysnes, Rene Larson
Next Election: November, 1982 (two year terms)

Administration

Chief Administrative Officer, J.R. Picherack
City Clerk, H.T. Kirk
Development Bureau, Director, G. McFadden
Thunder Bay Area Emergency Measures Org., 101 Waterloo St., (623-2711, ext. 392), Co-ordinator, E.A. Fallen
Director of Engineering & Operations, T. Fell
Director of Corporate Planning & Development, J.G. Rapino
Fire Chief, J.L. Bryant
Homes for the Aged, Administrator, D. O'Gorman
Parking Authority, Manager, F. Brown
Director of Community & Planning Development, I.P. Harper
Police Chief, T.R. Keep
Director of Administrative Services, A.J. Ingberg (responsible for purchasing)
Director of Community Services, D.R. MacLeod
Systems Manager, W. Bilyk
Manager of Public Transit, K. McLean
City Treasurer, S. Splawski
Public Affairs Manager, P. Drombolis
City Engineer, R.H. Wright

TORONTO

City Hall, Toronto, Ont. M5H 2N2
Incorporated: March 6, 1834
Area: Land, 101 sq. km; Water, 293 sq. km
Population: 630,487 (1980)
Information Contact: Information Office (phone: 416 367-7341)

Council

Mayor, Art Eggleton
Aldermen, Ward 1: Wm. Boytchuk, David White; Ward 2: Ben Grys, Chris Korwin-Kuczynski; Ward 3: Joseph J. Piccininni, Richard Gilbert; Ward 4: Joe Pantalone, Tony O'Donohue; Ward 5: Ying Hope, Ron Kanter; Ward 6: G.J. Chong, John Sewell; Ward 7: Gordon Cressy, David Reville; Ward 8: Frederick J. Beavis, Tom Clifford; Ward 9: Pat Sheppard, Dorothy Thomas; Ward 10: June Rowlands, Andrew Paton; Ward 11: Anne Johnston, Michael Gee
Next Election: November, 1982 (two year terms)

Administration

Heads of Depts.:
Audit, J. Rabinowitz, City Auditor
Buildings & Inspections, M. Nixon, Commr.
City Clerk's, Roy V. Henderson, City Clerk
City Legal, W.R. Callow, Q.C., City Solicitor
Com. of Adjustment, C.E. Taylor, Administrator & Secretary Treasurer
Finance, W.A. Wilford, Commr. of Finance & City Treasurer
Fire, B. Bonser, Chief
Housing, G.C. Cook, Commr.
Management Services, A.L. Stevenson, Executive Director
Mayor's Office, R. Cumberbatch, Administrative Officer
Parks & Recreation, Ivan B. Forrest, Commr.
Public Health, Dr. A.S. Macpherson, Medical Officer of Health
Public Works, R.M. Bremner, Commr.
Purchasing & Supply, D.G. Judd, Commr.
Planning & Development, S. McLaughlin, Commr.
Property, G. Emslie, Commr.

TROIS-RIVIERES

Hôtel de Ville, 1325 Place de l'Hôtel de Ville, Trois-Rivières, P.Q. G9A 5H3
Incorporated: 1855
Area: 32 sq. miles
Population: 50,600 (1979)

Counsel

Mayor, Gilles Beaudoin
Counsellors, Fernand Goneau, Léo Thibeault, Antoine Gauthier, Léopold Alarie, Gaston Vallières, Fernand Colbert, Jean-Guy Laferté, Lionel Julien

Next Election: November, 1982

Administration

Gérant, Jacques Charette (Manager)
Greffier, Me Jean Lamy (City Clerk)
Trésorier, Claude Doucet
Directeur des Services techniques, Origène Bellemare (Operations)
Directeur des Travaux publics, Yvon Poirier (Public Works)
Directeur des Services communautaires, Albert Morrissette (Community Planning)
Directeur du Service de Police & Incendie, G.-P. Simard (Police & Fire)
Directeur du personnel, Claude Gendron
Directeur des Achats, René Monfette (Purchasing)

VANCOUVER

453 W. 12th Ave., Vancouver, B.C. V5Y 1V4
Incorporated: 1886
Area: 44 sq. miles
Population: 410,000
Information Contact: R. Henry, City Clerk (phone: 604 873-7266)

Council

Mayor, Michael Harcourt
Aldermen, Donald Bellamy, Helen Boyce, May Brown, Nathan Divinsky, Bruce Eriken, Marguerite Ford, Warnett Kennedy, George Puil, Harry Rankin, Bruce Yorke
Elections: Every two years (November, 1982)

Administration

City Manager, F. Bowers
City Clerk, R. Henry
Director of Planning, R. Spaxman
Treasurer, D.J. Reid
Permits & Licences, Director, R.V. Hebert
Purchasing Agent, W. Ramsay
Parks Supt., V. Kondrosky
Fire Chief, N. Harcus
Chief Constable, R.J. Stewart
Director of Finance, P.D. Leckie
Director of Civic Buildings, A. Langley
City Engineer, W.H. Curtis
Deputy City Engineer, R.C. Boyes
Asst. City Engineer, Services & Sewers, T. Mulder
Asst. City Engineer, Electrical, H.P. Gibault
Asst. City Engineer, Traffic, D. Rudberg
Asst. City Engineer, Streets, E.A. West
Asst. City Engineer, Water, Sanitation & Materials, P.S. Herring

VICTORIA

No. 1, Centennial Sq., Victoria, B.C. V8W 1P6
Incorporated: August 2, 1862
Area: 4,641 acres
Population: 65,225 (1981)
Information Contact: Manager's Office (phone: 604 385-5711, Loc. 202)

Council

Mayor, Peter Pollen
Aldermen, J. Baird, R.K. Blencoe, G. Brewin, F.S. Carson, J.B. Cooper, M. Glazier, R. McKenzie, E. Simmons
Next Election: November 19, 1983 (two year terms)

Administration

Municipal Manager, James H. Bramley
Deputy Municipal Manager & City Clerk, Colin F.G. Crisp
Director of Community Development, G.J. Greenhalgh
City Engineer, John D. Sansom
Director of Finance, Mason A. Sheldrick
Fire Chief, M. Heppell
Chief Constable, Wm. Snowdon
Director of Recreation & Community Services, John B. Morgan
Director of Parks, A.I. Smith
Purchasing Agent, H.V. Robinson
Public Works Supt., R. Barnett

WATERLOO

City Hall, 20 Erb St. W. (Box 377, Waterloo, Ont. N2J 4A8)
Incorporated: January 1, 1948
Area: 6,645 hectares (25.6 sq. miles)
Population: 54,157
Phone: (519) 886-1550

Council

Mayor, Marjorie Carroll
Aldermen, Richard Biggs, Jim Erb, Robert Henry, Mary Jane Mewhinney, John Shortreed, Doreen Thomas, Charles Voelker, Glen Wright
Next Election: November, 1982 (two year terms)

Administration

City Clerk, R.C. Keeling
Commr. of Finance & City Treasurer, D.C. Schaefer
Commr. of Works & City Engineer, J.D. Willis
Chief Building Official, Guenter Trinkaus
Purchasing & Personnel Director, T.O. Hallman
Tax Collector, R.A. McKee
Community Services Director, K.P. Pflug
Planning Director, Tom Slomke
Fire Chief, John Staller
Solicitor & Corporation Counsel, W.H. White (Harper, Haney & White)

WHITEHORSE

2121 Second Ave., Whitehorse, Yukon Y1A 1C2
Incorporated: 1950
Area: 162 sq. miles
Population: 16,800
Phone: (403) 667-6401

Council

Mayor, Don Branigan
Aldermen, Art Deer, Bert Law, Joanne Linzey, Jon Pierce, Duncan Sinclair, Vern Toews (not updated to 1982)
Elections: Every two years, in November or December

Administration

City Manager, Dave Gairns
Director of Engineering, Ron Gourley
City Clerk, Jan McConachy
Director of Finance, Mrs. Sherron Jones
Engineer, Brian Laird
Fire Marshal, Fred Blaker
Fire Chief, Doug Row
Recreation Director, Barry Braun
Supt. of Works, Tom Walton
Chief Building Inspector, Marvin Amos
Bylaw Enforcement Suprv., Larry Leigh

WINDSOR

City Hall, 205 University Ave. E., Windsor, Ont. N9A 6S1
Incorporated: 1854
Area: 49.6 sq. miles
Population: 196,512 (1980)
Phone: (519) 255-6500

Council

Mayor, Bert Weeks
Aldermen, Ward 1: Peter Mackenzie, Michael Ray; Ward 2: Dr. Ronald Wagenberg, Peggy Simpson; Ward 3: Dr. Howard McCurdy, Frank Wansbrough; Ward 4: Elizabeth Kishkon, Thomas Toth; Ward 5: Al Santing, David Burr

Next Election: November, 1982 (two year terms)

Administration

City Administrator, Hilary Payne
Bldg. Dept., Commr., M. Mitchell
City Clerk's Dept., City Clerk, J.B. Adamac
(including Voters List, Assessment Rolls & Licence Bureau)
Emergency Planning, Director, R. Norwood
Finance Dept., Commr. of Finance, E.A. Agnew
Fire Dept., 815 Goyeau St., Fire Chief, K. Stewart
Landlords & Tenants Advisory Bureau, R. Norwood
Legal Dept., City Solicitor, A.S. Kellerman
Metro Windsor-Essex County Health Unit, 1550 Ouellette Ave., Medical Officer of Health, Dr. Joseph R. Jones

Parks & Recreation Dept., 2450 McDougall St., Commr., Lloyd Burridge
Personnel Dept., Director, A.P. Angus
Planning Dept., Commr., J. Atkins
Police Dept., 445 City Hall Sq., Chief of Police, John Shuttleworth
Property Dept., 68 Chatham St. E., Director, J.L. Boyer
Public Works Dept., Commr., G. Harding
Purchasing Dept., Director of Purchasing, P.J. Bolter
Social Services Dept., 755 Louis Ave., Director, R. Riddell
Traffic Engineering Dept., Director, E. Engelmann
Windsor-Essex County Development Commission, 80 Chatham St. E., Commr., J.R. Moore
Windsor Harbour Commission, 500 Riverside Dr. W., Secretary, C. Gress
Windsor Utilities Commission, 787 Ouellette Ave., General Manager, W.S. Mullin

WINNIPEG

Council Bldg., Civic Centre, Winnipeg, Man. R3B 1B9
Incorporated: November 8, 1873
Area: 220 sq. miles (140,980 acres)
Population: 592,482 (1977)
Information Contact: Dave Grant, Mayor's Office (phone: 204 946-0196)

Council

Mayor, William Norrie
Councillors:
City Centre-Fort Rouge
Notre Dame Ward: Alan C. Wade
Sargent Park Ward: Harvey R. Smith
Redboine Ward: Magnus Eliason
Memorial Ward: Frank Johnson
Corydon Ward: Harold Macdonald
Riverview Ward: Don Gerrie
Lord Selkirk-West Kildonan
Jefferson Ward: D.A. Yanossky
Sisler Ward: Alice Balsillie
Kildonan Park Ward: Helen Promislow
Mynarski Ward: William Chornopyski
Norquay Ward: Joseph Zuken
East Kildonan-Transcona
Henderson Ward: Don Mitchelson
Miles MacDonell Ward: Anne Jorowski
Elmwood Ward: Alf Skowron
Springfield Heights Ward: Jim Ragsdill
Transcona Ward: Philip A. Rizzuto
St. Boniface-St. Vital
Tache Ward: Guy M. Savoie
Langevin Ward: Evelyne Reese
Glenlawn Ward: Al Ducharme
Seine Valley Ward: Gerry Ducharme
Assiniboine Park-Fort Garry
University Ward: John Angus
Pembina Ward: Charles T. Birt
Crescent Heights Ward: Larry Fleisher
Tuxedo Heights Ward: Bill Neville
Charleswood Ward: Jim Moore
St. James-Assiniboia
St. Charles Ward: Ric Nordman
Grant's Mill Ward: Jim Ernst
Stevenson Ward: Pearl McGonigal
Deer Lodge Ward: Jae Eadie
Next Election: (Every 3 years) October 22, 1983

Administration

Assessment Division, 10 Fort St., City Assessor, D. Schmidt
Secretary, Board of Revision, Mrs. Carol Lyons
Audit Dept., Admin. Bldg., Civic Centre, City Auditor, L.E. Marks, C.A.
Board of Commrs., 3rd floor, Admin. Bldg., Chief Commr., N.W. Diakiw
Commr. of Finance, G.R. Evans
Commr. of Works & Operations, W.H. Finnbogason
Commr. of Environment, D.G. Henderson
Budget Bureau, 3rd floor, Admin. Bldg., Director, A.M. Duncan
City Clerk's Dept., Council Bldg., City Clerk, R.J. Fergusson
Civic Properties Dept., Council Bldg., Director, H.B. Young
Computer Services, Director, H.M. Beemer
Finance Dept., 3rd floor, Admin. Bldg., City Treasurer, L. Hutcheon
Fire Dept., Fire Chief, T.L. Moist
Health Dept., 280 William Ave., Medical Health Officer, Dr. D. Gemmill
Winnipeg Hydro, General Manager, K. Hallson
Land Surveys & Real Estate Dept., 4th floor, 10 Fort St., Director, J.H. Phillips
Law Dept., Council Bldg., City Solicitor, F.N. Steele
Operations Dept., Council Bldg., Director, R.J. McRae
Parks & Recreation, 2799 Roblin Blvd., General Manager, W.J. Swail (885-1500)
Director of Planning, Development & Central Services, G.A. Schoch
Director of Regional Parks & Operations, M. Benum
Director of Recreation & Community Parks, J. Spencer
Personnel Dept., 1st floor, Admin. Bldg., General Manager, A. Milroy
Planning Division, 100 Main St., Director, R.P. Darke
Police Dept., Public Safety Bldg., Chief, K.J. Johnston
Purchasing Dept., Admin. Bldg., Director, R.A. Ristock
Streets & Transportation Dept., 10 Fort St., Director, E.W.J. Clarke
Transit Dept., Director, R.L. Borland
Waterworks & Waste Disposal Dept., 1500 Plessis Rd., Director, A. Penman
Welfare Dept., Director, R.H.C. Hooper

Winnipeg Business Development Corp.

#400, 177 Lombard Ave., Winnipeg, Man. R3B OW7
General Manager, H.A. Fredericks

YELLOWKNIFE

Box 580, Yellowknife, N.W.T. X1A 2N4
Incorporated: January 1, 1970
Population: 10,500
Area: 13,857 hectares
Phone: (403) 873-2671

Council

Mayor, M.A. Ballantyne
Aldermen, Don Cooper, Bob Findlay, Everett Kasteel, Jo MacQuarrie, Pat McMahon, Don Sian, Ruth Spence, Richard Whitford
Next Election: December, 1983

Administration

City Administrator, Hugh Stevenson
City Clerk, Margaret Walton
Director of Community Services, Bill Newell
Director of Finance, Peter Tranter
Director of Public Safety, Gerry James
Director of Public Works, Ron Walton

MUNICIPAL GOVERNMENT Part 3 (Alphabetical List of Regional Municipalities in major population areas of British Columbia, Ontario and Quebec)

British Columbia:

For a complete list of Regional Governments in B.C. see Part 1 of this Section.

CAPITAL REGIONAL DISTRICT

524 Yates St. (P.O. Drawer 1000), Victoria, B.C. V8W 2S6
Incorporated: February 1, 1966
Area: 934 sq. miles
Population: 250,000 (1981)
Information Contact: Jack Fry, Information Officer (phone: 604 388-4421)
Member Areas within the District include: Central Saanich, Colwood, Esquimalt, Langford, Metchosin, North Saanich, Oak Bay, Outer Gulf Islands, Saanich, Salt Spring Island, Sidney, Sooke, Victoria, View Royal
Executive Director, Dennis A. Young
Treasurer, William Jordan
Health Services, Dr. A.S. Arneil
Hospital Planning, Murray Halkett

GREATER VANCOUVER REGIONAL DISTRICT

2294 W. Tenth Ave., Vancouver, B.C. V6K 2H9
Incorporated: June 29, 1967
Area: 1,004.9 sq. miles
Population: 1,085,242 (1976)
Information Contact: T. Dunlop, Asst. Secretary (phone: 604 731-1155)
Municipalities within the District include: Village of Belcarra, Dist. of Burnaby, Dist. of Coquitlam, Dist. of Delta, Village of Lions Bay, City of New Westminster, City of North Vancouver, Dist. of North Vancouver, City of Port Coquitlam, City of Port Moody, Dist. of Richmond, Dist. of Surrey, City of Vancouver, Dist. of West Vancouver, City of White Rock, and three electoral areas (Univ. Endowment Lands, Ioco-Buntzen, Bowen Is.)
Commr. of Operations, D.L. MacKay
Commr. of Finance & Admin., G.W. Carlisle
Commr. of Regional Development, W.T. Lane
Admr. of Hospital Planning, M.M. Walker
Admr. of Housing, R.M. Hall
Admr. of Parks, R.A. Hankin
Admr. of Planning, G.F. Farry
Admr. of Labour Relations, G. Leslie
Admr. of Finance, J. McLean
Chief Engineer, A. Purdon
Asst. Secretary, T.M. Dunlop
Comptroller, Accounting, J.M. Boyd

Ontario Regional Governments:

REGIONAL MUNICIPALITY OF DURHAM

605 Rossland Rd. E., Box 623, Whitby, Ont. L1N 6A3
Incorporated: January 1, 1974
Area: 1,000 sq. miles (247 km(2))
Population: 276,775 (1980)
Information Contact, Regional Clerk (phone: 416 668 7711)
Municipalities within the region include: Town of Ajax, Twp. of Brock, Town of Newcastle, City of Oshawa, Town of Pickering, Twp. of Scugog, Twp. of Uxbridge, Town of Whitby
Chief Administrative Officer, D.R. Evans
Regional Clerk, C.W. Lundy
Solicitor, S.K. Jain
Emergency Measures Division, Sgt. D. Matthews (579-1520)
Commr. of Personnel, T. Stevens
Manager, Business Development, M. Beauchamp
Commr. of Finance, J.L. Gartley (60 Bond St. W.)
Commr. of Planning, Dr. M. Michael (105 Consumers Dr., Whitby)
Commr. of Social Services, W.D. Johns (50 McMillan Dr.)
Commr. of Works, W.A. Twelvetrees (105 Consumers Dr., Whitby)

REGIONAL MUNICIPALITY OF HALDIMAND-NORFOLK

Box 2002, Cayuga, Ont. N0A 1E0
Incorporated: April 1, 1974
Area: 1,103 sq. miles
Population: 86,668
Information Contact: C.G. Douglas (phone: 416 772-3337)
Municipalities within the Region include: Twp. of Delhi, Town of Dunnville, Town of Haldimand, City of Nanticoke, Twp. of Norfolk, Town of Simcoe
Chief Administrator, C.G. Douglas
Clerk, MaryLou Johnston
Director of Finance & Treasurer, Robert Johnstone
Director of Engineering, William McDowell
Director of Planning, James Coughlin
Welfare Administrator, Donald MacLellan
Director of Building, Zoning & By-law Enforcement, A.J. Suprun
Personnel/Labour Relations Officer, D.W. McEntee
Medical Officer of Health, Dr. L. Grant
Solicitor, Thomas A. Cline
Administrator, Grandview Lodge, E.H. Montague
Administrator, Norview, R.S.J. Shortt
Economic Development Officer, Armas Pukala

REGIONAL MUNICIPALITY OF HALTON

1151 Bronte Rd., Box 7000, Oakville, Ont. L6J 6E1
Incorporated: January 1, 1974
Area: 381 sq. miles
Population: 247,311 (1980)
Information Contact: Garfield Brown, Regional Clerk (phone: 416 827-2151, ext. 354)
Municipalities within the Region include: City of Burlington, Town of Halton Hills, Town of Milton, Town of Oakville
Chief Administrative Officer, D.Y. Perlin
Personnel Director, D. Camm
Planning Director, R. Mohammed
Purchasing Agent, R. Higgins
Regional Clerk, Garfield Brown
Administrator, Social & Family Services, R.J. Vivian
Treasurer, G. Lawson
A/Administrator, Centennial Manor (185 Ontario St., Milton), G. Timbers
Chief of Police (1229 White Oaks Blvd., Oakville), W.J. Harding
Fire Co-ordinator (1167 Guelph Line, Burlington), W. Corp
Medical Officer of Health, Health Unit, Dr. P. Cole
Solicitor, K.S. Anderson
Director of Public Works, R.W.J. Moore
Director of Business Development, M. Fischer

REGIONAL MUNICIPALITY OF HAMILTON-WENTWORTH

100 Main St. E. (Box 910, Hamilton, Ont. L8N 3V9)
Incorporated: January 1, 1974
Area: 277,096 acres
Population: 407,758 (1979)
Information Contact: Mrs. Joan M. Gallipeau, Clerk (phone: 416 526-4140)
Municipalities within the Region include: Town of Ancaster, Town of Dundas, Twp. of Flamborough, Twp. of Glanbrook, City of Hamilton, Town of Stoney Creek
Co-ordinator, Cyril T.C. Armstrong
Commr. of Planning, vacant
Commr. of Social Services, William M. Carson
Commr. of Finance, Jack K. McAully
Commr. of Engineering, James Leach
Personnel Director, Lloyd R. Flemming
Solicitor, Ray Plant

Director of Economic Development, J. Morand

DISTRICT MUNICIPALITY OF MUSKOKA

Pine St., Box 1720, Bracebridge, Ont. POB 1CO
Incorporated: January 1, 1971
Area: 1,700 sq. miles
Population: 37,000 (1980)
Information: G.G. Williams, Clerk (phone: 705 645-2231)
Municipalities within the District include: Town of Bracebridge, Twp. of Georgian Bay, Town of Gravenhurst, Town of Huntsville, Twp. of Lake of Bays, Twp. of Muskoka Lakes
Regional Clerk, G.G. Williams
Treasurer, J. McRae
Engineer, G.L. Wilson
Social Services Administrator, I. Turnbull
Planning Director, Robert List
Solicitor, A.R. Black
Fire Co-ordinator, P. Mitchell
Land Division Committee Chairman, M. Kennedy

REGIONAL MUNICIPALITY OF NIAGARA

Box 3025, 150 Berryman Ave., St. Catharines, Ont. L2R 7E9
Incorporated: January 1, 1970
Area: 718 sq. miles
Population: 367,665 (1980)
Information Contact: Planning Dept. (phone: 416 685-1571)
Municipalities within the Region include: Town of Fort Erie, Town of Grimsby, Town of Lincoln, City of Niagara Falls, Town of Niagara-on-the-Lake, Town of Pelham, City of Port Colborne, City of St. Catharines, City of Thorold, Twp. of Wainfleet, City of Welland, Twp. of West Lincoln
Regional Solicitor, F.L. Walsh, Q.C.
Regional Clerk, W.J. Dawson
Director of Finance, S. Mowder
Director of Personnel, J.H. Yeo
Director of Engineering, C.H. Eidt
Director of Planning, A. Veale
Director of Social Services, M.F. Fraser
Director of Homes for the Aged, D.H. Rapelje
Emergency Measures Org., 227 Church St. (685-1571)

REGIONAL MUNICIPALITY OF OTTAWA-CARLETON

222 Queen St., Ottawa, Ont. K1P 5Z3
Incorporated: January 1, 1969
Area: 1,100 sq. miles
Population: 548,995 (1980)
Information Contact: (phone 613-563-2622), or write to Regional Clerk
Municipalities within the Region include: Twp. of Cumberland, City of Gloucester, Twp. of Goulbourn, City of Kanata, City of Nepean, Twp. of Osgoode, City of Ottawa, Twp. of Rideau, Village of Rockcliffe Park, City of Vanier, Twp. of West Carleton
Regional Clerk, W.H. Brunette
Executive Committee, Secretary, F. Perry
Finance Dept., Commr., J. Black
Legal Dept., Regional Solicitor, J.D. Cameron
Planning Dept., Commr., J.M. Wright
Transportation Dept., Commr., M.J.E. Sheflin
Works Dept., Commr., F.E. Ayers
Director, Homes for the Aged, Gary Armstrong (1 Porter's Island, Ottawa)
Social Services Dept., Commr., A.J. Pope (495 Richmond Rd.)
Emergency Measures Org., Co-ordinator, H. Tremblay (495 Richmond Rd.)

REGIONAL MUNICIPALITY OF PEEL

10 Peel Centre Dr., Brampton, Ont. L6T 4B9
Incorporated: October 15, 1973
Area: 484 sq. miles
Population: 464,491 (1980)
Information Contact: Infoservices, Regional Clerk's Dept. (phone: 416/791-9400, ext. 318)
Municipalities within the Region include: City of Brampton, Town of Caledon, City of Mississauga
Chief Administrative Officer, R.L. Frost
Commr. of Planning, Peter E. Allen
Commr. of Public Works, W.J. Anderson
Commr. of Finance, P.J. Marshall
Commr. of Social Services, J. Crozier
Regional Solicitor, J.K. Dundas
Regional Clerk, L.E. Button
Director of Personnel Services, Mrs. E. Lobo
Director of Labour Relations, S.G. Craig

REGIONAL MUNICIPALITY OF SUDBURY

Box 370, Civic Sq., Sudbury, Ont. P3E 4P2
Incorporated: January 1, 1973
Area: 1,088 sq. miles
Population: 160,116 (1979)
Information Contact: Regional Clerk (phone: 705 673-2171)
Municipalities within the Region include: Town of Capreol, Town of Nickel Centre, Town of Onaping Falls, Town of Rayside-Balfour, City of Sudbury, Town of Valley East, Town of Walden
Chief Administrative Officer, H.R. Akehurst
Regional Clerk, P. Philion
Regional Engineer, P. Morrow (act.)
Regional Planning Director, Klemens Dembek
Regional Treasurer, G. Skirda
Regional Personnel Director, G.H. Hatton
Regional Solicitor, J.J. Burns
Director, Homes for the Aged, K. Zinn
Director of Bldg. Controls, B. Fransen
Director of Operations, J. Mackay
Chief of Police, Regional Police Dept., J. Shilliday

MUNICIPALITY OF METROPOLITAN TORONTO

2nd floor, City Hall, Toronto, Ont. M5H 2N1
Incorporated: April 15, 1953
Area: 240 sq. miles
Population: 2,142,556
Information Contact: W.J. Lotto, Metro Toronto Clerk (phone: 416 367-8016)
Council includes 39 members from the Cities of North York and Toronto, and the Boroughs of East York, Etobicoke, Scarborough and York.
Chief Administrative Officer, John P. Kruger, 5th floor, West Tower, City Hall, Toronto
Dept. of Ambulance Services, General Manager, J. Dean, 4330 Dufferin St., Downsview (M3H 5R9)
Audit Dept., Allan G. Andrews, Auditor, 8th floor, West Tower, City Hall (M5H 2N1)
Clerk's Dept., Walter J. Lotto, Clerk, 2nd floor, City Hall (M5H 2N1)
Finance Dept., J.L. Pickard, Commr. of Finance & Treasurer, 10th floor, West Tower, City Hall (M5H 2N1)
Legal Dept., A.P.G. Joy, Q.C., Solicitor, 13th floor, West Tower, City Hall (M5H 2N1)
Management Information Systems Division, A. Orsava, Executive Director, 28th floor, The Simpson Tower, 401 Bay St.
Parks & Property Dept., Robert G. Bundy, Commr., 14th floor, East Tower, City Hall (M5H 2N1)
Personnel Dept., P.E. Ferguson, Commr. of Personnel, 7 King St. E., 18th floor
Planning Dept., R.J. Bower, Commr., 11th floor, East Tower, City Hall (M5H 2N1)
Roads & Traffic Dept., S. Cass, Commr., 30th floor, The Simpson Tower, 401 Bay St.
Community Services Dept., J.P. Kruger, Commr., 4th floor, East Tower, City Hall (M5H 2N1)
Treasury Dept., J.L. Pickard, Commr. of Finance & Treasurer, 10th floor, West Tower, City Hall (M5H 2N1)
Works Dept., F.J. Horgan, Commr., 10th floor, Phoenix House, 439 University Ave.
Board of Commrs. of Police

Administrative Offices, 590 Jarvis St., M4Y 2J5
Police Headquarters, 590 Jarvis St., M4Y 2J5, Chief of Police, J.W. Ackroyd; Chairman, Judge P.G. Givens, Q.C.
Canadian National Exhibition Association
Queen Elizabeth Bldg., Exhibition Park, M6K 3C3
General Manager, vacant
Catholic Children's Aid Society of Metro Toronto
26 Maitland St., M4Y 1C6
Executive Director, R. Arellano
Children's Aid Society of Metro Toronto
33 Charles St. E., M4Y 1R9
Executive Director, D.A. Barr
Community Information Centre of Metro Toronto
110 Adelaide St. E., M5C 1L1
Executive Director, Mrs. Elizabeth Wray
Convention & Tourist Bureau of Metro Toronto
Ste. 510, Eaton Centre Galleria, M5B 2H1
Executive Vice President, Wm. M. Duron
Licensing Commission
20 Holly St., M4S 2E6
General Manager, Wm. A. Barker
Metro Toronto Library Board
789 Yonge St., M4W 1G8
Director, Donald Meadows
Metro Toronto & Region Conservation Authority
5 Shoreham Dr., Downsview, M3N 1S4
General Manager, K.G. Higgs
Director of Planning & Policy, W. McLean
Metro Toronto Housing Co. Ltd.
110 Eglinton Ave. E., M4P 1A6
General Manager, Geo. A. Coleman
Toronto Area Industrial Development Board
11 King St. W., Room 1008, M5H 1A3
A/General Manager, W.J. Brennan
Toronto Transit Commission
1900 Yonge St., M4S 1Z2
Chief General Manager, Alfred H. Savage

Metro Toronto Boroughs (BOROUGH OF EAST YORK)

550 Mortimer Ave., Toronto, Ont. M4J 2H2
Incorporated: January 1, 1967
Area: 8.3 sq. miles
Population: 100,858 (1979)
Information Contact: Wm. Alexander, Jr. (phone: 416 461-9451)

Council

Mayor, A.A.S. Redway
Aldermen, Ward 1: J.D. Johnson, Cy Reader; Ward 2: M. Wyatt, N.S. Crone; Ward 3: G. Crann, K. Paige; Ward 4: P.E. Oyler, H. McGroarty
Next Election: November, 1982

Administration

Bldg. & Plumbing Dept., Director of Building, C. Bingham
Clerk's Dept., Borough Clerk, Wm. Alexander, Jr.
Finance Dept., Treasurer, D.C. Little
Fire Dept., Fire Chief, George Kerfoot
Legal Dept., Solicitor, J.R. Casey, Q.C.
Parks Dept., Director, R. Swain
Planning Commr., Don Baxter
Recreation Dept., Director, Don Wadlow
Works Commr., U. Luksep

Metro Toronto (BOROUGH OF ETOBICOKE)

Civic Centre, Etobicoke, Ont. M9C 2Y2
Incorporated: January, 1967
Area: 47.9 sq. miles
Population: 293,461 (Oct. 1976)
Information Contact: R.F. Cloutier (phone: 416 626-4270)

Council

Mayor, C. Dennis Flynn
Controllers, David Lacey, Dick O'Brien, Bruce Sinclair, Bill Stockwell
Aldermen, Ward 1: D.J. Sandford, Mrs. Helen Wursta; Ward 2: Mary Huffman, A.C. Marchetti; Ward 3: L. Allman, E.H. Farrow; Ward 4: Mrs. Lois Griffin, D. Robertson; Ward 5: Mrs. Ruth Grier, P.J. Keaveney
Next Election: November, 1982

Administration

Clerk, R.F. Cloutier
Borough Treasurer, T.G. Robinson
Borough Engineer, vacant
Fire Chief, B.N. Mitchell
Medical Officer of Health, A. Egbert
Bldg. Commr. & Zoning Administrator, G.K. Sutherland
Commr. of Works, B.W. Brunton
Commr. of Parks & Recreation Services, J.T. Riley
Personnel Director, J. de Vaal
Supt. of Municipal Properties, D.A. Conron
Planning Director & Secretary Treasurer of Planning Board, B.J. Morrison
Secretary Treasurer of Committee of Adjustment, Ms. D. Mungovan

Metro Toronto (CITY OF NORTH YORK)

See Cities Listings

Metro Toronto (BOROUGH OF SCARBOROUGH)

150 Borough Dr., Scarborough, Ont. M1P 4N7
Incorporated: 1850
Area: 72.5 sq. miles
Population: 409,592 (1979)
Information Contact: Clerk's Dept.

Council

Mayor, Gus Harris
Controllers, Brian Harrison, Ken Morrish, Joyce Trimmer, Carol Ruddell
Wards & Aldermen: 1: Bill Belfontaine; 2: Barry Christensen; 3: David Winkworth; 4: Jack Goodlad; 5: Frank Faubert; 6: Florence Cruikshank; 7: E.A. Fulton; 8: Shirley Eidt; 9: Doug Colling; 10: Maureen Prinsloo; 11: Ron Watson; 12: J.A. DeKort
Next Election: November, 1982

Administration

Bldg. Dept., Bldg. Commr., G.H. Fleming
Clerk's Dept., Borough Clerk, J.J. Poots
Development Dept., Commr. of Development, C.A. Tripp
Fire Dept., 740 Markham Rd., Fire Chief, W.E. Wretham
Health Dept., Medical Officer of Health, Dr. E.K. Fitzgerald
Law Dept., Solicitor, J.R. Ratchford
Personnel Dept., Personnel Commr., J.G. Griffin
Planning Dept., Planning Commr., K.J. Whitwell
Recreation & Parks Commr., B.F. Fleury
Treasury & Tax Dept., Treasurer, R.A. Arnold
Works Dept., Works Commr., R.K. Brown

Metro Toronto (CITY OF TORONTO)

See Cities Listings

Metro Toronto (BOROUGH OF YORK)

2700 Eglinton Ave. W., York, Ont. M6M 1V1
Incorporated: January 1, 1967
Area: 8 sq. miles
Population: 132,915 (1980)
Information Contact: I.F. Cronsberry, Director of Personnel & Public Relations (phone: 416 653-2700)

Council
Mayor, Gayle Christie
Controllers, F. Brown, P. White
Wards & Aldermen: 1: B. Nobleman; 2: T. Mandarano; 3: R. Bradd; 4: Pat Canavan; 5: C. Tonks; 6: J. Trimbee; 7: John Nunziata; 8: M. Waclawski
Next Election: November, 1982

Administration
Solicitor, J.H. Boland
Borough Clerk, C. Rodrigo
Medical Officer of Health, Dr. J.W. Mitchell
Commr. of Works, W.R. Hamilton
Treasurer, L.E. Hampson
Fire Chief, A.H. Beardshall
Hydro Manager, W.W.A. Secord
Director of Personnel & Public Relations, I.F. Cronsberry
Commr. of Planning, M. Christie
Commr. of Buildings, P. Hansen
By-law Enforcement & Property Standards Officer, W. Roxburgh
Commr. of Parks & Recreation, I. Thomson
Director of Recreation, D. Oitment
Director of Parks, R. Spraggett

REGIONAL MUNICIPALITY OF WATERLOO
20 Erb St. W., Waterloo, Ont. N2J 4G7
Incorporated: January 1, 1973
Area: 519.16 sq. miles
Population: 306,775 (1980)
Information Contact: Chief Administrative Officer (phone: 519 885-9425)
Municipalities within the Region include: City of Cambridge, City of Kitchener, Twp. of North Dumfries, City of Waterloo, Twp. of Wilmot, Twp. of Wellesley, Twp. of Woolwich
Chief Administrative Officer, R.F. Richardson
Regional Clerk, Mrs. E. Luhowy
Secretary Treasurer, Land Division Com., R.C. Dahmer
Regional Solicitor, E.L. Moore
Personnel Director, L.N. Lewis
Commr. of Finance, M. Gregg
Purchasing Officer, T.A. Moser
Commr. of Planning & Development, W.E. Thomson
Commr. of Engineering, C. Bauman
Director of Roads & Traffic, G.A. Thompson
Director of Engineering Operations, J. Pawley
Director of Design & Construction, W. Pyatt
Chief Environmental Engineer, G.H. Thompson
Manager, Laboratory Services, R. Luhowy
Commr. of Health & Social Services, G.P.A. Evans, M.D., M.O.H.

REGIONAL MUNICIPALITY OF YORK
Box 147, 62 Bayview Ave., Newmarket, Ont. L3Y 4W9
Incorporated: January 1, 1971
Area: 663 sq. miles
Population: 238,830 (1980)
Information Contact: Chief Administrative Officer (phone: 416 895-1231)
Municipalities within the Region include: Town of Aurora, Town of East Gwillimbury, Twp. of Georgina, Twp. of King, Town of Markham, Town of Newmarket, Town of Richmond Hill, Town of Vaughan, Town of Whitchurch-Stouffville
Chief Administrative Officer, A.J. Rettie
Solicitor, Edward Oakes
Regional Clerk, Robert N. Vernon
Regional Treasurer, John Hlynski
Commr. of Engineering, W.R. Hodgson
Commr. of Health & Social Services, Dr. J.O. Slingerland
Commr. of Planning, Hershel Weinberg
Chief of Police, Bruce A. Crawford

Quebec Regional Governments

MONTREAL URBAN COMMUNITY
2 Complexe Desjardins, Box 129, Montreal, P.Q. H5B 1E6
Incorporated: December 23, 1969
Area: 122,000 acres (49,000 hectares), or 190.88 sq. miles
Population: 1,855,093
Information Contact: J.-P. Blais, Deputy Secretary General (phone: 514 872-6811)
Municipalities within the Urban Community include: Anjou, Baie d'Urfé, Beaconsfield, Côte St-Luc, Dollard-des-Ormeaux, Dorval, Hampstead, Ile Bizard, Kirkland, Lachine, LaSalle, Montréal, Montréal-Est, Montréal-Nord, Montréal-Ouest, Mont-Royal, Outremont, Pierrefonds, Pointe-aux-Trembles, Pointe-Claire, Roxboro, Saint-Laurent, Saint-Léonard, Saint-Pierre, Sainte-Anne-de-Bellevue, Sainte-Geneviève, Senneville, Verdun, Westmount
Secretary General, Gérard Duhamel
Treasurer, Jean-Charles Desjardins
Valuation Commr., Conrad Cormier
Director of the Air Purification & Food Inspection Dept., Jean Marier
Director of the Metro. Transit Bureau, Gérard Gascon
Director of the Water Purification Dept., Jean R. Marcotte
Director of the Planning Dept., Guy Gravel
Director of the Economic Development Office, Marcel Marion
Director of the Police Dept., Henri-Paul Vignola

OUTAOUAIS REGIONAL COMMUNITY
25 rue Laurier, #500, Hull, P.Q. (Mailing: C.P. 2210, Succ. B, Hull, P.Q. J8X 3Z4)
Phone: (819) 770-1380
Population: 172,000 (1976)
Municipalities within the Region include: Aylmer, Buckingham, Gatineau, Hull, Hull Ouest, l'Ange-Gardien, La Pêche, Masson, Notre-Dame de la Salette, Pontiac, Val-des-Monts
Gérant/Secrétaire, Roland Stevens (Manager)
Directeur du Service du Génie, Léo Parent (Engineering)
Directeur du Personnel, Claude Lamarche
Directeur du Service de Planification, Nelson Tochon
Commissaire à l'Evaluation, Ronald St-Cyr
Trésorièr & Coordonnateur de l'informatique, Marc Chartier
Secrétaire adj., Jean Guy Gariépy
Co-ordonnateur des travaux d'épuration, Serge Lapointe

QUEBEC URBAN COMMUNITY
399 St-Joseph est, Québec, P.Q. G1K 8E2
Incorporated: December 23, 1969
Area: 575 sq. km
Population: 472,000 (1981)
Information Contact: Raymond Martin, Secretary to the President & Information Officer (phone: 418 681-9611)

Municipalities within the Urban Community include: City of Ancienne-Lorette, City of Beauport, Town of Boischatel, Town of Cap-Rouge, City of Charlesbourg, Town of Saint-Dunstan du Lac Beauport, Town of Lac Saint-Charles, City of Loretteville, City of Quebec, Town of Saint-Augustin, Town of Saint-Emile, City of Sainte-Foy, City of Sillery, Town of Val Belair, City of Vanier

General Manager, Gaston Meunier, ing.
Secretary General, Me Estelle Alain
Treasurer, Raynald Bédard, c.a.
Valuation Commissar, André St-Arnaud, ing.
Data Processing Director, Gilles Bélanger, M.Sc.
Industrial Development Director, Jacques Huot, ing.
Tourist & Convention Service Director, Chantal Gagnon, Adm. a.c., E.A.
Transport Commission President, Léonce Bouchard (Alderman, Québec City)
Engineering Dept., Water Pollution Control & Regional Incinerator Director, Hervé Aubin, ing.
Territorial Planning Service Director, Jean Guyard

Section B

ALMANAC INFORMATION

ASTRONOMICAL CALCULATIONS

Prepared for this publication by Margaret M. Heard and John R. Percy, Ph.D., of the David Dunlap Observatory of the University of Toronto.

ASTRONOMY IN CANADA

Canada possesses a number of major observatories and research institutes devoted to one phase or other of astronomical research. Some of these are operated by the National Research Council of Canada, others by Canadian universities.

Astronomical research in the National Research Council is controlled by the Herzberg Institute of Astrophysics which operates the following observatories: the Dominion Astrophysical Observatory at Victoria, possessing two major telescopes of 72-inch and 48-inch apertures; the Algonquin Radio Observatory at Lake Traverse in Algonquin Park which has, among others, a 150-foot steerable paraboloid; The Dominion Radio Astrophysical Observatory near Penticton which has an 85-foot paraboloid; the Ottawa River Solar Observatory; and the Spring Hill Meteor Observatory near Ottawa. The National Research Council also maintains Canada's Time Service in its Division of Physics.

A number of Canadian universities offer graduate training in astronomy. The Universities of Victoria and of British Columbia make use of the optical telescopes of the Dominion Astrophysical Observatory and the radio telescopes of U.B.C. The University of Alberta has a 20-inch telescope at a country site. The University of Calgary specializes in space studies, using rocket-borne instruments. The University of Toronto operates the David Dunlap Observatory at Richmond Hill with its 74-inch reflecting telescope and its 24-inch at the Las Campanas Observatory in the Chilean Andes—the only Canadian telescope in the Southern Hemisphere. The University of Western Ontario has a 48-inch reflector with unique accessories. Astronomers at the University of Waterloo and York University have small telescopes but rely largely upon observing facilities elsewhere. Queen's University specializes in radio astronomy. In the Province of Quebec the astronomical activities of the University of Montreal and of Laval University have been enhanced by the establishment of a new observatory at Mont Megantic which has a 60-inch reflector. In the Maritimes Saint Mary's University in Halifax operates the Burke-Gaffney Observatory which has a 16-inch telescope.

All Canadian astronomers share in the operation of a 3.6-metre telescope dedicated Sept 28, 1979, atop Mauna Kea on the island of Hawaii at an elevation of nearly 14,000 feet. This telescope is being shared both as to cost and operation by Canada, France and the State of Hawaii.

Observatories are open to the public as follows: Dominion Astrophysical Observatory, Victoria, May-August: Daily 9:15 a.m.-4:15 p.m. Sept-April: Monday to Friday, 9:15 a.m.-4:15 p.m. and Saturday evenings April 1 to October 31; Dominion Radio Astrophysical Observatory, Penticton, Sundays 2-5 July and August; University of Alberta by reservation (432-4201) Friday Evenings September to March; University of Saskatchewan Observatory, Saskatoon, Wednesday evenings; Hume Cronyn Observatory, London, according to an annual schedule published each fall; David Dunlap Observatory, Richmond Hill, Ont., Saturday evenings April through October by reservation (884-2112) and Tuesday mornings; York University, Downsview, Ont., Wednesday evenings mid-May through September; Burke-Gaffney Observatory, Halifax, Saturday evenings. Mont Mégantic, Notre-Dame-des-Bois, P.Q. May-September: Daily 2:00 p.m.-sunset. Saturday evening, May-August, by reservation.

There are the following planetariums, mostly with daily shows: MacMillan Planetarium, Vancouver; Queen Elizabeth Planetarium, Edmonton; Centennial Planetarium, Calgary; Manitoba Planetarium, Winnipeg; McLaughlin Planetarium, Toronto; Dow Planetarium, Montreal.

Most of Canada's enthusiastic amateur astronomers and telescope makers are members of the Royal Astronomical Society of Canada (see index) which has 19 Centres across Canada.

THE CALENDAR

The calendar is a method of identifying the passage of time and thereby regulating our civil life and religious observances.

Days, months, and years are based on astronomical periods. The day is the time it takes the earth to make one revolution on its axis, the month is associated with the period of orbiting of the moon around the earth, while the year has to do with the orbiting of the earth around the sun.

Many religious ideas and observances have been connected with the changes of the moon, and in ancient times the calendar took account of the moon rather than the seasons. From new moon to new moon is 29.530 days, and from one spring equinox to the next is 365.24219 days. Since the two are incommensurable, the modern calendar disregards the moon, except insofar as our months are roughly equal to a lunation.

THE JULIAN CALENDAR

When Julius Caesar came to power, the Roman Calendar was hopelessly confused. With the advice of the Alexandrian astronomer Sosigenes, Julius Caesar established the Julian Calendar. The length of the year was taken as 365¼ days, and in order to account for the ¼ day, an extra day was added every fourth year. From 45 B.C. each month has had its present number of days. In the old Roman Calendar which was based on the moon an extra month was inserted to straighten out the difference between twelve lunations 354.37 days, and 355 days, which they called a year. This was inserted when necessary after February 23rd. In the Julian Calendar the extra day was added by repeating the sixth day before the Kalends (1st) of March, whence comes our word bissextile for leap year.

No very significant change was made till the reform of Pope Gregory XIII in A.D. 1582.

The Julian Calendar is known as the "Old Style" whereas the calendar as improved by Pope Gregory is known as the "New Style". The difference between the two is now 13 days.

THE GREGORIAN CALENDAR

In that the Solar Year is 11 minutes, 12 seconds less than the Julian Year of 365¼ days, it followed in course of years that the Julian Calendar became inaccurate by several days, and in 1582 this difference amounted to 10 days. Pope Gregory XIII, at the suggestion of Aloysius Lilus, an astronomer of Naples, determined to rectify this, and devised the Calendar now known as the Gregorian Calendar. He dropped or cancelled these 10 days—October 5th being called October 15th—and made centurial years leap years only once in 4 centuries; so that whilst 1700, 1800 and 1900 were to be ordinary years 2000 would be leap year. This modification brought the Gregorian year into such close exactitude with the solar year that there is only a difference of 26 seconds, which amounts to a day in 3,323 years. This is the "New Style". The Gregorian Calendar was adopted in Italy, France, Spain, Portugal and Poland in 1582, by most of the German Roman Catholic states. Holland and Flanders in 1583, Hungary in 1587. The adoption in Switzerland began in 1584 and was not completed till 1812. The German and Dutch Protestant states generally, along with Denmark adopted it in 1700. British dominions in 1752, Sweden in 1753, Japan in 1873, China in 1912, Bulgaria in 1915, Soviet Russia in 1918, Yugoslavia in 1919, Romania and Greece in 1924, Turkey in 1927. The rules for Easter have not, however, been adopted by those oriental churches that are not subject to the Papacy.

The difference between the two "Styles" will remain 13 days until A.D. 2100.

THE JEWISH CALENDAR

The Jewish Calendar from the institution of the Mosaic Law downward was a lunar one, consisting of twelve months. The cycles of religious feasts commencing with the Passover depended not only on the month but on the moon; the 14th of the month of Abid or Nisan was coincident with the full moon; and the new moons themselves were the occasions of regular festivals; the commencement of the month was generally determined by observations of the new moon, but twelve lunar months would make but 354½ days, the years would be short twelve days of the true year and it was necessary that an additional month, Veader, be inserted about every third year.

The modern Jewish Calendar is based on fixed rules and not on observation. A common year may contain 353, 354 or 355 days and the leap year 383, 384 or 385 days. The intercalary month always contains 30 days and is inserted next before the month Adar which name and place it takes. Adar itself called second Adar or Veadar. Tishri 1 is the Jewish New Year and it cannot be a Sunday, Wednesday or Friday. Tishri 1 is not necessarily the day of new moon but is governed by a mean new moon which is calculated from the value of a mean lunation. It is complicated as compared with the Gregorian Calendar. The intercalary month is introduced seven times in every nineteen years.

The identification of the Jewish months with our own cannot be effected with precision on account of the variations existing between the lunar and solar month.

THE MOHAMMEDAN CALENDAR

The Mohammedan Calendar is called also the calendar of Hegira (i.e. Migration) and is attributed to the primary migration of Mohammed, the Prophet of Islam, on July 16th, 622 A.D. from Mecca, his native city in the land of Hejaz, Arabia, to the city of Medina in the north of the same land. In Medina the Prophet and Founder of the Islamic Faith died and was buried.

Each year consists of 12 lunar months, and since no intercalation is made the months go round the seasons in between 32 and 33 years.

The year 1403 according to the Hegira Calendar begins on October 19, 1982.

THE WEEK

The division of the week is found only among Aryan nations and in nations and in regions into which they have penetrated. The day is, for convenience, divided into 24 equal parts and is the period of a single rotation of the earth upon its own axis.

A solar or astronomical day commences at midnight, and is divided into two equal portions of 12 hours each—those before noon being termed (A.M.) those after noon (P.M.).

The Chinese week consists of 5 days, which are named after iron, wood, water, feathers and earth; they divide the day into 12 parts of 2 hours each.

The Anglo-Saxons named the days of the week after the following deities: Sunday, the Sun; Monday, the Moon; Tuesday, Tuesco (God of War); Wednesday, Woden (God of Storms); Thursday, Thor (God of Thunder); Friday, Freya (Goddess of Love); Saturday, Saturn (God of Time).

The word week is from Wikon (German); = change, succession.

THE SEASONS 1982

	Eastern Standard Time
Spring begins	March 20th 17 h 56 min
Summer begins	June 21st 12 h 23 min
Autumn begins	Sept 23rd 3 h 46 min
Winter begins	Dec. 21st 23 h 39 min

Eastern Standard time applies in Ontario and Quebec. Newfoundland time is one and one-half hours later than Eastern Standard time; in the Maritime Provinces, on Atlantic time, time is one hour later; in Manitoba and the eastern half of Saskatchewan, on Central time, time is one hour earlier; in Alberta and the western half of Saskatchewan, on Mountain time, time is two hours earlier; in British Columbia, on Pacific time, time is three hours earlier.

EPOCHS

The year 5743 of the Jewish era begins at sunset on September 18, 1982, Gregorian Calendar.

The year 1403 of the Mohammedan era, or the era of the Hegira, begins at sunset on October 19, 1982, Gregorian Calendar.

The thirty-first year of the reign of Queen Elizabeth II begins on February 6, 1982.

January 1, 1982, Julian Calendar, corresponds to January 14, 1982, Gregorian Calendar.

The 116th year of the Dominion of Canada begins July 1, 1982.

The 207th year of the Independence of the United States of America begins July 4, 1982.

The Julian Day 2,444,970 begins at Greenwich mean noon January 1, 1982, Gregorian Calendar.

CHRONOLOGICAL CYCLES

Golden Number	7	Solar Cycle	3	Roman Indiction	5
Epact	5	Dominical Letter	C	Julian Period	6695

Solar Cycle

In the Julian Calendar the days of the year recurred on the same days of the week in 7 x 4 years; 28 years was called the Solar Cycle. It is little used now.

The Cycle of the Indiction is a non-astronomical cycle of 15 years. Following Diocletian's reconquest of Egypt in A.D. 297 a provincial census was taken and repeated every 15 years.

Julian Period

This is a combination of the Solar Cycle of 28 years, the Metonic or Lunar Cycle of 19 years, and the Cycle of the Indiction, 15 years. These are all supposed to begin on January 1 of the Julian Calendar which was 4713 B.C. The Julian days are numbered consecutively from Greenwich mean noon on January 21, 4713 B.C.

Golden Number

The calendar for the phases of the moon is nearly the same every 19 years which is known as the Metonic Cycle. The Golden Number is its number in this Metonic Cycle. To find the Golden Number for 1982 add 1 to 1982 and divide by 19. The remainder, 7, is the Golden Number.

Epact is the age of the moon on some fixed day of the calendar year. (January 1 Gregorian Calendar).

Dominical Letter

The Roman Calendar makers placed the letters A.B.C.D.E.F.G. against the day of the year. The letter which stands against the Sundays is known as the Dominical Letter. In leap year since no letter is set opposite the added day one letter appears for January and February and the letter preceding for the remainder of the year.

Example—

	A	B	C	D	E	F	G
1980	Tues.	Wed.	Thu.	Fri.	Sat.	Sun.	Mon.
Jan.	1	2	3	4	5	6	7
Feb.	26	27	28	29			
	A	B	C	—	D	E	F
Mar.					1	2	3
	G	A	B	C			
	4	5	6	7			

Jan. 6 (Sun.) is F. F therefore is the Dominical letter for Jan. and Feb. Since no letter is assigned for Feb. 29, Sunday from then on comes under the letter E, which is the letter for the remainder of the year.

STANDARD TIME

Owing to the great breadth of Canada the difference in solar time in various parts of the country is adjusted by the creation of Standard Time Zones, one hour in width, fixed between arbitrary lines running approximately north and south, 15° of longitude apart, the time observed in each zone being an exact, except for Newfoundland, number of hours slow from Greenwich.

Example: When it is 8 a.m. by Pacific Time it is 12 noon by Atlantic Time and 4 p.m. at Greenwich.

There are seven zones divided as follows, reckoning from Greenwich:

Newfoundland Standard Time	Newfoundland, excluding Labrador, 3½ hours slow.
Atlantic Standard Time 60th Meridian Time	Labrador, New Brunswick, Nova Scotia, Prince Edward Island, and those parts of Quebec and N.W.T. east of the 63rd Meridian, 4 hours slow
Eastern Standard Time 75th Meridian Time	Quebec west of the 63rd Meridian and Ontario as far west as the 90th Meridian; N.W.T. between the 68th and 85th Meridian, 5 hours slow.
Central Standard Time 90th Meridian Time	Ontario west of the 90th Meridian, Manitoba, easterly part of Saskatchewan and N.W.T. between the 85th and 102nd Meridian, 6 hours slow.
Mountain Standard Time 105th Meridian Time	Western Saskatchewan (in winter); throughout Alberta and in N.W.T. west of the 102nd Meridian, 7 hours slow.
Pacific Standard Time 120th Meridian Time	Throughout most of British Columbia and in the Yukon 8 hours slow.

Railways and airways make up their schedules according to Standard Time in winter and Daylight Saving Time in summer. Solar time around the globe varies four minutes with each degree of longitude.

STANDARD TIME ZONES IN OTHER PARTS OF THE GLOBE

Northern and Mid-Europe	1	hour fast
Eastern Europe, Egypt, Palestine	2	hours "
Republic of South Africa	2	" "
Japan, Manchuria, Korea	9	" "
East China, Hong Kong, West Australia	8	" "
South Australia	9½	" "
Victoria	10	" "
New South Wales	10	" "
Queensland	10	" "
Tasmania	10	" "
New Zealand	12	" "
Fiji Islands	12	" "
United Kingdom, Ireland, Iceland, Maderia, Canary Islands	Greenwich	
Azores	1	hour slow
Cape Verde Islands, Eastern Greenland	2	hours slow
Eastern Brazil, Western Greenland	3	" "
Central Brazil, Argentina, Trinidad, Thule area of Greenland	4	" "
Western Brazil, Jamaica, Bahamas, Cuba	5	" "
Hawaiian Islands, Alaska	10	" "
Aleutian Islands	11	" "

1 hour "fast" means—6 o'clock at Greenwich = 7 o'clock at "fast" point

1 hour "slow" means—6 o'clock at Greenwich = 5 o'clock at "slow" point

A more complete list of Standard Times of the World is to be found in "Standard Time and Time Zones in Canada", by M.M. Thomson in the Journal of The Royal Astronomical Society of Canada, vol. 64, no. 3, p. 129, 1970.

TABLE FOR FINDING APPROXIMATE STANDARD TIME OF SUNRISE, SUNSET, MOONRISE, MOONSET FOR CANADIAN CITIES AND TOWNS

PLACE	Time Zone	FOR SUNRISE OR SUNSET Take value for	and apply correction	FOR MOONRISE OR MOONSET Take value for	and apply correction
Brandon	C	Winnipeg	+11 *m*	50°	+40 *m*
Brantford	E	Toronto	+ 4	45	+21
Calgary	M	Winnipeg	+ 8	50	+36
Charlottetown	A	Ottawa	+10	45	+13
Cornwall	E	Ottawa	− 4	45	− 1
Edmonton	M	Winnipeg	+ 6	50	+34
Fredericton	A	Ottawa	+24	45	+27
Gander	N	Vancouver	− 4	50	+ 8
Glace Bay	A	Ottawa	− 3	45	0
Goose Bay	A	Winnipeg	−26	50	+ 2
Granby	E	Ottawa	−12	45	− 9
Guelph	E	Toronto	+ 3	45	+21
Halifax	A	Ottawa	+11	45	+14
Hamilton	E	Toronto	+ 2	45	+19
Hull	E	Ottawa	0	45	+ 3
Kapuskasing	E	Vancouver	+17	50	+30
Kingston	E	Toronto	−12	45	+ 6
Kitchener	E	Toronto	+ 4	45	+22
London	E	Toronto	+ 8	45	+25
Medicine Hat	M	Winnipeg	− 4	50	+24
Moncton	A	Ottawa	+16	45	+19
Montreal	E	Ottawa	− 9	45	− 6
Moosonee	E	Winnipeg	− 6	50	+23
Moose Jaw	C	Winnipeg	+34	50	+62
Niagara Falls	E	Toronto	− 1	45	+16
North Bay	E	Ottawa	+14	45	+18
Ottawa	E	Ottawa	0	45	+ 3
Owen Sound	E	Ottawa	+21	45	+24
Penticton	P	Vancouver	−14	50	− 2
Peterborough	E	Toronto	− 4	45	+13
Prince Albert	C	Winnipeg	+36	50	+64
Prince Rupert	P	Winnipeg	+12	50	+40
Quebec	E	Ottawa	−18	45	−15
Regina	C	Winnipeg	+30	50	+58
St. Catharines	E	Toronto	0	45	+17
St. Hyacinthe	E	Ottawa	−11	45	− 8
Saint John, N.B.	A	Ottawa	+22	45	+24
St. John's, Nfld.	N	Vancouver	−11	50	+ 1
Sarnia	E	Toronto	+12	45	+30
Saskatoon	C	Winnipeg	+38	50	+66
Sault Ste Marie	E	Ottawa	+34	45	+37
Shawinigan	E	Ottawa	−12	45	− 9
Sherbrooke	E	Ottawa	−14	45	−12
Stratford	E	Toronto	+ 6	45	+24
Sudbury	E	Ottawa	+21	45	+24
Sydney	A	Ottawa	− 2	45	+ 1
The Pas	C	Winnipeg	+16	50	+44
Thunder Bay	E	Vancouver	+44	50	+57
Timmins	E	Vancouver	+13	50	+25
Toronto	E	Toronto	0	45	+18
Three Rivers	E	Ottawa	−12	45	− 9
Trail	P	Vancouver	−22	50	−10
Truro	A	Ottawa	+10	45	+13
Vancouver	P	Vancouver	0	50	+12
Victoria	P	Vancouver	+ 2	50	+14
Windsor	E	Toronto	+14	45	+32
Winnipeg	C	Winnipeg	0	50	+28

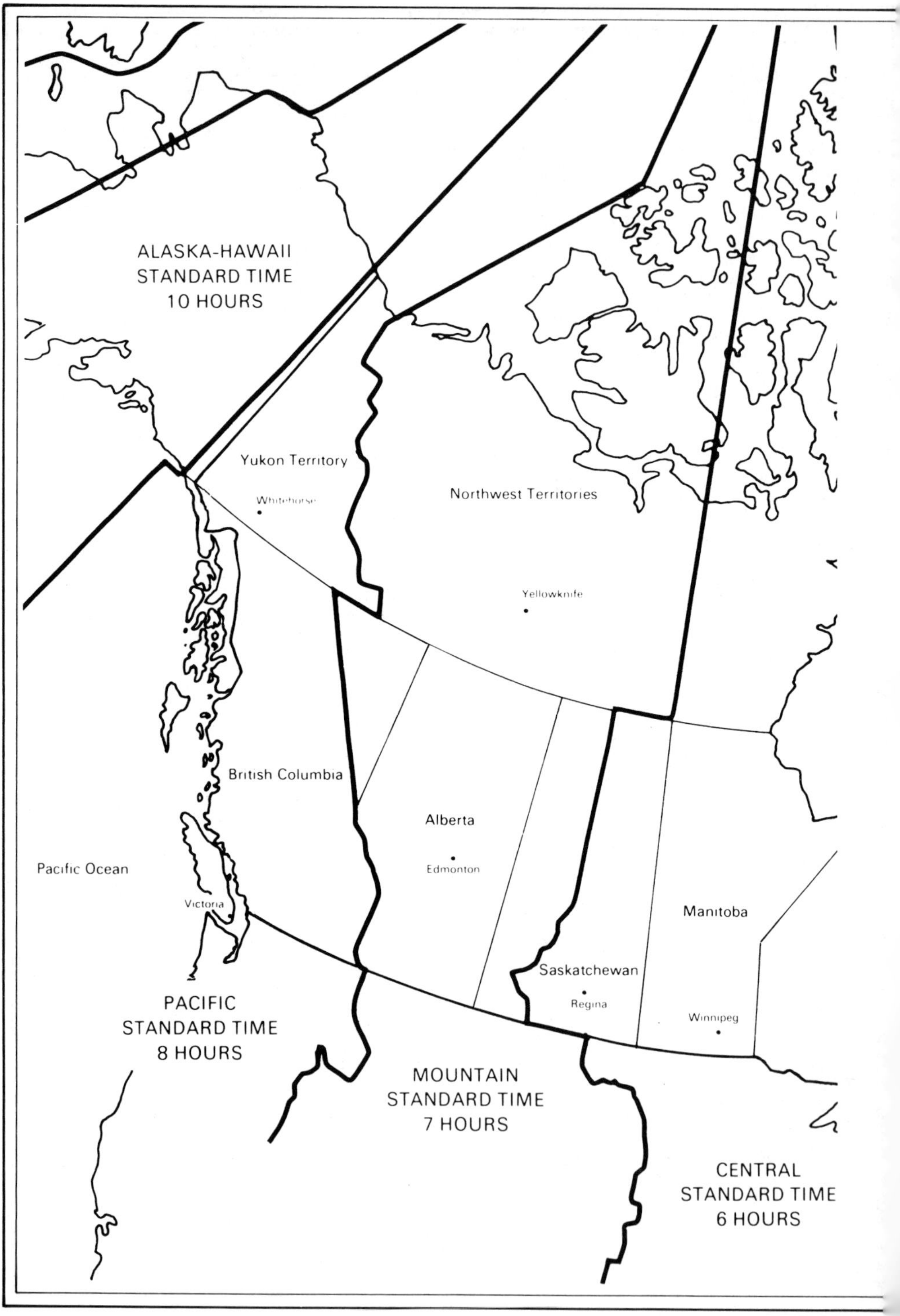
ALASKA-HAWAII
STANDARD TIME
10 HOURS
Yukon Territory
Northwest Territories
Yellowknife
British Columbia
Alberta
Edmonton
Pacific Ocean
Victoria
Manitoba
Saskatchewan
Regina
Winnipeg
PACIFIC
STANDARD TIME
8 HOURS
MOUNTAIN
STANDARD TIME
7 HOURS
CENTRAL
STANDARD TIME
6 HOURS

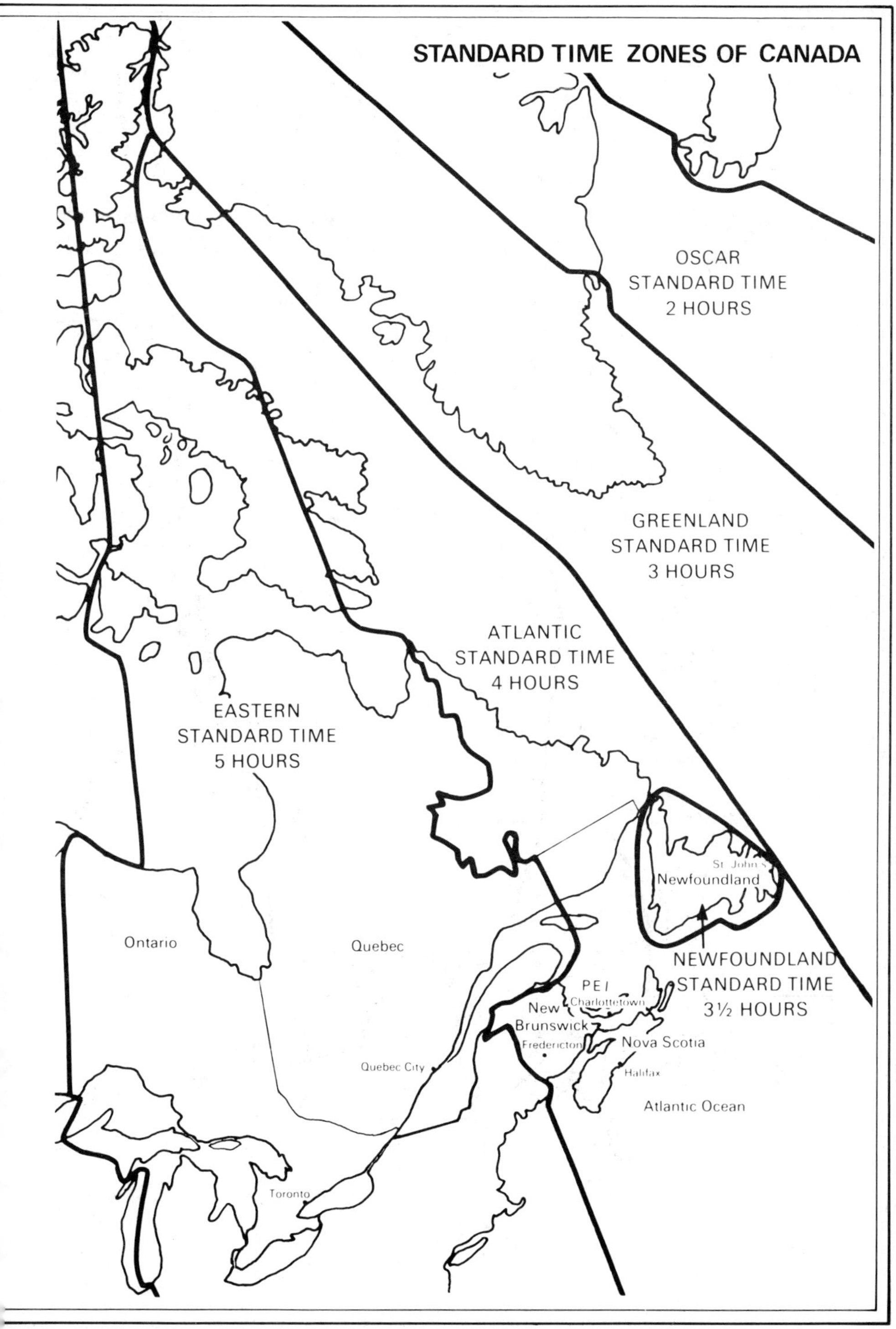
STANDARD TIME ZONES OF CANADA
OSCAR STANDARD TIME 2 HOURS
GREENLAND STANDARD TIME 3 HOURS
ATLANTIC STANDARD TIME 4 HOURS
EASTERN STANDARD TIME 5 HOURS
St. John's
Newfoundland
NEWFOUNDLAND STANDARD TIME 3½ HOURS
Ontario
Quebec
PEI
Charlottetown
New Brunswick
Fredericton
Nova Scotia
Halifax
Quebec City
Atlantic Ocean
Toronto

PACIFIC
STANDARD TIME
8 HOURS
MOUNTAIN
STANDARD TIME
7 HOURS
CENTRAL
STANDARD TIME
6 HOURS
Seattle
Olympia
Washington
Portland
Salem
Oregon
Montana
Helena
North Dakota
Bismarck
Boise
Idaho
South Dakota
Pierre
Wyoming
California
Nevada
Carson City
Salt Lake City
Cheyenne
Nebraska
Lincoln
Sacramento
San Francisco
Utah
Denver
Colorado
Kansas
Los Angeles
Arizona
Santa Fe
Albuquerque
New Mexico
Oklahoma
Oklahoma City
Phoenix
Dallas
Texas
Austin
Alaska
Hawaii
Juneau
Honolulu
ALASKA-HAWAII
STANDARD TIME
10 HOURS

STANDARD TIME ZONES OF THE UNITED STATES

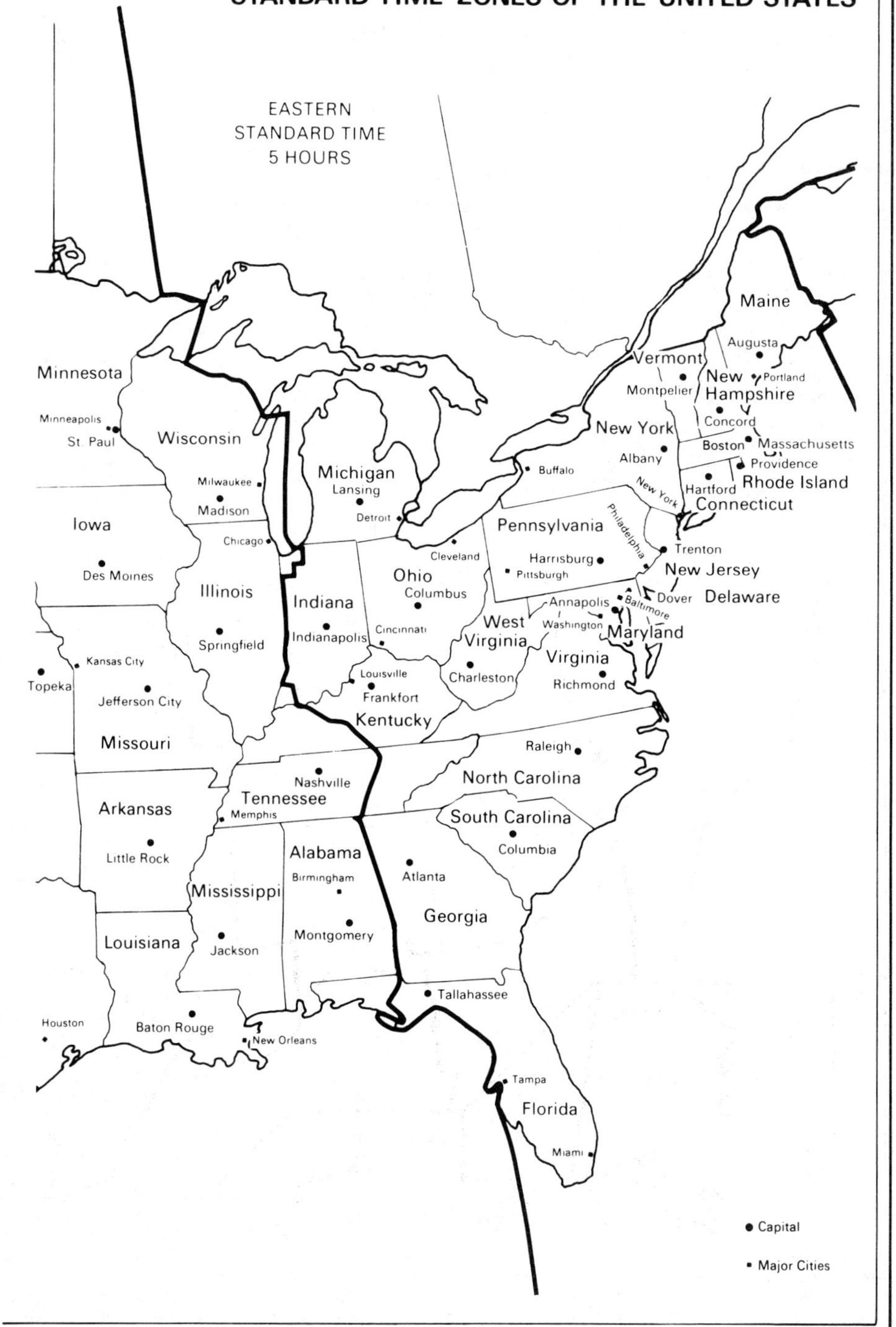
EASTERN
STANDARD TIME
5 HOURS
Minnesota
Minneapolis
St. Paul
Wisconsin
Milwaukee
Madison
Michigan
Lansing
Detroit
Iowa
Des Moines
Chicago
Illinois
Springfield
Indiana
Indianapolis
Ohio
Columbus
Cleveland
Cincinnati
Pennsylvania
Harrisburg
Pittsburgh
Philadelphia
New York
Albany
Buffalo
New York
Vermont
Montpelier
Maine
Augusta
Portland
New Hampshire
Concord
Boston
Massachusetts
Providence
Rhode Island
Hartford
Connecticut
Trenton
New Jersey
Dover
Delaware
Annapolis
Baltimore
Washington
Maryland
West Virginia
Charleston
Virginia
Richmond
Kansas City
Topeka
Jefferson City
Missouri
Louisville
Frankfort
Kentucky
Raleigh
North Carolina
Nashville
Tennessee
Memphis
Arkansas
Little Rock
South Carolina
Columbia
Alabama
Birmingham
Montgomery
Atlanta
Georgia
Mississippi
Jackson
Louisiana
Baton Rouge
New Orleans
Houston
Tallahassee
Tampa
Florida
Miami
Capital
Major Cities

AZIMUTHS OF THE POINTS OF RISING AND SETTING OF THE SUN FOR LATITUDES 43° N TO 52° N

In Degrees East of North for Rising and West of North for Setting

	43°N	44°N	45°N	46°N	47°N	48°N	49°N	50°N	51°N	52°N
Jan. 2 and Dec. 11	122	123	124	124	125	126	127	127	128	129
Jan. 10 and Dec. 3	121	121	122	123	123	124	125	126	127	127
Jan. 16 and Nov. 27	119	120	120	121	122	122	123	124	125	126
Jan. 21 and Nov. 22	118	118	119	120	120	121	121	122	123	124
Jan. 25 and Nov. 17	116	117	117	118	119	119	120	120	121	122
Jan. 29 and Nov. 14	115	115	116	116	117	118	118	119	119	120
Feb. 2 and Nov. 10	114	114	114	115	115	116	116	117	118	118
Feb. 5 and Nov. 6	112	113	113	113	114	114	115	115	116	116
Feb. 9 and Nov. 3	111	111	111	112	112	113	113	114	114	115
Feb. 12 and Oct. 31	109	110	110	110	111	111	112	112	113	113
Feb. 15 and Oct. 28	108	108	109	109	109	110	110	110	111	111
Feb. 18 and Oct. 25	107	107	107	107	108	108	108	109	109	110
Feb. 20 and Oct. 22	105	105	106	106	106	106	107	107	108	108
Feb. 23 and Oct. 19	104	104	104	104	105	105	105	106	106	106
Feb. 26 and Oct. 17	102	103	103	103	103	104	104	104	104	105
Mar. 1 and Oct. 14	101	101	101	102	102	102	102	102	103	103
Mar. 3 and Oct. 11	100	100	100	100	100	100	101	101	101	101
Mar. 6 and Oct. 9	98	98	98	99	99	99	99	99	100	100
Mar. 8 and Oct. 6	97	97	97	97	97	97	98	98	98	98
Mar. 11 and Oct. 4	95	96	96	96	96	96	96	96	96	96
Mar. 13 and Oct. 1	94	94	94	94	94	94	95	95	95	95
Mar. 16 and Sept. 28	93	93	93	93	93	93	93	93	93	93
Mar. 18 and Sept. 26	91	91	91	91	91	92	92	92	92	92
Mar. 21 and Sept. 23	90	90	90	90	90	90	90	90	90	90
Mar. 23 and Sept. 21	89	89	89	89	89	88	88	88	88	88
Mar. 26 and Sept. 18	87	87	87	87	87	87	87	87	87	87
Mar. 28 and Sept. 16	86	86	86	86	86	86	85	85	85	85
Mar. 31 and Sept. 13	85	84	84	84	84	84	84	84	84	84
Apr. 3 and Sept. 10	83	83	83	83	83	83	82	82	82	82
Apr. 5 and Sept. 8	82	82	82	81	81	81	81	81	80	80
Apr. 8 and Sept. 5	80	80	80	80	80	80	79	79	79	79
Apr. 11 and Sept. 2	79	79	79	78	78	78	78	78	77	77
Apr. 13 and Aug. 30	78	77	77	77	77	76	76	76	76	75
Apr. 16 and Aug. 28	76	76	76	76	75	75	75	74	74	74
Apr. 19 and Aug. 25	75	75	74	74	74	73	73	73	72	72
Apr. 22 and Aug. 22	73	73	73	73	72	72	72	71	71	70
Apr. 25 and Aug. 19	72	72	71	71	71	70	70	70	69	69
Apr. 28 and Aug. 16	71	70	70	70	69	69	68	68	67	67
May 1 and Aug. 12	69	69	69	68	68	67	67	66	66	65
May 5 and Aug. 9	68	67	67	67	66	66	65	65	64	63
May 8 and Aug. 5	66	66	66	65	65	64	64	63	62	62
May 12 and Aug. 2	65	65	64	64	63	62	62	61	61	60
May 16 and July 28	64	63	63	62	61	61	60	60	59	58
May 21 and June 24	62	62	61	60	60	59	59	58	57	56
May 26 and June 19	61	60	60	59	58	58	57	56	55	54
June 1 and July 12	59	59	58	57	57	56	55	54	53	53
June 10 and July 3	58	57	56	56	55	54	53	53	52	51

AZIMUTH OF THE SUN AT RISING AND SETTING

Only twice a year, namely about March 21 and September 23, does the sun rise and set more or less exactly in the east and west respectively. It is of interest and sometimes of value to know the position of Sunrise and Sunset at other times. The table above tabulates these in degrees east of north and west of north for Sunrise and Sunset respectively for a selection of latitudes and dates. For latitudes and dates other than those tabulated take simple proportions.

REFERENCES

The tables and charts in the Canadian Almanac are intended for simple astronomical observations. To make more extensive observations the following are recommended: The Observer's Handbook (obtainable from the Royal Astronomical Society of Canada, 124 Merton St., Toronto; Price $5.00); Astronomical Phenomena (obtainable from The Superintendent of Documents, U.S. Government Printing Office, Washington, D.C.; Price $2.40).

NOTES ON THE ASTRONOMICAL TABLES

The purpose of the following notes is to explain those tables which are not self-explanatory and to illustrate how they may be used for places other than those specified.

These tables give Standard Times of Sunrise and Sunset fo the four Canadian cities listed. When Daylight Saving Time is in effect, of course, one hour must be added to the listed times The calculations are for the upper limb (edge) of the sun and for the astronomical (sea) horizon. Accordingly the actua observation of Sunrise or Sunset will differ from the tabulated value if the observer is below or above the level of his visible horizon at the point of Sunrise or Sunset.

The listed times of Moonrise and Moonset (reproduced, with permission, from data supplied by the Science Research Coun cil, U.K.) have been calculated for places at the stated latitudes and for longitude 5 hours west.

To obtain the approximate times of Sunrise, Sunset, Moon rise and Moonset for other Canadian cities and towns procee as indicated in the table on page 906. The errors for Sunris and Sunset by this approximate method will seldom exceed 1 minutes in winter and summer or 4 minutes in spring and fal and for Moonrise and Moonset they will seldom exceed 1 minutes.

JANUARY
1982

☽	First Quarter	2 d 23 h 45 min	Moon's Phases E.S.T.
○	Full Moon	9 d 14 h 53 min	
☾	Last Quarter	16 d 18 h 58 min	
●	New Moon	24 d 23 h 56 min	

Day of Yr.	Day of Mo.	Day of Week	SUNRISE AND SUNSET Ottawa E.S.T. Rises	Ottawa Sets	Toronto E.S.T. Rises	Toronto Sets	Winnipeg C.S.T. Rises	Winnipeg Sets	Vancouver P.S.T. Rises	Vancouver Sets	MOONRISE AND MOONSET Local Mean Time Lat. 45° Rises	Lat. 45° Sets	Lat. 50° Rises	Lat. 50° Sets	Day of Week	Day of Mo.
			h m	h m	h m	h m	h m	h m	h m	h m	h m	h m	h m	h m		
1	1	Fri	7 43	16 30	7 52	16 51	8 27	16 37	8 08	16 24	11 25	22 56	11 31	22 51	Fri	1
2	2	Sat	7 43	16 31	7 52	16 52	8 27	16 38	8 08	16 25	11 51	—	11 53	—	Sat	2
3	3	Sun	7 43	16 32	7 52	16 53	8 27	16 39	8 08	16 26	12 18	0 05	12 16	0 05	Sun	3
4	4	Mon	7 43	16 33	7 52	16 54	8 27	16 40	8 08	16 28	12 47	1 16	12 40	1 20	Mon	4
5	5	Tue	7 43	16 34	7 52	16 55	8 27	16 41	8 08	16 29	13 19	2 30	13 08	2 38	Tue	5
6	6	Wed	7 43	16 35	7 52	16 56	8 26	16 43	8 07	16 30	13 56	3 45	13 41	3 59	Wed	6
7	7	Thu	7 43	16 36	7 52	16 57	8 26	16 44	8 07	16 31	14 41	5 02	14 23	5 19	Thu	7
8	8	Fri	7 43	16 37	7 52	16 58	8 26	16 45	8 07	16 32	15 35	6 15	15 15	6 35	Fri	8
9	9	Sat	7 42	16 38	7 51	16 59	8 26	16 46	8 06	16 33	16 39	7 22	16 19	7 42	Sat	9
10	10	Sun	7 42	16 39	7 51	17 00	8 25	16 48	8 06	16 34	17 49	8 19	17 31	8 38	Sun	10
11	11	Mon	7 42	16 40	7 51	17 01	8 25	16 49	8 06	16 36	19 02	9 05	18 47	9 21	Mon	11
12	12	Tue	7 41	16 41	7 50	17 02	8 24	16 50	8 05	16 37	20 14	9 44	20 03	9 56	Tue	12
13	13	Wed	7 41	16 42	7 50	17 03	8 23	16 52	8 05	16 39	21 24	10 16	21 17	10 24	Wed	13
14	14	Thu	7 40	16 44	7 50	17 04	8 22	16 53	8 04	16 40	22 31	10 43	22 28	10 48	Thu	14
15	15	Fri	7 40	16 45	7 49	17 06	8 22	16 54	8 03	16 42	23 35	11 08	23 37	11 09	Fri	15
16	16	Sat	7 39	16 46	7 48	17 07	8 21	16 56	8 02	16 43	—	11 33	—	11 29	Sat	16
17	17	Sun	7 38	16 47	7 48	17 08	8 20	16 58	8 01	16 45	0 38	11 57	0 43	11 50	Sun	17
18	18	Mon	7 38	16 49	7 47	17 10	8 19	16 59	8 00	16 46	1 39	12 23	1 48	12 12	Mon	18
19	19	Tue	7 37	16 50	7 47	17 11	8 18	17 01	8 00	16 48	2 40	12 51	2 52	12 37	Tue	19
20	20	Wed	7 36	16 51	7 46	17 12	8 17	17 02	7 59	16 49	3 40	13 23	3 55	13 06	Wed	20
21	21	Thu	7 35	16 53	7 45	17 13	8 15	17 04	7 58	16 51	4 38	14 00	4 56	13 41	Thu	21
22	22	Fri	7 35	16 54	7 45	17 15	8 14	17 05	7 57	16 52	5 33	14 43	5 54	14 23	Fri	22
23	23	Sat	7 34	16 56	7 44	17 16	8 13	17 07	7 56	16 54	6 25	15 33	6 46	15 13	Sat	23
24	24	Sun	7 33	16 57	7 43	17 17	8 12	17 08	7 55	16 55	7 12	16 29	7 31	16 10	Sun	24
25	25	Mon	7 32	16 58	7 42	17 19	8 11	17 10	7 54	16 57	7 53	17 30	8 10	17 13	Mon	25
26	26	Tue	7 31	17 00	7 41	17 20	8 10	17 12	7 52	16 59	8 29	18 34	8 43	18 21	Tue	26
27	27	Wed	7 30	17 01	7 40	17 21	8 09	17 14	7 51	17 00	9 00	19 40	9 11	19 31	Wed	27
28	28	Thu	7 29	17 03	7 39	17 22	8 07	17 15	7 50	17 02	9 29	20 48	9 36	20 43	Thu	28
29	29	Fri	7 28	17 04	7 39	17 24	8 06	17 17	7 49	17 04	9 56	21 56	9 59	21 55	Fri	29
30	30	Sat	7 27	17 06	7 38	17 25	8 05	17 18	7 48	17 05	10 22	23 06	10 21	23 09	Sat	30
31	31	Sun	7 26	17 07	7 37	17 26	8 03	17 20	7 46	17 07	10 50	—	10 45	—	Sun	31

FEBRUARY
1982

☽	First Quarter	1 d 9 h 28 min	Moon's Phases E.S.T.
○	Full Moon	8 d 2 h 57 min	
☾	Last Quarter	15 d 15 h 21 min	
●	New Moon	23 d 16 h 13 min	

Day of Yr.	Day of Mo.	Day of Week	SUNRISE AND SUNSET Ottawa E.S.T. Rises	Ottawa Sets	Toronto E.S.T. Rises	Toronto Sets	Winnipeg C.S.T. Rises	Winnipeg Sets	Vancouver P.S.T. Rises	Vancouver Sets	MOONRISE AND MOONSET Local Mean Time Lat. 45° Rises	Lat. 45° Sets	Lat. 50° Rises	Lat. 50° Sets	Day of Week	Day of Mo.
			h m	h m	h m	h m	h m	h m	h m	h m	h m	h m	h m	h m		
32	1	Mon	7 25	17 09	7 36	17 27	8 02	17 22	7 45	17 08	11 19	0 17	11 10	0 25	Mon	1
33	2	Tue	7 24	17 10	7 35	17 29	8 01	17 23	7 44	17 09	11 53	1 30	11 40	1 42	Tue	2
34	3	Wed	7 22	17 11	7 34	17 30	8 00	17 25	7 43	17 11	12 33	2 43	12 16	2 59	Wed	3
35	4	Thu	7 21	17 13	7 33	17 32	7 59	17 27	7 41	17 13	13 21	3 56	13 02	4 14	Thu	4
36	5	Fri	7 20	17 14	7 32	17 33	7 57	17 29	7 40	17 14	14 19	5 03	13 58	5 24	Fri	5
37	6	Sat	7 19	17 16	7 31	17 34	7 56	17 30	7 38	17 16	15 24	6 03	15 05	6 23	Sat	6
38	7	Sun	7 17	17 17	7 29	17 36	7 54	17 32	7 37	17 18	16 36	6 54	16 19	7 12	Sun	7
39	8	Mon	7 16	17 19	7 28	17 37	7 53	17 34	7 35	17 19	17 49	7 36	17 36	7 50	Mon	8
40	9	Tue	7 14	17 20	7 26	17 39	7 51	17 36	7 33	17 21	19 01	8 11	18 52	8 22	Tue	9
41	10	Wed	7 13	17 22	7 25	17 40	7 49	17 37	7 32	17 23	20 11	8 41	20 06	8 48	Wed	10
42	11	Thu	7 12	17 23	7 24	17 41	7 48	17 39	7 30	17 25	21 18	9 08	21 17	9 11	Thu	11
43	12	Fri	7 10	17 25	7 22	17 43	7 46	17 41	7 28	17 26	22 23	9 33	22 26	9 32	Fri	12
44	13	Sat	7 08	17 26	7 21	17 44	7 44	17 43	7 26	17 28	23 26	9 58	23 33	9 53	Sat	13
45	14	Sun	7 07	17 27	7 19	17 46	7 42	17 44	7 25	17 30	—	10 23	—	10 15	Sun	14
46	15	Mon	7 06	17 29	7 18	17 47	7 40	17 46	7 23	17 32	0 28	10 51	0 39	10 39	Mon	15
47	16	Tue	7 04	17 30	7 17	17 48	7 39	17 48	7 21	17 33	1 29	11 21	1 43	11 06	Tue	16
48	17	Wed	7 03	17 32	7 15	17 50	7 37	17 50	7 19	17 35	2 28	11 56	2 45	11 38	Wed	17
49	18	Thu	7 01	17 33	7 13	17 51	7 35	17 51	7 17	17 37	3 24	12 37	3 44	12 17	Thu	18
50	19	Fri	7 00	17 34	7 12	17 53	7 33	17 53	7 16	17 38	4 18	13 24	4 38	13 04	Fri	19
51	20	Sat	6 58	17 36	7 11	17 54	7 31	17 55	7 14	17 40	5 06	14 18	5 26	13 58	Sat	20
52	21	Sun	6 56	17 37	7 09	17 55	7 29	17 56	7 12	17 42	5 49	15 17	6 08	15 00	Sun	21
53	22	Mon	6 54	17 39	7 08	17 57	7 27	17 58	7 10	17 43	6 28	16 21	6 43	16 07	Mon	22
54	23	Tue	6 53	17 40	7 06	17 58	7 25	17 59	7 08	17 45	7 01	17 28	7 13	17 17	Tue	23
55	24	Wed	6 51	17 42	7 04	18 00	7 23	18 01	7 06	17 46	7 31	18 37	7 39	18 30	Wed	24
56	25	Thu	6 49	17 43	7 03	18 01	7 21	18 03	7 04	17 48	7 59	19 46	8 03	19 44	Thu	25
57	26	Fri	6 48	17 44	7 01	18 02	7 19	18 05	7 02	17 50	8 26	20 57	8 26	20 59	Fri	26
58	27	Sat	6 46	17 46	6 59	18 03	7 17	18 06	7 00	17 51	8 53	22 09	8 49	22 15	Sat	27
59	28	Sun	6 44	17 47	6 57	18 05	7 15	18 08	6 58	17 53	9 22	23 21	9 14	23 32	Sun	28

MARCH 1982

Moon's Phases E.S.T.
☽ First Quarter 2 d 17 h 15 min
○ Full Moon 9 d 15 h 45 min
☾ Last Quarter 17 d 12 h 15 min
● New Moon 25 d 5 h 17 min

SUNRISE AND SUNSET / MOONRISE AND MOONSET

Day of Yr.	Day of Mo.	Day of Week	Ottawa E.S.T. Rises	Sets	Toronto E.S.T. Rises	Sets	Winnipeg C.S.T. Rises	Sets	Vancouver P.S.T. Rises	Sets	Lat. 45° Rises	Sets	Lat. 50° Rises	Sets	Day of Week	Day of Mo.
			h m	h m	h m	h m	h m	h m	h m	h m	h m	h m	h m	h m		
60	1	Mon	6 42	17 48	6 56	18 06	7 13	18 10	6 56	17 54	9 54	—	9 42	—	Mon	1
61	2	Tue	6 41	17 50	6 54	18 07	7 11	18 11	6 54	17 56	10 31	0 34	10 16	0 49	Tue	2
62	3	Wed	6 39	17 51	6 52	18 08	7 09	18 13	6 52	17 58	11 16	1 46	10 57	2 04	Wed	3
63	4	Thu	6 37	17 52	6 51	18 09	7 07	18 14	6 50	17 59	12 08	2 54	11 48	3 14	Thu	4
64	5	Fri	6 36	17 54	6 49	18 11	7 05	18 16	6 48	18 01	13 09	3 55	12 49	4 15	Fri	5
65	6	Sat	6 34	17 55	6 48	18 12	7 03	18 18	6 46	18 02	14 17	4 47	13 59	5 06	Sat	6
66	7	Sun	6 32	17 56	6 46	18 13	7 01	18 19	6 44	18 04	15 28	5 31	15 13	5 47	Sun	7
67	8	Mon	6 30	17 58	6 44	18 14	6 59	18 21	6 42	18 06	16 40	6 08	16 29	6 20	Mon	8
68	9	Tue	6 28	17 59	6 42	18 15	6 57	18 23	6 40	18 07	17 50	6 40	17 44	6 48	Tue	9
69	10	Wed	6 26	18 01	6 40	18 17	6 55	18 25	6 38	18 09	18 59	7 07	18 57	7 11	Wed	10
70	11	Thu	6 24	18 02	6 38	18 18	6 52	18 26	6 36	18 10	20 05	7 33	20 07	7 33	Thu	11
71	12	Fri	6 22	18 04	6 37	18 19	6 50	18 28	6 33	18 12	21 10	7 58	21 16	7 54	Fri	12
72	13	Sat	6 20	18 05	6 35	18 20	6 48	18 30	6 31	18 13	22 14	8 23	22 24	8 16	Sat	13
73	14	Sun	6 19	18 06	6 33	18 21	6 46	18 31	6 29	18 15	23 16	8 50	23 29	8 39	Sun	14
74	15	Mon	6 17	18 08	6 31	18 23	6 44	18 33	6 27	18 17	—	9 19	—	9 05	Mon	15
75	16	Tue	6 15	18 09	6 29	18 24	6 41	18 34	6 25	18 18	0 17	9 52	0 33	9 35	Tue	16
76	17	Wed	6 13	18 10	6 28	18 26	6 39	18 36	6 23	18 20	1 15	10 31	1 34	10 11	Wed	17
77	18	Thu	6 11	18 12	6 26	18 27	6 37	18 37	6 21	18 21	2 09	11 15	2 30	10 54	Thu	18
78	19	Fri	6 09	18 13	6 24	18 28	6 35	18 39	6 19	18 23	2 59	12 05	3 20	11 45	Fri	19
79	20	Sat	6 07	18 14	6 22	18 30	6 33	18 40	6 17	18 24	3 44	13 02	4 04	12 43	Sat	20
80	21	Sun	6 05	18 16	6 20	18 31	6 31	18 42	6 15	18 26	4 24	14 04	4 41	13 48	Sun	21
81	22	Mon	6 03	18 17	6 18	18 32	6 29	18 44	6 13	18 28	4 59	15 10	5 13	14 57	Mon	22
82	23	Tue	6 01	18 18	6 16	18 33	6 26	18 45	6 11	18 29	5 31	16 18	5 41	16 10	Tue	23
83	24	Wed	5 59	18 19	6 14	18 34	6 24	18 47	6 09	18 31	5 59	17 29	6 05	17 24	Wed	24
84	25	Thu	5 58	18 21	6 12	18 36	6 22	18 49	6 06	18 32	6 27	18 41	6 29	18 41	Thu	25
85	26	Fri	5 56	18 22	6 11	18 37	6 20	18 50	6 04	18 34	6 54	19 54	6 52	19 59	Fri	26
86	27	Sat	5 54	18 23	6 09	18 38	6 18	18 52	6 02	18 35	7 21	21 09	7 16	21 18	Sat	27
87	28	Sun	5 52	18 25	6 08	18 39	6 15	18 53	6 00	18 37	7 54	22 24	7 43	22 38	Sun	28
88	29	Mon	5 50	18 26	6 06	18 40	6 13	18 55	5 58	18 38	8 30	23 38	8 15	23 55	Mon	29
89	30	Tue	5 48	18 27	6 04	18 41	6 11	18 56	5 55	18 40	9 13	—	8 55	—	Tue	30
90	31	Wed	5 46	17 29	6 02	18 42	6 08	18 58	5 53	18 41	10 03	0 48	9 43	1 08	Wed	31

APRIL 1982

Moon's Phases E.S.T.
☽ First Quarter 1 d 0 h 8 min
○ Full Moon 8 d 5 h 18 min
☾ Last Quarter 16 d 7 h 42 min
● New Moon 23 d 15h 29 min
☽ First Quarter 30 d 7 h 7 min

SUNRISE AND SUNSET / MOONRISE AND MOONSET

Day of Yr.	Day of Mo.	Day of Week	Ottawa E.S.T. Rises	Sets	Toronto E.S.T. Rises	Sets	Winnipeg C.S.T. Rises	Sets	Vancouver P.S.T. Rises	Sets	Lat. 45° Rises	Sets	Lat. 50° Rises	Sets	Day of Week	Day of Mo.
			h m	h m	h m	h m	h m	h m	h m	h m	h m	h m	h m	h m		
91	1	Thu	5 44	18 30	6 00	18 43	6 06	18 59	5 51	18 42	11 02	1 51	10 41	2 12	Thu	1
92	2	Fri	5 42	18 31	5 58	18 44	6 04	19 01	5 49	18 44	12 07	2 46	11 48	3 06	Fri	2
93	3	Sat	5 40	18 32	5 56	18 46	6 02	19 03	5 47	18 46	13 16	3 31	13 00	3 48	Sat	3
94	4	Sun	5 38	18 33	5 55	18 47	6 00	19 04	5 45	18 47	14 26	4 09	14 14	4 23	Sun	4
95	5	Mon	5 37	18 35	5 53	18 49	5 58	19 06	5 43	18 49	15 35	4 41	15 27	4 51	Mon	5
96	6	Tue	5 35	18 36	5 51	18 50	5 56	19 07	5 41	18 50	16 44	5 09	16 40	5 15	Tue	6
97	7	Wed	5 33	18 38	5 49	18 51	5 54	19 09	5 39	18 52	17 50	5 35	17 51	5 37	Wed	7
98	8	Thu	5 31	18 39	5 48	18 52	5 52	19 10	5 37	18 53	18 56	5 59	19 00	5 57	Thu	8
99	9	Fri	5 29	18 40	5 46	18 53	5 50	19 12	5 35	18 55	20 00	6 24	20 08	6 18	Fri	9
100	10	Sat	5 27	18 41	5 44	18 54	5 48	19 13	5 33	18 56	21 03	6 50	21 15	6 40	Sat	10
101	11	Sun	5 26	18 43	5 42	18 55	5 46	19 15	5 31	18 58	22 05	7 18	22 21	7 05	Sun	11
102	12	Mon	5 24	18 44	5 41	18 56	5 44	19 17	5 29	18 59	23 05	7 49	23 23	7 33	Mon	12
103	13	Tue	5 22	18 45	5 39	18 58	5 42	19 18	5 27	19 01	—	8 25	—	8 06	Tue	13
104	14	Wed	5 20	18 47	5 37	18 59	5 40	19 20	5 25	19 02	0 01	9 07	0 22	8 46	Wed	14
105	15	Thu	5 18	18 48	5 36	19 01	5 37	19 21	5 22	19 04	0 53	9 55	1 15	9 34	Thu	15
106	16	Fri	5 17	18 49	5 34	19 02	5 35	19 23	5 20	19 05	1 40	10 49	2 01	10 28	Fri	16
107	17	Sat	5 15	18 51	5 32	19 03	5 33	19 24	5 18	19 07	2 21	11 48	2 40	11 30	Sat	17
108	18	Sun	5 13	18 52	5 30	19 04	5 31	19 26	5 16	19 08	2 57	12 51	3 13	12 36	Sun	18
109	19	Mon	5 11	18 53	5 28	19 06	5 29	19 27	5 14	19 10	3 30	13 57	3 42	13 47	Mon	19
110	20	Tue	5 10	18 54	5 27	19 07	5 27	19 29	5 12	19 11	3 59	15 06	4 07	15 00	Tue	20
111	21	Wed	5 08	18 55	5 25	19 08	5 25	19 31	5 10	19 13	4 26	16 18	4 30	16 15	Wed	21
112	22	Thu	5 06	18 57	5 24	19 09	5 23	19 32	5 08	19 14	4 53	17 31	4 53	17 33	Thu	22
113	23	Fri	5 04	18 58	5 22	19 10	5 21	19 34	5 06	19 16	5 21	18 47	5 16	18 54	Fri	23
114	24	Sat	5 03	18 59	5 21	19 12	5 19	19 35	5 04	19 18	5 51	20 04	5 42	20 16	Sat	24
115	25	Sun	5 01	19 01	5 19	19 13	5 17	19 37	5 03	19 19	6 26	21 22	6 13	21 38	Sun	25
116	26	Mon	4 59	19 02	5 17	19 14	5 15	19 38	5 01	19 21	7 07	22 37	6 50	22 56	Mon	26
117	27	Tue	4 58	19 03	5 16	19 15	5 14	19 40	4 59	19 22	7 56	23 45	7 36	—	Tue	27
118	28	Wed	4 56	19 04	5 14	19 16	5 12	19 41	4 57	19 24	8 53	—	8 32	0 06	Wed	28
119	29	Thu	4 55	19 06	5 13	19 17	5 10	19 43	4 55	19 25	9 58	0 44	9 38	1 04	Thu	29
120	30	Fri	4 53	19 07	5 11	19 18	5 08	19 45	4 53	19 27	11 07	1 33	10 49	1 51	Fri	30

MAY 1982

○ Full Moon .... 7 d 19 h 45 min
☾ Last Quarter .... 16 d 0 h 11 min
● New Moon .... 22 d 23 h 40 min
☽ First Quarter .... 29 d 15 h 7 min

Moon's Phases E.S.T.

Day of Yr.	Day of Mo.	Day of Week	Ottawa E.S.T. Rises (h m)	Ottawa E.S.T. Sets (h m)	Toronto E.S.T. Rises (h m)	Toronto E.S.T. Sets (h m)	Winnipeg C.S.T. Rises (h m)	Winnipeg C.S.T. Sets (h m)	Vancouver P.S.T. Rises (h m)	Vancouver P.S.T. Sets (h m)	Moon Lat. 45° Rises (h m)	Moon Lat. 45° Sets (h m)	Moon Lat. 50° Rises (h m)	Moon Lat. 50° Sets (h m)	Day of Week	Day of Mo.
121	1	Sat	4 52	19 08	5 10	19 19	5 06	19 46	4 52	19 28	12 17	2 16	12 03	2 28	Sat	1
122	2	Sun	4 51	19 09	5 08	19 20	5 04	19 48	4 50	19 30	13 26	2 46	13 17	2 57	Sun	2
123	3	Mon	4 49	19 11	5 07	19 21	5 02	19 49	4 48	19 31	14 34	3 14	14 29	3 21	Mon	3
124	4	Tue	4 47	19 12	5 06	19 23	5 01	19 51	4 47	19 32	15 40	3 40	15 39	3 43	Tue	4
125	5	Wed	4 46	19 13	5 04	19 24	4 59	19 52	4 45	19 34	16 45	4 04	16 48	4 03	Wed	5
126	6	Thu	4 44	19 15	5 03	19 25	4 57	19 54	4 43	19 35	17 49	4 28	17 56	4 23	Thu	6
127	7	Fri	4 43	19 16	5 01	19 26	4 56	19 55	4 42	19 37	18 52	4 52	19 03	4 44	Fri	7
128	8	Sat	4 42	19 17	5 00	19 27	4 54	19 57	4 40	19 38	19 55	5 19	20 09	5 07	Sat	8
129	9	Sun	4 40	19 18	4 59	19 29	4 52	19 58	4 39	19 40	20 56	5 49	21 13	5 33	Sun	9
130	10	Mon	4 39	19 19	4 57	19 30	4 51	20 00	4 37	19 41	21 54	6 23	22 14	6 04	Mon	10
131	11	Tue	4 37	19 21	4 56	19 31	4 49	20 01	4 36	19 43	22 48	7 02	23 09	6 42	Tue	11
132	12	Wed	4 36	19 22	4 55	19 32	4 48	20 02	4 34	19 44	23 37	7 48	23 58	7 26	Wed	12
133	13	Thu	4 35	19 23	4 54	19 33	4 46	20 04	4 33	19 45	—	8 39	—	8 18	Thu	13
134	14	Fri	4 34	19 24	4 53	19 34	4 45	20 05	4 31	19 47	0 20	9 36	0 39	9 16	Fri	14
135	15	Sat	4 33	19 25	4 52	19 35	4 43	20 07	4 30	19 48	0 57	10 36	1 14	10 20	Sat	15
136	16	Sun	4 32	19 27	4 51	19 36	4 42	20 08	4 28	19 50	1 30	11 40	1 44	11 28	Sun	16
137	17	Mon	4 31	19 28	4 50	19 37	4 40	20 10	4 27	19 51	1 59	12 47	2 09	12 38	Mon	17
138	18	Tue	4 30	19 29	4 49	19 38	4 39	20 11	4 26	19 53	2 26	13 55	2 32	13 51	Tue	18
139	19	Wed	4 29	19 30	4 48	19 40	4 38	20 12	4 25	19 54	2 52	15 06	2 54	15 06	Wed	19
140	20	Thu	4 28	19 31	4 47	19 41	4 37	20 14	4 23	19 55	3 19	16 20	3 17	16 24	Thu	20
141	21	Fri	4 27	19 32	4 46	19 42	4 36	20 15	4 22	19 57	3 48	17 36	3 41	17 46	Fri	21
142	22	Sat	4 26	19 33	4 45	19 43	4 35	20 16	4 21	19 58	4 20	18 55	4 09	19 09	Sat	22
143	23	Sun	4 25	19 34	4 44	19 44	4 34	20 17	4 20	19 59	4 58	20 14	4 42	20 32	Sun	23
144	24	Mon	4 24	19 36	4 43	19 45	4 33	20 19	4 19	20 00	5 44	21 28	5 24	21 49	Mon	24
145	25	Tue	4 23	19 37	4 42	19 46	4 32	20 20	4 18	20 01	6 39	22 34	6 18	22 55	Tue	25
146	26	Wed	4 22	19 38	4 41	19 47	4 31	20 21	4 17	20 02	7 43	23 29	7 22	23 48	Wed	26
147	27	Thu	4 21	19 39	4 40	19 48	4 30	20 22	4 16	20 03	8 53	—	8 34	—	Thu	27
148	28	Fri	4 20	19 40	4 40	19 49	4 29	20 23	4 15	20 04	10 05	0 13	9 50	0 30	Fri	28
149	29	Sat	4 19	19 40	4 39	19 49	4 28	20 25	4 14	20 06	11 17	0 49	11 05	1 02	Sat	29
150	30	Sun	4 19	19 41	4 39	19 50	4 27	20 26	4 13	20 07	12 26	1 20	12 19	1 28	Sun	30
151	31	Mon	4 18	19 42	4 38	19 51	4 26	20 27	4 12	20 08	13 33	1 46	13 30	1 50	Mon	31

SUNRISE AND SUNSET — MOONRISE AND MOONSET, Local Mean Time

JUNE 1982

○ Full Moon .... 6 d 10 h 59 min
☾ Last Quarter .... 14 d 13 h 6 min
● New Moon .... 21 d 6 h 52 min
☽ First Quarter .... 28 d 0 h 56 min

Moon's Phases E.S.T.

Day of Yr.	Day of Mo.	Day of Week	Ottawa E.S.T. Rises (h m)	Ottawa E.S.T. Sets (h m)	Toronto E.S.T. Rises (h m)	Toronto E.S.T. Sets (h m)	Winnipeg C.S.T. Rises (h m)	Winnipeg C.S.T. Sets (h m)	Vancouver P.S.T. Rises (h m)	Vancouver P.S.T. Sets (h m)	Moon Lat. 45° Rises (h m)	Moon Lat. 45° Sets (h m)	Moon Lat. 50° Rises (h m)	Moon Lat. 50° Sets (h m)	Day of Week	Day of Mo.
152	1	Tue	4 18	19 43	4 38	19 52	4 25	20 28	4 12	20 09	14 38	2 10	14 39	2 11	Tue	1
153	2	Wed	4 17	19 44	4 37	19 53	4 24	20 29	4 11	20 10	15 41	2 34	15 47	2 30	Wed	2
154	3	Thu	4 16	19 45	4 37	19 54	4 24	20 30	4 11	20 11	16 44	2 57	16 54	2 50	Thu	3
155	4	Fri	4 16	19 46	4 36	19 54	4 23	20 31	4 10	20 12	17 47	3 23	18 00	3 12	Fri	4
156	5	Sat	4 16	19 46	4 36	19 55	4 22	20 32	4 09	20 13	18 48	3 51	19 05	3 37	Sat	5
157	6	Sun	4 15	19 47	4 35	19 56	4 21	20 33	4 09	20 14	19 47	4 23	20 07	4 06	Sun	6
158	7	Mon	4 15	19 48	4 35	19 56	4 21	20 34	4 08	20 14	20 43	5 00	21 04	4 40	Mon	7
159	8	Tue	4 14	19 49	4 34	19 57	4 20	20 34	4 08	20 15	21 34	5 44	21 55	5 22	Tue	8
160	9	Wed	4 14	19 49	4 34	19 57	4 20	20 35	4 07	20 16	22 19	6 33	22 39	6 11	Wed	9
161	10	Thu	4 14	19 50	4 34	19 58	4 20	20 36	4 07	20 17	22 58	7 28	23 16	7 08	Thu	10
162	11	Fri	4 14	19 50	4 34	19 59	4 19	20 37	4 06	20 18	23 32	8 27	23 47	8 09	Fri	11
163	12	Sat	4 13	19 51	4 34	19 59	4 19	20 37	4 06	20 18	—	9 29	—	9 15	Sat	12
164	13	Sun	4 13	19 51	4 33	20 00	4 19	20 38	4 06	20 19	0 02	10 33	0 14	10 23	Sun	13
165	14	Mon	4 13	19 52	4 33	20 00	4 18	20 38	4 06	20 19	0 29	11 39	0 37	11 33	Mon	14
166	15	Tue	4 13	19 52	4 33	20 01	4 18	20 39	4 06	20 20	0 54	12 47	0 58	12 45	Tue	15
167	16	Wed	4 13	19 53	4 33	20 01	4 18	20 39	4 06	20 20	1 20	13 57	1 19	14 00	Wed	16
168	17	Thu	4 13	19 53	4 33	20 02	4 18	20 40	4 06	20 21	1 46	15 10	1 42	15 17	Thu	17
169	18	Fri	4 13	19 54	4 33	20 02	4 18	20 40	4 06	20 21	2 15	16 26	2 06	16 38	Fri	18
170	19	Sat	4 13	19 54	4 33	20 03	4 18	20 41	4 06	20 21	2 49	17 45	2 36	18 01	Sat	19
171	20	Sun	4 13	19 55	4 34	20 03	4 18	20 41	4 06	20 22	3 30	19 02	3 13	19 22	Sun	20
172	21	Mon	4 13	19 55	4 34	20 03	4 19	20 41	4 06	20 22	4 21	20 14	4 00	20 35	Mon	21
173	22	Tue	4 14	19 55	4 34	20 03	4 19	20 41	4 06	20 22	5 22	21 16	5 00	21 37	Tue	22
174	23	Wed	4 14	19 55	4 34	20 04	4 19	20 42	4 06	20 22	6 31	22 07	6 11	22 25	Wed	23
175	24	Thu	4 14	19 55	4 34	20 04	4 19	20 42	4 07	20 22	7 45	22 48	7 28	23 02	Thu	24
176	25	Fri	4 14	19 55	4 35	20 04	4 20	20 42	4 07	20 22	9 00	23 21	8 47	23 31	Fri	25
177	26	Sat	4 15	19 55	4 35	20 04	4 20	20 42	4 08	20 23	10 13	23 50	10 04	23 56	Sat	26
178	27	Sun	4 15	19 55	4 36	20 04	4 21	20 42	4 08	20 23	11 22	—	11 18	—	Sun	27
179	28	Mon	4 16	19 55	4 36	20 03	4 21	20 42	4 08	20 23	12 29	0 15	12 29	0 17	Mon	28
180	29	Tue	4 16	19 55	4 36	20 03	4 22	20 42	4 09	20 23	13 33	0 39	13 38	0 37	Tue	29
181	30	Wed	4 16	19 55	4 37	20 03	4 22	20 42	4 10	20 22	14 37	1 03	14 45	0 57	Wed	30

SUNRISE AND SUNSET — MOONRISE AND MOONSET, Local Mean Time

JULY 1982

○ Full Moon .... 6 d 2 h 32 min
☾ Last Quarter .... 13 d 22 h 47 min
● New Moon .... 20 d 36 h 57 min
☽ First Quarter .... 27 d 13 h 22 min

Moon's Phases E.S.T.

Day of Yr.	Day of Mo.	Day of Week	SUNRISE AND SUNSET: Ottawa E.S.T.				Toronto E.S.T.				Winnipeg C.S.T.				Vancouver P.S.T.				MOONRISE AND MOONSET, Local Mean Time: Lat. 45°				Lat. 50°				Day of Week	Day of Mo.
			Rises		Sets		Rises		Sets		Rises		Sets		Rises		Sets		Rises		Sets		Rises		Sets			
			h	m	h	m	h	m	h	m	h	m	h	m	h	m	h	m	h	m	h	m	h	m	h	m		
182	1	Thu	4	17	19	55	4	37	20	03	4	23	20	41	4	10	20	22	15	39	1	27	15	51	1	18	Thu	1
183	2	Fri	4	17	19	54	4	38	20	03	4	23	20	41	4	11	20	22	16	41	1	54	16	56	1	41	Fri	2
184	3	Sat	4	18	19	54	4	38	20	02	4	24	20	41	4	11	20	21	17	41	2	25	17	59	2	09	Sat	3
185	4	Sun	4	19	19	54	4	39	20	02	4	25	20	41	4	12	20	21	18	38	3	00	18	59	2	41	Sun	4
186	5	Mon	4	20	19	54	4	40	20	02	4	25	20	40	4	13	20	21	19	31	3	41	19	52	3	20	Mon	5
187	6	Tue	4	20	19	54	4	40	20	02	4	26	20	40	4	14	20	20	20	18	4	29	20	39	4	07	Tue	6
188	7	Wed	4	21	19	53	4	41	20	02	4	27	20	39	4	14	20	20	20	59	5	22	21	18	5	01	Wed	7
189	8	Thu	4	22	19	53	4	42	20	01	4	28	20	38	4	15	20	19	21	35	6	20	21	51	6	02	Thu	8
190	9	Fri	4	23	19	52	4	42	20	01	4	29	20	38	4	16	20	18	22	06	7	21	22	18	7	06	Fri	9
191	10	Sat	4	23	19	52	4	43	20	00	4	30	20	37	4	17	20	18	22	33	8	25	22	42	8	13	Sat	10
192	11	Sun	4	24	19	51	4	44	20	00	4	31	20	36	4	18	20	17	22	59	9	30	23	04	9	22	Sun	11
193	12	Mon	4	25	19	51	4	45	19	59	4	32	20	35	4	19	20	16	23	23	10	36	23	24	9	32	Mon	12
194	13	Tue	4	26	19	50	4	46	19	59	4	33	20	34	4	20	20	15	23	48	11	43	23	45	11	44	Tue	13
195	14	Wed	4	27	19	49	4	46	19	58	4	34	20	34	4	21	20	15	—		12	53	—		12	58	Wed	14
196	15	Thu	4	28	19	49	4	47	19	58	4	35	20	33	4	22	20	14	0	18	14	05	0	08	14	15	Thu	15
197	16	Fri	4	28	19	48	4	48	19	57	4	36	20	32	4	23	20	13	0	45	15	20	0	34	15	34	Fri	16
198	17	Sat	4	29	19	47	4	49	19	56	4	37	20	31	4	24	20	12	1	21	16	36	1	06	16	54	Sat	17
199	18	Sun	4	30	19	46	4	50	19	56	4	38	20	30	4	25	20	11	2	06	17	50	1	47	18	11	Sun	18
200	19	Mon	4	31	19	45	4	51	19	55	4	39	20	29	4	27	20	10	3	01	18	57	2	39	19	18	Mon	19
201	20	Tue	4	32	19	45	4	52	19	54	4	41	20	28	4	28	20	09	4	06	19	54	3	45	20	13	Tue	20
202	21	Wed	4	33	19	44	4	53	19	53	4	42	20	27	4	29	20	08	5	19	20	40	5	00	20	56	Wed	21
203	22	Thu	4	34	19	43	4	54	19	52	4	43	20	26	4	30	20	07	6	35	21	18	6	20	21	30	Thu	22
204	23	Fri	4	36	19	42	4	55	19	52	4	45	20	24	4	32	20	06	7	51	21	50	7	41	21	57	Fri	23
205	24	Sat	4	37	19	41	4	56	19	51	4	46	20	23	4	33	20	04	9	04	22	17	8	59	22	20	Sat	24
206	25	Sun	4	38	19	40	4	57	19	50	4	47	20	22	4	34	20	03	10	14	22	42	10	16	22	41	Sun	25
207	26	Mon	4	39	19	39	4	58	19	49	4	49	20	21	4	36	20	02	11	22	23	06	11	24	23	02	Mon	26
208	27	Tue	4	40	19	38	4	59	19	48	4	50	20	19	4	37	20	01	12	27	23	31	12	34	23	22	Tue	27
209	28	Wed	4	41	19	36	5	00	19	47	4	51	20	18	4	38	19	59	13	30	23	57	13	41	23	45	Wed	28
210	29	Thu	4	42	19	35	5	01	19	46	4	53	20	16	4	39	19	58	14	33	—		14	47	—		Thu	29
211	30	Fri	4	44	19	34	5	02	19	45	4	54	20	15	4	41	19	56	15	33	0	26	15	51	0	11	Fri	30
212	31	Sat	4	45	19	33	5	03	19	44	4	56	20	13	4	42	19	55	16	32	1	00	16	52	0	42	Sat	31

AUGUST 1982

○ Full Moon .... 4 d 17 h 34 min
☾ Last Quarter .... 12 d 6 h 8 min
● New Moon .... 18 d 21 h 45 min
☽ First Quarter .... 26 d 4 h 49 min

Moon's Phases E.S.T.

Day of Yr.	Day of Mo.	Day of Week	SUNRISE AND SUNSET: Ottawa E.S.T.				Toronto E.S.T.				Winnipeg C.S.T.				Vancouver P.S.T.				MOONRISE AND MOONSET, Local Mean Time: Lat. 45°				Lat. 50°				Day of Week	Day of Mo.
			Rises		Sets		Rises		Sets		Rises		Sets		Rises		Sets		Rises		Sets		Rises		Sets			
			h	m	h	m	h	m	h	m	h	m	h	m	h	m	h	m	h	m	h	m	h	m	h	m		
213	1	Sun	4	46	19	31	5	04	19	43	4	57	20	12	4	43	19	53	17	26	1	39	17	47	1	19	Sun	1
214	2	Mon	4	47	19	30	5	05	19	41	4	58	20	10	4	45	19	52	18	15	2	24	18	36	2	03	Mon	2
215	3	Tue	4	48	19	29	5	06	19	40	4	59	20	09	4	46	19	50	18	58	3	16	19	18	2	55	Tue	3
216	4	Wed	4	49	19	28	5	08	19	39	5	01	20	07	4	47	19	49	19	36	4	13	19	53	3	54	Wed	4
217	5	Thu	4	50	19	26	5	09	19	38	5	02	20	06	4	49	19	47	20	08	5	14	20	22	4	58	Thu	5
218	6	Fri	4	52	19	25	5	10	19	36	5	04	20	04	4	50	19	46	20	37	6	17	20	47	6	05	Fri	6
219	7	Sat	4	53	19	24	5	11	19	35	5	05	20	03	4	52	19	44	21	03	7	22	21	09	7	14	Sat	7
220	8	Sun	4	54	19	22	5	12	19	33	5	07	20	01	4	53	19	43	21	28	8	28	21	30	8	24	Sun	8
221	9	Mon	4	55	19	21	5	13	19	32	5	08	19	59	4	54	19	41	21	52	9	35	21	51	9	34	Mon	9
222	10	Tue	4	56	19	19	5	14	19	30	5	10	19	57	4	56	19	39	22	18	10	43	22	12	10	47	Tue	10
223	11	Wed	4	57	19	17	5	15	19	29	5	11	19	55	4	57	19	37	22	46	11	53	22	36	12	01	Wed	11
224	12	Thu	4	58	19	16	5	16	19	27	5	12	19	53	4	59	19	36	23	19	13	05	23	05	13	18	Thu	12
225	13	Fri	5	00	19	14	5	18	19	26	5	14	19	52	5	00	19	34	23	58	14	19	23	40	14	35	Fri	13
226	14	Sat	5	01	19	13	5	19	19	24	5	15	19	50	5	01	19	32	—		15	31	—		15	51	Sat	14
227	15	Sun	5	02	19	11	5	20	19	23	5	17	19	48	5	03	19	30	0	47	16	39	0	26	17	01	Sun	15
228	16	Mon	5	03	19	10	5	21	19	21	5	18	19	46	5	04	19	28	1	45	17	39	1	24	18	00	Mon	16
229	17	Tue	5	05	19	08	5	22	19	20	5	20	19	44	5	06	19	26	2	54	18	30	2	34	18	48	Tue	17
230	18	Wed	5	06	19	06	5	24	19	18	5	21	19	42	5	07	19	25	4	09	19	12	3	51	19	26	Wed	18
231	19	Thu	5	07	19	05	5	25	19	17	5	23	19	40	5	09	19	23	5	25	19	46	5	12	19	56	Thu	19
232	20	Fri	5	08	19	03	5	26	19	15	5	24	19	38	5	10	19	21	6	41	20	15	6	33	20	21	Fri	20
233	21	Sat	5	10	19	01	5	27	19	14	5	26	19	36	5	12	19	19	7	54	20	42	7	50	20	43	Sat	21
234	22	Sun	5	11	18	59	5	28	19	12	5	27	19	34	5	13	19	17	9	04	21	07	9	05	21	04	Sun	22
235	23	Mon	5	12	18	58	5	29	19	11	5	29	19	32	5	15	19	15	10	12	21	32	10	17	21	25	Mon	23
236	24	Tue	5	13	18	56	5	31	19	09	5	30	19	30	5	16	19	13	11	18	21	58	11	27	21	47	Tue	24
237	25	Wed	5	14	18	54	5	32	19	07	5	32	19	28	5	18	19	11	12	22	22	26	12	35	22	12	Wed	25
238	26	Thu	5	16	18	52	5	33	19	05	5	33	19	26	5	19	19	08	13	24	22	58	13	41	22	41	Thu	26
239	27	Fri	5	17	18	51	5	34	19	04	5	35	19	24	5	20	19	06	14	23	23	36	14	43	23	16	Fri	27
240	28	Sat	5	18	18	49	5	36	19	02	5	36	19	22	5	22	19	04	15	19	—		15	41	23	57	Sat	28
241	29	Sun	5	19	18	47	5	37	19	00	5	38	19	20	5	23	19	02	16	10	0	19	16	32	—		Sun	29
242	30	Mon	5	20	18	45	5	38	18	58	5	39	19	18	5	24	19	00	16	56	1	08	17	16	0	46	Mon	30
243	31	Tue	5	22	18	43	5	39	18	57	5	41	19	16	5	26	18	58	17	35	2	03	17	54	1	43	Tue	31

SEPTEMBER 1982

Moon's Phases E.S.T.	
○ Full Moon	3 d 7 h 28 min
☾ Last Quarter	10 d 12 h 19 min
● New Moon	17 d 7 h 9 min
☽ First Quarter	24 d 23 h 7 min

SUNRISE AND SUNSET / MOONRISE AND MOONSET

Day of Yr.	Day of Mo.	Day of Week	Ottawa E.S.T. Rises	Sets	Toronto E.S.T. Rises	Sets	Winnipeg C.S.T. Rises	Sets	Vancouver P.S.T. Rises	Sets	Lat. 45° Rises	Sets	Lat. 50° Rises	Sets	Day of Week	Day of Mo.
			h m	h m	h m	h m	h m	h m	h m	h m	h m	h m	h m	h m		
244	1	Wed	5 23	18 41	5 40	18 55	5 42	19 14	5 27	18 56	18 10	3 03	18 25	2 46	Wed	1
245	2	Thu	5 24	18 39	5 41	18 54	5 44	19 12	5 29	18 54	18 40	4 07	18 51	3 53	Thu	2
246	3	Fri	5 25	18 38	5 42	18 52	5 45	19 10	5 30	18 52	19 07	5 12	19 14	5 02	Fri	3
247	4	Sat	5 26	18 36	5 43	18 50	5 47	19 08	5 32	18 50	19 32	6 19	19 35	6 13	Sat	4
248	5	Sun	5 27	18 34	5 44	18 48	5 48	19 06	5 33	18 48	19 56	7 26	19 56	7 25	Sun	5
249	6	Mon	5 29	18 32	5 45	18 47	5 50	19 03	5 34	18 46	20 22	8 35	20 17	8 38	Mon	6
250	7	Tue	5 30	18 30	5 46	18 45	5 51	19 01	5 36	18 44	20 49	9 45	20 40	9 52	Tue	7
251	8	Wed	5 31	18 28	5 47	18 43	5 53	18 59	5 37	18 42	21 20	10 57	21 07	11 08	Wed	8
252	9	Thu	5 32	18 26	5 48	18 41	5 54	18 57	5 39	18 40	21 56	12 09	21 39	12 25	Thu	9
253	10	Fri	5 34	18 25	5 50	18 39	5 56	18 55	5 40	18 38	22 40	13 21	22 20	13 40	Fri	10
254	11	Sat	5 35	18 23	5 51	18 38	5 57	18 52	5 42	18 36	23 34	14 29	23 12	14 51	Sat	11
255	12	Sun	5 37	18 21	5 53	18 36	5 59	18 50	5 43	18 33	—	15 31	—	15 52	Sun	12
256	13	Mon	5 38	18 19	5 54	18 34	6 00	18 48	5 45	18 31	0 37	16 23	0 16	16 43	Mon	13
257	14	Tue	5 39	18 17	5 55	18 32	6 02	18 46	5 46	18 29	1 48	17 07	1 29	17 23	Tue	14
258	15	Wed	5 40	18 15	5 56	18 30	6 03	18 44	5 48	18 27	3 02	17 43	2 47	17 55	Wed	15
259	16	Thu	5 42	18 13	5 57	18 29	6 05	18 42	5 49	18 25	4 17	18 14	4 07	18 21	Thu	16
260	17	Fri	5 43	18 11	5 58	18 27	6 06	18 39	5 51	18 23	5 31	18 41	5 26	18 44	Fri	17
261	18	Sat	5 44	18 09	6 00	18 25	6 08	18 37	5 52	18 20	6 43	19 06	6 42	19 05	Sat	18
262	19	Sun	5 45	18 07	6 01	18 23	6 09	18 35	5 54	18 18	7 53	19 31	7 56	19 26	Sun	19
263	20	Mon	5 47	18 05	6 02	18 21	6 11	18 32	5 55	18 16	9 01	19 57	9 08	19 48	Mon	20
264	21	Tue	5 48	18 03	6 03	18 19	6 12	18 30	5 57	18 14	10 07	20 25	10 19	20 12	Tue	21
265	22	Wed	5 49	18 01	6 04	18 17	6 14	18 28	5 58	18 12	11 11	20 55	11 27	20 39	Wed	22
266	23	Thu	5 50	17 59	6 05	18 15	6 15	18 26	6 00	18 09	12 11	21 31	12 32	21 11	Thu	23
267	24	Fri	5 52	17 57	6 06	18 13	6 17	18 24	6 01	18 07	13 11	22 12	13 32	21 50	Fri	24
268	25	Sat	5 53	17 55	6 08	18 11	6 18	18 22	6 02	18 05	14 04	22 59	14 26	22 37	Sat	25
269	26	Sun	5 54	17 54	6 09	18 10	6 20	18 20	6 04	18 03	14 52	23 52	15 13	23 30	Sun	26
270	27	Mon	5 55	17 52	6 10	18 08	6 21	18 18	6 05	18 01	15 33	—	15 53	—	Mon	27
271	28	Tue	5 56	17 50	6 11	18 06	6 22	18 15	6 07	17 59	16 09	0 50	16 26	0 31	Tue	28
272	29	Wed	5 58	17 48	6 12	18 04	6 24	18 13	6 08	17 56	16 40	1 52	16 54	1 36	Wed	29
273	30	Thu	5 59	17 46	6 14	18 02	6 25	18 10	6 10	17 54	17 08	2 57	17 18	2 45	Thu	30

OCTOBER 1982

Moon's Phases E.S.T.	
○ Full Moon	2 d 20 h 8 min
☾ Last Quarter	9 d 18 h 26 min
● New Moon	16 d 19 h 4 min
☽ First Quarter	24 d 19 h 8 min

SUNRISE AND SUNSET / MOONRISE AND MOONSET

Day of Yr.	Day of Mo.	Day of Week	Ottawa E.S.T. Rises	Sets	Toronto E.S.T. Rises	Sets	Winnipeg C.S.T. Rises	Sets	Vancouver P.S.T. Rises	Sets	Lat. 45° Rises	Sets	Lat. 50° Rises	Sets	Day of Week	Day of Mo.
			h m	h m	h m	h m	h m	h m	h m	h m	h m	h m	h m	h m		
274	1	Fri	6 00	17 44	6 15	18 01	6 27	18 08	6 11	17 52	17 34	4 04	17 39	3 56	Fri	1
275	2	Sat	6 01	17 42	6 16	17 59	6 29	18 06	6 13	17 50	17 59	5 12	18 00	5 08	Sat	2
276	3	Sun	6 03	17 40	6 17	17 57	6 31	18 04	6 14	17 48	18 24	6 21	18 21	6 23	Sun	3
277	4	Mon	6 04	17 39	6 19	17 55	6 33	18 02	6 16	17 46	18 51	7 33	18 43	7 38	Mon	4
278	5	Tue	6 05	17 37	6 20	17 53	6 34	18 00	6 17	17 44	19 21	8 46	19 09	8 56	Tue	5
279	6	Wed	6 06	17 35	6 21	17 52	6 35	17 58	6 19	17 42	19 56	10 00	19 40	10 15	Wed	6
280	7	Thu	6 08	17 33	6 23	17 50	6 37	17 56	6 20	17 40	20 38	11 13	20 18	11 32	Thu	7
281	8	Fri	6 09	17 31	6 24	17 48	6 38	17 53	6 22	17 38	21 28	12 24	21 07	12 45	Fri	8
282	9	Sat	6 10	17 30	6 25	17 46	6 39	17 51	6 23	17 36	22 28	13 27	22 06	13 49	Sat	9
283	10	Sun	6 12	17 28	6 26	17 45	6 41	17 49	6 25	17 34	23 36	14 21	23 16	14 42	Sun	10
284	11	Mon	6 13	17 26	6 28	17 43	6 43	17 47	6 26	17 31	—	15 06	—	15 24	Mon	11
285	12	Tue	6 14	17 24	6 29	17 41	6 45	17 45	6 28	17 29	0 47	15 44	0 31	15 57	Tue	12
286	13	Wed	6 15	17 22	6 30	17 39	6 46	17 43	6 29	17 27	2 01	16 15	1 49	16 24	Wed	13
287	14	Thu	6 17	17 20	6 32	17 37	6 48	17 41	6 31	17 25	3 14	16 43	3 06	16 48	Thu	14
288	15	Fri	6 18	17 18	6 33	17 36	6 49	17 39	6 33	17 23	4 25	17 08	4 22	17 09	Fri	15
289	16	Sat	6 19	17 17	6 34	17 34	6 51	17 37	6 34	17 21	5 35	17 32	5 36	17 29	Sat	16
290	17	Sun	6 21	17 15	6 36	17 33	6 53	17 35	6 36	17 19	6 43	17 57	6 49	17 49	Sun	17
291	18	Mon	6 22	17 13	6 37	17 31	6 54	17 33	6 37	17 16	7 50	18 23	8 01	18 12	Mon	18
292	19	Tue	6 23	17 12	6 38	17 29	6 56	17 31	6 39	17 16	8 56	18 53	9 10	18 38	Tue	19
293	20	Wed	6 25	17 10	6 39	17 28	6 57	17 29	6 40	17 14	10 00	19 26	10 18	19 08	Wed	20
294	21	Thu	6 26	17 08	6 41	17 26	6 59	17 27	6 42	17 12	11 01	20 05	11 21	19 44	Thu	21
295	22	Fri	6 27	17 06	6 42	17 25	7 00	17 25	6 43	17 10	11 57	20 49	12 19	20 26	Fri	22
296	23	Sat	6 29	17 05	6 43	17 23	7 02	17 23	6 45	17 08	12 47	21 40	13 09	21 18	Sat	23
297	24	Sun	6 30	17 03	6 44	17 21	7 04	17 21	6 47	17 06	13 30	22 36	13 51	22 16	Sun	24
298	25	Mon	6 31	17 02	6 46	17 20	7 06	17 19	6 49	17 04	14 08	23 36	14 26	23 19	Mon	25
299	26	Tue	6 33	17 00	6 47	17 18	7 07	17 17	6 50	17 02	14 41	—	14 56	—	Tue	26
300	27	Wed	6 34	16 59	6 48	17 17	7 09	17 15	6 52	17 00	15 09	0 39	15 20	0 25	Wed	27
301	28	Thu	6 36	16 57	6 49	17 15	7 11	17 13	6 54	16 59	15 37	1 45	15 43	1 35	Thu	28
302	29	Fri	6 37	16 56	6 50	17 14	7 12	17 12	6 55	16 57	16 00	2 52	16 03	2 43	Fri	29
303	30	Sat	6 38	16 54	6 51	17 13	7 14	17 10	6 56	16 55	16 25	4 01	16 24	4 00	Sat	30
304	31	Sun	6 40	16 52	6 52	17 11	7 15	17 08	6 58	16 54	16 51	5 12	16 45	5 16	Sun	31

NOVEMBER 1982

Moon's Phases E.S.T.

○ Full Moon .... 1 d 7 h 57 min
☾ Last Quarter .... 8 d 1 h 38 min
● New Moon.......... 15 d 10 h 10 min
☽ First Quarter .... 23 d 15h 5 min
○ Full Moon .... 30 d 19 h 21 min

SUNRISE AND SUNSET — MOONRISE AND MOONSET (Local Mean Time)

Day of Yr.	Day of Mo.	Day of Week	Ottawa E.S.T.				Toronto E.S.T.				Winnipeg C.S.T.				Vancouver P.S.T.				Lat. 45°				Lat. 50°				Day of Week	Day of Mo.
			Rises		Sets		Rises		Sets		Rises		Sets		Rises		Sets		Rises		Sets		Rises		Sets			
			h	m	h	m	h	m	h	m	h	m	h	m	h	m	h	m	h	m	h	m	h	m	h	m		
305	1	Mon	6	41	16	51	6	54	17	10	7	17	17	07	6	59	16	52	17	19	6	26	17	09	6	34	Mon	1
306	2	Tue	6	43	16	50	6	55	17	09	7	19	17	05	7	01	16	50	17	53	7	42	17	38	7	55	Tue	2
307	3	Wed	6	44	16	48	6	56	17	08	7	20	17	03	7	03	16	49	18	33	8	59	18	14	9	16	Wed	3
308	4	Thu	6	45	16	47	6	57	17	06	7	22	17	01	7	05	16	47	19	21	10	13	19	00	10	34	Thu	4
309	5	Fri	6	47	16	45	6	59	17	05	7	24	17	00	7	06	16	45	20	20	11	21	19	57	11	44	Fri	5
310	6	Sat	6	48	16	44	7	00	17	03	7	25	16	58	7	08	16	44	21	26	12	20	21	05	12	41	Sat	6
311	7	Sun	6	50	16	43	7	01	17	02	7	27	16	57	7	09	16	42	22	38	13	08	22	20	13	27	Sun	7
312	8	Mon	6	51	16	41	7	03	17	01	7	29	16	55	7	11	16	41	23	51	13	47	23	37	14	02	Mon	8
313	9	Tue	6	52	16	40	7	04	17	00	7	30	16	54	7	12	16	39	—		14	20	—		14	30	Tue	9
314	10	Wed	6	54	16	39	7	06	16	58	7	32	16	52	7	14	16	38	1	03	14	47	0	54	14	54	Wed	10
315	11	Thu	6	55	16	38	7	07	16	57	7	34	16	51	7	16	16	36	2	13	15	12	2	09	15	15	Thu	11
316	12	Fri	6	56	16	36	7	08	16	56	7	35	16	49	7	17	16	35	3	22	15	36	3	22	15	34	Fri	12
317	13	Sat	6	58	16	35	7	10	16	55	7	37	16	48	7	19	16	34	4	30	16	00	4	34	15	54	Sat	13
318	14	Sun	7	00	16	34	7	11	16	54	7	39	16	47	7	20	16	32	5	37	16	25	5	45	16	15	Sun	14
319	15	Mon	7	01	16	33	7	12	16	53	7	40	16	45	7	22	16	31	6	43	16	53	6	55	16	39	Mon	15
320	16	Tue	7	02	16	32	7	14	16	52	7	42	16	44	7	24	16	30	7	47	17	24	8	04	17	07	Tue	16
321	17	Wed	7	04	16	31	7	15	16	51	7	44	16	43	7	25	16	29	8	50	18	00	9	10	17	40	Wed	17
322	18	Thu	7	05	16	30	7	16	16	50	7	45	16	41	7	27	16	28	9	48	18	42	10	10	18	20	Thu	18
323	19	Fri	7	06	16	29	7	17	16	50	7	47	16	40	7	28	16	27	10	41	19	31	11	04	19	08	Fri	19
324	20	Sat	7	07	16	28	7	19	16	49	7	48	16	39	7	30	16	25	11	27	20	25	11	49	20	03	Sat	20
325	21	Sun	7	09	16	27	7	20	16	49	7	50	16	38	7	31	16	24	12	07	21	23	12	27	21	04	Sun	21
326	22	Mon	7	10	16	27	7	21	16	48	7	52	16	37	7	33	16	23	12	41	22	24	12	58	22	09	Mon	22
327	23	Tue	7	11	16	26	7	22	16	47	7	53	16	36	7	34	16	22	13	11	23	28	13	24	23	16	Tue	23
328	24	Wed	7	12	16	25	7	23	16	46	7	54	16	35	7	36	16	21	13	37	—		13	46	—		Wed	24
329	25	Thu	7	14	16	24	7	25	16	46	7	56	16	34	7	38	16	20	14	01	0	32	14	07	0	25	Thu	25
330	26	Fri	7	15	16	24	7	26	16	45	7	58	16	33	7	39	16	20	14	25	1	39	14	26	1	36	Fri	26
331	27	Sat	7	16	16	23	7	27	16	44	7	59	16	33	7	40	16	19	14	50	2	48	14	46	2	49	Sat	27
332	28	Sun	7	18	16	23	7	29	16	44	8	00	16	32	7	42	16	19	15	16	4	00	15	09	4	05	Sun	28
333	29	Mon	7	19	16	22	7	30	16	43	8	02	16	31	7	43	16	18	15	47	5	15	15	35	5	25	Mon	29
334	30	Tue	7	20	16	22	7	31	16	43	8	03	16	31	7	45	16	17	16	24	6	32	16	07	6	48	Tue	30

DECEMBER 1982

Moon's Phases E.S.T.

☾ Last Quarter .... 7 d 10 h 53 min
● New Moon.......... 15 d 4 h 18 min
☽ First Quarter .... 23 d 9 h 17 min
○ Full Moon .... 30 d 6 h 33 min

SUNRISE AND SUNSET — MOONRISE AND MOONSET (Local Mean Time)

Day of Yr.	Day of Mo.	Day of Week	Ottawa E.S.T.				Toronto E.S.T.				Winnipeg C.S.T.				Vancouver P.S.T.				Lat. 45°				Lat. 50°				Day of Week	Day of Mo.
			Rises		Sets		Rises		Sets		Rises		Sets		Rises		Sets		Rises		Sets		Rises		Sets			
			h	m	h	m	h	m	h	m	h	m	h	m	h	m	h	m	h	m	h	m	h	m	h	m		
335	1	Wed	7	22	16	21	7	32	16	42	8	05	16	30	7	46	16	17	17	09	7	50	16	49	8	10	Wed	1
336	2	Thu	7	23	16	21	7	33	16	42	8	06	16	30	7	47	16	16	18	05	9	04	17	43	9	27	Thu	2
337	3	Fri	7	24	16	20	7	34	16	42	8	07	16	29	7	48	16	16	19	11	10	11	18	49	10	32	Fri	3
338	4	Sat	7	25	16	20	7	36	16	42	8	09	16	29	7	50	16	15	20	24	11	04	20	04	11	25	Sat	4
339	5	Sun	7	26	16	20	7	37	16	41	8	10	16	28	7	51	16	15	21	39	11	48	21	23	12	05	Sun	5
340	6	Mon	7	27	16	20	7	38	16	41	8	11	16	28	7	52	16	14	22	53	12	23	22	42	12	36	Mon	6
341	7	Tue	7	28	16	19	7	39	16	41	8	12	16	28	7	53	16	14	—		12	53	23	59	13	01	Tue	7
342	8	Wed	7	29	16	19	7	40	16	41	8	13	16	27	7	54	16	14	0	05	13	18	—		13	22	Wed	8
343	9	Thu	7	30	16	19	7	41	16	41	8	14	16	27	7	55	16	14	1	14	13	42	1	12	13	42	Thu	9
344	10	Fri	7	32	16	19	7	42	16	41	8	15	16	27	7	56	16	13	2	21	14	05	2	24	14	01	Fri	10
345	11	Sat	7	32	16	19	7	42	16	41	8	17	16	27	7	57	16	13	3	28	14	29	3	35	14	21	Sat	11
346	12	Sun	7	33	16	19	7	43	16	41	8	18	16	27	7	58	16	13	4	33	14	55	4	44	14	43	Sun	12
347	13	Mon	7	34	16	19	7	44	16	41	8	19	16	27	7	59	16	13	5	37	15	25	5	53	15	09	Mon	13
348	14	Tue	7	34	16	19	7	45	16	41	8	20	16	27	8	00	16	13	6	40	15	59	6	59	15	40	Tue	14
349	15	Wed	7	35	16	20	7	46	16	42	8	20	16	27	8	01	16	13	7	40	16	39	8	02	16	17	Wed	15
350	16	Thu	7	36	16	20	7	46	16	42	8	21	16	27	8	02	16	14	8	35	17	25	8	58	17	02	Thu	16
351	17	Fri	7	37	16	20	7	47	16	42	8	22	16	27	8	02	16	14	9	24	18	17	9	47	17	55	Fri	17
352	18	Sat	7	37	16	20	7	48	16	43	8	22	16	28	8	03	16	14	10	06	19	14	10	27	18	53	Sat	18
353	19	Sun	7	38	16	20	7	48	16	43	8	23	16	28	8	04	16	15	10	42	20	14	11	00	19	57	Sun	19
354	20	Mon	7	39	16	21	7	49	16	44	8	24	16	29	8	05	16	15	11	13	21	16	11	27	21	02	Mon	20
355	21	Tue	7	39	16	21	7	49	16	44	8	25	16	29	8	05	16	16	11	40	22	19	11	51	22	09	Tue	21
356	22	Wed	7	40	16	22	7	50	16	44	8	25	16	30	8	06	16	16	12	04	23	23	12	11	23	18	Wed	22
357	23	Thu	7	40	16	22	7	50	16	45	8	26	16	30	8	06	16	17	12	27	—		12	30	—		Thu	23
358	24	Fri	7	41	16	23	7	51	16	45	8	26	16	31	8	07	16	17	12	50	0	29	12	49	0	28	Fri	24
359	25	Sat	7	42	16	24	7	51	16	46	8	27	16	31	8	07	16	18	13	15	1	37	13	09	1	40	Sat	25
360	26	Sun	7	42	16	24	7	52	16	46	8	27	16	32	8	08	16	19	13	42	2	48	13	32	2	56	Sun	26
361	27	Mon	7	42	16	25	7	52	16	47	8	27	16	32	8	08	16	19	14	15	4	02	14	00	4	15	Mon	27
362	28	Tue	7	42	16	26	7	52	16	48	8	27	16	33	8	08	16	20	14	55	5	19	14	36	5	37	Tue	28
363	29	Wed	7	43	16	27	7	52	16	48	8	28	16	34	8	08	16	21	15	45	6	36	15	23	6	57	Wed	29
364	30	Thu	7	43	16	27	7	53	16	49	8	28	16	35	8	08	16	22	16	47	7	48	16	24	8	11	Thu	30
365	31	Fri	7	43	16	28	7	53	16	50	8	28	16	36	8	09	16	23	17	59	8	50	17	38	9	12	Fri	31

JANUARY 1983

☾	Last Quarter .... 5 d 23 h 1 min	Moon's Phases E.S.T.
●	New Moon.......... 14 d 0 h 9 min	
☽	First Quarter .... 22 d 0 h 35 min	
○	Full Moon .... 28 d 17 h 27 min	

Day of Yr.	Day of Mo.	Day of Week	Sunrise and Sunset: Ottawa E.S.T. Rises (h m)	Ottawa Sets (h m)	Toronto E.S.T. Rises (h m)	Toronto Sets (h m)	Winnipeg C.S.T. Rises (h m)	Winnipeg Sets (h m)	Vancouver P.S.T. Rises (h m)	Vancouver Sets (h m)	Moonrise and Moonset (Local Mean Time): Lat. 45° Rises (h m)	Lat. 45° Sets (h m)	Lat. 50° Rises (h m)	Lat. 50° Sets (h m)	Day of Week	Day of Mo.
1	1	Sat	7 43	16 29	7 53	16 51	8 28	16 37	8 09	16 24	19 17	9 41	18 59	9 59	Sat	1
2	2	Sun	7 43	16 30	7 53	16 52	8 28	16 38	8 09	16 25	20 35	10 21	20 22	10 36	Sun	2
3	3	Mon	7 43	16 31	7 53	16 52	8 28	16 39	8 09	16 26	21 50	10 54	21 42	11 04	Mon	3
4	4	Tue	7 43	16 32	7 53	16 53	8 27	16 40	8 08	16 27	23 03	11 22	23 00	11 27	Tue	4
5	5	Wed	7 43	16 33	7 53	16 54	8 27	16 41	8 08	16 28	—	11 47	—	11 48	Wed	5
6	6	Thu	7 43	16 34	7 52	16 55	8 27	16 42	8 08	16 29	0 12	12 11	0 14	12 07	Thu	6
7	7	Fri	7 43	16 35	7 52	16 56	8 26	16 43	8 08	16 30	1 20	12 34	1 25	12 27	Fri	7
8	8	Sat	7 43	16 36	7 52	16 57	8 26	16 44	8 07	16 31	2 25	13 00	2 35	12 49	Sat	8
9	9	Sun	7 42	16 38	7 52	16 58	8 26	16 46	8 07	16 33	3 30	13 28	3 44	13 13	Sun	9
10	10	Mon	7 42	16 39	7 52	17 00	8 25	16 47	8 06	16 34	4 33	14 00	4 51	13 42	Mon	10
11	11	Tue	7 42	16 40	7 51	17 01	8 25	16 48	8 06	16 35	5 34	14 38	5 54	14 16	Tue	11
12	12	Wed	7 41	16 41	7 51	17 02	8 24	16 50	8 05	16 37	6 30	15 21	6 52	14 59	Wed	12
13	13	Thu	7 41	16 42	7 50	17 03	8 24	16 51	8 05	16 38	7 21	16 11	7 44	15 49	Thu	13
14	14	Fri	7 40	16 44	7 50	17 04	8 23	16 53	8 04	16 40	8 05	17 07	8 27	16 46	Fri	14
15	15	Sat	7 40	16 45	7 49	17 05	8 22	16 54	8 03	16 41	8 43	18 06	9 02	17 48	Sat	15
16	16	Sun	7 39	16 46	7 49	17 07	8 21	16 56	8 03	16 42	9 16	19 08	9 31	18 53	Sun	16
17	17	Mon	7 39	16 47	7 48	17 08	8 20	16 57	8 02	16 44	9 44	20 10	9 56	20 00	Mon	17
18	18	Tue	7 38	16 48	7 48	17 09	8 19	16 58	8 01	16 45	10 08	21 14	10 17	21 07	Tue	18
19	19	Wed	7 38	16 50	7 47	17 11	8 19	17 00	8 00	16 47	10 31	22 18	10 36	22 15	Wed	19
20	20	Thu	7 37	16 51	7 46	17 12	8 18	17 02	7 59	16 48	10 54	23 23	10 54	23 25	Thu	20
21	21	Fri	7 36	16 52	7 46	17 13	8 17	17 03	7 58	16 50	11 17	—	11 13	—	Fri	21
22	22	Sat	7 35	16 54	7 45	17 14	8 16	17 05	7 57	16 51	11 42	0 30	11 34	0 37	Sat	22
23	23	Sun	7 34	16 55	7 44	17 16	8 15	17 07	7 56	16 53	12 10	1 41	11 58	1 51	Sun	23
24	24	Mon	7 33	16 57	7 43	17 17	8 14	17 08	7 55	16 54	12 45	2 54	12 29	3 09	Mon	24
25	25	Tue	7 32	16 58	7 42	17 19	8 13	17 10	7 54	16 56	13 28	4 09	13 08	4 28	Tue	25
26	26	Wed	7 32	16 59	7 42	17 20	8 11	17 12	7 53	16 58	14 23	5 22	14 00	5 44	Wed	26
27	27	Thu	7 31	17 01	7 41	17 21	8 10	17 13	7 52	16 59	15 29	6 29	15 07	6 51	Thu	27
28	28	Fri	7 30	17 02	7 40	17 22	8 09	17 15	7 51	17 01	16 45	7 26	16 25	7 46	Fri	28
29	29	Sat	7 29	17 04	7 39	17 23	8 08	17 17	7 50	17 03	18 05	8 12	17 50	8 28	Sat	29
30	30	Sun	7 28	17 05	7 38	17 25	8 07	17 18	7 48	17 05	19 25	8 49	19 15	9 01	Sun	30
31	31	Mon	7 27	17 07	7 37	17 26	8 05	17 20	7 47	17 06	20 42	9 21	20 37	9 28	Mon	31

SYMBOLS AND ABBREVIATIONS

SUN, MOON AND PLANETS

☉ The Sun	♃ Jupiter
☾ The Moon	♄ Saturn
☿ Mercury	♅ Uranus
♀ Venus	♆ Neptune
⊕ The Earth	♇ Pluto
♂ Mars	

SIGNS OF THE ZODIAC

1. ♈ Aries	7. ♎ Libra
2. ♉ Taurus	8. ♏ Scorpius
3. ♊ Gemini	9. ♐ Sagittarius
4. ♋ Cancer	10. ♑ Capricornus
5. ♌ Leo	11. ♒ Aquarius
6. ♍ Virgo	12. ♓ Pisces

ASPECTS AND ABBREVIATIONS

☌ Conjunction, or having the same Longitude or Right Ascension

☍ Opposition, or differing 180° in Longitude or Right Ascension

Aphelion—Farthest from the sun

Perihelion—Nearest the sun

N.	North	′	Minutes of Arc
S.	South	″	Seconds of Arc
E.	East	h	Hours
W.	West	m	Minutes of Time
°	Degrees	s	Seconds of Time

PRINCIPAL ELEMENTS OF THE SOLAR SYSTEM

Object	Equatorial Diameter miles	Equatorial Diameter km	Mass (earth = 1)	Axial Rotation	Magnitude at brightest	Mean Dist. from Sun (mill. miles)	Mean Dist. from Sun (mill. km)	Per. of Revol.	Eccentricity	Inclination (deg.)
Sun	865,000	1,392,000	332,946	$24^d.7$	−26.8					
Moon	2,160	3,476	0.0123	$27^d.7^h.7$	−12.6					
Mercury	3,031	4,878	0.0553	58^d16^h	−1.9	36.0	57.9	88.0d	.206	7.0
Venus	7,521	12,104	0.8150	243^d(*retro*)	−4.4	67.2	108.1	224.7	.007	3.4
Earth	7,926	12,756	1.0000	$23^h56^m.1$		92.9	149.5	365.3	.017	
Mars.........	4,222	6,794	0.1075	$24^h37^m.4$	−2.8	141.5	227.8	687.0	.093	1.8
Jupiter......	88,729	142,796	317.89	9^h50^m	−2.5	483.3	778	11.86y	.048	1.3
Saturn	74,600	120,000	95.17	10^h14^m	−0.4	886	1427	29.46	.056	2.5
Uranus	31,600	50,800	14.56	$10.^h8$[1]	+5.7	1782	2869	84.01	.074	0.8
Neptune....	30,200	48,600	17.24	16^h[1]	+7.6	2792	4497	164.8	.009	1.8
Pluto	2,000[2]	3,000[2]	0.002[2]	$6^d9.^h3$	+14	3664	5900	247.7	.250	17.2

[1]New values, not yet confirmed.

[2]Figures uncertain.

PLANETARY CONFIGURATIONS, 1982

UNIVERSAL (GREENWICH) TIME

	d	h	
Jan.	4	11	Earth at perihelion
	9	14	Mercury 5°S. of Venus
	9	20	Eclipse of Moon
	16	12	Mercury greatest elong. E. (19°)
	21	10	Venus in inferior conjunction
	22	18	Mercury stationary in R.A.
Feb.	1	4	Mercury in inferior conjunction
	1	5	Saturn stationary in R.A.
	4	16	Pluto stationary in R.A.
	10	14	Venus stationary in R.A.
	12	22	Mercury stationary in R.A.
	21	5	Mars stationary in R.A.
	24	14	Jupiter stationary in R.A.
	25	1	Venus greatest brilliancy
	26	11	Mercury greatest elong. W. (27°)
Mar.	9	20	Uranus stationary in R.A.
	20	23	Vernal equinox
	29	17	Neptune stationary in R.A.
	31	10	Mars at opposition
Apr.	1	18	Venus greatest elong. W. (46°)
	5	7	Mars closest approach
	9	2	Saturn at opposition
	11	18	Mercury in superior conjunction
	15	21	Pluto at opposition
	26	0	Jupiter at opposition
May	9	0	Mercury greatest elong. E. (21°)
	13	5	Mars stationary in R.A.
	21	10	Mercury stationary in R.A.
	24	3	Uranus at opposition
June	1	20	Mercury in inferior conjunction
	13	21	Mercury stationary in R.A.
	17	5	Neptune at opposition
	19	12	Saturn stationary in R.A.
June	21	17	Summer solstice
	26	14	Mercury greatest elong. W. (22°)
	28	8	Jupiter stationary in R.A.
July	4	13	Earth at aphelion
	6	8	Eclipse of Moon
	10	0	Mars 3°S. of Saturn
	11	16	Pluto stationary in R.A.
	20	19	Eclipse of Sun
	25	8	Mercury in superior conjunction
Aug.	9	12	Uranus stationary in R.A.
	10	1	Mars 2°S. of Jupiter
Sept.	6	1	Neptune stationary in R.A.
	6	4	Mercury greatest elong. E. (27°)
	19	7	Mercury stationary in R.A.
	22	13	Mars 1.5°S. of Uranus
	23	9	Autumnal equinox
Oct.	2	5	Mercury in inferior conjunction
	10	13	Mercury stationary in R.A.
	17	18	Mercury greatest elong. W. (18°)
	18	21	Saturn in conjunction with Sun
	20	14	Pluto in conjunction with Sun
	25	6	Mars 3° S. of Neptune
Nov.	1	6	Mercury 0.7°S. of Saturn
	4	2	Venus in superior conjunction
	13	14	Jupiter in conjunction with Sun
	19	18	Mercury in superior conjunction
	27	11	Uranus in conjunction with Sun
Dec.	8	13	Mercury 3°S. of Neptune
	19	0	Neptune in conjunction with Sun
	22	5	Winter solstice
	30	12	Eclipse of Moon
	30	19	Mercury greatest elong. E. (20°)

METEORS, METEORITES, AND METEOR SHOWERS

A *meteor* or "shooting star" appears momentarily in the sky when a particle from beyond the earth enters the earth's atmosphere at a high velocity. Most visible meteors are caused by particles smaller than a grape or marble, and these small particles are completely vaporized in the atmosphere at a height of about 80 km. A spectacular meteor, known as a *fire-ball,* is caused by a larger body which may fall to the earth's surface in one or more pieces. Particles seen thus to fall, or subsequently found by analysis to be of this nature, are called *meteorites.*

The Herzberg Institute of Astrophysics, National Research Council, maintains a Camera network called the "Meteorite Observation and Recovery Project" on the Canadian Prairies. The network was successful in photographing and promptly recovering the Innisfree meteorite in 1977.

Meteorites may be divided into two main classes—the irons, which are almost pure nickel-iron, and the stones. Any freshly-fallen meteorite is characterized by a dark, smooth crust caused by the fusion of the outer part.

Meteors may be observed on any clear, moonless night at an average rate of about five an hour. At times there occur *meteor showers,* when meteors are seen with much greater frequency and appear to radiate from a particular part of the sky which is called the *radiant.* This is an effect of perspective, the radiant being the vanishing point of the parallel tracks of the meteors. Meteor showers usually repeat themselves annually, and in some cases have been associated with the orbits of comets. When the earth passes through or near the orbit of a comet it can intercept the small particles (meteoroids) which cause meteors. The principal meteor showers for the northern hemisphere are listed below.

The study of meteors and meteorites adds to our knowledge of the nature and origin of the solar system and also to our knowledge of the earth's outer atmosphere.

PRINCIPAL ANNUAL METEOR SHOWERS FOR THE NORTHERN HEMISPHERE (UNIVERSAL TIME)

Shower	Location of Radiant	Date of Maximum Frequency	Hourly Number	Duration (in days)
Quadrantids	Bootes	Jan. 3	40	1
Lyrids	Lyra	Apr. 22	15	2
Eta Aquarids	Aquarius	May 4	20	3
Delta Aquarids	Aquarius	July 28	20	–
Perseids	Perseus	Aug. 12	50	5
Orionids	Orion	Oct. 21	25	2
Taurids	Taurus	Nov. 2	15	–
Leonids	Leo	Nov. 17	15	–
Geminids	Gemini	Dec. 13	50	3
Ursids	Ursa Minor	Dec. 22	15	2

ECLIPSES DURING 1982

In 1982 there will be seven eclipses, four of the sun and three of the moon.

1. **A total eclipse of the moon** on January 9, not generally visible in North America.

2. **A partial eclipse of the sun** on January 24-25, visible only in Antarctica.

3. **A partial eclipse of the sun** on June 21, visible only in South Africa.

4. **A total eclipse of the moon** on the night of July 5-6, visible throughout most of North America.

Moon enters penumbra	July 5	23 22.2 E.S.T.
Moon enters umbra	July 6	0 32.8 E.S.T.
Total eclipse begins		1 37.7 E.S.T.
Middle of eclipse		2 30.9 E.S.T.
Total eclipse ends		3 24.1 E.S.T.
Moon leaves umbra		4 29.0 E.S.T.
Moon leaves penumbra		5 39.6 E.S.T.

5. **A partial eclipse of the sun** on July 20, visible only in the arctic regions of North America.

6. **A partial eclipse of the sun** on December 15, visible in most of Europe, North Africa and parts of Asia.

7. **A total eclipse of the moon** on the night of December 29-30, visible throughout North America.

Moon enters penumbra	December 30	3 51.9 E.S.T.
Moon enters umbra		4 50.4 E.S.T.
Total eclipse begins		5 58.2 E.S.T.
Middle of eclipse		6 28.7 E.S.T.
Total eclipse ends		6 59.3 E.S.T.
Moon leaves umbra		8 07.0 E.S.T.
Moon leaves penumbra		9 05.5 E.S.T.

QUARTERLY STAR MAP

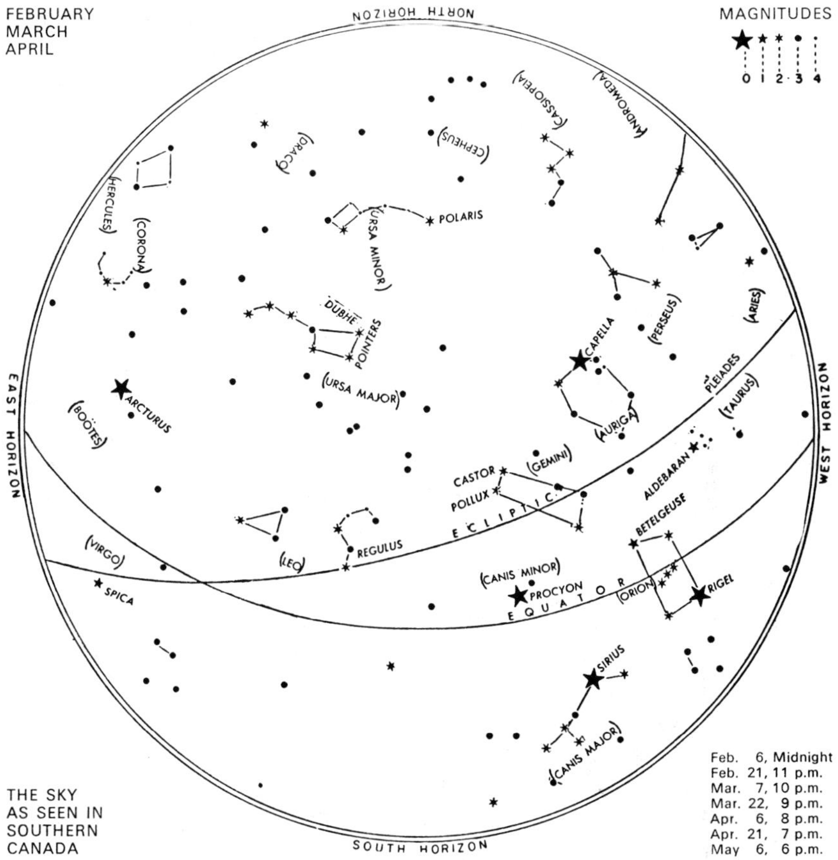

The centre of the map is the overhead point. The circumference is the horizon. To identify the stars, hold the map so that the part of the horizon you are facing is down. Constellation names are in brackets, other names are star names.

THE NAKED-EYE PLANETS FOR 1982

February

MERCURY can be seen at the end of the month, with great difficulty, very low in the east just before sunrise.

VENUS can be seen *very* low in the south-east just before sunrise.

MARS, in Virgo near *Spica*, rises in late evening and is low in the south-west at sunrise. Mars and Saturn are close; Mars is brighter and redder.

JUPITER, in Libra, rises in late evening and is in the south-west at sunrise.

SATURN, in Virgo near *Spica*, rises in mid-evening and is low in the south-west at sunrise. See also MARS above.

March

MERCURY can be seen at the beginning of the month, with great difficulty, very low in the east just before sunrise.

VENUS can be seen very low in the south-east just before sunrise.

MARS, in Virgo near *Spica*, rises in mid-evening and is very low in the south-west at sunrise. Mars and Saturn are close; Mars is brighter and redder.

JUPITER, in Libra, rises in mid-evening and is low in the south-west at sunrise.

SATURN, in Virgo near *Spica*, rises shortly after sunset and is very low in the south-west at sunrise.

April

MERCURY can be seen at the end of the month, low in the west just after sunset.

VENUS can be seen low in the south-east just before sunrise.

MARS, in Virgo, rises about sunset and sets about sunrise.

JUPITER, moving from Libra into Virgo, rises shortly after sunset and sets at sunrise.

SATURN, in Virgo near *Spica*, rises at sunset and sets at sunrise.

QUARTERLY STAR MAP

MAY
JUNE
JULY

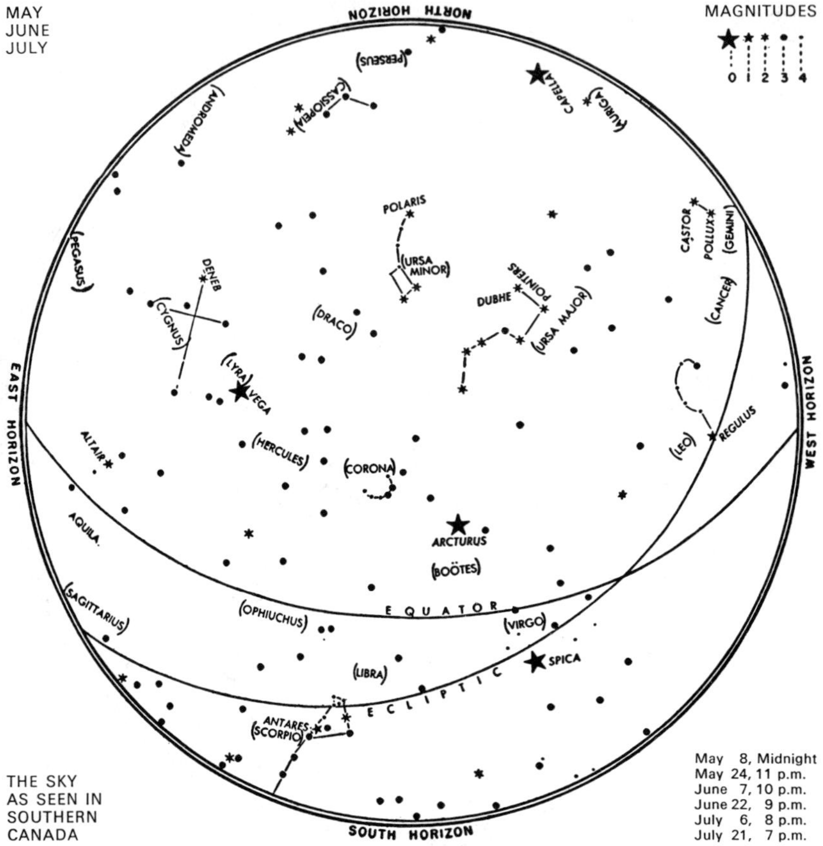

THE SKY
AS SEEN IN
SOUTHERN
CANADA

May 8, Midnight
May 24, 11 p.m.
June 7, 10 p.m.
June 22, 9 p.m.
July 6, 8 p.m.
July 21, 7 p.m.

The centre of the map is the overhead point. The circumference is the horizon. To identify the stars, hold the map so that the part of the horizon you are facing is down. Constellation names are in brackets, other names are star names.

THE NAKED-EYE PLANETS FOR 1982

May

MERCURY can be seen during the first half of the month, low in the west just after sunset.

VENUS can be seen very low in the south-east just before sunrise.

MARS, in Virgo, is high in the south-east at sunset and sets well before sunrise.

JUPITER, in Virgo, is in the south-east at sunset and sets shortly before sunrise.

SATURN, in Virgo near *Spica*, is well up in the south-east at sunset and sets an hour or two before sunrise.

June

MERCURY can be seen at the end of the month, very low in the east just before sunrise.

VENUS can be seen very low in the east, just before sunrise (higher and brighter than Mercury).

MARS, in Virgo, is in the south at sunset, and sets about 5 hours later. See also JUPITER below.

JUPITER, in Virgo, is in the south at sunset and sets shortly after midnight. It is east of Saturn and Mars.

SATURN, in Virgo near *Spica*, is in the south at sunset and sets at about midnight. See also JUPITER above.

July

MERCURY can be seen early in the month, very low in the east just before sunrise.

VENUS can be seen low in the east just before sunrise (higher and brighter than Mercury).

MARS, in Virgo, is well up in the south-west at sunset and sets about 3½ hours later. It passes just south of Saturn on the 10th and just north of *Spica* on the 21st.

JUPITER, in Virgo, is west of south at sunset, and sets before midnight. For the next month or so, Mars, Jupiter, Saturn and *Spica* form a line about 15° long.

SATURN, in Virgo near *Spica*, is in the south-west at sunset and sets about 3½ hours later. See also MARS and JUPITER above.

QUARTERLY STAR MAP

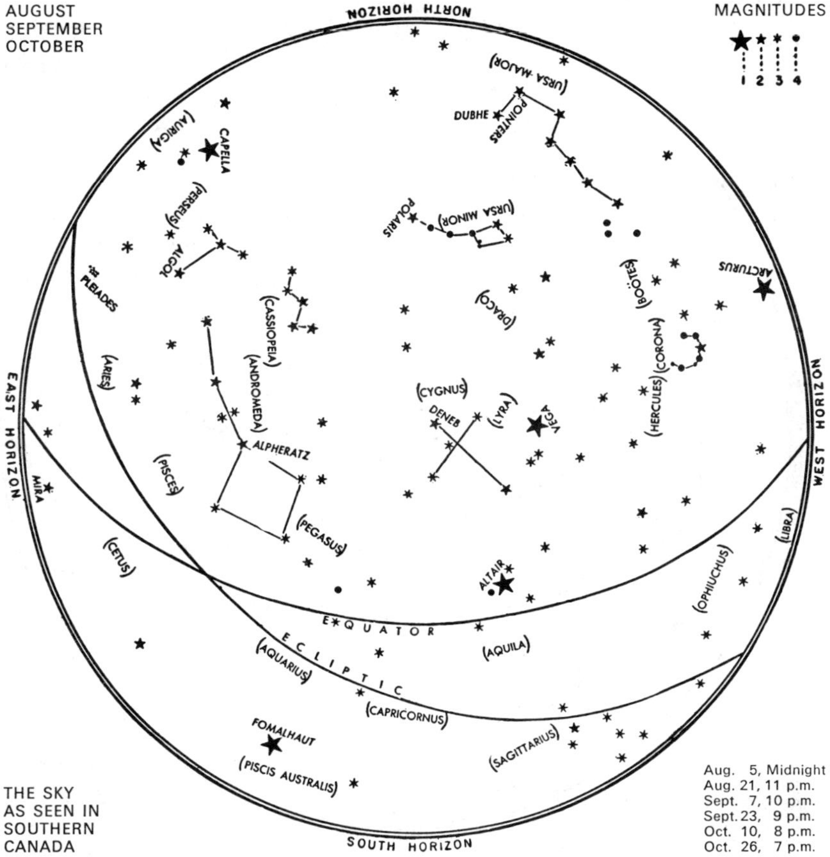

The centre of the map is the overhead point. The circumference is the horizon. To identify the stars, hold the map so that the part of the horizon you are facing is down. Constellation names are in brackets, other names are star names.

THE NAKED-EYE PLANETS FOR 1982

August	September	October
MERCURY may be seen at the end of the month, with very great difficulty, very low in the west just after sunset.	MERCURY may be seen at the beginning of the month, with very great difficulty, very low in the west just after sunset.	MERCURY can be seen starting in middle of the month, very low in the east just before sunrise.
VENUS can be seen low in the east just before sunrise.	VENUS can be seen at the beginning of the month, very low in the east just before sunrise.	VENUS is too close to the sun to be seen.
MARS, moving from Virgo into Libra, is low in the south-west at sunset and sets about 2½ hours later. Around the 10th, it passes 2° south of Jupiter.	MARS, moving from libra through Scorpius into Ophiuchus, is very low in the south-west at sunset, and sets about 2 hours later.	MARS, moving from Ophiuchus into Sagittarius late in the month, is very low in the south-west at sunset, and sets about 2 hours later.
JUPITER, in Virgo, is low in the south-west at sunset and sets about 2½ hours later. See also MARS above.	JUPITER, moving from Virgo into Libra early in the month, is very low in the south-west at sunset and sets about 2 hours later.	JUPITER, in Libra, may be seen at the beginning of the month, with great difficulty, very low in the south-west just after sunset.
SATURN, in Virgo near *Spica*, is low in the south-west at sunset and sets about 2 hours later.	SATURN, in Virgo, may be seen with great difficulty, very low in the south-west just after sunset.	SATURN is too close to the sun to be seen.

QUARTERLY STAR MAP

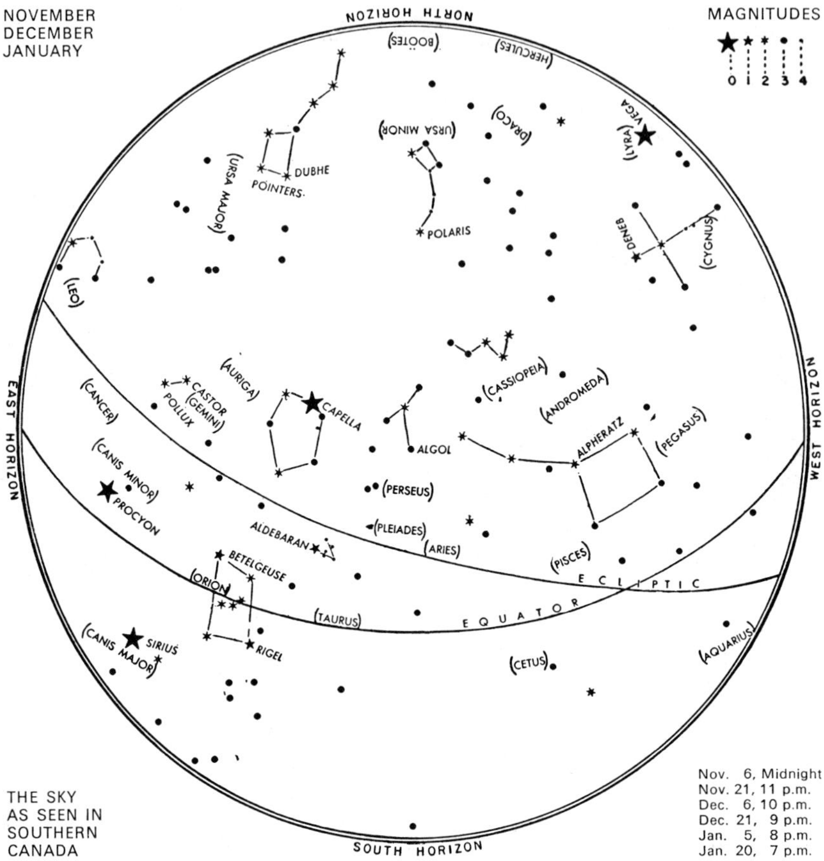

The centre of the map is the overhead point. The circumference is the horizon. To identify the stars, hold the map so that the part of the horizon you are facing is down. Constellation names are in brackets, other names are star names.

THE NAKED-EYE PLANETS FOR 1982

November	December	January 1983
MERCURY can be seen at the beginning of the month, very low in the south-east just before sunrise. It passes just south of Saturn on the 1st.	MERCURY can be seen at the end of the month, very low in the south-west just after sunset.	MERCURY can be seen at the beginning of the month, very low in the south-west just after sunset.
VENUS is too close to the sun to be seen.	VENUS may be seen at the end of the month with great difficulty, very low in the south-west just after sunset.	VENUS can be seen very low in the south-west, just after sunset.
MARS, in Sagittarius, is low in the south-west at sunset, and sets about 2½ hours later.	MARS, moving from Sagittarius into Capricornus, is low in the south-west at sunset and sets about 3 hours later.	MARS, moving from Capricornus into Aquarius, is low in the south-west at sunset and sets about 2½ hours later.
JUPITER is too close to the sun to be seen.	JUPITER, moving from Libra into Scorpius, can be seen at the end of the month, very low in the south-east just before sunrise.	JUPITER, in Scorpius, can be seen low in the south-east just before sunrise.
SATURN, in Virgo, can be seen low in the south-east just before sunrise. See also MERCURY above.	SATURN, in Virgo, rises a few hours before the sun and is well up in the south-east at sunrise.	SATURN, in Virgo, rises shortly after midnight and is in the south at sunrise.

MAGNETIC DECLINATION

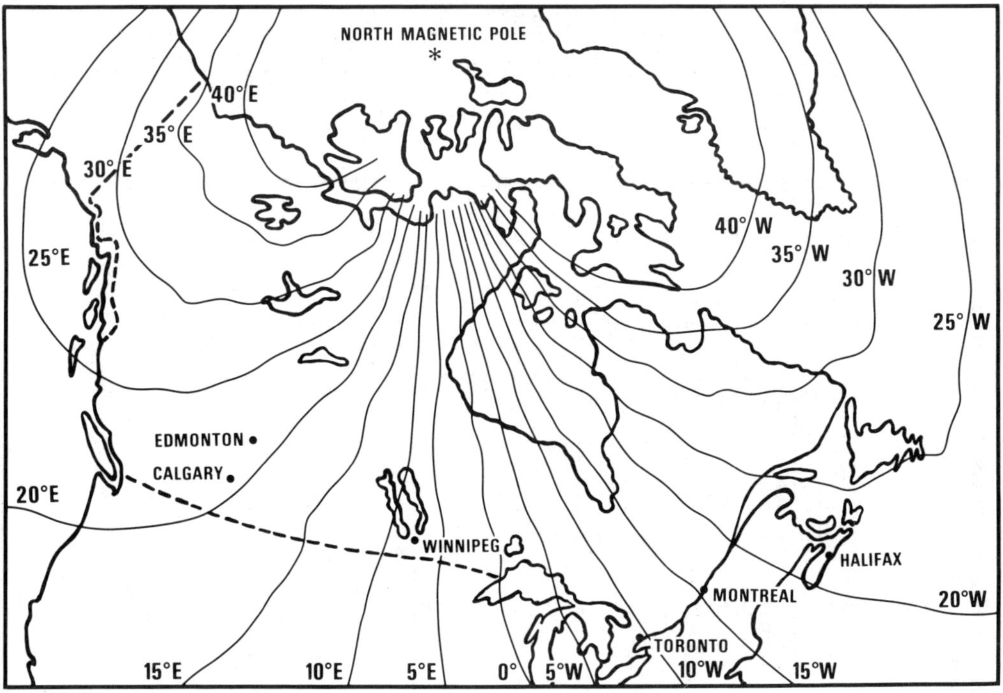

CHART OF MAGNETIC DECLINATION

A compass needle, even when unaffected by extraneous magnetic fields, does not in general point due north. The amount and direction by which its direction differs from true north is called magnetic declination or variation. The declination varies with the position of the observer and also varies slowly with time. The above chart gives the values of declination over Canada as of 1980.

Example: What is the direction of the compass needle at the southern tip of Lake Manitoba?

From the chart this point is about ¾ of the way from the line of 5°E declination towards the line of 10°E declination. Therefore the declination is 9°E, i.e., the needle points 9° east of true north.

The Isogonic Map of Canada MCR 701 (1980), revised every 5 years, a large map showing lines of Equal Magnetic Declination and Annual Change is obtainable from the Canada Map Office, 615 Booth St., Ottawa, Ont. K1A 0E9. Price $2.00 each.

TEMPERATURE AND PRECIPITATION DATA FOR REPRESENTATIVE STATIONS IN CANADA

AVERAGE OVER PERIOD 1941-1970

STATION (A = Airport)	Elevation Ft.	TEMPERATURE °C Mean Daily Ann.	Jan.	Apr.	July	Oct.	Extreme Max.*	Min.*	Average Frost Dates Last in Spring	First in Fall	AVERAGE TOTAL PRECIPITATION (mm.)‡ Jan.	Feb.	Mar.	Apr.	May	June	July	Aug.	Sept.	Oct.	Nov.	Dec.	Ann.	Aver. Am Snowfall (cm.)†
St. John's A Nfld.	463	4.9	−3.8	1.1	15.3	7.1	31	−23	June 3	Oct. 12	145.0	156.2	132.6	114.1	99.1	88.7	83.1	113.3	112.0	138.7	161.3	167.4	1511.5	363.9
Charlottetown A P.E.I.	186	5.5	−6.7	2.3	18.4	8.6	34	−28	May 17	Oct. 15	110.7	95.0	84.6	82.0	82.0	83.1	73.2	92.5	86.4	96.8	125.7	115.8	1127.8	305.6
Halifax Int. A N.S.	461	6.0	−5.9	2.9	18.1	9.0	34	−26	May 15	Oct. 15	136.9	127.5	103.6	108.0	98.6	79.0	79.5	108.0	94.5	118.4	163.1	178.6	1405.0	300.0
Sydney A N.S.	197	6.0	−4.4	2.2	17.9	8.9	35	−25	May 23	Oct. 16	137.2	118.6	119.4	95.3	99.6	80.8	78.5	99.6	99.1	111.8	161.3	139.7	1340.9	288.1
Yarmouth A N.S.	136	7.0	−2.7	4.6	16.4	9.8	30	−21	May 2	Oct. 24	140.7	115.8	101.9	98.6	100.8	87.4	73.9	96.5	86.1	108.5	138.9	134.1	1282.7	204.5
Chatham A N.B.	112	4.9	−9.3	2.9	19.2	7.5	38	−35	May 22	Sept. 21	97.0	90.7	83.8	75.7	80.3	83.6	75.7	83.6	87.1	88.4	112.3	93.0	1051.0	309.4
Fredericton A N.B.	74	5.5	−8.8	4.2	19.2	7.8	37	−37	May 21	Sept. 26	95.3	92.5	69.1	73.9	81.3	79.3	88.1	87.6	81.8	88.1	109.2	114.1	1060.3	28.4
Saint John A N.B.	352	5.0	−7.4	3.1	16.9	7.9	33	−37	May 18	Oct. 2	145.0	130.8	104.7	111.8	101.9	94.5	89.4	98.8	102.6	109.7	154.4	156.7	1400.3	296.7
Arvida, P.Q.	335	3.1	−15.0	2.8	18.4	6.6	36	−42	May 22	Sept. 19	68.1	60.5	51.1	50.6	66.3	94.5	115.3	90.2	101.1	74.9	73.7	79.3	924.8	278.1
Father Point, P.Q.	25	2.9	−10.9	1.7	15.4	6.0	32	−36	May 19	Sept. 28	58.4	53.9	49.0	53.3	69.1	106.2	124.5	100.3	106.9	77.0	73.9	73.4	945.1	272.0
Knob Lake, P.Q.	1681	−4.6	−22.7	−6.9	12.6	−0.9	32	−51	June 18	Aug. 31	41.2	36.6	36.8	34.8	44.7	79.0	88.7	98.0	82.8	70.1	63.8	46.0	721.5	335.5
Montreal Int. A P.Q.	98	6.5	−9.9	5.9	21.2	9.4	36	−38	May 5	Oct. 7	75.7	70.9	70.6	73.7	67.1	83.1	85.1	86.6	80.0	74.9	87.1	86.4	941.2	239.6
Quebec A P.Q.	245	4.4	−11.6	3.3	19.2	7.2	36	−36	May 18	Sept. 28	85.9	76.7	69.3	74.7	80.8	101.9	107.7	102.6	105.7	82.3	99.6	101.4	1088.6	326.7
Sherbrooke A P.Q.	782	4.0	−11.6	3.6	16.5	7.0	37	−39	June 1	Sept. 11	74.4	71.6	75.2	79.3	83.6	105.9	110.2	96.5	98.3	90.4	93.7	86.4	1065.5	279.3
Kapuskasing A Ont.	752	0.8	−18.2	0.7	17.0	5.3	36	−44	June 13	Sept. 5	53.3	47.5	53.9	55.9	79.3	85.3	95.5	92.2	92.2	78.2	87.4	55.9	871.2	321.8
London A Ont.	912	7.5	−6.0	6.6	20.5	9.9	37	−32	May 9	Oct. 6	76.2	65.3	71.9	78.2	74.9	81.0	81.3	73.4	78.7	74.2	82.8	86.6	924.5	201.1
Ottawa Int. A Ont.	413	5.8	−10.9	5.6	20.7	8.7	38	−36	May 11	Oct. 1	59.9	56.9	61.0	67.6	70.1	72.6	81.3	81.5	78.7	65.8	78.5	77.0	850.9	215.9
Thunder Bay A Ont.	644	2.4	−14.8	2.4	17.5	6.1	36	−41	May 31	Sept. 10	48.0	30.2	43.7	56.4	74.7	82.8	71.1	87.9	83.6	56.9	57.2	46.0	738.5	222.1
Toronto Ont.	379	8.9	−4.4	7.6	21.8	11.2	41	−33	Apr. 20	Oct. 30	62.5	56.6	65.5	67.3	72.9	63.0	80.8	67.3	61.2	61.5	67.3	64.0	789.9	141.1
Churchill A Man.	115	−7.3	−27.6	−11.0	12.0	−1.0	33	−45	June 22	Sept. 12	14.0	13.0	17.8	24.1	28.2	40.1	49.0	57.7	52.1	40.4	40.1	20.1	396.2	183.9
The Pas A Man.	894	−0.6	−22.4	−0.4	17.9	3.8	37	−49	May 28	Sept. 20	18.5	16.5	20.6	25.4	37.9	59.2	72.4	61.5	55.1	30.7	29.0	22.9	449.6	157.2
Winnipeg Int. A Man.	786	2.3	−18.3	3.3	19.7	6.6	41	−45	May 25	Sept. 21	23.6	19.1	26.2	37.3	57.2	80.3	80.3	73.7	52.6	34.8	27.2	22.9	535.2	131.3
Prince Albert A. Sask.	1414	0.1	−21.1	1.7	17.7	3.9	38	−50	June 5	Sept. 7	17.3	16.8	18.8	24.1	35.8	57.2	64.3	53.1	34.8	24.1	20.6	22.1	388.7	124.5
Regina A Sask.	1884	2.1	−17.3	3.3	18.9	5.3	43	−50	May 27	Sept. 12	18.0	17.3	18.3	23.4	40.9	82.6	57.9	49.8	36.3	19.1	18.0	16.3	397.9	114.8
Beaverlodge CDA Alta.	2500	1.8	−14.9	2.6	15.6	4.5	37	−48	May 22	Sept. 7	32.0	29.2	23.1	22.1	15.8	61.7	64.3	57.4	38.9	26.4	30.7	27.7	454.7	183.6
Calgary Int. A Alta.	3540	3.4	−10.9	3.3	16.5	5.7	36	−45	May 28	Sept. 12	17.0	19.8	20.3	29.5	49.8	91.7	68.3	55.9	35.3	18.8	16.0	14.7	437.1	153.9
Edmonton Int. A Alta.	2219	2.8	−14.7	4.0	17.5	5.4	34	−48	May 14	Sept. 19	25.2	20.1	16.8	23.4	37.3	74.7	83.3	71.6	35.8	18.5	18.5	21.3	446.5	132.1
Kamloops A B.C.	1133	8.4	−6.0	9.3	20.9	8.4	39	−37	May 5	Sept. 28	32.5	25.7	25.2	20.3	23.4	31.2	29.7	22.4	21.1	26.2	27.2	35.3	320.2	78.6
Prince George A B.C.	2218	3.2	−11.8	3.9	14.9	4.7	34	−50	June 10	Aug 28	59.2	42.9	31.5	29.5	42.2	58.2	57.9	73.4	55.9	61.0	54.9	54.1	620.7	233.4
Prince Rupert A B.C.	110	6.8	0.1	5.3	12.8	8.2	32	−21	May 8	Oct. 20	214.1	208.8	180.3	183.9	122.7	107.2	120.9	147.1	241.8	359.0	269.2	259.3	2428.0	113.0
Vancouver Int. A B.C.	16	9.8	2.4	8.9	17.4	10.1	33	−18	Mar. 31	Oct. 30	147.3	116.6	93.7	61.0	47.5	45.2	29.7	37.1	61.2	122.2	141.2	165.4	1068.1	52.4
Victoria Gonzales HTS B.C.	228	10.1	4.1	9.3	15.7	10.9	35	−16	Feb. 28	Dec. 9	106.9	75.7	49.0	34.3	21.3	21.3	12.5	19.6	33.0	73.9	94.7	114.8	657.0	32.8
Dawson Y.T.	1062	−4.7	−28.6	−1.8	15.5	−3.2	35	−58	May 26	Aug. 27	19.3	16.0	12.7	9.1	21.8	36.8	53.1	50.6	28.5	26.7	25.2	25.7	325.1	136.3
Whitehorse A Y.T.	2289	−0.9	−18.9	−0.1	14.1	0.7	34	−52	June 5	Sept. 1	18.5	14.0	14.7	10.7	13.5	28.7	33.3	36.1	29.0	19.8	22.4	19.6	260.3	127.8
Aklavik N.W.T.	30	−8.9	−28.6	−12.7	13.8	−7.1	34	−52	June 12	Aug. 30	11.9	10.7	11.2	8.1	8.1	18.3	33.8	36.1	20.1	32.3	21.1	24.4	236.0	136.9
Frobisher Bay A N.W.T.	68	−9.0	−26.2	−14.2	7.9	−4.7	24	−46	June 30	Aug. 29	24.4	27.9	20.6	22.4	22.9	37.9	53.1	57.9	43.4	41.7	36.8	26.2	414.0	246.9
Resolute A N.W.T.	209	−16.4	−32.6	−23.1	4.3	−14.7	18	−52	July 10	July 20	2.8	3.3	3.1	5.8	8.6	12.5	26.4	30.5	17.8	15.2	5.6	4.8	136.4	78.7
Yellowknife A N.W.T.	682	−5.6	−28.6	−7.8	16.0	−1.2	32	−51	May 30	Sept. 16	13.7	12.2	11.7	10.2	14.0	17.3	33.3	36.3	28.2	30.7	23.9	18.5	249.9	119.4

*Temperature extremes are for the total period of record to 1970. †1 in. = 25.4 mm. = 2.54 cm.

PERPETUAL CALENDAR FOR TWO THOUSAND YEARS

From January 1st 1 A.D. to December 31st 2000 A.D.

Find the Year of the Century, and for reference to the Indices below see Right-hand Columns under heading for the Century.

																		A.D. 1-100 701-800 1401-1500 1752-1800	A.D. 101-200 801-900 1501-1600	A.D. 201-300 901-1000 1601-1700 1801-1900	A.D. 301-400 1001-1100 1701-1752	A.D. 401-500 1101-1200 1901-2000	A.D. 501-600 1201-1300	A.D. 601-700 1301-1400
01	07	12	18		29	35	40	46		57	63	68	74		85	91	96	E	D	C	B	A	G	F
02		13	19	24	30		41	47	52	58		69	75	80	86		97	F	E	D	C	B	A	G
03	08	14		25	31	36	42		53	59	64	70		81	87	92	98	G	F	E	D	C	B	A
	09	15	20	26		37	43	48	54		65	71	76	82		93	99	A	G	F	E	D	C	B
04	10		21	27	32	38		49	55	60	66		77	83	88	94	100*	B	A	G	F	E	D	C
05	11	16	22		33	39	44	50		61	67	72	78		89	95	100†	C	B	A	G	F	E	D
06		17	23	28	34		45	51	56	62		73	79	84	90			D	C	B	A	G	F	E

*For use only for the years 1800 and 1900.
†For use for all 100th years except 1800 and 1900.

On September 14th, 1752, the New Style, or Gregorian Reform, Calendar came into use, September 3rd-13th being omitted from the almanac.

INDICES							January of Common Years	January of Leap Years	February of Common Years	February of Leap Years	March	April	May
A	B	C	D	E	F	G							
M	Tu	W	Th	F	Sa	Su	7 14 21 28	1 8 15 22 29	4 11 18 25	5 12 19 26	4 11 18 25	1 8 15 22 29	6 13 20 27
Tu	W	Th	F	Sa	Su	M	1 8 15 22 29	2 9 16 23 30	5 12 19 26	6 13 20 27	5 12 19 26	2 9 16 23 30	7 14 21 28
W	Th	F	Sa	Su	M	Tu	2 9 16 23 30	3 10 17 24 31	6 13 20 27	7 14 21 28	6 13 20 27	3 10 17 24	1 8 15 22 29
Th	F	Sa	Su	M	Tu	W	3 10 17 24 31	4 11 18 25	7 14 21 28	1 8 15 22 29	7 14 21 28	4 11 18 25	2 9 16 23 30
F	Sa	Su	M	Tu	W	Th	4 11 18 25	5 12 19 26	1 8 15 22	2 9 16 23	1 8 15 22 29	5 12 19 26	3 10 17 24 31
Sa	Su	M	Tu	W	Th	F	5 12 19 26	6 13 20 27	2 9 16 23	3 10 17 24	2 9 16 23 30	6 13 20 27	4 11 18 25
Su	M	Tu	W	Th	F	Sa	6 13 20 27	7 14 21 28	3 10 17 24	4 11 18 25	3 10 17 24 31	7 14 21 28	5 12 19 26

Example: *September 12th, 1759*
Under heading "1752-1800", and in line with the year of the century (59th), find the letter G. Index G is then the key to the whole of the Calendar for the year 1759, and this key shows that September 12th was on a Wednesday.

Copyright in Canada, Great Britain and the United States of America, by J. Thornton Cook

PERPETUAL CALENDAR FOR TWO THOUSAND YEARS—*Continued*

From January 1st 1 A.D. to December 31st 2000 A.D.

Find the Year of the Century, and for reference to the Indices below see Right-hand Columns under heading for the Century.

																		A.D. 1-100 701-800 1401-1500 1752-1800	A.D. 101-200 801-900 1501-1600	A.D. 201-300 901-1000 1601-1700 1801-1900	A.D. 301-400 1001-1100 1701-1752	A.D. 401-500 1101-1200 1901-2000	A.D. 501-600 1201-1300	A.D. 601-700 1301-1400
01	07	12	18		29	35	40	46		57	63	68	74		85	91	96	E	D	C	B	A	G	F
02		13	19	24	30		41	47	52	58		69	75	80	86		97	F	E	D	C	B	A	G
03	08	14		25	31	36	42		53	59	64	70		81	87	92	98	G	F	E	D	C	B	A
	09	15	20	26		37	43	48	54		65	71	76	82		93	99	A	G	F	E	D	C	B
04	10		21	27	32	38		49	55	60	66		77	83	88	94	100*	B	A	G	F	E	D	C
05	11	16	22		33	39	44	50		61	67	72	78		89	95	100†	C	B	A	G	F	E	D
06		17	23	28	34		45	51	56	62		73	79	84	90			D	C	B	A	G	F	E

*For use only for the years 1800 and 1900.
†For use for all 100th years except 1800 and 1900.

On September 14th, 1752, the New Style, Gregorian Reform, Calendar came into use, September 3rd-13th being omitted from the almanac.

INDICES													
A	B	C	D	E	F	G	June	July	August	September	October	November	December
M	Tu	W	Th	F	Sa	Su	3 10 17 24	1 8 15 22 29	5 12 19 26	2 9 16 23 30	7 14 21 28	4 11 18 25	2 9 16 23 30
Tu	W	Th	F	Sa	Su	M	4 11 18 25	2 9 16 23 30	6 13 20 27	3 10 17 24	1 8 15 22 29	5 12 19 26	3 10 17 24 31
W	Th	F	Sa	Su	M	Tu	5 12 19 26	3 10 17 24 31	7 14 21 28	4 11 18 25	2 9 16 23 30	6 13 20 27	4 11 18 25
Th	F	Sa	Su	M	Tu	W	6 13 20 27	4 11 18 25	1 8 15 22 29	5 12 19 26	3 10 17 24 31	7 14 21 28	5 12 19 26
F	Sa	Su	M	Tu	W	Th	7 14 21 28	5 12 19 26	2 9 16 23 30	6 13 20 27	4 11 18 25	1 8 15 22 29	6 13 20 27
Sa	Su	M	Tu	W	Th	F	1 8 15 22 29	6 13 20 27	3 10 17 24 31	7 14 21 28	5 12 19 26	2 9 16 23 30	7 14 21 28
Su	M	Tu	W	Th	F	Sa	2 9 16 23 30	7 14 21 28	4 11 18 25	1 8 15 22 29	6 13 20 27	3 10 17 24	1 8 15 22 29

Example: *September 12th, 1759*
Under heading "1752-1800", and in line with the year of the century (59th), find the letter G. Index G is then the key to the whole of the Calendar for the year 1759, and this key shows that September 12th was on a Wednesday.

Copyright in Canada, Great Britain and the United States of America, by J. Thornton Cook

ANNIVERSARIES AND HOLIDAYS

TABLE OF MOVABLE ECCLESIASTICAL FEASTS FOR A FIXED NUMBER OF YEARS

Year	Septuagesima Sunday	Ash Wednesday	Easter Sunday	Ascension Day (Thurs.)	Whit Sunday or Pentecost	Corpus Christi (Thurs.)	Sundays between Pentecost and Advent	First Sunday of Advent
1971	Feb. 7	Feb. 24	Apr. 11	May 20	May 30	June 10	25	Nov. 28
*1972	Jan. 30	Feb. 16	Apr. 2	May 11	May 21	June 1	27	Dec. 3
1973	Feb. 18	Mar. 7	Apr. 22	May 31	June 10	June 21	24	Dec. 2
1974	Feb. 10	Feb. 27	Apr. 14	May 23	June 2	June 13	25	Dec. 1
1975	Jan. 26	Feb. 12	Mar. 30	May 8	May 18	May 29	27	Nov. 30
*1976	Feb. 15	Mar. 3	Apr. 18	May 27	June 6	June 17	24	Nov. 28
1977	Feb. 6	Feb. 23	Apr. 10	May 10	May 29	June 9	25	Nov. 27
1978	Jan. 22	Feb. 8	Mar. 26	May 4	May 14	May 25	28	Dec. 3
1979	Feb. 11	Feb. 28	Apr. 15	May 24	June 3	June 14	25	Dec. 2
*1980	Feb. 3	Feb. 20	Apr. 6	May 15	May 25	June 5	26	Nov. 30
1981	Feb. 15	Mar. 4	Apr. 19	May 28	June 7	June 18	24	Nov. 29
1982	Feb. 7	Feb. 24	Apr. 11	May 20	May 30	June 10	25	Nov. 28
1983	Jan. 30	Feb. 16	Apr. 3	May 12	May 22	June 2	26	Nov. 27
*1984	Feb. 19	Mar. 7	Apr. 22	May 31	June 10	June 21	24	Dec. 2
1985	Feb. 3	Feb. 20	Apr. 7	May 16	May 26	June 6	26	Dec. 1
1986	Jan. 26	Feb. 12	Mar. 30	May 8	May 18	May 29	27	Nov. 30
1987	Feb. 15	Mar. 4	Apr. 19	May 28	June 7	June 18	24	Nov. 29
*1988	Jan. 31	Feb. 17	Apr. 3	May 12	May 22	June 2	26	Nov. 27
1989	Jan. 22	Feb. 8	Mar. 26	May 4	May 14	May 25	28	Dec. 3
1990	Feb. 11	Feb. 28	Apr. 15	May 24	June 3	June 14	25	Dec. 2

Days before Easter				Days after Easter			
Septuagesima Sunday	63	Quadragesima Sunday	42	Low Sunday	7	Whit Sunday	49
Quinquagesima Sunday	49	Palm Sunday	7	Rogation Sunday	35	Trinity Sunday	56
Ash Wednesday	46	Good Friday	2	Ascension Day	39	Corpus Christi	60

The First Sunday in Advent is the fourth Sunday before Christmas Day, and is therefore the nearest Sunday to November 30.
*Leap Years

FIXED AND MOVABLE FESTIVALS AND ANNIVERSARIES
(Gregorian Calendar)

(For dates of the Festivals of the Eastern Orthodox Church (based on the Julian Calendar) *Easter and other ecclesiastical feasts see Index. For Public Statutory Holidays, see Index.)*

	1982	1983	1984
JANUARY begins on	Fri.	Sat.	Sun.
New Year's Day	Jan. 1	Jan. 1	Jan. 1
Circumcision	Jan. 1	Jan. 1	Jan. 1
†Mary Mother of God	Jan. 1	Jan. 1	Jan. 1
†Solemnity of Epiphany	Jan. 3	Jan. 2	Jan. 8
Epiphany	Jan. 6	Jan. 6	Jan. 6
Church Unity Week begins on	Jan. 17	Jan. 16	Jan. 15
FEBRUARY begins on	Mon.	Tue.	Wed.
Accession of Queen Elizabeth II (1952)	Feb. 6	Feb. 6	Feb. 6
Ash Wednesday	Feb. 24	Feb. 16	Mar. 7
First Sunday of Lent	Feb. 28	Feb. 20	Mar. 11
MARCH begins on	Mon.	Tue.	Thu.
St. David	Mar. 1	Mar. 1	Mar. 1
World Day of Prayer	Mar. 5	Mar. 4	Mar. 2
St. Patrick	Mar. 17	Mar. 17	Mar. 17
St. Joseph (Patron Saint of Canada)	Mar. 19	Mar. 19	Mar. 19
Annunciation	Mar. 25	Mar. 25	Mar. 25
APRIL begins on	Thu.	Fri.	Sun.
Palm Sunday	April 4	Mar. 27	April 15
First Day of Passover (Pesach)	April 8	Mar. 29	April 17
Good Friday	April 9	April 1	April 20
Easter Sunday	April 11	April 3	April 22
Birthday of Queen Elizabeth (1926)	April 21	April 21	April 21
St. George	April 23	April 23	April 23
MAY begins on	Sat.	Sun.	Tue.
Rogation Sunday	May 16	May 8	May 27
Ascension	May 20	May 12	May 31
†Ascension Sunday	May 23	May 15	June 3
Victoria Day	May 24	May 23	May 21
Pentecost (Whitsunday)	May 30	May 22	June 10

	1982	1983	1984
JUNE begins on	Tue.	Wed.	Fri.
Trinity Sunday	June 6	May 29	June 17
Corpus Christi (Sunday)	June 13	June 5	June 24
Sacred Heart of Jesus	June 18	June 10	June 29
St. John Baptist	June 24	June 24	June 24
St. Peter and St. Paul	June 29	June 29	June 29
JULY begins on	Thu.	Fri.	Sun.
Dominion Day	July 1	July 1	July 1
AUGUST begins on	Sun.	Mon.	Wed.
Birthday of Queen Mother Elizabeth	Aug. 4	Aug. 4	Aug. 4
Transfiguration	Aug. 6	Aug. 6	Aug. 6
Assumption	Aug. 15	Aug. 15	Aug. 15
SEPTEMBER begins on	Wed.	Thu.	Sat.
Labour Day	Sept. 6	Sept. 5	Sept. 3
Hebrew New Year	Sept. 18	Sept. 8	Sept. 27
Day of Atonement (Yom Kippur)	Sept. 27	Sept. 17	Oct. 6
St. Michael	Sept. 29	Sept. 29	Sept. 29
OCTOBER begins on	Fri.	Sat.	Mon.
First Day of Feast of Tabernacles (Succuoth)	Oct. 2	Sept. 22	Oct. 11
Thanksgiving	Oct. 11	Oct. 10	Oct. 8
NOVEMBER begins on	Mon.	Tue.	Thu.
All Saints Day	Nov. 1	Nov. 1	Nov. 1
Remembrance Day	Nov. 11	Nov. 11	Nov. 11
First Sunday of Advent	Nov. 28	Nov. 27	Dec. 2
St. Andrew	Nov. 30	Nov. 30	Nov. 30
DECEMBER begins on	Wed.	Thu.	Sat.
First Day of Hanukah	Dec. 11	Dec. 1	Dec. 19
Christmas Day	Dec. 25	Dec. 25	Dec. 25
Last Day of Year (Dec. 31)	Fri.	Sat.	Mon.

†Revised Roman Catholic Liturgical Calendar – Years B:C:A:B.

PUBLIC STATUTORY HOLIDAYS IN CANADA

DOMINION OF CANADA.—

In accordance with the provisions of the Interpretation Act, the Bills of Exchange Act, and the Holidays Act, the holidays to be observed throughout Canada are as follows:

"(a) In all the provinces of Canada,

Sundays,	Dominion Day,
New Year's Day,	Labour Day,
Remembrance Day,	Good Friday,
Thanksgiving Day,	Easter Monday,
Christmas Day,	Victoria Day,

the birthday (or the day fixed by proclamation for the celebration of the birthday) of the reigning sovereign,

any day appointed by proclamation to be observed as a public holiday, or as a day of general prayer or mourning or day of public rejoicing or thanksgiving, throughout Canada,

(c) In any one of the provinces of Canada, any day appointed by proclamation of the Lieutenant-Governor of such province for a public holiday, or for a fast or thanksgiving within the same, and any non-juridical day by virtue of a statute of such province;

(d) In any city, town, municipality or other organized district, any day appointed as a civic holiday by resolution of the council, or other statutory body charged with the administration of the civic or municipal affairs of the city, town, municipality or district."

The Public Service Terms and Conditions of Employment Regulations further provide for one day in each year that, in the opinion of the deputy head, is recognized to be a provincial or civic holiday in the area in which an employee is employed or, in any area where, in the opinion of the deputy head, no day is recognized as a provincial or civic holiday, such other day as may be determined by the deputy head.

PROVINCIAL HOLIDAYS generally coincide with the Dominion list with the following additions:

BRITISH COLUMBIA, British Columbia Day, Aug. 7.

MANITOBA, Civic Holiday (usually first Monday in August).

NEWFOUNDLAND, (Holidays are usually observed on the nearest Monday to the anniversary date): St. Patrick's Day (Mar. 13); St. George's Day (Apr. 24); Commonwealth Day (May 24, or nearest Mon.); Discovery Day (June 26); Memorial Day; Orangemen's Day (July 10).

ONTARIO, Civic Holiday (usually first Monday in August)

QUEBEC, Quebec Day (June 24); any other day fixed by proclamation of the lieutenant governor in council.

SASKATCHEWAN, Civic Holiday (first Monday in August).

YUKON, Discovery Day (being the third Monday in August).

NORTHWEST TERRITORIES, Civic Holiday (usually first Monday in August).

SPECIAL DAYS IN 1982

New Year's Day	Friday	Jan.	1
Good Friday	Friday	Apr.	9
Easter Monday	Monday	Apr.	12
Victoria Day and the Sovereign's Birthday	Monday	May	24
Dominion Day	Thursday	July	1
Labour Day	Monday	Sept.	6
Thanksgiving Day	Monday	Oct.	11
Remembrance Day	Thursday	Nov.	11
Christmas Day	Saturday	Dec	25

When New Year's Day, Christmas Day, Dominion Day fall on Sunday the following day is observed as the holiday.

NATIONAL HOLIDAYS

Afghanistan -- National Day, Apr. 27
Algeria -- National Day, Nov. 1
Angola -- National Day, Nov. 11
Arab Republic of Egypt -- National Day, July 23
Argentina -- May Revolution, May 25
Australia -- Australia Day, Jan. 26
Austria -- National Day, Oct. 26
Bahamas -- Independence Day, July 10
Bahrain -- National Day, Dec. 16
Bangladesh -- Independence Day, Mar. 26
Barbados -- Independence Day, Nov. 30
Belgium -- Accession of King Leopold I, July 21
Benin -- National Day, Nov. 30
Bolivia -- Independence Day, Aug. 6
Botswana -- Independence Day, Sept. 30
Brazil -- Independence Day, Sept. 7
Britain -- See United Kingdom
Bulgaria -- National Liberation Day, Sept. 9
Burma -- Independence Day, Jan. 4
Burundi -- National Day, July 1
Cameroon -- National Day, May 20
Canada -- Dominion Day, July 1
Cape Verde -- National Day, July 5
Central African Republic -- Proclamation of Republic, Dec. 1
Chad -- National Day, Apr. 13
Chile -- Independence Day, Sept. 18
China (People's Republic) -- National Day, Oct. 1
Colombia -- Independence Day, July 20
Comoros -- National Day, July 6
Congo (Brazzaville) -- National Day, Aug. 15
Costa Rica -- Independence Day, Sept. 15
Cuba -- Day of Liberation, Jan. 1
Cyprus -- National Day, Oct. 1
Czechoslovakia -- National Day, May 9
Denmark -- Birthday of Her Majesty Queen Margrethe II, Apr. 16
Djibouti -- National Day, June 27
Dominica -- National Day, Nov. 3
Dominican Republic -- Independence Day, Feb. 27
Ecuador -- Independence Day, Aug. 10
El Salvador -- Independence Day, Sept. 15
Ethiopia -- National Day, Sept. (various)
European Communities -- Anniversary of the declaration of President Schuman, May 9
Fiji -- National Day, Oct. 10
Finland -- Independence Day, Dec. 6
France -- Bastille Day, July 14
Gabon -- National Day, Aug. 17
The Gambia -- Independence Day, Feb. 18
German Democratic Republic -- National Day, Oct. 7
German Federal Republic -- National Day, May 23
Ghana -- Independence Day, Mar. 6
Great Britain -- See United Kingdom
Greece -- Independence Day, Mar. 25
Grenada -- National Day, Feb. 7
Guatemala -- Independence Day, Sept. 15
Guinea -- Independence Day, Oct. 2
Guinea-Bissau -- National Day, Sept. 12
Guyana -- Republic Day, Feb. 23
Haiti -- Independence Day, Jan. 1
Holy See -- Coronation of His Holiness Pope John Paul II, Oct. 22
Honduras -- Independence Day, Sept. 15
Hungary -- Anniversary of the Liberation, Apr. 4
Iceland -- Proclamation of Republic, June 17
India -- Republic Day, Jan. 26
Indonesia -- Independence Day, Aug. 17
Iran -- National Day, Feb. 11
Iraq -- Establishment of Republic, July 14
Ireland -- St. Patrick's Day, Mar. 17
Israel -- Independence Day (various dates)
Italy -- Foundation of the Republic, first Sunday of June
Ivory Coast -- National Day, Dec. 7
Jamaica -- Independence Day, (1st Mon. in Aug.)

Japan -- Birthday of H.M. the Emperor, Apr. 29
Jordan -- National Day, May 25
Kenya -- National Day, Dec. 12
Kiribati, Republic of -- National Day, July 12
Korea -- National Day, Aug. 15
Kuwait -- National Day, Feb. 25
Laos -- National Day, Dec. 2
Lebanon -- Independence Day, Nov. 22
Lesotho -- Independence Day, Oct. 4
Liberia -- Independence Day, July 26
Libya -- National Day, Sept. 1
Liechtenstein -- National Day, Aug. 16
Luxembourg -- Birthday of H.R.H. the Grand Duke Jean, June 23
Madagascar -- Independence Day, June 26
Malaysia -- National Day, Aug. 31
Malawi -- Independence Day, July 6
Mali -- Proclamation of the Republic, Sept. 22
Malta -- National Day, Mar. 31
Mauritania -- Independence Day, Nov. 28
Mauritius -- National Day, Mar. 12
Mexico -- Independence Day, Sept. 16
Monaco -- National Day, Nov. 19
Mongolia -- People's Revolution Day, July 11
Morocco -- National Day, Mar. 3
Birthday of H.M., July 9
Mozambique -- Independence Day, June 25
Nepal -- National Day, Dec., various dates
Netherlands -- Birthday of H.M. Queen Juliana, Apr. 30
New Zealand -- New Zealand Day, Feb. 6
Nicaragua -- Independence Day, Sept. 15
Niger -- Republic Day, Dec. 18
Nigeria -- Independence Day, Oct. 1
Norway -- Constitution Day, May 17
Oman -- National Day, Nov. 18
Pakistan -- Pakistan Day, Mar. 23
Panama -- Independence Day, Nov. 3
Papua, N.G. -- Independence Day, Sept. 16
Paraguay -- Independence Day, May 14
Peru -- Independence Day, July 28
Philippines -- National Day, June 12
Poland -- National Liberation Day, July 22
Portugal -- National Day, June 10
Qatar -- Independence Day, Sept. 3
Romania -- Liberation Day, Aug. 23
Rwanda -- Independence Day, July 1
St. Lucia -- National Day, Feb. 22
Sao Tome and Principe -- National Day, July 12
Saudi Arabia -- Unification of the Kingdom, Sept. 23
Senegal -- Independence Day, Apr. 4
Seychelles -- National Day, June 5
Sierra Leone -- Republic Day, Apr. 19
Singapore -- National Day, Aug. 9
Solomon Islands -- National Day, July 7
Somalia -- Revolution Day, Oct. 21
South Africa -- Republic Day, May 31
Spain -- National Day, Oct. 12
Sri Lanka -- Independence Day, Feb. 4
Sudan -- Independence Day, Jan. 1
Suriname -- Independence Day, Nov. 25
Swaziland -- Independence Day, Sept. 6
Sweden -- National Day, June 6
Switzerland -- Confederation Day, Aug. 1
Syria -- Independence Day, Apr. 17
Tanzania -- Union Day, Apr. 26
Thailand -- Birthday of H.M., Dec. 5
Togo -- National Day, Apr. 27
Tonga -- Independence Day, June 4
Trinidad & Tobago -- National Day, Aug. 31
Tunisia -- National Day, June 1
Turkey -- Proclamation of the Republic, Oct. 29
Tuvalu -- National Day, Oct. 1
Uganda -- Independence Day, Oct. 9
Union of Arab Emirates -- National Day, Dec. 2
Union of Soviet Socialist Republics -- Revolution Day, Nov. 7
United Arab Emirates -- National Day, Dec. 2
United Kingdom -- Official Observation of the Birthday of H.M. Queen Elizabeth II, June (as proclaimed)
United States -- Independence Day, July 4
Upper Volta -- Republic Day, Dec. 11
Uruguay -- Independence Day, Aug. 25
Venezuela -- Independence Day, July 5
Viet-Nam -- Independence Day, Sept. 2
Western Samoa -- Independence Day, June 1
Yemen Arab Republic -- Proclamation of Republic, Sept. 26
Yemen (People's Democratic Republic) -- National Day, Oct. 14
Yugoslavia -- Proclamation of Republic, Nov. 29
Zaire -- Anniversary of Second Revolution, Nov. 24
Zambia -- Independence Day, Oct. 24

Notes:

Check Addenda at back of this book for late changes

Section C

CANADIAN INFORMATION AND STATISTICS

THE ARMORIAL BEARINGS OF CANADA AUTHORIZED 1957

The arms are those of England, Scotland, Ireland and France, with a "difference" to mark them as Canadian, namely on the lower third of the shield, a sprig of maple on a silver shield. The crest is a lion holding in its paw a red maple leaf, a symbol of sacrifice. The supporters are, with some slight distinctions, the lion and unicorn of the Royal Arms; the lion upholds the Union Jack, and the unicorn the ancient banner of France.

The motto — A MARI USQUE AD MARE — "From sea to sea" — is an extract from the Latin version of verse 8 of the 72nd Psalm — "He shall have dominion also from sea to sea, and from the river unto the ends of the earth."

O CANADA

O Canada! Our home and native land!
True patriot love in all thy sons command.
With glowing hearts we see thee rise, The True North strong and free!
From far and wide, O Canada, we stand on guard for thee.
God keep our land glorious and free!
O Canada, we stand on guard for thee.
O Canada, we stand on guard for thee.

O Canada! Terre de nos aieux!
Ton front est ceint de fleurons glorieux!
Car ton bras sait porter l'épée, Il sait porter la croix!
Ton histoire est une épopée Des plus brillants exploits.
Et ta valeur, de foi trempée,
Protégera nos foyers et nos droits,
Protégera nos foyers et nos droits.

from "Chapter 5, Statutes of Canada 1980; proclaimed July 1, 1980"

FATHERS OF CONFEDERATION

Three conferences helped to pave the way for Confederation —those held at Charlottetown (September, 1864), Quebec City (October, 1864) and London (December, 1866). As all the delegates who were at the Charlottetown conferences were also in attendance at Quebec, the following list includes the names of all those who attended one or more of the three conferences.

*Hewitt Bernard was John A. Macdonald's private secretary. He served as secretary of both the Quebec and London conferences.

DELEGATES TO THE CONFEDERATION CONFERENCES, 1864-1866

LEGEND: Charlottetown, 1 September, 1864 C
Quebec, 10 October, 1864 .... Q
London, 4 December, 1866 L

CANADA			
John A. Macdonald	C	Q	L
George E. Cartier	C	Q	L
Alexander T. Galt	C	Q	L
William McDougall	C	Q	L
Hector L. Langevin	C	Q	L
George Brown	C	Q	
Thomas D'Arcy McGee	C	Q	
Alexander Campbell	C	Q	
Sir Etienne P. Taché		Q	
Oliver Mowat		Q	
J. C. Chapais		Q	
James Cockburn		Q	
W. P. Howland			L
*Hewitt Bernard			
NOVA SCOTIA			
Charles Tupper	C	Q	L
William A. Henry	C	Q	L
Jonathan McCully	C	Q	L
Adams G. Archibald	C	Q	L
Robert B. Dickey		Q	
J. W. Ritchie			L
NEW BRUNSWICK			
Samuel L. Tilley	C	Q	L
J. M. Johnson	C	Q	L
William H. Steeves	C	Q	
E. B. Chandler	C	Q	
John Hamilton Gray	C	Q	
Peter Mitchell		Q	L
Charles Fisher		Q	L
R. D. Wilmot			L
PRINCE EDWARD ISLAND			
John Hamilton Gray	C	Q	
Edward Palmer	C	Q	
William H. Pope	C	Q	
A. A. Macdonald	C	Q	
George Coles	C	Q	
T. H. Haviland		Q	
Edward Whelan		Q	
NEWFOUNDLAND			
F. B. T. Carter		Q	
Ambrose Shea		Q	

CANADIAN PRIME MINISTERS SINCE 1867

1. Rt. Hon. Sir John A. Macdonald (Conservative)	From	July	1, 1867	to	Nov.	5,	1873
2. Hon. Alexander Mackenzie (Liberal)	From	Nov.	7, 1873	to	Oct.	16,	1878
3. Rt. Hon. Sir John A. Macdonald (Conservative)	From	Oct.	17, 1878	to	June	6,	1891
4. Hon. Sir John J. Abbott (Conservative)	From	June	16, 1891	to	Nov.	24,	1892
5. Rt. Hon. Sir John S. D. Thompson (Conservative)	From	Dec.	5, 1892	to	Dec.	12,	1894
6. Hon. Sir Mackenzie Bowell (Conservative)	From	Dec.	21, 1894	to	April	27,	1896
7. Rt. Hon. Sir Charles Tupper (Conservative)	From	May	1, 1896	to	July	8,	1896
8. Rt. Hon. Sir Wilfrid Laurier (Liberal)	From	July	11, 1896	to	Oct.	6,	1911
9. Rt. Hon. Sir Robert L. Borden (Conservative Administration)	From	Oct.	10, 1911	to	Oct.	12,	1917
10. Rt. Hon. Sir Robert L. Borden (Unionist Administration)	From	Oct.	12, 1917	to	July	10,	1920
11. Rt. Hon. Arthur Meighen (Unionist "National Liberal and Conservative Party")	From	July	10, 1920	to	Dec.	29,	1921
12. Rt. Hon. William Lyon Mackenzie King (Liberal)	From	Dec.	29, 1921	to	June	28,	1926
13. Rt. Hon. Arthur Meighen (Conservative)	From	June	29, 1926	to	Sept.	25,	1926
14. Rt. Hon. William Lyon Mackenzie King (Liberal)	From	Sept.	25, 1926	to	Aug.	6,	1930
15. Rt. Hon. Richard Bedford Bennett (Conservative) (Became Viscount Bennett, 1941)	From	Aug.	7, 1930	to	Oct.	23,	1935
16. Rt. Hon. William Lyon Mackenzie King (Liberal)	From	Oct.	23, 1935	to	Nov.	15,	1948
17. Rt. Hon. Louis Stephen St. Laurent (Liberal)	From	Nov.	15, 1948	to	June	21,	1957
18. Rt. Hon. John G. Diefenbaker (Progressive Conservative)	From	June	21, 1957	to	April	22,	1963
19. Rt. Hon. Lester Bowles Pearson (Liberal)	From	April	22, 1963	to	April	20,	1968
20. Rt. Hon. Pierre Elliott Trudeau (Liberal)	From	April	20, 1968	to	June	4,	1979
21. Rt. Hon. Charles Joseph Clark (Progressive Conservative)	From	June	4, 1979	to	Mar.	3,	1980
22. Rt. Hon. Pierre Elliott Trudeau (Liberal)	From	Mar.	3, 1980				

(Numbers 2, 4, 6, 20, 21 not members of U.K. Privy Council)

GOVERNORS GENERAL OF CANADA SINCE CONFEDERATION

	APPOINTED			ASSUMED OFFICE		
Viscount Monck, G.C.M.G.	June	1,	1867	July	1,	1867
Lord Lisgar, G.C.M.G., (Sir John Young)	Dec.	29,	1868	Feb.	2,	1869
The Earl of Dufferin, K.P., K.C.B., G.C.M.G.	May	22,	1872	June	25,	1872
The Marquis of Lorne, K.T., G.C.M.G.	Oct.	5,	1878	Nov.	25,	1878
The Marquis of Lansdowne, G.C.M.G.	Aug.	18,	1883	Oct.	23,	1883
Lord Stanley of Preston, G.C.B.	May	1,	1888	June	11,	1888
The Earl of Aberdeen, K.T., G.C.M.G.	May	22,	1893	Sept.	18,	1893
The Earl of Minto, G.C.M.G.	July	30,	1898	Nov.	12,	1898
Earl Grey, G.C.M.G.	Sept.	26,	1904	Dec.	10,	1904
Field-Marshal H.R.H. The Duke of Connaught, K.G.	Mar.	21,	1911	Oct.	13,	1911
The Duke of Devonshire, K.G., G.C.M.G., G.C.V.O.	Aug.	19,	1916	Nov.	11,	1916
General The Lord Byng of Vimy, G.C.B., G.C.M.G., M.V.O.	Aug.	2,	1921	Aug.	11,	1921
Viscount Willingdon of Ratton, G.C.S.I., G.C.I.E., G.B.E.	Aug.	5,	1926	Oct.	2,	1926
The Earl of Bessborough, G.C.M.G.	Feb.	9,	1931	Apr.	4,	1931
Lord Tweedsmuir of Elsfield, G.C.M.G., G.C.V.O., C.H.	Aug.	10,	1935	Nov.	2,	1935
Major-General The Earl of Athlone, K.G., P.C., G.C.B., G.C.M.G., G.C.V.O., D.S.O.	Apr.	3,	1940	June	21,	1940
Field Marshal The Rt. Hon. Viscount Alexander of Tunis, K.G., G.C.B., G.C.M.G., C.S.I., D.S.O., M.C., LL.D., A.D.C.	Aug.	1,	1945	Apr.	12,	1946
The Rt. Hon. Vincent Massey, C.H.	Jan.	24,	1952	Feb.	28,	1952
General The Rt. Hon. George Philias Vanier, P.C., D.S.O., M.C., C.D.	Aug.	1,	1959	Sept.	15,	1959
His Excellency The Rt. Hon. Roland Michener, P.C., C.C., C.M.M., C.D., Q.C.	Mar.	25,	1967	Apr.	17,	1967
His Excellency The Rt. Hon. Jules Léger, C.C., C.M.M., C.D.	Oct.	5,	1973	Jan.	14,	1974
His Excellency The Rt. Hon. Edward Schreyer, C.C., C.M.M., C.D.	Dec.	7,	1978	Jan.	22,	1979

FLORAL EMBLEMS

ALBERTA—Wild Rose *(Rosa Acicularis)*. Chosen in the Floral Emblem Act of 1930.

BRITISH COLUMBIA—Dogwood (*Cornus Nuttallii*, Audubon). Adopted under the Floral Emblem Act, 1956.

MANITOBA—Pasque Flower, known locally as Prairie Crocus *(Anemone Patens)*. Adopted 1906.

NEW BRUNSWICK—Purple Violet *(Viola Cuculata)*. Adopted by Order-in-Council, December 1, 1936, at the request of the New Brunswick Women's Institute.

NEWFOUNDLAND—Pitcher Plant *(Sarracenia Purpurea)*. Adopted in June 1954.

NOVA SCOTIA—Trailing Arbutus, also known as Mayflower *(Epigaea Repens)*. Adopted in April 1901.

ONTARIO—White Trillium *(Trillium Grandiflorum)*. Adopted March 25, 1937.

PRINCE EDWARD ISLAND—Lady's Slipper *(Cypripedium Acaule)*. Designated as the province's floral emblem by the Legislative Assembly in 1947. A more precise botanical name was included in an amendment to the Floral Emblem Act in 1965.

QUEBEC—White Garden (Madonna) Lily *(Lilium Candidum)*. Adopted in January 1963.

SASKATCHEWAN—Prairie Lily *(Lilium Philadelphicum Andinum)*. Adopted April 8, 1941.

NORTHWEST TERRITORIES—Mountain Avens *(Dryas Integrifolia)*. Adopted by the Council on June 7, 1959.

YUKON TERRITORY—Fireweed *(Epilobium Angustifolium)*. Adopted November 16, 1957.

THE GREAT SEAL OF CANADA

The first Great Seal of Canada was approved by Queen Victoria in 1868, and a new one has been approved for each succeeding reign. The present Great Seal of Canada was approved by Queen Elizabeth II in 1956. It is the first to have been designed and made in Canada. For the first time also the inscription is in both official languages, instead of the abbreviated Latin. The inscription reads: "•Elizabeth II•Reine du Canada• Elizabeth II•Queen of Canada.

The Governor General is the custodian of the Great Seal, but it is handed to the Registrar General of Canada for safekeeping. It is used on official documents such as Proclamations, Commissions of Judges, Grants of Land etc.

CANADIAN FLAGS AND COATS OF ARMS

THE NATIONAL FLAG

The National Flag of Canada, otherwise known as the Canadian Flag, was approved by Parliament and proclaimed by Her Majesty the Queen on February 15, 1965, and is described as a red flag of the proportions two by length and one by width, containing in its centre a white square the width of the flag, bearing a single red maple leaf.

The Flag is flown on land daily from sunrise to sunset at all federal government buildings, airports, and military bases and establishments within and outside Canada, and may appropriately be flown or displayed by individuals and organizations.

The Canada Shipping Act provides that the National Flag is the proper national colours for all Canadian ships and boats; and it is the flag flown on Canadian Naval vessels.

THE ROYAL UNION FLAG

The Royal Union Flag, generally known as the Union Jack, was approved by Parliament on December 18, 1964 for continued use in Canada as a symbol of Canada's membership in the Commonwealth of Nations and of her allegiance to the Crown. It will, where physical arrangements make it possible, be flown along with the National Flag at federal buildings, airports, and military bases and establishments within Canada on the date of the official observance of the Queen's birthday, the Anniversary of the Statute of Westminster (December 11th), and on the occasions of Royal Visits and certain Commonwealth gatherings in Canada.

FLAG OF THE GOVERNOR GENERAL

In 1930, King George V approved the design of a Flag for the Governor General of Canada that would be symbolic of the position of the Governor General as the Sovereign's personal representative. The Flag so approved is of the following description.

"On a blue field, the Royal Crest,—the Imperial Crown proper, thereon a Lion statant-guardant Or, crowned proper—subscribed 'CANADA' in block on a yellow scroll."

CANADIAN ARMED FORCES BADGE

The Canadian Armed Forces Badge was sanctioned by Her Majesty Queen Elizabeth II in May 1967. The description is as follows:

"Within a wreath of ten stylized maple leaves Red, a cartouche medium Blue edge Gold, charged with a foul anchor Gold, surmounted by Crusader's Swords in Saltire Silver and blue, pommelled and hilted Gold; and in front an eagle volant affronté head to the sinister Gold, the whole ensigned with a Royal Crown proper."

The Canadian Forces Badge replaces the badges of the Royal Canadian Navy, the Canadian Army, and the Royal Canadian Air Force.

ALBERTA

The Arms of the Province of Alberta were granted by Royal Warrant on May 30, 1907. The heraldic description is as follows: "Azure, in front of a Range of Snow Mountains proper, a Range of Hills Vert, in base a Wheat Field surmounted by a Prairie both also proper, on a Chief Argent the Cross of St. George."

The official flag of Alberta was adopted in 1968. It consists of the Arms of the Province on a royal ultramarine blue background. Proportions of the flag are two by length and one by width, with the Arms seven-elevenths of the width of the flag carried in the centre.

BRITISH COLUMBIA

The shield of British Columbia was granted by Royal Warrant on March 31, 1906. The crest and supporters have become part of the provincial Arms through usage. The heraldic description is as follows: "Argent, three Bars wavy Azure, issuant from the base of a demi-Sun in his splendour Or, on a Chief of the Union Device charged in the centre point with an antique Crown Or. Crest: the Royal Crown surmounted by a Lion stantant guardant Or, Langued Gules and Imperially crowned. The supporters are on the dexter a Wapiti, and on the sinister a Mountain Sheep, both rampant and proper." The motto reads "SPLENDOR SINE OCCASU" ("splendour without diminishment").

The flag of British Columbia was authorized by an Order-in-Council of June 20, 1960. The union Jack symbolizes the province's origins as a British colony, and the crown at its centre represents the sovereign power linking the nations of the Commonwealth. The sun sets over the Pacific Ocean. The original design of the flag was located in 1960 by Hon. W. A. C. Bennett at the College of Arms in London.

MANITOBA

The Arms of the Province of Manitoba were granted by Royal Warrant on May 10, 1905. The heraldic description is as follows: "Vert, on a rock a Buffalo statant proper, on a Chief Argent the Cross of St. George."

The flag of the Province of Manitoba was adopted under The Provincial Flag Act, assented to May 11, 1965, and proclaimed into force on May 12, 1966. It incorporates parts of the Royal Armorial Ensigns, namely the Union and Red Ensign; the badge in the fly of the flag is the shield of the arms of the province.

Description: A flag of the proportions two by length and one by width with the Union Jack occupying the upper quarter next the staff and with the shield of the armorial bearings of the province centred in the half farthest from the staff.

NEW BRUNSWICK

The Arms of New Brunswick were granted by Royal Warrant on May 26, 1868. The motto "SPEM REDUXIT" ("hope restored") was added by Order-in-Council in 1966, having been in use previously until Confederation. The heraldic description is as follows: "Or, issuant in base a Sea composed of flour Barrulets wavy Azure and Argent, thereon a Lymphad Sable, Sail set Argent, Ensigns and Pennant flotant to the dexter Gules, the Oars in action of the field, on a Chief Gules a Lion passant guardant Or langued of the Chief."

The flag of New Brunswick, adopted by Proclamation on February 24, 1965, is based on the Arms of the province. The chief and charge occupy the upper one-third of the flag, and the remainder of the armorial bearings occupy the lower two-thirds. The proportion is four by length and two and one half by width.

NEWFOUNDLAND

The Arms of Newfoundland were granted by Royal Letters Patent dated January 1, 1637. The heraldic description is as follows: "Gules, a Cross Argent, in the first and fourth quarters a Lion passant guardant crowned Or, in the second and third quarters an Unicorn passant Argent armed and crined Or, gorged with a Coronet and a Chain affixed thereto reflexed of the last. Crest: on a wreath Or and Gules a Moose passant proper. Supporters: two Savages of the clime armed and apparelled according to their guise when they go to war." The motto reads "QUAERITE PRIME REGNUM DEI" ("seek ye first the kingdom of God").

The official flag of Newfoundland, adopted in 1980, has primary colours of Red, Gold and Blue, against a White background. The Blue section on the left represents Newfoundland's Commonwealth heritage and the Red and Gold section on the right represents the hopes for the future with the arrow pointing the way. The two triangles represent the mainland and island parts of the province.

ET" ("loyal in the beginning, so it remained").

The flag of the Province of Ontario was adopted under the Flag Act of May 21, 1965. It incorporates parts of the Royal Armorial Ensigns, namely the Union and Red Ensign; the badge in the fly of the flag is the shield of the Arms of the province.

The flag is of the proportions two by length and one by width, with the Union Jack occupying the upper quarter next the staff and the shield of the armorial bearings of the province centred in the half farthest from the staff.

NOVA SCOTIA

The Arms of the Province of Nova Scotia were granted by Royal Warrant, January 19, 1929, to supercede the Armorial Ensigns granted May 26, 1868. The motto reads "MUNIT HAEC ET ALTERA VINCIT" ("one defends and the other conquers").

The flag of the Province of Nova Scotia is a blue St. Andrew's Cross on a white field, with the Royal Arms of Scotland mounted thereon. The width of the flag is three-quarters of the length.

The flag was originally authorized by Charles I in 1625. In 1929, on petition of Nova Scotia, a Royal Warrant of King George V was issued, revoking the modern Arms and ordering that the original Arms granted by Charles I be borne upon shields, banners, and otherwise according to the laws of Arms.

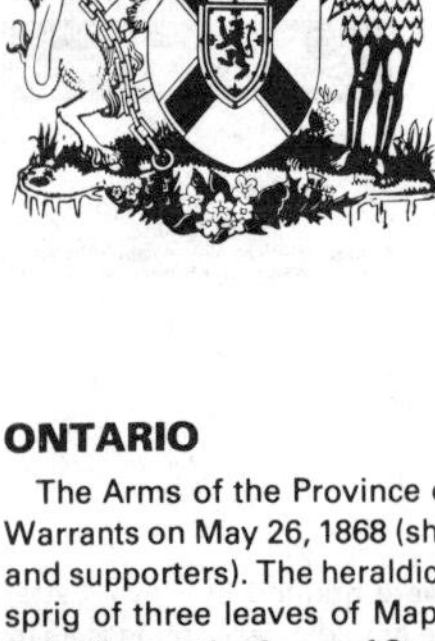

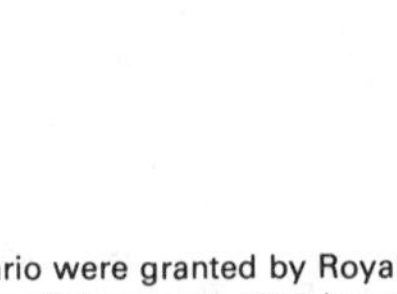

PRINCE EDWARD ISLAND

The Arms of the Province of Prince Edward Island were granted by Royal Warrant, May 30, 1905. The heraldic description is as follows: "Argent, on an Island Vert, to the sinister an Oak Tree fructed, to the dexter thereof three Oak samplings sprouting all proper, on a Chief Gules a Lion passant guardant Or." The motto reads: "PARVA SUB INGENTI" ("the small under the protection of the great").

The flag of the Province of Prince Edward Island was authorized by an Act of the Legislative Assembly, March 24, 1964. The design of the flag is that part of the Arms contained within the shield, but is of rectangular shape, with a fringe of alternating red and white. The chief and charge of the Arms occupies the upper one-third of the flag, and the remainder of the Arms occupies the lower two-thirds. The proportions of the flag are six, four, and one-quarter in relation to the fly, the hoist, and the depth of the fringe.

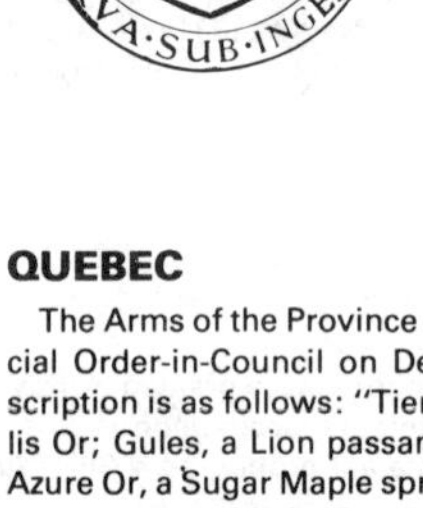

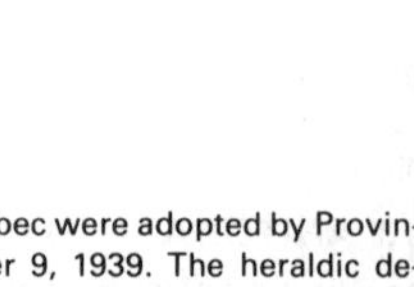

ONTARIO

The Arms of the Province of Ontario were granted by Royal Warrants on May 26, 1868 (shield), and February 27, 1909 (crest and supporters). The heraldic description is as follows: "Vert, a sprig of three leaves of Maple slipped Or nerved Sable, on a Chief Argent the Cross of St. George. Crest: upon a wreath Vert and Or a Bear passant Sable. The supporters are on the dexter side a Moose, and on the sinister side a Canadian Deer, both proper." The motto reads: "UT INCEPIT FIDELIS SIC PERMAN-

QUEBEC

The Arms of the Province of Quebec were adopted by Provincial Order-in-Council on December 9, 1939. The heraldic description is as follows: "Tierced in fess: Azure, three Fleurs-de-lis Or; Gules, a Lion passant guardant Or armed and langued Azure Or, a Sugar Maple sprig with three leaves Vert veined Or. Surmounted with the Royal Crown."

The official flag of the Province of Quebec was adopted by a Provincial Order-in-Council of January 1, 1948. The flag is generally known as the "fleurdelisé" flag. It is a white cross on a sky blue ground, with the fleur-de-lis in an upright position on the blue ground in each of the four quarters. The proportion is six units wide by four units deep.

SASKATCHEWAN

The Arms of the Province of Saskatchewan were granted by Royal Warrant, August 25, 1906. The heraldic description is as follows: "Vert, three garbs in fess Or, on a Chief of the last a lion passant guardant Gules armed and langued Azure."

The official flag of Saskatchewan was dedicated on September 22, 1969. The flag features the Arms of the province in the upper quarter nearest the staff, with the provincial floral emblem, "the Prairie Lily", in the half farthest from the staff. The upper green portion represents Saskatchewan forests, while the gold symbolizes prairie wheat fields. The basic design was adopted from the prize-winning entry of Anthony Drake of Hodgeville from a province-wide flag design competition.

NORTHWEST TERRITORIES

The Arms of the Northwest Territories were approved by Her Majesty Queen Elizabeth II on February 17, 1957. The crest consists of two gold narwhals guarding a compass rose, symbolic of the magnetic north pole. The white upper third of the shield represents the polar ice pack and is crossed by a wavy blue line portraying the Northwest Passage. the tree line is reflected by the diagonal line separating the red and green segments of the lower portion of the shield: the green symbolizing the forested areas south of the tree line, and the red standing for the barren lands north of it. The important bases of northern wealth, minerals and fur, are represented by gold billets in the green portion and the mask of a white fox in the red.

The official flag of the Northwest Territories was adopted by the Territorial Council on January 1, 1969. Blue panels at either side of the flag represent the lakes and waters of the Territories. The white centre panel, equal in width to the two blue panels combined, symbolizes the ice and snow of the North. In the centre of the white portion is the shield from the Arms of the Territories.

YUKON TERRITORY

The Arms of the Yukon Territory have the following explanation: The wavy white and blue vertical stripe represents the Yukon River and refers also to the rivers and creeks where gold was discovered. The red spire-like forms represent the mountainous country, and the gold discs the mineral resources. The St. George's Cross is in reference to the early explorers and fur traders from England, and the roundel in vair in the centre of the cross is a symbol for the fur trade. The crest displays a Malamute dog, an animal which has played an important part in the early history of the Yukon.

The Yukon flag, designed by Lynn Lambert, a Haines Junction student, was adopted by Council in 1967. It is divided into thirds: green for forests, white for snow, and blue for water; and carries the fireweed emblem and the Yukon Arms.

TABLE OF PRECEDENCE FOR CANADA

1. The Governor General or the Administrator. (Notes 1 and 1(a)).
2. The Prime Minister of Canada. (Note 2).
3. The Chief Justice of Canada.
4. The Speaker of the Senate.
5. The Speaker of the House of Commons.
6. Ambassadors, High Commissioners, Ministers Plenipotentiary. (Notes 3 and 4).
7. The Members of the Cabinet with relative precedence governed by the date of their appointment to the Queen's Privy Council of Canada.
8. The Leader of the Opposition. (Subject to Note 2).
9. The Lieutenant Governor of Ontario;
   The Lieutenant Governor of Quebec;
   The Lieutenant Governor of Nova Scotia;
   The Lieutenant Governor of New Brunswick;
   The Lieutenant Governor of Manitoba;
   The Lieutenant Governor of British Columbia;
   The Lieutenant Governor of Prince Edward Island;
   The Lieutenant Governor of Saskatchewan;
   The Lieutenant Governor of Alberta;
   The Lieutenant Governor of Newfoundland (Note 5).
10. Members of the Queen's Privy Council for Canada, not of the Cabinet, in accordance with the date of their appointment to the Privy Council.
11. The Primate of the Anglican Church of Canada, a Prelate of the Roman Catholic Church having high relative precedence in that Church in Canada, the Moderator of the United Church of Canada, the Moderator of the Presbyterian Church in Canada and the President of the Baptist Federation of Canada or their representatives, and a representative of the Jewish Faith in Canada. (Note 6).
12. The Premiers of the Provinces of Canada in the same order as the Lieutenant Governors (Note 5).
13. Puisne Judge of the Supreme Court of Canada.
14. The Chief Justice and the Associate Chief Justice of the Federal Court of Canada.
15. (a) The Chief Justice of the highest court of each province and territory; and
    (b) The Chief Justices of the other superior courts of the provinces and territories; including the Associate Chief Justice of the Superior Court of the Province of Quebec; with precedence within sub-categories (a) and (b) governed by the date of appointment as chief justice.
16. (a) Judges of the Federal Court of Canada.
    (b) Puisne Judges of the superior courts of the provinces and territories; with precedence within each sub-category to be governed by the date of appointment.
17. Members of the Senate.
18. Members of the House of Commons.
19. Consuls-General of countries without diplomatic representation.
20. The Chief of the Defence Staff. (Note 7).
21. Members of the Executive Councils, within their Provinces.
22. The Speakers of legislative assemblies within their Provinces.
23. Members of legislative assemblies within their Provinces.

NOTES

1. The presence of The Sovereign in Canada does not impair or supersede the authority of the Governor General to perform the functions delegated to him under the Letters Patent. The Governor General, under all circumstances, should be accorded precedence immediately after The Sovereign.
   (a) Precedence to be given immediately after the Chief Justice to former Governors General with relative precedence among them governed by the date of their leaving office.
2. Precedence to be given immediately after former Governors General to former Prime Ministers with relative precedence governed by the date of their first assumption of office.
3. Precedence among Ambassadors and High Commissioners, who rank equally, to be determined by the date of the presentation of their credentials.
4. Precedence to be given to Chargés d'Affaires immediately after Ministers Plenipotentiary.
5. This provision does not apply to such ceremonies and occasions as are of a Provincial nature.
6. The relative precedence of the Canadian ecclesiastical dignitaries to be governed by the date of their assumption of their present office, with their representatives to be given the same relative precedence.
7. This precedence to be given to the Chief of the Defence Staff on occasions when he has official functions to perform, otherwise the Chief of the Defence Staff to have equal precedence with Deputy Ministers with their relative position to be determined according to the respective dates of their appointments to office. The relative precedence of the Chief of the Defence Staff, Deputy Ministers and other high officials of the public service to be determined from time to time by the Secretary of State of Canada in consultation with the Prime Minister.

TABLE OF TITLES TO BE USED IN CANADA

1. The persons designated in Part 1 of the following Table shall be styled as set out in that Table.
2. The persons designated in Part 2 of the following Table are eligible to be granted permission by the Governor General on behalf of Her Majesty the Queen to retain the title of "Honourable" after they have ceased to hold office.

Part 1

1. The Governor General of Canada to be styled "Right Honourable" for life and to be styled during office "His Excellency" and his wife "Her Excellency", or "Her Excellency" and her husband "His Excellency", as the case may be.
2. A Lieutenant Governor of a Province to be styled "Honourable" and "His Honour" or "Her Honour" as the case may be, during tenure of office, and "Honourable" on retirement.
3. The Prime Minister of Canada to be styled "Right Honourable" for life.
4. The Chief Justice of Canada to be styled "Right Honourable" for life.
5. Privy Councillors of Canada to be styled "Honourable".
6. Senators of Canada to be styled "Honourable" during tenure of office and retired Senators of Canada to be styled "Honourable" for life.
7. The Speaker of the House of Commons to be styled "Honourable" during tenure of office.
8. The Judges of the Supreme and Federal Courts of Canada, and the Chief Justices and Judges of the undermentioned Courts in the Provinces and Territories of Canada
   Ontario—The Supreme Court of Ontario
   Quebec—The Court of Appeal and the Superior Court
   Nova Scotia—The Supreme Court of Nova Scotia
   New Brunswick—The Supreme Court of New Brunswick
   Manitoba—The Court of Appeal and the Court of Queen's Bench
   British Columbia—The Court of Appeal and the Supreme Court of British Columbia
   Prince Edward Island—The Supreme Court of Prince Edward Island
   Saskatchewan—The Court of Appeal and the Court of Queen's Bench
   Alberta—The Supreme Court of Alberta
   Newfoundland—The Supreme Court of Newfoundland
   Northwest Territories—The Supreme Court of Northwest Territories
   Yukon Territory—The Supreme Court of Yukon
   to be styled "Honourable" during tenure of office.
9. The Presidents and Speakers of the Legislatures of the Provinces to be styled "Honourable" during tenure of office.
10. Executive Councillors of the Provinces to be styled "Honourable" while in office.

Part 2

1. Speakers of the House of Commons on retirement.
2. The Chief Justices and Judges designated in item 8 of Part 1 of this Table on retirement.

ORDER OF PRECEDENCE OF ORDERS, DECORATIONS AND MEDALS

(Canadian Decorations in *italics*).

Canadian citizens wear their decorations in the following order:

Victoria Cross (VC)
George Cross (GC)
Cross of Valour (CV)
Companion of the Order of Canada (CC)
Officer of the Order of Canada (OC)
Order of Merit (OM)
Order of the Companions of Honour (CH)
Companion of the Order of the Bath (CB)
Companion of the Order of St. Michael and St. George (CMG)
Commander of the Royal Victorian Order (CVO)
Commander of the Order of the British Empire (CBE)
Commander of the Order of Military Merit (CMM)
Distinguished Service Order (DSO)
Member, Fourth Class, of the Royal Victorian Order (MVO)
Officer of the Order of the British Empire (OBE)
Imperial Service Order (ISO)
Member, Fifth Class, of the Royal Victorian Order (MVO)
Member of the Order of the British Empire (MBE)
Member of the Royal Red Cross (RRC)
Distinguished Service Cross (DSC)
Military Cross (MC)
Distinguished Flying Cross (DFC)
Star of Courage (SC)
Officer of the Order of Military Merit (OMM)
Medal of Bravery (MB)
Member of the Order of Canada (CM)
Member of the Order of Military Merit (MMM)
Air Force Cross (AFC)
Associate of the Royal Red Cross (ARRC)
Order of St. John of Jerusalem (all grades) (Grades in order: Bailiff/Dame Grand Cross; Knight/Dame of Justice; Knight/Dame of Grace; Commander (Brother) (Sister); Officer (Brother) (Sister); Officer (Brother) (Sister); Serving Brother/Sister)
Distinguished Conduct Medal (DCM)
Conspicuous Gallantry Medal (CGM - both Navy and Air Force)
George Medal (GM)
Distinguished Service Medal (DSM)
Military Medal (MM)
Distinguished Flying Medal (DFM)
Air Force Medal (AFM)
The Queen's Gallantry Medal (QGM)
British Empire Medal (BEM)

These are followed by war medals, including the *Canadian Volunteer Service Medal,* in order of the date of the campaign for which they were awarded; followed by the Polar Medals in order of the date on which they were awarded; followed by the Royal Victorian Medal and the Imperial Service Medal; followed by Coronation, Jubilee and other commemorative medals, including the *Centennial Medal* in order of the date on which they were awarded; followed by the following awards:

Long Service and Good Conduct Medal
Naval Long Service and Good Conduct Medal
Medal for Meritorious Service
Air Force Long Service and Good Conduct Medal
Royal Canadian Mounted Police Long Service Medal
Volunteer Officers' Decoration (VD)
Volunteer Long Service Medal
Efficiency Decoration (ED)
Efficiency Medal
Royal Naval Volunteer Reserve Decoration (VRD)
Royal Naval Volunteer Reserve Long Service and Good Conduct Medal
Air Efficiency Award
Queen's Medal for Champion Shots
Canadian Forces Decoration (CD)
Service Medal of the Order of St. John

CANADIAN HONOURS LIST

Compiled by Brian Donnellan, M.A.

The Victoria Cross was instituted by Queen Victoria at the close of the Crimean campaign, 1856. It is a Maltese cross, made of gun metal, with a Royal Crest in the centre and underneath it an escroll bearing the inscription "For Valour", and is awarded, irrespective of rank, to members of any branch of Her Majesty's services, either in the Imperial Forces or those of any British dominion, colony, dependency or protectorate, the Mercantile Marine, nurses or staffs of hospitals, or to civilians of either sex while serving in either regular or temporary capacity during naval, military, or air force operations. It is awarded only "for most conspicuous bravery or some daring or pre-eminent act of valour or self-sacrifice or extreme devotion to duty in the presence of the enemy." For additional conduct of similar bravery, a Bar is added. The ribbon was formerly red for the Army and blue for the Navy, but it is now crimson for all services. Since June 17th, 1943, the financial responsibility has been assumed by the Canadian Government. Since 1968 the annuity has been $300, payable $25.00 monthly.

V.C. (VICTORIA CROSS)

Major D. V. Currie, C.B.E.
Major the Reverend J. W. Foote
Lt.-Col. J. K. Mahony
Lt.-Col. C.C.I. Merritt, V.C., C.D.
Maj.-Gen. the Hon. G. R. Pearkes, P.C., C.B., D.S.O., M.C.
Captain C. B. Rutherford, M.C., M.M.
Sergeant E. A. Smith
Lt.-Col. H. Strachan, M.C.
Colonel F. A. Tilston

ROYAL HONOURS (COMMONWEALTH)

The Order of Baronets, the lowest Hereditary rank, was instituted in 1611; a Baronet is designated "Sir John Smith, Baronet"—the abbreviation Bt. is used in Court Circulars and has been generally adopted in lieu of "Bart." Taking precedence of Baronets are members of The Most Honourable Privy Council, who are addressed "Right Honourable."

The Most Noble Order of the Garter, instituted 1349.—K.G.

The Most Ancient and Most Noble Order of the Thistle, instituted 1687.—K.T.

The Most Honourable Order of the Bath, instituted in 1399, and revived in 1725, is divided into three classes—Knights Grand Cross, G.C.B.; Knights Commanders, K.C.B.; and Companions, C.B.

The Order of Merit, O.M., carries no title.

The Most Distinguished Order of St. Michael and St. George, instituted in 1818, has also three classes—Knights Grand Cross, G.C.M.G.; Knights Commanders, K.C.M.G.; Companions, C.M.G.

The Most Eminent Order of the Indian Empire instituted 1877, has three classes,—Knights Grand Commanders, G.C.I.E.; Knights Commanders, K.C.I.E.; Companions, C.I.E. (This Order has not been conferred since 1947.)

The Royal Victorian Order, instituted in 1896, has five classes—Knights Grand Cross, G.C.V.O.; Knights Commanders, K.C.V.O.; Commanders, C.V.O.; Members 4th and 5th classes—M.V.O. Ribbon; blue with red and white edges.

The Most Excellent Order of the British Empire, instituted in 1917, has five classes—Knights (or Dames) Grand Cross, G.B.E.; Knights Commanders, K.B.E.; Commanders, C.B.E.; Dames Commanders, D.B.E.; Officers, O.B.E.; and Members, M.B.E. Ribbon (Military) Rose pink, pearl grey edging, vertical pearl stripe in centre; O.B.E. (Civil) Rose pink, pearl grey edging and no central vertical stripe.

Knights Bachelors are gentlemen unconnected with any order who have received the honour of Knighthood, and are entitled to the prefix "Sir". They rank immediately after Knights Commanders of the British Empire.

The Companions of Honour, C.H., instituted in 1917 rank immediately after Knights (Dames) Grand Cross of the Order of the British Empire. Membership is limited; carries no title.

In all Orders of Knighthood the Knights Grand Cross and the Knights Commanders have the prefix "Sir" with the initials of their class following the name. Companions and Members bear no title, but have the letters C.B., C.M.G., M.V.O., as the case may be, attached to their names.

No new hereditary peerages and baronetcies have been created since 1964. Only life peerages are granted.

The Garter, the Thistle, The Order of Merit and the Royal Victorian Order are all in the personal bestowal of the Sovereign. Appointments to the other Orders are made by Her Majesty on recommendation of the Prime Minister.

G.C. (GEORGE CROSS)

Air Commodore A. Dwight Ross, G.C., C.B.E., C.D.
G. L. Bastian, G.C., M.B.E.
A.R.C. Butson, G.C., M.A., M.D., F.R.C.S.
John McClymont, G.C.
Doreen Ashburnham Ruffner, G.C.

MARQUESS

The Most Hon. the Marquess of Ely, Charles John Tottenham (Port Hope, Ont.) 8th Marquess.

EARL

The Right Hon. the Earl of Egmont, Frederick George Moore Perceval (Nanton, Alta.) 11th Earl and 15th Baronet.
The Right Hon. the Earl Grey, Richard Fleming George Charles Grey (Plymouth) 6th Earl.
The Right Hon. the Earl Winterton, Robert Chad Turnour (Delta, B.C.) 7th Earl.

OLD CANADIAN TITLE

The title of Baron de Longueuil existed prior to the Treaty of Paris (1763), and was duly recognized by Queen Victoria pursuant to that treaty.
Baron de Longueuil, Ronald Grant de Longueuil.

VISCOUNT

The Right Hon. the Viscount Charlemont, Charles Wilberforce Caulfield (Cumberland, Ont.)
The Right Hon. the Viscount Galway, Lt.-Cdr. George Rupert Monckton, R.C.N. (ret.) (London, Ont.) 12th Viscount.
The Right Hon. the Viscount Greenwood, David Henry Hamar Greenwood, F.R.G.S. (Qualicum Beach, B.C.) 2nd Viscount.
The Right Hon. the Viscount Hardinge, Henry Nicholas Paul Hardinge (Montreal, P.Q.) 5th Viscount.

BARONS

The Right Hon. the Lord Aylmer, Hugh Yates Aylmer (Victoria, B.C.), 12th Baron and 15th Baronet.
The Right Hon. the Lord Ashtown, Christopher Oliver Trench (Hamilton, Ont.) 6th Baron
The Right Hon. the Lord Chatfield, Ernle David Lewis Chatfield (Williamstown, Ont.) 2nd Baron.
The Right Hon. the Lord Greenhill, Stanley Ernest Greenhill, M.D., D.P.H., F.R.C.P. (Edmonton, Alta.) 2nd Baron.
The Right Hon. the Lord Rodney, John Francis Rodney (London) 9th Baron and 9th Baronet.
The Right Hon. the Lord Shaughnessy, William Graham Shaughnessy (Calgary) 3rd Baron.
The Right Hon. the Lord Strathcona and Mount Royal, Hon. Col. Donald Euan Palmer Howard (London) 4th Baron.
The Right Hon. the Lord Taylor, Stephen James Lake Taylor, M.D., F.R.C.P. (Llangollen) Life Peer.
The Right Hon. the Lord Thomson of Fleet, Kenneth Roy Thomson (London) 2nd Baron.

BARONETS

Sir Maxwell Aitken, D.S.O., D.F.C. (2nd Bt.).
Sir Fenton Gerald Aylmer (15th Bt.).
Sir Christopher Hilaro Barlow (7th Bt.).
Sir Harold Boulton (4th Bt.).
Sir Alexander Boyd (3rd Bt.).
Sir Lauder Brunton (3rd Bt.).
Sir Herbert Burbidge (5th Bt.).
Sir Michael Butler (3rd Bt.)
Sir Robert Cave-Brown-Cave (16th Bt.).
Sir George Reginald Chaytor (8th Bt.)
Sir Arthur Chetwynd (8th Bt.).
Sir Guy Cunard (7th Bt.).
Sir John Davis (3rd Bt.).
Sir Derek Dyke (9th Bt.).
Sir David Flavelle (3rd Bt.).
Sir Christopher Gibson, Bt. (3rd Bt.)
Sir George Philip Grant-Suttie (8th Bt.).
Sir Robert Gunning (8th Bt.).
Sir Charles Knowles (7th Bt.).
Sir Peter Johnson (7th Bt.).
Sir Richard Latham (3rd Bt.).
Sir Edwin MacGregor (7th Bt.).
Sir Allan MacKenzie, C.D. (4th Bt.).
Sir Harold Mitchell (1st Bt.).
Sir Christopher Oakes (3rd Bt.).
Sir Charles Piers (10th Bt.).
Sir Francis Price, Bt. (7th Bt.)
Sir John Beverly Robinson (7th Bt.).
Sir John James Michael Laud Robinson (11th Bt.)
Sir Julian Rose (5th Bt.).
Sir Charles Rugge-Price (9th Bt.).
Sir John Samuel (5th Bt.)
Sir Robert Shaw (7th Bt.).
Sir John Simeon (7th Bt.).
Sir Philip Stonhouse (18th Bt.).
Sir Adrian Stott (4th Bt.).
Sir John Stracey (9th Bt.).
Sir Philip Stuart (9th Bt.).
Sir Robert Synge (8th Bt.).
Sir Rodney Touche (2nd Bt.).
Sir Charles Hibbert Tupper (5th Bt.).
Sir Charles Wells, T.D. (2nd Bt.).
Sir Donald Williams (10th Bt.).
Sir Garnet Wolseley (12th Bt.).

G.C.B.

Air Chief Marshal Sir David Evans, G.C.B., C.B.E.
General Sir Charles Loewen, G.C.B., K.B.E., D.S.O.

G.C.M.G.

Sir John Shaw Rennie, G.C.M.G., O.B.E.

G.B.E.

Sir Peter Gadsden, G.B.E.
General Sir Neil Ritchie, G.B.E., K.C.B., D.S.O., M.C.

C.H.

Arnold Smith, C.H.

K.C.B.

Air Marshal Sir Richard Nelson, K.C.B., O.B.E., M.D.

K.C.M.G.

Sir Edwin Leather, K.C.M.G, K.C.V.O.
Sir Charles Stirling, K.C.M.G., K.C.V.O.
Sir Francis Aimé Vallat, K.C.M.G., Q.C.

K.C.V.O.

Sir Shuldham Redfern, K.C.V.O., C.M.G.

K.B.E.

Sir David Bate, K.B.E.
Air Marshal Sir Philip Livingston, K.B.E., C.B., A.F.C.
Air Vice-Marshal Sir Victor Tait, K.B.E., C.B.
Sir Edgar Vaughan, K.B.E., F.R.Hist.S.

KNIGHTS BACHELOR

Hon. Sir Joseph Luckhoo
Sir William McKie, M.V.O.

Col. Sir Leonard Cecil Outerbridge, C.C., C.B.E., D.S.O., C.D.
Sir William Samuel Stephenson, M.C., D.F.C.

C.B.

Herbert Wilfrid Ayers, C.B., C.B.E.
Rear-Admiral P.W. Brock, C.B., D.S.O.
Air Vice-Marshal George Brookes, C.B., O.B.E.
Maj.-Gen. Cecil Benfield Fairbanks, C.B., C.B.E.
Air Vice-Marshal Kenneth McGregor Guthrie, C.B., C.B.E., C.D.
Air Vice-Marshal F. V. Heakes, C.B.
Air Vice-Marshal George Roberts Howsam, C.B., M.C.
Air Vice-Marshal Thomas Albert Lawrence, C.B., C.D.
Air Vice-Marshal Frank Scholes McGill, C.B.
Air Vice-Marshal Arthur Laurence Morfee, C.B., C.B.E., C.D.
Maj.-Gen. the Hon. G. R. Pearkes, V.C., C.B., C.C., P.C., D.S.O., M.C., C.D.
Lt.-Gen. E. W. Sansom, C.B., D.S.O., C.D.
Air Marshal C. Roy Slemon, C.B., C.B.E., C.D.
Air Vice-Marshal L. F. Stevenson, C.B.
Air Vice-Marshal Sir Victor Tait, K.B.E., C.B., R.A.F.
Maj.-Gen. Christopher Vokes, C.B., C.B.E., D.S.O., C.D.
Maj.-Gen. E. G. Weeks, C.B., C.B.E., M.C., M.M., C.D.

C.M.G.

Binns, Howard Reed, C.M.G., O.B.E.
Borden, Henry, C.M.G., O.C., Q.C.
Campbell, James Grant, C.M.G.
Carmichael, H. J., C.M.G.
Cloutier, Edmond, C.M.G., B.A., L.Ph.
Cruikshank, John Merrill, C.M.G., O.B.E.
de Saintonge, Rolland Alfred Aime Chaput, C.M.G.
Duncan, The Hon. Air Commodore James Stuart, C.M.G.
Emery, Eleanor, C.M.G.
Finn, Donovan Bartley, C.M.G., M.Sc., Ph.D., F.R.S.C., F.C.I.C.
Heckle, Arnold, C.M.G.
Mackenzie, C.J., C.M.G., C.C., M.C., M.C.E., D.Sc., LL.D. F.R.S., F.R.S.C., M.E.I.C.
Mackenzie, Maxwell Weir, C.M.G., O.C.
Mackenzie, Dr. Norman Archibald MacRae, C.M.G., C.C., M.M., Q.C., B.A., LL.M., LL.D., D.C.L., F.R.S.C.
McIvor, George H., C.M.G.
McKinnon, Hector Brown, C.M.G., C.C.
Pelletier, Wilfrid, C.M.G., C.C.
Ross, Alexander, C.M.G.
Samples, Reginald McCartney, C.M.G., D.S.O., O.B.E.
St. Laurent, Joseph Emile, C.M.G.
Sim, David, C.M.G.
Smith, Ivor Otterbein, C.M.G., O.B.E.
Taylor, Edward Plunket, C.M.G.

C.I.E.

Major Frederick Wernham Gerrard, C.I.E.
Captain John Ryland, C.I.E., R.I.N.
Major Frederick Augustus Berrill Sheppard, C.I.E., O.B.E.

C.V.O.

Esmond Butler, C.V.O.
Brigadier P. S. Cooper, C.V.O., C.D.
Michel Gauvin, C.V.O., D.S.O.
John Reginald Gorman, C.V.O., C.B.E., M.C.
Lt.-Gen. Howard Graham, C.V.O., C.B.E., D.S.O., E.D., C.D., Q.C.
Captain Donald Curtis McKinnon, C.V.O., C.D., R.C.N.
Cdr. G.J. Manson, C.V.O., R.C.N.
Maj.-Gen. Roy Reid, C.V.O., M.C., E.D.

C.B.E.

William Eric Adams, C.B.E.
General Jean Victor Allard, C.C., C.B.E., D.S.O., E.D., C.D.
James Pomeroy Anderson, C.B.E.
Brigadier Gerald Gardiner Anglin, C.B.E., M.C., E.D.
Brigadier John Arthur Watson Bennett, C.B.E., C.D.
Brigadier John Francis Bingham, C.B.E.
Brigadier Dudley Kingdon Black, C.B.E., D.S.O.
Maj.-Gen. Mortimer Patrick Bogert, C.B.E., D.S.O.
George Herbert Bowler, C.B.E.
Garrett Brownrigg, C.B.E.
Air Vice-Marshal John George Bryans, C.B.E., C.D., R.C.A.F.
John Burke, C.B.E.
Air Marshal Hugh Lester Campbell, C.B.E., R.C.A.F.
Alfred Charpentier, C.B.E.
Howard Brown Chase, C.B.E.
John Horrell Collier-Wright, C.B.E.
Lt.-Gen. Samuel Findlay Clark, C.B.E., C.D.
Brigadier Frederick Graham Coleman, C.B.E.
Brig.-Gen. Alan Burton Connelly, C.B.E., C.D.
Air Commodore Martin Costello, C.B.E., R.C.A.F.
Brigadier A.J. Creighton, C.B.E.
Rear-Admiral Wallace Bourchier Creery, C.B.E., R.C.N.
Ian Douglas Davidson, C.B.E.
Arthur Davison, C.B.E.
Vice-Admiral Harry George De Wolf, C.B.E., D.S.O., D.S.C., R.C.N.
Lt.-Gen. Jacques Alfred Dextraze, C.B.E., D.S.O., C.D.
Hon. Charles Mills Drury, P.C., C.B.E., D.S.O., E.D.
Air Marshal Clarence Rupert Dunlap, C.B.E., C.D., R.C.A.F.
Brigadier Philip Earnshaw, C.B.E., D.S.O., M.C.
Philip Sydney Fisher, S.M., C.B.E., D.S.O., D.S.C., D.C.L., LL.D.
Conrad Trelawny Fitz-Gerald, C.B.E., M.D.
Brigadier Frank James Fleury, C.B.E.
Walter Leslie Forster, C.B.E.
Charles Gavsie, C.B.E., Q.C.
Gerald Godsoe, C.B.E., Q.C.
Air Vice-Marshal Harold Brandon Godwin, C.B.E., R.C.A.F.
Hon. Walter Lockhart Gordon, P.C., C.B.E.
Duncan Archibald Lamont Graham, C.C., C.B.E.
Lt.-Gen. Howard Douglas Graham, S.M., C.B.E., D.S.O., E.D., C.D., Q.C.
Alexander Grant, C.B.E.
Joseph Ernest Gregoire, C.B.E.
Frederick Grinke, C.B.E.
Frank Sydney Grisdale, C.B.E.
Raymond Gushue, S.M., C.B.E., Q.C.
Maj.-Gen. Lewis John Harris, C.B.E.
Wallace Bruce Haughan, C.B.E.
Brigadier Robert James Henderson, C.B.E.
Harold Ferguson Hodgson, C.B.E.
Rear-Admiral Frank Llewellyn Houghton, C.B.E.
Maj.-Gen. Gordon Byron Howard, C.B.E.
Wilbert Harvard Howard, C.B.E.
Captain Francis Deschamps Howie, C.B.E., D.S.O., R.N.
Alexander George Irvine, C.B.E.
Brigadier Ian Strachan Johnston, C.B.E., D.S.O., E.D., Q.C.
Eric Campbell Judd, C.B.E., M.V.O.
Lester Millman Keachie, C.B.E., Q.C.
Maj.-Gen. Ralph Holley Keefler, C.B.E., D.S.O., E.D.
Captain Thomas Douglas Kelly, C.B.E., R.C.N.R.
Air Vice-Marshal John Gordon Kerr, C.B.E., A.F.C., C.D.
D.F. Kershaw, C.B.E.
Maj.-Gen. George Kitching, C.B.E., D.S.O., M.C.
Brigadier J. A. de Lalanne, C.B.E., M.C., E.D.
Allan Collingwood Travers Lewis, C.B.E., Q.C.
Colonel Edward Raymond Lewis, C.B.E.
Wilfrid Bennett Lewis, C.B.E.
Gordon Clapp Lindsay, C.B.E.
Brigadier Frank Melville Lott, C.B.E.
Air Vice-Marshal Ralph Edward McBurney, C.B.E., C.D., R.C.A.F.
John Struthers McNeil, C.B.E.
Maj.-Gen. Clarence Churchill Mann, C.B.E., D.S.O., C.D.
Raymond Charles Manning, C.B.E.
David Ball Mansur, C.B.E.
John Emile Marks, C.B.E.
Cyril Herbert Alfred Marriott, C.B.E.
Walter Melvill Marshall, C.B.E.
James Matson, C.B.E.
Maynard Albert Metcalf, C.B.E.
Air Chief Marshal Frank Robert Miller, C.B.E., C.D., R.C.A.F.
Boyd Neel, C.B.E.
Air Vice-Marshal Walter Alyn Orr, C.B.E., C.D., R.C.A.F.

Brigadier Henri de Lotbiniere Panet, C.B.E.
Luke William Pearsall, C.B.E.
Maj.-Gen. Matthew Howard Somers Penhale, C.B.E., C.D.
Cyril Horace Frederick Pierrepont, C.B.E., E.D.
Air Vice-Marshal John Lawrence Plant, C.B.E., A.F.C., R.C.A.F.
Maj.-Gen. the Hon. Edward Chester Plow, C.B.E., D.S.O., C.D.
Louis Rasminsky, C.C., C.B.E.
Maj.-Gen. Norman Elliott Rodger, C.B.E.
Air Commodore Arthur Dwight Ross, G.C., C.B.E.
James Joseph Alexander Ross, C.B.E., C.D.
Mrs. Phyllis Gregory Ross, S.M., C.B.E.
Lynn Seymour, C.B.E.
Maj.-Gen. James Desmond Smith, C.B.E., D.S.O., M.C.
Air Vice-Marshal Douglas McCully Smith, C.B.E., C.D.
Brigadier Gerald Lucian Morgan Smith, C.B.E., C.D.
Maj.-Gen. Herbert Alan Sparling, C.B.E., D.S.O., C.D.
George Spence, C.B.E., LL.D.
William Leonard O'Brien Stallard, C.B.E.
Basil Otto Stevenson, C.B.E.
James Stewart, C.B.E.
Air Commodore Stanley Gibson Tackaberry, C.B.E.
Kenneth Wiffin Taylor, S.M., C.B.E.
George Gamlin Thomas, C.B.E.
Lyman Trumbull, C.B.E.
Cyrille Vaillancourt, C.B.E.
Mrs. Renee Vautelet, C.B.E.
Colonel the Hon. Clarence Wallace, C.B.E., C.D.
Frederick Baird Walls, C.B.E.
Lt.-Gen. Geoffrey Walsh, C.B.E., D.S.O., C.D.
Grace Elizabeth Watts, C.B.E.
Air Commodore James Roger Whelan, C.B.E., D.S.O., D.F.C., R.A.F.
Maj.-Gen. Arthur Egbert Wrinch, C.B.E., C.D.

I.S.O. (IMPERIAL SERVICE ORDER)

George Clayton Anderson
Robert Albert Andison
Arthur Barnstead
Avila Bedard
Peter Cooligan
Henri Fortier
Frank Henry French
Arthur Leigh Jolliffe
Edward Jost
Louis MacMillan
Walter Clifton Ronson
David John Scott
Ivan Vallee

ROYAL VICTORIAN CHAIN

Bestows no precedence, held by
The Right Hon. Roland Michener, P.C., C.C., C.M.M., C.D., Q.C.

HONOURS (CANADA)

For some years after Confederation awards were made of a few hereditary honours and some knighthoods and companionships in orders of chivalry, and this policy continued until the end of the first Great War.

On May 22, 1919, during the premiership of Sir Robert Borden, a resolution adopted by the House of Commons requested His Majesty to refrain from granting titular honours to Canadian citizens in the future. This policy was reversed in 1933 when, during the premiership of the Rt. Hon. R. B. Bennett, the Canadian Government recommended a number of such awards, which were duly granted on New Year's Day, 1934. Although titular honours were again conferred in 1935, the new administration which took office later that year under the premiership of the Rt. Hon. Mackenzie King revived the previous policy of the Government of 1919, and no titular honours have been recommended or awarded since that time.

On July 24, 1942, a Special Committee on Honours and Decorations reported to the House as follows:

"As a result of their deliberations your Committee desires to make the following recommendations:

(1) That His Majesty's subjects domiciled or ordinarily resident in Canada be eligible for the award of Honours and Decorations, including awards in the Orders of Chivalry, which do not involve titles.

(2) That his Majesty's Government in Canada consider a submission to His Majesty the King, of proposals of the establishment of an Order limited in number but not involving a title, for which His Majesty's subjects domiciled or ordinarily resident in Canada shall alone be eligible."

During World War II, decorations were awarded to several thousand members of Canada's Armed Forces and Canadians were appointed to both civil and military divisions of Orders of Chivalry in recognition of their war services. Similar awards were made during the campaign in Korea.

The hundredth anniversary of Confederation, July 1st, 1967, was the occasion on which the Order of Canada was created as the first component of a distinctly Canadian honours system.

In 1972, the Constitution of the Order of Canada was amended to provide for the appointment of a larger number of Canadians in recognition of achievement and service in all fields of human endeavour. The honours system was further enlarged at that time to include the Order of Military Merit and a series of three decorations, which are awarded in recognition of acts of bravery (The Cross of Valour, The Star of Courage, and the Medal of Bravery).

Subject to the provisions of regulations adopted in 1968, Canadians are eligible to receive honours from any country recognized by Canada, provided no title is included.

All matters relating to orders and decorations are the concern of the Secretariat of Honours at Government House in Ottawa. Nominations for the Order of Canada may be submitted by any individual or organization on behalf of Canadian citizens, by writing to the Registrar of Honours. Anyone may also submit the name of a person considered deserving of recognition for an act of heroism.

ORDER OF CANADA

Her Majesty The Queen is Sovereign of the Order of Canada and the Governor General is, by virtue of that office, Chancellor and Principal Companion. He is assisted in the administration of the Order by an Advisory Council which comprises:

a) the Chief Justice of Canada (Chairman)
b) the Clerk of the Privy Council
c) the Under Secretary of State
d) the Chairman of the Canada Council
e) the President of the Royal Society of Canada
f) the President of the Association of Universities and Colleges of Canada
g) where considered appropriate by the Governor General, not more than two other members can be appointed by him.

The Secretary to the Governor General is, by his office, Secretary General of the Order.

The Order of Canada is designed to honour Canadian citizens for outstanding achievement and service to the country or to humanity at large and also for distinguished service in particular localities and fields of actvity. The Order comprises three levels of membership: Companion, Officer, Member. Up to 15 Companions may be appointed annually, but the total number of living Companions may not exceed 150. Up to 40 Officers and 80 Members may be appointed annually with no over-al limit.

The Order includes no titles of honour and confers no specia privileges, hereditary or otherwise. Awards are made solely on the basis of merit. Members of the Order are entitled to place after their names the letters, for Companions: "C.C.", for Officers: "O.C.", for Members: "C.M."

Any person or organization may make nominations for appointment to the Order by writing to the Secretariat of Honours at Government House, in Ottawa. The Advisory Council submits to the Governor General lists of those nominees who, in the opinion of the Council, are of greatest merit. Appointments to the Order are made by the Sovereign of the Order on the recommendation of the Governor General as Chancellor of the Order, under an instrument sealed with the Seal of the Order.

Non-Canadians whom the Government desires to honour may be accorded honorary membership in the Order.

Companions of the Order of Canada
Compagnons de l'Ordre du Canada

(Appointed December 15th, 1980. For prior appointments refer to back editions of the Almanac).

M. le professeur Larkin Kerwin, C.C., D.Sc., Sillery, P.Q.
The Hon. Pauline M. McGibbon, C.C., LL.D., Toronto, Ont.

(Appointed June 22nd, 1981)

Dr. Margaret Atwood, C.C., LL.D., Toronto, Ont.
The Hon. Edward Milton Culliton, C.C., Q.C., D.C.L., Regina, Sask.
Mr. T.C. Douglas, C.C., D.C.L., Ottawa, Ont.

Officers of the Order of Canada
Officiers de l'Ordre du Canada

(Appointed July 1st, 1980. For prior appointments refer to back editions of the Almanac. Some Officers were formerly listed as recipients of the Medal of Service.)

Mr. Kenneth Douglas Taylor, O.C., Ottawa, Ont.

(Appointed December 15th, 1980)

Professor Murray Adaskin, O.C., D.Mus., Victoria, B.C.
Dr. Robert A. Bandeen, O.C., Ph.D., Westmount, P.Q.
M. le docteur André Barbeau, O.C., M.D., Montréal, P.Q.
Mrs. Shirley G.E. Carr, O.C., Ottawa, Ont.
The Hon. Charles Mills Drury, P.C., O.C., C.B.E., D.S.O., Q.C., Ottawa, Ont.
M. Yves O. Fortier, O.C., Ph.D., Ottawa, Ont.
Dr. Albert Welsey Johnson, O.C., Ph.D., Ottawa, Ont.
M. André Langevin, O.C., Frélighsburg, P.Q.
Le Révérend Père Emile Legault, c.s.c., O.C., Montréal, P.Q.
Dr. Ellen Signe McLean, O.C., LL.D., Eureka, N.S.
The Hon. John L. Nichol, O.C., Vancouver, B.C.
The Hon. Victor de B. Oland, O.C., E.D., C.D., D.C.L., Halifax, N.S.
Dr. L. Siminovitch, O.C., Ph.D., Toronto, Ont.
Dr. Ronald J. Thoms, O.C., LL.D., Scarborough, Ont.
M. Marc-Adélard Tremblay, O.C., M.Soc., Ste-Foy, P.Q.
Dr. Donald R. Wilson, O.C., M.D., Edmonton, Alta.
Dr. Harry Douglas Woods, O.C., LL.D., Fredericton, N.B.

(Appointed June 22nd, 1981)

Dr. Wilfred Gordon Bigelow, O.C., M.D., Toronto, Ont.
Mr. Gerald K. Bouey, O.C., B.A., Ottawa, Ont.
Professor J. Maurice S. Careless, O.C., Ph.D., Toronto, Ont.
M. le professeur Gilles G. Cloutier, O.C., B.Sc.A., Edmonton, Alta.
M. le professur Paul-André Crépeau, O.C., C.R., B.C.L., Montréal, P.Q.
Mrs. Betty Farrally, O.C., Kelowna, B.C.
Mrs. Mavis Gallant, O.C., Paris, France
Dr. James P. Gilmore, O.C., D.Sc., Victoria, B.C.
Professor George P. Grant, O.C., D.Phil., Halifax, N.S.
Dr. Robert Orville Jones, O.C., B.Sc., M.D., Halifax, N.S.
M. le docteur Fernand Labrie, O.C., M.D., Ste-Foy, P.Q.
Dr. J. Ross MacKay, O.C., D.Geog., Vancouver, B.C.
M. le professeur Paul Marmet, O.C., D.Sc., Ste-Foy, P.Q.
Mr. W. Earle McLaughlin, O.C., Westmount, P.Q.
Mr. Farley McGill Mowat, O.C., D.Litt., Port Hope, Ont.
Miss Susan Marie Nattrass, O.C., B.P.E., Edmonton, Alta.
Mr. Sydney Newman, O.C., F.R.S.A., Toronto, Ont.
M. Clermont Pépin, O.C., Outremont, P.Q.
M. Germain Perreault, O.C., Outremont, P.Q.
Mr. Michael Snow, O.C., LL.D., Toronto, Ont.
M. Roger Tassé, O.C., C.R., Chelsea, P.Q.
Mr. Patrick Watson, O.C., M.A., Smiths Falls, Ont.

Members of the Order of Canada
Membres de l'Ordre du Canada

(Appointed July 1st, 1980. For prior appointments refer to back editions of the Almanac).

Miss Laverna Dollimore, C.M., Ottawa, Ont.
Mr. Roger Lucy, C.M., Ottawa, Ont.
Miss Mary Catherine O'Flaherty, C.M., Ottawa, Ont.
Mr. John V. Sheardown, C.M., Ottawa, Ont.

(Appointed October 24th, 1980)

Mr. Edward Arunah Dunlop, O.B.E., C.M., G.M. (Deceased), Toronto, Ont.

(Appointed December 15th, 1980)

Mr. Ralph LeMoine Andrews, C.M., M.A., St. John's, Nfld.
M. Bona Arsenault, C.M., Sillery, P.Q.
M. le docteur Germain Bigué, C.M., M.D., Val d'Or, P.Q.
Mr. Harold (Slim) Byrnes, C.M., Cecil Lake, B.C.
Mr. Gordon Irwin Cameron, C.M., Whitehorse, Yukon
Mrs. Barbara V. Cormack, C.M., B.Ed., Sherwood Park, Alta.
Colonel Eric W. Cormack, O.B.E., C.M., E.D., C.D., Sherwood Park, Alta.
Colonel Georges-Henri Coulombe, C.M., C.D., Ville de la Baie, P.Q.
Dr. John Robert Dacey, M.B.E., C.M., Ph.D., Kingston, Ont.
Mr. Primo I. Di Luca, C.M., Islington, Ont.
Soeur Léonne Dumesnil, s.n.j.m., C.M., B.Ed., Winnipeg, Man.
Mr. Norman Alexander Dutton, C.M., Calgary, Alta.
Mr. R. Fraser Elliott, C.M., Q.C., Toronto, Ont.
M. Yves Gaucher, C.M., Montréal, P.Q.
Mr. Boniface Guimond, C.M., Pine Falls, Man.
Dr. R. Ben Gullison, C.M., M.B., Vancouver, B.C.
Mrs. Christie Harris, C.M., Vancouver, B.C.
The Rev. Canon William Edward Hart, C.M., B.A., Clifton Royal, N.B.
Mme Alphonsine Howlett, C.M., Montréal, P.Q.
Mr. Kalmen Kaplansky, C.M., Ottawa, Ont.
M. J.E. Raymond Lemay, C.M., Ville d'Anjou, P.Q.
Miss Dorothy A. Macham, C.M., Willowdale, Ont.
Dr. Margaret Scott McCready, C.M., Ph.D., Toronto, Ont.
Mrs. Mary Hamilton McInnis, C.M. (Deceased), Toronto, Ont.
Mrs. S. June Menzies, C.M., B.A., Ottawa, Ont.
Mlle Marie-Thérèse Paquin, C.M., Montréal, P.Q.
Mr. Lazar Peters, D.F.C., C.M., Westmount, P.Q.
Mr. E. Howard Radford, C.M., Town of Mount Royal, P.Q.
Le Révérend Père Albert Roger, c.s.c., C.M., Montréal, P.Q.
Mr. A. Gordon South, C.M., Melfort, Sask.
Son Honneur Mme Marcelle B. Trépanier, C.M., B.ès.S., Valleyfield, P.Q.
Mrs. Margaret Trott, C.M., Winnipeg, Man.
Mr. J. Bryan Vaughan, C.M., Toronto, Ont.
Miss Peggy Ann Walpole, C.M., R.N., Toronto, Ont.
The Reverend John G. Webb, C.M., M.S.W., Sydney, N.S.
Dr. Charles Morley Willoughby, C.M., LL.D., Regina, Sask.
Mr. William J. Withrow, C.M., C.D., M.A., Don Mills, Ont.
Mr. Ray D. Wolfe, C.M., B.A., Islington, Ont.

(Appointed June 22nd, 1981)

M. Maurice Allan, C.M., Dorval, P.Q.
Mr. Lewis Haldane Miller Ayre, C.M., St. John's, Nfld.
Mrs. Ruth Marion Bell, C.M., M.A., Nepean, Ont.
Mme Camille Bernard, C.M., Montréal, P.Q.
M. Victor Bouchard, C.M., LL.D., Québec, P.Q.
M. Gérard Brady, C.M., Laval, P.Q.
Mr. Walter T. Burns, C.M., M.Sc., Mount Lehman, B.C.
Mr. Neil William Campbell, C.M., Vineland Station, Ont.
Mr. Samuel Donaghey, C.M., Edmonton, Alta.
Dr. John G. Egnatoff, C.M., B.Ped., D.Ed., Saskatoon, Sask.
Mr. Mark Evaluarjuk, C.M., Igloolik, N.W.T.
Mr. Martin Wise Goodman, C.M., M.Sc., Toronto, Ont.
Soeur Mary Greene, f.m.a., C.M., Campbellton, N.B.
Mrs. Albert Hudec, C.M., R.N., Regina, Sask.
Mr. Ian K. Hume, C.M., Melbourne, P.Q.

Mr. Derek Arnold Inman, C.M., West Vancouver, B.C.
The Reverend Dr. Norman S. Johnston, C.M., Ottawa, Ont.
M. Roland Jomphe, C.M., Havre Saint-Pierre, P.Q.
Mr. Franz Kraemer, C.M., Ottawa, Ont.
Mr. Frank W. Laird, C.M., B.A., Penticton, B.C.
Mrs. Sarah Lavalley, C.M., Golden Lake, Ont.
Mr. John-Barbalinardo Lombardi, C.M., Toronto, Ont.
Dr. George Luscombe, C.M., LL.D., Toronto, Ont.
Mr. Hartland M. MacDougall, C.M., Belfountain, Ont.
Mrs. Josephine McCarthy, C.M., Toronto, Ont.
Mrs. Edna Hellen McIvor, C.M., Winnipeg, Man.
Mme Renée Morisset, C.M., Québec, P.Q.
Dr. Thomas Joseph Pashby, C.M., M.D., Don Mills, Ont.
Mrs. Leona D. Pedosuk, C.M., North Vancouver, B.C.
Mme Tania Plaw, C.M., Montréal, P.Q.
Lieut.-Col. G. Charles Rafter, C.M., C.D., Winnipeg, Man.
Mrs. Zena Kahn Sheardown, C.M. (Honorary Member), Ottawa, Ont.
Dr. Stuart Allen Smith, C.M., Ph.D., Mouth of Keswick, N.B.
Mr. Stan Stronge, C.M., North Vancouver, B.C.
M. le docteur Jean Taranu, C.M., M.D., Montréal, P.Q.
Dr. Patricia Taylor, C.M., Ph.D., New York, N.Y., U.S.A.
Lieut.-Col. Mark Tennant, C.M., E.D., C.D., Calgary, Alta.
Mr. Richard M. Veenis, C.M., Kabwe, Zambia, Africa

Commanders - Order of Military Merit
Commandeurs - Ordre du Merite Militaire

(Appointed December 8th, 1980. For prior appointments refer to back editions of the Almanac).

Lieut.-Gen. Harold Allison Carswell, C.M.M., C.D.
Vice-Admiral James Andrew Fulton, C.M.M., C.D.
Commodore Thomas Anthony McKenna Smith, C.M.M., C.D.

(Appointed June 15th, 1981)

Maj.-Gen. Douglas Roger Baker, C.M.M., C.D.
Rear-Admiral Daniel Nicholas Mainguy, C.M.M., C.D.
Brig.-Gen. William Rae Thompson, C.M.M., C.D.

Officers - Order of Military Merit
Officiers - Ordre du Merite Militaire

(Appointed December 8th, 1980. For prior appointments refer to back editions of the Almanac).

Lieut.-Cdr. Robert Benjamin Dougan, O.M.M., C.D.
Col. Robert James Ford, O.M.M., C.D.
Maj. James Henry Gebhardt, O.M.M., C.D.
Lieut.-Col. Joseph Edward Lawrence Gollner, O.M.M., C.D.
Col. Ormand Archibald Hopkins, O.M.M., C.D.
Maj. David Fairclough Ives, O.M.M., C.D.
Maj. Isaac Allen Kennedy, O.M.M., C.D.
Col. René Jean Marin, O.M.M., C.D.
Maj. Frank Hubert Mathew, O.M.M., C.D.
Col. Stuart Andrew Millar, O.M.M., C.D.
Lieut.-Col. Robert Earl Moore, O.M.M., C.D.
Lieut.-Col. Richard William Spencer, O.M.M., C.D.
Maj. Gordon Stanley Wallis, O.M.M., C.D.
Maj. Lorne Ellwood West, O.M.M., C.D.
Lieut.-col. Joseph Jules François Wilson, O.M.M., C.D.

(Appointed June 15th, 1981)

Col. John Raymond Allingham, O.M.M., C.D.
Lieut.-Col. Michael Davis Barr, O.M.M., C.D.
Maj. Kenneth Daniel Benner, O.M.M., C.D.
Maj. Donald Stewart Ethell, O.M.M., C.D.
Maj. Clifford Beaufort Fletcher, O.M.M., C.D.
Col. William Charles Gelling, O.M.M., C.D.
Maj. Albert Carl Hincke, O.M.M., C.D.
Lieut.-Col. William John Kitson, O.M.M., C.D.
Cdr. McGregor Fullerton MacIntosh, O.M.M., C.D.
Acting Col. Harold William Madsen, O.M.M., C.D.
Maj. (W) Elizabeth Marion Nicholson, O.M.M., C.D.
Maj. Dale Garnett Schott, O.M.M., C.D.
Col. Pierre Senecal, O.M.M., C.D.
Maj. Arthur Cluney Snow, O.M.M., C.D.
Lieut.-Col. Zenon Michael Zawislak, O.M.M., C.D.
Lieut.-Col. Frederick Taylor Zeggil, O.M.M., C.D.

Members - Order of Military Merit
Membres - Ordre du Merite Militaire

(Appointed July 1st, 1980. For prior appointments refer to back editions of the Almanac).

Master Corporal George Edward Brian, M.M.M., C.D.
Sergeant James Gordon Edward, M.M.M., C.D.
Sergent Claude Gauthier, M.M.M., C.D.

(Appointed December 8th, 1980)

Master Corporal Malcolm Bruce Bailey, M.M.M., C.D.
Master Warrant Officer Lawrence Nelson Bayley, M.M.M., C.D.
Chief Warrant Officer Donald Albert Brown, M.M.M., C.D.
Sergeant John Murray Bryson, M.M.M., C.D.
Sergeant Gordon Kenneth Bullock, M.M.M., C.D.
Master Warrant Officer William George Carnell, M.M.M., C.D.
Master Warrant Officer James Philip Chaston, M.M.M., C.D.
Chief Warrant Officer Willie Albin Colbourne, M.M.M., C.D.
Sergeant Joseph Henry Corbett, M.M.M., C.D.
Caporal chef Gérard Corneau, M.M.M., C.D.
Warrant Officer Dale Lloyd Dirks, M.M.M., C.D.
Chief Warrant Officer Terrance Benjamin Evans, M.M.M., C.D.
Chief Warrant Officer John William Russell Eveleigh, M.M.M., C.D.
Warrant Officer Lawrence Fish, M.M.M., C.D.
Capitaine Edgar Joseph Antoine Gagné, M.M.M., C.D.
Warrant Officer Raymond Arthur Gardner, M.M.M., C.D.
Chief Warrant Officer Philip James Graves, M.M.M., C.D.
Captain Joseph Albert Edmond Grenon, M.M.M., C.D.
Master Warrant Officer James Gerrard Hemlin, M.M.M., C.D.
Chief Warrant Officer George Anthony Henry Joseph Levesque, M.M.M., C.D.
Chief Petty Officer 1st Class Kenneth William McKendry, M.M.M., C.D.
Warrant Officer Joseph Lloyd Melanson, M.M.M., C.D.
Captain James Arthur O'Connor, M.M.M., C.D.
Adjudant-maitre Joseph Arthur Rosaire Parker, M.M.M., C.D.
Adjudant-maitre Noel Wilfred Pitre, M.M.M., C.D.
Chief Warrant Officer John Colin Stewart, M.M.M., C.D.
Warrant Officer Henrick Albert Verwey, M.M.M., C.D.
Master Warrant Officer Dudley Charles McCleave Winchester, M.M.M., C.D.
Chief Warrant Officer Erwin Karl Witt, M.M.M., C.D.

(Appointed June 15th, 1981)

Sergent Joseph Jean Paul Arsenault, M.M.M., C.D.
Chief Warrant Officer Bruce Barton, M.M.M., C.D.
Sergeant Stephen Cannon Burrell, M.M.M., C.D.
Adjudant-chef Peter Caissie, M.M.M., C.D.
Chief Warrant Officer Joseph James Casey, M.M.M., C.D.
Chief Warrant Officer Roland Bernard Edward Clark, M.M.M., C.D.
Chief Warrant Officer Norman Davis Colquhoun, M.M.M., C.D.
Adjudant Joseph Roger Doucet, M.M.M., C.D.
Adjudant-chef Joseph Gérard Fernand Drapeau, M.M.M., C.D.
Capitaine Joseph André Raymond Drouin, M.M.M., C.D.
Chief Warrant Officer Harry Newel Figenshaw, M.M.M., C.D.
Sergeant Dale Allan Frost, M.M.M., C.D.
Warrant Officer Ernest Horst Grossek, M.M.M., C.D.
Warrant Officer John James Ivany, M.M.M., C.D.
Adjudant-maitre Joseph Ronald Leblanc, M.M.M., C.D.
Chief Warrant Officer Michael James Lowe, M.M.M., C.D.
Master Corporal David McIntyre, M.M.M., C.D.
Corporal Robert Henry McLean, M.M.M., C.D.
Captain Robert Allen Nichols, M.M.M., C.D.
Lieut. (N) Garry Ivan Olmstead, M.M.M., C.D.
Adjudant-maitre Joseph Pierre Jacques Paradis, M.M.M., C.D.
Adjudant-chef Paul Pelletier, M.M.M., C.D.
Warrant Officer William Earle Pennington, M.M.M., C.D.
Chief Warrant Officer Erving William Ramsay, M.M.M., C.D.
Captain Stephen Leslie Ricketts, M.M.M., C.D.
Chief Warrant Officer Ross Joseph Roenspiess, M.M.M., C.D.
Master Warrant Officer Jurgen Rothenburg, M.M.M., C.D.
Master Warrant Officer Norman Joseph Saulnier, M.M.M., C.D.
Master Warrant Officer Allistair George Shand, M.M.M., C.D.
Major Bernard George Williams, M.M.M., C.D.
Chief Warrant Officer Garfield Kenneth Zinck, M.M.M., C.D.

Canadian Bravery Decorations
Decorations Canadiennes pour acte de bravoure

(Since publication of the last edition of the Almanac decorations for bravery have been awarded as follows):

Cross of Valour
Croix de la Vaillance

Mr. Lester Fudge, C.V., Salmonier, Nfld.
Mr. Harold Miller, C.V., Burgoyne's Cove, Nfld.
Mr. Martin Sceviour, C.V., Burgoyne's Cove, Nfld.

Star of Courage
Etoile du Courage

Mr. John Douglas Barnett, S.C., Beaverton, Ont.
M. Daniel Charlebois, E.C., Melocheville, P.Q.
Mr. Brian Mervyn Clegg, S.C., Niagara Falls, Ont.
Agent Claude Da Prato, E.C., Coteau du Lac, P.Q.
Mr. Frank Davall, S.C., Kingston, Ont.
M. André Denis, E.C., Québec, P.Q.
Mr. Michael Charles Fikis, S.C. (Posthumous), Thunder Bay, Ont.
M. Sylvain Fillion, E.C. (à titre posthume), Chicoutimi, P.Q.
Deputy Police Chief Thomas Grant Flanagan, S.C., Ottawa, Ont.
Captain Gary Louis Flath, S.C., Courtenay, B.C.
Mr. Robert Stephen Grant, S.C., Niagara Falls, Ont.
Mr. Martin Jerome Griffiths, S.C., Ship Harbour, Nfld.
Constable Ian Johnston Haimes, S.C., Winnipeg, Man.
Mr. Franklin John Hicks, S.C., Whitney, Ont.
Master Corporal Rodderick Warren Hipson, S.C., Shearwater, N.S.
Mr. Syed Jalaluddin, S.C. (Posthumous), Mississauga, Ont.
Mr. Owen Lorne Jones, S.C. (Posthumous), Beaverton, Ont.
Mr. John Stanley MacKinnon, S.C., Cape North, N.S.
Corporal David Albert Maloley, S.C., Lazo, B.C.
Petty Officer Patrick Garfield Marsh, S.C., Lower Sackville, N.S.
Chief Warrant Officer John Lorne McIntosh, S.C., Kingston, Ont.
Miss Jane Ellen Morrison, S.C., Owen Sound, Ont.
M. Joseph Albert Fernand Ouellet, E.C., Ste-Marthe-du-Cap, P.Q.
Agent Raymond Pitre, E.C., Vanier, Ont.
M. Euclide Lucien Prévost, E.C. (à titre posthume), Sudbury, Ont.
Constable John Ashley Robins, S.C., Winnipeg, Man.
Mr. Gordon Douglas Teeft, S.C., Halifax, N.S.
Mr. Brian John James Toney, S.C., Cambridge, N.S.
M. Vincent Vautour, E.C., Comté de Kent, N.B.

Medal of Bravery
Medaille de la Bravoure

M. Jasmin Asselin, M.B., Valleyfield, P.Q.
Corporal Marcel R.J. Bertrand, M.B., Edmonton, Alta.
Mr. Keith Bezanson, M.B., Ottawa, Ont.
Agent de police André Boivin, M.B., Vanier, Ont.
M. Marc Boucher, M.B., Dieppe, N.B.
Mr. Chris Boychuk, M.B., Saskatoon, Sask.
Able Seaman Richard Joseph John Broadhead, M.B., Victoria, B.C.
Mr. Lee Otis Brogan, M.B., Pugwash, N.S.
Mr. Robert Bull, M.B., Thunder Bay, Ont.
Sergeant George Enos Carpenter, M.B., Oromocto, N.B.
Mr. Robert William Carter, M.B., Mount Uniacke, N.S.
Mr. Jim Chrones, M.B., Saskatoon, Sask.
Mr. Gerald Henry Covell, Jr., M.B., Lombardy, Ont.
M. Robert Cree, M.B., Oka, P.Q.
M. Daniel Crépault, M.B., Ste-Foy, P.Q.
Mr. Russell Charles Cribb, M.B., Head Bay d'Espoir, Nfld.
Constable Daniel Desroches, M.B., Ottawa, Ont.
Mr. Joseph Ivan Lawrence Desroches, M.B., Summerside, P.E.I.
Constable Terrance Jeffrey DeGrood, M.B., Edmonton, Alta.
M. Réal Doucet, M.B., Comté de Kent, N.B.
Mr. Garth Murray Evans, M.B., West Vancouver, B.C.
Miss Jessie Ann Foote, M.B., Burin, Nfld.
M. Daniel Gélinas, M.B., St-Rédempteur, P.Q.
Master Corporal Joseph James Goetz, M.B., CFB Shilo, Man.
M. Luc Goudreault, M.B., Ottawa, Ont.
Constable Shamus Hall, M.B., Ottawa, Ont.
Mr. Ralph Stephen Hemphill, M.B., Dartmouth, N.S.
Mr. John Phillip Hiram, M.B., Maple Ridge, B.C.
Constable Allen Robert Hopper, M.B., Hudson Bay, Sask.
Miss Karen Olive Evelyn Jones, M.B., Moreton's Harbour, Nfld.
Mr. Henry Charles Kanouse, M.B., Maple Ridge, B.C.
Constable Richard Wilhelm Krenz, M.B., Squamish, B.C.
Mr. Paul Lawrence Labbie, M.B., Kingston, Ont.
M. Jean-François Lemay, M.B., Laval, P.Q.
Mr. Fraser Nelson MacLeod, M.B., Pugwash, N.S.
Mr. Murray Wayne Martin, M.B., Lantzville, B.C.
Mr. Robert Melis, M.B., Oshawa, Ont.
Master Seaman Ernest Alexander Nash, M.B., Victoria, B.C.
Mr. Lester John O'Neil, M.B., Ottawa, Ont.
M. Jean-Jacques Plante, M.B., Laval, P.Q.
Mrs. Judi Ritchey, M.B., Saskatoon, Sask.
Miss Colleen Lynn Serbyniuk, M.B., Winnipeg, Man.
Private Charles W. Stewart, M.B., Edmonton, Alta.
Mr. Joseph Szimanski, M.B., Oshawa, Ont.
Constable Eric Brian Thorne, M.B., Hudson Bay, Sask.
M. Joséphat Trottier, M.B., St-Joseph-du-Lac, P.Q.
Mr. George Richard Tucker, M.B., Pigeon Cove, Nfld.
M. Célime Vautour, M.B., Comté de Kent, N.B.
Mr. Joseph Waldner, M.B., Poplar Point, Man.
Mr. George Murray Wallace, M.B., Patricia, Alta.
Warrant Officer Arthur E. Warren, M.B., Lancaster Park, Alta.
Constable Dan Wiks, M.B., Saskatoon, Sask.
Mr. Eric Roy Willmott, M.B., Head Bay d'Espoir, Nfld.
Mr. Richard Wayne Winchester, M.B., Oxford, N.S.

MAJOR CANADIAN AWARDS

AGRICULTURAL INSTITUTE OF CANADA

#907, 151 Slater St., Ottawa, Ont. K1P 5H4
(613) 232-9459

FELLOWSHIPS

Awarded to members of the Institute for professional distinction associated with outstanding accomplishment in any field of agriculture.

GRINDLEY MEDAL

Awarded to a Canadian who has made a singular contribution to Canadian agriculture, the impact of which has been far-reaching and recognized within the past five years.

HONORARY MEMBERSHIPS

May be granted to non-members in recognition of distinction associated with outstanding and continuing accomplishment in, or contribution to, any field of Canadian agriculture.

INSTITUTE RECOGNITION AWARD

Awarded to a non-member or member who has rendered a special service to the Institute.

ALBERTA CULTURE

Film & Literary Arts Branch, 12th floor, CN Tower, Edmonton, Alta. T5J 0K5
(403) 427-2554

ALBERTA NON-FICTION AWARD

Established 1973. Awarded annually for the best non-fiction book of general interest written in English by an Alberta author and published within the calendar year. The award consists of a cash prize of $1,500.

Books entered for this award are not eligible for the Alberta Regional History Award.

ALBERTA REGIONAL HISTORY AWARD

Established 1973. Awarded annually for the best regional history written in English by an individual Alberta author, or a group, and published within the calendar year. The award consists of a cash prize of $1,000.

Books entered for this award are not eligible for the Alberta Non-Fiction Award.

NEW-ALBERTA-NOVELIST COMPETITION

Established 1972. The competition is held every two years in co-operation with the General Publishing Co. Ltd. The author of the winning manuscript receives a cash prize of $2,500 from the Government of Alberta and an advance on royalties of $1,500 plus a standard contract from General Publishing Company. Finalists may receive $1,000. In addition, General Publishing offer an advance of $500 with a standard contract to the author of any other manuscript they may wish to publish.

Entrants must be residents of Alberta and must never before have had a novel published.

THE ALBERTA WRITING-FOR-YOUNG-PEOPLE COMPETITION

Established 1980. In co-operation with Clarke, Irwin & Co., Alberta Culture is offering an award of $2,500 for the best publishable manuscript - fiction or non-fiction - in a competition for all Alberta authors of books for young readers. The author of the winning manuscript will receive an outright award of $1,500 from Alberta Culture and a non-refundable advance against royalties of $1,000 from Clarke Irwin.

In addition, any other manuscript entered in the Competition and accepted for publication by Clarke Irwin will receive a $500 award from Alberta Culture and a $500 non-refundable advance against royalties from Clarke Irwin.

The Competition is open to any author resident in Alberta.

ASSOCIATION OF CANADIAN ADVERTISERS

#1010, 180 Bloor St. W., Toronto, Ont. M5S 2V6

(416) 964-3805

ACA GOLD MEDAL

Established 1941. Awarded in recognition of outstanding achievement in advertising—for introducing new techniques or concepts; for significantly improving existing techniques or practices; or for contributions to enhancing the stature or improving the effectiveness of advertising. The purpose of the award is to encourage high standards of personal achievement by practitioners of advertising.

ASSOCIATION OF CANADIAN TELEVISION & RADIO ARTISTS

105 Carlton St., Toronto, Ont. M5B 1M2

(416) 977-6335

THE ACTRA AWARDS

The awards are presented at the Annual ACTRA Awards Dinner, the first of which was held in 1972. The ACTRA Award (the "Nellie"), presented to award winners for the first time in 1973, is a sculpture which was commissioned by ACTRA from the Canadian sculptor William McElcheran. At the 1981 Annual Dinner, the following awards were presented:

The John Drainie Award — for distinguished contribution to broadcasting. Established by ACTRA in 1968. The recipient is chosen each year by the previous recipients.

The Gordon Sinclair Award — for outspoken opinions and integrity in broadcasting. Established 1970.

The Earle Grey Award — for the best acting performance in television in a leading role.

The Andrew Allan Award — for the best acting performance in radio.

The Foster Hewitt Award — for excellence in sportscasting.

The du Maurier Award — for the best new performer in Canadian television.

Award for the best acting performance in a continuing role in television.

Award for the best acting performance in a supporting role in television.

Award for the best host/interviewer - television.

Award for the best host/interviewer - radio.

Award for the best writer - television drama.

Award for the best writer - radio drama.

Award for the best writer - television documentary/public affairs.

Award for the best writer - radio documentary/public affairs.

Award for the best writer - television variety.

Award for the best writer - radio variety.

Award for the best variety performance in television.

Award for the best variety performance in radio.

Award for the best television program of the year.

Award for the best radio program of the year.

THE ASSOCIATION OF PROFESSIONAL ENGINEERS OF ONTARIO

1027 Yonge St., Toronto, Ont. M4W 3E5

(416) 961-1100

THE PROFESSIONAL ENGINEERS GOLD MEDAL

Established 1947. Awarded to a member of the APEO who has spent some years working in the profession and has subsequently given outstanding public service to the country in the federal, provincial, educational, charitable, or other fields. The award winner receives a gold medal and an individually prepared citation.

THE PROFESSIONAL ENGINEERS CITIZENSHIP AWARD

Established 1970. Awarded to members of the APEO who have made a substantial contribution to humanity as citizens and members of the community—in such fields as education, the arts, medicine, law, and social service—while maintaining their identity as professional engineers. There is no limit to the number of these awards made each year. Award winners receive a gold medal.

THE ENGINEERING MEDAL

Established 1964. Awarded to members of APEO who have made a substantial contribution to the advancement of the technical side of the profession in any of its branches. There is no limit to the number of medals which may be awarded each year. Award winners receive a silver medal.

THE ORDER OF THE SONS OF MARTHA

The Order is an honorary Society of the Association of Professional Engineers, the purpose of which is to recognize and honour those professional engineers and others, who have rendered conspicuous service to the engineering profession in varying degrees and normally through the Association.

Awards are made in three classes: Member, Officer, and Companion. Honorary memberships are available to non-members.

V. G. SMITH AWARD

Established 1962. Awarded annually to a member of the Association who has achieved registration during the year by examination, with the highest standing of the candidates who have completed their examinations in that year.

S. W. WOLFE THESIS AWARD

Established 1965. Awarded to a member who has passed at least one of the Association examinations, and whose thesis has been awarded the highest mark of all those presented during the year.

ASTED (Association pour l'avancement des sciences et techniques de la documentation)

360, rue Lemoyne, Montréal, P.Q. H2Y 1Y3

(514) 844-8023

PRIX MARIE-CLAIRE-DAVELUY

Established 1970 (replacing the Prix Maxine which was awarded for the last time in 1965). Awarded every year to encourage young authors to write for young people, and to promote the production of Canadian writing for young people. The award is open to any French-speaking person, between 15 and 20 years, resident in Canada. There is a first prize of $700 and a second prize of $300.

BELL-NORTHERN RESEARCH LTD.

Box 3511, Stn. C, Ottawa, Ont. K1Y 4H7
(613) 596-2210

BNR STUDENT AWARDS

Established 1973. The awards are open to any pre-university student who has obtained highest honours in regional science fairs throughout Canada and has gone on to participate in the Canada-wide Science Fair sponsored by the Youth Science Foundation. One winner is selected from each participating province entered in the engineering or physical science categories. The award consists of a three-day field trip to the Ottawa laboratories of Bell-Northern Research (expenses paid), a cash prize of $200 per exhibit, and a special award citation.

BMI CANADA LTD.

See PERFORMING RIGHTS ORGANIZATION OF CANADA LTD.

BOOK PUBLISHERS' PROFESSIONAL ASSOCIATION

74 Lillian Dr., Scarborough, Ont. M1R 3W5

ROY BRITNELL AWARD

Established 1971. Awarded annually to a Canadian bookseller who has made an outstanding contribution to the business of bookselling and to the community served by that bookseller.

CANADA COUNCIL

255 Albert St., Box 1047, Ottawa, Ont. K1P 5V8
(613) 237-3400

CANADA-AUSTRALIA LITERARY PRIZE

(co-sponsored by the Canadian and Australian governments)

Established 1976. The $2,500 prize is awarded annually, in alternate years, to an English-language Canadian or Australian writer on the basis of his complete literary works.

CANADA-BELGIUM LITERARY PRIZE

(co-sponsored by the Canadian and Belgian governments)

Established 1970. The $2,500 prize is awarded annually, in alternate years, to a French-language Belgian or Canadian writer on the basis of his complete literary works.

CANADA-SWITZERLAND LITERARY PRIZE

(co-sponsored by the Swiss Foundation Pro-Helvetia)

Established 1980. The $2,500 prize is awarded annually, in alternate years, to a Canadian writer or a Swiss writer for a work published in French during the preceding eight years. Translations also included.

CANADA COUNCIL TRANSLATION PRIZES

Established 1974. Awarded annually for the best translations of Canadian books, one from English to French, and one from French to English. To be eligible, the books must be written and translated by Canadians or landed immigrants with five years residency in Canada. The award winners each receive a cash prize of $5,000.

CHILDREN'S LITERATURE PRIZES

Established 1976. Awarded annually to the authors or illustrators of two books (one in English, and one in French) which are judged to be the best of their kind published during the preceding calendar year. Books written by Canadians are eligible whether published in Canada or elsewhere. Each prize is worth $5,000.

GOVERNOR GENERAL'S LITERARY AWARDS

Established 1936. Up to six awards are made annually, three for English and three for French works, in the categories of poetry and drama, fiction and non-fiction. Each of the winners receives a cash prize of $5,000 from the Canada Council.

THE MOLSON PRIZES OF THE CANADA COUNCIL

Established 1963. Three $20,000 prizes are awarded annually to Canadian citizens to recognize outstanding contributions to the arts, humanities, or social sciences. They rank among the highest Canadian awards in the field of culture.

CANADA SAFETY COUNCIL

1765, blvd. St. Laurent, Ottawa, Ont. K1G 3V4
(613) 521-6881

GOLD/SILVER SEAL CERTIFICATES

Established by the Canadian Industrial Safety Association which became part of the Canada Safety Council upon its formation in 1968. The aim of these awards is to stimulate interest in the prevention of occupational accidents and diseases and to recognize meritorious achievement in resolving the problem. The award certificates are available on a non-competitive basis for in-plant recognition of a company's own injury-free record.

OCCUPATIONAL SAFETY & HEALTH ACHIEVEMENT AWARD

The objective of this award program is to provide a visible form of recognition to individuals for outstanding contribution to the prevention of death, injury and disease in the workplace in Canada. Full details re nominations for award are available from the Canada Safety Council.

AWARD FOR EXCELLENCE IN BROADCAST SAFETY MESSAGES

Established in 1978 and operated in co-operation with the Radio Bureau of Canada to recognize station-created safety messages broadcast as a public service by Canadian radio stations.

CANADIAN AERONAUTICS & SPACE INST.

Saxe Bldg., 75 Sparks St., Ottawa, Ont. K1P 5A5
(613) 234-0191

TRANS-CANADA (MCKEE) TROPHY

Established 1927. The Trans-Canada Trophy, generally known as the McKee Trophy, is the oldest aviation award in Canada. It is presented annually except when no qualified recipient is nominated for outstanding achievement in the field of air operations.

MCCURDY AWARD

Established 1954. The McCurdy Award is presented annually for outstanding achievement in art, science, and engineering relating to aeronautics and space.

The award consists of a trophy and a silver medal.

W. RUPERT TURNBULL LECTURE

Established 1955. The W. Rupert Turnbull Lecture is delivered annually at a major meeting of the Institute. The Lecturer is selected for his or her association with some significant achievement in the scientific or engineering fields of aeronautics or space research. The Lecturer receives a certificate and an honorarium.

F.W. (CASEY) BALDWIN AWARD

Established 1957. Awarded annually for the best article published in the *Canadian Aeronautics and Space Journal* and the *Canadian Journal of Remote Sensing* during the preceding year.

The award consists of a silver medal.

C.D. HOWE AWARD

Established 1966. Awarded annually for achievement in the fields of planning, policy making, and overall leadership in Canadian aeronautics and space activities. There is no restriction on the number of awards given in any year. The award consists of a silver plaque.

ROMEO VACHON AWARD

Established 1969. Awarded annually for outstanding contribution of a practical nature to the art, science, and engineering of aeronautics and space in Canada. The award consists of a bronze plaque.

CANADIAN ASSOCIATION OF BROADCASTERS

8th Floor, 165 Sparks St., Ottawa, Ont. K1P 5S2
(613) 233-4035

JOHN J. GILLIN JR. (AM STATION OF THE YEAR AWARD)

Established 1951. Awarded to the AM station making the greatest charitable or public service contribution within its community.

J. E. CAMPEAU (TV STATION OF THE YEAR AWARD)

Established 1962. The award honours the television station making the greatest single or continuing contribution to any form of community service.

LLOYD E. MOFFAT (FM STATION OF THE YEAR AWARD)

Established 1968. The award honours excellence and originality by the FM station making the greatest single or continuing contribution of outstanding value to any form of community service.

TED ROGERS SR./VELMA ROGERS GRAHAM AWARD

Established 1975. The award honours the person making the most significant single or continuing contribution to the Canadian broadcasting system, or for exceptional community service in a role as broadcaster.

THE CGE COLONEL KEITH S. ROGERS ENGINEERING AWARD

Established 1950 by Canadian General Electric. The award goes to the station or individual most successfully developing engineering or technical ideas, approaches, or methods to improve the extent or quality of service in technical terms, or to extend existing services.

H. GORDON LOVE TROPHY

Established 1968. Awarded to the station or individual most successfully meeting these requirements: Making a significant contribution to the improvement or availability of news material used by broadcasting stations in Canada; for helping make the public more conscious of the value of broadcast news; for the discovery, preparation, or presentation of news actually broadcast that has contributed significantly to public enlightenment or benefit in any field.

HARRY SEDGWICK AWARD

Established 1969. The award is designed to encourage and reward promising aspiring broadcasters. It goes to the top graduate in radio television arts at Ryerson Polytechnical Institute. The award is given by CFRB.

RAYMOND CREPAULT MEMORIAL SCHOLARSHIP

Established 1975. This $2,500 annual scholarship, offered by Radiomutuel Network, is open to any French-speaking Canadian citizen interested in improving radio and/or television skills through university training or the equivalent, on a full-time basis, in a Canadian institution.

RUTH HANCOCK MEMORIAL SCHOLARSHIP

Established jointly in 1975 by the Broadcast Executives Society and the CTV Television Network, in co-operation with the Canadian Assn. of Broadcasters, two $1,000 Scholarships are presented annually to two Canadian students enrolled in recognized communications courses in Canada.

Entries consist of 500 word (or less) essays outlining specifics of the communications course, hoped for goal and information on how the Scholarship will help achieve it, reasons for taking the course and a list of extra-curricular activities related to broadcasting.

The above awards are all presented annually at the Annual Meeting of the Canadian Association of Broadcasters.

CANADIAN ASSOCIATION OF MEDICAL RADIATION TECHNOLOGISTS

#410, 280 Metcalfe St., Ottawa, Ont. K2P 1R7
(613) 234-0012

DR. PETRIE MEMORIAL AWARD

Presented annually for the essay of the highest quality and standing submitted in any of the competitions by a Registered Technologist or student. The recipient receives an engraved scroll and a cash gift of $250.

THE CARTWRIGHT AWARD

Presented annually for the technical essay representing the highest quality and standing submitted by a Registered Technologist in good standing. The recipient receives an engraved scroll and a cash gift of $250.

THE HOOD AWARD

Presented annually for the essay of the highest quality and standing submitted by a Registered Technologist in good standing. The subject must be non technical in nature but related to the radiological health care system, i.e., Department Design or Administration, Economics, Supply or Training Systems. The recipient receives an engraved scroll and a cash gift of $250.

MALLINCKRODT AWARD

Presented annually to the technologist who receives the highest aggregate mark in the final C.A.M.R.T. examinations, in each of the three disciplines. Each winner receives a suitably inscribed certificate with a cash award of $200, contributed by the sponsor.

CANADIAN ASSOCIATION OF PATHOLOGISTS

Dept. of Pathology, Hotel Dieu Hospital, Kingston, Ont. K7L 3H6
(613) 544-3310, ext. 263

WILD-LEITZ JUNIOR SCIENTIFIC AWARD

(supported by Wild-Leitz Canada Ltd.)

Established 1965. Awarded annually for a meritorious scientific contribution to pathology. The work submitted may be in English or French and consist of either a paper or papers published or accepted for publication, or a thesis accepted by a faculty of medicine or of graduate studies. Applicants should be not over 35 years of age.

The award winner receives a plaque and a cash prize of $700, and is invited to present a paper at the Annual Scientific Program of the Association.

DONALD W. PENNER PRIZE

Established 1977. This award of $200 is made to the resident presenting the best paper at the annual meeting of the Canadian Congress of Laboratory Medicine.

CANADIAN AUTHORS ASSOCIATION

24 Ryerson Ave., Toronto, Ont. M5T 2P3
(416) 868-6916

THE VICKY METCALF AWARD

Established 1962. Awarded annually for a body of work of interest to Canadian youth. "The prize is given solely to stimulate writing for children...(it) is intended for a number of strictly children's books by any Canadian author. The books may be fiction, non-fiction, or even picture books." (Vicky Metcalf). The award consists of a cash prize of $1,000. There is also a new award of $500 for a short story for children.

CANADIAN BROADCASTING CORP.

Festivals and Special Events, CBC Radio Music, Box 500, Stn. A, Toronto, Ont. M5W 1E6

NATIONAL RADIO COMPETITION FOR YOUNG COMPOSERS

Established 1973. The Competition is sponsored every two years by the CBC and the Canada Council in co-operation with the Ontario Arts Council, le Ministère des Affaires Culturelles du Québec, Alberta Culture, the Saskatchewan Arts Board, the

Manitoba Arts Council, and the British Columbia Cultural Fund. Entrants must be Canadian citizens or landed immigrants 29 years of age and under. Candidates may submit up to three scores each.

Up to seven prizes are given: 1st prize: $4,000, 2nd prize: $3,000, in each of three classes: Electronic Music; 2 to 12 performers; a capella choir. Plus $5,000 Grand Prize.

A performance of the winning works is given on CBC English and French Radio Networks. Deadline is December 31, 1979.

NATIONAL RADIO COMPETITION FOR AMATEUR CHOIRS

Established 1975. Sponsored every two years by the CBC. Prizes are offered in the following classes: Children's, Youth, Adult Mixed, Adult Mixed Chamber, Adult Equal Voice, Adult Multi Cultural, and Contemporary Choral Music. Plus a special prize for best performance of a Canadian Work. Deadline is March 31, 1980.

CBC TALENT COMPETITION

The CBC Talent Competition is now held biennially (next competition 1980-81) as a competition for young Canadian singers and instrumentalists. The competition is open to Canadian citizens and landed immigrants between the ages of 15 and 30. There are five categories: voice; piano; string instruments; woodwind and brass instruments; and a rotating special category. First prize in each category is $2,500, with a $5,000 Grand Prize for the most promising soloist. Each finalist receives $500.

CBC RADIO MUSIC NATIONAL AUDITIONS

Established 1978. Semi-annually, professional individual musicians and ensembles may apply for audition, if they have not been heard nationally in the past two years. This program was devised for those not wishing to enter at the competitive level. The best of these will be broadcast nationally on the CBC Stereo Network.

ARTISTS' REGISTRY

A special service centre of the Festivals and Special Events Unit where Canadian artists and composers may submit their up-to-date resumés and repertoire for distribution to CBC music producers across the country.

CANADIAN COMMUNITY NEWSPAPERS ASSOCIATION

Jim Dills, Executive Director
Ste. 201, 12 Shuter St., Toronto, Ont. M5B 1A2
(416) 366-4277

These awards are open only to members of the Association (approx. 550 community newspapers across Canada). They are presented annually. The various provincial associations also make similar presentations during their annual meetings.

PREMIER AWARDS

Awards are presented in the following categories: Best Advertising Idea; Outstanding Columnist; Local Cartoon; Editorial Writing; and Community Service.

SPECIAL COMPETITIONS

Best Spot News Photo; Best Feature Photo; Best Sports Photo; Best Christmas Edition; Best Sports Page; Best Women's Content.

NEW AWARDS

Best News Story; Best Historical Story; Best Special Section; Best Newspaper Promotion; and Best Feature Story.

GENERAL NEWSPAPER COMPETITIONS

Awards are also given to newspapers for general excellence by circulation category, and include presentations to the Best All Round Newspaper; Best Front Page, and Best Editorial Page in both Broadsheet and Tabloid categories.

CANADIAN CONFERENCE OF THE ARTS

141 Laurier Ave. W., #707, Ottawa, Ont. K1P 5J3
(613) 238-3561

DIPLOME D'HONNEUR

Established 1954. Awarded annually for distinguished service to the arts in Canada.

The first Diplôme d'Honneur was awarded to Governor General Vincent Massey in recognition of the Massey Royal Commission on the Arts, Letters and Social Sciences.

CANADIAN COUNCIL OF CHRISTIANS & JEWS

49 Front St. E., Toronto, Ont. M5E 1B3
(416) 368-8026

BROTHERHOOD AWARD

This award is made to outstanding Canadians of all walks of life who have made a significant contribution towards bringing people together regardless of race, religion or social status, in an atmosphere of understanding and respect.

The award, made annually, is approved by a National Nominating Committee from the Board of Directors of the Canadian Council of Christians and Jews. Additional information can be supplied on request.

GOOD SERVANT MEDAL

Created to commemorate the retirement of Richard D. Jones, O.C., LL.D., after thirty years of continuous service to the Canadian Council of Christians and Jews, as founder and principal officer, 1947-1977. It recognizes individuals who have rendered extraordinary service to their community beyond the call of duty.

CANADIAN COUNCIL OF THE BLIND

96 Ridout St. S., London, Ont. N6C 3X4
(519) 434-4339

AWARD OF MERIT

Established 1952. Presented to a Canadian, blind or sighted, who has rendered outstanding work for the blind.

The award is in the form of a gold medal and clasp, bearing the words of the Council's motto, "Faith, Service, Fellowship." The award winner also receives a specially printed and bound citation, and an honorary life membership in the CCB.

BOOK OF FAME CITATION

The Book of Fame was donated to the Council in 1958 by the disbanded Comrades Club of Toronto. It contains the names and citations of outstanding blind Canadians selected yearly by the eight divisions and the National Board of Directors of the Council. Each recipient of a citation is presented with a framed photograph of the appropriate page in the Book.

CANADIAN COUNCIL OF PROFESSIONAL ENGINEERS

116 Albert St., #401, Ottawa, Ont. K1P 5G3
(613) 232-2474

CANADIAN ENGINEERS' GOLD MEDAL AWARD

Established 1972. This Award is the highest honour conferred by the engineering profession. It recognizes engineers who have made outstanding achievements in their chosen fields. The Award is not limited to members of any association, society or institute.

MERITORIOUS SERVICE AWARD

Established 1981 to recognize outstanding service and dedication to the Canadian engineering profession through Canadian professional, consulting or technical associations and societies, and to enhance the role of the associations and societies in the career of the professional engineer.

CANADIAN FICTION MAGAZINE

Box 946, Stn. F, Toronto, Ont. M4Y 2N9
(416) 534-1259

ANNUAL CONTRIBUTORS' PRIZE

Established 1975. $250 is awarded annually to a writer whose work is selected as the most outstanding original Canadian fiction appearing in French or English in the preceding four quarterly issues of the magazine. Previous winners include Leon Rooke, Ann Copeland, W.P. Kinsella, John Metcalf, Mavis Gallant, David Sharpe.

CANADIAN FOUNDATION FOR THE ADVANCEMENT OF PHARMACY

123 Edward St., #303, Toronto, Ont. M5G 1E2
(416) 979-2024

AUBREY A. BROWN MEMORIAL AWARD

Established 1967. An annual competition open to members of graduating classes of Canadian schools of pharmacy for the best paper of the library, archives and/or survey type (excluding laboratory or experimental work). The award winner receives a certificate of merit, and an award of $200.

E. L. WOODS MEMORIAL PRIZE IN PHARMACY

Established 1968. An annual competition open to graduating pharmacy students on the basis of experimental or laboratory work. The award winner receives a certificate of merit, and an award of $200.

GRADUATE FELLOWSHIPS IN HOSPITAL PHARMACY

Established 1956. The Fellowships are open to competition among Canadian pharmacy graduates and the awards (of $500 each) are to assist four candidates during a one-year residency program.

FELLOWSHIPS IN PROFESSIONAL PRACTICE

Established 1973. Four Fellowships (of $500 each) are offered annually to pharmacy graduates on a national competition basis to applicants presenting study programs in any professional area.

THE PAST PRESIDENTS' AWARD

Established 1966. Awarded to the most outstanding student in a Canadian school of pharmacy, on a rotational basis as to school, and based on (a) scholarship, (b) contribution to the undergraduate life of the school, and (c) likelihood of noteworthy contribution in the future toward the community and his/her profession.

The award winner (selected by the dean or director of the school) receives $250 and a certificate of merit.

FELLOWSHIPS IN INDUSTRIAL PHARMACY

Established 1977. Awarded to students registered in Canadian Schools of Pharmacy who have completed an Industrial Pharmacy Summer Studentship Program. Four Fellowships awarded at $250 each.

CANADIAN HISTORICAL ASSOCIATION

Public Archives of Canada, 395 Wellington St., Ottawa, Ont. K1A 0N3
(613) 233-7885

GARNEAU MEDAL

The Senior CHA Prize. Established 1977. Awarded every five years (the first award to be made in 1980, for the years 1973-1977) to a book which represents an outstanding Canadian contribution to history.

ALBERT B. COREY PRIZE

Established 1966 and jointly sponsored by the CHA and the American Historical Association.

Awarded every two years, with a prize of $2,000, to the best book dealing with the history of Canadian-American relations or the history of both countries.

JOHN A. MACDONALD PRIZE

Established 1976 and jointly sponsored by the CHA and the Manufacturers Life Insurance Co. A prize of $5,000 is given each year for the non-fiction work of Canadian history "judged to have made the most significant contribution to an understanding of the Canadian past".

THE WALLACE K. FERGUSON PRIZE

Established in 1978 (first award 1980 for the years 1977 and 1978) for the outstanding work in a field of history other than Canadian, published in a two-year period.

THE CHA CERTIFICATE OF MERIT

Awarded for outstanding work in the field of local or regional history.

CANADIAN HOSPITAL ASSOCIATION

#800, 410 Laurier Ave. W., Ottawa, Ont. K1R 7T6
(613) 238-8005

GEORGE FINDLAY STEPHENS MEMORIAL AWARD

Established 1949. Awarded in recognition of noteworthy service in the hospital field in Canada.

CANADIAN INSTITUTE OF FORESTRY

#815, 151 Slater St., Ottawa, Ont. K1P 5H3
(613) 234-2242

CANADIAN FORESTRY ACHIEVEMENT AWARD

Established 1966. A gold medal, a certificate, and an appropriate citation are presented annually in recognition of superior accomplishments in research in forestry, and/or of outstanding administrative leadership in management, research, affairs of professional and scientific societies, or education.

CANADIAN FORESTRY SCIENTIFIC ACHIEVEMENT AWARD

Established 1980. A gold medal, a certificate, and an appropriate citation are presented annually in recognition of superior accomplishments in scientific forestry.

CANADIAN INSTITUTE OF MINING & METALLURGY

#400, 1130 Sherbrooke St. W., Montreal, P.Q. H3A 2M8
(514) 842-3461

AIREY AWARD

(supported by the Noranda Group of Companies)

Established 1963. Awarded from time to time in recognition of highly significant contributions to the advancement of metallurgy in Canada, in the industrial field. The recipient must be domiciled in Canada and must be a member of the Institute.

ALCAN AWARD

Established 1966 by the Aluminum Company of Canada Ltd. Awarded from time to time in recognition of highly significant contributions to the advancement of metallurgy in Canada. The recipient must be domiciled in Canada and must be a member of the Institute.

BARLOW MEMORIAL MEDALS

Established 1926. Awarded annually for the best geological paper published in *CIM Bulletin* during the preceding year. Since 1941 the award has consisted of a gold medal.

SELWYN G. BLAYLOCK MEDAL

Established 1948. Awarded from time to time, within the membership of the Institute, for distinguished service to Canada through exceptional achievement in the field of Mining, Metallurgy, or Geology. The award consists of a gold medal.

DISTINGUISHED SERVICE AWARD OF THE PETROLEUM SOCIETY OF CIM

Established 1971. Awarded annually or from time to time as circumstances warrant for exceptional service to the Society or the industry.

DISTINGUISHED SERVICE MEDAL

Established 1957. Awarded from time to time for distinguished service to the Institute or the Mineral Industry (not necessarily of a technical or scientific nature). The award consists of a gold medal.

A.O. DUFRESNE AWARD

Established 1978. Awarded in recognition of exceptional achievements or distinguished contributions to mining exploration in Canada.

ROBERT ELVER AWARD

Established 1981 to commemorate the late Robert Elver. Awarded annually or from time to time in recognition of a significant contribution in the mineral economics field in Canada.

INCO MEDAL

Established 1933. Awarded from time to time as a mark of distinction and recognition to the person who has made a meritorious and practical contribution of outstanding importance to the mining and metallurgical industry of Canada. The award consists of a platinum medal, with a replica in nickel, donated by the International Nickel Company of Canada.

THE DONALD J. MCPARLAND MEMORIAL MEDAL

Established 1974. Awarded from time to time for outstanding performance in the mineral industry in the field of mechanical, electrical, or civil engineering design, general plant design, project engineering and/or management for mine plants. The award can be made to any person in Canada, or elsewhere, but preferably to a member of CIM.

MEDAL FOR BRAVERY

Established 1933. Awarded in recognition of great valour displayed to save life in mines or plants of Canadian mining companies. An award is made only in a case where a person knowingly risks his life in attempting to rescue a fellow worker. Each recipient of the medal receives also an embossed citation of his heroic conduct.

THE ORDER OF SANCTA BARBARA

Established 1968. Awarded to any woman who has made a significant contribution to the welfare of a mining community in Canada. The award consists of a silver medal depicting a portrait of the patron saint and protector of the mines of the world.

PAST PRESIDENTS' MEDAL

Established 1959. Awarded to a person not more than forty-five years of age who, by his attainments, has set an outstanding example to young members of the Institute and to young people contemplating a career in the mineral industry. The recipient must be a member of the Institute.

JOHN CAMPBELL SPROULE MEMORIAL PLAQUE

Established 1974. Awarded in recognition of eminent achievement or distinguished contributions to the exploration and development of Canada's mineral resources in the northern regions.

JOHN T. RYAN TROPHIES

(sponsored by The Mine Safety Appliances Company of Canada Ltd.)

Established 1941 to promote safe mining at Canadian mines. Awarded annually to the companies whose Canadian mines have achieved the lowest injury frequencies in the competition entry period.

The awards consist of three Canada Trophies, one each for Coal Mines, Metalliferous Mines, and Select Mines; and six Regional Trophies, two for the Coal Mining Industry (one each for mines in the Western Region, and the Maritime Provinces), and four for the Metalliferous Mining Industry (one each for mines in British Columbia and the Yukon Territory; the Prairie Provinces and the Northwest Territories; Ontario; and Quebec and the East).

DISTINGUISHED LECTURERS

CIM Distinguished Lecturers are selected on the basis of their distinguished service and accomplishments in scientific, technical, or administrative activities related to the mineral industries. Not more than seven Distinguished Lecturers are selected in any one year. Recipients are presented with an illuminated certificate and an award of $500.

BEST TECHNICAL PAPER

The Metallurgical Society of the CIM presents an annual award for the best technical paper published in the *Canadian Metallurgical Quarterly* in the preceding year. Award winners receive a certificate and a pewter tankard.

STUDENT ESSAY COMPETITION

(graduate and undergraduate competitions)

Established 1901, and since 1948 awarded at both graduate and undergraduate levels, the President's Gold Medal and a cash award are presented for the best essay in the Student Essay Competition. First and second prizes are also offered by the various Divisions and Societies within the CIM.

THE DOFASCO AWARD

Established 1979 by Dofasco Ltd. to recognize highly significant contributions in the field of materials engineering, and is administered by the Materials Engineering Section of the Metallurgical Society of CIM. Awarded from time to time by a senior official of Dofasco Ltd.

THE SHERRITT HYDROMETALLURGY AWARD

Established 1977 and awarded from time to time in recognition of significant contributions to the advancement of Hydrometallurgy through research, plant design and operations, education or CIM affairs. Recipients are to be CIM Members.

CANADIAN LIBRARY ASSOCIATION

151 Sparks St., Ottawa, Ont. K1P 5E3
(613) 232-9625

BOOK OF THE YEAR FOR CHILDREN MEDAL

Awarded annually for outstanding children's books, in English, written by a Canadian, resident in Canada. The award consists of a silver gilt medal.

AMELIA FRANCES HOWARD-GIBBON MEDAL

Established 1971. Awarded annually for the illustration of a children's book. The award consists of a silver gilt medal.

OUTSTANDING SERVICE TO LIBRARIANSHIP AWARD

May be given annually for distinguished service in the field of Canadian librarianship.

CLTA MERIT AWARD

Awarded annually to a Canadian Library Trustees' Association member for distinguished service. Award consists of a citation and plaque.

DISTINGUISHED SERVICE AWARD FOR SCHOOL ADMINISTRATORS

Awarded annually to a school administrator for an outstanding contribution to a resource centre program. Award consists of a citation and plaque.

MARGARET B. SCOTT AWARD OF MERIT

Awarded annually to an individual making an outstanding contribution to Canadian school librarianship. Award consists of a citation and plaque.

CANADIAN PUBLIC HEALTH ASSOCIATION

1335 Carling Ave., #210, Ottawa, Ont. K1Z 8N8
(613) 725-3769

DEFRIES AWARD

Presented in the form of a medal and citation, the Defries Award is the highest honour of CPHA. It is presented to the candidate who has made outstanding contributions in the broad field of public health. Preference is given to Canadian contributions and individuals who have substantially supported the objectives of CPHA. The Award carries with it an Honorary Life Membership.

HONORARY LIFE MEMBERSHIP

This membership is awarded for exceptional excellence as an educator, researcher or practitioner in the field of public health, as demonstrated by achievements, valuable and outstanding research or distinguished service in the advancement of public health knowledge and practice.

ORTHO AWARD

Presented to the candidate who has significantly advanced the cause, legitimized and stressed the responsibility and state of the art of public health.

CANADIAN REHABILITATION COUNCIL FOR THE DISABLED

#2110, One Yonge St., Toronto, Ont. M5E 1E5
(416) 862-0340

THE C. DOUGLAS TAYLOR AWARD

Established 1959. Awarded annually (if appropriate nomination received) in recognition of a person who, over a period of years, has demonstrated distinguished leadership in the development of services to the disabled in Canada.

The award winner receives a plaque.

THE TIMMY AWARD

Established 1959 by the Canadian Council for Crippled Children and Adults.

The award is in the form of a citation to an individual or organization who has rendered some outstanding service to crippled children, through the National Easter Seal Campaign.

THE ABILITY FUND AWARD

Established 1968. The award is in the form of a citation to an individual or organization who has rendered some outstanding service to disabled people through the National Ability Fund Campaign.

THE READER'S DIGEST AWARD

Established 1963 by the Reader's Digest Association (Canada) Ltd. The award is given to a national, provincial, regional, or local organization, agency, or institution, which over the preceding three years has significantly contributed to the development of more effective services for the rehabilitation of disabled persons. The award winner receives a framed certificate and $500.

THE CRCD AWARD

Established in 1969. Awarded in recognition of a disabled person, who through his/her own efforts, has successfully established him/herself and thereby has inspired others to do likewise. The award winner receives a plaque.

THE KEITH S. ARMSTRONG AWARD

Established 1976. The award is to be conferred from time to time to recognize and pay tribute to an individual professionally employed in the voluntary field relating to rehabilitation who over a period of years has provided exceptional service in the interests of the physically handicapped. The award winner receives a plaque.

CANADIAN SCIENCE WRITERS ASSOCIATION

c/o Bob Morrow, Ontario Hydro, 700 University Ave., Toronto, Ont. M5G 1X6

SCIENCE JOURNALISM AWARD

(sponsored by the Ministry of State for Science & Technology)

Awarded annually in recognition of an outstanding individual contribution, through the print medium, to science journalism in Canada. The award is intended to encourage better science writing and the extension of the general knowledge of science and technology. It is open to any writer resident in Canada and writing on any field of science and technology, whose entry has been published in a Canadian print medium during the preceding twelve months. The winner receives a scroll and $1,000.

THE BELL-NORTHERN RESEARCH AWARD OF EXCELLENCE FOR SCIENCE JOURNALISM IN THE ELECTRONIC MEDIA

(sponsored by Bell-Northern Research)

Established 1973. Awarded annually unless no outstanding submission has been made. The aim of the award is to honour an outstanding contribution to science reporting in the electronic media in Canada and to encourage continued excellence in this field. The award is open to any Canadian resident whose reporting in the general field of science (excluding medicine) is broadcast or transmitted by a Canadian radio or television station in French or English during the calendar year. The award consists of a citation and $1,000.

THE ORTHO MEDICAL JOURNALISM AWARD

(sponsored by Ortho Pharmaceutical (Canada) Ltd.)

The award is open to any Canadian resident whose writing in the general field of medicine is originally published in a Canadian print medium. The aim of the award is to honour an outstanding contribution to medical journalism in Canada and to encourage continued excellence in this field.

The award consists of a scroll, travel expenses, and $1000.

ELANCO JOURNALISM AWARD FOR AGRICULTURAL SCIENCES

(sponsored by Elanco Products Division, Eli Lilly & Co. (Canada) Ltd.)

Established 1979. Open to any Canadian resident who originally published in Canadian print media, in French or English, during the calendar year, articles dealing with research and development, regulatory trends, or the advancement of science in agriculture. The award consists of a plaque and $1,000.

CANADIAN SOCIETY OF HOSPITAL PHARMACISTS

123 Edward St., 3rd floor, Toronto, Ont. M5G 1E2
(416) 979-2049

CANADIAN SOCIETY OF HOSPITAL PHARMACISTS AWARD

(sponsored by Ortho Pharmaceutical (Canada) Ltd.)

Awarded annually to a hospital pharmacist for outstanding contribution in Hospital Pharmacy Practice.

The recipient receives travel expenses, a certificate and $1,000.

CANADIAN SOCIETY OF LABORATORY TECHNOLOGISTS

Box 830, Hamilton, Ont. L8N 3N8
(416) 528-8642

The Canadian Society of Laboratory Technologists' Award Program is intended to recognize and acknowledge individuals for meritorious achievement, and to assist members in pursuing advanced studies in medical laboratory technology. The following awards are available under the current program:

GOLD MEDAL AWARD

Awarded for an outstanding contribution to the advancement of medical laboratory technology. The winner receives a gold medal.

HONORARY MEMBERSHIP

Awarded for an outstanding contribution to the Canadian Society of Laboratory Technologists.

HONORARY AFFILIATE MEMBERSHIP

Awarded in recognition of services on behalf of the Canadian Society of Laboratory Technologists in advancing the aims and objectives of the Society.

FOUNDERS' FUND AWARD

Awarded for the purposes of allowing an applicant to obtain further education in medical laboratory technology at an advanced level. Award winners receive a cash allotment to a maximum of $250.

ESSAY COMPETITION AWARD

Awarded in recognition of a technologist who has submitted the best essay in accordance with designated topics as determined by the Canadian Society of Laboratory Technologists.

GRADUATE OF THE YEAR AWARD

(sponsored by I/B Maynard Diagnostics)

Awarded in recognition of the technologist achieving the highest aggregate mark in the General Certificate examinations in the year of the award selection. The award winner receives a plaque.

CYTOLOGY—HISTOLOGY AWARD

(sponsored by B D H Chemicals Ltd.)

Awarded in recognition of the technologist who has submitted the best scientific paper in the discipline of Cytology or Histology. The award winner receives a certificate and a cash prize.

CLINICAL MICROBIOLOGY AWARD

(sponsored by Becton, Dickinson & Co., Canada, Ltd.)

Awarded in recognition of the technologist who has submitted the best scientific paper in the discipline of Clinical Microbiology. The award winner receives a certificate and a cash prize.

HEMATOLOGY AWARD

(sponsored by Dade Division American Hospital Supply Corp.)

Awarded in recognition of the technologist who has submitted the best scientific paper in the discipline of Hematology. The award winner receives a certificate and a cash prize.

CLINICAL CHEMISTRY AWARD

(sponsored by Fisher Scientific Co. Ltd.)

Awarded in recognition of the technologist who has submitted the best scientific paper in the discipline of Clinical Chemistry. The award winner receives a certificate and a cash prize.

IMMUNOHEMATOLOGY AWARD

(sponsored by Ortho Diagnostic)

Awarded in recognition of the technologist who has submitted the best scientific paper in the discipline of Immunohematology. The award winner receives a certificate and a cash prize.

ANNUAL IMMUNOHEMATOLOGY AWARD

(sponsored by Ortho Diagnostics)

Awarded annually to the graduating student in Immunohematology with the highest marks in the C.S.L.T. Examination.

The award winner receives a cetificate, travel and accommodation expenses to attend the five-day postgraduate course in Immunohematology at the Ortho Education Center in Don Mills, Ontario.

AWARD IN CYTOTECHNOLOGY

(sponsored by Ortho Diagnostics)

Awarded annually for the best case study in Cytology presented by a student in Cytotechnology. The recipient receives a certificate and cheque for $50.

CANADIAN VETERINARY MEDICAL ASSOCIATION

360 Bronson Ave., Ottawa, Ont. K1R 6J3
(613) 236-1162

CVMA PLAQUE

Established 1969. Awarded annually in recognition of the student of veterinary medicine at each of the three Canadian veterinary colleges who has been judged by his/her classmates and faculty to combine most effectively the qualities of scholarship, leadership, and sportsmanship.

CVMA AWARD

Established 1966. The award of $250 is presented annually to a veterinary student in the third year at each of the three Canadian veterinary colleges. The recipient is selected by his/her classmates on the basis of achievement and leadership in student affairs.

CVMA YOUTH SCIENCE FAIR AWARD

Presented annually for the encouragement of scientific endeavour by Canadian Youth. The recipient is selected by the Youth Science Foundation from participants in the Annual Youth Science Fair. Amount of award is $100.

LE CERCLE DU LIVRE DE FRANCE

8955, blvd. Saint-Laurent, Montréal, P.Q. H2N 1M6
(514) 384-8760

PRIX ESSO DU CERCLE DU LIVRE DE FRANCE

Established 1949. Awarded annually for an original, unpublished work of fiction in French by a Canadian author who has not already won the Prix du Cercle du Livre de France. The award-winning work is subsequently published by le Cercle. The author receives a cash prize of $5,000.

PRIX JEAN BERAUD-MOLSON

(sponsored by Molson Brewery)

Established 1968. Awarded annually for an original, unpublished work of fiction in French by a Canadian author who has not already won Le Prix Jean-Béraud Molson. The award-winning work is subsequently published by le Cercle. The author receives a cash prize of $4,000.

CHEMICAL INSTITUTE OF CANADA, CANADIAN SOCIETY FOR CHEMICAL ENGINEERING, AND CANADIAN SOCIETY FOR CHEMICAL TECHNOLOGY

#906, 151 Slater St., Ottawa, Ont. K1P 5H3
(613) 233-5623

THE CHEMICAL INSTITUTE OF CANADA MEDAL

Established 1951. Awarded as a mark of distinction and recognition to a person who has made an outstanding contribution to the science of chemistry or chemical engineering in Canada.

The Medal is made of palladium and is provided by Inco Inc.

THE MERCK SHARP & DOHME LECTURE AWARD

Established 1955. Awarded annually to a scientist, under forty years of age, residing in Canada who has made a distinguished contribution in the fields of Organic Chemistry or Biochemistry while working in Canada. The award winner receives $1,000 provided by Merck Sharp & Dohme of Canada Ltd. The lecture is delivered at the Annual Conference of The Chemical Institute of Canada.

THE MONTREAL MEDAL

Established 1956. Awarded annually as a mark of distinction and honour to a resident of Canada who has shown significant leadership in or has made an outstanding contribution to the profession of chemistry or chemical engineering in Canada.

THE R.S. JANE MEMORIAL AWARD

Established 1960. Awarded annually to a person who while resident in Canada has made an exceptional achievement in the field of chemical engineering or industrial chemistry. The award winner is required to present a lecture at the Canadian Chemical Engineering Conference of the Canadian Society for Chemical Engineering, and receives a cash award.

THE UNION CARBIDE AWARD FOR CHEMICAL EDUCATION

Established 1961. Awarded annually as a mark of recognition of a person who has made outstanding contributions in Canada to education at any level in the field of chemistry or chemical engineering. It is accompanied by an honorarium of $750.

THE NORANDA LECTURE AWARD

Established 1963. Awarded annually to a scientist, under forty years of age, residing in Canada who has made a distinguished contribution in the field of Physical Chemistry while working in Canada. The award winner receives $1,000 provided by Noranda Mines Ltd. The lecture is delivered at the Annual Conference of The Chemical Institute of Canada.

THE JOHN LABATT LTD. AWARD

Established 1976. Presented annually for outstanding achievement in chemical or biochemical research or development pertinent to the food and beverage sciences. It is awarded to a scientist resident in Canada who has carried out the major portion of his applicable work in Canada. It is accompanied by an honorarium of $1,000.

THE CATALYSIS AWARD

Established 1976, to be presented to a person who has made a distinguished contribution in the field of catalysis while residing in Canada. The award consists of a rhodium-plated silver medal provided by Johnson, Matthey & Mallory Ltd.

THE FISHER SCIENTIFIC LECTURE AWARD

Awarded 1968. Awarded annually to a scientist residing in Canada who has made a distinguished contribution in the field of Analytical Chemistry while working in Canada. The award winner receives a framed scroll and $1,000 provided by Fisher Scientific Company Ltd. The lecture is delivered at the Annual Conference of the CIC.

THE ERCO AWARD OF THE C.S.Ch.E.

Established 1970. Awarded annually to a resident of Canada, under forty years of age, who has made a distinguished contribution in the field of chemical engineering while working in Canada. The award winner receives an engraved silver medallion and $500 provided by the Erco Industries Ltd.

THE DOMTAR AWARD OF THE CIC FOR HIGH SCHOOL CHEMISTRY TEACHERS

(formerly High School Chemistry Teaching Award)

The Domtar Award is offered as a means of recognizing excellence in the teaching of chemistry at the secondary level in Canada. Up to ten awards are offered each year. Membership in the Institute is not a prerequisite for this award.

STUDENT PRIZES

The CIC/C.S.Ch.E. awards annually an engraved medal and $50 to each of the students obtaining the highest academic standing in the penultimate year in chemical engineering and chemistry at universities across Canada in a course that qualifies for membership in the CIC/C.S.Ch.E.

A similar award of an engraved medal is given to each top student in chemistry at the institutes of technology in their final year and who are taking courses that meet the requirements of the CSCT Committee on Academic Qualifications for Technologists.

BEST STUDENT PAPER PRESENTED AT THE CANADIAN CHEMICAL ENGINEERING CONFERENCE

This award is for the best paper presented by a student during technical sessions of the Canadian Chemical Engineering Conference. The award consists of $200 and a certificate.

BEST PAPER PUBLISHED IN THE CANADIAN JOURNAL OF CHEMICAL ENGINEERING.

This award is for the author(s) of the best paper in a twelve-month period in *The Canadian Journal of Chemical Engineering.* The award consists of an engraved tankard and a certificate.

THE CIC FELLOWSHIP

The Fellowship of the CIC was created as a senior class of membership to recognize those who have made or who are clearly in the course of making a sustained and major contribution to the science or to the profession of chemistry or chemical engineering.

HONORARY FELLOWS

Honorary Fellows are persons to whom The Institute wishes to grant special recognition. The number of Honorary Fellows is limited to twenty at any one time.

ALCAN LECTURE AWARD

$1,000 is awarded for distinguished contributions to inorganic or electrochemistry. Sponsored by the Aluminum Co. of Canada Ltd.

POLYSAR AWARD

A scroll and $500 is awarded for chemical science teaching in community colleges and CEGEPs. Sponsored by Polysar Ltd.

DUNLOP AWARD

$500 and a scroll are awarded for macromolecular science or technology. Sponsored by Dunlop Research Centre.

PROTECTIVE COATINGS AWARD

$1,000 is awarded for protective coatings research or published contributions. Sponsored by the CIC Coatings Division.

CSChE AWARD IN INDUSTRIAL PRACTICE

$300 and a plaque is awarded for distinguished contributions in the application of chemical engineering or industrial chemistry to the industrial sphere.

NORMAN AND MARION BRIGHT MEMORIAL AWARD

An engraved medallion and honorarium is awarded for outstanding contributions in Canada to the furtherance of chemical technology.

ENVIRONMENTAL IMPROVEMENT AWARD

An artifact is awarded to an organization operating within Canada which has made significant contributions to environmental improvement. Sponsored by Beak Consultants Ltd.

COLLEGE OF FAMILY PHYSICIANS OF CANADA

4000 Leslie St., Toronto Ont. M2K 2R9
(416) 493-7513

POST GRADUATE STUDY AWARDS

Sixteen annual awards of $1,000 each, sponsored by the Schering & Upjohn pharmaceutical companies, for two-week post-graduate study sessions in North American hospital centres.

C.M. HINCKS SCHOLARSHIP IN PSYCHIATRY

Designed to meet the expenses of a College member for two weeks of continued education in Psychiatry. This $1,000 scholarship is provided through a memorial fund set up by the widow of the late Clarence Hincks, M.D., a former Director of the Canadian Mental Health Association.

CFP RESEARCH AWARD

Annual award of $1,000, sponsored by "Canadian Family Physician", to the author of the best article of original research published during the previous year in CFP.

ORTHO LITERARY AWARD

Awarded annually and sponsored by Ortho Pharmaceutical (Canada) Ltd., for the best article written by a family physician and published in the Journal of the College during the current year. The recipient received travel expenses, a certificate and a cheque for $500.

FAMILY PHYSICIAN-OF-THE-YEAR AWARD

Recipients of this award are physicians who have been in family practice for a minimum of fifteen years and members of the College for a least ten years, and who have made outstanding contributions to the College, to Family Medicine and to their communities. The award, sponsored by McNeil Laboratories (Canada) Ltd., is $1000 plus travel costs and accommodation for the recipient and spouse to attend the assembly at which the award is presented.

SUSTAINING FUND AWARDS

Awarded annually to CFPC members as follows:

Travelling Scholarships - to enable a CFPC member to undertake scholarly travel with a minimum of three weeks at a study site.

Clinical Traineeships - to enable a CFPC member to pursue clinical studies for a minimum of three weeks under the direction of a clinical department at a Canadian university.

Graduate Study Awards - to enable a CFPC member to pursue a course of study under the direction of a Canadian university for a period of at least six months on a part-time basis.

Awards for Research or Development - to provide "seed money" to a CFPC member to initiate or complete appropriate research or development projects in Family Medicine.

LE CONSEIL DE LA VIE FRANCAISE EN AMERIQUE

59, rue d'Auteuil, Québec, P.Q. G1R 4C2
(418) 692-1150

PRIX CHAMPLAIN

Established 1957. Awarded annually for a work on any subject written by a Franco-American or French Canadian resident outside of the Province of Quebec. If the author is resident in Quebec, the work must deal with Franco-Americans or French Canadians outside of Quebec. The winner receives a cash prize of $1,000.

CONSEIL DES ARTS DE LA COMMUNAUTE URBAINE DE MONTREAL

#2223, 2 Complexe Desjardins, Box 129, Montréal, P.Q. H5B 1E6
(514) 872-2074, 843-4142

GRAND PRIX LITTERAIRE DE LA COMMUNAUTE URBAINE DE MONTREAL

Established 1964. Awarded annually to the author of a literary work published in book form in Montreal in the preceding year. The author receives a cash prize of $3,000.

DELEGATION GENERALE DU QUEBEC (Les Services culturels)

66, rue Pergolese, Paris 16e, France

PRIX FRANCE-CANADA

Established 1961 by l'Association France-Canada, and the government of Québec. Awarded annually for a work, in any genre, published the preceding year in France or Canada by a Canadian. The winner receives a cash prize of 1,000 francs provided by the government of Québec.

PRIX FRANCE-QUEBEC JEAN-HAMELIN

Established 1965 by l'Association des Ecrivains de Langue Française, in collaboration with the government of Québec. Awarded annually for the work of a Canadian or American writer published in Québec or France during the preceding year. The winner receives a cash prize of 2,000 francs provided equally by l'Association des Ecrivains and the government of Québec.

DEPT. OF JUSTICE, OTTAWA

Programs & Law Information Section, Dept. of Justice, Justice Bldg., Ottawa, Ont. K1A 0H8

DUFF-RINFRET SCHOLARSHIP PROGRAM

The Department of Justice offers annually a number of scholarships for graduate studies at the Master's level in Canadian law schools in areas of law within federal jurisdiction. The scholarships are for one year and are valued at $7,700, plus tuition fees and travelling expenses.

FELLOWSHIPS IN LEGISLATIVE DRAFTING

Established 1970. Designed to encourage Canadian lawyers to enter the field of drafting statutes, subordinate legislation and legal instruments. Four fellowships of the value of $6,500 plus tuition are awarded each year, tenable at the Faculty of Law, University of Ottawa.

EDMONTON JOURNAL

Community Relations Dept., Box 2421, Edmonton, Alta. T5J 2S6
(403) 425-9120

EDMONTON JOURNAL LITERARY AWARDS

Established 1962. Prize money totalling $2,150 is awarded for the best entries in each of four categories: Fiction up to 3,000 words; Non-fiction up to 2,000 words; Poetry, maximum 72 lines; and One-Act Play, playing time 20 - 45 minutes. Purpose is to encourage the efforts of new writers. Entry is limited to residents of the Edmonton Journal's trading zone, which includes central and northern Alberta, the Peace River area of northern B.C., the Yukon and the Northwest Territories.

ETUDES FRANCAISES

Univ. de Montréal, Departement d'Etudes françaises, C.P. 6128, Montréal, P.Q. H3C 3J7
(514) 343-6207
(514) 343-6168

PRIX "ETUDES FRANCAISES"

Established 1966. Awarded annually for a literary work in French written by a French-speaking author who is resident in a country other than France. Only original and unpublished works are eligible for the award. The winner receives a cash prize of $2,000.

THE FIONA MEE FOUNDATION

59 Front St. E., Toronto, Ont. M5E 1B3
(416) 364-3333

LITERARY JOURNALISM AWARD

A $1,000 prize awarded annually, based on submissions of literary journalism published in the previous year in Canadian magazines and newspapers. The deadline for submissions is January 29 and entries are judged by a jury of book trade and library representatives.

HERITAGE CANADA FOUNDATION

Box 1358, Stn. B, Ottawa, Ont. K1P 5R4

AWARD OF HONOUR

Recognizes outstanding achievement in heritage conservation in Canada.

COMMUNITY SERVICE AWARD

Recognizes outstanding service to the community.

COMMUNICATIONS AWARD

Recognizes outstanding efforts to promote public awareness of Canada's heritage and the need to preserve it.

LIEUTENANT-GOVERNORS' MEDAL

Established 1979 to recognize outstanding work in architectural conservation on a provincial level by an individual or group. It must be demonstrated that the applicant's continuous efforts in the field of heritage conservation have benefitted the province where the Foundation's Annual Meeting is being held. Applications must be sponsored by an organized heritage group and/or elected officials at any level of government.

GABRIELLE LEGER MEDAL

Gabrielle Léger, wife of the Right Honorable Jules Léger, established a Heritage Canada medal to recognize outstanding work in architectural conservation in Canada. This is an annual national award to an individual who has contributed outstanding community services in the cause of heritage conservation.

IODE MUNICIPAL CHAPTER OF TORONTO

76 St. Clair Ave. W., Toronto, Ont. M4V 1N2
(416) 921-1197

IODE BOOK AWARD

Established 1975. Awarded annually to the author or illustrator of the best children's book written or illustrated by a Canadian resident in Toronto or surrounding area and published by a Canadian publisher within the preceding twelve months. The award winner receives an inscribed scroll and not less than $1,000.

JUNO AWARD PRESENTATIONS LIMITED

see RPM WEEKLY

LITTLE, BROWN & CO. (CANADA) LTD.

25 Hollinger Rd., Toronto, Ont. M4B 3G2
(416) 751-4520

THE LITTLE, BROWN CANADIAN CHILDREN'S BOOK AWARD

Established 1957. Awarded from time to time to the author of an original, unpublished work of fiction or non-fiction, in the English language, written for boys and/or girls of any age. The competition is open to any Canadian citizen or resident. The prize-winning manuscript is published simultaneously in Canada and the U.S., and the author receives $4,500 as a combined $1,000 cash prize and royalty advance.

NATIONAL COMPETITIVE FESTIVAL OF MUSIC

304-310 Donald St., Winnipeg, Man. R3B 2H4
(204) 943-6098

Underwritten as a public service by the Canadian Imperial Bank of Commerce, and organized by the Federation of Canadian Music Festivals in cooperation with the Canadian Bureau for the Advancement of Music and the Canadian National Exhibition.

Canadian Imperial Bank of Commerce Scholarships of $1,000, $500 and $250 are awarded to first, second and third place winners in each of six categories: voice, piano, strings, woodwinds, brass and ensemble. Ten separate provincial competitions are held throughout the early part of the year and the winners of these compete for national honours each September in Toronto. The Festival culminates in a gala concert at which a Canadian artist or ensemble of international renown appears with the top award-winners.

NATIONAL DESIGN COUNCIL, AND DEPT. OF INDUSTRY, TRADE & COMMERCE

Dept. of Industry, Trade & Commerce, Design Canada, Ottawa, Ont. K1A 0H5
(613) 992-4494

N.D.C. CHAIRMAN'S AWARD FOR DESIGN MANAGEMENT

Established 1970. Awarded annually to encourage Canadian enterprises to improve their design management activities. The Award recognizes the outstanding contribution made by a Canadian business enterprise in advancing the cause of good design by the application of effective design management.

Design management is the integration of design and related activities into a framework of policies and procedures which are reflected in the company's products, facilities, services, and corporate image.

The Award is presented to the Chief Executive Officer of the winning enterprise.

DESIGN CANADA SCHOLARSHIPS

Scholarships for advanced study in Canada or abroad in the field of graphic, industrial and interior design.

Relevant programs of study in engineering, business and education (teaching) are also available only to qualified candidates from the field of industrial design.

NATIONAL MAGAZINE AWARDS FOUNDATION

#300, 1240 Bay St., Toronto, Ont. M5R 2A7
(416) 922-3184

Awards are presented annually in twenty categories including General Magazine Articles, Humour, Business, Science and Technology, Sports, Politics, Agriculture, Fiction, Poetry, Culture, Travel, Religious Writing, Fashion Features, Comment, Magazine Illustration, Studio Photography, Photojournalism, Art Direction, Magazine Covers, and Outstanding Achievement by a Magazine.

Awards are gold or silver scrolls with $1,000 and $500 cash prizes respectively, given by corporate sponsors. All awards go to individual magazine writers, photographers, illustrators, or art directors, except Outstanding Achievement by a Magazine. Entries may be in English or French. Annual competition closes early in January, and a Magazine Awards Presentation Dinner is held in April or May.

THE PROVINCE OF ONTARIO

For nomination forms please write to: Executive Secretary, Ontario Medals, Office of the Premier, Room 463, Queen's Park, Toronto, Ont. M7A 1A1
(416) 965-9121

ONTARIO MEDAL FOR GOOD CITIZENSHIP

Established 1973 as a means of affording recognition and tribute to citizens who, through their selflessness, humanity, and kindness, make Ontario a better province in which to live.

ONTARIO MEDAL FOR POLICE BRAVERY

Established 1976 to recognize acts of superlative courage and bravery performed in the line of duty by members of Ontario's police forces.

ONTARIO MEDAL FOR FIREFIGHTERS BRAVERY

Established 1976 to recognize acts of superlative courage and bravery performed in the line of duty by members of Ontario's firefighting forces.

ONTARIO ARTS COUNCIL

151 Bloor St. W., Toronto, Ont. M5S 1T6
(416) 961-1660

THE CHALMERS AWARD

Established 1972 by the Floyd S. Chalmers Foundation and administered by the Ontario Arts Council. Awarded annually for the most outstanding Canadian-written play produced by any theatre organization in Canada and played in the area covered by the Toronto drama critics during the previous year. Emphasis is on new, full-length works. The value of the award is $5,000, with additional awards totalling $3,000.

THE JEAN A. CHALMERS AWARD IN CHOREOGRAPHY

Established 1974 by the Floyd S. Chalmers Foundation and administered by the Ontario Arts Council. The purpose of the award is to assist promising or deserving choreographers in improving their choreographic skills. Applicants must be Canadian citizens or landed immigrants. The value of the award is $5,000.

HEINZ UNGER SCHOLARSHIP

Established 1968. A competition is held annually and contestants are asked to conduct the University of Toronto Faculty of Music's Repertory Orchestra. Usually an award of up to $1,000 is made. Scholarship winners who are resident in Ontario may use the award to study conducting in Ontario or elsewhere; those who do not live in Ontario must use the award to study conducting in Ontario.

LESLIE BELL SCHOLARSHIP AWARD

Established 1973. Awarded annually in competition. The purpose of the award is to help young emerging conductors further their studies in the choral music field either in Canada or abroad. The winner receives up to $1,000 provided by the award fund and the Ontario Arts Council.

RUTH SCHWARTZ FOUNDATION AWARD

Presented annually to the best authored/illustrated Canadian children's book of the year. The winner receives a $2,000 award.

ONTARIO MINISTRY OF CULTURE & RECREATION

Huronia Historical Parks, Box 160, Midland, Ont. L4R 4K8
(705) 526-7838

THE SAINTE-MARIE PRIZE

Program currently under review.

PERFORMING RIGHTS ORGANIZATION OF CANADA LIMITED

41 Valleybrook Dr., Don Mills, Ont. M3B 2S6
(416) 445-8700

P.R.O. CANADA AWARDS

Established 1967 for the purpose of recognizing the P.R.O. Canada music creators and their contribution to Canadian music. They are presented at the annual Awards Dinner. Only P.R.O. Canada affiliated writers, composers and music publishers are eligible.

P.R.O. CANADA YOUNG COMPOSERS' COMPETITION

$6,000 presented annually.

P.R.O. CANADA ORCHESTRA AWARDS

$10,000 presented every two years to Canadian orchestras for the "imaginative programming of contemporary music."

P.R.O. CANADA COPYRIGHT AWARD

$2,500 presented annually to a law student or articling lawyer for essay on the subject of copyright and music.

THE WM. HAROLD MOON AWARD

Established 1974. The award recognizes the P.R.O. Canada affiliate who, in the opinion of the committee, has generated the greatest international influence for Canadian music in the past calendar year.

PERIODICAL DISTRIBUTORS OF CANADA

c/o Sheryll Reid, Argyle Communications, 322 King St. W., Toronto, Ont. M5V 1J2
(416) 977-9977

AUTHORS AWARDS

Established 1977 to encourage Canadian writing. A total of $4,500 in cash prizes is awarded annually in the following categories: 1) Paperback Book and Magazine Fiction, 2) Paperback Book Non-Fiction and Magazine Public Affairs, 3) Paperback Book and Magazine Cover Designs, and 4) Magazines- Humour, and Magazines- Personality Features.

PHARMACEUTICAL MANUFACTURERS ASSOCIATION OF CANADA

Room 1110, 141 Laurier Ave. W., Ottawa, Ont. K1P 5J3
(613) 236-9993

PMAC MEDAL OF HONOR

Established in 1945. Awarded periodically when an individual has made an invaluable contribution to the advancement of science in the world. The first award was made to Sir Alexander Fleming for his discovery of penicillin; the second award to Dr. Charles H. Best for his co-discovery of insulin.

PLANNED PARENTHOOD FEDERATION OF CANADA

151 Slater St., #200, Ottawa, Ont. K1P 5H3
(613) 722-3484

FAMILY PLANNING VOLUNTEER AWARD
(sponsored by Ortho Pharmaceutical (Canada) Ltd.)

The award has been established to recognize the outstanding contributions by a volunteer to the family planning movement in Canada.

The award consists of a certificate, travel expenses, and $500.

PROFESSIONAL INSTITUTE OF THE PUBLIC SERVICE OF CANADA

786 Bronson Ave., Ottawa, Ont. K1S 4G4
(613) 237-6310

PROFESSIONAL INSTITUTE GOLD MEDALS

Established 1937. Two gold medals are presented biennially, one in each of the following fields: a) pure or applied science; b) some field outside pure or applied science.

Those eligible for an award are scientific, professional or technical workers or groups of workers employed by the Federal, Provincial, or Municipal Public Service or the Armed Services of Canada who have made a contribution of outstanding importance to national or world well-being in either of the above fields.

INSTITUTE SERVICE AWARDS

Established 1970. Not more than five awards may be made annually to members of the Institute in any classification, or persons ineligible for membership, for outstanding service to the Institute.

The award consists of a brass plaque and a $25 book token.

QUEBEC DEPT. OF CULTURAL AFFAIRS

225 Grande Allée est, Québec, P.Q. G1R 5A5

LE PRIX DAVID

Established 1967. Le Prix David is the highest literary distinction conferred by the Government of Quebec. It is awarded to an author on the merit of his/her work as a whole. Canadian citizens domiciled in Quebec are eligible for the award. The winner receives the sum of $15,000 and an engraved medal.

The following five awards offer $15,000 bursaries and an engraved medal. They are awarded annually in a ceremony at the National Assembly.

LE PRIX BORDUAS

For a work in the visual arts (plastic arts, photography, artistic work, design and/or architecture).

LE PRIX DENISE PELLETIER

For a remarkable contribution in the performing arts (theatre, dance, music, lyrical arts and/or singing).

LE PRIX LEON GERIN

For works in the human sciences (moral science, philosophy, psychology, social sciences and/or the law).

LE PRIX MARIE-VICTORIN

For works in the pure sciences (physics, chemistry, biology and/or natural sciences).

LE PRIX ALBERT-TESSIER

For a remarkable contribution in the field of cinema.

ROYAL ARCHITECTURAL INSTITUTE OF CANADA

328 Somerset St. W., Ottawa, Ont. K2P 0J9
(613) 232-7165

RAIC ALLIED ARTS MEDAL

Established 1953. Awarded at intervals of not less than one year and not more than three years for outstanding achievement in the arts which are allied to architecture, such as mural paintings, sculpture, decoration, stained glass, industrial design. Awarded to an artist regardless of citizenship.

The award winner receives a silver medal.

RAIC GOLD MEDAL

Established 1930. May be awarded annually in recognition of a person of science or letters related to architecture and the arts, in addition to an architect, for great achievement and contribution to the architectural profession. Non-Canadians are eligible for the award.

The award winner receives a gold medal.

RAIC STUDENT MEDAL

Available to a student in each Canadian University School of Architecture in the graduating class for the degree of Bachelor of Architecture.

The award is made only to a student who, in the opinion of the School, has attained a high proficiency in the course and shows those qualities of character and ability which promise outstanding achievement in the profession.

ROYAL ASTRONOMICAL SOCIETY OF CANADA

124 Merton St., Toronto, Ont. M4S 2Z2
(416) 484-4960

GOLD MEDAL

The Gold Medal of the Society was established in 1905 as an encouragement to the study of astronomy. It is awarded to the graduating fourth year University of Toronto Arts & Science student who has both an A standing in his/her fourth year and the highest average mark in the two full courses and two half courses in astronomy which are contained in the Astronomy specialist program, provided this average is over 80%. If no student satisfies these criteria, the award is not made.

CHANT MEDAL

The Chant Medal of the Society was established in 1940 in appreciation of the great work of the late Professor C.A. Chant in furthering the interests of astronomy in Canada. This medal is awarded, not oftener than once a year, to an amateur astronomer resident in Canada on the basis of the value of the work which he/she has carried out in astronomy and closely allied fields of original investigation.

SERVICE AWARD MEDAL

The Service Award was established in 1959 and, on recommendation of a special committee of the National Council, this small bronze plaque is presented to members who have performed outstanding service to a Centre or to the National Society.

KEN CHILTON PRIZE

The Ken Chilton Prize was established in 1977 in memory of K. E. Chilton of Hamilton, and is awarded annually to an amateur astronomer resident in Canada, in recognition of a significant piece of work carried out or published during the year.

SIMON NEWCOMB AWARD

The Simon Newcomb Award was established in 1978 by the R.A.S.C. Halifax Centre, and is named after the distinguished Canadian-born astronomer Simon Newcomb. It is awarded annually for the best article on astronomy, astrophysics or space science submitted by a member of the Society during the year.

ROYAL BANK OF CANADA

Secretary, Selection Committee, Box 1102, Montreal, P.Q. H3C 2X9
(514) 874-6679

ROYAL BANK AWARD

Established 1967. The purpose of the Royal Bank Award is to honour outstanding achievements which contribute to human welfare and the common good. To be eligible a candidate must be a Canadian citizen or a person domiciled in Canada. Not necessarily conferred each year. Award may be shared. Institutions and corporations not eligible. The award consists of a gold medal and a cash payment of $100,000.

ROYAL CANADIAN GEOGRAPHICAL SOCIETY

488 Wilbrod St., Ottawa, Ont. K1N 6M8
(613) 236-7493

THE MASSEY MEDAL

Established 1959. Awarded annually for outstanding personal achievement in the exploration, development, or description of the geography of Canada. The award is limited to Canadian citizens (except in special circumstances). The award winner receives a silver gilt medal presented by the Massey Foundation.

ROYAL COLLEGE OF PHYSICIANS & SURGEONS OF CANADA

74 Stanley St., Ottawa, Ont. K1M 1P4
(613) 746-8177

THE ROYAL COLLEGE OF PHYSICIANS OF CANADA MEDAL, AND THE ROYAL COLLEGE OF SURGEONS OF CANADA MEDAL

Established 1946. Awarded annually for original scientific work judged best in the Division of Medicine and the Division of Surgery. The purpose of the awards is to provide national recognition to original work by young clinicians and investigators. The authors shall not have attained their 45th birthdays before Dec. 31 of the year in which his or her work is submitted. The awards are open to any graduate in Medicine of Canadian nationality; a graduate in Medicine of any nationality whose nomination is based on work done in Canada; any Fellow or certified specialist of the College. Award winners receive a bronze medal and a cash prize of $500, and are invited to present their papers at the time of the annual meeting. Travel and maintenance expenses of each award winner and spouse are paid. Deadline for receipt of applications and manuscripts is February 26th.

ROYAL SOCIETY OF CANADA

344 Wellington St., Ottawa, Ont. K1A 0N4
(613) 992-3468

CHAUVEAU MEDAL

Established 1951. Awarded every two years (since 1966) for a distinguished contribution to knowledge in the humanities other than Canadian literature and Canadian history. The winner receives a silver medal and $1,000.

FLAVELLE MEDAL

Established 1924. Awarded every two years (since 1966) for an outstanding contribution to biological science during the preceding two years or for significant additions to a previous outstanding contribution to biological science.

The winner receives a medal and $1,000.

INNIS-GERIN MEDAL

Established 1966. Awarded every two years for a distinguished and sustained contribution to the literature of the social sciences including human geography and social psychology. The winner receives a bronze medal and $1,000.

McLAUGHLIN MEDAL

Established 1978. Awarded yearly for important research of sustained excellence in any branch of medical science. The winner receives a medal and $1,000.

WILLET G. MILLER MEDAL

Established 1943. Awarded every two years for outstanding research in any branch of the earth sciences. The winner receives a medal and $1,000.

LORNE PIERCE MEDAL

Established 1926. Awarded every two years (since 1926) for an achievement of special significance and conspicuous merit in imaginative or critical literature written in either English or French, and preferably dealing with a Canadian subject. The winner receives a medal and $1,000.

HENRY MARSHALL TORY MEDAL

Established 1941. Awarded every two years (since 1947) for outstanding research in a branch of astronomy, chemistry, mathematics, physics, or an allied science. The winner receives a medal and $1,000.

TYRRELL MEDAL

Established 1927. Awarded from time to time for outstanding work in the history of Canada. The winner receives a medal and $1,000.

BANCROFT AWARD

Established 1968. Awarded every two years for publication, instruction, and research in the geological and geophysical sciences that have conspicuously contributed to public understanding and appreciation of the subject.

The winner receives a presentation scroll and $1,000.

HARRISON PRIZE

Established 1957. Awarded every three years for the best work on a bacteriological subject (medical bacteriology excluded).

The winner receives a scroll and $150.

RUTHERFORD MEMORIAL MEDALS

Established 1980. Two medals are awarded yearly for outstanding research, one in chemistry and one in physics. Some preference will be given to candidates whose age is not over 40 in the year of the medal.

SIR ARTHUR SIMS SCHOLARSHIP

Established 1952. The aim of the scholarship is to encourage Canadian students to undertake postgraduate work in Great Britain. It may be awarded for outstanding merit and promise in any subject of the humanities, social sciences, or natural sciences, and is open to graduates of Canadian universities who are British subjects. Awarded biennially. Tenure of two years, possibly three. The annual value of the scholarship is £650.

EADIE MEDAL

Established 1975. Awarded annually for a distinguished contribution to any field in Engineering or Applied Science. Preference would be given to achievements not eligible for other Awards of the Royal Society of Canada.

The winner receives a silver medal and $1,000.

JASON A. HANNAH MEDAL

Established 1976. Awarded yearly for an important publication in the history of medicine which is Canadian by reason of citizenship, residence or content. The winner receives a bronze medal and $1,000.

RPM WEEKLY
JUNO AWARD PRESENTATION LTD.

6 Brentcliffe Rd., Toronto, Ont. M4G 3Y2
(416) 425-0257
(Annual RPM Gold Leaf Award)

Established 1970, superceding the RPM Annual Music Poll which was inaugurated in 1964. The awards are administered by the Canadian Academy of Recording Arts and Sciences, and are presented on a live ninety minute CBC national telecast in honour of distinguished Canadian music figures, the top stars and craftsmen of the Canadian music and record industry. Awards are given in the following categories: top male vocalist; top female vocalist; top recording group; most promising male vocalist; most promising female vocalist; most promising recording group; top country male vocalist; top record producer; top composer; best album design; best selling single; and best-selling album. There are also awards for the best-selling international single and album in Canada. Selection of award winners is based equally on sales and votes (except for the last four categories).

Past award winners include: Anne Murray, Gordon Lightfoot, Stompin' Tom Connors, Backman-Turner Overdrive, The Guess Who, Pierre Juneau, Paul Anka, Bruce Cockburn, Murray McLauchlan.

SEAL BOOKS

60 St. Clair Ave. E., Toronto Ont. M4T 1N5
(416) 922-4970

$50,000 SEAL BOOKS FIRST NOVEL COMPETITION

Established 1977, the competition is open to Canadian citizens or Canadian landed immigrants who have not previously had a novel published anywhere in the world. The winner will receive a cheque for $50,000, $10,000 of which is an outright prize, $40,000 as a non-returnable advance against earnings under the publishing contract. The winning novel will be published in hardcover in Canada, in the U.S., and in the U.K. The subsequent paperback editions will be published by Seal Books in Canada, Bantam Books in the U.S., and by Corgi Books in the U.K. Manuscripts (not less than 60,000 words) must be written in English under the author's own name and submitted no later than December 31.

SOCIETY OF CHEMICAL INDUSTRY
Canadian Section

c/o D.W. Scott, Honorary Secretary, Celanese Canada Inc., Chemicals Division, Two Robert Speck Pkwy., #900, Mississauga, Ont. L4Z 1H8

SOCIETY OF CHEMICAL INDUSTRY CANADA MEDAL

Established 1939. Awarded every two years for outstanding services to the Canadian chemical industry.

STUDENT MERIT AWARDS

The awards are made at approved universities in Canada in courses qualified by The Chemical Institute of Canada in one of the fields of chemistry either alone or combined with another major course.

The merit award is a gold key bearing the likeness of the crest of the Society of Chemical Industry on the front, and the name of the winner, the University, and the year on the back.

SOCIETE DES ECRIVAINS CANADIENS

1161 boul. Vanier, Ville de Laval, P.Q. H7C 2N4
(514) 661-3064

PRIX LITTERAIRE AIR CANADA

Established 1976.

PRIX LITTERAIRE DE LA FONDATION LES AMIS DES ECRIVAINS INC.

(Section Saguenay/Lac Saint-Jean)

Established 1977.

PRIX LITTERAIRE ADRIENNE CHOQUETTE

(Section Québec)

Established 1980.

LA SOCIETE SAINT-JEAN-BAPTISTE DE MONTREAL

82 rue Sherbrooke ouest, Montreal, P.Q. H2X 1X3
(514) 843-8851

PRIX DUVERNAY

Established 1944. Awarded annually to a French Canadian in recognition of outstanding literary achievement in serving the higher interests of the French Canadian people. The award winner receives a cash prize of $1,500 and the medal "Bene Merenti de Patria".

PRIX PHILLIPE-HEBERT

Established 1971. Awarded annually to a French Canadian in recognition of outstanding achievement in the plastic arts in serving the higher interests of the French Canadian people. The award winner receives a cash prize of $1,500 and the medal "Bene Merenti de Patria".

PRIX OLIVAR-ASSELIN

Established 1955. Awarded annually to a French Canadian in recognition of outstanding achievement in journalism in serving the higher interests of the French Canadian people. The award winner receives a cash prize of $1,500 and the medal "Bene Merenti de Patria".

PRIX CALIXA-LAVALLEE

Established 1959. Awarded annually to a French Canadian in recognition of outstanding achievement in music in serving the higher interests of the French Canadian people. The award winner receives a cash prize of $1,500 and the medal "Bene Merenti de Patria".

PRIX VICTOR-MORIN

Established 1962. Awarded annually to a French Canadian in recognition of outstanding achievement in theatre, television, or film, in serving the higher interests of the French Canadian people. The award winner receives a cash prize of $1,500 and the medal "Bene Merenti de Patria".

PRIX ESDRAS-MINVILLE

Established 1978. Awarded annually to a French Canadian in recognition of outstanding achievement in Humane Science (History, Sociology, Economics, Politics, etc.), in serving the higher interests of the French Canadian people. The award winner receives a cash prize of $1,500 and the medal "Bene Merenti de Patria".

PRIX MAURICE-RICHARD

Established 1979. Awarded annually to a French Canadian in recognition of outstanding achievement in Sports and Athletics, in serving the higher interests of the French Canadian people. The award winner receives a cash prize of $1,500 and the medal "Bene Merenti de Patria".

SOCIETE ST-JEAN-BAPTISTE DE LA MAURICIE

3239, Papineau, C.P. 1059, Trois-Rivières, P.Q. G9A 5K5
(819) 375-4881

PRIX BENJAMIN-SULTE

Established 1972. Awarded to a person resident in the diocese of Trois-Rivières for a work of literature or journalism produced during the previous 12 months. The award consists of a medal, a certificate, and $100.

LE GRAND PRIX LITTERAIRE SSJB

Awarded, on the recommendation of a special committee, to recognize the whole body of work of an author.

This prize consists of a certificate, a carved statuette of Ludger Duvernay, founder of the Society in 1834, and $500.

SOUTHAM INC.

Southam Fellowships, Rm. 107, Simcoe Hall, University of Toronto, Toronto, Ont. M5S 1A1
(416) 925-2881

THE SOUTHAM FELLOWSHIPS FOR JOURNALISTS

Established 1962. Three or more awarded annually, tenable at The University of Toronto. Applicants must be working journalists with at least five years' experience in newspaper, magazine, radio or television. Individual awards are in an amount covering regular gross monthly salary, as at the date of the award, for the eight months of the University "year" up to a maximum gross salary ceiling that is specified for each annual competition.

E.W.R. STEACIE MEMORIAL FUND

c/o National Research Council of Canada, Ottawa, Ont. K1A 0R6
(613) 993-0286

THE STEACIE PRIZE

Established 1963. Awarded annually to a person under forty years of age for outstanding scientific work in a Canadian context. The prize consists of a certificate and a cash award of $5,000.

STEPHEN LEACOCK ASSOCIATES

Box 854, Orillia, Ont. L3V 6K8
(705) 325-6546 (Mrs. Jean Bradley, Chairman, Award Committee)

STEPHEN LEACOCK MEMORIAL MEDAL

Established 1946. The purpose of the award is to encourage the writing and publishing of humorous works in Canada. It is given annually for the best Canadian book of humour published in the previous year. The winner also receives a cash grant of $2000.

CITY OF TORONTO (Civic Honours)

City Clerk's Dept., City Hall, Toronto, Ont. M5H 2N2
(416) 367-7341

AWARD OF MERIT

In September, 1956, City Council established a policy of presenting Awards of Merit, in the form of a suitably inscribed medallion to persons who have attained distinction and renown in various fields of endeavour. To carry out this policy, City Council appointed a non-political Committee. In 1976, for the first time, citizens were invited to recommend nominees for the Award.

MEDAL OF SERVICE

Since 1971, City Council has presented Medals of Service in recognition of those citizens who have given freely and generously of their time and talents to serve on various City Boards and Commissions.

HISTORICAL BOARD AWARD OF MERIT

Established in 1974. Recipients are selected by the Board because of outstanding contributions to the preservation of the history of Toronto. Awards may be made to persons in the literary or visual arts field, to public-spirited individuals, groups or organizations, to persons involved in the various aspects of architectural preservation, or in such other areas as the Board may deem appropriate.

BOOK AWARDS

In 1973, City Council created a Book Award Selection Committee to select each year a winner or winners of a literary prize totalling $5,000. The Committee selects a short list of nominees whose books have been about Toronto and published that year. A winner(s) is chosen and the Award is presented by the Mayor on behalf of City Council, followed by a Civic Reception.

CIVIC HONOURS DAY

The aforementioned awards are presented each year in conjunction with the Anniversary of the Incorporation of Toronto on March 6. This date has been designated as Civic Honours Day and suitable celebrations of Toronto's Birthday are arranged.

CONSTANCE E. HAMILTON AWARD

Established 1979 to commemorate the 1929 Privy Council of Great Britain decision granting women status as persons within the British North America Act. Constance Hamilton was the first woman member of Toronto City Council. Recipients are persons whose actions have been significant in helping secure equitable treatment for Toronto women in various aspects of economic, social and cultural activities in Toronto.

CITY OF TORONTO SCHOLARSHIPS

To commemorate the visit of H.M. Queen Elizabeth II in 1973, the "City of Toronto Scholarship" in The George Brown College of Applied Arts & Technology is awarded to the most deserving student from a Toronto secondary school entering the course in Business Administration, and who is qualifying himself/herself for employment relating to Municipal Government.

To commemorate the visit of Her Majesty Queen Elizabeth The Queen Mother in 1981 the "City of Toronto Scholarship" in The National Ballet School is awarded to the most deserving student pursuing a career in ballet.

TORONTO PRESS CLUB

73 Richmond St. W., Toronto, Ont. M5H 1Z4
(416) 362-4266

NATIONAL NEWSPAPER AWARDS

Established 1949. Awarded annually to men and women employed regularly on the editorial staffs of Canadian daily newspapers and press associations for work published in a Canadian daily newspaper. (An exception to the rule of regular employment is made in the case of photography and cartooning.)

Nine awards were offered in 1980 for work in: Spot News Reporting; Feature Writing; Enterprise Reporting; Editorial Writing; Critical Writing; Sports Writing; Spot News Cartooning; Feature Photography; Spot News Photography. Award winners receive a cash prize of $500 or more.

NORMAN DePOE MEMORIAL SCHOLASTIC FUND

A bursary awards program to students in the media.

UNIVERSITY OF BRITISH COLUMBIA

UBC Awards Office, Vancouver, B.C. V6T 1W5

UBC MEDAL FOR POPULAR BIOGRAPHY

Established 1952. Awarded annually for the best popular biography written either about or by a Canadian and published in the previous year.

UNIVERSITY COLLEGE, UNIVERSITY OF TORONTO

15 King's College Circle, Toronto, Ont. M5S 1A1
(416) 978-3171

NORMA EPSTEIN FOUNDATION AWARDS

In the categories of drama, poetry, short story or other prose.

a) annual competition open to undergraduates of University College only, with awards totalling approximately $1,000. Entry date 15 January.

b) a biennial competition, open to undergraduates and graduates enrolled in any Canadian University, with a single award of $1,000. Entry date 15 May, 1981.

All manuscripts must be submitted in duplicate under a pseudonym to the College Registrar. Each entry must be covered by a separate entry form and a different pseudonym. Entry forms obtainable from the University College Registrar.

WRITERS' FEDERATION OF NOVA SCOTIA

Box 3608, Halifax South P.O., Halifax, N.S. B3J 3K6
(902) 423-8116

EVELYN RICHARDSON MEMORIAL LITERARY TRUST AWARD

Established 1978 to recognize outstanding work in the field of non-fiction by a Nova Scotian writer (native or resident), the annual award consists of a trophy and cash prize of $500.

Nominations consist of three copies of the book published in the previous calendar year. Deadline April 15.

ELECTION REGULATIONS IN CANADA

According to the Canada Elections Act, and subject to certain exceptions, the general rule as to the franchise of electors at a Federal election is that every person in Canada, man or woman, is qualified as an elector if such person

(a) is of the full age of 18 years or will attain such age on or before polling day at such election; and

(b) is a Canadian citizen.

Among persons disqualified are prisoners, and persons under restraint owing to mental disease.

Writs for a general election are issued about two months before the date fixed for polling day; at by-elections writs may be issued about 45 days before polling day.

Similar qualifications apply in the Provinces, for provincial elections. There is a residence requirement, usually twelve months before the date of issue of the writ of election. The age requirement is 18 years in all provinces except British Columbia, and the Territories, where it is 19 years.

To contact government election officers see Index, "Elections, Govt. Info. Sources".

MARRIAGE REGULATIONS IN CANADA

Divorce grounds in Canada: adultery; sodomy, bestiality, rape or homosexual act; bigamy; physical or mental cruelty; imprisonment (3 out of 5 years cumulative) (2 years of long term); gross addiction to alcohol or a narcotic (3 years); disappearance (3 years); non-consummation (1 year); separation (3 years); desertion by petitioner (5 years).

Alberta

Marriageable age:
- Without parental consent—18 years
- With parental consent—under 18 years

Blood test: required within 14 days before date of application for marriage licence.
Licence fee: $10.00

British Columbia

Marriageable age:
- Without parental consent—19 years
- With parental consent—16 to 18 years
- A court order of consent—under 16 years

Blood test: not required
Waiting period for licence: 2 full days
Licence fee: $5.00 (and an additional $7.50 fee for a civil ceremony)

Manitoba

Marriageable age:
- Without parental consent—18 years
- With parental consent—16 years*

Blood test: required
Waiting period for licence: none
Waiting period after issuance of licence: 24 hours
Licence fee:
- For residents of Manitoba—$10.00
- For non-residents—$10.00. Non-residents must complete special authorization applications also.

*Persons under 16 years of age can be married only with the consent of a judge of the Family Court.

New Brunswick

Marriageable age:
- Without parental consent—18 years
- With parental consent—under 18 years

Blood test: not required
Waiting period for licence: 5 days
Licence fee: $10.00

Newfoundland

Marriageable age:
- Without parental consent—19 years (excepting expectant mothers or mothers of illegitimate children)
- With parental consent—under 19 years

Blood test: not required
Marriage licence: none required unless by civil ceremony

Nova Scotia

Marriageable age:
- Without parental consent—19 years or over
- With parental consent—16 years

Blood test: not required
Waiting period for licence: 5 days
Licence fee: $10.00

Ontario

Marriageable age:
Without parental consent—18 years
With parental consent—16 years
Blood test: not required
Waiting period after issuance of licence: 3 days
Licence fee: $20.00
Marriage fee: $15.00

Prince Edward Island

Marriageable age:
- Without parental consent—18 years;
- With parental consent—under 18 years

Blood test: to be taken 5 days before licence is issued
Other requirements: birth certificates and Social Insurance Cards; in the case of a widow or widower, death certificate; in the case of a divorced person, certified copy of the Decree Absolute.
Waiting period for licence: 5 days
Licence fee: $5.00

Quebec

Marriageable age:
- Without parental consent—18 years
- With parental consent—men, 14 years
- With parental consent—women, 12 years

Blood test: not required
Other requirements and impediments: subject to the rules followed in the different churches and religious communities
Waiting period for licence: none
Fee for civil marriage: $40.00 ($65.00 on Saturday)
Divorce may be obtained before the Superior Court on grounds of adultery and other reasons as mentioned in the Divorce Act.

Saskatchewan

Marriageable age:
- Without parental consent—18 years
- With parental consent—16 to 18 years

Medical requirements: pre-marital medical examination, including blood test.
Licence fee: $10.00

For complete information, contact the Director of Vital Statistics, Department of Health, 3475 Albert St., Regina, Sask. S4S 6X6

Northwest Territories

Marriageable age:
- Without parental consent—19 years
- With parental consent—15 years

Blood test: not required
Waiting period for licence: none
Licence fee: $5.00

Yukon Territory

Marriageable age:
Without parental consent—19 years
(In the case of a self-supporting person apart from home for the preceding six months, 18 years)
With parental consent—15 years
Blood test: not required
Waiting period for licence: none
Waiting period after issuance of licence: 24 hours
Licence fee: $5.00

LIQUOR REGULATIONS IN CANADA

For names of personnel of the various Liquor Control Boards see index "Liquor Board, Commission, or Control,"

Alberta

Spirits, wines and beers are sold in Government liquor stores.
Legal drinking age is 18 years.

Beer in unopened bottles may be sold by licensed hotels to persons who are not disqualified under the Act, for consumption off the premises.

Liquor (including wine and beer) may be sold in a licensed Beverage Room, Canteen, Aircraft, Bus, Club, Dining Lounge, Lounge, Night Club, Train, Racetrack (closed stands), Recreational Facility, Theatre or Travellers' Lounge for consumption on the premises.

Beer, wine and liqueurs only may be sold in a licensed Restaurant.

Beer and cider only may be sold at concessions in a Racetrack (open stands) or Stadium (at professional soccer, football, hockey and baseball games). No sale is permitted in the stands.

Licensees may purchase liquor only from Government liquor stores and warehouses. Licences are issued for a maximum 12 month period. Fees vary with the type of licensed premises with an additional fee of 7 per cent of the purchase price of all wine and spirits purchased by a licensee.

Alberta Liquor Control Bd., 12360 142nd St., Edmonton, Alta. T5J 2R4

British Columbia

The Liquor Control and Licensing Branch may issue licenses to Dining Lounges, Dining Rooms, Lounges, Public Houses, "A" Pubs, Cabarets, Neighbourhood Public Houses, Recreational Centres and Special Occasion Licenses for special occasions.

B.C. Liquor Control & Licensing Branch, Box 640, Victoria, B.C. V8W 2P8

The Liquor Distribution Branch is solely responsible for the selection, purchasing, pricing and distribution of all alcohol beverages (wines, spirits and beer) throughout British Columbia, in a retail store system and to license holders. A portfolio of approximately 1,800 products is offered for sale to persons 19 years and older in more than 200 government liquor stores and over 50 agency stores in the province.

B.C. Liquor Distribution Branch, 3200 E. Broadway, Vancouver, B.C. V5M 1Z6 (604/254-5711)

Manitoba

Persons, resident in the province, transients and travellers, over the age of 18 years and who are not otherwise prohibited, may purchase and consume beer, wine and spirits in any premise licensed by the Liquor Control Commission, and may purchase from the Liquor Commission Stores, for consumption in a residence.

Beer may also be purchased from beer vendor depots located in most hotels throughout the province.

The Commission may authorize the sale of spirits of all kinds either unmixed or mixed only with water, soft drinks or fruit juices in a beverage room situated in a district in which the Commission may issue a cocktail room licence.

Parents dining with their children may purchase alcoholic beverages for the latter, for consumption with meals, only in licensed restaurants or dining rooms.

Beer parlors, beverage rooms and cocktail rooms must be vacated within 30 minutes after the hour at which sale of liquor must cease.

Man. Liquor Control Commn., 1555 Buffalo Place, Winnipeg, Man. R3C 2X1

New Brunswick

Intoxicating liquor is sold in sealed packages at Liquor Stores and by the glass in licenced dining rooms, restaurants, taverns, cabarets, lounges, beverage rooms, and clubs. It is not rationed and permits are not required. Age of majority is 19.

N.B. Liquor Corp., Box 20787, Fredericton, N.B. E3B 5B8

Newfoundland

The importation, manufacture, and sale of Alcoholic Beverages through Retail Liquor outlets is the responsibility of the Nfld. Liquor Corp.

The Nfld. Liquor Licensing Bd. is responsible for the issuing of all licenses, other than those to manufacture and to sell packaged beer, and enforcement of regulations including, but not limited to the following:

All alcoholic liquor sold in the hotel lounge shall be dispensed at the bar in such a manner that it may be viewed by persons using the lounge.

All liquor sold upon licensed premises shall be consumed thereon.

All liquor served in licensed premises shall be dispensed from the original container in which the liquor is purchased from or under the authority of the Liquor Corp.

Every person employed in serving liquor shall be in possession of a waiter's license which may be granted by the Board.

The drinking age in Newfoundland is 19 years.

Nfld. Liquor Corp., Box 8750, St. John's, Nfld. A1B 3P2; Nfld. Liquor Licensing Bd., Box 8550, St. John's, Nfld. A1B 3P2

Nova Scotia

Liquor can only be sold in sealed packages through the Government stores.

By local option vote, spirits can be sold by the glass and beer or wine by the glass or open bottle in licensed restaurants and dining rooms with meals, and in lounges with or without meals. Taverns in wet areas can sell beer only. Beverage rooms in wet areas may sell beer and wine to men or women.

Some hotels and restaurants are designated as resorts and are then not subject to local option vote.

The legal minimum drinking age is 19 years.

N.S. Liquor License Bd., 277 Pleasant St., Dartmouth, N.S. B2Y 4B7

Ontario

In accordance with the provisions of the Liquor Control Act of Ontario, the marketing and sale of liquor (spirits, wine or beer) is the responsibility of the Liquor Control Board of Ontario. No permit is required for individual purchases. Wines are retailed through Liquor Control Board Outlets and Wine Stores. Beer may be purchased through Liquor Control Board Stores and Brewers' Retail Stores without a permit.

Pursuant to the Liquor Licence Act of Ontario, the Liquor Licence Board of Ontario is responsible for the licensing of approved premises which sell liquor (spirits, wine or beer) by the glass to the general public. Liquor may be sold in licensed premises in municipalities where the municipal electors have decided in favour of such sale. Beer, wine and spirits are available in those establishments licensed as Lounges or Dining Lounges. Beer and wine only are sold in licensed Dining Rooms. Beer may be served for consumption on premises which are licensed as Public Houses. Clubs, theatres, railway trains, steamships, aircraft, military messes and recreational facilities may be issued various types of licenses for the sale of spirits, wine or beer. However, in clubs, the sale of liquor is restricted to members and their guests. In addition to the above, Special Occasion Permits may be issued in respect of individuals, groups and certain charitable or community functions which are held in approved non-licensed premises and which are not conducted for the purpose or with the intention of gain or profit.

The drinking age in Ontario is 19.

The Liquor Licence Bd. of Ont., 55 Lakeshore Blvd. E., Toronto, Ont. M5E 1A4

Liquor Control Bd. of Ont., 55 Lakeshore Blvd. E., Toronto, Ont. M5E 1A4

Prince Edward Island

Spirits, wines and beer in sealed packages may be purchased at Commission Stores throughout the Province by any person over the age of 18 who is not otherwise disqualified.

Spirits by the glass, and beer and wine by the open bottle or glass, may be purchased in dining rooms, cocktail lounges, clubs and military canteens licensed by the Commission.

P.E.I. Liquor Control Commn., 3 Garfield St., Parkdale, P.E.I. C1A 7M4

Quebec

Spirits and wines are sold and delivered by the Quebec Liquor Corporation stores only.

Spirits and wines so obtained may be sold to the public, by hotels, cafés and clubs under licenses, provided these are consumed on the premises.

Beer is obtained directly from the breweries and may be sold to the public by inns, taverns and restaurants under licenses, provided it is also consumed on the premises.

A grocery store duly licensed may sell beer at such store on condition: that not less than one bottle be sold; that beer be not consumed in that store or dependency thereof.

Municipalities may declare by by-law that no alcoholic liquor of any description may be sold within their territory.

In any place where the sale of alcoholic beverages is permitted, nobody being under 18 years old can purchase alcoholic beverages.

Que. Liquor Corp., C.P. 1058, Place d'Armes, Montreal, P.Q. H2Y 3J8

Saskatchewan

Beer, wine and spirits are sold in stores throughout the province operated by the Liquor Board under authority of The Liquor Act. The Act also provides for small liquor outlets in drug stores and other suitable business establishments at country points, operated as agencies under the supervision of the Liquor Board.

The minimum legal drinking age is 19.

No purchase permit required and no limitation on quantity purchased at retail liquor outlets.

Alcoholic Beverages are also sold in premises licensed by the Liquor Licensing Commission which agency has authority to grant Dining Room, Cocktail Room and Club licenses permitting the holder of the license to serve spirits, wine and beer; Restaurant licenses permitting the holder to serve wine and beer only; Beverage Room licenses permitting the holder to serve spirits, wine and beer. Hotel licensees holding a license to sell beer by the glass may also be granted a license to sell beer in closed packages to be consumed off the premises.

Premises meeting the requirements of The Liquor Licensing Act and Regulations and granted licenses by the Commission must purchase all spirits, wine and beer from the Liquor Board.

Sask. Liquor Bd., Box 5054, Regina, Sask. S4P 3M3

Northwest Territories

The Northwest Territories Act, Chapter 331 of the Revised Statutes of Canada, 1952, authorizes the Commissioner in Council of the Northwest Territories to make ordinances respecting intoxicants.

Under the Liquor Ordinance, Government operated stores are established at Hay River, Inuvik, Norman Wells, Frobisher Bay, and liquor agencies at Yellowknife, Fort Smith, Pine Point, Fort Simpson, and Cambridge Bay. Taverns, cocktail lounges, dining lounges, clubs and tourist lodges have been licensed in various communities.

A Liquor Licensing Board has been established to supervise and regulate the granting of licences and operation of the premises.

Several communities have asked for, and received, various types of alcohol control, ranging from complete prohibition to rationing.

Yukon Territory

The Yukon Act, Chapter Y-2 of the Revised Statutes of Canada, 1970, authorizes the Commissioner in Council, Yukon Territory, to make ordinances respecting intoxicants.

By virtue of Territorial Ordinance, liquor stores have been opened at Dawson, Mayo, Whitehorse, Haines Junction, Watson Lake and Faro and beer taverns, cocktail lounges, dining rooms, restaurants, clubs, canteens, special premises and aircrafts have been licensed throughout the Yukon Territory.

FORMS OF ADDRESS

(Salutations and closings have been used with the permission of The MacMillan Co. of Canada, from the book "Styles of Address", by Howard Measures.)

GOVERNMENT

THE GOVERNOR GENERAL:

If the name is used:

Address—His Excellency John M. Blank, Government House, Ottawa. If a member of the Queen's Privy Council for Canada—His Excellency the Honourable John M. Blank. If a member of Her Majesty's Most Honourable Privy Council (The United Kingdom Privy Council)—His Excellency the Right Honourable John M. Blank.

If the name is not used:

Address—His Excellency The Governor General, Government House, Ottawa.

Salutation and Closing—

(Sir)
I have the honour to be, Sir,
Your Excellency's obedient servant,

or, (Dear Governor General)
Believe me, Your Excellency,
Yours sincerely,

or, (My dear Governor General)
With kind regards,
Yours very sincerely,

Note: If the Governor General has military and other titles, the title His Excellency precedes the others. If the Governor General is a Prince or a Royal Duke, the title His Royal Highness and the salutation Your Royal Highness are used instead of His Excellency and Your Excellency. The wife of the Governor General is accorded the title Her Excellency. The Governor General and his wife together—Their Excellencies.

LIEUTENANT GOVERNOR OF A PROVINCE:

Address—His Honour, The Lieutenant Governor of (the Province of)______, Government House,______

or,

Address—His Honour the Hon. (name), Lieutenant Governor of (the Province of), Government House,______.

Salutation and Closing—

(Sir)
I am, Your Honour,
Yours very truly,
or, (Dear Sir)
Yours sincerely,
or, (My dear Lieutenant Governor)
I am, my dear Lieutenant Governor
Yours sincerely,
or, (Dear Mr. ...)
With kind regards,
Yours very sincerely,

Note: A lieutenant governor of a province of Canada retains the title Honourable for life.

THE PRIME MINISTER OF CANADA:

Address—The Right Honourable John M. Blank, P.C., M.P., Prime Minister of Canada, Ottawa.

Salutation and Closing—

(Dear Sir)
Yours very truly,
or, (Dear Mr. Prime Minister)
Yours sincerely,
or, (Dear Prime Minister)
With kind regards,
Yours sincerely,

Note: The Prime Minister of Canada is a member of the Queen's Privy Council for Canada and has the title "The Right Honourable" for life.

THE PREMIER OF A PROVINCE OF CANADA:

Address—The Honourable John M. Blank, M.L.A., Premier of the Province of______.

Salutation and Closing—

(Dear Sir)
Yours very truly,
or, (My dear Premier)
Believe me, my dear Premier,
Yours sincerely,
or, (Dear Mr. ...)
With kindest regards,
Yours sincerely,

Note: The Premier of a Province of Canada has the title "The Honourable" during his term of office. He is head of the government of the Province, i.e., the First Minister, he is generally the President of the Executive Council of the Province. In Quebec he is styled "Prime Minister" instead of "Premier" and members are styled M.P.P. in Ontario, and M.N.A. in Quebec instead of M.L.A.

MEMBER OF THE FEDERAL CABINET, MEMBER OF THE PRIVY COUNCIL NOT OF THE CABINET, AND MEMBER OF THE EXECUTIVE COUNCIL OF A PROVINCE:

Address—The Honourable John M. Blank, Minister of ______, ______.

Salutation and Closing—

(Dear Sir) (Dear Madam)
Yours very truly,
or, (Dear Mr. ...) (Dear Miss or Mrs. ...)
With kind regards,
Yours sincerely,

Note: If also a member of the United Kingdom Privy Council, he is addressed "The Right Honourable" for life. The letters P.C. are placed after the names of members of the Privy Councils of Canada and of the United Kingdom. One member of the Cabinet addressing another uses the salutation "My dear Colleague". Members of the Privy Council are appointed, and have the title "The Honourable", for life. Members of Executive Councils of the Provinces have the title of Honourable only during their terms of office.

MEMBER OF THE SENATE:

Address—The Honourable John M. Blank, *or* The Honourable Mary M. Blank, The Senate, Ottawa.

Salutation and Closing—

(Dear Sir)
Yours very truly,
or, (Dear Senator ...)
I am, dear Senator ...
Yours sincerely,
or, (My dear Senator)
Believe me,
Yours sincerely,

Note: A senator who is a member of the Canadian Privy Council is addressed "Senator the Honourable John M. Blank". A Senator who is a member of the United Kingdom Privy Council is addressed "Senator the Right Honourable John M. Blank".

MEMBER OF THE HOUSE OF COMMONS:

Address—John M. Blank, Esq., M.P., House of Commons, Ottawa.

Salutation and Closing—

(Dear Sir) (Dear Madam)
Yours very truly,
or, (Dear Mr. ...) (Dear Miss or Mrs. ...)
Yours sincerely,

DEPUTY MINISTER OF A DEPARTMENT:

Address—John M. Blank, Esq., Deputy Minister of______.

Salutation and Closing—

(Sir)
Yours truly,
or, (Dear Sir)
Yours sincerely,
or, (Dear Mr. ...)
With kind regards,
Yours sincerely,

MEMBER OF A PROVINCIAL GOVERNMENT:

Address—John M. Blank, Esq., M.L.A., Member of the Legislative Assembly, (Legislative Bldgs., Edmonton; Parliament Bldgs., Victoria; Legislative Bldg., Winnipeg; Legislative Bldg., Fredericton; Confederation Bldg., St. John's; Province House, Halifax; Parliament Bldgs., Toronto; Province Bldg., Charlottetown; Hotel du gouvernement, Quebec; Legislative Bldgs., Regina).

Salutation and Closing—

(Dear Sir)
Yours very truly,
or, (Dear Mr. ...)
Believe me,
Yours sincerely,

Note: In the case of the Province of Quebec use M.N.A. and Ontario use M.P.P. instead of M.L.A.

MAYOR OF A CITY OR TOWN:

If the name is used:

Address—His Worship Mayor John M. Blank, *or* Her Worship Mayor Joan M. Blank, City Hall.

If the name is not used:

His Worship the Mayor of ______. Her Worship the Mayor of ______.

Salutation and Closing—

(Dear Sir) (Dear Madam)
Yours very truly,
or, (Dear Mr. Mayor) (Dear Madam Mayor)
Believe me, dear Mr. Mayor,
Yours sincerely,

JUDGES

CANADA:

In Canada there are two broad classes of courts—superior courts and county (or district) courts. Judges of the superior courts are addressed "The Honourable Mr. Justice ______" and judges of the county or district courts are addressed "His Honour Judge ______". The Supreme Court of Canada and the Federal Court of Canada are also superior courts. The Supreme Courts of the Yukon and the Northwest Territories are superior courts.

There are two classes of Chief Justices—The Chief Justice of Canada or of a province on the one hand, and the Chief Justice of a court on the other. The Chief Justice of the Supreme Court of Canada is styled the Chief Justice of Canada; similarly, there is a Chief Justice for each of the provinces. Other courts in the provinces, namely, the trial courts, usually have a Chief Justice also and he is known as the Chief Justice of that court.

CHIEF JUSTICE:

The Chief Justice of Canada:

Address—The Right Honourable The Chief Justice of Canada, Supreme Court of Canada, Ottawa.

Or—The Right Honourable______, P.C., Chief Justice of Canada, Ottawa.

Salutation and Closing—

(Sir)
I am, Sir,
Yours very truly,
or, (Dear Sir)
Yours faithfully,

Chief Justice of a Province or Territory:

Address—The Honourable ______, Chief Justice of ______.

Salutation and Closing—

(Sir)
I am, Sir,
Yours very truly,
or, (Dear Sir)
I am, Sir,
Yours sincerely,
or, (Dear Mr. Chief Justice)
Believe me, dear Mr. Chief Justice,
Yours sincerely,

JUDGES:

Supreme Court of Canada, Federal Court of Canada, Courts of Appeal, Courts of the Queen's Bench, Superior Court of the Province of Quebec, Supreme Courts of the Provinces and Territories:

Address—The Honourable Mr. Justice John M. Blank, *or* The Honourable Madam Justice Mary M. Blank.

Salutation and Closing—

(Sir) (Madam)
I am, Sir, (Madam)
Yours very truly,
or, (Dear Mr. Justice ...)
Believe me,
Dear Mr. Justice ...
Yours sincerely,

JUDGES:

County and District Courts:

Address—His Honour Judge John M. Blank,

Salutation and Closing—

(Sir)
I am, Sir,
Yours very truly,
or, (Dear Judge Smith)
Believe me, dear Judge Smith,
Yours sincerely,

RELIGION

Anglican Church of Canada

ARCHBISHOP:

Address—The Most Reverend ______, D.D., Archbishop of ______.

Salutation and Closing—

(Most Reverend Sir)
I have the honour to be,
Most Reverend Sir,
Your obedient servant,
or, (Dear Archbishop)
Yours sincerely,

BISHOP:

Address—The Right Reverend ______, D.D., Bishop of ______.

Salutation and Closing—

(Right Reverend Sir)
I am, Right Reverend Sir,
Respectfully yours,
or, (Dear Bishop ...)
Believe me, dear Bishop ...
Yours sincerely,
or, (My dear Bishop)
Believe me, my dear Bishop,
Yours sincerely,

ARCHDEACON:

Address—The Venerable The Archdeacon of ______, *or*, The Venerable Archdeacon ______.

Salutation and Closing—

(Venerable Sir)
I am, Venerable Sir,
Yours sincerely,
or, (Dear Mr. Archdeacon)
I am, dear Mr. Archdeacon,
Yours sincerely,

DEAN:

Address—The Very Reverend John M. Blank, Dean of ______.

Salutation and Closing—

(Very Reverend Sir)
I am, Very Reverend Sir,
Yours very truly,
or, (Dear Mr. Dean)
Believe me, dear Mr. Dean,
Yours sincerely,

CANON:

Address—The Reverend Canon John M. Blank,

Salutation and Closing—

(Reverend Sir)
Yours very truly,
or, (Dear Canon ...)
Believe me, dear Canon ...
Yours faithfully,

MINISTER OF RELGION:

Address—The Reverend John M. Blank,

Salutation and Closing—

(Sir)
I am, Reverend Sir, (or, Sir),
Yours very truly,
or, (Reverend Sir)
Yours sincerely,
or, (Dear Mr. ...)
Believe me, dear Mr. ...
Yours sincerely,

MODERATOR (CANADA):

Address—The Right Reverend ______, D.D., Moderator of the ______ Church,

Salutation and Closing—

(Right Reverend Sir)
I am, Right Reverend Sir,

Yours sincerely,
or, (Dear Dr. ...)
Believe me, dear Dr. ...
Yours sincerely,

Roman Catholic

CARDINAL:

Address—His Eminence John Cardinal Blank, Archbishop of ______.

Salutation and Closing—
(Your Eminence)
I have the honour to be, Your Eminence,
Your obedient servant,
or, (Your Eminence)
I am, Your Eminence,
Yours sincerely,
or, (Dear Cardinal ...)
Believe me, dear Cardinal ...
Yours sincerely,

ARCHBISHOP:

Address—The Most Reverend John M. Blank, Archbishop of ______.

Salutation and Closing—
(Your Excellency)
I have the honour to be,
Your Excellency,
Respectfully yours,
(ecclesiastical use)
or, (Most Reverend Sir)
I am, Most Reverend Sir,
Yours very truly,
or, (Dear Archbishop)
Yours sincerely,

BISHOP:

Address—The Most Reverend John M. Blank, Bishop of ______. *(ecclesiastical use)*.
or, The Right Reverend John M. Blank, Bishop of ______.
Salutation and Closing—
(Your Excellency)
I am, Your Excellency,
Respectfully yours,
(ecclesiastical use)
or, (Right Reverend Sir)
I am, Right Reverend Sir,
Yours sincerely,
or, (Dear Bishop ...)
Believe me, dear Bishop ...
Yours sincerely,
or, (Dear Bishop)
With kind regards, dear Bishop,
Sincerely yours,

MONSIGNOR:

Address—The Right Reverend John M. Blank.
Salutation and Closing—
(Right Reverend Monsignor)
I am, Right Reverend Monsignor,
Yours sincerely,
or, (My dear Monsignor ...)
Believe me, my dear Monsignor ...
Yours sincerely,

CANON:

Address—The Very Reverend John M. Blank.
Salutation and Closing—
(Very Reverend Canon)
Very truly yours,
or, (My dear Canon ...)
Sincerely yours,

PRIEST:

Address—The Reverend John M. Blank.
Salutation and Closing—
(Reverend Sir)
Yours sincerely,
or, (Dear Father ...)
Believe me, dear Father ...
Yours sincerely,

MOTHER SUPERIOR:

Address—The Reverend Mother Superior, The Congregation of ______.
Salutation and Closing—
(Dear Madam)
I am, dear Madam,
Yours respectfully,
or, (Reverend Mother Superior)
I remain,
Reverend Mother Superior,
Yours sincerely,
or, (Dear Mother Superior)
Believe me, dear Mother, *or*
Believe me, dear Mother Superior,
Yours sincerely,

Jewish

CHIEF RABBI:

Address—The Very Reverend John M. Blank, Chief Rabbi.
Salutation and Closing—
(Dear Sir)
I remain, Sir,
Yours very truly,
or, (Dear Chief Rabbi)
I am, dear Chief Rabbi,
Sincerely yours,

RABBI:

Address—The Reverend Rabbi John M. Blank.
Salutation and Closing—
(Dear Sir)
I am, Sir,
Yours very truly,
or, (Dear Rabbi ...)
I am, my dear Rabbi ...
Yours sincerely,

PROFESSIONAL

ADVOCATE, NOTARY, PHYSICIAN, DENTIST, CHARTERED ACCOUNTANT, OPTOMETRIST, ETC.:

Address—John M. Blank, Esq., Q.C., John M. Blank, Esq., Advocate; Dr. John M. Blank, or J.M. Blank, Esq., M.D. (*Never* use both Dr. and M.D.); Dr. John M. Blank, or J.M. Blank, Esq., D.D.S. (*Never* use both Dr. and D.D.S.); J.M. Blank, Esq., C.A.; Optometrist John M. Blank, or J.M. Blank, O.D., or Dr. John M. Blank.

Salutation and Closing—
(Dear Sir)
Yours very truly,

DIPLOMATIC

AMBASSADORS of foreign countries in Canada:

Address—His Excellency John M. Blank, Ambassador of ______, Ottawa.
Salutation and Closing—
(Excellency)
Accept, Excellency, the assurances of my highest consideration,
or, (Excellency)
Yours very truly,
or, (Dear Mr. ...)
I am, dear Mr. ...
Yours sincerely,

HIGH COMMISSIONERS of British Commonwealth countries in Canada:

Address—His Excellency John M. Blank, High Commissioner for ______, Ottawa.

Salutation and Closing—

(Your Excellency)
Accept, Your Excellency, the assurances of my highest consideration,
or, (Dear Sir)
Yours sincerely,
or, (Dear Mr. ...)
With kind regards,
Yours very sincerely,

MINISTERS PLENIPOTENTIARY of foreign countries in Canada:

Address—His Excellency John M. Blank, Minister of ______, Ottawa.

Salutation and Closing—

(Excellency)
Accept, Excellency, the assurances of my highest consideration,
or, (Dear Mr. Minister)
I remain, dear Mr. Minister,
Yours sincerely,
or, (Dear Mr. ...)
Believe me, dear Mr. ...
Yours sincerely,

CANADIAN AMBASSADORS abroad from a Canadian citizen:

Address—John M. Blank, Esq., Canadian Ambassador to ______, ______.

Salutation and Closing—

(Dear Sir)
Yours very truly,
or, (Dear Ambassador)
I am, dear Ambassador,
Yours sincerely,
or, (Dear Mr. ...)
With kind regards,
Yours sincerely,

CANADIAN AMBASSADORS abroad from a foreign citizen:

Address—His Excellency John M. Blank, Canadian Ambassador to ______, ______.

Salutation and Closing—

(Your Excellency)
Accept, Your Excellency, the assurances of my highest consideration,
or, (Dear Mr. Ambassador)
I am, dear Mr. Ambassador,
Yours sincerely,
or, (Dear Mr. ...)
I am, dear Mr. ...
Yours sincerely,

CANADIAN HIGH COMMISSIONERS abroad:

Address—John M. Blank, Esq., High Commissioner for Canada.

Salutation and Closing—

(Dear Sir)
Yours very truly,
or, (Dear High Commissioner)
Believe me, dear High Commissioner,
Yours sincerely,
or, (Dear Mr. ...)
With kind regards,
Yours sincerely,

CANADIAN MINISTERS PLENIPOTENTIARY abroad from a Canadian citizen:

Address—John M. Blank, Esq., Canadian Minister to ______, ______.

Salutation and Closing—

(Sir)
I am, Sir,
Yours very truly,
or, (Dear Sir)
Yours very truly,
or, (Dear Mr. ...)
With kind regards,
Yours sincerely,

CANADIAN MINISTERS PLENIPOTENTIARY abroad from a foreign citizen:

Address—His Excellency John M. Blank, Canadian Minister to ______, ______.

Salutation and Closing—

(Your Excellency)
Accept, Your Excellency, the assurances of my highest consideration,
or, (Dear Mr. Minister)
I remain, dear Mr. Minister,
Yours sincerely,
or, (Dear Mr. ...)
Believe me, dear Mr. ...
Yours sincerely,

LIST OF ABBREVIATIONS

Indicating Academic, Ecclesiastical and other Degrees, membership in Societies and Institutions, etc., appearing in the Canadian Almanac and Directory. For other lists of abbreviations, see Index.

A.A.E.	Associate of Accountants' and Executives' Corp. of Canada
A.C.C.A.	—of Association of Certified Accountants
A.A.G.O.	—of the American Guild of Organists
A.A.S.A.	—of the Alberta Society of Artists
A.B.	Bachelor of Arts (Artium Baccalaureus)
A.C.	"Advanced Certification" Canadian Association of Medical Radiation Technologists
A.C.A.	Associate of Institute of Chartered Accountants (Eng.)
A.C.C.O.	—of Canadian College of Organists
AccS.C.R.P.	—of Canadian Public Relations Society Inc.
A.C.D.	—Archaeologiae Christianae Doctor (see Doct. Arch.)
A.C.G.I.	Associate of the City and Guilds of London Institute
A.C.I.C.	—of Canadian Institute of Chemistry
A.C.I.S.	—of Chartered Institute of Secretaries
A.C.S.M.	—of Cambourne School of Mines
A.F.R.A.S.	—Fellow of the Royal Aeronautical Society
Ag. de l'U (Paris)	Honorary Professor of University of Paris (Agrégé de l'Université Paris)
Ag. de Phil.	Professor of Philosphy (Agrégé en Philosophie Louvain)
A.G.S.M.	Associate of the Guildhall School of Music (London, Eng.)
A.I.C.	—of the Institute of Chemistry
A.I.I.C.	—of the Insurance Institute of Canada
A.K.C.	—of King's College
A.L.C.M.	—of London (Canada) Conservatory of Music
A.L.S.	Commissioned Alberta Land Surveyor
A.M.	Master of Arts (Artium Magister)
A.M.E.I.C.	Associate Member, Engineering Institute of Canada
A.M.I.C.E.	—Member, Institute of Civil Engineers
A.M.I.E.E.	—Member, Institute of Electrical Engineers

A.M.I.Mech.E.	—Member, Institution of Mechanical Engineers
A.Mus.	—of Music (McGill)
A.P.A.	—Member of Institute of Accredited Public Accountants
A.P.H.A.	—of Public Health Association
A.P.R.	Accredited Member, Canadian Public Relations Society
A.R.A.	Associate of the Royal Academy
A.R.C.C.O.	—of the Royal Canadian College of Organists
A.R.C.D.	—of Royal College of Dancing
A.R.C.M.	—of Royal College of Music
A.R.C.O.	—of the Royal College of Organists
A.R.C.Sc.	—of the Royal College of Science
A.R.C.T.	—of the Royal Conservatory of Toronto
A.R.C.V.S.	—of the Royal College of Veterinary Surgeons
A.R.D.S.	—of the Royal Drawing Society (London, Eng.)
A.R.I.B.A.	—of Royal Institute of British Architects
A.R.I.C.	—, Royal Institute of Chemistry
A.R.S.H.	—of Royal Society of Health
A.R.S.M.	—, Royal School of Mines
A.R.S.M.	—, Royal School of Music
Assoc. Inst. M.M.	—Institute of Mining and Metallurgy
A.T.C.L.	—, Trinity College, London (Eng.)
A.T.C.M.	—of Toronto Conservatory of Music
B.A.	Bachelor of Arts
B. Acc.	—of Accountancy
B.A.I.	—of Engineering (U. of Dublin)
B.A.O.	—of Obstetrics
B. Arch.	—of Architecture
B.A.Sc.	—of Applied Science
B.A.S.M.	—of Arts, Master of Science
B.A.Theo.	—of Arts in Theology
B.B.A.	—of Business Administration
B.C.D.	Bachelier en Chirurgie Dentale
B.Ch.	Bachelor in Surgery
B.Ch.E.	—in Chemical Engineering
B.C.L.	—of Civil Law
B.Com.(B. Comm.)	—of Commerce
B.D.	—of Divinity
B.D.C.	—of Canon Law (Bacc. Droit Canonique)
B.D.S.	—of Dental Surgery
B.E.	—of Engineering
B.Ed.	—of Education
B.E.E.	—of Electrical Engineering
B.Eng.	—of Engineering
B. en Ph.	Bachelier en Philosophie
B. en Sc. Com.	—en Science Commerciale
B. ès A.	—ès Arts
B. ès L.	—ès Lettres
B. ès Sc.	—ès Science
B. ès Sc. App.	—ès Science Appliquée
B.F.	Bachelor of Forestry
B.H.E.	—of Household Economics
B.H.Ec.	—of Household Economics
B.H.Sc.	—of Household Science
B.J.	—of Journalism
B.J.C.	—in Canon Law
B.L.	—in Literature (*or* of Laws)
B.Litt.	—of Letters *or* of Literature)
B.L.S.	—of Library Science
B.M.	—of Medicine
B.Mus.	—of Music
B.M.V.	Bachelier en Médecine Vetérinaire
B.N.	Bachelor of Nursing
B.N.Sc.	—of Nursing Science
B. Paed. (Péd.)	—of Pedagogy
B.P.A.	—of Public Administration
B.P.E.	—of Physical Education
B.Ph.	—of Philosophy
B.P.H.E.	—Physical and Health Education
B. Ps.	Baccalauréat en Psychologie
B.S.	Bachelor of Science (U.S.A.)
B.S.A.	—of Science in Agriculture
B.Sc.	—of Science
B.Sc.B.	Baccalauréat en Bibliothéconomie
B.Sc.Com.	Bachelor of Commercial Science
B.Sc.Dom.	Baccalauréat en Sciences Domestiques
B.Sc.F.	Bachelor of Science of Forestry
B.Sc.H.	Bachelier en Sciences Hospitalières
B.Sc.(P. & O.T.)	Bachelor of Science in Physical and Occupational Therapy
B.Sc.Phm.	—of Science in Pharmacy
B.Sc.Soc.	—of Social Science
B.S.C.E.	—of Science in Civil Engineering
B.S.Ed.	—of Science in Education
B.S.E.E.	—of Science in Electrical Engineering
B.S.F.	—of Science in Forestry
B.S.N.	—of Science in Nursing
B.S.P.	—of Science in Pharmacy
B.S.S.	—of Social Sciences
B.S.W.	—of Social Work
B.Th.	—of Theology
B.T.S.	—of Technological Science (Edinburgh)
B.V.Sc.	—of Veterinary Science
C.A.	Chartered Accountant
C.A.A.P.	Certified Advertising Agency Practitioner
C.A.P.	Certificat d'Aptitude Pedagogique
C.C.	Chartered Cartographer
C.E.	Civil Engineer
Cer.E.	Ceramic Engineer
C.E.S.	Certificat d'Etudes Secondaires (La Sorbonne)
C.G.A.	Certified General Accountant
Ch.B.	Bachelor of Surgery
Chan.	Chanoine (Canon)
Chem. Ing.	Ingénieur Chimiste Diplomé (Swiss Fed. Inst. Technology)
C.I.F.	Canadian Institute of Forestry
C.I.M.	Certificate in Management
C.I.M.	Certified Industrial Manager
C.I.S. & P.	Canadian Inst. of Surveying & Photogrammetry
C.L.U.	Chartered Life Underwriter
C.M.	Master in Surgery
Cdr.	Commander
C.L.S.	Canada Land Surveyor
C.O.A.	Certified Office Administrator
C.P.A.	—Public Accountant
C.P.P.O.	—Public Purchasing Officer
C.R. (or c.r.)	Conseiller de la Reine (Queen's Counsel)
C.S.R.	Chartered Stenographic Reporter
D.A.	Doctor of Art (Scotland)
D.A.	—of Archaeology (Laval)
D.A.Sc.	—in Applied Sciences
D.C.	—of Chiropractic
D.C.D.	Docteur en Chirurgie Dentale
D.C.L.	Doctor of Common (Civil) Law
D.D.	—of Divinity
D.D.C.	Doctorat Droit Canonique
D. de l'Un.	Doctorat de l'Université
D.D.S.	Doctor of Dental Surgery
D.D.T.	—of Drugless Therapy
D.Eng.	—of Engineering
D.F.Sc.	—of Financial Science (Laval)
D. en Méd. Vet.	Docteur en Médecine Vetérinaire
D. en Ph.	—en Philosophie
D. ès L.	—és Lettres (Doctor of Letters)
D. ès Sc. App.	Doctor of Applied Science
D.I.C.	Diploma of Imperial College of Science and Technology
Dip. Bact.	—in Bacteriology
Dip. d'E.	Diplome d'Etudes
Dip. de l'U. (P)	Diploma of the U. of Paris
Dip. d'E. Sup. Dip.E.S.	Diplome d'Etudes Supérieures, Paris
Dip. Ing.	Diploma in Engineering

D.J.C.	Doctor of Canon Law
D.L.	—in Civil Law
D. Lit.	—of Literature
D. Litt.	—of Letters
D.L.O.	Diploma in Laryngology and Otology
D.L.S.	see C.L.S.
D.M.	Doctorat Médecine
D.M.D.	Doctor of Dental Medicine
D. Ms.	—in Missionology
D. Mus.	Doctorat en Musique
D.M.R.(D.) or (T.)	Diploma in Medical Radiology (Royal Coll. of Surgeons, London)
D.M.T.	—in Tropical Medicine
D.M.T. & H. (Eng.)	—in Tropical Medicine and Hygiene
D.O.	Doctor of Osteopathy
Doct. Arch.	—of Christian Archaeology (Pontifical Institute, Rome)
D. Paed. (Péd.)	—of Paedagogy
D.P.E.	Diploma in Physical Education
D.Ph.	Doctor of Philosophy
D.P.Ec.	—of Political Economy
D.P.H.	—(or Diploma) of Public Health
D.P.Sc.	—of Political Science
D. Psych.	Diploma in Psychiatry
D.P.T.	Doctor of Physio-Therapy
D.R.	—of Radiology
Dr.Com.Sc.	—of Commercial Science
Dr. de l'U. (P)	—of the U. of Paris
Dr. ès Lettres	—of Letters (History of Literature)
Dr. jur.	—of Law (Dr. Juris)
Dr. rer. pol.	—of Political Economy (Dr. Rerum Politicarum) (Docteur des Sciences Politiques)
D.S.A.	Docteur ès Science Agricole
D.Sc.	Doctor of Science
D.Sc.Mil.	—of Military Science
D.S.L.	—of Sacred Letters
D.Sc.Com.	—of Commercial Science
D.Sc.Fin.	—of Financial Science
D.Sc.Nat.	—in Natural Science
D.Sc.Soc.	—of Social Science
D.Th.	—of Theology
D.V.M.	—of Veterinary Medicine
D.V.Sc.	—of Veterinary Science
Ed.D.	—of Education
Ed.M.	Master of Education (Harvard)
E.E.	Electrical Engineer
E.M.	Mining Engineer
E.T.C.M.	Graduate of Eastern Townships Conservatory of Music
F.A.A.O.	Fellow, American Academy of Optometry
F.A.A.O.Dip.	Diplomatic Fellow, American Academy of Optometry
F.A.C.D.	Fellow of American College of Dentists
F.A.C.P.	—of American College of Physicians
F.A.C.R.	—of American College of Radiology
F.A.C.S.	—of American College of Surgeons
F.A.E.	—of the Accountants' and Executives' Corp. of Canada
F.A.G.O.	—of the American Guild of Organists
F.A.G.S.	—of the American Geographical Society
F.A.I.A.	—of the American Institute of Actuaries (*or* of Architects)
F.A.O.U.	—of the American Ornithologists Union
F.A.P.H.A.	—of the American Public Health Association
F.A.P.S.	—of American Physical Society
F.A.S.	—of the Actuarial Society
F.B.A.	—of the British Academy
F.B.O.A.	—, British Association of Optometrists
F.C.A.	—of the Institute of Chartered Accountants
F.C.B.A.	—of the Canadian Bankers' Association
F.C.C.A.	—of the Association of Certified Accountants
F.C.C.O.	—of the Canadian College of Organists
F.C.C.T.	—of the Canadian College of Teachers
F.C.G.I.	—of the City and Guilds of London Institute
F.C.I.	—of the Canadian Credit Institute
F.C.I.C.	—of the Chemical Institute of Canada
F.C.I.I.	—of the Chartered Insurance Institute (London)
F.C.I.S.	—of the Chartered Institute of Secretaries
F.C.O.G.	—of the College of Obstetricians and Gynaecologists
F.C.A.M.R.T.	—of Canadian Association of Medical Radiation Technologists
F.E.	Forest Engineer
F.F.A.	Fellow of the Faculty of Actuaries (Scotland)
F.F.R.	—of the Faculty of Radiology
F.G.S.	Frater, (Fellow), Geological Society
F.G.S.A.	Fellow of the Geological Society of America
F.I.A.	—of the Institute of Actuaries (London)
F.I.C.	—of the Institute of Chemistry
F.I.I.C.	—of the Insurance Institute of Canada
F.I.L.	—of the Institute of Linguists
F.L.A.	—of the Library Association (Eng.)
F.M.S.A.	—of the Mineralogical Society of America
F.R.A.I.	—of the Royal Anthropological Institute
F.R.A.I.C.	—of the Royal Architectural Institute of Canada
F.R.A.M.	—of the Royal Academy of Music (London, Eng.)
F.R.A.S.	—of the Royal Astronomical Society
F.R.C.C.O.	—of the Royal Canadian College of Organists
F.R.C.M.	—of the Royal College of Music
F.R.C.O.	—of the Royal College of Organists
F.R.C.O.G.	—of the Royal College of Obstetrics and Gynaecology
F.R.C.P.	—of the Royal College of Physicians
F.R.C.S.	—of the Royal College of Surgeons
F.R.C.S.(E.)	—of the Royal College of Surgeons (Edinburgh)
F.R.G.S.	—of the Royal Geographical Society
F.R.Hist.S.	—of the Royal Historical Society
F.R.Hort.S.	—of the Royal Horticultural Society
F.R.I.B.A.	—of the Royal Institute of British Architects
F.R.I.C.S.	—of the Royal Institution of Chartered Surveyors
F.R.M.C.M.	—of Royal Manchester College of Music
F.R.M.S.	—of the Royal Meteorological Society
F.R.S.	—of the Royal Society
F.R.S.A.	—of the Royal Society of Arts
F.R.S.C.	—of the Royal Society of Canada
F.R.S.E.	—of the Royal Society of Edinburgh
F.R.S.H.	—, Royal Society of Health
F.R.S.L.	—of the Royal Society of Literature
F.S.A.	—of the Society of Actuaries
F.S.S.	—of Royal Statistical Society
F.T.C.L.	Frater, (Fellow), Trinity College of Music (London)
F.Z.S.	Fellow of the Zoological Society
G.J.	Graduate Jeweller
H.A.R.C.V.S.	Honorary Associate of Royal College of Veterinary Surgeons
Ing.E.T.P.	Diplome de l'Ecole Spéciale des Travaux Publiques
J.C.B.	Bachelor of Canon Law
J.C.D.	Doctor of Canon Law (*or* of Civil Law)
J.C.L.	Juris Canonici Licentiatus (Licentiate in Canon Law)
J.D.	Doctor of Jurisprudence
J.D.S.	—of Juridical Science
J.U.L.	Licentiate of Law in Utroque (both Civil and Canon Law)

Jur. utr. Dr.	Juris utriusque doctor, Equiv. to LL.D.
L.A.B.	Licentiate of the Associated Board of Royal Schools of Music (London, Eng.)
L.C.L.	—in Canon Law
L.C.M.I.	—, Cost and Management Institute
L.D.C.	—Droit Canonique
L.D.S.	—in Dental Surgery
L. ès L.	Licencié ès Lettres
L. ès Sc.	—ès Sciences
L.G.S.M.	Licentiate of Guildhall School of Music (London, Eng.)
Litt.D.	Doctorate ès Lettres
Litt.L.	Licence ès Lettres
L.J.C.	Licentiatus Juris Canonici
L.L.	License in Civil Law
L.L.B.	Bachelor of Laws (Legum Baccalaureus)
LL.D.	Doctor of Laws (Legum Doctor)
LL.L.	Licentiate in Laws
LL.M.	Master of Laws
L. Mus.	Licentiate of Music
L.M.U.S.	—in Music, U. of Saskatchewan
L. Mus. T.C.L.	—in Music, Trinity College, London
L.Péd.	Licence en Pédagogie
L.Ph.	—en Philosophie
L.Psych.	Licencié en Psychologie
L.R.A.M.	Licentiate, Royal Academy of Music (London)
L.R.C.M.	—of the Royal College of Music (London)
L.R.C.P.	—of the Royal College of Physicians
L.R.C.T.	—of the Royal Conservatory of Toronto
L.R.E.	—in Religious Education
L.R.S.M.	—of the Royal Schools of Music (London)
L.S.	Land Surveyor
L.S.A.	Licentiate in Agricultural Science
L.Sc.Com.	—in Commercial Science
L.Sc.O.	Licence in the Science of Optometry
L.S.Sc.	Licentiate in Sacred Scriptures
L.Sc.Soc.	Licence in Social Science
L.S.T.	Licentiate in Sacred Theology
L.T.C.L.	—, Trinity College of Music (London)
L.T.C.M.	—, Toronto Conservatory of Music
L.Th.	—in Theology
M.	Monsieur
M.A.	Master of Arts
M.A.C.F.	Membre de l'Académie canadienne française
M.A.I.E.E.	Member of American Institute of Electrical Engineers
M.A.I.M.E.	—of American Institute of Mining Engineers
M.A.L.S.	Master of Arts in Library Science
M.Arch.	—of Architecture
M.A.Sc.	—of Applied Science
M.A.S.C.E.	Member, American Society of Civil Engineers
M.A.S.M.E.	—, American Society of Mechanical Engineers
M. Aust. I.M.	—, Australian Institute of Mining and Metallurgy
M.B.	Bachelor of Medicine
M.B.A.	Master in Business Administration
M.C.E.	—of Civil Engineering
M.C.I.	Member, Credit Institute
M.C.I.C.	—of the Chemical Institute of Canada
M.C.I.F.	—of the Canadian Institute of Forestry
M.C.I.M.	—, Canadian Institute of Mining
M.C.I.M.M.	—, Canadian Institute of Mining and Metallury
M.Com.	Master of Commerce
M.D.	Doctor of Medicine
M.D.C.M.	—of Medicine and Master of Surgery
M.D.V.	—of Veterinary Medicine
Me	Maître
M.E.	Mechanical Engineer, Master of Engineering
M.Ed.	Master of Education
M.E.I.C.	Member of Engineering Institute of Canada
M.Eng.	Master of Engineering
M.F.	—of Forestry
M.F.A.	—of Fine Arts
Mgr.	Monsignor, Manager
M.H.A.	Master of Health Administration
M.I.C.E.	Member, Institution of Civil Engineers
M.I.C.I.A.	—, Industrial, Commercial and Institutional Accountants
M.I.E.E.	—, Institution of Electrical Engineers
M.I.M.M.	—of Institute of Mining and Metallurgy
M.I.N.A.	—of Institute of Naval Architects
M.I.R.E.	—of Institute of Radio Engineers
M.L.S.	Master of Library Science
M.M.	—of Music
M.P.E.	—of Physical Education
M.R.A.I.C.	Member of Royal Architectural Institute of Canada
M.R.C.O.G.	—of Royal College of Obstetricians and Gynaecologists
M.R.C.P.	—of Royal College of Physicians
M.R.C.S.	—of Royal College of Surgeons
M.R.C.V.C.(*or* S.)	—of Royal College of Veterinary Surgeons
M.R.S.C.	—of Royal Society of Canada
M.R.S.H.	—of Royal Society of Health
M.R.S.T.	—of the Royal Society of Teachers
M.S.	Master of Surgery
M.S.A.	—of Science in Agriculture
M.Sc.	—of Science
M.Sc.F.	—of Science in Forestry
M.Sc.(Med.)	—of Science in Medicine
M.S.(C.E.)	—of Science in Civil Engineering
M.S.Ed.	—of Science in Education
M.S.Litt.	—of Sacred Letters
M.S.P.E.	McGill School of Physical Education
M.S.R.C.	Membre Société Royale du Canada
M.S.S.	Master of Social Science
M.S.W.	—of Social Work
M.U.Dr.	Medecinae Universae Doctor (Prague) (Dentistry and Medicine)
Mus. Bac.	Bachelor of Music
Mus. Doc. (*or* D.)	Doctor of Music
Mus. G. Paed.	Musicae Graduatus Paedagogus (Graduate Teacher in Music)
M.V.	Médécin Vétérinaire
M.V.Sc.	Master of Veterinary Science
N.D.A.	National Diploma in Agriculture (Royal Ag. Soc. of Engineering)
N.D.D.	National Diploma in Dairying (Scotland)
N.P.	Notary Public
O.A.	Officier d'Académie (France)
O.D.	Doctor of Optometry
O.I.P.	Officier de l'Instruction Publique
O.L.S.	Ontario Land Surveyor
O.S.A.	Ontario Society of Artists
P.D.	Doctor of Parapsychology
P.E.	Professional Engineer
P.Eng.	Registered Professional Engineer
Ph.B.	Bachelor of Philosophy
Ph.C.	Philosopher of Chiropractic
Ph.D.	Doctor of Philosophy
Ph.T.D.	Physical Therapy Doctor
Ph.L.	Licentiate in Philosophy
Phm.B.	Bachelor of Pharmacy
P.L.S.	Professional Legal Secretary
P.Mgr.	—Manager
P.P.B.	—Public Buyer
P.T.I.C.	Patent & Trade Mark Institute of Canada
Q.C.	Queen's Counsel
Q.L.S.	Quebec Land Surveyor
R.A.	Royal Academy
R.A.M.	Royal Academy of Music (Budapest)
R.A.S.	Royal Aeronautical Society

R.B.A.	Member of the Royal Society of British Artists
R.C.A.	Royal Canadian Academy of Arts
R.C.A.M.	Royal College and Academy of Music (Budapest)
R.C.M.	Royal Conservatory of Music (Leipzig)
R.E.	Royal Engineers
R.I.A.	Registered Industrial and Cost Accountant
R.M.S.	Royal Miniature Society
R.M.T.	Registered Music Teacher
R.N.	—Nurse
R.O.I.	Member of Royal Institute of Painters in Oil Colours
R.P.	—of Royal Society of Portrait Painters
R.P.	Révérend Père (Reverend Father)
R.P.A.	Registered Public Accountant
R.P.Dt.	—Professional Dietitian
R.P.F.	—Professional Forester
R.R.L.	—Record Librarian
R.S.H.	Royal Society of Health
R.T.	Registered Technician, Canadian Association of Medical Radiation Technologists
S.C.	Senior Counsel (Eire) *equivalent* of Q.C.
Sc.D.	Doctorat ès Sciences
Sc.L.	Licence ès Sciences
Sc. Soc. B.	Bachelier Science Sociale
Sc. Soc. D.	Doctor of Social Science
Sc. Soc. L.	License in Social Science
S.J.	Society of Jesus
S.L.S.	Saskatchewan Land Surveyor
S.M.	Master of Science
S.S.B.	Bachelier en Science Sacrée
S.S.C.	Member of Sculptors' Society of Canada
S.S.L.	Licentiate in Sacred Scripture
S.T.B. (S.Th.B.)	Bachelor of Sacred Theology
S.T.D. (S.Th.D.)	Doctor of Sacred Theology
S.T.L. (S.Th.L.)	Sacrae Theologiae Licentiatus (Licentiate in Sacred Theology)
S.T.M.	Master of Sacred Theology
T.C.L.	Trinity College, London
T.M.M.G.	Teacher, Massage & Medical Gymnastics
Th.D.	Doctor of Theology
V.G.	Vicar-General
V.S.	Veterinary Surgeon

ABBREVIATIONS INDICATING HONOURS AND DECORATIONS

A.F.C.—Air Force Cross. Ribbon, wide diagonal stripes of white and red.

A.F.M.—Air Force Medal. Ribbon, narrow diagonal stripes of white and red.

A.M.—Albert Medal, gold (Sea). Ribbon, nine alternate narrow stripes of blue and white.

Albert Medal, gold (Land). Ribbon, nine alternate narrow stripes of red and white.

Albert Medal (Sea). Ribbon, blue ground with two wide stripes of white.

Albert Medal (Land). Ribbon, red ground with two wide stripes of white.

Albert Medals are posthumous awards.

B.E.M.—British Empire Medal.

C.B.—Companion of the Most Honourable Order of the Bath.

C.B.E.—Commander of the Order of the British Empire.

C.C.—Companion of the Order of Canada.

C.D.—Canadian Forces Decoration.

C.G.M.—Conspicuous Gallantry Medal; Navy and Air Force. It carries a cash grant. The Navy Medal ribbon is white with dark blue edges; the Air Force ribbon is light blue with dark blue edges.

C.H.—Member of the Order of the Companions of Honour.

C.I.E.—Companion of the Most Eminent Order of the Indian Empire.

C.M.—Member of the Order of Canada.

C.M.G.—Companion of the Most Distinguished Order of St. Michael and St. George.

C.M.M.—Commander of the Order of Military Merit.

C.S.I.—Companion of the Most Exalted Order of the Star of India.

C.V.—Cross of Valour, Canadian Bravery Decoration.

C.V.O.—Commander of the Royal Victorian Order.

D.C.M.—Distinguished Conduct Medal. Ribbon, red ground, dark blue stripe in centre.

D.F.C.—Distinguished Flying Cross. Ribbon, wide diagonal stripes of violet and white.

D.F.M.—Distinguished Flying Medal. Ribbon, narrow diagonal stripes of white and violet.

D.S.C.—Distinguished Service Cross. Ribbon, three broad bands, dark blue, white, dark blue.

D.S.M.—Distinguished Service Medal.

D.S.O.—Companion of the Distinguished Service Order. Instituted 1886. Ribbon, dark red with dark blue stripe at each end.

E.D.—Canadian Efficiency Decoration for Officers of Military Auxiliary Forces.

E.M.—Edward Medal. Posthumous award.

E.M.—Efficiency Medal.

G.B.E.—Knight Grand Cross or Dame Grand Cross of the Most Excellent Order of the British Empire.

G.C.—George Cross.

G.C.B.—Knight Grand Cross of the Most Honourable Order of the Bath.

G.C.I.E.—Knight Grand Commander of the Most Eminent Order of the Indian Empire.

G.C.M.G.—Knight Grand Cross of the Most Distinguished Order of St. Michael and St. George.

G.C.S.I.—Knight Grand Commander of the Most Exalted Order of the Star of India.

G.C.V.O.—Knight Grand Cross of the Royal Victorian Order.

G.M.—George Medal. Replaces, except in posthumous awards the A.M., E.M., the Queen's Fire Services Medal and the Queen's Police Medal.

I.S.M.—Imperial Service Medal.

I.S.O.—Companion of the Imperial Service Order. Instituted 1902.

K.B.E.—Knight Commander of the Most Excellent Order of the British Empire.

K.C.B.—Knight Commander of the Most Honourable Order of the Bath.

K.C.I.E.—Knight Commander of the Most Eminent Order of the Indian Empire.

K.C.M.G.—Knight Commander of the Most Distinguished Order of St. Michael and St. George.

K.C.S.I.—Knight Commander of the Most Exalted Order of the Star of India.

K.C.V.O.—Knight Commander of the Royal Victorian Order.

K.G.—Knight of the Most Noble Order of the Garter.

K.P.—Knight of the Most Illustrious Order of St. Patrick.

Kt.—Knight Bachelor.

K.T.—Knight of the Most Ancient and Most Noble Order of the Thistle.

M.B.—Medal of Bravery.

M.B.E.—Member of the Order of the British Empire.

M.C.—Military Cross. Instituted 1915, and Imperial award. Ribbon, white with broad band of blue in centre.

M. du C.—Canada Medal.

M.M.—Military Medal.

M.M.M.—Member of the Order of Military Merit.

M.V.O.—Member of the Royal Victorian Order.

O.B.E.—Officer of the Order of the British Empire.

O.C.—Officer of the Order of Canada.

O.M.—Member of the Order of Merit.
O.M.M.—Officer of the Order of Military Merit.
P.C.—Privy Counsellor.
R.R.C.—Royal Red Cross. Instituted 1883. Ribbon, dark blue with narrow band of dark red at each end.
S.C.—Star of Courage.
U.E.—Unity of Empire. Descendants of United Empire Loyalists.
V.C.—Victoria Cross.
V.D.—Auxiliary Forces (Volunteer) Officers' Decoration.

BUSINESS AND SHIPPING ABBREVIATIONS

As shipping terms vary in different countries, insurance or shipping agents should be consulted.
For other lists of abbreviations, academic, etc., see Index.

a/c	Account
Ad val.	Ad valorem
avoir	Avoirdupois
bbl.	Barrel
B/L.	Bill of Lading
b.m.	Board Measure
B.O.	Buyer's Option
B/P.	Bills Payable
B/R.	Bills Receivable
B/S.	Bill of Sale
c.	Hundred
C or Cent.	Centigrade
cf.	Compare
C. and F.	Cost and Freight
Cie	Compagnie
c.i.f.	Cost insurance and freight
C.L.	Car Load (of freight)
Co.	Company
C.O.D.	Cash on Delivery
C. of F.	Cost of Freight
Cr.	Credit
C.W.O.	Cash with Order
Cwt.	Hundredweight
D/A.	Documents Attached, also Deposit Account
Dis. (Disct.)	Discount
Dl. (or Tl.)	Double (or triple) first class
D.O.A.	Deliver Documents on Acceptance of Draft
D.O.P.	Deliver Documents on Payment of Draft
Dr.	Debit
D.V.	God willing (Deo volente)
e.g.	For example (exempli gratia)
E.&.O.E.	Errors and omissions excepted
Est. Wt.	Estimated Weight
et seq.	And the following (et sequens)
Ex. Div.	Without Dividend
Ex-Warehouse	Purchaser pays carriage charges and assumes risks from seller's warehouse
F.	Fahrenheit
F.a.a.	Free of Average (marine insurance)
F.A.S.	Free Alongside (Seller assumes risks and delivers goods to alongside of steamer free of carriage charges)
F.O.B.	Free on Board (Purchaser pays carriage charges and assumes risks from point specified)
F.P.A.	Free of Particular Average (Insured can recover only for a total loss, subject to other conditions of the contract)
Franco.	Pre-paid free of expense to point specified
G.A.	General Average (All owners of cargo and vessel share in any loss arising from expense incurred to preserve ship and contents from greater loss)
gm.	Grammes
gr.	Grain; grains, or gross
ibid.	In the same place (ibidem)
i.e.	That is (id est)
Inc.	Incorporated
Int.	Interest
K.D.	Knocked down
lb. (libra)	Pound
L/C.	Letter of Credit
L.C.L.	Less than Car Load (of freight)
Limited; Ltd.	Limited Liability (Shareholders are "limited" in liability to the amount of their subscribed stock in certain companies)
L.P.	List Price
M.	Thousand (Mille)
MS., MSS.	Manuscript(s)
N.E.S. (N.O.P.)	Not Otherwise Provided For (Customs)
N.O.S.	Not Otherwise Specified
N.S.F.	Not Sufficient Funds (re cheques)
Nstd.	Nested
O.K.	Correct
op. cit.	In the work quoted (opere citato)
O.R.	At Owner's Risk
O.R.B.	At Owner's Risk of Breakage
oz.	Ounce
P.A.	Particular Average (As used in Marine Insurance, means damage to the goods caused by perils insured against and named in the contract. This form is often written with a Franchise Clause, and means there will be no claim unless the loss exceeds the percentage named)
P/A.	Power of Attorney
P & D.	Pick Up and Deliver
pp.	Pages
Pro forma	As a Matter of Form
P.S.	Postscript
q.v.	Which see (quod vide)
R.R.	Rural Route (Postal delivery)
S.B.	Shipping Bill
s.s.	Steamship
s/o	Ship's Option, weight or measurement
S.U.	Set Up (meaning article is complete)
T.B.L.	Through Bill of Lading
Tare	Weight of Container (Deducting tare from "gross weight" gives "net weight")
Ton	2,000 (short ton) or 2,240 (long ton) lbs. avoirdupois. A cubic ton in marine freight = 40 cubic feet
Ton wt/M.	Ton, weight or measurement (ship's option)
vide	See
viz	Namely; to wit (videlicet)

POSTAL INFORMATION

NOTE:— The rates shown here were printed late in 1981. At that time the rates were proposed to come into effect on Jan. 1, 1982. Some new services not listed here are proposed, such as special rates for large mailings meeting detailed preparation requirements.

LETTERS OR POSTCARDS FOR DELIVERY WITHIN CANADA if posted unpaid or not fully prepaid, will be forwarded to destination charged with double deficiency. Envelopes and cards used for mailing purposes must not be less than 4 inches in length by 2¾ inches in width. The preferred minimum size is 70mm x 100mm 5½ inches length by 3½ inches height (140 mm by 90 mm).

POSTCARDS. The right-hand half of the face of the ordinary official postcards and of private postcards is to be strictly reserved for the address, postal directions and postage stamps. The left-hand half of the face and the entire back of the card are available for the purposes of the sender, subject to restrictions as to attaching articles to postcards.

THIRD CLASS mail includes all mailable matter not over 500 g in weight which does not require payment at the first class rates or is not acceptable at the second class rates. Included are:

Books, newspapers and magazines mailed by the public, catalogues, circulars, merchandise, etc. Christmas, Easter and other such greeting cards can be sent at the third class rate if they do not have more than five words of greeting added. Individually addressed third class mail posted in envelopes shall be sealed.

30¢ first 50 g.

15¢ each additional 50 g or fraction up to a maximum of 500 g.

Maximum Size—1 m in length, width or depth but the combined length and girth must not exceed 2 m. Packets of third class mail exceeding the dimensions above may be accepted for mailing provided no one dimension exceeds 2 m with a combined length and girth not exceeding 3 m. Such packets are subject to a surcharge of $2.00 in addition to the postage charge.

Special rates of postage apply to Newspapers and Periodicals (Mailed by the Publisher), and printed and published in Canada and posted from the office of publication.

FIRST CLASS RATES FOR DELIVERY IN CANADA

0- 30 g	30¢
30- 50 g	45¢
50-100 g	60¢
100-150 g	80¢
150-200 g	$1.00
200-250 g	$1.20
250-300 g	$1.40
300-350 g	$1.60
350-400 g	$1.80
400-450 g	$2.00
450-500 g	$2.20

REGISTRATION FEES (CANADA)

For indemnity up to $100, the fee is $1.85. For indemnity over $100 and up to $1,000, the fee is $1.85 first $100, plus 30¢ each additional $100 of coverage up to $1,000.

Registration will be restricted to items prepaid at the *first* class rates of postage only.

ACKNOWLEDGEMENT OF RECEIPT CARDS (AR) (CANADA)

) At time of mailing of a registered item .... 50¢
) Subsequent to the mailing of a registered item .... 75¢

INSURANCE FEES (CANADA)

(First, Third and Fourth Class mail only)

) not exceeding $10 .... 20¢
) exceeding $10, up to $50 .... 30¢
i) exceeding $50, up to $100 .... 35¢
/) exceeding $100, up to $1000 .... 30¢for each $100 coverage up to a maximum of $1000, except for Postpak where the maximum is $3500 per shipment.

SPECIAL DELIVERY FEES (CANADA)

First Class Mail only $1.00

C.O.D. FEE (CANADA)

Up to and including $100 .... $1.50
Over $100, up to and including $200 .... $1.80

The indemnity coverage is based on the C.O.D. fee paid at the time of mailing; additional coverage may be purchased by the sender at the rate of 30¢ per $100 up to a maximum of $1000 where the value of the item exceeds the indemnity coverage according to the C.O.D. fee paid. The limit of collection under the C.O.D. service remains at $200.

Collection, Remittance, Indemnity, C.O.D. service may be accorded all classes of mail.

BUSINESS REPLY MAIL

By prior arrangement with the Department, at the larger post offices firms sending out letters, enquiries and order forms to the Canadian public may enclose an addressed business reply envelope or card having printed on the face the words "Business Reply Mail, no postage stamp necessary if mailed in Canada. Postage will be paid by", and the name and address of the firm, and bearing a return postage impression. The return postage charges are collected, at the first class rate, on delivery from the addressee indicated thereon plus a surcharge of 3.5¢ per item.

CERTIFIED MAIL

Fees—$1.00 plus regular postage.

Embodies proof of delivery feature of Registered Mail, but does not include the indemnity feature of Registered Mail.

REDIRECTION SERVICE CHARGE

A service charge of $1 is levied for the Notice of Change of Address that is filed with the postmaster for each three (3) month period the customer requests his mail be redirected to the new address.

Change of Address Announcement Cards (form 33-086-037), used by the public to notify their correspondents, will continue to be free.

HOLD MAIL SERVICE

A service charge of $1.50 per month or any part thereof is levied on each customer to compensate for handling and storage costs.

PAPER FOR BLIND

Writing paper specially prepared for the use of the blind transmitted from a recognized Institution for the Blind in Canada to blind persons for their own use is allowed to pass free of postage.

PROHIBITED ARTICLES

It is forbidden to post for delivery or transmission by or through the post any explosive substances and inflammable liquids or solids, or any other dangerous substances such as compressed gas, corrosive liquids, oxidizing, toxic or radioactive matter, as well as any matter or thing which could endanger human life or injure persons or cause damage, intoxicating liquors and all matter subject to speedy decay, all obscene or immoral books, publications, pictures, etc., libellous post cards and letters the covers of which bear words of an offensive character, and letters and circulars relating to illegal lotteries or other fraudulent schemes. Enquiry should be made at the Post Office in regard to transmitting game, raw furs, skins, plumage, etc., by mail.

INTERNATIONAL REPLY COUPONS

International Reply Coupons may be purchased in Canada for 85¢ each and are exchangeable in any country of the Universal Postal Union for the minimum postage payable on an international unregistered surface letter or an international unregistered air mail letter upon presentation of a sufficient number of reply coupons. An International Reply Coupon is exchangeable at any Canadian post office for 85¢ in Canadian postage stamps.

REGISTRATION FEES—ALL COUNTRIES
(except the U.S., its Territories and Possessions)
Fee $2.00 .... $30.00 (Limit of Indemnity)
Acknowledgement of Receipt Card
At time of mailing ....50¢ each

INSURANCE FEES (parcel post only)
To most countries (See Postal Guide) except the U.S., its Territories and Possessions.
Insurance up to $50.00 ....30¢
Insurance over $50.00 to $100.00 ....50¢
Insurance over $100.00 to $200.00 ....$1.00
Plus 50¢ each additional $100.00 up to a maximum of $500.00

SPECIAL DELIVERY FEES (letter mail only)
To Australia, Belgium, France, Germany (Federal Republic of), Great Britain and Northern Ireland, Hong Kong, Israel, Netherlands, Sweden, Switzerland, United States, United States Possessions and Territories, Venezuela (only for items addressed to Caracas)—$1.00.

MONEY ORDER FEES
The money orders are to be drawn in Canadian currency for payment in CANADA and the countries listed below.

Anguilla, Antigua, Bahamas, Barbados, Belize, Cayman Islands, Dominica, Fiji, Jamaica, Nevis, St. Christopher (St. Kitts), St. Lucia, St. Vincent, Virgin Islands (Tortola)
and the fee is as follows:
From $0.01 to $200.00 inclusive ....40¢

The money orders are to be drawn in U.S. currency for payment in the UNITED STATES including:

Guam, Panama Canal Zone, Puerto Rico, Tutuila (Samoa), Virgin Islands of the United States
and the fee is as follows:
From $0.01 to $200.00 inclusive ....60¢

The money orders are to be drawn in £ currency for payment in the UNITED KINGDOM, the REPUBLIC OF IRELAND and the countries listed below:

Grenada, Guyana, Montserrat, Tobago, Trinidad
and the fee is as follows:
From £0.01 to £50.00 inclusive ....60¢ (plus 3% of value)

The money orders are to be drawn in Canadian currency for all OTHER COUNTRIES (except Mexico and Poland—U.S. currency)
and the fee is as follows:
From $0.01 to $200.00 inclusive $1.00

INTERNATIONAL AIR PARCEL POST
For postage rates, regulations and destinations to which International Air Parcel Post service is available enquire at Post Office.

REGISTRATION FEES—U.S.
Fees and Limit of Indemnity:
$2.00 ....$100.00
$2.50 ....$200.00

INSURANCE FEES (Parcel Post only)—U.S.
Insurance up to $10.00 ....20¢
Insurance over $10.00 to $50.00 ....30¢
Insurance over $50.00 to $100.00 ....35¢
Insurance over $100.00 to $200.00 ....65¢
Insurance over $200.00 to $300.00 ....95¢
Insurance over $300.00 to $400.00 ....$1.25
Insurance over $400.00 to $500.00 ....$1.50

POSTAL CODE
Canada's Postal Code is designed to speed up service. The first three characters represent a geographical area of Canada, and the last three specific delivery place within that area. Following is the correct procedure for use of the code.
1) Show the Code as the last item of the address. Leave a space between the first three and the last three characters.
2) Do not use punctuation or hyphens anywhere in the Code.
3) Wherever possible place the Code on a line by itself at the end of the address. Otherwise leave at least two character spaces and place the code on the last line, after the province.
4) All previous zone numbers are withdrawn and should not be used.

RATES TO THE UNITED STATES
its territories and possessions

LETTER MAIL AND POSTCARDS (airmail)

Up to	30 g $0.35	50 g $0.50	100 g $0.75	150 g $1.00	200 g $1.25	250 g $1.50
	300 g $1.75	350 g $2.00	400 g $2.25	450 g $2.50	500 g $2.75	

over 500 g mail becomes air parcels and the charge is $6.00 per 1st kg and $0.80 each additional .5 kg up to 30 kg maximum

PRINTED PAPERS (surface)

Up to and including

50 g	100 g	250 g	500 g
$0.30	0.45	0.90	$1.65

Maximum: 500 g
Over 500 g surface Parcel Post rates.
Direct Bags: (surface only) $3.00 each kg up to 30 kg maximum.

SMALL PACKETS

Up to and including

100 g	250 g	500 g
$0.45	0.90	$1.65

Small Packets is a category designed to provide an alternative and speedier service to Parcel Post for items weighing up to 500 g. Small Packets can be registered but not insured. Consult your Postmaster for further details on Small Packets. For Customs inspections please use Green Customs Declaration #185.

INTERNATIONAL RATES

LETTERS AND POSTCARDS
(All countries except the U.S.A., its territories and possessions, C.F.P.O.'s and F.M.O.'s)

WEIGHT STEPS	AIR MAIL
Up to 20 g	$0.60
Over 20 g up to 50 g	$0.93
Over 50 g up to 100 g	$1.45
Over 100 g up to 250 g	$2.92
Over 250 g up to 500 g	$5.60

MAXIMUM–500 g
Over 500 g: surface and air parcel post rates.

AEROGRAMMES
(All Countries) 60¢ each

PRINTED PAPERS
(Printed matter, newspapers, periodicals, greeting cards, books mailed *by the public*)
(All Countries except U.S.A., its territories and possessions, C.F.P.O's and F.M.O.'s)

WEIGHT STEPS	AIR MAIL	SURFACE MAIL
Up to 20 g	$0.45	$0.30
Over 20 g up to 50 g	$0.72	$0.44
Over 50 g up to 100 g	$1.12	$0.67
Over 100 g up to 250 g	$2.14	$1.22
Over 250 g up to 500 g	$3.89	$2.19

MAXIMUM–500 g
Over 500 g: surface and air parcel post rates.

Direct bags–surface only: $3.65 each kg up to 30 kg maximum

SMALL PACKETS
(All Countries except the U.S.A., its territories and possessions, C.F.P.O.'s and F.M.O.'s)

	AIR	SURFACE
Up to 20 g	$0.45	$0.67
Over 20 g up to 50 g	$0.72	$0.67
Over 50 g up to 100 g	$1.12	$0.67
Over 100 g up to 250 g	$2.14	$1.22
Over 250 g up to 500 g	$3.89	$2.19

MAXIMUM–500 g
Over 500 g: surface and air parcel post rates.

RATE CODES–FIRST & FOURTH CLASS–OVER 500 g

TABLE 1

The postage payable on first and fourth class mail weighing over 500 g shall be determined in accordance with the rate code that is based on the utilization of the first character of the postal code from the post office of mailing to the post office of destination, except for the "short haul" zone. The short haul zone takes precedence over the zone to zone rates when computing postage and is detailed on separate lists that are available on request at the local post office.

There are only two exceptions to the short haul zone; for all post offices in the Northwest Territories and for all air stage offices in Canada, the short haul rate will only apply to their immediate delivery area.

The rate code applicable to an item weighing over 500 g is the number appearing at the intersection of the horizontal line identifying the post office of mailing by the first character of the postal code and the vertical line showing likewise the first character of the postal code of the destination office, as shown on Table 1.

That code is used thereafter to determine the postage required, first class or fourth class, depending on the service that is requested, for a given item of a certain weight according to the scale of rates illustrated on Table 2.

RATE CODES From– To–	A	B	C	E	G	H	J	K	L	M	N	P	R	S	T	V	X	Y
NFLD.–A	1	3	3	3	4	5	5	5	6	6	6	6	7	8	8	9	10	9
N.S.–B	3	1	2	2	3	3	3	3	4	4	4	5	6	7	7	8	10	9
P.E.I.–C	3	2	1	2	3	3	3	3	4	4	4	5	6	7	7	8	10	9
N.B.–E	3	2	2	1	2	3	3	3	4	4	4	5	6	7	7	8	10	8
QUE.–G	4	3	3	2	1	2	2	2	2	2	3	4	5	6	7	7	10	8
QUE. (Mtl.)–H	5	3	3	3	2	1	2	2	2	2	2	3	5	6	6	7	10	8
QUE.–J	5	3	3	3	2	2	1	2	2	2	2	3	5	5	6	7	10	8
ONT.–K	5	3	3	3	2	2	2	1	2	2	2	2	5	5	6	7	10	8
ONT.–L	6	4	4	4	2	2	2	2	1	1	1	2	4	5	6	7	10	8
ONT. (Toronto)–M	6	4	4	4	2	2	2	2	1	1	1	2	4	5	6	7	10	8
ONT.–N	6	4	4	4	3	2	2	2	1	1	1	3	4	5	6	7	10	8
ONT.–P	6	5	5	5	4	3	3	2	2	2	3	1	3	3	5	6	10	7
MAN.–R	7	6	6	6	5	5	5	5	4	4	4	3	1	2	3	5	10	6
SASK.–S	8	7	7	7	6	6	5	5	5	5	5	3	2	1	3	4	10	5
ALTA.–T	8	7	7	7	7	6	6	6	6	6	6	5	3	3	1	3	10	4
B.C.–V	9	8	8	8	7	7	7	7	7	7	7	6	5	4	3	1	10	3
N.W.T.–X	10	10	10	10	10	10	10	10	10	10	10	10	10	10	10	10	10	10
YUKON–Y	9	9	9	8	8	8	8	8	8	8	8	7	6	5	4	3	10	1

NOTE: Before using the rate code outlined above, please consult the list that shows whether the post office of destination is comprised within the short haul zone. If enclosed therein, one must use the rate outlined on the first line of Table 2. Lists of post offices which make up the short haul zone are available at the local post office. Special rate charts for your originating zone are available from your local post office.

TABLE 2

RATE CODES	Kilograms Up to	1	1.5	2	2.5	3	3.5	4	6	8	10	12	14	16	18	20	22	24	26	28	30
Short Haul	First	$1.90	$2.30	$2.45	$2.60	$2.75	$2.90	$3.05	$3.35	$3.65	$3.95	$4.25	$4.55	$4.85	$5.10	$5.40	$5.70	$6.00	$6.30	$6.60	$6.90
	Fourth	1.10	1.20	1.30	1.45	1.60	1.75	1.90	2.10	2.35	2.90	3.20	3.55	3.90							
1	First	2.15	2.50	2.65	2.80	2.95	3.10	3.25	3.60	3.95	4.30	4.70	5.05	5.40	5.75	6.10	6.45	6.85	7.20	7.55	7.90
	Fourth	1.30	1.40	1.50	1.65	1.80	2.00	2.15	2.45	2.75	3.35	3.70	4.15	4.60							
2	First	2.30	2.55	2.80	3.00	3.25	3.50	3.75	4.30	4.85	5.35	5.90	6.45	7.00	7.50	8.05	8.60	9.15	9.65	10.20	10.75
	Fourth	1.30	1.40	1.50	1.65	1.80	2.00	2.15	2.45	2.75	3.35	3.70	4.15	4.60							
3	First	2.45	3.00	3.40	3.80	4.20	4.60	5.00	5.90	6.80	7.70	8.60	9.50	10.40	11.30	12.20	13.10	14.00	14.90	15.80	16.70
	Fourth	1.40	1.50	1.60	1.75	2.00	2.15	2.35	2.70	3.05	3.75	4.20	4.70	5.25							
4	First	2.65	3.50	4.00	4.50	5.00	5.50	6.00	7.20	8.40	9.60	10.80	12.00	13.20	14.40	15.60	16.80	18.00	19.20	20.40	21.60
	Fourth	1.50	1.60	1.75	1.95	2.10	2.35	2.50	2.95	3.35	4.20	4.80	5.40	6.00							
5	First	2.80	4.00	4.50	5.00	5.50	6.00	6.50	8.10	9.70	11.30	12.90	14.50	16.10	17.70	19.30	20.90	22.50	24.10	25.70	27.30
	Fourth	1.60	1.70	1.80	2.05	2.30	2.45	2.70	3.25	3.70	4.70	5.40	6.10	6.80							
6	First	3.10	4.50	5.10	5.70	6.30	6.90	7.50	9.60	11.70	13.80	15.90	18.00	20.10	22.20	24.30	26.40	28.50	30.60	32.70	34.80
	Fourth	1.70	1.75	2.05	2.30	2.55	2.85	3.10	3.65	4.40	5.10	5.90	6.70	7.40							
7	First	3.35	5.00	5.75	6.50	7.25	8.00	8.75	11.45	14.15	16.85	19.55	22.25	24.95	27.65	30.35	33.05	35.75	38.45	41.15	43.85
	Fourth	1.85	2.00	2.25	2.55	2.80	3.10	3.35	3.95	4.80	5.60	6.40	7.20	8.20							
8	First	3.60	5.50	6.50	7.50	8.50	9.50	10.50	14.00	17.50	21.00	24.50	28.00	31.50	35.00	38.50	42.00	45.50	49.00	52.50	56.00
	Fourth	2.00	2.35	2.70	3.05	3.35	3.70	4.00	4.60	5.50	6.30	7.10	8.00	8.90							
9	First	3.90	6.00	7.20	8.40	9.60	10.80	12.00	16.50	21.00	25.50	30.00	34.50	39.00	43.50	48.00	52.50	57.00	61.50	66.00	70.50
	Fourth	2.30	2.65	3.00	3.40	3.75	4.10	4.45	5.15	6.20	7.00	7.90	8.90	9.90							

ESTIMATED POPULATION BY PROVINCES AT JUNE 1, 1980**

The estimated population of Canada at June 1, 1980 was 23,914,400. This figure results from a population accounting which starts with the 1980 Census, adds births and immigration, and deducts deaths and an estimate of emigration based largely on United States and United Kingdom government statistics of immigration from Canada. For each province the same general method is used as for Canada. For purposes of estimating interprovincial migration, Family Allowances statistics and other data are used.

The 1980 estimate is distributed by provinces as follows:

Canada	23,914,400
Newfoundland	579,900
Prince Edward Island	124,300
Nova Scotia	852,500
New Brunswick	707,100
Québec	6,303,400
Ontario	8,570,400
Manitoba	1,028,300
Saskatchewan	969,200
Alberta	2,078,500
British Columbia	2,636,500
Yukon	21,400
Northwest Territories	43,000

**These figures are preliminary postcensal estimates.

PERCENTAGE DISTRIBUTION OF CANADIAN POPULATION, BY PROVINCES AND TERRITORIES, 1901 TO 1980

PROVINCE OR TERRITORY	1901	1941	1951	1961	1971	1979	1980(est.)
Newfoundland	—	—	2.58	2.51	2.42	2.42	2.42
Prince Edward Island	1.92	0.83	0.70	0.58	0.52	0.52	0.52
Nova Scotia	8.56	5.02	4.59	4.04	3.66	3.58	3.56
New Brunswick	6.16	3.97	3.68	3.28	2.94	2.96	2.96
Quebec	30.70	28.96	28.95	28.84	27.95	26.55	26.36
Ontario	40.64	32.92	32.82	34.19	35.71	35.92	35.84
Manitoba	4.75	6.34	5.54	5.05	4.58	4.36	4.30
Saskatchewan	1.70	7.79	5.94	5.07	4.29	4.05	4.05
Alberta	1.36	6.92	6.71	7.30	7.55	8.50	8.69
British Columbia	3.33	7.11	8.32	8.93	10.13	10.86	11.02
Yukon	0.51	0.04	0.06	0.08	0.09	0.09	0.09
Northwest Territories	0.37	0.10	0.11	0.13	0.16	0.18	0.18
Totals	100.00	100.00	100.00	100.00	100.00	100.00	100.00

POPULATION OF CANADA BY PROVINCES AND TERRITORIES

PROVINCE	1976 (Census)	1971 (Census)	1961 (Census)	1951 (Census)	1941 (Census)
Alberta	1,838,037	1,627,874	1,331,944	939,501	796,169
British Columbia	2,466,608	2,184,621	1,629,082	1,165,210	817,861
Manitoba	1,021,506	988,247	921,686	776,541	729,744
New Brunswick	677,250	634,557	597,936	515,697	457,401
Newfoundland	557,725	522,104	457,853	361,416	
Nova Scotia	828,571	788,960	737,007	642,584	577,962
Ontario	8,264,465	7,703,106	6,236,092	4,597,542	3,787,655
Prince Edward Island	118,229	111,641	104,629	98,429	95,047
Quebec	6,234,445	6,027,764	5,259,211	4,055,681	3,331,882
Saskatchewan	921,323	926,242	925,181	831,728	895,992
Yukon Territory	21,836	18,388	14,628	9,096	4,914
Northwest Territories	42,609	34,807	22,998	16,004	12,028
	22,992,604	21,568,311	18,238,247	14,009,429	11,506,655
Rural	5,638,965	5,157,525	5,537,857	5,381,176	5,254,239
Urban	17,353,640	16,410,785	12,700,390	8,628,253	6,252,416

Editor's note:- Urban population figures are incorporated in the municipal section of the Almanac.

POPULATION OF METROPOLITAN AREAS AS OF JUNE 1, 1976, CENSUS, WITH LATEST POSTCENSAL ESTIMATES

Editor's note:- Urban population figures are incorporated in the municipal section of the Almanac.

METROPOLITAN AREA	1976	1979(1)	Percentage Change over 1976
Calgary, Alta.	469,917	522,700	11.2
Chicoutimi-Jonquière, Qué.	128,643	130,000	1.1
Edmonton, Alta.	554,228	594,900	7.3
Halifax, N.S.	267,991	273,200	1.9
Hamilton, Ont.	529,371	538,600	1.7
Kitchener, Ont.	272,158	283,500	4.2
London, Ont.	270,383	275,300	1.8
Montréal, Qué.	2,802,485	2,818,300	0.6
Oshawa, Ont.	135,196	141,300	4.5
Ottawa-Hull, Ont., Qué.	693,288	738,600	6.5
Ontario (part)	521,341	556,900	6.8
Québec (part)	171,947	181,700	5.7
Québec, Qué.	542,158	559,100	3.1
Regina, Sask.	151,191	163,700	8.3
St. Catharines-Niagara, Ont.	301,921	307,300	1.8
St. John's, Nfld.	143,390	147,900	3.1
Saint John, N.B.	112,974	118,700	5.1
Saskatoon, Sask.	133,750	141,600	5.9
Sudbury, Ont.	157,030	153,400	–2.4
Thunder Bay, Ont.	119,253	121,200	1.6
Toronto, Ont.	2,803,101	2,864,700	2.2
Vancouver, B.C.	1,166,348	1,175,200	0.8
Victoria, B.C.	218,250	224,800	3.0
Windsor, Ont.	247,582	245,400	–0.9
Winnipeg, Man.	578,217	590,300	2.1

(1)preliminary estimates

VITAL STATISTICS COMPARED WITH OTHER COUNTRIES

COUNTRY	Infant Mortality (Rate per 1,000 Live Births)	Death Rate (per 1,000 Population)	Birth Rate (per 1,000 Population)
Australia	12.5 (1977)	7.6 (1978)*	15.7 (1978)*
Austria	14.8 (1979)*	12.2 (1979)*	11.5 (1979)*
Canada	10.9 (1979)	7.1 (1979)*	15.5 (1979)*
Denmark	8.9 (1978)*	10.4 (1978)*	12.2 (1978)*
Finland	9.1 (1977)	9.2 (1978)*	13.5 (1978)*
France	9.8 (1979)*	10.2 (1979)*	14.1 (1979)*
Germany, Federal Republic	14.7 (1978)	11.6 (1979)*	9.5 (1979)*
India	139.0 (1972)[1]	14.7 (1977)[1]	32.9 (1977)[1]
Italy	16.0 (1978)*	9.4 (1978)*	12.5 (1978)*
Japan	8.0 (1979)*	5.9 (1979)*	14.2 (1979)*
Netherlands	8.5 (1979)*	8.0 (1979)*	12.5 (1978)*
New Zealand	13.8 (1978)	8.2 (1979)*	16.9 (1979)*
Norway	9.2 (1977)	10.1 (1979)*	12.6 (1979)*
Portugal	38.9 (1975)	9.8 (1978)*	16.8 (1978)*
South Africa (Whites)	18.4 (1974)	8.4 (1974)	20.1 (1974)
Spain	15.1 (1978)*	7.9 (1978)*	17.2 (1978)*
Sweden	7.3 (1979)*	11.0 (1979)*	11.6 (1979)*
Switzerland	8.6 (1978)	9.1 (1978)	11.3 (1978)
United Kingdom	13.3 (1978)*	11.9 (1978)*	12.3 (1978)*
United States	13.0 (1979)*	8.7 (1979)*	15.8 (1979)*

*provisional [1]based on Sample Registration Scheme

BIRTH AND DEATH RATES, CANADA, 1979

PROVINCE	LIVE BIRTHS		DEATHS		INFANT DEATHS[1]	
	Number	Rate[2]	Number	Rate[2]	Number	Rate[3]
Newfoundland	10,170	17.7	3,136	5.5	109	10.7
Prince Edward Island	1,934	15.7	1,022	8.3	21	10.9
Nova Scotia	12,406	14.6	6,843	8.1	148	11.9
New Brunswick	10,848	15.5	5,172	7.4	124	11.4
Quebec	98,646	15.7	43,311	6.9	1,040	10.5
Ontario	121,655	14.3	61,468	7.2	1,247	10.3
Manitoba	16,242	15.7	8,217	8.0	211	13.0
Saskatchewan	16,944	17.7	7,369	7.7	194	11.4
Alberta	37,003	18.4	12,109	6.0	423	11.4
British Columbia	38,432	15.0	19,204	7.5	434	11.3
Yukon	501	23.2	127	5.9	8	16.0
Northwest Territories	1,283	29.6	205	4.7	35	27.3
Totals:	366,064	15.5	168,183	7.1	3,994	10.9

[1]children under one year of age [2]per 1,000 population [3]per 1,000 live births

CONSUMER PRICE INDEX

INDEX NUMBERS OF CONSUMER PRICES, 1962-1980, ALSO JULY, 1977 to MAY, 1981
(1971 = 100)

Year and Month	Food	Housing	Clothing	Trans-portation	Health and personal care	Recreation and reading	Tobacco and alcohol	All-Item Index
1963	80.0	74.8	80.3	76.9	73.5	75.4	78.9	77.2
1964	81.3	76.0	82.4	77.8	75.8	76.6	80.4	78.6
1965	83.4	77.3	83.8	80.7	79.4	77.9	81.7	80.5
1966	88.7	79.5	87.0	82.6	81.8	80.1	83.7	83.5
1967	89.9	82.9	91.4	86.1	86.0	84.1	85.8	86.5
1968	92.8	86.7	94.1	88.3	89.5	88.3	93.6	90.0
1969	96.7	91.2	96.7	92.4	93.8	93.5	97.2	94.1
1970	98.9	95.7	98.5	96.1	98.0	96.8	98.4	97.2
1971	100.0	100.0	100.0	100.0	100.0	100.0	100.0	100.0
1972	107.6	104.7	102.6	102.6	104.8	102.8	102.7	104.8
1973	123.3	111.4	107.7	105.3	109.8	107.1	106.0	112.7
1974	143.4	121.1	118.0	115.8	119.4	116.4	111.8	125.0
1975	161.9	133.2	125.1	129.4	133.0	128.5	125.3	138.5
1976	166.2	148.0	132.0	143.3	144.3	136.2	134.3	148.9
1977	180.1	161.9	141.0	153.3	155.0	142.7	143.8	160.8
1978	208.0	174.1	146.4	162.2	166.2	148.2	155.5	175.2
1979	235.4	186.2	159.9	178.0	181.2	158.4	166.7	191.2
1980	260.6	201.4	178.7	200.7	199.3	173.5	185.3	210.6
1977								
July	182.9	162.1	140.9	153.7	155.5	143.3	145.4	161.8
Aug.	183.9	163.2	141.8	153.3	156.7	143.9	146.1	162.5
Sept.	184.3	164.3	143.3	154.5	157.0	144.2	146.3	163.4
Oct.	186.9	166.6	144.7	153.9	158.4	145.6	146.6	165.0
Nov.	188.4	167.3	144.9	156.4	159.7	145.6	146.7	166.1
Dec.	191.5	167.8	145.5	156.7	160.0	145.4	148.6	167.2
1978								
Jan.	193.0	168.6	144.1	157.4	160.3	145.6	148.5	167.8
Feb.	194.3	169.6	145.3	158.9	161.4	145.7	149.1	168.9
Mar.	197.0	171.4	147.2	160.5	163.3	146.1	150.4	170.8
Apr.	200.4	171.3	143.2	159.8	163.3	145.8	154.0	171.2
May	207.1	172.1	143.5	160.3	164.7	146.3	157.0	173.6
June	211.2	172.9	144.5	160.7	165.0	146.9	157.4	175.1
July	219.7	173.8	144.4	161.3	166.2	148.5	157.5	177.7
Aug.	216.7	175.0	145.2	162.9	167.8	148.7	157.7	177.8
Sept.	211.6	176.5	146.9	164.0	168.2	149.4	157.9	177.5
Oct.	214.1	178.6	150.1	164.5	169.4	151.3	158.0	179.3
Nov.	214.8	179.3	151.0	168.4	172.0	151.9	159.1	180.8
Dec.	216.0	180.0	151.9	168.0	172.3	152.1	159.1	181.3
1979								
Jan.	220.2	181.2	150.8	169.3	172.9	152.4	159.1	182.7
Feb.	225.6	181.7	152.4	170.7	174.6	153.1	160.1	184.4
Mar.	231.3	182.7	155.5	171.4	177.7	153.6	161.6	186.6
Apr.	233.5	183.7	156.4	173.1	178.3	154.0	162.4	187.9
May	234.8	184.2	157.4	176.3	179.5	156.9	168.1	189.7
June	235.9	185.3	158.5	176.2	180.1	158.4	168.3	190.6
July	240.0	186.1	158.3	178.3	181.8	159.5	168.5	192.1
Aug.	238.4	187.0	160.5	179.3	183.9	160.5	169.7	192.8
Sept.	238.8	188.7	164.9	181.6	184.5	161.1	170.2	194.5
Oct.	240.4	190.1	166.5	183.1	185.2	163.0	170.3	195.9
Nov.	241.0	191.4	168.5	188.1	188.1	164.1	170.8	197.8
Dec.	244.3	192.2	169.4	188.7	188.4	164.2	171.0	199.0
1980								
Jan.	245.0	193.6	167.8	190.5	189.0	165.6	173.5	200.1
Feb.	248.4	194.6	171.1	190.9	191.2	167.0	175.9	201.8
Mar.	250.7	196.3	176.4	192.5	194.4	167.9	176.7	204.0
Apr.	251.5	197.3	177.5	195.3	195.0	168.4	178.0	205.2
May	253.8	198.6	178.3	197.3	197.5	172.5	185.1	207.6
June	259.5	200.1	178.8	199.4	198.2	173.2	187.9	209.9
July	261.8	201.6	178.5	202.2	199.8	174.6	188.2	211.5
Aug.	265.5	203.3	180.3	203.1	203.2	176.4	189.3	213.5
Sept.	269.8	205.0	182.5	203.5	204.0	176.6	190.0	215.4
Oct.	270.9	207.1	182.9	207.3	204.6	179.3	190.9	217.3
Nov.	273.9	208.7	185.0	213.1	207.1	180.0	193.2	220.0
Dec.	277.0	210.2	185.0	213.7	207.2	180.5	194.8	221.3
1981								
Jan.	278.5	213.1	184.1	221.4	207.9	183.1	194.4	224.1
Feb.	283.2	214.6	187.0	222.5	211.2	185.0	195.3	226.4
Mar.	285.1	217.9	188.9	227.1	216.7	186.3	197.3	229.4
Apr.	287.9	219.6	189.3	229.3	217.7	186.3	198.9	231.1
May	286.6	222.0	189.7	232.9	220.4	189.6	204.4	233.2

STATISTICS OF GROWTH AND PROGRESS IN CANADA

Compiled by Statistics Canada

Year	Population	Wheat Production	Acreage of Field Crops	Farm Cash Receipts for Field Crops[8]	Live Stock on Farms[1]	Dairy Factory[5] Production	Fisheries Production[2,7]
	'000 omitted	'000 bushels	'000 acres	$000,000	$000,000	$000	$000
1901	5,371	55,527	19,764	....	....	29,732	25,737
1911	7,207	132,078	30,556	....	615	39,048	34,668
1921	8,788	226,508	47,553	....	806	111,924	34,932
1931	11,381	321,325	58,862	178	514	104,482	30,517
1941	11,507	314,825	56,788	326	586	201,661	62,259
1951	14,009	552,657	60,862	1,151	1,912	440,798	203,663
1961	18,238	283,394	58,273	1,117	1,880	844,980	222,880
1970	21,297	331,579	55,671	1,428	2,990	1,369,206	426,601
1971	21,569	529,552	66,328	1,753	2,903	1,463,218	463,013
1972	21,802	533,288	63,854	2,137	3,549	1,573,723	546,138
1973	22,043	604,738	67,217	2,673	4,665	1,715,904	772,086
1974	22,364	488,513	64,247	4,169	4,742	2,083,009	708,161
1975	22,697	627,515	65,592	4,802	3,838	2,612,800	696,732
1976	22,993	866,672	67,559	4,617	4,056	2,811,178	975,835
1977	23,258	729,789	67,627	4,391	4,319	3,082,715	1,115,041[7]
1978	23,483	776,959	70,393	4,986	6,028	3,399,838	1,490,611
1979	23,672	631,423	70,735	5,923	8,699	3,789,563	1,717,165
1980	23,914	702,949	71,468	6,659	9,511	....	1,549,590

MINERAL PRODUCTION

Year	Crude Petroleum '000 BBL.	Copper Tons	Nickel Tons	Natural Gas Million Cu. Ft.	Iron Ore '000 Tons	Zinc Tons	Asbestos Tons	Cement '000 Tons	Value $000,000
1901	622[3]	18,914	4,595	....	314	....	40,217	79	66
1911	291[3]	27,824	17,050	11,644	210	1[4]	127,414	996	103
1921	188[3]	23,811	9,647	14,078	60	26,545	92,761	1,007	172
1931	1,534[3]	146,152	32,833	25,875	....	118,623	164,296	1,778	230
1941	10,134[3]	321,659	141,129	43,495	516	256,191	477,846	1,465	560
1951	47,616	269,971	137,903	79,461	4,681	341,112	973,198	2,976	1,245
1961	224,123	439,088	232,991	634,131	20,359	416,004	1,173,695	6,206	2,603
1970	461,180	672,717	305,881	2,277,109	52,314	1,251,911	1,661,644	7,946	5,722
1971	492,739	721,430	294,342	2,499,024	47,352	1,249,735	1,634,579	9,067	5,968
1972	554,328	800,621	256,467	2,851,630	43,710	1,323,647	1,692,000	10,010	6,403
1973	655,853	908,241	274,527	3,119,461	52,358	1,352,074	1,862,976	11,126	8,370
1974	614,777	905,417	296,600	3,045,506	51,571	1,242,314	1,811,938	11,436	11,711
1975	520,810	808,906	266,958	3,089,530	49,486	1,163,104	1,163,674	10,985	13,338
1976	480,782	805,712	265,464	3,095,323	61,086	1,082,533	1,693,250	10,609	15,448
1977	481,900	837,120	256,301	3,230,672	59,107	1,180,041	1,672,603	10,626	18,473
1978	480,448	726,842	141,437	3,128,056	47,323	1,176,058	1,567,275	11,639	20,261
1979	546,915	701,492	139,423	3,333,338	66,716	1,212,461	1,646,100	12,969	26,081
1980	529,849	780,895	214,893	2,979,440	56,070	986,100	1,472,000	11,571	32,369

Year	Gross Value of Manufacturing Shipments[6]	Employees in Manufacturing	Pig Iron Production	Imports of Raw Sugar	Imports of Crude Natural Rubber (excluding Latex)	Imports of Raw Cotton (including Linters)	Imports of Crude Petroleum
	$000,000	'000	'000 short tons[9]	'000 tons	'000 lb.	'000 lb.	'000 gals.
1901	481	339	274	....	....	....	....
1911	1,166	515	917	....	....	....	....
1921	2,489	439	663	....	....	....	....
1931	2,555	529	470	465	56,611	103,324	1,020,762
1941	6,076	961	1,528	536	149,305	268,522	1,637,465
1951	16,392	1,258	2,553	533	107,549	214,028	2,914,911
1961	23,439	1,353	4,946	743	66,411	208,378	4,663,718
1970	46,382	1,648	9,086	1,046	113,054	182,788	7,267,157
1971	50,276	1,640	8,616	991	113,512	213,280	8,574,012
1972	56,191	1,680	9,364	1,000	130,953	209,334	9,858,246
1973	66,674	1,775	10,511	1,061	143,710	202,268	11,464,733
1974	82,455	1,838	10,386	941	122,380	166,651	10,189,191
1975	88,462	1,755	10,096	1,032	136,086	142,188	10,444,772
1976	98,084	1,773	10,803	953	176,067	148,444	9,675,602
1977	108,998	1,775	10,649	1,169	193,358	139,206	8,468,266
1978	129,247	1,804	11,396	1,134	175,453	128,379	8,105,744
1979	151,729	1,874	12,021	1,112	197,645	160,403	7,751,380
1980	165,788	1,851	10,893	946	159,948	161,774	7,163,831

[1] Not including poultry and animals on fur farm. [2] Includes Newfoundland from 1951. [3] Includes natural gasoline.
[4] Excludes refined zinc. [5] From 1968, figures include Process Cheese Manufacturers.
[6] New series beginning in 1952, gross value of Products was replaced by value of factory shipments.
[7] New series beginning in 1977 includes marketed values for sea fisheries only. [8] Excludes Newfoundland from 1979.
[9] From 1980 metric tons.

Year	Exports, (including Re-exports)	Imports	Industry Selling Price Indexes for Manufacturing (1971 = 100)	Railway Gross Revenues*	Railway Operating Expenses*	Tons of Revenue Freight Carried One Mile*	Freight Carried on Welland Canal	Vessels other than Coastal Entered & Cleared[2]
	$000,000	$000,000		$000,000	$000,000	'000,000	'000 tonnes	'000 reg. net tons
1901	[1]	[1]	....	73	50	....	562	26,030
1911	[1]	[1]	....	189	131	16,048	2,302	47,430
1921	814	799	....	458	423	26,622	2,792	54,649
1941	1,640	1,449	....	538	404	49,982	12,002	64,766
1951	3,963	4,085	....	1,089	978	64,300	14,696	100,259
1961	5,896	5,771	82.4	1,156	1,053	65,828	28,489	156,987
1970	16,819	13,952	98.1	1,672	1,570	108,210	57,035	217,621
1971	17,820	15,618	100.0	1,797	1,693	119,412	57,206	228,561
1972	20,140	18,669	104.4	1,843	1,750	119,135	58,236	243,376
1973	25,301	23,303	116.1	2,029	1,935	125,471	60,959	244,466
1974	32,441	31,692	138.1	2,476	2,394	133,554	47,501	227,175
1975	33,245	34,691	153.7	2,619	2,669	131,048	54,295	231,354
1976	38,397	37,444	161.6	3,058	2,927	132,599	58,369	248,502
1977	44,554	42,156	174.3	3,388	3,186	137,745	65,079	264,425
1978	53,183	30,102	190.4	3,723	3,526	141,737	65,671	277,433
1979	65,514	62,724	217.9	4,601	4,259	152,085	66,165	301,562
1980	75,515	68,710	247.2	5,174	4,832	156,247	....	....

*6 major railways representing about 95% of the industry in terms of operating revenues and other performance indicators.

Year	Motor Vehicle Registrations	Telephones in Use	Post Office and Money Order Revenue[3]	Index Numbers of Weekly Earnings[5] 1961 = 100	Strikes and Lockouts[4] Employees Affected	Strikes and Lockouts[4] Time Lost Working Days	Federal Finance[3] Total Revenue	Federal Finance[3] Total Expenditure	Federal Finance[3] Net Debt
	'000	'000	$000		'000	'000	$000,000	$000,000	$000,000
1901	....	....	3,421	....	24	738	53	58	268
1911	22	303	9,147	....	29	1,821	118	123	340
1921	465	902	26,331	....	28	1,049	436	528	2,341
1931	1,201	1,364	30,416	....	11	204	356	442	2,262
1941	1,573	1,562	40,383	34.1	87	434	872	1,250	3,649
1951	2,872	3,114	90,455	64.0	103	902	3,113	2,901	11,645
1961	5,517	6,014	202,004	100.0	98	1,335	5,618	5,958	12,437
1970	8,497	9,750	444,069	162.8	262	6,540	12,321	11,928	16,943
1971	9,022	10,269	432,911	176.7	240	2,867	12,803	13,182	17,322
1972	9,481	10,987	504,211	191.4	706	7,754	14,227	14,841	17,937
1973	10,158	11,677	563,159	205.4	348	5,776	16,602	16,121	17,456
1974	11,002	12,454	591,133	227.6	581	9,255	19,383	20,056	18,128
1975	11,443	13,165	617,743	261.7	506	11,480	24,909	26,055	19,275
1976	11,786	13,885	568,190	295.8	*1,571	11,685	29,956	33,978	23,296
1977	12,547	14,488	774,860	326.2	218	3,742	32,721	39,011	29,586
1978	12,975	15,172	945,763	350.3	402	7,393	32,866	42,902	39,622
1979	13,338	15,839	1,108,543	381.6	463	7,834	35,216	46,923	55,807
1980	....	....	1,483,211	419.6	441	8,975	40,054	52,364	68,595

*This figure includes 830,000 affected by "day of protest".

Year	Bk of Can. Notes in Circulation	Chartered Banks: Assets	Chartered Banks: Liabilities excluding Capital and Reserves	Chartered Banks: Demand Deposits	Chartered Banks: Notice Deposits	Chartered Banks: Total Loans	Net Amount Life Insurance in Force Dec. 31[6]
	$000,000	$000,000	$000,000	$000,000	$000,000	$000,000	$000,000
1901	28	532	420	95	222	338	464
1911	99	1,303	1,098	305	569	927	950
1921	272	2,842	2,556	552	1,289	1,781	2,935
1931	153	3,066	2,742	579	1,438	1,764	6,622
1941	406	4,008	3,712	1,088	1,616	1,403	7,349
1951	1,361	9,385	9,020	2,712	4,593	3,496	17,235
1955[7]	1,738	12,702	12,146	3,915	6,096	5,489	25,452
1956	1,869	13,428	12,781	4,180	6,451	6,192	29,087
1961	2,147	19,153	18,091	4,701	8,547	9,007	48,284
1970	3,632	47,307	45,723	7,038	21,065	24,509	111,116
1971	4,103	54,428	52,705	8,436	23,997	28,830	121,891
1972	4,806	63,222	61,237	9,772	27,592	34,100	136,405
1973	5,551	79,754	77,548	11,100	33,887	42,457	153,610
1974	6,290	97,015	94,557	11,570	40,999	54,551	177,120
1975	7,283	108,378	105,478	14,254	46,594	63,989	208,079
1976	7,813	126,403	123,066	13,373	58,136	75,251	242,690
1977	8,639	150,477	146,642	15,613	65,858	87,954	278,139
1978	9,540	189,100	184,366	16,840	77,468	105,414	313,433
1979	10,315	229,151	223,484	17,293	98,236	131,052	357,478
1980	11,108	281,244	272,835	18,513	109,000	164,094	403,047

[1]Calendar year figures are not available.
[2]Fiscal years ended March 31 to 1940.
[3]Fiscal year ended March 31.
[4]Compiled by the Department of Labour.
[5]In manufacturing.
[6]Compiled by the Department of Insurance.
[7]As at the end of December for 1955 and subsequent years.

IMPORTS AND EXPORTS — CANADA

Value of merchandise imported and exported during the twelve months ended December 31st, 1980.

Countries	IMPORTS ($000)	EXPORTS ($000)
Commonwealth and Preferential Countries		
Australia	507,133	663,485
Bahamas	38,537	23,806
Bahrain	10	5,629
Bangladesh	11,575	74,500
Barbados	11,509	33,453
Belize	1,752	3,828
Bermuda	1,180	28,045
Britain	1,970,536	3,192,634
British Oceania, n.e.s.	3	456
Commonwealth Africa, n.e.s.	97	1,944
Cyprus	779	4,516
Falkland Islands	2	12
Fiji	30,642	3,674
Gambia	10	198
Gibraltar	376	97
Ghana	5,068	23,995
Guyana	35,720	15,033
Hong Kong	574,372	192,875
India	94,263	348,157
Ireland	100,105	111,388
Jamaica	49,908	62,498
Kenya	17,773	14,041
Leeward & Windward Islands	2,340	28,313
Malawi	476	21,033
Malaysia	83,389	93,015
Malta	2,005	1,477
Mauritius and Dependencies.	41	805
New Zealand	146,950	112,281
Nigeria	41,750	102,424
Pakistan	15,386	58,501
Papua, N.G.	957	2,437
Qatar	104	8,742
Republic of South Africa	349,918	201,935
Rhodesia	60	593
Sierra Leone	27	870
Singapore	149,584	198,139
Sri Lanka	16,923	24,885
Tanzania	4,777	21,751
Trinidad & Tobago	11,246	119,603
Uganda	992	175
Zambia	26	11,708
Foreign Countries		
Afghanistan	184	335
Albania	850	100
Algeria	12,076	393,083
Angola	17,542	2,374
Argentina	36,145	226,166
Austria	95,561	68,463
Belgium and Luxembourg	250,684	986,827
Benin	4	3,391
Bolivia	16,681	6,948
Brazil	347,772	893,225
Bulgaria	4,677	5,100
Burma	165	2,610
Cameroun Republic	691	13,157
Chile	95,382	108,695
China, People's Republic of	154,911	866,420
Colombia	101,494	185,112
Costa Rica	35,238	30,064
Cuba	157,315	415,298
Czechoslovakia	63,332	126,933
Denmark	119,981	85,463
Dominican Republic	17,485	51,658
Ecuador	40,642	82,414
Egyptian Arab Republic	10,721	128,126
El Salvador	26,911	15,331
Ethiopia	845	19,395
Finland	66,660	138,135
France	770,050	996,659
French Africa, n.e.s.	2,924	8,301
French Guiana	4	255
French Oceania	261	4,460
French West Indies	240	5,019
Gabon Republic	6,704	3,115
Germany, Federal Republic of	1,448,595	1,636,825
Germany, East	9,620	9,924
Greece	30,938	126,826
Greenland	2,090	10,076
Guatemala	25,078	21,701
Guinea, Republic of	39,946	1,456
Haiti, Republic of	6,583	26,636
Honduras	39,622	22,933
Hungary	25,823	10,622
Iceland	6,016	8,234
Indonesia	28,913	212,993
Iran	3,444	41,338
Iraq	254,465	152,880
Israel	54,387	101,106
Italy	609,657	981,479
Ivory Coast	3,177	18,744
Japan	2,792,160	4,370,465
Jordan	18	13,986
Korea, North	508	18
Korea, South	414,116	504,086
Kuwait	167,555	71,072
Khmer Rep.—Laos	4	15
Lebanon	1,045	39,522
Liberia	4,217	5,160
Libya	231	72,118
Madagascar	849	23,364
Mauritania	6	898
Mexico	345,296	482,903
Morocco	11,086	67,290
Mozambique	3,183	14,117
Netherlands	262,911	1,427,888
Netherlands Antilles	77,419	9,994
Nicaragua	31,502	14,708
Norway	80,373	334,897
Oman (Muscat)	—	3,233
Panama	45,663	35,989
Paraguay	4,541	1,931
Peru	94,141	54,713
Philippines	101,416	107,896
Poland	72,071	345,533
Portugal	51,676	100,159
Portuguese Africa, n.e.s.	5	2,434
Portuguese Asia	5,202	6
Puerto Rico	102,930	93,700
Romania	37,792	21,364
Saudi Arabia	2,445,804	310,509
Senegal	1,586	8,140
Somalia	6	2,037
Spain	186,613	224,167
Spanish Africa	42	1,511
St. Pierre and Miquelon	95	19,459
Sudan	1,029	7,925
Surinam	7,321	4,822
Sweden	414,912	269,350
Switzerland	521,119	372,729
Syria	2,543	20,869
Taiwan	557,301	251,060
Thailand	24,688	141,602
Togo	3	1,260
Tunisia	282	58,563
Turkey	11,258	39,705
United Arab Emirates	62,163	44,367
United States	48,414,134	46,825,396
United States Oceania	19	3,228
United States Virgin Islands	314	2,879
Uruguay	8,438	17,599
U.S.S.R. (Russia)	59,290	1,534,861
Venezuela	2,190,263	652,924
Viet-Nam	62	358
Yemen North	—	81
Yemen South	52	30,033
Yugoslavia	32,968	68,734
Zaire	8,356	25,714
Total (all countries)	68,979,364	74,228,694

n.e.s. not elsewhere specified

PRINCIPAL TRADING PARTNERS IN 1980

COUNTRY	($000) IMPORTS	($000) EXPORTS
United States	48,414,134	46,825,396
Japan	2,792,160	4,370,465
United Kingdom	1,970,536	3,192,634
Saudi Arabia	2,445,804	310,509
Venezuela	2,190,263	652,924
Germany West	1,448,595	1,636,825
Netherlands	262,911	1,427,888
Russia	59,290	1,534,861
France	770,050	996,659
Italy	609,657	981,479
Belgium and Luxembourg	250,684	986,827
Australia	507,133	663,485

GUIDE TO THE METRIC SYSTEM

Source: Metric Commission Canada, Box 4000, Ottawa, Ont. K1S 5G8

An uncomplicated guide to most of the things you really need to know about the Metric System.

The metric usage in this section has been reviewed by the Metric Screening Office of the Canadian Government Specifications Board.

METRIC VOCABULARY

1. **Mass**

tonne (t)	A tonne is used for measuring large masses — like what a van or pickup can carry.
kilogram (kg)	Kilograms are big — like turkeys, hams, bags of sugar, etc.
gram (g)	Grams are smaller than kilograms — turkey legs, slices of ham.
milligram (mg)	You are most likely to run across milligrams in your pharmacy — prescription drugs, household remedies.

2. **Volume**

litre (L)	Most things that come in litres pour, splash and spill — like milk and juices.
millilitre (mL)	If it's less than a litre and pours, splashes and spills, it'll probably be measured in millilitres.

3. **Temperature**

degrees Celsius (°C)	It indicates to you whether you're hot or cold.

4. **Distance**

kilometre (km)	Most people would use their cars to cover distances in kilometres.
metre (m)	It's about an average man's long step.
centimetre (cm)	A stack of 10 dimes is about 1 cm in height.
millimetre (mm)	One dime is as thick as a millimetre.

SIMPLE EXPLANATION OF METRIC VOCABULARY

1. Kilograms are big — like turkeys and hams and roasts and things.

t (tonne)	Tonnes are bigger than kilograms. It takes 1000 kg to make a tonne. A mass of 1 t is what a van or pickup could carry.
g (gram)	Many foods will be sold in packages measured in grams. Grams are not as heavy as kilograms. Potato chips, ham slices, turkey legs — any food that's usually weighed in kilograms, smaller portions of it will be weighed in grams. 1000 g = 1 kg.

2. Most things that come in litres pour, splash and spill.

L (litre)	Many products such as gasoline, paint, cooking oil, juices will be sold in litres. Milk containers in the range of 1 to 4 L could be the most common sizes for this product.
mL (millilitre)	It takes 1000 mL to make 1 L. 5 mL is about a teaspoon. Metric kitchen measures come in millilitres.

3. Canada's weather temperature reports are being given in degrees Celsius only . . .
It's really very simple. On the Celsius scale, water freezes at 0°C; 20°C is room temperature; and 30°C is a hot summer day. When the temperature is −10°C you might like to go skating; at −30°C you could have trouble starting your car.

4. Most people would use their car to cover distances in kilometres and their feet to cover distances in metres.

km (kilometre)	We use kilometres to measure longer distances. The distance from one city or town to another would be measured in kilometres. Car speeds are measured in kilometres per hour (km/h). For wind speeds km/h is used.
m (metre)	A metre is about an average man's long step. The average door opening is a little over 2 m high and a door handle is approximately 1 m from the floor. 1000 m = 1 km
cm (centimetre)	A convenient unit for shorter lengths is the centimetre. The widest part of your little fingernail is about 1 cm wide. Snowfall is measured in cm (centimetre). 100 cm = 1 m
mm (millimetre)	The thickness of a dime is about 1 mm and 10 mm or 1 cm is equal to the stack of 10 dimes.

BASE UNIT TABLE

Quantity	Unit	Symbol
Length	metre	m
Mass	kilogram	kg
Time	second	s
Current	ampere	A
Temperature	kelvin	K
Luminosity	candela	cd
Amount of substance	mole	mol

SUPPLEMENTARY UNIT TABLE

Quantity	Unit	Symbol
Plane Angle	radian	rad
Solid Angle	steradian	sr

PREFIX SYMBOL TABLE

Prefix	Factor	Symbol
mega	10^6	M
kilo	10^3	k
hecto	10^2	h
deca	10	da
deci	10^{-1}	d
centi	10^{-2}	c
milli	10^{-3}	m
micro	10^{-6}	μ

SIMPLE CONVERSION TABLE OF AREA

Square Inches	1	2	3	4	5	6	7	8	9	10
Square Centimetres	6.45	12.90	19.36	25.81	32.26	38.71	45.16	51.61	58.06	64.52
Square Feet	1	2	3	4	5	6	7	8	9	10
Square Metres	0.09	0.19	0.28	0.37	0.46	0.56	0.65	0.74	0.84	0.93
Acres	1	2	3	4	5	6	7	8	9	10
Square Metres	4,047	8,094	12,141	16,187	20,234	24,281	28,328	32,375	36,422	40,469

SIMPLE CONVERSION TABLE OF TEMPERATURE

Degrees Fahrenheit	0	10	20	30	32*	40	50	60	70	80	90	100	200	212	400
Degrees Celsius	−17.8	−12.2	−6.7	−1.1	0*	4.4	10.0	15.6	21.1†	26.7	32.2	37.8	93.3	100.0	204.4‡

*(Water Freezes) †(Room Temperature) ‡(Hot Oven)

SIMPLE CONVERSION TABLE OF VOLUME

Ounces (fl.)	1	2	3	4	5	6	7	8	9	10	11	12	13	14	15	16
Millilitres	28.4	56.8	85.2	113.7	142.1	170.5	198.9	227.3	255.7	284.1	312.5	341.0	369.4	397.8	426.2	454.6
Ounces (fl.)	17		18		19		20									
Millilitres	483.0		511.4		539.8		568.3		(approx. 0.57 L)							
Pints	1	2	3	4	5	6	7	8	9	10						
Litres	0.57	1.14	1.70	2.27	2.84	3.41	3.98	4.55	5.11	5.68						
Gallons	1	2	3	4	5	6	7	8	9	10						
Litres	4.5	9.1	13.6	18.2	22.7	27.3	31.8	36.4	40.9	45.5						

	Items	Customary Units	Metric Units
1.	Clothing	inches sizes by numbers	centimetres sizes by numbers
2.	Cooking Utensils	spoons	millilitres
3.	Wall paper	yards	metres
4.	Paints	quarts pints gallons	litres litres litres
5.	Carpets and Tiles	yards feet inches	metres metres centimetres
6.	Yard Goods for Drapes, Bedding and Table Cloths	inches feet yards	centimetres metres metres
7.	Sports such as track and field, horse racing, football, baseball	yards	Will probably stay the same for a time, but eventually change to metres
8	Shoes	Sizes based on inches	Sizes based on centimetres by international agreement
9.	Groceries such as: Meats Cans Bottles Milk Butter	 pounds ounces (fluid) ounces (fluid) quarts pounds	 kilograms grams millilitres litres kilograms
10.	Baked Goods, Fruits and Vegetables	ounces (wt.) pounds	grams grams
11.	Hardware and Lumber	inches feet	grams metres
12.	Paper for writing and wrapping	inches	centimetres and millimetres

TABLES OF WEIGHTS AND MEASURES

THE INTERNATIONAL SYSTEM OF UNITS (SI)

Source: National Standard of Canada, CAN3 Z234.1-79, Canadian Metric Practice Guide.

Base Units

The International System of Units is founded on seven base units.

SI BASE UNITS

Quantity	Name	Symbol
length	metre	m
mass	kilogram	kg
time	second	s
electric current	ampere	A
thermodynamic temperature	kelvin	K
amount of substance	mole	mol
luminous intensity	candela	cd

Supplementary Units

For the time being this class contains only two purely geometrical units: the SI unit of plane angle, the *radian* and the SI unit of solid angle, the *steradian.*

SI SUPPLEMENTARY UNITS

Quantity	Name	Symbol
plane angle	radian	rad
solid angle	steradian	sr

Derived Units

Derived units are expressed algebraically in terms of base units and/or supplementary units. Their expressions in symbolic form are obtained by means of the mathematical signs of multiplication and division; for example, the SI unit for velocity is metre per second (m/s or $m{\cdot}s^{-1}$) and the SI unit for angular velocity is radian per second (rad/s or $rad{\cdot}s^{-1}$).

SI DERIVED UNITS WITH SPECIAL NAMES

Quantity	Name	Symbol	Typical Form*	In Base Units
frequency†	hertz	Hz	s^{-1}	s^{-1}
force	newton	N	$m{\cdot}kg{\cdot}s^{-2}$	$m{\cdot}kg{\cdot}s^{-2}$
pressure, stress	pascal	Pa	N/m^2	$m^{-1}{\cdot}kg{\cdot}s^{-2}$
energy, work, quantity of heat	joule	J	N·m	$m^2{\cdot}kg{\cdot}s^{-2}$
power, radiant flux	watt	W	J/s	$m^2{\cdot}kg{\cdot}s^{-3}$
quantity of electricity, electric charge	coulomb	C	s·A	s·A
electric potential, potential difference, electromotive force	volt	V	W/A	$m^2{\cdot}kg{\cdot}s^{-3}{\cdot}A^{-1}$
electric capacitance	farad	F	C/V	$m^{-2}{\cdot}kg^{-1}{\cdot}s^4{\cdot}A^2$
electric resistance	ohm	Ω	V/A	$m^2{\cdot}kg{\cdot}s^{-3}{\cdot}A^{-2}$
electric conductance	siemens	S	A/V	$m^{-2}{\cdot}kg^{-1}{\cdot}s^3{\cdot}A^2$
magnetic flux	weber	Wb	V·s	$m^2{\cdot}kg{\cdot}s^{-2}{\cdot}A^{-1}$
magnetic flux density	tesla	T	Wb/m^2	$kg{\cdot}s^{-2}{\cdot}A^{-1}$
inductance	henry	H	Wb/A	$m^2{\cdot}kg{\cdot}s^{-2}{\cdot}A^{-2}$
Celsius Temperature●	degree Celsius	°C	K	K
luminous flux	lumen	lm	cd·sr	cd·sr‡
illuminance	lux	lx	lm/m^2	$m^{-2}{\cdot}cd{\cdot}sr$‡
activity of radionuclides	becqueral	Bq	s^{-1}	s^{-1}
absorbed dose of ionising radiation	gray	Gy	J/kg	$m^2{\cdot}A^{-2}$

*The formulae for derived units are not necessarily unique. For example, the volt may be defined as one joule per coulomb.

†The SI unit of frequency, the hertz, is one cycle per second. The reciprocal of the frequency is the period. The hertz should not be used as a measure of discrete items per unit of time, e.g. 5 boxes per second on an assembly line would not be referred to as 5 hertz, but may be referred to in terms of the reciprocal second i.e. $5s^{-1}$.

●The Celsius temperature scale (previously called Centigrade, but renamed to avoid confusion with "centigrade", associated with the centismal system of angular measurement) is the commonly used scale, except for certain scientific and technological purposes where the thermodynamic temperature scale is preferred. Note the use of uppercase C for Celsius.

‡In this expression the steradian (sr) is treated as a base unit.

SI PREFIXES

Multiplying Factor	Prefix	Symbol
1 000 000 000 000 000 000 = 10^{18}	exa	E
1 000 000 000 000 000 = 10^{15}	peta	P
1 000 000 000 000 = 10^{12}	tera	T
1 000 000 000 = 10^9	giga	G
1 000 000 = 10^6	mega	M
1 000 = 10^3	kilo	k
100 = 10^2	hecto	h
10 = 10^1	deca	da
0.1 = 10^{-1}	deci	d
0.01 = 10^{-2}	centi	c
0.001 = 10^{-3}	milli	m
0.00 001 = 10^{-6}	micro	µ
0.000 000 001 = 10^{-9}	nano	n
0.000 000 000 001 = 10^{-12}	pico	p
0.000 000 000 000 001 = 10^{-15}	femto	f
0.000 000 000 000 000 001 = 10^{-18}	atto	a

Multiples of SI Units

The prefixes given (SI prefixes) and their symbols are used to form names and symbols of decimal multiples and sub-multiples of the SI units.

The multiple can usually be chosen so that the numerical values will be between 0.1 and 1000.

Examples:

1.2×10^4 N can be written as 12 kN
0.003 94 m can be written as 3.94 mm
1 401 Pa can be written as 1.401 kPa
3.1×10^{-8} s can be written as 31 ns

CONVERSION OF YARD/POUND UNITS TO THE INTERNATIONAL SYSTEM OF UNITS (SI)

Length

1 ångstrom	= 0.1 nm
1 arpent (French measure)*	= 58.471 31 m
1 astronomical unit	= 149.6 Gm
1 chain (66 feet)	= 20.116 8 m
1 ell (45 inches)	= 1.143 m
1 fathom	= 1.828 8 m
1 foot	= 0.304 8 m
1 foot (French measure)*	= 0.324 841 m
1 foot (US survey, limited usage)	= 0.304 800 6 m
1 furlong	= 0.201 168 km
1 inch	= 25.4 mm
1 league (International nautical)	= 5.556 km
1 league (UK nautical)	= 5.559 552 km
1 league (US)	= 4.828 032 km
1 link (1/100 chain)	= 0.201 168 m
1 mile	= 1.609 344 km
1 mile (International nautical)	= 1.852 km
1 mile (UK nautical)	= 1.853 184 km
1 mile (US nautical)	= 1.852 km
1 mil (0.001 inch)	= 25.4 μm
1 microinch	= 25.4 nm
1 parsec	= 30.857 Pm
1 light year	= 9.4605 Pm
1 perch	= 5.029 2 m
1 perch (French measure)*	= 5.847 131 m
1 pica (printers)	= 4.217 518 mm
1 point (printers)	= 0.351 459 8 mm
1 pole	= 5.029 2 m
1 rod	= 5.029 2 m
1 yard	= 0.914 4 m

*Measures formerly used to describe certain land in the Province of Quebec.

Mass

1 cental (100 lb)	= 45.359 237 kg
1 coal tub (100 lb, Newfoundland)	= 45.359 237 kg
1 drachm (apothecary)	= 3.887 935 g
1 dram (apothecary, US)	= 3.887 935 g
1 dram (avoirdupois)	= 1.771 845 g
1 grain	= 64.798 91 mg
1 hundredweight (100 lb)	= 45.359 237 kg
1 hundredweight (long 112 lb, UK)	= 50.802 345 kg
1 ounce (avoirdupois)	= 28.349 523 g
1 ounce (troy or apothecary)	= 31.103 476 8 g
1 metric carat	= 200 mg
1 pennyweight	= 1.555 174 g
1 pound (avoirdupois)	= 0.453 592 37 kg
1 pound (troy or apothecary)	= 373.241 721 6 g
1 quarter (28 lb, UK)	= 12.700 58 kg
1 scruple (apothecary, 20 grains)	= 1.295 98 g
1 slug	= 14.593 9 kg
1 stone (14 lb, UK)	= 6.350 293 kg
1 ton (2240 lb, UK)	= 1.016 046 908 8 Mg
1 ton (short, 2000 lb)	= 0.907 184 74 Mg
1 unified atomic mass	= $1.660\ 44 \times 10^{-27}$ kg

Area

1 acre	= 0.404 685 6 ha
1 arpent (French measure)*	= 0.341 889 4 ha
1 circular mil	= 506.7 μm^2
1 legal subdivision (40 acres)	= 0.161 874 2 km^2
1 perch (French measure)*	= 34.188 94 m^2
1 rood (1210 square yards)	= 0.101 171 4 ha
1 section (1 mile square, 640 acres)	= 2.589 988 km^2
1 square foot	= 929.030 4 cm^2
1 square foot (French measure)*	= 0.105 521 m^2
1 square inch	= 645.16 mm^2
1 square mile	= 2.589 988 km^2
1 square yard	= 0.836 127 4 m^2
1 township (36 sections)	= 93.239 57 km^2

*Measures formerly used to describe certain land in the Province of Quebec.

Capacity

1 barrel (36 UK gallons)	= 0.163 659 m^3
1 barrel (US dry, 7056 in^3)	= 0.115 627 m^3
1 barrel (Oil, 42 US gallons)	= 0.158 987 3 m^3
1 barrel (US dry, cranberries, 5826 in^3)	= 95.471 dm^3
1 bushel	= 36.368 72 dm^3
1 bushel (UK)	= 36.368 74 dm^3
1 bushel (US dry, 2150.42 in^3)	= 35.239 07 dm^3
1 fluid dram	= 3.551 633 cm^3
1 fluid dram (US measure)	= 3.696 691 cm^3
1 fluid drachm (UK measure)	= 3.551 634 cm^3
1 fluid ounce	= 28.413 062 cm^3
1 fluid ounce (UK)	= 28.413 08 cm^3
1 fluid ounce (US)	= 29.573 53 cm^3
1 gallon*	= 4.546 09 dm^3
1 gallon (UK)†	= 4.546 092 dm^3
1 gallon (US)	= 3.785 412 dm^3
1 gill (UK)	= 0.142 065 dm^3
1 gill (US)	= 0.118 294 dm^3
1 minim (UK)	= 59.193 9 mm^3
1 minim (US)	= 61.611 5 mm^3
1 peck	= 9.092 180 dm^3
1 peck (UK)	= 9.092 184 dm^3
1 peck (US dry)	= 8.809 768 dm^3
1 pint	= 0.568 261 dm^3
1 pint (UK)	= 0.568 262 dm^3
1 pint (US dry)	= 0.550 610 dm^3
1 pint (US liquid)	= 0.473 176 dm^3
1 quart	= 1.136 522 dm^3
1 quart (UK)	= 1.136 523 dm^3
1 quart (US dry)	= 1.101 221 dm^3
1 quart (US liquid)	= 0.946 353 dm^3
1 ton (register)	= 2.831 685 m^3

*The Australian gallon is the same as the Canadian gallon. The term "Imperial gallon" is frequently used when the correct expression is "Canadian gallon" or simply "gallon" when from the context the intent is clear.

†Also referred to as the "Imperial gallon".

Pressure or Stress (Force per Area)

1 atmosphere, standard (= 760 torr)	= 101.325 kPa
1 atmosphere, technical (= 1 kgf/cm^2)	= 98.066 5 kPa
1 bar	= 100 kPa
1 foot of water (39.2°F, 4°C)	= 2.988 98 kPa
1 inch of mercury (conventional 32°F)	= 3,386 39 kPa
1 inch of mercury (60°F)	= 3.376 85 kPa
1 inch of mercury (68°F, 20°C)	= 3.374 11 kPa
1 inch of water (conventional)	= 249.089 Pa
1 inch of water (39.2°F, 4°C)	= 249.082 Pa
1 inch of water (60°F)	= 248.843 Pa
1 inch of water (68°F, 20°C)	= 248.641 Pa
1 ksi (1000 lbf/in^2)	= 6.894 757 MPa
1 poundal per square foot	= 1.488 164 Pa
1 pound-force per square foot	= 47.880 26 Pa
1 pound-force per square inch (psi)	= 6.894 757 kPa
1 ton-force per square inch	= 13.789 514 MPa
1 ton-force (UK) per square inch	= 15.444 3 MPa
1 torr	= 133.322 Pa

EXAMPLE OF SI DERIVED UNITS WITHOUT SPECIAL NAMES

Quantity	Description	Unit Symbols Typical form	In Base Units
area	square metre	m^2	m^2
volume	cubic metre	m^3	m^3
speed — linear	metre per second	m/s	m/s
— angular	radian per second	rad/s	rad/s
acceleration — linear	metre per second squared	m/s^2	m/s^2
— angular	radian per second squared	rad/s^2	rad/s^2
wave number*	reciprocal metre	m^{-1}	m^{-1}
density, mass density	kilogram per cubic metre	kg/m^3	kg/m^3
concentration (of amount of substance)	mole per cubic metre	mol/m^3	mol/m^3
specific volume	cubic metre per kilogram	m^3/kg	m^3/kg
luminance	candela per square metre	cd/m^2	cd/m^2
dynamic viscosity	pascal second	Pa·s	$m^{-1}\cdot kg\cdot s^{-1}$
kinematic viscosity	square metre per second	m^2/s	$m^2\cdot s^{-1}$
moment of force	newton metre	N·m	$m^2\cdot kg\cdot s^{-2}$
surface tension	newton per metre	N/m	$kg\cdot s^{-2}$
heat flux density, irradiance	watt per square metre	W/m^2	$kg\cdot s^{-3}$
heat capacity, entropy	joule per kelvin	J/K	$m^2\cdot kg\cdot s^{-2}\cdot K^{-1}$
specific heat capacity, specific entropy	joule per kilogram kelvin	J/(kg·K)	$m^2\cdot s^{-2}\cdot K^{-1}$
specific energy	joule per kilogram	J/kg	$m^2\cdot s^{-2}$
thermal conductivity	watt per metre kelvin	W/(m·K)	$m\cdot kg\cdot s^{-3}\cdot K^{-1}$
energy density	joule per cubic metre	J/m^3	$m^{-1}\cdot kg\cdot s^{-2}$
electric field strength	volt per metre	V/m	$m\cdot kg\cdot s^{-3}\cdot A^{-1}$
electric charge density	coulomb per cubic metre	C/m^3	$m^{-3}\cdot s\cdot A$
surface density of charge, flux density	coulomb per square metre	C/m^2	$m^{-2}\cdot s\cdot A$
permittivity	farad per metre	F/m	$m^{-3}\cdot kg^{-1}\cdot s^4\cdot A^2$
current density	ampere per square metre	A/m^{-2}	$A\cdot m^{-2}$
magnetic field strength	ampere per metre	A/m	$A\cdot m^{-1}$
permeability	henry per metre	H/m	$m\cdot kg\cdot s^{-2}\cdot A^{-2}$
molar energy	joule per mole	J/mol	$m^2\cdot kg\cdot s^{-2}\cdot mol^{-1}$
molar entropy, molar heat capacity	joule per mole kelvin	J/(mol·K)	$m^2\cdot kg\cdot s^{-2}K^{-1}\cdot mol^{-1}$
radiant intensity	watt per steradian	W/sr	$m^2\cdot kg\cdot s^{-3}\cdot sr^{-1}$
radiance	watt per square metre steradian	$w/(m^2\cdot sr)$	$kg\cdot s^{-3}sr^{-1}$
exposure	coulomb per kilogram	C/kg	$A\cdot s\cdot kg^{-1}$
absorbed dose rate	gray per second	Gy/s	$m^2\cdot s^{-3}$

*The wave number is the reciprocal of the wavelength, expressed in metres, of an electromagnetic radiation.

NOTE: The values of certain so-called dimensionless quantities, as for example refractive index, relative permeability or relative permittivity are expressed by pure numbers.

Temperature

Celsius* temperature = temperature in kelvins—273.15
Fahrenheit temperature = 1.8 (temperature in kelvins)—459.67
Rankine temperature = 1.8 (temperature in kelvins)
Fahrenheit temperature = 1.8 (Celsius temperature) + 32

*"Celsius" replaced "Centigrade" in 1948 to eliminate confusion with the word centigrade associated with angular measure.

*Measures Having Household Usage**

1 cup (Canadian, 8 fluid ounces	= 227 mL
1 cup (US, 8 fluid ounces)	= 236 mL
1 drop (1/100 teaspoon, Canadian hospital usage)	= 0.05 mL
1 tablespoon (Canadian, ½ fluid ounce)	= 14.21 mL
1 tablespoon (Canadian hospital usage)	= 15 mL
1 tablespoon (UK, ⅝ fluid ounce)	= 17.8 mL
1 tablespoon (US, ½ fluid ounce)	= 14.8 mL
1 teaspoon (Canadian, 1/6 fluid ounce)	= 4.74 mL
1 teaspoon (Canadian hospital usage)	= 5 mL
1 teaspoon (UK, 5·24 fluid ounce)	= 5.92 mL
1 teaspoon (US, 1/6 fluid ounce)	= 4.93 mL

*1 mL = 1 cm^3. Refer also to CGSB standard CAN 2-26·3-M77, COOKING MEASURES, METRIC and CAN 2-26·4-M77 Medicine Spoon, Metric

Volume

1 acre foot	= 1 233.482 m^3
1 board foot	= 2.359 737 dm^3
1 cord (128 ft^3, 4 ft x 4 ft x 8 ft, stacked wood)	= 3.624 6 m^3
1 cubic foot	= 28.316 85 dm^3
1 cubic inch	= 16.387 064 cm^3
1 cubic yard	= 0.764 555 m^3
1 cunit (100 ft^3, solid timber)	= 2.831 68 m^3
1 Petrograd standard (165 ft^3, sawn timber)	= 4.672 28 m^3

FAHRENHEIT AND CELSIUS THERMOMETER SCALES COMPARED

	Fahrenheit (in	Celsius degrees)	From Fahrenheit to Celsius	
Boiling	212	100		
	104	40	Subtract	32
	86	30	Multiply by	5
	68	20	Divide by	9
	50	10	From Celsius to Fahrenheit:	
Freezing	32	Zero		
	14	– 10		
	Zero		Add	32
	–4	–20	Multiply by	9
	–22	–30	Divide by	5

ENVIRONMENT CANADA—NAVIGATION CANALS

Name	Location	Length of Channel	Locks			
			Minimum Dimensions			
			No.	Length	Width	Depth
		km		m	m	m
ATLANTIC AREA—						
St. Peters	St. Peter's Bay to Bras d'Or Lakes, Cape Breton, N.S.	0.80	1	91.4	14.4	5.2
Richelieu River—						
St. Ours	St. Ours, Que.	0.24	1	103.3	13.7	3.7
Chambly	Chambly to St. Jean, Que.	18.95	9	38.4	7.1	1.9
Ottawa and Rideau Rivers—						
Ste. Anne	Junction of St. Lawrence and Ottawa Rivers	0.59	1	61	13.7	2.7
Carillon	Carillon Rapids, Ottawa River	0.8	1	57.3	40.8	2.7
Rideau	Ottawa to Kingston	198.8	48	40.8	10	1.7
	Rideau Lake to Perth (Tay Branch)	9.85	2	40.8	10	1.7
Lake Ontario to Georgian Bay—						
Trent	Trenton to Peterborough Lock, Peterborough	142.8	18	53.3	10	2.4
	Peterborough lock to Swift Rapids	218.4	24	40.8	10	1.8
	Swift Rapids to Big Chute	12.87	—	—	—	1.2
	Big Chute to Port Severn	13.05	1	30.5	7.6	1.8
	Sturgeon Lake to Lindsay (Scugog Br.)	16.09	1	43.3	10	1.8
	Lindsay to Port Perry (Scugog Br.)	40.23	—	—	—	1.2
Murray	Isthmus of Murray, Bay of Quinte	12.12	—	—	—	2.9

FACTORS GOVERNING THE TRANSIT OF VESSELS THROUGH THE ST. LAWRENCE SEAWAY LOCKS, CANALS AND CHANNELS BETWEEN MONTREAL AND LAKE ERIE

Channel widths vary from a minimum of 61 m between bridge abutments and canals flanked by two embankments, to at least 137 m in open reaches.

Minimum vertical overhead clearance of structures and cables crossing the Seaway is 36 m above High Water.

MAXIMUM VESSEL DIMENSIONS

Length.....................222.50 m overall
Beam.......................23.15 m extreme breadth including permanent fenders

The channels and canals in the Deep Waterway between Port of Montreal and Lake Erie are designed for a minimum controlling depth of 8.23 m.

In the Seaway canals the maximum permitted draught will be currently prescribed by The St. Lawrence Seaway Authority and the Saint Lawrence Seaway Development Corporation.

The present maximum permissible draught is 79.25 dm.

Lock	Normal Lift in Metres	Usable Length in Metres	Width in Metres	Usable Length Lower Ent. in Metres	Usable Length Upper Ent. in Metres
St. Lambert (Montreal Hr.)	4.5	222.5	24.38	653	456
Cote Ste. Catherine	10.0	222.5	24.38	319	223
Lower Beauharnois	12.2	222.5	24.38	379	498
Upper Beauharnois	11.3	222.5	24.38	498	575
Snell	14.0	222.5	24.38	449	212
Eisenhower	11.8	222.5	24.38	210	330
Iroquois	0.2	222.5	24.38	240	686

Minimum depth on Lock Gate Sills is 9.14 m.

WELLAND CANAL LOCKS

Lock No.	Type	Usable Length in Metres	Width in Metres	Normal Lift in Metres	Mileage From Port Weller (Nautical Miles)*	Usable Length Lower Ent. in Metres	Usable Length Upper Ent. in Metres
1	Single	222.5	24.38	14	1.7	840	448
2	Single	222.5	24.38	14	3.2	458	507
3	Single	222.5	24.38	14	5.5	445	482
4	Double	222.5	24.38	15	6.8	290	—
5	Double	222.5	24.38	15	6.8	—	—
6	Double	222.5	24.38	13	6.8	—	275
7	Single	222.5	24.38	14	7.5	275	404.5
Guard Gate	Single	—	24.38	—	8.3	739	680
8	Single	350	24.38	2	21.3	346	380

*Distances are shown in nautical miles in keeping with an international maritime agreement. One nautical mile equals 1,852 km.

LAND AND FRESH WATER AREA OF CANADA BY PROVINCES AND TERRITORIES

Province or Territory	Land Sq. km	Fresh Water Sq. km	Total Sq. km	Per Cent. of Total Area
Newfoundland	370,486	22,687	393,173	4.1
Prince Edward Island	5,656	–	5,656	0.1
Nova Scotia	52,841	2,650	55,491	0.6
New Brunswick	72,093	1,344	73,437	0.7
Quebec	1,356,797	183,890	1,540,687	15.4
Ontario	891,198	177,389	1,068,587	10.7
Manitoba	548,497	101,593	650,090	6.5
Saskatchewan	570,271	81,632	651,903	6.5
Alberta	644,392	16,796	661,188	6.6
British Columbia	930,533	18,068	948,601	9.5
Yukon	478,036	4,481	482,517	5.4
Northwest Territories	3,246,404	133,294	3,379,698	33.9
Franklin	1,403,140	19,425	1,422,565	14.3
Keewatin	565,811	25,123	590,934	5.9
Mackenzie	1,277,453	88,746	1,366,199	13.7
Totals	12,413,608	877,118	13,290,726	100.0

NOTE:- 1 sq. km equals 2.590 sq. miles.

DISTANCES BETWEEN PRINCIPAL POINTS IN CANADA

VIA RAIL OR WATER

Approximate distances by rail or water (miles)	Nfld. St. John's	N.S. Halifax	P.E.I. Charlottetown	N.B. Saint John	N.B. Fredericton	Que. Quebec	Que. Montreal	Ont. Ottawa	Ont. Toronto	Ont. Thunder Bay	Man. Winnipeg	Sask. Regina	Sask. Saskatoon	Alta. Calgary	Alta. Edmonton	B.C. Vancouver	B.C. Victoria	B.C. Pr. Rupert
St. John's	0	930	1041	1081	1094	1466	1563	1675	1897	2521	2797	3153	3268	3531	3646	4262	4362	4543
Halifax	930	0	239	279	292	664	761	873	1095	1719	1995	2351	2466	2729	2844	3460	3560	3741
Charlottetown	1041	239	0	215	230	600	684	795	1018	1653	1950	2305	2421	2772	2751	3413	3498	3707
Saint John	1081	279	215	0	67	425	482	594	816	1470	1894	2250	2374	2726	2699	3368	3324	3655
Fredericton	1094	292	230	67	0	403	454	565	788	1423	1753	2108	2224	2575	2554	3216	3301	3510
Quebec City	1466	664	600	425	403	0	164	276	498	1152	1521	1877	1992	2353	2323	2995	2898	3279
Montreal	1563	761	684	482	454	164	0	112	334	988	1357	1713	1828	2244	2151	2886	2900	3115
Ottawa	1675	873	795	594	565	276	112	0	247	887	1301	1658	1772	2133	2098	2775	2789	3054
Toronto	1897	1095	1018	816	788	498	334	247	0	809	1233	1590	1704	2065	2030	2707	2755	2986
Thunder Bay	2521	1719	1653	1470	1423	1152	988	877	809	0	424	781	895	1256	1221	1898	1967	2177
Winnipeg	2797	1995	1950	1894	1753	1521	1357	1301	1233	424	0	356	471	832	797	1474	1548	1753
Regina	3153	2351	2305	2250	2108	1877	1713	1658	1590	781	356	0	161	476	487	1118	1193	1443
Saskatoon	3268	2466	2421	2374	2224	1992	1828	1772	1704	895	471	161	0	399	326	1097	1131	1282
Calgary	3531	2729	2772	2726	2575	2353	2244	2133	2065	1256	832	476	399	0	195	642	727	1151
Edmonton	3646	2844	2751	2699	2554	2323	2151	2098	2030	1221	797	487	326	195	0	771	846	956
Vancouver	4262	3460	3413	3368	3216	2995	2886	2775	2707	1898	1474	1118	1097	642	771	0	85	546
Victoria	4362	3560	3498	3324	3301	2898	2900	2789	2755	1967	1548	1193	1131	727	846	85	0	631
Prince Rupert	4543	3741	3707	3655	3510	3279	3115	3054	2986	2177	1753	1443	1282	1151	956	546	631	0

NOTE:- Convert to km by multiplying by 1.609344

VIA AIR CANADA

From	To	km	Miles	From	To	km	Miles
Gander	Montreal	1,664	1,109	Montreal	Vancouver	3,666	2,444
Gander	Toronto	2,241	1,494	Montreal	Windsor	782	521
Halifax	Moncton	180	120	Ottawa	Winnipeg	1,761	1,174
Halifax	Montreal	857	571	St. John's, Nfld.	Montreal	1,721	1,147
Halifax	North Bay	1,551	1,034	Sydney	Halifax	300	200
Halifax	Ottawa	998	665	Toronto	Chicago, U.S.A.	653	435
Halifax	Toronto	1,346	897	Toronto	Cleveland, U.S.A.	293	195
Halifax	Vancouver	4,523	3,015	Toronto	Edmonton	2,540	1,693
Halifax	Winnipeg	2,840	1,893	Toronto	New York, U.S.A.	563	375
Lethbridge	Calgary	186	124	Toronto	Tampa, U.S.A.	1,679	1,119
Lethbridge	Edmonton	452	301	Toronto	Vancouver	3,177	2,118
Montreal	Boston, U.S.A.	1,167	778	Toronto	Winnipeg	1,413	942
Montreal	Edmonton	3,029	2,019	Vancouver	Victoria	71	47
Montreal	Goose Bay	1,236	824	Winnipeg	Calgary	1,125	750
Montreal	Moncton	677	451	Winnipeg	Edmonton	1,130	753
Montreal	New York, U.S.A.	525	350				
Montreal	Ottawa	141	94				
Montreal	Toronto	489	326				

Information obtained through the courtesy of Air Canada.

MILEAGE GUIDE

	BANFF	BRANDON	CALGARY	CHARLOTTETOWN	CHICOUTIMI	CORNERBROOK	DAWSON CREEK	EDMONTON	FLIN FLON	FORT SMITH	FREDERICTON	GANDER	GASPÉ	HALIFAX	HAMILTON	JASPER	KENORA	LETHBRIDGE	LONDON	MONCTON	MONTREAL	NIAGARA FALLS	NORTH BAY	OTTAWA	PORT AUX BASQUES	PRINCE ALBERT	PRINCE GEORGE	PRINCE RUPERT	QUEBEC	REGINA	RIVIÈRE-DU-LOUP	ROUYN	SAINT JOHN	ST. JOHN'S	SASKATOON	SAULT STE. MARIE	SEPT-ILES	SHERBROOKE	SUMMERSIDE	SYDNEY	THE PAS	THUNDER BAY	TORONTO	VANCOUVER	VICTORIA	WHITEHORSE	WINDSOR	WINNIPEG	YARMOUTH	YELLOWKNIFE
BANFF	•	782	80	3147	2702	3484	633	266	846	1094	2924	3725	2997	3225	2256	178	1037	216	2327	3047	2406	2299	2059	2288	3356	567	393	853	2574	555	2687	1960	2990	3932	465	1794	2980	2503	3131	3356	920	1354	2214	577	618	1562	2457	910	3055	1205
BRANDON	782	•	702	2392	1920	2714	1082	715	451	1543	2142	2943	2215	2447	1474	944	255	622	1545	2292	1624	1517	1277	1506	2574	454	1159	1619	1792	227	1905	1178	2208	3152	387	1012	2198	1721	2349	2574	357	572	1432	1359	1400	2011	1677	128	2273	1654
CALGARY	80	702	•	3055	2622	3404	553	186	766	1011	2832	3633	2917	3133	2176	258	957	136	2247	2955	2326	2219	1979	2208	3264	487	473	933	2494	475	2607	1880	2898	3842	385	1714	2900	2423	3051	3264	840	1274	2134	657	698	1482	2377	830	2963	1125
CHARLOTTETOWN	3147	2392	3055	•	552	368	3442	3075	2787	3903	223	597	516	144	1143	3304	2105	3014	1184	100	736	1147	1083	854	228	2814	3519	3979	587	2587	460	1136	192	804	2747	1348	531	706	39	228	2749	1788	1071	3719	3760	4371	1303	2232	257	4014
CHICOUTIMI	2702	1920	2622	552	•	901	3002	2635	2347	3463	329	1130	402	544	673	2864	1665	2542	744	452	296	716	643	414	761	2374	3079	3539	128	2147	92	696	383	1357	2307	908	385	261	536	761	2277	1348	631	3279	3320	3931	858	1792	460	3574
CORNERBROOK	3484	2714	3404	368	901	•	3791	3424	3136	4252	572	229	865	402	1462	3653	2454	3336	1534	449	1085	1500	1432	1203	140	3163	3868	4328	936	2936	809	1485	541	436	3096	1697	911	1055	407	140	3071	2137	1420	4068	4109	4720	1652	2581	566	4363
DAWSON CREEK	633	1082	553	3442	3002	3791	•	367	1020	640	3224	4020	3297	3525	2556	467	1337	689	2627	3342	2706	2599	2359	2588	3651	741	252	712	2874	855	2987	2260	3290	4227	695	2094	3280	2803	3426	3651	1013	1654	2514	747	788	929	2731	1210	3343	751
EDMONTON	266	715	186	3075	2635	3424	367	•	653	828	2857	3653	2930	3158	2189	229	970	322	2260	2975	2339	2232	1992	2221	3284	374	444	904	2507	488	2620	1893	2923	3860	328	1727	2913	2436	3059	3284	646	1287	2147	773	814	1296	2364	843	2988	939
FLIN FLON	846	451	766	2787	2347	3136	1020	653	•	1481	2569	3365	2642	2870	1901	882	682	862	1972	2687	2051	1944	1704	1933	2996	279	1097	1557	2219	467	2332	1605	2635	3572	381	1439	2625	2148	2771	2996	94	999	1859	1423	1464	1949	2086	555	2700	1592
FORT SMITH	1094	1543	1011	3903	3463	4252	640	828	1481	•	3685	4480	3758	3986	3017	995	1798	1150	3083	3803	3167	3055	2820	3049	4112	1202	892	1352	3335	1316	3448	272	3751	4692	1156	2555	3741	3264	3887	4112	1474	2115	2975	1387	1428	1569	3192	1671	3816	443
FREDERICTON	2924	2142	2832	223	329	572	3224	2857	2569	3685	•	801	435	215	895	3086	1887	2764	966	123	518	938	865	636	432	2596	3301	3761	364	2369	237	918	66	1008	2529	1130	481	483	207	432	2499	1570	853	3501	3542	4153	1080	2014	131	3796
GANDER	3725	2943	3633	597	1130	229	4020	3653	3365	4480	801	•	1094	631	1691	3882	2683	3560	1762	678	1314	1734	1661	1432	369	3392	4097	4557	1165	3165	1038	1714	770	207	3325	1926	1140	1284	636	369	3300	2366	1649	4297	4338	4949	1881	2810	795	4592
GASPÉ	2997	2215	2917	516	402	865	3297	2930	2642	3758	435	1094	•	587	968	3159	1960	2837	1039	416	591	1011	938	709	725	2669	3374	3834	437	2442	310	991	501	1301	2602	1203	299	556	500	725	2572	1643	926	3574	3615	4226	1153	2087	566	3869
HALIFAX	3225	2447	3133	144	544	402	3525	3158	2870	3986	215	631	587	•	1196	3387	2188	3065	1267	171	819	1239	1166	937	262	2897	3602	4062	567	2670	452	1214	149	838	2830	1431	628	698	188	262	2800	1871	1154	3802	3843	4454	1381	2315	217	4097
HAMILTON	2256	1474	2176	1143	673	1462	2556	2189	1901	3017	895	1691	968	1196	•	2418	1219	2096	84	1013	377	43	250	290	1322	1928	2633	3093	545	1701	658	431	961	1898	1861	462	951	474	1097	1322	1831	902	42	2833	2874	3485	198	1346	1026	3128
JASPER	178	944	258	3304	2864	3653	467	229	882	995	3086	3882	3159	3387	2418	•	1199	394	2489	3204	2568	2461	2221	2450	3513	603	215	675	2736	717	2849	2122	3152	4089	557	1956	3142	2665	3288	3513	875	1516	2376	544	585	1396	2635	1072	3217	1106
KENORA	1037	255	957	2105	1665	2454	1337	970	682	1798	1887	2683	1960	2188	1219	1199	•	877	1290	2005	1369	1262	1022	1251	2314	709	1414	1874	1537	482	1650	923	1953	2890	642	757	1943	1466	2089	2314	612	317	1177	1614	1655	2266	1404	127	2018	1909
LETHBRIDGE	216	622	136	3014	2542	3336	689	322	862	1150	2764	3560	2837	3065	2096	394	877	•	2167	2882	2246	2139	1899	2128	3191	623	609	1069	2414	395	2527	1800	2830	2767	412	1626	2820	2343	2966	3191	768	1194	2054	710	751	1618	2297	750	2902	1261
LONDON	2327	1545	2247	1184	744	1534	2627	2260	1972	3083	966	1762	1039	1267	84	2489	1290	2167	•	1084	448	126	321	361	1393	2009	2704	3164	616	1772	729	502	1032	1969	1932	533	1022	545	1166	1393	1902	973	113	2904	2945	3548	126	1417	1097	3199
MONCTON	3047	2292	2955	100	452	449	3342	2975	2687	3803	123	678	416	171	1013	3204	2005	2882	1084	•	636	1056	983	754	309	2714	3419	3879	487	2487	360	1036	92	885	2647	1248	462	606	84	309	2649	1688	971	3619	3660	4271	1203	2132	157	3914
MONTREAL	2406	1624	2326	736	296	1085	2706	2339	2051	3167	518	1314	591	819	377	2568	1369	2246	448	636	•	420	347	118	945	2078	2783	3243	168	1851	281	400	584	1521	2011	612	574	97	720	945	1981	1052	335	2983	3024	3635	562	1496	649	3278
NIAGARA FALLS	2299	1517	2219	1147	716	1500	2599	2232	1944	3055	938	1734	1011	1239	43	2461	1262	2139	126	1056	420	•	293	333	1365	1971	2676	3136	588	1744	701	474	1004	1941	1904	505	983	517	1140	1365	1874	945	85	2876	2917	3528	241	1389	1069	3171
NORTH BAY	2059	1277	1979	1083	643	1432	2359	1992	1704	2820	865	1661	938	1166	250	2221	1022	1809	321	983	347	293	•	229	1292	1731	2436	2896	515	1504	628	181	931	1868	1664	265	921	444	1067	1292	1634	705	208	2636	2677	3280	435	1149	996	2931
OTTAWA	2288	1506	2208	854	414	1203	2588	2221	1933	3049	636	1432	709	937	290	2450	1251	2128	361	754	118	333	229	•	1063	1960	2665	3125	286	1733	399	343	702	1639	1893	494	692	215	838	1063	1863	934	248	2865	2906	3517	475	1378	767	3160
PORT AUX BASQUES	3356	2574	3264	228	761	140	3651	3284	2996	4112	432	369	725	262	1322	3513	2314	3191	1393	309	945	1365	1292	1063	•	3023	3728	4188	796	2796	669	1345	401	576	2956	1557	771	915	267	0	2931	1997	1280	3928	3969	4580	1512	2441	426	4223
PRINCE ALBERT	567	454	487	2814	2374	3163	741	374	279	1202	2596	3392	2669	2897	1928	603	709	623	2009	2714	2078	1971	1731	1960	3023	•	818	1278	2246	227	2359	1632	2662	3599	102	1466	2652	2175	2798	3023	272	1026	1896	1144	1185	1670	2082	582	2727	1313
PRINCE GEORGE	393	1159	473	3519	3079	3868	252	444	1097	892	3301	4097	3374	3602	2633	215	1414	609	2704	3419	2783	2676	2436	2665	3728	818	•	460	2951	932	3064	2337	3367	4304	772	2163	3357	2880	3503	3728	1090	1731	2591	495	536	1181	2850	1287	3432	1003
PRINCE RUPERT	853	1619	933	3979	3539	4328	712	904	1557	1352	3761	4557	3834	4062	3093	675	1874	1069	3164	3879	3243	3136	2896	3125	4188	1278	460	•	3411	1392	3524	2797	3827	4764	1232	2623	3817	3340	3963	4188	1550	2191	3051	955	996	1641	3310	1747	3892	1463
QUEBEC	2574	1792	2494	587	128	936	2874	2507	2219	3335	364	1165	437	567	545	2736	1537	2414	616	487	168	588	515	286	796	2246	2951	3411	•	2019	127	568	418	1372	2179	780	406	133	571	796	2149	1220	503	3151	3192	3803	730	1664	495	3446
REGINA	555	227	475	2587	2147	2936	855	488	467	1316	2369	3165	2442	2670	1701	717	482	395	1772	2487	1851	1744	1504	1733	2796	227	932	1392	2019	•	2132	1405	2435	3372	160	1231	2425	1948	2571	2796	373	799	1659	1132	1173	1784	1902	355	2507	1427
RIVIÈRE-DU-LOUP	2687	1905	2607	460	92	809	2987	2620	2332	3448	237	1038	310	452	658	2849	1650	2527	729	360	281	701	628	399	669	2359	3064	3524	127	2132	•	681	303	1245	2292	893	231	246	444	669	2262	1333	616	3264	3305	3916	843	1777	368	3559
ROUYN	1960	1178	1880	1136	696	1485	2260	1893	1605	2721	918	1714	991	1219	431	2122	923	1800	502	1036	400	474	181	343	1345	1632	2337	2797	568	1405	681	•	984	1921	1565	446	974	497	1120	1345	1535	606	389	2537	2578	3189	616	1050	1049	2832
SAINT JOHN	2990	2208	2898	192	383	541	3290	2923	2635	3751	66	770	501	149	961	3152	1953	2830	1032	92	584	1004	931	702	401	2662	3367	3827	418	2435	303	984	•	977	2595	1196	547	537	176	401	2565	1636	919	3567	3608	4219	1146	2080	65	3862
ST. JOHN'S	3932	3152	3842	804	1357	436	4227	3860	3572	4692	1008	207	1301	838	1898	4089	2890	2767	1969	885	1521	1941	1868	1639	576	3599	4304	4764	1372	3372	1245	1921	977	•	3532	2133	1347	1491	843	576	3507	2573	1856	4504	4545	5156	2088	3017	1012	4799
SASKATOON	465	387	385	2747	2307	3096	695	328	381	1156	2529	3325	2602	2830	1861	557	642	412	1932	2647	2011	1904	1664	1893	2956	102	772	1232	2179	160	2292	1565	2595	3532	•	1391	2585	2108	2731	2956	346	959	1819	1042	1083	1624	2036	515	2660	1267
SAULT STE. MARIE	1794	1012	1714	1348	908	1697	2094	1727	1439	2555	1130	1926	1203	1431	462	1956	757	1626	533	1248	612	505	265	494	1557	1466	2163	2623	780	1231	893	446	1196	2133	1391	•	1186	709	1332	1557	1369	440	420	2363	2404	3015	647	884	1261	2666
SEPT-ILES	2980	2198	2900	531	385	911	3280	2913	2625	3741	481	1140	299	628	951	3142	1943	2820	1022	462	574	983	921	692	771	2652	3357	3817	406	2425	231	974	547	1347	2585	1186	•	539	515	771	2555	1626	909	3557	3598	4209	1136	2070	612	3852
SHERBROOKE	2503	1721	2423	706	261	1055	2803	2436	2148	3264	483	1284	556	698	474	2665	1466	2343	545	606	97	517	444	215	915	2175	2880	3340	133	1948	246	497	537	1491	2108	709	539	•	690	915	2078	1149	432	3080	3121	3732	659	1593	614	3375
SUMMERSIDE	3131	2349	3051	39	536	407	3426	3059	2771	3887	207	636	500	188	1097	3288	2089	2966	1166	84	720	1140	1067	838	267	2798	3503	3963	571	2571	444	1120	176	843	2731	1332	515	690	•	267	2706	1772	1053	3703	3744	4355	1287	2216	241	3998
SYDNEY	3356	2574	3264	228	761	140	3651	3284	2996	4112	432	369	725	262	1322	3513	2314	3191	1393	309	945	1365	1292	1063	0	3023	3728	4188	796	2796	669	1345	401	576	2956	1557	771	915	267	•	2931	1997	1280	3928	3969	4580	1512	2441	426	4223
THE PAS	920	357	840	2749	2277	3071	1013	646	94	1474	2499	3300	2572	2800	1831	875	612	768	1902	2649	1981	1874	1634	1863	2931	272	1090	1550	2149	373	2262	1535	2565	3507	346	1369	2555	2078	2706	2931	•	929	1789	1388	1429	1942	2008	485	2630	1585
THUNDER BAY	1354	572	1274	1788	1348	2137	1654	1287	999	2115	1570	2366	1643	1871	902	1516	317	1194	973	1688	1052	945	705	934	1997	1026	1731	2191	1220	799	1333	606	1636	2573	959	440	1626	1149	1772	1997	929	•	860	1931	1972	2583	1087	444	741	2226
TORONTO	2214	1432	2134	1071	631	1420	2514	2147	1859	2975	853	1649	926	1154	42	2376	1177	2054	113	971	335	85	208	248	1280	1896	2591	3051	503	1659	616	389	919	1856	1819	420	909	432	1053	1280	1789	860	•	2791	2832	3435	227	1304	984	3086
VANCOUVER	577	1359	657	3719	3279	4068	747	773	1423	1387	3501	4297	3574	3802	2833	544	1614	710	2904	3619	2983	2876	2636	2865	3928	1144	495	955	3151	1132	3264	2537	3567	4504	1042	2363	3557	3080	3703	3928	1388	1931	2791	•	41	1676	3034	1487	3632	1498
VICTORIA	618	1400	698	3760	3320	4109	788	814	1464	1428	3542	4338	3615	3843	2874	585	1655	751	2945	3660	3024	2917	2677	2906	3969	1185	536	996	3192	1173	3305	2578	3608	4545	1083	2404	3598	3121	3744	3969	1429	1972	2832	41	•	1717	3053	1528	3673	1539
WHITEHORSE	1562	2011	1482	4371	3931	4720	929	1296	1949	1569	4153	4949	4226	4454	3485	1396	2266	1618	3548	4271	3635	3528	3280	3517	4580	1670	1181	1641	3803	1784	3916	3189	4219	5156	1624	3015	4209	3732	4355	4580	1942	2583	3435	1676	1717	•	3660	2190	4284	1680
WINDSOR	2457	1677	2377	1303	858	1652	2731	2364	2086	3192	1080	1881	1153	1381	198	2635	1404	2297	126	1203	562	241	435	475	1512	2082	2850	3310	730	1902	843	616	1146	2088	2036	647	1136	659	1287	1512	2008	1087	227	3034	3053	3660	•	1547	1211	3303
WINNIPEG	910	128	830	2232	1792	2581	1210	843	555	1671	2014	2810	2087	2315	1346	1072	127	750	1417	2132	1496	1389	1149	1378	2441	582	1287	1747	1664	355	1777	1050	2080	3017	515	884	2070	1593	2216	2441	485	444	1304	1487	1528	2190	1547	•	2145	1782
YARMOUTH	3055	2273	2963	257	460	566	3343	2988	2700	3816	131	795	566	217	1026	3217	2018	2902	1097	157	649	1069	996	767	426	2727	3432	3892	495	2507	368	1049	65	1012	2660	1261	612	614	241	426	2630	741	984	3632	3673	4284	1211	2145	•	3927
YELLOWKNIFE	1205	1654	1125	4014	3574	4363	751	939	1592	443	3796	4592	3869	4097	3128	1106	1909	1261	3199	3914	3278	3171	2931	3160	4223	1313	1003	1463	3446	1427	3559	2832	3862	4799	1267	2666	3852	3375	3998	4223	1585	2226	3086	1498	1539	1680	3303	1782	3927	•

This Guide produced by the Geographical Services Directorate of the Surveys & Mapping Branch, Energy, Mines & Resources Canada.

KILOMETRE GUIDE

	BANFF	BRANDON	CALGARY	CHARLOTTETOWN	CHICOUTIMI	CORNERBROOK	DAWSON CREEK	EDMONTON	FLIN FLON	FORT SMITH	FREDERICTON	GANDER	GASPÉ	HALIFAX	HAMILTON	JASPER	KENORA	LETHBRIDGE	LONDON	MONCTON	MONTREAL	NIAGARA FALLS	NORTH BAY	OTTAWA	PORT AUX BASQUES	PRINCE ALBERT	PRINCE GEORGE	PRINCE RUPERT	QUEBEC	REGINA	RIVIÈRE-DU-LOUP	ROUYN	SAINT JOHN	ST. JOHN'S	SASKATOON	SAULT STE. MARIE	SEPT-ILES	SHERBROOKE	SUMMERSIDE	SYDNEY	THE PAS	THUNDER BAY	TORONTO	VANCOUVER	VICTORIA	WHITEHORSE	WINDSOR	WINNIPEG	YARMOUTH	YELLOWKNIFE
BANFF	•	1259	129	5065	4348	5607	1019	428	1362	1761	4706	5995	4823	5190	3631	286	1669	384	3745	4904	3872	3700	3314	3682	5401	912	632	1373	4142	893	4324	3154	4812	6328	748	2887	4796	4028	5039	5401	1481	2179	3563	929	995	2514	3954	1465	4917	1939
BRANDON	1259	•	1130	3850	3090	4368	1741	1151	668	2483	3447	4736	3565	3938	2372	1519	410	1001	2486	3689	2614	2441	2055	2424	4142	731	1865	2606	2884	365	3066	1896	3553	5073	623	1629	3537	2770	3780	4142	575	921	2305	2187	2253	3236	2699	206	3658	2662
CALGARY	129	1130	•	4917	4220	5478	890	299	1233	1627	4558	5847	4694	5042	3502	415	1540	219	3616	4756	3743	3571	3185	3553	5253	784	761	1502	4014	764	4196	3026	4664	6183	620	2758	4667	3899	4910	5253	1352	2050	3434	1057	1123	2385	3825	1336	4768	1811
CHARLOTTETOWN	5065	3850	4917	•	888	592	5539	4949	4485	6281	359	961	830	232	1839	5317	3388	4851	1905	161	1184	1846	1743	1374	367	4529	5663	6404	945	4163	740	1828	309	1294	4421	2169	855	1136	63	367	4424	2878	1724	5985	6051	7034	2097	3592	414	6460
CHICOUTIMI	4348	3090	4220	888	•	1450	4831	4241	3777	5573	529	1819	647	875	1083	4609	2680	4091	1197	727	476	1152	1035	666	1225	3821	4955	5695	206	3455	148	1120	616	2184	3713	1461	620	420	863	1225	3664	2169	1015	5277	5343	6326	1381	2884	740	5752
CORNERBROOK	5607	4368	5478	592	1450	•	6101	5510	5047	6843	921	369	1392	647	2353	5879	3949	5369	2469	723	1746	2414	2305	1936	225	5090	6225	6965	1506	4725	1302	2390	871	702	4983	2731	1466	1698	655	225	4942	3439	2285	6547	6613	7596	2659	4154	911	7022
DAWSON CREEK	1019	1741	890	5539	4831	6101	•	591	1642	1030	5189	6470	5306	5673	4114	752	2152	1109	4228	5378	4355	4183	3796	4165	5876	1193	406	1146	4625	1376	4807	3637	5295	6803	1118	3370	5279	4511	5514	5876	1630	2662	4046	1202	1268	1495	4395	1947	5380	1209
EDMONTON	428	1151	299	4949	4241	5510	591	•	1051	1333	4598	5879	4715	5082	3523	369	1561	518	3637	4788	3764	3592	3206	3574	5285	602	715	1455	4035	785	4216	3046	4704	6212	528	2779	4688	3920	4923	5285	1040	2071	3455	1244	1310	2086	3804	1357	4809	1511
FLIN FLON	1362	668	1233	4485	3777	5047	1642	1051	•	2383	4134	5415	4252	4619	3059	1419	1098	1387	3174	4324	3301	3129	2742	3111	4822	449	1765	2506	3571	752	3753	2583	4241	5749	613	2360	4225	3457	4459	4822	151	1608	2992	2290	2356	3137	3357	893	4345	2562
FORT SMITH	1761	2483	1627	6281	5573	6843	1030	1333	2383	•	5930	7210	6048	6415	4855	1601	2894	1851	4962	6120	5097	4917	4538	4907	6618	1934	1436	2176	5367	2118	5549	4379	6037	7551	1860	4112	6021	5253	6256	6618	2372	3404	4788	2232	2298	2525	5137	2689	6141	713
FREDERICTON	4706	3447	4558	359	529	921	5189	4598	4134	5930	•	1289	700	346	1440	4966	3037	4448	1555	198	834	1510	1392	1024	695	4178	5312	6053	586	3813	381	1477	106	1622	4070	1819	774	777	333	695	4022	2527	1373	5634	5700	6684	1738	3241	211	6109
GANDER	5995	4736	5847	961	1819	369	6470	5879	5415	7210	1289	•	1761	1015	2721	6247	4318	5729	2836	1091	2115	2791	2673	2305	594	5459	6593	7334	1875	5094	1670	2758	1239	333	5351	3100	1835	2066	1024	594	5311	3808	2654	6915	6981	7965	3027	4522	1279	7390
GASPÉ	4823	3565	4694	830	647	1392	5306	4715	4252	6048	700	1761	•	945	1558	5084	3154	4566	1672	669	951	1627	1510	1141	1167	4295	5430	6170	703	3930	499	1595	806	2094	4188	1936	481	895	805	1167	4139	2644	1490	5752	5818	6801	1856	3359	911	6227
HALIFAX	5190	3938	5042	232	875	647	5673	5082	4619	6415	346	1015	945	•	1925	5451	3521	4933	2039	275	1318	1994	1876	1508	422	4662	5797	6537	912	4297	727	1962	240	1349	4554	2303	1011	1123	303	422	4506	3011	1857	6119	6185	7168	2223	3726	349	6593
HAMILTON	3631	2372	3502	1839	1083	2353	4114	3523	3059	4855	1440	2721	1558	1925	•	3891	1962	3373	135	1630	607	69	402	467	2128	3103	4237	4978	877	2737	1059	694	1547	3055	2995	744	1530	763	1765	2128	2947	1452	68	4559	4625	5609	319	2166	1651	5034
JASPER	286	1519	415	5317	4609	5879	752	369	1419	1601	4966	6247	5084	5451	3891	•	1930	634	4006	5156	4133	3961	3574	3943	5654	970	346	1086	4403	1154	4585	3415	5073	6581	896	3148	5057	4289	5292	5654	1408	2440	3824	875	941	2247	4241	1725	5177	1780
KENORA	1669	410	1510	3388	2680	3949	2152	1561	1098	2894	3037	4318	3154	3521	1962	1930	•	1411	2076	3227	2203	2031	1645	2013	3724	1141	2276	3016	2474	776	2655	1485	3143	4651	1033	1218	3127	2359	3362	3724	985	510	1894	2597	2663	3647	2260	204	3248	3072
LETHBRIDGE	384	1001	219	4851	4091	5369	1109	518	1387	1851	4448	5729	4566	4933	3373	634	1411	•	3487	4638	3615	3442	3056	3425	5135	1003	980	1720	3885	636	4067	2897	4554	4453	663	2617	4538	3771	4773	5135	1236	1922	3306	1143	1209	2604	3697	1207	4670	2029
LONDON	3745	2486	3616	1905	1197	2469	4228	3637	3174	4962	1555	2836	1672	2039	135	4006	2076	3487	•	1745	721	203	517	581	2242	3233	4352	5092	991	2852	1173	808	1661	3169	3109	858	1645	877	1876	2242	3061	1566	182	4674	4740	5710	203	2280	1765	5148
MONCTON	4904	3689	4756	161	727	723	5378	4788	4324	6120	198	1091	669	275	1630	5156	3227	4638	1745	•	1024	1699	1582	1213	497	4368	5502	6243	784	4002	579	1667	148	1424	4260	2008	744	975	135	497	4263	2717	1563	5824	5890	6874	1936	3431	253	6299
MONTREAL	3872	2614	3743	1184	476	1746	4355	3764	3301	5097	834	2115	951	1318	607	4133	2203	3615	721	1024	•	676	558	190	1521	3344	4479	5219	270	2979	452	644	940	2448	3236	985	924	156	1159	1521	3188	1693	539	4801	4867	5850	904	2408	1044	5275
NIAGARA FALLS	3700	2441	3571	1846	1152	2414	4183	3592	3129	4917	1510	2791	1627	1994	69	3961	2031	3442	203	1699	676	•	472	536	2197	3172	4307	5047	946	2807	1128	763	1616	3124	3064	813	1582	832	1835	2197	3016	1521	137	4628	4694	5678	388	2235	1720	5103
NORTH BAY	3314	2055	3185	1743	1035	2305	3796	3206	2742	4538	1392	2673	1510	1876	402	3574	1645	3056	517	1582	558	472	•	369	2079	2786	3920	4661	829	2420	1011	291	1498	3006	2678	426	1482	715	1717	2079	2630	1135	335	4242	4308	5279	700	1849	1603	4717
OTTAWA	3682	2424	3553	1374	666	1936	4165	3574	3111	4907	1024	2305	1141	1508	467	3943	2013	3425	581	1213	190	536	369	•	1711	3154	4289	5029	460	2789	642	552	1130	2638	3046	795	1114	346	1349	1711	2998	1503	399	4611	4677	5660	764	2218	1234	5086
PORT AUX BASQUES	5401	4142	5253	367	1225	225	5876	5285	4822	6618	695	594	1167	422	2128	5654	3724	5135	2242	497	1521	2197	2079	1711	•	4865	6000	6740	1281	4500	1077	2165	645	927	4757	2506	1241	1473	430	0	4717	3214	2060	6322	6387	7371	2433	3928	686	6796
PRINCE ALBERT	912	731	784	4529	3821	5090	1193	602	449	1934	4178	5459	4295	4662	3103	970	1141	1003	3233	4368	3344	3172	2786	3154	4865	•	1316	2057	3615	365	3796	2626	4284	5792	164	2359	4268	3500	4503	4865	438	1651	3051	1841	1907	2688	3351	937	4389	2113
PRINCE GEORGE	632	1865	761	5663	4955	6225	406	715	1765	1436	5312	6593	5430	5797	4237	346	2276	980	4352	5502	4479	4307	3920	4289	6000	1316	•	740	4749	1500	4931	3761	5419	6927	1242	3481	5403	4635	5638	6000	1754	2786	4170	797	863	1901	4587	2071	5523	1614
PRINCE RUPERT	1373	2606	1502	6404	5695	6965	1146	1455	2506	2176	6053	7334	6170	6537	4978	1086	3016	1720	5092	6243	5219	5047	4661	5029	6740	2057	740	•	5489	2240	5671	4501	6159	7667	1983	4221	6143	5375	6378	6740	2494	3526	4910	1537	1603	2641	5327	2812	6264	2354
QUEBEC	4142	2884	4014	945	206	1506	4625	4035	3571	5367	586	1875	703	912	877	4403	2474	3885	991	784	270	946	829	460	1281	3615	4749	5489	•	3249	204	914	673	2208	3507	1255	653	214	919	1281	3458	1963	810	5071	5137	6120	1175	2678	797	5546
REGINA	893	365	764	4163	3455	4725	1376	785	752	2118	3813	5094	3930	4297	2737	1154	776	636	2852	4002	2979	2807	2420	2789	4500	365	1500	2240	3249	•	3431	2261	3919	5427	257	1981	3903	3135	4138	4500	600	1286	2670	1822	1888	2871	3061	571	4035	2297
RIVIÈRE-DU-LOUP	4324	3066	4196	740	148	1302	4807	4216	3753	5549	381	1670	499	727	1059	4585	2655	4067	1173	579	452	1128	1011	642	1077	3796	4931	5671	204	3431	•	1096	488	2004	3689	1437	372	396	715	1077	3640	2145	991	5253	5319	6302	1357	2860	592	5728
ROUYN	3154	1896	3026	1828	1120	2390	3637	3046	2583	4379	1477	2758	1595	1962	694	3415	1485	2897	808	1667	644	763	291	552	2165	2626	3761	4501	914	2261	1096	•	1584	3092	2519	718	1568	800	1802	2165	2470	975	626	4083	4149	5132	991	1690	1688	4558
SAINT JOHN	4812	3553	4684	309	616	871	5295	4704	4241	6037	106	1239	806	240	1547	5073	3143	4554	1661	148	940	1616	1498	1130	645	4284	5419	6159	673	3919	488	1584	•	1572	4176	1925	880	864	283	645	4128	2633	1479	5741	5807	6790	1844	3347	105	6215
ST. JOHN'S	6328	5073	6183	1294	2184	702	6803	6212	5749	7551	1622	333	2094	1349	3055	6581	4651	4453	3169	1424	2448	3124	3006	2638	927	5792	6927	7667	2208	5427	2004	3092	1572	•	5684	3433	2168	2400	1357	927	5644	4141	2987	7248	7314	8298	3360	4855	1629	7723
SASKATOON	748	623	620	4421	3713	4983	1118	528	613	1860	4070	5351	4188	4554	2995	896	1033	663	3109	4260	3236	3064	2678	3046	4757	164	1242	1983	3507	257	3689	2519	4176	5684	•	2239	4160	3392	4395	4757	557	1543	2927	1677	1743	2614	3277	829	4281	2039
SAULT STE. MARIE	2887	1629	2758	2169	1461	2731	3370	2779	2360	4112	1819	3100	1936	2303	744	3148	1218	2617	858	2008	985	813	426	795	2506	2359	3481	4221	1255	1981	1437	718	1925	3433	2239	•	1909	1141	2144	2506	2203	708	676	3803	3869	4852	1041	1423	2029	4291
SEPT-ILES	4796	3537	4667	855	620	1466	5279	4688	4225	6021	774	1835	481	1011	1530	5057	3127	4538	1645	744	924	1582	1482	1114	1241	4268	5403	6143	653	3903	372	1568	880	2168	4160	1909	•	867	829	1241	4112	2617	1463	5724	5790	6774	1828	3331	985	6199
SHERBROOKE	4028	2770	3899	1136	420	1698	4511	3920	3457	5253	777	2066	895	1123	763	4289	2359	3771	877	975	156	832	715	346	1473	3500	4635	5375	214	3135	396	800	864	2400	3392	1141	867	•	1110	1473	3344	1849	695	4957	5023	6006	1061	2564	988	5432
SUMMERSIDE	5039	3780	4910	63	863	655	5514	4923	4459	6256	333	1024	805	303	1765	5292	3362	4773	1876	135	1159	1835	1717	1349	430	4503	5638	6378	919	4138	715	1802	283	1357	4395	2144	829	1110	•	430	4355	2852	1695	5959	6025	7009	2071	3566	388	6418
SYDNEY	5401	4142	5253	367	1225	225	5876	5285	4822	6618	695	594	1167	422	2128	5654	3724	5135	2242	497	1521	2197	2079	1711	0	4865	6000	6740	1281	4500	1077	2165	645	927	4757	2506	1241	1473	430	•	4717	3214	2060	6322	6387	7371	2433	3928	686	6796
THE PAS	1481	575	1352	4424	3664	4942	1630	1040	151	2372	4022	5311	4139	4506	2947	1408	985	1236	3061	4263	3188	3016	2630	2998	4717	438	1754	2494	3458	600	3640	2470	4128	5644	557	2203	4112	3344	4355	4717	•	1495	2879	2234	2300	3125	3232	781	4233	2551
THUNDER BAY	2179	921	2050	2878	2169	3439	2662	2071	1608	3404	2527	3808	2644	3011	1452	2440	510	1922	1566	2717	1693	1521	1135	1503	3214	1651	2786	3526	1963	1286	2145	975	2633	4141	1543	708	2617	1849	2852	3214	1495	•	1384	3108	3174	4157	1749	715	1193	3582
TORONTO	3563	2305	3434	1724	1015	2285	4046	3455	2992	4788	1373	2654	1490	1857	68	3824	1894	3306	182	1563	539	137	335	399	2060	3051	4170	4910	810	2670	991	626	1479	2987	2927	676	1463	695	1695	2060	2879	1384	•	4492	4558	5528	365	2099	1584	4966
VANCOUVER	929	2187	1057	5985	5277	6547	1202	1244	2290	2232	5634	6915	5752	6119	4559	875	2597	1143	4674	5824	4801	4628	4242	4611	6322	1841	797	1537	5071	1822	5253	4083	5741	7248	1677	3803	5724	4957	5959	6322	2234	3108	4492	•	66	2697	4883	2393	5845	2411
VICTORIA	995	2253	1123	6051	5343	6613	1268	1310	2356	2298	5700	6981	5818	6185	4625	941	2663	1209	4740	5890	4867	4694	4308	4677	6387	1907	863	1603	5137	1888	5319	4149	5807	7314	1743	3869	5790	5023	6025	6387	2300	3174	4558	66	•	2763	4913	2459	5911	2477
WHITEHORSE	2514	3236	2385	7034	6326	7596	1495	2086	3137	2525	6684	7965	6801	7168	5609	2247	3647	2604	5710	6874	5850	5678	5279	5660	7371	2688	1901	2641	6120	2871	6302	5132	6790	8298	2614	4852	6774	6006	7009	7371	3125	4157	5528	2697	2763	•	5890	3524	6894	2704
WINDSOR	3954	2699	3825	2097	1381	2659	4395	3804	3357	5137	1738	3027	1856	2223	319	4241	2260	3697	203	1936	904	388	700	764	2433	3351	4587	5327	1175	3061	1357	991	1844	3360	3277	1041	1828	1061	2071	2433	3232	1749	365	4883	4913	5890	•	2490	1949	5316
WINNIPEG	1465	206	1336	3592	2884	4154	1947	1357	893	2689	3241	4522	3359	3726	2166	1725	204	1207	2280	3431	2408	2235	1849	2218	3928	937	2071	2812	2678	571	2860	1690	3347	4855	829	1423	3331	2564	3566	3928	781	715	2099	2393	2459	3524	2490	•	3452	2868
YARMOUTH	4917	3658	4768	414	740	911	5380	4809	4345	6141	211	1279	911	349	1651	5177	3248	4670	1765	253	1044	1720	1603	1234	686	4389	5523	6264	797	4035	592	1688	105	1629	4281	2029	985	988	388	686	4233	1193	1584	5845	5911	6894	1949	3452	•	6320
YELLOWKNIFE	1939	2662	1811	6460	5752	7022	1209	1511	2562	713	6109	7390	6227	6593	5034	1780	3072	2029	5148	6299	5275	5103	4717	5086	6796	2113	1614	2354	5546	2297	5728	4558	6215	7723	2039	4291	6199	5432	6418	6796	2551	3582	4966	2411	2477	2704	5316	2868	6320	•

This Guide produced by the Geographical Services Directorate of the Surveys & Mapping Branch, Energy, Mines & Resources Canada.

Notes:

Check your addenda at back of this book for up to date information.

Section **D**

CANADIAN LAW FIRMS AND LAWYERS

DIRECTORY OF LAW FIRMS IN CANADA

BARRISTERS AND SOLICITORS IN ALBERTA

AIRDRIE, Calgary
Hashizume, R.J., 125 Main St.
Wilson, M.J., #5, 400 Main St. n.

ALDER FLATS, Wetaskiwin
Jensen, P.A., Box 221

ATHABASCA, Edmonton
Davies & Chamberlain, Percy G. Davies, Q.C., L. C. Chamberlain
Smith, Gawlinski & Co. (also Edmonton)

BANFF, Calgary
MacKay, Karras, Rathbone & Gould, Box 899, J.A. Karras, D.G. Rathbone, D.G. Gould, K.L. Wood
Shuler, D.R., Box 1600

BARRHEAD, Edmonton
MacCallum & Ritter, Box 69, E. P. MacCallum, K. G. Ritter, S.M. Ritter
Skinner, J.G., Box 158

BASHAW, Wetaskiwin
Schmidt & Farnham (also Camrose)

BASSANO, Medicine Hat
Plumer, B.R., Box 188 (also Medicine Hat)

BEAUMONT, Wetaskiwin
Zalapski, Walker & Co. (also Leduc)

BLACKIE, Calgary
Heseltine, C. H. (also High River)

BLAIRMORE, Macleod
Costigan, T. J., Q.C., Box 395
King & Young, Box 450, S.G. King, D.G. Young
Paterson & Co. (also Lethbridge)

BONNYVILLE, Edmonton
Fowle, Fraser & Co., Box 1410, W.R. Fowle, A.W. Fraser
Meunier, M.D., Box 1170
Wood & Wiebe, 4917 51st St., J. Wiebe, B.G. Wood

BOW ISLAND, Lethbridge
Virtue & Co. (also Lethbridge)

BROOKS, Medicine Hat
Bell, D.H., Box 1900
Crerar, Lutes & Shantz, Box 670, D.C. Crerar, K.W. Lutes, O.B. Shantz, D.H. Bell (also Vauxhall)
Kay, Kay & Riggins, Bag 1227, G. W. Kay, A. S. Kay, R.G. Riggins
Plumer, B.R., Box 2049

CALGARY, Calgary
Adamson, W., 200, 905 7th Ave. s.w.
Adamson & Willoughby, #204, 5401 Temple Dr. n.e., V.A. Adamson, S.A. Willoughby
Alberstat & Co., 304, 409 8th Ave. s.w., L. Alberstat, M.M. Wolfe
Armitage, R.E., 1019 4th Ave. s.w.
Atkinson McMahon, #750, 606 4th St. s.w. (T2P 1T1), M. G. Atkinson, Q.C., T. F. McMahon, Q.C., R. D. Tingle, B. W. Harrison, W. T. Corbett, M. F. Casey, J. B. McCashin, R.D. Boettger, J.F. Costello, Adelle Fruman, N.G. Cameron, D.E. Greenfield, S.R. Miller, K.D. Macleod, J.K. Reid, R.R.E. DeFilippi, M. Ann McLean, G.S. Dunnigan; Consultant, Hon. J.V.H. Milvain, Q.C.(E.P. Lougheed, Q.C.)
Ballem, McDill & MacInnes, #3600, 700 2nd St. s.w. (T2P 2W2), J. B. Ballem, Q.C., M. V. McDill, W. B. MacInnes, S. Carscallen, P.S. Jull, O.A. Pyrcz, J.F. Newman, L.L. Fryers, J.A. Paterson, G.J. Forrest, W.R. Lonsdale, N.S. Rudovics
Barkwell, J.J., #1600, 840 7th Ave. s.w.
Barron McGown, #2900, 400 4th Ave. s.w. (T2P 0J4), W. C. Barron, Q.C., M.D. McGown, N.R. Hess, W.J. Johnson, R.W. Devries, Wendy E. Best, Marina S. Paperny
Barron, R. H., Q.C., #300, 9705 Horton Rd. s.w.
Beaumont Proctor, 606 7th Ave. s.w. (T2P 0Y7), H.M. Beaumont, Q.C., R.M. Proctor, S.A. Church, L.W. Scott, J.C. DePaoli, R.W. Thompson, Cheryl C. Gottselig, G.W. Faulkner, P.G. Saranchuk, D.M. Goldenberg, J.M.B. Clark, F. Zinkhofer, G.J. Alexander, A.G. Waller, R.T. Shrieves, S.K.J. Kirk. Counsel: R.M. Nesbitt, Q.C.
Bell, Felesky, Iverach, Flynn & Struck, #1605, 311 6th Ave. s.w., R.D. Bell, Q.C., B.A. Felesky, R.J. Iverach, G.W. Flynn, J.D.A. Struck, H.G. McKenzie, E.B. Switzer, M.J. Beninger, C.A. Calverley, M.L. Edelson. Assoc. Counsel: K.H. Lambert
Beninger, R.E., 503 6th St. s.w.
Benjamin & Hooker, #220, 1121 Centre St. n., R.R.A. Benjamin, C.J. Hooker, Diane Ablonczy
Bennett Jones, #3200, 400 4th Ave. s.w. (T2P 0X9), M.E. Jones, Q.C., H.F. Gain, Q.C., H.D. Wyman, Q.C., E.J. Chambers, D.O. Sabey, Q.C., W.G. Brown, J.C. Major, Q.C., W.B. O'Donoghue, Q.C., G.C. Johnson, C.D. O'Brien, W.L. Britton, J.C. Armstrong, J.F. Curran, L.A. Johnson, D.H. McDermid, R.J. Pitt, J.G. Martland, D.G. Anderson, M.A. Carten, A.A. Phillips, H.M. Kay, D.Y. Urban, R.B. Low, R.K. Laing, S.J. LoVecchio, S.C.R. Mah Toy, J.D.B. McDonald, R.B. Sirkis, W.S. Rice, W.R. Whitlock, B.R. Libin, D.A. Ast, B.K. O'Ferrall, A.W. Rubin, R.M. Wilkinson, C.M. Ryer, R.P. Desbarats, B.G. Nemetz, P.D. Backman, A.L. Friend, J.F. Cordeau, P.L. Goldman, D.T. Gallagher, R.T. Booth, T.D. Kerrigan, E.S. Moir, J.E. Killam, J. Richels, F.R. Dearlove, B.W. Aitken, M.F. Gazzara, P.D. Edwards, G.N. Stapon, T.J. Hopwood, P.M. Farion, K.S. MacFarlane, H.H. Decter, B.B. de Jonge, R.V. Milligan, M.A. Lambert, E.L. Miller, M.H. Lockwood, M. Wayne, B.R. Emes, N.E. Glaister, J. Roy, P.E. Carr, M. Lemay, L. Carson, B.A. Burns, J. Strekaf, A.J. Hudec, K.M. Horner, J.G. Smeltzer. Counsel: J.J. Saucier, Q.C.
Berezowski, Crosland & Co., 629 7th Ave. s.w., D.B. Berezowski, R.A. Rivard, W.R. Hicks
Bhadresa, M. N., 210, 355 Heritage Dr. s.e.
Bishop, A.A., #100, 635 6th Ave. s.w.
Bixby, Molnar, Managh, 631 7 Ave. s.w., C.D. Bixby, G.G. Molnar, A.R. Managh, S.E. Faulknor, J.A. Leroy
Black & Co., #2902, 425 1st St. s.w., R.G. Black, Q.C., B.R. Cheeseman, G.P. Vernon, L.T. Forbes, J.C. McCartney, D.S. Ewens, D.M. Paton, R.A. Shaw, E.P. Kerwin, G.B. Cowper-Smith, P.D. Quinn, B.T. McManus, R.E. Nowack
Blaine, Mrs. S.L., Box 1164
Bolton, E.R., #6, 101 25th Ave. s.w.
Bourassa, Conway & Soltysiak, #200, 1216 Centre St. n., R.W. Bourassa, J.W. Conway, H.M. Soltysiak
Bowes, Switzer & Kerr, 1-1019 17th Ave. s.w., L.E. Bowes, S. Switzer, W.C. Kerr
Bridges, D.M., 3527 18th St. s.w.
Brown & Curran, #316 Mayfair Pl., 6707 Elbow Dr. s.w., W.Z. Brown, R.J. Curran
Brown, M.W., 4303 17th Ave. s.e.
Brownlee, J.S., Q.C., 1019 4th Ave. s.w.
Brunnen, J.P., #305, 1220 Kensington Rd. n.w.
Burge, David R., #113, 3501 Charleswood Dr. n.w.
Burgess & Kennedy, #775, 404 6th Ave. s.w., H. McD. Burgess, W.H. Kennedy, A.N. Kolias, J.C. Darling
Burnet, Duckworth & Palmer, 32nd floor, 425 1st St. s.w. (Box 280, Stn. M, T2P 2H9), F.L. Burnet, Q.C., T.J. Duckworth, Q.C., J.S. Palmer, Q.C., D.R. Haigh, R. F. Newby, M.L.J. Morin, A.W. Macdonald, Jr., J. D. Rooke, P.M. Clark, M.J. Feldman, A. R. Twa, H. S. Campbell, J. R. Quigley, G. M. Schulhauser, J.R. Paget, K.E.G. Taves, C.D. Johnson, R.J. Thrasher, C.S.L. Hoffmann, E.N. Vink, R.L. Spackman, B.D. Kinney, P.J. McIntyre, Barbara E. Romaine, T.T. Mudry, S.H. Halperin, Patricia H. Forrest, A.T. Pettie, Rosemary E. Nation, T.M. Livermore, R.J. Macknight, Katherine E. Sibold, C.C.v. Vegesack, G.R. Pauling, B.R. Newby, D.R. DiPaolo, J.H. Cuthbertson, E.J. Evans, S. Donalda Macbeath, R.E. Quesnel, A.J. Hilling, C.W. Nixon, J.S. Schwarz, K.S. Stickland, Linda J. Hirst, B.G. Poznanski, R.A. Ferguson, John Wilmot, D.H. Parken, Virginia M. May
Burstall & Co., 540 5th Ave. s.w., V.F. Burstall, A.F. Coady, A.H. Trawick, Mrs. H.M. Bonnycastle, D.J. Barber, H.R. Ward, M.A. Hughes, B.G. Hilchey, R.N. Depoe
Butlin & Biggs, 307, 120 17 Ave. s.w., J.A. Butlin, R.D. Biggs, J.R. Ferguson
Cairns, R.A., #204, 1330 8th St. s.w.
Callanan, E.C., #209, 5403 Crowchild Trail n.w.
C.P.R. Law Dept., 205 9th Ave. s.e.
Carson, J.F., 2711 17th Ave. s.w.
Chenger & Heming, #1510, 1 St. s.e., B.L. Chenger, B.P. Heming, K.C. Johnston, H.W. White
Chumir, S.M., 210, 639 5th Ave. s.w.
City Solicitors, D.O. Kvemshagen, J. deWolfe, A.A. Abougoush, B.R. Inlow, M. A. Bell, M. Peters, C.R. Meyers, W.J.A. Lenhardt, L.J.P. Offrowich, P.L. Tolley, D.L. Windjack, G.W. Payne, D.N. Larson
Clark, B.N., #209, 2411 4th St. n.w.
Clark, Young & Assoc., #830, 808 4th Ave. s.w., W.D. Clark
Code Hunter, 640 7th Ave. s.w., T2P 3A6, W. E. Code, Q.C., A. D. Hunter, A.V.M. Beattie, G. L. Ford, J. S. Steel, J.P. Peacock, N. C. Wittmann, J. B. Katchen, C. S. Brooker, B. E. Emes, R. M. Eeson, Glenn Cameron, R.G. Stevens, A.J. Jordan, J.A. Malcolm, E.R. Holden, L.A. Wagar, M.N. Woolstencroft, I.H. Lamoureux, T.D. Hamill, R.L. Pruitt, N.K. Machida, Elizabeth T. Callaghan, R.W. Myers, Judy N. Boyes, Eva M. Stutz, Carol D. Pennycook, J.B. Laycraft, J.S. Peacock
Colton, D.J., #209, 2411 4 St. n.w.
Condin, J.R., #206, 495 36th St. n.e.
Conrad Blain Bloomenthal Carruthers, #1400, 505 3rd St. s.w., W.R. Blain, E.K. Conrad, A. Bloomenthal, E.R.R. Carruthers, R.A. Wilson, W.D. Hawley, A.G. Loucks, T.G. Lidster, D.E. Prasow, T.W. Robinson, Barbara Widdowson,

Carol Conrad, Q.C., W.M. Brown, F.A. Mason, J.A. Helm, Laura Safran, M.M. Schoenemann, C.J. Goldie, M.Y. Chow, J.S. Charnock, Judith Hanebury, Laurie Dunbar, R.J. Simmons, M.J. Perkins, G.J. Shields
Cook & Jordan, #509, 5920 Macleod Trail s.w., Lynn Cook, Karen Jordan
Cook, Snowdon & Laird, 17th floor, 444 5th Ave. s.w., (Box 2468, T2P 2M7), H.G. Cook, Q.C., T.W. Snowdon, Q.C., D.R. Laird, B.F. Thurgood, W.J. Armstrong, G.A. Thornton, F.G.V. Marshall, Barbara J. Snowdon
Cooper, W.E., 6535 Bowness Rd.
Couch, R.G., 609 25th Ave. n.e.
Crawford, C.E.H., 4011 26th Ave. n.e.
Creighton, L.H.A., 4935 40th Ave. n.w. (K.J. Rogers)
Crump, R.J., #200, 940 17th Ave. s.w.
Cumming & Cumming, #830, 610 8th Ave. s.w., S. Cumming, Q.C., J.S. Cumming
Darwent, C.R., #200, 905 7th Ave. s.w.
Davey, R.E., #460, 640 12 Ave. s.w.
Davis, T.O., 1109 17th Ave. s.w.
Densmore, H. R., 410, 603 7th Ave. s.w.
Diamond, L. M., 717 7th Ave. s.w.
Diamond, A.F., #301, 836 5th Ave. s.w.
Dick, T.S., 3527 18th St. s.w.
Docken, C.G., #410, 999 8th St. s.w.
Donahue, Lister & Russell, 223 17th Ave. s.e., J.W.G. Donahue, W.B. Lister, D.S. Russell
Downton, McDonald, Plotkins & Co., 5th fl., 640 8th Ave. s.w. (T2P 1G7), W. H. Downton, J.A.S. McDonald, Q.C., R.W. Jull, L.J. Plotkins, B.E. Higgs, P.L. Sveen, J.L. Straith, L.G. Lien, J.W. Morin, N.S. Ramsay, H.L. Goldford
Dudelzak & Landry, #325, 4400 Macleod Trail s.w., R. Dudelzak, J.A. Landry
Dukeshire, J.E., 570, 407 8th Ave. s.w.
Dworkin, Zinner & Heumann, #745, 401 9 Ave. s.w., D.L. Dworkin, G.I. Zinner, H.W.B. Heumann, H.M. Joffe
Dymond, G.A., #714, 603 7th Ave. s.w.(G.R. Auck)
Dziadyk & Co., 1609 Kensington Rd. n.w., J. Dziadyk, G.F. Quigley
Eamon, Vickers & Gillis, #530, 11012 Macleod Trail s.e., G.M. Eamon, H.R. Vickers, D.K. Reid, W.D. Gillis
Ebbels, J.C., 814 Prospect Ave. s.w.
Eden & Pirie, #300, 615 3rd Ave. s.w., R. W. Eden, J.D. Pirie, W.R. Pepler, M.J. Tadman
Edmison Spence, #450, 706 7th Ave. s.w., J.K. Edmison, C.D. Spence
Evans, Rowe & Bascom, #401, 604 1st St. s.w., C.D. Evans, Q.C., D.W. Rowe, J.D. Bascom, P.V. Groarke
Faber, Gurevitch, 2nd floor, 1501 1st St. s.w., L. Faber, B.L. Gurevitch, I.K. Gurevitch, S.A. Klinger, D.M. Bickman, E.B. Corenblum, N.C. Conrad, Julia A. Turnbull
Facey, A. W., 414, 630 8th Ave. s.w.
Fejtek, Beatrice, #570, 407 8th Ave. s.w.
Fenerty, Robertson, Fraser & Hatch, 39th floor, Bow Valley Square 2, 205 5th Ave. s.w., T2P 2V7, J. M. Robertson, Q.C., R. P. Fraser, Q.C., D.T. Hatch, B.E. Scott, B. H. Jackson, L. R. Duncan, E.D.D. Tavender, Q.C., S.B. Green, F. M. Saville, A.D. Castle, D.A. McDermott, E.J. Durand, T.G. Millar, J.W. Rose, G.F. Scott, C.K. Yates, M.F. Belich, R.A. Coad, P.G. Kingstone, R.C. Dixon, H.D. Lloyd, C.H. Fryers, A.L. McLarty, M.A. Hurst, D.R. Brown, K.R. Mullback, G.M. Deyell, W.H. Winters, J.N. Thom, K.H.P. Ham, R.J. Hall, L.A. Westersund, J.D. Merrett, D.R. Lewthwaite, L.J. Holmes, D.L. Droppo, Susan E.A. Trylinski, R.A. Neufeld, D.G. Samuelson, Brian Mainwaring
Fetherston, D.W., #200, 1216 16th Ave. n.w.
Fixler Zimmerman, 3012 17th Ave. s.e., G.N. Fixler, M.S. Zimmerman
Fleming, Kambeitz & Pottinger, #500, 600 6th Ave. s.w., F. J. Fleming, Q.C., R. Kambeitz, R.E. Pottinger, E.H. Schuster, W.M. Gray
Foster Wedekind, #444, 4935 40th Ave. n.w., R.S. Foster, M.A. Wedekind, W.J. Cummings
Fradsham, S.E., 5865 Dalcastle Dr. n.w.
Freitag & Wiechert, #217, 7015 Macleod Trail s.w., E. Freitag, B.W. Wiechart, M.A. McConaghy
Gee, R.W., 229 Chinook Professional Bldg.
German & Co., 224 9th Ave. s.w., N.V. German, Q.C., C. Maureen Campbell
Gerwing & Johnson, #800, 5920 Macleod Trail s.w., H.C. Gerwing, B.C. Johnson
Ghitter & Co., #400, 1010 8th Ave. s.w., R.D. Ghitter, Q.C., T.D. Hetherington, J. C. Soby, B. Rogers, P.B.H. Rondeau, D.F. Guenther, E.G. Kelly
Gill, W.B., Q.C., #1401, 1800 4th St. s.w.
Goett, G.V., #202, 4600 Crowchild Trail n.w.
Goldman, I., #1411, 1800 4th St. s.w.
Goodfellow MacKenzie, #300, 255 17th Ave. s.w., W.D. Goodfellow, J.V. MacKenzie, A.B. Cameron, J.B. Marshall, J.H. Welbourn, P. Pastewka
Goodman, Abboud, #900, 1520 4 St. s.w., Y. Goodman, M. Porat
Goss & Larder, #515, 500 4th Ave. s.w., R.F. Goss, D.A. Larder
Gregg & Co., #300, 611 10th Ave. s.w., H.T.R. Gregg, Q.C., D. G. McA. Anglin, R.A. Mackie, Maggie Collins
Grey, E. N., #305, 4723 1st St. s.w. (D.H. Raniseth)
Grier, Green & McIlhargey, #420, 444 5th Ave. s.w., D.D. Grier, J.D. Green, P.M. McIlhargey
Guild, H., #502, 5920 1A St. s.w.
Hagel & Harrison, #4, 2009 33rd Ave. s.w., B.F. Hagel, J.M. Harrison
Hallgren, A.N., 2122 Kensington Rd. n.w.
Hanson & Co., #410, 301 14th St. n.w., G.E. Hanson, E. Zimmer, P.K. Smith-Grayton
Harris & Co., 8820A Macleod Trail s.w., A.L. Harris
Harris, G.R., #302, 634 6th Ave. s.w.
Harris, O.W., 610 8th Ave. s.w.
Harrison, Tims, 613 11 Ave. s.w., M.E. Harrison, M.D. Tims, J.K. Lawson
Hassett, B.D., #209, 1235 17 Ave. s.w. (H.R. Eamon)
Helmer, K.E., #210, 534 17th Ave. s.w.
Henbury & Co., #380, 624 36th St. n.e., M.A. Henbury, Terry Sturgeon
Henders & Co., #262, 1632 14th Ave. n.w., G.R. Henders, R.B. Collins
High Wo & Verstraten, #219, 222 16th Ave. n.e., C.R. Hi Wo, M.J. Verstraten
Hirst, T.E., #3002, 425 1st St. s.w.
Hoffman & Dorchik, #100, 4816 Macleod Trail s.w., G.J. Hoffman, M.J. Dorchik
Holdsworth, R.F., #750, 999 8th St. s.w.
Homme Baker, #1500, 202 6th Ave. s.w., R.A. Homme, K.R. Baker, J.G. Shea, W.B. Woods, R.D. Shannon, M.A. Mason, L.B. McCarten, W.B. Woods, B.J. Hughson, A.Z. Brietman, I.C. Schofield, D.L. Nerland, D.J. Blackett, B.R. Crump
Howard, J.A.L., #206, 424 10th St. n.w.
Howard, Mackie, #300, 330 5th Ave. s.w. (T2P OL4), W.A. Howard, Q.C., J.A.N. Mackie, Q.C., T.J. Hopwood, Q.C., P. T. Kueber, D. H. Mitchell, W. W. Stanford, E. F. McRory, M. J. O'Brien Kelly, R.G. Powers, G.C. Hawco, H. D. Williamson, G.E. Anderson, F. R. Foran, A.D. Nielsen, J.P. Petch, R.A. Reaburn, P.T. McCarthy, D.F. Mackie, J.W. Surbey, S.P. Sibold, F.W.T. Somerville, D.A. Follett, D.J. Pettie, M.J. Hill, B.E. Roberts, J.E. Fletcher, M.A. Smith, J.L. Ircandia, H.Q. Wong, B.A. Yaworski, I. Ash, M.D. Sharpe, N.E. Hall, B.E. Cotton, J.E. Tyrrell. Counsel: E.M. Bredin, Q.C., M.H. Patterson, Q.C.
Hughes, J.C., #650, 999 8th St. s.w.
Hurov, H.J., 750, 404 6th Ave. s.w.
Hutchings & Fric, 920 36th St. n.e., L.F. Hutchings, W.H. Fric
James, Pieschel & Taylor, #330, 1201 5th St. s.w., J.D. James, W.R. Pieschel, A.D. Taylor
James, W.L., #800, 703 6th Ave. s.w.
Jamison, M.M., 3527 18th St. s.w.
Jellis, Kravinchuk & Bayrak, 615 36th St. n.e., T.L. Babie (also Edmonton)
Jermyn, D. E., 211, 1711 4th St. s.w.
Johnson, I.S., #116, 8220 Simons Valley Dr. n.e.
Jones, D.S., 1760, 717 7th Ave. s.w.
Jumaga, G.M., 2411 4 St. n.w.
Kahanoff, Fern, #1250, 321 6th Ave. s.w.
Karasick, Blitt & Lirenman, 1505 15th Ave. s.w., V.A. Karasick, M. Blitt, J.H. Welbourn, W. Lirenman
Kelly & Kelly, 2424, 715 5th Ave. s.w., M. J. Kelly, R. J. Kelly, P. C. Pyra, T. A. B. Jolliffe
Kenney & Co., #300, 1121 Centre St. n., D. T. Kenney, E. V. Anderson, K. Kaleva
Kerr & Kolinsky, 1034 8th Ave. s.w., R. D. Kerr, A. M. Kolinsky
King, J. A., 740, 610 8th Ave. s.w.
Korman, H.C., #520, 2424 4th St. s.w.
Lagasse, C. E., 505 8th Ave. s.w.
Landerkin Dunphy Calvert Minchin, #950, 602 12 Ave. s.w., H.F. Landerkin, Q.C., J.H. Dunphy, R.W. Calvert, J.F. Minchin, R.B. Waller, D.D. Ellert
Laven & Co., #300, 1010 8th Ave. s.w., D. L. Laven, Q.C., A. J. Harben, W.T. Aaron, P. Meyers. Counsel: B.N. Laven, Q.C.
Lee, R.T., #404, 540 12 Ave. s.w.
Leech & Shyba, #210, 1610 37th St. s.w., K.W. Leech, G.A. Shyba
Lennie, De Bow & Martin, #228, 4935 40th Ave. n.w., W.J. Hope-Rose, (also Edmonton)
Limpert de Morin, B.L., 348 14th St. n.w.
Lindsay, N.N., #800, 805 8th Ave. s.w.
Litwiniuk & Co., #205, 4020 17th Ave. s.e., L.A. Litwiniuk, R.C. Davidson, G.S. Lynas
Livergant, M. B., 10928 Willowfern Dr. s.e.
Lockwood & Shields, 303, 409 8th Ave. s.w., C.W. Lockwood, B. A. Shields
Lomow & Assoc., #303, 1609 14th St. s.w., J.G. Lomow
Loster, Teed & McLeod, #508, 8500 Macleod Trail s.e., G.J. Loster, D.E. Teed, D.J. McLeod
Low & Glenn, #119, 2640 52 St. n.e., S.A. Low, T.F. Glenn
Low, J.P., #203, 7403 Macleod Trail s.w.
Low, Leonard & Dalton, #17, 6624 Centre St. s., R.A. Low, Sharon J. Dalton, M.T. Leonard, M.W. Gruman
Lutz, Westerberg, O'Leary, Fenerty, Beland & MacDonald, #200, 639 5th Ave. s.w., A. M. Lutz, J. I. Westerberg, W. E. O'Leary, R.L. Fenerty, J.C. Belland, J.A. MacDonald, D.R. Skeith, S.R. MacMillan, D.M. Sefcik
Lyle, Smith & Davison, #1150, 707 7 Ave.

s.w., R. L. Lyle, B.A.R. Smith, J.E. Davison, R.D. McManus, G.B. Davison, G.M. Sherritt, A. Buckingham

Macdonald, A.W., Sr., #202, 634 6th Ave. s.w. (P.J. Lamont)

MacInnes, C.M., #3600, 700 2nd St. s.w.

MacKay, M.D., #225, 495 36th St. n.e.

MacKimmie Matthews, #700, 401 9th Ave. s.w., Box 2010 (T2P 2M2), F. R. Matthews, Q.C., S. H. Wood, Q.C., J. R. Smith, Q.C., E. A. Hutchinson, Q.C., J.A. Millard, M. A. Putnam, Q.C., H.B. Johnson, R.M. Cairns, H.A. McQueen, I.M. Robison, T.M. Ryder, T.H. Ferguson, R.T. Malcolm, R.L. McKinnon, J.A. Stewart, G.S. Griffiths, D.S. MacKimmie, R.E. Davis, R.G. Cormie, J.R. Matthews, J.D. McCartney, J.H. Courtright, E.O. McAvity, A.A. Fradsham, R.J. Engbloom, R.G. Knox, B.L. Rawlins, C.G. Mack, J.R. Houghton, J.H. Selby, H.L. Winger, J.R. Norman, R.G. Polson, R.J. Guthrie, M.J. Flatters, G.G. Turnbull, L.C. Fontaine, R.E. Pelzer, G.J. McKibben, D.L. Friesen, S.W. James, R.P. Griese. Counsel: R.A. MacKimmie, Q.C.

Macleod Dixon, 1500 Home Oil Tower, 324 8th Ave. s.w. (T2P 2Z2), K. S. Dixon, Q.C., R. J. Burns, Q.C., R. B. Love, Q.C., R.A.F. Montgomery, Q.C., J.C.F. Casey, Q.C., C. A. Rae, W. H. Bonney, D. G. Hart, D. P. Hays, J. J. Marshall, R. G. Rowley, J. S. Burns, G. F. Dixon, K. B. Potter, A. D. Macleod, W. Mirosh, D. A. Graham, B. D. Sherman, D. H. Watkins, J. H. Coleman, E.J. Brown, S.L.H. McDonald, D.A. McGillivray, A.G. Vickery, G.F. Graham, E.A. Leew, D.W. Ross, V.A. MacDonald, S.G. Raby, D.L. Baxter, C.M. Jones, D.G. Davies, P.K. Matkin, W.F. Quigley, G.F. Faass, M.J. McWilliams, J.L. Treleaven, W.Y. Shaw, H.A. Jacques, J.G. Hanley, J.I. Parker, D.E. Nesbitt, W.C. Hunter, J.J. Park, G.J. Cochrane, D.N. Duke, D. Guichon, Jr., S.A. Lloyd, L.M. Kwinter, J.G. McKee

MacPhail & Cowper-Smith, #350, 1121 Centre St. n., D.E. MacPhail, M.A. Cowper-Smith

MacPherson & Assoc., #400, 602 11th Ave. s.w., J.A. MacPherson, Q.C., T.C. Semenuk, A. Hepner, Donna J. Martinson, Patricia A. Davis

MacPherson, Kelly, O'Neil & McNiven, #1600, 840 7th Ave. s.w., J. L. MacPherson, Q.C., J.G. McNiven, D. J. Kelly, R. H. O'Neil, W. L. Severson, L. B. Robinson, J.G. Greenan, W.M. LeClair, K.J. Martens, B.L. Hodgan, Susan Robinson, Linda Threet

Magnus, Blewett & Co., 501, 736 8th Ave. s.w., J. G. Magnus, D.G. Blewett, J.H. Uhma, J.L. Harms

Mahony & Dawson, 914 8th Ave. s.w., J.J. Mahony, F. S. Dawson

Major & Caron, #420, 1210 8th St. s.w., W.J. Major, Q.C., P. J. Caron, J.P. Stopa, M.J. Major, M.J. McDonald

Manolescu, Zaozirny & Arkell, #207, 495 36th St. n.w., J.N. Manolescu, M. M. Manolescu, J.B. Zaozirny, M.J. Arkell, W.J. Kunicki, G. Vinci, J.W. Kovitz

Mason & Co., #1110, 205 5th Ave. s.w., D. B. Mason, Q.C., D. I. MacLeod, Q.C., M.S. McManus, J.D. Miles, M.C. Anderson, J.B. Rooney, J.T. McCarthy, R.B. Mainwood, D.J. McDonald, J.D. Thomson, J.R. MacInnes, D.D. Peterson, D.A. Hickey, J.D. McFarlane, R.D. Maxwell, J.E. Prentice, D.R. Armstrong, Barbara Follett

McCaffery & Co., 1700, 633 6th Ave. s.w., P. J. McCaffery, Q.C., M. T. McCaffery, D.V. McCaffery, T.T. McCaffery, B.B. Norton, R.V.T. Boyden, Heather Lamoureux, W.C. Ranson, D.P.E. Fournier, B.R. Lane, G.K. Savage, A.R. Robertson

McClelland & Armstrong, #14, 3616 52nd Ave. n.w., K.W. McClelland, D.S. Armstrong

McCombe Cameron, 901, 441 5th Ave. s.w., B.G. McCombe, N.G. Cameron, C. Millar, B.E. Slater

McConnell, K.F., #301, 4015 Macleod Trail s.e.

McCormick, E. J., Q.C., 745, 610 8th Ave. s.w.

McDonald, D.P., Q.C., #420, 444 5th Ave. s.w.

McDonald & Hayden, 510, 444 5th Ave. s.w., J.G. McDonald, J.C. Crawford, P.R. Hayden (also Toronto)

McKay, N.R., #203, 636 11th Ave. s.w. (E.A. Gabille)

McLaws & Co., 6th fl., 407 8th Ave. s.w., T2P 1E6, D.P. McLaws, Q.C., J. E. Prothroe, Q.C., G. L. Crawford, Q.C., R. V. Deyell, Q.C., D.W. Hilland, J.P. Floyd, Q.C., J. S. Moore, Q.C., J. Stein, G.R.D. Goulet, A.G. Park, L.M. Sali, J.B.D. Malone, A. S. Hollingworth, S.W. Ingram, P.A. Stone, C.W. Walker, I.L. MacLachlan, M.C. Crowe, D.C. Edie, W.H. Smith, Peggy A. McDonald, G.M. Adams, W.G. Hopkins, F.W. Dent, G.E. Parker, Kathleen M.T. Luna, J.G. Friesen, R.J. Martin, E.A. Dolden, D.B. Reesor, L.D. Revitt, Marilyn E. Martin, R.D. Matheson, E.S. Shipman. Counsel: J.L. Lebel, Q.C.; Patent Agent: G.H. Dunsmuir

McLeod Conner, #350, 11012 Macleod Trail s.w., R.J. McLeod, R.D. Conner

McLeod & Ferner, 600 6th Ave. s.w., D. F. McLeod, Q.C., P. Ferner, J.M. Bruni

McMurchie & Webber, #200, 306 10th St. n.w., L.J. McMurchie, B.O. Webber

Melville, R.J., #105, 2885 80th Ave. s.e.

Meronek & Blumell, #230, 1620 29th St. n.w., W.M. Meronek, C.R. Blumell, R.C. Blumell, T.P. Friesen

Metz & Smith, 348 14th St. n.w., M.J. Metz, J.A. Smith

Meurin & Isbister, #604, 1040 7th Ave. s.w., G.R. Meurin, R.B. Isbister, R.B. Simpson

Miles, R.A., 210, 9919 Fairmount Dr. s.e.

Millar, B.A., #104, 2885 80th Ave. s.e.

Millard, Johnson & Maxwell, 309 8th Ave. s.w., C. Johnson, R. C. Maxwell, N.T. De Meza

Milne, Davis & Nicholson, 600, 700 2nd St. s.w., G. Milne, A. M. Davis, E. M. Nicholson, J.D. Phillips

Milne, Papp, #204, 10601 Southport Rd. s.w., W.D. Milne, R.G. Papp

Milner & Steer, 1125 IBM Bldg., 606 4th St. s.w., A.S. Williamson, Q.C., J.M. Thomson, Q.C., R.W. Poffenroth, G.N. McDermid, J.A. Bancroft, D.G. Loader, H.J. Shore, D.J. De Grandis (also Edmonton)

Mintoft, J.F., #101, 927 14th Ave. s.w.

Moore Martin, #665, 800 6th Ave. s.w., J.F. Moore, Q.C., D.C. Martin, G.C. Collver, G.J. Daniel, A.M. Pilling, P.T. Stevenson; W.D. Dickie, Q.C.

Moreau & Ogle, #401, 515 11th Ave. s.w., J.M. Moreau, J.J. Ogle, B.E. Mahoney

Munholland, J.B., #210, 4014 Macleod Trail s.e.

Murphy, K.P., #103, 3501 Charleswood Dr. n.w.

Muskath, R.L., #1605, 1800 4th Ave. s.w.

Naimish, V. M., #1200, 640 8th Ave. s.w. (D.J. Campbell)

Nelson & Steele, 258, 1632 14th Ave. n.w., B.H. Nelson, Q.C., D.V. Steele

Nesbitt, A.J., 365 Wildwood Dr. s.w.

Nielsen, D.M., #307, 1305 11th Ave. s.w.

O'Brien, Devlin, Markey, #480, 602 12th Ave. s.w., N.C. O'Brien, B.E. Devlin, J.J. Markey, D.W. MacLeod, M.L.L. Ho

O'Connor, Iredale & Maitland, 600 6th Ave. s.w., J. B. O'Connor, Q.C., N.R. Iredale, Q.C., H. Vincent O'Connor, C.V. Burns, R.V. O'Connor, J.N. Ireland, A.G. Maitland, V.H. Vogel, W.G. Webb, Linda Broskie

Oughton & Co., #920, 401 9th Ave. s.w., C.D. Oughton, K.S. King

Owens, Sattin & Co., 5th fl., 1011 1st St. s.w., E.L. Owens, A.J. Sattin, W.A.T. Coultry

Parlee, Irving, Henning, Mustard & Rodney, 21st fl., 300 5th Ave. s.w., J.A. Cox, B.P. O'Leary, W.R. Shouldice, C.G. Watkins, A.B. Sulatycky, C.S. Phillips, R.G. Matthews, R.D. Freeman, R.L. Dawson, D.J. Adams (also Edmonton)

Pearce & Smyth, 1850 14th St. s.w., A.F. Pearce, R.C.P. Smyth, H.J. Wiebe

Perraton, Masuch, Macdonald, #100, 805 9th St. s.w., J.R. Perraton, G.E. Masuch, M.W.L. Macdonald, I.R. MacDonald, R.J.N. Gilborn, J.A. Drummond, A.J. Rynd

Petrasuk & Co., 404, 6th Ave. s.w., W.A. Troughton, M.R. Bradshaw

Pickton & Co., #990, 1520 4 St. s.w., C.B. Pickton, T.W. Bardsley, A.N. Inkpen

Pipella & Co., 285, 444 7th Ave. s.w., E.S. Pipella, M.B. Warren

Porat & Schlittner, #900, 1520 4th St. s.w., M. Porat, D. Schlittner

Prodanchuk & Dickson, #250, 999 8th St. s.w., D. J. Prodanchuk, R. G. Dickson, J.M. Switzer

Pulak Price & Fulton, Plaza 2-A, 840 7th Ave. s.w., G. Pulak, G.E. Price, J.G. Fulton

Purdy, R.L., 1603 10 Ave. s.w.

Ramsay & Ramsay, #407, 3630 Morley Trail n.w., J.T. Ramsay, M.J. Ramsay

Redling, G.F., 734, 550 6th Ave. s.w.

Reiman, G.B.E., 306, 4600 Crowchild Trail n.w.

Rollins, W.W., 624 9th Ave. s.w.

Ross, Chernichen, Durham, Peterson & Clark, 2nd fl., 755 Lake Bonavista Dr. s.e., L.L. Ross, D.J. Chernichen, J.T. Durham, R.M. Peterson, R.T. Clark, S.T. MacIsaac, Helen Timmons

Ross & Murphy, #204, 1632 14th Ave. n.w., N.A. Ross, K.F. Murphy

Ryan, J.E., 308 23rd Ave. s.w.

St. Pierre, J.P., #207, 239 Midpark Way s.e.

Salmon & Co., #333, 509 8th Ave. s.w., J.D. Salmon, D.J. Salmon, G.N. Reddekopp

Scott & Smith, #550, 1414 8th St. s.w., F.L. Scott, C.M. Smith, Karen D. Jacobson

Scott, J. F., O.B.E., Q.C., 2320 8th St. s.w.

Scott, Thomas & Co., #606, 7015 Macleod Trail s.w., T. H. Scott, C. G. Thomas, R.B. Carlyle

Scurfield, R.D., 226 11A St. n.w.

Selinger & Tottrup, #216, 3715 51st St. s.w., J.P. Selinger, K.E. Tottrup

Semmens Ney, 1121 Centre St. n., E.L. Semmens, S.G. Ney

Shachnowich, W.J., 211, 212 7th Ave. s.w.

Shepherdson, W.J.E., #500, 706 7th Ave. s.w.

Shymka & Co., 401, 239 8th Ave. s.w., E.R. Shymka, A.M. Mears, T.S. Van Aalst

Silver, B., #304, 1550 8 St. s.w.

Sinclair, McGeough, Lilburn, 1011 6th

Ave. s.w., D. H. Sinclair, Q.C., G. McGeough, R. E. Lilburn, M.B. Woods, H. Lowenstein, M.J. McRae, R.A. Kaplan
Skene, Gorman, Stewart & Stewart, 213, 1610 37th St. s.w., J. C. Gorman, Q.C., G.C. Stewart, P.S. Stewart, L.I.F. Gorman
Smith, Carole I., 210, 534 17th Ave. s.w.
Smith, J.T., #202, 636 11th Ave. s.w.
Spackman, Matt, Halliday & Co., 1501 1st St. s.w., R.E. Spackman, L.A. Matt, B.A. McCullough, B.J. Halliday, C.R. Stewart
Spier, J. A., #1005, 505 5 St. s.w.
Starchuk, Basaraba, 5915 1A St. s.w., K.G. Starchuk, B.M.W. Basaraba
Starr, M.N., #204, 1330 8th St. s.w.
Stemp, W.R., #100, 608 7th St. s.w.
Stengl, Everard & Ratcliffe, #212, 1935 32 Ave. n.e., R.R. Stengl, R.J. Everard, R.B. Ratcliffe
Stephen & Co., #211, 4616 Valiant Dr. n.w., T.R.B. Stephen, D.R.C. Ebbert, D.J. Jenkins, C.L. Kenny, B.F. Pomerance
Stilwell & St. Louis, #617, 205 9 Ave. s.e., W. V. Stilwell, K. A. St. Louis
Stinchcombe & Thoms, 5th fl., 1011 1st St. s.w., W.B. Stinchcombe, G.S. Thoms
Stobo, G.H., #304B, 7301 4A St. s.w.
Strilchuk, J.N.M., 451, 131 9th Ave. s.w.
Sugimoto, Bilyk & Groves, #310, 3016 5 Ave. n.e., T.S. Sugimoto, G.E. Bilyk, K.F. Groves, C.B. Fowler
Sullivan, W.P., #750, 2424 4th St. s.w.
Sutherland & Geselbracht, 4303 17th Ave. s.e., J.A. Sutherland, W.W. Geselbracht
Sutherland, P., 5032 16 Ave. n.w.
Szmolyan, L.G., #601, 2303 4th St. s.w.
Tagg & Card, #110, 3016 5th Ave. n.e., M.J. Tagg, J.N. Card
Taylor & Schultz, #224, 100 Anderson Rd. s.e., V.M. Taylor, A.C. Schultz
Tharp & Wildeman, #800, 933 17 Ave. s.w., R. S. Tharp, L. W. Wildeman, L.S. Matthews
Thompson, Ball, Anderson & Hough, #201, 358 58th Ave. s.w., G.V. Thompson, G.S. Ball, D.H. Anderson, D.D. Hough
Tighe, K.D., #100, 2411 4th St. n.w.
Tompkins, D.J., 825 8th Ave. s.w.
Townsend & Christensen, 310, 534 17th Ave. s.w., A. M. Townsend, C. O. Christensen
Trobst, Patterson, 238 21st Ave. s.w., K.H.H. Trobst, J. S. Patterson
Uniacke & Yanko, 4710 17th Ave. s.e., E.J. Uniacke, D.G. Yanko, I.M. Schachter
Vallance & Co., 1400, 606 4th St. s.w., P.S. Vallance, D.P. Vallance, Barbara Vallance
Vavra, S., #714, 603 7 Ave. s.w.
Viccars, T.K., #242, 10816 Macleod Trail s.e.
Visser, J.C., 2548 Toronto Cres. s.w.
Vogel, Butler & Kazakoff, #810, 11012 Macleod Trail s.e., V.H. Vogel, G.F. Butler, P.A. Kazakoff
Wakerich, Heald, Allen & Stirling, #504, 4600 Crowchild Trail n.w., W.M. Wakerich, L.S. Heald, M.D. Allen, R.M. Stirling, S.A. Barker
Walsh, W.L., #104, 2885 80th Ave. s.e.
Walsh Young, 15th floor, Guinness House, 727 7th Ave. s.w., T2P OZ8, T. J. Walsh, Q.C., G. W. Pittman, R.A.M. Young, G. J. Clark, R.J. Wilkins, R.C. Smith, Q.C., G.J. Burrell, D.R. Bouey, M.J. Webb, H.C. MacDonald, J.N. Shaw, D.R. Worden, G.M. Meagher, Elaine L. Lenz, D.I.D. McLean, M.R. Théroux, R.G. Hunt, E.P. Newcombe, R.G. Mitchell, J.R. Kitsul, L.W. Sloan, F.R. Fenwick, W.T. Spence, Debbie M. Underdahl
Warren, Raymaker & Stewart, 441 5th Ave. s.w., W. J. Warren, D. J. Raymaker, F.A. Stewart, Q.C., P.L. Ridley, J.D. Poole, D.G. Tettensor, C.J. Kakish, J.E. Polley, J.B. Amantea, R.A. Benson. Counsel: E.E. McNally
Watkins, S.R., 3631 12th St. s.w.
Watson & McIntosh, 1717 Macleod Trail s.e., K. G. Watson, H. N. McIntosh, R.S. Johnson, M.A. Gottlieb
Watts, Gottlieb, #8, 5602 4th St. n.w., D.M. Gottlieb, V.K. Watts
Webb, J.S., #3, 1019 17th Ave. s.w.
Webb, Lerner, Kutz & Dyck, #271, 1632 14th Ave. n.w., D. A. Lerner, R. F. Kutz, P. Dyck, J.C. Cohen, C.N.D. Hotzel
Webber, D.J., 2712 32nd Ave. s.w.
Wilson, Staroszik & Daniels, #200, 1414 8th St. s.w., J.H. Wilson, K.E. Staroszik, G.A. Daniels
Witwicki, B.T., 227 12th Ave. s.e.
Wolfman & Co., 108 8th Ave. s.w., E. L. Wolfman, S.M. Hirji, R.S. Johnson, D.P. Maguire
Wolsey & Wilde, #206, 8404 Elbow Dr. s.w., J.B. Wolsey, J.B. Wilde
Wong-Ken, D.N., #63, 6103 Madigan Dr. s.e.
Woolliams, Korman, Moore & Wittman, 10th fl., 640 8th Ave. s.w., E.M. Woolliams, Q.C., D.G. Korman, Q.C., M.L. Moore, D. Wittman, B.O. Phillips, Dorothy Sunde
Wuttunee, W.I.C., #612, 206 7th Ave. s.w.
Yuzda, Boulton & Ritter, #920, 401 9th Ave. s.w., L.W. Yuzda, J. D'A. Boulton, B.P. Ritter, A.S.W. Stiles
Zenith, Klym & Hookenson, #311, 6707 Elbow Dr., L.M. Zenith, W.S. Klym, C.J. Hookenson, T.J. Boyle

CAMROSE, Wetaskiwin
Andreasson, Ziebart & Olson, 4870 51st St., H.P.D. Andreasson, R. Ziebart, V. Olson, W. Andreasson
Batke & Co., 4814 50 Ave., T.L. Batke, J. Schaffter
Gaede, Fielding & Rostad, #201, 5015 50 Ave., H. D. Gaede, A.D. Fielding, K.L. Rostad, H.A. Syed
Knaut, Johnson & Sawle, Box 1630, G. R. Knaut, Q.C., L.J. Johnson, D.A. Sawle
Schmidt & Farnham, 4886 50th St., K. Schmidt, S. Farnham

CANMORE, Calgary
Elliott, R., 822 8th St.
Evans & Rencz, 713 8th St., B.J. Evans, D.B. Rencz

CARBON, Drumheller
Schumacher, Madden & Co. (also Drumheller)

CARDSTON, Lethbridge
Fletcher, Norton & Co. (also Lethbridge)
Matkin, T.M., Box 1209
Stringam & Co. (also Lethbridge)

CLARESHOLM, Macleod
Burton, F.D., 133 49th Ave. w.
Welbourn, Maloney & Tysowski, Box 1300, D.J. Welbourn, F.L. Maloney, G. Tysowski

CLYDE, Edmonton
Davies, P. G., Q.C. (also Athabasca)

COALDALE, Lethbridge
Boras, Hogan & Co., 1713 20th Ave. (also Lethbridge)
Fast, L.D., Box 1360

COCHRANE, Calgary
Anderson & Leach, Box 1210, D.W. Anderson, G.C. Leach
Wifley, G.M., #104, 127 1st Ave. n.w.

CORONATION, Red Deer
Sloan, MacNaughton & Co. (also Stettler)

CROSSFIELD, Calgary
Benjamin & Hooker (also Calgary)

DAYSLAND, Wetaskiwin
Schmidt & Farnham (also Camrose)

DEVON, Wetaskiwin
Taylor & Taylor, 6 Athabasca Ave., D.J. Taylor, M.E.G. Taylor

DIDSBURY, Calgary
Fisher, J.S., Box 1027

DRAYTON VALLEY, Edmonton
Smith, Gawlinski & Co. (also Edmonton)
Thomas, Prentice & Hubbell, Box 2130, D.D. Thomas, M.D. Prentice, J.E. Hubbell, A.G. Hall

DRUMHELLER, Drumheller
Ross, Todd & Co., 3 Ross Bldg., R.D. Ross, Q.C., D.B. Todd, W.H. Gough, E.D. Chapelski, W.A. Herman
Schumacher, Madden & Sparling, 180 Riverside Dr. e., S.S. Schumacher, P.J. Madden, J.L. Sparling

EDMONTON, Edmonton
Abbey, D.H., #2710, 9925 Jasper Ave.
Abbott, D.W., 11846B 145 Ave.
Ackroyd, Bradley & Piasta, 7th fl., 10242 105 St., A.O. Ackroyd, Q.C., R.W. Bradley, Q.C., E. Piasta, D.R. Ackroyd, D.B. Roth, D.S. Day, A.F. Ganser, V. Roth, D.W. Matson, D.M. Robinson, Janet Franklin, D'A. Depoe, J.E. Cregan
Acorn, Elliott, #313, 11523 100 Ave., G.W. Acorn, Q.C., D.C. Elliott
Agard & Co., #1313, 10025 Jasper Ave., R.W. Agard, M. Kaylor
Agrios, J.N., Q.C., #700, 10150 100th St.
Albert & Cook, #1140, 5555 Calgary Trail, A.L. Albert, B.J.D. Cook
Amerongen, Burger, Spencer & Ross, #900, 10024 Jasper Ave., Gerard Amerongen, Q.C., John T. Burger, D. C. Spencer, D.W. Ross, P. Loong
Andrew & Donahoe, #302, 10310 102 Ave., W.S. Andrew, J.J. Donahoe
Andrews, L.T., #2703, 10004 Jasper Ave.
Archibald Edwards, #1010, 3 Sir Winston Churchill Sq., T.A. Edwards
Ares & Murdoch, #300, 10351 Whyte Ave., L.M.E. Ares, B.J. Murdoch, A.G.M. Grant
Askin, Sciur & Wilson, #301, 9662 42nd Ave., J.H. Askin, G.D. Sciur, P.D. Wilson
Averback, D.C., #403, 10169 104th St.
Baker & Purdon, #2710, 10004 104 Ave., I.H. Baker, P.G. Purdon
Baker, Semonick & Hay, #2066, 10303 Jasper Ave., P.R.W. Semonick, I.C. Hay
Barber, S., Box 26
Barr Wensel Nesbitt & Reeson, #300, 11745 Jasper Ave., G.E.W. Barr, S.V. Wensel, J.R.W. Nesbitt, R.T.G. Reeson
Bassie, Shymko & Kantor, #1700, 10123 99 St., J. Bassie, Q.C., W. J. Shymko, T.H. Kantor, T.E. Plupek, Sharon Oleszkowicz
Bell, Felesky, Iverach, Flynn & Struck, #2102, 10235 101 St., G.W. Flynn, H.G. McKenzie, M.J. Beninger (also Calgary)
Bercov, A.A., #1700, 10235 101st St.
Berger & Hanington, #902, 10080 Jasper Ave., R.L. Berger, Q.C., P.C. Hanington
Berman, B.R., #403, 10089 Jasper Ave.
Berndt & McKee, #226, 3210 118 Ave., H. Berndt, T.L. McKee
Bernstein, L., #101, 10025 115 St.

Berzins, Willemse & Co., #200, 8723 82nd Ave., M. Berzins, C.A. Willemse
Biamonte, Harper & Cairo, #630, 10038 Jasper Ave., R. J. Biamonte, S. L. Harper, A. Cairo
Binsky & Munro, #203, 10136 100th St., H. Binsky, J.A. Munro
Bishop & McKenzie, 2200 Royal Trust Bldg. (T5J 1V3), E. E. Bishop, Q.C., K.A. McKenzie, Q.C., T. Jackson, Q.C., P. M. Bentley, D. P. Sharpe, J. P. Warner, J. J. Kane, A. J. Moss, B.J. Kickham, B.D. Hirsche, D.B. Fenny, G.R. McKenzie, E.A. Hee, C.J. Miller, C.P. Russell, R.D. Kneteman, R.H. Kennedy, Linda Richardson, S.D. Laird, R.I. Macdonald, N.J.K. Bishop, J.A. Thygesen
Bourbonnais, Cleall, Sussman & St. Pierre, 404, 10240 124 St., R. M. Bourbonnais, K.F.S. Cleall, B.S. Sussman, M.J. St. Pierre, G.J. Morrison
Bowker & Pontin, #303, 10160 112 St., H.N. Bowker, T.F. Pontin
Boyle, J.M., 500 One Thornton Ct.
Braithwaite, Kolthammer & Vigen, 8713 156 St., K.J. Braithwaite, C.K.W. Kolthammer, R.D. Vigen, G.R. Ludwig. Counsel: S.C. McGoey
Braul, Gaffney, Watson, Galbraith, 2170, 10123 99th St., W. Braul, Q.C., H. K. Gaffney, K.M. Watson, R. D. Galbraith, J.T. McEvoy, K.T. Mott
Brennand, B.R., 10540 97th St.
Brett, M.S., 10004 104th Ave.
Brinsmead & Midanik, 24 Centennial Village Shopping Mall, W.M. Brinsmead, D.M. Midanik
Broda, Cox & Co., 800 Canada Trust Bldg., 10150 100th St., P. R. Broda, Q.C., J. A. Cox, Q.C., J. T. Trofimuk, Q.C., J.L. Oake, J.C. Van Doesburg, J.W. Jackie
Broda, I., #8, 15333 Castle Downs Rd.
Brosseau, Odishaw, Hansen & Turfus, #1900, 9803 102A Ave., G. R. Brosseau, Q.C., J.H. Odishaw, Dolores Hutton-Hansen, Margaret R. Turfus, N. St. Arnaud, Ingrid Meier
Brownlee Fryett, 803 Chancery Hall, 3 Sir Winston Churchill Sq. (T5J 2C9), G. Fryett, Q.C., E. J. Walter, W. S. Sowa, P. G. Sully, M. C. Welsh, L. E. Malin, S. Fialkow, H. B. Madill, P. T. Costigan, L.J. Burgess, D.R. Syme, L.H. Whittaker, G.W. Sharek, J. McIsaac, R.C. Purdy
Bryan Andrekson, 900 Chancery Hall, 3 Sir Winston Churchill Sq. (T5J 2E1), A. Andrekson, Q.C., W. E. Wilson, Q.C., D. H. Ostry, J. A. Bryan, D. J. Boyer, L. W. Olesen, J. G. Easton, D. W. Hagg, B.D. Young, M. W. Crozier, N.F.W. Picard, B.F. Romanko, D.J. Pelkie, K.B. Blasius, R.J. MacKay, E.D. Young, J.P. Bond, J.P.J. Rossall
Bubel, L.J., #701, 10136 100th St.
Campbell, A.F., #204, 10136 100 St.
Campbell & Beckwith, 1720 Sun Life Place, 10123 99th St., S.M. Campbell, D. A. Beckwith
Campbell & Bulmer, #300, 10230 142 St., C.E. Campbell, Susan Bulmer
Chapman & Chapman, 10425 Whyte Ave., J. L. Chapman, Q.C., V. Darlene Chapman
Chapman, Finlay, McKenzie, MacPherson, Gawne, #2332, 10235 101 St., K.J. Chapman, D.G. Finlay, D.G. McKenzie, L.W. MacPherson, G.B. Gawne
Chipman, W. G., Q.C., 516 McLeod Bldg., 10136 100th St.
Chopra, R.S., #711, 10136 100th St.
Christensen, R.P., 11450 124 St.
City Solicitors, A. Konye, C.E. Frost, M.A. Massing, E.L. Pritchard, D.L. Davidson, J.A. Hughes, J.H. Pratt, J.R. Muller, M.P. Sherk, L.B. Chrzanowski
Cole, R.A., #701, 10136 100th St.
Coley & Gustafson, 115, 8905 51st Ave., N.D. Coley, C.O. Gustafson
Cooke, D. J., 627 Tegler Bldg.
Cooke, Shandling, #500, 10004 Jasper Ave., A.T. Cooke, Q.C., H.I. Shandling, D.N. Jardine, T.G. Cooke, J.C.G. Kennedy, S.L. Livergant, B.M. King
Cooper & Patrick, #200, 10020 101A Ave., G. K. Cooper, G.A. Patrick, E.L. Parker, J.M. Mutchmor
Corbett, Benkendorf, Hodgson & Lachambre, 600 Cambridge Bldg., 10024 Jasper Ave. (T5J 1R9), J. H. Corbett, Q.C., W. L. Benkendorf, A. S. Hodgson, P. K. Lachambre, B. P. Kaliel, D. R. McCalla, A.A.E. Wilson, Heather L. Jenkins
Cormie Kennedy, #1600, 10024 Jasper Ave. (T5J 1S3), D. M. Cormie, Q.C., J. W. Kennedy, Q.C., S. T. Fitch, L. A. Patrick, E. S. Cook, G. G. Campbell, K.J. Brown, R.L. Duke, B.W.L. Tod, W.S. Connauton, B.R. Garriock, R.T. McKall, D.C.P. Stachnik, W.I. Kennedy, J.A. Cross, G.S. Marr, D.D. Lewis, Jr., B.S. Hunt
Cousineau, C.D., #2, 11751 124 St.
Covey & Behm, 357, 10310 Jasper Ave., A.A. Covey, L.J. Behm, R.G. Horne
Covlin, Alton & Macdonald, 11211 76 Ave., R.W. Covlin, W.D. Alton, C.S. Macdonald
Cross, E.E., Q.C., #505, 10102 101st St.
Cruickshank Phillips, 9797 45 Ave., R.H. Cruickshank, G.J. Yakemchuk, P.F.A. Jasper, R.H. Phillips, R.J. Bishop, N. Kangles, A.J. Hladyshevsky, A.R. Anderson, R.B. Kuzyk, Donna Shelley, K.J. Jenkins, W.K. McIntosh
Cullen, M.D., 11206 101st St.
Cummings, Andrews, Wilton & Mackay, #500, 10150 100 St., R.G. Cummings, D.J. Andrews, P.B. Wilton, F.C. Mackay, J.D. MacEachern, C.M. Brodsky
Darby, D.E., #419, 10201 104 St.
Davidson, B.L., 39 Sundance, Riverdale
Davidson, R.H., 10138 121st St.
Davies, R., 287 Bonnie Doon Shop. Centre (R.W. Derrah)
Davies, T. F., 77 St. George's Cres.
Day, R. C., 307, 10012 Jasper Ave.
Decore & Co., 9636 102A Ave., J. V. Decore, Q.C., L. G. Decore, L. L. Decore, B.H.P. Kwan, R.F. Raitz, R.J. Normey, A.G. Hawrelak
Demco, A. D., 712, 10024 Jasper Ave.
Dickson, Dickson & Masson, 503 Tegler Bldg., 10189 101st St., A.H. Dickson, Q.C., J. Masson
Dlin, Breitkreuz & Bosse, 10126 118th St., G. A. Dlin, W. Breitkreuz, T.D. Bosse, D.B. Harker, M.L. Gordon
Doehring, H.J.R., 500 One Thornton Court
Dolsky & Evans, #310, 11044 51 Ave., R.M. Dolsky, R.D. Evans
Donnelly, M.M., Box 39, Site 11, R.R. 5
Doz, J. & Assoc., #315, 10180 102 St. (D. W. McGechie, B.K. Yiu, B. Karrel)
Doz & Dean, Suite 200, 15205 Stony Plain Rd., S. Doz, H.J. Dean, E.M. Crane
Dumont, Mrs. J.B., 15612 75th Ave.
Duncan & Craig, #1900, 10020 101A Ave., D. D. Duncan, Q.C., J.W.D. Craig, Q.C., D.J. Horne, L. E. Nemirsky, J. Hope, D. Heighington, S.J. Rolingher, W. A. Scott, R. W. Dutchak, D. J. Lobay, D.A. Boyd, F.D. Cook, D.P. Gahn, L.J. Smith, J.P. Poirier, L.J. Smith, E.F. Macklin
Duncan, L.F., 9529 100A St.
Durocher, Ares, Manning & Lynass, 5th floor, 10355 Jasper Ave., H.H. Durocher, G.A. Ares, D.J. Manning, D.A. Lynass, R.M. Simpson, Marjorie Mooney
Elford, E.A.O., 50 Westridge Rd.
Embury & McFayden, 10439 82 Ave., L.C. McFayden
Emery, Jamieson, 1700 Oxford Tower, 10235 101st St., H.T. Emery, Q.C., J. H. Jamieson, Q.C., S. Bercov, J. L. Lewis, L. W. Drewry, M. Dumont, H. B. Martin, R. B. Drewry, W. P. Sharek, R.W. Thompson, G. A. Riskin, Phyllis Smith, A.R. Hudson, R.J. Cotter, Wendy M. Young, G.D. Sustrik, D.R. Abbey, Shirley McNeilly, M.J. Penny; Hon. M. Lambert, Q.C., M.P.
Estrin, S., #900, 9707 110 St.
Faulkner, J.E., 10138 121st St.
Feehan, F.M., Q.C., 602 Chancery Hall, 3 Sir Winston Churchill Sq., F.M. Feehan, Q.C
Ferguson, Switzer & Mah, 12323 113th Ave., F.B. Ferguson, A.R.F. Switzer, S. Mah
Ferguson, Mrs. R., Q.C., 12019 Windsor Rd.
Field & Field, #2000, 10235 101 St. (T5J 3G1), H. G. Field, Q.C., H.A. Bodner, Q.C., T.S. Millman, M.G. Stevens-Guille, W. M. Wintermute, C. P. Clarke, E. L. Boyd, R. H. Teskey, M.C. Elias, S. D. Hillier, Myra B. Bielby, Christine G. Rapp, D.K. Neeland, R.S. Peacock, S.C. Potts, B.C. Howell, D.P. Carroll, J.D. McInnes, J.J. Oakes, S.I. Palmer, D.A. Kennedy
Fontaine, G.J., #221, 10106 11th Ave.
Foster Chatwin, #1907, 9803 102A Ave., Nina Foster, B.A. Chatwin, R.P. Belzil
Fraser, Mintz & McGuire, #101, 17510 107 Ave., R.C. Fraser, B. E. Mintz, B.C. McGuire, W.G. Plewes
Freeland, Robb, Royal, McCrum & Browne, #215, 8204 104 St., Halyna C. Freeland, J.C. Robb, P.J. Royal, T.A. McCrum, Beverley A. Brown (also NWT Bar)
Frolich, Irwin & Rand, 1984 Century Place, 9803 102A Ave., G.V. Frolich, H.J.L. Irwin, R.W. Rand, M.T. Moreau
Gall, C.L., 13316 110th Ave.
Game, B.R., #425, 10036 Jasper Ave.
Geddes, W.G., 10580 113th St. (D.A. Miller, M.R. Hetherington)
Gellert, R., #2040, 10123 99th St.
Gibb & Joosse, 15620 11th Ave., D.W. Gibb, J.W. Joosse
Gillespie, Anderson, Mar & Carter, #204, 4445 Calgary Trail, R.D. Gillespie, H.J. Anderson, L.G.L. Mar
Gledhill, Johnson & Reid, 10458 Mayfield Rd., I.H. Gledhill, B.W. Johnson, G.D. Reid, C.J. Clark
Greaves, H.R., 632 Tegler Bldg.
Grotski & Hochachka, 701 Chancery Hall, 3 Sir Winston Churchill Sq., J. Grotski, F. Hochachka, K.M. Kunicki-Tadman
Gunn & Co., #240, 10123 99 St., P.B. Gunn, J.M. Walker
Haljan, P.L., 308, 10004 Jasper Ave.
Hall & Burchak, 12026 102 Ave., F.I.A. Hall, R.D. Burchak, R.J. Hall
Hankinson & Lippe, #207, 10734 107th Ave., R.J. Hankinson, M.R. Lippe
Hardy, G.A., 2nd fl., 10619 103 Ave.
Hattersley & Hendrickson, 1200 Centennial Bldg., 10015 103rd Ave., J.M. Hattersley, L.W. Hendrickson, Teresa M. Mitchell, A.H. Channer
Haufe, T.E., 10912 81st Ave.
Hauptman, Hart & Cherkawsky, 1-9301 50th St., J.L. Hauptman, K.M. Hart, R.J. Cherkawsky
Hayduk, M.F., 14623 110A Ave.
Hayward & Romaniuk, 292 Saddleback Rd., D.R. Hayward, D.C. Romaniuk

Heaton, M.A., #3, 9837 44th Ave.
Henderson, C.C., 830, 10025 Jasper Ave.
Hewitt, Mrs. A. M., Q.C., 7304 95th Ave.
Hladun, Blakely, 440 One Thornton Court, R.W. Hladun, R.R. Blakely, W.A. Dushenski, E.L. Oddliefson, R. Gariepy, G.L. Lintz
Hoff, A.C., 2512 132nd Ave.
Holmes & Collins, #204, 11520 100th Ave., C.D. Holmes, A.R. Collins
Horbay, Miss H., 10912 97th St.
Hunt, R.A., 132, 6325 103rd St.
Illsley & Co., 202, 15241 Stony Plain Rd., G. E. Illsley, V.M. Anthonysamy
Ingersoll & Ingersoll, #606, 10179 105 St., G.G. Ingersoll, D.K. Ingersoll, W.M. Faulkner
Jackson, Arlette, MacIver & Skitsko, #1001, 10080 Jasper Ave., L. P. Arlette, Q.C., A. N. MacIver, J.L.G. Skitsko, D.S. Bulmer, Irene Kmet, I.D. Logan
Jellis, Kravinchuk & Bayrak, 10328 121 St., E.A. Jellis, I.S. Kravinchuk, D.E. Bayrak
Jenkins, J.D., #900, 10089 Jasper Ave.
Johnson, Mariash, Majeski, #400, 10004 Jasper Ave., W.A. Johnson, D.G. Mariash, J.E.A. Majeski, A.A. Marchesich, R.J. Kennedy, M.T. Johnson, P.P. Wiedman, M.D.E. Sereda, D.K. Handerek
Johnston, C.C., 14547 107A Ave.
Joly & Ayers, #202, 10115 150 St., J.A.R. Joly, L.D. Ayers (also Stony Plain)
Jones & Empson, #205, 12910 50th St., B.W. Jones, G.C. Empson, R.N. Fotty
Jorgenson & Co., 205, 11714 95th St., J. P. Jorgenson, M.S.D. Smith, P.G. Bresee
Kampitsch, R.E., 500 One Thornton Ct.
Kempo, J., 10160 118 St.
Kempo, W., Q.C., 10105 125 St.
Kiss & Davidson, 15807 102 Ave., R.A. Kiss, J.C. Davidson, B.J. Herring
Kitt, G.M., 300, 10036 Jasper Ave.
Klemen, V.J., #308, 10004 Jasper Ave.
Knaak, P., #330, 10160 112th St.
Koshman & Johnson, #700, 10117 Jasper Ave., J.C. Koshman, E.E.P. Johnson
Kroetch, L.P., 704, 10135 116th St.
Kruger, O. H., 200, 10237 98th St.
Kuckertz, H.W., #2B, 9959 82 Ave.
Kuehn, P.M.W., #719, 10136 100th St.
Kvill, Henderson, #1, 1510B Lake Wood Shopping Centre, P.E. Kvill, P.M. Henderson
Larson, Henderson & Co., #208, 15132 Stony Plain Rd., D.W. Larson, E.A. Henderson, K.H. Conradi, B.L. Fish
Lavallee & Buchanan, 705, 10240 124th St., B. D. Lavallee, D. J. Buchanan, E. W. Onusko, P.C. Lefebvre, J.K. Coutts
Lavallee, G.D., Q.C., Site 5, R.R. 6
Lawson, S.B., #202, 15132 Stony Plain Rd.
Lazarenko, J.M., Q.C., #420, 10189 101st St.
Lazarowich, Pidruchney & Co., 1330 Royal Trust Tower, T5J 2Z2, W.T. Pidruchney, I.W. Nicholson
Lefsrud, Cunningham & Patrick, #300, 10232 112 St., E. S. Lefsrud, Q.C., L.R. Cunningham, J.R. Patrick, W. G. Patrick, D. R. Wray, J.D. Coulter, J.B. Kerby, C.W. Wood, G.R. Ulveland, B.A. Murray, J.M. Devlin, L.J. Chilibeck, K.G. Senda
Lennie, DeBow & Martin, 1110 One Thornton Ct., M.D. Lennie, G.R. DeBow, B.R. Martin, J.C. Mah, J.C. Campbell, D.A. Fennell, Helen Turner, P.F. Piroth, D.F. Dunwoodie, Y.E. Byl
Lesniak, F.P., 290 Northtown Mall
Leviston, C. W., 262 10012 Jasper Ave.
Lieber, Koch, #516, 10136 100 St., F. Lieber, Q.C., A.E. Koch, R.M. Borchert
Lister, P.G., 203 McLeod Bldg., 10136 100 St.
Littlechild & Goodson, #536, 10303 Jasper Ave., J.W. Littlechild, T.R. Goodson
Lucas, Edwards & Bishop, #1501, Toronto Dominion Bank Tower, 10004 Jasper Ave., G.A. Lucas, G.K. Edwards, R.A. Weeks, Q.C., D.G. Bishop, C.A. Fraser, G.E. Bowker, R.B. White, D.J. Stratton, C.I. Johnstone, J.R. Day, J.E. Power, F.P. Layton, M. O'Byrne, J.A. Knebel, D.R. Cranston, K.P. Weeks, K.A. Cawkell, E.A. Johnson, R.C. Stemp, J.M. Enzle, J.C. Copp, E.M. Kaminski, N.J. Pollock, L.G. McFadden
Lyons, MacKenzie & Brimacombe, 311, 10310 Jasper Ave., M. Lyons, Q.C., M.I. MacKenzie, A. G. Brimacombe, G. Bailey
Maccagno, T.R., #1900, 9803 102A Ave.
Macdonald, A.G., Q.C., 900 Bank of Montreal Bldg.
MacDonald, B.H., 11203 53rd Ave.
MacKay & Coffey, #110, 12310 105th Ave., C.D.L. MacKay, J.M. Coffey
Malhotra & Watzke, #315, 10909 Jasper Ave., R. Malhotra, R.F. Watzke
Marriott, D.C., #1, 10745 85 Ave.
Matheson & Co., 10410 81st Ave., R. S. Matheson, Q.C., D. R. Matheson, Q.C., D. G. Ingram, L. Ewanchuk, D. Rode, D.S. Serink, M.A. Mittelstadt, L.R. Fleming, D.G. Hancock, S. English, Betty Young
Matheson, J.A., 11914 129 Ave. (W.J. Watson)
Mazzolini, E., 500 One Thornton Ct.
McBean, Becker & Cochard, #228, 9119 82nd Ave., J.M. McBean, R.L. Becker, R.M.R. Cochard
McCallum, D.L., 670 One Thornton Ct.
McCuaig, Desrochers, 1824 Royal Trust Tower, T5J 2Z2, E.A.D. McCuaig, Q.C., L. A. Desrochers, Q.C., J. A. Beckingham, Q.C., B. Schepanovich, R.M. Curtis, R.D. Murray, L.B. Dawson, Anne de Villars, F.F. Slatter, J.J. Gill
McGee & Co., #1301, 5555 Calgary Trail, J.E. McGee, S.L. Scragg
McGinnis, A.L., #200, 5008 86th St.
McGoey, S.C., 14430 McKenzie Dr.
McKay, A.G., #160, 4445 Calgary Trail s. (I.A. Nicol)
McLaws & Co., #907, 10100 106 St., D. McLaws, Q.C., J.E. Prothroe, Q.C., G.L. Crawford, Q.C., R.V. Deyell, Q.C., D.W. Hilland, J.P. Floyd, Q.C., J.S. Moore, Q.C., B.V. Reed, Q.C., J. Stein, G.R.D. Goulet, L.M. Sali, A.S. Hollingworth, S.W. Ingram, J.B. Malone, P.A. Stone, C.W. Walker, I.L. McLachlan, M.C. Crowe, D.C. Edie, W.H. Smith, G.M. Adams, W.G. Hopkins, F.W. Dent, Kathleen Luna, R.J. Martin, J.G. Friesen, G.E. Parker, E.A. Dolden, D.B. Reesor, L.D. Revitt, Marilyn Martin, R.D. Matheson, E.S. Shipman. Counsel: J.L. Lebel, Q.C.
McLennan Ross, #600, 12220 Stony Plain Rd. (Box 12040, T5J 3L2), R.A. McLennan, Q.C., D.J.R. Ross, J.E. Enright, J. Sterk, P.P. Taschuk, P.G. Ponting, D.M. Gunderson, D.B. Becker, B.R. Burrows, F.A. Day, B.A. Beresh, T.M. Kulasa, H.J.D. McPhail, M. Okubo, G.J. Bigg
McPhail & Clark, #205, 10435 12th St., R.J. McPhail, C.H. Clark
Meikle, I.L., 304 Kingsway Garden Mall
Melnechuk, A.J., 10472 172nd St.
Melnyk, McCord & Meiklejohn, 11054 86 Ave., A.M.S. Melnyk, Mrs. S. A. McCord, May M. Melnyk, L.R. Meiklejohn, W.K. Backhaus
Michaels & Co., #501, 10012 Jasper Ave., J.J. Michaels, S.L. Ingrey
Midgley, H.C., #105, 11147 82nd Ave.
Milner & Steer, 9th floor, Milner Bldg., 10040 104th St., T5J 0Z7, P.L.P. Macdonnell, C.M., Q.C., A.S. Williamson, Q.C., J. D. Cregan, Q.C., J. M. Thomson, Q.C., T. Mayson, Q.C., J. W. Beames, Q.C., Agnes Y. Fleming, Q.C., J.E. Redmond, Q.C., P.L. Herring, Q.C., R.A. Lundrigan, M.H. Dale, G.A. Verville, R.W. Poffenroth, D. R. Bailey, D.R. Thomas, R.L. Leclerc, G.A. Salembier, K. D. Hope, R. H. Sharplin, C.R. Allard, G.N. McDermid, J. T. Prowse, A.W.A. Bellstedt, R. J. Turner, E.H.J. Phoa, R.M. Fulton, H.R. Zechel, K.D. Wakefield, G.J. Draper, D.R. Sommerfeldt, R.A. Speidel, K.G. Nielsen, M. Gluckman, J.A. Bancroft, K.P. Feehan, L.D. Lutic, R.A. Miller, S.M. MacLellan, H.J. Shore, D.T. Robottom, J.T. Henderson, D.G. Loader, B. Zalmanowitz, D.J. Degrandis, M.D. Obert, K.C. Day, R.F. Redgrave, L.A. Wong (also Calgary)
Minsos & McLeod, #200, 8723 82 Ave., O. Minsos, R.J. McLeod, J.W. Mandick
Mitchell, W. R., 205, 10204 125th St.
Molstad & Gilbert, #200, 9990 Jasper Ave., E.H. Molstad, P. L. Gilbert, J. MacLean, G.B. Romanchuk, T.M. Engel, K.A. Pazder
Morris, Ian, 9728 141st St.
Morrison, B.P., #900, 10024 Jasper Ave.
Morse & Reay, #309, 10179 105th St., T.J. Morse, D.F. Reay
Mosychuk, N., 502, 10012 Jasper Ave.
Moxam, Mrs. M.Y., 10993 138 St.
Murphy, P.N., #230, 9751 51st Ave.
Neuman Thompson, #2, 11503 100th Ave., R.O. Neuman, Q.C., B.M. Thompson
Newson, Brumlik, 700 Chancery Hall, 3 Sir Winston Churchill Sq., F. J. Newson, Q.C., J.P. Brumlik, Q.C., J. A. Weir, M. L. Bowen, L.M.A. Lees, H.O. Moffet, P.J. McAllister, E.M. McInnis
Nicholl & Akers, #200, 10187 104 St., J.K. Nicholl, G. H. Akers, M.W. Fitzmaurice, M.E. Lindskoog
Nickerson, Roberts & Hilborn, 300 Toronto Dominion Bank Bldg., 10004 Jasper Ave., J.R. Nickerson, T.B. Roberts, C.R. Hilborn, C.D. Gardner, A.A. Holinski, D.B. Mercer
Nugent, T.J., #220, 11 Fairway Dr.
Ogilvie & Co., #700, 10150 100th St., T.W. Gallant, R. V. Lloyd, J. D. Neilson, L. N. Boddy, R.W. Odynski, B.J. Willis, R.P. Assaly, E.K. Boddy, J.J. Flaman, D.M. Peddicord, J.R. Vaage, M.J. McCabe, J.W. Murphy, L.J. Ruzicka, J.D. Blair
Olekshy & Co., 10832 82nd Ave., R. Olekshy, R.D. Karoles
Oluk, J.D., #705, 10109 106th St.
Oshry & Co., #1970, 10123 99th St., A. Oshry, A.J. Semotiuk, I.M. Stillman
Owen, P.M., Q.C., #570, 10123 99 St.
Pahl, D.R., 10430 178 St.
Park, M.M., 10119 107 Ave.
Parker, P.G., #316, 109 St. & Kingsway Ave.
Parker, R.L., 8923 187 St.
Parlee, Irving, Henning, Mustard & Rodney, #1800, 10405 Jasper Ave. (T5J 3N4), W. O. Parlee, Q.C., H. L. Irving, Q.C., W.J.M. Henning, Q.C., W. M. Mustard, Q.C., M. C. Rodney, Q.C., A. T. Murray, Q.C., C. H. Kerr, J.A. Cox, L. S. Witten, R. A. Newton, M. D. MacDonald, T.A. Cockrall, K. F. Bailey, J. T. Byrne, E. L. Bunnell, R. J. Butler, S. F. Goddard, C. R. Henning, M. J. Trussler, H. D. Montemurro, J. D. Karvellas, A.B.

Sulatycky, R.B. Davison, F.J. Niziol, W.J. Kenny, D.J. Adams, F.R. Haldane, R.G. Matthews, R.W. Wilson, M.J. Burch, B.P. O'Leary, P.E.J. Curran, D.A. Ball, R.L. Dawson, A. Du Heaume, J.A. Whitmore, D.W. Lutz, D.H. Field, K.A. Ferguson, B.J. Larbalestier, C.G. Watkins, C.R. Head, C.S. Phillips, J.K. McFadyen, R.G. McBean, B.M. Roth, R.D. Freeman, J.D. McCormick, N.J. Cavanagh, W.R. Shouldice, R.C. Secord, F.L. Zinger, R.I. Tennant, D.B. Karasick, J.A. Head, N.P. Kent, B.E. Olsen, R.C. Dunseith, A.K. Maciag, D.R. Spackman
Pawlowski, F.F., #107, 11831 123 St.
Pecover & Peck, 980, 10020 101A Ave., J.F.Pecover, S.G. Peck
Pedicaris, G., #457, 10310 Jasper Ave.
Perreault Hayward, #609, 10240 124th St., G.A. Perreault, R.R. Hayward
Peterson Ross, #2700, 10004 104 Ave. (T5J 0K1), G.P. Peterson, Q.C., J.D. Ross, J.A. Hustwick, G.G. Wetsch, D.W. Batchelor, D.M. Russell, R.O. Langley, Johanne Amonson, R.C. Heil, D.J. McKay, A.A. Robinson, J.A. Moffat, W.J. McKenna. Counsel: J.T. Joyce, Q.C.
Phelan, P.J., 500 One Thornton Ct.
Philp, R.A., 11122 66th St.
Pirani, S., #202, 9074 51 Ave.
Polack, Meindersma & Smith, 10316 121 St., G. R. Polack, D. W. Meindersma, K. J. Smith
Ponich, L.V.M., 1806 Cambridge Bldg., 10024 Jasper Ave.
Poole, Becker & Larocque, #900, 10080 Jasper Ave., R. J. Poole, D. B. Becker, R. G. Larocque
Powelson, R.G., #2240, 10123 99th St.
Power, G.E., #1110, 10177 Jasper Ave.
Pringle, Brimacombe & Sanderman, #200, 10201 104th St., A.D. Pringle, J.D. Brimacombe, S.M. Sanderman
Prodor, Whiting & Co., #300, 10209 97th St., L.B. Prodor, R.W. Poitras, R.E. Marr, F.W. Whiting, R.J. Sachs
Prowse, Chowne, Prowse & Mallon, #138A, 6325 103rd St., J.C. Prowse, R.G. Chowne, J.C. Prowse, D.P. Mallon
Prowse & Dzenick, 920 Centennial Bldg., T5J 0H1, R.L. Dzenick, Q.C., M.K.L. Leung
Pundit, G.S., #725, 10189 101st St.
Ralston, D.J., #240, 10123 99th St.
Randall, L.W.R., #206, 10441 124 St.
Reich, H.M., 500 One Thornton Ct.
Reid, P.A., #302, 4209 99 St.
Remesz & Co., 820, 10015 103 Ave., L.C. Remesz, J.I. Fraser
Revai, E.S., 288 Kingsway Garden Mall
Reyda, J., Q.C., #460, 10250 101st St.
Reynolds, Mirth & Côté, #1700, 9803 102A Ave. (T5J 2C7), D. V. Reynolds, Q.C., E.W.S. Kane, E. Mirth, J. E. Côté, W. N. Richards, R. A. Farmer, A. H. Lefever, R.A. Graesser, F.C.R. Price, D.R. Stollery, R.W. Ewasiuk, Linda M. Sherwood, W.L. Russell, E.E. Gillese, D.R. Noel
Robertson, Hartridge, Rennick, #360, 10036 Jasper Ave., G.W. Robertson, R.B. Hartridge, G. DiPinto, R.S. Rennick
Roddick, R.F., 10232 112th St.
Romaine, S.G., #805, 10080 Jasper Ave.
Romanchuk, A.S., #295, 10149 109th St.
Rowand, Lopatka & Savich, 12304 107 Ave., D.S. Rowand, V.J. Lopatka, D.M. Savich
Rudko, J., 9222 90 St.
Rusnak, K. J., 2040, 10123 99th St.
Rutley, W.B., #719, 10136 100th St.
Saddy, E., 704, 10024 Jasper Ave.
St. Pierre & Legg, #100, 9808 42 Ave., R.J.G. St. Pierre, L.S. Legg
Savaryn, P., Q.C., #721, 10189 101st St.
Saxton, G.H., Q.C., #2550, 10123 99 St.
Schloss & Co., 5th fl., 10036 Jasper Ave., B.M. Schloss, G.J. Davies, K.J. Anderson
Schwab, Hansen, 9908 106th St., V. Schwab, Q.C., D. L. Hansen, I. Grape, W.A.C. Rowe
Schwartz, D.L., #420, 10201 104th St.
Scott, Stromsmoe, #600, 10004 Jasper Ave., J.R. Scott, Marcia Stromsmoe, R.G. Bradford
Semeniuk, R.A., #212, 10189 101st St.
Shandro, Fuller, 10709 105th St., W. Shandro, H.W.A. Fuller, P.J. Maher, T.M. Walter
Shaw & Tamke, #282, 8170 50 St., W.R. Shaw, K.G. Tamke
Shewchuk & Co., 701 Chancery Hall, 3 Sir Winston Churchill Sq., T5J 2C3, P.N. Shewchuk, L. Markevych
Shoctor, Hill, Mousseau & Starkman, 10123 99th St., J.H. Shoctor, Q.C., J.D. Hill, Q.C., P.J. Mousseau, H.L. Starkman, Margaret Bonar, S.M. Margolis, R.G. Ferguson, B.K. Rattan, J.R.B. Shortreed, Jr., E.T. Spink, Doris Wilson, P.J. Faulds, K.D. Caskenette, M.N. Shoctor
Shtabsky & Tussman, 1200 Cambridge Bldg., 10024 Jasper Ave., A. Shtabsky, Q.C., M. Tussman, D.G. Groh, G.A. Reist, J. Bouthillier, P.G. Yearwood, Ching-Wo Ng, Kim Girtel, J.C. Busheikin
Sieben, J.C., 13507 102nd Ave.
Silverman & Shafir, #1104, 10117 Jasper Ave., N. H. Silverman, Q.C., J.M. Shafir
Sim, Reid & Birenbaum, #821, 10189 101st St., A. Sim, S.H. Birenbaum, E.A. Reid
Simons & Co., #403, 10240 124 St., N. W. Simons, W.R. Dueck, J.T. Pemberton, J. Keller, J.R. Taitinger
Simpson, W. E., Q.C., 407 Macdonald Hotel, 10065 100 St.
Sims & Kent, 11936 100th Ave., A.C.L. Sims, C.A. Kent, L.T. Callaghan
Singer, F.M., 207, 12907 97 St. (L.N. Hiller)
Sitko, L.A., 12909 97th St.
Smith, Gawlinski, Parkatti, Paton & Olthuis, 10025 Jasper Ave. and 2420 No. 3 McCauley Plaza, A. G. Smith, S. Gawlinski, D. Parkatti, Linda Paton, W. Olthuis, T. Croll, Teresa Smith
Smith, P.F., #206, 14925 111 Ave.
Smith, R.P., #632, 10189 101 St.
Smith-Tadman, #203, 5405 99th St., K.D. Smith, D.M. Tadman, A.J. Trevoy
Smithwick, B.A., 500 One Thornton Court
Snaychuk & Stefanik, #401, 10036 Jasper Ave., L.M. Snaychuk, R.N. Stefanik
Spitz & Combe, #900, 10089 Jasper Ave., D. Spitz, P.V. Combe, J.W. Carr
Stainton, J.T.A., #1004, 10024 Jasper Ave.
Stewart & McKay, #300, 10446 122 St., D. A. Stewart, W. N. McKay, T.G. Kaklin, R.D. Albert, J.N.G. Mitchell, S.C. Edge
Stewart, R. E., 12421 118th Ave.
Stothert, B.L., #302, 4209 99 St.
Stuffco & Olsen, 11440 Kingsway Ave., P.R. Stuffco, M.K. Olsen
Swist, Jones, #2300, 10123 99th St., R.C. Swist, A. B. Jones, G.C. Bolton, D.J. Sullivan, Sara Graziani
Syska, E.S., 305, 8540 109th St.
Taylor, C., #2733, 10004 Jasper Ave.
Taylor, P.L., 1103, 9816 112th St.
Thachuk, M.D., #440, 10020 101A Ave.
Thiele & Graziano, #1105, 10830 Jasper Ave., Valerie Graziano, F. Roth
Thompson, D.B., #627, 10189 101st St.
Thomson, J.A., #302, 4209 99 St.
Thurston, Long & Logan, #100, 10612 124 St., D.E. Thurston, D.C. Long, D.B. Logan, D.W. Hrycun, A.R. Schayler
Tkachuk & Assoc., #230, 10130 112 St., R.I. Tkachuk, M.B. Yonge
Touchings, B.R., #401, 10310 102 Ave.
Trott, Robertson & Co., 700 One Thornton Court, G.E. Trott, H.A. Robertson, J.K. Wheatley, R.M. Kelcher, C.C. Ward, D.K. Cox, K.A. Platten
Tussman, M.M., 1116 64th St.
Tymoczko, H.S., 13216 79th St.
Ulan & Assoc., 606 Chancery Hall, 3 Sir Winston Churchill Sq., J.F. Ulan, K.M. Leslie
Veale, Snyder, Flint & Bridges, #2000, 10065 Jasper Ave., H.W. Veale, Q.C., B.W. Westerman, R.A. Flint, H.A. Bridges, S.C. Snyder, E.A. Bridges, W.S. McKall, M.G. Parker, K. Gessert, D.S. Welsh
Wachowich & Co., 600 Chancery Hall, 3 Sir Winston Churchill Sq., E.R. Wachowich, Q.C., P.R. Chomicki, Q.C., M.T.J. Koziak, R.G. Baril, L.M. Dolgoy, S.L. Miller, N.D. Koziak
Werbicki & Venkatraman, 8432 182nd St., J.F. Werbicki, P. Venkatraman
Wheatley, Sadownik & Co., #330, 10621 100 Ave., R.G. Wheatley, R. Sadownik, Ferne L. Onusko, U. Welz, B. Freeman
Wiber, D.R., #408, 10136 100 St.
Wiese, W.A., 303, 8540 109 St.
Williams & Cooper, 406, 10454 82 Ave., L. G. Cooper
Williamson, H.D., #122, 4440 Calgary Trail
Witten, Vogel, Binder & Lyons, #2300, 10025 Jasper Ave., N. L. Witten, Q.C., B. C. Vogel, M.A. Binder, R.J. Lyons, D.E. Grossman, D.J. Tilley, R. M. Craddock, R.D. Schachter, M. Calof, D.B. Margolus, D. Lee, J.D. Snowdon, R.S. Abells, B.A. McNally, D. Zalmanowitz, G.E. Howorth, D.J. Patterson, A. Veylan
Wolff, Elgert, Budnitsky, Davies & Nichols, #2000, 10123 99th St., H.G. Wolff, R.H. Elgert, H.J. Budnitsky, B.J. Davies, N.W. Nichols, M.L. New, A.J. Kwasniak, B.A. Ramage
Wood, Allford, Caffaro & Gower, 1000 Chancery Hall, 3 Sir Winston Churchill Sq., J. Allford, S.E. Wood, P.M. Caffaro, L.N. Gower, B.J. Massing, Donna Oliver Dyck, R.A.N. Watkiss
Wright, Chivers & Co., #301, 10328 81 Ave., G.S.D. Wright, A.B.C. Chivers, J.C. Worton, R.M. Fulton, M. Pollock, Sheila J. Greckol, M.P. Stone, W.L. Hunter, F. McMenemy
Wright, Jacques & Bent, 9333 50 St., J.R. Jacques, P.A. Wright, P.D. Bent
Young & Kahlke, 8603 104th St., R.J. Young, E. Kahlke
Zariski Kramer Kosak, #500, 10201 104 St., A.M. Zariski, D.J. Kramer, G.R. Kosak
Zuk & Co., #203, 10611 Kingsway Ave., W.J. Zuk, T.L. Hodgkinson
Zwikstra, A.A., #305, 10036 Jasper Ave.

EDSON, Edmonton
Anderson & Co., Box 519, R.W. Anderson, K.A. Oyler
Catterall & Co., Box 460, D.H. Catterall, D.C. Calvert

ELK POINT, Edmonton
Bayduza, G.N., Box 748
Fowle, Fraser & Co. (also Bonnyville)

ENTWHISTLE, Edmonton
Maynard, L., Q.C., Box 250

FAIRVIEW, Peace River
Byers, H.A., Box 75

FALHER, Peace River
Campbell & Co. (also Peace River)

FOREMOST, Lethbridge
Virtue & Co. (also Lethbridge)

FORESTBURG, Wetaskiwin
Knaut & Johnson (also Camrose)

FORT MACLEOD, Macleod
Davis, J. C.
Gaschler, G.J., 249 24th St.
Moodie & Co. (also Lethbridge)
Welbourn & Maloney (also Claresholm)

FORT MCMURRAY, Edmonton
Campbell, Germain, Liteplo & Crick, 212 Morrison Centre, R. J. Campbell, A. W. Germain, R.J. Liteplo, C.G. Crick, T.A. Cooper
Mason, S.N., 104, 10012 Franklin Ave.
Mills & Boyd, #200, 10011 Franklin Ave., H.F.E. Mills, T.H. Boyd, R.L.J. Bouvier
Simons & Co., 36 Riedel St. (also Edmonton)
Spence Halley, 10003B Biggs Ave., J.C.M. Spence, S. Halley

FORT SASKATCHEWAN, Edmonton
Valens & Jenkins, 10509 100 Ave., J.C. Valens, D.I. Jenkins, P.M. Hartman
Wiebe, W. H., 10307 100 Ave.

GRAND CENTRE, Edmonton
Kowalski & Lovatt, Box 480, W. Kowalski, W. Lovatt, M. Clancy
Todd & Co., Box 908, R.M. Todd

GRANDE CACHE, Edmonton
Rooneem, R., Box 90

GRANDE PRAIRIE, Grande Prairie
Bang & McNaught, #203, 10029 Richmond Ave., Karen Bang, A. McNaught
Burgess & Gurevitch, #104, 9934 Richmond Ave., S.F. Burgess, C. Gurevitch
Carter, Lock & Repka, 200, 9803 101st Ave., D. Carter, T.T. Lock, J. Zurcher, R. Carter, B. Stefura
Coutu & Myroniuk, 9731 Richmond Ave., Jacqueline Coutu, B.W. Myroniuk
Gauk, Kay & Dobko, 9835 101 Ave., O. W. Gauk, Q.C., G. G. Dobko, I.B. Kay, F.J. Lewis, R.G. McVey, H.L. Franklin, T.D. Clackson
Hendery, R., #201, 10017 101 Ave.
Innes, G.R., #104, 9835 101st Ave.
Lewis, R.M., Box 688
Logan, Watson & Walisser, Box 1178, J.A. Watson, B.B. Walisser, J.R. Gordon, S.L. Shavers
MacDonell & Sutcliffe, #202, 9934 Richmond Ave., C.A. MacDonell, C. Sutcliffe
Rodnunsky, Pollick & Smith, 10009 101 Ave., S. Rodnunsky, R.S. Pollick, R. Smith
Shipley, K.A., #300, 10104 101 Ave.

HANNA, Hanna
Kush, Eugene, Q.C., Box 369
Ross, Todd & Co., D. B. Todd (also Drumheller)

HARDISTY, Wetaskiwin
Knaut, Johnson etc. (also Camrose)

HIGH LEVEL, Peace River
Campbell, Marceau & Co. (also Peace River)
Welligan & Follett, Box 269, C.B. Welligan, T. Follett

HIGH PRAIRIE, Peace River
Hennessey, J.P., Box 787
Sillito & Cobban, Box 1355, G.E. Sillito, C.P. Cobban

HIGH RIVER, Calgary
Andresen, W.J., Box 2080
Arnold & Arnold, Box 250, P.D. Arnold
Heseltine, C. H., Box 39
Robbins & Co., Box 1000, E.C. Robbins, D. Peters
Thompson, Ball etc., Box 1720 (also Calgary)

HINTON, Edmonton
Borys, Hope & Thom, Box 1160, S.N. Borys, R.M. Hope, B.E. Thom
Bowes, D.M., Box 1034
Catterall & Co. (also Edson)
Woods & Robson, Box 2598, R.S. Woods, W.C.M. Robson, Sandra Hamilton

INNISFAIL, Red Deer
Johnson, Miller & Lehane, Box 699, D.L. Johnson, J.G. Miller, J.J. Lehane
McFetridge, MacInnis, Box 2340 (also Olds)
Page & Tulloch, Box 999, M.M. Page, C.J. Tulloch

IRRICANA, Calgary
Henricks, A. W., Q.C.

JASPER, Edmonton
Oyler, K.A., Box 130 (L.A. Rodger)

KILLAM, Wetaskiwin
Gaede, Fielding (also Camrose)
Knaut & Co. (also Camrose)

KITSCOTY, Vegreville
Reynolds & Crerar (also Vermilion)

LAC LA BICHE, Edmonton
Koziak & Kozina, Box 1439, D.M. Koziak, J.W. Kozina, J.L. Booth
Quantz, P.W., Box 1530

LACOMBE, Red Deer
Advani, Rose & Cruickshank, Box 129, G.M. Advani, Q.C., A. Rose, K.C. Cruickshank, C. Lowden, R. Hicks
Holteen, R.C., Box 639
Rumbles, R., Box 178

LANGDON, Calgary
Farrell, J.M., Box 1

LEDUC, Wetaskiwin
MacLaren, W.H.R., Box 1276
Wolff, Elgert & Co. (also Edmonton)
Young & Kahlke (also Edmonton)
Zalapski, Walker & Pahl, 5304 50th St., L.W. Zalapski, D.G. Walker, B.R. Pahl

LETHBRIDGE, Lethbridge
Babki, Legrandeur, Millar & Thiessen, 817 4th Ave. s., R.F. Babki, J.N. Legrandeur, D.D. Millar, R.L. Thiessen, A.E. Dahl
Boras, Hogan & Co., 740 4th Ave. s., J.I. Boras, L.B. Hogan, V.A. Lammi
City Solicitor: D.S. Hudson
Davidson & Williams, 410 9th St. s., W.P. Davidson, Q.C., R. W. Williams, W.C.R. Davidson, H. R. Beswick, R.A. Jerke
Elander & Moffatt, 507 Canada Trust Bldg., R.W. Elander, D.M. Moffatt
Evans & Rice, 1216 3rd Ave. s., D.J. Evans, E.E. Rice, Mrs. S.M. Kubara
Fletcher, Norton & Pollock, 315 Woodward Tower, R.W. Fletcher, B.H. Norton, D.L. Pollock, R.W. Sugden, D.C. Thompson
Higa & Wood, 519 7th St. s., L. Higa, Q.C., J.A. Wood, R.E. Pocock, J.C. Woods
Huckvale, Wilde & Krushel, 612 3rd Ave. s., R. D. Wilde, A. R. Krushel, H. Heil, C.L. Chiste, R.A. Low
Huzil & Peta, 318B 13th St. n., J.T. Huzil, F.S. Peta
Ives & Carleton, #200, 542 7th St. s., T. O. Ives, Q.C., B. G. Carleton
Keebler & Shapiro, #807, 400 4th Ave. s., P.J. Keebler, D.I. Shapiro, N.H. Clair
Maxwell, Larson & Co., 1000 Woodward Tower, W.D. Maxwell, A.N. Larson, Susan Smith
Milne Hepburn McCallum, 1111 Woodward Tower, J.B. Milne, D.B. Hepburn, D.H. McCallum
Moodie & Co., 506 4th Ave. s., H.N. Moodie, S.L. Redel
Paterson North, 407 Mayor Magrath Dr., J.D. Paterson, R.P.M. North, D.R. Lint, W.C. Petersen, Lori G. Andreachuk, A.G. McKay, F.A. de Walle
Peterson & Purvis, 537 7th St. s., W. D. Peterson, K. J. Purvis, R.A. Byrne, Jane McDonald
Pritchard & Stokes, 740 4th Ave. s., F. M. Pritchard, Q.C., S. C. Stokes
Scholdra, R., 219 12th St. s.
Spanos, T., Q.C., Box 671
Stringam & Co., 900 Woodward Tower, S. Denecky, R. E. Baines, R. F. Llewellyn, T. G. Hironaka, E.W. Peterson, P. Pharo, R.G. Bissett
Virtue & Co., 601 Woodward Tower, W.S. Russell, Q.C., F. J. Morgan, Q.C., C.G. Virtue, Q.C., G.M. Morrison, W.V. Hembroff, Q.C., K.G. Torry, K. H. Lewis, L.J. Abells, M.I. Wylie, Brenda M. Gash, T.B. MacLachlan

LLOYDMINSTER, Vegreville (and Battleford, Sask.)
Bugg & Assoc., Box 1440, T.F. Bugg, J.H. Sunstrum
Clements & Ballegooyen, 5010 46 St., D.W. Clements, J.V. Ballegooyen
Johnston & Bennett, 5105 49th St., P.T. Johnston, B. Colleen Bennett
Macrae & Lonsdale, 5014 50th Ave., J.A. Macrae, F.R. Lonsdale
Politeski, L.F., Drawer 1100 (D.G. Milen)
Robertson, Baynton, Moskal, Stolniuk & Strilchuk, Drawer 20, A.G. Robertson, G.W. Baynton, Q.C., W.A. Moskal, P.C. Stolniuk, M.I. Strilchuk, Margaret Wheat, G.D. Heinrichs, K.A.B. Locke, B.E.J. Piller

MAGRATH, Lethbridge
Fletcher, Norton, etc. (also Lethbridge)

MAYERTHORPE, Edmonton
Mitchell, J.N.G.

MEDICINE HAT, Medicine Hat
Biddell, Fisher & Link, Cedar Sq. Bldg., K.R. Biddell, D.J. Fisher, R.E. Link, K.C. Reeder
Hamilton, I., 414 6th Ave. s.e.
MacDonald, E.W.N., Q.C., 414 6th Ave. s.e.
MacLean, Wiedemann, Rombough & Pitcher, 525 2nd St. s.e., D. J. MacLean, Q.C., R. J. Wiedemann, G. H. Rombough, D.L. Pitcher, R.W. Jensen
McCartney, Gordon, 378 1st St. s.e., M. McCartney, L.R. Gordon, D.J. Smith, D.F. McCrimmon
Niblock & Co., 420 Macleod Trail Law Chambers, W.J. Anhorn, W.B. Thorsteinson, R.B. Baba, R.B. Miskuski
Plumer, B.R., Box 2049
Pritchard, Lerner & Co., Professional Bldg., J. M. Pritchard, Q.C., S. J. Lerner, L. D. Wilkins, R. D. Bolton, M.F. Pritchard, Janis M. Pritchard, P.M. Bishop
Sihvon, A.M., #204, 1741 Dunmore Rd. s.e.
Wahl, H.F., #102, 520 2nd St. s.e.

MILK RIVER, Lethbridge
Babki & Co. (also Lethbridge)
Paterson North (also Lethbridge)
Virtue & Co. (also Lethbridge)

NANTON, Macleod
Bishop, D.G., Box 849
Roddie & Gordon, Box 100, R.G. Roddie, L.M. Gordon, L.K. McLellan

NISKU, Wetaskiwin
Barrett & Konik, Box 162, P.J. Barrett, E.E. Konik

NORTH COOKING LAKE, Vegreville
Abercrombie, W.D., Crescent Island

OKOTOKS, Calgary
Heseltine, C. H. (also High River)
Landerkin Dunphy etc., 2 McRae St. (also Calgary)
Robbins & Co. (also High River)
Simper, E.D., Box 1117

OLDS, Calgary
Fowler, Cardwell (also Red Deer)
Galvon, H. F., Box 848
McFetridge, MacInnis & Martinson, Box 2340, T.D. McFetridge, J.L. MacInnis, D.S. Martinson
Yuzda & Boulton, J.D. Boulton (also Calgary)

PEACE RIVER, Peace River
Campbell, Marceau, Gilbert, Mathieu & Hryniuk, Box 1210, R.P. Marceau, W.N. Gilbert, G.C. Mathieu, L.P. Hryniuk, G.L. Teeling, G.W. Paul
Freeland & Co., Box 940, J. W. Freeland, D.W. Freeland, Margaret R. Perrotta
Mann, L.G., Box 3478
Marshall, Norheim & Riemer, Box 2188, E.A. Marshall, Q.C., D.C. Norheim, E.D. Riemer, P. Van Winssen
Sisson & McIntosh, Box 820, H.C. Sisson, Q.C., J.R. McIntosh

PICTURE BUTTE, Lethbridge
Keebler & Shapiro (also Lethbridge)
Paterson & Co. (also Lethbridge)

PINCHER CREEK, Macleod
Ives & Carleton (also Lethbridge)
Keebler & Shapiro (also Lethbridge)
McGurk, W.M.K., Box 1598
Paterson & Co. (also Lethbridge)
Turcott & Co., G. A. Turcott, J.A. Oman, G.L. Jasman, R.M. Oxman

PONOKA, Wetaskiwin
Advani, Rose & Co., Box 1048, C.B. Lowden (also Lacombe)
Noble & Kidd, Box 1150, H. J. Noble, W.J. Kidd
Wyrozub, R.D., Box 354

PROVOST, Wetaskiwin
Ackroyd & Co. (R. W. Bradley) (also Edmonton)

RAYMOND, Lethbridge
Fletcher, Norton & Co. (also Lethbridge)
Jones, W.L., Box 629

RED DEER, Red Deer
Altvater, N., 4909 Gaetz Ave.
Armstrong, A. B., 302, 4820 Gaetz Ave.
Capeling Gerig, #501, 4901 48 St., G.D. Capeling, A.F. Gerig, G.W. Neufeld, L.E. Goddard
Chapman, T.H., 208, 4808 Ross St. (Lenore Harris, D.J. Simpson)
Correll, R.J., #27, 4917 48th St.
Crowe, Duhamel & Manning, 5233 49th Ave., D.W. Crowe, D.M. Duhamel, D.J. Manning, B.D. Neeland, K.R. Laycock, D.A. Petersen, G.W. Wanless
Fielding, H., Q.C., 4811 48 St.
Flanagan, Sully & Surkan, 4825 47 St., P.G. Flanagan, A. R. Sully, R.N. Surkan
Foster, Lizee, #202, 5000 Gaetz Ave., J.L. Foster, Q.C., L.R. Lizee, B.K. Adair, C.R. Warren, K.L. Sisson
Fowler Cardwell, #301, 4943 Ross St., J.W. Fowler, F.G. Cardwell
Gross, D.A., 212, 4919 59 St. (M. Jones)
Hamilton, B.W., #402, 4901 48th St.
Hawthorne, J.N., #307, 4822 50 St. (P. MacSween)
Johnston, Ming, Scammell, Manning, Lamb & Lee, Royal Bank Bldg., J.M. Johnston, Q.C., J.T. Mah Ming, R.H. Scammell, Q.C., D.M. Manning, K.R. Lamb, J.E. Lee, J.B. Mitchell, D.R. Moore, G.E. Deck
Lockerby, Siewert, 4921 49 St., N. W. Lockerby, W. H. Siewert, B.N. Bothwell
Loney, H.R., 4808 Ross St.
MacDonald & Boris, 4919 59 St., D.A. MacDonald, G. Boris
Murphy, E.F., Q.C., #404, 4812 Ross St.
Robinson, J.L., 4920 Gaetz Ave.
Schnell, Lawrence, MacSween & Hardy, 4808 Ross St., R. E. Schnell, N. P. Lawrence, Q.C., D.L. Hardy, J.I. MacSween
Sinclair, D.J., #215, 4711 51 Ave.
Vanden Brink & Wilson, 5005 Gaetz Ave., B. Vanden Brink, B.M. Wilson

REDWATER, Edmonton
Smith, Gawlinski & Co. (also Edmonton)
Thurston, Long etc. (also Edmonton)

RIMBEY, Wetaskiwin
Advani, Rose & Co. (also Lacombe)
Hawley, Donna Lea, Box 808

ROCKY MOUNTAIN HOUSE, Red Deer
Johnston, Ming (also Red Deer)
Lockerby, Siewert (also Red Deer)
Wilson, L.G., Box 100 (B.C. Bishop)
Woollard & Symington, Box 700, S. Woollard, D.C. Symington

RYCROFT, Grande Prairie
Logan & Co. (also Grande Prairie)

ST. ALBERT, Edmonton
Herfst & Goldsman, #131, 7 St. Anne St., A.J. Herfst, A. Goldsman
Rowand, Fowler & Dalsin, 7 St. Anne St., T.A. Rowand, R.S. Fowler, C.E. Dalsin
Rusnak, O., 7 Perron St.
Weary, D.B., #116, 7 St. Anne St.

ST. PAUL, Edmonton
Holeton, Langager, Box 2350, R.R. Holeton, L.E. Langager
Kawulych, M. W. (also Vegreville)
Webb, C.A., Box 1690 (D.L. Wilson)

SEDGEWICK, Wetaskiwin
Batke & Co. (also Camrose)

SHERWOOD PARK, Edmonton
Ashton Hinz, 2 Athabascan Ave., J.G. Ashton, Wendy L. Hinz
Dunn, R.A., 80 Chippawa Rd.
McClelland & Spratlin, 363 Sioux Rd., J.R. McClelland, T.E. Spratlin
Morrow, O.T.G., #113, 2020 Sherwood Dr.
Nigro, Ahlstrom & Wright, 20 Main Blvd., R.B. Nigro, L.E. Ahlstrom, G.R. Wright, C.S. McAfee, J.D. Watson, D.A. Miller

SLAVE LAKE, Peace River
Schimpf, L.W., Box 818 (J.C. Jordan)

SMOKY LAKE, Edmonton
Dolsky & Evans (also Edmonton)

SPRUCE GROVE, Edmonton
Peterson Ross, Box 2370, A.A. Robinson (also Edmonton)
Wallace & Spitz, Box 2850, R.C. Wallace, P.D. Spitz

STETTLER, Red Deer
Grant, Alton & Pfau, Box 430, G. G. Grant, W.L. Alton, D.R.T. Pfau
Grindley, J.M., Box 1785
Sloan, MacNaughton, Box 1630, R. W. Sloan, Q.C., D. P. MacNaughton, R.V. Stretch, D.C. Ellis, H.M. Landman

STONY PLAIN, Edmonton
Amerongen & Burger (also Edmonton)
Joly & Ayers, 5000 53 Ave., R.A. Joly, L.D. Ayers, D.A. Hill, M.C. Birdsell (also Edmonton)
Nickerson & Co. (also Edmonton)

STRATHMORE, Calgary
Freeman, D.A., Box 420

TABER, Lethbridge
Higa & Wood (also Lethbridge)
Peterson & Purvis, 5317 50th Ave. (also Lethbridge)
Stringam & Co. (also Lethbridge)
Wilkinson, D.C., Box 1029

THORHILD, Edmonton
Thurston, Long, etc. (also Edmonton)

THORSBY, Wetaskiwin
Olekshy & St. Pierre (also Edmonton)
Pyper, M.M., Box 496

THREE HILLS, Calgary
Tainsh, N.L., Box 266

TOFIELD, Vegreville
Braul, Gaffney & Co. (also Edmonton)

TROCHU, Calgary
Lockerby, Siewert (also Red Deer)

TURNER VALLEY, Calgary
McKillop & Co., Box 570, D.L. McKillop, M.S. McKay

TWO HILLS, Vegreville
Blonsky & Co. (also Vegreville)
Fowle, Fraser etc. (also Bonnyville)

VALLEYVIEW, Grande Prairie
MacMillan, A.G., Box 1588

VAUXHALL, Lethbridge
Crerar & Co. (also Brooks)
Keebler & Shapiro (also Lethbridge)

VEGREVILLE, Vegreville
Blonsky & Co., 4925 50 St., J.A. Blonsky
Himsl, D.D., Box 1838
Kawulych, M. W., Box 989
Starko, L.M., Box 1178

VERMILION, Vegreville
Reynolds, Crerar & Hurdle, Box 925, J.H. Reynolds, D.F. Crerar, R. Hurdle

VIKING, Vegreville
Hunter, J.D., Box 110
Schmidt & Farnham (also Camrose)

VULCAN, Calgary
Murphy, A. J.

WAINWRIGHT, Vegreville
Rodnunsky & Marchant, Box 1560, A Marcia Rodnunsky, G.C. Marchant

WARNER, Lethbridge
Paterson, North (also Lethbridge)
Virtue & Co. (also Lethbridge)

WESTLOCK, Edmonton
Kobie, C. J., 10611 100 Ave.
Logan & Smart, Box 57, R.B. Logan, W.W Smart
Murphy, J.V.

WETASKIWIN, Wetaskiwin
Adilman, Sirrs, Watson & Deckert, 520 51st Ave., P.L. Adilman, D. A. Sirrs, J.S Watson, A.H. Deckert
Gallinger, G.F., Box 6600
Goodson & Littlechild (also Edmonton)
Pike & Sockett, #100, 5108 50 Ave., D.W Pike, K.R. Sockett, G.G. Yake
Vickerson & Watson, Box 6600, R. K. Vickerson, Q.C., G.G. Watson

WHITECOURT, Edmonton
Gould & Braun, Box 760, L.J. Gould M.J.H. Braun
Stocco & Co., Box 960, J.A. Stocco, R.W Koski

BARRISTERS AND SOLICITORS IN BRITISH COLUMBIA

ABBOTSFORD, Westminster
Beaubier, J.D., 202, 2702 Ware St.
Fuller, G.T.H., 2224 Broadway
Kuzminski & Heringa, #205, 33119 s. Fraser Way, L.M. Kuzminski, E.B. Heringa, E.R. Swedahl
Miner, J.A., 2296 McCallum Rd. (G.E. Palmer)
Robertson & Griffin, #301, 33695 s. Fraser Way, D.A. Robertson, R.W. Downe, P.M. Griffin, F.M. Mullally. Assoc. Counsel: J.W. Conroy
Rosborough & Co., 33832 s. Fraser Way, F. S. Rosborough, J. Koot, J.M. Burke, G.J. Dykstra, P.J. Keighley, W.W. Norris
Siemens & Co., 2459 Pauline St., E. Siemens, C.D., W. M. Siemens, C.R. Temple
Wilson, L. H., 2644 Montrose St. (T.J. Hordal)

AGASSIZ, Westminster
Rowell, F.N.A., Box 649

ALDERGROVE, Westminster
Brawn & Randall, 206, 27115 Fraser Hwy., J.L. Randall (also Surrey)
Filkow, S., 25162 40th Ave.
Hall, R.J., 209, 3100 272nd St.
Major, G.A., 201, 27211 30th Ave. (M.E. Rae)

ARMSTRONG, Yale
Lawrence, H.C., Box 545
Pattie, Mitchell & Helm, Box 69 (also Vernon)

BARRIERE, Cariboo
Mair, Janowsky & Co. (also Kamloops)

BRENTWOOD BAY, Vancouver Island
MacDonald & Tindall, Box 425, R.I.T. MacDonald, L. Wong (also Victoria)

BURNABY, Westminster
Andru, J., 3799 Garden Grove Dr.
Bakony, C. E., 5000 Kingsway
Becker & Mathers, 5679 Imperial St., A.J. Becker, W.M. Mathers
Bergmann, W. E., 4550 e. Hastings St.
Cotton & Gourlay, 4259 e. Hastings St., W.M. Cotton, J.L. Gourlay
Dohm, Jaffer, #1, 7257 Kingsway, Hon. T.A. Dohm, Q.C., M.S.B. Jaffer
Doig, Baily, McLean, Greenbank & Murdoch, 7297 Kingsway, H. Doig, F. M. Baily, B.A. McLean, D.L. Greenbank, W.D. Murdoch, R.C.C. Barratt, T.M. Mullen
Edwards, Edwards, Edwards & Maskall, #510, 5021 Kingsway, Robert Edwards, Dudley Edwards, J. H. Edwards, Yvonne Edwards, D.W. Maskall, J.A. Dunne, H.W. Hunter
Emerson, Sutherland, #200, 4411 e. Hastings St., A.T. Emerson, J.D. Sutherland
ox, R.B., 4946 Canada Way
Greiner & Co., #202, 5501 Kingsway, G.J. Greiner, V.E. Pigeon, D.T. Forsyth, B.L. Gibbard
Harris, Campbell & Threlfall, 4729 e. Hastings St., G.J. Harris, C.K. Campbell, J.J. Threlfall, G.M. Rideout, L.B. O'Neill
Hawthorne & Piggott, 1899 Willingdon Ave., E. A. Hawthorne, G. A. Piggott
Hean & Wylie, #600, 4211 Kingsway, A.F.C. Hean, Q.C., T.M. Wylie. B.D. Stewart, C.H. Bergen, Anne L.B. Kober, P. Schlosser-Moller, Irene Leonard, K.A. Bowman, D.H. Bentley, Marie Johnson
ierans, M.J., 7946 Edmonds Ave.
Koole, L., 6035 Sussex Ave.
Lorimer, J.G., 4857 Kingsway
Lowe, M. N., 4536 e. Hastings St.
McGovern, F. T. D., 4795 Kingsway
McGuire, W.F., 6637 Kingsway
Motiuk, J.W., #222, 5000 Kingsway (E.A. Pedersen)
Ogilvie & Co., 150 Lougheed Mall, C. Ogilvie, C.W. Sunderland
Peach, DeStefanis & Co., #2, 7375 Kingsway, T.S. Peach, F.G. DeStefanis, V.A. Ishkanian
Peterson, Stark & Fowler, #340, 9940 Lougheed Hwy. (also Vancouver)
Prentice, T.B., 4012 e. Hastings St.
Raetzen, M.S., #315, 5000 Kingsway
Shamanski, Cheevers, 360, 9940 Lougheed Hwy., H.R. Shamanski, J.P. Cheevers
Smitton, F. A., 4429 Kingsway
Yamasaki, G.C., #102, 5868 Olive Ave.

BURNS LAKE, Prince Rupert
Low, R.R., Box 389

CACHE CREEK, Cariboo
Littlewood, N., Box 69

CAMPBELL RIVER, Vancouver Island
Barker, Tees & Clare, 1260 Island Hwy., D. G. Barker, D.J.F. Tees, M.C.A. Clare
Brown, G.D., 161 Beech St.
Burrows, M.L., Box 157
Grant, Saunderson, Keighley, Wickham & Orobko, 964 Island Hwy., J.F. Grant, B.H. Saunderson, I.M. Keighley, D.A.J. Wickham, W.P. Orobko
Lazerte, McVea & Shook, #1, 918 Island Hwy., M.A. McVea, S.S. Shook, T.J. Bishop
Naknakin, R.V., 1441A n. Island Hwy.
Sinnott, Stamp & Stein, 920 Alder St., G. P. Sinnott, B. A. Stamp, W. H. Stein, G. A. Lloyd, R.P. Stewart
Thompson, Stewart & Murdoch, 400 10th Ave., P.M. Thompson, A.G.M. Stewart, B.G. Murdoch, J.A. Sharpe

CASTLEGAR, W. Kootenay
Dalton, T.M., 820 8th Ave.
Moran, Carpenter, Piket, Box 3008, J.C. Carpenter, Diane Piket, J.M. Young, T.H. Thompson
Polonicoff, Jones & Perehudoff, 1115 3rd St., J.P. Polonicoff, Mrs. A.M.N. Jones, A. Perehudoff
Spilker, Bridgeman, Box 3490, R. Spilker, L.J. Bridgeman

CAWSTON, Yale
Dawson, R.F., R.R. 1 (also Vancouver)

CHASE, Yale
McTavish, D.S., Box 428
Mair, Janowsky & Co., Squires Mall (also Kamloops)

CHETWYND, Cariboo
Cochrane, E.R., Box 1480
Wills, R.A. & Co., 4713 51st St.

CHILLIWACK, Westminster
Adair, D.B., 123 Main St.
Baker, Newby & Co., 123 Main St., J.D. Baker, W.M.R. Newby, J.C. Lee, A.A. Purdy, L.R. Stinson, D.M. Renwick, F. Jensen, R.A. Kelly
Barlow & Co., 12 College St., R.W. Barlow, B.E. Sloan
Erickson, Patten & Barrett, 131 Main St., J. Erickson, D.N. Patten, L.E. Barrett, L.A. MacDonald
Jesperson, S.K., Box 363
Rempel, Kaye, Toews & Verbrugge, 142 Young St. s., W.J. Rempel, R. M. Kaye, J.R. Toews, M.S. Verbrugge, W.G. Grist
Thome & Hoy, 12 College St., P.A. Thome, B.G. Hoy
Thompson, W.J., #201, 31 Yale Rd. e.

CLEARBROOK, Westminster
Abrams, G.W.D., 32056 s. Fraser Way
Cope, Martyn, #210, 32112 s. Fraser Way, S.T. Cope, M.J. Martyn, T.F. Strocel
Janzen, Anderson and Holmes, 32086 s. Fraser Way, E. J. Janzen, J. O. Anderson, O.B. Holmes. Counsel: A.L. Balakshin
Linley, Duignan, Wattie & Brown, 2548 Clearbrook Rd., P.B. Linley, J.L. Duignan, R. A. Wattie, R.N. Brown, R.W. Howarth, R.W. Greenwood
Rosborough & Co., #203, 31943 s. Fraser Way, W.W. Norris (also Abbotsford)

CLEARWATER, Cariboo
Mair, Janowsky & Co., Brookfield Plaza (also Kamloops)

COMOX, Vancouver Island
Carten, J.F., 204 Port Augusta Rd.
Reddin, H.M., R.R. 2, Anderton Rd.
Welsh, J.E., 2267 McKenzie Ave.

COQUITLAM, Westminster
Antifaev, K.W., #108, 3020 Lincoln Ave.
Burke, Tomchenko, Duprat, #200, 1034 Austin Ave., B.H. Burke, O.H. Tomchenko, L.M.J. Duprat, K.W. Thornicroft
Davies, R.B., 955 Brunette Ave. (S.J. Morris)
Edwards, C.G., 1130C Austin Ave.
Girard, M.M., 307 Blue Mountain St.
Goddard, E.J., 566 Lougheed Hwy.
Nixon, R.L., #200, 1046 Austin Ave.
Parks, Feller, Anstey, Meyer, #200, 1106 Austin Ave., J.M. Parks, C.J. Meyer, B.R. McArthur, D.A. Drysdale, B.D. Bennett (also Vancouver & Port Coquitlam)
Spraggs & Co., #202, 1030 Westwood St., T.L. Spraggs, J.M. Schwarz
Taylor & Bardal, 2, 1111 Austin Ave., J.D. Taylor, B.P. Bardal, E.G. Dorchester
Thomas, K.R., 1319 Johnson St.
Way, D.R., #302, 566 Lougheed Hwy.
Welch, L. F., 508 Clarke Rd.
Zipp & Forshaw, 204 Blue Mountain Rd., A.H. Zipp, S.B. Forshaw, R.W. Miller

COURTENAY, Vancouver Island
Chesterley, E.K., 505 5th St.
Dow, Muir & Co., 468 3rd St., J.E. Dow, W.G. Muir, Z. Tabaczuk-Porter, C.R. Sinclare
Gibson, D.L., 505 5th St. (M.S. Kelly)
Gordon & Morris, 949 Fitzgerald Ave., C.H.L. Morris, J.C. Holland
Holekamp, Cunliffe & Greyson, 512 4th St., E.A. Holekamp, D.S. Cunliffe, P.A. Greyson
Huibers, H., 449 Cumberland Rd.
MacIvor, H., 1, 450 5th St.
Olstead, D.W., 968 Fitzgerald Ave. (I.A. Brand)
Pouss, R. W., 243 4th St.
Swift, Datoo, Doherty, 536 5th St., R.J.S. Swift, A.N. Datoo, P.M. Doherty
Tabbernor, P., 460 6th St. (R.D. Miller)
Trotter, W. M., Box 3224

CRANBROOK, E. Kootenay
Buddenhagen, R.G., #205, 14A 13th Ave. s.
Gansner, H.L., 1629 Baker St.
Graham, P., 122 11th Ave. s.
Hislop & Co., 220 Royal Bank Bldg., F.C. Hislop, G.J. Lazenby, T.G. Colgur, L.A.

Best, D.J. Sliva, P.L. Summers, K.F. Delamont, B.K. Kluge, M. Lott
Memory, C.S., 824 Baker St.
Rella Docking, 6 10th Ave. s., A. Rella, T. Docking, G. Mamen
Steidl, Kambeitz, Melnick, Niedermayer & Donald, #201, 828D Baker St., K.R. Steidl, G.J. Kambeitz, T.J. Melnick, D.P. Niedermayer, W.I. Donald, R.C. McLeod

CRESTON, W. Kootenay
Lindsay, A.G.
Smith & Smith, Box 1174, J.W. Scott
Urban & Baumgartner, Box 2040, D.L. Urban, R.M. Baumgartner

DAWSON CREEK, Cariboo
Cosburn, Karen, Plenert & Co., 201, 1136 103rd Ave., R.S. Cosburn, M.M. Karen, W.N. Plenert, W. Pope
Gibb & Syal, #201, 10312 12th St., P.A. Gibb, B.C. Syal, S.M. Soll
Masters & Dollis, 1022 103rd Ave., L.G. Masters, Lynne Dollis
Mitchell, Schuller & Co., 2, 933 103 Ave., D.J. Mitchell, J. Schuller, L. Dellow, G.A.P. Stasiuk, M.G. Emery
Seyl, D.P., 10208 10th St. (Sandra Seale)
Valair & Kawano, Royal Bank Chambers, 10302 10th St., D.C. Valair, D.N. Kawano, B.G. Kiddle

DELTA, Westminster
Basile, A.W., 4624 54th St.
Buckley & Buckley, 9453 120th St., G. J. Buckley, J.W. Buckley, G. McPherson
Hrytsak & Co., 9349 120th St., D. J. Hrytsak, I.J. Kaminsky, Rose DeFrancesco
Hutton, D.M., 935 Pacific Ave.
Ivens & MacDonald, 1234 56th St., J.B.M. Ivens, C.R. MacDonald, V.G. Panchmatia
Ivens, McGuire, Souch & Ottho, 4837 Delta St., D.A. Souch, U.K. Ottho, R.B. Adler, R.A. ter Borg
Kane, Shannon & Weiler, 201, 6950 Nicholson Rd., J. G. Kane, C. R. Shannon, W. G. Weiler
Millichamp, T.D., #2, 1323 56th St.
Piters, R.E., 5090 48th Ave.
Sisett & Sauer, 4832 Delta St., I.R. Sisett, D.W. Sauer, Sarah Davis
Smith, P.A., 5094 48 Ave.
Stasiuk, R.A., 203, 1255 56th St. (D.P. Hoyt)
Stevenson, W.W., 6702 Kent Cres.
Zaruby & Grimson, 1133 56th St., E.B. Zaruby, M.J. Grimson

DENMAN ISLAND, Vancouver Island
Campbell, S.S., Northwest Rd.

DUNCAN, Vancouver Island
Brewin, Milne & Morley, 225 Canada Ave. (also Victoria)
Coleman LaCroix Nesbitt O'Shea Wright, 271 Ingram St., M.G. Coleman, G.C. LaCroix, R.J.P. Nesbitt, L.J. O'Shea, D.F. Wright, C.J. Askew
Kuta & Mabley, #206, 435 Trunk Rd., L.C. Kuta, D.J. Mabley
Lines, T.H., 127 Ingram St.
MacDonald, A. I., 225 Canada Ave.
McDaniel, R.B., #204, 55 Canada Ave.
Taylor, Newcomb & Ridgway, 166 Station St., D.E. Taylor, K.R. Newcomb, G.G. Ridgway, P.L. Lawson
Whittaker, J.B., 1100 Herd Rd.
Whittome, J. L., 122 Station St.
Williams, Davie, Orchard, Singh & MacCarthy, 170 Craig St., D.R. Williams, Q.C., J.C. Davie, D.R. Orchard, T.M. Singh, J.P. MacCarthy, B.R. McCutcheon, Laura Nield

ELKFORD, East Kootenay
Majic, Patel & Leffler (also Fernie)

ENDERBY, Yale
Pattie & Co., Box 377 (also Vernon)
Sivertz & Brecknell (also Salmon Arm)

ERRINGTON, Vancouver Island
Seaton, P.E., Box 143

FERNIE, E. Kootenay
Graham, P. (also Cranbrook)
Hislop, Lazenby & Co., D. Sliva, P. L. Summers (also Cranbrook)
Majic, Patel & Leffler, Box 369, G.S. Majic, B. N. Patel, G. Leffler, R. Bentley, B. Erickson

FORT LANGLEY, Westminster
Nundal, Cherrington & Easingwood, 9067 Church St., D.L. Nundal, J.A. Cherrington, R.H. Easingwood

FORT NELSON, Cariboo
Schuck & Merritt, Box 1137, A.P. Schuck, W.P. Merritt

FORT ST. JOHN, Cariboo
Bruhaug & Co., 10139 100th St., I.J. Bruhaug, S.M. Bruhaug, B.A. Daley
Callison & Co., 10419 100th St., G.S. Callison, B.D. Currie. Counsel: C.R. Maclean
Chapman, W.W., 10233 100th St.
Hoffman & Co., 10740 100 St., C.D. Hoffman, J.D. Lewis
Kelly, J. J., 10136 100th Ave.
Pomeroy & Harrison, 9947 100th Ave., G.B. Pomeroy, D.J. Bosley
Smith, B.W., 10 Princess Cres.
Walsh & MacAdams, 9940 104th Ave., P.D. Walsh, S.L. MacAdams, Mary Fus, C.D. Cleaveley

GANGES, Vancouver Island
McConnan, Bion etc., Ganges Centre Bldg. (also Victoria)
Sloan, G.B., Box 248 (L.J. Oldroyd)

GIBSONS, Vancouver
Luke, H.C., Box 710
Reid & Assoc., Box 649, R.C. Reid, R.F. Crum

GOLDEN, E. Kootenay
Apps, R.E.C. (also Kimberley)
Pope & Ewan, Box 429, D.B. Pope, G. Ewan

GRAND FORKS, W. Kootenay
Brothers, D.L., Q.C., Christina Lake
Butterfield, O.T., Box 2557
Geronazzo, D.D., Box 1030
Soberlak, P.J., Box 2440
Somerville, P., Box 1016

HOPE, Westminster
Kennedy, P.D., Box 1719

HORSEFLY, Cariboo
Best, D.N., Box 160

INVERMERE, E. Kootenay
Hubbard & Co., 1229 7th Ave., C.A.W. Hubbard
MacDonald, W.J., Box 2400
McRoberts, R.K., Box 1049

KAMLOOPS, Yale
Allik-Petersenn, P., #36, 750 Fortune Dr.
Berna, Horne & Marr, 345 Victoria Ave., A.S. Berna, J.A. Horne, D.J. Marr
Bianco, Bailey & Co., 131 Victoria St., P.R. Bianco, G.S. Bailey, R.W. Gray
Brown, R.M., 264 3rd Ave.
City Solicitor: W.P. Turlock, 210, 175 2nd Ave.
Coates, D.P., #540, 175 2nd Ave.
Coutlee, G., 219 Victoria St.
Gnitt, J.G., 810 Seymour St.
Hunter, Jebson, Howard, 248 2nd Ave., R.B. Hunter, D. Jebson, M.D. Howard, D.L. Clarke, B.D. Ross, N.B. Kulla, H.R. Dreyer, D.T. Knapp, L.R. Backman, D.A. Handy, F.R. Scordo, R. Cundari, G. Woitas
Jensen, Mitchell & Co., #300, 125 4th Ave., L.P. Jensen, C.A. Mitchell, R. Fischer, R. Watson, P. Henry
Kurta, J., 141 Victoria St. (D.J. Cruickshank)
Mair, Janowsky, Blair, #305, 186 Victoria St., R.D. Janowsky, R.M.L. Blair, I.F. Kaatz, R.H. Jensen, Daphne M. Smith, S.D. Smith, J.B. Carter, S.D. Dley, T.B. Bepple, K. Sommerfeld, R.C. Adkin, S.R. Harrison, F.I. Ritchie
Moore, Jensen, McAllister, Berg, 790 Seymour St., G.L. Moore, K.P. Jensen, C.G. McAllister, D.R. Berg, P.J. Maher, D. McDougall
Murphy, B.I., 256 Seymour St.
Plested, R.R., 618 Tranquille Rd.
Riley, Taylor, Kong, Patrick, 153 Seymour St., G. Taylor, D.N. Riley, V.M. Kong, K.H. Patrick, W.A. Blair, R.E. Powers, B.W. Eremko, D.J. Bilkey, E. Epp, F. Quinn
Robinson Morelli, Chertkow, #300, 180 Seymour St., R. Robinson, M. Chertkow, R. Morelli, G. W. Griffiths, D. L. Donaldson, J. M. Hogg, R.D.C. Campbell, M.J. Smith, M.E. MacGregor, R.M. McDiarmid, K.W. Dever
Rogers & Hyslop, #460, 175 2nd Ave., D. Rogers, Hope Hyslop
Ryan, Schaefer & Co., 950, 175 2nd Ave., J.W. Ryan, J.F. Schaefer, D.W. Mann. Assoc. Counsel: N. Fetterly
Saucier, Goar, #35, 750 Fortune Dr., R.J. Saucier, D.J. Goar
Tessovitch, K., 4, 237 6th Ave.
Walley, D.G., #501, 235 1st Ave.
Webber & Co., #200, 121 St. Paul St., J.R. Webber, D.W. Gillespie, R.A. Renkema, R. Burke, F.S.M. Barnett, J.E. Broadway
Woodruff, K.G., 785 Seymour St.
Wozniak & Walker, 1212 Battle St., W. J. Wozniak, K. M. Walker

KASLO, West Kootenay
Watson, E.E., Box 1049

KELOWNA, Yale
Beairsto, R.E., #100, 1449 St. Paul St.
Bilsland, A.W., 1654 Ellis St.
Finkelstein, T., 260 Harvey Ave.
Fretwell & Mossman, 1470 St. Paul St., H R. Fretwell, D. R. Mossman
Gregory, A., #15, 1638 Pandosy St.
Gunnlaugson, L.C., 3034 Pandosy St.
Hayman, R. M., 3017 Tutt St.
Ibbetson & Boon, 1638 Pandosy St., J.D. Ibbetson, D.K. Boon
Larson, Smith & Henderson, 200, 21 Lawrence Ave., C.H. Larson, L.L. Smith B.R. Henderson
MacDonald, J.B., 665 Lawrence Ave.
McAfee, Harder & Co., #301, 1475 Elli St., J.A. McAfee, D.B. Harder, J.M. Harnah, R.O. Levin, D.J. Rutherford, R.H Montgomery, P.L. Mitchell, R.J. Pushor, M.W. Baron (also Rutland)
Peacock, Porter & Mahoney, 1641 Pandosy St., J.C. Peacock, R.S. Porter, R.F Mahoney
Peyton & Co., #200, 1420 St. Paul St A.E. Peyton, G.J. McDade
Phelps, R.G., 202, 1636 Pandosy St.
Ramsay, Smith & Co., #202, 1433 St. Pa St., J. Ramsay, T.W. Smithwick, Smith, G.H. Barnett, J.D. Van Blarcom
Salloum, Doak & Co., #200, 537 Leo Ave., L.T. Salloum, Q.C., M.R. Dirk, G. Shirreff, A.W. Donaldson, J.C Hardwick, L.F. Thomas, R.A. Basse M.D. Johnson, R.T. Solmer, D.W. Wel er, M.A. Braaten. Counsel: J.C. Doa Q.C.
Sigurgeirson, D.S., 544 Bernard Ave.
Stewart, Ward & Schlosser, #100, 58

Leon Ave., W.A.M. Stewart, J.T. Ward, J.W. Schlosser, K.G. Schlosser
Thiessen, W.J., #103, 1610 Bertram St.
Tinker & Kueng, 1573 Ellis Ave., R.P. Tinker, R.P. Kueng
Tymchuk, Brown & Hattori, 147 Park Rd. (Rutland), W.M. Tymchuk, D. Brown, J.T. Hattori
Wageman, Bailey & Glazier, 260 Harvey Ave., R.L. Wageman, D.R. Bailey, M.D. Glazier, D.J. Johnson
Warren, Ladner, Berge & Co., #101, 346 Lawrence Ave., D.T. Warren, H.G. Ladner, H.R. Berge, K.W. Purvin-Good, M.R. Bishop, J.D. Flannigan, B.M. Davies. Assoc. Counsel: D.C. Fillmore, Q.C.
Weddell, Horn & Co., 389 Queensway, J.T.F. Horn, F.E. Reagh, J. McLellan, G.R. Holland, B. MacKenzie, M.D. Johnson
Wilkinson, Pihl, #201, 1636 Pandosy St., C.W. Wilkinson, D.H. Pihl
Wilson, Bauman & Staples, 215 Lawrence Ave., R.J. Bauman (also Victoria)

KIMBERLEY, E. Kootenay
Apps, R.E.C., 230 Spokane St.
Graham & Co. (also Cranbrook)
Heflin, W.J., 200, 290 Wallinger Ave.
Mayne Maciborski, 167 Deer Park Ave., R. Mayne, R. Maciborski, M. Luchenko
Smaill, Van Steinberg, #200, 144 Deer Park Ave., Sandra Smaill, J.H. Van Steinberg
Steidl, Kambeitz etc., 495 Wallinger Ave. (also Cranbrook)

KITIMAT, Prince Rupert
Douglas, K.P., 369 City Centre
Wozney & Co., 366 City Centre, R. W. Wozney, R.S. Donaldson

LADYSMITH, Vancouver Island
Bohun, J.A.D., 225 Bayview St. (J.R. Down)
Luff, B.D., Box 370 (J.T. Martin)
Taylor, Newcomb & Co., 10 High St. (also Duncan)

LANGLEY, Westminster
Babb, R.R., #302, 20644 Eastleigh Cres.
Bell, D.G., 203, 20644 Eastleigh Cres. (C.A.G. Meugens, R.M. Meugens)
Bryenton & Douglas, 202, 20218 Fraser Hwy., G.M. Bryenton, J.F. Douglas, P.J. Faminoff, M.K. Sloane
Burton, S.E., 21641 48th Ave.
Fleming, Olson & Co., 20051 40th Ave., G.K. Fisher-Fleming, J.S.A. Olson
Forbes, Nielsen & Co., 202, 20558 Fraser Hwy., T.A.S. MacCallum (also Richmond)
MacDonald & Boyle, 20450 Fraser Hwy., J. A. MacDonald, M. Boyle
McDonald, R.B., 3128 208th St.
McEwen & Campbell, 21641 48th Ave., J.A. McEwen, J.J. Campbell, C.A. Pritchard
Minten & McCallum, 221, 20316 56th Ave., P.V. Minten, H.J. McCallum
Nundall, Cherrington, Easingwood & MacEachern, 20570 56th Ave., D.L.L. Nundall, J.A. Cherrington, R.H. Easingwood, L.J. MacEachern, B.A. Scott (also Fort Langley)
Prodor & Co., 20410 Fraser Hwy., J.M. Prodor, C.R. Van Duffelen
Severide, Staplin & Co., 20432 Douglas Cres., O.P.L. Staplin, J.B. Hira, D.A. Critchley, A.K. Seabrook, Barbara Gamlin. Assoc. Counsel: N. Severide
Shore, M.A., #212, 20316 56th Ave.
Wood, M.D., 7807 199 St.

LLOOET, Cariboo
Boeujon, G.A., 102, 674 Main St.
Fraser, R.K., 416 Main St.
Blair, Janowsky & Co. (also Kamloops)

LOGAN LAKE,
Robinson Morelli Chertkow, Box 580 (also Kamloops)

LUMBY, Yale
Davidson & Co., Box 760, W.E. Catlin (also Vernon)
Kidston, Davis & Adams (also Vernon)

MADEIRA PARK, Vancouver
Malkus, B.M., Box 178

MAPLE RIDGE, Westminster
Baird, M.R., 22515 Dewdney Trunk Rd.
Becker & Langdon, #304, 11965 Fraser St., E.J. Becker, G.C.N. Langdon
Meighen, R.W., 103, 11743 224th St. (C.D. Lazar)
Nicholson, D. M., 7, 22374 Lougheed Hwy.
Norquist, Shantz & Davies, 22371 Dewdney Trunk Rd., J.B. Norquist, R. D. Shantz, T.A. Davies, J.J. Lenaghan, Rosalyn Manthorpe
Vernon & Thompson, 23311 119th Ave., F.D.S. Vernon, A.C. Thompson, L. W. Anderson, B. R. Marshall, T.E. Dinsley
Webb, B.R., 22312 Dewdney Trunk Rd.

MERRITT, Yale
Eagles, R.S., #4, 2139 Quilchena Ave.
Merry & Co., #203, 1970 Quilchena Ave., P.J. Merry, A. Chaster
Robinson Morelli Chertkow, 2196 Quilchena Ave., M.E. McGregor (also Kamloops)

MILL BAY, Vancouver Island
Lathrop & Gibson, Box 145, T.H. Lathrop, P.J.T. Gibson

MISSION, Westminster
Blacklock, P.S., Box 3339
Blane, R.D., 7311D James St.
Boyle & Lacusta, 4, 33132 1st Ave., F.A. Boyle, D.E. Lacusta
Conroy, J. W., R.R. 3, 12699 Stave Lake Rd.
Dobell & Rands, 7311B James St., E.R. Dobell, J.E. Rands
Gill, N.S., 32934 4th Ave.
Gordy, W., 33056 1st Ave.
Haber, Taylor & Tait, 33066 1st Ave., B.J. Haber, G.D. Taylor, J.G. Tait, C.R. Temple
Leedham, Walker & Co., Box 3250, D. A. Leedham, G. W. Walker, G.B. Goodfellow

NAKUSP, West Kootenay
Gegenberg, B., Box 800

NANAIMO, Vancouver Island
Bergen, G.S., 55 Front St.
Cunliffe & Cunliffe, 82 Commercial St., D.M. Cunliffe, Q.C., J.D. Macfarlane
Ewert, J.D., 87 Wharf St. (R. Petley-Jones)
Green, Sinclair, Gray & Hobbs, 2150 Bowen Rd., C.G. Green, J.A. Sinclair, M.A. Gray, B.R. Hobbs
Groos, C.E.D., 149 Wallace St.
Harris, R. G., 304 235 Bastion St.
Heath, Taylor, Shabbits, Giovando & Downs, 111 Wallace St., H. B. Heath, J.D. Taylor, S. J. Shabbits, P.J. Giovando, K.K. Downs
Henderson, G.E., 575 Terminal Ave. (S.S. Ollek)
Hogan, S.M., 515 Campbell St.
Jones & Assoc., #23, 111 Wall St., D.G. Jones, P.W. Avis
King, Dunn, Sutton & Hope, 10 Commercial St., A.E. King, J.N. Dunn, B.D. Sutton, J.D. Hope
MacIsaac, Clark & Co., 30 Front St., R.F. MacIsaac, S.G. Clark, G.B. Sinclair, R. McNeil, E.A. Bamford, B.R. Vining, J.S. Godfrey, D.M. Traill, B.J. Senini, J.A. Vanstone, Deborah Acheson, E.B. Shaw
MacLeod, D.A., 17 Church St.
Martin, McAfee & Co., 155 Commercial St., J. B. Martin, A.R. McAfee
McBride Ramsay Thompson Lampman, 1611 Bowen Rd., R.D. McBride, D.P. Ramsay, K.W. Thompson, J.W. Lampman, J.W. Mackie
McEwen & Co., #303, 155 Skinner St., N.P. McEwen, D.D. Windross
McIntosh, D.A., 10 Church St.
Morrison, B.D., 44 Church St.
Mulligan, D.J., 149 Wallace St.
Saunders, Fabris & Murphy, 40 Cavan St., F.H. Saunders, N. Fabris, J.J. Murphy, M.W. McKeachie
Sproule & Assoc., 17 Church St., L.H. Sproule, J.W. Horn, W.R. Mullan, C.V. Allin
Strongitharm, Currie & Co., 94 Commercial St., E. D. Strongitharm, Q.C., W. G. Currie, A.E. Rushworth, L.E. Krog, J.E. Hamilton
Van Alstine, Owen & Cowling, 41 Chapel St., S.S. Van Alstine, G.F. Owen, J.D. Cowling

NELSON, West Kootenay
Enderton, Kent, 606 Front St., S. W. Enderton, B.F. Suffredine, D.B. Burianyk, Susan Wallach
Hamilton, Brown & Co., Box 80, W.R. Brown, P. M. Nasmyth, W.A. Morrow, P.M. Goody
Lanyon, S., 514 Hall St.
McEwan & Harrison, #208, 507 Baker St. (also Trail)
Singleton & Wyllie, 373 Baker St., M.K. Singleton, K.M. Wyllie

NEW WESTMINSTER, Westminster
Anderson, H.A., #322, 604 Columbia St.
Baumgartel, Tretiak & Co., 550 Sixth St., B. W. Baumgartel, R.S. Tretiak, F.M. Kassam, D.J. Gable
Bondoreff & Nottingham, #202, 713 Columbia St., G.J. Bondoreff, A.M. Nottingham
Cassady, Insley, Lauener & Burgess, #330, 552 Seventh St., J. R. Insley, G. P. Cassady, J. P. Lauener, E.A. Burgess, D.D. Mainland, P.C. MacDonald
Chipperfield, J.L., 319 Columbia St.
Cox, W. L., #2, 704 6th St.
Eirikson & Gould, 314 Sixth St., E. Eirikson, G.B. Gould
Ferbey, E.A., #104, 630 Columbia St.
Goodwin & Mark, 217, 713 Columbia St., J.R. Goodwin, D.T. Mark, J. J. Michalski, H.V. Freeman, A. Sweezey
Hogarth, D.A., Q.C., #317, 713 Columbia St.
Hughes, M. J., 550 Sixth St.
Johnson & McLellan, 713 Columbia St., M. Johnson, D.D. McLellan
McQuarrie Hunter, 713 Columbia St. (Box 249, V3L 4Y6), C. D. McQuarrie, Q.C., J. G. Gates, B. J. Pettenuzzo, T. G. Pearce, H. B. Dixon, Marlene H. Scott, W.A.O. McQuarrie, R. Crawford, M.G. Tyler, D.J. Brine, M. Kendler, P.E. Levy, Vikki Bell, C.J. Huggett, Kim Floeck, A.C. McQuarrie, R. Molstad
Milne, Carmichael, Corbould & Todd, 604 Columbia St., D.D.G. Milne, D. W. Carmichael, B. B. Corbould, R.L. Hugh, R.E. Turner, R.S. McLeod
Mollison, J.J., #104, 773 6th St.
Munro, G.R., 711 5th Ave.
Nordman, V., 348 Columbia St.
Nyack & Co., 514 Sixth Ave., K.L. Nyack, D. Persad. Assoc. Counsel: G.B. Walker
Oliver, Hughes, Drabik, 725 Carnarvon

St., M.G. Oliver, R.J. Hughes, R.E. Drabik, L.R.E. Taneda, K.D. Crider
Pilkington, L., 515 4th St.
Rhodes, McShane, 604 Columbia St., G.E. McShane, M.J. Rhodes
Ross, D.M., #105, 765 6th St. (J.A. MacGregor)
Selkirk, R.B., 713 Columbia St.
Somers, G.L.F., #107, 765 6th St.
Thompson & MacDonald, 422 Sixth St., W.C. MacDonald, W. R. Thompson, B.J. Omichinski
Todd, R.T., 604 Columbia St.
Westaway & Edwards, 607 Columbia St., R.J. Westaway, M.J. Edwards
Williams, N. W., 774 Columbia St.

NORTH VANCOUVER, Vancouver
Anderson, Rush & Lockwood, #214, 255 w. 1st St., K.J. Anderson, G.B. Rush, J.E. Lockwood
Ardagh, J.V., #105, 133 w. 15th St.
Biedler, E. E., 1500 Marine Dr.
Bradbrooke, Crawford & Green, #36, 1199 Lynn Valley Rd., W. H. Bradbrooke, J.D. Crawford, G. R. Green, Orla Cousineau
Collier, Hanson & Milos, 133 w. 17th St., D.J. Collier, B.A. Hanson, D.S. Milos
Croft & Finlay, #22, 1501 Lonsdale Ave., J.M. Croft, D.B. Finlay, T.R. Bjurman, R.W. Corbett
Davis & Romilly, 465 Dollarton Hwy., J.E. Davis, V. Romilly
Dulian, A.M., #3, 1348 Marine Ave.
Faminow, P.S., 743 Roslyn Blvd.
Forrest, Gray, Munro & Lewis, 149 e. 15th St., G. N. Munro, R. T. Lewis
Hamilton, R.K., 2008 Fullerton Ave.
Hanrahan, G.T., 5123 Redonda Dr.
Higgins & Pozer, #203, 1401 Lonsdale Ave., B.J. Higgins, J.W.N. Pozer
Hollander, M., #204, 1420 Marine Dr.
Jabour, D.E., 142A w. 15th St.
Jackson, R. F., #200, 132 e. 14th St.
Kroon, E. B., 132 e. 14th St.
MacEwan, W.G., #308, 150 e. 5th St.
Mutrie, D.E., 1067 n. Keith Rd.
Perkins, H.M.F., 986 Beachview Dr.
Perrick, R.W., #480, 145 w. 17th St.
Poyner & Co., 924 w. 16th St., J.M. Poyner, J.H. Bayntun
Ratcliff & Co., 103, 133 w. 15th St., R.A. Kitchen, J.P. Reecke, B.E. Miller, J.A. Ruddy, B.J. Buan, H.A. Slade, R.I. Vaage, Louise Johnston, W.B. Campbell, S. Turner
Riches, C.R., 5189 Madeira Ct.
Shepard, M.W., Waterfront Place
Spurr, Mrs. L. G., 3070 Edgemont Blvd.
Stein, C.G., #305, 140 w. 15th St. (A.J. Lakes)
Taschuk, K.N., 3046 Edgemont Blvd.

OLIVER, Yale
Maier, E., 411 Main St.
Murphy, Jessica M.D., Box 258
Pugh, D.V., Box 8

ONE HUNDRED MILE HOUSE, Cariboo
Messner & Foster, 255 Birch Ave., P.U.D. Messner, W.A. Foster, R.L. Stevens

OSOYOOS, Yale
Cooper, J.R., 8506 Main St.
Holland, W.D., 8318A 76th Ave.

PARKSVILLE, Vancouver Island
Davis, G.W., Box 1600
Donald, K.E., 166 Island Hwy. e.
Fenton, C.E., Box 1840
Ruddell, D. R., 152 Morrison Ave.

PEACHLAND, Yale
Gilmour, Noonan (also Summerland)
Salloum & Co. (also Kelowna)

PENTICTON, Yale
Anderson, D.N., 65 Wade Ave. e.
Boyle & Co., 284 Main St., E. Dewdney, F.A. Lloyd, G.M. Handford, T.R. Brooke, B.M. Preston, J.G. Marshall, D. King, E.R. Hill, Jolene Fletcher. Assoc. Counsel: F.C. Christian
Drossos, N.A., 341 Main St.
Gilchrist, Sinclair & Campbell, 208 Main St., R.W. Gilchrist, G.G. Sinclair, D.J. Campbell
Halbauer, Albas, Keene & Adams, 498 Ellis St., L.D. Halbauer, C.L. Albas, J.A. Keene, B.P. Adams
Kinsman & Co., 166 Main St., P.S. Mott, M.J.R. Ross, M.F. Smith, R. W. Rutherford, R.P. Thompson, R.R. Walsh, J.D. Thomas, G.C. Baldwin, M.F. Davie
McDougall, G.F., #1, 311 Main St.

PITT MEADOWS, Westminster
Routley & Sprague, #202, 12165 Harris Rd., K.T. Routley, T.E. Sprague

PORT ALBERNI, Vancouver Island
Badovinac, Scoffield & Mosley, 3290 3rd Ave., G. Badovinac, R. A. Scoffield, E.J. Mosley, Mary Margetis
Beavan, R., 5053 Johnston St.
Beckingham, W., & Co., 5029 Argyle St., W. Beckingham, R.C. Wallensteen
Pearson, W. S., 4853 Angus St.
Sabean, Stofer & Co., 5169 Argyle St., C.P. Sabean, D.A. Stofer, Barbara Smith, Joan Stirling

PORT COQUITLAM, Westminster
Beavo, W. A., 2288 Elgin Ave.
Garton & Harris, 1536 Prairie Ave., M.M. Garton, W.J. Harris, J.E. Bethel
Kapelus, G.A., 2239 e. McAllister
Lesyk, E., 1, 2628 Shaughnessy St.
Levenson, R.J., 2311 Whyte Ave.
Parks, Feller, etc., #1, 2311 Whyte Ave., Lynda Casey, Rose De Francesco (also Vancouver)
Way, D.R., #302, 566 Lougheed Hwy.

PORT HARDY, Vancouver Island
Iverson & Nowosad, Box 1289, E.L. Iverson, D.J. Nowosad

PORT McNEILL, Vancouver Island
Evans & Dick, 5 & 6, 1547 Beach Ave., J.F.E. Evans, R.W. Dick

PORT MOODY, Westminster
MacLeod, Thorson, 3190 St. John's Rd., J.S.M. MacLeod, Christine Thorson
Marr & Hyde, 2402 St. John's St., R. F. Marr, P. A. Hyde, J.D. Baird

POWELL RIVER, Vancouver
Giroday & Co., 4571 Marine Ave., M.R. Giroday, Shirley E. Giroday
Hayden, F. S., 6239 Walnut St.
Johnston & Garling, 4717 Marine Ave., A.R.M. Johnston, H.D.S. Garling
McKenzie, D.L., 7050 Field St.
Roberts, L.G., 4721 Willingdon Ave.
Stedham, G.M., #4, 4471 Joyce Ave.

PRINCE GEORGE, Cariboo
Aartsen & Morrison, #505, 280 Victoria St., K.C. Aartsen, M. Morrison, Lee Hawkins
Archambault, Harris, #260, 444 Victoria St., D.P. Archambault, J.M. Harris
Bate & Co., 1274 5th Ave., Allan Bate, S. Wood
Bogle & Curtis, #515, 1488 4th Ave., J.H. Bogle, V.R. Curtis, W.J. Farr, R.A. Clarke, F.F. Fatt
Cluff, J.H., Box 2406
Coleman & Co., 1, 1515 2nd Ave., J. T. Coleman, N. R. Nose, E. S. Mieske, D.W. Manders, R.A. Traxler, R.W. Haines, L.R. Brack
Dungate & Co., 1209 4th Ave., J.K. Dungate, D.M. Marcotte, R.G. Nicholson
Gibbs, R.C., #904, 299 Victoria St.
Heather, Sadler, Hughes & Jenkins, #700, 550 Victoria St. (V2L 2K1), J. R. Heather, W. M. Sadler, G. C. Hughes, D.E.M. Jenkins, W.R. Hibbard, D.J. Daley, A.H.G. Johnsen, P.D. Warner, G.C. Starr, J.A. Davis, R.G.P. Brown, J. Christiansen, G.G. Walters, Dick Byl, L.R. Brack
Heinrich, J.H., #507, 1448 4th Ave.
Hogan, P.V., #20, 444 Victoria St.
Hope, Heinrich & Hansen, 1598 6th Ave., H. A. Hope, C. O. Hansen, G. R. Brown, R.B. Macfarlane, E.G. Chamberlist, W. G. Parrett, T. V. Cole, G. C. Coole, A. W. Lightfoot, D. E. Jones, C.E.L. Ongman, P.M. Pakenham, Edna Ritchie, A.R. Elliot, T.P. Matte
Howard-Gibbon, F.A., #600, 550 Victoria St. (H.M. McSheffrey)
Krantz, A.K., 435 Quebec Ave.
Leverman & Watt, #810, 550 Victoria St., J.R. Leverman, A.P. Watt
MacLatchy, E. B., 1370 7th Ave.
Meiklem & Harrison, 608, 1488 4th Ave., I.C. Meiklem, C.E. Harrison
Mooney, J.A., #901, 299 Victoria St.
Prefontaine, M.K., Box 1511, Stn. A
Ramsay & Stelmock, #310, 1488 4th Ave., D. Ramsay, Donna Stelmock
Smith, D., 1378 5th Ave.
Ter Heide, M.J., #901, 299 Victoria St.
Welwood, L.K., #502, 550 Victoria Ave. (T.B. Townrow)
Wilbur, Madill & McDonald, #200, 1110 6th Ave., D.S. Wilbur, R.W. Madill, N.G. McDonald
Wilson, King & Co., 299 Victoria St., H. B. King, Q.C., G. W. Baldwin, Q.C., R.M. Dick, J. H. Outhet, D.B. McGaughey, C.T.F. Hughes, W. J. Duncan, D.V. Wade, R.J. Stewart, M.J. Hargreaves, F.W. Hansford, W.B. Donn, J.F. Galati, D.S. Mulroney, Diane Stuart

PRINCE RUPERT, Prince Rupert
Clendening, Johnston & Punnett, #7, 222 Third Ave. w., S.T. Clendening, P.M. Johnston, R.D. Punnett, N.A. Campbell
Errico, Silversides, Wilson, Mars & Seidemann, 330 Second Ave. w., R. T. Errico, D. A. Silversides, A.F. Wilson, D.J. Mars, H.J. Seidemann III, G.P. Gould, R.A. Currie, Kristina Robinson
Johnstone & Co., 325 4th Ave. e., B.W. Johnstone, M.J. Shaw
Sestak & Smith, 342 Third Ave. w., D.J. Sestak, B.R. Smith

PRINCETON, Yale
Turner, Stanley G., Box 568

QUALICUM BEACH, Vancouver Island
Hossack, J.A., 129 w. 2nd Ave.
Poole, W. N., Box 158

QUEEN CHARLOTTE CITY, Prince Rupert
Sutton, R.J., Box 520

QUESNEL, Cariboo
Bate & Co., 242 Reid St., P. Gulbransen (also Prince George)
Coffey & Quinn, 164 Front St., E.A. Coffey, G.C. Quinn
Main, D.A., 897 Moffat St.
Quinn, G.C., 2020 Felspar Ave.
Shkuratoff, Pearce & Murray, 531 Reid St., A. M. Shkuratoff, M. L. Pearce, G.D. Murray, T.L.S. Landry

REVELSTOKE, Yale
Bernacki, S.G., Box 2699
Collicutt, D.B., Box 2160
Lavallee, B.C., 300 1st St. w.
Lundberg, R.A., Box 2490
Stiell, Jennifer, #201, 101 1st St. e.

RICHMOND, Vancouver
Bardos, M.A., #2, 8311 Steveston Hwy.
Bergstrom, W. L., 6411 Buswell St.

Brodie, M.D., 8055 Anderson Rd.
Brown, A.D.E., #230, 8136 Park Rd.
Carvalho, V.N.J., 10895 Springmont Gate
Cohen, Frost & Quon, #204, 4940 No. 3 Rd., G.M. Cohen, M.S. Frost, J.W. Quon
Comeau, G., 8331 River Rd.
Crane, Paterson, Graves, #205, 8171 Park Rd., D.G. Crane, D.T. Paterson, D.B. Graves
Dayan, Levitt & Van Ochten, #200, 8136 Park Rd., G.C. Dayan, M.A. Levitt, F.K. Van Ochten
DeCario & Co., 8040 Cook Rd., G.J. DeCario
Ewachniuk, A.T., 8331 River Rd.
Forbes, Nielsen, Lambert, MacCallum, #207, 7031 Westminster Hwy., V6X 1A3, D.H. Forbes, A. O. Nielsen, M.E.J. Lambert, A.S. MacCallum, C.J. McIntyre, F.T. Williamson, J.St.J.F. Shotton
Friesen & Epp, #220, 8120 Granville St. (also Vancouver)
Graham, D.J.T., #303, 6411 Buswell Rd. (W.H. Mackie)
Gray, Green, Hoodekoff & Pocock, #300, 8055 Anderson Rd., C. B. Gray, A. M. Green, B. Hoodekoff, C.L. Pocock
Holman, S.J., 6731 No. 5 Rd.
Hughes, W.G., #217, 8055 Anderson Rd.
Johnstone & Co., 8331 Ackroyd St., W.C. Johnstone, P.W. Watson
Kahn, Zack, Hammerberg & Ehrlich, #340, 8120 Granville Ave., L.A. Kahn, D.A. Zack, S. Hammerberg, P.S. Ehrlich
Lawson & Krag, 6860 No. 3 Rd., P.G. Lawson, K.B. Krag
Lee, G. N., 8055 Anderson Rd.
Moseley, Campbell, Froh & May, 204, 6055 No. 3 Rd., L.A.T. Moseley, W. A. Campbell, R.P. Froh, R.A. May, E.J. Rice, R.A. Hamilton, F.E. Bronson, Jr., R.A. Doran, T.C. Vos
Mulholland, Webster & Co., 211, 8171 Park Rd., W. H. Mulholland, R.B. Webster, M.B. Mulholland, J. Fairburn
Municipal Solicitors: 6911 No. 3 Rd., T.D. Nicholls, P.E. Kendrick, R.F. Schultz
Sigurgeirson, W.J., 11200 4th Ave.
Simmonds, Pryke, Leathley & Wright, #4, 8111 Anderson Rd., R.A. Simmonds, F.R.M. Pryke, J.L. Leathley, K.B. Panton, R.H. Wright, G.P.G. Johnsen, A.D.C. Ross, K.A. Jones
Spry & Hawkins, 6411 Buswell St., F. R. Spry, G. J. Hawkins
Stark, Christian & Henderson, #211, 4800 No. 3 Rd., M.N. Stark, J.F. Christian, R.S. Henderson, D.N. Paul, J.B. Donovan, B.G. Livingston
Tonstad & Eadie, 204, 10151 No. 3 Rd., M.P. Tonstad, F.R. Eadie, J.D.G. Buchan
Walker & McTavish, 6531 Buswell St., I.F. McTavish, D.L. Takahashi

ROSSLAND, West Kootenay
Dahlstrom, A.R., Box 699

RUTLAND, Yale
McAfee, Harder & Co., 200, 270 Hwy. 33 w., R.J. Pushor, M.W. Baron (also Kelowna)

SAANICHTON, Victoria
Griffiths, J.R., 8129 Lochside Dr.

SALMON ARM, Yale
Robertson & Brooke, 370 Front St. n.e., P.G. Robertson, G.M. Brooke, R.D. McManus, L.R. Jackson
Scharf, A. G., Box 2128
Sivertz, Brecknell & Kiehlbauch, Box 190, H. G. Sivertz, E. R. Brecknell, L.D. Kiehlbauch
Wynne & Bartlett, Box 910, G. N. Wynne, H. R. Bartlett

SARDIS, Westminster
Nickel, W.J., Box 310

SECHELT, Vancouver
Gordon, C.H.J., Box 130 (R.C. Bledsoe)

SICAMOUS, Cariboo
Hillier, H.L., Box 422

SIDNEY, Vancouver Island
Finall, Alice, #103, 9790 2nd St.
Henley, Robertson & Walden, #201, 2377 Bevan Ave., D.R. Henley, J.W. Robertson, M.A. Walden
McKimm, Lott & deRosenroll, #201, 9830 Fourth St., G.F. McKimm, N.W. Lott, M.A. deRosenroll, C.S. Lott, B.W. Scott-Montcrief
Woods, W., 9771 4th St.

SKIDEGATE, Prince Rupert
Linde, W.C.

SMITHERS, Prince Rupert
Buri, Milne & Co., Box 847, T.R. Buri, J.R. Milne, B.A. Bruser
Perry & Co., Box 790, L.W. Perry, J.L. Perry
Toews, Greene & Takahashi, #200, 3790 Alfred St., G.R. Toews, M. Takahashi, G. Greene

SOOKE, Vancouver Island
Dinning & Vallance, 6689 Sooke Rd. (also Victoria)
Hallgren, M.W., 6605 Sooke Rd.
McIntyre, J.H., 6642 Sooke Rd.

SPARWOOD, E. Kootenay
Hislop, Lazenby & Co. (also Cranbrook)
Majic, Patel & Leffler, Box 1618 (also Fernie)

SQUAMISH, Vancouver
Paul & Race, Box 1850, J.H.W. Paul, D.A. Race
Wilson, V.D.R., Box 1910

SUMMERLAND, Yale
Gilmour, Noonan & Co., Box 520, W.A. Gilmour, R.B. Noonan, Nina Green

SURREY, Westminster
Brawn & Randall, #101, 17702 56th St., D.H. Brawn, J.L. Randall
Campbell, J.C., #3, 10715 135A St.
David, S.S., #305, 10252 135th St.
Davidson, J.L., 10715 135A St.
Elchuk, K.G., 1331 129A St.
Gatley & Assoc., 9333 120A St., D.R. Gatley, S.A. Bowers, J. Dearman, V.M. Fisher
Hamilton, Duncan & Armstrong, 13639 108th Ave., B.C. Duncan, T.C. Armstrong, J.B. Stewart. Assoc.: R.G. Walkem
Harris, Stuart & Tomyn, 8620 120th St., D.G. Harris, L.M. Stuart, H.F. Tomyn
Howden, G. A., 5720 176A St.
Jacobs, R.W., 13553 105th Ave.
Joe, MacDonald, Watchorn & McLellan, 310, 15225 104 Ave., Barry Joe, W.G. MacDonald, A.W. Watchorn, L.I. McLellan
Kaine, G.B., #201, 13638 Grosvenor Rd.
Kelso, J., 1256 Guilford Town Centre
Lawrenson, L.M., 8865 Roslin Rd.
MacMillan & McKinnon, 17679 57th Ave., J. L. MacMillan, R. A. McKinnon, A.H. Blackmore
Mark & Rehnby, 15344 Fraser Hwy., E.G. Mark, K. Rehnby
McAndrew, A.L., 13692 72nd Ave.
McQuarrie, Hunter & Co., 10619 King George VI Hwy. (also New Westminster)
Mosher & Treleaven, 13762 72nd Ave., P. F. Mosher, W. J. Treleaven
Newton, D.W., #234, 7449 140th St.
Norquist, Shantz, etc., #200, 10330 152nd St. (also Maple Ridge)
Pelzman, P.B., 305 Ranmore Cres.
Peterson, Stark & Fowler, 10451A e. Whalley Ring Rd., D.N. MacKinnon (also Vancouver)
Rhodes, R.E., #201, 13638 Grosvenor Rd.
Richards, J., 14819 108th Ave.
Ross, R.W., #204, 7188 King George VI Hwy.
Roy & Maier, #205, 13541 102nd Ave., G.J. Roy, H.H. Maier
Scott & Smith, 5752 176th St., G.D. Scott, G.R. Smith, J.J. Tucker
Skands, E.H., 10246B 152nd St.
Soronow & Soronow, #305, 10252 135th St., B.I. Soronow, M. Soronow
Stilling & Moss, 201, 7188 King George VI Hwy., W.E. Stilling, K.L. Moss
Virani, Z.K.N., 10447 137th St. (J.A. Jaffer)
Worthington & Simm, 13655 104th Ave., D.L. Worthington, D.C.E. Simm, D.R. Gardner

TERRACE, Prince Rupert
Crampton & Brown, #3, 4623 Park Ave., G. L. Crampton, D. Brown, Claire F. Guest
Pratt, C.C., 4509 Lakelse Ave.
Robertson & Co., #201, 4630 Lazelle Ave., M.R. Robertson, D.A. Halfyard, J.R. Arndt
Talstra & Co., 4722 Lakelse Ave., J.J. Talstra, E. De Walle, D. Warner

TRAIL, W. Kootenay
Barlow & Sperry, 1247 Cedar Ave., M.C.W. Barlow, D.L. Sperry. Assoc.: W.J.S. Bell
Fabbro, R. G., 1460 Bay Ave.
Geronazzo & Thompson, 1199 Cedar Ave., M.P. Geronazzo, T.H. Thompson
McEwan Harrison & Co., 1432 Bay St., T.M. McEwan, G.L. Harrison, M.T. Kew

VANCOUVER, Vancouver
Achtem, A.J., #1205, 701 w. Georgia St.
Adams, B.R., #102, 1005 w. Georgia St.
Adelaar, Shapiro, Assoc., 520 Hornby St., J.A. Adelaar, M.H. Shapiro
Ainsworth & Co., Box 10022, 700 w. Georgia St., A. H. Ainsworth, W. S. Henson, D. G. Purvis, P. Williams, J. Yazdi. Assoc. Counsel: Senator Jack Austin
Alexander, Guest, Holburn & Beaudin, 700 w. Georgia St., Box 10057 (V7Y 1B8), E.A. Alexander, Q.C., G.T. Guest, W.M. Holburn, E.C. Beaudin, G.R. Whitelaw, M.P. Ragona, F.S. Lang, J.G. Sanderson, I.D. Robertson, L.J. Gwozd, T.A. Roper, D.A. Gooderham, J.A. Dowler, M.J. Weiler, M.C. Scholz, R.G. Payne, A.H. Merkley, L.C. Boulton, Patricia J. Armstrong, J.B. Hall, S.F. Lee
Alexander, W.J., 700 w. Georgia St.
Allan & Lougheed, #1200, 777 Hornby St., D.V. Allan, W.E. Lougheed, D.G. Nairne, D.R. Burton, A.A. Leir, G.J. Fretwell
Allard & Co., #600, 815 Hornby St., P.A. Allard, M.S. Thompson, M.E. Brown
Allen, W.G., #840, 770 Hornby St.
Alliston, S.R.D., 4 Gaolers Mews
Altman & Co., #1770, 700 w. Georgia St., H. Altman, Q.C., J. M. Altman, M. Altman
Ames, J.M., 1030 w. Georgia St.
Anderegg, R.V., 505 Burrard St.
Anderson, G.R., 405, 550 Burrard St.
Anderton, J.T., 1393 Commercial Dr. (M.E. Anderson)
Andree, A.S., #1157, 409 Granville St.
Angelomatis, G.P., #400, 68 Water St.
Annable, G.M., #915, 525 Seymour St. (J.P. Sanders)

Armstrong, G.A., Box 12508, 1066 w. Hastings St.

Armstrong, W.F., #102, 2211 Wall St.

Assaly & MacPhail, 5862 Cambie St., L.B. Assaly, D.R. MacPhail

Atkins, Evans, Munroe & Baillie, #2850, 555 w. Hastings St., R.L. Atkins, H.A. Evans, R.N. Munroe, G.C.B. Baillie

Atkinson, B.K., 2876 w. 49th Ave.

Atmore, W.M., #603, 1260 Nelson St.

Au, K.T., 193 e. Hastings St.

Auxier, N.J., #301, 1 Alexander St.

Aydin, K.T., #305, 510 w. Hastings St.

Baigent & Jackson, #410, 198 w. Hastings St., J. Baigent, Marguerite Jackson, W. Rilkoff, D. Blair, A. Pape, J. Rogers

Baker & Young, #1200, 701 w. Georgia St., J.B. Baker, R.E. Young

Ballem, P.C., 1243 Hornby St. (Anne Adrian)

Banno & Mitchell, #1106, 1166 Alberni St., D.Y. Banno, G.K. Mitchell

Barbeau, McKercher, Collingwood & Hanna, 1066 w. Hastings St. (V6E 3X1), J. Barbeau, J.S. McKercher, T.A. Collingwood, K.G. Hanna, G. Sutherland, K.G. Hanna, T.D. Devitt, G.H. Ellis, M.F. Welters, C.S. Bird, C.V. Forth, G.G. Briant, D.J. Weaver, G.F. Bartels, C.D. Thomas, R. Wahl, M.R. Reeves, C. Falk, J. Wagner, B.D. Galbraith, G.H. Scott

Barrett & Oddy, 789 w. Pender St., J.L. Barrett, N.R. Oddy

Barrigar & Oyen, #280, 505 Burrard St., R.H. Barrigar, G.O.S. Oyen, L.A. Turlock, Blake Wiggs

Batist, D.G., 807 Drake St.

Beadle, L.W., #300, 2025 w. 42nd Ave.

Beaty, R.J., 2831 w. 22nd Ave.

Beaumont, G.M., #1700, 1066 w. Hastings St.

Beck, Dorothy, #918, 925 w. Georgia St.

Beck, Robinson & Co., 135 e. 8th Ave., W.P. Beck, R.C. Robinson, M.R. Elson, A.H. Mohamedali

Behrens, Stabler & McAfee, #1120, 675 Howe St., G. Behrens, P.J. Stabler, D.R. McAfee

Bellows, R.W., 1151 w. 8th Ave.

Bennett, C.F., 4207 Dunbar St.

Berger, Syberg-Olsen, #702, 1055 w. Georgia St., P.G. Berger, E. Syberg-Olsen, J.F. Poulsen, S.J. Lein

Bhuler, A.K., #203, 190 e. 48th Ave.

Bieg, P.P., #301, 455 Granville St.

Birnie, Sturrock & Bowden, #510, 1030 w. Georgia St., D.A.G. Birnie, C.C. Sturrock, G.T.W. Bowden, R.P. Reble, J.T.K. Fraser

Bisaro & Pinsky, #206, 131 Water St., G.L. Bisaro, B.I. Pinsky

Bitney, G.J., #404, 675 w. Hastings St.

Blaxland, M.T.L., #214, 131 Water St.

Boggild, K.E., #20, 1601 Comox St.

Bonner & Fouks, #2000, 1055 w. Georgia St., R.W. Bonner, Q.C., A. Fouks, Q.C.

Bonner & McNair, #1734, 1055 Dunsmuir St., R.Y. Bonner, R.B. McNair

Booth, A.R., #6, 5729 West Blvd.

Borsa, Leona, #405, 535 w. Georgia St.

Bose, D.D., #218, 2416 w. 3rd Ave.

Boucher, Shrimpton & Wlodyka, 1325 Kingsway, J.M. Boucher, D.A. Shrimpton, A.Z. Wlodyka

Boughton & Co., 16th fl., 1100 Melville St. (V6E 4B4), L.R. Peterson, Q.C., A.B. Ferris, Q.C., D. R. Dunfee, Cyril White, Q.C., D.L. Vaughan, Q.C., R.R. Wollen, W.B. McAllister, R.K. Yardley, G.V. Anderson, A.C. Schultz, C.D. MacKinnon, K.J. Learn, W.D. MacRae, G.E.H. Cadman, J.C.R. Cumming, D.S. Pedlow, Nicole J. Garson, G.A. Fulton, B.E. Morley, Sharon E. White. Counsel: J.E. Boughton, Q.C.

Bourne, Lyall, Davenport & Herbert, #1180, 505 Burrard St. (V7X 1B8) after Apr. 1, '82: #3000, 595 Burrard St., V7X 1H3, G.C. Lyall, D.C. Davenport, F.H. Herbert, Q.C., D.H. Risk, W.A. Randall, G.M. Catherwood, R.H. Watts, A.M. Mersey, N.K. Trerise, P.C. Marshall, R.J. McClellan, L.C. Webber, J.B. Myers. Counsel: J.A. Bourne, Q.C.

Boyle, T.W., 1350 e. 8th Ave.

Boytinck, W.J.W., #1490, 1055 w. Hastings St.

Braidwood, Nuttall, MacKenzie, Brewer, Greyell & Co., #1500, 510 w. Hastings St. (V6B 1M6), T. R. Braidwood, Q.C., G.C. MacKenzie, D.S.C. Nuttall, R.W. Brewer, B. M. Greyell, G.A. Goyer, R. W. Stevenson, R.R. Sugden, K.F. Warner, C.V. Winch, E.D. Crossin, J.S. Harvey, G.S. Funt, S.E. Wood, W.E. Knutson, R.E. Groves, D.G. Seaton, M. Patricia Gallivan, R.D. Husdon, R.E. Breivik. Counsel: Hon. A.E. Branca, Q.C.

Brail, R.A., 52 Powell St.

Brawner & Phillips, 700 w. Georgia St., Box 10091, K.L. Brawner, G.J. Phillips

Brennan, Jarvis & Co., #802, 535 Thurlow St., R.J. Brennan, K.C. Jarvis, J.R. Gerbrandt, J.E. Whiteley

Brenner, D.I., #202, 1107 Seymour St. (H.A. Barends)

Bridal, J.F.C., 12 Gaolers Mews

Brown, Benson & Fiddes, #1450, 701 w. Georgia St., E. Brown, K.R. Benson, J.C. Fiddes, R.A. Deering, T.J. Corbett

Brown & Burns, 982 w. 21st Ave., P.W. Brown, T.E. Burns

Brown, R.A., #210, 1665 w. Broadway

Bruk, J., #330, 355 Burrard St.

Buell Ellis, #770, 777 Hornby St., J.W. Seddon, H.M. Suiker, E.P.J. Chibber, M.D. Sawyer, R. W. Jenkins, T.I. Mitha, J.R. Pollard, M.J. Skapski

Bull, Housser & Tupper, Box 11130, Royal Centre (V6E 3R3), D. Tupper, J.W. Walsh, I.B. Quinn, D.B. Smith, H.R. Bowering, H.C. Murray, H. C. Cameron, H.A. Hollinrake, F. Low-Beer, E. F. Horsey, W.C. Bice, B. O'N. Dryvynsyde, J.T. Lau, J.D.L. Morrison, R. J. Orr, A. K. MacKinnon, D. A. Webster, W. G. Gooderham, G.A. Urquhart, P.B. Webber, J. A. Hargrave, R. E. P. Maurice, B. Shapiro, M.C. Fairweather, M.D.B. Paine, R.S. Angus, N.E. Daugulis, M.E. Boyd, R.B. Wallace, J.M. MacKenzie, J.S. Sigurdson, M.A. Fitch, D.J. Haslam, M.M. Koenigsberg, D.G. Morrison, G.K. Weaver, J.G. Dives, R.W. Hunter, J.W. Stout, J.F. Koenig, W.J. McFetridge, Marilynn Nash, C.D. Howe, R. Elizabeth Friedman, Lynn Panar, L.G. Schafer, D.B. Wende, J.C. Grauer, J.S. Haythorne, Holly Robertson, C.G. Speakman, S.B. Hankinson, Ann Gourley, Susan Hamilton. Assoc. Counsel: C.C.I. Merritt, Q.C., J. Guy

Burnet & Fenton, #463, 1155 w. Georgia St., R.J. Fenton, K.A. Price, M.F.J. Smith, J. Klassen

Bush, R.W., 4457 w. 13th Ave.

Cameron, E.A., #1102, 207 w. Hastings St.

Campbell, A.P.B., 3841 w. 22nd Ave.

Campbell, R.S., #2170, 1066 w. Hastings St.

Campbell, T.J., Q.C., 543 Granville St.

Campney & Murphy, Box 49190, 595 Burrard St., V7X 1K9, W.R. Mead, W.D.C. Tuck, J.B. Watson, A.F. Campney, D.W.H. Creighton, J.S. Clyne, E.G.D. Cant, M. M. Soule, R.I.A. Smith, M.F.M. Hermann, David Roberts, Boon Siong Lee, J.J.B. Gilliland, D. J. McKinlay, Jr., E.J. Harris, R.F. Hungerford, K.A. Cameron, P.D. Lowry, J.D. Kinzie, L. W. Goddard, D. I. Knowles, D. Zacks, D. D. Kermode, H. Wiebach, Marianne Shannon, B.R. Bronk, R.J. MacRae, R.D. Standerwick, M.A. Clemens, Wendy D. Piggott, P.A. Csiszar, G.W. Brooke-Taylor, T.J. Nichols, R.A. Francis, J.N. Arnold, Bruce Tattrie, C.K. Haines, John Marquardt, Wendy J. Devine, Howie Caldwell, F. Tam

Canadian National Railway, Regional Legal Dept., #217, 1150 Station St.

Canadian Pacific Ltd., Regional Legal Dept., #360, 601 w. Cordova St.

Candido, L.M., #1190, 700 w. Georgia St.

Carr, J.A., 535 w. Georgia St.

Carter, Joan, J., #1519, 925 w. Georgia St.

Cashman, H.L., 640 w. Broadway

Chamberlain & Guinn, #500, 190 Alexander St., S.R. Chamberlain, W.F. Guinn

Chambers & Co., 1313 w. Pender St., M. Chambers

Chan, M. Y., 2nd fl., 178 e. Pender St.

Chan, Martin & Lerch, #750, 999 w. Broadway, R. Chan, G.K. Martin, B.A. Lercher

Chapman & Co., #1, 2140 w. 41st Ave., G.G. Chapman, P.A. Chapman

Charland, W.R.G., 131 Water St.

Chee, R.T.T., #710, 650 w. Georgia St.

Chen, R.P., #202, 475 Main St.

Chertkow, D.A., 470 Granville St.

Christie & Murphy, Box 11147, 1055 w. Georgia St., D.E. Christie, T.E.G. Murphy

City Law Dept., 453 w. 12th Ave., J.L. Mulberry, T. R. Bland, R. G. Jackson, J.N. Stubbs, P.J.V. Gilbert, Mrs. Maureen Ryan, B.J. Porter, D.C. Creighton

Clare, J., #1225, 200 Granville St.

Clark, Wilson, #1700, 750 w. Pender St (V6C 2B8), D.M. Clark, Q.C., G.W Young, W.J. Esselmont, O.C. Dolan K.M. Noble, B.C. Irwin, J. M. Halley D.W. Buchanan, D.J. Mullan, F.W Shandro, W.G. Nugent, J.F. Dixon, R.S Wells, D.W. Donohoe, R.R.J. Mueller C.H. Fultz, F.R. Dorchester, A.N. Robertson, P.J. MacAulay, P.N. Grant, P.S Cowan, D.J. Wedge, K.G. Teskey, R.P Hamilton, Sam Szajman, B.D. Woolley K.G. Downing, Judith B. Downes, Alexander Petrenko, R.W. Reid, C.M. Dean D.K. Fitzpatrick, W.D. Holder, R.A. Nieuwenburg, D.J. Rowntree, Jill M. Callan D.A. Coulson, W.C. Helgason, Carol A Lee

Clarke, A.T., #950, 505 Burrard St.

Clarke, Covell & Banks, 1109 Robson St J.B. Clarke, R.D. Covell, J.D. Banks

Clarke & McRae, 1045 Howe St., J.F Clarke, A.D. McRae

Cofman, M.E., #2000, 650 w. Georgia St.

Coleman, J.M.B., 8 Gaolers Mews

Comparelli, D.E., #704, 510 w. Hasting St.

Conrad, J.M., #403, 1431 Howe St.

Constantini, A.G., 409 Granville St. (P.D Taberner, C.M. Trower)

Cook, N.B., 999 w. Hastings St.

Corrigan, Bernardino & Co., #220, 331 Kingsway, D.R. Corrigan, C.M. Bernardino, C.D. Baker, K.H. Dorman

Cove, Jesse, 923 Denman St. (V6G 2L9)

Cowan & Co., 475 Howe St., R.S. Thorpe D.F. MacDonald

Craig, J.A., #720, 1441 Creekside Dr.

Cram, J.N., #301, 1 Alexander St.

Cramer, S.R., #108, 12 Water St. (H.K Cramer)

Cranston, G.C., 234 Abbott St.
Crosby, H., 5316 Victoria Ave. (G.H. Dowding)
Cumming, Richards, Underhill, Fraser, Skillings, #600, 900 w. Hastings St. (V6C 1G1), G.S. Cumming, Q.C., P.C.G. Richards, W.R.D. Underhill, B.F. Fraser, M.L. Leckie, A.D.P. MacAdams, K.H. Priebe, M.A. Cummings, T.A. Dunn, B.M. Joyce, J.E. Rogers, C.A. Yip, P.T. McGivern, S.O. Youngman. Assoc. Counsel: R.J.G. Richards, R.K. Baker, Q.C. (also Victoria)
Dafoe, P.L., 475 Howe St.
Dallas, Kinney & Co., 852 Seymour St., G.D. Dallas, E.P. Kinney, V.J. LeBlanc
Danderfer, K.J., #1220, 609 Granville St.
Daniells & Herman, #601, 207 w. Hastings St., S.C.M. Daniells, R.S. Herman
Davidson, D.M. & Co., #101, 2182 W. 12th Ave. (G.Y. Davidson, L.H. McInnes)
Davies, R.K., 1154 Robson St.
Davis, A.R., 1754 w. 68th Ave.
Davis & Co., 1030 w. Georgia St. (V6E 3C2), A.J.F. Johnson, Q.C., David Hossie, H.C. Millham, G.K. Fujisawa, D.W. Shaw, A.W. Sutherland, D.H.C. Paterson, J.R. MacKay, W.J. Wright, D.M. Johnston, S.R. Basford, P.C., Q.C., J. Pearson, A.C. Robertson, P.W. Bogardus, P.J. Furlong, J.M. Pelrine, R.T. Banno, I.G. Nathanson, J.M.D. Tootill, R.E. Marriott, M.R.V. Storrow, P. J. Gordon, Larry Page, R.B.D. Swift, R.K. McLeod, D.R. Clark, G.D. Burnyeat, W. Schwegler, Jacqueline A. Kelly, R. Ellison, D.C. Morley, V. Morgan, R.R. Senft, Anne M. Stewart, M.P. Carroll, R.K. Ward, J.G. Fitzpatrick, P.C. Lee, D.G. Sanderson, Joan I. McEwen, J.J.L. Hunter, P.G. Morgan, W.H. Downs, J.I. McLean, S.R. Schachter, Wendy G. Baker, F.S. Borowicz, P.A. Shandro, R.A. Snow, L.F. Harvey, P.R. Albi, S.B. Morrow, J.I. Reynolds, Linda Parsons, D.W. Cooper, K.L.H. Embree, E.M. Myers, Janine L. Thomas, R.T. Groves, Beverley Silver-Corber, Catherine C. Galloway, Susan B. Merrill, S.G. Thompson. Assoc. Counsel: C.W. Brazier, Q.C., A.T.R. Campbell, Q.C., A.W. Fisher, Q.C., E.S. Thorne
Deane, Miss W., 2788 w. 1st Ave.
DeBou & Co., #400, 1152 Mainland St., R.G. DeBou, L.E. Maerov, H.C. Wood, S.A. Schwartz, N. Wexler
DeMeulemeester, A.J., #501, 68 Water St.
Dent & Crestani, #1, 2519 e. Hastings St., R. Dent, F.S. Crestani
Dent, D.E., 4467 w. 11th Ave.
Derpak, White & Co., 1933 w. Broadway, K.W. Derpak, D.S. White, P.R. Kerr
Deverell, Harrop & Co., Two Goalers Mews, W.H. Deverell, J.F. Harrop, J. Wood, W. R. Powell, D.W. Gibbons, J.F.R. Chouinard, R.J. Charlton, P.F. Buxton
Dharney, B.K., 17th fl., 100 w. Pender St.
Dickson, G.B., #112, 736 Granville St.
Dillon, J.R., Box 10091, 700 w. Georgia St.
Dobbin & Assoc., 510 w. Hastings St., J.W. Dobbin, N.S. Ganapathi
Doolan, K.J., 807 Drake St.
Dosanjh & Pirani, #202, 5887 Victoria Dr., U.D. Dosanjh, M.M. Pirani
Douglas, Symes & Brissenden, 409 Granville St. (V6C 1V1), P.R. Brissenden, Q.C., R.A.C. Douglas, R.D. Plommer, Q.C., W.G. Essex, D.H. Bell-Irving, K.B. Carruthers, W.S. Armstrong, W.R. Adamson, N.H. Scherf, J.W. Elwick, P.E. Armstrong, A.K. Wooster, M.G. King, E.A. Bence, D.H. Clarke, C.G. Weiler, D. Martin, R.B. Carrothers, M.P. Tindle, M.V. Vidal-Ribas, J.J. Casey, G.B. MacRae
Doust & Smith, 1045 Howe St., L.T. Doust, K.J. Smith, P.R. Lawrence, W.B. Smart, A.F. Cullen, C.M. Powell
Draeseke, G.L., 658 Leg in Boot Sq.
Drost, I.L., Box 10030, Pacific Centre
Du Moulin, Black, #1004, 595 Howe St., M.L. Du Moulin, W.D. Black, G.R. Brazier, J.E. Hall, S.H. Berner, K.W. Ball, D.A. Schwartz, Cheri Nataros
Dunn, R.M., 123 Main St.
Easton, C.F., 2676 w. 13th Ave.
Eastwood & Co., #306, 540 Burrard St., M.C. Eastwood, H.W. Jones, G.J. Bennett
Eberhardt, Caplan, LaCroix & Silverman, #900, 409 Granville St., K.C. Eberhardt, A.R. Caplan, D.C. LaCroix, A.H. Silverman, L.S. Blaschuk
Eckardt, L.S., #201, 8041 Granville St.
Edwards, Kenny & Bray, 1030 w. Georgia St., J.T. Edwards, B.D. Kenny, C.O.D. Branson, S.D. Gill, R.G. Ward, A.M. Ross, G. Bird, T.G. Stewart, G.A. Letcher, D.P. Bellwood, D.B. McLean, B.G. McLean, J.D. McInnis, Rosalind Foucault, Kari Boyle
Edwards & Martin, #315, 890 w. Pender St., J.P.L. Edwards, J.T. Martin
Egolf, Anas & Associates, #103, 2590 Granville St., G. Egolf, A. J. Anas
Elias, Raynier, Pinsky, 885 Dunsmuir St., V.J. Elias, J. Raynier, H. Pinsky
Ellis, W.E., #201, 1665 w. Broadway
Ellis, Roadburg, #300, 1111 w. Georgia St., R.J. Ellis, E.M. Roadburg
Evans, Cantillon & Goldstein, #210, 717 w. Pender St., G.M. Evans, P.R. Cantillon, G.G. Goldstein, R.J. Ludgate, G.B. Starr
Fader, S.A., #208, 1929 w. 3rd Ave.
Falconer, R.J., Box 10281, 700 w. Georgia St.
Fan, Harry & Co., 279 e. Pender St. (A.D. Baria)
Farber & Folk, #1245, 700 w. Georgia St., A.E. Farber, Felicia S. Folk
Farris, H.D., 200 Granville St.
Farris, K.B., #1015, 837 w. Hastings St.
Farris, Vaughan, Wills & Murphy, Box 10026, Pacific Centre, 700 w. Georgia St. (V7Y 1B3), C.F. Murphy, B.S. Evans, A.D. Pool, P.W. Butler, J.M. Giles, J.F. Richardson, G.P. Bancroft, R.C. Holmes, A.K. Mitchell, Elizabeth Harrison, A.J. Hamilton, G.K. Macintosh, J.J. Swift, H.M. Matthews, D.F. Tysoe, D.F. Jackie, B.T. Gibson, H.D. Dodd, R.H. MacKay-Dunn, J.A. Angus, D.B. Pope, Karen Davis, P.S. Richardson, D. Lunny, S.S. Dunlop
Fayers & Co., 496 w. 40th Ave., K. Fayers, B. Fayers
Fedyk, J.J., #920, 777 Hornby St.
Fee, T.P., #1001, 470 Granville St.
Field & Uzelac, #1103, 805 w. Broadway, A.H. Field, M. Uzelac
Fisher, H.E.B., 736 Granville St.
Flader, Phelps & Paczkowski, #512, 2525 Willow St., L.C. Flader, D.B. Phelps, N. Paczkowski
Fogal, C.C., #401, 207 w. Hastings St.
Forsyth, R.B., #103, 2590 Granville St.
Fox & Morgan, #1405, 1166 Alberni St., R.G. Fox, J.G. Morgan, M.J. Slater, K.G. Phillips
Fraser & Co., #900, 777 Hornby St., D.K. Fraser, M.J. Steven, R.D. Rabson, G.W. Hardy
Fraser Hyndman, Box 49360, #3200, 1055 Dunsmuir St. (V7X 1P2), P.D.K. Fraser, M.N. Gifford, W. A. Ferguson, J.H.R. Robertson, M. D. Akerly, B.D. Robson, A.R. Okazaki, A.B. Hudson, J. Webster, W.G. Robinson, H.C.R. Clark, A.J. Coombe, D.C. Quinlan, Eva-Lisa Helin, P.S. Hyndman
Fraser & Leask, #444, 601 w. Cordova St., P. Fraser, P. Leask, F.E. Howard
Fratkin, R.D., #500, 68 Water St.
Freeman & Co., 16th fl., 1030 w. Georgia St. (V6E 3C4), H. Freeman, D.A. Freeman, Q.C., D.L. Silvers, M. Koffman, D. Huberman, H. M. Loomer, L.S. Bobroff, H.M. Karby, Sandra D. Sutherland, H. Shapray, C.D. Goddard, M.M. Kalef, H.S. Silber, L. Getz, J.S. Mackoff, Carol A. Kerfoot, E.N. Kornfeld, B.W. Goldberg, Sunny Rothschild, D. Pangman, Elizabeth Nicholls, M.H. Altman, S. Wong, M.H. Smith, G.S. Segal
Friesen & Epp, #4, 3103 Kingsway, E. Friesen, H.B. Epp
French, F.S., #201, 2250 Commercial Dr.
Frith, H.G.N., 198 w. Hastings St.
Fung, T., Jr., #315, 409 Granville St.
Gaff, K. E. G., #208, 409 Granville St.
Gagnon, D.A., #315, 409 Granville St.
Gallagher, T.E., #315, 409 Granville St.
Gamiet, Z., #215, 1956 w. Broadway
Gardner, Mrs. E.M., #305, 207 w. Hastings St.
Gardner & Assoc., 831 Helmcken St., W. Moore, R.C. Gardner, G.S. Snarch, H.R. Anderson
Gargrave, A.J., #1770, 700 w. Georgia St.
Gedye, Guenther, 245 Main St., Judi Gedye, Stan Guenther
Geller, D.B., #1900, 355 Burrard St.
Geraghty, Sarava & Conner, #402, 68 Water St., G.C. Geraghty, H.K. Sarava, K. Conner
Gilbert, S.M., #203, 1620 Burnaby St.
Glazier, R.F., 100 w. Pender St.
Gibbons, R.P., #1190, 700 w. Georgia St.
Goldenberger, J., #582, 885 Dunsmuir St.
Goldman & Co., #1422, 1055 w. Georgia St., N.M. Goldman, S.M. Mathiesen, D.J. Bilinsky
Goldman, P.L., #2302, 1501 Haro St.
Goldsmith, A., #602, 626 w. Pender St.
Goldsmith, Hartshorne, Hira & Campbell, Box 11505, 650 w. Georgia St., D. Goldsmith, R.K. Hartshorne, R.N. Hira, I.R. Campbell, W.N. Fritz
Good, P.A., 40 Powell St.
Gorham, W.C., #268, 2025 w. 42nd Ave.
Gorick, P.C., 2676 w. 1st Ave.
Gourlay & Spencer, #200, 1104 Hornby St., R.W. Gourlay, P.A. Spencer
Gove & Senior, 1001, 601 w. Broadway, T. J. Gove, R. L. Senior, D.R. Pendleton, R.D.J. Brown, W.A. McLachlan
Gowan, Victor, 5670 Yew St.
Gracey & Morton, 595 Howe St., K.A. Gracey, J. N. Morton
Grant, M.H., #1650, 777 Hornby St.
Gray, D.A., #200, 1663 w. 7th Ave.
Gray, H.D., 4850 Selkirk St.
Greenberg, H., 3450 w. 16th Ave.
Gregg, P.D., 408 e. 20th Ave.
Griffiths & Co., #1880, 1055 w. Hastings St., T.O. Griffiths, G.W. Kereluk, S.G. Vickers
Groberman, H.S., 1260 w. 46th Ave.
Gropper, M.H., 999 w. Hastings St.
Grossman & Stanley, #700, 925 w. Georgia St., E.H. Grossman, P.W. Stanley
Grunberg, G., #305, 1037 w. Broadway
Guichon, T.K., 1064 Balfour Ave.
Guild, Yule, Schmitt, Lane, Sullivan & Finch, #1680, 505 Burrard St. (V7X 1C9), G.R. Schmitt, W.G. Lane, W.J.

Sullivan, L.S.G. Finch, K. C. Mackenzie, R. R. Holmes, D.W. Yule, J.D. Truscott, F. J. Slivinski, S. L. Enticknap, I.J. Stirling, G.B. Roy, M.M. Moseley, J.A. Hardy, C.G. Herb, D.F. Sutherland, G.L. Manuel, P.W. Walker, B.R. Rose, G.C. Blanchard, S.R. Cameron
Guisti, R.F., #720, 789 w. Pender St.
Guy, D. M., #304, 190 Alexander St.
Hager, Kaplan & Waddell, #102, 2590 Granville St., D.C. Hager, F.S. Kaplan, D.G.D. Waddell, P.R. Meyers
Hanano, F.Y., #304, 4464 w. 10th Ave.
Hanson, L.C., 704 Denman St.
Hara, T.H., #303, 190 Alexander St. (G.F. Hara)
Harcourt, M.F., 1134 w. 7th Ave.
Harowitz & Tick, #1870, 777 Hornby St., L.E. Harowitz, S.H. Tick
Harper, Grey, Easton & Co., Box 11504, 650 w. Georgia St. (V6B 4P7), A. M. Harper, Q.C., H.J. Grey, Q.C., M.D. Easton, D.V. Whitworth, A. D. Thackray, D.A. McDonald, R. Weddigen, L. N. Matheson, T. C. O'Brien, W.J. McJannet, L.M. Blond, J. M. Lepp, B.G. Baynham, J.B. Brown, C.E. Hinkson, B.M. Gordon, Jr., G.G. Hilliker, M.M. Skorah, T.W. Barnes, S.E. McKellar, G.B. Butler, G.J. Te Hennepe, D.G. Keeling, M.B. Rutherford; David Sigler, Q.C.; Associate Counsel: Hon. C. W. Tysoe, Q.C.
Hart, D.D., 1982 McNicoll Ave.
Hart, P.A., 15th fl., 100 w. Pender St.
Hauff, B.L., 3001 Point Grey Rd.
Hayward, S.H., 2880 w. 32nd Ave.
Hazlewood & Co., #1620, 777 Hornby St., G.A. Hazlewood
Helgason, A.G., #800, 777 Hornby St.
Helsing, J.E., 1775 Nanaimo St.
Hemsworth, Schmidt, 555 Howe St., H.B. Hemsworth, W.E. Schmidt
Henderson & Baxter, #602, 626 w. Pender St., D.J. Henderson, K.J. Baxter
Henshall Cottick, #50, 200 Granville St., W.R. Cottick, R.H. Swadden, J.A. Henshall, P.A. Cote
Hine, H.R., Q.C., 777 Hornby St.
Hodges, D.B., 1041 w. 8th Ave.
Hogan & Co., #1205, 1177 w. Hastings St., J. O'L. Hogan, P.J. Reardon, W.J. Rodgers
Hogan & Co., 5th fl., 195 Alexander St., J.W. Hogan, L.D. Myers, R.G. Keefer
Hogan & Webber, #890, 777 Hornby St., P. E. Hogan, D. G. Webber
Holland, Sharp & McGinley, #612, 475 Howe St., A. C. Sharp, F. G. McGinley
Hood, P., #220, 475 Main St.
Horembala & Smith, 6 Gaolers Mews, E.J. Horembala, M.L. Smith
Hoy, B.D., #209, 539 Main St.
Huberman, J.J., #203, 1148 Hornby St.
Huberman, Cristall & Co., #501, 796 Granville St., S. Huberman, K. Cristall, G.C. Bird, L.D. Rainaldi
Hundert & Warren, #105, 1104 Hornby St., Roberta Hundert, Catherine Warren
Hunter & Hunter, #606, 796 Granville St., D.L. Hunter, B.D. Hunter
Hunter, H.D.C., 505 Burrard St.
Hutchinson & Einarsson, #601, 796 Granville St., J.C. Hutchinson, N.F. Einarsson
Hyman, L.N., #306, 1111 w. Georgia St.
Ince, J.G., #1103, 207 w. Hastings St.
Irving, L.M., 1131 e. 23rd Ave.
Israels & Ballantyne, 14th fl., 100 w. Pender St., R.T. Israels, R.D. Ballantyne
Jabour, D.E., 1555 Robson St. (C.C. Harris)
Jackson & Westlake, 15th fl., 100 w. Pender St., J.B. Jackson, K.S. Westlake, H.K. Brown, A.B. Bartram
Jacobsen, L.H., 2170 w. 4th Ave.
Jacobsen, R.B., #820, 777 Hornby St.
James, J.D., 1014 Howe St.
Jatko, R.A., 3825 Arbutus St. (M.J. Kierans, A.R. Lazare)
Jeffery & Calder, #601, 815 Hornby St., M. Jeffery, G.E. Calder, S. Mackoff, J.L. Simmonds
Jeletzky, A., #230, 2609 Granville St.
Jestley Kirstiuk, #1900, 1055 w. Hastings St., J. Kirstiuk, P. J. Jones, E.B. Bromley, W.F. Murray
Joe, Chong & Yee, 124 e. Pender St., A.W.Y. Joe, D. Chong, W.F.W. Yee, A.N. Barbour
Johns & Diebel, #760, 475 w. Georgia St., M.E. Johns, D.H. Diebel
Johnson, A.W., 470 Granville St.
Johnson, P.H., #1227, 510 w. Hastings St.
Johnson, R.,
Jordan & Gall, #1120, 1176 w. Georgia St., D.J. Jordan, P.A. Gall, L.D. Russell, W.C. Kaplan
Joyce & Co., #1040, 650 w. Georgia St., P.B. Joyce
Jung, D., 416 Columbia St.
Jussa, R.N., 4673 Main St.
Kagna, E.W., #310, 837 w. Hastings St.
Kanji, A.J., #301, 850 w. Hastings St.
Karton, Lazare, #202, 1104 Hornby St., M. Karton, A.R. Lazare
Katz, B.A., #300, 800 w. Pender St.
Kelly, S.M., #310, 2150 w. Broadway
Kendall & Sumpton, #270, 5655 Cambie St., T.G. Kendall, J.M. Sumpton
Kennedy, C.R., #305, 190 Alexander St.
Ker, Ross, 2021 w. 41st Ave.
Kerbel & Co., 2020 Comox St., J.A. Kerbel, J.N. Rodgers
Kerfoot & Co., #301, 5511 West Blvd., B.B. Kerfoot, F. Yehia, J.E.D. Cameron
Kershaw, B.H., 6311 Wiltshire St.
Kich, Wm., #501, 470 Granville St.
Killam, Whitelaw & Twining, #200, 321 Water St., G.J. Killam, D.J. Whitelaw, R.R.C. Twining
Kilpatrick & Gavin Assoc., #1115, 207 w. Hastings St., Diane Kilpatrick, Gayle Gavin
Kinahan, C.M., #206, 2121 w. 38th Ave.
Kincaid, Epstein & Co., Box 10019, Pacific Centre, G. Kincaid, I. Epstein, R.A. Logie, C.H.L. Hughes, J.R. Allin, S.M. Allen
King, Arnold & Co., #800, 777 Hornby St., L.A. King, G.R. Arnold
King, W.N., 409 Granville St.
Kitchen, W.J., 10 Gaolers Mews
Kliman, N.C., 736 Granville St.
Klopping, J.R., #802, 535 Thurlow St.
Knott, Pollard & Morgan, #2910, 700 w. Georgia St., W.W.L. Knott, C.J. Pollard, N.R.M. Morgan, R.A. Easton, D.F. Gormican, D.W. Wilcox
Kornfeld, A.C., #582, 885 Dunsmuir St.
Kornfeld, E.L., #1116, 736 Granville St.
Koval, J., #528, 470 Granville St.
Kowarsky & Co., #600, 535 w. Georgia St., B.A. Russell, J.B. Kowarsky, T.E. Hodson, M.W. Morrow, A.G. Sandilands, K.N. Brayley
Krautter, Anne-Marie, #348, 5740 Cambie St.
Kroll, G.R.R., Box 10097, Pacific Centre
Kuchta, T., #1150, 777 Hornby St.
Kussin, I., #1900, 355 Burrard St.
La Charite, Alteman & Blasina, #300, 131 Water St., D.T. La Charite, G.A. Alteman, R.B. Blasina
Ladner, Downs, #2100, 700 w. Georgia St. (V7Y 1A8), T.E. Ladner, Q.C., P.G. Lenox, W.M. Carlyle, J.H. Noble, H.B. Hareid, A.M. Edwardson, W.R. Miles, R. Brock, C.R.L. Peers, G.S. Cross, K.M. Bagshaw, G.P. Reilly, B.I. Cohen, W.T. Wilson, R.D.C. Malcolm, E.C. Chiasson, J.J. Camp, D.B. McIntyre, C.J. Pines, P.M. Archibald, R.W. Lusk, M.D. Donner, R.G. Howay, J.D. Rose, G.W.J. Ghikas, G.R. Switzer, R.L. Bozzer, P.J. Lowry, S.J. Mulhall, R.B. Zien, H.G. Stark, W.F. Sirett, M.V. Newbury, V.R. Orchard, S.K. Gudmundseth, D.P. Mydske, P.G. Foy, O.H. Nowak, C.J. O'Connor, R.D. Conchie, J.L. Fletcher, T.D.J. Schiller, N. deGelder, K.J. MacLise, T.R. Sehmer, M.E. Saunders, B.D. Chase, J. Margolis, F.J. Connell, J.D. Morrison, P.J. Scheer, R.C. Baker, M.L. Thompson, R.J. Arseneau, D.L. Browning, P.D. MacDonald, S.K. Strachan, P.G. Voith, I.M. Stewart, D.K. Camp, S.M. Tratch, J.C. Mowatt, L.R. Sandrin
Lakes, J.R., #503, 470 Granville St.
Lam, V., 1850 Comox St.
Lam, Y., 200 e. Pender St.
Lando & Co., #1734, 1055 Dunsmuir St., E. Lando, Q.C., H. Frydenlund, M. I. Huculak, L.H. Aasen
Lau, P.T.K., 940 w. King Edward St.
Laurin, G.B., #8, 1465 w. 14th Ave.
LaVan MacKinlay, 10th fl., 1285 w. Pender St., J.R. LaVan, J.D. MacKinlay. Assoc. Counsel: J.A. Rubenstein, Barbara Armstrong
Lawrence, R.E., 4154 w. 11th Ave.
Lawrence & Shaw, Box 49200, 595 Burrard St. (V7X 1L1), B.W.F. McLoughlin, Q.C., C.P. Daniels, Q.C., J.W. Lawrence, J.H. Konst, W.M. Swanson, L.J. Creery, H.H. Ridgway, D.T. Hopkins, G.C. Stevens, J.F. Tollestrup, D.L. Larson, D.W. Tokarek, C.B. Coutts, D.J. Ross, G.B. Finlayson, J.D. Helmcken, K.E. Gustafson, A.H.S. Knight, K.E. Clark, R.C. Strother, G.A. MacDonald, Julia H. Cross, Deborah C. Lytle, Jacqueline Aulinger, L.S. Hughes, R.G. Kuhn, L.G. Montpellier, Diana R. Reid
Lawson, Lundell, Lawson & McIntosh, Box 11506, #2800, 650 w. Georgia St. (V6B 4R7), G.B. McIntosh, J.M. Tennant, R.J.L. Worthington, D.G. Sweet, D.J. Smith, R. J. Mair, J.O.E. Lundell, D. E. Gillanders, C.H. McKee, W. F. Dickson, L. D. Peterson, J. G. Trueman, B. J. Wallace, D.M. Thompson, A.G. Miller, D.L. Rice, W. M. Everett, D.F. Robinson, S. McCullough, J.H. Fraser, A.W. Ryan, P.D. Bradley, C.G. Baldwin, Susan Murphy, J.M. Kyle, C.W. Sanderson, G.M. Craig, J.E. Gouge, J.W. Peters, Kate D. Pollock, K.R. Doyle, Lenore R. Rowntree, B.D. Fulton, L.N. Marshall, G.C. Weatherill, S.B. Armstrong. Associate Counsel: Oscar F. Lundell, Q.C., R.J. Gibbs, Q.C.
Laxton & Co., 10th fl., 1285 w. Pender St., J.N. Laxton, D.K. Pidgeon, F.A. Schroeder, Miriam Gropper
Layne, G.C., #900, 925 w. Georgia St.
LeBlanc & Co., 1826 e. Broadway, R.L. LeBlanc, K.S. Specht
Lecovin, Millar & Co., #1000, 777 Hornby St., G.J. Lecovin, C.A. Millar, Suzan D. Beattie
Ledding, G.J., #502, 535 w. Georgia St.
Lee, J.L., 501 Main St.
Lee, R.A., #102, 100 w. Pender St.
Legge & Co., #605, 815 Hornby St., B.M. Legge, L.E. Kancs, G.D. McLaren
Leighton, J.F., 2626 w. 36th Ave.
Leslie, D.F., #1200, 609 Granville St.
Leung, M.M., 1774 w. 36th Ave.
Levey & Glasner, #306, 1111 w. Georgia St., G.S. Levey, K.J. Glasner
Levine & Leslie, 1120 Hornby St., S.L. Levine, M.L. Leslie
Lew, C., #1010, 207 w. Hastings St.

Lew, H.H., #302, 2695 Granville St.
Lew & Lee, 166 e. Pender St., F.C.M. Lew, A.J. Lee
Libby, Blair, Moss & Beirne, 3rd fl., 157 Alexander St., H.D. Libby, J.M.B. Blair, D.E. Moss, P.J. Beirne, J.F. Rowan
Lindsay Kenney, #800, 475 Howe St., R.B. Lindsay, J.T.W. Kenney, L.J. Hogg, F.G. Potts
Litsky, P., #205, 190 Alexander St.
Little, G.B., #101, 2044 w. 3rd Ave.
Lo, K.A., 501 Main St.
Long, A.D., #305, 1030 w. Georgia St.
Long & Long, #200, 8675 Granville St., C.F. Long
Long, Miller & Co., #300, 595 Howe St., G.R. Long, Jr., J.M. Miller
Long, R.H. & Co., #560, 2609 Granville St., R. H. Long, W.H. Lim, R.E. Noble, C.K. Iwata, W.D.O. Bees
Louie, Lam & Co., #220, 193 e. Hastings St., R.D. Louie, B.S.K. Lam, R.D. Carr-Harris, R.B. Frith
Lytwyn, J.R., 572 w. 22nd Ave.
Macaulay McColl, #1650, 700 w. Georgia St., J.A. Macaulay, B.H. McColl, D.L. Campbell, K.N. Affleck, J.K. Irving
Macdonald, A.B., Q.C., Box 10117, Pacific Centre
MacDonald & Co., #1120, 800 w. Pender St., W.E. MacDonald, M.G. Gayman, D.M. MacPhail
Macdonald, D.G., #1530, 1176 w. Georgia St.
Macdonald, Kwan & Lewis, #401, 698 Seymour St., R.W. Macdonald, E.H. Kwan, T.G. Lewis, J.N. Paton, R.P. Taylor, B.Y.F. Dong
Macey, J.K., #205, 190 Alexander St.
Macfarlane & Co., 960 Howe St., R.F. Macfarlane, I.G. McKenzie, R.J. Scardina, J.K. Logan, J. Eddy, N.M. Kassam, A.H. Brown
Macfarlane, Pearkes, Smiley & Guthrie, 3066 Arbutus St., D.J. Macfarlane, J.A. Pearkes, L.I. Smiley, R.J. Guthrie, M.A. Benton
MacKay & Dwor, #201, 1271 Howe St., R.B. MacKay, M.S. Dwor
Mackay, J.D., #2660, 650 w. Georgia St.
MacKenzie, I.F.A., 1665 w. 68th Ave.
MacKenzie, Lidstone, #1860, 505 Burrard St., R.M. MacKenzie, D. Lidstone, Sandra Watson
MacKenzie, R.H., #2000, 658 w. Georgia St.
Mackey, Petancic & Co., #1230, 800 w. Pender St., J. M. Mackey, A. Petancic
MacKinnon, T., 4309 Osler St.
Mackrow, John P., #1112, 409 Granville St.
MacLachlan, Mrs. D.R., 6989 Arbutus St.
MacLean, S.C., #1770, 700 w. Georgia St.
MacLeod, E.J., #702, 1055 w. Georgia St.
MacLeod, J.R., #1240, 701 w. Georgia St.
MacQuarrie, Hobkirk, McCurdy, Schuman, Culhane & van Eijnsbergen, #2020, 777 Hornby St., A.B. MacQuarrie, D.A. Hobkirk, K.B. McCurdy, J.A. Schuman, G.F. Culhane, H. van Eijnsbergen
Macrae, Montgomery & Cunningham, 555 Burrard St., 15th fl., V7X 1H8, J.R. Cunningham, J.D. Montgomery, J.L. Jessiman, P.G. Bernard, R.V. Burns, J.W. Perrett, F.G. Kraemer, J.R. Coleman, M.J. MacEwing, S.E. Milne, M.S. Goetze, R.J. Kincaid
Maddaugh, J.E., 3521 w. 42nd Ave.
Maddin, Suderman, Malach & Bowes, Box 49212, 595 Burrard St., C.H. Maddin, E.A. Suderman, B.J. Malach, E.E. Bowes
Mah, W., Box 11118, Royal Centre
Maitland & Co., #901, 470 Granville St., R.C. McCutcheon, B.A. Mason, N.W. Dowad, M.L. Seifert, C.J. Butler
Maltby, D.H.J., 3730 w. Broadway
Mann & Loptson, #655, 555 Burrard St., D.E. Mann, T.R. Loptson
Manning, H.E., 496 w. 40th Ave.
Margach, J.A., #1880, 1055 w. Hastings St.
Marinakis & Frank, #2753, 595 Burrard St., A. S. Marinakis, M. J. Frank
Marshall, W.E., 777 Hornby St. (Joan Snape)
Marshall, W.L., 3728 w. 24th Ave.
Martin, D.R., 2443 Kingsway (D.E. Leahy)
Martin, W.R., 2nd fl., 4371 Fraser St.
Mason, D.D., #2620, 1066 w. Hastings St.
Mass, M.V., #302, 2695 Granville St.
Mawhinney & Kellough, #1850, 1055 w. Hastings St., J.D.S. Mawhinney, H.J. Kellough, W.J. Baillie, J.G.R. Third, G.W. Esau, Janine Thomas
Maxwell, F.E., #1060, 1090 w. Georgia St.(B.E. Bulmer)
Maykut, J.C., #900, 1050 w. Pender St.
Mazurchuk, M.E., 3933 Parkway Dr.
McAlpine, Roberts & Hordo, #3050, 700 w. Georgia St., J.D. McAlpine, Q.C., D.W. Roberts, R.J.R. Hordo, Catherine Wedge, P. Hildebrand
McCallum, T.V., #300, 1148 Hornby St. (Law Society Secretary)
McCandless, Palkowski & Burns, 15th fl., 409 Granville St., H.A. McCandless, R.J. Palkowski, D.E. Burns, Rose Mok, T.A. Beechinor, W. Gray, R.J. Allan, G.A. Wasko, G.A. Marhas
McCloy Mackay & Rust, #450, 890 w. Pender St., R.H. McCloy, R.W. Mackay, J.T. Rust, G.K. Steele
McClusky, Joanne, #1155, 409 Granville St.
McCrossan, J.A., 3615 w. 19th Ave.
McCrum, J.G., #1470, 1176 w. Georgia St.
McCrum, K.W., #1470, 1176 w. Georgia St.
McCulloch, R.G., #1160, 1090 w. Georgia St.
McInnes & Neumann, #1620, 701 w. Georgia St., J.E. McInnes, G. J. Neumann, K.A. Christofferson
McIntyre, J.J., 456A w. 18th Ave.
McKenzie & Co., #422, 837 w. Hastings St., F.J. McKenzie, R.D. Bellamy
McKitrick, R.M., 2695 Granville St.
McLaughlin, H.P., #1001, 750 w. Pender St.
McLean, Hungerford & Simon, Two Bentall Centre, 555 Burrard St., D.G.A. McLean, G.W. Hungerford, R.A. Simon, M.D. Corday, D.F. Gurney, E.E. Macchi
McLeod, J.F., #800, 777 Hornby St.
McMaster, Bray, Cameron & Jasich, 355 Burrard St., G.F. McMaster, M. Bray, T.P. Cameron, A.J. Jasich
McNeney Morrison, 17th fl., 100 w. Pender St., E.J. McNeney, K. Morrison, Susan Brandreth-Gibbs
McOuat, W.G., Box 11557, 650 w. Georgia St.
McTaggart, Ellis & Co., 885 Dunsmuir St., D.G. Melvin, R.E. Cocking, R.K. McDonald, A.G. Radcliff, S.B. Hatch, Lorraine Shore, Jan Coplick
Medland & White, #312, 1281 w. Georgia St., J.R.E. Medland, J.M. White
Meredith & Co., #1700, 777 Hornby St., T.C. Marshall, B.J. McConnell, P.G. Ferber, Theresa Hartshorne, J.D. Spears
Michelson, B.E., 123 Main St.
Millar, J.W., 680C Leg in Boot Sq.
Millward, C.J., #816, 602 w. Hastings St.
Mint, E.T., 928 w. King Edward (D.A. Nuyts)
Moglove, C.I.,
Moir, D.S., Box 10051, Pacific Centre (C. Allevato, R.L. Nash, S.S. Swartz)
Molson, J.B., #36, 566 Cardero St.
Montaine, Black & Co., #201, 1111 w. Georgia St., L.A. Montaine, P.G.S. Bush, P. Owen
Mortimer, M.E., 1116 Hornby St. (F.M.C. Lowther)
Moseley, E.P.G., #1103, 475 Howe St.
Mueller, R.J., 750 w. Pender St.
Muldoon, D.W., #103, 1104 Hornby St.
Mulhern, E.F., 1784 w. Georgia St.
Mulligan, M.W., 223 Main St.
Munro & Crawford, 5670 Yew St., W.S. Munro, P.N. Crawford
Murphy, M.P., #301, 2255 w. 8th Ave.
Murray, D.H., #908, 207 w. Hastings St.
Murray, R.D., 3003 w. 3rd Ave.
Nash, A.B., #1614, 675 w. Hastings St.
Nathanson, S.B., 211 w. 49th Ave.
Nellis, T., #230, 2609 Granville St.
Nelson, B.J., 3rd fl., 1247 Hornby St.
Nichols & Co., #2715, 650 w. Georgia St., K.R. Nichols, T.C. Arsenault
Nicol, G.J., 3349 Kingsway
Norby, D.M., #700, 925 w. Georgia St.
Nordlinger, K.F., 1247 Hornby St.
Norton, Stewart, Norton, Cave & Scarlett, #1200, 1055 w. Georgia St., D.H. Norton, T.W. Stewart, J.W. Norton, D.A. Cave, D.W. Scarlett, K.D. Landels, G.W. Dunn, G.M. Harasym, J.D. Burns, D.J. Manson, D.H. Pedlow, K.A. Dangerfield, K.T. Marsden, Cindy Lombard, K.S.F. Lee
O'Connor, T.G., 1220 Homer St.
Oland, A.B., #2000, 650 w. Georgia St.
Oliver, Waldock & Richardson, #1011, 1030 w. Georgia St., H.A.D. Oliver, H.E. Waldock, J.O. Richardson, R.B. Donaldson
Oreck & Chernoff, #1460, 701 w. Georgia St., P.G. Oreck, Y. M. Chernoff, A.M. Abramson, H.A. Oreck, A.H. Grunfeld
Oreck, N.L., 1331 w. 48th Ave.
Orris, LaLiberte & Co., 123 Main St., G. Orris, T.E. LaLiberte. Assoc. Counsel: Nancy Morrison
Osten & Osten, #2753, 595 Burrard St., Max Osten, W.R. Osten
Owen, Bird, Box 49130, 595 Burrard St. (V7X 1J5), J.I. Bird, Q.C., W.O. Forbes, D.S. Owen, D.A. Farac, W.E. Ireland, D.H. Standfield, F.M.P. Warren, D.B. Kirkham, W.K. Hanlin, R.C. Macfarlane, J.D. Dunn, R.H. Hamilton, M.J. Bird, W.G. Farish, R.J. Argue, T.S. Robbins, Jo Ann Carmichael, D.G. Fredricksen, R.A. Davis, D.C.A. De Vuyst, T.L. Vazakas, Gretchen H. Cleveland
Paine, Edmonds, Dudley & Woodley, #304, 717 w. Pender St., W.H.K. Edmonds, Q.C., L.C. Dudley, J.L. Woodley, E.A. Yusep, J.C. Taylor, L.G. Harris, S.H. Heringa, O.G. Jones
Pandya, R., #204, 717 w. Pender St.
Parker & Wylie, #204, 3540 w. 41st Ave., Hon. John Parker
Parks, Feller, Anstey, Meyer, #930, 1066 w. Hastings St.
Parsons & Seymour, #304, 2425 Quebec St., I.R. Seymour, A.D. Adams
Pashos, L.L., 550 Hornby St.
Patterson, Price, #207, 1039 Richards St., C.E. Patterson, M.T.C. Price
Pedrini, H., 1045 Howe St.
Perry, J.L., 1710 Knox Rd.
Peterson, Stark & Fowler, 1177 w. Broadway, J.B. Peterson, S.R. Stark, K.R. Fowler, D.N. MacKinnon, T.R.I. Dusevic, A. Visram, W.J. Baker, Margaret Ostrowski, Joanne Lentsch, J.D. Osborne
Petronio, A.A., 1714 e. Broadway
Phippen, F.H., 1250 w. Broadway

Pinkus, Ruth, #901, 525 Seymour St.
Pontius, H.A., #1603, 1320 Bute St.
Potter, J.E., #250, 1465 w. 7th Ave.
Poulus, H., 18th fl., 1500 w. Georgia St.
Prowse, D.C., 700 w. Georgia St.
Prowse, W.C., 520 Seymour St.
Prowse, Williamson & Whitman, #603, 736 Granville St., J.E. Prowse, L.P. Williamson, J.E. Whitman
Puhach, M., #200, 8675 Granville St.
Pyrgos, N., 1090 w. Georgia St.
Raibmon, Young, Campbell & Goulet, #355, 555 Burrard St., R.L. Raibmon, K.G. Young, J.K. Campbell, L.W. Goulet
Rand & Edgar, #400, 750 w. Pender St., W.A. Rand, B.D. Edgar
Rankin, Robertson & Donald, 195 Alexander St., H. Rankin, D. Morgan, T.L. Robertson, R. Russell, R. Peck, I. Donald, Patricia Howard, K. Moore, B. Laughton
Rankin, Stone & McMurray, 157 Alexander St., P.C. Rankin, D. Stone, P.S. McMurray, D.L. Jang, E.J. Bond
Raphanel, G.A., 2776 w. 10th Ave.
Ray, Wolfe, Connell, Lightbody & Reynolds, 18th fl., 1030 w. Georgia St. (V6E 3C1), W.P. Lightbody, J.G. Connell, I.M. Wolfe, J.J. Reynolds, M.H. Heller, D.F. McEwen, G.R. Pellatt, L.H. Polsky, D.P. Baron, T.E. Baillie, S.H. Lipetz, Janet M. Biga, J.S. Cheng, M.R. Steven, R.M. Young, Raquel M. Goncalves, Paul Daltrop, D.G. Schmitt, W.C. Wakely, E.G. Kroft, Suzanne K. MacGregor, Pauline M. Cusack
Redekop, D.G., 3330 w. 12th Ave.
Rich, R.A., #135, 3473 e. 49th Ave.
Ritchie, Taylor, 5th fl., 195 Alexander St., K.P. Ritchie, G.C. Taylor
Robertson, I.L., #424, 925 w. Georgia St.
Roell, M.A., #200, 43 Powell St.
Rogers, J.L., #201, 2309 w. 41st Ave.
Romeril, P.E.A., 4464 w. 13th Ave.
Rosenberg, Rosenberg & Woodward, 671 Market Hill, P.S. Rosenberg, D.M. Rosenberg, E.J. Woodward
Rosenbloom, McCrea & Leggatt, 75 Alexander St., D.J. Rosenbloom, D.G. McCrea, S. Leggatt, J.R. Aldridge
Rosner, J.H., #770, 475 w. Georgia St.
Ross, J.Y., 6057 Willow St.
Ross, R.S., 4741 w. 2nd Ave.
Roth, K., #405, 535 w. Georgia St.
Rothe, Lipetz & Assoc., 11th fl., 1090 w. Georgia St., R.O. Rothe, A.L. Lipetz, J.A. Swanson, A. Wade
Rounthwaite, Ann, 2444 w. 45th Ave.
Rowles & Assoc., #701, 2695 Granville St., M. Anne Rowles, Alison MacLennan, Kathleen Keating, J.W. Bradley
Roza-Pereira, M., 3066 e. 19th Ave.
Rubin, Belkin & Arbour, #1150, 701 w. Georgia St., H. Rubin, E.J. Belkin, G.J. Arbour
Ruryk, E.B., #307, 736 Granville St.
Rush, S.A., #610, 207 w. Hastings St.
Russell & Betts, #1200, 609 Granville St., B.C.E. Russell, L. Betts
Russell & DuMoulin, 1075 w. Georgia St. (V6E 3G2), D. McK. Brown, Q.C., E.D.H. Wilkinson, Q.C., R.E. Ostlund, D.A. Williamson, D.M.M. Goldie, Q.C., R.B. Harvey, R.H. Guile, B.W.F. Fodchuk, B.B. Trevino, A. E. Harvey, J.G. Smith, S.W. Hood, G.W. Forster, L. Amighetti, J. T. Steeves, J.B.L. Robertson, P.H. Stafford, A.P. Pantages, R.A. Ross, J.T. English, W.S. Berardino, G.H.G. Hume, J.G. Carphin, M.W. Hunter, J.M. McCormick, C.E. Barnes, C.B. Johnson, C. Harvey, D.G.S. Rae, H.L. Brown, B.A. Dyer, J.D. Piers, P.R. Sheen, A. McDonell, P.F. Parsons, G.J. May, R.A. Goodrich, Kirsti M. Gill, Norah J. Hall, B.V. Slutsky, K.P. O'Neill, B.R. Grist, D.M. Dalik, R.J. Rose, J.H. MacMaster, Katherine J. Heller, Marion J. Allan, G.R. Sollis, Patricia L. Janzen, J.W. Stelmaszczuk, D.B. Gleadle, D.M. Tevlin, A.A. Abdula, W.I. Cassie, Elaine Reynolds, G.P. Holeksa, W.S. Martin, C.F. Willms, M.A. Thomas, H.K. Johannsen, T.R. Manson, A.D. Winter, M.J. Peerson, Susan M. Eyre, T.I. McAuley. Associate Counsel: L. St. M. DuMoulin, Q.C., R. T. DuMoulin, Q.C., Hon. J.O. Wilson, Q.C., Hon. A.B. Robertson, Q.C.
Salter, R., #610, 207 w. Hastings St.
Samuels, S.N., #501, 796 Granville St.
Sandberg, C.A., #108, 2786 w. 16th Ave.
Sanderson & Ranson, 3rd fl., 1151 w. 8th Ave., Samantha Sanderson, Joanne Ranson
Sara, I., #6, 6325 Fraser St.
Scarisbrick, P.N., 234 Abbott St.
Schacter, B., #415, 700 w. Georgia St.
Schiffer, R.C., #1422, 1055 w. Georgia St.
Schneiderman, S.M., 850 w. Hastings St.
Seaton Promislow, #801, 850 w. Hastings St., B.J. Promislow
Seifred & Roth, 52 Powell St., E.A. Seifred, R.D. Roth
Semorad, F. J., 3389 Kingsway
Serka & Shelling, 1151 w. 8th Ave., A.P. Serka, L.J. Shelling
Shah, R.K., #211, 717 w. Pender St.
Shelton, S.S., 2245 Commercial Dr.
Shier & Buchan, 1151 w. 8th Ave., P. Shier, Niki Buchan, Linda Thayer
Shortt & Co., #320, 625 Howe St., M. D. Shortt, E.B. Norman, S.A. Moore
Shrum, Liddle & Hebenton, #1300, 999 w. Hastings St., V6C 2W5, G.B. Shrum, S. Hebenton, R.P. Beckmann, W.K. Derby, J.W. Lutes, R.J. Sewell, R.N. Stern, J.W. Pearson, L. Smith, A. B. Gibson, T.A. Zacks, T.W. Bell, Rosemarie Wertschek, G.M. Quijano, J.A. Titerle, A.F. Hilliard, Pamela Kirkpatrick, K.E. Burrell, Diane Mason, Julia Ryan, D.T. Winnett, A.B. Kerr, M.E. Mitchell, Heather Holmes, P.B. O'Neal, P. Pagnan, E.G. Phillips, F.L. Sharp, Donna Cooke, D.A. Knox, R.B. Fraser, P.D. Fairey. Assoc. Counsel: Hon. J.L. Farris, Q.C.
Shulman, S.R.W., #302, 2695 Granville St.
Siddall, H.K., #100, 535 w. 10th Ave.
Sier, H.N., Box 11554, 650 w. Georgia St.
Sikula, Yager, Werbes & Longpre, 1199 w. Pender St., M.M. Sikula, W. D. Yager, K. Werbes, G.B. Longpre, M.E. Brown
Silbernagel, S.H., #760, 1111 Melville St.
Simon, Wener, Gutkin & Adler, #101, 1632 w. 7th Ave., S.D. Simon, J.A. Wener, R.K. Gutkin, J.S. Adler, Anne Wallace
Simons, S.B., 40 Powell St. (J. Andersen)
Simpson, B., #950, 999 w. Broadway
Small, D.W., #2000, 650 w. Georgia St.
Smilie, Henry, 5740 Cambie St.
Smilsky, P.T., #1115, 207 w. Hastings St.
Smith, H.M., #206, 207 w. Hastings St.
Smith, R.W., 17th fl., 100 w. Pender St.
Sobolewski Anfield, 7th fl., 609 Granville St., S.D. Anfield, B.D. Speton, S. Sobolewski, L.G. Wilson, L.A. Gold, J.W. Tarnowski, J.N. Rodgers, D.A. Lyons
Sokol, D.B.L., 15th fl., 100 w. Pender St.
Somers, M.S.D., #208, 2760 w. Broadway
Spring, Brammall & Gemmill, 2774 Granville St., R.H. Spring, H.R. Brammall, J.A. Gemmill. Counsel: H.C.F. Spring
Stanton, R.V., 4132 Tytahun Cres.
Steinberg & Co., #200, 2609 Granville St., K.R. Steinberg, Beverley Muller
Steinberg, D.M.B., #500, 68 Water St.
Stephens, Cheryl, 1340 Burrard St.
Stephens, V.A., 2578 Burrard St.
Stewart, Saunders & Aulinger, #404, 515 w. 10th Ave., A.B. Stewart, A.D. Saunders, R.J. Aulinger, J.P. Taylor, K.R. Ditta, R.A. Kasting, C.M. Emslie
Street, W.A., #102, 853 Richards St. (N.A. Morrison)
Stromberg-Stein, S.S., 1998 Quilchena Cres.
Sun Paterson, #701, 1285 w. Pender St., C.M. Sun, J.C. Paterson
Sutherland & Sutherland, #1502, 736 Granville St., J.J. Sutherland, Mrs. A.M. Sutherland
Sutherland, T.M., 1045 Howe St.
Sutton, Braidwood, #1900, 609 Granville St., Box 10020, O.J. Hall, A. H. Fyfe, C.S. Hopkins, L.C. Luther, J.D. Vilvang, R.P.T. Geopel, R.J. Cameron, G.J. Wilson, R.D. Watson, T.G. Keast, J.M. Munsie, D.J. Livingston, D.A. Liden, A.P. Czepil. Assoc. Counsel: D.T. Braidwood, Q.C.
Sutton, D.A., #1160, 1090 w. Georgia St.
Swinton & Co., #1300, 1090 w. Georgia St. (V6E 3X9), A.H. Swinton, B. Williams, R.R. Dodd, R.H. Stewart, G.E. Rose, E.A. Odishaw, K.N. Burnett, R.J. Rogers, D.J. Stuart, B.T. Ross, S.E. Dadson, D.J. Sorochan, F.L. Waldbillig, D.C. Harbottle, P.N.M. Glass, Lynn Ramsay, M.A. Coady, S.R. Ross, P.W. Hammond, R.W. Taylor, G. Walsh, D.G. Walley, D.L. Richardson, P.J. Dadson, Sharon Morrisroe, T.V. Seibold, A.A. Hobkirk, M.M. Mangan, D.J. Rand, B.W. Tyzuk. Assoc. Counsel: Mary F. Southin, Q.C.
Symons, L.T., 950, 505 Burrard St.
Taylor, John & Associates, #404, 1111 w. Georgia St., J.R. Taylor, F.R. Whiteside, B.M. Isman
Thompson, A.J., 3895 w. 23rd Ave.
Thompson, H.W., #2020, 777 Hornby St.
Thompson & Elliott, #401, 601 w. Broadway, R.K. Thompson, G.M. Elliott
Thompson, Guthrie, Casilio, #800, 1200 Burrard St., B.A. Thompson, I.W. Guthrie, G.D. Casilio
Thompson & McConnell, 4005 Cambie St., W.C. McConnell, A.J. McConkey, A.R. Adlem, K.A. Blair
Thomson, J.G., #608, 1033 Davie St.
Thorne & Co., 904 Helmcken St., A.C. Thorne, I.J. Tindale
Thorpe, Bonnie L., #201, 1045 w. 13th Ave.
Thorsteinsson, Mitchell, Little, O'Keefe & Davidson, 595 Burrard St., P.N. Thorsteinsson, W.J.A. Mitchell, L.M. Little, M.J. O'Keefe, A.B. Davidson, I.H. Pitfield, J.H.G. Roche, R.E. Levine, C.E. Beil, L.A. Green, C.C. Baird, D.D. Gibbs
Todd, E.C.E., 1866 Wesbrook Cres.
Torrie, R.B., 1211 Bidwell St.
Townsend, J.A., #800, 777 Hornby St.
Tuck, D.T., 5629 Angus Dr.
Tufts, B.D., #603, 601 w. Broadway
Tupper, Jonsson, Shroff & Zink, #1710, 1177 w. Hastings St., C.R. Jonsson, H. Shroff, M. Zink, L.S. Tupper, G.R. Yeadon, G.A. Harmel, H.W. Tupper, M. Kurschner
Turco, Moscovich, Sabatino & Aikenhead, #101, 1109 Commercial Dr., F.M. Turco, M.H. Moscovich, P. Sabatino, I.D. Aikenhead. Assoc. Counsel: G.V. Lauk
Van der Horst & Co., #601, 850 w. Hastings St., A.L. Van der Horst, L.E. Guno
Van Hof, J.O., 1014 Howe St.

Van Heukelom, A., #1480, 1055 w. Hastings St.
Van Roggen, G.C., #602, 1285 w. Pender St.
Verdicchio & Co., 11th fl., 510 w. Hastings St., F. Verdicchio, M.C. Babey
Vermette, C.W., #456, 409 Granville St.
Vertlieb, Anderson & Co., #1005, 750 w. Pender St., A.E. Vertlieb, C.L. Anderson, J. Bomhof, R.O. Klassen
Vick & McPhee, #309, 1111 w. Georgia St., M.D. Vick, R.A. McPhee
Volrich, Eades & Mott, 1st fl., 960 Howe St., R.E. Eades, G.H. Mott, R.J. Beadle, B.E. Mark, G. Taylor. Assoc. Counsel: J.J. Volrich, J.E. Eades, Q.C.
Von Dehn, W.A., #760, 1111 Melville St.
Vorvis, E.J., #401, 1395 Beach Ave.
Wai, T.W., 475 Main St.
Walden, Miss P.S., #913, 736 Granville St.
Walker & Brown, #1240, 1176 w. Georgia St., A.G. Walker, J.A. Brown, M.A. Lakhani
Warner & Thompson, #202, 640 w. Hastings St., W.L. Warner, D.B. Peterson, J.G. Nelson, K.J. Stupich
Warren, E., 40 Powell St.
Warren, T.P., 1247 Hornby St.
Wasson & Wasson, #801, 525 Seymour St., E.E. Wasson, Q.C., G.C. Wasson
Watson, Martin, 1663 w. 7th Ave., E.E. Watson, J.G. Martin, D.M. Tanack, J.D. Kadlec
Watts, Burns & Davis, #950, 999 w. Broadway, P.D. Watts, M.P. Burns, G.E. Davis
Watts, R.H., 505 Burrard St.
Welch, J.S., #1408, 207 w. Hastings St.
Wesik, P., #460, 2609 Granville St.
Whist, J.A.B., #1290, 999 w. Hastings St.
White, A.C., #205, 2105 w. 38th Ave.
White, H.A., #2600, 1055 w. Georgia St.
White, R.A., #2600, 1055 w. Georgia St.
Whittall, W.E., #802, 475 Howe St.
Wicks, R.R., #1105, 1030 w. Georgia St. (R.W. Dresser)
Wickson, M.C.J., 3396 Cambie St.
Wilder & Co., #2160, 1066 w. Hastings St., M.D. Wilder, P.K. Jensen
Williams & Ross, #980, 789 w. Pender St., Mrs. E. Williams Ross, H. V. Ross
Williamson, H.E., 1148 Hornby St.
Williamson, P., #603, 736 Granville St.
Wilson, R., #600, 815 Hornby St.
Wing, Stewart & Co., #401, 796 Granville St., J.T. Wing, S.B. Stewart, J.E. Atkinson
Wismer, J., #3, 1447 Hornby St.
Wong, P.L., #340, 2609 Granville St.
Wong, S.G., 6330 Fraser St. (D.E. Smith)
Wong, S.R., #8, 4335 w. 10th Ave.
Wong & Verbrugge, 2nd fl., 550 Burrard St., G.E. Wong, N.M.A.R. Verbrugge, V.A. Chen, V.M.C. Cox
Wong, W.G., 2nd fl., 145 Keefer St.
Worrall, Page & Scott, #1000, 609 w. Hastings St., W.J. Worrall, L.P. Page, G.E. Scott, E.B. Rutledge, K.S. Campbell, E.R. Watkins, D.R. Garrod, D.E. Cameron
Wosk, S.L., #950, 625 Howe St.
Yang, Anderson & Abraham, #600, 1285 w. Pender St., V.J. Yang, C.A. Anderson, B. Abraham, Betty Tsui, T.M. Nabata, Ka Cheung Li
Yaremovich, P.L., #113, 404 e. 8th Ave.
Young, M.R., 1030 w. Georgia St.
Young, W.S.L., #627, 925 w. Georgia St.
Youngson, D.L., 924 w. King Edward
Yue, L.C.L., #212, 475 Main St.
Zlotnik, DuMoulin, Lowes & Boskovich, 520 Seymour St., J.A. Boskovich, A.B.P. DuMoulin, J.K. Lowes, M.D. Zlotnik, J.E. Murphy, Rose-Mary Liu Basham, B.S. Koonar, G. Battista, F.L. Morris, S.E. Smith

VANDERHOOF, Cariboo
Wingham, C.K., Box 1489 (D.G.O. Smith)

VERNON, Yale
Barker & Usher, 3105 30th Ave., J.D. Barker, R.R. Usher
Danyliu, Kenny & Co., 3009 28th St., P.C. Danyliu, E.F. Kenny, K. Diebert, Marnee Pearce
Davidson & Co., #3205, 32nd Ave., N.A. Davidson, Q.C., B.L. Willows, R. J. Gillespie, K.L. Christensen, M.R. Mondin, W.E. Catlin, F.W. Cole, T.D.A. Fletcher, K.R. Kurbis, G.J. Schroeder, F.A. Kern
Fiddes, K.R., #204, 2802 30th St.
Kidston & Co., 3104 32nd Ave., R.S. Adams, K.W. Tollestrup, K.B. Allan, R.C. Bernhardt
Lawrence, H.C., 7600 Ormsby Dr. (also Armstrong)
Nixon, Wenger, Watts, Wagner, Einfeld, Williamson, 3317 30th Ave., D.P. Nixon, D.P. Wenger, R.D. Watts, G.W. Wagner, D.G. Einfeld, R.E. Williamson, G.P. Weatherill
Orr & Clarke, 3109 34th Ave., R.M.J.D. Orr, G.C. Clarke
Pattie, Mitchell & Helm, 2915 28 Ave., B.L. Pattie, D.H. Mitchell, D.A. Helm, B.K. Loewen
Sigalet & Maguire, 2743 30th St., D.J. Sigalet, J.S. Maguire
Steiner, Nagy & Morin, 3107A 31st Ave., A. W. Steiner, J. S. Nagy, G.M. Morin

VICTORIA, Vancouver Island
Achtem, Alexander, 1175 Douglas St., E.D.J. Achtem, R.S. Alexander, M.S. Greene, D.A. Brindle, P.J. Delsey, D.P.J. Lawton, L.B. Jamieson
Ashurst, Main & Bircher, 1020 McKenzie Ave., D.E. Ashurst, J.C.M. Main, R.J. Bircher
Aujula, S.S., 2951 Tillicum Rd.
Baldini, M.A., 758 Queen's Ave.
Bigelow, A.E., 1510 Monterey
Bolton, D.H.W., 620 View St.
Botterell, Mrs. M.E., 533 Transit Rd.
Brennan, C.W.A., 425 Constance Ave.
Brewin, Milne & Morley, 1208 Wharf St., J.F. Brewin, R.G. Milne, J.B. Morley
Brock & Co., 853 Burdett Ave., C.J.H. Brock, T.A.C. Schober
Buckler, Fast, Brown & Smith, 1031 Vancouver St., T.L. Brown, L.R. Fast, R.B. Buckler, C.M. Huddart, I.C.B. Smith, E.B. Kluge, C.E. MacDonald
Buffam, R.B., 1640 Oak Bay
Butler, Angus, 736 Broughton St., M. Butler, Q.C., J.A. Angus, D. Cowan
Cameron, Burns & Co., 620 View St., D.G. Cameron, A.J. Burns
Campbell, Donegani & Wood, #305, 1020 Government St., F.T. Donegani, J. F. Wood, J. R. McMillan
Cardinal, Edgar, Emberton & Macaulay, 2244 Sooke Rd., R.J.A. Cardinal, D.C. Edgar, B.T. Emberton, M.D. Macaulay, H.J. Rusk, Kathryn Berge
Chard, R.W., 645 Fort St.
Christie, D.H., 810 Courtney St.
City Solicitors, 1 Centennial Sq., J.S. DeVilliers, G.A. Durand
Clapp, J.R., 848 Fort St. (L.W. Roberts)
Clark, Wilson etc., Bank of N.S. Bldg. (also Vancouver)
Clay & Co., 837 Burdett St., E.A. Popham, J.A. Bond, P.A. Murray, J.T. Alexander, P.G. Scambler, W.R. Philps. Assoc. Counsel: R.J. Harvey, Q.C.
Cook, Roberts & Whittaker, 777 Fort St., R.C. Cook, A.M. Roberts, M.J. Whittaker, A.D. Macfarlane, P.C.M. Freeman, P. Marson, C.R. Pearson, R.C. Claus, R.A. Fashler
Cooper, C., #503, 777 Blanshard St.
Cowper-Smith, D., 608 Yates St.
Cox, Taylor, Bryant, 26 Bastion Sq., A.L. Cox, R.J.E. Taylor, R.T. Bryant, M.J. Holmes, R.F. Barber, R.T.C. Johnston, C.E. Hanman, S.F.B. Carson, R.F. Barbour
Crawford & Hunter, #201, 895 Fort St., G.A. Crawford, R.F. Hunter
Crease & Co., #800, 1070 Douglas St., D.J. Lawson, Q.C., J.C. Scott-Harston, Q.C., R.B. Hutchison, R.N. Samson, R. Lou Poy, J.D. Patterson, P.W. Klassen, R.T. Taylor, G.C. Whitman, J.E.D. Savage, J.K. Greenwood, J.I.D. Joe, B.D. Kell
Cumming, Richards & Co., 880 Douglas St., C.D. Skillings, G.B. Sauder, L.H. Berry (also Vancouver)
Davies, J.S., 2230A Oak Bay Ave.
DiCastri, J.V., Q.C., 902 Foul Bay Rd.
Dinning & Vallance, 328 Goldstream Ave., C. Corners, B.E. Dinning, N.W. Vallance, B.H. Neff
Dunne, S.J., 531 Quadra St.
Easdon, G., #411, 620 View St. (R.J. Getz)
Ferne, H.C., #44, 4061 Larchwood Dr.
Fetterly, D.G., 1070 Douglas St.
Fisher & Cowan, 947 Fort St., C.W. Cowan, P. Nikolic, L.F.W. Mounce. Assoc. Counsel: J.D. Fisher
Giles, V.R., #250, 727 Johnson St.
Goult, McElmoyle & Wilson, #201, 2255 Oak Bay Ave., J.B.E. Goult, W.P. McElmoyle, C.R.W. Wilson, S. Manning
Hallatt, H.F., 848 Fort St.
Harling, J.K., 3561 Shelbourne St.
Harman & Co., 645 Fort St., J.N. McIllree, H.L. Henderson, R.M. McKay, R.H.G. Harman, S.M. Johnson, D.C. Brown, R.L. Spooner, P.C. Harrison, G.E. McDonald, J.R. Pennington
Heath & Co., 3371 Oak St., R.G. Heath, R.J. Irving, F.K. Walton, J.T. Leroy
Hitch & Co., 848 Courtney St., W.M. Hitch, G.F. Poole, R.H.M. Stewart
Holmes & Isherwood, 1192 Fort St., T.F. Isherwood, Constance D. Isherwood
Horne, Coupar, Manson & Shaw, #302, 612 View St., I.M. Horne, Q.C., R.B. Coupar, R.S. Manson, G.D. Shaw, W.J. Fensom, M. Horne, T.L. Thomson
Howard, S.F., 2041 Oak Bay Ave.
Hubbard, J.M., 611 Courtney St.
Humphries, MacKenzie & Johnson, 817 Fort St., D.A. Humphries, B.D. MacKenzie, L.T.D. Johnson
Illington, J.K., 2nd fl., 506 Fort St.
Jackson & Co., 25 Bastion Sq., A.B. Russ, W.G. McIntosh, F.J. Hansen, A.K. Fraser
Jawl & Bundon, 1007 Fort St., M.S. Jawl, P.M. Bundon, Lynne Eversole, J.R. Phillips, J.J. McLean
Johnson & Lee, #212, 1595 McKenzie Ave., E.M. Johnson, E.M. Lee
Jones, Emery & Carfra, #200, 1175 Douglas St., G.F. Jones, E.H.A. Emery, J.S. Carfra, D.W. Johns, W.R. Southward, G.P. Macdonald, R.D. Glazier, G.D. Walton, Martha E. McNeely, R.T. Horne, B.A. Barrington-Foote
Jones, R.E.M., 1518 Oak Crest Dr.
Jorre de St. Jorre, E.D., 1207 Douglas St.
Kelliher, S.M., 819 Fort St.
King & Hills, #310, 1205 Broad St., R.E. King, J.A.J. Hills
Kirchner & Co., 1070 Douglas St., D.C. Kirchner, C.J. Wilson
Ladner, Downs, 1175 Douglas St., D.H. Vickers (also Vancouver)
Latham, D.A., 612 View St.

Lee, M.M., 2224 Sooke Rd.
MacIsaac, Clark & Co., #201, 2067 Cadboro Bay Rd. (also Nanaimo)
MacMinn, Izard & Trann, 612 View St., E.G. MacMinn, I.D. Izard, R.A.W. Trann
Maddock, C.D.R., 1026 Meakes St.
Mah Ming, Chaperon & Hall, #203, 660 Fort St., B.W. Mah Ming, L.F.E. Chaperon, F.J.S. Hall, D.A. Logan
Marchant & Gillis, 844 Courtney St., J.H.L. Gillis
Matthews, Bryden & Co., 818 Douglas St., H.L. Matthews, R.K. Bryden, W.E. Oppel
McCallum, W.C., 1105 Oscar St. (D.W. Stewart)
McConnan, Bion, O'Connor & Peterson, 837 Burdett St., B.R. McConnan, P.E. Bion, M.J. O'Connor, A.J. Peterson, E.A. Moyes, W.S. Johnson
McMartin & Morrison, #201, 3749 Shelbourne St., P.O.H. McMartin, D. J. Morrison. Assoc. Counsel: C.P. Kehler
McMicken, Benn, Kjellander & Shaver, 3490 Saanich Rd., M.G. McMicken, G.W. Benn, K.C. Kjellander, J.A. Shaver
Milton & Munch, 2420 Douglas St., E.V. Milton, G.R. Munch
Monrad & Whitson, 1175 Cook St., B. Monrad, D. Whitson
Mundhenk, C.F., 841C Goldstream Ave.
O'Connor, T.G., 3420 Beach Dr.
O'Grady, T.P., Q.C., 1175 Douglas St. (R.E. McLarty)
Owen-Flood, Turnham, Green & Higinbotham, 844 Courtney St., D. D. Owen-Flood, H.F. Turnham, J.B. Green, R.A. Higinbotham, C.M. Considine, A.T. Milne, Barbara J. Yates, A.R. Woodland, J.W. Green, J.D. Waddell
Parsons & Bugeaud, 714A Goldstream Ave., P.L. Parsons, S.I. Bugeaud
Patterson, A.N., 645 Fort St.
Pearlman & Lindholm, 736 Broughton St. (V8W 2W6), L.F. Lindholm, G.A. Neely, J.F.N. Paget, D.A.M. Patterson, D.A. Farquhar, V.P. Reilly, J.W. Kenny, W.D. Murray, P. Pearlman, A.R. Tryon, D.I. Johannessen, J.K. Bracken
Price, Boyes & Co., #M-15, 635 Humbolt St., R.A. Price, L.B. Boyes, Fiona Hunter, E.W. Daigneault
Randall, Meyer & Pollard, #103, 1006 Fort St., C.G. Randall, R.J. Meyer, E. St. J. Pollard, R.C. DiBella
Roberts, B.C., 1175 Douglas St. (J.F. McGee)
Rogers, E.O., 1920 Sooke Rd.
Salmond, L., 1315 Esquimalt Rd., R.J. Salmond, D.E. Linge
Simeoni, V.W., 727 Johnson St.
Sinott & Simpson, #308, 645 Fort St., V.A. Simpson, T.H. MacLachlan
Smith & Co., 848 Courtney St., R.H. Smith, E.J. Woodhouse, J.R. Impett
Smith, G.P.H., 506 Fort St.
Smith, Hutchison & Gow, 747 Fort St., G.J. Smith, J.J. Gow, J.M. Hutchison, E.J. Partridge
Stevenson, Doell & Co., 999 Fort St., M.M. Stevenson, R.C. Doell, Jane Henderson, B. Kitzke, Mavis Ray
Stewart, I.H., 1175 Douglas St.
Stewart, Stewart & Trowbridge, #300, 1111 Blanshard St., R.N. Stewart, A. Stewart, B. Trowbridge
Straith & Co., 1070 Douglas St., W.A. Buchan, M.B.M. Ellis, M.D.W. Young, J.B. Garrison. Assoc. Counsel: H.C.K. Housser
Sullivan, G.J., #114, 3490 Saanich Rd.
Sweeney & Hatter, #320, 560 Johnson St., P.M. Sweeney, D.J. Hatter, E.C. Blake, R.J. Fahlman, R.S. Margetts
Tindall & Assoc., 3491 Saanich Rd., G.M. Tindall, D.E. Stuart
Tomlinson, E.G.L., 1162 Fort St.
Turner, R.J.A., 4400 Saanich Rd. w.
van Cuylenborg & Gray, 850 Courtney St., W. van Cuylenborg, D.H. Gray, R.D. Wilson, M.R. Birmingham, D.B. Adams, K.D. Jacques, B.G. Browning, U.O. Anniko, T.F. Lott
Williams, Eayrs & Darling, 990 Fort St., H.O. Williams, B.J. Eayrs, C.R. Darling, T.E. Dunford
Wilson, Bauman, Staples, #212, 895 Fort St., J.G. Wilson, Lorena Staples (also Kelowna)
Wilson, Marshall, 1005 Broad St., D.R. Wilson, S. Marshall
Woods & Adair, #201, 4500 w. Saanich Rd., D. Woods, R.D. Adair
Wootton, Anna, 620 View St.

WEST SUMMERLAND, Yale
Boyle & Co. (also Penticton)

WEST VANCOUVER, Vancouver
Allgaier, G., Box 91312
Balshine, L.I., 1084 Highland Dr.
Blackburn, W.E., #503, 100 s. Park Royal
Brady, M.A., 1497 Marine Dr.
Brister, D.E., 285 17th St.
Cave, W.H., 605 Clyde Ave.
Collins, D.S., 2146 Ottawa Ave.
Gillette, K.J., 2242 Marine Dr.
Goluboff, Mazzei & Schmidt, #201, 585 16th St., R.M. Goluboff, W.G. Mazzei, R.J. Schmidt
Hillman, K.A.L., 1318 Cammeray Rd.
Humphreys Merrifield, 605 Clyde Ave., R.G. Humphreys, S. S. Merrifield
Johnson, McCrea & Co., #410, 545 Clyde Ave., R.W. Johnson, B.E. McCrea, H.G. Cullen, Shelley Williams
Mathieson, D.L., 2020 Bellevue Ave.
Millan, M., 940 Keith Rd.
Monroe, R.N., 2204 Bellevue Rd. (also Vancouver)
Rapanos, G. P., 767 Eyremont Dr.
Stewart, P.C., 2337 Marine Dr.
Sweeney, Mrs. A.M., 1590 Bellevue Ave.
Topham & Laker, 285 17th St., L.W. Topham, J.C. Laker

WESTBANK, Yale
Brown, H.L., Box 548

WHISTLER, Westminster
Kraumanis, V.R., Box 172
Paul & Race (also Squamish)
Stacey, R.A.

WHITE ROCK, Westminster
Auerbach & Green, 1480 Foster St., V.K. Auerbach, R.H. Green
Bateman, J.H., #201, 1561 Russell St.
Beuhler, Carmen, #208, 15261 Russell Ave.
Blewett, J.C., 14468 Marine Dr.
Donald, Adams & Kruse, #305, 1656 Martin Dr., P.R.E. Adams, G.C. Kruse
Flesher, W.R., 13808 Marine Dr.
Ginther & Hardy, 15245 16th Ave., J.L. Ginther
Hambrook & Co., 15245 North Bluff Rd., R.A. Hambrook, Jane Purdie
Neen, W.A., 15125 16th Ave.
Petrunia, J., 14935 Marine Dr.
Taylor, R.L., #205, 1812 152nd St.
Thompson & McConnell, 15240 Thrift Ave., A.K. Thompson, W.C. McConnell, M.H. Thomas, A.J. McConkey, M.A. Parsons, R.C.P. Walker, A.R. Adlem, K.A. Blair, D.S. Fenton, R.K. Oliver, J.D. Bradford (also Vancouver)

WILLIAMS LAKE, Cariboo
Brackenbury, S.B.K., 150 Oliver St.
Crook & Oliver, 235 Oliver St., W.F. Crook, S.J. Oliver
Gardiner, L.R., 481 6th Ave. n.
Grant, K., #1, 72A s. 2nd Ave.
Rhodes, T.A.T., 197 n. 2nd Ave.
Vanderburgh, Scott & D'Arcy, #5, 123 Borland St., A.E. Vanderburgh, T.M. Scott, M.G.N. D'Arcy, L.T. Halpin, D.R. McLeod

BARRISTERS AND SOLICITORS IN MANITOBA

ALTONA, Winnipeg
Duncan & Co. (also Morden)
Wiens & Cole, 108 Main St., H.J. Wiens, P.J.E. Cole

ARBORG, Winnipeg
Walker, Cristall etc., Credit Union Bldg. (also Winnipeg)

ASHERN, Winnipeg
Geisler, D.E., Counsel: J.F. Anderson

BEAUSEJOUR, Beausejour
Bellan, Schroeder, Baker & Wasylin, 632 Park Ave. e., J. Bellan, Q.C., V. Schroeder, F.J. Baker, M.M. Wasylin
Middleton, Boni, Hawranik, Box 1150, W.C. Middleton, Q.C., J.F. Boni, G. Hawranik

BIRTLE, Russell
Butcher & Assoc., Box 190, M.D. Butcher, W. Langford

BOISSEVAIN, Killarney
George, J.A.H., Box 900

BRANDON, Brandon
Brawn, G.D., 227 10th St.
Carroll, Mullally, Paterson, 260 8th St., H. N. Carroll, Q.C., J. A. Mullally, D.A.S. Paterson
Clement, Potter & Co., 1202 Princess Ave., W.C. Pearson, Q.C., J.W. Potter, G.T. Williams, D.R. Hudson, J.D. Cram, B. Juce. Counsel: R.A. Clement, Q.C.
Hirschfield, Hunt, Fjeldsted & Miller, 148 8th St., A. A. Hirschfield, Q.C., D.S. Fjeldsted, G. T. Miller, J.H. Combs, D. Campbell
Meighen, Haddad & Co., #110, 119 11th St., F. O. Meighen, Q.C., J. Haddad, Q.C., R.L.R. Bidinosti, C.O. Meighen, Q.C., D.J. Pratt, W.G. Barber, L.W. Donald, B.J. Rodrigue
Sheldon, Singleton, Midwinter, Donald, 421 9th St., D.J. Sheldon, R.W. Singleton, B.C. Midwinter, D.R.C. Donald
Thornborough, Roy & Johnston, Box 605, L.J. Thornborough, P. Roy, R.H. Johnston

CARBERRY, Brandon
Agrawal, R.K., 122 Main St.
Clement, Potter & Co., 46 Main St. (also Brandon)

CARMAN, Morden
McKenzie, Mooney & Braun, R.S. McKenzie, T.R. Mooney, Mona Braun
Wilson, Selinger & Co., Box 219, J. W. Wilson, G.T. Selinger

CRYSTAL CITY, Morden
Treble & Morrison, Box 10, J.H. Treble, R.W. Morrison

DAUPHIN, Dauphin
Dawson & Parrot, 38 First Ave., R.W. Dawson, J. Parrot
Hawkins, McKenzie & Sanderson, Box 552, E.W. Hawkins, Q.C., P.M.A. McKenzie, G.H. Sanderson
Irwin Law Office, 108 1st St. n.w., E.B. Irwin
Johnston, Oliphant, Van Buekenhout & Deans, Box 551, I.R. Johnston, J.J. Oliphant, Q.C., T.J.J. Van Buekenhout, J.D. Deans, J. Menzies
Valiant, M.J., 7 Tuxedo Dr.

DELORAINE, Killarney
Meighen, Haddad & Co., W.G. Barber (also Brandon)
North, G. H.

DUGALD, Winnipeg
Holland, J. D.

ELIE, Portage la Prairie
Miller, Miller & Co. (also Portage la Prairie)

ELKHORN, Virden
Aitken, Alex & Co. (also Virden)

EMERSON, St. Boniface
Forrester & Forrester, W. R. Forrester, Q.C.

ERICKSON, Minnedosa
Brawn & Co. (also Minnedosa)
McTavish, Golightly (also Winnipeg)
St. John & St. John (also Minnedosa)

FLIN FLON, Flin Flon
Black Law Firm, 35 Main St., R.K. Black
Ginnell, Gregoire & Sardiwalla, 35 Main St., J.M. Ginnell, Q.C., R.J.C. Gregoire, O.F.I. Sardiwalla

GILBERT PLAINS, Dauphin
Johnston & Co. (also Dauphin)

GLADSTONE, Portage la Prairie
Christianson & Christianson (also Portage la Prairie)

GLENBORO, Brandon
Meighen & Co. (also Brandon)

GRANDVIEW, Dauphin
Hawkins & Co. (also Dauphin)

HAMIOTA, Minnedosa
Buckingham & Co. (also Virden)
Perlmutter, S.

HOLLAND, Morden
Meighen, Haddad & Co. (also Brandon)

KILLARNEY, Killarney
Gardiner & Harrison, Wm. Harrison, E.G. Harrison
Heming, K.I.M., Box 304

LAC DU BONNET, Beausejour
Besel, W.B., Box 566
Fillmore, Riley (also Winnipeg)
Kushner, B. (also Winnipeg)
Tolton & Co. (also Winnipeg)

LORETTE, St. Boniface
Wyrzykowski, C.L. (also Winnipeg)

MACGREGOR, Portage la Prairie
Christianson & Christianson (also Portage la Prairie)

MANITOU, Morden
Scurfield & Selby, Box 27, W.E. Scurfield, L.J. Selby

MELITA, Killarney
Smeltz & Holmes, Main & Souris Sts., M.H. Smeltz, R.A. Holmes

MINNEDOSA, Minnedosa
Brawn, Taylor, Cummings, Box 460, R.D. Brawn. Assoc. Counsel: C.D. Taylor, R.G. Cummings
St. John & St. John, Box 428, D.D. St. John, Q.C.

MORDEN, Morden
Duncan & Co., Box 70, D.A. Duncan, Q.C., J.A. Duncan, Q.C., K.R. Hanssen, G.J. Hoeschen
Westwood & Dykman, Box 20, F.S. Westwood, J.A. Dykman

MORRIS, Winnipeg
Braun, Schmidt & Gregory, Box 578, S. E. Braun, G. B. Schmidt, B.D. Gregory

NEEPAWA, Minnedosa
Bass & Berg, 390 Mountain Ave., G.N. Bass, A.L. Berg
Brawn, Taylor, Cummings, Box 309, C.D. Taylor, R.G. Cummings. Assoc.: R.D. Brawn

PILOT MOUND, Morden
Clark, A. E.
Treble & Morrison, Box 240 (also Crystal City)

PORTAGE LA PRAIRIE, Portage la Prairie
Anderson & Beaulieu, 232½ Saskatchewan Ave. e., J. Anderson, G.C. Beaulieu
Christianson & Christianson, 316 Saskatchewan Ave. e., C.C. Christianson, B. Christianson
Greenberg & Greenberg, 231 Saskatchewan Ave. e., G. D. Greenberg, B. R. Greenberg. Associate: H. I. Pollock, Q.C. (also Winnipeg)
Miller, Miller & Pressey, Box 368, J. C. Miller, Q.C., B. Miller, Q.C., O.W. Pressey
Sing & Sing, Box 548, Carol P. Sing
Troniak, D.M., 2401 Saskatchewan Ave. w.

RAPID CITY, Minnedosa
St. John & St. John (also Minnedosa)

RESTON, Virden
Buckingham & Co. (also Virden)
Forrest & Forrest (also Souris)

RIVERS, Brandon
Clement, Potter & Co., 505 2nd Ave. (also Brandon)
Perlmutter, S. (also Hamiota)

ROBLIN, Dauphin
Demkiw, E. W., Box 963
Gregoire, M., 204 Main St.

RUSSELL, Russell
Coppleman, D.D.S., 346 Main St.
Wilson, J.E.N., Box 70

ST. ADOLPHE, Eastern
McTavish, Golightly (also Winnipeg)

ST. BONIFACE, St. Boniface
Avanthay, F. R., 185 Provencher Blvd.
Deniset, P.J.R., #305, 400 Tache (also Winnipeg)
Marcoux, Betournay, etc., 200, 170 Marion St. (also Winnipeg)
Teffaine, Monnin, Hogue, Teillet & Sharp, #201, 185 Provencher Blvd., R. E. Teffaine, Q.C., M. Monnin, A.J. Hogue, L.V. Teillet, Carol W. Sharp

ST. CLAUDE, Winnipeg
Troniuk & Co. (also Portage la Prairie)

STE. ROSE DU LAC, Dauphin
Hawkins & Co. (also Dauphin)

SELKIRK, Selkirk
Israel, M., 357 Main St. (also Winnipeg)
Kitchen, D.W., 2 Main St.
Parker, Sarbit & Co., 379A Arena Plaza (also Winnipeg)
Szewczyk, R. H., 371 Eveline St.
Taylor & Co., 347 Main St. (also Winnipeg)
Walker, Cristall, etc., 345 Main St. (also Winnipeg)
Wasel, L.D., 339 Main St.
Wawrykow & Kohaykewych, 413 Main St., M.D. Kohaykewych
Williams, D.F., 407 Main St., A. Scramstad. Counsel: J.R. Glowacki, Q.C.

SHOAL LAKE, Minnedosa
Brawn, R.D., Box 430 (also Minnedosa)
Lauman, G. A., Q.C.

SOMERSET, Morden
Marcoux & Co. (also Winnipeg)

SOURIS, Brandon
Forrest & Forrest, H. W. Forrest, B. H. Forrest

STEINBACH, St. Boniface
Dyck, Smith & Neufeld, Box 1267, E. R. Dyck, R.P. Smith, J.E. Neufeld, B.D. Stewart
Goossen, E. R., Box 2320
Oliver & Derksen, #203, 333A Main St. (also Winnipeg)
Plett, D. J.

STONEWALL, Winnipeg
Binkley Assoc., Box 1158, J.R. Binkley
Goodman, T.A. & Co., T.A. Goodman, D.W. Grantham
Lyons, J. M., 364 Main St.

SWAN RIVER, Swan River
Bjornsson Law Office, 510 Main St. e., D.G. Bjornsson, D.N. Gray
Carroll Jamieson, Box 340, K.R. Carroll, D.W. Jamieson
Sloane & Palsson, Box 1238, E.J. Sloane, B.G. Palsson

THE PAS, The Pas
Barton & Giesbrecht, 229 Fischer Ave., R.W. Barton, L. Giesbrecht
MacIver, D.N. & Assoc., 163 Edward Ave.
Mercredi & Buhay, Otineka Mall, O. Mercredi, S.M. Buhay
Premachuk, Wight & Knight, 237 Fischer St., E. Premachuk, L. Wight, D.R. Knight
Watkins, N., 215 Fischer St.

THOMPSON, Thompson
Bancroft, Whidden, Mayer & Buzza, 7 Selkirk Ave., W. R. Whidden, R. A. Mayer, T.R.J. Buzza, Holly Beard
Drapack & Howell, 309, 83 Churchill Dr., J. P. Drapack, M.W. Howell

TREHERNE, Portage la Prairie
Miller & Miller (also Portage la Prairie)

VIRDEN, Virden
Aitken & Co., Box 1780, A. Aitken (also Elkhorn)
Buckingham, McNeill, Smith, Poole & Co., Box 520, C. W. Buckingham, Q.C., R.M. McNeill, R.T. Smith, S.R. Poole, E.J. Sims, N.H. Sims

WHITEMOUTH, Beausejour
Middleton & Boni (also Beausejour)

WINKLER, Morden
Duncan & Duncan (also Morden)
Dyck & Co. (also Steinbach)
Gilmour, Partington & Assoc., Box 1238, G.R. Gilmour, T. Partington

WINNIPEG, Eastern
Abrams, W., 117 Regent Ave. w. (Transcona)
Adelman, B., 504 Main St.

Aikins, MacAulay & Thorvaldson, 3rd floor, 333 Broadway Ave. (R3C OT1), A.L. Campbell, C.D., Q.C., W.S. Martin, Q.C., J.S. Lamont, Q.C., R.J. Hansell, Q.C., M.J. Mercury, Q.C., A.J. Mercury, M.H. Freedman, Q.C., A.C. Tough, J.E. Foran, K.B. Foster, Q.C., A.J. Irving, E.B. MacDonald, R.G. Smellie, Q.C., L.N. Mercury, M.E. Rothstein, Q.C., R.H.G. Flett, J.T. Samson, C.G. Labman, L.R. Crane, R.B. Dias, C.L. Chappell, C.R. MacArthur, R.E. Stephenson, G.D. Parkinson, F.M. Statham, D.G. Hill, E.B. Parker, S. Jane Evans, Judith M. Blair, D.L. Voechting, M.M. Monnin, Diane E. Jones, S.H.I. Wilder, D.J. Rosin, M.N. Trachtenberg, W.S. Gange, G.B. Taylor, R.L. Yaffe, R.G. Siddall, W.A. Simms. Assoc. Counsel: Hon. R.S. Bowles, Q.C.
Allen & Riley, 253 Hugo St., H.L. Allen, G.P.S. Riley, L.P. Allen
Alsip & Tracy, 137 Scott St., S.D. Alsip, M.T. Tracy, D. Zyla
Appleby, Hedley & McCandless, #340, 125 Garry St., W.R. Appleby, J.W. Hedley, M.W. McCandless, D.H. Jordan
Arenson, A.C., #201, 834 Ellice Ave.
Arenson, M., 2055 McPhillips St.
Arpin & Co., 1100, 444 St. Mary Ave., M.J. Arpin, Q.C., A.A. Rich, Q.C., K.A. Filkow, Q.C., R.M. Rice, Helen M. Arpin, J. Keyzer, J.E. Crane
Baker, A.P., #704, 283 Portage Ave.
Baker, Zivot, Radcliffe, Murray & Sinnock, #300, 360 Main St., R.H.C. Baker, Q.C., A. M. Zivot, Q.C., M.F.C. Radcliffe, W.R. Murray, G.J. Sinnock, L.B. Cherrett
Barker, W.L., #900, 294 Portage Ave.
Beehler & Co., 1754 Main St., M.J. Beehler
Beley, T.P., 390 York Ave.
Bernstein & Hirsch, #800, 283 Portage Ave., M. Bernstein, E. Hirsch
Besko & Assoc., 171 River Ave., T.P. Besko
Billinkoff, Meltzer, 175 Carlton St., M.M. Meltzer, E. I. Essers, M.A.N. Goldberg, A. L. Kussin, M.D. Kay, O.G. Ament, L.M. Smordin
Birt, C.T., 2571 Pembina Hwy.
Booth, Kripiakevich, Dennehy, Parfeniuk & Ernst, 387 Broadway Ave., D.A. Booth, N.A. Kripiakevich, G.M. Dennehy, E. Parfeniuk, D.B. Ernst, P.F. Lasko, W.R. Van Walleghem. Counsel: D.B.W. Forrester, Q.C.
Bowman & Bowman, 200, 116 Edmonton St., D.E. Bowman, Myrna Bowman
Braker, S. B., 228 Notre Dame Ave.
Breen & Breen, 200 Osborne St. n., Samuel Breen, Q.C., Helen D. Breen, D.M. Griffin
Brotman, Cramer & Braunstein, #1018, 363 Broadway Ave., E.A. Brotman, Q.C., Caroline Cramer, M. Braunstein
Buchwald, Asper, Henteleff, #1900, 155 Carlton St., R3C 3H8, H. Buchwald, Q.C., A.A. Sarchuk, Q.C., R.G.S. Shead, Y. Lerner, E.D. Brown, M.K. Fingold, A.D.M. Orgaranko, D.W. Regelous, R.M. Leipsic, N. Promislow, R.M. Gray, Y.M. Henteleff, B. Kushner, L.B. Nasberg, A.M. Kaufman, M.S. Palay, Carol Cockshott, D.M. Ehringer. Counsel: I.H. Asper, Q.C.; Assoc.: S.B. Zitzerman
Bunn, T.A., 300 Assiniboine St.
Campbell, Maxwell, Kozminski, Jackiew & Reimer, #400, 208 Edmonton St., F. G. Campbell, R. V. Maxwell, R. M. Kozminski, W.R. Jackiew, G.P. Reimer
Canadian National Railways, 360, 123 Main St., Regional Counsel: G. H. Nerbas
Canadian Pacific Ltd., 181 Higgins Ave., Regional Counsel: J.L. Bowles
Canadian Wheat Board, 423 Main St., H. B. Monk, Q.C.
The Chapman Company, 1864 Portage Ave., G. E. Chapman, C. A. Chapman, A.R. Goddard, T.B. Kumka. Counsel: G.T. Chapman, Q.C.
Charne, T.C., Q.C., #200, 185 Carlton St.
Chasanoff, J., 129 McDermot Ave. e.
Cherniak, S.M., Q.C., 333 St. John's Ave.
Cholakis, L., 1800, 275 Portage Ave.
Christie, DeGraves, MacKay, 400, 433 Portage Ave., N. C. Christie, Q.C., W. R. DeGraves, Q.C., M. MacKay, Q.C., C. C. Settle, Q.C., D. G. Unruh, A. W. Eyolfson, A.B. Graham, G.M. Wood, B.E. Pydee
City Solicitors, Winnipeg Law Dept., Council Bldg., Civic Centre, F.N. Steele, City Solicitor; H.R.R. Klapecki, Asst. City Solicitor; T.L.O. Thomas, M.S. Samphir, S.K. Treon, N.D. Bodnarchuk, V.P. Bahl, W.R. Stovel, L.E. Strijack, D.W. Buhr, G.R. Carnegie, U.B. Goeres
Clifford & Freed, #200D, 338 Broadway Ave., G.C. Clifford, M. Freed
Clubine, H.P., 807, 294 Portage Ave.
Cohan, S., #201, 379 Broadway Ave.
Cohen, T.C., 207 Academy Rd.
Corne & Corne, #700, 259 Portage Ave., A.S. Corne, M.S. Corne, Q.C. Counsel: H.I. Corne
Corrin, B. M., 857 Sargent Ave.
Cowan, J., Q.C., 269 Yale Ave.
Crawford, J.L., Q.C., 202, 460 Main St.
Cuddy, N.A., #606, 228 Notre Dame Ave. (R.J. Strahl)
D'Arcy & Deacon, 300, 286 Smith St. (R3C 1K6), J. C. Kirby, Q.C., H. K. Irving, Q.C., G.T. Haig, Q.C., R.G. Smethurst, Q.C., R. Anderson, J.E. Deacon, C. Pappas, J.G. Harley, D.A. Young, B.P. Metcalfe, R.W. MacNeil, R.J. Graham, R.G. Wookey, Bonnie-Kay McPhee, P.R. Anderson
Dattani, T.V., 2101 One Evergreen Place
Deeley, Fabbri & Sellen, 6th floor, 386 Broadway Ave., R.K. Deeley, R.R. Fabbri, D.R. Sellen, D.A. Lampe-Adams
DeLucia & DeLucia, 228 Notre Dame Ave., G. O. DeLucia
Deniset, P.J.R., 674 Langevin St.
Dettman, A.B., 31 Carriere Ave.
Diamond & Adleman, 1300 Plessis Rd., H.D. Diamond, S. Adleman
Dowhan, W., #1610, 330 Portage Ave.
Drache, S.J., Q.C., Penthouse A, 21 Mayfair Place
Dunlop, D.M., #200, 1120 Grant Ave.
Dzinkowski, K., 305, 209 Notre Dame Ave.
Eadie & Assoc., 1907 Portage Ave., W.S. Eadie
Einarson & Einarson, 1105, 444 St. Mary Ave., G.J. Einarson, B.J. Einarson
Enns, C. (Neil), 1522, 363 Broadway Ave.
Eyrikson, Clay & Co., 298 St. Anne's Rd., H.J. Eyrikson, G.R. Clay, D.A. Flett
Fainman, F., #900, 294 Portage Ave.
Falk, Warkentin, Van Den Bosch, Thiessen & Jensen, #1800, 360 Main St., P.J. Falk, E.L. Warkentin, G. Van Den Bosch, W. Thiessen, P.L. Jensen
Federsel, G.J., 214, 504 Main St.
Feuer & Jacobson, 312, 352 Donald Ave., M. Feuer, M. Jacobson, J.S. Gill
Fillmore & Riley, #1700, 360 Main St., E.R. Yarnell, Q.C., D.H. Ringstrom, W.G. Ryall, R.B. Goodwin, R.I. Good, M.K. Christie, R.D. McDonald, J. Carlson, R.B. McNicol, M.M. Rutherford, D.W. Leslie, W.P. Fillmore, D.I. Christie, D.S. Norquay, Colleen Suche, D.N. Kruk, R.A. Simpson, R.S. Ade, Louise Lamb
Fineman, A., 711 Portage Ave.
Fishman, L.R., 200, 116 Edmonton St.
Fitch, E. L., #205, 259 Portage Ave.
Follett, R. L., 200, 1135 Henderson Hwy. (J.K. Reid, J.R. Braemer)
Freedman, M., #601, 330 Portage Ave.
Friesen, David, Q.C., & Associates, 711, 213 Notre Dame Ave. (B. Albrecht, R.L. Friesen)
Furgale & Co., #155K, 1485 Portage Ave., T.C. Furgale, H.A. Henning, J.R. Chamberlain
Galbraith, P.M., 392 Waterloo St.
Genik, N., 708, 294 Portage Ave.
George & Assoc., 108 Regent Ave. e., J.D. George, P.C. Patel
Gindin, Soronow & Malamud, #200, 297 Smith St., J. Gindin, S.G. Soronow, S. Malamud, R.G.C. Allard, R.L. Gutkin, J. Werier, D.I. Friedman
Glowacki, Libitka & Janicki, #600, 228 Notre Dame Ave., J.R. Glowacki, V.W. Libitka, V.S. Janicki
Goldberg, S., 1212, 363 Broadway Ave.
Golsof, Pullan, Guld & Satran, 800, 259 Portage Ave., N. B. Golsof, G. M. Pullan, N. M. Satran, E. A. Guld, P.E. Kammerlock
Goodman, H. G., 501, 228 Notre Dame Ave.
Gotti, J., 807, 294 Portage Ave.
Gould, Norman S., & Assoc., 175 Carlton St., H.L. Tennenhouse, D.E. McDonald
Grafton & Co., 304, 213 Notre Dame Ave., T. D. Grafton, R. S. Rosenberg
Greenberg & Co., 9th fl., 363 Broadway Ave., L.C. Greenberg, Q.C., R. Stachurski
Grubert, O. B., 175 Hargrave St.
Gunn, J.L., #900, 259 Portage Ave.
Halprin & Halprin, 310, 213 Notre Dame Ave., R.K. Halprin
Halter, Aubrey J., 604, 265 Portage Ave.
Halter, G. Sydney, Q.C., 614, 294 Portage Ave.
Harasym, J.I., 161 Stafford St.
Heppenstall & Habing, 3303A Portage Ave., L.F. Heppenstall, R.M. Habing
Hillhouse, T.P., Q.C., 354 Scotia St. (W. Kildonan)
Hnidan, J. R., 603, 265 Portage Ave.
Hoffer, A.D., #900, 363 Broadway Ave.
Hoffman, Allan A., 1212, 363 Broadway Ave.
Houston & MacIver, 1522, 363 Broadway Ave., K.G. Houston, A.J. MacIver
Hretzay, E.N., 125 Higgins St.
Huppe, Harold A., Q.C., 929 St. Mary's Rd.
Inkster, Walker, Westbury, Irish, Rusen & Hughes, 219 Kennedy St., J. B. Hughes, Q.C., W.C. Irish, P.W.A. Westbury, G. D. Walker, Q.C., C. L. Inkster, M. S. Rusen, J. D. Barnsley, J.L. Henteleff
Ironquill Meadmore, M., #900, 294 Portage Ave.
Isaacs & Isaacs, 265 Portage Ave., Max Isaacs, Q.C., Manly Isaacs
Israel & Assoc., #900, 363 Broadway Ave., M.W. Israel, P.D.M. Smith, L.A. Bubis
Johnson, F.A.G., 607, 386 Broadway Ave.
Juravsky, Sharfe & Associates, 704, 213 Notre Dame Ave., W. Juravsky, L. Sharfe
Karasevich & Associates, 179 Henderson Hwy., J.G. Karasevich. Counsel: J.G. Karasevich, Q.C.
Kelekis, L. C. & Associates, 101, 189 Henderson Hwy., L.C. Kelekis, G. Minuk
Kennedy, J.S.,
Kerr, B.N., 402, 259 Portage Ave.
Khanuja, S.S., 1373 Portage Ave.
Kimmel, A. K., 701, 228 Notre Dame Ave.

Kirby, E. J., Q.C., #403, 209 Notre Dame Ave.
Klein & Co., #718, 363 Broadway Ave., K.D. Klein, R.A. Ward, S.J. Pierce
Kohm, H., 204, 228 Notre Dame Ave.
Koshowski, W.D., #5, 1311 Portage Ave.
Krawchuk, Galanchuk, 401, 213 Notre Dame Ave., B. E. Krawchuk, K. J. Galanchuk, A.W. Bellhouse, A.F. Huck, A.B. Warbanski
Kress, B., #220, 530 Kenaston Blvd.
Kushner & Gordon, 500, 338 Broadway Ave., C.N. Kushner, Q.C., H.E. Gordon
Kushnier, R.N., 232 Henderson Hwy.
Labbus, Frances R., 61 Moore Ave.
Lamont, Mary, 900, 294 Portage Ave.
Law Office, 100M, 1485 Portage Ave., Alice Steinbart
Lawrence, A.G., 4910 Roblin Blvd.
Lawrence, F., 507, 283 Portage Ave.
Lerner, H., #205, 175 Hargrave St.
Levin & Soronow, #200, 297 Smith St., R.I. Soronow, Q.C.
Levine, Naomi, #1522H, 363 Broadway
Lindgren, E., 21 St. Annes Rd.
Loewen & Martens, 1110 Henderson Hwy., V.G. Loewen, R.G. Martens
Ludlow, H. J. L., 708, 294 Portage Ave.
MacDonald, Macmillan, #1445, 444 St. Mary Ave., I.R.A. Macmillan, J.A. MacDonald, T. Fultz, G.A. Cudney, F.A. Lee, J.E. Rutley, Jr.
MacInnes, Burbidge & Co., 191 Lombard Ave., F.L. Cvitkovitch, T. R. McDowell, Donna E. Matthews
MacKenzie, A.J., #508, 428 Portage Ave.
Mackling, A.H., Q.C., 1874 Portage Ave.
Marantz, W., 1383 Pembina Hwy., Fort Garry
Marcoux, Betournay, La Bossiere, #200, 170 Marion St. (St. Boniface), L. G. Marcoux, Q.C., R. L. Betournay, D.J. La Bossiere, F.W. DuVal
Margolis, Kaufman, Cassidy, Zaifman, Swartz, #201, 379 Broadway Ave., D. Marolis, M. Kaufman, R.L. Cassidy, K.S. Zaifman, P. Swartz, B. Bonney, F.S. Wilder. Counsel: M.E. Kopstein, Q.C.
Martens, W., Q.C., #601, 330 Portage Ave.
Masciuch, Moss & Bortoluzzi, 700, 228 Notre Dame Ave., Y.O. Mascuich, P.J. Moss, F.E. Bortoluzzi, E.S. Waskiw
Matas, D., #200, 116 Edmonton St.
Mauer, J.O., 433 Stradbrook Ave.
McCreedy & Co., 931 Nairn Ave., K.W.A. McCreedy, M. Knight
McDonald, J.H., #1014, 363 Broadway Ave.
McGonigal, M., #900, 294 Portage Ave.
McManus, T.J., #310, 283 Portage Ave.
McRoberts, Henderson Law Offices, 919 Notre Dame Ave., R.J.D. McRoberts, R.J. Henderson
McTavish & Golightly, 1002 Pembina Hwy., D.N. McTavish, G.E. Golightly
Michel, H. E. & Co., 502 Paris Bldg.
Miller, Irene, #206, 428 Portage Ave.
Minuk, R., #200, 297 Smith St.
Monk, Goodwin & Co., #500, 232 Portage Ave., H. B. Monk, Q.C., W.F. Smith, R.R. Goodwin, Q.C., E.M. Shewchuk, R. Hucal, J.H. Dixon, R.N. Hoeschen, G.E. Ulyatt, C.J. Phelan, C. Lynn Romeo, L.J. Roy, B.L. Gorlick
Morkin, Hayes & Dobrowolski, #920, 363 Broadway, D. W. Hayes, Q.C., A. Dobrowolski, K.R.P. Kirby, G.T. Hodgson
Musick, B., 20 Wordsworth Way
Namak & Kovnats, #207, 83 Sherbrooke St., G.S. Namak, D.B. Kovnats
Nemy, Brown & Roy, 200, 2727 Portage Ave., M.H. Nemy, J.C. Brown, B.A. Roy. Assoc.: J.M. Rabkin
Newman & Co., #601, 386 Broadway Ave., D.G. Newman, A. Morton, Alexandra Gunson, V.J. Duke
Newman, MacLean, 436 Main St., G. Arron, L.J. Lucas, V.L. Baird, Q.C., G.C. MacLean, Q.C., M. Neuman, Q.C., V.F. Janzen, W.A. Redekopp, G.W. Katelnikoff, H.E. Suderman, W.J. Kehler, R.D. Steinburg, R.B. King, Jennifer Cooper
Nozick, M.J., 175 Hargrave St.
Nozick, Sinder & Assoc., #800, 283 Portage Ave., S. Nozick, B. Sinder, M. Kucher, M. Manko
Numerow, K., #804, 363 Broadway Ave.
Nusgart, D. M., 213 Notre Dame Ave.
Ogaranko & Iwanchuk, #200, 952 Main St., M.J. Ogaranko, C.W. Iwanchuk, N. Trusewych
Olesky, R.L., #500, 338 Broadway Ave.
Oliver & Derksen, 433 Stradbrooke Ave., Jill D. Oliver, Mary Rose Derksen, April D. Katz, Monique Bicknell Danaher. Counsel: Janet Baldwin
Olynyk, R. P., #103, 2639 Portage Ave.
Parashin & Co., 404 McGregor St., P. Parashin, Katherine L. Lamont, R. P. Parashin
Parker, J.H., #500, 211 Portage Ave.
Parker, Sarbit, Lorenc, 1708 Richardson Bldg., One Lombard Place, B. S. Parker, S. D. Sarbit, C. Lorenc, E.G. Strell, G. Funk
Pauls, Pedlar & Preston, #201, 323 Portage Ave., B.A. Pauls, Dorothy Pedlar, T. Preston
Pearlman, D. M., 203, 265 Portage Ave.
Peikoff, L.A.M., #202, 309 Hargrave St.
Perlov, D., #200, 297 Smith St.
Peterson, Mrs. M. G., 3224 Portage Ave.
Pitblado & Hoskin, 19th floor, Richardson Bldg., One Lombard Place (R3B 2L8), G. R. Hunter, Q.C., D.J. Jessiman, Q.C., W.C. Gardner, Q.C., W.M. Coghlin, Q.C., D. Proctor, R.W. McMurray, T.M. Glowacki, Q.C., I.L. Jessiman, Q.C., W.L. Palk, Q.C., P.M. Ramsay, J.B. Fraser, W.C. Kushneryk, F.W. Christie, D.D. Jessiman, R.A. Dewar, J.R. Toone, B.G. Bergh, W.S. Gardner, R.J. Handlon, E.J. Guercio, R.M. Jessiman, E.W. Peever, P.G. Guy, Catherine Dunn, K.R. Bolt, J.A. Ferguson, W.E. Skelly, R.P. Sokalski. Counsel: Keith Turner, Q.C., E.A. Braid
Pittarelli, A.P., 904, 211 Portage Ave.
Pollock & Co., 1610, 155 Carlton St., H.I. Pollock, Q.C., B. Steinfeld, C.N. Guberman, Brenda L. Keyser
Pollock, Kravetsky & Alexander, 711, 259 Portage Ave., G.C. Pollock, N.H. Kravetsky, A.D. Alexander, J.S. Michaels, Sandra Polinsky, R.Z. Potash
Posner, G.S., #200, 938 Corydon Ave.
Pybus, Chornous, Smith, Green, Romaniw, Davidson & Gabor, 310 Edmonton St., C. W. Pybus, Q.C., E. G. Chornous, J. G. Smith, L. Green, W. O. Romaniw, L.A. Davidson, R. Gabor
Rachman, Wm., 203, 504 Main St.
Radchuk & Peters, 1114, 330 Portage Ave., S. Radchuk, Q.C., K.B. Peters
Regier, Stewart, 1540, 155 Carlton St., K.P. Regier, Q.C., A.L.V. Stewart, G.W. Saunders, I. Hamilton
Regnier, L. A., 265 Portage Ave.
Restall, J. H., Q.C., #1610, 330 Portage Ave.
Robertson & Bond, 807, 294 Portage Ave., J.E. Bond
Robinson, R. S., #707, 213 Notre Dame Ave.
Rosen, A., #603, 504 Main St.
Rosenbaum, Murray & Potkonjak, #201, 2211 McPhillips St., H.J. Rosenbaum, D.G. Murray, E. Potkonjak, M.L. Skremetka, R.C. Rutman
Ross & Kasloff, #912, 363 Broadway Ave., C. Ross, T.L. Kasloff
Ross & Skinner, 641 St. Mary's Rd., J.G. Ross, D.J. Skinner, M.H.D. Green
Rusimovich, R.M., 247 Knowles Ave.
Rutledge & Unger, #214, 2281 Portage Ave., R. F. Rutledge, A. I. Unger
Sansome, J. H., 438 Woodlands Cres.
Saper, J.H., #203, 1345 Pembina Hwy. (T.W. Hadaller)
Scarth, Simonsen, Dooley, Olson & Wiens, 386 Broadway Ave., A. Scarth, Q.C., V. Simonsen, T. P. Dooley, E. W. Olson, J. T. Wiens, Barbara Hamilton, G. McKinnon, H.J. Peters
Schafer, D., 820 Queenston St.
Schoen, F.S., 1037 Garfield St. n.
Schulman & Schulman, 816, 294 Portage Ave., M.M. Schulman, P.W. Schulman, Q.C.
Schwartz, D.G., #402, 259 Portage Ave.
Schwartz, McJannet, Weinberg, Riley, 5th fl., 175 Carlton St., R3C 3H9, S.I. Schwartz, J.T. McJannet, Q.C., A.L. Weinberg, W.P. Riley, A. Anhang, A.H. Adam, E.A. Wehrle, M. Kravetsky, E.P. Zinman, M.D. Werier, G.J. Orle, D.J. Nelko, J.A. Schnoor, N.F. Trenholm, D.M. Willcock, S.Z. Tessler, Sherryl Steinberg, D.M.R. Cheop, Sylvia Guertin, L.K. Vickar
Schwartzwald, M. H., 912, 363 Broadway Ave.
Seipp, L.A., #507, 283 Portage Ave.
Sharfe, L., #704, 213 Notre Dame Ave.
Sheps, S. G. & Associates Ltd., 673 Oak St., S.G. Sheps
Shewchuk & Assoc., 2645 Portage Ave., J. Shewchuk, Brenda Armstrong
Shuckett, B. A., 203, 209 Notre Dame Ave.
Shuckett, N., #603, 265 Portage Ave.
Silden, M., #500, 338 Broadway Ave.
Simkin, Gallagher, 6th floor, 363 Broadway Ave. (R3C 1L2), A. L. Simkin, Q.C., A. P. Cantor, Q.C., J.M. Chapman, Q.C., N.S. Goltsman, M. L. Rosenberg, A.R. McGregor, P.M. Sheps, S.F. Kohn, D. Morry, J.L. Dudeck, B.C.M. Simkin, D.A. Primeau, C.M. Fien, R.F. Doolan, Sandra C. Gordon, Janice Y. Sylvestre, P.S. Teskey, D.R. James, D.M. Shrom, Celia E. Kaufman, R.B. Giesbrecht, Mira J. Thow. Counsel: J.E. Hershfield. Assoc.: Raymond Kives
Sinclair & Assoc., 221, 1120 Grant Ave., J.L. Sinclair, G.W. Edmond, G.G. Parker, R.A. Bennell
Skwark, Myers, Baizley & Weinstein, #204, 215 Portage Ave., M. Skwark, Q.C., Mel Myers, Q.C., P. Bromley, D.G. Baizley, Q.C., H. Weinstein, L.W. Ring, D.M. Baczynsky, D.P. Bryk, R.L. Pollock, L. Cherniak, Vivian Hilder. Assoc.: G. Pollock, Q.C., Marva Smith
Slusky & Slusky, 1212, 363 Broadway Ave., M. A. Slusky, I. H. Slusky
Smith, J.R., #202, 1383 Pembina Hwy.
Smith, Remi, #900, 363 Broadway Ave.
Sokolov, Klein & Co., 220 Portage Ave., D. I. Sokolov, Q.C., B. D. Klein, M. Newman
Solomon, Earl, 914, 363 Broadway Ave.
Spivak & Spivak, #607, 386 Broadway Ave., S.J. Spivak, Q.C.
Strange, Miles & Assoc., 205, 93 Lombard Ave., J.D.F. Strange, D.S. Miles, M.G. Tadman
Stefanyshyn, R., #205, 52 Donald St.
Stubbs, Stubbs & Stubbs, 504, 283 Portage Ave., G. St. G. Stubbs
Suffield & Denaburg, #504, 294 Portage Ave., S.G. Denaburg
Sukhan, J. S., 1158 Clarence Ave.

Swystyn & Co., #102, 5 Donald St. s., N.W. Swystyn, J.H. Restall, Jr., J.G. Webster, R.C. Jenion, T.L. Luchak
Tallin & Kristjansson, 300, 232 Portage Ave., C.K. Tallin, Q.C., A.F. Kristjansson, Q.C., B.N. Johannson
Tapper, M.H., 804, 363 Broadway Ave.
Tax, W. S., 228 Notre Dame Ave.
Taylor Brazzell McCaffrey, 4th fl., 386 Broadway Ave., R3C 3R6, G.T. Brazzell, Q.C., R. Carr, R.L. Coke, J.H. Cook, G.M. Erickson, D.E. Finkbeiner, P.B. Forsyth, Nicole Garson, S. Greenberg, D.C. King, J.A. King, E.G. Lister, Jacqueline Lowe, D.J. Mackenzie, D.I. Marr, D'A. McCaffrey, Q.C., L.G.C. Milne, G. Mitchell, H.S. Riley, R.C. Roy, C.A. Sherbo, S.G. Sigurdson, G.R. Smith, J.F.R. Taylor, Q.C., Shelley Weiss. Counsel: C.G. Dilts, Q.C.; Assoc.: R.M. Akman
Tepley & Pooley, 401, 460 Main St., J.H. Tepley, W.B.K. Pooley
Thompson, Dorfman, Sweatman, #500, 3 Lombard Place (R3B 1N4), D. A. Thompson, Q.C., I. Dorfman, Q.C., A. Sweatman, Q.C., W. L. Ritchie, Q.C., R.A.L. Nugent, Q.C., F.J. DeVrieze, Hon. Nathan Nurgitz, Q.C., B.S. Thompson, R. J. Scott, Q.C., A.D. MacInnes, Q.C., D.A. Balfour, P. M. Sinclair, A.L. Clearwater, B.W. Hall, G.V. Brickman, Q.C., G.S. Farwell, W.G. Percy, M.T. Green, W.D. Hamilton, J.A. Weinstein, R.H.G. Adams, R.J.M. Adkins, H.J. Arkin, D.N. Abra, D.G. Douglas, T.W. Kirk, M.E. Bakal, P.J. Brett, J.D. Brett, Cheryl M. Hall, W.J. Burnett, G.J. Tallon, D.H. Kells, F. Lavitt, Ellen P. Leibl, R.M. Kersey, K.S. Maclean, J.A. Ripley, Fern Carr
Thorarinson, S. A., 708, 294 Portage Ave.
Thullner, J.F., #100, 52 Donald St.
Tolton & Williams, #301, 275 Portage Ave., R. Tolton, Beverly Williams
Troniuk & Watson, 3313 Roblin (Charleswood) (also Portage la Prairie)
Tupper & Adams, 4th fl., 200 Portage Ave., R.K. Adams, A.A. Adams, R.E. Rivalin, N.G. MacKay, D.L. Fraser, J.A. Davidson, D.C. Brock, D.G. Ward, H.A. Adams, A.L. Dyker, J.E. Fielder, D.G. Meighen
Turnbull, K., 3717 Roblin Blvd.
Twaddle, A.K., 1522A, 363 Broadway Ave., A.K. Twaddle, Q.C., E.R. Dawson, L. Pettit
Udow & Co., #900, 363 Broadway Ave., S.N. Udow, P.A. Rose
Urbanowski, R.N., 167 St. Mary's Rd.
Walker, Cristall, Pandya, Mezzanine, 283 Portage Ave., J. S. Walker, Q.C., B.E. Cristall, H.D. Pandya
Walsh, Micay & Co., 7th floor, 211 Portage Ave., H. Walsh, Q.C., A. R. Micay, Q.C., G.G. Brodsky, Q.C., R.K. Vohora, R.J. Wolson, D. Donen, J.M. Stoffman, A.G. Slayen, S. Katz, H. Glinter, A. Dalmyn, M.W. Billinkoff, Linda Kerr, M. Fenson, S.Z. Katz, S.B. Simmonds
Walsh, Prober, Yard, Gutkin, McManus, Petryshyn, 205 Edmonton St., P.V. Walsh, J. Prober, D.D. Yard, T.A. Gutkin, Mary Susan McManus, J.S. Petryshyn
Werier, A.M., 235 Cambridge St.
Wilder, Wilder & Langtry, 1500 One Lombard Place, J. J. Wilder, S. I. Wilder, D.W. Langtry
Williamson, J.R., 712, 283 Portage Ave.
Wilson, Yerex, Young & Webster, #200, 296 Garry St., J.W. Wilson, R.A. Yerex, W.G. Webster. Assoc.: K.B. Young
Windsor & Berman, 556 Academy Rd., S.K. Windsor, I.L. Berman, A.E. Finkel
Winnipeg, City Legal Dept., *see* City Solicitors
Wolch, Pinx, Tapper, Scurfield, Martin & Wyant, #804, 363 Broadway Ave., H.E. Wolch, S.E. Pinx, R.L. Tapper, J.M. Scurfield, G.E. Martin, R.E. Wyant, Heather Leonoff, G.R. Rodin, T. Killeen, I.R. Malkin
Wolchock, Levine, Levene, Ludwig & Golub, #404, 310 Broadway Ave., S.R. Wolchock, D.M. Levine, D.S. Levene, I.A. Ludwig, D.C. Golub, S.A. Levene, J.K. Knowlton
Wolinsky, Liffmann, Wolinsky, 400, 228 Notre Dame Ave., M. Wolinsky, Q.C., H. Liffmann, D. Wolinsky
Wortzman, A., #503, 294 Portage Ave.
Wyrzykowski, C.L., 390 York Ave.
Yanofsky, D.A. & Assoc., 500, 211 Portage Ave., D.A. Yanofsky, O.C., Q.C., B. Kelsch
Young & Rose, #501, 228 Notre Dame Ave., J.M. Young, J.F.C. Rose
Zaslov, M., 912, 363 Broadway Ave.
Zimmerman & Zimmerman, #503, 294 Portage Ave., R.B. Zimmerman
Zuken, Penner, Savino & Assoc., 208, 323 Portage Ave., J. Zuken, Q.C., R. Penner, Q.C., V.S. Savino, K.G. Kaminski, D.B. Deutschen

BARRISTERS AND SOLICITORS IN NEW BRUNSWICK

ATHOLVILLE, Co. Restigouche
LeBlanc, L., 95A Mair Ave., Box 447

BATHURST, Co. Gloucester
Boisvert, G.W., 1755 Carl Dr.
Boudreau, R.M., 1154 St. Peter's Ave. (B.F. Aube)
Byrne, Riordon, Lenihan, Williamson & Theriault, 281 St. George St., T.W. Riordon, T.P. Lenihan, B.D. Theriault, H.H. Williamson
Hazen, Leblanc & Assoc., 240 King Ave., J.D. Hazen, D. J. Leblanc, C.R. Leblanc
Richard, C.J., 260 Main St.
Richard, J.J., 273 St. George St.
Robichaud, Godin, Robichaud, Gallagher & Dumaresq, 270 Douglas Ave., A. J. Robichaud, Q.C., R. Godin, M.A. Robichaud, R.E. Dumaresq, T.M. Gallagher, P.J. Veniot, C.H. Johnstone
Tremblay, Landry, Landry & Bujold, 548 King Ave., P.T. Tremblay, J.F. Landry, A. Landry, J.R. Bujold
Whelton, McGinley & Chiasson, 378 King Ave., V. J. Whelton, Q.C., E. McGinley, J. G. Chiasson

BLACKLAND, Co. Restigouche
MacIvor, L., Box 81

BUCTOUCHE, Co. Kent
LeBlanc, Boucher & Rodger (also Moncton)
Leger & Robichaud, Irving Blvd.
Michaud, LeBlanc & Co. (also Shediac)

CAMPBELLTON, Co. Restigouche
Doucet, F., 25 Water St.
Dube, F., Q.C., Box 126
Dumont, G., 58 Water St.
Dykeman, P. J., 64 Water St. (T. H. Delaney, S.M. Hutchinson)
Larlee, J.D., 74 Roseberry St.
McBrearty, T., 123 Water St.
Senechal & McBrearty, 193 Roseberry St., J.H.W. Senechal, T. McBrearty
Tingley, Humphrey & Blanchard, 78 Roseberry St., R.J. Tingley, J.D. Humphrey, E.P. Blanchard

CAP PELE, Co. Westmorland
Richard & Cormier, Box 339, B. Richard, J.A. Cormier

CARAQUET, Co. Gloucester
Hazen, Leblanc etc., Place St. Pierre (also Bathurst)
LeBouthillier, Alie A., 295 Boul. St-Pierre w., A. Bouthillier, J.A.R. Leger, C. Poirier
Robichaud, B., 9 du Voilier

CHATHAM, Co. Northumberland
Lordon, P.B., Q.C., Box 220
Martin, Lordon, McKenna, Martin & Bowes, 13 Henderson St., J. R. Martin, T.D. Lordon, F. McKenna, G.W. Martin, J.M. Bowes, Ellen Cook
Trevors & Walsh, Box 342, J. Trevors, J.J. Walsh. Assoc.: W.B. Richards

DALHOUSIE, Co. Restigouche
Dube, R., Box 1900
Hayes, D.P., 414 Adelaide St.
McIntyre & McIntyre, 103 Brunswick St., J. R. McIntyre, P.E. McIntyre, P.W. Arseneault
Whalen, T.M.G., Box 852

DOAKTOWN, Co. Northumberland
Mills, R.A.

EAST RIVERSIDE, Co. Kings
Baird-Filliter, B.L., 132 Wiljac St.
Baxter, J.B.M., Q.C., 143 Green Rd.
Filliter, G.P., 132 Wiljac St.

EDMUNDSTON, Co. Madawaska
Angers & McLaughlin, 56 Church St., F. Angers, G.J. McLaughlin
Charest, Poitras & Bourque, 174 Church St., G. G. Charest, R. D. Poitras, M.F. Bourque
Cyr, J.B., 58 Church St.
Dionne, J.-M., 106 Church St.
Jessop, M.A., 73 Rice St.
Martin, J. G., 56 Church St.
Michaud, J.-M., Q.C., 2 Hill St.
Morneault, J.P., 55 Emerson St.
Pelletier, P. E., Q.C., 2 Hill St.
Pichette, Pichette & Seheult, 81 Church St. (also Grand Falls)
Rice, Valcourt & Assoc., 11 Costigan St., R. C. Rice, Q.C., B. Valcourt, L.P. Picard
Thibodeau, Shaw & LaVigne, 77 Church St., G.C. Thibodeau, R.G. Shaw, L.A. LaVigne
Tweedie, E. T., Q.C., 10 Emerson St. Counsel: F. D. Tweedie, Q.C.

FLORENCEVILLE, Co. Carleton
Crocco, Hunter, etc., Box 99 (also Woodstock)
MacElwain & Renouf, Box 148, R.D. MacElwain, R. Renouf

FREDERICTON, Co. York
Armstrong, A.M., 266 Winslow St.
Ashfield, DeWitt & LeBlanc, 470 York St., R. J. Ashfield, R. L. DeWitt, J.M. LeBlanc
Astle, J.A., 41 Michener Court

Atkinson & Atkinson, 108 Queen St., F. E. Atkinson, Q.C., Sherron J.L. Hughes, W.K. Lebans, T.A. Bishop
Barrett, J.J., 126 Victoria St.
Beaton & Stephen, 181 Westmorland St., J.G. Beaton, W.G. Stephenson
Blue, Janette, 860 Regent St.
Brewer & MacPherson, 565 Priestman Centre, E.A. Brewer, R.W. MacPherson, C.S. McAllister
Brown, H.W., 165 Cambridge Cres.
Bryden, DiPaolo & Breen, 346 Brunswick St., J.G. Bryden, J. A. DiPaolo, R.D. Breen
Budovitch, A.R., 525 Prospect St. e.
Calabrese & Whitehead, 154A Main St., H.F. Calabrese, Allison Whitehead, Marilyn Evans
Carrier, M.A., 181 Westmorland St.
Chase, S.A., 604 York St.
Clark, A. J., 364 York St.
Clark & Peterson, 623 King St., D.R. Clark, D.L.E. Peterson, P. Hawkins
Cochrane, Sargeant & Co., 98 Prospect St., R. B. Cochrane, Q.C., C.A. Sargeant, D.W. McCormack
D'Arcy, L.D., Q.C., Needham & Regent Sts. (D.W. McConkey)
Eddy & McElman, 224 Brunswick St., R.B. Eddy, F.C. McElman
Fenton, Neill, Janssens & Miller, 340 Brunswick St., M.W. Fenton, J.B. Neill, P. Janssens, G. Miller
Forbes, D.P., 474 York St.
Forestell, M.D., 57 Carleton St.
Freeze, Walker, Lourensse & Lee, 212 Queen St., R. St. John Freeze, Q.C., W. T. Walker, R. Lourensse, Janet C. Lee, L.C. Neilson, K.D. Bettle
Garvie, L., Q.C., 115 Prospect St. w.
Gilliss & Constable, 461 King St., M.C. Gilliss, R.W. Constable
Gorman, M.D., 641 York St.
Hamilton, V.C.M., 225 Stanley St.
Hanson, Hashey & Scott, 61 Carleton St. (E3B 4Y9), H. A. Hanson, Q.C., D. T. Hashey, Q.C., D.M. Norman, Q.C., J. M. Hanson, P.J. Adams, W. D. Vail, M. E. Bowlin, R.J. Scott, B.D. Hatfield, J.A.G. Dickson, D.G. Bell, A.W. MacLeod
Harper Buchanan, 88 Prospect St. w., J.D. Harper, J.A. Buchanan
Hilborn & Hilborn, 92 Regent St. (Box 472), Mildred B. Hilborn, Susan E. Hilborn
Hollowell, L.B., 377 Saint John St.
Howie, J. R., 57 Carleton St.
Hughes, Cooper & Assoc., 551 Charlotte St., C.D. Hughes, W.E. Cooper, Judy L. Clendening
Kelly, D.H., Box 1254
Kenny, Jackson & Murray, 228 Brunswick St., R. L. Kenny, R. L. Jackson, A.I. Murray, G.A. Grant
Khoury, C.J., Box 1525
Levesque, C.B., Box 1115
Levesque, P.C., Box 220
MacKenzie, S.M., 242 York St.
MacPhee, J. S., 469 King St.
Matthews & Assoc., 255 Main St., W.J. Matthews, Sharon Cupples
McGinley, E.C., 756 Smythe St.
McNair, J. C., Q.C., 780 King St.
McNally, A.N., 763 Union St.
Mockler, Allen & Dixon, 836 Churchill Row, E.J. Mockler, G.K. Allen, R.W. Dixon, Lorraine King, P.E. Hurley, A.F. Wood, M.N.K. Toor, Carole McLennan, D.R. Oley, Myrna Athey
Noble & Noble, 560 Queen St., G.A. Noble, B.A. Noble
Ogilvie, D., 146 Waterloo Row
Paul-Elias, M. C., 355 George St.
Petrie & Richmond, 191 Prospect St. w., J. G. Petrie, G. R. Richmond, R.B. Jackson, D.E. MacPherson
Quinn, McKnight & Yeamans, 147 Westmorland St., M.P. Quinn, S.D.G. McKnight, G.T. Yeamans, J.W. Cabel
Ruben & Kingston, 391 Brunswick St., A.M. Ruben, C. Kingston, G.A. McAllister
Ryan, Graser & Smith, 57 Carleton St., P.A.A. Ryan, Q.C., W. Graser, Q.C., D. L. Smith, J.D. Townsend, Leslye Fraser, J.H. Campbell, Lorna MacKenzie
Shaw, B.E., Box 10, Site 26, S.S. #2
Smart, B.T., 763 Union St.
Smith & Irvine, #103, 212 Queen St., D.L. Smith, A.G.D. Irvine
Stevenson & Yerxa, 158 Brunswick St., D.J. Stevenson, P.L. Yerxa
Warner, J.E., Q.C., 634 Queen St. (J.J. Wilby)
Watters, D.C., Box 3105, Stn. B
Wilby, A. E., II, 679 Churchill Row
Wilby, A.E., Q.C., 526 Queen St.
Williamson, K.E., Box 1417

GRAND BAY, Co. Kings
O'Connell, R.G., Box 120

GRAND FALLS, Co. Victoria
Duffie, Friel & Godbout, Box 747, J.C. Friel, G.J. Godbout, P.E. Duffie
McLaughlin, H.E., Box 650 (Marie McLaughlin)
Pichette, Pichette & Seheult, 257 Broadway, Hon. J.A. Pichette, Q.C., G.A. Pichette, P. Seheult

GRAND MANAN, Co. Charlotte
Larsen, Prince (also St. George)

HAMPTON, Co. Kings
Day, Lutz & Co., Box 500, J.A. Day, D.M. Lutz, D. Smith, J.S. Dubbin

KESWICK RIDGE, Co. York
Haines, C.L., Crock's Point

LAMEQUE, Co. Gloucester
Noel, R.A.

MINTO, Co. Sunbury
Lawson, W. L., Box 369
Thorne, Sheila R., 24 Queen St., Box 383

MONCTON, Co. Westmorland
Anderson, Savoie & DeWitt, 860 Main St., J.E. Anderson, S.J. Savoie, M.S. DeWitt, C.B. Allaby, M.S. Sheehan. Counsel: H.B. Trites, Q.C.
Arsenault, P. J., #102, 720 Main St.
Bingham, Bingham & Macklem, 28 John St., G. J. Bingham, Q.C., W. R. Bingham, T. D. Macklem
Boudreau, P.A., 770 Main St.
Brison & LeBlanc, 97 Botsford St., C.E. Brison, B.A. LeBlanc
Bujold, G.E., Box 713
Cohen, H. R., Q.C., 1111 Main St., D.D. Smith
Couturier, G.G., 98 Church St.
Cyr & LeBlanc, 225 Lutz St., L.H. Cyr, Q.C., R. LeBlanc
Devereux, G.J., 735 Mountain Rd.
Diamond, S.D., Box 1362
Forbes, Radford & Mellish, 100 Cameron St., F. H. Forbes, Q.C., R. E. Radford, R.L. Mellish, B.F. Forbes, M.J. Richards
Fowler & Fowler, #11, 885 Main St., J.E. Fowler, S.F. Fowler
Godin, P.J.M., 236 St. George St. (R. Basque)
Goodwin & Ellsworth, 879 Main St., D.C. Ellsworth, G.S. Ellsworth
Innes, Bosse & Mills, 9 Dominion St., D. S. Innes, M. A. Bosse, C.A. Mills
Jewett & MacLennan, 108 Highfield St., J.G.G. Jewett, J.W. MacLennan
Johnson, Attis, 777 Main St., R. B. Johnson, J. Attis, M. McKee, M.J. LeBlanc, P.H. Pugsley, G.S. McAllister, M.J. LeBlanc
Jones, L.C., 63 Church St.
Landry & McIntyre, 770 Main St., A.R. Landry, Q.C., D.H. McIntyre
LeBlanc, B.O., 97 Botsford St.
LeBlanc, Boucher & Rodger, 756 Main St., L. F. LeBlanc, J. A. Boucher, N. S. Rodger, Catherine LeBlanc
Letcher & Murray, Box 608, J.C. Letcher, J.W. Murray
Lupien, A., 195½ Maple St.
MacLean, Chase, McNichol & Blair, 85 Bonaccord St., G.B. MacLean, J.G. Chase, W.J. McNichol, P.F. Blair, H.J. Murphy, E.G. Ehrhardt
MacLean, D., 64 Archibald St.
MacNeill, G.H., 12 Duke St.
MacPherson, Judith F., 115 Queen St.
Maxwell, W.J. & Assoc., 90 Weldon St.
Mitton, Durling & Mix, 52 Weldon St., H.M. Mitton, G.M. Durling, P.C. Mix, D.A. Morley
Mix, Ruth A., 232 Highfield St.
Murphy, Murphy & Mollins, 89 Church St., J. E. Murphy, Q.C., R. W. Mollins, G.E. Murphy
Rideout, McGrath, 19 Church St., G.S. Rideout, E.J. McGrath, J.E. Weir, P.A. Lennox, A.K. Robinson, R.L. Tuck, P.J. Landry
Rinzler, Sutherland & Steeves, 75 Botsford St., M.M. Rinzler, C.C.W. Sutherland, J.A. Steeves
Roth, R.A., 1199 Main St.
Roy, Losier, Lampert & Gaudet, 192 Church St., C. H. Roy, Q.C., A. J. Losier, I. E. Lampert, J. E. Gaudet, G.L. Algee
Savoie, Drapeau & Assoc., 64 Wesley St., R. Savoie, J.E. Drapeau, B.M. Robichaud
Schelew, A.D., 803 Main St.
Scobie, Marriner & Girvan, 190 Cameron St., P. D. Scobie, D.J.M. Marriner, S.C. Girvan
Stewart & Cooper, 50 Cameron St., G.B. Cooper, Q.C., W.B. White, D.B. McCartney, R.E. DeBow, J.C. Nagle, R.J. Newton
Tedford, Delehanty & Mills, 1616 Main St., E. E. Tedford, K.F. Delehanty, E.E. Mills
White, J.F., Box 961
Yeoman, Savoie, LeBlanc & Assoc., 86 Church St., M.M. Yeoman, Q.C., M. A. Savoie, Q.C., S.A. LeBlanc, R.J. LeBlanc

NACKAWIC, Co. York
Carrier, M.A. (also Fredericton)

NELSON-MIRAMICHI, Co. Northumberland
Dolan, H.E.

NEWCASTLE, Co. Northumberland
Burchill, W. J., 283 Pleasant St.
Martin, Lordon & McKenna, 142 Castle St. (also Chatham)
McAllister, J. L., Box 442 (C.T. Prince)
Morris, D., Box 40
Morrissy, T.W., 247 Pleasant St.
Smith & Smith, 155 Pleasant St., G. A. Percy Smith, Q.C., G. F. Smith, D. G. Smith

OROMOCTO, Co. Sunbury
Calabrese & Co., 54 Broad R. (also Fredericton)
Clark, A.J., 101 Hersey St. (also Fredericton)
McKay & Whittaker, 101 Hersey St., B. McKay, B.J. Whittaker
Roach & Morris, Box 232, R.L. Roach, R.E. Morris

PERTH-ANDOVER, Co. Victoria
Johnson, M.C., Box 698

Peters, R. J., Main St., Box 545
Shaw, G.S., Main St.

PETITCODIAC, Co. Westmorland
Beardsworth & Wright (also Riverview)
Scobie, Marriner, etc. (also Moncton)

PETIT-ROCHER, Co. Gloucester
Boudreau, R.M. (B.F. Aube) (also Bathurst)

RICHIBUCTO, Co. Kent
Michaud, LeBlanc & Co., J.C. Robichaud (also Shediac)
Vatour, Richard & Assoc., Box 520, J.C. Vatour, J.C. Richard

RIVERVIEW, Co. Albert
Beardsworth & Wright, 350 Coverdale Rd., P.J. Beardsworth, P.M. Wright
MacGregor, S.R., 406 Coverdale Rd.

ROGERSVILLE, Co. Northumberland
LeBlanc, Boucher & Rodger (also Moncton)

ROTHESAY, Kings
Clain, E.J., Box 136
Higgins, W.E., Box 855

SACKVILLE, Co. Westmorland
Bissell, J. D., Box 1829 (also Amherst)
Crosby, Veniot, etc., 505 No. 1 Hwy. (also Halifax)
Meldrum, Wynn W., 11 Bridge St.
Samuelsen, O.B., Box 1797

ST. ANDREWS, Co. Charlotte
Larsen, Prince (also St. George)
Nicholson, Nicholson, Turner & Walker, 177 Water St., D.C. Walker (also St. Stephen)

STE. ANNE DE KENT, Co. Kent
Daigle, G.

ST. ANTOINE, Co. Kent
Richard, J. C.

ST. GEORGE, Co. Charlotte
D'Arcy, L.D., Q.C., Main St. (D.W. McConkey) (also Fredericton)
Larsen, Prince, 4 Main St., G.J. Larsen, Nadene Prince
Nicholson, Nicholson & Turner (also St. Stephen)

SAINT JOHN, Co. Saint John
Associated Attorneys, 133 Prince William St., A.J. Ritchie, D.R. Patterson
Baker & Poley, 9 Main St. w., G.S. Baker, R.D. Poley, R.A. Northrup
Barry, O'Neil & Co., 85 Charlotte St., J.P. Barry, Q.C., D.G. Barry, T.G. O'Neil, R.B. Costello, Paulette Nason, H.A. Spalding, P.T. Zed
Broderick, R. J., 50 Princess St.
Byrne & Brown, 77 Germain St., A.M. Byrne, D.M. Brown
Casey & Cullinan, 35 Charlotte St., G.T. Casey, B. A. Cullinan
Chase, D.P.F., 186 Adelaide St.
Clark, Drummie & Co., 40 Wellington Row (Box 6850, Stn. A, E2L 4S3), T. B. Drummie, Q.C., D.P. Pappas, Q.C., D.F. MacGowan, A.D. Case, W.M. Jenkins, W. A. Anderson, M.R. Jette, B.R. Morrison, H.J. Flemming, T.W. Hutchinson, F.P. Hamm, P.J.P. Ervin. Counsel: G.T. Clark, Q.C.
Clarke, W.E., Q.C., 573 Dunn Ave. w.
Cliff, F. S., 50 Princess St.
Collier, G.C., 30 King St.
Colwell, Ryan & Co., 30 Wellington Row, H.G. Colwell, Brenda Lutz
Cormier, D.J., 43 Simpson Dr.
Drost, B.A., Box 6593
Gilbert, McGloan, Gillis, 133 Prince William St. (Box 7174, Stn. A, E2L 4S6), A.B. Gilbert, Q.C., R.J. Gillis, D.M. Gillis, Q.C., D.A.M. Evans, Thomas L. McGloan, Q.C., G.D. Hubley, A.G.W. Gilbert, D.H. Russell, K.R. Costello, R.K. MacCallum, W.B. Gandy, Joanne O'-Reilly. Counsel: T. Louis McGloan, Q.C.
Gorman, Nason, Farrell & Ljungstrom, 121 Germain St., G.P. Gorman, Lynn Nason, Lynda Farrell, G.B. Ljungstrom, R.P. Gorman
Hatty, P. D., 82 Germain St.
Hines & McLennan, 21 Canterbury St., R.L. Hines, W.E. McLennan
Howes, J.D., 87 Prince William St.
Lahey, E. J., 108 Prince William St.
Landers, M.J., Box 6903
Lawson & Lawson, 40 Charlotte St., G.B. Lawson, G.M. Lawson
Marquis, Faloon & Grant, 53 King St., H.J. Marquis, R.G. Faloon, W.T. Grant
McCluskey, M.L., 50 Princess St.
McInerny, H.J., 102 Black St.
McKelvey, Macaulay, Machum, 44 Prince William St. (Box 7289, Stn. A, E2L 4S6), E. N. McKelvey, Q.C., W. D. Macaulay, Q.C., L. M. Machum, Q.C., A. Elizabeth Hoyt-Brown, R. G. Lister, Q.C., J.I.M. Whitcomb, D. L. Cullinan, W. R. Chapman, Levi E. Clain, D. H. Aiton, F. D. Toole, R. W. MacKenzie, G.S. McMackin, R.G. Vincent, W.B. Goss, K.B. McCullogh, Lynne M. Burnham, M.D. Wennberg, Barbara Bonham, G.S. Sinclair, J.R. Willett, J.F. LeMesurier
McKenna, H. P., 35 Charlotte St.
McLellan, Allaby, Allman & Holland, 107 Germain St., H. H. McLellan, C. D. Allaby, A. Allman, Mary Anne Holland
Meltzer, W., 50 Princess St.
Palmer, O'Connell, Leger, Turnbull & Turnbull, 1600 One Brunswick Sq., (Box 1324, E2L 4H8), G.F. O'Connell, Q.C., F. O. Leger, Q.C., J. W. Turnbull, W. S. Turnbull, R. J. Guerette, M. B. Roderick, P. S. Glennie, J. D. Wallace, M. J. Giberson, R.F. Glennie, W.F. O'Connell, B.H. McIntyre, P.R. Forestell, W.H. Teed, C.D. Whelly, Anne F. Duffie
Purnell & Brien, 98 Main St. w., L.F.D. Purnell, Q.C., A. H. Brien, G. M. Fulton, H.A. Cannell, P.G. Blackmore
Riley, Mosher & Stanton, 186 Adelaide St., J. G. Riley, B. W. Mosher, R. D. Stanton, W.S.R. Chedore, M.D. Fineberg
Ring, S.D., 94 Prince William St.
Shalala, R.E., 20 Charlotte St.
Sherwood, A.A., 10 Peel St.
Spencer, E.E., Q.C., 111 Prince William St.
Stephen, R. J., 135 Douglas Ave.
Swanton, C. Y., 11 Canterbury St.
Teed, Teed & McPhee, 133 Prince William St., E. L. Teed, Q.C., R. McPhee, P.E.L. Teed, T.L.S. Teed, M. Shannon
Tippett, W. R., 186 Adelaide St.
Whelly & Whelly, 40 Charlotte St., A.W. Whelly, Q.C., C. F. Whelly, Q.C., S.B. Murphy, J.A. Whelly
Wilson, T.E., 28 Germain St.
Zed, D., 6 Queen Sq.
Zed, T.J., 35 Charlotte St.

ST. JOSEPH, Co. Westmorland
Gauthier, J.J., Box 440, R.R. 1

ST. QUENTIN, Co. Restigouche
Deschenes, L.J.

ST. STEPHEN, Co. Charlotte
Cockburn, G.W.N., Q.C., 120 Water St.
Hansen & MacDonald, 184 King St., J. Hansen, G. MacDonald
Nicholson, Nicholson, Turner & Walker, 46 Milltown Blvd., G. Fred Nicholson, Q.C., D.C. Nicholson, G. M. Turner, D.C. Walker
Sutherland, R.W., 71 King St.

SHEDIAC, Co. Westmorland
Goguen & Donelle, Box 1628, J.M. Goguen, B. Donelle
Landry, A. R., Q.C., 44 Sackville St. (also Moncton)
Michaud, LeBlanc, Robichaud & Deschenes, Main St., J. C. A. Michaud, J. G. Y. LeBlanc, J. C. Robichaud, A. Deschenes
Robichaud, J.T., 9 Victoria St.
Storey, J., Box 1658

SHIPPEGAN, Co. Gloucester
Godin, Lizotte & Co., Box 190, G. A. Godin, G. J. Lizotte

SUSSEX, Co. Kings
Gerrish-Smith, 488 Main St., J.D. Gerrish, G. B. Smith, T.A. Gerrish
Hunt, R.W., 684 Main St. (J.J. Forbes)
Purnell & Brien, 55 Broad St., L.F.D. Purnell, Q.C., A.H. Brien, G.M. Fulton, H.A. Cannell, P.G. Blackmore

TABUSINTAC, Co. Northumberland
Munroe, W.
Stymiest, A.R.J.

TRACADIE, Co. Gloucester
Bertrand, M.J., Box 110
Young & Doiron, Box 1120, M.D. Young, L.J. Doiron, G. Paulin

WOODSTOCK, Co. Carleton
Crocco, Hunter, Purvis & Depow, 105 Connell St., D.G. Hunter, I.S. Purvis, H.R. Depow, P.E. Crocco
Holmes, M.D., 645 Main St.
MacLauchlan, K. E., Q.C., 104 Queen St.
Maddox & MacInnis, 664 Main St., P.B. Maddox, Q.C., I.D. MacInnis
Rose, N.J., South St.
Wills, M.E., 104 Queen St.

BARRISTERS AND SOLICITORS IN NEWFOUNDLAND

BAY ROBERTS
Moores & Finn, Box 806 (also Harbour Grace)

CARBONEAR
Brewer, R. A., Box 190

CLARENVILLE
Hussey, A.W.
Mills & Dymond, O.C. Mills, W.G. Dymond

CORNER BROOK
Dicks, Dicks & Watton, Royal Bank Bldg., P.D. Dicks, Maureen D. Dicks, G.C. Watton, C.J. Price, C.D., D. King
Gushue, G., 47 West Valley Rd.
Martin, G.J., #320 Millbrooke Mall

Martin, Woolridge, Poole, Althouse & Clarke, 49-51 Park St., L. A. Martin, Q.C., F.R. Woolridge, Q.C., E. P. Poole, Q.C., D. P. Althouse, O.N. Clarke, C.R. Thompson, L. L. Thomas, J.S. Hutchings, B.K. Wentzell, D.W. Hillier
Ozon, E.R., Box 1166
Robinson, Vivian & Faour, 50-52 Main St., A.N. Robinson, J.L. Vivian, A.E. Faour
Sweetland, J.C., 100 West St.
Wells, Monaghan & Co., 17 West St., M.J. Monaghan, A.C. Seaborn, T.W. Marshall, D.M. Roberts. Counsel: C.K. Wells, Q.C.

GANDER

Bonnell, R.A., 143 Bennett Dr.
Easton, Easton, Facey & Dawe, 61 Elizabeth Dr., G.G. Easton, Q.C., L.F. Easton, E. C. Facey, J.V. Dawe
Power & MacMillan, 328 Elizabeth Dr., D.E. Power, W.J. MacMillan

GRAND FALLS

Baggs, L. E., Q.C., 11 Hill Rd.
Dwyer, Locke & Schwartz, 7 High St., C. J. Dwyer, J. R. Locke, A. Schwartz, K. Goulding
Griffin, M.J., Box 400
Matthews, Blackmore & LeBlanc, 2 Mill Rd., R.M. Matthews, B. Blackmore, R.D. LeBlanc
Sweezey, G.G., 28 Grenfell Heights

HARBOUR GRACE

Moores & Finn, Thompson Prof. Bldg., D.B. Moores, J.W. Finn

KELLIGREWS

Noonan & Chalker, Box 237 (also St. John's)

LABRADOR CITY

Miller & Hearn, Box 129, A. F. Miller, E. M. Hearn
White, R.S., Bruno Plaza

MARYSTOWN

Handrigan, G.A., Box 1176
MacBeath, D.A., Box 218

PORT AUX BASQUES

Parsons, K.L., Box 695
Wells, Monaghan & Co., 112A Main St. (also Corner Brook)

ST. JOHN'S

Aylward, Morris & Pittman, 261 Duckworth St., F. J. Aylward, Q.C., R.K. Morris, R.P. Pittman
Baird, Carter & Parker, 333 Duckworth St., J.D. Baird, P.R. Carter, D.T.R. Parker
Barry & Smyth, 288 Water St., D. G. Barry, J. J. Smyth, J.L. Fardy
Bootwala, A. K. G., Box 1701
Brown & Rorke, 174 Water St., G.D. Brown, J.F. Rorke
Browne, The Hon. W. J., P.C., Q.C., 97 Rennie's Mill Rd.
Buffett, D.G.L., 21 Church Hill
Cashin, R.J., Box 5158
Caule, A. F., Q.C., Box 9393
Chalker, Green & Rowe, Royal Trust Bldg., Water St., J.R. Chalker, Q.C., J. M. Green, W. G. Rowe, G. P. Horan, E.J. Kipnis, J.L. Atkinson, J.L. O'Dea, R.A. Brait
City Solicitor, City Hall: P.R. Stapleton
Clarke & Fahey, Box 8306, Stn. A, G.W. Clarke, Q.C., R.D.J. Fahey
Coady, H.F., 198 Water St.
Curtis, Dawe, Russell, Bonnell, Winsor & Stokes, #1101, Royal Trust Bldg., Water St., D.W.K. Dawe, Q.C., D. L. Russell, A. L. Bonnell, F. B. Winsor, P. R. Stokes, Christine A. Fagan, I.F. Kelly, W.G. Morrow
Fowler, Mercer, Kendell, The Murray Premises, Harbour Dr., F.P. Fowler, Q.C., K. Mercer, T.R. Kendell, L.A. Horwood
French & Roil, 329 Duckworth St., J.B.V. French, J.F. Roil, W.J. Clarke, F.G. Crockett
Gillies, W. P., 170 Water St.
Goodridge, A.M., 57 Military Rd.
Greene Law Office, Box 5217, R. Greene, Q.C., J.G. Kelly, J.A. Henheffer
Halley, Hunt, 1 Church Hill, D.C. Hunt, Q.C., E. Roberts, Q.C., A.W. Carter, Leo Barry, Q.C., R.M. Hall, J.P. Adams, D.J. Black, R.M. Sinclair, J.C. Oakley, J.P. Andrews, J.A. Bruce. Counsel: J.J. Halley, Q.C.
Jewell, Mary, 283 Duckworth St.
Kennedy, P.J., Royal Trust Bldg.
Learmonth & Harding, 280 Duckworth St., R.B. Learmonth, Gloria Harding
Lewis, Day, Cook & Sheppard, 261 Duckworth St., Hon. P. D. Lewis, Q.C., D. C. Day, Q.C., J.D. Cook, C. Sheppard, Jr., J.D.B. Eaton
Lewis & Sinnott, 339 Duckworth St., P. J. Lewis, Q.C., J.R. Sinnott, Elizabeth Heneghan
Marshall, White, Ottenheimer & Green, Royal Trust Bldg., W. W. Marshall, Q.C., C.W. White, J.D. Green, J.A. Baker, R.P. Whalen, G.D. Butler. Counsel: G.R. Ottenheimer
Martin, Whalen & Hennebury, 15 Church Hill, G.D. Martin, N.J. Whalen, J.A. Hennebury, K.F. Stamp, Maria McIntyre, Dana Lenehan
McDonald, T.F., 74 O'Leary Ave.
McGrath, J., 170 Water St.
Mercer, MacNab & Vavasour, 70 Portugal Cove Rd., I. Mercer, Q.C., R. Mercer, G. MacNab, J. Vavasour
Mercer, Spracklin, Heywood & McKay, 159 Water St., D.A. Mercer, Q.C., W.F. Spracklin, Lynn E. Spracklin, B. Heywood, D.D. McKay, Paula Howatt
Murray, M.A., 2 LeMarchant Rd.
Noonan & Chalker, 339 Duckworth St., E.P. Noonan, T.J. Chalker, D. Orr
Nurse, J. E., Q.C., 70 Portugal Cove Rd.
O'Brien, Hurley & Coffey, The Murray Premises, Beck's Cove, G.F. O'Brien, D.F. Hurley, B.M. Coffey
O'Dea, Greene, 263 Duckworth St., Hon. F. A. O'Dea, Q.C., J.J. Greene, Q.C., W.J. English, B.F. Furey, Dianne Fraser
O'Neill, Riche, O'Reilly & Noseworthy, 323 Duckworth St., J. J. O'Neill, Q.C., D. G. Riche, Q.C., T.J. O'Reilly, Q.C., R.S. Noseworthy, R.H. Brown, R.C. Snelgrove, D.R. Robbins, R. Smith, D. Sword
Parsons, Dunne & Co., 280 Duckworth St., R.A. Parsons, P.M. Dunne, K.J. O'-Hara
Parsons & O'Neill, 155 Water St., R.A. Parsons, Q.C., H. O'Neill, Q.C.
Philpott, Mary, 15 Cherry Hill Rd.
Pike & Collins, 272 Duckworth St., F.A.D. Pike, W. A. Collins
Pratt, C.C., Box 1346
Puddester/Orsborn, 211 LeMarchant Rd., H.J. Puddester, D.B. Orsborn, J.P. Benson, G.A. Wells
Smallwood, W.R., Q.C., 119 Portugal Cove Rd. (D. Harvey)
Sparkes, B.R., 70 Portugal Cove Rd.
Sparkes, D.B., 283 Duckworth St.
Stirling, Ryan, Reid, Harrington, Andrews & Lilly, Royal Trust Bldg., Water St., G. M. Stirling, Q.C., F. J. Ryan, Q.C., E. G. Reid, M. F. Harrington, L. B. Andrews, A.G. Lilly, H.M. Smith, G.E. Browne, J.P. Frecker, Janet Henley, K.A. Templeton, B.C. Grant
Strong, Andrews & O'Dea, Royal Trust Bldg., Water St., P. W. Strong, R. B. Andrews, W.G. O'Dea, K.L. Baggs
Stuck, G.B., 331 Duckworth St.
Thistle, W.W., Memorial Univ.
Thoms, Rowe & Rose, Box 5007, L. R. Thoms, W. N. Rowe, K. F. Rose
Tucker, D. D., Box 1241
Wells, O'Dea, Halley, Earle, Shortall & Burke, 319 Duckworth St., R. Wells, Q.C., M. F. O'Dea, R. J. Halley, V. R. Earle, E. J. Shortall, T.J. Burke
Williams, D.E., 6 Logy Bay Rd.
Williams, Joy & Chambers, 6 Logy Bay Rd., T.E. Williams, Q.C., J.L. Joy, B.W. Chambers
Wood, E.C., 367 Duckworth St.

STEPHENVILLE

Gallant, W.J., Box 447
Stagg & Stagg, 28 Main St., F.R. Stagg, B.C. Stagg
Wells, E. J., P.O. Drawer 388
Wells, Monaghan & Co., 165 Main St. (also Corner Brook)

BARRISTERS AND SOLICITORS IN NOVA SCOTIA

AMHERST, Co. Cumberland

Archibald, Bissell & Morley, 77 Victoria St. (Box 192, B4H 3Z2), R.B. Archibald, J.D. Bissell, A.J. Morley
Bent, M.D., 14 Electric St.
Fairbanks, Fairbanks & Fairbanks, 77 Victoria St. (Box 103, B4H 3Y6), J.O. Fairbanks, Q.C., W. B. Fairbanks, D. A. Fairbanks
Hicks, LeMoine, Haugg & Christie, 23 La Planche St. (Box 279, B4H 3Z2), E. C. Hicks, Q.C., J.J. LeMoine, Q.C., M. J. Haugg, D. H. Christie, Beryl A. MacDonald, C.A. Ellis
MacNeill, G. H., Q.C., 11 Princess St. (M.T. Taj)
McKim, L., Q.C., 39 Victoria St.
Milner, Shatford, Creighton, 14 Electric St., D.A. Milner, D.B. Shatford, B.S. Creighton. Counsel: A.C. Milner, Q.C.

ANNAPOLIS ROYAL, Co. Annapolis

Armstrong & Armstrong, 240 St. George St., D.M. Armstrong, Q.C., J.H. Armstrong
Batiot, J.-L., Box 388
MacArthur, R.K., Box 366 (Patricia Buchholz)

ANTIGONISH, Co. Antigonish

Cameron & Emery, 86 College St., J.A. Cameron, Anne Emery
MacIsaac, D. J., 256D Main St.

MacPherson, J.C., Q.C., 42 West St. (L.D. MacDougall, C.M. MacNeil)
Meehan, W.F. & Assoc., 195 Main St., W.F. Meehan, R.J. MacKinnon
Murphy, W.F., Q.C., 222 Main St.
Richard & MacDonald, 18 Church St., A. G. MacDonald, D.J. Chisholm

ARICHAT, Co. Richmond
Doyle, P. C.

BADDECK, Co. Victoria
Hudson, R. F., Q.C.
Hutchison, W., Box 329

BARRINGTON, Co. Shelburne
Eldridge, G.D. & Assoc., Box 157

BEDFORD, Co. Halifax
Baldwin, D.S.T., Box 769
Hopkins, W.E., Bedford Place Mall (Constance Rusk)
Innes, Matheson & Curran, Box 580, Bedford Tower, J.A. Innes, W.A. Matheson
MacInnes, Wilson & Hallett, Sunnyside Plaza (also Halifax)
McGrath, D.J. & Assoc., Sunnyside Plaza (also Windsor)
Rhindress, Cameron & Assoc., 1496 Bedford Hwy.

BERWICK, Co. Kings
Hall & Stewart, 191 Commercial St., D.M. Hall, Q.C., R.C. Stewart
Waterbury, Newton & Co., 202 Commercial St. (also Kentville)
Weir, D.

BRAS D'OR, Co. Cape Breton
Andrea, L.A., Q.C., Box 189

BRIDGETOWN, Co. Annapolis
Hatherly, D. H., Q.C., Box 269
Orlando & Hicks, 3 Queen St., D.J. Cottenden, J.R. Cameron. Counsel: Hon. H.D. Hicks, Q.C.

BRIDGEWATER, Co. Lunenburg
Bardon & Conrad, 51 Dufferin St., G. C. Bardon, Q.C., B. L. Conrad, T.J. Feindel
Brown, A.W., 557 King St.
Coughlan & Coughlan, 48 Pleasant St., C. R. Coughlan, Q.C., C. Richard Coughlan, K.O. Thomas
Kenney, Theakston, Allen & Hole, Box 370, K.J. Kenney, Q.C., J.D.F. Theakston, Q.C., W.K. Allen, T.J. Hole, M.A. Burke
Milner, H. W., 66 Pleasant St.
Morris, J.P., 463 King St.
Romney & Power, 158 Dufferin St., G.F.P. Romney, M.K. Power, Holly MacDougall

CANNING, Co. Kings
Knight, V.M., Box 33

CHESTER, Co. Lunenburg
Fraser, D. S., Q.C., Box 4
Hennigar, Wells & Lamey, 36 Pleasant St., D.M. Wells, S.R. Lamey. Counsel: R.E. Hennigar, Q.C.

CHESTER BASIN, Co. Lunenburg
Black, R.M., Q.C.
Preeper, B.J., Box 99

DARTMOUTH, Co. Halifax
Aronson & MacDonald, #305, 277 Pleasant St., S.J. Aronson, L. MacDonald
Boyne, Jones, Murrant & Young, 33 Queen St., T.O. Boyne, R. Murrant, J.A. Young, G.F. Proudfoot, A.L. Graham
Claman, Dietrich, Clark, Bright & MacInnis, 660 Portland St., M. Dietrich, D.W. Clark, W.R. Clark, H.J. Dietrich, J.L. Connors
Cleary, C.M. & Assoc., 270 Wyse Rd., C.M. Cleary, Q.C., M.J. Cleary
Cote, L.E., 33 Overdale Lane
Davidson, G.H., Q.C., 34 Queen St.
Davis, Clark, Dunsworth & Assoc., 44 Portland St., F. E. Clark, E.T. Dunsworth, W.J. Chisholm, R.V. Penny, Elizabeth Mullaly. Counsel: T.B. Davis, Q.C.
Drury, Huestis, Anderson, Dickie & Kydd, Royal Bank Bldg., J. S. Drury, Q.C., R.S. Huestis, Q.C., D.D. Anderson, Q.C., E.K. Dickie, Q.C., W. H. Kydd, R. B. Gibson, G.R. Baker, N.J. Bateman, S.M. Hood, M.H. Moreash, L. Labelle, M.L. Cohen
Duplak, R.R. & Assoc., Box 1159 (W.P. Thomson)
Foot, Helen, 8 Amelia Place
Grant, D., Box 457
Horne, Langille & MacIntyre, 159 Portland St., F. K. Horne, Q.C., K. Langille, A. A. MacIntyre, W.B. MacKinnon, Jennifer March
Jones, Tyler & Assoc., 156 Wyse Rd., D. I. Jones, Q.C., G.R. Rankin
Landry & McGillivray, 700, 45 Alderney Dr., P.M. Landry, M.G. McGillivray, M.F. LeBlanc, N.B. Hill
Livingstone & Cox, 82 Portland St., D.J. Livingstone, C.F. Cox, A.V. McBride
MacInnes, Wilson & Hallett, 140 Portland St. (also Halifax)
McInnes, Mont & Randall, Box 2069/E, S.K. Mont, C. Randall
Metcalf & Holm, 50 Tacoma Dr., F. Metcalf, C.A. Holm, M. J. Ritch, W.M. Penfound, T. Hayashi, M.G. Tompkins, Rose Anne MacGillivray. Counsel: Dr. E. Gold
Ruck & Mitchell, 1706 Argyle Rd., D.G. Ruck, B.H. Mitchell
Smith, Gay, Evans & Assoc., Box 852, W.B. Smith, J. Gay, B.W. Evans
Waterfield & Waterfield, 34 Queen St., G. S. Waterfield, Q.C. (Counsel), B. C. Waterfield, Q.C. Associates: V.L. Pettipas, G.B. Stanford
Weldon & Misener, 19 Portland St., R. L. Weldon, C.M. Misener, Q.C., P.L. Casey, J.A. Gass, P.R. Covert, M.J. Beeler
Wolfson, Schelew, Green & Zatzman, #603, 73 Tacoma Dr., A.S. Wolfson, J.L. Schelew, S.G. Zatzman

DIGBY, Co. Digby
Bradshaw, M.H., 26 Water St. (also Yarmouth)
Haliburton & Comeau, 68 Water St., C. E. Haliburton, Q.C., J. D. Comeau, Rebecca Wheeler
Outhouse, J.L., 9 Water St.

ENFIELD, Co. Hants
Crowe, Thompson, Haynes & Co., Box 277, D.F. English, J.M. Haughn

GLACE BAY, Co. Cape Breton
Crosby, Keliher & Broderick, 38 Union St., R.M. Crosby, C.J. Keliher, C. Broderick, W.R. Burke
Fergusson, N. L., Q.C., Bank of N.S. Bldg.
Matheson, J.R., 5½ Commercial St.
McIntyre, MacDonald & Gillis, 65 Minto St., S.J. MacDonald, F.G. Gillis

GREENWOOD, Co. Kings
Durland, Gillis & Parker, Box 629, C. Parker (also Middleton)
Tidman & Dyer (also Kingston)

GUYSBOROUGH, Co. Guysboro
Biggs, W., 313 Main St. (C.M. Campbell)
Gillis, D.J., Box 205
Grant, C.W., Q.C., Box 36

HALIFAX, Co. Halifax
Barnett, H.B., 6270 Jubilee Rd.
Barss, Hare & Turner, 1657 Barrington St., A. E. Hare, Q.C., A. J. Turner
Block, Prossin & MacLean, 6243 Quinpool Rd., M.C. Block, B.Y.S. Prossin, J.G. MacLean
Blois, Nickerson, Palmeter & Bryson, 1568 Hollis St., R.H.N. Blois, Q.C., B.M. Nickerson, Q.C., I.H.M. Palmeter, Q.C., S.D. Bryson, Q.C., W. Strug, S.B. Outhouse, Elizabeth A. Roscoe, Roberta Clarke, R.J. Williams, M.B. Sherar, J.D. Hurst
Blufarb, B., 1246 Hollis St.
Burchell, Jost, MacAdam, Hayman & Merrick, 1646 Barrington St., W.H. Jost, Q.C., C.W. Burchell, Q.C., A.D. MacAdam, A.G. Hayman, J.P. Merrick, T.J. Burchell, R.F. Reens, R.L. Barnes, W.A. Harvey, K.A. MacInnis
Burris, G.D., 1391 Henry St.
Burton, Lynch, Armsworthy & Ward, 1888 Brunswick St., R.W. Burton, M. Lynch, G.R. Armsworthy, R.B. Ward, J.M. O'Neil
Charlton, J.B., 505A Market St. Mall
City Solicitors, Box 1670, D.F. Murphy, Q.C., W. Anstey, B. S. Allen, G.J. Goneau, Mary E. Donovan, B. Macdonald
Claman, Dietrich, Clark, Bright & Clarke, 6178 Quinpool Rd., P. Claman, M. Dietrich, D.W. Clark, D.J. Bright, W. R. Clarke, D. A. Copp, H.J. Dietrich, J.L. Connors
Clancy, Mary, 6064 Coburg Rd.
Clarke, D.J., 2973 Oxford St.
Cohen, Gaudet, Sharma, Williams & Associates, 6156 Quinpool Rd., H.L. Cohen, G.L. Gaudet, B.H. Sharma, C.F.H. Williams
Connor, J.D., 1584 Chestnut St.
Cooper & McDonald, 702, 1660 Hollis St., T.R. Cooper, R.A. McDonald, R.S. Riddell, Nancy MacLean
Corbett, Corinne R., 1521 Dresden Row
Corkum, W.R., 337D Herring Cove Rd.
Cox, Downie, Nunn & Goodfellow, 800 Barrington Tower, Scotia Sq., (Box 2380, Stn. M, B3J 3E5), A. W. Cox, Q.C., R. J. Downie, Q.C., G.M. Mitchell, Q.C., D.M. Nunn, Q.C., W.R.E. Goodfellow, Q.C., D.McD. Mann, J. M. Barker, J. R. Grant, R. G. MacKeigan, M. S. Ryan, D. M. Campbell, J. W. Arnold, G. I. North, D. C. Campbell, D.F. Gallivan, P.W. Gurnham, T.P. Donovan, F.P. Crooks, T.L. Roane, A.L. Chapman
Cragg, R. G., 645, 5991 Spring Garden Rd.
Crawford & Boudreau, 1568 Hollis St., K.D. Crawford, A.P. Boudreau
Crowe, Thompson, Haynes & Ashworth, 19, Bayers Rd. Shopping Centre, A.M. Crowe, H.D. Thompson, R.H. Haynes, D. Ashworth, D.F. English, J.M.J. Cooper, K.H.A. Robinson, J.M. Haughn
Daley, Black & Moreira, 1791 Barrington St., A. R. Moreira, Q.C., J. W. Alward, Q.C., E.C. Harris, Q.C., J.M. MacGowan, Q.C., R.W. Cregan, R. W. Wright, B. W. Piercey, P. J. MacKeigan, A. S. Beveridge, M. Jill Hamilton, A.W. Moreira, A.L. Bishop
Dillon & Blackburn, #202, 264 Bedford Hwy., J.M. Dillon, B.A.N. Blackburn
Donahoe, Davies, Watson, Gregg & McGillivray, #1800, 1791 Barrington St., A.R. Donahoe, J.F.L. Davies, M.A. Watson, J.A. Gregg, Carol McGillivray
Doucet, Kelly, Evans & MacIsaac, #812, 1660 Hollis St., Fiona Imrie (also Port Hawkesbury)
Epstein, H., 1722 Granville St. (Ann Diego)
Evans, R. D., 5991 Spring Garden Rd.
Filliter & Filliter, 6464 Chebucto Rd., J.D. Filliter, R.J. Filliter
Fleig, R.A., 6097 Jubilee Rd.
Forgeron, S.T., 6443 Almon St.
Franklin, Mitton, Fountain & Thompson, 5162 Duke St., N.W. Franklin, R.B. Mit-

ton, F.S. Fountain, J.W. Thompson, M.A. Argand
Fraser, P.M., Q.C., 1036 Maritime Centre
Gaum, S.L., #202, 6169 Quinpool Rd.
Goldberg, Goldberg & Ehrlich, #1314, 1809 Barrington St., P. Goldberg, V. Goldberg, D.S. Ehrlich
Green & Zatzman, 433 Roy Bldg., S.G. Zatzman
Hutton, Cooke & Assoc., 6464 Chebucto Rd., J.M. Hutton, Q.C., W.M. Cooke, R.J. Filliter, D.E. Gillis, J.K. Hathaway
Iosipescu, M.I., 1781 Chestnut St.
Jordan, J. W., 2745 Dutch Village Rd.
Kanigsberg, Cordon, Stern & Freeman, 400, 1526 Dresden Row, F.W. Cordon, Q.C., A.J. Stern, L.A. Freeman, Jane E. Holmes. Counsel: R.A. Kanigsberg, Q.C.
Kelsie, W.M., 1529 Dresden Row
Kent, G.N., 1579 Granville St.
Khattar, T.J., 1541 Barrington St. (R.F. Wagner, M.W. Burke)
Kitz, Matheson, Green & MacIsaac, #1600, 5151 George St. (Box 247, B3J 2N9), L.A. Kitz, Q.C., P.G. Green, J.D. MacIsaac, F.J. Dickson, Q.C., P.M. Murphy, F.J. Powell, R.N. Rafuse, G.J. McConnell, R.A. Pink, D.R. Feindel, J.C. MacPherson, R.F. Larkin, A.D. Tupper, J.E. Fichaud, D.I. Pink, Dara L. Wiseman, D.A.R. Thompson. Counsel: K.E. Eaton, Q.C.
Lienaux, C.D., 1526 Dresden Row
MacConnachie, I., 1569 Brunswick St.
MacInnes, Wilson & Hallett, 1819 Granville St., W. J. MacInnes, Q.C., K. G. Wilson, Q.C., J. Y. Hickman, Q.C., E. J. Flinn, Q.C., F. B. Wickwire, Q.C., W. L. MacInnes, R. N. Calder, J.D. Thompson, J.W. Chandler, B. MacLellan, Dawna Ring, M.M. Kennedy
MacNeil, Church & MacDonald, Bayers Rd. Shopping Centre, #102, E.J. MacNeil, J.B. Church, N.B. MacDonald
McInnes, Cooper & Robertson, 1673 Bedford Row (B3J 2V1), Donald McInnes, Q.C., J. H. Dickey, Q.C., G. B. Robertson, Q.C., L. A. Bell, Q.C., H. F. Jackson, Q.C., R. A. Cluney, Q.C., H. McInnes, Q.C., H. E. Wrathall, Q.C., J. M. Davison, Q.C., S. McInnes, Q.C., L. J. Hayes, Q.C., J.A.F. Macdonald, G.T.H. Cooper, J.G. Cooper, D. B. Ritcey, P. J. E. McDonough, J. E. Gould, D. H. Reardon, G. W. MacDonald, E.B. Durnford, R. G. Belliveau, M. I. King, C.P. McLellan, W.W. Spicer, F.V.W. Penick, Linda L. Oland, J.D. Stringer, C.C. Robinson, H.L. Morrison, G.J. Arsenault, N.A. Pittas, T.E. Hart, B.G. Johnston, D.A. Graves
Medjuck & Medjuck, One Sackville Place, R. M. Medjuck, Q.C., F. D. Medjuck
Metcalf & Holm, 1809 Barrington St., F. Metcalf, C.A. Holm, M.J. Ritch, W.M. Penfound, T. Hayashi, M.G. Tompkins, Rose Anne MacGillivray. Counsel: Dr. E. Gold (also Dartmouth)
Moore, MacDonald & Davis, 2194 Gottingen St., C.W. Moore, Q.C., G.W. Davis, Q.C.
Newman, Routledge & Weldon Assoc., 7071 Bayers Rd., R.W. Newman, D.L. Routledge, S. Weldon
Paton & Paton, 1529 Granville St., H. M. Paton, Q.C., A.P.D. Chandler, W.P. Moore, W.A. Sutherland, D.S. Johnson, R.J.R. Stinson, B.H. Wildsmith, M. Rosen
Paul, Clyde A. & Assoc., 4, 378 Herring Cove Rd., C.A. Paul, V.F. Lambie
Potts-Meadows, S.C., 5991 Spring Garden Rd.
Power & Co., 1521 Dresden Row, T.P. Power, L. MacDougall
Quackenbush & Thomson, #210, 6021 Young St., D.W. Quackenbush, E.F.G. Thomson, D.W. MacDonald
Rafuse, J. P., Q.C., 200, 6265 Quinpool Rd.
Rockwell & Moore, 5991 Spring Garden Rd., G.W. Rockwell, M.C. Moore, P.D. Wedlake, B.J. Butler
Ross, E. A., & Assoc., 1577 Granville St., E.A. Ross, J.B. Pachai, Sheila Ray
Roza, J.S., #200, 6208 Quinpool Rd.
Rozovsky, L.E., 2044 Armcrescent
Scaravelli, L.W., 1806 Upper Water St.
Seaman, G.H., 6956 Chebucto Rd.
Shaw, J. F., 121 Roy Bldg.
Silverman, A. J., 1541 Barrington St.
Smith, A.M., Q.C., 102 Main Mall, Bayers Rd. Shopping Centre
Spencer & Co., Historic Properties, P.F. Spencer, F.A. Mason, W.M. Leahey, Alison Scott
Stewart, H. L., 208 Roy Bldg.
Stewart MacKeen & Covert, 1583 Hollis St. (Box 997, B3J 2X2), F.M. Covert, Q.C., J.W.E. Mingo, Q.C., H.B. Rhude, Q.C., D.R. Chipman, Q.C., J.D. Moore, Q.C., R.N. Pugsley, Q.C., J.T. MacQuarrie, Q.C., D.A. Stewart, Q.C., G.A. Caines, Q.C., B. Flemming, Q.C., D.H. Oliver, Q.C., G.D.N. Covert, J.S. Cowan, D.H. McDougall, J.G. Godsoe, Jr., H.K. Smith, J.E. Pink, J.S. McFarlane, W.L. Ryan, R.K. Jones, C.G. McCormick, D.A. Miller, D.J. Mathews, J.D. Murphy, Deborah A. Carver, D.S. Green, Mary E. Meisner, T.C. Matthews, Barbara S. Penick, Karin A. McCaskill, Debora H. Zatzman, R.G. Grant, M.E. MacDonald. Counsel: D.A. Kerr, Q.C.
Thompson, P.L., 981 Marlborough Wood
Veniot Jessome Kelly, 1828 Upper Water St., M.J. Veniot, L.R. Jessome, G.R. Kelly. Counsel: H.E. Crosby, Q.C.
Walker, Catherine, 1828 Upper Water St.
Walker, Dunlop, 5670 Spring Garden Rd., A. L. Caldwell, Q.C., G. G. Simms, T.P. Sodero, C.B. Havey, Q.C., W.C. Matthews, W.G. MacArthur, M. Heather Robertson, W.D. Dunlop, D.G. Peverill, A.J. Fraser. Counsel: W.C. Dunlop, Q.C., J.E. Godwin, Q.C.
Wedderburn, H.A.J., 7001 Mumford Rd.
White & Co., 9 Bobolink St., J.J. White
Wolfson, Schelew, Green, etc., #433, 1657 Barrington St. (also Dartmouth)
Wood, J.D., 1579 Granville St.

HANTSPORT, Co. Hants
Day, J.G., Box 31

KENTVILLE, Co. Kings
Taylor, MacLellan & Cochrane, 23 Cornwallis St., K. L. Taylor, Q.C., J. P. Cochrane, Q.C., E. B. Chase, L. M. Lenethen, G. C. Gordon, G.R. Lohnes, Margaret J. Stewart
Thompson-Sheppard, Dianne E., Drawer 578
Thorpe, Buntain, Muttart & Forse, 20 Cornwallis St., V.N. Thorpe, Q.C., R.P. Muttart, M. G. Forse, G. Steele, A.T. Tufts, H.T. Wheeldon
Waterbury, Newton & Johnson, 469 Main St., W. Newton, R.W. Johnson, E.O. Sturk, H.A.R. Simpson, L.M. Walsh. Counsel: D.J.C. Waterbury, Q.C., S.R. Enman

KINGSTON, Co. Kings
Tidman & Dyer, Box 267, G.A. Tidman, Q.C., W.J. Dyer, D.I. Carmichael

LIVERPOOL, Co. Queens
Clements, Tutty, Box 760, S.F. Clements, W.Y. Tutty, B.F. Bailey
Freeman, G.B., Q.C., Box 1600 (Anne Crawford)
Milford, C.S., Q.C., Box 1390

LOWER SACKVILLE, Co. Halifax
Dillon & Blackburn, 265 Old Windsor Hwy.
Farwell & Hines, Box 351, Downsview Mall, D. F. Farwell, R. C. Hines
Miller & Fitt, Box 239 (also New Glasgow)
Murtha, R.A., 505 #1 Hwy. (D.C. Melnick, J.A. Feehan)
Prossin, B.Y.S., 787 #1 Hwy. (also Halifax)

LUNENBURG, Co. Lunenburg
Brattson, D.W.T., Box 1415
Cook, W. W., 6 King St.
Hebb & Burke, Box 549, R.C. Hebb, Q.C., P.A. Burke
Parish & Macdonald, 258 Lincoln St., A.V. Parish, D.K. Macdonald
Saunders, E.R., Q.C., Box 412 (G.L. Graham)

MAHONE BAY, Lunenburg
Parish & Macdonald, Box 279, V. Haysom (also Lunenburg)

METEGHAN, Co. Digby
Deveau, R. A.

MIDDLETON, Co. Annapolis
Dowell, C.H., Q.C., Box 910
Durland, Gillis & Parker, 76 Commercial St., C.H. Durland, Q.C., W.B. Gillis, C. Parker. Counsel: Hon. K. L. Crowell, Q.C.

NEW GERMANY, Co. Lunenburg
Walker & Taylor, Box 28, D.F. Walker, Q.C., D.S. Taylor

NEW GLASGOW, Co. Pictou
Langley, J.G., 130 George St.
MacIntosh, MacDonnell & MacDonald, 174 Archimedes St., H. J. MacDonnell, Q.C., R. B. MacDonald, Q.C., C. F. MacDonald, D. Wallace, B.T. MacIntosh, N.M. Scaravelli. Counsel: T.C. Sedgwick, Q.C.
MacKay, H.E., 465 Westville Rd.
MacKay, I.A., 610 e. River Rd. (Dana MacKay)
Margeson & Wilson, 133A Provost St., T. E. Margeson, J. C. Wilson
Miller & Fitt, 210 Archimedes St., P.B. Miller, J.W. Fitt, E.M. MacKay, Q.C.
Proudfoot, J.G., 260 Westville Rd.
Roddam, Goodman, etc., 483 River Rd., R.S. Goodman, J.G. MacDonald (also Pictou)
White, Stroud & Assoc., 559 e. River Rd., R.J. White, R.A. Stroud, H.E. Patterson

NEW MINAS, Co. Kings
MacDonald & Assoc., 1147½ Commercial St., P.G. Griffiths (also Wolfville)

NEW WATERFORD, Co. Cape Breton
Crosby, Keliher & Broderick, 3353 Plummer Ave., C. Broderick (also Glace Bay)
Hinchey & Hinchey, M.J. Hinchey, Q.C., M.S. Hinchey
Sullivan, Smith, etc., 455 Smith St. (also Sydney)

NORTH SYDNEY, Co. Cape Breton
Boudreau, Beaton & LaFosse, 310 Commercial St., A.P. Ross (also Sydney)
Burchell, W.P., 258 Commercial St. (J. Di-Persio)
Dinault, A.J., Box 272
Macdonald, J. M., Q.C., 321 Commercial St.
MacLennan, C.H., 2 Archibald Ave.
Ryan & Ryan, 262 Commercial St., M. J. Ryan, Q.C., D. J. Ryan, M. Ryan

PARRSBORO, Co. Cumberland
Fullerton, W.B., Q.C., Box 365

PICTOU, Co. Pictou
MacKay, H.E., 465 Westville Rd.
MacLean & MacDonald, 16 Coleraine St., I.H. MacLean, E.A. MacDonald
Roddam, Goodman, MacDonald & Scanlan, 94 Church St., K.E.W. Roddam, Q.C., J.G. MacDonald, J.E. Scanlan

PORT HAWKESBURY, Co. Inverness
Doucet, Kelly, Evans & MacIsaac, Church St., G.J. Doucet, Q.C., F.B.W. Kelly, L.K. Evans, Harold MacIsaac, Hugh MacIsaac, Fiona Imrie, Margaret MacDonald
Leblanc & Assoc., Box 700, A.J. Leblanc, G.A. MacDonald, A. Pickup, Louise Campbell
MacIsaac, P.G., Box 961
Williams, G.H., Q.C., Box 389

PORT HOOD, Inverness
MacDonald, M.L., R.R. 2

PUGWASH, Co. Cumberland
Tait, R.C., Box 275

RIVER PHILIP, Co. Cumberland
McCunn, R. F., Q.C.

SHELBURNE, Co. Shelburne
Clements, Tutty & Co. (also Liverpool)
Foster, G.R.
Harding, J.M., Q.C., John St., Box 549
Rideout, W.S.

SHERBROOKE, Co. Guysborough
Archibald, R.W., Box 176

SHUBENACADIE, Co. Hants
Carruthers, R.A., Box 280

SPRINGHILL, Co. Cumberland
Filliter & Filliter, Box 2440, J.D. Filliter (also Halifax)
Hicks & Co., 49 Main St. (also Amherst)

STELLARTON, Co. Pictou
Baker, J.B., Q.C., 253 Foord St.
Graham, Skoke-Graham, Box 850, P. Graham, R.M. Skoke-Graham
O'Blenis, R.E., Box 1500

SYDNEY, Co. Cape Breton
Boudreau, Beaton & LaFosse, 50 Dorchester St., J. B. Boudreau, G. W. Beaton, G. LaFosse, A.P. Ross, J.M. MacDonald. Counsel: T.J.K. Gillis, Q.C.
Elman & Kuna, 327 Charlotte St., F.L. Elman, Q.C., J. M. Kuna, M.F. Hannem
Goduto, D., 106 Townsend St.
Gunn, A.O., Q.C., 111 Park St.
Kellerman, Joanne, 235 Charlotte St.
Khattar & Khattar, 378 Charlotte St., S.J. Khattar, Q.C., G.S. Khattar, J.V. MacDonald, M.B. Campbell
Lorway & Muise, 217 Charlotte St., C.R. Lorway, Jr., D.N. Muise
MacLellan, MacDonald & Haley, 80 Crescent St., R.G. MacLellan, W.P. MacDonald, K.C. Haley
McIntyre, R.R., Q.C., 205 Charlotte St.
McIntyre & Khattar, 463 Prince St., H.F. McIntyre, J.G. Khattar
McLeod, H.R., 200 Charlotte St.
Murphy, G. F., Q.C., 200 Charlotte St.
Nathanson, H. S., Q.C., 268 Charlotte St. (R.B. Campbell)
Parsons, D.L., 54 Prince St.
Rosenblum, C. M., Q.C., 200 Charlotte St.
Salter, J.L., 223 Esplanade St.
Sullivan, Smith, McMahon & Gillis, Bank of N.S. Bldg., G.A.S. Smith, Q.C., N.F. McMahon, G.R. Sullivan, J.D. Gillis
Walsh, E.C., 235 Charlotte St.

SYDNEY MINES, Co. Cape Breton
Brogan, N.T., Box 129

TATAMAGOUCHE, Co. Colchester
Hamilton, D. F.
Kennedy, W.R. (also Truro)

TRURO, Co. Colchester
Archibald & Lederman, 187 Queen St., Jeanne Archibald, P. Lederman
Burchell, MacDougall & Gruchy, 710 Prince St., R. L. MacDougall, Q.C., D.W. Gruchy, Q.C., J.R. Winters, Q.C., J.R.M. Akerman, R.B. MacLellan, M.W. Stokoe, J.W. Stonehouse, J.G. MacDougall, J.T. Rafferty, J.W. Stanley, B.S. Russell, C.D. MacDougall
Kennedy, W.R., 56 Elm St.
MacLean & Assoc., 188 Queen St., M.J. MacLean, A.D. MacNeill, K.E. Grant
McLellan, Nichols & Richards, 795 Prince St., D. A. Nichols, Q.C., J. F. Richards
Patterson, Smith, Matthews & Grant, 10 Church St., (Box 1068, B2N 5B9), Hon. G.I. Smith, Q.C., K. M. Matthews, Q.C., D.J. MacDonald, Q.C., J. C. Leefe, Q.C., D. R. Hubley, D. A. Caldwell, C.A. Beckett, J.W.S. Saunders, J. R. Creighton, G.L. White, L.E. Barnhill, R.M. Purdy, S.R. Morse, R.M. MacLeod, J.M. McCrea, A.C. MacLean, D. Suzan Frazer
Retson & Curtis, 64 Inglis St., J.C. Retson, D.F. Curtis
Scanlan & Co., 789 Prince St., G.P. Scanlan

WESTERN SHORE, Co. Lunenburg
Preeper, B. (also Chester Basin)

WESTVILLE, Co. Pictou
Facey, S.C., 2008 College St.

WINDSOR, Co. Hants
Adams & Co., 87 Gerrish St., H.G.S. Adams, M.C. Chisholm, M.C. Jones
Hughes & Nelson, 533 Albert St., Barbara D. Hughes, Q.C., G.L. Nelson
Lawrence & Bigelow, Box 788, W.R. Lawrence, Q.C., J. Bigelow
Macdonald & Alexander, Water St., A. G. Macdonald, Q.C., B.J. Alexander
McGrath & MacKenzie, Box 280, D.J. McGrath, R.M. MacKenzie
Romans, J.D., 140 King St.

WOLFVILLE, Co. Kings
DeMont & Dewar, Box 1449, E.G. DeMont, Q.C., J.E. Dewar
Hatfield, B.M., Q.C., 215 Main St. (also New Minas)
How, Smith & Kimball, Box 670, L.M. Smith, Q.C., D.J. Kimball
MacDonald & Associates, Box 490, G. C. MacDonald, Q.C. (also New Minas)

YARMOUTH, Co. Yarmouth
Bradshaw, M. H., 17 Porter St.
Chipman, Fraser, Pink & Nickerson, 341 Main St., D.L. Chipman, Q.C., H.J. Fraser, M.J. Pink, A.S. Nickerson. Counsel: A.B. MacGillivray, Q.C.
Forbes & Wickens, 348 Main St., R. Forbes, D. Wickens, R.B. Vaughan
Hood & Assoc., 381 Main St., S.C. Hood, R.M. Prince
Pink, Macdonald, Caldwell, Warner, 379½ Main St., I.C. Pink, Q.C., I.H. Macdonald, Patricia E. Caldwell, G. M. Warner
Reardon, J.D., Q.C., 3 Glebe St.
Ross, J.G., 381 Main St.

BARRISTERS AND SOLICITORS IN ONTARIO

ACTON (Halton Hills), Halton
Braida & Valeriote, 67 Mill St. e. (also Guelph)
MacKenzie & Chapman, 28 Main St. n., Margaret MacKenzie, G.R. Chapman

AGINCOURT, York
Braganca & Lee, 4271 Sheppard Ave. e., J.S. Braganca, M.Y. Lee
Cohen, L.M., 11a Glenwatford Dr.
Cohen & Saul, #201, 1001 Sandhurst Circle, B.C. Cohen, K.H. Saul
Goldstein & Grubner, 3428 Sheppard Ave. e., M1T 3K4, K.B. Goldstein, I. Grubner
Greenberg & Levine, 2245 Kennedy Rd., H. Greenberg, M. Levine
Hicks, D., 30 Emblem Ct.
Kates & Goldkind, 206, 3850 Sheppard Ave. e.(see Toronto)
Papernick, S. A., 4433 Sheppard Ave. e.
Silverberg & Weisberg, 4240 Sheppard Ave. e., L.A. Silverberg, H. Weisberg
Topp & Zaretsky, 2547 Pharmacy Ave., D.M. Topp, M.R. Zaretsky
Wong, W.H., 4455 Sheppard Ave. e.

AILSA CRAIG, Middlesex
Judson & Co. (also London)

AJAX, Durham
Berg, L.A., Q.C., 152 Harwood Ave. s.
Cohen, L.M., 70 Harwood Ave. s.
Fromstein, R. J., 61 Commercial Ave.
Morris, M.J., 158 Harwood Ave. s.
Parish & Bloodworth, 158 Harwood Ave. s., S. Parish, T.W. Bloodworth
Polak, McKay & Balena, 158 Harwood Ave. s., H.S. Polak, Q.C., D.J. Balena, L.A. Seguin, R.J. Hawkshaw. Counsel: D.W. McKay
Singh, P. G., 158 Harwood Ave. s.

ALEXANDRIA, Glengarry
Bergeron, Follon & Co. (also Cornwall)
Lefebvre, Bellefeuille, 39 rue Principale n., J.-M. Lefebvre, R.E. Bellefeuille
Macdonald & Aubry, G. G. Aubry
MacDonald & MacPhee (also Cornwall)

ALLISTON, Simcoe
Bowerman, Cochrane, Long, Assoc., 44 Victoria St. w., J.D. Bowerman, Q.C., P. E. Cochrane, N.E. Long
Corbett, Montgomery & Assoc., 30 Victoria St. w. (also Newmarket)
Greenfield, Service, 146 Victoria St. w., G.A. Greenfield, D.R. Service
Ritchie & Feehely, 59 Victoria St. e. (also Tottenham)
Smith, McLean, 22 Church St. s., J.N. Darling, Q.C., J. W. Smith (also Barrie)

ALMONTE, Lanark
Chapman, L.G.W., Box 362
Galligan, M.J., 63 Bridge St.
Galway, P., 58 Mill St.

ALVINSTON, Lambton
Weed, R.F., 514 River St. (also Sarnia)

AMHERSTBURG, Essex
Bondy, Kirwin & Co. (also Windsor)
DiPierdomenico, L., 290 Sandwich St. s.
Fee, Colleen A., 138 Laird Ave.
Hall, Wm. J.

McCready, G.R.
Willson & Barat (also Windsor)

AMHERSTVIEW, Lennox & Addington
Mylks, H.G.
Vince, W. E. M.

ANCASTER, Hamilton-Wentworth
McKeon, Wilkins, etc., 245 Wilson St. e., R.J. Wilkins, R.J. Horodyski (also Hamilton)

ANNAN, Grey
McCubbin, J., Q.C., R.R. 2

ARKONA, Lambton
Carpeneto, J.J. (also Sarnia)

ARNPRIOR, Renfrew
Abbott & Lemay, #15, 55 Daniel St. n., D.A. Abbott, Pamela R. Lemay
Coady, C. J., Box 6
Colbert, T.B., 375 Daniel St. s.
McLean & Moore, Box 8, A.A. McLean, J.D. Moore
Mulvihill, Murray & Merla, 102 John St. n., D.S. Murray, C.P. Merla

ARTHUR, Wellington
Smith & Jenzen, D.D. Smith, R.G. Jenzen

ATHENS, Leeds
Flood, R. W. (also Brockville)

ATIKOKAN, Rainy River
Phillips, McKillop, 112 Gorrie St. (also Fort Frances)
Wolder & McLennan, 103 Main St. (also Fort Frances)

AURORA, York
Bailey, W.H.C., 33 Victoria St.
Binnington, A.A., 24 Yonge St. s.
Corner & Switzer, 47 Yonge St. s., B.W. Switzer, J.M. Whyte
Leighton, R.G., 59 Yonge St. s.
Mark & Singer, 11 Mosely St., L. Mark, R.N. Singer
McPherson & Shugart, 34 Yonge St. s., T. McPherson, K.R. Shugart
Russell, G.A., Q.C., Box 126
Shortill, T.D., 109 Yonge St. n.
Smith, Thompson & Assoc., 50 Yonge St. s., C.G. Smith, P.M. Thompson

AVONMORE, Stormont
Fennell, Rudden & Co. (also Cornwall)

AYLMER, Elgin
Gloin & Assoc. (also St. Thomas)
Johnston, Doyle & Prendergast, 10 Sydenham St., B.V. Johnston, Q.C., M. Doyle, D.J. Prendergast

AZILDA, Sudbury
Steinberg, Renzini & Co., Azilda Shopping Centre (also Sudbury)

BANCROFT, Hastings
Anderson, O. G., Q.C., Box 700
Lincoln, R.
Plater, L.C.

BARRIE, Simcoe
Bell, June, 15 Collier St.
Bell, Temple, 58 Collier St., P. Archibald, P.H. Lamprey (also Toronto)
Boys, Seagram & Rowe, 13 Owen St., C. J. Seagram, Q.C., O.J. Rowe, Q.C., I.J. Rowe, G.L. Craig
Bryson, T., 91 Bayfield St.
Burns, F.E., 118 Collier St.
Carroll, D.K., 118 Collier St.
Coffey, J. D., 110 Little Ave.
Conder, Sugg, 23 Owen St., G.W.E. Conder, Q.C., D.J. Sugg, J.G. Currie, Q.C.
Corbett, Montgomery & Assoc., 110 Dunlop St. w., Carolyn Jones (also Newmarket)
Cowan & Carter, 107 Collier St., G. A. R. Cowan, L. Carter
Graham, Wilson & Green, 17 Poyntz St., J. D. D. Graham, E. M. Green, T. S. Wilson, R.F. McDonald
Hogben, Mayhew & Van Lange, 39 Owen St., D. T. A. Hogben, E. P. Mayhew, I.J. Van Lange
Horton, F., 33 Murray St.
Jacoby, K.N., 17 Owen St.
Kenny, Bigelow, Reed, 23 Owen St., W.A. Kenny, B.J. Bigelow, M.E. Reed
Livingston, Myers & Cockburn, 89 Collier St., J. A. Livingston, Q.C., E. J. Myers, J. R. Cockburn, A. R. Elliott, D.F. Smith, K.J. Levison
Luhowy, G.W., 3 Berczy St.
McMaster, M., 80 Maple Ave.
Menzies, J.M., 118 Collier St.
Miller, A., 23 Owen St.
Moorby, J.W., Box 626
Norman, G.E., 99 Bayfield St.
Oatley, Purser, 1 Berczy St., R. G. Oatley, A. R. Purser
Otton, J. S., Q.C., 15 Owen St.
Owen, Burgar, Hamilton & Dart, 26 Owen St., B. A. Owen, J. Burgar, T. Dart, G.D. Krelove, G.A. Knight, P.E. Dickey
Paisley, G.W., 30 Owen St.
Palmer, G.V., 9 Owen St.
Ruttan, C., 30 Owen St.
Scharf, M., 103 Collier St.
Smith, McLean, 20 Owen St., H. E. Smith, Q.C., P. Howden, Q.C., A.A. Peckham, C. H. Style, L. R. Gray
Stewart, Esten, 100 Collier St., P.A. Mills, Q.C., A. W. J. Dick, P. G. M. Hermiston, Q.C., D. S. White, W.J. Leslie, S.W. Lemesurier, Wendy Miller
Stewart, J., 2 Fred Grant Sq.
Taves, E., 2 Owen St.
Thompson, W. M., Q.C., 37 Peel St.
Wall-Armstrong, D.L., 252 Yonge St.
Wessenger & McCreary, 9 Owen St., P.D. Wessenger, R.F. McCreary
Wildman, Mitchell, 40 Clapperton St., E. C. Wildman, R. J. Mitchell
Wilson, C.L., Q.C., 118 Collier St.
Wrigley, J. R., 129 Worsley St.

BARRY'S BAY, Renfrew
Howe, R.B., Box 790

BATH, Lennox
Wynn, G.G., R.R. 1 (also Picton)

BAY RIDGES, Durham
Greening, W.J., 927 Liverpool Rd. s. (also Toronto)

BEACHBURG, Renfrew
Huckabone & O'Brien, Main St. (also Pembroke)

BEAMSVILLE, Niagara North
Allen & Vandeyar, 72 King St. w., L.R. Allen, M. Vandeyar
Reid, McNaughton & Co. (also St. Catharines)

BEAVERTON, Durham
Calder, C. C.
Eady, R.
Tomlinson, I. G.

BEETON, Simcoe
Ritchie & Feehely, 58 Main St. (also Tottenham)

BELLE RIVER, Essex
Comartin & Deziel, Box 226 (also Windsor)
Mousseau Law Firm (also Windsor)
Mullins & Mullins (also Windsor)

BELLEVILLE, Hastings
Argue, W., Q.C., 256½ Front St. (G. K. Murray)
Bailey, J.W., 257 Pinnacle St.
Barrett, Lally & Wright, 25 Campbell St., R. E. Barrett, Thos. J. Lally, P.J. Wright
Bateman, D. H., Q.C., 175 Front St.
Bates, B., 400 Dundas St. e.
Boyle & Keilty, 49 Campbell St., D.P. Boyle, Q.C., W.J. Keilty
Butler & Graydon, #101, 146 Front St., R.L. Graydon
Cameron & Ord, 175 Front St., G. R. Cameron, R. J. Ord, W.P.H. Procter
Cass, R. W., Q.C., 17 Campbell St.
Collins & Collins, 153 Front St., B.R. Collins
Corbett, J.R., 308 n. Front St.
Desaulniers, D. W., 210 Church St.
Follwell, Follwell & Macleod, 24 Catherine St., E. E. Follwell, Q. C., R.E. Follwell
Girard & Black, 199 Front St., A.P. Girard, M.A. Black
Kaufmann, R., 187b n. Front St.
Ketcheson, R.R., 212½ Front St.
Maraskas, L., Q.C., 212½ Front St.
McLeod, A.J., 257 Pinnacle St.
Miller, J.C., 218 Front St.
Murray, S. I., 30 Bridge St. e.
O'Flynn, Weese, Burns & Walker, #530, Century Place, S. A. Weese, Kathryn Burns, W.W. Walker
Reynolds, Hunter, Sullivan & Kline, 219 Front St., R.J. Reynolds, S.J. Hunter, I.B. Sullivan, Janet M. Kline, R. Hainsworth, E. Kuglin-Alyea
Ross, J.D.M., 175 Front St.
Russell, P., 4 Bridge St. w.
Scott, R.F., 470 Dundas St. e.
Tausendfreund, W.U., #400, Century Place
Temple, R., 15 Campbell St.
Templeman, Brady, Menninga & Kort, 208 John St., I.W. Brady, W. Menninga, K.W. Kort, D.W. Fairbrother, R.M. Renz
Van Huizen, B., 210 Church St.

BLENHEIM, Kent
Kerr & Wood, J. M. Kerr, N. E. Wood, Q.C.
Warwick & Glenn, T.R. Warwick, L.C. Glenn

BLIND RIVER, Algoma
Berthelot & Gagnon, 16 Woodward Ave. (also Elliot Lake)
Cameron, G. D., Q.C
Peterson & Peterson (also Bruce Mines)
Pigeon, A. A. J.

BLYTH, Huron
Crawford, Mill & Co. (also Wingham)

BOBCAYGEON, Victoria
McQuarrie, Hill & Co., E.C. Hill, Q.C. (also Lindsay)
Walker, R.J., 75 Bolton St.

BOLTON, Peel
Carberry, Mrs. J.P., 4 Queen St. n.
Conte, A., 49 Queen St. n.
Jones, Marilyn Conway, 60 Owen Dr.
Palmateer, R.B.G., 4 Queen St. s. Assoc.: P.G. Muise
Penfold, M.E., 23 King St. w.
Walsh & Walsh (also Toronto)

BOWMANVILLE, Durham
Barber, D. J.
Kelly, M. B.
Mason, L. C., Q.C.
Strike & Strike, W. R. Strike, Q.C., A. A. H. Strike
Van Nest & Assoc., 118 King St. e., J.K. Van Nest, J.J. Chalmers

BRACEBRIDGE, Muskoka
Black, A. R., Pine St.
Lee, Roche, Kelly & Jacques, 6 Dominion St., N.B. Roche, M. S. Kelly, B. G. Jacques
Pinckard, T.C., 58 Dominion St., E.R. McGowan (also Huntsville)
Reid, W.B., 9 Chancery Lane
Strongitharm, R.G., 95 Manitoba St.
Sugg & Fitton, 5 Chancery Lane, H.E.S. Sugg, Q.C., M. Fitton

Tweedie & Wood, 47 Quebec St., R. A. Tweedie, T.M. Wood
Wyjad, D.J., 39 Dominion St.

BRADFORD, Simcoe
Corbett, Montgomery & Assoc., 95 Holland St. w., G.A. Hunter (also Newmarket)
Evans & Evans, 21 Holland St. w., B. M. Evans, Q.C., T.E. Evans, Q.C., R.F. Evans, Q.C.. Counsel: C.T.S. Evans, Q.C.
Gordon, W. R., 57 Holland St., Box 1660
Losell, C.

BRAMALEA, Peel
Dalzell, W.R., One City Centre
Forrester, J., #302, 44 Peel Centre Dr.
McLennan, N.D., One City Centre Dr.
Offman & Raby, 30 Melanie Dr., L. Offman, R.B. Raby
Podkowa, S. A., 41 Bramalea Rd. (S. J. Repa)
Pratt & Logan, 44 Peel Centre Dr., J.H. Pratt, D.F. Logan
Speigel & Nichols, 44 Peel Centre Dr., J.D. Speigel, B.S. Nichols
Stockey, R.C., 111D Bramalea City Centre

BRAMPTON, Peel
Acri, Seeback & Longfield, 134 Queen St. e., L. S. Acri, D. E. Seeback, R.A. Longfield, W.R.H. Fader, C.K. Waite
Batchelar & Carey, 350 Rutherford Rd. s., B.D. Batchelar, T.J.P. Carey
Bowyer, Greenslade & Hall, 6 George St. s., C. B. Bowyer, E. W. Greenslade, T. G. Hall, K.L. Webster, Linda Peckitt-Roszell, R.D. Allison
Cohen, D. M., 24 Queen St. e.
Cooke, Callahan & Leschied, 60 Queen St. e., W.M. Cooke, R.V. Callahan, Q.C., R.S. Leschied
Davis, Webb, 41 George St. s., R.K. Webb, Q.C., T.M. Dunn, Q.C., C.G. Schulze, B. W. Tinsley, J.D. Ostler, J.R. Inglis. Counsel: B.T. Clark, Q.C.
Greenbaum, S., 41 Kennedy Rd. n.
Heller & Weinstock, 25, 239 Queen St. e., M. Heller, F. Weinstock
Hendy, T.C., 113 Queen St. e.
Hillier, S.L. & Assoc., 145 Queen St. e. (Ava Hillier)
Hollinrake, A., Q.C., 14 Nelson St. w.
Kiss, J.P., 1 City Centre
Lawrence, Lawrence & Stevenson, 43 Queen St. w., W. C. Lawrence, Q.C., B.J. Stevenson, Q.C., D.F. Cole, Q.C., J.R. Kelly, Q.C., J.F. Macdonald, L. N. Shapiro, K. F. McCabe, Brenda Duncan, A. Orr, J.M. Simmons, R.J. Weiler, R.A. Filkin, G.D. Fitzhenry, J.C. Gaskin, C.L. Moon, J.P. Mullen
Lent, D.R., 38 Queen St. w.
Mackie, W.D., 14 Nelson St. w.
MacPherson, C.G., 113 Queen St. e.
Marsden, Gerald H., Q.C., 11 Queen St. e.
Matheson, H. A., 134 Queen St. e.
McIntyre & Assoc., 181 Queen St. e., R.D. McIntyre, Q.C., P.W. Jeffries
Monro, H. D., 8 Main St. s.
Morris, W.H., 118 Queen St. w.
Neiman & Edward, 24 Queen St. e., C.M. Neiman, D.G. Edward, P.W. Read, T.W.G. Pratt. Counsel: Hon. Joan Bissett Neiman
Prouse, Dash & Prouse, 20 Nelson St. w., R. E. Prouse, Q.C., R.D. Prouse, D.A. Dash
Richardson, Schnall & Sanderson, 13 Queen St. e., G. Schnall, J. R. Sanderson
Samuel & Paul, 41 Kennedy Rd. n., L. F. Samuel, J. M. Paul
Simmons, Shuster & da Silva, 499 Main St. s., H. S. Simmons, N.A. Nolasco da Silva, E.J. Sinton. Counsel: R. Shuster
Smith, G.P., 24 Queen St. e.
Szumlanski, V., 11 Queen St. e.
Tannahill & Lockhart, 284 Queen St. e., D.D. Tannahill, J.S. Lockhart, T.A. Clark
Upshall, MacKenzie & Kelday, 24 Queen St. e., P.C. Upshall, A.D.K. MacKenzie, E. M. Kelday, G. Struk, G.T. Snowdon, D.R. Lane, S.M. Harrington
Wainwright, A., 24 Queen St. e.
Walsh, M.J., 181 Queen St. w.
West & Robb, 34 Queen St. w., K.D. Robb, Q.C., B.W. Stephenson, C.P. Stobie, G.J. Nikota
Zuker & Dale, 24 Queen St. e., A. M. Zuker, E. Dale, F. Streiman

BRANTFORD, Brant
Ainsworth, D.C., 40 Nelson St.
Ballachey, Moore, Beyer & Harrow, 88 Nelson St., P. A. Ballachey, Q.C., H. C. Moore, Q.C., K.K. Beyer, W.D. Harrow, D.J. Partridge
Boddy, Ryerson, Houlding, Clarke, Thompson & Hart, 42 Wellington St., R. I. Ryerson, Q.C., G. R. Houlding, Q.C., E.F. Clarke, Q.C., R.M. Thompson, T.F.M. Hart, R.L. Parsons
Calder & Goold, 57 Chatham St., D. C. Calder, C. D. Goold
Canning, J.S., 112 Market St.
City Solicitor, C. D. Wilson, 100 Wellington Sq.
Claridge & Cook, 105 George St., B.L. Claridge, R.M. Cook
Duce, Forbes, Hitchon & Quinlan, 39 Nelson St., W. Duce, P. B. Forbes, J.A. Hitchon, P.M. Quinlan
Frost & Smits, 37 Wellington St., S.C. Frost, I.G.T. Smits
Hart, Parkhill & Reeves, 134 Charing Cross St., J.M. Hart, L. E. Parkhill, D.O. Reeves
Jaychuk, N.V., 93 Pearl St.
Lawrence, Davies, 73 Chatham St., J.W.G. Lawrence, J.S. Davies
Lefebvre & Lefebvre, 80 Chatham St., M. E. Lefebvre, K. P. Lefebvre, Q.C., R.J. Lefebvre, J.M.A. Lefebvre
Leslie & St. Amand, 111 George St., J.G. Leslie, L. St. Amand
Macdonald, Binkley & Daboll, 83 Chatham St., A.L. Binkley, Q.C., M.B. Daboll, Q.C.
McIntosh, Kindon & James, 101 Wellington St., R.G.S. McIntosh, Q.C., R.L. Kindon, P.A.M. James
Miller, Miller & Hospodar, 148 Dalhousie St., G. E. Miller, J. M. Hospodar, P. Holyoake
Painter, E.W., 47 Charing Cross St.
Painter, W.S., 417 St. Paul Ave.
Pennell, Underwood & Ion, 109 George St., B. T. Pennell, W. H. Underwood, J.G. Ion
Pope, R.B.A., 293 Dalhousie St.
Read, Innes, Verity & Gregory, 34 Wellington St., P. D. Read, Q.C., R. L. Verity, Q.C., D. J. Gregory
Slemin, Wynn, 90 Nelson St., J.A. Wynn, Q.C., D.E. Spicer
Staats & Harris, 82 Charlotte St., H. E. Staats, Q.C., Sandra J. Harris
Thompson, P. J., 30 King St.
Trepanier, Hagey, Kneale & Wiacek, 63 Charlotte St., M.G. Kneale, Q.C., J. M. Wiacek, H. L. Hagey, K.G. Lenz
Vandervet, P., 107 Wellington St.
Waterous, Holden, Kent & Amey, 20 Wellington St., R. N. Waterous, H. C. Holden, J. Kent, P. D. Amey, T. R. Sheldon, P.R. Corless, J.A. Renwick, D.K. Davis
Whitbread, T. A., 22 Sky Acres Dr.
Wray, B. F., R.R. #8
Wyatt, Purcell, Will, Stillman & Scott, 103 Darling St., S. E. Wyatt, Q.C., J. A. Purcell, G. B. Will, P. M. Stillman, Margaret Scott
Zaltz, S.G., 40 Nelson St.

BRIDGENORTH, Peterborough
Devitt, H.G., Box 269 (also Peterborough)

BRIGDEN, Lambton
McEachran & Co. (also Sarnia)

BRIGHTON, Northumberland
Banbury, J. T., Box 868
Staddon, P.S., Box 65
Thompson & Thompson, T.C. Thompson, Q.C., D.J. Thompson

BROCKVILLE, Leeds
Anderson, Wilson, 3 Court Terrace, C. D. Anderson, W. R. Wilson
Beale, Macintosh & Lewis, 2 Court House Ave., J. H. Macintosh, Q.C., D. C. Lewis
Fitzpatrick & Culic, 9 Pine St., C.H. Culic
Flood, R.W., 20 Broad St.
Fraser/Best, 9 Pine St., D.C. Fraser, Q.C., G.O. Best
Hain, D.A., 84 King St. w.
Henderson, A.B., 14 King St. w.
Henderson, Hart, Johnston & Fournier, 61 King St. e., J. E. Henderson, Q.C., H. R. Hart, N. C. Johnston, P. J. Fournier, R.D. Hammond
McFarland, J.H., 37 King St. w.
Preston, H.R., 84 King St. w.
Stewart, Corbett, Musclow, Barr, O'Shaughnessy & Simpson, 21 Court House Ave., J. T. Corbett, Q.C., C. H. Musclow, Q.C., R. A. Barr, Q.C., M.J. O'Shaughnessy, J.D. Simpson
Wyatt, D.W., 96 King St. w.

BRUCE MINES, Algoma
Peterson & Peterson, Box 100, L.D. Peterson, Patricia Peterson, E.D. McCooeye

BRUSSELS, Huron
Crawford, Mill & Co. (also Wingham)
Goodall, J.T. (also Wingham)

BURFORD, Brant
Wyatt, Purcell & Co. (also Brantford)

BURK'S FALLS, Parry Sound
Heyder, L.M., Box 360
Morley, R.J., Box 541, R.J. van den Wijst (also South River)
Powell, Cunningham & Co. (also Parry Sound)

BURLINGTON, Halton
Brechin, G.A., 694 Walker's Line
Breen, C.C., & Assoc., 3400 Fairview St., N.N. Fur
Bridle & Bridle, 392 John St., J. A. Bridle, L. K. Bridle
Brown, D.C., 426 Brant St.
Cameron, G.W., 1956 Waterdown Rd.
Cleaver, Crawford, Gall & Brooks, 2019 Caroline St., E. N. Crawford, Q.C., W. Gall, Q.C., A. Brooks
Corvese, J., 501 John St.
Craig & Matthews, 204, 4031 Fairview St., C. V. Craig, L. W. Matthews
Cruickshank, W., 498a Brant St.
Dean, H.F., 440 Elizabeth St.
Dingle & Charlebois, 2021 James St., J.P. Charlebois, Q.C. Counsel: W.G.J. Swybrous
Feltmate, Kusinski, 760 Brant St., M.G. Feltmate, S.R. Kusinski
Gibson, C. D., Q.C., 440 Elizabeth St.
Haber, C.J., 214, 4031 Fairview St. (Catherine Haber)
Hallatt, H.A., 802 Hager Ave.
Hastings & Charlebois, 3027 Harvester Rd., L.A. Hastings, H.J. Charlebois
Hourigan, J.P., Q.C., 2078 Pine St.
Hourigan, W.E., Q.C., 2063 Caroline St.
Kerr & Hawken, 201, 377 Brant St., G.A. Kerr, Q.C., W.C. Hawken, Q.C.
Kosterski, R. R., 3016 New St.

Little, Forbes, Thatcher & Culver, 440 Elizabeth St., C.M. Little, R.M. Forbes, W.L. Thatcher, T.A. Culver
Littlejohn, G.M., 471 Burlington Ave.
Martin, Dunlop, Hillyer & Assoc., 2122 Lakeshore Rd., R. S. Martin, H. B. Hillyer, W.D. Dunlop, A.R. Snelius, M.V. O'Malley, S.J. Serena
McLeod, McLellan, 3077 New St., A.K. McLeod, J.C. McLellan
Milligan, Cass & Barradas, 2012 James St., D. J. Milligan, Q.C., P. H. Cass, E.M. Barradas
Muir, D.W., Q.C., 468 Elizabeth St.
Pichelli & Turingia, 620 Brant St., J. Pichelli, J. Turingia
Ralfe, Green Germann, 518 Brant St., E.G. Ralfe, D.G. Green, R.N. Bates, B.W. Green, G.P. Germann, F.L. Forsyth
Savchuk, J.C., 3425 Harvester Rd.
Simpson, Rich, 473 Brant St., G. Simpson, G.D. Rich
Sutherland, T.R., Q.C., 730 Brant St.
Watters, J. B., 482 Elizabeth St.
Zahoruk, H. W., 3077 New St.

CALEDON EAST, Peel
Jenney, G.W., 9 Airport Rd. s.
Neiman & Co., Airport Rd. at Church (also Brampton)

CALEDONIA, Haldimand
Arrell, Brown, Osier & Murray, 5 Caithness St. w., F.J. Brown, P.J. Osier, W.P. Murray
Humenik, L.S.
Jones, W.B., Q.C. (D.V. Ferguson)

CALLANDER, Parry Sound
Scott & Parslow, Box 340, D.A. Scott, A.C. Parslow

CAMBRIDGE, Waterloo
Copp, Cosman & Pavey, 29 Dickson St., V. B. Copp, Q.C., J. V. Cosman, D.W. Pavey
Cougler, E.O., #201, 624 King St.
Dufresne & Dufresne, 30 George St. n., P. A. Dufresne, A.P. Dufresne
Dyer, W.T., 649a King St. e.
Fogo, B.E., 48 George St. n.
Goad & Goad, 65 Cambridge St., G.S. Goad, T.G. Goad, J.T. Lynch
Grant, D.W., 2 Water St. n.
Hancock, Kidd & Charlton, 17 Cambridge St., W. H. Kidd, Q.C., D. F. Charlton, Diane Tinker
Hardman, P.A., 999 King St. e.
Hilborn, T.J., 18 Queen St.
Isaacksz, C., 1434 King St. e.
Johnson, C.G., 57 Ainslie St. n.
Kao, R., 15 Main St.
Kopinak, J., 654 King St.
Korz, Foell, Ratcliffe & Tikkala, 780 King St. e., William Korz, Q.C., Barbara C. Foell, Linda L. Ratcliffe, D.A. Tikkala
Lavergne, D.K., 99 King St. e.
Loker & Clement, 43 Cambridge St., G. E. Loker, G. J. Clement
Mann & Beagan, 635 Coronation Blvd., P.M. Mann, Lorraine Beagan
Matlow, Miller, Harris, 39 Dickson St., M. Matlow, R.J. Miller, J.M. Harris, D. St. C. Bond
Onorato, Hauser, 708 Duke St., G.J. Onorato, G.E.J. Hauser
Parrott, M.G.F., 15 Main St.
Pearson, Flynn, Sturdy, Martiniuk & Tugender, 553 King St. e., P. R. Sturdy, Q.C., D.M. Tugender, J.F. Lennox
Pettitt, Schwarz, 65 Dickson St., W.K. Schwarz, R.C. Pettitt, R.F. Woynarski
Rivers, C.M., 170 Water St. n.
Shields, H.R., 15 Main St.
Simmers, Edwards, Jenkins, 19 Thorne St., P. J. Simmers, Q.C., R. A. Edwards, Q.C., J. H. Jenkins, Q.C., M. J. Somerville, C. T. LeBrun, G. R. Carpenter, R. H. Clark, R. C. Logan, J.C. Spearn, L.J. Palvetzian, R.C. Snyder, R.F. Earnshaw, T.R. Williston, J.A. MacLeod, P.M. Koch
Thompson, D.A., 2 Water St. n.
Wiegand, J.W., 631 Franklin Blvd.
Wilson, J.C., 2 Water St. n.
Wraight, W.C., 15 Main St.

CAMPBELLFORD, Northumberland
Baker, W.E., 79 Bridge St. e.
Burgess, N.R.H., 64 Front St.
Carter & Brown, J.A. Carter, W. Brown
Smith & Buck, 32 Pellissier St., P. M. G. Smith, J. W. Buck

CANNINGTON, Durham
Miller, D.J., Q.C., 17 Cameron St. w.

CAPREOL, Sudbury
Thomas & Poulson, 41 Young St. (also Sudbury)

CARDINAL, Grenville
Gorrell & Grenkie, Box 580 (also Morrisburg)

CARLETON PLACE, Lanark
Bruun & Bennett, 74 Bridge St., K.B. Bruun, K.J. Bennett
Courtice, P.D., 164 Bridge St.
Dempsey & Jones, 92 Bridge St., D.W. Dempsey, N.A. Jones

CAVAN, Peterborough
Trerise, V.M., R.R. 1

CAYUGA, Haldimand
Marshall, Thibideau & Rous, Box 508, T.D. Marshall, L. P. Thibideau, F.C. Rous
Slimon & Gallagher, H.M. Slimon, J.B. Gallagher

CHATHAM, Kent
Archibald, Ms. Margaret N., Q.C., Box 214
Arnold, Watson & Comiskey, 55 Centre St., J.B. Watson, J.B. Comiskey
Bedford, Myers & Hansen, 186 Wellington St., W. M. Myers, Q.C., K. Hansen, Q.C., J.E.S. Allin
Benoit, Van Raay, Spisani & Fuerth, 124 Thames St., G.L. Benoit, J. F. Van Raay, S. Spisani, S.J. Fuerth
Campbell, Wickett & Trinca, 75 Thames St., T.D. Campbell, J. Wickett, J.B. Trinca
Carscallen, Reinhart, Mathany & Nagle, 111½ St. Clair St., D.J. Reinhart (also Wallaceburg)
Giffen, Pensa, 48 5th St., D.W. Blair (also London)
Goodal, B.J., 36 4th St.
Hinnegan & Babcock, 72 Victoria Ave., K. A. Hinnegan, L. R. Babcock
Juba & Kuchta, Box 848, M.M. Juba, M.E. Kuchta
Kee, Ross & Robertson, 29 3rd St., D. T. Kee, Q.C., K. Ross, R. Robertson
Lachance, D.R., 5 6th St.
Magee, W.P., 36 4th St.
Mayes, S.G., 117 Keil Dr. s.
McDonnell, D.C.A., 5 6th St.
McFalls, Stevens & Sulman, 93 Centre St., R.L. McFalls, R.C. Stevens, D.A. Sulman
McGuire, McFarlane & Thomas, 26 5th St. s., P.L. McGuire, R.J. McFarlane, B.G. Thomas
McNevin, Gee & O'Connor, 43 William St. n., F. R. Gee, Q.C., L. G. O'Connor, Q.C., J. B. Gee, B.W. Knott
Mitchell & Mitchell, 4 6th St., T.P. Mitchell, Q.C., B.P. Mitchell
Myers & Wakely, 177 Grand Ave. w., S.J. Wakely
Nixon, P.A., 5 6th St.
O'Brien, D. J., 226 Wellington St. w.
O'Brien, Kirby & Jacklin, 214 Queen St., H. J. O'Brien, R. Kirby, D.E. Jacklin, J.F. O'Brien
Pascoe, J.R., 26 5th St. s.
Peifer, E.C., 26 5th St. s.
Pockele, G.A., 93 Centre St.
Pugh, F.V., 10 Third St. s.
Rankin, R.K., 93 William St. n.
Rhodes & Asher, 121 Oshawa Dr., K.W. Rhodes, D.H. Asher
Shen, P.M., 180 Keil Dr. s.
Walker & Walker, 65 Adelaide St. s., Shirley Walker, G.C. Walker
Woods, W.A., 57 Harvey St.

CHELMSFORD, Sudbury
Mailloux & Gray, Box 1347, M.C. Mailloux (also Sudbury)
Pharand, Kuyek & Lebel (also Sudbury)

CHESLEY, Bruce
Loucks & Garcia, Box 430, G. C. Loucks, Q.C., R. W. Garcia

CHESTERVILLE, Dundas
Cass & Workman, F. M. Cass, Q.C. (also Winchester)

CLIFFORD, Wellington
McKenzie, D. M.

CLINTON, Huron
Hiltz, D. G., 52 Huron St. (D.A. Aiken)
Menzies, E.B., Q.C., 49 Albert St.

COBALT, Dist. Timiskaming
Gibson, P.S. (also Haileybury)
Ross, D.C., 21 Silver St. (also New Liskeard)

COBDEN, Renfrew
Leach, B. (also Pembroke)
McNab & Stewart (also Renfrew)

COBOURG, Northumberland
Brent, Purvis, 17 King St. e., H.M. Brent, Q.C., D.G.A. Purvis, C.G. Kay
Clarke, Stewart & Mitchell, 92 King St. w., J.H. Clarke, Q.C., D.I. Stewart, Q.C., R. F. Mitchell
Cooper & Menear, Box 188, R.F. Cooper, M.A. Menear, N.L. Ralph
Funnell, J. P., Q.C., 304 Division St.
Irvine & Irvine, 24 Covert St., J. A. Irvine, Q.C., J. R. Irvine
MacDonald & Bernhardt, Box 72, H. MacDonald, K.G. Bernhardt
Macklin, Van Duzer & Halls, 20 King St. w., P.H. Macklin, J.H. Van Duzer, J.B. Halls
Stokes, D. E., 3A King St. w.
Targon, Hustler & Lifeso, 1 King St. w., V. W. Targon, P. A. Hustler, W.C. Lifeso

COCHRANE, Cochrane
Evans, Bragagnolo & Co. (also Timmins)
Karam & Mino, 153 3rd St., N.M.J. Karam, G.A. Mino

COLBORNE, Northumberland
Bell, K.D.

COLDWATER, Simcoe
Wilson, A. S. C.

COLLINGWOOD, Simcoe
Bellamy, Besse, Augaitis & Vandergust, 50 Hume St., P.C. Bellamy, A. E. Besse, V.J. Augaitis, V.L. Vandergust, T.P. Merrifield
Corcoran, Thompson, Bulmer & Loton, 150 Hurontario St., R. C. Thompson, Q.C., J. D. Bulmer, M.A. Loton
Jacks, R., Q.C., 31 Simcoe St.
Lant & Greasley, 60 Hume St., L.E. Lant, B. Greasley
McKay, D., Hurontario St.
Noble, L., 246 Hurontario St.
Shaw, McLellan, Melitzer, 104A Hurontario St., P.I. Shaw, B.R. McLellan, D.R. Melitzer

Young, E., 168 Hurontario St.

CONCORD, York
Betcherman, I.I., 1531 Langstaff Rd.
Fraser, Atwell & Jones, 7777 Keele St., D.K. Fraser, W.G. Atwell, C.D. Jones
Newman, M.D., 8161 Keele St.
Rosen, S.A., 635 Oster Lane
Sonshine, B., 111 Rayette Rd.

CORNWALL, Stormont
Adams, Sherwood & Swabey, 305 2nd St. e., R. J. Adams, Q.C., H. H. Sherwood, Elizabeth MacLennan, T.R. Swabey, J.O. Leduc
Arthur, M.C., 12A 2nd St. w.
Bergeron, Follon & Filion, 103 Sydney St., R.G.A. Bergeron, H.S. Follon, A.L. Filion
Bergeron & Royer, 340 2nd St. e., K.J. Bergeron, D.J. Royer
Castle, E.C., 214 Marlborough St.
Dube, R., 26 9th St. e.
Fennell, Rudden, Campbell & Stevenson, 35 2nd St. e., S. E. Fennell, Q.C., P. V. Rudden, Q.C., J. R. Campbell, Q.C., G.W. Stevenson, W.L. McDermid
Guindon, MacLean & McDonald, 50 2nd St. e., P.M. Guindon, W.R. MacLean, J.H. McDonald
Lafrance-Cardinal, J., 204 Montreal Rd.
Lamoureux & Gauthier, 132 2nd St. e., G.F. Gauthier
MacDonald, Lemieux & Kovinch, 15 4th St. e., A.M. MacDonald, P.S. Lemieux, V.M. Kovinch
MacDonald & MacPhee, 126 Sydney St., D.J. MacDonald, Q.C., B.E. MacPhee
McDougall, Dancause, Shields & McDerby, 119 Sydney St., H. A. V. Dancause, Q.C., B. J. Shields, P. J. McDerby, R.J. Airey
Parisien, R. W., 214 Marlborough St. n.
Poirier & Donihee, 4 Montreal Rd., A.G. Poirier, T.T. Donihee
Renner, S. A. B., 225 Second St. e.
Ross & Duncan, 120 Sydney St., D. R. Ross, R. W. Duncan
Salhany, M. R., 109 Pitt St. (R.G. Willis)
White, D.J., 700 Montreal Rd.
Wilson & McClelland, 132 2nd St. w., B.M. Wilson, R.G. McClelland
Wise & Burns, 11 4th St. w., W.J. Wise, E.P. Burns

CORUNNA, Lambton
Brock, Allan

CREEMORE, Simcoe
Bellamy & Co. (also Collingwood)
Calder, C. C. (also Beaverton)

CUMBERLAND, Ottawa-Carleton
MacRae, D.J., Box 280

DEEP RIVER, Renfrew
Leconte, G.
Roche & Dakin, Box 1240, T.E. Roche, L.A. Dakin

DELHI, Haldimand-Norfolk
Hanselman, J. R.
Harrison & Harrison, Box 98, J. H. Harrison, Q.C., J. L. Harrison
Kapusta, Sayeau & Aicken, J. D. Kapusta, D. E. Sayeau, L.J. Aicken, D.M. Atkinson

DESERONTO, Hastings
Butler & Graydon, 324 Main St. (also Belleville)

DORCHESTER, Middlesex
Cromarty, D. A. (also London)
Gent & Park, 21 Catherine St. e. (also London)

DRAYTON, Wellington
Wade, Waters, etc., Main St., S.C. Lichty (also Elmira)

Wilson, Jack & Co. (also Fergus)

DRYDEN, Kenora
McAuley, Burns & Platana, 4 Whyte Ave., N. F. McAuley, Q.C., P.A. Burns, J. B. Burns, T. A. Platana, A.A. Mazurski
Vermeer & Van Walleghem, 29 King St., W.J. Vermeer, M.G. Van Walleghem

DUNDALK, Grey
Harris & Dunlop (also Markdale)
Shepherd & Osyany, Box 10 (also Shelburne)

DUNDAS, Hamilton-Wentworth
Hines, Sapiano & Stevens, Box 280, H.M. Hines, Q.C., D.L. Stevens
Hinton & Johnson, #11, 33 King St. e., K.S. Johnson, Q.C., M.L. Castle
Lee & Lee, 63 King St. w., D'Arcy R. Lee, Q.C., David R. Lee, Q.C.
Mahony, J. F., Q.C., 161 King St. w.
Orme, J., 177 Hatt St.
Paci, L.T., 163 King St. w.
Ramsbottom, D.J., 2 Cross St.

DUNNVILLE, Haldimand-Norfolk
Chambers, G.D.
Collins & Watterworth, 110 Lock St. e., V. B. Collins, Q.C., W. R. Watterworth
Hedley, G.B., 311 Broad St. e.
Jacob & Jacob, J. J. Jacob

DURHAM, Grey
Fallis & Fallis, 195 Lambton St., C. E. Fallis, Q.C., P. T. Fallis, J.P. Twohig, Kim Twohig
Harris & Dunlop, K.G. Prosser (also Markdale)

DUTTON, Elgin
Stirling & Faussett (also Ridgetown)

EAR FALLS, Patricia
Meadows, D.R. (R.B. Smart) (also Red Lake)

EARLTON, Temiskaming
Smith, Glaude & Co., Mun. Bldg. (also New Liskeard)

ECHO BAY, Algoma
Peterson & Peterson (also Bruce Mines)

EDEN MILLS, Wellington
Estrin, D. (S.R. Garrod)

EGANVILLE, Renfrew
Chown & Chown (also Renfrew)
Lavigueur, H.S., Box 9 (also Pembroke)

ELGIN, Leeds
Monaghan, J.T., Box 190

ELLIOT LAKE, Algoma
Aube, R.H., Box 310
Berthelot & Gagnon, 13 Elizabeth Walk, A.L.J. Berthelot, M.L. Gagnon
Brown, Dougherty & Rose, 11 Manitoba Rd., W.C. Brown, R.G. Dougherty, J.W. Rose
Gale & Montrose, 4 Elizabeth Walk, J. Gale, A.L. Montrose
Mantello Scott etc., 136 Ontario St. (also Sault Ste. Marie)
Wishart, Noble (also Sault Ste. Marie)

ELMIRA, Waterloo
Snyder & Zinszer, 51 Arthur St. s. (also Kitchener)
Teahen, D.S., 11 Arthur St. n.
Wade, Waters, Haney & Lichty, 21 Arthur St. s., R.H. Waters, P.F. Haney, S.C. Lichty
Woods & Clemens, Box 216, J.A. Woods, W.G. Clemens

ELMVALE, Simcoe
French, G.E., Queen St. w.
Heacock, J., 12 Queen St. w.

ELORA, Wellington
Hebner, M.P., Box 846

McElderry, Morris & Co. (also Guelph)

EMBRUN, Ottawa-Carleton
Baribault, Beseau & Campbell, Box 480, J.W. Baribault, P.D. Beseau, J.D. Campbell, P.R. McCuaig
Lalonde, M., Box 519

ENGLEHART, Temiskaming
Ramsay, Ramsay & Co., Box 517 (also New Liskeard)

ERIN, Wellington
Campbell, G.
Harper, R.

ESPANOLA, Sudbury
Thomas & Poulson, 71 Centre St. (also Sudbury)
Wilkins, DiSalle etc. (also Sudbury)

ESSEX, Essex
Bondy & Rossi, 78 Talbot St. (also Windsor)
Hickey & Brown, 14 Centre St., C. E. Hickey, E. J. Brown
Kendrick, W. K. (also Windsor)
Quinn, Ouellette (also Windsor)

EXETER, Huron
Deane & Laughton, 417 Main St., R.J. Deane; Counsel: C.V. Laughton, Q.C.
Little & Evans, 493 Main St., J.C. Little, R. Evans
Raymond, McLean & Gray, 387 Main St., P. L. Raymond, K. I. McLean, G.G.H. Gray

FENELON FALLS, Victoria
Glass & Co. (also Lindsay)
McIntyre, Ann, Box 607
McQuarrie, Hill & Co. (also Lindsay)
Webster, J.R. (also Lindsay)

FERGUS, Wellington
Wilson, Jack & Grant, Box 128, D. H. Jack, Q.C., R. D. Grant, W. Corby, C.B. Acheson
Wolfe & Smith, J.C. Wolfe, D. Smith, C. Forster

FINCH, Stormont
Martin-Hrycak, C.A., Box 170

FLESHERTON, Grey
Harris & Dunlop (also Markdale)

FONTHILL, Niagara South
Goldring, G. F. D.

FOREST, Lambton
Crozier, L.M., Q.C.
Walden, J.P. (also Thedford)

FORT ERIE, Niagara South
Miller & Hurren, 549 Garrison Rd., R.B. Miller, D.A. Hurren, J.R. Henderson
Ruch & Williams, 43 Jarvis St., G. Ruch, L.C. Williams
Teal & Jacobi, Box 247, J.T. Teal, D.J. Jacobi
Willson, Girdlestone & Marchand, 29 Jarvis St., R.F. Girdlestone, Q.C., G.A. Marchand, G.M. Berman
Ziff & George, 139 Niagara Blvd., Louis Ziff, Q.C., M. L. George

FORT FRANCES, Rainy River
Eustace, L.A., 510 Portage Ave.
McCormack, C. S., 418 Portage Ave.
Phillips, McKillop, 237 Church St., L.G. Phillips, B.H. McKillop
Watt, C. J.
Wolder & McLennan, 356 Church St., T. Wolder, I.J. McLennan

FRANKFORD, Hastings
Parsons, D.J., 13 Mill St.

GANANOQUE, Leeds
Knotek, H. J.
Laidlaw, G.G.G.

MacFarlane, Clarke & Wright, R.M. MacFarlane, Q.C., H.C.J. Clarke, Q.C., C.E. Wright
Steacy & Delaney, 110 Stone St. s., L.L. Steacy, F.R. Delaney

GEORGETOWN (Halton Hills), Halton
Arnold & Banbury, 232A Guelph St., H.T. Arnold, C.D. Banbury
Belleghem, J.R., 18 Church St.
Dodokin, R.R., Q.C., 90 Main St. s.
Helson & Kogan, 132 Mill St., F.A. Helson, Q.C., A.W. Kogan, J.R. McMillan, M.K. Jarvis, T.B. Anderson, D. Ashbee
Howitt, R.T., Q.C., 37 Main St. s.
Hyde, M.T., 33 Main St. s.
Isaac, D.G., 10 Mountainview Rd. s.
Manderson, W.H., 112 Main St. s.
Sopinka, W.J., 145 Mill St. (W.C. Kort)
Walinga, J.T., 33 Main St. s.

GERALDTON, Thunder Bay
Kovanchak & Co. (also Thunder Bay)
Ward & Ward, Box 1180, G.M. Ward, L.L. Ward

GLENCOE, Middlesex
Moss, Morris & Merritt, 199 Main St., B.K. Morris, G.R. Merritt. Counsel: W.D.J. Moss, Q.C.

GODERICH, Huron
Carey & Ottewell, 50 North St., G.R. Carey, J.R. Ottewell
Donnelly & Murphy, 18 The Square, J. M. Donnelly, Q.C., D. J. Murphy, Q.C., T. Murphy
Hunter, Parker & Rivers, 44 North St., W.J.E. Parker, J. P. Rivers
Pickell, N.B., 58 South St.
Prest & Egener, 33 Montreal St., W. M. Prest, Q.C., W. J. M. Egener
Troyan & Fincher, 1 Nelson St. e., T.J. Troyan, E.A. Fincher

GOODERHAM, Haliburton
Goff, S.A.

GORE BAY, Manitoulin
Armstrong & Land, Box 90, B.R. Armstrong, T.E. Land
Edmonstone & Lane, Box 60, R.H. Edmonstone, R. Lane
Greenspoon, J.L., R.R. #1

GORRIE, Huron
Crawford, Mills & Davies (also Wingham)

GRAND BEND, Lambton
Deane & Laughton (also Exeter)

GRAVENHURST, Muskoka
Aiken, Christensen & Heath, 195 Muskoka Rd. n., G. H. Aiken, Q.C., J. A. Christensen, Q.C., P. C. Heath
Graves, P.G., 101 Muskoka Rd. n.
Malvern, J.C., 130 Muskoka Rd. n.
Stuart & Cruickshank, 195 Church St., P. B. Stuart, Q.C., J. W. Cruickshank, W.G. Beatty
Sullivan & Weekes, 225 Muskoka Rd. s., L.A. Sullivan, R.N. Weekes

GRIMSBY, Niagara North
King, M. K., 6 Main St. e.
Lillico & Higson, 32 Main St. e., K.J. Higson
Lovett, J. C., 66 Main St. e. (W.J. Marinac)
Nicholls, C.P.Z., 18 Ontario St.
Schaming & Meldrum, 15 Main St. e., G. Schaming, M.G. Meldrum
Sinclair, Murakami & Loney, 55 Main St. w., R.A. Sinclair, W. Murakami, D. C. Loney
Tisdall, H.M., Q.C., 18 Ontario St.
Wolfe, J.L., 63 Main St.

GUELPH, Wellington
Acker, A. A., Q.C., 18 Douglas St. (K.H. Richardson, J.A. Mann)
Braida & Valeriote, 28 Paisley St., A. Braida, J. Valeriote, R. K. Henry, F.M. Valeriote
Dunbar, Goetz & Dunbar, 32 Douglas St., A. Dunbar, Q.C., G. W. Goetz, Q.C.
Flesher & Stuart, 210 Norfolk St., S. M. Flesher, A. J. Stuart
Hastings, D.E., Q.C., 166 Woolwich St. (K.W. Hogg)
Howitt & Goldie, 5 Douglas St., J. L. Goldie, Q.C.
Hungerford, Guthrie & Berry, 15 Douglas St., R. B. Hungerford, Q.C., H. Guthrie, Q.C., J. Berry
James & Starr, 62 Yarmouth St., M.E. James, D.T. Starr
Kearns, McKinnon, 20 Douglas St., C. L. McKinnon, Q.C., A. N. Kearns, Q.C., P. A. Gifford, Q.C., W. C. Hamilton, Q.C., D.M.B. Bean, G. F. Hearn, R.R. Berry, J.A. Wright
Maiocco, C.A., 19 Prospect St.
Maxwell & Rinne, 191 Woolwich St., G.P. Maxwell, I.K. Rinne
McElderry, Morris, 84 Woolwich St., P. J. Morris, Q.C., J. W. Matthews, Q.C., G. H. Murphy, R. G. Sansom, R. D. Noble, J. E. Morris
Moon, Heath, Hamilton & Farley, 16 Douglas St., A. J. Moon, Joan E. Heath, C. Hamilton, T.S. Farley
Morrow, Nicholson & Doney, 185 Woolwich St., R.R. Morrow, J.R. Nicholson, D.G. Doney
Moyer & Malak, 17 Cork St. w., F. P. Moyer, Q.C., T. Malak, T.B. Jackman
Nelson, Watson, 183 Norfolk St., P. J. Nelson, J.A. Watson, S.W. Pettipiere
Payne, Smith, Smith, Campbell & Gazzola, 285 Woolwich St., B. E. Payne, Q.C., D. C. Smith, P. Smith, G. A. Campbell, R.A. Gazzola
Punnett, W. G., Box 431
Runions, Brewster & McCann, 3 Paisley St., J. A. Runions, F.O. Brewster, B. McCann, S.J. Manera
Smart, J.G., 115 Woodwich St.
Toole, G.W., Q.C., 59 Woolwich St.
Vorvis, Anderson & Gray, 5 Douglas St., W. Vorvis, P. D. Anderson, B.A. Gray
Woolfrey, C.R., 31A Wyndham St.

HAGERSVILLE, Haldimand-Norfolk
Baxter, J.R., 25 Church St. e.
Hewitt, D.J., 16 Main St.
Munro & McCarthy, 27 King St. w., K. B. Munro, Q.C., C. E. McCarthy, M.W. Fowler

HAILEYBURY, Temiskaming
Clark, Dawn, Box 273
Dean, Gordon & Byck, I.M. Gordon, Q.C., T. Byck
Gibson, P.S., 439 Ferguson Ave.

HALIBURTON, Haliburton
Bishop & Rogers, D. Bishop, F.A. Rogers
Selbie, R.G.

HALTON HILLS, Halton
See Acton, Georgetown

HAMILTON, Hamilton-Wentworth
Adler, E. W., 135 James St. s.
Agro & Bartolini, 195 Main St. e., A. J. Agro, Q.C., M. A. Bartolini
Agro, Zaffiro, Parente, Orzel, Hubar & Baker, 15 King St. w. (L8N 3G6), J. L. Agro, Q.C., N. J. Zaffiro, Q.C., J. A. Parente, Q.C., E. J. Orzel, Q.C., W. J. Hubar, Q.C., M. L. Baker, M. A. Levy, S. P. Jaskot, D.R. Dempster, F.A. DeSantis, J.W. Logan, I.P. Newcombe, M.D. Parayeski, J.M. Riley
Allan & Chrolavicius, 131 John St. s., D.C. Allan, J.M. Chrolavicius
Baker & Dechert, 636 Upper James St., G.R. Baker, K.W. Dechert
Barrs, R.B., 636 Upper James St.
Bartkiw & Rosart, #222, 550 Fennell Ave. e., R. Bartkiw, C.J. Rosart
Basciano, T.N., 72 James St. n.
Beasley, A. Z., #806, 15 King St. w.
Beckett, J. R., Q.C., 20 Jackson St. w.
Beckett, Harris & Henderson, 92 King St. e., T. A. Beckett, Q.C., C. R. Harris, B.S. Henderson, H.E. Huffman
Bennett & Bennett, 42 James St. s., Miss M. M. Bennett
Borkovich, Ingrassia & Borkovich, 939 Main St. e., N. Borkovich, J. Ingrassia, P. Borkovich
Bowlby, Luchak, Thoman, Lofchik, Soule, 46 Jackson St. e., J. D. Bowlby, Q.C., F. Luchak, Q.C., J.D. Thoman, T. R. Lofchik, J. A. Soule, G. Gage, R. McGlynn
Braden & Braden, 1430 King St. e., H. O. E. Braden, Jr.
Bradley, D.J., #312, 20 Jackson St. w.
Brown, Scarfone, Fernihough, Brown, 414 Main St. e., J.C. Brown, J. A. Scarfone, E. W. Fernihough, R.S. Brown
Buckle, G. D., 124 James St. s. (R. Buchanan)
Burns, Vasan, Christmas, McLeod, Chaimovitz, #406, 15 King St. w., A.D. Burns, F.H. Christmas, R.M. McLeod, J.J. Chaimovitz. Counsel: S.R. Vasan
Byrne, Martin & Bedford, 166 John St. s., N. E. Byrne, Q.C., K. E. Martin, Q.C., B. H. Bedford
Cain, Gzik & Dandie, 340 Main St. e., E. F. Cain, Q.C., E. A. Gzik, G.W. Dandie
Campling, Gordon & Greer, 225 Main St. w., C.G. Campling, P.J. Gordon, Linda Greer
Canary, W.F., Q.C., 42 James St. n.
Caskie, R.B., 8 Main St. e.
Castellani, R.W., 90 John St. s.
Castrodale, P., 502 King St. e.
Charko, R., 1059 Upper James St.
Chertkoff, G., Q.C., 20 Jackson St. w.
Child & Smith, #250, 100 Main St. e., A.J. Child, J.N. Smith
Christilaw, Wigle & Milne, 50 King St. e., F. E. Wigle, Q.C., P. D. Milne, G.T. Gibson
City Solicitor, K.A. Rouff, City Hall, 71 Main St. w.
Cohen, L.J., 502, 20 Hughson St. s.
Cohen, M. V., 77 Sherman Ave. s.
Connor & Connor, 1104 Fennell Ave. e., R. J. Connor, P. K. Connor
Cooper & Cooper, 42 James St. s., W. W. Cooper, Q.C., W. G. Cooper
Corner, F.J.W., 25 Hughson St. s.
D'Angelo, T., 1059 Upper James St.
Davis & Baldwin, 20 Hughson St. s., R. H. Davis, S. A. Baldwin
DeRubeis, A.F., 1362 Main St. e.
DeRubeis & Chetcuti, #206, 131 John St. s., B. DeRubeis, P. Chetcuti
DiPietro, J., 72 James St. n.
Dodson, J., 63 John St. s.
D'Ortenzio, E., 120 Hughson St. s.
Drennan, M. J., 112 Catharine St. s.
Dubeck & Assoc., 172 Main St. e., J. Dubeck, J. Cvetkovic
Dunham, Manek, 660 Fennell St. e., J.H.F. Dunham, A.M. Manek
Dudzic, S.F., 172 Main St. e.
Dzwiekowski, D.C., 1286 Barton St. e. (also Toronto)
Easterbrook, R. B., 150 James St. s.
Eddy & Montcalm, 329 Ottawa St. n., D. Montcalm
Ellis, J.F., 2328 King St. e.
Ennis & Tick, 108 John St. n., P.H. Ennis, Q.C., S.M. Tick, Q.C., K.L.M. Hope, M.J. Semple
Evans, Husband, 20 Hughson St. s., J.R. Husband, Q.C., E.L. Cranfield, Q.C., F.J.

Lee, C.D., R.W. Hayman, J.D. Higginson, P.S. Dixon
Fazakas, Nash, 942 King St. w., R.L. Fazakas, M.A.I. Nash
Fedak & Fedak, 1320 Barton St. e., Emil Fedak, E.B. Fedak, Q.C.
Ferguson, C.E., 168 John St. s.
Ferro, L.A., #100, 149 Main St. e.
Findlay, D.R., #220, 20 Jackson St. w.
Findlay, J., #200, 20 Jackson St. w.
Foreman, Bennett & Rosenblatt, #909, 105 Main St. e., A.I. Foreman, Q.C., N. Bennett, Q.C., M. Rosenblatt, S. Frankel
Gaasenbeek, R. F., 131 John St. s.
Gage, Campbell & Gardner, 15 King St. w., N.A. Campbell, G.T. Gardner
Genesee & Genesee, 143 Main St. e., F.E. Genesee, Danielle Genesee
Godo, G. J., 686 Main St. e.
Halford, C.D., 801 Mohawk Rd.
Halpern, S. M., 38 Ottawa St. n.
Hammond, J. W., 152 James St. s.
Harper, R.J., 212 James St. s.
Hazell, Gay & White, 20 Hughson St. s., W. J. C. White, E. H. Palmer
Helson, J. D., 92 King St. e.
Hinchey, E.J., #1501, 25 Main St. w.
Holmes & Morwick, 25 Hughson St. S., J.T.D. Holmes, Q.C., E.J. Morwick
Horlacher, D.E., #209, 1059 Upper James St.
Hovius, J., #425, 135 James St. s. (Anne Crawford)
Howell & Howell, 105 Main St. e., G. W. Howell, Q.C., R. C. Howell, Q.C.
Inch, Easterbrook & Shaker, 15 King St. w., E. A. Shaker, Q.C., R. K. Broadfoot, P.D.V. Cannon, J.S. Kelly, B.L. Paul, J.R. Carruthers
Inch, D.L.L., Q.C., 1164 Barton St. e.
Jackson, K.W., #101, 681 Upper James St.
Jaksa, F., 1871 King St. e.
Jaskula & Kostyk, 678 Main St. e., J. L. Jaskula, Q.C., J. T. Kostyk, C. Sherk
Jazvac, W., 263 John St. s.
Jennis, R., 150 James St. s.
Johnston & Peart, #403, 20 Hughson St. s., R. S. Johnston, Q.C., J. E. Peart
Jovanovich, A., 25 Hughson St. s.
Judd, A., 105 Main St. e.
Katz, H.E., #900, 105 Main St. e.
Katz, H.J., 14 Hess St. s.
Keesmaat, H., 75 Hunter St. e.
Kemeny, M.J., 151 John St. s.
Kennedy, P.D., 40 Mohawk Rd. e.
Koskey, Kevey, Q.C., 63 John St. s.
Kronas, E., 370 Main St. e.
Kurds, Joana, 360A Queenston Rd.
Kuska, A.V., 90 John St. s.
Lambier & Lambier, 42 James St. n., L. Lambier, Q.C., J.F. Lambier
Lamont & Tidball, 105 Main St. e., M.J. Lamont, W.J. Tidball, N.G. Lamont
Landeg, G. G., Q.C., 1005, 20 Hughson St. s. (J.R. Park)
Langs, Binkley, O'Neal & Smith, 8 Main St. e., J. G. Langs, Q.C., R. C. O'Neal, Q.C., B. M. Smith
Lanza, A. A., 50 King St. e.
Lazier & Lazier, 42 James St. s., C.G. Lazier, P.J. Sullivan
Lees & Lees, 15 King St. w., W. F. Lees, Q.C., G.W. Hutton, Q.C., R. W. Lees. Counsel: C.S. Lees, Q.C.
Levy, C., #640, 110 King St. w.
Levy, J.S., #640, 110 King St. w.
Lishman, A. K., 531 Upper Wellington St.
Livesay, Shaughnessy & Pazaratz, 117 Hunter St. e., G.R. Livesay, T.G. Shaughnessy, A. Pazaratz
Logan, C.E., 1239 Main St. e.
Lowe & Arsenault, 20 Hughson St. s., J.F. Arsenault, Q.C., C.A. Brennan
Lypka, M.J., 1306 Barton St. e.
Madronich, E.R., 230 James St. s.
Mahan & Shipton, 103 John St. s., J.W. Shipton, K.J. Mahan
Malcolm, W. J. I., 20 Hughson St. s.
Marck & Marck, 42 James St. n., H. P. Marck
Marshall & McCormick, 5 Empress Ave., P.A. Marshall, J.L. McCormick
Martin & Martin, 15 King St. w., Argue Martin, Q.C., H. A. Martin, Q.C., D. S. Scott, Q.C., G.M. Luxton, Q.C., D.G. Luxton, Q.C., Mary Lou Dingle, L. Bremner, Patricia Poole
Maziarz, J., 20 Jackson St. w.
Mazza, Mazza, Mazza, 143 Main St. e., R.J. Mazza, P.D. Mazza
McEniry, R.M., #203, 90 John St. s.
McHugh, Mowat, Szpirglas, Whitmore, 335 Queenston Rd., M. J. McHugh, B. A. Mowat, A. M. Szpirglas, R.S. Whitmore
McKeon, Wilkins, Wynne & Horodyski, 20 Jackson St. w., J.D. McKeon, Q.C., R.J. Wilkins, R.G. Wynne, R. Horodyski
McLaren, J., 1278 Barton St. e.
McLelland & Dean, 15 King St. w., J. F. McLelland, Q.C., J. M. Dean
McMillan & Dimitry, 101 Hunter St. e., D.J. McMillan, L.M. Dimitry
Meisner, D., 8 Fennell Ave. w.
Mewburn, Marshall & Reesor, 25 Main St. w., J. S. Marshall, Q.C., J. F. Reesor, Q.C., J. M. Reesor
Millar, Alexander, Tokiwa & Isaacs, 15 King St. w., J. S. Millar, Q.C., P.Y. Tokiwa, P.R.W. Isaacs
Miller, H.N., 189 Hughson St. s.
Milligan, Gresko & Murphy, #315, 100 King St. w., G.P. Murphy, G.J. Gresko, J.G. Milligan. Counsel: A.T. Marshall, Q.C.
Mills, A.V., #203, 8 Main St. e.
Mitchnick & Mitchnick, 42 James St. s., D. Mitchnick, Q.C., Leslie Mitchnick
Mohideen, F., 152 Locke St. n.
Momotiuk W., Q.C., 42 James St. n.
Morgan, Stewart, #205, 131 John St. s., M.P.D. Morgan. Counsel: J.L. Stewart
Moriarity & Harrington, 540 Concession St., C. L. Harrington, J. J. Malik
Morison, B.W.B., Q.C., #2121, 25 Main St. w. (Judith Jacob)
Morley, J. J., 32 James St. s.
Morreale, Lorraine, 49 Maplewood Ave.
Morris, D.E., 334 Upper Ottawa St.
Morris & Lewis, 151 John St. s., W. Morris, Q.C., M.J. Lewis, Q.C., P.H. Robinson
Morris & Morris, 20 Hughson St. s., Mrs. A. M. Malcolm
Morton, D. G. F., 307 Charlton Ave. w.
Murgatroyd, Callaghan & Wilkins, 11 Forest Ave., W.N. Callaghan, Q.C., W.J. Wilkins
Nicholson, J. W., 117 Hunter St. e.
Nolan, Nolan & McLean, 20 Jackson St. w., J.H. Nolan, D.P. Nolan, M. Constance McLean
Okuloski & Okuloski, 928 King St. e., Helen F. Okuloski, Q.C., R.R. Skibinski
Olenski, J.Z., 1638 Upper James St.
Orr, R.M., 40A Centennial Pkwy. n.
Palumbo, R., 75 Hunter St. e.
Panek, L.H.P., 105 Main St. e.
Paquette & McCreadie, 886 King St. e., R. M. Paquette, Q.C., R. N. McCreadie
Parker, G.J., 172 Main St. e.
Peacock & Peglar, 32 James St. s., T. Peacock, S. Peglar
Pelech, Turnbull, Otto & Powell, 149 Main St. e., J. C. Pelech, J. R. Turnbull, R. A. Otto, A. J. B. Powell
Pepe, A.M.J., #220, 20 Jackson St. w.
Perl, A.K., 131 John St. s.
Perozak, Winchie & Lennon, 112 Hughson St. s., M. J. Perozak, T. L. Winchie, P.D. Lennon, M. Mychailyshyn
Petrini, Rubenstein & Waxman, 242 James St. s., G. Petrini, M. N. Rubenstein, G. L. Waxman
Philp, Gordon, Leggat, Evans, Pigott & Culver, 39 James St. s., P.G. Philp, Q.C., W.I. Gordon, Q.C., B.H. Leggat, J.F. Evans, Q.C., J.M. Pigott, L.G. Culver, R.H. Rogers
Piliste, T., 445 Dundas St. w.
Price, L., 143 James St. s.
Radigan, J. B., 204, 1030 Upper James St.
Rayner, Oliver & Colman, 59 John St. s., G.C. Rayner, J.W. Oliver, G.C. Colman, J.S. Cimba
Robinson, McCallum, McKerracher & Dingwall, #1010, 20 Hughson St. s., I.R.A. McCallum, Q.C., H.F. McKerracher, Q.C., M.A. Dingwall
Rocchi, Cassano & Rocchi, 120 Hughson St. s., F. Rocchi, V.J. Cassano, Q.C., J.P. Rocchi
Rosenblatt, J.N., #608, 105 Main St. e.
Rosenblood & Renaud, 1221, 25 Main St. w., B.P. Rosenblood, L.P. Renaud
Ross & McBride, 1 James St. s., Box 907 (L8N 3P6), C. W. Robinson, Q.C., E. D. Hickey, Q.C., S. F. Ross, Q.C., D. Goldberg, Q.C., C. D. McCallum, Q.C., D. M. Mann, Q.C., R. L. Robinson, T. A. Hickey, R. M. Morris, G. B. Aggus, R.W. Shields, P.D. Paradis, J.S. Hall, R.B. Campbell, Aida Sullivan. Counsel: Wm. G. Charlton
Ross & Ross, #700, 142 James St. s., L.S. Ross, Q.C., J.J. Ross
Roy, Godard & Buchanan, 350 Kenilworth Ave. n., D.R. Roy, D.S. Godard, S.J. Buchanan
Schreiber, Bordonaro & Yanover, 126 Jackson St. e., T.A.J. Bordonaro, S.S. Yanover, J.S. Nadel
Schreiber, H.L., Q.C., 288 Ottawa St. n. (B. E. Smurlick)
Schroeder & Hawkins, 40 Forest Ave., D. B. Schroeder, D. B. Hawkins
Scime, C. S., 278 James St. n.
Scoccia, Castura, 263 John St. s., T.R. Scoccia, L. Castura
Sharpe, Inglis, Litwiller, #2121, 25 Main St. w., R.E. Inglis, Q.C., W.J. Litwiller, B.J. Inglis
Shekter, B.B., Q.C., 103 John St. s.
Shinehoft, Mihailovich & Czutrin, 1020, 135 James St. s., J.S. Shinehoft, M.M. Mihailovich, G. Czutrin
Silver, A. B., 900, 105 Main St. e.
Simpson, Duncan, Hamel & Jackson, #501, 32 James St. s., J. B. Simpson, Q.C., G.A.C. Simpson, Q.C., R. T. Hamel, D.J. Jackson, P.F. Ryan
Simpson, J.R., 950 King St. w. (N.S. Watson)
Simpson, S., 20 Hughson St. s.
Skarica, T., #200, 8 Main St. e.
Smith, J. I., Q.C., 1416 King St. e. (I.D. Smith)
Smith & Channan, 1257 King St. e., L.H. Smith, Q.C. (Consultant), K.K. Channan
Snyder & Guyatt, 1151 Main St. e., G. N. Guyatt, Q.C.
Sondola, F.P., 25 Hughson St. s.
Soule, H., #490, 110 King St. w.
Spears, J.W., 910 King St. e.
Spitale, C., 44 Summer Place
State & Garman, 1036 Upper James St., J. State, T. Garman
Steadman & Jones, 19 Augusta St., J.J. Steadman, N. Jones
Stephen, L., 640 Barton St. e.
Stringer, M.P., Q.C., 20 Hughson St. s.
Sullivan, Festeryga, Lawlor & Arrell, 29

Augusta St., J. F. Sullivan, Q.C., W. J. Festeryga, Q.C., J. J. Lawlor, H.S. Arrell
Swierszcz, H.P., #105, 131 John St. s.
Sworden, P.J., 42 James St. s.
Tharen, E., 1234 Barton St. e.
Tice, P.R., #100, 149 Main St. e.
Tkach, F. J., 646 Main St. e.
Treleaven, Milne & van der Woerd, 75 Hunter St. e., J. van der Woerd
Turkstra, Dore, 15 Bold St., H. Turkstra, K.R. Dore, R.B. Munroe, D. Ivey, Margaret McCarthy
Tuvikene, M., 100 King St. w.
Vance & Vance, 32 James St. s., H. M. Vance, Q.C., J. P. Vance (also Waterdown)
Vine, F., 272 Kenilworth Ave. n.
Violin, R. B., 1164 Barton St. e.
Walkling, D.W., #1200, 92 King St. e.
Wallace & Cassady, 135 James St. s., Patricia Wallace, Catherine Cassady
Waller & Homer, 25 Hughson St. s., J.W. Homer, Q.C.; Consultant, A.M. Waller, Q.C.
Wasserman, R.G., #1400, 105 Main St. e.
Watson, S., 1084 King St. e.
Weisz & Assoc., 292 Main St. e., T.J. Weisz, T.J. Rocchi, M.A. Scholes
Welby & Sweetlove, 20 Jackson St. w., J.A. Sweetlove
Wellenreiter, A., Q.C., 46 Forest Ave.
West, Szpiech, 533 King St. e., W.C. West, Q.C., H.E. Szpiech
Westland, H.L.G., Q.C., 231 St. Clair Blvd.
Whelan, T. A., 131 John St. s.
White, Mackesy & Smye, 117 Hughson St. s., J.G. White, Q.C., W.P. Mackesy, D.F. Smye, R. Grilli
White, N.R., 120 Hughson St. s.
Williams, N. F., 42 James St. s.
Yachetti, Lanza & Restivo, 105 Main St. e., R.D. Yachetti, Q.C., F.A. Lanza, J.S. Restivo, J.I. Marini, Elena M. Szamosvari, B.E. Zabel
Yates & Yates, 15 King St. e., G. Yates, Q.C.
Zimmerman, A. C., Q.C., 36 James St. s.
Zimmerman, Davis, 100 Main St. e., J.W. Davis, W. Zimmerman, D.J. Sherman

HANMER, Sudbury
Lanteigne, N.M., Dennie St.
Paquette, Campbell & Lalande, N. N. Paquette, N. J. Campbell, R. W. Lalande, J.J. Paquette (also Sudbury)

HANOVER, Grey
Crockford, Duffy & Halpin, 282 10th St., G. K. Crockford, K.P.Duffy, T.C. Halpin
Easto & Sweet, 451 10th St., J.A. Easto, B.R. Sweet
Leifso, D.R., 215 10th St.
Loucks & Garcia, Box 37, P. Loucks (also Chesley)
MacDonald, P.V., Q.C., 302 10th St.
Neilson, D. R., 320 10th St.

HARRISTON, Wellington
Grant & Deverell, 2 Elora St., P. Grant, G. Deverell, R. Lemaich (also Mount Forest)

HARROW, Essex
Golden, J. J.
Karry, Salem & Melinz, 105 Queen St. (also Kingsville)
Meleg, R., 51 King St. e.

HASTINGS, Northumberland
Clarke, Stewart & Co. (also Cobourg)

HAWKESBURY, Prescott
Langlois/Wilkins, 178 Main St. e., G. E. Langlois, R.K. Wilkins, R.E. Tolhurst, N.J. Berthiaume
Montpetit & Charbonneau, 482 Main St. e., Y. Montpetit, M.Z. Charbonneau
Parisien, M., 69 Main St. e. (L. Michaud)

Smith, R.J., 151 Main St. e.
Woods Lapalme Shelly, 115 Main St. e., J.J.E. Woods, Q.C., Roger Lapalme, D.R. Shelly, J.-C.A. Gelinas

HEARST, Cochrane
Boivin, G.R., 826 George St.
Matwichuk & Agar, 9th & Front (also Kapuskasing)
Perras, Brisson, 15 9th Ave. (also Kapuskasing)

HILLSBURGH, Wellington
Robertson, D.S., Q.C., 89 Main St.

HUNTSVILLE, Muskoka
Cochran, A.B., 110 Main St. e.
Colvin, B.N., Box 2040
Ireland, J.C., 8 West St. s.
Jones, L.A., 106 Main St. e.
Pinckard, T.C., 110 Main St. e. (also Bracebridge)
Schuch, F.B., Q.C., 110 Main St. e.
Smith, G.A., 8 West St. s.
Thoms & Currie, 6 Main St. w., J.D. Thoms, D.R. Currie
Tobias & Bagshaw, 64 Main St. e., P.B. Tobias, Q.C., J.R. Bagshaw, J.S. Anderson

HYDE PARK, Middlesex
Eberhard, Morden & Farley, Box 54, N0M 1Z0, J.J. Eberhard, M.L. Morden, P.F. Farley

IGNACE, Kenora
McAuley, Burns & Co. (also Dryden)

INGERSOLL, Oxford
McBride & Carr, 167 Thames St., J.C. McBride, Q.C., J.P. Carr, M.L.M. Lamers
Start, Marshall, Parker, Ross & Borndahl, 36 King St. e., T.R. Parker, K.E. Ross, M.R. Borndahl, I.R. Blain

INGLESIDE, Stormont
Guest & Syrduk (also Lancaster)
Gorrell & Grenkie (also Morrisburg)

INNERKIP, Oxford
Calder, G.A., Q.C. (also Woodstock)

IROQUOIS, Dundas
Gorrell & Grenkie (also Morrisburg)
McInnis & MacEwen (also Morrisburg)

IROQUOIS FALLS, Cochrane
Cousineau, Alexander, 328 Main St. (also Timmins)
McGrath, Susan, 89 Ambridge Dr.

JARVIS, Haldimand-Norfolk
Kelly, W. E.

KANATA, Ottawa-Carleton
Publow & Sagle, #18, 462 Hwy. 7 & 15, C.J. Publow, A.M. Sagle
Simser & Wyatt, 3 Beaverbrook Rd., G.R. Simser, J.H. Wyatt
Tetro, P.B., 62 Pentland Cres.
Tucker, Roche & Bregman, 411 Beaufort Dr., R.B. Tucker, E.M. Roche, P.G. Bregman

KAPUSKASING, Cochrane
Matwichuk & Agar, 36 McPherson Ave., Bill Matwichuk, G.R. Agar
Perras, Brisson, 7 Cain Ave., R. Perras, Q.C., J.F.G. Brisson

KEMPTVILLE, Grenville
Miller, Dubinsky (also Ottawa)
Shaw, R. G.
Warren & Childs, 215 Van Buren St., E.J.W. Warren, Q.C., P.H.R. Childs

KENORA, Kenora
Doner, J. K., Box 1360
Elliott, D.J., 225 Main St. w.
Findlay, Hook & Seller, 114 Main St. s., B.H. Findlay, E.J.T. Hook, W.R.F. Seller

Fraser & Little, 136 Main St. s., D.G. Fraser, J.P. Little
MacDonell & Ormiston, 102 Matheson St. s., D. F. MacDonell, B. A. J. Ormiston, W.M. Peterson
O'Flaherty, T. A., Q.C., 115 Chipman St. (D.E. Gibson)
Posner, G. S., 222, 128 Main St. s.
Roy, D.D., 136 Main St. s.
Swancar, Compton & Shewchuk, 101 Chipman St., D. L. Swancar, L. P. Compton, Q.C., R.W. Shewchuk

KESWICK, York
Armour, M.L., 273 Parkway Ave.
Bailey, R.W., 4 Queensway s.
Dales, J.O., Q.C., 314 Queensway s.
Green, C.C., Box 37
McChesney & Rogers, 28 Queensway n., Sherrill M. Rogers (also Newmarket)

KILLALOE, Renfrew
Chown & Chown (also Renfrew)

KINCARDINE, Bruce
Farr D. (also Walkerton)
Shepherd & Laschuk, N. A. Shepherd, J. L. Laschuk
Wilson, F.S.
Wright, T.A.

KING CITY, York
Burgess & Co. (also Toronto)
Findlay, D. M., Q.C., 22 Keele St. s.
Geisler, J.A., Q.C., R.R. 31
Stevens & Stevens, S.M. Stevens, Q.C., N.M. Stevens, Q.C. (also Toronto)

KINGSTON, Frontenac
Amell, G.A., 727 Gardiners Rd.
Balme, C.N., #205, 10 Montreal St.
Bishop, W. J. F., 354 Montreal St.
Black, Atkinson & Coull, 225 Bagot St., J.A. Black, Q.C., D.J. Atkinson, K.J.M. Coull
Black, E.C., Q.C., 223 Bagot St.
Bourassa, R.M., #213, 800 Princess St.
Breau, S.C., 119 Barrack St.
Bruce & Johnston, 45 Johnson St., K.R. Bruce, J.W. Johnston
Cartwright & Cartwright, 89 Clarence St., H.L. Cartwright, K.E.B. Cartwright
Chadwick & Lukezich, 211 Division St., N. Chadwick, J.I.F. Lukezich
Chong & Lloyd, 95 Clarence St., J.W. Chong, G.E. Lloyd
Chown, J.B., 159 Wellington St.
City Solicitor: N.C. Jackson, City Hall
Clarke, K.L., 797 Princess St.
Cooper, R. K., 166 Queen St.
Crouchman, J. R., 420 MacDonnell St.
Cunningham, Little, Bonham & Milliken, #500, 259 King St. e., D. G. Cunningham, Q.C., R.A. Little, Q.C., J.D. Cunningham, Q.C., P.A.S. Milliken, D.H. Bonham, G.W. Tranmer
Donnelly, J. F., 221 King St. e.
Gerretsen, Lord, Conacher, 195 Sydenham St., J.P. Gerretson, R.B. Conacher, R.G. Lord
Good & Elliott, 153 Brock St., D.B. Good, E.S. Elliott
Gorham, M.B., 164 Queen St.
Griffith, McCue & Olson, 104 Queen St., B.W. Griffith, M.A. McCue, P.M. Olson, J.L. Steele
Hardtman & Martin, 11 Princess St., D.L. Hardtman, Q.C., V.A. Martin, Q.C.
Harris, Keachie & Co., 464 Princess St. (also Toronto)
Headrick, W.R.J., 770 Bath Rd.
Heder, B.R.A., 80 Johnson St.
Herrington, J. R., 830B Development Dr.
Hickey & Hickey, 93 Clarence St., M.G. Hickey, Q.C.
Jacob, Macpherson, Stewart & Hogan, 235-237 Queen St., G. R. Jacob, D. R.

Macpherson, H. S. W. Stewart, J.T. Hogan
Kamin, L.S., #213, 800 Princess St.
Kennedy & Crowe, 45 Johnson St., R.R. Kennedy, J.D. Crowe
McCullough, P.S., 279 King St. e.
McDiarmid, G.Y., 3 Rideau St.
McFadyen, D.M., 327 King St. e.
McKeown, Tarnowecky & Schlichter, Canada Trust Sq., J. McKeown, Y. Tarnowecky, D.G. Schlichter
Oaks, R.C., Q.C., 45 Johnson St.
O'Connor, Ecclestone, 159 Welington St., F.J. O'Connor, C.E.J. Ecclestone
O'Hara, Cromwell & Wilkin, #4, 179 Sydenham St., T.G. O'Hara, T.A. Cromwell, T.J. Wilkin. Counsel: H.R.S. Ryan, Q.C.
Prevost, O. G., 279 King St. e.
Pryal, G.T., 770 Bath Rd.
Quintin, P.DeB., 173 Princess St.
Radley, McNeely, 279 King St. e., P.J. Radley, G.C. McNeely
Rayner, D. G., 464 Princess St.
Reilly, M.W., 346½ Princess St.
Rosen, H.M., Box 1055
Sampson, J.E., Q.C., Regional Crown Attorney, Court House (K7L 2N4)
Sands, Pattenden, Gay & Kemp, 119 Barrack St., J.G.W. Sands, Q.C., D. Pattenden, W. C. Gay, Peter Kemp
Sheppard, H. R., 18 Market St.
Slack, D. M., 620 Princess St.
Smith, A. B., Q.C., 80 Johnson St.
Speal, Viner & Kennedy, 74 Brock St., G. N. Speal, Q.C., W. W. Viner, Q.C., P. S. Kennedy, D.R. Haunts
Swain, E. V., Q.C., 194 Ontario St. (D.R. Hurley)
Swan, Carty, Belch & Ryan, 172 Ontario St., P.G.D. Swan, Q.C., M.W. Carty, Q.C., D. M. Belch, P. C. Ryan
Tait & Kaminer, 520 Gardiner Rd., T.J. Tait, Q.C., J.J. Kaminer
Tepper, L. H., Q.C., 461 Princess St. (Geraldine Tepper)
Thomson, A.G., 151 Wellington St.
Thorne, I.G., 174 Ontario St.
Troughton, T.W., 164 Queen St.
Trousdale & Trousdale, #2, 179 Wellington St., P.J. Trousdale, A.C. Trousdale
Trumpour & Drummond, 89 Clarence St., B.W. Trumpour, Q.C., D.R. Drummond
Webster & Webster, 33 Brock St., R. C. Webster, Q.C.
Wilcox & McNeill, 264 King St. e., T. R. Wilcox, Q.C., V. J. McNeill
Willoughby, L. S., Q.C., 295 Brock St., Helen King
Wilson, J.C.A., 1412 Princess St.
Woogh, J.M., 159 Wellington St.
Yearsley, M.J., 3 Rideau St.

KINGSVILLE, Essex
Clark & O'Neill, W. N. Clark, P. M. O'Neill
Dunnion, P.J., 7 Main St. w.
Karry, Salem & Melinz, 25 Main St. e., G. J. Karry, Q.C., W. A. Salem, K. G. Melinz
McGregor & Sims, 58 Main St. e., W. L. McGregor, Q.C., T. L. Sims

KIRKLAND LAKE, Temiskaming
Boissonneault, R.P., 26 Government Rd. w.
Evans, D.B., Box 366
Parry & Ellies, 6 Government Rd. w., F.J. Parry, Q.C., M.N. Ellies, Q.C., G. Shorrock

KITCHENER, Waterloo
Amos, G.C., 276 Frederick St.
Artindale & Whitfield, 7 Duke St. w., W. R. Artindale, Q.C., D. S. Whitfield, R. Van Buskirk, G.E. Flaxbard, E.M.E. Elstner
Askin, J.S., Q.C., 97 Frederick St.
Barron, Zimmer, Schafer & Horman, 141 Ontario St. n., A.D. Barron, D.S. Zimmer, G.W. Schafer, W. Horman
Bellingham, S., 684 Belmont Ave. w.
Bergstein, S.S., Q.C., 39 Weber St. e. (M.J. Morrison)
Billo, T.J., Royal Bank Tower
Bitter, D.H., 520 Queen St. s.
Brock & Brock, 520 Queen St. s., G.R. Brock, D.P. Olsen, P.R. Weiner, S.H. Rotberg, T.L. Brock
Bryson, R. C., 305 King St. w.
Buie, D., 45 Weber St. e.
Casey, White & Steinkraus, 233 Frederick St., S. O. Casey, Q.C., A. D. White, D. U. Steinkraus
Chris, Chris & Volpini, 194 Weber St. e., G.S. Chris, T.C. Chris, F.R. Volpini
Claxton, E.W., #102, 678 Belmont Ave. w.
Clement, Eastman, Dreger, Martin & Meunier, 277 King St. w. (N2G 4J9), J.G. Martin, Q.C., R.G. Meunier, Q.C., S.R. Cameron, D.C. Downie, Q.C., W.R. Greenwood, F.S. Finch, R.L. Warren, J.J.K. Martin, M.W. McCarter, P.E. Grespan, C.M. Robson. Counsel: G.E. Eastman, Q.C., F.L. Dreger, Q.C.
Cody & Ross, 71 Weber St. e., W.P. Cody, J.G. Ross
Coleman, J.D., 115 Victoria St. n.
Conley, K., 151 Frederick St.
Cooke, D.R., 7 Duke St. w.
Cooper, R.A., 280 Frederick St. (R.B. Carter)
Cox, H. J., 91 Church St.
Crawford, N.A., 1444 King St. e.
Farhood, E.W., 222 Frederick St. (R.B. Martin)
Fitzpatrick, L., 276 Frederick St.
Flynn & Sorbara, 460 Frederick St., P.J. Flynn, S.O. Sorbara
Giesbrecht, T.G., 60 College St.
Giffen & Lee, 50 Queen St. n., J.P. Giffen, B.L. Lee, B.R. Wagner
Goebel, C.W.J., 102 Weber St. n.
Gothard & Breithaupt, 151 Frederick St., J. C. M. Gothard, J. R. Breithaupt, Q.C., E.S. Barker
Gould, R. W., Q.C., 151 Frederick St.
Gower & Assoc., 239 Frederick St., T.A. Gower, A. Burk
Grant, R.S., 305 King St. w.
Greatrex, Reaume, 106 Young St., G.L. Greatrex, R. Reaume
Guy, J.R., 245 Frederick St.
Haalboom & Hambly, 22 Frederick St., R.R. Haalboom, P.B. Hambly
Hare, R.J., 741 King St. w. (Barbara Mincer)
Hummel, J. J., 155 Frederick St.
Hunt, T. N., Corporation Sq.
Kay, S.J., 95 College St.
Kelleher, Hoskinson, 74 Queen St. n., T.S. Kelleher, W.C. Hoskinson, C.H. Thompson
Keller, T.A., 100 King St. e.
Kelly, Morley & LaRocque, 500 Corporation Sq., J. J. Kelly, Q.C., J. S. Morley, D.J. LaRocque
Kling, M.B., 306 Fischer Dr.
Kosky, S., 71 Weber St. e.
Kruse, Lawson & Haller, 289 Frederick St., P. D. Kruse, R. N. Lawson, S.P. Haller
Lackenbauer, Hertzberger, 639 King St. w., B. Lackenbauer, G.C. Hertzberger
Lackowicz, P.W., 280 Frederick St.
Lang, Lang & Ziegler, 678 Belmont Ave. w., J. E. Lang, P.W. Lang, J. Ziegler, M.R. Doering
Lawrence, R.G., 97 Frederick St.
Lieberman, Jos. W., Q.C., 47 King St. w.
Lisso, D. R., 71 Weber St. e.
Lochead, Sills, 235 King St. e., G. H. Lochead, Q.C., R. C. Sills, Q.C., W.H.P. Madorin, Q.C., H.W. Snyder, J. R. Culley, F.W. McGrath, F.D. Carere, J.H. Bennett
Ludwig, Lichtenheldt & Eby, 97 Frederick St., G.R. Ludwig, B.A. Lichtenheldt, B.P. Eby
Mackay, Kirvan, Seitz, #510, 101 Frederick St., G.A. Mackay, Q.C., F.T. Kirvan, P.L. Seitz, F.E. Tessaro, G.A. Mackay, Jr.
MacKinnon & Schnurr, 18 Weber St. w., G. MacKinnon, D.W. Schnurr
Makarchuk, M., 24 Amherst St.
Mank & Atkinson, 50 Queen St. n., S.R. Mank, Q.C., D.M. Atkinson
Marentette, J.J., #301, 7 Water St. n.
McCormick, W.R., 97 Frederick St.
McIntyre, D.A., 100 King St. e.
McMurray, S.F., 235 King St. e.
Miller, Voll, 28 Weber St. w., H.L. Miller, Q.C., Margaret Anne Voll
Mollison, Boehler, McCormick, 71 Weber St. e., M.T. Mollison, W.L. Boehler, W.F. McCormick, B.G. Wolf
Morscher & Fehrenbach, 22 Frederick St., A. A. Morscher, J. Fehrenbach
Munk, J. J., 257 Frederick St.
Murphy, T. V., 151 Frederick St.
Neeb, J.W.W., Q.C., Royal Bank Tower
Nowak, F.H., 82 Weber St. e.
Nowak Voisin, 421 Greenbrook Dr., M.T. Nowak, G.G. Voisin
Paquette & Travers, 127 Frederick St., B.T. Paquette, D.J. Travers
Potwarka, R. C., 18 Irvin St.
Reisler, S., 95 College St.
Roetsch & Ward, 684 Belmont Ave. w., U.W. Roetsch, J.G. Ward
Rosenberg, M. A., Q.C., 35 Roy St.
Sanderson, M., 309 Lancaster St. w.
Semple, D.E., 159 Frederick St.
Shannon, J. D. E., 30 Spetz St.
Sherman, K.L., 678 Belmont Ave. w.
Shuh & Reinhart, 25 Bruce St., F.J. Shuh, R.W. Reinhart, D.T. Bogden
Sims & McKinnon, 22 Frederick St., P. H. Sims, Q.C., W. W. McKinnon, D. L. Varey, J. J. Griggs, R.J. Trafford, G.L. Robson
Smith, Graham, Hunt, Royal Bank Tower, Corporation Sq., J. H. Smith, Q.C., J.D.C. Graham, R. M. Hunt, S. Adler
Smyth, Hobson, 7 Water St. n., H.A. Smyth, T.O. Hobson
Snelgrove, J. G., 7 Clarence Place
Snyder & Zinszer, 133 Frederick St., R. O. Snyder, J. A. Zinszer, T.C. Dueck
Somer, Nanson, 181 Frederick St., M.M. Somer, Q.C., J.D. Nanson
Somerville, P.G., 22 Water St. s.
Speyer & Glithero, 15 Weber St. e., C.M. Speyer, C.S. Glithero
Stark & McGee, 737 King St. w., M.E. McGee
Strype, R.B., 228 Frederick St.
Sutherland, Hagarty & Mark, 22 Water St. s., R. A. Sutherland, P. T. Hagarty, R. E. Mark, P.G. Somerville
Tait, McDonald, 195 King St. w., J.H. Tait, B.F. McDonald
Trotter, C.D., 27 Roy St.
Villemaire, M.J., 82 Weber St. e. (M.V. Parks)
Walters, Sutton, Gubler, 151 Frederick St., M.M. Walters, Q.C., J.D. Sutton, A. Gubler
Watson, D.W., 22 Frederick St.
Weston, C.R., 28 Weber St. w.
Wunder, H. L., 151 Frederick St.
Zalagenas, Irene, 235 Frederick St.
Zalman, W. R., #202, 678 Belmont St. w.
Zinkann, J., 684 Belmont St. w.

LAKEFIELD, Peterborough
Booth, G.A., 36 Bridge St.
Cole, T.E., 25 Queen St.

LAMBETH, Middlesex
Chapman & Fowler, 12 Talbot Rd. s. (also London)
Kew, R. W., 5 Main St. e.

LANARK, Lanark
O'Donnell, Dulmage, etc. (also Perth)

LANCASTER, Glengarry
Guest & Syrduk, 10 Oak St., C.S. Guest, P.D. Syrduk, G.W. Fournier

LANSDOWNE, Leeds
Henderson, A. B. (also Brockville)

LEAMINGTON, Essex
Cartlidge, R.D., 42 Mill St. w.
Gordner & Mossman, 91 Talbot St. w. (also Windsor)
Gulyas, D.R., 65 Talbot St. e.
McGrath, R., 75 Erie St. s.
Odette, T. C., Jr., Q.C., 3 Erie St. n.
Patterson, W.W., 91 Talbot St. e.
Pearsall & Marshall, 22 Queens Ave., S.L. Pearsall, Q.C.,E.B. Marshall
Scaddan, B.D., #105, 9 Princess St.
Spettigue & de Jong, 21 Talbot St. e., C.O. Spettigue, J. de Jong
Willson, Gallagher, Reynolds & Collins, 64 Talbot St. w., H. H. Willson, Q.C., G.A. Gallagher, Q.C., G.B. Reynolds, B.D. Collins

LINDSAY, Victoria
Calverley, R.W., Q.C., 6 Durham St. e.
Cornell, R.D., #22, 24 Peel St.
Evans, J.W., 22-24 Peel St.
Flett & Mortlock, 74 Lindsay St. s., D.M. Flett, A.W. Mortlock
Frost, Frost & Gorwill, 169 Kent St., J. R. Gorwill, Q.C.
Gardiner, E.J., 136 Kent St. w.
Glass, Farn & Reynolds, 6 Albert St. n., B. Glass, R. Farn, I. Reynolds. Counsel: R.G. Thomas, Q.C.
McEachern, I.T., 18 Cambridge St. n.
McQuarrie, Hill, Walden, Chester, McLean, 64 Lindsay St. s., J.A. McQuarrie, Q.C., E.C. Hill, Q.C., J.D. Walden, L.E. Chester, L.R. McLean
Patterson, A. B., Q.C., Box 791
Scott & Gemmill, 189 Kent St. w., W.A.W. Scott, Q.C., D.R. Gemmill
Staples & Swain, 10 William St. s., J. L. Staples, Q.C., R.J. Swain
Starr, A.E., 10 William St. s.
Ward & Sillberg, 1 William St. s., E.B. Ward, J.H. Sillberg
Warner, Cork & Siegel, 22 Peel St., D.J. Warner, A.R. Cork, L.S. Siegel
Webster, J.R., 18 Cambridge St. n.
Winsor, W. G., 22-24 Peel St.

LISTOWEL, Perth
Benson & Carter, E. Carter, M. Reid
Giller & MacLennan, D.A. Giller, J.A. MacLennan
Johns, R.S., 218 Main St. w. (S.F. Mather)
Pratt & Pratt, 280 Inkerman St. w., W.M. Pratt, Q.C., D.W. Pratt. Assoc.: E.D. Bell, Q.C.

LITTLE CURRENT, Manitoulin
Edmonstone & Lane, Water St. (also Gore Bay)

LONDON, Middlesex
Ambrogio, F., 505 Talbot St.
Annett, R.D., 2 Kenneth Ave.
Arvai, K., 383 Richmond St.
Bangarth, D.J.S., 687 Dundas St.
Banting, Ashford & McKinnon, 326 Queen's Ave., G.T. Banting, D.J. Ashford, R.J. McKinnon
Barnes, S.C., 536 Queen's Ave.
Bates, Aitken, 207, 795 Wonderland Rd., T. A. Bates, N. M. Aitken
Beccarea, R.A., 536 Queen's Ave.
Beechie, Kerr & Madison, 439 Waterloo St., J. A. Beechie, J. G. Kerr, Q.C., T.J. Madison
Behr, P.M., 121 Queen's Ave. (J. Vigars)
Belanger, Cassino & Benson, 153, 759 Hyde Park Rd., T. J. Belanger, D.P. Cassino, J.C. Benson
Belecky & Belecky, 45 King St., J. F. Belecky, A. J. Belecky
Biderman, M.B., 176 Albert St.
Bitz, M.A., 526 Adelaide St. n.
Bock, G., 468 Ridout St. n.
Boyer, R.C., 410 Queen's Ave.
Braund, D., 505 Talbot St.
Brister & Assoc., 148 York St., S.B. Brister, Linda Carey, K.B. Cribbie
Brown, Beattie, Dillon & King, 220 Dundas St., C.W. Brown, W.E. Beattie, Q.C., J.M. Dillon, A. G. King, J.R. Fisher, M.F. Loebach
Brown, J.M., 400 Ridout St. n.
Browne, Burgard, Robinson & Venutti, 585 Talbot St. n., E. R. Browne, Q.C., M.F.J. Burgard, Q.C., Anne Robinson, J. Venutti
Bryant, A.W., 199 Cheapside St.
Caldwell, R.C., #304, 361 Richmond St.
Chapman & Fowler, 540 Queen's Ave., K.A. Chapman, L.D. Fowler, V.R. M'Garry
Chapman, Lisowski, 66 King St., P.B. Chapman, J.R. Lisowski
Chinneck, Thomson, 1067 Wellington Rd. s., J.M. Chinneck, S.G. Thomson
Chizmar, Walker, 636 Wellington St., W.G. Chizmar, P.D. Walker
Circelli, L., 28, 505 Talbot St.
City Solicitor: Box 5035, R. A. Blackwell, Q.C.
Clarke, C.R., 275 Dundas St.
Clayton & Uren, 82 Wellington St., W.R. Clayton, T.C. Uren
Cockburn, Foster, Cudmore & Kiteley, 551 Waterloo St., C. M. Cockburn, B.A. Foster, G.D. Cudmore, P.D. Kiteley, B.C. Cleaver, J.R. Townsend. Counsel: J.G. McLeod
Cohen, Melnitzer, 600, 137 Dundas St., H. W. Cohen, J. Melnitzer, D.F. Dawson, P.G. Vogel, C.A.W. Bentley
Cooper, J. W., 1555 Glenora Drive
Coveney, D.C., 390 Wharncliffe s.
Cram & Associates, 200 Queen's Ave., J.W. Cram, Q.C., G.L. Flannigan, R. Furlonger
Crawford, D.H., 275 Dundas St.
Danilunas, M.J., 481 Talbot St.
Dean & Monteith, 120 Carling St., T.G. Dean, W.R. Monteith, J.M. Phillips
Dewar, W.L., 479 Talbot St.
Dickie, Wheable, 365 Richmond St., R.W. Dickie, A.E. Wheable
Dionysakopoulos, Mary, 326 Tecumseh Ave. e.
Dobson, A.C., 25 Baseline Rd. w.
Dockstader & Dockstader, 428 Richmond St., D.C. Dockstader, C.M. Dockstader
Downs, M.P., 487 Talbot St.
Duggan, K., #31, 170 Dundas St.
Dunlop, Mantz, Steacy, #700, 171 Queen's Ave., J.W. Dunlop, P.R. Steacy, D.R. Mantz, J.B. Phillips
Dyer, Brown, 495 Richmond St., N. C. Brown, Q.C., D. H. Proudfoot, Q.C., J. R. Cowan, Q.C., D.D. Organ, W. W. Holmes, J.W. Makins, B. J. Sullivan, I.M. Boundy, P.M. Macaulay, B.C. Fick, A.R. McIntyre, G.G. Wade
Egener, D.M., 1 Carrothers Ave.
Evans & Polishuk, 1602, 275 Dundas St., D.G. Evans, Q.C., A.P. Polishuk, D.L. Brown
Farrington, R.D., 400 Ridout St. n.
Fee, C.H., 753 Lorne Ave.
Fitzgerald, G.E., 419 Dundas St.
Fleming, C.W., 383 Richmond St.
Fox, J.P., 505 Talbot St.
Fraser, H., 493 Adelaide St. n.
Fulton & Rivett, 625 Wellington St., D.W. Fulton, D.W. Rivett
Gent & Park, 380 Ridout St. n. (Box 252), L. J. Gent, Q.C., H.R. Park, D.B. McArdle
Getliffe, Cousins & Trudell, 782 Richmond St., J. L. Getliffe, I. R. K. Cousins, P. Trudell
Gibson, T.W.I., 321 Central Ave.
Giffen, Pensa, 478 Waterloo St., J.A. Giffen, Q.C., C.M.V. Pensa, Q.C., D. W. Lewis, G. D. Wilson, P. M. Ledroit, G.L. Bladon, K.M. Trussler, E.M. Perlmutter, D.B. Williams
Gray, Laura I., Q.C., 354 Waterloo St.
Hagarty, W. B., 517 Dufferin Ave.
Hamilton, D. J., 107, 294 Dundas St.
Handelman, M., 470 Ridout St. n. (A.R. Patton)
Harding, J.G., 536 Queen's Ave.
Harris, K.M., 506 Oxford St. e.
Harrison, Elwood, 450 Talbot St., J. D. Harrison, Q.C., E. C. Elwood, Q.C., H.A. Gregory, Q.C., H.E. Fleming, S.N. Adams, Q.C., P.R. Lockyer, J.D.M. Scott, D. R. Ross, E. L. Elwood, F. A. Highley, R.J. Israel, J.A. Clark, T.D. Little, P.C. Johnson, L.C. Leitch, J. Smart, I.C. Wallace
Haskett, D., 79 Ridout St. s.
Haskett, Dalton, Whaley & Assoc., #200, 145 Wharncliffe Rd. s., C. P. Haskett, Q.C., L. R. Dalton, Q.C., J.A. Whaley, Q.C., M.S. Wolfe
Hassan & Toon, 545 Talbot St. n., M.H. Hassan, W. Toon
Hennick, H.L., 170 Dundas St.
Hill, J.L., 526 Oxford St.
Horn, J.D., 481 Talbot St.
Horricks, Greenaway, 481 Talbot St., B.A. Horricks, D.G. Greenaway
Hueston, Connie, 176 Albert St.
Irwin & Hartley, #16, 425 1st St., J.W. Irwin, Susan Hartley
Ivey & Dowler, 380 Wellington St. (N6A 5B5), R. M. Ivey, Q.C., J.E. Adamson, P.H.E. Schwartz, G.R.C. Barker, G. B. Carmichael, J. C. Campbell, R. C. Delanghe, R.M. Gasparotto, D.M. Ross, F.G. Jones, R.G. Hatt, J.D. Fischer, R.K.W. Goldstein, K.J. McGill, D.J. Oliver
Janjua, M.M.A., 572 Dundas St.
Jefferson, G., 505 Talbot St.
Jeffery & Jeffery, 174-180 King St., Box 2095, Joseph Jeffery, O.B.E., C.D., Q.C., A. H. Jeffery, Q.C., A. E. Jeffery, G. D. Jeffery, A. M. Jeffery, J.G. O'Grady, W. C. Nursey, S.P. Pearson, R.C. Stoddart, R.A. Hayes
Johnston & Wanger, 468 Ridout St. n., J.G. Johnston, L.A. Wanger
Joy & Oatman, #303, 291 King St., D.L. Oatman
Judson, Coughlin & Kennedy, 441 Ridout St. n., J.W.T. Judson, B.J. Coughlin, W.R. Kennedy, C.A. MacDonald
Keating, R. D. W., Q.C., 170 Dundas St.
Keele, P.M., 466 Ridout St. n.
Kendall, K. H., 470 Dundas St.
Khawly, R., 383 Richmond St.
Kirk, C. B., Q.C., 385 Dufferin Ave.
Koprowski, K.W., 133 Kent St.
Kramer, B.B., 128 Thornton Ave.
Lamon & McGrath, 800, 383 Richmond St., R. J. Lamon, Q.C., E. J. McGrath, D.W. Kilpatrick, G.A.R. Grant, R.A. Braiden
Lawrence, B. H., 135 Albert St.
Leahy, D., #210, 795 Wonderland Rd.
Lee, F.B., 311 Central Ave.
Leitch, C.D., 120 Carling St.
Lepine, P.F., 400 Ridout Stn. n.

Lerner & Associates, 80 Maple St. (Box 2335, Stn. A, N6A 4G4), S. Lerner, Q.C., P. E. Bradley, E. A. Cherniak, Q.C., B. T. Granger, Q.C., Janet Stewart, J. C. Kennedy, V.J. Calzonetti, M.M. Lerner, R.D. Dale, M.D. Lerner, G. A. Ste. Marie, S.J. Stefanko, Mary Anne Sanderson, S.M. Robertson, N.G. Gilby, S.E. Haller, J.R. Morse, L.S. Smith
Lesser & Lipson, 410 Queen's Ave., D.J. Lipson
Libis, V., 400 Ridout St. n.
Litterick & Ison, 1620 Dundas St., J.M. Litterick, L.J. Ison
Little, Gillespie & Reeves, 412 King St., P. C. Gillespie, C. H. Reeves, Q.C., A. H. Little, R. H. Mahoney, S.M. Jarrett, J.W. Hart, Glenda Bishop; F.H. Little, Q.C.
Littlejohn & Elliott, #902, 272 Dundas St., H. Littlejohn, Q.C., J.D. Elliott, M.R.G. Best, M. Eisenstein
Livingstone, Carrier, 174 Wellington Rd. s., R. B. Livingstone, R. G. Carrier
Lockwood & Blackburn, 834 Richmond St., J. R. Lockwood, R. A. Blackburn
MacDonald, MacKenzie, 365 Richmond St., C.C. MacDonald, B.J. MacKenzie
Mackenzie, C.L., Q.C., #4, 175 Dundas St. (A. Steepe)
MacKenzie, J.K., Q.C., 430 King St. (K. Dungavell)
MacKewn, Smeenk, 383 Richmond St., C. F. MacKewn, F.C. Smeenk, R.F. Leach, D.A. Broad
Mackin, F.J., 461 Ridout St. s.
Mamo, A.A., 480 Talbot St. (L.M. Waxman)
Mann, E.J., 540 York St.
Mantz & Phillips, 215 Piccadilly St., D.R. Mantz, J.B. Phillips
Marcus & Tobin, 330 Central Ave., M.A. Marcus, B.M. Tobin
McCarron, M., 355 Ridout St. n.
McClean, Arntfield & Aston, 400 Ridout St. n., R.M. McClean, D.G. Arntfield, D.R. Aston, D.E. Burns
McCormack & Van Dop, 25 Base Line Rd. w., B.W. McCormack, R. Van Dop, A.J. Dobson
McLeish, J.W., 241 Queen's Ave.
McLennan, Flinn & Driesman, 383 Richmond St. (Box 3173, N6A 4J4), D.L. McLennan, Q.C., J.M. Driesman, R.G. Inglis, H.J. Wood, C.G. Dickie. Counsel: H.R. Davidson, Q.C.
Meren, J. A., 400 Ridout St. n.
Mills, M., 631 Commissioners Rd. e.
Mitchell, E. W., 171 Dundas St.
Mitchell, Hockin & Dawson, 560 Wellington St., H.W. Hockin, Q.C., C.G.S. Dawson, Q.C., P. B. Hockin, M. M. Pellarin, B. McCall, D.G. Dawson
Mitchell & Mitrow, 204 Central Ave., M.R. Mitchell, V. Mitrow
Mitches & Mitches, 350 Ridout St. s., P. T. Mitches
Morgan, H. D., 300 Princess Ave.
Morrison, Hanes & Buchner, 783 Richmond St., A. J. Hanes, Wm. R. Buchner, Q.C., R. I. Morrison, J. P. Hanes, L.A. Hipfner, W.J. Buchner
Morrow, A., 200 Queen's Ave.
Murphy & Brown, 311 Dufferin Ave., C. A. Brown, F. J. Murphy, G.T. Hopcroft
Murphy, Durdin & McNamara, 267 Dundas St., O. W. Durdin, Q.C., D. J. McNamara
Myers, J.E., 131 Wharncliffe Rd. s.
Neilson, J.M., 479 Talbot St.
Nelligan & Nelligan, 267 Dundas St., T.B. Nelligan, B.F. Nelligan
Newman & Shanfeld, 380 York St., S. S. Newman, L. Shanfeld
Nicholson, Seabrook & Epstein, 120 Carling St., R.R. Nicholson, R.E. Seabrook, M.J. Epstein
O'Donnell, J.R., 484 Richmond St.
O'Donovan & Hutton, 505 Dundas St., B.V. O'Donovan, R.E. Hutton, M.E. Marshman, P.B. Morrissey, S.L. Schuessler, C.F. Joles
Oliver & Wright, 369 Hamilton Rd., Wendy Oliver, B. Wright
Peel, N., 466 Ridout St. n.
Petrie, Forrester, Glanville, 30 Picton St., W.A. Petrie, J.T. Forrester, G.M. Glanville
Poole, Porter, 444 Waterloo St., W.R. Poole, Q.C., H.D. Porter, Q.C., J. C. Drake, T. W. Hainsworth, H. Berg, Eleanor Schnall
Portis, M.F., #302, 483 Richmond St.
Ramkelawan, H.P., 1225 Wonderland Rd.
Reed, R., 205½ Dundas St.
Richardson, R.O., 850 Dundas St.
Richmond, Richmond, Stambler & Mills, 400, 200 Queen's Ave., E. Richmond, Q.C., A. Richmond, Q.C., M. Stambler, Q.C., R.D. Mills, J.R. Kennedy
Rohrer, R.D., 631 Commissioners Rd. e.
Ronsky, N., 286 Central Ave.
Ross, Bennett & Lake, 511 Talbot St., C.F.M. Ross, M. Bennett, M.A. Lake
Russell, D.D., 1045 Flintlock Ct.
Sawchuk, E., 30 Elmgrove Cres.
Scarfe, C.G., 560 Adelaide St.
Sengbusch, H.P., 89 Dundas St.
Shepherd, McKenzie, Plaxton, Little & Jenkins, #1200, 380 Wellington St. (N6A 5B5), A.L. McKenzie, Q.C., G.F. Plaxton, Q.C., J. H. Little, Q.C., W. A. Jenkins, Q.C., J. F. McGarry, Q.C., R. A. Parker, R. J. Haines, T. M. Conway, J.M. Kierans, F. Boniferro, D.R. Nash, D.K. Livingstone, D.S. Bryant, G.T. Tillman, K.I. Beach
Siskind, Cromarty, 471 Waterloo St., N6B 2P5, D. A. Cromarty, P. M. Siskind, Q.C., J.R. Caskey, Q.C., R.G. Siskind, Q.C., J.S.M. Mitchell, C.S. Ritchie, G.H. Kleiman, P.R.J. Noble, B.R. Scott, P.E. Knill, N.W. Fursman, O. Colosimo, J.D. Virtue, G.A. Richardson, C.L. Daniel, P.C. Strickland, J.A. Higgins, E.P. Heyninck
Smugler & Steven, 190 Wortley Rd., J.S. Smugler, R.P. Steven
Sommerfreund, J., 400 Ridout St. n.
Storry, D., 291 King St.
Swinnen, F. E., 365 Richmond St.
Taggart, H.S., Q.C., 487 Talbot St.
Thomas, Groom, 355 Ridout St. n., W.L. Thomas, L.K. Thomas, J.H. Groom
Thompson, F. L., 424 Wellington St.
Tovey, J. E., 205 Sydenham St.
Underhill & Underhill, 379 Dufferin Ave., Mrs. B. L. Underhill
Unger, E.H., 200 Queen's Ave.
Valassis, D., 579 Talbot St.
Walker & Wood, 69 Dundas St., G. W. Walker, Q.C., R. J. Wood
Weekes & Weekes, 396 Ridout St. n., R.N. Weekes, Q.C.
Winder, Winder & McNeil, 135 Albert St., E.D. Winder, P.L. Learmonth
Winninger, D., 483 Richmond St.
Wohl, T., 91 Runnymede Cres.
Wright, J.D., 480 Talbot St.
Wright, Davies, 612, 383 Richmond St., A. C. Wright, S.R.R. Davies, D.S. Scott
Wright, Kelly, Merrifield, 382 Ridout St. n., D.G. Wright, T.J. Kelly, S.M. Merrifield
Yormak & Yormak, 176 Albert St., J.L. Yormak, S.R. Yormak

L'ORIGNAL, Prescott
Proulx, Henri, Q.C.
Seguin, Landriault & Co. (also Ottawa)

LUCAN,
Benner & Hope, 240 Main St., J.R. Benner, J.R. Hope

LUCKNOW, Bruce
Andrew, R. W. (also Listowel)
Brophy, G.J., Box 610
Crawford, Mill & Co. (also Wingham)

MADOC, Hastings
Bailey, J.W. (also Belleville)

MANOTICK, Ottawa-Carleton
Hamilton, D., Q.C., 7 Main St. (Janet Kelly)
Wilson, Ross & Co., Box 429 (also Ottawa)

MAPLE, York
Walsh & Walsh (also Toronto)

MARKDALE, Grey
Harris & Dunlop, W.E. Harris, Q.C., J.A. Dunlop, Q.C., E.J.R. Willis, J.L. Ferris

MARKHAM, York
Black & Read, 7358 Woodbine Ave., R.W. Black, E.M.D. Read
Bongard, M.B., 10 Washington St.
Burstein, E., & Assoc., #2, 50 Don Park Rd., M.B. Koreen, P.T. Zoldhelyi
Cattanach, Hindson, Sutton & Hall, 52 Main St. n., J.L. Cattanach, Q.C., D. C. Hindson, Q.C., L.R.S. Sutton, Q.C., G.H. Hall, S.D. Brown
Cohen, H.C., 27 Wellington St. w.
Fagan, M., 60 Esna Park Dr.
Gamble & Garbe, 72 Wellington St. w., J.A. Gamble, E.A. Garbe
Matthews, Irene L., #104, 7225 Woodbine Ave.
Mingay & Associates, 81 Main St. n., P.W.J. Mingay, Q.C., S. C. Aranha, P.F. Smith, R.W. Wilson, D.W. Wells
Moad, G.A. & Assoc., 72 Wellington St. w. (E.B. Solomon)
Noik, Wall & Midanik, #203, 7240 Woodbine Ave., B.H. Noik, V. Wall, B.N. Midanik
Parnes, R., 72 Wellington St. w.
Starzynski, D.M., 27 Wellington St. w.
Tsubouchi, D.H., 59 Main St. n.
Wigdor & Assoc., #200, 7050 Woodbine Ave., R.J. Wigdor, G.A. Chornenki, J.M. Swift
Wilson, L.D., 27 Wellington St. w.

MARMORA, Hastings
Philpot, A.M.

MATTAWA, Nipissing
Hurtubise & Legault, 374 Main St. (also North Bay)

MAXVILLE, Dundas
Adams & Sherwood (also Cornwall)

MEAFORD, Grey
McKay & Scheifele, Box 1090, J. I. McKay, Q.C., D. G. Scheifele, Q.C.

MIDLAND, Simcoe
Blake, J., 366 First St.
Gorman, J.P., 518 Elizabeth St.
Hacker, Gignac & Rice, 226 King St., F.W. Hacker, J.L. Gignac, G.A. Rice. Counsel: D.G. Haig, Q.C.
Kendall, E.B., 262 King St.
Lunnie, J., 298 1st St.
MacKinnon, DeVillers & Horton, 476 Elizabeth St., J. R. MacKinnon, P.J. DeVillers, P.R. Deacon. Counsel: F.E. Horton, Q.C.
Peet, Prost, 323 Midland Ave., D.S. Peet, M.J. Prost, J.J. Yaworsky
Symons & Grise, 525 Elizabeth St., E.F. Symons, F. Grise
Teskey, Heacock, Ferguson, 361 King St., G. Teskey, Q.C., W.R. Heacock, R.S. Ferguson, R. Main, B.M. Richardt

MILLBROOK, Peterborough
Howell, Fleming etc., 21 King St. e. (also Peterborough)
Irvine & Irvine (also Cobourg)

MILTON, Halton
Flannagan, R., 13 Charles St.
Furlong, R., #27, 55 Ontario St. s. (R.W. Collins)
Greenwood, L.D., 165 Main St.
Grieves, H., 369 Main St.
Gunding, N.A., 165 Main St. e.
Holden, Ford, 196 Main St. (also Oakville)
Hutchinson, Thompson & Henderson, 264 Main St., B.L. Henderson, H.I. Mott
McWilliams, P.K., Q.C., 264 Main St.
Nichols & Servos, 207 Mary St., A.J. Nichols, Q.C., J. Servos
Sproule & Girouard, 17 Wilson Dr. (also Mississauga)

MILVERTON, Perth
Byers & Kenny (also Stratford)
Stratton & Co. (also Stratford)

MINDEMOYA, Manitoulin
Armstrong & Land, Box 46 (also Gore Bay)

MINDEN, Haliburton
Adamson, B.F.
Evans, J.W. (also Lindsay)
Finn, D. J.
Gardiner, E.J. (also Haliburton)

MISSISSAUGA, Peel
Allan, Harris, Cousins, #200, 2 Robert Speck Pkwy., L4Z 1H8, J.H. Allan, K.R. Harris, D.F. Cousins
Ball, D.G., #203, 3040 Palstan Rd.
Bannon, J.P., #255, 33 City Centre Dr.
Bennett, R.T., 94 Lakeshore Rd. e.
Black, Margaret, 187 Queen St. s., L5M 1L4 (Marla Vachon)
Blaney, Pasternak, etc., #601, 201 City Centre Dr. (also Toronto)
Blenkarn, Roche, Kerr, Jeffery & Shadlock, 39 Lakeshore Rd. e., D. A. Blenkarn, Q.C., J. P. Roche, Q.C., H. G. Kerr, K.R. Shadlock, Q.C., W.G. Jeffery, J. Fantl, E.K. Mann. Counsel: J.G. Reid, Q.C.
Brazys, J.G., 3189 Cawthra Rd.
Broadhurst & Ball, Two Robert Speck Pkwy., P. A. Broadhurst, J. J. Ball, G.D. Walkden, D.A. Allport, Beverley Znidar-Martel
Buchanan & Cutler, 1454 Dundas St. e., T.H. Buchanan, L.R. Cutler
Buckman, D.E., 2168 Dundas St. e.
Burrow & Dixon, 1250 South Service Rd., D.G. Burrow, Q.C., J.H. Dixon
Carter, R., #1401, 2235 Hurontario St.
Chapman & Salomaa, 377 Burnhamthorpe Rd. e., J.C. Chapman, T.D. Salomaa
Cooke, P.G.B., 470 Hensall Circle
Cowan, I.B., #103, 424 Hensall Circle
Cunningham, A.L., #112B, 377 Burnhamthorpe Rd. e.
Davidson, D.M., 15A Dundas St. w.
DeCosimo, M.G., 7 Helene St. s.
Diamond, A. E., 7205 Goreway Dr.
Dyer, K.F., #255, 33 City Centre Dr.
Eades, L.M., 57 Queen St. s. (M.J. Day)
Elbirt, R., 94 Lakeshore Rd. e.
Erlich, H., 90 Dundas St. w.
Fellman, R.A., 2114 Hurontario St.
Ford & Fuller, #408, 2000 Argentia St., J.K. Ford, D.L. Fuller
Foster, M. C., 205 Queen St. s.
Garvey, M.T., 987 Clarkson Rd. s.
Gelman, L., 55 Dundas St. w.
Gelman, S., 2114 Hurontario St.
Genereux & Associates, 1057 Dundas St. w., R.J. Genereux, A.E. Genereux
Gillespie, R.K., 230 Lakeshore Rd. e.
Godfrey, E., 2564 Confederation Pkwy.
Gogek & Associates, 470 Hensall Circle, M. Gogek, R. Baytor, J.J. Press, N. Bartels, S.R. Biss, C.A. Agard
Goldberg, Wilson, 15A Dundas St. w. (also Toronto)
Goodman & Griffin, #675, 33 City Centre Dr., J.C. Goodman, M.J. Griffin
Gray, Offer & David, #6, 3105 Glen Erin Dr., S. Offer, A. David (also Toronto)
Handelman, Korman, 90 Dundas St. w., A.S. Handelman, J. S. Korman
Harris & Hardacre, 2 Robert Speck Pkwy., J.E. Harris, Q.C., D.F. Hardacre
Hilger, W., 2170 Stanfield Rd.
Horwood, R.A., #403, Plaza 2, 2000 Argentia Rd.
Iggers, D.P., 41A Dundas St. e.
Jackson, Watson, Gillespie & Lane, 230 Lakeshore Rd. e., R. H. Watson, Q.C., R. M. Gillespie, Q.C., S.G.J. Lane, Q.C.
Kamin, Goodman, Gardner, 165 Dundas St. w., S. Goodman, Q.C., B.J. Kamin, Q.C., D.A. Gardner, J. Goldberg, G.L. Wiseman
Keller & Treloar, 5170 Dixie Rd., J.B. Keller, Jennifer Treloar
Kennedy, S.J., 7152 Airport Rd.
Keyser, Mason, Coleman, McTavish & Lewis, #701, 201 City Centre Dr., C.I. Mason, Q.C., J.B. Keyser, Q.C., W.A. McTavish, Q.C., B.G. Coleman, J.E. Lewis, Q.C., G.A. Lane, S.S. Seppi
Korman, M., 67 Lakeshore Rd. e.
Lafferty, D., Box 337, Clarkson
Lawrie & Leckie, 2114 Hurontario St., R. G. Lawrie, R.D. Leckie
Lokash, P.E., 1515 Matheson Blvd.
Longo, G.P., 5220 Bradco Blvd.
MacColl, A., #200a, 77 City Centre Dr. (J.L. Robinson)
Malicki & Malicki, 3020 Kirwin Ave., S. Malicki, M.S. Malicki, A.M. Dyach
Mazzucco & Boguski, 700 Dundas St. e., M. Mazzucco, S.F. Boguski
McNeely & Crouch, #103, 3040 Palstan Rd., R.A. McNeely, R.B. Crouch
Morra, R.A., 1715 Lakeshore Rd. w.
Moss, Bensette, Thompson, Squires, #1000, Two Robert Speck Pkwy., L4Z 1H8, W.D. Moss, R.L. Bensette, G.V. Thompson, P.D. Squires, R.A. Masson, P.R. Hammond, T.L. Leier, M.N. Kimber
Mossip, N.M., #309, 5170 Dixie Rd.
Murphy & Ghalioungui, 3060A Hurontario St., K.P. Murphy, J.M.P. Ghalioungui
Nicholson, E.B., 41A Dundas St. e.
Novak, W.S., 2200 Dundas St. e. (D.A. Newport)
O'Marra & O'Marra, 181 Lakeshore Rd. e., A. J. O'Marra, Q.C., T. E. O'Marra, B.P. O'Marra
O'Neail, M. D. J., 121 Lakeshore Rd. e.
Outhet, R. A., Q.C., 94 Lakeshore Rd. e.
Ovenden, H. D., 2547A Hurontario St. (R.K. Ovenden)
Pallett, Valo, Barsky & Hutcheson, #1450, 2 Robert Speck Pkwy., J.C. Pallett, Q.C., S. Valo, L. Barsky, G.K. Hutcheson, K.J. Yolles, T. Furst, D.J. Brown, D.C. Pallett, Jill McLeod
Plener & Nadler, 2445 Dunwin Dr., L.R. Plener, E. Nadler, I.R. Marples
Press & Reininger, 470 Hensall Circle, J.J. Press, H.W. Reininger
Rawding, Lindsay, 3415 Dixie Rd., H. G. H. Rawding, Victoria A. Lindsay
Ross, D.F., 1150 Lorne Park Rd.
Rowland, P. M., 10 Stavebank Rd. n.
Saltzman, J., 7205 Goreway Dr.
Seheult, M.M.R., 2170 Stanfield Rd.
Selley, J.H., 93 Dundas St. w.
Shaw, D.N., Q.C., #306, 130 Dundas St. e.
Sheldon, F.W., #201, 1945 Dundas St. e. (also Toronto)
Shulman, A., 2225 Erin Mills Pkwy. (G.G. McClelland)
Soloway, A. D., 7205 Goreway Dr.
Somers, M., 68 Dundas St. w.
Sproule & Girouard, #403, Plaza 2, 2000 Argentia Rd., T. Sproule, P.A. Girouard, M.E. Howard. Assoc.: H.C. Funk (also Milton)
Stabins, A., 12 Thomas St.
Strickland, J.K., 2596 Kinnerton Cres.
Switzer, Shaw, 77 City Centre Dr., J.H. Switzer, Q.C., J.V. Shaw, W.E. Mathers, M.H. Senderowitz, R.A. Macrae, J.K. Brownridge
Talsky & Alter, 2921A Derry Rd. e., M. Talsky, M.E. Alter
Varcoe, Luby, 2393 Dunwin Dr., B.J. Varcoe, W.P. Luby, C.A. Letman
Warren, D. P., 150 Lakeshore Rd. w.
Watson, B.M., #105, 3034 Palstan Rd.
Weir & Assoc., #204, 101 Queensway s., M.E. Weir, Q.C., S.D. Braithwaite, P.P. Kolassa
Weseloh, R.T., 6541 Mississauga Rd.
Wheeler & Trainer, 203, 106 Lakeshore Rd. e., J.S.B. Wheeler, W.G. Trainer
Willis, R.J., Q.C., #355, 33 City Centre Dr.

MITCHELL, Perth
Ferguson, J. D.
Wilson, W. E.

MORRISBURG, Dundas
Bayne, N., Box 855
Beavers, G. P. A.
Gorrell & Grenkie, Box 820, J.D. Grenkie, Q.C., R.T. Leroy, P.J. Remillard
McInnis & McEwen, Box 733, C.F. McInnis, Q.C., P.H. McEwen, Q.C., R.R. Mills

MOUNT ALBERT, York
Turville, W. D. (also Newmarket)

MOUNT BRYDGES, Middlesex
Little, Gillespie & Co. (also London)

MOUNT FOREST, Wellington
Fallis & Fallis, 150 Main St., J.P. Twohig (also Durham)
Grant & Deverell, 166 Main St. s., W.P. Grant, G.W. Deverell, Q.C., R.J. Lemaich, R.W. Barclay, R.M. Grant, Q.C. (also Harriston)

NAPANEE, Lennox & Addington
Dempster, G.G., 21 Market Sq.
Grange, W. A., Box 26 (J. M. Grange)
Hogle & Doreleyers, 35 Dundas St. e., H.W. Hogle, C.F. Doreleyers, R.G. Smart
Madden, Sirman & Zeran, 110 John St., J. E. Madden, W.G. Sirman, B.E. Zeran
Pearce & Olson, 32 Dundas St. e., J.K. Pearce, Q.C., R.A. Olson

NEWCASTLE, Durham
Brooks, Harrison, Jones & Mann, 29 King St. w., Catherine Cornwall, Mary Ormerod (also Port Hope)
Ewert & MacGregor, Box 9, C.C. Ewert, J.D. MacGregor

NEW HAMBURG, Waterloo
Brookes, T. A. F.
Mahlstedt, H.C., 82 Huron St.
Snyder & Zinszer, 59 Huron St. (also Kitchener)
Thomas, N.A., Box 1000

NEW LISKEARD, Temiskaming
Hoyles, J.D.V., Box 760
Ramsay, Ramsay, Kemp & Andrew, Box 1540, W. R. Ramsay, Q.C., P. R. Ramsay, G. W. Kemp, W.A. Andrew
Ross, D.C., Q.C., 7 Armstrong St.
Smith, Glaude & Kearney, 22 Paget St., O.J.R. Smith, Q.C., G.N. Glaude, N.J. Kearney

NEWMARKET, York
Corbett, Montgomery & Assoc., 18 Main St. s., P.E. Montgomery, R.B. Corbett, J.G. Herlihy, Penelope E. Bryan, G.H. Hunter, Maureen Love. Counsel: Marie Corbett
Day, McDonald, Pollock & Fysh, 204 Main St. s., M.J. McDonald, W.H. Fysh, R.E. Pollock
DiCecco, A. M., 496 Davis Dr.
Dunsmuir, B.G., 56 Prospect St.
Faed, D.M., 187 Main St. s.
Koster, Nancy, 60 Hamilton Dr.
Linton, Leck & Monteith, 597 Davis Dr., R. B. Linton, Q.C., R. D. Leck, D.W. Monteith, R.W. Sedore
McChesney & Rogers, 69 Main St. s., D.B. McChesney, J.S. Rogers, Sherrill M. Rogers, Patricia McCann-Smith. Counsel: W.S. Rogers, Q.C.
McKee, D.J., 47 Main St. s.
Otton, J. D., Q.C., 236 Main St.
Schneider, A., 637 Davis Dr.
Stiver Vale, 195 Main St., Wm. Errington, Q.C., A. M. Mills, Q.C., P.S. Oliver, Susan Plamondon, K.C. Hill, Kathryn Boyd. Counsel: K.M.R. Stiver, Q.C.
Stone, Glasner & Caroline, 38 Main St., P.H. Caroline, A. Christopher. Counsel: C.A. Stone, Q.C., A. Glasner
Turville, W. D., 34 Eagle St. e.

NIAGARA FALLS, Niagara South
Beresh, C.W., 5234 Victoria Ave.
Booth, W. G., 5979 Lundy's Lane
Broderick, McLeod, Clifford, Marinelli & Amadio, 4365 Queen St., J. J. Broderick, Q.C., D. M. McLeod, E. R. Clifford, W. A. Amadio, D. F. Marinelli, P.D. Sullivan
Den Ouden & McKay, 4673 Ontario Ave., J.L. Den Ouden, N.A. McKay, Q.C., P.R. Heath, K.B. Harris
Di Paolo, P.V., 5001 Victoria Ave.
Douglas, K., 4683 Queen St.
Fraser & Fraser, 4669 St. Lawrence Ave., F. A. Fraser
Galloway, C. A., 4485 Queen St.
Gampel, S., 5896 Main St.
Hopkins & Kirkham, 4683 Queen St., J.B. Hopkins, G.A. Kirkham
Jaluvka & Sauer, 4231 Portage Rd., J.D. Jaluvka, E.A. Sauer
Knight & McDonald, 4683 Queen St., S. J. Knight, Q.C., D. J. McDonald
Lococo, P.C., 5079 Victoria Ave.
Mann & Stockton, 3950 Portage Rd., P.S. Mann, M.A. Stockton
Martin, Sheppard, 4607 Huron St., A. F. Sheppard, Q.C., J.R. Boyce, J. A. Sissons, R.J. Kajan, D.L. Brown
Matthews & Matthews, 5146 Victoria Ave., F.J. Matthews, Q.C.
McBurney, Durdan, Henderson & Corbett, 4759 Queen St., R. S. Durdan, A. D. Henderson, R.E. Corbett
McNab, G., 3950 Portage Rd.
Minov, N., 5235 Victoria Ave.
Nicoletti, J. L., 5001 Victoria Ave. (P. De Paul)
Rocca, J., 4904 Victoria Ave.
Ryall, C. J., 4579 Huron St. (J.D. Conte)
Sharpe & Sharpe, 4700 St. Clair Ave., N.F. Sharpe
Slovak, Sinclair, Crowe, 4786 Queen St., W. Slovak, Q.C., B. N. Sinclair, D. A. Crowe
Ungaro & Barycky, 5274 Victoria Ave., G. Ungaro, G. Barycky
Walker, G.F., 4624 Ontario Ave.
Walker, Pamela, 4999 Victoria Ave.
Waterhouse & Goslin, 5627 Main St., D. Waterhouse, D.A. Goslin
Young, H.R., Q.C. (City Solicitor)

NIAGARA-ON-THE-LAKE, Niagara North
Bracken, W.J.G., 91 Queen St.
Dodson, J., 36 Queen St.
King, W.R., 91 Queen St.
Lampard, Ellis & Walsh, 129 Queen St. (also St. Catharines)

NIPIGON, Thunder Bay
Young, P.G.F., 64 Front St. (also Thunder Bay)

NOBLETON, York
Johnston & Douglas, Box 789 (also Toronto)

NORTH BAY, Nipissing
Birnie & McMillan, 116 McIntyre St. w., P. C. Birnie, Q.C., R. G. McMillan
Bowness & Murray, 348 Fraser St., R.B. Bowness, P.J. Murray
Colvin & Colvin, 149 Main St. w., R.A. Colvin, S.N. Colvin
D'Iorio, Duchesneau-McLachlan & Boland, 269 Main St. w., J.F.L. D'Ioria, Louisette Duchesneau-McLachlan, M.F. Boland
Donnelly, Denomme, Souter & Larsh, 116 McIntyre St. w., R. F. Donnelly, Q.C., F. C. Denomme, J. W. Souter, P.D. Larsh
Froud, J.L., 440 Ferguson St.
Galipeau, R. C., 269 Main St. w.
Gorman, Martyn & Ferguson, 374 Fraser St., J.B. Gorman, R.J. Martyn, D. Ferguson
Hurtubise & Legault, 240 Algonquin Ave., L.M. Hurtubise, P. Legault
Inch, J.A., Q.C., 251 Cassells St.
Klein, Falconi & Assoc., 387 Fraser St., A. E. Klein, Q.C., F.M. Falconi, P.W. Rutland, L.J. Klein
Lucenti, Rivard & Manning, 373 Main St. w., R.S. Lucenti, P.U. Rivard, F.L. Manning
McIntosh & O'Hagan, 109 Main St. e., J. R. McIntosh, E. A. O'Hagan
McLachlan, Sangster, 222 McIntyre St. w., H.C. McLachlan, W.A. Sangster
McWha, A. E., 881 McIntyre St. w.
O'Connell, Wood & Woltz, #202, 387 Fraser St., T. O'Connell, D.W. Wood, D.D. Woltz
Olah & Olah, 251 Cassells St., G.D. Olah, Lydia Olah
Parslow, A. C., 191 McIntyre St. w.
Tafel & Friedrich, 477 Sherbrooke St., R.D. Tafel, S.L. Friedrich
Trussler & McTavish, 304 Worthington St. w., J. H. C. Trussler, I. R. McTavish
Valin, Valin, Brunton & Wellard, 140 Main St. w., K. M. Valin, Q.C., G.T.S. Valin, W.A. Brunton, B.M. Wellard
Wallace & Carr, 225 McIntyre St. w., G. E. Wallace, Q.C., R. T. Carr, J. A. Wallace, D. C. Wallace, R.M. Thompson

NORWICH, Oxford
Graham, White & Co. (also Woodstock)
Treleaven, R.L., Q.C. (also Woodstock)

NORWOOD, Peterborough
Campbell, I.W., Box 130
Hughes, J.D., Box 190
Lech, Lightbody & Co. (also Peterborough)

OAK RIDGES, York
Burlew, E.L., Box 909
Mitchell, K.D., 12800 Yonge St.

OAKVILLE, Halton
Adamson, M. T., 274 Kerr St.
Ateah, C.D., 117 Lakeshore Rd. w.
Baggs, D.D., 228 Lakeshore Rd. e.
Black, D.S., 292 Lakeshore Rd. e.
Clarke, S.D., 155 Church St.
Crittenden, J.D., 305 Lakeshore Rd. e.
Day, R. B., 305 Lakeshore Rd. e.
Depew, J.H.H., Q.C., Box 249
Edwards, G. M., 461 Trafalgar Rd.
Elias, W., 132 Allan St.
Fenton, F. M., 132 Dunn St.
Gallagher & McKenna, 2452 Lakeshore Rd. w., N. L. McKenna
Gardner, J. B., 228 Lakeshore Rd. e.
Gonet, Milne, Allan & Peterson, 2448 Lakeshore Rd. e., W.S. Gonet, Q.C., B.W. Milne, W.J.N. Allan, N. Peterson
Ham, J. H., Q.C., 228 Lakeshore Rd. e.
Hanna, B.J., 288 Lakeshore Rd. e.
Holden, Ford, 125 Navy St., T.M. Holden, Q.C., J.P.H. Ford, Q.C.
Jackson, L.S., 123 Maurice Dr.
Kavanagh, T.M., 40 Brentwood Rd.
Kerr, W. B., 292 Lakeshore Rd. e.
King, B. W., 407 Speers Rd.
Knox, A., 2368 Lakeshore Rd. w.
Lush, Bowker & Bowker, 261 Lakeshore Rd. e., R.G. Lush, Q.C., D.C. Bowker, L.R. Bowker
MacLeod & Watts, 1226 White Oaks Blvd., W.J. MacLeod, K.W. Watts
Marshall, D. G., Q.C., 235 Church St.
Marshall, T. H., 296 Randall St.
McAskie, E.J., 292 Lakeshore Rd. e.
McConachie, D.A., Q.C., 345 Lakeshore Rd. e.
McCrea, W., 292 Lakeshore Rd. e.
McKenzie, D.L., 235 Church St.
Murphy, F.A., 345 Lakeshore Rd. e.
O'Connor, Leitch, Hays & Gangbar, 300 Hopedale Mall, T.P. O'Connor, Q.C., F.E. Leitch, Q.C., T.C. Hays, L.S. Gangbar, Louise McKillop
O'Reilly, J. G., 187a Lakeshore Rd. e.
Perras, P.W., Jr., 284 Lakeshore Rd. e.
Renison, K.E., 191A Lakeshore Rd. e.
Ryrie & Davidson, 103 George St., R. Ryrie, Q.C., P. R. Davidson
Serafini, A.A., 284 Lakeshore Rd. e.
Sher, D., Q.C., 1515 Rebecca St.
Vokes, M., 155 Church St.
Weiss, W. B., 345 Lakeshore Rd. e. (F.M St. Clair)
Zambosco, F.G., 407 Speers Rd.

OMEMEE, Victoria
Warner, Cork & Co. (also Lindsay)

ORANGEVILLE, Dufferin
Allison, C.A., 75 1st St.
Butler, J., 205 Broadway St.
Church, R.G., 192 Broadway St.
Church, W., Q.C., 192 Broadway St. (Margot Hornseth)
Evans & Adams, 107 Broadway, H. C. Adams, Q.C.
MacKenzie, Wood etc., 279 Broadway w (also Toronto)
McAlpine, A. D., 70 First St.
Parkinson, Parkinson & Maund, 147 Broadway, B. T. Parkinson, Q.C., P. T Parkinson, D.B. Maund
Perets, H.H., 70 First St.
Stutz & Bourque, 76 Broadway St., W.W Stutz, P.N. Bourque, S.F. White
Wardlaw, Wardlaw & Mullin, 235 Broadway St., J.J. Wardlaw, Q.C., G. T. Mullin, T.S. Carter, D.G. Thwaites

ORILLIA, Simcoe
Algie, R. B., 6 West St. n.
Bourne, Jenkins, Michener & French, 27 Peter St. n., C. H. Bourne, Q.C., D.W Jenkins, G. Michener, R.C.A. French
Clarke, Zwicker, Sparks, Evans, Earle & Lewis, 93 Coldwater St. e., R.N. Clarke M.W. Zwicker, R. G. Sparks, G. T. Evans, Jr., A.E.I. Earle, J.R. Lewis
Clegg & Drury, 31 Peter St. n., G. Clegg M.J. Drury
Crawford, Farr, Lewis, Worling, Ewart & McKenzie, 40 Coldwater St. e., D. J Crawford, Q.C., J. E. Farr, Q.C., D.H Worling, H.D. Ewert, K.W. McKenzie Counsel: D.G. Lewis

Donnelly, H.B., 41 Coldwater St. e.
Downard, G. G., Q.C., 40 Coldwater St. e.
Eberhard, M.P., #204, 2 Mississaga St. e.
Ford, A.J.F., 110 Neywash St.
Haidle, R. M., 13 Mississaga St. w.
Hamilton, W.H., 32 Matchedash St. n.
Holdsworth, W.M., 32 Matchedash St. n.
Lindsey, S., 32 Matchedash St. n.
Marshall, Russell, Waite & Christie, 66 Coldwater St. e., W. D. Russell, Q.C., R. B. Waite, D. S. Christie, M.B. Miller
McLean, W.G., 17A Mississaga St. w.
Mulligan, G. M., 18 West St. n.
Owen, A.E., 18 West St. n.
Trivett, W.L.S., Q.C., 27 Front St. n.

ORLEANS, Ottawa-Carleton
Altimas, F. J., 200, 2744 St. Joseph Blvd.
Brisebois, L., 2442 St. Joseph Blvd.
Dust, G.A., 1101 Champlain St.

ORONO, Durham
Lycett, W. K., Q.C.

OSHAWA, Durham
Affleck, Sosna & Shaughnessy, 57 Simcoe St. s., W.B. Affleck, Q.C., A. Sosna, J.B. Shaughnessy, P. Farquharson
Aitchison, Starzynski & Shine, 115 Simcoe St. s., J.N. Aitchison, J.G. Starzynski, S. Shine
Allore & Assoc., 11 Simcoe St. n., L.S. Allore, W.N. McKinnon
Berk, A., 650 King St. e. (Kay Carlson)
Bolotenko, A.G., 13 John St. w.
Boychyn & Boychyn, 36½ King St. e., G.S. Boychyn, Q.C., R.G. Boychyn, D.P. Boychyn
Couch, H. J. (City Solicitor), 50 Centre St. s.
Creighton, Victor, Alexander & Hayward, 235 King St. e., J. C. Victor, Q.C., R. A. Alexander, R. J. Hayward, G.C.S. Morison
Crotin & Palter, 219 King St. e., L.E. Crotin, J.R. Palter
Diamond & Fischman, 58 Rossland Rd. w., M.N. Diamond, S.M. Fischman
Drynan, G. K., Q.C., #1001, 44 Bond St. w.
Elliott, Kitchen & Kitchen, 86 Simcoe St. s., G.L. Elliott, R.J. Kitchen, G.G. Kitchen
Fletcher, McKay, Mack & Kisbee, 146 Simcoe St. n., J. P. Fletcher, J.N. McKay, P.D. Mack, N.M. Kisbee. Counsel: R.J. Harris
Greer, Seiler, Fisher, 54B Centre St. n., T.H. Greer, Q.C., R.F. Seiler, P.G. Fisher, J.G. Brown
Humphreys & Hillman, 36½ King St. e., W. A. Hillman, Q.C., J. D. Humphreys, Q.C. Counsel: R.D. Humphreys, Q.C.
Jewell, Angus & Michael, 11 Simcoe St. n., P.R. Jewell, Q.C., A.D. Angus, D.B. Thomas (also Toronto)
Jones & Jones, 130 King St. e., R. S. Jones, F. R. Jones, D.S. Jones
Kelly, Jermyn, Zuly, 114 King St. e., T. V. Kelly, Q.C., T. H. Jermyn, Q.C., S.V. Zuly, I.P. Greenway, M. Fowler, A.J. Bruce
Koziar, A., 72 Centre St. n.
Lancaster, K.L., 56 Division St.
Laskowsky & Neubauer, 73 Centre St. s., A. E. Laskowsky, J. Neubauer
Macdonald & Lack, 286 King St. w., J.A. Macdonald, M.L. Lack
Mackey, Bailey & Higgins, 17 Simcoe St. n., B.V. Mackey, Q.C., E.G. Bailey, T.P. Higgins
Magda, P. Z., 96 King St. e.
Mangan, J. P., Q.C., 14½ King St. e.
Marks & Valcour, Box 35, Ernest Marks, Q.C., Edward Marks, G.F. Valcour
Matthews, R.G., 96 King St. e.
Mazar, R.J., 96 King St. e.
McGibbon, Bastedo, Armstrong & Armstrong, 32 Simcoe St. s., E. F. Bastedo, Q.C., G. H. Armstrong, W.M. Armstrong
McLaughlin, J.D., 36½ King St. e.
Michaels & Michaels, 50 Colborne St. e., L. Michaels, B.H. Michaels
Minich, F., 194 King St. w.
Murphy, O'Brien & Vella, 187 King St. e., R.J. Murphy, Q.C., B.F. O'Brien, G.R. Vella, M.J.G. Gillen
Parkhill & Yanch, 69 King St. e., J. A. Yanch, Q.C., L. A. Yanch
Pollit, Walters & Halikowski, 70 Bond St. w., G. J. Pollit, B. Walters, D.J. Halikowski
Risen & Espey, 57 Simcoe St. s., A.J. Risen, R. Espey
Salmers & Furlong, 63 King St. w., Z. T. Salmers, Q.C., A. Furlong
Stelmach, B.P.,
Sproule, J., 1050 Simcoe St. n.
Stein & Price, 136 Simcoe St. n., S.P. Stein, G.G. Price
Stolwyk, F. H. M., 15 Charles St. (F. Reid)
Swartz & Swartz, 231 Simcoe St. n., R. L. Swartz, H. S. Swartz
Wallace, R. A., Q.C., 112 Simcoe St. n.
Worboy, R.F., 153 Simcoe St. n.
Zubkavich & Wilbur, 16 Lloyd St., S.M. Zubkavich, J. Wilbur

OTTAWA, Ottawa-Carleton
Abell & Moore, 22 Metcalfe St., P.D. Abell, R.J. Moore
Abelson, A.D., Q.C., #402, 30 Metcalfe St.
Adam, Forbes, Singer, #905, 141 Laurier Ave. w., J. D. Adam, B. N. Forbes, D. B. Singer, M.E. Marshall
Addelman, Cohen & Edelson, 300, 126 York St., R. Addelman, J. L. Cohen, M.D. Edelson, R.F. Meagher
Aitken, Greenberg, #706, 116 Lisgar St., C.D. Aitken, S. Greenberg
Anders, K. W., 1580 Merivale Rd.
Anderson & Goss, 157 McLeod St., S.L. Anderson, J.D. Goss
Appleton, R.B., 52 Scrivens Ave.
Apse, Janis, #1820, 112 Kent St.
Aronson, L.S., 130 Albert St.
Assaly & Richard, #402, 77 Metcalfe St., L.C. Assaly, Q.C., T. Richard
Asselin, Jacqueline, #802, 261 Cooper St.
Bales, R., #100, 56 Sparks St.
Barnard, K.E., 78 Daly Ave. (D. Ward)
Barnes, G.M., #220, 126 York St.
Barnhart, M.E., 77 Metcalfe St.
Barrette, R., 1651 Montreal Rd. (Vanier)
Barrigar & Oyen, #700, 130 Slater St., R.H. Barrigar, G.O.S. Oyen, L.A. Turlock, J.R. Morrissey, J.E. Hopkins, D.J. Martin, B.M. Green, R.S. Mitchell
Batt, R.F., #411, 77 Metcalfe St.
Baumgarten & Freeborn, 200, 344 O'Connor St., R. Baumgarten, B. Freeborn
Beale, C.E., #503, 116 Lisgar St.
Beament, Green, York, 100 Sparks St., J. W. York, Jr., Q.C., W.T. Green, Q.C., J.H. Haydon, C.D. McKinnon, W.L. Riley, W.C.V. Johnson, C.A., J.B. Hebert, J.R. Read. Counsel: G. E. Beament, Q.C.
Beckett, J., 65 Centennial Blvd.
Bell, Baker, #500, 116 Lisgar St. (K2P 0C2), Hon. R. A. Bell, P.C., Q.C., J.C. Clarke, Q.C., D.C. Thompson, Q.C., Judith M. Oyen, Q.C., P.A. Webber, J.H. Deacon, J.R. McIninch. Counsel: E.H. Charleson, Q.C., Hon. W.D. Baker, P.C., Q.C.
Bell, J.S., 261 Cooper St.
Berthiaume, Adele, 1137 Richard Ave.
Binks, Chilcott & Simpson, 19 Daly Ave., K. C. Binks, Q.C., W. D. Chilcott, Q.C., W. J. Simpson, Q.C., B.F. Simpson, C.T. Hackland. Counsel: Hon. L.A. Landreville, Q.C.
Blaney, Pasternak, Smela & Watson, 255 Albert St., H.T. McGovern, J.A. Emond, L.A. Roine, W.O. Murphy, J.A. Brule, Q.C. (also Toronto)
Bogue, J., #701, 99 Bank St.
Bosada & Assoc., 222 Somerset St. w., R. J. Bosada, C.W. Stroud, C. Moore, M.A. Weller, Q.C.
Bourassa, A., Q.C., 280 Metcalfe St.
Bowley, J.N., #606, 1 Nicholas St.
Boyd, Susan, 538 MacLaren St.
Boyle & Boyle, 130 Albert St., R. N. Boyle, B. J. Boyle
Brennan, Tunney & McGurk, 77 Metcalfe St., L. Brennan, Q.C., B. L. Tunney, R.J. McGurk, P.A. Niebergall, Dianne Nicholas
Bunning, L.B., #606, 1 Nicholas St.
Burchill, J.F., 919 Glasgow Ave.
Burke-Robertson, Chadwick & Ritchie, 130 Albert St., W. G. Burke-Robertson, Q.C., J. B. Chadwick, Q.C., R. A. Ritchie, J. E. Smith, W. C. Kent, W.T. Langley, J.R.M. Gautreau, Q.C., T.C. Barber, D.C. Silverson, W.R. Edgar, Jennifer Mackinnon, Sharon Rosentzveig, E.H. Masters, L.L. Herman. Patent Attorney: W. I. Haskett
Burritt, Grace & Neville, #500, 77 Metcalfe St., S.J. Grace, M.J. Neville, A.F. Burritt, Q.C., K.G. Hall, W.J.S. Elliott
Button, R.W., #400, 77 Metcalfe St.
Callan, Ryan, 136 Lewis St., J.J. Callan, S.J. Ryan
Carleton, R., #503, 30 Metcalfe St.
Carroll, W.J., #1510, 1 Nicholas St.
Chan, Judie, 100 Renfrew Ave.
Charlebois, Charron, #205, 126 York St., G. Charlebois, L. Charron
Charles, Merovitz & Potechin, 2660 Southvale Cres., D.L.E. Charles, C.L. Merovitz, B. Potechin
Chartrand, J.V., 275 Slater St.
Chenier & LeBel, 445 Cumberland St., J.M. Chenier, M.P. LeBel
Cherner, S., #1, 201 McLeod St.
Chiarelli, Karr & Cramer, 2019 Carling Ave., R. Chiarelli, B. Karr, R.W. Graw, H. Connelly, K.H. Cramer, H. Witteveen
Chinkiwsky, M., 2668 Alta Vista Dr.
Chisholm, J.R., #304, 260 Metcalfe St.
Citron, M., #201, 116 Lisgar St.
City Solicitors, City Hall, #406, 111 Sussex Dr., F.C. Askwith, City Solicitor
Coady, M.M., #1000, 77 Metcalfe St.
Cogan & Cogan, 170 Laurier Ave. w., F.T. Cogan, J.A. Cogan, Q.C., S.P. Horwitz
Coll, N.E., 36 Herridge St.
Conlin & McAlpin, 1678 Bank St., P. J. Conlin, S.W. McAlpin
Cooligan, Ryan, McNeely, Montague & Connolly, 237 Argyle Ave., G. J. Cooligan, Q.C., M. E. Ryan, H. R. McNeely, R. J. Montague, T. P. Connolly
Cuffari, J.C., #606, 1 Nicholas St.
Curran, Gibson & McNab, 350 Sparks St., J. Curran, D.K. Gibson, J.J. McNab
Cuzner, MacQuarrie, #1003, 116 Albert St., R. H. Cuzner, Q.C., R. W. MacQuarrie, Q.C., G. R. Gordon, M.A. Chambers. Counsel: A.D. Wilson
Dehler, D., Q.C., #1104, 100 Bronson
Dent, G.M., 312 Cooper St.
Dick, Nichols & Loeb, #700, 141 Laurier Ave. w., P.W. Dick, Q.C., J.H. Nichols, K.J. Loeb, Margaret Smith
Dixon, Bulger & Young, 1245 Wellington St., R. B. Dixon, Q.C., W. B. Bulger, K. V. Young, J. J. Cardill, D.S. Duncan
Doraty & Noble, #255, 39 Highway 7 (Nepean), J. A. Doraty, D.K.S. Noble, D.J. Gadient

Drache, Goldstein, #400, 130 Slater St., A.B.C. Drache, S.W. Goldstein
Dunlap & Assoc., 1716 Woodward Ave., J. G. Dunlap, Q.C., M. A. Dunlap, W.T. McInenly
Ebbs, J.B., Q.C., 958 Merivale Rd. (J.D. Guay, J.S. Paul)
Filion, DeGagne, 235 Montreal Rd. (Vanier), J.P. Filion, P. DeGagne, Q.C., J.P. Gascon, G. Charbonneau
Finn, T. D'A., 1284 Parkhill Circle
Forrest, D. G., 951 Bronson Ave.
Fortey & Scott, #420, 1335 Carling Ave., J.B. Fortey, J.R. Scott
Francis, J.P., 3 Starwood Ave. (Nepean)
Fraser, Kathleen, #207, 2948 Baseline Rd. (Nepean)
Frink, G., #204, 190 Somerset St. w.
Fry, Daphne, #3, 305 Waverley St.
Gennis, P.H., 2019 Carling Ave.
Gold, Gasparini, Fera & Denison, 299 Richmond Rd., B.B. Gold, R.O. Gasparini, N.M. Fera, W.T. Denison
Goldberg, S.I., 427 Gilmour St.
Goldberg, Shinder, Gardner, Kronick & Tavel, 307 Gilmour St., A. Goldberg, Q.C., S.B. Shinder, Q.C., C.J. Gardner, Q.C., J.I. Tavel, Q.C., R. Kronick, G. L. Steinberg, D.C. Kardash, R.I. Steinberg, R. Prehogan, M.Z. Black
Goulet, C.H., Q.C., #502, 45 Rideau St.
Gour, Guenette & Roy, 255 Montreal Rd. (Vanier), R. Gour, G. Guenette, A. Roy, Q.C.
Gowling & Henderson, 160 Elgin St., (Mail address: Box 466, Terminal A) (K1N 8S3), E. G. Gowling, Q.C., G. F. Henderson, O.C., Q.C., C. F. Scott, Q.C., David Watson, Q.C., E. P. Newcombe, Q.C., R. G. McClenahan, Q.C., R. W. Cleary, Q.C., J. D. Richard, Q.C., B. A. Crane, Q.C., W. B. Spooner, Q.C., C. E. O'Connor, R. J. Laughton, G. A. Macklin, Q.C., K.H.E. Plumley, R. J. Redmond, Robert Chevrier, Rose-Marie Perry, Elisabeth Slasor, D. E. Clarke, D. G. Casey, Y.A.G. Hynna, R. J. Ostiguy, R.D. Chapman, T. D. Beynon, G. E. Fisk, A.R. O'Brien, D.C. Gavsie, W.A. Joyce, R.M. Nelson, K. G. Evans, G. F. Windsor, H.R. Cowan, T.W. Peterman, P. Richard, Allyne Thomson, R.G. Gravelle, G.E. Kaiser, A.I. Fors, R.W. Groulx, J.-M. Raymond, E.S. Binavince, F.A.W. Ault, B.E. Morgan, T.G. O'Neill, P.T. Taggart, D.C. Woods, Margaret Ross, L.T. Lederman, P.D. Blanchard, G.J. David, R.R. Hahn, Lynn Harnden, P.A. Millican, A. Trotta, R.S. Jolliffe, P.W. Jones, G.N. Addy, J.C. Avis, R.G. Dearden, D.M. Woody, Jane Steinberg, S.P. Whitehead, Jennifer Ward, H.S. Brown, A.G. Creber, Bernadette Eischen, Emma Hill, M.A. Holowack, Jan Matejcek, L.R. Milrod, D.C. Simmonds, E.M. Singer, M.J. Szczepaniak, G.W. Wall, Victoria Wong, R.W. Zinn, S.M. Eaton. Counsel: J.C. Osborne, Q.C., B.M. Alexander, Q.C.; Patent Agents: E.J. McKhool, W.N. Mace, Vivian Wickham, B. Dudley, J.W. Ross, R.F. Delbridge, F.I. Pole, I. Straznicky, K.G. Curry, W.G. Currie; Trade Mark Agents: D.A. Smyth, Jane Myers, R. Colbert, W.O. Hunt
Grant & Wake, 400, 77 Metcalfe St., D.G. Grant, J.D. Wake
Guertin, B., Q.C., 1 Nicholas St.
Guertin, J.P., Q.C., #330, 333 River Rd. (Vanier)
Guertin, R., #1512, 1 Nicholas St.
Gusella, M., 50 Southern Dr.
Habib, D., 1390 Prince of Wales Dr.
Hall, Hall & Ray, 359 Kent St., J. H. Hall, Q.C., J. S. Hall, D. E. Ray
Hamilton/Ray, 100 Sparks St., J.E. Hamilton, T.D. Ray, S.A. Appotive, M.G. Cochrane, Marilyn Stanley
Hanson, J.C., Q.C., 35 Beechwood Ave.
Harbic, J.D., #1402, 1 Nicholas St.
Harris, Holly, 31 Russell Ave.
Hendin & Hendin, #902, 130 Albert St., S.E. Hendin, Judith Hendin, S. Waxman, E.M. Appotive, G.G. Boyd
Herridge, Tolmie, 116 Albert St., J. Ross Tolmie, Q.C., R. G. Gray, Q.C., J. M. Coyne, Q.C., J. G. Fogo, R. G. Belfoi, Q.C., F. Lemieux, K.L.W. Boland, M.L. Phelan, Barbara A. McIsaac, J.H. Smellie, K.S. McLean, R.C. Cheng, G.A. Bloom, Penny Bonner, G.G. Buchan
Hewitt, Hewitt, Nesbitt, Reid, 75 Albert St. (K1P 5E7), A. T. Hewitt, Q.C., P. P. Hewitt, Q.C., J. L. Nesbitt, Q.C., J. Reid, Q.C., P.D. Rasmussen, D.F. Smith, H. B. Starr, C. A. Murphy, A.H.A. Keenleyside, P.R. Hughes, M.S. Ruddy, R.R. Hurtubise
Honey, E., #503, 785 Carling Ave.
Honeywell, Pascoe & Garay, #703, 1355 Bank St., W.J. Honeywell, L.S. Pascoe, W.A. Garay, D.D.G. Stel
Honeywell, Wotherspoon, #500, 90 Sparks St. (K1P 5B4), Hon. J. J. Connolly, Q.C., A.B.R. Lawrence, Q.C. (Counsel); S.F.M. Wotherspoon, Q.C., L. M. Joyal, Q.C., J.G.M. Hooper, Q.C., E. L. Gladu, Q.C., P. W. Fortier, J. M. Connolly, J. M. Scott, G.H. Robichon, R.V. Crozier, M.E. Panet, G.A. Howard, E. Montenegrino
Honsl, J.V., 2277 Riverside Dr. e.
Hough, T. H., 65 Bank St.
Houlahan & Baldwin, 1115, 130 Albert St., J.R. Houlahan, R.W. Baldwin, J.W. Hiscock
House & Plaskacz, #400, 30 Metcalfe St., G. House, Q.C.
Howe, Eglington, Watt & Guay, #201, 75 Albert St., O. Howe, Q.C., G. Eglington, G. Watt, A. Guay
Hughes, Laishley, Touhey & Sigouin, 116 Lisgar St., R. A. Hughes, Q.C., R.K. Laishley, Q.C., J. W. Touhey, Q.C., J.R. Sigouin, Q.C., J. C. Barnabe, T.C. Jameson, P. Santini
Hunter, T.R., #200, 344 O'Connor St.
Irani, E., #3A, 101 Rideau St.
Jabour, T., 170 Laurier Ave. w.
Jackman, R., 352 MacLaren St.
Johnston & Buchan, #1500, 275 Slater St., C.C. Johnston, R.J. Buchan, D.E. Osborn, L.J. Dunbar
Jones, A.S., 322 Waverly St.
Jones, M.W., #1, 201 McLeod St.
Karam, Tannis, Greenspon & Scapilatti, 328 Frank St., B. Karam, E.G. Tannis, L. Greenspon, D.A. Scapilatti
Kaye, L., #505, 77 Metcalfe St.
Kealey, G., 2249 Carling Ave.
Kealey & Lafrange, 451 Metcalfe St., R. J. Kealey, Q.C., Pat Lafrange
Kebe/Cannon, 120 Hwy. 7, J. Kebe, J.T. Cannon, M.A. Henry
Kee & Langford, 185 Rideau St., J. Kee, S. Langford
Kelly, Doering & Morrow, 265 Carling Ave., L.P. Kelly, R.L. Doering, R.C. Morrow, D.R. Good
Kelly, H.K., #420, 396 Cooper St.
Kelly, Kelly & Manthorp, B3, 2323 Riverside Dr., P. Kelly, T.M.E. Kelly, E. Manthorp
Kemp, J., #2, 480 Oakhill Rd.
Kennedy, Sweet, Shouldice & Whyte, 130 Albert St., Ralph D. Sweet, Q.C., D.F. Shouldice, B.A. Whyte, J.E. Merner
Kerr, J. K., Q.C., 65 Bank St.
Kershman, S.J., #200, 344 O'Connor St.
Kertzer, M. M., 141 Laurier Ave. w.
Kierdorf, J.W., 322 Waverley St.
Kimmel, Victor, Ages & Rothman, #904, 255 Albert St., D. Kimmel, S. Victor, M.M. Ages, S. Rothman, S. Srivastava
Kirvan, M.A., #1010, 1435 Prince of Wales Dr. (M.J. Kirvan)
Kos-Rabcewicz-Zubkowski, L., 214 Roger Rd. (K1H 5C6)
Lafleur & Aubin, 45 Rideau St., J. C. Aubin, Q.C.
Lalonde, Chartrand & Co., 234 Montreal Rd., R.F. Lalonde, R. Chartrand, P.F. Lalonde, R.H. Gouin
Lamoureux, S., 345 Queen St. e.
Latour, B., 2249 Carling Ave.
Lazarovitz, M., 343 Somerset St. w.
Levencrown, Robertson, #1007, 130 Albert St., L. Levencrown, S.M. Robertson, G.K. Blaney, E.M. Lieff
Lieff & Nicholson, #404, 151 Sparks St., J. Lieff, Q.C., D. E. Nicholson, R. W. Wight, N.B. Lieff
Lithwick, H.A., 204, 880 Lady Ellen Place
Livingstone-Pickett, K., 134 Hawthorne St.
Low, Murchison, Burns, Thomas & McCay, 141 Laurier Ave. w., K. A. Murchison, Q.C., D. C. Burns, J. W. Thomas, G. J. McCay, P.A.J. Hargadon, D.W.J. Smyth
Lynch, Jennifer, 249 McLeod St. (Barbara Kincaid)
Lynch & McCormack, #503, 130 Slater St., D.P. Lynch, Hilary McCormack
Macdonald, Affleck, 100 Sparks St. (K1P 5B7), A. Macdonald, Q.C., R.W.D. Affleck, Q.C., R.E.B. Brocklesby, Q.C., R. C. McLaughlin, J. L.D. King, G. P. Kelly, G.E. Schreider, Q.C., D.P. Burke, Susan Klassen, B. Stockfish. Counsel: Hon. George McIlraith, P.C., Q.C.
Macera & Jarzyna, #505, 350 Sparks St., J.S. Macera, A.K. Jarzyna
MacKay, Gnys, Morgan & Co., #300, 171 Nepean St., R.D. MacKay, A. Gnys, R. Morgan, S.L. Sanderson
MacKinnon & Phillips, #701, 99 Bank St., R.W. MacKinnon, H. Phillips
Maclaren, Corlett, Tanner & Greenwood, 30 Metcalfe St., M.E. Corlett, Q.C., F.G. Tanner, G.B. Greenwood, J.L. McCauley. Assoc. Counsel: G.F. Maclaren, Q.C.
MacLeod, A.C., #501, 77 Metcalfe St.
Macleod, N.E., #606, 1 Nicholas St.
MacMillan, F., #505, 785 Carling Ave.
Mantha, H.E., #2170, 320 Queen St.
Manton & Hebert, #605, 170 Laurier Ave w., B.J. Manton, M. Hebert
Marcus, Parnega, McNamara, #305, 185 Somerset St. w., B. Marcus, Q.C., B Parnega, J.E. McNamara
Mattar, Menczer, Savage, #900, 325 Dalhousie St., G.A. Mattar, M. Menczer Nancy Savage, H.L. Fraser, F.M. Falsetto
Max, L., Q.C., #900, 325 Dalhousie St.
McCann, Bayne & Sellar, #525, 126 York St., P. F. D. McCann, D. B. Bayne, R.G Sellar, N.D. Boxall, S.M. Bayne
McCarthy & Hollander, #803, 116 Albert St., W.G.D. McCarthy, J.A. Hollander
McCauley/Toneguzzi, #302, 1755 Woodward Ave., T. McCauley, B. Toneguzzi
McCloskey McCloskey, 2087 Montreal Rd., P.K. McCloskey, R.E. McCloskey
McCulloch, J., 401, 2249 Carling Ave.
McDonald & Landry, 1511 Merivale Rd. H.R. McDonald, M. Landry
McGuire & Mills, 1 Nicholas St., D. H McGuire, P. N. Mills, Q.C., W.D. Harrington
McGuire & Assoc., 100 Sparks St., F.M McGuire, D. Keilty

McHugh, Devine, McArthur & Rouatt, 182 Isabella St., J.P. Devine, C.H. McArthur, J.E. Rouatt
McKechnie, I.L., #702, 325 Dalhousie St.
McKenna & Peterson, #1403, 1 Nicholas St., J.E. McKenna, P.E. Peterson, J.L. Sprague
McKimm, Keeler & McFarlane, 701, 99 Bank St., R.W. McKimm, R.W. Keeler, J.N. McFarlane
McKinley, McKinley & Bradley, 900 Greenbank Rd., B. McKinley, R. McKinley, R.K. Bradley
McLachlan, P., #2, 84 Third Ave.
McLeod, D.G., #306, 1580 Merivale Rd.
McMahon, J.R., #250, 130 Slater St.
McMichael & Owens, #705, 77 Metcalfe St., G.T. McMichael, Q.C., M.D. Owens
McNaughton & Curley, #303, 2255 Carling Ave., J.P. McNaughton, B.G. Curley, M.H. Arbique
McTaggart, Adams & Martin, #703, 100 Sparks St., R. P. McTaggart, D. R. Adams, S. H. Martin
Mender, S., #101, 427 Gilmour St.
Meredith & Finlayson, 77 Metcalfe St., Wm. R. Meredith, Q.C., D. G. Finlayson, J.C. Singlehurst, R. Ahluwalia
Metrick, T. P., Q.C., #1508, 1 Nicholas St. (M.D. Scott)
Miller, Dubinsky, 116 Albert St., T. H. Miller, G. L. Dubinsky
Milloy, S., #303, 185 Somerset St. w.
Mirsky & Sage, 39 Highway 7 (Nepean), P.S. Mirsky, R.W. Sage
Monaghan/Robb, 205, 1355 Bank St., M.F. Monaghan, B.J. Robb
Moore, J.C., #204, 126 York St.
Morrison (A.L.) & Assoc., #200, 815 Somerset St. w., A.L. Morrison
Mount, Wright & Gilhooly, #101, 1899 Baseline Rd., R. Mount, J.P. Wright, D.G. Gilhooly
Munro, D.D., 201 McLeod St.
Murphy, A.P., #208, 1725 St. Laurent Blvd.
Nelligan/Power, 77 Metcalfe St., J. P. Nelligan, D.J. Power, W. F. Burrows, C. Callan-Jones, J. E. Johnson, A. R. O'-Brien, Janice B. Payne, Catherine H. MacLean, P.J. Cronyn, D.J. Jewitt, D.H. Chick
Nicol, O'Connor & Lazier, #203, 331 Cooper St., W.M. Nicol, J.P. O'Connor, R.D. Lazier
Nolan, P.J., #105, 45 Rideau St.
Oakes & Marshall, #217, 703 Bank St., F.G. Oakes, Kay Marshall
O'Brien, J., 40 Acacia Rd.
O'Byrne, K.M., #402, 77 Metcalfe St.
O'Connor, M.J., #1402, 1 Nicholas St.
O'Donnell, D. J., 150 Gloucester St.
O'Neill, G. J., 2249 Carling Ave.
Paradis, J.C., #1216, 1 Nicholas St.
Paris, Mercier & Sirois, 291 Dalhousie St., R.G. Paris, P. Mercier, J. C. Sirois, Q.C., R. Lajoie, Jacqueline Fitzgibbons
Patenaude, J.M., 1072 Cyrville Rd.
Perley-Robertson, Panet, Hill & McDougall, 99 Bank St., G. Perley-Robertson, Q.C., A. deLotbiniere Panet, Q.C., D. H. Hill, T. A. McDougall, Q.C., T.C. Klotz, C. A. Fournier, P. B. Kane, G.A. Jameson, M.J. Siddons, J.P. Manley, J.B. West, M.G. Peacock, Lynn D. Ratushny, R.J. Kearns, J.R. Hendry, Janice Vauthier
Piazza, Allard, 66 Lisgar St., J.B. Piazza, R.D. Allard, S. Polowin, P.R. Brooks, S.E. Cumming
Pope, K., #100, 56 Sparks St.
Prachter, W. F., 130 Albert St.
Pyper & Farrell, 185 Rideau St., P. Pyper, M.J. Farrell
Quain, Dioguardi, 400 Cumberland Ave., H. Quain, Q.C., P. Dioguardi, J.B. Barnes, W.J. Sammon, G. Barnes
Radnoff, Pearl, Pearl & Slover, 100 Gloucester St., K. Radnoff, Q.C., H. W. Pearl, B. S. Pearl, N. S. Slover, D.Y. Dwoskin
Reid, Janet, #1800, 130 Albert St.
Rice & Rice, 303 Waverley St., B.F.L. Rice, Mary Jane Binks Rice, G.C. McKechnie
Richard, J. T., Q.C., 48 Sparks St.
Richer & Richer, #702, 325 Dalhousie St., J.L. Richer, S.A. Richer
Ritchie & Evans, #300, 311 Richmond Rd., S.A. Ritchie, Christine Evans
Rock, P., 355 Waverley St. (C.J. McCorriston)
Ross, D., #700, 77 Metcalfe St.
Ross & Baston, #404, 130 Albert St., K.J. Ross, A.M. Baston
Rotenberg, C.M., #400, 130 Slater St.
Ryan, H., 355 Waverley St.
Saint Jacques, H.O., Q.C., 1 Nicholas St.
Samek & Forsythe, #202, 7 Slack Rd. (Nepean), L.J. Samek, D.H. Forsythe
Schwartz, M., #9, 1419 Carling Ave.
Scott & Aylen, 170 Laurier Ave. w., J. G. Aylen, Q.C., D. W. Scott, Q.C., L.J. Rasmussen, P.C.P. Thompson, Q.C., J. G. Potvin, B.A. Carroll, G. D. Hunter, J. I. Minnes, J.B. Carr-Harris, T.J. McManus, M. Jolicoeur, D.A. Aylen. Assoc. Counsel: J.A. Aylen, Q.C., C. Scott, Q.C.
Segal, M., 1305 Richmond Rd.
Seguin, Landriault, Lamoureux, 233 Gilmour St., R. Landriault, P.R. Lamoureux, D.E. Faulkner, R.G. Julien. Counsel: R.N. Seguin, O.C., Q.C.
Shaikh, M.S., #210, 85 Sparks St.
Shanbaum, H.R., #700, 77 Metcalfe St.
Shapiro, N. R., Q.C., Box 2705, Stn. D (J.C. Cohen, S.C. McCormack)
Shinder & Ages, #1516, 1 Nicholas St., B.M. Ages
Shore, L.M., Q.C., #1512, 1 Nicholas St. (A.P. Davis)
Sigler, H., Q.C., 116 Albert St.
Sim & Morrison, 130 Albert St., D. C. Sim, J. P. Morrison, Q.C.
Simester, G.A., #15, 99 5th St.
Simpson, Rosemary, 1 Wick Cres.
Simser & Wyatt, Box 369 (Kanata)
Smart & Biggar, 70 Gloucester St., R.S. Smart, Q.C., J. J. Ellis, D. A. Hill, J. D. Kokonis, Q.C., J.A. Devenny, Q.C., P.L. Beck, N.H. Fyfe, A. R. Campbell, A.D. Morrow, R.D. Gould, T.R. Kelly, J. Bochnovic, Joy Harding, A.M. Troicuk, W.L. Webster. Counsel: E.L. Medcalf, Q.C.
Smith & Janigan, 727 Somerset St. w., J.M. Smith, M. Janigan
Snipper, Cohen & Murray, 210 Gladstone Ave., D. R. Snipper, Q.C., E. M. Cohen, Q.C., R. E. Murray, Q.C., J. D. Snipper
Soloway, Wright, Houston, Greenberg, O'Grady, Morin, 170 Metcalfe St. (K2P 1P3), H. Soloway, Q.C., M. W. Wright, Q.C., I. Greenberg, M. J. O'Grady, G. R. Morin, Q.C., A. Feinstein, R.E. Houston, Q.C., J. L. Shields, F.J. Holmes, P.N. Leamen, Susan M. Gibson, A.E. Honeywell, G.J. Rip, Lyon Gilbert, S.C. Guest, T.J. Marlay, W.T. Houston, L.J. Soloway, A.K. Cohen, Janet Bradley, A.J. Raven, P.G. Hagen, Monique Metivier, Lyon Lightstone
Sorensen, R.B., Q.C., #408, 151 Sparks St.
Spice, Patricia, #803, 370 Metcalfe St.
Sterling & Clark, 1510 Merivale Rd. (Nepean), A.E. Clark
Stoller, Sabey & McCarthy, 120 Holland Ave., K.W. Sabey, T.J. McCarthy
Stout, D.A., #220, 126 York St.
Taylor, B.R., 1580 Merivale Rd.
Tennant, E. W., 3754 Richmond Rd.
Thomas, Thomas & Winship, 273 Bank St., R. C. Thomas, A. R. Winship
Thompson, R.W., #15, 99 Fifth Ave.
Tietolman, R.H. #204, 126 York St.
Tomosk, Mayhew, Peart & Johnston, #300, 441 MacLaren St., R. Tomosk, T.J. Mayhew, J.D. Peart, R.C. Johnstone
Vanasse, A., #416, 1435 Prince of Wales Dr.
Vanier, R.A., #306, 1580 Merivale Rd. (Nepean)
Vice & Hunter, 344 Frank St., J.P. Vice, Q.C., W.R. Hunter, Brenda Vice, D.G. Martin
Vincent, Choquette, Dagenais & Marks, #600, 325 Dalhousie St., L. Choquette, Q.C., L. Vincent, R. R. Dagenais, R.R. Marks, M. Gauthier, J.V. Chartrand
Wakefield, R., 1 Nicholas St.
Wallace, M., 136 Lewis St.
Ward, L., #1510, 1 Nicholas St.
Warren, G.D., 157 McLeod St.
Watson & Farber, 330 Churchill Ave., P. Watson, I. Farber, E.N. Fry
Watson, Hughes, Fontana & Coulson, 429 MacLaren St., P. Watson, Q.C., Donnell J. Hughes, J.A. Fontana, David J. Hughes, P.H. Coulson, Ellen Beall
Webb & Heeley, 107 4th Ave., R.T. Webb, D.G. Heeley
Wentzell, J.D., #204, 190 Somerset St. w.
Williams, McEnery & Davis, #401, 116 Lisgar St., E.R. Williams, P.T. McEnery. Counsel: W.M. Davis
Wilson, Dubuc, Ryan & Whillans, #503, 141 Laurier Ave. w., R.C.E. Wilson, Q.C., A.J. Dubuc, J.C. Ryan, R.A. Whillans, P.J. Bishop
Wiseman, C., #1104, 1435 Prince of Wales Dr.
Wiseman, Swedco, #512, 90 Sparks St., C.S. Wiseman, N. Swedco
Wolf, N.W., 322 Waverley St.
Wyatt, Menczer, Savage, Fraser & Falsetto, #900, 325 Dalhousie St.
Young, W.D., 1745 St. Laurent Blvd.

OWEN SOUND, Grey
Alisauskas & Boyce, 836 2nd Ave. w., A. Alisauskas, H.E. Boyce
Grace, D.A., 949 2nd Ave. w.
Greenfield & Barrie, 142 10th St. w., D.R. Greenfield, B.D. Barrie
Horton, Middlebro', Stevens, 1390 2nd Ave. w., R. P. Horton, Q.C., J. H. E. Middlebro', E. P. Horton, E.J. Stevens
Keon, M. C., #216, 945 3rd Ave. e.
Laing, Meanwell, 935 2nd Ave. w., J.F. Laing, Q.C., Catherine Meanwell
Lendon & Lovell, 167 10th St. w., H. A. Lendon, D. L. Lovell, S.P. Harrison
McKerroll & Murray, 945 3rd Ave. e., D.M. McKerroll, Q.C., W.L. Murray, J.A. McKerroll
Telford, Van Wyck, Kirby & McGibbon, 945 3rd Ave. e., H. L. Van Wyck, Q.C., J.L. Van Wyck, J.A. Kirby, J.D. McGibbon
Whitten, A.C.R., 1101 2nd Ave. e.

PAINSWICK, Simcoe
Wall-Armstrong, Deborah, 252A Yonge St.

PAISLEY, Bruce
Kelly, P.L.J., Box 190

PALMERSTON, Wellington
Fallis & Fallis, K.M. Twohig (also Mount Forest)

PARIS, Brant
Barron, G. R., Q.C., 24 St. George St.
Buck, T.H., 120 Grand River St. n.
Tarrison & Hunter, 19 William St., M. J. Tarrison, G. R. Hunter

PARKHILL, Middlesex
Lamon & McGrath (also London)
Walden, J. P.

PARRY SOUND, Parry Sound
Douglas, L.W., 16 Seguin St. (J.D. McLellan)
Green & Eves, 7 Miller St., W. H. Green, Q.C., E. L. Eves, D.J. Fraser
Holmes, D.A., 22 James St.
McTurk, D.J., 51B James St.
Piddington, A.W., 33 James St.
Powell, Cunningham, Kennedy & Grandy, 88 James St., F. D. Powell, Q.C., W. B. Cunningham, J. W. Kennedy, D. R. Grandy
Powell & Powell, 34 Mary St., J.R. Powell, F. C. Powell, Q.C.
Stone, G.D., Q.C., 33 James St.
Wilson, J.B., 97 James St.

PEMBROKE, Renfrew
Bradley, H.J., Q.C., 196 Victoria St.
Felhaber & Reiche, 10 Pembroke St. w., B.L. Felhaber, R.C. Reiche
Fortier, M. J., Box 758
Garretto & Campbell, 79 Pembroke St. w., A.S. Garretto, A. Campbell
Huckabone, O'Brien, Radley-Walters & Shushack, 284 Pembroke St. e., F. A. Huckabone, Q.C., S.G. Radley-Walters, D.A. O'Brien, Q.C., Mary Shushack
Johnson, Fraser, 259 Pembroke St. e., H. B. Johnson, Q.C., J.W. Fraser
LaFrance, Shaw & LaFrance, 182 MacKay St., L. P. LaFrance, Q.C., H.W. Shaw, P.L. LaFrance
Lavigueur, H.S., Box 155
Leach, B., Box 546
McCann & Sheppard, 290 Pembroke St. e., T.V. McCann, R.B. Sheppard
Millette, E.R., 270 Lake St.
Sauriol, R. L., 238 Pembroke St. w.
Walsh, Greenberg, 220 Pembroke St. e., H. G. Walsh, Q.C., J.S. Greenberg

PENETANGUISHENE, Simcoe
Devillers, Elise, 1 Simcoe St.
Hacker, Gignac & Rice, 9B Simcoe St. (also Midland)
MacKinnon, DeVillers & Co., 90 Main St., P.R. Deacon (also Midland)
Rubens, A.W., 67A Robert St. w.

PERTH, Lanark
Barker, Butterworth & Woodwark, 32 Foster St., R. G. Barker, Q.C., R. D. Butterworth, P.C.W. Woodwark, D.C. Stevens
O'Donnell, Dulmage, Bond, March & Anderson, 83 Gore St. e., J.M. Bond, S.A.J. March, G.W. Anderson. Counsel: Hon. R. Frith, Q.C.
Rubino & Chaplin, Box 338, G. Chaplin (also Smiths Falls)
Shrybman, S.L., 53 Gore St. e.
Smith, K.W., 27 Foster St.
Willson, James, Cuddy & Scott, 47 Gore St. e., J.E. Willson, D. B. James, K.D. Cuddy, R.G. Scott. Counsel: B.A. Percival, Q.C., H.C. Willson, Q.C.

PETAWAWA, Renfrew
Huckabone & O'Brien (also Carleton Place)
Riemer, R.A., Box 148
Roche & Dakin (also Deep River)

PETERBOROUGH, Peterborough
Burgess, R.F., 408 Water St.
Cameron & Johnston, 816 Lansdowne St. w., F.S. Cameron, R.E. Johnston
Corkery, J. W., Q.C., 164 Hunter St. w.
Coros, G.W., 329 Rubidge St.
Crook, J.J., 418A Sheridan St.
Davidson, W. A., 172 Hunter St. w. (Lois Davidson)
Devitt, H.G., 806 Chemong Rd.
Dunn & Dunn, 469 Water St., J. F. Dunn, Q.C., J. R. Dunn, G.R. Collins
Ebbs, Taillon & Nichols, 340 George St. n., D. A. Ebbs, R. P. Taillon, J. D. Nichols
Elliott, Wood & Lockington, 349 Reid St., J.C.E. Wood, W. S. Lockington
Farquharson & Daly, 161 Hunter St. w., G. H. T. Farquharson, Q.C., J. J. Daly, A. S. McMichael
Fitzpatrick, J.E., Q.C., 425 Water St.
Foster & Clark, 401 McDonnel St., F.G. Foster, Q.C., R. Clark
Fox & Potts, 371 George St. n., W.H. Fox, J.L.R. Potts
Galvin & Murphy, 466 George St. n., P. D. Galvin, M.G. Murphy
Gariepy & Murphy, 176 McDonnel St., A.W. Gariepy, S.M. Murphy
Gordon & Lillico, 163 Hunter St. w., J.B. Lillico, Q.C., S.L. Barrett, P.B. Lillico
Gowland, Boriss, Peterborough Square, A. Gowland, R. Boriss
Grant, Carruthers & Whetung, 457 Water St., W.C. Grant, W.M. Carruthers, T.E. Whetung
Guerin & Howson, 418A Sheridan St., Joan Guerin, R. Howson
Hall & Gillespie, 444 George St. n., J. A. Gillespie
Harries, A.S., 308 Park St. n.
Hauraney, J., 387 George St. s.
Howell, Fleming, Bark, Rishor, White & Pakenham, 415 Water St., W. H. Howell, Q.C., A. Fleming, Q.C., W. D. Bark, Q.C., G. G. Rishor, D. D. White, R. E. Pakenham, M. Wendy Robson, S.G. Bazuk, S.P. Kylie
Johnston, F.A., 333 Reid St.
Lech, Lightbody & O'Brien, 425 Water St., W.C. Lech, Q.C., R.D. Lightbody, M.R. O'Brien
Leipciger, I., 469 Water St.
MacDougall, B.G., 430 Sheridan St.
McCarney, J.G., Q.C., 351 Reid St.
McNeely, G.G., #402, 340 George St.
McVicar, R.J., 314 Rubidge St.
Millard & McGillen, 469 Water St., P. Millard, R.C. McGillen
Moldaver & Burgis, 121 George St. n., J.S. Moldaver, R.C. Burgis
Moser, M.B., 184 Charlotte St.
Robertson & Robertson, 191 Hunter St. w., H. W. Robertson, J. S. Robertson
Ross, D. W., 408 Water St.
Steffler, F.G., 184 Charlotte St.
Usher, Dwyer, Whittington & Jordan, 359 Aylmer St. n., G.H. Usher, M.J. Dwyer, J.R. Whittington, E.J. Jordan
Walker, D.F., 308 Park St. n.

PETROLIA, Lambton
Edward, F.J. (also Sarnia)
Kilby, P.J.
Oliver, W. R.

PICKERING, Durham
Edmiston, G.W., 1281 Commerce St.
Fisher, A., 94 Kingston Rd. e.
Greening, W.J., 924 Liverpool Rd.
Howes & Head, Pickering Corporate Centre, J.G. Howes, M.F. Head, R. Banik
Huxley & Chodak, 364 Kingston Rd., J.M. Huxley, E.W. Chodak
Lawson & Clark, W. D. Clark
Robertson, P.A., 92 Church St. s. (B. Dowling)
Rubinoff, R. A., Sheridan Mall
Storm, H., 1360 Kingston Rd.
Stroud, M.D., 364 Kingston Rd., M.D. Stroud, R.P. Kaufman
Tesluk, M.J., 1305 Sheridan Mall Pkwy.
Vanular, G.P., 867 Liverpool Rd.
Walker, Wright & Rowsell, 75 Kingston Rd. e., W.F. Walker, G.D. Wright, A.R. Rowsell

PICTON, Prince Edward
Bezaire, J.
Byers & Williams, 199 Main St., R. G. Byers, C. D. L. Williams
Campbell, B.F., 194 Main St.
McFarland & Martin, 6 Ross St., M.J. McFarland, W.M. Martin
McLoughlin, H., Q.C.
Mowat, D.T., 165 Main St.
Walmsley & Walmsley, G. D. Walmsley
Ward, J. H.

PORT BURWELL, Elgin
Farlow & Little (also Woodstock)

PORT CARLING, Muskoka
Wyjad, D.J., Maple St. (also Bracebridge)

PORT COLBORNE, Niagara South
Cash, Reilly & Quinn, 518 King St., R.H.H. Reilly, J. W. Quinn
Davies & Ebert, 190 Elm St., B.P. Davies, Q.C., W.K. Ebert, Q.C.
Gibbs, F. N., 232 Catherine St.
Macdonald & Tuck, 196 West St., G.S. Macdonald, Q.C., J.D. Tuck, G.R. Alderson
Maloney & Maloney, 178 Clarence St., J.D. Maloney, T. Maloney

PORT DOVER, Haldimand-Norfolk
Gaunt & Driscoll, 110 St. Andrew St., Lee Gaunt
Stahl, O. W.
Winter, H. A., 517 Main St.

PORT ELGIN, Bruce
Bainbridge, J.S., 490 Goderich St.
Dollar & King, R. S. Dollar, J. D. King
Ryder, L.D.
Tomlinson, Gruetzner, 667 Goderich St., G. D. Gruetzner

PORT HOPE, Northumberland
Brooks, Harrison, Jones & Mann, 114 Walton St., G. Brooks, M. C. J. Harrison, C. M. Jones, J.D. Mann
Carr & Coleman, 50 Walton St., R.N. Carr, B.H. Coleman
Day & Wormington, 17 Ontario St., W.A. Day, D. Wormington
Good & Parker, 11 Mill St. n., A.R. Good, H.J. Parker
Kelly & O'Connor, 25 Walton St., G. C. Kelly, C. B. O'Connor

PORTLAND, Leeds
Willson & Co. (also Perth)

PORT PERRY, Durham
Bridgewater, R.D., 647 Scugog St.
Harris, Fletcher, etc., 230 Queen St., W.T. Harris (also Oshawa)
Kelly, Jermyn & Co., 217 Queen St., M.L. Fowler (also Oshawa)
Smith & Sutherland, 226 Queen St., G.L. Smith, R. Sutherland

POWASSAN, Parry Sound
Morley, R.J. (also South River)

PRESCOTT, Grenville
Adams, P.R., 513 King St. w.
Arthurs, R. K.
Beaumont & Laushway, Loring Bldg., H. Beaumont, Q.C., B.D. Laushway
Tobin, R. M.

RAINY RIVER, Rainy River
Wolder & McLennan, 211 4th St. (also Fort Frances)

RED LAKE, Kenora
Meadows, D.R., Discovery Rd. (R.S. Smart)

RENFREW, Renfrew
Chown & Chown, S. M. Chown, Q.C., W. S. E. Chown
Cooke, Dickinson, 191 Plaunt St. s., G.B. Cooke, Q.C., R.H. Dickinson

Dawe & Edmondstone, K. S. Dawe, Q.C., T. G. Edmondstone
Gallagher, L., Box 481
Garlough, B.B., Box 69
McNab, Stewart & Prince, Box 338, A.A. McNab, D.A. Stewart, T.J. Prince
Stewart, H. P., Q.C., Box 310
Wilson, N.J., 7 Lorne St. s.

RICHMOND HILL, York
Ashton, A., 14 Church St. s.
Chauhan, J., 10350 Yonge St.
Fienberg, S.P., 10225 Yonge St.
Hengen, P.C., 10239 Yonge St.
Herman, M.M., 9350 Yonge St. (G.E. Watkin)
Hobson, J.D., 10239 Yonge St.
Lawlor & LeClaire, 10265 Yonge St., J. J. Lawlor, J. LeClaire
Levine, G.E., 10620 Yonge St.
May, P.L., 14 Church St. s.
Plaxton & Mann, 10350 Yonge St., D.G. Plaxton, W.E.N. Mann
Raciunas, Z.T., 10350 Yonge St.
Rumack, M.K.I., 10225 Yonge St. (also Toronto)
Rumble, W.A., 10211 Yonge St.
Steinberg & Steinberg, 9350 Yonge St., R. Steinberg, D. Steinberg
Stong, Blackburn & Machon, 10350 Yonge St., A.J. Stong, R.H. Blackburn, B.E. Machon
Wechselmann, P.A., 10023 Yonge St.
Winemaker, Dorsey, Hartman & Todd, 10023 Yonge St., E.J. Winemaker, H.S. Dorsey, M.A. Hartman, N.A. Todd
Wintraub, M.E., 10225 Yonge St.

RIDGETOWN, Kent
Shaw & Shaw, 64 Main St. e., G. H. Shaw, D.B. Nicol
Stirling, Faussett, 43 Main St. w., F.E. Faussett
Watson & Walker, C. R. Watson, G.C. Walker

RIDGEWAY, Niagara South
Jones, Jamieson & Redekop, 288 Ridge St., T. O. Jones, Q.C., T. Jamieson, W. Redekop
Parker, G.T., 333 Ridge St. n. (A. Parker)

RIPLEY, Bruce
Crawford, Mill & Co. (also Wingham)

RODNEY, Elgin
Popovich, E. W. (also St. Thomas)
Stirling & Faussett (also Ridgetown)

ST. CATHARINES, Niagara North
Babij, O. D., 217 King St.
Bakker, Atamanuk, Taylor & Wenglowski, 60 James St., A. J. Bakker, Q.C., R. W. Atamanuk, C.R. Taylor, P.B. Wenglowski
Bench, Keogh, Rogers & Grass, 15 Church St. (Box 307, L2R 6V2), M.D. Kriluck, A.J. Crossingham, R. N. Brady, M.K. Douglas, M.R. McDonald, P. Janzen
Black, G.L., 170 Church St.
Charlebois, J. R., 38 James St.
Chorozy, E.E., 255 St. Paul St. w.
Chown, Cairns, 110 James St., M.A. Chown, Q.C., R. Cairns, Q.C., R. B. Edgar, Q.C., D. J. Taliano, E.M. Werner, R.J. Gillen, D.M. Kerr, D.R. Thomas. Counsel: S.K. Learie, Q.C.
Coy, Barch, 46 Ontario St., E.P. Coy, Q.C., R.H. Barch, R.D. Nicholson, A.W. Hawryluk, P.B. Robinson
Dohnberg, S.H., Q.C., 61 James St.
Doidge, Vicki, 18 Lake St.
Doliszny, B. W., Q.C., 69 Queen St.
Dube, M. J., 19 Wellington St.
Elliott & Vyse, 195 King St., P.J. Elliott, D.T. Vyse
Foley, S.F., 10 Court St.
Forster, Lewandowski & Cords, 82 Lake St., L.C. Forster, Q.C., R. Lewandowski, D.F. Cords
Forster, Morgan, Lafontaine, 15 King St., J.T. Morgan, Q.C., C.P. Lafontaine, R.A. Dilts
Freeman, Frayne & Morningstar & Reid, 9 Raymond St., R. H. Frayne, R.J. Morningstar, R.B. Reid
Fullerton & Fullerton, 43 Church St., C. W. Fullerton, Q.C., D. W. Fullerton, H.C. MacNaughton
Gordon, R.A., Q.C., 63 Ontario St.
Greenspoon, R., 259 St. Paul St.
Gullett & Banfield, 1 Church St., J.W.J. Gullett, B.A. Banfield
Harris, Barr, Hildebrand, Daniel & Wilson, 39 Queen St., H. E. Harris, Q.C., J. R. Barr, Q.C., J. Hildebrand, Q.C., H. J. Daniel, Q.C., R. A. Wilson, P.J. Lingard, K.I. Weaver, P.M. Barr, R.S. Franklin
Hawkins, B., 158 King St.
Heelis & Williams, 4 Garden Park, W.E. Heelis, R.S. Williams, H.A.P. Little
Hendin, G.S., 71 King St.
Hetherington, Kerwin & Henderson, 8 Church St., P. K. Kerwin, Q.C., L. R. Allen, D.M. Henderson
Hicks, J. A., Pen Centre
Huska, W.A., 12 King St.
Kray, C. M., 27 William St.
Kroeker, Kratzmann & Martens, 344 Lake St., L.H. Kroeker, P.H. Kratzmann, R.E. Martens
Lampard, Ellis & Walsh, 51 Queen St., Stuart Ellis, Q.C., Peter R. Walsh, K. Atkinson, Sherry M. Wiesner
Lancaster, Mix, Welch, Thorsteinson & Edwards, 154 James St., R.S. Welch, Q.C., H.E. Thorsteinson, Q.C., D.L. Edwards, J.B. Hanna, R.W.P. Welch
Maley, H.G., 11 Duke St.
Marotta & Brooks, 21 Duke St., F.M. Marotta, R.H. Brooks
Mascarin & Toppari, 15 King St., A.J. Mascarin, D.G. Toppari
McClelland, G.R., 158 King St.
McGarvie, A., 150A King St.
McKaig & McKaig, 12 King St., W.B. McKaig, L.M. McKaig
Monson, D., Q.C., #201, 15 King St.
Murphy, J.E., 361 Merritt St.
O'Neill, A.G., 17 Wellington St.
Partington, Abbey & Wormald, 72 Welland Ave., P. Partington, Q.C., R.J. Abbey, Q.C., B.S. Wormald
Pedwell, K.G., 2 Church St. (D.M. Hummell)
Pongray & Caplan, 13 Wellington St., T. Pongray, F. Caplan
Reed, W.R., 12 King St.
Reid, McNaughton, Martin, Zabek, Sachdeva, Liboiron, Pickering, McNaughton, 63 Ontario St., J. L. Reid, Q.C., J. G. McNaughton, Q.C., W.P. Martin, Q.C., J.J. Zabek, Om P. Sachdeva, A. Liboiron, D. Pickering, B. McNaughton, E.J. Kok
Roberts, G.S., 18 Lake St.
Robins, W.H., Q.C., 30 Duke St.
Rogers, H., 158 Ontario St.
Ross, R.K., Q.C., 18 South Dr.
Sayles, D.F., 154 King St.
Secord, D. B., Q.C., 15 James St.
Shantz, D.S., 259 St. Paul St.
Shapiro, I.D., 150 King St.
Shea, M.J., 10 Court St.
Smith, B.C., 5 St. Paul Cres.
Sullivan, Mahoney, Graves, Matheson & Muratori, 14 King St., L2R 6Z2, C.H. Mahoney, Q.C., E.W. Graves, Q.C., B.H. Matheson, V. F. Muratori, Q.C., P.B. Bedard, G. A. Wiggins, P. T. Banwell, P.M. Sheehan, J. Dallal, R.F. Miller, Anne Bain
Tessmer, A.E., 15 Church St.
Tolonen, A., 177 James St.
Trasewick, E. W., 1 Cherry St.
von Anrep & Repei, 172 James St., M. von Anrep, G. W. Repei
Walters, Maddalena & Cunnison, 205 King St., L.M. Walters, Theresa Maddalena, J.A. Cunnison
Wilson, J. E., 61 James St.
Wilson, Miller, Radford, 40 Queen St., R. A. Wilson, Q.C., F. L. Miller, Q.C., B. M. Radford

ST. GEORGE, Brant
Ballachey, Moore (also Brantford)

ST. ISIDORE DE PRESCOTT, Prescott
Seguin, Landriault & Co. (also Ottawa)

ST. MARYS, Perth
Grose, E.
Waghorn, Stephens & de Young, 21 Wellington St. n., D. H. Waghorn, R. G. Stephens, H. de Young
White & Galloway, 12a Queen St. e., R.J. White, W.J. Galloway

ST. THOMAS, Elgin
Arnold, R.W., 16 Pearl St.
Bowsher, Williams, 132 Centre St., K.S. Bowsher, J.R. Williams
Cameron & Cameron, 6 Hincks St., H. C. Cameron, Jr.
Carrie & O'Dea, 555 Talbot St., J.R. Carrie, M. P. O'Dea, D.Z. Belanger
Cyr, R. F., 35 William St.
Dewsnap, R.J., 19 Glanworth Ave.
Fordham, M.F., 300 Talbot St.
Gloin, Hall & Assoc., 12 Pearl St., P. J. Gloin, Q.C., R.O. Hall, M.L.D. Roberts, M.A. Shields, B.J. Reade
Graham & McKillop, 110 Centre St., D. C. McKillop
Gundry, J.A., 170 Centre St.
Gunn, Upsdell, Dick & Eitel, 108 Centre St., D. G. Gunn, Q.C., R. J. Upsdell, W.I. Dick, W.D. Eitel, Denise Korpan
Hennessey, M.J., 108 Centre St.
Herold, W. O., Q.C., 130 Centre St.
Johnson, W. W., 458 Talbot St. (A.I. Pellitier)
Kempster & Scott, Box 220, B.W. Kempster, B.D. Scott
Laing, R., 651 Talbot St.
McKay, McKay & VeDova, 344 Talbot St., W. S. McKay, Q.C., W. K. A. McKay, G. R. VeDova, J.A. Collins
McNabb, G. A., Q.C., 498 Talbot St.
Morrison, D.K., 142 Centre St.
Popovich, E. W., 24 Curtis St.
Por & McColl, 16 Pearl St., T.A. Por, D. McColl
Riddell, M.L., 488 Talbot St.
Sanders & Cline, 14 Southwick St., E.F.S. Sanders, Q.C., R.F. Cline, R.J. Foster
Smith, L.D.N., 142 Centre St.
Stafford, H.E., Q.C., 458 Talbot St.
Walsh, E.M., 22 Spackman Blvd.
Watterworth, D.C., 651 Talbot St.

SARNIA, Lambton
Beatty, D.W., 103 Mitton St. s.
Beaudet, Hornblower & Ruffilli, 193 Wellington St., P.R. Beaudet, G.M. Hornblower, J.A. Ruffilli
Brown, R., 278 n. Front St.
Carpeneto, J.J., 166 Ross St.
Curran, L. F., Q.C., 116 Front St. s.
Dally & Elliott, 500 Exmouth St., F.C. Dally, Q.C., D.J.C. Elliott
Dawson, W.M., Q.C., 805 n. Christina St. (Sandra Gabruss)
Donohue, J.M., 521 n. Christina St. (D. Henderson)
Donohue, R.V., 274 n. Christina St.
Eddy, A.L., Q.C., 425 n. Christina St.
Edward, F.J., 145 Wellington St.

Elliott, Porter & McFadyen, 1298 Exmouth St., D. A. Elliott, G. G. Porter, G.F. McFadyen, D.R. Canton
Farina, J.A., 300 n. Christina St.
Fleck, Sartor, Gray & Bruce, 1166 London Rd., C.E. Fleck, Q.C., A. Sartor, R.B. Gray, Ian Bruce
Galloway, R., 442 n. Christina St.
Gaviller, D., 265 Exmouth St.
Heath, W.P., 103 s. Mitton St.
Hockin, D.G., 345 n. Christina St.
Kirby & Robbins, 119 s. Christina St., D.J. Kirby, B.G. Robbins
Kovac, J. J., 219 Lochiel St.
Lang, W.B., 242 Indian Rd. s.
Lockhart, Wyrzykowski & Higgins, 272 n. Christina St., O. M. Lockhart, Q.C., R. F. Wyrzykowski, W.F. Higgins, Jr.
Lockyer, A.M., Box 1086
McEachran & Associates, 2 Ferry Dock Hill, J.D. George, Q.C., J. F. Foreman, Q.C., R.G. Murray, Q.C., W.N. Shipley, W.E. Tennyson, R.W. Bildfell, D'A. W. Bell, J.G. Kohlmeier
McFadden, R., 560 Exmouth St.
McGrath, B. A., 137 Wellington St.
McMillin, J.D., 103 s. Mitton St.
Melnychuk, P.E., 635 Cathcart St.
Merchant, Dawson & Donovan, 1323 Exmouth St., P.R. Merchant, G.T. Dawson, D.B. Donovan
Minifie, W.H., 345 n. Christina St.
Nanton, J., 141 Wellington St.
Phillips, R.F., 425 n. Christina St.
Robb, T.L., 300 n. Christina St.
Rowcliffe & Houston, 27 n. Front St., R.E. Rowcliffe, Q.C., Susan Houston
Ryan, L.E., 274 n. Christina St.
Stoner, K.G., 10 Derby Lane
Stuart, J.M., Q.C., 145 Wellington St.
Taylor, W.E., Q.C., 160 George St.
Trusler, J. E., Box 910
Weed, R., 103 s. Mitton St.
Westfall, P., 346½ n. Christina St.
Whitnall, R. A., 345 n. Christina St.
Wing, J. M., Q.C., 141 Wellington St.

SAULT STE MARIE, Algoma
Allemano, M.C., 224 Queen St. e.
Bondar, Aldona V., 482 McDonald Ave.
Bortolussi, Palombi, 168 East St., P.L. Bortolussi
Caputo, Sarlo, Irwin, Aiello, Vaillancourt & Whalen, 116 Spring St., F. R. Caputo, Q.C., R. Irwin, Q.C., F.S. Sarlo, A. V. Aiello, C. H. Vaillancourt, W.L. Whalen, M.S. O'Neill
Culina & Smyth, 183 Brock St., J.J. Culina, Q.C., K. Smyth
Darou, F.E., #202, 616 Queen St. e.
Fabbro, D.A.J., #201, 616 Queen St. e.
Falkins & Willson, 75 Elgin St., R.J. Falkins, C.B. Willson
Fratesi, J.M., 189 East St.
Gaetz & Stableforth, 446 Albert St. e., N.D. Gaetz, Q.C., N.L. Stableforth
Hamilton, Nixon & Marchand, 67 Elgin St., R.I. Hamilton, Q.C., J.D. Nixon, Q.C., C. Marchand, Q.C.
Harry, Alexander C., Q.C., 138 Brock St.
Holder & Pardu, 123 East St., G. D. Holder, Q.C., G.I. Pardu
Hornstein, E.R., 527 Queen St. e.
Hugill, I.D., 421 Bay St. (K.R. Davies)
Kelleher, Walker & Laidlaw, 421 Bay St., J. F. Kelleher, Q.C., J.C. Walker, D.B. Laidlaw, M. Hollingsworth, H.N. Macdonald
Kozak & Delorenzi, 224 Queen St. e., L.C. Kozak, Q.C., R.J. Delorenzi
Lang, H. M., Q.C., 157 East St. (F. Baxter, C. FitzGerald, B.R. Campbell)
Maich, G.P., 434 Albert St. e.
Mantello, F.N., 224 Queen St. e.
McCurry, P.M., 103 Old Hwy. 17 n.
Peres, R. C., Q.C., 212 Queen St. e.
Peterson & Peterson, 118 March St., L.D. Peterson, Patricia Peterson, E.D. McCooeye (also Bruce Mines)
Pilo & Ferranti, 464 Albert St. e., J.G. Pilo, Q.C., A. Ferranti
Priddle, Pawelek & Lawson, 604 Queen St. e., G.W. Priddle, Q.C., M.J. Pawelek, O.K. Lawson
Pritchard, B.F., #3, 118 Brock St.
Provenzano, Provenzano & McMillan, 422 Albert St. e., F. J. Provenzano, C. Provenzano, I.S. McMillan
Virene, A.T., 183 Brock St.
Wishart, Noble, 390 Bay St., C. B. Noble, Q.C., G. E. Nori, Q.C., Ross Reilly, Q.C., J. de Pencier Wright, J. A. Bisceglia, R.W. Paciocco, G.P. Acton

SEAFORTH, Huron
McConnell, Stewart & Devereaux, 64 Main St. s., D.I. Stewart, Q.C., K.A. Devereaux, R.E. Smith
Menzies, Ross (also Clinton)

SHELBURNE, Dufferin
Shepherd & Osyany, Box 760, G. H. Shepherd, A. Osyany
Timmerman, J.F., 305 Owen Sound St. (L.W. Haskell)

SIMCOE, Haldimand-Norfolk
Brimage, Tyrrell, Van Severen & Homeniuk, 21 Norfolk St. n., J.R. Tyrrell, Q.C., R. Van Severen, T. F. Homeniuk, R. K. Simpson, F.A.C. Madill, J.A. Boll, B.G. Mooney
Cline, Backus & Nightingale, 28 Colborne St. n., T.A. Cline, Q.C., J.A. Backus, R.J. Nightingale
Cobb & Jones, 92 Norfolk St. s., M. E. Cobb, K. M. Jones
Hogan, B.J., Colborne St.
Pohoresky, H.M., 191 Queensway West
Sheppard, Sheppard, MacIntosh & Harlow, 58 Peel St., J. D. Sheppard, W. G. Sheppard, D. G. MacIntosh, R.D. Harlow, A.G. Lados
Smelko & Marra, 46 Norfolk St. n., A.E. Smelko, M.J. Marra
Tisdale, Reid & Stead, 39 Kent St. n., F.M. Reid, Q.C., J.E. Tisdale, Q.C., W.B. Stead
Winter & Winter, 68 Peel St., A. W. Winter, Nora M. Winter

SMITHS FALLS, Lanark
Dixon & Johnston, 40 Main St. w., N.D. Dixon, M.M. Johnston
Kirkland, Murphy & Zielinski, 15 Russell St. e., J. S. Kirkland, W.A.J. Murphy, Q.C., L.J. Zielinski
McLean & Howard, 11 William St. w., H. McLean, P. Howard
Quigley, Ross & Cliffen, 30 Russell St. e., M.J. Quigley, M.V. Ross, M.R. Cliffen
Rubino & Chaplin, 69 Beckwith St. n., G.A. Rubino (also Perth)

SMITHVILLE, Niagara North
Davis, J. Nickle

SOUTHAMPTON, Bruce
Forsyth, R.E., Box 779

SOUTH PORCUPINE, Cochrane
Girones & Co. (also Timmins)

SOUTH RIVER, Parry Sound
Morley, R.J., Box 430 (R.J. Van der Wijst)

SPRINGFIELD, Elgin
Riddell, M.L. (also St. Thomas)

STAYNER, Simcoe
Bumstead & Demery, A.R. Bumstead, G.V. Demery
Robinson, G. L.
Service & Greenfield, 236 William St., D.G. Stehl

STIRLING, Hastings
Cameron & Ord (also Belleville)
Miller, J.C. (also Belleville)

STONEY CREEK, Hamilton-Wentworth
Coombs, Woolcott & Startek, 6 Lake Ave s., R. M. Coombs, Q.C., N. P. Woolcott, R. P. Startek
Fallis, G.D., Ste. A, 99 Hwy. 8
James, R.T., 21 King St. w. (J. Jakub)
Mazza, M.R., #202, 115 Hwy. 8 (also Hamilton)
O'Brien, F.A., 26 King St. e.
Orr, R.M., 40A Centennial Pkwy. n.
Peacock & Peglar, 286 Barton St. (also Hamilton)
Rogala, A.R., Box 296
Smith, K.I.M., 40A Centennial Pkwy. n.

STOUFFVILLE, York
Button, Armstrong & Ness, 6 Main St. e., J. M. Armstrong, Q.C., G. C. Ness, E. R. Button, J.P. Nevins
Goodbrand, K.C., 135 Main St. w.
Kimura, D.I., 155 Main St. w.
Parson, W., 120 Main St. w.

STRATFORD, Perth
Anderson, R.J., Albert St.
Byers & Kenny, 25 William St., W.E. Byers, Q.C., W.S. Kenny, A.P. Parlee
Dilks, A.P., Ontario St.
Fair, M., 22 Erie St.
Goodwin, A. G., 4 Ontario St.
Gregory, McDonald, Linley & Buechler, 168 Ontario St., W. P. Gregory, Q.C., H. D. McDonald, R. J. Linley, W.J. Buechler
Lusk, R., Brunswick St.
Mountain, Mitchell, Hill, Monteith & Hastings, 56 Albert St., R. E. Mountain, M. E. Mitchell, P. C. Hill, S. C. Monteith, E. W. Hastings, G. Burdett, G.E. Stewart
Neilson, Bell, Skinner & Rogerson, 1 Ontario St., J.C. Neilson, D.A. Bell, J.M. Skinner, Q.C., R.W. Rogerson
Stratton, Barenberg & Van Drunen, 20 Ontario St., J. H. Stratton, Q.C., D.J. Barenberg, H. Van Drunen
Sylvester, W. E., 15 Downie St.
Waller, L. R., 21 Albert St.

STRATHROY, Middlesex
Jones, M.E.H., Q.C., 39 Front St. w. (J.M. Gibbons)
Little, Gillespie & Co., 52 Frank St. (also London)
Ramkelawan, H.P., 79 Caradoc St. (also London)
Siskind, Cromarty, 81 Frank St. (also London)
Somerville, E. C., Q.C., 18 Front St. e.
Swinnen, F.A., 79 Caradoc St. (also London)
Waters & Sinker, 72 Frank St., R.G. Waters, G.E. Sinker

STROUD, Simcoe
Fenik, McLellan, Box 211, Z.J. Fenik, M.F. McLellan
Gibson & Adams, Box 100, G.W. Gibson, M. Adams
Graham, Wilson, etc., 198 Victoria St. (also Barrie)

STURGEON FALLS, Nipissing
Galipeau, R.C. (also North Bay)
Hurtubise & Legault, 194 Main St. (also North Bay)
Proulx, C., 49 Queen St.
Stewart, B., 229 Main St.

SUDBURY, Sudbury
Auvinen, H.A., 67 Elm St. e.
Bailey, S., 235 Elm St. w.
Beach, W.G., 194 Elm St. w.
Best & Desotti, #302, 210 Cedar St., D.P. Best, J. Desotti

Caldarelli & Bubba, 235 Elm St. w., E. J. Caldarelli, J. V. Bubba
Chmara, W., 4 Elgin St. s.
City Solicitor: F. Dean, 200 Brady St.
Conlon, C. P., 312 Pine St.
Conroy, Trebb, Scott, 69 Elm St. w., E. J. Conroy, R.V. Trebb, M.A. Scott
De Diana, Eloranta & Longstreet, 219 Pine St., A.J. De Diana, Q.C., T. A. Eloranta, J. M. Longstreet
Desmarais, Keenan, Beaudry, Cull, Mahaffy & Young, 4 Durham St. n., H. P. Beaudry, Q.C., R. B. M. Keenan, R. C. Desmarais, Q.C., P. J. Cull, Q.C., W. G. Mahaffy, J.M. Young, M.S. James, D.J. Bamberger. Counsel: J. N. Desmarais, Q.C.
Doig & Pitura, 100 Elm St. w., H.A. Doig, Q.C., J.P. Pitura
Dumont, McAndrew, 238 Elm St. w., B.A. Dumont, Q.C., G.E. McAndrew
Edmonstone & Lane, 210 Cedar St. (also Little Current)
Ferguson & MacMillan, 69 Elm St. w., W. A. Ferguson, C. N. R. MacMillan
Fortier & LeBlanc, 139 Pine St., B.F. Fortier, J.R. LeBlanc
Goodearle, Barth & Fouriezos, 144 Elm St. w., J.A. Goodearle, Q.C., F. Barth, C.T. Fouriezos, Q.C.
Guy & Assoc., 153 Spruce St., R. Guy, M.A. Hastings, P. Zylberberg, B. Gervais, Susan DeGruchy
Hawkins, J.E., 260 Cedar St.
Hinds, Sinclair & Holub, 18 Alder St. s., J. S. Hinds, Q.C., M. D. Sinclair, Q.C., D.B. Holub
Horeck, Beckett, Bobesich & Whitehead, McAndrew & Bobesich, 204 Pine St., R.N. Horeck, R.J. Beckett, G.J.Z. Bobesich, R.J. Beckett
Howe, B.N., 235 Elm St. w.
Hurtubise & Plaunt, 7 Cedar St., G. Hurtubise, D. Plaunt
Jakabfy, J. R., 767 Barrydowne Rd.
Lacroix, Forest & Del Frate, 182 Larch St., A. Lacroix, N. J. Forest, R.G.S. Del Frate, A. Arkilander, H.D. Bray
Mailloux & Gray, 67 Elm St. e., M.C. Mailloux, J.E.R. Gray
Mensour & Mensour, 69 Elm St. w., M.S. Mensour, P.E. Mensour
Miller, Maki, 176 Elm St. w., W.A. Inch, Q.C., D.H. Mulligan, T.E. Maki, M.P. O'-Hara, J.S. O'Neill, C.F. Reil, W.L. Neville. Counsel: K.E. Maki, Q.C.
Paquette, Campbell & Lalande, 218 LaSalle Blvd. (also Hanmer)
Parise & Hennessy, 218 City Centre, M. Hennessy, R. Parise, Kathleen Howes
Pharand, Kuyek, Lebel & McDonald, 229 Elm St. w., R. A. Pharand, D. P. Kuyek, J.-G. Lebel, S. McDonald, J.P. Marcuccio
Reid & Keast, 238 Elm St. w., J. R. Reid, Q.C., J. D. Keast
Rolston, Humphrey & Babij, 45 Elm St. e., B.T. Rolston, Q.C., R.A. Humphrey, W.M. Babij
Ryan, J., 238 Elm St. w.
Slater, S.A., 146A Elm St. w.
Sopha, E.W., Q.C., 144 Elm St. w.
Steinberg, Renzini & Fabbro, 4 Elgin St. s., M. Steinberg, Q.C., R.G. Renzini, R. L. Fabbro
Stoner & Fesyk, 88 Larch St., N.G. Stoner, B.J. Fesyk
Sullivan, Horton & Orendorff, 213 Pine St., R. Sullivan, S. D. Horton, T.L.W. Orendorff
Temelini & Zito, 146A Elm St. w., P.D.N. Temelini, J. Zito, M. Joanisse, L.T. Roslyn, C.A. Dawe
Thomas & Poulson, 159 Pine St., S.J. Thomas, B.J. Poulson, M.I. Twocock, M.B. Middleton
Toffoli, A., 250 Elm St. w.
Topp, R.C., 146A Elm St. w. (Lisa Stevens)
Valin, Innes & Carroll, 105 Durham St. s., L. J. Valin, Q.C., J. D. Innes, Q.C., T.C.K. Carroll
Vere & Gray, 208 Elm St. w., V. F. Vere, S. Elizabeth Gray, P.B. Bland
Weaver, Simmons, 69 Elm St. w., Mary P. Weaver, Q.C., J.C. Simmons, F.A. Donnelly, D.S. Cooper, B.L. Montgomery, D.J. Los, P.B. Keaney, M.E. Mottonen, L.H. Sola, J.P. Arenburg, J.W. Luczak
Wilkins, Di Salle, Poupore & Wilkins, 128 Larch St., W.M.D. Wilkins, Q.C., M.C. Di Salle, J.S. Poupore, A. D. Wilkins, L.A. Arseneau

SUNDERLAND, Durham
McQuarrie & Co., River St. (also Lindsay)

SUNDRIDGE, Parry Sound
Smith, G.D., Box 234

SUTTON, York
Fahey & Reeder, 100 High St., P.J.J. Fahey, P.A. Reeder

SUTTON WEST, York
Day, McDonald, etc., Box 507 (also Newmarket)
Nasello, S., Box 820 (P.C. Finley)

TARA, Bruce
Loucks & Garcia (also Chesley)

TECUMSEH, Essex
Baillargeon, M. D.
Gervais, G.M., 12213 Riverside Dr.
Levesque, G. P.

TEESWATER, Bruce
McTavish, A. H.

TEMAGAMI, Nipissing
Grant, R.F., Box 516

TERRACE BAY, Thunder Bay
Paget, E.W., Simcoe Plaza, Box 10
Stewart, Deborah, Box 220

TERRA COTTA, Peel
Smith, D.L.A., R.R. 1

THAMESVILLE, Kent
Suffield, L. O.

THEDFORD, Lambton
Walden, J. P., Box 121

THORNBURY, Grey
Carr, E. C., Q.C.
Metras, J.

THORNDALE, Middlesex
McBirnie, P.S., 160 King St.

THORNHILL, York
Adelson, M., #216, 2900 Steeles Ave. e.
Deane, J.F., 8779 Yonge St.
Drew, J.H., 7061 Yonge St.
Gray, Offer & Co., 39 Glen Cameron (also Toronto)
Hippler, J.B., 7039 Yonge St.
Iseman, Pettle, #216, 2900 Steeles Ave. e., L3T 41X, S. Iseman, S. Pettle
Jackson, A.L., 136 Willowbank St.
Johnston, D.B., 7290 Leslie St.
MacKillop, D.J., 7039 Yonge St.
Mandel & Hirsch, #218, 180 Steeles Ave. w., A.H. Mandel, J.R. Hirsch
McDougall, Janet, 68 Riverside Blvd.
McGill, E., 7039 Yonge St.
Merritt, R.G., 7061 Yonge St.
Mulholland, J.N., Q.C., 21 Uplands Ave.
Parker, S. P., Q.C., Box 29
Rubinoff, L., 300 John St.
Rumack, W., 8185 Yonge St.
Somjen & Suter, Markham Market Place (also Toronto)
Speciale, Anthony & Assoc., 72 Steeles Ave. w., I.R. Thornhill, B.I. Fisher
Steinberg & Waldman, 12 Centre St., S.H. Steinberg, H.L. Waldman
Swern & Fish, 8131 Yonge St., L. H. Swern, B. M. Fish, C.K. Beernink

THOROLD, Niagara South
McManamy & Jurmain, 21½ Front St. s., J.V. McManamy, P. Jurmain
Sherk, S.E., 63 Front St.
Young, McNamara, 18 Albert St. e., N.R.H. Young, Q.C., J.J. Simon, Jill Anthony, N.R.P. Young

THUNDER BAY, Thunder Bay
Atwood, Shaw & Labine, #108, 105 s. May St., J.W. Atwood, D.C. Shaw, G.L. Labine
Baig & Assoc., 34 n. Cumberland St., B.L. Baig, Dianne P. Baig
Black, B.I., Q.C., 401 Chapple Bldg.
Brown, R.A., 204 s. Syndicate Ave.
Buset, R.J., 1020 Victoria Ave.
Carrel, Pustina, Zelinski, Whent, Knutsen & Thrasher, Box 638, J. B. Carrel, Q.C., N. J. Pustina, Q.C., R. E. Zelinski, Q.C., K.A. Whent, K. H. Knutsen, D.J. Thrasher, J.N.M. Jamieson, S. Di Gregorio
Cheadle, Bryan, 510 Chapple Bldg. (Box 429, P7C 4V9), D. S. Cheadle, Q.C., W. E. Bryan, W.G. Shanks
Christie, Kislock, 581 Red River Rd., D.J. Christie, D.W. Kislock, G.B. Fillmore
Colborne, D.R., 195 Park St.
Filipovic & Young, 8A n. Cumberland, J.P. Filipovic, D.S. Young, P. Hurrell
Gilbart, T.L., 278 Bay St.
Gordon, Carter & Johnson, #204, 215 Red River Rd., P. A. Gordon, M. B. Carter, D.E. Johnson
Illingworth, R.I., 104 n. Syndicate Ave. (J.G. Illingworth)
Kostyshyn, G.W., 415 e. Victoria Ave.
Kovanchak, Ferris & Ross, 79 n. Court St., S.G. Kovanchak, A.D. Ferris, P.D. Ross, M.L. Bode
Lannon & Climenhage, 1023 Victoria Ave. e., P.N. Lannon, D.W. Climenhage, J.H. Mathieson
Lauder, R.E., 278 Bay St.
Lees, D.J., 1820 Victoria Ave.
Lester, R.B., 34 n. Cumberland St.
Lucas, P.G., 47 n. Cumberland St.
Lukinuk, Halabisky & McKenzie, 516 Victoria Ave. e., S.W. Lukinuk, R.A. Halabisky, I. McKenzie
Macgillivray, Poirier, 217 Van Norman St., R.D. Macgillivray, R.J. Poirier
Martin & Lenardon Assoc., 28 n. Cumberland St., D.A. Martin, D.J. Lenardon, R.A. Young, L.S.S. Scrimshaw, Julaine Palmer
McCartney, Judge, Murray, 1103 Victoria Ave., J. F. McCartney, R. B. Judge, J.L. Murray
McKitrick, Erickson, Jones & Shanks, 17A s. Cumberland St., A. G. McKitrick, J. W. Erickson, A. G. Jones, J.D. Shanks, G.V. Hutchinson, D.G. Nattress
McNeill, S.N.F., #511, 34 n. Cumberland St.
Murray, R.W., 101 n. Syndicate Ave.
O'Leary, H.G., 4 s. Court St.
Petrone, Hatherly, Hornak & Associates, 22 n. Cumberland St., A. A. Petrone, Q.C., J. W. Hatherly, Q.C., J. H. Hornak, J.A. Johnston
Pugsley, S. D., 103 Cuthbertson Block
Reitberger, C.M., 34 n. Cumberland St.
Seaman, Kajander, Blanchard & Conway, 76 n. Algoma St., A. A. Kajander, Q.C., H. G. Blanchard, Q.C., M.D. Conway, S.K. Paivalainen
Shaffer, Jobbitt & Stead, 105 s. May St.,

B. Shaffer, Q.C., K. J. F. Jobbitt, R.E. Stead
Somerleigh, Erickson, 500A River St., R.E. Somerleigh, K.E. Erickson
Stasiv, Mitton & Smith, 305 Chapple Bldg. (Box 173, P7C 4V8), T.C. Mitton, G.P. Smith. Counsel: W.B. Stasiv, Q.C.
Stewart, K.A., Q.C., 105 n. May St. (A.D. Stewart)
Tilson, K.R., 4A Court St.
Watkinson, T.G., 134 Frederica St. w.
Weiler, Maloney, Nelson, 2nd floor, 101 n. Syndicate Ave., G.B. Weiler, Q.C., V. L. Maloney, Q.C., D. F. Nelson, Q.C., E. W. Stach, D. J. Livesey, F. J. W. Bickford, P.T. Deighton, B.P. Jasiura, G.L. Firman, J.A. Cyr
Wieckowski, W.C., #702, 34 n. Cumberland St.
Welch & Mullen, 316 n. May St., G.J. Welch, R. Mullen, R.F. Karlstedt
Young, F. H., 230 Lower Van Norman St.
Young, J.D., 1204A Roland St.
Young, P.G.F., 244 Camelot St., G.H. Young, Q.C., P.G.F. Young, W.H. McIlwain
Zaitzeff, Cancade, Arnone, Larson, Desimone & Di Guiseppe, 115 n. May St., R.E.E. Larson, G.P.P. Cancade, W. Desimone, G.L. Arnone, S.A. Zaitzeff, Marilyn Zaitzeff, D. Di Guiseppe

TILBURY, Kent
Jutras, R.M., 10 Fort St.
Odette, T. C., Jr., Q.C., 13 Queen St. n. (also Leamington)
Taylor & Delrue, 39 Queen St. n., J.C. Taylor, G. Delrue

TILLSONBURG, Oxford
Brown & Brown, 30 Brock St. e., G.C. Brown, Q.C., C. Brown
Gibson, Linton, Toth & Campbell, 36 Broadway, D.M. Gibson, Q.C., I. R. Linton, Q.C., B. Toth, S.K. Campbell
Groom & Mansell, 1C Library Lane, R.G. Groom, Q.C., G.J. Mansell
Innanen, L.J., 27 Brock St. w.
Mandryk & Heeney, 65 Bidwell St., O. Mandryk, Q.C., T.A. Heeney
Morris, Holmes, Jenkins, 19 Ridout St. e., T. D. Morris, J. Holmes, G. D. L. Jenkins
Odorjan, D., 35 Harvey St.
Tillson & Tillson, 17 Brock St. w., E.V. Tillson, J.G. Battin
Weir, W.J., Q.C., 25 Harvey St.

TIMMINS, Cochrane
Cousineau, Alexander, 47 Pine St. s., J.K. Alexander, J.A. Cousineau
Evans, Bragagnolo, Sullivan & Carlesso, 131, 101 Mall, Pine St. n., G. C. Evans, Q.C., R. C. Bragagnolo, Q.C., G. J. Sullivan, Q.C., S.A. Carlesso, J.W. Clarke, R.A. Minard
Girones & Ciccone, 12 Cedar St. s., L.J.A. Girones, A. S. Ciccone, M. Clements
Moscoe & Brooks, 83 Pine St. s., S. Brooks, J. Rothel, A.E. Montgomery
Pope & Bracken, 121, 38 Pine St. n., A.W. Pope, J.K. Bracken
Racicot, Bonney, Grandbois, Aube, 15 Balsam St. s., G.L. Racicot, G.G. Bonney, D.A. Grandbois, J.F. Aube, Louise Gauthier
Riopelle, Evans, Chornyj & Carr, 137 Pine St. s., R.A. Riopelle, G.B. Chornyj, J.D. Evans, R.E.W. Carr
Ristimaki, A., 273 Third Ave.
Rowe, R., 21 Cedar St. n.
Thalheimer, P. F., 273 Third Ave.

TORONTO, York
Aaron & Aaron, 372 Bay St., Irving Aaron, Q.C., Robert Aaron, Deborah Aaron
Abbass, C. J., 347 Bay St., M5H 2R7
Abbott, W.T., 85 Richmond St. w., #506, M5H 2C9
Abraham, Duggan, Hoppe, Niman, Stott, #512, 214 King St. w., M5H 1K4, S.R. Abraham, S.C. Duggan, C.C. Hoppe, H. Niman, P.J. Stott, M. Faubert
Ackerman & Silver, 620 Wilson Ave. (Downsview, M3K 1Z3), C. S. Ackerman, N. Silver
Adair, G.D.E., Box 83, First Canadian Place
Adams, W. J., 2773 Lakeshore Blvd. w., M8V 1H4
Addy & Addy, 85 Richmond St. w., J.P.G. Addy
Adelman, Miss B., 98 Roberta Dr.
Adelson, M., 101 Richmond St. w.
Adler, C., Q.C., 700 Bay St., M5G 1Z6
Adler, Leo, 2404, One Dundas St. w.
Ahee, A.J., #702, 121 Richmond St. w.
Aiken & Boyko, 812 Wilson Ave. (Downsview), M.H. Aiken, N.L. Boyko
Aiken, Capp, #1000, 2 St. Clair Ave. e., M4T 2T5, I. J. Aiken, Q.C., H. Capp, Q.C., W. L. Mandel, Q.C., E.M. Futerman, Q.C., W. A. Lipson, A. Altschuler, N.L. Winton, J. M. Futerman, M.R. Kestenberg, A. Siegal, D.M. Cohn, L.M. Lipkus
Aird & Berlis, 145 King St. w., M5H 2J3, D.A. Berlis, Q.C., J.D.S. Bohme, Q.C., C.T. Grant, Q.C., J.M. Lewis, G.D. Worley, Q.C., R.S. Paddon, Q.C., J.P. Terry, M.S. Bistrisky, H.R. Berry, Q.C., R.N. Granger, Q.C., J.D. Sharples, W.S. Vaughan, J.P. Dawson, R.D. Dalgarno, J.G. Matthews, G.D.F. Skerrett, T.E.R. Butcher, J.J. Pizale, P.Y. Atkinson, A.J. Milstein, E. Smith, W.G. Vanderburgh, A. Bell, G.W. Dawson, J.A. Barnes, R.J. Howe, D.L. West, P.V. McCallen, E.J. Bennett, G.A. Bragg, R.L. Hines, L.J. Morgan, F.D. Cass, L.F. Cornett, Peter McCarter, Barbara Uhlir, B.G. Wright, J.A. Connidis, K.J. Harild, M.D. Smith. Counsel: J. G. Edison, Q.C.
Akai, M.V.B., #204, 3459 Sheppard Ave. e. (Scarboro)
Alexandrowicz, G. W., 618A Queen St. w.
Alfred, E. J. E., Toronto Dominion Centre, Box 326
Allan & Clark, #1104, 330 Bay St., G. F. Allan, G.B. Clark
Allen & Fiszauf, #200, 425 University Ave., J.E. Allen, A. Fiszauf
Alpert, H.J., #900, 1 St. Clair Ave. e.
Altman, S.L., #2404, 1 Dundas S.t. w., M5G 1Z3
Altwerger, Lapowich, 347 Bay St., #400, M5H 2R7, S. Altwerger, D.H. Lapowich, A.J. Esterbauer
Ambrozic, A., 861 College St.
Amourgis & Amourgis, 65 Queen St. w., C. Amourgis, Julie Amourgis
Amsterdam & Peroff, 122 Patrick St., R.R. Amsterdam, D.A. Peroff, G. Brown
Anders, K., 100 Richmond St. w.
Anderson, R.M., #1108, 85 Richmond St. w.
Anderson, Rosalind, 443 Hillsdale Ave. e., M4S 1V1
Anderson, Sinclair, Walters & Associates, 3416 Dundas St. w., M6S 2S1, E. J. Walters, Q.C., S.E. McClennan, R.F.D. Swaine
Andreansky, R., 38 Baycrest Ave.
Angus, Peace & Marshall, 80 Richmond St. w., I.W.M. Angus, J.W. Peace, Lauren Marshall, L.J. Burns. Counsel: J.A.W. Whiteacre, Q.C.
Anisio, R.A., #400, 67 Richmond St. w.
Anklewicz, L., 542 Mount Pleasant Rd.
Antflyck, M.I., 738 Spadina Ave.
Antonette, S.J., 455 Spadina Ave., M5S 2G8
Apelbaum, S.J., 4599 Kingston Rd. (Scarboro)
Appell, Lenkinski, #802, 27 Queen St. e., Cheryl Appell, Esther Lenkinski
Applebaum, J., 1006B Eglinton Ave. w.
Aprile, F. A., 2563 Danforth Ave., M4C 1L4
Arbus, S. J., 615A Bloor St. w.
Archibald, C. E., 817 Bloor St. w.
Argiris, G.L., 572 Danforth Ave.
Armstrong, B.J., 5100 Dundas St. w. (Islington)
Armstrong, Kemp, Young, Burrows & Grant, 1606, 141 Adelaide St. w. (M5H 1V7), R.G. Burrows, Q.C., G.V. Armstrong, Q.C., D.R. Grant, Q.C., J.F. MacCarthy, R.D. Owen. Counsel: K.W. Kernaghan, Q.C.
Armstrong, Schiralli & Cleary, #420, 181 University Ave., M. Armstrong, Q.C., R.A. Schiralli, J.A. Cleary, A.S. Raphael, Anne McGarrigle
Arn, D.W., 380 Bathurst St.
Aronoff, M.S., 15 Gervaise Dr. (Don Mills)
Ash & Fenster, 55 Eglinton Ave. e., #704, M4P 1G8, Wm. Ash, A. Fenster
Ashby & Rapaport, #206, 660 Eglinton Ave. e., P.F.C. Ashby, R.S. Rapaport
Atkinson, J.R., 45 Richmond St. w.
Atlin, Goldenberg, Cass, Cohen, Lissaman & Armel, #2200, 439 University Ave. (M5G 1Y8), Gordon Atlin, Q.C., I. Cass, Q.C., J. C. Goldenberg, Q.C., Charles B. Cohen, Q.C., D.H. Lissaman, Q.C., Murray Armel, Q.C., S. Stieber, R.C. Belsito, G. Warner, Linda Pittaway, J. Agostino, Jo Ann Kurtz, H. Perlis, M. Engelberg, S.M. Cass. Assoc.: D.W. Eryou
Atlin, G., 65 Queen St. w.
Au, J., #1008, 180 Dundas St. w.
Ault & Ault, 19 Richmond St. w., M5H 1Y9, W. A. Ault
Austin, F., #32, 485 Duplex Ave.
Austin, J.W., #404, 19 Richmond St. w.
AvRuskin, S.J., 101 Charles St. e.
Axton & Dexter, #802, 111 Richmond St. w. (M5H 2G4), N.S. Axton, R. Dexter, Caron E. Wishart. Counsel: H. Cravit, Q.C.
Aylesworth, Thompson, Royal Bank Plaza, Box 15, J. C. Denison, Q.C., J.W.V. Craig, Q.C., J.D. Simmons, Q.C., S.J. Wallace, D.R. Hamilton, J.M. O'Connor, P.R. Welsh, M.J. Neirinck., D.A. Smith. Counsel: Sir Allen Aylesworth, Q.C., Hon. J.B. Aylesworth, Q.C.
Baerg, J.W., #1001, 110 Yonge St.
Bain, H.R.R., #810, 40 University Ave.
Bain, W.N., #1601, 65 Queen St. w.
Baker & Baker, #900, 500 University Ave., M5G 1V7, Anne Baker, D.S. Baker
Baker, Blakely, Freeman & Reim, #514, 111 Richmond St. w., R.H. Baker, R.W. Blakely, J.M. Freeman, R.I. Reim
Baker & Cuttler, 794 Bathurst St., M.A. Baker, H.K. Cuttler
Baker, G.R., 180 Dundas St. w.
Baker & Parker, 1106, 20 Eglinton Ave. w., F.A.A. Baker, S.A. Parker
Balder, P.O., #1408, 330 Bay St., M5H 2S8
Baldwin & Baldock, 598 St. Clair Ave. w., Elizabeth Baldwin, J.C. Baldock
Banack, L.A., #2305, 180 Dundas St. w.
Band, P.E., Q.C., 668 Briar Hill Ave.
Banik & Breault, 951 Queen St. e., R.J. Banik, D.A. Breault
Banks & Chapnik, #407, 11 Yorkville Ave., M4W 1L2, L.A. Banks, S. Chapnik
Bardyn, Zalucky & Tyssiak, #303, 330 Bay St., I.W. Bardyn, L.E. Zalucky, A.V. Tyssiak
Barkin & Epstein, 374 Bloor St. w., Kiva Barkin, A. Epstein

Barlow, Peck & O'Donoghue, 365 Bay St., M5H 2V1, H.R. Barlow, I.L.B. Peck, J.J. O'Donoghue, A. Baldanza, I. Kleiner
Barrett, Anne, 111 Elizabeth St.
Barron, H., 2986 Danforth Ave.
Barrs, J.R., 372 Bay St.
Basman & Dougherty, #200, 12 Sheppard St., M5H 3A1, M. Basman, R.G. Dougherty, I. Basman, R.H. Saunders, S.B. Eisen, J.W. Rose
Bassel, Sullivan & Leake, Box 351, Commerce Court West (M5L 1H4), J.P. Bassel, Q.C., G.A.R. Leake, Q.C., M.E. Sullivan, Q.C., A. Bennett, Q.C., R.S. Romanick, Q.C., J.M. Davison, N.A. Best, G. E. Burson, Q.C., R.D. Finlayson, R. D. Wilson, R.M. Zarnett, L.A. Pick, F.A. O'Neill, M.L. McGowan, R.B. Thibodeau, R.L. Lee
Bassel & Bassel, #804, 111 Richmond St. w., W.P. Bassel, Q.C., Angeline Bassel
Basserman, R.J., #1405, 480 University Ave.
Bastedo, Cooper, Kluwak & Shostack, 508, 330 University Ave. (M5G 1S1), T.G. Bastedo, G.W.M. Cooper, G.R. Kluwak, B.F. Shostack, E.L. McGivney, B.E.T. Derby, J.P. Gauthier, D.A.R. Sheldon, D.B. Prentice, R.P. Edmonds, G.C. Thomas
Batcher & Associates, 2452 Dufferin St., M6E 3T1, T. Batcher. Counsel: A. Lang
Baum, B., #322, 2788 Bathurst St.
Bazos, A.C., 25 St. Mary St.
Beaman, Fitchett & Owen, #200, 171 Dundas St. w., A.S. Beaman, G.I. Owen
Beard, Winter, Gordon, 200 University Ave., M5H 2K4, D.L.D. Beard, Q.C., R.I.R. Winter, M. Gordon, J.A.B. Macdonald, D.K. Robinson, Q.C., K.J. Bialkowski, M. Gula, J.A. Olah, J.P. Wearing, J.C.F. Hunt, T.A. Stefanik, Leilah Edroos, P.K. Guselle, T.C. Wilson. Counsel: E.A. Sabol, Q.C.
Beatty, Wood, 101 Richmond St. w., E.S. Beatty, F.H. Wood, F.I. Liebeck
Beaudoin & Pepper, #800, 439 University Ave., M5G 1Y8, Elliott R. Pepper, Q.C., Mary E. Atkinson, J.M. Straitman
Beck, F.A., Q.C., 330 University Ave., M5G 1S1
Beckett, E., 108 Willow Ave.
Belisle, A.J., 260 Scarlett Rd.
Bell, D.C., Box 361, First Canadian Place
Bell, M.W., #410, 101 Richmond St. w.
Bell, Temple, 481 University Ave., J.D. Bell, Q.C., J.W. Temple, V.I. Rogers, R.C. Lee, Q.C., T. Laar, M. R. Fernandes, R. A. Calder, P. D. Archibald, C.C.R. Godden, D. G. Cormack, D.A. Tompkins, S.R. Bell, M.G. Lichty, R.A. Wood, P.H. Lamprey
Bellissimo, S., #503, 121 Richmond St. w.
Belman, Toby, #1104, 20 Queen St. w.
Belyea, K.W., Q.C., #701, 20 Victoria St., M5C 1Y1
Ben & Petryshyn, 1134 Dundas St. w., M6J 1X2, V.W. Petryshyn. Counsel: M.J. Haesler, Q.C.
Benedetto, S.M., Q.C., 55 Eglinton Ave. e., M4P 1G8
Benson, E.J., #902, 35 Ormskirk Ave.
Benson, M., Q.C., 100 Adelaide St. w.
Benson, McMurtry, Percival & Brown, 101 Richmond St. w., #2210, M5H 1W3, P.W. Benson, Q.C., B.A. Percival, Q.C., B.D. Brown, Q.C., J.J. Walsh, J.E. Doyle, H. Klein, P.B. McCabe
Berens, Zimmerman, #701, 2161 Yonge St., M4S 3A6, M.L. Berens, G. Zimmerman, M. Sosnovitch
Bergart, P., 120 Eglinton Ave. e., M4P 1B8
Bergel, H., 1000 Finch Ave. w. (Downsview, M3J 2V5) (A.H. Zweig)
Bergstein, N.N., 113 Davenport Rd.
Berlin, E., #505, 335 Bay St.
Berman, Louise, #801, 121 Richmond St. w.
Bernhard, H.D., Q.C., & Assoc., 330 Bay St., M5H 2S8, H. Dieter-Bernhard, Q.C., J. Holzman
Berman & Wharton, #26, 165 Spadina Ave., H.M. Berman, M.E.J. Wharton
Bernholtz, J.I., 28 Admiral Rd.
Besant & Murray, 165 Carlton St., D.C. Besant, R.K. Murray
Best & Gray, #1202, 390 Bay St., R.A. Best, Q.C., J.F.H. Gray, Q.C., H. Tevel, B.M. Leck
Betel, M., 89 Chestnut St.
Biback, W.W., #703, 80 Richmond St. w.
Bickerton, A.J., 65 Queen St. w.
Bielski, C.M.B., Q.C., 226 Roncesvalles Ave.
Bigelow, Hendy, Shirer & Uukkivi, 789 Don Mills Rd. (Don Mills, M3C 1T5), Robt. Bigelow, Q.C., R.I. Hendy, Q.C., J.W. Shirer, Q.C., I. Uukkivi, A. Olvet, U. Suits
Biggar, G., 67 Yonge St.
Biggs, S.C., Q.C., #711, 330 University Ave.
Biles & Wratten, #502, 10 King St. e., L.E. Wratten, Q.C., C.A. Murray
Birenbaum, Steinberg, 2 Bloor St. w., #1900, M4W 3J9, J.N. Bienbaum, H. Steinberg, K. Lee-Whiting, D.K. Langer, J.A. Howlett, J.A. Wahl. Counsel: N. Borins, Q.C.
Birks, Langdon & Elliott, 101 Richmond St. w., M5H 1T1, H.D. Langdon, Q.C., R.J. Elliott, D.H. Simpson
Biro, S., 394 Bloor St. w., M5S 1X4
Bjarnason & Copeland, #1701, 110 Yonge St., M5C 2R5, S.A. Bjarnason, Q.C., G.W. Copeland, Q.C.
Black & Cook, 2 Bloor St. w., J. Black, J. G. Cook
Black, H.A., Q.C., #504, 85 Richmond St. w.
Black, J.A., #1800, 65 Queen St. w.
Black, Osborne, McMahon, #901, 111 Richmond St. w. (M5H 2J4), D. B. Black, Q.C., S.V. McMahon, D.J. Thompson, M.A. Osborne
Black, S., 3500 Dufferin St.
Black, Worrall & Price, 372 Bay St., M5H 2W9, J.J. Black, G.C. Price, Q.C.
Blackwell, Law, Spratt, Armstrong & Grass, 110 Yonge St., M5C 1V2, W.H. Grass, Q.C., R.W. Spratt, Q.C., W.J. Stewart, R.J. Armstrong, Robert Law, Q.C., C.R. Spencer, Q.C., Glorianne F. Stromberg, D.R. Arthurs, Marni Whitaker, J.S. McKeown, C.D. Stewart, W.B. Clark, M.T. Garland. Counsel: M. P. Hyndman, O.C., Q.C.
Blaier & Albert, #400, 347 Bay St., H. Blaier, S. Albert
Blake, Cassels & Graydon, Commerce Court West, Box 25 (M5L 1A9), P.S. Osler, Q.C., D.M. Grimshaw, Q.C., N.M. Simpson, Q.C., A.J. MacIntosh, Q.C., J.M. Hodgson, Q.C., W.O.C. Miller, Q.C., B.B. Lockwood, Q.C., J.F. Howard, Q.C., R.W. Stevens, Q.C., W.E. Brown, Q.C., A.L. Davies, Q.C., P.M. Harvie, Q.C., S. Heighington, Q.C., G.W. Hately, Q.C., R.C. Brown, J.B. Tinker, Q.C., L.J. Goffart, Q.C., J.W. Brown, Q.C., J.R. Weir, J.F. Heal, B.H. Kellock, Q.C., J.D. Brownlie, J.W. Garrow, Q.C., E.L. Donegan, D.M. O'Rorke, W.M.H. Grover, Q.C., J.S. Hausman, D.W. Milne, R.A. Donaldson, J.T. Evans, G.R.W. Gale, G.W. Borden, D.J. McRae, B.C. Westlake, R.A. Thompson, D.J.M. Brown, D.J. Kee, G.F.G. Pooley, T.N. Unwin, R.D. Weiler, J.P. Dube, J.W. Mik, J.M. Stewart, R.A. Bondy, E.S. Langdon, E.B. Leonard, R.E.H. Macdonald, J.M. Solursh, J.A. Doyle, M. Fingerhut, J.R. Collins, I.M. Douglas, J.A. Hodgson, P.J. Lewarne, E.L. McNaughton, J. Shafer, P.W. Gilchrist, R.S. Bruser, J.D. DeSipio, J.D.A. Jackson, G.F. Leslie, K.N. Feldman, H.J. Kesten, R.C. McIvor, D.C. Ross, C.S. Goldman, J.H. Phillips, D.L. Rogers, D.J. Sharpless, J.W. Teolis, M.J. Bevan, D.E. Burt, J.M. Fraser, G.M. Frenette, J.S. Hilton, B.G. McGee, R.J. McGillis, J.D. Murphy, P.K. Tamaki, D. Wahl, R.K. Watson, J.R. Christie, P.C. Kalbfleisch, J.K. McDonald, M.L. Paterson, P.A. Love, P.H. Ortved, E.W. Purdy, L.D. Robinson, B. MacL. Rogers, E.R. Weinheimer, D.G. Benson, E.R. Elvidge, B.W. Holmes, R.S. Michna, A.J. Stewart, A.M. Heisey, D.A. Intrator, C.C. Taylor, S.M. Grundy, W.J. Millar, P.G. Neilson, J. Richler, R.B. Smith, B.A. Tough, G.D. Lilley, F.L. Buckland, P.C. Finnerty, D.P. Hughes, J. Nicol, A.D. Brands, A.F. Brown, V.P. Lalonde, P.L. Loughlan, J.L. Ronson, D.H. Rowat, F.M. Rowe. Counsel: B. B. Osler, Q.C., W.E.P. DeRoche, Q.C., D. G. Guest, Q.C., W.H.C. Boyd, Q.C., R.A. Kingston, Q.C., T.A. King, Q.C.
Blake, Edith M., 85 Ellesmere Rd. (Scarboro, M1R 4B8)
Blaney, Pasternak, Smela & Watson, #1400, 20 Queen St. w., J.W. Blaney, Q.C., I.W. Pasternak, Q.C., J.A. Brulé, Q.C., R.H. Smela, Q.C., R.J. Watson, Q.C., S.H. Aarons, Q.C., J.H. Clarke, Q.C., J.S. Ublansky, E.J. Freyseng, Q.C., A.A. Mesbur, R.L.K. Smith, R. Cohen, J. Defalco, A.B. Tulk, D.M. Jamieson, H.J. Kirsh, D.G. Lash, R.J. Potts, B.A. Schnurr, H.T. McGovern, L.A. Roine, E.K. Rowan-Legg, J.R. Dingle, J.A. Emond, J.L. Freelan, R.S.W. Winsor, D. Meehan, W.O. Murphy, H.B. Radomski, E. Sachs, G.R. Banfai, V.R. Upans, S.A. Ritchie, J.C. Shepherd, R.J. Fujarczuk, K.A. Milne, G. Steinhart. Counsel: Wm. R. McMurtry, Q.C.; L.D. Cadsby, Q.C.
Blankstein, M.E., 20 Eglinton Ave. w.
Bliss, Kirsh, 133 Richmond St. w., H.J. Bliss, Q.C., S.E. Kirsh, F.J. Burns, S.I.J. Salcman, A. Herschorn
Bloomenfeld, J.L., 330 Bay St.
Blooval, M.H., #2200, 390 Bay St.
Bocknek, H., 460 College St.
Bodnaruk & Capone, 720 Spadina Ave., B.H.Y. Bodnaruk, P. Capone
Bogart, Campbell, Robertson, Box 250, Commerce Court n., J.D. Bogart, Q.C., B.M. Campbell, G.A. Robertson, T.A. Bogart, Patricia Hennessy
Bolton & Webster, #12A2, 2 Clair Ave. w., J.M. Bolton, Q.C., J.D. Webster, Q.C.
Bombier, R. E., 1366 Dundas St. w., M6J 1Y2
Bomza, G.H., 500 University Ave.
Bonder & Bouroukis, #304, 1110 Finch Ave. w. (Downsview), P.R. Bonder, P. Bouroukis
Book, I.E., 1436 Kingston Rd. (Scarboro)
Bookman & Assoc., #204, 45 Richmond St. w., M5H 1Z2, S.M. Bookman, J.M. Clarke, J.R. Atkinson, E.F. Gutstein. Counsel: R. Wise
Boraks, R., 98 Dupont St. (V. Boraks)
Borden & Elliot, 250 University Ave. (M5H 3E9), B.V. Elliot, Q.C., J.T. Johnson, Q.C., H.R. MacEwen, Q.C., W.L.N. Somerville, Q.C., R.C. Meech, Q.C., W.S. Robertson, Q.C., D.W. Falconer, Q.C., G.W. Chapin, B. Forman, Q.C., R.A.F. Sutherland, Q.C., D.A.L. Britnell,

Q.C., G. Dunnet, Q.C., I. A. McEwan, Q.C., K. W. Scott, Q.C., D. M. Harley, Q.C., J.D. Holding, Q.C., G. Manning, Q.C., J. A. Coates, W. R. Murray, Q.C., N. J. Munn, G. Cihra, Q.C., R. A. Stradiotto, Q.C., J.D. Hylton, J. D. Brooks, J. H. McC. McNair, J. P. Borden, Q.C., J. Dimoff, Q.C., R. L. Woods, S. B. Scott, T. A. Sweeney, D. L. Macdonald, L. A. Wright, J.F.T. Warren, H.J.B.A. Dickie, G. E. Thompson, A.W. Oughtred, B. Lisowski, W.P. McCarten, P. R. Braund, E. A. Ayers, W. T. Pashby, D. S. Ferguson, G.E. Petch, L.H. Saltman, W.J. McNeill, J.G. Chipman, B.C. Keith, T.P. Bates, R.P. Hutchison, J.F. Mann, R.S. Echlin, W.D.T. Carter, M.J. Dermer, R.W. Kitchen, E.M. Krasa, S.F. Waque, M.J. Lang, P.G. Findlay, B.H. Bresner, E.N. Schneider, J.D. Dean, G.B. Morawetz, R.B. Bell, Marguerite Mooney, M.K. McKelvey, W.D.R. Beamish, R.V. Wright, T.G. Andrews, S.C. Borlak, Anne Corbett, Mary M. Fox, B.D. Mulroney, A.L.J. Page, Larissa Tkachenko, S. Weir. Counsel: E.R.E. Carter, Q.C., C.A. Morawetz, Q.C., Dennis O'Connor, Q.C.; Patent Counsel: G.J.M. Shearn

Borden, H., Q.C., Commerce Court West, Box 125, M5L 1E2

Borenstein & Shnier, #304, 3335 Yonge St., M4N 2M1, H.J. Borenstein, R.M. Shnier

Borins & Borins, 1512 Danforth Ave., S.D. Borins, Q.C., A.E. Borins

Borman, A., 330 Bay St.

Borski, N., 201, 2256B Bloor St. w.

Botiuk, Y.R., 794 Bathurst St. (S.M. Werbowyj)

Boudreau, D.J., 942 Gerrard St. e.

Bourdon, Burgess, 2333 Dundas St. w., W. R. Burgess

Bovard, J.W., 110 Yonge St.

Bowden, J.F., #305, 1992 Yonge St.

Bowlby & Bowlby, 330 Bay St., M5H 2S8, R. A. Bowlby, Q.C.

Bowman, Farber & Ceresney, #110, 2100 Ellesmere Rd. (Scarboro), Eric Bowman, Q.C., S. H. Farber, M.A. Ceresney

Boyce, Mary, 11 Prince Arthur Ave., M5R 1B2

Boyes, N.W.R., Q.C., 514, 85 Richmond St. w., M5H 2E3

Bradburn & Powell, #306, 2 Dunbloor Rd., R. Bradburn, R.W. Powell

Bradbury, D.C., 2920 Bloor St. w., M8X 1B6

Braden, J.R., #603, 347 Bay St.

Bradley, P.G., 1051 Tapscott Rd. (Scarboro)

Braithwaite, P.D., #1502, 55 Queen St. e.

Braverman, W., 771 St. Clair Ave. w.

Breglia & Breglia, 688 Coxwell Ave., J.R. Breglia, A.F. Breglia

Brenner, Susan, 1405, 480 University Ave., M5G 1V2

Bresver, Scheininger & Davis, 390 Bay St., #2902, M5H 2Y2, D. H. Bresver, L. Scheininger, M.A. Davis, R. Goldberger

Brigden, G. W., Q.C., 80 Richmond St. w., M5H 2A7

Brigham & Mills, 94 Laird Dr., R. Brigham, D. H. Mills

Bright, V.C., #1601, 65 Queen St. w.

Brissenden, B.A., #200, 1017 Wilson Ave. (Downsview)

Bristow, Catalano, Moldaver & Gilgan, #2714, 130 Adelaide St. w., M5H 3P5, D. I. Bristow, Q.C., D.J. Catalano, Q.C., R.B. Moldaver, J.E.G. Gilgan, J.R. Connolly, G.H. Doak, D.W. Glaholt, S.A. Brunswick, M.T. Tamblyn. Counsel: H.G. Bristow, Q.C., G.B. Bagwell, Q.C., M. Shafir

Brodey, Waclawski & Smolkin, 78 Charles St. w., M5S 1K8, P.E. Brodey, M. Waclawski, S.A. Smolkin, B.E. Slocum

Brodkin, Fridson & German, 39 Pleasant Blvd., H.M.A. Brodkin, A. Fridson, S.E. German, M. Zanini

Broley, M.W., Q.C., 1119 O'Connor Dr.

Bromley, H.E., 62 Glengarry Ave.

Bromstein, R.M., #2212, 401 Bay St.

Brooks, D.A., 372 Bay St.

Broughton, R., 2903 Bloor St. w., M8X 1B3

Brown & Forbes, #201, 73 Richmond St. w., E.L. Brown, Q.C., D.S. Forbes, Q.C., M.A. Chochla, A.P.P. Trebuss

Brown, F.M.C., #201, 663 Yonge St.

Brown, Geoffrey, #133, 17 Queen St. e.

Brown, G.P., 9 Lapsley Rd. (Scarboro)

Brown & Grushka, 1267A St. Clair Ave. w., E. O'D. Brown, I. Grushka

Brown, H.D., 36 King St. e., M5C 1E5

Brown, Mannie, 401 Bay St., Box 5, M5H 2Y4

Brown, M.A., Q.C., 14 Isabella St., M4Y 1N1 (G.R. Wise)

Brown, M.S., 161 Eglinton Ave. e.

Brown & Manchee, #620, 500 University Ave., M5G 1V7, Constance Brown, Melanie Manchee

Brown, Masters & Brown, 65 Queen St. w., M.J. Brown, Q.C., R.M. Masters, Q.C., J. Brown, L. R. Mitz, J.J. Weinstein. Counsel: R. Lobl

Brown & Mazin, 1620, 439 University Ave., K.J. Brown, R.M. Mazin

Brudner, J., 2753 Eglinton Ave. e. (Scarboro, M1J 2C7)

Bryce, D.G., #101, 31 Wellesley St. e.

Buckman, Fritz, Fox & Rechtsman, #400, 491 Lawrence Ave. w., R.A. Fritz, M.I. Fox, H.S. Buckman, H.L. Rechtsman

Budd, L.G., Box 288, Commercial Union Tower

Budd, S.R., 334 Yonge St.

Budi, E.S., 94 Walmer Rd.

Budnick, P.G., #1205, 180 Bloor St. w.

Bukovac, M.J., 129 John St., M5V 2E2

Burden & Burden, #1100, 27 Queen St. e., B.C. Burden, Q.C.

Burgess & Macdonald, #1960, Box 152, Royal Bank Plaza, M5J 2J4, R.B. Burgess, J.W. Macdonald, Q.C., S.J. Gray, A. Riswick, G.N. Feldman, F.W. Sheldon

Burke, Thorne, 290 The West Mall (Etobicoke, M9C 1C6), J.J. Burke, W.J. Thorne

Burke, Pancer & Bloom, 161 Eglinton Ave. e., M4P 1J5, A. G. Pancer, J. Bloom

Burke, R.H., Q.C., #151, 7 Queen St. e.

Burkham, H.R., Box 227, Toronto Dominion Centre (J.M. Novak)

Burnett & Assoc., 65 Queen St. w., M5H 2M5, T.F. Burnett, M. Jacobson, C.M. McEachern

Burt, Burt, Wolfe & Bowman, 85 Richmond St. w., R.G. Burt, Q.C., M. S. Wolfe, Q.C., F.R. Bowman, W.P. McCarten

Burton, B., 500 University Ave. (M.T. Frydman)

Burton, D.M., #810, 111 Richmond St. w.

Burton, R. L., 155 Eglinton Ave. e., M4P 1G8

Busby, W. C., 1884 Eglinton Ave. e. (Scarboro, M1L 2L1)

Bussin & Bussin, 285 Yonge St., M5B 1R3, J.J. Bussin, Q.C., M.A. Bussin, B.E. Bussin

Butler, J.C.S., 212 Douglas Ave.

Butterill, G.C., #305, 121 Richmond St. w.

Byers, K.R., #800, 1867 Yonge St.

Bynoe, B.C., Q.C., 111 Elizabeth St.

Byrne, T.F., 8 King St. e., M5C 1B5

Caccia, Mrs. M. E., 349 St. Clair Ave. e., M4T 1P3

Cadsby, P.S., 1501 Ellesmere Rd. (Scarboro)

Caley & Wray, #1205, 111 Richmond St. w., H.F. Caley, D.J. Wray, D.A. McKee, M.A. Church, B.W. Adams

Cameron, Brewin & Scott, 181 University Ave., M5H 3M7, A.J.P. Cameron, Q.C., I.G. Scott, Q.C., J.A. Ryder, Q.C., D.A. Rubin, Q.C., S. T. Goudge, C.G. Paliare, I.J. Roland, S. M. Grant, R. Anand, R. Wells; Counsel: F. A. Brewin, Q.C.

Cameron, H.D., #1002, 18 King St. e.

Cameron, W.W., #515, 159 Bay St.

Campbell, A.M., 181 Eglinton Ave. e.

Campbell, C.A., #208, 111 Richmond St. w.

Campbell, C.A., #1402, 372 Bay St.

Campbell, Godfrey & Lewtas, Box 36, Toronto Dominion Centre (M5K 1C5), D.G.C. Menzel, Q.C., J.A. Geller, Q.C., J.A. Bradshaw, Q.C., R.G. Doe, Q.C., C.R. Thomson, Q.C., G. Tiviluk, Q.C., D.J. Steadman, I. MacGregor, E.A. Tory, B.J. Hutzel, K.W. McCracken, D. J. Deacon, R.E. Smolkin, J.T. Morin, J.W. Sabine, Karen F. Trotter, S.S. Ruby, K.C. Morlock, W.J. Palmer, L. Rose, D.E. Short, S.R. Rickett, M.A. Richardson, T.B. Baker, L. Price, D.G. Kelly, G. MacKenzie, Joan M.H. Weppler, R.J. McCloskey, P.W. Vair, M.P. Frawley, G.R.M. Haynen, J.S. Leon, P.J. Barbetta, Cornelia Schuh, D.E. Grundy, Elizabeth Johnson, P.R. Trethewey, A.G. Beach, D.S. Moles, W.J.D. Scott, N.J. Smitheman, M.F. Brown. Counsel: Hon. J.M. Godfrey, Q.C., T.B.O. McKeag, Q.C.

Campbell, H.B., #901, 111 Richmond St. w.

Campbell, Jarvis, McKenzie & Fulton, 372 Bay St., H. E. Fulton, Q.C.

Campbell, Mills, 8 King St. e., J. R. Campbell, Q.C., J.T.M. Mills, W. J. Palmer, Q.C.

Campbell, R.S.W., 7 Queen St. e.

Campione & Vaturi, #204, 1183 Finch Ave. w. (Downsview), D. Campione, M. Vaturi

Canadian Manufacturers Association, One Yonge St., M5E 1J9

Canadian National Railways, 505 University Ave., M5G 1X4, Regional Counsel: A. G. Lennon

Canadian Pacific Railway, 40 University Ave., M5J 1T1, Regional Counsel: N.A. Chalmers, Q.C.

Cancilla, G. H., 1516, 401 Bay St.

Caney & Klowak, #514, 111 Richmond St. w., M5H 2H3, Gloria R. Klowak

Cannings, R.J., 80 Richmond St. w., M5H 2A4 (J.E. Gross)

Canton, Miss R., 761 Jane St., M6N 4B4

Caplan, R., 40 Hayden St.

Cappe & Cappe, 365 Bay St., N. R. Cappe, Q.C., J. Cappe

Card, P.C., #204, 330 Bay St.

Caroline, M.W., #1807, 8 King St. e.

Carruthers, F.L., #1405, 480 University Ave.

Carson, Poultney, Box 33, 401 Bay St., M5H 2Y4, J.C. Carson, Q.C., I.F.H. Rogers, Q.C., H.R. Poultney, Q.C., S.P. Ponesse, A.F. Marshall, Sandra G. Birnbaum, C.E. Wilson

Carter & Powell, #200, 425 University Ave., R.J. Carter, Q.C., C.M. Powell, Q.C., A.M. Mandell, R.J. Climie

Carter & Wong, 386 Spadina Ave., Carol Carter, P.S.G. Wong

Caruso, J.F., 65 Queen St. w.

Casey, J.E., 120 Adelaide St. w., #902, M5H 3P7
Casey, J.R., Q.C., 401 Bay St., M5H 2Y4
Casey, J.S., #1516, 401 Bay St.
Caskie, Beck, Box 159, Royal Trust Tower, M5K 1H1, T.W. Caskie, C.S. Beck
Cass & Miller, #100, 272 Lawrence Ave. w., M5M 4M1, M.E. Cass, M.B. Miller, J.H. Cunningham, M. Fenson, P. Kupferstein
Cass, G.M., 2034 Queen St. e.
Cassels, Brock, 130 Adelaide St. w. (M5H 3C2), Donald Guthrie, Q.C., J.W. Graham, Q.C., Hamilton Cassels, Q.C., D. A. Anderson, Q.C., Hon. R.J.H. Stanbury, Q.C., D.G. Kilgour, S. World, Q.C., J. T. DesBrisay, Q.C., Pierre Genest, Q.C., H.D. Guthrie, Q.C., I.L. McCulloch, Q.C., E.R. Murray, Q.C., Helen L. Murray, Q.C., A.A. Russell, Q.C., R.J. Pirie, Q.C., G.G. Dickson, B.A. Thomas, Q.C., W.M. Bowen, Q.C., D.H. Milman, G.E.H. Betts, I.A. Blue, P.E. Steinmetz, W.G. Scott, K.G. Crompton, D.R. Angelson, B. Torno, W.G. Beach, K.C. Cancellara, L.R. Hepburn, B.T. McNeely, T.W. Ouchterlony, J.M. Parks, G.S. Rossiter, J.W.R. Day, Lois Andal, R.J. Clayton, W.E. Pepall, S. Plener, J.A. Easto, P.S. Rouleau, Elizabeth Atcheson, A.G.R. Conant, N.B. Holmes, R. Kligman, M. Manly, J.D.T. Pinos, K.G. Singer, R.B. Viner, C. Diamond, Nora Gillespie, J.P. McMahon, E.M. O'Brien
Cassels, Mitchell, Somers, Dutton & Winkler, #1800, 390 Bay St. (M5H 2G3), W.G. Cassels, Q.C., J.F. Mitchell, W.P. Somers, Q.C., W.G. Dutton, Q.C., W.K. Winkler, Q.C., M.J. Mitchell, Q.C., J.D. Gilfillan, Q.C., B.J.E. Brock, Q.C., R.C. Filion, C.M. MacIntyre, T.J. Collier, D.I. Wakely, L.H. Gilbertson, G.B. Kilpatrick, S.J. MacDonald, Felicia Salomon, S.W. Morris, B.P. Smeenk
Catzman & Wahl, 133 Richmond St. w., M5H 2L8, F.M. Catzman, Q.C., J.K. Wahl, Q.C., I.N. Roher, D.N. Dunsmuir
Cengarle & Counter, 1 Greensboro Dr. (Rexdale, M9W 1C8), L.E. Cengarle, W.R. Counter
Chambers, E.J., 2876 Dundas St. w., M6P 1Y8
Chaplick, E., #601, 1 St. Clair Ave. e.
Chapman, R.G., #707, 339 University Ave.
Chapnick, J.J., #609, 85 Richmond St. w.
Chappell, Bushell & Stewart, 101 Richmond St. w., M5H 1T1, H. G. Chappell, Q.C., June M. Bushell, Q.C., H.D. Stewart, Q.C., M.G. Appel, P.R. Henry, J.G. Goodwin, H.N. Shuster, M.L. Benotto
Chatarpaul, K.S., #502, 2065 Finch Ave. w. (Downsview)
Chen, T.T.P., #1530, 180 Dundas St. w.
Chernin & Kirsh, 1497 Yonge St., I. S. Kirsh
Chernovsky, M., 165 Spadina Ave.
Chetner, J.P., 20 Eglinton Ave. w.
Chilco, M.T., 1710 Dufferin St.
Chisholm, R.W., Q.C., 330 University Ave.
Christie, Herron, Stephenson, Saccucci & Matthews, 3902 Royal Trust Tower, Box 68, M5X 1K7, E.A. Christie, Q.C., J.S. Herron, R.F. Stephenson, V.M. Saccucci, F.J. Matthews, J.E. Weppler, B.V. Hatt
Christie, K.A., Q.C., 365 Bay St.
Chusid, Rakowsky, Polson, Friedman & Shapero, 702, 1000 Finch Ave. w. (Downsview, M3J 2V5), A.B. Polson, A.A. Rakowsky, A.L. Shapero, W. Friedman, M.D. Silverberg, J.T. Syrtash, M.P. Marsh, S. Letofsky, J. Ditkofsky. Counsel: M.H. Chusid
Ciccia, R., #207, 1055 Wilson Ave.
Chykaliuk, W., 1058A Albion Rd. (Rexdale)
Ciglen, G.J., #1800, 700 Bay St.
Cimetta & Cimetta, 55 Bloor St. e., A. P. Cimetta, S. D. Cimetta
Cirone, D.J., #401, 294 Main St.
City Legal Department, City Hall, City Solicitor: W. R. Callow, Q.C., Deputy City Solicitor: M. E. Fram, Q.C., Corporation Counsel: M.J. Winer
Clapp & Gibson, 22 Erskine Ave., M4P 1Y2, S.G. Clapp, J.R. Gibson
Clark, Harriet, 44 Foxbar Rd.
Clarke, M.J., 217 Carlton St.
Clow, Brenda, #1108, 85 Richmond St. w.
Clyne, L.P., #502, 360 Bloor St. w.
Coates, R.G., #20, 146 Dundas St. w.
Coatsworth, Richardson & Hart, 85 Richmond St. w., M5H 2C9, I. C. Hart, Q.C., L.K. Porter
Cobban, Ash, Mogan & Patterson, 604, 75 The Donway w. (Don Mills), H.J. Ash, P.J. Mogan, A.B. Patterson. Counsel: W.A. Cobban, Q.C., J.J.P. McDermott, Q.C.
Cocomile, Feldman & Battiston, 1710 Dufferin St., J.A. Cocomile, Q.C., M. Feldman, E.J. Battiston
Code & Green, 11 Prince Arthur Ave., M. Code, M. Green
Cogen, D.J., Box 501, Stn. Z
Cogliano, M.G., #205, 133 Richmond St. w.
Cohen & Chasse, 2971 Lakeshore Blvd. w., M8V 1J5, G. Cohen, Wm. Chasse
Cohen, D., 347 Bay St.
Cohen, H.B., Q.C., 10 Foxbar Rd.
Cohen, H.H., Q.C., #605, 45 Richmond St. w.
Cohen, H.W., #800, 1867 Yonge St.
Cohen & Saul, #202, 133 Richmond St. s. (also Agincourt)
Cohen & Weissglas, #1202, 121 Richmond St. w., S.S. Cohen, W.W.B. Weissglas
Cohen & Wolpert, 354 Bathurst St., Marion Cohen, M. Wolpert
Cole, D.P., 11 Prince Arthur Ave.
Colebourn, V.K., Q.C., 85 Richmond St. w., Suite 506, M5H 2C9
Coles & Gringorten, #1306, 330 Bay St., A.H. Coles, G.S. Gringorten, G. Machtinger, Shelley Pohjola
Collins, J., #400, 101 Richmond St. w., M5H 1T1
Conn, G. C., #205, 133 Richmond St. w.
Connor, J.A., #2101, 65 Queen St. w.
Conrad, D.H., 100 Adelaide St. w.
Coon, D.A., 80 Richmond St. w.
Cooney, R.P.P., 401 Bay St., Box 46
Cooper, A.M., Q.C., #600, 111 Richmond St. w. (M.J. Sandler)
Cooper & Cooper, #1216, 100 Adelaide St. w., G.B. Cooper, K.R. Cooper
Cooper, Jarvis, #801, 121 Richmond St. w., A.S. Cooper, Q.C., D.A. Jarvis, Patricia Rogerson
Cooper, Schwartz, 148 Yorkville Ave., M.H. Cooper, I. Schwartz, S.M. Cohen
Copeland, I., #605, 111 Peter St.
Copeland, Liss, 31 Prince Arthur Ave., M5R 1B2, P.D. Copeland, J. Liss
Copeland, McKenna & Kerba, 3638 Lakeshore Blvd. w., J.W. McKenna, J.A. Copeland, S.N. Kerba, K.D. Nelson
Copelovici, J., 1 St. Clair Ave. e.
Corbin & Ellis, #700, 27 Queen St. e., K.M. Corbin, S.A. Ellis
Cornish, King & Sachs, 320, 111 Richmond St. w., M5H 3N6, Mary Cornish, Lynn King, Harriet Sachs
Corse, Willa J., 78 Shields Ave., M5N 2K4
Cosman & Fingold, #206, 4250 Weston Rd. (Weston), L.E. Fingold, M.L. Cosman
Costa, F.D., 1389 Dundas St. w.
Cousins, D.B., #300, 111 Elizabeth St.
Couto, A.V., Q.C., 2481A Bloor St. w. (N.E. Kostyniuk, D.N. Hawreliak)
Coutts, Crane, Ingram, 7th fl., 111 Elizabeth St., E.E. Coutts, Q.C., R.A. Crane, M.B. Ingram, R.M. McLean
Cowan, A.C., Q.C., 2 Carlton St., M5B 1J5
Cowitz, R., 794 Bathurst St.
Cox, Armstrong & Smith, 19 Richmond St. w., M5H 1Y9, W.D. Cox, Q.C., J.S. Armstrong, R.I. Smith
Cozzi & Cozzi, 538 Parliament St., P.B. Cozzi, P.D.J. Cozzi, G.E. Shapiro, Riva Rotter
Crabtree & Crabtree, Box 379, Commerce Court North, A. H. Crabtree, Q.C., J.L. Ringer
Crane, J.D., Q.C., 330 University Ave. (C.U. Simco)
Crawford & Scott, #1101, 67 Yonge St., C.R. Crawford, Elizabeth Scott
Creed, R.S., #212, 1415 Lawrence Ave. w.
Creighton, J.L., 3500 Eglinton Ave. w.
Cremer & Kudrac, 1593 Wilson Ave. (Downsview), F. H. Cremer, E.M. Kudrac
Cronish & Zwicker, #2828, 2 Bloor St. e., M4W 1A8, R.C. Cronish, J.S. Zwicker
Crown Trust Co., Legal Dept., Box 38, One First Canadian Place
Crum-Ewing, P.A., 133 Davenport Rd. (H.G. Zweig)
Cugelman, B., #300, 111 Elizabeth St.
Cundari, G.A.J., 1684 Dufferin St.
Cunningham & Sutherland, 9 Bloor St. e., W.A. Sutherland, Q.C.
Curran, G.W., 217 Carlton St.
Curtis, Carole, #1003, 80 Richmond St. w.
Cutler, E.H., 160 Duncan Mill Rd. (Don Mills)
Czajkowski, T.P., 714A College St.
Dale, H.A., 3 Sultan St.
Dales, B.S., 12 Sheppard St.
D'Alimonte & Reino, #103, 1111 Albion Rd. (Rexdale), E.L. D'Alimonte, A. Reino
Dalla Rosa, R., 147 Oakwood Ave.
Damery & Mamak, 2440 Bloor St. w., J. W. Damery, S. A. Mamak
Damiani & Furguiele, #202, 1013 Wilson Ave., A.L. Furguiele, G.C. Damiani
Daniels, P., 2145 Avenue Rd.
Danielson, D.A., #1910, 101 Richmond St. w.
Danson & Zucker, #2010, 390 Bay St., K.B. Danson, S. Zucker, T.S.B. Danson, B.G. Freesman, Q.C.
Danylchuk, B.J., 50 Richmond St. e.
Danyliw, W.G., 401 Bay St., Box 31
Daris, J., 743 Queen St. e.
Dashwood, J., 961 Kingston Rd.
Davey, L.J., #1104, 20 Queen St. w.
David & David, #229, 900 Dufferin St., T. David. Counsel: H. David
David, R., #1900, 65 Queen St. w.
Davidson, A.E., 101 Richmond St. w.
Davidson & Davidson, 17 Queen St. e., M5C 1P9, R. W. Davidson
Davidson, L., 21 Dundas Sq.
Davies, D., 1963A Queen St. e.
Davies, Ward & Beck, Box 147, Commerce Court West (M5L 1G8), D.A. Ward, Q.C., H.L. Beck, Q.C., C.K. Overland, L.B. Heath, Q.C., T.I.A. Allen, D.J. Watchorn, H.G. Emerson, D.A. Brown, D.W. Smith, M.C. Cullity, Q.C., C.H. Foster, N.J. Leblovic, D.C. Stanbury, M.J. Rochwerg, B.R. Carr, W.M. O'Reilly, J.A. Swartz, A.S. Shiff, J.P. Bisnaire, W.N. Gulla, G.E. Taylor, G.W. Voorheis, J.F. Bankes, T.H. Bowman, M. Disney, G.R.K. Myers, J.M. Ulmer, J.A. Zinn
Davis, J.L., #707, 44 Eglinton Ave. w.
Davison, Marie, 43 Eglinton Ave. e.

Day, Ault & White, 401 Bay St., Box 101, M5H 2Y4, E.F. Ault, Q.C., M.J. White, L. Naymark; H.S. Day, Q.C.
Day, B.D., #241, 17 Queen St. e.
Day, Wilson, Campbell, 250 University Ave. (M5H 3E7), T.J. Day, Q.C., R.F. Wilson, Q.C., W.C. Campbell, R.S. McCreath, Q.C., D.F. McDonald, Q.C., R.Y.W. Campbell, J.K. Smith, M.J. Wheldrake, Q.C., C. E. Woollcombe, Q.C., W. Filipiuk, E.B. Russell, Q.C., H.M. Kelly, Q.C., G.F. Day, Q.C., R.L. Falby, W.D. Barton, H. P. Hands, T. J. Tone, A. Paton, F.T. Richmond, R.E. Lean, Linda Bertoldi, J.P. Dillon, Dawn McConnell, W.M. Pigott, Mary Porjes, G.R. Shiff, P.D. Lauwers, B.G. McKenna
Deacon, Benevides & Thomson, 335 Bay St., E.A. Benevides, Q.C., T.H. Thomson, T.E. Storus
Deakon, W.C., 19 Richmond St. w.
DeFaria & DeFaria, 1261 Dundas St. w., C. DeFaria, R. DeFaria
de Kenedy, A.B., #1403, 55 Queen St. e.
Delany, J. E., 85 Richmond St. w. (B. J. Jolly)
DeLucia & DiGregorio, 682 Wilson Ave. (Downsview), W.C. DeLucia, B.N. DiGregorio
DelZotto, Zorzi, Applebaum, 951 Wilson Ave. w. (Downsview), E. L. DelZotto, F.J.T. Zorzi, M.I. Applebaum, Q.C., D.R. Rothwell, P. Neubauer, H. Herskowitz, H.W. Isenberg, J.S.P. Martinello, R.C. Harason, E.P. Micheli, M. Gottheil, B.R. Leve, D. Rubin, A.W. Snider
Demianenko, P., 347 Bay St.
Demon & Ciaschini, #604, 330 Bay St., M.D. Demon, L.L. Ciaschini, L. Colt
Dempsey, A.M., 533 Queen St. e.
Dennis, D.L., Q.C., 76 St. Clair Ave. w.
Derry, P.G., 145 Adelaide St. w.
DeRubeis, M.S., 65 Queen St. w.
Deutch, W.G., Q.C., 67 Yonge St.
Devlin, J.P., 2376 Kingston Rd. (Scarboro)
DeVuono, F.J., #207, 1055 Wilson Ave. (Downsview)
Dewar, Graham & Johnson, 4889 Dundas St. w., J.D. Dewar, J.J. Graham, Q.C., I.C. Johnson
Dewart, L.S., 14 Prospect St.
Dewji, I.I., #900, 43 Eglinton Ave. e.
Diamond, M.R., #500, 51 Eglinton Ave. e.
Dicker, E., Q.C., 111 Peter St.
Dickler, Irvine P., Q.C., 80 Richmond St. w.
Dier, Tara, 129 John St.
Dillon, Cronin & Lamb, #1002, 111 Richmond St. w., M5H 2G4, J. L. Cronin, Q.C., B.F. Lamb, Q.C.
Di Monte, Di Paolo, 1700 Wilson Ave. (Downsview), P. Di Monte, M.A. Di Paolo
Direnfeld & Nurgitz, 4999 Yonge St. (Willowdale), N. Direnfeld, Naomi B. Nurgitz
Diwan, K.C., 1412A Gerrard St. e.
Doan, H.J., #204, 1240 Bay St., M5R 2A7
Doidge, T.R., Q.C., 25 Overlea Blvd.
Dolman, C.H., Q.C., 2797 Eglinton Ave. e. (Scarboro, M1J 2E1)
Donnelly, B.P., 347 Bay St.
Donnelly & Daigneault, 101 Charles St. e., T.J. Donnelly, S.J. Daigneault
Donnelly, B.J., 1165A St. Clair Ave. w.
Downey, Shand & Herold, 1243 Islington Ave., C. E. Shand, Q.C., C.N. Herold, Q.C. Counsel: C.C. Downey, Q.C.
Doyle, E.E., #905, 27 Queen St. e.
Draimin, W.C., 40 St. Clair Ave. w.
Dranoff, Linda S., 390 Bay St.
Drebin, S.L., #705, 133 Richmond St. w.
Drevnig, V.L., Q.C., #810, 111 Richmond St. w.
Drexler & Budd, 1033 Pape Ave., H. Drexler, P. J. Budd
Druck, S.B., 603 Briar Hill Ave.
Drynan & McGregor, 2281 Yonge St., D. A. Drynan, D. R. McGregor
Duco, Geist & Chodos, #120, 1315 Finch Ave. w. (Downsview), P.A. Duco, M.S.N. Geist, M.E. Chodos
Duffy, P.S., Q.C., 85 Richmond St. w.
Dukovich, S., #201, 2 Toronto St.
Durbin, N.L., 2530 Jane St. (Downsview)
Durno & Shea, 919 Ellesmere Ave., R.G. Durno, M.E. Shea
Dutrizac, R.J., 1977 Avenue Rd.
DuVernet, Stewart, #1720, 180 Dundas St. w., E.A. DuVernet, Q.C., J.S. Stewart, Q.C., T.J. Treloar, P.P.E. DuVernet, M.A. Wilkinson
Dyment & Small, 330 Bay St., #1008, M5H 2S8, A.D. Dyment, Q.C., B.S. Small, H.S. Dyment
Dyson, N., Q.C., 100 Richmond St. w. (M.F. Kacaba)
Dzwiekowski, D.C., 257A Willard Ave.
Eagleson, R.A., Q.C., 65 Queen St. w., #1000, M5H 2M5 (H. Ungerman)
Easser, P., 111 Richmond St. w., #912, M5H 2G4
Eastman, B.L., Q.C., 121 Richmond St. w.
Edelstein, M., 625 Sheppard Ave. w. (Downsview)
Edgar, J.M., Q.C., 2901 Bloor St. w.
Edmonds, G.W., Q.C., 514, 85 Richmond St. w.
Elaschuk, G.J., Q.C., 372 Bay St.
Elgie, Walsh & Dhanani, 145 Adelaide St. w., J.G. Walsh, T.I. Dewji
Elia, J., 401 Bay St., Box 59
Elkind & Lipton, 15th fl., 69 Yonge St., S.W. Elkind, Q.C., M.D. Lipton, Q.C., M.H. Greenglass, H. Hochman, Ruth Rapoport, S.F. Sklar, L.W. Fedchun
Elliott & Champagne, #912, 390 Bay St., G.D. Elliott, D.C. Champagne, C.G. James
Elliott, Warne, Carter, 401 Bay St., Box 105, H.H. Elliott, Q.C., T.C. Warne, R.J. Carter, R.L. Steele, J.G. Richardson, M. Mason, R.C. Taylor, P.B. Sahagian, P. Lukasiewicz. Corporate Counsel: R.J. Hassard, Q.C.
Ellwood, R.D., 2857 Lakeshore Blvd. w.
Enfield, Hemmerick, Henry, Lyonde & Wood, Toronto Dominion Centre, Box 284, F.A. Enfield, Q.C., W.J. Hemmerick, Q.C., J.V. Henry, Q.C., G.E. Wood, L.A. Enfield, D.R. Miller
Engle, R.S., 102 Bloor St. w., #200, M5S 1M8 (E.W. Gross)
Epstein, Cole, #1608, 390 Bay St., P.M. Epstein, K.A. Cole, D.S. Starkman
Epstein, A., 666 Burnhamthorpe Rd. (Etobicoke)
Erts, V.M., #1403, 55 Queen St. e.
Eustace, M.A., 1 Sultan St.
Evans & Christoff, 600 Sherbourne St., B.N. Christoff, J.P. Evans
Evans, L.S., Q.C., 101 Richmond St. w., #2122, M5H 1T1
Ezrin, S., #805, 27 Queen St. e.
Fagan, S. J., Q.C., 58 Greenbrook Dr.
Fair & Siegel, 1818 Eglinton Ave. w., M. R. Siegel
Faivish, J., 133 Richmond St. w., #403, M5H 2L3
Faraci, J., 620 Wilson Ave. (Downsview, M3K 1Z3) (A.H. Mandel)
Farano, Green & Brans, #1202, 2 St. Clair Ave. e., R. J. Farano, Q.C., W. S. Green, D.M. Brans, P.R. Brown, W.S. Bernstein
Farb, Snitman & Bergman, 2313A Bloor St. w., D. D. Farb, I. Snitman, M. B. Bergman
Farberman, P., #142, 144 Davenport Rd.
Fargnoli, V., 834A Danforth Ave.
Farquhar, A., 165 Spadina Ave.
Fasken & Calvin, Box 30, Toronto Dominion Bank Tower (M5K 1C1), F.M. Fell, Q.C., R. M. Sutherland, Q.C., R. N. Robertson, Q.C., A.J. Cavan, Q.C., Georgia M. Bentley, A.D.T. Givens, Q.C., F. D. Gibson, Q.C., R.D. Wilson, Q.C., R.B. Tuer, Q.C., R. J. Rolls, Q.C., R. L. Shirriff, Q.C., J. W. Huckle, Q.C., T. E. Brooks, Q.C., W. A. Kelly, Q.C., R.W. Gardner, Q.C., K.J.C. Harries, D. S. Affleck, Q.C., J. H. Hough, J. M. Robinson, Q.C., R.B. Potter, D. G. Marwick, P. J. Green, N. T. Norris, A. M. Schwartz, S.T.P. Risk, W. R. Passi, G. C. Glover, Jr., R. W. McDowell, A.M. Rock, D. R. Scott, R. W. McInnes, P. E. Brent, J. A. Campion, R. W. Cosman, R. S. Harrison, Anne E. Armstrong, S. B. Blain, J. A. Levin, W.J. Bies, P.L. Roy, J.R. Varley, D.C. New, E.A. Cronk, R.A. Lomas, D.G. Stinson, Patricia I. Thomas, M.S.F. Watson, P.J. Rowcliffe, J.W.W. Hick, Gloria J. Adair, D.N. Corbett, A.C. Dekany, C.L. Sugiyama, D.K. Bruce, P.R. Greene, M.E. Hoffstein, J.F.S. Thomson, D.A. Cannon, Barbara Miller, D.E. Milner, L. Ricchetti, J.D. Vincent. Counsel: B.R. MacKenzie, Q.C., J.C. Risk, Q.C.
Fass & Kilian, 810 Midland Ave. (Scarboro), K. Fass, C. W. Kilian
Faust, Rovan & Hacker, 727 Ossington Ave., M6G 3T6, J.J. Faust, D.M. Rovan, H.H. Hacker
Fay, F.X., Q.C., #403, 330 Bay St.
Fecser, P.R., 5146A Dundas St. w.
Feigman & Chernos, 141 Adelaide St. w., #509, M5H 3L5, L. Feigman, Q.C., B. Chernos, Q.C., R.H. Raphael, J. P. Conway, D.V. Hutchinson, T. Nemetz, C.P. Gryski, C.A. Harnick, C.B. Davis, P.E. McInnis, B. Teichman
Feintuch, Balitsky & Alter, 894A St. Clair Ave. w., B. Feintuch, J.S. Balitsky, I.H. Alter
Feldman, F.F., #205, 951 Queen St. e.
Feldman & Weisbrot, 43 Eglinton Ave. e., #900, M4P 1A2, I. Feldman, Q.C., A. Weisbrot
Fellowes, T.E.G., Q.C., 372 Bay St. (J. S. McNeil, C.J. Freedlander, J.W. Strype)
Fenson, A., 172 Major St.
Ferguson, A., 2470A Yonge St.
Field, Turner, Dunn & Lynch, #707, 330 University Ave., D.G. Field, J.R.A. Turner, B.R. Dunn, P.M. Lynch
Fields, G.S., #500, 51 Eglinton Ave. e.
Fienberg, W., Q.C., 175 Keewatin Ave.
Figol, Gray, #520, 1110 Finch Ave. w. (Downsview), M. Figol, R.J. Gray
Fine, A., #205, 1011 Dufferin St.
Fine, D.M., #805, 1240 Bay St.
Fineberg, C.E., #1400, 390 Bay St.
Fingerhut, R. M., 390 Bay St.
Fink & Bornstein, 354 Bathurst St., R.A. Fink, E.T. Bornstein
Finkelstein, A. C., 89 Elizabeth St., M5G 1P4
Finkelstein & Birken, 199 Richmond St. w., H. Finkelstein, R. Birken
Finlayson, Smith, #1100, 27 Queen St. e., D. A. Smith, Q.C.
Fisch, J. Y., 368 College St.
Fisch & Tweyman, 1593 Ellesmere Rd. (Scarborough), W. Fisch, M. Tweyman
Fisher, Kugelmass, 180 Dundas St. w., B.D. Fisher, S. Kugelmass
Fitch & Gotlieb, #101, 14 Prince Arthur Ave., A. Fitch, Q.C., S. Fitch, N. Gotlieb
Fitzpatrick & Poss, Box 226, Commercial Union Tower, J. J. Fitzpatrick, Q.C., H. Poss, R.J. Halfnight, M.D.E. Duder, Sheila Corey

Fitzsimmons & MacFarlane, #2403, 180 Dundas St. w., R.G. Fitzsimmons, R.H. MacFarlane, D.S. Johnson, B.E. Slocum, Angela Costigan
Flaccavento, G., #300, 2017A Danforth Ave. (W.E. Hildreth)
Fleischmann, I., 110 Yonge St.
Fleming, J.C., 1520, 390 Bay St.
Fleming, Smoke, Burgess & Phillips, Toronto Dominion Bank Tower, Box 60, M. Fleming, Q.C., A. C. Burgess, Q.C., D. N. Phillips, E.G. Spong, O.D. Young
Flisfeder, A.M., #202, 560 Danforth Ave.
Flom & Geller, 1992 Yonge St., M4S 1Z7, R. Flom, G.R. Geller
Florence & Fodor, 598 St. Clair Ave. w., L.N. Florence, J.W. Fodor
Floszmann, F., 360 Bloor St. w.
Fong, F.W., #615, 425 University Ave.
Foreht, C., Q.C., 2780 Jane St. (Downsview)
Formusa, L.I., 700 University Ave.
Forrest, D. W., 3495 Lawrence Ave. e. (Scarboro)
Fors, A.I., #2010, 8 King St. e.
Foster, L.A., 1000 Gerard St. e.
Fox, B., #201, 89 Chestnut St.
Fox, W., #432, 100 Richmond St. w.
Fram, D.A., #508, 1 Yorkdale Rd.
Franklin, D., 425 University Ave.
Fraser, A.M., #404, 50 Richmond St. e.
Fraser & Beatty, Box 100, First Canadian Place (M5X 1B2), D. A. McIntosh, Q.C., J. A. Mullin, Q.C., Z.G.C. Lash, Q.C., L. Hynes, Q.C., S. E. Edwards, Q.C., J. W. deC. O'Grady, Q.C., A. Conway, Q.C., C. H. Hollingshead, Q.C., W.J.E. Beverley, Q.C., J. B. Gillespie, Q.C., W. J. Whittaker, Q.C., H. Sutherland, Q.C., G. W. Owen, Q.C., D. B. Horsley, Q.C., G.D. Scroggie, R.W.W. Fraser, A. G. Richmond, Q.C., W. A. Corbett, Q.C., C. M. McKeown, Q.C., J. B. McLellan, W. O. Francis, J.B. MacAulay, R. J. Murphy, D. F. Pounsett, R. J. Fraser, Q.C., J. S. Elder, J.G.N. Johnston, P.S.A. Lamek, Q.C., J. M. Bradley, C. C. Finley, C. Stoyan, J. M. Fuke, C.H.H. McNairn, I.C.B. Currie, E. A. Peters, W. D. Chambers, J.L. McDougall, Q.C., D.G. Fuller, J. H. Whiteside, R. B. Foster, T. H. Young, J. W. Adams, J. M. Langs, D.J.T. Mungovan, N. A. Ross, H.M. McKinlay, P. P. Ginou, E. A. Horton, R. P. Quinlan, R. B. Freeman, R. A. Goldenberg, A. B. Lorriman, J. D. Pennal, P.W. Hand, L.A.H. Franklin, G.R. Hiseler, M.J. Penman, S.J. Simpson, P.F. Baston, W.H. Gravely, B.A. O'Byrne, P.D. McCutcheon, R.W. Walker, P.J. Williams, J.P. Boyer, B.E. LeVasseur, R.B. Budd, E. Goldfarb, J.L. Lewy, I.V.B. Nordheimer, W.K. Orr, H.A. Zimmerman, B.L. Croll, F.M. Deacon, R.C. Heintzman, C.I. Mackiw, I.E. Peters, P.D. Shantz, P.M. Emmons, S.E. Fremes, A.E. Holland, T.A. Houston, J.I. Mackintosh, R.J. Matheson, P.E. Murphy, P.A. Shiroky, L.A. White, R.L. Armstrong, D.B. Fuller, D.F. Hirsh, D.S.D. Hobson, A.F. Lin, G. Turner, C.D. Woodbury. Counsel: P.B.C. Pepper, Q.C.
Fraser & Stratton, #1450, 25 King St. w., B.C.F. Fraser, Q.C., J.B. Stratton
Freedman, A. H., #902, 357 Bay St.
Freedman, H., 111 Richmond St. w. (R.N. Vale, M.G. Koller)
Freedman, I.P., #102, 2780 Jane St. (Downsview, M3N 2J2)
Freedman, L.S., #514, 111 Richmond St. w.
Freedman, N.J., 390 Bay St.
Freedman, S., 37 Prince Arthur Ave.
Freeman, D.V., 25 Lesmill Rd. (Don Mills)
Freeman, J.J., Q.C., 312 Dundas St. w., M5T 1G5
Freeman, Miller, 9 Bloor St. e., W. E. Miller, Q.C., M.J. Singer
Fried, J., 202 Ossington Ave.
Friedman, J., Q.C., #2600, 20 Queen St. w.
Frolick & Frolick, 80 Richmond St. w., S. W. Frolick, Q.C., L. G. Frolick, V.M. Frolick
Frost, R.J., #400, 67 Richmond St. w.
Frost & Redway, 3080 Yonge St., C.S. Frost, Q.C., A.A.S. Redway, Q.C.
Frymer, H., #320, 100 Richmond St. w.
Futerman, H., 448 Wilson Ave. (Downsview)
Fyles, F.M., #1502, 80 Richmond St. w.
Gabriel, F.A., #515, 159 Bay St.
Gaertner & Math, 187 King St. e., M5A 1J5, A. Gaertner, P.H. Math, A.M. Anthony
Gaglione, G.J., 229 Glen Park Ave.
Gain, T.G., 121 Richmond St. w.
Gambin, Bratty, Chiappetta, Morassutti, Caruso, 1055 Wilson Ave. (Downsview, M3K 1Y9), R. P. Bratty, Q.C., E. J. Gambin, Q.C., M. A. Morassutti, J. A. Chiappetta, Q.C., M. E. Caruso, Q.C., N.A.J. Volpe, H. L. Wisebrod, E.H. Richardson, M.H. Goodman, M. N. Durisin, H. Berholz, C.M. Bush, R. Belluz, S.J. Marano, Celeste Iacobelli, C.R. Piersanti
Gangbar & Stancer, 45C Hazelton Ave., S. Gangbar, Q.C., R. Stancer
Ganz, F. H., Q.C., #1102, 27 Queen St. e.
Gardiner & Crozier, #805, 65 Queen St. w., J.R. Gardiner, L.J. Crozier
Gardiner, Roberts, 120 Adelaide St. w. (M5H 1T5), H. D. Roberts, Q.C., J. B. Conlin, Q.C., J. F. McCallum, Q.C., M. J. Mowbray, Q.C., J. G. Parkinson, Q.C., P. Webb, Q.C., W. Liber, Q.C., J. R. Miller, B. W. Webb, Q.C., R. R. MacDougall, R. G. Goodwin, R. Rossow, C.B. Tarshis, D.E. Fine, J.B. Casey, R.G. Doumani, I.J. Lord, J.G. McMehen, L.F. Longo, A.C. Gluek, J.H. Wigley, B.A. Farlinger, D.C. Poynton, Gina Brannan. Counsel: F. G. Gardiner, Q.C.
Gardiner, Shelley, 2 St. Clair Ave. e.
Garfin, Zeidenberg, 3995 Bathurst St. (Downsview), M.E. Garfin, M.K. Zeidenberg, Suzanne Garfin, P.A. Grunwald, R.C. Henderson. Assoc.: A.J. Garfinkel, P.L. Rosenberg
Garfinkle, Biderman, Brown & Blustein, #1201, 121 Richmond St. w., R.P. Biderman, A. W. Brown, M.G. Blustein, D.R. English
Garnick, M., 2167 Yonge St.
Garton, N., #1505, 330 Bay St.
Garvey, Ferriss, Royal Bank Plaza, Box 56, H. J. Murphy, Q.C., H. J. Bruce, Q.C., D.J. Green, Joanne Murphy, P.J. Avis. Counsel: R.J. McComb
Gavendo, L., #1402, 80 Richmond St. w.
Geffen & Chernoff, 2907 Kennedy Rd. (Scarboro), L.B. Geffen, S.A.M. Chernoff
Gemmell, J. W., Q.C., Box 379, Commerce Court Postal Stn.
Gemmell, J.M., 11 Prince Arthur Ave.
Gershman, S., 1684 Dufferin St.
Gerstl, A.C., 505, 133 Richmond St. w.
Gibson, E., #207, 1 Yorkdale Rd.
Gilbert, D. R., Q.C., 67 Richmond St. w.
Gilbert & Hartley, 1983 Queen St. e., W. Gilbert, J. Hartley
Gilbert, J.A., Q.C., #405, 122 St. Patrick St.
Gilbert, Wright & Flaherty, 301, 155 University Ave., S. A. Gilbert, T. C. Wright, J. M. Flaherty, Christine Elliott
Giles, Percy, 2 Carlton St., W.H. Giles, Q.C., J.L. Percy, G.B. Shorser
Ginsberg, S.B., 390 Bay St.
Giuffrida, D., 16 Barton Ave.
Glasner, A., 286 Danforth Ave.
Glasner, E., 100 Richmond St. w.
Glass, A.A., 390 Bay St.
Glass, L., 293 Eglinton Ave. e.
Glatt, L., 2354 Danforth Ave.
Glick, Marilynne, 158 the Esplanade
Glinert & Assoc., 120 Avenue Rd., M5R 2H4, E.L. Glinert, M.L. Lewis
Glober, Cohen & Reisler, 121 Richmond St. w., S.I. Glober, M.A. Cohen, A.C.J. Reisler
Gludish, W.J., 5233 Dundas St. w. (Islington) (M.Z. Goose)
Godfrey & Corcoran, 55 Queen St. e., Celia E. Corcoran
Godfrey, S.J., 3rd fl., 49 Front St. e.
Gold, A.D., Box 137, 401 Bay St.
Gold & Assoc., 593 Bloor St. w., K.L. Gold, G.A. Rudnik, A.B. Shusterman
Gold, Hildebrand, #2224, 130 Adelaide St. w., P.M. Gold, E.G. Hildebrand
Goldberg, Wilson, 1509, 180 Dundas St. w., M5G 1Z8, (also Mississauga), S.D. Goldberg, D.S. Wilson
Golden, Levinson, #1908, 101 Richmond St. w., A. E. Golden, M. L. Levinson, P.A. Sigurdson, M. A. Green, P. J. J. Cavalluzzo, J.K.A. Hayes, W.C. Bartlett, E.J.S. Lennon, D.K.L. Starkman
Goldfarb, Schwartz, #840, 439 University Ave., C.S. Goldfarb, C. Schwartz
Goldhar & Nemoy, #2312, 101 Richmond St. w., S. N. Goldhar, Q.C., M. B. Nemoy, Q.C., G.M. Gampel, A.H. Nemoy
Goldkind, H. A., 45 Richmond St. w.
Goldman, Litwack, Norsworthy & Nash, #502, 365 Bay St., N.L. Goldman, A.D. Litwack, H.G. Norsworthy, S.H. Nash
Goldman, R.M., 351 Wellesley St. e.
Goldsmith, I., Q.C., #504, 330 University Ave., #504, M5G 1R7
Goldstein, A.I., 325 Eglinton Ave. e.
Goldstein, K., 19 Richmond St. w.
Goldstein, L., #1605, 80 Richmond St. w.
Goldstein & Rosen, 1648 Victoria Park Ave., A. Goldstein, I. A. Rosen
Goldstein, T., #505, 335 Bay St.
Goldstick & Goldstick, #802, 2 Regal Rd., Miss I. S. Goldstick
Goodenough, McDonnell & Anderson, #1507, 320 Bay St., M5H 2P2, L. G. Goodenough, Q.C., W. S. McDonnell, Q.C., R.N. Starr, Q.C., T.K. Anderson
Goodman and Carr, 2800 York Centre, 145 King St. w. (M5H 3K1), W. D. Goodman, Q.C., D. Carr, Q.C., G. E. Cooper, Q.C., J.G. Casse, Q.C., Leonard Fine, Q.C., A. D. Silver, B. A. Spiegel, Saul Shulman, Allen Karp, J. Goldenberg, S. J. Messinger, David Moscovitz, S.L. Goldenberg, M.R. Wasserman, J. J. Fineberg, E. I. Miller, H. A. Shapiro, M. Winton, J. M. Blidner, H. M. Carr, J. M. Clow, M. J. Perelman, S.J. Wax, J.L. Cummings, B.H. Naiberg, G.H. Fox, L.N. Ginsler, A. Sternberg, Paula D. Stark, Susan Eng, L.S. Chernin, K.H. Kadonoff, L.M. Geringer, A.E. Kauffman, M.E. Kovnats, A.J. Trebilcock, L.R. Kohn, Joanne Swystun, Elizabeth Ellis, R.S. Green, G.H. Luftspring, J. Ditkofsky, Paula Mannone, Ariella Rohringer
Goodman & Fefergrad, 1200, 121 Richmond St. w., D.M. Goodman, I.W. Fefergrad, M.J. Gersht
Goodman & Goodman, #3000, Box 30, 20 Queen St. w. (M5H 1V5), E.A. Goodman, Q.C., N. H. Schipper, Q.C., H. H. Solway, Q.C., K.N. Karp, Q.C., S. Silver, Q.C., P. Schwartz, Q.C., G. Ross, Q.C., S.N. Filer, Q.C., C. J. Schwartz, Q.C., L.

Waisberg, D.G. Pierce, Q.C., C. Gail Cornwall, C.C. Lax, G. I. Kirke, A.O. Jacques, N. H. Harris, A. Leibel, W.V. Alcamo, M. Kathryn Robinson, J.A. Keefe, J.S. Schachter, M.S. Steinberg, Diane Harris, Patricia Robinson, Gale Rubenstein, J. Shier, S. Diamond, K.H. Kadonoff, A.P. Reich, A.P. Shanoff, R. Storrey, E.J. Fish, Roslyn Houser, L. Kushnir, Juli Morrow, M.S. Myers, E.I. Rotman, D.B. Fairbairn, A.S. Shapiro

Goodman & Hartney, 330 Bay St., H. G. Goodman

Goodman, I., 85 Richmond St. w.

Goodman, L., 29 Pleasant Blvd.

Goodman, Sheldon, 120 Avenue Rd.

Gora, J. L. Z., 85 Richmond St. w.

Gordon, Traub & Rotenberg, 5th floor, 390 Bay St., W. Gordon, Q.C., W.M. Traub, J.B. Rotenberg, D. Gordon, K.M. Kagan, S.I. Pearlstein, Leor Margulies. Counsel: Norman May, Q.C.

Gorewich, W.A., #2404, 1 Dundas St. w.

Gorrie, T.G., Q.C., #1100, 27 Queen St. e.

Gosbee, R.A., #200, 1081 Bloor St. w.

Gossin, E.B., 546 St. Clair Ave. w., M6C 1A5

Gottlieb, G. L., 600 Bay St.

Gottlieb, S., Q.C., 85 Richmond St. w.

Gould, M. A., 230 Bloor St. w.

Gould, M.J., #1212, 2 St. Clair Ave. e.

Gowling & Henderson, #5260, One First Canadian Place (also Ottawa)

Graham & Bourque, #503, 2065 Finch Ave. w. (Downsview), C.D. Graham, R.C.J. Bourque

Graham, M.W., #706, 44 Eglinton Ave. w.

Graham, Parsons & Liscombe, 372 Bay St., M5H 2W9, W. Liscombe, Q.C.

Graner, H., Q.C., 111 Richmond St. w.

Grant, D.L., Q.C., 111 Richmond St. w.

Gray, Offer & David, #204, 89 Chestnut St., M5G 1R1, W.D. Gray (also Mississauga)

Green, D.J., 399 Spadina Ave.

Green & Dunn, 1801 Eglinton Ave. w., N. Green, Q.C., V. P. Dunn, Q.C.

Green, E., #1402, 2 Carlton St.

Green, Pauline, #700, 27 Queen St. e.

Green & Spiegel, 390 Bay St., M. M. Green, Q.C., H. Spiegel, Q.C., M. E. Drukarsh, A.C. Van Houten, J.S. Guberman, I. Fox

Green, W. F., Q.C., 360 Bay St., #804, M5H 2W2 (E.J.A. Gierczak)

Greenberg, B.S., 347 Bay St.

Greenberg, J., #200, 25 Imperial St.

Greenglass & Grosman, #2000, 390 Bay St., M5H 2Y2, M. Greenglass, Q.C., B.A. Grosman, Q.C., N.A. Kaufman, P.D. Schmidt, G. Gold, S.H. Marcus

Greenley, R.H., 2100 Ellesmere Rd. (Scarboro)

Greenspan & Arnup, #2800, 130 Adelaide St. w., M5H 3P5, B.H. Greenspan, C.J. Arnup

Greenspan, Moldaver, 1110, 390 Bay St., M5H 1T7, E.L. Greenspan, M.J. Moldaver, Marc Rosenberg, C.N. Buhr

Greenstein, Rose, 861 College St.

Greer, L.H., 7 Coxwell Ave.

Gresik, E. J., 131 Bloor St. w.

Griesdorf, A. H., 111 Richmond St. w.

Griesdorf, Chertkoff, Levitt & Assoc., #502, 2200 Yonge St., N.D. Griesdorf, Q.C., S.B. Chertkoff, Q.C., A.J. Levitt, Q.C., A.C. Reinstein

Griffiths, P., 901, 110 Yonge St.

Grimanis, C., 904 Logan Ave.

Grimson, S.L., 2970 Lakeshore Blvd. w.

Groll & Groll, 112 St. Clair Ave. w., B. Groll, R. Groll

Grosberg, J.J., #151, 7 Queen St. e.

Grosberg, R.M., #203, 133 Richmond St. w.

Gross, A.H., 861 College St.

Grossi, P.A., 1385 Queen St. w.

Grossman, Helen, Q.C., 100 Adelaide St. w.

Grossman, J. M., 372 Bay St., Suite 900, M5H 2W9

Grudeff, Berg & Gold, 1595 Bloor St. w., S.J. Berg, L.S. Gold

Grupp, G., 111 Elizabeth St.

Gunn, D. D., Q.C., 555 Burnhamthorpe Rd. (Etobicoke)

Guoba, J.M., 113 Davenport Rd.

Gurland, A., 20 Madison Ave.

Hadbavny, L., #404, 1415 Lawrence Ave. w.

Haffey, Sherwood, 401 Bay St., Suite 2508, M. J. Haffey, Q.C., W. R. Sherwood, Q.C., L.M. Foy, D.A. Herceg

Hahn, K. A., 5230 Dundas St. w. (Islington)

Halberstadt, Weisman, 794 Bathurst St., M. Halberstadt, Q.C., G.S. Weisman

Hale, K.J., 1215 St. Clair Ave. w.

Haley & Martin, 200 University Ave., W.D. Martin

Hall, Baker, Berman, Rosenblatt & Goodman, 390 Bay St., R.R. Hall, Q.C., L.B. Baker, Q.C., J. Berman, Q.C., R.M. Rosenblatt, Q.C., E. Goodman, B. Schneider, J. Berkow, R.J. Molson, G.W. Kinasz, M.L. Wolfe, E.F. Gutstein, G.E. Cohen, D.M. Bereskin

Hall, Barbara, 113 Davenport Rd.

Halman, Pilzmaker & Ament, #1102, 20 Queen St. w., W.I. Halman, L.W. Ament, M.S. Pilzmaker, H. Bloom, S. Austin

Halpern, F., 94 Overbrook Place (Downsview)

Ham, G.C., #2404, 1 Dundas St. w.

Hames, C.M., Q.C., #2914, 390 Bay St.

Hamilton, J.F., #1001, 110 Yonge St.

Hamilton, Torrance, Stinson, Campbell, Nobbs & Woods, 196 Adelaide St. w., M5H 1W7, J. B. Hamilton, Q.C., F. W. Torrance, Q.C., F. C. Stinson, Q.C., W. A. Campbell, Q.C., E. T. Nobbs, Q.C., R. O. Woods, Q.C., G. F. Reid, W. F. Clark, Miriam Kavanagh. Counsel: G.L. Rooke, Q.C.

Hamilton, Wilkie, #200, 425 University Ave., D. J. Hamilton, P. H. Wilkie

Hammond, C. A., Q.C., 2390 Eglinton Ave. e. (Scarboro)

Hans & Hans, 10 Foxbar Rd., S.W. Hans, Q.C., Judith Hans, T.A. Kelly

Harasymowycz, G.M., #202, 2490 Bloor St. w.

Hare, W.R., 4174 Dundas St. w. (Islington)

Harries, Houser, Ste. 700, 145 King St. w. (M5H 2B6), Elmore Houser, Q.C., J. S. Brown, Q.C., D. T. Bennett, Q.C., D. N. Macklem, Q.C., R. W. Henry, Q.C., D. E. Baird, Q.C., R. M. Loudon, Q.C., M. D. O'Reilly, Q.C., M. D. Syron, P. D. Wendling, N. G. Powell, G.I. Ferguson, R. D. Walker, R. R. Neville, Shirley Perdue, F. Bennett, R. W. Nainby, Mary Lou Parker, R. J. Morris, H. M. Fogul, S. J. Butts, P.R. Basso, T.J. Matz, M.B. Rotsztain, D.R. Dowdall, P.D. MacMillan, R.G. Watkin, Joyce Kaplan, A.L. Morin, A.J. Kent, D.A. Palmateer, Evelyn Moskowitz, R.M. Slattery, P.A. Anderson, H.W. Sterling, Jennifer Powell

Harrington, A.L.B., 67 Yonge St.

Harrington, M. P., 1723a Bayview Ave.

Harris & Brennen, #405, 1 Greensboro Dr. (Rexdale), R. A. Harris, D. C. Brennen, E. Kent

Harris & Darragh, 390 Bay St., M. H. Harris, Q.C., S. E. Darragh, Q.C.

Harris, G., 4140 Bathurst St. (Downsview)

Harris & Jones, 422 Dundas St. e., P.J. Harris, P.J. Jones

Harris, Keachie, Garrow, Davies & Hunter, 181 University Ave., #300, M5H 3M7, R. W. Davies, Q.C., J. R. Hunter, Q.C., A. M. Huycke, W.J. Smith, J.H. Lytle, F.L. Gardner, Jane Demaray. Counsel: J.T. Garrow, Q.C.

Hart, Bulwa, #1201, 100 Adelaide St. w., R. S. Hart, J. Bulwa

Hartley, J.M., 1980 Queen St. e. (C.A. Brand)

Hartrick & Sclodnick, #507, 11 Adelaide St. w., M.D. Hartrick, H.L. Sclodnick, H.B. Robertson

Hass & Floras, 401 Bay St., Box 91, L. A. Hass, Q.C., F. Floras, Q.C., B.D. Murray, B. Panning

Havrlant, Robinson, Bateman, #304, 347 Bay St., M5H 2R8, A. Havrlant, A. M. Robinson, W. E. Bateman, Anne Roberts

Haxell & Snelgrove, #520, 1110 Finch Ave. w. (Downsview), D.K. Haxell, Susan Snelgrove

Hayhurst, Dale & Deeth, 2300, 101 Richmond St. w. (M5H 2J7), W.L. Hayhurst, Q.C., W.E.H. Dale, Q.C., D.N. Deeth, B.W. Gray, S. Burshtein, J.R. Lake. Patent & Trade Mark Agents: A.L. Grove, Margaret H. Miskelly, G.P. Orleans, P.E. McArdle, R.A.R. Parsons, P.K. Holland. Counsel: D.J. Wright, Q.C.

Hazel, J. J., 2489 Bloor St. w.

Headford, S. J., 14 Kew Beach Ave., M4L 1B7

Heather & Eaton, #1200, 8 King St. e., M5C 1B5, D.R.H. Heather, Q.C., J.C. Eaton, Q.C.

Hebb, M.D., 24 Ryerson Ave., M5T 2P3

Heifetz, Crozier & Schelew, #1400, 65 Queen St. w., G. Heifetz, D.C. Crozier, M. Schelew

Heinrich, Kovach & Pazulla, #216, 2323 Bloor St. w., M6S 4W1, G.A. Heinrich, Q.C., M.W. Kovach, W.J. Pazulla, Fern Silverman

Hemsworth and Thom, #1555, 55 University Ave., G.N. Hemsworth, S. Thom

Hennessey, I. S., #101, 31 Wellesley St. e., M4Y 1G7

Henderson, A., #1812, 2 Carlton St.

Henry & Brown, #2300, 390 Bay St., P. Henry, Q.C., R. Brown, Q.C., L. H. Iron, Q.C., L.G.A. Bassin, A.T. Neuman. Counsel: J.A. Stevenson, Q.C., J.M.H. Lamont

Henry, R.A., #511, 37 King St. e.

Herberman, H., 648 Danforth Ave.

Herman, M.J., #202, 2 Gloucester St.

Herman, M. M., Q.C., 66 Collier St.

Herman, Peirce, 25 Lesmill Rd. (Don Mills), L.I. Herman, D.H. Peirce, P.E. Mallon, D.V. Freeman

Herman, W. B., Q.C., #205, 11 Adelaide St. w.

Hermant, L., Q.C., 169 Yonge St.

Hershorn, Wm., 964 Albion Rd., Rexdale (D. Fuochi)

Hertz, J.L., #116, 1000 Finch Ave. w., Downsview (Anita Lerek)

Hetherington, Fallis, Park, Watt & Carriere, 365 Bay St., J. R. Hetherington, Q.C., G. A. Fallis, Q.C., A. Park, Q.C., R. C. Watt, J. S. H. Carriere

Hicks, Morley, Hamilton, Stewart, Storie, Box 371, Toronto Dominion Centre (M5K 1K8), R. V. Hicks, Q.C., C. A. Morley, F. G. Hamilton, Q.C., B. H. Stewart, Q.C., T. F. Storie, Q.C., C.G. Riggs, H.A. Beresford, R.J. Drmaj, J.C. Murray, D.K. Gray, R.R. Dunsmore, D.W. Brady, Janice Baker, Corinne Murray, W.M. Kenny, M.P. Moran, W.J. Hayter, Susan Biggs

Higgins, J.R., #307, 80 Richmond St. w.

Hill, A., #1906, 401 Bay St.

Hill, Friend & Reilly, 120 Adelaide St. w., R. D. Hill, Q.C., D. G. Friend, Q.C., J.D. Reilly, Q.C.
Hills & Pilon, 1168 Warden Ave. (Scarboro), R.G. Hills, M.W. Pilon
Himel, I., Q.C., #305, 121 Richmond St. w.
Himel, S., 455 Spadina Ave.
Hinkson (W.E.) & Assoc., #310, 100 Richmond St. w., W.E. Hinkson, A.L. Gagner
Hlinka, M., 1486 Dundas St. w., M6K 1T5
Hodgson, J.B., 2346 Danforth Ave.
Hoffman, N., Q.C., 1810 Avenue Rd.
Hogg, D. T., #1012, 123 Edward St.
Holden, Murdoch & Finlay, Box 80, First Canadian Place (M5X 1B1), P. C. Finlay, Q.C., W. D. Jordan, Q.C., C. G. Cowan, Q.C., J. F. Logan, Q.C., K.G.R. Gwynne-Timothy, Q.C., L. M. Keay, J.J. Murphy, Q.C., D. W. Wright, Q.C., A. Abramson, P.J. Clarke, A.M. McLennan, J.H. Craig, J.F. Rook, P.E. Harvey, Verna E. Cuthbert, J.A. Little, L.J. Abramson, H. Ulster, B.D. Wynn, G. Hoy, Sandra B. Kidd, M.I. Young, A.W. Macdonald, M.P. Thompson. Counsel: W.S. Walton, Q.C., S.H. Robinson, Q.C., J.F. Lake, Q.C., Oscar Rechtshaffen
Holden, R. L., 390 Bay St.
Holmested & Sutton, 7 King St. e., D. L. Campbell, Q.C., A. R. MacDonald, Q.C., D. E. Hill, Q.C., L. W. Scott, Q.C., J. A. Baird, T.H. Grygiencza, R. Diakun. Counsel: G.E. Hill, Q.C.
Holoboff, C., #241, 17 Queen St. e.
Honeyford & Honeyford, #1100, 27 Queen St. e., R. H. Honeyford, Q.C.
Hoolihan, Rollo & Johnston, #400, 425 University Ave., J. A. Hoolihan, Q.C., D. E. Rollo, Q.C., Karen Johnston
Hopperton, P.G., #1108, 330 Bay St.
Horan, M. G., #707, 330 University Ave.
Horkins, W.B., #400, 120 Adelaide St. w.
Horne, R.J., 390 Bay St.
Hornsby, B. J., 120 Eglinton Ave. e.
Horodeckyj, S., 129 John St.
Horwitz, M., Q.C., 390 Bay St.
Hotz, J. E., 2221 Yonge St.
House & Hall, #32, 165 Spadina Ave., J.A. House, L.A. Hall
Housley, M.K., 3329 Bloor St. w.
How, W. G., Q.C., 2028 Avenue Rd.
Howell, W.T., #2010, 8 King St. e.
Howse, W.D., #205, 133 Richmond St. w.
Hryn, P., 165 Spadina Ave.
Hrynkiw & Buchan, 2105, 401 Bay St., O. W. Hrynkiw, J. S. Buchan. Counsel: P.F. Schindler
Hubbard, P., 142 King St. e., M5C 1G7 (J. Favaro)
Hubscher, F.F., #1712, 390 Bay St.
Hughes, Amys, 2800, 390 Bay St. (M5H 2Y2), W. S. Wigle, Q.C., D. G. Duke, Q.C., L. G. Harlock, Q.C., M.T.J. McGoey, B. R. Madigan, M.M. Smith, P.M. Stevens, R.F. Horak, J.F. Fitch, D.J. Ross, M.S. Teitelbaum
Hughes, Archer, Suite 1500, 372 Bay St. (M5H 2X8), R. A. Hughes, Q.C., W. L. Archer, Q.C., R. R. Anger, D.L. Dorsch
Hughes, F.T.L.
Hughes, I.M., 1110 Finch Ave. w. (Downsview)
Hughes, J.E., Q.C., 132 Buckingham Ave.
Hugo, J.R.Y., #1104, 20 Queen St. w.
Hui, Hune & Wong, 180 Dundas St. w., H.K.S. Hui, G. Hune, C.K.S. Wong
Hume, Martin & Timmins, 110 Church St., F. R. Hume, Q.C., R. I. Martin, Q.C., J. H. Timmins, Q.C., D.E. Martin, D.G. Higgins
Humeniuk, W., #1207, 330 Bay St., #1207, M5H 2S8
Humphrey, Ecclestone & Durno, 3 Sultan St., D. G. Humphrey, Q.C., G. W. Ecclestone, Q.C., S. B. Durno
Hunt, D.J., #208, 1940 Eglinton Ave. e. (Scarboro)
Hunter, J. W. G., Q.C., 131 Bloor St. w.
Hunter & Johnston, 1550 Queen St. w., T. Hunter, W. A. Johnston
Hurowitz, S.G., 144 Davenport Rd. (R.A. Rubinoff)
Hutchinson, Tackaberry, #707, 44 Eglinton Ave. w., P.A. Hutchinson, J.A. Tackaberry
Hyde, Pollit & Arnold, 40 Dundas St. e., E. G. Hyde, Q.C., H. M. Pollit, L. C. Arnold, S.L. Stewart
Ontario Hydro, 700 University Ave. (Legal Dept.)
Hynes, D.L., 2874 Keele St. (Downsview)
Iglar & Lebo, 2605 Eglinton Ave. e. (Scarboro), E. E. P. Iglar, H. W. Lebo
Iler, B.E., 280 Bloor St. w.
Inch, A.B., 40 Gerrard St. e.
Irish, C.E., 85 Ellesmere Rd. (Scarboro)
Irvine, S.H., #304, 80 Richmond St. w.
Isaac, Dr. Richard, #605, 190 St. George St.
Isenberg, Miriam, 180 Bloor St. w.
Iwasykiw & Renton, #505, 2 Jane St., J.A. Iwasykiw, R.J. Renton
Jackson, D. F., 35 Astley Ave.
Jacobs, M.H., #505, 133 Richmond St. w.
Jacobs, Zigelstein & Macdonald, #1640, 439 University Ave., P. Jacobs, S.H. Zigelstein, R. Macdonald
Jacques, V.A., 330 Bay St.
Jaffey, J.M., 3080 Yonge St.
James & Assoc., 112 Merton St., K. James, Gloria Balaban, H.I. Shain
James, P.A., 55 Queen St. e.
Jamieson, N.J., 951 Queen St. e.
Jamieson, W.S., Q.C., #501, 133 Richmond St. w.
Janoscik & Janoscik, 1576 Bloor St. w., J. J. Janoscik, R. Janoscik
Jarson, G.O., #2, 3077a Bloor St. w., M8X 1C8
Jarvis, Blott, Fejer, Pepino, 2200 Yonge St., #400, M4S 2C6, R. E. Jarvis, Q.C., A. S. Blott, Q.C., B. W. Fejer, N. J. Pepino, P.J. Devine, S.M. Brooks, D.B. Quick. Counsel: J.S. Stewart, Q.C.
Jeffery, Jeffery, Robertson, #1812, 2 Carlton St., M5B 1J3, I.R. Robertson, N.P. Watson, P.R. Pendrith
Jemmott, M.M., #200, 914 St. Clair Ave. w.
Jewell, Angus & Michael, #700, 390 Bay St., P.R. Jewell, Q.C., A.D. Angus, D.B. Thomas, R.A. Stewart, M. Obradovich, G.M. Scarcella
John, A.S., 10 Trinity Sq., M5G 1B1
Johnston & Douglas, 140 Islington Ave., M8V 3B7, J. I. Johnston, Q.C., J. R. Douglas
Johnston, I. S., Q.C., Royal Bank Plaza, Box 11, M5J 2J1
Johnston, M. S., Q.C., #903, 347 Bay St.
Johnston, R.T., 85 Richmond St. w., #1111, M5H 2C9
Johnstone, G.P., #1012, 123 Edward St.
Jonas, G.F., 1607, 80 Richmond St. w., M5H 2C2 (D.S. Dignam)
Jonas, S., 559 College St.
Jones, B., 100 Richmond St. w.
Jones, G., #300, 111 Elizabeth St.
Jones, K., 284 Sherbourne St.
Jones, Waugh, #1908, 101 Richmond St. w., R. B. Jones, D. B. Waugh, M.J. Angevine, B.A. Sargeant
Jupp, E. A., Q.C., 65 Queen St. w.
Kafun, A.P., 20 Ben Hur Cres.
Kagan, L., 2171 Avenue Rd.
Kagan, Marsha, 2171 Avenue Rd.
Kalen, M., 354 King St. e.
Kallmeyer, R. B., 2896 Dundas St. w., M6P 1Y8
Kan, Mark & Poon, 8th floor, 111 Elizabeth St., M5G 1P7, R.S.T. Mark, F.K.C. Kan, S.S.L. Poon, J.W.P. Mo, O.C. Wong, C.R. Nowlan, J.L. Davies
Kang, C.Y., 484 Bloor St. w.
Kapelos, N.P., 500 Danforth Ave. (P.S. Carlisi)
Kaplan, A.I., 40 Hayden St.
Kaplan, J., Q.C., 1104, 45 Richmond St. w.
Kaplan, Murray, Q.C., 801 Eglinton Ave. w.
Kaplan, Sidney, 111 Richmond St. w.
Kappy, J. H., 45 Richmond St. w., #404, M5H 1Z2
Karal, N. H., Q.C., 55 Eglinton Ave. e.
Karas, J.G., 560 Danforth Ave. (M. Jurjans)
Karfell, R. S., 2 Carlton St.
Karfilis, J., 85 Richmond St. w.
Kasman, H. B., 731A Danforth Ave.
Kasman, S. L., 1622 Eglinton Ave. w. (R.H. Shay)
Kassirer, B.M., Q.C., 45 Richmond St. w., M5H 1Z3
Kates & Goldkind, #206, 3850 Sheppard Ave. e. (Agincourt), C.B. Kates, Q.C., H.S. Goldkind, Q.C.
Katz & Solnicki, 180 Bloor St. w., A. Katz, V. Solnicki
Kavanagh, J.M., 2390 Eglinton Ave. e. (Scarboro)
Kay, B. L., #2404, 1 Dundas St. w.
Kayfetz, D. H., 1000, 6 Adelaide St. e.
Kazdan, Yager, #700, 2 Bloor St. w., J.F. Kazdan, L. Yager
Kazman & Sidenberg, 1110 Lodestar Rd. (Downsview), S. Kazman, M. L. Sidenberg, C.M. Rutter
Keith, Katzman & Kramer, 401 Bay St., Box 49, C. A. Keith, Q.C., M. M. Katzman, Q.C., M.S. Kramer, D.P. Brannan
Kellermann, J.R., #4, 165 Spadina Ave.
Kellermann & Shier, 80 Richmond St. w., M5H 2A4, M. W. Kellermann, Q.C., S. I. Shier
Kelly, H.M., Q.C., 2828 Dufferin St. (R.A. Boccia)
Kelly, J.V., 609, 85 Richmond St. w.
Kelly, Miriam, #2600, 390 Bay St.
Kelman, F.S., 1818 Eglinton Ave. w.
Kelner, S.B., 65 Queen St. w.
Kelsey, B.M., Q.C., #300, 70 Richmond St. e. (I. Marks)
Kennedy, Sherman, Marin, #102, 300 The East Mall, R.R. Kennedy, B.A. Sherman, J. Marin, F.D. Weinstock, D.N. Beavis
Kennedy, V.R., #507, 80 Richmond St. w.
Kentish, J.W., 14 Elgin Ave.
Kerbel, H.E., 11 Prince Arthur Ave.
Kerbel, M.L., #1601, 65 Queen St. w.
Kerbel, M., Q.C., #706, 347 Bay St.
Kerekes, Collins, #1212, 2 St. Clair Ave. e., M4T 2T5, A. Z. Kerekes, I. J. Collins
Kerr, D.W., 3 Strathearn Rd.
Kerr, John E., Q.C., 133 Richmond St. w.
Kerr, Oster & Wolfman, 14 Madison Ave., J.D.L. Kerr, F.P. Oster, L.A. Wolfman
Kert & Feige, #208, 111 Richmond St. w., M5H 2G4, R.B. Kert, R.E. Feige
Kert & Kert, 825 Eglinton Ave. w., S. Kert
Kerzner, A., 90 Eglinton Ave. w.
Kesten, L. I., 887 Queen St. e. (Ann Gibson, M. Takatsch)
Kettner, Miskin & Edelstein, #801, 500 University Ave., D. L. Kettner, Q.C., J.S. Miskin, E.M. Edelstein
Keyfetz, C.K., Q.C., #1919, 390 Bay St., M5H 2Y2
Kho, H.S.T., #2400, 180 Dundas St. w.
Kidd, J. Kenneth, Q.C., #604, 85 Richmond St. w., Miss Anne B. Wright
Kielb, T.J., 250 University Ave.

Kimberley & Associates, 1937 Gerrard St. e., M4L 2C2, H. E. Kimberley, J.W. Vaillancourt, F.H. Vanston
Kimel, R.S., 444 Adelaide St. w.
King, E. O., Q.C., 372 Bay St., #1400, M5H 2W9
King, G.P., #700, 2 Bloor St. w.
King, W.A., 120 Eglinton Ave. e.
Kingsmill, Jennings, 4700, 1 First Canadian Place, Box 124, M5X 1G1, R. D. Jennings, Q.C., Wm. W. Barrett, Q.C., Duncan Finlayson, Q.C., G. C. Hollyer, Q.C., Lorraine Gotlib, Q.C., W.B. Ivany, Q.C., J.R.R. Jennings, Q.C., F.E. Cappell, H.W. Cares, K.D. Graham, M.N. Silver, Graysanne Bedell
Kirsch, Fern, #803, 11 Adelaide St. w.
Kirsh, Sheila, 800, 181 University Ave., M5H 2E5
Kitamura Yates & Margolis, #1702, 11 King St. w., A.R. Kitamura, J.B. Yates, W.M. Lehun, M.S. Appel, J.W. Wright, B.B. Green, A.N. Burke. Counsel: M.N. Margolis
Klady, B., #513, 159 Bay St.
Klassen, R. J.
Klein, M., 344 Bloor St. w., #306, M5S 1W9
Klemencic, A., 770 Browns Line (Etobicoke)
Kligerman, Bortnick, #507, 44 Eglinton Ave. w., R. Kligerman, T.J. Bortnick
Klymko, A.W., 100 Richmond St. w.
Knazan, Jackman & Goodman, #33, 165 Spadina Ave., B. Knazan, B. Jackman, N. Goodman
Knopf, H.P., #200, 102 Bloor St. w.
Koffman, Cohen, Lapedus, #200, 101 Yorkville Ave., B. Koffman, M. Cohen, M. A. Lapedus, M.L. Siegel, M.H. Viner
Kolas, S.A., #117, 1000 Finch Ave. w. (Downsview)
Kopparath, P.G., #114, 747 Don Mills Rd. (Don Mills)
Kopyto, H., 121 Richmond St. w.
Koroloff & Huckins, #1000, 88 University Ave., G.P. Koroloff, P.M. Huckins
Korzen, E.C, #2200, 390 Bay St.
Koskie & Minsky, #2500, 130 Adelaide St. w. (M5H 2M2), R. Koskie, Q.C., A.M. Minsky, S.B.D. Wahl, M. Zigler, B.S. Fishbein
Kosoy, Gordin & Schiller, #202, 89 Bloor St. w., D. Kosoy, P. Gordin, L.I. Schiller
Kostuk, R.M., Q.C., 2195 Bloor St. w.
Kotick & Assoc., #909, 2 Carlton St., S.O. Kotick, M. Brown, S. Laufer
Kott, B., 20 Queen St. w.
Koury, H., 347 Bay St.
Kozak, A. E., 26 Lia Cres. (Don Mills)
Kravetz, S.B., #333, 85 Bloor St. w.
Kreiger, J.H., 700 Bay St.
Kremer & Associates, 845 St. Clair Ave. w., E. A. Kremer
Krepakevich, S., Q.C., 85 Richmond St. w.
Kroll, G., Q.C., 607, 80 Richmond St. w.
Kronby, Chercover, 88 Avenue Rd., M. G. Kronby, Q.C., J. L. Chercover, Q.C., G.R. Davis, L.I. Barrington-Corres, R.V. Zaldin, N.L. Backhouse
Kruger & Givertz, 1 Yorkdale Rd., A. H. Kruger, M. Givertz, B.C. Atherton
Krupnik, S.E., #505, 44 Eglinton Ave. w.
Kutney, A.N., #205, 133 Richmond St. w., M5H 2L3
Kuz, S., #205, 2 Jane St., M6S 4W3
Kuzma, O.S., #105, 31 Wellesley St. e., M4Y 1G7
Kuzmochka, J., 89 Elizabeth St.
Kwinter, S., #1550, 439 University Ave. (G.D. Goldman)
Kyser, W.H., #700, 360 Bay St.
Laan, T.R., #705, 133 Richmond St. w.
LaBrie, F. E., Q.C., 330 University Ave.
Lackie, B.F., 364A King St. e.
Lackner, K. D. L., 696A Coxwell Ave.
Laforme, H.S., #507, 122 St. Patrick St.
Laird & Laird, #1900, 700 Bay St., B. K. Laird, Hon. J. K. M. Laird, Q.C.
Laird, W. W., Q.C., 99 Avenue Rd.
Laker, B., Q.C., 121 Westgate Blvd. (Downsview)
Lalka, W.N., #200, 3031 Bloor St. w.
Lalla, T.K., 1205 Bloor St. w.
Lalonde & Eisen, 360 Bay St., D.W. Lalonde, M.D. Eisen
Lamb, L.C., 100 Richmond St. w.
Lamerton, W. W., Q.C., 1262 Don Mills Rd. (Don Mills)
Lamey, L., #201, 330 Bay St., M5H 2S8
Lamont & Lamont, 372 Bay St., D. H. L. Lamont, Q.C., Mrs. M. Lamont, Mary Brennan, D.D.W. Lamont, D.F. Lamont
Lamourie, G., 640 Bloor St. w., M5G 1K9
Landau & Glicksman, #211, 44 Eglinton Ave. w., S.I. Landau, H. Glicksman
Lane, Breck, 55 University Ave., M5J 2H7, E.M. Lane, A.W. Breck, W.J. Melko, R.J. Allen, D.B. Garrow, N.C. Jones
Lang, Michener, Cranston, Farquharson & Wright, Box 10, First Canadian Place (M5X 1A2), R.A. Cranston, Q.C., J.H.O. Peppler, Q.C., G. M. Farquharson, Q.C., W.P.G. Allen, T.C. Douglas, Q.C., L. Levenstein, R. J. Wright, Q.C., A. B. Doran, Q.C., R.M. McDerment, Q.C., A. Englander, J.G. Sinclair, Q.C., D.N. Plumley, W.S.R. Seyffert, A.F.M. Reid, G. W. Footit, B. C. McDonald, A. Gnat, D. H. MacOdrum, W. F. Carney, R. J. Metcalfe, R. F. Mossman, W.J.V. Sheridan, Barbara A. Suzuki, C. R. Vernon, J. D. Wilson, M. R. Gray, R. D. Archibald, D. W. Pamenter, R. N. Waterman, J. L. Dillman, Jennifer Leddy, G. B. Lewis, W. B. Drake, Marsha Onyett, R.R. Cranston, W.B. Keevil, Nancy Deshaw, M.K. Eisen, B.A. Kirkwood, D.B. Merrick, Anne L. Sone, F. Palmay, Gaylanne Phelan, Rebecca Regenstreif, P.E.J. Wells, J. Alpert, M.E.P. Cavanaugh, G.D. Courage, T. Ann Devitt, Joanne Wildgoose, B.W. Cameron, H.J. Cheesman, Alexandra Hoy, G. Myers, J.B. Simpson, Carole Trethewey, T.J. Hunter. Associate Counsel: Rt. Hon. Roland Michener, P.C., Q.C., Hon. D. A. Lang, Q.C.; Counsel: D. J. Wright, Q.C.
Lang, S.E., #406, 347 Bay St.
Langer, S. J., 374 Brooke Ave.
Lantos, G., 66 Wellesley St. e.
Lapowich, J., 347 Bay St.
Larin, G. A., 4180 Dundas St. w.
Lash, Johnston, 2400 Royal Bank Plaza, North, M5J 2J1, D. M. Pringle, Q.C., J.B. Clements, Q.C., G. I. Pringle, Q.C., D.R. Cameron, Q.C., W.L. Hooey, Q.C., T. G. Jamieson, Q.C., B.L. Remus, K. Soomer, M.M.K. Fitzpatrick, J.C. Dunlop, D.B. Smith, D. Hager, J.D. Wright, D.M.W. Young, J.S. Mannone, B.A. McKenna, R.A.B. Devenney, P.E. Reiss, W.B. Binions, R.E. Glass, G.A. Meiklejohn, P.J. Watson. Counsel: T. Sheard, Q.C., P. D. Isbister, Q.C., H. Rowan, Q.C., W.M. Temple, Q.C., H.R. Douglas, Q.C., J.A. Campbell, Q.C.
Laski & Simpson, #402, 372 Bay St., W.S. Laski, B.A. Simpson
Laskin, Jack, Horton & Harris, 612, 390 Bay St., J.I. Laskin, D.H. Jack, W.G. Horton, Joyce Harris
Laufer, J.S., #505, 133 Richmond St. w.
Lawlor, P. D., Q.C., 154 Lake Promenade
Lawson, McGrenere, Wesley, Jarvis & Rose, 902, 120 Adelaide St. w., R.B. Lawson, Q.C., W.T. McGrenere, Q.C., J.R. Wesley, Q.C., P.G. Jarvis, Q.C., R.F.L. Rose, T.H. Clemenhagen, J.L. Davis
Laxton, Glass & Swartz, #502, 80 Richmond St. w., J.T. Glass, Q.C., F. A. Swartz, S. C. Tessis, L.J. Rutherford, K.E. Wise
Lea, Chas., Q.C., 1381 Queen St. w. (M. Goldstein)
Lee, Fireman, Regan, 199 Richmond St. w., P. A. Lee, Q.C., J. J. Fireman, J. M. Regan, R. J. Kram, J.C. Blouin, L. Samis, J.E. Dunn, Debra E. Rolph, C.R. MacColl, J.W. Scott, D.I. Reisler, C.M. Berry
Lee, S., 283 Spadina Ave.
Legeti, E.B., 435A Montrose Ave.
Legge & Legge, 60 St. Clair Ave. e., Miss L. Legge, Q.C., B. J. Legge, Q.C., W.E. Gatward, D.J. Richardson
Leggett, A., 290 St. Clair Ave. w.
Leibel, J. L., Q.C., 3089 Bathurst St.
Leibel & Leibel, 390 Bay St., #1220, M5H 2Y2, J.S. Leibel, A.D. Leibel
Lemire, J.C., #3000, 390 Bay St.
Lencki, W. A., 100 Adelaide St. w.
Lende, Clayman & Wortsman, 89 Chestnut St., S. J. Lende, B. Clayman, H. Wortsman
Lerek, Anita, #802, 190 St. George St.
Letterio, B.J.B., Q.C., 201, 1279 St. Clair Ave. w.
Leve & Zeiler, 27 Queen St. e., A. Z. Leve, J. I. Zeiler
Levenson, H.S., 146 Davenport Rd.
Levine, P., 165 Spadina Ave.
Levine, R.M., 484 Bloor St. w.
Levinter & Levinter, #810, 111 Richmond St. w., B.V. Levinter, Q.C., L.L. Reznick, Adele Belanger, Linda Lamoureux
Levitt, Lightman, 2 Dunbloor Rd. (Islington), F. Levitt, M.E. Lightman. Counsel: S.H. Levitt
Levitt, Shekter, Direnfeld, #1604, 20 Queen St. w., E.N. Levitt, R.H. Shekter, A.D. Direnfeld
Levy, A. D., 40 Hayden St.
Levy, E. J., Q.C., 100 Richmond St. w.
Lewis & Birenbaum, 3889 Keele St. (Downsview), M. J. Lewis, I. Birenbaum
Lewis, F.A., #1704, 2180 Yonge St.
Lewis, J. E., 43 Eglinton Ave. e.
Lewis, Marrus & Finkler, 145 King St. w., E. L. Marrus, Q.C., Bruce A. Finkler, Q.C., I. Wenus, F.S. Turton, A.J. Frank
Lichtman, H.I., 377 Ridelle Ave.
Lieberman, R.M., 2 Gloucester St.
Lieberman, S.J., 2900 Warden Ave. (Scarboro)
Ligeti, E.B., #202, 280 Bloor St. w.
Lindberg, C., 123 Edward St.
Lindberg, C. O., 191 Eglinton Ave. e.
Linden & Linden, #1508, 330 Bay St., H.J. Linden, H.D. Linden, J.M. Magder
Linden, S. B., Q.C., 390 Bay St.
Lindenberg & Lindenberg, 121 Richmond St. w., G.E. Lindenberg, N. Lindenberg
Lindsay, E.S., 501, 360 Bloor St. w.
Lindzon, I.S., 401 Bay St., Box 62
Linett & Karoly, 110 Bond St., M. Linett, R. Karoly
Lipman, Zener & Waxman, #302, 2200 Yonge St., A.L. Lipman, W.S. Zener, M.H. Waxman, A.J. Turko
Lipton, C. H., Q.C., #808, 40 University Ave., M5J 1T1
Lipton, M. M., 212, 8 King St. e.
Litowitz, G. E., 2020 Bathurst St., M5P 3L1
Litowitz, P., 1403 Bathurst St.
Livingstone & Welwood, #202, 80 Richmond St. w., M5H 2A4, L. Anne Welwood
Lockwood, Bellmore & Moore, #1440, 439 University Ave., T. J. Lockwood, B. P. Bellmore, D.C. Moore
Loconte & Isenberg, 1729 Eglinton Ave. w., F. Loconte, A. Isenberg

LoFaso & Assoc., 1205 St. Clair Ave. w., #201, M6E 1B5, G. LoFaso, D.C. Bird
LoFranco & Gollom, #200, 51 Eglinton Ave. e., R.C. LoFranco, P.P. Gollom, D.F. Longley
Loftus, B. D., 600, 347 Bay St.
Lomer, M., #400, 425 University Ave.
Loopstra, Nixon & McLeish, 145 Rexdale Blvd. (Rexdale), C. M. Loopstra, J. A. Nixon, J. A. McLeish, J.R. Hall, R.B. Cohen, J.C. Hubble
Lopes, B.J., 939 Mount Pleasant Rd., M4P 2L7
Lorenzetti & Wolfe, 133 Richmond St. w., N. L. Lorenzetti, Q.C., H. Wolfe, P. Alter, J. C. Riddell
Loreto, F., 3329 Bloor St. w.
Lovas, S.I., #1103, 141 Adelaide St. w.
Low, W., #800, 1867 Yonge St.
Lubell, Kreitzer, 55 Eglinton Ave. e., J.B. Lubell, A.A. Kreitzer
Lucas, J.D., Q.C., 55 Harper Ave.
Luck, E.H., Q.C., 1 Greensboro Dr. (Rexdale)
Luftspring, A.J., 2300 Yonge St.
Lukasewich, P., 3386 Lakeshore Blvd. w.
Lundy, A., 65 Queen St. w.
Lutes, E. L., 557 Danforth Ave.
Lynde, S. W., 85 Richmond St. w.
Lyons, Arbus, Toronto Dominion Centre, Box 291, J. S. Lyons, Q.C., B.S. Arbus, V. I. Balaban, P.M. Iacono, H.P. Brown, D.L. Zifkin, P.D. Slan, M.S. Slan, C.M. Harpur, D. Chong. Counsel: D.P. Smith
Macartney, G. A., Q.C., 365 Bay St., M5H 2V1
Macaulay, J.M., 1436 Kingston Rd. (Scarboro, M1N 1R3)
Macaulay, Lipson & Joseph, #1800, 2180 Yonge St., B.D. Lipson, H.I. Joseph, P.R. O'Donoghue, R.N. Siddall, P. Beglaubter, R.D. Sheaffer, J.L. Davies, R.R. Elliott, M.F. Freedman, R.B. Melvin, J.S. Teichman, M.A. Eustace. Counsel: R.W. Macaulay, Q.C., Richard Rohmer, Q.C.
MacBeth & Johnson, 133 Richmond St. w., D. S. Johnson, Q.C., S. Anissimoff, J.W. Carson, P.D. Salsbury
MacBride, B.A., 8 King St. e.
Macdonald, E.M, 372 Bay St. (E. Cody-Rice)
MacDonald & Ferrier, #1500, 401 Bay St., M5H 2Y4, J. C. MacDonald, Q.C., L. K. Ferrier, Q.C., E. R. Kruzick, C. S. Nelson
Macdonald, Kennedy & Pandell, #1103, 330 Bay St., G.S. Macdonald, Q.C., L. Pandell, L.M. Marshall
MacDonald, W. E., Q.C., #104, 85 The East Mall, M8Z 5W4
MacGregor, R.G., #300, 111 Elizabeth St.
MacGregor, Wilson & MacKerrow, 3416 Dundas St. w., R. E. MacKerrow
MacKay, R., #320, 100 Richmond St. w.
Mackenzie, Wood & Magill, #620, 85 Richmond St. w., J. N. Magill, J.P. Burk, Q.C., J.V. O'Donnell, J.W. Waters, Margot Hallman, V.A. Sgro. Counsel: H.S. Mackenzie, Q.C.
MacLean & Chercover, 85 Richmond St. w., #615, M5H 2H1, L. A. MacLean, Q.C., B. Chercover, L. Maureen Kenny, S. Krashinsky
MacLean, H. J., 100 Yorkville Ave.
MacLennan, D.J., Q.C., #2914, 390 Bay St.
MacMahon, J. W., Q.C., 2842 Bloor St. w.
MacMaster, Poolman, #915, 1075 Bay St., W.G. Poolman, L. De Vries. Counsel: H.M. MacMaster, Q.C.
MacMillan, Rooke, Avery & Boeckle, 365 Bay St., C.F. MacMillan, Q.C., G. L. Rooke, Q.C., W. M. Avery, Q.C., P.K. Boeckle, B. R. Robinson, J.D. Tomlinson
MacNamara, G.R., 25 Severn St.
Macnaughton & Macnaughton, #1101, 27 Queen St. e., A.M. Macnaughton, Q.C.
MacRobie, Alan C., Q.C., #2200, 20 Eglinton Ave. w., M4R 1K8
Magerman & Page, 2141 Jane St. (Downsview), A. S. Magerman, Q.C., A. Page, Q.C., G.M. Kuzmarov, M.M. Bines
Magwood, Pocock, Rogers, O'Callaghan, 44 King St. w., J. M. Magwood, Q.C., J. A. Pocock, Q.C., I. MacF. Rogers, Q.C., J. E. O'Callaghan, J.H. Marler, B.W. Brucker, J.C. Ruderman
Maksymiw, Tokar & Hrycyna, #200, 1081 Bloor St. w., R.A. Maksymiw, G.O. Tokar, T. Hrycyna
Malcolm, D. I., #705, 330 University Ave.
Malcolm, T.R.A., #1120, 100 King St. w. (also Montreal)
Male, W.H., Q.C., 270 Kennedy Ave.
Mallin, Anna, 457 Woburn Ave.
Malo, Pilley, 1067 Bloor St. w., G. Malo, Q.C., B. P. Pilley, D. Lee
Maloney, Arthur, Q.C., #400, 120 Adelaide St. w. (G. Hainey)
Maloney, P.M., 467 Church St.
Mandel, H.M., #1102, 27 Queen St. e.
Mandell, H.S., Q.C., 175 Bloor St. e.
Mandell, J., #705, 55 Queen St. e. (P.H. Mandell, E.L. James)
Mang & Steinberg, 573A College St., I.R. Mang, G.S. Steinberg
Manley, Grant & Camisso, 390 Bay St., M5H 2W7, John S. Grant, Q.C., A. Camisso, Q.C., M. W. Manley, J. S. Grant, Jr.
Manning & Assoc., #2900, 390 Bay St., M. Manning, Q.C., Ingrid Myers, S. Labow
Manning, Bruce, Macdonald & Macintosh, Commerce Court West, Box 33, M. Bruce, Q.C., P.H.H. Ridout, Q.C., H.F. Kimber, Q.C., J.M. Banfill, R.D. Poupore, Q.C., I.C.C. Balfour, E.F. Merringer, D.C. Ross, D.L. Todd, J.M. McEown. Counsel: Charles C. Mark
Marchildon, P. F., #2200, 390 Bay St.
Marcos, Bouchard & Cusmariu, 1618 Dundas St. w., E. Marcos, M.G. Bouchard, J.J. Cusmariu
Marks, H.D., Q.C., #1001, 110 Yonge St.
Marks, I., #300, 70 Richmond St. e.
Marler & Assoc., #2308, 44 King St. w., J.H. Marler, H. Jarvlepp
Marron, G. A., #403, 330 Bay St.
Marshall, F.R., Q.C., 111 Richmond St. w.
Marszewski, E.E., #307, 347 Bay St.
Martin, Ben, 469 Queen St. e.
Martin, E.J.S., 4214 Dundas St. w.
Martin & Fyshe, 113 Davenport Rd., D.L. Martin, G.J. Fyshe
Martin, M., 577 Jarvis St.
Martin, McGill, 600 Church St., C. Martin, Q.C., Roberta McGill
Martin, S.L., #2200, 390 Bay St.
Martin, T., 490 College St.
Martin, W.W., #221, 1884 Eglinton Ave. e. (Scarboro)
Marzec, E., 1234 Royal York Rd. (Islington)
Massey, W. J., 85 Ellesmere Rd. (Scarboro)
Massie, R. D. A., 29 Golden Gate Court (Scarboro)
Mastin, A.J.R., #1908, 101 Richmond St. w.
Mathews, Dinsdale & Clark, Box 36, 401 Bay St. (M5H 2Z7), S.E. Dinsdale, Q.C., J. P. Sanderson, Q.C., B. W. Binning, W. S. Cook, Wm. G. Phelps, R.A. Werry, B.R. Baldwin, S.C. Bernardo, W. J. McNaughton, J.D. Carrier, G.H. Grossman, R.M. Parry, P.M. Rusak, M.D. Contini, D.J. Forbes-Roberts. Counsel: N.L. Mathews, Q.C.
Maubach, D.J., 731 Queen St. e.
Maxwell, Vickery, #505, 133 Richmond St. w., W.R. Maxwell, Q.C., P.B. Vickery
May, May & McCreary, 709, 2300 Yonge St., R. F. May, Q.C., L. A. May, Q.C., W. P. McCreary, J.W. May
May, J.W., #503, 121 Richmond St. w.
Maynard, W.E., 204, 330 Bay St.
Mayne, D.C., 577 Jarvis St.
Mayzel, H., 401 Bay St.
Mazza, Mazza, #2901, 390 Bay St. (also Hamilton)
McAlpine, A. D., Q.C., 65 Queen St. w., #1105, M5H 2M5
McBey, R.A., #301, 460 Eglinton Ave. e.
McBride, Wallace & Laurent, 2405 Lakeshore Blvd. w., J. M. McBride, M. F. Wallace, P. R. Laurent
McCallum McClean, #800, 111 Richmond St. w., A.D. McCallum, D.K. McClean
McCarthy, D.V., 1810 Avenue Rd.
McCarthy & McCarthy, Box 48, Toronto Dominion Centre, Beverley Matthews, Q.C., James W. Walker, Q.C., J. W. Blain, Q.C., John H. C. Clarry, Q.C., D. G. Milne, Q.C., I. Douglas, Q.C., G. F. Hayden, Q.C., P.H.G. Walker, Q.C., J. B. Lawson, Q.C., B. R. Cheeseman, Q.C., G. D. Finlayson, Q.C., G.P.H. Vernon, Q.C., Hon. D.S. Macdonald, D.K. Laidlaw, Q.C., H. W. Macdonell, Q.C., P. G. Beattie, Q.C., R. Robertson, Q.C., D. J. Donahue, Q.C., Michael Croghan, Q.C., J. H. Francis, Q.C., R. E. Sobier, Q.C., D.F.O. Hersey, R. L. Butters, L.T. Forbes, Q.C., S.C. Smith, D. E. Smith, C.L. Campbell, Q.C., A.R.A. Scace, Q.C., B. Tait, Q.C., G.A. Halladay, Q.C., W.J. Cornwall, D.H. Gordon, T.G. Heintzman, B. Crawford, J.C. McCartney, P.S. Grant, A.J. Lenczner, D.E. Gilmore, T.H. Bjarnason, D.G. Cooper, D.S. Ewens, D.L. Robinette, D.M. Paton, R.G. Slaght, D.H. Wood, D.G. Gibson, J.B. Noonan, Susan Greer, M.E. Royce, G.G. MacArthur, E.P. Kerwin, R.A. Shaw, V.P. Alboini, P.D. Quinn, G.B. Cowper-Smith, N.S. Rankin, J.R. Wilson. Associates: M.M. Johnston, Mary L. Dickson, E.A. McNeill, W.N. Ortved, G.S. Clarke, L.P. Salzman, D.M. Harley, F.D. Rounthwaite, G.A. Smith, A.R. Szibbo, Judith M. Woods, R.E. Forbes, F.P. Morrison, K.R. Peel, J.J. Colangelo, G.M. Girvan, S.D.A. Clark, J.L. Finlay, Shanon O.N. Grauer, G.P. Sadvari, P.L. Sanford, R.R. Sorell, R.W.F. Stephenson, Elizabeth M. Stewart, F.B. Wright, T.B. Akin, Linda J. Betts, C.A. Montague, G.S. Sato, D.M. Armstrong, Susan Bisset, Elizabeth Fisher, P.H. Griffin, G.J. Howard, Judith Kingston, R.B. Miner, M.G. Quigley, Cheryl Belkin, C.J. Birchall, K. Chown, B.D. Edmonds, D.I. Hamer, O.A. Johnson, D. Langer, R.A. MacPherson, H.C.G. Underwood. Counsel: J.J. Robinette, Q.C., D.R.C. Harvey, Q.C., T.M. Dolan; Associate Counsel: Hon. Salter A. Hayden, Q.C., W.C. Terry, Q.C.
McCaw, L.M.I., 8 King St. e.
McClintock, Devry & Deeth, 40 Wynford Dr. (Don Mills), W. R. McClintock, H. R. Devry, Q.C., F.T. Deeth, W.J. Smith
McClyment, S.A., 1571 Sandhurst Circle (Scarboro)
McCombs, J.D., 65 Queen St. w.
McCulla, W., 326 Bathurst St.
McDermott, McGarry & Rafferty, #509, 212 King St. w., F.T. McDermott, D.E. McGarry, D.P. Rafferty

McDonald & Hayden, #1900, 155 University Ave., J. G. McDonald, Q.C., P.R. Hayden, Q.C., D.C. Nathanson, J. H. Burns, D.R. Street, J.J. McDermott, B.N. McLellan, C.M. Goldlist, Wendy Posluns. Counsel: J.I. Laskin
McDonald, J. J., 2180 Danforth Ave., M4C 1K3
McElwain & Assoc., 41 Hazelton Ave., J.D. McElwain, Q.C., Joanne Rusnell, K.D. Stout
McFadden, Marrocco & Parker, 480 University Ave., D. J. McFadden, F. N. S. Marrocco, R. H. Parker, B. Weagant, G.R. Laidlaw
McGarry & McKeon, 401 Bay St., Box 30, C. F. McKeon, Q.C., R. W. Heather, Q.C., S.M. Lynham
McGrath, Joy, Box 105, 401 Bay St.
McGraw, B. J., Q.C., 17 Queen St. e.
McGregor, J., #402, 19 Richmond St. w.
McGuire, B., 2643 Eglinton Ave. w.
McIver, T. P., Q.C., 44 King St. w. (L.C. Wesson)
McKague & McKague, 401 Bay St., Box 47, A. E. McKague, Q.C., B. H. McKague
McKechnie & Jurgeit, 655 Dixon Rd. (Rexdale), G.W. McKechnie, H.M. Jurgeit
McKeown, C.G.S., 155 Broadview Ave.
McKeown, M.C., 32 Westrose Ave.
McKeown, Yoerger, Spearing, #401, 121 Richmond St. w., M5H 2K2, M.P.S. Spearing, P.M. Gordon. Counsel: G.R. Green
McKillop, D.J., Q.C., 2161 Yonge St. (J.E. Bowden)
McLachlan, Winter & Czernik, 19 Madison Ave., M.S. McLachlan, M. Winter, A.M. Czernik
McLaren, D.A., Q.C., 1240 Bay St., #606, M5R 2A7
McLaughlin, H.E.L., 1268 Weston Rd.
McLaughlin, Soward, Markle, 200 University Ave. (M5H 3E1), R. H. Soward, Q.C., A.D. McFall, R. N. McLaughlin, Q.C., J. H. McLaughlin, Q.C., W. W. Markle, Q.C., D.E.G. Phibbs, P. Virginia Holmes, Karon C. Bales, D.B. Leith. Counsel: W.D.S. Morden, Q.C.
McLean, G. W., 121 Richmond St. w.
McLean & Kerr, 372 Bay St., W.E. McLean, Q.C., H.C. Kerr, Q.C., Wm. E. Paterson, Q.C., R. B. Cumine, Q.C., R. J. Roberts, J. W. Handiak, R. J. Arcand, H.J. Blake, Q.C., W.R. Stevenson, R. J. Goodman, M. A. Sear, L. Alksnis, Suzanne J. Johnston, J.A. Ballard, Reeva M. Finkel
McMaster, McIntyre & Smyth, 2859 Dundas St. w., J.A. Smyth, P.J. Crowe, G.L. Wright, W.A. McIntyre
McMaster & Meighen, Box 191, First Canadian Place, M.A. Meighen, P.E. Lockie, R.B. Matthews, J.D. Stirling, S.J. Harrington, N.A. Saibil, Marilyn Bartlett, A. Whiteley. Counsel: F.G. Felkai
McMaster Montgomery, 133 Richmond St. w. (M5H 2L9), J. W. McMaster, Q.C., D. A. Mackenzie, K.J.C. Dean, W. P. Butler, D.W. Croft, P.K. Foulds. Counsel: H.L. Steele, Q.C.
McMillan, Binch, Box 38, Royal Bank Plaza (M5J 2J7), W. A. Macdonald, Q.C., J. S. Farquharson, Q.C., J.N. Turner, P.C., Q.C., F.O. Gerity, Q.C., M. B. Jameson, Q.C., K.B. McMillan, Nancy L. Carnwath, R. M. Turnbull, Q.C., S.G. Fisher, Q.C., P.F.M. Jones, D. I. Matheson, Q.C., C.T. Loughrin, G.E. Whyte, Q.C., C.D. Macdonald, Q.C., P.G. Cathcart, Q.C., E.K. Weir, J. A. Paterson, J. S. Peterson, T.E. McDonnell, W.D. McCordic, R.K. McDermott, W. Woloshyn, J.W. Craig, R.N. Gilmore, H. Lenore Roszell, J.W.F. Rowley, J.G. Armstrong, J.C. Osborne, T.J. O'Sullivan, Alice-Anne Morlock, D.G. Butler, G.L. Jacobs, J.A. Kazanjian, L.T. Taman, M.J. Davies, R.G. Keel, B.F. Little, D.J. Packer, G.K.S. Payne, M.M. Yaksich, T.W. McBride, B.W. Burkett, S.E. Pepall, J.E.A. West, D.A. Giannini, L. Macchione, D.S. McLean, M.M. Trask, F.A. Archibald, J.S. Drance, B.C. Hoyes, I.G. McLeod, T.E. Scott, J.M. Stransman, S.W. Bowman, C.I. Simpson, C.J. Sinclair
McNish & McNish, 2221 Yonge St., J. D. McNish, Q.C., N. D. McNish, I. H. McNish
McPhail, I.D.C., #905, 27 Queen St. e.
McRae, N. D., Q.C., 401 Bay St., Box 74
McTaggart, Potts, Stone, Winters & Herridge, #2600, 390 Bay St. (M5H 2Y2), D. H. McTaggart, Q.C., D. Winters, Q.C., J.H. Potts, Q.C., A. J. Stone, Q.C., Wm. R. Herridge, Q.C., Elizabeth Julian, W.I.C. Binnie, Q.C., T.J. Dunne, L. Kozak, R. D. Peck, R. J. Sharpe, J.B. Love, J.R. Cade, G.R. Strathy, O.V. Gray, J.D. Gregory, Elizabeth J. Forster, Kristine Connidis, L.H. Dudley, J.P. Groia, E.W. Wright
Meagher, Shaw, #1704, 8 King St. e., R.J. Meagher, R.J. Shaw
Medland, D. H., 141 Adelaide St. w., M5H 3L5
Meech, R. G., Q.C., Commerce Court West, Box 127, M5L 1E2
Melnik & Saunders, #400, 70 Richmond St. e., D. Melnik, Q.C., H. W. Saunders, Q.C., D. A. Hendler, Marion J. Stendon, G.H. Harris, A.C. Dymond, P. Draper, Kathi Arkin, D.N. Ross. Counsel: B.A. Kelsey, Q.C.
Mendelson, H.L., Q.C., 260 8th St.
Menzies, J. A., Q.C., 1071B Bloor St. w. (L.A. von Bogen)
Merenda, S., 29 Beatrice St.
Merkur, D.I., 1801 Avenue Rd.
Merrick, Pollack, Grubner, #1201, 180 Bloor St. w., Paul Merrick, L. Pollack, A. Grubner. Counsel: J.D. Sloan
Mesbur, Ruth E., 1108, 85 Richmond St. w., M5H 2C9
Metropolitan Toronto Legal Dept., City Hall, A. P. G. Joy, Q.C., Solicitor; J. B. Davis, Deputy Solicitor; R. M. Parker, Corporation Counsel
Metzler, W.J., 100 Richmond St. w. (D.G. LeFeuvre)
Meyer, W. J., Q.C., #1202, 20 Eglinton Ave. w., M4R 1K8
Meyrick, D.F., Q.C., #508, 372 Bay St., M5H 2W9 (M.J. Kennedy)
Midanik, Starkman & Rose, 401 Bay St., Box 4, J.S. Midanik, Q.C., S.H. Starkman, S.M. Rose, J.M. Rubinoff
Mikitchook, Y., #203, 229 Yonge St.
Miller, G.R., #804, 161 Eglinton Ave. e.
Miller & Miller, 1622 Bloor St. w., A. Miller, L. Miller
Miller, Stohn, Mills, #205, 47 Colborne St., M5E 1E3, T.S. Mills, Q.C., G.C. Miller, J.S. Stohn, S. Schneiderman
Miller, Thomson, Sedgewick, Lewis & Healy, 20 Queen St. w., M5H 3S1 (branch office at 7050 Woodbine Ave., Markham), J.H. Thomson, Q.C., R.M. Sedgewick, Q.C., C. W. Lewis, Q.C., J.W. Healy, Q.C., D. Churchill-Smith, Q.C., J. A. Langford, Q.C., M. A. Mogan, Q.C., J. E. Sheppard, Q.C., D. C. Matheson, Q.C., W.L. McAuley, R. J. Fuller, D.J. Moxon, T.K. Billings, L. Bertuzzi, A. M. Gans, J.T. Beamish, J. D. Whiteside, J.D.M. Fraser, R.D. McGregor, F.M.E. Maréchaux, E.G. Nazzer, E.M.F. McCallum, M.A. Fredricks, J.L. Burns, R.G. Weppler, M.J. Pace, R.T. Rocchi, J.A. Roffey, J.R. Sproat, M.J. Addario, K.M. Tamaki, P.F. Kiborn, L.H. Macleod, M.L. Shell. Counsel: J.A.F. Miller, Q.C.
Mills & Mills, 401 Bay St., Box 20, M5H 2Y4, P. H. Mills, Q.C., Ralph S. Mills, Q.C., D. S. Mills, Q.C., R. N. Rudan, Q.C., R. A. Cobham, J. P. Mills, J.B. Kutcy, G. R. Reid, P. J. Westlake, D.A. Quirt
Millward, D'Oliveira, Berman, #1904, 390 Bay St., M5H 2Y2, A.C. Millward, D.A.J. D'Oliveira, R.R. Berman
Milrad & Agnew, #1104, 20 Queen St. w., A.M. Milrad, E.M. Agnew
Milrad, L.H., 204, 2 Gloucester St.
Minden, A., 428 Dundas St. w., M5T 1G7
Minden, Gross, Grafstein & Greenstein, #600, 111 Richmond St. w., M5H 2H5, M. A. Gross, Q.C., J. S. Grafstein, Q.C., H.J. Greenstein, Q.C., M. L. Ainsley, J. S. Posen, H. R. Nathan, M. S. Sable, L. Klug, L.A. Lebovic, M.S. Lazarus, R.J. Armstrong, Ellen Cohen, P. Israel, P.D. Howe, M.R. Blidner, M. Maierovits, G.A. Maldoff, G.M. Caplan, R. Rapuch. Counsel: P. J. Brunner
Minsky, J.J., Q.C., 17 Queen St. e.
Mintz, A., 100 Richmond St. w., #434, M5H 3K6
Mircheff, N., 364A King St. e.
Miskin & Flancman, 1286 Kennedy Rd. (Scarboro), L. S. Miskin, M. H. Flancman, I.I. Frisch
Mitchell, R., Q.C., 245 College St.
Mitchell, Robinson, Anderson & Phelan, 101 Richmond St. w., G.G. Robinson, Q.C., J.E. Anderson, T.P. Phelan
Mohideen & Power, 2969 Kingston Rd. (Scarboro), A.K. Mohideen, G.M. Power
Moledina, G.A., 2938 Danforth Ave.
Monaco, E.L., 1710 Dufferin St.
Monaghan, B. J., 3080 Yonge St.
Montgomery & Gardner, 8 King St. e., M5C 1B5, M. Montgomery, Q.C., J. H. Gardner, Q.C.
Montgomery, Gary, 1729 Bloor St. w.
Morlock & Associates, #1104, 18 King St. e., M5C1C4, J. H. Morlock, Q.C., N.J.F. Steenberg, J.G. Griffiths, D.G. Flood, M.J.B. Wood
Morris & Assoc., 1295A St. Clair Ave. w., C.L. Morris, Q.C.
Morris/Bright/Rose, 2600, 145 King St. w., H. G. Morris, Q.C., J. C. Bright, Q.C., J. M. Rose, R.A. Blair, M. F. Ledgett, J. Hahn, J. A. Kilgour, J.G. McPherson, R.C. Wright, Christine E. Hart, Roslyn Maian, B.F. Kinahan, B. Lokash, Patricia Conway, R.G. Schipper
Morris, D. S., 129 John St.
Morris & Morris, 85 Richmond St. w., M5H 2C9, W.J.H. Morris, Q.C., R.W. Morris, J. W. Morris
Morris, Morris & Morris, #1506, 65 Queen St. w., Brian M. Morris, Saul Morris, Carol Wolkove. Counsel: L.J. Morris
Morris & Westman, #422, 131 Bloor St. w., L.J. Morris, C.R. Westman
Morrison, D.A., 2773 Lakeshore Blvd. w.
Morrison, S.R., #10, 401 Champagne Dr. (Downsview)
Mortimer Clark, Gray & Martin, 85 Richmond St. w., Mary E. Martin. Counsel: R.H.R. Gray, Q.C.
Moscoe & Moscoe, 80 Richmond St. w., H. R. Moscoe, Q.C., S. Moscoe, Q.C.
Moses, L. E., 525 Mt. Pleasant Rd.
Moses, Spring, Greenbaum & Pang, 20 Madison Ave., M5R 2S1, A. Moses, Q.C., H. Spring, D. M. Greenbaum, Q.C., J.C.L. Pang

Mostyn & Mostyn, 845 St. Clair Ave. w., #303, L. Mostyn, Q.C., A. Mostyn, L. Wayne
Mott-Trille, F. R., #1003, 111 Elizabeth St., M5G 1P7
Mowat, Maclennan & Titus, 120 Adelaide St. w., E. B. Titus, Q.C.
Mucha, S.M., #1205, 180 Bloor St. w.
Muir, Robert, Q.C., 3464 Kingston Rd., Scarboro
Murphy, A. J., #1101, 27 Queen St. e.
Murphy, Moise & Grayson, 19 Richmond St. w., W.G. Murphy, J.P. Moise, B.M. Grayson, Q.C.
Murphy, R. J., 55 Nugget Ave. (Scarboro)
Murray, Ellen, 33, 165 Spadina Ave.
Murray, J. A., 390 Bay St.
Muskat, Clara, 45 Richmond St. w.
Nakelsky, D.L., #210, 372 Bay St., M5H 2W9
Napier, W.M., #202, 80 Richmond St. w., M5H 2A4
Nasello, F.G., 2737 Danforth Ave.
Nashman, H. B., #211, 825 Eglinton Ave. w., M5N 1E7
Naumovich, J., 813 Broadview Ave.
Nawrocki, Coviensky, #406, 133 Richmond St. w., J.R. Nawrocki, A. Coviensky
Naylor, W. E. M., 372 Bay St., #900, M5H 2W9
Neal & Smith, #202, 2950 Birchmount Rd. (Scarboro), R.R. Neal, B.H. Smith
Neinstein & Singer, 1183 Finch Ave. w. (Downsview), M. Neinstein, E. Singer
Nelson, McNamee, , J.C. Nelson, J. McNamee
Nemis, R., 436 Adelaide St. w.
Neuman & Grant, #520C, 131 Bloor St. w., I.J. Neuman, G.D. Grant
Nevels, W.M., 425 Jane St.
Newey & Newey, 824 Wilson Ave. (Downsview), D. D. Newey
Newhouse, G.W., #32, 165 Spadina Ave.
Newman, D. H., 347 Bay St.
Newman (Harry A.) & Newman, #1101, 27 Queen St. e., Thomas A. Newman, Q.C.
Newman, J. L., #300, 106 Adelaide St. w.
Newman, Reiber & Weinstock, 43 Eglinton Ave. e., N. Reiber, A. Weinstock, Eva Lake
Newman, S. H., 706, 347 Bay St.
Nicol, A.R., #502, 145 Adelaide St. w.
Niebler, D., #900, 372 Bay St.
Niejadlik, R. A., 409 Roncesvalles Ave.
Noble, W. H., Q.C., 55 Charles St. e.
Norman, J.D., #1708, 390 Bay St.
Novak, J.M., Box 227, Commercial Union Tower
O'Connor, D., #322, 100 Richmond St. w.
O'Connor & Gold, 1 Sultan St., M5S 1L6, F. D. O'Connor, G. Gold
O'Donnell & Frank, #2108, 101 Richmond St. w., R.A. O'Donnell, Q.C., E. Eva Frank
O'Donnell, J.F., #1704, 8 King St. e.
O'Donohue, White & Christo, #2010, 401 Bay St., M. O'Donohue, Q.C., R.C. White, Q.C., P.R. Christo, M.W. Price, W.P. Brown
Offman, M.E., 2131 Yonge St.
Offman & Raby, 2020 Bathurst St., M2L 2E1, L. Offman, R.B. Raby
Ogden, C.R., 881 Eglinton Ave. w.
Oiye, K. G., Q.C., 2 Carlton St.
Okell, Greenblatt, Weisman & Feldman, #100, 345 Wilson Ave. (Downsview, M3H 1T1), N.K. Okell, D.P. Greenblatt, D.A. Weisman, S.B. Feldman
O'Kell, J.R., Q.C., 3500 Royal Bank Plaza
Olanick, M. K., Q.C., 1081 Bloor St. w.
Olch, Torgov, Cohen & Kent, 111 Richmond St. w., H. W. Olch, Q.C., M. L. Torgov, M. M. Cohen, P.J. Kent, P.R. Bonenfant
Oldreive, J.C., #133, 111 Richmond St. w.
Olkovich, E.F., #801, 111 Richmond St. w.
Olmstead, E.B., #2108, 401 Bay St.
O'Malley, W. D., Q.C., 401 Bay St., Box 48
Omatsu, M., 840 Palmerston Ave.
O'Neill, Browning, Box 373, Commerce Court Postal Stn., T. E. O'Neill, Q.C., B. A. Browning, S.P. Pineau
O'Neill, P.F., #345, 100 Richmond St. w.
Ongley & Blair, 85 Richmond St. w., #207, M5H 2C9, D. J. Ongley, Q.C., D'A. Blair, Q.C.
Onizuka, T. T., Q.C., 201, 425 University Ave.
Opekokew, D.M.A., #202, 280 Bloor St. w.
Orbach, Katzman & Roth, 417 Parliament St., C. Orbach, Q.C., H.P. Katzman, F.L. Roth, S. Herschorn
O'Reilly, Moll & Libman, #1002, 330 Bay St., M5H 2S8, C. I. O'Reilly, D. J. Moll, P.K. Libman
Orkin, Jaffary, #1700, 390 Bay St., M.M. Orkin, Q.C., K.D. Jaffary, Q.C., R.A.M. Ikeda
Orliffe, Turner, Brooks, 1530 Albion Rd. (Rexdale), S. Turner, P. Brooks
Orzech, M.C., 4121 Lawrence Ave. e. (Scarboro)
Osak, Grossman, #300, 2788 Bathurst St., S. Osak, S.Z. Grossman
Osler, Hoskin & Harcourt, Box 50, First Canadian Place (M5X 1B8), Deborah M. Alexander, F.R. Allen, D.R. Allgood, S.V. Arnold, R.G. Atkey, Q.C., W.B.C. Bailey, J.M. Baker, L.A.J. Barnes, B.R. Bawden, A.L. Beattie, Q.C., F.R. Berrill, A.S. Blair, H.K. Boylan, Q.C., W.M. Bryden, Q.C., B.D. Bucknall, Sheila Budd, Nancy D. Chaplick, M. J. Coombs, P. Crawford, Q.C., Jean M. DeMarco, P. J. Dey, Ann D. Dillon, J. K. Doran, Q.C., D.W. Drinkwater, M.L.J. Edwards, M. Field-Marsham, J.E. Fordyce, C. Alicia Forgie, Q.C., Heather A. Frawley, J. G. Goodwin, Q.C., J.N. Grieve, Q.C., J. D. Ground, Q.C., J.R. Hassell, E.A. Heakes, L.D. Hebb, A. O. Hendrie, H.D. Hodgson, E.J.M. Huycke, Q.C., F.A.M. Huycke, Q.C., T.R. Judge, G. E. Julian, Q.C., Krista Kehl, J.F. Kennedy, J. T. Kennish, D. Lane, Q.C., J.F. Layton, J.B.G. Ledger, Julie Lee, B.M. Levitt, R.F. Lindsay, Q.C., J.H. Lisson, N.C. Loveland, S.W. Luff, D.L. Marston, E.T. McDermott, Barbara McGregor, F.W. McIntosh-Janis, I.J.F. McSweeney, B. Morgan, M. Mraz, B. Murray, C.R. Osler, Q.C., E. Pascutto, D.F. Pattison, Q.C., B.M.W. Paulin, Q.C., J.F. Petch, C. Portner, A.D.G. Purdy, W.R. Rauenbusch, F.L. Reid, Nancy Riley, J.M. Roland, P.U. Schmidt, J.E. Sexton, Q.C., P. Siller, S.B. Smart, J.M. Steiner, G.J. Stewart, D.C.A. Tay, Carol Tennenhouse Diamond, Wendy Thompson, G.T. Tsampalieros, J.G. Vesely, D.E. Wakefield, Diane E. Walker, J.G. Ware, P. White, F. Zaid; Counsel: R. G. Ferguson, Q.C., H.C.F. Mockridge, Q.C., B. M. Osler, Q.C., W.S. Rogers, Q.C., S. Thom, Q.C., P. White, Q.C.
Osmak, O.J., 269 Riverside Dr.
Ostrowski, J.A., #2403, 180 Dundas St. w.
Outerbridge, #3000, 390 Bay St. (M5H 2Y2), T.W. Outerbridge, Q.C., W.H.O. Mueller, S. Lavine, W.A. Landon, R.E. Carr, F.A. Platt, C.R.C. Sefton, K.E. Rubin, R.P. Bowles
Pacevicius, A.S., 300 The East Mall (Islington)
Pacey & Deacon, 1810, 181 University Ave., M5H 3M7, G.R. Pacey, J.A. Deacon, M.A. Spears, P.L. Spears
Page, Cooper & Skryzlo, 401 Bay St., Box 6, M. B. Page, Q.C., G. Cooper, S. J. Skryzlo, W.E. Dourley, R.A. Klotz
Page & Strange, #17, 2885 Jane St. (Downsview), S.J. Page, E.A. Strange
Paisley, H.S.D.
Paisley, V.S., 390 Bay St.
Palamar, W., Q.C., 17 Queen St. e.
Palermo, V.L., 1055 Wilson Ave. (Downsview)
Palmer, B. D., Q.C., 229 Yonge St.
Palmer, M.L., Q.C., #902, 372 Bay St.
Panchenko, L.A., 390 Bay St.
Pantazis, D., #202, 751 Pape Ave.
Pape, P.J., #2901, 390 Bay St.
Papernick & Papernick, #224, 4580 Dufferin St., H. Papernick, Q.C., B. W. Papernick
Papoff, L.J., 951 Queen St. e., M4M 1J9
Paradiso, J., & Assoc., 1225 St. Clair Ave. w., M.Q. Chowdhry
Park, F., 347 Bay St.
Parker, F.T., 2 Bloor St. w. (L.A. Rotenberg)
Parkinson & Parkinson, 372 Bay St., T. M. Parkinson
Parkinson, R.A., Q.C., 14 Carlton St.
Partyka, R.A., #920, 250 Bloor St. e.
Paskaleff, V. L., 671 Danforth Ave.
Pasternak, S.B., 600 Church St.
Paterson, MacDougall, Commerce Court North, Box 411, A. R. Paterson, Q.C., D. B. MacDougall, V.R.P. Bersenas, W. M. McIntosh, C.E. McCall, N.H. Frawley, G.R. Hejduk
Patterson, P., 3 Sultan St.
Paul & Andrews, 7 Queen St. e., M5C 1P6, N. P. Paul, Q.C., W. Andrews, Q.C., S. Kanellos, J.J. Doane
Paul, J.G., 40 Dundas St. e.
Paul, R.A., #505, 133 Richmond St. w.
Payne, Marc, Box 23, Adelaide St. Stn.
Payne, Murray, 3329 Bloor St. w.
Pazulla, W.J., 2323 Bloor St. w.
Pearl, E.H., 4 Prince Arthur Ave.
Pease, E.G., #501, 133 Richmond St. w.
Peck, M., 133 Richmond St. w.
Peikes & Halpert, #300, 44 Eglinton Ave. w., S.M. Peikes, A.S. Halpert. Counsel: N.A. Endicott
Pelensky, M., 2 Toronto St.
Perdue, Baker & Whittaker, #1810, 65 Queen St. w., R.R. Perdue, M.D. Baker, W.G. Whittaker
Perkins, Kenney & Ballard, 2 Billingham Rd., J.H. Perkins, W.O.S. Ballard, G.J. Kenney, R.D. Stewart
Perkins, R. D., 41 Roxborough St. e.
Perry, Farley & Onyschuk, Box 451, Toronto Dominion Centre (M5K 1M5), V.R.E. Perry, Q.C., F.A. Rush, Q.C., G.M. Deacon, J.M. Farley, T. Kerzner, Q.C., B.S. Onyschuk, Q.C., P.H. Harris, B.G. Armstrong, R.A. MacDermid, B.B. Papazian, J.R. Boxma, C.B. MacFarlane, M.J. Campbell, R.R. Arblaster, A.P.C. Dean, J.P. Maggisano, R.Z. Kowalyk, A.P.C. Dean, W.D. Templeton, A.M. McLauchlan. Counsel: Hon. Royce Frith, Q.C.
Peters & Kestelman, 245 Coxwell Ave., D. Peters, Q.C., A. Kestelman
Peterson & D'Andrea, 2352 Dufferin St., D. R. Peterson, F. M. D'Andrea
Petricone, I.F., 11 Prince Arthur Ave.
Petropoulos, P., 2200 Yonge St., #604, M4S 2C6
Phelan, O'Brien, Shannon & Lawer, 101 Richmond St. w. (M5H 1W1), Brendan O'Brien, Q.C., J.V. Lawer, Q.C., L.P. Shannon, Q.C., A.G.F. Macdonald,

M.D.R. O'Brien, W. P. Cipollone, M.H. Miskin
Phillips & Phillips, 65 Queen St. w., Howard A. Phillips, Q.C., B. C. North, Q.C.
Philp & Fonseca, 425 University Ave., J. D. Philp, O. A. J. Fonseca
Phipps, N. E., Q.C., 330 University Ave.
Picov, Joseph & Kleinberg, 164 Eglinton Ave. e., K.I. Picov, G.S. Joseph, B.H.J. Kleinberg
Pidruchny, W., 171 Yonge St.
Pih, G.C.W., #201, 94 Cumberland St.
Piller, L.A., 3 Sultan St.
Pinkofsky, Lockyer & Martin, #1550, 439 University Ave., J.L. Pinkofsky, J. Lockyer, D. Martin
Piscelli & Faieta, 856 The Queensway, G. Piscelli, N. Faieta
Pitt, R.W.M., 201, 360 Bloor St. w.
Pivnick, Morrow, #1800, 101 Richmond St. w., M.R. Morrow, Q.C., J.M. Pivnick
Platt, P., #1807, 8 King St. e.
Poch, D.I., 293 Eglinton Ave. e.
Polla, F., 1684 Dufferin St.
Pollack, A. S., 111 Richmond St. w.
Pollock & Eisen, 3625 Dufferin St. (Downsview), J. H. Pollock, M. Eisen
Pollock, J., 1415 Lawrence Ave. w.
Pomer & Zeppieri, 3255 Dufferin St., D.M. Pomer, E. Zeppieri
Pomerant & Devlin, 3360 First Canadian Place, J.B. Pomerant, Q.C., Jane Devlin, Y. Timol, D.R. Beardall, M.Z. Tufman, B. Daley, Kai Wing Tsang, L. Phillips
Pomerantz, H.M., #412, 170 Bloor St. w.
Poole & Perreault, 219 Avenue Rd., A.F.N. Poole, B. Perreault, Eileen Martin
Popovski, W., 45 Overlea Blvd.
Porter & Posluns, Commerce Court North, Box 365, Julian Porter, Q.C., D. Posluns, R.B. Kennedy
Posner, G.S., 3646 Lawrence Ave. e. (also Kenora)
Posthumus & Abols, #1900, 700 Bay St., W.G. Posthumus, G. Abols, S.M. Jusyp
Potter, S.J., 640 Bloor St. w., M6G 1K9 (R.J. Tyndorf)
Powell, D.M., #904, 347 Bay St.
Prattas, Z.J.C., 3 Chester St.
Prendergast, D'A. J., 15 St. Andrews Gardens
Preobrazenski, C.G., #1001, 100 Yonge St.
Preszler, R. P., 45 Richmond St. w., #1003, M5H 1Z2
Price, A.S., #1800, 2180 Yonge St.
Price, S., 2404, 1 Dundas St. w., M5G 1Z3
Prince, D.J., 1421 Danforth Ave.
Proctor, D.R., 229 Yonge St.
Prousky & Biback, 2 Toronto St., N. Biback, Q.C., V. Prousky, H. M. Lewin. Counsel: M. Prousky, Q.C.
Purcell & Walton, 893 O'Connor Dr., V. E. Purcell, Q.C., M. R. Walton
Purvis & Purvis, 95 St. Clair Ave. w., G. I. Purvis, Q.C.
Puteris, A., #200, 3031 Bloor St. w.
Pyne, R.G., 3329 Bloor St. w.
Qualer, N., 245 Coxwell Ave.
Quirk, McGillicuddy & Sutton, 1661 Dufferin St., H. McGillicuddy, F. B. Sutton
Rabinovitch, M.D., #3100, 390 Bay St.
Rachlin, Wolfson & Malach, 390 Bay St., T. H. Rachlin, Q.C., H. Wolfson, Q.C., S. M. Malach, J.T. Fidler, D.B. Scanlon
Radford, A.J., #1700, 11 King St. w.
Radomski, D.H., #1004, 60 St. Clair Ave. e.
Radomsky, Freedman, #601, 121 Richmond St. w., L. Radomsky, G.M. Freedman, S.J. Brannan
Raftopoulos, A., #117, 1000 Finch Ave. w. (Downsview)
Rainer, Niebler, #900, 372 Bay St., M.C. Rainer, D. Niebler
Raisbeck, W.A., M.D., Commerce Court w., Box 98 (V.W. Hamra)
Raman, A. M., 1944A Eglinton Ave. w.
Ramsay, A.M., 372 Bay St., M5H 2W9
Raphael, Wheatley & MacPherson, #200, 77 Elizabeth St., B. Raphael, Q.C., B.H. Wheatley, Q.C., G.A. MacPherson, Q.C., S.H. Raphael, P.A. Daley, R.E. Sugar
Rash & Back, 3420 Finch Ave. e. (Scarboro), H. Rash, K. Back
Raymond, H., 1477 Eglinton Ave. w.
Raymond & Honsberger, 85 Richmond St. w., M5H 2C9, John D. Honsberger, Q.C., R. B. Watt, L.P. Straub, H.I. Lewis
Ready, E.A., #1004, 60 St. Clair Ave. e., M4T 1N5
Reble & Townend, #111, 1 Eva Rd. (Etobicoke), J.H. Reble, G.M. Townend
Reed, P.D., #400, 243 Queen St. w.
Reeve, D.J., 6th fl., 111 Elizabeth St.
Regan, F. V., Q.C., 65 Queen St. w., M5H 2M5
Reid, W. H., Q.C., 2938 Danforth Ave., M4C 1M5, C. R. Langdon, Q.C.
Reilly, Mrs. Dorothy J., 701 Coxwell Ave.
Reingold, J., Q.C., 3080 Yonge St., M4N 3N1
Reinhardt, P.H., 165 Spadina Ave.
Reisman, S., #1012, 123 Edward St.
Reiter & Assoc., 86 Avenue Rd., M. Reiter, Q.C., M.S. Korn, Susan Anderson
Reiter & Rain, 410 Adelaide St. w., E. Reiter, M. Rain, S.R.C. Schnurr
Rekai, Judyth, 45 Nanton Ave.
Reycraft & Saunders, 330 Bay St., M5H 2S8, J. S. Reycraft, G. W. Saunders
Richardson, L. J., #705, 133 Richmond St. w., M5H 2L3
Riches, McKenzie & Herbert, #2900, 2 Bloor St. e., M4W 3J5, G. H. Riches, Q.C., C. R. Riches, R. D. McKenzie, Paul Herbert, L.L. Annett, R.B. Latham
Rickerd, D.S., Q.C., Box 122, Toronto Dominion Centre
Ricketts, Farley & Lowndes, 181 University Ave., T. S. Farley, Q.C., J. M. Lowndes, Q.C., R. D. Preston, J.D. Gibson, G.I. Leckie, C.A. Nelson
Roach, Smith, 688 St. Clair Ave. w., C.C. Roach, M.F. Smith, M. Roulston, R.S. Richardson
Robb, M., Q.C., Box 365, Commerce Court North, M5L 1G2
Roberts & Drabinsky, Box 82, First Canadian Place, #6965, M5X 1B1, R.J. Roberts, Q.C., G.H. Drabinsky, S.D. Elliott, S.T. Selznick, Susan G. Cavan
Robertson & Keith, 2481 Kingston Rd. (Scarboro, M1N 1V4), A.R. Keith
Robertson, N.S., Q.C., 105 Adelaide St. w.
Robertson, Perrett, #1720, 180 Dundas St. w., John F. Perrett, Q.C., D. D. Hague, P.A. Adams, Q.C.; Counsel: N. S. Robertson, Q.C., E.A. DuVernet, Q.C.
Robins & Partners, 130 Adelaide St. w., H. Robins, Q.C., H.G. Kotler, Q.C., R. Appleby, J.M. Banks, G.M. Taub, Q.C., R.P. Miller, L. C. Larry, L.J. Levine, J.R. Bergman, M. Gotlieb, D.H. Shlagbaum, B.H. Somer, Alison Manzer, A.L. Greenspoon, G.A. Levitan
Robins, S.M., 45 Richmond St. w.
Robinson & Haines, 372 Bay St., J. A. Haines, Q.C.
Robinson, Williams & Burn, 390 Bay St., M5H 2Y2, H. H. Robinson, Q.C., J. C. Williams, D. W. Burn
Robinson, W.K., 731 The Queensway, W. K. Robinson, B.J. Lange
Robson, T., 37 Gormley Ave.
Rocca & Rowatt, 1415 Lawrence Ave. w., F. Rocca, J. Rowatt
Rochester, B.L., #701, 121 Richmond St. w.
Rodney, R. A., 85 Scollard St.
Roebuck, L.D., #1608, 390 Bay St. (M.L. Solomon)
Roebuck & Roebuck, 9 Richmond St. e., M5C 1N4, M.H. Roebuck, Q.C., Sydney Smith, Q.C., J. Gold
Roebuck & Walkinshaw, 372 Bay St., D. R. Walkinshaw, Q.C.
Roger, Fiksel & Sloan, #302, 372 Bay St., H.J. Sloan, E.P. Fiksel, H.S. Roger
Rogers, Bereskin & Parr, Box 313, Commerce Court Postal Stn., M5L 1G1, D. M. Rogers, Q.C., D. R. Bereskin, R. J. Parr, H.R. Hart, C.L. Sarginson, M. Waraksa, Cynthia Rowden, K.E. Sharpe, D.M. Cameron, M. Korenberg. Counsel: H.L. Morphy, Q.C.
Rogers, J.R., #400, 914 St. Clair Ave. w.
Rogers, Rogers, Moore, #3000, 390 Bay St., M5H 2Y2, W.P. Rogers, Q.C., D.H. Rogers, J.P. Moore, J.D. Strung, Diane McDowell
Rogers & Rowland, 133 Richmond St. w., M5H 2M1, W. M. Rowland, Q.C., A. D. Rogers, E.J.W. Walker
Rogers, Smith, Dick & Thomson, #2606, 2 Bloor St. w., G.T. Rogers, Q.C., N.A. Smith, Q.C., R.C. Dick, Q.C., B.A. Thomson
Rolston, G. A., 20 Eglinton Ave. w., M4R 1K8
Romanick, M. B., Q.C., 80 Richmond St. w.
Romanko, J., Q.C., 372 Bay St.
Roopchand, P., 717 Pape Ave.
Rosati & Di Zio, 968 Wilson Ave. (Downsview, M3K 1E7), J. Rosati, A. Di Zio
Rose, J.M., Box 614 (Don Mills)
Rose, Persiko, Arnold, Gleiberman, Box 12, Toronto Dominion Centre, A. C. Rose, Q.C., B. J. Persiko, Q.C., M.S. Arnold, Q.C., I. Gleiberman, H. Litowitz, L. Balaban, J.C. Goldberg. Counsel: W.V. Sasso
Rose, W. C., Q.C., 100 Richmond St. w.
Rosemay, V. T., 4202 Dundas St. w., M8X 1Y6
Rosen, A. C., #904, 27 Queen St. e.
Rosen, G. M., 14A Hazelton Ave.
Rosen, J.M., 1520, 390 Bay St., M5H 2Y2
Rosen, S. L., 2933 Dufferin St.
Rosenberg, H., 269 Queen St. w.
Rosenberg, I., 535 Glengarry Ave.
Rosenberg, Smith, Paton, Hyman & Matlow, #1800, 120 Adelaide St. w., M5H 1S8, A.B. Rosenberg, Q.C., S. D. Paton, M.M. Smith, Q.C., G.D. Hyman, Q.C., P.T. Matlow, Q.C., H.C. Sobel, C.F. Shnier, Mary G. Critelli, Margaret Silver
Rosenfarb, Millstone, #204, 2100 Ellesmere Rd. (Scarboro, M1H 3B7), S. Rosenfarb, D.J. Millstone
Rosenfeld, Malcolmson, Lampkin, Levine & Johnson, 65 Queen St. w., M5H 2M5, J. Rosenfeld, Q.C., A. C. Schwartz, Q.C., H. A. Malcolmson, W. P. Rosenfeld, V.A.R. Lampkin, J.R. Johnson, M.A. Levine, P.C. Birnbaum, S.S. Levitan, J.J. O'Hoski, J.H. Flanders, Joanne Lewis. Counsel: Samuel Gotfrid, Q.C., R. David
Rosenthal, H., Q.C., #1807, 8 King St. e., M5C 1B5
Ross, L.H., 609 Bloor St. w.
Ross, R.M., #816, 181 University Ave.
Ross & Ross, 111 Elizabeth St., J.D.L. Ross
Rossman, Sinclair, 1272 Dundas St. w., A.M. Rossman, N.V. Sinclair
Rossman, H.M., 418 Richview Ave.
Rotenberg, C.L., Q.C., #202, 1500 Don

Mills Rd. (Don Mills) (H.D. Rotenberg, Yolanta Lewis, D.E. Ferguson)
Rotenberg, J.S., 810A Queen St. e.
Rothman, Sigal, 606, 347 Bay St., R. Rothman, Q.C., M. Sigal, C.B. Ticker
Rovazzi & Mancini, 2000 Eglinton Ave. w., M6E 2J9, L. Rovazzi, A.C. Mancini
Rovet & Assoc., #614, 214 King St. w., M5H 1K4 (B.B. Fisher, M.L. Powell)
Rowan & Temple, Royal Bank Plaza, Box 11, H. W. Rowan, Q.C., W.M. Temple, Q.C., J.T. Pepall
Rowland (G.A.) & Assoc., 2389A Bloor St. w., M6S 1P6, G.A. Rowland, P.M. Feldman
Ruben, S., #211, 31 Wellesley St. e.
Rubenstein, D.A., 90 Eglinton Ave. w.
Rubinoff & Rubinoff, 401 Bay St., Box 26, M5H 2Y6, M. P. Rubinoff, P. Meretsky, S. S. Cohen, D.G. Bent, Sharon Landsman, G.C. Grierson
Ruby & Edwardh, 11 Prince Arthur Ave., C.C. Ruby, M.A. Edwardh, M. Green, M. Code
Rudolph & Ittleman, #501, 164 Eglinton Ave. e., S. Rudolph, R.M. Ittleman
Rumack & Gold, 66 Isabella St., H.I. Rumack, Q.C., L.M. Rumack, H. Gold
Rumack, M.K.I., Law Firm of, #202, 2 St. Clair Ave. e., M.K.I. Rumack
Rusak, H., 8 Beamish Dr. (Islington)
Rusek & Richardson, 1644 Bloor St. w., R. E. Rusek, T. D. Richardson
Russell & Sands, 663 Greenwood Ave., R.M. Russell, D.A. Sands
Rush, G. C., 2970 Lakeshore Blvd. w.
Russo & Soppelsa, 797 Wilson Ave. (Downsview), R.S. Russo, F.A. Soppelsa
Ryan & Hogan, 1863 Danforth Ave., S. P. Ryan, Q.C., J. H. Ryan, Q.C., R. M. Hogan
Rye & Partners, #1200, 65 Queen St. w., R.E. Rye, W.G. Kuplowsky, T.S. Turner, J.M. Gartenburg, A.H. Kessel
Sachter, R. L., Q.C., #402, 801 Eglinton Ave. w., M5N 1E3
Sack, Charney, Goldblatt & Mitchell, 181 University Ave., J. Sack, G.J. Charney, Q.C., H. Goldblatt, C.M. Mitchell, R.K. Rae, J. Egner, E. Poskanzer, M. Kainer, Naomi Duguid, Sandy Price
Sack, M., 347 Bay St.
Sacks & Leich, 1776 Danforth Ave., P. M. Leich, G. D. Sacks
Saffrey, R. H., 439 University Ave., M5G 1V8
Saginur, H., #901, 701 Evans Ave. (Etobicoke, M9C 1A3)
Sahaidak, T.T., Q.C., #911, 1243 Islington Ave.
Sainaney, R. A., #205, 1011 Dufferin St.
Salamon & Moskowitz, 740 Spadina Ave., B. Salamon, S. S. Moskowitz
Salem & Bryant, 85 Richmond St. w., H.M. Salem, Q.C., A.G. Bryant
Salter, Apple, Cousland & Kerbel, 10 King St. e., B. Nixon Apple, Q.C., R.P.K. Cousland, Q.C., H. M. Kerbel, Q.C., H. P. Unroth, D. Sorffer, R.B. Borchiver
Salter, M.E.B., 81 Woodlawn Ave. w.
Saltman, M., #1555, 55 University Ave.
Salvatori & Kirby, #101, 3675 Keele St. (Downsview), E. Salvatori, P. Kirby
Samuel, D.M., #1900, 2 Bloor St. w.
Samulovitch, G., 4 Prince Arthur Ave.
Sanderson, Cochrane & Gastmeier, 8 King St. e., M5C 1B5, C. F. Sanderson, Q.C., I. D. Cochrane, Q.C., D. J. Gastmeier
Sandler, Gordon & Saperia, 2 Bloor St. w., Lillian Sandler, J. A. Gordon, L.P. Saperia
Sanwalka, S. K., 429 Donlands Ave., M4J 3S4
Sarafian, E., 167 Belsize Dr.
Saul, MacLeod & Madras, #600, 102 Bloor St. w., D. Saul, C.D. MacLeod, M.L. Madras, Wenda Yenson, R.D. Kneebone, Clara Kisko
Savage, H.S., #602, 2 Bloor St. w.
Savage, R.B., 2065 Finch Ave. w. (Downsview)
Sax, Isaacs, 12 Sheppard St., L. Sax, A. Isaacs, L.B. Goldapple
Sac (M.M.) & Assoc., #1800, 700 Bay St., M.M. Sax, Alexandra Ngan
Scandiffio & Cassidy, #301, 443 University Ave., N.F.A. Scandiffio, Q.C., W. P. Cassidy
Scandiffio, J.F., 509 Bloor St. w.
Scandiffio, P.M., 794 Bathurst St.
Schacter, Leo E., Q.C., #808, 123 Edward St.
Schell, S.J., 1199 Weston Rd.
Scherer, B., 3768 Bathurst St. (Downsview)
Schnall, I., 372 Bay St.
Schoenborn, M., 31 Wellesley St. e.
Schofield, E. L., 607, 141 Adelaide St. w., M5H 3L5
Schorr, A.S., 111 Bond St., M5B 1Y2
Schrieder, J.P., Q.C., 2280 Eglinton Ave. w.
Schwartz, A., 40 Hayden St.
Schwartz, H.A., 1110 Lodestar Rd. (Downsview)
Schwartz & Jacobson, 3089 Bathurst St., S. Schwartz, H. Jacobson
Schwarz, J.B., #403, 133 Richmond St. w.
Scott, A.E., #501, 133 Richmond St. w.
Scott, E.W.V., Q.C., 2094 Yonge St., M4S 2A3
Scott, N. D., 4 Richmond St. e.
Scott, Susan, 11 Prince Arthur Ave.
Scott, W. A., 4945 Dundas St. w. (Islington, M9A 1B6)
Scully, B.M., 127 John St., M5V 2E2
Scully & Olkovich, #904, 111 Richmond St. w., G.P. Scully, G. Olkovich, T.D. Prest
Scully, P. B., 31 Prince Arthur Ave. (R.F.S. Plain)
Seabrook & Assoc., #3300, Box 33, First Canadian Place, M5X 1A9, V. M. Seabrook, Q.C., J. P. Gunning, G.D.R. Finlay, M.J. Braun, P.W. Thomas
Searles, E. M., Q.C., 501 Yonge St. (F. A. Beckles)
Secord, S.L., #901, 111 Richmond St. w.
Sector, J. A., 1365 Yonge St.
Seed, Howard, Cook & Caswell, 220 Bay St., M5J 1P8, J.R. Howard, G.A. Cook, R.S. Caswell, Q.C., D.D. McPherson, Moira Caswell, Q.C., J.A. Graham, Helen Keeley, K.P. Murray. Counsel: J. Sedgwick, C.C., Q.C.; Assoc. Counsel: J.A. Seed, Q.C.
Segal, Signer & Rotenberg, 1240 Bay St., G.L. Segal, T.B. Rotenberg, B.N. Signer
Seguin, J.H., #1505, 330 Bay St. (F.W. White)
Seltzer & Seltzer, #607, 2161 Yonge St., B. Seltzer, E.S. Seltzer
Semonovs, A., 1039 Woodbine Ave.
Senyk, N.A., #1200, 8 King St. e.
Seon, Gutstadt, Goldman & Fisher, #318, 3701 Chesswood Dr. (Downsview, M3J 2P6), S.D. Seon, Eli Gutstadt, A. Goldman, R.A. Fisher, S.A. Kichler
Sequeira, I. St. C., 2970 Lakeshore Rd. w.
Shah & Haque, #406, 91 Yonge St., S.B. Shah, Z. Haque
Shanahan, F. J., 123 Queen St. w., #407, M5H 2M9
Shankman, J.P., #503, 121 Richmond St. w.
Shapiro, P.H., 45 Richmond St. w. (H.S. Goody, J.M. Levy)
Shapiro, S.H., 1977 Finch Ave. w., Downsview, M3N 2V3 (J. Cirillo)
Shapiro & Shapiro, #211, 875 Eglinton Ave. w., S.J. Shapiro, L.A. Shapiro
Sharma, R.N., 942 Gerrard St. e., M4M 1Z2
Sharp, R. C., Q.C., 495 Wellington St. w.
Shaughnessy, B.R., 709 Markham St.
Shaul, A.J., Q.C., #208, 1940 Eglinton Ave. e. (Scarboro)
Shaw, J. E., 1867 Yonge St., #800, M4S 1R2
Shaw, M. A., #505, 60 St. Clair Ave. e., M4T 1N5
Shayne, J., #1101, 27 Queen St. e.
Shelley, G., #202, 2 St. Clair Ave. e.
Sheppard & Thomas, P.A. Sheppard, S. Thomas
Sherizen, Lily I., Q.C., 212, 455 Spadina Ave.
Sherman & Baum, 1018, 111 Richmond St. w., N. Sherman, Q.C., D. Baum
Sherman, I.H., Q.C., #112, 2100 Ellesmere Rd. (Scarboro)
Sherman, S.L., 2645 Eglinton Ave. e. (Scarboro)
Sherwin & Liberman, 1616, 120 Adelaide St. w., N. Sherwin, Q.C., J. Liberman, D.G. Merner, N.I. Kahn
Shewchuk & Martynowicz, 555 Burnhamthorpe Rd. (Etobicoke), M. D. Shewchuk, A. Martynowicz
Shibley, Righton & McCutcheon, 401 Bay St., Box 32 (M5H 2Z1), R. E. Shibley, Q.C., R. F. Righton, Q.C., J. W. McCutcheon, Q.C., J. M. Judson, Q.C., R. E. Anka, B. S. Wortzman, L.S. Mason, Dez Windischmann, J.P. Bell, T.J. Rock, G.J. Corn, P.H. Smith, V.R. Morrison, P.J. Pitcher, J.P. Malette, A.L. Bromstein, M.C. Birley, P.C. Williams, G.P. Ditomaso, B.D. Katchen, B. McGarva, Joan Gilmour, N. Shopsowitz, Christine Walsh, C.I. Cole. Counsel: J.T. Clement, Q.C., M.L. O'Brien, Q.C.
Shields, A., #401, 51 Eglinton Ave. e.
Shier, B.S., 942 Gerrard St. e.
Shiff, Gross, 1867 Yonge St., #800, M4S 1R2, M.G. Gross, R.A. Applebaum, S.N. Iczkovitz, G.S. Kay, S.B. Bush, E.S. Heiber, A.J. Pivnick, M.B. Shopiko, S.B. Pottins, R.M. Shiff. Counsel: J.R. Shiff, Q.C.
Shiff, R., 2788 Bathurst St.
Shiffman, G., 505 Eglinton Ave. w.
Shifman & Hart, #238, 2375 Steeles Ave. w. (Downsview), M.B. Shifman, M.J. Hart
Shifrin, White, Michela & Gord, #703, 121 Richmond St. w., L.B. White, M.C. Gord, G. Michela, A. Shifrin, Q.C.
Shime, O. B., Q.C., 401 Bay St., Box 42
Shoihet, E. I., 100 Adelaide St. w.
Shore, M.H., #1104, 390 Bay St., M5H 2Y2
Shortliffe, G.E., 47½ Lee Ave.
Shour, Fedorsen & McBurney, #1403, 55 Queen St. e., M5C 1R5, R.A.L. Shour, F.S. Fedorsen, E.C. McBurney
Shtal & Birnbaum, 1530 Albion Rd. (Rexdale), M.J. Shtal, I.I. Birnbaum
Shub, Levstein & Bradshaw, 1543 Victoria Park Ave. (Scarboro), S.H. Shub, I. Levstein, P. Bradshaw, I. Wolkowicz, C.A. Morrison
Shuber, Gluckstein, 500, 102 Bloor St. w., S. Shuber, Q.C., B. L. Gluckstein, Q.C., G. Neinstein, G. Smith, W. Stasyshyn, Florene Shuber, Philippa Samworth
Shulman, J.D., #404, 45 Richmond St. w.
Shupac, J.M., 243 Queen St. w.
Shuyler, Ecclestone, Green & Chykaliuk, 110 Yonge St., A. M. Ecclestone, Q.C., C. R. Green, Q.C., M. Chykaliuk, M. A. Siegel, W.M. Forsythe, A.E. Allan

Siegal, Fogler, 390 Bay St., L.S.D. Fogler, Q.C., M.H. Appleton, Q.C., S.N. Conn, R.A. Bain, E. Sonshine, A.M. Schwartz, L. G. Dollinger, M. L. Middlestadt, S.B. Norris, M.R. Kaplan, R.S. Sutin, B. Zarnett, J.B. Goldenberg, Arlene Wolfe, M.S. Wolfish, Evelyn Brown, R.I. Druker, J. Wiesenfeld
Siegel, M. H., 133 Richmond St. w.
Sillery, P.W., 1810 Avenue Rd.
Silver, L. D., Q.C., 100 Richmond St. w.
Silver, M. I., 3768 Bathurst St., #206, Downsview, M3H 3M7
Silverberg, N.P., #1102, 27 Queen St. e.
Silverman & Freed, 19th floor, 700 Bay St., M5G 1Z6, S.J. Silverman, L.J. Freed
Silverman, J. C., 57 Ossington Ave.
Silverman, S.N., 1205, 45 Richmond St. w., M5H 1Z2; Counsel: B. Haines, Q.C.
Silverman & Silverman, 535 Glengarry Ave., H.W. Silverman, Q.C., Anne M. Silverman
Silverstein, L.M., #725, 1075 Bay St. (D. Himelfarb)
Silverstein & Silver, #201, 3284 Yonge St., A.G. Silverstein, M.J. Silver
Sim, D. F., Q.C., 330 University Ave., M5G 1R7, R. T. Hughes, Toni Polson Ashton, R.E. Dimock, Colleen Spring, K.D. McKay
Simbrow, L., #1450, 439 University Ave.
Simmonds, M. M., Q.C., 401 Bay St.
Simon, M., Q.C., #912, 111 Richmond St. w., M5H 2G4
Simonelis, P.C., #200, 3031 Bloor St. w.
Singer, B.M., Q.C., 2 Bloor St. w.
Singer, I., 906, 101 Richmond St. w.
Singer, Keyfetz, Crackower & Saltzman, 806, 1240 Bay St., M5R 2A7, A. Singer, Q.C., M. L. Keyfetz, Q.C., L.S. Crackower, Q.C., K.L. Saltzman, G.F. Vella
Singer, Kwinter, 360 Bloor St. w., M.A. Singer, A. Kwinter, M.A. Fischer
Sintzel, J. R. N., Q.C., 133 Richmond St. w., #505, M5H 2L3
Sinukoff, S.H., #1800, 2180 Yonge St.
Skala, J., 110 Yonge St.
Skells, J.T., Q.C., 372 Bay St.
Skolnik, S.H., 102, 868 Markham Rd. (Scarboro)
Slater, Huston, 644 Evans Ave., J. R. Slater, W. P. Huston
Slater, V.W., 555 Burnhamthorpe Rd. (Etobicoke)
Slocombe, P., 805, 1240 Bay St.
Slone, E.K., #800, 1867 Yonge St.
Smiley & Allingham, 80 Richmond St. w., R.V. Smiley, Q.C., N.W. Allingham, Q.C., J.L. MacFarland, Diane C. Stortini, Livia Singer, D.E. Crabbe
Smith, A., 695 Markham Rd. (Scarboro)
Smith, A.L., #1400, 65 Queen St. w.
Smith, B.A., 120 Eglinton Ave. e.
Smith, Brzezinski, #840, 439 University Ave., M.R. Smith, L. Brzezinski
Smith, C., Q.C., 2490 Bloor St. w., M6S 1R3
Smith & Harper, 2405 Lakeshore Blvd. w., M8V 1C6, B. J. Smith, Q.C., D. G. Harper
Smith, K. D., 277 Brunswick Ave.
Smith, Lyons, Torrance, Stevenson & Mayer, Box 420, Exchange Tower, Two First Canadian Place (M5X 1E3), H.B. Mayer, Q.C., J.D. Stevenson, Q.C., J.G. Torrance, Q.C., J.C. Lyons, Q.C., R.A. Smith, Q.C., J.R.C. Cermak, Q.C., R.G. Marantz, Q.C., J.R. Finley, Q.C., T.G. Deacon, Q.C., R.W. Comish, F.K. Roberts, Q.C., P.A. Carroll, R.G. Witterick, D.W. Mutch, T.R. Hawkins, J.G. Myers, J.S. Brown, J.H. Farrell, J.M. Potwin, R.E. Milnes, R.W.J. Seyffert, A. Birnbaum, S.L. Dunbar, R.J. Carew, L.T. Gord, R.H. Chartrand, W.J. Miller, R.M. Richler, I.C. Harrison, G.D. Peacock, H.J. Marin, R.T. Bauer, S.P. Mantini, D.E. Wires, P.D. Fox, B.M. Graham, N.E.J. Dietrich, S.R. Coxford, D.G. Hatch, S.L. Ewart, D.F. Bell, P.H. Harricks, S.L. Scheuermann, J.M. Macdonald, C.D. Sloan, J.M. Prior, R.G.S. Hull, D.A. Clément, D.L. Tripodi. Counsel: C.E. Walden
Smith, M.I., 3016 Danforth Ave.
Smith, Shaver, Selzer & McLuskie, 200 University Ave., G.R.H. Shaver, G.K. Selzer, H.W. Keyes, Q.C., J.R. McLuskie, S.W. Brett, D.M. Campbell, J.O. Connolly
Smith, W. M., 2606, 401 Bay St.
Smither, S., #1204, 1 St. Clair Ave. w., M4V 1K6
Smokorowski, Anne, #30, 165 Spadina Ave.
Smookler, Smookler & Assoc., #607, 2221 Yonge St., K.M. Smookler, F. Smookler, M.T. Ross, M.M. Roefe, A.L. Bowland
Sneath, Wilkins & Assoc., 44 Victoria St., M5C 1Z5, A. J. Sneath, Q.C., J. C. Wilkins, Q.C., A.P. Riley, T.M. Lowman, R.H. Hickman
Snider & Collins, 951 Queen St. e., G.M. Snider, A. Collins
Snider, D.B., 978 Kingston Rd.
Solish & Fellen, 111 Bond St., L. Solish, Q.C., P. A. Fellen
Solnik & Goldman, 2991 Dundas St. w., M6P 1Z4, S. Solnik, J. W. Goldman
Solnik, S., 2991 Dundas St. w.
Solomon, Farmer, #1400, 180 Bloor St. w., B.H. Solomon, R.A. Farmer
Solomon, G.R., #503, 121 Richmond St. w.
Solomon, H., 354 Bathurst St.
Solomon & Harnum, #810, 111 Richmond St. w., C.M. Solomon, M.G. Harnum
Solomon, I.S., #1920, 401 Bay St.
Solomon & Solomon, #411, 85 Richmond St. w., J.N. Solomon, Q.C.
Soloway & Wylde, 401 Bay St., Box 22, M5H 2Y4, G. M. Soloway, H.H. Wylde
Solway, M., #2514, 130 Adelaide St. w.
Somers, Kronis & Rotsztain, #1200, 20 Eglinton Ave. w., A. Somers, Q.C., J.N. Kronis, J.A. Rotsztain, Andrea Margles, B.D. Cappel
Somjen & Suter-McEwen, 94 Cumberland St., J.J. Somjen, H. Suter-McEwen
Sommers & Roth, 268 Avenue Rd., R.J. Sommers, Q.C., R. Roth, E.E.H. Birk
Sommerville, Scace, White & Lamson, 120 Bloor St. e., W. F. Lamson, Q.C., I. C. White, Q.C.
Sommerville & Sommerville, 890, 151 Bloor St. w., T.J. Sommerville, D.F. Sommerville, J.C. Ruderman
Sonenberg, L.S., 2280 Eglinton Ave. w.
Sosna, L. B., 2627 Eglinton Ave. e. (Scarboro)
Sotos, J.M., #1202, 100 Adelaide St. w.
Sparham, F. J., Q.C., 52 Cuffley Cres. n. (Downsview)
Sparling, C.J., #504, 133 Richmond St. w.
Speciale, A.M. & Assoc., 332 Browns Line (Etobicoke, M8W 3T6), A.M. Speciale, P. Meier
Spencer, Romberg, 21 Dundas Sq., L. W. Spencer, Q.C., H. L. Romberg, Q.C., M. Barkin, Q.C., S. C. Esbin, A. E. Resnick, J.S. Klein, B. Rubinoff
Spensieri, Cirillo, 1977 Finch Ave. w., M.A. Spensieri, J. Cirillo
Spiegel, B.N., #1400, 180 Bloor St. w.
Spina, J., #1420, 123 Edward St.
Spiro, S., 11 King St. w.
Spiro & Wisebrod, #200, 2949 Bathurst St., M. Spiro, Avi Wisebrod
Spodek, L., #607, 2221 Yonge St.
Sproule & Girouard, #1620, 44 Victoria St., A.R. Sproule, Q.C.
Spurr & Levine, #706, 44 Eglinton Ave. w., T.B. Spurr, L. Levine
Stabile, Maniaci, Di Poce & Angeletti, #401, 1055 Wilson Ave., M3K 1Y9, S. Stabile, A. Maniaci, T. Di Poce, F.A. Angeletti. Counsel: L.G. Stortini
Stafford, C.A., 1036 Coxwell Ave., M4C 3G5
Stainton, R. H., 3036A Bloor St. w., M8X 1C4
Stainton, R. K., Q.C., 1624 Bayview Ave., M4G 3B7 (J. M. A. Little)
Stapells & Sewell, Box 113, First Canadian Place, W. S. Sewell, Q.C., R. B. Stapells, Q.C., H. R. Patterson, Q.C., D. J. MacKay, R. H. Krempulec, Q.C., A. K. Crossley, S. K. Mann, B. T. Grant, W.S. Gray, P. Spencer, C.W. Spratt, D.W. Salomon, Sherri Reinstein, D.S. Wilson, J.R. Miller, T.W. Maich, Joan Garson, Carol MacPherson, P.A. Salvatore, K.W. Chalmers
Stark, B.C., #2007, 2 Bloor St. w.
Starkman, S. H., 401 Bay St.
Statton & Webster, 390 Bay St., M5H 2Y2, R.B. Statton, W.C. Webster
Stefoff & Brown, #1505, 80 Richmond St. w., M5H 2C1, J. Stefoff, P. L. Brown
Steidman, M.M., Q.C., #505, 335 Bay St.
Stein, F. P., 439 University Ave.
Stein, H.W., 398 Bloor St. w.
Stein, S.
Steinberg, Friedman & Michael, #100, 8 Appleton Ave., M6E 3A3, I. Steinberg, E. Friedman, A. Kviesis, F. Michael, S. Ouanounou, Janice Clarfield, J.W. Burton
Steinberg, R.B., #1900, 2 Bloor St. w.
Steinberg, W.A., 88 Bloor St. e.
Steiner, Leslie, 2 Gloucester St.
Steiner, S. J., 100 Richmond St. w.
Steinman, S., 2 Bloor St. w.
Stenzler, M.S.,
Stephens, French, McKeown, #400, 120 Adelaide St. w., M5H 1T1, J.W.V. Stephens, Q.C., W.P. McKeown, P.L.J. French, R.F. Tighe, A.G. Sinclair
Stephens, J. H., Q.C., 242 Runnymede Rd.
Steponaitis, H. P., 1613 Bloor St. w., M6P 1A6
Sterling, A.T., 2488A Kingston Rd. (Scarboro)
Stern, J., #1212, 2 St. Clair Ave. e.
Stern & Stern, #2016, 390 Bay St., P.D. Stern, R. Stern
Sternberg, G., 66 Charles St. e., M4Y 1T1
Stevens & Stevens, 3560 Commerce Court w., Box 67, M5L 1B9, Hon. S.M. Stevens, N.M. Stevens, Q.C. (also King City)
Stevenson, Anna, Q.C., #1230, 180 Dundas St. w.
Stevenson, W. G., 44 St. Clair Ave. e.
Stewart, A.G., #400, 199 Bay St., M5J 1L4
Stewart, R.A., 47 Main St.
Stikeman, Elliott, Robarts & Bowman, 4950 Commerce Court West, Box 85 (M5L 1B9), H.H. Stikeman, Q.C., R.F. Elliott, C.M., Q.C., Hon. J.P. Robarts, P.C., C.C., Q.C., G.T. Tamaki, Q.C., D.G.H. Bowman, Q.C., E. J. Arnett, Q.C., F.R. von Veh, T.C.H. Baldwin, S.N. Lederman, W.E. Shaw, L.M. Hess, M. Yontef, J.C. Davis, R. Couzin, D.N. Finkelstein, D.B. Buchanan, J.D. Weir, W.B. Rose, R.E. Clark, M.S. Allen, W.I. Innes, R.F. Barrett, R. Rueter, J.A.M. Judge, R.K. Durand, S.J. McCormack, J.A. Riley,

Kathryn Chalmers, Maralynne Monteith, R.B. Pollock, J.R. Dow, D.B. Houston, I. Roxan, Kathleen Ward, R.E. Burgess. Counsel: J. Sopinka, Q.C.
Stikeman, Lee & Chenoweth, Toronto Dominion Centre, Box 66, M5K 1E7, H.R.H. Stikeman, D.V. Lee, F.W. Chenoweth
Stikuts, A.M., #620, 85 Richmond St. w.
Stitt, Baker & McKenzie, 112 Adelaide St. e., M5C 1K9, H.J. Stitt, Q.C., S.M. Sigel, Q.C., S.R. Baker, H. Margles, E.J. Kowal, Q.C., R.K. Kusano, S.M. Borraccia, Mary C. Hall, S.D. Saxe, Janice McAuley, Tamara Parschin-Rybkin, R.B. Warren, B.D. Segal, R.P. McLaughlin, F.P. Monteleone, Betty Ho, D.G. Loucks, R.O. Lee, J.M. Stitt, J.F. Caruso, W.R. Watson, J.K. Kivisto
Stoangi, R.J., 1267A St. Clair Ave. w.
Stockwood, D., Q.C., #410, 101 Richmond St. w. (N.J. Spies)
Stone & Stiff, 330 Broadview Ave., C. A. Stone, Q.C., J.K.H. Stiff, P.T. Willis
Storm, H., #606, 347 Bay St. (also Pickering)
Stortini, L.G., 533 Queen St. e.
Strachan, I.J., #401, 425 University Ave.
Strashin, D.S., 2323 Yonge St.
Strathy, Archibald & Seagram, Commerce Court West, Box 438 (M5L 1J3), C.M.A. Strathy, Q.C., C.R. Archibald, Q.C., N.O. Seagram, Q.C., M. Gunn, R. S. Thomson, Q.C., G. A. Wilson, Q.C., R.D.S. Hunter, H. R. VanderLugt, S. R. Clarke, L.A. Wittlin, K.R. Aalto, W.J. Burden, G. Vukelich, J.M. Whyte, D.D. Langley, W.J. Walker, S.P. Johnston, Elizabeth Waight, L.J. Jacques, D.B. Light, J.C. London, K.T. Rosenberg. Counsel: T.F.C. Cole, Q.C.
Strauss Associates, 360 Bay St., #900, M5H 2V6, L.A. Strauss, H. Ritchie, M.J. Fingret, H.N. Little, J.A. Geisler, Q.C., W. Sehr. Counsel: H.D. Pitch
Strauss, Cooper, #800, 347 Bay St., I. Cooper, A.A. Strauss, Q.C., L.A. Weinstein. Counsel: N. Strauss, Q.C.
Stren, S. J., 1185 Eglinton Ave. e. (Don Mills)
Strigberger, M., #808, 123 Edward St.
Stringer, Brisbin, 390 Bay St., M5H 2Y2, E.L. Stringer, Q.C., D.L. Brisbin, C.E. Humphrey, P.J. Wolfenden
Stroz, J. F., Q.C., 2275 Dundas St. w., M6R 1X6
Struyk, J.A.F., 1144 Queen St. e.
Sugarman, A., 1300 Bay St.
Sukerman, S., #1900, 2 Bloor St. w.
Sullivan, Grimson, #100, 2970 Lakeshore Blvd. w., D. Sullivan, S.L. Grimson
Sullivan, P.J., Q.C., Box 33, First Canadian Place, M5H 1A9
Summerville & Leibel, 2084 Danforth Ave., W.A. Summerville, J.M. Leibel
Suppa, S., 833 The Queensway
Sutton, R. A., 1674 Eglinton Ave. w.
Svami, N., 310 Tweedsmuir Ave.
Swadron & Brown, 243 Queen St. w., M5V 1Z4, B. B. Swadron, Q.C., A.C. Brown, M.C. Cascone, Susan G. Himel, D.R. Draper
Swartz, H.A., 1110 Lodestar Rd. (Downsview)
Swartz, H. M., Q.C., 80 Jarvis St., M5C 2A3
Swayze & Holmes, 350 Bay St., R.J. Swayze, J.T. Holmes, D.F. McCrae
Swenarchuk, M., #205, 121 Richmond St. w.
Symes, Kiteley & McIntyre, #307, 347 Bay St., Beth Symes, F.P. Kiteley, Elizabeth McIntyre
Tadman, E.J., 185B Strachan Ave.
Tait, J. G., Q.C., #902, 120 Adelaide St. w., M5H 3P7
Tan & Mah, #1503, 180 Dundas St. w., P.-T. Tan, M.Y. Mah
Tanenbaum, H.A., #401, 55 Adelaide St. e.
Tanna, K.P., 105 Carlton St., M5B 1M2
Tanner, R. C., 3240 Bloor St. w., M8X 1E4
Tanzola & Sorbara, 2950 Keele St. (Downsview), J. M. Tanzola, J. D. Sorbara, G.R. McClellan, A. Scauzillo, M.J. Callahan. Assoc.: M.A. Handler
Tarum, M., 75 Cottonwood Dr. (Don Mills)
Taube, L., 793 Bathurst St.
Taube, S., #1005, 21 St. Clair Ave. e.
Taylor, Joy & McKague, 145 King St. w., G. G. Baker, Q.C., J. H. Rodd, Q.C., W. D. Lessmann, Q.C., D.R. Freeman, W.A. Doyle. Counsel: E. V. McKague, Q.C.
Taylor, P.C., 79 Shuter St.
Taylor, R.C.
Taylor, R.R., #201, 2608 Yonge St.
Telfer, W. E., #605, 74 Victoria St.
Temins, I.D., Q.C., 69 Yonge St.
Tencer, J.E., 1034A Bloor St. w.
Teplitsky, M., Q.C., #800, 1867 Yonge St. (R.L. Colson, W. Low)
Tepper, B., Q.C., 460 College St.
Tepper, K., 801 York Mills Rd. (Don Mills)
Terry, Helen L., #1640, 439 University Ave.
Tershakowec, S.I., 8 Savalon Court (Islington)
Texaco Canada, Legal Dept., 90 Wynford Dr. (Don Mills)
Thomas, R. G., Q.C., 110 Yonge St., #1001, M5C 1V6
Thompson, P.M., 85 Richmond St. w.
Thompson, Tooze & McLean, 347 Bay St., Clair Tooze, Q.C., R. D. McLean, Q.C., R. N. Kostyniuk, Q.C., J.D. Withrow, J.J. Keaney, C.R. Carter
Thompson, W. H., 330 University Ave.
Thomson, R.G., Q.C., Box 113, First Canadian Place
Thomson, Rogers, #3100, 390 Bay St. (M5H 1W2), K.E. Howie, Q.C., D.W. Goudie, Q.C., R. O. Howie, Q.C., W. D. Lilly, Q.C., J. A. Sawers, Q.C., L.H. Mandel, Q.C., D.B. Greenspan, R.T. Beaman, D. H. Dixon, D. R. Neill, J.J. Prince, J. F. Sagel, W.L.C. Roland, T.D. Sagel, F.E.P. Bowman, M.J. Silver, W.P. McCague, F.K. Gomberg, J. Liswood, J.M. Macchione, L.C. Brown, J.R. Howie, S.E. Maloney, L.J. Bradley, D.G. Dunnet, A.A.A. Farrer, T.M. Macdonald, C.J. Morgan, J.G. Norton. Counsel: L. R. Freeman, O.B.E., Q.C.
Thornley-Hall & Watson, 45 Charles St. e., I. deB. Thornley-Hall, S. Watson
Thornton, D. H., Q.C., 2670 Danforth Ave.
Thurston, R.W., #1010, 480 University Ave.
Tikal & Associates, 390 Bay St., M.A. Tikal, Q.C., W. von Teichman, R.D. Howell, M. Mueller, J.H. Lowry
Tilley, Carson & Findlay, 44 King St. w. (M5H 1G4), A. Findlay, Q.C., A.S. Kingsmill, Q.C., J.G. Middleton, Q.C., G.R. Mackie, Q.C., N. MacL. Rogers, Q.C., F.W. Benn, G.G. Sedgwick, Q.C., C.J. Hayhoe, B.W. Earle, F.J.C. Newbould, G.A. Park, W.S. Robertson, J.R. Wood, M. Sclisizzi, B.B. Campbell, H.J.P. Wiercinski, S.W. Ireland, E.F. Spindler, J.D. Marshall, R.M.J. Werbicki, J.H. Archer, Susan Clarke, W.I. Scott, G.F. Willcocks, A.J. Skinner, Heather Douglas, P.A.D. Mingay, J.D.G. Douglas, T.J. Pryor
Timms, D.R., 49 Wellington St. e.
Tinianov, P., #606, 347 Bay St.
Titherington, M.K., 82 Tyrrel Ave.
Tkatch, M., 20 Madison Ave.
Tobias, Krawec, Rosenbaum, 503, 121 Richmond St. w., W.W. Tobias, P. Krawec, H. Rosenbaum
Tomlinson, P. V., #705, 330 University Ave.
Tonello, E., #1420, 123 Edward St.
Toomath & Assoc., #444, 100 Richmond St. w., E.H. Toomath, J.T. Riley, G.H. Erikson
Toome, R., #207, 1 Yorkdale Rd.
Topp & Zaretsky, 2700 Kipling Ave., Rexdale (also Agincourt)
Torkin, Manes & Cohen, 2800, 130 Adelaide St. w., M5H 3R2, R.D. Manes, B.A. Cohen, L.A. Torkin, S. Schwartz, J. Feldman, L.H. Wolfson, S. Troister, D.H. Rosen, Madelaine Hare, J.E. Fulcher, R.D. Malen, I.J. Tod
Toronto Transit Commn., 1900 Yonge St., M4S 1Z2
Tory, Tory, DesLauriers & Binnington, Box 20, Royal Bank Plaza, M5J 2K1, John A. Tory, Q.C., James M. Tory, Q.C., W. J. DesLauriers, Q.C., A.A. Binnington, Q.C., Anne R. Dubin, Q.C., Douglas Andison, Q.C., A.A. Kennedy, Q.C., B.W. Shields, Q.C., D.J. Mackey, J. T. Eyton, Q.C., R.L. Kennedy, J.C. Baillie, Q.C., J.G. Coleman, Q.C., M. G. Thorley, C.M. Burton, J.G. Pink, Q.C., R.W. Torrens, P. M. Moore, R. P. Armstrong, Q.C., J.M. Spence, R. G. Macdonald, S.P.H. Robinson, P.D. Maddaugh, B.M. Flood, G.R. Cunningham, E. P. Salsberg, R. J. Hamilton, V. Peters, G.G.S. Takach, W. J. L'Heureux, E.G. Haythorne, Sheila R. Block, P.E.S. Jewett, Patricia J. Myhal, C. F. Scott, W. M. Estey, L.A. Pattillo, Mary Eberts, S.R. Richardson, B.J. Johnson, B.A. Leon, J.E.A. Turner, G.J.R. Dyer, B.C. Barker, R.W. Ivey, J.H. Loosemore, H.J. Wilton-Siegel, S. Sellers, D.C. Betts, R.S. Wernham, J.H. Butler, Marlene J. Davidge, Patricia D. Jackson, S. Sharpe, T.W. Leishman, R.C. van Banning, J.W. McIninch, R.S. Blumenstein, S.J. Donovan, Pamela Hughes, D.B. Roger, J.H. Tory, J. Unger, R.J. Balfour, Anne Molloy, Kathleen Keller-Hobson, D.E. Thring. Counsel: H.L. Morphy, Q.C.
Townshend, E., 330 Bay St.
Traversy, P.J., 16A Isabella St.
Trickey, G. A., 10 Checkers Court
Trofimenko, M.B., Box 200, 401 Bay St.
Trudell, W.M., 7 Draper St.
Tugwood, A., 3458 Danforth Ave. (Scarboro)
Tureck, Wengle & Lewis, 67 Richmond St. w., L.A. Tureck, L. Wengle, J. M. Lewis
Turk, N.W., 38 Elderwood Dr., M5P 1W7
Turner, P.D., Q.C., #409, 85 Richmond St. w.
Tytler & Sproule, 44 Victoria St., John L. Tytler
Udell, S., 880 Ellesmere Rd. (Scarboro)
Ulrich & Sherr, #202, 2978 Islington Ave.
Underhay, B. M., 806, 159 Bay St.
Urman, H. S., 2857 Lawrence Ave. e. (Scarboro)
Usprech, I., 21 Dundas Sq.
Valenti, P. M., 1110a Wilson Ave. (Downsview)
Valentine, R., #300, 111 Elizabeth St.
Van Dyke, D.A., #2004, 80 Richmond St. w.
Vanek, S.C., #1001, 110 Yonge St.
Vano, G., 528 St. Clair Ave. w.
Vasilaros, L., 509 Bloor St. w. (D. Vasilaros)
Vass, F., Q.C., 245 College St.
Vaughan, K.C., #514, 85 Richmond St. w.

Vaughan, Willms, 73 Richmond St. w., #200, M5H 1Z4, M.B. Vaughan, J. Willms, Donna S.K. Shier, H. Poch, J.A. Smale
Velanoff & Velanoff, 55 Eglinton Ave. e., R. T. Velanoff, D. Velanoff
Verbeek, L., 964 Albion Rd. (Rexdale)
Verchere, Noel & Eddy, 6400 First Canadian Place, B. Verchere, R.B. Eddy, M. Noel, M.F. Menard, D.B. Morris, Guy Dube, Guy DuPont, S.C. Kerr, G. Lawson, K. Russell, S. Tardif, Janice McCart, P. Martin. Counsel: W.R. Jackett
Vero, R.F., 797 Wilson Ave. (Downsview)
Vesa, P. A., Q.C., 1028 Danforth Ave.
Vine, D. R., Q.C., 80 Richmond St. w., #1003, M5H 2A4
Vine, L.R.
Vipavec, C., 401 Bay St., Box 200
Voege, J.F., #212, 385 The East Mall (Etobicoke)
von Ketelhodt, E., #2, 425 Jane St., M6S 3Z7
Wade, M. G., 181 Eglinton Ave. e.
Wadsworth, M. A., 400, 120 Adelaide St. w.
Wadsworth, M. T., 1252 Lawrence Ave. e. (Don Mills)
Wagman & Sherkin, 898 Queen St. e., M4M 1J3, C. Wagman, Francine Sherkin
Wainberg, J.M., Q.C., #1708, 372 Bay St., M5H 2W9
Wainberg, M., 158 the Esplanade
Waisberg, S., #204, 330 Bay St.
Wakim, S.A., 25 Adelaide St. e.
Waldin, de Kenedy, #1403, 55 Queen St. e., J.P. Waldin, A.B. de Kenedy
Waldman & Beckmann, #205, 121 Richmond St. w., Geraldine Waldman, Carol Beckmann
Walfish, D., Q.C., 156 Danforth Ave.
Walfish, Henry, 169 Yonge St.
Walker, Ellis & Pezzack, 7 King St. e., M.N. Ellis, Q.C., R.J. Pezzack, Q.C., I.M. Thompson, D. V. Thomson, G. L. Hill, Shelley Mitchell
Walker, L.I., #1002, 347 Bay St.
Walker, Poole, Milligan, #1800, 700 Bay St., J.A. Walker, Q.C., R.N. Poole, P.A. Milligan, J.D. Elliott, M.S. Georgas, Yvonne Hamlin. Assoc.: S.F. Troster
Wall, T.H., 1081 Bloor St. w.
Wallace, J.H.G., 551 Gerrard St. e.
Walsh & Walsh, 85 Richmond St. w., F. P. Walsh, J. F. Walsh
Wanigasekera, G., 747 Don Mills Rd. (Don Mills)
Wappel, Rethy & Wappel, 226 Queen St. w., #210, M5V 1Z6, T.W. Wappel, G.W. Regasz-Rethy, R.D.J. Wappel
Warner, J.P., #1600, 372 Bay St.
Warren, C.B., #500, 51 Eglinton Ave. e.
Warren, H.E., 609 Bloor St. w.
Wasserman, M., 627A Dufferin St., M6K 2B2
Watson, M. O., 199 Richmond St. w., M5V 1V3
Weatherhead & Weatherhead, 19 Richmond St. w., D.B. Weatherhead, P.A.B. Weatherhead, J.R. Ward
Weatherill, J.F.W., 36 King St. e.
Webb, I.D.A., #1000, 65 Queen St. w.
Webster, J.H., Q.C., 2600 Danforth Ave., E.M. Webster
Weekes, J. M., Q.C., #509, 335 Bay St.
Weiler, C. J., 207 McCaul St.
Weinberg, A.W., 20 Madison Ave.
Weinreb, A.W., 942 Gerrard St. e.
Weinstein & Starkman, 243 Queen St. w., B. Weinstein, N. D. Starkman
Weinstock, G., 155 Balliol St.
Weir & Foulds, 330 University Ave. (M5G 1S2), K.A. Foulds, Q.C., H.S.O. Morris, Q.C., R. B. Robinson, Q.C., J. P. Hamilton, A. McN. Austin, M. S. Archibald, Q.C., J. J. Carthy, Q.C., J. D. McKellar, Q.C., G. J. Smith, Q.C., M.J. McQuaid, Q.C., N.W.C. Ross, W.T.R. Wilson, B. Finlay, R. W. Rosenman, S. B. Stein, L. J. O'Connor, W.A.D. Millar, R.R. Wozenilek, L.C.E. Brown, R.S. Sleightholm, P.M. Perell, J.G. Cowan, J.L. Lax, J.D. Winberg, B. Hebert, D.R. Elver, M.A. Gray, J.S. Prypasniak, G.J. Tzekas, J.D. Campbell, K. Prehogan, J.M. Buhlman
Weir, J.D., Box 105, 401 Bay St.
Weisfeld, R.A., 220 Wildcat Rd. (Downsview, M3J 2N5)
Weisman, S.J., Q.C., 3802 Bloor St. w. (Islington)
Weiss, E. J., #305, 2788 Bathurst St.
Weldon & Sproule, 17 Queen St. e., J.A. Sproule, Q.C., C.A. Carroll
Wengle & Assoc., 106 Adelaide St. w., H.H. Wengle, Q.C., S.C. Wengle
Werb, R.M., #906, 150 Neptune Dr.
West, Rebecca, #1107, 7 Jackes Ave.
Westell & Hanley, 120 Eglinton Ave. e., R. L. Westell, L. E. Hanley
Wetmore, D.A., #333, 85 Bloor St. e.
Wexler, Fleet & Pelman, #503, 122 St. Patrick St., A.I. Wexler, D.G. Fleet, P.S. Pelman
White, F.W., #507, 11 Adelaide St. w.
Whitelaw, A. B., Q.C., 100 Adelaide St. w.
Whittaker, A.H., #1702, 11 King St. w.
Whittaker, W.G., #1810, 65 Queen St. w.
Whitzman, S., #1550, 439 University Ave.
Widman & Burns, #808, 123 Edward St., B.B. Widman, A.L. Burns
Wiens & Pukitis, 885 Dundas St. w., O. J. Pukitis, H. J. von Monteton
Wiley, J.T., #300, 1081 Bloor St. w.
Wilkinson, M.A., #1720, 180 Dundas St. w.
Willard & Devitt, 155 Roncesvalles Ave., G. C. Devitt
Willmot, J.D., 165 Carlton St.
Willoughby, S.I., 939 Mount Pleasant Rd.
Wills, N. A., 330 University Ave.
Wilson, A.C., Q.C., 1810 Avenue Rd.
Wilson, A.J., Q.C., 12 Richmond St. e.
Wilson, B.J., #314, 3701 Chesswood Dr. (Downsview)
Wilson & Bartlett, #904, 27 Queen St. e., A.H. Bartlett, Q.C.
Wilson, Jeffery, 49 Wellington St. e.
Wilson, Marie, Q.C., 6 Adelaide St. e.
Wilson, T.H., #2000, 372 Bay St.
Winch, Martin & Gasee, 200, 80 Richmond St. w., M5H 2A5, J.W. Winch, D.G. Martin, B.B. Gasee, K.J. Cohen
Winer, C.F., Q.C., 3232 Bloor St. w. (Islington)
Winkler, Filion & Wakely, #1800, 390 Bay St., W.K. Winkler, Q.C., R.C. Filion, D.I. Wakely, B.P. Smeenk
Wise, B., 821 Eglinton Ave. w., M5N 1E6
Wise, L. A., 314 Dundas St. w.
Wolfe & Bernstein, #1007, 111 Richmond St. w., H. B. Wolfe, M. J. Bernstein
Wolicki, N., 2323 Bloor St. w., #206, M6S 4W1
Wolman, W., Q.C., 372 Bay St.
Wong, R.S.D., 150 Dundas St. w.
Wood, J. R., 933 St. Clair Ave. w., A. A. Khalifa
Woodruff & Stich, 1 Kingsmill Rd., A.M. Woodruff, I. Stich
Woolf, R.L.H., 646 St. Clair Ave. w.
Woolfson, E. S., Q.C., 1678a Eglinton Ave. w.
Woolley, Dale & Dingwall, Box 65, Toronto Dominion Centre (M5K 1E7), D.W.M. Cooper, Q.C., L. Guolla, Q.C., T.P. O'Gorman, Q.C., D.C. Woolley, Q.C., W.G. Dingwall, Q.C., K.A. Lund, Q.C., R.E. Dale, Q.C., P.J.V. Stevens, Q.C., J.W.C. Macfarlane, J.D. McPhail, P.J. Roche, T.D. Brady, W.A. McLauchlin, W.T. Perks, C.A., D.E. Clark, W.A. Knights, P.G. Bevans, R.P. Quance. Counsel: Rodney Hull, Q.C.
Wootten, Rinaldo, Rosenfeld, 901, 701 Evans Ave. (Etobicoke, M9C 1A3), M. Rinaldo, S. Rosenfeld, G. Wootten, J. Bailey, R. Lund
Wray, Russell, Sands, 663 Greenwood Ave. (M4J 4B4), R.M. Russell, D.A. Sands
Wright, K.E., 65 Queen St. w.
Yang, S., 208 Spadina Ave.
Yaskin & Stein, #206, 4580 Dufferin St., G.B. Yaskin, L.C. Stein
Yee & Zapf, 794 Bathurst St., W.K. Yee, C.P. Zapf
Yip, K. Dock, 600 Bay St.
York, J.C., #607, 141 Adelaide St. w.
Young & Owens, 229 Yonge St., M5B 1N9, J.E. Young, Q.C., D. Owens
Youngs, G. R., Q.C., 1884 Eglinton Ave. e. (Scarboro)
Zadorozny, D. R., 4195 Dundas St. w., M8X 1Y4 (D. Fiske, D. Morrison)
Zaduk, M.P., #320, 100 Richmond St. w., M5H 3K6
Zahumeny, Stephen, 1007, 330 Bay St.
Zaldin, Fine & Siskind, 181 University Ave., A. H. Zaldin, Q.C., I. J. Fine, G.E. Siskind, M.A. Turner. Counsel: B. Sischy, Q.C.
Zaldin, L.D., 2637 Eglinton Ave. e. (Scarboro)
Zammit, Dash & Semple, #307, 1240 Bay St., M5R 2A7, P.M.A. Zammit, R.M. Dash, S.W. Semple
Zammit, M., 396 Pacific Ave.
Zarowksy, B. B., Q.C., 2198a Bloor St. w.
Zekavica, D., #1105, 85 Richmond St. w.
Zeldin, Collin, 23 Bedford Rd., M5R 2J9, J.L. Zeldin, Q.C., S.D. Collin
Zelewicz, S., 1275 Dundas St. w.
Zeller, M.L., 505 Consumers Rd. (Willowdale)
Zender & Klotz, 1175 Weston Rd., A.B. Zender, Q.C., S. Klotz
Zinko, P., 1444 Queen St. w., M6K 1M2
Zinman, B.M., #1102, 330 Bay St.
Zisman, R., 347 Bay St., #706, M5H 2R7
Zuker & Zuker, 292 Spadina Ave., L. J. Zuker, Q.C.
Zutis, A., 17 Queen St. e., M5C 1N1
Zyla, B.E., #505, 2 Jane St.

TOTTENHAM, Simcoe
Keyes, J.M., 15 King St. n.
Ritchie & Feehely, 5 Mill St., J.C.L. Ritchie, J.J. Feehely, P.F. Gastaldi
Smith, R.D.L., 8 Queen St. s.

TRENTON, Hastings
Bonn, G. W., 80 Division St.
Campbell & Garrett, 21 Quinte St., R. S. Campbell, Q.C., B. R. Garrett
Davis, V.R., 499 Dundas St. w.
Fleming & Valentine, 82 Division St., T.H. Fleming, T.M. Valentine
Gazley, Johnston, 23 Dundas St. w., A.E. Johnston
Karten & Winkler, 80 Division St., B.B. Karten, A. Winkler
Reynolds, Hunter etc., 80 Division St. (also Belleville)
Robertson, J.S., 92 Dundas St. e. (B. Mitchell)
Standon, P.S., 499 Dundas St. w. (also Brighton)
Weston, W. G., 42 Dundas St. w.

TWEED, Hastings
Jackson, Marilyn E., 312 Victoria St. n.

UNIONVILLE, York
Hoy, G., 3927 #7 Hwy.

Parnes, R., 4480 #7 Hwy.
Thomas, W.B., 4701 #7 Hwy.

UXBRIDGE, Durham
Bailey, W.H.C. (also Aurora)
Harris, Fletcher, etc., 9 Main St. s., R.J. Harris (also Oshawa)
Wilson, D.E., Box 1420

VAL CARON, Sudbury
Desmarais, Keenan & Co. (also Sudbury)
Fortier & Leblanc, Box 340 (also Sudbury)

VANIER, Ottawa-Carleton
Firms listed with Ottawa

VIRGIL, Niagara North
Kroeker & Kratzmann (also St. Catharines)

WALKERTON, Bruce
Farr, D.A.
McCray, Johnston & Linley, 240 Durham St. e., D.O. McCray, G. Johnston, B.R. Linley
Mosser, H.C., Q.C., Box 670
Reichenbach, J.A., 3 Colborne St.
Waechter, Magwood & MacKenzie, 215 Durham St., J. D. Waechter, Q.C., G. C. Magwood, R.S. MacKenzie, B.J. van de Vyvere

WALLACEBURG, Kent
Bowsher & Cree, 121 Camp St., W.D. Bowsher, D.S.H. Cree
Burgess & Burgess, 218 Duncan St., J. W. Burgess, Q.C., J.A. Burgess
Carscallen, Reinhart, Mathany & Nagle, 631 James St., C. Carscallen, Q.C., D.J. Reinhart, J.E. Mathany, J.J. Nagle
Hyde & Hyde, 233 Creek St., F. A. Hyde, Q.C., G. Hyde
Irwin, R.L., Q.C., 402 Wellington St.

WARREN, Sudbury
Pharand, Kuyek etc., 38 Rutland St. (also Sudbury)

WASAGA BEACH, Simcoe
Squires, F.D.R., Mosley & 21st St.

WATERDOWN, Hamilton-Wentworth
Hays & Adamson, 61 Nelson St., T.C. Hays, M.T. Adamson
Vance & Vance (also Hamilton)
Welby & Sweetlove, 11 Mill St. s. (also Hamilton)

WATERFORD, Haldimand-Norfolk
Birnie, I. A.
David, L.

WATERLOO, Waterloo
Amy, Appleby & Brennan, 55 Erb St. e., D.G. Amy, W.R. Appleby, P. Brennan
Bauer, P. H., 308 Waterloo Sq.
Biggs, Sloan & Axler, 92 Erb St. e., R. Biggs, J.W. Sloan, J.R. Axler
Burns, D.A., 120 Park St.
Doerner, F. T., 124 King St. n. (K. Doerner)
Gehl, Nowak, 421 King St. n., N.E. Gehl, E.I. Nowak
Harper, Haney & White, 45 Erb St. e. (Box 457, N2J 4B5), J.M. Harper, Q.C., R.A. Haney, Q.C., W.H. White, Q.C., A.L. Ostner, Hilde M. English, J.D. Linton, D.A. Thomson, T.M. Fleming
Heimbecker, F., 28 Young St. e.
Hobson, Wood, Jenkins, Duncan, Wellhauser & Taylor, 172 King St. s., R.J. Hobson, Q.C., O.C. Wood, W.D. Jenkins, I.A. Duncan, E.L. Wellhauser, G.E. Taylor
Kominek, Gladstone, Godden, 601 Waterloo Sq., R. Kominek, G. W. Gladstone, D. A. Godden
McDowell & Hafemann, 156 King St. s., D.J.S. McDowell, E. S. Hafemann, L.P. Welch
McGibbon & Woodworth, #215, 50 Westmount Rd. n. (N2L 2R5), J.G. McGibbon, Q.C., S. Woodworth
Miller, P.M., #412, 75 King St. s.
Miller, W.D., 128 King St. w.
Richardson, L. R., Box 546
Sauer, L.E., 496 Albert St.
Schneider & Krakovsky, 380 King St. n., H. Schneider, J.M. Krakovsky
Toolsie, J.V., 55 Erb St. e.
Underwood, R.G., #29, 279 Weber St. n.
Weber, J.R., 35 King St. n.
Weylie, Shortt, Buck & Hanbidge, 7 Union St., W.J.D. Weylie, D.M. Shortt, C.R. Buck, K. Hanbidge, E. Reidel. Counsel: E.J.B. Martin
Whitney, M.J., 35 King St. n.

WATFORD, Lambton
Carpeneto, J.J., 625 Broadway St. (also Sarnia)
Heath, W.P., 331 Main St. (also Sarnia)

WAWA, Algoma
Wishart, Noble, etc. (also Sault Ste. Marie)

WELLAND, Niagara South
Brooks, Macfarlane & Bielby, 76 Division St., G. F. Brooks, Q.C., D. M. Macfarlane, T.A. Bielby, J.M. Patus
Flett, Beccario, Crouch, Morrison & D'-Amico, 190 Division St., C.D. Beccario, Q.C., P. Crouch, Q.C., W.D. Morrison, Q.C., A. D'Amico
Forestell, Talmage, Stratton & Latinovich, 221 Division St., M. P. Forestell, Q.C., C. A. Talmage, M.S. Stratton, S.N. Latinovich
Gibbs, F. N., 59 Empire St.
Gordon, J. W., 800 Niagara St. s. (R.F. Adams)
Gowan, Green, Fleury & Leon, 136 Main St. e., D. H. Gowan, Q.C., G.R. Green, J. J. Fleury, P.D. Leon
Humphries, D.G., Q.C., 136 Main St. e.
Kormos, P., 675 King St. (J.M. Gillespie)
Lacavera, A. T., 233 Division St.
LaRose & Taylor, 149 Main St. w., M. LaRose, P.A. Taylor
Luciani, P., Q.C., 163 Division St.
MacInnes & Blackadder, 24 Dorothy St., E.A. Blackadder, H. Keenan, H.R. Stephen
Macoomb, Houghton, Sloniowski & Marion, 170 Division St., G. J. Macoomb, Q.C., R.D.A. Houghton, J.E. Sloniowski, R.A. Marion
Nash, G.A., Q.C., 76 Division St.
Railton, J.V., Lincoln St.
Riou & Frith, 76 Division St., D.A. Riou, W.D. Frith
Rose & Banks, 191 Division St., G.C.M. Banks
Smith & Keenan, #301, 76 Division St. (also St. Catharines)
Spencer, Anderson, Anderson, 171 Division St., T. G. Spencer, Q.C., R.B. Burns, Q.C., R. T. Anderson, W.S. Anderson
Sullivan, J. L., 76 Division St.
Swayze & Swayze, 170 Division St., J. F. Swayze, Q.C., C. D. Swayze
Tolmie, Johnston & Marotta, 189 Main St. e., D.R. Tolmie, Q.C., D.K. Johnston, B.K. Marotta

WEST HILL, York
Brown & Kaplan, #309, 255 Morningside Ave., M. Brown, R. Kaplan
Cairns, L. A., 305 Port Union Rd.
Fleury, Comery & Pearson, 215 Morrish Rd., E. R. Fleury, Q.C., Wm. F. Comery, Q.C., M. D. Pearson
Milrod & Ellison, 4121 Lawrence Ave. e., R. P. Milrod, M. L. Ellison
O'Donnell, F. L., 6107 Kingston Rd.
Posen, E.G., #311, 255 Morningside Dr.
Tatham, W. G., 5524 Lawrence Ave. e.
Von Buchwald, C.D., #204, 4121 Lawrence Ave. e.

WEST LORNE, Elgin
Graham & McKillop (also St. Thomas)
Moss, Morris & Merritt, 173 Main St. (also Glencoe)
Por & McColl (also St. Thomas)

WESTON, York
Ashbourne & Caskey, 2077 Lawrence Ave. w., H. G. Ashbourne, C. W. Caskey, Q.C.
Botnick & Botnick, #53, 2300 Finch Ave. w., S.P. Botnick, R.S. Botnick. Counsel: H.P. Botnick
Braithwaite, L. A., Q.C., 1500 Royal York Rd.
Capo, Srgo & DiLena, 1680 Jane St., J.A. Capo, F.C. Srgo, A. DiLena
Citron, D., 235 Dixon Rd.
Cosentino, J.A., Q.C., 120 Widdicombe Hill Blvd.
Cosman & Fingold, 4250 Weston Rd., M.L. Cosman, L.E. Fingold
Day, McDonald, etc., 1941 Weston Rd. (also Newmarket)
Fraser & Simms, 1944 Weston Rd., R. E. Simms
Freedman, J.P., 1716 Jane St.
Heakes, A. C., 1920 Weston Rd.
Henderson & Abramsky, 3433 Weston Rd., R.E. Henderson, J. Abramsky
Herman, A. H., Q.C., 1948 Weston Rd.
Koplovic & Ram, 1969 Weston Rd., B. Koplovic, H. Ram
Laughlin & Hartley, 1180 Weston Rd., S.E. Hartley
MacDonald & MacDonald, 1923 Weston Rd., D. J. MacDonald, B. J. MacDonald
McLaughlin, H.E.L., 1268 Weston Rd.
Merkur, Naftolin & Cappel, 1735 Kipling Ave., E.N. Merkur, S. Naftolin, B.L. Cappel, T.D. Prest
Penman & Penman, 1938 Weston Rd., W.R.J. Penman, W.W. Wintar
Peterson & Peterson, 1920 Weston Rd., C. R. Peterson, M.J. Leach
Saltzman, J., 2159A Weston Rd.
Warga & Margel, 2365 Finch Ave. w., D. Warga, H.S. Margel

WESTPORT, Leeds
Willson & Co. (also Perth)

WHITBY, Durham
Aaron, S.H., 400 Dundas St. w.
Bagg, F.B., 113B Dundas St. w.
Coath, Livingstone & Johnston, 101 Dundas St. w., E.P. Coath, Q.C., W.J.R. Livingstone, J.W.P. Johnston
Dixon, F.R., 458 Brock St. s.
Evans, B.L., 1615 Dundas St. e.
Gillespie, D.J., 214 Dundas St. e.
Goodaire, D.G., 101 Brock St. s.
Morton, Burch, 185 Brock St. n., R. Morton, M. Burch
Nichol & Irwin, 201 Byron St. s., H.T. Nichol, Q.C., W.G. Irwin
Peleshok, S.F., 105 Dundas St. w.
Schilling & Evans, 121 Brock St. n., N. Schilling, Q.C., B.K. Evans
Schneider, H., 122A Brock St. s.
Shewan, G.A. & Assoc., 149 Brock St. n., G. A. Shewan, R. Whittington
Sims, Brady & McInerney, 117 King St., D. Sims, Q.C., J.F. Brady
Smith, R.J., 112 Athol St. (D. Franklin)
Wootton & Wootton, 304 Dundas St. w., J. W. Wootton

WIARTON, Bruce
Dykstra, P. S.
Hendry, H.R., 343 William St.
Pegg, P.

WILLOWDALE, York
Adourian, R.P., #302, 121 Willowdale Ave.
Altman, H., 68 Garnier Court
Baker, W. G., 5179 Yonge St.
Bars, I.J., 43 Alamosa Dr.
Baxter, J.R., 5740 Yonge St.
Braund, G. K. C., Q.C., 3333 Bayview Ave., M2K 1G4
Bredin & Pivnick, 2175 Sheppard Ave. e., C.P. Bredin, M.J. Pivnick
Brown, J.A.L., 5803 Yonge St.
Brown, M.H., 11 Goldfinch Court
Brown, Peck & Lubelsky, 4881 Yonge St., M.R. Brown, I.L. Peck, S. Lubelsky
Bunn & Assoc., 4 Finch Ave. w., H.A. Bunn, W.D. Devenney
Burnside & Dawson, 4881 Yonge St., D.J. Burnside, Faye Dawson
Cale, D.D., 4141 Yonge St.
Cappe, S.L., 6013 Yonge St.
Carleton, R., 4881 Yonge St.
Caroe, L.C., #404, 47 Sheppard Ave. e.
Cass & Miller, 2942 Finch Ave. e. (also Toronto)
Chadwick, Walerstein, 505 Consumers Rd., P. Chadwick, D.J. Walerstein
Chaiton & Chaiton, #200, 4800 Yonge St., C. Chaiton, A.S. Chaiton
Chapman, B.J., 200 Consumers Rd.
Cochrane, J.S., #308, 121 Willowdale Ave.
Cooper, H. S., 45 Sheppard Ave. e.
Cornacchia, Virgilio & Argier, 2810 Victoria Park Ave., J. Cornacchia, J.C. Argier, J. Virgilio, M. Roberts. Counsel: E.A. Conway
Cowle, M.J., 258 Sheppard Ave. e.
Daniels & Kutner, 1110 Sheppard Ave. e., J.M. Daniels, H.S. Kutner
Davidson, R., 4881 Yonge St.
Dineen, T.S., 255 Yorkland Blvd.
Domovitch, M., 34 Elise Terrace
Dunn, B.A., 1 Madeline Rd.
Epstein, N., 45 Sheppard Ave. e.
Eubank, B.L., 47 Northdale Rd.
Fagan & Egan, 6013 Yonge St., J.F. Fagan, M.J. Egan, D. Strykowski
Fieldstone, D.M., 400 Woodsworth Rd.
Filipovich, Nielsen, 3333 Bayview Ave., R.C. Filipovich, P.J.B. Nielsen
Fishman & Miller, 5987 Bathurst St., I. Fishman, J.L.M. Miller
Fleisher, Kieselstein & Kochberg, 4824 Yonge St., J.G. Fleisher, L. Kieselstein, P. Kochberg, J. Stone
Ford, A.L., 5740 Yonge St.
Freedman & Recht, 601, 2 Sheppard Ave. e., A.M. Freedman, A. Recht, I.M. Samis
Friedland, A., #212, 3555 Don Mills Rd.
Gariepy, Kanbergs & Black, 5859 Yonge St., K. A. Gariepy, Q.C., A. V. Kanbergs, D. D. Black
Gelgoot, Fox, 250 Consumers Rd., R.M. Gelgoot, H.I. Fox
Goldman, D.S., 1 Sparks Ave.
Goldstein & Merifield, #202, 1 Elmhurst Ave., H.S. Goldstein, E.H. Merifield
Gottlieb, Hoffman, Chaiton & Kumer, 4881 Yonge St., M.W. Gottlieb, D. Chaiton, B.S. Weinrib, R.D. Harris, I. Kumer. Counsel: R. Hoffman
Grant, D.J., 26 Deepglade Cres.
Grant, Grant & Fraser, 5740 Yonge St., T.O. Fraser, Q.C.
Harbin, N.J., 250 Consumers Rd.
Hardy, D.K., 127 Gypsy Roseway
Heisler, A., 2772 Victoria Park Ave.
Herman, T. S., 2175 Sheppard Ave. e.
Hitch & Assoc., 5740 Yonge St., D. Phillips, Q.C., C. Shifman, R. Shuster, S. Bloom
Hopkins, R. F., 250 Consumers Rd.
Itzkovitch, S., 2175 Sheppard Ave. e.
Janes, F.G., 5527 Yonge St.
Junger, P. C., #280, 5 Fairview Mall Dr.
Juriansz, H.K., 5590 Yonge St.
Kates, C.J.N., 32 Elliotwood Court
Kaufman, B.M., #608, 505 Consumers Rd.
Kirsh, E. J., 738 Sheppard Ave. e. (L. Stulberg)
Krauss, L., 5075 Yonge St. (Arlene Godfrey)
Kuchar & Nesker, 5332 Yonge St., G.M. Kuchar, J.M. Nesker, J.W. Hope
Lagowski, L., 255 Yorkland Blvd.
Laimon, Landy & Taveroff, #1005, 2 Sheppard Ave. e., K.S. Laimon, K.M. Landy, B.M. Taveroff
Lambert & Lambert, 6307 Yonge St., R.M.S. Lambert, J.S. Lambert
Landra, H., Q.C., 72 Lesgay Cres.
Leggett, MacDonald & Morrow, #311, 45 Sheppard Ave. e., A.B.P. Leggett, J.T. Morrow, M. MacDonald
Leitch, R.P., 5385 Yonge St.
Levin, H.A., 4141 Yonge St.
Levine & Morris, 4985 Yonge St., H.H. Levine, G.J. Morris
Lewchuk, G.W., 121 Willowdale Ave.
Lipton, H., 1800 Sheppard Ave. e.
Litman, Lash & First, 47 Sheppard Ave. e., C.H. Litman, S.J. First, R.A. Lash, M. Garnick. Counsel: Igor Ellyn
Markowitz & Stone, 1110 Finch Ave. w., C.Z. Markowitz, R.R. Stone
McGee, J.G., 6013 Yonge St.
McMahon, Raine, 145 Sheppard Ave. e., L. Raine, D.J. McMahon
Melnick, N.J.P., 52 Sheppard Ave. w.
Metcalfe, Blainey & Burns, #435, 5 Fairview Mall, W.J. Blainey, Q.C., E.B. Burns, Q.C.
Meyer, Wassenaar & Banach, 4865 Yonge St., W.J.B. Meyer, Q.C., S.L. Wassenaar, M. Banach
Moore & Costello, 5 Fairview Mall Dr., G.R. Moore, R.E.A. Costello, K.F. Pollard
Morayniss, S.G., 51 Wynn Rd.
Noor, M., 4817 Leslie St.
Otto, S., 4881 Yonge St.
Parkinson, J.R., 5740 Yonge St.
Prentice, J. L., Q.C., 1404, 6 Forest Laneway
Prydatok, I., 5 Fairview Mall Dr.
Ralph, B. M., 8a Finch Ave. w.
Reinstein, P., 2 Twin Circle Court
Richman, A.S., 1800 Sheppard Ave. e. (A. Lane)
Richman, R. R., Q.C., 4824 Yonge St.
Rose & Rose, 45 Sheppard Ave. e., A.A. Rose, B.C. Rose
Rusonick, M.H., 4824 Yonge St.
Sera, S.D., 47 Sheppard Ave. e.
Service, J. D., 6 Courtwood Place
Shone-Pelman, 505 Consumers Rd., P. Shone, I.R. Pelman, R.C. Campbell, D. Demille
Shuken, B. A., 100 Sheppard Ave. w.
Siegel, R.L. #207, 2175 Sheppard Ave. e.
Sitzer & Sitzer, 738 Sheppard Ave. e., S. J. Sitzer, P. Sitzer, C.D. Jones
Stanbrook, R.J., 4999 Yonge St.
Stein, D.A., #502, 5075 Yonge St.
Steinberg, W.A., 6013 Yonge St.
Sugar, R. M., 305 Finch Ave. w.
Tanney & Panter, 6460 Yonge St., M. Tanney, Q.C., J. H. Panter
Tucker, M.L., 67 Newton Dr.
Ulster, R., #301, 200 Consumers Rd.
Weinstein & Kirshin, 5799 Yonge St., A. Weinstein, B.L. Kirshin
Weisfeld, R.A., S11, Town & Country Sq.
Wengle, L., 313 Homewood Ave.
Wetstein, G.I., 4881 Yonge St. (L.W. Shulman)
White & White, #302, 4985 Yonge St., E.A. White, H.L.E. White
Wilson & Wilson, 5803 Yonge St., A.S.C. Wilson
Wood, H.F., 245 Fairview Mall Dr.
Young, M.L., 6 Allenwood Cres.
Young, Sokolsky, #608, 505 Consumers Rd., A. Young, A.M. Sokolsky
Zaraska, E. J., 5795 Yonge St.
Zeller, M.L., #608, 505 Consumers Rd.
Zupan, S.R., #309, 121 Willowdale Ave.

WINCHESTER, Dundas
Barnhart, D. J. (also Ottawa)
Cass, Workman, Box 390, F. M. Cass, Q.C., W.J.S. Workman
Lamb, R., Box 850

WINDSOR, Essex
Abramson, H. L., 901 Canada Trust Bldg., 176 University Ave. w.
Appel, R.M., 1183 Lauzon Rd.
Baksi & Baksi, 829 Ottawa St., N.W. Baksi, R.W. Baksi, F. Dickens
Baldassi & Campigotto, 380 Ouellette Ave., R.J. Baldassi, G. Campigotto
Ballance, R.J.M., 251 Goyeau St. (G. Goulin)
Balsamo, S., 447 Wyandotte St. e.
Bartlet & Richardes, 1000 Canada Bldg., 374 Ouellette Ave., J.N. Bartlet, Q.C., F. W. Knight, Q.C., F. D. Wilson, Q.C., M. H. Grant, R. C. Gates, Q.C., C.F. Dodd, D.S. Jovanovic, L.R. McRae
Bear, J.A., 251 Goyeau St.
Bell & MacEachern, 1922 Wyandotte St. e., C. A. Bell, Q.C., D. MacEachern
Bentley & Koss, 241 Dougall Ave., J.T. Bentley, M.R. Koss
Berecz, Anita, #505, 500 Ouellette Ave.
Bondy & Csiszar, 100 Ouellette Ave., D.A. Bondy, Q.C., E. Csiszar, C. Stevenson
Bondy & Rossi, 100 Ouellette Ave., C.M. Bondy, J.L. Rossi
Bondy, R. J., Canada Trust Bldg., 176 University Ave. w.
Bourgard, T. R., 202, 7610 Tecumseh St. e.
Bowman, G. W., Q.C., Bartlet Bldg.
Brockenshire, Wilson & Morin, 380 Ouellette Ave., W.S. Brockenshire, R.B. Wilson, L.R. Morin
Brophey, T. R., Sr., 68 Chatham St. e.
Brophey, T.R., Jr., 909 Canada Trust Bldg., 176 University Ave. w.
Brudner, E.C., 3062 Dougall Ave.
Burnell, R. E., Q.C., 910 Canada Trust Bldg., 176 University Ave. w.
Carefoot, Helen M., 251 Goyeau St.
Carten, T., 380 Ouellette Ave.
Charters & Brockenshire, 700 Canada Trust Bldg., 176 University Ave. w., D.E. Charters, Q.C., J.H. Brockenshire, Q.C., R.G. Copland
Chartier & Farrell, 2 Eugenie St. e., W. F. Chartier, F. G. Farrell
City Solicitor, City Hall, A. S. Kellerman
Cohn, B., Q.C., Canada Bldg., 374 Ouellette Ave.
Cole, D.M., 29 Park w.
Comartin & Deziel, 480 Goyeau St., J.J. Comartin, J.L. Deziel, A.I. Sorensen
Corrent & Macri, 76 University Ave. w., J.P. Corrent, J. Macri
Cottrell, G. M., 480 Goyeau St.
Cowan, McWilliams, Laird & Salvador, 100 Ouellette Ave., W.A. Cowan, Q.C., D.I. McWilliams, Q.C., S. Laird, S. Salvador. Counsel: Hon. Keith Laird, Q.C.
Croll & Croll, Canada Bldg., 374 Ouellette Ave., C.R. Croll, Q.C.
Cusinato, Gatti & Wright, 500 Ouellette Ave., A. E. Cusinato, A. R. Gatti, W.F. Wright, R.M. Godard, B.H. Jane, M.R. Steffes

DeMarco, G. C., 1011 Canada Trust Bldg., 176 University Ave. w.
Des Rosiers, R.J., Q.C., 408 Canada Trust Bldg., 176 University Ave. w.
Dodick & Brodsky, 711 Canada Trust Bldg., 176 University Ave. w., K.I. Dodick, Q.C., M.R. Brode
Donaldson, Shulgan, Kuker, Greenaway, 904 Canada Bldg., 374 Ouellette Ave., C.W. Donaldson, Q.C., W.K. Donaldson, M.W. Shulgan, P.J. Kuker, W.M. Greenaway
Easton, R. R., Q.C., 602 Canada Trust Bldg., 176 University Ave. w.
Fazio Law Firm, 185 City Hall Sq. s., F.F. Fazio, L.M. Beneteau, S.E. Bukhari
Fodor, Julie, 1922 Wyandotte St. e.
Fox, Mary, 374 Ouellette Ave.
Furlong & Brown, #908, 100 Ouellette Ave., P. G. Furlong, Q.C., D.D.A. Brown, J.M. Skipper
Garson, J. J., 650 Goyeau St.
Gignac, Sutts, #600, 251 Goyeau St., A. F. Gignac, Q.C., C. N. Sutts, Q.C., H.M. Taub, J.K. Ball, J.C. Holland, R.R. Istl. Counsel: R.E. Barnes, Q.C., H.T. Strosberg
Gordner & Mossman, 359 Goyeau St., M.A. Gordner, S.A. Mossman, R. Gardner
Grant, G. M., Q.C., 604 Security Bldg.
Hochberg, Slopen, 691 Ouellette Ave., T. J. Hochberg, Q.C., J. M. Slopen, Doris A.M. Gaspar, S.F. Miller
Holden, J. A., Q.C., Canada Bldg., 374 Ouellette Ave.
Horrocks & Koski, 586 Ouellette Ave., R.L. Horrocks, G.W. Koski
Kamen, S.C., 267 Pelissier St.
Kamin, Fisher & Burnett, 42 Pitt St. w., M. Kamin, Q.C., I.R. Fisher, R. E. Burnett, D.W. Ziriada
Kamin, S., 307 Canada Bldg., 374 Ouellette Ave.
Kendrick, W. K., 500 Ouellette Ave.
Kirwin & Gordon, 411 Riverside Dr. e., J.C. Kirwin, D. Gordon
Klein & Branoff, 359 Goyeau St., G.L. Klein, D. Branoff
Kuzak & Levasseur, 1255 Grand Marais w., G. Kuzak, T. Levasseur, M.D. Hurst
Levesque, G. P., 52 Chatham St. w.
Lyons & Goldberg, 139 University Ave. w., L. Lyons, J. Goldberg
Macdonald, I., Q.C., 309 Canada Bldg., 374 Ouellette Ave.
MacDonnell, D.A., 3737 Tecumseh St. e.
MacMillan & MacMillan, 251 Goyeau St., A. W. MacMillan, A. R. MacMillan, W. A. MacMillan
MacPhee, Burnett, 100 Ouellette Ave., P. B. Burnett, Q.C., N. J. MacPhee, Q.C.
MacPhee, N.C., 3658 Church St.
Maleyko & D'Hondt, 993 Ottawa St., B. A. Maleyko, B. A. D'Hondt, B. M. Maleyko, D. A. Connor
Mariotti, A. R., 805 Security Bldg., 267 Pelissier St.
McKerrow & Osmun, 403 Westcourt Place, R. D. McKerrow, R. A. Osmun
McMahon, R.J.C., 545 Ouellette Ave.
McPherson, Prince & Geddes, 200 Canada Bldg., 374 Ouellette Ave., L.Z. McPherson, Q.C., W.H. Prince, Q.C., H.B. Geddes, Q.C., R.H. Penfold, D.S. Foulds
McTague, Clark, 200 Canada Trust Bldg., 176 University Ave. w., N9A 5P2, Helen M. McTague, Q.C., C.J. Clark, Q.C., M.F. Coughlin, Q.C., J.H. McGivney, Q.C., L. R. Mailloux, R.A. Skinner, J.D. Lawson, L.P. Kavanaugh, A.R. Szalkai, C.F. Clark, L.A. Innocente, R.M. Clark, J. Coughlin, S. Cohen, R.M. Beaudoin, G.E. Skillings
Meconi, N., Q.C., 447 Wyandotte St. e.
Meconi, T., 349 Wyandotte St. e.
Meretsky & Muroff, 205 Paramount Bldg., 327 Ouellette Ave., M.C. Meretsky, Q.C., M. A. Muroff, L. Belowus, Laurie Tuttle
Monforton, Robitaille, #201, 52 Chatham St. w., G.J. Monforton, B.J. Robitaille
Montello & Vucinic, 251 Goyeau St., F.J. Montello, Q.C., S.S. Vucinic
Moorehouse, D.K., #802, 374 Ouellette Ave.
Moroun, P.J., 3204 Sandwich St.
Mousseau Law Firm, Canada Trust Bldg., 176 University Ave. w., M.N. Mousseau, Q.C., A.F. DeLuca, R. P. Hilbers, R.A. Dinham, D.W. Phillips, T.R. Porter, Diane Favot
Mullins & Mullins, 7843 Tecumseh St. e., Paul Mullins, L. Mullins, B. Ducharme
Nairn, B.M., 251 Goyeau St.
Nesseth & Winbaum, 1499 Ouellette Ave., P.C. Nesseth, D. Winbaum
Nolan & Dumont, #300, 380 Ouellette Ave., B.P. Nolan, R.J. Dumont, A.R. Jane. Counsel: R.D. Thrasher, Q.C.
Odette, T. C., Jr., Q.C., Box 3113, Walkerville (also Leamington)
Ohler, Mingay & Riggs, 134 University Ave. w., J.G. Ohler, P.M. Mingay, H.J. Riggs
Ozimac, J., 1011 Ouellette Ave.
Pape, Hopkins, 1451 Ouellette Ave., B.T. Pape, E.P. Hopkins
Paroian, Courey, Cohen & Houston, 875 Ouellette Ave., L. Paroian, Q.C., G.J. Courey, C.S. Cohen, Q.C., A.D. Houston, Q.C., K.W. Cheung, A. M. Paton, H.D. Bryant, R.G. Colautti, D.E. Cavill, J.T. Comstock, P.M.T. Kondruk
Patterson, Eberlie, Millson, 586 Ouellette Ave., T.L.J. Patterson, P.D. Eberlie, R.G. Millson, S.M. Baker
Perfect, E.A., 311 Chatham St. w. (A.T. Costaris)
Pugsley, J.R., 2501 Tecumseh Rd. w.
Quinn, Ouellette & McCullough, 2855 Howard Ave., J.G. Quinn, G.G. Ouellette, P.D. McCullough
Ray, M., 85 Wyandotte St. w.
Revait, D.R., #302, 586 Ouellette Ave.
Rivait & Ducharme, 185 City Hall Sq., R.G. Rivait, P.J. Ducharme
Rogin, S., 185 City Hall Sq.
Rohaly, K.B., 100, 1511 Ouellette Ave.
Rubin, B., 635 Tecumseh Rd. w.
Schott, M., Q.C., Canada Bldg., 374 Ouellette Ave.
Schwartz, Udell & Shanfield, 670 Goyeau St., S.L. Schwartz, J.B. Udell, S.L. Shanfield, M.S. Kirsch
Sherwell, B., 827 Pillette Rd.
Sinclair, M., 85 Wyandotte St. w.
Spooner, S.B., 1060 University St. w.
Steeves, R.M., 683 Ouellette Ave.
Stoyka & Chodola, 500 Goyeau St., M.F. Stoyka, A.S.J. Chodola, R. Reynolds
Sutton, R.A., 251 Goyeau St.
Thomson, G.I., 108 McDougall St.
Tuck, G.S., #402, 374 Ouellette Ave.
Valentinis, F.B., #1207, 374 Ouellette Ave.
Watters, M., 85 Wyandotte St. w.
Weingarden & Hawrish, 100 Ouellette Ave., A. B. Weingarden, R. A. Hawrish, J.M. Sereda
Wellman, Bonn & Wilkki, #201, 302 Ouellette Ave., G.M. Wellman, Gabriella S. Bonn, G.A. Wilkki
Wigley-Mueller, U., 1199 Front Rd., LaSalle
Willson & Barat, 251 Goyeau St., W. A. Willson, Q.C., A. M. Barat, A. H. Stevenson, Q.C., D. Stainton, A. Farlam, S.S. Bondy, L. DeShield
Wilson, Walker, Morga & Leschied, 251 Goyeau St. (Box 1390, N9A 6R4), R.R. Walker, Q.C., Gino Morga, D.W. Leschied, G.P. Charette, V.L. Lipnicki
Wortley, G. W., 2490 Talbot Rd.
Wunder, M.H., Canada Trust Bldg., 176 University Ave. w. (W.C. Chapman)
Yates & Oxley, 380 Ouellette Ave., G.A. Yates, J.W. Oxley
Yuffy & Yuffy, 900 Canada Trust Bldg., 176 University Ave. w., B.H. Yuffy, Q.C., M. Yuffy, Q.C.
Zalev, F., 2776 Whelpton St.
Zeron & Zeron, 402, 251 Goyeau St., J. M. Zeron

WINGHAM, Huron

Crawford, Mill, Davies & Elston, 217 Josephine St., J. Harley Crawford, Q.C., A.R.M. Mill, R. E. Davies, M.J. Elston
Goodall, J.T., Box 730 (J.W. Schenk)

WOODBRIDGE, York

Borgatti & Piccin, 7055 Islington Ave., F. Borgatti, G. Piccin
Finley, Mrs. J.D.T., R.R. #2
Pede, M., 7955 Kipling Ave.
Poot & Vroom, 7955 Kipling Ave., J. Poot, J. Vroom

WOODSTOCK, Oxford

Beatty, D.J., 487 Princess St.
Bishop, G.H., 527 Adelaide St.
Calder, G.A., Q.C., 77 Light St.
Crockett, B.E., 45 Light St.
Dow, L. E., Q.C., 69 Light St.
Farlow, R., Q.C., 13 Light St.
Giffen, Pensa, J.D. Little, J.D. Searle (also London)
Graham, White, Coad & Patience, 5 Wellington St. n., A.M. Graham, Q.C., R.G. White, R.A. Coad, T.W. Patience. Counsel: W.B. Calder
Haskett, Dalton, Whaley & Assoc., 39 Light St., J.A. Whaley, M.S. Wolfe (also London)
Hewson, Thompson, 48 Vansittart St., W. L. Hewson, T. Thompson
Hutchinson, J. F., 395 Dundas St.
Lewonas, C.J., 40 Wellington St. s.
McIntyre, P.D., 442 Dundas St.
McManamy, T. V., 25 Wellington St. n.
Nesbitt, Coulter, Legate & Micacchi, 30 Wellington St. n., M.L. Coulter, Barbara Legate, E. Micacchi
Stock, D.J.B., Q.C., 530 Adelaide St.
Treleaven & Mould, 19 Riddell St., R.L. Treleaven, Q.C., G. Mould
Wolyniuk, R.B., 487 Princess St.

WOODVILLE, Victoria

McEachern, I.T., King St. (also Lindsay)

WYOMING, Lambton

Dawson, W.M., Q.C. (also Sarnia)
Elliott & Porter (also Sarnia)

ZURICH, Huron

Carey & Ottewell (also Goderich)
Deane & Laughton (also Exeter)

BARRISTERS AND SOLICITORS IN PRINCE EDWARD ISLAND

CHARLOTTETOWN, Queens Co.
Campbell & MacPhee, 159 Kent St., L.C. Campbell, A.J. MacPhee
Campbell, Lea, Cheverie & Michael, 75 Rochford St., B.G. Campbell, Q.C., W.G. Lea, W.D. Cheverie, P.D. Michael
Carver, Matheson & Matheson, 106 Kent St., H.B. Carver, Q.C., T.A. Matheson, Jacqueline Matheson
Dalzell & Bailey, Box 1850, R.V. Dalzell, I.W.H. Bailey
Farmer & Farmer, 83 Queen St., M. A. Farmer, Q.C., M.A. Farmer, G.W. Stewart, J.B. Fortier
Foster, O'Keefe, 129 Water St., G. R. Foster, Q.C., J.A. O'Keefe, G. Campbell, J.T. Beckett
Holmes, J. J., 150 Richmond St.
Large, D.P., 37 Grafton St.
MacDougall, J., 82 Fitzroy St.
MacLeod & Carr, 131 Water St., R.G. MacLeod, Q.C., J.A. Carr, J.G. MacKay
MacLeod, D.E., 82 Fitzroy St.
MacLeod, MacMillan & Tweel, 112 Kent St., I.M. MacLeod, Q.C., R.H. MacMillan, T.D. Tweel, R.B. Langille
MacNutt, J.W., 134 Richmond St. (Daphne Dumont, Beverly Mills Stetson)
Mullally, P., 135 Kent St. (Maureen Gregor)
Reagh (Theodore & Elizabeth), 17 West St.
Scales, Ghiz, Jenkins & McQuaid, 70 Kent St., A. K. Scales, Q.C., J. A. Ghiz, S. D. H. Jenkins, J. A. McQuaid, S.A. Murphy, E.P. Rossiter, Linda P. St. Jean, J.C. Travers
Shaw & McCabe, 53 Grafton St., D.C. Shaw, C.C. McCabe
Trainor & O'Donnell, 162 Richmond St., L. P. O'Donnell, Q.C.
Tweedy, Ross, #605, 134 Kent St., G.G. Tweedy, Q.C., N.D. Ross, P.J.D. Mullin, J.F. Keaveny, J.R.A. Douglas, D.W. Hooley, E.S. Murphy, Barbara Stevenson, Rosemary Scott. Counsel: Hon. George J. Tweedy, C.M., Q.C., A.J. Haslam, Q.C.

CORNWALL, Queens Co.
Tweedy, Ross (also Charlottetown)

CRAPAUD, Queens Co.
Campbell, McEwen (also Summerside)

MONTAGUE, Kings Co.
Foster, O'Keefe (also Charlottetown)
Fraser, A. K., Box 516
Tweedy, Ross (also Charlottetown)

O'LEARY, Prince Co.
Campbell, McEwen etc. (also Summerside)
Ramsay, Campbell (also Summerside)

SOURIS, Kings Co.
Fraser, A. K. (also Montague)
McQuaid & Mullally, G. J. Mullally

SUMMERSIDE, Prince Co.
Campbell, McEwen & McLellan, 37 Central St., J.M. Campbell, Q.C., W.A. McEwen, B.V. McLellan, G.A. Walker
Hinton & Lyle, Box 1326, R.S. Hinton, Q.C., G.A. Lyle, D.D. Key
MacDonald, G. B., Q.C., 247 Water St.
MacLeod & Clark, 235 Water St., N.R. MacLeod, Q.C., J.K. Clark
MacNaught & MacNaught, Smallman Bldg., J. W. MacNaught, Q.C., J. W. MacNaught
McCabe & Taylor, 268 Water St., B. St.C. McCabe, Q.C., B.B. Taylor
McMahon & Hammond, 293 Water St., D. Hammond
Ramsay, Campbell & Riley, 307 Water St., J.L. Ramsay, Diane Campbell, D.B. Riley

ADVOCATES IN THE PROVINCE OF QUEBEC

ACTON VALE, Dist. St. Hyacinthe
Ratte, G., 1015 Beaugrand (also Drummondville)

ALMA, Dist. Roberval
Abud & Harvey, 540 Sacre-Coeur St. w., M. Abud, L. Harvey
Fleury, Bergeron & Paradis, 625 o., Sacre-Coeur, J. V. Fleury, A. Bergeron, Y. Paradis
Gagnon & Larouche, 85 St. Joseph St. s., B. Gagnon, R. Larouche
Pedneault, G., 580 Sacre Coeur St. w.
Simard, M., 415 Collard w.

AMOS, Dist. Abitibi
Barbes & Barbes (also Val d'Or)
Bigue, Claude
Bigue, L.
Cossette, C.
Fauteux, P.
Frignon & Gagnon
Gauthier, M., 741 1st St. w.
Leduc, D.
Lemay, M.
Provost, J.
St. Julien, Tessier & Co., 261 1st Ave. w., I. St. Julien, G. Tessier (also Val d'Or)
Viens, Godbout & Gagnon, J. Viens, F. Godbout. Counsel: G. Gagnon, Hon. H. Drouin

AMQUI, Dist. Rimouski
Blouin, J., 20 Adrien St. (also Baie Comeau)
Gagnon, Ouellet & Chamberland, 21 St. Benoit Blvd., M. Gagnon, J. J. Ouellet, J.-P. Chamberland (also Matane)

ARTHABASKA, Dist. Arthabaska
Baril, Belisle, Lassonde, Roy, Nault, 67 Girouard St., S. Baril, P. Belisle, J. Lassonde, C. Roy, J.-M. Nault
Moisan, Bellevance, Aubert, Labbe, 702 boul. Bois-Francs sud, Y. Moisan, J. M. Bellevance, C. Aubert, P. Labbe (also Daveluyville and Plessisville)

ARVIDA, Dist. Chicoutimi
Blanchet, A.
Roy & Gauthier
Tremblay & Tremblay, C.P. 1217, J.-Y. Tremblay, P. Tremblay

ASBESTOS, Dist. St. Francois
Boudreau, G.G. (also Sherbrooke)
Geoffroy & Geoffroy (also Sherbrooke)
Lamontagne, F.
Tardif, A.F.

AYLMER, Dist. Hull
Byrne, D.J., Box 642
Guitard, M., #3, 21 Park St.

BAIE COMEAU, Dist. Hauterive
Dufour & Coulombe, 92 LaSalle Blvd., J.C. Dufour, H. Coulombe
Rouleau, Carrier, Blouin, Carrier & Dostie, 67 Place LaSalle, G. Rouleau, Q.C., A. Carrier, O. Carrier, J. Blouin, G. Dostie
Sabourin, Corriveau, Nadeau, Tremblay, Francoeur & Assoc., 231 LaSalle Blvd., P. Sabourin, P. Corriveau, S. Francoeur, J. Nadeau, C. Tremblay (also Quebec)

BEACONSFIELD, Dist. Montreal
Anctil, J., 130 Beaconsfield Blvd.
Boyd, F.S., 444 Beaconsfield Blvd., Ste. 8, H9W 4C1

BEAUCEVILLE, Dist. Beauce
Cliche, D.
Gagne, A.
Poulin, J.R.

BEAUHARNOIS, Dist. Beauharnois
Lecompte, LaGarde & Marleau, 57 Ellice St., M. Lecompte, G. LaGarde, R. Marleau (also Valleyfield)

BEDFORD, Dist. Bedford
Cambrini, M., 7 Place d'Estrie (M. Desruisseaux)
Levesque, F., 7 Place d'Estrie (A. Hachimi)
Paradis & Paradis, C.P. 930, D. Paradis, P. Paradis, L. Lord, M. Lemieux-Pierce, J.C. Beauchamp, A. Bedard
Parent, R., Box 1562
Raymond, G., Box 1562

BELOEIL, Dist. St-Hyacinthe
Dubreuil, R., 166 Brunelle (M. Charbonneau)

BERTHIERVILLE, Dist. Joliette
Sylvestre, Lacroix & Yanakis, 600 Frontenac St., A. Sylvestre, L. Lacroix, P. Yanakis

BLACK LAKE, Dist. Frontenac
Lefebvre, R.

BOUCHERVILLE, Dist. Montreal
Cousineau, R., 16 Desmarteau Ave.
Heppell-Morin, S., 25 des Seigneurs
Lalancette, J.P., 216 Thomas Pepin St.
Lefebvre, B., 1090 de Belleme

BROSSARD, Dist. Montreal
Leclerc & Alie, 6185 Taschereau, N. Leclerc

BUCKINGHAM, Dist. Hull.
Gauthier, G., 399 Principale
Joanisse, P., 106 Maclaren St.
Montreuil, D., 143 St. Joseph
Sauve, Osborne, etc., 517 Gauthier St. (also Gatineau)

CABANO, Dist. Kamouraska
Thivierge, Nicole, 14 rue Pelletier

CAMPBELL'S BAY, Dist. Pontiac
Lavallee, D., Box 59
Leclerc & Gravel, McLellan St., R.P. Leclerc, F. Gravel (also Hull)

St-Amand & Desjardins, Box 219, J.-P. St-Amand, G. Desjardins, C. Juneau. Counsel: M. Boisvert, Q.C., C. Belleau (also Hull)

CAP CHAT, Dist. Gaspé
Julien & Tremblay, R. Julien, G. Tremblay

CAP-DE-LA MADELEINE, Dist. Trois Rivieres
Lamothe, Ayotte, 283 Ste. Madeleine Blvd., B. Lamothe, C. Ayotte
Pinsonneault, Roy, Lambert, Mercier & Lambert, 399A Ste. Madeleine Blvd., A. Roy, R. Lambert, J. Pinsonneault, J. Mercier, L. Matteau

CARLETON, Dist. Bonaventure
Cormier, N., Perron Blvd.
Lacroix, L., C.P. 306

CHANDLER, Dist. Gaspé
Becu & Roy, C.P. 489, J. Becu, P. Roy
Gaul, G., 461 Rehel St.
Hayes, R.

CHATEAUGUAY, Dist. Beauharnois
Chevrefils, P., 75 St. Jean Baptiste St.
Costigan, J., 255 d'Anjou
Francoeur, J., 119 Ashmore St.
Montanbault, J., 370 Salaberry n.
Trudeau, M., Q.C., 88 Salaberry s.

CHICOUTIMI, Dist. Chicoutimi
Aubin, Bedard, Fillion, Brisson, Fournier & Cote, 110 Racine St. e., G. Aubin, Q.C., M. A. Bedard, A. Fillion, E. Brisson, L.-C. Fournier, A. Cote, D. Cote
Bergeron, Cain, Lamarre, Casgrain, Wells & Lachance, 110 Racine St. e., P. Bergeron, Q.C., M. Cain, Q.C., F. Lamarre, P. Casgrain, G. Wells, C. Lachance, C. Gauthier, P. Simard, F.G. Tremblay, A. Tremblay, Rita Vaillancourt, J. Dauphinais, R. Bergeron, F. Bouchard
Bouchard, Larouche, Brassard, Gauthier & Babin, 393 Racine St. e., Lucien Bouchard, C. Larouche, R. Brassard, L. Gauthier, J. Babin
Brodeur & Girard, 121 Racine St. e., J.R. Brodeur, C. Girard
Cote, Gilbert, Lortie & St-Gelais, 52 Racine St. e., R. Cote, N. Gilbert, P. Lortie, L. St-Gelais. Counsel: Roland Bergeron, Q.C.
Cote, M., 106 Garon St.
Dufour, Cote & Laperriere, 23 Racine St. e., R. Dufour, G. M. Cote, Y. Laperriere
Gagnon, M., 1 Place du Royaume
Lambert & Lambert, 31 Racine St. w., R. Lambert, G. Lambert
Lapointe, B., #101, 100 Racine St. e.
Lavoie, J.M., 110 Racine St. e.
Morin, Gaudreault & Dumais, 23 Racine St. e., A. Morin, C. Gaudreault, D. Dumais
Prevost, Girard, 901 Talbot Blvd., C. Girard, G. Prevost
Tremblay, D.M., 413 Racine St. e.
Truchon, A., #107, 247 Racine St. e.

COATICOOK, Dist. St. Francois
Larocque, L.
Morisette, A.

CONTRECOEUR,
Lemoine, M., 7738 rte Marie-Victorin

COWANSVILLE, Dist. Bedford
Bachand & Assoc., 106 Principale, A. Bachand, F. Bourassa
Champagne, Y., 218A Principale
Hackett, Campbell & Co., 314 Principale, P. Turner, D. Bissonnette (also Sherbrooke)
Hamann, C., 436 South St. (M. Lacasse)
Mercure & Bachand, 817 Principale, G. Mercure, P. Bachand

DAVELUYVILLE, Dist. Arthabaska
Moisan, Bellevance & Co. (also Arthabaska)

DOLBEAU, Dist. Roberval
Bouchard & Voyer, G.H. Bouchard, C. Voyer
Legare & Beaumier, 1313 Walberg S.I., Jacquelin Legare

DONNACONA, Dist. Quebec
Dussault, C., 299 Notre Dame St.
Fournier, C., 309 de l'Eglise

DORION, Dist. Beauharnois
Perron, Schmidt & Legault, 176 Harwood St., G. Perron, Y. Schmidt, A. Legault

DORVAL, Dist. Montreal
Amaron, Stead & Viberg, 280 Dorval Ave., A.C.S. Stead, R.C. Amaron, H. R. Viberg
Bousquet, G., Q.C., 285 Malcolm Circle
Glazaille, S., 1 Lilas St.

DRAGON-RIGAUD, Dist. Montreal
Gauthier, M., 262 Ch. de l'Anse (also Amos)

DRUMMONDVILLE, Dist. Drummond
Baril, Lahaie, Lahaie & Parenteau, 150 Heriot St., J.C. Baril, G. Lahaie, S. Lahaie, A. Parenteau
Biron, P., 302 Lindsay St.
Blais & Lafreniere, 215 Lindsay St., R. Blais, M. Lafreniere
Bolduc, Leduc & Martin, 234 St. Marcel St., Y. Bolduc, R. Leduc, P. Martin
Clair, Laplante & Cote, 186 Heriot St., R. Clair, M. Laplante, J. Cote
Corriveau & Lagace, 108 Marchand St., N. Corriveau, J.-C. Lagace
Hinse & Parenteau, 147 Lindsay St., J.-P. Hinse, R. Parenteau, G. Gagnon
Jutras, Houle & Assoc., 449 Heriot St., G. Jutras, M. Houle, N. Jutras
Prince, J., 480 Lindsay St.
Ratte, G., 183 Lindsay St.

EAST ANGUS, Dist. St. Francois
Desrochers, Y.

FARNHAM, Dist. Bedford
Paradis, G., 448 Hotel de Ville (M. Plouffe, M. Turcot)

FORESTVILLE, Dist. Hauterive
Lafleur & Assoc., 2 7th St., J. Lafleur, J.P. Bedard
Lapointe & Simard, 31 rte 138, J. Lapointe, J.L. Simard
Lavoie, Verret & Assoc., 59 rte 138 (also Hauterive)

GASPE, Dist. Gaspé
Joncas, R., rue de la Reine
Michaud & Cote, 147 rue de la Reine, J.R. Michaud, Suzanne Cote
Pidgeon, R., rue de la Reine
Poupart & Leliene, Y. Poupart, G. Leliene

GATINEAU, Dist. Hull
Dagenais, Lewis & Cayen, 159 2nd Ave., J. R. Dagenais, M. Lewis, G. Cayen, L. Ducharme
Gauthier & Ouellette, 278 Notre Dame, P. Gauthier, M. Ouellette
Kehoe, Blais & Robinson, 340 Maloney Blvd. e., J. J. Kehoe, P. Blais, C. Robinson
Lapointe, LeBlanc & Assoc., 365 Greber Blvd., R.R. Lapointe, C.M. Lapointe, R.M. LeBlanc
Roy, R., 576 Maloney Blvd. e. (R. Mantha, Colette Sabourin)
Sauve, Osborne & Bastien, 277 Notre Dame, J. Sauve, J.-P. Osborne, R. Bastien
Seguin, Ouellette, Lalonde & Assoc., 151 LaBrosse Blvd., R. Seguin, R. Ouellette, J.P.R. Lalonde, R. Belanger, Annette Paris
Tache, Pharand & Assoc., 355 Greber Blvd. (also Hull)

GENTILLY, Dist. Trois-Rivieres
Poisson, R., 2820 Becancour Blvd.

GEORGEVILLE, Dist. St. Francois
Kohl, G.G., Q.C., Box 55

GRANBY, Dist. Bedford
Arsenault, Robichaud, Guay, Guertin, Lapierre, 50 Centre St., G. Arsenault, Y. Robichaud, A. Guay, J. Guertin, Gisele Lapierre
Choiniere, R., 26 Court St.
Delorme & Denis, 102 Principale, Johanne Denis, J. Delorme
Gaudet, G., 25 Dufferin St.
Gerin, Rancourt & Lavallee, 50 Centre St., D. Lavallee (also Sherbrooke)
Grignon, Brun & Mireault, 18 Court St., L.-B. Grignon, M. Brun, Suzanne Mireault
Normandin, Brisebois & Laflamme, 35 Dufferin St., L. Normandin, R.D. Brisebois, D. Laflamme. Counsel: G. Normandin, Q.C
Robert, M., 135 Principale (C. Dionne)
Savoie, J.M., 2 Court St. (D. Giard, P. Smith)

GRANDE RIVIERE, Dist. Gaspé
Gendron, G.

GRAND'MERE, Dist. St. Maurice
Brault, Marguerite, 644 4th St.
Champagne, J.M., 1133 6th Ave.
Goulet & Cote, 602 6th Ave., A. Goulet
Goulet, P., 1671 6th Ave.
Venne, M., 561 5th St.

HAUTERIVE, Dist. Hauterive
Hebert, G., 864 de Puyjalon
Lavoie, Verret, Houde & Langlois, 1295 Blanche St., A. Lavoie, S. Verret, F. Houde, Y. Langlois
Maltais, P., 625 Lafleche Blvd. (M. Martin, L. Hinse)

HULL, Dist. Hull
Allard & Assoc., 241 Papineau St., J.E. Allard, J. Coutu, R. Trudel
Beauchamp, C.N., 162 Wellington St.
Beaudry, Bertrand, 25 Laurier, Marcel Beaudry, Q.C., Michel Beaudry, J. C. Sarrazin, L. Bertrand, P. Bertrand, Y. Letellier, Monique Bourgon, J. Pigeon, C. Dupont, C. La Salle, Francine Dupont, Mona Rivest-Beaudry. Counsel: J. Bertrand, Q.C., P.H. Foran, Q.C., A. Larouche, C.M. Dalfen
Bedard & Leduc, 277 St. Joseph Blvd., M. Bedard, P. Leduc, J.P. Vianna
Beland, J., 6 Thibault St.
Belanger, R., 98 St. Joseph Blvd.
Belanger & Marchildon, 145 Champlain St., J. Belanger, L. Marchildon
Belec & Associates, 30 Dumas St., R. Belec, C. Boulanger, Renee Joyal, R. Belec, Nicole Gibeault
Bergeron & Gaudreau, 167 Notre Dame, Batonnier V. Bergeron, Q.C., R. Gaudreau, C. Payant, Marcia Pinet
Boucher, L., 76 Desjardins St.
Bourget & Bourget, 73 Laurier St., M. Bourget, Q.C., P. Bourget, R. Bourget, L. Poupart
Brisebois, R., 341 St. Joseph Blvd.
Brochu, Gratton & Assoc., 733 St. Joseph Blvd., D. Brochu, C. Gratton, J. Tessier
Charette, H.M., Q.C., 18 Decosse St.
Courval, H., 79 Hotel de Ville
D'Aoust & Prefontaine, 65 Begin St., A. D'Aoust, R. Prefontaine
Findlay, H.T., 285 Laurier St.
Hamon, Dufour & Isabelle, 768 Boul. St-

Joseph, F. Hamon, P. Dufour, P. Isabelle, M. Isabelle, Carole Theberge
Lavery, O'Brien, 25 Eddy St., B. Courtois, Y. Mayrand, A. Lufty (also Montreal)
Leclerc & Gravel, #102, 165 Wellington St. (also Campbell's Bay)
Legere, R., 6 Ste-Marie (M. Legere, Suzanne Ricard)
Marcil-Bourgoin, M.T., 47 Pharand St.
Moreau, Paquette & Paradis, 365 St. Joseph Blvd., M. Moreau, R. Paquette
Noel, Decary, Aubry & Assoc., 95 Victoria St., S. Noel, R. Decary, J.P. Aubry, G. Lehoux, C. Alain, M. Roy. Counsel: Hon. Camil Noel, Q.C.
Quain & Quain, 200, 95 Victoria Ave. (also Ottawa)
St-Amand & Desjardins, 102 Promenade du Portage (also Campbell's Bay)
St. Marie, J., Q.C., 36 Tache Blvd.
Ste. Marie, M., 132 Champlain St.
Scott & Aylen, 170 Laurier Ave. w., Ottawa, J. A. Aylen, Q.C., J. G. Aylen, Q.C.
Tache, Pharand & Assoc., 166 Wellington St., P. Tache, Q.C., M. Pharand, Francine R. Pharand-Robillard, R.W. Waddell, P. Dallaire, G. Belanger
Theriault, J., 53 Moncion St.
Voyer, A., 6 Villeneuve St.

HUNTINGDON, Dist. Beauharnois
Alary, R., 16 Prince St.
Martin, E. C.

IBERVILLE, Dist. Iberville
Forget, A., Q.C., 525 1st St.
Gingras, P.B., 789 2nd St.

ILE-PERROT, Dist. Beauharnois
Bourassa & Savoie, 91 Grand Blvd., G. Bourassa, M. Savoie

JOLIETTE, Dist. Joliette
Asselin, Beaulieu & Perrault, 569 Archambault St., A. Asselin, Luc Beaulieu, P. Perrault
Desrochers, M., 51 St. Charles n.
Dugas, Dugas & Pauze-Forest, 643 Manseau St., C. Dugas, Q.C., Michele Pauze-Forest, M. Dugas
Gagnon, Bazinet, Quenneville, Beausejour & Vincelette, 820 Notre Dame St., J.H.D. Gagnon, A. Bazinet, S. Quenneville, R. Beausejour, Claudette Vincelette
Genereux, Frechette, 35 St. Charles n., A. Genereux, M. Frechette
Landry, R., 439 Manseau Blvd., M. Brisson, B. Jolicoeur
Laporte & Ferland, 70 Place Bourget s., L. Laporte, M. Ferland
Pinault, R., #6, 334 Marsolais
Ratelle, Ratelle, Sylvestre, Preville, Belair, Ratelle & Loranger, 685 Manseau Blvd., G. Ratelle, L. Ratelle, Monique Sylvestre, Marie-E. Preville, M. Belair, D. Ratelle, P.D. Loranger
Trudel, Fontaine, Roy & Laporte, 386 Manseau Blvd., C. Trudel, A. Fontaine, A. Roy, R. Laporte

JONQUIERE, Dist. Chicoutimi
Angers, J.J., 357 St. Jules St.
Begin, Gauthier, Simard, Ouellet, Mazurette & Tremblay, 509 Boul. Harvey, D. Begin, J. Bte. Gauthier, S. Simard, A. Ouellet, P. Mazurette, Estelle Tremblay, R. Gaudreault
D'Auteuil, P., 166 St. Dominique St.
Dion, Girard & Beaudoin, 372 St. Dominique St., R. Dion, G. Girard, R. Beaudoin
Godin, L., 372 St. Dominique St.
Roy & Gauthier, 263 Mellon Blvd., C. Roy, Françoise Gauthier
Turcotte, Gauthier & Fortin, 65 King George St. (Kenogami Section), J. J. Turcotte, Q.C., R. Gauthier, B. Fortin

KENOGAMI, Dist. Chicoutimi
Turcotte, Gauthier & Fortin, 65 King George (also Jonquiere)

KNOWLTON, Dist. Bedford
Stairs, J., Q.C., Box 808

LA BAIE, Dist. Saguenay
Aubain, Fillion, etc., 1262 6th Ave. (also Chicoutimi)

LAC DES SEIZE ILES, Dist. Terrebonne
Lajeunesse, R., Box 56

LACHINE, Dist. Montreal
Cardinal & Major, 26th Ave., A. Cardinal, Roselyne Major
Gaston & Tabak, 1375 Notre Dame Ave., P. Gaston, G.E. Tabak
Neuer, M., 1024 Notre Dame Ave.
St. Amour & Beauchamp, 1155 Notre Dame Ave., Louise St. Amour, Huguette Beauchamp

LACHUTE, Dist. Terrebonne
Beaudoin, D., 537 Principale
Chartrand, M. J. J., 415 Principale
Paquin, J. C., 597 Principale
Poisson, Denis, 514 Principale
Steeves, W. M. C., 18 Providence Blvd.

LAC MEGANTIC, Dist. St. Francois
Greffard & Aubut, 5284 Frontenac, P. Greffard, M. Aubut
Paradis & Giguere, 5109 Frontenac, C. Paradis, R. Giguere
Turgeon, A., 5175 Frontenac

La CONCEPTION, Dist. Labelle
Letourneau, J., Q.C.

La MALBIE, Dist. Saguenay
Lapointe & Simard, J. Lapointe, J.L. Simard, R. Tremblay
Martineau, D.
Savard & Dumas, P.-P. Savard, A. Dumas
Tremblay, P.

LA POCATIERE, Dist. Kamouraska
Chamard, R., 706 Quatrieme Ave.

LAPRAIRIE, Dist. Montreal
Brisson, G., 320 St. George St.
Dulude, P., 220 St. Ignace St.
Lanctot, C., 1410 Elizabeth Blvd. (J. Dessureault)
Lavallee, J.M., 751 St. Jean Rd.
Lussier, M., 514 St. Jean Rd.

LA SARRE, Dist. Abitibi
Gagnon & Breton, M. Gagnon, Nicole Breton
Grimard, Desjardins (also Rouyn)
Lambert, M., 62 5th Ave. e.
St. Pierre, C.

LA TUQUE, Dist. St. Maurice
Carrier, J.-M.
Levesque, J.
Ouellet, R.

LEVIS, Dist. Quebec
Belanger, R., Q.C., 109 St. George St. (also Quebec)
Boivin, Lagace, Poulin, Lessard, Jessop, 95, rue St.-Georges, C. Boivin, J. Lagace, C. Poulin, G. Lessard, W. Jessop, R. Turgeon, M. Patry, A. Roy, L. Dignard
Forgues, Brochu, 67 Cote du Passage, J. Forgues, R. Brochu, Francine Neron, J. Doyon
Genest, Lacroix & Laflamme, 124 St. Georges, J.C. Genest, A. Lacroix, M. Laflamme, J. Ouellet (also Quebec)
Girard & Lacombe, 2 Trans Canada Hwy. w., A. Girard, J.-F. Lacombe
Gosselin & Assoc., 67 Cote du Passage, M. Gosselin, J. Marceau, G. Poitras
Kronstrom, Turmel, Desjardins & Villeneuve, 52 Cote du Passage, S. Kronstrom, E. Turmel, J. Y. Desjardins, J. G. Villeneuve, A. Robitaille, P. Cloutier, R. Ramsay, B. Godbout, Y. Rochette, B. Vachon, M. Gravel, R. St. Pierre, L. Godbout
Savard, Cayer & Assoc., 56 Cote du Passage, Y. Savard, R. Cayer, G. Gourde, D. Dutil

LONGUEUIL, Dist. Montreal
Bernard, Girard, Despatis & Cormier, 1470 chemin Chambly, G. Girard, M. Bernard, P. Despatis, J.C. Cormier
Brassard, D. & Assoc., 2154 Ch. Tremblay
Brissette, St-Jacques, Trepanier, Lamarre, 3 St. Charles St. w., D. Brissette, Q.C., Ginette Trepanier, P. Lamarre, L. de L'Etoile, J. Chandonnet, F. Bissette, N. Gibeau, J. Sasseville, F. Bosse. Counsel: A. Cote, L. Laprade, Q.C.
Brochu, Drolet, Lavoie, 99 Place Charles Lemoyne, L. Drolet, L. Lavoie
Chiquette, Bissonnette & Girard, 90 Ste Foy Blvd., G. Chiquette, J. Bissonnette, G. Girard
Cimone & Poupart, 365 St. Jean St., P. Cimone, S. Poupart
Ferland & Archambault, 720 St. Lawrence w., J.H. Ferland, G. Archambault, Louise Comeau
Jodoin, C., 1050 Cure Poirier St.
Lapalme-Boucher & Bourbeau, 580 rue Ste. Foy, O. Lapalme-Boucher, S. Bourbeau
Lariviere, Brault & Dury, 482 Ste. Helene, J. Lariviere, S. Brault, R. Dury
Proulx & Lacoste, 460 St. Charles St. w., R.J. Proulx, M. Lacoste
Tremblay, M., 162 St. Charles St. w.

LOUISEVILLE, Dist. Trois-Rivieres
Boulay, F.
Dubeau, S., 21 St. Marc St.
Gagnon, S.

MAGOG, Dist. St. Francois
Beaudry, Allaire & Vaillancourt, 155 Main St. w., J. Beaudry, G. Allaire, S. Vaillancourt
Bergeron, L., 22 St. Patrice St. e.
Galipeau, L.-P., 737 Main St. w.
Gosselin, C., 9 Main St. w.
St. Pierre, H., R.R. 2

MANIWAKI, Dist. Labelle
Lefebvre, C., 163 Laurier

MANSONVILLE, Dist. Bedford
Cote, Nicole, R.R. 4

MARIEVILLE, Dist. St. Hyacinthe
Chiquette, Bissonnette & Girard, 394 Claude de Ramezay (also Longueuil)
Gervais & Major, 1368 Dupont St., L. Gervais, Micheline Major, P. Adam
Lesarge, L., 800 Ouelette St.

MATANE, Dist. Rimouski
Begin & Brind'Amour, M. Begin, M. Brind'Amour
Deschenes & Doiron, 352 St. Jerome Ave., J. Deschenes, J.-M. Doiron
Gagnon, Ouellet & Chamberland, 159 St. Pierre, J.P. Chamberland (also Amqui)
Tremblay, B.V., 100 St. Pierre

METABETCHOUAN, Dist. Roberval
Tremblay, N. (also Alma)

MISTASSINI, Dist. Roberval
Boivin, G.

MONT JOLI, Dist. Rimouski
Pelletier, Y., 1555 boul. J.-Cartier

MONT LAURIER, Dist. Labelle
Chartrand, P., 620 de la Madone
Courtemanche, Hon. H., P.C. (also Val d'-Or)
Lauzon, J.
Ouellette, D.

Rancourt, R.
Roy, J. M.
Simard, M.A., 1138 Aristide Masse
Therrien, V., Q.C.

MONTEBELLO, Dist. Hull
Desmarais, P., Box 397

MONTMAGNY, Dist. Montmagny
Daveluy, R., 46 St. Jean Baptiste e.
Garant, R., 77 Ave. de la Gare
Morin, Lemieux & Blais, 41 St. Jean Baptiste e., M. Morin, A. Lemieux, P. Blais
Paquin & Dumontier, 121 St. Thomas, S. 101, L. Paquin, P. Dumontier

MONTREAL, Dist. Montreal
Aaron, J., 200 Bates Rd.
Abbey, M., Q.C., 4115 Sherbrooke St. w. (M. Slapack, Q.C.)
Ackermann, V., 1117 St. Catherine St. w.
Adessky, Kingstone, Zerbisias, Poulin, Gervais & Bier, 1010 Sherbrooke St. w., I. L. Adessky, Q.C., D. Kingstone, Q.C., D. Zerbisias, G. Poulin, R. Gervais, E.L. Bier, Carol A. Fitzwilliam, E.S. Brott, Irene Papvisal, Micheline McDuff. Counsel: H.D. Clarke
Ahern, Nuss & Drymer, 4111 Stock Exchange Tower, Place Victoria, J.R. Nuss, Q.C., F. Lalonde, Q.C., E. H. Drymer, J. A. Silcoff, J. Dery, G.H. Waxman, B. Riordan
Alarie, Legault, Nadon & Quevillon, 3431 St. Hubert St., L. Alarie, A. Legault, Odette Nadon, P.-A. Quevillon
Alepin & Bigras, 1688 Laurentides Blvd. (Vimont), F. Alepin, D. Bigras
Alguire, W.G., 5015 Sherbrooke St. w.
Allaire, P., 12,017 Pasteur St.
Allen & Beauvais, 112 Giroux Ave. (Laval), R. Allen, R. Beauvais
Amsel & Maliniak, 355 St. James St., R. Amsel, L. Maliniak
Amyot, Lesage, Bernard, etc., #3411, 1 Place Ville Marie (also Quebec)
Antonuk, A., 3500 St. Hubert St.
Appel, Golfman, Lehrer & Castonguay, 1 Westmount Sq., D. Appel, H. Lehrer, R. M. Cooper, J. Castonguay, W.R. Golfman. Counsel: Lilian Reinblatt
Apple, M., 2030 Crescent St.
Archambault, Boucher & Associates, 10 St. James St., C. F. Archambault, R. Boucher
Arsenault, Pelletier & Gregoire, 4 Notre Dame St. e., G. Arsenault, F. Pelletier, L. Gregoire
Arslanian, C.-P., 5064 Park Ave.
Asselin, Cadieux, Cadieux & Chartrand, 1198 de la Montagne, E.T. Asselin, Pierre Cadieux, P.H. Cadieux, L. Chartrand. Counsel: P. Ferland, Q.C.
Aster & Aster, 1010 St. Catherine St. w., M. A. Aster, Margaret A. Aster
Audet, F., 4 Notre Dame St. e.
Awada & Sumbulian, 1010 Sherbrooke St. w., M. Awada, H. Sumbulian
Ayoup, R., 1255 Phillips Sq.
Baer, Debra, 355 St. James St.
Baker, Nudleman, Lamontagne & Dupont, 1155 Dorchester Blvd. w. (H3B 2J3), H. Baker, Q.C., R. E. Baker, G. Nudleman, Lise-Anne Dupont, Tetiana Gerych, G.R. Lamontagne, R.L. Renaud, P. Audet
Baron, Piasetski & Abrams, 5180 Queen Mary Rd., B. Baron, M. Piasetski, G. Abrams
Barriere-Carfagnini, Suzanne, 1227 Sherbrooke St. w.
Barron, Picard & Geoffrion, 1405 Henri Bourassa Blvd. w., Y. Barron, R. Picard, L. Geoffrion
Bastien, Brosseau & Bastien, 6070 Sherbrooke St. e., R. Bastien, P. Brosseau, M. Bastien
Batshaw, L. D., 1010 St. Catherine St. w.
Beaudet, Robert, 5331 Bannatyne
Beaule & Lafortune, 359 St. Pierre St., R. Beaulne, Ginette Lafortune
Beaulieu, Boisvert, Szemenyei, Paiement & Semeniuk, 1420 Sherbrooke St. w., R. Beaulieu, Q.C., G.E. Boisvert, L. Szemenyei, J. R. Paiement, J. P. Semeniuk
Beaupré, Trudeau, 2 Complexe Desjardins, G. Beaupré, Q.C., M. Trudeau, Q.C., Y. Sylvestre, B. Taillefer, J. Berkowitz, M. Richer, P. Brunet, Luc Lamarre
Beausejour, J.G., 6907 St. Denis St.
Bedard, J., Q.C., 2085 Guy St.
Bedard & Poirier, 451 St. Sulpice St., P. Bedard, F. Poirier
Bedard & Vadeboncoeur, 360 St. James St. w., R. Bedard, P.G. Vadeboncoeur, Q.C.
Beique, J., 300 Decarie Blvd.
Belanger Bissonnette Belanger, 5835 Leger St. (Montreal North), A. J. Belanger, Guy Belanger, Elaine Bissonnette
Belanger, Claudette, 6879 de Marseille St.
Belanger, Leclerc, 800 Victoria Sq., G. Belanger, J. Leclerc
Belanger, Mongeau & Brunet, #300, 31 St. James St., A. Belanger, Q.C., J. Mongeau, Q.C., M. Brunet
Belhassen, E., #101, 240 St. James St.
Belhumeur, A., #506, 1030 Cherrier St.
Bell, Cytrynbaum & Solloway, 1010 St. Catherine St. w., M. Bell, S. Cytrynbaum, I. Solloway
Bellaiche, J.M., #304, 1500 Stanley St.
Bellavance & Hogue, #201, 5800 Chambly Rd. (St. Hubert), P. Bellavance, G. Hogue
Belleau, Madeleine, 10 St. James St.
Benoit, Hykawy & Raiche, 2315 Ontario St. e., J.B. Benoit, J. Hykawy, C. Raiche
Berger & Winston, 2102, 3410 Peel St., E. Michael Berger, Q.C., E.J. Winston, Martin Berger
Bergeron, J., 1641 St. Hubert St.
Bergman, M.N., #211, 1255 Phillips Sq.
Bernard, J.Y., 1 Notre Dame St. e.
Bernier, B., 2600 St. Joseph Blvd. e.
Bernier, J.-M., 3860 Notre Dame (Chomedey)
Bernstein, C.D., 302 Place d'Youville
Bernstein, Feifer, Beaupre, Roussy, Blanchard, Steinberg & Savoyan, 1080 Beaver Hall Hill, M. A. Feifer, D. M. Bernstein, J.G. Roussy, J.B. Blanchard, M. Steinberg, G. I. Beaupre, A. Savoyan, A. Gaulin, J. Mercier, R. Bernatchez, C.C. Gagnon, J. Rouleau
Bernstein & Schnitzer, #880, 231 St. James St., B. Bernstein, H. Schnitzer
Berthiaume, J., 4020 Delorimier St.
Bertrand, Guerard, Tetreault & Bleau, 3 Place Laval (Laval), J. Bertrand, G. Guerard, J. Tetreault, P. M. Bleau
Beullac, R.A., Q.C., 1645 de Maisonneuve Blvd. w.
Biega, A. Q.C., 276 St. James St. w.
Bierbrier, E.G., #305, 10 St. James St.
Binda, R., 6895 Jarry St. e.
Bisson, Archambaut, Suicco, Lapierre, Caron, Robitaille, 1851 Sherbrooke St. e., F. Bisson, M. Archambault, A. Suicco, G. Lapierre, Jacquelin Caron, C. Robitaille
Bissonnette, Christine, 618 Outremont Ave.
Blain, Papillon & Assoc., 315 Dorchester Blvd. e., J. Blain, Y. Papillon, J.-R. Dufresne
Blain, Piché, Emery & Assoc., 1010 Sherbrooke St. w. (H3A 1S6), M. Piché, O.C., Q.C., G. Emery, Q.C., P.-E. Blain, Q.C., J. Guérin, Q.C., F. Guérette, P. Tessier, S. Bourque, G. Doss, R. Page, J.J. O'-Reilly, P.P. Lavoie, P.D. Richard, M. St-Pierre, R. de Gage Rochette, B. Emery, Doris Jacques. Counsel: J. Blain, Q.C.; Maurice D. Godbout, Q.C.
Blank, H., Q.C., 1255 University St. (J. Rosenfeld)
Blanshay, Blanshay & Eidinger, #360, 901 Bleury St., I.E. Blanshay, L.J. Blanshay, R.L. Eidinger, F. Barette. Counsel: Philippe Ferland, Q.C.
Blau, S., 5725 Notre Dame de Grace
Bless, J.S., 210 St. Catherine St. e.
Blond-Frank, Joyce, 275 St. James St.
Bloomfield & Bloomfield, #2020, 1080 Beaver Hall Hill, L.M. Bloomfield, Q.C., H.J.F. Bloomfield
Blouin, Guy, #700, 1980 Sherbrooke St. w.
Bobrove, J. B., Q.C., 1010 St. Catherine St. w.
Bogante, M.D., 666 Sherbrooke St. w.
Boies, C., 5800 St. Denis
Boisclair, Kozina, Sasseville & Pellerin, 4906 Gouin Blvd. e., R. Boisclair, M. Kozina, Micheline Sasseville, P. Pellerin
Boisclair, Lamoureux & Brizard, #2604, 800 Place Victoria, F. Boisclair, J. L. Lamoureux, Y. Brizard, J. Biron, G. Duranleau, R. Tessier, R. Proulx, J.-M. Clement
Boissoneault, A., #1001, 3555 Berri St.
Boissoneault, G., 1 Notre Dame St. e.
Boisvert, Menard & Roberge, 345 Cremazie w., M. Boisvert, M. Menard, P. Roberge
Boivin, A., 11553 Brunet Ave.
Boivin, D., 5712 des Grandes Prairies
Boivin, Fortin, Gaudreau, #305, 110 Cremazie w., P. Boivin, D. Fortin, M. Gaudreau
Bolduc, Lavigne & Malouin, 6070 Sherbrooke St. e., M. Bolduc, M. Lavigne, J. Malouin
Bonin, G., #2020, 500 Place d'Armes
Bouchard, Pothier & Cytrynbaum, 4141 Sherbrooke St. w., P. Bouchard, J.C. Pothier, S. L. Cytrynbaum
Bouchard, R., 84 Duvernay St.
Boucher, Gariepy, Moreault, 1030 Cherrier St., S. Boucher, J. Gariepy
Boucher, J.P., 1816 Sherbrooke St. e.
Boudrias, Frechette, Gelinas & Pasini, 276 St. James St., D. Boudrias, J. Frechette, M.G. Gelinas, M. Pasini
Bourbonnais, Y., 2115 Lapiniere St. (Brossard)
Boulianne, J.R., 1641 St. Hubert St.
Boxer & Feldman, 10 St. James St., M. Boxer, M. Feldman
Boyd, F.S., 444 Beaconsfield Blvd. (Beaconsfield, H9W 4C1)
Boyer, Laverdure, Boule & Lamontagne, 152 Notre Dame St. e., J.P. Boyer, J. Laverdure, M. Lamontagne, P. Boule
Boyer, Roland, 10 St. James St.
Brabant, A., #200, 210 St. James St.
Brassard, P., 5199 Sherbrooke St. e.
Brisset, Bishop, Davidson & Davis, 620 St. James St. w., J. Brisset, Q.C., T. H. Bishop, P. W. Davidson, M. Davis, R. J. Cypihot
Brisson, M., 359 St. Peter St.
Brisson, Y.
Brodeur, Matteau, Barrette & Toupin, 1312 Sherbrooke St. e., Y. Brodeur, Colette Matteau, J. Barrette, R. Toupin
Brodie & Polisuk, 1010 St. Catherine St. w., I. S. Brodie, Q.C., T. H. Polisuk, E.F. Balangero, R.W. Lord
Bronstetter, Wilkie, Penhale, Donovan, Giroux & Charbonneau, 1 Place Ville

Marie, #3411, H3B 3N7, W.E. Bronstetter, Q.C., N.J.K. Donovan, D.B. Wilkie, J.A. Penhale, Andrée-Anne Charbonneau, D.I. Penhale, L. Giroux, R.A. Bradley, J.-G. Campeau, I.T. Chapman, J.C.M. Donovan, J.N. Schwartz, G. Michalk. Counsel: R. deW. MacKay, Q.C., W.P. Keating
Brouillard, R., 4 Notre Dame St. e.
Brouillette, M., 2927 Concorde Blvd. (Laval)
Brule, J., 2933 Masson St.
Bruneau, Morin & LeBer, 10 St. James St., J. Bruneau, S. Morin, C. LeBer
Brunet, J., 3714 Ontario St. e.
Brunet, Paquin, Danis & Brunet, 440 Dorchester Blvd. w., R. Brunet, L.P. Paquin, M. Danis, S. Brunet
Budyk, Harry M., Q.C., 715 Victoria Sq.
Buisson, C.P., 750 Laurentien Blvd.
Buller, I., 168 Notre Dame St. e.
Bureau, Champagne & Parisien, 1400 Metcalfe St., A. Bureau, Liette Champagne, J. Parisien
Byers Casgrain, C.P. 27, Tour de la Bourse (H4Z 1A6), *Partners:* J. Bazin, D.N. Byers, R.S. Carswell, P. Casgrain, P.F. Dingle, P. Fournier, P. Langlois, R.E. Lawson, C.E. Leduc, V.F. Lefebvre, J.F. Lemieux, P.R. Marchand, A.A. Mass, H.B. McNally, C. Richer B1 *Associates:* M. Deschamps, S. Deslauriers, P. D'Etcheverry, Catherine Duff-Caron, G. Dugré, W. Hart, Sandra Markman, D. McAusland, Darlene Pearson, Lilia Pouliot, Anne-Marie Senécal, M. Towner
Cadieux & Sauve, 60 St. James St., J.D. Cadieux, M. Sauve, Q.C.
Campbell & Assoc., #1002, 800 Victoria Sq., B.L. Campbell, F. Gillman
Campbell, Pepper, Laffoley, 1 Place Ville Marie (H3B 2B3), A. J. Campbell, Q.C., J. J. Pepper, Q.C., J. R. Laffoley, J.M. Thomas, F. T. Legault, P.J. Habib, Diane Skiejka, M.J. Kushnir, M. Osterman
Canadian National Railways, Legal Dept., 935 Lagauchetiere St. w.
Canadian Pacific Railway, Legal Dept., Windsor Station
Canuel, Quidoz, Tremblay & Blier, 31 St. James St., G. Canuel, C. Quidoz, A. Tremblay, D. Blier
Capelovitch, L., 1 Westmount Sq.
Caplan, N.I., 5800 Cavendish St.
Cardinal, S., #1607, 3550 Jeanne Mance St.
Carisse, J.B., #1607, 3550 Jeanne Mance St.
Caron, B., 4150 St. Martin Blvd. w. (Laval)
Carouzet, J. & Assoc., #201, 315 Dorchester Blvd. e.
Carriere, G., 360 St. James St.
Carriere, P., 3 Place Bellerive
Carrieres, Y., 1100 Cremazie est
Cartwright, Kennedy & Gossack, 555 Dorchester Blvd. w., R. Cartwright, J.T. Kennedy, Q.C., H. Gossack, D. Kujan
Caumartin, J., 6688 Christophe Colomb
Cayer, V., 11903 St. Gertrude St. (Montreal North)
Cazelais, Pauline, Q.C., 2339 Guindon Terrace
Centorno, D., 800 Maisonneuve Blvd. e.
Cerini, Salmon, Watson, Souaid & Harris, 1010 St. Catherine St. w., J.M. Cerini, Q.C., H. C. Salmon, I. Watson, N. Souaid, I. E. Harris, R.E. Reynolds, D.G. Ironside
Cerundolo & Nivoix, 1819 Jean Talon St. e., E. Cerundolo, R. Nivoix
Chabot, Downs, Laurier & Cere, 356-90th Ave. (Lasalle), G. Chabot, K. Downs, J. Laurier, C. Cere
Chaikelson & Spector, 1255 Phillips Sq., Morris Chaikelson, Mortimer Chaikelson, C. Spector
Chait, Salomon, Gelber, Reis, Bronstein, Litvack, Echenberg & Lipper, 1 Place Ville Marie, Ste. 1901 (H3B 2C3), Samuel Chait, Q.C., N. H. Salomon, Nahum Gelber, Q.C., A. I. Bronstein, Bernard Reis, R. S. Litvack, G. L. Echenberg, C. R. Lipper, S.J. Klein, A. M. Sanft, D. H. Kauffman, N. Amyot, D. Lessard, R.M. Auclair, R.H. Levy, Sylvia B. Litvack, D.G. Masse, Judith G. Shenker, J.-F. Ménard
Chait, Sternthal, Katznelson & Michelin, 1020 Place du Canada, J. Michelin, J.S. Chait, D. Sternthal, D. Katznelson, D.R. Michelin, Monique Dupuis
Chalifoux, J., 10 St. James St.
Champagne, Dionne, Desy, Ferland, Roy, 3425 St. Hubert St., P. Champagne, Q.C., Mrs. Luce Dionne-Bourassa, N. Desy, Miss A. Ferland, Francine Massy-Roy, G. Ferland
Chapados, Chevalier & Gaul, 1010 Sherbrooke St. w., F. Chapados, A. Chevalier, I. Gaul, R. Primeau, Denise C. Lafortune
Charbonneau, Francine, 507 Place d'Armes
Charbonneau, G., 3270 Langelier St.
Charness & Charness, 615 Dorchester Blvd. w., I. J. Charness, Q.C., G. N. F. Charness
Charron, A., Q.C., 360 St. James St.
Chasse, R., 3714 Ontario St. e.
Chaurette & Thibault, 10800 Lajeunesse St., D. Chaurette, Johanne Thibault
Chenard, M., 5174 Cote des Neiges Rd.
Chicoyne, Helene F., 5400 Lacordaire Blvd.
Choquette & Groszman, 5064 Park Ave., J. Choquette, Q.C., E.L. Groszman
Chouinard, P., 410 St. Nicholas St.
City Attorneys: City Hall, J. Peloquin, Q.C., Chief City Attorney
Clarke & Kooiman, 606 Cathcart St., H. D. Clarke, H. Kooiman
Clement, C., 10785 Pie IX Blvd.
Clement & Slawner, 1010 Sherbrooke St. w., P. Clement, A. Slawner
Cloutier, Chamard, Sabourin & Associates, 837 Gilford St., P. Cloutier, A. Chamard, R. Sabourin
Cloutier, J.F., #302, 520 Cherrier St.
Cloutier, R., 6317 Gouin Blvd. e.
Coblentz & Coblentz, 555 Dorchester Blvd. w., M. Coblentz, Q.C., R.E. Coblentz
Cohen, Abraham, #1150, 555 Dorchester Blvd. w.
Cohen, B.Z., 1015 Beaver Hall Hill
Cohen, D., #809, 1110 Sherbrooke St. w.
Cohen, Fraid, 1310 Greene Ave., D.L. Cohen, S. Fraid
Cohen, P. B., 4000 de Maisonneuve Blvd. w. (Westmount)
Cohen, R., 3514 Park Ave.
Colby, Rioux, Demers & Smiley, 1155 Dorchester Blvd. w., J.H.E. Colby, Q.C., M.E. Rioux, Q.C., P.M. Demers, C.L. Smiley, W.G. Whittaker, Monique Dionne, R.E. Charbonneau, D.P. Crevier, F.J. Pepin, M.C. Martin, P. Labelle, Vera Mesenzew
Coleman & Greenberg, 1255 Phillips Sq., A.B. Coleman, M.J. Greenberg
Colpron, B., 4 Notre Dame St. e.
Comeau, A.R., #1104, 666 Sherbrooke St. w.
Constantine, M. J., 1117 St. Catherine St. w.
Cooke, E., Q.C., 1117 St. Catherine St. w.
Cooperstein, S., 400 de Maisonneuve Blvd. w.
Corbeil, C., 3530 Jean Talon w.
Corbeil, F., 2125 Jean Talon e.
Corbeil, Groleau & Dufresne, #100, 31 St. James St., G. Corbeil, B. Groleau, J. Dufresne
Corbeil, Howard, Marchand & Gagne, 4139 Amiens St., M. Corbeil, B. Howard, P. Marchand, P. Gagne
Corbeil, Meloche, Lariviere & Laberge, 250 Place d'Youville, G. Corbeil, B. Meloche, J.M. Lariviere, D. Laberge
Corbeil, N., 50 Place Cremazie
Cossette, G., #1420, 3555 Berri St.
Cote, L.M., 5083 St. Denis St.
Cote, Louise, 1030 Cherrier St.
Cote, M.C., #1300, 1801 McGill College Ave.
Cote, Miller, Simard, Talbot & Assoc., #600, 2525 Daniel Johnson Blvd. (Laval), A. Cote, M.M. Dagenais, R. Lalonde, R. Talbot, J. Methot, N.P. Miller, Suzanne Racine, J.G. Simard
Coulanges, M., 2125 Jean Talon St. e.
Coulombe, R., 2045 Stanley St.
Coulourides, D., Q.C., 10 St. James St. w.
Courtois, Clarkson, Parsons & Tétrault, 630 Dorchester Blvd. w. (H3B 1V7), J. Archambault, R.A. Beaulieu, Y. Bériault, Anne Bétournay, P.E. Bisaillon, Q.C., M. Boodman, R.J. Chénier, R.T. Clarkson, Q.C., M. Côté, Q.C., E.J. Courtois, Q.C., T.R.M. Davis, M. Dennis, J.M. Deschamps, J.R. Doyle, B. Ducharme, J.O. Duchesneau, Q.C., C.J.M. Flavell, G. Fortin, F.S. Freedman, A.P. Gauthier, J.-R. Gauthier, W.M. Goodman, Hon. J.-P. Goyer, P.C., Q.C., N. Grou, D.A. Hanson, Q.C., A.R. Hilton, R.T. Huot, C.K. Irving, J. Jeansonne, Jocelyne Drouin Knoppers, L. Lacoursière, H.T. Lacroix, P.M. Laing, Q.C., J.S. Lanctôt, P.D. Leblanc, Hélène Leroux, M.D. Levinson, P. Malo, Louise Martin, P.S. Martin, L.A. Miller, G. Nesbitt, R.E. Parsons, Q.C., A.J. Payeur, M.M. Peterson, L. Picard, P.E. Poirier, Y. Pratte, Q.C., A. Prévost, F. Rioux, P.-Y. Roy, L. Sarna, R.B. Schubert, L.J. Telfer, L. Terriault, J. Tétrault, Q.C., G.R. Tremblay, D.P. Ulin, M. Vallée, L.R. Wilson. Counsel: R. Caron, Q.C.
Cousineau, Beauchemin & Beauvais, 1843 St. Catherine St. e., R. Cousineau, A. Beauvais, J. Beauchemin
Coutu, P., 3100 Cartier Blvd.
Coutu, R., #2810, 800 Victoria Sq.
Crepeau & Beauregard, 1251 St. Joseph Blvd. e., R. Crepeau, J.M. Beauregard
Crete, L., 1 Notre Dame St. e.
Crystal & Adler, #505, 455 St-Antoine St. w., H. J. Crystal, N. A. Adler
Cyr & Globensky, 11920 Notre Dame St. e. (Pointe aux Trembles), J. Cyr, G. Globensky
Cyr, Weldon & Parizeau, #4281A Notre Dame w., P. Cyr, J.P. Weldon, F. Parizeau
Dagenais & Desormeau, 680 Labelle (Chomedey), M. Dagenais, P. Desormeau, C. Bovet
Dagenais & Wolfe, 581 des Laurentides (Laval), G. Dagenais, M. Wolfe
Dansereau, G., 60 St. James St.
Danis, J.C., #410, 345 Victoria Ave.
Dansereau & Lacoste, 200 St. James St., J.P. Dansereau, P. Lacoste
Daoust, G., #304, 4 Notre Dame St. e.
Daoust, Duceppe, Beaudry, Jolicoeur & Associates, 1595 St. Hubert St., R. Daoust, Q.C., A. Duceppe, G. Beaudry, E. Jolicoeur, M. Pinsonnault, Jr., J. Marquis, M. Duceppe, Y. Duceppe
David & Touchette, 1010 St. Catherine St. w., M. V. David, R. Touchette

Decary, Beauchemin, Giguere & Gosselin, 3467 St. Hubert St., A. Decary, Mona Beauchemin, M. Giguere, G. Gosselin
deDongo, P. J., #621, 1440 St. Catherine St. w.
Defoy, R., 9263 St. Denis St.
de Grandpre, Colas, Deschenes, Godin, Paquette, Lasnier & Alary, 2501 Tour de la Bourse, Place Victoria, Pierre de Grandpre, Q.C., E. Colas, Q.C., B.M. Deschenes, Q.C., G. Godin, Q.C., R.-C. Alary, Q.C., B. Lasnier, Q.C., A. Paquette, Q.C., J. Crepeau, Q.C., J.J. Gagnon, O. Prat, R. David, L.-A. Toupin, M. Desjardins, G. Fafard, J.L. Perron, G. Kordovi, A.P. Asselin, Claudette Blondeau, P. Mercille, A. Robichaud, B. Corbeil, M. Christine L. Papillon, J. Laurin, P. Chesnay, Victoria A. Percival, L. Roberge, M. Simard, Anne-R. Guimond, Y. Poirier, J. Luciani, F. Beauchamp, Andree Lauzon Ratelle; Counsel: Le Batonnier E. Poissant, Q.C., J. Landry, Q.C.
Deguire, R., Q.C., 60 St. James St. w.
De La Grave, Carole, 1800 Bercy St.
de la Madeleine, C., 3600 Henri Bourassa St. e.
Demers, Bigras, 10 St. James St., A. Demers, Y. Bigras
Demers & Huot, #200, 787 St. Elizabeth (Laprairie), Y.J. Demers, R. Huot
De Michele & Bissonnet, #860, 6020 Jean Talon St. e., A. De Michele, M. Bissonnet, A. DiCiocco, Louise Lefebvre
de Muszka, A., Q.C., 269 McDougall Ave.
Deniger & Beaudry, #701, 4 Notre Dame St. e., C. Deniger, M. Beaudry
Denis, C.-J., #1603, 1155 Sherbrooke St. w.
Department of Justice (Federal), 500 Place d'Armes
Deschamps, J., 10735 St. Lawrence Blvd.
Descoteaux, Jarry, Hebert, #202, 790 Laurentien Blvd., S. Descoteaux, Monique Jarry, G.P. Hebert
Descoteaux & Tranquille, 3323 Henri Bourassa St. e., Y. Descoteaux, Guillet Diane Tranquille
Desjardins, J.G., 3 Complexe Desjardins
Desjardins, Ducharme, Desjardins & Bourque, #1200, 635 Dorchester Blvd. w. (H3B 1R9), G. Desjardins, Q.C., C. Ducharme, Q.C., P. Bourque, Q.C., J. A. Desjardins, Q.C., C. Tellier, Q.C., J. P. Zigby, P. A. Michaud, Q.C., A. Lortie, A. Brossard, Q.C., F. Bélanger, M. Roy, J.-A. Maranda, M. Laurendeau, C. Bédard, P.G. Rioux, D. Bellemare, R. Lizotte, D. St-Onge, C. F. Couture, J. Paquin, M.A. Léonard, G. Coulombe, A. Loranger, J.-M. Saulnier, Anne-Marie L. Lizotte, L. Payette, A. Wéry, R.J. Phénix, E. Boulva, S.R. Tison, L. Bigaouette, P.R. Granda, S. Gloutney, M. Mongrain, M. McMillan, P. Legault, D. Bénay, A. Aznar, P. Marcotte, Danièle Mayrand, F. Garneau, F.A. Cheftechi, D. Francoeur, Louise Lalonde. Counsel: Counsel: C. J. Gélinas, Q.C.
Desjardins, Robt., 4515 Notre Dame St. w.
Deslongchamps, Johanne, 5800 St. Denis St.
Desmarais & Hargreaves, #201, 410 Henri Bourassa Blvd. e., R. Desmarais, L. Hargreaves
Desormeau, J., 60 Henri Bourassa Blvd. w.
Desrosiers, J. M., 4192 Girouard St.
Desrosiers, Josee, #402, 59 St. James St.
di Francesco, D., 6000 Monk Blvd.
Diner, L., 325, 4141 Sherbrooke St. w.
Dion, P.-E., #1104, 666 Sherbrooke St. w.
Di Tullio, D., #100, 8754 St. Michel Blvd.
Doheny, Mackenzie, Grivakes, Gervais & Le Moyne, 5 Place Ville Marie, D. O'C. Doheny, Q.C., D. Mackenzie, Q.C., J. Greenstein, Q.C., T. G. Grivakes, Q.C., P.A. Gervais, Q.C., R. LeMoyne, P.C. Casey, D. M. Doubilet, L. LaRochelle, I. B. Taylor, S. Brassard, G.R. Thibaudeau, P. Richardson, M.A. Brunet, Francoise Brais, G.M. Gillman, L. Lemire, V.A. Buffoni, Grace Strusberg-Hazanovitz, P. LeFevre, M. Patry, F. Tutino. Counsel: G. H. Day, Q.C., J. G. Thomka-Gazdik, Q.C.
Dolman, Hart & Assoc., 1010 St. Catherine St. w., R. H. Dolman, B. H. Hart
Dore, G., #803, 4 Notre Dame e.
Dorget, Danielle, 10 St. James St.
Doyle, J., #750, 276 St. James St.
Drouin, Sirois, Papineau, Arseneault & Gariepy, 2275 Jean-Talon St. e., A. Drouin, Q.C., C. Sirois, C. Papineau, Y. Arseneault, P.G. Gariepy. Counsel: Camille Antaki
Druker, Freed & Oiknine, 1255 Phillips Sq., E. J. Druker, G.G.E. Freed, Danielle Oiknine, S.B. Apel
Drummond, G., Q.C., 1117 St. Catherine St. w.
Dubuc, Trudeau & Assoc., #2060, 500 Place d'Armes, C. Dubuc, M. Trudeau
Dugas & Allard, 1415 Jarry St. e., L. Dugas, R. Allard
Duguay, Salois & Associates, 425 St. Sulpice St., G. Duguay, J.R. Salois, Lorraine Duguay
Dulude & Dufour, 272 de la Concorde Blvd. w. (Laval), A. Dulude, R. Dufour
DuMesnil, M., #1500, 505 Dorchester Blvd. w.
Duong, M., 1967 Mount Royal St. e.
Dupre, J., Q.C., 1600 St. Martin Blvd. (Laval)
Dupont-Lacroix, Marcelle, 3000 Lacombe
Duquette, P., 5311 Park Ave.
Duval, N., 50 Cremazie w.
Ethier, G., 2610 Henri Bourassa St.
Even, F., 6993 St. Denis St.
Eymard, L., 6095 Metropolitain (St. Leonard)
Fargnoli & Allen, 7170 St. Laurent Blvd., A. Fargnoli, J.W. Allen
Farley, J. G., 2544 Rosemont Blvd.
Favreau, Asselin, Dupaul & Lalande, #108, 276 St. James St., D. Favreau, Q.C., A. Asselin, R. Dupaul, Daniele Lalande
Feinstein, B., 615 Dorchester Blvd. w.
Ferland, P., Q.C., 417 St. Peter St.
Fetherstonhaugh, J., Q.C., 6600 Trans Canada Hwy.
Figlarz, E., 1435 St. Alexander St.
Filiatreault, J., 4237 St. Hubert St.
Finkelberg, W.H., 1350 Sherbrooke St. w.
Finkelstein, Fournelle, Berku & Paquin, 3459 St. Hubert St., Z. Finkelstein, M. Fournelle, D. Berku, D. Paquin
Fisher & Hanna, 388 St. James St., S.A. Fisher, M. Hanna
Fiske, Emery, Breton & Kanner, #660, 615 Dorchester Blvd. w., C. A. Fiske, C. E. Emery, M. Breton, Ava Kanner
Flanagan, R., #200, 1400 Metcalfe St.
Fleming, I. D., 1440 St. Catherine St. w.
Flynn, Rivard, etc., 2020 University St. (also Quebec)
Fortin, J., 4 Notre Dame e.
Fortin, L'Anglais, Trudel, #500, 261 St. James St., J.Y. Fortin, Y. L'Anglais, J. Trudel, F. Cossette
Fortugno, P., #2800, 500 Place d'Armes
Francescucci, F., 10,340 Christophe Colomb
Frankel & Frankel, 10 St. James St., I. A. Frankel, Q.C., H. Frankel
Franklin & Franklin, 4141 Sherbrooke St. w., M. H. Franklin, Q.C., M. Franklin, D. Franklin
Freedman, L., Q.C., 6595 Mackle Rd.
Fridhandler, B., 1010 Sherbrooke St. w.
Friedman, Berbrier & Cappel, 1010 St. Catherine St. w., H. Friedman, Q.C., B. J. Berbrier, B. Cappel
Frumkin, Feldman & Glazman, 1155 Place du Canada, A. E. Feldman, H. Frumkin, B. Glazman
Fusey, Robert E., 2226 Sherbrooke St. e.
Gadoury, S., 1199 Bleury St.
Gagne, Gagne & Assoc., #600, 59 St. James St., J. Gagne, Q.C., J. Y. Gagne, L. Beauchemin, N. Chaput
Gagnon, Bourdages & Sauve, #801, 1130 Sherbrooke St. w., J.H. Gagnon, P.P. Bourdages, D. Sauve
Gagnon, H., 1030 Cherrier St.
Gagnon, Jean, Q.C., 6380 Cote de Liesse Rd.
Gagnon, R., #803, 152 Notre Dame e.
Garber & Reinblatt, #1004, 1010 St. Catherine St. w., H.Y. Garber, S. Reinblatt, R.G. Wolfe, R.M. Mailhot, M.J. Abramowitz
Gareau, Grey & Pohoryles, #2406, 1110 Sherbrooke St. w., R. Gareau, J.H. Grey, Vivian Pohoryles
Gasco, Linteau & Grignon, #5, 1010 St. Catherine St. w., R. Gasco, L. Linteau, C.-H. Grignon, Judith Lifshitz
Gaudette, M., 561 Cremazie e.
Gelfand, S., 189 Hymus (Pointe Claire)
Gelinas, P., Q.C., 10 St. James St. w.
Genereux, Gauthier & Maruca, 276 St. James St., P. Genereux, G. Gauthier, R. Maruca
Genet, P., 500 Place d'Armes
Geoffrion, Duchesne, Bernier & Barbeau, 210 St. Catherine St. e., J. Geoffrion, Q.C., G. Duchesne, P. Bernier, R. Barbeau, M. Perreault
Geoffrion, Prud'homme, 500 Place d'Armes (H2Y 2W4), F. Aquin, G. Geoffrion, Q.C., R. Beaulac, J.-J. Goulet, Hilary Bennett, G. Guèvremont, J.-P. Cardinal, Q.C., R.B. Holden, Q.C., Marie Chevrier Gervais, Jocelyne Jarry, M. Cogger, M. Jetté, R. David, C. Leblanc, J.-P. Dépelteau, P.C. Lemoine, J.P. Dorais, J. Marchessault, Q.C., A. Dugas, Raymonde Verreault, R. Dulude, Q.C.; Counsel: J.-L. Baudouin, Q.C., Hon. L. Chevrier, P.C., C.C., Q.C.
Geoffroy, Luc, 3555 Berri St.
Geoffroy, P., #307, 3414 Park Ave.
Gervais & Lepine, 276 St. James St., G. F. Gervais, P. Lepine
Gibeault, A., 360 St. James St.
Gilbert, Magnan, Marcotte, Simard, Tremblay & Forget, #1600, 2020 University St. G. Gilbert, Q.C., P. Magnan, G. Marcotte, A. Simard, J. Tremblay, Y. Forget, L. Dufresne, J. Bourque, P. Rouleau, P.R. Sicotte, B. Roussy, L. Dick. Counsel: L'Hon. L. Tremblay, Q.C.
Giroux, R. B., 800 Maisonneuve Blvd. e.
Gitman, L., #1106, 440 Dorchester Blvd. w.
Gliserman, Ackman, Cutler & Bernfeld, 625 President Kennedy Blvd., I. Gliserman, Q.C., M. Ackman, Q.C., S. Cutler, E.H. Bernfeld, Q.C.
Godin, Tellier, 800 Victoria Sq., R.P. Godin, P.R. Tellier, M.S. Raymond, S.R. Charest, J.F. Hudon, N.L. Bindman, V. Chenard, R. Hebert, C. Gendron, P.R. Slaughter, L.D. Chamberland
Gohier, J.M., 662 St. Croix Blvd.
Goldenberg, Hon. H. C., Q.C., 1010 St. Catherine St. w.
Goldfield, Miss E., 4519 Van Horne Ave.
Gomberg, A., 1010 St. Catherine St. w.

Gonzales, L., 1500 Stanley St.
Gotlieb, J. J., Q.C., 200 St. James St. w.
Gottlieb, Kaylor, Swift & Stocks, #1005, 1010 St. Catherine St. w., R.S. Gottlieb, J.A.A. Swift, M. Kaylor, R.J. Stocks, M. Greenberg, A.G. Marcil, A.J. Elbaz. Counsel: H.E. Feigelson, Q.C., R.W. Agard, T.R.A. Malcolm
Gougeon, G., 800 Maisonneuve Blvd. e.
Gould, G. C., Q.C., 3940 Cote des Neiges
Goulet & St. Amour, 3250 Jean Talon St. e., Y. Goulet, N. St. Amour, Diane Chartrand
Goulston, P., 2029 St. Hubert St.
Gourd & Brunet, 1200 McGill College Ave., A. Gourd, Jr., C. Brunet, L. Bertrand, Louise Paul, J. Richstone. Counsel: D. Hardy
Gourd & Monette, 1010 St. Catherine St. w., J. J. Gourd, Q.C., J. Monette, Q.C.
Grana, Goldman, Assh & Associates, #200, 245 St. James St., V.J. Grana, L.M. Goldman, I.D. Assh, S.M. Altshul
Granich, Krymalowski & Assoc., #503, 355 St. James St., B. Granich, M. Krymalowski
Grant, Martin, Gerard, Chartrand, 1852 Rachel St. e., C. Grant, G. Martin, D. Gerard, Francine Chartrand
Gravenor & Keenan, #1150, 2001 University St., C.A. Gravenor, Jr., J.T. Keenan, L. Beck, M. Labry
Greenbaum, I., 800 Dorchester Blvd. w.
Greenblatt, Ginsberg, 1440 Towers St., Suite 100, S. Greenblatt, Q.C., H. Ginsberg, H. Barza, S. Finkelstein, R. Landry, R. Resin; G. Glazer (Tel-Aviv Office)
Greenwood, J. L., 1396 St. Catherine St. w.
Gregoire, Ranger, Mailhot & Aubry, 440 Dorchester Blvd. w., F. Gregoire, J.R. Ranger, P.F. Mailhot, Michele Aubry
Gregory & Robitaille, 1801 McGill College Ave., H. D. J. Gregory, J. P. Robitaille. Counsel: G.D. McKay, Q.C.
Grief, H., 4950 Queen Mary Rd.
Gross, M., Q.C., 4300 de Maisonneuve Blvd. w.
Gualtieri, Rosa-Bianca, #350, 4150 St. Catherine St. w.
Guay, L.-P., Q.C., 4 Notre Dame St. e.
Guevremont, G., #600, 200 St. James St.
Guilbault, P., 4880 Bellechasse St.
Gurman, Marcovitch & Aumais, #308, 10 St. James St., A. Gurman, S. Marcovitch, A. Aumais
Guy, Mercier, Bertrand, Bourgeois & Laurent, #2306, 1010 Sherbrooke St. w., H3A 2R7, G. Bertrand, Hélène Boudreau, M. Bourgeois, Anne-Marie Bourgouin, Y.J.A. Brisson, M. Décary, Y. Desjardins Siciliano, R. Dorion, M. Fleury, J.-M. Fortier, M. Gagnon, P. Gariépy, J. Guy, D. Johnston, J. Laurent, Y. Lebrun, C.G. Leduc, J. Lefrançois, C.J. Melançon, P. Mercier, Q.C., N. Petitclerc, M. Rochefort, R.J. Roy, M. Savoie
Gyulai, Mrs. B., Q.C., 2 McCulloch Ave. (Outremont)
Hadjis & Feng, 1117 St. Catherine St. w., J. S. Feng, E. A. Hadjis
Handelman & Handelman, 1255 University St., S. Handelman, I. M. Handelman
Hardy, T., #2314, 500 Place d'Armes
Harper, S., 615 Dorchester Blvd. w.
Harris, G.I., Q.C., 3410 Peel St.
Harris, H.H., 231 St. James St. w.
Hebert & Heroux, 435 de la Gauchetiere e., J.-P. Hebert, M. Heroux
Heenan, Blaikie, Jolin, Potvin, Trepanier & Cobbett, 4 Place Ville Marie, K.S. Atlas, G. Audet, N. Bacal, Claudette Bellemare, M.R. Bernard, P.M. Blaikie, Y. Bolduc, J.-P. Breard, S.H. Cobbett, G. Dufort, R.D. Farley, Janice Gerson, Y. Hebert, R.L. Heenan, P. Jolin, D.J. Kaufer, Michelle LeFrancois, R. Legault, D.J. Levinson, C. Martin, P. McClemens, B. McNiven, J. Potvin, D. Rochefort, Suzanne Thibaudeau, G. Tremblay, P. Trepanier, R. Lewin
Helfield, E. S., 1247-1 Westmount Sq.
Heller, Landy & Mauer, #1010, 1253 McGill College Ave., W.B. Mauer, M.E. Heller, B. Landy, A.E. Benzakein, W. Friedman
Hemens, Harris, Thomas, Mason, Schweitzer & McNeill, 505 Dorchester Blvd. w. (H2Z 1A8), J.W. Hemens, Q.C., R.C.T. Harris, Q.C., W. D. Thomas, Q.C., Kathryn H. Mason, Q.C., A.C. Schweitzer, D.I. McNeill, Ginette Piché, J.B. Cornish, N. Quesnel, D. Levac, C.E. Bertrand, Joan Hazen Ornstein, R. Gauthier. Counsel: L.G. McDougall, Q.C., H.J. Hemens, Q.C.
Hendler, J., #602, 388 St. James St.
Herman, M. C., 355 St. James St. w.
Hetu, G., 6718 Christophe Colomb
Hogue, Chouinard, Gouin & Assoc., 276 St. James St., P. Hogue, Y. Chouinard, M. Gouin
Hollinger, M., #1250, 400 Maisonneuve Blvd. w.
Houle & Labelle, 388 St. James St., M. Houle, P. Labelle
Houle, S., 3541 Hochelaga St.
Hutchins & Soroka, 4th fl., 245 St. James St., P.W. Hutchins, Diane H. Soroka
Isganaitis, R., 4 Notre Dame St. e.
Iuticone, E.R., #704, 10 St. James St.
Iuticone, R.W., 1030 Cherrier St.
Jacobs, A.B., Q.C., 360 St. James St.
Jasmin, Rivest, Castiglio, Castiglio & Lebel, 441 De La Gauchetiere St. e., M. Jasmin, M. Rivest, R. Castiglio, G. Castiglio, Helene Lebel
Joffe, Pennee, Gagne & Silverstone, 4898 de Maisonneuve Blvd. w., Paul Joffe, B. Pennee, G. Gagne, S. Silverstone
Julien, Raymond, Q.C., 1800 St. Joseph Blvd. e.
Kalnitsky & Kalnitsky, 276 St. James St., H. Kalnitsky, J. Kalnitsky
Kandestin, Kugler & Partners, #2204, 800 Victoria Sq., S. Kandestin, Q.C., G. Kugler, J.A. Costin, M.H. Kay, B. Stern, G.F. Kandestin, R. Kandestin, R. Prevost. Counsel: M. Gameroff, Q.C., S. Fenster, Q.C.
Kaufman, I.H., 1255 Phillips Sq.
Kaufman, Respitz, 715 Victoria Sq., M. S. Kaufman, Q.C., O. Respitz, Q.C., S. Sederoff, S. Steinman, P. Shugar, E. S. Segal, S. M. Shein, R. Laramee, Michele Rouillard, Anne Cartier, L.M. Cytrynbaum
Kelada, H., 3785 Cote de Liesse
Kessner, N. S., 2020 University St.
Kierans & Guay, 606 Cathcart St., P. E. Kierans, Q.C., P. J. Guay, Q.C., C. Turianskyj, P.E. Kierans, D.B. Kierans, B. Charron. Counsel: J.F. Stairs, Q.C., L. Kos-Rabcewicz-Zubkowski
King, Haberkorn, #2114, 1010 Sherbrooke St. w., J. King, M. Haberkorn, J. Kuhnreich, H. Madar
Kirshenblatt & Crestohl, #940, 1010 St. Catherine St. w., D. Kirshenblatt, Q.C., H. Crestohl, P. Light, Yolande Lemire
Klein, Roth, 1010 St. Catherine St. w., M.L. Klein, Q.C., S.J. Roth
Kliger & Kliger, 1255 Phillips Sq., H. H. Kliger, Q.C., L. Kliger
Kolodny, Mildred B., 5151 Cote Ste-Catherine Rd.
Korda, S., 2320, 2 Complex Desjardins
Kouri, D., 3925 St. James St.
Kragaris, A., #1008, 300 Leo Pariseau St.
Kravitz & Kravitz, #415, 515 St. Catherine St. w., L. Kravitz, B. Kravitz, M. Latendresse
Kronish, M.S., 1255 Phillips Sq.
Lachapelle, L., #525, 276 St. James St.
Lachapelle & Lachapelle, 5569 Gatineau St., P. A. Lachapelle, R. Lachapelle, Q.C.
Lack, D. M., Q.C., #616, 1255 University St. (P. R. Lack)
Lackstone & Turner, 2360 Lucerne Rd. (Mount Royal), M. Lackstone, H.P. Turner
Laferriere, B., #4205, 800 Victoria Sq.
Lafleur, Brown, de Grandpre, 800 Victoria Sq. (Box 214, Tour de la Bourse, H4Z 1E4), L.P. de Grandpre, C.C., Q.C., H. Wilson, Q.C., J. B. Claxton, Q.C., C.S. Bradeen, Jr., Q.C., J.B. McMullan, J.-M. Tardif, A. K. Ham, P. Sébastien, Q.C., A. B. Sharp, D. H. Tingley, P. A. R. Townsend, J. E. Labelle, Leonard Serafini, Pierre Flageole, P. Boyer, Marzia Frascadore, S.F. Norych, K.L. Erlick, L. Lissoir, P.D. McCallum, M. Bantey, D. Lacelle, R.J. Montcalm, I. de Grandpre, R.P.D. Birrell. Counsel: H. G. Lafleur, Q.C., B. Culver, Q.C.
Lafleur, MacDougall & Dubuc, #555, 515 St. Catherine St. w., G. Lafleur, J. B. MacDougall, C. Dubuc, France Duhamel. Counsel: L.I.C. MacDougall, Q.C.
Lafleur & Menard, 2085 Union Ave., G. Lafleur, Jocelyne Menard
Laforest, P., 2525 Daniel Johnson
Lagarde, G., 1554 Mont Royal e.
LaHaye, Ferrari & Filteau, 4 Notre Dame St. e., R. LaHaye, J. Ferrari, Christiane Filteau
Lalande & Provencher, 242 Ste. Rose Blvd. (Laval), M. Lalande, R. Provencher
Lalonde, P. P., 10426 Grande Allee
Lamarche, P., 1000 St. Denis
Lamontagne, Mongeau, One Westmount Sq., P. Lamontagne, Q.C., R. Mongeau, P. Roy, Anne Letellier de St. Just
Lamoureux, Rousseau, 276 St. James St., J. Lamoureux, D. Rousseau, Christiane Mathieu
Langevin, P., 210 St. James St.
Langlois, Drouin etc., 290 Place d'Youville (A. Brault) (also Quebec)
Lanthier, Roustan & Shee, 751 Victoria Sq., J. P. Lanthier, W.J. Roustan, N. D. Shee
Lapalme, G.E., Q.C., 165 Cote St. Catherine Rd.
Lapin, May & Steinberg, 615 Dorchester Blvd. w., M. Lapin, Q.C., N.M. May, H. Steinberg
Lapointe Rosenstein, #923, 1117 St. Catherine St. w. (H3B 1H9), B.M. Gelfand, P.L. Lapointe, M. M. Rosenstein, A.S. Konigsberg, P.F. Delorme, T.A. Lavin, H.W. Dermer, R. Massicotte, D. Boudreault, J. Rossignol, C. Bergeron, P. Martel, J.D. Holmested, P. Barnard, N. Issley, R.D. Lauzon, N.A. Rishikoff; R. Brouillette (Patent Agent). Counsel: A. J. Rosenstein, Q.C., A. Paré, Q.C.
Lapointe, Schachter & Champagne, #1885, 500 Place d'Armes, G. Lapointe, Q.C., R.H. Schachter, A. Champagne, M. Talbot, J.T. Pepper
Laporte, S., 3236 Masson St.
Laramee & Cordeau, 500 St. Jean Baptiste St., M. Laramee, A. Cordeau
Lariviere & Archambault, 511 Place d'Armes, A. Lariviere, R. Archambault
Larue, R., 31 St. James St.

Lattimer, E. J., Q.C., #1108, 1010 St. Catherine St. w.
Lattoni, M.E., Q.C., 7170 St. Laurent Blvd.
Laurence, A., Q.C., 500 Place d'Armes
Laurin, J., 1816 Sherbrooke St. e.
Laurin, Laplante & Laplante, 60 St. James St., R. Laurin, P. Laplante, M. Laplante
Laurin, M., 500 Place du Canada
Laverdiere, Y., 4984 Place de la Savane
Lavery, O'Brien, 31st floor, 2 Complexe Desjardins (H5B 1G4), C. Lavery, Q.C., R.G. Chauvin, Q.C., M.C. Johnston, Q.C., R.S. O'Brien, Q.C., J.C. Smyth, Q.C., J.V. O'Donnell, Q.C., P.P. Carrière, M.K. Smyth, D.S. Pryde, R.W. Mason, J. Bélanger, J.F. Martin, J. Guibault, G. Lemay, J. Nols, A. René, E. Baudry, A. Lutfy, P. Caron, B.A. Courtois, A. Laurin, J.F. de Grandpré, P. Cartier, J. Pomminville, J.P. Casavant, J. Chamberland, C. Baillargeon, J. Hébert, I. Rose, P. Paradis, M.-J. Vachon, Y. Mayrand, R.A. Hinse, J.M. Saint-Denis, Hélène Langlois, J. Audette, A. Gascon, D.M. Eramian, D.A. Dagenais, D.R. McCarty, R.F. Dolan, R. Wagner, Louise Cérat, J. Gauthier. Counsel: G.W. Hall, Q.C.
Laviolette & Lamquin, 450 Cherrier St., Paula Laviolette, Michele Lamquin
Lavoie, Francine, 4246 St. Denis St.
Lavut, L. D., 400 de Maisonneuve St. w.
Lazare & Altschuler, 3201, 1 Place Ville Marie, H. Lazare, H.R. Altschuler
Lazarovitz, Cannon, etc., 666 Sherbrooke St. w. (also Quebec)
Lazarus, Heft, Charbonneau & Herman, #505, 606 Cathcart St., M. Lazarus, A.H. Heft, M. Charbonneau, L. Herman, J. Charron
Lebeau, C., 168 Notre Dame St. e.
Lebeau, F., #700, 1980 Sherbrooke St. w.
Lebeau, G., 819 Decarie Blvd.
LeBel & Westmorland-Traore, 210 St. Catherine St. e., G.A. LeBel, Juanita Westmorland-Traore
LeBlanc, G., 1753 Jacques Lemaistre Ave.
Leblanc, L. R., Q.C., 60 St. James St. w.
Leblanc, R., 950 Cherrier St.
Leboeuf, R., 5111 Sherbrooke St. e.
Lebovics & Cytrynbaum, 615 Dorchester Blvd. w., T. J. Lebovics, A. Cytrynbaum, G. Peizler, H. Djihanian
Lebrun-Sylvestre, Micheline, 301 Deguire Blvd.
Lecavalier, Liette, 1199 Bleury St.
Lecavalier, R., #930, 800 Dorchester Blvd. w.
Lechter & Segal, 1440 St. Catherine St. w., A. A. Lechter, N. H. Segal
Lechter & Melnikoff, 2015 Drummond St., J. Lechter, M. V. Melnikoff
Leduc, Guay, Martel & Leboeuf, 1390 Sherbrooke St. w., B. Leduc, R.F. Guay, A. Martel, G. Leboeuf
Leduc, Jacqueline, 777 Laurentien Blvd.
Leduc, J., Q.C., 250 St. Joseph Blvd. e.
Lefebvre, Marie-C., 10830 Grande Allée
Lefrancois & Benoit, 5325 Jean-Talon St. e., R. R. Lefrancois, R. M. Benoit
Legault, Longtin, Legault, Joly, 363 St. Francois Xavier, P.E. Legault, D. Longtin, R. Legault, C. Joly
Leger, Robic & Richard, 1514 Dr. Penfield Ave., J.A. Leger, G. Robic, H. Richard, L. Carriere, Michele Craig, F. Grenier
Legris & Boyer, 276 St. James St., R. Legris, F. Boyer, R. Baril
Legris, Y.M., 4 Notre Dame St. e.
Leithman & Glazer, 1255 Phillips Sq., E. Leithman, Q.C., V. H. Glazer
Leithman, Goldenberg, Guberman, Lafontaine & Girouard, #405, 1255 Phillips Sq., S. Leithman, S.D. Goldenberg, J.L. Guberman, J. Lafontaine, C. Bluteau, C. Girouard, F. Brabant
Lemay & Jodoin, #303, 465 St. Jean St., H.-P. Lemay, Q.C., P.-A. Jodoin
Lerner, Y., 275 St. James St.
Leroux, Seguin, 1030 Cherrier St., M. Leroux, H. Seguin
Lette, Marcotte, Sutto, 615 Dorchester Blvd. w., R. Lette, Q.C., L. C. Marcotte, Q.C., J. P. Sutto, P. Lette, P. Normandin, Q.C., R. Favreau, F. Deslierres, J.G. Robert, C. Bujold, F. Montonaro, Joyce Cornfield-Mazur, B. Lette
Levesque, F., 4 Notre Dame St. e.
Lewandowski, B. A., Q.C., 2740 Sherbrooke St. e.
L'Heureux, Nadeau, Bureau & Assoc., 630 Sherbrooke St. w., J.J. L'Heureux, Q.C., R. Nadeau, J.C. Bureau, G. Gamache, Q.C., P. Donati, J.Y. Lalonde, R. Maisonneuve, M. Robin
L'Heureux, P., Q.C., 276 St. James St.
Liberman, Segall, Finkelberg, Pelletier & Greenspoon, 1303 Greene Ave., #401, J. L. Liberman, Q.C., A.N. Segall, Q.C., I. I. Finkelberg, G.R. Pelletier, A.A. Greenspoon
Lightstone, Riback & Hamerman, #621, 1440 St. Catherine St. w., J. Lightstone, Q.C., M. Riback, Q.C., A. Hamerman
Lindsay, F.R., 1 Place Ville Marie
Linetsky, Leblanc & Assoc., 1255 Phillips Sq., D. Linetsky, M. Leblanc
Litovsky, A., Q.C., 5616 Park Ave.
Liverman & Liverman, 1450 City Councillors St., L. Liverman, F. S. Liverman
Losier, Trudeau, Raiche & Bernatchez, 31 St. James St., N. Losier, P.A. Trudeau, P.J. Raiche, G. Bernatchez
Lussier & Beliveau, 3355 Queen Mary Rd., J.P. Lussier, P. Beliveau. Counsel: J. Bellemare
Lustgarten, L.S., 1285 Place St. Croix
Luterman, Stotland & Davis, #350, 4150 St. Catherine St. w., S. Luterman, G. Stotland, D.S. Davis, C. Bedard
Major, A.J., 772 Sherbrooke St. w.
Malcolm, T.R.A., #1005, 1010 St. Catherine St. w. (also Toronto)
Maranda & Meloche, 325 St. Joseph Blvd. e., J.H. Maranda, G. Meloche
Maranda, L. R., 3500 St. Hubert St.
Marchand & Assoc., #1008, 300 Leo Pariseau St., L.H. Marchand
Marchand, Jasmin & Melancon, 507 Place d'Armes, M. Marchand, P. Jasmin, P.A. Melancon, B. Paiement, F. Shanks. Counsel: J.E. Gervais, Q.C.
Marchand & Kosorwich, 1255 University St., M. Marchand, J. Kosorwich
Marcus & Feiner, 1015 Beaver Hall Hill, A. Marcus, Q.C., A. Feiner, Q.C.
Margolian, H., 1410 Stanley St.
Marinacci, N., #801, 625 President Kennedy Blvd.
Marsolais, J., 2 Complexe Desjardins
Martel & Cantin, 800 Victoria Sq., M. Martel, Q.C., J. Cantin, Q.C., H. Cantin, M. Cantin, Paul Martel, Luc Martel
Martel, J.F., 1200 St. Martin Blvd.
Martin, A., Q.C., 276 St. James St.
Martin, C., 2995 St. Zotique St. e.
Martineau Walker, 3400 Stock Exchange Tower, (Box 242, Victoria Sq., H4Z 1E9), G. A. Allison, Q.C., R. L. Beaulieu, Q.C., P.R.D. MacKell, Q.C., Guy Gagnon, Q.C., A.J. Clermont, Q.C., J. H. Gomery, Q.C., R. A. Hope, Q.C., J. L. Toupin, Q.C., R. Reinhardt, J.H. Lafleur, Q.C., Bertrand Lacombe, F. M. Gagnon, C.S. Cheasley, R.J.F. Bowie, J. R. Miller, S. D. Tremblay, R.M. Skelly, M.A. Forget, R. Martel, S.S. Heller, R. Forget, Pierrette Rayle, C. LeCorre, D. W. Salomon, S. Fortin, A. T. Mécs, J.G. Wright, S. F. Guérette, A. Larivée, L.P. Yelin, L. Bernier, J.-F. Buffoni, M. Messier, W. C. Décarie, R. B. Issenman, M. Nadon, Andrea Francoeur Mécs, D.M. Hendy, C. Désy, P.B. Bélanger, P.G. Thibeault, F. Rolland, G. Nevin, J. Masson, D.P. Griffin, A. Durocher, R.J. Clare, A. Contant, M. Giguère, E.M. Maldoff, X.C. Martis, R.J. McRobie, D. Powell, R.G. Grudev, R. Trudeau, R. Paré, R. Lacoursière, Marie-France Bich, D.W. Boyd, P.J. Deslauriers, Brigitte Gouin, D. Picotte, J. de l'Etoile, J. Rajotte, Lucie Roy, Anne Hood-Metzger, Joy Goodman-Mailhot, J.R. Sproule, M.L. Paquet, Diane Terrault, M.E. Goldbloom, M.D. Walker, G. Artinian, J.A. Coleman, R.A. Ford, Joan Monahan, G.J. Pollack, Lieba Shell. Counsel: Jean Martineau, C.C., Q.C., R.H.E. Walker, Q.C., The Hon. Alan A. MacNaughton, P.C., Q.C., Marcel Cinq-Mars, Q.C., Fernand Guertin, Q.C.
Masse, Briskin, Bouchard & Assoc., #1010, 10 St. James St., J. Masse, J. Briskin, Q.C., P. Bouchard, G. Laframboise, C. Lapointe, Carole Doyon
Massey, Huot & Beauchamp, #900, 152 Notre Dame e., J.H. Massey, J. Huot, J.-C. Beauchamp
Massicotte, Sullivan, Lagace, Goloff & Bilodeau, #826, 276 St. James St., J. Massicotte, Q.C., W. Sullivan, Monique J. Lagace, A. Bilodeau, Y. Georges
Melancon, A., 1671 St. Denis St.
McAllister, Blakely, Turgeon & Hesler, 1230 Place du Canada, W.R. McAllister, Q.C., J.A. Blakely, Q.C., J. Turgeon, Nicole Duval-Hesler, C.K. LaPierre, Mireille Tremblay-Noel, G.D.D. Morrison, P. Baillargeon, C. Massicotte, F. Catalano, A. Leduc. Counsel: E. Buchanan, Q.C.
McConomy, Burke & Boisse, #1400, 800 Dorchester Blvd. w., R.J. McConomy, G.C. Burke, Louise B. Boisse, Pierrette Sevigny-McConomy
McDougall, Lemay, #1501, 666 Sherbrooke St. w., J. McDougall, Q.C., C. Lemay, A. Campeau, G.A. Bey, M. Mueller, J.O. Caron, M.A. Goulet, Catherine Muraz, P.E. Graham, Q.C., Michele Pineau, G.P. Latulippe, Ruby Quane, C. St. Laurent, S. Wernstein
McGilton & Johnston, 1350 Sherbrooke St. w., G.L. McGilton, R.W. Johnston, Penny Westman
McLeod, Lamorey & Levesque, 1 Place Ville Marie, A.W. McLeod, D.H. Lamorey, Louise Levesque
McMaster, Meighen, 630 Dorchester Blvd. w., H3B 4H7, A. S. Hyndman, Q.C., R. C. Legge, Q.C., T. C. Camp, Q.C., A. K. Paterson, Q.C., R. J. Riendeau, Q.C., J. Brien, W.E. Stavert, R. J. Plant, H. Senécal, T. R. Carsley, M. A. Meighen, A.P. Bergeron, S.J. Harrington, G. P. Barry, N. A. Saibil, J. A. Laurin, B.M. Schneiderman, D. Ayotte, J. H. Scott, R.W. Shannon, M.A. Pinsonnault, E.A. Mitchell, M. Charbonneau, W.J. Demers, J.P. Thomson, E.H. Straus, J. Almaleh, P.J. Bolger, B.M. Provost, R.M. Peck, D. Quenneville. Counsel: D.R. McMaster, Q.C., A.M. Minnion, Q.C., R.A. Patch, Q.C., T.P. Howard, Q.C.
Melancon, Helie, Marceau, Grenier & Sciortino, 210 St. Catherine St. e., C.G. Melancon, J. Helie, G. Marceau, P. Grenier, G. Sciortino
Menard & Hebert, 500 Place d'Armes, S. Menard, J.-C. Hebert
Menard, P., 152 Notre Dame St. e.

Mendelsohn, Rosentzveig, Shacter, #600, 1010 St. Catherine St. w., S.L. Mendelsohn, Q.C., Leo Rosentzveig, Q.C., Manuel Shacter, Q.C., Jack Shayne, Stanley Taviss, William Levitt, B.J. Woloshen, Q.C., M. Mendelsohn, E.E. Aronoff, L.M. Blumenstein, M.A. Charlap, W. Fraiberg, B.P. Stein, C.A., J. Weitzman, I.R. Rudnikoff, L.B. Erdle, F. Zylberberg, F.L. Carsley, D. Rosentzveig, S. Roy, J. Brossard, M. Ludwick
Mendelson Gross Pinsky Dizgun Zelman, 1212 One Westmount Sq., J. A. Mendelson, Q.C., M. Gross, J. A. Pinsky, H. Dizgun, G. Zelman, M. A. Segal, B.L. Mintz, N. Lindover. Counsel: S.E. Berger, Q.C.
Mercier, J., 2382 Sherbrooke St.
Mercure, Poliquin, Coutu, Bernier, Simon & Dayan, #1800, 507 Place d'Armes, Y. Poliquin, Q.C., Y. Coutu, C. Bernier, H. Simon, G. Dayan, J.F. Mercure, M. Coutu, R. Proschek. Counsel: B. Nantel, Q.C.
Meyerovitch, Goldstein, Flanz & Fishman, #1800, 300 Leo Parizeau St., P. Meyerovitch, Q.C., Y. Goldstein, L.W. Flanz, A. Fishman, M. Schrager, G. Paquin, M.E. Melano
Michaud, P.G., Q.C., 620 Cathcart St.
Michon, Moss, Moreau, Robillard & Gagnon, 210 St. James St., P. Michon, R. Moss, G. Moreau, L. Robillard, B. Gagnon
Miller, A., 388 St. James St.
Miller, I.I., 8350 Jeanne Mance St.
Miller, J. P., 168 Notre Dame St. e.
Miller, Green & Assoc., #305, 276 St. James St., W.I. Miller, Q.C., G.Y. Green, Doreen Brown, A. Adel, J.M. Brunette
Millette, Renée, 1825 Champlain St.
Minc, M.S., 1010 St. Catherine St. w.
Mochon & Ouellette, 202 Sauve St. w., J. Mochon, C. Ouellette, D. Courcy
Moisan & Lasalle, 450 Sherbrooke St. e., Pierrette Moisan, Raymonde Lasalle
Mondello, R., 12270 Taylor Blvd.
Mondor, Rousseau & Fournier, 50 Cremazie Blvd. w., P. Mondor, C. Rousseau, J.R. Fournier
Monet, Hart, Saint-Pierre & Des Marais, 1200 McGill College Ave., J. Monet, Q.C., S.D. Hart, M. Saint-Pierre, J. Des Marais, J. Delage, J. Goldberg, Nina Cherney
Monette, C., 1385 Mount Royal e.
Monette, Clerk, Barakett, Levesque, Bourque & Pedneault, 1850 Place du Canada (H3B 2R6), G. Monette, Q.C., S. Clerk, Q.C., A. Michaud, R. Barakett, J. Levesque, G. Bourque, R. Pedneault, G. Monette, G. Duguay, H. Poulin, J. M. Gagne, L.A. Lafreniere, P. Laramee, G. Theoret, J. L. Gagnon, Carole Lariviere, P. Douville
Montcalm, N., 1717 Dorchester Blvd. e.
Morris, D., Q.C., #406, 1255 Phillips Sq.
Morris & Morris, #402, 2075 University St., W.G. Morris (also Toronto)
Mousseau, L., 31 St. James St.
Murray, A., 1450 Springland St.
Muszynski, Barbara, 10 St. James St.
Myszka, I., 4781 Van Horne Ave.
Nadon & Lebrun, 495 St. Martin w. (Chomedey), J. Nadon, R. Lebrun
Narvey, I., #801, 625 President Kennedy St.
Nasadiuk, N., 5290 10th Ave.
Nesbitt, A.R.D., 2075 University St.
Noiseux, R., 4936 Verdun Ave.
Nolin & Cuerrier, 400 Cure Labelle Blvd. (Laval), P.C. Nolin, Madeleine Cuerrier
Normandeau, P.E., #600, 2120 Sherbrooke St. e.
Normandin, G., 507 Place d'Armes
Notkin, L. I., 1010 St. Catherine St. w.
Nourry, L., 3239 Edouard Montpetit St.
Ogilvy, Renault, 1 Place Ville Marie, H3B 1Z7, T.H. Montgomery, Q.C., P.F. Renault, Q.C., B.F. Clarke, Q.C., J.G. Kirkpatrick, Q.C., F.B. Common, Jr., Q.C., M.S. Hannon, Q.C., K.S. Howard, Q.C., P.W. Gauthier, Q.C., W.A. Grant, Q.C., J.C. Couture, Q.C., Joan Clark, Q.C., W.S. Tyndale, Q.C., J. Bishop, Q.C., M.G. Bergeron, Q.C., J.C.C. Chipman, Q.C., J.A. Ogilvy, Q.C., P.D. Walsh, Q.C., P. Legrand, Q.C., L.Y. Fortier, Q.C., R.L. Munro, D.F. Cope, J.G. Chamberland, T.P. O'Connor, A.D. Guthrie, R.J. Cowling, R. Crevier, M.A. Gagnon, A.J. Chagnon, C. Fontaine, T.S. Gillespie, B.A. Roy, P.M. Amos, M.E. McLeod, D.A. Riendeau, P.R. Matthews, Y.W. Brunet, J.J. O'Connor, J.A. Savard, C.M. Bloom, G. Rochon, P.G. Côté, A.H. Campeau, W. Hesler, G.B. Maughan, G. Touchette, J.N. Landry, D.H. Tees, R. Monette, D.I. Lack, L. Bergeron, D.H. Bunker, P. Pronovost, P. Hébert, P.Y. Lamarre, Céline April, A. Papillon, R. Favreau, S. Gravel, M. Savard, P. Chaput, L.J. Gouin, R.P. Charlton, A. Fleming, S.V. Potter, Hélène Lalonde Martin, P.-Y. Châtillon, M. Goudreau, N.M. Steinberg, Rémi Gagnon, O.F. Kott, L.-P. Cullen, Ann Phillips, Y.V. Raic, Suzanne Renault, L.H. Renault, Louise Laplante, Marc Duquette, Christine Carron, Hélène Floch, Johanne Gauthier, Hélène Lefebvre, A.D. Pouliot, Isabelle Cantin, C.M. Gohier, J.I.S. Nicholl, Johanne Savard, Danièle Boutet, Anne Leydet. Counsel: F.C. Cope, Q.C., J.G. Porteous, Q.C., H. Hansard, Q.C., J. de M. Marler, Q.C., R.E. Morrow, Q.C.
Oligny & Jacques, 7231 St. Denis St., F. Oligny, G. Jacques
O'Reilly & Grodinsky, 245 St. James St., J. A. O'Reilly, W.S. Grodinsky, J.D. Hurley, R. Mainville, A. Gauthier. Counsel: R.A. Pratt
Orenstein, Ruby & Orenstein, 3rd fl., 2015 Peel St., L. Orenstein, Q.C., J. Ruby, A. P. Orenstein, I.M. Greenberg, Susan Orenstein
Orlando, F., 5325 Jean Talon St. e.
Ouellette, S.J., #304, 4 Notre Dame St. e.
Oulousian, A., 440 Dorchester Blvd. w.
Overland, Wekarchuk, Gold & Rosenzveig, 1010 Sherbrooke St. w., K.H. Overland, W. Wekarchuk, P.M. Gold, D. Rosenzveig
Page, Duchesne, Desmarais & Picard, #2525, 500 Place d'Armes, R. Page, Q.C., J. Duchesne, Q.C., M. Desmarais, P. Picard, Jean Lariviere, M. Garceau, A. Pasquin, P. Page, P. Viens
Pageau, C., 1460 Sauve St. e.
Panet-Raymond, E., 4545 Pierre de Coubertin Ave.
Panneton, Philippe, 4 Notre Dame St. e.
Panneton, Pierre, 4350 Coolbrook Ave.
Papachristou, B., 1010 Sherbrooke St. w.
Paquet, Galardo & Nantais, 800 Place Victoria, J.M. Paquet, P. Galardo, R. Nantais, M. Hebert
Paquette, Paquette, Perreault, Rivet & Assoc., 200, rue St-Jacques, A. R. Paquette, Q.C., M. Paquette, F. Perreault, B. Rivet, Celine Trudeau, Loraine Vibert
Paquette, Godin, Simard & Boisvert, #1500, 505 Dorchester Blvd. w., C. Paquette, A. Godin, F. Simard, P. Boisvert, M. Fortier, R. L'Abbe, M. Rivard, P. de Niverville
Paquette, M., 1 Notre Dame St. e.
Paradis, Nicole, 686 Outremont Ave.
Parcigneau, J.L., 210 St. James St.
Parent & Girard, 333 St-Antoine St. e., L. Parent, Q.C., M. R. Girard
Parent, J., 152 Notre Dame St. e.
Parenteau, Vallee, Laroche & Coulombe, 1030 Cherrier St., G. Parenteau, E. Vallee, R. Larouche, S.L. Coulombe
Pascal, Garonce, Cohen & Devine, 625 President Kennedy Ave., D. L. Pascal, M.L. Garonce, E. S. Cohen, D.M. Devine, M.I. Leiter, S.J. Frishman. Counsel: P.S. Garonce, Q.C.
Pateras & Iezzoni, 500 Place d'Armes, B. J. Pateras, Q.C., F.B. Iezzoni, P.J. Beauchamp, M.J. Paci; A. Ouellet, M.P.
Paul, D.R., 1671 St. Denis St.
Paul, Jocelyne, 932 St. Joseph Blvd. e.
Payette, Josee, 3903 St. Denis St.
Pearl & Prud'homme, 1400, 2001 University St., R. Pearl, A. Prud'homme
Pelletier, E., Q.C., 4 Notre Dame St. e.
Pelletier, Yves, Q.C., 60 St. James St. w.
Peloquin, Badeaux, etc. (City Attorneys)
Peloquin, Daniel, 4840 Henri Bourassa Blvd. e.
Pepin, Létourneau & Associates, #2200, 500 Place D'Armes (H2Y 3S3), P. Forest, Q.C., G. Raymond, Q.C., A. Létourneau, Q.C., G. Pepin, Q.C., R. de Tremblay, René Roy, B. Faribault, G. Brunelle, M. Saucier, D. Létourneau, D. Mandron, P. Journet, A. Laviolette, P. Bélanger, G. Legris, M. Beauregard, D. Latour, B. Roy, A. Cadieux, R. Bock, Line Durocher, Daniele Gruffy, D. Archambault, Isabelle Parizeau, S. Lachapelle. Counsel: Hon. G.E. Rinfret, P.C., Q.C., Yvon Bock, Q.C.
Perigny & Sanche, 7755 Louis H. Lafontaine Blvd. (Anjou), Y. Perigny, P. Sanche. Counsel: C. Beland
Perras & Perras, 440 Sherbrooke St. e., Y. Perras, Q.C., P. Y. Perras
Perrault, Archambault & Fournier, #1210, 2075 University St., P.J. Perrault, J.L. Archambault, M. Fournier
Perreault, A., 50 Place Cremazie
Petrin, J.L., 3270 Langelier Blvd.
Philibert, F., 6850 Sherbrooke St. e.
Phillips, F. R., 4080 Wellington St., Suite 5 (Verdun)
Phillips, Halperin, 1400 Place du Canada, H3B 2P8, M. Greenblatt, Q.C., S. Godinsky, Q.C., S. Phillips, Q.C., I.J. Halperin, Q.C., W. M. Friedman, Q.C., H.W. Ashenmil, Q.C., J. Kotler, Q.C., A. A. Garvis, S.R. Shuster, M.S. Schiff, R. Uditsky, H. Nemeroff, G.J. Analytis. Counsel: L. Sperber, Q.C.; N. N. Genser, Q.C.
Phillips & Vineberg, Ste. 930, 1 Place Ville Marie (H3B 2A5), Hon. L. Phillips, O.B.E., Q.C., P. F. Vineberg, O.C., Q.C., N. F. Phillips, Q.C., J. L'Anglais, Q.C., I. E. Phillips, M.H. Klein, D. S. Miller, A. Z. Golden, D.C. Robertson, R.S. Vineberg, E.W. Rubin (Hong Kong), M.D. Vineberg, P.A. Gélinas (Paris), S.P. Mendell, R. Mongeon, G.R. Hendy, S. Minzberg, P.-A. Themens, S. Horn, P. Harris, R.G. Ventura, S. Lussier, W. Brock, R.J. Abrams, M. Pelletier, Peggy Ross-Bybelezer, J.-D. Roy, P.E. Brace (Hong Kong)
Picard, Claude, 10 St. James St.
Piche & Saint Pierre, 6664 St. Denis St., A. Piche, J. Saint-Pierre
Pilon, Lagace & Major, 3303 Ontario St. e., J. P. Pilon, J. Lagace, Y. Major
Pilote, L., #128, 276 St. James St.
Pilote, O., 4403 Beaubien St. e.
Pinker, H., #2320, 2 Complexe Desjardins
Pinsonnault, M., 360 St. James St. w.
Pion, P., 3742 Levesque Blvd. (Laval)
Plante & Blackburn, 6984 St. Denis St., M. Plante, S. Blackburn
Poisson, Nicole, #723, 50 Cremazie w.

Pollack, A., 1130 Sherbrooke St. w.
Pollack, Teitelbaum & Cohen, #1410, 800 Dorchester Blvd. w., B. Pollack, Q.C., M. Teitelbaum, Q.C., Rhea Cohen
Pominville & Vachon, 818 Sherbrooke St. e., J. Pominville, M.-J. Vachon
Popovici, Parizeau & Terroux, 10 St. James St., A. Popovici, Micheline Parizeau-Popovici, F. Terroux
Portugais, M., 909 Dorchester Blvd. w.
Postelnik, G.W., #1008, 300 Leo Pariseau St.
Postelnik & Phaneuf, 465 St. Jean St., C.S. Postelnik, Ginette Phaneuf
Poulin, R., 1250 Pine Ave. w.
Pouliot, Dion, Guilbault, Caron, Prevost, 300 Leo Parizeau St., G. Pouliot, Q.C., M. Dion, M.G. Guilbault, J.G. Caron, J. Prevost, M.C. Belisle
Pouliot, Mercure, LeBel, Desrochers, Legault & Dancosse, 1155 Dorchester Blvd. w. (H3B 3S6), G. A. Pouliot, Q.C., L. Mercure, Q.C., J. LeBel, Q.C., S. Desrochers, J. Legault, G.P. Dancosse, A. Nadon, D. Charest, M. LaRoche, J.T. Tousignant, C. Laporte, P.L. Baribeau, L.A. Leclerc, P. Daviault, Carol Anne Laramée, J. Paul-Hus, Norma Desmarais, A. Robichaud, Michèle St-Onge, M. Gélinas, M. D'Amours, L.-M. Tremblay, Barbara Winters, J.-C. Cherrier, D. Gagné, Luc Audet, P. Paquet
Poupart, Thomas, Lesage & Paquet, 255 St. James St. w., A. Poupart, Q.C., P. Thomas, S. Fortier, Jules Lesage, J. Paquet
Pozza, J.L., 5120 Metropolitain Blvd. e.
Prazoff, I.R., Q.C., #1150, 555 Dorchester Blvd. w.
Price & Fine, 1 Place Ville Marie, S.G. Price, P.E. Fine
Proulx, Barot & Dupuis, #1007, 1255 Phillips Sq., M. Proulx, Danielle Barot, J.P. Dupuis, R. Masson
Prupas, Engels & Martz, 1310 Greene Ave., M. Prupas, D. Engels, A. Martz
Quesnel, Brunelle & Bertrand, 1 Place Ville Marie, A. Quesnel, Q.C., A. Brunelle, Y. Bertrand, B. Lemay
Racine, Michele, 210 St. Catherine St. e.
Raider, A., 615 Dorchester Blvd. w.
Rancourt, J., 484 McGill St. (also St. Jean)
Ranger, J., 5694 Laurendeau St.
Rappaport, Whelan, Bessner, Feldman & Ross, 1080 Beaver Hall Hill, #1800, N.L. Rappaport, Q.C., G. Whelan, Q.C., M. Bessner, J. M. Feldman, A.J. Ross, P. Lelarge
Reich, L., 5745 Pare St.
Reitman, J.H., 250 Sauve St. w.
Renaud, J. P. A., Q.C., 2382 Sherbrooke St. e.
Renaud & Renaud, 10 St. James St., J. O. Renaud, Q.C., A. Renaud
Renaud, Y., 1561 St. Joseph Blvd. e.
Retty, Stephanie, 4476 Maisonneuve Blvd. w.
Rheault, S., 7579 Centrale
Richard, J., 827 Decarie Blvd.
Richter, S., 455 St-Antoine St. w.
Riopel, P., 7331 De La Roche St.
Rivard, Hickson, #606, 1010 Sherbrooke St. w. (also Quebec)
Robert & Champagne, 302 Place d'Youville, P. Robert, Francine Champagne
Robert, Dansereau, Barre, Marchessault & Lauzon, 1211, 1 Complexe Desjardins, M. Robert, L. Dansereau, L. Barre, Carmelle Marchessault, Y. Lauzon, Louyse Cadieux, A. Sasseville, Luc Martineau, R. Vaillancourt
Robert, Jean, 4 Notre Dame St. e.
Robinson, Cutler, Sheppard, Borenstein, Shapiro, Langlois, Flam & Green, #612, 800 Place Victoria (C.P. 322, Tour de la Bourse, H4Z 1H6), J. J. Robinson, P. Cutler, Q.C., C.-A. Sheppard, B. H. Shapiro, C.J. Borenstein, P. Langlois, C. E. Flam, M. Green, N. Helfield, Herbert Z. Pinchuk, J. P. Renault, Y. Cousineau, P. Henry, Lynne Kassie, Nicole Laflamme, H. Graton, Solange Pau, Debra Blackwell
Robitaille, Malo, #1980, 500 Place d'Armes, M.G. Robitaille, Q.C., J. Malo, Q.C., P. Dansereau, A. Brunet, J.-J. Croteau, L. Trempe, Q.C., G. Cyr, P. Desaulniers, P. Larue, S. Dube, J. Bruyere, J.-P. Gagne, G. Robert, B. Themens, Y. Maranda, C. Beauvais, D. Champagne, C. Violette; Le Batonnier B.E. Blanchard
Rolfe, C.J., 5032 Clanranald Ave.
Rosenhek & Machlovitch, 1700 One Westmount Sq., M. Rosenhek, S. Machlovitch, W.S. Kravitz. Counsel: C. Rosenhek, D. Litner, Q.C.
Rothman, J. L., 1010 Sherbrooke St. w.
Rouleau, G., 5340 Industrial St.
Rousseau, Andree, 4341 Delorimier St.
Rousseau & Assoc., 530 Cherrier St., R. Rousseau, R. Bernier
Roy & Charbonneau, 484 McGill St., G. Roy, J. M. Charbonneau
Roy, F., 6840 D'Avila St.
Roy, G. A., Q.C., 1745 Cedar Ave.
Roy, Wingender, Laplante, 68 Cartier Blvd. (Laval), J.R. Roy, R. Wingender, B. Laplante
Roy, Therrien & Plante, 1435 St. Martin Blvd. w. (Chomedey), B. Roy, C. Therrien, Y. Plante
Ruby, G.L., #1900, 300 Leo Pariseau
Rudick, Posman, Tannenbaum, Liebman & Strasser, 10 St. James St., I. Rudnick, C.J. Posman, L. Tannenbaum, I.I. Liebman, S. Strasser
Sabloff, L. I., 1255 Phillips Sq.
St. Cyr & Demers, 154 St. Paul St. e., M. St. Cyr, L. Demers
Saint-Louis & Lippel, #201, 210 St. Catherine St. e., R.G. Saint-Louis, Katherine Lippel, Suzanne Guillet
St. Michael, J.J.J., #620, 1801 McGill College Ave.
St. Pierre, Drapeau & Alarie, 3730 Cremazie e., G. St. Pierre, M. Drapeau, J.M. Alarie
Saint Pierre, L.-A., 276 St. James St.
Saint Pierre, M., 3460 Place Decelles
St. Pierre, P., Q.C., 505 de Maisonneuve e.
Salomon, K.F., 1 Place Ville Marie
Samuels & Assoc., 1 Place Ville Marie, K.S. Samuels, Q.C., M. Brossard
Sand, G.G., 1010 St. Catherine St. w.
Saulnier, J., 7190 St. Denis St.
Schatia, D.I., #920, 1310 Greene Ave.
Schiff & Zilbert, #414, 276 St. James St., L. Schiff, A. Zilbert
Schlesinger & Schlesinger, 1010 St. Catherine St. w., J.M. Schlesinger, Q.C. (Counsel), F.M.E. Schlesinger
Schnaiberg & Schnaiberg, 2050 Mansfield St., H. L. Schnaiberg, Q.C., I. Schnaiberg
Schmolka, V., 1870 Baile St.
Schneider, B. K., 450 St. Joseph Blvd. e.
Schwartz, N., 1255 Phillips Sq.
Schwartz, W. D., 1010 St. Catherine St. w. (A. Kramer)
Schwisberg, Benson & MacKay, #804, 1010 St. Catherine St. w., C. E. Schwisberg, Q.C., B. R. Benson, Q.C., Louise Boucher MacKay
Sciascia, Corbeil, Messina & Scalasse, 2125 Jean Talon St. e., A. Sciascia, F. Corbeil, P. Messina, R. Scalasse
Seal & Associates, 2015 Drummond St., D.W. Seal, Q.C., P. Shaposnick, G. Moscowitz, P. Nadler, L.E. Seidman, S. Danino. Counsel: L. Tinkoff, Q.C.
Segal, A., 1440 St. Catherine St. w.
Seguin & Beaudoin, 2486 Jean Talon St. e., P. Seguin, M. Beaudoin
Selick, A.D., Q.C., 1200 McGill College Ave.
Selig & Jedeikin, #1009, 625 President Kennedy Blvd., G.M. Selig, L. Jedeikin
Selinger & Lengvari, 1 Place Ville Marie, S. L. Selinger, G. F. Lengvari, Jr., F.A. Braman, P. Trudel, M. Boivin, A.K. Kazandjian, J. Durocher, R. Fontaine, R. Barbacki, B. Moreau, A. Zoltowski. Counsel: Julien Savignac, Q.C.
Senecal, J., 336 Redfern St.
Seton, L. A., Q.C., 388 St. James St.
Shadley, Melancon, Boro & Heller, #303, 1255 Phillips Sq., R. E. Shadley, C. Melancon, J. K. Boro, B. Heller, B. Henry, J. Muskatel
Shaffer, H. E., 666 Sherbrooke St. w.
Shapiro, Green & Beinhaker, 1200, One Westmount Sq., I. Shapiro, M. Green, Ezra Beinhaker
Shaw, W. P., 477 St. Francois Xavier St.
Shoofey, Morneau, Blais, Rolland, Pariseau & Poupart, 1030 Cherrier St., F.D. Shoofey, C. Olivier, R. Blais, P. Morneau, G. Pariseau, J. Rolland, M. Poupart, R. Dore, M. Massicotte, R. Charbonneau, Marguerite Mancini
Shriar, Polak, Cooperstone & Shenker, Suite 6620, 1010 St. Catherine St. w., S. H. Shriar, H. M. Cooperstone, M. Shenker, M. Polak, Q.C.
Shulman, Goldman & Boileau, 4115 Sherbrooke St. w., A. I. Shulman, A. L. Goldman, A. Boileau
Shuster, Glazer & Gagnon, 1255 Phillips Sq., A. Shuster, Q.C., L. Glazer, R. Gagnon
Silver & Lamarche, 510 St. Lawrence Blvd., J. Silver, Stephanie Lamarche
Simard, A., 3469 Henri Julien St.
Simard & Desjardins, 1405 Peel St., A.S. Simard, Q.C., B. Desjardins, Q.C.
Simcoe, L., 1117 St. Catherine St. w.
Sirota, L., 10 St. James St.
Sivak, B., 1 Westmount Sq.
Sklar, M.J., 10 St. James St.
Skolnik, P., #505, 1117 St. Catherine St. w.
Slattery, McQuillan & Lafleur, 360 St. James St., T. P. Slattery, Q.C., W. J. McQuillan, Q.C., R. J. Lafleur, T.J. McQuillan, G. Broderick, Q.C.
Smiley, S. J., 1396 St. Catherine St. w.
Smith, E.M., 1460 Crescent St.
Smith, Lussier & Saint-Martin, 615 Dorchester Blvd. w., M.W. Smith, R. Lussier, P. Saint-Martin, J.-P. Morin, M. Richard, J.-F. Chicoine
Smolka, V., 1860 Baile St.
Solomon, F.L., #103, 4300 de Maisonneuve Blvd. w.
Solomon, Linda, 4281A Notre Dame St. w.
Solomon, H., Q.C., 1155 Dorchester Blvd. w.
Somers, Sylvia, 388 St. James St.
Spagnoli, A., 505 Jean Talon St. w.
Sperlich, R. H., 1445 Bishop St.
Spiegel & Kravetz, 1155 Dorchester Blvd. w., M.B. Spiegel, Q.C., D. Kravetz, Q.C., D.H. Sohmer, J.E. Khazzam, A. Miller, J. Matte, C. Peloquin, D.N. Kattan, R. Raich, C.M. Ravinsky, J. Bernstein, Cecile Solomon, J. Goldman. Counsel: R. Spector, Q.C.
Steckler, A. H., 5115 de Gaspe St.
Stein & Stein, 800 Dorchester Blvd. w., A.

L. Stein, Q.C., S. Stein, Q.C., A. M. Stein, N. H. Stein, H. Neufeld, D. Poirier, B.D. Stein
Steinberg-Drobin, M., 407 Lazar St.
Stern & Blumer, 305, 630 Sherbrooke St. w., M. M. Stern, R. Blumer
Stewart, McKenna, Gauthier, #1010, 606 Cathcart St. (H3B 1L8), J. G. Stewart, Q.C., T. J. McKenna, Q.C., O. Gauthier, Francine P. Deschamps, M. Deslauriers, M. Belanger, J. Duchastel, R.T. Quinn. Assoc.: E. Tannage, Q.C.
Stikeman, Elliott, Tamaki, Mercier & Robb, #3900, 1155 Dorchester Blvd. w., H3B 3V2, H. H. Stikeman, Q.C., R. F. Elliott, C.M., Q.C., G. T. Tamaki, Q.C., F. Mercier, O.C., Q.C., J. A. Robb, Q.C., M. A. Régnier, Q.C., J. A. Grant, W. D. Angus, S. H. Hartt, M. L. Richards, H. P. Gordon, A.P.F. Cumyn, M. Vennat, M. G. Freiheit, M. C. Lepage, V. M. Prager, R. W. Pound, C. P. Desaulniers, J. N. Wyatt, Yvon Martineau, P. Fortin, P.R. O'Brien, M. Prévost, Claudette Picard-Lavallée, J.-P. Ouellet, D.W. Colson, Elinore J. Richardson, C. Salbaing, D.N. Finkelstein, M. De Man, R. Couzin, G.A. Cranker, J.-P. Belhumeur, J.-J. Chabot, D. Lachance, R. Hackett, R. Langlois, J.A. Woods, P. Archambault, M.H. Scheim, D.G. Barbeau, A.R. Dorais, A.E. Aust, L.P. Bélanger, F.H. Ouimet, L. Fortier, P. Raymond, F. Sixt, B. Arnould, C. Rovinescu, G. Masson, Louise Pelly, G. Sarault, M. Casavant, J.W. Leopold, E. Skelton, L. Ouellet, P.J. Setlakwe. Counsel: The Hon. M. Riel, Q.C.
Stojak, D., 2020 University St.
Strauber, R., 666 Sherbrooke St. w.
Sutton, R.G., #608, 3460 Peel St.
Sweibel, S., 1 Westmount Sq.
Synott, M., 209 St. Paul St. w.
Taillefer, Taillefer & Pigeon, #1020, 276 St. James St. w., G. Taillefer, C. Taillefer, R. Pigeon, S.S. Sheitoyan
Talbot & Clement-Talbot, #208, 1255 Laird Blvd. (Mount Royal), N. Talbot, Catherine Clement-Talbot
Talbot, R., 1015 Beaver Hall Hill
Tannenbaum & Lefebvre, 276 St. James St., L. Tannenbaum, Q.C., R. Lefebvre, N. Lazare, J.-Y. Desjardins
Tardi, P., 10 St. James St. w.
Tellier, DeSeve, 827 Decarie Blvd. (St. Laurent)
Tessier, Corbeil, Bourbeau & Gilbert, 1155 Sherbrooke St. w., G. Tessier, Micheline Corbeil, J.P. Bourbeau, M. Gilbert, R.P. Saucier, M. Proulx, P. Hudon. Counsel: J.E. Lamontagne
Tetreault, N., 5480 St. Denis St.
Theoret, R., 225 Fleury St. w.
Toulch & Strohl, 1117 St. Catherine St. w., H. Toulch, A. Strohl
Trahan, M., 892 Sherbrooke St. w.
Tremblay & Ferland, 3425 St. Hubert St., G. Tremblay, G. Ferland
Tremblay, P., 7042 Pie IX Blvd.
Trevick, D. I., 1255 Phillips Sq.
Trinque, C., 231 St. James St.
Trudeau, Dufresne & Peloquin, 10802 Lajeunesse St., P.L. Trudeau, C. Dufresne, D. Peloquin
Trudeau, Leduc, Lavoie & Martel, #400, 1200 St. Martin Blvd. w. (Laval), P. Trudeau, Q.C., P. Leduc, J.M. Duranceau, G. Lavoie, J.-F. Martel, P.Y. Leduc, Louise Belanger, L. Villiard, S. Lalonde
Trudel, Nadeau, Lesage, Cleary & Menard, #200, 1259 Berri St., L. C. Trudel, G. Nadeau, P. Lesage, R. Cleary, Louise Menard, L. Roy, N. Beaulieu, R. Bertrand, F. Cote, Y. Saint-Andre, France Saint-Laurent, Ginet Touzel
Trudel, R., 3566 Clark St.
Truesdell, C., 440 Dorchester Blvd. w.
Tucci, S., 201 St. Zotique St. e.
Turcotte, M., 3530 Jean Talon St. w.
Unterberg, Boyer & Bonin, 1980 Sherbrooke St. w., P. G. Unterberg, R. Boyer, Y. Bonin, Lise Labelle
Valiquette, Blouin & Kochenburger, 630 Sherbrooke St. w., A. Valiquette, M. Blouin, D.M. Kochenburger, J. Normand, F. Rivest
Valois, M., 1200 McGill College Ave.
Velentzas, A., 1255 University St.
Verchere, Noel & Eddy, #1600, 1 Place Ville Marie, B. Verchere, R.B. Eddy, M. Noel, M.F. Menard, D.B. Morris, G. Dube, G. Du Pont, S. Kerr, G. Lawson, K. Russell, S. Tardif, Janice McCart, P. Martin. Advisory Counsel: W.R. Jackett
Vermette, Dunton, Rusko, De Wever, Caron & Rainville, #2104, 800 Victoria Sq., C. Vermette, Q.C., J.W. Dunton, J. Ciaccia, M.P.J. Rusko, Q.C., M. de Wever, J.P. Saintonge, M. Caron, J.-J. Rainville, R. Caron. Counsel: E. Brais, Q.C.
Veronneau, L.
Vezina, C., 2150 Maisonneuve Blvd. w.
Viau, Bélanger & Assoc., 2810 Stock Exchange Tower (H4Z 1E6), R. Adam, R.G. Alain, Christine Béland, M. Bélanger, Q.C., A. Bergeron, J. Berkowitz, R. Boyer, G. Caisse, M. Cantin, A. Comeau, R. Coutu, M. Delorme, Y. Denault, A. Denis, A.-C. Desforges, S. Devito, R. Dostie, P. Dozois, C.J.E. Dupont, M. Dupuy, Aline Grenon, G. Hébert, Q.C., J. Hurlet, Diane Larose, L. Lefebvre, J.P. Legault, P. LePage, N. Martin, C. Nadeau, Carole Julien-Rocheleau, P. Roy, P. Sauvé, Le Batonnier J. Viau, O.C., Q.C.
Viau & Delisle, 500 Place d'Armes, P. Viau, C. Delisle, J. Tanguay
Villeneuve, Pigeon, Clement, Guilbeault, Laurendeau & Hebert, #501, 235 Dorchester Blvd. e., A. Villeneuve, Q.C., R. Pigeon, J. Clement, Q.C., J. Guilbeault, O. Laurendeau, J. Hebert
Virag, P.G., 360 St. James St.
Vlahos, N., 7200 Hutchison St.
Waxman, Flahiff, Houle, Champagne & Proulx, 407 McGill St., L. Waxman, R. Flahiff, A. Houle, G. Champagne, J.-P. Proulx
Weber, S. W., Q.C., 1000 Pratt St.
Weigel, M., 5126 Park Ave.
White, J.-P., 2309 Ontario St. e.
Wolfson, C., Q.C., 1010 St. Catherine St. w.
Wolofsky, J. L., 2 Complexe Desjardins
Woloshen & Axelrod, 1010 St. Catherine St. w., J. H. Woloshen, A. Axelrod
Wood, Aaron & Henry, 615 Dorchester Blvd. w., D. H. Wood, W. S. Aaron, P. C. Henry
Worsoff, Mass & Teitelbaum, #725, 360 St. James St., M. Worsoff, I. Mass, R. Teitelbaum
Yanofsky, Brull & Assoc., #1235, 2020 University St., A. Yanofsky, Q.C., Ellen Walfish Amdursky, J.A. Brull, Leila Heller
Yarosky, Fish, Zigman, Isaacs & Daviault, #1103, 1255 Phillips Sq., H. W. Yarosky, M. J. Fish, Natalie F. Isaacs, J. J. Zigman, F. Daviault, M. Hartman
Zaitlin, A.H.J., Q.C., 2 Complexe Desjardins
Zascinski, J., 200 St. James St.
Zaurrini & Semeteys, 360 St. James St., D. Zaurrini, M. Semeteys
Zimmerman, Blitt & Jarry, #410, 345 Victoria Ave., A. Zimmerman, Q.C., P.E. Blitt, R.A. Jarry
Zimmerman, M., 1450 City Councillors St.

NEW CARLISLE, Dist. Bonaventure
Grenier, Grenier & Grenier, Box 519, L. Grenier, Q.C., R. Grenier, D. Grenier
Levesque & Landry, Box 727, J.-R. Landry, G.D. Levesque

NICOLET, Dist. Trois-Rivieres
Beaubien, M., 78 Place 21 Mars
Pelletier, A., 1888 Ls. Frechette Blvd.
Verrier, J., 181 Notre Dame (also Sorel)

OTTERBURN PARK, Dist. Richelieu
Robillard, P., 380 Ostiguy St.

PAPINEAUVILLE, Dist. Hull
Saulnier, D., 326 Papineau St.

PASPEBIAC, Dist. Bonaventure
Lemarquand, A.
Moulin & Moulin, B. Moulin, J.G. Moulin

PIERREFONDS, Dist. Montreal
Chauret, C., 4393 Pascal St.

PLESSISVILLE, Dist. Arthabaska
Baril, Belisle & Assoc. (also Arthabaska)
Houde, E., Q.C.
Moisan, Bellevance & Co. (also Arthabaska)
Provencher & Provencher (also Victoriaville)

POINTE GATINEAU, Dist. Hull
Birtz & Laporte, 151 St. Antoine, S. Birtz, Agnes Laporte
Boucher & Legault, 149 ch. de la Savane, J.C. Boucher, L. Legault, Louise Archambault, M. Heyendal, Martine Nantel
Chevrier-Beauregard & Major, 195 Greber Blvd., C. Chevrier-Beauregard, H. Major
Lapointe & Assoc., 365 Greber Blvd., R.R. Lapointe, J.P. Aubry, R. Leblanc, J. Morel, C. Lapointe
Vaillant, Rainville, 151 St. Antoine, J. Vaillant, F. Rainville

PORT ALFRED, Dist. Chicoutimi
Ouellet, J.C., 1960 du Port Ave.
Page, Girard, etc., 1402 5th Ave. (also Chicoutimi)
Tremblay, R., 520 2nd St.

PORT CARTIER, Dist. Mingan
Bouchard, S.
Dionne, Gauthier & Belanger (also Sept Iles)
Fillion, Berthi, 5 Lebel St.

PRINCEVILLE, Dist. Arthabaska
Baril, Belisle & Assoc. (also Arthabaska)

QUEBEC, Dist. Quebec
Amyot, Lesage, Bernard, Drolet & Assoc., 55 D'Auteuil (G1R 4T5), R. Amyot, Q.C., R. Lesage, Q.C., P. Lesage, B. Bernard, G. Drolet, J.-P. Bussieres, L. Lamarre, P. Boulanger, J.P. Cantin, A. Rochon, D. Lavoie, M. Messely, A. Levesque, M. Fortier, P. Rousseau, P. Boivin. Counsel: Hon. P. Lesage, Q.C., Rene Dussault
Anglehart, Bussieres & Royer, 1725 1st Ave., F. Anglehart, A. Bussieres, A. Royer, P. Montreuil
Beaudet, Piuze & Assoc., 2100 Charest Blvd. w., P. Beaudet, B. Piuze
Beaudry, H., Q.C., 105 Cote de la Montagne
Beauvais, Truchon & Aubut, #736, 2 Place Quebec, O. Carter, Q.C., J. Beauvais, R. Truchon, M. Aubut, G. Thiboutot, J. Pelletier, C. Cote, E. Payne, J. Reeves, P. Picard, M. Parent, Y. Lepage, A. Reinhardt, D. O'Brien, B. Lepage
Bedard, H., 51 Desjardins

Belanger & Belanger, 71 rue St. Pierre, R. Belanger, Q.C., M. Belanger
Belanger, Gagnon & Assoc., 61 d'Auteuil, P. Belanger, N. Gagnon
Bernatchez, A., #35, 132 St. Pierre St.
Bernatchez & Assoc., 675 Marguerite-Bourgeois Rd., Y. Bernatchez, E. Taschereau, R. Bernatchez, J. Bernatchez, M. Rinfret
Bernier & Gosselin, 2891 1er Ave., P. Bernier, R. Gosselin
Bertrand, Otis & Grenier, #42, rue Ste-Anne, G. Bertrand, Louise Otis, G. Grenier
Bherer, Bernier, Cote, Ouellet, Cantin & Poliquin, 580 Grande Allee e., W. Bherer, Q.C., J.-P. Bernier, Q.C., J. Cote, R. Ouellet, D. Houle, J. Cantin, G. Poliquin, P. Cote, P. Leboeuf, P. Darveau, G. Legris, J. Beaudoin. Counsel: R. Cote, Q.C.
Bherer, J.-C., #400, 2 Place Quebec
Blanchet & Blanchet, 1235 Galipeault Ave., B. Blanchet, Q.C.
Blouin, P., 1217 Royale Ave. (Beauport)
Boivin, Lagace, Poulin, etc., #240, 900 d'-Youville (also Levis)
Brochet, Fortin & Assoc., 649 Grande Allee e., A. J. Brochet, J. Fortin, G. Richer, R. Voyer, M. Dussault
Brochu, J., 11 St. Pierre St.
Cantin, Christiane, #100, 2475 Laurier Blvd.
Bronstetter, Wilkie, Penhale, etc., 55 rue d'Auteuil (also Montreal)
Cardinal, Paquet, Racine, Hendriks & Brodeur, #100, 35 Grande Alee e., R.J. Cardinal, J. Paquet, J.-L. Racine, F. Hendriks, M.-J. Brodeur
Caron, Gingras, Goulet, Grenier & Gilbert, 8 de la Fabrique St., M. Caron, P.G. Gingras, R. Grenier, S. Goulet, J.-G. Gilbert
Chabot & Assoc., 401 Grande Allee e., M. C. Chabot, M. Giroux. Counsel: Hon. P. Miquelon, Q.C.
Charest, Labrecque, Levesque, Vallerand & Laroche, 900 d'Youville, G. Charest, G. Labrecque, V. Levesque, S. Barma, J. Vallerand, B. Laroche
City Attorneys, #216, 2 Desjardins, Brochu, Roy, Boutin & Ouimet, J.-C. Brochu, G. Roy, D. Boutin, P. Ouimet
Clermont, Croteau & Binet, 1070 ch. Ste-Foy, Micheline Clermont-Marceau, M. Croteau, R. Binet
Cloutier, Cartier & Assoc., 537 est Charest boul., A. Cloutier, A.C. Cartier, C. Boulanger, R. Lavoie, Anne Turgeon, D. Boudreau
Coderre & Courtemanche, 220 Grande Allee e., Mireille Coderre, Claire Courtemanche
Corriveau, Bouchard, Corriveau & Assoc., #2, 51 rue Desjardins, L. Corriveau, Q.C., J. Bouchard, Anne Duchesnay, R.L. Corriveau, C. Belanger, Susan Corriveau
Cote, R., 1445 Maine St.
Daigneault, P., #306, 56 St. Pierre
Delisle, M., 7 d'Auteuil St.
Demers, Gosselin & Robitaille, 425 e., boul. Charest, J. Demers, M. Gosselin, Carol Robitaille. Counsel: G. de L. Demers, Q.C.
Des Rivieres, Vermette & Berube, 71 rue St. Pierre, G. Des Rivieres, Q.C., S. Vermette, C. Berube, R. Thivierge, F. Fava, L.-M. Lavoie, M. Germain, G. Fortier, L. Legare
De Turris, C.A., 1260 St. Cyrille w.
Dion & Cote, #200, 210 Charest Blvd. e., P. Dion, D. Cote
Dionne, Noreau, Cliche & Gravel, 689 Grande Allee e., R.F. Dionne, G.-M. Noreau, N. Cliche, M. Gravel
Dorion, Jolin & Associates, 150 St-Cyrille e., L. Dorion, P. Jolin, P. Le Gallais, J.R. Gingras, R. Lesperance, J. Valois, D. Desaulniers
Doyon, J., #101, 515 Grande Allee e.
Dugal, Fortier, Robert, Matte & Assoc., 800 ch. Ste-Foy, M.N. Dugal, J. Fortier, R. Robert, D. Matte, M.T. O'Neil, J.-A. Lemieux
Dumas, M., 425 Charest Blvd. e.
Duplessis, Bernier, Brochu & Assoc., #1405, 8 Jardins Merici, R. Beaudry, J. Bedard, M.-C. Bernier, R. Brochu, M.L. Duplessis, A. Levesque, M. Normand, P. Rioux, M. Turgeon
Dupont & Assoc., 6 Jardins Merici, J. Dupont, Monique Ducharme, Christine Samson, Lucie Lupine
Falardeau, Brosseau & Parent, 1327 Maguire St., A. Falardeau, J. Brosseau, D. Parent
Flynn, Rivard & Assoc., 2, av. Chauveau, L. Baillargeon, J. Lavoie, M. LeBlond, J. Croteau, J. LeMay, G. Dussault, R.W. Lessard, Hon. J. Flynn, Q.C., F. Folot, C. Ouellet, R. Gouge, P. Proulx, C. Jean, H. Renault, J. Langlois, J. Rivard, Q.C., P. Latreille, P. Laurin, F. Rouette. Counsel: Hon. A. Rivard, Q.C., G. Gilbert
Forgues, Brochu, 515 Grande Allee e., J. Forgues, R. Brochu, Francine Neron, J. Doyon
Fortier, F.G., Box 305, Stn. B
Fortin, Dallaire, Fortier & Champagne, 30 Grande Allee w., C. Fortin, Y. Dallaire, J. Fortier, Danielle Champagne
Fournier, Vaillancourt & Assoc., 2815 Boul. Laurier (Ste Foy), L. Fournier, J. L. Vaillancourt, M. Gagnon, J. Riou, L.P. Dore; Senator Martial Asselin
Gagne, Letarte, Royer, Gauthier, Lacasse & Boily, 2, av. Chauveau, J.-H. Gagne, Q.C., G. Letarte, Q.C., J.-C. Royer, P. Gauthier, A. Lacasse, G. Boily, B. Mailloux, G. Plante, F. Barbeau, M. Heroux, M. Gagne, J.-M. Gagne, Louise Letarte
Gagnon, de Billy, Cantin, Martin, Beaudoin & Lesage, Suite 1700, 800 d'Youville (G1R 4W8), J. de Billy, Q.C., G. de Billy, Q.C., A. Gagnon, Q.C., E. Martin, P. Beaudoin, M. Lesage, P. Cantin, L.-M. Cossette, P.-C. Gagnon, C. Larose, Michele Bolduc, M.J. Edwards, Helene Gauvin, J. Provencher, S. Letourneau, T. Zamuner, C.R. Drolet, C. Jarry, M. Dorion, P. Carter
Garneau, Gauvin, Turgeon, Doyon & Guimont, 65 Ste Anne St., R. Garneau, J. Gauvin, A. Turgeon, L. Guimont, M. Doyon, P. Samson, J. Barakatt, M. Martin, J. Gascon, Elisabeth Pinard. Assoc.: J. L'Heureux
Gaudreau & St. Cyr, 75 d'Auteuil, P. Gaudreau, Carol St. Cyr
Gaudry, G., Q.C., #7, 48 Place Philippe
Genest, Laflamme, Ouellet & Beauchamp, 81 St. Pierre St., J.-C. Genest, M. Laflamme, J. Ouellet, M. Beauchamp
Gignac & Morneau, #220, 5350 Henri Bourassa (Charlesbourg), J.-P. Gignac, C. Morneau
Gonthier & Duval, 2590 Laurier Blvd. (Ste-Foy), Y. Gonthier, R. Duval, Y. Ferland
Goodwin, De Blois, Parent & Assoc., #602, 2 Place Quebec, R. Goodwin, R. De Blois, Monique Parent Dufour, R. Gauthier, F. Samson. Counsel: Hon. H. Lapointe, P.C., O.C., Q.C.
Grondin, LeBel, Poudrier, Isabel, Morin & Gagnon, 1 Parc Samuel Holland, Le Batonnier H. Grondin, L. LeBel, J. Poudrier, M.-A. Isabel, J. Morin, R. P. Gagnon, L. Giroux, G. Gaumond, J. F. Keable, L. Vaillancourt, P. Ouellet, D. Bradet, M. Racine, France Thibault, J. White, D. Jacques, Isabelle Paquet
Guerin, M., 360 Charest Blvd. e.
Hogue, Chouinard & Gouin, 35 Grande Allee e., Y. Chouinard
Huot, M., Q.C., 351 6th St. (Limoilou)
Joli-Coeur & Moisan, 250 Grande Allee w., P. Joli-Coeur, F. Moisan
Kronstrom, Turmel, Desjardins & Villeneuve, 1085 de la Tour, S. Kronstrom, E. Turmel, J. Y. Desjardins, J.-G. Villeneuve, A. Robitaille, P. Cloutier, R. Ramsay, B. Godbout, Y. Rochette, B. Vachon, M. Gravel, R. St. Pierre, L. Godbout (also Levis)
Lachapelle & Bedard, 5555 3rd Ave. (Charlesbourg), S. Lachapelle, R. Bedard
Lamonde, D., 105 Cote de la Montagne
Langlois, Drouin & Assoc., 126 rue St. Pierre, Senator L. Langlois, Q.C., Batonnier R. Drouin, Q.C., I.C. Pollack, C.M., Q.C., R. Drouin, Q.C., L. Remillard, Q.C., R. Langlois, J.N. Henry, M. Boulianne, J.-P. Roy, M. Frechette, A. Joli-Coeur, F.G. Barakett, L. Trudeau, G. Mathieu, R. Gaudreau, P. Tourigny, R. Chartier, G. Vaillancourt, G.H. Marier, C. Laflamme, L. Masson, F.X. Simard, Jr., A. Brault, A. Asselin, M. St. Pierre, P. Lamontagne, Francine Cote, G.-M. Henry, France Simard, Line Despres, R. Levesque, H. Lanctot, C. Joli-Coeur, Lisette Roy, C. Verge, R. Maltais, Celine Garneau, B. Gravel
Langlois, Vallee & Landry, 220 Grande Allee e., Maxine Langlois, M. Vallee, Leandre Landry
Laperrierre, Tardif & Assoc., 51 Desjardins, A. Laperriere, M. Tardif, P. Nadeau, M. Baribeau
Lapointe, Lord & Boutin, 1433 4th Ave., P. Lapointe, G. Lord, R. Boutin
Laroche, L.N., Q.C., 350 Charest e.
Lazarovitz, Cannon, Lemelin & Rourke, 980 Holland, Le Batonnier S. Lazarovitz, Q.C., D.L. Cannon, J. Lemelin, R. Rourke, M.J. Longpre, M. Hebert, R. Leblanc
Lemieux, J., 525 de l'Eglise
Lemieux, Lacroix, Routhier, Gagnon, Beaupre & Assoc., 65 Ste-Anne, M. Lemieux, C. Lacroix, P. Routhier, P. Gagnon, J. Beaupre, C. Morissette
Lesage, Paquet, #1800, 150 St-Cyrille e., R. Paquet, L. Paradis, G. Morency, D. St-Pierre. Counsel: J.-C. Sirois, Q.C.
Letourneau & Stein, 65 rue Ste-Anne, Batonnier R. Letourneau, Q.C., C. Stein, Q.C., A. Monast, Q.C., C. Pratte, Q.C., P. Marseille, Q.C., J. Delisle, Q.C., P. LaRue, Q.C., J. Marier, P. Cimon, J. Gingras, P. Pelletier, J. Deblois, R. Vallieres, L. Huot, J. Houle, M. Dupont, C. Girard, M. Demers, M. Letourneau, H.L. Fortin, C. Rochon, J. Audet
Levasseur, Ouellet & Plourde, #336, 2 Place Quebec, G. Levasseur, G. Q. Ouellet, P.B. Plourde, J. Larochelle, Julie Dutil
Levesque, A., 34 Cote de la Fabrique
Maltais, A., Q.C., 2219 Mgr. Gosselin
Maranda, J., 220 Grande Allee e.
Marcoux, J.R., 775 de Longpre (Ste Foy)
Mariost, R., 448 Langelier
Marquis, Jessop, Gagnon, Huot, Belanger & Laflamme, 500 Grande Allee e., J. Marquis, Q.C., M. Jessop, Q.C., Y. Gagnon, L. P. Huot, G. Belanger, R. Laflamme

Martin, Pare & Alain, 67 Ste Ursule St., P. Martin, B. Pare, Y. Alain. Conseil: C. Rochette, F. Sauvageau
McNicoll & Parent, 1170 de Salaberry, J. NcNicoll, G.N. Parent, B.L. Charron. Counsel: S.G. Parent, Q.C.
Mercier, J., Q.C., 1165 Bougainville Ave.
Morisset, R., 1307 Fontenay St.
Morissette & Robitaille, 350 Charest Blvd. e., J.-M. Morissette, J. Robitaille
Morneau, L., Q.C., 350 e. boul. Charest
Neron, Blais, Belzile & Assoc., 771 St. Joseph e., P. Neron, R. Blais, Y. Belzile, J. Carrier, N. Auger, R. Bouchard, M. Robert
Pare, Daigle & Boyer, #501, 265 de la Couronne, Ellen Pare, J. Daigle, M. Boyer
Petit & Lahoud, 2835 Chemin Gomin (Ste Foy), D. Petit, Y. Lahoud, G. Martel
Picard, Marineau & Asselin, 175 Benoit XV, J. Picard, G. Marineau, M. Asselin
Pothier, Begin, Delisle, Veilleux, Sauvageau, Gobeil, Paquet, Lemay, Tremblay, 977 Route de l'Eglise, R.D. Pothier, P. Begin, P. Delisle, C.A. Veilleux, C. Sauvageau, B. Gobeil, J. Paquet, D. Beaulieu, D. Dinan, J. Tremblay, N. Morin
Poulin, Valin & Lemay, #203, 2835 Chemin Gomin, Ste. Foy, M. Poulin, P. Valin, Y. Lemay
Pouliot, G., 879 Place Beloeil (Ste Foy)
Proulx, Fontaine & Garneau, 45 Ste. Ursule St., Narcisse Proulx, W. Fontaine, G. Garneau
Proulx, Marquis & Roy, 120 St-Jean, P. Proulx, M. Marquis, G. Roy
Provencher, C., 6 Jardins Merici
Ratte & Bergeron, 1033 Cote de l'Eglise (Ste-Foy), J. Ratte, R. Bergeron
Richer, Rousseau & Lapointe, 1112 St. Vallier St. e., G. Richer, P.-A. Rousseau, J. Lapointe
Rivard, Hickson, #636, 2 Place Quebec, G. Rivard, Q.C., M. E. Hickson, Q.C., J. Sirois, G. Samson, P.M. Bouchard, Y. Descoteaux, J. St. Laurent, M. Cordeau, N. Gagne, F. Poulin, L.R. Lavallee, L. Bond, A. Chauvin. Conseil: E. Rivard, Q.C.
Rivard & Morency, 2750 Chemin Ste-Foy, J. R. Rivard, J. Morency, C. Morency, L.E. Roy
Robitaille & Robitaille, 51 rue des Jardins, P. E. Robitaille, Q.C., P. Robitaille
Roussy, Blanchard & Assoc., 425 St. Cyrille w., J.G. Roussy, J. Blanchard, A. Gaulin, R. Bernatchez, J. Rouleau, A. Morand, M. Bernatchez, M. Bilodeau, J.-P. Anglehart, J. Mercier
Roy, Savard, Tremblay & Assoc., 7 Jardins Merici, L.L. Roy, G. Savard, P. Jacques, J. Tremblay, B. Legal, Louisette Proulx
Sabourin, Savard, Corriveau, Nadeau, Tremblay, Kallis, Francoeur & Jobin, #401, 34 de la Fabrique St., P. Sabourin, G. Savard, Q.C., P. Corriveau, J. Nadeau, C. Kallis, S. Francoeur, M. Jobin, C. Tremblay (also Baie Comeau)
St. Hilaire, DeBlois, Leclerc, Gingras & Delage, 200 Grande Allee e., M. St. Hilaire, L. DeBlois, B. Leclerc, D. Gingras, M. M. Delage, P. Leblanc, J. Richard
Simard, I., Q.C., 360 Charest e.
Simard, Picard, Boulet, Rogerge & Leboeuf, 67 Ste. Ursule St., M. Simard, J.G. Picard, M. Roberge, C. Boulet, J. Leboeuf
Sirois, Blanchard & Beaudet, 220 Grande Allee e., G. Sirois, C.A. Blanchard, J. Beaudet, M. Watters
Sirois, Lapointe & Begin, 2900 Quatre Bourgeois, D. Sirois, R. Lapointe, P. Begin, L. Cote
Thibaudeau & Assoc., 71 rue St. Pierre, R. Thibaudeau, Q.C., A. Thibaudeau, P. Bradley
Tremblay, Morisset, Bois & Mignault, 1195 rue Lavigerie (Ste-Foy), C. Tremblay, Q.C., A. Morisset, A. Bois, A. Mignault, Liliane G. Duperrey, A. Lemay, R. Talbot, J.G. Morency, P. Giroux, M. Boulanger, A. Michaud, L. Harvey. Counsel: T. Tremblay, S.M., Q.C.
Tremblay, R., 1319 ch. Ste-Foy
Vachon, Michaud, Laroche & Wallot, 1720 de la Canardiere, L.M. Vachon, J.P. Michaud, A. Laroche, C. Wallota
Vezina, Pouliot, 2535 Laurier Blvd. (Ste-Foy), L. Vezina, P. Vezina, P. F. Pouliot, G. L'Ecuyer, P. Morin, F. Pelletier, M. Jobidon, Lise Lambert, D. Bureau, Lise Cote, R. Mainguy, Michele Lacroix, M. Jacob, C. Marchand

RACINE, Dist. Bedford
Beaulieu, D., R.R. 2

REPENTIGNY, Dist. Joliette
Dupuis, J., 522 Notre Dame St. (M. Duval)
Duval, H., 577 Notre Dame St.
Forest & Renaud, 224 Notre Dame St., G. Forest, A. Renaud
Imbeault, P., 577 Notre Dame St.
Lefebvre, J.E., 51 Terrasse de Bienville
Savoie, C., 215 Notre Dame St.
Thouin & Brochu, 577 Notre Dame St., G. Thouin, M. Brochu

RICHMOND, Dist. St. Francois
Grenier, Bessette, etc. (also Sherbrooke)
Martel, M. A.

RIMOUSKI, Dist. Rimouski
Berube, R., 66 St. Marce
Blouin, J., 216 de la Cathedrale
Bouchard, Ringuet & Laprise, 6 St. Jean St., G. Bouchard, G. Ringuet, G. Laprise, A. Provencher
Casgrain, Crevier, Blanchet, Gagnon & Desrosiers, 184 de la Cathedrale, A. P. Casgrain, Q.C., Marcel Crevier, G. Blanchet, G. Gagnon, G. Desrosiers, G. Voyer, A. Begin
Chasse, J.-M., 10 Eveche St. e.
Desrosiers & Gagne, 125 Rene Lepage, M. Desrosiers, V. Gagne
Gagnon, J.-C., Q.C., Box 230
Gendreau, Pelletier, Langis, Berube & Savoie, 41 Eveche St. w., M. Pelletier, C. H. Gendreau, D. Langis, D. Lavallee, J. Berube, L. Savoie
Roy, J.H., 148 St. Barnabe St.
Tessier, M., 116 Germain St. w.

RIVIERE DU LOUP, Dist. Kamouraska
Belzil, Dumas & Deschenes, 2 rue de la Cour, A.H. Belzil, S.Y. Dumas, G. Deschenes
Chasse & Boucher, 126 rue Lafontaine, P. Chasse, J. P. Boucher, L. Dufresne
Chasse, Laforest & Assoc., 30 rue de la Cour, H. Chasse, Q.C., G. Laforest, G. Morneau, A. Dube
Lebel, Pelletier, Rioux & Bosse, 12 rue de la Cour, G. Lebel, Q.C., G. Pelletier, D. Rioux, N. Bosse, C. Masse, G. Moreau
Lemieux & LeBlond, 6 rue de la Cour, F. Lemieux, D. LeBlond

ROBERVAL, Dist. Roberval
Cote, Gilbert, etc., 773 St. Joseph Blvd. (also Chicoutimi)
Simard & Amireault, 822 St. Joseph Blvd., J. Simard

ROCK FOREST, Dist. St. Francois
Daigle, Y., 4300 Bourque blvd.
Delorme & LeBel, 5104 Bourque blvd., R.E. Delorme, R. LeBel
Duval, H., 5104 Bourque

ROCK ISLAND, Dist. St. Francois
Hackett, Campbell & Co., P. Bouchard (also Sherbrooke)

ROUYN, Dist. Rouyn-Noranda
Coutu, Fortin, Bedard & Assoc., 50 Perreault St. w., J. Coutu, J. Fortin, R. Bedard, Q.C.
Gagne, J.C., 175 Principale
Grimard, Desjardins, Guertin, Lavallee, Grimard, 155 Dallaire St., N. Grimard, Q.C., G. Desjardins, Q.C., L. Guertin, P. Lavallee, M. Grimard (also La Sarre)
Larouche, C., 145 rue Principale
McNally, F. J., Q.C., 49 Principale
St. Julien, Tessier & Assoc., 145 Principale (also Val d'Or)

STE. ADELE, Dist. Terrebonne
Boivin, Fortin, Gaudreau, 916 Ste Adele Blvd. (also Montreal)
Champagne, G., 1285 Dumouchel St.
Genest, G., Q.C., 893 Ste. Adele Blvd.

ST. ADOLPHE DE HOWARD, Dist. Terrebonne
Parent, R., C.P. 381

STE. AGATHE DES MONTS, Dist. Terrebonne
Demers, M., 107 St. Vincent
Gelinas & Gelinas, 22 Ste Agathe St., P. Gelinas, Q.C., M.P. Gelinas
Godard, Belisle, Collin & Bertrand, 3 Prefontaine, Guy Godard, A. A. Belisle, R. Collin, F. Bertrand
Paquin, G.-M., 107 St. Vincent St.

STE ANNE DES MONTS, Dist. Gaspe
Pelletier, R.
Robert, J.M.

ST. CONSTANT, Dist. Montreal
Lefebvre, S., 277 St. Pierre
Veilleux, G., 21 Ste. Marie St.

ST. EUSTACHE, Dist. Terrebonne
Belanger & Blais, 148 St. Louis, L. Belanger, A. Blais
Blouin & Saulnier, 149 St. Eustache, C. Blouin, G. Saulnier
Desjardins, R., 102 St. Eustache
Drouin & Assoc., 140 St. Eustache, L. Raymond (also Montreal)
Forget, B., 148 St. Louis St.
Gravel, J., 350 Sauve Blvd.
LaCharite, R., Q.C., 183 Sauve Blvd.
Terreault, M., 349 Villeneuve

ST. FELICIEN, Dist. Roberval
Brassard, R.

ST GEORGES, Dist. Beauce
Dutil & Assoc., R. Dutil, G. Garneau, M. Deblois
Jolicoeur, R., 11725 1st Ave.
Lebel Poirier, 11720 1st Ave., G. Lebel, J. Poirier
LeMay-Lavoie, Therese, Q.C., #11, 145 7th Ave.
Lessard & Morin, 12285 1st Ave., R. Lessard, P.A. Morin
Morin & Pepin, P.W. Morin, S. Pepin
Parent, Doyon & Rancourt, 11660 1st Ave., G. Parent, R. Doyon, J. D. Rancourt
Thibaudeau, Thibaudeau, 12045 1st Ave., C. Thibaudeau, Q.C., B. Thibaudeau, Anne Thibaudeau

ST-GEORGES WEST, Dist. Beauce
Morin & Roy, M. Morin, J. Roy
Turcotte & Begin, J.R. Turcotte, L. Begin

ST. GERTRUDE, Dist. Trois-Rivieres
Villeneuve, J., 7165 Industrial Park Blvd.

ST. HYACINTHE, Dist. St. Hyacinthe
Beaudoin, J.-R., 900 Hotel de Ville
Bousquet & Bousquet, 755 du Palais St.,

F. Bousquet, J.P. Bousquet, C. Gourdeau
Brodeur, J., 515 St. Denis St.
Brodeur, L., 1555 Girouard St.
LaBrie, H. P., 515 St. Denis St.
Locas, Boileau & Boucher, 1555 Girouard St., J.P. Boileau, R. Boucher, G. Locas
Poirier, Diane, 955 Palais St.
Pothier, J., 1653 Girouard St. w.
Senecal, J. P., 515 St. Denis St.
Sylvestre & Matte, 1600 Girouard St., J. Sylvestre, B. Matte

ST. JEAN, Dist. Iberville
Beaudry, J., 266 Champlain
Boulais, L., 439 Blvd. du Seminaire
Cartier, J., 215 Jacques-Cartier St.
Demers, M., 26 St. Jacques St.
Denault, C., 209 Richelieu St.
Dureault, Bowlerice & Dupuis, 525 Blvd. du Seminaire, P. Dureault, G. Bowlerice, D. Dupuis
Fournier & Meunier, 232 Longueuil St., G. Fournier, A. Meunier
Gregoire & Gravel, G. Gregoire, A. Gravel
Lanteigne, R., 123 St. Jacques St.
Lauzon, C., 160 Longueuil St.
Lorrain, P., 170 Longueuil St.
Mercier, P. E., 62 St. Jacques St.
Rancourt, J., 123 St. Jacques St.
Rivest, P., 192 Richelieu St.
Tremblay, Roy, Bedard & Massignani, 112 St. Jacques St., R. Tremblay, Q.C., L. Roy, M. Bedard, E. Massignani
Trudeau, C., 123 St. Jacques St.

ST. JEROME, Dist. Terrebonne
Auclair, G., 444 Labelle St.
Beaudoin, F., 60 de Martigny w.
Boismenu, R., 48 de Martigny w.
Boivin, Fortin & Gaudreau, 85 de Martigny w., D. Fortin
Boucher, Marc, 300, rue Labelle
de Martigny, C. L., Q.C., 440 du Palais
Filfe, Paquin, Filion, Larue & Laferriere, 316 St. Georges St., J. Y. Filfe, M. Paquin, A. Filion, J. Larue, J. Laferriere
Forget, Rochon, Prevost & Auclair, 85 de Martigny w., A. Forget, A. Rochon, A. Prevost, C. Auclair, Ginette Galipeau, J. Marquis
Guerin, J., Q.C., 444 Labelle St.
Levac & Cotte-Levac, 450 Laviolette St., J.M. Levac, L.-A. Cotte-Levac, S. Lepage
Lord, Lalonde, Goupil, Gendron & Riendeau, 450 Laviolette St., R. Lord, C. Lalonde, M.F. Goupil, R. Gendron, N. Riendeau
Marchand, J.C., Q.C., 501 du Palais
Morin, Perras & Bergevin, 60 de Martigny w., R. Morin, R. Perras, M. Bergevin, P. Morin, C. Castonguay
Piche, Diane, 227 St. Georges
Racicot & Richard, 336 Labelle St., G. Racicot, P. Richard
Ross & Geraghty, 480 St. Georges St., G. Ross, D. Geraghty
Roy, G., 450 Laviolette St.
Simard, Simard & Boucher, 300 Labelle St., M. A. Simard, P. Simard, J. Boucher

ST. JOSEPH DE BEAUCE, Dist. Beauce
Cliche & Laflamme, rue Verreault, P. Laflamme, Richard Cliche, Diane Loubier
Cliche, Cloutier & Labbe, Ave. du Palais, N. Cliche, G. Cloutier, H. Labbe
Giroux & Couture, 808 Ave. du Palais, M. Giroux, H. Couture
Poulin, C., 849 Ave. du Palais

ST. JOVITE, Dist. Terrebonne
Paquin & Paquin, 972 Ouimet (also Ste. Agathe)

ST. LAMBERT, Dist. Montreal
Dureault, G. H., Q.C., 333 Riverside Dr.

STE MARIE, Dist. Beauce
Ferland & Ferland, C.P. 665, L.-C. Ferland. Counsel: L.-A. Ferland, Q.C.
Sylvain, Parent, Gobeil & Assoc., C.P. 40, D. Sylvain, J. G. Parent, G. Gobeil

ST. PROSPER (DORCHESTER), Dist. Beauce
Sylvain, M.

ST. ROMUALD D'ETCHEMIN, Dist. Quebec
Dorval & Rancourt, 10 de l'Eglise, M. Dorval, P. Rancourt

ST. SAUVEUR DES MONTS, Dist. Terrebonne
Boivin, Fortin & Gaudreau, 216 Principale (also Montreal)

STE SOPHIE DE LEVRARD, Dist. Trois-Rivieres
Mayrand, A., Rg. St. Antoine

STE THERESE DE BLAINVILLE, Dist. Terrebonne
Deziel, Brazeau & Gregoire, 8 Roux, M. Deziel, G. Brazeau, A. Gregoire
Dorais, Lamontagne, Teasdale & Dorais, 33 Blainville w., B. Dorais, J. Lamontagne, C.R., P. Teasdale, Danielle Dorais
Duquette & Beauchamp, 21 St. Charles St., J.-P. Duquette, G. Beauchamp
Hotte, A., 39 Turgeon St.
Lamarre, Marguerite, 821 Carre Hotte
Morrisette, J.M., 19 St. Charles
Royal, D., 212 Labelle
Vachon, J., 36 Turgeon St.
Vadeboncoeur, P.G., 39 Turgeon

SENNETERRE, Dist. Abitibi
Bolduc, P.

SEPT-ILES, Dist. Mingan
Blanchette, Lapointe & Boissoneault, 106 Napoleon St., G. Blanchette, P. Lapointe, P. Boissoneault
Caron, Bergeron & Lefort, B. Bergeron, J.-Y. Caron, P. Lefort
De Pokomandy, Besnier & Parvu, 865 Laure Blvd., G. De Pokomandy, H. Besnier, A. Parvu
Desrosiers & Boucher, 500 Brochu Ave., C. H. Desrosiers, R. Boucher
Dionne, Gauthier, Belanger & Nepveu, 690 Laure St., J. Dionne, A. Gauthier, P. Belanger, R. Nepveu
Landry & Lemieux, 390 Brochu Ave., F. Landry, B. Lemieux
Lemieux, R., Plage Routhier
Pettigrew & Simard, 439 Brochu Ave., G. Pettigrew, Q.C., C. Simard
Roy & Gauthier, 350 Smith St., M. Roy, R. Gauthier

SHAWINIGAN, Dist. St. Maurice
Deschenes, Pronovost & Garceau, 772 5th St., P. Deschenes, R.W. Pronovost, Y. Garceau
Germain & Marchand, 637 5th St., G. Germain, F. Marchand
Grenier, Leclerc & Goulet, 794 5th St., R. Grenier, R. Leclerc, C. Goulet
Poudrier, R., 2425 5th St., Shawinigan South
Sanschagrin, J. L., 559 5th st.
Trudel, Dugre & Giroux, 228 7th St., C. Trudel, P. Dugre, M. Giroux

SHERBROOKE, Dist. St. Francois
Beauchamp, C., 111 King St. w.
Beauchemin & Dussault, 108 Wellington St. n., M. Beauchemin, M. Dussault
Belanger, R.R., 18 Wellington St. n.
Boily, Fontaine, Panneton & Pelletier, 32 Wellington St. n., P. Boily, G. Fontaine, L. Panneton, L. Pelletier
Boudreau, G., 92 Wellington St. n.
Bourque, R., 111 King St. w.
Chapdelaine, G., 67 King St. w.
Denis, A., 18 Wellington St. n.
Desmarais & Pariseau, 108 Wellington St. n., G. E. Desmarais, M. Pariseau
Desy & Houle, 1040 King St. w., A. Desy, Helene Houle
Dube, G., 144 Wellington St. n.
Durand & Daigle, 234 Dufferin St., V.M. Durand, L. Daigle, P. Proulx, P. Lessard
Fournier, Demers, Barnard & Assoc., #200, 165 Wellington St. n., P.C. Fournier, J.L. Demers, F. Barnard, M. Bureau, M. Lacroix, L. Borduas, Roseline Alric, Jovette Letourneau. Counsel: J. Fournier, Q.C., C. Leblanc, Q.C.
Frechette, Blanchette, Gobeil & Gaudette, 13 Wellington St. n., R. Frechette, J. Blanchette, G.A. Gobeil, J. Gaudette
Geoffroy & Geoffroy, #4, 204 Wellington St. n., P.G. Geoffroy, J.G. Geoffroy
Gerin, Rancourt & Lavallee, 144 Wellington St. n., F. Gerin, J.P. Rancourt, D. Lavallee
Girard, Soucy & Allard, 32 Wellington St. n., M.-A. Girard, M.-A. Soucy, Micheline Allard, J. Bellehumeur
Grenier, Bessette, Martel, O'Bready & Guerin, 25 Wellington St. n., G. Grenier, M. Bessette, M.-A. Martel, J. O'-Bready, D. Guerin
Hackett, Campbell, Turner, Bissonnette & Bouchard, 80 Peel St., J.E. Hackett, D.B. Campbell, D. Bissonnette, C.P. Turner, P. Bouchard, M. Despres, Jacqueline Kouri
Hebert, Marcheterre, 25 Wellington St. n., D. Hebert, R. Marcheterre, J. Trudel
Huard & Bureau, Box 187, P. Huard, P. Bureau, Johanne Lafleur
Joncas, M., 25 Wellington St. n.
Labrecque & Germain, 117 Wellington St. n., G. Labrecque, P. Germain. Counsel: C. Lemieux
Lafrance & Letourneau, 31 King St. w., G. Lafrance, M. Letourneau
Lamoureux, R., 520 Bowen St. s.
Leblond, Montplaisir & Chapdelaine, #310, 234 Dufferin St., C. Leblond, M. Montplaisir, C. Chapdelaine
Lemieux, J. P., 1585 Desnoyers
Messier, Y., 18 Wellington St. n.
Monty, Coulombe, Pepin, Fecteau, Fournier, Gilbert, Landry & Assoc., 234 Dufferin St., R. Monty, G. Coulombe, R. Fecteau, B. Gilbert, H. Pepin, R.A. Fournier, G.R. Landry, P.-M. Bellevance, J.-M. Fortin, R. Veilleux, D.L. Blouin, C. Labonte, Helene Simoneau, A. Gauthier, S. Dubois. Counsel: A. Langlais, Q.C., W.H. Bradley, Q.C.
Nadeau, A., Q.C., 111 King St. w.
Nadeau, C., 205 Continental Bldg.
Richer & Deschenes, 138 Wellington St. n., G. Richer, P. Deschenes, M. St. Cyr
Scott, Cote & Laskin, 7 Camirand St., L.R. Scott, Danielle Cote, R. Laskin
Steinman, S., 111 King St. w.
Zaor, Boutin, Gauthier, 25 Wellington St. n., D. Zaor, J. C. Boutin, M. Gauthier

SOREL, Dist. Richelieu
Ally & Ally, 53 Georges St., P. E. Ally, Q.C., R. Ally
Forcier, Fournier & Boucher, 75 George St., L. A. Forcier, J. Fournier, B. Boucher
Gauthier, Frappier, 26 Place d'Entraide, G. Gauthier, Q.C., J. Frappier, C. Crevier
Guertin, J., 26 Place d'Entraide
Lavallee, G., 50B Hotel-Dieu

Lepage, Dupuis, 96 George St., Carole Lepage, Monique Dupuis
Martin, C., 79 Prince St.
Poupart, L., 37 George St.
Quintal, R., 50B Hotel-Dieu
Verrier, J., 56 Charlotte St.

TERREBONNE, Dist. Terrebonne
Lallier, Marthe, 1238 Hall St.
Laurence & Assoc., 455 boul. des Seigneurs, J.R. Laurence, A. Marcoux

THETFORD MINES, Dist. Frontenac
Beaudoin, Antonio, Q.C., 95 Notre Dame St. n.
Bergeron, M., 238 Notre Dame St. s.
Ferron, J., 189 Notre Dame St. s. (K. Binette)
Paradis, Chabot & Paquet, 257 Notre Dame St. s., P. Paradis, J.-C. Chabot, M. Paquet
Roy, Lefebvre & Gosselin, 179 Notre Dame St. s., R. Roy, R. Lefebvre, N. Gosselin
Setlawke, R. C., 188 Notre Dame St. s.
Warren & Ouellet, 14 Dumais St. e., M. Warren, G. Ouellet

TRACY, Dist. Richelieu
Roussel, M., 2225 St. Louis Blvd.

TROIS RIVIERES, Dist. Trois Rivieres
Beaumier, Richard, Normand & St. Pierre, 90 des Casernes, M.J.G. Beaumier, M. Richard, J. Normand, M. St. Pierre, P.H. Vincent, R. Desormeaux
Biron & Spain, 154 Radisson St., M. Biron, P. Spain
Boisvert & Mayrand, 167 Laviolette St., M. Boisvert, L. Mayrand
Bourbeau, M., 1117 Ste-Louise
Chartier, M., 197 Bonaventure St.
Chorel, G., 118 Radisson St.
Comeau, L., Q.C., 849 des Ursulines
Cossette, J.-P., 250 Laviolette St.
Dessureault, J., 1481 Notre Dame St.
Godin & St. Amant, 190 Bonaventure St., D.P. Godin, P. St. Amant
Godin, Lacoursiere & Girard, 1185 Hart St., I. Godin, G. Lacoursiere, L. Girard. Counsel: J. L. Marchand, Q.C.
Heroux, G., 795 des Plaines
Huard, R. P., 118 Radisson St.
Lajoie, Desaulniers, Lajoie, 940 Notre Dame, R. Lajoie, Q.C., J. Desaulniers, F. Lajoie, B. Heon
Legris, Legris & Michaud, 282 Radisson St., Real Legris, Q.C., Robert Legris, M. Michaud
Lupien, M., 144 Bonaventure St.
Marchildon, Joseph, Q.C., 1001 Laviolette St.
Rioux & Rioux, 1240 Royale St., R. Rioux, J. Rioux
Roberge, R., 220 Dunant St.
Tremblay, P., 4340 Barthe St.

VAL D'OR, Dist. Abitibi
Cliche & Cliche, 1121 6th St., Normand Cliche, Georges Cliche, Nicole Cliche, A. Lortie, Lucien Cliche, Jr. Counsel: Hon. Lucien Cliche, Q.C., J. Deslauriers
Courtemanche & Cossette, H. Courtemanche, Q.C., C. Cossette
Dufour, France, 760 3rd Ave.
Frignon, J., 888 3rd Ave.
Provost, J., 888 3rd Ave.
St. Julien, Tessier & Assoc., 855 3rd Ave., I. St. Julien, G. Tessier, J. R. Beaulieu, D. Petitclerc, R. Lapointe, G. Reny, J. McGuire, G. Bruno, L. Cossette

VALLEYFIELD, Dist. Beauharnois
Barrette, C., 39 Jacques Cartier St.
Blanchard, Vinet & Plante, 70 Nicholson St., C. Blanchard, J. Vinet, J.-C. Plante, M. Bourbonnais
Cosette, J. P., 52 chemin Larocque
Daoust, A., 110 Ch. Larocque
Demers, C., 59 Jacques Cartier St.
Hebert, Lafontaine & Mercier, 139 Salaberry, G. Hebert, R. Lafontaine, M. Mercier, P.E. L'Ecuyer
Lafontaine, R., 50 Jacques Cartier St.
Lecompte & LaGarde, 50 Jacques Cartier St., M. Lecompte, M. LaGarde (also Beauharnois)
Lemieux, Lemieux & Lamarche, 23 Ste. Helene, A. Lemieux, P. Lemieux, G. Lamarche
Morin, R., 39 rue Jacques Cartier
Perron, Odette, 47 Jacques Cartier St.
Renaud, F., 47 Jacques Cartier St.
Vachon & Martin, 83 St. Jean Baptiste, F. Vachon, C. Martin
Villeneuve, M.-A., 19 du Marche

VARENNES, Dist. Richelieu
Chicoine & Belanger, 2082 Marie Victorin, C.H. Chicoine, Dominique Belanger

VAUDREUIL, Dist. Beauharnois
Asselin, Cadieux, Cadieux & Chartrand, 415 Roche Blvd., P. Cadieux, L. Chartrand (also Montreal)

VERDUN, Dist. Montreal
Cadieux, G., 5035 Verdun Ave.
Cohen, R.N., 3988 Wellington St.
Phillips, F. R., 4080 Wellington St.
Rudinskas, V.E., 4701 Bannatyne St.

VICTORIAVILLE, Dist. Arthabaska
Dallaire, Lavigne & Vallieres, 100 Notre Dame St. e., J. C. Dallaire, D. Lavigne, C. Vallieres
Denault, Allard, Dubois, Caron, 120 Notre Dame est, P. Denault, Le Batonnier J. Allard, J.-G. Dubois, C. Caron
Provencher, Provencher & Comtois, 42 Carignan Blvd., J. L. Provencher, J. G. Provencher, C. Comtois

VILLE-MARIE, Dist. Temiscamingue
Frigon & Gagnon (also Amos)
Grimard & Co. (also Rouyn)

WAKEFIELD, Hull
St-Laurent & Ouellet, 174 River Rd., J.R. Ouellet, P.L. St-Laurent

WARWICK, Dist. Arthabaska
Gagnon & St. Pierre, 5 rue St-Joseph (C.P.307), J. Gagnon, B. St. Pierre

WATERLOO, Dist. Bedford
Jolin, L., Q.C., 417 Court St. (City Hall)
Lafrenaye-Bedard, A., 4784 Foster St.

BARRISTERS AND SOLICITORS IN SASKATCHEWAN

ALAMEDA, Estevan
Wartman, G.D., Box 176

ALLAN, Saskatoon
Averbach, G. (also Saskatoon)

ARBORFIELD, Melfort
Taylor & Fitzpatrick (also Nipawin)

ARCOLA, Estevan
Hill, McLellan & Co. (also Estevan)

ASSINIBOIA, Assiniboia
Leslie & Marlin (also Regina)
Lewans & Assoc., P.J. Lewans
MacDonald-Mountain Law Firm, Box 459, T.V. Mountain. Counsel: R.E. MacDonald, Lynn MacDonald

BATTLEFORD, *See* North Battleford

BENGOUGH, Assiniboia
MacDonald-Mountain (also Assiniboia)

BIGGAR, Kerrobert
Busse, S. A., 302 Main St.

BIRCH HILLS, Prince Albert
Eggum, Abrametz & Co. (also Prince Albert)

BLAINE LAKE, Saskatoon
Averbach, G. (also Saskatoon)

BROADVIEW, Melville
Moore, G. G., Box 610

CANORA, Yorkton
Kyba, S.G. (also Yorkton)
Matsalla, L.A. (also Melville)
Ozirny & Co. (also Melville & Yorkton)
Seidle, A.L.W., Box 309

CARLYLE, Estevan
Hill, McLellan & Co. (also Estevan)

CARNDUFF, Estevan
Hill, McLellan & Co. (also Estevan)
Ignatiuk & Tessem (also Estevan)

CARROT RIVER, Melfort
Taylor & Fitzpatrick (also Nipawin)

CUT KNIFE, Battleford
Sallows, Osborn & Co. (also N. Battleford)

DAVIDSON, Saskatoon
Coxworth & Ulmer, J.I. Ulmer

DODSLAND, Kerrobert
MacDermid & Co. (also Saskatoon)

EASTEND, Shaunavon
Wilson, MacBean etc. (also Swift Current)

EATONIA, Kerrobert
Chinn, T.S. (also Kindersley)

ELROSE, Kerrobert
Chinn, T.S. (also Kindersley)

ESTERHAZY, Melville
Mackenzie & Mackenzie, 465 Main St., D. A. Mackenzie, Q.C., D. K. Mackenzie
Ozirny & Co. (also Melville)

ESTEVAN, Estevan
Hill, McLellan, Ball, Cundall & Bridges, Drawer 609, G. D. Hill, G. P. McLellan, D.P. Ball, L.V. Cundall,. B.D. Bridges, G.A. Chicoine
Ignatiuk & Tessem, Box 460, D. Ignatiuk, G.F. Tessem
Kohaly & Elash, Drawer 580, R. Kohaly, Q.C., P.D. Elash, R.M. Peet
Komarnicki Law Firm, Drawer 725, E.A. Komarnicki, P.A. Bishoff

ESTON, Kerrobert
Caskey, R. J., Box 399

FOAM LAKE, Wynyard
Paulson, W. (also Wynyard)

FORT QU'APPELLE, Regina
Hall, W.

FRONTIER, Shaunavon
Wilson, MacBean & Co. (also Swift Current)

GLASLYN, Battleford
Shury, Migneault & Co. (also North Battleford)

GRAVELBOURG, Gravelbourg
Dauphinais, G.J., Box 480
Stringer, L. E.

GRENFELL, Melville
Rendek, Toews (also Regina)

GULL LAKE, Swift Current
Weston, Marlene, Box 518
Wilson & Co. (also Swift Current)

HAFFORD, Battleford
Maher & Lindgren (also North Battleford)

HERBERT, Swift Current
Krueger, McLaughlin & Co. (also Swift Current)

HODGEVILLE, Gravelbourg
Bader, R.G. (also Swift Current)

HUDSON BAY, Melfort
Price Jones, R. (also Melfort)

HUMBOLDT, Humboldt
Holt, Munkler & Halderman, 607 9th St., D.F. Holt, R.A. Munkler, B.D. Halderman
Sutherland, Behiel & Scott, 623 7th St., S.M. Sutherland, B. Behiel, Marilyn M. Scott
Weninger, E., 816 7th Ave.

IMPERIAL, Humboldt
Shirkey & Shirkey (also Regina)

INDIAN HEAD, Regina
Toews Kaufman (also Regina)

KAMSACK, Yorkton
Rosowsky & Campbell, 445 Second St., O. Rosowsky, T.P. Campbell

KELVINGTON, Wynyard
Koch, Bertram & Co. (also Regina)

KERROBERT, Kerrobert
Chinn, T.S. (also Kindersley)

KINDERSLEY, Kerrobert
Chinn, T.S., 111 1st Ave. w.
Gares, B. L., Drawer 1567
Roberts & Setrakov, Box 1510, D.J. Roberts, Q.C., Judith Setrakov

KINISTINO, Melfort
Dokken & Eberle (also Melfort)

KIPLING, Weyburn
Komarnicki & Co. (also Estevan)

KYLE, Swift Current
Wilson & Co. (also Swift Current)

LAFLECHE, Assiniboia
Lewans & Assoc. (also Assiniboia)

LANGENBURG, Yorkton
Wentzell, M. D. (also Yorkton)

LANGHAM, Saskatoon
Gold & Stockan, I. H. Stockan, Q.C.

LANIGAN, Humboldt
Averback, G. (also Saskatoon)
Holt, Munkler & Co. (also Humboldt)

LA RONGE, Prince Albert
Eggum, Abrametz & Co. (also Prince Albert)

LEADER, Swift Current
Schmidt, J. M., Box 189

LIPTON, Regina
Halford, N. (also Regina)

LLOYDMINSTER, Battleford
(*see* Alberta)

LOREBURN, Saskatoon
Baker, W. A.

MAIDSTONE, Battleford
Maher, Lindgren & Co. (also North Battleford)
Sallows, Osborn & Co. (also North Battleford)

MAPLE CREEK, Swift Current
Kosolofski, J. C.
Krueger, McLaughlin & Co. (also Swift Current)
Orr, W. R.
Wilson, MacBean & Co. (also Swift Current)

MEADOW LAKE, Battleford
Cariou, Partyka & Francis, 306 Centre St., R.G. Cariou, B.J. Partyka, L. Francis
Kuebler, F. G.
Lamontagne, D., 118 Centre St.

MELFORT, Melfort
Carson & Co., 803 Main St., G. Carson, J.A. Louis, R. Smith
Dokken, Eberle & Annand, 204 Main St., M.H. Dokken, Q.C., D.R. Eberle, M.R. Annand
Eisner & Eisner, Box 238, J. Eisner, Q.C., S. Eisner
Kapoor & Selnes, Box 2200, A. Kapoor, W.A. Selnes
Price Jones, R., 108 Burrows Ave. w.

MELVILLE, Melville
Hillson, J.D., Box 2200
Mattsala, L.A., Box 2620
Ozirny, Wrubell, Fisher & Tourney, Cameo Block, C.M. Ozirny, R.C. Wrubell, M.K. Fisher, B.W. Tourney, A.C. Hjelte, R.C.A. Neville
Rathgeber & Schmidt, 131 3rd Ave. e., R.A. Rathgeber, G. J. Schmidt

MILESTONE, Regina
Murphy, B.F. (also Regina)

MOOSE JAW, Moose Jaw
Chow, Ocrane, Walper & Assoc., 133 Ominica St. w., K.R. Chow, T.W. Ocrane, B.A. Walper. Assoc. Counsel: W.G. Gardner, Q.C.
Craik, Curran & Hagan, 54 Ominica St. w., B.R. Craik, L.W. Curran, R.G. Hagan
Dickinson, R.A., Q.C., & Assoc., 414 Hammond Bldg., R. A. Dickinson, Q.C., J.C. Zimmer
Dubinsky, B., Q.C., 314 Hammond Bldg.
Falconer, B.G., 54 Stadacona St. w.
Grayson, Rushford, Cooper, Nidesh & Arendt, 350 Langdon Cres., R.J. Rushford, J.D. Cooper, M.W. Nidesh, R.L. Arendt
Whittaker, Acton, Wheatley & Beck, 69 High St. w., M. D. Acton, C. B. Wheatley, D.K. Beck

MOOSOMIN, Moosomin
Goliath & Osman, W. V. Goliath, D. J. Osman

MORSE, Swift Current
Krueger, McLaughlin & Co. (also Swift Current)

NAICAM, Humboldt
Dokken & Eberle (also Melfort)

NIPAWIN, Melfort
Eremko, J., Q.C., Box 250 (D.J. Eremko)
Taylor & Fitzpatrick, Box 850, J.W.R. Taylor, B.M. Fitzpatrick
Treleaven & Treleaven, 116 1st Ave. e., R.G. Treleaven, G. A. Treleaven

NOKOMIS,
Averbach, G. (also Saskatoon)

NORTH BATTLEFORD, Battleford
Cameron, White & Lawrence, 1161 99 St., D.A. Cameron, T.W. White, J. Lawrence
Cawood-Walker, Box 905, H.G. Walker, R.G. Cawood, D.F. Woloshyn, S.J. Demmans, Sandra Kochan
Conroy, D. D., 1062 100th St. (Susan J. Campbell)
Dahlem & Frank, 1281 100th St., H.H. Dahlem, I.S. Frank
Lojek, J., 1102 103 St. (L. Jones)
Maher, Lindgren & Blais, 1301 101 St., R. D. Maher, E.B. Lindgren, R.J. Blais, S. Bartlett
Millar, N. F., 1641 100th St.
Sallows, Osborn & Wilhelm, 1391 101st St., A. F. Sallows, Q.C., H.A. Osborn, Q.C., D.A. Wilhelm, Q.C., M.E. Greenwood
Shury, Migneault & Miller, 1371 100th St., D.W. Shury, K. Migneault, J.S. Miller

OUTLOOK, Saskatoon
Clark, C.J., Box 1040

OXBOW, Estevan
Hill, McLellan & Co. (also Estevan)

PONTEIX, Gravelbourg
Dauphinais & Brown (also Gravelbourg)
Krueger, McLaughlin & Co. (also Swift Current)
Stringer, L. (also Gravelbourg)

PREECEVILLE, Yorkton
Rosowsky & Campbell (also Kamsack)

PRINCE ALBERT, Prince Albert
Agnew, T.D., 220 Mitchell Block (D.H.J. Welsh)
Balon, G., 4050 2nd Ave. w.
Bekolay, Maksymiuk & Meekma, 1002 1st Ave. w., T.B. Bekolay, J.P. Maksymiuk, V.H. Meekma
Carson, Siwak, 1109 Central Ave., I.B. Carson, H.L. Siwak
Cherkewich, Pinel & Bockus, 1005 Central Ave., R. Cherkewich, L. Pinel, P. Bockus
Chetty, P.C., 12th St. & 1st Ave. e.
Dutchak, Balicki & Co., #201, 29 11th St. e., S. Dutchak, L. Balicki, J. Kernaghan
Dynna, D.M., 118 12th St. e.
Eggum, Abrametz & Mills, 100 Royal Bank Bldg., K. Eggum, P. V. Abrametz, R.J. Mills, J.S. Wytosky, L.W. Zuk
Harradence, Longworth & Zatlyn, 1102 1st Ave. w., J.H.C. Harradence, Q.C., V.J. Longworth, Q.C., L.J. Zatlyn, R.J. Lane, G.J. Moran, D.E. Winsor
Kirkby, G. W., 100, 48 12th St. e.
Loewen, S.D., 3300 2nd Ave. w.
Pereverzoff, M. A., 107 Tadman Bldg.
Pradzynski, R.E., 110 11th St. e.
Sanderson & Wilkinson, 27 11th St. w., J.H.W. Sanderson, Q.C., Ysanne Wilkinson
Simonot, Hansen & Co., 101 Professional Bldg., M. Simonot, S. Hansen, Barbara Cram

RADISSON, Saskatoon
Gold, Stockan & Co. (also Langham)

RADVILLE, Weyburn
MacDonald Law Firm, Drawer 24 (also Weyburn)
Wilson, Drummond & Co. (also Regina)

REDVERS, Moosomin
Goliath & Osman (also Moosomin)
Komarnicki, E.A. (also Estevan)

REGINA, Regina
Alexander, Kruzeniski, Goudie & McLaren, 2207 Smith St., R.J. Kruzeniski, A.J. Goudie, H.D. McLaren. Assoc.: F.J. Flynn
Andrews & Gordon, D.W. Andrews, M. Gordon, J. McMahon, D.C. Knoll
Armstrong, Gritzfeld, Embury, #305, McCallum-Hill Bldg., G.H.M. Armstrong, Q.C., E.R. Gritzfeld, Q.C., J.M. Embury,

J.R.B. Hobbs, I.T. Tulloch, Sheila Johnson
Avrum Law Office, 2124 Broad St., L. Avrum
Balfour, Moss, Milliken, Laschuk, Kyle, Vancise, 1850 Cornwall St., E.J. Moss, Q.C., Hon. R.J. Balfour, Q.C., R.A. Milliken, Q.C., R.B. Laschuk, Q.C., L.A. Kyle, W.J. Vancise, Q.C., F.C. McBeth, B.J. Scherman, D.E.W. McIntyre, Barbara Shourounis, J.L. Garvie, J.T. Lyon, L. Softley, D.R. Doan
Barr, R.M., Q.C., #204, 1771 Rose St.
City Solicitors, T.A. Leier, L. Shaw, E. Morrison
Davidson & Co., 2230 Lorne St., J. R. Davidson, Q.C., L.A. Kirk
de la Gorgendiere, Randall, Pederson, Pinch & Turnbull, 1960 Albert St., M. de la Gorgendiere, C.H. Randall, W. Pederson, Bonnie Donlevy, G.J. Pinch, W. Turnbull, D. Jahnke, Charlen Werry (also Saskatoon)
Duncan, P.A., 2343 Broad St.
Findlay & Neufeld, #2, 1540 Albert St., D.J. Findlay, E.J. Neufeld
Gates & Herle, 452 Albert St. n., R.G. Gates, W.J. Herle
Gerrand, McLellan & Mulatz, #201, 1822 Scarth St., G.L. Gerrand, Q.C., I.D. McLellan, M.F. Mulatz, D.A. Gerrand, F.H.L. Chad Smith, J.M. Hall
Graf, Zarzeczny, Linka & LePage, 2132 Broad St., T.G. Graf, T.C. Zarzeczny, Jr., R.W. Linka, R.J.F. LePage
Griffin, Beke & Thorson, #300, 2220 12th Ave., J.A. Griffin, Q.C., A. J. Beke, Q.C., Kim Thorson, Q.C., R.K. Ottenbreit, W.D. Baldwin, A.J. Koschinsky, D.J. Maddigan, T.R. Strutt, M.L.E. Schoenfeld
Halford, N., 2131 Broad St.
Hleck, Kanuka, Thuringer, Semenchuck, Sandomirsky, Boyd & Baker, #1500, 2500 Victoria Ave. (S4P 3X2), P. Hleck, Q.C., J. W. Kanuka, Q.C., P. E. Thuringer, G.G.W. Semenchuck, N. S. Sandomirsky, K. D. Boyd, R. J. Baker, L.J. Yakimowski, Carol-Anne Cockburn, J. Elizabeth Sargeant, M.H. Gabruch, K.D. Skilnick, P.H.A. Korpan, J.S. Ehmann. Assoc. Counsel: R. L. Pierce, Q.C.
Husk, Elaine, 2269 Hamilton St.
Jakeman, A. H., 2036 St. John St.
Jameson Law Office, 2062 Cornwall St., J.A. Jameson, Q.C., H.B. Wellsch
Koch, Bertram, Scrivens & Prior, 2002 Victoria Ave., J.D. Koch, R. H. Bertram, D. M. Scrivens, K.W. Prior, Coralie Geving, J.R. Hoffart
Kraus & McKay, 2031 Albert St., G.M. Kraus, I.D. McKay
Kuziak & Gray, 1872 Angus St., M.A. Kuziak, G.J. Gray
Lane & Whitmore Law Offices, 2100 Smith St., J.G. Lane, P.A. Whitmore, D.D. Kowalishen
Laurin Law Office, #106B, 5875 Rochdale Blvd., L.R. Laurin
Leslie & Marlin, 2002 Victoria Ave., L.E. Leslie, G.B. Marlin
MacKay & McLean, 2144 Cornwall St., D.G. MacKay, S.G. McLean
MacLean, Keith, McDonald & Love, 2398 Scarth St., D.A.K. MacLean, R.L. Keith, P.N. McDonald, K.G. Love, S.J. Arsenych, W.T. Stodalka. Counsel: D.M. Keith, Q.C.
MacPherson, Leslie & Tyerman, 2161 Scarth St. (S4P 2V4), W. M. Elliott, Q.C., D. K. MacPherson, Q.C., S. A. Arsenych, W. R. Matheson, Q.C., R. L. Barclay, Q.C., H.H. MacKay, Q.C., J. Klebuc, C.A.P. Wagner, Marjorie A. Gerwing, R. B. Pletch, A. R. Garden, F.J. Kovach, M.O. Laprairie, D.K. Wilson, L.B. LeBlanc, J.T. Nilson, Janis D. Busse, R.N. MacKay, Darla Hunter, G.R. Baudais, W.D. Mulholland, L.D. Andrychuk, G.D. Crossman. Counsel: D.M. Tyerman, Q.C.
McDougall, Ready, Wakeling, 2010 11th Ave., W.F. Ready, Q.C., T.C. Wakeling, Q.C., E. Youck, G. J. Kuski, R.N. Millar, L.A. Smith, R.S. Smith, K.A. Ready, L.M. Schwann, M.W. Milani. Counsel: J.L. McDougall, Q.C.
Morgan, Khaladkar & Skinner, 2220 Albert St., L. Morgan, V. Khaladkar, R.D. Skinner, M. Pappas
Murphy, B.F., 1919 Rose St.
Naylen, Morris & Bourassa, #200, 1919 Rose St., G.E. Naylen, R.B. Morris, J.P. Bourassa, R.B. Braun, M.F. Martinez
Neill Law Office, #568, 2020 11th Ave., G.J.K. Neill, S.C. Amrud
Noble, K.W., 454 McCarthy Blvd. n. (K.J. Karwandy)
Olive, Waller, Zinkhan & Waller, 2255 13th Ave., W.H. Olive, T.J. Waller, F.C. Zinkhan, W.R. Waller, D.G. Schindel, A. Kirsten Logan, R.E. Langgard
Pedersen, Norman, McLeod & Todd, 403, 2045 Broad St., C. L. Pedersen, Q.C., S.J. Norman, Q.C., D. G. McLeod, Q.C., D. A. Todd, E. F. A. Merchant, C.G. Morris, W.R. Pelton, W. Schoenroth, G.W. Kinar, E. Lysyk, G.A. Swanson, Elaine Moser, R.T. Molaro
Rendek Toews Kaufman, 2042 Cornwall St., R.P. Rendek, C.H. Toews, N.A. Kaufman, H.H.G. Dahlem, R.D. McCrank, P.W. Glendinning, D.A. Halvorsen, D.A. Canham, J.G. Garden, D.G. Orr, Anna Maria Crugnale-Reid. Counsel: J.J. Kerr, Q.C.
Robb, J.E., 2050 Scarth St.
Robinson, E. C., 2164 Smith St. (S4P 2P2)
Safian, S. J. & Associates, 200 Bank of Canada Bldg., S. J. Safian, Q.C.
Scheibel, Thompson, Rath & Oledzki, 1853 Hamilton St., E.A. Scheibel, R.J. Rath, G.J. Oledzki, F.W. Johnson
Segal, S.G., 2220 Albert St.
Shillington, N., 2343 Broad St.
Shirkey Law Firm, 1540, 2002 Victoria Ave., R.E. Shirkey, D.A. Shirkey, A.G. McIntyre
Shumiatcher, M.C., Q.C., 2100 Scarth St. (A.A. Fox, R.A. Watson, L.A. Kram, R.B. Hunter, J.A. McInnis)
Simard, R.M. Louise, 2343 Broad St.
Stewart, Harmel, Kelly & Martin, 1, 1945 Scarth St., E. B. Stewart, E. T. Harmel, Sharon A. Martin, P.A. Kelly
Thauberger, J.J., 1960 Albert St.
Tkach, G. J., 2500 13th Ave.
Trudelle, Sheppard, Beke & Singer, Guaranty Trust Bldg., 2020 11th Ave., P.G. Trudelle, W.J. Sheppard, A.P. Beke, B.E. Singer
Tufts, W.C., #11, 4601 Albert St.
Tulloch, N.J., #322, 845 Broad St.
Tyerman & Egan, #306, 2101 Scarth St., P.J.D. Tyerman, W.D. Egan
Walker, M. R., 1872 Angus St.
Wellman, Andrews, 1771 Rose St., W. R. Wellman, D.R. Andrews
Willows, Howe & Willows, #200, 806 Victoria Ave., W.A. Willows, W.R. Howe, G.G. Willows, W.T. Jennings
Wilson, Drummond, 1560 Avord Tower, G. Wilson, Q.C., G.J. Drummond, T.S. Quinlan

ROSETOWN, Kerrobert
Aseltine, M.G., 106 Main St.
Skelton & Spencer, Drawer 1120, D.R. Skelton, C.L. Spencer

ROSTHERN, Saskatoon
Simpson, R. M., Q.C., 601 1st Ave.

ST. BRIEUX
Dokken, Eberle & Co. (also Melfort)

SASKATOON, Saskatoon
Agnew, Nykyforuk, Purdy & Young, 279 3rd Ave. n., A.Q. Agnew, W. Nykyforuk, Q.C., W.B. Purdy, K.J. Young, W. Burianyk, J.A. Davis
Averback, G., 210 Birks Bldg., S7K 3K1
Balfour, Moss, Milliken, etc., #410, 22nd St. e. (also Regina)
Belsher, M.M.R.,
Bodnar & Wanhella, 812 Spadina Cres. e., M.P. Bodnar, G.P. Wanhella, G.C. Courtney
Burlingham & Co., 1043 8th St. e., E.R. Burlingham, A.F. McLeod, D.R. Morgan, D.A. Leland
Butschler, M.A., 115 20th St. w.
Cherneskey, M.T., #509, 105 21st St. e.
City Solicitors, City Hall, M.D. Irwin, H.G. Dirauf, D.D. Angene, R. McLeod, Theresa Dust, W.J. Davern
Crowe & Crowe, 812 Spadina Cres. e., G.E. Crowe, R.G. Crowe
Cuelenaere, Beaubier, Walters & Kendall, #302, 210 21st St. e., M. Cuelenaere, Q.C., D.W. Beaubier, Q.C., C.D. Walters, D.J. Kendall, N.B. Fisher
de la Gorgendiere, Randall, Pederson, Pinch & Turnbull, #300, 333 3rd Ave. n., M. de la Gorgendiere, C. H. Randall, W. Pederson, Bonnie Donlevy, G.J. Pinch, W.G. Turnbull, D.B. Jahnke, Charlen Werry (also Regina)
Dokken, Scharfstein & Co., #200, 241 2nd Ave. s., M.H. Dokken, Q.C., J.F. Scharfstein, G.J. Scharfstein
Ewing, Leila M., 1222 Elliott St.
Finley & Assoc., #501, 333 3rd Ave. n., R.G. Finley, T.G. Hymers, M. Brayford, Jane Rooney
Gauley & Co., #300, 701 Broadway, D.E. Gauley, Q.C., J.J.A. Dierker, H.H. Dahlem, Q.C., P. Foley, L. F. Seiferling, D. J. McKeague, W.J. Shaw, K. R. Robertson, J. R. Manning, R.G. Kennedy, R.M. Beaton, N.E. Hopkins, J.E. Seibel, D.K. Reid
Goldenberg, Taylor, Randall, Buckwold & Halstead, 301 Investors' Bldg., 402 21st St. e., J.M. Goldenberg, Q.C., G.J.D. Taylor, Q.C., Gwen K. Randall, Q.C., I. Buckwold, Bette Halstead, W.G. Craik, T.J. Koskie
Goldstein & Goldstein, #303, 728 Spadina Cres. e., B. Goldstein, Q.C., S. Goldstein, Q.C., R.D. Jackson, R.J. Gibbings
Halyk & Allbright, 500 Spadina Cres. e., S.E. Halyk, Q.C., G.N. Allbright
Haubrich & Borden, 309 Canada Bldg., A.M. Haubrich, R.L. Borden, Catherine M. Zuck
Hawrish & Hawrish, #605, 402 21st St. e., A. Hawrish, E.A. Hawrish, G.G. Walen, B.G. Miller
Henderson, Donlevy, Campbell & Loewen, 239 20th St. e., M.W. Henderson, W.R. Donlevy, W.J. Campbell, D.P. Loewen
Hnatyshyn, Sandstrom & Co., #601, 402 21st St. e., Hon. R.J. Hnatyshyn, P.C., Q.C., G.W. Sandstrom, V.M. Hnatyshyn, D.M. Hnatyshyn, W.B. Gough, K.W. Scott, Patricia Blacklock, D.A. Shapiro, D.W. McIver
Holizki & Houston, #201, 111 2nd Ave. s., T.A. Holizki, D.L. Houston
Huebert, A.J., 812 Spadina Cres. e.
Jamieson, Lavoie & Rourke, #801, 119 4th Ave. s., R.L. Jamieson, D.A. Lavoie,

B.J. Rourke, G.N. Bains, G.P. Molnar, Susan Mak
Kloppenburg & Kloppenburg, 220 3rd Ave. s., H.R. Kloppenburg, C.L. Kloppenburg, Penny Tallis
Lamarsh, Emigh, Preston & Carey, 200, 420 24th St., A.G. Lamarsh, Q.C., R.B. Emigh, W. Preston, B.P. Carey, K. Ziegler, D. G. Linn, T.E. Turple
MacDermid & Co., #905, 201 21st St. e., W.T. Molloy, C. J. W. Biss, P. J. Bitz, G.M. Chad, G.A. Zabos, W.N. Beckman, J.H. Gillis, G.J. Herman, W.F. Smith. Associate Counsel: F. F. MacDermid, Q.C.
MacPherson, Leslie & Tyerman, #200, 224 4th Ave. s. (also Regina)
Mah & Merry, 608 33rd St. w., B. Mah, J.T. Merry
Mathiason, Trach & Valkenburg, 106 Ross Block, A.W. Mathiason, L.F. Trach, B.C. Valkenburg
McCalla, W.C., 706 Trent Cres.
McCallum, G. M., 238 3rd Ave. s.
McKercher, McKercher, Stack, Korchin & Laing, 3rd fl., 374 3rd Ave. s. (S7K 1M5), D. S. McKercher, Q.C., R. H. McKercher, Q.C., J. A. Stack, L. J. Korchin, R. D. Laing, N. G. Gabrielson, B. W. Wilkinson, L. Larson, D.B. Richardson, J.R. Beckman, L.J.D. Batten, W.R. Rooke, P.J. Haidenger-Bains, B.W. Wirth, B.H. Rossmann, D. Dobni, J.D.D. Pelletier
Mitchell-Ching, #1003, 201 21st St. e., R.W. Mitchell, D.R. Ching, D.T. Kovatch, R.C. Touet, H.D. Mattison
Palynchuk, D. W., 414A Spadina Cres. e.
Partridge & Roe, #1110, 606 Spadina Cres. e., E.C. Partridge, W.H. Roe
Platzer, A., 316 6th Ave. n.
Plaxton & Wright, #202, 220 3rd Ave. s., D.S. Plaxton, J.L. Wright
Posner, G.S., 1801, 241 5th Ave. n. (also Kenora)
Priel, Stevenson, Hood & Thornton, 902 Spadina Cres. e., L.T. Priel, K.A. Stevenson, W.F.J. Hood, R.F. Thornton, Tamara Buckwold
Prosser Goldenberg, #308, 220 3rd Ave. s., L.W. Prosser, I. Goldenberg
Quon & Ferguson, #207, 115 2nd Ave. n., D.I. Quon, D. Ferguson
Rees, Newsham & Ansell, #303, 402 21st St. e., H. C. Rees, Q.C., D.S. Newsham, Q.C., Diane Ansell
Robertson, H.M.L., 201, 110 21st St. e. (A.M. Lees, D. Murrison)
Robertson, Muzyka, Bell, Robertson & Nieman, 311 20th St. e., J.L. Robertson, Q.C., G. Muzyka, Q.C., R. G. Bell, R.A. Robertson, T.J. Nieman, Kathryn Ford, C.P. Thagard, B.E. Salte, G.M. Currie. Associate Counsel: C. G. Schmitt, Q.C.
Schulman, Morrison, Boryski & Gall, 308 Birks Bldg., M. Schulman, J. H. Morrison, A. L. Boryski, R. G. Gall
Serne, McKenzie, Weir, Miller & Katzman, 1011B 8th St. e., W.J. Serne, G.D. McKenzie, S.F. Weir, D.B. Miller, R.K. Katzman
Sherstobitoff, Hrabinsky, Stromberg & Young, #300, 128 4th Ave. s., N.W. Sherstobitoff, Q.C., Paul Hrabinsky, Q.C., E. R. Stromberg, G.D. Young, K. Lucille Lamb, M.L. Riou, Martha Carter
Singer & Beckie, #409, 220 3rd Ave. s., B.M. Singer, S.D. Beckie, W.A. Wiegers
Sonnenschein, E., 313 20th St. e.
Soonias & Pennington, #A5, 116 103rd St., R. Soonias, R.A. Pennington
Stevenson, R.L., 109 Poplar Cres.
Surtees, L. A., #228, 220 3rd Ave. s.
Trunks, Lane & Leibel, #405, 128 4th Ave. s., M.T. Trunks, H.W. Lane, R.J. Leibel
Walker, Kaiser, Walker & Carter, #502, 224 4th Ave. s., R.A. Walker, Q.C., D.J. Kaiser, K.G. Walker, S.C. Carter
Windels, Chow, Manton & Beerling, #315, 220 3rd Ave. s., D. Windels, K.W. Chow, B. Manton, W. Beerling

SHAUNAVON, Shaunavon
Benison, J., 407 Centre St.
Dermody, D. J.

SHELLBROOK, Prince Albert
Bradley & Gibbons, Box 820, K.G. Bradley, R.A. Gibbons
Pereverzoff, M.A. (also Prince Albert)

SPIRITWOOD, Battleford
Sallows, Osborn & Co. (also North Battleford)

STOUGHTON, Weyburn
Komarnicki & Co. (also Estevan)

STRASBOURG, Regina
Hleck, Kanuka & Co. (N.S. Sandomirsky) (also Regina)

SWIFT CURRENT, Swift Current
Anderson, Nimegeers, Walter & Gibbings, 40 Cheadle St. w., J. G. Anderson, C. M. Nimegeers, M. K. Walter, N. G. Gibbings, Jacelyn A. Ryan, M.A. Froslee, T.J. Keene
Bader, R.G., Box 1614
Busch & Heinricks, 327 Central Ave. n., J.J. Busch, D.J. Heinricks
Holland, W. J., 106 Chaplin St. e.
Krueger, McLaughlin, Forrester & Rittinger, #9, 244 1st Ave. n.e., D.K. Krueger, H.M. McLaughlin, G.E. Forrester, D.W. Rittinger
Nakonechny, M.S., #5, 244 1st Ave. n.e.
Vause & Jackson, 276 2nd Ave. n.e., C.W. Vause, W.E. Jackson
Wiensz, T.H., Box 1717
Wilson, MacBean, Maurice, McIntosh & Wiebe, Calex Bldg., G. T. Wilson, F.A. MacBean, G.A.F. Maurice, J.H. McIntosh, J.D. Wiebe

TISDALE, Melfort
Saretzky & Klimm, 10005 102nd Ave. e., R.N. Saretzky, G.L. Klimm
Woolard & Aseltine, Box 760, W. B. Woolard
Zurowski, F. B., Box 995

TURTLEFORD, Battleford
Cawood & Walker (also North Battleford)
Sallows, Osborn & Co. (also North Battleford)
Wooff, D. S.
Wooff, H. G.

UNITY, Kerrobert
Hepting, H.T., Box 600
Young, J.E., 107 Main St.

URANIUM CITY, Prince Albert
Carson, Siwak & Co. (also Prince Albert)

WADENA, Wynyard
Kotyk & Zawislak, P.L. Kotyk, P.W. Zawislak

WAKAW, Prince Albert
Eggum, Abrametz & Co. (also Prince Albert)

WATROUS, Humboldt
Lannan, B.H., Box 580

WATSON, Humboldt
Sutherland, Weninger & Co. (also Humboldt)

WAWOTA, Moosomin
Goliath & Osman (also Moosomin)

WELDON, Melfort
Paine, Harold

WEYBURN, Weyburn
Hardy, G.N., 102 Coteau Ave. n.e.
MacDonald Law Firm, Drawer 97, L.B. MacDonald, R.E. MacDonald
Mazer, R.J., 28 Coteau St.
Nimegeers, Schuck, Wormsbecker & Bobbitt, Drawer 8, S. E. Nimegeers, T. A. Schuck, R. J. Wormsbecker, D.G. Bobbitt
Stinson & Assoc., 8 4th St. n.e., W.R. Stinson, D.M. Stinson, G.M. Berscheid, D.G. Kohlenberg

WHITEWOOD, Moosomin
Goliath & Osman (also Moosomin)

WILKIE, Battleford
Bieber, W., Q.C.

WYNYARD, Wynyard
Paulson, W., Drawer 460
Pillipow & Owen, Drawer 1120, W.J. Pillipow, D. Owen

YORKTON, Yorkton
Bright, Kolenick & Sommervill, 41 Broadway St. w., D.B. Bright, P.S. Kolenick, G.P. Sommervill
Dellow & Greenhorn, #2, 35 Broadway St. e., W.A. Dellow, L.G. Greenhorn
Kyba, S.G., 41 Betts Ave.
Morrison, Hornung, Stamatinos & Leland, 38 4th Ave. n., R.I. Hornung, J.L. Stamatinos, R.A. Leland
Ozirny, Wrubell, Fisher & Tourney, 35 Broadway St. e. R. C. Wrubell, B.W. Tourney (also Melville)
Rusnak, Balacko & Kachur, 7 Broadway St. e., W.M. Rusnak, R.J. Balacko, R.P. Kachur
Wasylyshen & Johnson, 44 Broadway St. e., K.W. Wasylyshen, G. Johnson
Weisberger, R. (also Melville)
Wentzell, M. D., 2A Smith St.

BARRISTERS AND SOLICITORS IN THE TERRITORIES

FORT SIMPSON, NWT
Sibbeston, N.G., Box 560

HAY RIVER, NWT
Boyd & Tancock, Box 1419, G.J. Boyd, L.C. Tancock, D.J. MacDonald, Cheryl Meikle, Jean Morris

WHITEHORSE, YT
Anton, Asquith & Campion, #200, 204 Lambert St., J.N.P. Anton, Q.C., G. Asquith, C.B. Campion, R.G. Macdonald, D.M. Florence, M.D. Perry, R.M. Zboril, Penelope Cawn. Counsel: Hon. Erik Nielsen, P.C., Q.C.
Boylan, Preston, Kidd & O'Brien, 2093 2nd Ave., T. W. Boylan, T. S. Preston, D.G. Kidd, P.S. O'Brien, B.L. Willis, M.J. Leitch, Ann King, B.C. Bell
Cable, Veale, Morris & Claxton, 3081 3rd Ave., I. J. Cable, R. S. Veale, B.L. Morris, D.N. Claxton, D.J. Avison

Dalziel & Co., #200, 100 Main St., R.R. Dalziel, G. Kilpatrick. Counsel: D.W. Pelton

Ernewein, B., #102, 107 Main St.

Phelps, Willard L., #203, 107 Main St.

Pitzel, R.B., 207 Lambert St.

Smith, Joe & Kimmerly, #205, 4133 4th Ave., M. Smith, D. Joe, R. Kimmerly, Lynn Gaudet

Walters & Walters, #8, 204 Main St., R.D. Walters, Edith Walters, M.W. Dale

YELLOWKNIFE, NWT

Boyd & Tancock, Box 2910, G.J. Boyd, L.C. Tancock, D.J. MacDonald, Cheryl Meikle, Jean Morris

Carter & Fuglsang, #301, 4920 47th St., G.N. Carter, P.C. Fuglsang

Cooper, Johnson & Wilson, 4908 Franklyn Ave., D.M. Cooper, E.D. Johnson, R.M.E. Wilson, A.J. Wey, L.E. Erickson

Richard, Kingsmill & Vertes, 5108 Franklin Ave., J.E. Richard, J.E. Kingsmill, J.Z. Vertes, Katherine R. Peterson, Gabriella I. Lang, Patricia Spence, B.J. Jensen, G.K. Phillips

INDEX

EDITOR'S NOTE:- Wherever possible the listings in this Index are arranged alphabetically according to the main word in each entry. Thus the Canadian Bankers Association is listed under "Bankers Assn., Cdn.", and the National Harbours Board is listed under "Harbours Bd., Ntl.". Government Departments are listed under the name of the Department, and not under the names of provinces. Thus if you are looking for the Ontario Transportation Department, look under "Transportation, Depts.," not under "Ontario".
Occasionally a listing (such as the International Boundary Commission) has been duplicated when it was difficult to determine which word a subscriber might consider to be the main one, or where it was felt a subscriber would look for an entry under a title that is well-known (such as the National Arts Centre).

A

C

Listings are by main word. See note at beginning of Index.

D

E

Listings are by main word. See note at beginning of Index.

F

Listings are by main word. See note at beginning of Index.

G

H

Listings are by main word. See note at beginning of Index.

J

K

L

Listings are by main word. See note at beginning of Index.

M

N

O

P

Q

R

Listings are by main word. See note at beginning of Index.

Listings are by main word. See note at beginning of Index.

S

T

U

V

W

Y

Z

ADDENDA

Page 1: Letters patent have been issued, or are pending, for incorporation of the following new banks in Canada, according to the Bank Act, 1980:

ABN Bank Canada, Hq. to be Toronto, Ont.

Banca Nazionale del Lavoro of Canada, Hq. to be Toronto, Ont. (For information contact hq. at Via Veneto, 119, Rome, Italy)

Bank of America Canada, Hq. to be Toronto, Ont. (For information contact #1900, North Tower, Royal Bank Plaza, Toronto, Ont.)

Bank Hapoalim (Canada), 1 First Canadian Place, Toronto, Ont.

The Bank of Tokyo Canada, #2075, South Tower, Royal Bank Plaza, Toronto, Ont. M5J 2J1

Banque Nationale de Paris (Canada), #3500 Stock Exchange Tower, Place Victoria, Montreal, P.Q.

Barclays Bank of Canada, #3505, Commerce Court West, Toronto, Ont.

BT Bank of Canada, #1600, North Tower, Royal Bank Plaza, Toronto, Ont. M5J 2J2

The Chase Manhattan Bank of Canada, #3605, Commerce Court West, Toronto, Ont. M5L 1G1

Chemical Bank of Canada, #200, 181 University Ave., Toronto, Ont.

Citibank Canada, #3400, First Canadian Place, Toronto, Ont. M5X 1C3

Continental Illinois Bank (Canada), Hq. to be Toronto, Ont. (For information contact R.L. Clute, 14 Dublin St., Apt. 7-F, Markham, Ont. L3P 1M7)

Crédit Suisse Canada, Hq. to be Toronto, Ont. (For information contact M.K. Cartier, Apt. 1904, 625 Avenue Rd., Toronto, Ont. M4V 2K7)

Dai-Ichi Kangyo Bank (Canada), Hq. to be Toronto, Ont. (For information contact hq. at 1-5 Uchisaiwai-cho, 1 chome, Chiyoda-ku, Tokyo 100, Japan)

Deutsche Bank (Canada), Hq. to be Toronto, Ont. (For information contact hq. at Postfach 26 31, D-6000, Frankfurt, Germany)

First Interstate Bank of Canada, #3101, South Tower, Royal Bank Plaza, Toronto, Ont. M5J 2J1

The First National Bank of Chicago, #2200, Commerce Court North, Toronto, Ont.

Fuji Bank Canada, Hq. to be Toronto, Ont. (For information contact hq. at 5-5, Otemachi 1-chome, Chiyoda-ku, Tokyo, Japan)

Hanil Bank Canada, 26th floor, Bentall 4, 1055 Dunsmuir St., Vancouver, B.C. V6C 1A8

Hong Kong Bank of Canada, #1818, 200 Granville St., Vancouver, B.C. V6C 1L3

The Industrial Bank of Japan, Hq. to be Toronto, Ont. (For information contact hq. at 3-3 Marunouchi 1-chome, Chiyoda-ku, Tokyo, Japan)

Israel Discount Bank of Canada, Hq. to be Toronto, Ont. (For information contact hq. at 27-31 Yehuda Halevi St., Tel Aviv, Israel)

Korea Exchange Bank of Canada, 2 First Canadian Place, Toronto, Ont. M5X 1B5

Lloyds Bank International Canada, #2500, Commerce Court North, Toronto, Ont. M5L 1H8

The Mitsui Bank of Canada, Hq. to be Toronto, Ont. (For information contact hq. at 1-2, Yurakucho 1-chome, Chiyoda-ku, Tokyo 100, Japan)

National Bank of Detroit, #895, North Tower, Royal Bank Plaza, Toronto, Ont. M5J 2S3

National Westminster Bank of Canada, #2060, South Tower, Royal Bank Plaza, Toronto, Ont.

Société Générale (Canada), Hq. to be Montréal, P.Q. (For information contact Jean-Michel Le Petit, 87 Summit Cres., Westmount, P.Q.)

Standard Chartered Bank of Canada, #5150 Commerce Court West, Toronto, Ont. M5L 1G4

Swiss Bank Corporation (Canada), Hq. to be Toronto, Ont. (For information contact SBC Financial Ltd., 800 Dorchester Blvd. W., Montréal, P.Q.)

Wells Fargo Bank Canada, Hq. to be Calgary, Alta. (For information contact Wells Fargo & Co., #4045, 1 First Canadian Place, Toronto, Ont.)

Page 23: Cdn. Health Libraries Assn.:

Remove treasurer's name, address & phone. New address is: Box 983, Stn. B, Ottawa, Ont. K1A 5R1

Page 38: Legislative Library, Winnipeg: Postal Code is R3C 0V8; Phone is 944-3784; Librarian is Mrs. Joyce Irvine

Page 65: Central Baptist Seminary Library is called "Dr. W. Gordon Brown Memorial Library" (address etc. is correct)

Page 70: Confederation Centre Library, Charlottetown: Librarian is William Masselink

Page 78: Add to Pointe Claire:

Forest Engineering Research Institute of Canada Library/Bibliotheque Institut canadien de recherches en génie forestier, 143 Place Frontenac, Pointe Claire, P.Q. H9R 4Z7 – (514/694-1140) – Christel Mukhopadhyay

Page 87: Indian & Northern Affairs Librarian (Yellowknife) is Don A. Albright

Page 101: Add:

Canho Enterprises, Box 249, Vernon, B.C. V1T 6M2; (604/545-8723); ISBN 0-919289

Page 105: New address for McGill-Queen's is 849 Sherbrooke St. W., Montréal, P.Q. H3A 2T5 (phone # is same)

Page 144: Add to Ottawa-Hull:

Kent, Walter, 33 Spring Garden Ave., Nepean, Ont. K2G 3B1 (613/225-2508; 996-1321) *Russ.-Eng.*

Page 148: J.-P. Partensky has a new office number (bur. 103) and a new phone number (514/767-4541)

Page 166: To the list of repeater stations of CKCW Moncton add:

CKCW-TV, Channel 2, Caledonia Mtn., N.B.
CKLT-TV, Channel 9, Mount Champlain, N.B.
CKCW-TV-1, Channel 8, Tyrone, P.E.I.

Page 192: Correct Anglican Church listings as follows:

Archbishops: Change Most Rev. T.D. Somerville to Most Rev. D.W. Hambidge, #101, 325 Howe St., Vancouver, B.C. V6C 1Z7; Change Most Rev. R.L. Seaborn to Most Rev. H.L. Nutter, 791 Brunswick St., Fredericton, N.B. E3B 1H8

Bishops: Caledonia: Change Rt. Rev. D.W. Hambidge to Rt. Rev. J.E. Hannen (same address)

Fredericton: Change Rt. Rev. Nutter to *Most* Rev.

New Westminster: Change Most Rev. T.D. Somerville to Most Rev. D.W. Hambidge (same address)

Ontario: Change Rt. Rev. H.G. Hill to Rt. Rev. A.A. Read (same address)

Ottawa: Change Rt. Rev. W.J. Robinson to Rt. Rev. E.K. Lackey (same address)

Yukon: Change Rt. Rev. J.T. Frame to Rt. Rev. R.C. Ferris

Toronto: Delete Rt. Rev. A.A. Read; and add: Rt. Rev. A.D. Brown, Suffragan Bishop, Aurora Conference Centre, R.R. 2, Aurora, Ont. L4G 3G8; Rt. Rev. D.C. Hunt, Suffragan Bishop, 135 Adelaide St. E., Toronto, Ont. M5C 1L8; Rt. Rev. G.H. Parke-Taylor, Suffragan Bishop, 135 Adelaide St. E.; Rt. Rev. B. Tonks, Suffragan Bishop, 123 Prince George Dr., Islington, Ont. M9B 2Y3

Huron: Delete Rt. Rev. G.H. Parke-Taylor

Niagara: Add Rt. Rev. C.M. Mitchell, Suffragan Bishop (same address as Bothwell)

Under Program of General Synod: Add Media Officer, Rev. R.J. Berryman; Delete Ecumenical Officer, Rev. James Boyles

Church Statistics 1979
Total Parish enrolment - 952,489
Total Number of Clergy - 2,955
Total Number of congregations - 3,212
Total Number of Dioceses - 30

Page 211: Alta. Assn. of Agricultural Societies: Secretary is Carol Armtzen; Address is the same; Phone is 403/427-2174

Page 212: Cdn. Consulting Agrologists' Assn. has a new address & phone: 89 Queensway W., #200, Mississauga, Ont. L5B 2V2 (416/270-7751)

Page 213: Cdn. Soc. for Horticultural Science officers are:
President, Dr. J.M. Molnar, Director, Agric. Canada Research Stn., 8801 E. Saanich Rd., Sidney, B.C. V8L 1H3
Secretary Treasurer, Dr. I.V. Hall, Agric. Canada Research Stn., Kentville, N.S. B4N 1J5

Page 218: Add: Arbitrators' Institute of Canada, Inc., 234 Eglinton Ave. E., #411, Toronto, Ont. M4P 1K5 (416/487-8433); Executive Director, J.A. Tuck

Page 224: Delete Assn. of Counties & Regions. Now part of Association of Municipalities of Ontario, page 225

Page 226: The Assn. des Realisateurs de Films du Que. is now called: "Association des réalisateurs et réalisatrices de film du Québec" and the new president is André Théberge (address the same)

Page 228: New address for the Canadian Blind Sports Assn. is 4364 W. 12th Ave., Vancouver, B.C. V6R 2R1. The Executive Director is Phil de Leeuw

Page 229: Cdn. Lawn Bowling Council officers are:
President, Tom Holness, 253 E. 11th St., North Vancouver, B.C. V7L 2G8
Secretary Treasurer, James Carter, 1695 Playfair Dr., Apt. 1121, Ottawa, Ont. K1H 8J6 (res: 613/523-4258)

Page 238: Add: Canada Association of Legal Secretaries, c/o Mrs. Janet E. Bradley, 1075 Prince George Rd., London, Ont. N6H 4E2

Page 241: Add: Canadian Association of Professional Conservators, c/o Cdn. Museums Association, 331 Cooper St., #400, Ottawa, Ont. K2P 0G5

Page 274: The new Rm. # for Alta. Federation of Home & School Associations is #8. (balance of address, & phone # is unchanged)

Page 278: Institut Canadien d'Education des Adultes is confirmed. All information correct

Page 280: Add: Prince George Naturalist Club, Box 1092, Stn. A, Prince George, B.C. V2L 4V2

Page 280: Add: Richmond Anti-Pollution Association, Box 204, Richmond, B.C. V6Y 2A3 (604/274-7655)

Page 281: Add: Durham Region Field Naturalists, Box 354, Oshawa, Ont. L1H 7L3

Page 282: Add: Ontario Wolf League, Box 177, Stn. S, Toronto, Ont. M5M 4L7 (416/889-7426)

Page 293: Ancaster Twp. Hist. Soc.: PO Box # is 7163

Page 299: Add: International Relief Agency Inc., 2675 Dominion Blvd., Windsor, Ont. N9E 2M7; Executive Director, A.A. Budzanowski

Page 303: The new secretary for the B.C. Goat Breeders' Assn. is Marilyn Cumming, R.R. 1, Tappen, B.C. V0E 2X0 (604/835-8309)

Page 306: With Cdn. Simmental Assn., add the following provincial associations:
British Columbia: Secretary Dorothy Warner, Box 10, Fort Langley, B.C. V0X 1J0 (604/888-1944)
Alberta: Secretary Doris Burrington, Box 605, Red Deer, Alta. T4N 5G5
Saskatchewan: Secretary, Marlin Moore, Box 178, Chaplin, Sask. S0H 0V0
Manitoba: Secretary, Archie Londry, Rapid City, Man. R0K 1W0
Ontario: Secretary, Marion McArthur, R.R. 1, Stayner, Ont. L0M 1S0
Quebec: Secretary, Armand Pellerin, 479 Rte 138, St-Augustin, P.Q. G0A 3B0

Page 314: Add: Canadian Association of Teachers of Accordion, c/o Boris Borgstrom, 6 Glengrove Circle, St. Catharines, Ont. L2T 2Y9

Page 316: Add: Okanagan Symphony Soc., Box 1120, Kelowna, B.C. V1Y 7P8 (604/763-4500); Executive Director, R.R. Johnson

Page 316: Add: Prince Edward Island Symphony Orchestra Society, c/o General Manager, Norman Osborne, Box 185, Charlottetown, P.E.I. C1A 7K4 (902/892-4121)

Page 316: Add: Prince George Symphony Orchestra, Box 43, Prince George, B.C. V2L 4R9 (604/562-0800); President, Des Parker; Conductor, Kerry Stratton; Manager, Andrew Thompson

Page 323: Ontario Sheet Metal & Air Handling Group has a new address & phone: 1110 Sheppard Ave. E., #310, Willowdale, Ont. M2K 2W2 (416/226-5533)

Page 328: Add: The Progressive Party, c/o Sidney Green, Legislative Bldg., Winnipeg, Man. R3C 0V8

Page 328: Add: The Unparty, Ntl. Hq., Box 6069, Stn. A, Toronto, Ont. M5W 1P5; Ont. Hq., 111 Queen St. E., #402, Toronto, Ont. M5C 1S2; Phone, 416/361-0630; Ntl. President, Wm. A. McDonald

Page 328: Add: Postal History Society of Canada, c/o Secretary Treasurer, A. Palochik, Box 3461, Stn. C, Ottawa, Ont. K1Y 4J6 (613/728-2907)

Page 332: Rocky Mountain Ramblers new address is 713 23 Ave. N.W., Calgary, Alta. T2M 1T1 (phone # same)

Page 333: Delete Rural Ont. Municipal Assn. Now part of Association of Municipalities of Ontario, page 225.

Page 335: Add: La Société de Géographie de Québec, a/s Faculté des Lettres, Université Laval, Québec, P.Q. G1K 7P4; Président, Me Paul Bouchard

Page 337: New address for Toronto Film Society is #212B, 1430 Yonge St., Toronto, Ont. M4T 1Y6; Phone numbers for Helen Arthurs are 485-8474 & 921-7309

Page 341: New PO Box for Union of Manitoba Municipalities is 397; Postal Code is R1N 3B7

Page 351: Camrose Lutheran College is confirmed. All information is correct

Page 351: Coralwood Academy is confirmed. Address & phone are correct

Page 363: King's-Edgehill is confirmed. All information is correct

Page 370: Add to Agricultural Colleges: Alfred College of Agric. Tech., C.P. 580, Alfred, Ont. K0B 1A0; Principal, M. Paulhus

Page 373: Loretto Abbey is confirmed. All information is correct

Page 387: Victoriaville (CEGEP): Remove C.P. #; Postal Code is G6P 4B3; Phone is 819/758-6401

Page 389: University of Saskatchewan:
Chairman, Bd. of Governors is Christine Devrome, B.A.
Arts & Science Dean is A.R. Knight
Commerce Dean is W.J. Brennan
Education Dean is Naomi Hersom
On page 390, Principal of Emmanuel & St. Chad is Very Rev. J. Russell Brown

Page 449: The Alberta Dept. responsible for Energy Conservation is: Energy Conservation Branch, Alta. Energy & Natural Resources, 7th floor, 9915 108 St., Edmonton, Alta. T5K 2C9 (403/427-6902) There is no provincial residental grant program for insulation or up-grading heating systems in Alberta.

Page 461: The address of the Queen's Printer of Saskatchewan is 14th floor, Avord Tower, Regina, Sask. S4P 3V7

Page 476: The High Commissioner of the Solomon Islands is H.E. Francis Bugotu, C.B.E., c/o Ministry of Foreign Affairs, Box 910, Honiara, Solomon Islands

Page 477: The correct address for the Belgian Consulate in Halifax is #233, 1657 Barrington St. (Box 1590, Stn. M, Halifax, N.S. B3J 2Y3); phone: 902/423-6323
The correct address in St. John's is Finger Pier, Harbour Dr. (Box 1506, St. John's, Nfld. A1C 5N8); phone 709/726-8948

Pages 571-580: Preliminary results of election in Manitoba on November 17, 1981 are as follows:
Executive Council (not announced at Almanac press time)
Party Standings: New Democratic Party (N.D.P.) 34; Progressive Conservative (P.C.) 23; Total 57.
Premier, Howard Pawley
Leader of Opposition, Sterling Lyon
Speaker, (not announced at Almanac press time)

Members elected (preliminary list):
Arthur: James Downey, P.C.
Assiniboia: Ric Nordman, P.C.
Brandon East: Leonard Evans, N.D.P.
Brandon West: Henry Carroll, N.D.P.
Burrows: Conrad Santos, N.D.P.
Charleswood: Sterling Lyon, P.C.
Churchill: Jay Cowan, N.D.P.
Concordia: Peter Fox, N.D.P.
Dauphin: John Plohman, N.D.P.
Ellice: Brian Corrin, N.D.P.
Elmwood: Russell Doern, N.D.P.
Emerson: Albert Driedger, P.C.
Flin Flon: Jerry Storie, N.D.P.
Fort Garry: Bud Sherman, P.C.
Fort Rouge: Roland Penner, N.D.P.
Gimli: John Bucklaschuk, N.D.P.
Gladstone: Charlotte Oleson, P.C.
Inkster: Don Scott, N.D.P.
Interlake: Bill Uruski, N.D.P.
Kildonan: Mary Dolin, N.D.P.
Kirkfield Park: Gerrie Hammond, P.C.
Lac du Bonnet: Samuel Uskiw, N.D.P.
Lakeside: Harry Enns, P.C.
La Verendrye: Robert Banman, P.C.
Logan: Maureen Hemphill, N.D.P.
Minnedosa: David Blake, P.C.
Morris: Clayton Manness, P.C.
Niakwa: Abe Kovnats, P.C.
Osborne: Muriel Smith, N.D.P.
Pembina: Donald Orchard, P.C.
Portage la Prairie: Lloyd Hyde, P.C.
Radisson: Gerard Lecuyer, N.D.P.
Rhineland: Arnold Brown, P.C.
Riel: Doreen Dodick, N.D.P.
River East: Phil Eyler, N.D.P.
River Heights: Warren Steen, P.C.
Roblin-Russell: Wallace McKenzie, P.C.
Rossmere: Victor Schroeder, N.D.P.
Rupertsland: Elijah Harper, N.D.P.
St. Boniface: Laurent Desjardins, N.D.P.
St. James: Alvin Mackling, N.D.P.
St. John's: Donald Malinowski, N.D.P.
St. Norbert: Gerald Mercier, P.C.
St. Vital: James Walding, N.D.P.
Ste. Rose: A.M. Adam, N.D.P.
Selkirk: Howard Pawley, N.D.P.
Seven Oaks: Eugene Kostyra, N.D.P.
Springfield: Andrew Anstett, N.D.P.
Sturgeon Creek: J.F. Johnston, P.C.
Swan River: Douglas Gourlay, P.C.
The Pas: Harry Harapiak, N.D.P.
Thompson: Steve Ashton, N.D.P.
Transcona: Wilson Parasiuk, N.D.P.
Turtle Mountain: Brian Ransom, P.C.
Tuxedo: Gary Filmon, P.C.
Virden: Harry Graham, P.C.
Wolseley: Myrna Phillips, N.D.P.

Page 596: The new address for the N.S. Processing Pea Marketing Board is R.R. 1, Port Williams. All other information is the same.

Pages 622-626: The new premier of Prince Edward Island is James Lee. The new leader of the Liberal Party is Joe Ghiz. New cabinet positions are as follows:
Premier, and President of the Council, Hon. James Lee
Minister of Fisheries & Labour, Hon. Patrick Binns
Minister of Finance, Hon. Lloyd G. MacPhail
Minister of Community Affairs, Hon. Horace Carver
Minister of Justice & Attorney General, Hon. George McMahon
Minister of Agriculture & Forestry, Hon. Prowse G. Chappell
Minister of Education, Hon. Frederick L. Driscoll
Minister of Tourism, Industry & Energy, Hon. Barry R. Clark
Minister of Health & Social Services, Hon. Albert Fogarty
Minister of Highways & Public Works, Hon. Roddy Pratt

Page 893: Summerside (add):
Mayor, Ross Lefurgey
Councillors: Norman Gallant, Michael Gallant, Melville Campbell, Donald Beairsto, Wendell Morrison, Edward Dillon
Next Election: November, 1982